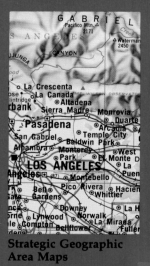

RAND McNALLY

The New International Atlas
Der Neue Internationale Atlas
El Nuevo Atlas Internacional
Le Nouvel Atlas International
O Nôvo Atlas Internacional

RAND McNALLY & COMPANY CHICAGO / NEW YORK / SAN FRANCISCO

ADVISERS AND CONSULTANTS

The editors wish to express their special appreciation to these geographers, cartographers, and regional specialists who assisted in the refinement of the basic concepts of the atlas or who participated in the review of many of the regional maps.

ALLGEMEINE UND KARTOGRAPHISCHE BERATER

Die Herausgeber möchten ihren besonderen Dank den Geographen, Kartographen und Landeskundlern aussprechen, die mitgeholfen haben bei der Klärung des Atlaskonzepts oder beteiligt waren an der Durchsicht vieler Regionalkarten.

ASESORES Y CONSULTORES

Los redactores quieren expresar su más profundo agradecimiento a los geógrafos, cartógrafos y especialistas en mapas regionales, que han colaborado en la determinación exacta de los conceptos básicos del atlas o que han participado en la revisión de gran número de los mapas regionales.

CONSEILLERS ET CONSULTANTS

Les éditeurs veulent exprimer ici leur gratitude aux géographes, cartographes et spécialistes régionaux qui ont collaboré à la mise au point de la conception de base de l'Atlas ou qui ont participé à la révision de nombreuses cartes régionales.

CONSELHEIROS E CONSULTORES

Os editores desejam expressar seu profundo agradecimento aos geógrafos, cartógrafos e especialistas regionais que assistiram no refinamento dos conceitos básicos do atlas ou que tenham participado na revisão de um grande número de mapas regionais.

International Planning Conference
Internationale Planungskonferenz
Conferencia Internacional de Consultores
Conférence Internationale de Planning
Conferência Internacional de Consultores

Dr. MANLIO CASTIGLIONI
Italy

Dr. ARCH C. GERLACH
United States

Dr. Ir. CORNELIS KOEMAN
Netherlands

Dr. ANDRÉ LIBAULT
Brazil

Brig. D. E. O. THACKWELL
United Kingdom

ROBERT J. VOSKUIL
United States

Dr. AKIRA WATANABE
Japan

Map Advisers
Kartographische Berater
Consejeros Cartográficos
Conseillers Cartographes
Conselheiros Cartográficos

Europe
Prof. Dr. EMIL MEYNEN
Germany

Dr. SANDOR RADO
Hungary

Asia
Dr. HISASHI SATO
Japan

Australia
R. O. BUCHANAN
United Kingdom

Anglo-America
Dr. ARCH C. GERLACH
United States

Latin America
Dr. ANDRÉ LIBAULT
Brazil

Dra. CONSUELO SOTO MORA
Mexico

Dr. JORGE A. VIVÓ ESCOTO
Mexico

Metropolitan Area Maps
Prof. HAROLD M. MAYER
United States

The New International Atlas

Library of Congress Catalog Card Number: 87-60460
Printed in the United States of America.

International Atlas Staff
Redaktion des Internationalen Atlasses
Personal del Atlas Internacional
Personnel de l'Atlas International
Redação do Atlas Internacional

RAND McNALLY & COMPANY, Chicago

Publisher
Andrew McNally III

Editorial and Cartographic Direction
Russell L. Voisin
Jon M. Leverenz

Art and Design Direction
Chris Arvetis
Gordon Hartshorne

Coordination
Victor P. Healy
John E. Zych
David B. Gattorna

Geographic Research
Joseph C. Smutnik
Kerstin Thielen
Keith Jennerjohn

Cartographic Editorial
Visvaldis Smits
Robert K. Argersinger
William L. Abel

Cartographic Compilation
Esther A. Grene, Lynn N. Jasmer,
Ernest A. Dahl, Han Sik Lee,
Larry K. Tyler

Cartographic Production
Raymond J. Nitch, Wasyl Szwec,
Adolph Bravi, Ronald Peters,
Walter E. Erck, Dorothy M. Cundiff,
Robert Mancic, Joseph H. Funke,
Ruthe Garner

Index
Donald R. Schultz

Terrain Illustrators
Ivan Barcaba
Evelyn Mitchell

Corporate Advisory Group
Thomas J. Hermes
Dennis O'Shea
Carl Mapes
Bruce C. Ogilvie
Paul T. Tiddens

MONDADORI McNALLY GmbH, Stuttgart

General Manager
Helmut Schaub
and Cartographic Staff

CARTOGRAPHIA, Budapest

Coordinator
Ervin Földi
and Cartographic Staff

ESSELTE MAP SERVICE, Stockholm

Editorial and Cartographic Direction
Paul R. Kraske,
Jürgen Jansch,
and Cartographic Staff

GEORGE PHILIP & SON, London

Editorial and Cartographic Direction
Harold Fullard,
A. G. Poynter,
and Cartographic Staff

TEIKOKU-SHOIN CO., LTD., Tokyo

Supervisor
Kimio Moriya
and Cartographic Staff

Foreword

THE HISTORY OF MAPS is as old as travel, discovery, and curiosity about the world. Since the earliest times, cartographers have served mariners with guidance for their explorations, monarchs with portraits of their territories, and scholars with a record of the earth's surface. Today, maps play an even more important role by providing men with the evidence of the ties which link the world's countries and peoples to one another.

The prime function of a map is to portray the earth's surface and the patterns of human occupance that have developed upon it. If a map were no more than an objective record, it would not need revision; however, a map is more than just a simple picture. Greatly reduced in scale from the reality it represents, it must abstract and generalize from that reality, selecting and interpreting the facts deemed to be of greatest significance. Thus, not only must cartography map new regions of the world, but it must also reflect a steady improvement in the techniques of portraying geographic information for the user.

The present century has offered a great challenge to map makers. Not only has it witnessed the increasing demand for specialized map information from governments, teachers, and scientists, it has also seen growing numbers of non-specialists eager to use maps in their business, for travel, or simply for enjoyment.

The Editors of *The International Atlas* feel, then, that a new work should be more than an updated version of older ones. The goal should be to produce an atlas of the greatest possible value and interest to a wide range of specialists and laymen. In this Foreword, we call the attention of users to several aspects which are new to the traditional framework of atlas publishing. The two most significant of these are the internationality of its planning and execution, and the designing of the maps as components of five distinctive series.

From the beginning, this Atlas has been international in concept, planning, editorial policy, and production. It was felt by Rand McNally & Company that there would be important gains in source material and expertise from the participation of organizations with previous cartographic experience in widely varying regions of the world. The advice and guidance of the senior personnel of these organizations has borne out this belief, although Rand McNally & Company as publisher has retained prime responsibility.

The editorial policies of the Atlas have been established with international use in mind, being designed for those whose native tongue is German, Spanish, French or Portuguese, as well as English. This international approach has been carried into the maps through the utilization of the metric system of measurement, and particularly by a strong emphasis on the use of local forms for geographic names. Essentially all names are in the local language, and English is used only for names of major features which extend across international borders. The names of countries appear on most of the maps both in English and in the locally official forms.

Generic terms for physical features (mountain, island, cape, etc.) also appear in their local forms, not in English. Short glossaries translating the most common of these terms appear in the margins of most maps. There is also a comprehensive glossary of all the generic terms. In the index to the Atlas, translation of generic terms is aided by the use of a system of symbols.

The coverage of the world's regions has also been planned with international utilization in mind. The space allotted to each region reflects its relative economic and cultural significance on the world scene, as well as its total population and area. There is an approximate balance between Anglo-America, Europe, and Asia, each with over one-fifth of the total map pages. Africa, Oceania, and Latin America together account for the remaining one-third. The index maps on pages xiii-xv show the map coverage according to scale.

The second of the Atlas' significant new aspects is the planning of the maps as components of five separate series. Each series has a distinctive style and content. In the first of these series, the continents are portrayed at 1:24,000,000 in natural colors, as they might appear from about 4,000 miles in space. The series also includes maps of the oceans at 1:48,000,000 and the world at 1:75,000,000.

In the next series, the major world regions are uniformly portrayed at 1:12,000,000 (190 miles to the inch). These maps are primarily political in style and content. The third series covers virtually the entire inhabited area of the earth at either 1:6,000,000 (95 miles to the inch), for the less dense regions, or 1:3,000,000 (47 miles to the inch), for Europe, most of North America, and the densest portions of South and East Asia. Physical and cultural detail are given approximately equal emphasis in this series.

In the fourth series, the scale of 1:1,000,000 (16 miles to the inch) has been used to portray key regions in each continent, selected for their exceptional importance, high population density, or complexity of development. The emphasis is on cultural detail, though shaded relief also appears. A final series maps the world's major urban areas at 1:300,000 (4.7 miles to the inch). This series emphasizes the complex patterns characteristic of large urban areas, omitting relief portrayal.

Each of the map series is comprehensive in a significant sense. The first three are territorially comprehensive, except for a few remote areas, and the last two are comprehensive for the most densely settled regions of the earth.

The sequence of maps in the Atlas begins with the series of world, continent, and ocean maps. Next are the three series of regional maps, arranged within major regions from smallest scale (1:12,000,000) to largest scale (1:1,000,000). The metropolitan map series (1:300,000) are kept together in one section following the regional maps.

The individual map layouts have usually been planned to portray geographic and economic regions rather than individual countries. Thus there are maps of the Iberian Peninsula and of Southeastern Europe, but no separate maps of Portugal or Romania. In a few instances, this has necessitated the omission of some small portion of the region or country described in the map title. Inset maps have also been avoided, though exceptions have been made to portray some isolated islands or island groups.

The map symbols used for given features (Legend to Maps, pages x-xii) are generally alike on all of the map scales, though reduced in size on smaller scales. The symbols most often used have been arranged on page xi.

No aspect of map design has shown more dramatic advances in recent years than the cartographic rendering of relief. The Editors believe that the most effective method to depict this is the bird's-eye view or hill shading technique, which uses variation from light through dark tones to indicate slope and shape of relief features pictorially. This Atlas uses shaded relief on all but one of its five map series. On the 1:6,000,000 and 1:3,000,000 maps, it appears in combination with altitude tints, which show variations in elevation by means of light reflection, hue and intensity.

In the concluding portion of the Atlas are various tables and summaries for general reference. The World Scene (pages 289-320) is a separate section of topical maps. These maps summarize the patterns of man's physical environment and some of his more important economic activities, political alignments, and cultural distributions. This section is based on the most recent information available, taken from a variety of sources and adapted by the editors. Next is the comprehensive glossary of geographic terms (pages 321-327). The World Information Table (pages 328-331) lists the area, population, and political status for each major political unit. The world's largest metropolitan areas are listed on page 332, followed by a comprehensive list of the world's major cities with population (pages 333-348). Finally, the Index provides map location references—map page, latitude and longitude—for more than 160,000 names.

Vorwort

DIE GESCHICHTE DER KARTE ist so alt wie das Reisen, die Entdeckungsfahrten und die Wissbegier über die Welt. Seit alten Zeiten haben Kartographen den Seefahrern mit Unterlagen für ihre Erkundungen gedient, den Herrschern Aufnahmen ihres Besitzes und den Gelehrten Darstellungen der Erdoberfläche geliefert. Heute spielen Karten eine noch bedeutendere Rolle, weil sie den Menschen vor Augen führen, wie eng die Länder und Völker der Welt miteinander verbunden sind.

Wichtigste Aufgabe einer Karte ist es, die Oberfläche der Erde und die vom Menschen geschaffenen Formen darzustellen. Wäre eine Karte nichts anderes als eine objektive Bestandsaufnahme, brauchte sie nicht bearbeitet zu werden; eine Karte ist jedoch mehr als nur ein Bild. Da sie eine vielfache Verkleinerung der Wirklichkeit wiedergibt, muss sie abstrahieren und durch Auswahl und Symbolisierung der wesentlichsten Tatsachen vereinfachen. So hat die Kartographie neue Regionen der Erde aufzunehmen und den neuesten Stand der Darstellung geographischer Informationen für den Benutzer aufzuzeigen.

Unser Jahrhundert bedeutet für die Kartographen eine grosse Herausforderung. Karten werden nicht nur in zunehmendem Masse von Regierungen, Wissenschaftlern und Pädagogen gefordert, sondern auch von interessierten Laien, die in ihrem Beruf, auf Reisen oder einfach zu ihrer Freude Karten benutzen.

Die Herausgeber des *Internationalen Atlas* meinen, dass ein neues Atlaswerk mehr sein sollte als nur die laufend gehaltene Ausgabe eines alten. Das Ziel sollte sein, einen Atlas von höchstem Gebrauchswert und Interesse sowohl für Fachleute wie auch Laien zu schaffen.

In diesem Sinne möchten wir auf Besonderheiten hinweisen, die sich von dem traditionellen Aufbau eines Atlas wesentlich unterscheiden. Die beiden wichtigsten sind die Internationalität in Planung und Ausführung sowie die einheitliche Gestaltung der Karten zu fünf Gruppen.

Von Anfang an war dieser Atlas international in Planung, Redaktion und Herstellung. Rand McNally & Company war überzeugt, dass die Beteiligung von Partnern aus verschiedenen Teilen der Welt mit ihrer kartographischen Erfahrung einen grossen Gewinn an Quellen und Rat ergeben würde. Der Rat und die Mitarbeit dieser Fachleute haben diese Ansicht voll bestätigt, wobei Rand McNally als Verleger die letzte Entscheidung zufiel.

Die redaktionelle Bearbeitung des Atlas erfolgte mit Blick auf einen internationalen Interessentenkreis, vor allem aber für Benutzer, deren Muttersprache Deutsch, Spanisch, Französisch, Portugiesisch oder Englisch ist. Diese internationale Einstellung zeigt sich im Karteninhalt selbst, in der Benutzung des metrischen Masssystems und vor allem in der Bevorzugung der lokalen Schreibweise geographischer Namen. Grundsätzlich werden alle Namen in der Landessprache wiedergegeben; nur Namen grösserer Objekte, die sich über nationale Grenzen erstrecken, erscheinen in Englisch. Die Ländernamen stehen auf den meisten Karten sowohl in Englisch als auch in der offiziellen nationalen Form.

Namen für physische Objekte (Berg, Insel, Kap usw.) sind ebenfalls in ihrer lokalen Form wiedergegeben, nicht in Englisch. Die am häufigsten vorkommenden Begriffe stehen am Rande der meisten Karten erläutert. Der Atlas enthält ausserdem ein umfangreiches Verzeichnis aller Gattungsbegriffe. Im Register wird das Verständnis dieser Gattungsbegriffe durch ein System von Symbolen erleichtert.

Die Kartenausschnitte der verschiedenen Regionen der Erde wurden gleichfalls mit Blick auf einen internationalen Benutzerkreis gewählt. In diesem Atlas entspricht der einer Region zugemessene Kartenanteil ihrer relativen wirtstshaftlichen und kulturellen Bedeutung in der Welt wie ihrer Gesamtbevölkerung und Fläche. Auf Anglo-Amerika, Europa und Asien entfällt mit je etwas mehr als einen Fünftel der Gesamtkartenzahl ungefähr der gleiche Anteil. Das verbleibende Drittel teilen sich Afrika, Australien, Ozeanien und Lateinamerika. Auf den Seiten XIII-XV sind die Kartenschnitte den Massstäben entsprechend auf Übersichtskarten ersichtlich.

Die zweite wesentliche Besonderhiet des Atlas ist seine Gliederung der Karten in fünf charakteristische Gruppen. Jede Gruppe ist gekennzeichnet durch einen bestimmten Stil und Inhalt. In der ersten Gruppe werden die Kontinente (1:24 Mill.) abgebildet, wie sie sich aus einer ungefähren Entfernung von 6 500 km aus dem Weltraum darbieten. Diese Gruppe schliesst Karten der Ozeane (1:48 Mill.) und der Erde (1:75 Mill.) ein. In der folgenden Gruppe werden Grossregionen einheitlich (1:12 Mill.) dargestellt. Diese Karten sind in erster Linie politische Karten. Die dritte Serie deckt im wesentlichen das bewohnte Gebiet der Erde, entweder 1:6 Mill. für weniger dicht besiedelte Gebiete oder 1:3 Mill. für Europa, den Grossteil von Nordamerika und die dichtest besiedelten Teile Süd- und Ostasiens. Physische und kulturgeographische Einzelheiten werden in ungefähr gleichem Umfang wiedergegeben.

Für die vierte Gruppe wurde der Massstab 1:1 Mill. gewählt, um zentrale Räume jedes Kontinents abzubilden; sie sind entsprechend ihrer aussergewöhnlichen Bedeutung, hohen Bevölkerungsdichte oder komplexen Entwicklung gewählt. Betont werden kulturgeographische Einzelheiten, dazu enthalten die Karten eine Reliefschummerung. Die letzte Gruppe umfasst die bedeutendsten Stadtregionen der Erde (1:300 000). Diese Serie hebt das charakteristische, komplexe Gefüge grosser städtischer Ballungsgebiete hervor; auf Reliefdarstellung wurde verzichtet.

Jede der Kartenserien ist in sich abgeschlossen: Die ersten drei sind in Bezug auf die Landflächen umfassend, ausgenommen einige entlegene Gebiete; die zwei letzten sind es hinsichtlich der Darstellung der dichtest besiedelten Räume der Erde.

Der Atlas beginnt mit der Gruppe der Welt-, Kontinent- und Ozeankarten. Es folgen drei Gruppen Regionalkarten, innerhalb jeder Grossregion geordnet vom kleinsten Massstab (1:12 Mill.) zum grössten (1:1 Mill.). Die Serie der Stadtregionen (1:300 000) wurde in einem einzigen Kapitel zusammengefasst, im Anschluss an die Regionalkarten.

Die Festlegung der einzelnen Kartenausschnitte zielte gewöhnlich mehr darauf ab, geographische und wirtschaftliche Regionen darzustellen als einzelne Staaten. Es gibt daher eine Karte der Iberischen Halbinsel oder von Südosteuropa, aber keine Einzelkarte von Portugal oder Rumänien. In einigen Fällen sind hierdurch kleinere Flächen des Landes oder der Region nicht erfasst, die im Kartentitel genannt sind. Die Verwendung von Einsatzkärtchen wurde möglichst vermieden, dennoch waren Ausnahmen erforderlich, um entlegene Inseln oder Inselgruppen darstellen zu können.

Die Kartensignaturen für bestimmte Objekte (Zeichenerklärung Seite X-XII) gleichen sich im allgemeinen in allen Massstäben, auch wenn sie in Karten kleinerer Massstäbe verkleinert sind. Die am häufigsten vorkommenden Signaturen sind auf Seite XI dargestellt.

Auf kaum einem Gebiet der Kartengestaltung gab es in den vergangenen Jahren so eindrucksvolle Fortschritte wie auf dem der Geländedarstellung. Die Herausgeber glauben, dass die wirkungsvollste Darstellungsmethode die Reliefschummerung ist. Sie benutzt Tonabstufungen von Hell zu Dunkel, um Neigungen und Geländeformen plastisch hervorzuheben. Dieser Atlas bringt die Schummerung bei vier der fünf Kartenserien. In den Karten 1:6 und 1:3 Mill. wird sie kombiniert mit farbigen Höhenschichten, die unterschiedliche Höhenlagen durch ihren Farb- und Tonwert abgestuft wiedergeben.

Der letzte Teil des Atlas enthält zahlreiche Tabellen und Übersichten. Die Welt von Heute (Seite 289-320) ist ein selbständiges Kapitel mit thematischen Karten. Sie geben einen Überblick über die physischen Grundlagen des Siedlungsraumes des Menschen, seine wichtigsten wirtschaftlichen Tätigkeiten, die politischen Grenzen und Gruppierungen und sonstige Kulturgeographische Erscheinungen. Als Grundlage dienten die neuesten erhältlichen Daten verschiedenster Herkunft. Auf Seite 321-327 folgt eine Zusammenstellung geographischer Begriffe. In einer Länderübersicht (Seite 328-331) sind Daten über Fläche, Bevölkerung und politischen Status der wichtigsten politischen Einheiten zusammengefasst. Die grössten Stadtregionen der Erde werden auf Seite 332. Weiter folgt eine umfangreiche Liste der wichtigsten Weltstädte mit Einwohnerzahlen (Seite 333-348). Im Register werden für über 160 000 Namen die Kartenseite sowie die geographische Länge und Breite aufgeführt.

Prefacio

LA HISTORIA DE LOS MAPAS es tan antigua como la de los viajes, los descubrimientos y la curiosidad del hombre por el mundo. Desde hace mucho tiempo los cartógrafos han proporcionado guías a los navegantes en sus exploraciones, descripciones de sus territorios a los monarcas y registros de la superficie de la tierra a los eruditos. Más importante todavía es el papel que desempeñan los mapas en la actualidad, proporcionando al hombre en todas partes prueba de los lazos que vinculan entre sí a los diferentes países y pueblos del globo.

La función primordial de un mapa es la representación de la superficie de la tierra y de los patrones de ocupación humana que se han desarrollado sobre ella. Si un mapa no fuera sino un registro objetivo, no necesitaría ser revisado; sin embargo, un mapa es algo más que una simple representación gráfica. Representando una realidad enormemente reducida a escala, el mapa, forzosamente, debe abstraer y generalizar de esa realidad, seleccionando e interpretando los hechos que se juzguen de mayor significación. En consecuencia, la cartografía no debe limitarse al trazo de mapas de las nuevas regiones del mundo, sino que debe reflejar en ellos un continuo adelanto en las técnicas de representación de la información geográfica en provecho de quien los utiliza.

El siglo actual ha venido a presentar a los cartógrafos una desafiante tarea. Es época que no sólo ha presenciado una creciente demanda de información cartográfica especializada por parte de los gobiernos, maestros y científicos, sino que durante ella ha surgido un público cada vez mayor de gentes no especializadas, ávidas de aprovechar los mapas en sus negocios y viajes o que los adquieren simplemente por placer.

Los directores del *Atlas Internacional* consideran, por lo tanto, que una nueva obra debe ser algo más que una versión al día de trabajos anteriores. El objetivo debe ser producir un atlas del mayor valor e interés posibles para un vasto número de especialistas y de legos en la materia. En este prefacio, queremos llamar la atención de quienes consulten esta obra sobre varias innovaciones introducidas en el diseño tradicional de un atlas. De ellas, las más significativas son la internacionalidad de su preparación, y el diseño de los mapas como componentes de cinco series con características propias.

Desde un principio, este atlas ha tenido carácter internacional en cuanto a su concepto básico, su planeamiento, política editorial y producción. Rand McNally y Compañía consideró que con la participación de organizaciones con experiencia en cartografía en una gran variedad de regiones del mundo, se obtendría importante progreso en cuanto a fuentes de material y de conocimientos. Esta creencia originó el asesoramiento y guía recibidos del personal directivo de estas organizaciones, aunque Rand McNally y Compañía ha retenido la responsabilidad principal como casa editora.

Las normas o política editorial del atlas se ha establecido teniendo en cuenta su uso internacional, y éste ha sido diseñado para el público de habla alemana, española, francesa, portuguesa e inglesa. Este carácter internacional se introdujo en los mapas mediante la utilización del sistema métrico y en particular, dando marcada preferencia al uso de vocablos locales en la nomenclatura. Virtualmente todo nombre se da en el idioma de la localidad, usándose el inglés únicamente en la identificación de elementos geográficos de mayor importancia que se extienden a través de las fronteras internacionales. En la mayoría de los mapas, los nombres de los países aparecen en inglés y en la forma oficial localmente utilizada.

Los términos genéricos de geografía física (montañas, islas, cabos, etc.), también aparecen en el idioma local, no en inglés. Al margen de la mayoría de los mapas se incluyen breves glosarios con la traducción de los más comunes de dichos términos. Se incluye también un glosario completo de los términos genéricos y en el índice del atlas, mediante un sistema de símbolos, se facilita la traducción de los mismos.

Igualmente, la amplitud que el atlas da a las distintas regiones del mundo, fue preparada con un criterio de utilización internacional. El espacio asignado a cada región refleja su posición económica y cultural relativa dentro del escenario mundial, así como su población y superficie. El resultado de esto ha sido el equilibrio aproximado resultante entre Angloamérica, Europa y Asia, ocupando, cada cual, más de la quinta parte del total de páginas dedicadas a mapas. Africa, Oceanía y América Latina juntas, cubren el resto del volumen. Los mapas índices, en las páginas xiii a xv, muestran, a escala, la extensión de las regiones que los mapas comprenden.

El segundo de los nuevo aspectos significativos del atlas, es el planeamiento de los mapas como componentes de cinco series separadas. Cada serie tiene un estilo y contenido propios. En la primera de estas series, los continentes están representados a una escala de 1:24 000 000, en colores naturales, como aparecerían al observar la tierra desde el espacio a una distancia de cerca de 6 500 kilómetros. La serie incluye también mapas de los océanos a escala 1:48 000 000 y del mundo a escala 1:75 000 000.

En la serie siguiente, las principales regiones del mundo están uniformemente representadas a escala 1:12 000 000 (120 km por cm). Estos mapas son básicamente políticos en su estilo y contenido. La tercera serie cubre prácticamente el total de la superficie habitada de la tierra, a una de dos escalas: 1:6 000 000 (60 km por cm), para las regiones menos densas, o 1:3 000 000 (30 km por cm), para Europa, la mayor parte de Norteamérica y las regiones de mayor densidad de población del Sur y Sureste de Asia. En esta serie se hace aproximadamente igual énfasis a los detalles de orden físico y cultural.

En la cuarta serie se ha usado la escala 1:1 000 000 (10 km por cm), para representar las regiones más notables en cada continente, seleccionadas por su excepcional importancia, alta densidad de población o complejidad de desarrollo. Acá, el énfasis es en el detalle cultural aunque también aparece el relieve utilizando la técnica de sombreado. La serie final la componen los mapas de las principales áreas urbanas del mundo a una escala de 1:300 000 (3 km por cm). Esta serie recalca los complejos patrones culturales característicos de las grandes áreas urbanas, omitiendo la representación del relieve.

Cada una de las series es en sí una serie integral desde el punto de vista de significación. Las tres primeras, con excepción de unas cuantas áreas remotas, son territorialmente completas; las dos últimas, son completas en cuanto a las regiones más densamente pobladas de la tierra.

La sucesión de los mapas en el atlas principia con la serie del mundo, los continentes y los océanos. Luego vienen las tres series de mapas regionales distribuídos dentro de cada región principal, de la escala menor, (1:12 000 000), a la escala mayor, (1:1 000 000). La serie de mapas de áreas metropolitanas (1:300 000), se ofrece en una sección, inmediatamente después de los mapas regionales.

En general, el trazado de cada mapa se hizo con miras a representar regiones geográficas y económicas, y no necesariamente países individuales. Así, el atlas contiene mapas de la Península Ibérica y de Europa Sudoriental, pero no mapas separados de Portugal o de Rumania. En unos pocos casos, esto impuso la necesidad de omitir alguna pequeña porción de la región o país descrito en el título del mapa. También se evitó la inserción de mapas detallando determinada área, aunque se hicieron excepciones para representar algunas islas o grupos de islas.

Los símbolos utilizados para ciertos elementos (Leyenda para Mapas, páginas x a xii), son en general similares en todas las escalas, aunque reducidos en tamaño en los mapas de escala más pequeña. Los usados más frecuentemente se encuentran en la página xi.

En ningún aspecto del diseño cartográfico se han hecho progresos tan notables en años recientes como en la representación del relieve del terreno. Los editores opinan, sin embargo, que el método más efectivo en este sentido es la vista a vuelo de pájaro o técnica de sombreado: la variación de tonos claros a obscuros indica gráficamente la pendiente y la configuración del relieve. Este atlas utiliza el sombreado en cuatro de las cinco series de mapas. En los mapas a escala 1:6 000 000 y 1:3 000 000, el sombreado se combina con tintes que indican los cambios de altitud mediante reflexión de la luz, colorido e intensidad variables.

En la última parte del atlas se ofrecen varias tablas y resúmenes para consulta. La Escena Mundial, (páginas 289 a 320), es una sección separada de mapas los cuales resumen los patrones del medio ambiente del hombre y algunas de sus más importantes actividades, alineaciones políticas y distribuciones culturales. Esta sección se basa en la información disponible más reciente tomada de diversas fuentes y compendiada por los editores. En seguida se encuentra un glosario completo de términos geográficos (páginas 321-327). La Tabla de Información Mundial, (páginas 328-331), muestra el área, la población y la situación de cada una de las principales unidades políticas. La lista de las áreas metropolitanas más grandes del mundo aparece en la página 332, y está seguida por una lista completa de las principales ciudades del mundo con indicación del número de habitantes, (páginas 333-338). Finalmente, el índice ofrece referencias para localizar en los mapas más de 160 000 nombres: página del mapa, latitud y longitud.

Avant-propos

L'HISTOIRE DES CARTES géographiques remonte aussi loin que celle des voyages, des découvertes et du sentiment de curiosité touchant le globe terrestre. Depuis les temps les plus reculés, les cartographes ont servi les marins en les aidant à s'orienter dans leurs voyages d'explorations, les monarques en leur fournissant des représentations de leurs territoires, les savants en les documentant sur la surface terrestre. De nos jours, les cartes jouent un rôle plus important encore, en ce qu'elles procurent aux hommes l'évidence tangible des liens joignant les uns aux autres peuples et nations du monde.

La fonction primordiale d'une carte consiste à représenter la surface du globe et la répartition des concentrations humaines qui s'y sont développées. Une carte ne fût-elle qu'un document objectif, point ne serait besoin de la réviser; mais justement, elle constitue bien davantage qu'une simple image. Considérablement réduite relativement à la réalité qu'elle représente, elle doit abstraire et généraliser à partir de cette réalité, par la sélection et l'interprétation des données jugées les plus significatives. De sorte que la cartographie doit non seulement établir les cartes des nouvelles régions du globe, mais il lui faut en outre refléter les progrès constants des techniques d'exposé de la documentation géographique à l'intention du lecteur.

Le siècle actuel a porté un défi suprême aux cartographes. Non seulement en ce que l'on y est témoin d'une demande toujours croissante de cartes à l'usage des spécialistes, de la part des gouvernements, des professeurs et des savants, mais aussi bien en ce que l'on y constate une proportion de plus en plus élevée de non-initiés avides d'utiliser des cartes de vulgarisation pour leurs affaires, leurs voyages, ou simplement leur plaisir.

Les Editeurs de *L'Atlas International* estiment, dès lors, qu'un nouvel ouvrage se doit d'être plus qu'une ancienne version mise à jour. Le but qu'ils se proposent consiste à sortir un atlas qui soit du plus haut intérêt et de la plus profonde valeur pour un vaste public de spécialistes et de profanes. Les Editeurs attirent l'attention des lecteurs sur plusieurs innovations apportées ici au cadre traditionnel de publication des atlas. Deux des plus significatives de ces innovations résident dans l'internationalisation de la conception et de l'exécution d'une part, d'autre part dans la disposition des cartes réparties en cinq séries distinctives. Envisagé et entrepris sur un mode international dès le début, cet Atlas s'est développé selon une conception, une forme éditoriale et une réalisation du même ordre. Rand McNally & Company jugeait que de sérieux avantages—apports importants en matériaux de documentation et en connaissances spécialisées faisant autorité—résulteraient d'une collaboration avec des organisations possédant de longue date une expérience cartographique des régions les plus diversifiées du globe. Les avis et les opinions émanant du personnel de cadres de ces organisations ont corroboré cette conviction, encore que Rand McNally en tant que société d'édition en assume la responsabilité principale.

D'usage international, destiné à des lecteurs de langue allemande, espagnole , française ou portugaise, tout autant qu'anglaise, cet Atlas a dû être édité sous une forme qui tînt compte de sa raison d'être. Cette conception internationale de l'Atlas a été réalisée sur les cartes elles-mêmes avec d'une part l'utilisation du système métrique, avec d'autre part l'emploi délibéré des noms géographiques sous leur forme nationale. Essentiellement, tous les noms apparaissent sous leur forme nationale, l'anglais n'étant utilisé que pour les noms d'importantes structures du relief qui s'étendent par-delà les frontières internationales. Sur la plupart des cartes, les noms des pays apparaissent à la fois en anglais et sous leur forme nationale officielle.

Les termes génériques désignant des structures de relief (montagne, île, cap, etc.) apparaissent également sous leur forme nationale, et non pas en anglais. En marge de la plupart des cartes, de courtes listes lexicales donnent la traduction des plus communs de ces termes. En outre, un glossaire donne tous les termes génériques dont la traduction se trouve par ailleurs facilitée grâce au système de symboles décrit dans l'Index de l'Atlas.

La répartition des régions du globe a été également déterminée en tenant compte de l'usage international qu'il sera fait de l'Atlas. L'espace attribué à chaque région reflète son importance économique et culturelle relative dans le monde, aussi bien que sa superficie et sa population. Il y a un équilibre approximatif entre l Amérique du Nord, l'Europe et l'Asie, chacune avec plus d'un cinquième de la totalité des pages. L'Afrique, l'Océanie et l'Amérique du Sud occupent le tiers restant. Les cartes index des pages xiii-xv présentent la répartition des cartes en fonction de l'échelle à laquelle elles sont reproduites.

La seconde des innovations importantes de cet Atlas réside dans la conception des cartes en tant qu'éléments constitutifs de cinq séries séparées. Style et contenu distinctifs caractérisent nettement chacune de ces cinq séries. Dans la première, les continents sont représentés à l'échelle de 1:24 000 000, en couleurs naturelles, tels qu'ils apparaîtraient, vus de l'espace, à 6 500 km. Cette série comprend également les cartes de océans à l'échelle de 1:48 000 000 et du monde à l'échelle de 1:75 000 000.

Dans la série suivante, les régions majeures du globe sont représentées de facon uniforme à l'échelle de 1:12 000 000 (120 km au cm). Par leur style et leur contenu, celles-ci sont essentiellement des cartes politiques. Dans la troisième série, virtuellement toute las surface habitée de la terre est représentée, soit à l'échelle de 1:6 000 000 (60 km au cm) pour les régions de moindre densité de population, soit à l'échelle de 1:3 000 000 (30 km au cm) pour l'Europe, la plus grande partie de l'Amérique du Nord et les portions de plus forte densité du Sud et de l'Est de l'Asie. Dans cette série, une importance à peu près égale a été accordée aux détails physiques et aux détails culturels.

Dans la quatrième série, l'échelle de 1:1 000 000 (10 km au cm) a été employée pour représenter certaines régionsclefs de chaque continent, choisies pour leur importance exceptionnelle, leur densité de population, ou la complexité de leur développement. L'accent porte sur les détails culturels, bien que le relief ombré apparaisse également. Une série finale souligne la répartition culturelle complexe, caractéristique des vastes zones urbaines, omettant le relief.

Chacune de ces séries est complète dans un mode significatif. Les trois premières sont complètes du point de vue territorial, exception faite de quelques lointaines contrées, et les deux dernières sont complètes en ce qui concerne les régions du globe de plus forte densité de population.

La succession des cartes de l'Atlas s'ouvre avec la série qui comprend les cartes du monde, des continents, et des océans. A sa suite, viennent les trois séries de cartes régionales disposées pour chaque région principale depuis les plus petites échelles (1:12 000 000), aux plus grandes (1:1 000 000). La série des cartes métropolitaines est groupée en une section qui fait suite aux cartes régionales.

La répartition individuelle des cartes a généralement été conçue en fonction des régions géographiques et économiques, plutôt qu'en fonction des frontières politiques nationales. De sorte qu'il y a des cartes de la Péninsule Ibérique et de l'Europe du Sud-Est, mais pas de cartes séparées pour le Portugal ou la Roumanie. Dans quelques cas, ceci a nécessité l'omission de quelque petite portion de la région ou du pays décrit dans le titre de la carte. Les insertions d'extensions ont également été évitées, encore que plusieurs exceptions aient été faites pour représenter certaines îles isolées ou certains groupes d'îles.

Les symboles employés sur les cartes sont en général identiques pour toutes les échelles de cartes, quoique de taille réduite sur les cartes à petite échelle. Les symboles les plus fréquemment employés ont été réunis à la page xi.

Aucun de aspects de la réalisation des cartes n'a fait de progrès plus prodigieux durant ces dernières années que la représentation cartographique du relief. Les Editeurs estiment que la méthode la plus efficace est celle de la "vue à vol d'oiseau", ou technique du relief ombré; celle-ci utilise toute la gamme des tons, des plus clairs aux plus foncés, pour indiquer picturalement l'inclinaison des pentes et la forme des structures du relief. Le relief ombré apparaît sur quatre des cinqu séries de cartes. Sur les cartes au 1:6 000 000e et au 1:3 000 000e, il apparaît en combinaison avec les teintes d'altitude qui indiquent les variations d'élévation au moyen de la réflexion de la lumière, de la nuance et de l'intensité.

Dans la dernière partie de l'Atlas, qui constitue sa conclusion, se trouvent divers tableaux de récapitulations et de références. La Scène du Monde (pages 289-320) occupe une section à part avec se cartes de sujets particuliers. Ces carte récapitulent les répartitions de l'environnement physique de l'homme, ainsi que certaines de ses activités économiques les plus importantes, les limite politiques et les distributions culturelles. Cette section s'appuie sur la plus récente documentation disponible provenant de sources diverses et adaptée par les editeurs. A sa suite se trouve le lexique complet des termes géographiques (pages 321-327). Puis une table d'informations mondiales donne la liste de toutes les unités politiques principales, avec superficie, population et statut politique de chacune (pages 328-331). La liste des plus importants centres urbains du monde est à la page 332. A la suite de cette table se trouve une liste complète des principales villes du monde avec leur population (pages 333-348). Enfin, l'Index fournit des références de cartes—numéros de pages, longitude et latitude—pour permettre de situer plus de 160 000 noms géographiques.

Prefácio

A HISTÓRIA DOS MAPAS é tão antiga quanto as das viagens, descobertas, e curiosidades sobre o mundo. Desde os primórdios tempos, cartógrafos têm servido à marinheiros orientando-os em suas explorações, monarcas com reproduções dos seus territórios, e acadêmicos com o registro da superfície da terra. Hoje, os mapas têm um papel mais importante-ainda, fornecendo ao homem provas das ligações que unem os países e os povos do mundo.

A função fundamental do mapa é de retratar a superfície da terra e os padrões da ocupação humana que sobre ela se desenvolveu. Se o mapa não fosse nada mais que um registro objetivo, não necessitaria de revisão; contudo, um mapa é mais do que um simples retrato. Grandemente reduzido em escala, em relação à realidade que representa, ele deve absorver e ao mesmo tempo generalizar a realidade, selecionando e interpretando os fatos supostamente de maior significado. Portanto, não somente é preciso que o cartógrafo registre novas regiões do mundo, mas também tente refletir um melhoramento contínuo nas técnicas de retratamento de informação geográfica para o usuário.

O século atual tem oferecido um grande desafio para confeccionadores de mapas. Não há somente o testemunho da crescente demanda por mapas de informações especializadas, pelos governos, professores e cientistas, mas também tem-se notado um número crescente de leigos, ansiosos em usar mapas em seus negócios, viagens, ou simplesmente como-passatempo.

Os Editores do *Atlas Internàcional* sentem, que um novo trabalho deveria ser maiś do que uma versão renovada dos trabalhos anteriores. O objetivo deveria ser de produzir um atlas de máximo valor e interêsse possível, para uma grande gama de especialistas e leigos. Neste prefácio, chamamos a atenção dos usuários para os vários aspectos-que são novos para os esquemas tradicionais de publicação de atlas. Os dois mais significantes são: a internacionalidade do seu planejamento e execução, e o arranjo de mapas como componentes de cinco séries distintas.

Desde o início, o atlas tem sido internacional em conceito, planejamento, política editorial e produção. Rand McNally & Company sentiu que haveriam ganhos importantes na fonte de material e conhecimento, pela participação de organizações com experiências cartográficas anteriores, nas mais diversas regiões do mundo. O conselho e orientação do quadro pessoal dessas organizações têm comprovado esta crença, apesar da Rand McNally & Company, como editor, ter retido a responsabilidade principal.

As políticas editoriais do Atlas têm sido estabelecidas visando o uso internacional, sendo designado para aqueles cuja língua nativa é Alemão, Espanhol, Francês ou Português, bem como Inglês. Essa técnica internacional tem sido executada em mapas, através da utilização do sistema métrico de medidas, e particularmente, pela grande ênfase no uso dos estilos locais para nomes geográficos. Essencialmente, todos os nomes estão em linguagem local, e o Inglês é usado somente para nomes de acidentes geográficos importantes, que se extendam através de fronteiras internacionais. Os nomes dos países-aparecem na maioria dos mapas, em Inglês, e em linguagem oficial local.

Termos genéricos para características físicas (montanhas, ilhas, cabos, etc.) aparecem também nas suas formas locais, não em Inglês. Pequenos glossários traduzindo estes têrmos mais comuns aparecem nas margens da maioria dos mapas. Há também um glossário completo de todos os termos genéricos. No índice dos atlas, a tradução dos termos genéricos é auxiliada pelo uso de um sistema de símbolos.

A cobertura das regiões do mundo tem sido visando a utilização internacional. O espaço atribuído para cada região reflete seu relativo significado econômico e cultural no cenário mundial, bem como sua população e área. Há um balanço aproximado entre Anglo-América, Europa e Ásia, cada qual com mais de um quinto do total de páginas. África, Oceania e América Latina, juntos, contam com o restante um terço. O mapa índice nas páginas xiii-xv mostra a cobertura do mapa de acordo com a escala.

Um novo aspecto secundário do Atlas, é o planejamento de mapas como componentes de cinco séries separadas. Cada série tem um estilo e conteúdo distinto. Na primeira dessas séries, os continentes são ilustrados em 1:24 000 00 em cores naturais, tal como elas apareceriam a 6.500 km de espaço. A série também inclui mapas dos oceanos em 1:48 000 000 e do mundo em 1:75 000 000.

Na série seguinte, as regiões principais do mundo estão uniformemente ilustradas em 1:12 000 000 (120 km por cm). Estes mapas são principalmente políticos no estilo e conteúdo. A terceira série virtualmente, cobre toda a área habitada da terra em 1:6 000 000 (60 km por cm) para as regiões menos densas, ou 1:3 000 000 (47 km por cm) para Europa, maioria da América do Norte, e a mais densa porção do Sul e Leste da Ásia. É dado ênfase de igual valor aos detalhes físicos e culturais nesta série.

Na quarta série, a escala de 1:1 000 000 (10 km por cm) tem sido usada para ilustrar regiões chaves em cada continente, selecionado pela sua excepcional importância, alta densidade populacional ou complexidade de desenvolvimento. A ênfase está no detalhe cultural, apesar de relêvo sombreado também aparecer. A série final mapeia as principais áreas urbanas mundiais em 1:300 000 (3 km por cm). Esta série enfatiza padrões complexos característicos de grandes áreas urbanas, omitindo a ilustração do relêvo.

Cada série de mapas é completa em um determinado senso. As três primeiras são territorialmente completas, exceto as poucas áreas remotas, e as duas últimas são também completas para as regiões mais densamente habitadas da terra.

A sequência de mapas no Atlas começa com a série de mapas do mundo, continentes e oceanos. Em seguida, estão as três séries de mapas regionais, arranjados dentro de regiões principais de escala mínima (1:12 000 000) para escala máxima (1:1 000 000). As séries de mapas metropolitanos (1:300 000) têm sido mantidas juntas em uma secção seguindo os mapas regionais.

As apresentações individuais dos mapas têm sido normalmente planejadas para ilustrar regiões geográficas e econômicas em vez de países individuais. Portanto, existem mapas da Península Ibérica e do Sudeste Europeu, mas não existem mapas separados para Portugal ou Romênia. Em alguns casos, foi necessária a omissão de pequena porção de uma região ou país, descrito no título do mapa. Têm sido evitados os mapas embutidos, apesar de terem sido feitas exceções para ilustrar algumas ilhas ou grupos de ilhas isolados.

Os símbolos dos mapas usados para as características dadas (legendas para mapas, páginas x-xii) são geralmente semelhantes em todas as escalas dos mapas, apesar de serem reduzidos em tamanho nas escalas menores. Os símbolos mais usados foram dispostos na página xi.

Nenhum aspecto de apresentação de mapas, mostrou-se mais dramático recentemente, do que a reprodução cartográfica do relêvo. Os editores acreditam que o método mais efetivo para representá-lo é a reprodução vista do alto ou a técnica do sombreamento das colinas, que usa variações de tonalidades claras para escuras, para indicar o declive e a forma dos aspectos dos relêvos, por meio de ilustrações. Este Atlas usa relêvo sombreado em todas as cinco séries de mapas, com exceção de uma. Nos mapas de 1:6 000 000 e 1:3 000 000, aparece em combinação com variações de cores das altitudes, que mostram variações em elevação por meio de reflexão da luz, matiz e intensidade.

Na porção conclusiva do Atlas, estão várias tabelas e sumários para referências gerais. O cenário do mundo (páginas 289-320) é uma secção separada dos mapas especializados. Estes mapas sintetizam os padrões do ambiente físico do homem e alguma das suas mais importantes atividades econômicas, tendências políticas e distribuições culturais. Esta secção está baseada nas mais recentes informações disponíveis, tomadas de uma variedade de fontes, e adaptadas pelos editores. Em seguida, está um glossário completo de termos geográficos (páginas 321-327). A tabela de informação mundial (páginas 328-331) registra a área, população e "status" político para cada unidade política principal. As maiores áreas metropolitanas do mundo, estão relacionadas na página 332. É seguido por uma lista completa das principais cidades do mundo, com as respectivas populações (páginas 333-348). Finalmente, o índice dá referências para a localização do mapa—página do mapa, latitude e longitude—com mais de 160 000 nomes.

SUMMARY OF CONTENTS

INHALTSVERZEICHNIS

SUMARIO DEL CONTENIDO

TABLE DES MATIÈRES

SUMÁRIO

List of Maps

WORLD, OCEAN, and CONTINENT MAPS

REGIONAL MAPS

Europe

Union of Soviet Socialist Republics

Asia

Africa

Australia/Oceania

Anglo America

Latin America

METROPOLITAN AREA MAPS (1:300,000)

***Scale in millions**

Kartenverzeichnis

WELTKARTEN, KARTEN DER OZEANE UND ERDTEILE

REGIONALKARTEN

EUROPA

Union der Sozialistischen Sowjetrepubliken

Asien

Afrika

Australien/Ozeanien

Anglo-Amerika

Latein-Amerika

KARTEN VON STADTREGIONEN (1:300 000)

***Im massstäb millionen**

Lista de Mapas

MAPAS DEL MUNDO, OCÉANOS Y CONTINENTES

***Escala en millones**

MAPAS REGIONALES

Europa

Unión de Repúblicas Socialistas Soviéticas

MAPAS DE LAS ÁREAS METROPOLITANAS (1:300 000)

Liste des Cartes

CARTES DU MONDE, DES OCÉANS ET DES CONTINENTS

CARTES RÉGIONALES

*Echelle en millions

Amérique Latine

CARTES DES ZONES MÉTROPOLITAINES (1 :300 000)

Lista de Mapas

MAPAS DO MUNDO, DOS OCEANOS E DOS CONTINENTES

MAPAS REGIONAIS

Europa

União das Repúblicas Socialistas Soviéticas

Ásia

África

Austrália/Oceania

América Anglosaxônica

América Latina

MAPAS DAS ÁREAS METROPOLITANAS (1 :300 000)

*Escalas em milhões

Legend to Maps/Zeichenerklärung
Leyendas Para Mapas/Légende des Cartes/Legendas dos Mapas

The design and color of the map symbols are consistent throughout the Regional and Metropolitan Area maps, although the size of the symbol varies with scale. An asterisk marks those symbols which appear only on the 1:300,000 scale maps. Symbols for inhabited localities, boundaries, and capitals are given on page xi.

The symbol 80-81 in the margin of a map directs the reader to a map of the adjoining area.

A separate legend on page 1 identifies the land and submarine features which appear on the World, Ocean, and Continent maps.

Der·Entwurf und die Farbe der Kartensymbole sind einheitlich für alle Regionalkarten und Karten von Stadtregionen, während die Grösse des Symbols sich mit dem Massstab ändert. Ein Stern kennzeichnet diejenigen Symbole, welche nur auf den Karten im Massstab 1:300 000 erscheinen. Symbole für bewohnte Orte, für Grenzen und Hauptstädte sind auf Seite xi angeführt.

Kennzeichen 80-81 am Rande einer Karte ist ein Hinweis für den Leser, die Karte eines angrenzenden Gebietes nachzuschlagen.

Eine andere Legende auf Seite 1 identifiziert die Land- und untermeerischen Phänomene, die auf den Weltkarten, Karten der Ozeane und Erdteile erscheinen.

El diseño y el color de los símbolos cartográficos son uniformes para todas los mapas regionales y de las áreas metropolitanas, aunque el tamaño del símbolo varía según la escala. Un asterisco distingue los símbolos que aparecen sólo en los mapas a 1:300 000. Los símbolos de lugares poblados, de límites y de capitales se hallan en la página xi.

El símbolo 80-81 al margen de un mapa dirige al lector a un mapa del área adyacente.

Otra leyenda, en la página 1, identifica la topografía terrestre y submarina que se encuentra en los mapas del Mundo, Océanos y Continentes.

La couleur et la forme des symboles cartographiques des cartes régionales et des cartes des zones métropolitaines sont identiques, bien que la grandeur des signes varie selon l'échelle. Un astérisque accompagne les symboles qui n'apparaissent que sur les cartes au 1:300 000. La légende des signes conventionnels pour les lieux habités, les frontières et les capitales se trouve à la page xi.

Le symbole 80-81 en marge d'une carte renvoie le lecteur à une carte de la région voisine.

Pour les cartes du monde, des océans et des continents une légende séparée, à la page 1, donne le sens des symboles représentant les paysages continentaux et les formes de relief sous-marin.

A cor e a forma dos símbolos cartográficos dos mapas regionais e das áreas metropolitanas são idênticos, ainda que a dimensão do símbolo varie segundo a escala. Um asterisco distingue os símbolos que só aparecem nos mapas da escala de 1:300 000. As legendas dos símbolos convencionais dos lugares povoados, fronteiras e capitais encontram-se à pág. xi.

O símbolo 80-81 à margem de um mapa, remete o leitor a um mapa da região vizinha.

Nos mapas do mundo, dos oceanos e dos continentes uma legenda separada, na pág. 1, indica o sentido dos símbolos representativos das paisagens continentais e das formas do relevo submarino.

Hydrographic Features / Hydrographische Objekte / Elementos Hidrográficos
Données Hydrographiques / Acidentes Hidrográficos

Shoreline/Uferlinie
Línea costanera/Trait de côte
Linha costeira

Undefined or Fluctuating Shoreline
Unbestimmte oder Veränderliche Uferlinie
Línea costanera indefinida o fluctuante
Trait de côte indéfini ou fluctuant
Linha costeira indefinida ou flutuante

Amur
River, Stream/Fluss, Strom
Río, Corriente/Rivière, Cours d'eau
Rio, curso d'água

Intermittent Stream/Periodischer Fluss
Corriente intermitente/Cours d'eau périodique
Rio, curso d'água intermitente

SALTO ANGEL
Rapids, Falls/Stromschnellen, Wasserfälle
Rápidos, Cascadas/Rapides, Chutes d'eau
Corredeiras, quedas d'água

764 ▿
Depth of Water/Wassertiefe
Profundidad del agua/Profondeur bathymétrique
Profundidade da água

8428 ▾
Greatest Depth (Atlantic, Indian, Pacific oceans)
Grösste Tiefe (Atlantischer, Indischer, Pazifischer Ozean)
Profundidad más grande (Océanos Atlántico, Índico, Pacífico)
Profondeur maximum (océans Atlantique, Indien, Pacifique)
Profundidade máxima (oceanos Atlântico, Índico, Pacífico)

Canal du Midi
Navigable Canal/Schiffbarer Kanal
Canal navegable/Canal navigable
Canal navegável

Irrigation or Drainage Canal
Be- oder Entwässerungskanal
Canal de irrigación o desagüe
Canal d'irrigation ou de drainage
Canal de irrigação ou drenagem

Los Angeles Aqueduct
Aqueduct/Aquädukt
Acueducto/Aqueduc
Aqueduto

Pier, Breakwater/Landungsbrücke, Wellenbrecher
Embarcadero, Rompeolas/Jetée, Brise-lames
Cais, Quebra-mar

GREAT BARRIER REEF
Reef/Riff
Arrecife/Récif
Recife

Kumdah
Uninhabited Oasis/Unbewohnte Oase
Oasis deshabitado/Oasis inhabitée
Oásis desabitado

L. Victoria
Lake, Reservoir/See, Stausee
Lago, Embalse/Lac, Réservoir
Lago, reservatório (represa)

Intermittent Lake, Reservoir
Periodischer See, Stausee
Lago o Embalse intermitente
Lac ou Réservoir périodique
Lago, reservatório (represa) **intermitent**

Tuz Gölü
Salt Lake/Salzsee
Lago salado/Lac salé
Lago salgado

Dry Lake Bed/Trockener Seeboden
Lecho de lago seco/Fond de lac asséch
Leito de lago seco

The Everglades
Swamp/Sumpf
Pantano/Marais
Pântano

RIMO GLACIER
Glacier/Gletscher
Glaciar/Glacier
Geleira

(395)
Lake Surface Elevation
Seehöhe
Elevación del lago
Cote du niveau du lac
Altitude do nível do lago

Topographic Features / Topographische Objekte / Elementos Topográficos
Données Topographiques / Acidentes Topográficos

Matterhorn △ 4478
Elevation Above Sea Level
Höhe über dem Meeresspiegel
Elevatión sobre del nivel del mar
Cote au-dessus du niveau de la mer
Altitude acima do nível do mar

76 ▿
Elevation Below Sea Level
Höhe unter dem Meeresspiegel
Elevación bajo del nivel del mar
Cote au-dessous du niveau de la mer
Altitude abaixo do nível do mar

Mount Cook ▲ 3764
Highest Elevation in Country
Höchster Punkt des Landes
Elevación más alta en el país
Cote la plus élevée d'un pays
Altitude mais elevada de um país

133 ▾
Lowest Elevation in Country
Tiefster Punkt des Landes
Elevación más baja en el país
Cote la plus basse d'un pays
Altitude mais baixa de um país

(106)
Elevation of City
Höhenangabe einer Stadt
Elevación de ciudad
Altitude d'une ville
Altitude de uma cidade

Khyber Pass 1067
Mountain Pass/Pass
Paso/Col de montagne
Passo (de montanha)

*
Rock/Fels
Roca/Rocher
Rocha

Lava/Lava
Lava/Lave
Lava

Sand Area/Sandgebiet
Area de arena/Région sableuse, Erg
Região arenosa, Erg

Salt Flat/Salzebene
Salar/Dépression salée
Depressão salgada

Elevations and depths are given in meters
Höhen und Tiefen sind in Metern angegeben
Elevaciones y profundidades se dan en metros
Cotes et profondeurs sont indiquées en mètres
Altitudes e profundidades são apresentadas em metros

A N D E S
KUNLUNSHANMAI
Mountain Range, Plateau, Valley, etc.
Gebirge, Hochebene, Tal, usw.
Sierra, Meseta, Valle, etc.
Chaîne de montagnes, Plateau, Vallée, etc.
Cadeia de montanhas. Planalto, Vale etc.

BAFFIN ISLAND
NUNIVAK ISLAND
Island
Insel
Isla
Île
Ilha

POLUOSTROV KAMČATKA
CABO DE HORNOS
Peninsula, Cape, Point, etc.
Halbinsel, Kap, Landspitze, usw.
Península, Cabo, Punta, etc.
Péninsule, Cap, Pointe, etc.
Península, Cabo, Ponta etc.

Highest Elevation and Lowest Elevation of a continent are underlined
Höchster und tiefster Punkt innerhalb eines Erdteils sind unterstrichen
Elevación más alta y más baja de un continente se subrayan
La cote la plus haute et la cote la plus basse d'un continent sont soulignées
As altitudes mais e menos elevadas de um continente são sublinhadas

Legend to Maps / Zeichenerklärung
Leyendas Para Mapas / Légende des Cartes / Legendas dos Mapas

Inhabited Localities / Bewohnte Orte / Lugares Poblados / Lieux Habités / Lugares Habitados

The symbol represents the number of inhabitants within the locality / Die Signatur entspricht der Einwohnerzahl des Ortes
El símbolo representa el número de habitantes dentro del lugar / Le symbole représente le nombre d'habitants de la localité
O símbolo representa o número de habitantes do lugar

1:300,000 / 1:3,000,000 / 1:1,000,000 / 1:6,000,000		1:12,000,000		1:24,000,000 / 1:48,000,000	
·	0—10,000	·	0—50,000	·	0—100,000
○	10,000—25,000	◉	50,000—100,000	◉	100,000—1,500,000
◉	25,000—100,000	▣	100,000—250,000	■	>1,500,000
▣	100,000—250,000	▣	250,000—1,000,000		
▣	250,000—1,000,000	■	>1,000,000		
■	>1,000,000				

The size of type indicates the relative economic and political importance of the locality
Die Schriftgrösse entspricht der relativen wirtschaftlichen und politischen Bedeutung des Ortes
El tamaño del tipo de imprenta indica la relativa importancia económica y política del lugar
La dimension des caractères indique l'importance économique et politique relative d'une localité
A dimensão dos caracteres tipográficos indica a importância econômica e política relativa do lugar

Écommoy	Lisieux	**Rouen**
Trouville	**Orléans**	**PARIS**

Hollywood ▫ *Westminster* — Section of a City, Neighborhood / Stadtteil, Nachbarschaft
Sección de una ciudad, Barrio / Arrondissement, Quartier
Seção de uma cidade, Bairro

Northland Center ■ — * Major Shopping Center / Haupteinkaufszentrum / Mercado principal
Centre commercial important / Centro comercial importante

BYRD ▫ — Scientific Station / Wissenschaftliche Station / Estación científica
Station scientifique / Estação científica

Bi'r Safājah ° — Inhabited Oasis / Bewohnte Oase / Oasis habitado
Oasis habitée / Oásis habitado

Kumdah ° — Uninhabited Oasis / Unbewohnte Oase / Oasis deshabitado
Oasis inhabitée / Oásis desabitado

Urban Area (area of continuous industrial, commercial, and residential development)
Stadtgebiet (ausgedehntes industrie-, Geschäfts- und Wohngebiet)
Zona urbanizada (área de desarrollo industrial, comercial y residencial)
Zone urbanisée (zone d'occupation continue par des industries, des commerces, des habitations)
Zona urbanizada (área de ocupação contínua por indústrias, estabelecimentos comerciais e habitações)

* Major Industrial Area / Hauptindustriegebiet / Zona principal industrial
Région industrielle importante / Zona industrial importante

* Wooded Area / Wald / Área de bosque
Région boisée / Área verde

* Local Park or Recreational Area / Park oder Erholungsgebiet
Parque municipal o área de recreo / Parc municipal ou zone de loisirs
Parque municipal ou área de lazer

Political Boundaries / Politische Grenzen / Límites Políticos / Frontières Politiques / Fronteiras e Limites

International (First-order political unit) / **Staatsgrenze** (Politische Einheit erster Ordnung)
Internacionales (Unidad política de primer orden) / **Internationales** (Entités politiques de premier ordre)
Internacionais (Unidade política de primeiro nível)

1:300,000 / 1:1,000,000 / 1:3,000,000 / 1:6,000,000 — 1:24,000,000 / 1:48,000,000 — 1:12,000,000

HUNGARY — Demarcated, Undemarcated, and Administrative
Markiert, unmarkiert, verwaltungstechnisch
Demarcado, No demarcado, y Administrativo
Délimitées, Non-délimitées, Administratives
Delimitados, Não delimitados, Administrativos

Disputed de facto / Umstritten de facto
Disputado de hecho / Contestées de facto
Contestados de fato

Disputed de jure / Umstritten de jure
Disputado de derecho / Contestées de jure
Contestados de direito

Indefinite or Undefined / Unklar oder Unbestimmt
Indefinido o No determinado / Imprécises ou Non définies
Imprecisos ou Não definidos

Demarcation Line / Demarkationslinie
Línea de demarcación / Ligne de démarcation
Linha de demarcação (utilizada na Coréia)

Capitals of Political Units
Hauptstädte politischer Einheiten
Capitales de Unidades Políticas
Capitales d'Entités Politiques
Capitais de Unidades Políticas

BUDAPEST — Independent Nation
Unabhängiger Staat
Nación independiente
État indépendant
Estado independente

Cayenne — Dependency (Colony, protectorate, etc.)
Abhängiges Gebiet (Kolonie, Protektorat, usw.)
Dependencia (Colonia, protectorado, etc.)
Territoire dépendant (Colonie, protectorat, etc.)
Dependência (Colônia, protetorado, etc.)

GALAPAGOS (Ecuador) — Administering Country
Verwaltender Staat
País administrador
Pays administrateur
País administrador

Internal / Verwaltungsgrenze / Internos / Intérieures / Limites Internos

PERNAMBUCO — **State, Province, etc.** (Second-order political unit)
Land, Provinz, usw. (Politische Einheit zweiter Ordnung)
Estado, Provincia, etc. (Unidad política de segundo orden)
État, Province, etc. (Subdivision administrative de deuxième ordre)
Estado, Província, etc. (Unidade política de segundo nível)

Recife — State, Province, etc. / Land, Provinz, usw.
Estado, Provincia, etc. / État, Province, etc.
Estado, Província, etc.

WESTCHESTER — **County, Oblast, etc.** (Third-order political unit) / **Grafschaft, Oblast, usw.** (Politische Einheit dritter Ordnung)
Condado, Oblast, etc. (Unidad política de tercer orden)
Comté, Oblast, etc. (Subdivision administrative de troisième ordre)
Condado, Oblast, etc. (Unidade política de terceiro nível)

White Plains — County, Oblast, etc. / Grafschaft, Oblast, usw.
Condado, Oblast, etc. / Comté, Oblast, etc.
Condado, Oblast, etc.

ISERLOHN — **Okrug, Kreis, etc.** (Fourth-order political unit) / **Okrug, Kreis, usw.** (Politische Einheit vierter Ordnung)
Okrug, Kreis, etc. (Unidad política de cuarto orden)
Okrug, Kreis, etc. (Subdivision administrative de quatrième ordre)
Okrug, Kreis, etc. (Unidade política de quarto nível)

Iserlohn — Okrug, Kreis, etc. / Okrug, Kreis, usw.
Okrug, Kreis, etc. / Okrug, Kreis, etc.
Okrug, Kreis, etc.

City or Municipality (may appear in combination with another boundary symbol)
Stadt oder Gemeinde (kann zusammen mit einem anderen Begrenzungssymbol erscheinen)
Ciudad o Municipio (puede aparecer en combinación con otro símbolo de límite)
Ville ou Municipalité (peut paraître en combinaison avec un autre symbole de limites politiques)
Cidade ou Municipalidade (Pode aparecer em combinação com outro símbolo de limite político)

ANDALUCÍA — **Historical Region** (No boundaries indicated)
Historische Landschaft (Grenzen werden nicht gezeigt)
Región Histórica (Sin indicación de límites)
Région Historique (Sans indication de frontières)
Região Histórica (Sem indicação de fronteiras)

Legend to Maps/Zeichenerklärung
Leyendas Para Mapas/Légende des Cartes/Legendas dos Mapas

Transportation /Verkehr /Transporte /Transports /Transporte

Road/Strasse/Camino/Route/Rodovia	1:300,000	1:1,000,000	1:3,000,000 1:6,000,000	1:12,000,000
Primary/Erster Ordnung/Principal/de premier ordre/Principal	PASSAIC EXPWY. (I-80)	PENNSYLVANIA TURNPIKE		
Secondary/Zweiter Ordnung/Secundario/de second ordre/Secundária	BERLINER RING			
Tertiary/Dritter Ordnung/Terciario/de troisième ordre/Terciária				
Minor Road, Trail/Weg, Pfad Rodera, Vereda/Route secondaire, Piste/Caminho, trilha				

Railway/Eisenbahn/Ferrocarril/Voie ferrée/Ferrovia

Primary/Hauptbahn/Principal/Principale/Principal — CANADIAN NATIONAL — SANTA FE

Secondary/Sonstige Bahn/Secundario/Secondaire/Secundária

*Rapid Transit/Schnellverkehr/Tránsito rápido/Métro/Trânsito rápido (metrô)

Airport/Flughafen/Aeropuerto/Aéroport/Aeroporto — LONDON (HEATHROW) AIRPORT — DULLES INTERNATIONAL AIRPORT

*Rail or Air Terminal/Bahnhof oder Flughafengebäude
Terminal ferroviaria o aéro/Gare ou aérogare
Terminal ferroviário ou aéreo (estação) — SÜD-BAHNHOF

REICHS-BRÜCKE — Bridge/Brücke/Puente/Pont/Ponte

GREAT ST. BERNARD TUNNEL — Tunnel/Tunnel/Túnel/Tunnel/Túnel

Houston Ship Channel — Shipping Channel/Schiffahrtsrinne
Canal maritimo/Chenal maritime
Canal marítimo

Canal du Midi — Navigable Canal/Schiffbarer Kanal
Canal navegable/Canal navigable
Canal navegável

Intracoastal Waterway/Küstenschiffahrtsweg
Via fluvial Intracostera/Canal côtier
Via costeira interna

TO MALMÖ — Ferry/Fähre
Balsadera/Bac
Balsa

Miscellaneous Cultural Features / Sonstige Objekte / Elementos Culturales Misceláneos
Éléments Culturels Divers / Acidentes Culturais Diversos

PARQUE NACIONAL LANÍN — National or State Park or Monument
National- oder Naturpark oder Denkmal
Parque o Monumento nacional o provincial
Parc ou Monument national ou régional
Parque ou Monumento nacional ou regional

EDISON NAT. HIST. SITE — National or State Historic(al) Site, Memorial
Historische Stätte, Gedenkstätte
Sitio histórico nacional o provincial, Monumento
Site historique national ou régional, Mémorial
Sitio histórico nacional ou regional, Monumento histórico

SEMINOLE IND. RES. — Indian Reservation/Indianerreservation
Reserva de indios/Réserve indienne
Reserva indígena

FORT DIX — Military Installation/Militäranlage
Instalación militar/Installation militaire
Instalação militar

GREENWOOD CEMETERY — * Cemetery/Friedhof
Cementerio/Cimetière/Cemitério

SORBONNE — **Point of Interest** (Battlefield, museum, temple, university, etc.)
Sehenswürdigkeit (Schlachtfeld, Museum, Tempel, Universität, usw.)
Punto de interés (Campo de batalla, museo, templo, universidad, etc.)
Curiosité (Champ de bataille, musée, temple, université, etc.)
Pontos de interesse (Campo de batalha, museu, templo, universidade, etc.)

STEPHANSDOM — Church, Monastery/Kirche, Kloster
Iglesia, Monasterio/Église, Monastère
Igreja, Mosteiro

UXMAL — Ruins/Ruinen/Ruinas/Ruines/Ruínas

WINDSOR CASTLE — Castle/Burg, Schloss/Castillo/Château/Castelo

* Lighthouse/Leuchtturm
Faro/Phare/Farol

ASWĀN DAM — Dam/Damm/Presa/Barrage
Represa (barragem)

* Lock/Schleuse/Esclusa
Écluse/Eclusa

Crib — * Water Intake Crib/Wasseraufnahmestation
Toma de agua/Prise d'eau/Captação de água

Quarry or Surface Mine
Steinbruch oder Tagebau
Cantera o Mina de hoyo abierto
Carrière ou Mine à ciel ouvert
Pedreira ou mina a céu aberto

Subsurface Mine/Bergwerk
Mina subterránea/Mine souterraine
Mina subterrânea

* Oil Well/Ölbohrturm
Pozo de petróleo/Puits de pétrole
Poço de petróleo

Metric-English Equivalents / Umrechnung metrischer Masse in englische Masse / Métrico-Equivalentes Ingleses
Equivalences métriques des mesures anglaises / Equivalentes métricos das medidas inglesas

Areas represented by one square centimeter at various map scales
Flächen die einem cm² in den verschiedenen Kartenmassstäben entsprechen
Áreas representados por un centímetro cuadrado a varias escalas de mapas
Surface représentée par un cm² aux échelles indiquées
Áreas representadas por cm² nas escalas indicadas nos mapas

Meter=3.28 feet — Meter² (m²)=10.76 square feet
Kilometer=0.62 mile — Kilometer² (km²)=0.39 square mile

1:300,000 9 km² 3.48 square miles	1:6,000,000 3,600 km² 1,390 square miles	1:48,000,000 230,400 km² 88,934 square miles
1:1,000,000 100 km² 39 square miles	1:12,000,000 14,400 km² 5,558 square miles	
1:3,000,000 900 km² 348 square miles	1:24,000,000 57,600 km² 22,234 square miles	

Elevation tints shown only on 1:3,000,000 and 1:6,000,000 scale maps
Höhenschichten erscheinen nur auf Karten im Massstab 1:3 000 000 und 1:6 000 000
Se indica las tintas de elevación sólo en los mapas de escala 1:3 000 000 y 1:6 000 000
Teintes hypsométriques exprimées seulement sur cartes à 1:3 000 000 et 1:6 000 000
Indicaram-se as graduações de cor hipsométricas somente nos mapas de escalas 1:3 000 000 e 1:6 000 000

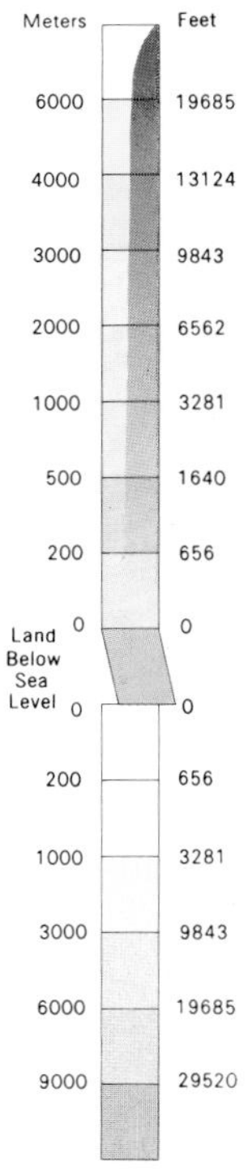

Meters
Feet
6000
19685
4000
13124
3000
9843
2000
6562
1000
3281
500
1640
200
656
Land Below Sea Level
0
0
0
0
200
656
1000
3281
3000
9843
6000
19685
9000
29520

Alternate Names / Alternative Namensformen / Nombres Alternativos
Variantes Toponymiques / Variantes Toponímicas

MOSKVA
MOSCOW

Basel
Bâle

English or second official language names are shown in reduced size lettering
Englische Namen oder Namen in einer zweiten offiziellen Sprache erscheinen in kleineren Schriftgrössen
Los nombres en inglés o un segundo idioma oficial se muestran en tipo de imprenta mas pequeño
Les toponymes en anglais ou dans la seconde langue officielle sont indiqués en caractères plus petits
Os topônimos em inglês ou num segundo idioma oficial aparecem em tipologia menor

VOLGOGRAD
(STALINGRAD)

Ventura
(San Buenaventura)

Historical or other alternates in the local language are shown in parentheses
Historische oder alternative Namensformen einheimischen Sprache erscheinen in Klammern
Los nombres históricos y alternativos locales se muestran en paréntesis
Les noms historiques de lieux ou les variantes toponymiques locales sont mis entre parenthèses
Os topônimos históricos ou as variantes toponímicas locais aparecem entre parênteses

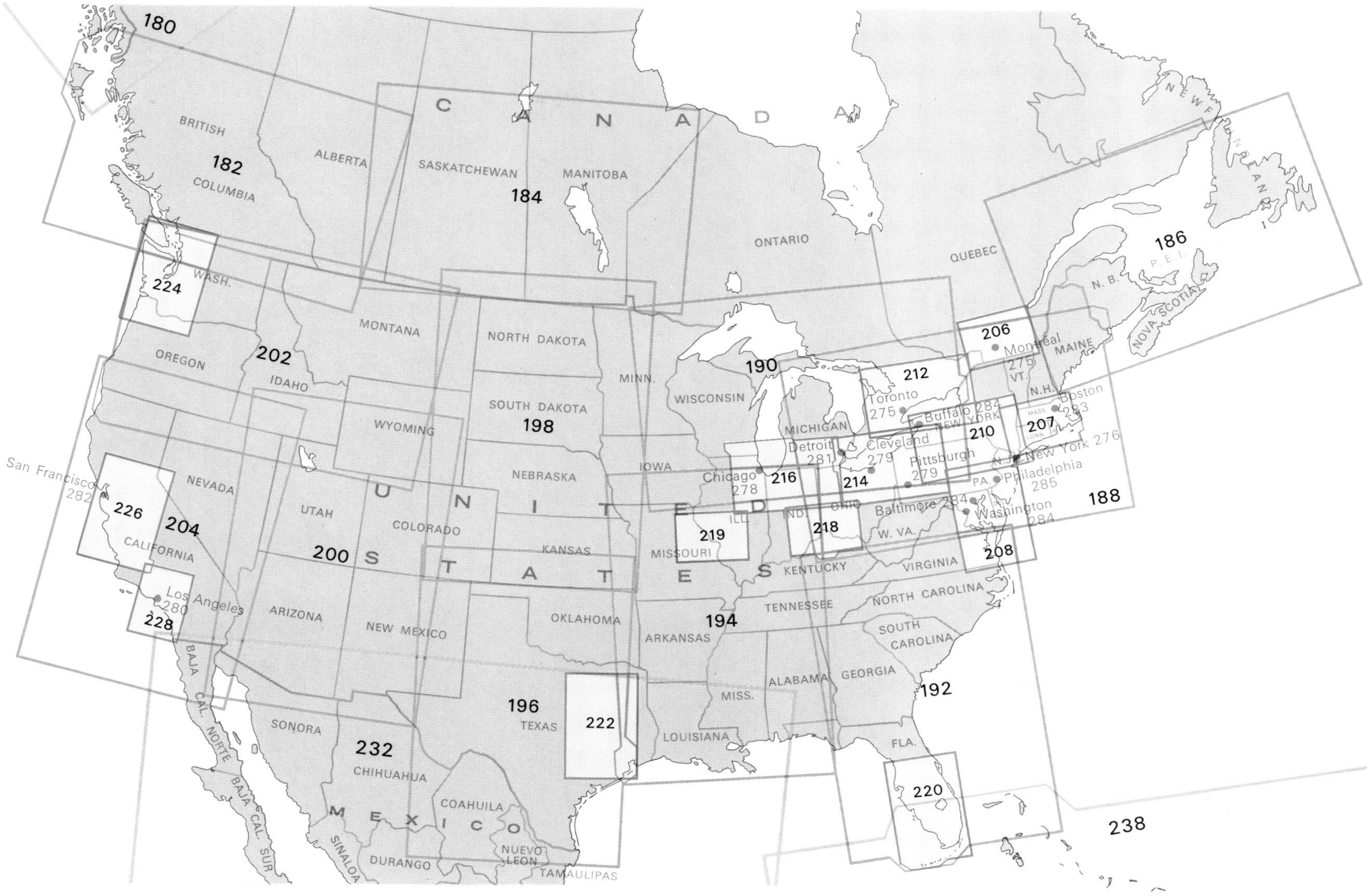
180
BRITISH
182
COLUMBIA
ALBERTA
C A N A D A
SASKATCHEWAN
MANITOBA
184
ONTARIO
QUEBEC
186
N.B.
P.E.I.
NOVA SCOTIA
NEWFOUNDLAND
224
WASH.
MONTANA
NORTH DAKOTA
OREGON
202
IDAHO
MINN.
190
WISCONSIN
206
Montreal
275
MAINE
212
Toronto
275
Boston
283
207
N.H.
VT.
SOUTH DAKOTA
198
WYOMING
MICHIGAN
Buffalo 284
NEW YORK
210
Detroit
281
Cleveland
279
Pittsburgh
279
New York 276
San Francisco
282
NEVADA
NEBRASKA
IOWA
Chicago
278
216
214
PA.
Philadelphia
285
226
204
UTAH
U N I T E D S T A T E S
COLORADO
ILL.
IND.
OHIO
Baltimore 284
Washington
284
188
CALIFORNIA
200
KANSAS
MISSOURI
219
218
W. VA.
208
Los Angeles
280
228
ARIZONA
NEW MEXICO
OKLAHOMA
KENTUCKY
VIRGINIA
TENNESSEE
NORTH CAROLINA
194
ARKANSAS
SOUTH CAROLINA
ALABAMA
GEORGIA
MISS.
192
BAJA CAL. NORTE
196
TEXAS
222
SONORA
LOUISIANA
232
CHIHUAHUA
FLA.
COAHUILA
220
M E X I C O
BAJA CAL. SUR
SINALOA
DURANGO
NUEVO LEON
TAMAULIPAS
238

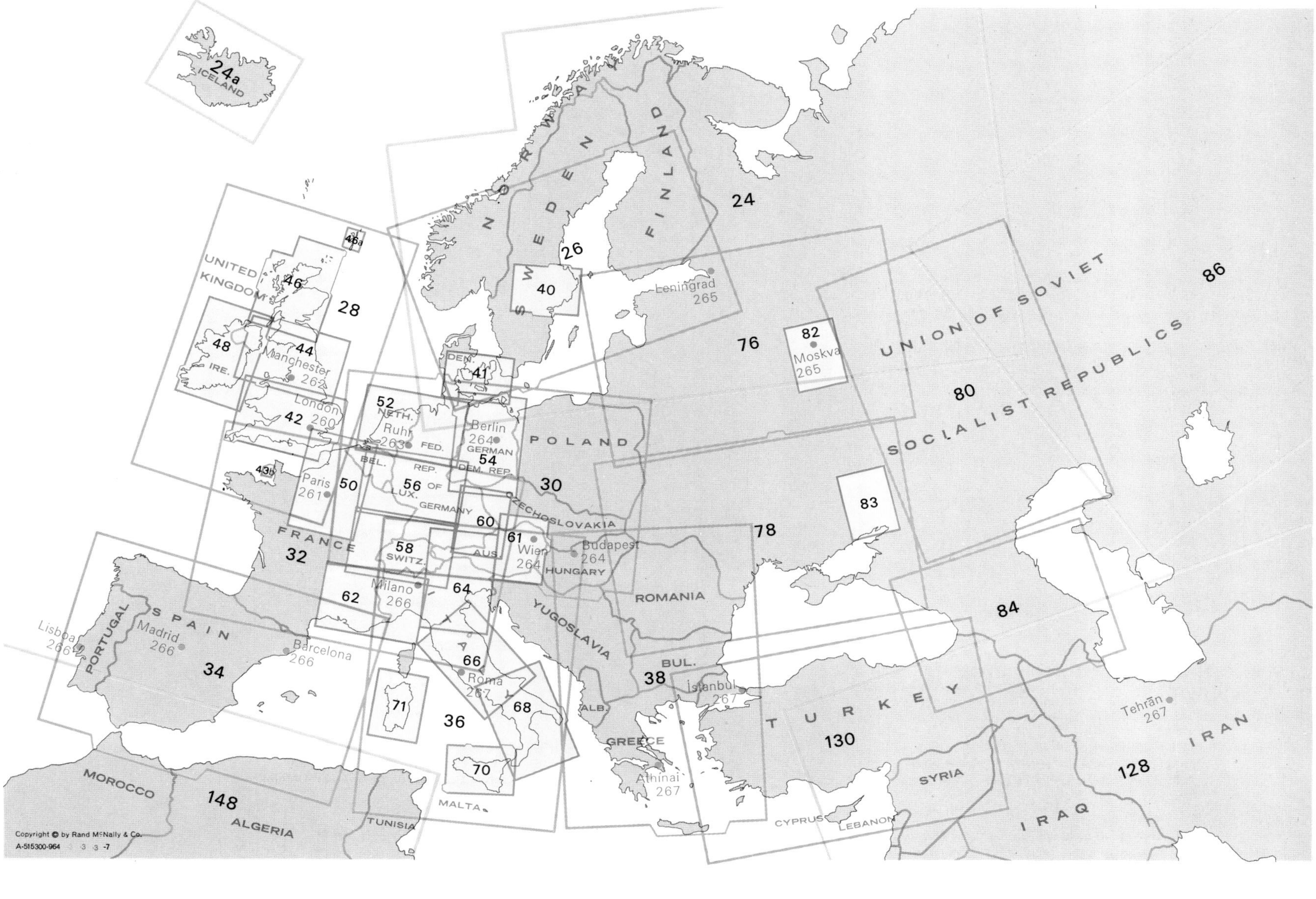
24a
ICELAND
N O R W A Y
S W E D E N
F I N L A N D
24
46a
UNITED KINGDOM
46
28
26
40
Leningrad
265
48
IRE.
44
Manchester
262
82
Moskva
265
76
UNION OF SOVIET
SOCIALIST REPUBLICS
86
80
DEN.
41
52
NETH.
London
260
Berlin
264
42
Ruhr
263
FED.
REP.
OF
GERMANY
GERMAN
DEM. REP.
54
POLAND
43b
BEL.
LUX.
Paris
261
50
56
30
CZECHOSLOVAKIA
83
60
F R A N C E
61
78
32
58
SWITZ.
AUS.
Wien
264
Budapest
264
HUNGARY
Milano
266
64
62
ROMANIA
84
Lisboa
266
PORTUGAL
S P A I N
Madrid
266
Barcelona
266
I T A L Y
YUGOSLAVIA
BUL.
66
Roma
267
38
İstanbul
267
T U R K E Y
34
71
36
68
ALB.
Tehrān
267
GREECE
130
I R A N
70
Athínai
267
SYRIA
128
MOROCCO
148
MALTA
ALGERIA
TUNISIA
CYPRUS
LEBANON
I R A Q

MAP COVERAGE / KARTENAUSSCHNITTE
CONTENIDO DEL ATLAS / TABLEAU D'ASSEMBLAGE
ABRANGÊNCIA DO MAPA

Map Scale

Manila 269 • 1:300,000

1:1,000,000

1:6,000,000

1:3,000,000

1:12,000,000

148 Page Reference / Seitenangabe
Página de Referencia / Page de Référence / Página de Referência

Enlarged maps of Anglo-America and Europe on page xiii.
Vergrösserte Karten von Anglo-Amerika und Europa auf Seite xiii.
Mapas aumentados de América Anglosajona y Europa, página xiii.
Cartes à grande échelle de l'Amérique anglo-saxonne et de l'Europe à la page xiii.
Mapas ampliados da América Anglo-saxônica e da Europa, página xiii.

World, Ocean, and Continent maps on pages 2-19.
Weltkarten, Karten der Ozeane und Erdteile auf Seiten 2-19.
Mapas del Mundo, Océanos y Continentes, páginas 2-19.
Cartes du Monde, des Océans et des Continents aux pages 2-19.
Mapas do Mundo, dos Oceanos e dos Continentes, páginas 2-19.

Additional Pacific Ocean Island maps on pages 174-175.
Zusätzliche Karten der Inseln des Pazifischen Ozeans auf Seite 174-175.
Mapas adicionales de las Islas del Océano Pacifico, páginas174-175.
Cartes supplémentaires des Îles de l'Océan Pacifique aux pages 174-175.
Mapas suplementares das ilhas do Oceano Pacífico, páginas 174-175.

UNION OF SOVIET SOCIALIST REPUBLICS
24
76
80
86
88
89
78
Black Sea
Caspian Sea
84
85
TURKEY
130
MONGOLIA
CHINA
KOREA
92
94
96
98
104
105
Beijing (Peking) 271
Seoul 271
Shanghai 269
106
100
102
107
93b
174m
175d
T'aipei 269
TAIWAN
Hong Kong
SYRIA
CYPRUS
LEBANON
ISRAEL
JORDAN
IRAQ
128
IRAN
Tehrān 267
AFGHANISTAN
PAKISTAN
123
120
NEPAL
Delhi 272
124
INDIA
Calcutta 272
126
BURMA
LAOS
VIETNAM
THAILAND
Krung Thep (Bangkok) 269
KAMPUCHEA
Thanh-pho Ho Chi Minh (Saigon) 269
110
Bombay 272
122
SRI LANKA
132
142
EGYPT
SAUDI ARABIA
OMAN
Red Sea
140
SUDAN
YEMEN
P.D.R. OF YEMEN
DJIBOUTI
144
ETHIOPIA
SOMALIA
KENYA
UGANDA
RWANDA
BURUNDI
TANZANIA
154
COMOROS
157a
MALAWI
MOZAMBIQUE
ZAMBIA
ZIMBABWE
MADAGASCAR
157b
157c
MAURITIUS
REUNION
SWAZILAND
LESOTHO
Indian Ocean
Pacific Ocean
175c
TRUK ISLANDS
175b
PALAU ISLANDS
Manila 269
116
PHILIPPINES
MALAYSIA
114
SUMATRA
Singapore 271
BORNEO
112
CELEBES
INDONESIA
Jakarta 269
115a
115b
JAVA
LESSER SUNDA ISLANDS
PAPUA NEW GUINEA
NEW GUINEA
164
SOLOMON ISLANDS
175e
VANUATU
NEW CALEDONIA
175f
175g
FIJI
AUSTRALIA
162
166
171a
168a
168b
170
Sydney 274
171b
169
Melbourne 274
TASMANIA
NEW ZEALAND
172

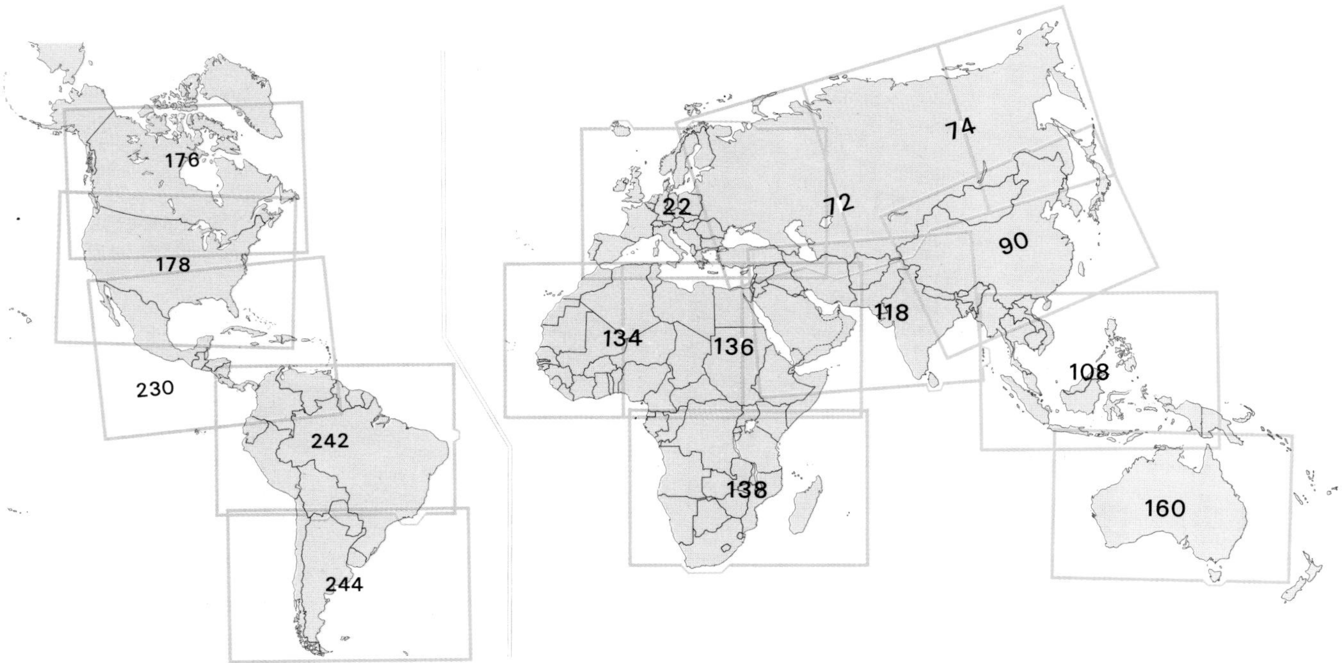
176
178
230
242
244
22
72
74
90
134
136
118
108
138
160

THIS SECTION OPENS with World Political and World Physical maps at the scale of 1:75,000,000. There follow maps of the Pacific, Indian, and Atlantic oceans at the scale 1:48,000,000, the largest scale at which the total expanse of these bodies of water could be portrayed. Finally, a series of continent relief maps at the scale of 1:24,000,000 show a global view of the earth as it would appear from about 4,000 miles in space. The Azimuthal Equal-Area projection is used for the 1:24,000,000 maps, the scale being approximately that of a globe 20 inches in diameter.

The colors of the continent maps portray the land areas as if viewed from space during the growing season, without regard to the fact that the growing seasons are not concurrent in all areas. Underwater features and varying water depths are represented by shaded relief and different color tones. The result is a strong physical portrait of the earth's major land and submarine forms. The legend below shows how these different kinds of terrain and vegetation have been represented. The names of physical features—plateaus, basins, mountain ranges, seas, rivers, lakes, gulfs, trenches, bays, islands—predominate on these maps.

DIESER KARTENTEIL BEGINNT mit politischen und physischen Weltkarten im Massstab 1:75 Millionen. Dann folgen Karten des Pazifischen, Indischen und Atlantischen Ozeans in 1:48 Millionen, dem grössten Massstab, in dem diese Wasserflächen in ihrer ganzen Ausdehnung abgebildet werden konnten. Schliesslich folgt eine Reihe von Reliefkarten der Erdteile in 1:24 Millionen. Sie geben eine Übersicht der Erde, wie sie aus einer Entfernung von ungefähr 6 400 Kilometer aus dem Weltraum gewonnen würde. Den Karten im Massstab 1:24 Millionen liegt ein flächentreuer azimutaler Entwurf zugrunde, dieser Massstab entspricht ungefähr dem eines Globus von 50 cm Durchmesser.

Die Farben der Erdteilkarten bilden jedes Landgebiet so ab, wie es in der Vegetationsperiode aus der Vogelperspektive erschiene, ohne zu berücksichtigen, dass die Vegetationsperioden nicht in allen Gebieten gleichzeitig eintreten. Die Gliederung des Meeresbodens und die unterschiedlichen Meerestiefen werden durch Schummerung und verschiedene Farbstufen dargestellt. Das Ergebnis ist eine anschauliche physische Darstellung der wichtigsten terrestrischen und untermeerischen Formen der Erde. Die untenstehende Zeichenerklärung zeigt, wie diese verschiedenen Geländeformen und Vegetationsgebiete veranschaulicht werden. Namen physischer Objekte—Hochebenen, Becken, Gebirgszüge, Meere, Flüsse, Seen, Buchten, Gräben, Inseln—herrschen in diesen Karten vor.

ESTA SECCIÓN DA PRINCIPIO con los Mapas Políticos y Físicos del Mundo, a una escala de 1:75 000 000. A continuación están los mapas de los océanos Pacífico, Indico y Atlántico a una escala de 1:48 000 000, que es la mayor escala utilizable para la representación de esas masas de agua en toda su extensión. Por último, una serie de mapas del relieve de los continentes, a una escala de 1:24 000 000, proporcionan una vista global de la tierra tal como se apreciaría desde el espacio a una distancia aproximada de 6 400 kilómetros. La proyección azimutal equiárea se usa, para los mapas de 1:24 000 000, a una escala según la cual la tierra se reduciría a un globo de unos 50 cm de diámetro.

Los colores utilizados en los mapas de los continentes representan las diversas regiones de la tierra tal como se verían desde el espacio durante la estación en que la vegetación se desarrolla, sin tomar en cuenta que este fenómeno no se produce simultáneamente en todas las áreas. Las estructuras características del fondo marino y las variaciones de profundidad de los océanos se representan mediante relieve sombreado y distintos matices de color. El resultado es una imagen elocuente de las formas terrestres y submarinas más notables del planeta. La leyenda abajo explica cómo se representan estos diferentes tipos de terreno y vegetación. En estos mapas predomina la nomenclatura de elementos físicos: mesetas, cuencas, sierras, mares, ríos, lagos, golfos, bahías, trincheras, islas.

CETTE PARTIE comprend d'abord des cartes du monde politique et du monde physique à l'échelle de 1:75 000 000. Viennent ensuite les cartes des océans Pacifique, Indien et Atlantique à l'échelle de 1:48 000 000, la plus grande échelle qui a permis la reproduction complète de ces étendues d'eau. Pour terminer, une série de cartes en relief des continents à l'échelle de 1:24 000 000 donne une vue globale de la terre, telle qu'elle apparaîtrait vue de l'espace à une distance d'environ 6 400 kilomètres. La projection azimutale équivalente a été utilisée pour les cartes au 1:24 000 000[c], dont l'échelle équivaut à celle d'un globe de 50 cm de diamètre environ.

Les couleurs des cartes font apparaître les continents tels qu'on les verrait de l'espace, pendant la saison de croissance végétale, mais sans tenir compte du fait que cette saison n'apparaît pas partout simultanément. Le relief sous-marin est représenté par un estompage et la profondeur des océans par une variation de la couleur. Il en résulte une reproduction vigoureuse des principaux paysages continentaux et des principales formes sous-marines. La légende ci-dessous indique de quelle façon ils sont cartographiés. Les noms d'éléments topographiques tels que plateaux, bassins, chaînes de montagnes, mers, cours d'eau, lacs, golfes, baies, crêtes, îles et fosses océaniques, prédominent dans ces cartes.

ESTA SEÇÃO PRINCIPIA com os mapas políticos e físicos do Mundo, em escala de 1:75 000 000. Seguem-se os mapas dos oceanos Pacífico, Índico e Atlântico na escala de 1:48 000 000, a maior escala que se pode utilizar para a representação dessas massas de água em toda a sua extensão. Finalmente, uma série de mapas de relevo dos continentes, na escala de 1:24 000 000, proporciona uma visão global da Terra tal como apareceria do espaço a uma distância aproximada de cerca de 6 400 km. A projeção azimutal equiárea foi usada para os mapas da escala de 1:24 000 000, segundo a qual a Terra se apresentaria como um globo de cerca de 50 cm de diâmetro.

As cores utilizadas nos mapas dos continentes representam as massas terrestres tal como apareceriam vistas do espaço durante a estação do crescimento vegetal, sem levar em conta que este fenômeno não se produz simultaneamente em todas as regiões. As características do fundo do mar e as variações de profundidade das águas são representadas por um relevo sombreado e por diferentes matizes de cor. O resultado proporciona uma imagem física eloqüente das principais formas terrestres e submarinas da Terra. As legendas abaixo explicam como foram representados os diversos tipos de terreno e de vegetação. Nestes mapas predomina a nomenclatura dos elementos físicos: planaltos, bacias, cadeias de montanhas, mares, rios, lagos, golfos, baías, fossas, ilhas.

Land Features / Land Phänomene / Elementos de la Tierra
Paysages Continentaux / Acidentes Continentais

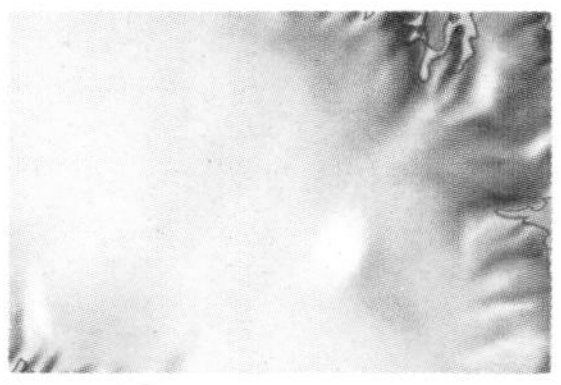

Ice and Snow
Eis und Schnee
Hielo y nieve
Glace et neige
Gelo e neve

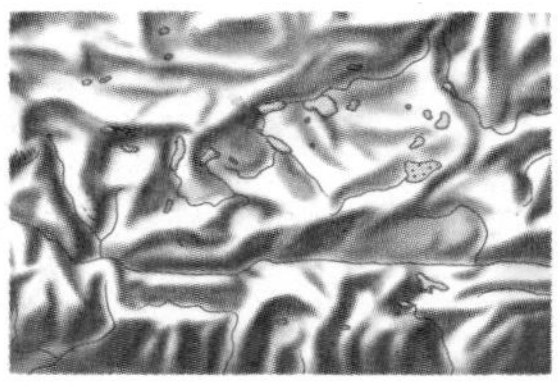

High Barren Area
Hochgebirgswüste
Alta zona árida
Région haute et aride
Alta zona árida

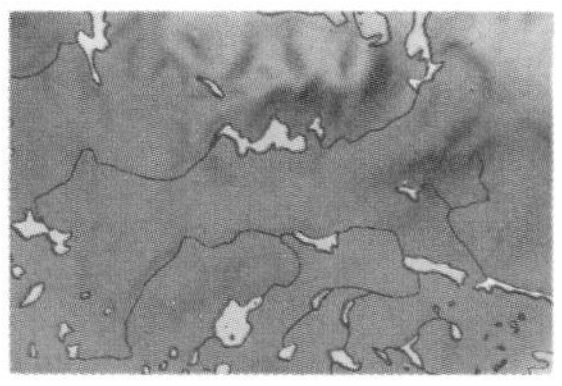

Tundra and Alpine
Tundra und Alpine Vegetation
Tundra y alpina
Toundra et végétation alpine
Tundra e vegetação alpina

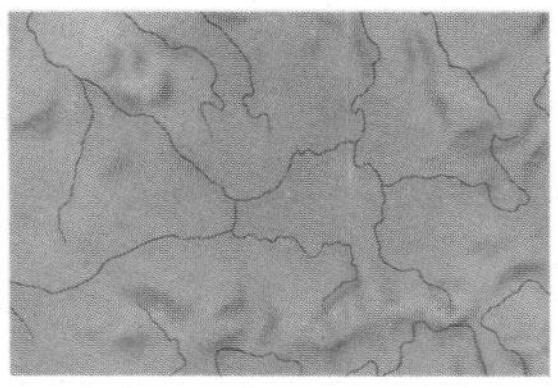

Needleleaf Trees
Nadelwälder
Coníferas
Forêt de conifères
Coníferas

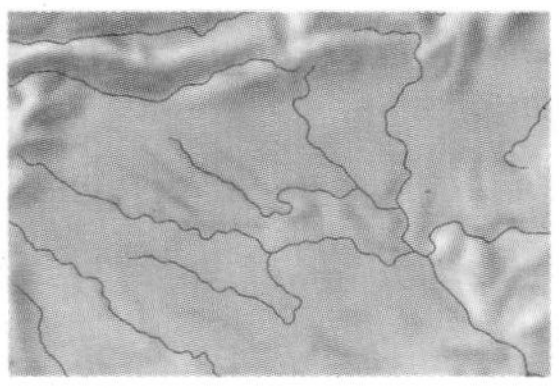

Broadleaf Trees
Laubwälder
Árboles de hojas anchas
Forêt à feuilles caduques
Árvores de folhas caducas

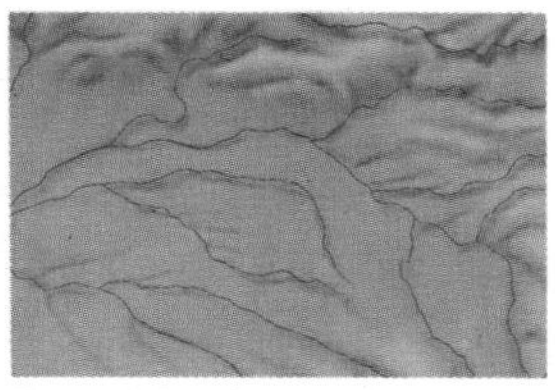

Tropical Rainforest
Tropischer Regenwald
Bosque tropical lluvioso
Forêt tropicale humide
Floresta tropical úmida

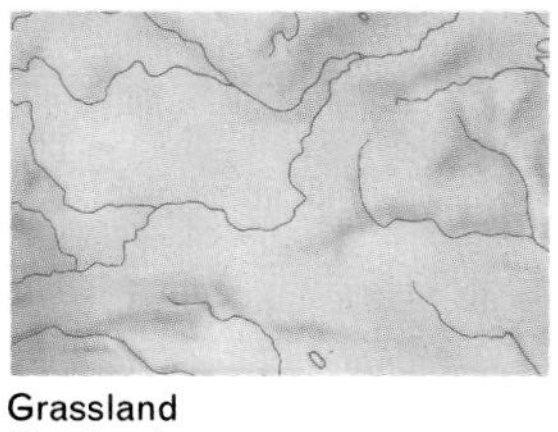

Grassland
Grasland
Pradera
Formations herbacées
Pradaria

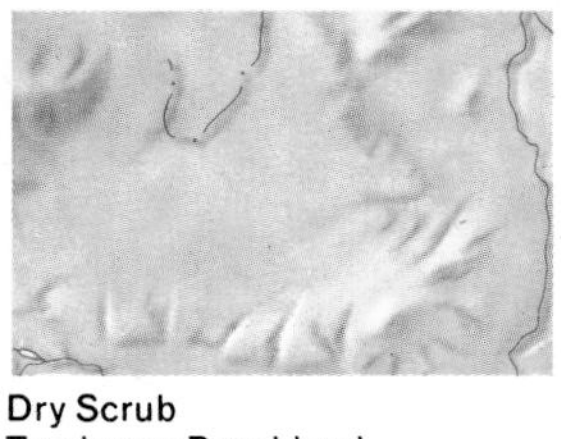

Dry Scrub
Trockenes Buschland
Matorral
Brousse sèche
Caatinga

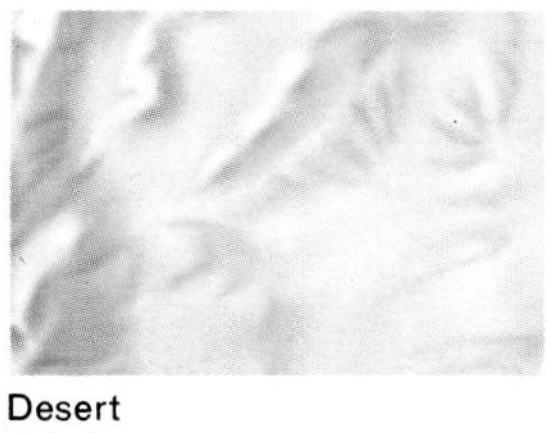

Desert
Wüste
Desierto
Désert
Deserto

Submarine Features / Untermeerische Phänomene
Elementos Submarinos / Formes de Relief Sous-marin / Acidentes do Revelo Submarino

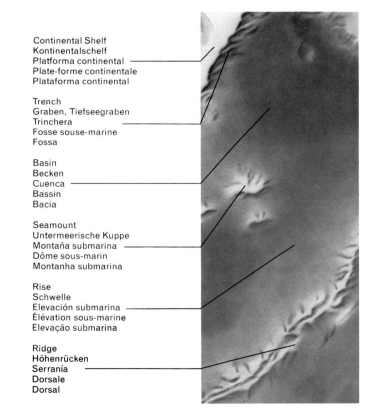

Continental Shelf
Kontinentalschelf
Platforma continental
Plate-forme continentale
Plataforma continental

Trench
Graben, Tiefseegraben
Trinchera
Fosse sousе-marine
Fossa

Basin
Becken
Cuenca
Bassin
Bacia

Seamount
Untermeerische Kuppe
Montaña submarina
Dôme sous-marin
Montanha submarina

Rise
Schwelle
Elevación submarina
Élevation sous-marine
Elevação submarina

Ridge
Höhenrücken
Serranía
Dorsale
Dorsal

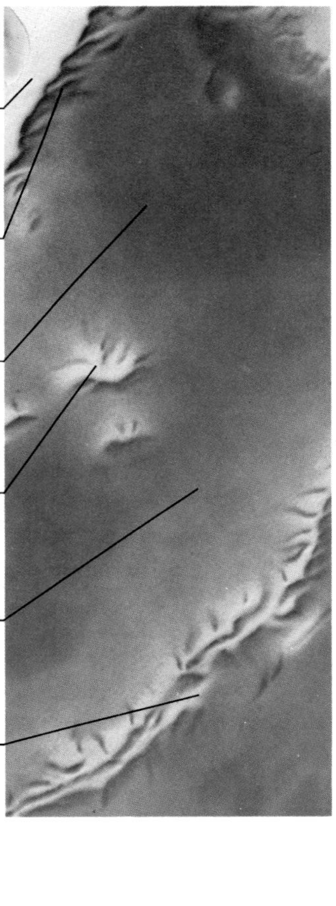

ARCTIC OCEAN
Beaufort Sea
GREENLAND
(Den.)
Baffin Bay
BAFFIN ISLAND
VICTORIA ISLAND
Godhavn
Godthåb
Davis Strait
Angmagssalik
Reykjavík
ICELAND
U.S.S.R.
UNITED STATES
Nome
Fairbanks
Inuvik
Mount McKinley 6194
Anchorage
Yellowknife
Bering Sea
Gulf of Alaska
Juneau
Hudson Bay
Churchill
ALEUTIAN ISLANDS
CANADA
ROCKY MOUNTAINS
Edmonton
Calgary
Goose Bay
Vancouver
Winnipeg
NEWFOUNDLAND
Seattle
St. John's
Portland
Minneapolis
Ottawa
Montréal
Québec
Halifax
NORTH AMERICA
DETROIT
Toronto
Boston
CHICAGO
Salt Lake City
Denver
NEW YORK
PHILADELPHIA
Washington
APPALACHIAN MOUNTAINS
SAN FRANCISCO
UNITED STATES
St. Louis
ATLANTIC OCEAN
Glasgow
Dublin
IRELAND
Porto
PORTUGAL
Lisboa
GIBRALTAR (U.K.)
Rabat
Casablanca
MOROCCO
AÇORES AZORES (Port.)
ARQUIPÉLAGO DA MADEIRA (Port.)
PACIFIC OCEAN
LOS ANGELES
San Diego
Phoenix
El Paso
Dallas
Atlanta
BERMUDA (U.K.)
MIDWAY ISLANDS (U.S.)
Houston
New Orleans
Miami
BAHAMAS
ISLAS CANARIAS CANARY ISLANDS (Sp.)
Gulf of Mexico
Tropic of Cancer
Monterrey
WESTERN SAHARA
HAWAIIAN ISLANDS (U.S.)
Honolulu
CABO SAN LUCAS
MEXICO
La Habana
CUBA
MAURITANIA
Guadalajara
CIUDAD DE MÉXICO
DOMINICAN REPUBLIC
HAITI
PUERTO RICO (U.S.)
Port-au-Prince
Santo Domingo
San Juan
JAMAICA
Kingston
Nouakchott
JOHNSTON ATOLL (U.S.)
GUATEMALA
BELIZE
GUADELOUPE (Fr.)
CAPE VERDE
SENEGAL
Dakar
GAMBIA
Banjul
Guatemala
HONDURAS
Tegucigalpa
San Salvador
MARTINIQUE (Fr.)
EL SALVADOR
NICARAGUA
BARBADOS
Caribbean Sea
TRINIDAD AND TOBAGO
GUINEA-BISSAU
Managua
Port of Spain
ÎLE CLIPPERTON (Fr. Poly.)
San José
Caracas
GUINEA
COSTA RICA
Panamá
GUYANA
Georgetown
Conakry
SIERRA LEONE
Freetown
PANAMA
VENEZUELA
Medellín
Paramaribo
Bogotá
FRENCH GUIANA
Monrovia
LIBERIA
SURINAME
Cali
COLOMBIA
LINE ISLANDS
Equator
Quito
ECUADOR
ARCHIPIÉLAGO DE COLÓN GALÁPAGOS ISLANDS (Ec.)
Guayaquil
Manaus
Belém
PHOENIX ISLANDS
Iquitos
Fortaleza
CABO DE SÃO ROQUE
Natal
Recife
TOKELAU (N.Z.)
ÎLES MARQUISES
Trujillo
BRAZIL
WALLIS AND FUTUNA (Fr.)
W. SAMOA
AM. SAMOA
Apia
PERU
Lima
SOUTH AMERICA
Salvador
ATLANTIC OCEAN
ÎLES TUAMOTU
FIJI
ÎLES DE LA SOCIÉTÉ SOCIETY ISLANDS
POLYNESIA
Arequipa
La Paz
BOLIVIA
Goiânia
Brasília
NIUE (N.Z.)
COOK ISLANDS (N.Z.)
FRENCH POLYNESIA
Sucre
TONGA
PARAGUAY
Belo Horizonte
Tropic of Capricorn
SÃO PAULO
RIO DE JANEIRO
PITCAIRN (U.K.)
Antofagasta
Santos
ISLA SAN AMBROSIO (Chile)
Asunción
Curitiba
International Date Line
ISLA DE PASCUA EASTER ISLAND (Chile)
CHILE
Co. Aconcagua 6958
Córdoba
Porto Alegre
Valparaíso
Santiago
Rosario
URUGUAY
ARCHIPIÉLAGO JUAN FERNÁNDEZ (Chile)
BUENOS AIRES
Montevideo
ARGENTINA
ANDES
Concepción
Mar del Plata
Bahía Blanca
CHATHAM ISLANDS (N.Z.)
FALKLAND ISLANDS ISLAS MALVINAS (U.K.)
Punta Arenas
SOUTH GEORGIA (Falk. Is.)
CABO DE HORNOS CAPE HORN
Drake Passage
SOUTH ORKNEY ISLANDS (B.A.T.)
Antarctic Circle
ANTARCTIC PENINSULA
Bellingshausen Sea
Weddell Sea
Ross Sea
MARIE BYRD LAND
ROSS ICE SHELF
Vinson Massif 4897
ANTAR

ARCTIC OCEAN
UNION OF SOVIET SOCIALIST REPUBLICS
EUROPE
ASIA
MONGOLIA
CHINA
JAPAN
INDIA
PAKISTAN
IRAN
IRAQ
TURKEY
SAUDI ARABIA
EGYPT
LIBYA
SUDAN
ETHIOPIA
KENYA
ZAIRE
ANGOLA
ZAMBIA
ZIMBABWE
BOTSWANA
NAMIBIA
MOZAMBIQUE
SOUTH AFRICA
MADAGASCAR
AFRICA
PHILIPPINES
MALAYSIA
INDONESIA
PAPUA NEW GUINEA
AUSTRALIA
NEW ZEALAND
TASMANIA
MICRONESIA
MELANESIA
PACIFIC OCEAN
INDIAN OCEAN
Bay of Bengal
Arabian Sea
South China Sea
Philippine Sea
Sea of Okhotsk
Bering Sea
Coral Sea
Tasman Sea
Tropic of Cancer
Equator
Tropic of Capricorn
Arctic Circle
Antarctic Circle
International Date Line
ENDERBY LAND
WILKES LAND
ANTARCTICA
Copyright © by Rand McNally & Co.
Map prepared by Rand McNally & Co.
Kilometers 0 1000 2000 3000 Km.
Statute Miles 0 1000 2000 3000 Mi.

One centimeter represents 750 kilometers.
One inch represents approximately 1200 miles.
Robinson Projection
Scale 1:75,000,000

ARCTIC OCEAN
ELLESMERE ISLAND
GREENLAND
Baffin Bay
Beaufort Sea
Greenland Sea
ICELAND
Hudson Bay
Labrador Sea
LABRADOR BASIN
CANADA
NORTH AMERICA
UNITED STATES
ROCKY MOUNTAINS
APPALACHIAN MOUNTAINS
GREAT PLAINS
Gulf of Alaska
Bering Sea
ALEUTIAN BASIN
ALEUTIAN TRENCH
Chukchi Sea
U.S.S.R.
Arctic Circle
Mount McKinley 6194
Mount Logan 5951
Lake Athabasca
Lake Winnipeg
Lake Superior
Pikes Peak 4301
LOS ANGELES
CHICAGO
NEW YORK
Houston
Mississippi
Gulf of Mexico
MEXICO
Tropic of Cancer
CUBA
GREATER ANTILLES
WEST INDIES
Caribbean Sea
VENEZUELA
COLOMBIA
SOUTH AMERICA
BRAZIL
BOLIVIA
PERU
ANDES
Amazon
Equator
SÃO PAULO
RIO DE JANEIRO
BUENOS AIRES
URUGUAY
PARAGUAY
PAMPA
PATAGONIA
Cerro Aconcagua 6959
Santiago
Lima
Recife
Belém
Tropic of Capricorn
FALKLAND ISLANDS
Drake Passage
SOUTH GEORGIA
SCOTIA RIDGE
Scotia Sea
Weddell Sea
Bellingshausen Sea
Amundsen Sea
Ross Sea
ROSS ICE SHELF
MARIE BYRD LAND
Vinson Massif 4897
Antarctic Circle
PACIFIC OCEAN
CENTRAL PACIFIC BASIN
POLYNESIA
HAWAIIAN ISLANDS
HAWAIIAN RIDGE
MENDOCINO FRACTURE ZONE
MURRAY FRACTURE ZONE
CLARION FRACTURE ZONE
CLIPPERTON FRACTURE ZONE
EAST PACIFIC RISE
CHILE RISE
SOUTHWEST PACIFIC BASIN
SOUTHEAST PACIFIC BASIN
International Date Line
ATLANTIC OCEAN
MID-ATLANTIC RIDGE
NORTH AMERICAN BASIN
NEWFOUNDLAND BASIN
GUIANA BASIN
ARGENTINE BASIN
CAPE VERDE BASIN
AZORES
PORTUGAL
MAURITANIA
180° 165° 150° 135° 120° 105° 90° 75° 60° 45° 30° 15°

Kilometers 0 1000 2000 3000 Km.
Statute Miles 0 1000 2000 3000 Mi.

One centimeter represents 750 kilometers.
One inch represents approximately 1200 miles.
Robinson Projection
Scale 1:75,000,000

GREENLAND
Greenland Sea
Barents Sea
NORWEGIAN BASIN
Arctic Circle
Norwegian Sea
ICELAND
FAEROE IS.
SWEDEN
FINLAND
LENINGRAD
Helsinki
Stockholm
Oslo
Baltic Sea
UNITED KINGDOM
IRELAND
North Sea
DENMARK
København
LONDON
PARIS
FRANCE
BERLIN
POLAND
Warszawa
HUNGARY
Budapest
ROMANIA
Bucureşti
YUGO.
BULGARIA
Sofija
Roma
Barcelona
MOSKVA
URAL'SKIJE GORY
URAL MOUNTAINS
UNION OF SOVIET SOCIALIST REPUBLICS
ZAPADNO-SIBIRSKAJA RAVNINA
SREDNESIBIRSKOJE PLOSKOGORJE
SIBERIA
Black Sea
Caspian Sea
Aral'skoje more
KAZACHSKIJ MELKOSOPOČNIK
MONGOLIA
GOBI
A S I A
TIEN SHAN
ALTAI
CHINA
KUNLUN SHAN
QING ZANG GAOYUAN
HIMALAYAS
BEIJING
SHANGHAI
KOREA
Sea of Japan
JAPAN
TŌKYŌ
Yellow Sea
East China Sea
TURKEY
ASIA MINOR
İstanbul
Ankara
CYPRUS
SYRIA
LEBANON
ISRAEL
JORDAN
IRAQ
Baghdād
IRAN
Tehrān
AFGHANISTAN
HINDU KUSH
PAKISTAN
INDIA
NEPAL
BHUTAN
BNGL.
Delhi
CALCUTTA
BOMBAY
Madras
SRI LANKA
BURMA
Rangoon
THAILAND
INDOCHINA
VIET-NAM
KAM.
MALAYSIA
Singapore
PHILIPPINES
Manila
TAIWAN
HONG KONG
SAUDI ARABIA
ARABIAN PENINSULA
AR-RUB' AL-KHĀLI
YEMEN
P.D.R. OF YEMEN
OMAN
UNITED ARAB EMIRATES
QATAR
KUWAIT
LIBYA
EGYPT
SAHARA
Tropic of Cancer
NUBIAN DESERT
SUDAN
ETHIOPIA
SOMALIA
KENYA
UGANDA
TANZANIA
ZAMBIA
MOZAMBIQUE
ZIMBABWE
BOTSWANA
SOUTH AFRICA
MADAGASCAR
AFRICA
MEDITERRANEAN SEA
Red Sea
Gulf of Aden
ARABIAN SEA
Bay of Bengal
ARABIAN BASIN
SOMALI BASIN
MALDIVES
SEYCHELLES
MID-INDIAN BASIN
INDIAN OCEAN
NINETY EAST RIDGE
CARLSBERG RIDGE
CHAGOS-LACCADIVE PLATEAU
MASCARENE PLATEAU
MAURITIUS
Mozambique Channel
Tropic of Capricorn
WHARTON BASIN
MID-INDIAN RIDGE
SOUTHWEST INDIAN RIDGE
MADAGASCAR BASIN
CROZET BASIN
AGULHAS BASIN
SOUTHEAST INDIAN RIDGE
SOUTH INDIAN BASIN
ATLANTIC-INDIAN RIDGE
ATLANTIC-INDIAN BASIN
KERGUELEN PLATEAU
BROKEN RIDGE
PERTH BASIN
NORTH AUSTRALIAN BASIN
SOUTH AUSTRALIAN BASIN
Great Australian Bight
GREATER SUNDA ISLANDS
INDONESIA
SUMATERA
BORNEO
JAWA
JAKARTA
JAVA TRENCH
SUNDA SHELF
South China Sea
Philippine Sea
PHILIPPINE BASIN
NEW GUINEA
Arafura Sea
Timor Sea
Gulf of Carpentaria
AUSTRALIA
GREAT SANDY DESERT
GIBSON DESERT
GREAT VICTORIA DESERT
GREAT DIVIDING RANGE
Sydney
Melbourne
Adelaide
Perth
TASMANIA
Antarctic Circle
ENDERBY LAND
ANTARCTICA
WILKES LAND
AMERICAN HIGHLAND
PRINCESS MARTHA COAST
AMERY ICE SHELF

ARCTIC OCEAN
Beaufort Sea
Chukchi Sea
BERING SEA
ALEUTIAN BASIN
Gulf of Alaska
ROCKY MOUNTAINS
CANADA
Hudson Bay
Labrador Sea
LABRADOR BASIN
GREENLAND (Den.)
ATLANTIC
NORTH AMERICA
UNITED STATES
GREAT PLAINS
APPALACHIAN MOUNTAINS
NEWFOUNDLAND BASIN
NORTH AMERICAN BASIN
OCEAN
Gulf of Mexico
MEXICO
PACIFIC OCEAN
EMPEROR SEAMOUNTS
MENDOCINO FRACTURE ZONE
MURRAY FRACTURE ZONE
MIDWAY ISLANDS (U.S.)
HAWAIIAN RIDGE
HAWAIIAN ISLANDS (U.S.)
Honolulu
Tropic of Cancer
CLARION FRACTURE ZONE
Caribbean Sea
WEST INDIES
CUBA
BAHAMAS
GUATEMALA
HONDURAS
NICARAGUA
COSTA RICA
PANAMA
COLOMBIA
VENEZUELA
ECUADOR
PERU
BOLIVIA
PARAGUAY
CHILE
ARGENTINA
URUGUAY
BRAZIL
SOUTH AMERICA
CENTRAL PACIFIC BASIN
MARSHALL ISLANDS
GILBERT ISLANDS
KIRIBATI
TUVALU
Equator
POLYNESIA
FRENCH POLYNESIA
COOK ISLANDS (N.Z.)
AMERICAN SAMOA
TONGA
FIJI
VANUATU
NEW ZEALAND
NORTH ISLAND
SOUTH ISLAND
Tropic of Capricorn
PERU BASIN
EAST PACIFIC RISE
CHILE RISE
SOUTHWEST PACIFIC BASIN
SOUTHEAST PACIFIC BASIN
PACIFIC-ANTARCTIC RIDGE
ARGENTINE BASIN
FALKLAND ISLANDS
Drake Passage
Scotia Sea
ATLANTIC-INDIAN BASIN
Antarctic Circle
Bellingshausen Sea
Amundsen Sea
Ross Sea
Weddell Sea
International Date Line
Kilometers 0 400 800 1200 1600 Km.
Statute Miles 0 400 800 1200 1600 Mi.
Scale 1:48,000,000 at 35° latitude.
One centimeter represents 480 kilometers.
One inch represents approximately 760 miles.
Modified Cylindrical Projection
Copyright © by Rand McNally & Co.
Map prepared by Rand McNally & Co.

8 Atlantic Ocean / Atlantischer Ozean
Océano Atlántico / Océan Atlantique
Oceano Atlântico

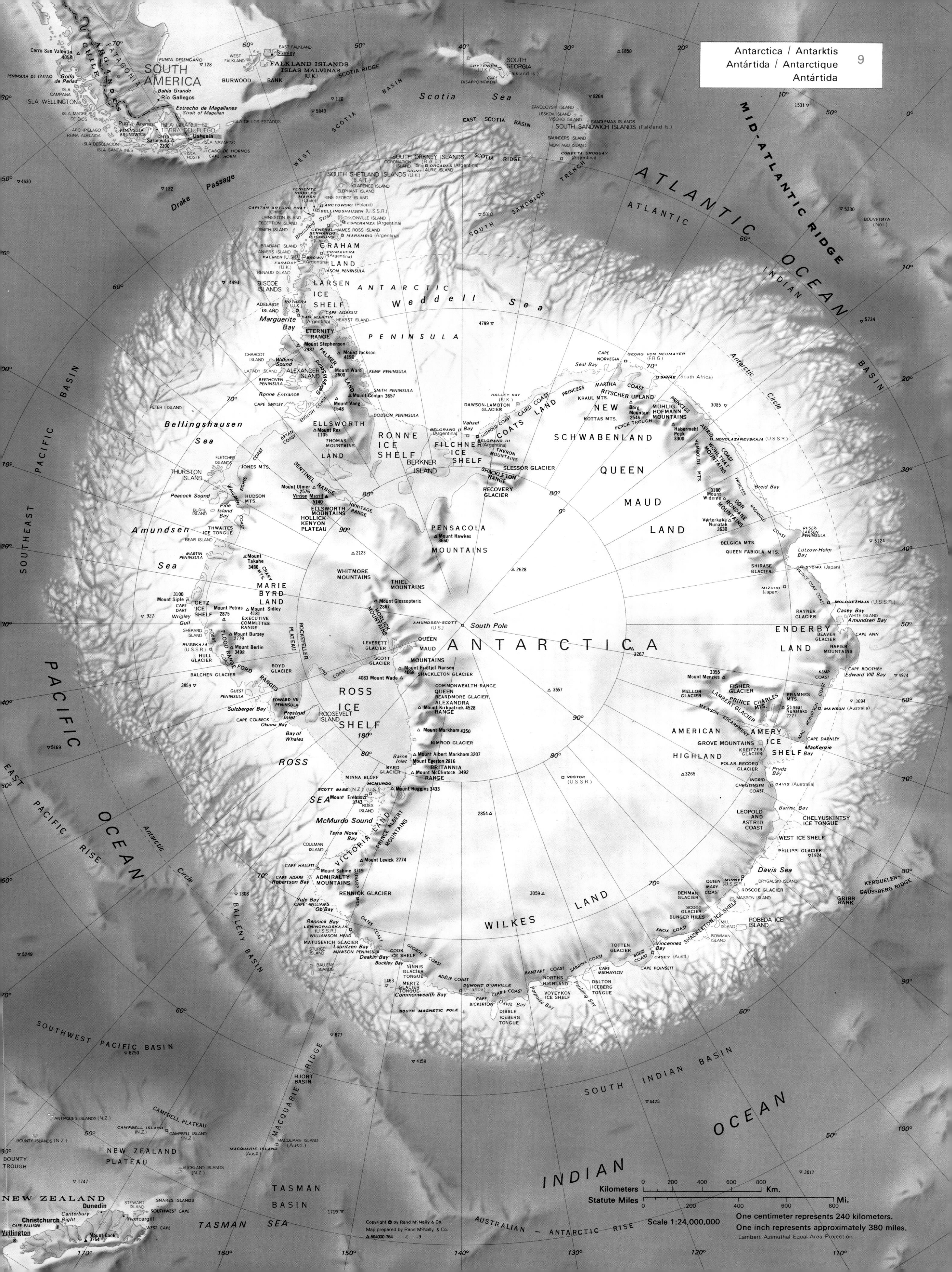
SOUTH AMERICA
PATAGONIA
CHILE
ARGENTINA
ANDES
Cerro San Valentín 4058
PENÍNSULA DE TAITAO
Golfo de Penas
ISLA WELLINGTON
Bahía Grande
Río Gallegos
Estrecho de Magallanes
Strait of Magellan
Punta Arenas
ISLA GRANDE DE TIERRA DEL FUEGO
Ushuaia
ISLA DE LOS ESTADOS
CABO DE HORNOS
CAPE HORN
FALKLAND ISLANDS
ISLAS MALVINAS
(U.K.)
Stanley
BURWOOD BANK
SCOTIA RIDGE
SOUTH GEORGIA
(Falkland Is.)
Scotia Sea
EAST SCOTIA BASIN
SOUTH SANDWICH ISLANDS (Falkland Is.)
SOUTH SANDWICH TRENCH
WEST SCOTIA BASIN
Drake Passage
SOUTH ORKNEY ISLANDS
SOUTH SHETLAND ISLANDS
MID-ATLANTIC RIDGE
ATLANTIC OCEAN
ATLANTIC-INDIAN BASIN
BOUVETØYA (Nor.)
GRAHAM LAND
LARSEN ICE SHELF
ANTARCTIC PENINSULA
Weddell Sea
Marguerite Bay
ALEXANDER ISLAND
PALMER LAND
Bellingshausen Sea
SOUTHEAST PACIFIC BASIN
ELLSWORTH LAND
RONNE ICE SHELF
FILCHNER ICE SHELF
BERKNER ISLAND
Vinson Massif 5140
ELLSWORTH MOUNTAINS
PENSACOLA MOUNTAINS
Amundsen Sea
MARIE BYRD LAND
WHITMORE MOUNTAINS
THIEL MOUNTAINS
South Pole
AMUNDSEN-SCOTT (U.S.)
ANTARCTICA
QUEEN MAUD MOUNTAINS
ROSS ICE SHELF
ROOSEVELT ISLAND
Bay of Whales
ROSS SEA
McMurdo Sound
Mount Erebus 3743
VICTORIA LAND
TRANSANTARCTIC MOUNTAINS
Mount Kirkpatrick 4528
COATS LAND
NEW SCHWABENLAND
QUEEN MAUD LAND
PRINCESS MARTHA COAST
PRINCESS ASTRID COAST
PRINCESS RAGNHILD COAST
PRINCE OLAV COAST
Lützow-Holm Bay
ENDERBY LAND
Amundsen Bay
KEMP COAST
MAC. ROBERTSON COAST
AMERY ICE SHELF
PRINCE CHARLES MTS.
LAMBERT GLACIER
AMERICAN HIGHLAND
VOSTOK (U.S.S.R.)
INGRID CHRISTENSEN COAST
LEOPOLD AND ASTRID COAST
WEST ICE SHELF
Davis Sea
QUEEN MARY COAST
SHACKLETON ICE SHELF
KNOX COAST
BUDD COAST
SABRINA COAST
BANZARE COAST
WILKES LAND
ADÉLIE COAST
CLARIE COAST
GEORGE V COAST
OATES COAST
SOUTH MAGNETIC POLE
BALLENY ISLANDS
BALLENY BASIN
PACIFIC-ANTARCTIC RISE
EAST PACIFIC OCEAN
KERGUELEN-GAUSSBERG RIDGE
SOUTH INDIAN BASIN
INDIAN OCEAN
SOUTHWEST PACIFIC BASIN
MACQUARIE RIDGE
HJORT BASIN
CAMPBELL PLATEAU
NEW ZEALAND PLATEAU
BOUNTY TROUGH
TASMAN BASIN
TASMAN SEA
AUSTRALIAN - ANTARCTIC RISE
NEW ZEALAND
Dunedin
Christchurch
Wellington
Invercargill
Mount Cook 3764
Antarctic Circle
Kilometers 0 200 400 600 800 Km.
Statute Miles 0 200 400 600 800 Mi.
Scale 1:24,000,000
One centimeter represents 240 kilometers.
One inch represents approximately 380 miles.
Lambert Azimuthal Equal-Area Projection
Copyright © by Rand McNally & Co.
Map prepared by Rand McNally & Co.
A-594000-764

CANADA
GREENLAND (Den.)
ICELAND
Reykjavik
Labrador Sea
LABRADOR BASIN
IRMINGER BASIN
REYKJANES RIDGE
ICELAND BASIN
ROCKALL RISE
Davis Strait
Denmark Strait
Arctic Circle
GREENLAND BASIN
Greenland Sea
LOFOTEN BASIN
NORWEGIAN BASIN
Norwegian Sea
SPITSBERGEN
SVALBARD (Nor.)
Barents Sea
ATLANTIC OCEAN
MID-ATLANTIC RIDGE
WEST EUROPEAN BASIN
AZORES-GIBRALTAR RIDGE
CANARY BASIN
AZORES
North Sea
Baltic Sea
Bay of Biscay
English Channel
EUROPE
NORWAY
SWEDEN
FINLAND
DENMARK
UNITED KINGDOM
IRELAND
FRANCE
SPAIN
PORTUGAL
ITALY
POLAND
CZECHOSLOVAKIA
AUSTRIA
HUNGARY
ROMANIA
YUGOSLAVIA
BULGARIA
ALBANIA
GREECE
TURKEY
ASIA MINOR
UNION OF SOVIET SOCIALIST REPUBLICS
URAL'SKIJE GORY
URAL MOUNTAINS
ASIA
ZAPADNO-SIBIRSKAJA RAVNINA
MOSKVA
MOSCOW
LENINGRAD
KIJEV
Helsinki
Stockholm
Oslo
København
Warszawa
BERLIN
Praha
WIEN
BUDAPEST
Beograd
București
Sofija
ROMA
PARIS
LONDON
MADRID
Lisboa
İSTANBUL
Black Sea
Caspian Sea
Aral'skoje more
Mediterranean Sea
Adriatic Sea
Tyrrhenian Sea
Ionian Sea
Aegean Sea
BOL'ŠOJ KAVKAZ
CAUCASUS
TEHRAN
BAGHDAD
DIMASHQ
Bayrūt
LEBANON
SYRIA
IRAQ
IRAN
ISRAEL
JORDAN
CYPRUS
KUWAIT
SAUDI ARABIA
ARABIAN PENINSULA
UNITED ARAB EMIRATES
QATAR
BAHRAIN
Persian Gulf
Red Sea
AL-QĀHIRAH
CAIRO
EGYPT
LIBYA
TUNISIA
ALGERIA
MOROCCO
WESTERN SAHARA
MAURITANIA
SAHARA
ATLAS MOUNTAINS
EL DJAZAÏR
ALGIERS
Tunis
Țarābulus
Rabat
CASABLANCA
Tropic of Cancer
CAPE VERDE

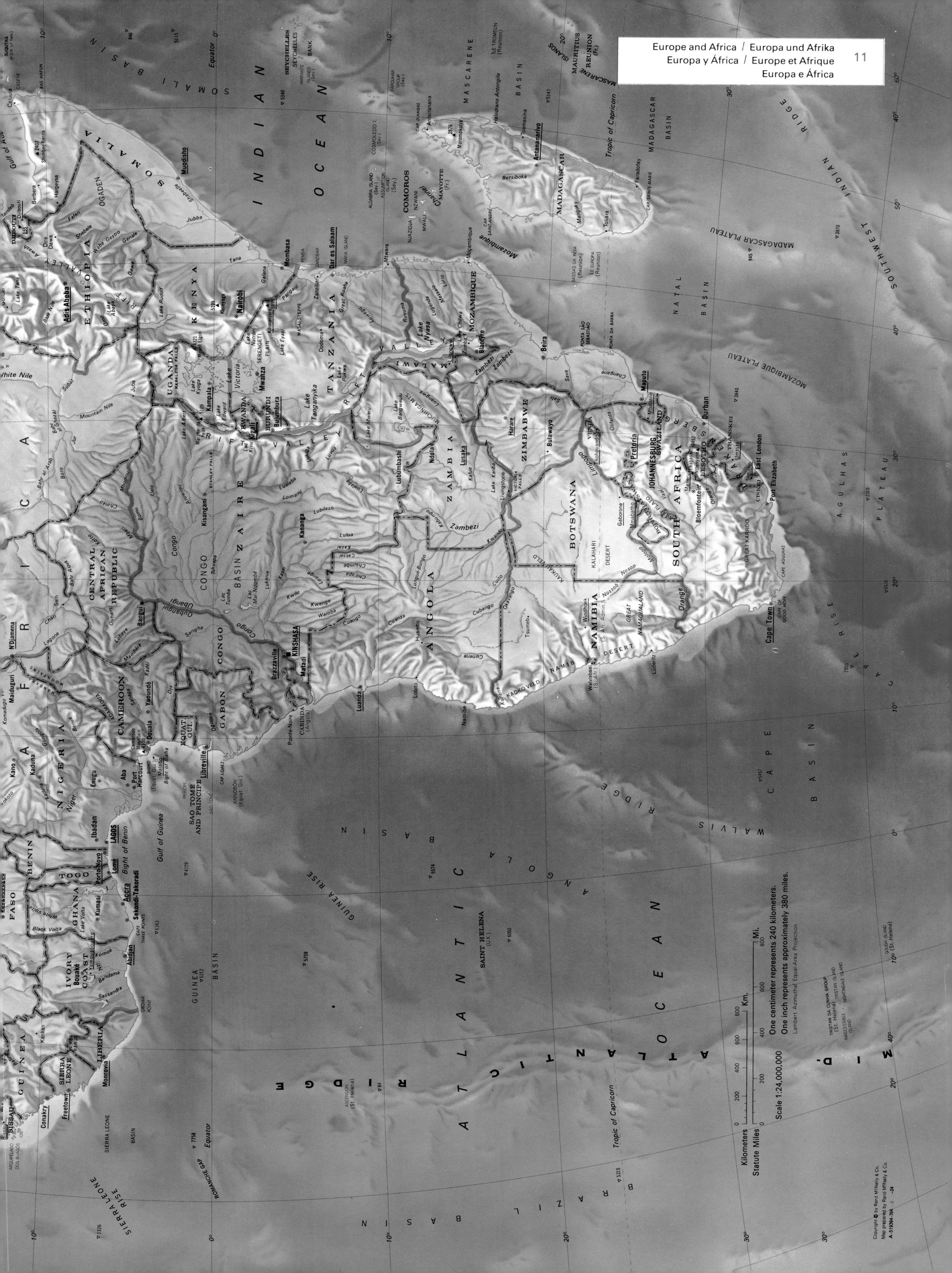
ATLANTIC OCEAN
INDIAN OCEAN
AFRICA
ZAIRE
ANGOLA
NAMIBIA
BOTSWANA
SOUTH AFRICA
ZIMBABWE
ZAMBIA
MOZAMBIQUE
TANZANIA
KENYA
UGANDA
ETHIOPIA
SOMALIA
MADAGASCAR
NIGERIA
CAMEROON
GABON
CONGO
CENTRAL AFRICAN REPUBLIC
GHANA
TOGO
BENIN
IVORY COAST
LIBERIA
SIERRA LEONE
GUINEA
BURUNDI
RWANDA
LESOTHO
SWAZILAND
MALAWI
COMOROS
Kinshasa
Luanda
Lusaka
Harare
Pretoria
Johannesburg
Cape Town
Maputo
Dar es Salaam
Nairobi
Mogadisho
Adis Abeba
Antananarivo
Lagos
Accra
Abidjan
Libreville
Brazzaville
Windhoek
Gaborone
Tropic of Capricorn
Equator
Gulf of Guinea
Mozambique Channel
Scale 1:24,000,000
One centimeter represents 240 kilometers.
One inch represents approximately 380 miles.
Lambert Azimuthal Equal-Area Projection
Kilometers
Statute Miles
Copyright © by Rand McNally & Co.
Map prepared by Rand McNally & Co.

ARCTIC OCEAN
North Pole
ATLANTIC OCEAN
GREENLAND (Den.)
ICELAND
Reykjavík
Greenland Sea
Norwegian Sea
Barents Sea
Kara Sea
Laptev Sea
East Siberian Sea
Chukchi Sea
Bering Sea
Sea of Okhotsk
Sea of Japan
Caspian Sea
Black Sea
Baltic Sea
North Sea
SVALBARD
FRANZ JOSEPH LAND
SEVERNAJA ZEML'A
UNITED KINGDOM
IRELAND
LONDON
NORWAY
SWEDEN
FINLAND
POLAND
CZECHOSLOVAKIA
HUNGARY
ROMANIA
BULGARIA
TURKEY
ASIA MINOR
SYRIA
IRAQ
IRAN
UNION OF SOVIET SOCIALIST REPUBLICS
EUROPE
ASIA
SIBERIA
MONGOLIA
GOBI
CHINA
JAPAN
NORTH KOREA
SOUTH KOREA
UNITED STATES
Bering Strait
MOSKVA
LENINGRAD
KIEV
VOLGOGRAD
SVERDLOVSK
Novosibirsk
Irkutsk
Vladivostok
ULAN BAATAR
BEIJING
TIANJIN
SHANGHAI
TEHRĀN
BAGHDĀD
TAŠKENT
URAL'SKIJE GORY
URAL MOUNTAINS
ZAPADNO-SIBIRSKAJA RAVNINA
SREDNESIBIRSKOJE PLOSKOGORJE
TIEN SHAN
KUNLUN SHAN
ALTAI
KAVKAZ
CAUCASUS
TARIM PENDI
KURIL ISLANDS
ALEUTIAN ISLANDS

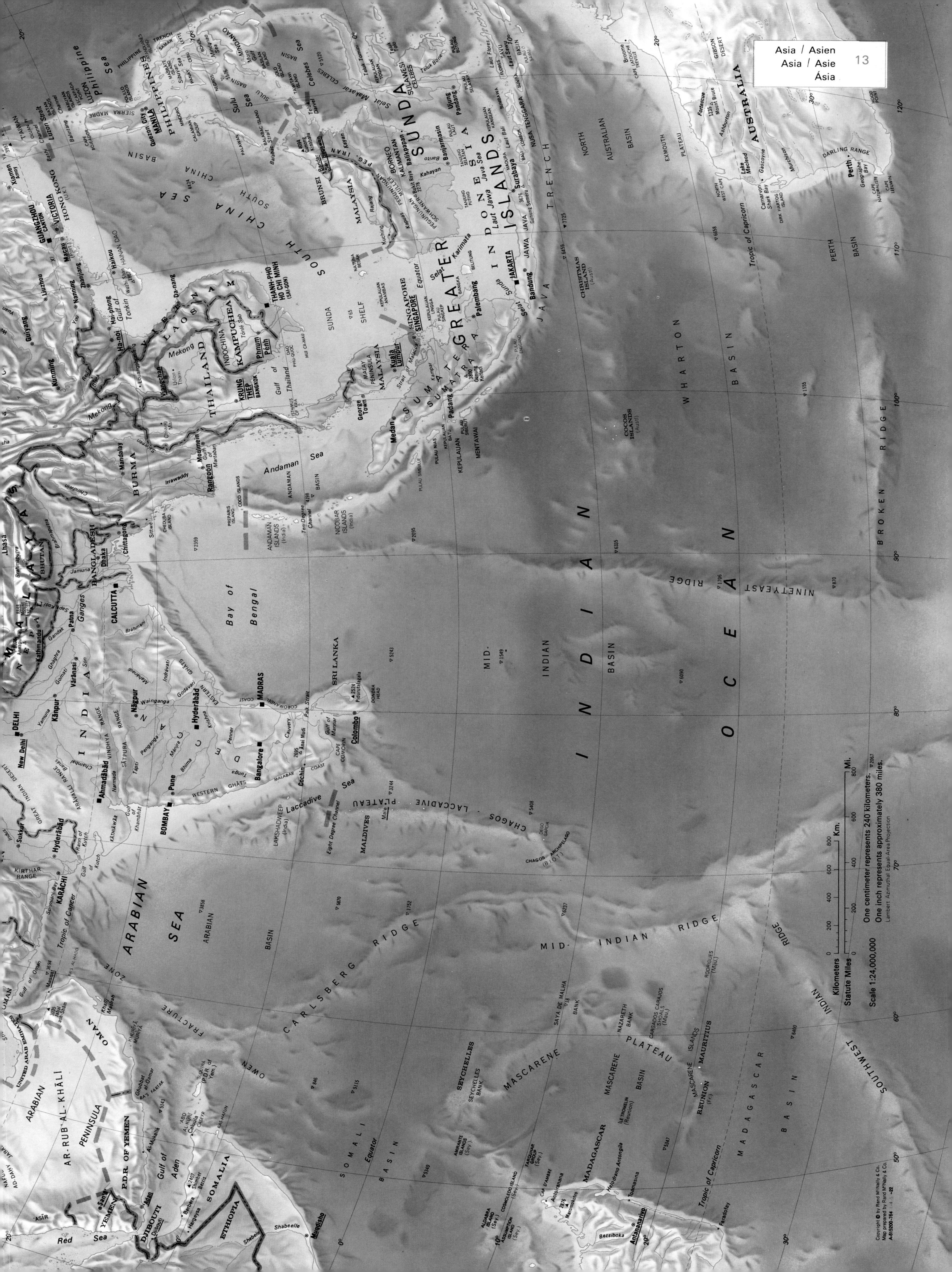
INDIAN OCEAN
ARABIAN SEA
Bay of Bengal
Andaman Sea
SOUTH CHINA SEA
Philippine Sea
Java Sea
Laccadive Sea
Red Sea
Gulf of Aden
Gulf of Oman
Gulf of Thailand
Gulf of Tonkin
INDIA
BURMA
THAILAND
LAOS
VIETNAM
KAMPUCHEA
MALAYSIA
INDONESIA
PHILIPPINES
BANGLADESH
BHUTAN
NEPAL
SRI LANKA
MALDIVES
SOMALIA
ETHIOPIA
DJIBOUTI
YEMEN
P.D.R. OF YEMEN
OMAN
UNITED ARAB EMIRATES
MADAGASCAR
SEYCHELLES
MAURITIUS
REUNION
AUSTRALIA
GREATER SUNDA ISLANDS
SUMATERA
JAWA
BORNEO
KALIMANTAN
SULAWESI
MINDANAO
ARABIAN PENINSULA
AR-RUB' AL-KHALI
DECCAN
WESTERN GHATS
EASTERN GHATS
THAR DESERT
HIMALAYAS
NEW DELHI
DELHI
BOMBAY
CALCUTTA
MADRAS
KARACHI
Colombo
Dhaka
Rangoon
KRUNG THEP (BANGKOK)
THANH-PHO HO CHI MINH (SAIGON)
SINGAPORE
JAKARTA
MANILA
HONG KONG
VICTORIA
Kuala Lumpur
Phnum Penh
Ha-noi
Perth
Antananarivo
Muqdisho
Aden
ARABIAN BASIN
CARLSBERG RIDGE
MID-INDIAN RIDGE
MID-INDIAN BASIN
NINETYEAST RIDGE
WHARTON BASIN
JAVA TRENCH
SOMALI BASIN
MASCARENE BASIN
MASCARENE PLATEAU
MADAGASCAR BASIN
SOUTHWEST INDIAN RIDGE
OWEN FRACTURE ZONE
LACCADIVE PLATEAU
CHAGOS
BROKEN RIDGE
PERTH BASIN
NORTH AUSTRALIAN BASIN
SUNDA SHELF
Equator
Tropic of Cancer
Tropic of Capricorn
Scale 1:24,000,000
One centimeter represents 240 kilometers.
One inch represents approximately 380 miles.
Lambert Azimuthal Equal-Area Projection
Kilometers
Statute Miles
Copyright © by Rand McNally & Co.
Map prepared by Rand McNally & Co.

ASIA
CHINA
HIMALAYAS
INDIA
BURMA
LAOS
VIETNAM
THAILAND
INDOCHINA
KAMPUCHEA
MALAYSIA
SINGAPORE
BRUNEI
PHILIPPINES
INDONESIA
GREATER SUNDA ISLANDS
MALUKU
NUSA TENGGARA
NEW GUINEA
PAPUA NEW GUINEA
AUSTRALIA
TAIWAN
CHONGQING
Changsha
Nanchang
Wenzhou
Guiyang
Fuzhou
Kunming
Liuzhou
Xiamen
GUANGZHOU
CANTON
VICTORIA
HONG KONG (U.K.)
Macau (Port.)
Nanning
Zhanjiang
Haikou
HAINAN DAO
Mandalay
Ha-noi
Hai-phong
Louangphrabang
Viangchan
Udon Thani
Chiang Mai
Da-nang
Moulmein
KRUNG THEP
BANGKOK
Phnum Penh
THANH-PHO HO CHI MINH
(SAI-GON)
T'AIPEI
Naha
MANILA
Quezon City
Cebu
MINDANAO
George Town
Medan
Kuala Lumpur
Kuching
Balikpapan
Banjarmasin
Padang
Palembang
JAKARTA
Bandung
Surabaya
Ujung Pandang
Manado
Jayapura
Port Moresby
Lae
Rabaul
Darwin
Broome
Mount Isa
Alice Springs
Cairns
Townsville
Rockhampton
Brisbane
Newcastle
SYDNEY
Canberra
MELBOURNE
Adelaide
Perth
Kalgoorlie
Hobart
Launceston
Broken Hill
Birdum
East China Sea
South China Sea
Gulf of Tonkin
Gulf of Thailand
Sulu Sea
Celebes Sea
Java Sea
Laut Banda
Arafura Sea
Timor Sea
Gulf of Carpentaria
Coral Sea
Bismarck Sea
Solomon Sea
Gulf of Papua
Great Australian Bight
Torres Strait
Bass Strait
Luzon Strait
Taiwan Strait
Strait of Malacca
Selat Karimata
PHILIPPINE SEA
PHILIPPINE BASIN
WEST MARIANA BASIN
MARIANA ISLANDS
NORTHERN MARIANA ISLANDS
GUAM (U.S.)
Challenger Deep 11034
TRUST TERRITORY OF THE PACIFIC ISLANDS (U.S.)
CAROLINE ISLANDS
WEST CAROLINE BASIN
EAST CAROLINE BASIN
FEDERATED STATES OF MICRONESIA (T.T.P.I.)
BELAU PALAU (T.T.P.I.)
OGASAWARA-GUNTŌ
BONIN ISLANDS (Japan)
KAZAN-RETTŌ
NANSEI-SHOTŌ
RYUKYU ISLANDS (Japan)
RYUKYU TRENCH
PHILIPPINE TRENCH
KYUSHU-PALAU RIDGE
WEST MARIANA RIDGE
MARIANA TRENCH
BISMARCK ARCHIPELAGO
NEW BRITAIN
NEW IRELAND
BOUGAINVILLE
SUNDA SHELF
SAHUL SHELF
ARAFURA SHELF
JAVA TRENCH
TIMOR TROUGH
CHRISTMAS ISLAND (Austl.)
COCOS ISLANDS (Austl.)
NORTH AUSTRALIAN BASIN
WHARTON BASIN
EXMOUTH PLATEAU
PERTH BASIN
SOUTH AUSTRALIAN BASIN
BROKEN RIDGE
DIAMANTINA FRACTURE ZONE
SOUTH TASMAN RISE
INDIAN OCEAN
KIMBERLEY PLATEAU
ARNHEM LAND
CAPE YORK PENINSULA
BARKLY TABLELAND
GREAT SANDY DESERT
TANAMI DESERT
GIBSON DESERT
GREAT VICTORIA DESERT
SIMPSON DESERT
STURT DESERT
NULLARBOR PLAIN
MACDONNELL RANGES
GREAT DIVIDING RANGE
GREAT BARRIER REEF
QUEENSLAND PLATEAU
CORAL SEA BASIN
FLINDERS RANGES
DARLING RANGE
Lake Eyre
Lake Torrens
Lake Frome
Mount Kosciusko 2228
Mount Woodroffe 1439
Mount Bruce 1235
Mount Wilhelm 4509
Puncak Jaya 5030
Gunong Kinabalu 4094
Tropic of Cancer
Tropic of Capricorn
Equator
TASMANIA
Kilometers 0 200 400 600 800 Km.
Statute Miles 0 200 400 600 800 Mi.
Scale 1:24,000,000
One centimeter represents 240 kilometers.
One inch represents approximately 380 miles.
Lambert Azimuthal Equal-Area Projection
Copyright © by Rand McNally & Co.
Map prepared by Rand McNally & Co.
A-580000-764

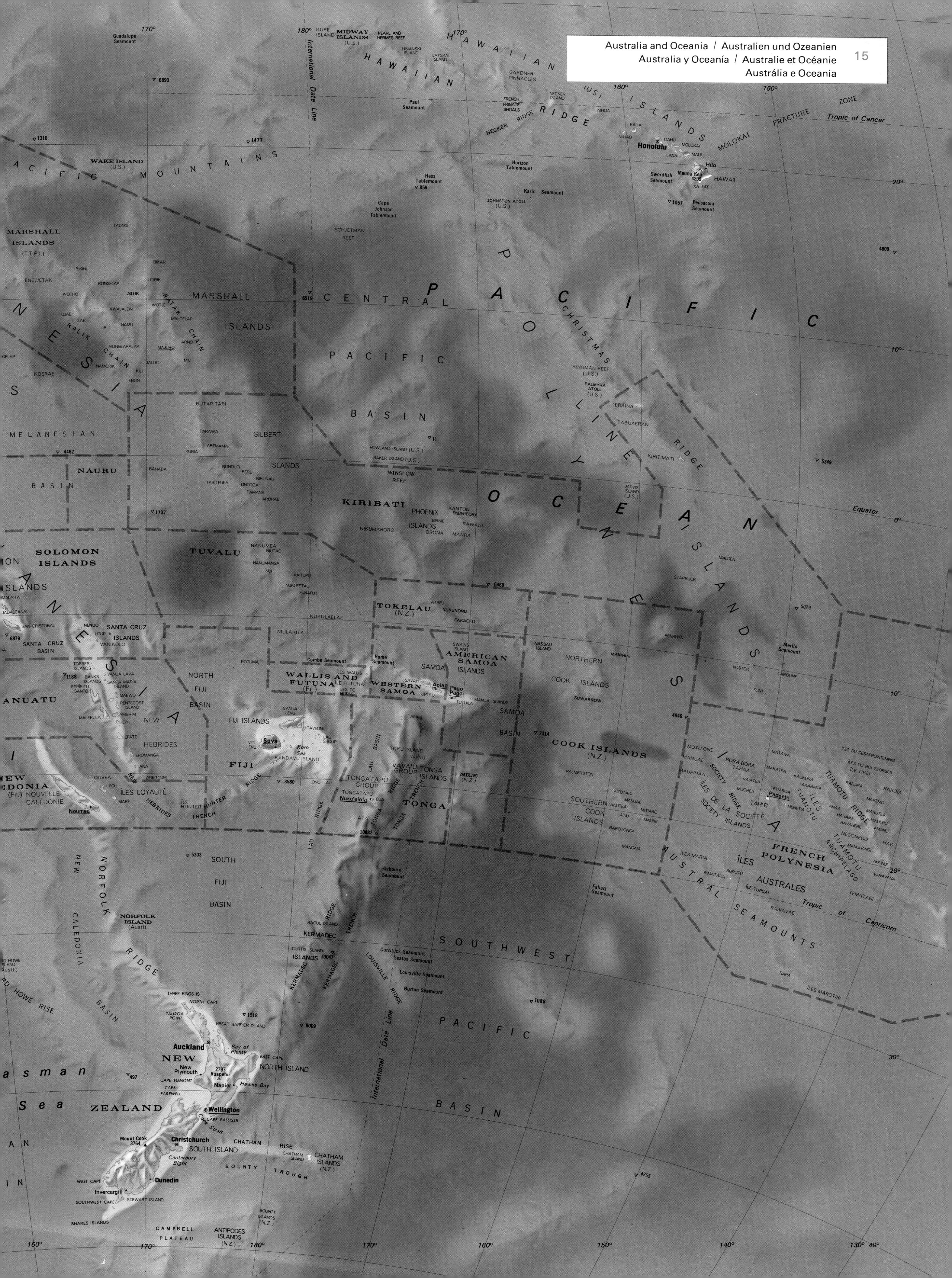
P A C I F I C   O C E A N
P O L Y N E S I A
M E L A N E S I A
HAWAIIAN ISLANDS (U.S.)
HAWAIIAN RIDGE
Honolulu
Hilo
Mauna Kea 4205
HAWAII
MOLOKAI FRACTURE ZONE
Tropic of Cancer
MIDWAY ISLANDS (U.S.)
KURE ISLAND
PEARL AND HERMES REEF
LISIANSKI ISLAND
LAYSAN ISLAND
GARDNER PINNACLES
NECKER ISLAND
NECKER RIDGE
FRENCH FRIGATE SHOALS
NIHOA
KAUAI
NIIHAU
OAHU
MOLOKAI
LANAI
MAUI
KA LAE
Paul Seamount
Horizon Tablemount
Hess Tablemount 859
Karin Seamount
JOHNSTON ATOLL (U.S.)
Swordfish Seamount
Pensacola Seamount
Cape Johnson Tablemount
SCHJETMAN REEF
Guadalupe Seamount
International Date Line
WAKE ISLAND (U.S.)
MID-PACIFIC MOUNTAINS
MARSHALL ISLANDS (T.T.P.I.)
TAONGI
BIKINI
ENEWETAK
RONGELAP
AILUK
UTIRIK
BIKAR
WOTHO
WOTJE
KWAJALEIN
MALOELAP
ARNO
MAJURO
MILI
JALUIT
EBON
KILI
NAMORIK
AILINGLAPALAP
NAMU
UJAE
LAE
LIB
RATAK CHAIN
RALIK CHAIN
KOSRAE
MARSHALL ISLANDS
CENTRAL PACIFIC BASIN
CHRISTMAS RIDGE
LINE ISLANDS
KINGMAN REEF (U.S.)
PALMYRA ATOLL (U.S.)
TERAINA
TABUAERAN
KIRITIMATI
JARVIS ISLAND (U.S.)
MALDEN
STARBUCK
PENRHYN
VOSTOK
CAROLINE
FLINT
Merlin Seamount
Equator
BUTARITARI
TARAWA
ABEMAMA
KURIA
GILBERT ISLANDS
BANABA
NONOUTI
BERU
NIKUNAU
TABITEUEA
ONOTOA
TAMANA
ARORAE
NAURU
MELANESIAN BASIN
KIRIBATI
HOWLAND ISLAND (U.S.)
BAKER ISLAND (U.S.)
WINSLOW REEF
PHOENIX ISLANDS
KANTON
ENDERBURY
BIRNIE
RAWAKI
NIKUMARORO
ORONA
MANRA
TUVALU
NANUMEA
NUTAO
NANUMANGA
NUI
VAITUPU
NUKUFETAU
FUNAFUTI
NUKULAELAE
NIULAKITA
TOKELAU (N.Z.)
ATAFU
NUKUNONU
FAKAOFO
SWAINS ISLAND
AMERICAN SAMOA
SAMOA ISLANDS
WESTERN SAMOA
SAVAI'I
Apia
UPOLU
Pago Pago
TUTUILA
MANUA ISLANDS
SAMOA BASIN
WALLIS AND FUTUNA (Fr.)
ÎLES WALLIS
ÎLE FUTUNA
ÎLES DE HORNE
Combe Seamount
Home Seamount
ROTUMA
SOLOMON ISLANDS
MALAITA
GUADALCANAL
SAN CRISTOBAL
NENDO
UTUPUA
VANIKOLO
SANTA CRUZ ISLANDS
SANTA CRUZ BASIN
TORRES ISLANDS
BANKS ISLANDS
VANUA LAVA
SANTA MARIA ISLAND
ESPIRITU SANTO
MAEWO
PENTECOST ISLAND
AMBRYM
MALEKULA
EPI
EFATE
ERROMANGA
TANA
ANEITYUM
VANUATU
NEW HEBRIDES
NORTH FIJI BASIN
FIJI ISLANDS
FIJI
VANUA LEVU
TAVEUNI
VITI LEVU
Suva
Koro Sea
LAU GROUP
KANDAVU ISLAND
LAU BASIN
LAU RIDGE
HUNTER RIDGE
ÎLE HUNTER
HUNTER TRENCH
HEBRIDES TRENCH
NEW CALEDONIA (Fr.)
NOUVELLE-CALÉDONIE
Nouméa
ÎLES LOYAUTÉ
OUVEA
LIFOU
MARÉ
TOKU ISLAND
VAVA'U GROUP
TONGA ISLANDS
TONGATAPU GROUP
TONGATAPU
Nuku'alofa
EUA
ONO-I-LAU
ATA
TONGA
TONGA RIDGE
TONGA TRENCH
NIUE (N.Z.)
NORTHERN COOK ISLANDS
NASSAU ISLAND
MANIHIKI
SUWARROW
COOK ISLANDS (N.Z.)
PALMERSTON
AITUTAKI
MANUAE
TAKUTEA
MITIARO
ATIU
MAUKE
RAROTONGA
MANGAIA
SOUTHERN COOK ISLANDS
FRENCH POLYNESIA
MOTU ONE
BORA-BORA
TAHAA
MAUPIHAA
RAIATEA
MOOREA
TAHITI
Papeete
TETIAROA
MEHETIA
SOCIETY RIDGE
ÎLES DE LA SOCIÉTÉ
SOCIETY ISLANDS
MATAIVA
MAKATEA
RANGIROA
KAUKURA
FAKARAVA
ANAA
HARAIKI
RAVAHERE
ÎLES DU DÉSAPPOINTEMENT
ÎLES DU ROI GEORGES
ÎLE TIKEI
TUAMOTU RIDGE
TUAMOTU ARCHIPELAGO
ÎLES TUAMOTU
RAROIA
MAKEMO
MARUTEA
HIKUERU
AMANU
NEGONEGO
MANUHANGI
HAO
AHUNUI
VANAVANA
TEMATAGI
ÎLES MARIA
RIMATARA
RURUTU
ÎLES AUSTRALES
ÎLE TUBUAI
RAIVAVAE
AUSTRAL SEAMOUNTS
Tropic of Capricorn
RAPA
ÎLES MAROTIRI
Fabert Seamount
SOUTH FIJI BASIN
NORFOLK ISLAND (Austl.)
NORFOLK RIDGE
NEW CALEDONIA BASIN
LORD HOWE RISE
LORD HOWE ISLAND (Austl.)
Ozbourn Seamount
RAOUL ISLAND
KERMADEC RIDGE
KERMADEC TRENCH
CURTIS ISLAND
KERMADEC ISLANDS
Currituck Seamount
Seafox Seamount
Louisville Seamount
Burton Seamount
LOUISVILLE RIDGE
SOUTHWEST PACIFIC BASIN
THREE KINGS IS.
NORTH CAPE
TAUROA POINT
GREAT BARRIER ISLAND
Auckland
Bay of Plenty
EAST CAPE
NEW ZEALAND
New Plymouth
Ruapehu 2797
Napier
Hawke Bay
CAPE EGMONT
NORTH ISLAND
CAPE FAREWELL
Wellington
CAPE PALLISER
Cook Strait
Tasman Sea
Mount Cook 3764
Christchurch
SOUTH ISLAND
Canterbury Bight
CHATHAM RISE
CHATHAM ISLAND
CHATHAM ISLANDS (N.Z.)
BOUNTY TROUGH
Dunedin
WEST CAPE
Invercargill
SOUTHWEST CAPE
STEWART ISLAND
SNARES ISLANDS
CAMPBELL PLATEAU
ANTIPODES ISLANDS (N.Z.)
BOUNTY ISLANDS (N.Z.)
6890
1316
1477
6519
4809
5349
11
4462
1737
6469
5029
6879
1188
3580
7314
4846
10882
5303
10047
1088
1518
8009
497
4755
160°
170°
180°
150°
140°
130°
40°
30°
20°
10°
0°

ARCTIC
OCEAN
North Pole
3910
ASIA
SIBERIA
SIBIR'
UNION OF SOVIET SOCIALIST REPUBLICS
EUROPE
URAL'SKIJE GORY
URAL MTS.
Arctic Circle
Chabarovsk
Komsomol'sk-na-Amure
Jakutsk
Lensk
Aldan
Tommot
ALDANSKOJE NAGORJE
STANOVOJ CHREBET
VERCHOJANSKIJ CHREBET
CHREBET ČERSKOGO
CHREBET DŽUGDŽUR
Verchojansk
Žigansk
Tiksi
Ochotsk
Ajan
Magadan
Kazačje
Jamsk
Sea of Okhotsk
OKHOTSK BASIN
1644
OSTROV SACHALIN
Nikolajevsk
Aleksandrovsk-Sachalinskij
Ocha
Tatarskij proliv
SICHOTE-ALIN'
Amur
POLUOSTROV KAMČATKA
zaliv Šelichova
SREDINNYJ CHREBET
Petropavlovsk-Kamčatskij
vulkan Kl'učevskaja Sopka 4750
Palana
OSTROV KARAGINSKIJ
KOMANDORSKIJE OSTROVA
Kavača
gora Led'anaja 2562
Markovo
Anadyr'
Uel'kal'
ANADYRSKOJE PLOSKOGORJE
JUKAGIRSKOJE PLOSKOGORJE
Srednekolymsk
Ambarčik
Kolyma
Omolon
Indigirka
gora Pobeda 3147
Vostočno-Sibirskoje more
East Siberian Sea
more Laptevych
Laptev Sea
NOVOSIBIRSKIJE OSTROVA
OSTROV KOTEL'NYJ
OSTROV VRANGEL'A
OSTROV AJON
Chukchi Sea
ALEUTIAN BASIN
BERING SEA
Anadyrskij zaliv
MYS NAVARIN
Bering Strait
MYS DEŽNEVA
SAINT LAWRENCE ISLAND
SAINT MATTHEW ISLAND
PRIBILOF ISLANDS
NUNIVAK ISLAND
UNIMAK ISLAND
BOWERS RIDGE
ALEUTIAN ISLANDS
ALEUTIAN TRENCH
KISKA
CAPE WRANGELL ATTU ISLAND
Unalaska
UNITED STATES
ALASKA
ALASKA RANGE
BROOKS RANGE
Yukon
Barrow
POINT BARROW
POINT HOPE
Nome
SEWARD PENINSULA
Norton Sound
Bethel
Bristol Bay
ALASKA PENINSULA
Fairbanks
Anchorage
Seward
KODIAK ISLAND
WRANGELL MOUNTAINS
Gulf of Alaska
GULF OF ALASKA SEAMOUNT PROVINCE
PATTON SEAMOUNTS
Beaufort Sea
Mackenzie Bay
Inuvik
MACKENZIE MOUNTAINS
SELWYN MOUNTAINS
OGILVIE MOUNTAINS
PELLY MOUNTAINS
Whitehorse
Juneau
STIKINE RANGES
COAST MOUNTAINS
ROCKY
Prince Rupert
Ketchikan
QUEEN CHARLOTTE ISLANDS
Prince George
Dawson Creek
Fort Nelson
CARIBOU MOUNTAINS
HORN PLATEAU
Norman Wells
Great Bear Lake
Great Slave Lake
Yellowknife
Pine Point
Uranium City
Lake Athabasca
CANADA
Hudson Bay
Churchill
York Factory
Reindeer Lake
Lynn Lake
Nelson
BELCHER ISLANDS
PÉNINSULE D'UNGAVA
Ungava Bay
Schefferville
Smallwood Reservoir
Happy Valley-Goose Bay
Hamilton Inlet
Strait of Belle Isle
CAPE BAULD
FLEMISH CAP
Hudson Strait
SOUTHAMPTON ISLAND
COATS ISLAND
MANSEL ISLAND
Repulse Bay
Foxe Basin
PRINCE CHARLES ISLAND
MELVILLE PENINSULA
KING WILLIAM ISLAND
Gulf of Boothia
SOMERSET ISLAND
PRINCE OF WALES ISLAND
VICTORIA ISLAND
Cambridge Bay
Coronation Gulf
Amundsen Gulf
BANKS ISLAND
MELVILLE ISLAND
PRINCE PATRICK ISLAND
BATHURST ISLAND
CORNWALLIS ISLAND
Viscount Melville Sound
Parry Channel
Lancaster Sound
DEVON ISLAND
BYLOT ISLAND
QUEEN ELIZABETH ISLANDS
ELLEF RINGNES ISLAND
AXEL HEIBERG ISLAND
NORTH MAGNETIC POLE
ELLESMERE ISLAND
Barbeau Peak 2604
CAPE COLUMBIA
Lincoln Sea
Nares Strait
Etah
Thule
Melville Bugt
KAP YORK
BAFFIN ISLAND
Baffin Bay
BAFFIN BASIN
Davis Strait
Cumberland Sound
Frobisher Bay
Godthåb
Godhavn
DISKO
Labrador Sea
LABRADOR BASIN
GREENLAND (Den.)
PEARY LAND
KAP MORRIS JESUP
NORDOST-RUNDINGEN
Gunnbjørn Fjeld 3700
Mont Forel 3360
Angmagssalik
Julianehåb
KAP FARVEL
Denmark Strait
KAP BREWSTER
GREENLAND-ICELAND RISE
IRMINGER BASIN
REYKJANES RIDGE
ICELAND BASIN
ICELAND
Reykjavík
Hvannadalshnúkur 2119
ROCKALL RISE
ATLANTIC OCEAN
NORWEGIAN BASIN
JAN MAYEN (Nor.)
JAN MAYEN RIDGE
WEST JAN MAYEN RIDGE
GREENLAND BASIN
Greenland Sea
MOHNS RIDGE
LOFOTEN BASIN
Norwegian Sea
FAEROE ISLANDS (Den.)
SHETLAND ISLANDS (U.K.)
ORKNEY ISLANDS
HEBRIDES
UNITED KINGDOM
Edinburgh
Glasgow
North Sea
NORWEGIAN TRENCH
Bergen
Stavanger
Glittertind 2470
NORWAY
Trondheim
Oslo
DENMARK
København
Göteborg
SWEDEN
Stockholm
Kiruna
Narvik
Hammerfest
FINLAND
Oulu
Helsinki
Gulf of Bothnia
Gulf of Finland
Baltic Sea
Kaliningrad
Klaipėda
Riga
Tallinn
Vilnius
Minsk
LENINGRAD
Smolensk
MOSKVA
Tula
Kursk
Char'kov
Voronež
Doneck
Rostov-na-Donu
Gor'kij
Jaroslavl'
Vologda
Kalinin
Archangel'sk
Kirov
Kotlas
Murmansk
SVALBARD (Nor.)
SPITSBERGEN
EDGEØYA
NORDAUSTLANDET
BJØRNØYA BEAR ISLAND (Nor.)
SPITSBERGEN BANK
BARENTS TROUGH
Barents Sea
MURMANSK RISE
NORDKAPP
ZEML'A FRANCA-IOSIFA
FRANZ JOSEPH LAND
NOVAJA ZEML'A
EAST NOVAYA ZEMLYA TROUGH
WEST NOVAYA ZEMLYA TROUGH
OSTROV KOLGUJEV
OSTROV VAJGAČ
Karskoje more
Kara Sea
Dikson
OSTROV BELYJ
POLUOSTROV JAMAL
Obskaja guba
Salechard
Vorkuta
Dudinka
Noril'sk
PLATO PUTORANA
SEVERO-SIBIRSKAJA NIZMENNOST'
POLUOSTROV TAJMYR
SEVERNAJA ZEML'A
MYS ČEL'USKIN
OSTROV BOL'ŠOJ BEGIČEV
Chatanga
Lena

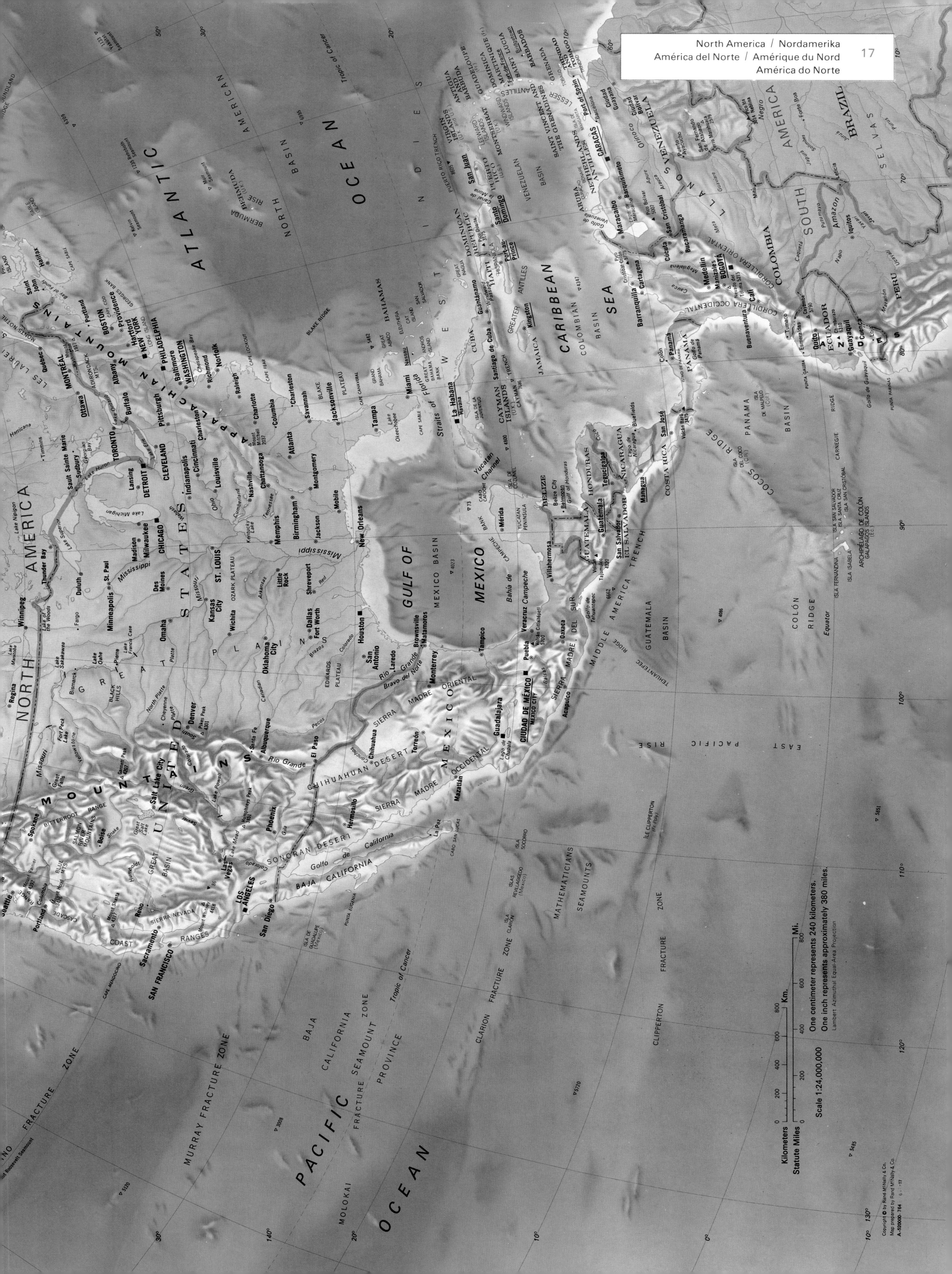
NORTH AMERICA
UNITED STATES
ATLANTIC OCEAN
PACIFIC OCEAN
GULF OF MEXICO
CARIBBEAN SEA
WEST INDIES
SOUTH AMERICA
APPALACHIAN MOUNTAINS
ROCKY MOUNTAINS
GREAT PLAINS
SIERRA MADRE ORIENTAL
SIERRA MADRE OCCIDENTAL
SIERRA MADRE DEL SUR
MIDDLE AMERICA TRENCH
EAST PACIFIC RISE
COLÓN RIDGE
Tropic of Cancer
Equator
Kilometers
Statute Miles
Scale 1:24,000,000
One centimeter represents 240 kilometers.
One inch represents approximately 380 miles.
Lambert Azimuthal Equal-Area Projection
Copyright © by Rand McNally & Co.
Map prepared by Rand McNally & Co.

NORTH AMERICA
UNITED STATES
ROCKY MTS.
APPALACHIAN MOUNTAINS
GREAT PLAINS
OZARK PLATEAU
EDWARDS PLATEAU
CHICAGO
CLEVELAND
NEW YORK
PHILADELPHIA
WASHINGTON
Baltimore
Pittsburgh
Indianapolis
Cincinnati
Charleston
Louisville
Richmond
Norfolk
Raleigh
Nashville
Chattanooga
Charlotte
Columbia
Memphis
Atlanta
Birmingham
Montgomery
Savannah
Jacksonville
Tampa
Miami
Des Moines
Omaha
Kansas City
ST. LOUIS
Wichita
Denver
Cheyenne
Pikes Peak 4301
Santa Fe
Albuquerque
Oklahoma City
Little Rock
Dallas
Fort Worth
Shreveport
Jackson
Mobile
New Orleans
Houston
San Antonio
Laredo
Brownsville
El Paso
MEXICO
SIERRA MADRE ORIENTAL
SIERRA MADRE DEL SUR
Monterrey
Matamoros
Torreón
Tampico
Guadalajara
Lago de Chapala
CIUDAD DE MÉXICO
Puebla
Veracruz
Volcán Citlaltépetl 5700
Oaxaca
Acapulco
Villahermosa
Mérida
YUCATAN PENINSULA
Bahía de Campeche
CAMPECHE BANK
GULF OF MEXICO
MEXICO BASIN
Yucatan Channel
Straits of Florida
CUBA
La Habana
Havana
Santiago de Cuba
Guantánamo
BAHAMAS
Nassau
GREAT BAHAMA BANK
CAYMAN ISLANDS
JAMAICA
Kingston
HAITI
Port-au-Prince
HISPANIOLA
DOMINICAN REPUBLIC
Santo Domingo
Pico Duarte 3175
PUERTO RICO
San Juan
PUERTO RICO TRENCH
VIRGIN ISLANDS (U.K. and U.S.)
ANTIGUA AND BARBUDA
MONTSERRAT
GUADELOUPE (Fr.)
DOMINICA
MARTINIQUE (Fr.)
Fort-de-France
SAINT LUCIA
BARBADOS
Bridgetown
SAINT VINCENT AND THE GRENADINES
GRENADA
TRINIDAD AND TOBAGO
Port of Spain
WEST INDIES
GREATER ANTILLES
LESSER ANTILLES
NETHERLANDS ANTILLES
ARUBA
CARIBBEAN SEA
VENEZUELAN BASIN
COLOMBIAN BASIN
BELIZE
Belize City
Belmopan
Gulf of Honduras
GUATEMALA
Guatemala
HONDURAS
Tegucigalpa
EL SALVADOR
San Salvador
NICARAGUA
Managua
Lago de Nicaragua
COSTA RICA
San José
PANAMA
Panamá
Colón
MIDDLE AMERICA TRENCH
GUATEMALA BASIN
TEHUANTEPEC RIDGE
COCOS RIDGE
PANAMA BASIN
CARNEGIE RIDGE
COLÓN RIDGE
ARCHIPIÉLAGO DE COLÓN
GALAPAGOS ISLANDS (Ec.)
Equator
NORTH AMERICAN BASIN
BERMUDA (U.K.)
ATLANTIC OCEAN
MID-ATLANTIC RIDGE
AZORES PLATEAU
AÇORES
AZORES (Port.)
Tropic of Cancer
CAPE VERDE BASIN
GUIANA BASIN
Great Meteor Tablemount
Kelvin Seamount
Muir Seamount
Yakutat Seamount
Rehoboth Seamount
SOUTH AMERICA
VENEZUELA
CARACAS
Maracaibo
Barquisimeto
Barcelona
Ciudad Bolívar
Ciudad Guayana
COLOMBIA
BOGOTÁ
Medellín
Cali
Barranquilla
Cartagena
Cúcuta
Bucaramanga
Manizales
Buenaventura
CORDILLERA OCCIDENTAL
CORDILLERA ORIENTAL
LLANOS
GUYANA
Georgetown
SURINAME
Paramaribo
FRENCH GUIANA
Cayenne
ECUADOR
Quito
Guayaquil
Cuenca
PERU
LIMA
Iquitos
Trujillo
Chiclayo
ANDES
PERU-CHILE TRENCH
BRAZIL
SELVAS
Manaus
Belém
São Luís
Fortaleza
Natal
João Pessoa
Recife
Maceió
Aracaju
Salvador
Teresina
Amazon
Orinoco
Negro
Madeira
Purus
Tocantins
Xingu
ILHA DE MARAJÓ
CHAPADA DOS PARECIS
SA. DO RONCADOR
Mato Grosso

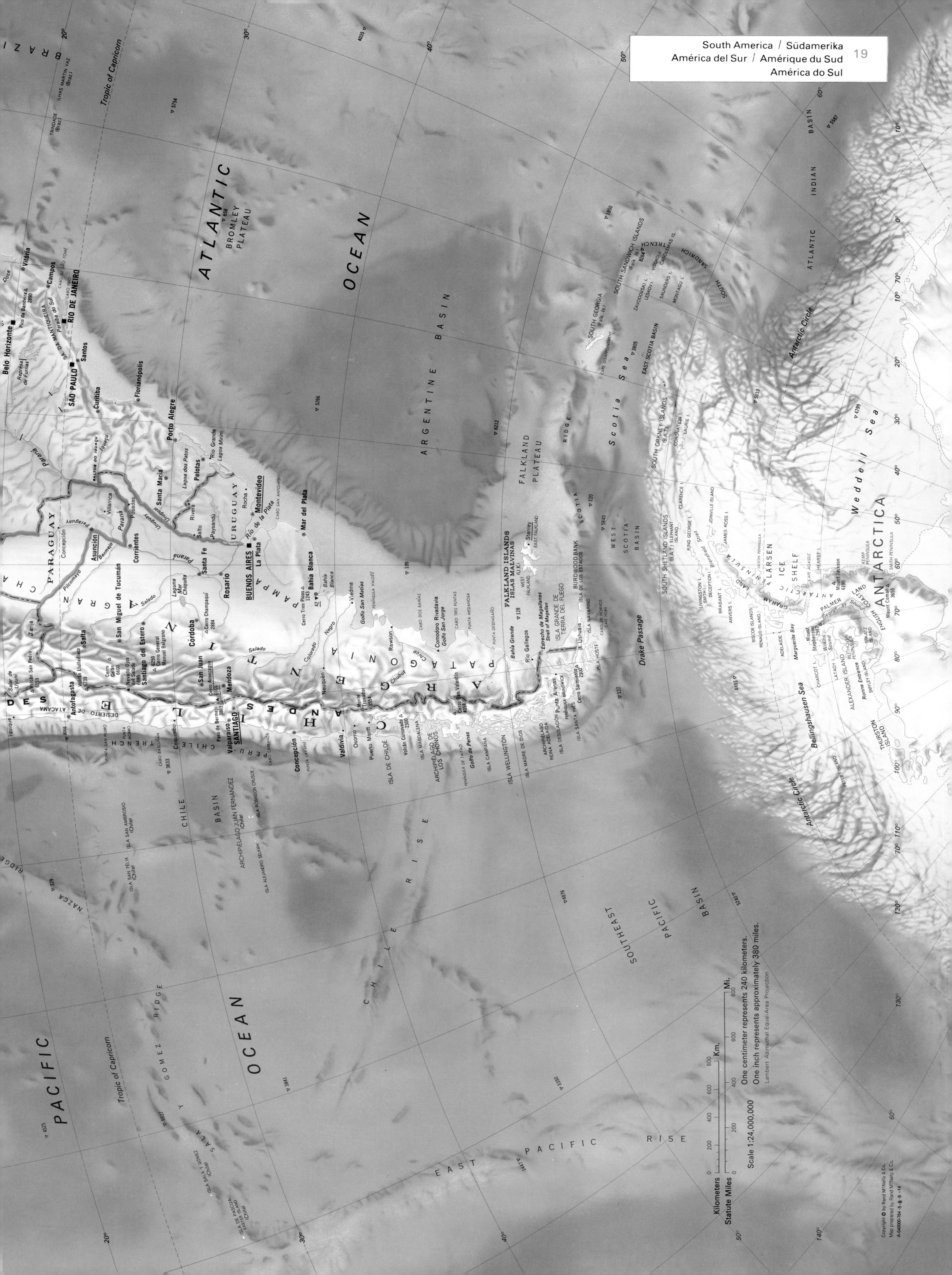
ATLANTIC OCEAN
PACIFIC OCEAN
ARGENTINE BASIN
BROMLEY PLATEAU
FALKLAND PLATEAU
Scotia Sea
Weddell Sea
ANTARCTICA
Bellingshausen Sea
Drake Passage
SOUTHEAST PACIFIC BASIN
EAST PACIFIC RISE
CHILE RISE
CHILE BASIN
NAZCA RIDGE
SALA Y GOMEZ RIDGE
Tropic of Capricorn
Antarctic Circle
ATLANTIC INDIAN BASIN
SOUTH SANDWICH TRENCH
EAST SCOTIA BASIN
WEST SCOTIA BASIN
FALKLAND ISLANDS
ISLAS MALVINAS
SOUTH GEORGIA
SOUTH SANDWICH ISLANDS
SOUTH ORKNEY ISLANDS
SOUTH SHETLAND ISLANDS
ANTARCTIC PENINSULA
LARSEN ICE SHELF
PARAGUAY
URUGUAY
PATAGONIA
PAMPA
ANDES
BUENOS AIRES
Montevideo
SANTIAGO
SÃO PAULO
RIO DE JANEIRO
Asunción
Córdoba
Rosario
Mendoza
Porto Alegre
Mar del Plata
Bahía Blanca
Valparaíso
Concepción
Valdivia
Puerto Montt
Punta Arenas
Ushuaia
Río Gallegos
ISLA GRANDE DE TIERRA DEL FUEGO
Estrecho de Magallanes
Kilometers
Statute Miles
Scale 1:24,000,000
One centimeter represents 240 kilometers.
One inch represents approximately 380 miles.
Lambert Azimuthal Equal-Area Projection
Copyright © by Rand McNally & Co.

THE REGIONAL MAPS consist of three basic series, each distinctive in style, but using common symbols to ensure ease of understanding (see Legend to Maps, pages x-xii). Every major land region, continent or subcontinent, is introduced by one or more maps at the scale of 1:12,000,000. There follow maps at 1:6,000,000 and 1:3,000,000 which cover the region in sections, in greater detail. Except for scale, the 1:6,000,000 and 1:3,000,000 maps are alike. Finally, selected areas of special importance in the region are shown at 1:1,000,000. Each scale is identified by a color bar, and a locater map with the same color may be found in the margin of the map page. A sample area at each of the scales, including centimeter-kilometer and inch-mile equivalents, appears on page 21.

The three basic series differ in content and emphasis. The 1:12,000,000 maps, which are primarily political, present an overview of each region. They show national boundaries and, in some cases, subordinate administrative subdivisions as well. These introductory maps make it possible to compare location, areal extent, and shape among the nations of the world. The distribution of cities, towns and metropolitan areas is shown in the context of broad physical configurations. A selection of the most important railways and highways also appears.

The 1:6,000,000 and 1:3,000,000 maps together constitute about half of the map pages and provide the basic reference coverage of the Atlas. They show sections of regions in great detail—in some cases individual countries (Japan and New Zealand), in others, parts of countries (central Mexico), in still others, larger regions (the Middle East). The more densely settled areas appear at the larger 1:3,000,000 scale, the remaining areas at 1:6,000,000. Maps at these two scales present political and cultural information against the background of a detailed physical portrait of the terrain, which is depicted by both shaded relief and a spectrum of altitude tints. Bathymetric tints are used to show offshore water depths. The transportation pattern shown includes major railways, two classes of roads, and airports that offer either international or jet service. The names and boundaries of political subdivisions are given for selected countries.

In the 1:1,000,000 series, strategic areas that are of special interest because of economic importance, dense settlement, or both, appear in even greater detail. This series is designed to show the pattern of cities, towns, roads, railways, bridges, airports, dams, reservoirs, and other interrelated features reflecting man's dense occupancy in these areas. The most important parks, places of historical interest, and recreational facilities are indicated. Three classes of highways and two classes of railways are shown, and major roads are named. All features are portrayed against a topographic background of shaded relief.

Inhabited places on the regional maps are classified in two distinct ways. Cities and towns of different *population size* are distinguished by the *size and shape of the symbol* that locates the place. The symbol reflects the population within the municipal or corporate limits, exclusive of any suburbs. In countries where the limits of a municipality include rural areas, the symbol represents only the urban or agglomerated population. The *relative political and economic importance* of a place which may be independent of the number of its inhabitants, is indicated by the *size of type* in which its name appears.

A key to all symbols and type sizes is shown on page xi of the Legend to Maps.

DIE REGIONALKARTEN bestehen aus drei Serien, die im Stil verschieden sind, der besseren Lesbarkeit halber aber gemeinsame Kartensignaturen verwenden (siehe "Zeichenerklärung" S. x-xii). Jede Grossregion, jeder Kontinent oder Subkontinent wird durch eine oder mehrere Karten im Massstab 1:12 Millionen eingeleitet. Es folgen sodann Karten in den Massstäben 1:6 und 1:3 Millionen, welche die Region in Teilen und grösseren Einzelheiten darstellen. Die Karten in 1:6 Millionen und 1:3 Millionen unterscheiden sich nur im Massstab. Schliesslich werden ausgewählte Gebiete von besonderer Bedeutung innerhalb der Region in 1:1 Million dargestellt. Jede Massstabsangabe ist durch ein Farbfeld gekennzeichnet, und ein Lagekärtchen in derselben Farbe erscheint am Rand der Kartenseite. Kartenausschnitte als Beispiele für jeden dieser Massstäbe mit Angabe des Verhältnisses Zentimeter zu Kilometer und Zoll zu Meilen sind auf Seite 21 aufgeführt.

Die drei Kartenreihen unterscheiden sich in Inhalt und Betonung. Die Karten in 1:12 Millionen, die vor allem politische Karten sind, geben einen Überblick über jede Region. Sie zeigen die Staatsgrenzen und in manchen Fällen auch die Grenzen von nachgeordneten Verwaltungseinheiten. Diese einführenden Karten ermöglichen einen Vergleich der Lage, Ausdehnung und Gestalt der Staaten der Erde. Die Verteilung der städtischen Ballungsgebiete, Grossstädte und Städte wird in ihrem Zusammenhang mit dem grossräumigen Formenschatz des Reliefs gezeigt. Gezeigt wird auch eine Auswahl der wichtigsten Eisenbahnlinien und Fernverkehrsstrassen.

Die Karten 1:6 Millionen und 1:3 Millionen machen zusammen mehr als die Hälfte der Kartenseiten aus und bilden den grundlegenden Teil des Atlasses. Sie zeigen sehr inhaltsreiche Ausschnitte von Regionen—in einigen Fällen einzelne Länder (Japan und Neuseeland), in anderen Landesteile (Zentralmexiko) und weider anderen Grossräume (Mittlerer Osten).

Die dichter besiedelten Gebiete sind in 1:3 Millionen dargestellt, die übrigen Gebiete in 1:6 Millionen. Die Karten in diesen beiden Massstäben liefern politische und kulturgeographische Informationen vor dem Hintergrund einer detaillierten Geländedarstellung, gekennzeichnet durch Reliefschummerung und eine Skala von Höhenschichten. Tiefenstufen werden verwendet, um die Wassertiefen jenseits der Küsten zu gliedern. Das abgebildete Verkehrsnetz umfasst wichtige Eisenbahnlinien, zwei Klassen von Strassen und Flughäfen, die entweder im internationalen Verkehr oder von Düsenflugzeugen angeflogen werden. Die Verwaltungsgliederung wird für eine grosse Zahl von Staaten gezeigt.

In der Kartenserie 1:1 Million sind mit noch zahlreicheren Einzelheiten zentrale Räume dargestellt, denen infolge ihrer wirtschaftlichen Bedeutung, dichten Besiedlung oder durch beide Faktoren bedingt, besonderes Interesse zukommt. Diese Kartenserie wurde entwickelt, um die Verteilung der Grossstädte, Städte, Strassen, Eisenbahnen, Brücken, Flughäfen, Dämme, Stauseen und anderer Objekte zu zeigen, die Ausdruck sind für die dichte Besiedlung. Verzeichnet sind auch die wichtigsten Parks, Örtlichkeiten von historischem Interesse und Erholungsstätten. Drei Strassenklassen und zwei Klassen von Eisenbahnlinien werden unterschieden. Die Darstellung ist unterlegt durch eine Reliefschummerung.

Die Siedlungen auf den Regionalkarten sind auf zwei bestimmte Arten klassifiziert. Grossstädte und Städte unterschiedlicher *Einwohnerzahl* sind durch *Grösse und Form der Signatur* unterschieden, die den Ort lokalisiert. Die Signatur entspricht der Zahl der Einwohner innerhalb der Stadtgrenzen, schliesst also nicht eingemeindete Vororte aus. In Staaten, in denen ländliche Gebiete in die Stadtgemeinden einbezogen sind, entsprechen die Signaturen nur der in den zentralen Siedlungen ansässigen Bevölkerung. Die *relative politische und wirtschaftliche Bedeutung* eines Ortes, die von der Zahl seiner Einwohner unabhängig sein kann, ist ausgedrückt durch die *Schriftgrösse*, in welcher der Ortsname erscheint.

Ein Schlüssel zu allen Signaturen und Schriftgrössen findet sich auf Seite xi der "Zeichenerklärung".

LOS MAPAS REGIONALES integran tres series básicas, cada una con su estilo propio; pero los símbolos usados son en todas los mismos para facilitar su comprensión (véanse las Leyendas para Mapas, páginas x-xii). Cada una de las grandes regiones, continentes o subcontinentes, se presenta a través de uno o varios mapas a la escala de 1:12 000 000. A continuación hay mapas a escalas de 1:6 000 000 y 1:3 000 000 que presentan la región correspondiente en secciones, con mayores detalles. Con excepción de su escala, los mapas de 1:6 000 000 y 1:3 000 000 tienen las mismas características. Por ultimo, aparecen a la escala de 1:1 000 000 áreas de cada región seleccionadas por su importancia. Cada escala se identifica por una barra de color, y un mapa-guía con el mismo color se presenta en el margen de la página de cada mapa. La página 21 ofrece como ejemplo un área-muestra a cada una de las escalas, incluyendo equivalentes en centímetros-kilómetros y pulgadas-millas.

Las tres series básicas son diferentes en contenido y en énfasis. Los mapas a escala de 1:12 000 000, fundamentalmente políticos, ofrecen una vista general de cada región. Indican las fronteras nacionales y, en algunos casos, las subdivisiones administrativas secundarias. Son mapas introductivos que permiten comparar la ubicación, extensión territorial y forma de las distintas naciones. La distribución de ciudades, poblados y áreas metropolitanas se aprecia en un contexto físico esbozado a grandes rasgos. Los detalles incluyen una selección de las vías férras y las carreteras más importantes.

Las series de mapas a 1:6 000 000 y a 1:3 000 000 ocupan entre ambas cerca de la mitad de los mapas del atlas y en ellas se concentra el material de consulta básico de la obra. Los mapas muestran secciones de regiones en gran detalle: en algunos casos países enteros, como Japón y Nueva Zelandia; en otros, partes de países, como el centro de México; y en otros, regiones mas extensas, como el Medio Oriente. Las áreas con mayor densidad de establecimientos humanos se presentan a una escala mayor, la de 1:3 000 000, y las demás a la escala de 1:6 000 000. En estas dos escalas los mapas contienen información política y cultural, sobre un fondo que ilustra en detalle la configuración física del terreno, utilizando sombreado para el relieve y toda una gama de tintes para indicar las altitudes. Un colorido batimétrico señala las variaciones de profundidad en el suelo marino. El esquema de las vías de comunicación incluye las principales vías férreas, dos clases de caminos, y los aeropuertos que ofrecen servicio nacional o internacional de jets. Las subdivisiones políticas secundarias se dan para una selección de varios países.

En la serie de mapas de 1:1 000 000, las áreas estratégicas de especial interés por su importancia económica, su densidad de población, o ambos factores combinados, aparecen aún con mayor detalle. Esta serie se diseñó para mostrar la distribución de ciudades, poblados, caminos, vías férreas, puentes, aeropuertos, presas, embalses y otros elementos similares, que reflejan la densidad de la ocupación humana. También se consignan los parques más importantes, los sitios de interés histórico, los campos de recreo, tres clases de carreteras, y dos de ferrocarriles, se da los nombres de los caminos más importantes. Todos estos elementos aparecen sobre un fondo topográfico de relieve sombreado.

En los mapas regionales se hacen dos clasificaciones distintas de los lugares habitados. Las ciudades y las poblaciones *de diferente densidad de habitantes* se distinguen por la *forma y tamaño del símbolo* que las localiza en el mapa. Este símbolo refleja el tamaño de la poblacióin dentro de sus límites municipales, sin tomar en cuenta los suburbios. En los países donde los límites de una municipalidad incluyen áreas rurales, el símbolo se limita a representar el conglomerado urbano de habitantes. La *importancia económica y política de un lugar*, la cual puede ser independiente del número de sus habitantes, se indica mediante el *tamaño del tipo de imprenta* en que aparece su nombre.

La clave de los símbolos y el valor de los tamaños de las letras se dan en la página xi de las Leyendas para Mapas.

LES CARTES RÉGIONALES sont de trois types principaux, chacun d'un style différent mais avec des symboles communs pour faciliter la compréhension (voir la légende des cartes pages x-xii). Chaque grande région, continent ou subcontinent, est représentée par une ou plusieurs cartes à l'échelle de 1:12 000 000e. Viennent ensuite des cartes au 1:6 000 000e et au 1:3 000 000e qui couvrent la région par sections plus détaillées; hormis la différence d'échelle, ces cartes sont semblables. Enfin, des secteurs particulièrement importants sont représentés au 1:1 000 000e. À chaque échelle correspond une bande colorée et une carte repère de même couleur, dans la marge de chaque page. Un échantillon de cartes aux diverses échelles est représenté à droite. Chaque carte est accompagnée d'une double échelle graphique donnant les rapports centimètre/kilomètre et inch/mille correspondants.

Les trois catégories de cartes diffèrent par le contenu et par ce qu'elles mettent en relief. Les cartes au 1:12 000 000e, qui sont essentiellement politiques, donnent un apercu général de chaque région. Elles indiquent les frontières nationales et, dans certains cas, les subdivisions administratives intérieures. Ces cartes d'introduction permettent de comparer la localisation, la superficie et la forme des pays du monde. La répartition des villes et des zones métropolitaines y apparaît dans le cadre des grandes régions naturelles. Les routes et les voies ferrées les plus importantes y figurent également.

Les cartes au 1:6 000 000e et au 1:3 000 000e forment la moitié de l'Atlas et en constituent la série cartographique essentielle. Elles représentent de façon plus détaillée une partie de pays (centre du Mexique), ou encore des régions plus vestes (Moyen-Orient) ou, parfois, des pays entiers (Japon, Nouvelle-Zélande). Les régiones les plus peuplées sont représentées à plus grande échelle (1;3 000 000e) que les autres (1:6 000 000e). Ces cartes offrent des informations d'ordre politique et culturel sur un fond topographique précis où le relief est indiqué à la fois par un estompage et par des variations de couleur. Différentes teintes de bleu sont utilisées pour symboliser les profondeurs marines. Les réseaux de transport représentés comprennent les principales voies ferrées, deux catégories de routes et les aéroports internationaux ou desservis par des avions à réaction. Les subdivisions politiques d'un certain nombre de pays sont aussi tracées.

Dans la série de cartes au 1:1 000 000e, des régions très importantes, soit du fait de leur densité de population, soit du fait de leur rôle économique, sont représentées d'une manière encore plus détaillée. L'objectif de cette série de cartes est de montrer la répartition des villes, routes, voies ferrées, ponts, aéroports, barrages, lacs de barrages et autres données associées qui traduisent la densité de l'occupation humaine dans ces régions. Les parcs les plus importants, les sites historiques essentiels et les centres de loisirs sont indiqués. Toutes les informations se détachent sur un fond topographique où le relief apparaît en estompage.

Les centres urbains des cartes régionales sont classés de deux manières différentes. *L'importance de la population* des villes est indiquée par *la dimension et la forme du symbole* qui les situe sur la carte. Seule la population comprise dans les limites municipales est prise en considération; dans les pays où des espaces ruraux sont inclus dans les limites d'une municipalité, seule la population urbaine entre en ligne de compte. *L'importance politique et économique relative* d'une ville, qui n'est pas nécessairement liée au nombre d'habitants, est indiquée par la dimension des caractères qui composent son nom.

La signification de tous les symboles utilisés dans les cartes régionales est donnée par la légende des cartes aux pages x-xii.

OS MAPAS REGIONAIS compreendem três séries básicas, cada uma em estilo diferente, mas que empregam os mesmos símbolos para facilitar sua compreensão (Ver as *Legendas dos mapas*, pág. x-xii). Os mapas de cada uma das principais regiões terrestres, continentes ou subcontinentes, são introduzidos por um ou mais mapas na escala 1:12 000 000. Em seguida, vêm mapas, nas escalas de 1:6 000 000 e 1:3 000 000, que apresentam, com maiores detalhes, seções da região considerada. Exceto quanto à escala, os mapas de 1:6 000 000 e 1:3 000 000 têm as mesmas características. Finalmente, aparecem, na escala de 1:1 000 000, os mapas das áreas mais importantes da região considerada. A cada escala corresponde uma barra colorida e um indicador da mesma cor, que se encontra à margem da página de cada mapa. À página 21, acha-se um exemplo de cada escala, bem como a equivalência das relações centímetro/quilômetro e polegada/milha.

As três séries básicas de mapas são diferentes quanto ao conteúdo e à apresentação. Os mapas em escala de 1:12 000 000, que são essencialmente políticos, oferecem uma visão geral de cada região. Indicam as fronteiras nacionais e, em alguns casos, as subdivisões administrativas internas. Esses mapas servem de introdução e permitem avaliar e comparar a posição, superfície e forma dos países do Mundo. Neles está claramente indicada a distribuição das cidades e outros centros urbanos, bem como as principais características da configuração do solo. Encontra-se neles também uma seleção das ferrovias e rodovias mais importantes.

A série de mapas das escalas de 1:6 000 000 e de 1:3 000 000 constituem o principal material de referência do Atlas e representa cerca de metade do conjunto de mapas. Entre eles há mapas detalhados de parte de um país (centro do México), de um país inteiro (Japão e a Nova Zelândia) ou de uma região mais extensa (Oriente Médio). As áreas de maior densidade demográfica são apresentadas em escala maior, a de 1:3 000 000, e as demais, na de 1:6 000 000. Nessas duas escalas, os mapas fornecem informações de ordem política e cultural sobre um fundo que indica a configuração detalhada das particularidades físicas do solo, cujo relevo se destaca por contrastes de sombras e cores. Diversos matizes do azul traduzem o mapa batimétrico da profundidade ao largo das costas. Indicam também os aeroportos internacionais, as principais ferrovias, duas categorias de rodovias. As subdivisões políticas internas de numerosos países estão igualmente assinalados.

Na série de mapas da escala de 1:1 000 000, certas áreas, de interesse estratégico conjugado à importância econômica, densidade demográfica, ou ambos os elementos combinados, aparecem em forma ainda mais detalhada. O objetivo dessa série é representar a distribuição dos grandes centros urbanos, cidades, rodovias, ferrovias, pontes, aeroportos, represas, reservatórios e outras características associadas às grandes densidades demográficas. Indicam-se, também, os parques mais importantes, os lugares de interesse histórico, as áreas de lazer, três categorias de rodovias, e duas de ferrovias; e a nomenclatura dos grandes itinerários rodoviários. Todos esses elementos destacam-se sobre um fundo topográfico do relevo, executado em matizes das diversas cores.

Nos mapas regionais, assinalam-se os centros urbanos de dois modos. A *grandeza da população* das grandes cidades e dos centros urbanos secundários é representada pela *dimensão e forma do símbolo* que as localiza no mapa. O símbolo só reflete a população situada dentro de limites administrativos, sem levar em conta os subúrbios. Nos países onde os limites de uma municipalidade incluem zonas rurais, o símbolo representa apenas a população. A *importância política e econômica* de uma cidade, que não se relaciona necessariamente com o número de seus habitantes, é indicada pela *dimensão* dos caracteres tipográficos com que se compõe o seu nome.

A chave dos símbolos e caracteres tipográficos empregados figura na pág. xi, nas *Legendas dos mapas*.

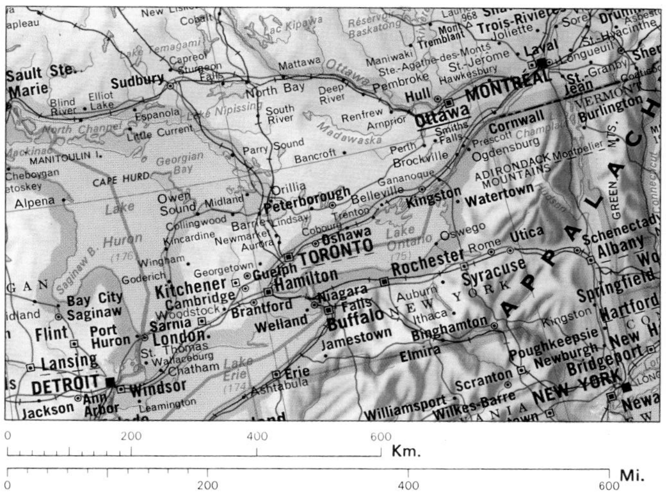

Scale 1:12,000,000
One centimeter represents 120 kilometers.
One inch represents approximately 190 miles.

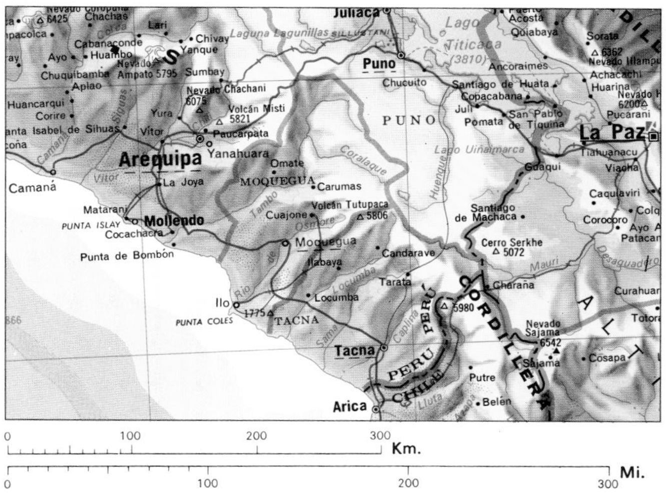

Scale 1:6,000,000
One centimeter represents 60 kilometers.
One inch represents approximately 95 miles.

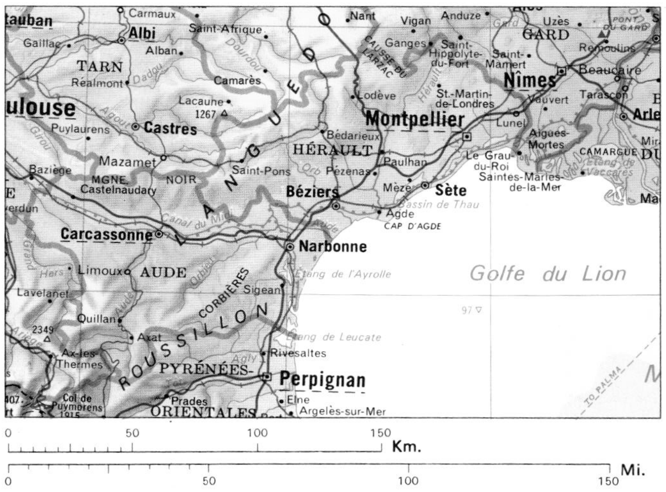

Scale 1:3,000,000
One centimeter represents 30 kilometers.
One inch represents approximately 47 miles.

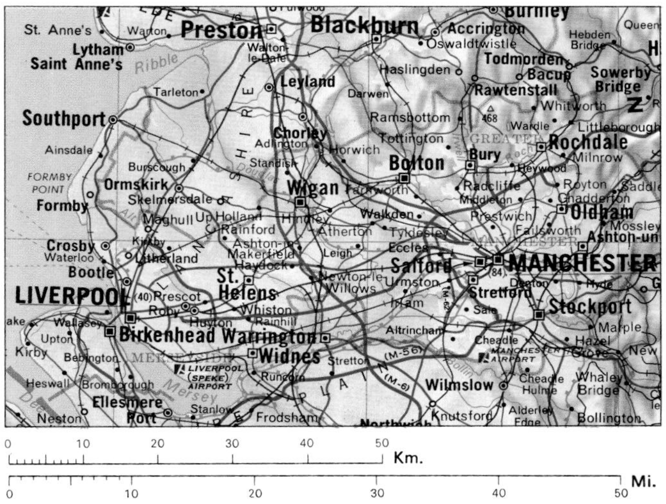

Scale 1:1,000,000
One centimeter represents 10 kilometers.
One inch represents approximately 16 miles.

134 - 137

MAP FORM	-älven	gora	île	islands	-øya	ozero	sea	vodochranilišče
ENGLISH	river	mountain	island	islands	island	lake	sea	reservoir
DEUTSCH	Fluss	Berg	Insel	Inseln	Insel	See	Meer	Stausee
ESPAÑOL	río	montaña	isla	islas	isla	lago	mar	embalse
FRANÇAIS	rivière	montagne	île	îles	île	lac	mer	réservoir
PORTUGUÊS	rio	montanha	ilha	ilhas	ilha	lago	mar	reservatório

BARENTS SEA
Murmansk
Archangel'sk
Beloje more
White Sea
FINLAND
Helsinki
LENINGRAD
Tallinn
Riga
Vilnius
Minsk
MOSKVA
Gor'kij
Kazan'
Kujbyšev
Saratov
Volgograd (Stalingrad)
Astrachan'
Perm'
Sverdlovsk
Čel'abinsk
Ufa
Orenburg
Kijev
Char'kov
Odessa
Rostov-na-Donu
Doneck
Dnepropetrovsk
Krasnodar
Tbilisi
Jerevan
Baku
Istanbul
Ankara
București
Sofija
Athínai
TEHRĀN
Baghdād
RUSSIAN SOVIET FEDERATIVE SOCIALIST REPUBLIC
UNION OF SOVIET SOCIALIST REPUBLICS
URAL'SKIJE GORY
URAL MOUNTAINS
ZAPADNO SIBIRSKAJA RAVNINA
BOL'SOJ KAVKAZ
CAUCASUS
BLACK SEA
CASPIAN SEA
Aral'skoje more
Azovskoje more
TURKEY
IRAN
IRAQ
SYRIA
CYPRUS
ROMANIA
BULGARIA
KAZACHSKAJA S.S.R.
UKRAINSKAJA S.S.R.
BELORUSSKAJA S.S.R.
UZBEKSKAJA S.S.R.
TURKMENSKAJA S.S.R.
72-75
118-119

Kilometers 0 200 400 600 Km.
Statute Miles 0 200 400 600 Mi.

Scale 1:12,000,000

One centimeter represents 120 kilometers.
One inch represents approximately 190 miles.
Miller Oblated Stereographic Projection

a

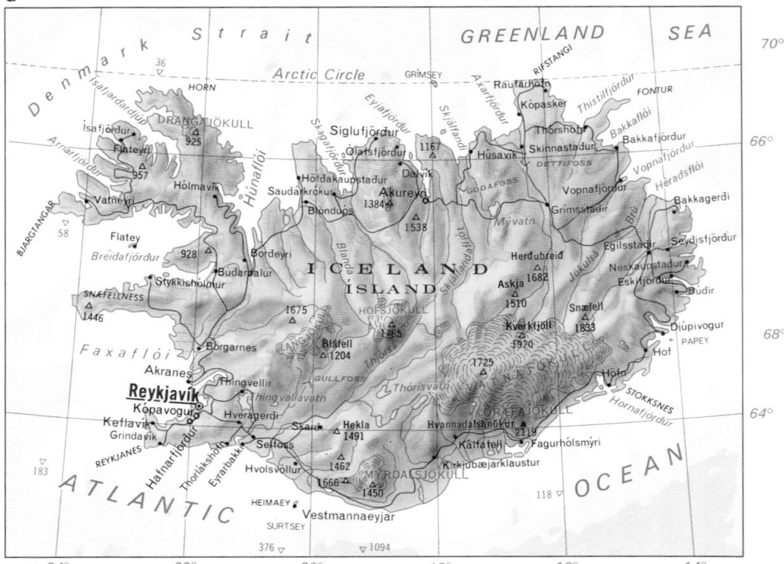

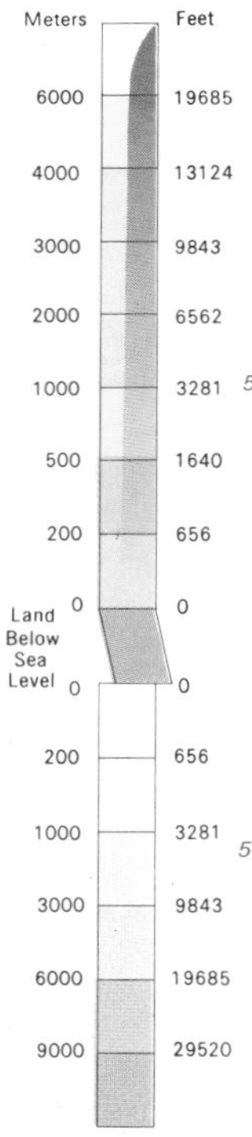

MAP FORM	-älven	-fjorden	guba	-joki	-jökull	lääni	-øya	ozero
ENGLISH	river	fjord, lake	bay	river	glacier	province	island	lake
DEUTSCH	Fluss	Fjord, See	Bucht	Fluss	Gletscher	Provinz	Insel	See
ESPAÑOL	rio	fiordo, lago	bahia	rio	glaciar	provincia	isla	lago
FRANÇAIS	rivière	fjord, lac	baie	rivière	glacier	province	île	lac
PORTUGUÊS	rio	fiorde, lago	baia	rio	geleira	provincia	ilha	lago

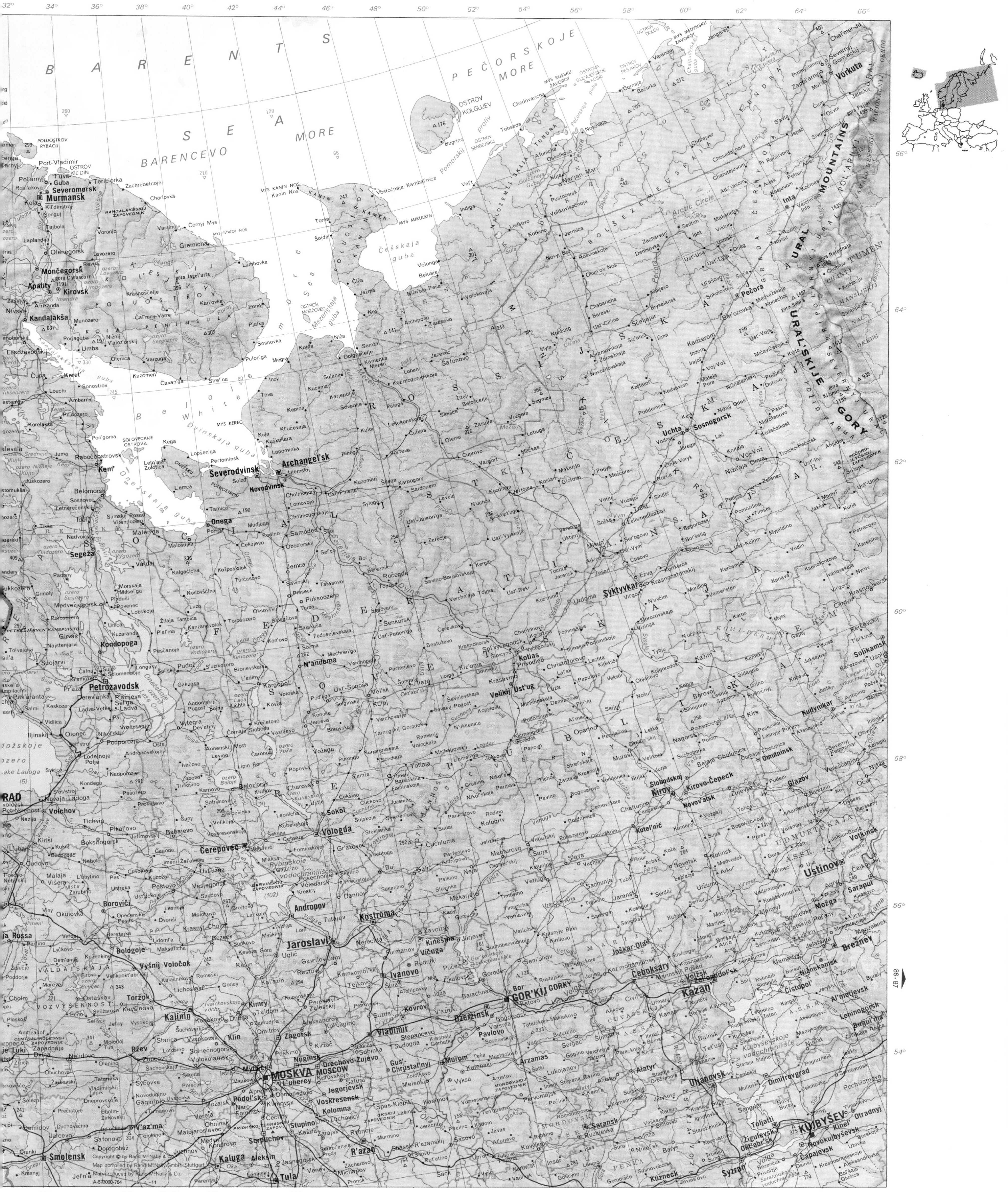

Kilometers 0 100 200 300 Km.

Statute Miles 0 100 200 300 Mi.

Scale 1:6,000,000

One centimeter represents 60 kilometers.
One inch represents approximately 95 miles.
Lambert Conformal Conic Projection

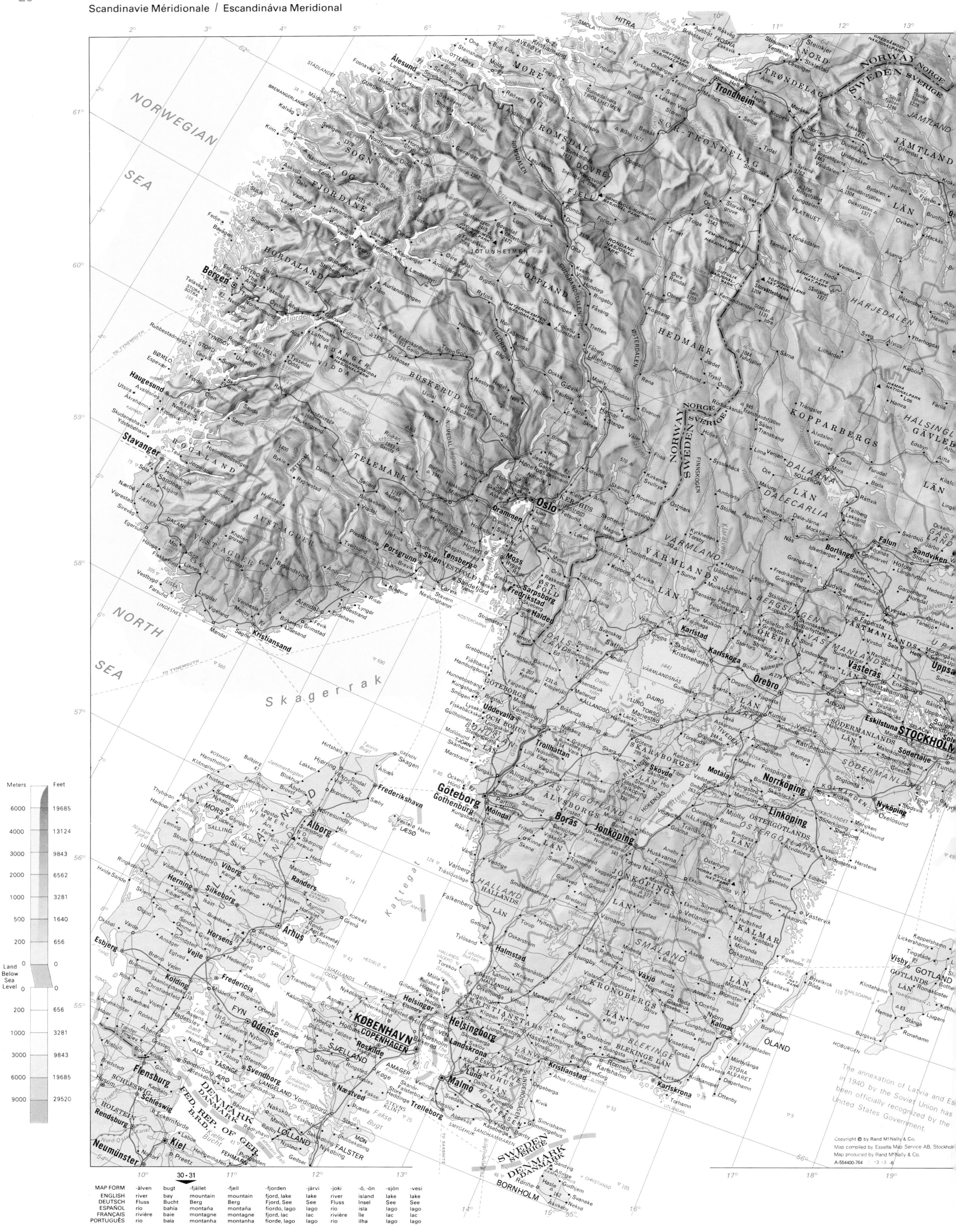

30 - 31

MAP FORM	-älven	bugt	-fjället	-fjell	-fjorden	-järvi	-joki	-ö, -ön	-sjön	-vesi
ENGLISH	river	bay	mountain	mountain	fjord, lake	lake	river	island	lake	lake
DEUTSCH	Fluss	Bucht	Berg	Berg	Fjord, See	See	Fluss	Insel	See	See
ESPAÑOL	río	bahía	montaña	montaña	fiordo, lago	lago	río	isla	lago	lago
FRANÇAIS	rivière	baie	montagne	montagne	fjord, lac	lac	rivière	île	lac	lac
PORTUGUÊS	rio	baía	montanha	montanha	fiorde, lago	lago	rio	ilha	lago	lago

Kilometers 0 50 100 150 Km.
Statute Miles 0 50 100 150 Mi.

Scale 1:3,000,000

One centimeter represents 30 kilometers.
One inch represents approximately 47 miles.
Conic Projection, Two Standard Parallels

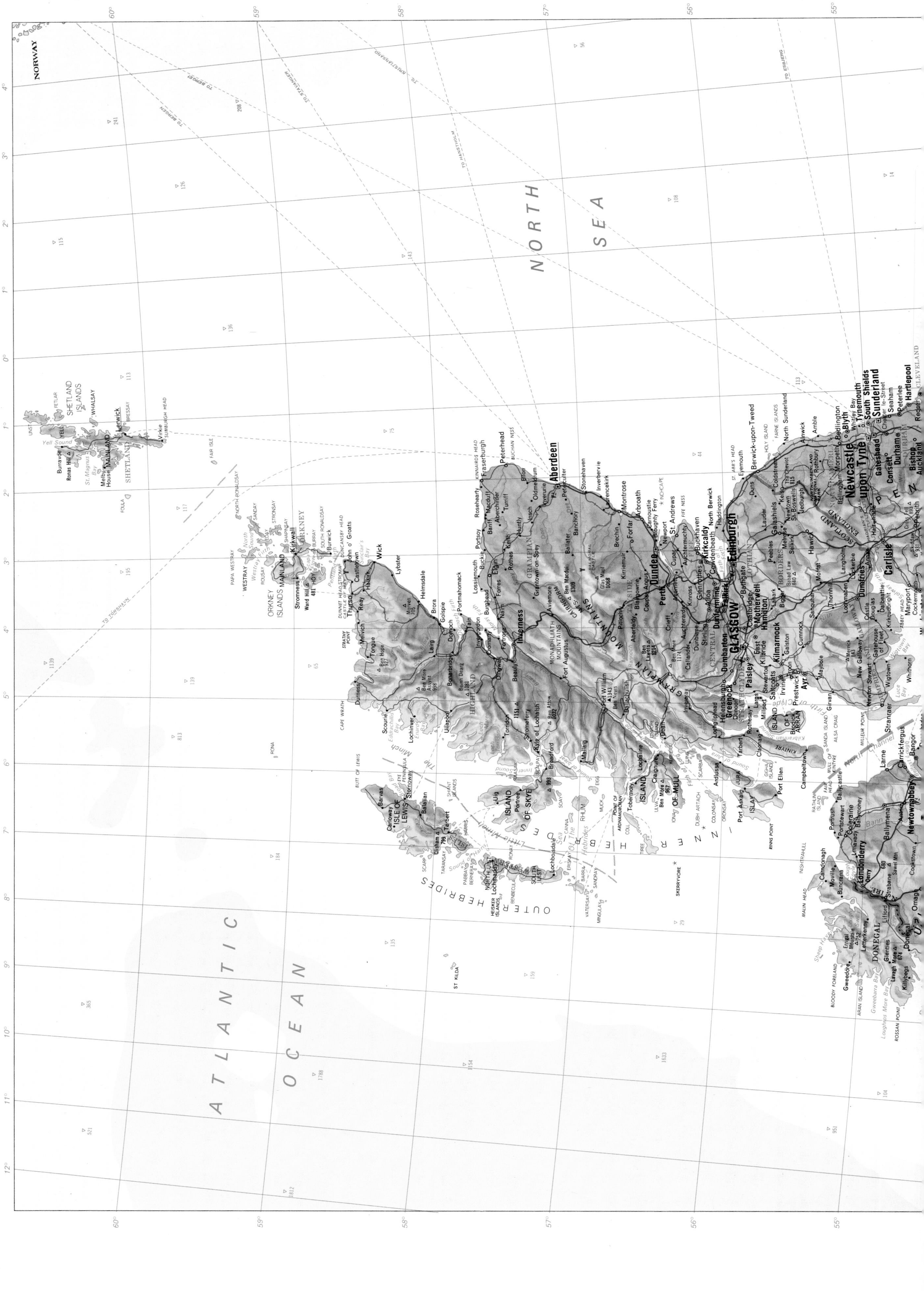
NORWAY
NORTH SEA
ATLANTIC OCEAN
SHETLAND ISLANDS
Lerwick
ORKNEY ISLANDS
Kirkwall
Thurso
Wick
Inverness
Aberdeen
Peterhead
Fraserburgh
Dundee
Perth
Edinburgh
GLASGOW
Paisley
Kilmarnock
Ayr
Carlisle
Newcastle upon Tyne
Sunderland
South Shields
Tynemouth
Gateshead
Hartlepool
Londonderry
Coleraine
Carrickfergus
Newtownabbey
Bangor
Larne
Stornoway
ISLE OF LEWIS
ISLAND OF SKYE
OUTER HEBRIDES
ST KILDA
Fort William
Oban
Campbeltown
DONEGAL
Omagh
Dumfries
Stranraer

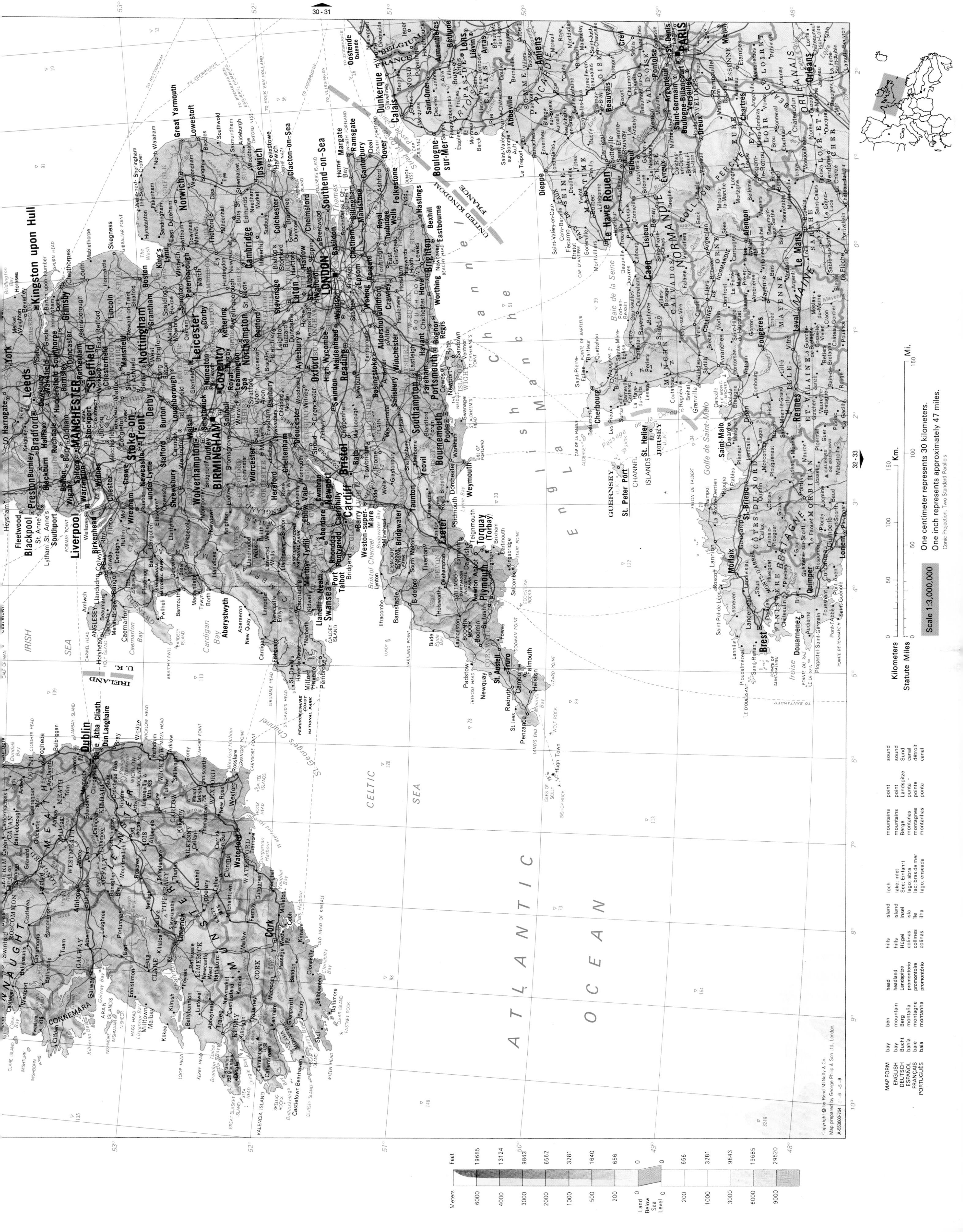
ATLANTIC OCEAN
CELTIC SEA
IRISH SEA
English Channel
La Manche
Scale 1:3,000,000
One centimeter represents 30 kilometers.
One inch represents approximately 47 miles.
Conic Projection, Two Standard Parallels
Kilometers
Statute Miles
MAP FORM
ENGLISH
DEUTSCH
ESPAÑOL
FRANÇAIS
PORTUGUÊS
Copyright © by Rand McNally & Co.
Map prepared by George Philip & Son Ltd, London.

Central Europe / Mitteleuropa / Europa Central
Europe Centrale / Europa Central

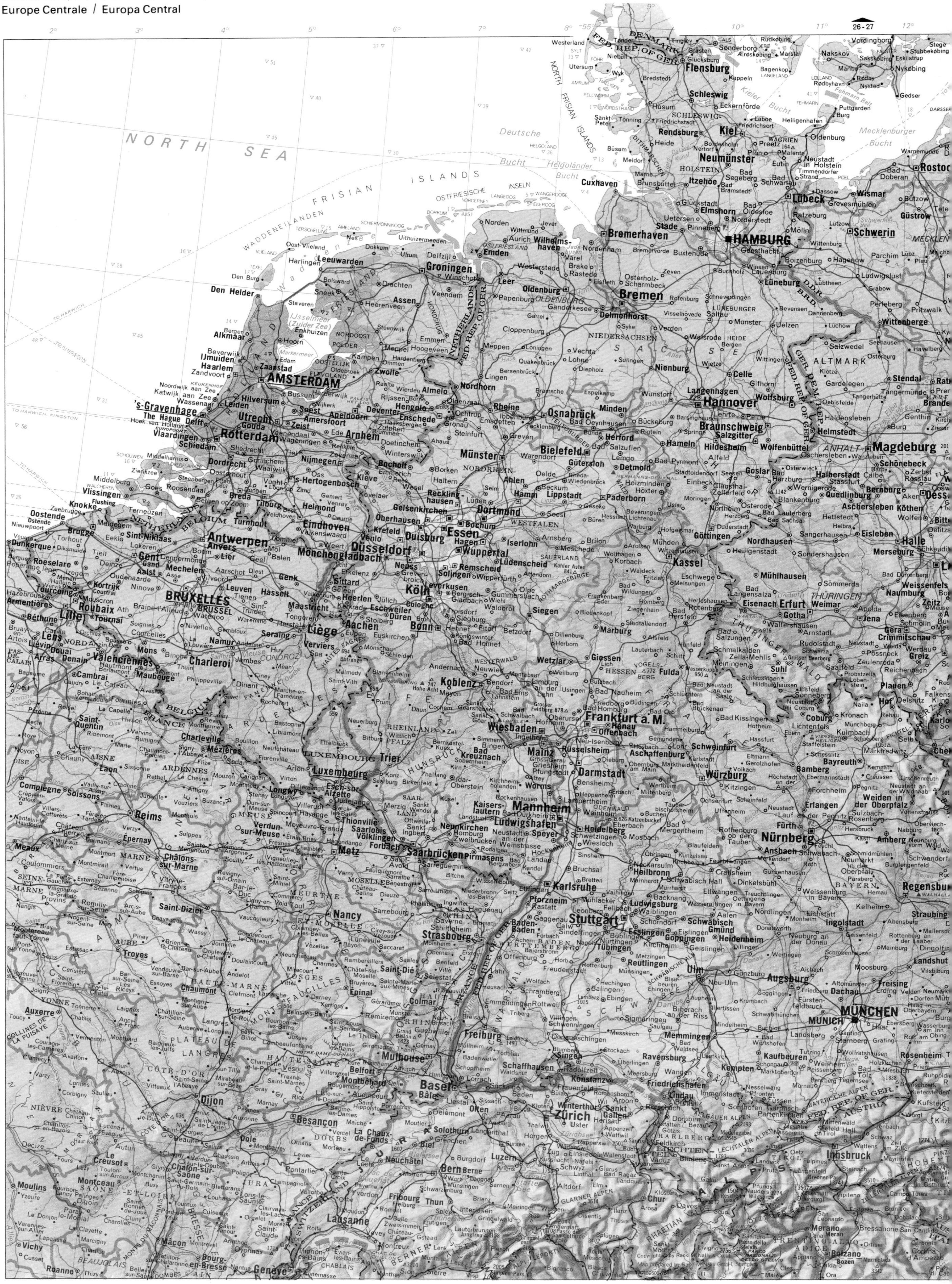

Meters | Feet

Meters	Feet
6000	19685
4000	13124
3000	9843
2000	6562
1000	3281
500	1640
200	656
0	0
Land Below Sea Level 0	0
200	656
1000	3281
3000	9843
6000	19685
9000	29520

MAP FORM	Bucht	Gebirge	jezioro	Kanal	park narodowy	See	Wald
ENGLISH	bay	range	lake, lagoon	canal	national park	lake	forest, mountains
DEUTSCH	Bucht	Gebirge	See, Haff	Kanal	Nationalpark	See	Wald
ESPAÑOL	bahía	sierra	lago, laguna	canal	parque nacional	lago	bosque, montañas
FRANÇAIS	baie	chaîne	lac, lagune	canal	parc national	lac	forêt, montagnes
PORTUGUÊS	baía	serra	lago, laguna	canal	parque nacional	lago	floresta, montanhas

Kilometers 0 50 100 150 Km.

Statute Miles 0 50 100 150 Mi.

Scale 1:3,000,000

One centimeter represents 30 kilometers.

One inch represents approximately 47 miles.

Conic Projection, Two Standard Parallels.

BALTIC SEA
Gdańsk
(Danzig)
Gdynia
Kaliningrad
(Königsberg)
Szczecin
(Stettin)
Bydgoszcz
Toruń
Białystok
Poznań
Warszawa WARSAW
Łódź
Wrocław
(Breslau)
Częstochowa
Kraków
Katowice
Lublin
Kielce
Radom
Dresden
PRAHA
PRAGUE
Brno
Ostrava
Bratislava
WIEN
VIENNA
Linz
Graz
BUDAPEST
Debrecen
Miskolc
Szeged
Pécs
Košice
Prešov
Žilina
C A R P A T H I A N   M O U N T A I N S
ÖSTERREICH
HUNGARY
POLAND
Brest
Grodno
Kaunas
Oradea
Arad
Subotica

76-77
78-79

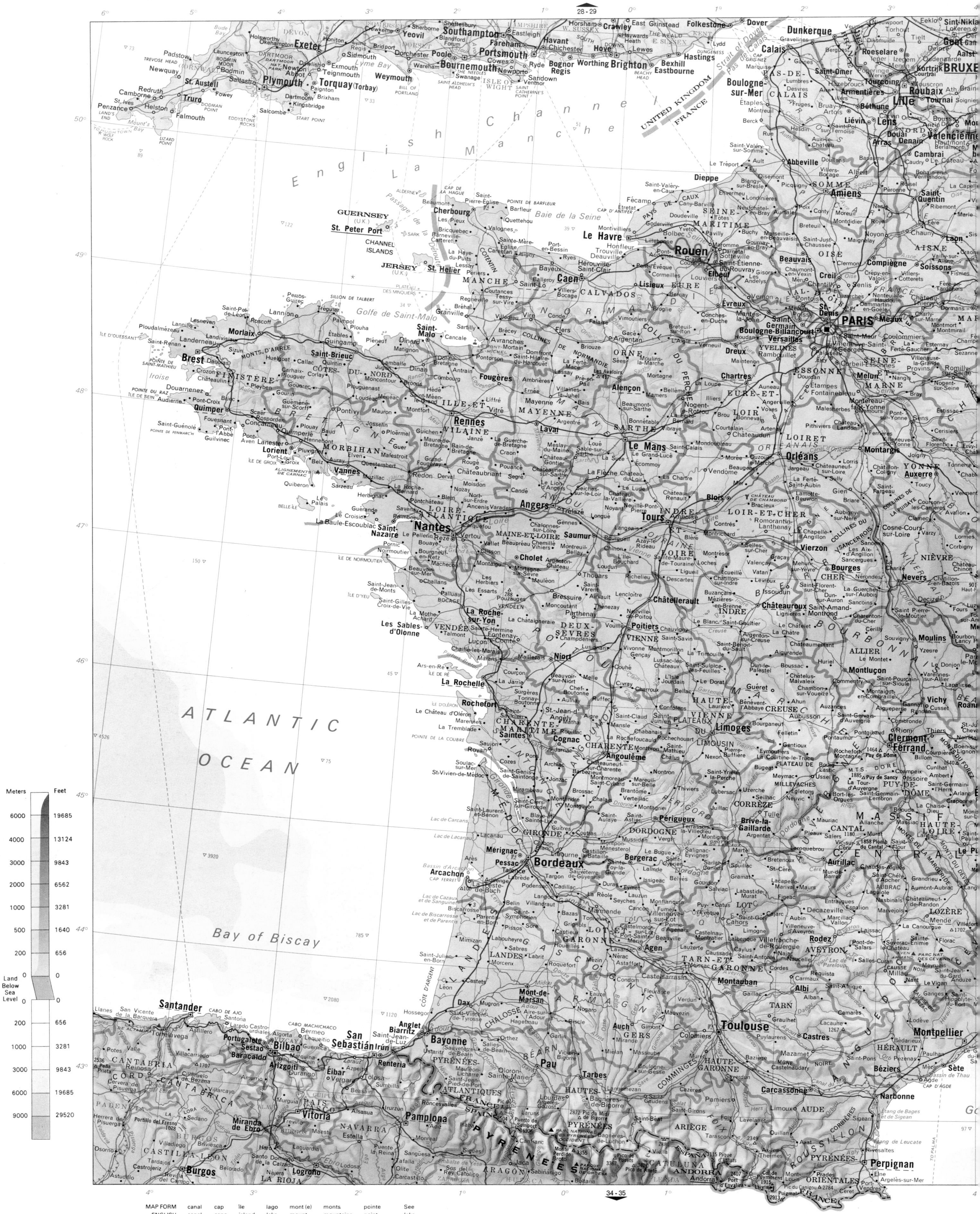

MAP FORM	canal	cap	île	lago	mont (e)	monts	pointe	See
ENGLISH	canal	cape	island	lake	mount	mountains	point	lake
DEUTSCH	Kanal	Kap	Insel	See	Berg	Berge	Landspitze	See
ESPAÑOL	canal	cabo	isla	lago	monte	montes	punta	lago
FRANÇAIS	canal	cap	île	lac	mont	monts	pointe	lac
PORTUGUÊS	canal	cabo	ilha	lago	monte	montes	ponta	lago

Kilometers 0 50 100 150 Km.
Statute Miles 0 50 100 150 Mi.

Scale 1:3,000,000

One centimeter represents 30 kilometers.
One inch represents approximately 47 miles.
Lambert Conformal Conic Projection

Spain and Portugal / Spanien und Portugal / España y Portugal
Espagne et Portugal / Espanha e Portugal

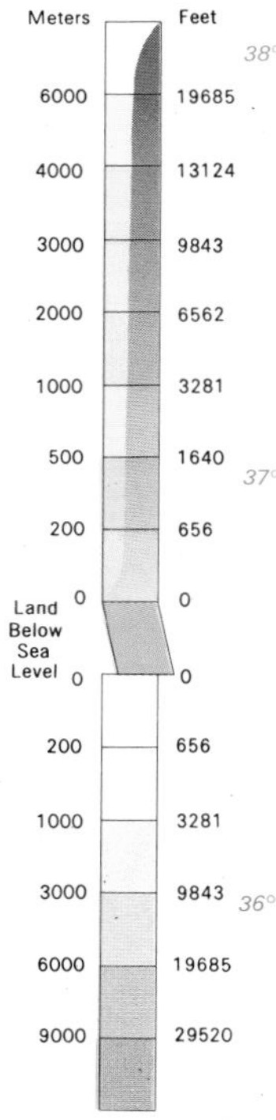

ESPAÑOL	bahía	cabo	isla	embalse	puerto	punta	ría	sierra
ENGLISH	bay	cape	island	reservoir	port	point	estuary	mountains
DEUTSCH	Bucht	Kap	Insel	Stausee	Hafen	Landspitze	Trichtermündung	Berge
FRANÇAIS	baie	cap	île	réservoir	port	pointe	estuaire	montagnes
PORTUGUÊS	baía	cabo	ilha	reservatório	porto	ponta	estuário	serra

Kilometers 0 50 100 150 Km.
Statute Miles 0 50 100 150 Mi.

Scale 1:3,000,000

One centimeter represents 30 kilometers.
One inch represents approximately 47 miles.
Conic Projection, Two Standard Parallels

38 • 39

30 • 31

32 • 33

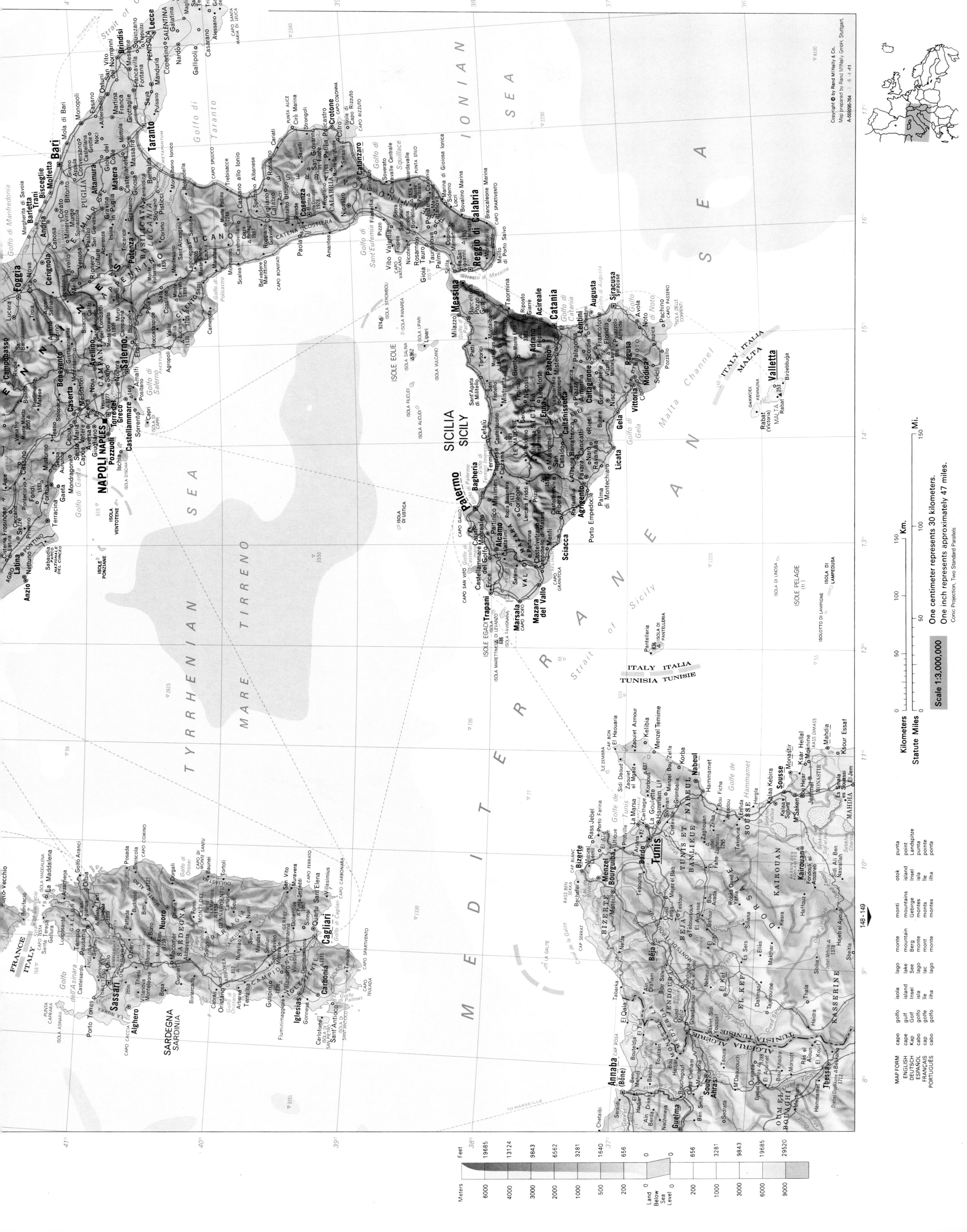
TYRRHENIAN SEA
MARE TIRRENO
IONIAN SEA
MEDITERRANEAN SEA
Strait of Sicily
Malta Channel
Strait of Otranto
Golfo di Taranto
SICILIA
SICILY
SARDEGNA
SARDINIA
ITALY ITALIA
TUNISIA TUNISIE
ITALY ITALIA
MALTA
FRANCE
ITALY
NAPOLI NAPLES
Palermo
Messina
Catania
Cagliari
Tunis
Valletta
Bari
Taranto
Reggio di Calabria
Scale 1:3,000,000
One centimeter represents 30 kilometers.
One inch represents approximately 47 miles.
Conic Projection, Two Standard Parallels
Kilometers
Statute Miles
Km.
Mi.
Copyright © by Rand McNally & Co.
Map prepared by Rand McNally GmbH, Stuttgart.
148-149
MAP FORM capo golfo isola lago monte monti otok punta
ENGLISH cape gulf island lake mountain mountains island point
DEUTSCH Kap Golf Insel See Berg Gebirge Insel Landspitze
ESPAÑOL cabo golfo isla lago monte montes isla punta
FRANÇAIS cap golfe île lac mont monts île pointe
PORTUGUÊS cabo golfo ilha lago monte montes ilha ponta
Feet
Meters
Land
Below
Sea
Level

Kilometers 0 50 100 150 Km.
Statute Miles 0 50 100 150 Mi.

Scale 1:3,000,000

One centimeter represents 30 kilometers.
One inch represents approximately 47 miles.
Conic Projection, Two Standard Parallels

MAP FORM	akra	kólpos	lacul	limni	manastir	munţii	prohod	sea
ENGLISH	cape	bay	lake	lake	monastery	mountains	pass	sea
DEUTSCH	Kap	Bucht	See	See	Kloster	Berge	Pass	Meer
ESPAÑOL	cabo	bahía	lago	lago	monasterio	montañas	paso	mar
FRANÇAIS	cap	baie	lac	lac	monastère	montagnes	col	mer
PORTUGUÊS	cabo	baía	lago	lago	mosteiro	montanhas	passo	mar

30-31
78-79
36-37

130-131
AEGEAN SEA
MEDITERRANEAN SEA
IONIAN SEA
ADRIATIC SEA
IONIAN ISLANDS
Strait of Otranto
ITALY
KIKLÁDHES
CYCLADES
DHODHEKÁNISOS
DODECANESE
KRÍTI
CRETE
Kritikón Pélagos
Sea of Crete
Marmara Denizi
Sea of Marmara
ATHÍNAI
ATHENS
Piraiévs
Thessaloníki
Salonika
İSTANBUL
İzmir
Bursa
Edirne
Tiranë
Durrës
Vlorë
Kérkira
Pátrai
Iráklion
Khaniá
Ródhos
Rhodes
Lárisa
Vólos
Ioánnina
Kaválla
Sérrai
Kalámai
LÉSVOS
LESBOS
KHÍOS
CHIOS
SÁMOS
NÁXOS
TÍNOS
ÁNDROS
LÍMNOS
THÁSOS
EVVOIA
KÁRPATHOS
KEFALLINÍA
ZÁKINTHOS
LEVKÁS
KÉRKIRA
CORFU
PELOPÓNNISOS
PELOPONNESUS
TURKEY
TÜRKIYE
GREECE
ELLÁS
Copyright © by Rand McNally & Co.
Map prepared by Rand McNally GmbH, Stuttgart.
Feet
Meters
Land Below Sea Level
19685
13124
9843
6562
3281
1640
656
0
6000
4000
3000
2000
1000
500
200
29520
9000

MAP FORM	ENGLISH	DEUTSCH	ESPAÑOL	FRANÇAIS	PORTUGUÊS
-älven	river	Fluss	río	rivière	rio
-ån	river	Fluss	río	rivière	rio
-berget	hill	Hügel	colina	colline	colina
-fjärden	fjord	Fjord	fiordo	fjord	fiorde
-ö	island	Insel	isla	île	ilha
-sjön	lake	See	lago	lac	lago
slott	castle	Burg	castillo	château	castelo

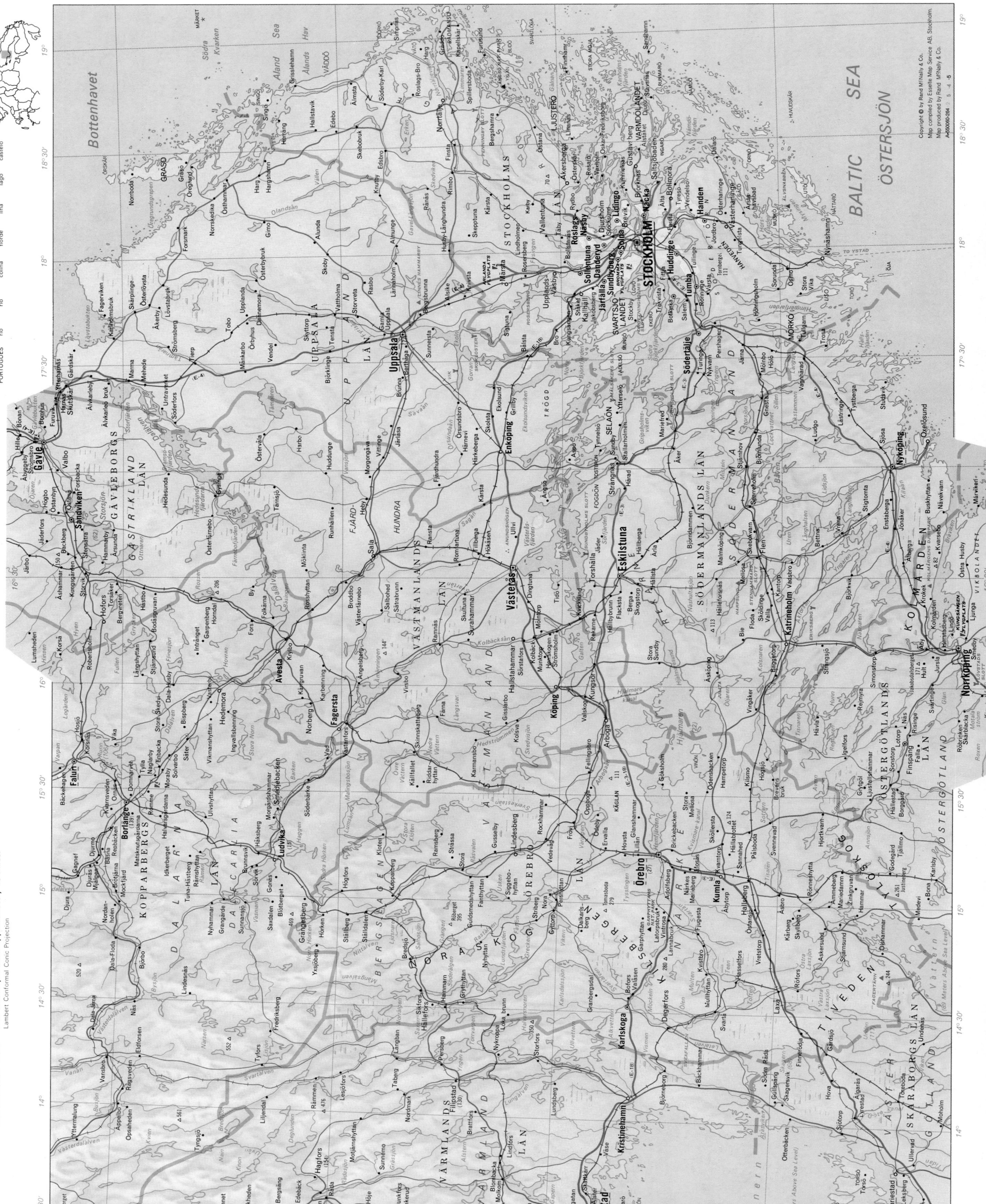

Kilometers 0 10 20 30 40 50 Km.
Statute Miles 0 10 20 30 40 50 Mi.

Scale 1:1,000,000

One centimeter represents 10 kilometers.
One inch represents approximately 16 miles.
Lambert Conformal Conic Projection

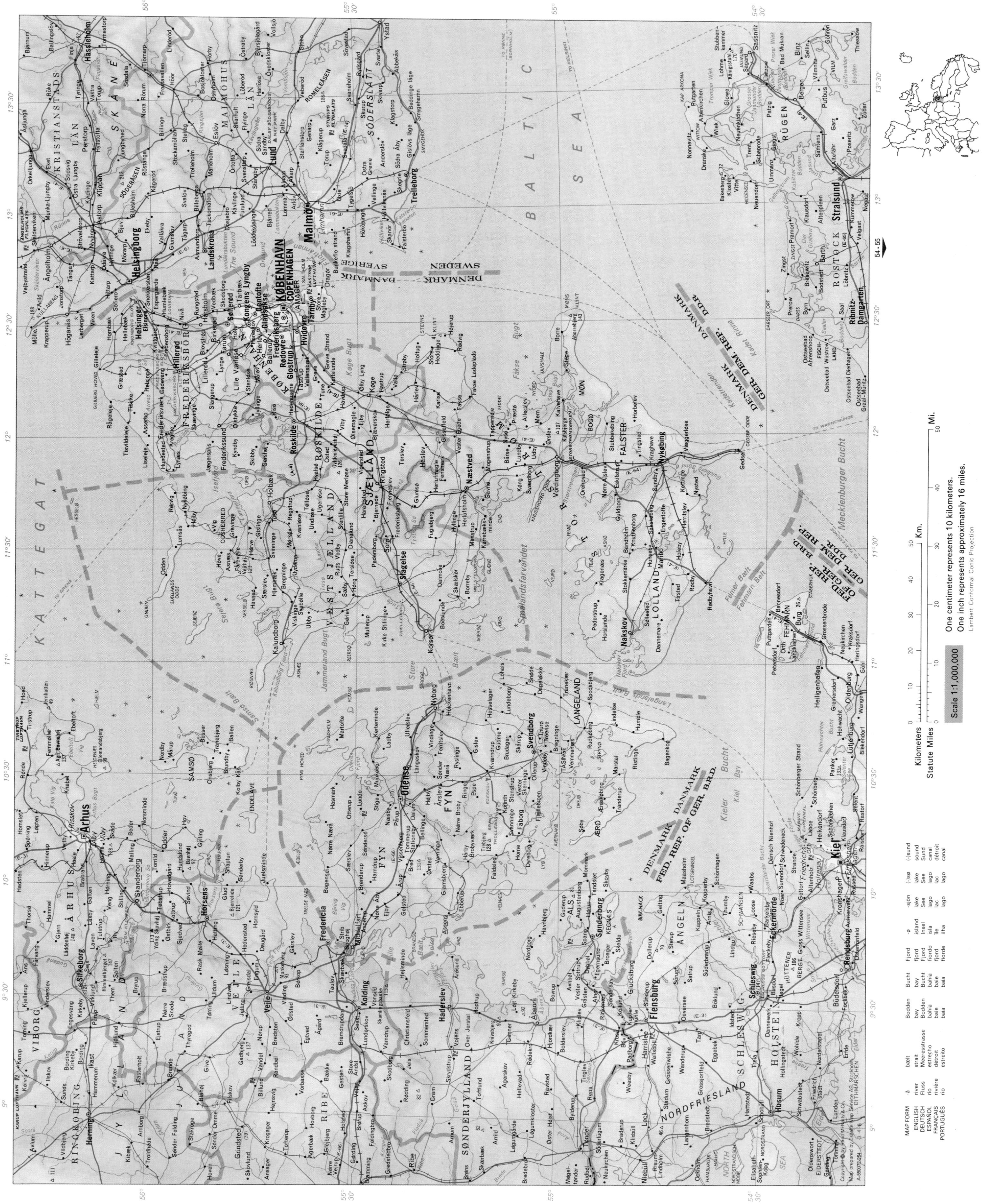
KØBENHAVN COPENHAGEN
Malmö
Kiel
KATTEGAT
BALTIC SEA
SJÆLLAND
FYN
LOLLAND
FALSTER
MØN
RÜGEN
FEHMARN
DANMARK
SWEDEN
SVERIGE
DDR
GER. DEM. REP.
FED. REP. OF GER.
B.R.D.
Scale 1:1,000,000
Kilometers
Statute Miles
Km.
Mi.
One centimeter represents 10 kilometers.
One inch represents approximately 16 miles.
Lambert Conformal Conic Projection
MAP FORM: -å, bælt, Bodden, Bucht, Fjord, -ø, -sjön, (-)sø, (-)sund
ENGLISH: river, strait, bay, bay, fjord, island, lake, lake, sound
DEUTSCH: Fluss, Meeresstrasse, Bodden, Bucht, Fjord, Insel, See, See, Sund
ESPAÑOL: río, estrecho, bahía, bahía, fiordo, isla, lago, lago, canal
FRANÇAIS: rivière, détroit, baie, baie, fjord, île, lac, lac, détroit
PORTUGUÊS: rio, estreito, baía, baía, fiorde, ilha, lago, lago, canal

ENGLISH	bay	drain	forest	head	hill	isle	marsh	point	vale
DEUTSCH	Bucht	Abzugsgraben	Wald	Landspitze	Hügel	Insel	Marsch	Landspitze	Tal
ESPAÑOL	bahia	acquia	bosque	promontorio	colina	isla	pantano	punta	valle
FRANÇAIS	baie	drainage	forêt	promontoire	colline	île	marais	pointe	dépression
PORTUGUÊS	baía	drenagem	floresta	promontório	colina	ilha	pântano	ponta	vale

Kilometers 0 10 20 30 40 50 Km.

Statute Miles 0 10 20 30 40 50 Mi.

Scale 1:1,000,000

One centimeter represents 10 kilometers.

One inch represents approximately 16 miles.

Lambert Conformal Conic Projection

46-47
48-49
North Channel
IRISH SEA
NORTHERN IRELAND
SCOTLAND
IRELAND ÉIRE
UNITED KINGDOM
ISLE OF MAN (U.K.)
ISLAND OF ARRAN
KINTYRE
DONEGAL
MONAGHAN
CAVAN
LOUTH
MEATH
DUBLIN-FINGAL
KILDARE
WICKLOW
WICKLOW MOUNTAINS
CARLOW
WEXFORD
MOURNE MTS.
ANGLESEY
GALLOWAY
CARRICK
THE RHINS
THE MACHARS
THE MOORS
THE GLENKENS
CUNNINGHAME
CLYDESDALE
NITHSDALE
ANNANDALE
LOWTHER HILLS
PENTLAND HILLS
SNOWDONIA
LLEYN PENINSULA
Dublin
Baile Átha Cliath
Belfast
Londonderry
Derry
Newry
Dundalk
Dún Dealgan
Drogheda
Droichead Átha
Dún Laoghaire
Bray
Wicklow
Arklow
Larne
Bangor
Newtownards
Lisburn
Portadown
Armagh
Ballymena
Coleraine
Douglas
Stranraer
Ayr
Kilmarnock
Irvine
Dumfries
Workington
Whitehaven
Barrow-in-Furness
Holyhead
Caernarfon
Llandudno
Rhyl
Colwyn Bay
Lough Neagh
Lough Foyle
Strangford Lough
Dundalk Bay
Luce Bay
Solway Firth
Caernarfon Bay
Tremadog Bay
Slieve Donard 850
Snaefell 621
Snowdon 1085
Lugnaquillia Mountain 926
BOYNE BATTLESITE (1690)

Copyright © by Rand McNally & Co.
Map prepared by Rand McNally & Co.
A-556800-264 -4 -7 -8 -10

MAP FORM	bay	dale	firth	forest	head	loch	moor	water
ENGLISH	bay	dale	estuary	forest	head	lake; inlet	moor	water (lake, river)
DEUTSCH	Bucht	Weites Tal	Trichtermündung	Wald	Landspitze	See; Einfahrt	Moor	See, Fluss
ESPAÑOL	bahía	valle	estuario	bosque	promontorio	lago; abra	páramo	lago, río
FRANÇAIS	baie	vallée	estuaire	forêt	promontoire	lac; bras de mer	lande	lac, rivière
PORTUGUÊS	baía	vale	estuário	floresta	promontório	lago; enseada	pântano	lago, rio

Kilometers 0 10 20 30 40 50 Km.

Statute Miles 0 10 20 30 40 50 Mi.

Scale 1:1,000,000

One centimeter represents 10 kilometers.

One inch represents approximately 16 miles.

Lambert Conformal Conic Projection

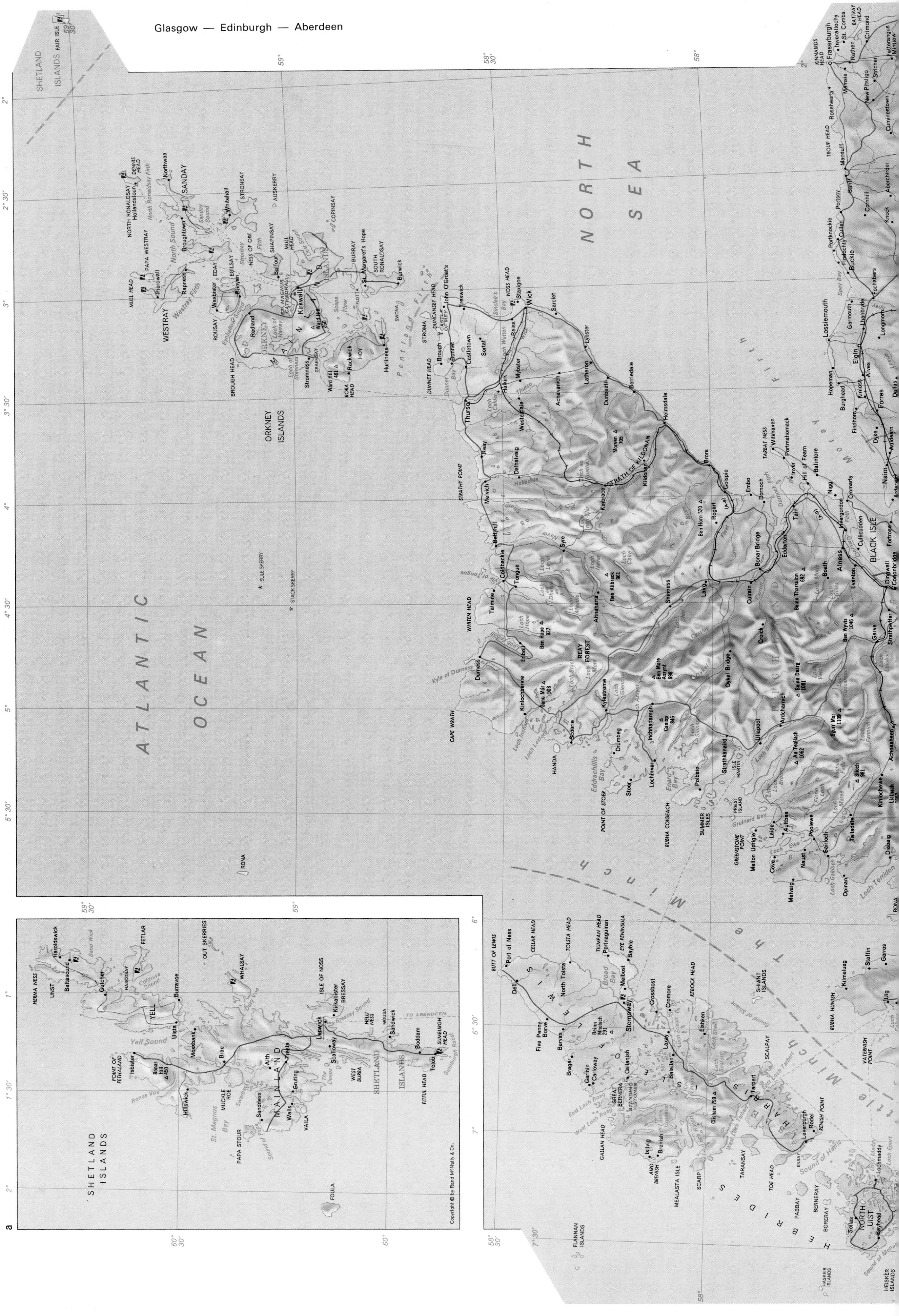
ATLANTIC OCEAN
NORTH SEA
ORKNEY ISLANDS
SHETLAND ISLANDS
Pentland Firth
Moray Firth
The Minch
Little Minch
HEBRIDES
Dunnet Head
Cape Wrath
Thurso
Wick
Kirkwall
Stromness
Lerwick
Stornoway
Ullapool
Dornoch
Fraserburgh
Elgin
Nairn
Butt of Lewis
North Uist
Fair Isle
Foula
Rona
Sule Skerry
Stack Skerry
Flannan Islands
Shiant Islands
Copyright © by Rand McNally & Co.

48-49

44-45

MAP FORM	bay	ben, beinn	firth	head	loch	sound	water
ENGLISH	bay	mountain	estuary	head	lake; inlet	sound	water (river)
DEUTSCH	Bucht	Berg	Trichtermündung	Landspitze	See; Einfahrt	Sund	Fluss
ESPAÑOL	bahía	montaña	estuario	promontorio	lago; abra	canal	río
FRANÇAIS	baie	montagne	estuaire	promontoire	lac; bras de mer	détroit	rivière
PORTUGUÊS	baía	montanha	estário	promontório	lago; enseada	canal	rio

Kilometers 0 10 20 30 40 50 Km.

Statute Miles 0 10 20 30 40 50 Mi.

Scale 1:1,000,000

One centimeter represents 10 kilometers.
One inch represents approximately 16 miles.

Lambert Conformal Conic Projection

ATLANTIC
OCEAN
IRISH
SEA
North Channel
SCOTLAND
NORTHERN IRELAND
U.K.
IRELAND
EIRE
ULSTER
DONEGAL
MONAGHAN
CAVAN
LOUTH
SLIGO
ROSCOMMON
MAYO
Belfast
Londonderry
Derry
Armagh
Omagh
Sligo
Sligeach
Dundalk
Dún Dealgan
Drogheda
Droichead Átha
Newry
Lisburn
Lurgan
Portadown
Bangor
Newtownards
Larne
Ballymena
Coleraine
Strabane
Letterkenny
Enniskillen
Ballina
Castlebar
Westport
Cavan
Monaghan
Lough Neagh
Lough Foyle
Lough Swilly
Donegal Bay
Sligo Bay
Clew Bay
Dundalk Bay
Strangford Lough
SPERRIN MTS.
MOURNE MTS.
BLUE STACK MTS.
DERRYVEAGH MTS.
SLIEVE GAMPH
NEPHIN BEG RANGE
INISHOWEN
ACHILL ISLAND
CLARE ISLAND
MULL OF KINTYRE
MALIN HEAD
BLOODY FORELAND
BLACK ROCK
44-45
46-47

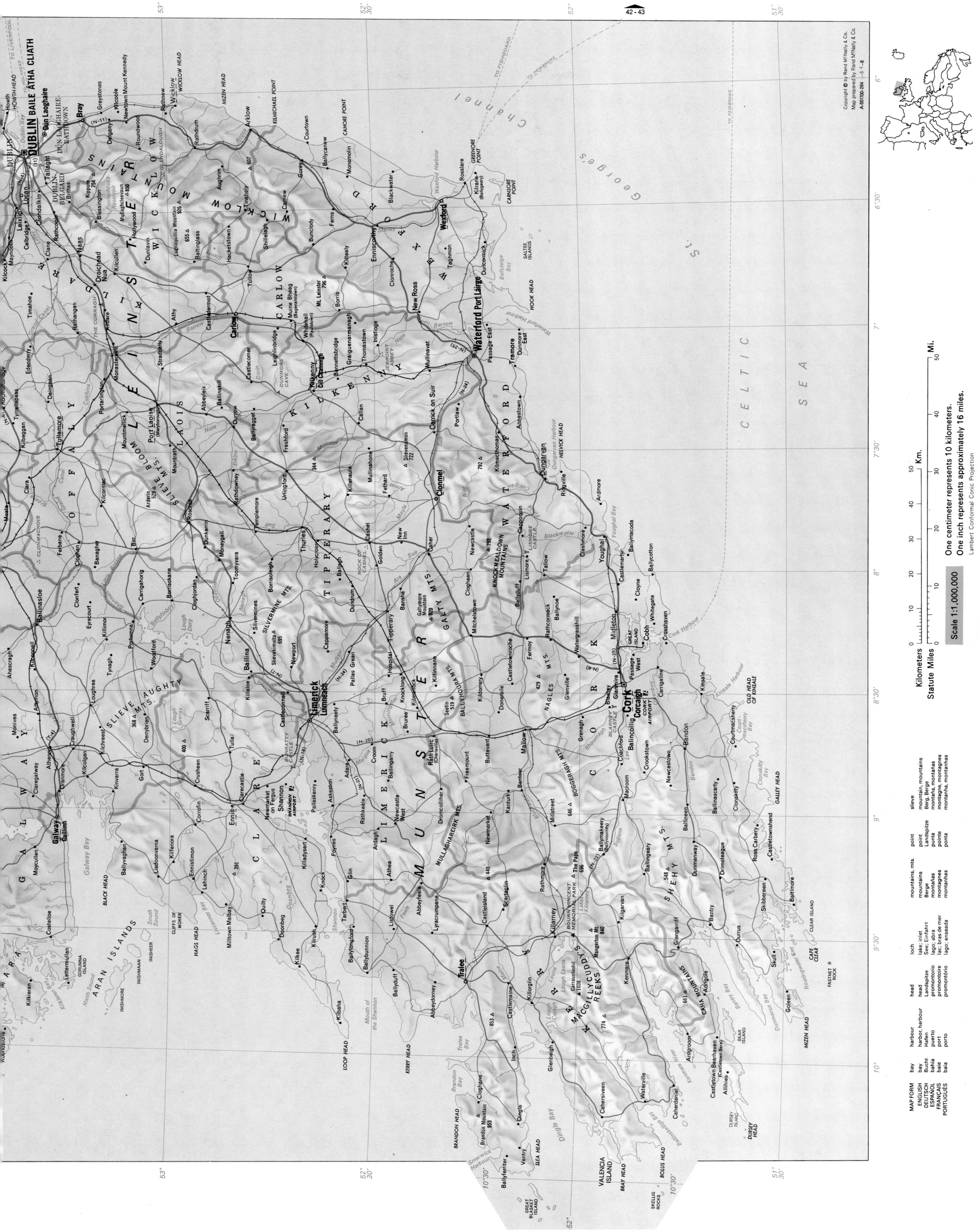
Scale 1:1,000,000
One centimeter represents 10 kilometers.
One inch represents approximately 16 miles.
Lambert Conformal Conic Projection
Kilometers
Statute Miles
Copyright © by Rand McNally & Co.
Map prepared by Rand McNally & Co.
CELTIC SEA
St. George's Channel
LEINSTER
MUNSTER
Dublin
Cork
Limerick
Waterford
Galway

56-57

52-53

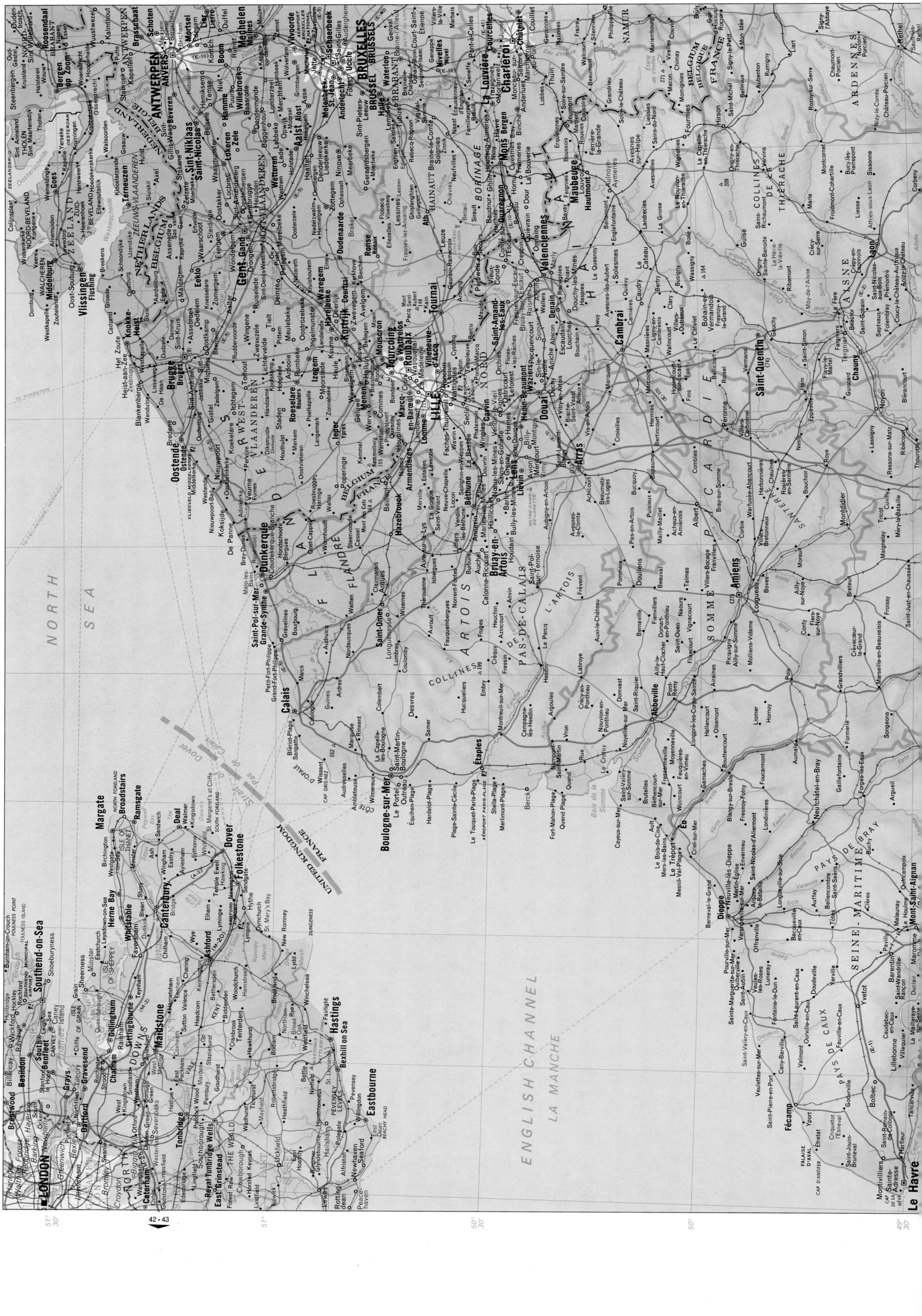

42-43

58-59

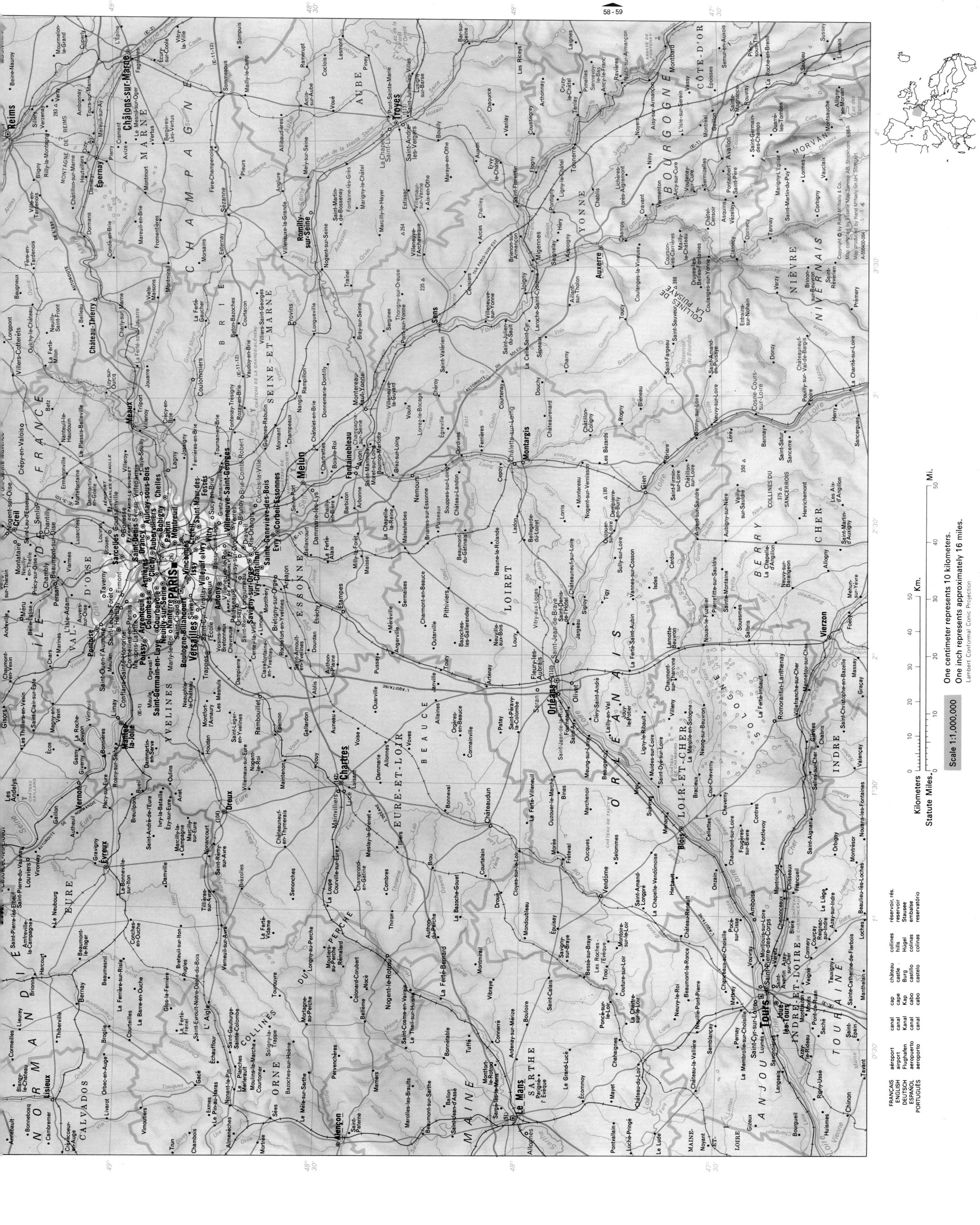
Scale 1:1,000,000
One centimeter represents 10 kilometers.
One inch represents approximately 16 miles.
Lambert Conformal Conic Projection
Kilometers
Statute Miles
Km.
Mi.
FRANÇAIS aéroport canal cap château collines réservoir, rés.
ENGLISH airport canal cape castle hills reservoir
DEUTSCH Flughafen Kanal Kap Burg Hügel Stausee
ESPAÑOL aeropuerto canal cabo castillo colinas embalse
PORTUGUÊS aeroporto canal cabo castelo colinas reservatório
PARIS
Reims
Châlons-sur-Marne
Troyes
Orléans
Chartres
Tours
Le Mans
Auxerre
Versailles
Melun
Fontainebleau
Sens
Blois
Évreux
Alençon
Lisieux
Dreux
Montargis
Vierzon
Meaux
ÎLE-DE-FRANCE
CHAMPAGNE
BOURGOGNE
ORLÉANAIS
NORMANDIE
TOURAINE
MAINE
ANJOU
BEAUCE
SOLOGNE
BERRY
LOIRET
LOIR-ET-CHER
EURE-ET-LOIR
SEINE-ET-MARNE
YONNE
AUBE
MARNE
CÔTE-D'OR
NIÈVRE
SARTHE
ORNE
EURE
YVELINES
ESSONNE
CHER
INDRE
INDRE-ET-LOIRE

DEUTSCH	Gebirge	Kanal	Moor	Naturpark	Stausee	Talsperre	Wald
ENGLISH	range	canal	moor	reserve	reservoir	dam	forest, mountains'
ESPAÑOL	sierra	canal	páramo	reserva	embalse	presa	bosque, montañas
FRANÇAIS	chaîne	canal	lande	réserve	réservoir	barrage	forêt, montagnes'
PORTUGUÊS	serra	canal	pântano	reserva natural	reservatório	represa	floresta, montanhas

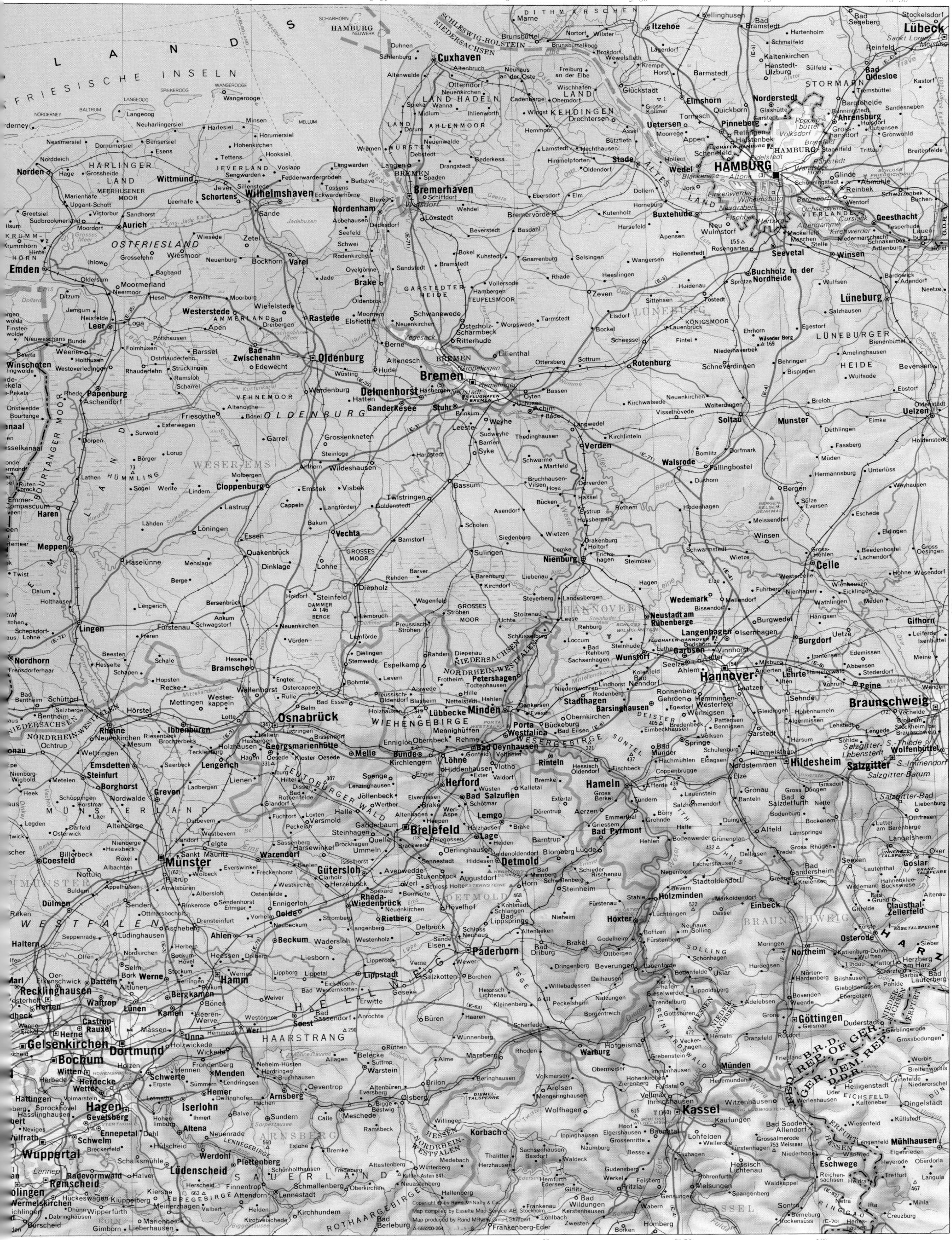

Kilometers 0 10 20 30 40 50 Km.

Statute Miles 0 10 20 30 40 50 Mi.

Scale 1:1,000,000

One centimeter represents 10 kilometers.
One inch represents approximately 16 miles.
Lambert Conformal Conic Projection

BALTIC SEA
Pomeranian Bay
Mecklenburger Bucht
Kieler Bucht
Szczecin (Stettin)
Police
Goleniów
Stargard Szczeciński (Stargard in Pommern)
Świnoujście (Swinemünde)
Kamień Pomorski
Rostock
Stralsund
Greifswald
Wismar
Lübeck
Kiel
HAMBURG
Schwerin
Güstrow
Neubrandenburg
Neustrelitz
Demmin
Anklam
Wolgast
Prenzlau
Schwedt
Angermünde
Eberswalde
Oranienburg
BERLIN (WEST) (OST)
Strausberg
Falkensee
Hennigsdorf
Nauen
Rathenow
Stendal
Neuruppin
Wittstock
Pritzwalk
Perleberg
Wittenberge
Salzwedel
Lüneburg
Uelzen
Gifhorn
Wolfsburg
Parchim
Ludwigslust
Waren
Malchin
Teterow
Ribnitz-Damgarten
Bergen
Sassnitz
Barth
Rügen
Usedom
Wolin
Fehmarn
Neustadt in Holstein
Eutin
Bad Oldesloe
Ahrensburg
Ratzeburg
Mölln
Geesthacht
Bad Segeberg
Norderstedt
Kostrzyn
BALTIC SEA
VORPOMMERN
MECKLENBURG
MECKLENBURGISCHE SEENPLATTE
UCKERMARK
PRIGNITZ
ALTMARK
WENDLAND
HAVELLAND
BARNIM
GER. DEM. REP. / FED. REP. OF GER.
GER. DEM. REP. / POLAND
POLSKA / D.D.R.
NIEDERSACHSEN
MAGDEBURG

41
52-53

Scale 1:1,000,000
One centimeter represents 10 kilometers.
One inch represents approximately 16 miles.
Lambert Conformal Conic Projection
Kilometers
Statute Miles

56-57

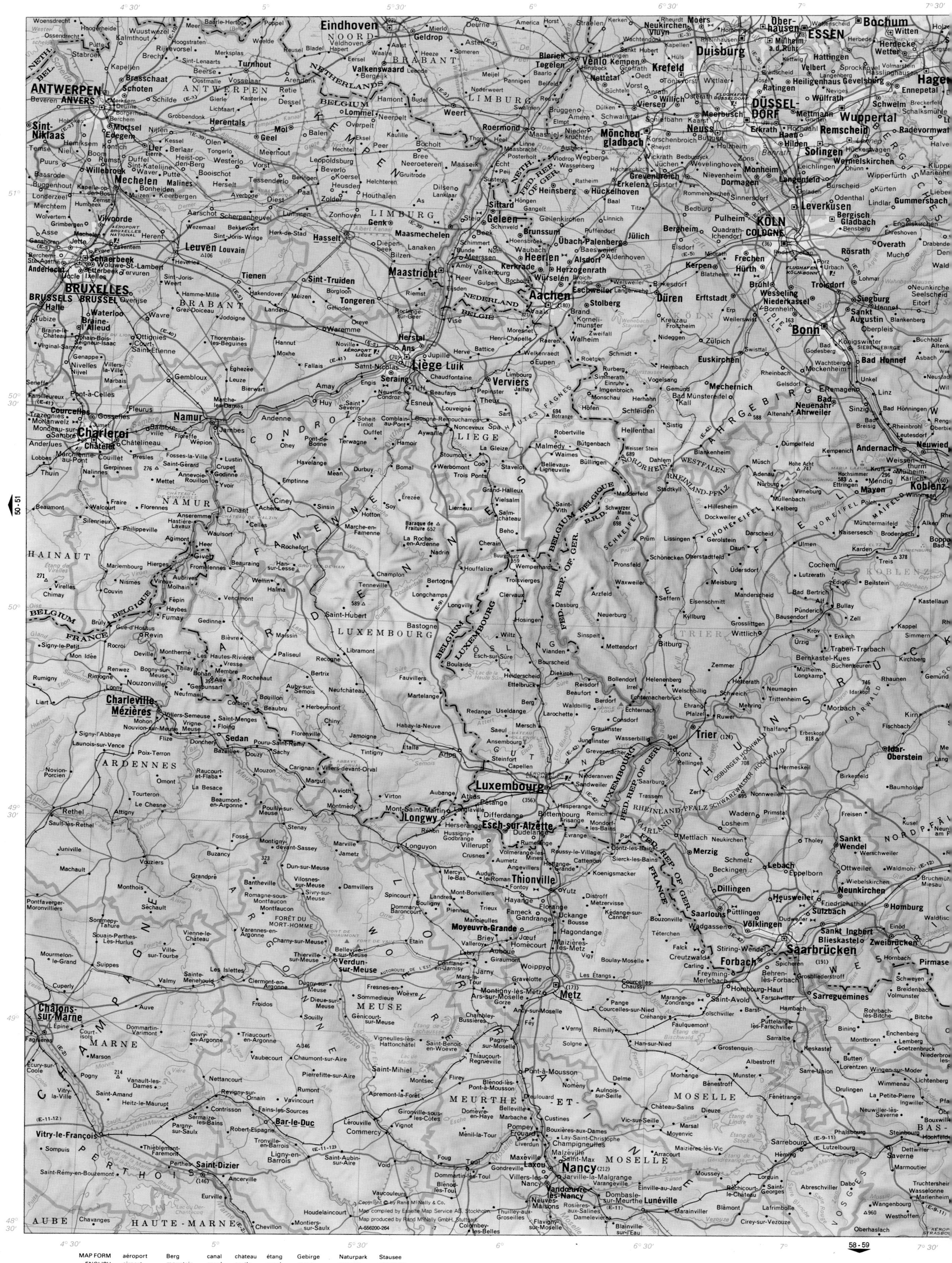

50-51
58-59

MAP FORM	aéroport	Berg	canal	chateau	étang	Gebirge	Naturpark	Stausee
ENGLISH	airport	mountain	canal	castle	pond	range	reserve	reservoir
DEUTSCH	Flughafen	Berg	Kanal	Burg	Teich	Gebirge	Naturpark	Stausee
ESPAÑOL	aeropuerto	montaña	canal	castillo	charca	cordillera	reserva	embalse
FRANCAIS	aéroport	montagne	canal	château	étang	chaîne	réserve	réservoir
PORTUGUÊS	aeroporto	montanha	canal	castelo	lagoa	cordilheira	reserva	reservatório

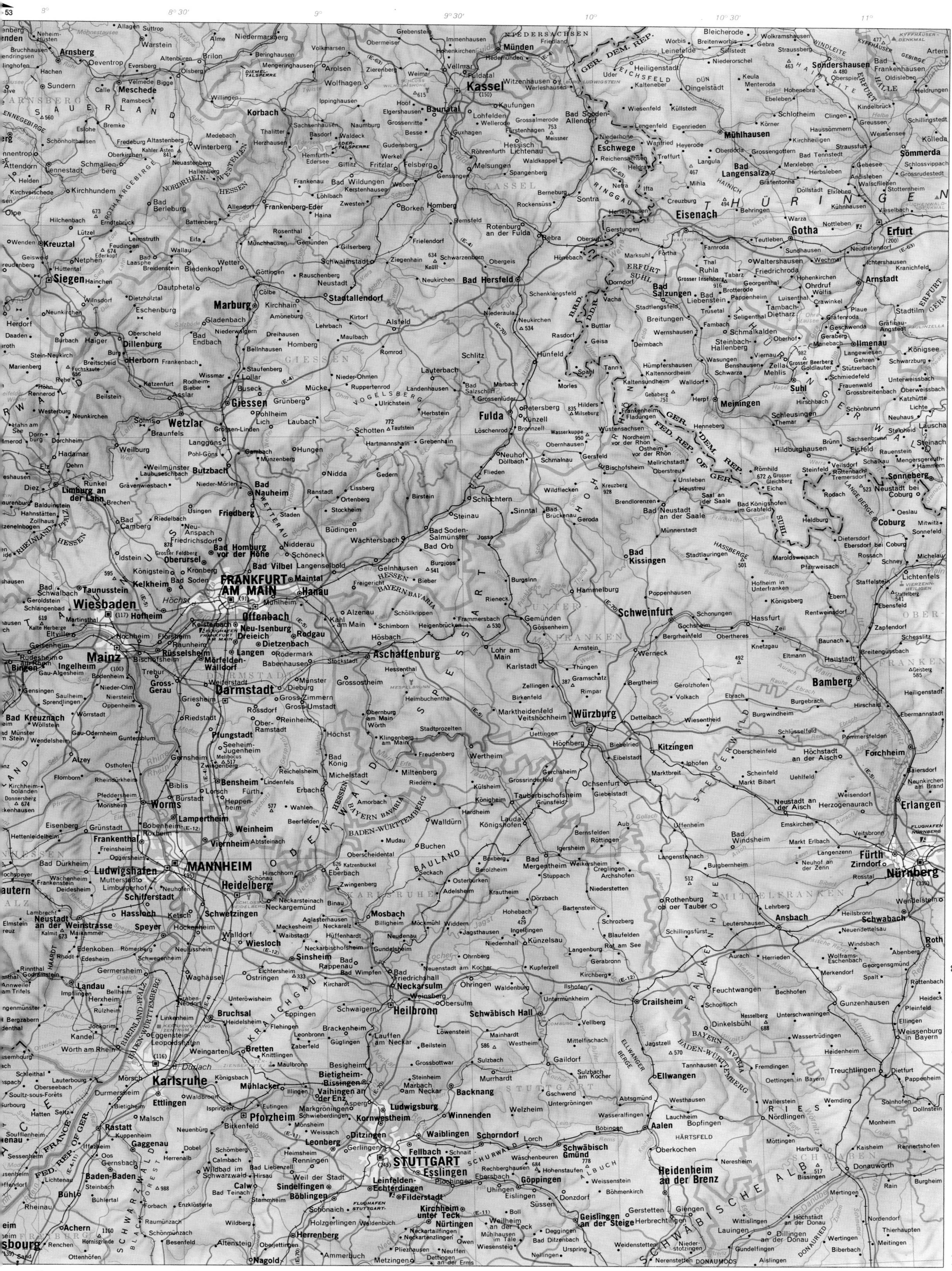

Kilometers 0 10 20 30 40 50 Km.

Statute Miles 0 10 20 30 40 50 Mi.

Scale 1:1,000,000

One centimeter represents 10 kilometers.
One inch represents approximately 16 miles.
Lambert Conformal Conic Projection

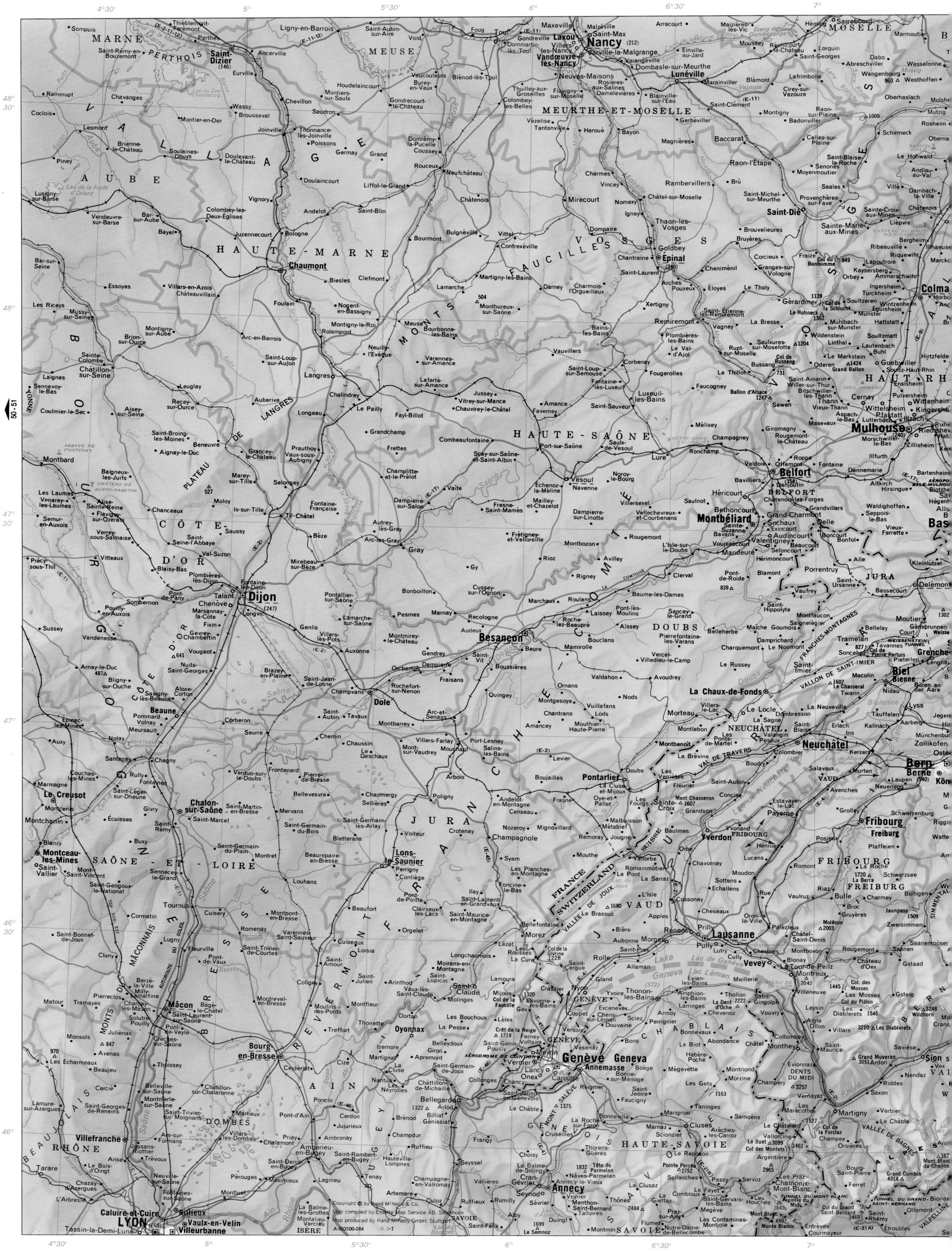

MAP FORM	col	Horn	lago	mont	passo	piz, -zo	See	Spitze	val
ENGLISH	pass	peak	lake	mount	pass	peak	lake	peak	valley
DEUTSCH	Pass	Horn	See	Berg	Pass	Gipfel	See	Spitze	Tal
ESPAÑOL	paso	pico	lago	monte	paso	pico	lago	pico	valle
FRANÇAIS	col	cime	lac	mont	col	cime	lac	cime	val
PORTUGUÊS	passo	pico	lago	monte	passo	pico	lago	pico	vale

Kilometers 0 10 20 30 40 50 Km.

Statute Miles 0 10 20 30 40 50 Mi.

Scale 1:1,000,000

One centimeter represents 10 kilometers.
One inch represents approximately 16 miles.
Lambert Conformal Conic Projection

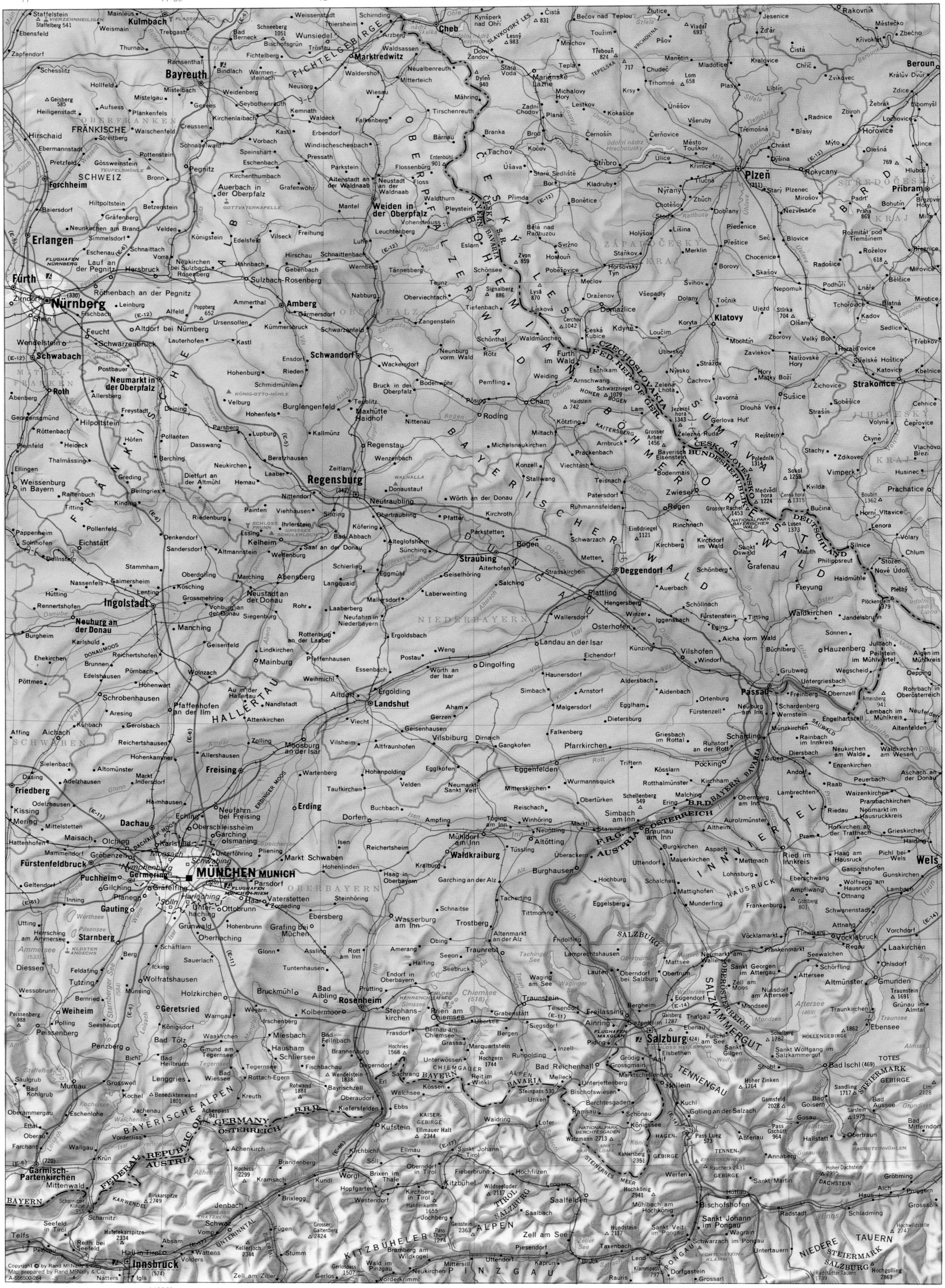

DEUTSCH	Berg	Gebirge	Pass	Schloss	See
ENGLISH	mountain	range	pass	castle	lake
ESPAÑOL	montaña	sierra	paso	castillo	lago
FRANÇAIS	montagne	chaîne	col	château	lac
PORTUGUÊS	montanha	serra	passo	castelo	lago

Kilometers 0 10 20 30 40 50 Km.

Statute Miles 0 10 20 30 40 50 Mi.

Scale 1:1,000,000

One centimeter represents 10 kilometers.
One inch represents approximately 16 miles.
Modified Polyconic Projection

DEUTSCH	Alpe, -n	Berg	Gebirge	Sattel	Schloss	Wald
ENGLISH	mountains	mountain	range	saddle	castle	forest; mountains
ESPAÑOL	montañas	montaña	sierra	paso	castillo	bosque; montañas
FRANÇAIS	montagnes	montagne	chaîne	col	château	forêt; montagnes
PORTUGUÊS	montanhas	montanha	serra	passo	castelo	Floresta; montanhas

Kilometers 0 10 20 30 40 50 Km.

Statute Miles 0 10 20 30 40 50 Mi.

Scale 1:1,000,000

One centimeter represents 10 kilometers.
One inch represents approximately 16 miles.

Lambert Conformal Conic Projection

MAP FORM	abbaye	capo	col	île, î.	lac, l.	monte	passo	pic	val (-le)
ENGLISH	abbey	cape	pass	island	lake	mountain	pass	peak	valley
DEUTSCH	Abtei	Kap	Pass	Insel	See	Berg	Pass	Gipfel	Tal
ESPAÑOL	abadía	cabo	paso	isla	lago	montaña	paso	pico	valle
FRANÇAIS	abbaye	cap	col	île	lac	montagne	col	cime	val
PORTUGUÊS	abadia	cabo	passo	ilha	lago	montanha	passo	pico	vale

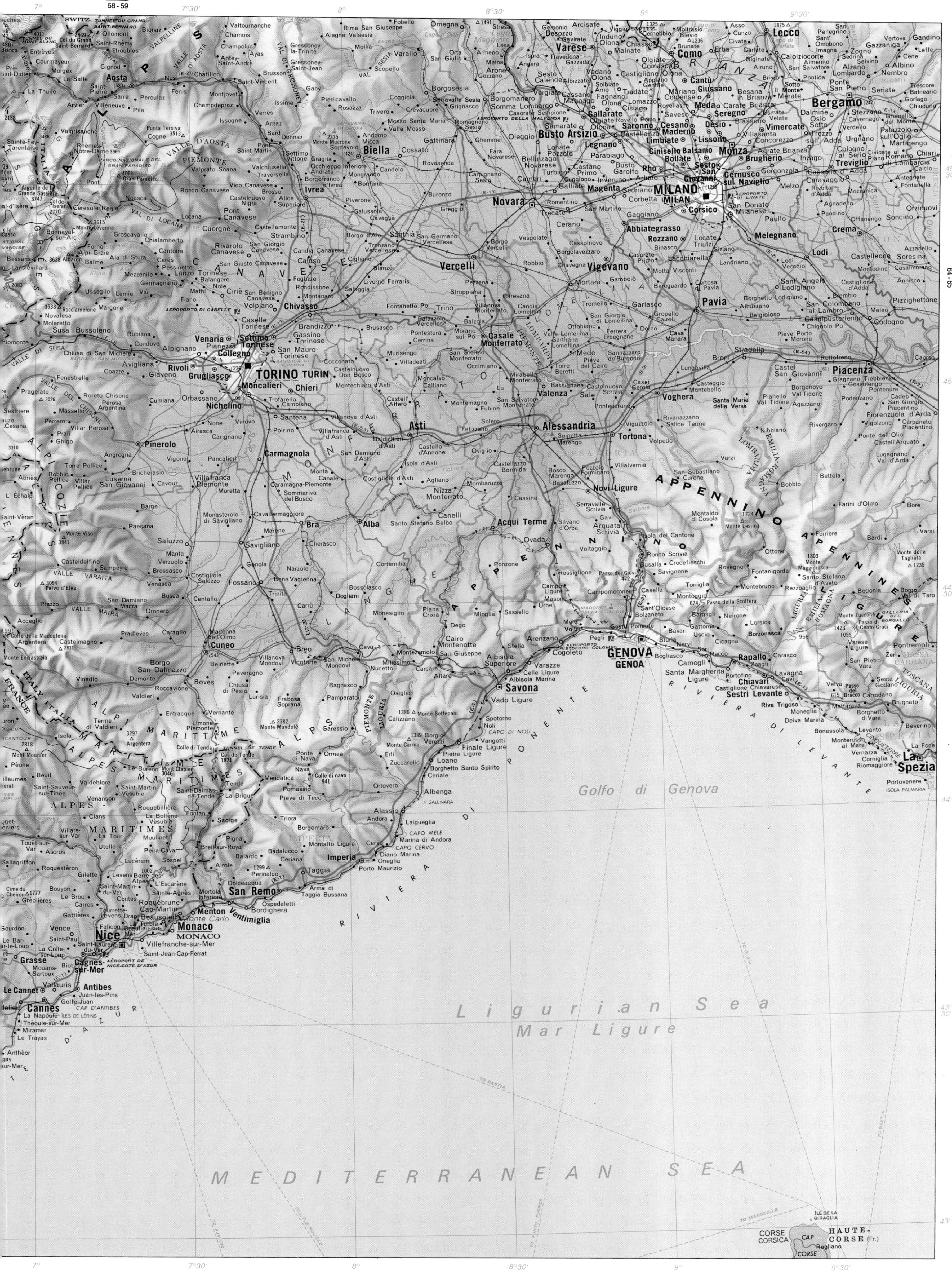

Kilometers 0 10 20 30 40 50 Km.

Statute Miles 0 10 20 30 40 50 Mi.

Scale 1:1,000,000

One centimeter represents 10 kilometers.

One inch represents approximately 16 miles.

Lambert Conformal Conic Projection

61

60

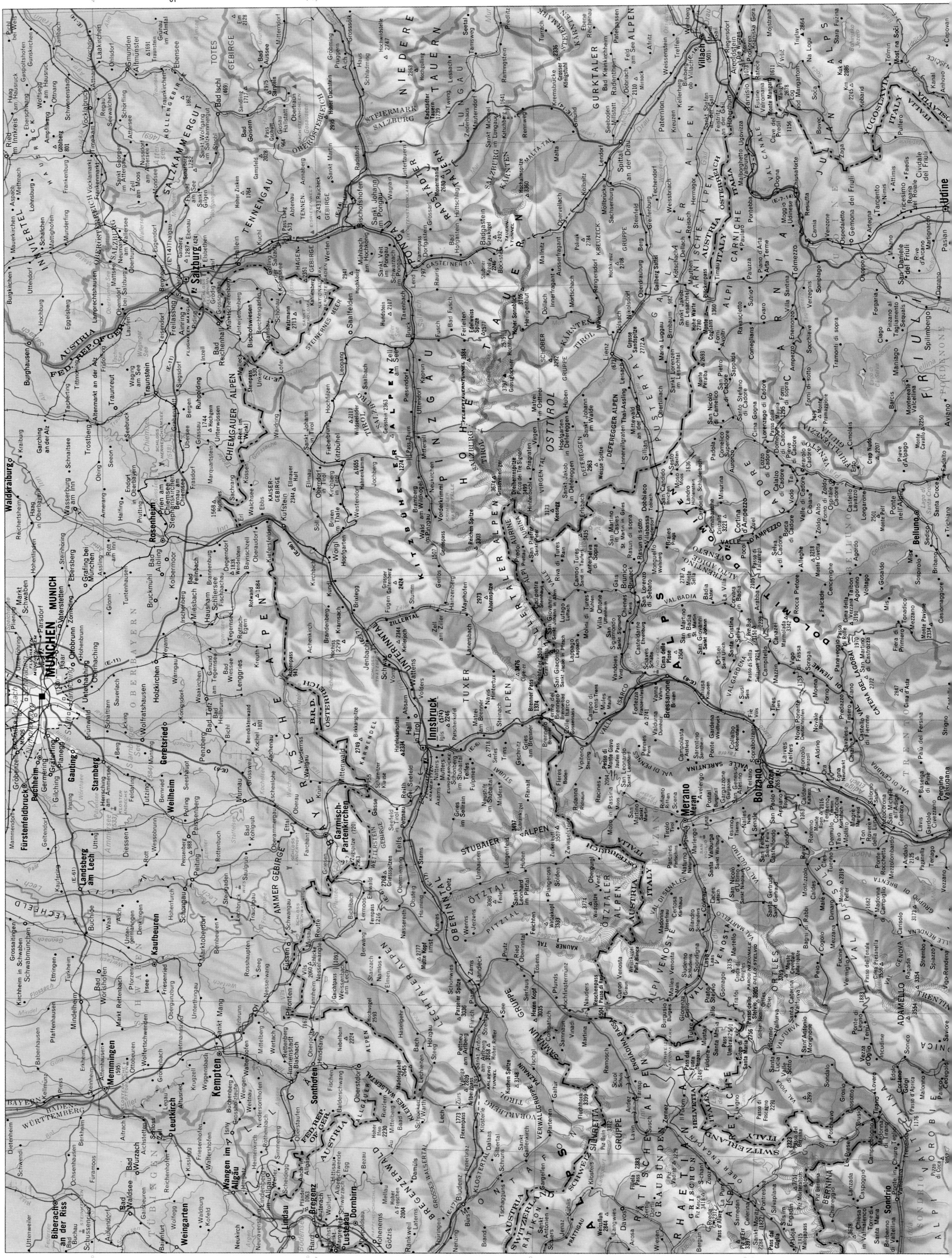
MÜNCHEN
MUNICH
Innsbruck
Salzburg
Bolzano
Merano
Belluno
Udine
Kempten
Lindau
Bregenz
TIROL
SALZBURG
KÄRNTEN
AUSTRIA
ITALY
SWITZERLAND

58-59

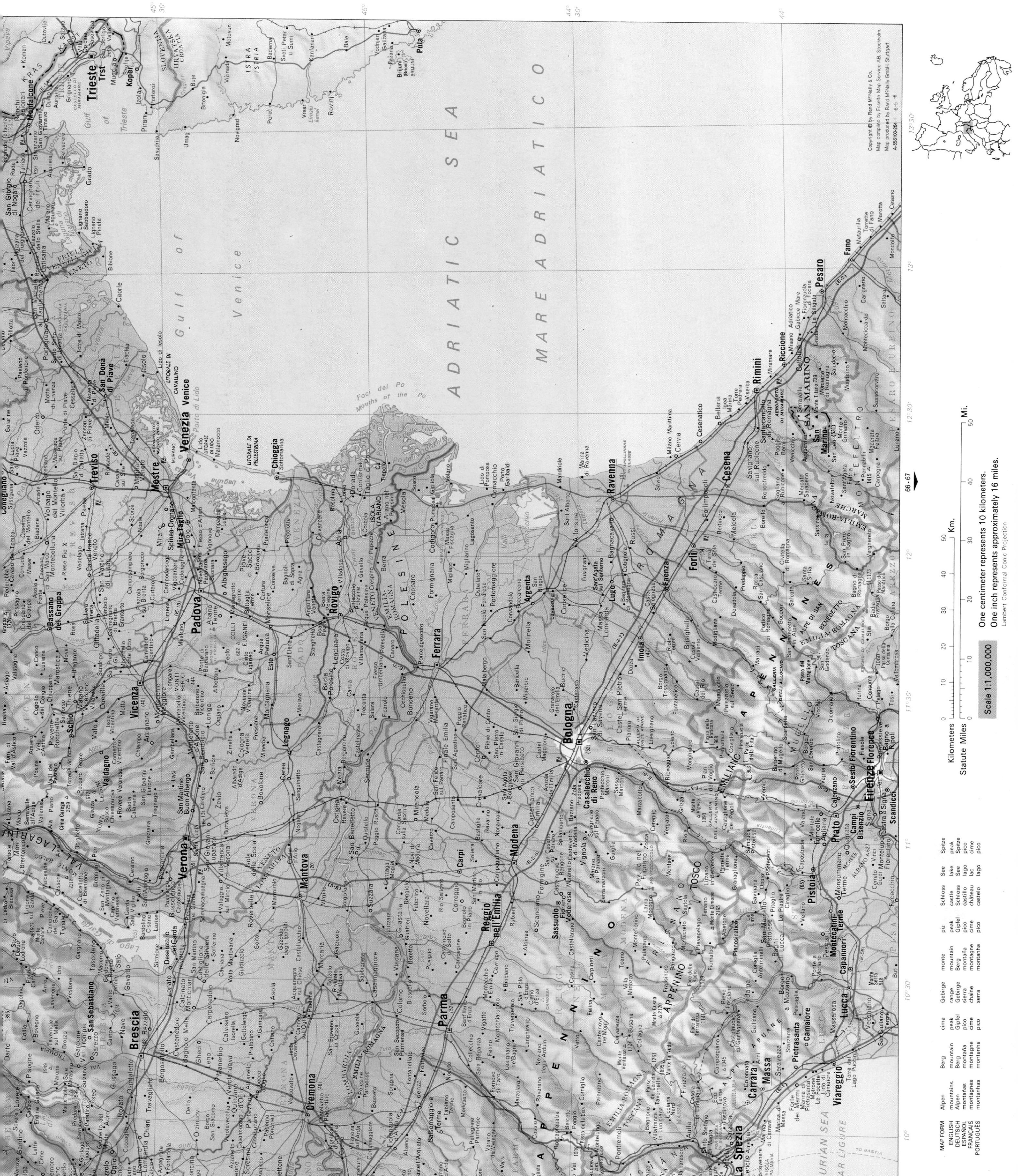
ADRIATIC SEA
MARE ADRIATICO
Gulf of Venice
LIGURIAN SEA
MAR LIGURE
Venezia Venice
Trieste Trst
Bologna
Ferrara
Padova
Verona
Vicenza
Treviso
Mantova
Modena
Parma
Cremona
Brescia
Rimini
Ravenna
Forlì
Pesaro
Firenze Florence
Prato
Pistoia
Lucca
La Spezia
Viareggio
San Marino
66-67
62-63
Scale 1:1,000,000
One centimeter represents 10 kilometers.
One inch represents approximately 16 miles.
Lambert Conformal Conic Projection
Kilometers
Statute Miles

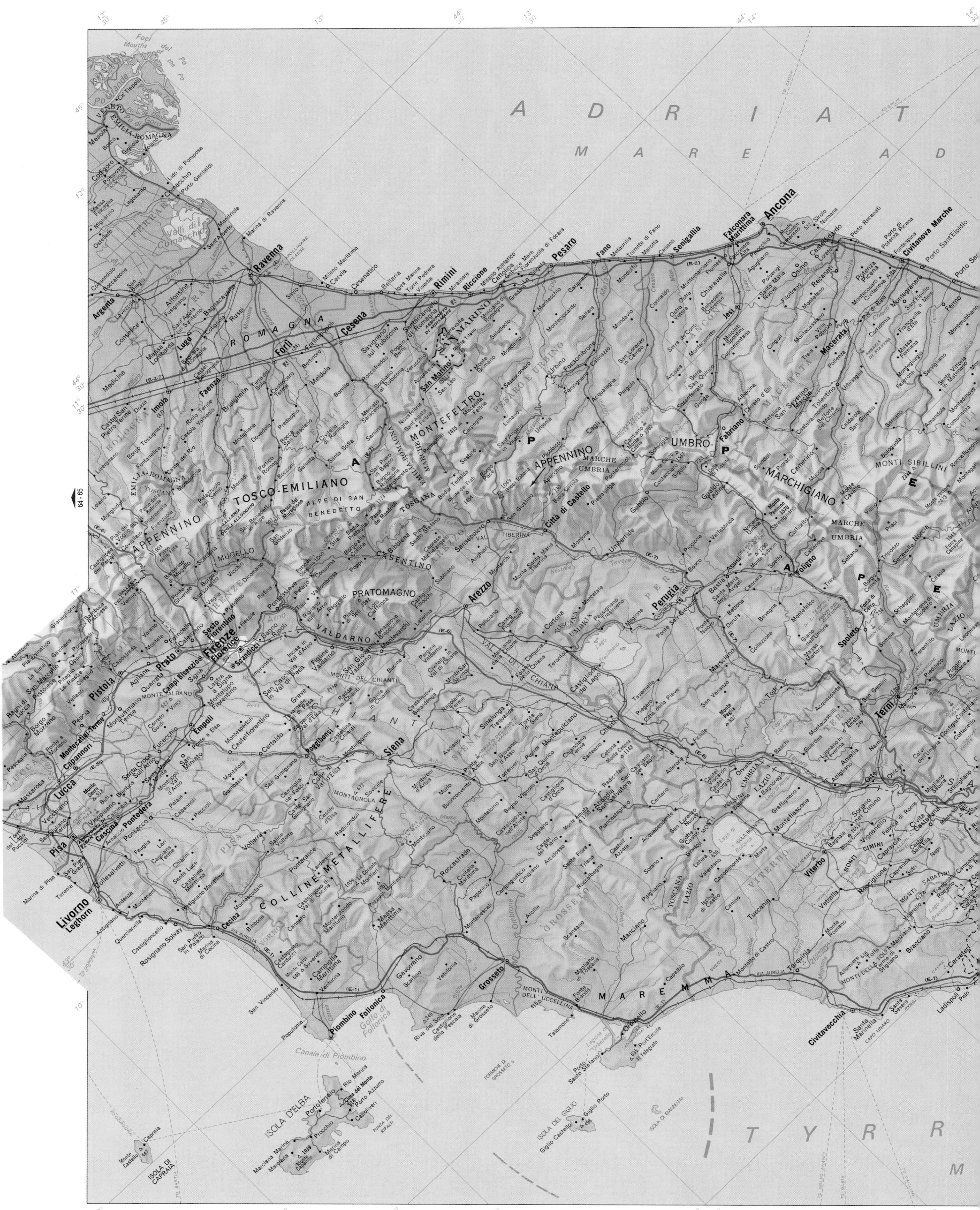

MAP FORM	golfo	isola	lago	monte	monti	passo	punta
ENGLISH	gulf	island	lake	mountain	mountains	pass	point
DEUTSCH	Golf	Insel	See	Berg	Berge	Pass	Landspitze
ESPAÑOL	golfo	isla	lago	montaña	montañas	paso	punta
FRANÇAIS	golfe	île	lac	montagne	montagnes	col	pointe
PORTUGUÊS	golfo	ilha	lago	montanha	montanhas	passo	ponta

Kilometers 0 10 20 30 40 50 Km.
Statute Miles 0 10 20 30 40 50 Mi.

Scale 1:1,000,000 One centimeter represents 10 kilometers.
One inch represents approximately 16 miles.
Lambert Conformal Conic Projection

MAP FORM	capo	golfo	isola	lago	monte	monti	punta
ENGLISH	cape	gulf	island	lake	mountain	mountains	point
DEUTSCH	Kap	Golf	Insel	See	Berg	Berge	Landspitze
ESPAÑOL	cabo	golfo	isla	lago	montaña	montañas	punta
FRANÇAIS	cap	golfe	île	lac	montagne	montagnes	pointe
PORTUGUÊS	cabo	golfo	ilha	lago	montanha	montanhas	ponta

70

Kilometers 0 10 20 30 40 50 Km.

Statute Miles 0 10 20 30 40 50 Mi.

Scale 1:1,000,000

One centimeter represents 10 kilometers.
One inch represents approximately 16 miles.

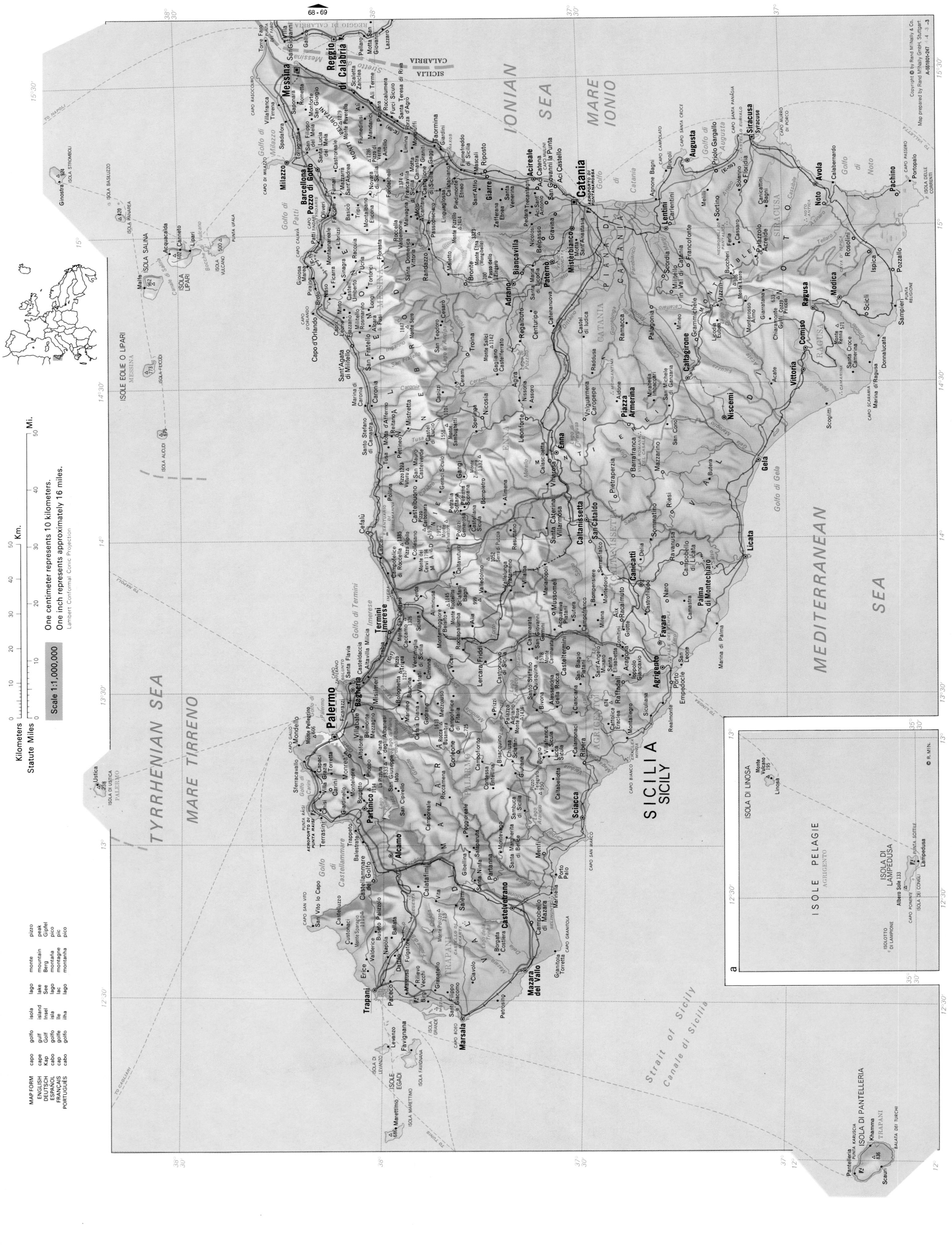
68 - 69
TYRRHENIAN SEA
MARE TIRRENO
IONIAN SEA
MARE IONIO
MEDITERRANEAN SEA
SICILIA
SICILY
Palermo
Catania
Messina
Reggio di Calabria
Siracusa
Agrigento
Trapani
Marsala
Caltanissetta
Enna
Ragusa
Strait of Sicily
Canale di Sicilia
ISOLE EOLIE O LIPARI
ISOLE EGADI
ISOLE PELAGIE
ISOLA DI PANTELLERIA
ISOLA DI LAMPEDUSA
ISOLA DI LINOSA
Scale 1:1,000,000
One centimeter represents 10 kilometers.
One inch represents approximately 16 miles.
Lambert Conformal Conic Projection
Kilometers
Statute Miles

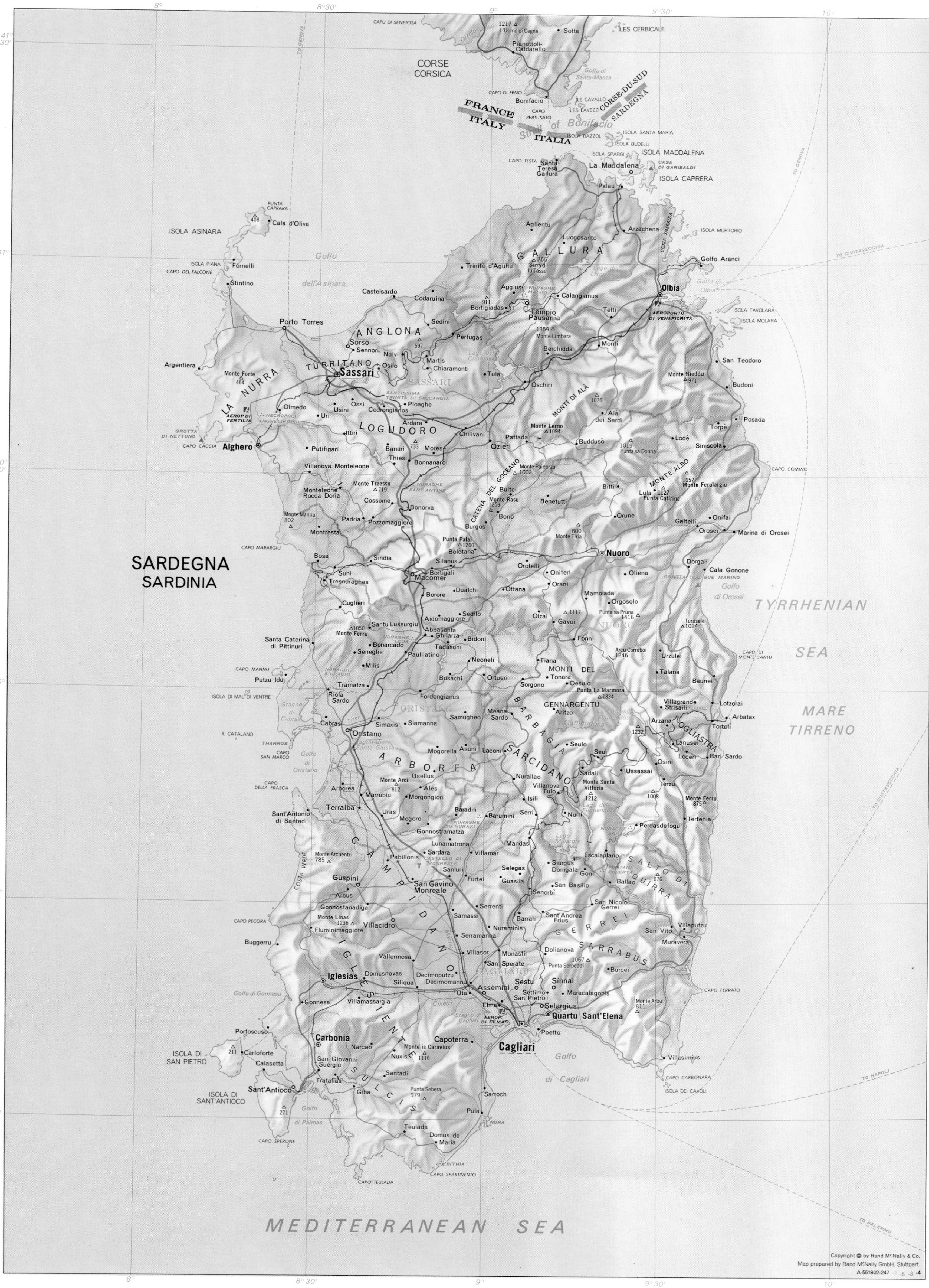
CORSE
CORSICA
FRANCE
ITALY
ITALIA
CORSE-DU-SUD
SARDEGNA
Strait of Bonifacio
Bonifacio
Sotta
Pianottoli-Caldarello
ILES CERBICALE
ISOLA MADDALENA
La Maddalena
ISOLA CAPRERA
Santa Teresa Gallura
Palau
Arzachena
ISOLA MORTORIO
Golfo Aranci
Olbia
AEROPORTO DI VENAFIORITA
ISOLA TAVOLARA
ISOLA MOLARA
San Teodoro
Budoni
Posada
Torpè
Siniscola
Lodè
ISOLA ASINARA
Cala d'Oliva
Fornelli
Stintino
Golfo dell'Asinara
Castelsardo
Porto Torres
ANGLONA
Sorso
Sennori
Sassari
Osilo
TURRITANO
Argentiera
LA NURRA
Olmedo
Alghero
CAPO CACCIA
LOGUDORO
Ozieri
Chilivani
Tempio Pausania
GALLURA
Luogosanto
Aglientu
Trinità d'Agultu
Calangianus
Berchidda
Monti
Telti
Oschiri
Pattada
Buddusò
MONTI DI ALÀ
Alà dei Sardi
Bitti
Lula
Orune
Nuoro
Orosei
Galtellì
Onifai
Marina di Orosei
Dorgali
Cala Gonone
Golfo di Orosei
Oliena
Orgosolo
Mamoiada
Fonni
Gavoi
Ottana
Macomer
Bosa
Suni
Tresnuraghes
Cuglieri
SARDEGNA
SARDINIA
TYRRHENIAN SEA
MARE TIRRENO
Santa Caterina di Pittinuri
Abbasanta
Ghilarza
Paulilatino
Busachi
Fordongianus
Oristano
Cabras
Simaxis
Samugheo
Sorgono
Tonara
Desulo
Aritzo
GENNARGENTU
Punta La Marmora 1834
BARBAGIA
Tortolì
Arbatax
Lanusei
Bari Sardo
OGLIASTRA
Ussassai
Jerzu
Tertenia
Perdasdefogu
SARCIDANO
Laconi
Isili
Nurri
Barumini
Arborea
ARBOREA
Terralba
Marrubiu
Uras
Mogoro
Sardara
Sanluri
San Gavino Monreale
Guspini
Arbus
CAMPIDANO
Villacidro
Fluminimaggiore
Buggerru
Iglesias
Domusnovas
Siliqua
Decimomannu
Assemini
Elmas
Cagliari
Quartu Sant'Elena
Poetto
Selargius
Sinnai
Monastir
Serramanna
Samassi
Senorbì
Dolianova
SARRABUS
GERREI
SALTO DI QUIRRA
San Vito
Muravera
Villaputzu
Villasimius
CAPO CARBONARA
Golfo di Cagliari
Capoterra
Sarroch
Pula
Teulada
Domus de Maria
CAPO SPARTIVENTO
CAPO TEULADA
Carbonia
Gonnesa
Portoscuso
Carloforte
ISOLA DI SAN PIETRO
Calasetta
Sant'Antioco
ISOLA DI SANT'ANTIOCO
Giba
Santadi
Narcao
IGLESIENTE
SULCIS
Golfo di Palmas
MEDITERRANEAN SEA
Copyright © by Rand McNally & Co.
Map prepared by Rand McNally GmbH, Stuttgart.
A-551802-247

MAP FORM	capo	golfo	isola	lago, l.	monte
ENGLISH	cape	gulf	island	lake	mountain
DEUTSCH	Kap	Golf	Insel	See	Berg
ESPAÑOL	cabo	golfo	isla	lago	montaña
FRANÇAIS	cap	golfe	île	lac	montagne
PORTUGUÊS	cabo	golfo	ilha	lago	montanha

Kilometers 0 10 20 30 40 50 Km.
Statute Miles 0 10 20 30 40 50 Mi.

Scale 1:1,000,000

One centimeter represents 10 kilometers.
One inch represents approximately 16 miles.
Lambert Conformal Conic Projection

22-23
118-119

MAP FORM	chrebet	gora	guba	mys	ostrov	ozero	poluostrov	proliv	vodochranilišče
ENGLISH	range	mountain	bay	cape	island	lake	peninsula	strait	reservoir
DEUTSCH	Gebirge	Berg	Bucht	Kap	Insel	See	Halbinsel	Meeresstrasse	Stausee
ESPAÑOL	sierra	montaña	bahía	cabo	isla	lago	península	estrecho	embalse
FRANÇAIS	chaîne	montagne	baie	cabo	île	lac	péninsule	détroit	réservoir
PORTUGUÊS	serra	montanha	baía	cabo	ilha	lago	península	estreito	reservatório

90 - 91

14 - 75

Kilometers 0 200 400 600 Km.

Statute Miles 0 200 400 600 Mi.

Scale 1:12,000,000

One centimeter represents 120 kilometers.
One inch represents approximately 190 miles.
Lambert Conformal Conic Projection

Eastern and Central Soviet Union / Östliche und zentrale Sowjetunion / Unión Soviética Oriental y Central
Union Soviétique Orientale et Centrale / União Soviética Oriental e Central

72-73
90-91

MAP FORM	chrebet	gora	guba	mys	ostrov	ozero	poluostrov	proliv	vodochranilišče
ENGLISH	range	mountain	bay	cape	island	lake	peninsula	strait	reservoir
DEUTSCH	Gebirge	Berg	Bucht	Kap	Insel	See	Halbinsel	Meeresstrasse	Stausee
ESPAÑOL	sierra	montaña	bahía	cabo	isla	lago	península	estrecho	embalse
FRANÇAIS	chaîne	montagne	baie	cap	île	lac	péninsule	détroit	réservoir
PORTUGUÊS	serra	montanha	baía	cabo	ilha	lago	peninsula	estreito	reservatório

Kilometers 0 200 400 600 Km.
Statute Miles 0 200 400 600 Mi.

Scale 1:12,000,000

One centimeter represents 120 kilometers.
One inch represents approximately 190 miles.
Lambert Conformal Conic Projection

ALASKA
UNITED STATES
Bering Strait
Chukchi Sea
OSTROV VRANGEL'A
SAINT LAWRENCE ISLAND
NUNIVAK ISLAND
SAINT MATTHEW ISLAND
VOSTOČNO-SIBIRSKOJE MORE
EAST SIBERIAN SEA
OSTROVA DE-LONGA
OSTROV NOVAJA SIBIR'
OSTROV KOTEL'NYJ
OSTROV BOL'ŠOJ L'ACHOVSKIJ
ČUKOTSKIJ POLUOSTROV
EKIATAPSKIJ CHREBET
ANADYRSKOJE PLOSKOGORJE
AN'UJSKIJ CHREBET
KOLYMSKAJA NIZMENNOST'
JUKAGIRSKOJE PLOSKOGORJE
KOR'AKSKOJE NAGORJE
PENŽINSKIJ CHREBET
Bering Sea
Anadyrskij zaliv
KOMANDORSKIJE OSTROVA
MOMSKIJ CHREBET
CHREBET ČERSKOGO
SIBERIA
CHREBET SUNTAR-CHAJATA
CHREBET SETTE-DABAN
CHREBET DŽUGDŽUR
REPUBLICS
ALDANSKOJE NAGORJE
STANOVOJ CHREBET
Jakutsk
Magadan
Ochotsk
Ajan
zaliv Šelichova
POLUOSTROV KAMČATKA
SREDINNYJ CHREBET
Petropavlovsk-Kamčatskij
SEA OF OKHOTSK
OCHOTSKOJE MORE
OSTROV SACHALIN
SAKHALIN
Južno-Sachalinsk
KURIL'SKIJE OSTROVA
KURIL ISLANDS
Habomai, Shikotan, Kunashiri, and Etorofu, occupied by the U.S.S.R. since 1945, are claimed by Japan pending a final peace treaty.
Komsomol'sk-na-Amure
Chabarovsk
Blagoveščensk
SICHOTE-ALIN'
BUREINSKIJ CHREBET
La Perouse Strait
HOKKAIDŌ
Sapporo
Hakodate
JAPAN
HONSHŪ
PACIFIC OCEAN
SEA OF JAPAN
Vladivostok
Nachodka
Harbin
Qiqihar Tsitsihar
HEILONGJIANG
MANCHURIA
CHINA
NEI MONGGOL ZIZHIQU
DA HINGGAN LING
XIAO HINGGAN LING

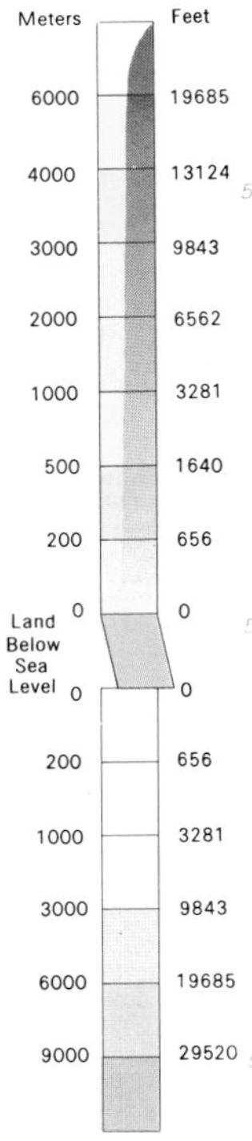

MAP FORM	gr'ada	ostrov, o.	ozero, o.	vodochranilišče, vdchr.	vozvyšennost', vozv.	zaliv	zapovednik, zapov.
ENGLISH	ridge	island	lake	reservoir	upland	gulf; bay	reserve
DEUTSCH	Höhenrücken	Insel	See	Stausee	Bergland	Golf; Bucht	Reservat
ESPAÑOL	lomerío	isla	lago	embalse	tierras altas	golfo; bahía	reserva
FRANÇAIS	crête	île	lac	réservoir	hautes terres	golfe; baie	réserve
PORTUGUÊS	cordilheira	ilha	lago	reservatório	terras altas	golfo; baía	reserva

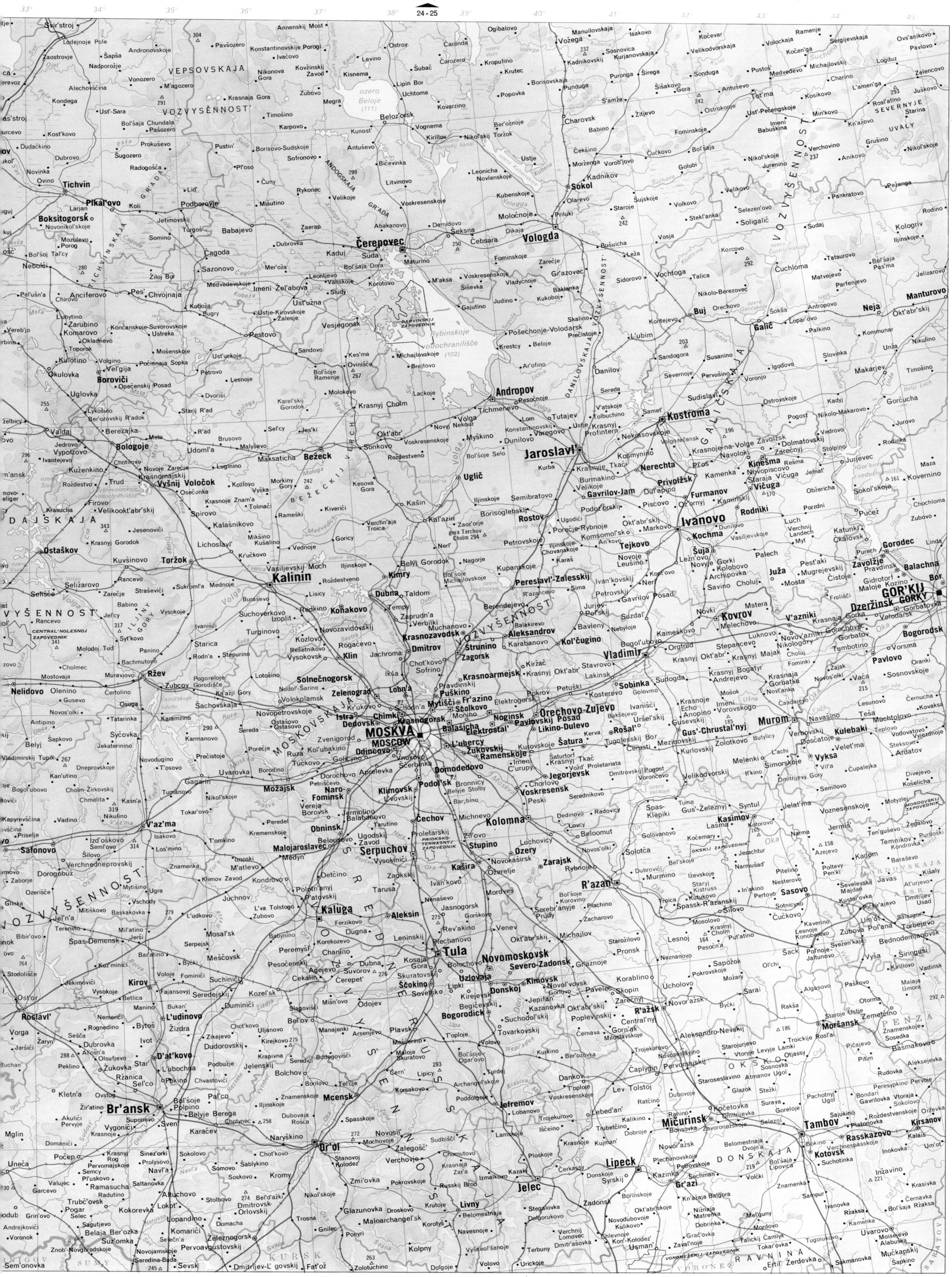

Kilometers 0 50 100 150 Km.
Statute Miles 0 50 100 150 Mi.

Scale 1:3,000,000

One centimeter represents 30 kilometers.
One inch represents approximately 47 miles.
Lambert Conformal Conic Projection

Ukraine / Ukraine / Ucrania
Ukraine / Ucrânia

MAP FORM	gora	liman	mys	nizmennost', nizm.	ozero	vozvyšennost', vozv.	zaliv
ENGLISH	mountain	bay	cape	plain	lake	upland	bay
DEUTSCH	Berg	Bucht	Kap	Ebene	See	Bergland	Bucht
ESPAÑOL	montaña	bahía	cabo	llanno	lago	tierras altas	bahía
FRANÇAIS	montagne	baie	cap	plaine	lac	hautes terres	baie
PORTUGUÊS	montanha	baia	cabo	planície	lago	terras altas	baia

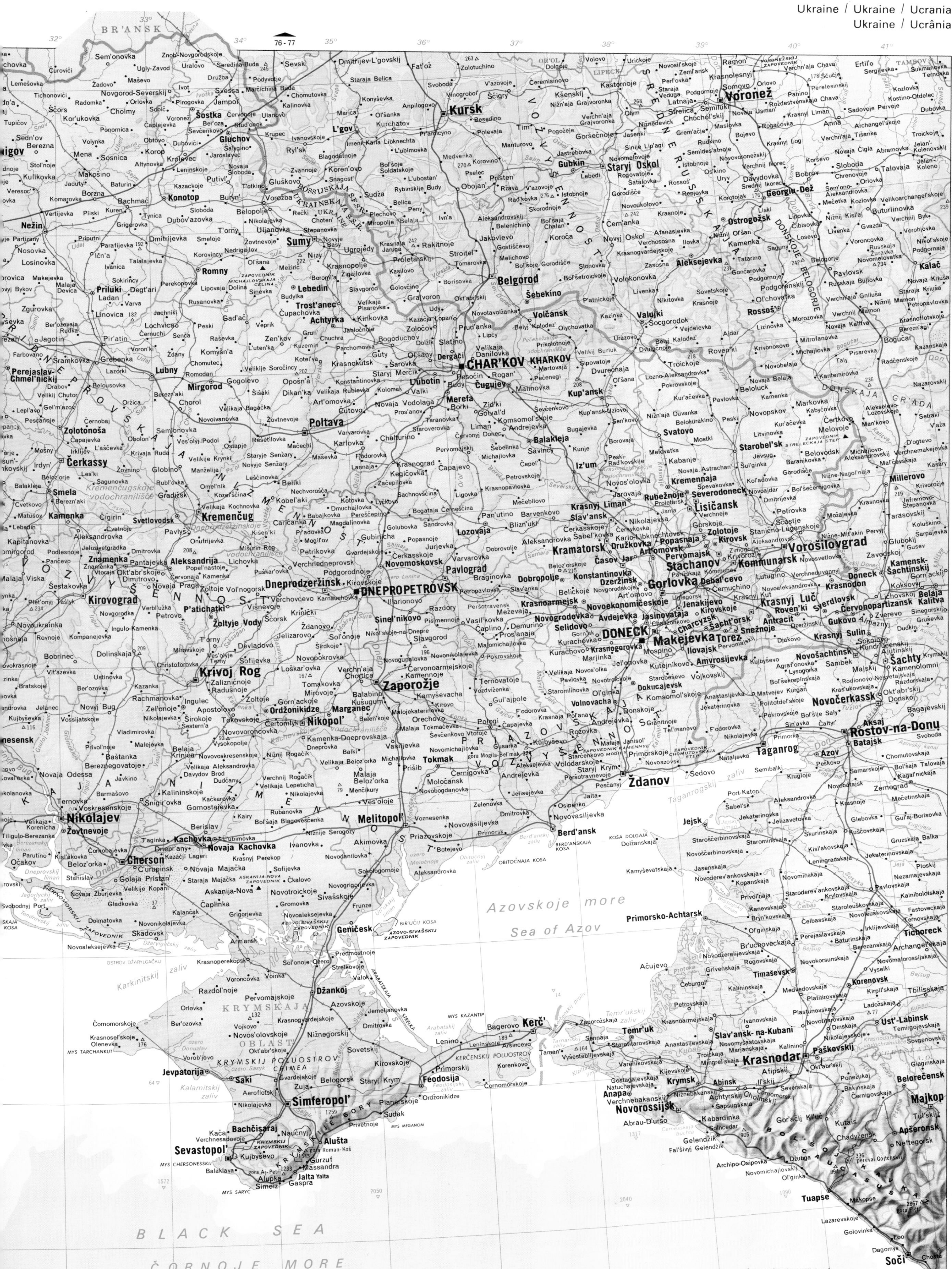
76 - 77
80 - 81
84
BR'ANSK
Kursk
Voronež
Sumy
Belgorod
CHAR'KOV KHARKOV
Poltava
Kremenčug
DNEPROPETROVSK
Dneprodzeržinsk
Zaporožje
Krivoj Rog
Kirovograd
Nikolajev
Cherson
Melitopol'
DONECK
Gorlovka
Makejevka
Vorošilovgrad
Ždanov
Taganrog
Rostov-na-Donu
Novočerkassk
Krasnodar
Novorossijsk
Simferopol'
Sevastopol'
Feodosija
Kerč'
Jevpatorija
Tuapse
Soči
Azovskoje more
Sea of Azov
BLACK SEA
ČORNOJE MORE
KRYMSKAJA OBLAST
KRYMSKIJ POLUOSTROV
CRIMEA
Copyright © by Rand McNally & Co.
Map compiled by Cartographia, Budapest.
Map produced by Rand McNally & Co.
A-571900-764

Kilometers 0 50 100 150 Km.

Statute Miles 0 50 100 150 Mi.

Scale 1:3,000,000

One centimeter represents 30 kilometers.
One inch represents approximately 47 miles.
Lambert Conformal Conic Projection

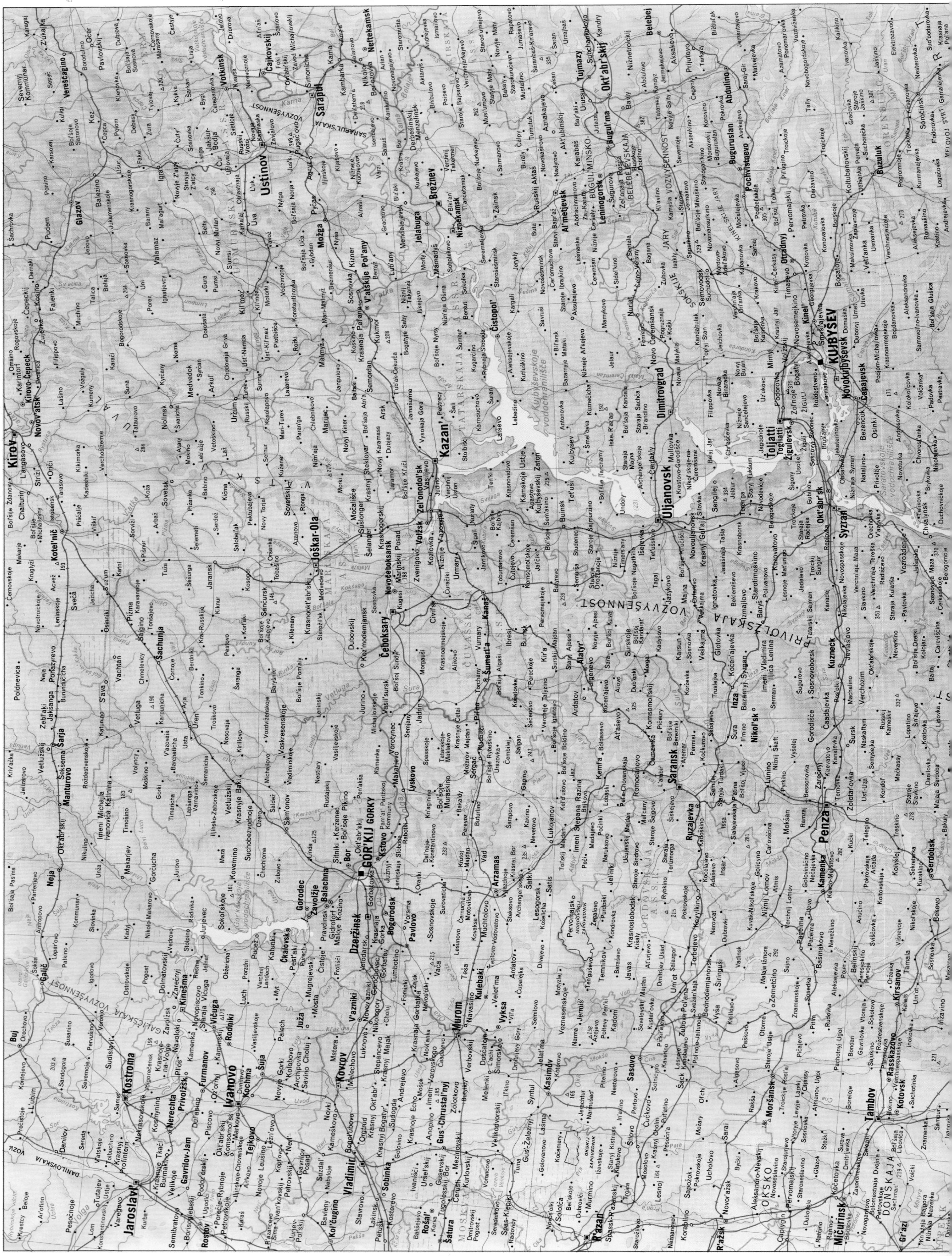
Kirov
Kazan'
Ul'janovsk
Kujbyšev
Penza
Saransk
Gor'kij Gorky
Čeboksary
Joškar-Ola
Jaroslavl'
Kostroma
Ivanovo
Vladimir
Murom
Tol'jatti
Syzran'
Dimitrovgrad
Ustinov
Votkinsk
Tambov
Mičurinsk
R'azan'
Buzuluk
Kuzneck

24-25

76-77

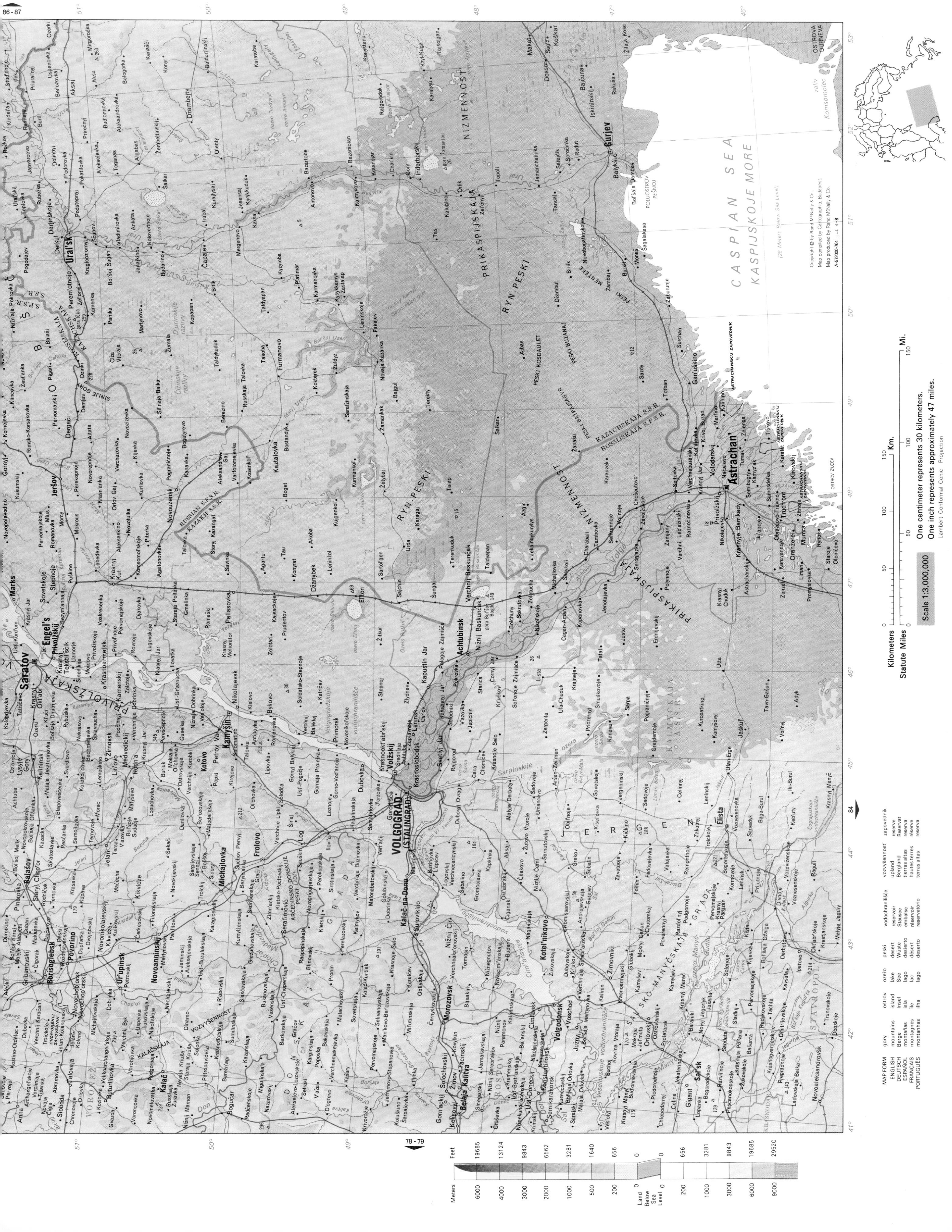
CASPIAN SEA
KASPIJSKOJE MORE
VOLGOGRAD (STALINGRAD)
Saratov
Astrachan
Ural'sk
Gurjev
Elista
Scale 1:3,000,000
One centimeter represents 30 kilometers.
One inch represents approximately 47 miles.
Lambert Conformal Conic Projection
Kilometers
Statute Miles
Copyright © by Rand McNally & Co.
Map compiled by Cartographia, Budapest.
Map produced by Rand McNally & Co.
A-572000-764 -4 -4 -8
MAP FORM
ENGLISH
DEUTSCH
ESPAÑOL
FRANÇAIS
PORTUGUÊS
Meters
Feet
Land
Below Sea Level

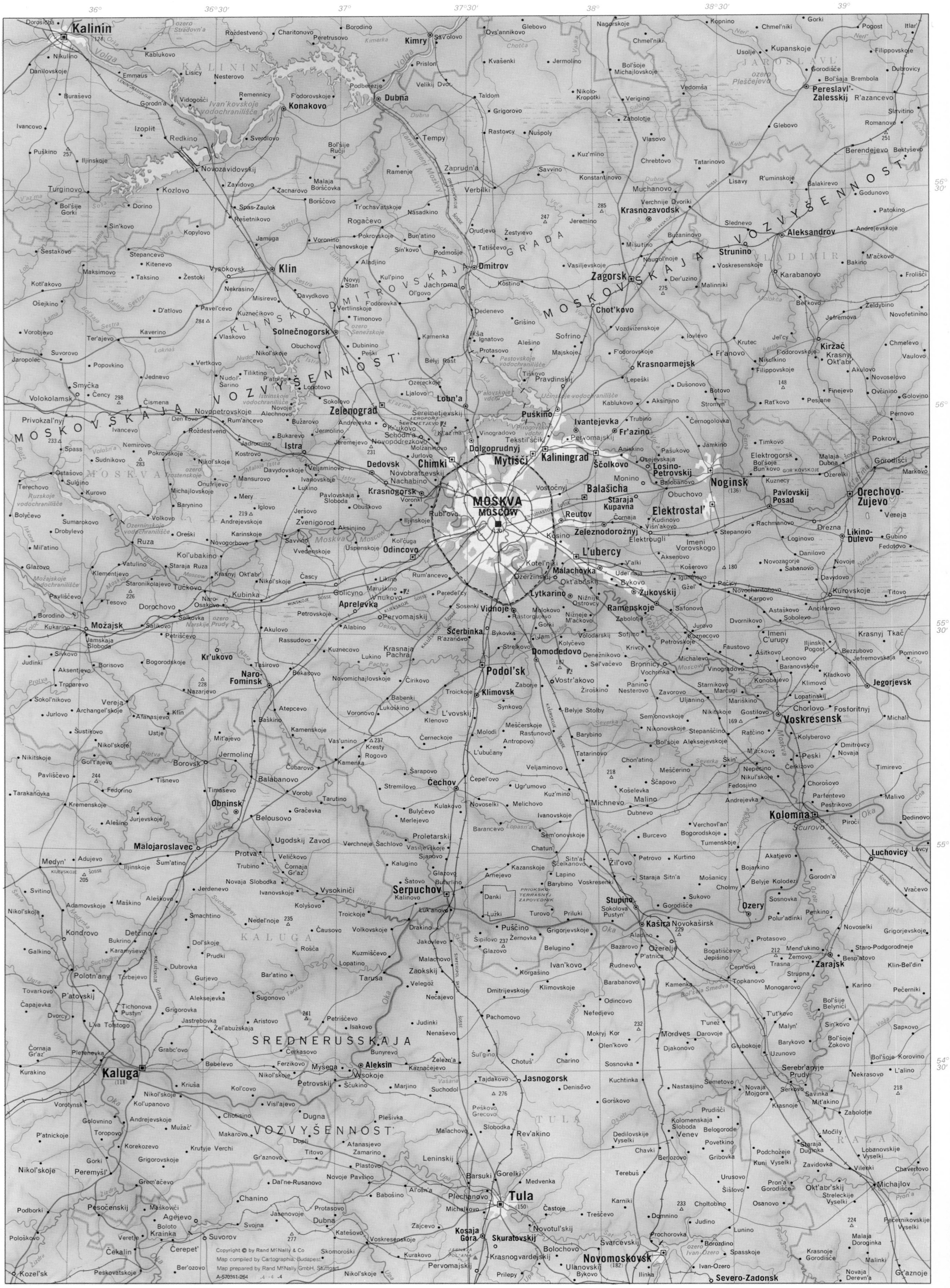

MAP FORM	gr'ada	ozero	vodochranilišče, vdchr.	vozvyšennost'	zapovednik
ENGLISH	ridge	lake	reservoir	upland	reserve
DEUTSCH	Höhenrücken	See	Stausee	Bergland	Reservat
ESPAÑOL	lomerio	lago	embalse	tierras altas	reserva
FRANÇAIS	crête	lac	réservoir	hautes terres	réserve
PORTUGUÊS	cordilheira	lago	reservatório	terras altas	reserva

Kilometers 0 10 20 30 40 50 Km.
Statute Miles 0 10 20 30 40 50 Mi.

Scale 1:1,000,000

One centimeter represents 10 kilometers.
One inch represents approximately 16 miles.
Lambert Conformal Conic Projection

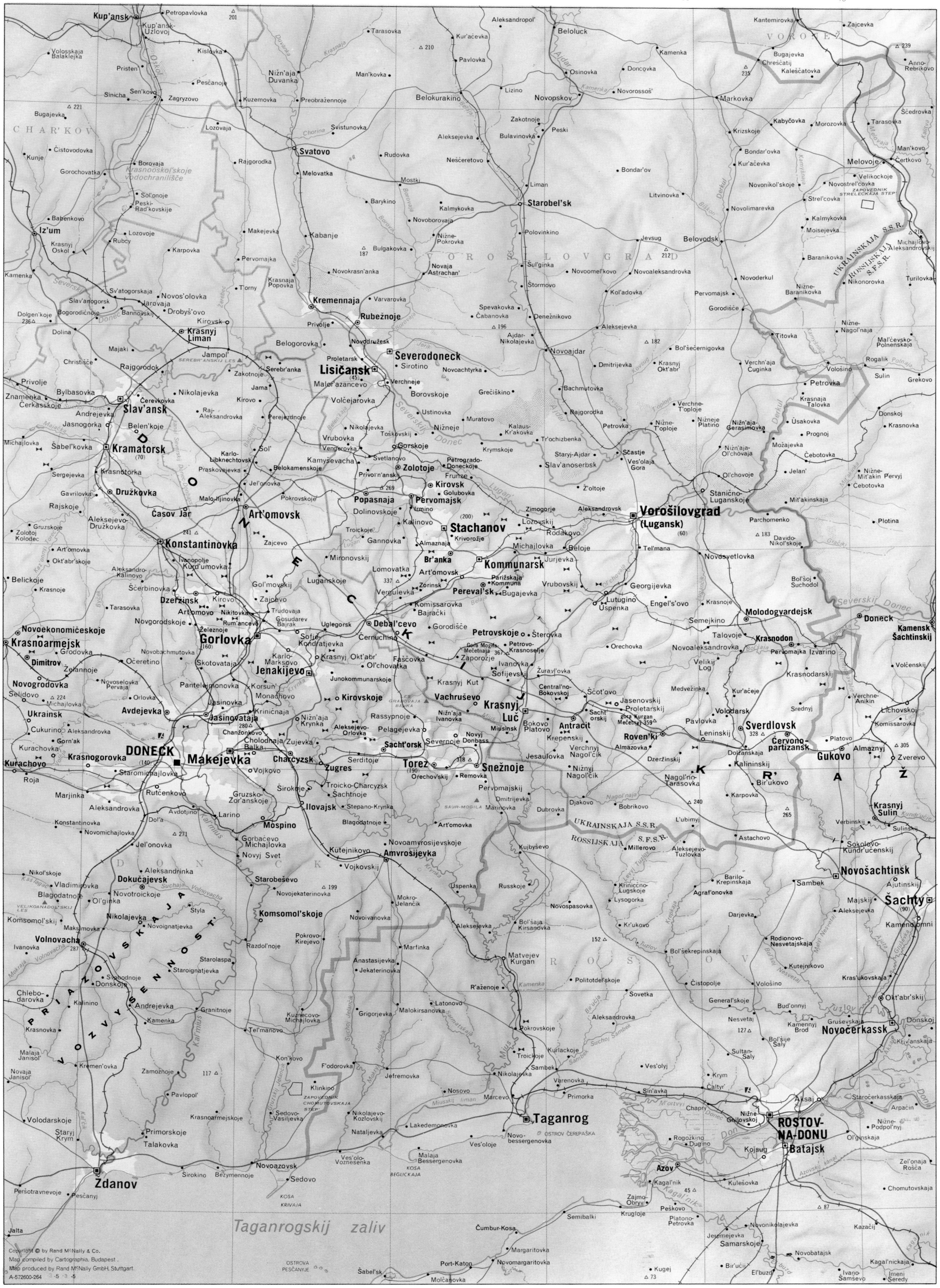

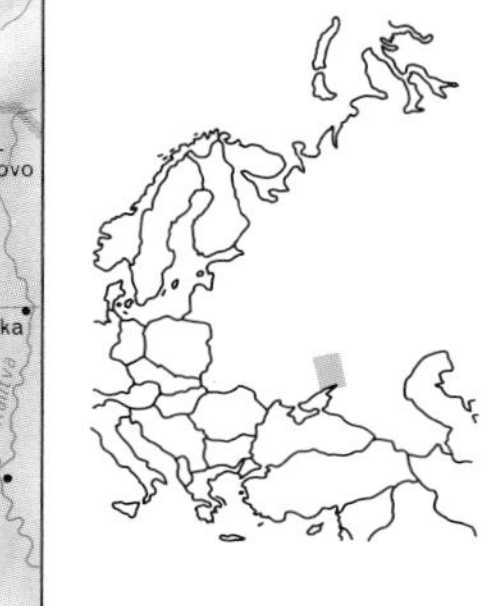

MAP FORM	kosa	ostrov, o.	vodochranilišče, vdchr.	vozvyšennost', vozv.	zaliv	zapovednik, zapov
ENGLISH	spit	island	reservoir	upland	bay	reserve
DEUTSCH	Landzunge	Insel	Stausee	Bergland	Bucht	Reservat
ESPAÑOL	lengua de tierra	isla	embalse	tierras altas	bahía	reserva
FRANÇAIS	flèche	île	réservoir	hautes terres	baie	réserve
PORTUGUÊS	ponta de terra	ilha	reservatório	terras altas	baía	reserva

Kilometers 0 10 20 30 40 50 Km.

Statute Miles 0 10 20 30 40 50 Mi.

Scale 1:1,000,000

One centimeter represents 10 kilometers.

One inch represents approximately 16 miles.

Lambert Conformal Conic Projection

Caucasus and Transcaucasia / Kaukasus und Transkaukasien / Cáucaso y Transcaucasia
Caucasie et Transcaucasie / Cáucaso e Transcaucásia

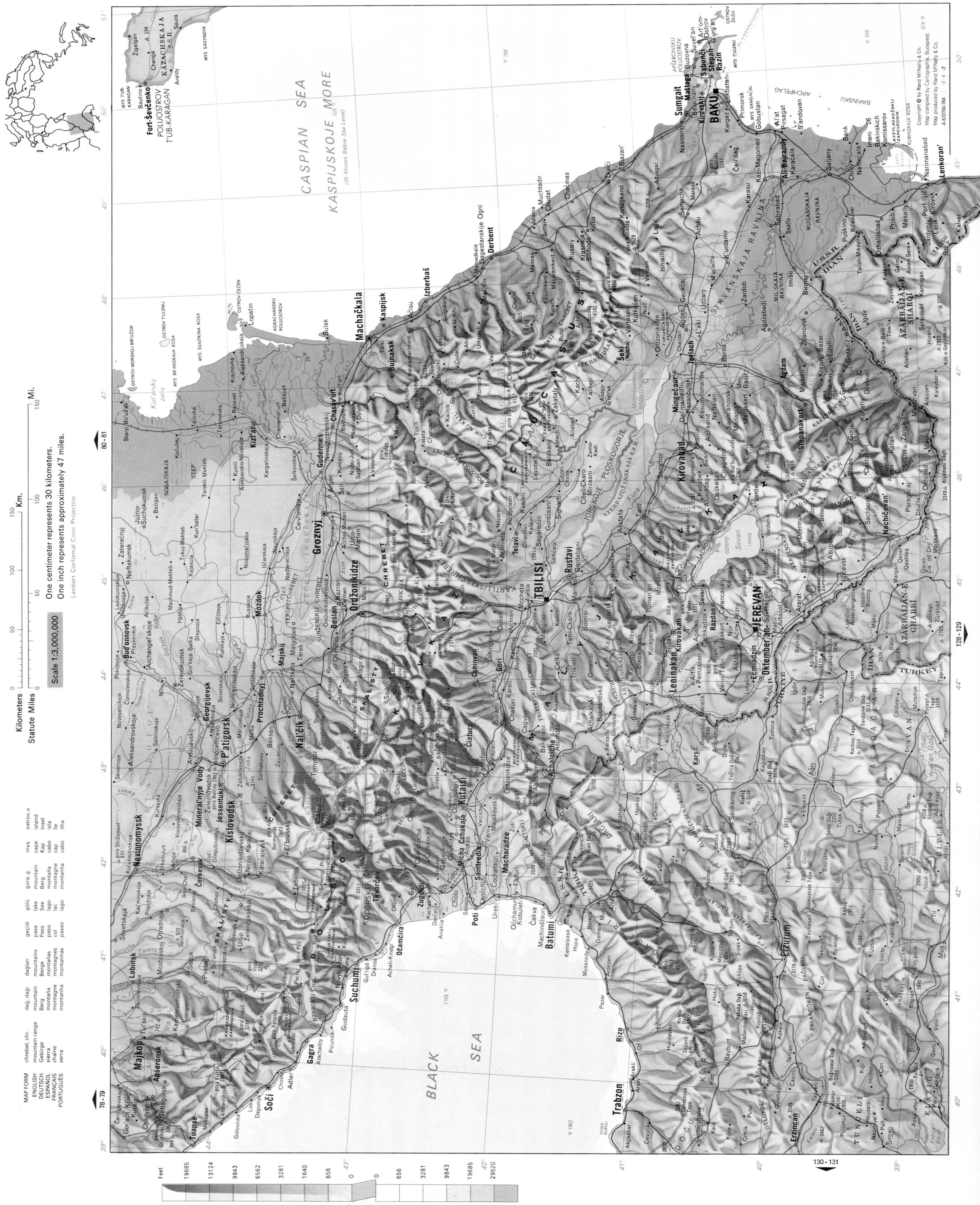

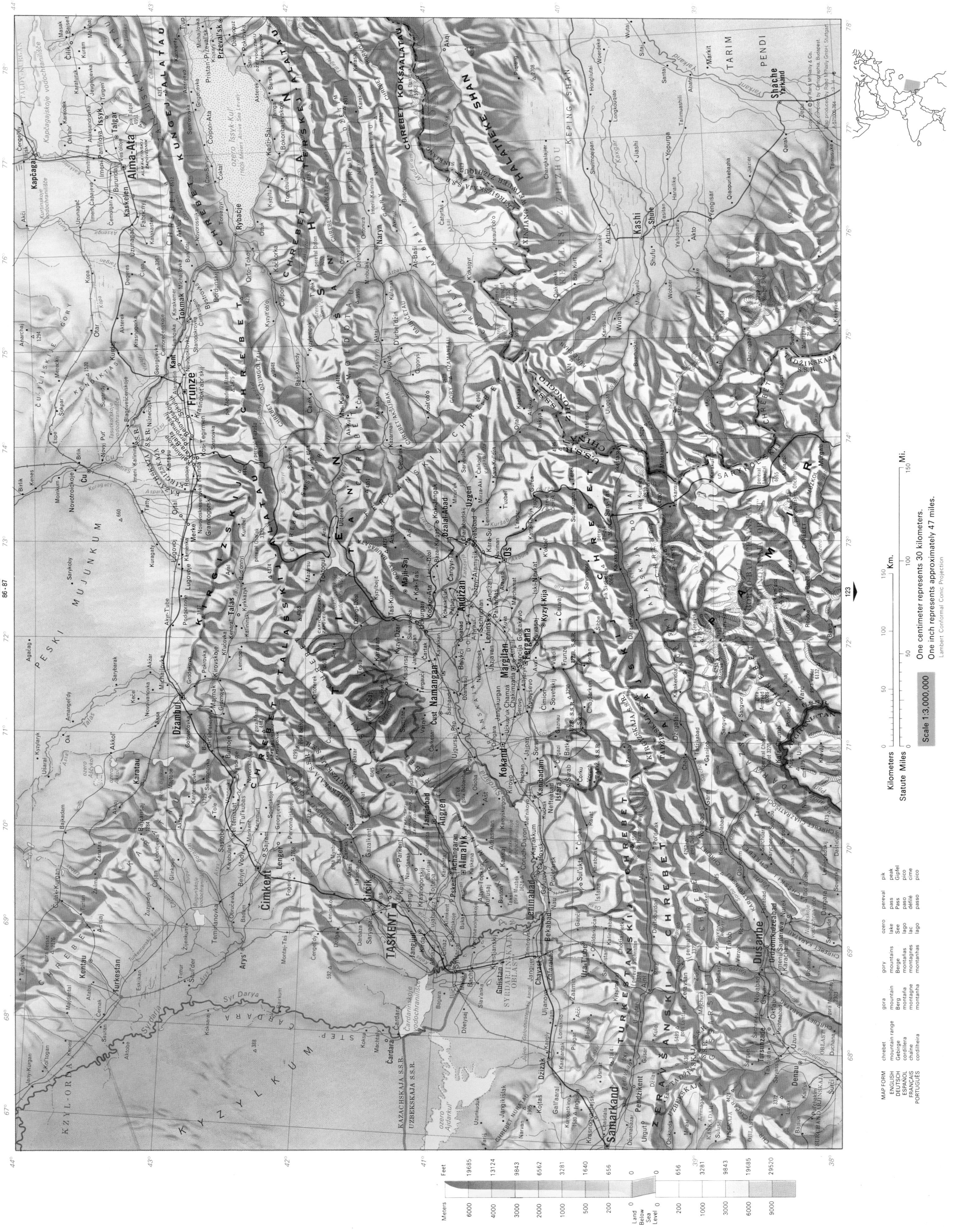
Scale 1:3,000,000
One centimeter represents 30 kilometers.
One inch represents approximately 47 miles.
Lambert Conformal Conic Projection
Kilometers 0 50 100 150 Km.
Statute Miles 0 50 100 150 Mi.
MAP FORM / ENGLISH / DEUTSCH / ESPAÑOL / FRANÇAIS / PORTUGUÊS
chrebet / mountain range / Gebirge / cordillera / chaîne / cordilheira
gora / mountain / Berg / montaña / montagne / montanha
gory / mountains / Berge / montañas / montagnes / montanhas
ozero / lake / See / lago / lac / lago
pereval / pass / Pass / paso / défilé / passo
pik / peak / Gipfel / pico / cime / pico
Feet 19685 13124 9843 6562 3281 1640 656 0 0 656 3281 9843 19685 29520
Meters 6000 4000 3000 2000 1000 500 200 0 Land Below Sea Level 0 200 1000 3000 6000 9000
86-87
123
TAŠKENT
Alma-Ata
Frunze
Samarkand
Dušanbe
Kashi
Čimkent
Džambul
Leninabad
Kokand
Andižan
Namangan
Fergana
Oš
Przeval'sk
Rybač'e
Naryn
Kapčagaj
Turkestan
Kentau
Karatau
Shache Yarkand
Syr Darya
ozero Issyk-Kul'
PESKI MUJUNKUM
KYZYLKUM
T'IEN SHAN
KYRGYZSKIJ ALATAU
TALASSKIJ ALATAU
TURKESTANSKIJ CHREBET
ZERAVŠANSKIJ CHREBET
ALAJSKIJ CHREBET
PAMIR
TARIM PENDI
KAZACHSKAJA S.S.R.
UZBEKSKAJA S.S.R.
KIRGIZSKAJA S.S.R.
TADŽIKSKAJA S.S.R.

Central Soviet Union / Sowjet-Mittelasien / Unión Soviética Central
Union Soviétique Centrale / União Soviética Central

72-73

24-25

80-81

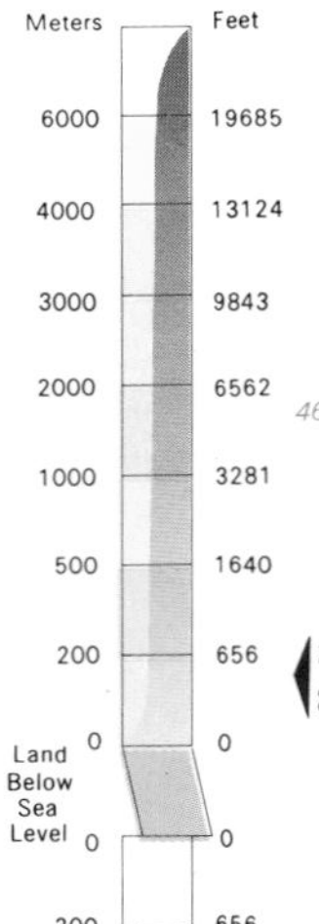

85

MAP FORM	chrebet	gora	hu	ozero	plato	porog
ENGLISH	mountain range	mountain	lake	lake	plateau	waterfall
DEUTSCH	Gebirge	Berg	See	See	Hochebene	Wasserfall
ESPAÑOL	cordillera	montaña	lago	lago	meseta	cascada
FRANÇAIS	chaîne	montagne	lac	lac	plateau	chute d'eau
PORTUGUÊS	cordilheira	montanha	lago	lago	planalto	queda d'água

Kilometers 0 100 200 300 Km.
Statute Miles 0 100 200 300 Mi.

Scale 1:6,000,000

One centimeter represents 60 kilometers.
One inch represents approximately 95 miles.
Lambert Conformal Conic Projection

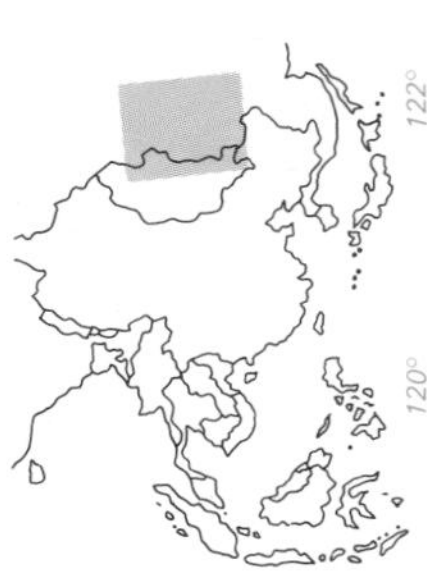

Scale 1:6,000,000
One centimeter represents 60 kilometers.
One inch represents approximately 95 miles.
Lambert Conformal Conic Projection

MAP FORM	chrebet	gora	nuruu	nuur	ozero, o.	porog	uul
ENGLISH	mountain range	mountain	mountain range	lake	lake	waterfall	mountains
DEUTSCH	Gebirge	Berg	Gebirge	See	See	Wasserfall	Berge
ESPAÑOL	cordillera	montaña	cordillera	lago	lago	cascada	montañas
FRANÇAIS	chaîne	montagne	chaîne	lac	lac	chute d'eau	montagnes
PORTUGUÊS	cordilheira	montanha	cordilheira	lago	lago	queda d'agua	montanhas

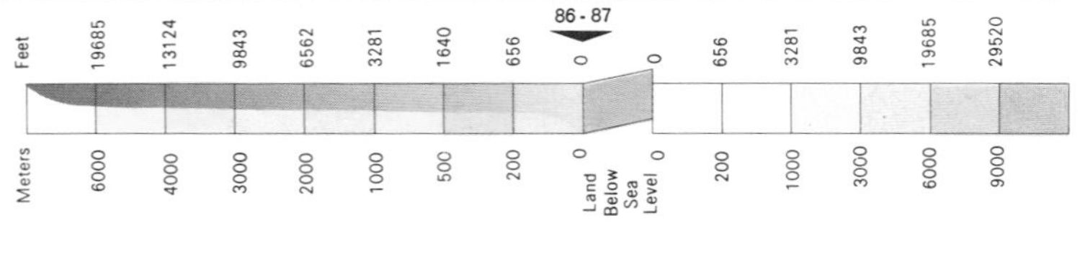

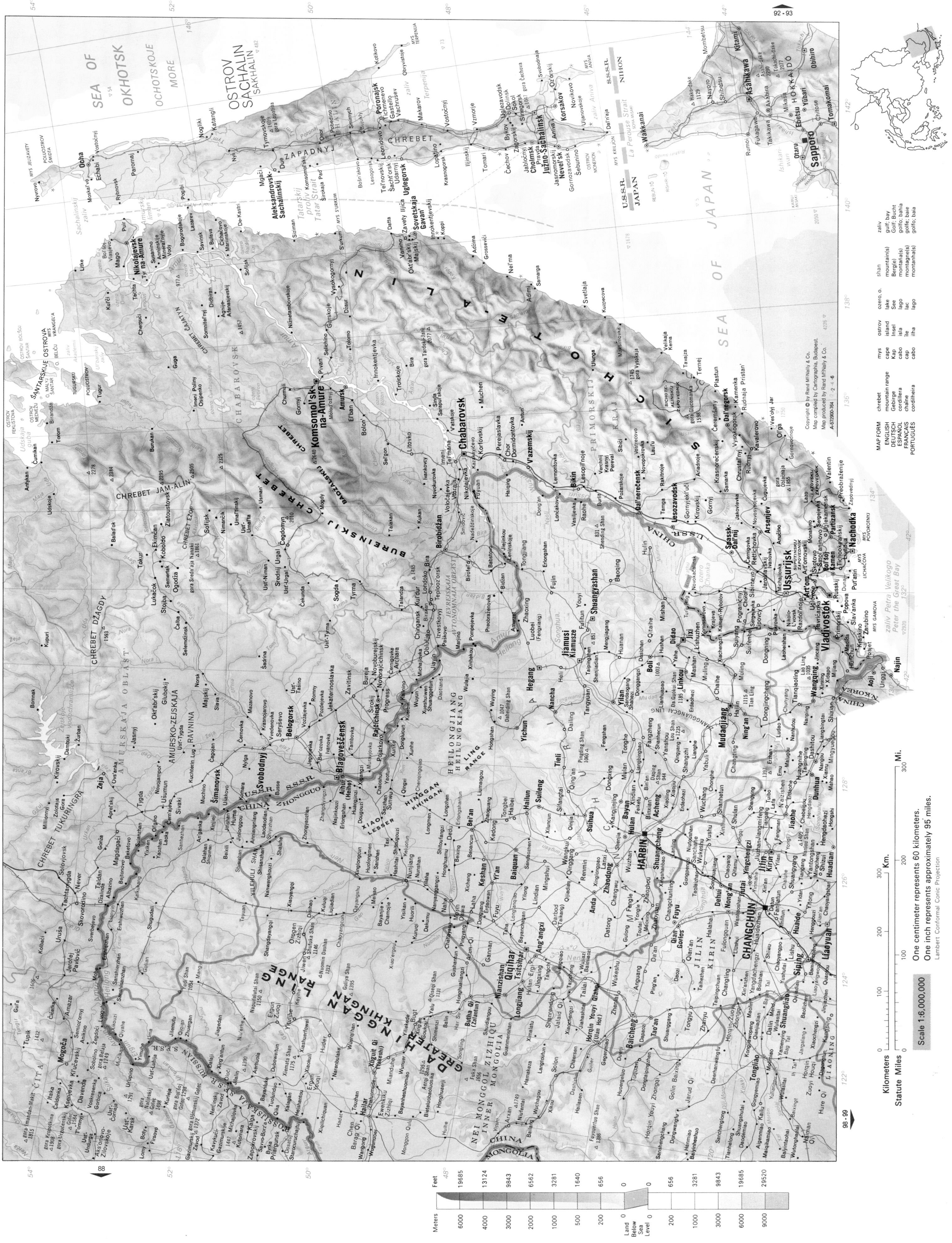
92 - 93
74 - 75
88
98 - 99
SEA OF OKHOTSK
OCHOTSKOJE MORE
OSTROV SACHALIN
SAKHALIN
SEA OF JAPAN
Komsomol'sk-na-Amure
Chabarovsk
Vladivostok
Nachodka
Ussurijsk
Blagoveščensk
Svobodnyj
Birobidžan
Južno-Sachalinsk
Sapporo
HARBIN
CHANGCHUN
Qiqihar
Jiamusi
Mudanjiang
Jilin
GREAT KHINGAN RANGE
DA HINGGAN LING
LESSER KHINGAN RANGE
XIAO HINGGAN LING
CHREBET DŽAGDY
BUREINSKIJ CHREBET
SICHOTE-ALIN'
CHINA
U.S.S.R.
Scale 1:6,000,000
One centimeter represents 60 kilometers.
One inch represents approximately 95 miles.
Lambert Conformal Conic Projection
Kilometers
Statute Miles
Copyright © by Rand McNally & Co.
Map compiled by Cartographia, Budapest.
Map produced by Rand McNally & Co.
A-572000-764
MAP FORM
ENGLISH
DEUTSCH
ESPAÑOL
FRANÇAIS
PORTUGUÊS
Feet
Meters
Land Below Sea Level

MAP FORM	bandao	dao	hu	-jima	pendi	shan	-shima
ENGLISH	peninsula	island	lake	island	basin	mountain(s)	island
DEUTSCH	Halbinsel	Insel	See	Insel	Becken	Berg(e)	Insel
ESPAÑOL	peninsula	isla	lago	isla	cuenca	montaña(s)	isla
FRANÇAIS	péninsule	île	lac	île	bassin	montagne(s)	île
PORTUGUÊS	peninsula	ilha	lago	ilha	bacia	montanha(s)	ilha

U. S. S. R.
ROSSIJSKAJA S.F.S.R.
Čita
Blagoveščensk
Chabarovsk
Južno-Sachalinsk
OSTROV SACHALIN
SEA OF OKHOTSK
La Perouse Strait
HOKKAIDŌ
Sapporo
Asahikawa
Hakodate
Vladivostok
Ussurijsk
Nachodka
MANCHURIA
HEILONGJIANG
Harbin
Qiqihar
Jiamusi
Mudanjiang
Changchun
Jilin
DA HINGGAN LING
XIAO HINGGAN LING
SICHOTE-ALIN
NEI MONGGOL ZIZHIQU
INNER MONGOLIA
Hohhot
Baotou
SHENYANG
MUKDEN
Fushun
Anshan
LIAONING
Dandong
Lüda
Dairen
BEIJING
PEKING
TIANJIN
Tangshan
Shijiazhuang
Taiyuan
SHANXI
HEBEI
SHANDONG
Jinan
Qingdao
Bo Hai
Korea Bay
NORTH KOREA
P'yŏngyang
Ch'ŏngjin
Kimch'aek
Hamhŭng
SOUTH KOREA
SEOUL
Inch'ŏn
Taegu
Pusan
Kwangju
Taejŏn
SEA OF JAPAN
JAPAN
HONSHŪ
TŌKYŌ
Yokohama
Kawasaki
Nagoya
Kyōto
Kōbe
ŌSAKA
Hiroshima
Niigata
Sendai
SHIKOKU
KYŪSHŪ
Fukuoka
Kitakyūshū
Nagasaki
Kagoshima
Yellow Sea
JIANGSU
Nanjing
SHANGHAI
Hangzhou
Wuhan
Zhengzhou
Kaifeng
Luoyang
HENAN
ANHUI
Hefei
HUBEI
HUNAN
Changsha
Nanchang
JIANGXI
ZHEJIANG
Ningbo
Wenzhou
FUJIAN
Fuzhou
Xiamen
Amoy
GUANGDONG
GUANGZHOU
CANTON
Shantou
Swatow
Kowloon
Victoria
HONG KONG
Macau
Haikou
EAST CHINA SEA
RYUKYU ISLANDS (Japan)
OKINAWA-JIMA
Naha
TAIWAN
T'aipei
Kaohsiung
Tropic of Cancer
PACIFIC OCEAN
Bashi Channel
Luzon Strait
PHILIPPINE SEA
PHILIPPINES
LUZON
SOUTH CHINA SEA
Copyright © by Rand McNally & Co.
Map prepared by Esselte Map Service AB, Stockholm.
A-569700-264

108 - 109

Kilometers 0 200 400 600 Km.
Statute Miles 0 200 400 600 Mi.

Scale 1:12,000,000

One centimeter represents 120 kilometers.
One inch represents approximately 190 miles.
Lambert Conformal Conic Projection

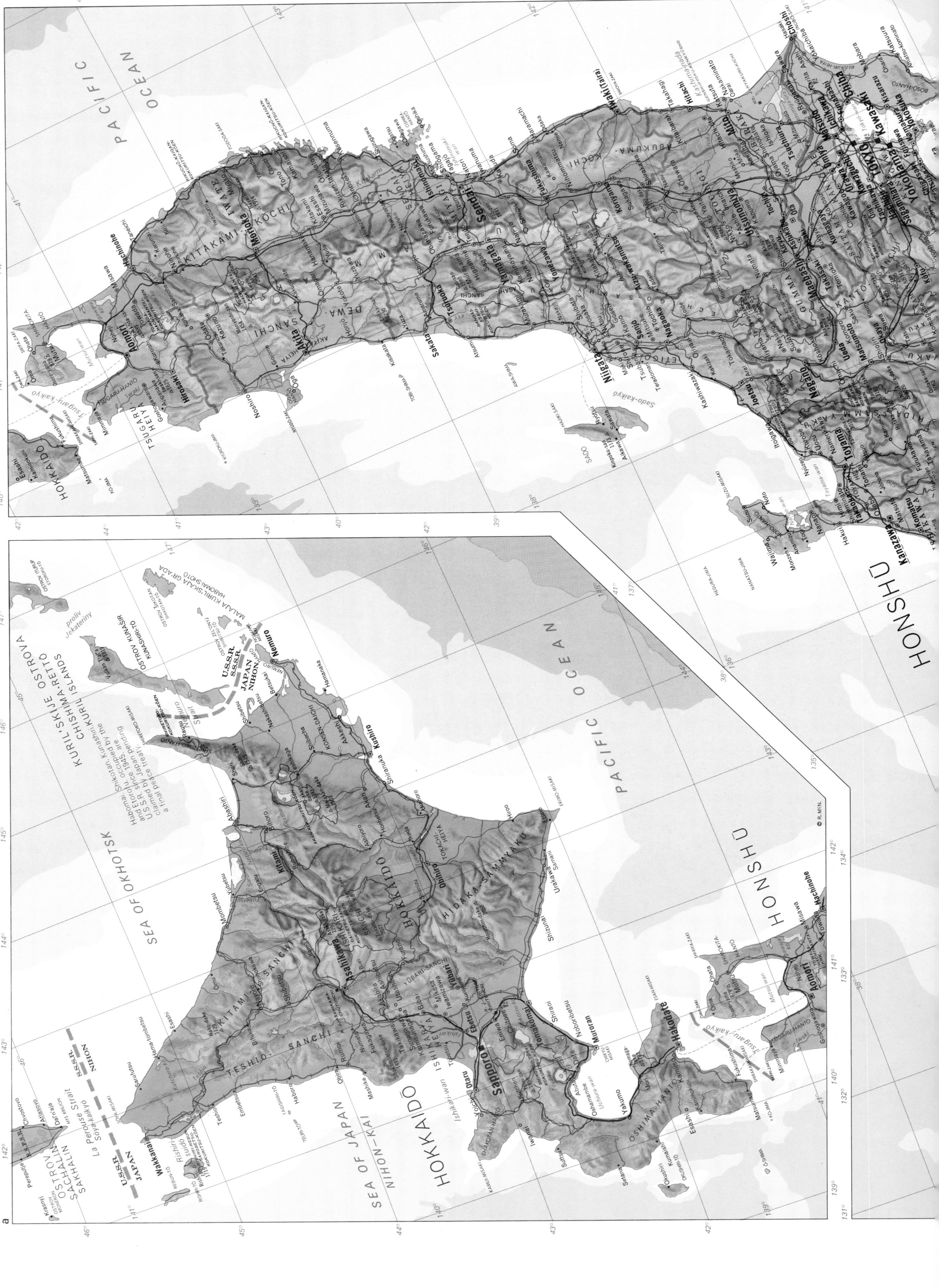
PACIFIC OCEAN
HONSHŪ
SADO
HOKKAIDŌ
SEA OF JAPAN
NIHON-KAI
SEA OF OKHOTSK
KURIL'SKIJE OSTROVA
CHISHIMA-RETTO
KURIL ISLANDS
Habomai, Shikotan, Kunashiri, and Etorofu occupied by the U.S.S.R. since 1945, are claimed by Japan pending a final peace treaty.
La Perouse Strait
Sōya-kaikyō
Tsugaru-kaikyō
Sapporo
Hakodate
Asahikawa
Kushiro
Aomori
Sendai
Niigata
Tōkyō
a

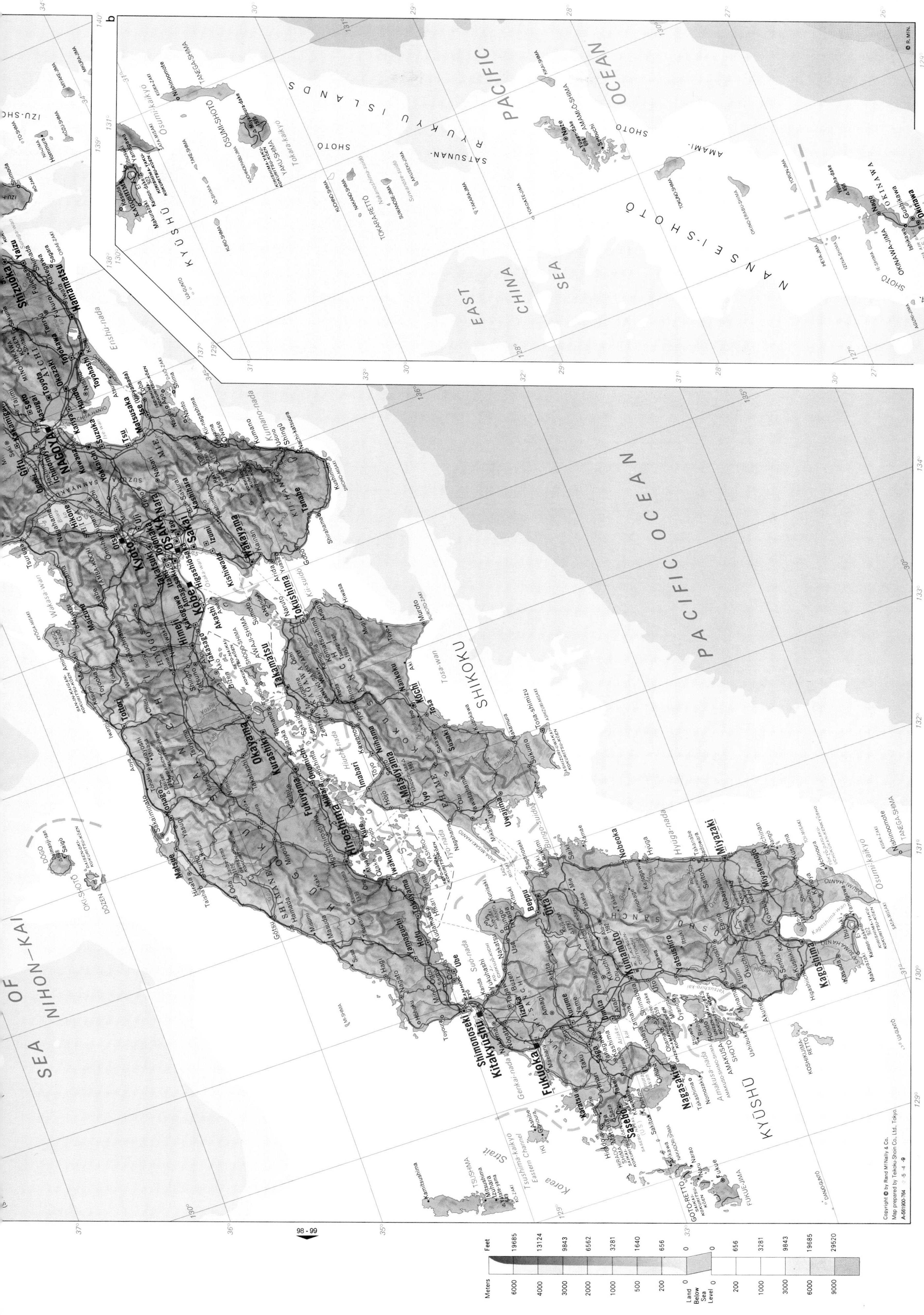
SEA OF
NIHON-KAI
PACIFIC OCEAN
SHIKOKU
KYŪSHŪ
EAST CHINA SEA
RYUKYU ISLANDS
NANSEI-SHOTŌ
OKINAWA
Naha
Kagoshima
Fukuoka
Kitakyushu
Hiroshima
Okayama
Kobe
OSAKA
Kyoto
NAGOYA
Shizuoka
Matsuyama
Kochi
Tokushima
Nagasaki
Kumamoto
Miyazaki
b
Meters
6000
4000
3000
2000
1000
500
200
0
Feet
19685
13124
9843
6562
3281
1640
656
0
Land Below Sea Level
0
200
1000
3000
6000
9000
0
656
3281
9843
19685
29520
98 - 99
Scale 1:3,000,000
Kilometers 0 50 100 150 Km.
Statute Miles 0 50 100 150 Mi.
One centimeter represents 30 kilometers.
One inch represents approximately 47 miles.
Lambert Conformal Conic Projection
MAP FORM / ENGLISH / DEUTSCH / ESPAÑOL / FRANÇAIS / PORTUGUÊS
-dake mountain Berg montaña montagne montanha
-hantō peninsula Halbinsel península péninsule península
-heiya plain Ebene llanura plaine planície
-jima island Insel isla île ilha
-kokuritsu-kōen national park Nationalpark parque nacional parc national parque nacional
-san mountain Berg montaña montagne montanha
-shima island Insel isla île ilha
-wan bay Bucht bahía baie baía
Copyright © by Rand McNally & Co.
Map prepared by Teikoku-Shoin Co., Ltd. Tokyo
A-561900-764 -5-4-9

MAP FORM	-dake	-hantō	-kokutei-kōen	-misaki	-san	-tōge	-wan	-yama	-zaki
ENGLISH	mountain	peninsula	national park	cape	mountain	pass	bay	mountain	point
DEUTSCH	Berg	Halbinsel	Nationalpark	Kap	Berg	Pass	Bucht	Berg	Landspitze
ESPAÑOL	montaña	península	parque nacional	cabo	montaña	paso	bahía	montaña	punta
FRANÇAIS	montagne	péninsule	parc national	cap	montagne	col	baie	montagne	pointe
PORTUGUÊS	montanha	península	parque nacional	cabo	montanha	passo	baía	montanha	ponta

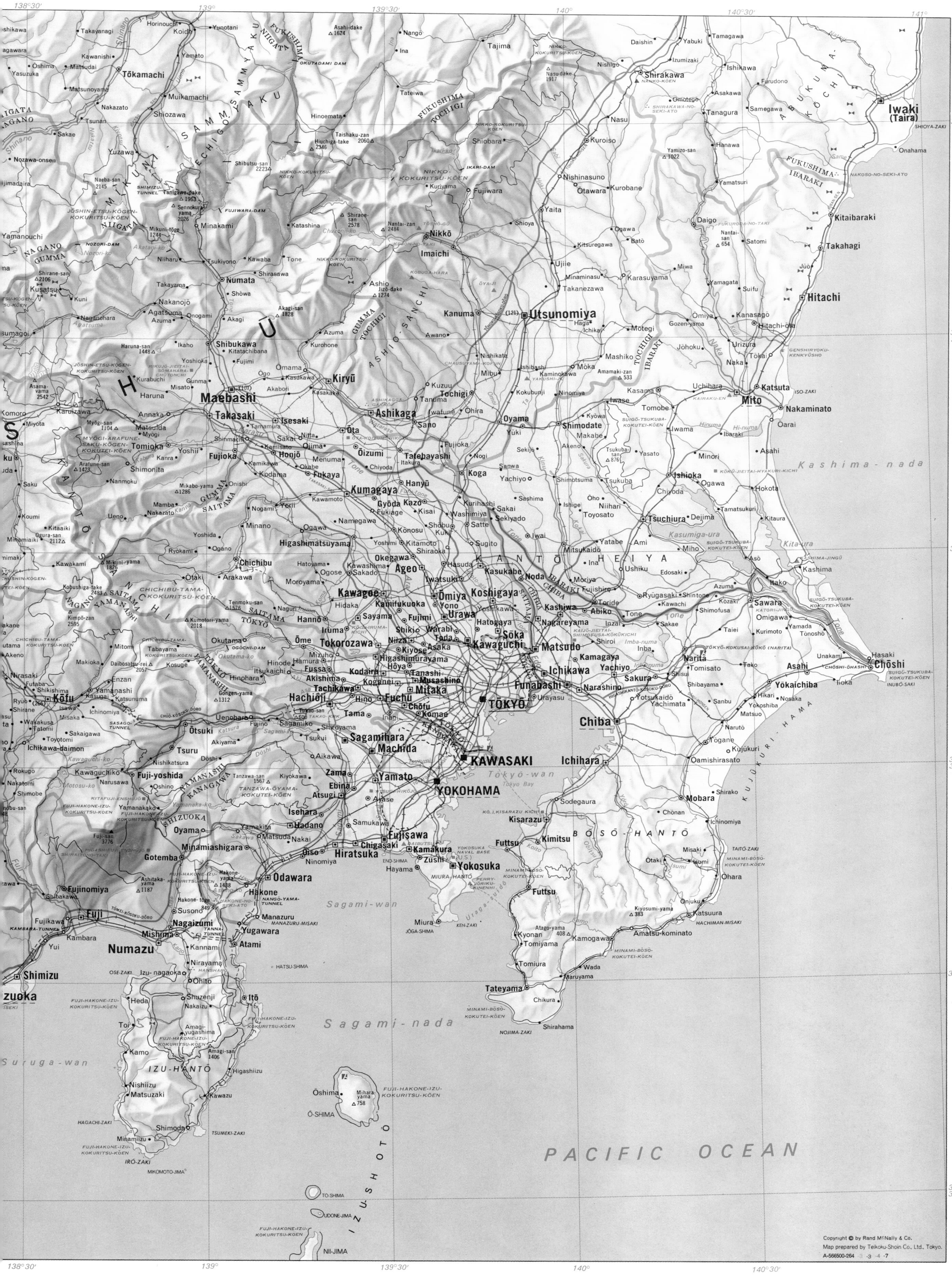

Kilometers 0 10 20 30 40 50 Km.

Statute Miles 0 10 20 30 40 50 Mi.

Scale 1:1,000,000

One centimeter represents 10 kilometers.
One inch represents approximately 16 miles.
Lambert Conformal Conic Projection

MAP FORM	-jima	-misaki	-san	-sen	-shima	-tōge	-yama	-zen
ENGLISH	island	cape	mountain	mountain	island	pass	mountain	mountain
DEUTSCH	Insel	Kap	Berg	Berg	Insel	Pass	Berg	Berg
ESPAÑOL	isla	cabo	montaña	montaña	isla	paso	montaña	montaña
FRANÇAIS	île	cap	montagne	montagne	île	col	montagne	montagne
PORTUGUÊS	ilha	cabo	montanha	montanha	ilha	passo	montanha	montanha

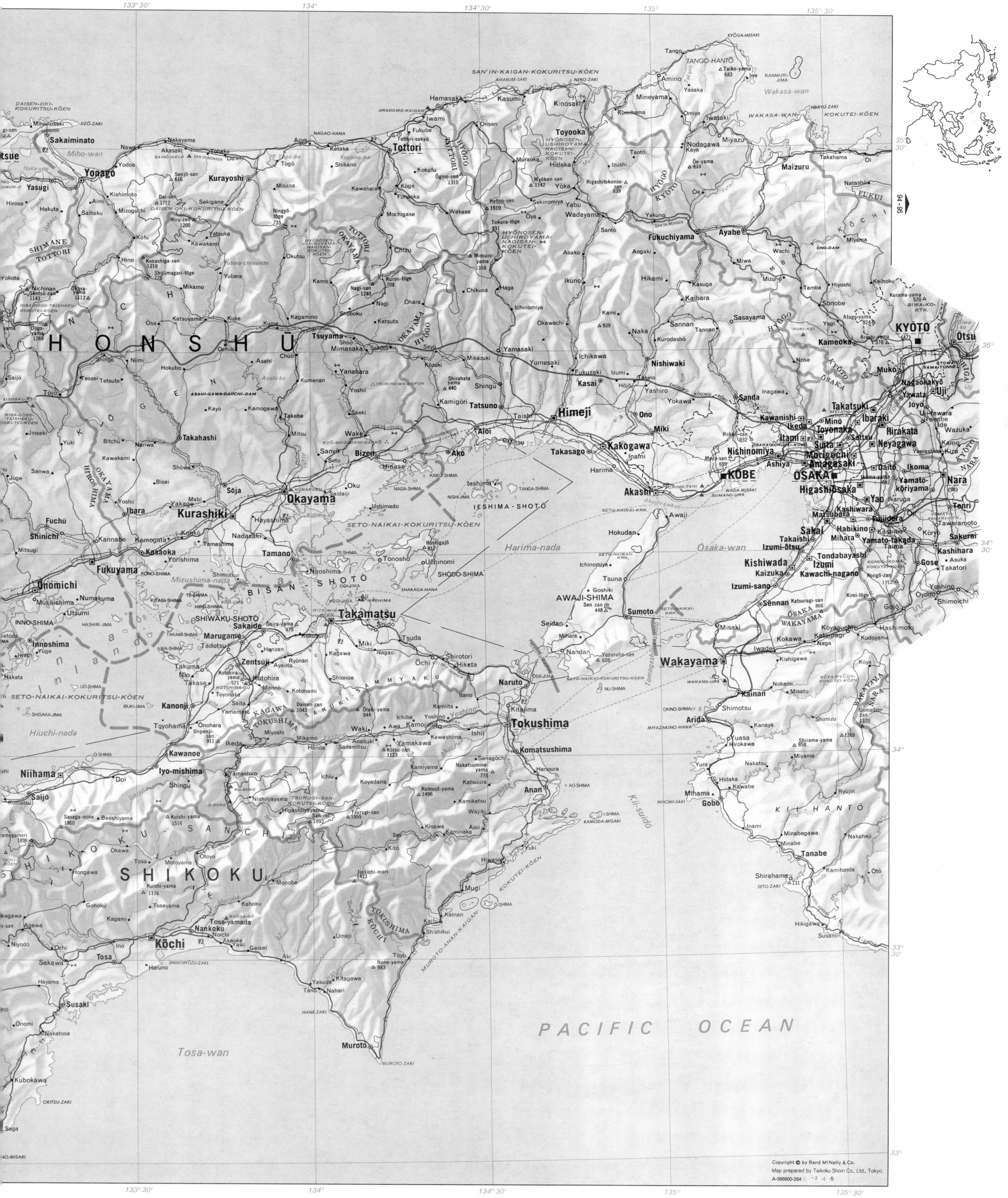

Kilometers 0 10 20 30 40 50 Km.

Statute Miles 0 10 20 30 40 50 Mi.

Scale 1:1,000,000

One centimeter represents 10 kilometers.
One inch represents approximately 16 miles.
Lambert Conformal Conic Projection

Northeast China and Korea / Nordostchina und Korea / China Nor-oriental y Corea / Nord-Est de la Chine et Corée / Nordeste da China e Coréia

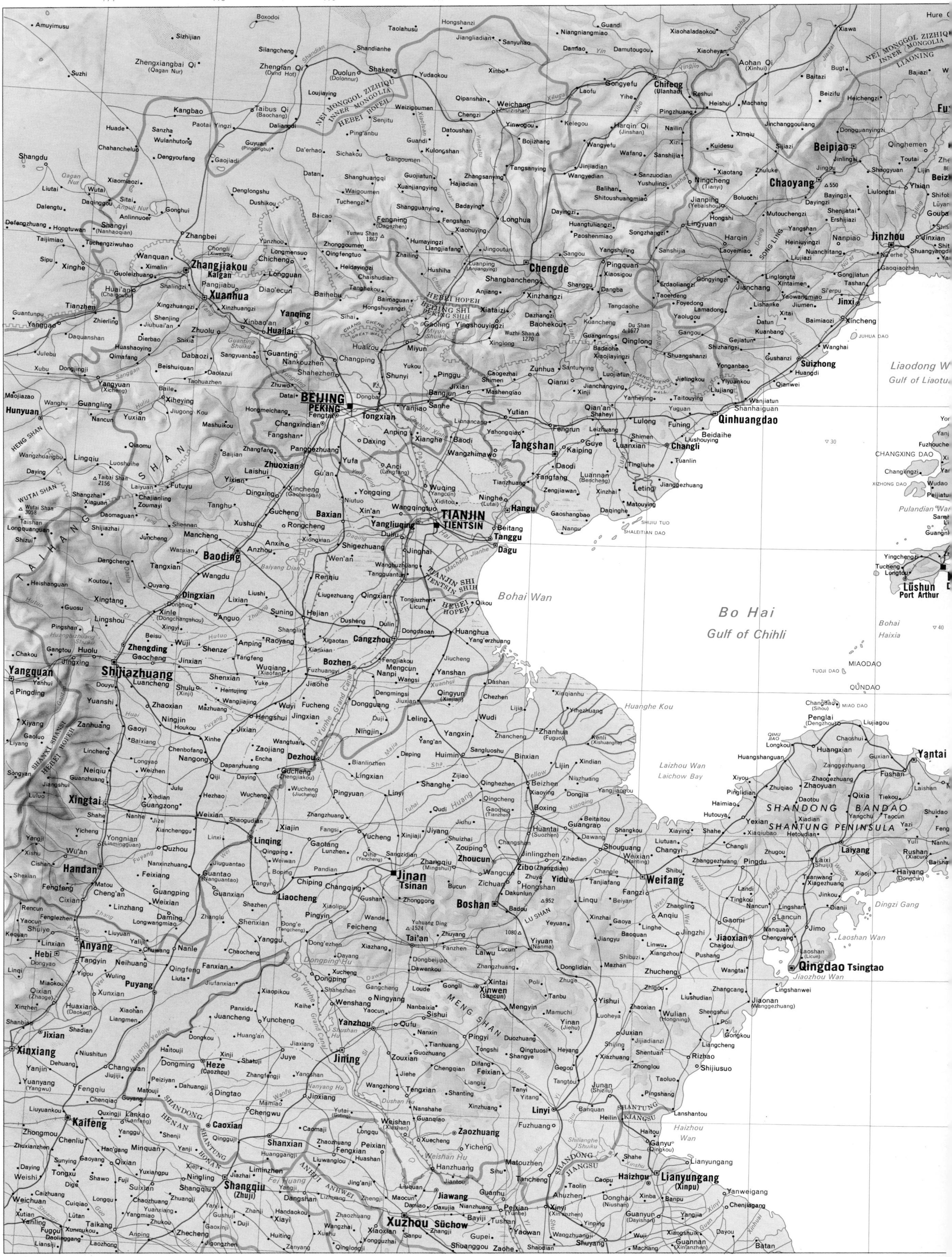

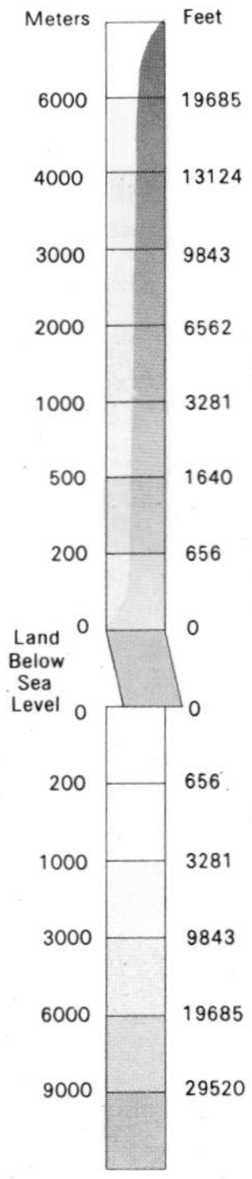

MAP FORM	dao	-do	-gang	hu	kukrip kongwŏn	-san	shan	wan
ENGLISH	island	island	river	lake	national park	mountain	mountain(s)	bay
DEUTSCH	Insel	Insel	Fluss	See	Nationalpark	Berg	Berg(e)	Bucht
ESPAÑOL	isla	isla	río	lago	parque nacional	montaña	montaña(s)	bahía
FRANÇAIS	île	île	rivière	lac	parc national	montagne	montagne(s)	baie
PORTUGUÊS	ilha	ilha	rio	lago	parque nacional	montanha	montanha(s)	baía

MANCHURIA
CHINA
NORTH KOREA
SOUTH KOREA
SEA OF JAPAN
Korea Bay
YELLOW SEA
Korea Strait
Western Channel
Tsushima-kaikyō
Eastern Channel
U.S.S.R.
JAPAN
NIHON
TSUSHIMA
LIAODONG BANDAO
LIAOTUNG PENINSULA
HAMGYŎNG PUKDO
HAMGYŎNG NAMDO
YANGGANG DO
CHAGANG DO
P'YŎNGAN PUKDO
P'YŎNGAN NAMDO
HWANGHAE PUKDO
HWANGHAE NAMDO
KANGWŎN DO
KYŎNGGI DO
CH'UNGCH'ŎNG PUKDO
CH'UNGCH'ŎNG NAMDO
KYŎNGSANG PUKDO
KYŎNGSANG NAMDO
CHŎLLA PUKDO
CHŎLLA NAMDO
HAMGYŎNG SANMAEK
T'AEBAEK SANMAEK
SOBAEK SANMAEK
NANGNIM SANMAEK
KANGNAM SANMAEK
MYOHYANG SANMAEK
CHANGBAI SHAN
Sŏjosŏn-man
Tongjosŏn-man
Kyŏnggi-man
SHENYANG
MUKDEN
FUSHUN
Anshan
Liaoyang
Benxi
Dandong
Tonghua
Yanji
P'yŏngyang
Namp'o
Sinŭiju
Kaesŏng
Haeju
Wŏnsan
Hamhŭng
Hŭngnam
Ch'ŏngjin
Kimch'aek
SŎUL
SEOUL
Inch'ŏn
Suwŏn
Sŏngnam-si
Ch'unch'ŏn
Wŏnju
Ch'ŏngju
Taejŏn
Chŏnju
Kunsan
Kwangju
Mokp'o
Taegu
P'ohang
Ulsan
Masan
Chinju
Pusan
Yŏsu
Paektu-san 2744
Copyright © by Rand McNally & Co.
Map compiled by Cartographia, Budapest.
Map produced by Rand McNally & Co.
A-564400-764

Kilometers 0 50 100 150 Km.

Statute Miles 0 50 100 150 Mi.

Scale 1:3,000,000

One centimeter represents 30 kilometers.
One inch represents approximately 47 miles.
Lambert Conformal Conic Projection

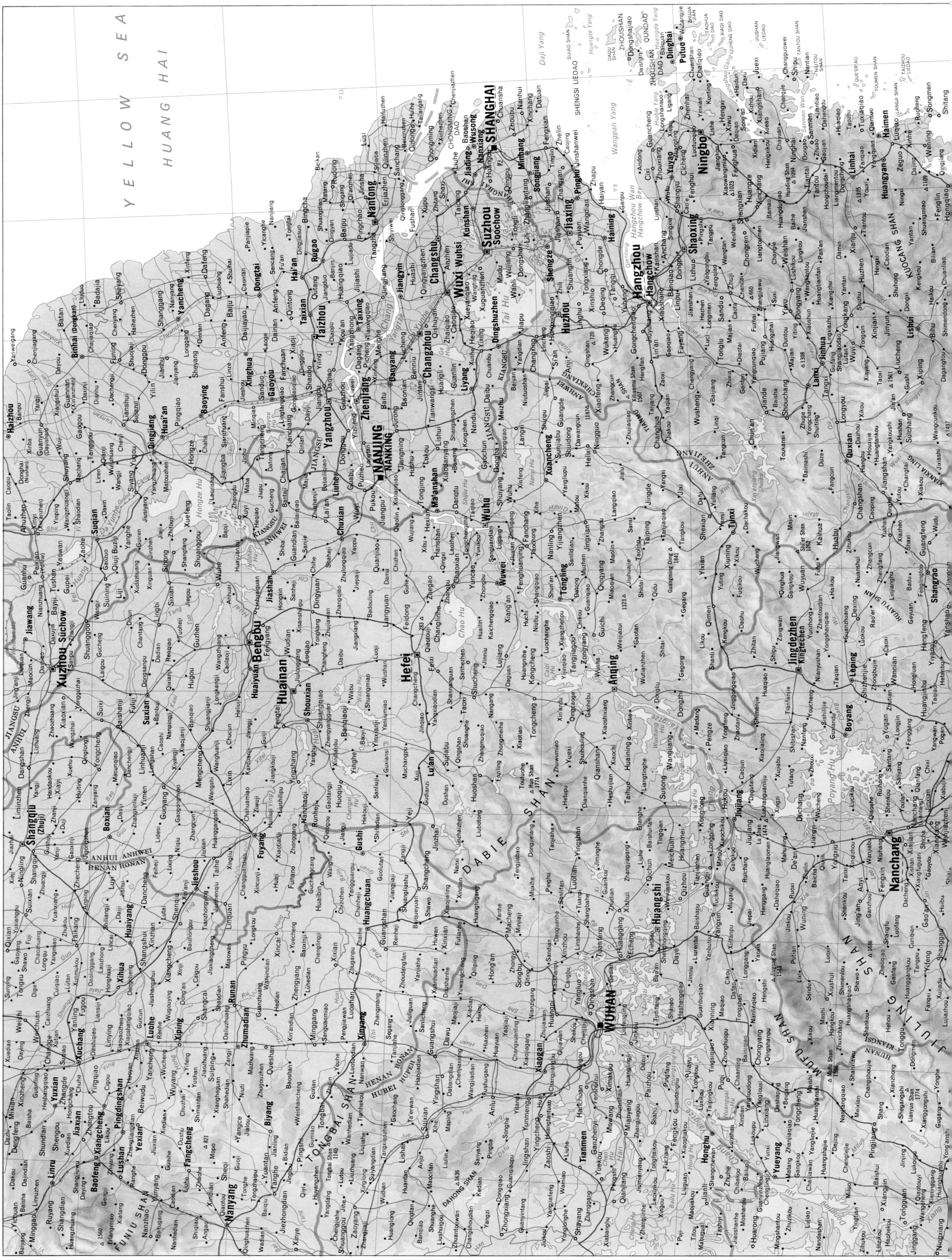
YELLOW SEA
HUANG HAI
SHANGHAI
NANJING
NANKING
WUHAN
Hangzhou
Suzhou
Hefei
Nanchang
Ningbo
DABIE SHAN
TONGBAI SHAN
FUNIU SHAN
JIULING SHAN
MUFU SHAN
Tai Hu
Chao Hu
Poyang Hu
ANHUI
JIANGSU
HENAN
HUBEI
ZHEJIANG
JIANGXI

98 - 99
102 - 103

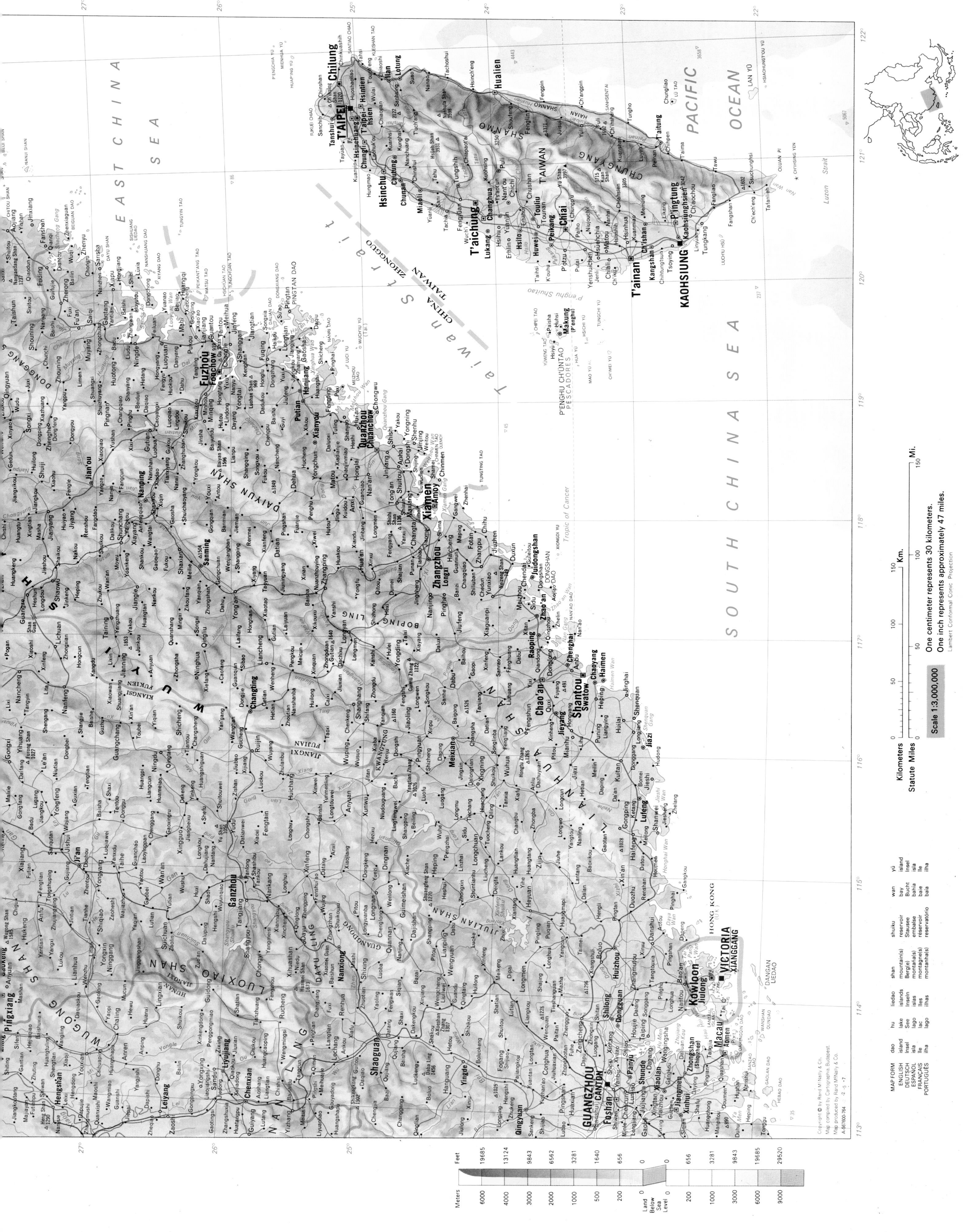
EAST CHINA SEA
SOUTH CHINA SEA
PACIFIC OCEAN
Taiwan Strait
TAIWAN
GUANGZHOU (CANTON)
Fuzhou (Foochow)
Xiamen (Amoy)
Shantou (Swatow)
T'AIPEI
KAOHSIUNG
VICTORIA
HONG KONG
Macau
Scale 1:3,000,000
One centimeter represents 30 kilometers.
One inch represents approximately 47 miles.
Lambert Conformal Conic Projection
Kilometers
Statute Miles

98 - 99

88

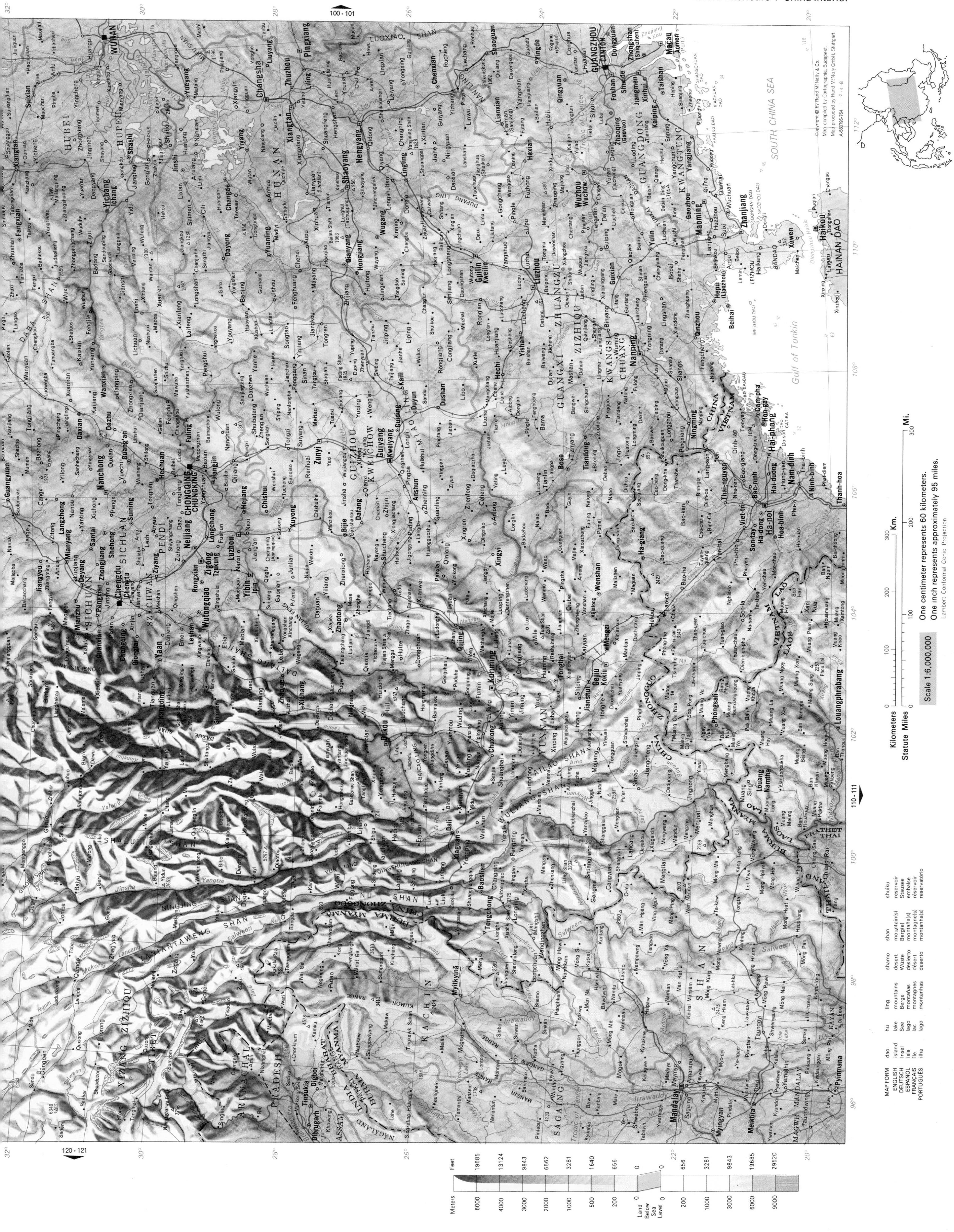
100 - 101
110 - 111
120 - 121
SOUTH CHINA SEA
Gulf of Tonkin
HAINAN DAO
Scale 1:6,000,000
One centimeter represents 60 kilometers.
One inch represents approximately 95 miles.
Lambert Conformal Conic Projection
Kilometers 0 100 200 300 Km.
Statute Miles 0 100 200 300 Mi.
MAP FORM / ENGLISH / DEUTSCH / ESPAÑOL / FRANÇAIS / PORTUGUÊS
dao: island, Insel, isla, île, ilha
hu: lake, See, lago, lac, lago
ling: mountains, Berge, montañas, montagnes, montanhas
shamo: desert, Wüste, desierto, désert, deserto
shan: mountain(s), Berg(e), montaña(s), montagne(s), montanha(s)
shuiku: reservoir, Stausee, embalse, réservoir, reservatório
Copyright © by Rand McNally & Co.
Map compiled by Cartographia, Budapest.
Map produced by Rand McNally GmbH, Stuttgart.
A-560795-764
Meters: 6000, 4000, 3000, 2000, 1000, 500, 200, 0, Land Below Sea Level, 0, 200, 1000, 3000, 6000, 9000
Feet: 19685, 13124, 9843, 6562, 3281, 1640, 656, 0, 0, 656, 3281, 9843, 19685, 29520

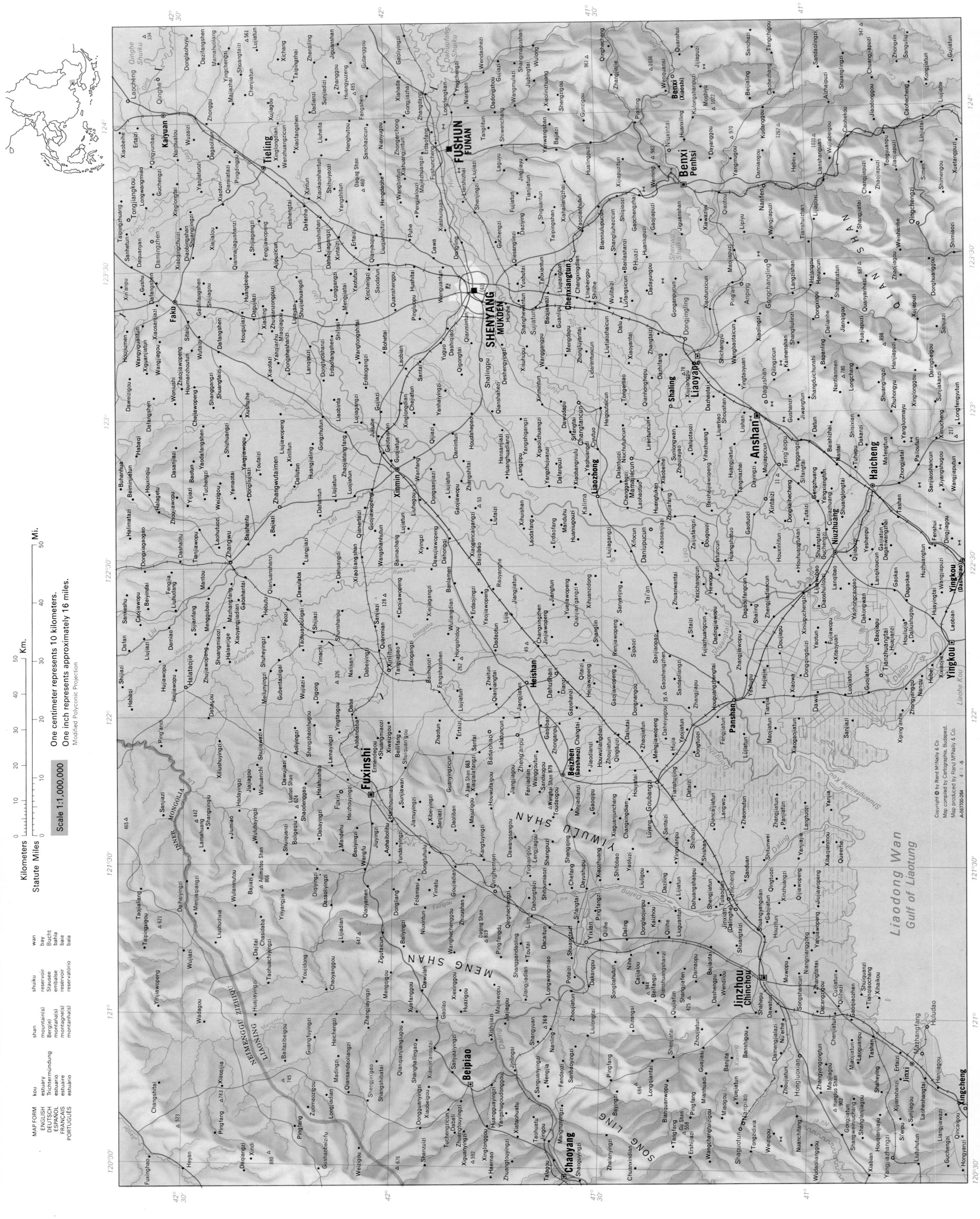
Scale 1:1,000,000
One centimeter represents 10 kilometers.
One inch represents approximately 16 miles.
Modified Polyconic Projection
Kilometers
Statute Miles
Km.
Mi.
MAP FORM kou shan shuiku wan
ENGLISH estuary mountain(s) reservoir bay
DEUTSCH Trichtermündung Berg(e) Stausee Bucht
ESPAÑOL estuario montaña(s) embalse bahía
FRANÇAIS estuaire montagne(s) réservoir baie
PORTUGUÊS estuário montanha(s) reservatório baía
SHENYANG
MUKDEN
FUSHUN
FUNAN
Benxi
Penhsi
Anshan
Liaoyang
Fuxinshi
Jinzhou
Chinchou
Yingkou
Haicheng
Tieling
Kaiyuan
Chaoyang
Beipiao
Heishan
Panshan
Xinmin
Faku
Liaodong Wan
Gulf of Liaotung
MENG SHAN
YIWULU SHAN
SONG LING
QIAN SHAN
LIAONING
NEIMENGGU ZIZHIQU
INNER MONGOLIA
Copyright © by Rand McNally & Co.
Map compiled by Cartographia, Budapest.
Map produced by Rand McNally & Co.

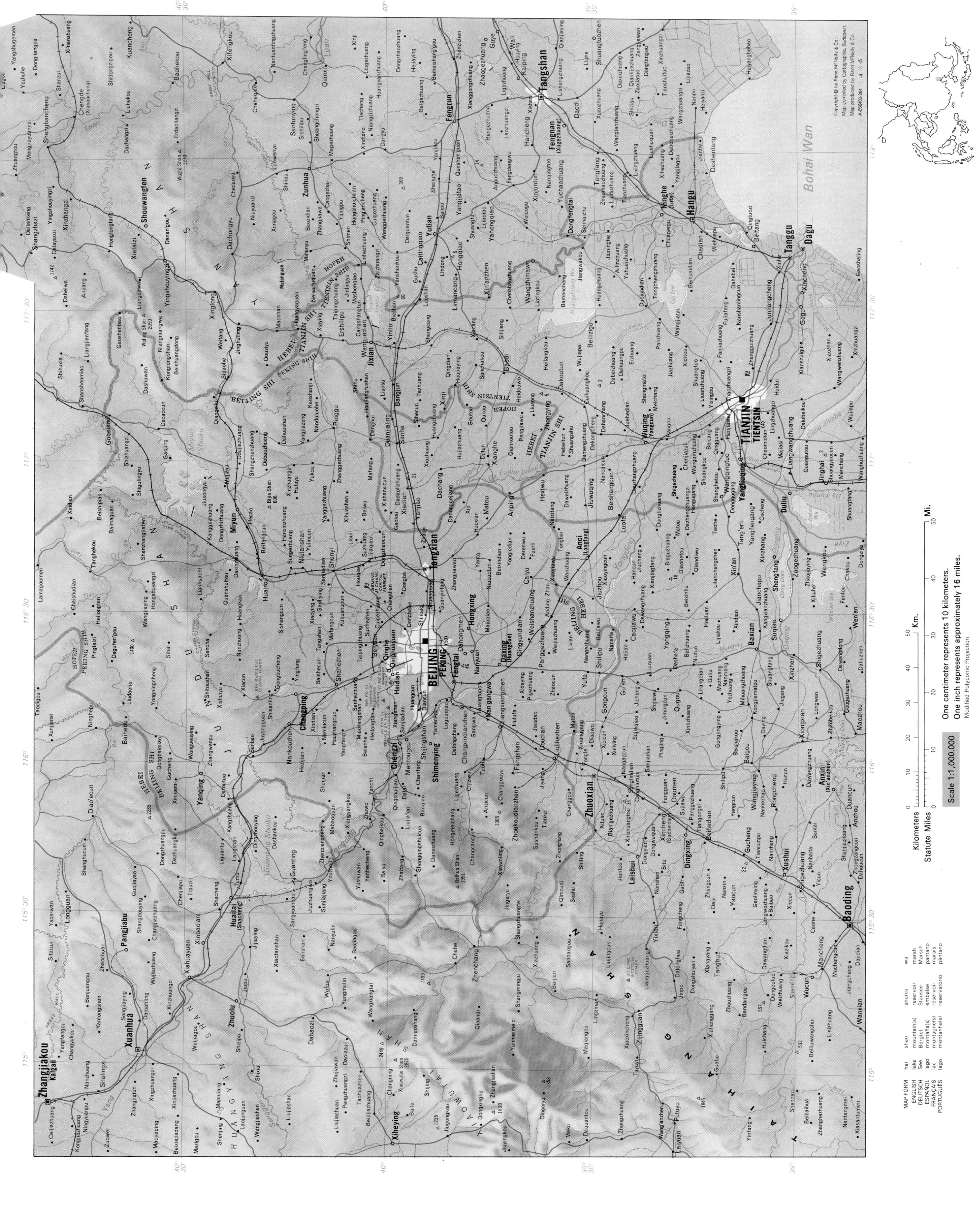
BEIJING
PEKING
TIANJIN
TIENTSIN
Tangshan
Baoding
Zhangjiakou
Kalgan
Tanggu
Dagu
Hangu
Bohai Wan
Kilometers
Statute Miles
Scale 1:1,000,000
One centimeter represents 10 kilometers.
One inch represents approximately 16 miles.
Modified Polyconic Projection
MAP FORM hai shan shuiku wa
ENGLISH lake mountain(s) reservoir marsh
DEUTSCH See Berg(e) Stausee Marsch
ESPAÑOL lago montaña(s) embalse pantano
FRANÇAIS lac montagne(s) réservoir marais
PORTUGUÊS lago montanha(s) reservatório pântano
Copyright © by Rand McNally & Co.
Map compiled by Cartographia, Budapest.
Map produced by Rand McNally & Co.

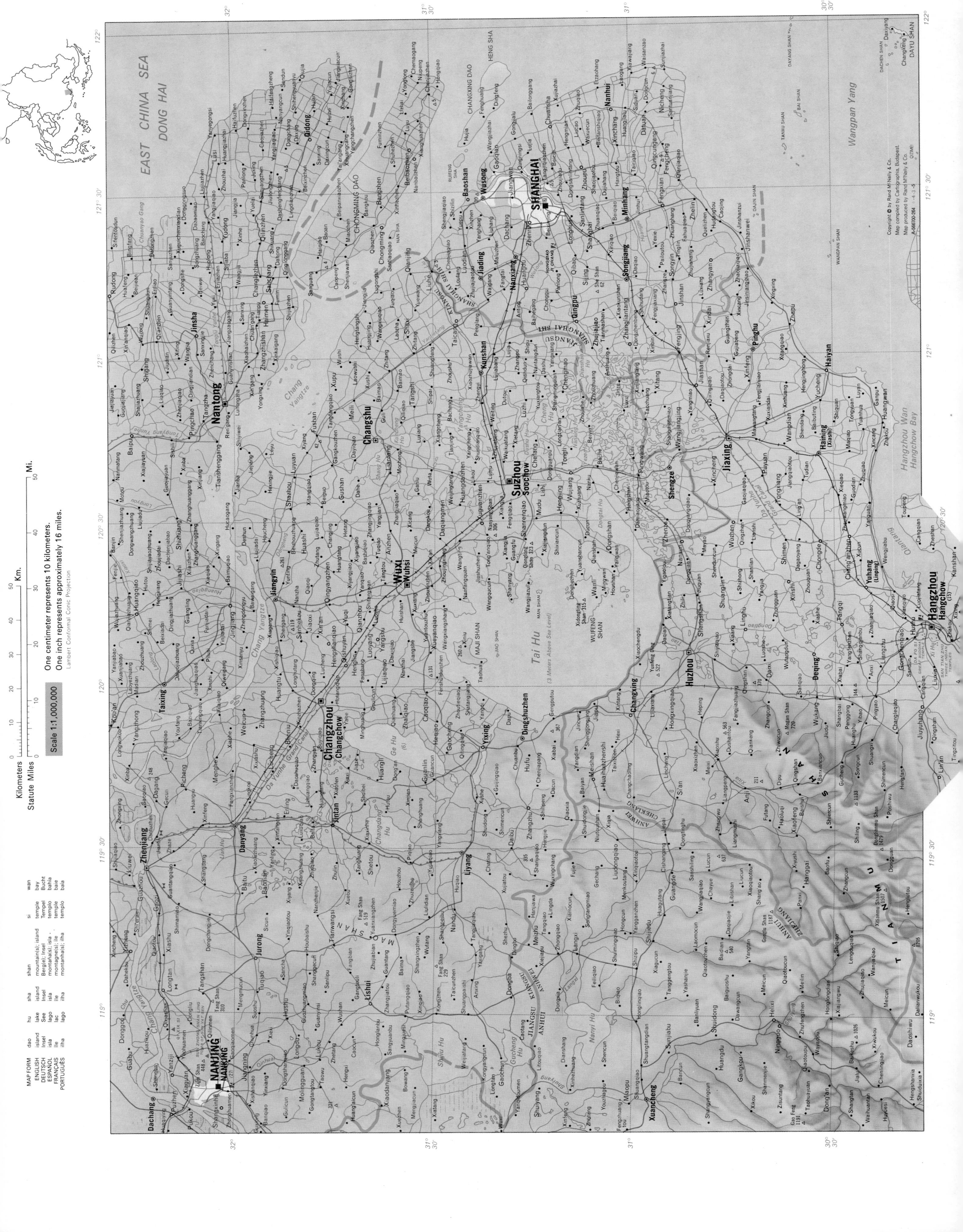
Scale 1:1,000,000
One centimeter represents 10 kilometers.
One inch represents approximately 16 miles.
Lambert Conformal Conic Projection
Kilometers
Statute Miles
Km.
Mi.
MAP FORM dao hu sha shan si wan
ENGLISH island lake island mountain(s); island temple bay
DEUTSCH Insel See Insel Berg(e); Insel Tempel Bucht
ESPAÑOL isla lago isla montaña(s); isla templo bahía
FRANÇAIS île lac île montagne(s); île temple baie
PORTUGUÊS ilha lago ilha montanha(s); ilha templo baía
EAST CHINA SEA
DONG HAI
SHANGHAI
NANJING
NANKING
Suzhou
Soochow
Wuxi
Changzhou
Changchow
Hangzhou
Hangchow
Nantong
Zhenjiang
Tai Hu
Hangzhou Wan
Hangchow Bay
Wangpan Yang
CHONGMING DAO
Chang Yangtze
JIANGSU
ANHUI
ZHEJIANG
Copyright © by Rand McNally & Co.
Map compiled by Cartographia, Budapest.
Map produced by Rand McNally & Co.

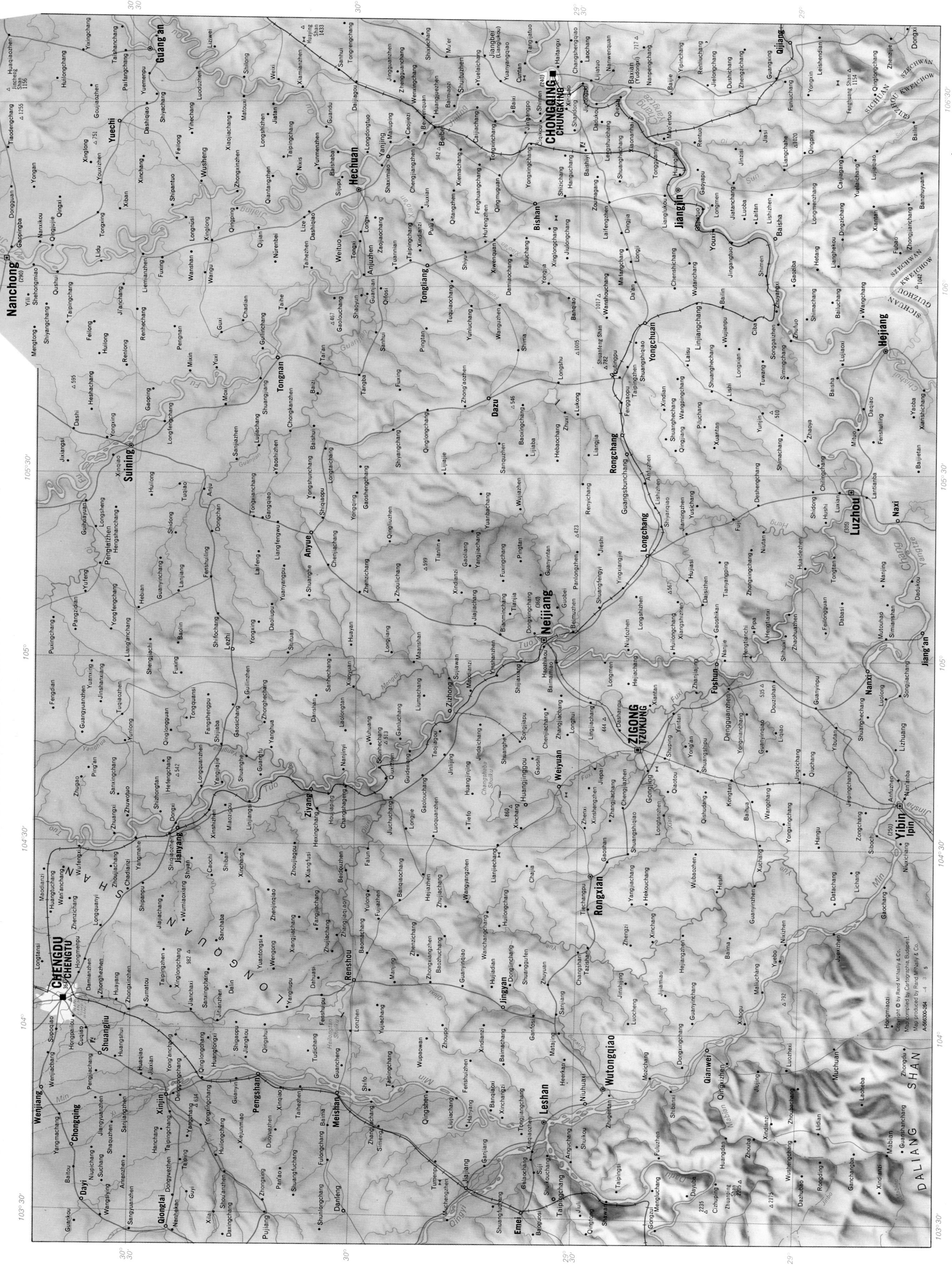

Kilometers 0 10 20 30 40 50 Km.

Statute Miles 0 10 20 30 40 50 Mi.

Scale 1:1,000,000

One centimeter represents 10 kilometers.
One inch represents approximately 16 miles.

Modified Polyconic Projection

MAP FORM	shan	shuiku
ENGLISH	mountain(s)	reservoir
DEUTSCH	Berg(e)	Stausee
ESPAÑOL	montaña(s)	embalse
FRANÇAIS	montagne(s)	réservoir
PORTUGUÊS	montanha(s)	reservatório

Southeast Asia / Südostasien / Asia Sud-oriental
Asie du Sud-Est / Śudeste Asiático

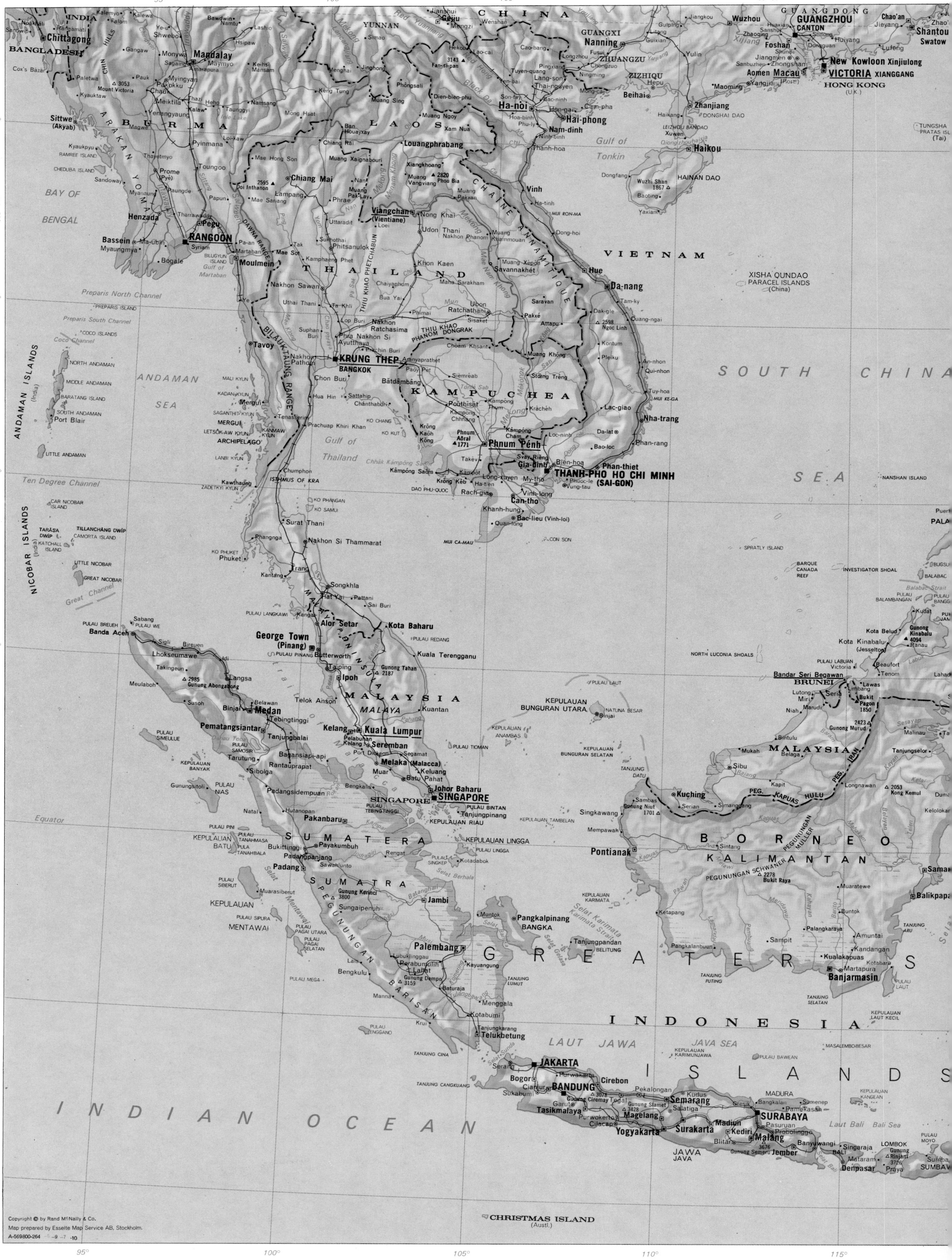

MAP FORM	gulf	gunung	island	kepulauan	pulau	sea	selat	strait
ENGLISH	gulf	mountain	island	islands	island	sea	strait	strait
DEUTSCH	Golf	Berg	Insel	Inseln	Insel	Meer	Meeresstrasse	Meeresstrasse
ESPAÑOL	golfo	montaña	isla	islas	isla	mar	estrecho	estrecho
FRANÇAIS	golfe	montagne	île	îles	île	mer	détroit	détroit
PORTUGUÊS	golfo	montanha	ilha	ilhas	ilha	mar	estreito	estreito

160 - 161

Kilometers 0 200 400 600 Km.
Statute Miles 0 200 400 600 Mi.

Scale 1:12,000,000
One centimeter represents 120 kilometers.
One inch represents approximately 190 miles.
Lambert Conformal Conic Projection

Kilometers 0 100 200 300 Km.
Statute Miles 0 100 200 300 Mi.

Scale 1:6,000,000

One centimeter represents 60 kilometers.
One inch represents approximately 95 miles.
Lambert Conformal Conic Projection

MAP FORM	gunung	island	-jiang	kepulauan	khao	kyun	pulau	-shan
ENGLISH	mountain	island	river	islands	mountain	island	island	mountain
DEUTSCH	Berg	Insel	Fluss	Inseln	Berg	Insel	Insel	Berg
ESPAÑOL	montaña	isla	río	islas	montaña	isla	isla	montaña
FRANÇAIS	montagne	île	rivière	îles	montagne	île	île	montagne
PORTUGUÊS	montanha	ilha	rio	ilhas	montanha	ilha	ilha	montanha

102-103

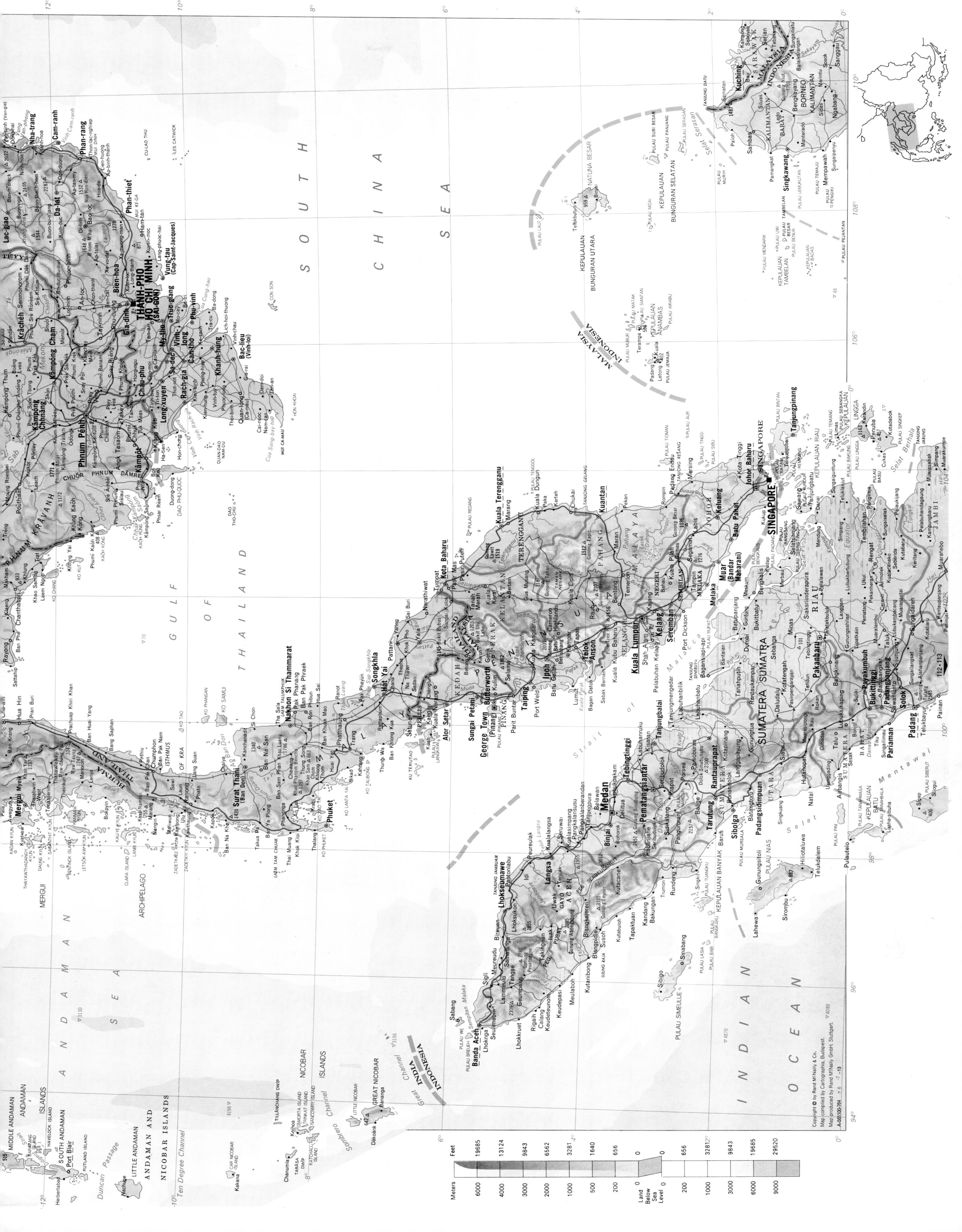
SOUTH CHINA SEA
GULF OF THAILAND
ANDAMAN SEA
INDIAN OCEAN
Strait of Malacca
MALAYA
SUMATERA
SINGAPORE
Kuala Lumpur
Medan
Padang
Pakanbaru
Melaka
Kuantan
Kuala Terengganu
Kota Baharu
George Town (Pinang)
Alor Setar
Hat Yai
Songkhla
Nakhon Si Thammarat
Surat Thani
Phuket
Phnum Pénh
THANH-PHO HO CHI MINH (SAI-GON)
Kuching
Banda Aceh
Port Blair
ANDAMAN AND NICOBAR ISLANDS
GREAT NICOBAR
Copyright © by Rand McNally & Co.
Map compiled by Cartographia, Budapest.
Map produced by Rand McNally GmbH, Stuttgart.
Meters
6000
4000
3000
2000
1000
500
200
0
Land Below Sea Level
0
200
1000
3000
6000
9000
Feet
19685
13124
9843
6562
3281
1640
656
0
0
656
3281
9843
19685
29520

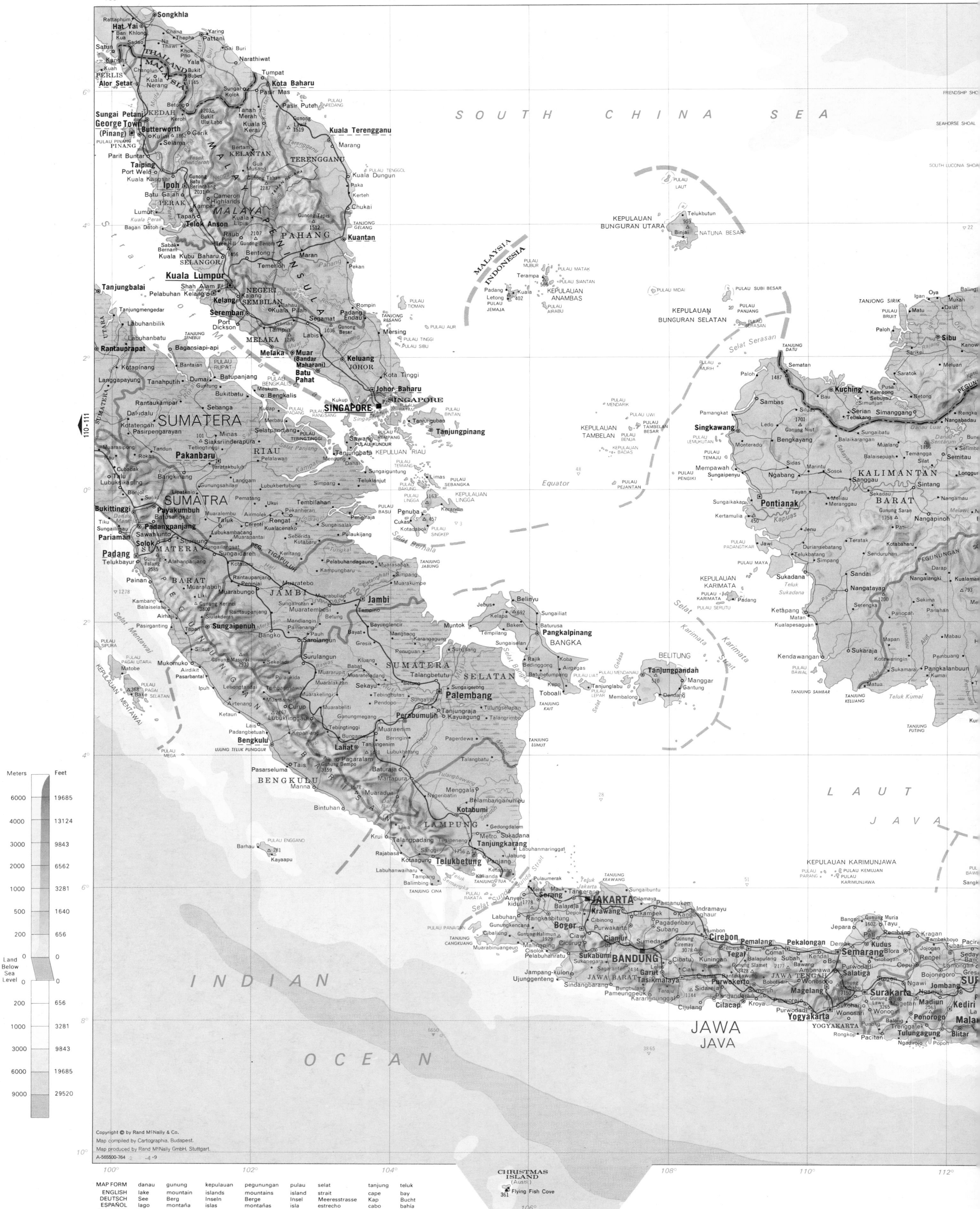

Map compiled by Cartographia, Budapest.
Map produced by Rand McNally GmbH, Stuttgart.
A-565500-764

MAP FORM	danau	gunung	kepulauan	pegunungan	pulau	selat	tanjung	teluk
ENGLISH	lake	mountain	islands	mountains	island	strait	cape	bay
DEUTSCH	See	Berg	Inseln	Berge	Insel	Meeresstrasse	Kap	Bucht
ESPAÑOL	lago	montaña	islas	montañas	isla	estrecho	cabo	bahía
FRANÇAIS	lac	montagne	îles	montagnes	île	détroit	cap	baie
PORTUGUÊS	lago	montanha	ilhas	montanhas	ilha	estreito	cabo	baía

SULU SEA
CELEBES SEA
Moro Gulf
SULU ARCHIPELAGO
BORNEO
KALIMANTAN
SABAH
BRUNEI
Bandar Seri Begawan
Kota Kinabalu (Jesselton)
Sandakan
Tawau
Zamboanga
Jolo
Davao
MINDANAO
General Santos
KALIMANTAN TIMUR
KALIMANTAN SELATAN
KALIMANTAN TENGAH
Samarinda
Balikpapan
Banjarmasin
Makasar Strait
Selat Makasar
SULAWESI
CELEBES
SULAWESI UTARA
SULAWESI TENGAH
SULAWESI SELATAN
SULAWESI TENGGARA
Manado
Gorontalo
Palu
Teluk Tomini
Teluk Bone
Ujung Pandang (Makasar)
Kendari
Baubau
LAUT MALUKU
MOLUCCA SEA
MALUKU
KEPULAUAN SULA
BURU
LAUT BANDA
BANDA SEA
Laut Flores
Flores Sea
Laut Bali
Bali Sea
JAWA TIMUR
BALI
Denpasar
LOMBOK
Mataram
SUMBAWA
FLORES
SUMBA
TIMOR
Kupang
Dili
TIMOR TIMUR
NUSA TENGGARA BARAT
NUSA TENGGARA TIMUR
Laut Sawu
Savu Sea
TIMOR SEA
Equator
PHILIPPINES
MALAYSIA
INDONESIA
116-117
164-165
Kilometers 0 100 200 300 Km.
Statute Miles 0 100 200 300 Mi.
Scale 1:6,000,000
One centimeter represents 60 kilometers.
One inch represents approximately 95 miles.
Mercator Projection

Malaya, Singapore and Northern Sumatra / Malaya, Singapur und Nordsumatra / Malaya, Singapur y Sumatra Septentrional
Malaya, Singapour et Sumatra Septentrional / Malaia, Cingapura e Sumatra Setentrional

MAP FORM	gunung	krueng	pegunungan	pulau	selat	tanjong	teluk	ujung
ENGLISH	mountain	river	mountains	island	strait	cape	bay	cape
DEUTSCH	Berg	Fluss	Berge	Insel	Meeresstrasse	Kap	Bucht	Kap
ESPAÑOL	montaña	rio	montañas	isla	estrecho	cabo	bahia	cabo
FRANÇAIS	montagne	rivière	montagnes	île	détroit	cap	baie	cap
PORTUGUÊS	montanha	rio	montanhas	ilha	estreito	cabo	baía	cabo

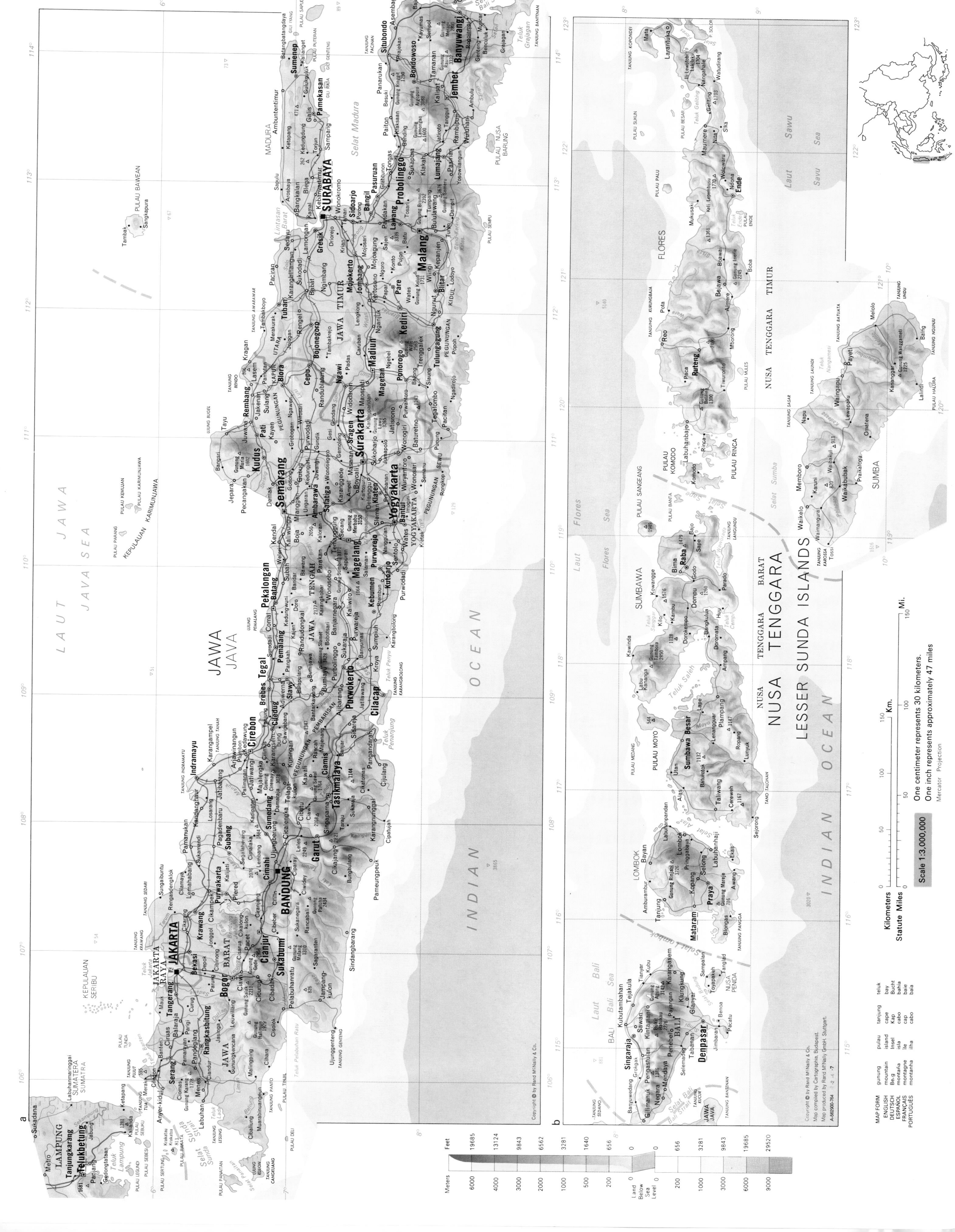
a
b
JAWA
JAVA
LAUT JAWA
JAVA SEA
INDIAN OCEAN
MADURA
Selat Madura
JAWA BARAT
JAWA TENGAH
JAWA TIMUR
JAKARTA RAYA
JAKARTA
BANDUNG
SEMARANG
SURABAYA
Yogyakarta
Surakarta
Malang
BALI
LOMBOK
SUMBAWA
FLORES
SUMBA
NUSA TENGGARA BARAT
NUSA TENGGARA TIMUR
LESSER SUNDA ISLANDS
Laut Sawu
Savu Sea
Laut Flores
Flores Sea
LAMPUNG
SUMATERA
SUMATRA
Selat Sunda
Feet
Meters
Land and Below Sea Level
Scale 1:3,000,000
Kilometers
Statute Miles
One centimeter represents 30 kilometers.
One inch represents approximately 47 miles
Mercator Projection
MAP FORM gunung pulau tanjung teluk
ENGLISH mountain island cape bay
DEUTSCH Berg Insel Kap Bucht
ESPAÑOL montaña isla cabo bahía
FRANÇAIS montagne île cap baie
PORTUGUÊS montanha ilha cabo baía
Copyright © by Rand McNally & Co.
Map compiled by Cartographia, Budapest.
Map produced by Rand McNally GmbH, Stuttgart.

22-23

134-137

MAP FORM	gulf	-he	jabal	jazirat	range	ra's	-shan	-shanmai
ENGLISH	gulf	river	mountain	island	range	cape	mountain(s)	mountains
DEUTSCH	Golf	Fluss	Berg	Insel	Gebirge	Kap	Berg(e)	Berge
ESPAÑOL	golfo	rio	montaña	isla	sierra	cabo	montaña(s)	montañas
FRANÇAIS	golfe	rivière	montagne	île	chaîne	cap	montagne(s)	montagnes
PORTUGUÊS	golfo	rio	montanha	ilha	serra	cabo	montanha(s)	montanhas

Kilometers 0 200 400 600 Km.
Statute Miles 0 200 400 600 Mi.

Scale 1:12,000,000

One centimeter represents 120 kilometers.
One inch represents approximately 190 miles.
Lambert Conformal Conic Projection

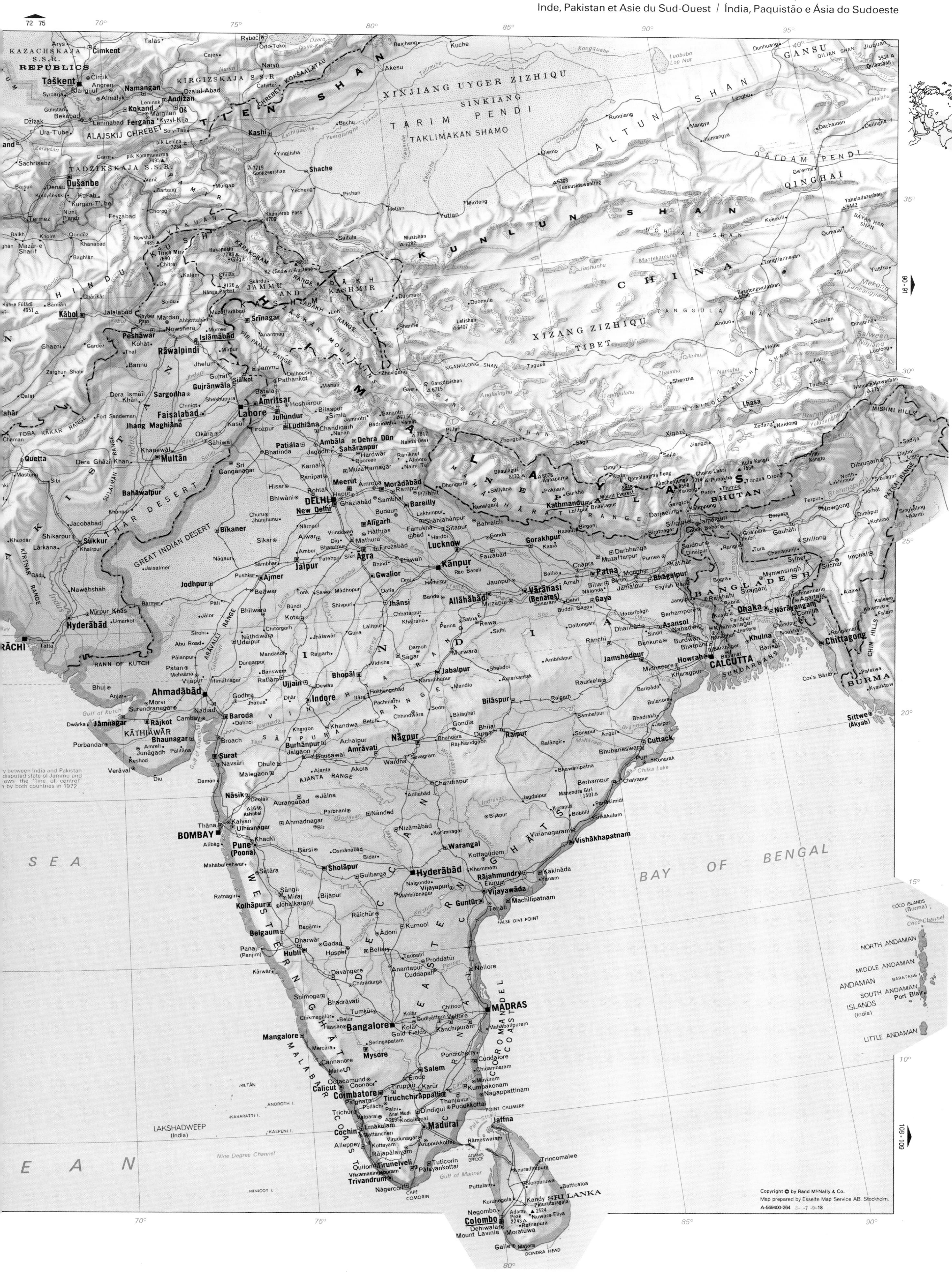
XINJIANG UYGER ZIZHIQU
SINKIANG
TARIM PENDI
TAKLIMAKAN SHAMO
TIEN SHAN
ALTUN SHAN
KUNLUN SHAN
QAIDAM PENDI
QINGHAI
GANSU
CHINA
XIZANG ZIZHIQU
TIBET
TANGGULA SHAN
HINDU KUSH
KARAKORAM RANGE
JAMMU AND KASHMIR
LADAKH RANGE
ZASKAR MOUNTAINS
PIR PANJAL RANGE
HIMALAYAS
NEPAL
BHUTAN
BANGLADESH
BURMA
PAKISTAN
INDIA
THAR DESERT
GREAT INDIAN DESERT
RANN OF KUTCH
KATHIAWAR
ARAVALLI RANGE
VINDHYA RANGE
SATPURA RANGE
AJANTA RANGE
DECCAN
WESTERN GHATS
EASTERN GHATS
MALABAR COAST
COROMANDEL COAST
SEA
BAY OF BENGAL
OCEAN
LAKSHADWEEP (India)
ANDAMAN ISLANDS (India)
NORTH ANDAMAN
MIDDLE ANDAMAN
SOUTH ANDAMAN
LITTLE ANDAMAN
Port Blair
COCO ISLANDS (Burma)
SRI LANKA
Colombo
Jaffna
Trincomalee
Kandy
DELHI
New Delhi
Islāmābād
Kābol
Kathmandu
Lhasa
Dhaka
CALCUTTA
BOMBAY
MADRAS
Bangalore
Hyderābād
Lahore
Karāchi
Taškent
Dušanbe
Kāshi
Nāgpur
Ahmadābād
Kānpur
Lucknow
Jaipur
Patna
Vārānasi (Benares)
Chittagong
Sittwe (Akyab)
Pune (Poona)
Cochin
Madurai
Trivandrum
Mangalore
Vishākhapatnam
Mount Everest
Palk Strait
Gulf of Mannar
Gulf of Kutch
Nine Degree Channel
Coco Channel
Copyright © by Rand McNally & Co.
Map prepared by Esselte Map Service AB, Stockholm.
A-569400-264

Northern India and Pakistan / Nordindien und Pakistan / India Septentrional y Pakistán
Inde Septentrionale et Pakistan / Índia Setentrional e Paquistão

Meters	Feet
6000	19685
4000	13124
3000	9843
2000	6562
1000	3281
500	1640
200	656
0	0
Land Below Sea Level 0	0
200	656
1000	3281
3000	9843
6000	19685
9000	29520

MAP FORM	-chi	-he	-hu	-kou	range	-shan	-shanmai
ENGLISH	lake	river	lake	pass	range	mountain	mountains
DEUTSCH	See	Fluss	See	Pass	Gebirge	Berg	Berge
ESPAÑOL	lago	rio	lago	paso	sierra	montaña	montañas
FRANÇAIS	lac	rivière	lac	col	chaîne	montagne	montagnes
PORTUGUÊS	lago	rio	lago	passo	serra	montanha	montanhas

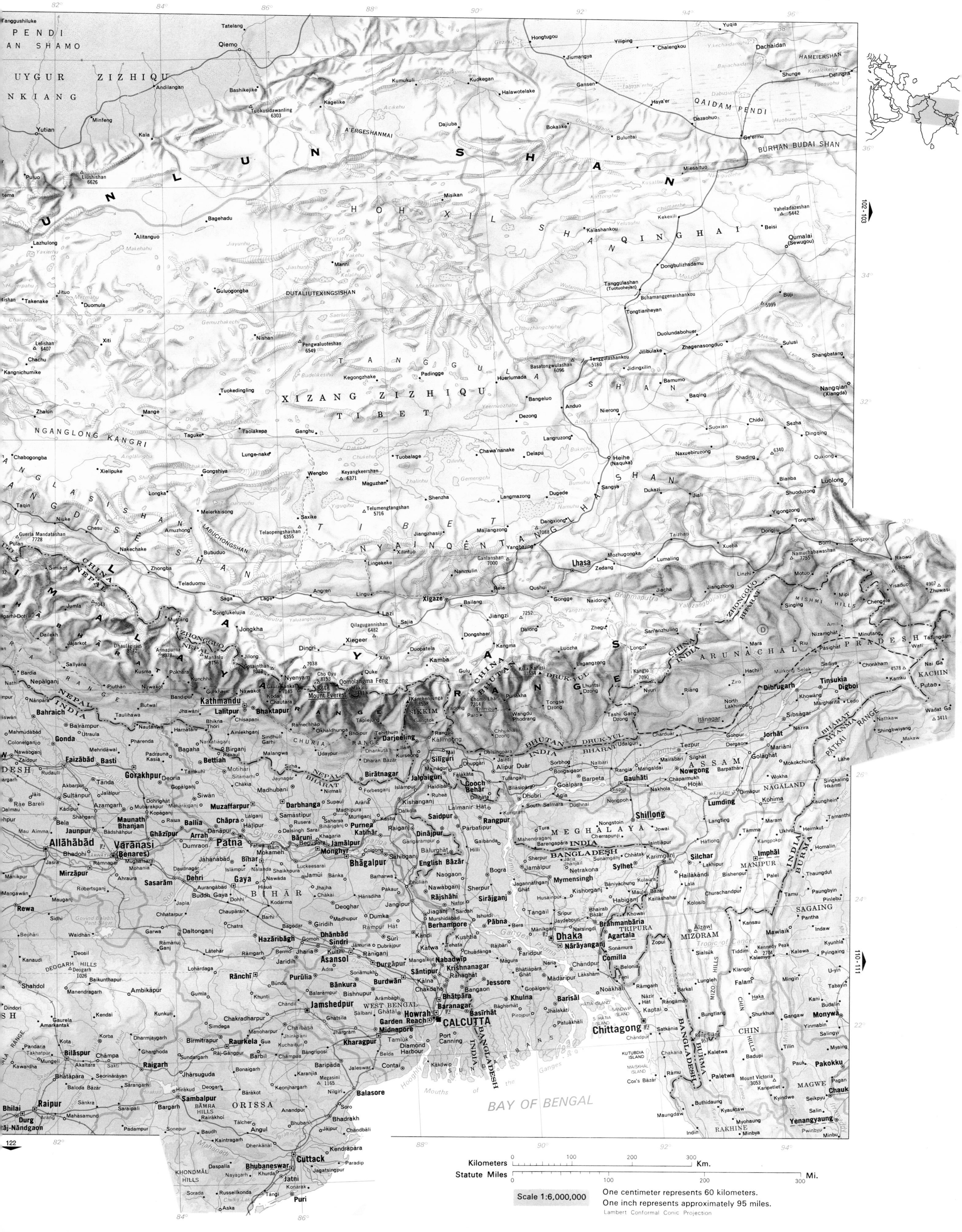
KUNLUN SHAN
XIZANG ZIZHIQU
TIBET
TANGGULA SHAN
QAIDAM PENDI
BURHAN BUDAI SHAN
HOH XIL SHAN
QINGHAI
NYAINQÊNTANGLHA SHAN
GANGDISE SHAN
NGANGLONG KANGRI
HIMALAYA
CHINA
NEPAL
INDIA
BHUTAN
DRUK-YUL
SIKKIM
BANGLADESH
BURMA
ASSAM
MEGHALAYA
ARUNACHAL PRADESH
NAGALAND
MANIPUR
MIZORAM
TRIPURA
WEST BENGAL
BIHAR
ORISSA
BAY OF BENGAL
Lhasa
Kathmandu
Dhaka
CALCUTTA
Patna
Varanasi (Benares)
Allahabad
Chittagong
Shillong
Mount Everest
Qomolangma Feng
Kilometers 0 100 200 300 Km.
Statute Miles 0 100 200 300 Mi.
Scale 1:6,000,000
One centimeter represents 60 kilometers.
One inch represents approximately 95 miles.
Lambert Conformal Conic Projection
102-103
110-111
122

Southern India and Sri Lanka / Südindien und Sri Lanka / India Meridional y Sri Lanka
Inde Méridionale et Sri Lanka / Índia Meridional e Sri Lanka

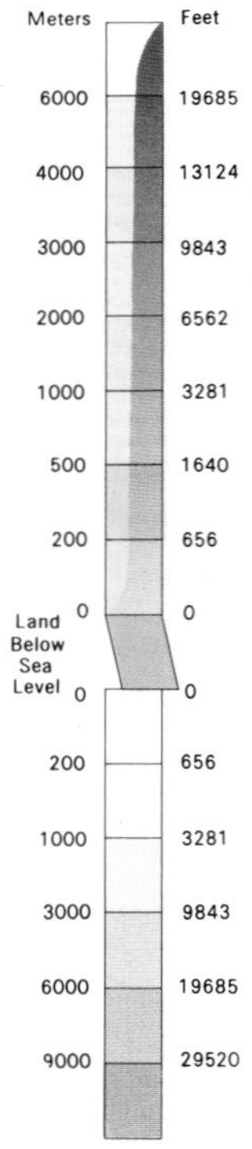

ENGLISH	atoll	hills	island	lagoon	lake	range	reservoir
DEUTSCH	Atoll	Hügel	Insel	Haff	See	Gebirge	Stausee
ESPAÑOL	atolón	colinas	isla	laguna	lago	sierra	embalse
FRANÇAIS	atoll	collines	île	lagune	lac	chaîne	réservoir
PORTUGUÊS	atol	colinas	ilha	laguna	lago	serra	reservatório

Kilometers 0 100 200 300 Km.
Statute Miles 0 100 200 300 Mi.

Scale 1:6,000,000

One centimeter represents 60 kilometers.
One inch represents approximately 95 miles.
Lambert Conformal Conic Projection

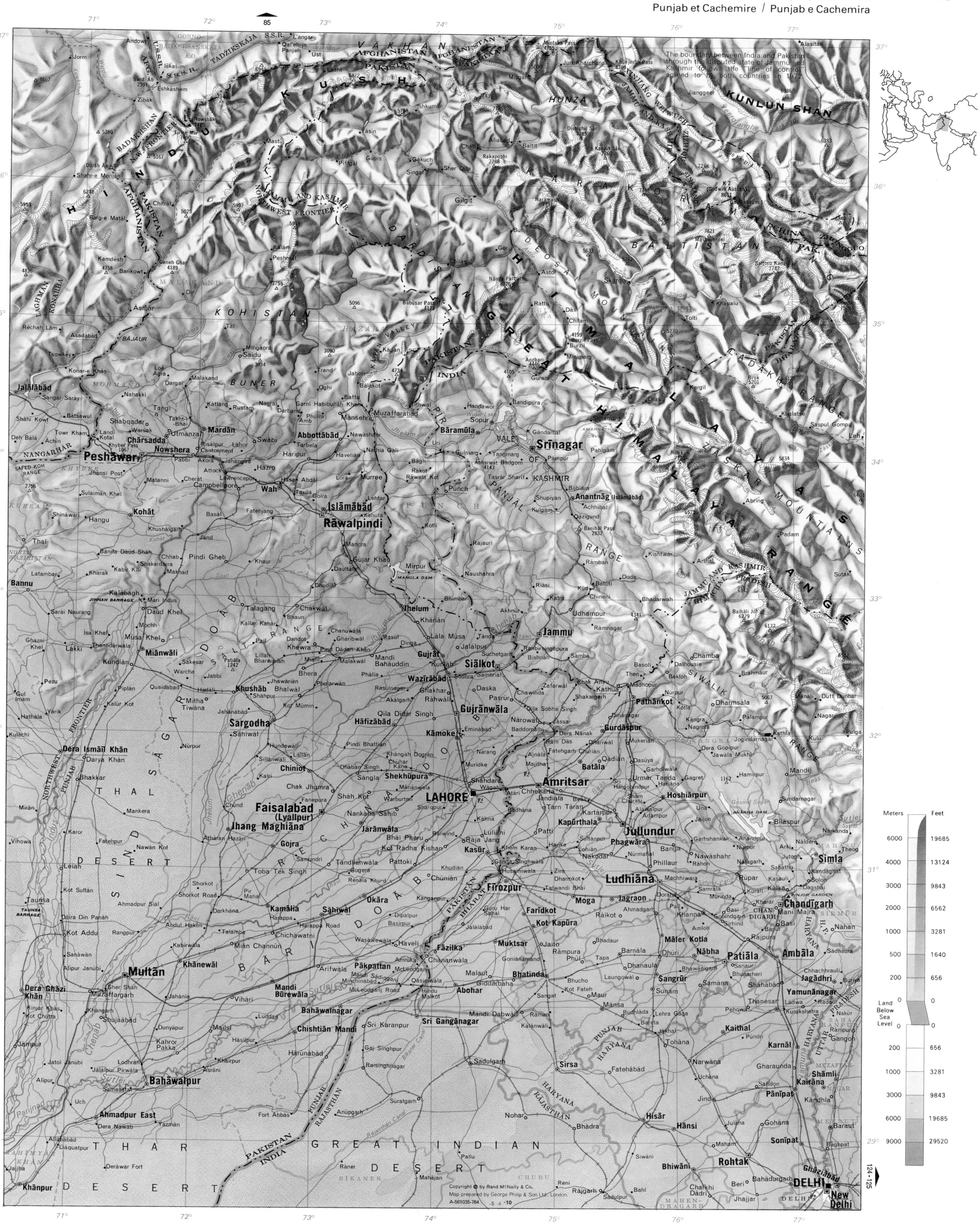

MAP FORM	airport	doāb	glacier	pass	range	sar
ENGLISH	airport	upland	glacier	pass	range	mountain
DEUTSCH	Flughafen	Bergland	Gletscher	Pass	Gebirge	Berg
ESPAÑOL	aeropuerto	tierras altas	glaciar	paso	sierra	montaña
FRANÇAIS	aéroport	hautes terres	glacier	col	chaîne	montagne
PORTUGUÊS	aeroporto	terras altas	geleira	passo	serra	montanha

Kilometers 0 50 100 150 Km.
Statute Miles 0 50 100 150 Mi.

Scale 1:3,000,000

One centimeter represents 30 kilometers.
One inch represents approximately 47 miles.
Lambert Conformal Conic Projection

Ganges Lowland and Nepal / Gangestiefland und Nepal / Llanuras del Ganges y Nepal
Plaine du Gange et Népal / Planicie do Ganges e Nepal

123

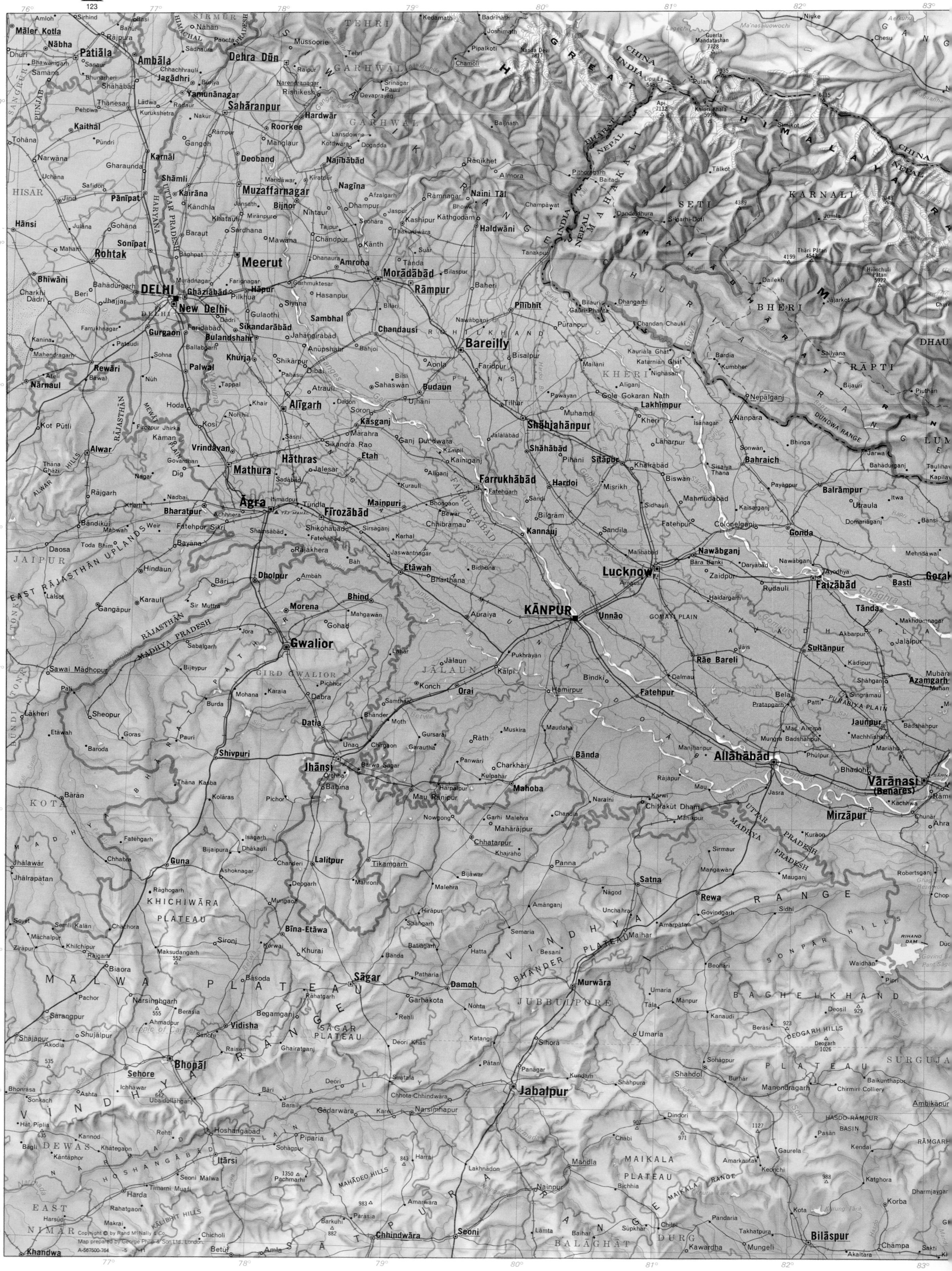

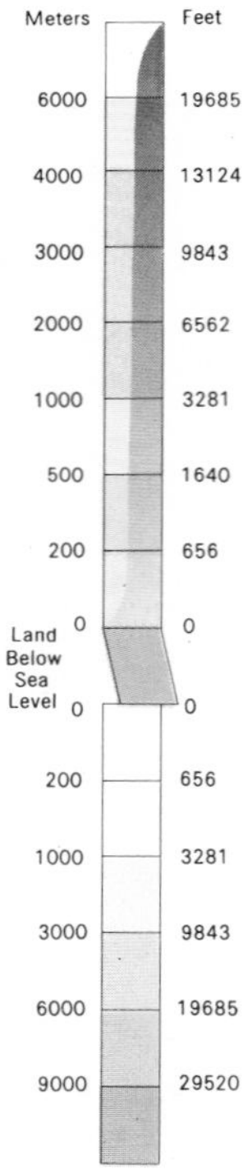

MAP FORM	hills	-hu	plains	plateau	range	-shan
ENGLISH	hills	lake	plains	plateau	range	mountains
DEUTSCH	Hügel	See	Ebenen	Hochebene	Gebirge	Berge
ESPAÑOL	colinas	lago	llanos	meseta	sierra	montañas
FRANÇAIS	collines	lac	plaines	plateau	chaîne	montagnes
PORTUGUÊS	colinas	lago	planícies	planalto	serra	montanhas

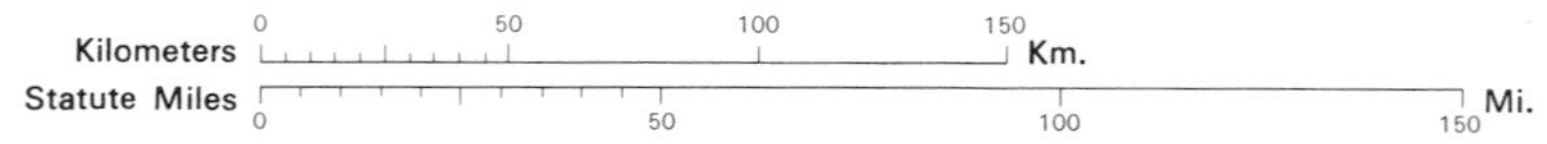

Scale 1:3,000,000

One centimeter represents 30 kilometers.
One inch represents approximately 47 miles.

Lambert Conformal Conic Projection

Lhasa
GANGDISI SHAN
XIZANG
TIBET
Qomolangma Feng
Mount Everest
Kathmandu
Bhaktapur
Lalitpur
BAGMATI
NĀRĀYANI
JANAKPUR
SAGARMATHA
KOSI
MECHI
Darjeeling
Kālimpong
SIKKIM
Gangtok
Thimbu
BHUTAN
DRUK-YUL
Siliguri
Jalpaiguri
Cooch Behār
Dhubri
ASSAM
MEGHALAYA
Biratnagar
Madhubani
Darbhanga
Muzaffarpur
Chāpra
Patna
Monghyr
Bhāgalpur
Gaya
Purnea
Katihār
Sahibganj
Dinājpur
Rangpur
Bogra
Rājshāhi
Pābna
Mymensingh
Dhaka
Nārāyanganj
Comilla
Chāndpur
Faridpur
Jessore
Khulna
Barisāl
Kushtia
Berhampore
Krishnanagar
Burdwān
Asansol
Dhanbād
Hazāribāgh
Rānchi
Purūlia
Bānkura
Jamshedpur
Raurkela
Kharagpur
Midnapore
Howrah
CALCUTTA
GANGES DELTA
SUNDARBANS
Mouths of the Ganges
BAY OF BENGAL
Tropic of Cancer
HAZĀRIBĀGH PLATEAU
RĀNCHI PLATEAU
HIMALAYA RANGE
NEPAL
INDIA
BHARAT
BANGLADESH
WEST BENGAL
BIHAR
ORISSA
84°
85°
86°
87°
88°
89°
90°
91°
22°
24°
25°
26°
27°
28°
29°

MAP FORM	bay	canal	char	delta	island	plain
ENGLISH	bay	canal	island	delta	island	plain
DEUTSCH	Bucht	Kanal	Insel	Delta	Insel	Ebene
ESPAÑOL	bahia	canal	isla	delta	isla	llanura
FRANÇAIS	baie	canal	île	delta	île	plaine
PORTUGUÊS	baia	canal	ilha	delta	ilha	planície

Kilometers 0 10 20 30 40 50 Km.

Statute Miles 0 10 20 30 40 50 Mi.

Scale 1:1,000,000

One centimeter represents 10 kilometers.
One inch represents approximately 16 miles.

Lambert Conformal Conic Projection

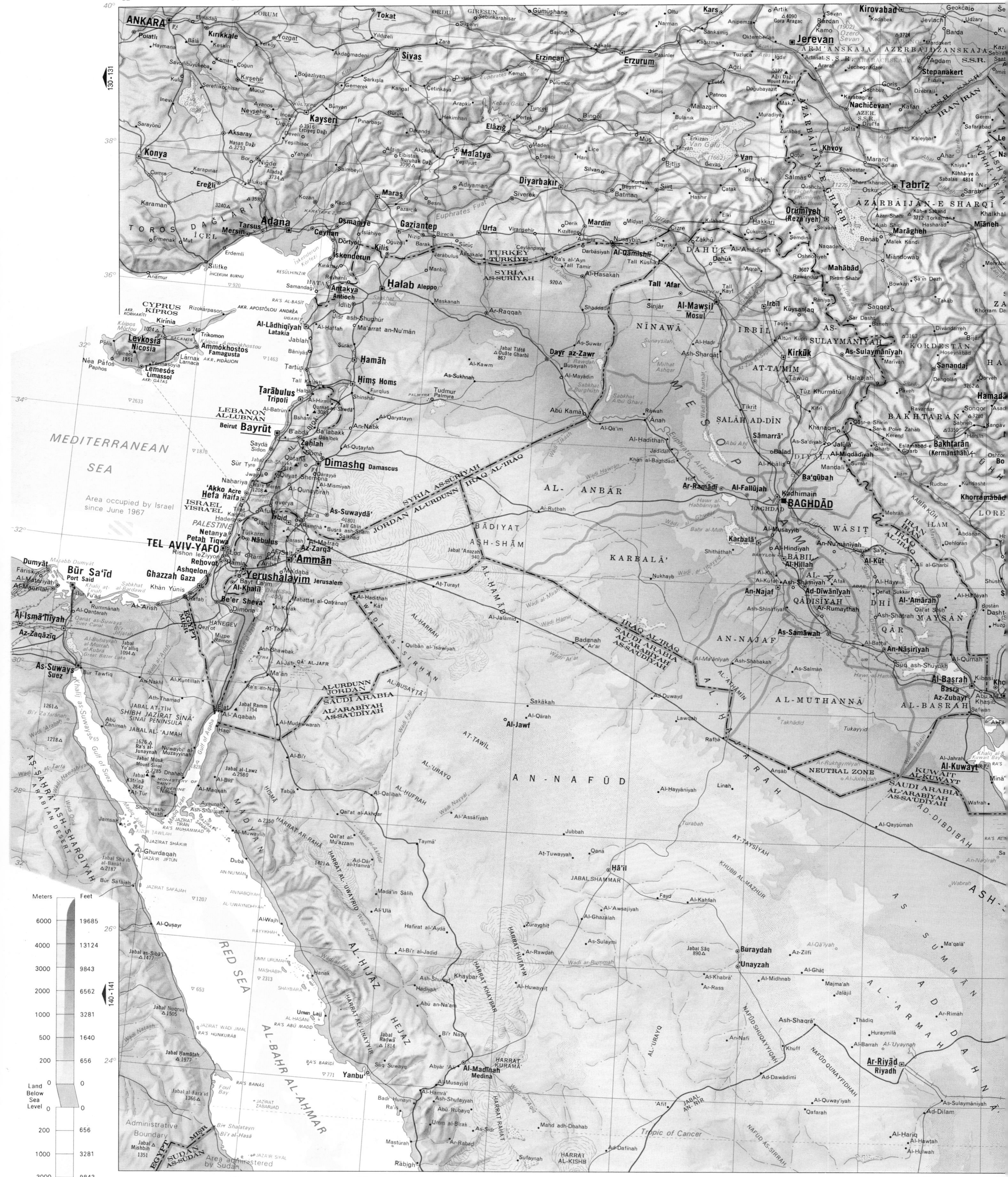

MAP FORM	harrat	jabal	jazīreh	kūh	ra's	sabkhat	wādī
ENGLISH	lava flow	mountain	island	mountain	cape	salt marsh	wadi
DEUTSCH	Lavastrom	Berg	Insel	Berg	Kap	Salzmarsch	Wadi
ESPAÑOL	corriente de lava	montaña	isla	montaña	cabo	pantano salado	uadi
FRANÇAIS	coulée de lave	montagne	île	montagne	cap	marais salé	wadi
PORTUGUÊS	corrente de lava	montanha	ilha	montanha	cabo	pântano salgado	uádi

Kilometers 0 100 200 300 Km.

Statute Miles 0 100 200 300 Mi.

Scale 1:6,000,000

One centimeter represents 60 kilometers.

One inch represents approximately 95 miles.

Lambert Conformal Conic Projection

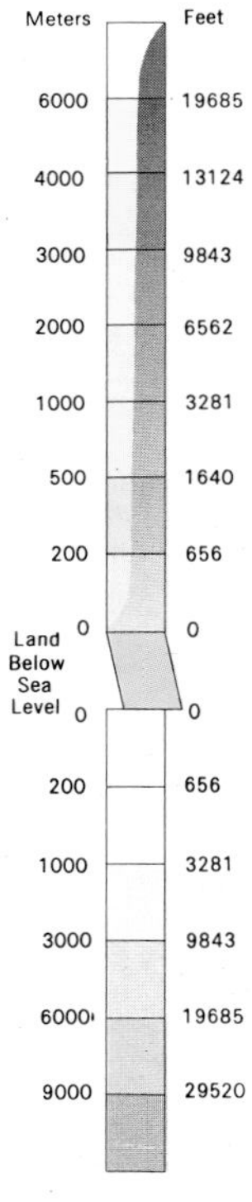

MAP FORM	burnu	dağ, dağı	dağları	gölü	jabal	körfezi	sabkhat
ENGLISH	cape	mountain	mountains	lake	mountains	bay, gulf	salt marsh
DEUTSCH	Kap	Berg	Berge	See	Berge	Bucht, Golf	Salzmarsch
ESPAÑOL	cabo	montaña	montañas	lago	montañas	bahía, golfo	pantano salado
FRANÇAIS	cap	montagne	montagnes	lac	montagnes	baie, golfe	marais salé
PORTUGUÊS	cabo	montanha	montanhas	lago	montanhas	baía, golfo	pântano salgado

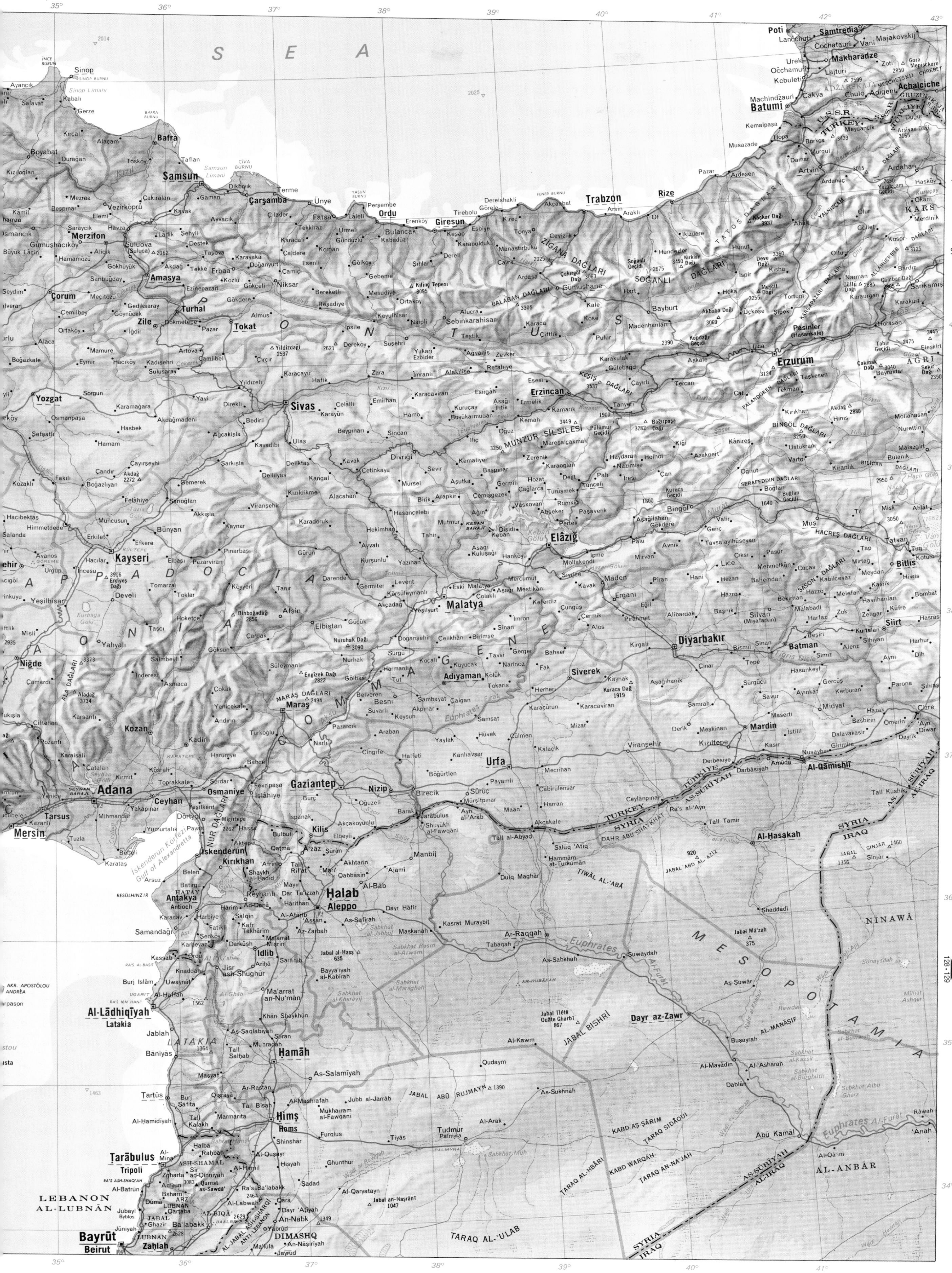

Kilometers 0 50 100 150 Km.
Statute Miles 0 50 100 150 Mi.

Scale 1:3,000,000

One centimeter represents 30 kilometers.
One inch represents approximately 47 miles.
Conic Projection, Two Standard Parallels

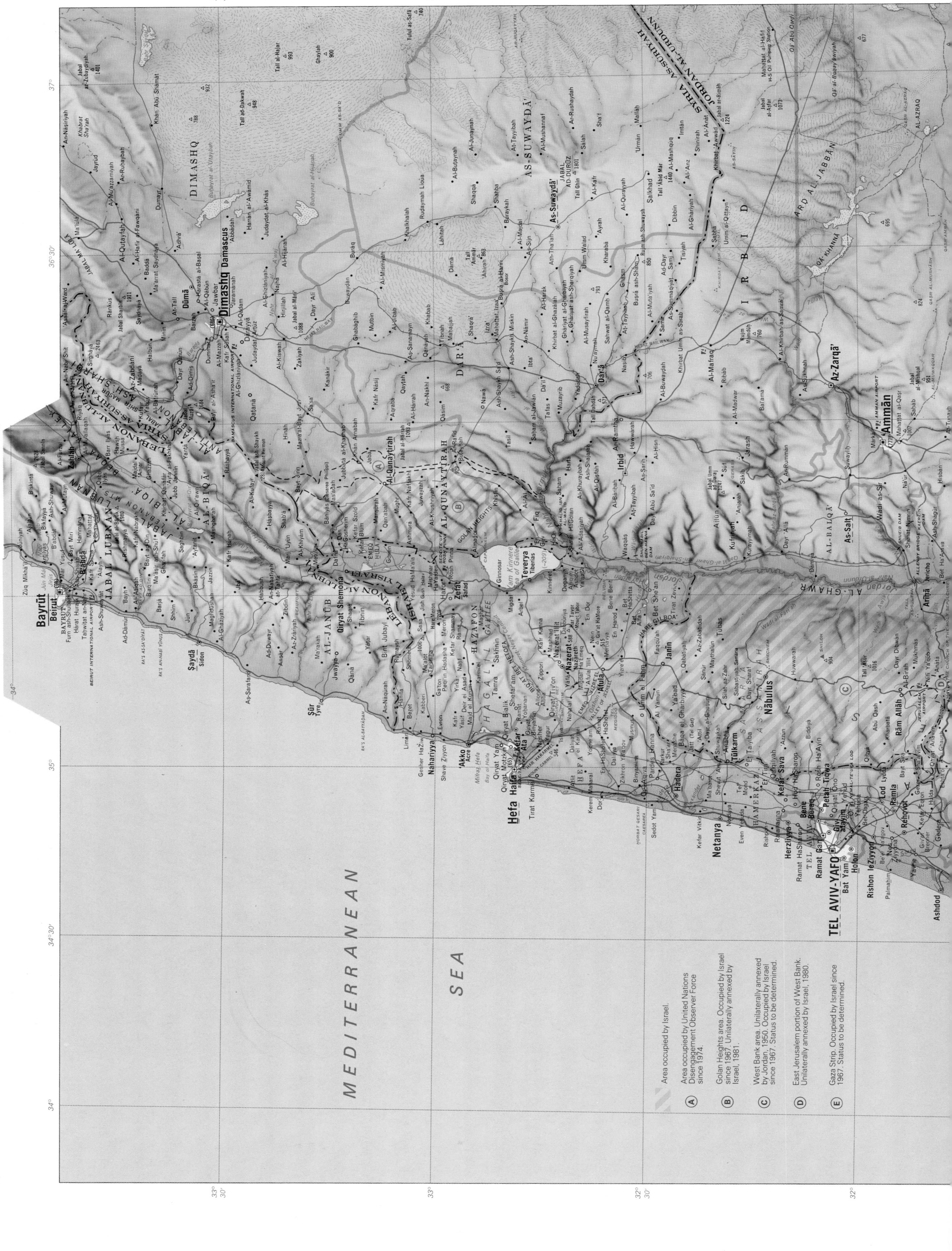
MEDITERRANEAN
SEA
Area occupied by Israel.
A Area occupied by United Nations Disengagement Observer Force since 1974.
B Golan Heights area. Occupied by Israel since 1967. Unilaterally annexed by Israel, 1981.
C West Bank area. Unilaterally annexed by Jordan, 1950. Occupied by Israel since 1967. Status to be determined.
D East Jerusalem portion of West Bank. Unilaterally annexed by Israel, 1980.
E Gaza Strip. Occupied by Israel since 1967. Status to be determined.

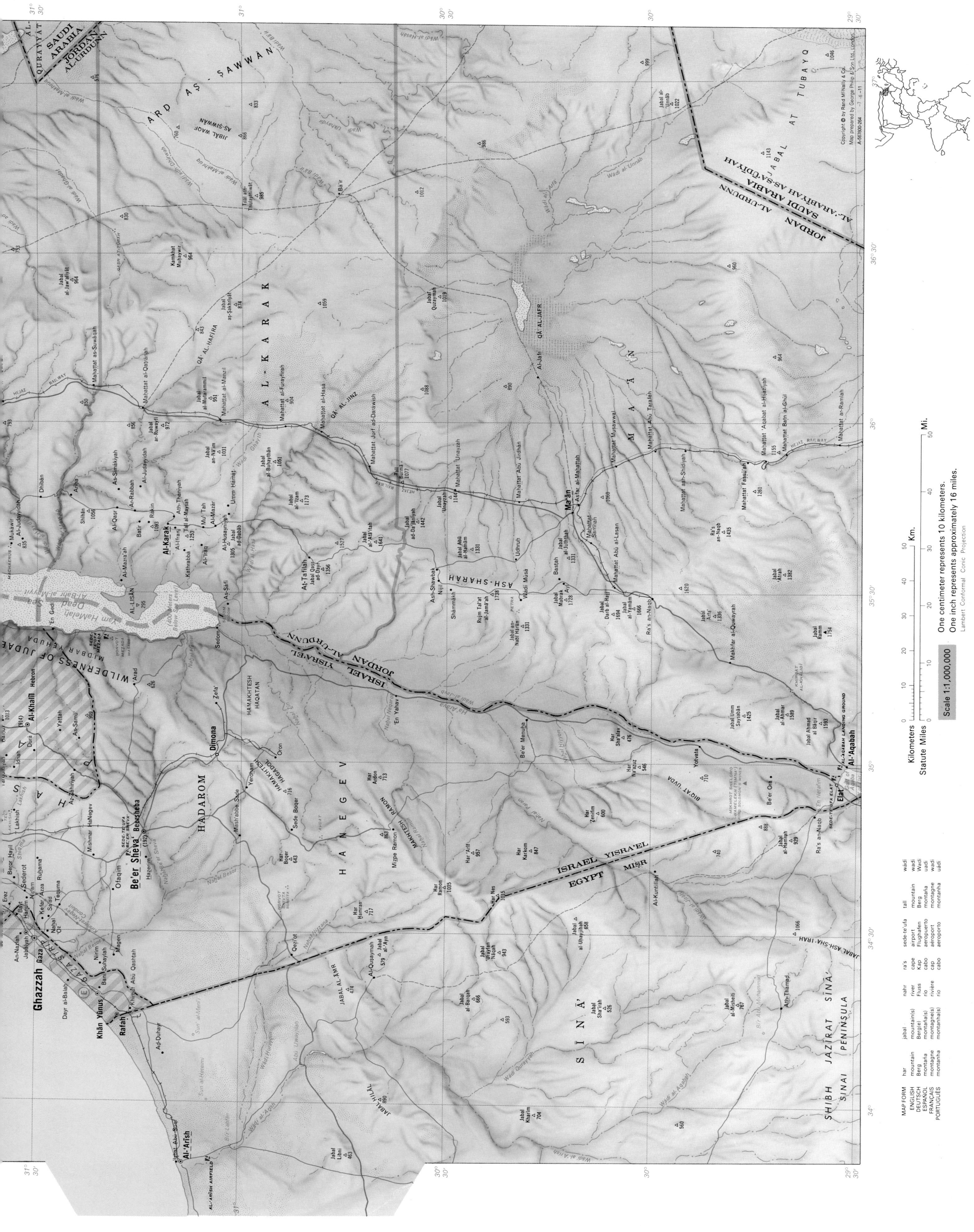
Kilometers
Statute Miles
Scale 1:1,000,000
One centimeter represents 10 kilometers.
One inch represents approximately 16 miles.
Lambert Conformal Conic Projection
MAP FORM | har | jabal | nahr | ra's | sede-te'ufa | tall | wadi
ENGLISH | mountain | mountain(s) | river | cape | airport | mountain | wadi
DEUTSCH | Berg | Berg(e) | Fluss | Kap | Flughafen | Berg | Wadi
ESPAÑOL | montaña | montaña(s) | río | cabo | aeropuerto | montaña | uadi
FRANÇAIS | montagne | montagne(s) | rivière | cap | aéroport | montagne | wadi
PORTUGUÊS | montanha | montanha(s) | rio | cabo | aeroporto | montanha | uadi
Copyright © by Rand McNally & Co.
Map prepared by George Philip & Son Ltd., London
JORDAN AL-URDUNN
SAUDI ARABIA AL-'ARABIYAH AS-SA'ŪDĪYAH
ISRAEL YISRA'EL
EGYPT MIŞR
ARD AŞ-ŞAWWAN
AL-KARAK
MA'ĀN
JABAL AT TUBAYQ
HANEGEV
HADAROM
SĪNĀ'
SHIBH JAZĪRAT SĪNĀ'
SINAI PENINSULA
WILDERNESS OF JUDEA
Dead Sea
Yam HaMelah
Al-Bahr al-Mayyit
Ghazzah
Gaza
Khān Yūnus
Rafah
Al-'Arīsh
Be'er Sheva'
Beersheba
Dimona
Al-Karak
Ma'ān
Al-'Aqabah
Elat
Al-Khalīl
Hebron
At-Tafīlah
Qā' al-Jafr
Yeroham
Mizpe Ramon
HEJAZ RAILWAY

MAP FORM	bahr, baḥr	chott	jabal	lake	mountains	oued	wahât
ENGLISH	river, sea	salt marsh	mountain(s)	lake	mountains	wadi	oasis
DEUTSCH	Fluss, Meer	Salzmarsch	Berg(e)	See	Berge	Wadi	Oase
ESPAÑOL	río, mar	pantano salado	montaña(s)	lago	montañas	uadi	oasis
FRANÇAIS	rivière, mer	marais salé	montagne(s)	lac	montagnes	wadi	oasis
PORTUGUÊS	rio, mar	pântano salgado	montanha(s)	lago	montanhas	uádi	oásis

Kilometers 0 200 400 600 Km.

Statute Miles 0 200 400 600 Mi.

Scale 1:12,000,000

One centimeter represents 120 kilometers.
One inch represents approximately 190 miles.
Miller Oblated Stereographic Projection

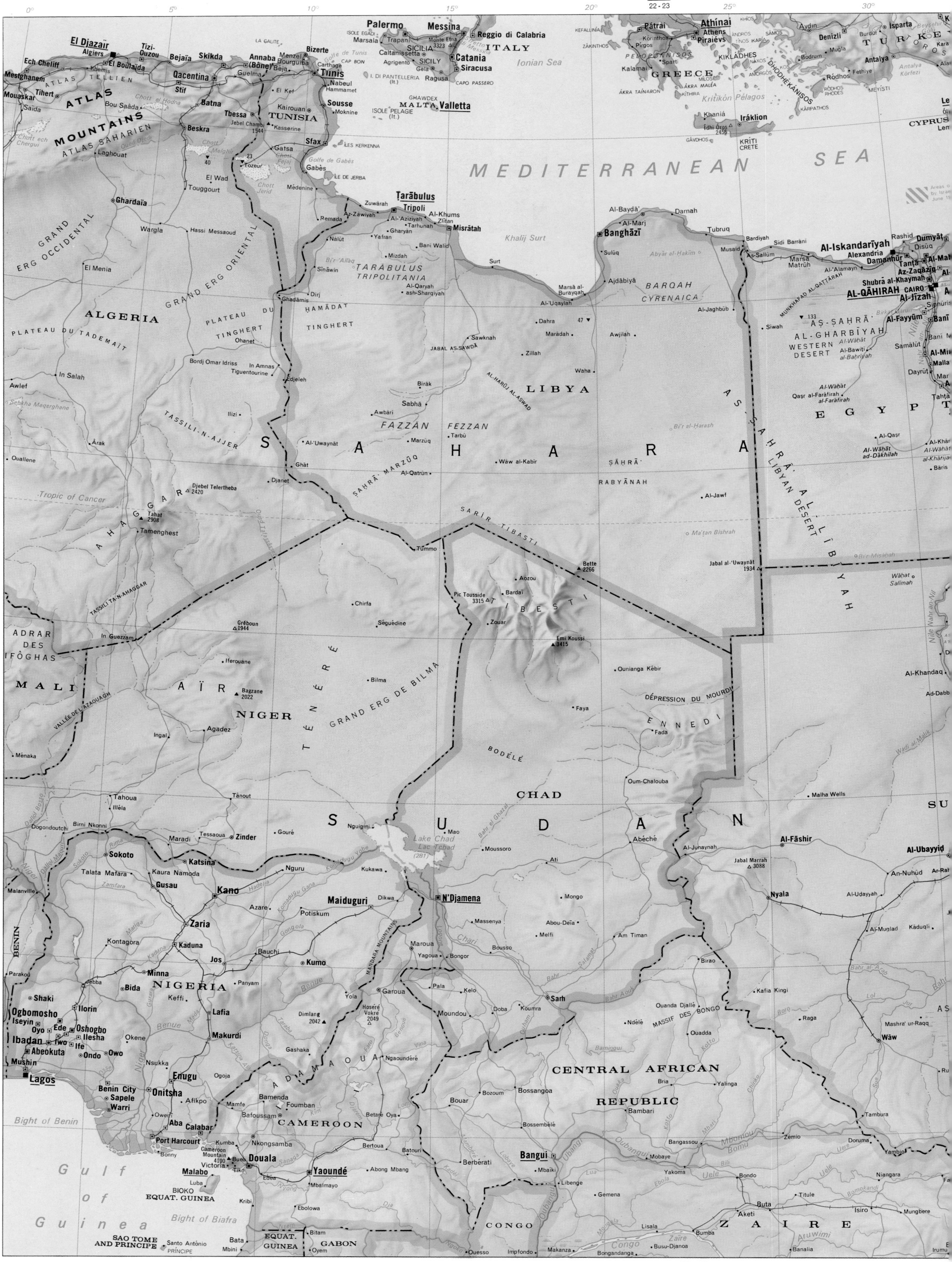

MAP FORM	bahr, baḥr	chott	jabal	lake	mountains	oued	ra's; ras	wāhāt
ENGLISH	river, sea	salt marsh	mountain(s)	lake	mountains	wadi	cape	oasis
DEUTSCH	Fluss, Meer	Salzmarsch	Berg(e)	See	Berge	Wadi	Kap	Oase
ESPAÑOL	río, mar	pantano salado	montaña(s)	lago	montañas	uadi	cabo	oasis
FRANÇAIS	rivière, mer	marais salé	montagne(s)	lac	montagnes	wadi	cap	oasis
PORTUGUÊS	rio, mar	pântano salgado	montanha(s)	lago	montanhas	uádi	cabo	oásis

Kilometers 0 200 400 600 Km.
Statute Miles 0 200 400 600 Mi.

Scale 1:12,000,000

One centimeter represents 120 kilometers.
One inch represents approximately 190 miles.
Miller Oblated Stereographic Projection

MAP FORM	cape	île	island	lake	mountains	plateau
ENGLISH	cape	island	island	lake	mountains	plateau
DEUTSCH	Kap	Insel	Insel	See	Berge	Hochebene
ESPAÑOL	cabo	isla	isla	lago	montañas	meseta
FRANÇAIS	cap	île	île	lac	montagnes	plateau
PORTUGUÊS	cabo	ilha	ilha	lago	montanhas	planalto

INDIAN OCEAN
SOMALIA
KENYA
Nairobi
Mombasa
Kisumu
Nakuru
Machakos
Arusha
Moshi
Tanga
Zanzibar
Dar es Salaam
Dodoma
Morogoro
Iringa
Lindi
Mtwara
MASAI
STEPPE
SERENGETI
PLAIN
YATTA PLATEAU
Kilimanjaro
Equator
SEYCHELLES
Victoria
MAHÉ ISLAND
AMIRANTE ISLANDS
(Sey.)
ALDABRA ISLAND
(Sey.)
COSMOLEDO I.
(Sey.)
PROVIDENCE ISLAND
(Sey.)
FARQUHAR GROUP
(Sey.)
AGALEGA ISLANDS
(Mauritius)
COMOROS
Moroni
ARCHIPEL DES COMORES
MAYOTTE
(Fr.)
Dzaoudzi
MADAGASCAR
Antananarivo
Antsiranana
Mahajanga
Toamasina
Antsirabe
Fianarantsoa
Toliara
Morondava
Maroantsetra
Antalaha
Sambava
Manakara
Farafangana
Faradofay
CAP D'AMBRE
CAP SAINTE-MARIE
MASSIF DU TSARATANANA
Maromokotro ▲ 2876
ÎLE TROMELIN
(Reunion)
MOZAMBIQUE
Nampula
Nacala
Quelimane
Beira
Blantyre
Zomba
Lake Nyasa
MALAWI
Mozambique Channel
BASSAS DA INDIA
(Reunion)
ÎLE EUROPA
(Reunion)
Port Louis
Curepipe
Mahébourg
MAURITIUS
Saint-Denis
REUNION
(Fr.)
MASCARENE
ISLANDS
Tropic of Capricorn
INDIAN OCEAN
Copyright © by Rand McNally & Co.
Map prepared by Esselte Map Service AB, Stockholm.
A-589200-264

Kilometers 0 200 400 600 Km.
Statute Miles 0 200 400 600 Mi.

Scale 1:12,000,000

One centimeter represents 120 kilometers.
One inch represents approximately 190 miles.
Miller Oblated Stereographic Projection

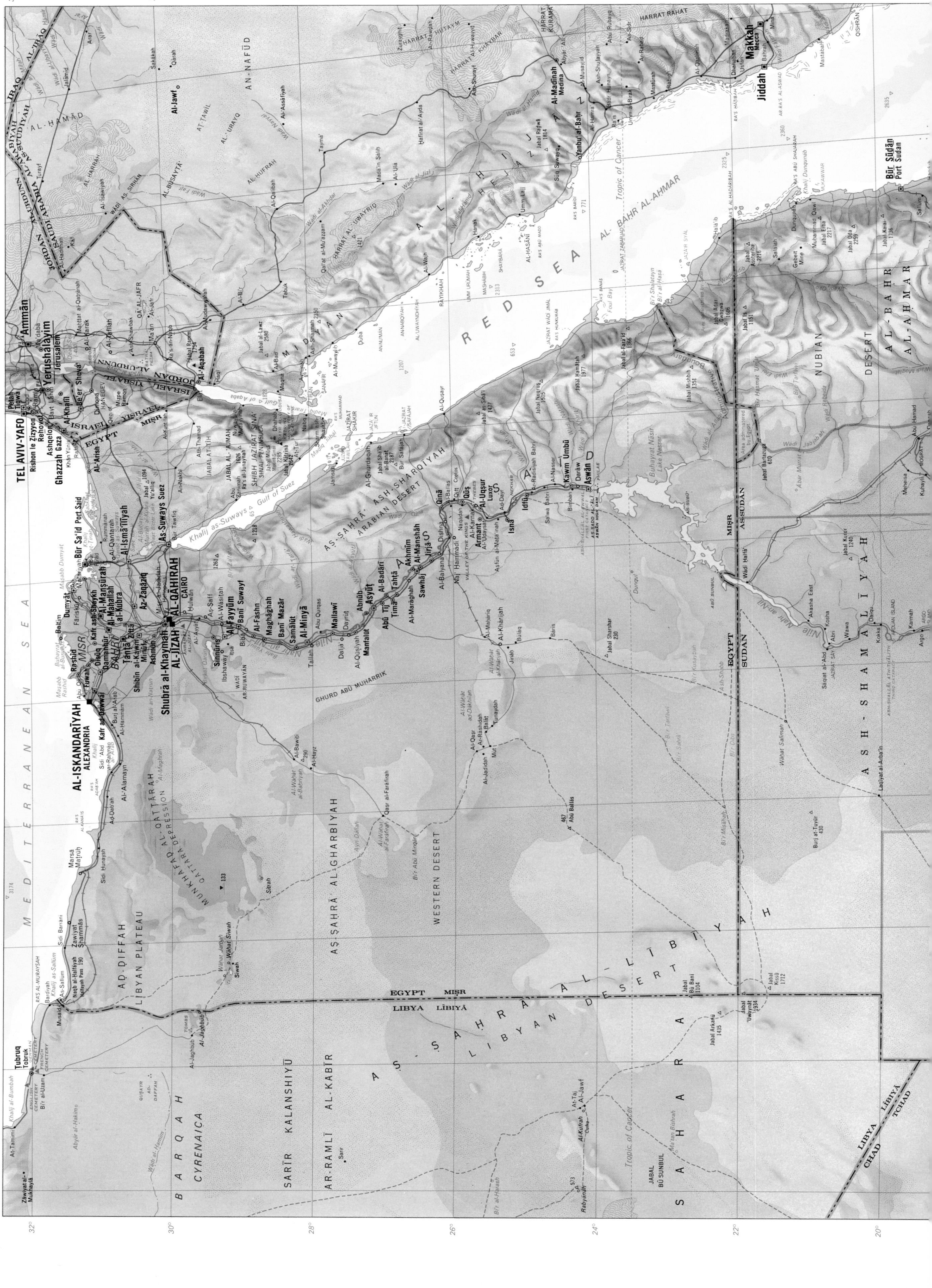
MEDITERRANEAN SEA
RED SEA
AL-BAHR AL-AHMAR
AL-ISKANDARIYAH
ALEXANDRIA
AL-QAHIRAH
CAIRO
AL-JIZAH
Shubrā al-Khaymah
Būr Sa'īd Port Said
As-Suways Suez
Al-Ismā'īlīyah
Az-Zaqāzīq
Al-Manṣūrah
Ṭanṭā
Dumyāṭ
Al-Fayyūm
Banī Suwayf
Al-Minyā
Asyūṭ
Sawhāj
Qinā
Al-Uqṣur
Luxor
Aswān
Isnā
Idfū
Kawm Umbū
Marsā Maṭrūḥ
Sīwah
As-Sallūm
TEL AVIV-YAFO
Yerushalayim
Jerusalem
'Ammān
Ghazzah Gaza
Al-'Aqabah
Al-Madīnah
Medina
Makkah
Mecca
Jiddah
Yanbu' al-Baḥr
Būr Sūdān
Port Sudan
Wādī Ḥalfā
Tubruq
Tobruk
EGYPT
MIṢR
LIBYA
LĪBIYĀ
SUDAN
AS-SUDAN
ISRAEL
YISRA'EL
JORDAN
SAUDI ARABIA
AS-SA'ŪDĪYAH
CHAD
TCHAD
WESTERN DESERT
ARABIAN DESERT
NUBIAN DESERT
LIBYAN DESERT
LIBYAN PLATEAU
AD-DIFFAH
AŞ-ŞAḤRĀ' AL-GHARBĪYAH
AŞ-ŞAḤRĀ' ASH-SHARQĪYAH
AŞ-ŞAḤRĀ' AL-LĪBĪYAH
SAHARA
CYRENAICA
BARQAH
SARĪR KALANSHIYŪ
AR-RAMLĪ AL-KABĪR
MUNKHAFAḌ AL-QAṬṬĀRAH
QATTARA DEPRESSION
AL-HIJĀZ
AN-NAFŪD
AL-ḤAMĀD
SINAI PENINSULA
SHIBH JAZĪRAT SĪNĀ'
Gulf of Suez
Gulf of Aqaba
Tropic of Cancer
Nile
Lake Nasser
Buḥayrat Nāṣir
ASH-SHAMĀLĪYAH
AL-BAHR AL-AHMAR

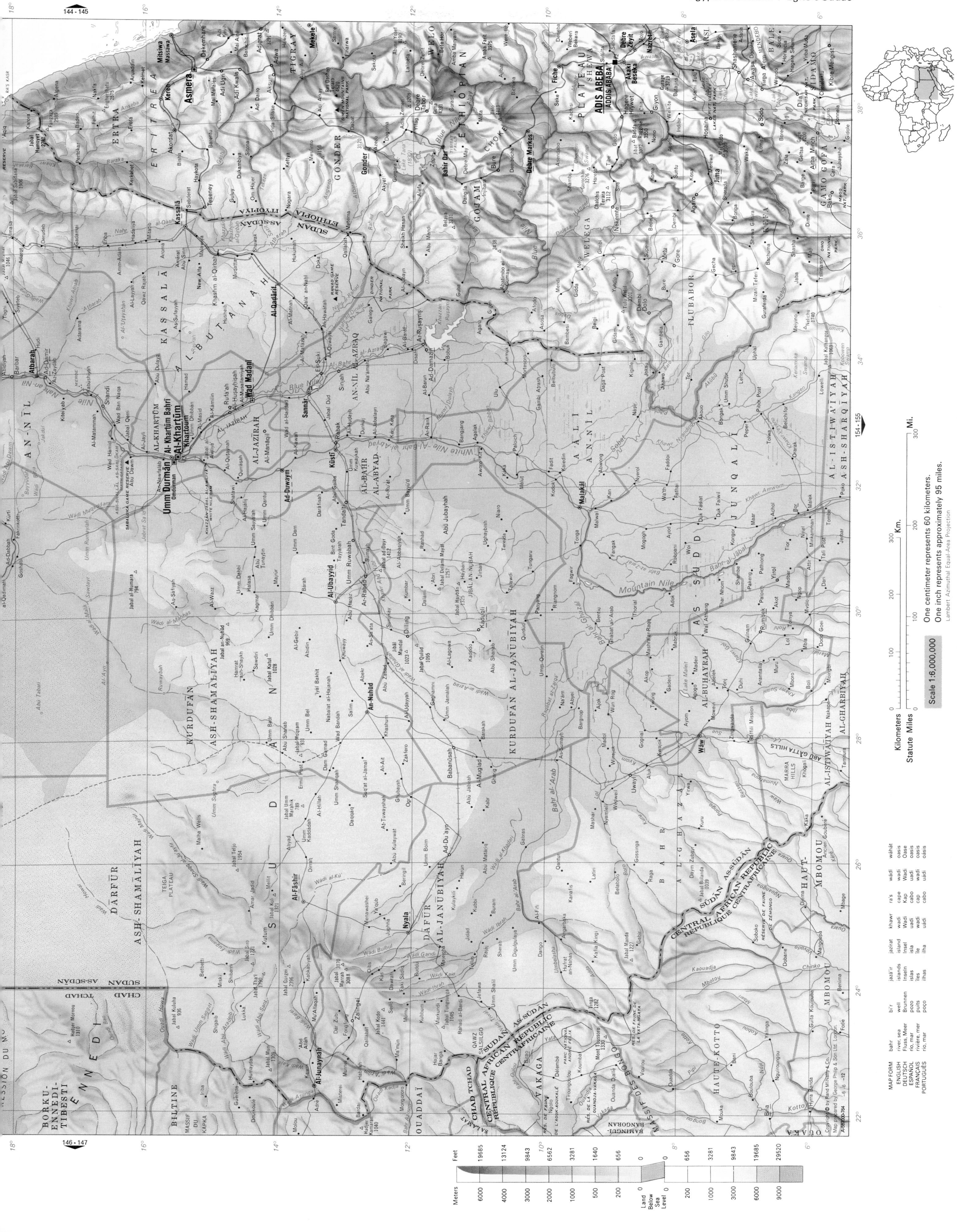
144 - 145
146 - 147
154 - 155
Scale 1:6,000,000
One centimeter represents 60 kilometers.
One inch represents approximately 95 miles.
Lambert Azimuthal Equal-Area Projection
Kilometers
Statute Miles
Km.
Mi.
MAP FORM
ENGLISH
DEUTSCH
ESPAÑOL
FRANÇAIS
PORTUGUÊS
Meters
Feet
Land Below Sea Level
SUDAN
AS-SŪDĀN
ETHIOPIA
ITYOPIYA
ERTRA
ERITREA
CHAD
TCHAD
CENTRAL AFRICAN REPUBLIC
RÉPUBLIQUE CENTRAFRICAINE
Al-Kharṭūm
Khartoum
Umm Durmān
Omdurman
Al-Kharṭūm Baḥrī
Asmera
ADIS ABEBA
Wad Madanī
Kassalā
Al-Fāshir
Nyala
Al-Ubayyiḍ
Kūstī
Malakāl
Wāw
Atbarah
Gonder
Bahir Dar
Mitsiwa
Massawa
White Nile
Blue Nile
Mountain Nile
Baḥr al-'Arab
Baḥr al-Ghazāl
DĀRFŪR
KURDUFĀN
AS-SUDD
BORKU-ENNEDI-TIBESTI
BILTINE
OUADDAÏ
VAKAGA
ILUBABOR
WELEGA
GOJAM
GONDER
TIGRAY
WELO
SHEWA
ARSI
SIDAMO
KEFA
GAMO GOFA
HAUT-MBOMOU
HAUTE-KOTTO
MBOMOU

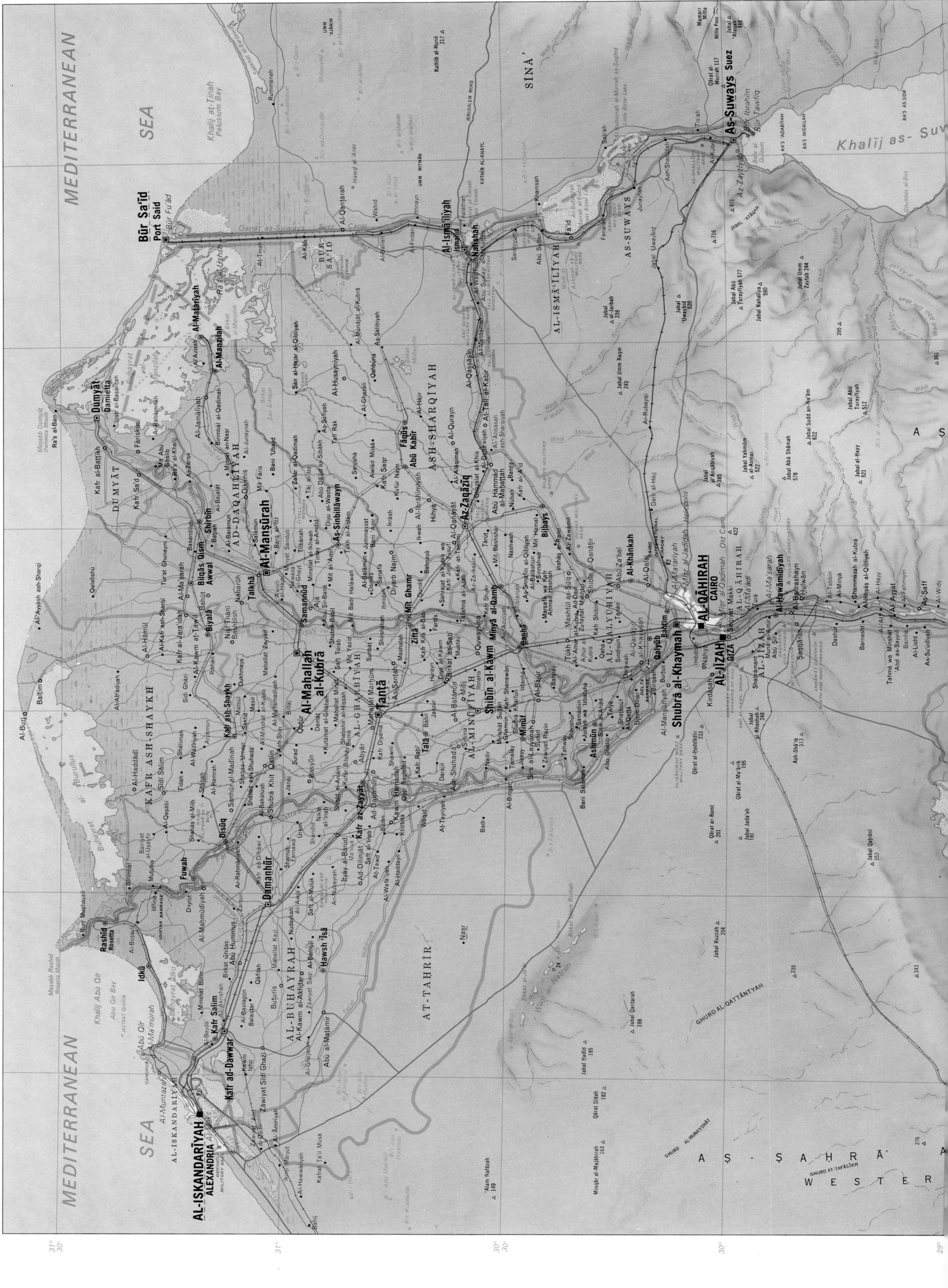
MEDITERRANEAN SEA
AL-ISKANDARĪYAH
ALEXANDRIA
Kafr ad-Dawwār
Rashīd
Rosetta
Dumyāṭ
Damietta
Būr Sa'īd
Port Said
Al-Manṣūrah
Al-Maḥallah al-Kubrā
Ṭanṭā
Damanhūr
Az-Zaqāzīq
Al-Ismā'īlīyah
AL-QĀHIRAH
CAIRO
AL-JĪZAH
GIZA
Shubrā al-Khaymah
As-Suways
Suez
Khalīj as-Suways
SĪNĀ'
AṢ-ṢAḤRĀ' AL-GHARBĪYAH
WESTERN
AT-TAḤRĪR
AL-BUḤAYRAH
KAFR ASH-SHAYKH
AD-DAQAHLĪYAH
ASH-SHARQĪYAH
AL-GHARBĪYAH
AL-MINŪFĪYAH
AL-QALYŪBĪYAH
AL-ISMĀ'ĪLĪYAH
AS-SUWAYS
DUMYĀṬ
BŪR SA'ĪD
AL-ISKANDARĪYAH
Qanāt as-Suways
Suez Canal

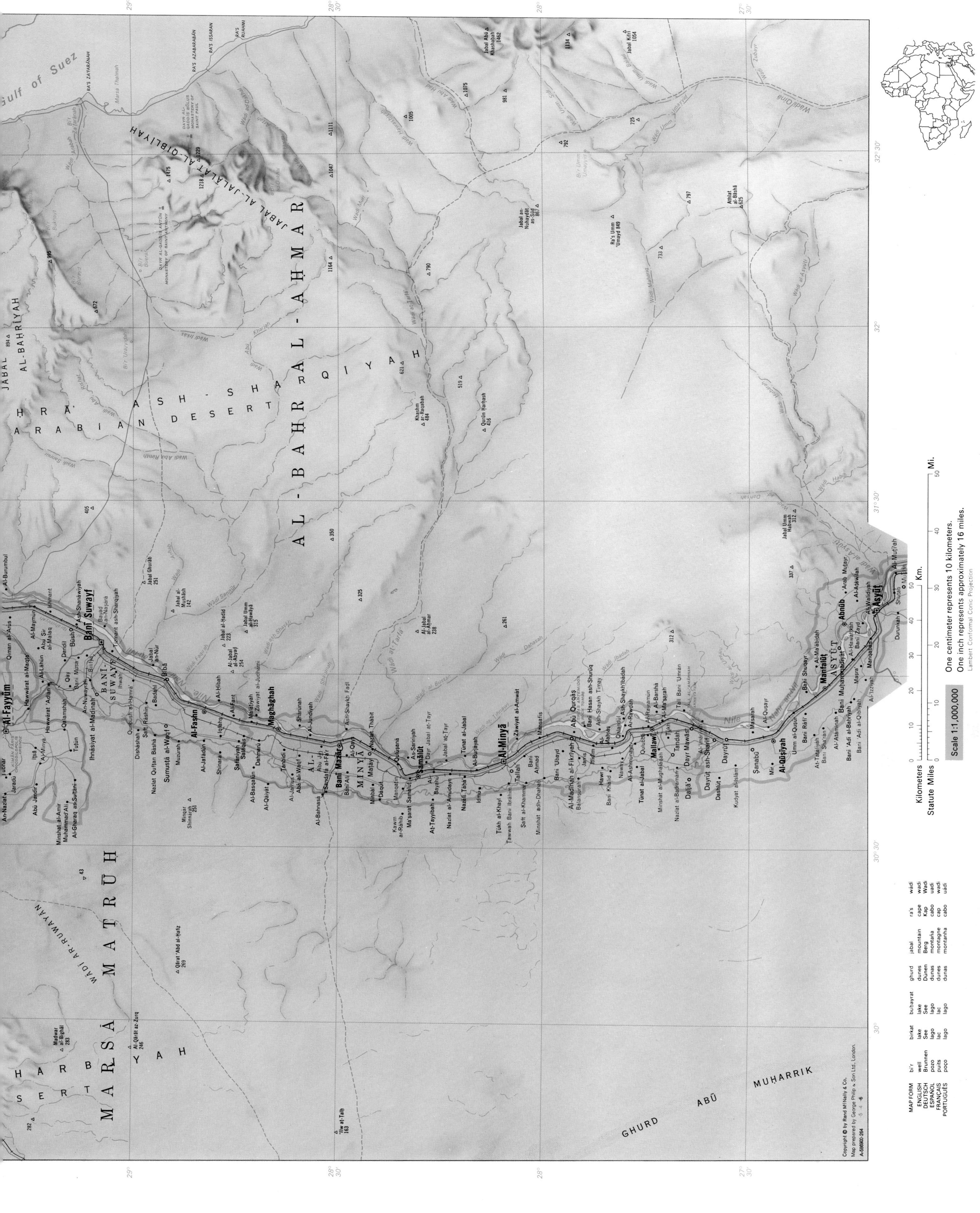
Gulf of Suez
JABAL AL-JALĀLAT AL-QIBLĪYAH
AL-BAḤR AL-AḤMAR
ASH-SHARQIYAH
ARABIAN DESERT
MARSĀ MATRŪḤ
WADI AR-RUWAYAN
GHURD ABŪ MUḤARRIK
Al-Fayyūm
Banī Suwayf
Al-Fashn
Maghāghah
Banī Mazār
Al-Minyā
Samālūṭ
Mallawī
Dayrūṭ
Al-Qūṣīyah
Manfalūṭ
Asyūṭ
Abnūb
Nile
Scale 1:1,000,000
One centimeter represents 10 kilometers.
One inch represents approximately 16 miles.
Lambert Conformal Conic Projection
Kilometers
Statute Miles
Km.
Mi.
MAP FORM bi'r birkat buḥayrat ghurd jabal ra's wādī
ENGLISH well lake lake dunes mountain cape wadi
DEUTSCH Brunnen See See Dünen Berg Kap Wadi
ESPAÑOL pozo lago lago dunas montaña cabo uadi
FRANÇAIS puits lac lac dunes montagne cap wadi
PORTUGUÊS poço lago lago dunas montanha cabo uadi
Copyright © by Rand McNally & Co.
Map prepared by George Philip & Son Ltd., London.

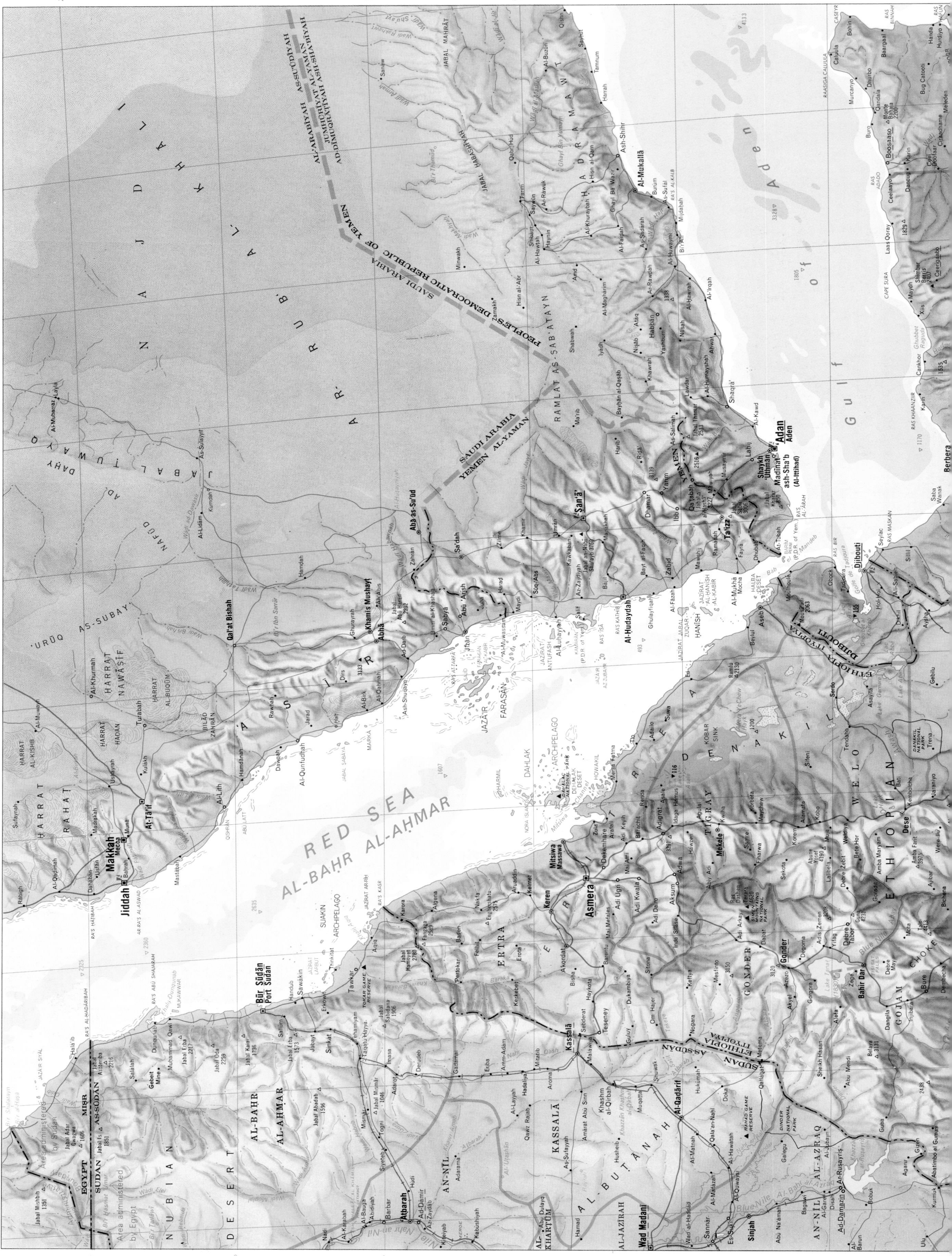

128 · 129
140 · 141

INDIAN OCEAN
Equator
ADIS ABEBA
Harer
Mugdisho
Mogadishu
Kismaayo
Nairobi
Nazret
Asela
Jima
Kisumu
Nakuru
Eldoret
Nyeri
Thika
Kilimanjaro
ETHIOPIA
SOMALIA
KENYA
UGANDA
TANZANIA
OGADEN
HARERGE
SIDAMO
BALE
GEDO
BAKOOL
BAY
HIIRAAN
GALGUDUUD
MUDUG
NUGAAL
TOGDHEER
SHABEELLAHA DHEXE
SHABEELLAHA HOOSE
JUBBADA DHEXE
JUBBADA HOOSE
NORTH EASTERN
RIFT VALLEY
CHALBI DESERT
LOTIKIPI PLAIN
154-155
Kilometers
Statute Miles
Km.
Mi.
Scale 1:6,000,000
One centimeter represents 60 kilometers.
One inch represents approximately 95 miles.
Lambert Azimuthal Equal-Area Projection
Copyright © by Rand McNally & Co.
Map prepared by George Philip & Son, Ltd. London.
A-587100-764
MAP FORM
ENGLISH
DEUTSCH
ESPAÑOL
FRANÇAIS
PORTUGUÊS
Meters
Feet
Land Below Sea Level

MEDITERRANEAN SEA
Khalīj Surt
Gulf of Sidra
Ţarābulus
Tripoli
Banghāzī
Misratah
Tubruq
Tobruk
Darnah
Al-Bayḑā'
Surt
Ajdābiyā
Sabhā
Marzūq
Ghāt
Al-Kufrah
Al-Jaghbūb
EGYPT MIṢR
LIBYA LĪBIYĀ
SUDAN
ALGERIA ALGÉRIE
TUNISIA TUNISIE
NIGER
CHAD TCHAD
AD-DIFFAH
LIBYAN PLATEAU
MUNKHAFAD AL-QAṬṬĀRAH
BARQAH
CYRENAICA
SARĪR KALANSHIYŪ
AR-RAMLĪ AL-KABĪR
AṢ-ṢAḤRĀ' AL-LĪBIYAH
LIBYAN DESERT
JABAL BŪ SUNBUL
ṢAḤRĀ' RABYĀNAH
AL-HARŪJ AL-ASWAD
JABAL BIN GHUNAYMAH
SARĪR TIBASTĪ
TRIPOLITANIA
ṬARĀBULUS
AL-ḤAMĀDAH AL-ḤAMRĀ'
JABAL NAFŪSAH
FEZZAN
FAZZĀN
ṢAḤRĀ' MARZŪQ
ḤAMĀDAT MARZŪQ
ḤAMĀDAT ZEGHER
ṢAḤRĀ' AWBĀRĪ
ḤAMĀDAT TINGHERT
PLATEAU DU TINGHERT
GRAND ERG ORIENTAL
RMEL EL ABIOD
TASSILI N'AJJER
ERG D'ADMER
TAMENGHEST
WARGLA
BESKRA
GABÈS
MÉDENINE JEFFARA
PLATEAU DU TCHIGAÏ
PLATEAU DU MANGUÉNI
PLATEAU DU DJADO
TÉNÉRÉ DU TAFASSÂSSET
Tropic of Cancer
Bette 2266
Jabal al-'Uwaynat 1934
Jabal Arkanū 1435

148 - 149

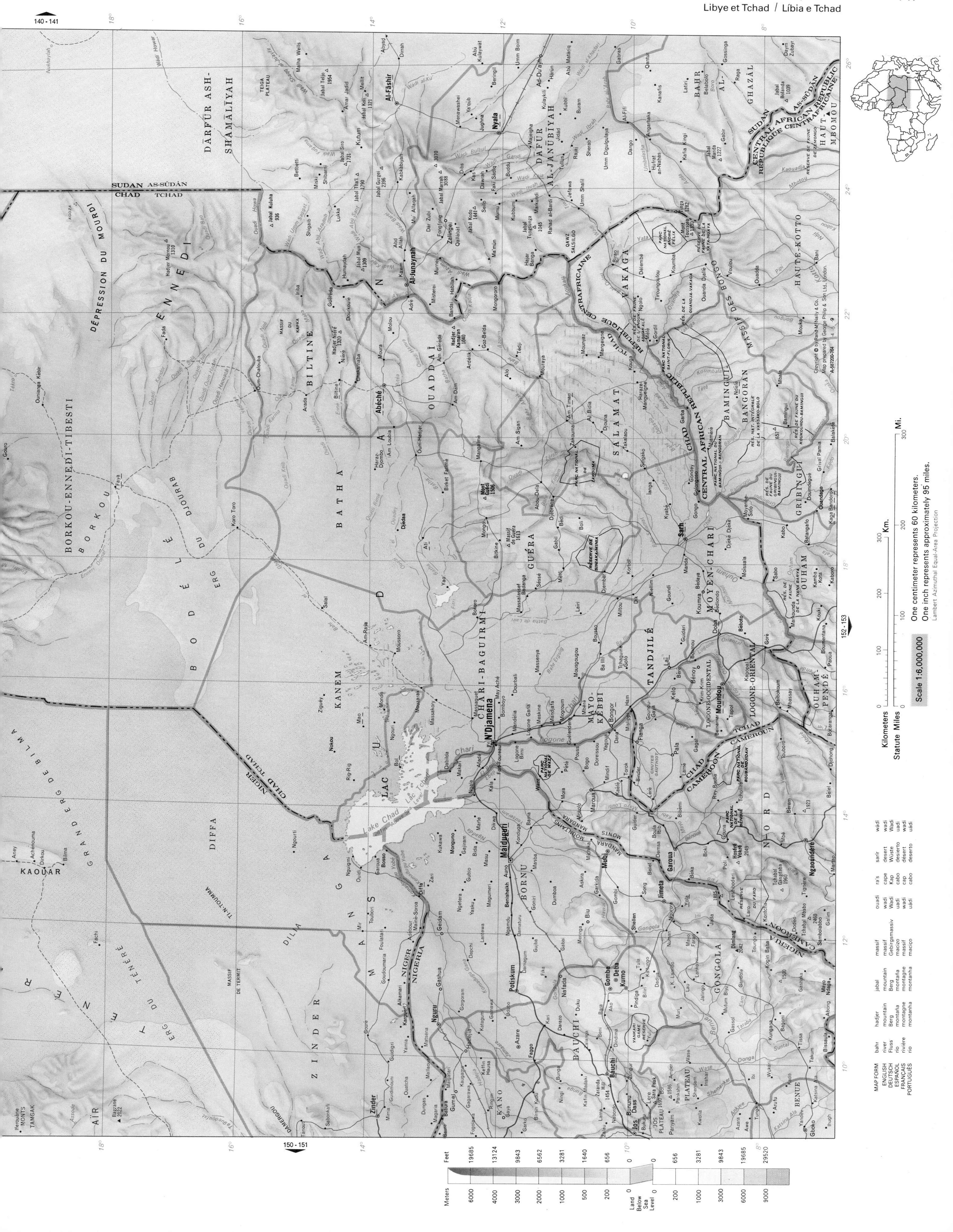
Scale 1:6,000,000
One centimeter represents 60 kilometers.
One inch represents approximately 95 miles.
Lambert Azimuthal Equal-Area Projection
Kilometers
Statute Miles
Km.
Mi.
140 - 141
150 - 151
152 - 153
SUDAN AS-SŪDĀN
CHAD TCHAD
N'Djamena
Abéché
Sarh
Moundou
Al-Fāshir
Nyala
Al-Junaynah
Maiduguri
Zinder
Lake Chad
LAC TCHAD
KANEM
BATHA
OUADDAÏ
BILTINE
GUÉRA
SALAMAT
MOYEN-CHARI
LOGONE-OCCIDENTAL
LOGONE-ORIENTAL
TANDJILÉ
MAYO-KEBBI
CHARI-BAGUIRMI
BORKOU-ENNEDI-TIBESTI
CENTRAL AFRICAN REPUBLIC
RÉPUBLIQUE CENTRAFRICAINE
CAMEROON
CAMEROUN
NIGER
NIGERIA
Land Below Sea Level
Meters
Feet
MAP FORM
ENGLISH
DEUTSCH
ESPAÑOL
FRANÇAIS
PORTUGUÊS

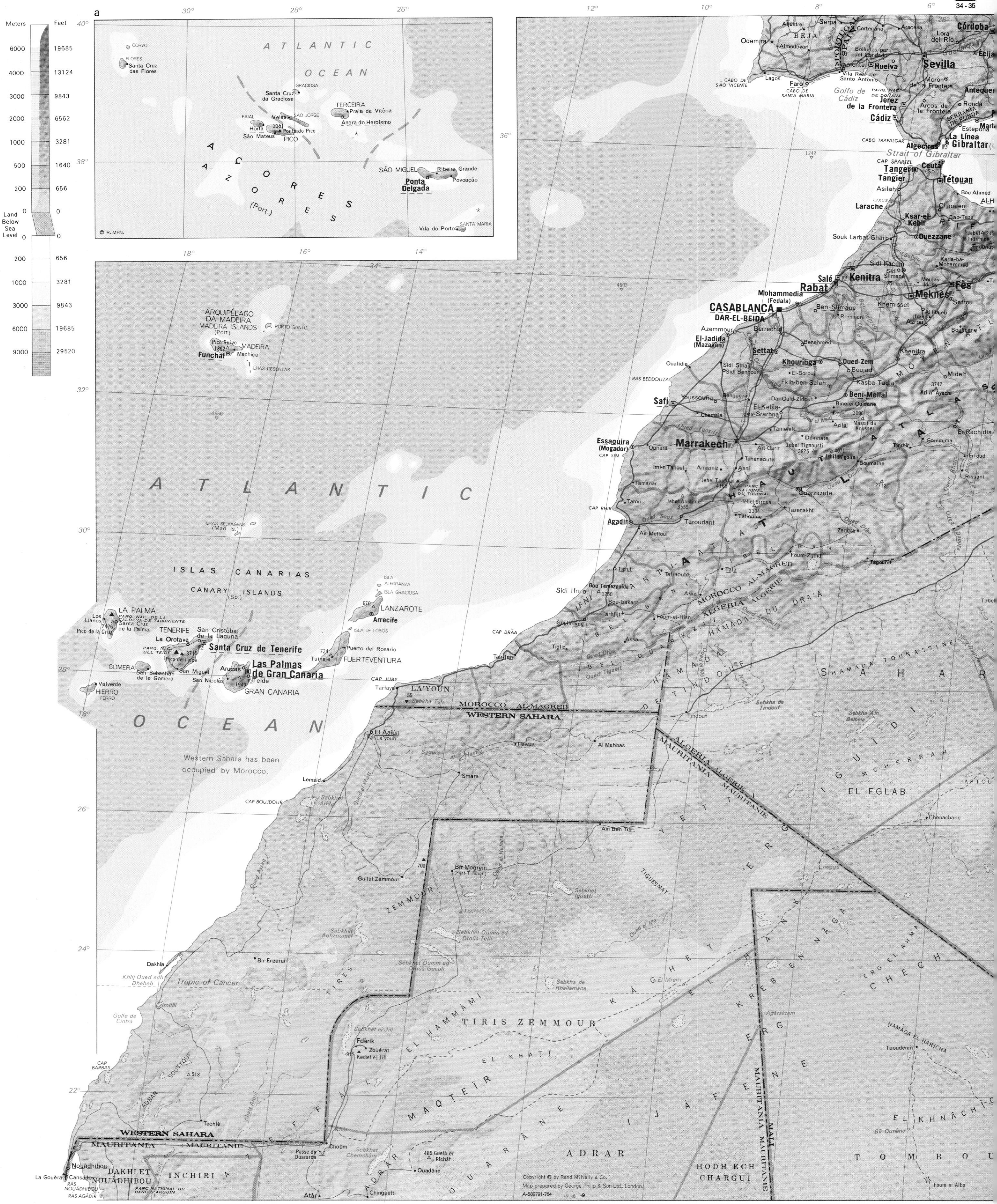

MAP FORM	cap	chott	djebel	erg	hamada	jbel	oued	sebkha
ENGLISH	cape	intermittent lake	mountain	sand desert	desert	mountain	wadi	salt flat
DEUTSCH	Kap	periodischer See	Berg	Sandwüste	Wüste	Berg	Wadi	Salzebene
ESPAÑOL	cabo	lago intermitente	montaña	desierto arenoso	desierto	montaña	uadi	salar
FRANÇAIS	cap	lac périodique	montagne	désert de sable	désert	montagne	wadi	saline
PORTUGUÊS	cabo	lago intermitente	montanha	deserto arenoso	deserto	montanha	uádi	salina

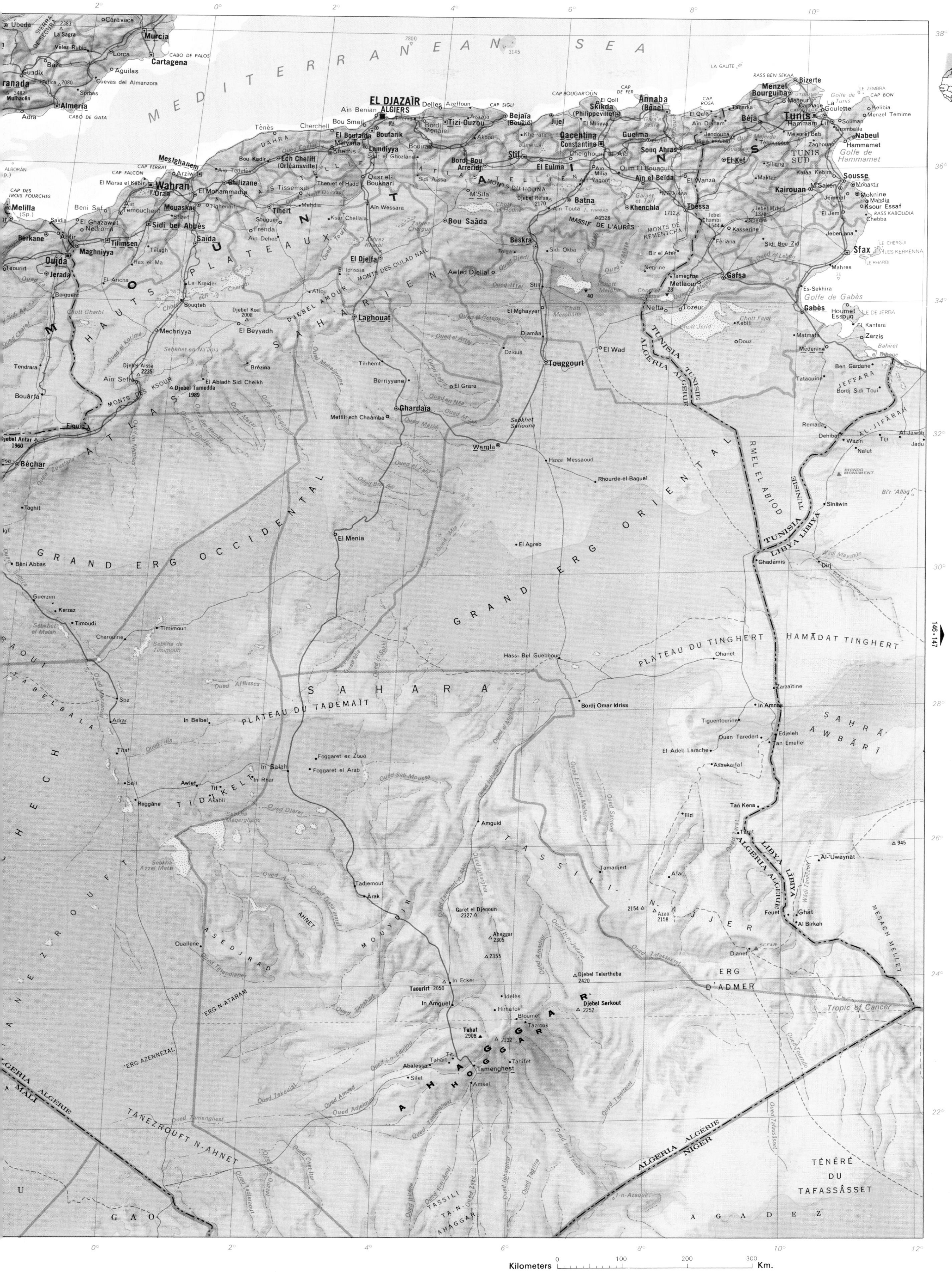

Kilometers 0 100 200 300 Km.
Statute Miles 0 100 200 300 Mi.

Scale 1:6,000,000

One centimeter represents 60 kilometers.
One inch represents approximately 95 miles.
Lambert Azimuthal Equal-Area Projection

West Africa / Westafrika / África Occidental
Afrique Occidentale / África Ocidental

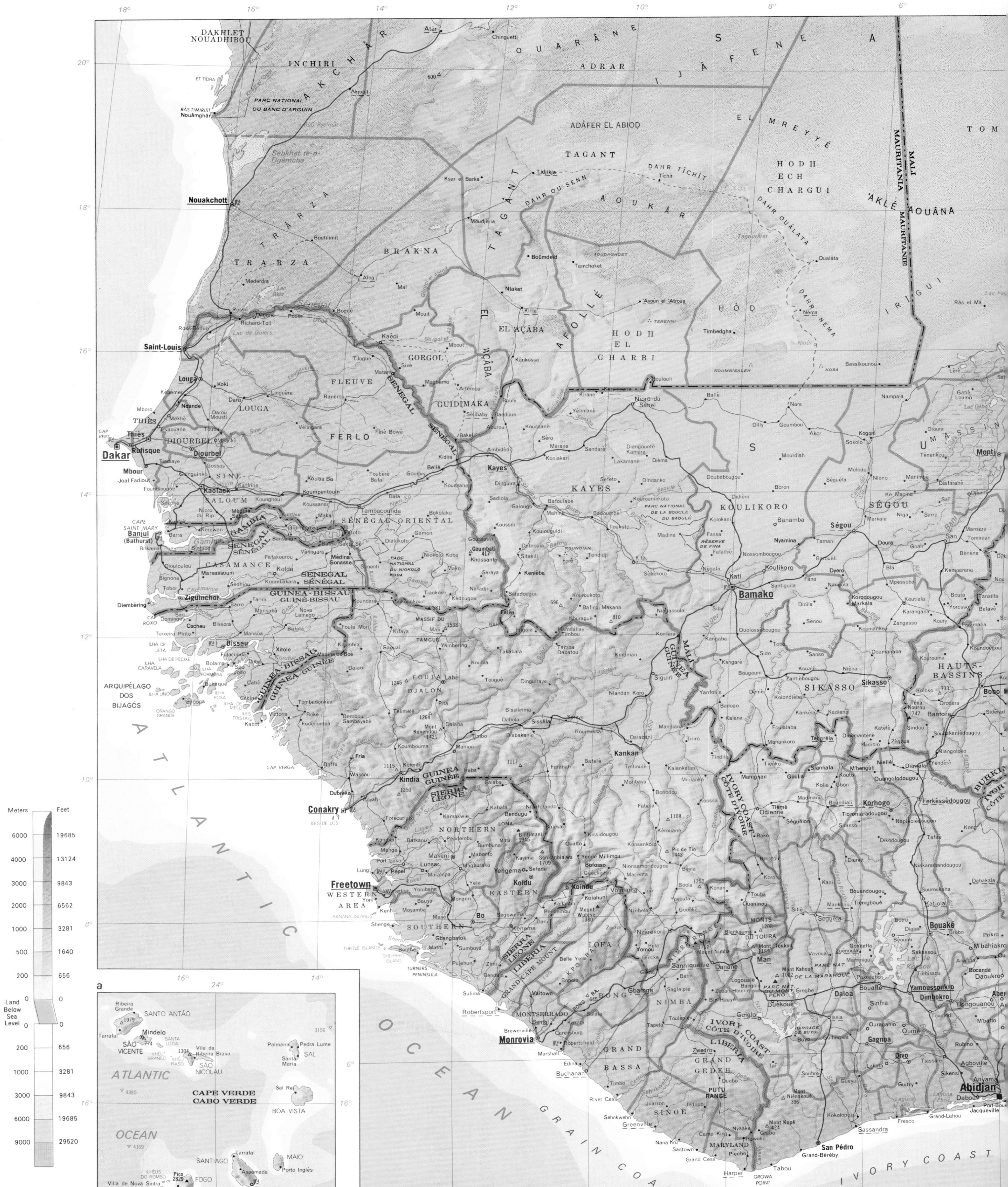

MAP FORM	coast	dhar	game reserve	ilha	lac	monts	mountains	vallée
ENGLISH	coast	escarpment	game reserve	island	lake	mountains	mountains	valley
DEUTSCH	Küste	Landstufe	Wildpark	Insel	See	Berge	Berge	Tal
ESPAÑOL	costa	escarpa	vedado de caza	isla	lago	montes	montañas	valle
FRANÇAIS	côte	escarpement	réserve à gibier	île	lac	monts	montagnes	vallée
PORTUGUÊS	costa	escarpa	reserva de caça	ilha	lago	montes	montanhas	vale

Scale 1:6,000,000

One centimeter represents 60 kilometers.

One inch represents approximately 95 miles.

Lambert Azimuthal Equal-Area Projection

CENTRAL AFRICAN REPUBLIC
CAMEROON
CONGO
ZAIRE
GABON
EQUATORIAL GUINEA
SAO TOME AND PRINCIPE
NIGERIA
Bangui
Yaoundé
Douala
Libreville
Brazzaville
KINSHASA (LÉOPOLDVILLE)
Mbandaka (Coquilhatville)
Port Gentil
Malabo
Bight of Biafra
Gulf of Guinea
Equator
146-147
150-151

154 - 155

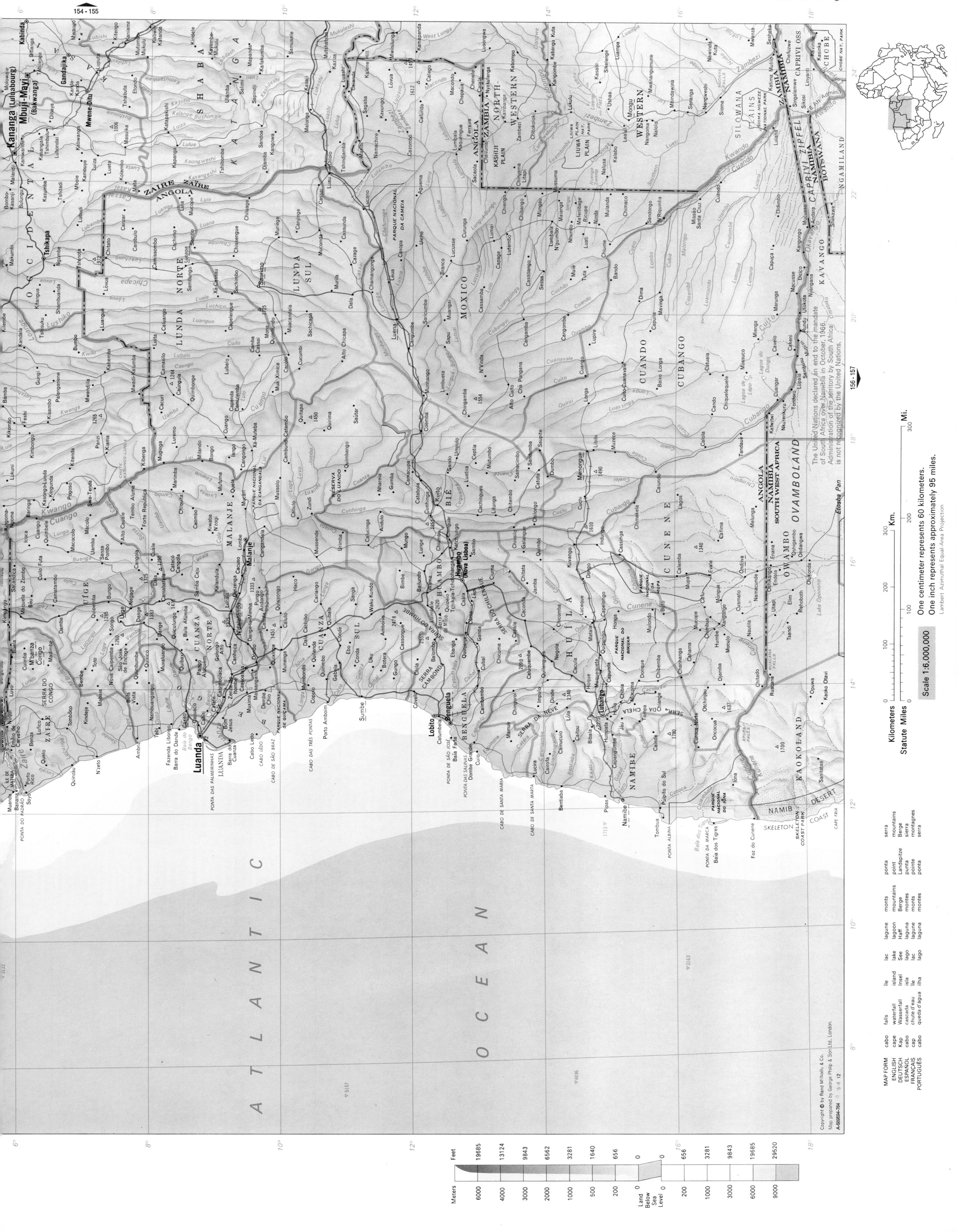
ATLANTIC OCEAN
ANGOLA
ZAIRE
ZAMBIA
NAMIBIA
SOUTH WEST AFRICA
BOTSWANA
Luanda
Lobito
Benguela
Huambo (Nova Lisboa)
Lubango
Namibe
Malanje
Kananga (Luluabourg)
Mbuji-Mayi (Bakwanga)
Tshikapa
Mwene-Ditu
The United Nations declared an end to the mandate of South Africa over Namibia in October, 1966. Administration of the territory by South Africa is not recognized by the United Nations.
156 - 157
Scale 1:6,000,000
One centimeter represents 60 kilometers.
One inch represents approximately 95 miles.
Lambert Azimuthal Equal-Area Projection
Kilometers
Statute Miles
Km.
Mi.
MAP FORM cabo falls île lac lagune monts ponta serra
ENGLISH cape waterfall island lake lagoon mountains point mountains
DEUTSCH Kap Wasserfall Insel See Haff Berge Landspitze Berge
ESPAÑOL cabo cascada isla lago laguna montes punta sierra
FRANÇAIS cap chute d'eau île lac lagune monts pointe montagnes
PORTUGUÊS cabo queda d'água ilha lago laguna montes ponta serra
Copyright © by Rand McNally & Co.
Map prepared by George Philip & Son Ltd, London.
Meters
Feet
Land Below Sea Level

East Africa and Eastern Congo Basin / Ostafrika und Östliches Kongobecken / África Oriental y Cuenca Oriental del Congo
Afrique Orientale et Bassin du Congo, partie Orientale / África Oriental e Bacia Oriental do Congo

Kilometers 0 100 200 300 Km.

Statute Miles 0 100 200 300 Mi.

Scale 1:6,000,000

One centimeter represents 60 kilometers.
One inch represents approximately 95 miles.

Lambert Azimuthal Equal-Area Projection

ENGLISH	DEUTSCH	ESPAÑOL	FRANÇAIS	PORTUGUÊS
falls	Wasserfall	cascada	chute d'eau	queda d'água
game reserve	Wildreservat	vedado de caza	réserve à gibier	reserva de caça
island	Insel	isla	île	ilha
lake	See	lago	lac	lago
mountains	Berge	montañas	montagnes	montanhas
national park	Nationalpark	parque nacional	parc national	parque nacional
plain	Ebene	llano	plaine	planície
swamp	Sumpf	pantano	marais	pântano

MOZAMBIQUE CHANNEL
MOZAMBIQUE
TANZANIA
ZAMBIA
MALAWI
ZIMBABWE
BOTSWANA
SOUTH AFRICA
NAMIBIA
ZAIRE
Lake Malawi
Lusaka
Harare (Salisbury)
Lubumbashi (Élisabethville)
Bulawayo
Blantyre
Lilongwe
Beira
Nampula
Livingstone
156 - 157
Copyright © by Rand McNally & Co.
Map prepared by George Philip & Son Ltd. London.
Feet
Meters
Land Below Sea Level

Southern Africa and Madagascar / Südafrika und Madagaskar / África Meridional y Madagascar
Afrique Méridionale et Madagascar / África Meridional e Madagascar

MAP FORM	bay	berg, berge	cape	game reserve	ilha	lake	national park
ENGLISH	bay	mountain, mountains	cape	game reserve	island	lake	national park
DEUTSCH	Bucht	Berg, Berge	Kap	Wildpark	Insel	See	Nationalpark
ESPAÑOL	bahía	montaña, montañas	cabo	vedado de caza	isla	lago	parque nacional
FRANÇAIS	baie	montagne, montagnes	cap	réserve à gibier	île	lac	parc national
PORTUGUÊS	baía	montanha, montanhas	cabo	reserva de caça	ilha	lago	parque nacional

Kilometers 0 100 200 300 Km.

Statute Miles 0 100 200 300 Mi.

Scale 1:6,000,000

One centimeter represents 60 kilometers.
One inch represents approximately 95 miles.

Lambert Azimuthal Equal-Area Projection

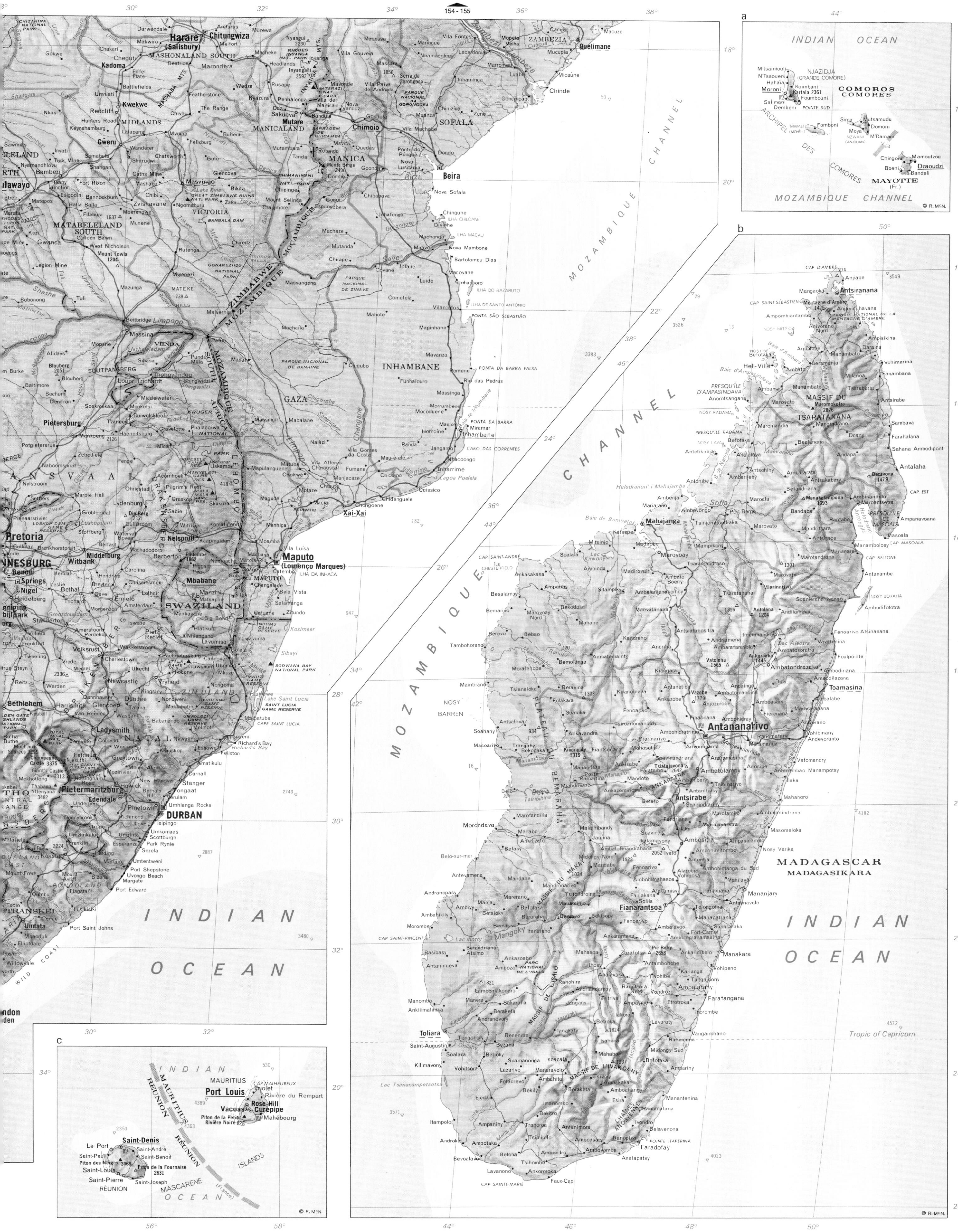
154 - 155
Harare (Salisbury)
Chitungwiza
Kadoma
Kwekwe
Gweru
Masvingo
Mutare
Chimoio
Beira
Quelimane
ZAMBEZIA
SOFALA
MANICA
INHAMBANE
GAZA
Maputo (Lourenço Marques)
Xai-Xai
Pretoria
Pietersburg
Mbabane
SWAZILAND
Nelspruit
DURBAN
Pietermaritzburg
Ladysmith
Bethlehem
Umtata
ZIMBABWE
MOZAMBIQUE
MOZAMBIQUE CHANNEL
INDIAN OCEAN
a
INDIAN OCEAN
COMOROS
COMORES
Moroni
MAYOTTE (Fr.)
Dzaoudzi
MOZAMBIQUE CHANNEL
b
Antsiranana
Mahajanga
Toamasina
Antananarivo
Antsirabe
Fianarantsoa
Toliara
Morondava
MADAGASCAR
MADAGASIKARA
INDIAN OCEAN
Tropic of Capricorn
c
INDIAN OCEAN
MAURITIUS
Port Louis
Saint-Denis
REUNION
MASCARENE ISLANDS
© R. MEN.

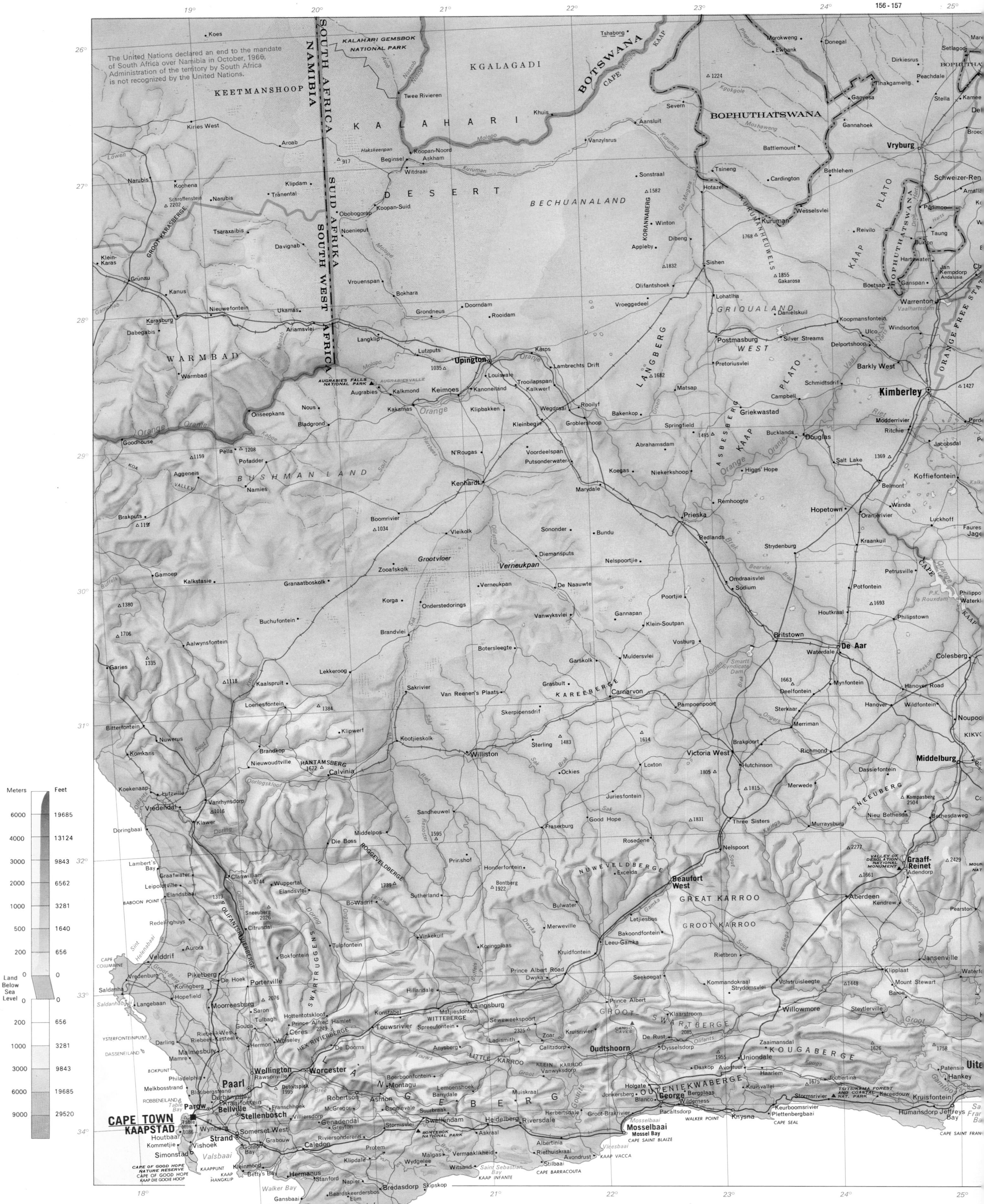

MAP FORM	bay	berge	cape	dam	game reserve	national park	pass	point
ENGLISH	bay	mountains	cape	dam	game reserve	national park	pass	point
DEUTSCH	Bucht	Berge	Kap	Damm	Wildpark	Nationalpark	Pass	Landspitze
ESPAÑOL	bahía	montañas	cabo	presa	vedado de caza	parque nacional	paso	punta
FRANÇAIS	baie	montagnes	cap	barrage	réserve à gibier	parc national	col	pointe
PORTUGUÊS	baía	montanhas	cabo	represa	reserva de caça	parque nacional	passo	ponta

Pretoria
Johannesburg
Soweto
Krugersdorp
Germiston
Benoni
Springs
Vereeniging
Potchefstroom
Klerksdorp
Kroonstad
Welkom
Virginia
Bethlehem
Harrismith
Ladysmith
Newcastle
Dundee
Maseru
LESOTHO
Pietermaritzburg
DURBAN
Mbabane
SWAZILAND
Manzini
Maputo
(Lourenço Marques)
MOZAMBIQUE
MOÇAMBIQUE
Piet Retief
Standerton
Ermelo
Middelburg
Witbank
DRAKENSBERG
TRANSKEI
Umtata
Queenstown
King William's Town
East London
Oos-Londen
Grahamstown
Port Alfred
Elizabeth
Port Shepstone
Richard's Bay
Stanger
Empangeni
INDIAN
OCEAN
WILD COAST
ZULULAND
CISKEI
Copyright © by Rand McNally & Co.
Map prepared by George Philip & Son Ltd., London.

Kilometers 0 50 100 150 Km.
Statute Miles 0 50 100 150 Mi.

Scale 1:3,000,000

One centimeter represents 30 kilometers.
One inch represents approximately 47 miles.
Lambert Conformal Conic Projection

ENGLISH	bay	cape	island	lake	mount	point	range	reef
DEUTSCH	Bucht	Kap	Insel	See	Berg	Landspitze	Gebirge	Riff
ESPAÑOL	bahía	cabo	isla	lago	montaña	punta	cordillera	arrecife
FRANÇAIS	baie	cap	île	lac	mont	pointe	chaîne	récif
PORTUGUÊS	baía	cabo	ilha	lago	monte	ponta	cordilheira	recife

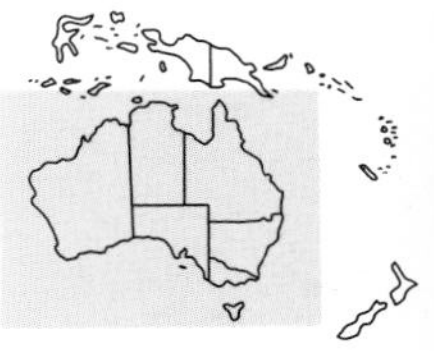

Kilometers 0 200 400 600 Km.
Statute Miles 0 200 400 600 Mi.

Scale 1:12,000,000

One centimeter represents 120 kilometers.
One inch represents approximately 190 miles.
Lambert Conformal Conic Projection

Western and Central Australia / West-und Mittelaustralien / Australia Centro-occidental
Australie Occidentale et Centrale / Austrália Ocidental e Central

INDIAN OCEAN
GREAT SANDY DESERT
GIBSON DESERT
WESTERN AUSTRALIA
Tropic of Capricorn
Meters
Feet
6000 19685
4000 13124
3000 9843
2000 6562
1000 3281
500 1640
200 656
0 0
Land Below Sea Level
200 656
1000 3281
3000 9843
6000 19685
9000 29520
Perth
Fremantle
Geraldton
Kalgoorlie
Bunbury
Albany
Esperance
Carnarvon
Port Hedland
Broome
Derby
Shark Bay
Lake Carnegie
Lake Disappointment
Hamersley Range
Kennedy Range
Stirling Range
Copyright © by Rand McNally & Co.
Map prepared by George Philip & Son Ltd., London.
A-590294-764

ENGLISH	bay	cape	creek, cr.	island, i.	lake, l.	mount	point	range
DEUTSCH	Bucht	Kap	Bach	Insel	See	Berg	Landspitze	Gebirge
ESPAÑOL	bahía	cabo	riachuelo	isla	lago	montaña	punta	cordillera
FRANÇAIS	baie	cap	crique	île	lac	mont	pointe	chaîne
PORTUGUÊS	baía	cabo	riacho	ilha	lago	monte	ponta	cordilheira

Kilometers 0 100 200 300 Km.
Statute Miles 0 100 200 300 Mi.
Scale 1:6,000,000
One centimeter represents 60 kilometers.
One inch represents approximately 95 miles.
Lambert Conformal Conic Projection

Northern Australia and New Guinea / Nordaustralien und Neuguinea / Australia Septentrional y Nueva Guinea / Australie Septentrionale et Nouvelle Guinée / Austrália Setentrional e Nova Guiné

MAP FORM	bay	cape	island	kepulauan	mount	pulau	range	tanjung
ENGLISH	bay	cape	island	islands	mount	island	range	cape
DEUTSCH	Bucht	Kap	Insel	Inseln	Berg	Insel	Gebirge	Kap
ESPAÑOL	bahía	cabo	isla	islas	montaña	isla	cordillera	cabo
FRANÇAIS	baie	cap	île	îles	mont	île	chaîne	cap
PORTUGUÊS	baía	cabo	ilha	ilhas	monte	ilha	cordilheira	cabo

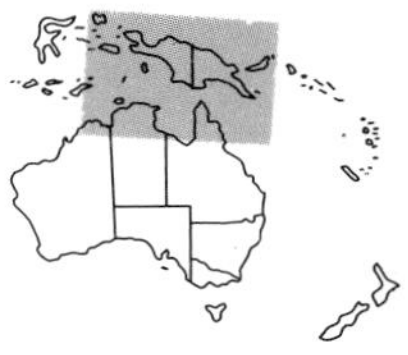

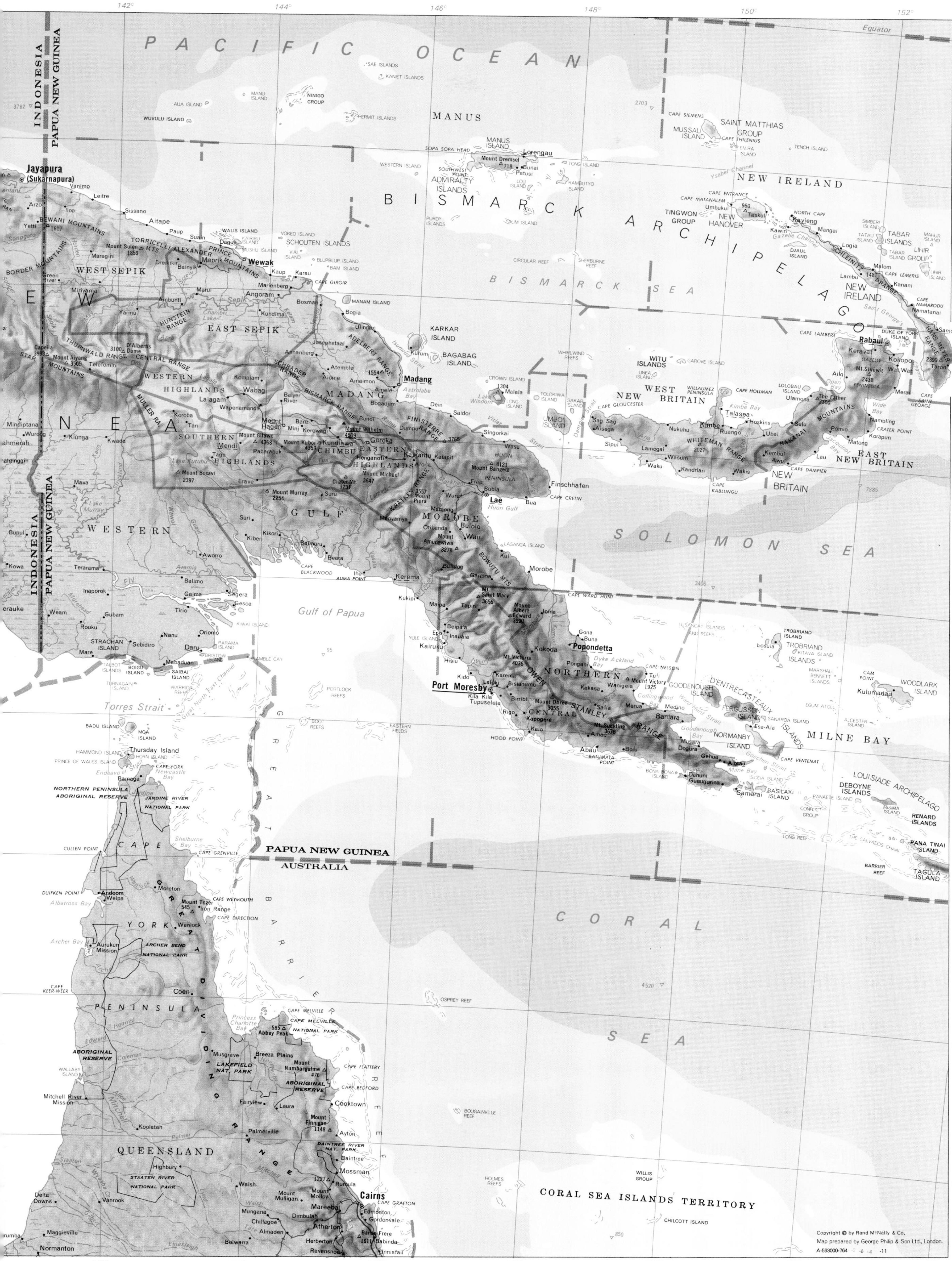

166 - 167

Kilometers 0 100 200 300 Km.
Statute Miles 0 100 200 300 Mi.

Scale 1:6,000,000
One centimeter represents 60 kilometers.
One inch represents approximately 95 miles.
Lambert Conformal Conic Projection

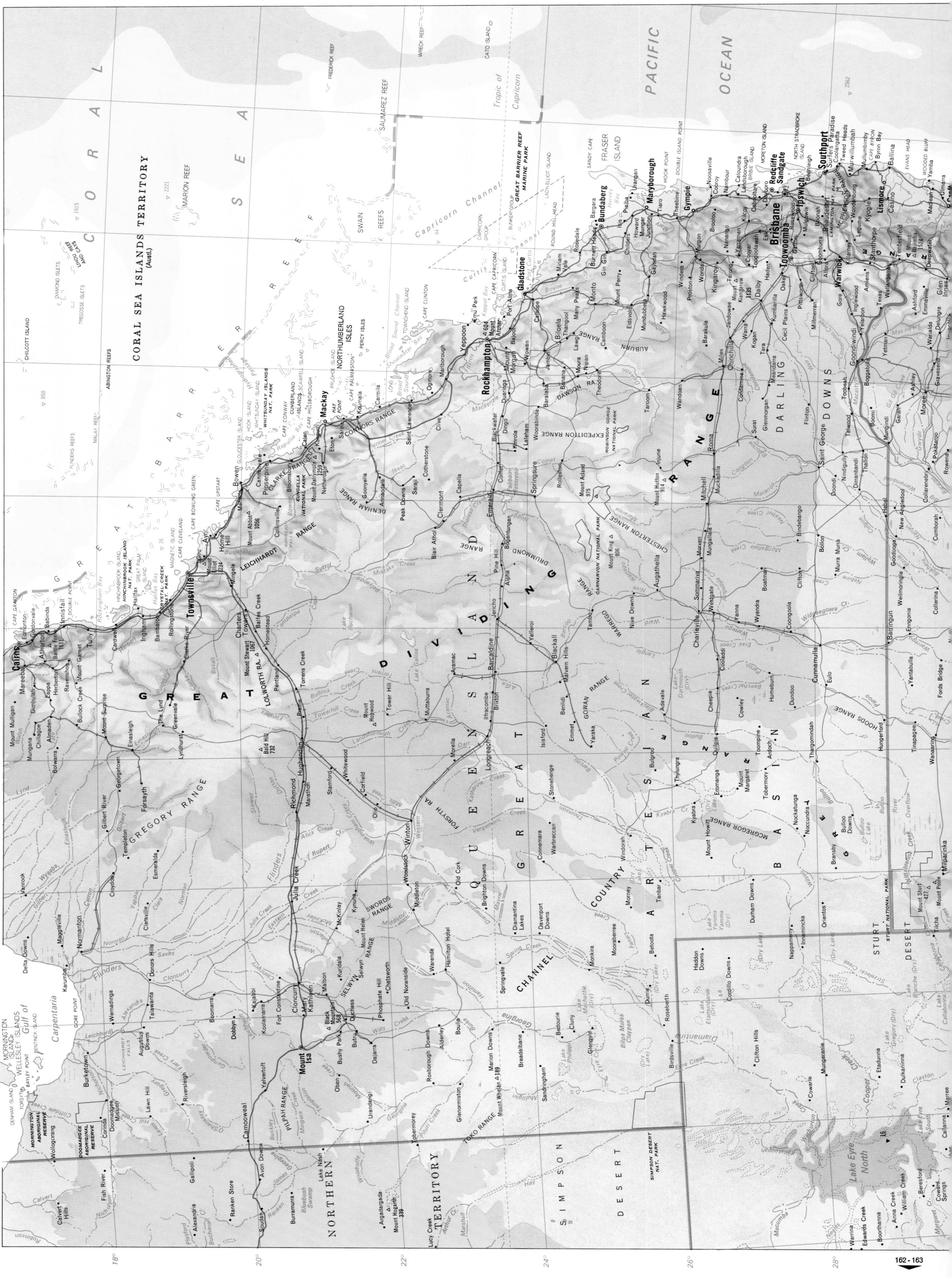

164-165
162-163

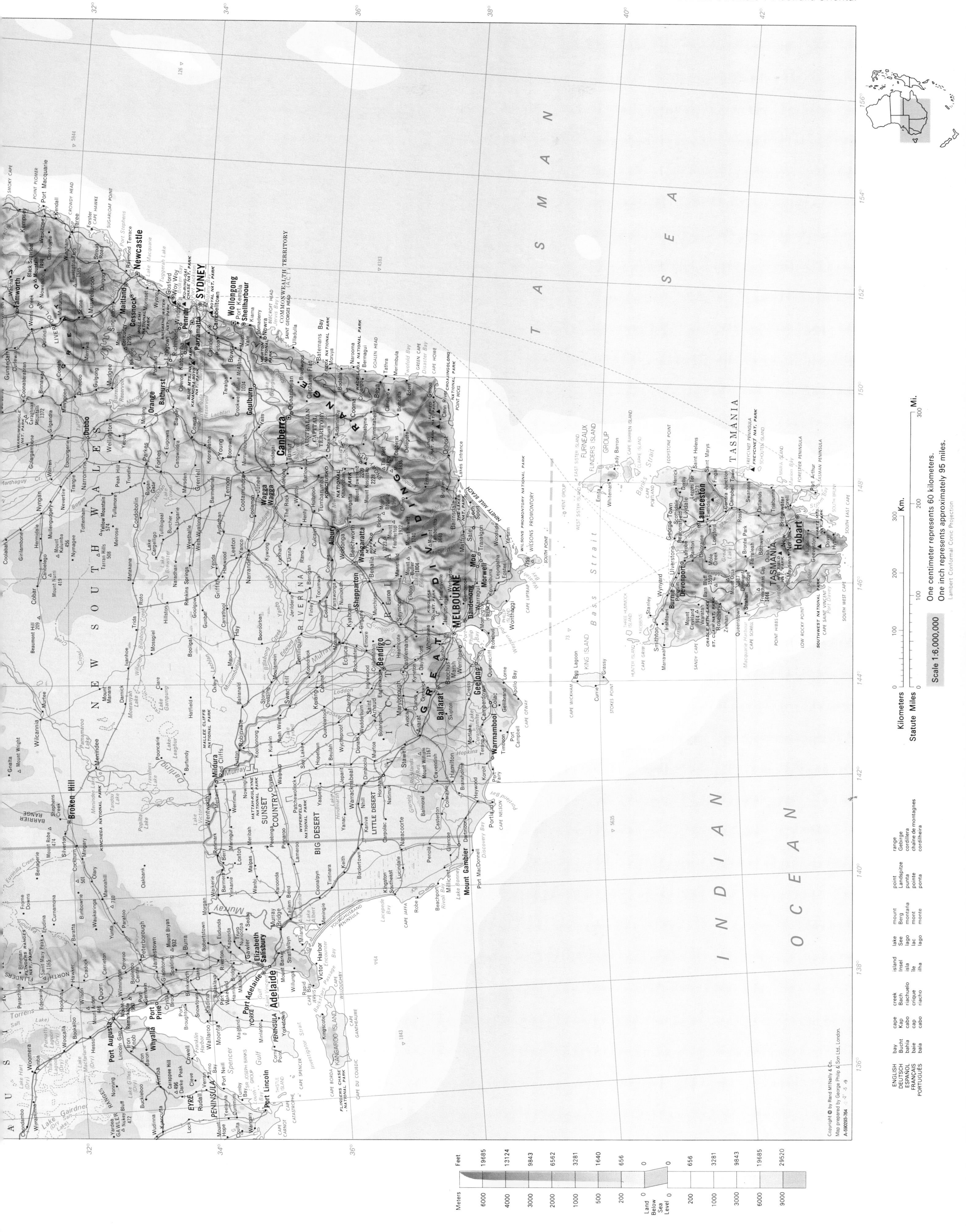
SYDNEY
Newcastle
Wollongong
Canberra
AUSTRALIAN CAPITAL TERRITORY
MELBOURNE
Geelong
Ballarat
Bendigo
Adelaide
Broken Hill
Port Augusta
Whyalla
Port Lincoln
Mount Gambier
Hobart
Launceston
TASMANIA
NEW SOUTH WALES
VICTORIA
GREAT DIVIDING RANGE
T A S M A N S E A
I N D I A N O C E A N
Bass Strait
KING ISLAND
FURNEAUX GROUP
FLINDERS ISLAND
KANGAROO ISLAND
Kilometers
Statute Miles
Km.
Mi.
Scale 1:6,000,000
One centimeter represents 60 kilometers.
One inch represents approximately 95 miles.
Lambert Conformal Conic Projection
ENGLISH bay cape creek island lake mount point range
DEUTSCH Bucht Kap Bach Insel See Berg Landspitze Gebirge
ESPAÑOL bahía cabo riachuelo isla lago montaña punta cordillera
FRANÇAIS baie cap crique île lac mont pointe chaîne de montagnes
PORTUGUÊS baía cabo riacho ilha lago monte ponta cordilheira
Copyright © by Rand McNally & Co.
Map prepared by George Philip & Son Ltd, London.
Feet
Meters
Land Below Sea Level
19685 13124 9843 6562 3281 1640 656 0
6000 4000 3000 2000 1000 500 200 0
656 3281 9843 19685 29520
200 1000 3000 6000 9000

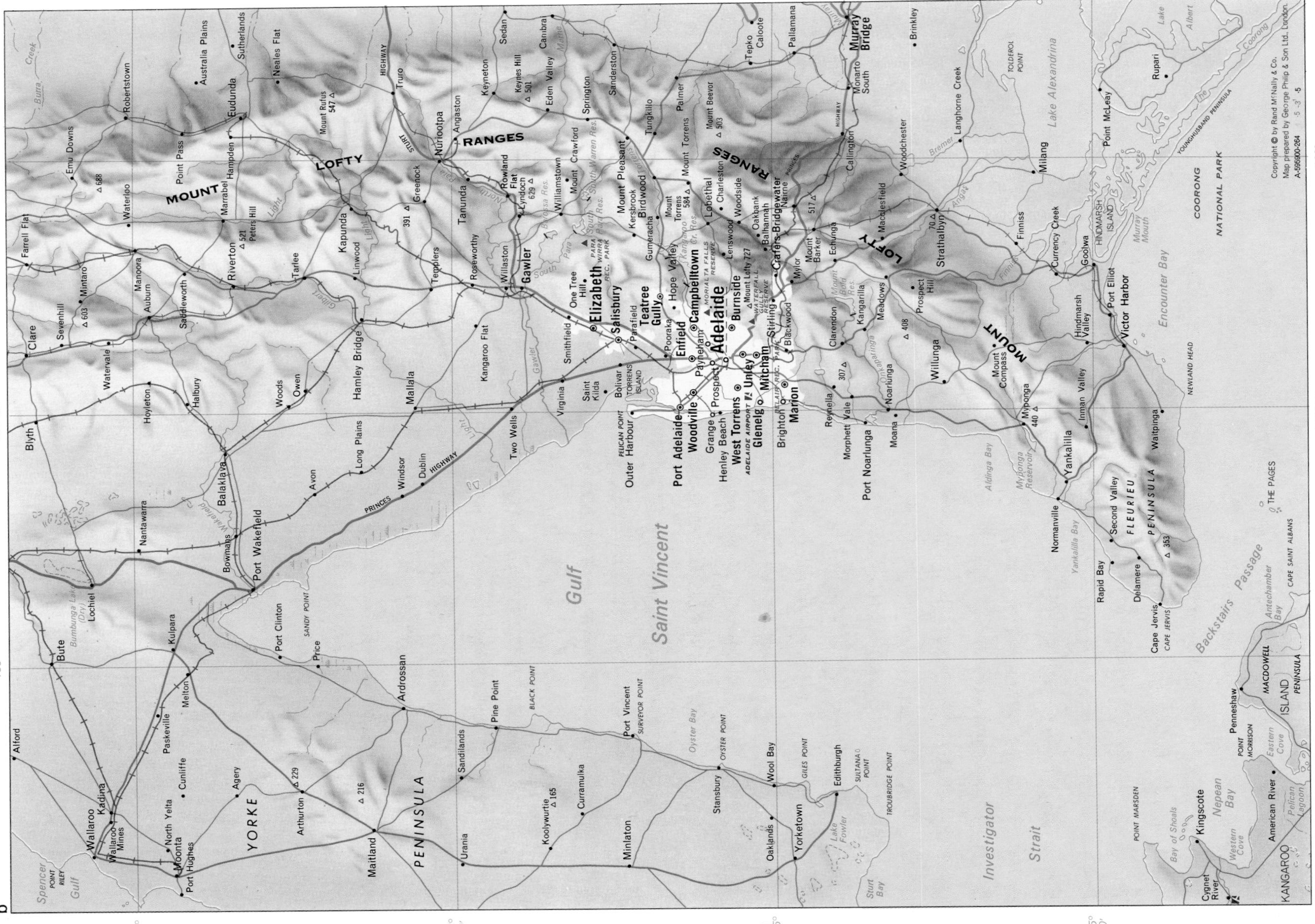

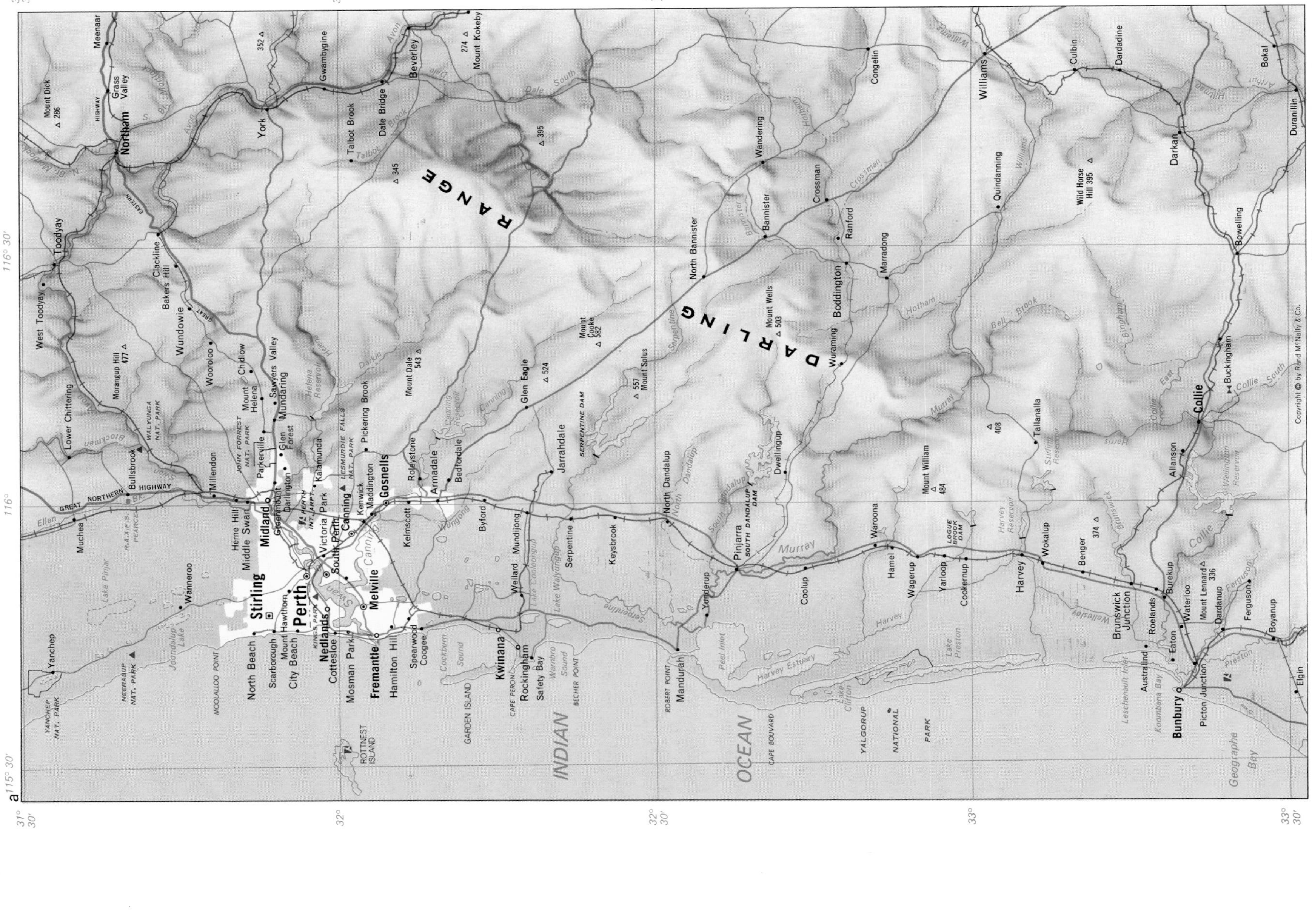

ENGLISH	bay, b.	cape	dam	gulf	island	lake, l.	peninsula	point
DEUTSCH	Bucht	Kap	Damm	Golf	Insel	See	Halbinsel	Landspitze
ESPAÑOL	bahía	cabo	diques	golfo	isla	lago	península	punta
FRANÇAIS	baie	cap	barrage	golfe	île	lac	péninsule	pointe
PORTUGUES	baía	cabo	barragem	golfo	ilha	lago	península	ponta

Kilometers 0 10 20 30 40 50 Km.

Statute Miles 0 10 20 30 40 50 Mi.

Scale 1:1,000,000

One centimeter represents 10 kilometers.
One inch represents approximately 16 miles.
Lambert Conformal Conic Projection

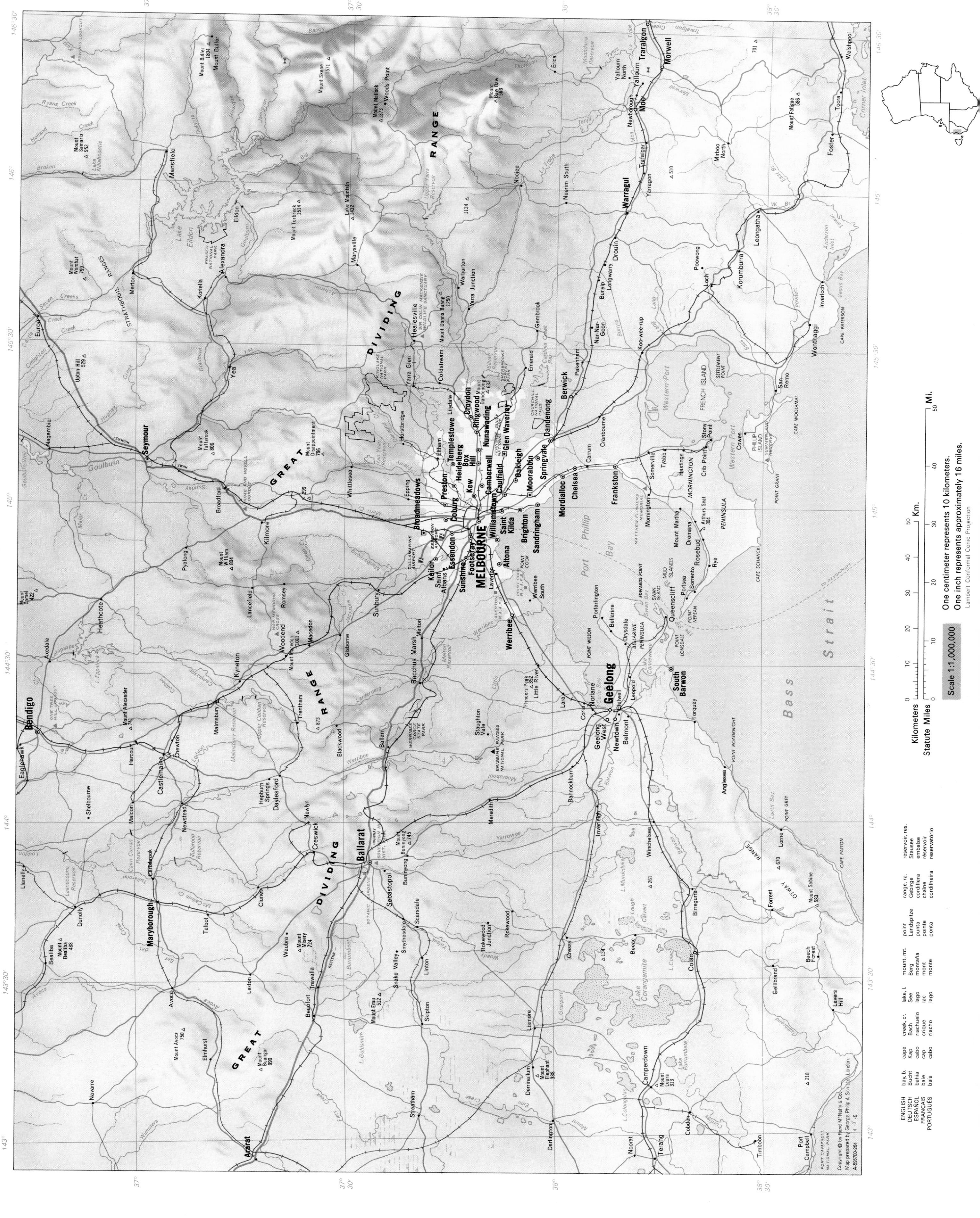
Scale 1:1,000,000
One centimeter represents 10 kilometers.
One inch represents approximately 16 miles.
Lambert Conformal Conic Projection
Kilometers
Statute Miles
Bass Strait
Port Phillip Bay
MELBOURNE
Geelong
Ballarat
Bendigo
GREAT DIVIDING RANGE
ENGLISH bay, b. cape creek, cr. lake, l. mount, mt. point range, ra. reservoir, res.
DEUTSCH Bucht Kap Bach See Berg Landspitze Gebirge Stausee
ESPAÑOL bahía cabo riachuelo lago montaña punta cordillera embalse
FRANÇAIS baie cap crique lac mont pointe chaîne reservoir
PORTUGUÊS baía cabo riacho lago monte ponta cordilheira reservatório
Copyright © by Rand McNally & Co.
Map prepared by George Philip & Son Ltd. London.

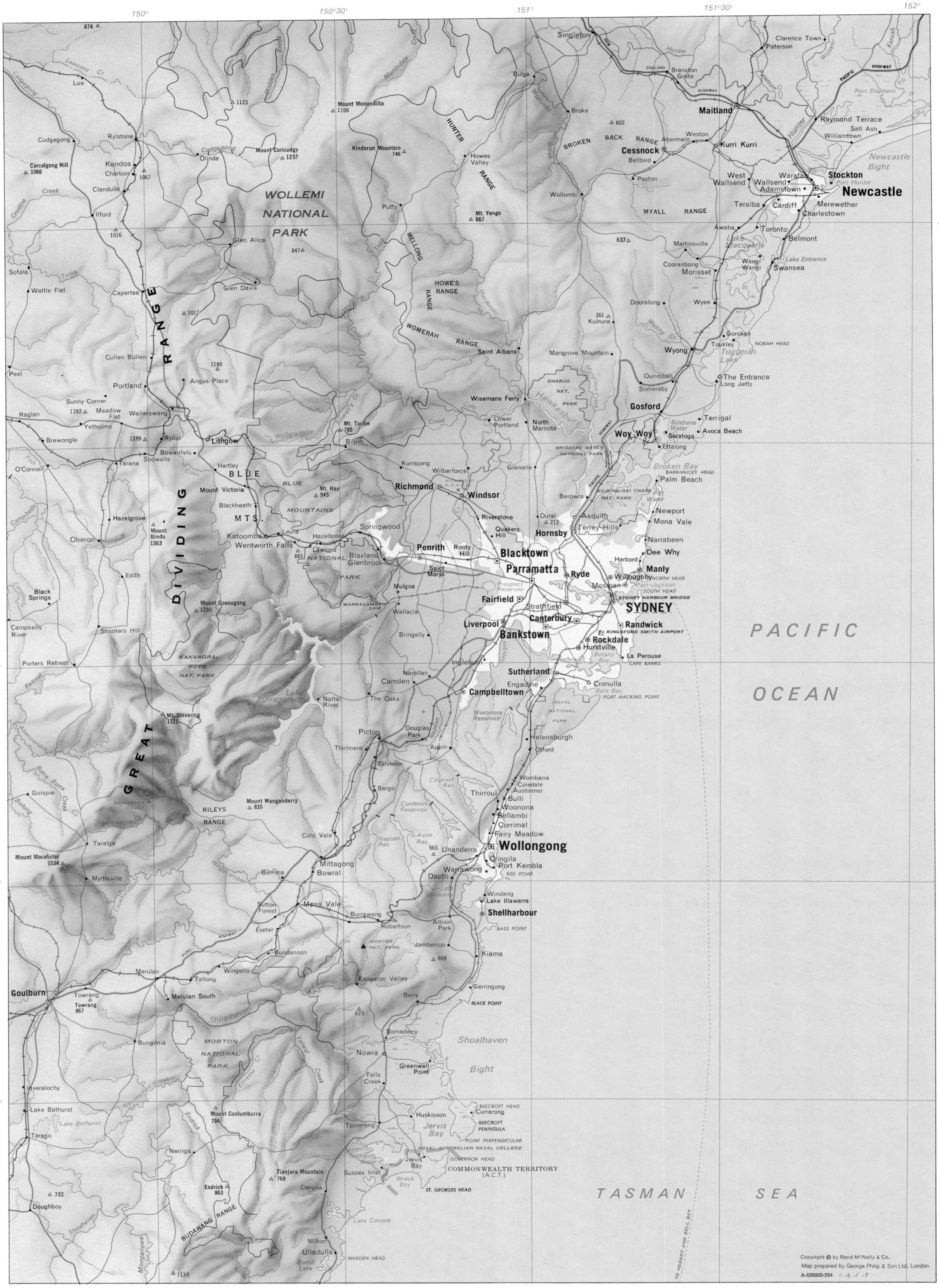

ENGLISH	bight	creek, cr.	head	mount	range	reservoir, res.
DEUTSCH	Bucht	Bach	Vorgebirge	Berg	Gebirge	Stausee
ESPAÑOL	ensenada pequeña	riachuelo	promontorio	montaña	cordillera	estanque
FRANÇAIS	anse	crique	promontoire	mont	chaîne	réservoir
PORTUGUÊS	enseada	riacho	promontório	monte	cordilheira	reservatório

Kilometers 0 10 20 30 40 50 Km.

Statute Miles 0 10 20 30 40 50 Mi.

Scale 1:1,000,000

One centimeter represents 10 kilometers.
One inch represents approximately 16 miles.

Lambert Conformal Conic Projection

a

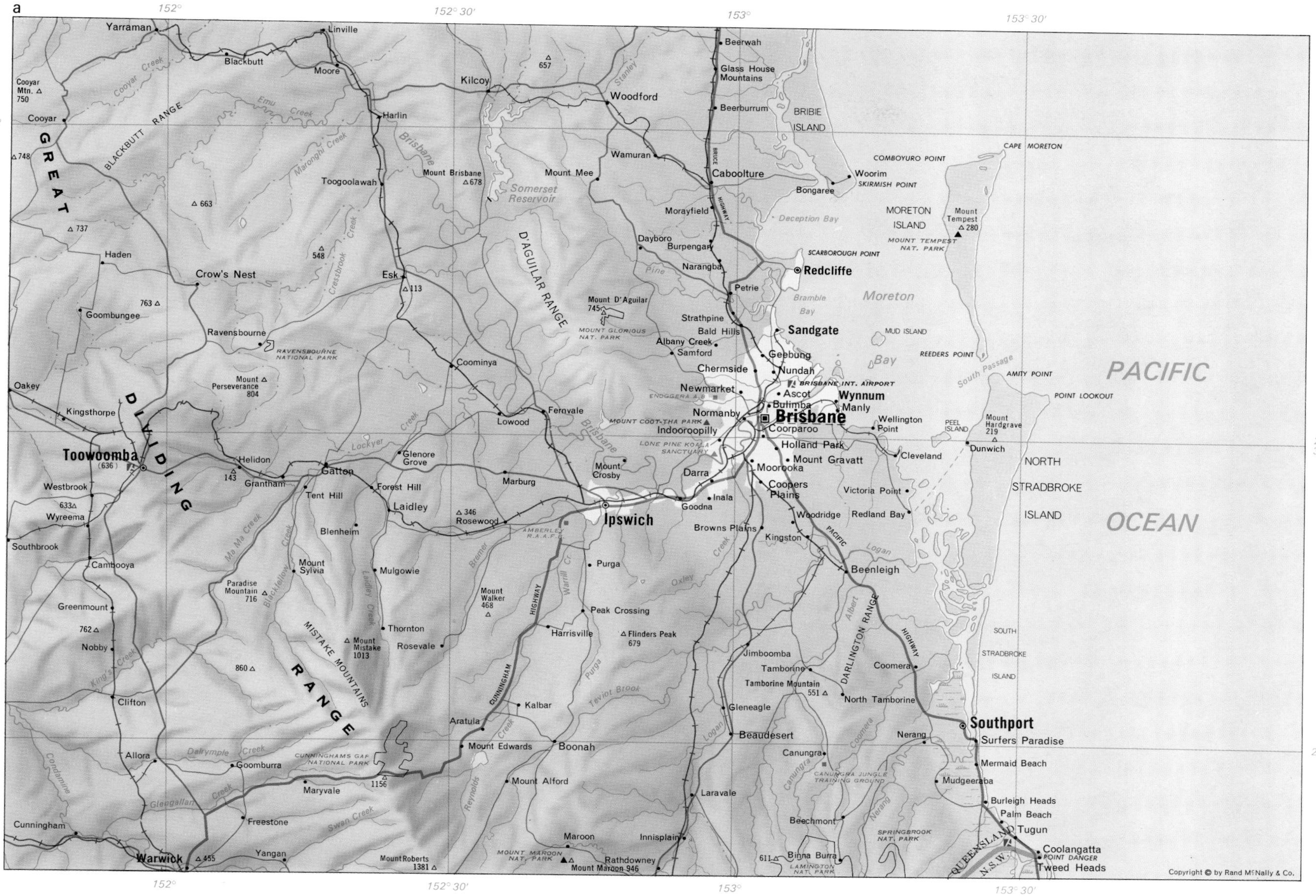

b

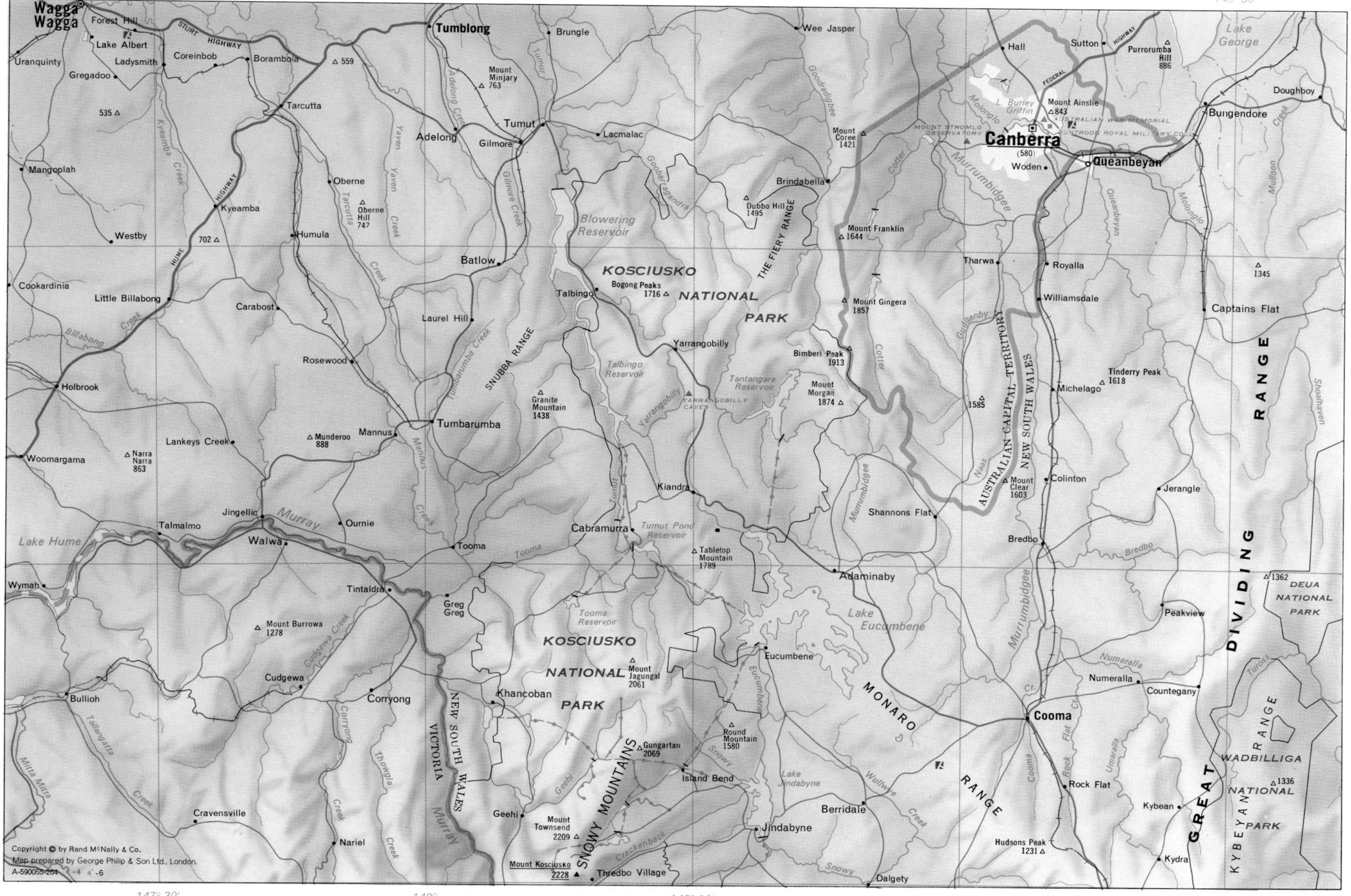

ENGLISH	creek	island	mount	peak	point	range	reservoir
DEUTSCH	Bach	Insel	Berg	Gipfel	Landspitze	Gebirge	Stausee
ESPAÑOL	riachuelo	isla	montaña	pico	punta	cordillera	embalse
FRANÇAIS	crique	île	mont	cime	pointe	chaîne	réservoir
PORTUGUÊS	riacho	ilha	monte	pico	ponta	cordilheira	reservatório

Kilometers 0 10 20 30 40 50 Km.

Statute Miles 0 10 20 30 40 50 Mi.

Scale 1:1,000,000

One centimeter represents 10 kilometers.
One inch represents approximately 16 miles.

Lambert Conformal Conic Projection

New Zealand / Neuseeland / Nueva Zelanda
Nouvelle Zélande / Nova Zelândia

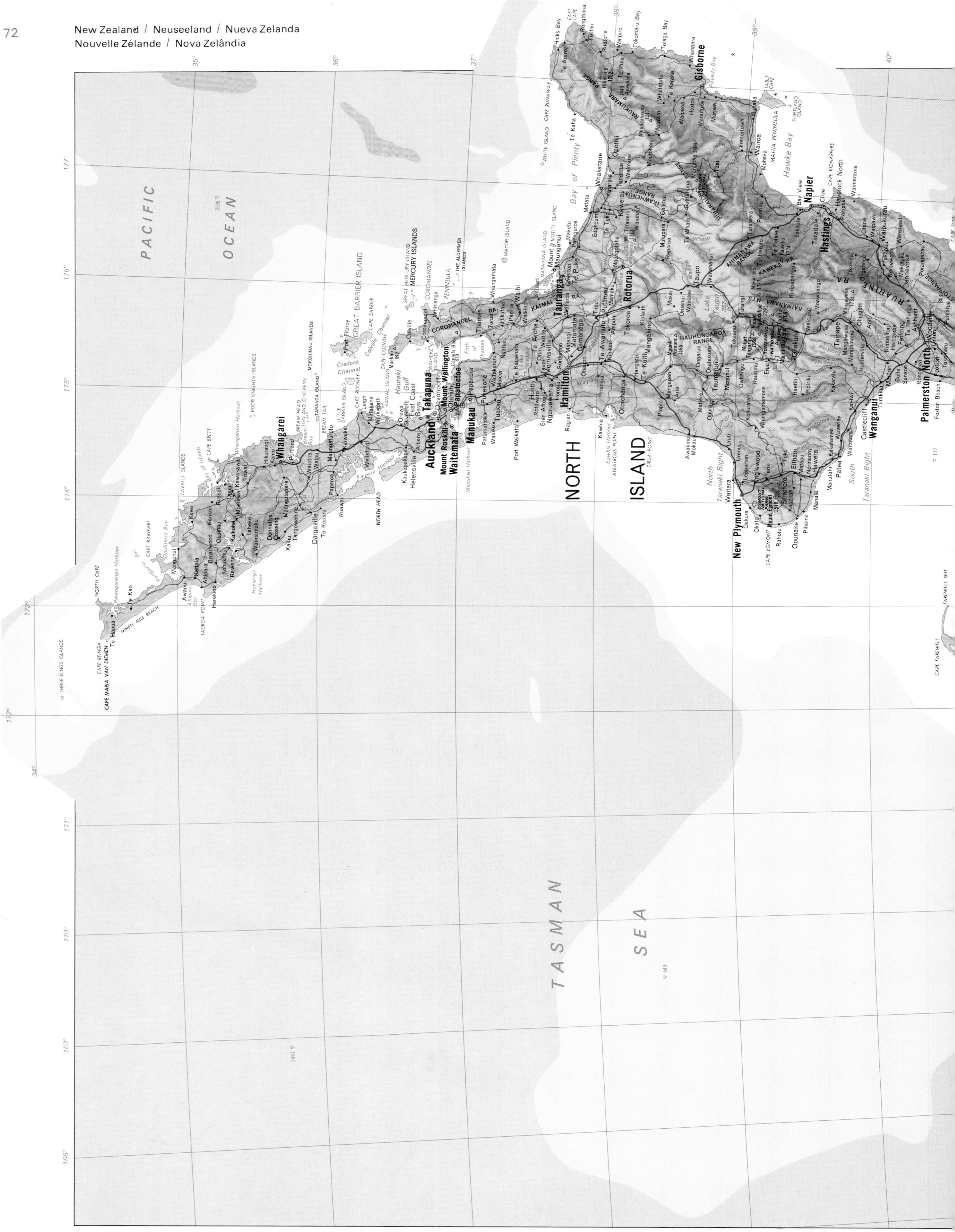
PACIFIC
OCEAN
TASMAN
SEA
NORTH
ISLAND
Auckland
Manukau
Hamilton
Tauranga
Rotorua
Gisborne
Napier
Hastings
Whangarei
New Plymouth
Wanganui
Palmerston North
Bay of Plenty
Hawke Bay
North Taranaki Bight
South Taranaki Bight
GREAT BARRIER ISLAND
Hauraki Gulf
Firth of Thames
Lake Taupo
CAPE MARIA VAN DIEMEN
NORTH CAPE
EAST CAPE
CAPE EGMONT
THREE KINGS ISLANDS
MERCURY ISLANDS
COROMANDEL PENINSULA
Kaipara Harbour
Manukau Harbour

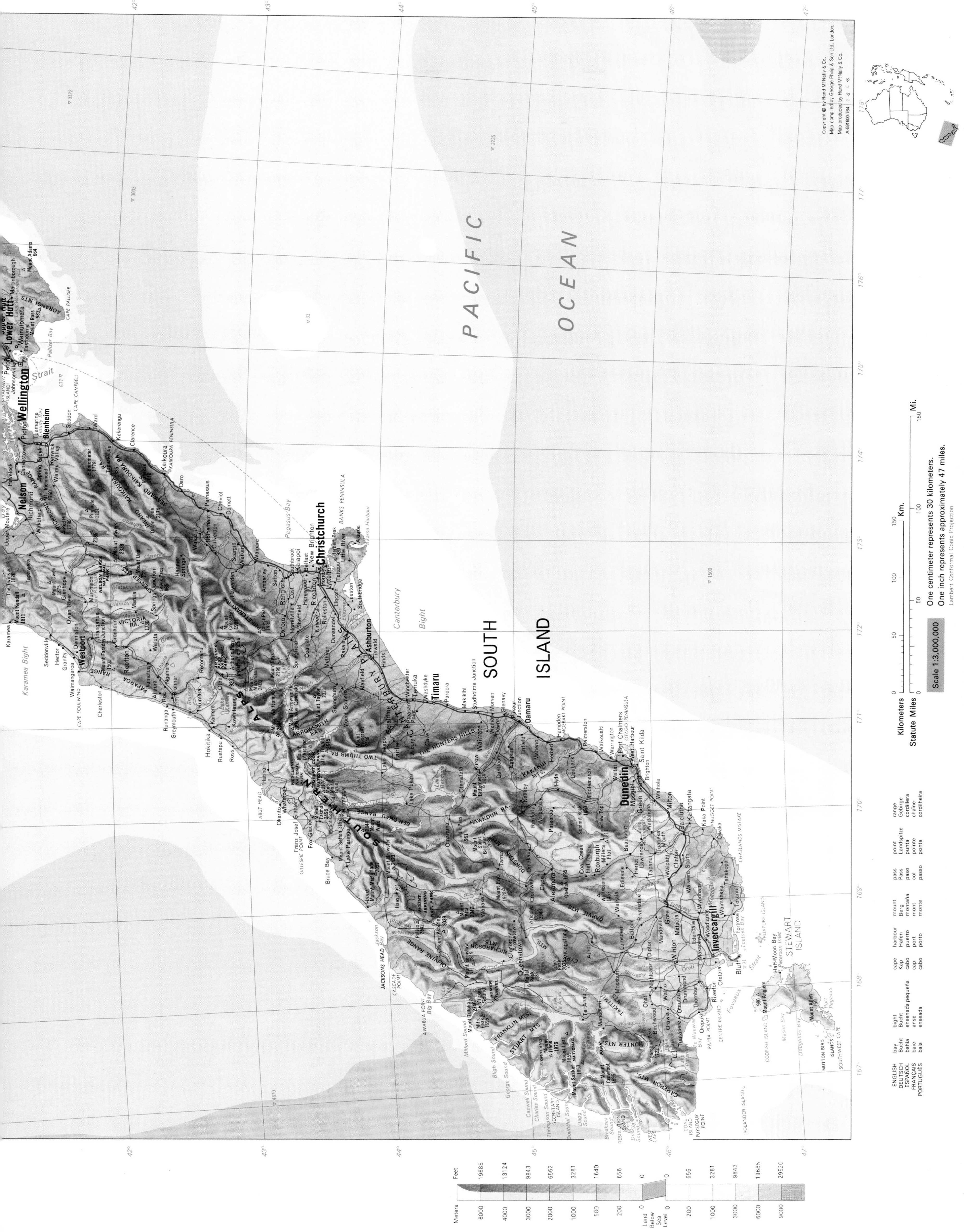
PACIFIC
OCEAN
SOUTH
ISLAND
STEWART
ISLAND
Canterbury
Bight
Pegasus Bay
Karamea Bight
Strait
Foveaux
Wellington
Lower Hutt
Nelson
Blenheim
Kaikoura
Christchurch
Ashburton
Timaru
Oamaru
Dunedin
Invercargill
Queenstown
Greymouth
Westport
Hokitika
Bluff
SOUTHERN ALPS
BANKS PENINSULA
KAIKOURA PENINSULA
Copyright © by Rand McNally & Co.
Map compiled by George Philip & Son Ltd. London.
Map produced by Rand McNally & Co.
A-591600-784
Scale 1:3,000,000
One centimeter represents 30 kilometers.
One inch represents approximately 47 miles.
Lambert Conformal Conic Projection
Kilometers
Statute Miles
Km.
Mi.
ENGLISH bay cape harbour mount pass point range
DEUTSCH Bucht Kap Hafen Berg Pass Landspitze Gebirge
ESPAÑOL bahía cabo puerto montaña paso punta cordillera
FRANÇAIS baie cap port mont col pointe chaîne
PORTUGUÊS baía cabo porto monte passo ponta cordilheira
Feet
Meters
Land Below Sea Level

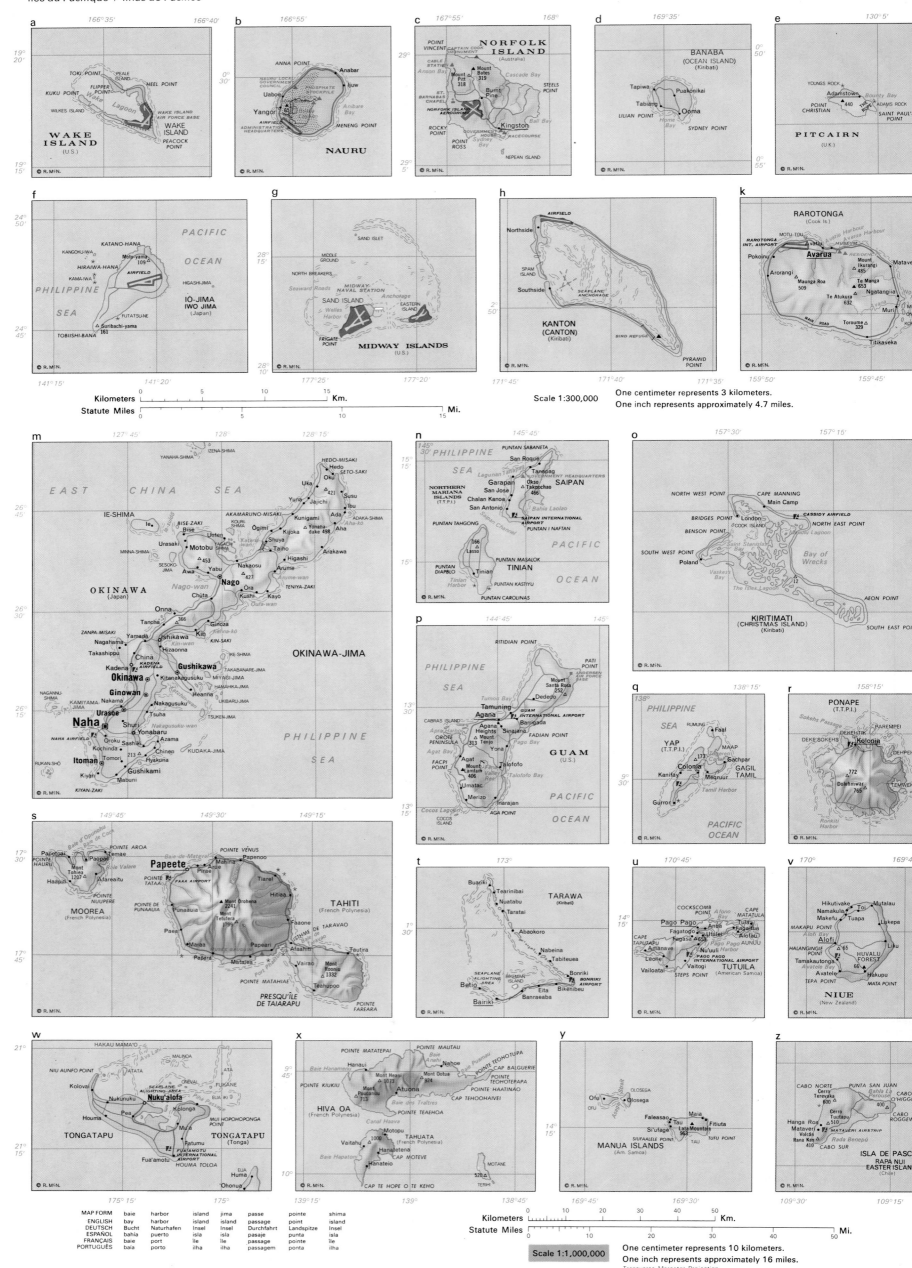

Islands of the Pacific / Pazifische Inseln / Islas del Pacífico
Îles du Pacifique / Ilhas do Pacífico

a

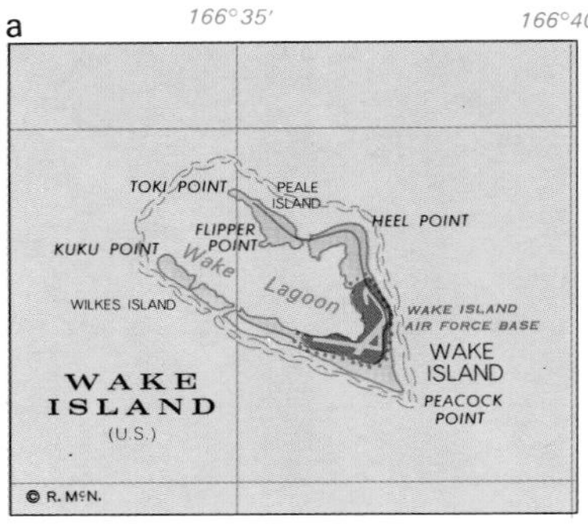

b

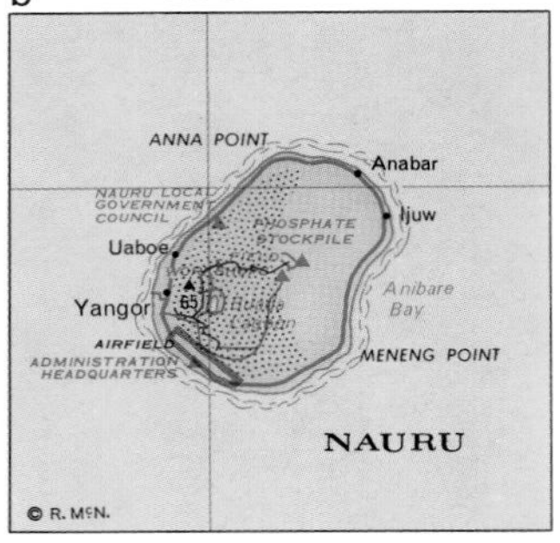

c

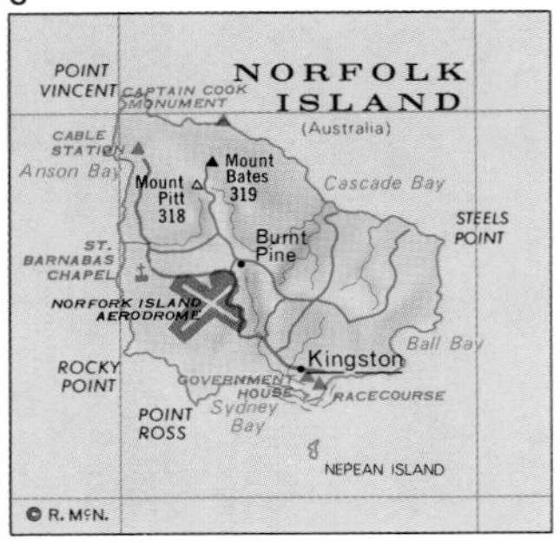

d

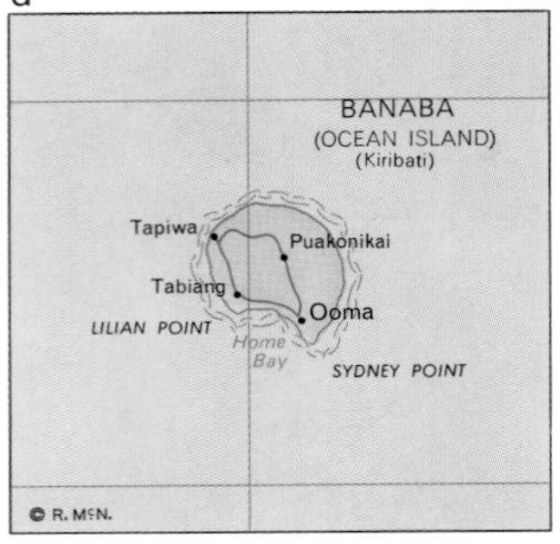

e

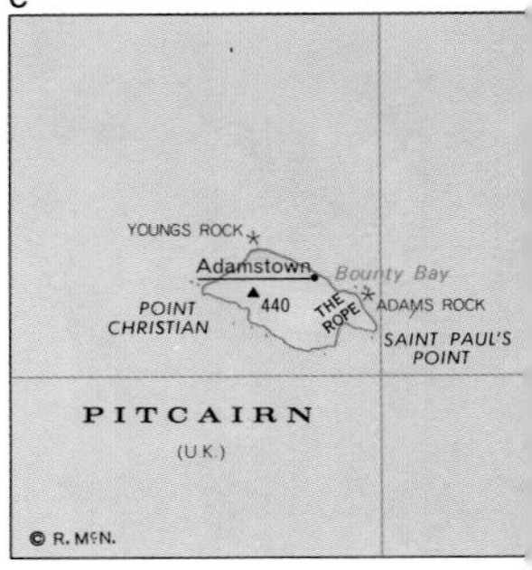

f

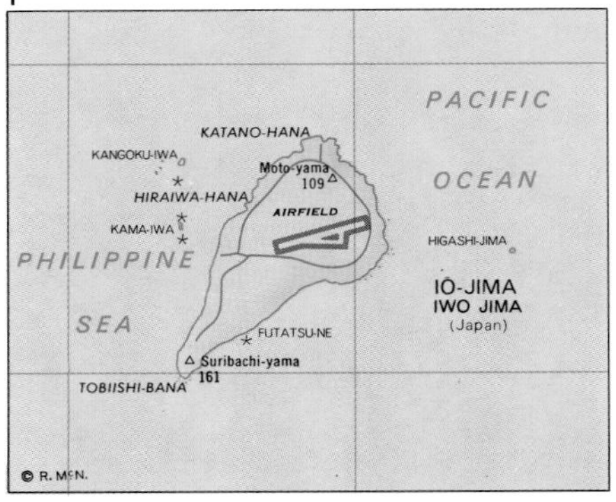

g

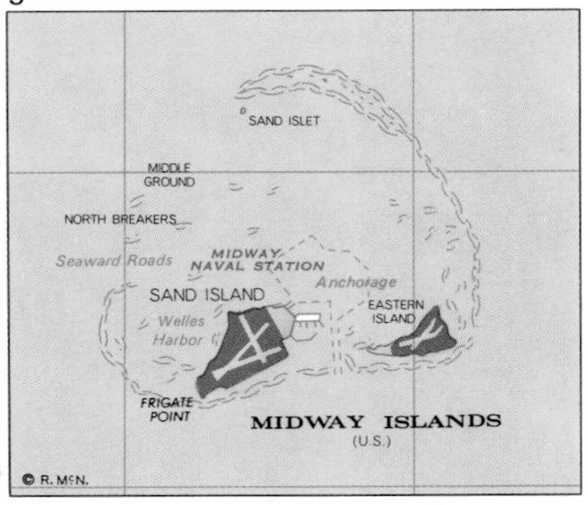

h

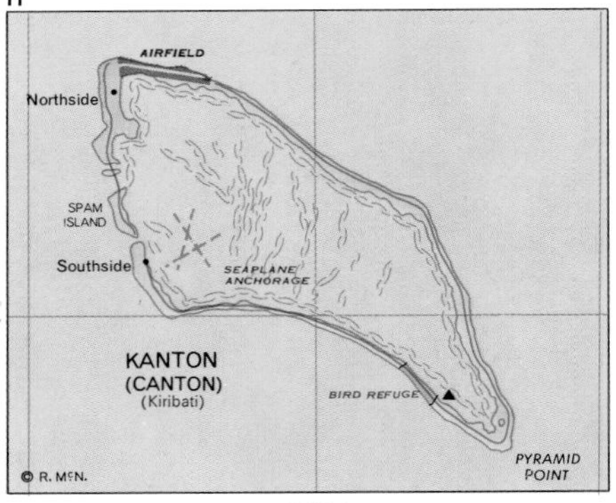

k

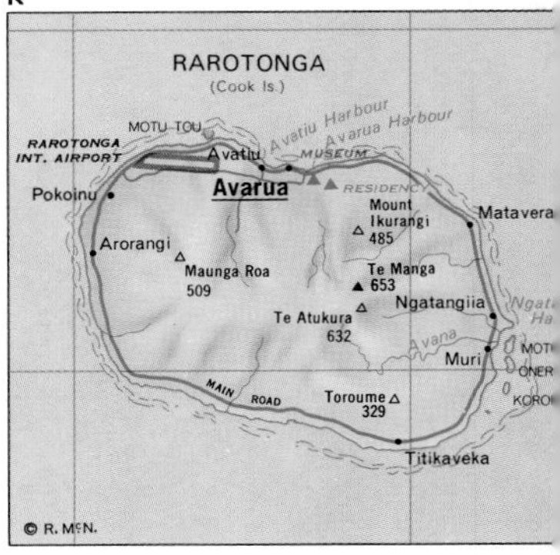

141°15′ 141°20′ 177°25′ 177°20′ 171°45′ 171°40′ 171°35′ 159°50′ 159°45′

Kilometers 0 5 10 15 Km.
Statute Miles 0 5 10 15 Mi.

Scale 1:300,000
One centimeter represents 3 kilometers.
One inch represents approximately 4.7 miles.

m

n

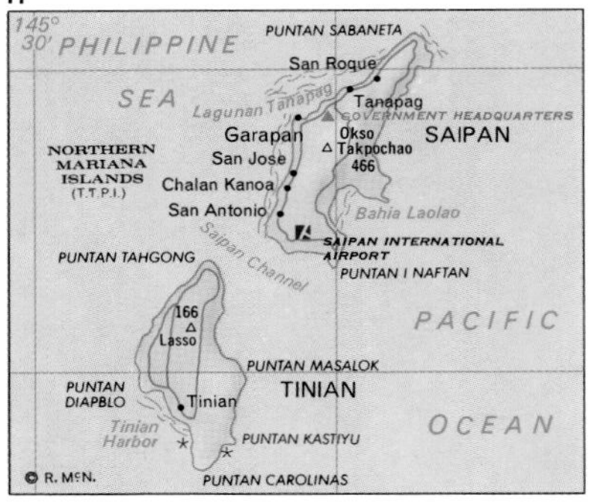

o

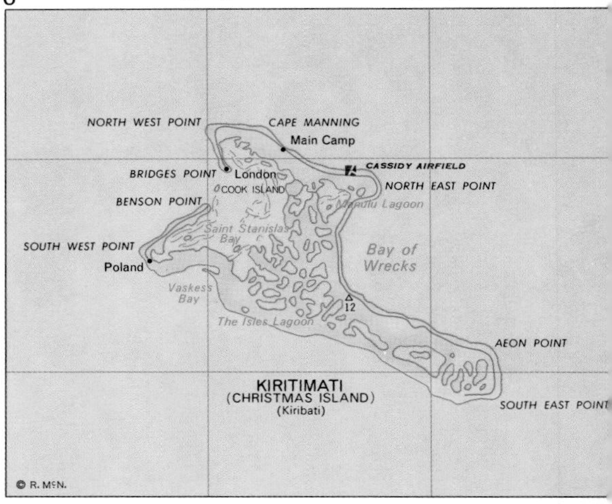

p

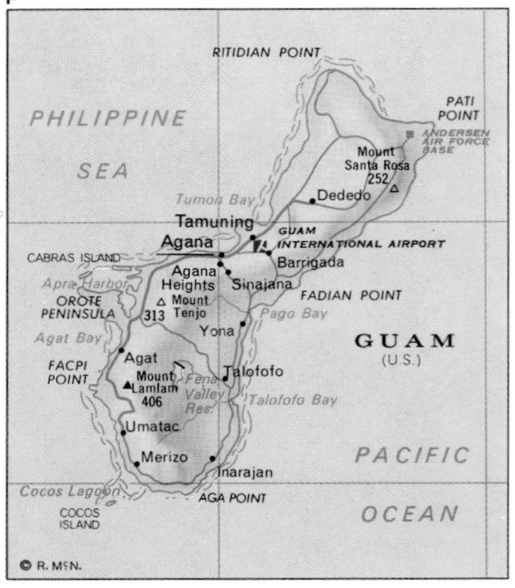

q

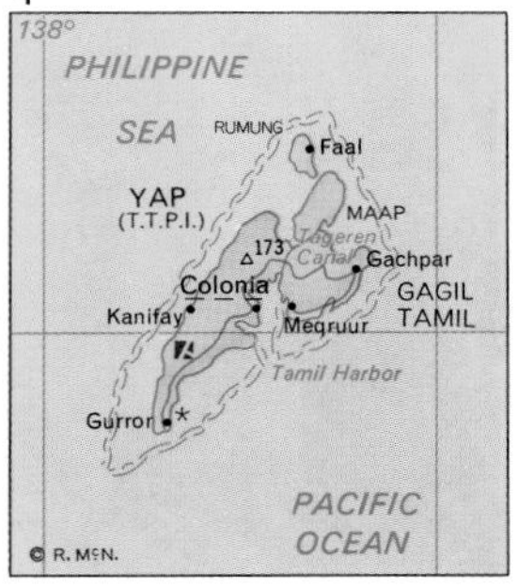

r

s

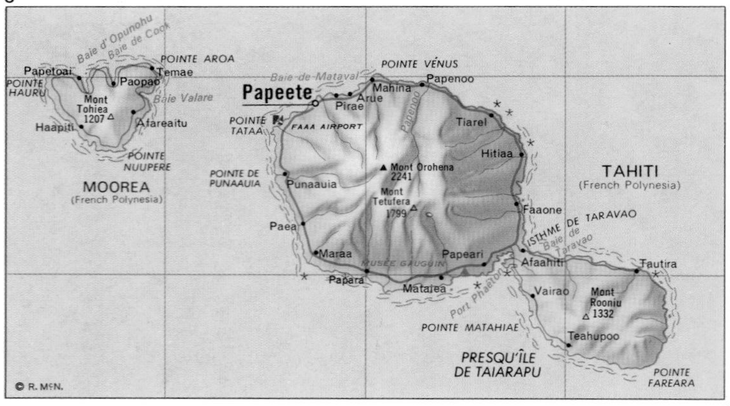

t

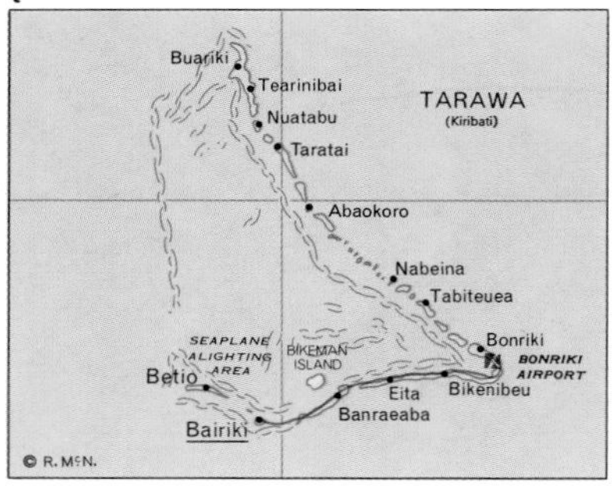

u

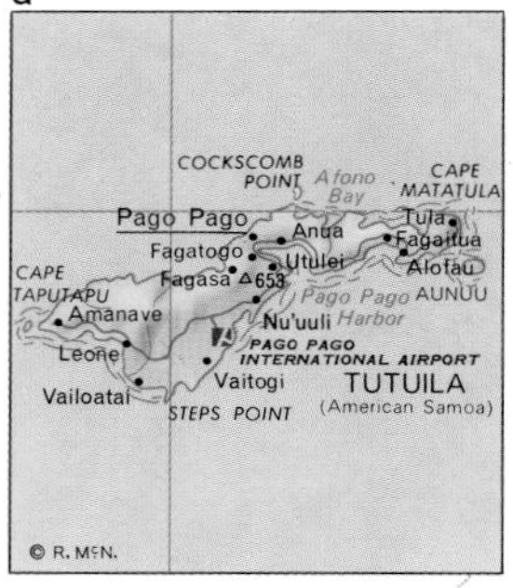

v

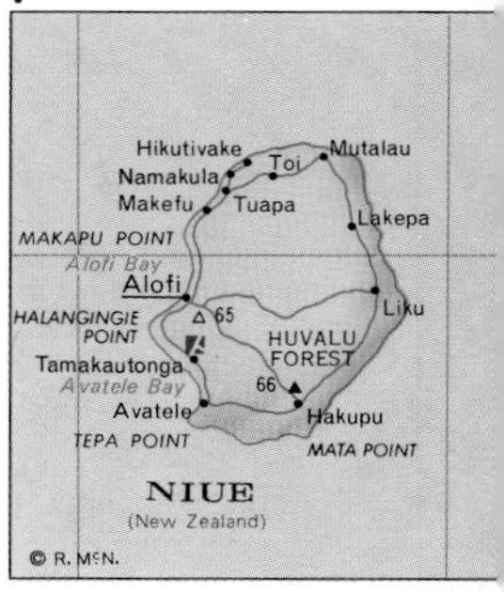

w

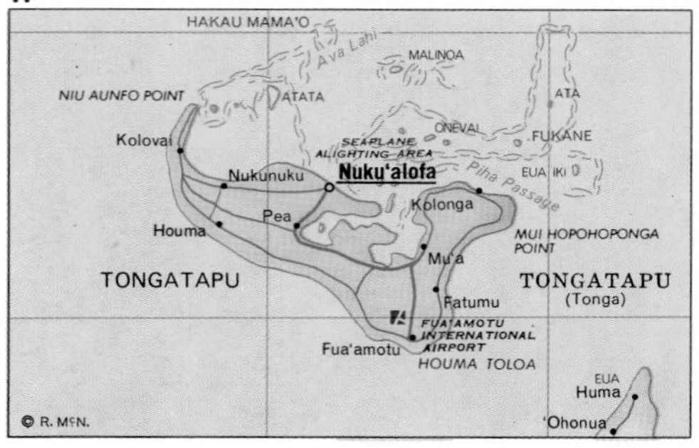

x

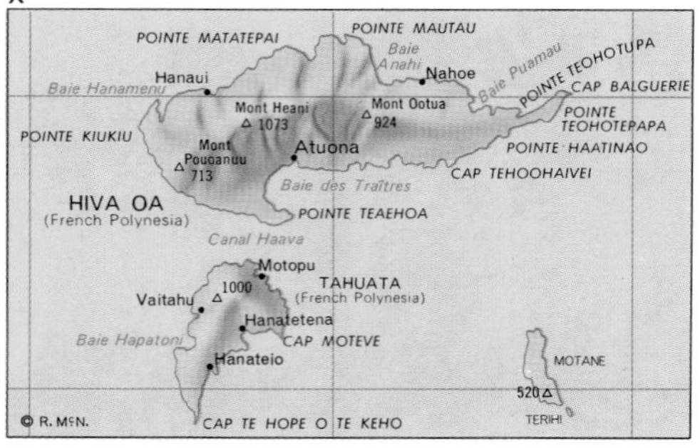

y

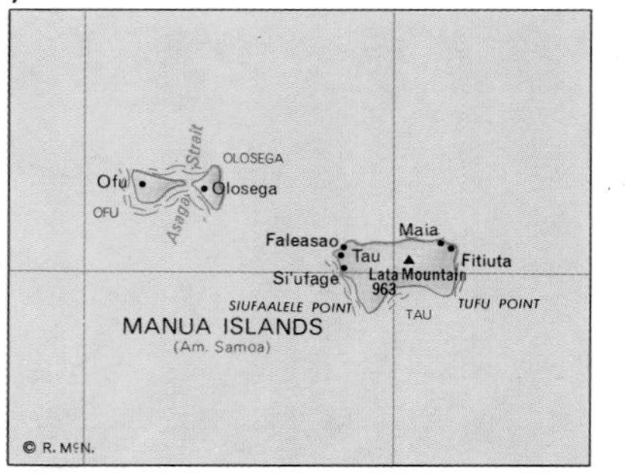

z

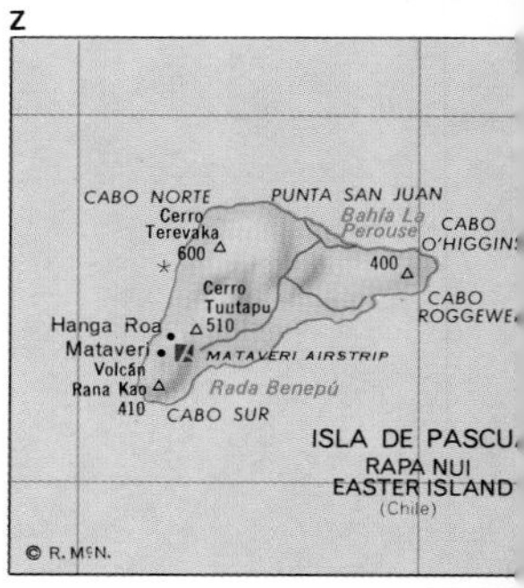

175°15′ 175° 139°15′ 139° 138°45′ 169°45′ 169°30′ 109°30′ 109°15′

MAP FORM	baie	harbor	island	jima	passe	pointe	shima
ENGLISH	bay	harbor	island	island	passage	point	island
DEUTSCH	Bucht	Naturhafen	Insel	Insel	Durchfahrt	Landspitze	Insel
ESPAÑOL	bahía	puerto	isla	isla	pasaje	punta	isla
FRANÇAIS	baie	port	île	île	passage	pointe	île
PORTUGUÊS	baía	porto	ilha	ilha	passagem	ponta	ilha

Kilometers 0 10 20 30 40 50 Km.
Statute Miles 0 10 20 30 40 50 Mi.

Scale 1:1,000,000
One centimeter represents 10 kilometers.
One inch represents approximately 16 miles.
Transverse Mercator Projection

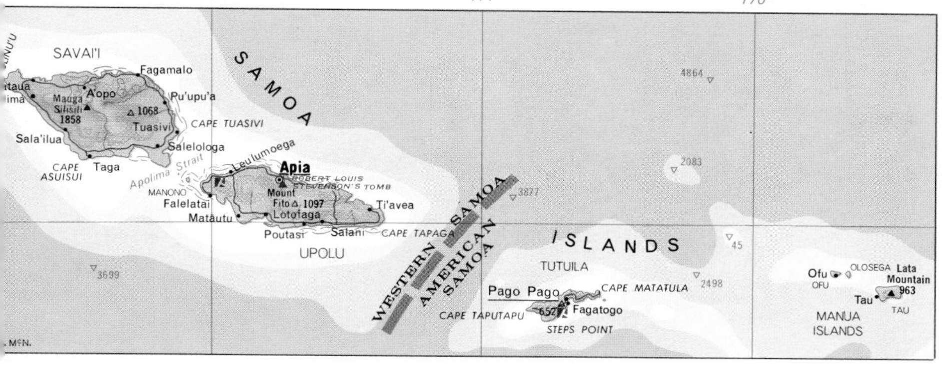

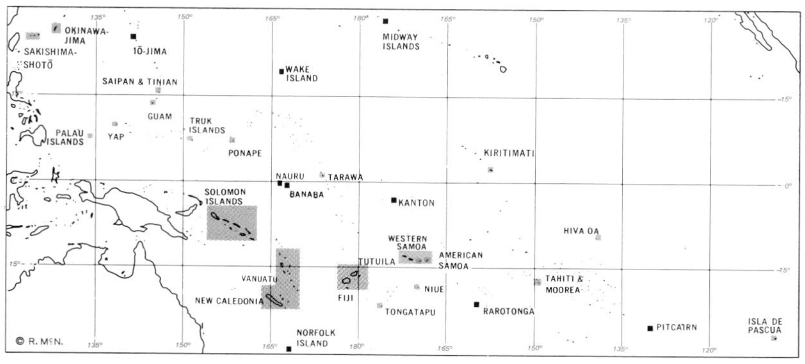

c

d

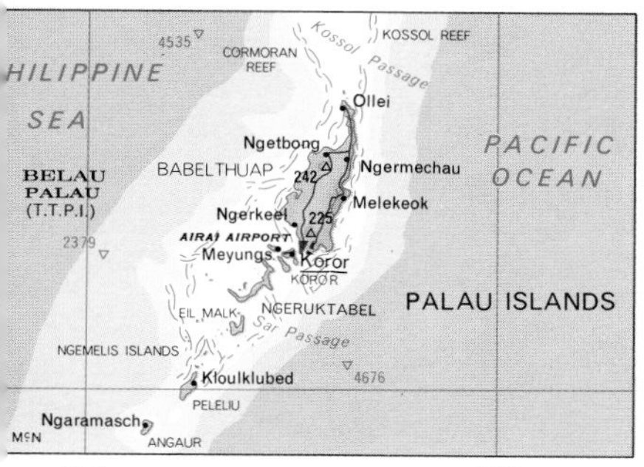

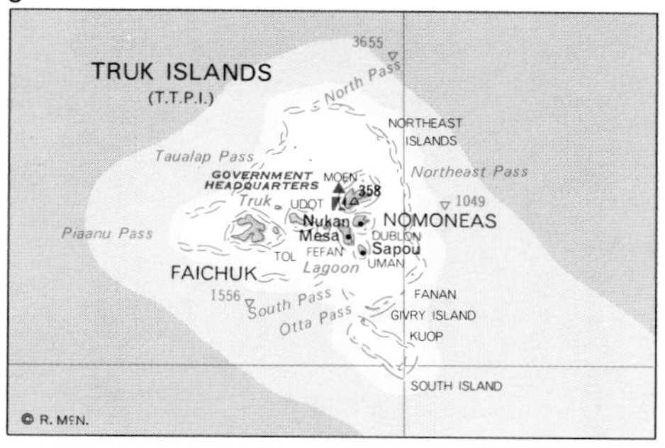

Kilometers 0 50 100 150 Km.
Statute Miles 0 50 100 150 Mi.

Scale 1:3,000,000
One centimeter represents 30 kilometers.
One inch represents approximately 47 miles.
Lambert Conformal Conic Projection

f

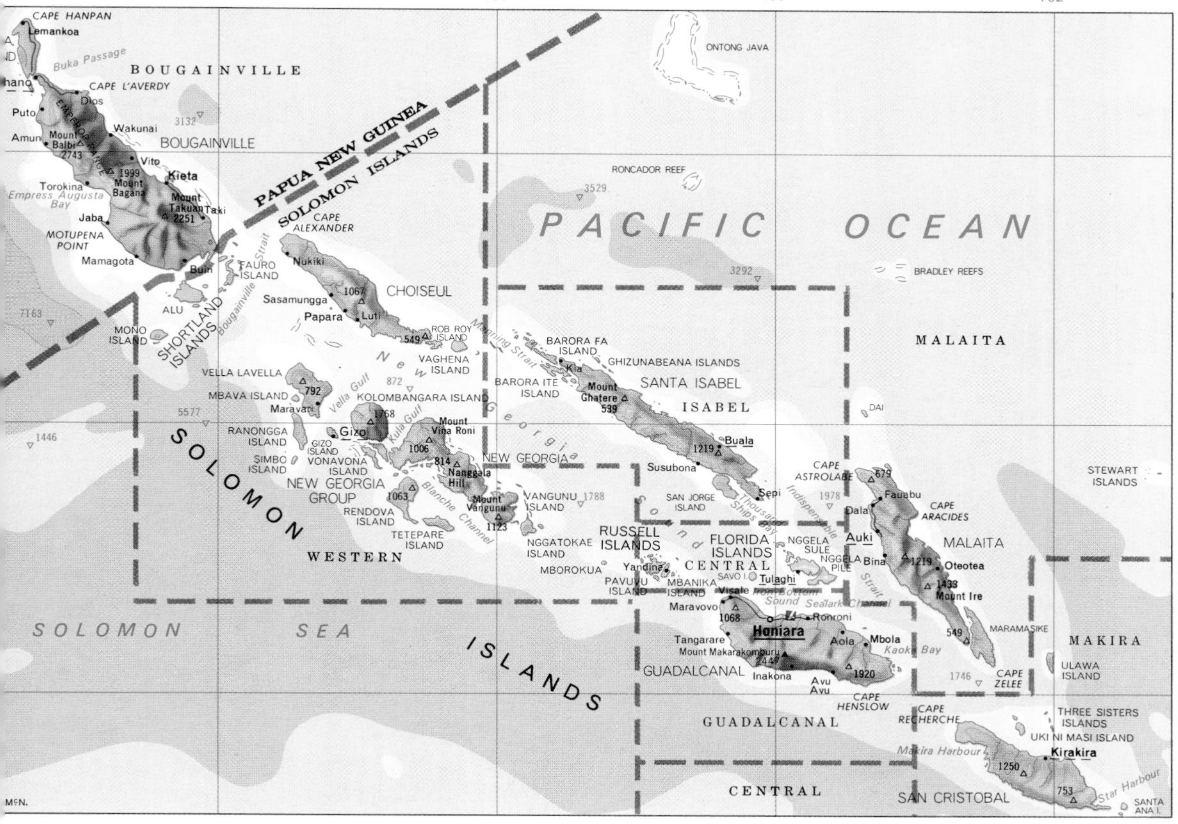

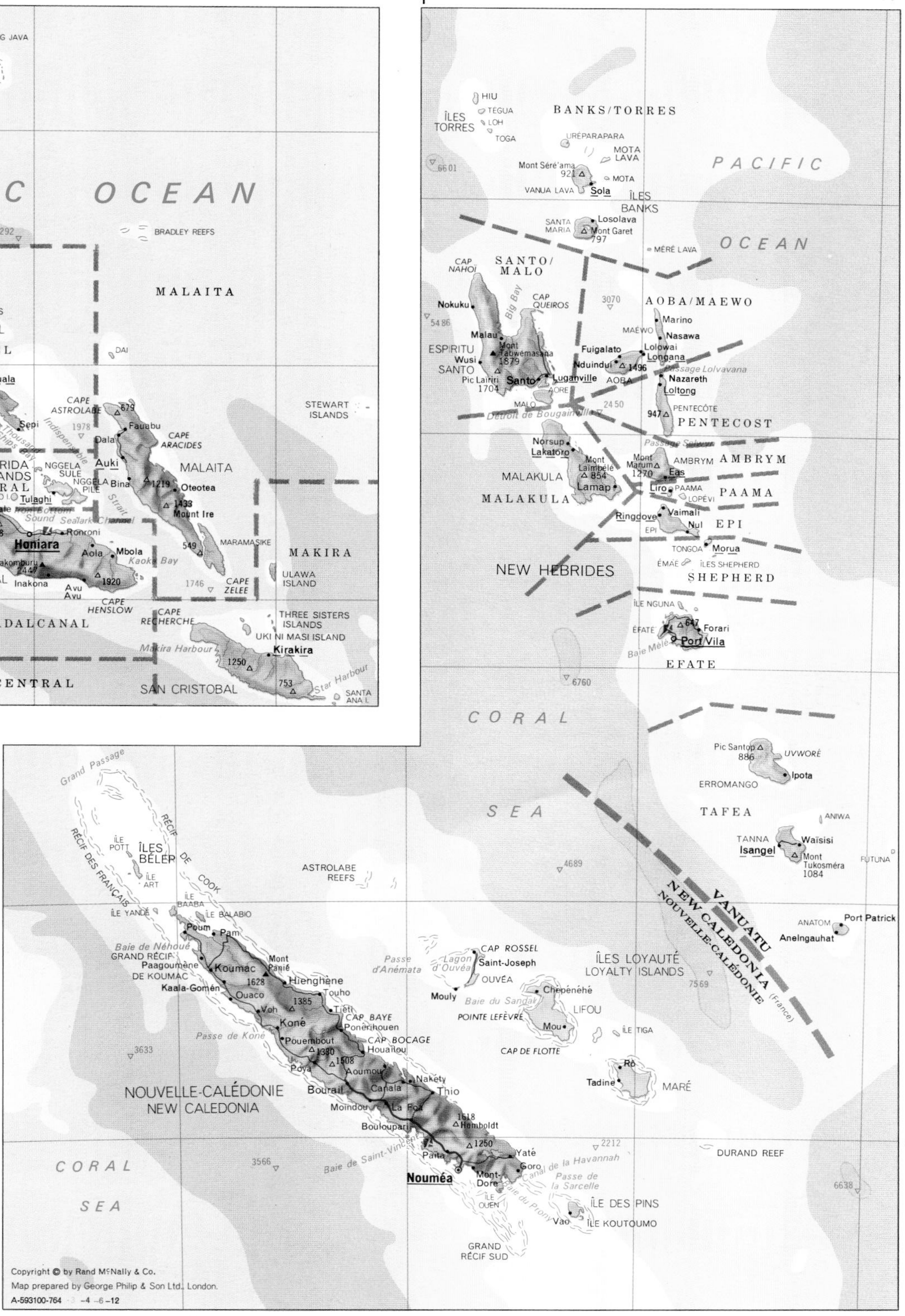

Meters	Feet
6000	19685
4000	13124
3000	9843
2000	6562
1000	3281
500	1640
200	656
0	0
Land Below Sea Level	
0	0
200	656
1000	3281
3000	9843
6000	19685
9000	29520

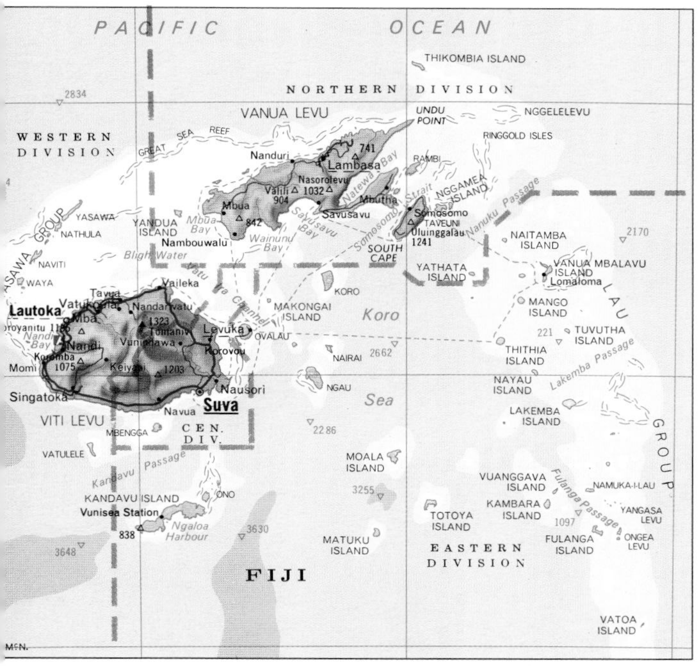

MAP FORM	bay	cape	île	lagoon	mount	point	passage	strait
ENGLISH	bay	cape	island	lagoon	mount	point	passage	strait
DEUTSCH	Bucht	Kap	Insel	Haff	Berg	Landspitze	Durchfahrt	Meeresstrasse
ESPAÑOL	bahía	cabo	isla	laguna	montaña	punta	pasaje	estrecho
FRANÇAIS	baie	cap	île	lagune	mont	pointe	passage	détroit
PORTUGUÊS	baía	cabo	ilha	laguna	monte	ponta	passagem	estreito

Kilometers 0 100 200 300 Km.
Statute Miles 0 100 200 300 Mi.

Scale 1:6,000,000
One centimeter represents 60 kilometers.
One inch represents approximately 95 miles.
Lambert Conformal Conic Projection

178 - 179

ENGLISH	bay	cape	island	lake, l.	mountains, mts.	point	range	strait
DEUTSCH	Bucht	Kap	Insel	See	Berge	Landspitze	Gebirge	Meeresstrasse
ESPAÑOL	bahía	cabo	isla	lago	montañas	punta	sierra	estrecho
FRANÇAIS	baie	cap	île	lac	montagnes	pointe	chaîne	détroit
PORTUGUÊS	baía	cabo	ilha	lago	montanhas	ponta	serra	estreito

Kilometers 0 200 400 600 Km.

Statute Miles 0 200 400 600 Mi.

Scale 1:12,000,000

One centimeter represents 120 kilometers.
One inch represents approximately 190 miles.
Lambert Conformal Conic Projection

Copyright © by Rand McNally & Co.
Map prepared by Rand McNally & Co
A-520500-264

ENGLISH	bay	cape	desert	island	lake	mountains	peak	range
DEUTSCH	Bucht	Kap	Wüste	Insel	See	Berge	Gipfel	Gebirge
ESPAÑOL	bahía	cabo	desierto	isla	lago	montañas	pico	sierra
FRANÇAIS	baie	cap	désert	île	lac	montagnes	cime	chaîne
PORTUGUÊS	baía	cabo	deserto	ilha	lago	montanhas	pico	serra

230-231

176 - 177

Kilometers 0 200 400 600 Km.
Statute Miles 0 200 400 600 Mi.

Scale 1:12,000,000

One centimeter represents 120 kilometers.
One inch represents approximately 190 miles.
Albers Conical Equal-Area Projection

Alaska and Yukon / Alaska und Yukon / Alaska y Yukón
Alaska et Yukon / Alasca e Yukon

ENGLISH	bay	cape	island, i.	lake, l.	mount, mt.	peak, pk.	point	vo
DEUTSCH	Bucht	Kap	Insel	See	Berg	Gipfel	Landspitze	Vu
ESPAÑOL	bahía	cabo	isla	lago	monte	pico	punta	vo
FRANÇAIS	baie	cap	île	lac	mont	cime	pointe	vo
PORTUGUÊS	baía	cabo	ilha	lago	monte	pico	ponta	vu

Kilometers 0 100 200 300 Km.
Statute Miles 0 100 200 300 Mi.

Scale 1:6,000,000

One centimeter represents 60 kilometers.
One inch represents approximately 95 miles.
Lambert Conformal Conic Projection

ENGLISH	creek	Indian reserve	inlet	island	lake, l.	mountain	peak	provincial park	sound
DEUTSCH	Bach	Indianerreservation	Einfahrt	Insel	See	Berg	Gipfel	Provinz-Park	Sund
ESPAÑOL	riachuelo	reserva de Indios	abra	isla	lago	montaña	pico	parque de provincia	sonda
FRANÇAIS	crique	réserve indienne	bras de mer	île	lac	montagne	cime	parc provincial	détroit
PORTUGUÊS	riacho	reserva indígena	enseada	ilha	lago	montanha	pico	parque provincial	estreito

184 · 185

202 · 203

Kilometers 0 50 100 150 Km.

Statute Miles 0 50 100 150 Mi.

Scale 1:3,000,000

One centimeter represents 30 kilometers.
One inch represents approximately 47 miles.
Lambert Conformal Conic Projection

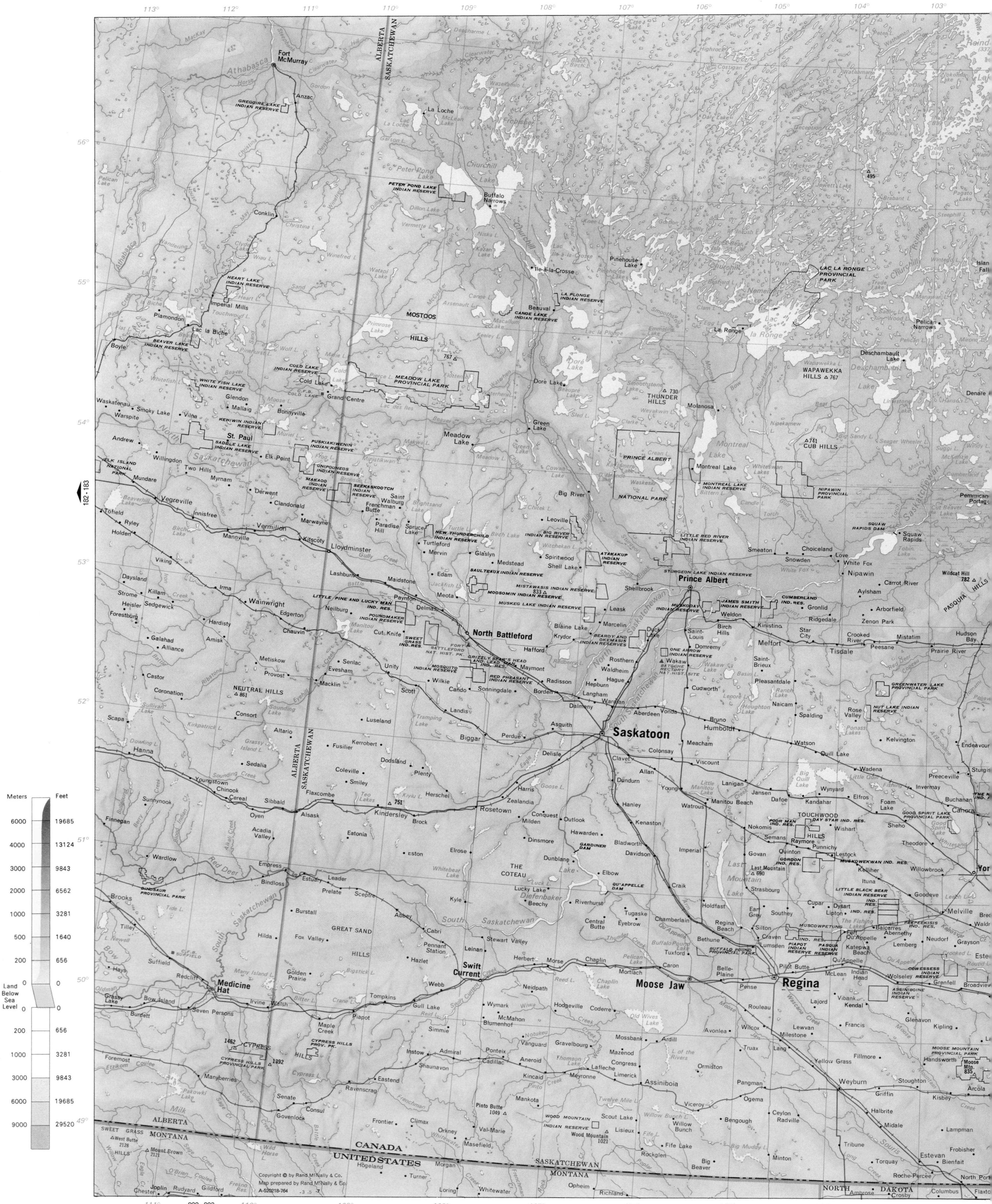

ENGLISH	creek, cr.	hills	Indian reserve	island, i.	lake, l.	provincial park
DEUTSCH	Bach	Hügel	Indianerreservation	Insel	See	Provinz-Park
ESPAÑOL	riachuelo	colinas	reserva de Indios	isla	lago	parque de provincia
FRANÇAIS	crique	collines	réserve indienne	île	lac	parc provincial
PORTUGUÊS	riacho	colinas	reserva indígena	ilha	lago	parque provincial

182 · 183
202 - 203
198 - 199

Kilometers 0 50 100 150 Km.

Statute Miles 0 50 100 150 Mi.

Scale 1:3,000,000

One centimeter represents 30 kilometers.

One inch represents approximately 47 miles.

Lambert Conformal Conic Projection

Southeastern Canada / Südostkanada / Canadá Sud-oriental
Sud-Est du Canada / Canadá: Sudeste

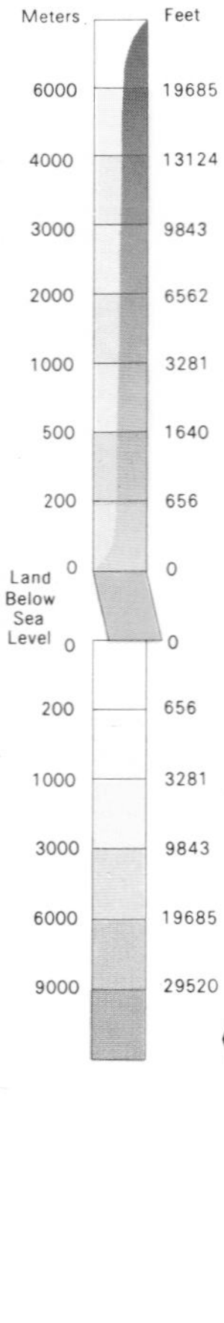

188-189

ENGLISH	bay	cape	dam	island	lake, l.	mountain	point	strait
DEUTSCH	Bucht	Kap	Damm	Insel	See	Berg	Landspitze	Meeresstrasse
ESPAÑOL	bahía	cabo	presa	isla	lago	montaña	punta	estrecho
FRANÇAIS	baie	cap	barrage	île	lac	montagne	pointe	détroit
PORTUGUÊS	baía	cabo	represa	ilha	lago	montanha	ponta	estreito

Kilometers 0 50 100 150 Km.

Statute Miles 0 50 100 150 Mi.

Scale 1:3,000,000

One centimeter represents 30 kilometers.
One inch represents approximately 47 miles.
Lambert Conformal Conic Projection

Northeastern United States / Nordöstliche Vereinigte Staaten / Nor-este de los Estados Unidos
Nord-Est des États-Unis / Estados Unidos: Nordeste

190-191

194-195

192-193

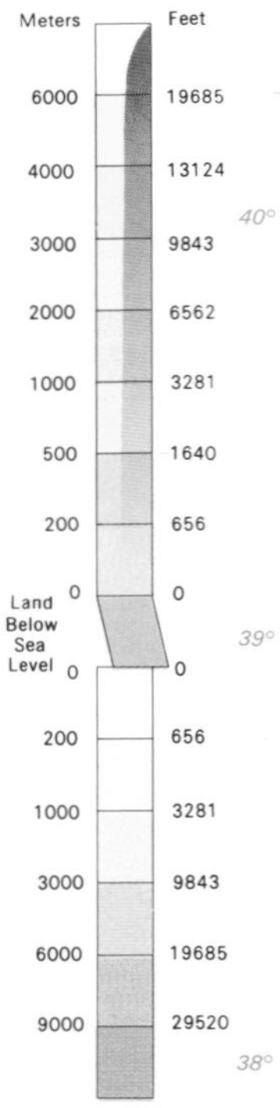

ENGLISH	bay	creek, cr.	island, i.	lake, l.	mountain, mtn.	point, pt.	reservoir, res.	state park, s.p.
DEUTSCH	Bucht	Bach	Insel	See	Berg	Landspitze	Stausee	Staatspark
ESPAÑOL	bahía	riachuelo	isla	lago	montaña	punta	embalse	parque del estado
FRANÇAIS	baie	crique	île	lac	montagne	pointe	réservoir	parc régional
PORTUGUÊS	baía	riacho	ilha	lago	montanha	ponta	reservatório	parque estadual

Kilometers 0 50 100 150 Km.
Statute Miles 0 50 100 150 Mi.

Scale 1:3,000,000

One centimeter represents 30 kilometers.
One inch represents approximately 47 miles.
Albers Conical Equal-Area Projection

Great Lakes Region / Grosse Seen-Region / Región de los Grandes Lagos
Région des Grands Lacs / Região dos Grandes Lagos

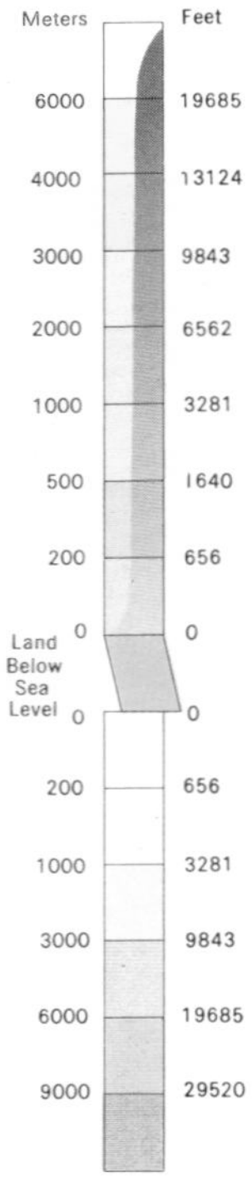

ENGLISH	bay	creek, cr.	Indian reservation	island, i.	lake, l.	point	reservoir, res.	state park, s.p.
DEUTSCH	Bucht	Bach	Indianerreservation	Insel	See	Landspitze	Stausee	Staatspark
ESPAÑOL	bahía	riachuelo	reserva de Indios	isla	lago	punta	embalse	parque del estado
FRANÇAIS	baie	crique	réserve indienne	île	lac	pointe	réservoir	parc régional
PORTUGUÊS	baía	riacho	reserva indígena	ilha	lago	ponta	reservatório	parque estadual

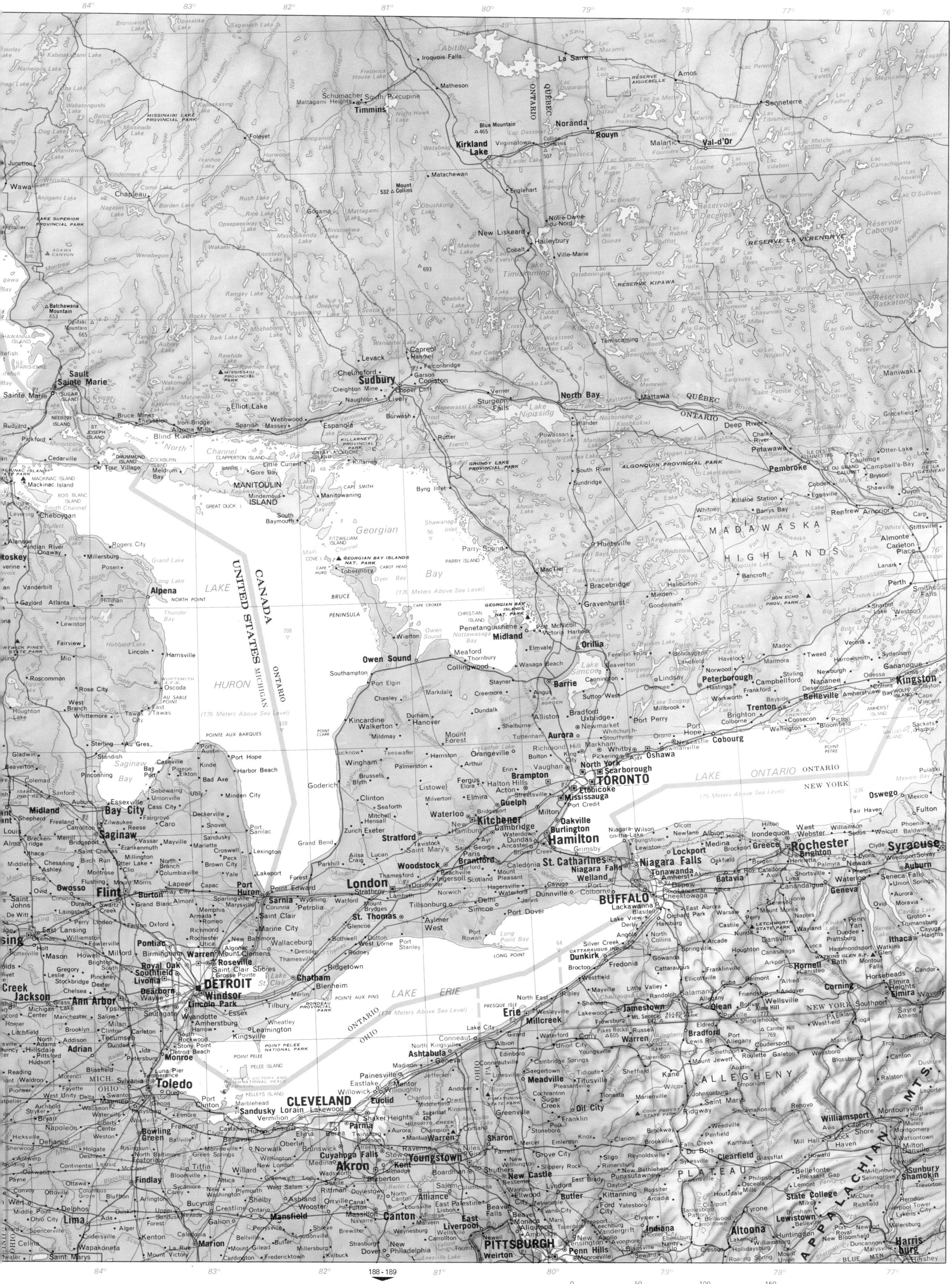

188 - 189

Kilometers 0 50 100 150 Km.
Statute Miles 0 50 100 150 Mi.

Scale 1:3,000,000

One centimeter represents 30 kilometers.
One inch represents approximately 47 miles.
Albers Conical Equal Area Projection

Southeastern United States / Südöstliche Vereinigte Staaten / Sud-este de los Estados Unidos
Sud-Est des États-Unis / Estados Unidos: Sudeste

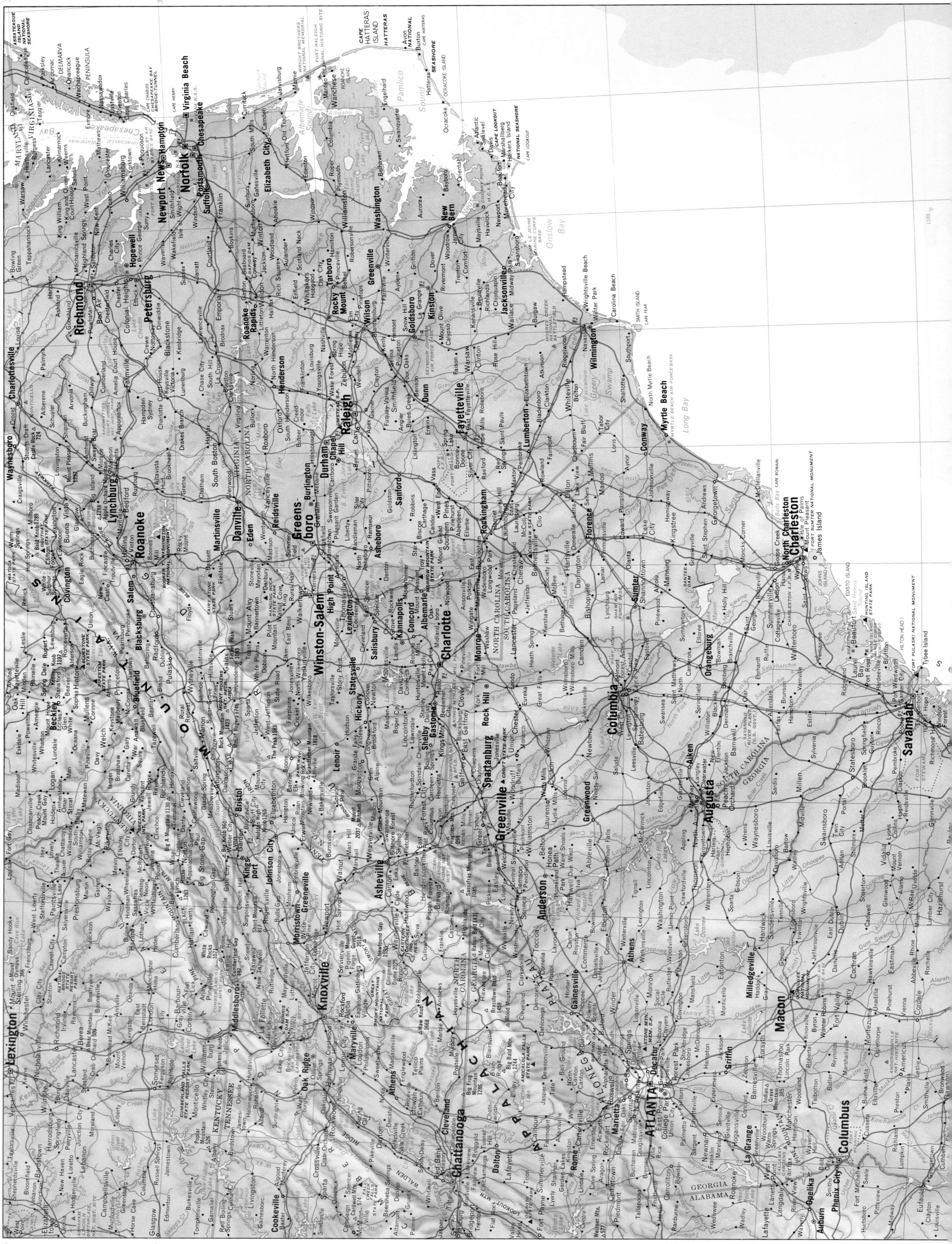

188 · 189

194 · 195

Kilometers 0 50 100 150 Km.
Statute Miles 0 50 100 150 Mi.

Scale 1:3,000,000

One centimeter represents 30 kilometers.
One inch represents approximately 47 miles.
Albers Conical Equal-Area Projection

ENGLISH	bay	cape	creek, cr.	dam	island, i.	lake, l.	mountain, mtn.	state park, s.p.
DEUTSCH	Bucht	Kap	Bach	Damm	Insel	See	Berg	Staatspark
ESPAÑOL	bahía	cabo	riachuelo	presa	isla	lago	montaña	parque del estado
FRANÇAIS	baie	cap	crique	barrage	île	lac	montagne	parc régional
PORTUGUÊS	baía	cabo	riacho	represa	ilha	lago	montanha	parque estadual

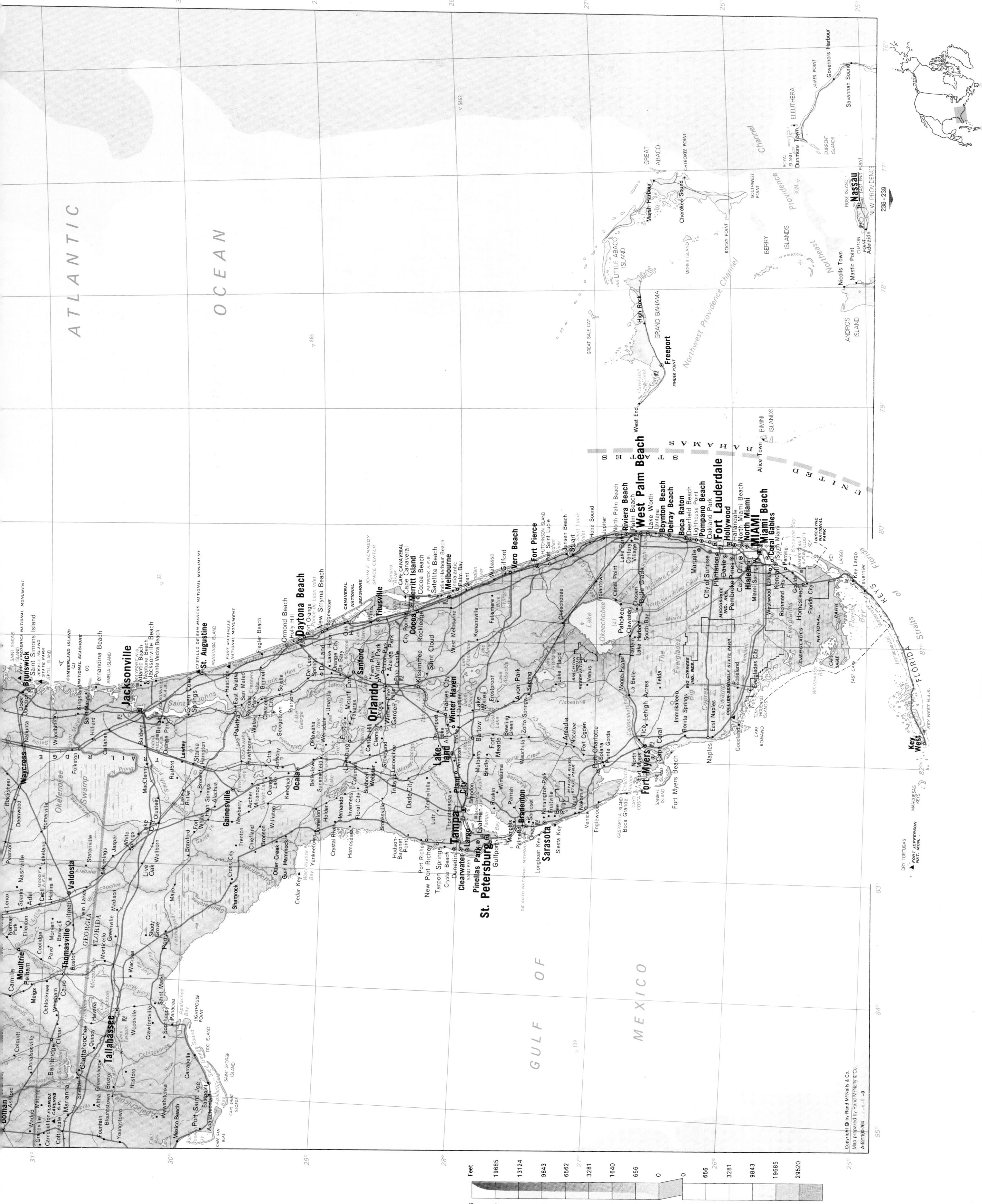
ATLANTIC
OCEAN
GULF OF MEXICO
Jacksonville
St. Augustine
Daytona Beach
Orlando
Tampa
St. Petersburg
Clearwater
Sarasota
Fort Myers
West Palm Beach
Fort Lauderdale
MIAMI
Key West
Tallahassee
Gainesville
Ocala
Nassau
Freeport
GRAND BAHAMA
BAHAMAS
UNITED STATES
Feet
19685
13124
9843
6562
3281
1640
656
0
0
656
3281
9843
19685
29520
Meters
6000
4000
3000
2000
1000
500
200
0
Land Below Sea Level
0
200
1000
3000
6000
9000

188 - 189

190 - 191

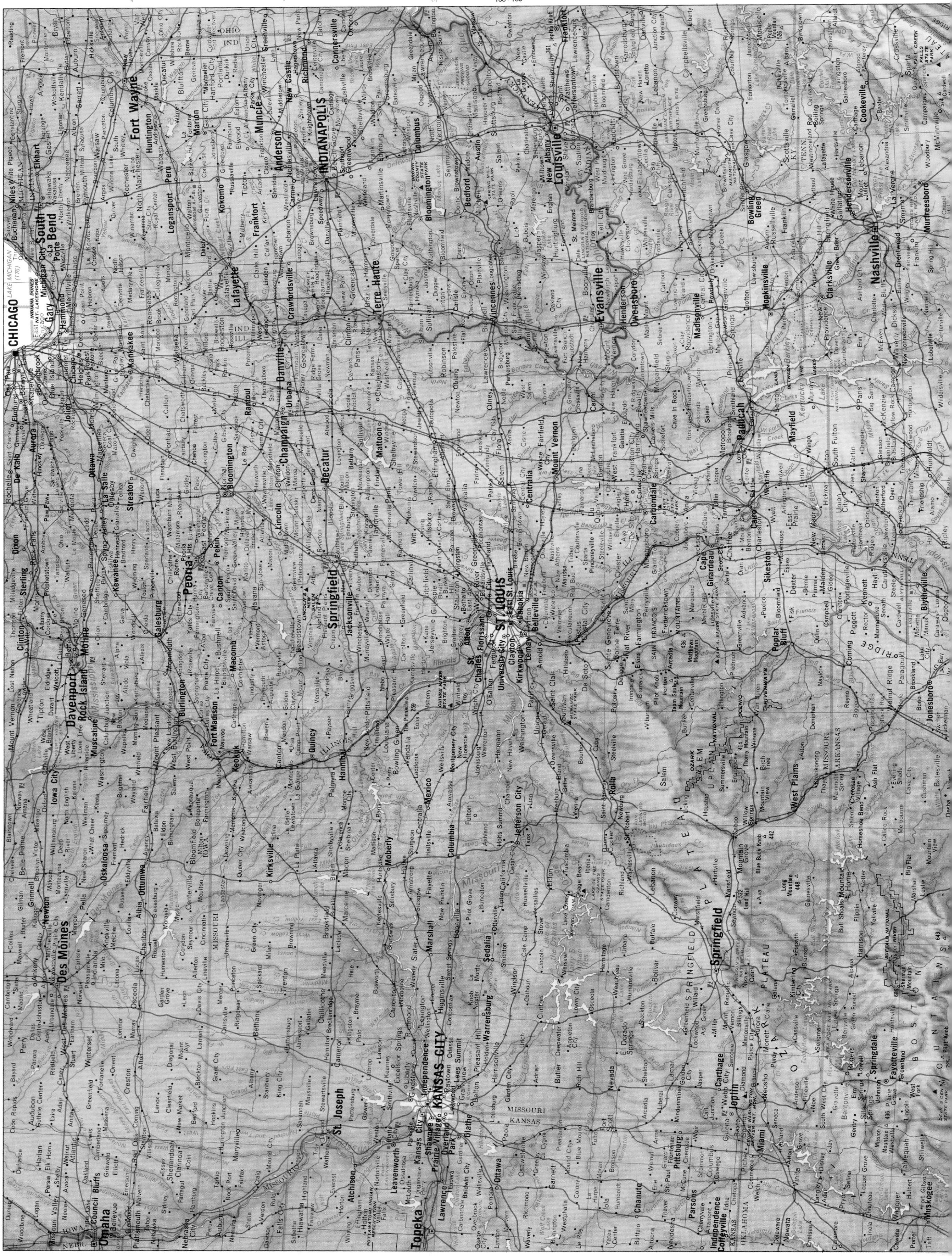

198 - 199

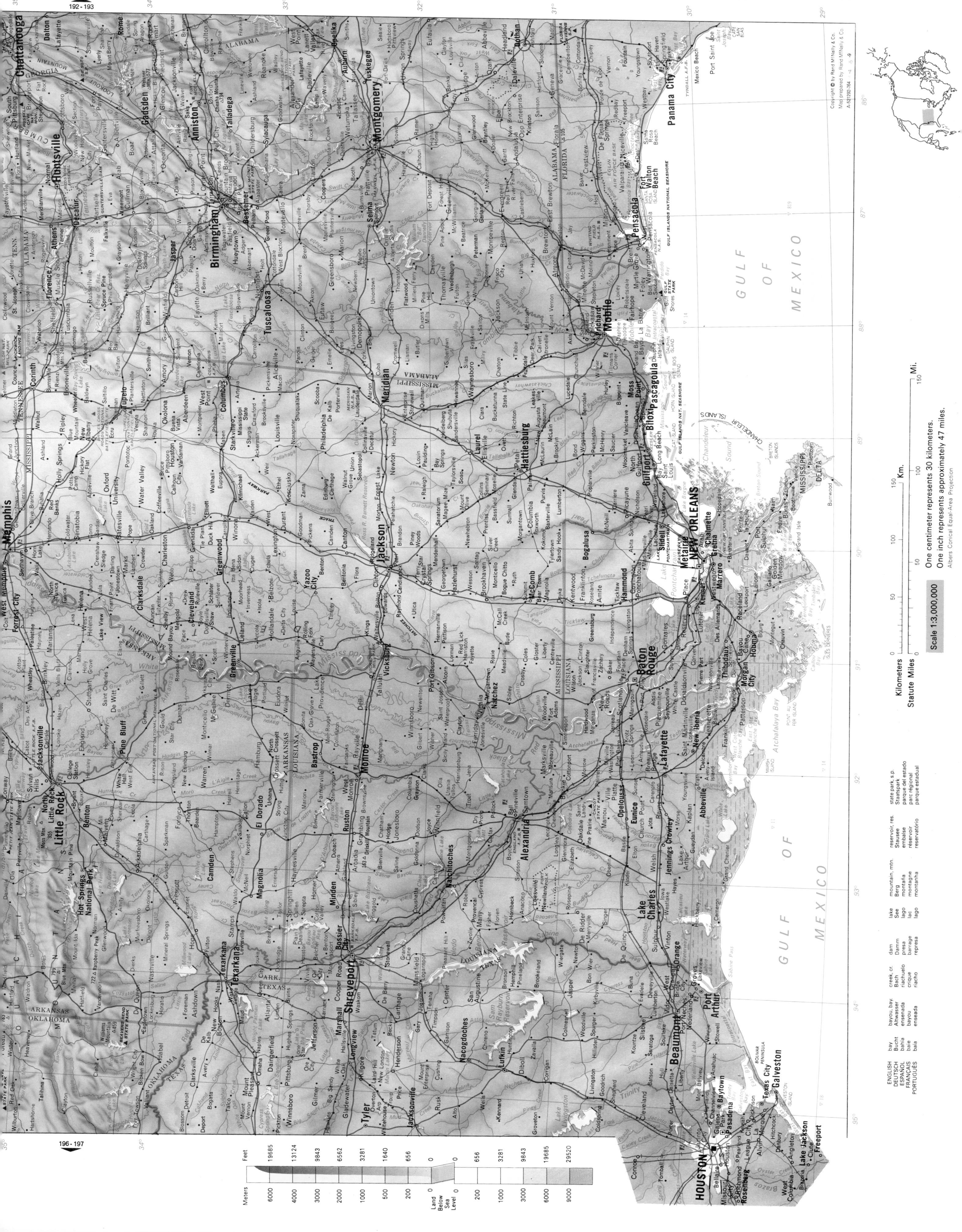
192-193
196-197
GULF OF MEXICO
Memphis
Birmingham
Montgomery
Jackson
New Orleans
Baton Rouge
Shreveport
Little Rock
Houston
Mobile
Scale 1:3,000,000
One centimeter represents 30 kilometers.
One inch represents approximately 47 miles.
Albers Conical Equal-Area Projection
Kilometers
Statute Miles
ENGLISH DEUTSCH ESPAÑOL FRANÇAIS PORTUGUÊS
bay Bucht bahía baie baía
bayou, bay. Altwasser ensenada bayou enseada
creek, cr. Bach riachuelo crique riacho
dam Damm presa barrage represa
lake See lago lac lago
mountain, mtn. Berg montaña montagne montanha
reservoir, res. Stausee embalse réservoir reservatório
state park, s.p. Staatspark parque del estado parc régional parque estadual
Feet
Meters
Land Below Sea Level

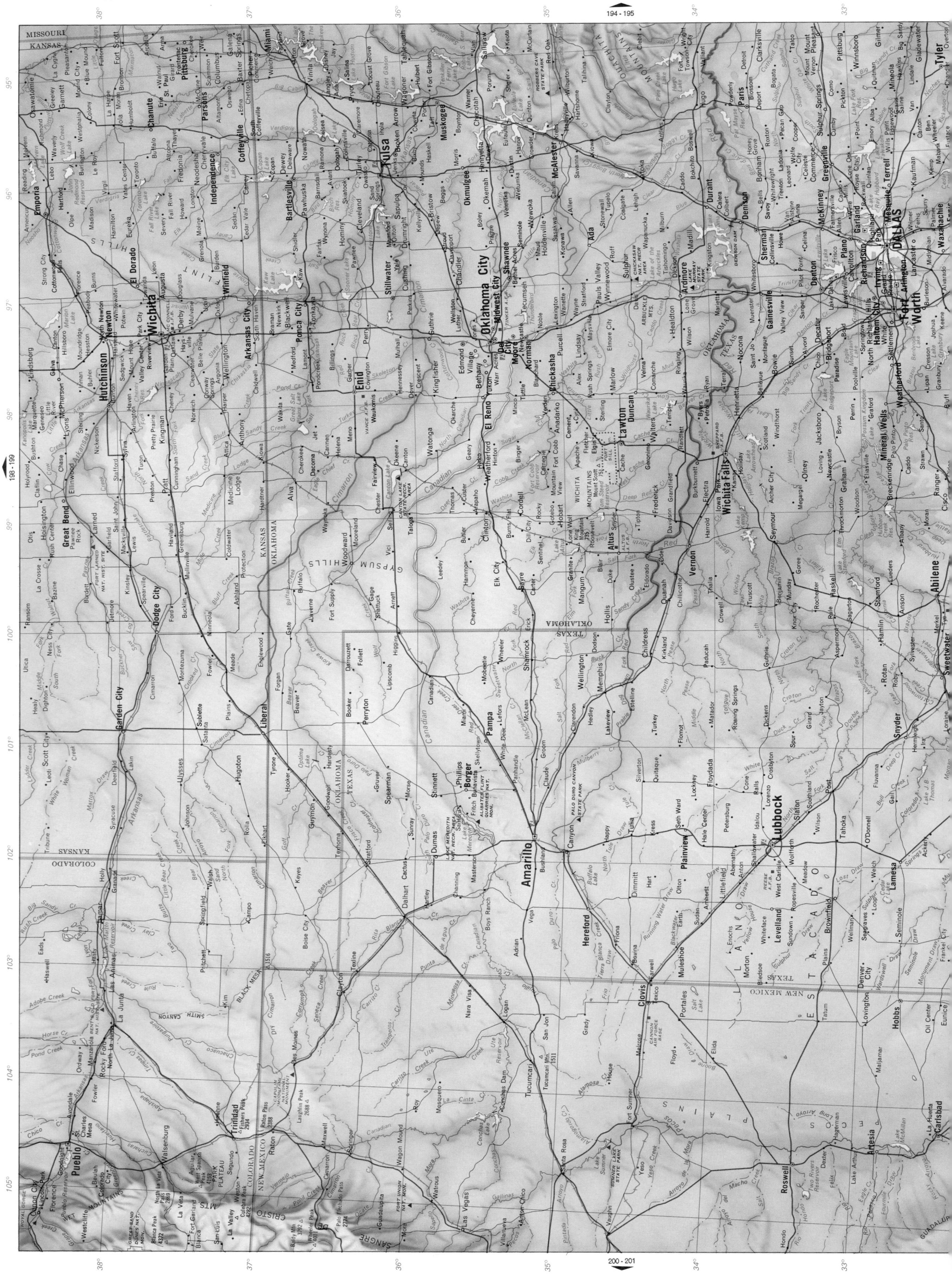
194 - 195
198 - 199
200 - 201
38°
37°
36°
35°
34°
33°
95°
96°
97°
98°
99°
100°
101°
102°
103°
104°
105°
MISSOURI
KANSAS
OKLAHOMA
TEXAS
COLORADO
NEW MEXICO
Wichita
Hutchinson
Oklahoma City
Tulsa
Amarillo
Lubbock
Wichita Falls
Lawton
DALLAS
Fort Worth
Abilene
Pueblo
Trinidad
Raton
Clovis
Roswell
Dodge City
Garden City
Liberal
Enid
Norman
Denton
Sherman
Tyler
GYPSUM HILLS
FLINT HILLS
LLANO ESTACADO
PLAINS
SANGRE DE CRISTO MTS
WET MOUNTAINS

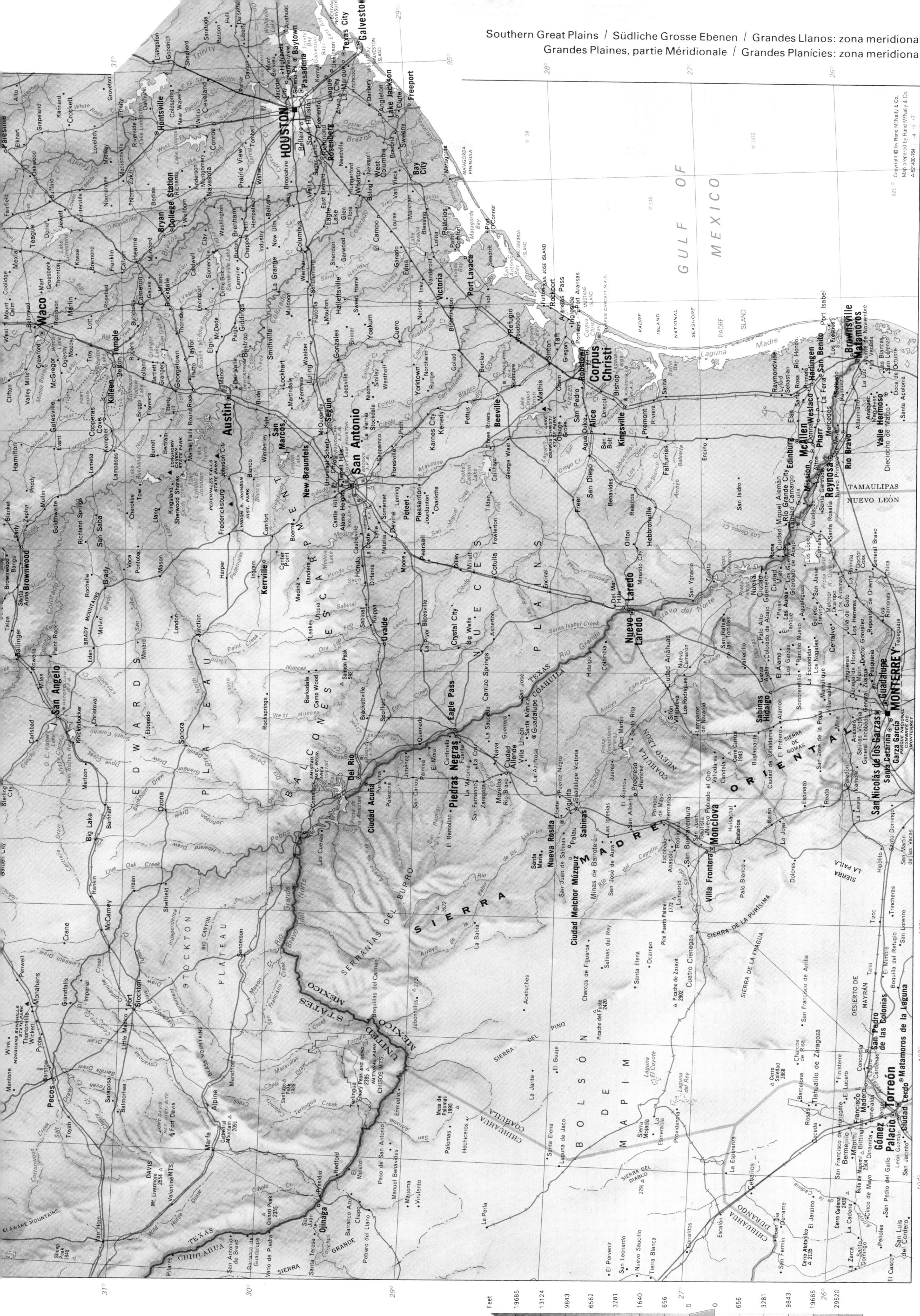
GULF OF MEXICO
HOUSTON
San Antonio
Austin
Corpus Christi
MONTERREY
Torreón
EDWARDS PLATEAU
STOCKTON PLATEAU
BALCONES ESCARPMENT
NUECES PLAINS
SIERRA MADRE ORIENTAL
BOLSÓN DE MAPIMÍ
SERRANÍAS DEL BURRO
UNITED STATES
MEXICO
TEXAS
COAHUILA
CHIHUAHUA
DURANGO
TAMAULIPAS
NUEVO LEÓN

Scale 1:3,000,000
One centimeter represents 30 kilometers.
One inch represents approximately 47 miles.
Albers Conical Equal-Area Projection

Kilometers 0 50 100 150 Km.
Statute Miles 0 50 100 150 Mi.

Copyright © by Rand McNally & Co.
Map prepared by Rand McNally & Co.
A-521400-764 -4 -5 -7

ENGLISH	bay	creek, cr.	draw	lake	mountains, mts.	peak	reservoir, res.	state park, s.p.
DEUTSCH	Bucht	Bach	Schlucht	See	Berge	Gipfel	Stausee	Staatspark
ESPAÑOL	bahía	riachuelo	arrastre	lago	montañas	pico	embalse	parque del estado
FRANÇAIS	baie	crique	vallée	lac	montagnes	cime	réservoir	parc régional
PORTUGUÊS	baía	riacho	vale	lago	montanhas	pico	reservatório	parque estadual

Feet	19685	13124	9843	6562	3281	1640	656	0	0	656	3281	9843	19685	29520
Meters	6000	4000	3000	2000	1000	500	200	0	Land Below Sea Level 0	200	1000	3000	6000	9000

190 - 191

184 - 185

202 - 203

194-195

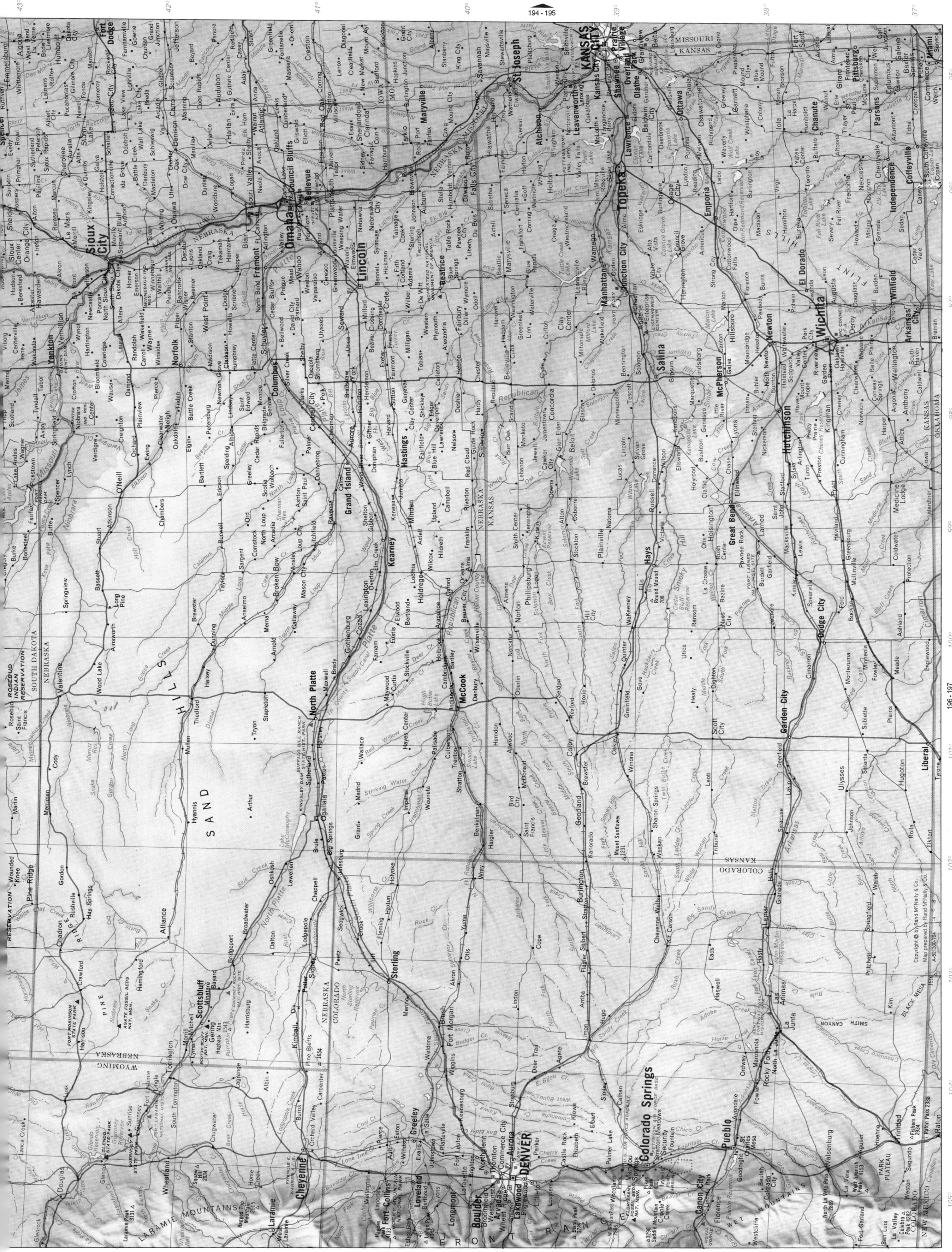

196-197

200-201

ENGLISH	DEUTSCH	ESPAÑOL	FRANÇAIS	PORTUGUÊS
creek, cr.	Bach	riachuelo	crique	riacho
dam	Damm	presa	barrage	barragem
Indian reservation, Ind. res.	Indianerreservation	reserva de Indios	réserve indienne	reserva indígena
lake, l.	See	lago	lac	lago
mountain, mtn.	Berg	montaña	montagne	montanha
peak	Gipfel	pico	cime	pico
reservoir, res.	Stausee	embalse	réservoir	reservatório
state park	Staatspark	parque del estado	parc régional	parque estadual

Copyright © by Rand McNally & Co.
Map prepared by Rand McNally & Co.

Scale 1:3,000,000

Kilometers 0 50 100 150 Km.
Statute Miles 0 50 100 150 Mi.

One centimeter represents 30 kilometers.
One inch represents approximately 47 miles.
Albers Conical Equal-Area Projection

Feet	Meters
19685	6000
13124	4000
9843	3000
6562	2000
3281	1000
1640	500
656	200
0	0
Land Below Sea Level	
0	0
656	200
3281	1000
9843	3000
19685	6000
29520	9000

198 - 199

202 - 203

204 - 205

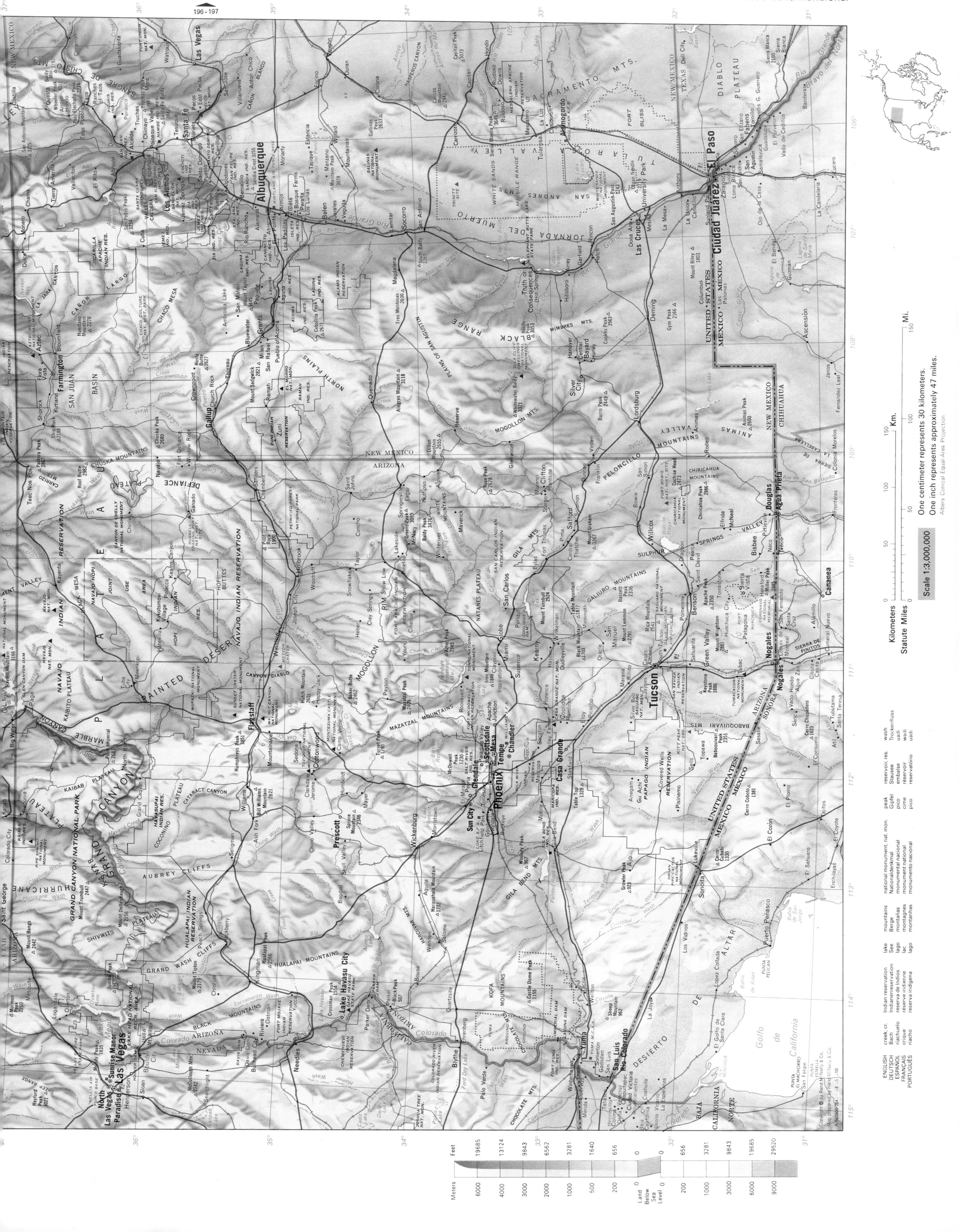
196-197
Scale 1:3,000,000
One centimeter represents 30 kilometers.
One inch represents approximately 47 miles.
Albers Conical Equal-Area Projection
Kilometers
Statute Miles
ENGLISH
creek, cr.
Indian reservation
lake
mountains
national monument, nat. mon.
peak
reservoir, res.
wash
Copyright © by Rand McNally & Co.
Meters
Feet
Land Below Sea Level

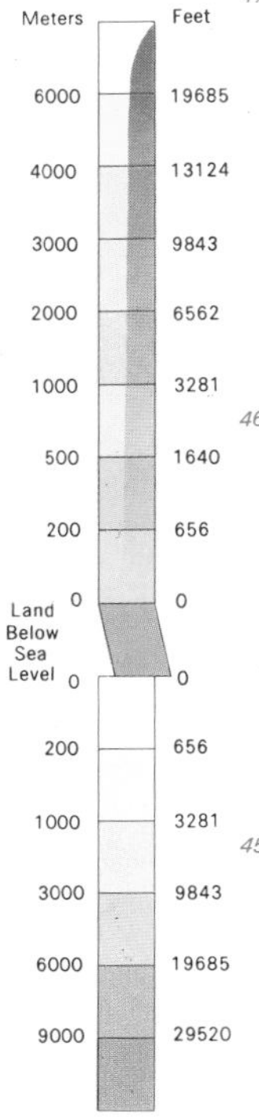

ENGLISH	creek, cr.	Indian reservation	lake, l.	mountain, mtn.	pass	peak	range	reservoir, res.
DEUTSCH	Bach	Indianerreservation	See	Berg	Pass	Gipfel	Gebirge	Stausee
ESPAÑOL	riachuelo	reserva de Indios	lago	montaña	paso	pico	sierra	embalse
FRANÇAIS	crique	réserve indienne	lac	montagne	col	cime	chaîne	réservoir
PORTUGUÊS	riacho	reserva indígena	lago	montanha	passo	pico	serra	reservatório

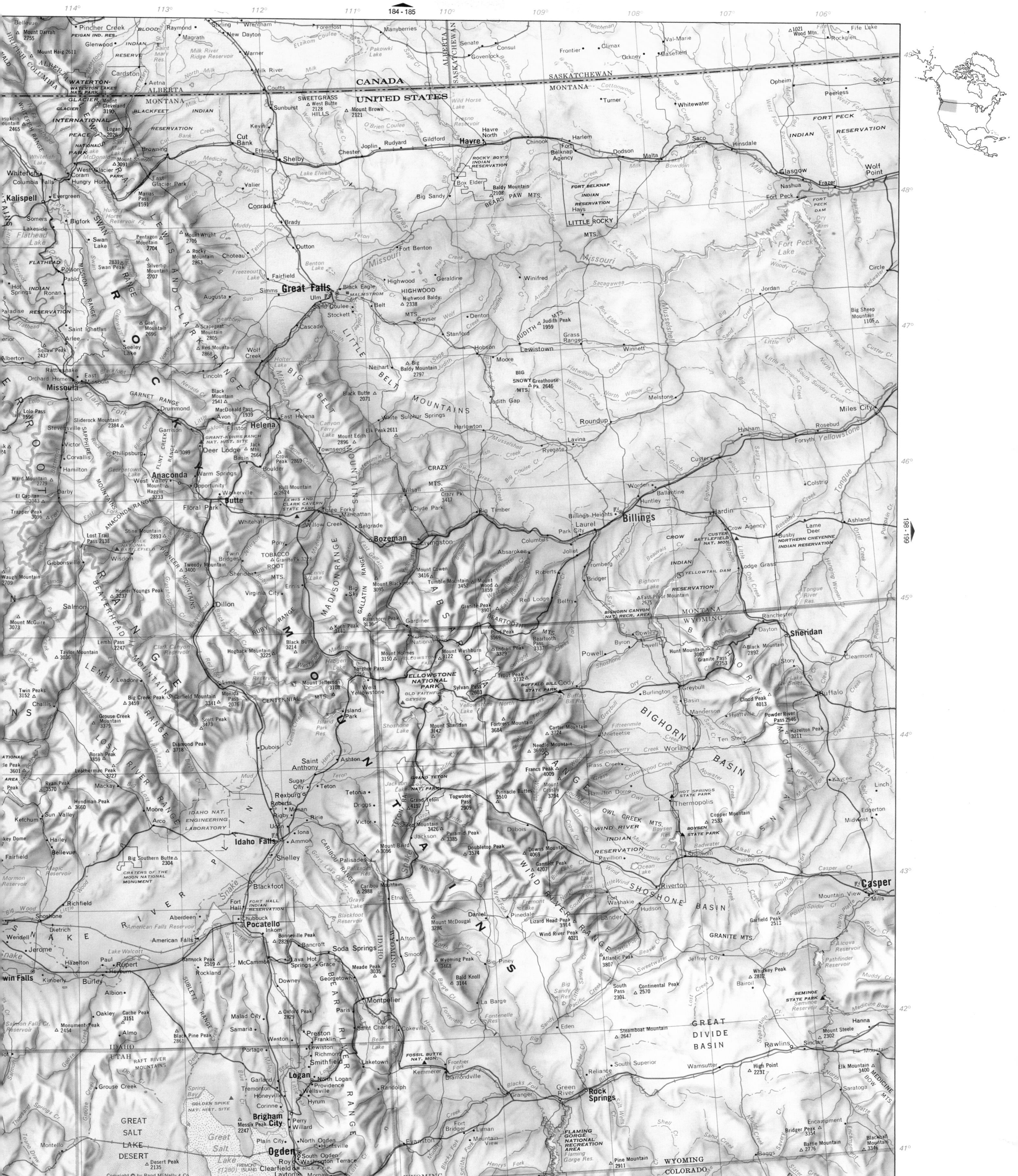

Kilometers 0 50 100 150 Km.

Statute Miles 0 50 100 150 Mi.

Scale 1:3,000,000

One centimeter represents 30 kilometers.

One inch represents approximately 47 miles.

Albers Conical Equal-Area Projection

200 - 201

202 - 203

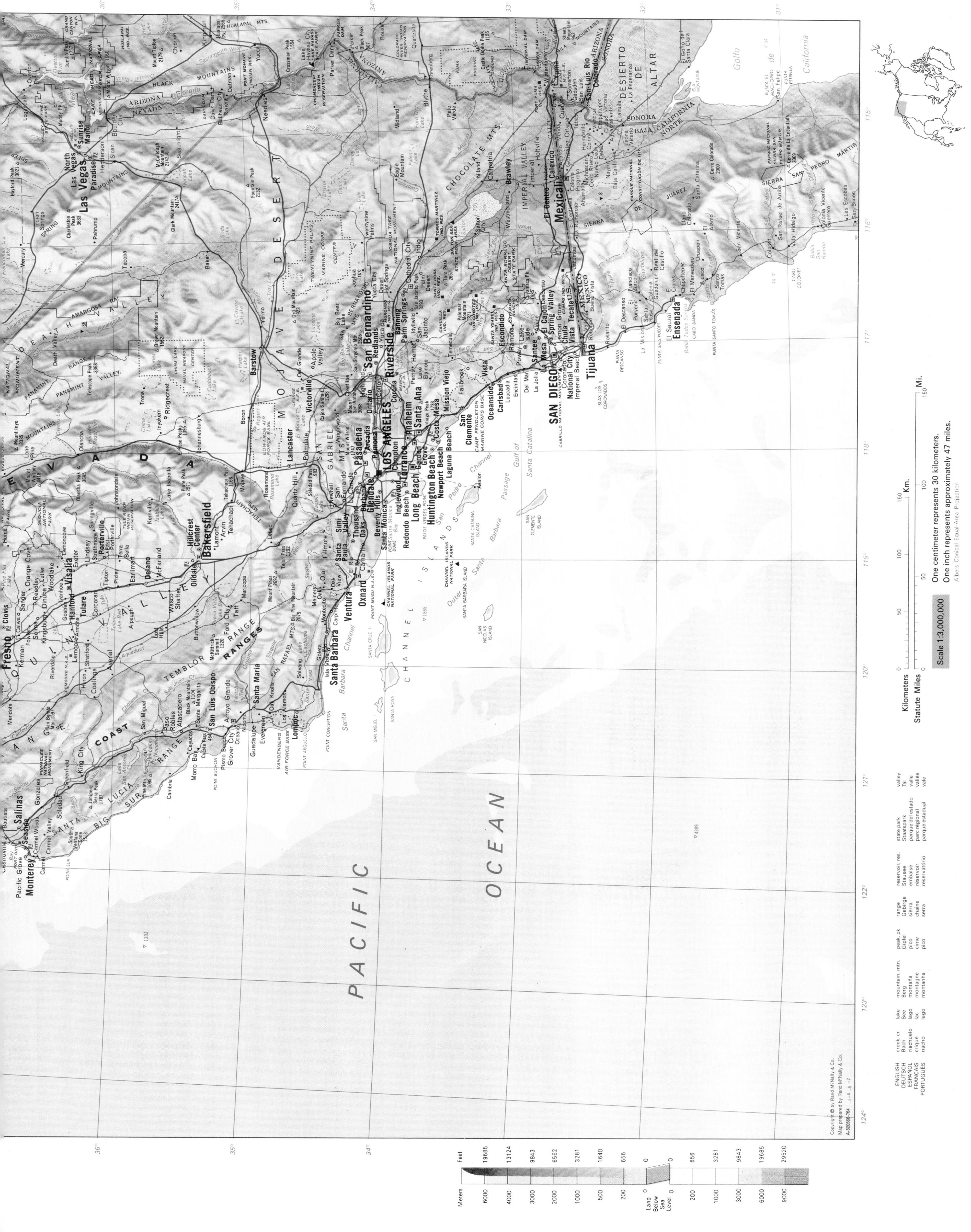
PACIFIC OCEAN
MOJAVE DESERT
DEATH VALLEY
SIERRA NEVADA
COAST RANGES
IMPERIAL VALLEY
CHANNEL ISLANDS
DESIERTO DE ALTAR
BAJA CALIFORNIA NORTE
SONORA
ARIZONA
NEVADA
CALIFORNIA
MEXICO
U.S.
LOS ANGELES
SAN DIEGO
Las Vegas
Bakersfield
Fresno
Santa Barbara
Ventura
Oxnard
San Bernardino
Riverside
Long Beach
Anaheim
Santa Ana
Pasadena
Tijuana
Mexicali
Ensenada
Salinas
Monterey
San Luis Obispo
Barstow
Lancaster
Palmdale
Victorville
Needles
El Centro
Yuma
Scale 1:3,000,000
One centimeter represents 30 kilometers.
One inch represents approximately 47 miles.
Albers Conical Equal-Area Projection
Kilometers
Statute Miles
Km.
Mi.
ENGLISH DEUTSCH ESPAÑOL FRANÇAIS PORTUGUÊS
creek, cr. Bach riachuelo crique riacho
lake See lago lac lago
mountain, mtn. Berg montaña montagne montanha
peak, pk. Gipfel pico cime pico
range Gebirge sierra chaîne serra
reservoir, res. Stausee embalse réservoir reservatório
state park Staatspark parque del estado parc régional parque estadual
valley Tal valle vallée vale
Copyright © by Rand McNally & Co.
Map prepared by Rand McNally & Co.
Feet
19685
13124
9843
6562
3281
1640
656
0
Meters
6000
4000
3000
2000
1000
500
200
0
Land Below Sea Level
200
1000
3000
6000
9000
29520

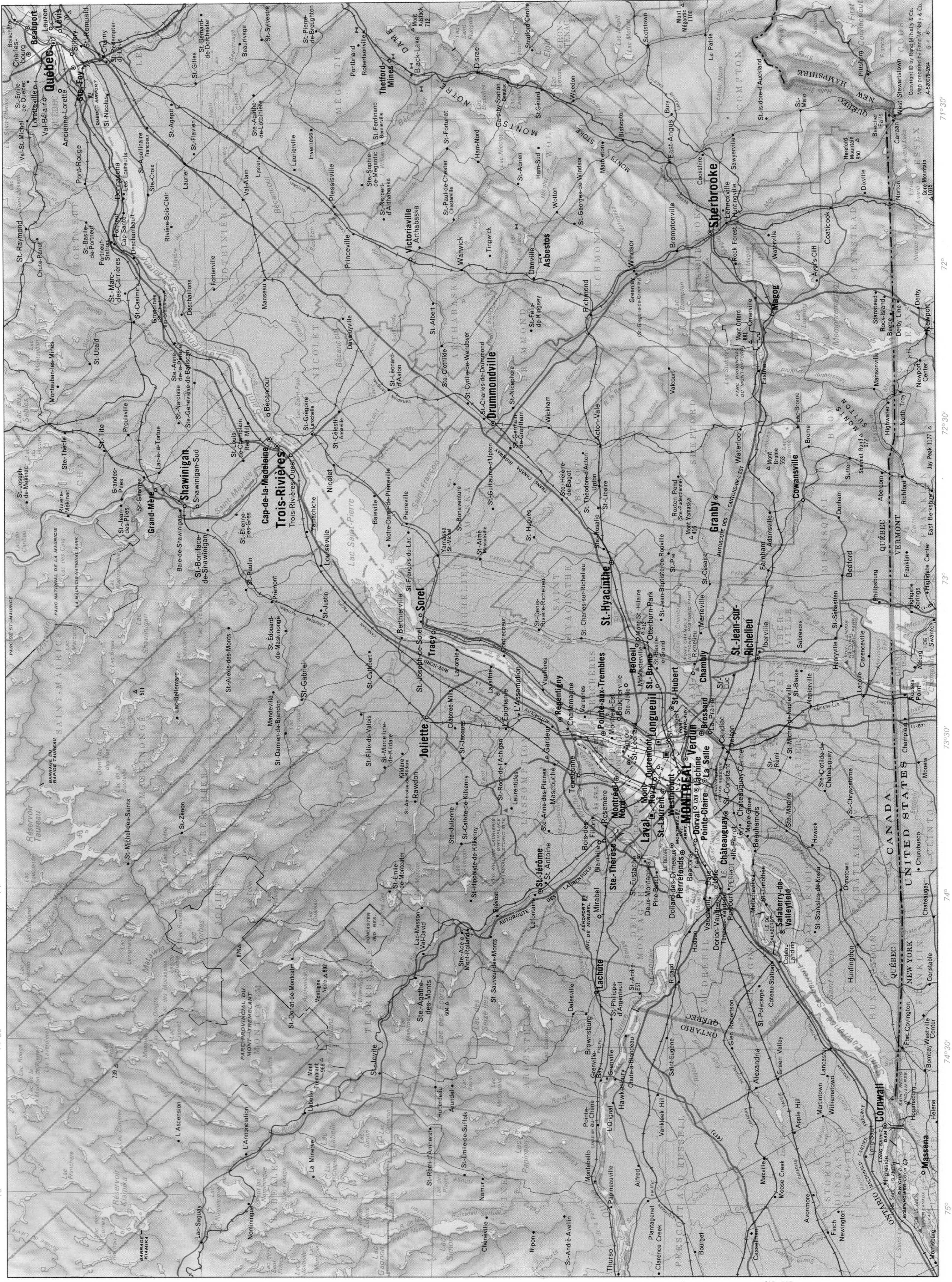

FRANÇAIS	ENGLISH	DEUTSCH	ESPAÑOL	PORTUGUÊS
aéroport	airport	Flughafen	aeropuerto	aeroporto
barrage	dam	Damm	presa	represa
île	island	Insel	isla	ilha
lac	lake	See	lago	lago
montagne	mountain	Berg	montaña	montanha
parc	park	Park	parque	parque
réservoir, rés.	reservoir	Stausee	embalse	reservatório
rivière, r.	river	Fluss	rio	rio

Kilometers 0 10 20 30 40 50 Km.

Statute Miles 0 10 20 30 40 50 Mi.

Scale 1:1,000,000

One centimeter represents 10 kilometers.
One inch represents approximately 16 miles.
Lambert Conformal Conic Projection

212-213

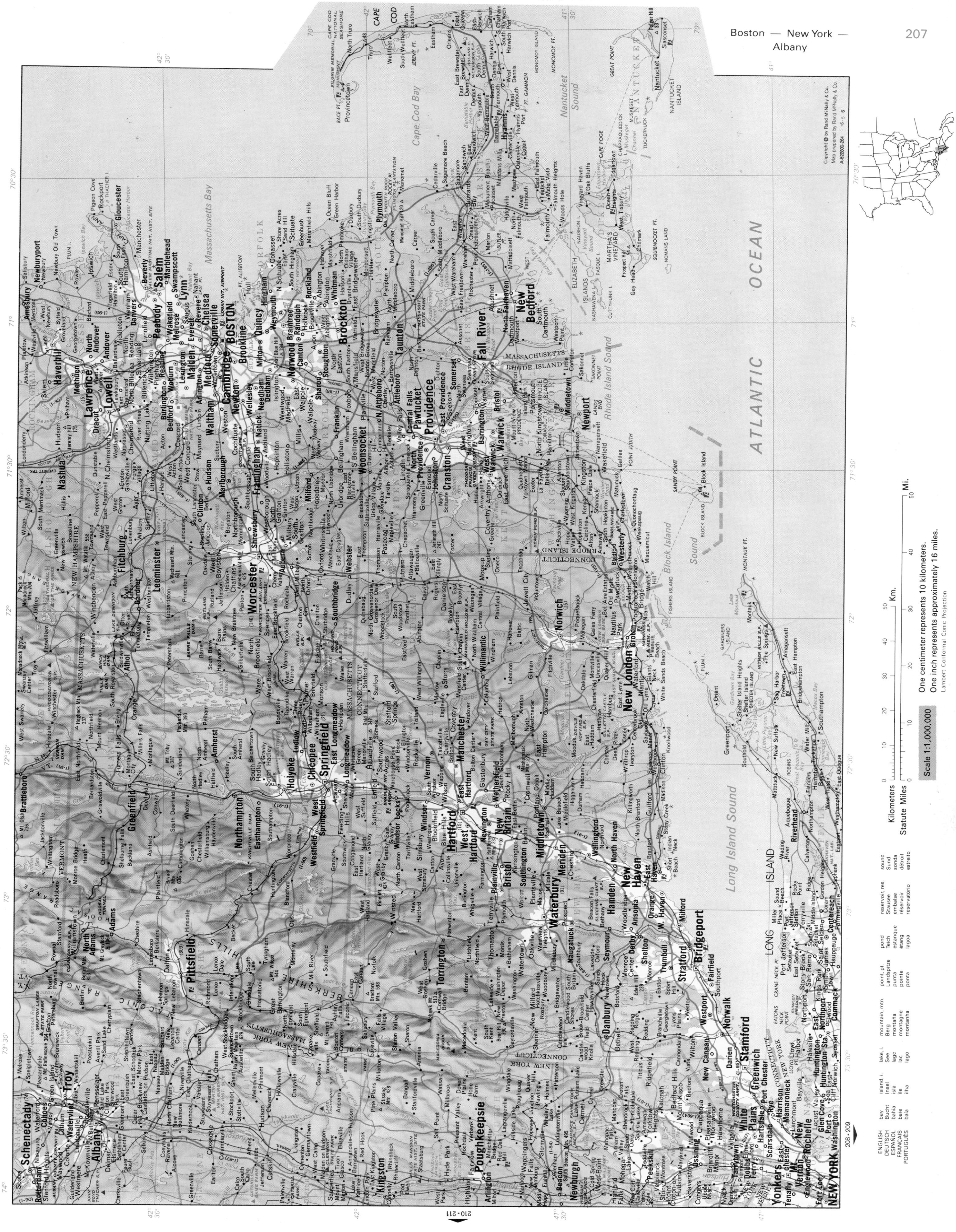
Scale 1:1,000,000
One centimeter represents 10 kilometers.
One inch represents approximately 16 miles.
Lambert Conformal Conic Projection
Kilometers
Statute Miles
ATLANTIC OCEAN
BOSTON
NEW YORK
Albany
Providence
Hartford
Long Island Sound
Massachusetts Bay
Cape Cod Bay
Nantucket Sound
Rhode Island Sound
Block Island Sound
208 · 209
210 · 211
Copyright © by Rand McNally & Co.

210-211

NEW YORK
NEWARK
Jersey City
Elizabeth
Trenton
PHILADELPHIA
Camden
Wilmington
Atlantic City
Allentown
Bethlehem
Reading
Lancaster
Harrisburg
York
BALTIMORE
WASHINGTON
Alexandria
Annapolis
Dover
Vineland
Delaware Bay
DELMARVA
APPALACHIAN
MOUNTAINS

ATLANTIC
OCEAN
Chesapeake Bay
PENINSULA
Salisbury
Ocean City
Fredericksburg
Richmond
Petersburg
Hopewell
Williamsburg
Newport News
Hampton
Norfolk
Portsmouth
Chesapeake
Virginia Beach
Suffolk
Cape Charles
CAPE HENRY
CHESAPEAKE BAY BRIDGE-TUNNEL
ASSATEAGUE ISLAND NATIONAL SEASHORE
MARYLAND
VIRGINIA
NORTH CAROLINA
Kilometers 0 10 20 30 40 50 Km.
Statute Miles 0 10 20 30 40 50 Mi.
Scale 1:1,000,000
One centimeter represents 10 kilometers.
One inch represents approximately 16 miles.
Lambert Conformal Conic Projection
ENGLISH airport, arpt. bay creek, cr. inlet island, i. mountain point, pt. reservoir, res. state park
DEUTSCH Flughafen Bucht Bach Einfahrt Insel Berg Landspitze Stausee Naturpark
ESPAÑOL aeropuerto bahía riachuelo abra isla montaña punta embalse parque provincial
FRANÇAIS aéroport baie crique bras de mer île montagne pointe réservoir parc régional
PORTUGUÊS aeroporto baía riacho enseada ilha montanha ponta reservatório parque estadual
Copyright © by Rand McNally & Co.
Map prepared by Rand McNally & Co.

ENGLISH	airport, arpt.	bay	creek, cr.	hill	Island	lake	mountain	reservoir	state park, s.p.
DEUTSCH	Flughafen	Bucht	Bach	Hügel	Insel	See	Berg	Stausee	Naturpark
ESPAÑOL	aeropuerto	bahía	riachuelo	colina	isla	lago	montaña	embalse	parque provincial
FRANÇAIS	aéroport	baie	crique	colline	île	lac	montagne	réservoir	parc régional
PORTUGUÊS	aeroporto	baía	riacho	colina	ilha	lago	montanha	reservatório	parque estadual

Kilometers 0 10 20 30 40 50 Km.

Statute Miles 0 10 20 30 40 50 Mi.

Scale 1:1,000,000

One centimeter represents 10 kilometers.

One inch represents approximately 16 miles.

Lambert Conformal Conic Projection

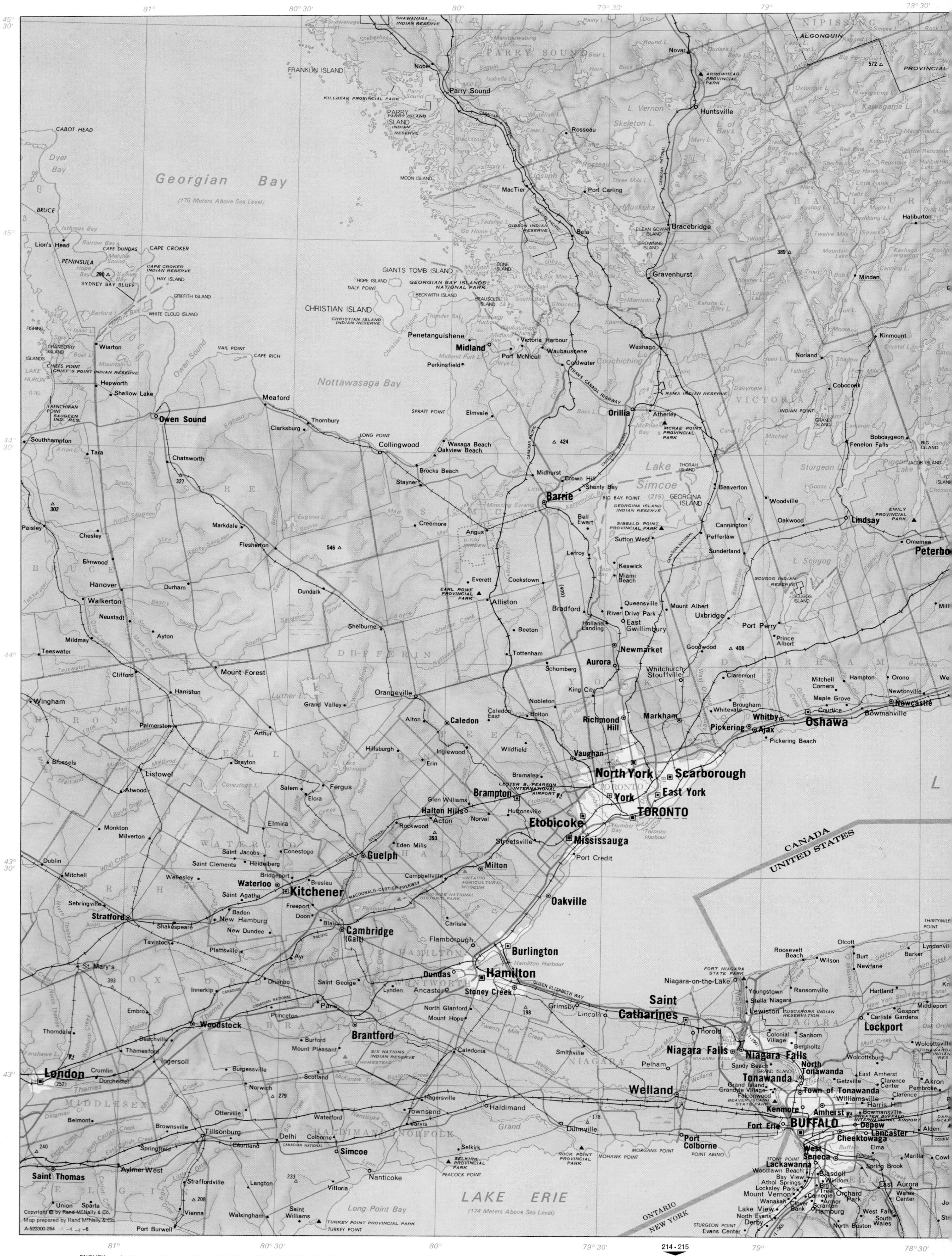

ENGLISH	airport	bay	canal	channel	creek, cr.	Indian reservation	island	lake, l.	point
DEUTSCH	Flughafen	Bucht	Kanal	Kanal	Bach	Indianerreservation	Insel	See	Landspitze
ESPAÑOL	aeropuerto	bahía	canal	canal	riachuelo	reserva de Indios	isla	lago	punta
FRANÇAIS	aéroport	baie	canal	canal	crique	réserve indienne	île	lac	pointe
PORTUGUÊS	aeroporto	baía	canal	canal	riacho	reserva indígena	ilha	lago	ponta

214-215

Kilometers 0 10 20 30 40 50 Km.

Statute Miles 0 10 20 30 40 50 Mi.

Scale 1:1,000,000

One centimeter represents 10 kilometers.
One inch represents approximately 16 miles.
Lambert Conformal Conic Projection

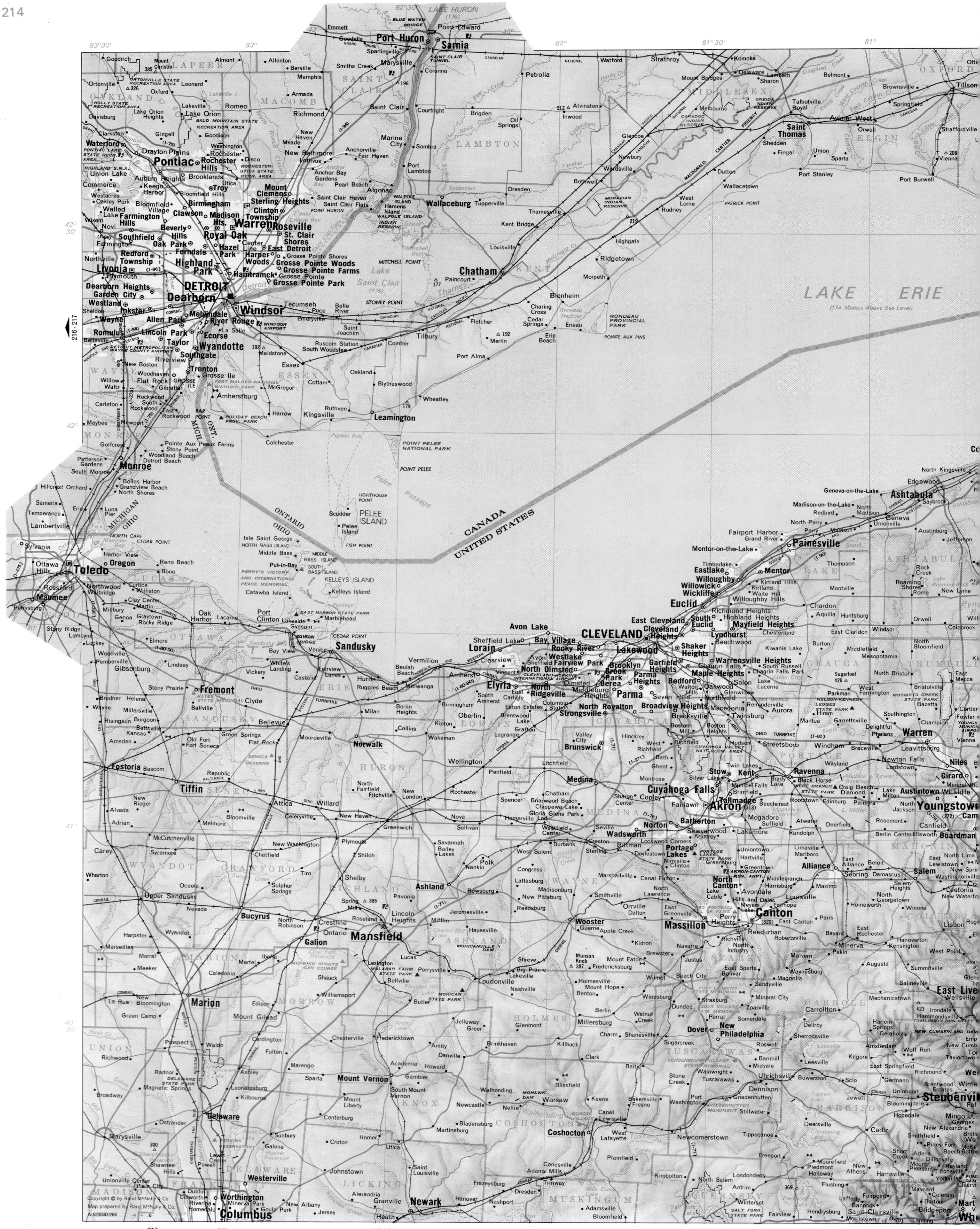

ENGLISH	airport	creek, cr.	hill	lake, l.	mountain, mtn.	point, pt.	reservoir, res.	state park
DEUTSCH	Flughafen	Bach	Hügel	See	Berg	Landspitze	Stausee	Naturpark
ESPAÑOL	aeropuerto	riachuelo	colina	lago	montaña	punta	embalse	parque provincial
FRANÇAIS	aéroport	crique	colline	lac	montagne	pointe	réservoir	parc régional
PORTUGUÊS	aeroporto	riacho	colina	lago	montanha	ponta	reservatório	parque estadual

Kilometers 0 10 20 30 40 50 Km.

Statute Miles 0 10 20 30 40 50 Mi.

Scale 1:1,000,000

One centimeter represents 10 kilometers.

One inch represents approximately 16 miles.

Lambert Conformal Conic Projection

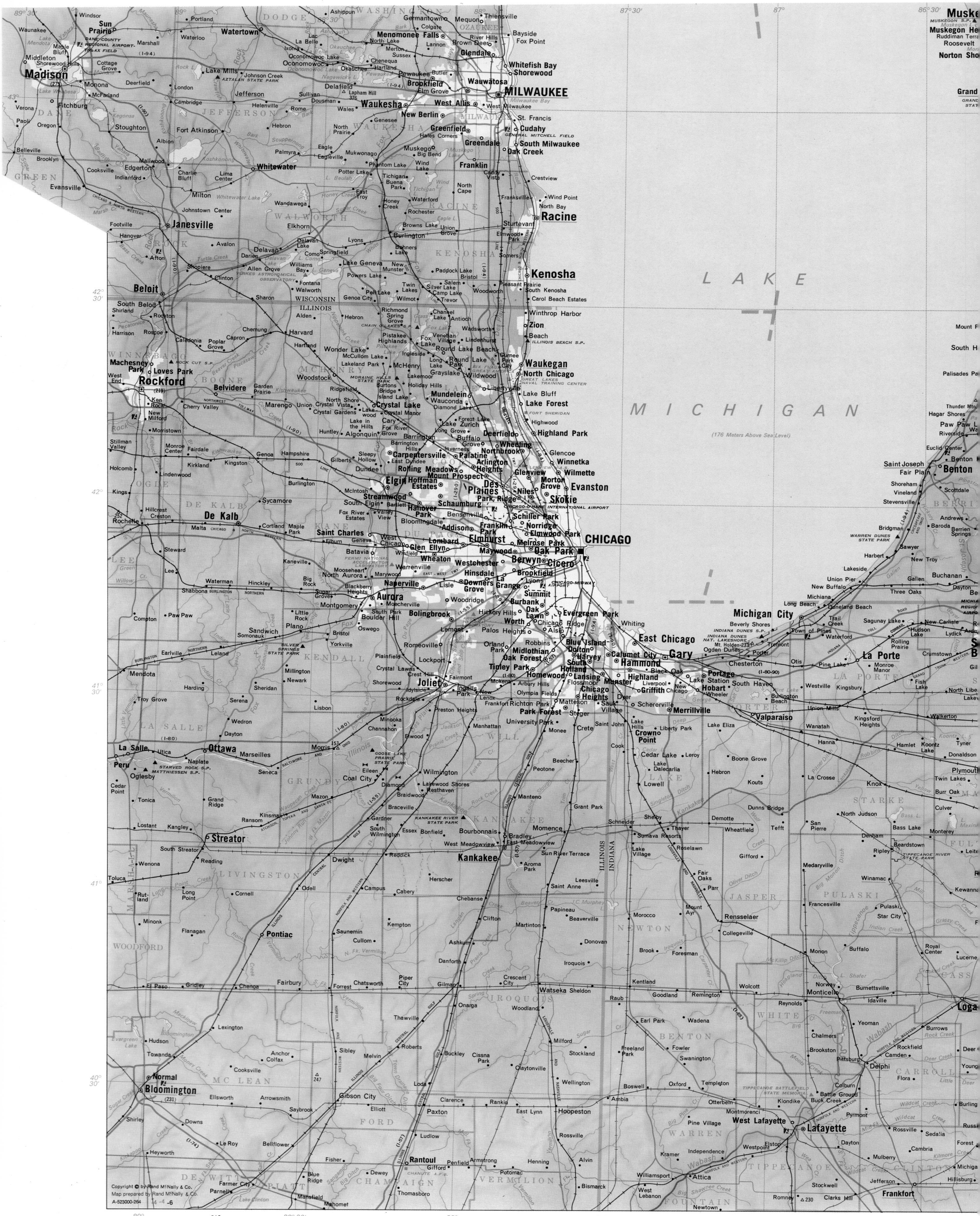

219

ENGLISH	airport	creek, cr.	ditch	lake, l.	reservoir	state park, s.p.
DEUTSCH	Flughafen	Bach	Graben	See	Stausee	Naturpark
ESPAÑOL	aeropuerto	riachuelo	acequia	lago	embalse	parque provincial
FRANÇAIS	aéroport	crique	fossé	lac	réservoir	parc régional
PORTUGUÊS	aeroporto	riacho	fosso	lago	reservatório	parque estadual

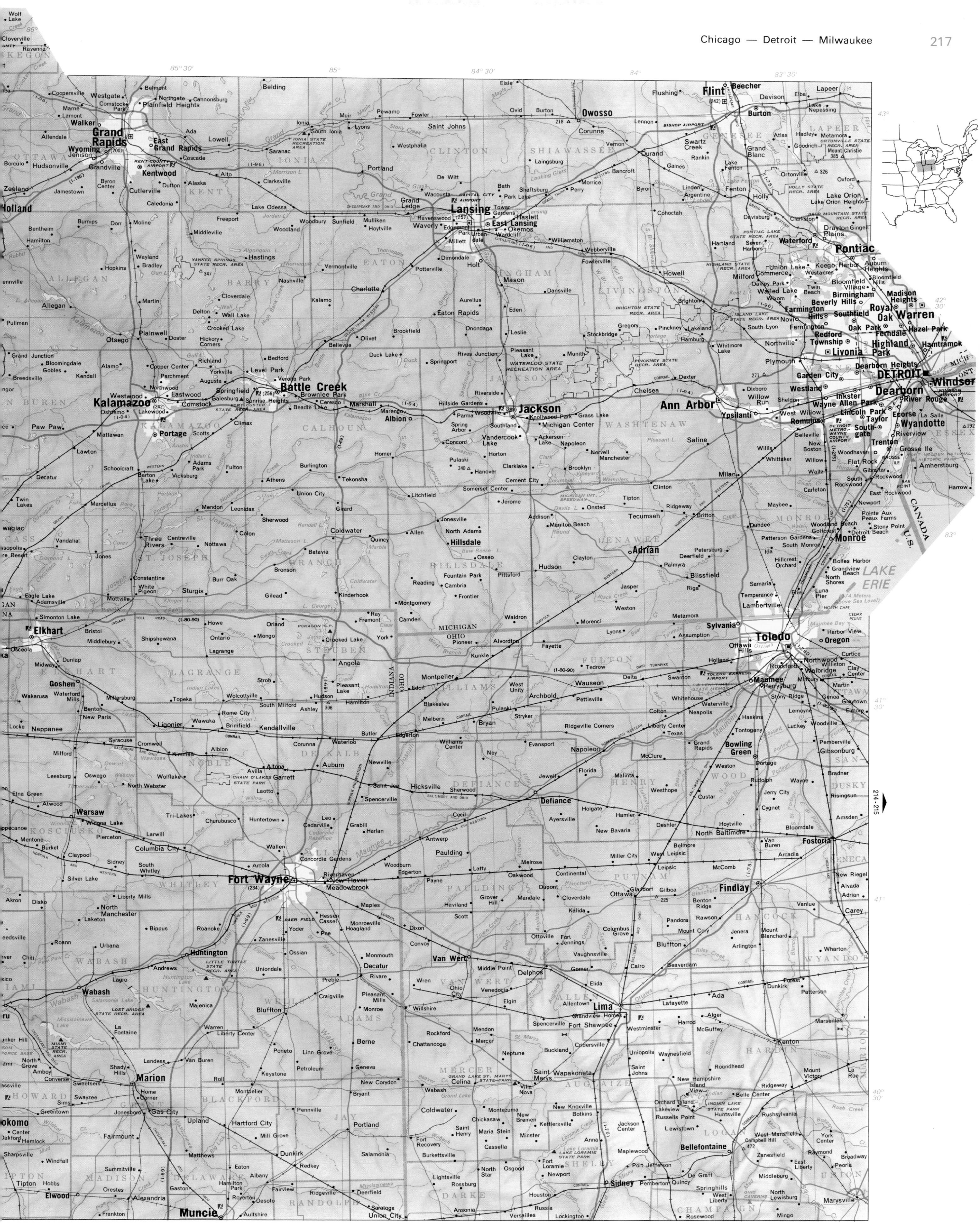

Kilometers 0 10 20 30 40 50 Km.

Statute Miles 0 10 20 30 40 50 Mi.

Scale 1:1,000,000

One centimeter represents 10 kilometers.

One inch represents approximately 16 miles.

Lambert Conformal Conic Projection

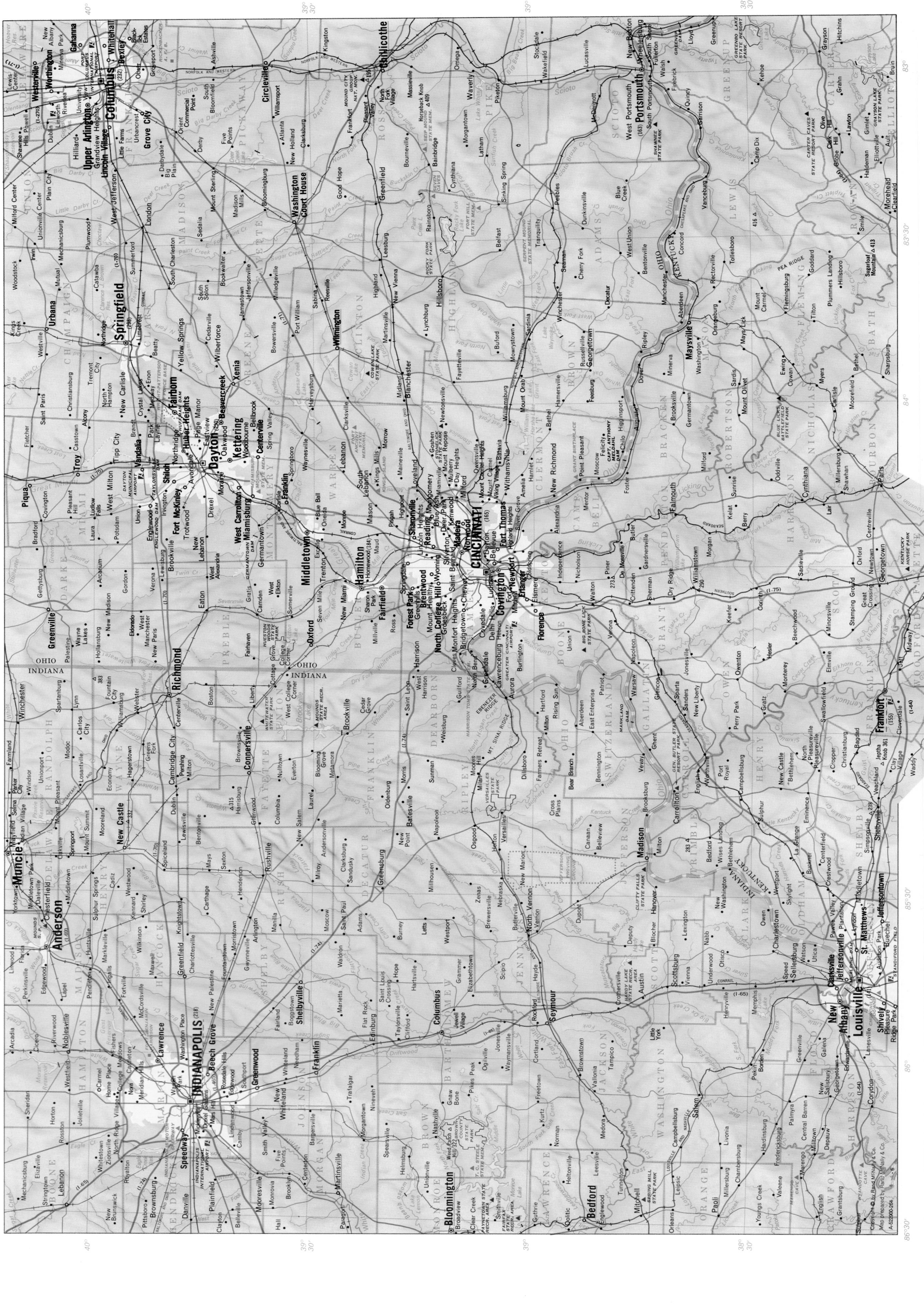

Kilometers 0 10 20 30 40 50 Km.

Statute Miles 0 10 20 30 40 50 Mi.

Scale 1:1,000,000

One centimeter represents 10 kilometers.
One inch represents approximately 16 miles.
Lambert Conformal Conic Projection

ENGLISH	airport	creek, cr.	dam	lake	reservoir, res.	ridge	state park
DEUTSCH	Flughafen	Bach	Damm	See	Stausee	Hohenrucken	Naturpark
ESPAÑOL	aeropuerto	riachuelo	presa	lago	embalse	serrania	parque provincial
FRANÇAIS	aéroport	ruisseau	barrage	lac	réservoir	crête	parc régional
PORTUGUÊS	aeroporto	riacho	represa	lago	reservatório	cordilheira	parque estadual

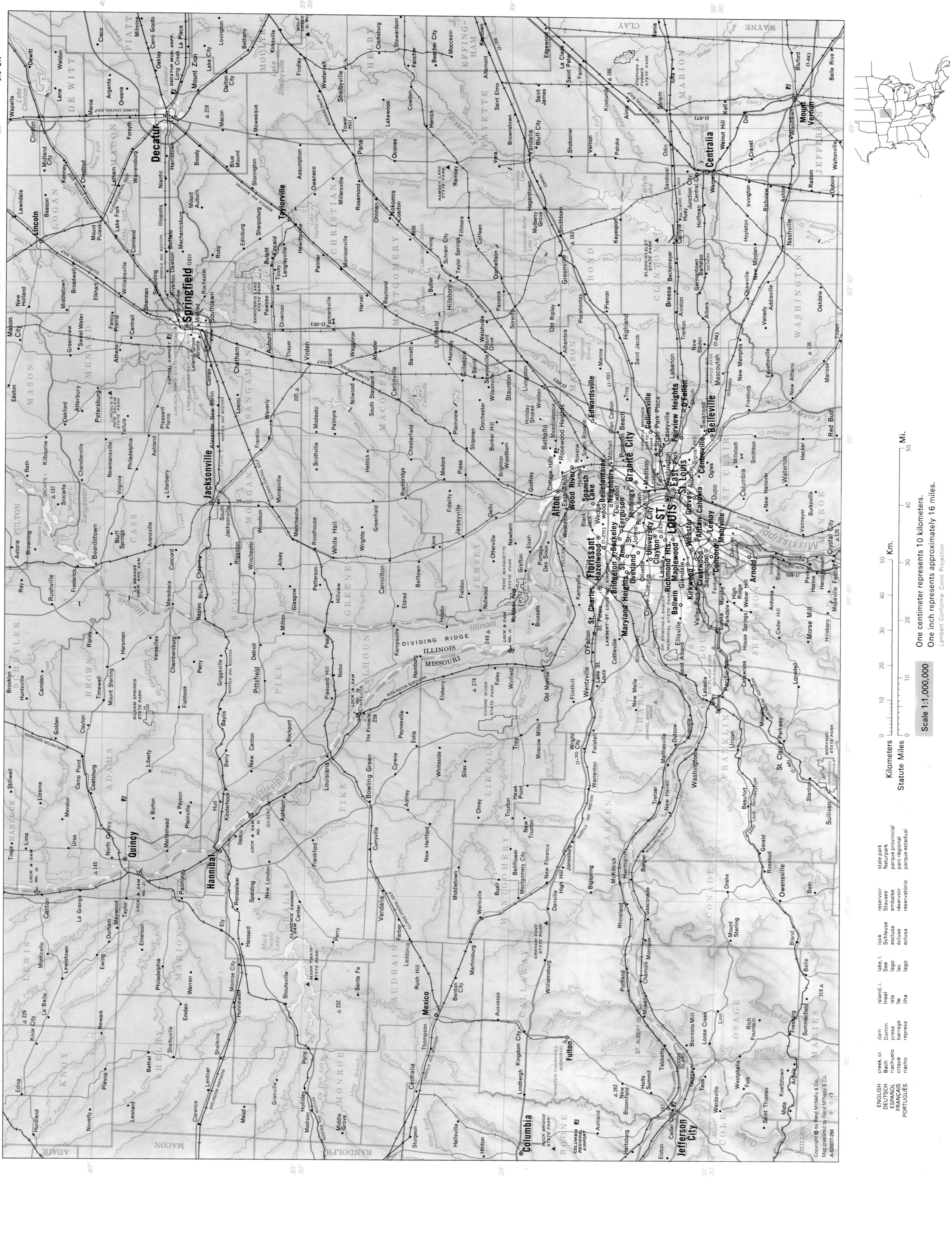
216-217
Scale 1:1,000,000
One centimeter represents 10 kilometers.
One inch represents approximately 16 miles.
Lambert Conformal Conic Projection
Kilometers
Statute Miles
Km.
Mi.
Copyright © by Rand McNally & Co.
Map made by Rand McNally & Co.

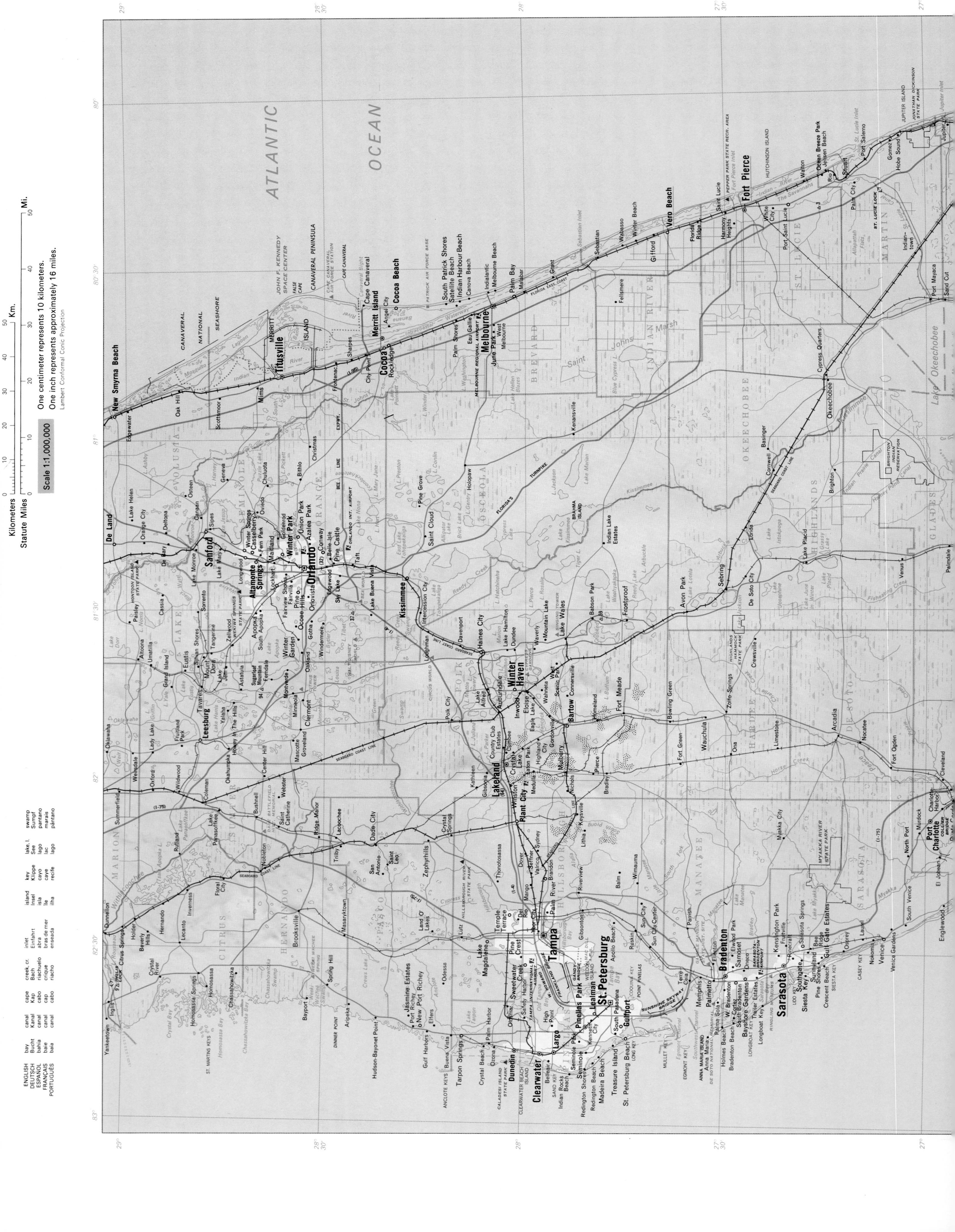
ATLANTIC
OCEAN
Scale 1:1,000,000
Kilometers
Statute Miles
Km.
Mi.
One centimeter represents 10 kilometers.
One inch represents approximately 16 miles.
Lambert Conformal Conic Projection

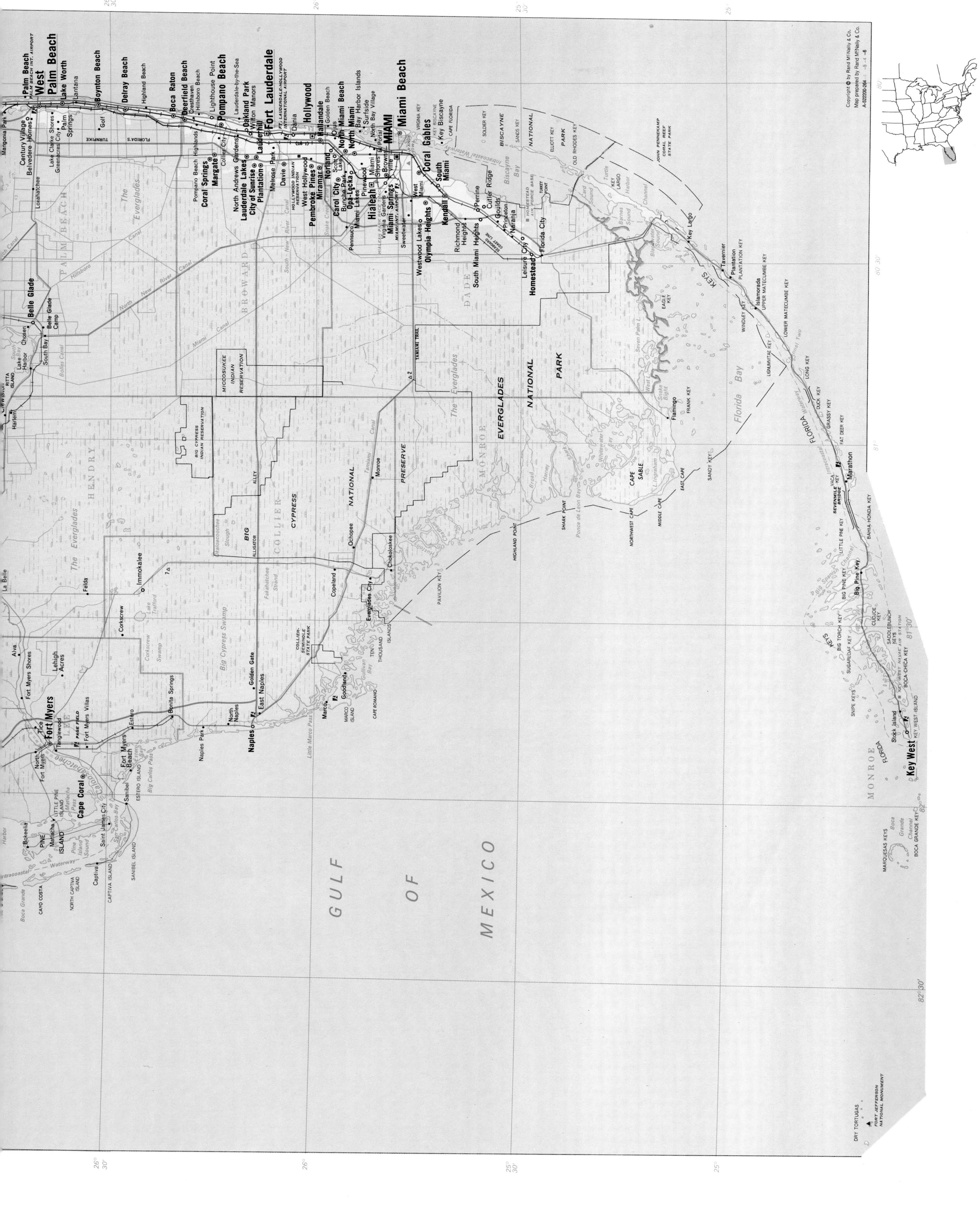
West Palm Beach
Palm Beach
Lake Worth
Lantana
Boynton Beach
Delray Beach
Highland Beach
Boca Raton
Deerfield Beach
Pompano Beach
Lighthouse Point
Fort Lauderdale
Hollywood
Dania
Hallandale
North Miami Beach
North Miami
Miami Beach
MIAMI
Coral Gables
Key Biscayne
South Miami
Hialeah
Miami Springs
Opa-Locka
Carol City
Kendall
Olympia Heights
Westwood Lakes
Perrine
Cutler Ridge
Goulds
Homestead
Florida City
Leisure City
Coral Springs
Margate
Plantation
Lauderhill
Davie
Pembroke Pines
Miramar
Belle Glade
South Bay
Fort Myers
North Fort Myers
Cape Coral
Fort Myers Beach
Sanibel
Captiva
Naples
East Naples
Golden Gate
Bonita Springs
Estero
Lehigh Acres
Immokalee
Felda
La Belle
Everglades City
Chokoloskee
Ochopee
Copeland
Marco
Goodland
Flamingo
Key Largo
Tavernier
Plantation
Islamorada
Marathon
Big Pine Key
Key West
Stock Island
PALM BEACH
BROWARD
DADE
COLLIER
HENDRY
LEE
MONROE
EVERGLADES NATIONAL PARK
BIG CYPRESS NATIONAL PRESERVE
BISCAYNE NATIONAL PARK
MICCOSUKEE INDIAN RESERVATION
BIG CYPRESS INDIAN RESERVATION
JOHN PENNEKAMP CORAL REEF STATE PARK
TAMIAMI TRAIL
The Everglades
Florida Bay
Biscayne Bay
GULF OF MEXICO
FLORIDA KEYS
CAPE SABLE
TEN THOUSAND ISLANDS
DRY TORTUGAS
FORT JEFFERSON NATIONAL MONUMENT
MARQUESAS KEYS
Copyright © by Rand McNally & Co.
Map prepared by Rand McNally & Co.

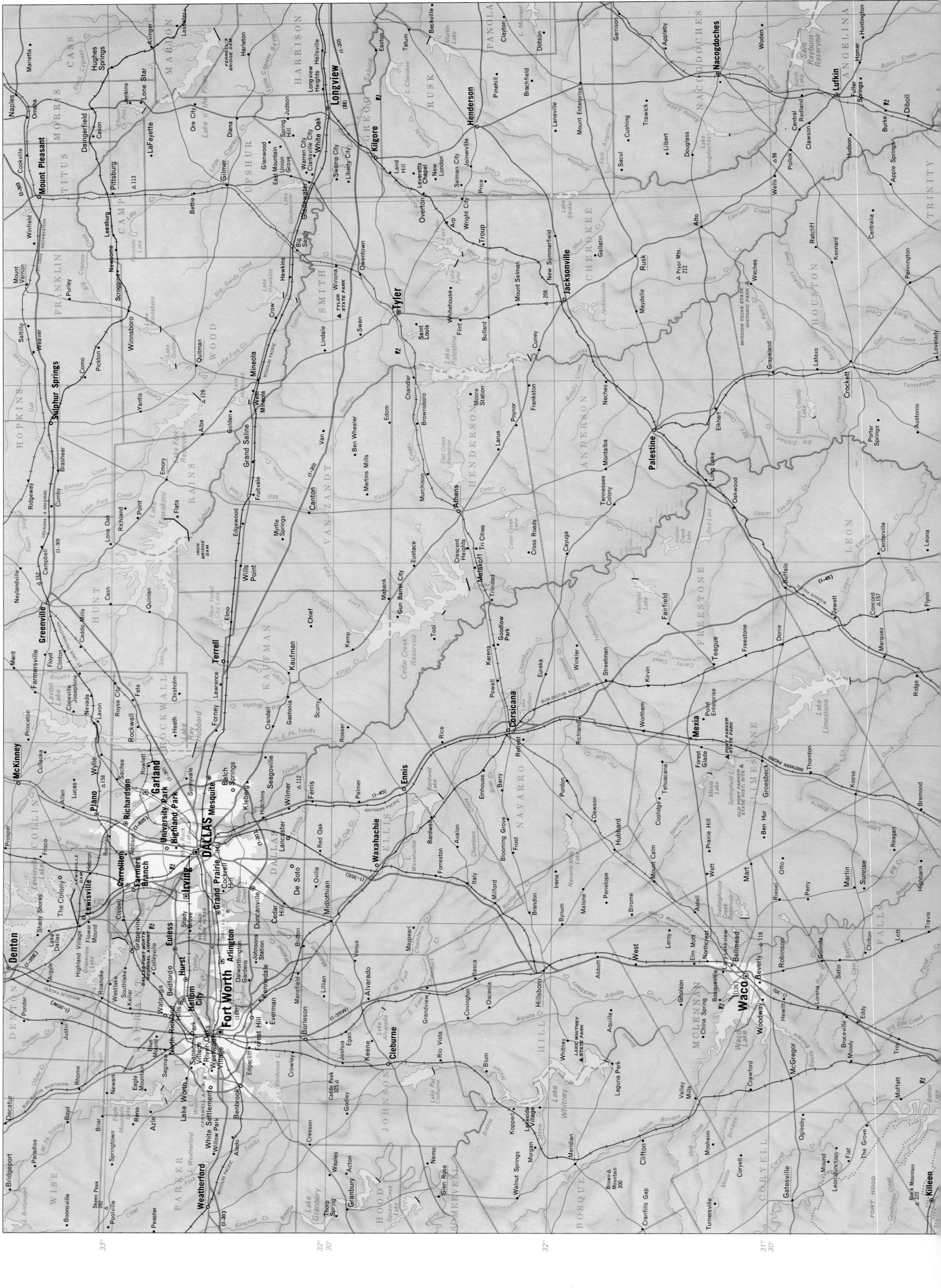
DALLAS
Fort Worth
Waco
Tyler
Longview
Palestine
Corsicana
Denton
McKinney
Greenville
Sulphur Springs
Mount Pleasant
Kilgore
Henderson
Nacogdoches
Lufkin
Jacksonville
Athens
Terrell
Waxahachie
Ennis
Cleburne
Weatherford
Hillsboro
Mexia
Killeen
Garland
Irving
Arlington
Mesquite
Grand Prairie
Richardson
Plano
Lewisville
Carrollton
Crockett
Rusk
Fairfield
Teague
Marlin
Groesbeck
Canton
Mineola
Gilmer
Pittsburg
Kaufman
Cedar Creek Reservoir
Lake Whitney
Lake Palestine
Lake Tawakoni
Lake Limestone
Navarro Mills Lake
DENTON
COLLIN
HUNT
HOPKINS
FRANKLIN
TITUS
MORRIS
CASS
MARION
HARRISON
UPSHUR
CAMP
WOOD
RAINS
ROCKWALL
KAUFMAN
VAN ZANDT
SMITH
GREGG
RUSK
PANOLA
NACOGDOCHES
CHEROKEE
ANDERSON
HENDERSON
NAVARRO
ELLIS
JOHNSON
HILL
FREESTONE
LIMESTONE
LEON
HOUSTON
TRINITY
ANGELINA
MCLENNAN
BOSQUE
SOMERVELL
HOOD
PARKER
WISE
CORYELL
FALLS
33°
32° 30'
32°
31° 30'
94° 30'
95°
95° 30'
96°
96° 30'
97°
97° 30'

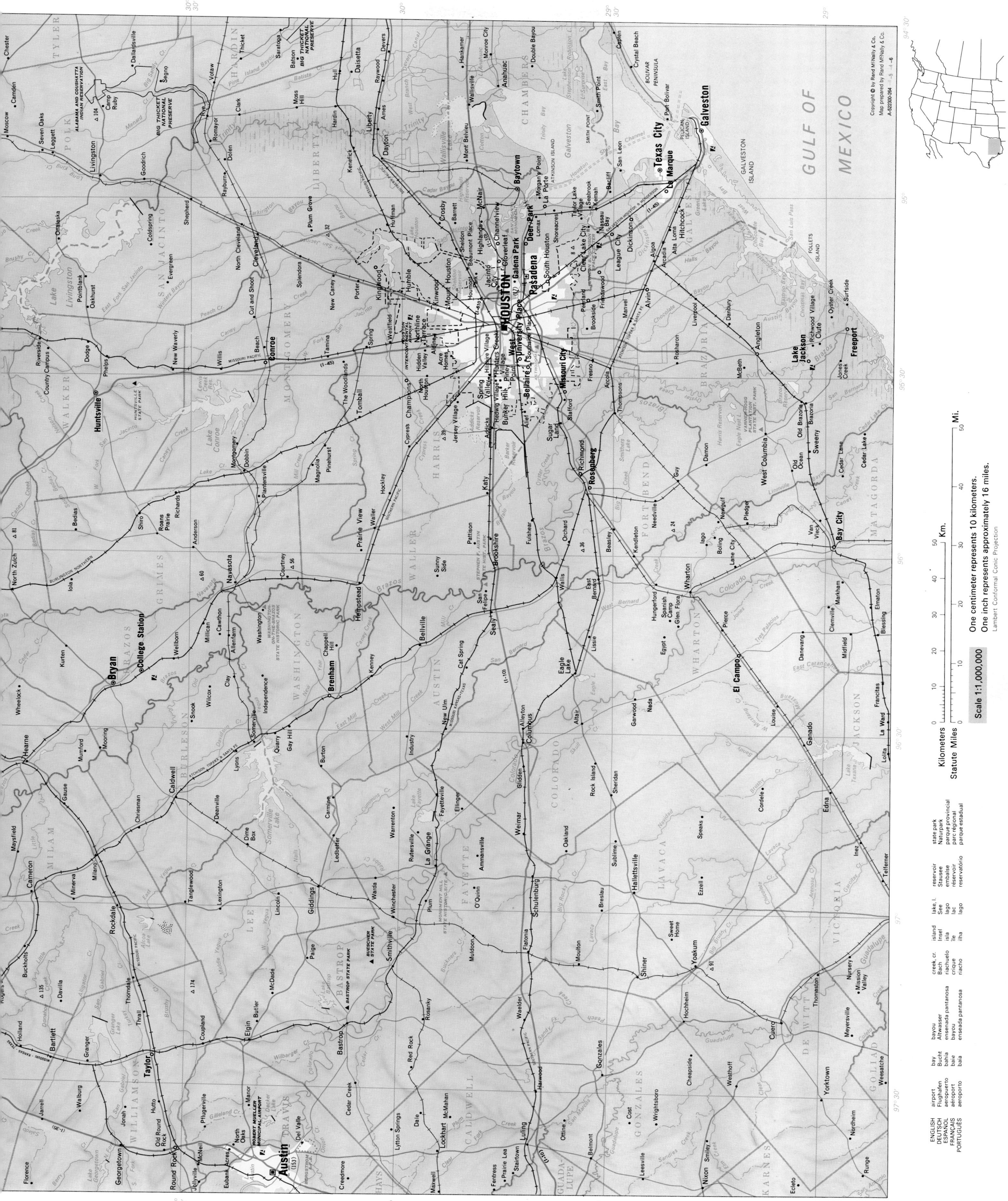
GULF OF MEXICO
HOUSTON
Galveston
Austin
Bryan
College Station
Scale 1:1,000,000
One centimeter represents 10 kilometers.
One inch represents approximately 16 miles.
Lambert Conformal Conic Projection
Kilometers 0 10 20 30 40 50 Km.
Statute Miles 0 10 20 30 40 50 Mi.
ENGLISH airport bay bayou creek, cr. island lake, l. reservoir state park
DEUTSCH Flughafen Bucht Altwasser Bach Insel See Stausee Naturpark
ESPAÑOL aeropuerto bahia ensenada pantanosa riachuelo isla lago embalse parque provincial
FRANÇAIS aéroport baie bayou cirque île lac réservoir parc régional
PORTUGUÊS aeroporto baía enseada pantanosa riacho ilha lago reservatório parque estadual
Copyright © by Rand McNally & Co.
Map prepared by Rand McNally & Co.

VANCOUVER
North Vancouver
Burnaby
New Westminster
Richmond
Victoria
Esquimalt
Oak Bay
Nanaimo
Port Alberni
Chilliwack
Bellingham
Mount Vernon
Anacortes
Everett
SEATTLE
Tacoma
Bremerton
Port Angeles
Port Townsend
CASCADE MOUNTAINS
OLYMPIC MOUNTAINS
VANCOUVER ISLAND
Strait of Georgia
Strait of Juan de Fuca
SAN JUAN ISLANDS
BRITISH COLUMBIA
WASHINGTON
CANADA
UNITED STATES
OLYMPIC NATIONAL PARK
NORTH CASCADES NATIONAL PARK
WENATCHEE MOUNTAINS
Haro Strait
Puget Sound
Saratoga Passage
Mt. Baker
Mt. Olympus

Scale 1:1,000,000

One centimeter represents 10 kilometers.
One inch represents approximately 16 miles.
Lambert Conformal Conic Projection

Kilometers 0 10 20 30 40 50 Km.

Statute Miles 0 10 20 30 40 50 Mi.

ENGLISH	bay	cape	channel	creek, cr.	island, i.	lake, l.	mount	peak	strait
DEUTSCH	Bucht	Kap	Kanal	Bach	Insel	See	Berg	Gipfel	Meeresstrasse
ESPAÑOL	bahía	cabo	canal	riachuelo	isla	lago	monte	pico	estrecho
FRANÇAIS	baie	cap	canal	crique	île	lac	mont	cime	détroit
PORTUGUÊS	baía	cabo	canal	riacho	ilha	lago	monte	pico	estreito

Reno
Sparks
Carson City
South Lake Tahoe
Lake Tahoe
SIERRA NEVADA
PINE NUT MOUNTAINS
CARSON RANGE
CARSON VALLEY
SWEETWATER MTS.
CATHEDRAL RANGE
Yosemite National Park
Sacramento
West Sacramento
Davis
Woodland
Yuba City
Marysville
Oroville
Roseville
Citrus Heights
Fair Oaks
Rancho Cordova
Stockton
Lodi
Manteca
Tracy
Modesto
Turlock
Fairfield
Vacaville
Vallejo
Napa
Santa Rosa
Petaluma
Novato
Concord
Walnut Creek
Oakland
Berkeley
Alameda
Hayward
Fremont
Livermore
Pleasanton
San Leandro
SAN FRANCISCO
Daly City
San Mateo
Pacifica
SACRAMENTO VALLEY

ENGLISH	bay	canal	creek, cr.	lake, l.	mountain, mtn.	pass	range	reservoir	slough
DEUTSCH	Bucht	Kanal	Bach	See	Berg	Pass	Gebirge	Stausee	verlandene Wasserfläche
ESPAÑOL	bahía	canal	riachuelo	lago	montaña	paso	sierra	embalse	pantano
FRANÇAIS	baie	canal	crique	lac	montagne	col	chaîne	réservoir	fondrière
PORTUGUÊS	baía	canal	riacho	lago	montanha	passo	serra	reservatório	pântano

Kilometers 0 10 20 30 40 50 Km.
Statute Miles 0 10 20 30 40 50 Mi.

Scale 1:1,000,000

One centimeter represents 10 kilometers.
One inch represents approximately 16 miles.
Lambert Conformal Conic Projection

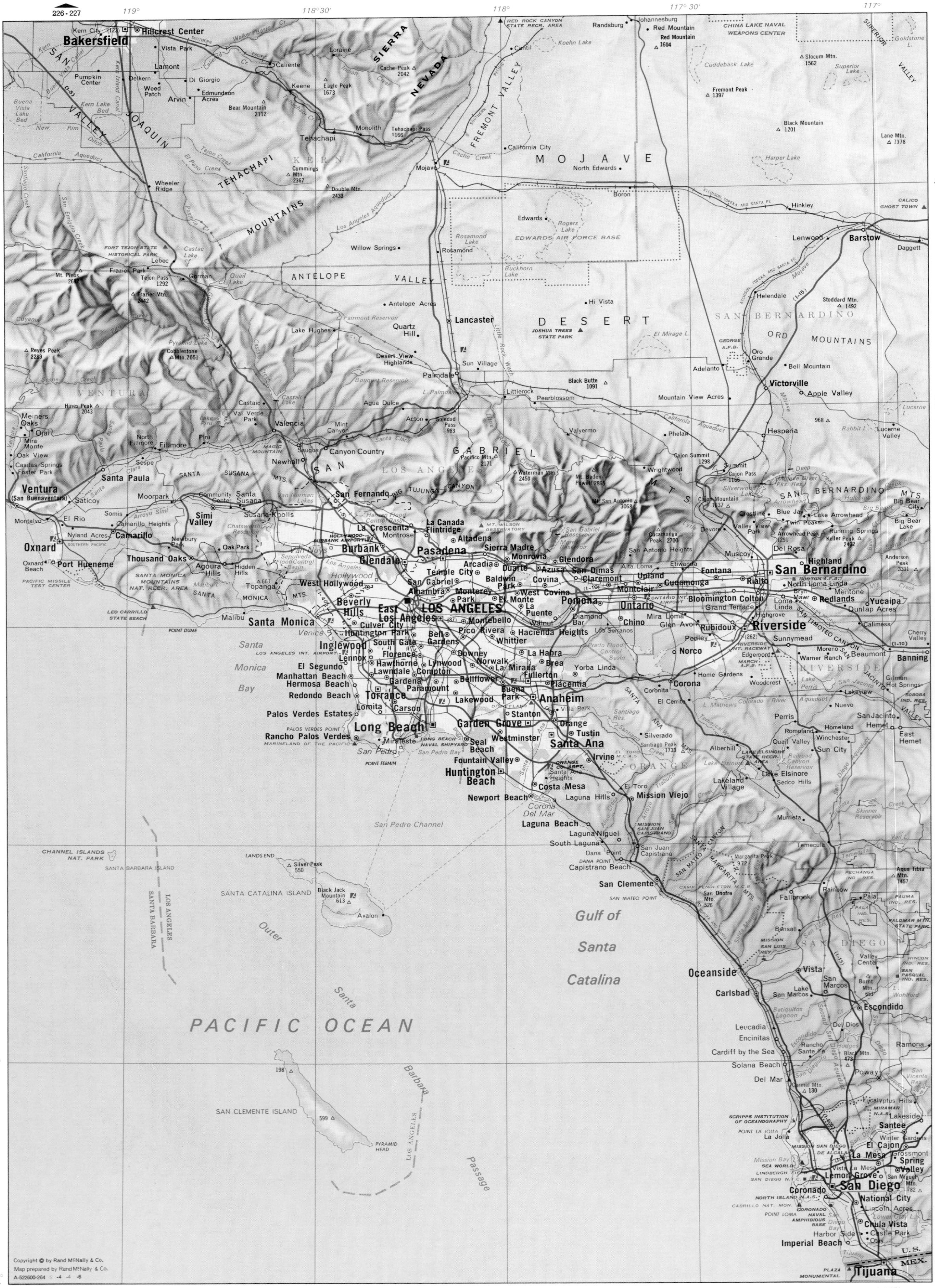

ENGLISH	canyon	creek, cr.	lake, l.	mountain, mtn.	pass	peak	point	reservoir, res
DEUTSCH	Cañon	Bach	See	Berg	Pass	Gipfel	Landspitze	Stausee
ESPAÑOL	cañón	riachuelo	lago	montaña	paso	pico	punta	embalse
FRANÇAIS	canyon	crique	lac	montagne	col	cime	pointe	réservoir
PORTUGUÊS	canhão	riacho	lago	montanha	passo	pico	ponta	reservatório

Kilometers 0 10 20 30 40 50 Km.

Statute Miles 0 10 20 30 40 50 Mi.

Scale 1:1,000,000

One centimeter represents 10 kilometers.
One inch represents approximately 16 miles.

Lambert Conformal Conic Projection

a

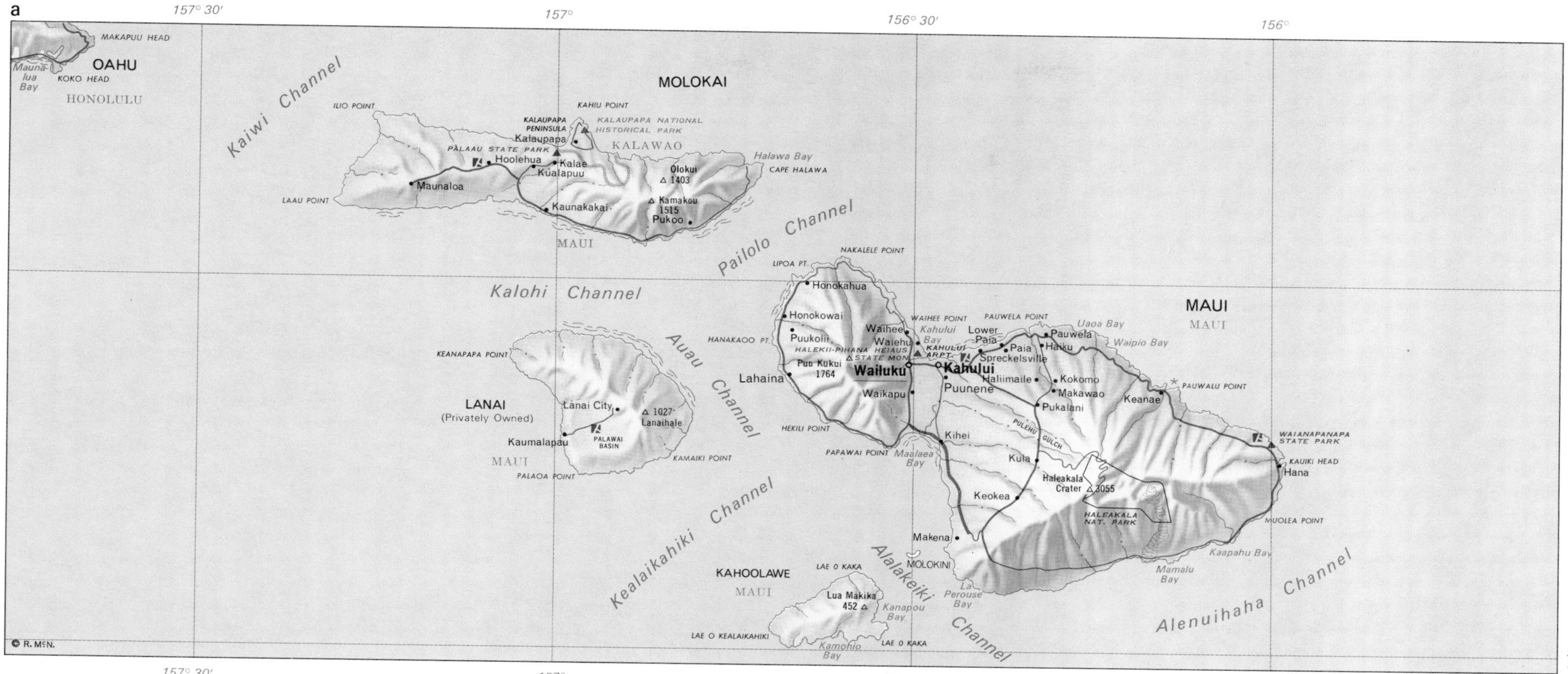

b

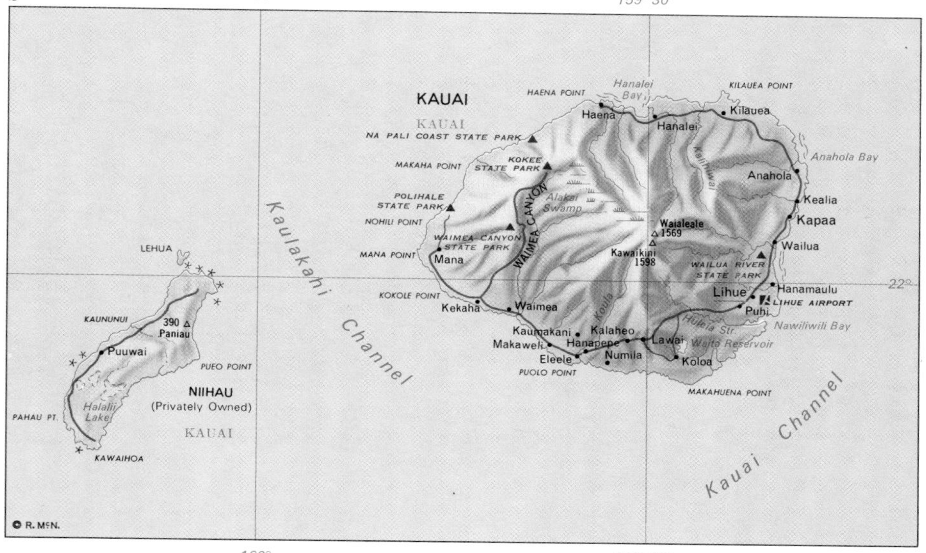

c

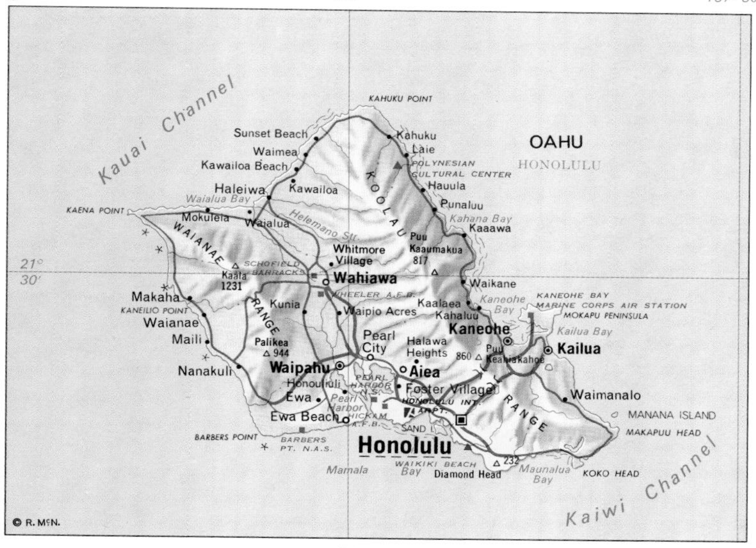

Kilometers 0 10 20 30 40 50 Km.
Statute Miles 0 10 20 30 40 50 Mi.

Scale 1:1,000,000

One centimeter represents 10 kilometers.
One inch represents approximately 16 miles.
Lambert Conformal Conic Projection

d

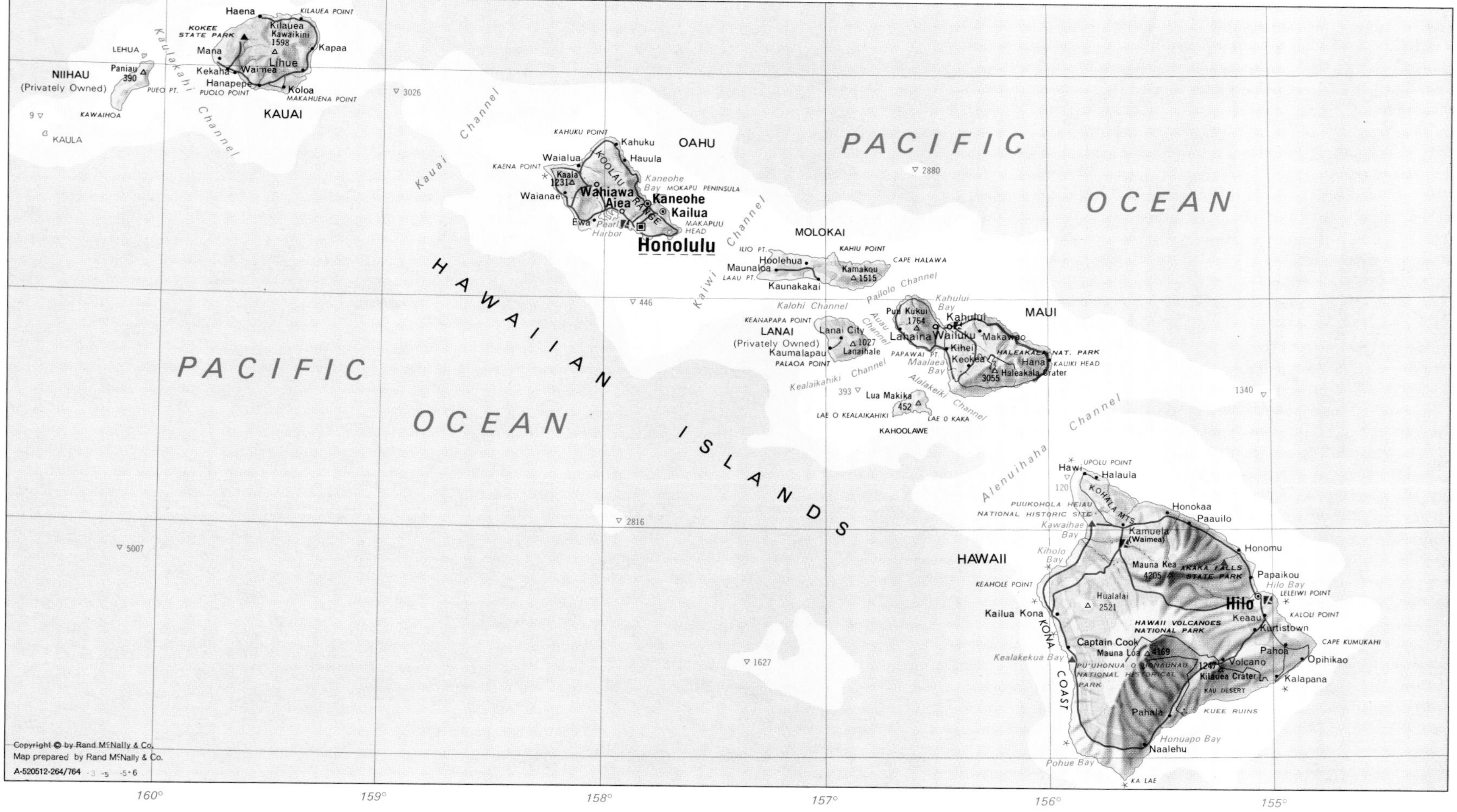

Meters	Feet
6000	19685
4000	13124
3000	9843
2000	6562
1000	3281
500	1640
200	656
0	0
Land Below Sea Level	
0	0
200	656
1000	3281
3000	9843
6000	19685
9000	29520

ENGLISH	bay	channel	head	mount	point	state park, s.p.
DEUTSCH	Bucht	Kanal	Landspitze	Berg	Landspitze	Staatspark
ESPAÑOL	bahía	canal	promontorio	monte	punta	parque del estado
FRANÇAIS	baie	détroit	promontoire	mont	pointe	parc régional
PORTUGUÊS	baía	canal	promontório	monte	ponta	parque estadual

Kilometers 0 50 100 150 Km.
Statute Miles 0 50 100 150 Mi.

Scale 1:3,000,000

One centimeter represents 30 kilometers.
One inch represents approximately 47 miles.
Lambert Conformal Conic Projection

ESPAÑOL	cabo	cordillera	golfo	isla, i.	lago, l.	punta	sierra	volcán, vol.
ENGLISH	cape	mountains	gulf	island	lake	point	mountains	volcano
DEUTSCH	Kap	Berge	Golf	Insel	See	Landspitze	Berge	Vulkan
FRANÇAIS	cap	montagnes	golfe	île	lac	pointe	montagnes	volcan
PORTUGUÊS	cabo	cordilheira	golfo	ilha	lago	ponta	serra	vulcão

Kilometers 0 200 400 600 Km.
Statute Miles 0 200 400 600 Mi.
Scale 1:12,000,000
One centimeter represents 120 kilometers.
One inch represents approximately 190 miles.
Oblique Conic Conformal Projection

242-243

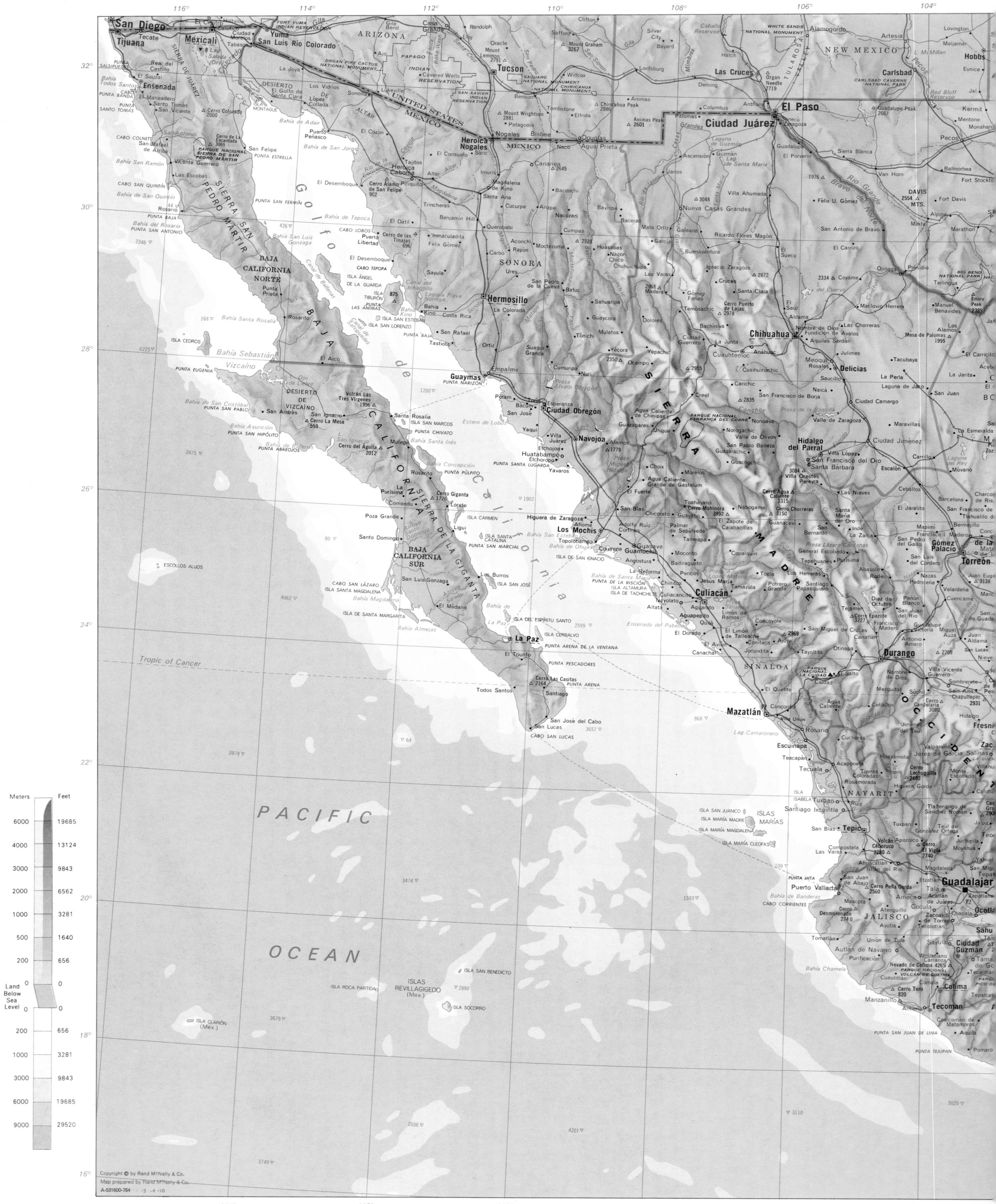

ESPAÑOL	bahía	cerro	isla	laguna	presa	punta	río	sierra
ENGLISH	bay	mountain	island	lagoon	reservoir	point	river	mountains
DEUTSCH	Bucht	Berg	Insel	Haff	Stausee	Landspitze	Fluss	Berge
FRANÇAIS	baie	montagne	île	lagune	réservoir	pointe	rivière	montagnes
PORTUGUÊS	baía	montanha	ilha	laguna	reservatório	ponta	rio	serra

Kilometers 0 100 200 300 Km.
Statute Miles 0 100 200 300

Scale 1:6,000,000

One centimeter represents 60 kilometers.
One inch represents approximately 95 miles.
Lambert Conformal Conic Projection

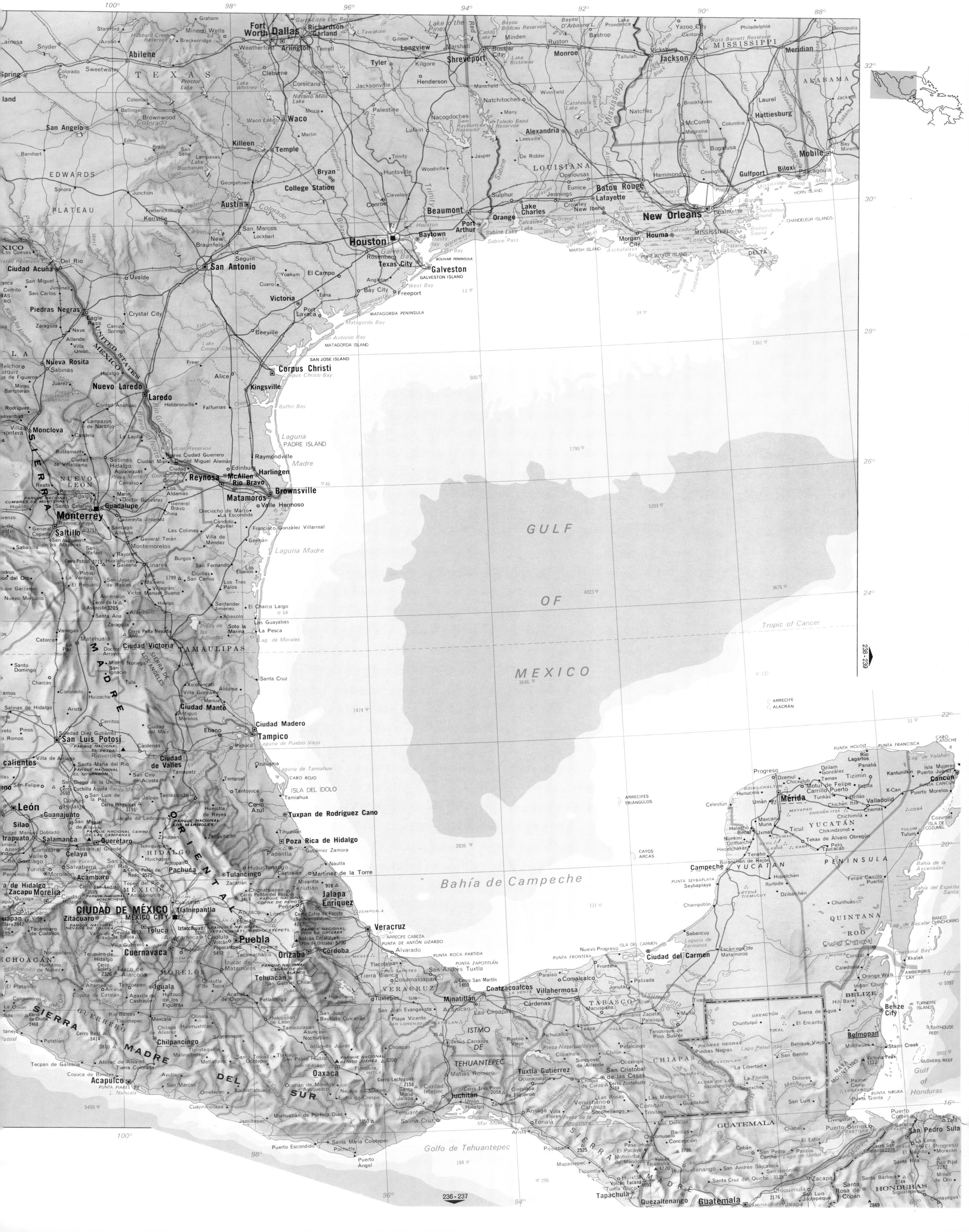
GULF
OF
MEXICO
Bahía de Campeche
Golfo de Tehuantepec
Tropic of Cancer
T E X A S
LOUISIANA
MISSISSIPPI
ALABAMA
TAMAULIPAS
NUEVO LEÓN
HIDALGO
MÉXICO
MORELOS
VERACRUZ
TABASCO
CHIAPAS
YUCATÁN
CAMPECHE
QUINTANA ROO
GUATEMALA
BELIZE
HONDURAS
EDWARDS PLATEAU
SIERRA MADRE
SIERRA MADRE ORIENTAL
SIERRA MADRE DEL SUR
ISTMO DE TEHUANTEPEC
YUCATAN PENINSULA
Dallas
Fort Worth
Houston
San Antonio
Austin
Corpus Christi
Galveston
Beaumont
Shreveport
Baton Rouge
New Orleans
Jackson
Mobile
Monterrey
Saltillo
Nuevo Laredo
Laredo
Reynosa
Matamoros
Brownsville
Ciudad Victoria
Tampico
San Luis Potosí
León
Querétaro
Pachuca
CIUDAD DE MÉXICO
MEXICO CITY
Puebla
Toluca
Cuernavaca
Veracruz
Jalapa Enríquez
Orizaba
Oaxaca
Acapulco
Chilpancingo
Coatzacoalcos
Villahermosa
Ciudad del Carmen
Campeche
Mérida
Cancún
Belize City
Belmopan
Tuxtla Gutiérrez
Tapachula
Guatemala
Quezaltenango
San Pedro Sula
Gulf of Honduras
236 - 237
238 - 239

ESPAÑOL	arroyo	boca	cerro	lago	laguna	punta	río	sierra	volcán
ENGLISH	brook	entrance	butte	lake	lagoon	point	river	ranges	volcano
DEUTSCH	Bach	Einfahrt	Restberg	See	Haff	Landspitze	Fluss	Bergketten	Vulkan
FRANÇAIS	ruisseau	entrée	butte	lac	lagune	pointe	rivière	chaîne	volcan
PORTUGUÊS	riacho	entrada	cerro	lago	laguna	ponta	rio	serra	vulcão

99°
98°
97°
96°
95°
94°
93°
24°
23°
22°
21°
20°
19°
18°
17°
16°
Tropic of Cancer
GULF OF MEXICO
Bahia de Campeche
Golfo de Tehuantepec
Ciudad Victoria
Ciudad Mante
Tampico
Ciudad Madero
TAMAULIPAS
SAN LUIS POTOSÍ
VERACRUZ
HIDALGO
PUEBLA
SIERRA AZUL
La Pesca
Soto la Marina
Altamira
Pánuco
ISLA JUANA RAMIREZ
CABO ROJO
Tempoal
Tantoyuca
Naranjos
Cerro Azul
Tuxpan de Rodríguez Cano
Poza Rica de Hidalgo
Papantla
Pachuca
Tulancingo
Martínez de la Torre
Teziutlán
Misantla
Jalapa Enríquez
CIUDAD DE MÉXICO
MEXICO CITY
Puebla
Atlixco
Orizaba
Córdoba
Ciudad Mendoza
Veracruz
Alvarado
Tehuacán
Izúcar de Matamoros
Tierra Blanca
San Andrés Tuxtla
Cosamaloapan
Coatzacoalcos
Minatitlán
Villahermosa
Frontera
Oaxaca
Juchitán
Salina Cruz
Tehuantepec
ISTMO DE TEHUANTEPEC
OAXACA
CHIAPAS
TABASCO
GUERRERO
MORELOS
SIERRA MADRE DEL SUR
SIERRA MADRE
Tuxtla Gutiérrez
San Cristóbal de las Casas
Arriaga
Tonalá
Puerto Escondido
Puerto Ángel
Pinotepa Nacional
Huajuapan de León
Miahuatlán de Porfirio Díaz
Ejutla de Crespo
Matías Romero
Acayucan
232-233
236-237

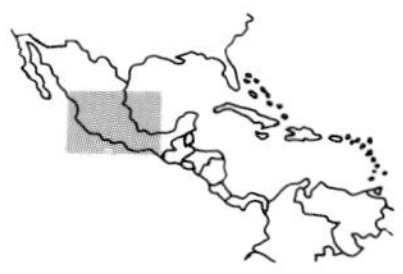

Kilometers 0 50 100 150 Km.
Statute Miles 0 50 100 150 Mi.

Scale 1:3,000,000

One centimeter represents 30 kilometers.
One inch represents approximately 47 miles.
Lambert Conformal Conic Projection

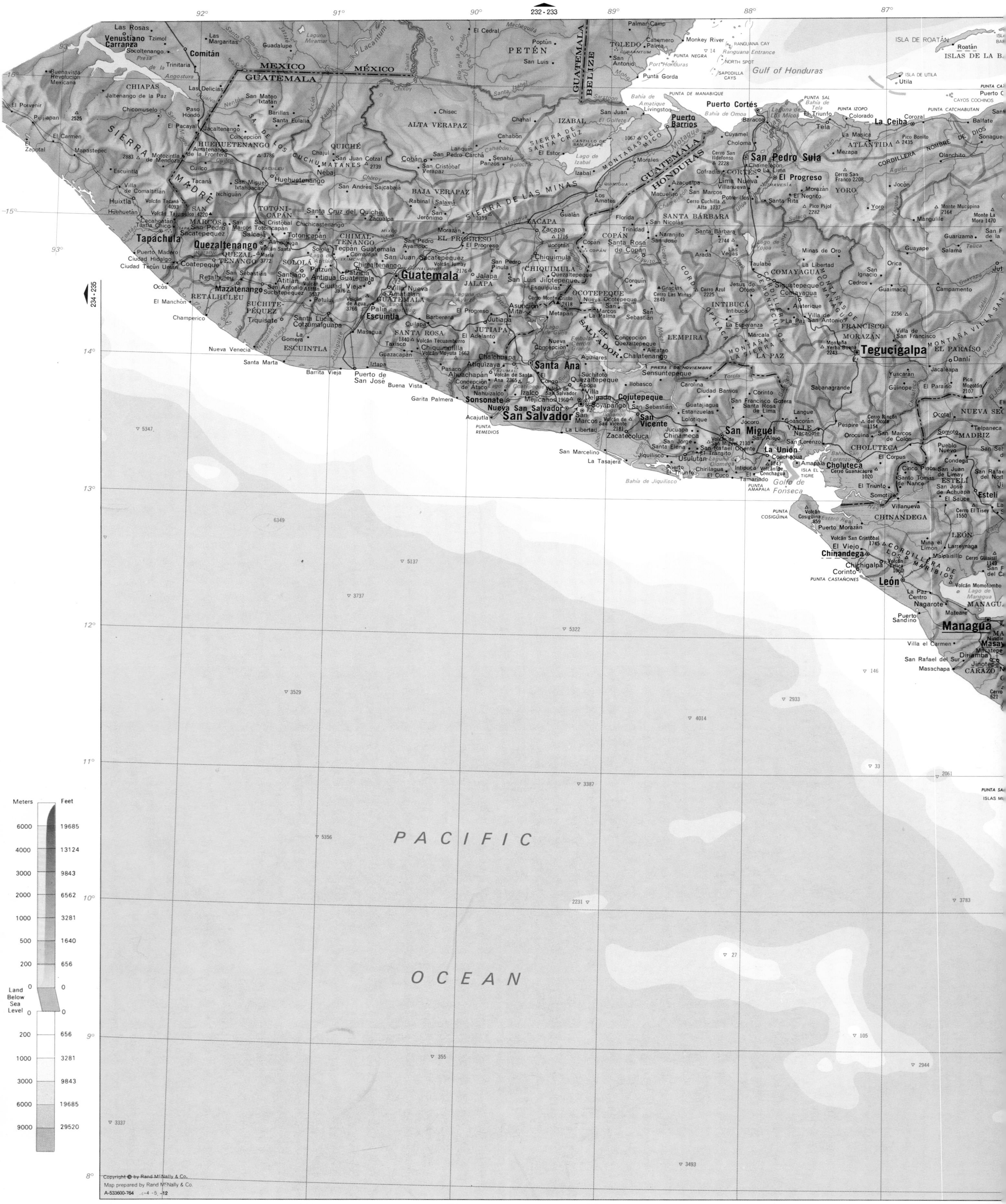

ESPAÑOL	bahía	cerro	cordillera	isla	lago	laguna	punta	sierra	volcán
ENGLISH	bay	mountain	mountains	island	lake	lagoon	point	mountains	volcano
DEUTSCH	Bucht	Berg	Berge	Insel	See	Haff	Landspitze	Berge	Vulkan
FRANÇAIS	baie	montagne	montagnes	île	lac	lagune	pointe	montagnes	volcan
PORTUGUÊS	baía	montanha	cordilheira	ilha	lago	laguna	ponta	serra	vulcão

Kilometers 0 50 100 150 Km.

Statute Miles 0 50 100 150 Mi.

Scale 1:3,000,000

One centimeter represents 30 kilometers.
One inch represents approximately 47 miles.
Lambert Conformal Conic Projection

MAP FORM	bahia	cabo	cerro	channel	golfo	isla	passage	pico	punta
ENGLISH	bay	cape	mountain	channel	gulf	isle	passage	peak	point
DEUTSCH	Bucht	Kap	Berg	Kanal	Golf	Insel	Durchfahrt	Gipfel	Landspitze
ESPAÑOL	bahía	cabo	cerro	canal	golfo	isla	pasaje	pico	punta
FRANÇAIS	baie	cap	montagne	détroit	golfe	île	passage	cime	pointe
PORTUGUÊS	baía	cabo	montanha	canal	golfo	ilha	passagem	pico	ponta

ATLANTIC
OCEAN
Tropic of Cancer
TURKS AND CAICOS ISLANDS
(U.K.)
CAICOS ISLANDS
TURKS ISLANDS
Grand Turk
GREAT INAGUA
Mouchoir Passage
Silver Bank Passage
SILVER BANK
NAVIDAD BANK
INDIES
HAITI
HAÏTI
Cap-Haïtien
Gonaïves
Golfe de la Gonâve
Port-au-Prince
Jacmel
HISPANIOLA
Santiago
San Francisco de Macorís
Santo Domingo
San Pedro de Macorís
La Romana
DOMINICAN REPUBLIC
REPÚBLICA DOMINICANA
ISLA SAONA
ISLA BEATA
Canal de la Mona
PUERTO RICO
(U.S.)
SAN JUAN
Arecibo
Mayagüez
Ponce
Caguas
Bayamón
VIRGIN ISLANDS
(U.S.)
(U.K.)
Charlotte Amalie
Road Town
SAINT CROIX
Christiansted
Frederiksted
LEEWARD
ANGUILLA
The Valley
SAINT MARTIN
SINT MAARTEN
Philipsburg
Marigot
SAINT CHRISTOPHER-NEVIS
Basseterre
Charlestown
ANTIGUA AND BARBUDA
Saint Johns
MONTSERRAT
Plymouth
(U.K.)
LESSER
ANTILLES
GUADELOUPE
(Fr.)
Pointe-à-Pitre
Basse-Terre
DOMINICA
Roseau
MARTINIQUE
(Fr.)
Fort-de-France
Saint Lucia Channel
SAINT LUCIA
Castries
SAINT VINCENT AND THE GRENADINES
Kingstown
Bridgetown
BARBADOS
GRENADA
Saint George's
WINDWARD ISLANDS
ISLA DE AVES
(Ven.)
SEA
ARUBA
(Neth.)
Oranjestad
NETHERLANDS ANTILLES
NEDERLANDSE ANTILLEN
CURAÇAO
Willemstad
BONAIRE
Kralendijk
LESSER ANTILLES
PENÍNSULA DE LA GUAJIRA
LA GUAJIRA
Golfo de Venezuela
Punto Fijo
Coro
FALCÓN
Maracaibo
Lago de Maracaibo
ZULIA
COLOMBIA
VENEZUELA
LARA
Barquisimeto
Valencia
Maracay
CARACAS
La Guaira
Maiquetía
MIRANDA
ARAGUA
CARABOBO
COJEDES
PORTUGUESA
GUÁRICO
ANZOÁTEGUI
Barcelona
Puerto la Cruz
Cumaná
SUCRE
Carúpano
MONAGAS
Maturín
ISLA DE MARGARITA
NUEVA ESPARTA
DELTA AMACURO
Port of Spain
TRINIDAD AND TOBAGO
TRINIDAD
TOBAGO
San Fernando
Gulf of Paria
Serpents Mouth
Dragons Mouth
Orinoco
72°
70°
68°
66°
64°
62°
60°
24°
22°
20°
18°
16°
14°
12°
10°
246-247

Kilometers 0 100 200 300 Km.
Statute Miles 0 100 200 300 Mi.

Scale 1:6,000,000

One centimeter represents 60 kilometers.
One inch represents approximately 95 miles.
Lambert Conformal Conic Projection

a

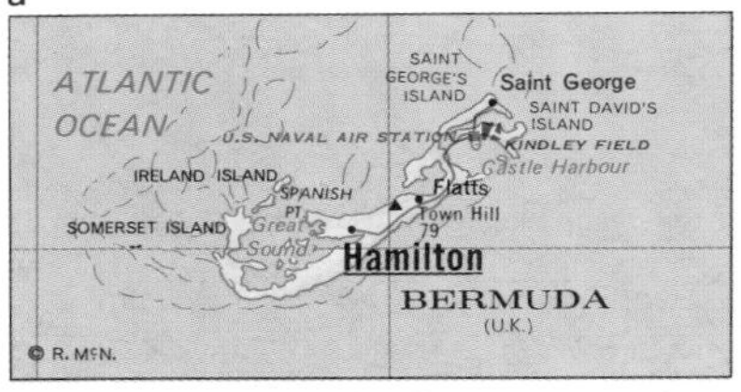

b

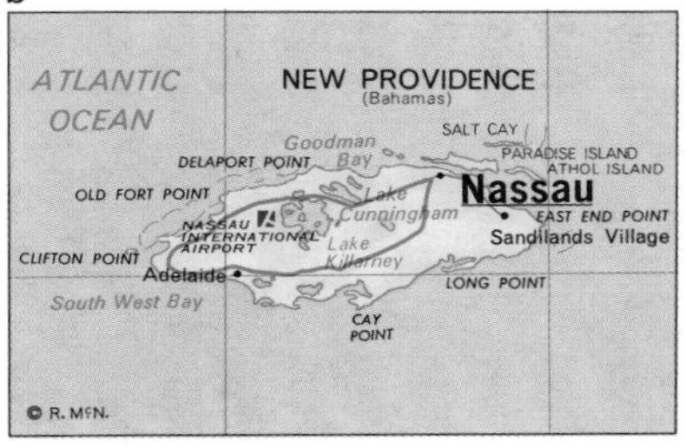

c

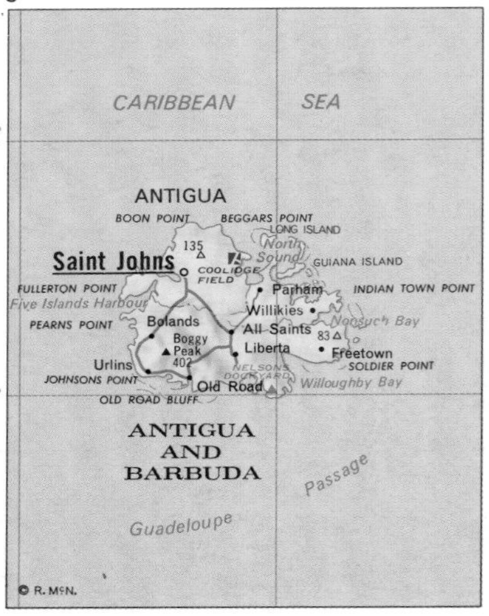

d

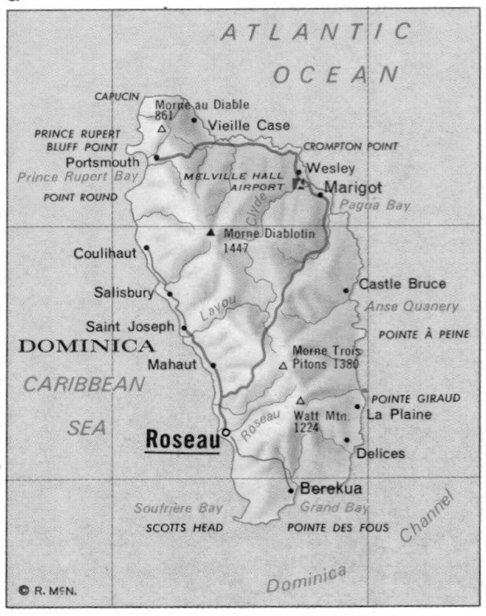

e

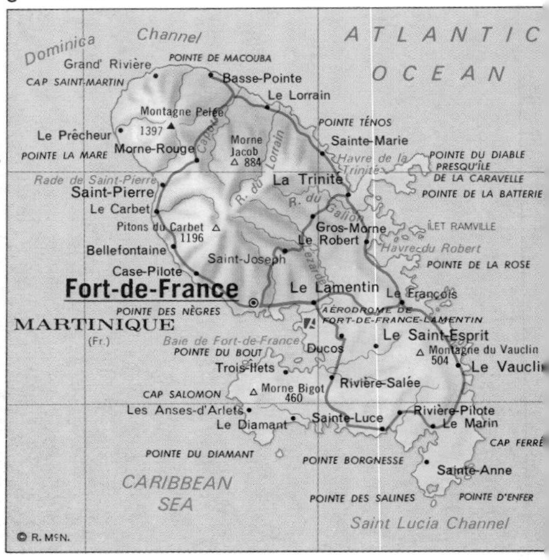

m

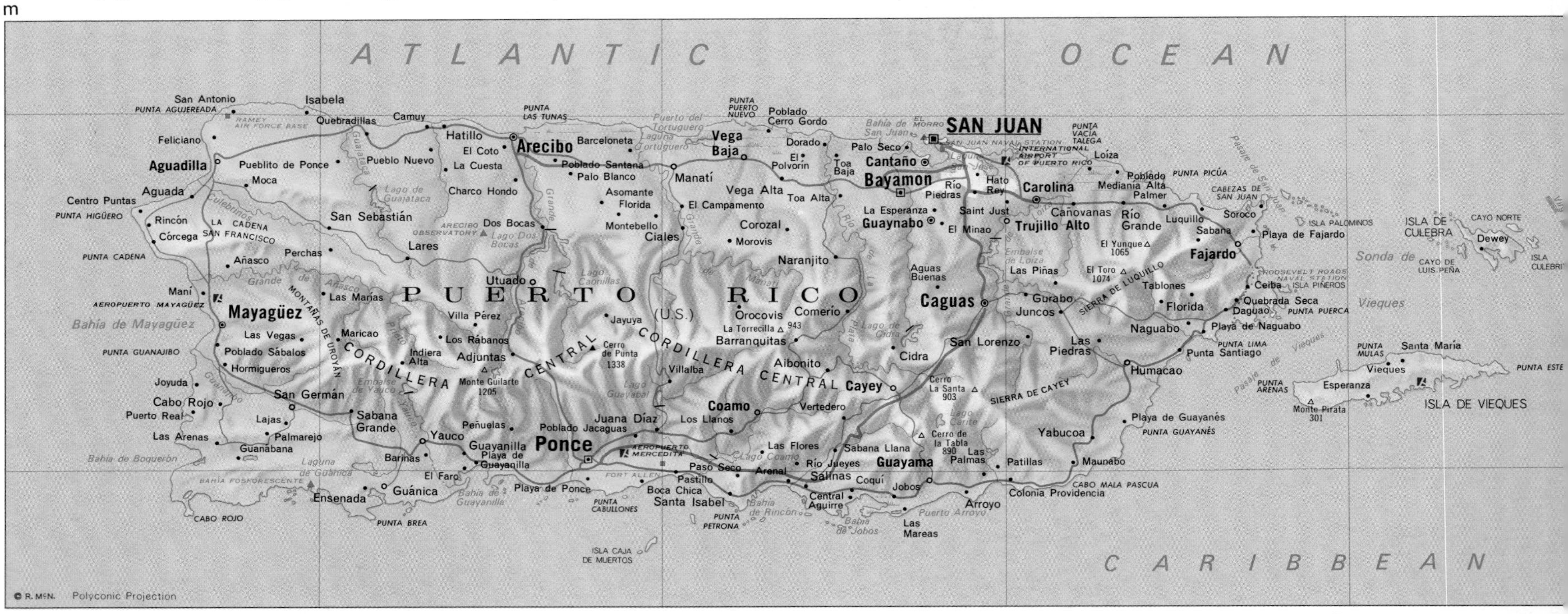

p

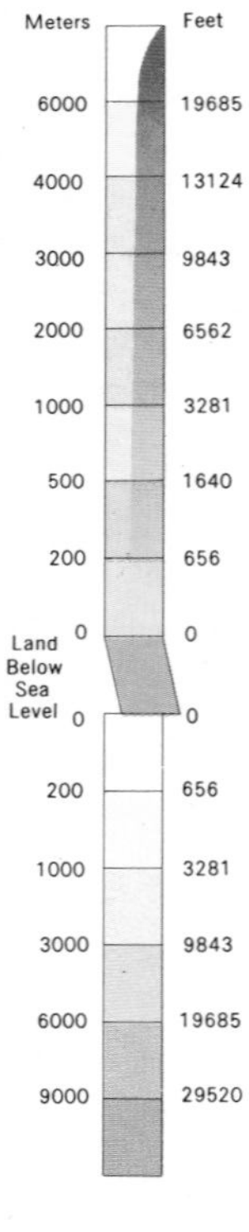

MAP FORM	bahía	cayo	channel	ensenada	golfo	island	mount	passage	point
ENGLISH	bay	cay	channel	bayou	gulf	island	mount	passage	point
DEUTSCH	Bucht	Klippe	Kanal	Altwasser	Golf	Insel	Berg	Durchfahrt	Landspitze
ESPAÑOL	bahía	cayo	canal	ensenada	golfo	isla	montaña	pasaje	punta
FRANÇAIS	baie	caye	détroit	bayou	golfe	île	mont	passage	pointe
PORTUGUÊS	baía	baixio	canal	enseada	golfo	ilha	montanha	passagem	ponta

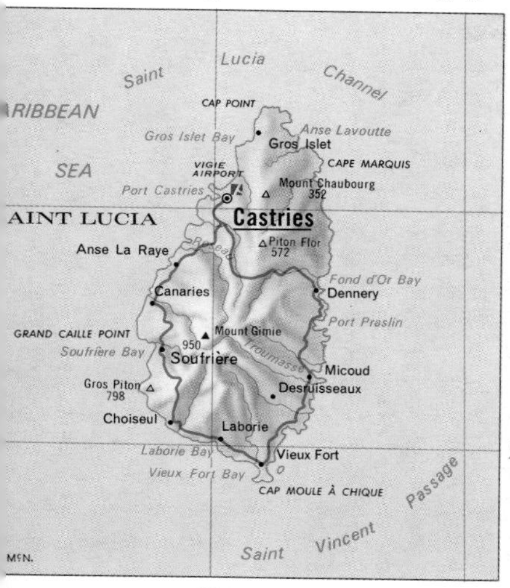

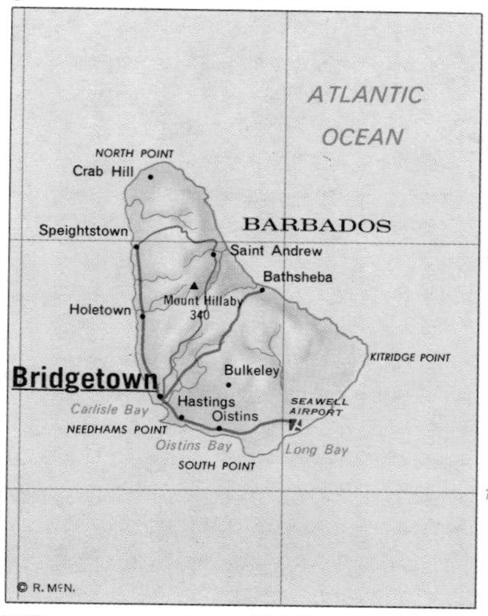

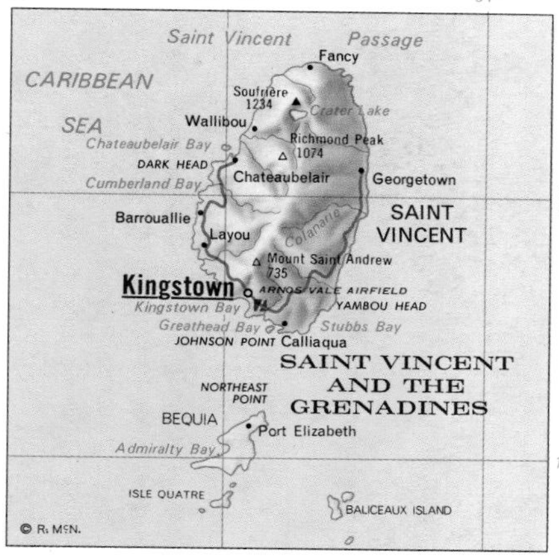

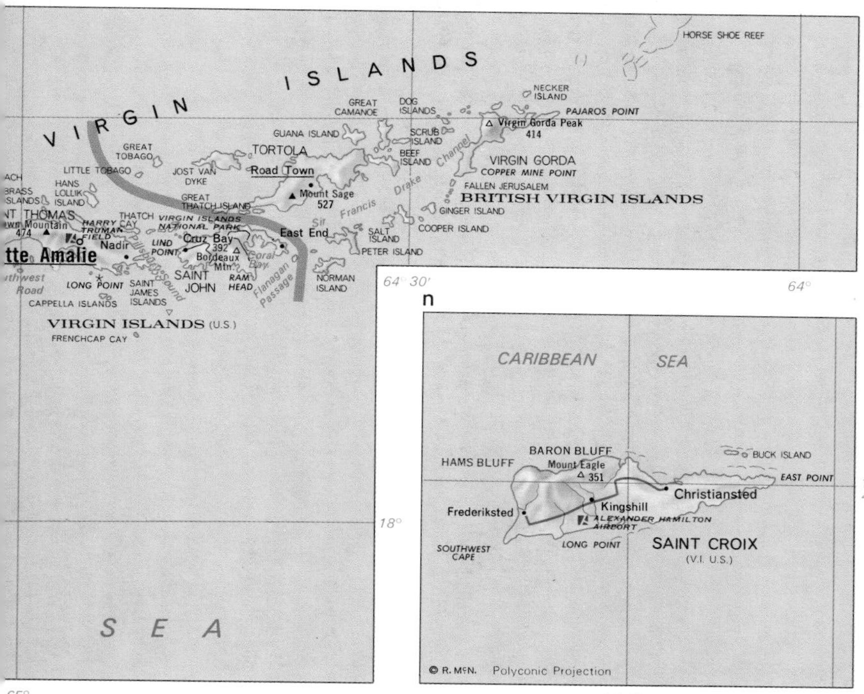

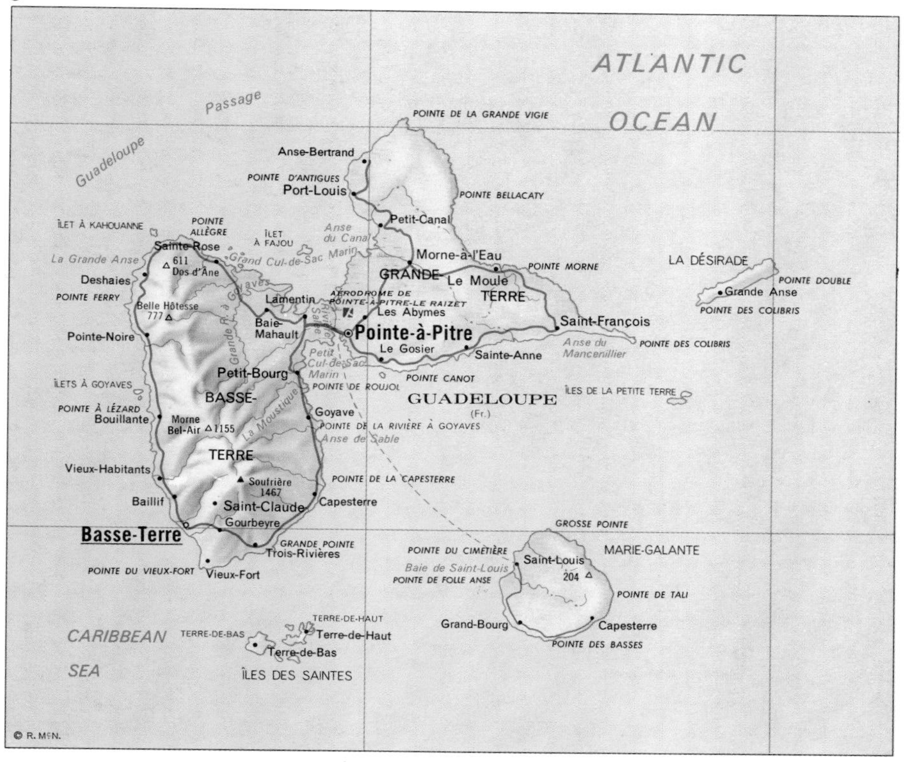

Kilometers 0 10 20 30 40 50 Km.
Statute Miles 0 10 20 30 40 50 Mi.

Scale 1:1,000,000

One centimeter represents 10 kilometers.
One inch represents approximately 16 miles.
Transverse Mercator Projection (except as noted)

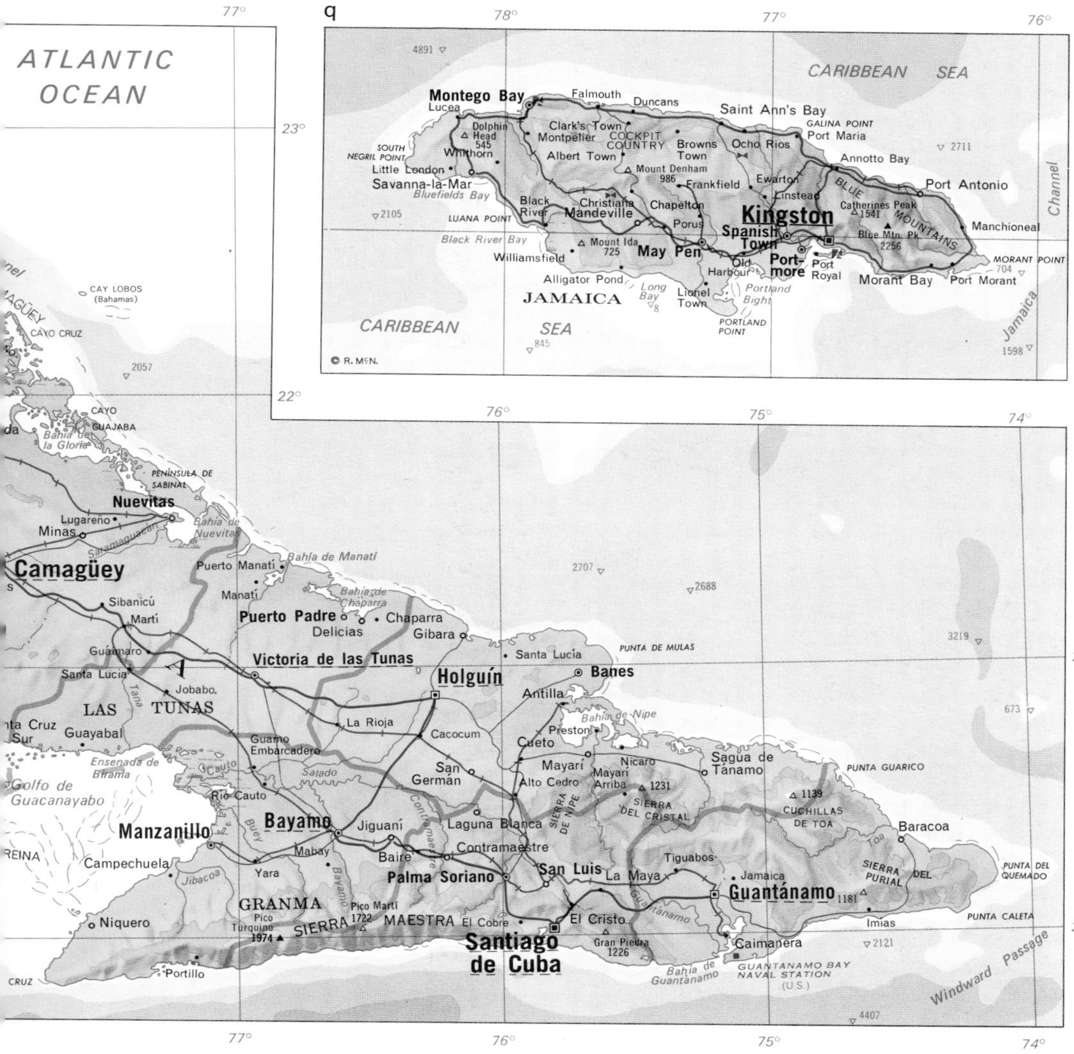

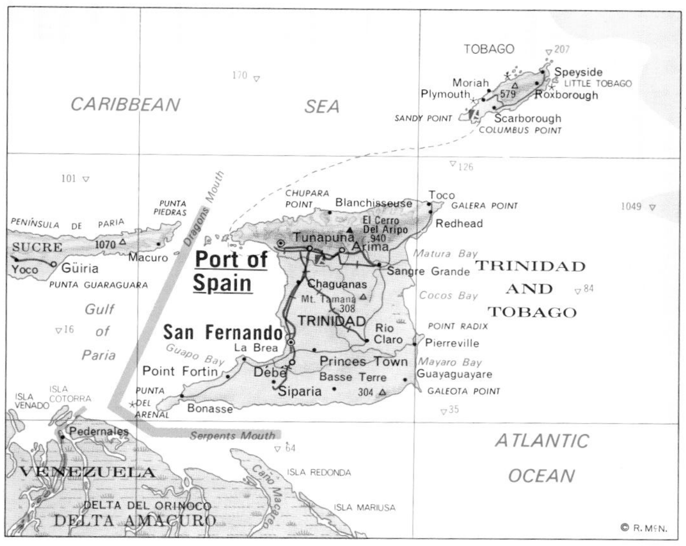

Kilometers 0 50 100 150 Km.
Statute Miles 0 50 100 150 Mi.

Scale 1:3,000,000

One centimeter represents 30 kilometers.
One inch represents approximately 47 miles.
Lambert Conformal Conic Projection

Kilometers 0 200 400 600 Km.
Statute Miles 0 200 400 600 Mi.

Scale 1:12,000,000
One centimeter represents 120 kilometers.
One inch represents approximately 190 miles.
Oblique Conic Conformal Projection

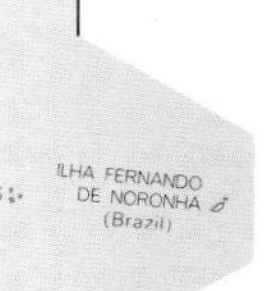

ATLANTIC OCEAN
Equator
Tropic of Capricorn
SURINAME
FRENCH GUIANA
BRAZIL
Georgetown
Paramaribo
Cayenne
Belém
São Luís
Fortaleza
Natal
João Pessoa
Recife
Olinda
Maceió
Aracaju
Salvador
Teresina
Brasília
Goiânia
Cuiabá
Campo Grande
Belo Horizonte
Vitória
RIO DE JANEIRO
SÃO PAULO
Santos
ILHA DE MARAJÓ
ILHA DO BANANAL
TUMUC-HUMAC MTS.
ACARAI MTS.
SERRA DO CACHIMBO
SERRA DO RONCADOR
SERRA DOS CARAJÁS
PLANALTO DO MATO GROSSO
PLANALTO CENTRAL
SERRA DO ESPINHAÇO
CHAPADA DAS MANGABEIRAS
Amazonas
Amazon
Tocantins
Araguaia
Xingu
Tapajós
São Francisco
Paraná
ATOL DAS ROCAS
ILHA FERNANDO DE NORONHA (Brazil)
CABO DE SÃO ROQUE
CABO ORANGE
CABO FRIO
244 - 245

MAP FORM	cerro	cordillera	ilha	lago	nevado	peninsula	serra
ENGLISH	mountain	range	island	lake	mountain	peninsula	mountains
DEUTSCH	Berg	Gebirge	Insel	See	Berg	Halbinsel	Berge
ESPAÑOL	montaña	cordillera	isla	lago	montaña	península	montañas
FRANÇAIS	montagne	chaîne	île	lac	montagne	péninsule	montagnes
PORTUGUÊS	montanha	cordilheira	ilha	lago	montanha	península	montanhas

242 - 243

MAP FORM	cerro, co.	golfo	ilha	isla	lago	lagoa	monte	salar
ENGLISH	butte	gulf	island	isle	lake	lake	mountain	saltflat
DEUTSCH	Restberg	Golf	Insel	Insel	See	See	Berg	Salzebene
ESPAÑOL	cerro	golfo	isla	isla	lago	lago	montaña	salobral
FRANÇAIS	butte	golfe	île	île	lac	lac	montagne	salina
PORTUGUÊS	colina	golfo	ilha	ilha	lago	lago	montanha	salina

Kilometers 0 200 400 600 Km.
Statute Miles 0 200 400 600 Mi.

Scale 1:12,000,000

One centimeter represents 120 kilometers.
One inch represents approximately 190 miles.
Oblique Conic Conformal Projection

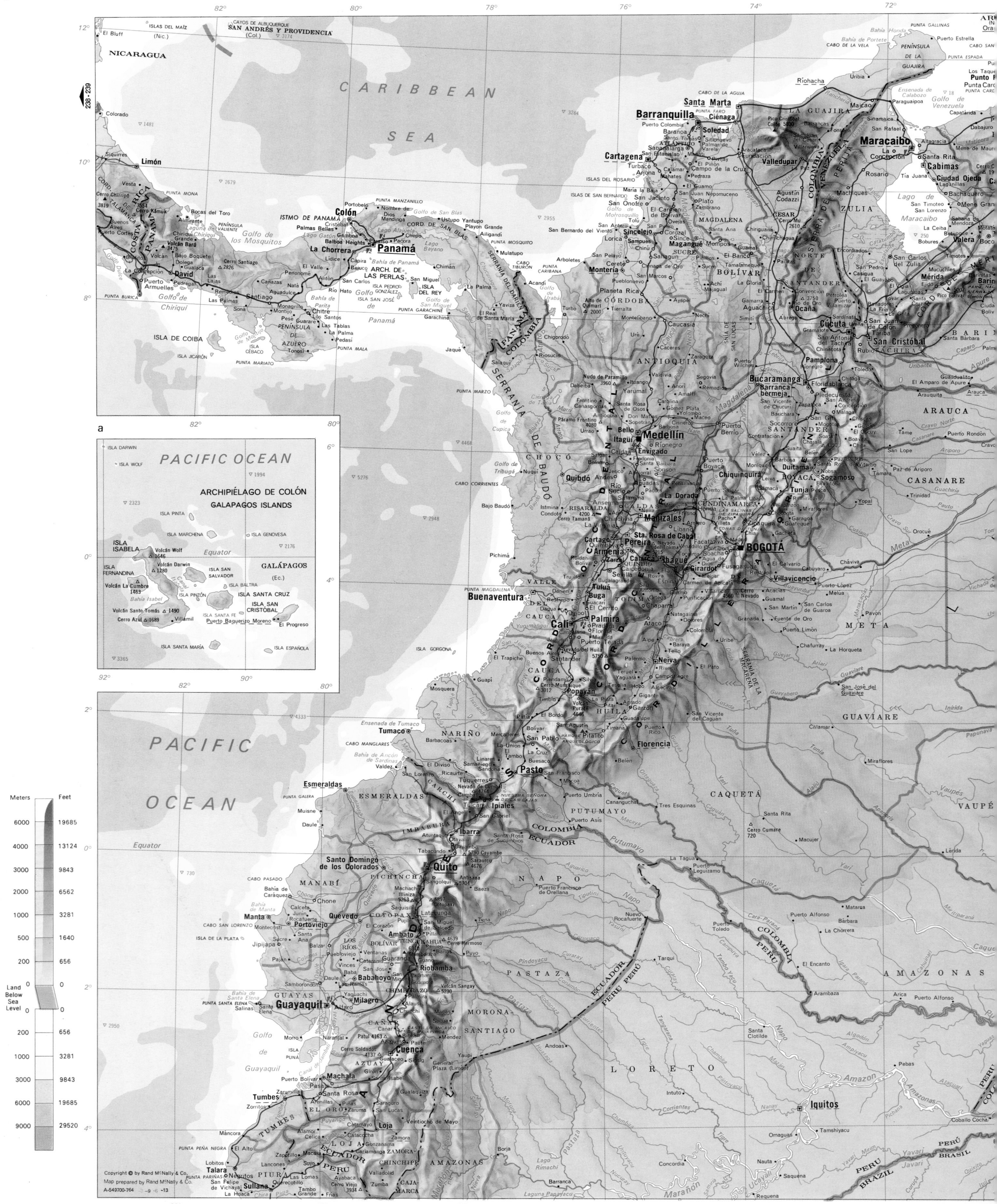

238-239

248-249

MAP FORM	bahía	cabo	cerro, co.	golfo	igarapé	isla, i.	lago, l.	punta	volcán, vol.
ENGLISH	bay	cape	butte	gulf	river	island	lake	point	volcano
DEUTSCH	Bucht	Kap	Restberg	Golf	Fluss	Insel	See	Landspitze	Vulkan
ESPAÑOL	bahía	cabo	cerro	golfo	río	isla	lago	punta	volcán
FRANÇAIS	baie	cap	butte	golfe	rivière	île	lac	pointe	volcan
PORTUGUÊS	baía	cabo	colina	golfo	rio	ilha	lago	ponta	vulcão

238 - 239

250 - 251

Kilometers 0 100 200 300 Km.
Statute Miles 0 100 200 300 Mi.

Scale 1:6,000,000
One centimeter represents 60 kilometers.
One inch represents approximately 95 miles.
Oblique Conic Conformal Projection

PACIFIC
OCEAN
CORDILLERA OCCIDENTAL
CORDILLERA CENTRAL
CORDILLERA ORIENTAL
ANDES
DESIERTO DE SECHURA
LORETO
UCAYALI
ACRE
MADRE DE DIOS
CUZCO
PUNO
AREQUIPA
LIMA
Callao
Chiclayo
Trujillo
Chimbote
Huancayo
Ayacucho
Cuzco
Arequipa
Pucallpa
Yurimaguas
Iquitos
Piura
Arica
Iquique
Tocopilla
Meters
Feet
6000 19685
4000 13124
3000 9843
2000 6562
1000 3281
500 1640
200 656
0 0
Land Below Sea Level
0 0
200 656
1000 3281
3000 9843
6000 19685
9000 29520
Copyright © by Rand McNally & Co.
Map prepared by Rand McNally & Co.
A-549792-764

MAP FORM	cerro	cordillera	isla, i.	lago, l.	nevado	punta	río	serra
ENGLISH	mountain	mountains	island	lake	mountain	point	river	mountains
DEUTSCH	Berg	Berge	Insel	See	Berg	Landspitze	Fluss	Berge
ESPAÑOL	montaña	montañas	isla	lago	nevado	punta	río	sierra
FRANÇAIS	montagne	montagnes	île	lac	montagne	pointe	rivière	montagnes
PORTUGUÊS	montanha	montanhas	ilha	lago	pico nevado	ponta	rio	serra

Kilometers 0 100 200 300 Km.
Statute Miles 0 100 200 300 Mi.

Scale 1:6,000,000
One centimeter represents 60 kilometers.
One inch represents approximately 95 miles.
Oblique Conic Conformal Projection

MAP FORM	cabo	cachoeira, cach.	ilha, i.	lago, l.	riacho	ribeirão, rão.	rio, r.	serra, sa.
ENGLISH	cape	waterfall	island	lake	creek	creek	river	mountains
DEUTSCH	Kap	Wasserfall	Insel	See	Bach	Bach	Fluss	Berge
ESPAÑOL	cabo	cascada	isla	lago	riachuelo	riachuelo	río	montañas
FRANÇAIS	cap	chute d'eau	île	lac	crique	crique	rivière	montagnes
PORTUGUÊS	cabo	queda d'água	ilha	lago	riacho	riacho	rio	montanhas

ATLANTIC OCEAN
Equator
FORTALEZA
RECIFE
Natal
João Pessoa
Maceió
Aracaju
Teresina
Olinda
Campina Grande
Caruaru
Mossoró
Parnaíba
Juàzeiro
Petrolina
Paulo Afonso
Arapiraca
Garanhuns
Arcoverde
Crato
Juàzeiro do Norte
Sobral
Crateús
Caxias
Floriano
Picos
Patos
Alagoinhas
CEARÁ
PIAUÍ
PERNAMBUCO
PARAÍBA
RIO GRANDE DO NORTE
ALAGOAS
SERGIPE
BAHIA
FERNANDO DE NORONHA
ATOL DAS ROCAS
ILHA FERNANDO DE NORONHA
CABO DE SÃO ROQUE
CHAPADA DO ARARIPE
SERRA GRANDE
SERRA DA IBIAPABA
Copyright © by Rand McNally & Co.
Map prepared by Rand McNally & Co.
A-540396-764

Kilometers 0 100 200 300 Km.
Statute Miles 0 100 200 300 Mi.

Scale 1:6,000,000

One centimeter represents 60 kilometers.
One inch represents approximately 95 miles.
Oblique Conic Conformal Projection

248 - 249

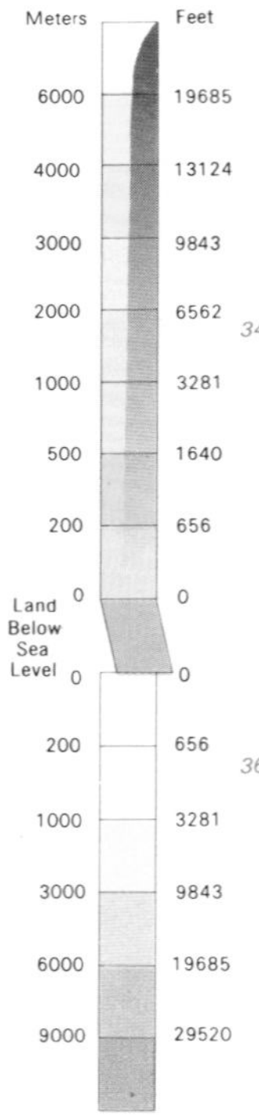

254

MAP FORM	cabo	cerro	cuchilla	ilha	laguna	punta	salar	sierra	volcán
ENGLISH	cape	mountain	hills	island	lagoon; lake	point	saltflat	mountains	volcano
DEUTSCH	Kap	Berg	Hügel	Insel	Haff; See	Landspitze	Salzebene	Berge	Vulkan
ESPAÑOL	cabo	cerro	cuchilla	isla	laguna	punta	salobral	sierra	volcán
FRANÇAIS	cap	montagne	collines	île	lagune; lac	pointe	salina	montagnes	volcan
PORTUGUÊS	cabo	montanha	colina	ilha	laguna	ponta	salina	serra	vulcão

255

Kilometers 0 100 200 300 Km.
Statute Miles 0 100 200 300 Mi.

Scale 1:6,000,000
One centimeter represents 60 kilometers.
One inch represents approximately 95 miles.
Oblique Conic Conformal Projection

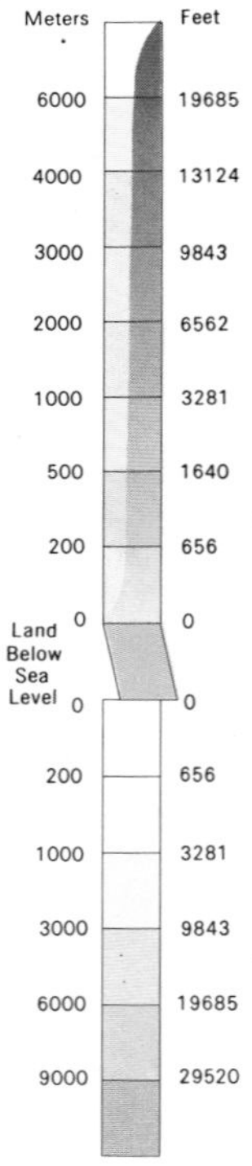

MAP FORM	bahía	cabo	cerro	isla	lago	monte	punta
ENGLISH	bay	cape	mountain, hill	isle	lake	mountain	point
DEUTSCH	Bucht	Kap	Berg, Hügel	Insel	See	Berg	Landspitze
ESPAÑOL	bahía	cabo	cerro	isla	lago	monte	punta
FRANÇAIS	baie	cap	montagne, colline	île	lac	montagne	pointe
PORTUGUÊS	baía	cabo	montanha, colina	ilha	lago	monte	ponta

Kilometers 0 100 200 300 Km.
Statute Miles 0 100 200 300 Mi.

Scale 1:6,000,000

One centimeter represents 60 kilometers.
One inch represents approximately 95 miles.
Oblique Conic Conformal Projection

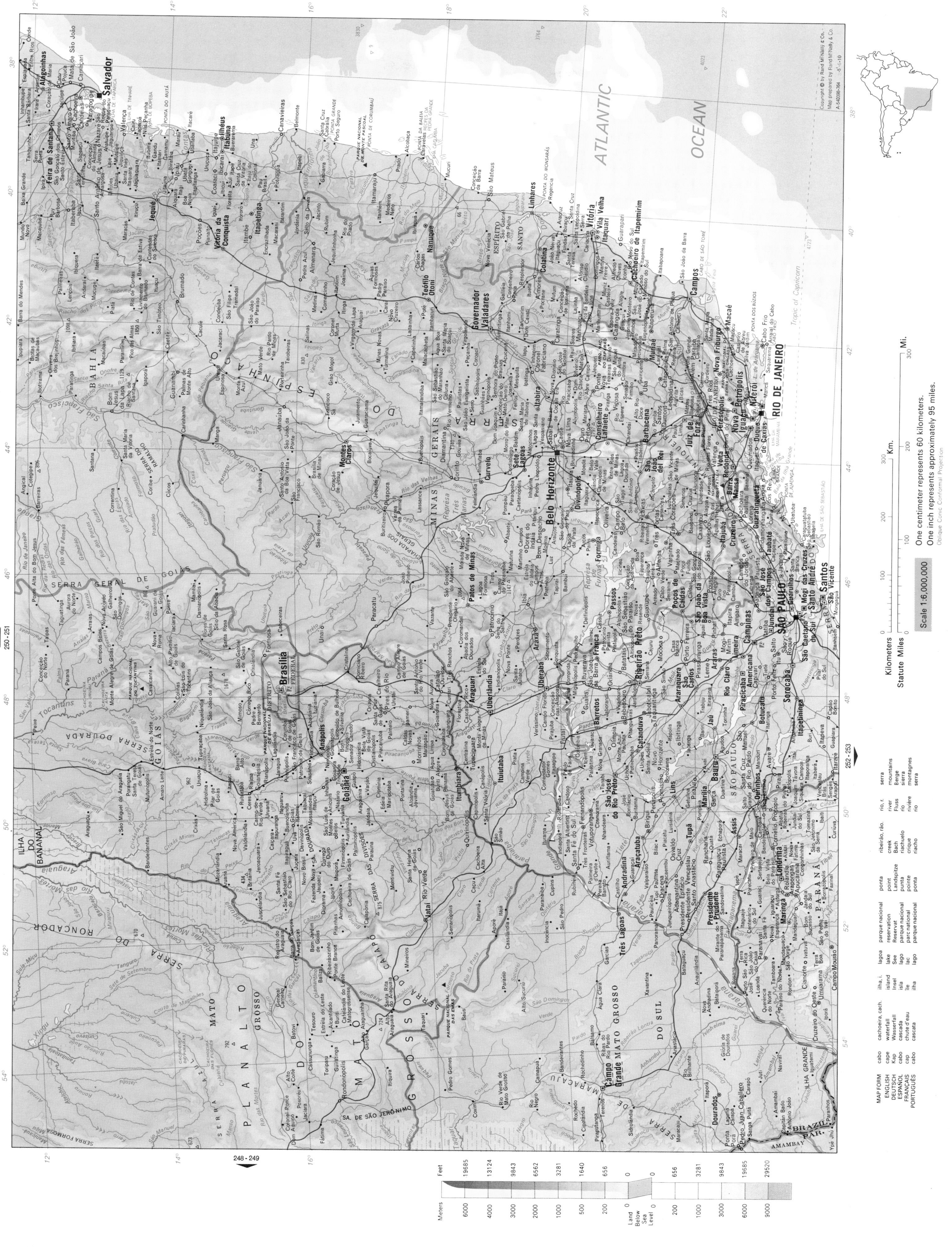
ATLANTIC
OCEAN
Salvador
Brasília
Belo Horizonte
RIO DE JANEIRO
SÃO PAULO
Santos
Campinas
Campo Grande
MINAS GERAIS
SÃO PAULO
MATO GROSSO DO SUL
Tropic of Capricorn
250-251
252-253
248-249
Scale 1:6,000,000
One centimeter represents 60 kilometers.
One inch represents approximately 95 miles.
Oblique Conic Conformal Projection
Kilometers
Statute Miles
MAP FORM: cabo, cachoeira, cach., ilha, i., lagoa, parque nacional, ponta, ribeirão, rio, r., serra
ENGLISH: cape, waterfall, island, lake, reservation, point, creek, river, mountains
DEUTSCH: Kap, Wasserfall, Insel, See, Reservat, Landspitze, Bach, Fluss, Berge
ESPAÑOL: cabo, cascada, isla, lago, parque nacional, punta, riachuelo, río, sierra
FRANÇAIS: cap, chute d'eau, île, lac, parc national, pointe, crique, rivière, montagnes
PORTUGUÊS: cabo, cascata, ilha, lago, parque nacional, ponta, riacho, rio, serra
Feet
Meters
Land Below Sea Level
Copyright © by Rand McNally & Co.
Map prepared by Rand McNally & Co.

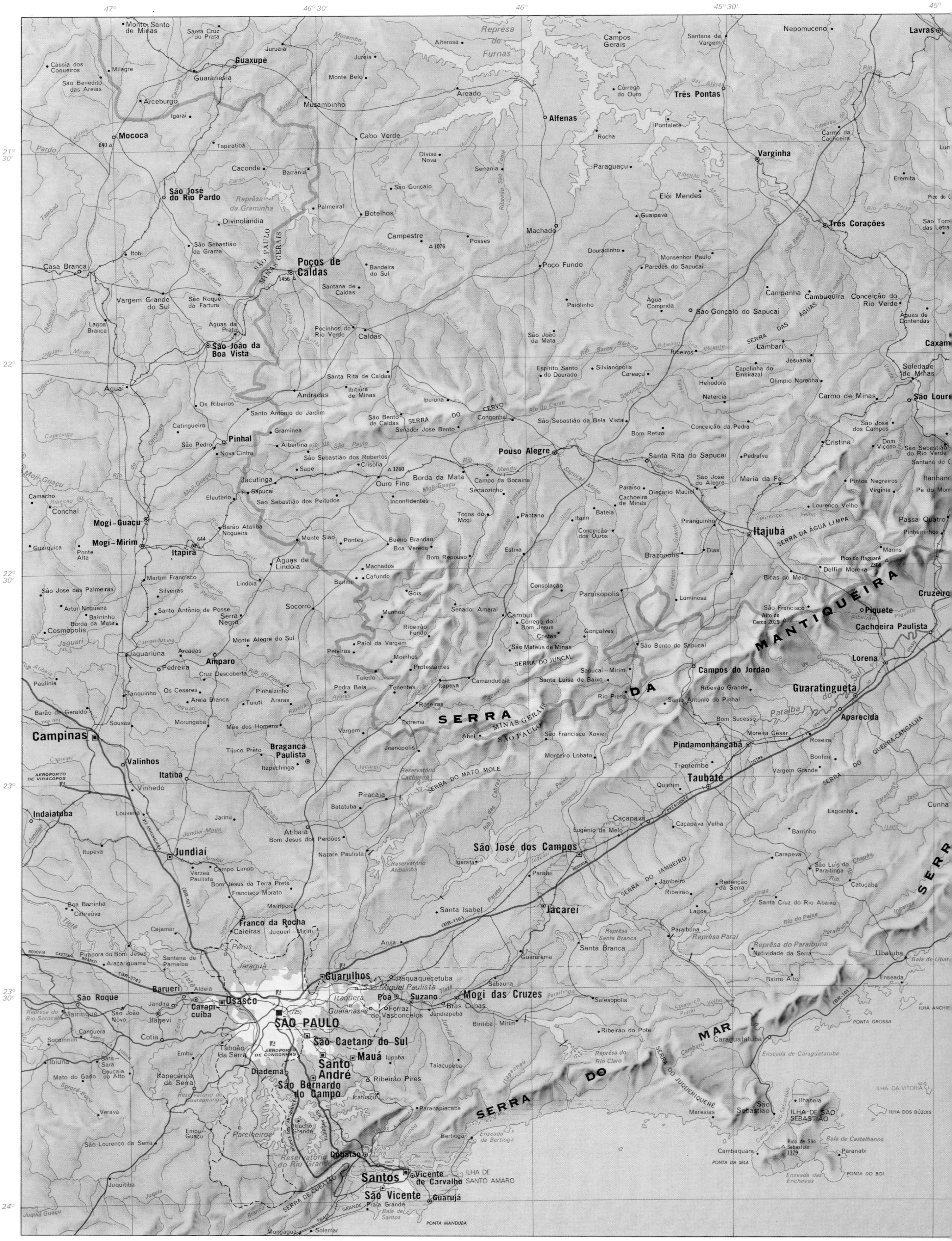

MAP FORM	baía	enseada	ilha	pico	ponta	represa	ribeirão	rio	serra
ENGLISH	bay	bay	island	peak	point	reservoir	stream	river	mountains
DEUTSCH	Bucht	Bucht	Insel	Gipfel	Landspitze	Stausee	Bach	Fluss	Berge
ESPAÑOL	bahía	bahía	isla	pico	punta	estanque	corriente de agua	río	sierra
FRANÇAIS	baie	baie	île	cime	pointe	réservoir	cours d'eau	rivière	montagnes
PORTUGUÊS	baía	enseada	ilha	pico	ponta	represa	ribeirão	rio	serra

Kilometers 0 10 20 30 40 50 Km.

Statute Miles 0 10 20 30 40 50 Mi.

Scale 1:1,000,000

One centimeter represents 10 kilometers.
One inch represents approximately 16 miles.

Polyconic Projection

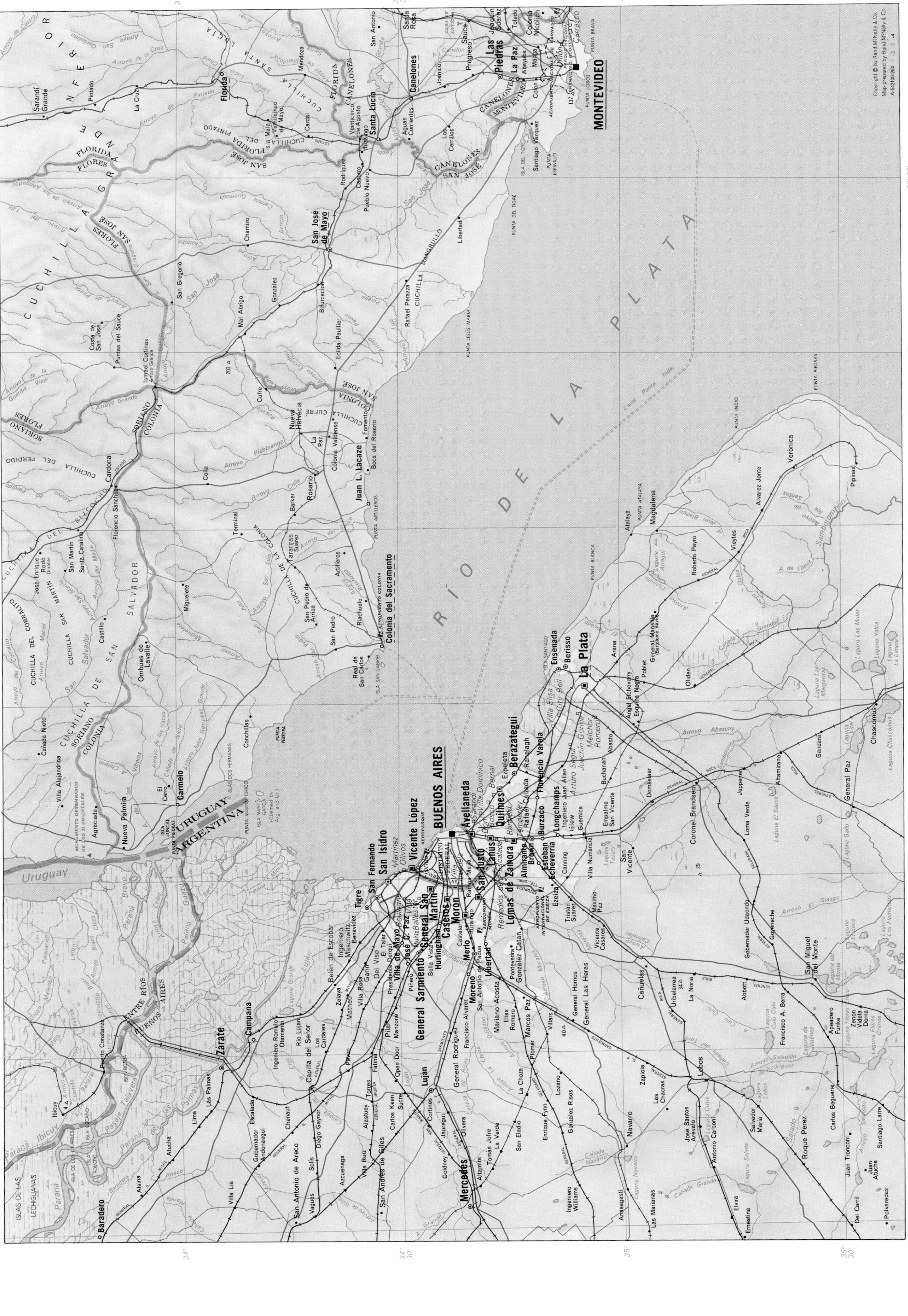

ESPAÑOL	ENGLISH	DEUTSCH	FRANÇAIS	PORTUGUÊS
aerodromo	airport	Flughafen	aéroport	aeroporto
arroyo, a.	brook	Bach	ruisseau	arroio
cañada	brook	Bach	ruisseau	riacho
cuchilla	hills	Hügel	collines	colina
isla	island	Insel	île	ilha
laguna	lake	See	lac	laguna
punta	point	Landspitze	point	ponta

Kilometers 0 10 20 30 40 50 Km.

Statute Miles 0 10 20 30 40 50 Mi.

Scale 1:1,000,000

One centimeter represents 10 kilometers.

One inch represents approximately 16 miles.

Gauss-Krüger Projection

THIS SECTION CONSISTS of 60 maps of the world's major metropolitan areas, at the scale of 1:300,000. The maps show the generalized land-use patterns in and around each city—the total urban extent, major industrial areas, parks and preserves, and wooded areas. Airports are shown, as are many details of the highway and rail transportation networks. Selected points of interest appear, such as Fisherman's Wharf and Chinatown in San Francisco, the Welcome monument in Jakarta, the Temple of the Jade Buddha in Shanghai, and the Cristo Redentor statue in Rio de Janeiro.

The maps name and locate a great number of towns, villages, and suburbs, and also sections or neighborhoods within limits of the larger cities. Prominent physical features, including elevations, named and unnamed, have been indicated to give a general impression of the local topography. Shaded relief has been omitted, however, to permit display of such details as streams, parks, airport runways, important public buildings and monuments, and the names of major streets. The corporate limits of major cities are also outlined. For the symbols used on these maps see the Legend to Maps, pages x-xii.

Maps of major world cities usually vary widely in scale, and heretofore have not been consistent in design and coverage. For this section, a special effort has been made to portray these varied metropolitan areas in as standard and comparable a fashion as possible. However, for a few cities (notably several in Asia) there has not been adequate source material to include certain information, such as major industrial areas and corporate limits.

The order of presentation is generally regional, with some exceptions where for ease of comparison major capitals or industrial centers or cities located in similar physical surroundings have been juxtaposed. Many American cities and some European cities, with their lower densities and more extensive areas, require larger maps than do Asiatic cities of comparable population. The total land area and population within the confines of each map are stated in the margin as a further aid to comparison.

DIESER KARTENTEIL UMFASST 60 Karten der bedeutendsten Stadtregionen der Erde im Massstab 1:300 000. Die Karten zeigen in generalisierter Form die Landnutzung in und um jede Stadt: die gesamte Ausdehnung des verstädterten Gebietes, wichtige Industriegebiete, Parks, Landflächen in Gemeinbesitz und Wald. Flughäfen werden ebenso dargestellt wie viele Einzelheiten des Strassen- und Eisenbahnnetzes. Bekannte Sehenswürdigkeiten sind eingetragen wie die "Fisherman's Wharf" und "Chinatown" in San Francisco, das Willkomm-Denkmal in Jakarta, der Tempel des Jade-Buddhas in Shanghai und die "Cristo Redentor"-Statue in Rio de Janeiro.

Die Karten verzeichnen Name and Lage einer grossen Zahl von Städten, Dörfern, Vororten ebenso wie eingemeindete Ortsteile bei grösseren Städten. Hervortretende physische Formen wie benannte und unbenannte Erhebungen sind aufgenommen, um eine allgemeine Vorstellung des lokalen Reliefs zu geben. Auf die Schummerung wurde jedoch verzichtet, um klar solche Einzelheiten wie Flüsse, Parks, Start- und Landebahnen der Flughäfen, bedeutende öffentliche Gebäude und Denkmäler sowie die Namen der wichtigsten Strassen herausstellen zu können. Eingetragen sind ferner die Gemeindegrenzen der wichtigsten Städte. Zu den auf diesen Karten verwendeten Signaturen siehe "Zeichenerklärung" Seite x-xii.

Karten der bedeutendsten Weltstädte differieren normalerweise sehr stark in ihren Massstäben und sind daher uneinheitlich in ihrer Gestaltung und Begrenzung. Deshalb wurde in diesem Kartenteil besonderer Wert darauf gelegt, die verschiedenen städtischen Ballungsgebiete in möglichst einheitlicher und vergleichbarer Form darzustellen. Für einige Städte, vor allem mehrere asiatische, war das Quellenmaterial jedoch nicht ausreichend genug, um gewisse Informationen wie Hauptindustriegebiete oder Stadtgrenzen einzutragen.

Im allgemeinen sind diese Karten nach regionalen Gesichtspunkten geordnet. Um Vergleiche zu erleichtern wurden einige Ausnahmen gemacht, indem wichtige Hauptstädte, Industriezentren oder Städte in vergleichbarer landschaftlicher Lage einander gegenübergestellt wurden. Viele amerikanische und einige europäische Städte mit ihrer geringen Bevölkerungsdichte, aber ausgedehnteren Fläche erfordern eine grössere Kartenfläche als asiatische Städte von vergleichbarer Bevölkerungszahl. Die gesamte Landfläche und die Bevölkerung innerhalb des dargestellten Gebietes ist am Kartenrand verzeichnet als ein weiteres Hilfsmittel für Vergleiche.

INTEGRAN ESTA SECCION 60 mapas de las áreas metropolitanas más importantes del mundo, a la escala de 1:300 000. Los mapas muestran los patrones de uso del suelo dentro de cada ciudad y en sus alrededores—la extensión total del conglomerado urbano, las principales áreas industriales, parques y reservas, y zonas boscosas. Aparecen los aeropuertos, así como muchos otros detalles de las redes de carreteras y ferrocarriles. Se seleccionaron también puntos de interés, como el Muelle de los Pescadores y el Barrio Chino de San Francisco, el monumento de Bienvenida de Jakarta, el Templo del Buda de Jade de Shanghai y la estatua del Cristo Redentor de Rio de Janeiro.

Los mapas incluyen los nombres y la ubicación de gran número de ciudades, poblaciones menores, suburbios, e inclusive barrios y distritos de algunas de las ciudades más importantes. Las características físicas sobresalientes, e incluso algunas elevaciones con o sin nombre, están indicados para dar una impresión general de la topografía local. Se omitió sin embargo el relieve sombreado, lo cual permite mostrar detalles como ríos y arroyos, parques, pistas de aterrizaje, edificios y monumentos públicos notables y los nombres de las calles principales. También están marcados los límites territoriales de las ciudades más grandes. Para la interpretación de los símbolos usados en estos mapas, véanse Leyendas para Mapas en las páginas x-xii.

Los mapas de las ciudades más importantes del mundo varían generalmente en escala, y hasta ahora no han sido consistentes ni en diseño ni en contenido. En esta sección hemos hecho un esfuerzo de presentar las distintas áreas metropolitanas en la forma más uniforme posible, para facilitar sus comparaciones. Para algunas ciudades (la mayoría de ellas en Asia), no fué posible obtener de las propias fuentes material adecuado para la inclusión de ciertos datos, tales como las mayores áreas industriales y los límites municipales.

Los mapas de áreas metropolitanas se presentan por regiones, a excepción de unos cuantos que aparecen yuxtapuestos para facilitar la comparación entre grandes capitales, o centros comerciales, o ciudades ubicadas en contextos físicos similares. Muchas ciudades de América y algunas ciudades de Europa, por su baja densidad de población y su área extensa, requieren mapas más grandes que los ocupados por ciudades asiáticas con poblaciones comparables. Al margen de cada mapa se anotaron el área total y la población de territorio representado, lo cual facilita también las comparaciones.

CETTE PARTIE COMPREND 60 cartes des principales zones métropolitaines à l'échelle du 1:300 000e. Les cartes représentent les principaux types d'occupation du sol des villes et de leurs environs, c'est-à-dire de toute la zone urbanisée, les principales zones industrielles, les parcs et réserves naturelles, et les régions boisées. Les aéroports sont aussi représentés ainsi que de nombreux éléments des réseaux routier et ferroviaire. Certains lieux particulièrement intéressants sont indiqués, tels que le quai des pêcheurs et la ville chinoise à San Francisco, le monument de la Bienvenue à Jakarta, le temple du Bouddha de Jade à Shanghai et la statue du Christ Rédempteur à Rio de Janeiro.

Les cartes permettent de localiser un grand nombre de villes, villages et banlieues, ainsi que des quartiers de grandes villes. Les caractéristiques topographiques notables, comme les hauteurs sont indiquées même si elles ne portent pas de nom, pour donner une idée du site de l'aire métropolitaine. L'estompage du relief est omis cependant pour permettre de représenter cours d'eau, parcs, pistes d'envol des aéroports, monuments et bâtiments publics importants, noms des principales rues, ainsi que les limites municipales des grandes villes. (Pour la signification des symboles voir légende, pages x-xii.)

En général, les échelles des cartes des grandes villes du monde varient considérablement, et jusqu'ici la présentation et le contenu de ces cartes n'étaient pas comparables. Dans cette partie de l'Atlas, un effort spécial a été fait pour représenter les diverses zones métropolitaines de manière aussi homogène que possible. Cependant, dans certains cas (en Asie notamment), les documents de base n'étaient pas assez complets pour qu'il fût possible d'inclure avec précision des données comme les zones industrielles et les limites municipales.

L'ordre de présentation est régional, avec des exceptions quand, pour faciliter les comparaisons, de grandes capitales de grands centres industriels ou encore des villes possédant un même environnement naturel, sont juxtaposés. Beaucoup de villes américaines et quelques villes européennes ont une faible densité de population et une étendue considérable; elles requièrent, par conséquent, des cartes plus grandes que des villes asiatiques de population similaire. La superficie et la population de chaque carte sont indiquées dans la marge.

INTEGRAM ESTA SEÇÃO 60 mapas das áreas metropolitanas mais importantes do mundo, em escala de 1:300 000. Os mapas mostram os principais tipos de uso do solo em cada cidade e seus arredores, seja, a extensão total da zona urbanizada, as principais áreas industriais, os parques e reservas, e as áreas florestais. Mostram os aeroportos, e muitos detalhes das redes rodo e ferroviária. Indicam também pontos de interesse, selecionados, tais como o Cais dos Pescadores e o Bairro Chinês de San Francisco, o monumento de Boasvindas, em Jakarta, o templo do Buda de Jade, em Shanghai, e a Estátua do Cristo Redentor, no Rio de Janeiro.

Os mapas apresentam o nome e a localização de grande número de cidades, vilas e subúrbios, e incluem bairros das cidades mais importantes. Foram indicadas as características físicas principais, inclusive elevações, com ou sem nome, com o objetivo de proporcionar uma idéia geral da topografia local. No entanto, omitiu-se o sombreado do relevo, para permitir a indicação de detalhes tais como cursos d'água, parques, pistas de aeroportos, edifícios públicos e monumentos notáveis, e os nomes das principais ruas, bem como os limites municipais das grandes cidades. Para a interpretação dos símbolos usados nesses mapas, ver as *Legendas dos mapas*, nas pág. x-xii.

Os mapas das cidades mais importantes do mundo variam consideravelmente, de modo geral, quanto à escala, e até o presente não são comparáveis nem na forma de apresentação nem no conteúdo. Nesta seção, fez-se um esforço especial para representar as diversas áreas metropolitanas do modo mais uniforme e comparável possível. No entanto, para algumas cidades, a maioria das quais da Ásia, não foi possível obter fontes fidedignas de informações, tais como áreas industriais principais e limites municipais.

A ordem de apresentação dos mapas das áreas metropolitanas é geralmente regional, exceto em certos casos em que, para facilidade de comparação, capitais ou centros industriais e cidades importantes localizadas em meio físico semelhante foram justapostos. Muitas cidades da América e algumas da Europa, por sua baixa densidade demográfica e áreas mais extensas, exigem mapas maiores que as cidades asiáticas de população comparável. À margem de cada mapa indicam-se a área terrestre e a população total do território representado, também para maior facilidade de comparação.

Kilometers 0 5 10 15 Km.
Statute Miles 0 5 10 15 Mi.

Scale 1:300,000
One centimeter represents 3 kilometers.
One inch represents approximately 4.7 miles.

ENGLISH	DEUTSCH	ESPAÑOL	FRANÇAIS	PORTUGUÊS
aerodrome	Flughafen	aeropuerto	aéroport	aeroporto
canal	Kanal	canal	canal	canal
castle	Burg	castillo	château	castelo
palace	Palast	palacio	palais	palácio
park	Park	parque	parc	parque
race course	Rennbahn	hipódromo	champ de course	hipódromo
road	Landstrasse	camino	route	rodovia
station	Bahnhof	estación	gare	estação

AREA 6,400 km²
POPULATION 10,325,000

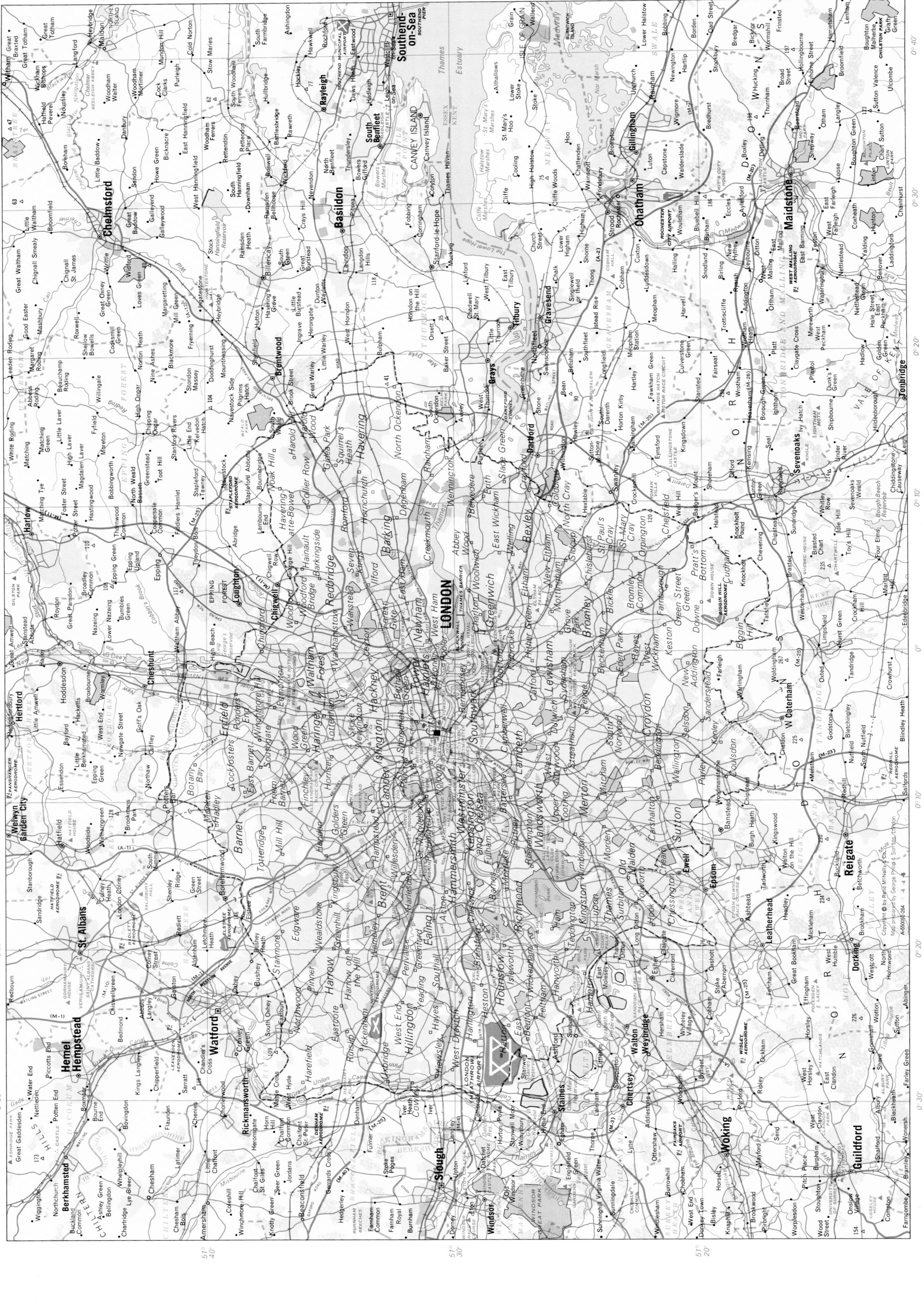

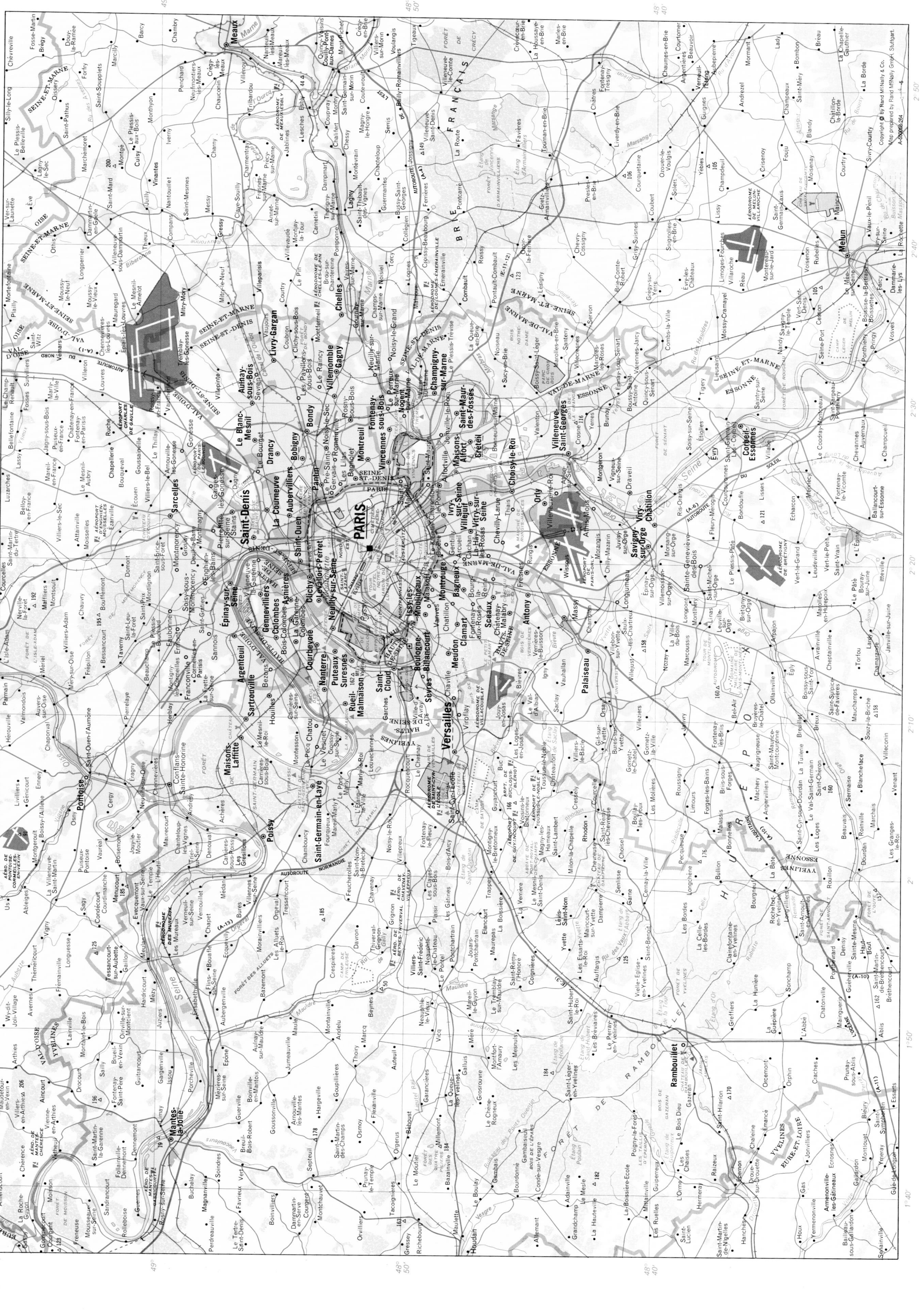

Kilometers 0 5 10 15 Km.

Statute Miles 0 5 10 15 Mi.

Scale 1:300,000

One centimeter represents 3 kilometers.
One inch represents approximately 4.7 miles.

FRANÇAIS	aérodrome	bois	château	étang	forêt	ruisseau
ENGLISH	airport	woods	castle	pond	forest	brook
DEUTSCH	Flughafen	Gehölz	Burg	Teich	Wald	Bach
ESPAÑOL	aeropuerto	bosques	castillo	charca	bosque	arroyo
PORTUGUÊS	aeroporto	bosques	castelo	lagoa	floresta	arroio

AREA 6,500 km²
POPULATION 9,800,000

Kilometers 0 5 10 15 Km.
Statute Miles 0 5 10 15 Mi.

Scale 1:300,000
One centimeter represents 3 kilometers.
One inch represents approximately 4.7 miles.

ENGLISH	DEUTSCH	ESPAÑOL	FRANÇAIS	PORTUGUÊS
bank	Bank	banco	banc	banco
canal	Kanal	canal	canal	canal
hill	Hügel	colina	colline	colina
moor	Ried	páramo	lande	charneca
park	Park	parque	parc	parque
railway station	Bahnhof	terminal ferroviaria	gare	estação ferroviária
reservoir	Stausee	estanque	réservoir	reservatório
tower	Turm	torre	tour	torre

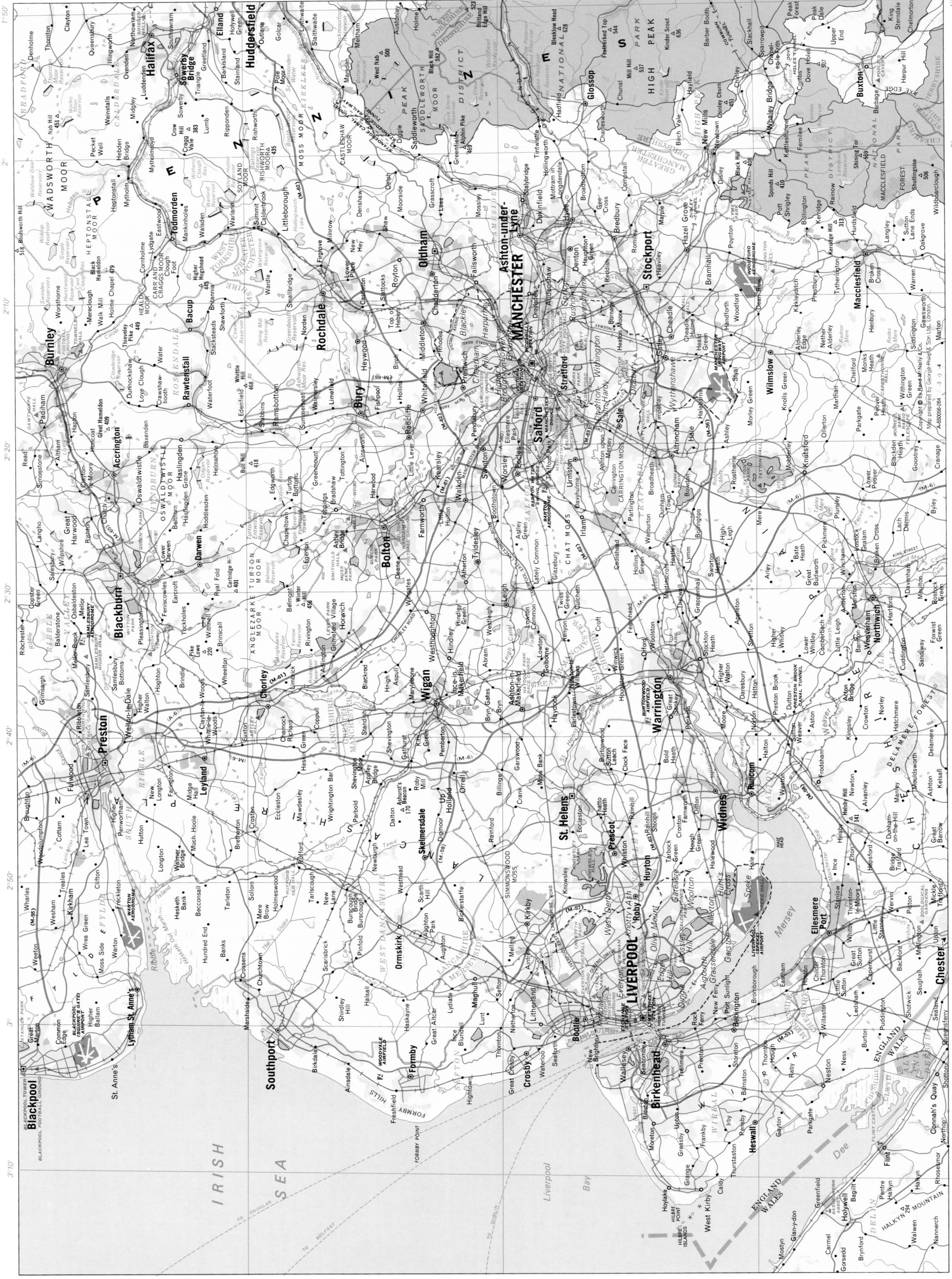

AREA: 5,650 km²
POPULATION: 6,275,000

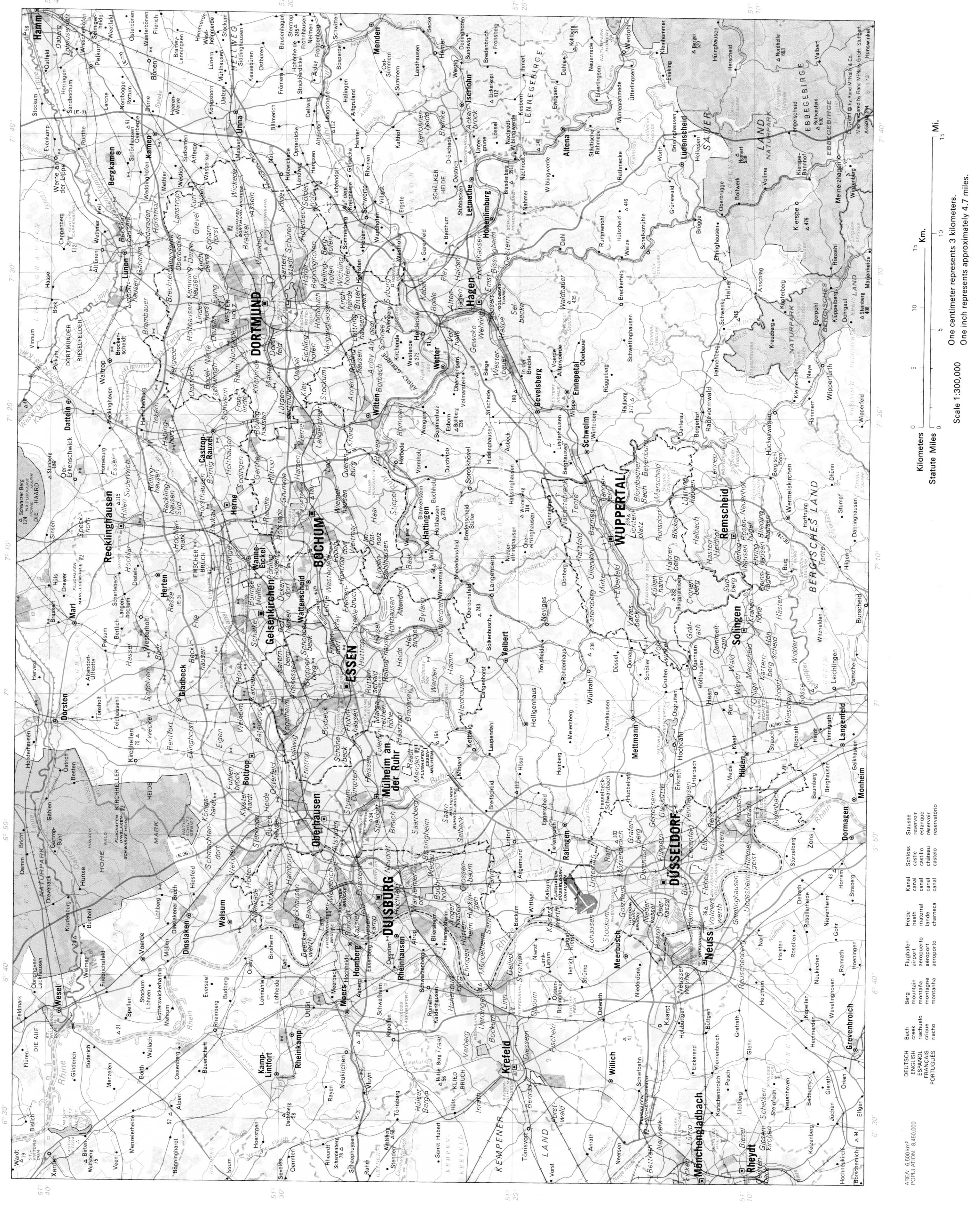
Scale 1:300,000
One centimeter represents 3 kilometers.
One inch represents approximately 4.7 miles.
Kilometers
Statute Miles
Km.
Mi.
AREA 6,500 km²
POPULATION 8,450,000
DEUTSCH Bach Berg Flughafen Heide Kanal Schloss Stausee
ENGLISH creek mountain airport heath canal castle reservoir
ESPAÑOL riachuelo montaña aeropuerto matorral canal castillo estanque
FRANÇAIS crique montagne aéroport lande canal château réservoir
PORTUGUÊS riacho montanha aeroporto charneca canal castelo reservatório
Copyright © by Rand McNally & Co.
Hamm
Unna
Kamen
Bergkamen
Lünen
Dortmund
Hagen
Iserlohn
Menden
Lüdenscheid
Altena
Wetter
Witten
Bochum
Herne
Castrop-Rauxel
Recklinghausen
Datteln
Marl
Herten
Gelsenkirchen
Wanne-Eickel
Wattenscheid
Essen
Gladbeck
Bottrop
Oberhausen
Mülheim an der Ruhr
Duisburg
Dinslaken
Dorsten
Wesel
Moers
Rheinhausen
Homberg
Kamp-Lintfort
Rheinkamp
Krefeld
Willich
Mönchengladbach
Rheydt
Neuss
Düsseldorf
Ratingen
Velbert
Hattingen
Sprockhövel
Schwelm
Gevelsberg
Ennepetal
Wuppertal
Remscheid
Solingen
Hilden
Langenfeld
Mettmann
Monheim
Dormagen
Grevenbroich
Wülfrath
Haan
Hohenlimburg
Letmathe
Schwerte
Kierspe
Meinerzhagen
BERGISCHES LAND
EBBEGEBIRGE
SAUERLAND
LENNEGEBIRGE
Rhein
Ruhr
Lippe
Emscher

a

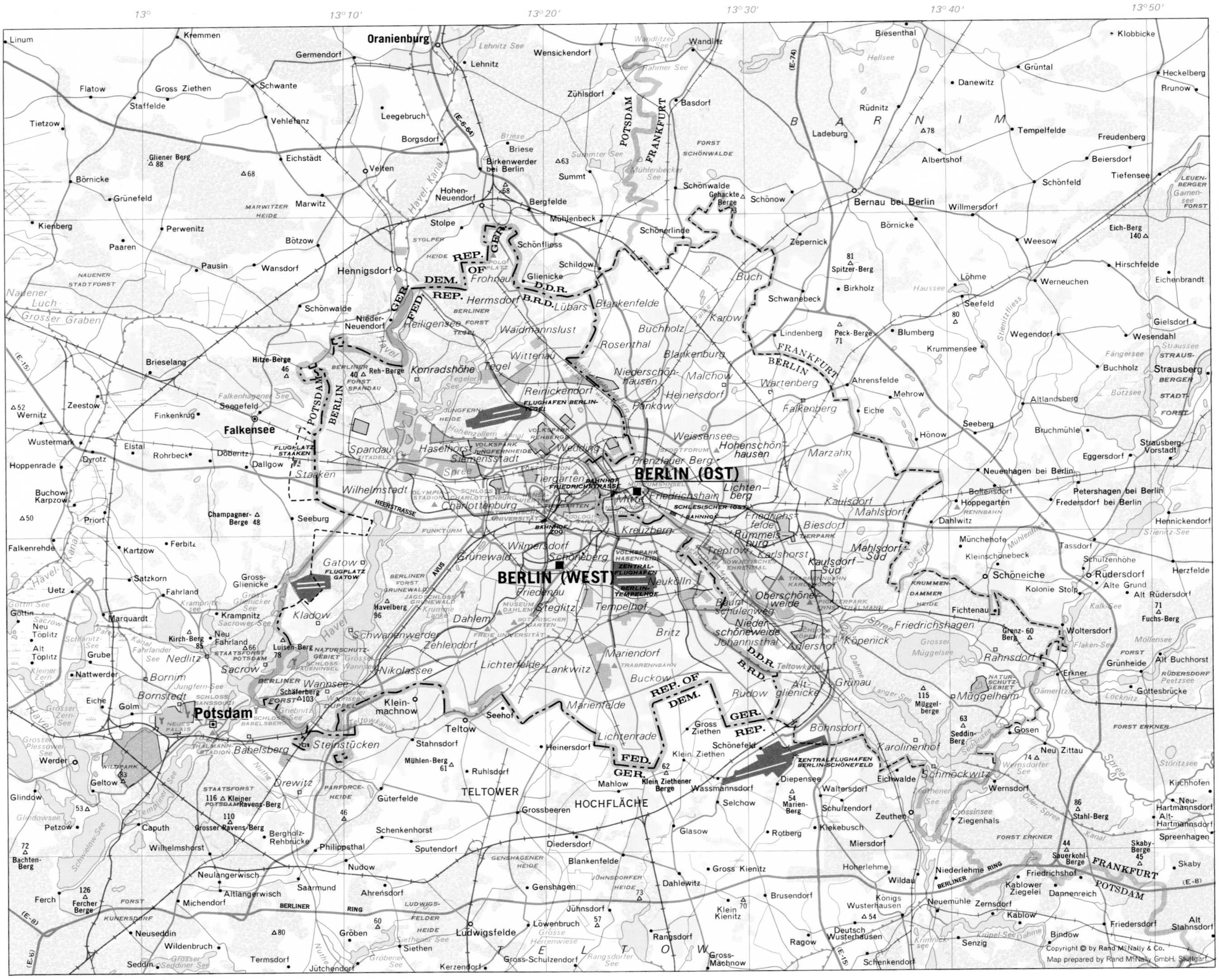

b

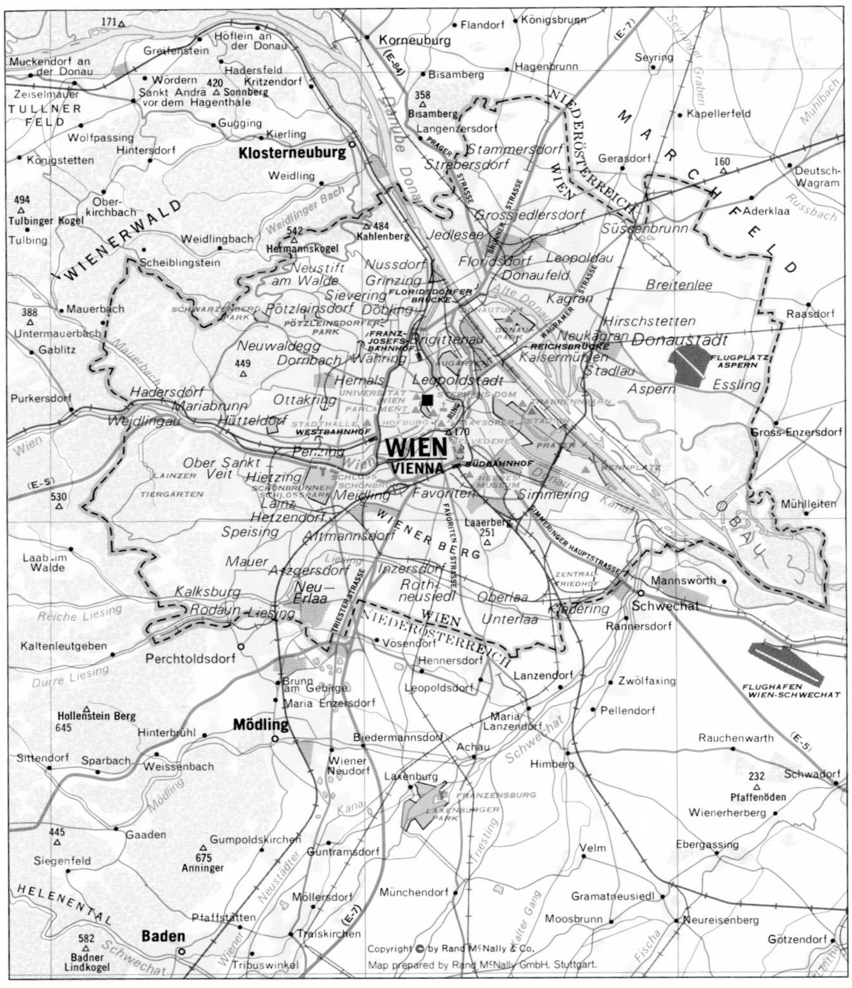

c

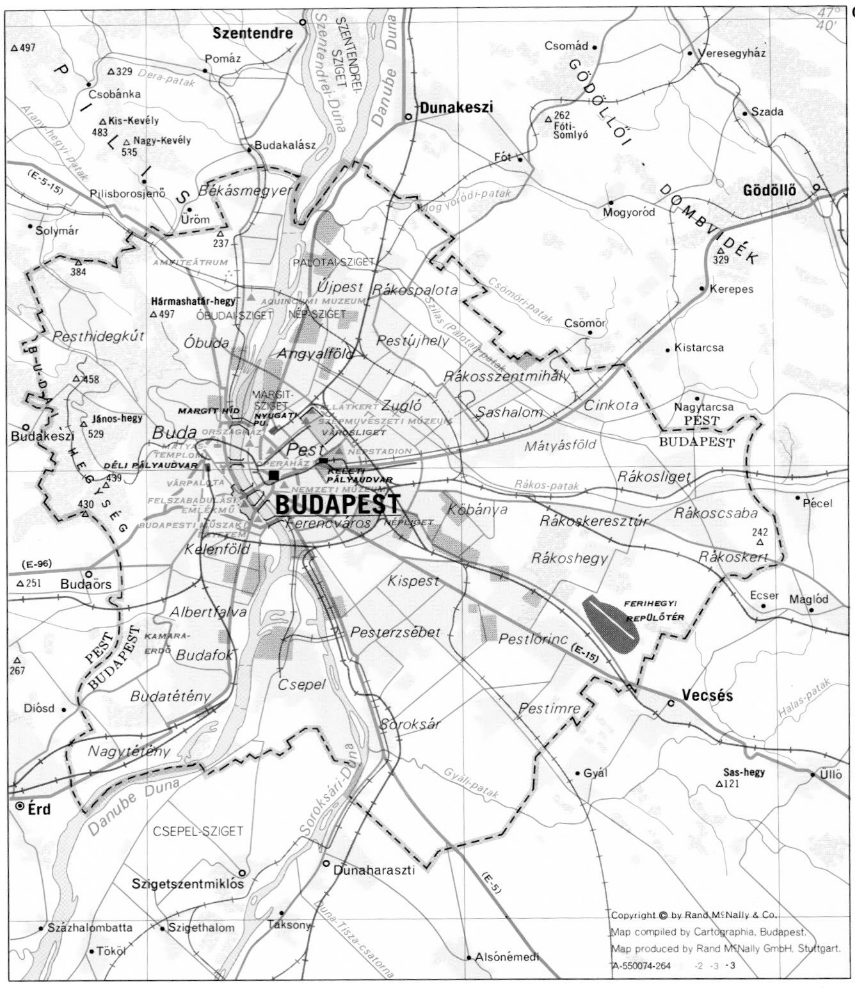

	AREA (km²)	POPULATION
BERLIN	3,700	3,550,000
WIEN	1,300	1,825,000
BUDAPEST	1,300	2,450,000

MAP FORM	Berg	Berge	hegy	Heide	Schloss	See	sziget
ENGLISH	hill	hills	mountain	heath	castle	lake	island
DEUTSCH	Berg	Berge	Berg	Heide	Schloss	See	Insel
ESPAÑOL	colina	colinas	montaña	matorral	castillo	lago	isla
FRANÇAIS	colline	collines	montagne	lande	château	lac	île
PORTUGUÊS	colina	colinas	montanha	charneca	castelo	lago	ilha

Kilometers 0 5 10 15 Km.

Statute Miles 0 5 10 15 Mi.

Scale 1:300,000

One centimeter represents 3 kilometers.
One inch represents approximately 4.7 miles.

a

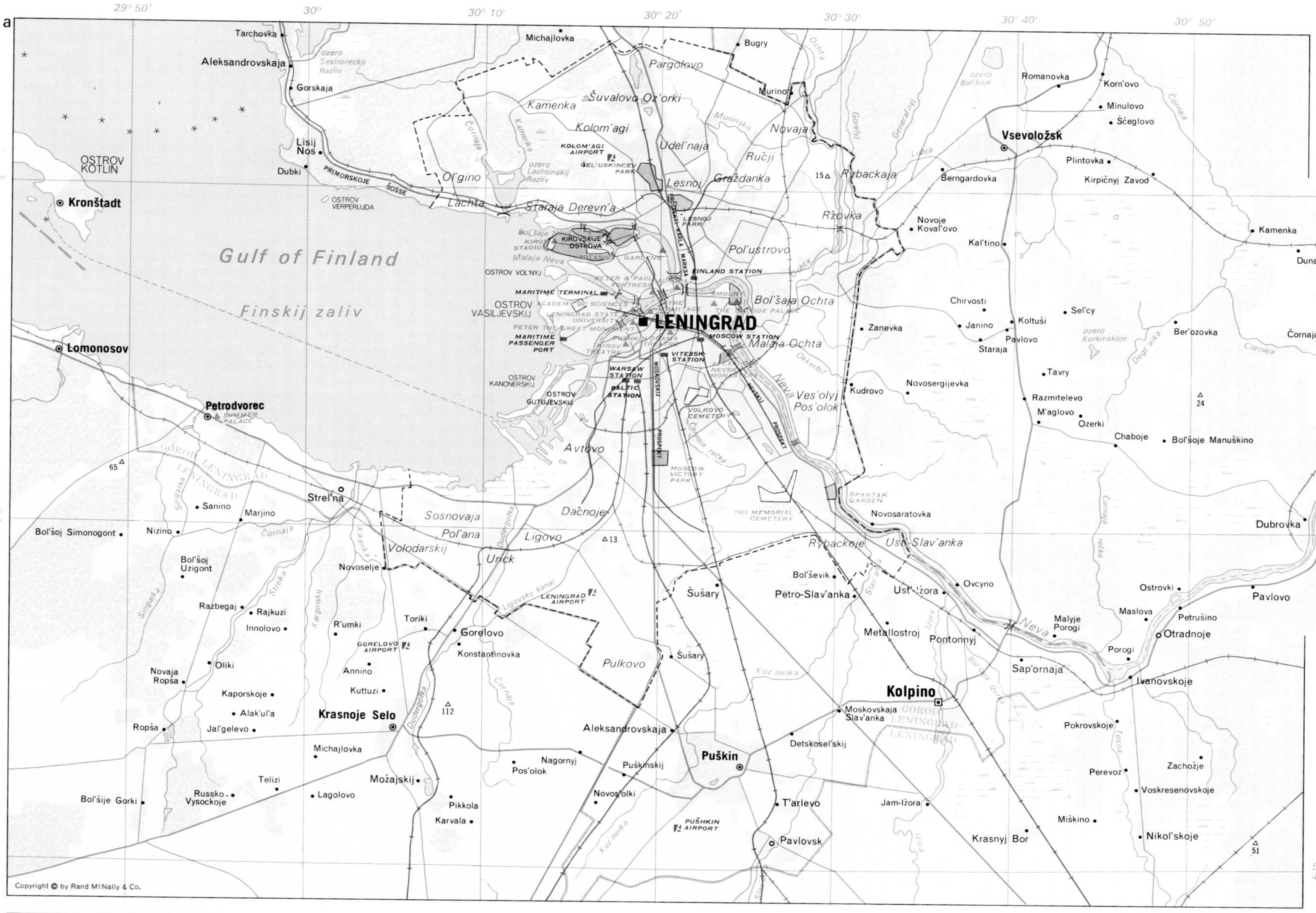

b

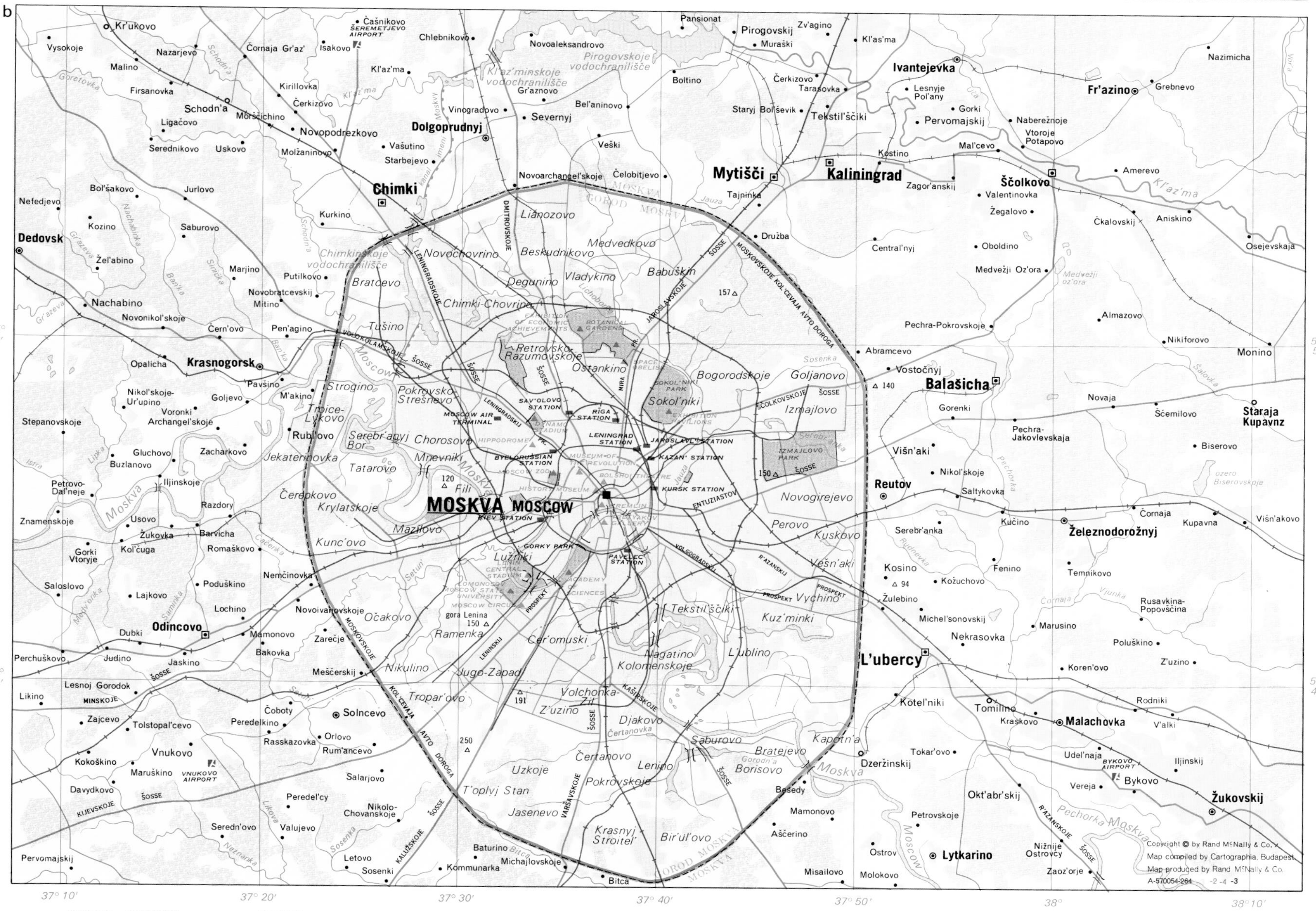

	AREA (km²)	POPULATION
LENINGRAD	2,800	4,850,000
MOSKVA	3,200	9,950,000

MAP FORM	ostrov	ozero	stadion	vodochranilišče	vokzal
ENGLISH	island	lake	stadium	reservoir	rail terminal
DEUTSCH	Insel	See	Stadion	Stausee	Bahnhof
ESPAÑOL	isla	lago	estadio	estanque	terminal ferroviaria
FRANÇAIS	île	lac	stade	réservoir	gare
PORTUGUÊS	ilha	lago	estádio	reservatório	estação ferroviária

Kilometers 0 5 10 15 Km.

Statute Miles 0 5 10 15 Mi.

Scale 1:300,000

One centimeter represents 3 kilometers.

One inch represents approximately 4.7 miles.

Kilometers 0 5 10 15 Km.

Statute Miles 0 5 10 15 Mi.

One centimeter represents 3 kilometers.
One inch represents approximately 4.7 miles

Scale 1:300,000

	AREA (km²)	POPULATION
MADRID	1,250	3,875,000
MILANO	1,900	3,975,000
LISBOA	1,150	2,150,000
BARCELONA	950	3,825,000

MAP FORM	aeroporto	arroyo	estación	ponta	ribeira	riera
ENGLISH	airport	brook	station	point	creek	creek
DEUTSCH	Flughafen	Bach	Bahnhof	Landspitze	Bach	Bach
ESPAÑOL	aeropuerto	arroyo	estación	punta	riachuelo	riera
FRANÇAIS	aéroport	ruisseau	gare	pointe	crique	crique
PORTUGUÊS	aeroporto	arroio	estação	ponta	riacho	riacho

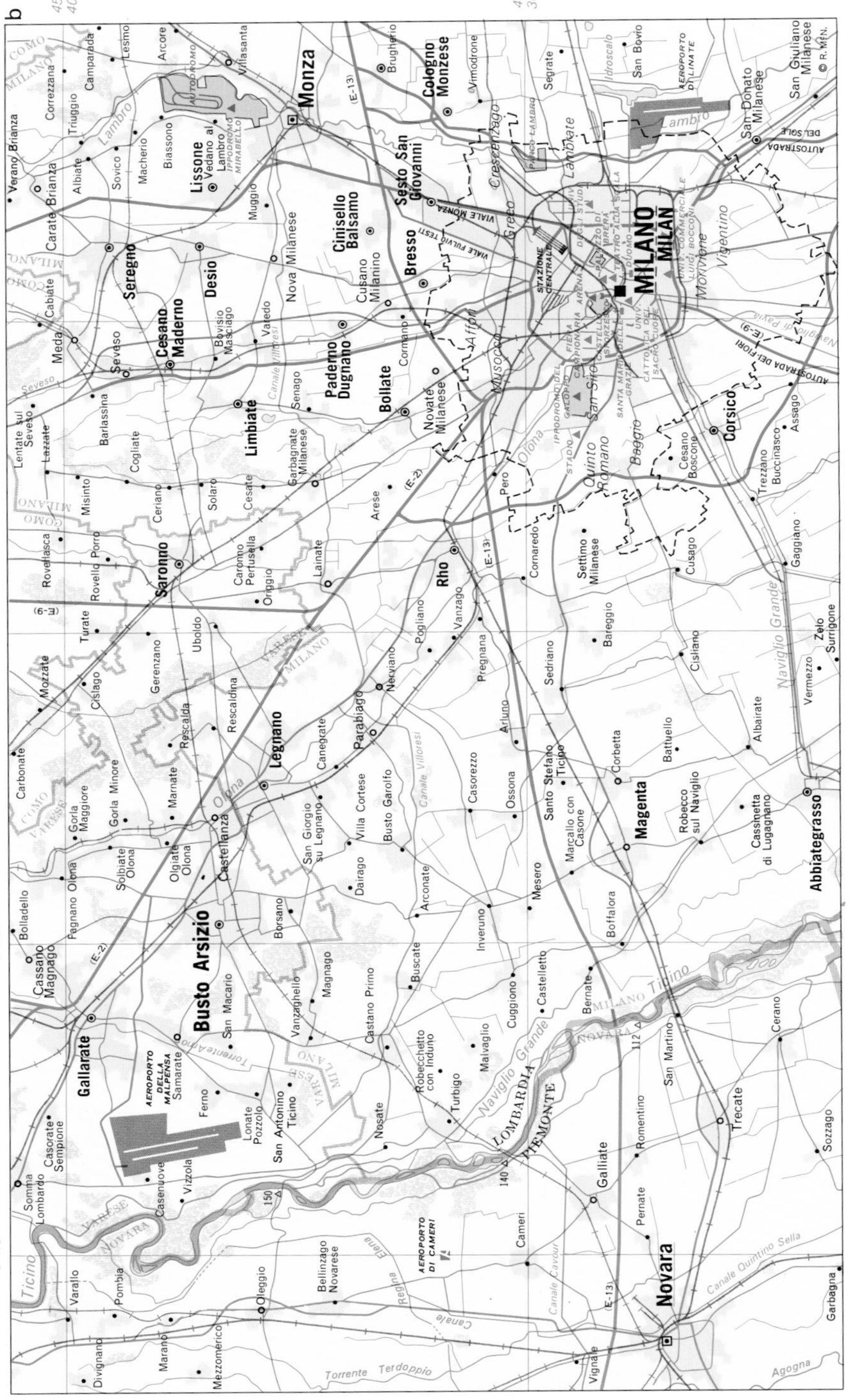

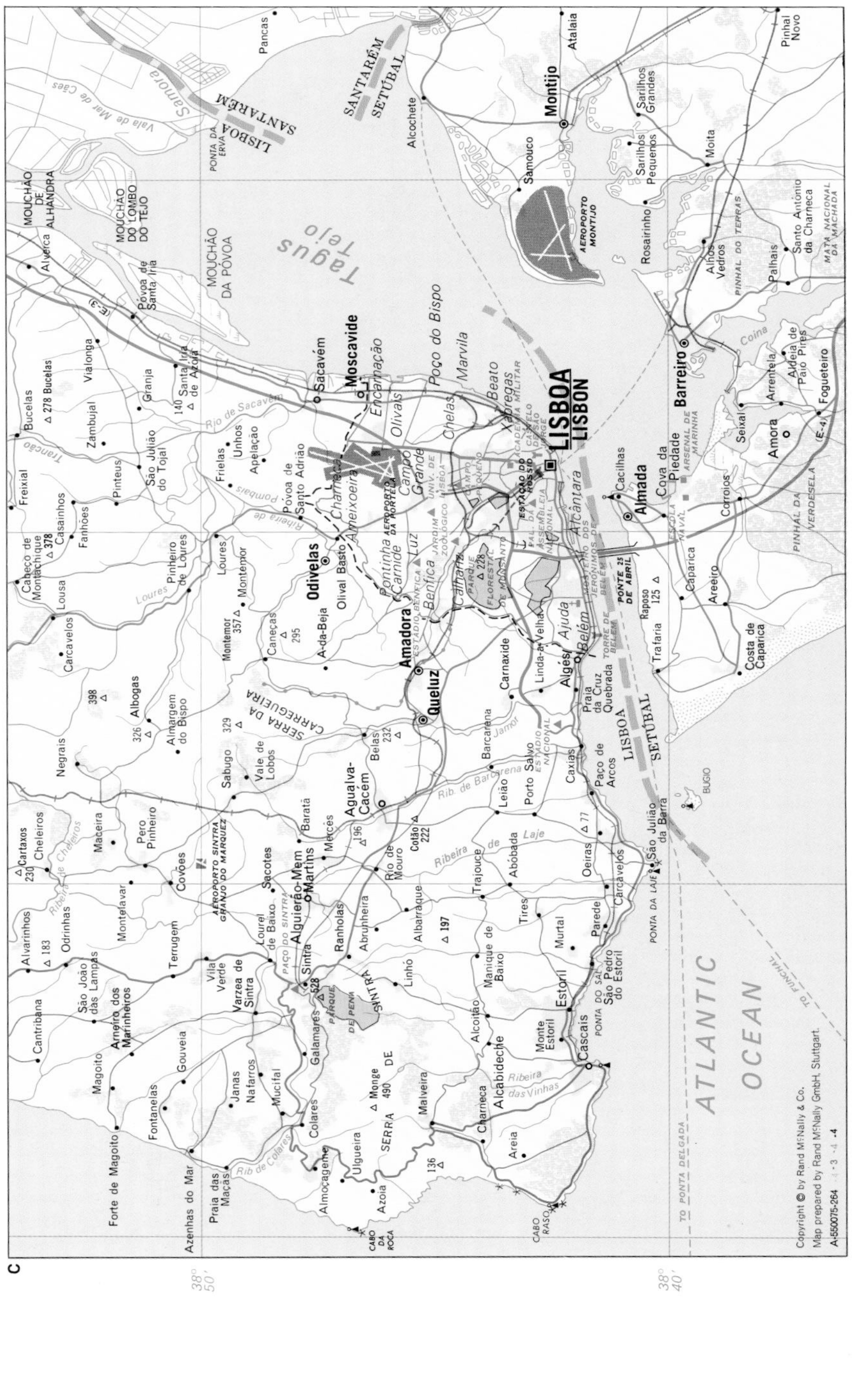

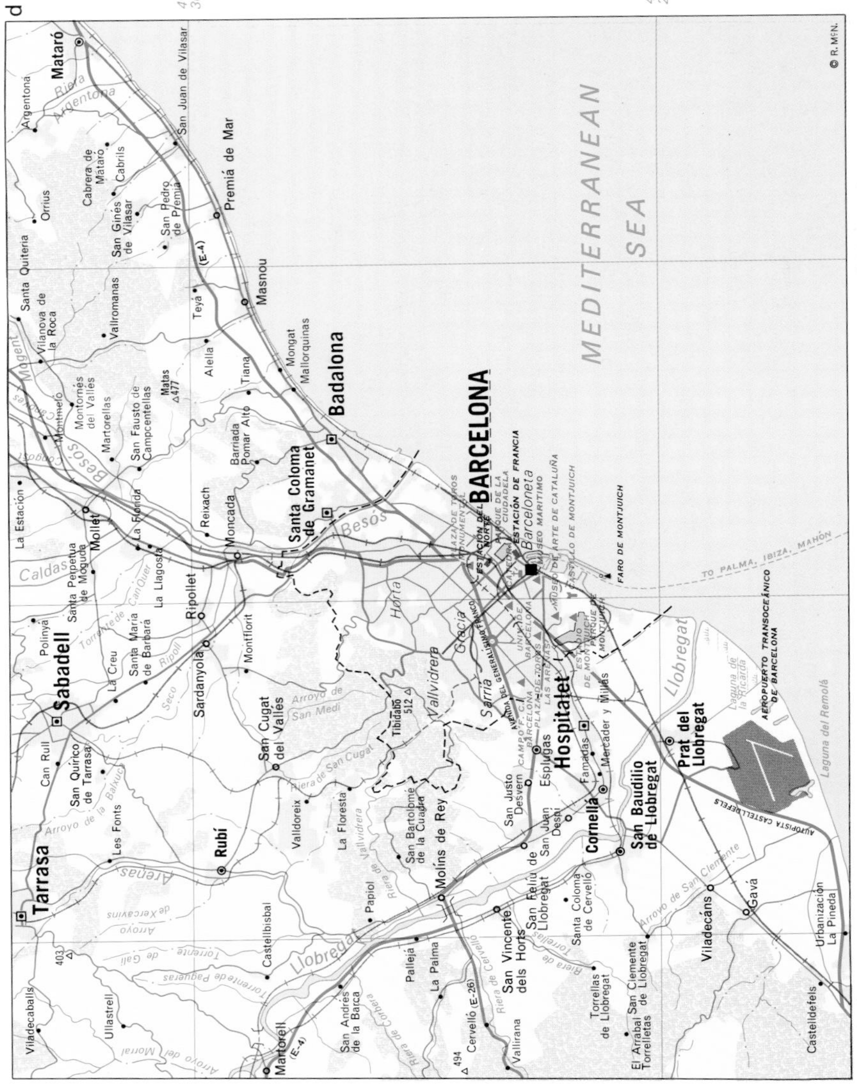

a

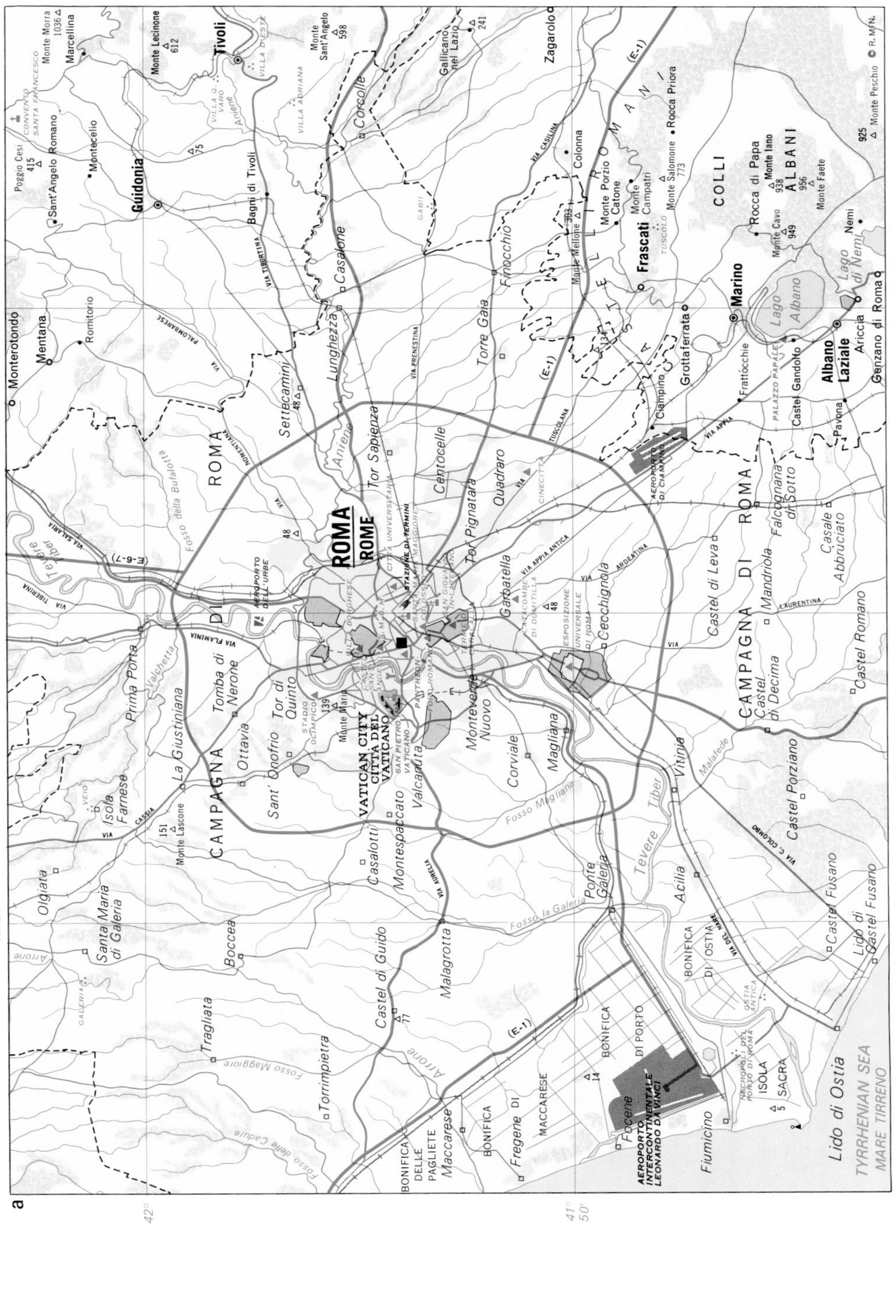

b

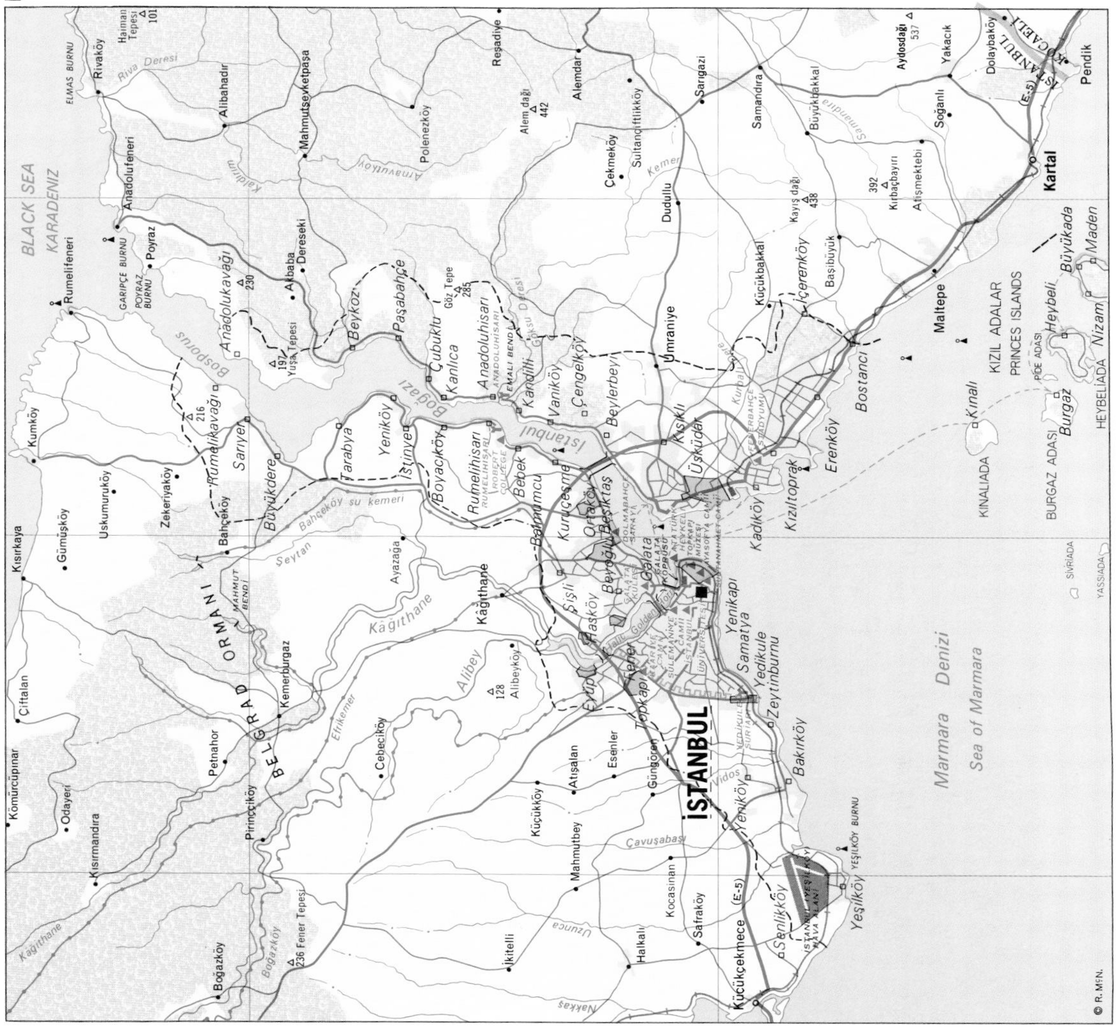

c

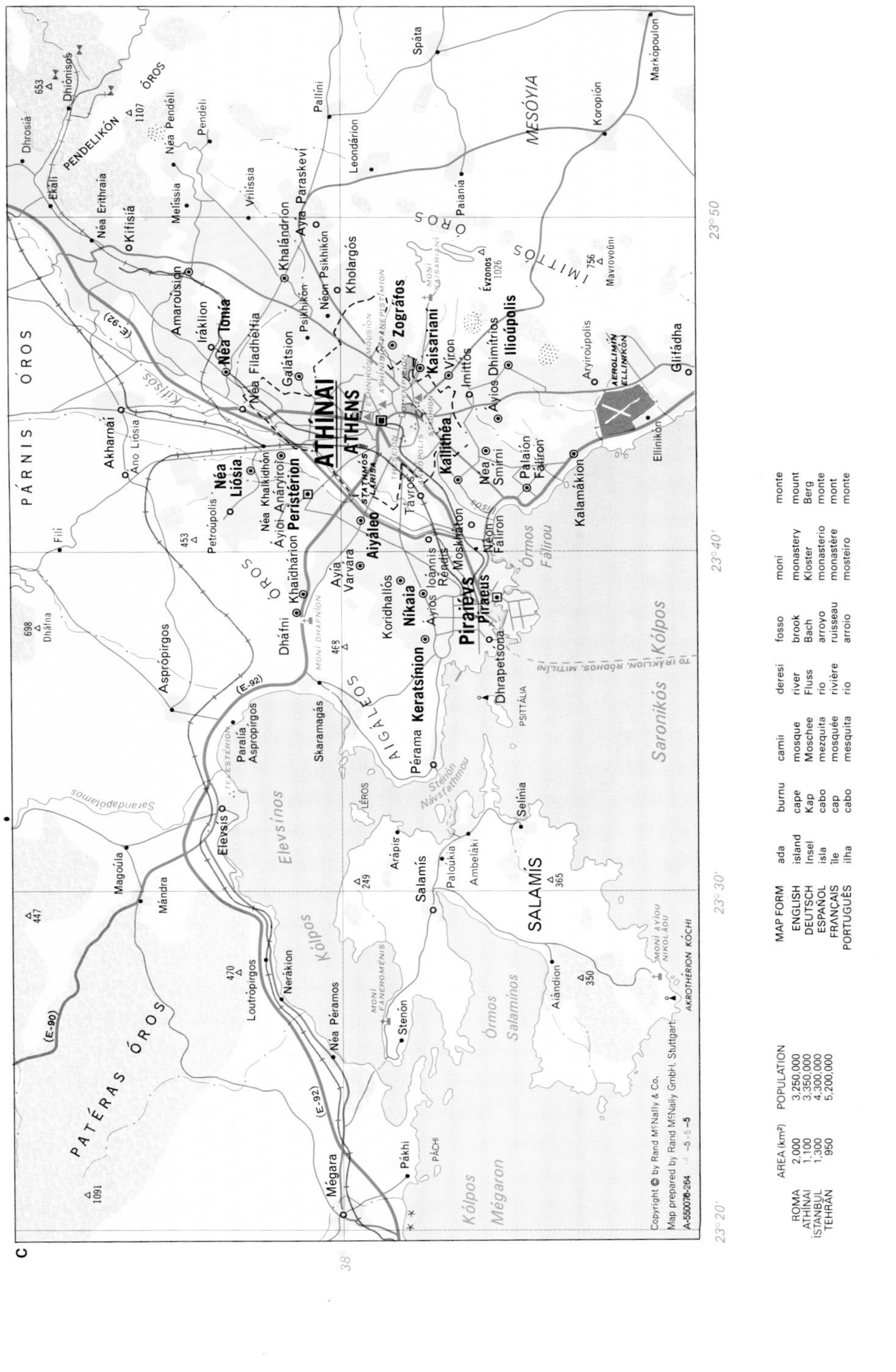

d

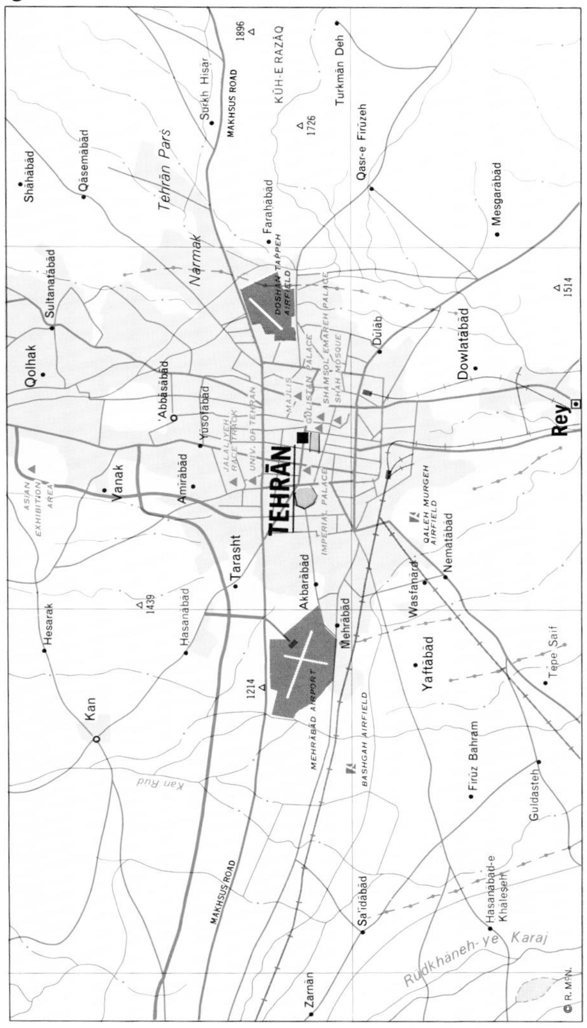

	AREA (km²)	POPULATION
ROMA	2,000	3,250,000
ATHÍNAI	1,100	3,350,000
İSTANBUL	1,300	4,300,000
TEHRĀN	950	5,200,000

MAP FORM	ada	burnu	camii	deresi	fosso	moni	monte
ENGLISH	island	cape	mosque	river	brook	monastery	mount
DEUTSCH	Insel	Kap	Moschee	Fluss	Bach	Kloster	Berg
ESPAÑOL	isla	cabo	mezquita	río	arroyo	monasterio	monte
FRANÇAIS	île	cap	mosquée	rivière	ruisseau	monastère	mont
PORTUGUÊS	ilha	cabo	mesquita	rio	arroio	mosteiro	monte

Scale 1:300,000
One centimeter represents 3 kilometers.
One inch represents approximately 4.7 miles.

Copyright © by Rand McNally & Co.
Map prepared by Rand McNally GmbH, Stuttgart.

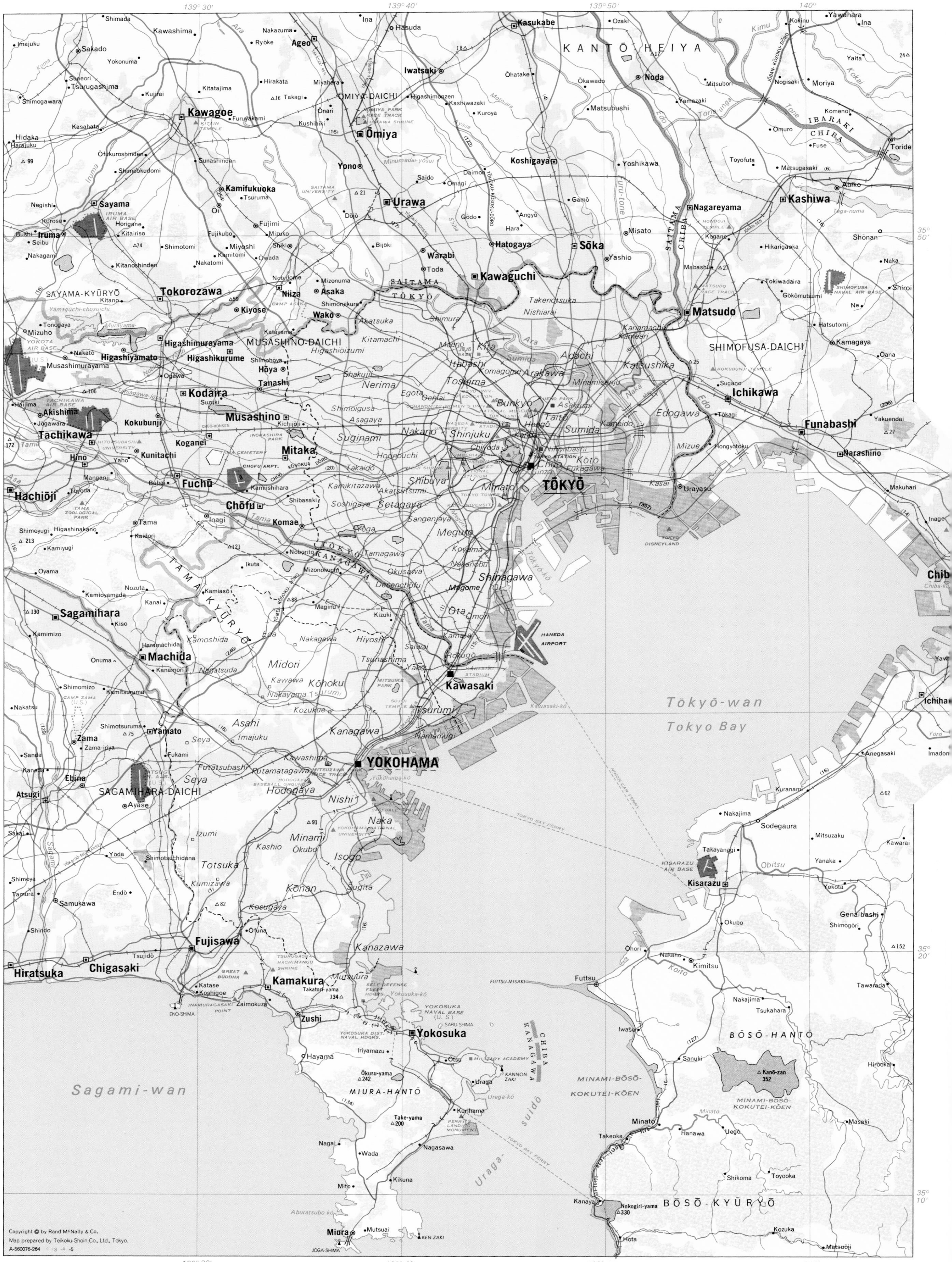

AREA (km²): 5,350
POPULATION: 24,350,000

MAP FORM	air base	camp	-daichi	-kō	-shima	temple	-yama
ENGLISH	air base	camp	plateau	harbor	island	temple	mountain
DEUTSCH	Luftstützpunkt	Lager	Hochebene	Hafen	Insel	Tempel	Berg
ESPAÑOL	base aérea	campo	meseta	puerto	isla	templo	montaña
FRANÇAIS	base aérienne	camp	plateau	port	île	temple	montagne
PORTUGUÊS	base aérea	campo	planalto	porto	ilha	templo	montanha

Kilometers 0 5 10 15 Km.
Statute Miles 0 5 10 15 Mi.

Scale 1:300,000
One centimeter represents 3 kilometers.
One inch represents approximately 4.7 miles.

a

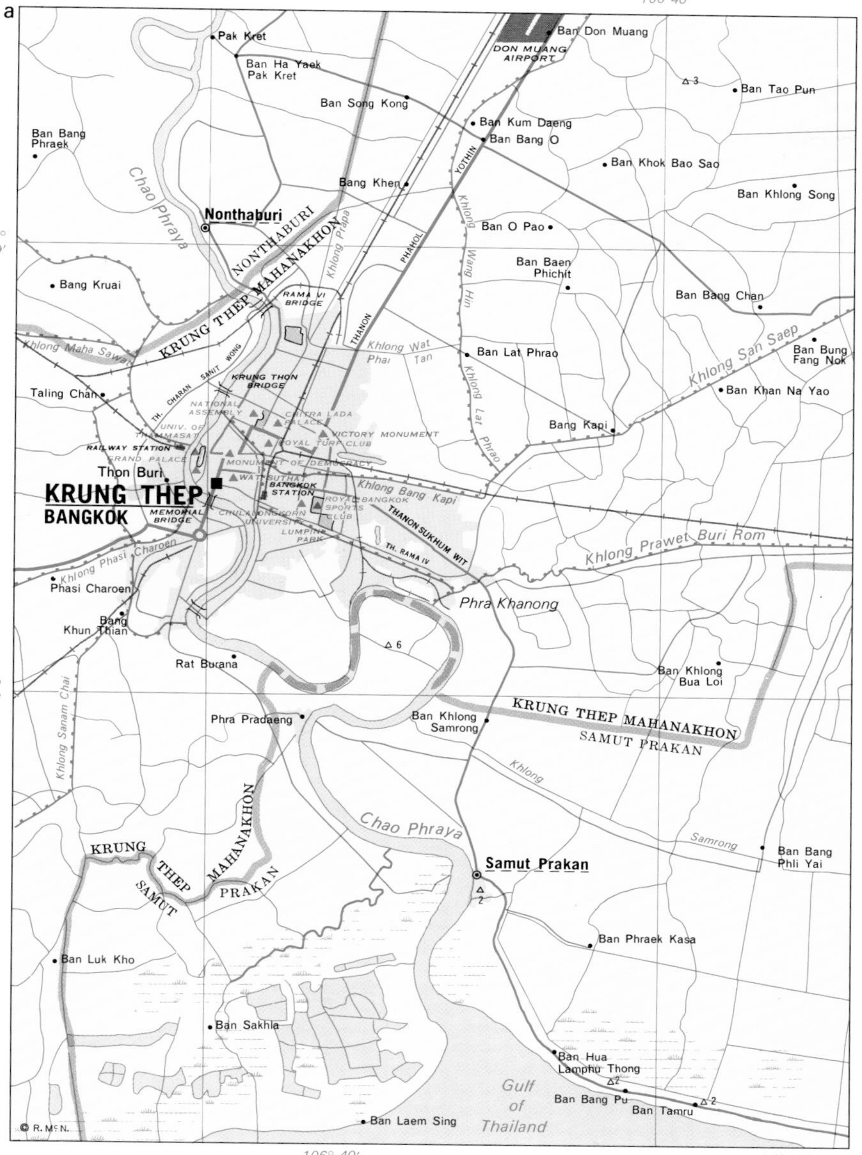
KRUNG THEP
BANGKOK
Thon Buri
Nonthaburi
Pak Kret
Ban Don Muang
DON MUANG AIRPORT
Ban Tao Pun
Ban Song Kong
Ban Kum Daeng
Ban Bang O
Ban Khok Bao Sao
Ban Khlong Song
Bang Khen
Ban O Pao
Ban Baen Phichit
Ban Bang Chan
Bang Kruai
Ban Lat Phrao
Ban Bung Fang Nok
Ban Khan Na Yao
Taling Chan
Bang Kapi
Chao Phraya
Khlong San Saep
Khlong Prawet Buri Rom
Phasi Charoen
Khun Thian
Phra Khanong
Rat Burana
Ban Khlong Bua Loi
Phra Pradaeng
Ban Khlong Samrong
KRUNG THEP MAHANAKHON
SAMUT PRAKAN
NONTHABURI
Samut Prakan
Ban Bang Phli Yai
Ban Phraek Kasa
Ban Luk Kho
Ban Sakhla
Ban Hua Lamphu Thong
Ban Bang Pu
Ban Tamru
Ban Laem Sing
Gulf of Thailand
RAILWAY STATION
VICTORY MONUMENT
MEMORIAL BRIDGE
© R.McN.

b

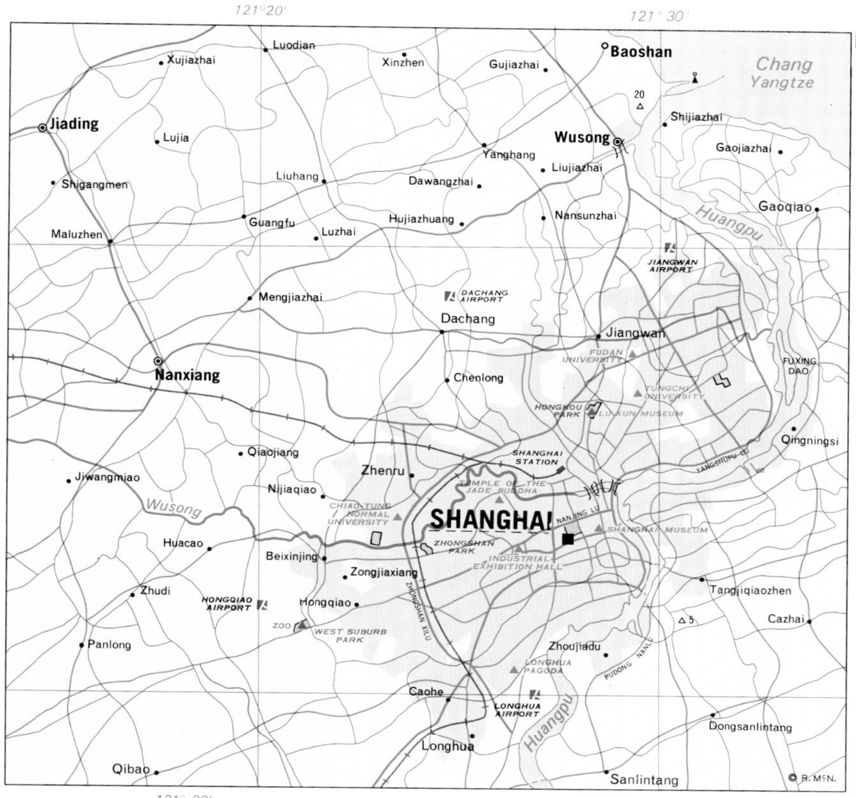
SHANGHAI
Baoshan
Chang Yangtze
Luodian
Xinzhen
Gujiazhai
Xujiazhai
Jiading
Shijiazhai
Wusong
Gaojiazhai
Lujia
Yanghang
Liujiazhai
Shigangmen
Liuhang
Dawangzhai
Gaoqiao
Nansunzhai
Guangfu
Hujiazhuang
Maluzhen
Luzhai
Huangpu
JIANGWAN AIRPORT
DACHANG AIRPORT
Mengjiazhai
Dachang
Jiangwan
FUXING DAO
Nanxiang
Chenlong
Qingningsi
SHANGHAI STATION
Qiaojiang
Zhenru
Jiwangmiao
Nijiaqiao
Wusong
Huacao
Beixinjing
Zongjiaxiang
HONGQIAO AIRPORT
Hongqiao
Zhudi
Tangjiqiaozhen
Cazhai
Panlong
Zhoujiadu
LONGHUA PAGODA
Caohe
LONGHUA AIRPORT
Longhua
Dongsanlintang
Qibao
Sanlintang
© R.McN.

c

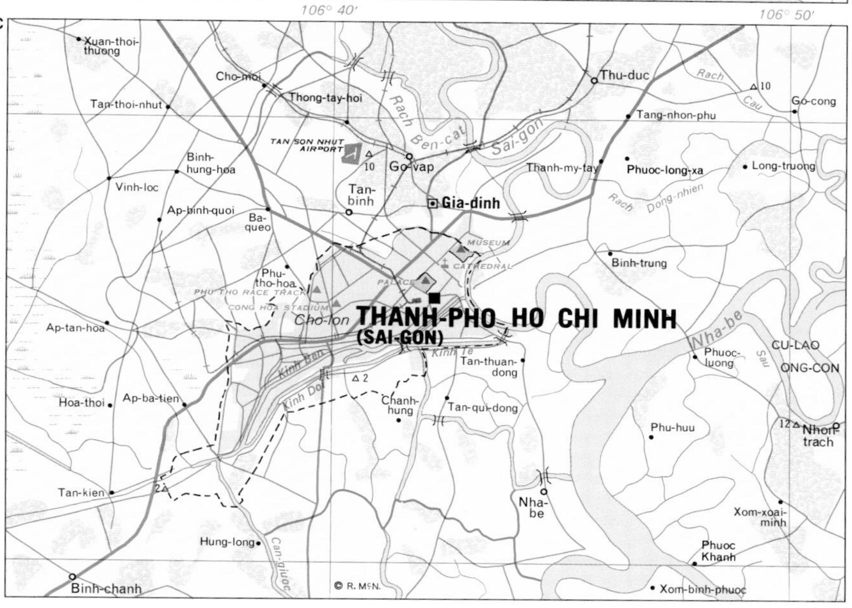
THANH-PHO HO CHI MINH
(SAI-GON)
Xuan-thoi-thuong
Cho-moi
Thu-duc
Tan-thoi-nhut
Thong-tay-hoi
Go-cong
Tang-nhon-phu
TAN SON NHUT AIRPORT
Binh-hung-hoa
Go-vap
Thanh-my-tay
Phuoc-long-xa
Long-truong
Vinh-loc
Tan-binh
Gia-dinh
Ap-binh-quoi
Ba-queo
Binh-trung
Phu-tho-hoa
Cho-lon
Ap-tan-hoa
Khanh Hoi
Tan-thuan-dong
Phuoc-luong
CU-LAO
ONG-CON
Hoa-thoi
Ap-ba-tien
Chanh-hung
Tan-qui-dong
Phu-huu
Nhon-trach
Tan-kien
Nha-be
Xom-xoai-minh
Hung-long
Phuoc Khanh
Binh-chanh
Xom-binh-phuoc
© R.McN.

d

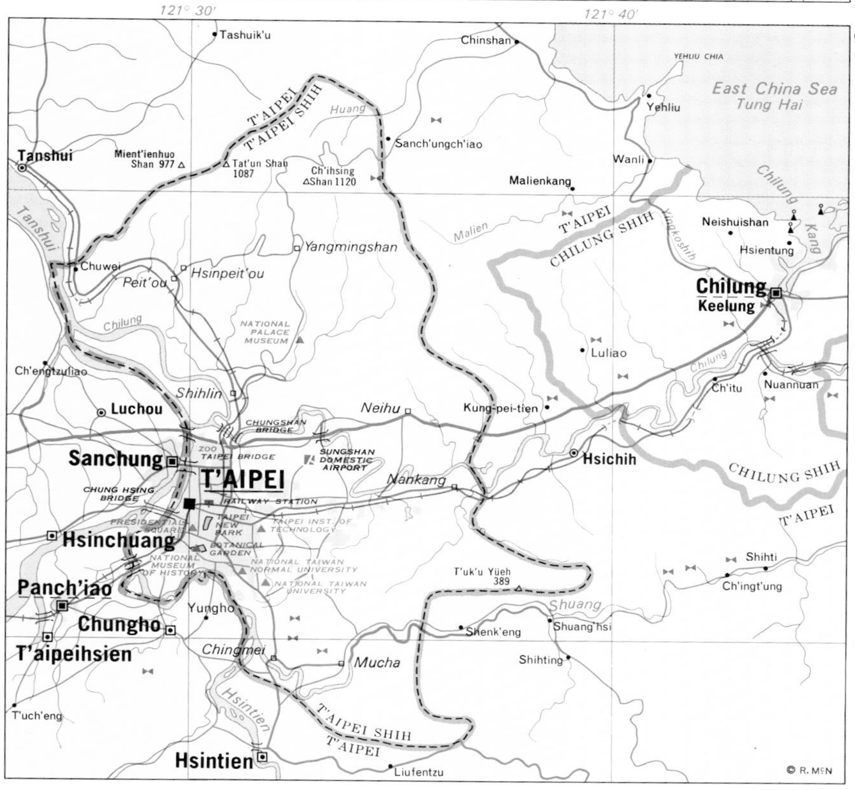
T'AIPEI
Tashuik'u
Chinshan
East China Sea
Tung Hai
Yehliu
Tanshui
Sanch'ungch'iao
Wanli
Malienkang
Neishuishan
Hsientung
Yangmingshan
Chilung
Keelung
Hsinpeit'ou
Peit'ou
Luliao
Ch'engtzuliao
Shihlin
Luchou
Neihu
Kung-pei-tien
Ch'itu
Nuannuan
Sanchung
Hsichih
Nankang
Hsinchuang
Shihti
Ch'ingt'ung
Panch'iao
Yungho
Chungho
Shenk'eng
Shuang'hsi
T'aipeihsien
Chingmei
Mucha
Shihting
T'uch'eng
Hsintien
Liufentzu
T'AIPEI SHIH
CHILUNG SHIH
© R.McN.

e

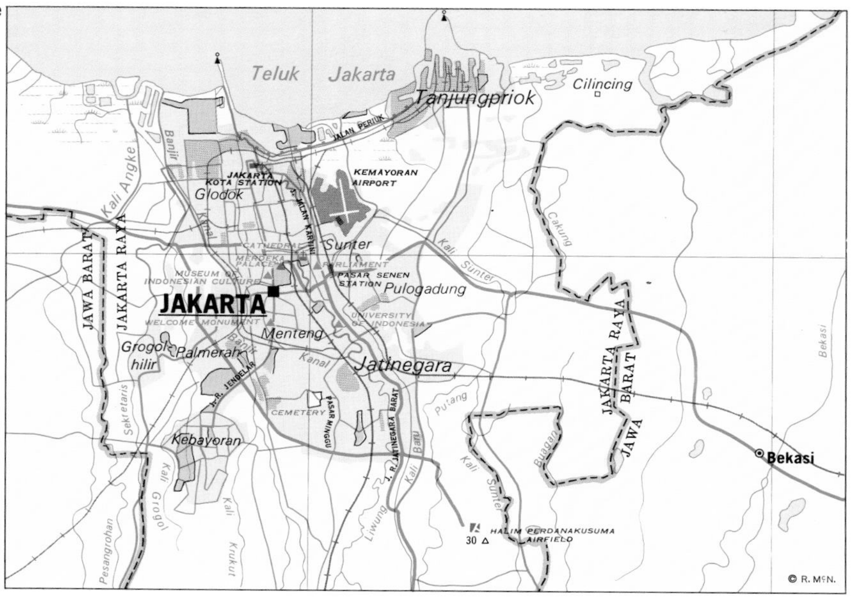
Teluk Jakarta
Tanjungpriok
Cilincing
KEMAYORAN AIRPORT
JAKARTA
Glodok
Sunter
Pulogadung
Palmerah
Grogol
Menteng
Jatinegara
Kebayoran
Bekasi
HALIM PERDANAKUSUMA AIRFIELD
JAWA BARAT
JAKARTA RAYA
© R.McN.

f

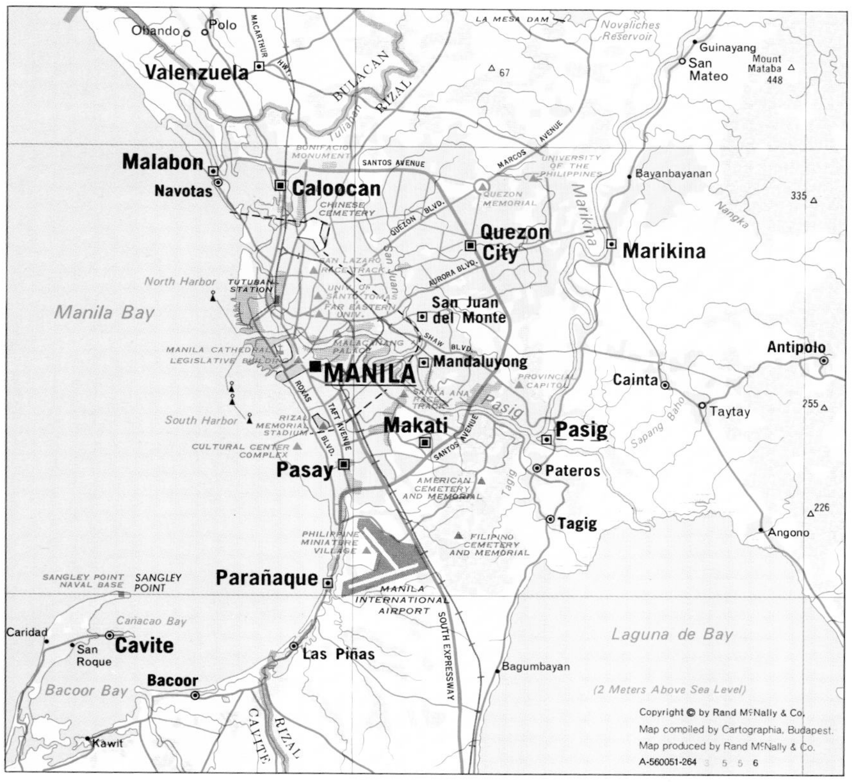
Polo
Obando
Valenzuela
Novaliches Reservoir
Guinayang
San Mateo
Mount Mataba 448
BULACAN
RIZAL
Malabon
Navotas
Caloocan
Bayanbayanan
Quezon City
Marikina
North Harbor
Manila Bay
San Juan del Monte
Antipolo
MANILA
Mandaluyong
Cainta
Taytay
South Harbor
Makati
Pasig
Pasay
Pateros
Tagig
Angono
Parañaque
MANILA INTERNATIONAL AIRPORT
SANGLEY POINT
Cavite
San Roque
Caridad
Las Piñas
Bacoor
Bacoor Bay
Laguna de Bay
(2 Meters Above Sea Level)
Bagumbayan
Kawit
CAVITE
RIZAL
Copyright © by Rand McNally & Co.
Map compiled by Cartographia, Budapest.
Map produced by Rand McNally & Co.
A-560051-264 5 5 6

	AREA (km²)	POPULATION
KRUNG THEP (BANGKOK)	1,450	5,300,000
SAI-GON	750	2,400,000
JAKARTA	700	6,450,000
SHANGHAI	1,000	8,400,000
T'AIPEI	950	4,125,000
MANILA	650	5,900,000

MAP FORM	kali	khlong	monument	shan
ENGLISH	stream	stream	monument	mountain
DEUTSCH	Bach	Bach	Denkmal	Berg
ESPAÑOL	corriente de agua	corriente de agua	monumento	montaña
FRANÇAIS	cours d'eau	cours d'eau	monument	montagne
PORTUGUÊS	corrente de água	corrente de água	monumento	montanha

Kilometers 0 5 10 15 Km.
Statute Miles 0 5 10 15 Mi.

Scale 1:300,000
One centimeter represents 3 kilometers.
One inch represents approximately 4.7 miles.

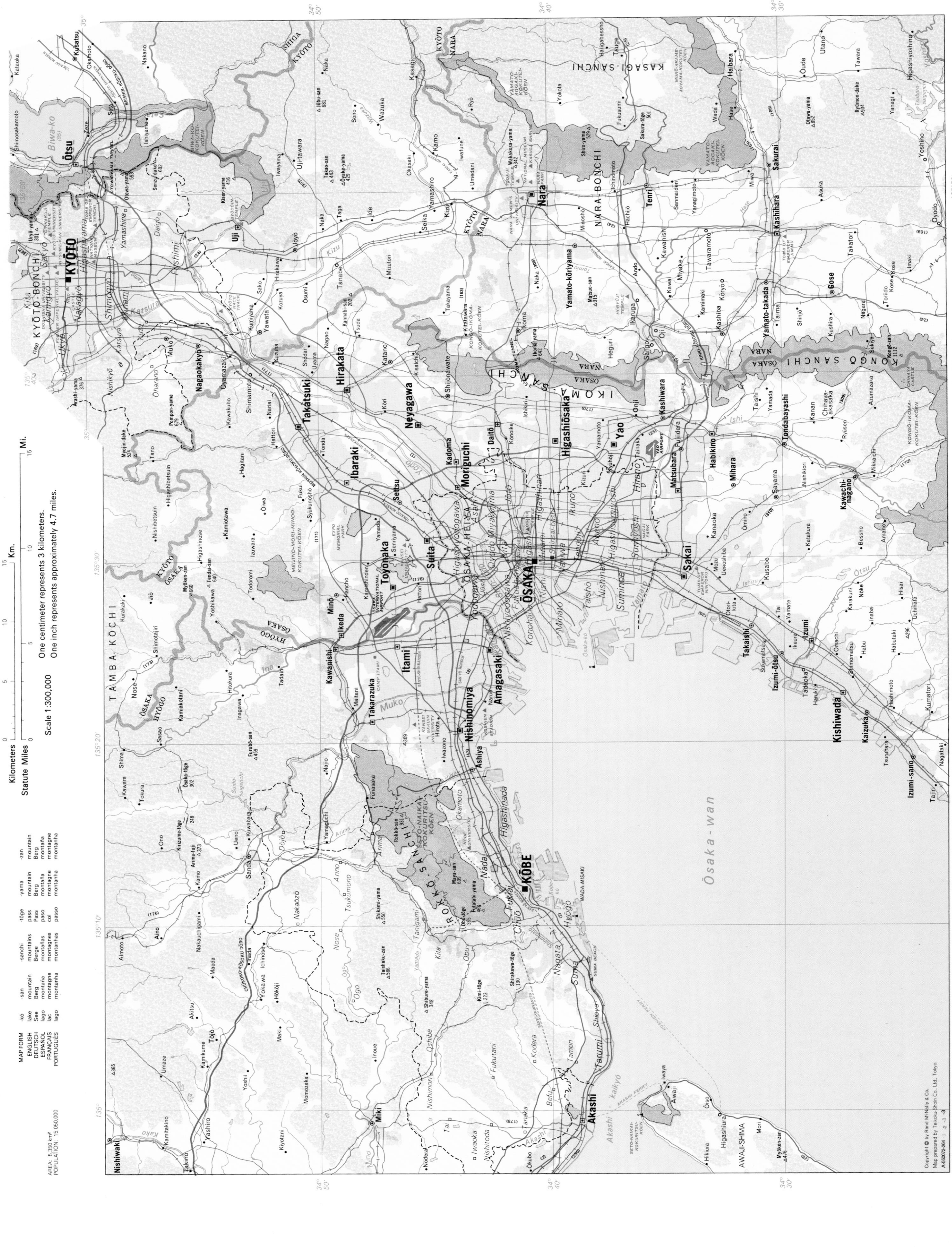
Kilometers 0 5 10 15 Km.
Statute Miles 0 5 10 15 Mi.
Scale 1:300,000
One centimeter represents 3 kilometers.
One inch represents approximately 4.7 miles.
MAP FORM kō -san -sanchi -tōge -yama -zan
ENGLISH lake mountain mountains pass mountain mountain
DEUTSCH See Berg Berge Pass Berg Berg
ESPAÑOL lago montaña montañas paso montaña montaña
FRANÇAIS lac montagne montagnes col montagne montagne
PORTUGUÊS lago montanha montanhas passo montanha montanha
AREA 5,350 km²
POPULATION 15,050,000
KYŌTO
Ōtsu
Biwa-ko
Nara
ŌSAKA
KŌBE
Sakai
Akashi
Kishiwada
Ōsaka-wan
NARA-BONCHI
KYŌTO-BONCHI
ŌSAKA-HEIYA
TAMBA-KŌCHI
ROKKŌ-SANCHI
IKOMA-SANCHI
KONGŌ-SANCHI
KASAGI-SANCHI
AWAJI-SHIMA
Copyright © by Rand McNally & Co.
Map prepared by Teikoku-Shoin Co., Ltd. Tokyo.

a

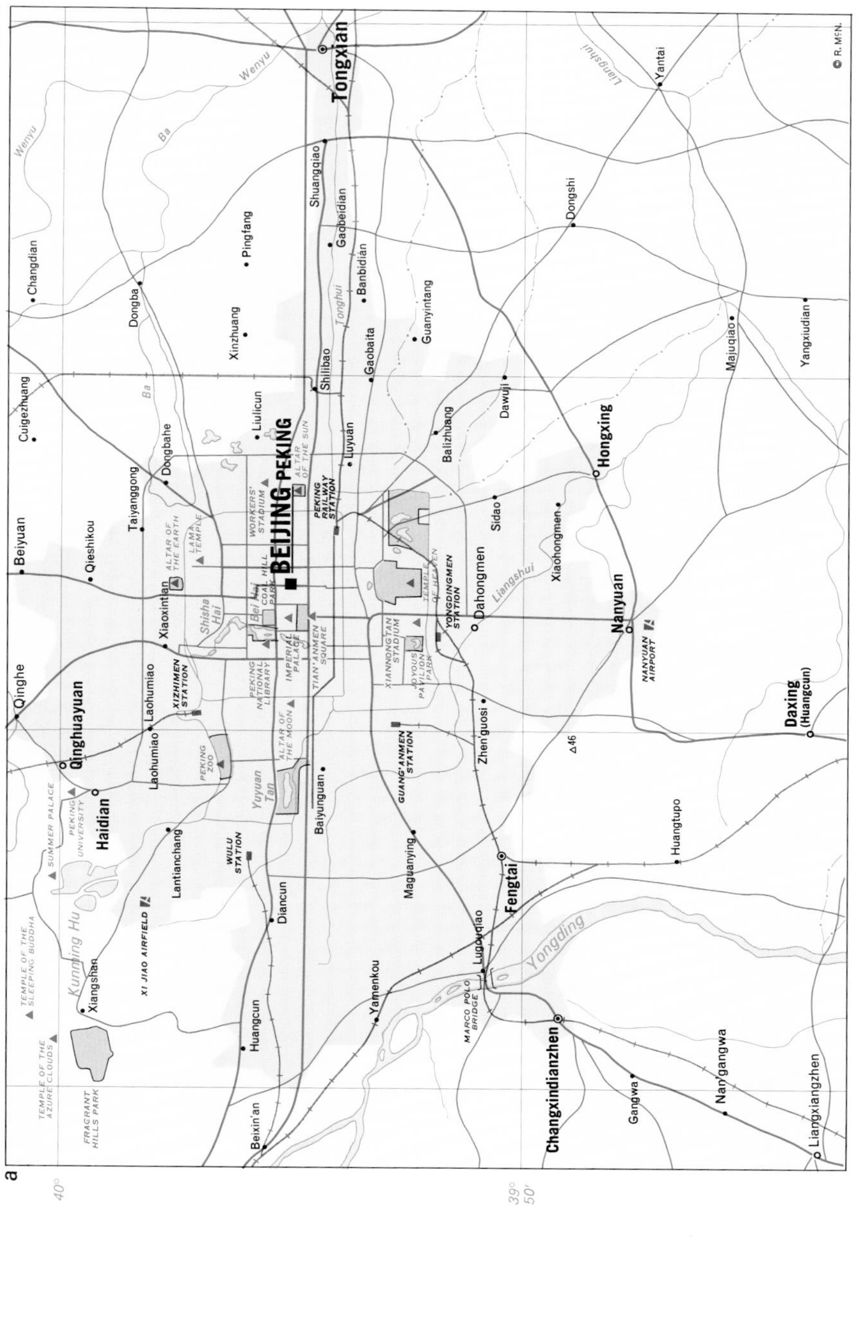
BEIJING-PEKING
Tongxian
Fengtai
Nanyuan
Daxing (Huangcun)
Changxindianzhen
Haidian
Qinghuayuan

b

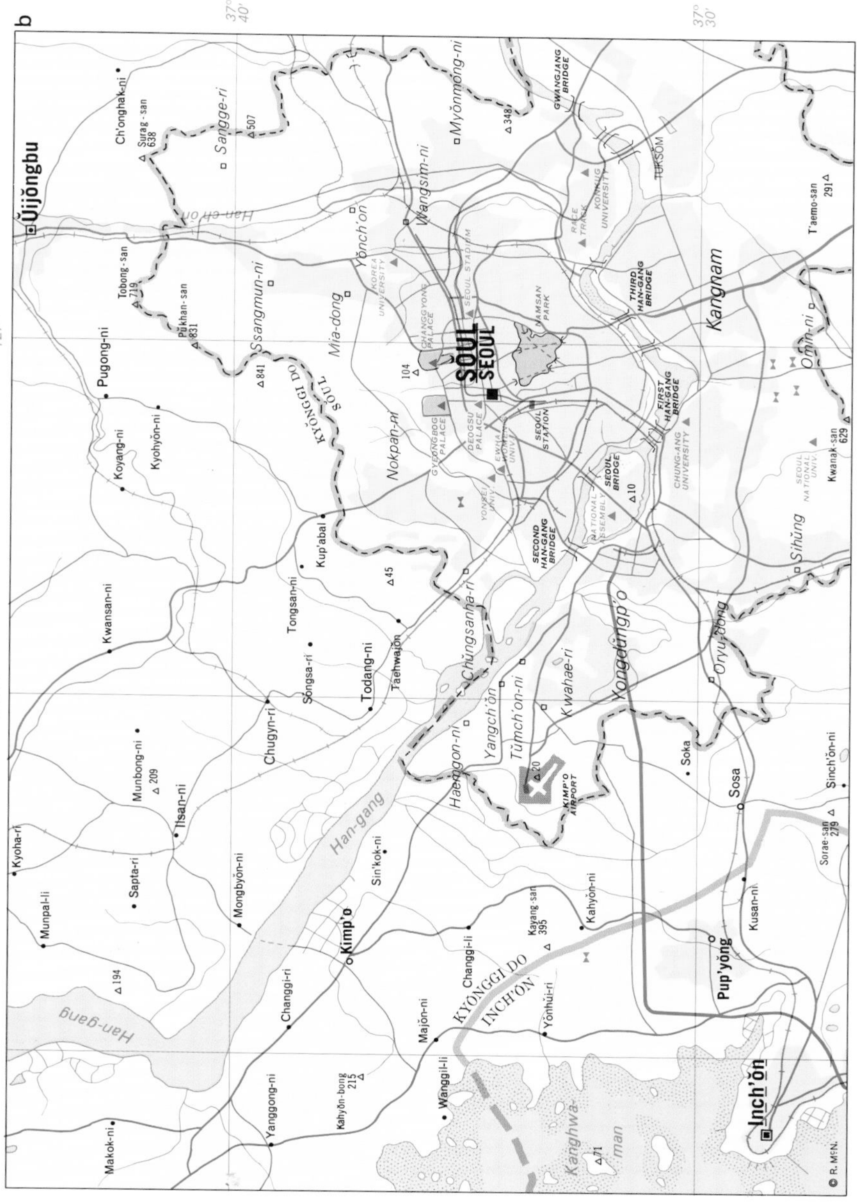
SŎUL
SEOUL
Ŭijŏngbu
Inch'ŏn
Kimp'o
Kangnam
KYŎNGGI-DO
Han-gang

c

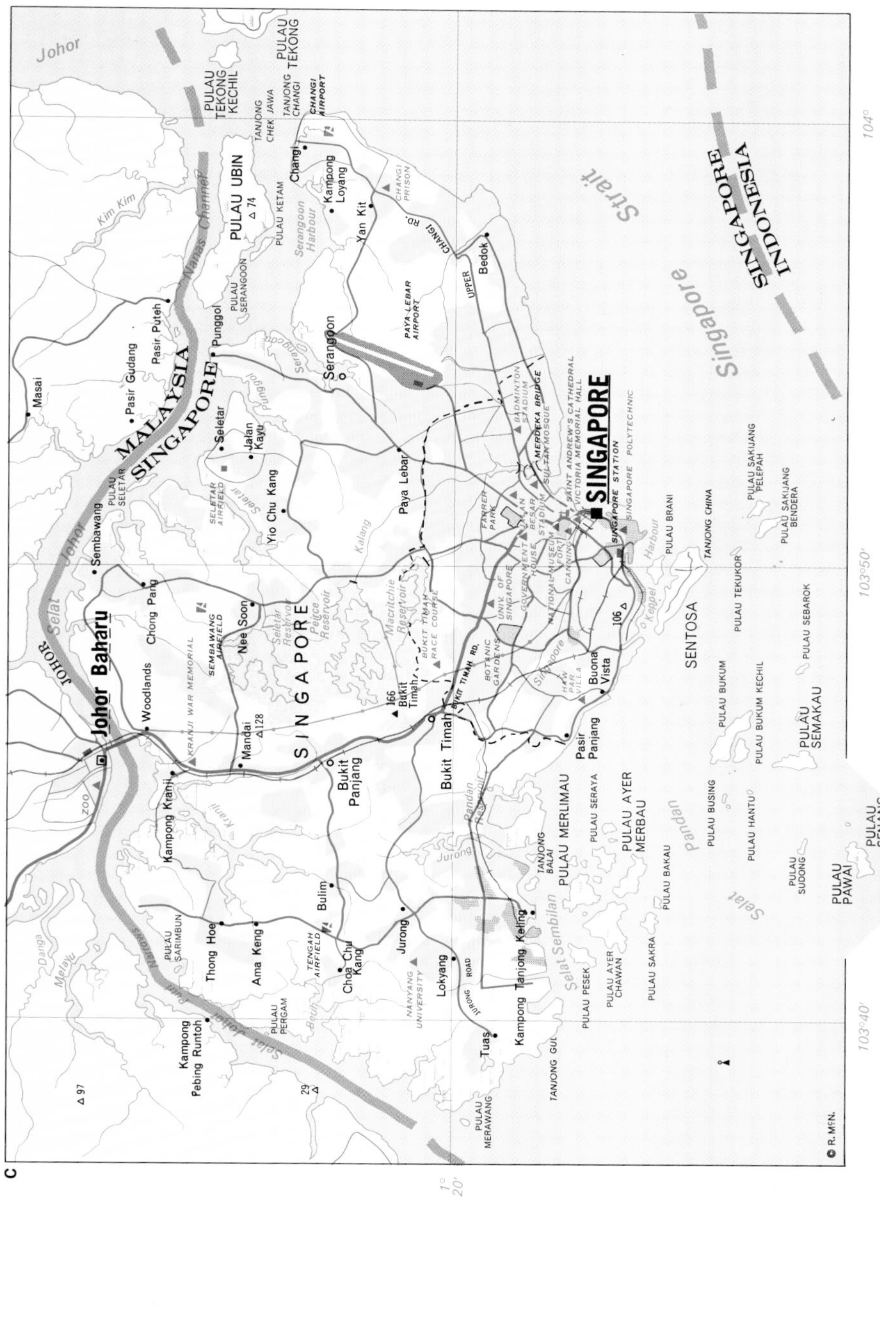
SINGAPORE
Johor Baharu
MALAYSIA
SINGAPORE
INDONESIA
Singapore Strait

d

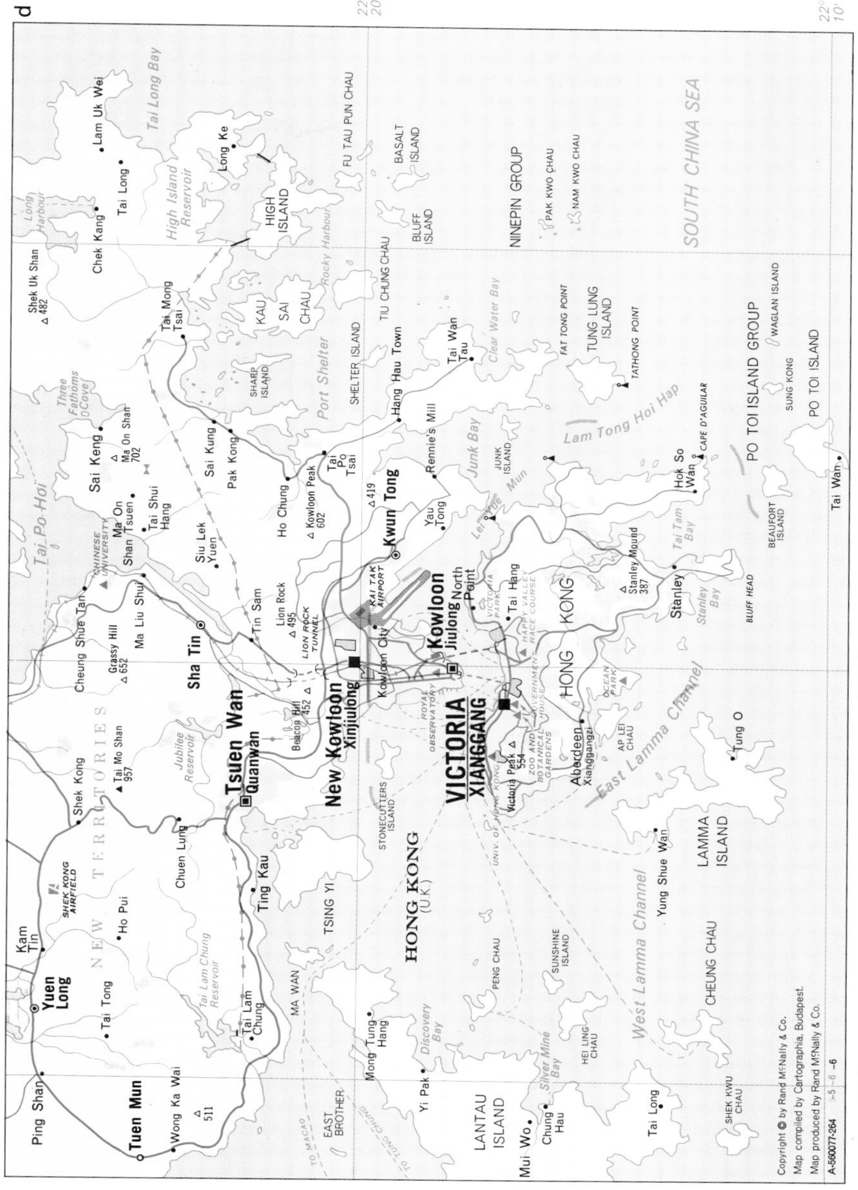
VICTORIA
XIANGGANG
Kowloon
Jiulong
New Kowloon
Xinjiulong
Tsuen Wan
Quanwan
Sha Tin
Tuen Mun
Yuen Long
HONG KONG (U.K.)
LANTAU ISLAND
SOUTH CHINA SEA
NEW TERRITORIES
Copyright © by Rand McNally & Co.
Map compiled by Cartographia, Budapest.
Map produced by Rand McNally & Co.

Kilometers 0 5 10 15 Km.
Statute Miles 0 5 10 15 Mi.

Scale 1:300,000

One centimeter represents 3 kilometers.
One inch represents approximately 4.7 miles.

	AREA (km²)	POPULATION
BEIJING (PEKING)	1,550	5,300,000
SŎUL	1,450	9,300,000
SINGAPORE	900	2,600,000
HONG KONG	650	4,450,000

MAP FORM	airport	chau	island	park	peak	reservoir	wan
ENGLISH	airport	island	island	park	peak	reservoir	bay
DEUTSCH	Flughafen	Insel	Insel	Park	Gipfel	Stausee	Bucht
ESPAÑOL	aeropuerto	isla	isla	parque	pico	estanque	bahía
FRANÇAIS	aéroport	île	île	parc	cime	réservoir	baie
PORTUGUÊS	aeroporto	ilha	ilha	parque	pico	reservatório	baía

Kilometers 0 5 10 15 Km.
Statute Miles 0 5 10 15 Mi.

Scale 1:300,000
One centimeter represents 3 kilometers.
One inch represents approximately 4.7 miles.

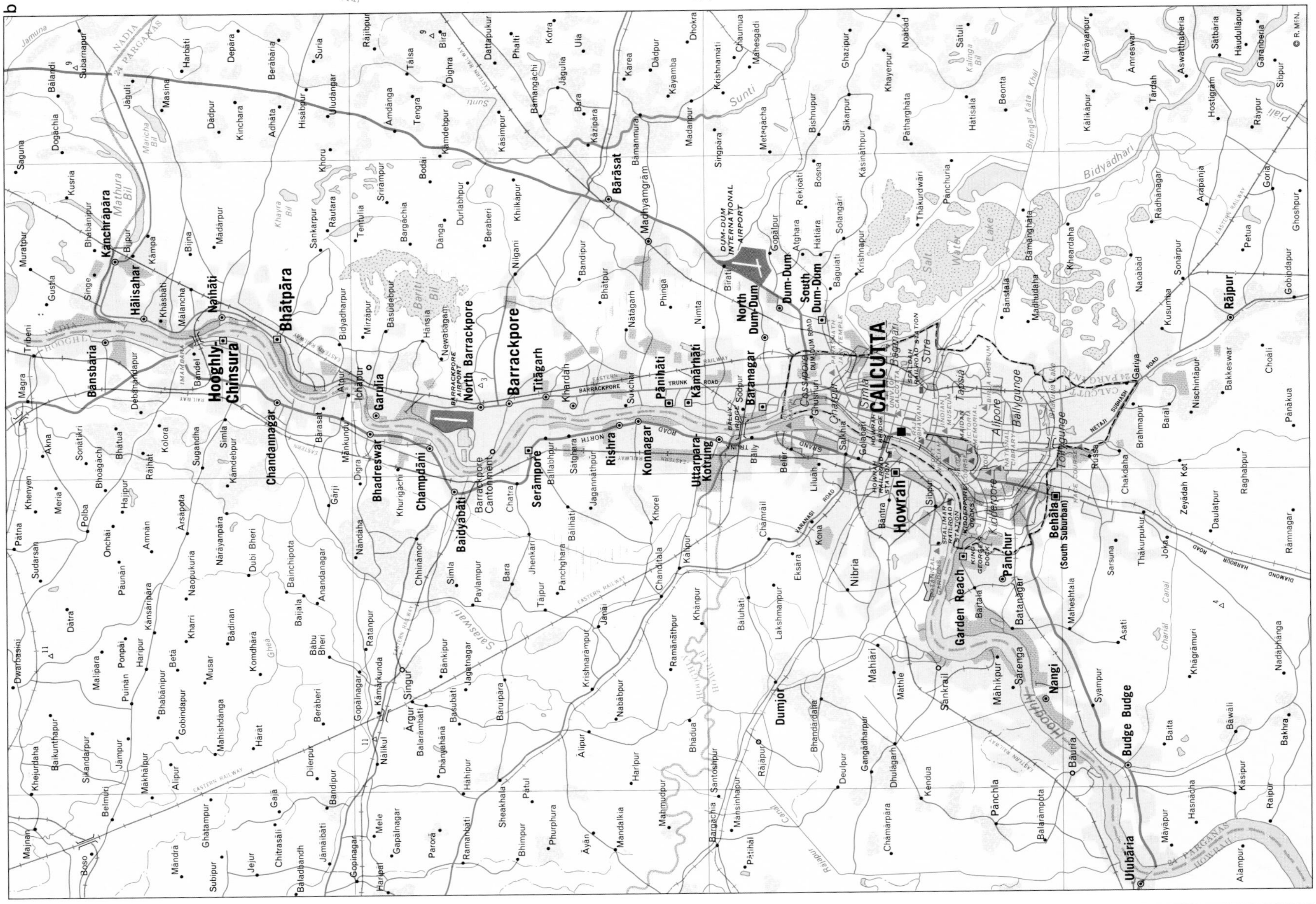

	AREA (km²)	POPULATION
DELHI	1,400	5,500,000
BOMBAY	1,050	8,250,000
CALCUTTA	3,100	11,200,000

ENGLISH	DEUTSCH	ESPAÑOL	FRANÇAIS	PORTUGUÊS
airport	Flughafen	aeropuerto	aéroport	aeroporto
dock	Dock	muelle	quai	cais
island	Insel	isla	île	ilha
lake	See	lago	lac	lago
point	Punkt	punta	pointe	ponta
railroad station	Bahnhof	terminal ferroviaria	gare	estação ferroviária
road	Landstrasse	camino	route	rodovia
temple	Tempel	templo	temple	templo

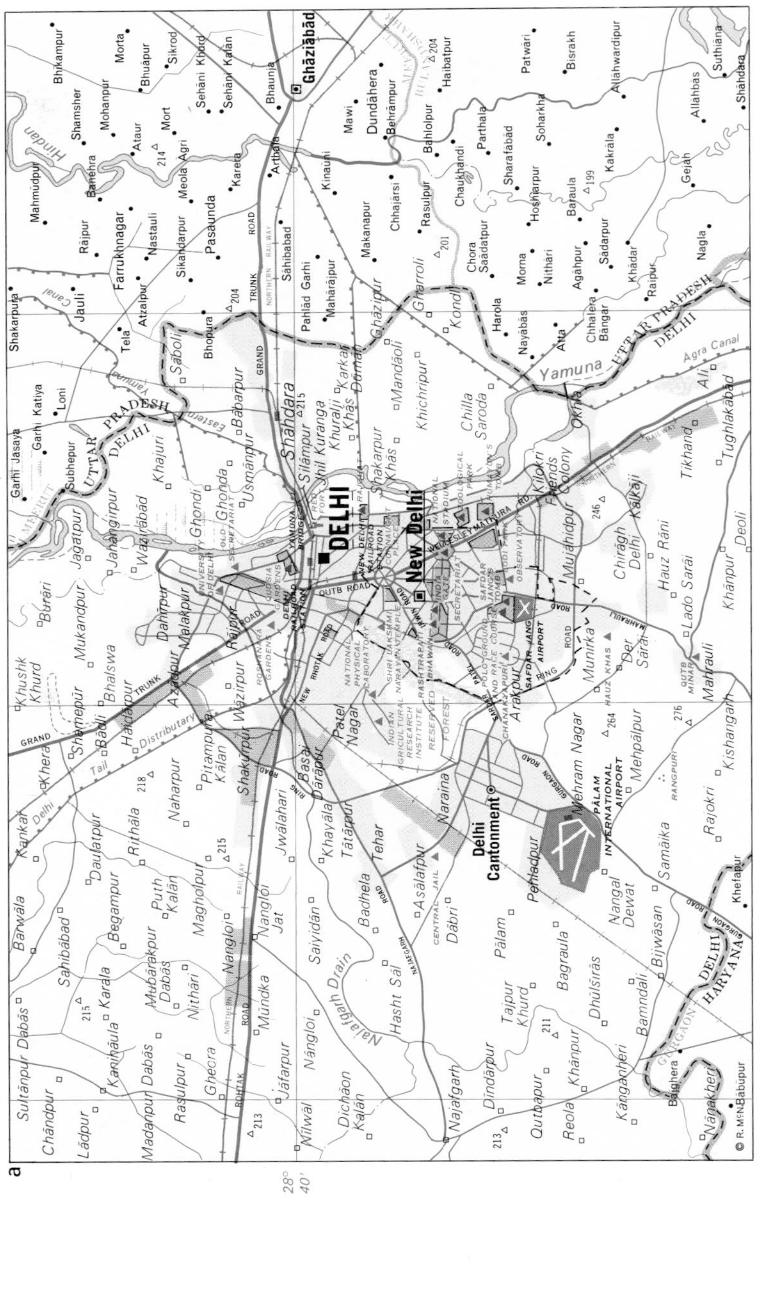

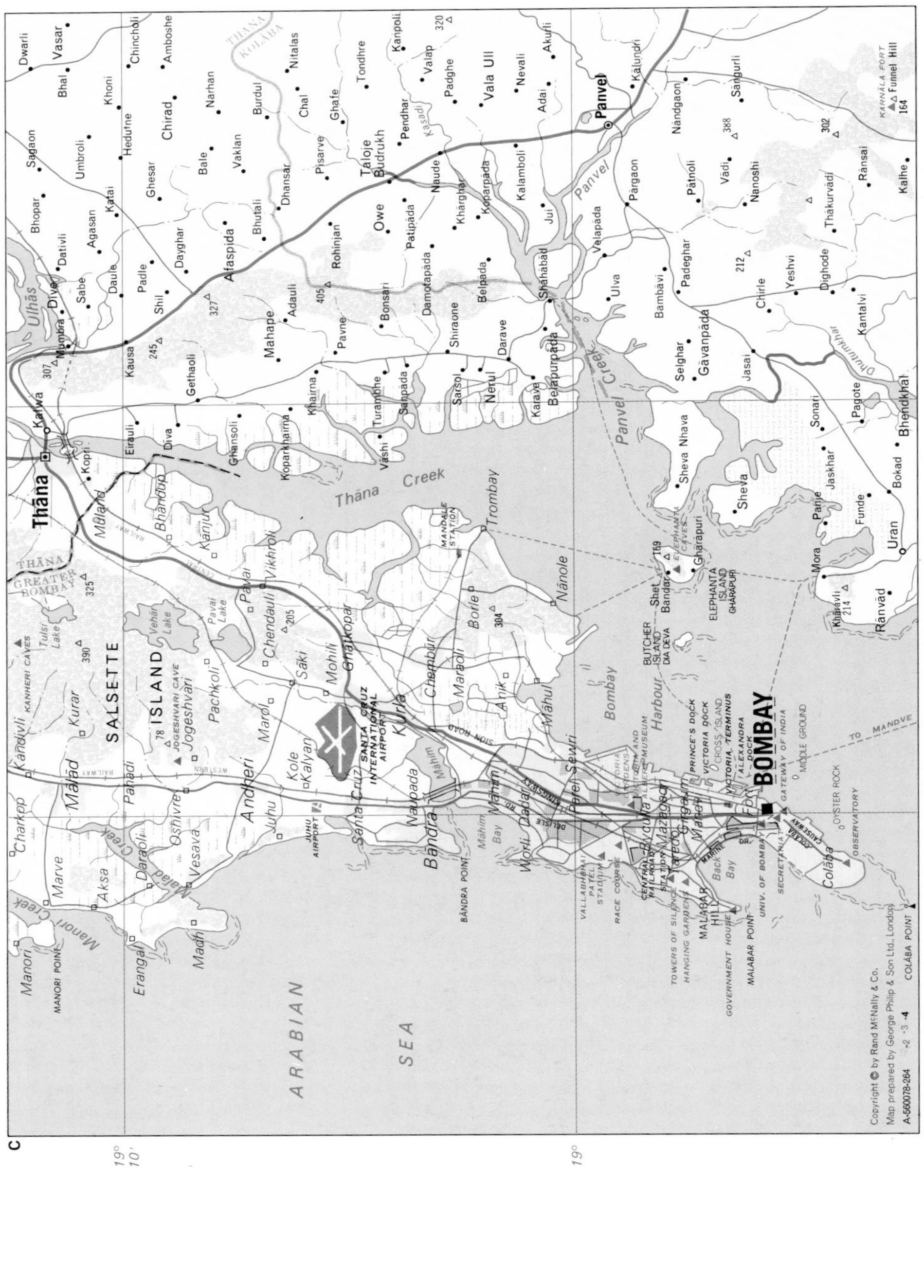

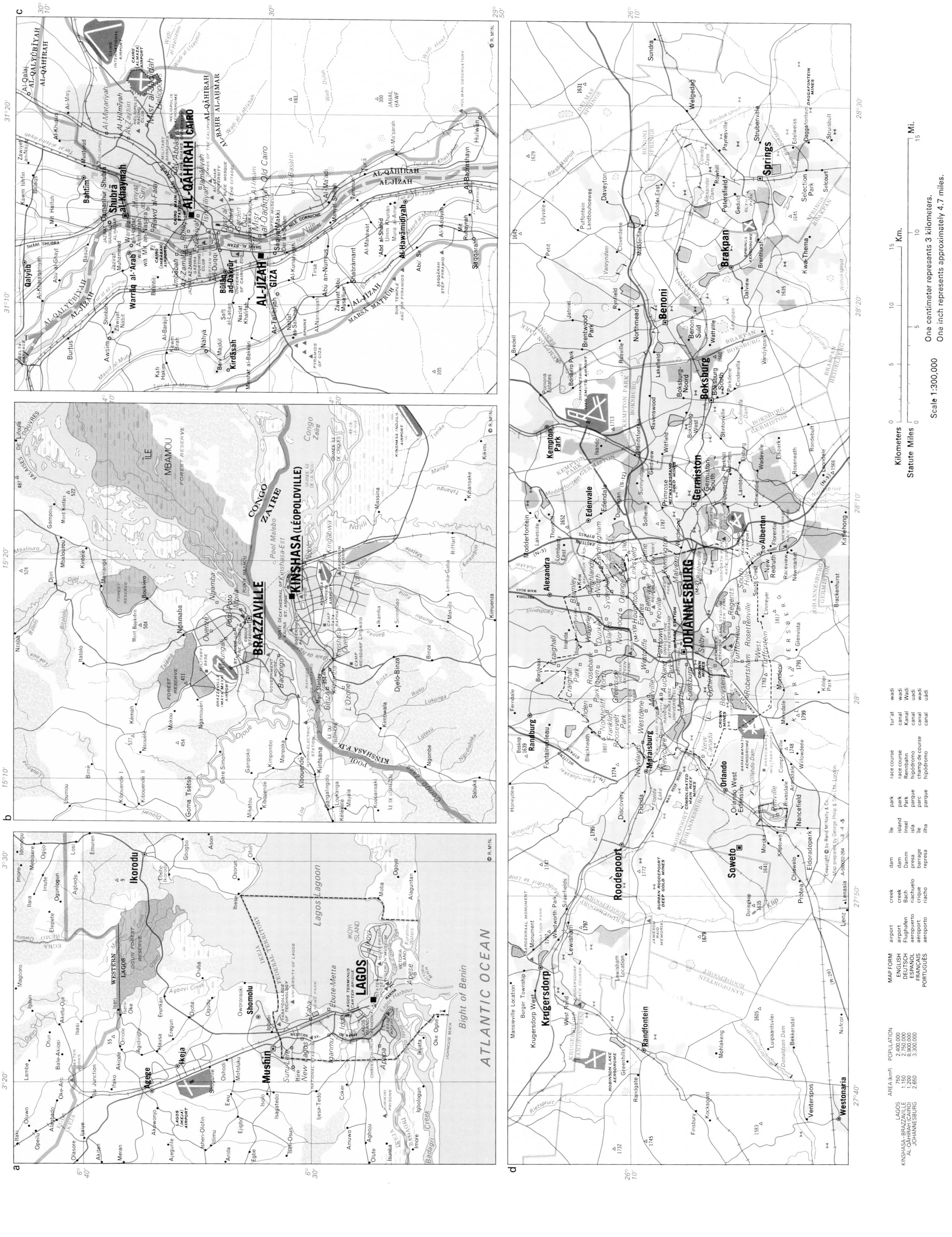
a
b
c
d
ATLANTIC OCEAN
Bight of Benin
Lagos Lagoon
LAGOS
Ikeja
Mushin
Ikorodu
BRAZZAVILLE
KINSHASA (LÉOPOLDVILLE)
CONGO ZAIRE
Pool Malebo
AL-QĀHIRAH CAIRO
AL-JĪZAH GIZA
JOHANNESBURG
Soweto
Germiston
Benoni
Springs
Brakpan
Krugersdorp
Roodepoort
AREA (km²) POPULATION
LAGOS 750 2,400,000
KINSHASA-BRAZZAVILLE 1,150 2,750,000
AL-QĀHIRAH (CAIRO) 1,200 8,900,000
JOHANNESBURG 2,650 3,300,000
Scale 1:300,000
One centimeter represents 3 kilometers.
One inch represents approximately 4.7 miles.
Kilometers
Statute Miles

a

b

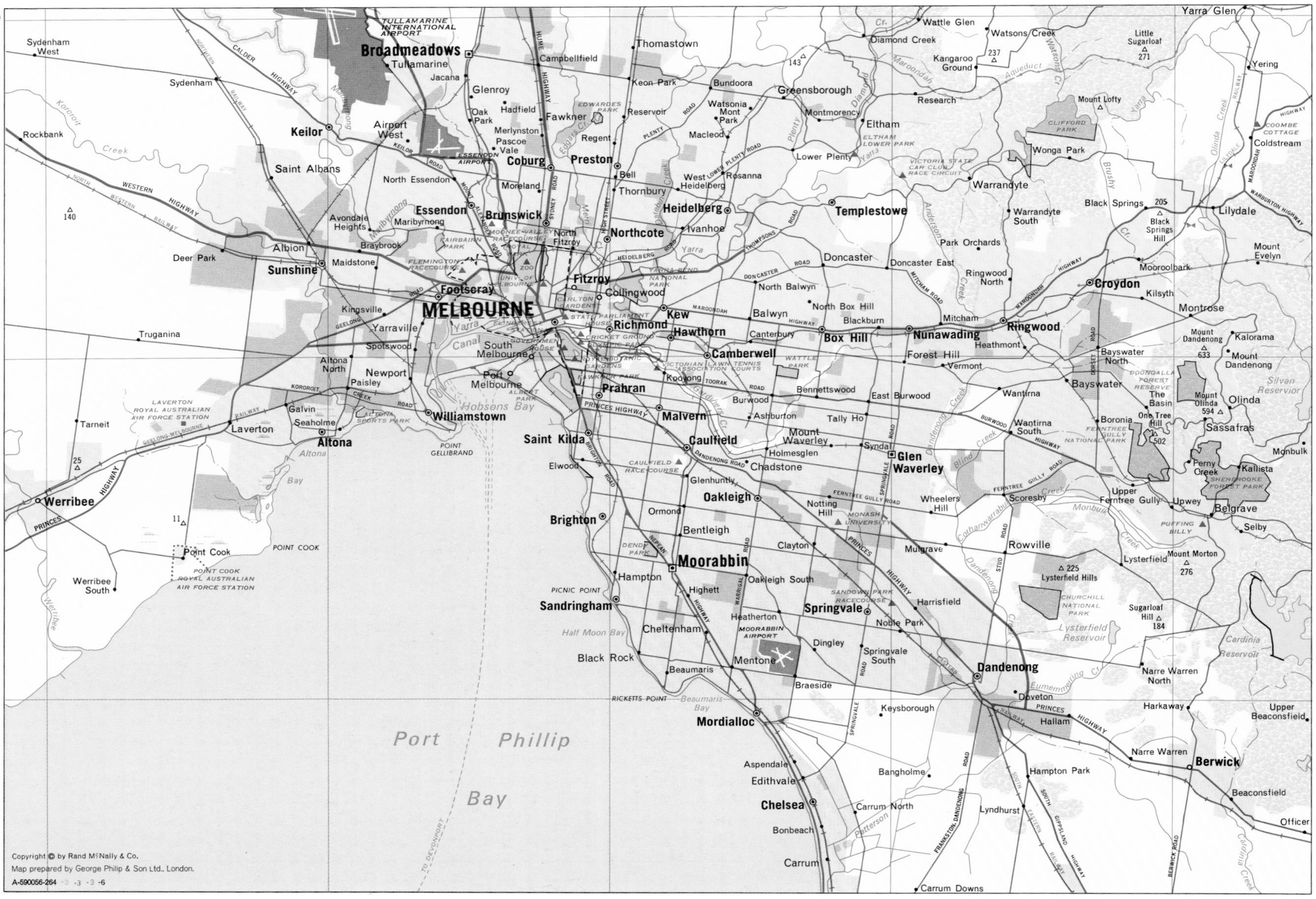

	AREA (km²)	POPULATION
MELBOURNE	2,600	2,425,000
SYDNEY	2,800	2,850,000

ENGLISH	bay, b.	bridge	creek, cr.	highway	point	road
DEUTSCH	Bucht	Brücke	Bach	Landstrasse	Landspitze	Landstrasse
ESPAÑOL	bahía	puente	riachuelo	camino	punta	camino
FRANÇAIS	baie	pont	crique	route	pointe	route
PORTUGUÊS	baía	ponte	riacho	rodovia	ponta	rodovia

Kilometers 0 5 10 15 Km.
Statute Miles 0 5 10 15 Mi.

Scale 1:300,000

One centimeter represents 3 kilometers.
One inch represents approximately 4.7 miles.

a

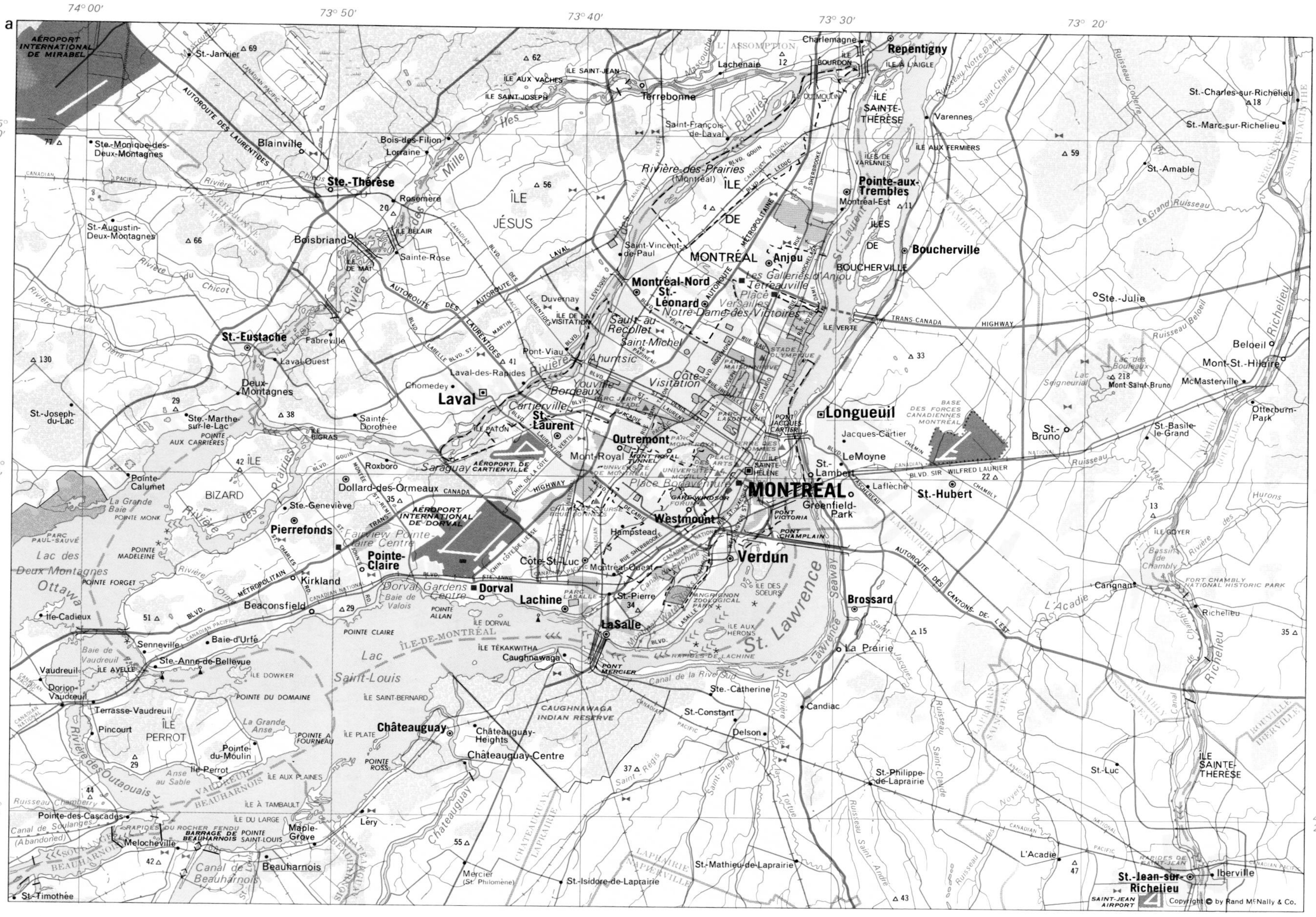

b

	AREA (km²)	POPULATION
MONTRÉAL	3,100	2,875,000
TORONTO	2,100	2,850,000

MAP FORM	île	park	rapides	rivière	ruisseau
ENGLISH	island	park	rapids	river	brook
DEUTSCH	Insel	Park	Stromschnellen	Fluss	Bach
ESPAÑOL	isla	parque	rápidos	río	arroyo
FRANÇAIS	île	parc	rapides	rivière	ruisseau
PORTUGUÊS	ilha	parque	rápidos	rio	arroio

Kilometers 0 5 10 15 Km.

Statute Miles 0 5 10 15 Mi.

Scale 1:300,000

One centimeter represents 3 kilometers.
One inch represents approximately 4.7 miles.

AREA: 8,900 km²
POPULATION: 15,800,000

ENGLISH	bay	brook, br.	creek	harbor	island	lake, l.	point	pond
DEUTSCH	Bucht	Bach	Bach	Hafen	Insel	See	Landspitze	Teich
ESPAÑOL	bahía	arroyo	riachuelo	puerto	isla	lago	punta	charca
FRANÇAIS	baie	ruisseau	crique	port	île	lac	pointe	étang
PORTUGUÊS	baía	arroio	riacho	porto	ilha	lago	ponta	lagoa

Kilometers 0 5 10 15 Km.

Statute Miles 0 5 10 15 Mi.

Scale 1:300,000

One centimeter represents 3 kilometers.
One inch represents approximately 4.7 miles.

AREA: 4,500 km²
POPULATION: 6,700,000

ENGLISH	airport	creek, cr.	harbor	lake, l.	park	woods
DEUTSCH	Flughafen	Bach	Hafen	See	Park	Gehölz
ESPAÑOL	aeropuerto	riachuelo	puerto	lago	parque	bosques
FRANÇAIS	aéroport	crique	port	lac	parc	bois
PORTUGUÊS	aeroporto	riacho	porto	lago	parque	bosques

Kilometers 0 5 10 15 Km.
Statute Miles 0 5 10 15 Mi.

Scale 1:300,000

One centimeter represents 3 kilometers.
One inch represents approximately 4.7 miles.

a

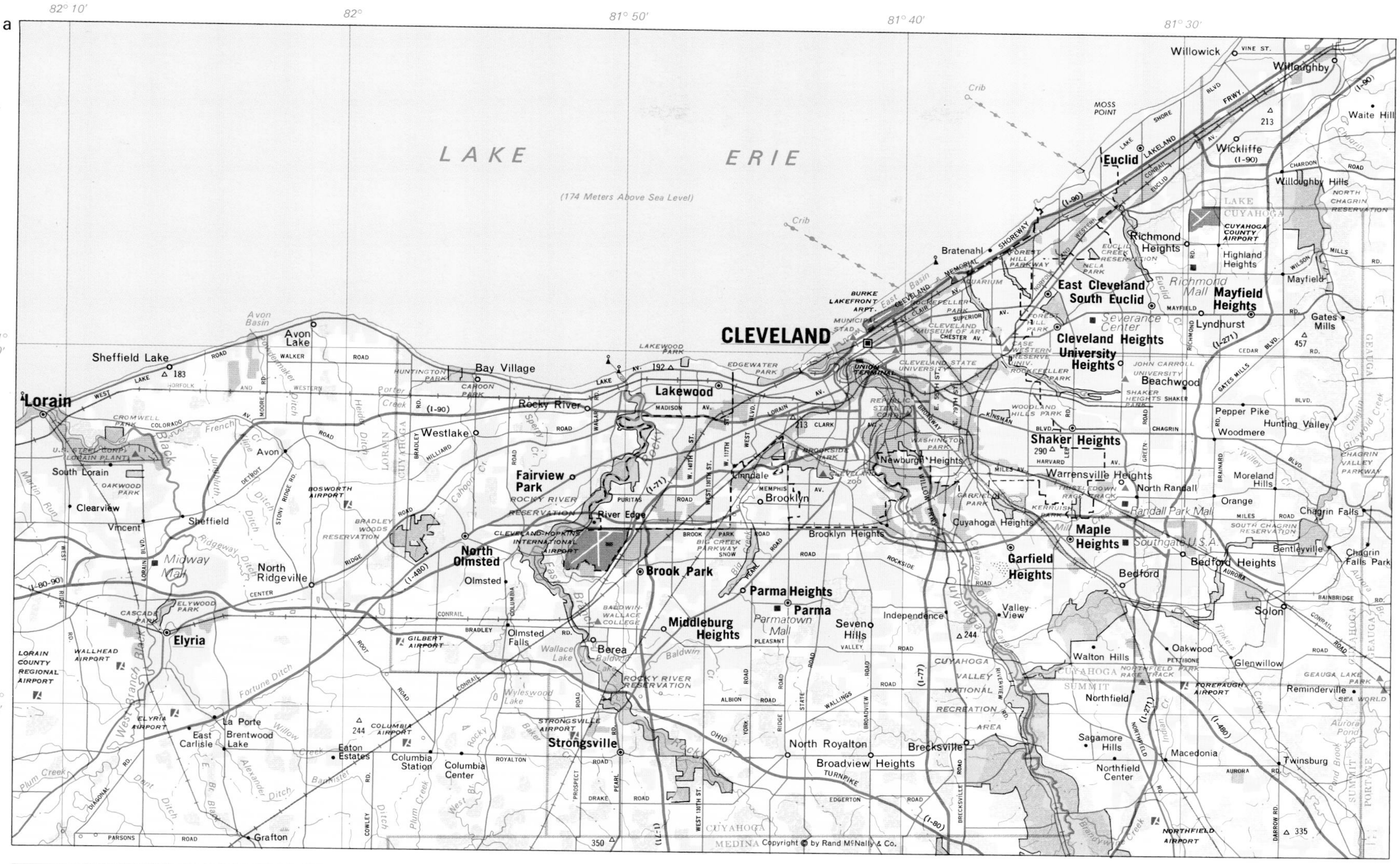

b

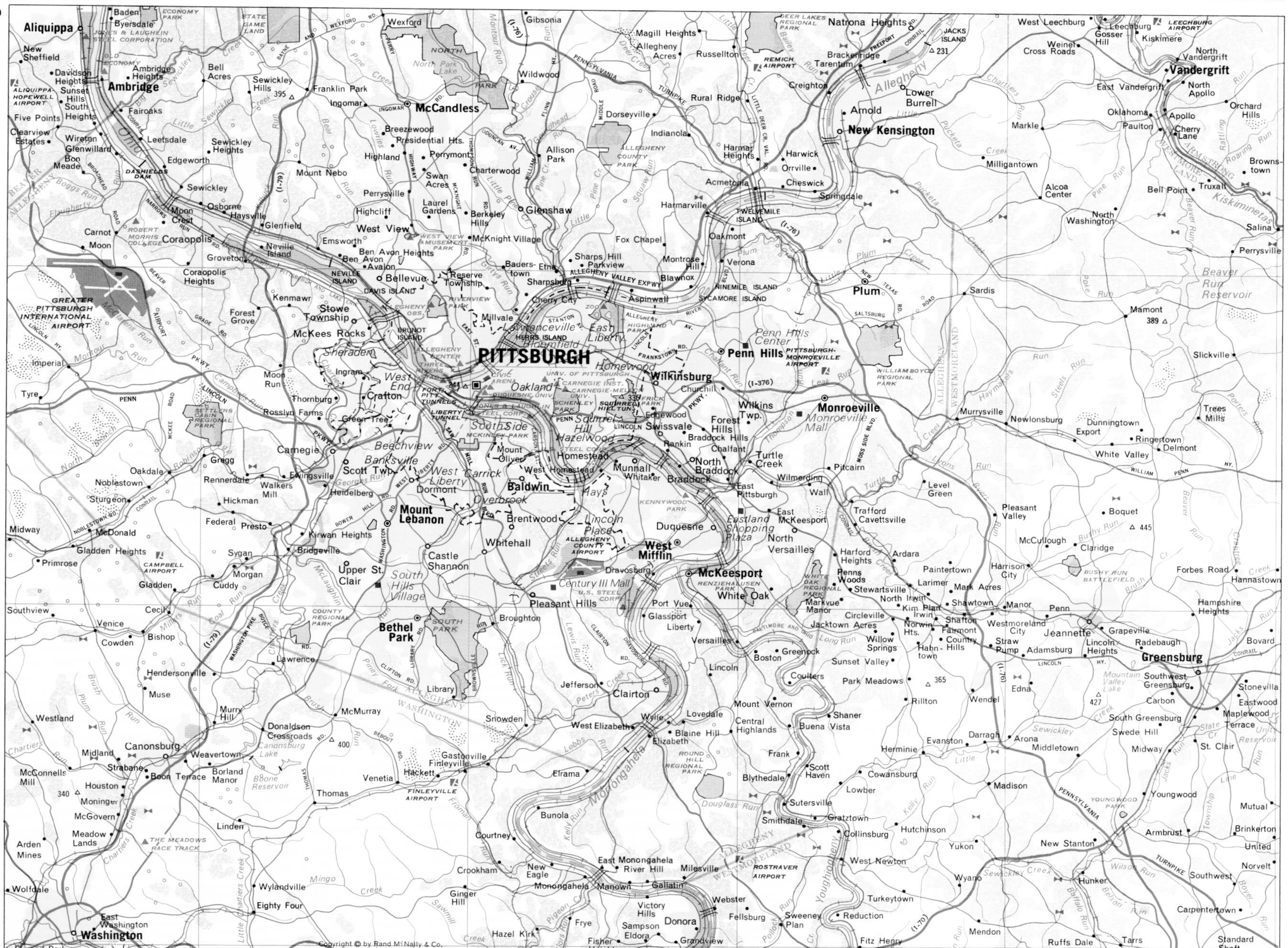

	AREA (km²)	POPULATION
CLEVELAND	1,900	1,850,000
PITTSBURGH	3,800	1,950,000

ENGLISH	creek, cr.	ditch	island	lake, l.	park	reservoir	run
DEUTSCH	Bach	Graben	Insel	See	Park	Stausee	Bach
ESPAÑOL	riachuelo	acequia	isla	lago	parque	embalse	arroyo
FRANÇAIS	crique	fossé	île	lac	parc	réservoir	ruisseau
PORTUGUÊS	riacho	fosso	ilha	lago	parque	reservatório	córrego

Kilometers 0 5 10 15 Km.
Statute Miles 0 5 10 15 Mi.

Scale 1:300,000
One centimeter represents 3 kilometers.
One inch represents approximately 4.7 miles.

Kilometers 0 5 10 15 Km.
Statute Miles 0 5 10 15 Mi.

Scale 1:300,000
One centimeter represents 3 kilometers.
One inch represents approximately 4.7 miles.

ENGLISH	canyon	college	creek	dam	hills	mount	park	peak	reservoir
DEUTSCH	Cañon	College	Bach	Damm	Hügel	Berg	Park	Gipfel	Stausee
ESPAÑOL	cañón	escuela	riachuelo	diques	colinas	montaña	parque	pico	estanque
FRANÇAIS	canyon	collège	crique	barrage	collines	mont	parc	cime	réservoir
PORTUGUÊS	canhão	colégio	riacho	represa	colinas	monte	parque	pico	reservatório

AREA: 5,900 km²
POPULATION: 8,375,000

Kilometers 0 5 10 15 Km.
Statute Miles 0 5 10 15 Mi.

Scale 1:300,000

One centimeter represents 3 kilometers.
One inch represents approximately 4.7 miles.

ENGLISH	DEUTSCH	ESPAÑOL	FRANÇAIS	PORTUGUÊS
bay	Bucht	bahía	baie	baía
channel	Kanal	canal	canal	canal
creek, cr.	Bach	riachuelo	crique	riacho
island	Insel	isla	île	ilha
lake, l.	See	lago	lac	lago
point	Landspitze	punta	pointe	ponta

AREA 5,550 km²
POPULATION 4,425,000

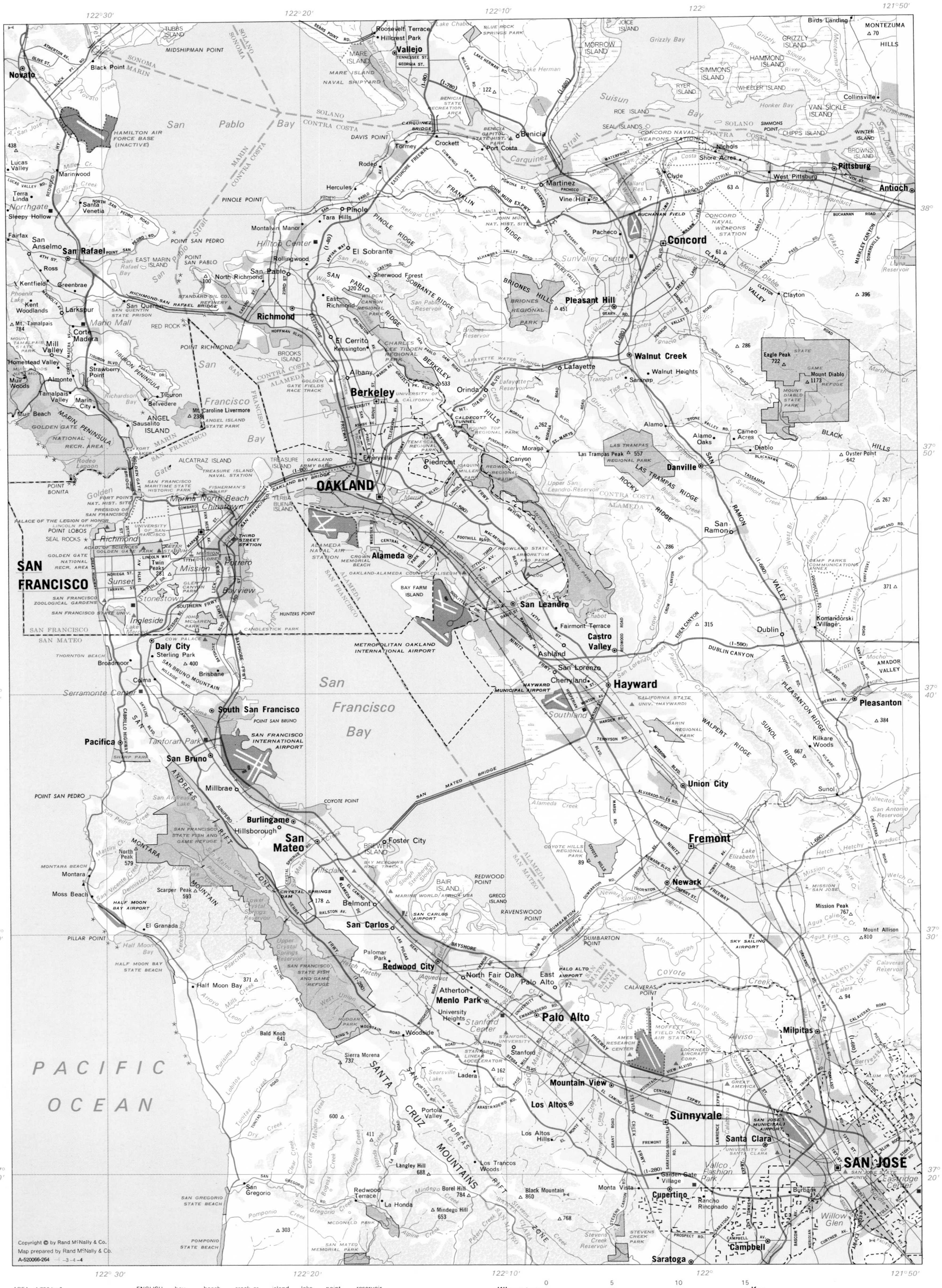

Copyright © by Rand McNally & Co.
Map prepared by Rand McNally & Co.
A-520066-264 -1-3-4-4

AREA 4,750 km²
POPULATION 4,175,000

ENGLISH	bay	beach	creek, cr.	island	lake	point	reservoir
DEUTSCH	Bucht	Strand	Bach	Insel	See	Punkt	Stausee
ESPAÑOL	bahía	playa	riachuelo	isla	lago	punta	estanque
FRANÇAIS	baie	plage	crique	île	lac	pointe	réservoir
PORTUGUÊS	baía	praia	riacho	ilha	lago	ponta	reservatório

Kilometers 0 5 10 15 Km.
Statute Miles 0 5 10 15 Mi.

Scale 1:300,000
One centimeter represents 3 kilometers.
One inch represents approximately 4.7 miles.

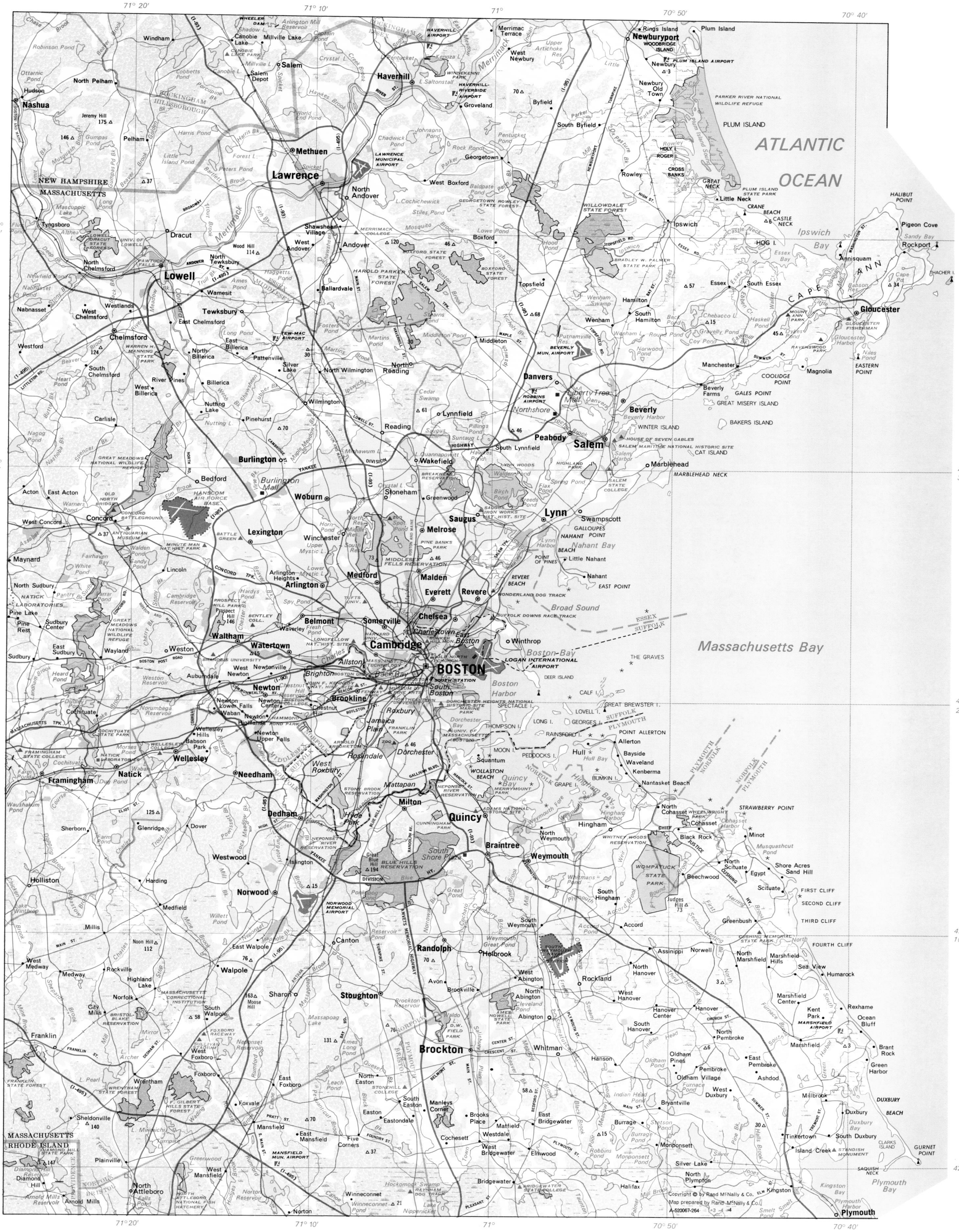

AREA: 5,150 km²
POPULATION: 3,625,000

ENGLISH	bay	brook	island, i.	lake, l.	point	pond	reservation
DEUTSCH	Bucht	Bach	Insel	See	Landspitze	Teich	Reservat
ESPAÑOL	bahía	arroyo	isla	lago	punta	charca	parque nacional
FRANÇAIS	baie	ruisseau	île	lac	pointe	étang	réservation
PORTUGUÊS	baia	arroio	ilha	lago	ponta	lagoa	reservation

Kilometers 0 5 10 15 Km.
Statute Miles 0 5 10 15 Mi.

Scale 1:300,000
One centimeter represents 3 kilometers.
One inch represents approximately 4.7 miles.

Kilometers 0 5 10 15 Km.
Statute Miles 0 5 10 15 Mi.

Scale 1:300,000
One centimeter represents 3 kilometers.
One inch represents approximately 4.7 miles.

	AREA (km²)	POPULATION
BUFFALO	2,550	1,450,000
BALTIMORE	1,150	1,500,000
WASHINGTON	1,550	2,225,000

ENGLISH	airport	bridge	creek, cr.	island, i.	park	point	run	university
DEUTSCH	Flughafen	Brücke	Bach	Insel	Park	Landspitze	Bach	Universität
ESPAÑOL	aeropuerto	puente	riachuelo	isla	parque	punta	arroyo	universidad
FRANÇAIS	aéroport	pont	crique	île	parc	pointe	ruisseau	université
PORTUGUÊS	aeroporto	ponte	riacho	ilha	parque	ponta	córrego	universidade

b

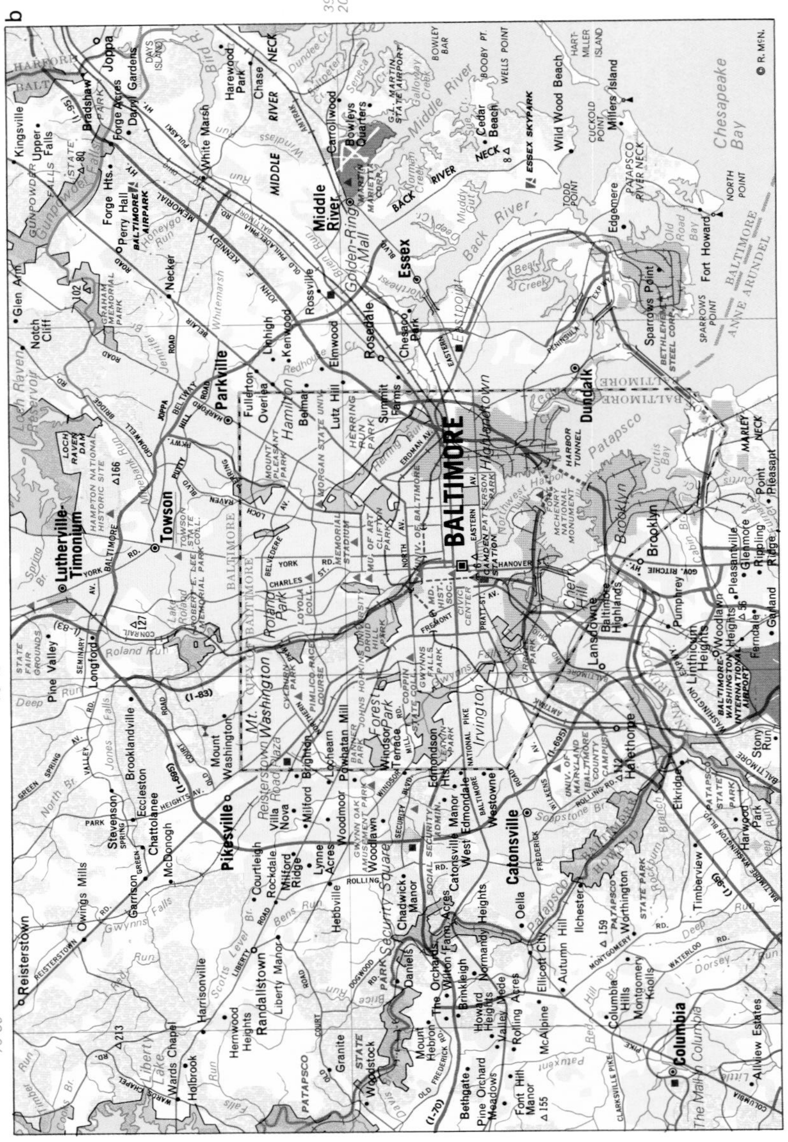

c

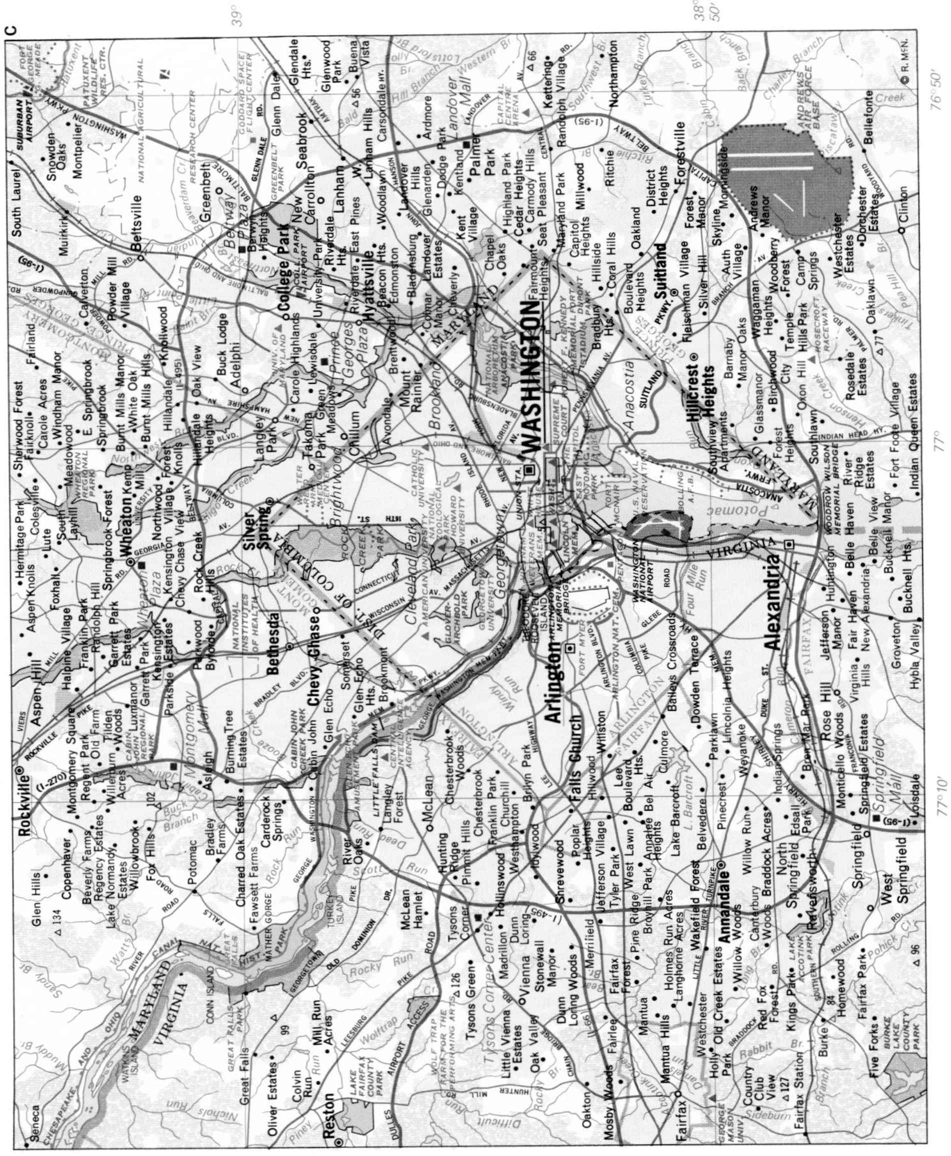

a

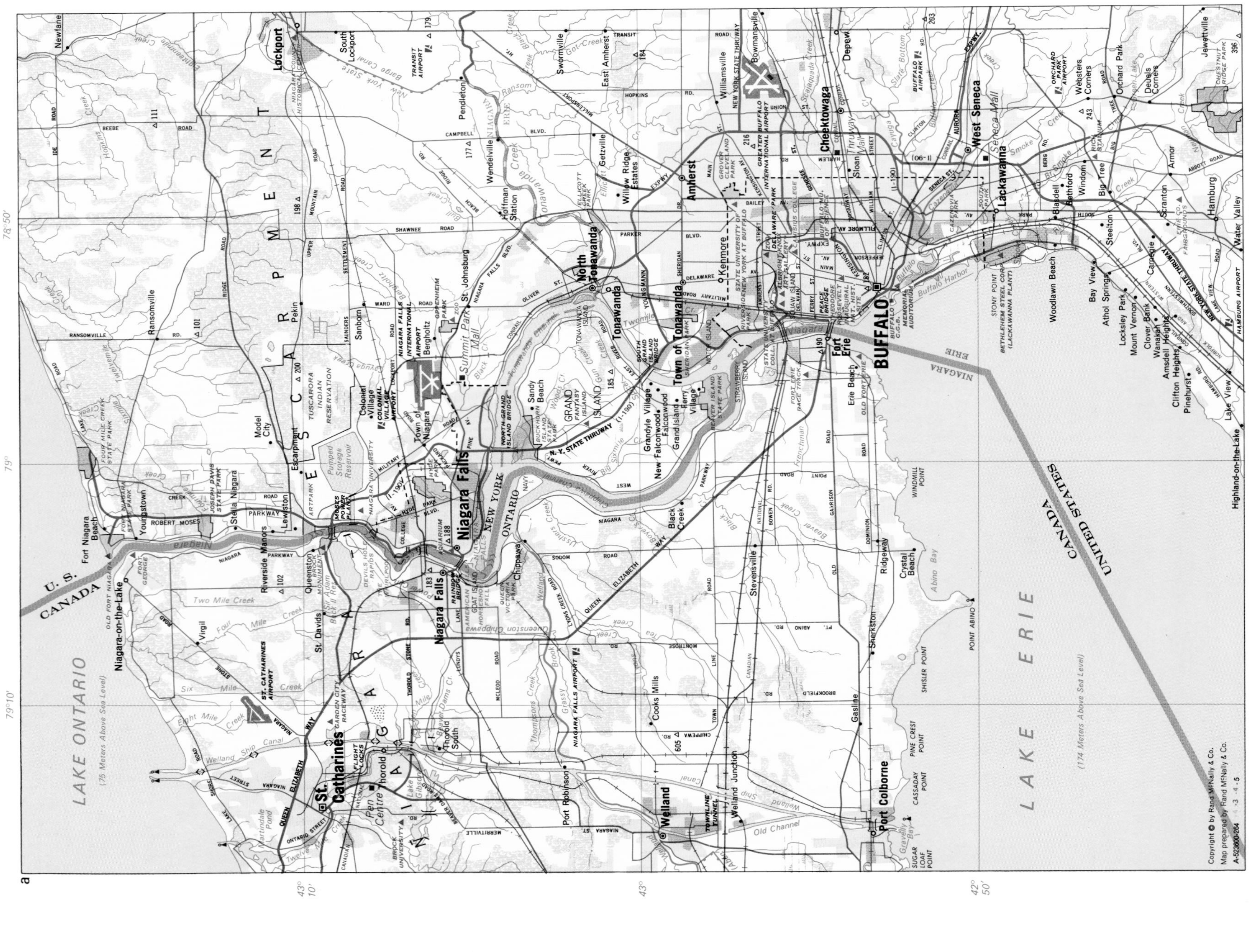

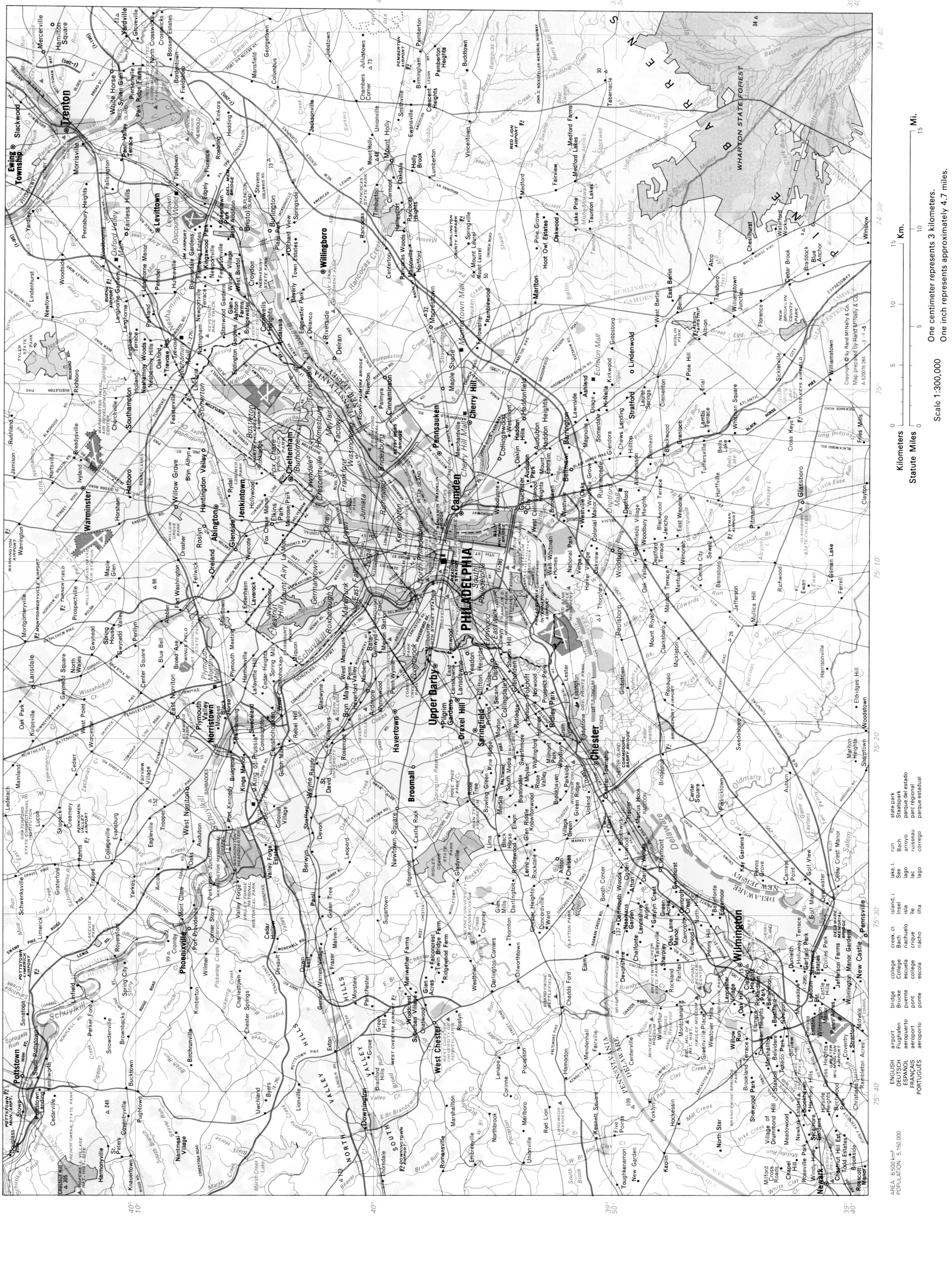
PHILADELPHIA
Kilometers
Statute Miles
Scale 1:300,000
One centimeter represents 3 kilometers.
One inch represents approximately 4.7 miles.
AREA 6,500 km²
POPULATION 5,150,000
ENGLISH airport bridge college creek, cr. island, i. lake, l. run state park
DEUTSCH Flughafen Brücke Collège Bach Insel See Bach Staatspark
ESPAÑOL aeropuerto puente escuela riachuelo isla lago arroyo parque del estado
FRANÇAIS aéroport pont collège crique île lac ruisseau parc régional
PORTUGUÊS aeroporto ponte escola riacho ilha lago córrego parque estadual
Copyright © by Rand McNally & Co.

a

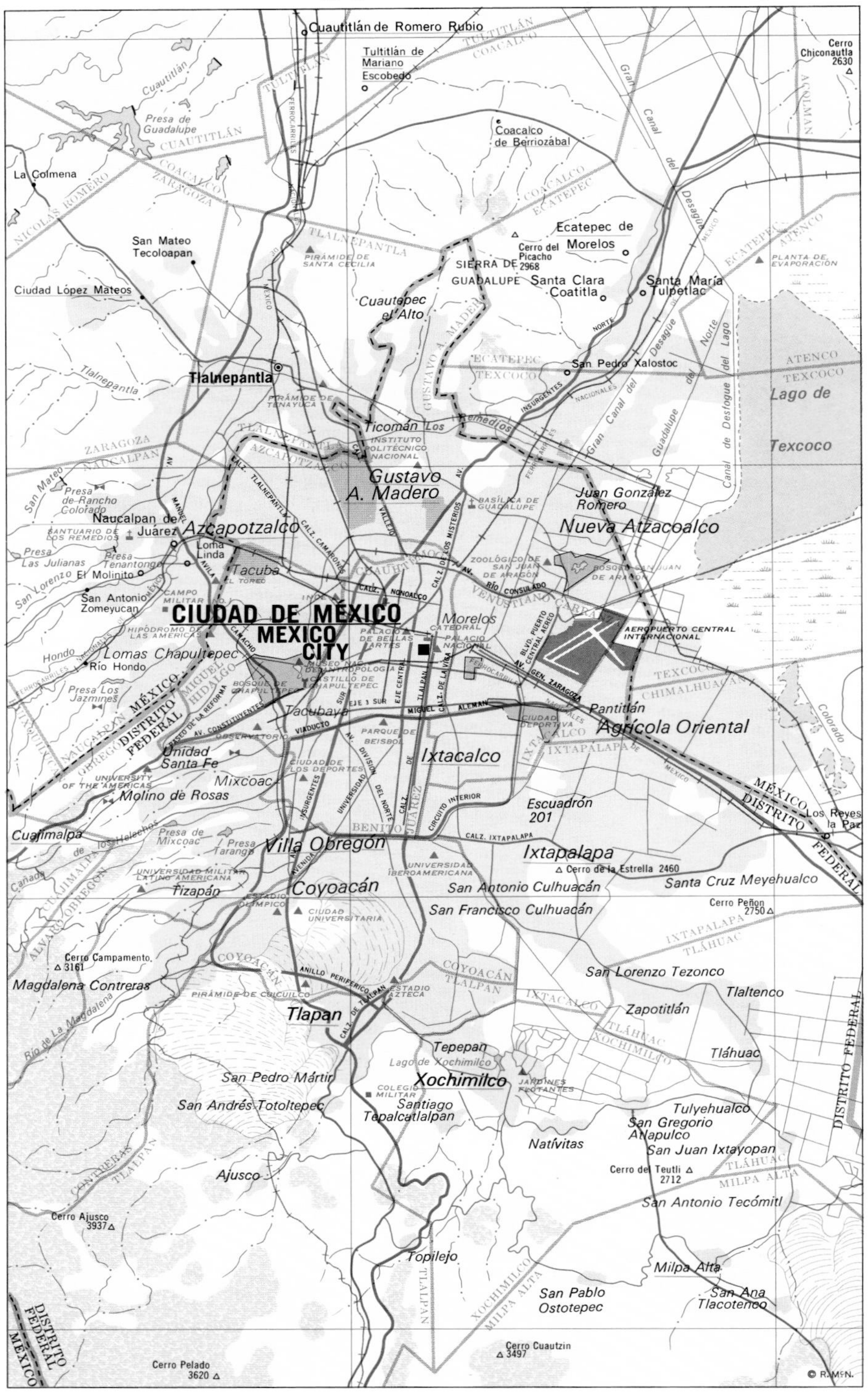

b

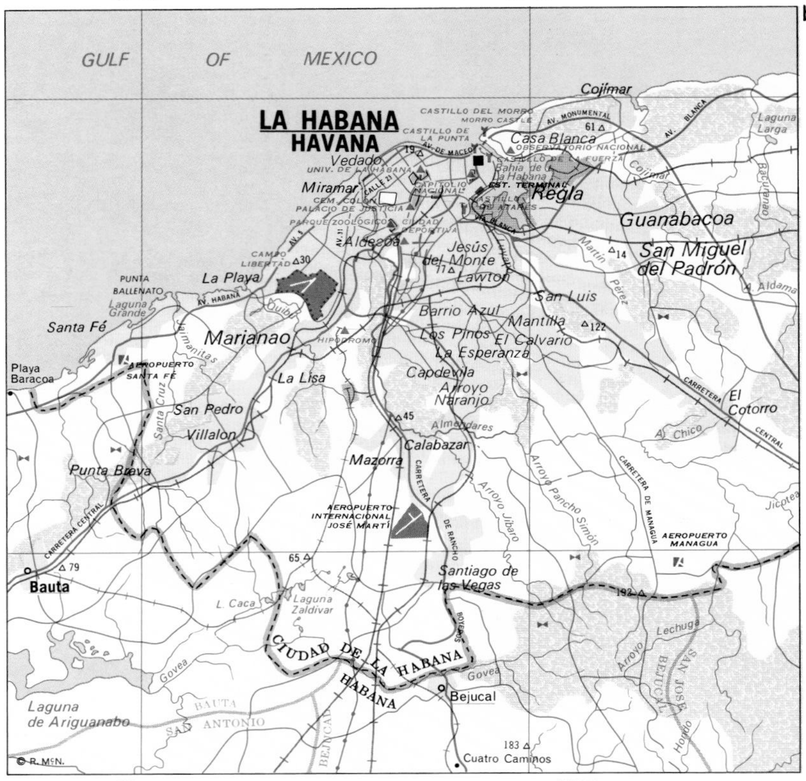

c

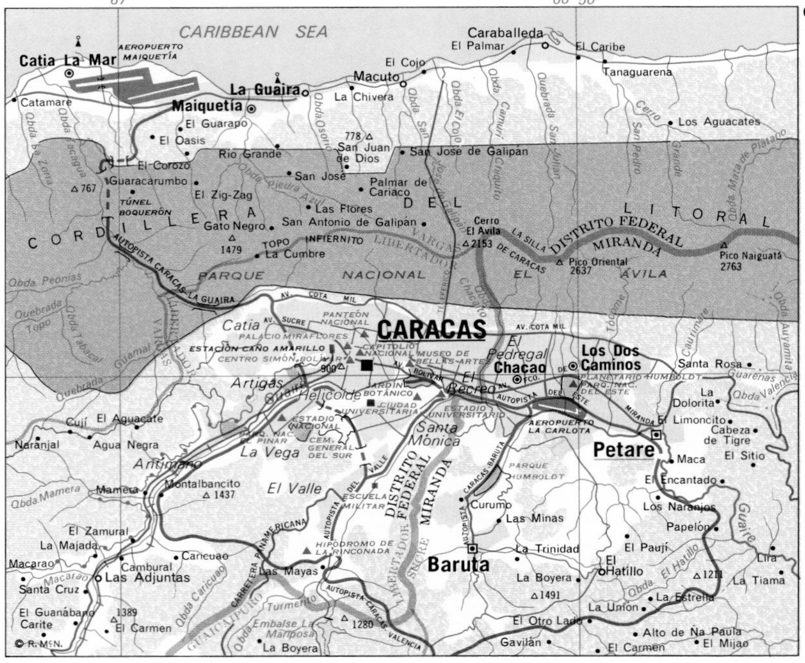

d

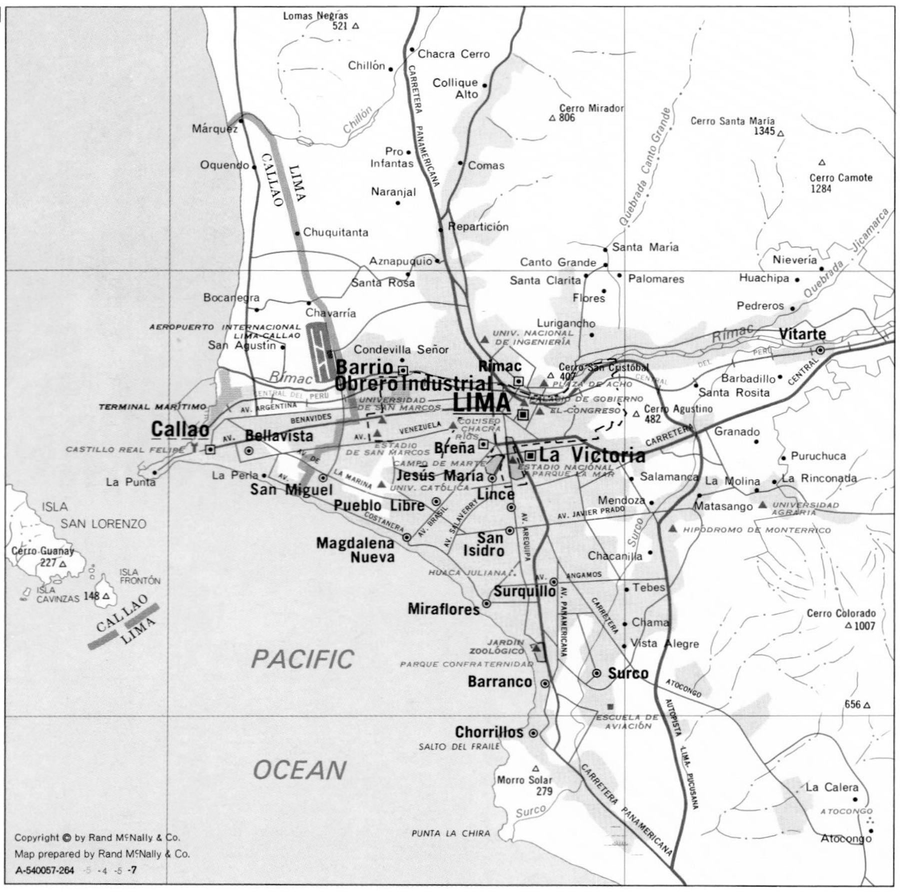

e

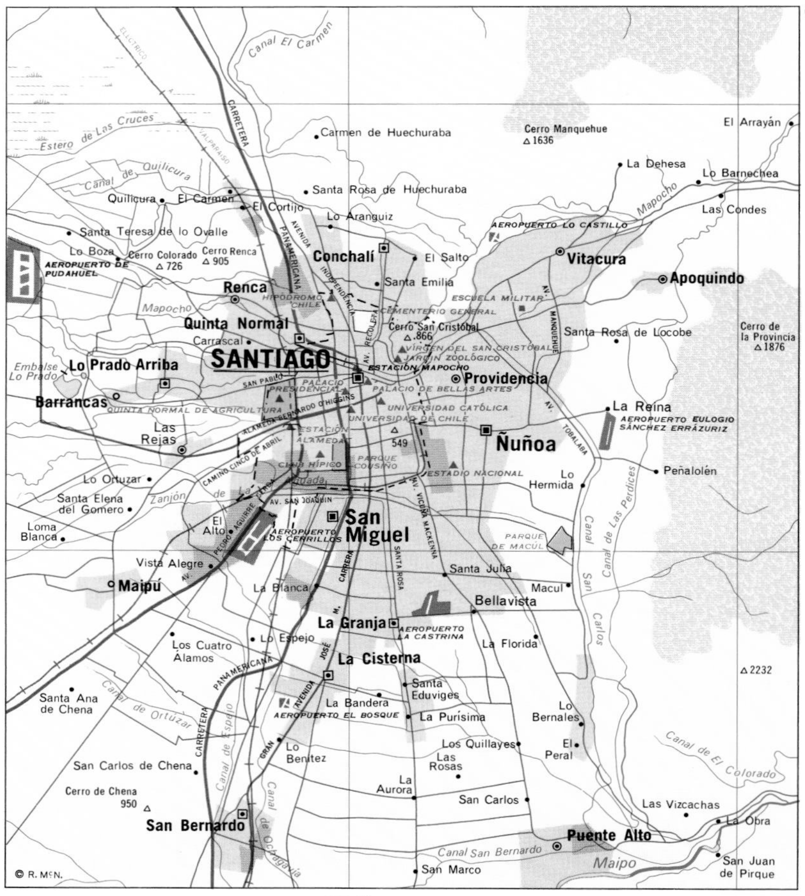

	AREA (km²)	POPULATION
CIUDAD DE MÉXICO	2,050	13,250,000
LA HABANA	750	2,050,000
CARACAS	750	2,950,000
LIMA	750	4,300,000
SANTIAGO	1,100	3,700,000

ESPAÑOL	arroyo	castillo	isla	laguna	presa	quebrada
ENGLISH	brook	castle	island	lagoon	reservoir	creek
DEUTSCH	Bach	Burg	Insel	Haff	Stausee	Bach
FRANÇAIS	ruisseau	château	île	lagune	réservoir	crique
PORTUGUÊS	arroio	castelo	ilha	laguna	reservatório	riacho

Kilometers 0 5 10 15 Km.
Statute Miles 0 5 10 15 Mi.

Scale 1:300,000
One centimeter represents 3 kilometers.
One inch represents approximately 4.7 miles.

a

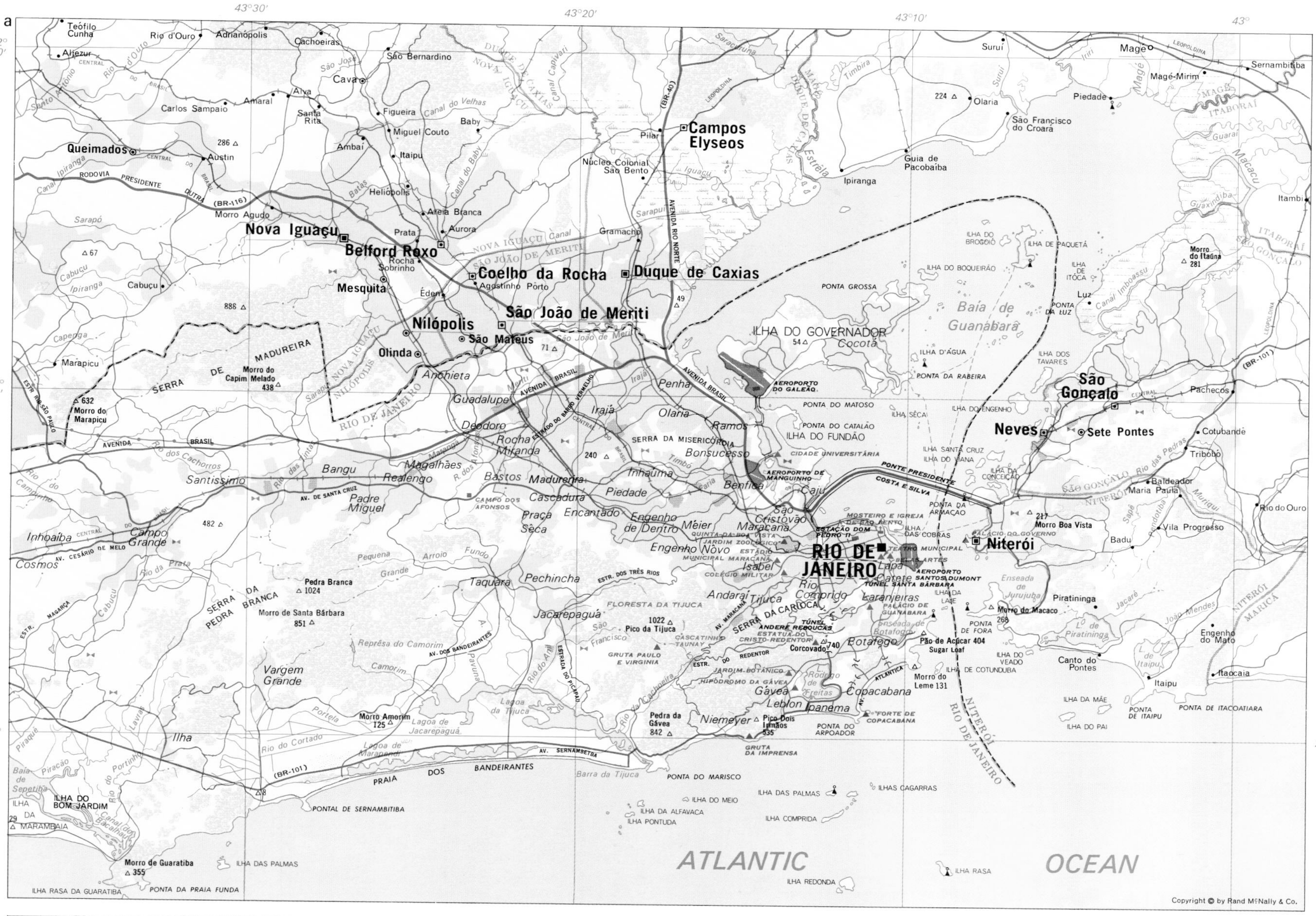

b

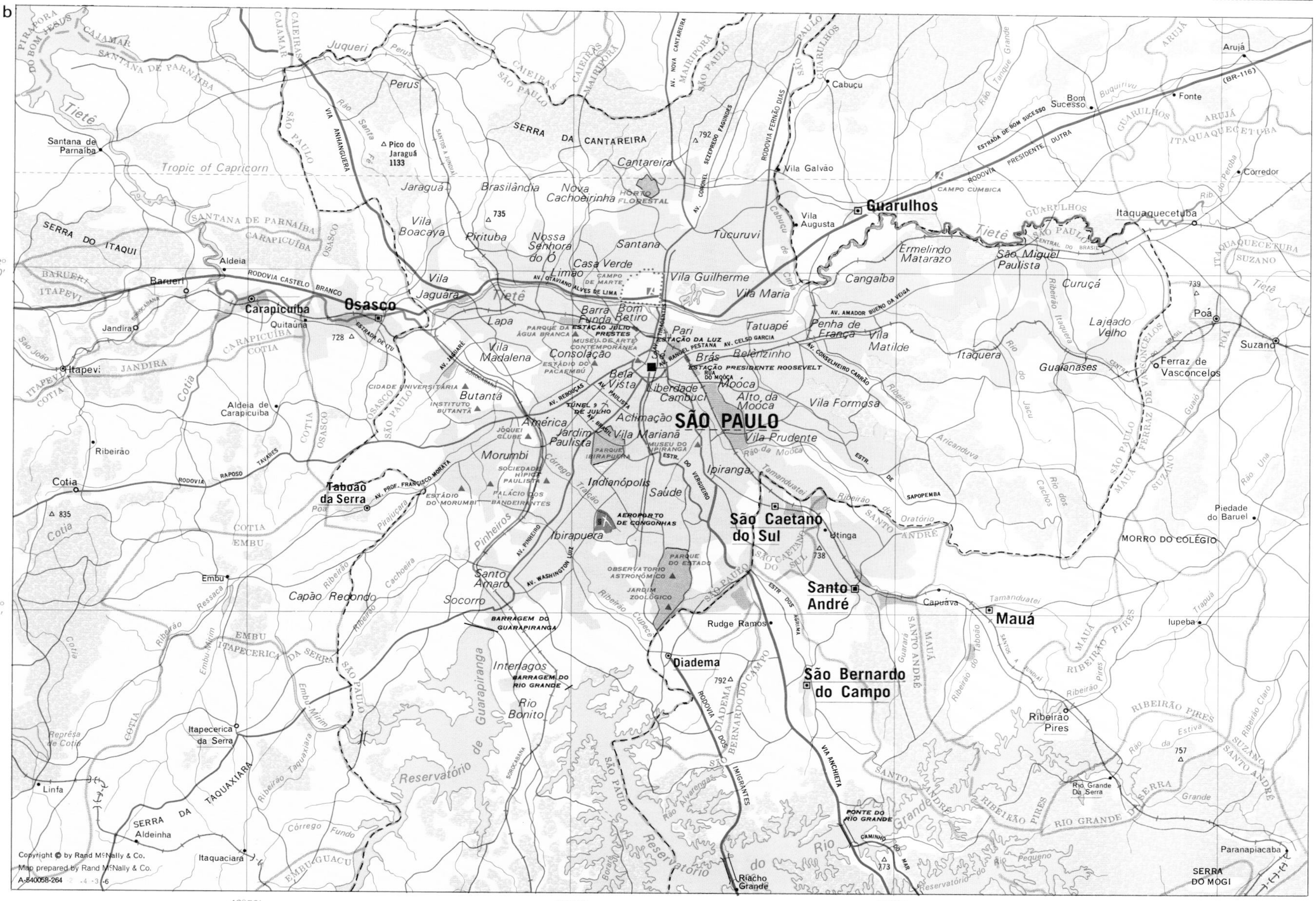

	AREA (km²)	POPULATION
RIO DE JANEIRO	2,200	8,200,000
SÃO PAULO	3,200	11,000,000

PORTUGUÊS	ilha	lagoa, l.	morro	ponta	reservatório	ribeirão, raõ.
ENGLISH	island	lagoon	hill	point	reservoir	creek
DEUTSCH	Insel	Haff	Hügel	Landspitze	Stausee	Bach
ESPAÑOL	isla	laguna	colina	punta	embalse	riachuelo
FRANÇAIS	île	lagune	colline	pointe	réservoir	crique

Kilometers 0 5 10 15 Km.
Statute Miles 0 5 10 15 Mi.

Scale 1:300,000

One centimeter represents 3 kilometers.
One inch represents approximately 4.7 miles.

AREA 4,700 km²
POPULATION 8,850,000

MAP FORM	ENGLISH	DEUTSCH	ESPAÑOL	FRANÇAIS	PORTUGUÊS
aeródromo	airport	Flughafen	aeropuerto	aéroport	aeroporto
arroyo	creek	Bach	riachuelo	crique	riacho
canal	navigation canal	Schiffahrtskanal	canal de navegación	canal	canal navegável
estación	station	Bahnhof	estación	gare	estação
isla	island	Insel	isla	île	ilha
parque	park	Park	parque	parc	parque
punta	point	Landspitze	punta	pointe	ponta

Kilometers 0 5 10 15 Km.
Statute Miles 0 5 10 15 Mi.

Scale 1:300,000
One centimeter represents 3 kilometers.
One inch represents approximately 4.7 miles.

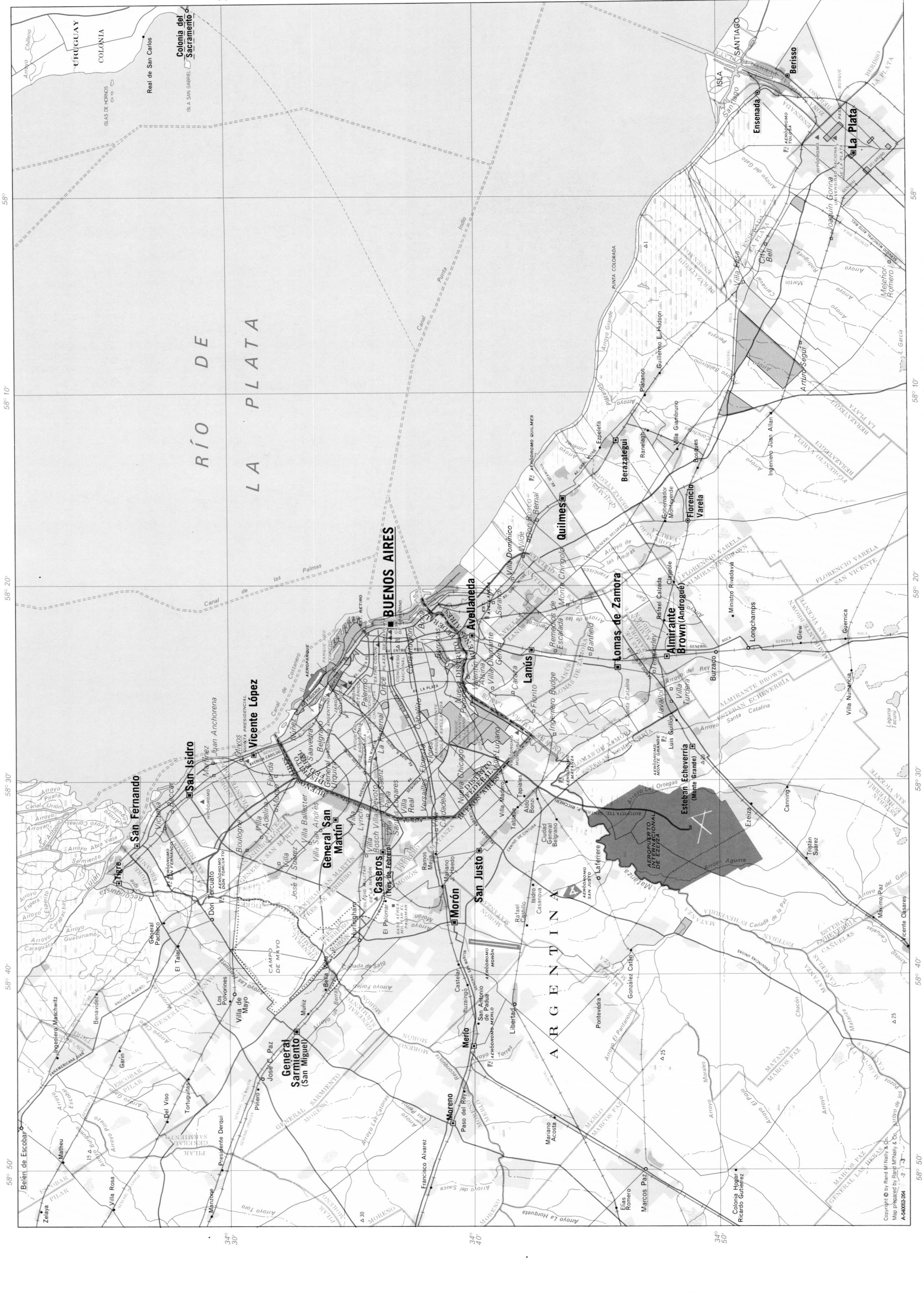

RÍO DE LA PLATA
URUGUAY
COLONIA
Colonia del Sacramento
Real de San Carlos
BUENOS AIRES
ARGENTINA
La Plata
Ensenada
Berisso
Quilmes
Berazategui
Florencio Varela
Avellaneda
Lanús
Lomas de Zamora
Almirante Brown (Adrogué)
Esteban Echeverría (Monte Grande)
San Justo
Morón
Merlo
Moreno
General Sarmiento (San Miguel)
General San Martín
Caseros (Tres de Febrero)
Vicente López
San Isidro
San Fernando
Tigre

World Scene

World Scene

Table of Contents

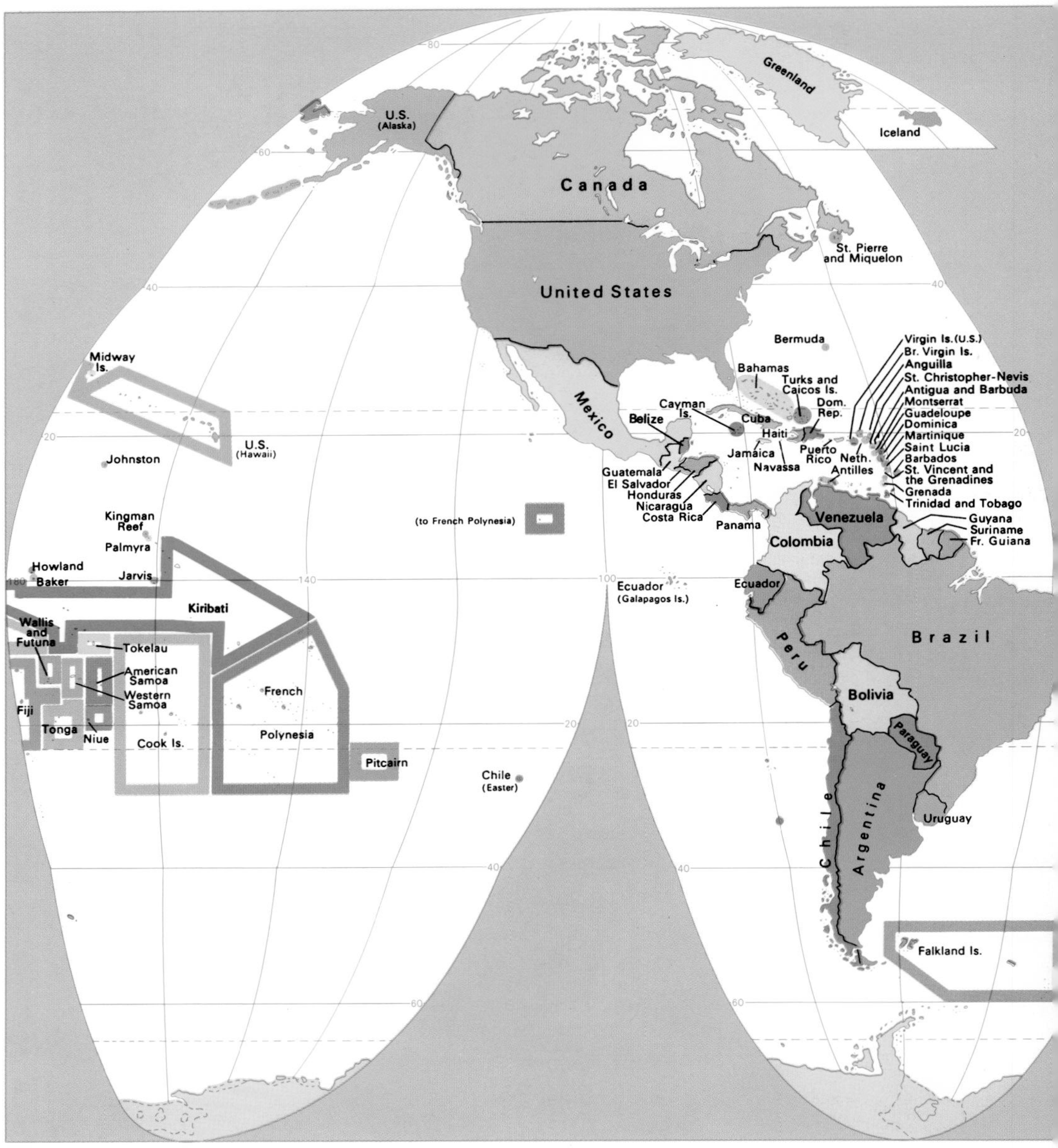

The World January 1, 1988

Every political entity that has a separate administration, whether it is independent or dependent, is named here and is distinguished from adjacent units by color. In all, over 200 political units are named. A noncontiguous part of a country has the same color as the country. If it lies at any distance, it is identified (for example, Alaska, a state of the United States), but if it lies close by, it is not (for example, the island of Corsica, which comprises two departments of France).

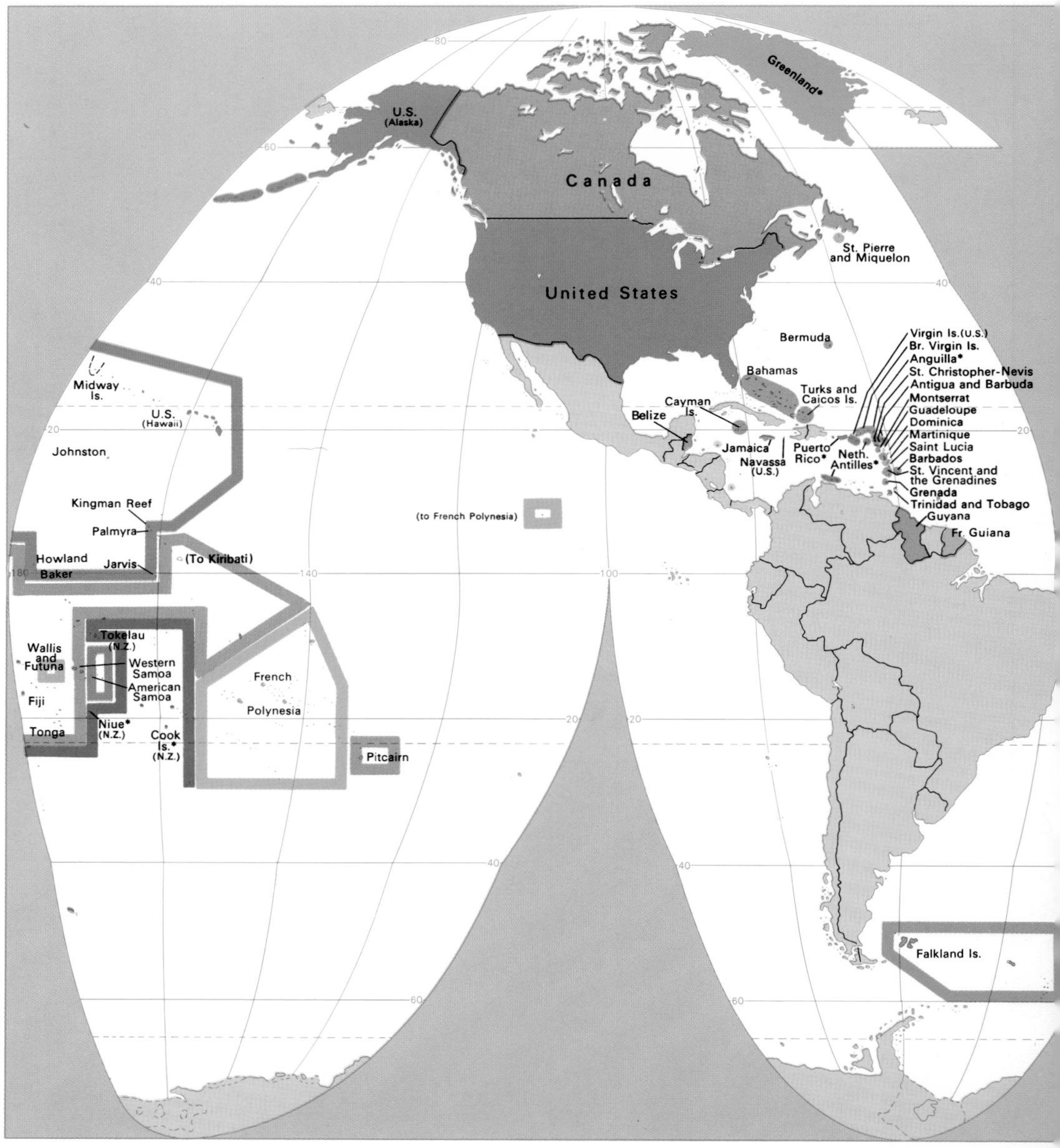

Politically Related Areas

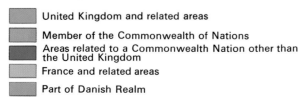

- United Kingdom and related areas
- Member of the Commonwealth of Nations
- Areas related to a Commonwealth Nation other than the United Kingdom
- France and related areas
- Part of Danish Realm
- Part of Netherlands Realm
- United States and related areas

*Virtually independent: major country primarily responsible for foreign relations and defense.

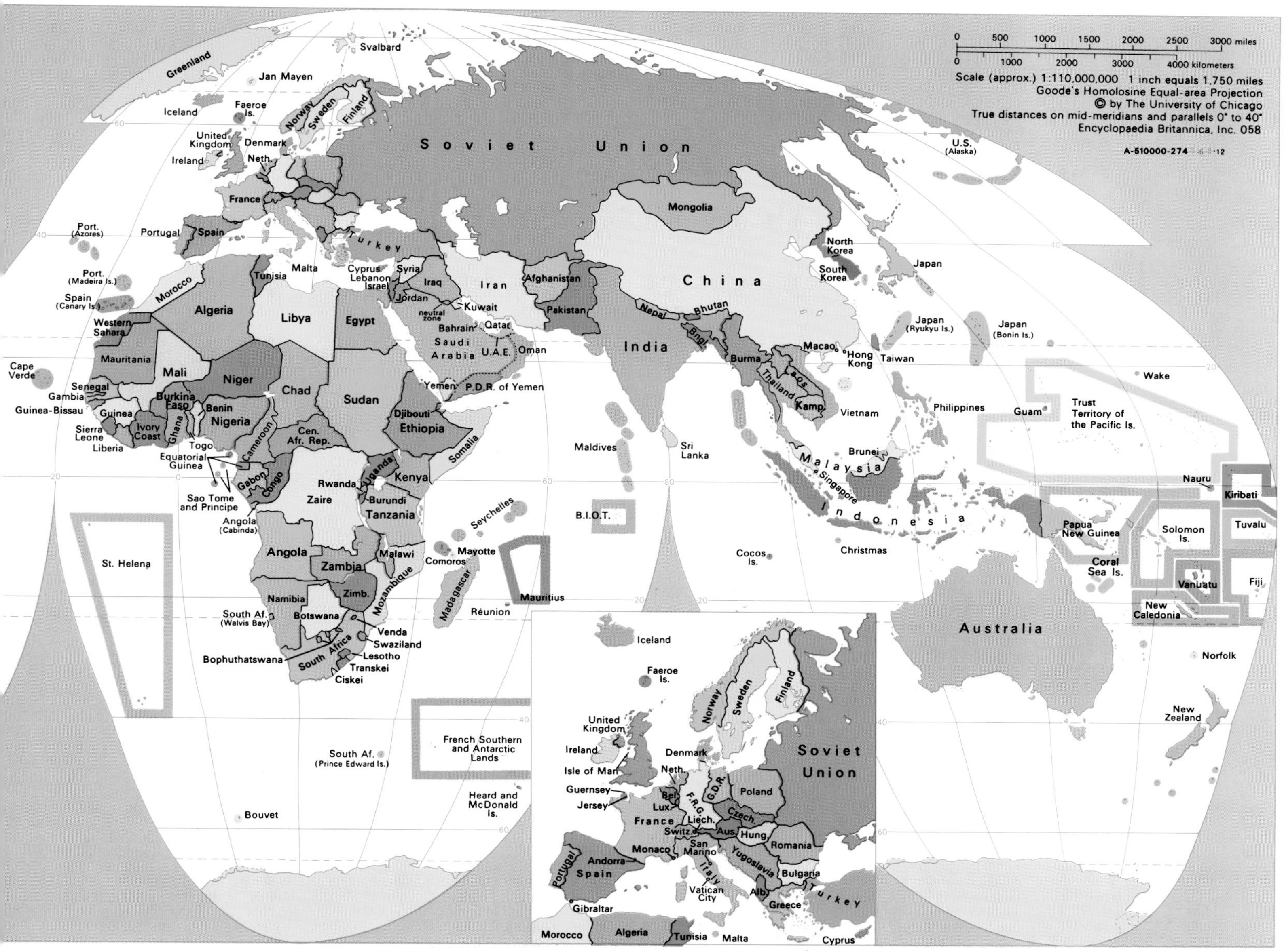

0 500 1000 1500 2000 2500 3000 miles
0 1000 2000 3000 4000 kilometers
Scale (approx.) 1:110,000,000 1 inch equals 1,750 miles
Goode's Homolosine Equal-area Projection
© by The University of Chicago
True distances on mid-meridians and parallels 0° to 40°
Encyclopaedia Britannica, Inc. 058
A-510000-274
Greenland
Svalbard
Jan Mayen
Iceland
Faeroe Is.
Norway
Sweden
Finland
United Kingdom
Ireland
Denmark
Neth.
France
Soviet Union
U.S. (Alaska)
Mongolia
Port. (Azores)
Portugal
Spain
Turkey
North Korea
South Korea
Japan
Port. (Madeira Is.)
Spain (Canary Is.)
Morocco
Tunisia
Malta
Cyprus
Lebanon
Israel
Syria
Iraq
Iran
Afghanistan
China
Algeria
Libya
Egypt
Jordan
neutral zone
Kuwait
Qatar
Bahrain
Saudi Arabia
U.A.E.
Oman
Pakistan
Nepal
Bhutan
Bngl.
India
Japan (Ryukyu Is.)
Japan (Bonin Is.)
Western Sahara
Mauritania
Cape Verde
Mali
Niger
Chad
Sudan
Yemen
P.D.R. of Yemen
Burma
Laos
Thailand
Kamp.
Vietnam
Macao
Hong Kong
Taiwan
Philippines
Wake
Guam
Trust Territory of the Pacific Is.
Senegal
Gambia
Guinea-Bissau
Guinea
Sierra Leone
Liberia
Burkina Faso
Ghana
Ivory Coast
Togo
Benin
Nigeria
Cameroon
Cen. Afr. Rep.
Djibouti
Ethiopia
Somalia
Equatorial Guinea
Sao Tome and Principe
Gabon
Congo
Zaire
Uganda
Kenya
Rwanda
Burundi
Tanzania
Angola (Cabinda)
Maldives
Sri Lanka
Brunei
Malaysia
Singapore
Indonesia
Nauru
Kiribati
Papua New Guinea
Solomon Is.
Tuvalu
Seychelles
B.I.O.T.
St. Helena
Angola
Zambia
Malawi
Comoros
Mayotte
Cocos Is.
Christmas
Coral Sea Is.
Vanuatu
Fiji
New Caledonia
Namibia
Zimb.
Mozambique
Madagascar
Mauritius
Réunion
South Af. (Walvis Bay)
Botswana
Venda
Swaziland
Lesotho
Transkei
Ciskei
South Africa
Bophuthatswana
Australia
Norfolk
New Zealand
French Southern and Antarctic Lands
South Af. (Prince Edward Is.)
Heard and McDonald Is.
Bouvet
Iceland
Faeroe Is.
Norway
Sweden
Finland
United Kingdom
Ireland
Isle of Man
Guernsey
Jersey
Denmark
Neth.
Bel.
Lux.
F.R.G.
G.D.R.
Poland
Soviet Union
France
Liech.
Switz.
Aus.
Czech.
Hung.
Romania
Monaco
San Marino
Italy
Yugoslavia
Bulgaria
Andorra
Portugal
Spain
Vatican City
Alb.
Greece
Turkey
Gibraltar
Morocco
Algeria
Tunisia
Malta
Cyprus

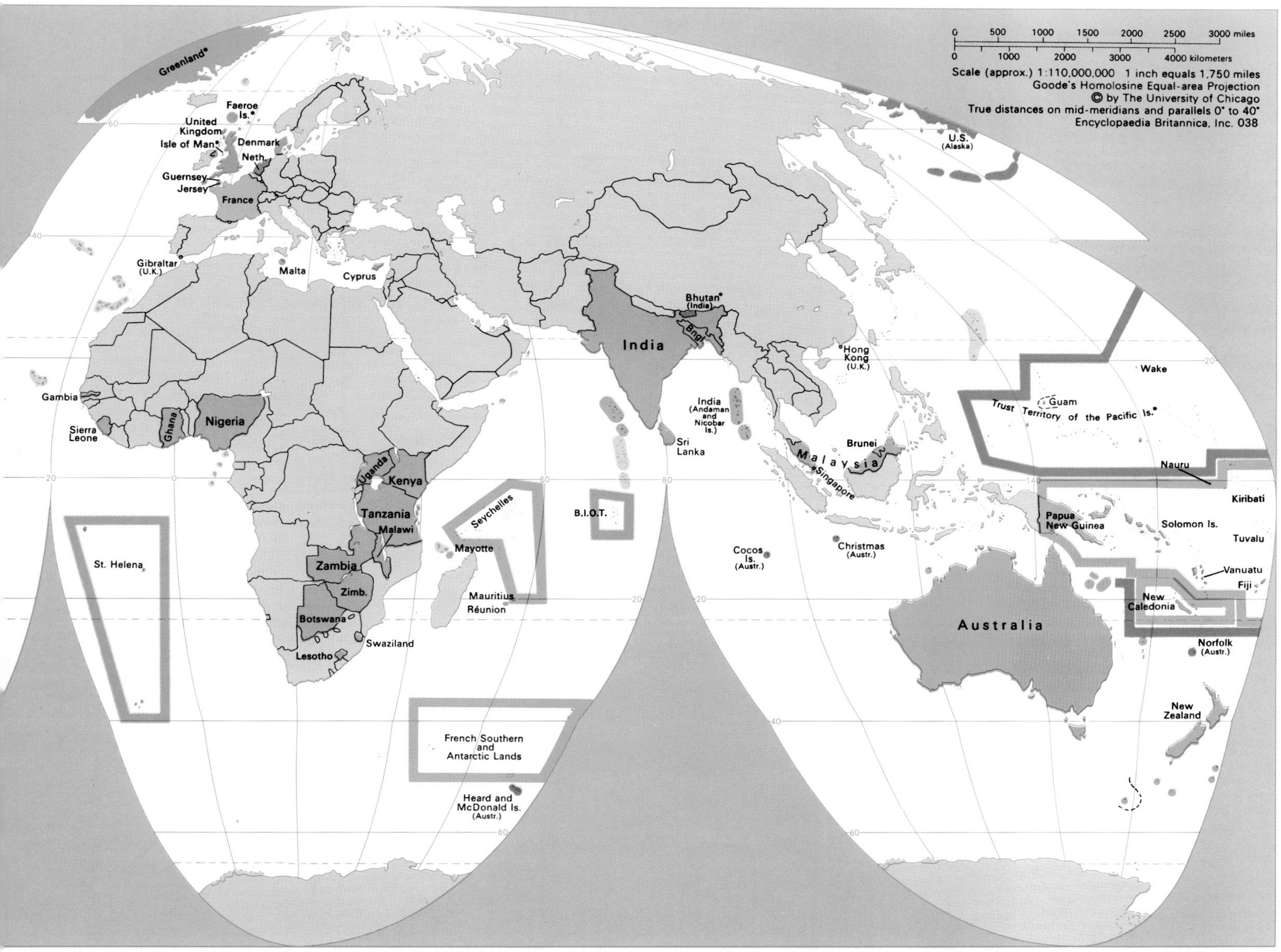

0 500 1000 1500 2000 2500 3000 miles
0 1000 2000 3000 4000 kilometers
Scale (approx.) 1:110,000,000 1 inch equals 1,750 miles
Goode's Homolosine Equal-area Projection
© by The University of Chicago
True distances on mid-meridians and parallels 0° to 40°
Encyclopaedia Britannica, Inc. 038
Greenland
Faeroe Is.
United Kingdom
Isle of Man
Denmark
Neth.
Guernsey
Jersey
France
U.S. (Alaska)
Gibraltar (U.K.)
Malta
Cyprus
Bhutan (India)
Bngl.
India
Hong Kong (U.K.)
Wake
Gambia
Sierra Leone
Ghana
Nigeria
India (Andaman and Nicobar Is.)
Sri Lanka
Guam
Trust Territory of the Pacific Is.
Brunei
Malaysia
Singapore
Nauru
Kiribati
Uganda
Kenya
Tanzania
Malawi
Seychelles
B.I.O.T.
Papua New Guinea
Solomon Is.
Tuvalu
St. Helena
Mayotte
Zambia
Cocos Is. (Austr.)
Christmas (Austr.)
Vanuatu
Fiji
Zimb.
Mauritius
Réunion
New Caledonia
Botswana
Swaziland
Lesotho
Australia
Norfolk (Austr.)
New Zealand
French Southern and Antarctic Lands
Heard and McDonald Is. (Austr.)

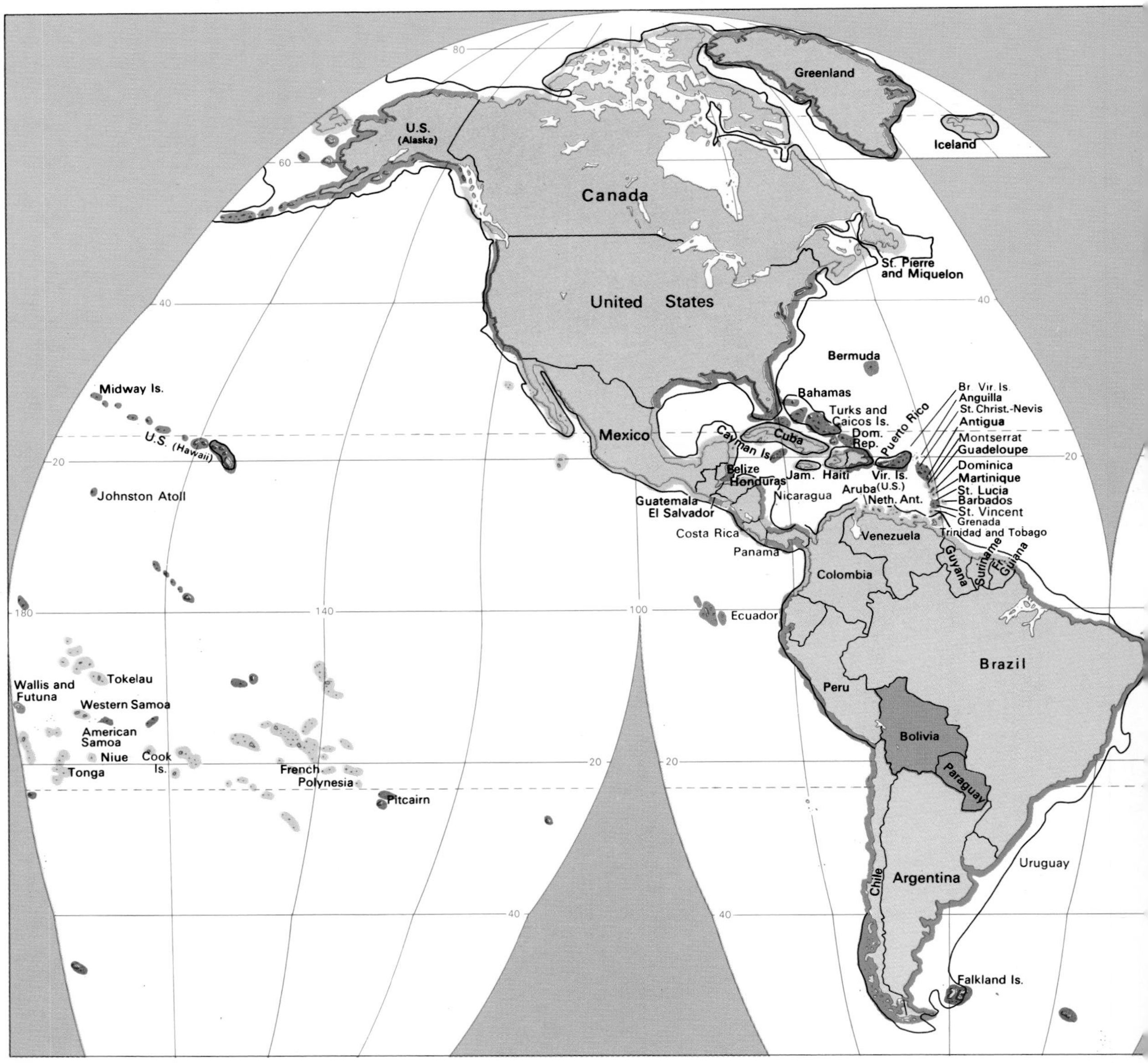

Seaward Claims

Common territorial sea claims

- 3 nautical miles
- 6 nautical miles
- 12 nautical miles

Less common claims

- 4 nautical miles
- 10 nautical miles
- Over 12 nautical miles
- Unusual claim

Other features

- Landlocked countries
- Continental shelf

Note: Territorial claims of outlying islands to their offshore waters are the same as those of the administering country.

The growth of international law on the legal status of the portions of the seas claimed by coastal states probably began in the early 17th century, when conflicting claims to parts of the high seas by colonial and exploring European sea powers induced the Dutch jurist Hugo Grotius to write *Mare liberum* (1609), on the concept of the "free, or open, sea." His work was answered in 1617-18 by John Selden's *Mare clausum*, proposing that the seas were as subject to property rights and claims as land areas. The first successful synthesis of the two positions was Cornelis van Bynkershoek's *De dominio maris* (1702) in which he suggested that the seaward limit of a national claim should be that of its effective land-based control (the distance of a cannon-shot, three nautical miles). Though never universally accepted, that standard persisted well into the twentieth century.

After World War II, however, both traditional sea-based economic activity—fishing, commercial navigation—and activities made newly possible or intensified by technological change—exploitation of the seabed, pollution, scientific investigation—led coastal states to make increasingly wider claims to both territorial seas, those wholly subject to national law, and to zones in which some, but not all, sovereign rights were claimed, usually to protect economic, but especially fishing, interests. The first Law of the Sea Conference in 1958 attempted under UN auspices to codify international law in these areas. More than 14 years later at the final meeting of the Third Conference, a text representing the efforts of some 150 countries was opened for signature on Dec. 10, 1982 as the *United Nations Convention on the Law of the Sea*. Accessions were deposited that day by 119 states to a document providing definitions, guidelines, procedures, and institutions to govern a wide range of maritime law and activities.

Among the subjects relating to sovereignty delimited by the Convention were sections defining the rights, jurisdiction, and duties of coastal states in matters relating to the territorial sea, the right of innocent passage, international straits, archipelagic (island) states, exclusive economic zones (EEZ's), the continental shelf, the high seas, as well as access to, and use of, areas of the sea beyond the jurisdiction of a single national power.

Territorial sea may be claimed up to a distance of 12 nautical miles (n.m.) from either the shoreline of a coastal state (measured from low water on navigational charts), or from a straight baseline defined by the state when its shoreline is very irregular, as is that of Norway. Waters directly connected to the sea behind this baseline are called internal waters, and include bays (which may be closed at the mouth by a single baseline if they are less than 24 n.m. wide, and river mouths and estuaries. A zone contiguous to the territorial sea not wider than 24 n.m. beyond the baselines defining the territorial sea is defined in which states may exercise *limited* control for customs, immigration, fiscal, or sanitary reasons. Another zone, defined in relation to the continental shelf (the seaward prolongation of the coastal landmass beneath the sea) permits extension of the national sovereignty over the seabed and subsoil of the zone to the edge of the continental margin (the lower termination of the continental slope and rise) for purposes of exploration, scientific study, or economic exploitation of either biological or mineral resources.

In areas of the seas where coastal states lie in close proximity, the seaward extension of a national boundary may necessitate the drawing or negotiation of an international boundary in the sea. Where claims permissible under the Convention overlap, as in the Persian Gulf, median lines must be drawn so as to accommodate each state's maximum claim without disadvantaging bordering states.

The table opposite provides a description of the nature of current national claims to territorial seas and of the economic, usually fishing, zones that have been declared *within* the permissible 200-n.m. limits of the potential EEZ permitted by the Convention.

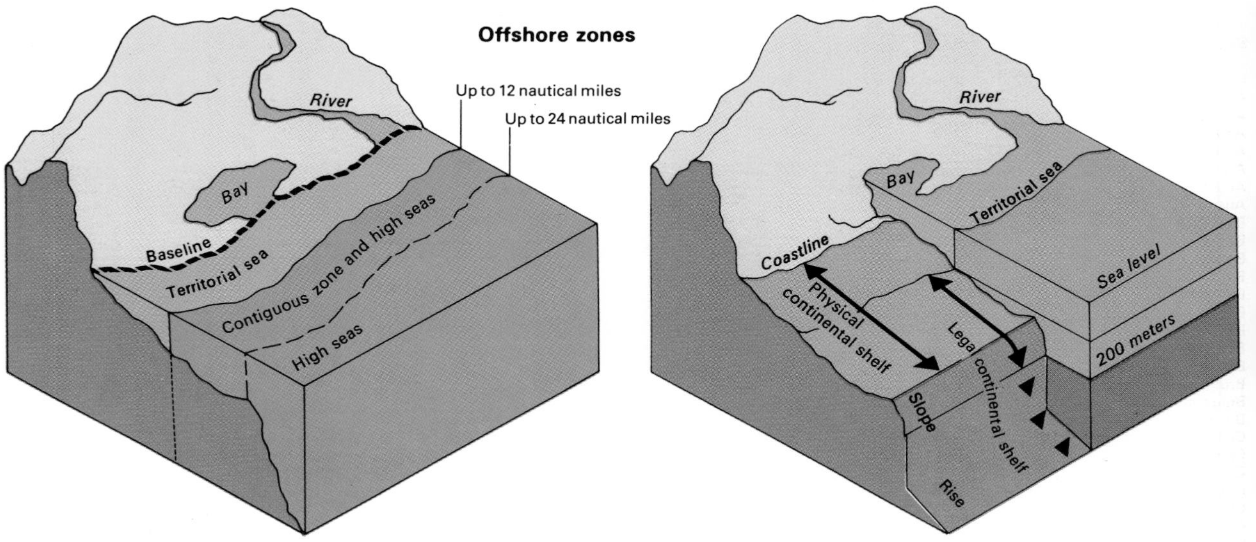

Irregular coastline of Norway

Norway measures its territorial sea from a straight baseline, which in general runs along the outer fringe of offshore islands and coastal promontories. The Law of the Sea Convention permits this type of claim in the case of highly irregular coastlines fringed with islands. In other cases the coastal features do not justify such claims to additional waters, and the claims may not be recognized.

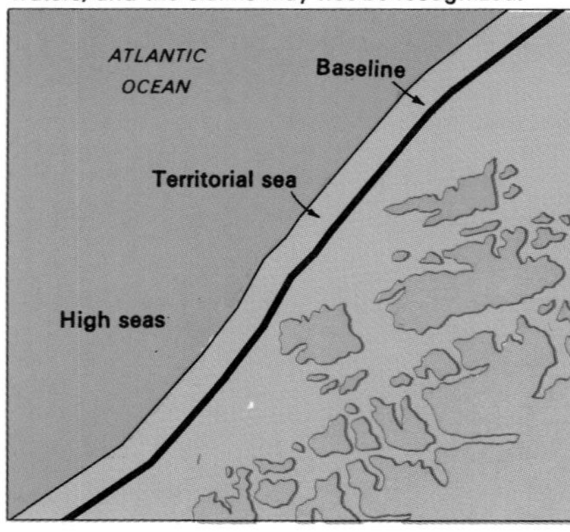

Overlapping claims in the Persian Gulf

The waters of the Persian Gulf are less than 200 meters in depth and the entire seabed is continental shelf. To determine the extent of jurisdiction that each state has over the resources of the seabed beyond its territorial sea, the Law of the Sea Convention provides for median lines, measured from the same baseline as the territorial sea. The median lines divide the continental shelf between opposite and adjacent states.

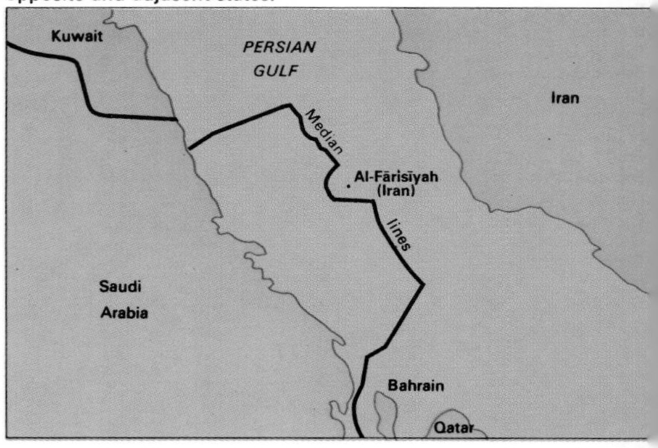

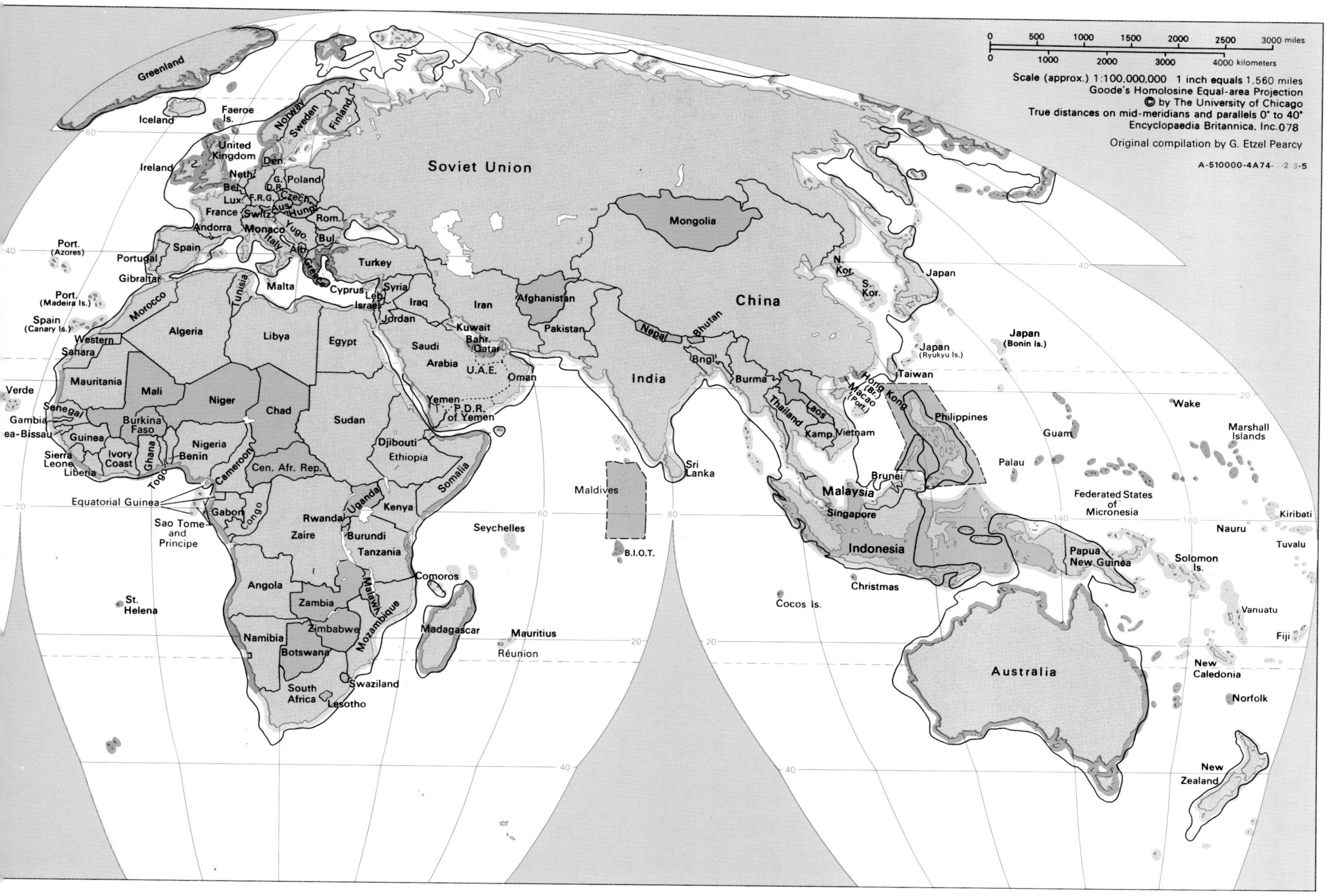

Political unit	Territorial sea claim*	Fishing claim*†
Albania	15 A	
Algeria	12	
Angola	20	200
Antigua and Barbuda	12	200D
Argentina	200 A	
Aruba	12	
Australia	3 A	200
Bahamas	3	200
Bahrain	3	
Bangladesh	12 A	200D
Barbados	12	200D
Belgium	3	200
Belize	3	
Benin	200	
Bermuda	3 B	200
Brazil	200 A	
Brunei	12	200
Bulgaria	12	
Burma	12 A	200D
Cameroon	50 A	
Canada	12 A	200
Cape Verde	12 C	200D
Chile	24	200
China	12 A	
Colombia	12	200D
Comoros	12	200D
Congo	200	
Cook Islands	12 B	200D
Costa Rica	12	200D
Cuba	12 A	200D
Cyprus	12	
Denmark	3 A	200
Djibouti	12	200D
Dominica	12	200D
Dominican Republic	6 A	200D
Ecuador	200 A	
Egypt	12 A	200D
El Salvador	200	
Equatorial Guinea	12	
Ethiopia	12 A	
Faeroe Islands	3 B	200
Falkland Islands	3	200
Fiji	12 C	200D
Finland	4 A	12
France	12 A	200D
French Guiana	12 B	200D
French Polynesia	12 B	200D
Gabon	100 A	150
Gambia	200	
German Dem. Rep.	12 A	200
Germany, Fed. Rep. of	3 A	200
Ghana	200	
Gibraltar	3 B	

Political unit	Territorial sea claim*	Fishing claim*†
Greece	6	
Greenland	3 B	200
Grenada	12	200D
Guatemala	12 A	200D
Guinea	12 A	200D
Guinea-Bissau	12	200D
Guyana	12	200
Haiti	12 A	200D
Honduras	12	200D
Hong Kong	3 B	
Iceland	12 A	200D
India	12	200D
Indonesia	12 C	200D
Iran	12 A	50
Iraq	12	
Ireland	3 A	200
Israel	6	
Italy	12	
Ivorv Coast	12	200D
Jamaica	12	
Japan	12	200
Jordan	3	
Kampuchea	12 A	200D
Kenya	12 A	200D
Kiribati	12	200
Korea, North	12	200D
Korea, South	12 A	
Kuwait	12	
Lebanon	12	
Liberia	200	
Libya	12 A	
Madagascar	50 A	150D
Malaysia	12 A	200D
Maldives		35–300
Malta	12 A	25
Marshall Islands	3 B	200D
Mauritania	70 A	200D
Mauritius	12 A	200D
Mexico	12 A	200D
Micronesia, Fed. States of	3 B	200D
Monaco	12	
Morocco	12	200D
Mozambique	12 A	200D
Namibia	6	12
Nauru	12	200
Netherlands	12	200
Netherlands Antilles	12	
New Caledonia	12 B	200D
New Zealand	12	200D
Nicaragua	200	
Nigeria	30	200D
Northern Mariana Islands	3 B	200D
Norway	4 A	200D

Political unit	Territorial sea claim*	Fishing claim*†
Oman	12 A	200D
Pakistan	12	200D
Palau	3 B	200D
Panama	200 A	
Papua New Guinea	12 C	200D
Peru	200	
Philippines		200D
Poland	12 A	200
Portugal	12 A	200D
Puerto Rico	3 B	200
Qatar	3	200D
Romania	200	
St. Christopher—Nevis	12	200D
St. Lucia	3	12
St. Pierre and Miquelon	12 B	200D
St. Vincent and the Grenadines	3	12
Sao Tome and Principe	12 C	200D
Saudi Arabia	12 A	
Senegal	12 A	200
Seychelles	12	200D
Sierra Leone	200	
Singapore	3	12
Solomon Islands	12 C	200D
Somalia	200 A	
South Africa	12	200
Soviet Union	12 A	200D
Spain	12	200D
Sri Lanka	12 A	200D
Sudan	12 A	
Suriname	12	200D
Sweden	12 A	200
Syria	35 A	
Taiwan	12	200D
Tanzania	50 A	
Thailand	12 A	200D
Togo	30	200D
Tonga	12	200D
Trinidad and Tobago	12	200D
Tunisia	12	
Turkey	6–12 A	
Tuvalu	12	200D
United Arab Emirates	3 or 12	200D
United Kingdom	3 A	200
United States	3	200D
Uruguay	200	
Vanuatu	12 C	200D
Venezuela	12 A	200D
Vietnam	12	200D
Western Samoa	12	200D
Yemen	12	
Yemen, P.D.R.	12	200D
Yugoslavia	12 A	
Zaire	12	200

* Nautical miles.
† When claim is beyond the territorial sea.

A. Measured from a straight (or extended) baseline.
B. Same as that of administering country.
C. Extends beyond a perimeter drawn around archipelago.
D. Extended economic zone.

Dissolution of the Ottoman Empire

Ottoman Empire 1913

Administrative boundaries (1923) as a result of WW I settlements; dotted are indefinite

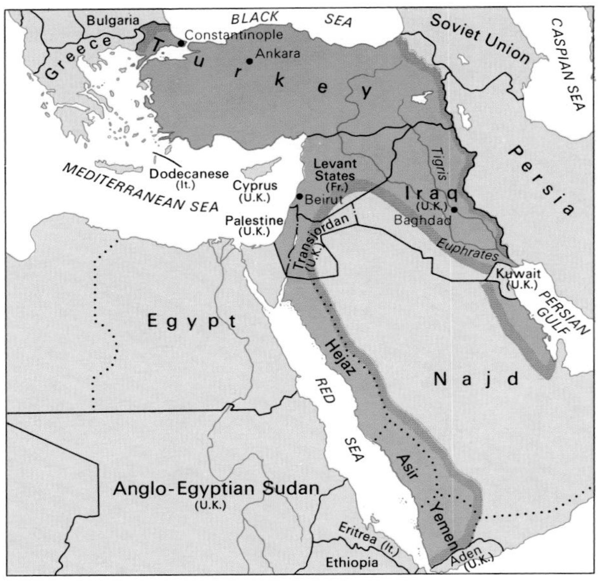

Dissolution of Austria-Hungary

Austria-Hungary 1913

Administrative boundaries (1923) as a result of WW I settlements

Japanese Expansion World War II

Japan 1939

Japanese dependencies 1939

Maximum occupation

Neutral states

States joining Allies 1945

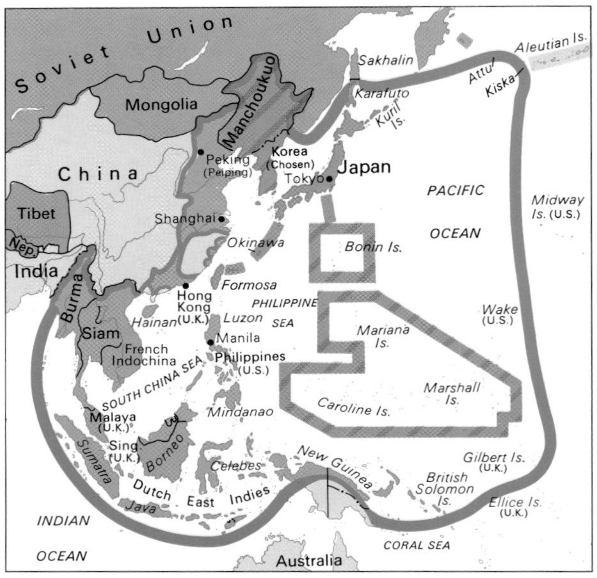

Axis Expansion World War II

Germany 1939

Other Axis Powers 1940-45

Maximum occupation

Neutral states

States joining Allies 1943-45

*Occupied by Allies

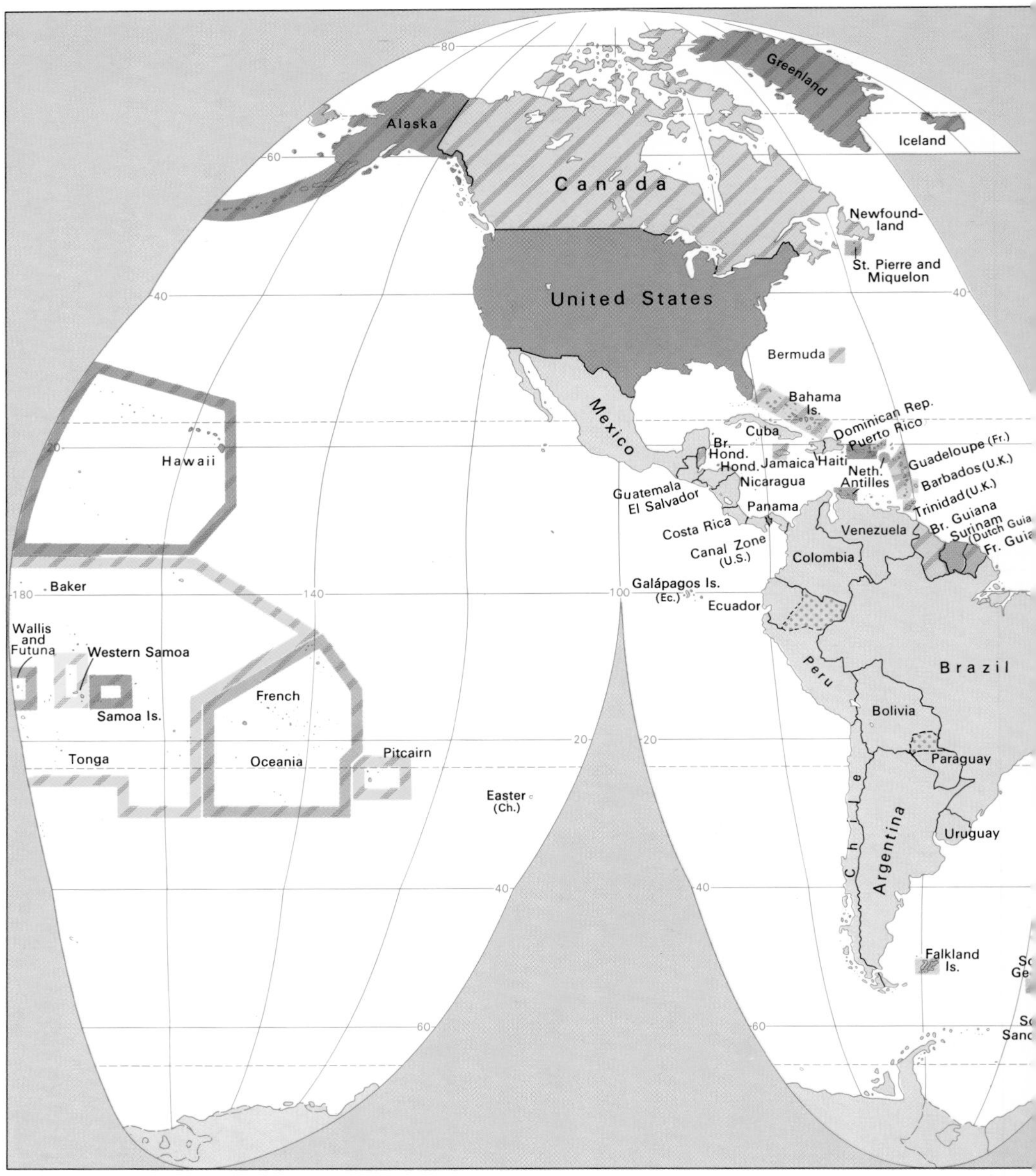

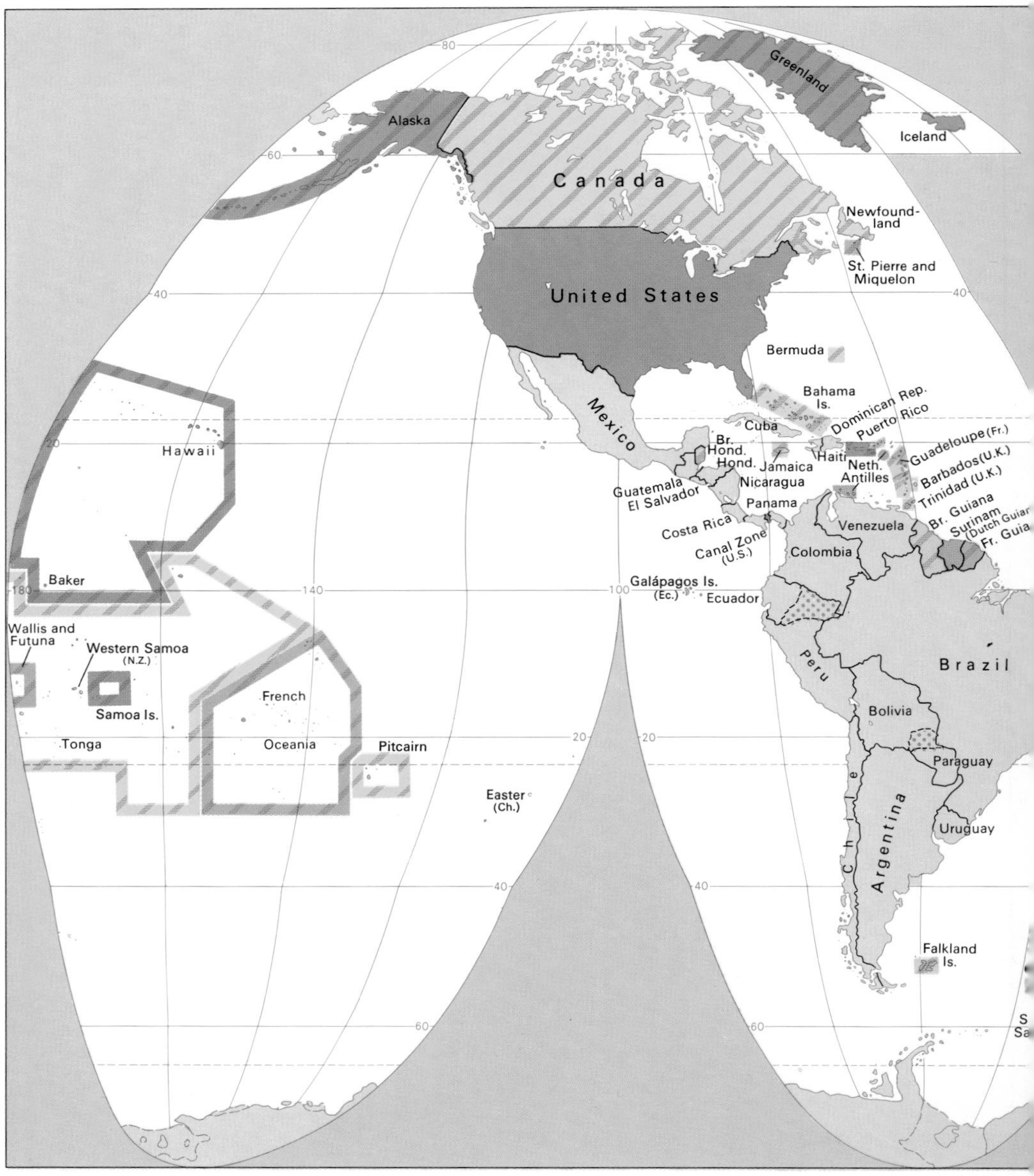

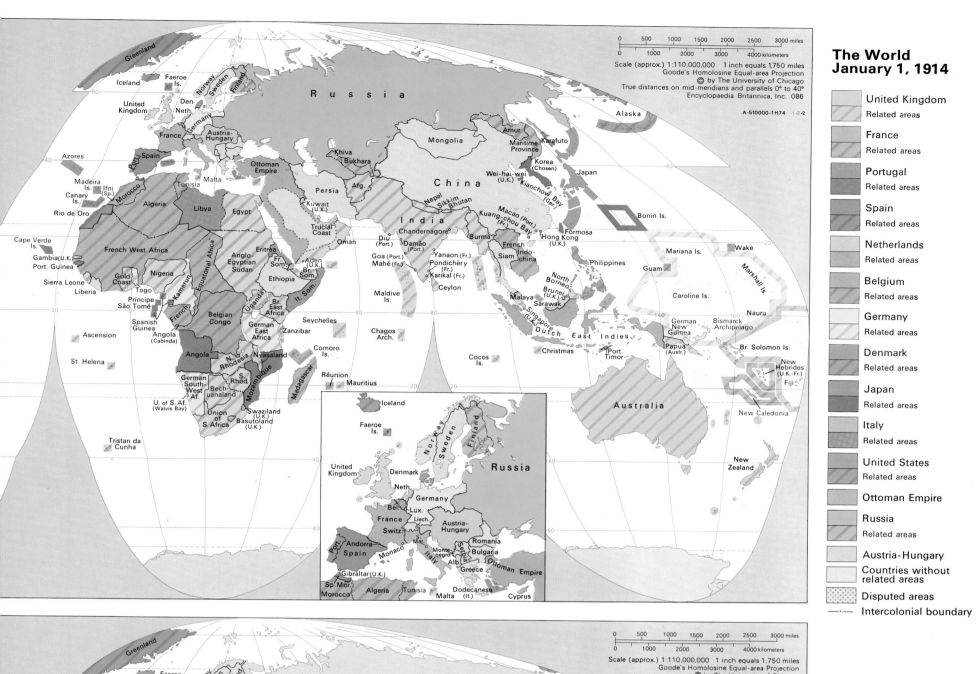

The World January 1, 1914

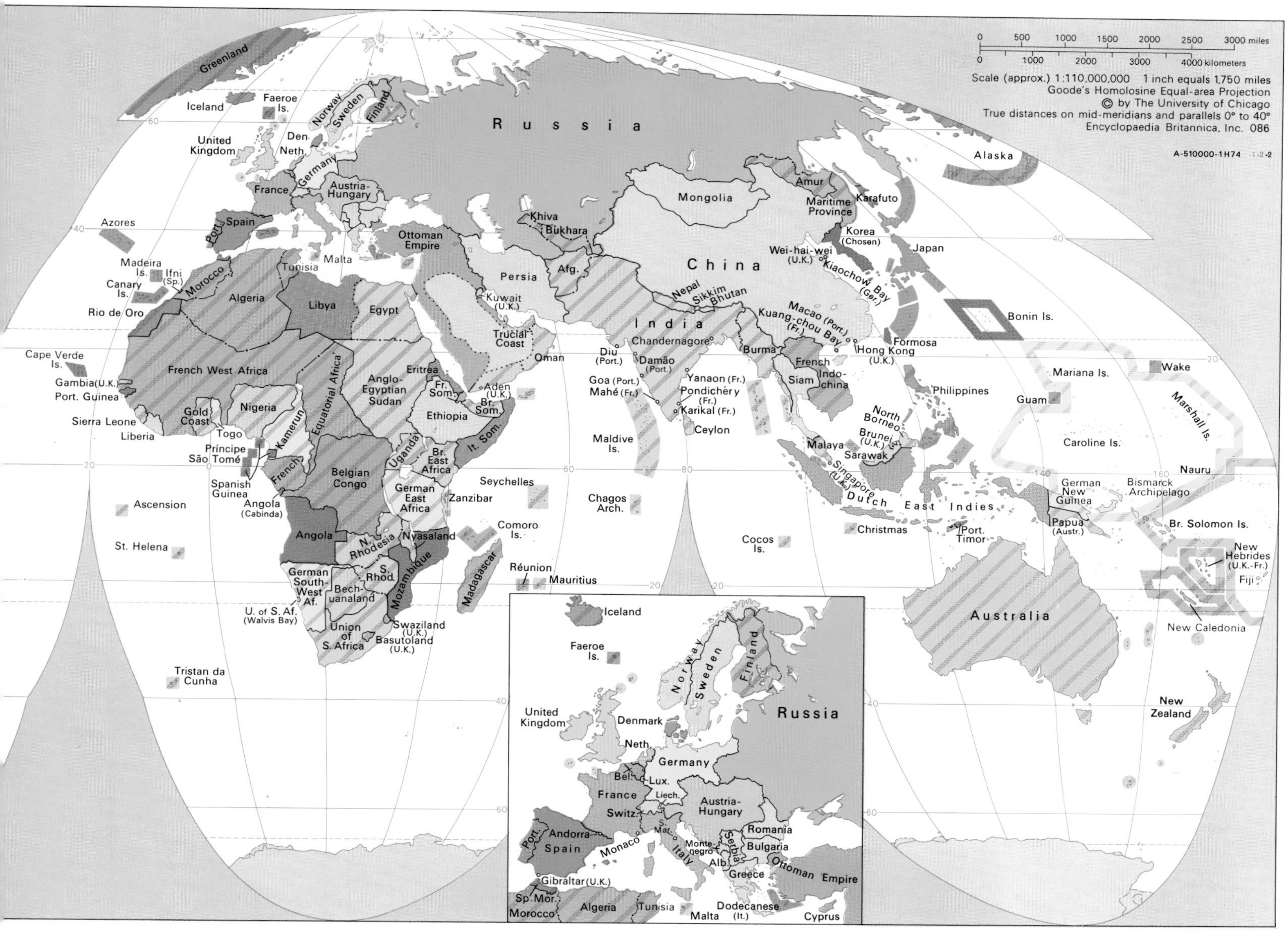

- United Kingdom
  - Related areas
- France
  - Related areas
- Portugal
  - Related areas
- Spain
  - Related areas
- Netherlands
  - Related areas
- Belgium
  - Related areas
- Germany
  - Related areas
- Denmark
  - Related areas
- Japan
  - Related areas
- Italy
  - Related areas
- United States
  - Related areas
- Ottoman Empire
- Russia
  - Related areas
- Austria-Hungary
- Countries without related areas
- Disputed areas
- Intercolonial boundary

The World January 1, 1937

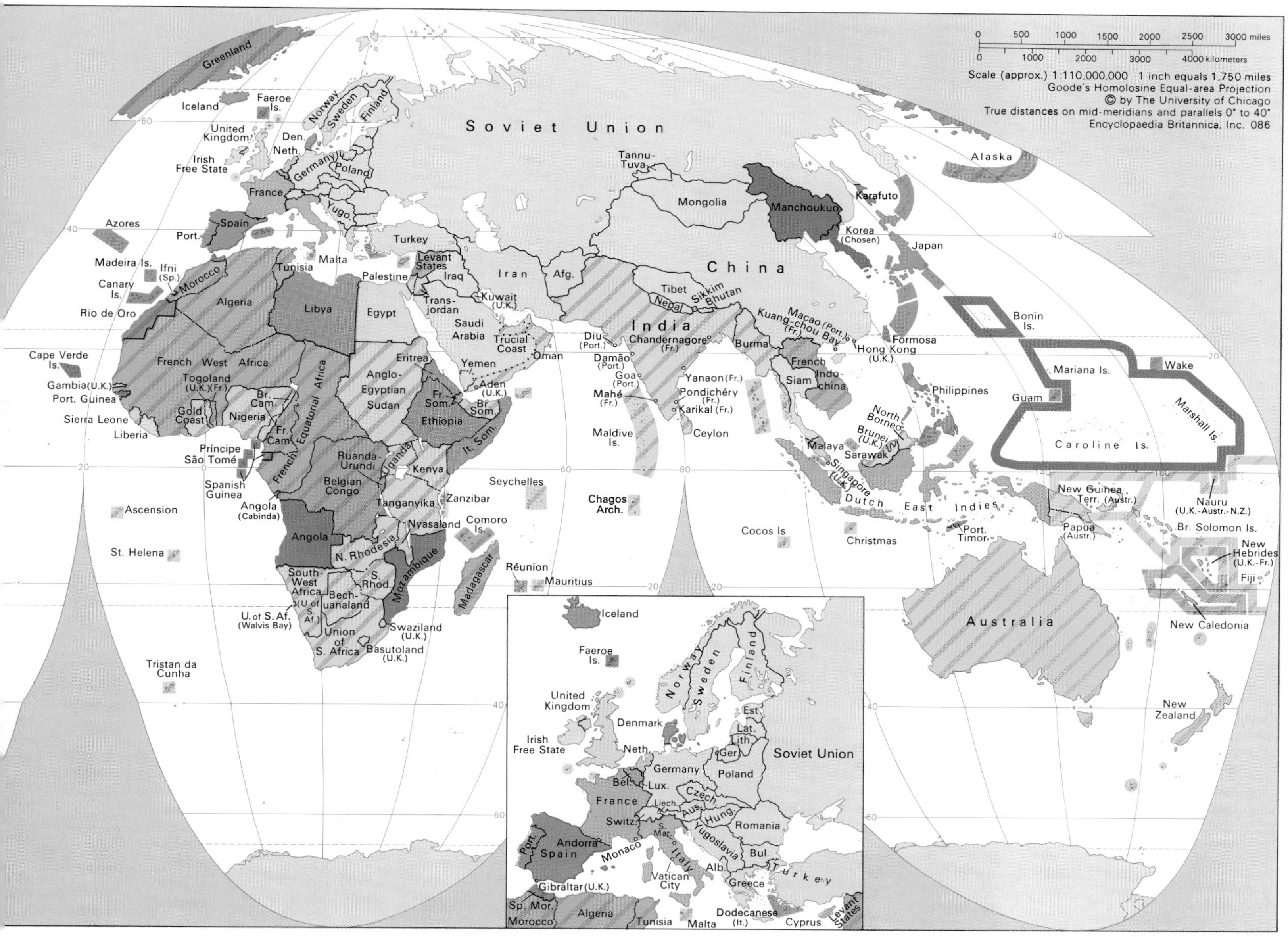

- United Kingdom
  - Related areas
- France
  - Related areas
- Portugal
  - Related areas
- Spain
  - Related areas
- Netherlands
  - Related areas
- Belgium
  - Related areas
- Denmark
  - Related areas
- Japan
  - Related areas
- Italy
  - Related areas
- United States
  - Related areas
- Countries without related areas
- Disputed areas
- Intercolonial boundary

Population

Extent of urbanization
Percent of total population urban

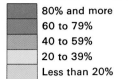

- 80% and more
- 60 to 79%
- 40 to 59%
- 20 to 39%
- Less than 20%

Major metropolitan areas

- 5,000,000 and more persons
- 3,000,000 to 4,999,999
- 2,000,000 to 2,999,999

The increase in the proportion of urban to total population reflects the change from a dispersed pattern of human settlement to a concentrated one. In industrialized countries the proportion of people living in cities increases mainly through movement from country to city, due to the attraction of higher wages and greater opportunities, a process which in most cases started about 100 years ago. In the underdeveloped countries, where in recent years the number of people living in cities has risen sharply, the proportion of urban population has not increased appreciably; here the urban growth is generally due not so much to rural-urban migration as it is to the natural population increase in both urban and rural areas, and to the decline in the urban mortality rate.

In population studies the definitions of "urban" differ from country to country, but generally take into account the total number of people in a settlement and the percent of the population engaged in nonagricultural activities. The map shows the degree of urbanization (the proportion of urban to total population), considering as urban those communities having no fewer than 2,000 inhabitants, more than half of them dependent on nonfarm occupations. Also indicated are selected metropolitan areas where cities have expanded beyond their boundaries into the surrounding regions in patterns of continuous settlement oriented toward the central cities.

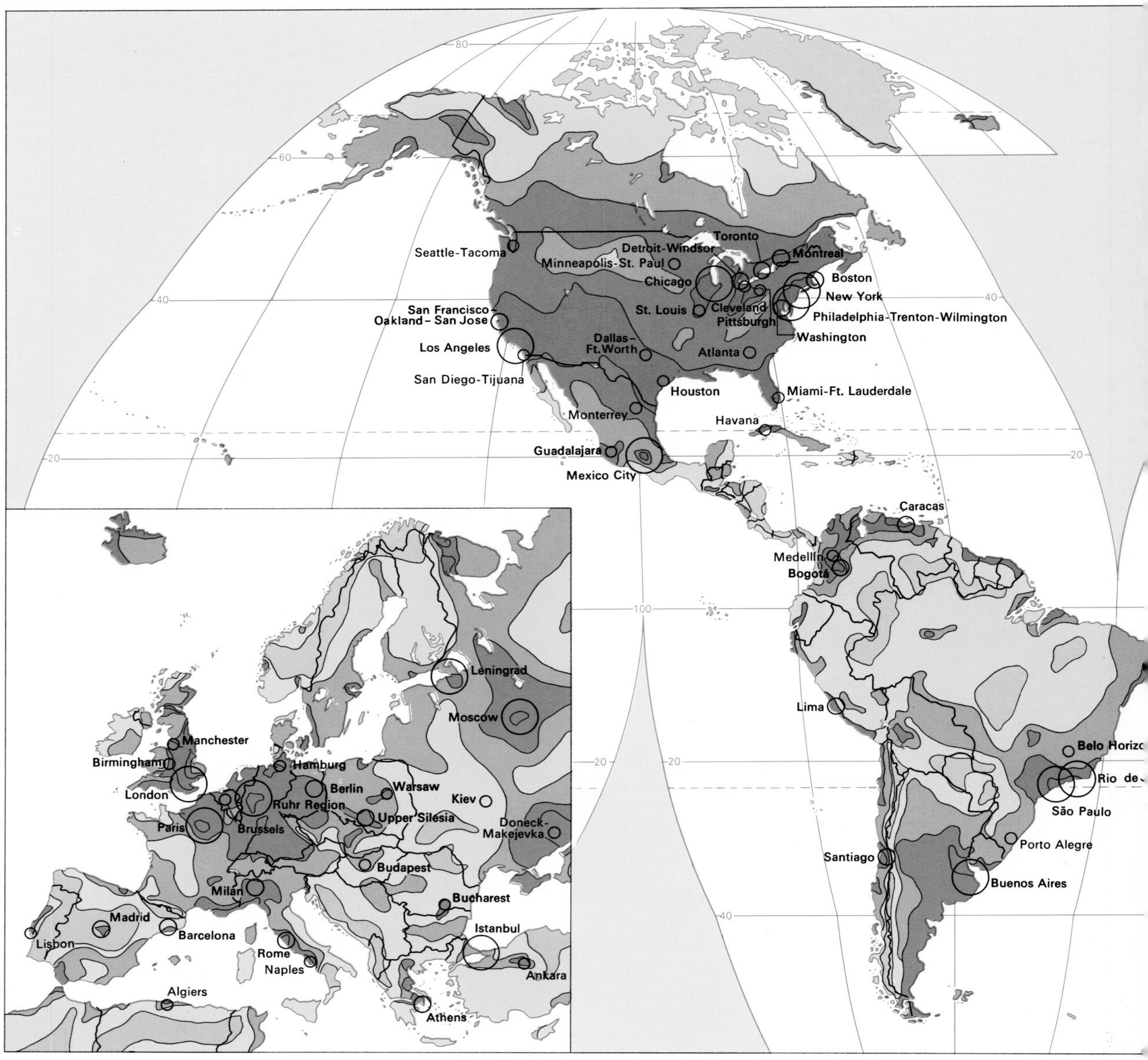
Seattle-Tacoma
Minneapolis-St. Paul
Detroit-Windsor
Toronto
Montreal
Chicago
Boston
New York
Cleveland
Pittsburgh
Philadelphia-Trenton-Wilmington
Washington
St. Louis
San Francisco-Oakland-San Jose
Los Angeles
Dallas-Ft. Worth
Atlanta
San Diego-Tijuana
Houston
Miami-Ft. Lauderdale
Havana
Monterrey
Guadalajara
Mexico City
Caracas
Medellín
Bogotá
Lima
Belo Horizo
Rio de
São Paulo
Porto Alegre
Santiago
Buenos Aires
Leningrad
Moscow
Manchester
Birmingham
Hamburg
Berlin
London
Warsaw
Ruhr Region
Kiev
Paris
Brussels
Upper Silesia
Doneck-Makejevka
Budapest
Milan
Bucharest
Madrid
Barcelona
Lisbon
Istanbul
Rome
Naples
Ankara
Algiers
Athens

Age and sex composition

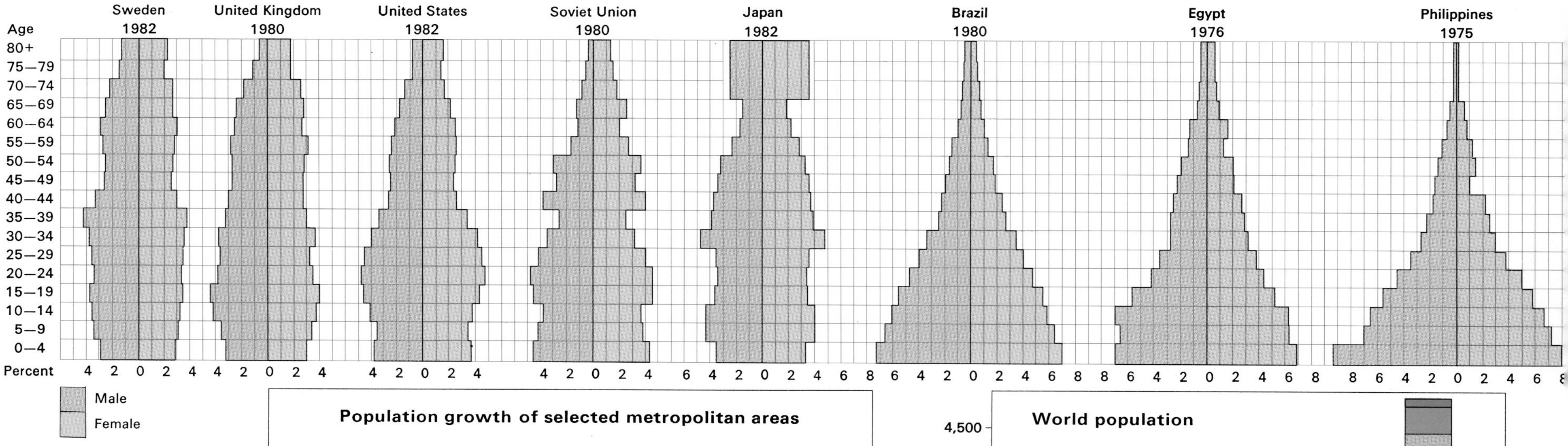
Sweden 1982
United Kingdom 1980
United States 1982
Soviet Union 1980
Japan 1982
Brazil 1980
Egypt 1976
Philippines 1975
Age
80+
75–79
70–74
65–69
60–64
55–59
50–54
45–49
40–44
35–39
30–34
25–29
20–24
15–19
10–14
5–9
0–4
Percent
Male
Female

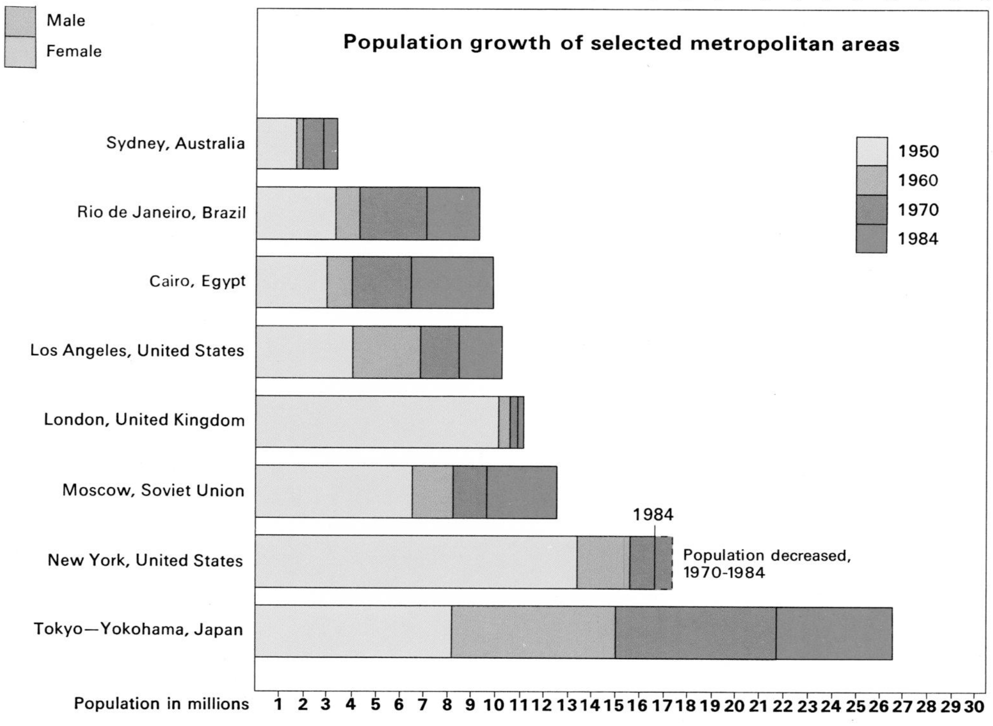
Population growth of selected metropolitan areas
Sydney, Australia
Rio de Janeiro, Brazil
Cairo, Egypt
Los Angeles, United States
London, United Kingdom
Moscow, Soviet Union
New York, United States
Tokyo—Yokohama, Japan
1950
1960
1970
1984
1984
Population decreased, 1970-1984
Population in millions
1 2 3 4 5 6 7 8 9 10 11 12 13 14 15 16 17 18 19 20 21 22 23 24 25 26 27 28 29 30

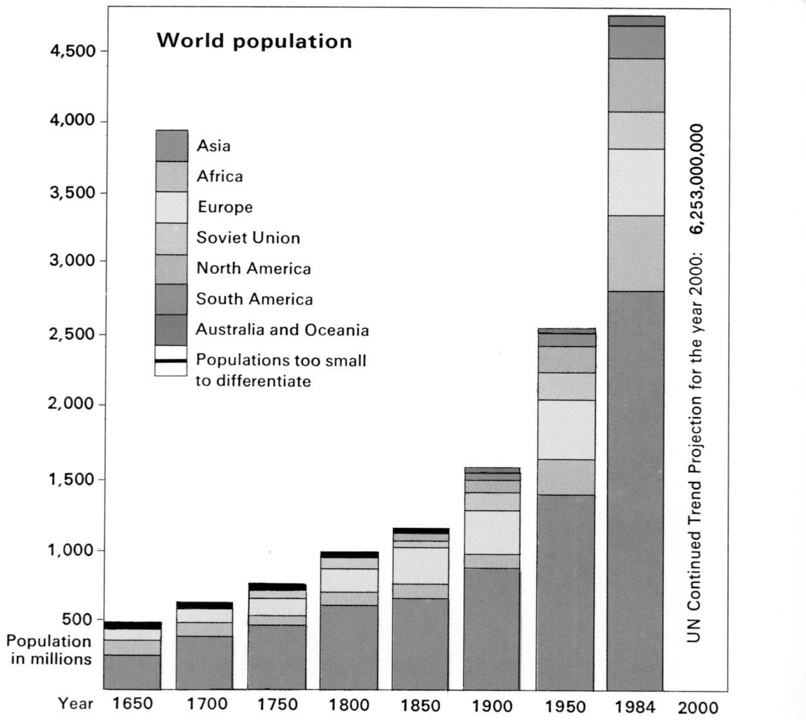
World population
Asia
Africa
Europe
Soviet Union
North America
South America
Australia and Oceania
Populations too small to differentiate
4,500
4,000
3,500
3,000
2,500
2,000
1,500
1,000
500
Population in millions
Year 1650 1700 1750 1800 1850 1900 1950 1984 2000
UN Continued Trend Projection for the year 2000: 6,253,000,000

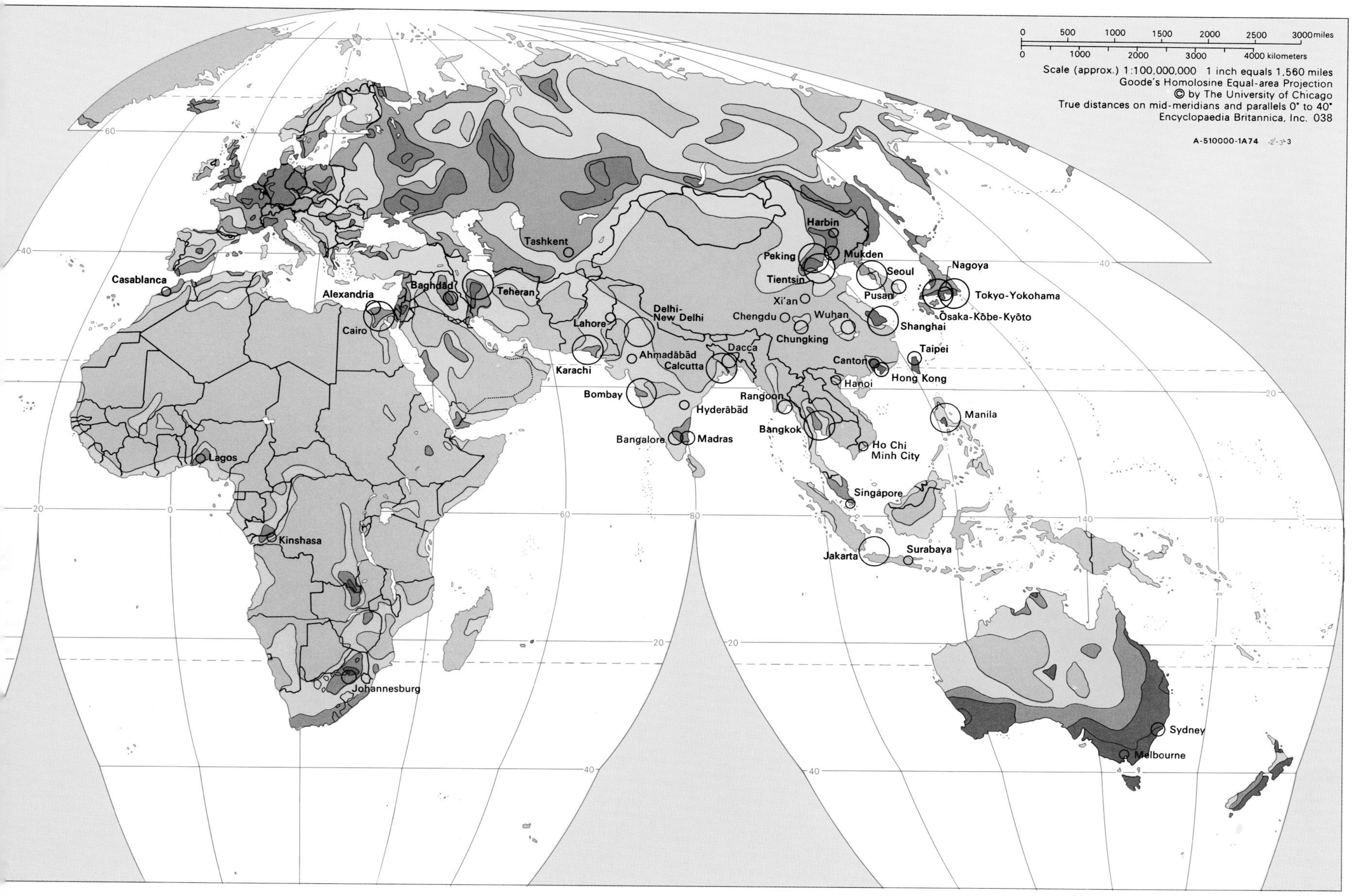

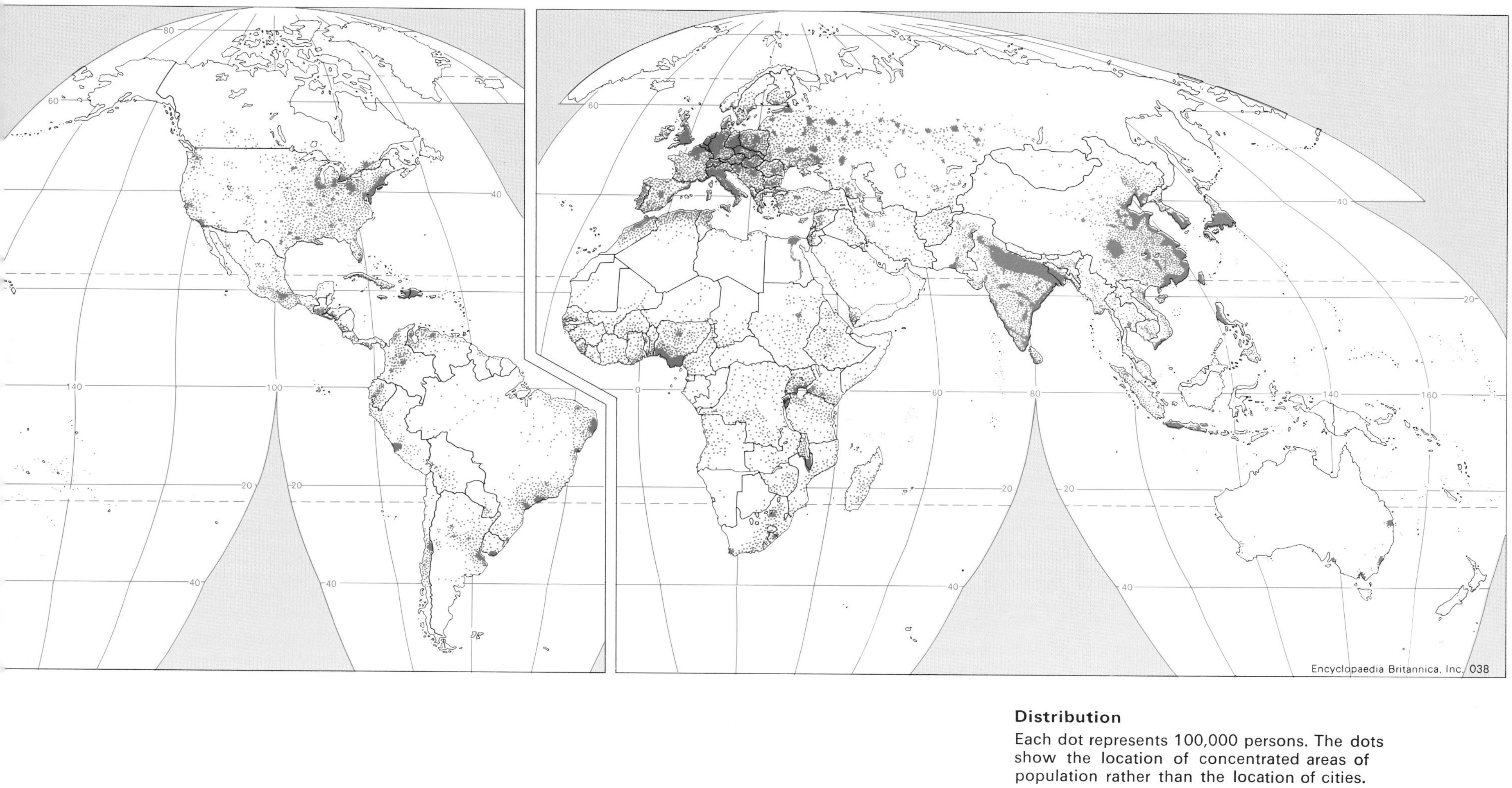

Distribution

Each dot represents 100,000 persons. The dots show the location of concentrated areas of population rather than the location of cities.

Religions

The majority of the inhabitants in each of the areas colored on the map share the religious tradition indicated. Letter symbols show religious traditions shared by at least 25% of the inhabitants within areal units no smaller than one thousand square miles. Therefore minority religions of city-dwellers have generally not been represented.

- R Roman Catholicism
- P Protestantism
- E Eastern Orthodox religions (including Armenian, Coptic, Ethiopian, Greek, and Russian Orthodox)
- M Mormonism
- C Christianity, undifferentiated by branch (chiefly mingled Protestantism and Roman Catholicism, neither predominant)
- I Islam, predominantly Sunni
- Sh Islam, predominantly Shia
- Theravada Buddhism
- L Lamaism
- H Hinduism
- J Judaism
- Ch Chinese religions*
- Ja Japanese religions*
- Korean religions*
- Vietnamese religions*
- T Simple ethnic (tribal) religions
- Sk Sikhism
- Countries under Communist regimes; traditional religions often subject to restraint
- Uninhabited

*In certain Eastern Asian areas, most of the people have plural religious affiliations. Chinese, Korean, and Vietnamese religions include Mahayana Buddhism, Taoism, Confucianism, and folk cults. The Japanese religions include Shinto and Mahayana Buddhism.

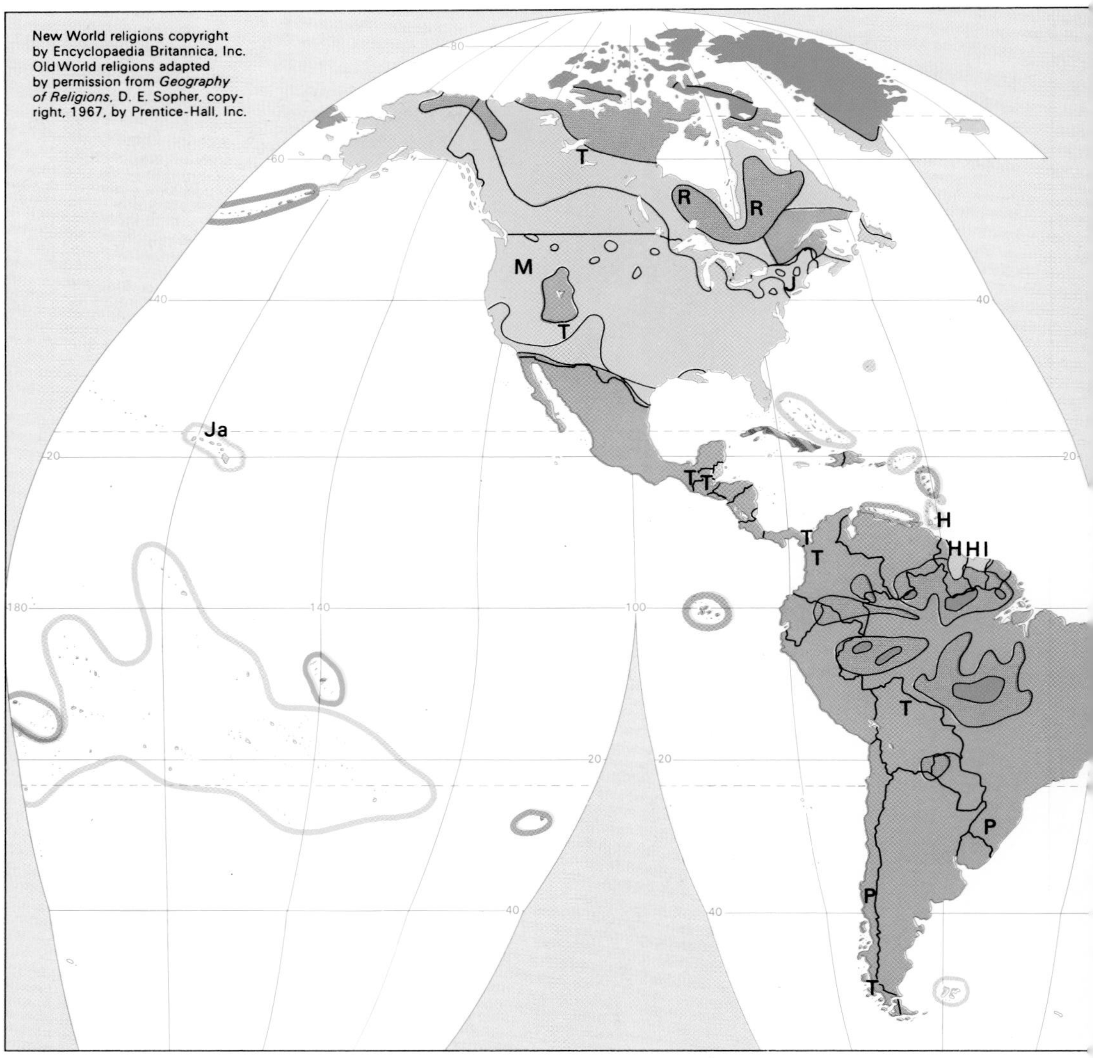
New World religions copyright
by Encyclopaedia Britannica, Inc.
Old World religions adapted
by permission from *Geography of Religions*, D. E. Sopher, copyright, 1967, by Prentice-Hall, Inc.
T
R
R
M
T
Ja
H
HHI
P
P

Languages

Languages of Europe

The following languages are ranked in descending order by number of speakers. Languages spoken by more than 4.5 million people are indicated by color. Others listed, spoken by fewer than 4.5 million persons, are named on the map.

Russian, German, Italian, English, French, Ukrainian, Polish, Spanish, Romanian, Serbo-Croatian, Dutch-Flemish, Hungarian, Portuguese, Czech, Belorussian, Greek, Bulgarian, Swedish, Catalan, Danish, Turkish, Slovak, Albanian, Finnish, All others

Norwegian, Lithuanian, Chuvash, Slovenian, Macedonian, Latvian, Mordvinian, Estonian, Breton, Basque, Irish-Gaelic, Mari, Welsh, Friulian, Komi, Frisian, Sardinian, Maltese, Karelian, Icelandic, Adyge, Scots-Gaelic, Romansh, Lappish, Lusatian, Ladin

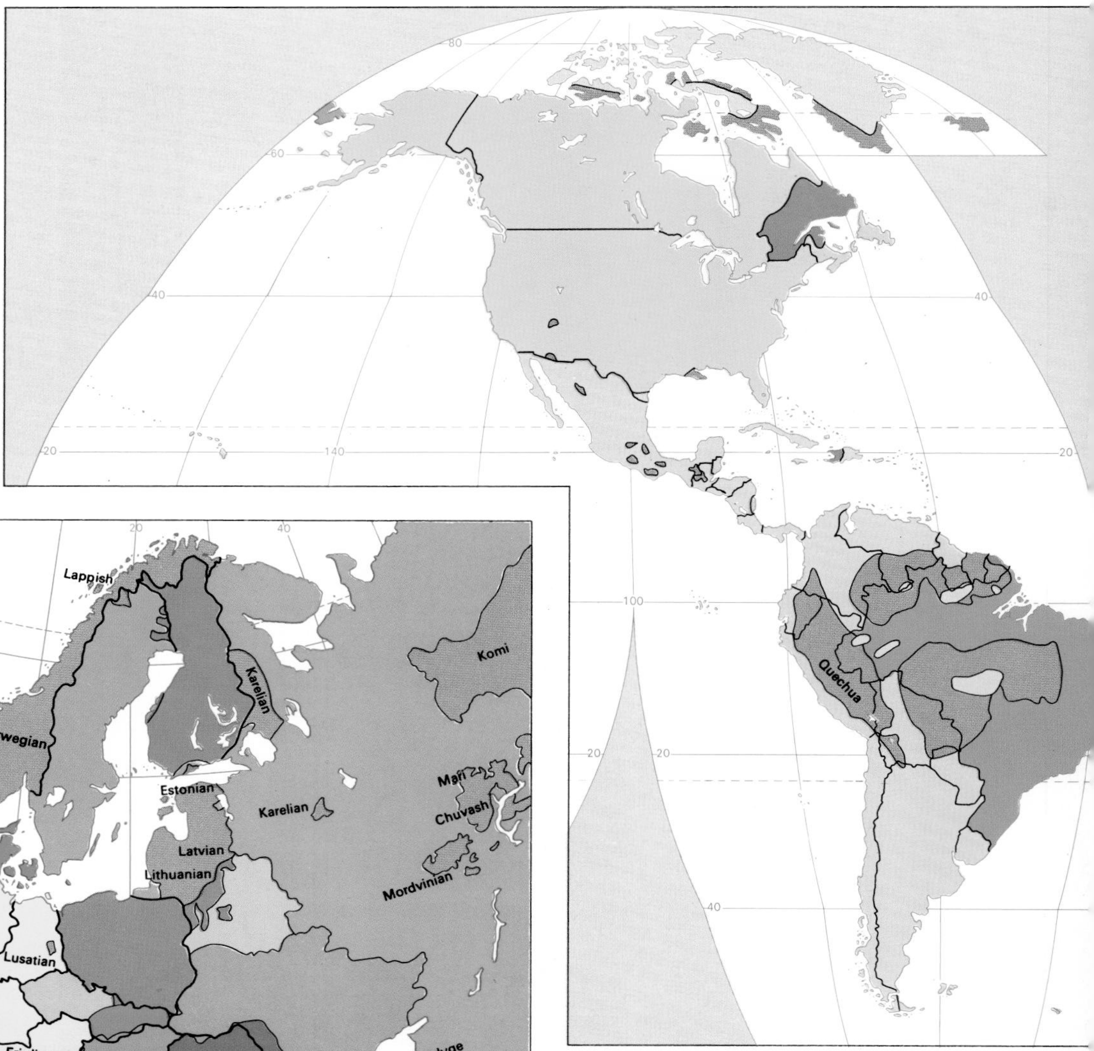
Quechua

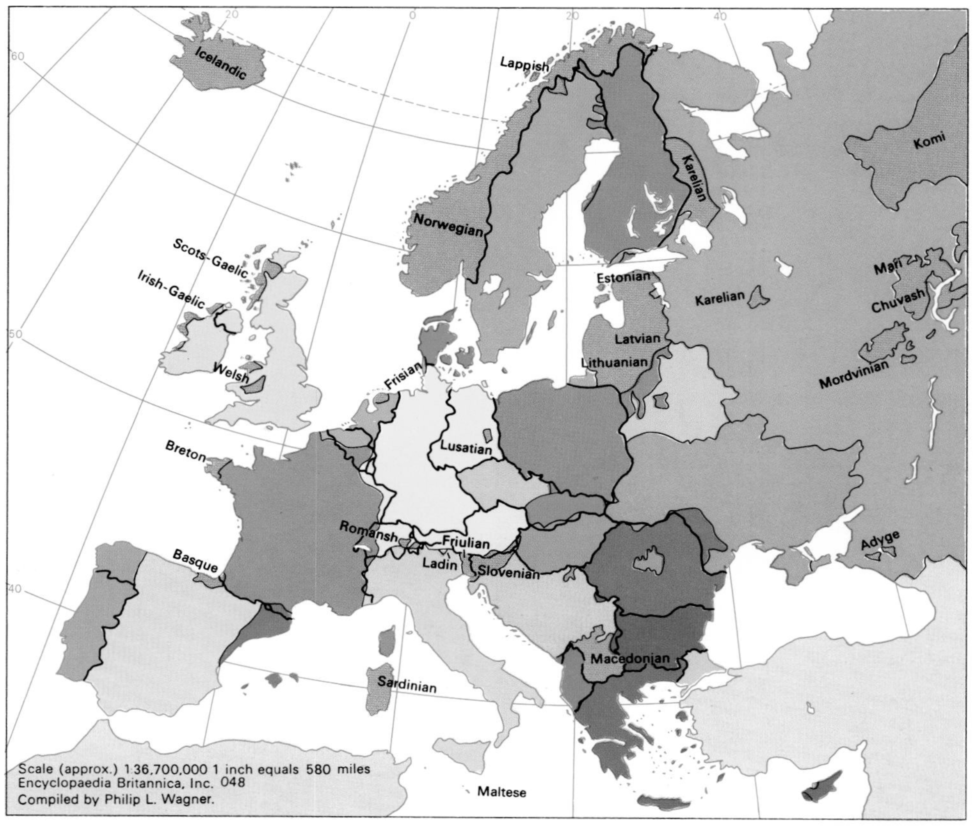
Icelandic
Lappish
Karelian
Komi
Norwegian
Scots-Gaelic
Irish-Gaelic
Estonian
Karelian
Mari
Chuvash
Latvian
Lithuanian
Welsh
Frisian
Mordvinian
Lusatian
Breton
Romansh
Friulian
Ladin
Slovenian
Basque
Adyge
Macedonian
Sardinian
Maltese
Scale (approx.) 1:36,700,000 1 inch equals 580 miles
Encyclopaedia Britannica, Inc. 048
Compiled by Philip L. Wagner.

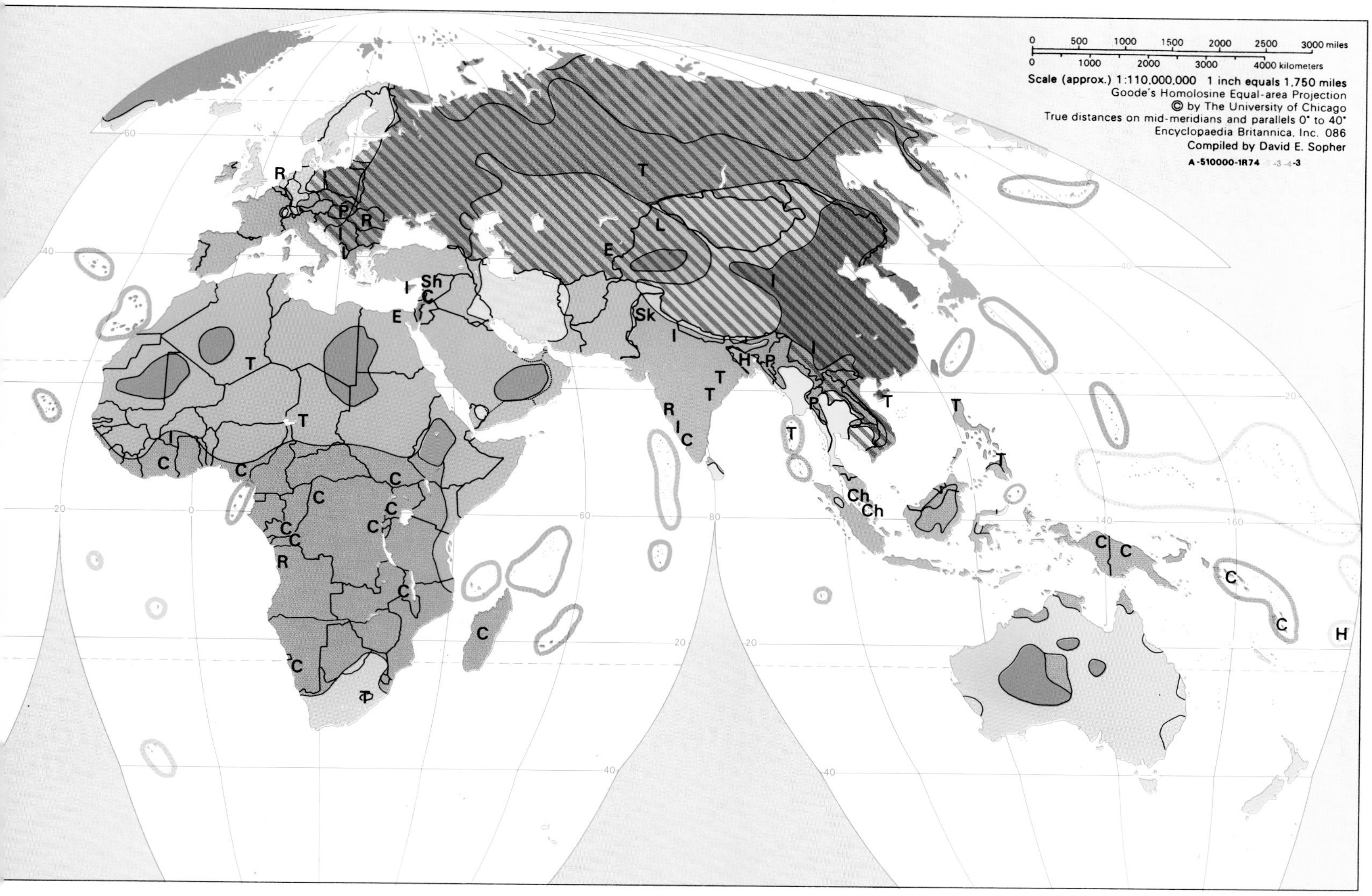

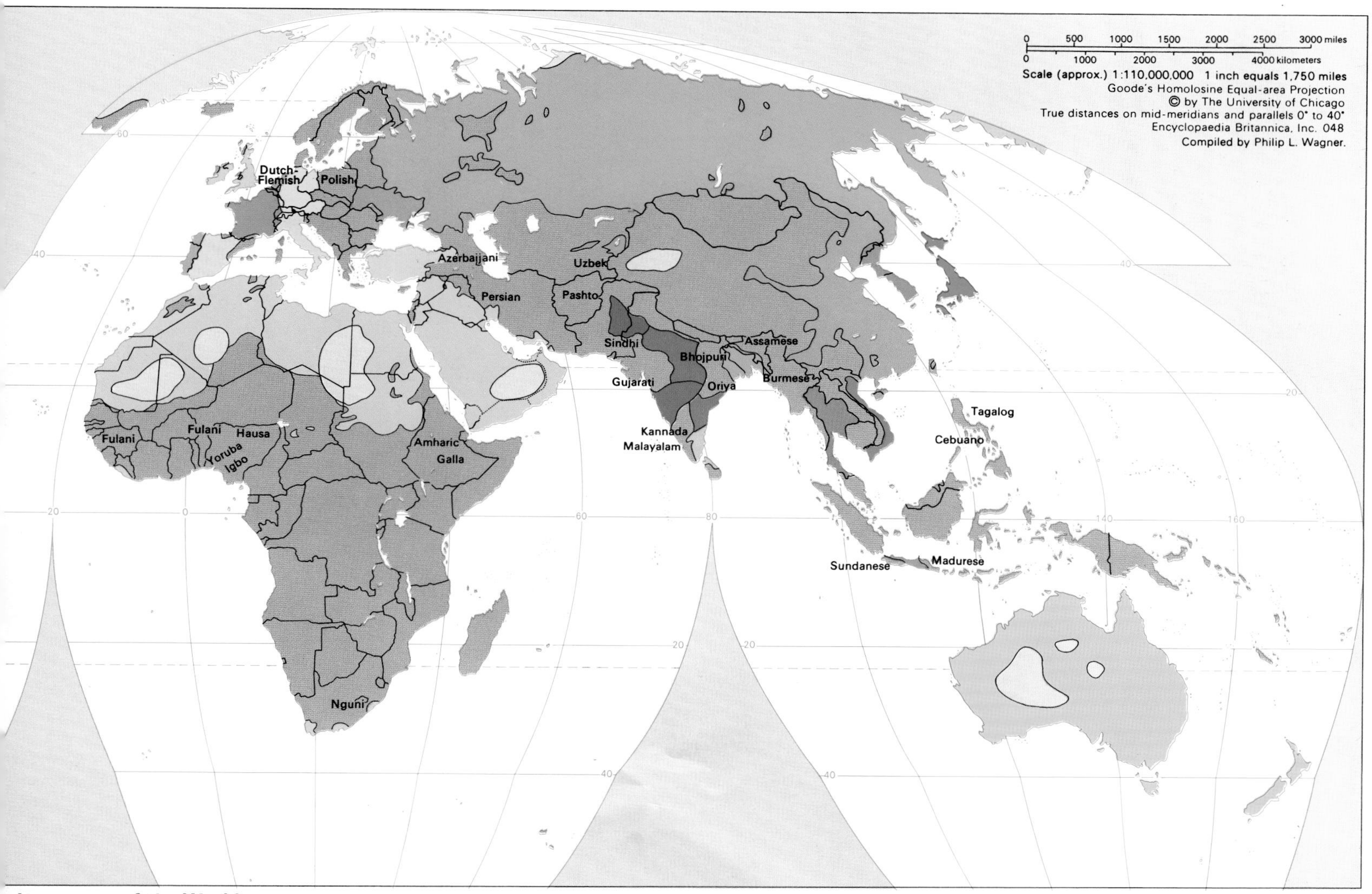

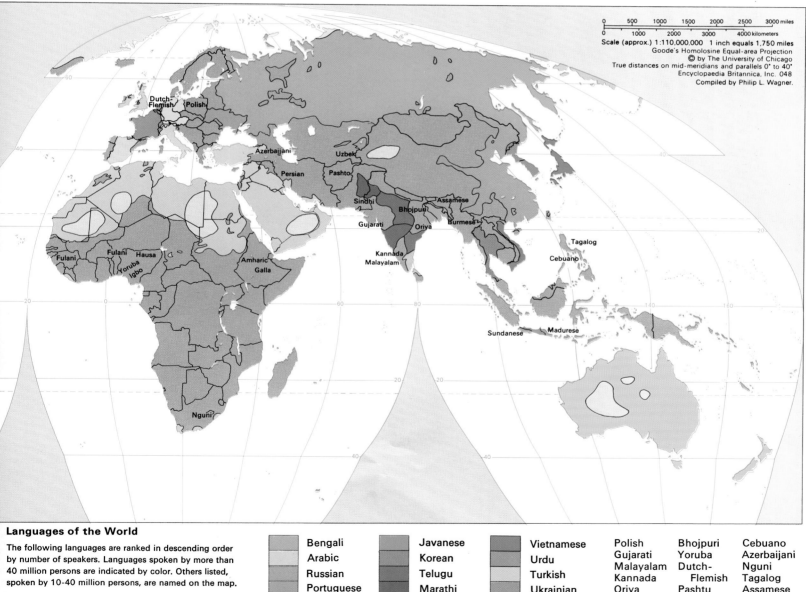

Languages of the World

The following languages are ranked in descending order by number of speakers. Languages spoken by more than 40 million persons are indicated by color. Others listed, spoken by 10-40 million persons, are named on the map.

- Chinese
- Spanish
- English
- Hindi
- Bengali
- Arabic
- Russian
- Portuguese
- Japanese
- German
- Punjabi
- Javanese
- Korean
- Telugu
- Marathi
- French
- Italian
- Tamil
- Vietnamese
- Urdu
- Turkish
- Ukrainian
- Thai
- All others
- Uninhabited

Polish
Gujarati
Malayalam
Kannada
Oriya
Burmese
Persian
Hausa
Sundanese
Bhojpuri
Yoruba
Dutch-Flemish
Pashtu
Fulani
Igbo
Uzbek
Galla
Cebuano
Azerbaijani
Nguni
Tagalog
Assamese
Sindhi
Amharic
Madurese

Agricultural Regions

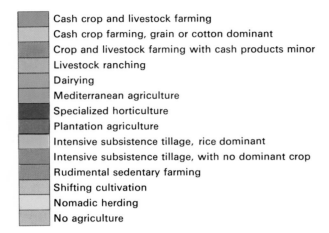

- Cash crop and livestock farming
- Cash crop farming, grain or cotton dominant
- Crop and livestock farming with cash products minor
- Livestock ranching
- Dairying
- Mediterranean agriculture
- Specialized horticulture
- Plantation agriculture
- Intensive subsistence tillage, rice dominant
- Intensive subsistence tillage, with no dominant crop
- Rudimental sedentary farming
- Shifting cultivation
- Nomadic herding
- No agriculture

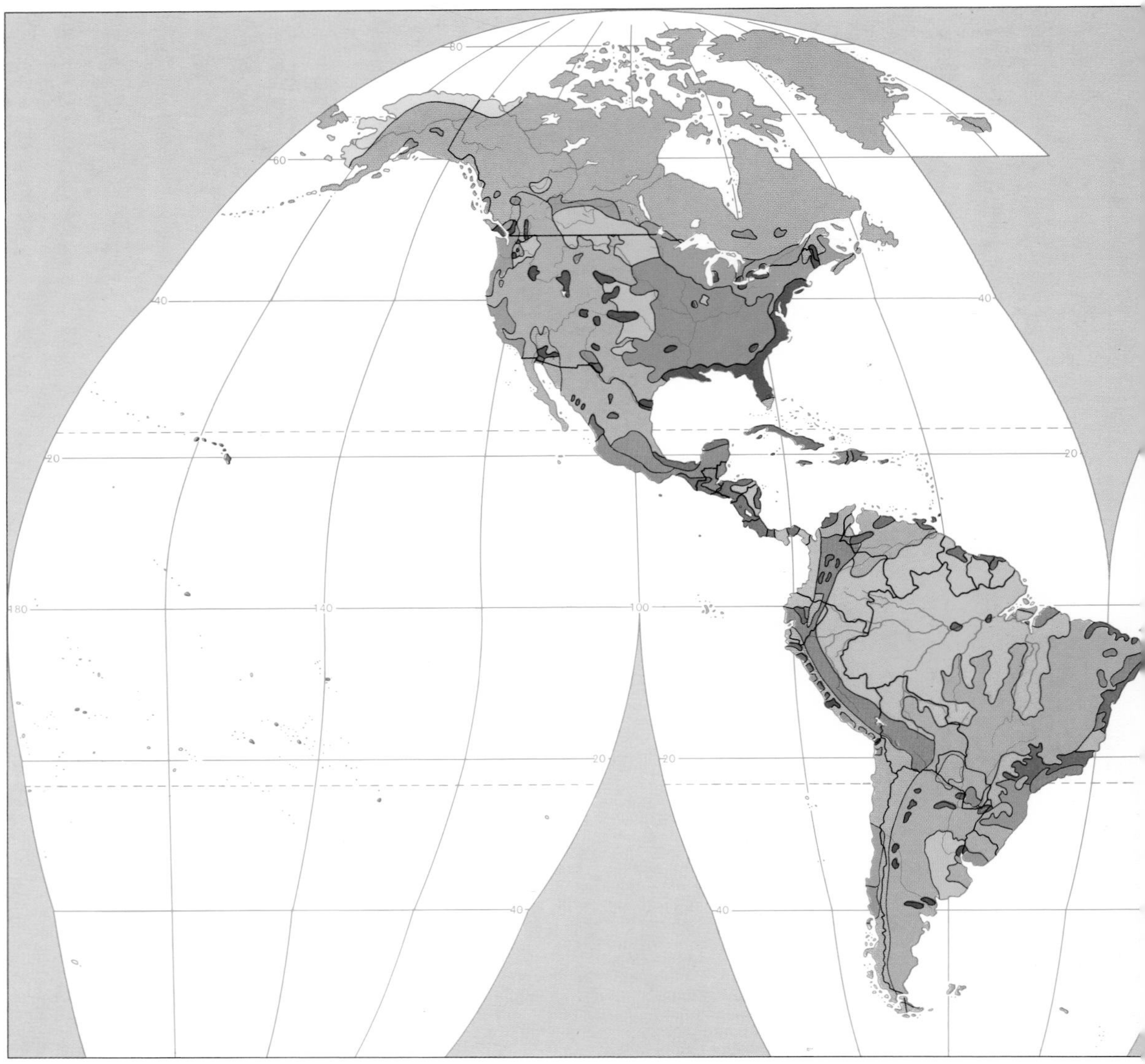

Forests and Fisheries

Forests

- Conifers: cedar, fir, hemlock, pine, redwood, spruce
- Regions of exploitation
- Tropical hardwoods: ebony, mahogany, rosewood, teak
- Regions of exploitation
- Temperate hardwoods: hickory, maple, oak, poplar, walnut, and some mixed hardwoods and conifers
- Regions of exploitation

Fisheries

- Pelagic fishing regions: anchoveta, anchovy, herring, menhaden, pilchard, sardine, sprat, tuna
- Ground fishing regions: cod, haddock, hake, horse mackerel, mackerel, pollack, redfish
- Mixed ground and pelagic fishing regions
- Shellfish: clam, crab, lobster, mussel, oyster, scallop, shrimp, squid
- Whales: blue, fin, minke, pilot, sei, sperm. Each represents an average annual catch of about 300 whales; Each represents an average annual catch of less than 200 whales
- Fishing regions showing percentage of world catch (excluding whales)

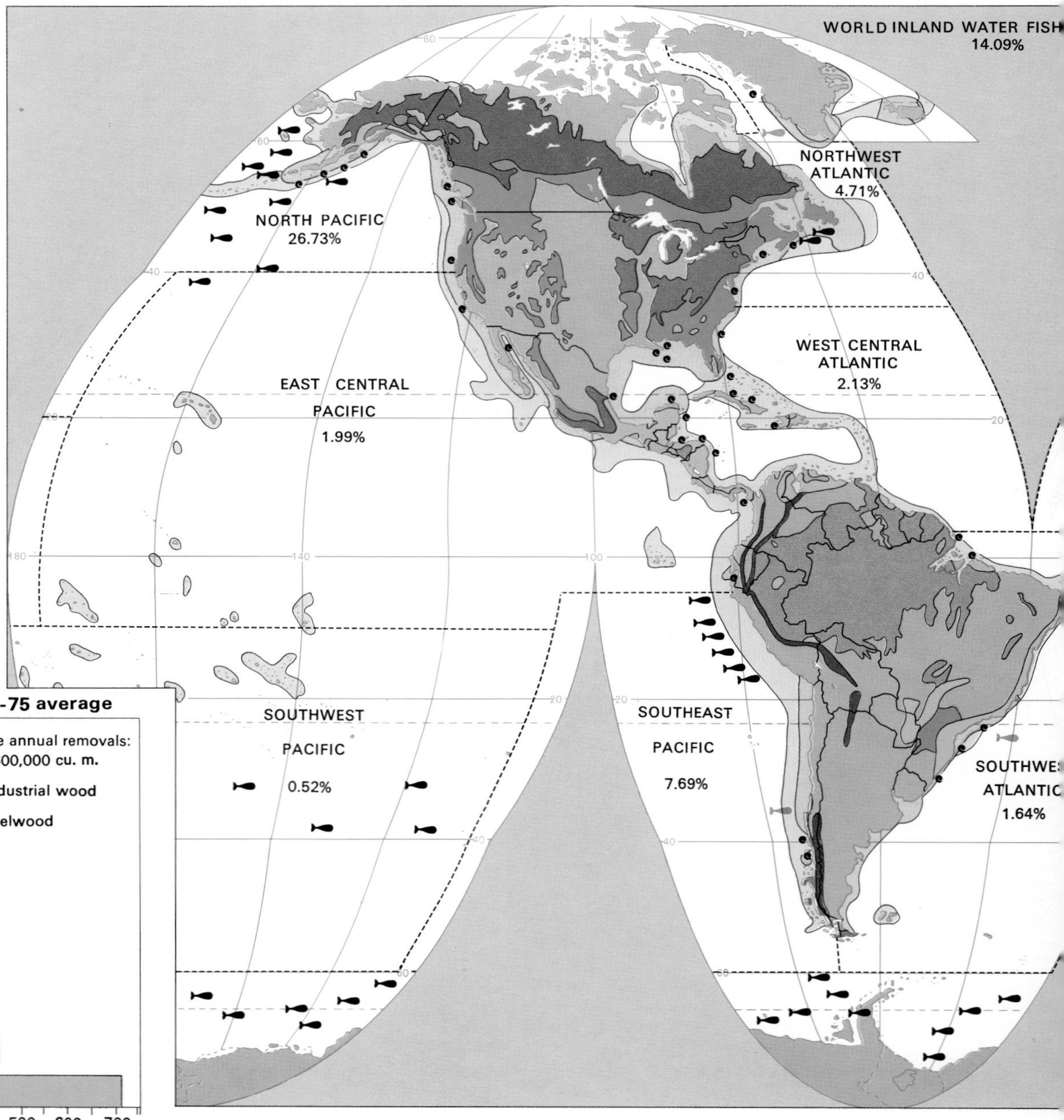
WORLD INLAND WATER FISH
14.09%
NORTHWEST ATLANTIC
4.71%
NORTH PACIFIC
26.73%
WEST CENTRAL ATLANTIC
2.13%
EAST CENTRAL PACIFIC
1.99%
SOUTHWEST PACIFIC
0.52%
SOUTHEAST PACIFIC
7.69%
SOUTHWE ATLANTIC
1.64%

Fishing catch (live weight) 1971-75 average

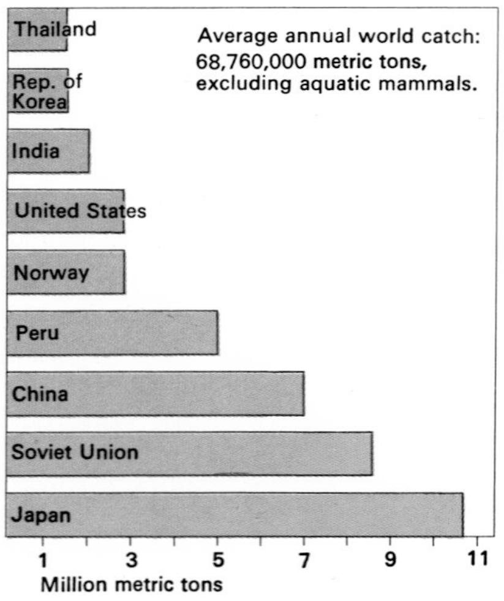
Average annual world catch: 68,760,000 metric tons, excluding aquatic mammals.
Thailand
Rep. of Korea
India
United States
Norway
Peru
China
Soviet Union
Japan
1
3
5
7
9
11
Million metric tons

Forest removals 1971-75 average

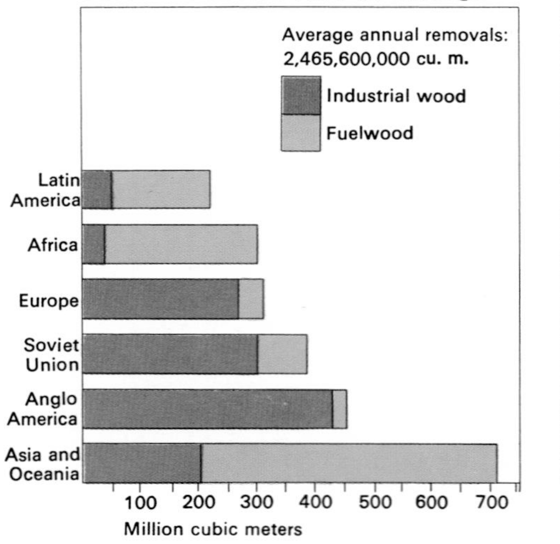
Average annual removals: 2,465,600,000 cu. m.
Industrial wood
Fuelwood
Latin America
Africa
Europe
Soviet Union
Anglo America
Asia and Oceania
100
200
300
400
500
600
700
Million cubic meters

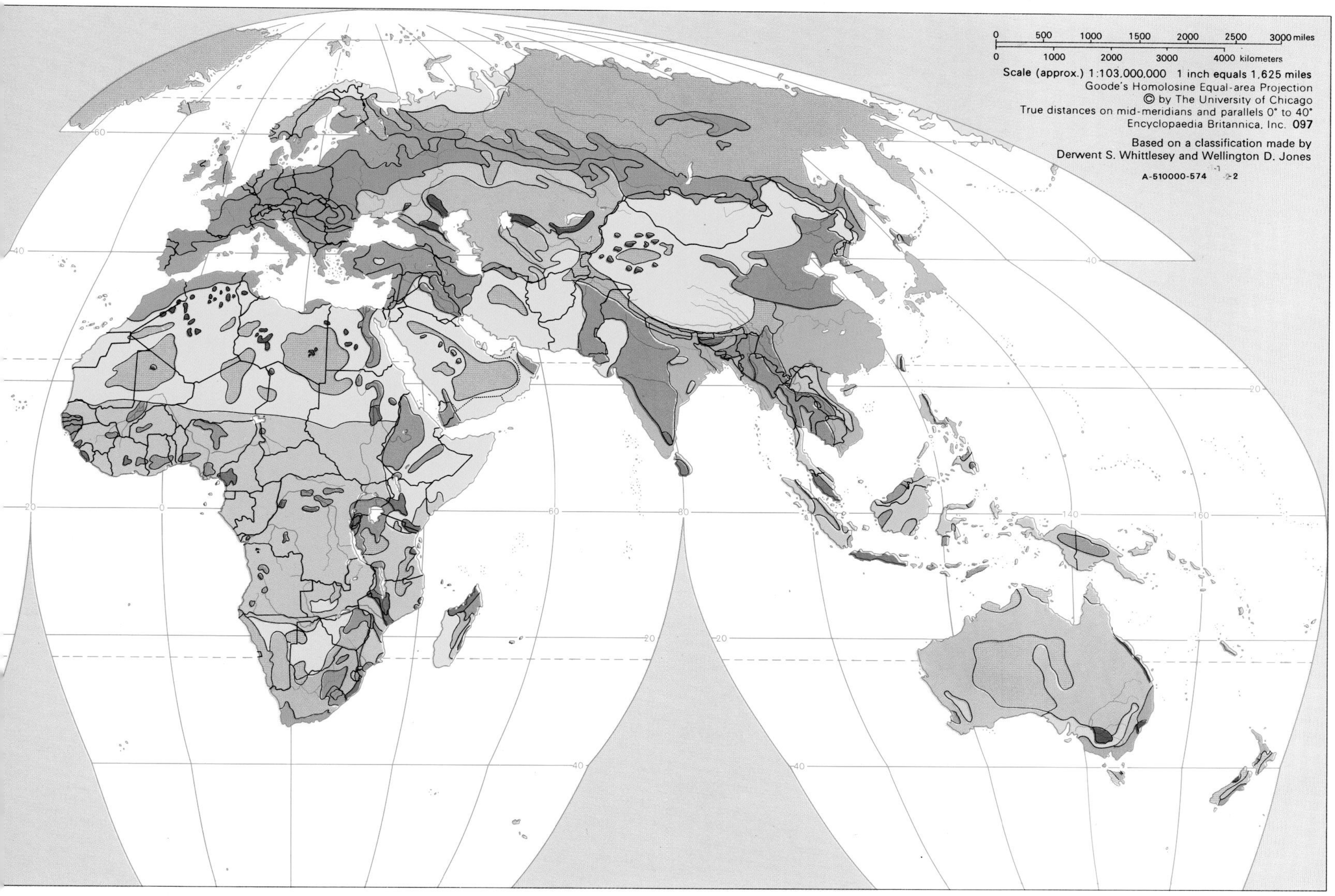
0 500 1000 1500 2000 2500 3000 miles
0 1000 2000 3000 4000 kilometers
Scale (approx.) 1:103,000,000 1 inch equals 1,625 miles
Goode's Homolosine Equal-area Projection
© by The University of Chicago
True distances on mid-meridians and parallels 0° to 40°
Encyclopaedia Britannica, Inc. 097
Based on a classification made by
Derwent S. Whittlesey and Wellington D. Jones
A-510000-574

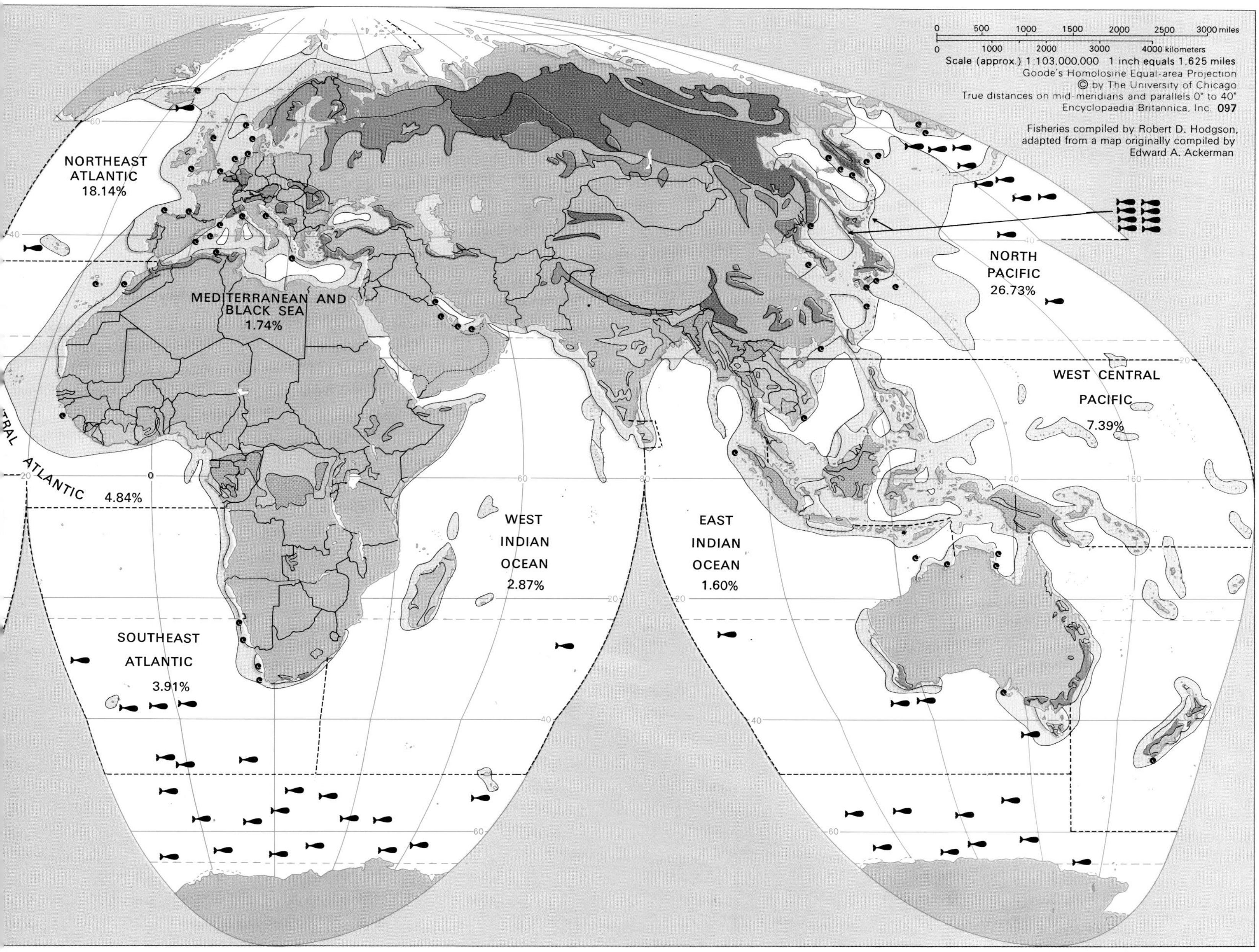
0 500 1000 1500 2000 2500 3000 miles
0 1000 2000 3000 4000 kilometers
Scale (approx.) 1:103,000,000 1 inch equals 1,625 miles
Goode's Homolosine Equal-area Projection
© by The University of Chicago
True distances on mid-meridians and parallels 0° to 40°
Encyclopaedia Britannica, Inc. 097
Fisheries compiled by Robert D. Hodgson,
adapted from a map originally compiled by
Edward A. Ackerman
NORTHEAST ATLANTIC 18.14%
MEDITERRANEAN AND BLACK SEA 1.74%
NORTH PACIFIC 26.73%
WEST CENTRAL PACIFIC 7.39%
ATLANTIC 4.84%
WEST INDIAN OCEAN 2.87%
EAST INDIAN OCEAN 1.60%
SOUTHEAST ATLANTIC 3.91%

Minerals

4-year world average production shown in graphs. Producing areas shown on maps

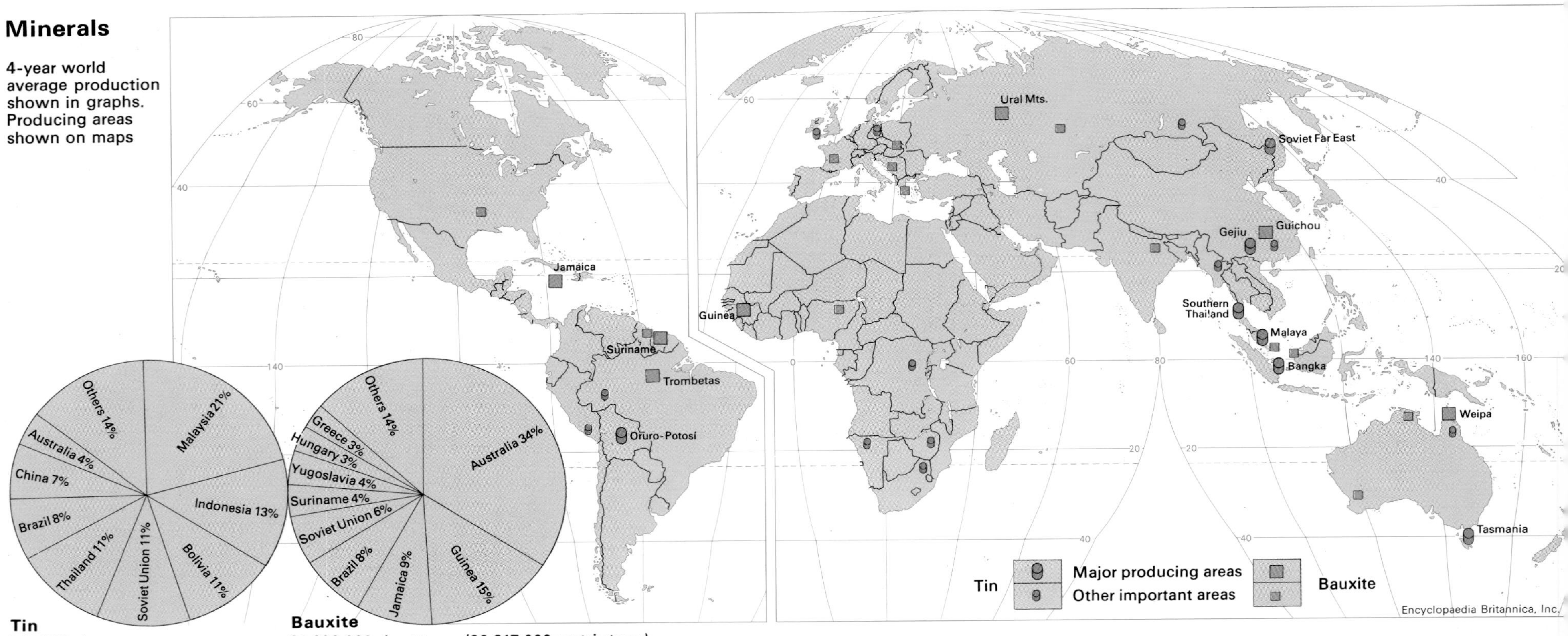

Others 14%
Malaysia 21%
Indonesia 13%
Bolivia 11%
Soviet Union 11%
Thailand 11%
Brazil 8%
China 7%
Australia 4%
Others 14%
Australia 34%
Guinea 15%
Jamaica 9%
Brazil 8%
Soviet Union 6%
Suriname 4%
Yugoslavia 4%
Hungary 3%
Greece 3%
Ural Mts.
Soviet Far East
Gejiu
Guichou
Southern Thailand
Malaya
Bangka
Weipa
Tasmania
Jamaica
Guinea
Suriname
Trombetas
Oruro-Potosí
Tin
Major producing areas
Other important areas
Bauxite
Encyclopaedia Britannica, Inc.

Tin
222,200 short tons
(201,600 metric tons)

Bauxite
91,290,000 short tons (82,817,000 metric tons)

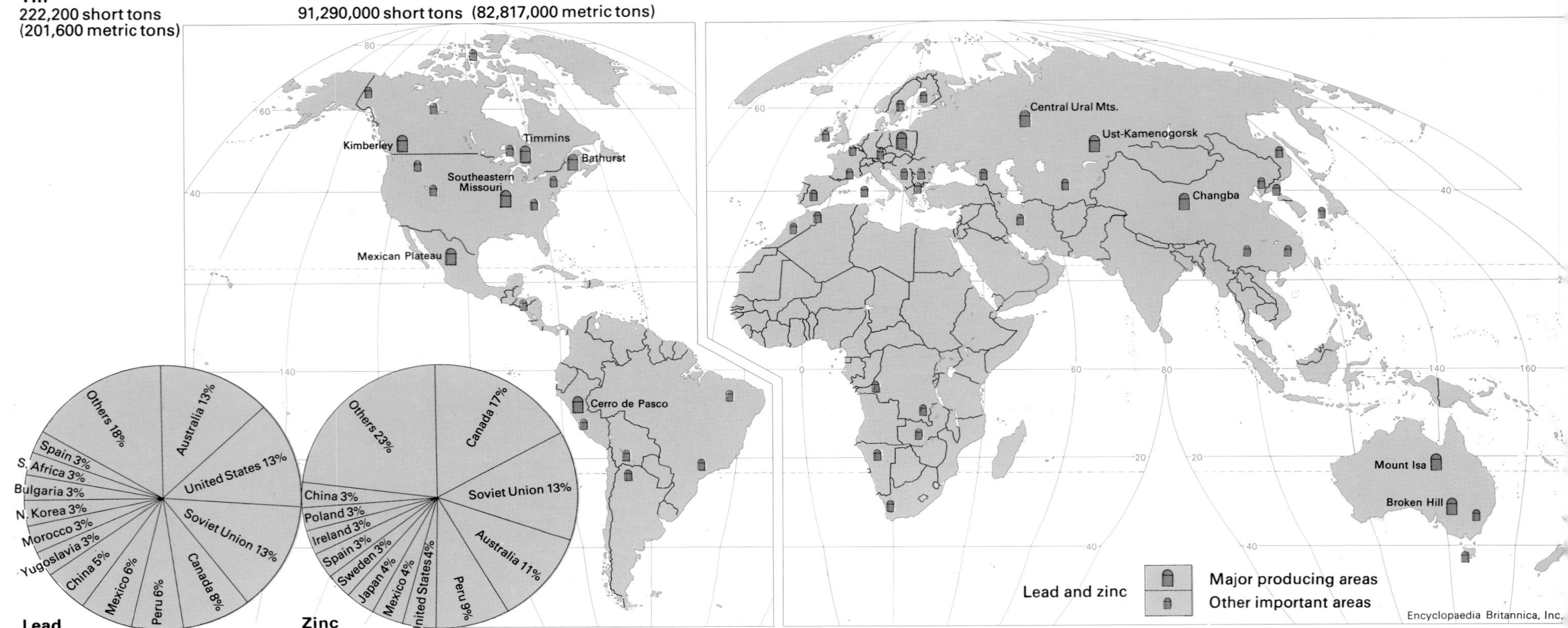

Others 18%
Australia 13%
United States 13%
Soviet Union 13%
Canada 8%
Peru 6%
Mexico 6%
China 5%
Yugoslavia 3%
Morocco 3%
N. Korea 3%
Bulgaria 3%
S. Africa 3%
Spain 3%
Others 23%
Canada 17%
Soviet Union 13%
Australia 11%
Peru 9%
United States 4%
Mexico 4%
Japan 4%
Sweden 3%
Spain 3%
Ireland 3%
Poland 3%
China 3%
Kimberley
Timmins
Bathurst
Southeastern Missouri
Mexican Plateau
Cerro de Pasco
Central Ural Mts.
Ust-Kamenogorsk
Changba
Mount Isa
Broken Hill
Lead and zinc
Major producing areas
Other important areas
Encyclopaedia Britannica, Inc.

Lead
3,700,600 short tons
(3,357,200 metric tons)

Zinc
7,081,300 short tons (6,424,100 metric tons)

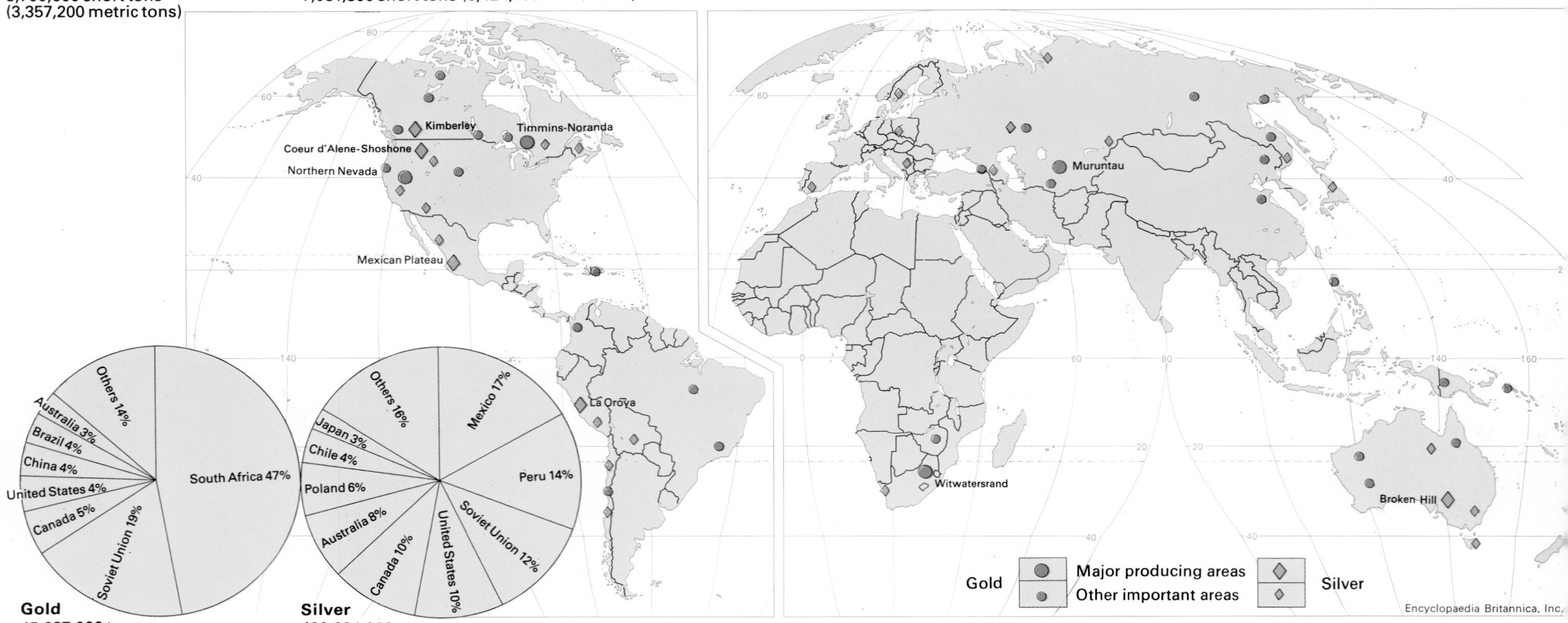

Others 14%
South Africa 47%
Soviet Union 19%
Canada 5%
United States 4%
China 4%
Brazil 4%
Australia 3%
Others 16%
Mexico 17%
Peru 14%
Soviet Union 12%
United States 10%
Canada 10%
Australia 8%
Poland 6%
Chile 4%
Japan 3%
Kimberley
Timmins-Noranda
Coeur d'Alene-Shoshone
Northern Nevada
Mexican Plateau
La Oroya
Muruntau
Witwatersrand
Broken Hill
Gold
Major producing areas
Other important areas
Silver
Encyclopaedia Britannica, Inc.

Gold
45,687,000 troy ounces
(1,421,000 kilograms)

Silver
400,634,000 troy ounces
(12,461,000 kilograms)

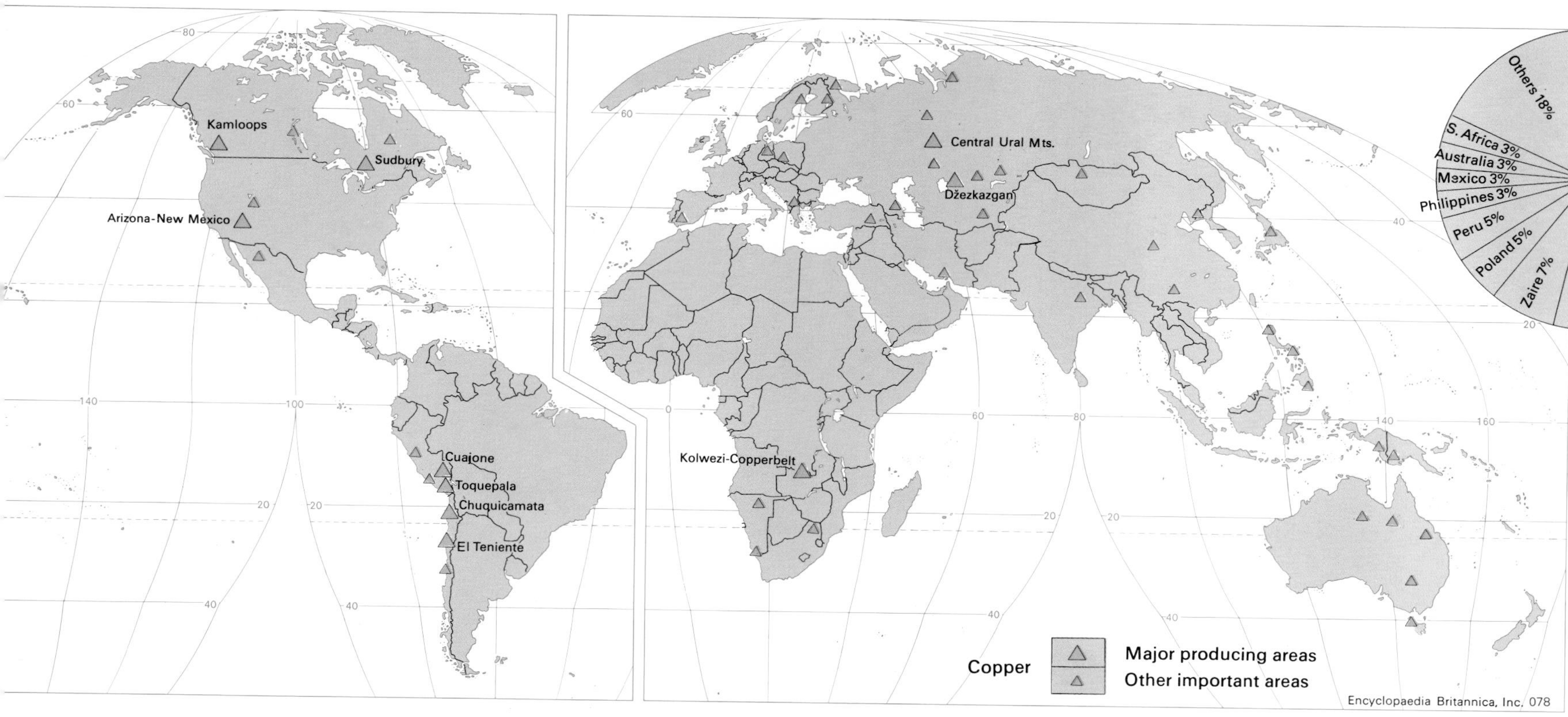
Kamloops
Sudbury
Arizona-New Mexico
Cuajone
Toquepala
Chuquicamata
El Teniente
Central Ural Mts.
Džezkazgan
Kolwezi-Copperbelt
Copper
Major producing areas
Other important areas
Encyclopaedia Britannica, Inc. 078

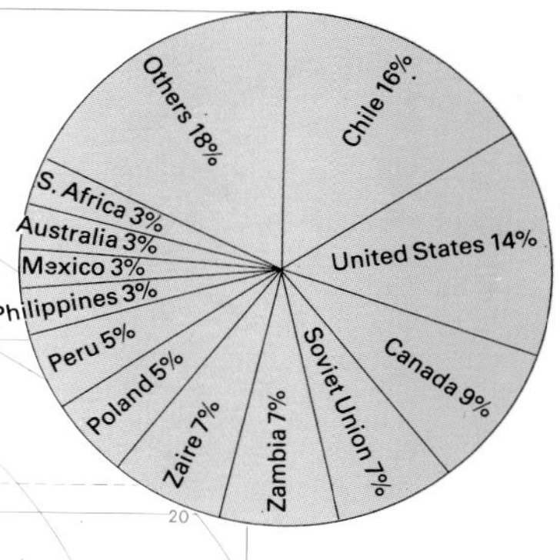
Others 18%
Chile 16%
United States 14%
Canada 9%
Soviet Union 7%
Zambia 7%
Zaire 7%
Poland 5%
Peru 5%
Philippines 3%
Mexico 3%
Australia 3%
S. Africa 3%

Copper
8,661,600
short tons
(7,857,700
metric tons)

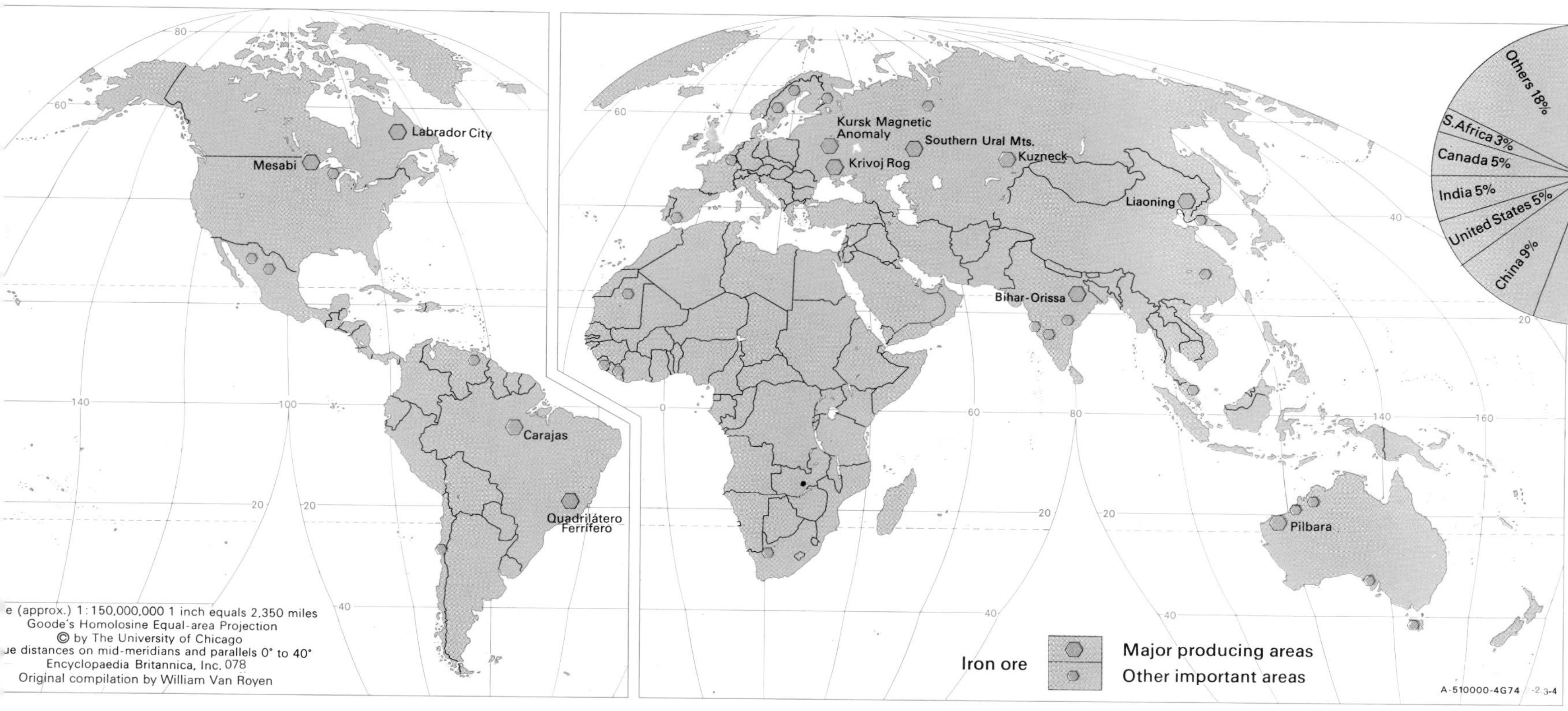
Labrador City
Mesabi
Kursk Magnetic Anomaly
Krivoj Rog
Southern Ural Mts.
Kuzneck
Liaoning
Bihar-Orissa
Carajas
Quadrilátero Ferrífero
Pilbara
e (approx.) 1:150,000,000 1 inch equals 2,350 miles
Goode's Homolosine Equal-area Projection
© by The University of Chicago
ue distances on mid-meridians and parallels 0° to 40°
Encyclopaedia Britannica, Inc. 078
Original compilation by William Van Royen
Iron ore
Major producing areas
Other important areas
A-510000-4G74

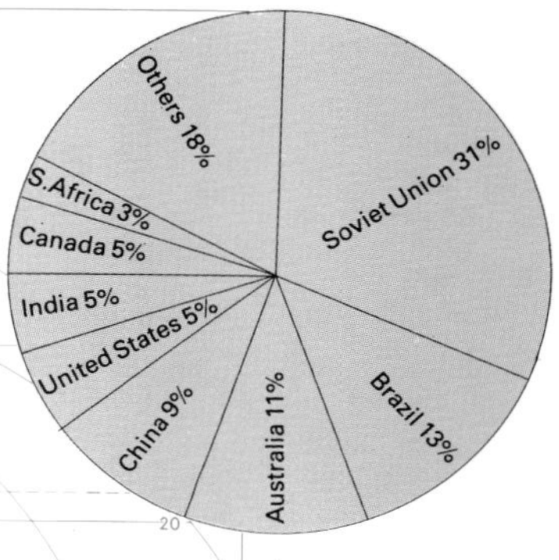
Others 18%
Soviet Union 31%
Brazil 13%
Australia 11%
China 9%
United States 5%
India 5%
Canada 5%
S.Africa 3%

Iron ore
883,984,900
short tons
(801,937,600
metric tons)

Ferroalloying Minerals

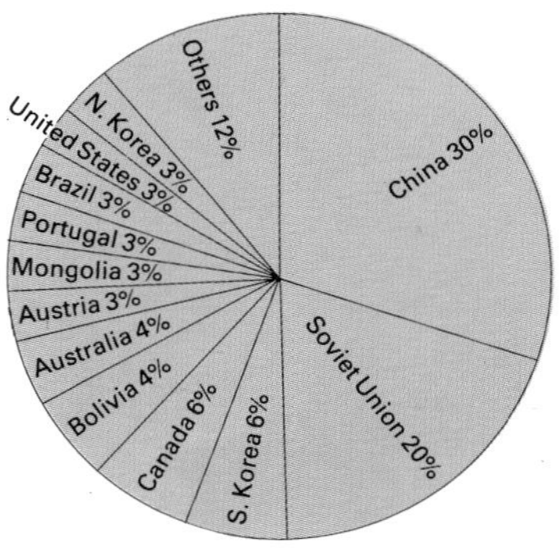
Others 12%
China 30%
Soviet Union 20%
S. Korea 6%
Canada 6%
Bolivia 4%
Australia 4%
Austria 3%
Mongolia 3%
Portugal 3%
Brazil 3%
United States 3%
N. Korea 3%

Tungsten
49,900 short tons
(45,300 metric tons)

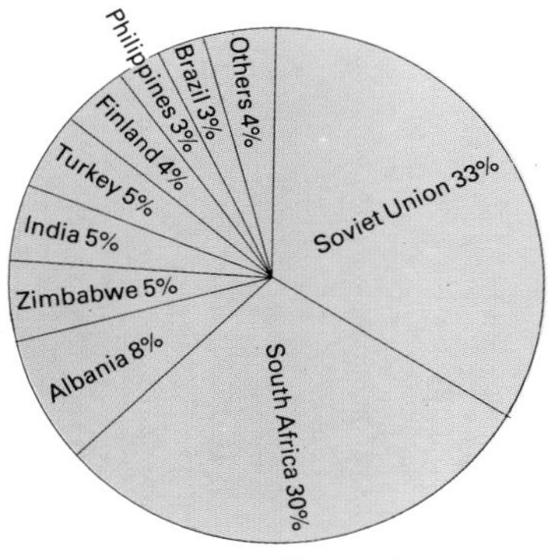
Others 4%
Soviet Union 33%
South Africa 30%
Albania 8%
Zimbabwe 5%
India 5%
Turkey 5%
Finland 4%
Philippines 3%
Brazil 3%

Chromite
9,779,500 short tons
(8,871,800 metric tons)

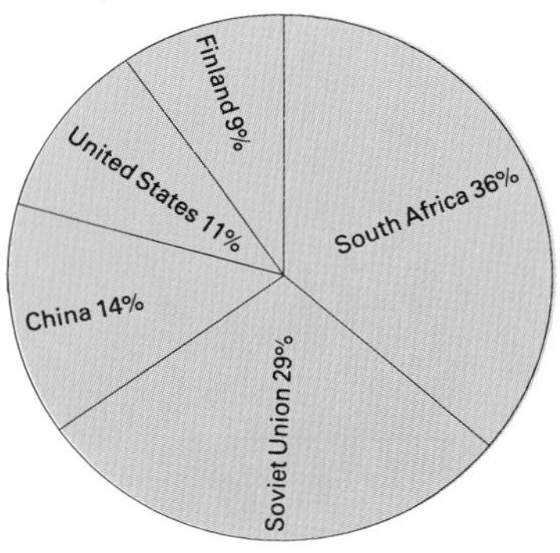
Finland 9%
South Africa 36%
Soviet Union 29%
China 14%
United States 11%

Vanadium
36,200 short tons
(32,900 metric tons)

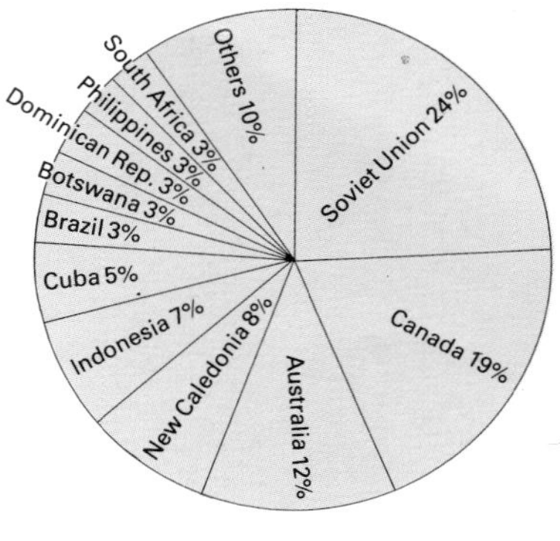
Others 10%
Soviet Union 24%
Canada 19%
Australia 12%
New Caledonia 8%
Indonesia 7%
Cuba 5%
Brazil 3%
Botswana 3%
Dominican Rep. 3%
Philippines 3%
South Africa 3%

Nickel
776,600 short tons
(704,500 metric tons)

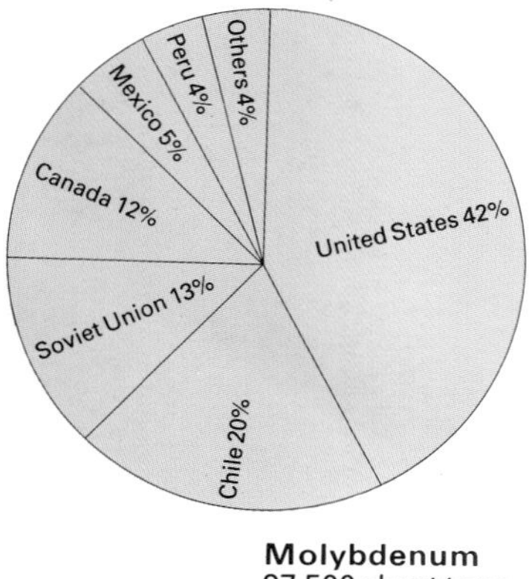
Others 4%
United States 42%
Chile 20%
Soviet Union 13%
Canada 12%
Mexico 5%
Peru 4%

Molybdenum
97,500 short tons
(88,400 metric tons)

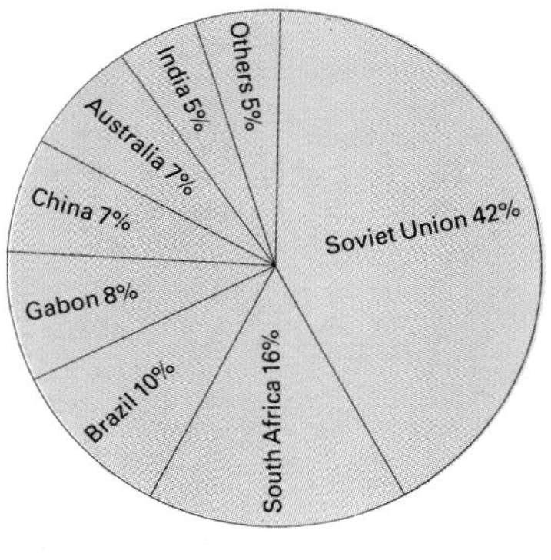
Others 5%
Soviet Union 42%
South Africa 16%
Brazil 10%
Gabon 8%
China 7%
Australia 7%
India 5%

Manganese
25,960,000 short tons
(23,550,500 metric tons)

Energy Production and Consumption

Unit of measure is metric tons coal equivalent (m.t.c.e.)

Production

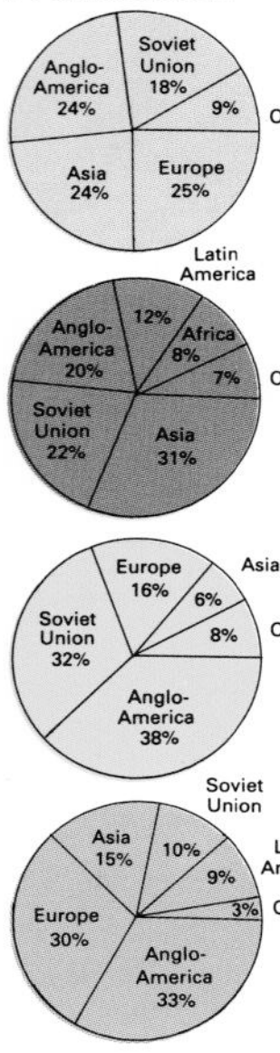
Anglo-America 24%
Soviet Union 18%
9%
Others
Asia 24%
Europe 25%
Latin America
Anglo-America 20%
12%
Africa 8%
7%
Others
Soviet Union 22%
Asia 31%
Europe 16%
Asia
6%
Soviet Union 32%
8%
Others
Anglo-America 38%
Soviet Union
Asia 15%
10%
Latin America
9%
3%
Others
Europe 30%
Anglo-America 33%

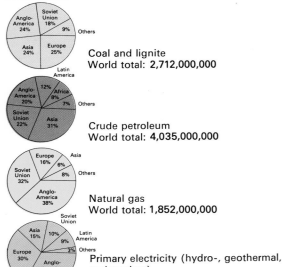

Coal and lignite
World total: **2,712,000,000**

Crude petroleum
World total: **4,035,000,000**

Natural gas
World total: **1,852,000,000**

Primary electricity (hydro-, geothermal, and nuclear)
World total: **334,000,000**

Table of equivalents

Coal, anthracite and bituminous	1 metric ton = 1.0 m.t.c.e.
Lignite	1 metric ton = 0.3 – 0.6 m.t.c.e.
Petroleum	1 metric ton = 1.5 m.t.c.e.
Natural gas	1,000 cubic meters = 1.33 m.t.c.e.
Hydro-, geothermal, and nuclear electricity	1.0 megawatt-hour = 0.125 m.t.c.e.

Potential energy of 1 metric ton of coal equals 28,000,000 B.T.U.

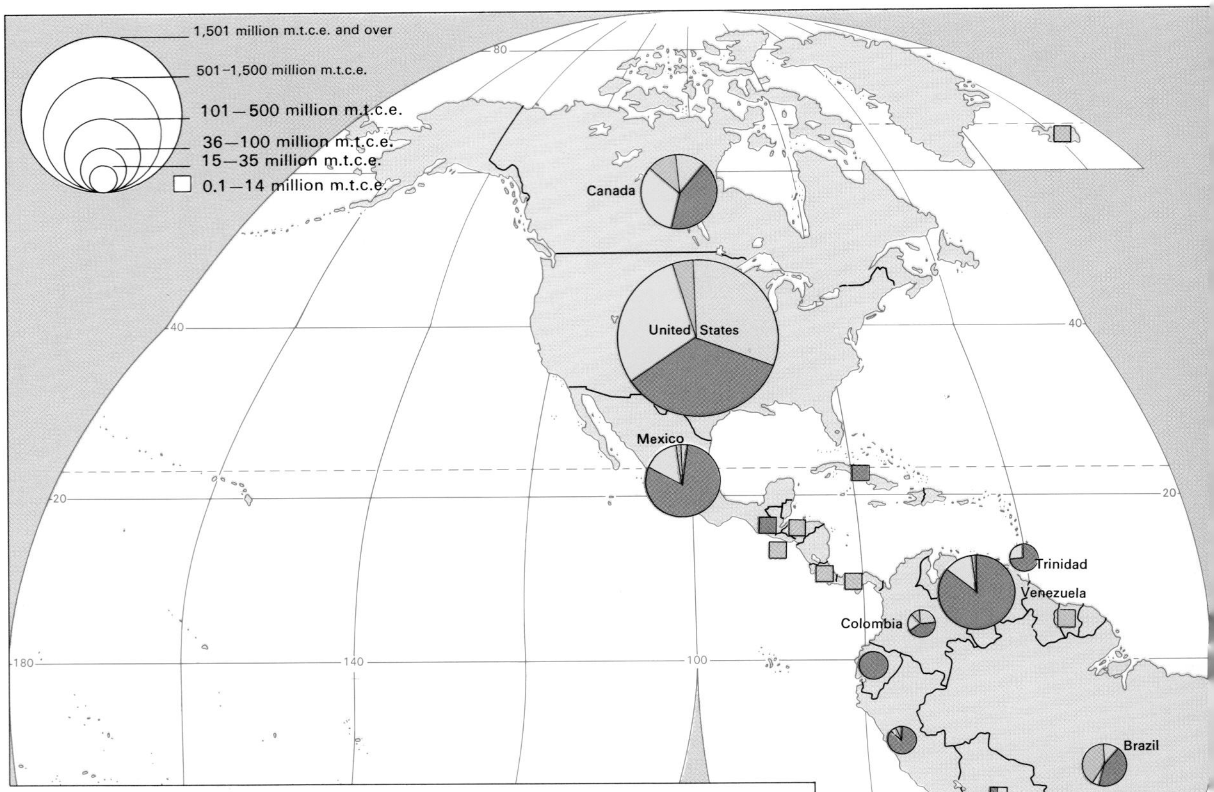
1,501 million m.t.c.e. and over
501–1,500 million m.t.c.e.
101 – 500 million m.t.c.e.
36 – 100 million m.t.c.e.
15 – 35 million m.t.c.e.
0.1 – 14 million m.t.c.e.
Canada
United States
Mexico
Trinidad
Venezuela
Colombia
Brazil

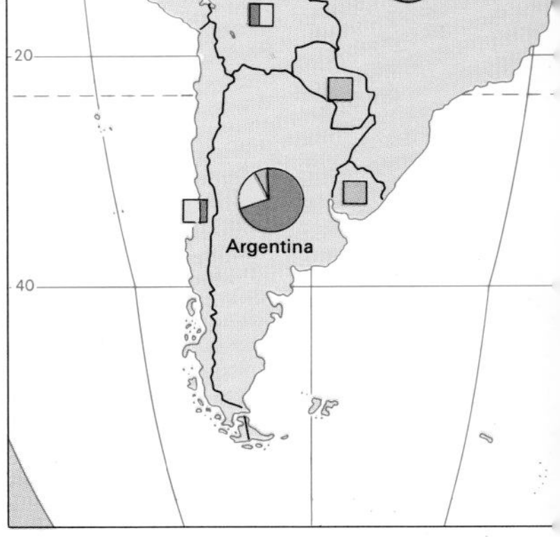
Argentina

Electricity production 1982

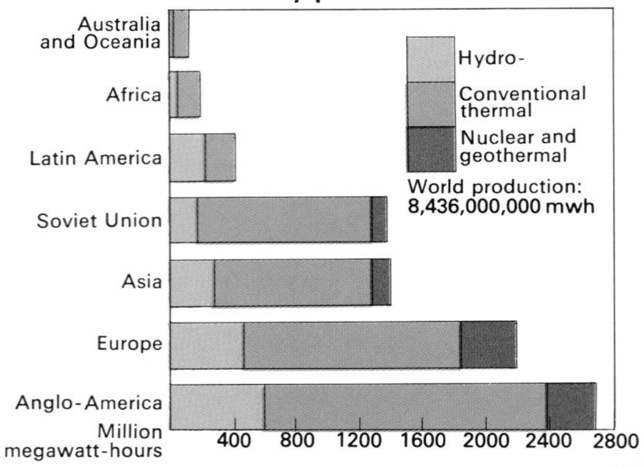
Australia and Oceania
Africa
Latin America
Soviet Union
Asia
Europe
Anglo-America
Hydro-
Conventional thermal
Nuclear and geothermal
World production: 8,436,000,000 mwh
Million megawatt-hours
400
800
1200
1600
2000
2400
2800

World production 1982

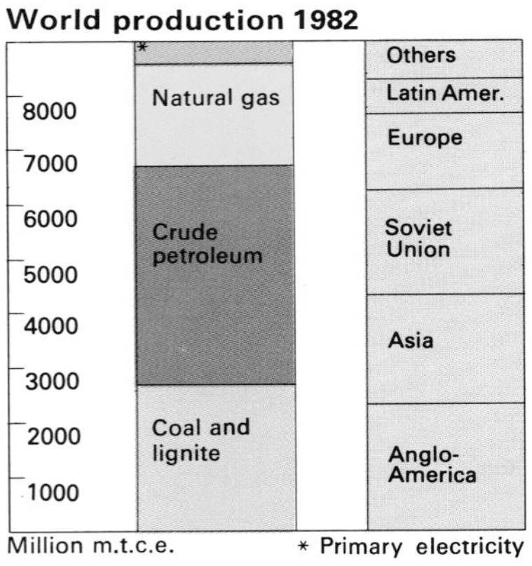
8000
7000
6000
5000
4000
3000
2000
1000
*
Natural gas
Crude petroleum
Coal and lignite
Others
Latin Amer.
Europe
Soviet Union
Asia
Anglo-America
Million m.t.c.e.
* Primary electricity

Consumption

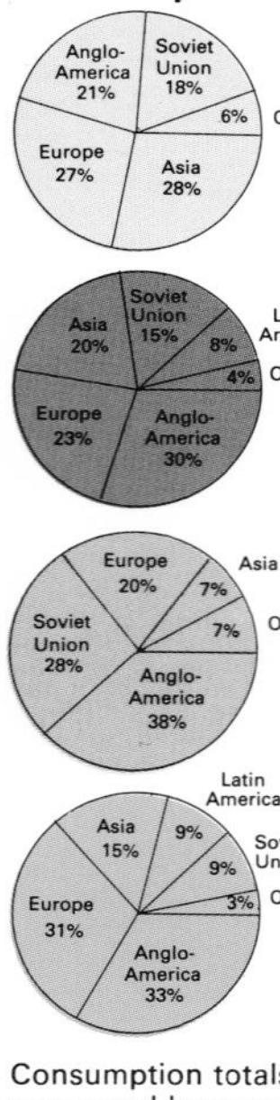
Anglo-America 21%
Soviet Union 18%
6%
Others
Europe 27%
Asia 28%
Soviet Union 15%
Latin America
Asia 20%
8%
4%
Others
Europe 23%
Anglo-America 30%
Europe 20%
Asia
7%
Soviet Union 28%
7%
Others
Anglo-America 38%
Latin America
Asia 15%
9%
Soviet Union
9%
3%
Others
Europe 31%
Anglo-America 33%

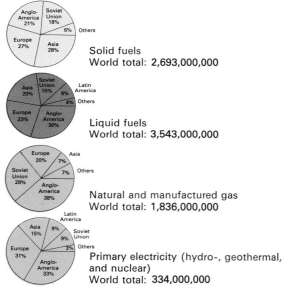

Solid fuels
World total: **2,693,000,000**

Liquid fuels
World total: **3,543,000,000**

Natural and manufactured gas
World total: **1,836,000,000**

Primary electricity (hydro-, geothermal, and nuclear)
World total: **334,000,000**

Consumption totals exclude noncommercial fuels, fuels consumed by vessels engaged in international trade, and nonfuel petroleum products.

Per capita consumption

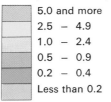

- 5.0 and more
- 2.5 – 4.9
- 1.0 – 2.4
- 0.5 – 0.9
- 0.2 – 0.4
- Less than 0.2

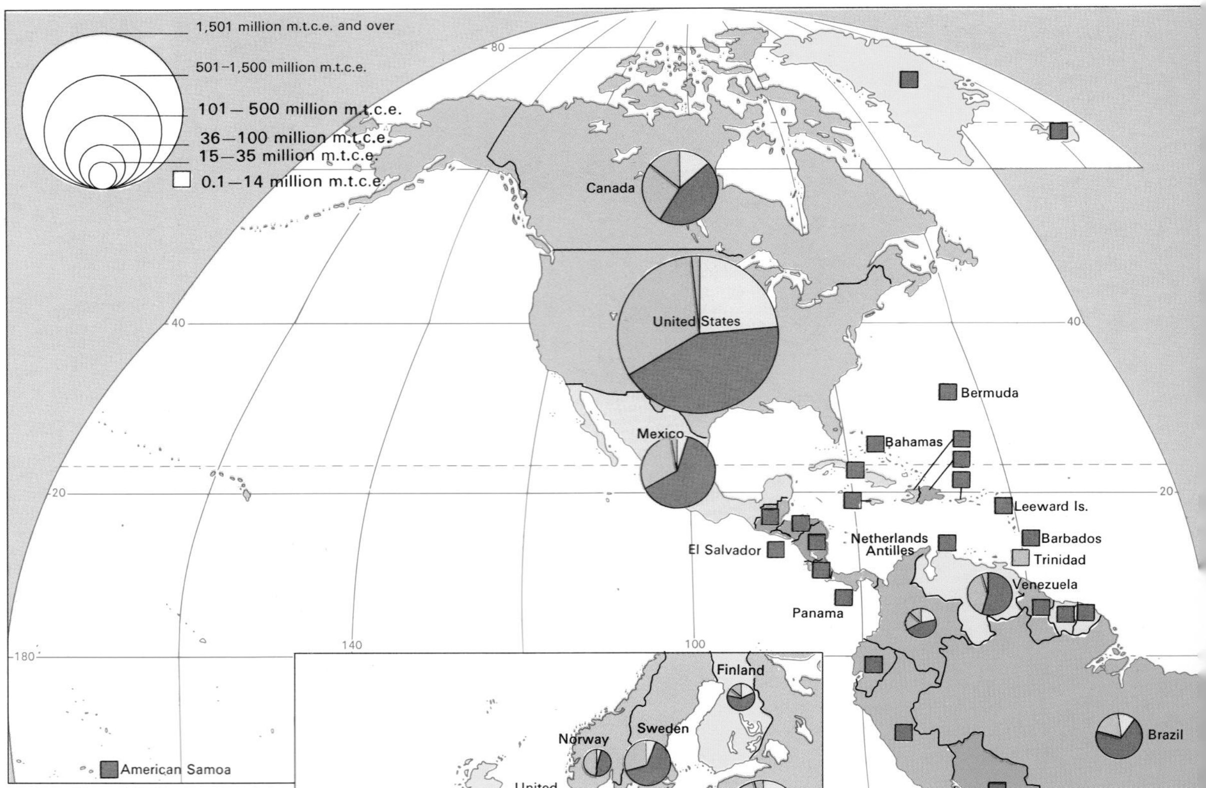
1,501 million m.t.c.e. and over
501–1,500 million m.t.c.e.
101 – 500 million m.t.c.e.
36 – 100 million m.t.c.e.
15 – 35 million m.t.c.e.
0.1 – 14 million m.t.c.e.
Canada
United States
Mexico
Bermuda
Bahamas
Leeward Is.
Barbados
Trinidad
Netherlands Antilles
El Salvador
Venezuela
Panama
Brazil
Argentina
American Samoa

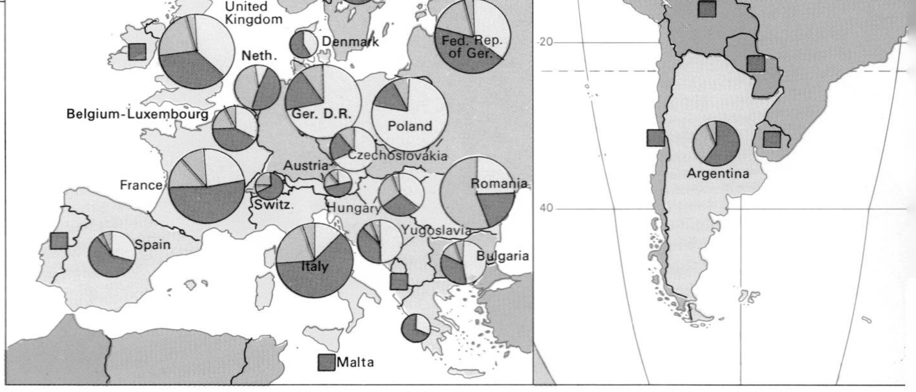
Finland
Norway
Sweden
United Kingdom
Denmark
Neth.
Fed. Rep. of Ger.
Belgium-Luxembourg
Ger. D.R.
Poland
Czechoslovakia
France
Austria
Switz.
Hungary
Romania
Yugoslavia
Spain
Italy
Bulgaria
Malta

World consumption 1982

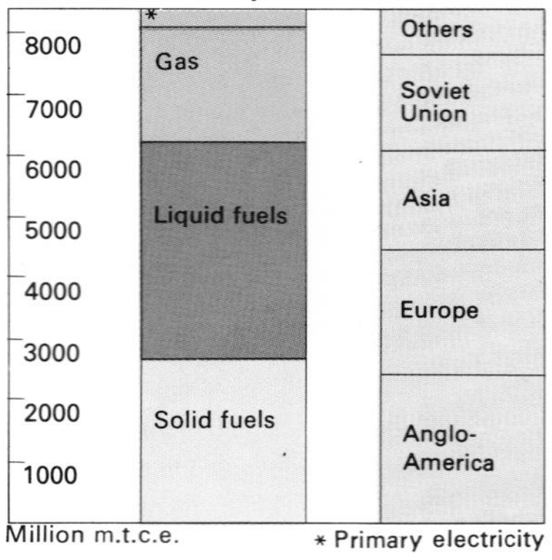
8000
7000
6000
5000
4000
3000
2000
1000
*
Gas
Liquid fuels
Solid fuels
Others
Soviet Union
Asia
Europe
Anglo-America
Million m.t.c.e.
* Primary electricity

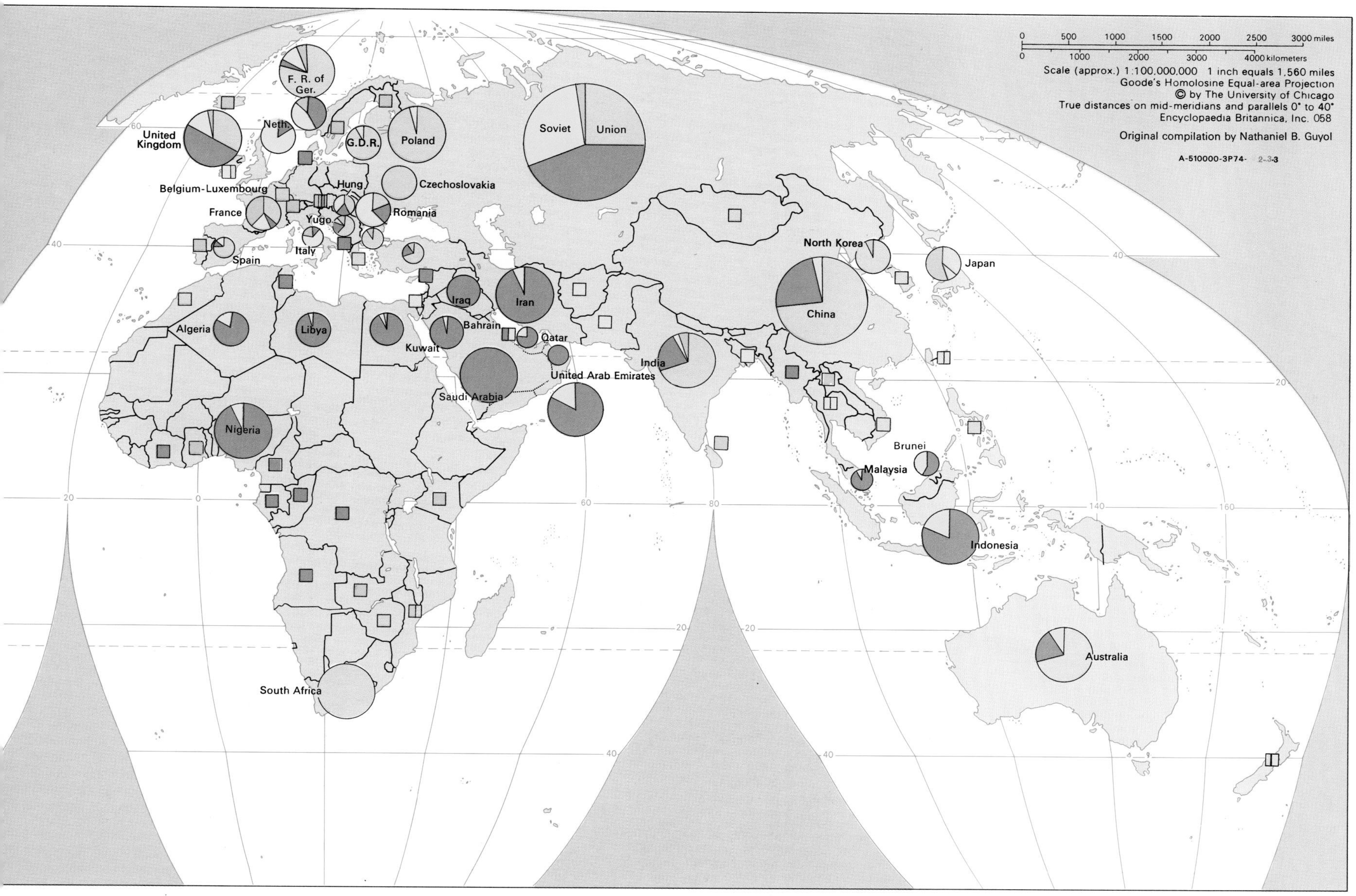

0 500 1000 1500 2000 2500 3000 miles
0 1000 2000 3000 4000 kilometers
Scale (approx.) 1:100,000,000 1 inch equals 1,560 miles
Goode's Homolosine Equal-area Projection
© by The University of Chicago
True distances on mid-meridians and parallels 0° to 40°
Encyclopaedia Britannica, Inc. 058
Original compilation by Nathaniel B. Guyol
A-510000-3P74-
F. R. of Ger.
United Kingdom
Neth.
G.D.R.
Poland
Czechoslovakia
Belgium-Luxembourg
Hung.
France
Yugo.
Romania
Italy
Spain
Soviet Union
North Korea
Japan
China
Iraq
Iran
Algeria
Libya
Bahrain
Qatar
Kuwait
United Arab Emirates
Saudi Arabia
India
Nigeria
Brunei
Malaysia
Indonesia
Australia
South Africa

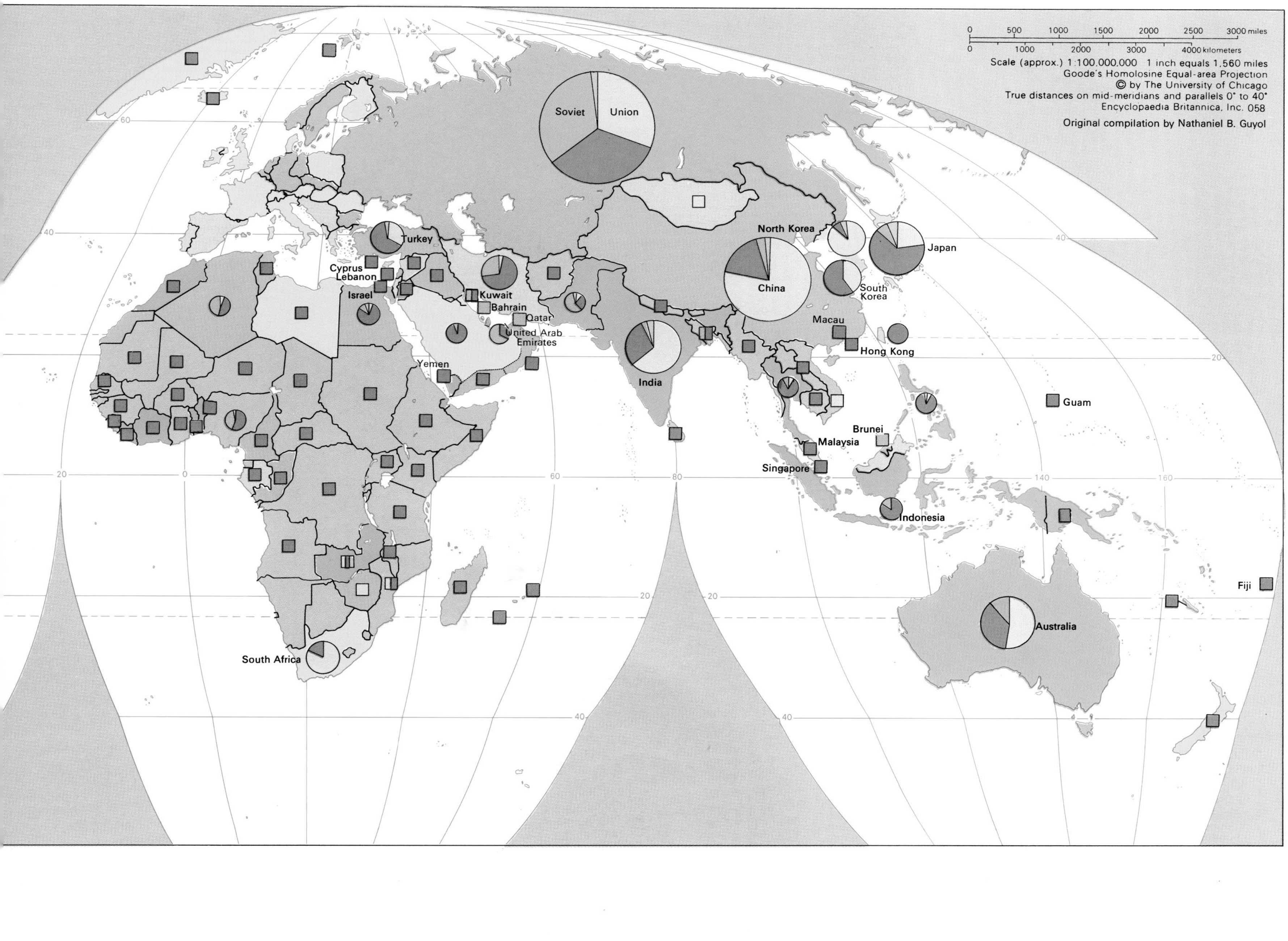

0 500 1000 1500 2000 2500 3000 miles
0 1000 2000 3000 4000 kilometers
Scale (approx.) 1:100,000,000 1 inch equals 1,560 miles
Goode's Homolosine Equal-area Projection
© by The University of Chicago
True distances on mid-meridians and parallels 0° to 40°
Encyclopaedia Britannica, Inc. 058
Original compilation by Nathaniel B. Guyol
Soviet Union
Turkey
North Korea
Japan
China
South Korea
Cyprus
Lebanon
Israel
Kuwait
Bahrain
Qatar
United Arab Emirates
Yemen
Macau
Hong Kong
India
Guam
Brunei
Malaysia
Singapore
Indonesia
Fiji
Australia
South Africa

Gross National Product

Total per country at market price — In billions of U.S. dollars	Number of countries
300–3,670	9
50–300	27
10–50	28
3–10	34
1–3	33
Less than 1	21
No data available	

Per capita — In U.S. dollars	Number of countries
■ 10,000–22,300	18
▮▮ 3,000–10,000	35
◗ 1,000–3,000	32
▲ 400–1,000	30
♥ 200–400	27
● Less than 200	15

International Trade

Total per country — In billions of U.S. dollars	Number of countries
100–560	10
30–100	19
10–30	25
3–10	19
1–3	34
Less than 1	46
No data available	

Per capita — In U.S. dollars	Number of countries
■ 10,000–45,000	11
▮▮ 3,000–10,000	25
◗ 1,000–3,000	28
▲ 500–1,000	19
♥ 200–500	36
● Less than 200	39

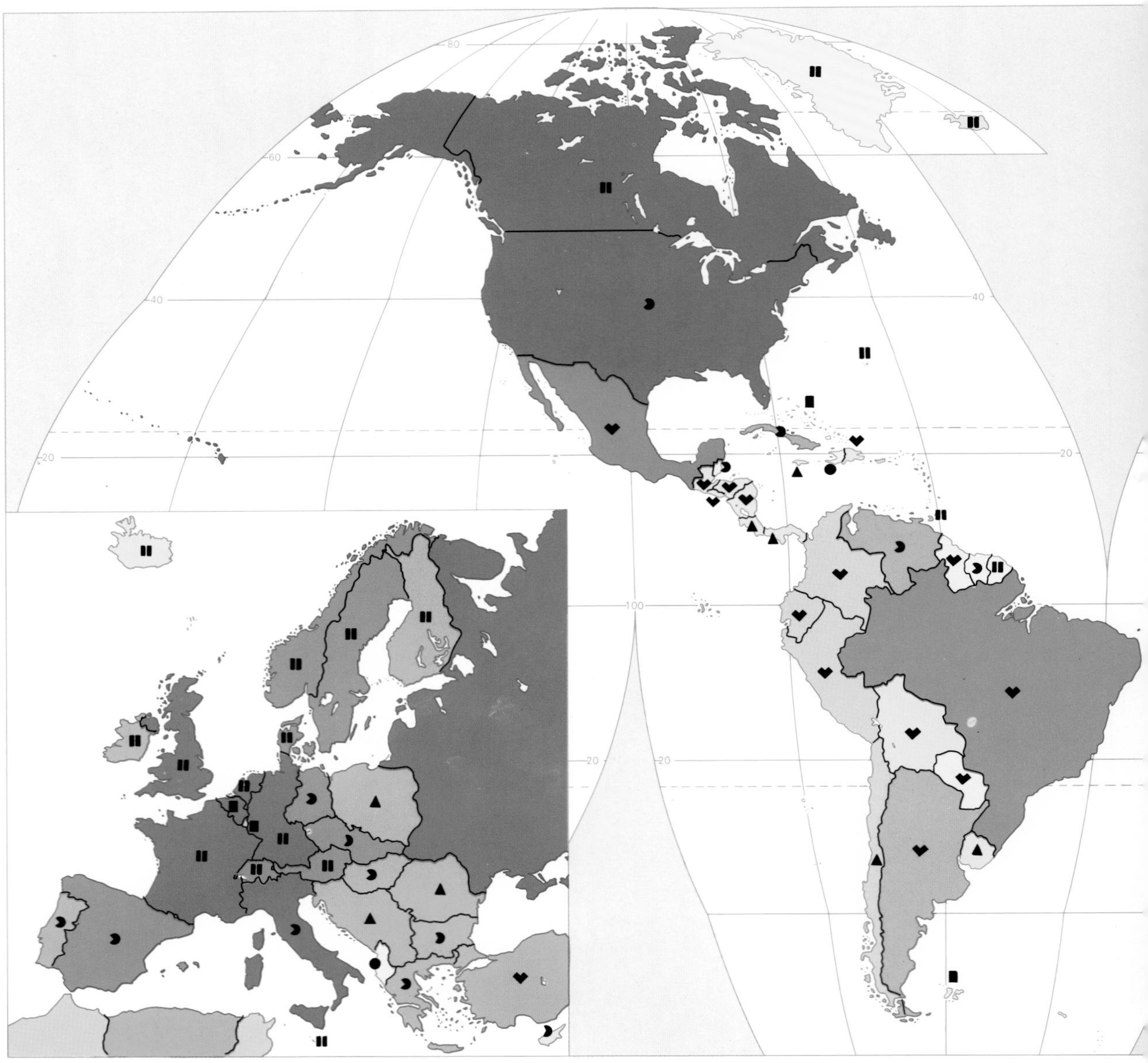

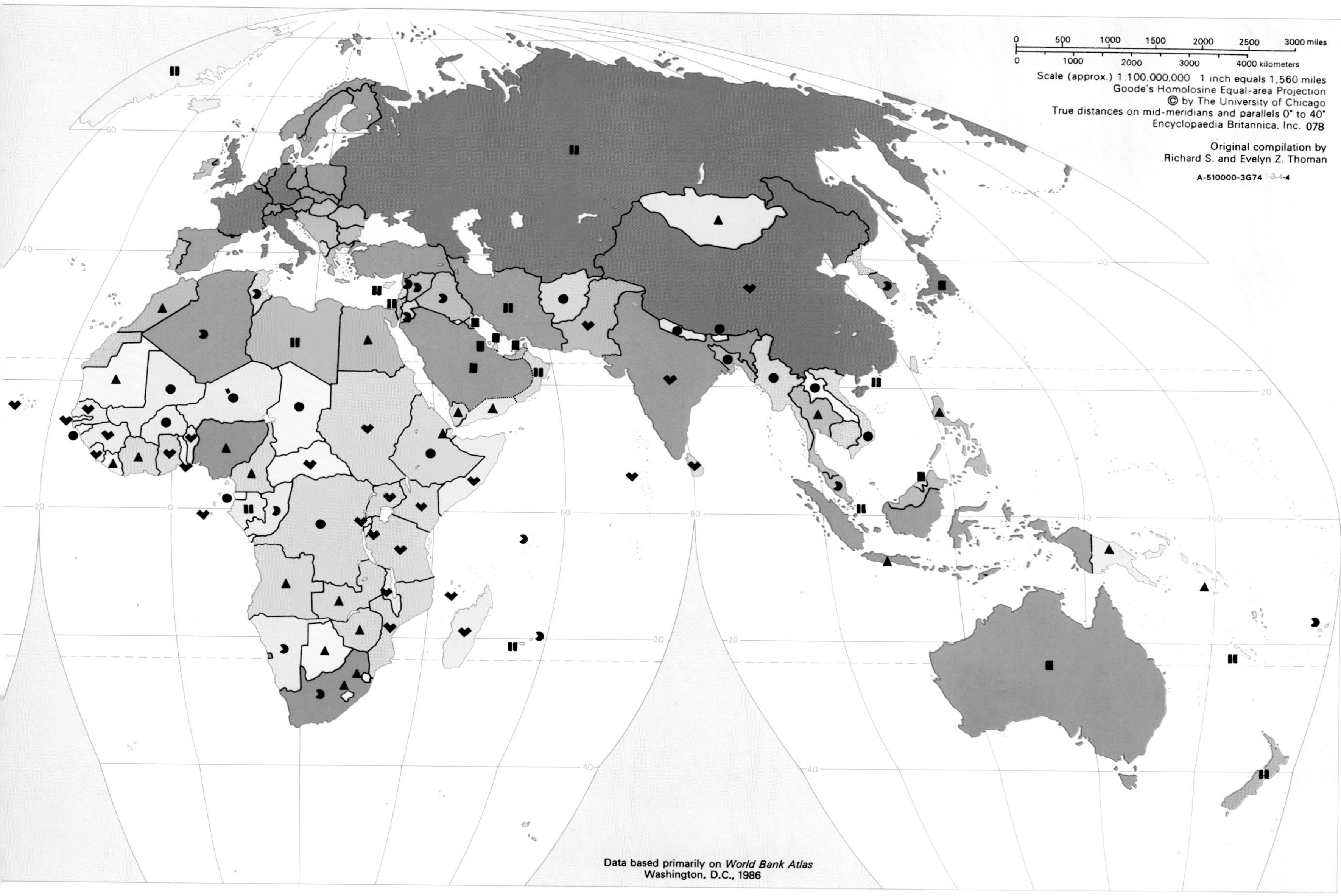
0 500 1000 1500 2000 2500 3000 miles
0 1000 2000 3000 4000 kilometers
Scale (approx.) 1:100,000,000 1 inch equals 1,560 miles
Goode's Homolosine Equal-area Projection
© by The University of Chicago
True distances on mid-meridians and parallels 0° to 40°
Encyclopaedia Britannica, Inc. 078
Original compilation by
Richard S. and Evelyn Z. Thoman
A-510000-3G74

Data based primarily on *World Bank Atlas*
Washington, D.C., 1986

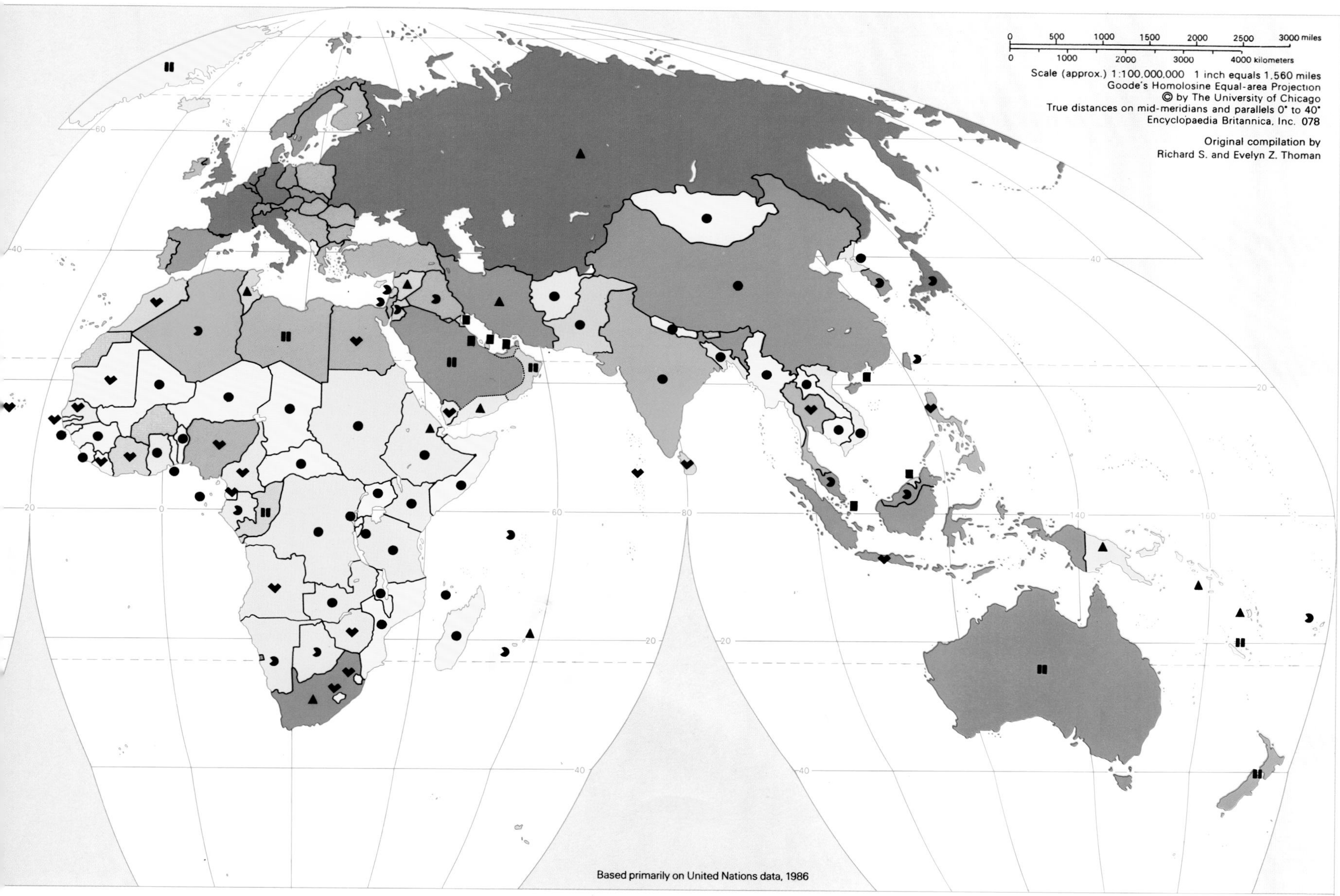
0 500 1000 1500 2000 2500 3000 miles
0 1000 2000 3000 4000 kilometers
Scale (approx.) 1:100,000,000 1 inch equals 1,560 miles
Goode's Homolosine Equal-area Projection
© by The University of Chicago
True distances on mid-meridians and parallels 0° to 40°
Encyclopaedia Britannica, Inc. 078
Original compilation by
Richard S. and Evelyn Z. Thoman

Based primarily on United Nations data, 1986

Intercontinental Air Connections

Scale (approx.) 1:70,000,000 1 inch equals 1100 miles
Center: 45° North Latitude, 10° East Longitude
Briesemeister Elliptical Equal-area Projection
Adapted by permission from the American Geographical Society
Encyclopaedia Britannica, Inc. 028
A-510000-4D74 -2 -2

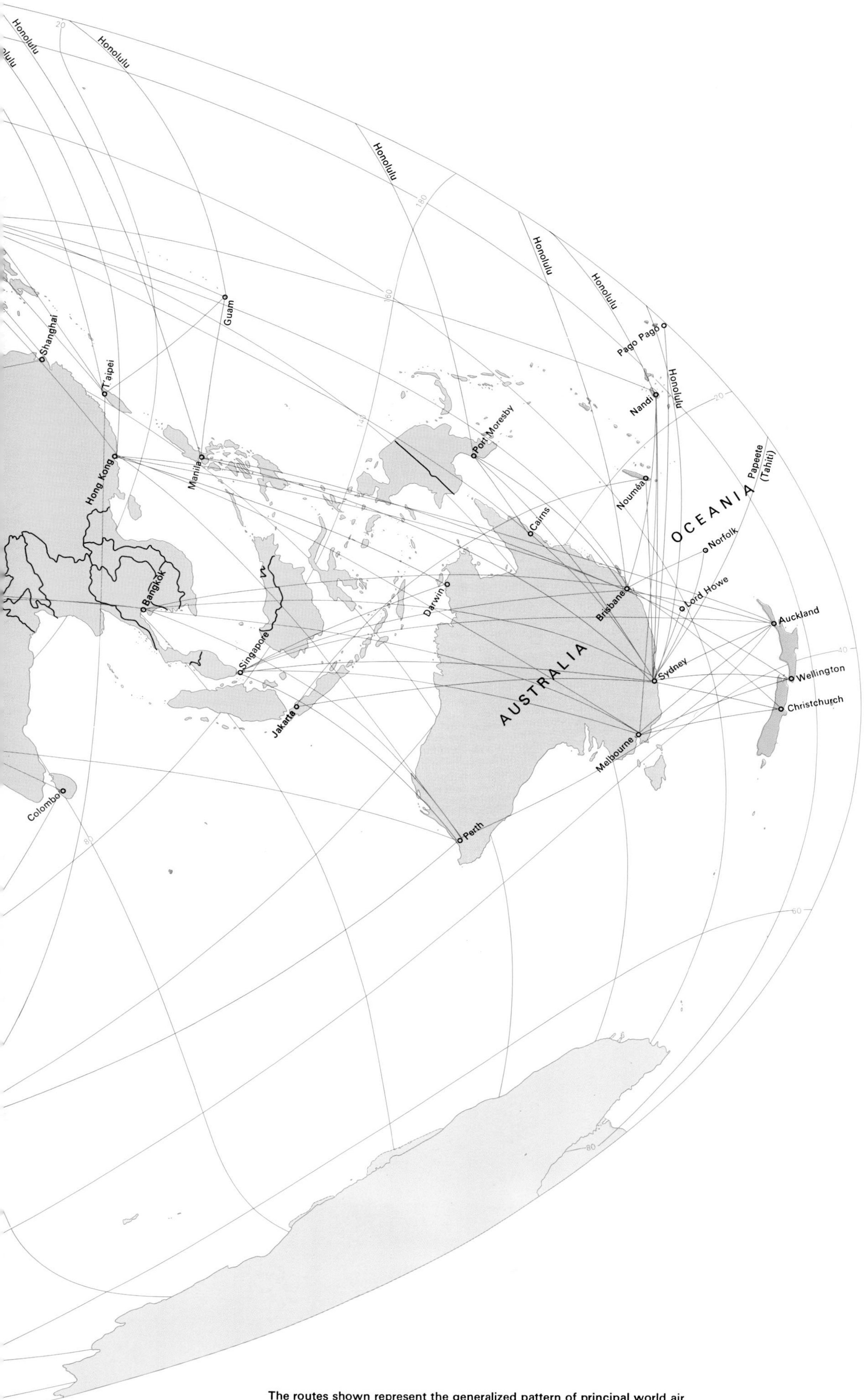

The routes shown represent the generalized pattern of principal world air flights between continents showing points of departure and arrival. Connecting flights between points on the same continent are not shown. The data are taken primarily from the *Official Airline Guide*, Worldwide edition (R. H. Donnelley Corp.), and *Air Distances Manual* (International Air Transport Association).

Great Circle Distances

	Statute miles	Kilo-meters
Beirut to Belgrade	1,107	1,782
Lagos	2,784	4,481
Paris	1,980	3,186
Rome	1,377	2,216
Cairo to Colombo	3,524	5,671
London	2,192	3,528
Moscow	1,808	2,910
Teheran	1,214	1,954
Caracas to Guatemala City	1,609	2,590
Las Palmas	3,540	5,696
Madrid	4,349	6,999
Miami	1,361	2,190
Copenhagen to Anchorage	4,310	6,935
Montreal	3,604	5,799
Sondre Stromfjord	2,129	3,427
Tel Aviv-Yafo	1,953	3,143
Dakar to Geneva	2,567	4,132
Madrid	1,964	3,161
New York	3,800	6,115
Recife	1,980	3,186
Honolulu to Brisbane	4,694	7,554
Los Angeles	2,551	4,106
Manila	5,292	8,515
Tokyo	3,846	6,189
Karachi to Addis Ababa	2,167	3,486
Athens	2,684	4,320
Cairo	2,210	3,556
Nairobi	2,713	4,367
Lima to Kingston	2,069	3,330
Miami	2,619	4,215
New York	3,642	5,861
Panama City	1,465	2,357
Lisbon to Luanda	3,588	5,774
Montreal	3,261	5,248
Paramaribo	3,679	5,920
Rio de Janeiro	4,791	7,710
London to Bermuda	3,428	5,514
Chicago	3,941	6,343
Los Angeles	5,439	8,753
Tunis	1,137	1,830
Los Angeles to Panama City	3,007	4,840
Papeete	4,105	6,607
Paris	5,659	9,108
Tokyo	5,473	8,808
Mexico City to Chicago	1,689	2,718
Lima	2,635	4,241
Vancouver	2,448	3,940
Washington, D.C.	1,879	3,024
Moscow to Amsterdam	1,330	2,142
Delhi	2,709	4,360
Peking	3,606	5,802
Teheran	1,545	2,486
New York to Bogotá	2,481	3,993
Brasília	4,238	6,821
London	3,440	5,536
Rome	4,263	6,861
Panama City to Brasília	2,754	4,433
Houston	1,772	2,852
Los Angeles	3,007	4,840
Quito	640	1,029
Paris to Colombo	5,292	8,516
Fort-de-France	4,255	6,848
Kano	2,559	4,115
Moscow	1,541	2,479
Rio de Janeiro to London	5,746	9,248
Monrovia	2,994	4,818
New York	4,800	7,725
Panama City	3,289	5,293
Rome to Delhi	3,685	5,929
Lagos	2,490	4,007
Nairobi	3,353	5,396
Tel Aviv-Yafo	1,416	2,280
Sydney to Auckland	1,341	2,159
Manila	3,888	6,258
Pago Pago	2,733	4,399
Singapore	3,912	6,296
Tokyo to Anchorage	3,457	5,563
San Francisco	5,145	8,280
Seattle	4,790	7,708
Wake	1,983	3,192

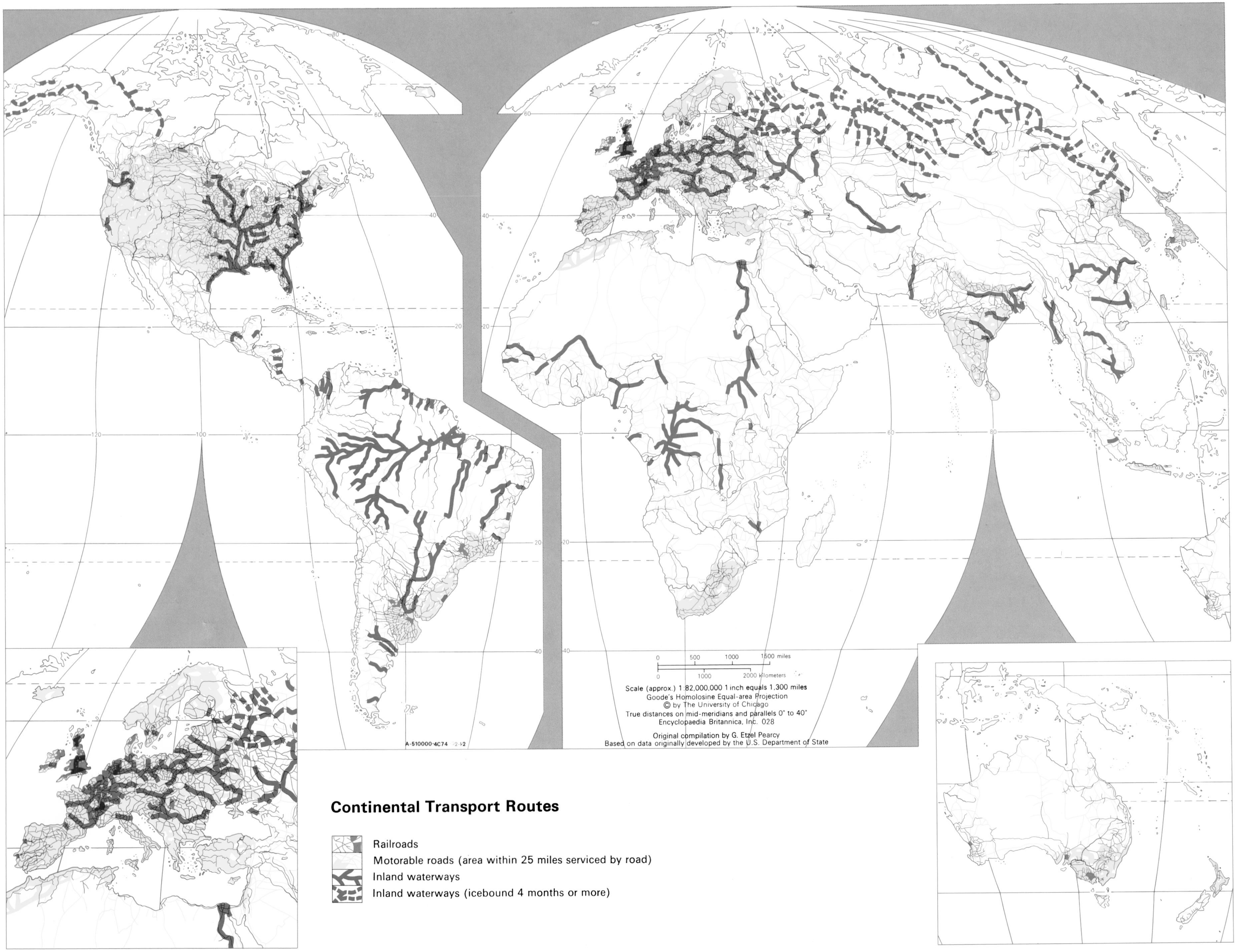

Railroads
Motorable roads (area within 25 miles serviced by road)
Inland waterways
Inland waterways (icebound 4 months or more)
0 500 1000 1500 miles
0 1000 2000 kilometers
Scale (approx.) 1:82,000,000 1 inch equals 1,300 miles
Goode's Homolosine Equal-area Projection
© by The University of Chicago
True distances on mid-meridians and parallels 0° to 40°
Encyclopaedia Britannica, Inc. 028
Original compilation by G. Etzel Pearcy
Based on data originally developed by the U.S. Department of State
A-510000-4C74

Continental Transport Routes

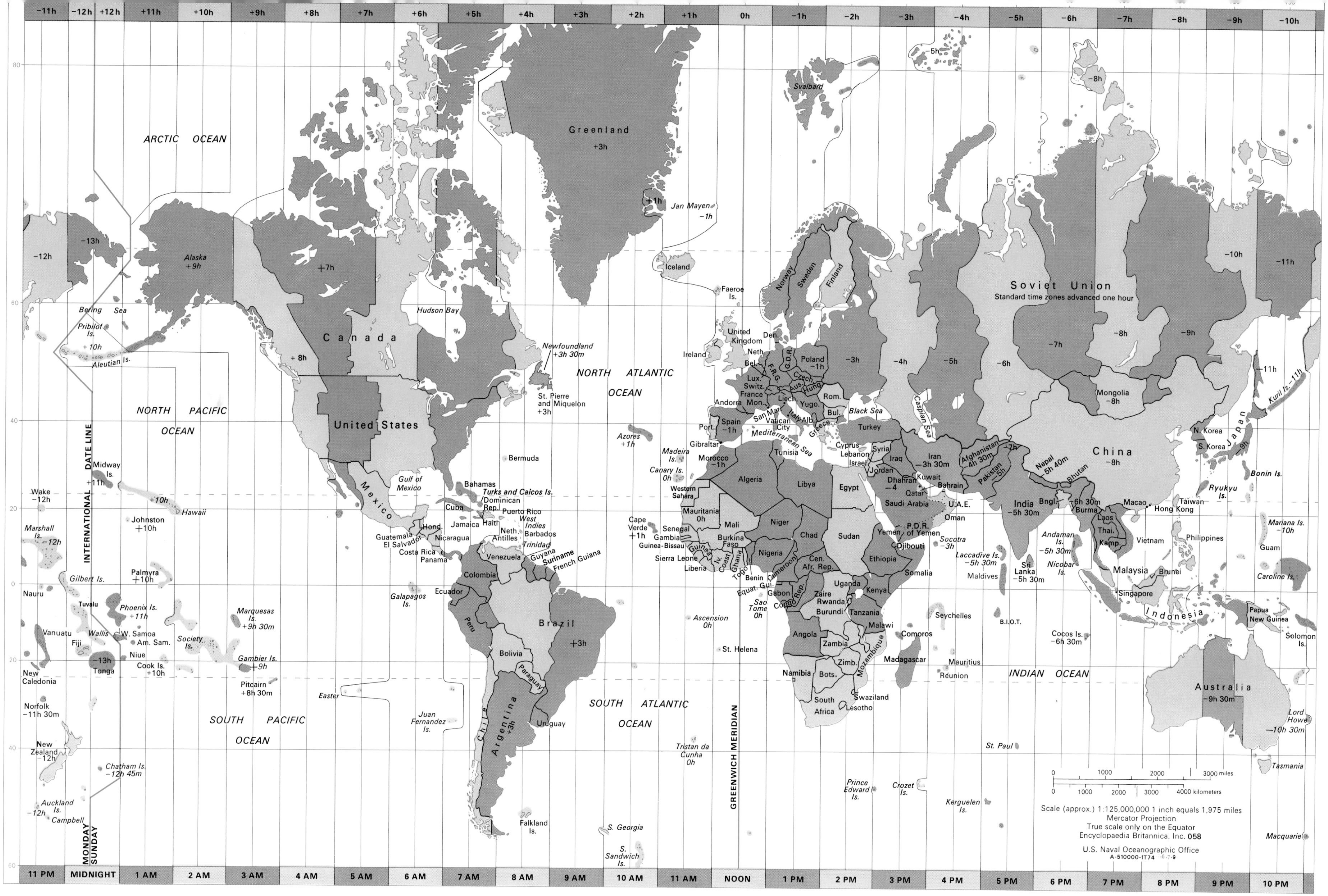

Time Zones

- Standard time zone of even-numbered hours from Greenwich time
- Standard time zone of odd-numbered hours from Greenwich time
- Time varies from the standard time zone by half an hour
- Time varies from the standard time zone by other than half an hour

h m hours, minutes

The standard time zone system, fixed by international agreement and by law in each country, is based on a theoretical division of the globe into 24 zones of 15° longitude each. The mid-meridian of each zone fixes the hour for the entire zone. The zero time zone extends 7½° east and 7½° west of the Greenwich meridian, 0° longitude. Since the earth rotates toward the east, time zones to the west of Greenwich are earlier, to the east, later.
Plus and minus hours at the top of the map are added to or subtracted from local time to find Greenwich time. Local standard time can be determined for any area in the world by adding one hour for each time zone counted in an easterly direction from one's own, or by subtracting one hour for each zone counted in a westerly direction. To separate one day from the next, the 180th meridian has been designated as the international date line.
On both sides of the line the time of day is the same, but west of the line it is one day later than it is to the east.
Countries that adhere to the international zone system adopt the zone applicable to their location. Some countries, however, establish time zones based on political boundaries, or adopt the time zone of a neighboring unit. For all or part of the year some countries also advance their time by one hour, thereby utilizing more daylight hours each day.

Climate Graphs

Each graph below shows temperature and rainfall at a weather station that was selected to illustrate one of the climate regions described in the legend at the right. The weather stations are keyed by number to the maps. The elements of the graphs are identified in the sample graph at the top, with a temperature scale in degrees Fahrenheit and Celsius (Centigrade), and a precipitation scale in inches and millimeters.

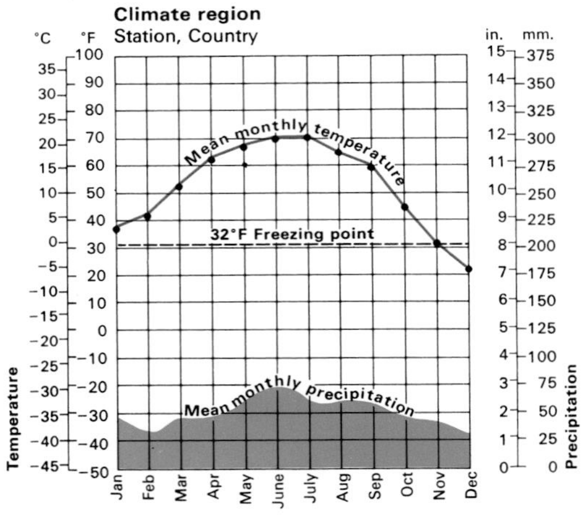

1 Rainy tropical
Manaus, Brazil

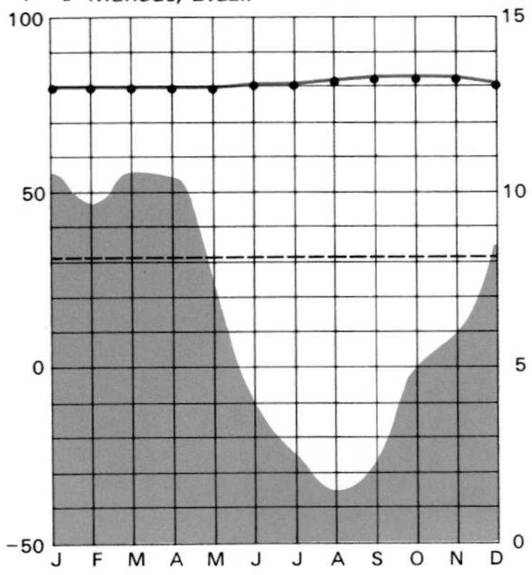

2 Wet and dry tropical
Madras, India

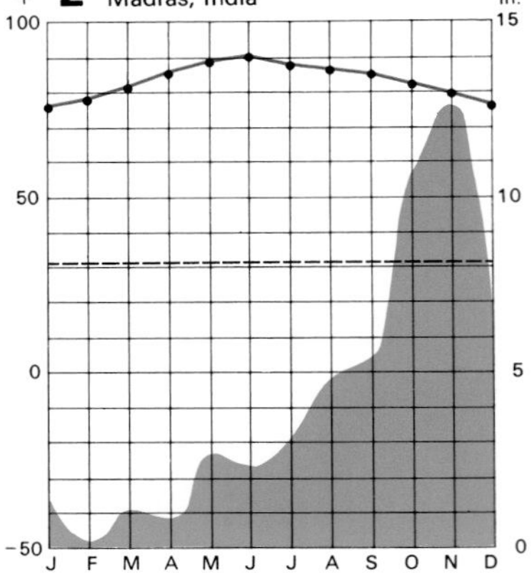

3 Semiarid tropical
Cloncurry, Australia

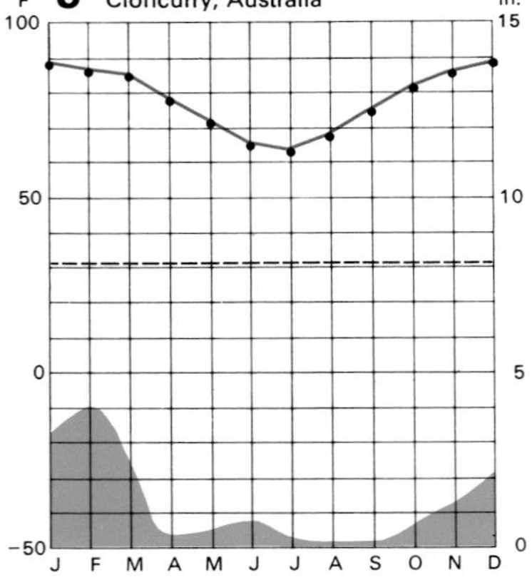

4 Hot arid
Aswan, Egypt

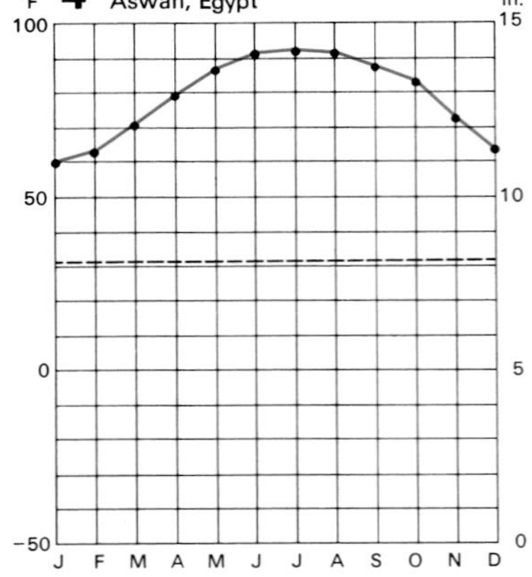

5 Humid subtropical
Tokyo, Japan

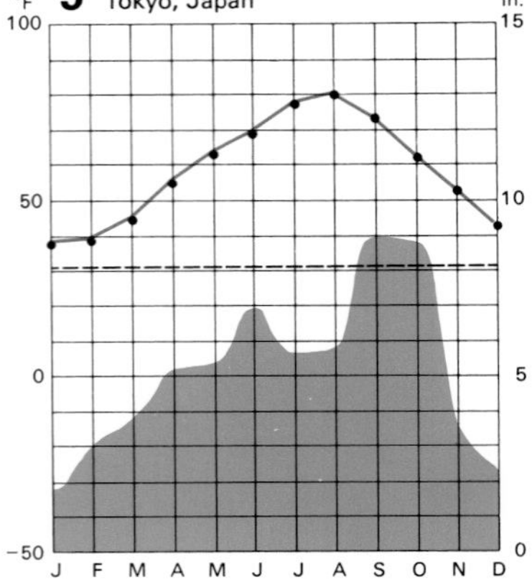

6 Dry subtropical
Oran, Algeria

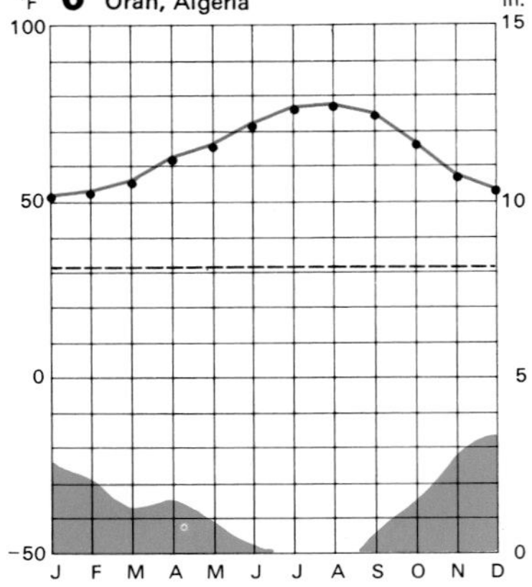

7 Humid mid-latitude
Chicago, United States

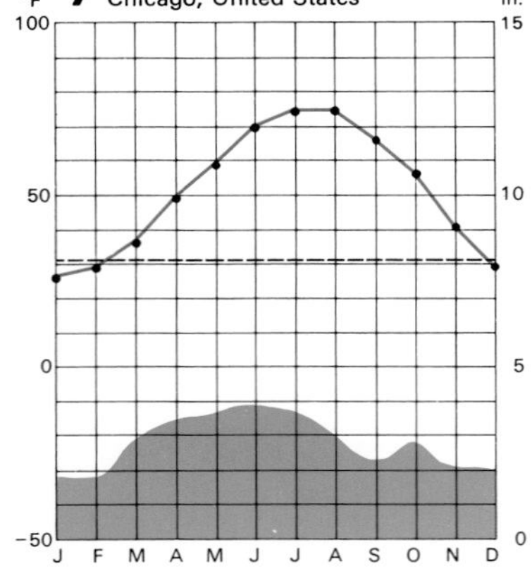

8 Temperate marine
Amsterdam, Netherlands

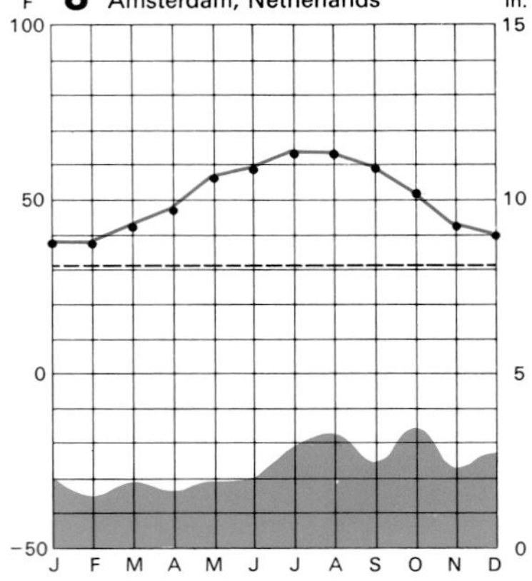

9 Semiarid mid-latitude
Ankara, Turkey

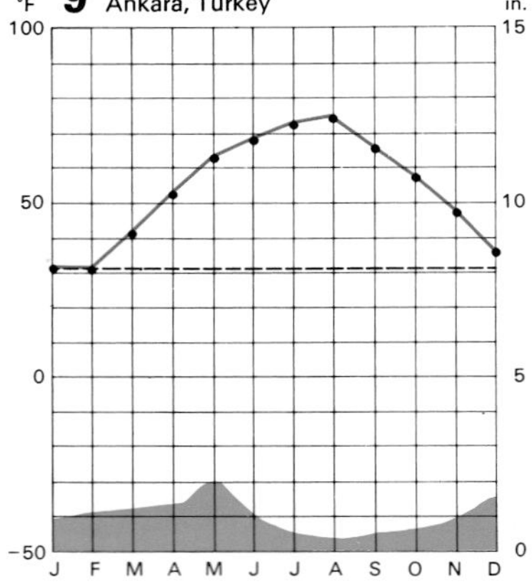

10 Arid mid-latitude
Las Vegas, United States

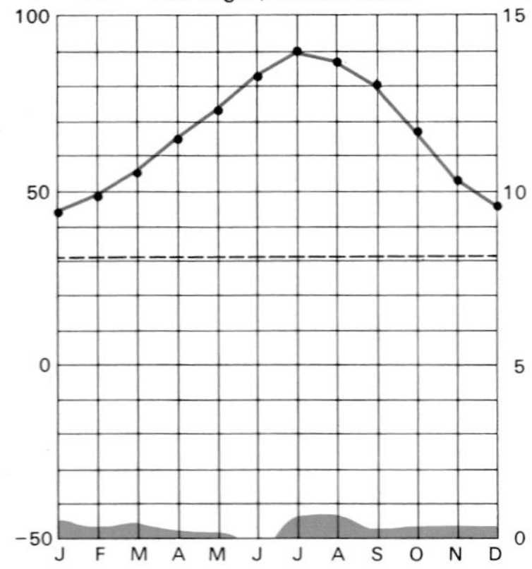

11 Subarctic
Yakutsk, Soviet Union

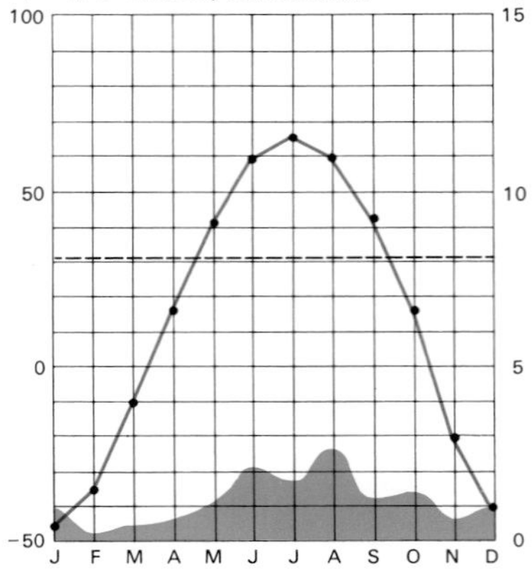

12 Arctic margin
Dikson, Soviet Union

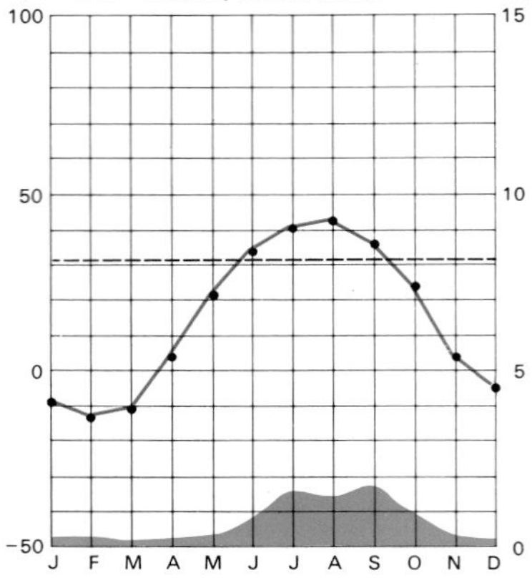

Climate Regions

- **Rainy tropical** At most, one or two dry months; all months warm or hot
- **Wet and dry tropical** A well-developed dry season with one or two rainy seasons; all months warm or hot
- **Semiarid tropical** Light precipitation, rapid evaporation; all months warm or hot
- **Hot arid** Negligible precipitation, rapid evaporation; all months warm or hot
- **Humid subtropical** Precipitation in all seasons with maximum in summer; long warm summers, cool winters
- **Dry subtropical** Hot dry summers; cool, moderately rainy winters
- **Humid mid-latitude** Precipitation in all seasons with maximum in summer; warm or hot summers, cold winters
- **Temperate marine** Numerous rainy days in all seasons with moderate total precipitation, higher precipitation in highland areas; warm summers, cool winters
- **Semiarid mid-latitude** Light precipitation; warm or hot summers, cool or cold winters
- **Arid mid-latitude** Extremely light precipitation; warm or hot summers, cool or cold winters
- **Subarctic** Light precipitation; short cool summers, long very cold winters
- **Arctic margin** Extremely light precipitation; very short cold summers, extremely long cold winters
- **High altitude** Climate varies with elevation, latitude, and exposure

Mean Annual Temperature

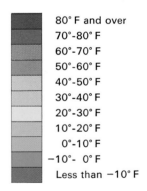

- 80° F and over
- 70°-80° F
- 60°-70° F
- 50°-60° F
- 40°-50° F
- 30°-40° F
- 20°-30° F
- 10°-20° F
- 0°-10° F
- −10°- 0° F
- Less than −10° F

Mean Annual Precipitation

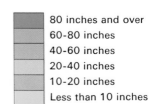

- 80 inches and over
- 60-80 inches
- 40-60 inches
- 20-40 inches
- 10-20 inches
- Less than 10 inches

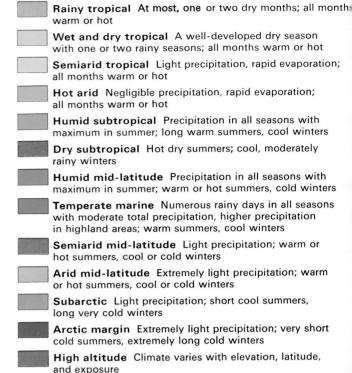

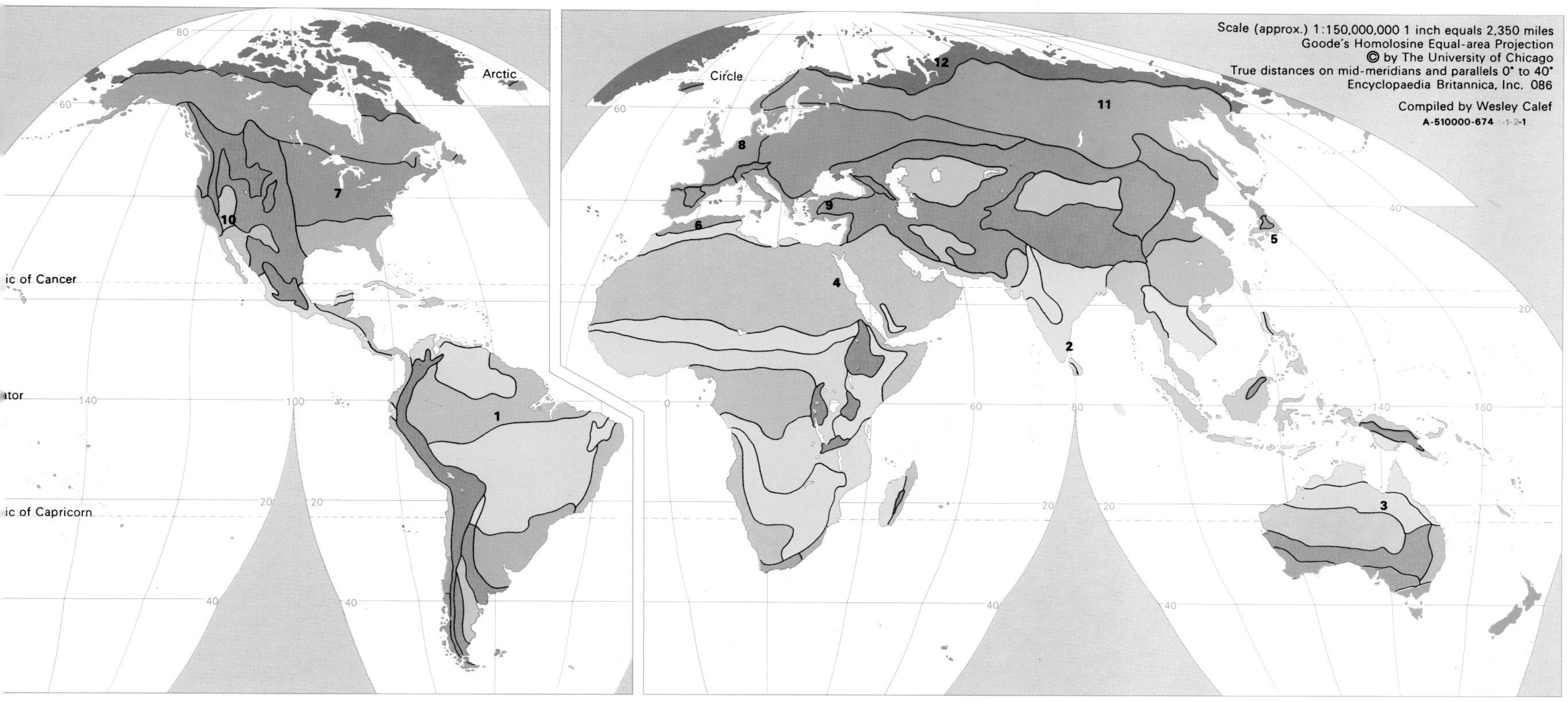
Scale (approx.) 1:150,000,000 1 inch equals 2,350 miles
Goode's Homolosine Equal-area Projection
© by The University of Chicago
True distances on mid-meridians and parallels 0° to 40°
Encyclopaedia Britannica, Inc. 086
Compiled by Wesley Calef
A-510000-674 -1-2-1
Arctic
Circle
ic of Cancer
ator
ic of Capricorn
1
2
3
4
5
6
7
8
9
10
11
12

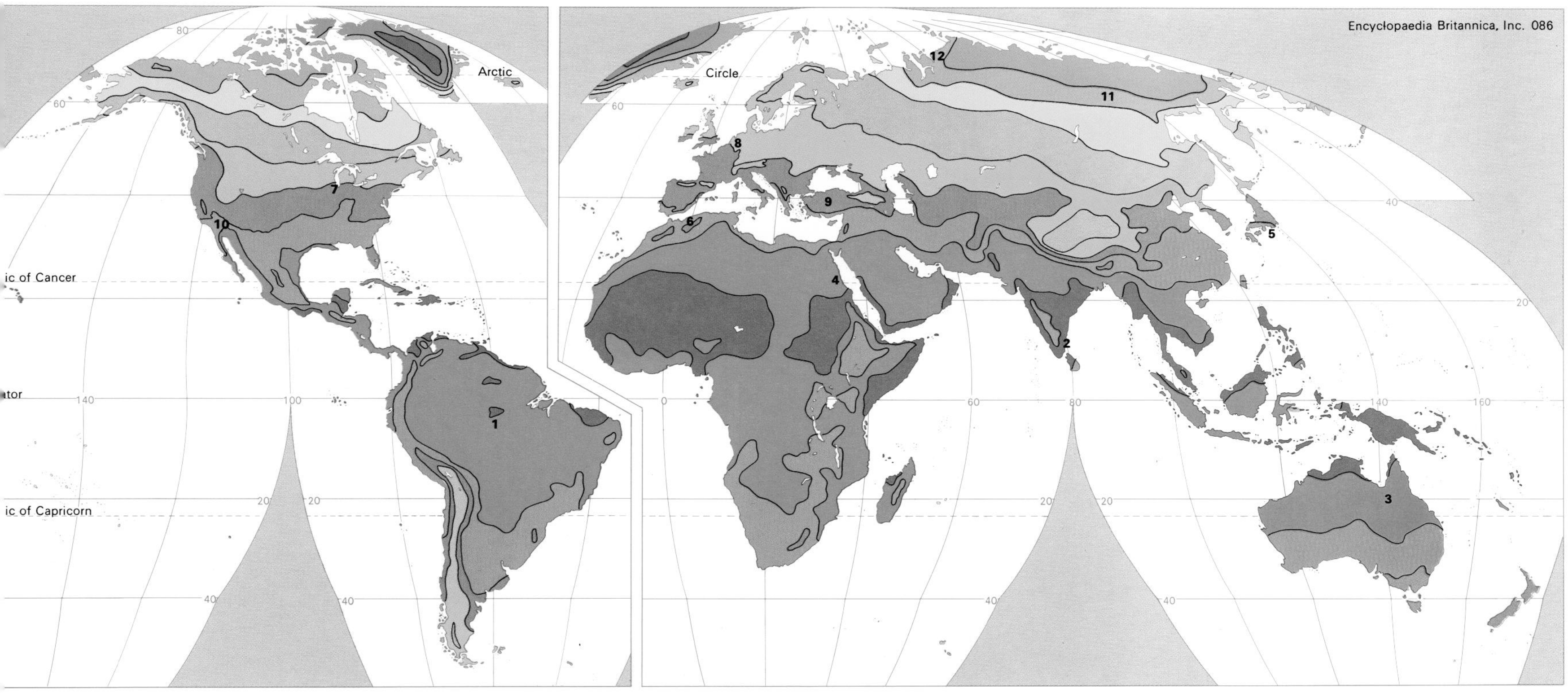
Encyclopaedia Britannica, Inc. 086
Arctic
Circle
ic of Cancer
ator
ic of Capricorn
1
2
3
4
5
6
7
8
9
10
11
12

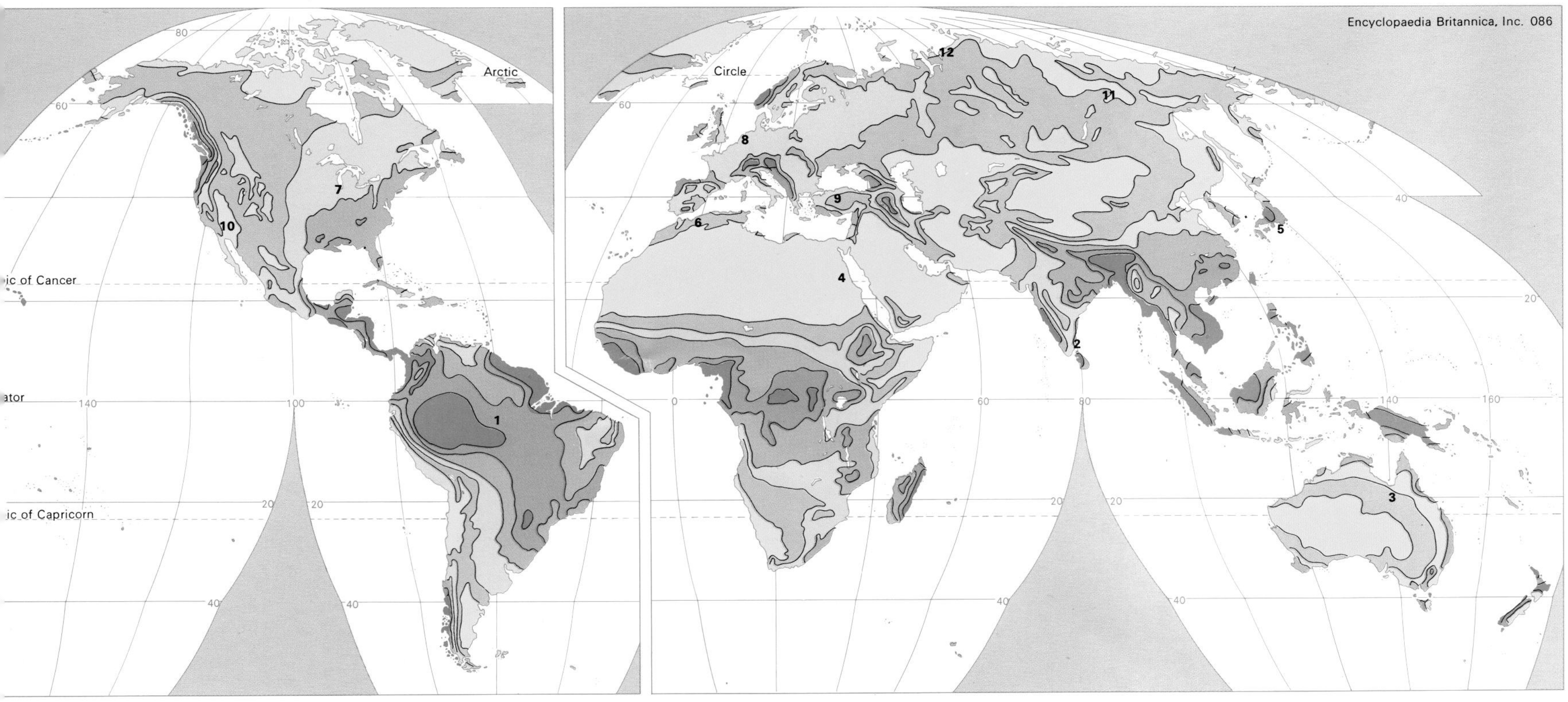
Encyclopaedia Britannica, Inc. 086
Arctic
Circle
ic of Cancer
ator
ic of Capricorn
1
2
3
4
5
6
7
8
9
10
11
12

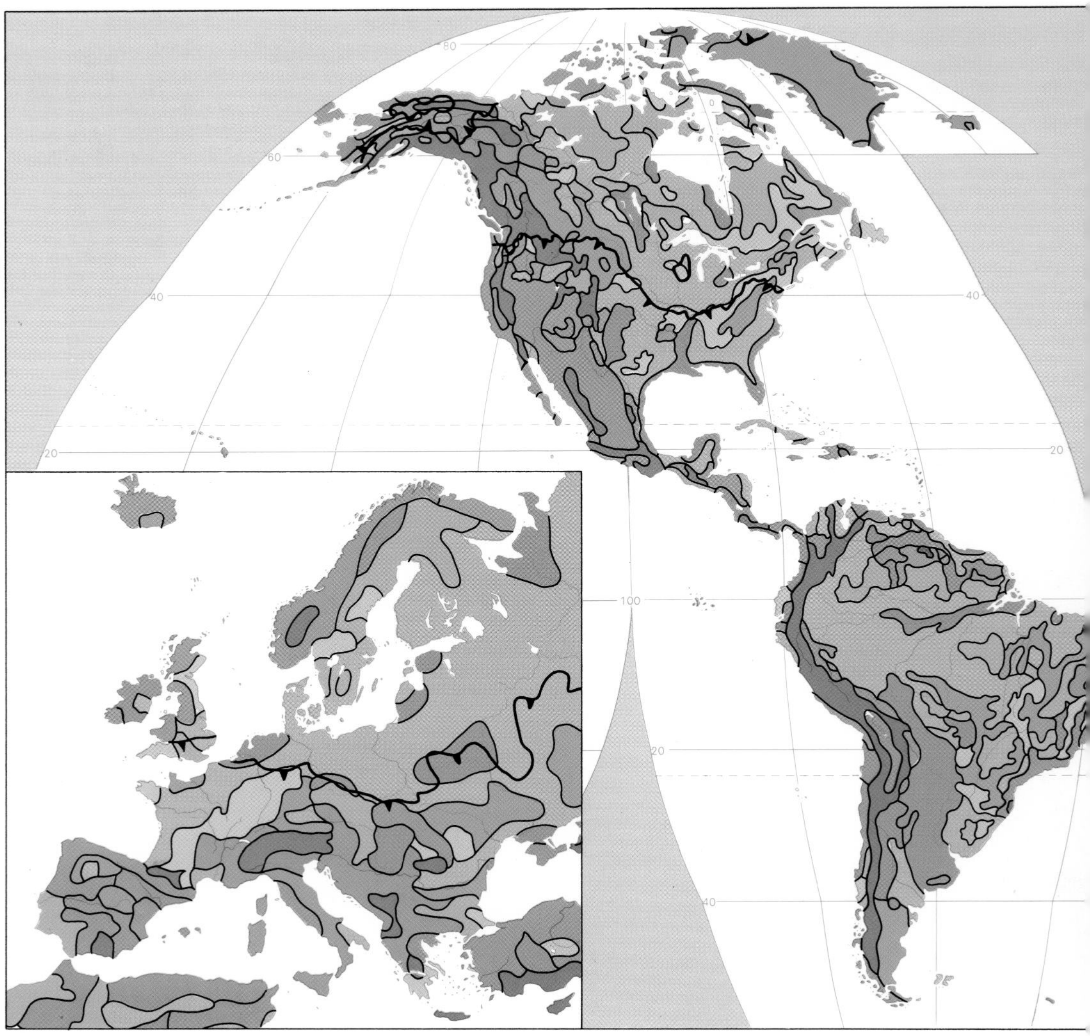

Surface Configuration

Smooth lands

- Level plains: nearly all slopes gentle; local relief less than 100 ft. (30 m.)
- Irregular plains: majority of slopes gentle; local relief 100-300 ft. (30-90 m.)

Broken lands

- Tablelands and plateaus: majority of slopes gentle, with the gentler slopes on the uplands; local relief more than 300 ft. (90 m.)
- Hill-studded plains: majority of slopes gentle, with the gentler slopes in the lowlands; local relief 300-1,000 ft. (90-300 m.)
- Mountain-studded plains: majority of slopes gentle, with the gentler slopes in the lowlands; local relief more than 1,000 ft. (300 m.)

Rough lands

- Hill lands: steeper slopes predominate; local relief less than 1,000 ft. (300 m.)
- Mountains: steeper slopes predominate; local relief 1,000-5,000 ft. (300-1,500 m.)
- Mountains of great relief: steeper slopes predominate; local relief more than 5,000 ft. (1,500 m.)

Other surfaces

- Ice caps: permanent ice
- Maximum extent of glaciation

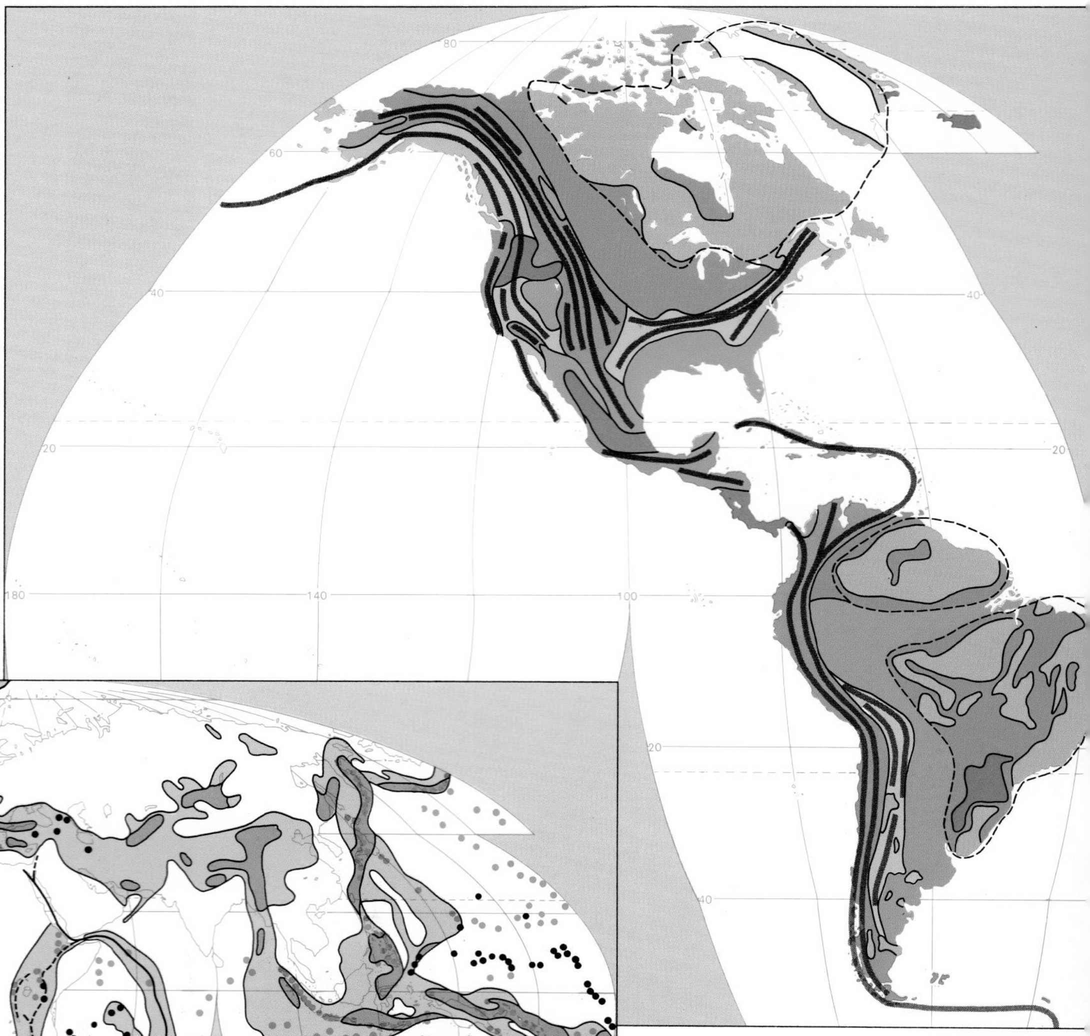

Earth Structure and Tectonics

- Precambrian stable shield areas
- Exposed Precambrian rock
- Paleozoic and Mesozoic flat-lying sedimentary rocks
- Principal Paleozoic and Mesozoic folded areas
- Cenozoic sedimentary rocks
- Principal Cenozoic folded areas
- Lava plateaus
- Major trends of folding

Geologic time chart

Precambrian—from formation of the earth (at least 4 billion years ago) to 600 million years ago

Paleozoic—from 600 million to 200 million years ago

Mesozoic—from 200 million to 70 million years ago

Cenozoic—from 70 million years ago to present time

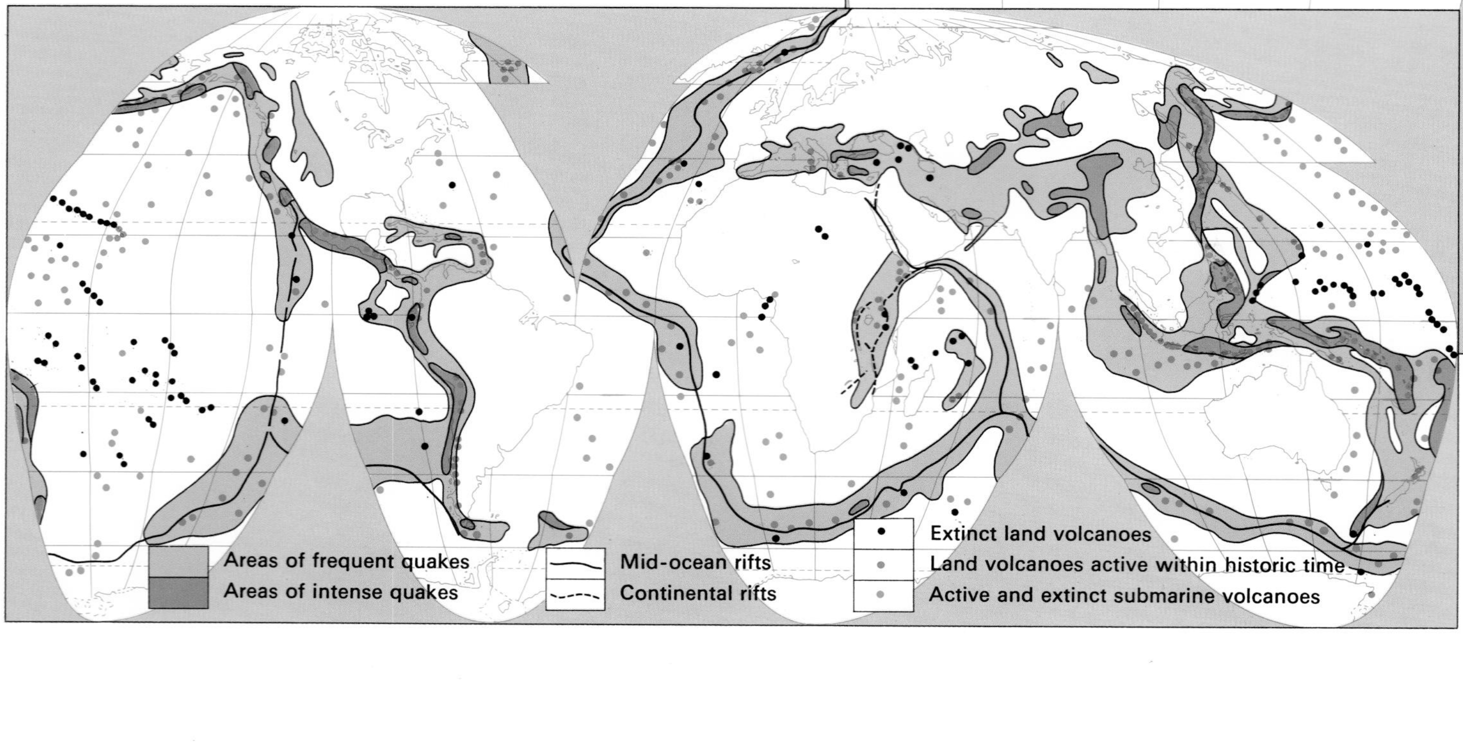
Areas of frequent quakes
Areas of intense quakes
Mid-ocean rifts
Continental rifts
Extinct land volcanoes
Land volcanoes active within historic time
Active and extinct submarine volcanoes

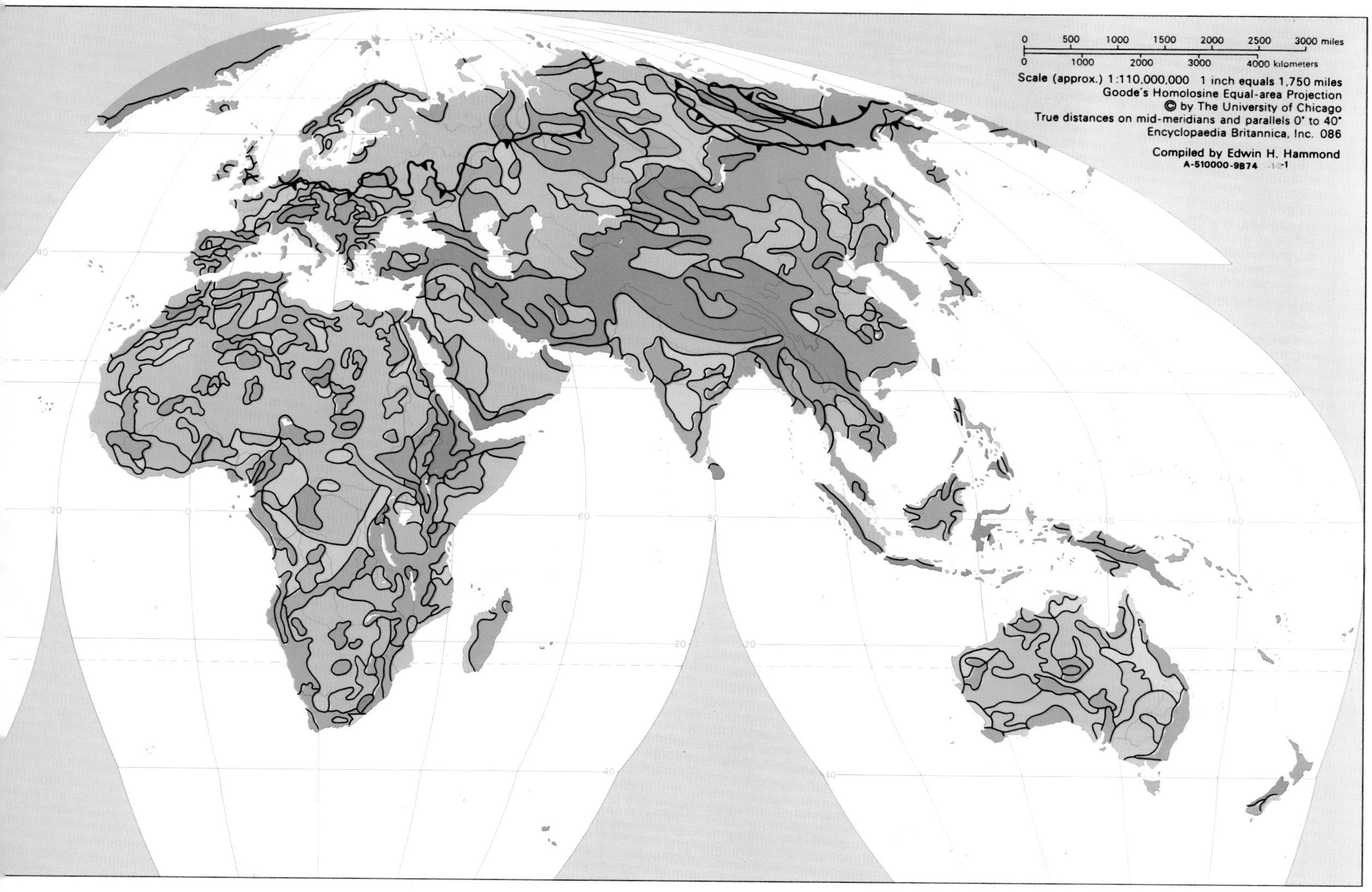
0 500 1000 1500 2000 2500 3000 miles
0 1000 2000 3000 4000 kilometers
Scale (approx.) 1:110,000,000 1 inch equals 1,750 miles
Goode's Homolosine Equal-area Projection
© by The University of Chicago
True distances on mid-meridians and parallels 0° to 40°
Encyclopaedia Britannica, Inc. 086
Compiled by Edwin H. Hammond
A-510000-9874

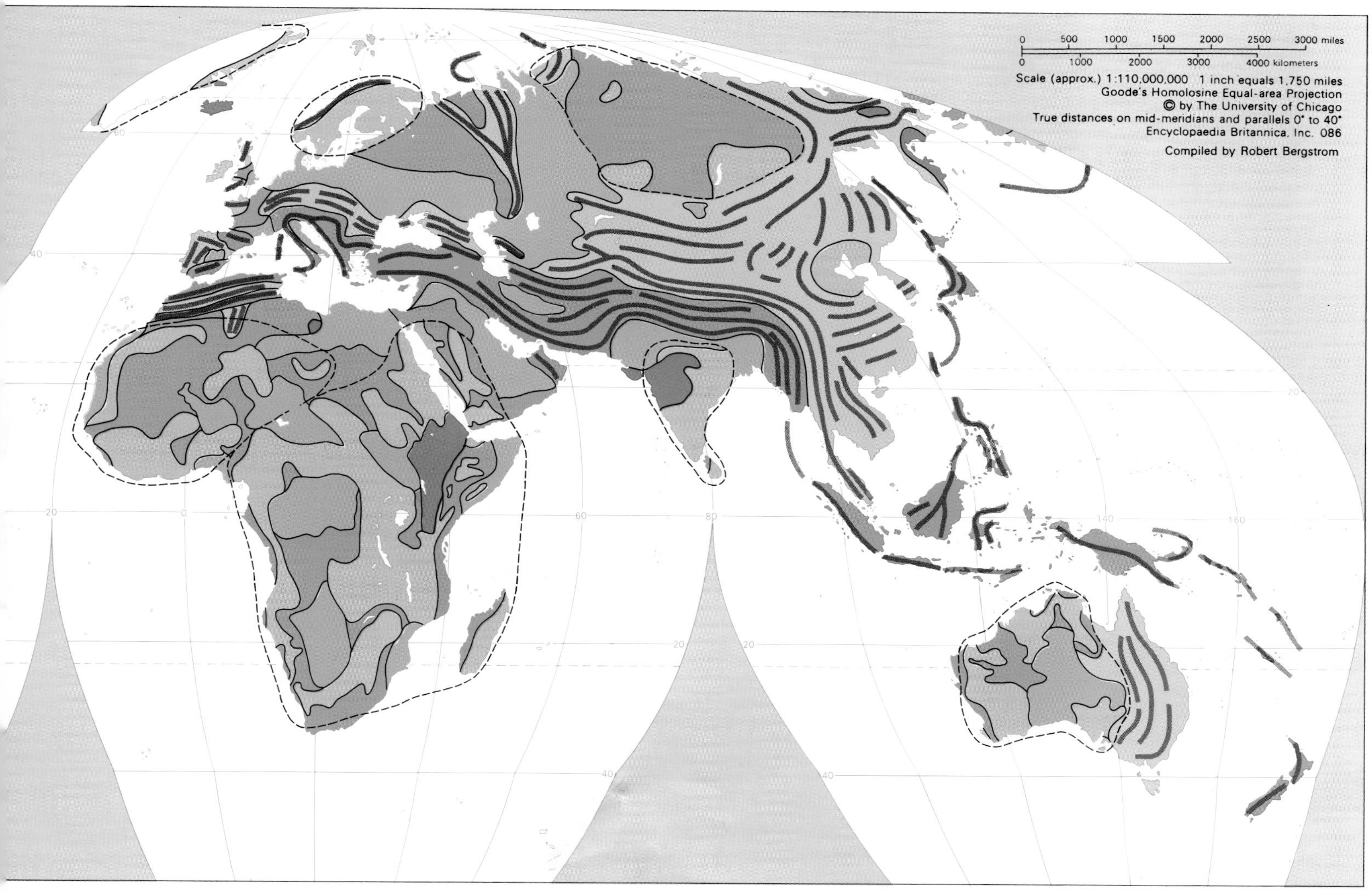
0 500 1000 1500 2000 2500 3000 miles
0 1000 2000 3000 4000 kilometers
Scale (approx.) 1:110,000,000 1 inch equals 1,750 miles
Goode's Homolosine Equal-area Projection
© by The University of Chicago
True distances on mid-meridians and parallels 0° to 40°
Encyclopaedia Britannica, Inc. 086
Compiled by Robert Bergstrom

Development of the earth's structure

The earth is in process of constant transformation. Movements in the hot, dense interior of the earth result in folding and fracture of the crust and transfer of molten material to the surface. As a result, large structures such as mountain ranges, volcanoes, lava plateaus, and rift valleys are created. The forces that bring about these structural changes are called *tectonic forces*.

The present continents have developed from stable nuclei, or *shields*, of ancient (Precambrian) rock. Erosive forces such as water, wind, and ice have worn away particles of the rock, depositing them at the edges of the shields, where they have accumulated and ultimately become sedimentary rock. Subsequently, in plaees, these extensive areas of flat-lying rock have been elevated, folded, or warped, by the action of tectonic forces, to form mountains. The shape of these mountains has been altered by later erosion. Where the forces of erosion have been at work for a long time, the mountains tend to have a low relief and rounded contours, like the Appalachians. Mountains more recently formed are high and rugged, like the Himalayas.

The map above depicts some of the major geologic structures of the earth and identifies them according to the period of their formation. A geologic time chart is included in the legend. The inset map shows the most important areas of earthquakes, rifts, and volcanic activity. Comparison of all the maps will show the close correlation between present-day mountain systems, recent (Cenozoic) mountain-building, and the areas of frequent earthquakes and active volcanoes.

Natural Vegetation

Broad-leaved evergreen vegetation
- Broad-leaved evergreen forest
- Broad-leaved evergreen shrub formation
- Scattered broad-leaved evergreen shrubs
- Scattered broad-leaved evergreen dwarf shrubs

Broad-leaved deciduous vegetation
- Broad-leaved deciduous forest
- Broad-leaved deciduous shrub formation
- Scattered broad-leaved deciduous shrubs
- Scattered broad-leaved deciduous dwarf shrubs

Coniferous vegetation
- Needle-leaved evergreen forest
- Scattered needle-leaved evergreen trees
- Needle-leaved deciduous forest

Mixed vegetation without grass
- Forest of broad-leaved evergreen and deciduous trees
- Forest of broad-leaved and needle-leaved evergreen trees
- Broad-leaved deciduous forests with broad-leaved evergreen shrubs
- Forest of broad-leaved deciduous and needle-leaved evergreen trees

Mixed vegetation with grass
- Grassland with scattered broad-leaved evergreen trees
- Grassland with broad-leaved evergreen shrubs
- Grassland with scattered broad-leaved deciduous trees
- Grassland with broad-leaved deciduous shrubs

Grassland, tundra, barren
- Grassland
- Patches of grass
- Lichens and grasses
- Lichens and mosses
- Barren

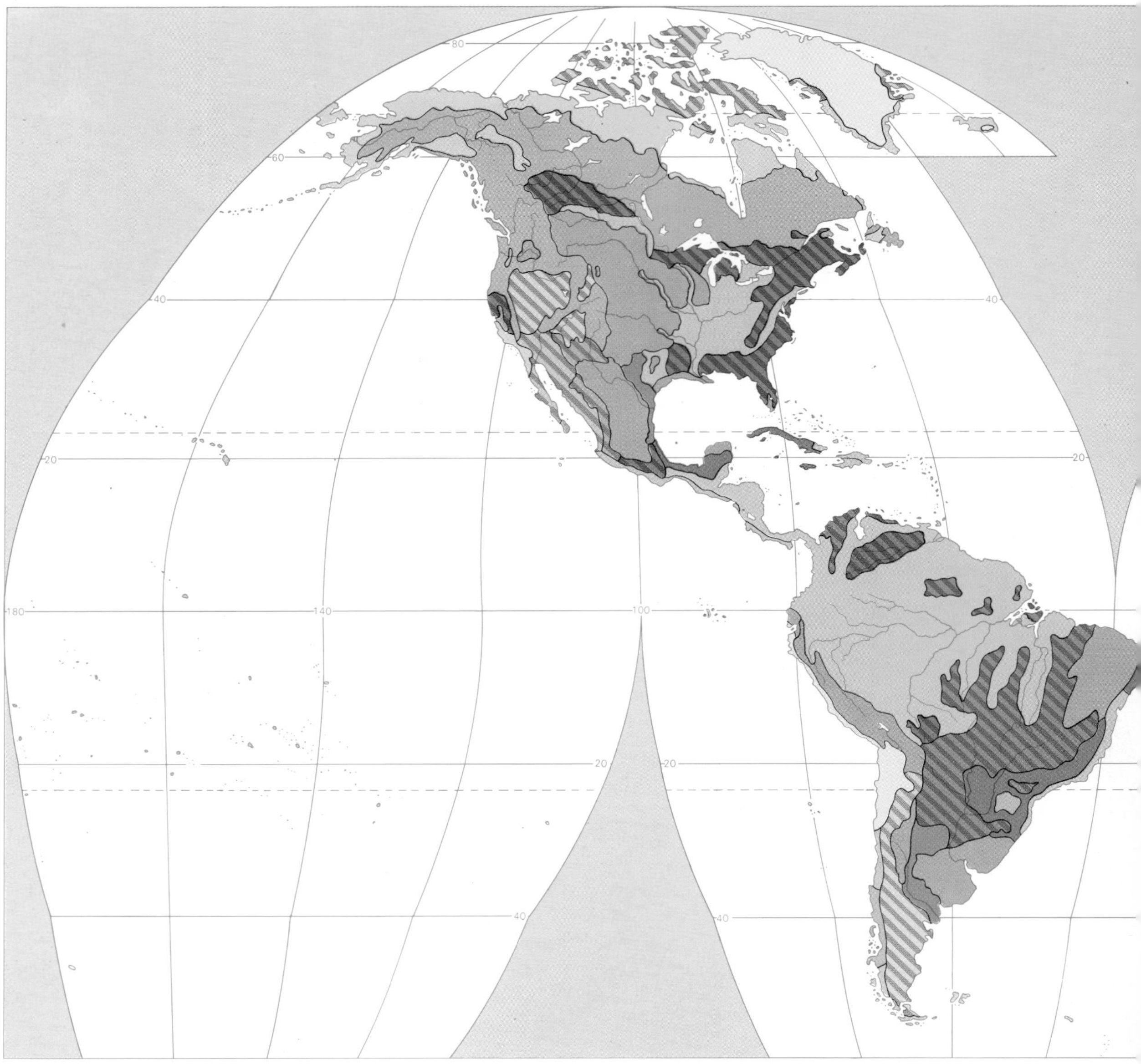

Soils

- Tundra soils of frigid climates; commonly with permanently frozen subsoil; supports dwarf shrubs, mosses, and lichens; some used for reindeer pasture
- Podzolic soils of humid, cool climates; covered with predominantly coniferous forest; some farming, mainly subsistence
- Podzolic soils of humid, temperate climates; originally covered with predominantly deciduous forest, much of it removed to accommodate extensive general farming, industry, and cities
- Podzolic soils of humid, warm climates; covered with coniferous or mixed forest; general farming
- Chernozemic soils of subhumid and semiarid, cool to tropical climates; supports mainly grasslands; extensive grain and livestock farming
- Latosolic soils of humid or wet-dry tropical and subtropical climates; supports forest or savanna; shifting cultivation with some plantation agriculture
- Grumusolic soils of humid to semiarid and temperate to tropical climates, with distinct wet and dry seasons; mainly grass-covered; livestock and grain farming
- Desertic soils of arid climates; includes many areas of shallow, stony soils; sparse cover of shrubs and grass, some suitable for grazing; fertile if irrigated; dry farming possible in some areas
- Mountain soils of all climates; shallow, stony; barren, grass-covered, or forested, depending on climate; includes many areas of other soils
- Alluvial soils of all climates; deposited by water in flood plains and deltas of rivers; intensive farming in most temperate and some tropical regions (many smaller areas not shown)
- Ice cap of polar regions

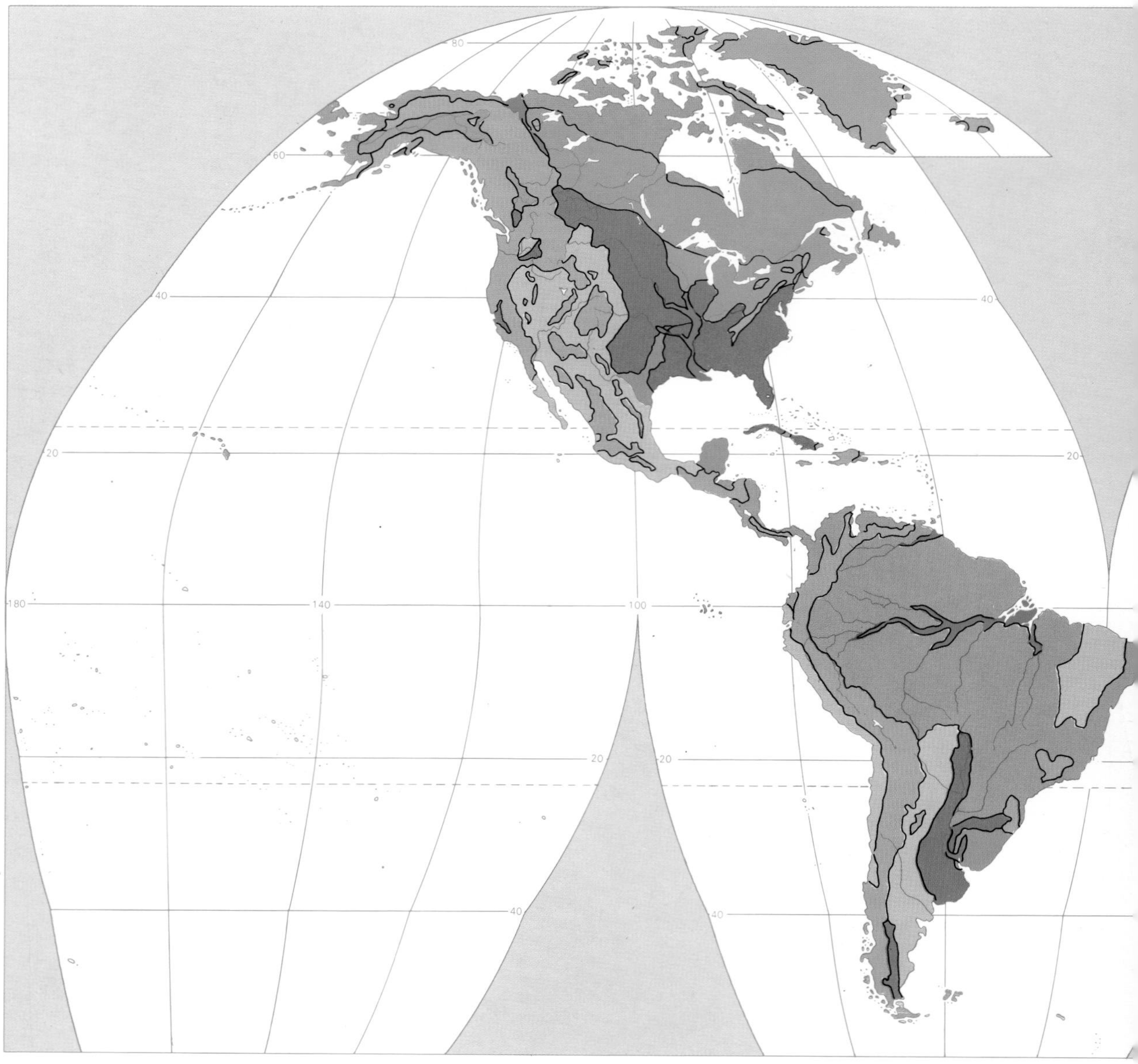

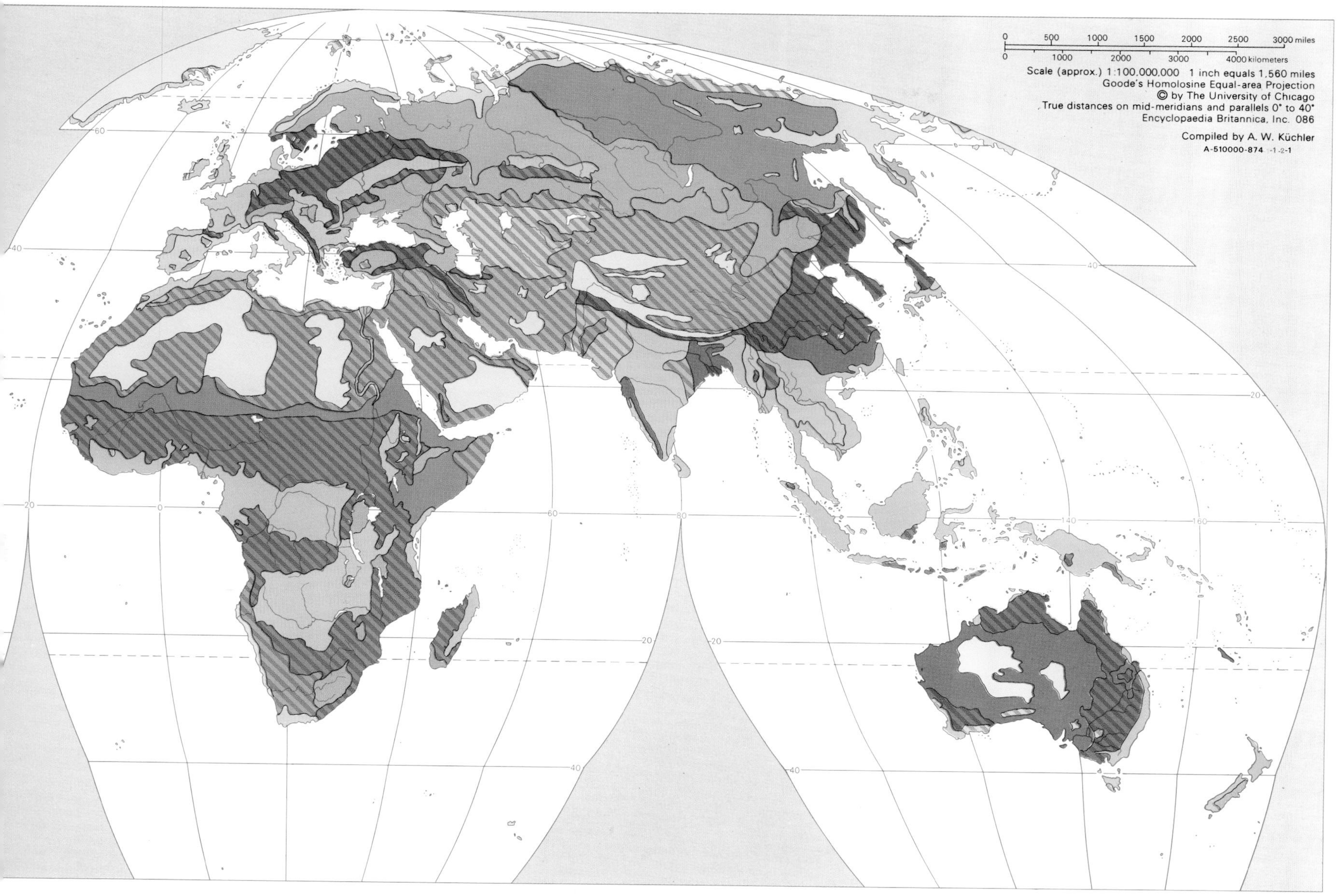
0 500 1000 1500 2000 2500 3000 miles
0 1000 2000 3000 4000 kilometers
Scale (approx.) 1:100,000,000 1 inch equals 1,560 miles
Goode's Homolosine Equal-area Projection
© by The University of Chicago
True distances on mid-meridians and parallels 0° to 40°
Encyclopaedia Britannica, Inc. 086
Compiled by A. W. Küchler
A-510000-874 -1-2-1

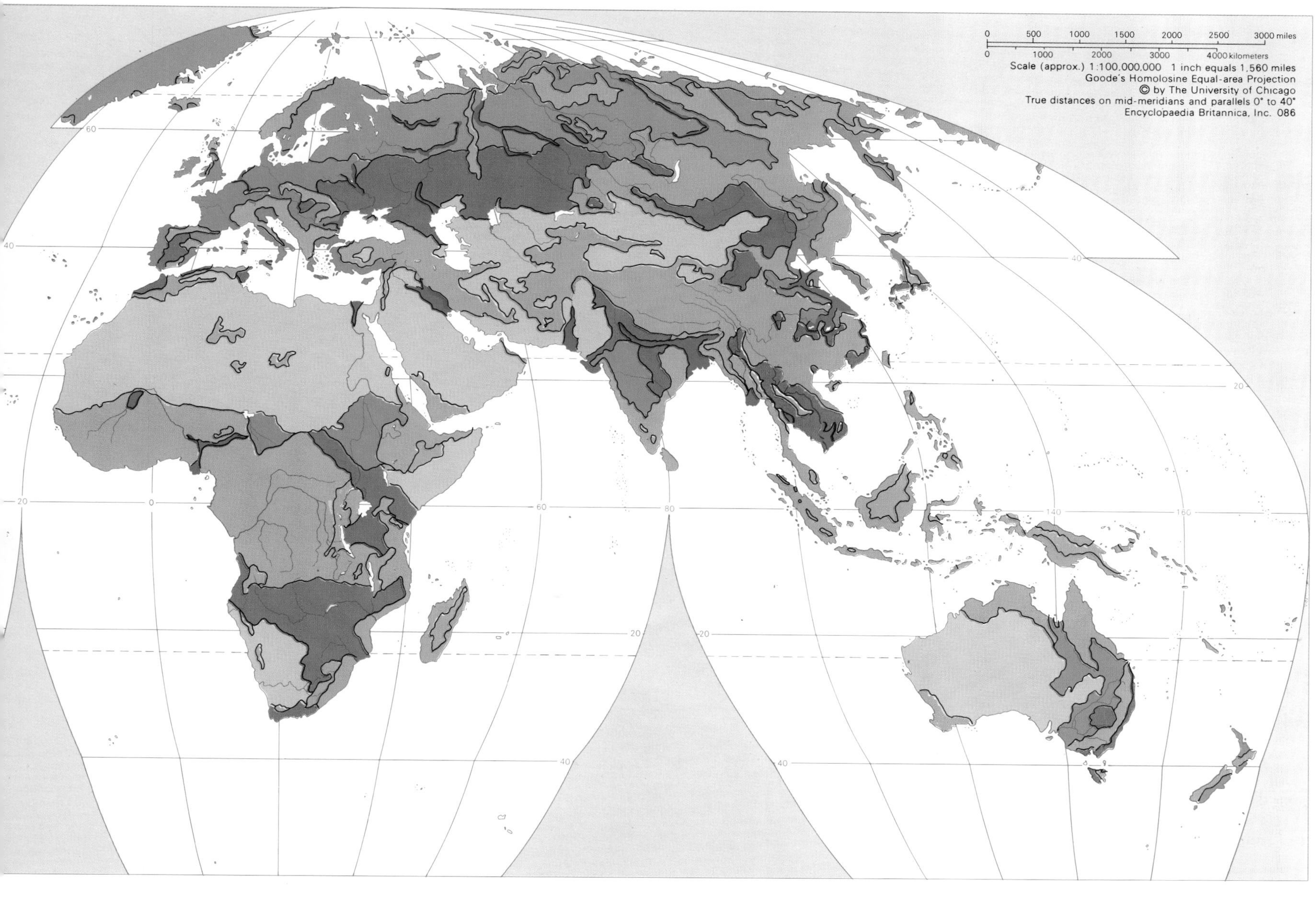
0 500 1000 1500 2000 2500 3000 miles
0 1000 2000 3000 4000 kilometers
Scale (approx.) 1:100,000,000 1 inch equals 1,560 miles
Goode's Homolosine Equal-area Projection
© by The University of Chicago
True distances on mid-meridians and parallels 0° to 40°
Encyclopaedia Britannica, Inc. 086

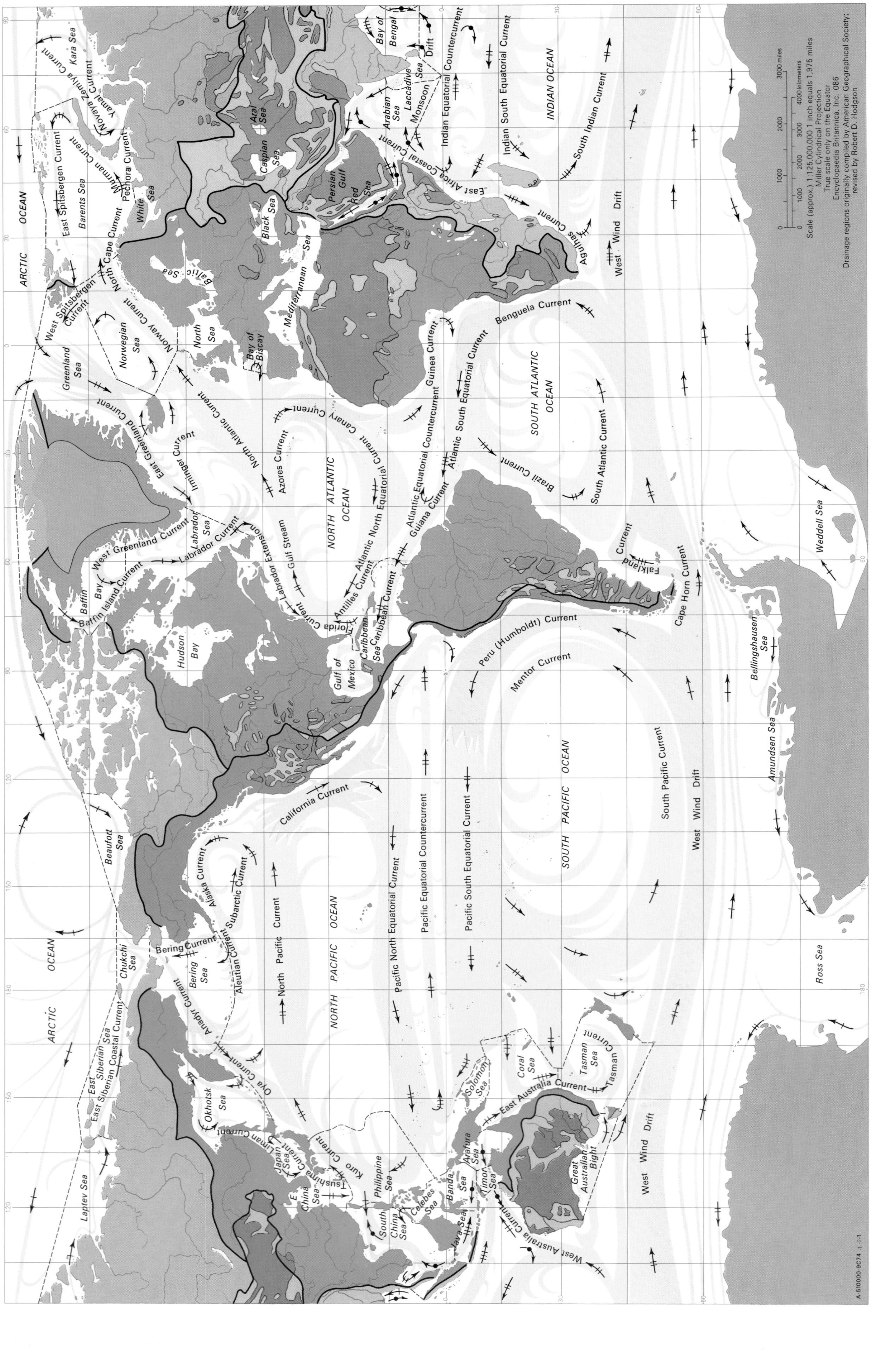

Drainage Regions and Ocean Currents

Currents during Northern Hemisphere winter

- Cold current
- Warm current
- Indicates a current that reverses direction during Northern Hemisphere summer

Speed of current
(1 knot=1 nautical mile[6,076 ft.] per hour)

- Less than 0.5 knots
- 0.5—0.8 knots
- Greater than 0.8 knots
- Limits of seas

Drainage regions
Surface drainage reaching an Ocean

- Outline of oceanic drainage regions
- Atlantic Ocean
- Pacific Ocean
- Indian Ocean
- Arctic Ocean
- Surface drainage not reaching an ocean
- Arid regions
- Ice cap

THE MAP FORM column of the Glossary lists in alphabetical order the geographical terms, including any abbreviations, that appear on the maps. Terms preceded by a hyphen are those which commonly appear as endings in map names (for example, -san in Fuji-san, -älven in Dalälven). The languages of the terms are identified by abbreviations in *italics* (see Abbreviations of Language Names below). The Glossary provides the English, German, Spanish, French, and Portuguese equivalent for each term.

As a rule, the translations were made from the map form to English, then from English into the other four languages. Since the glossary terms and translations refer to specific map features, some may vary from the customary dictionary definitions of the terms.

IN DER SPALTE "Geographische Begriffe" werden alle Begriffe und Abkürzungen in alphabetischer Ordnung aufgeführt, die in den Karten erscheinen. Begriffe mit vorgesetztem Bindestrich erscheinen normalerweise als Wortendungen in Kartennamen (z.B. -san in Fuji-san, -älven in Dalälven). In *Kursivschrift* sind die jeweiligen Abkürzungen angegeben für die Sprachen, in denen der Begriff wiedergegeben ist (siehe unten: Abkürzungen der Sprachen). Das Verzeichnis gibt für jeden Begriff den entsprechenden Ausdruck in englisch, deutsch, spanisch, französisch, und portugiesisch.

In der Regel wurde der Begriff in der Karte ins Englische übersetzt und dann vom Englischen in die vier anderen Sprachen. Da die Begriffe und Übersetzungen sich auf bestimmte Objekte in der Karte beziehen, können einige von ihnen von den in den üblichen Wörterbüchern aufgeführten Begriffsbestimmungen abweichen.

LOS TÉRMINOS GEOGRÁFICOS que aparecen en los mapas, incluyendo abreviaciones, son presentados en la columna de Términos Geográficas del Glosario, en orden alfabético. Los términos que están precedidos por un guión aparecen frecuentemente como terminaciones de los nombres en los mapas (por ejemplo, -san en Fuji-san, -älven en Dalälven). Los idiomas que representan los términos están identificados por medio de abreviaciones en *cursiva* (véase abajo, Abreviaciones de los Idiomas Extranjeros). El Glosario provee el equivalente para cada término en inglés, alemán, español, francés y portugués.

Generalmente las traducciones están hechas de las formas originales de la terminología de los mapas que aparecen primero en inglés, y luego se traducen a las otras cuatro lenguas. Algunos términos y traducciones pueden aparecer distintas a las usadas en los diccionarios generales porque se refieren a los rasgos particulares de los mapas.

LE GLOSSAIRE cite par ordre alphabétique les termes géographiques et les abréviations utilisées. Les mots précédés d'un tiret sont des suffixes (par exemple -san dans Fuji-san, -älven dans Dalälven). La langue d'origine du nom cité est indiquée par une abréviation en *italique* (voir Abréviations des noms de langues, ci-dessous). Le Glossaire donne chaque nom en anglais, allemand, espagnol, français, et portugais.

En général, les termes géographiques des cartes ont d'abord été traduits en anglais, puis de l'anglais dans les quatre autres langues. Les définitions de certains termes sont adaptées aux particularités de l'Atlas. Il peut arriver qu'elles diffèrent des définitions habituelles données par les dictionnaires.

A COLUNA 'TERMINOLOGIA', do *Glossário*, contém todos os termos geográficos que figuram nos mapas, em ordem alfabética e com as respectivas abreviações. Os termos precedidos por um hífen são os que freqüentemente aparecem nos mapas como sufixos de nomes tais como *-san* (em Fuji-san), *-älven* (em Dalälven). As línguas em que os termos são expressos estão identificadas por abreviações em *grifo* (ver abaixo, 'Abreviações das línguas estrangeiras'). O Glossário fornece o equivalente de cada termo em inglês, alemão, espanhol, português e francês.

De modo geral, as traduções foram feitas das formas originais da terminologia usada nos mapas para o inglês, e, em seguida, do inglês para as outras quatro línguas. Uma vez que os termos geográficos e traduções do *Glossário* referem-se a acidentes específicos de cada mapa, é possível que algumas definições sejam diferentes das consignadas nos dicionários gerais das línguas.

Abbreviations of Language Names / Abkürzungen der Nationalsprachen / Abreviaciones de los Idiomas Extranjeros / Abréviations des Noms de Langues / Abreviações dos Idiomas Estrangeiros

	ENGLISH	DEUTSCH	ESPAÑOL	FRANÇAIS	PORTUGUÊS
Afk.	Afrikaans	Afrikaans	Africano	Afrikaans	Afrikaans
Alb.	Albanian	Albanisch	Albanesa	Albanais	Albanês
Ara.	Arabic	Arabisch	Árabe	Arabe	Árabe
Ber.	Berber	Berberisch	Bereber	Berbère	Berbere
Ben.	Bengali	Bengali	Bengali	Bengali	Bengali
Blg.	Bulgarian	Bulgarisch	Búlgaro	Bulgare	Búlgaro
Bur.	Burmese	Burmanisch	Birmano	Birman	Birmanês
Cat.	Catalan	Katalanisch	Catalán	Catalan	Catalão
Cbd.	Cambodian	Kambodschanisch	Camboyano	Cambodgien	Cambojano
Ch.	Chinese	Chinesisch	Chino	Chinois	Chinês
Czech	Czech	Tschechisch	Checo	Tchèque	Tcheco
Dan.	Danish	Dänisch	Danés	Danois	Dinamarquês
Du.	Dutch	Niederländisch	Holandés	Néerlandais	Holandês
Eng.	English	Englisch	Inglés	Anglais	Inglês
Est.	Estonian	Estnisch	Estonio	Esthonien	Estoniano
Finn.	Finnish	Finnisch	Finés	Finnois	Finlandês
Flm.	Flemish	Flämisch	Flamenco	Flamand	Flamengo
Fr.	French	Französisch	Francés	Français	Francês
Gae.	Gaelic	Gälisch	Gaélico	Gaélique	Gaélico
Ger.	German	Deutsch	Alemán	Allemand	Alemão
Gr.	Greek	Griechisch	Griego	Grec	Grego
Hau.	Hausa	Haussa	Hausa	Haoussa	Haussa
Heb.	Hebrew	Hebräisch	Hebreo	Hébreu	Hebraico
Hung.	Hungarian	Ungarisch	Húngaro	Hongrois	Húngaro
Ice.	Icelandic	Isländisch	Islandés	Islandais	Islandês
Indon.	Indonesian	Indonesisch	Indonesio	Indonésien	Indonésio
It.	Italian	Italienisch	Italiano	Italien	Italiano
Jap.	Japanese	Japanisch	Japonés	Japonais	Japonês
Kor.	Korean	Koreanisch	Coreano	Coréen	Coreano
Lao.	Laotian	Laotisch	Laosiano	Laotien	Laosiano
Lapp.	Lappish	Lappisch	Lapón	Lapon	Lapão
Latv.	Latvian	Lettisch	Letón	Letton	Letão
Lith.	Lithuanian	Litauisch	Lituano	Lithuanien	Lituano
Mal.	Malay	Malaiisch	Malayo	Malais	Malaio
Mong.	Mongolian	Mongolisch	Mogol	Mongol	Mongol
Nor.	Norwegian	Norwegisch	Norvego	Norvégien	Norueguês
Pas.	Pashto	Paschtu	Pushtu	Pachtou	Pachtu
Per.	Persian	Persisch	Persa	Persan	Persa
Pol.	Polish	Polnisch	Polaco	Polonais	Polonês
Poly.	Polynesian	Polynesisch	Polinesio	Polynésien	Polinésio
Port.	Portuguese	Portugiesisch	Portugués	Portugais	Português
Rom.	Romanian	Rumänisch	Rumano	Roumain	Romeno
Rus.	Russian	Russisch	Ruso	Russe	Russo
S./C.	Serbo-Croatian	Serbokroatisch	Servio-croata	Serbo-croate	Servo-croata
Sin.	Sinhalese	Singhalesisch	Cingalés	Cinghalais	Cingalês
Slo.	Slovak	Slowakisch	Eslovaco	Slovaque	Eslovaco
Sp.	Spanish	Spanisch	Español	Espagnol	Espanhol
Swe.	Swedish	Schwedisch	Sueco	Suédois	Sueco
Thai	Thai	Thai	Tai	Thaï	Tailandês
Tib.	Tibetan	Tibetisch	Tibetano	Tibétain	Tibetano
Tur.	Turkish	Türkisch	Turco	Turc	Turco
Viet.	Vietnamese	Vietnamesisch	Vietnamita	Vietnamien	Vietnamita
Welsh	Welsh	Walisisch	Galés	Gallois	Galês

ENGLISH	DEUTSCH	**Map Form / Geographische Begriffe / Términos Geográficos / Termes Géographiques / Termos Geográficos**	ESPAÑOL	FRANÇAIS	PORTUGUÊS
		A			
river	Fluss	**-å** *Dan., Nor., Swe.*	río	rivière	rio
brook	Bach	**a., arroyo** *Sp.*	arroyo	ruisseau	córrego
river	Fluss	**āb** *Per.*	río	rivière	rio
army base	Heeresstützpunkt	**a.b., army base** *Eng.*	base del ejército	base d'armée	base militar
well	Brunnen	**ābār** *Ara.*	pozo	puits	poço
abbey	Abtei	**abb., abbazia** *It.*	abadía	abbaye	abadia
abbey	Abtei	**abbaye** *Fr.*	abadía	abbaye	abadia
abbey	Abtei	**abbazia** *It.*	abadía	abbaye	abadia
abbey	Abtei	**abbey** *Eng.*	abadía	abbaye	abadia
aboriginal reserve	Eingeborenenschutzgebiet	**aboriginal reserve** *Eng.*	zona de aborígenes	réserve des indigènes	reserva indígena
abbey	Abtei	**Abtei** *Ger.*	abadía	abbaye	abadia
ditch	Graben	**acequia** *Sp.*	acequia	fossé	fosso
reservoir	Stausee	**açude** *Port.*	embalse	réservoir	açude
island(s)	Insel(n)	**ada(lar)** *Tur.*	isla(s)	île(s)	ilha(s)
island	Insel	**adası** *Tur.*	isla	île	ilha
mountains	Berge	**adrar** *Ber.*	montañas	montagnes	montanhas
Atomic Energy Commission	Atomenergiekommission	**A.E.C., Atomic Energy Commission** *Eng.*	Comisión de Energía Atomica	Commission de l'Énergie Atomique	Comissão de Energia Atômica
airport	Flughafen	**aérd., aérodrome** *Fr.*	aeródromo	aérodrome	aeródromo
airport	Flughafen	**aeródromo** *Port., Sp.*	aeródromo	aérodrome	aeródromo
airport	Flughafen	**aeroparque** *Sp.*	aeroparque	aéroport	aeroporto
airport	Flughafen	**aéroport** *Fr.*	aeropuerto	aéroport	aeroporto
airport	Flughafen	**aeroporto** *It., Port.*	aeropuerto	aéroport	aeroporto
airport	Flughafen	**aeropuerto** *Sp.*	aeropuerto	aéroport	aeroporto
air force base	Luftwaffenstützpunkt	**a.f.b., air force base** *Eng.*	base aeronáutica	base aérienne	base aérea
wadi	Wadi	**ahzar** *Ara.*	uadi	wadi	uádi
peak	Gipfel	**aiguille** *Fr.*	pico	aiguille	pico
air base	Luftstützpunkt	**air base** *Eng.*	base aérea	base aérienne	base aérea
airfield	Flugplatz	**airfield** *Eng.*	camp de aviación	aérodrome	campo de pouso
air force base	Luftwaffenstützpunkt	**air force base** *Eng.*	base aeronáutica	base aérienne	base aérea
airport	Flughafen	**airport** *Eng.*	aeropuerto	aéroport	aeroporto
cape	Kap	**ákra, akrotírion** *Gr.*	cabo	cap	cabo
hill	Hügel	**'alam, 'alāmat** *Ara.*	colina	colline	colina
avenue	Allee	**alameda** *Sp.*	alameda	avenue	avenida
alps	Alpen	**alpes** *Fr.*	alpes	alpes	alpes
alps	Alpen	**alpi** *It.*	alpes	alpes	alpes
mountains, hills	Berge, Hügel	**altos** *Sp.*	altos	montagnes, collines	montanhas, colinas
river	Fluss	**-älv, -älven** *Swe.*	río	rivière	rio
amusement park	Vergnügungspark	**amusement park** *Eng.*	parque de diversiones	parc récréatif	parque de diversões
river	Fluss	**-ån** *Swe.*	río	rivière	rio
anchorage	Ankerplatz	**anchorage** *Eng.*	ancladero	ancrage	ancoradouro
bay	Bucht	**angra** *Sp.*	angra	baie	baía
cove	kleine Bucht	**anse** *Fr.*	ensenada	anse	enseada
bay	Bucht	**ao** *Thai*	bahía	baie	baía
aqueduct	Aquädukt	**aqueduc** *Fr.*	acueducto	aqueduc	aqueduto
aqueduct	Aquädukt	**aqueduct** *Eng.*	acueducto	aqueduc	aqueduto
archipelago	Archipel	**archipel** *Fr.*	archipiélago	archipel	arquipélago
archipelago	Archipel	**archipelag** *Rus.*	archipiélago	archipel	arquipélago
archipelago	Archipel	**archipelago** *Eng.*	archipiélago	archipel	arquipélago
archipelago	Archipel	**archipiélago** *Sp.*	archipiélago	archipel	arquipélago
arm	Arm	**arm** *Eng.*	brazo	bras	braço de rio
army base	Heeresstützpunkt	**army base** *Eng.*	base del ejército	base d'armée	base militar
airport	Flughafen	**arpt., aéroport** *Fr.* **aeroporto** *It., Port.* **aeropuerto** *Sp.* **airport** *Eng.*	aeropuerto	aéroport	aeroporto
archipelago	Archipel	**arquipélago** *Port.*	archipiélago	archipel	arquipélago
reef	Riff	**arrecife** *Sp.*	arrecife	récif	recife
brook	Bach	**arroyo** *Sp.*	arroyo	ruisseau	córrego, arroio
hills	Hügel	**-ås,-åsen** *Swe.*	colinas	collines	colinas
ridge	Höhenrücken	**'assâbet** *Ara.*	sierra	crête	serra
atoll	Atoll	**atol** *Port.*	atolón	atoll	atol
atoll	Atoll	**atoll** *Eng., Fr.*	atolón	atoll	atol
auditorium	Auditorium	**aud., auditorium** *Eng.*	auditorio	auditorium	auditório
race course	Rennbahn	**autodrome** *Fr.*	autódromo	autodrome	autódromo
race course	Rennbahn	**autodromo** *It.*	autódromo	autodrome	autódromo
expressway	Autobahn	**autopista** *Sp.*	autopista	autoroute	via expressa
avenue	Allee	**av., avenida** *Port., Sp.* **avenue** *Eng., Fr.*	avenida	avenue	avenida
channel	Kanal	**ava** *Poly.*	canal, estrecho	canal, détroit	canal, estreito
avenue	Allee	**avenida** *Port., Sp.*	avenida	avenue	avenida
avenue	Allee	**avenue** *Eng., Fr.*	avenida	avenue	avenida
spring	Quelle	**'ayn** *Ara.*	manantial	source	manancial, fonte

B

ENGLISH	DEUTSCH	Map Form / Geographische Begriffe / Términos Geográficos / Termes Géographiques / Termos Geográficos	ESPAÑOL	FRANÇAIS	PORTUGUÊS
bay	Bucht	**baai** *Du.*	bahía	baie	baía
strait	Meeresstrasse	**bab** *Ara.*	estrecho	détroit	estreito
brook, creek	Bach	**Bach** *Ger.*	arroyo, riachuelo	ruisseau, crique	córrego, arroio
hill	Hügel	**-backen** *Swe.*	colina	colline	colina
desert	Wüste	**bādiyat** *Ara.*	desierto	désert	deserto
strait	Meeresstrasse	**bælt** *Dan.*	estrecho	détroit	estreito
bay	Bucht	**bahía** *Sp.*	bahía	baie	baía
inlet	Einfahrt	**bahiret** *Ara.*	abra	bras de mer	enseada, estuário
railroad station	Bahnhof	**Bahnhof** *Ger.*	estación de ferrocarril	gare	estação ferroviária
river; sea	Fluss; Meer	**bahr, baḥr** *Ara.*	río; mar	rivière; mer	rio; mar
reservoir	Stausee	**baḥrat** *Ara.*	embalse	réservoir	reservatório
bay	Bucht	**baía** *Port.*	bahía	baie	baía
bay	Bucht	**baie** *Fr.*	bahía	baie	baía
reef, sand bar	Riff, Sandbarre	**bajo** *Sp.*	bajo	récif, banc de sable	recife, banco de areia
gorge	Schlucht	**balka** *Rus.*	garganta	gorge	garganta
dome	Kuppe	**ballon** *Fr.*	domo	ballon	domo
marsh	Marsch	**balta** *Rom.*	pantano	marais	pântano
cape	Kap	**-bana** *Jap.*	cabo	cap	cabo
marsh	Marsch	**bañados** *Sp.*	bañados	marais	pântano
island	Insel	**-banare** *Jap.*	isla	île	ilha
bank	Bank	**banco** *Sp.*	banco	banc	banco
peninsula	Halbinsel	**-bandao** *Ch.*	península	péninsule	península
bank	Bank	**bank** *Eng.*	banco	banc	banco
shoal	Untiefe	**-banken** *Swe.*	bajo	haut-fond	escolho
sand bar	Sandbarre	**barra** *Sp.*	barra	banc de sable	banco de areia
dam	Damm	**barrage** *Fr.*	presa	barrage	represa
ravine	Tobel	**barranca** *Sp.*	barranca	ravin	ravina
air base	Luftstützpunkt	**base aérea** *Sp.*	base aérea	base aérienne	base aérea
basilica	Basilika	**basílica** *Sp.*	basílica	basilique	basílica
basilica	Basilika	**basilique** *Fr.*	basílica	basilique	basílica
basin	Becken	**basin** *Eng.*	cuenca	bassin	bacia
basin	Becken	**bassin** *Fr.*	cuenca	bassin	bacia
marsh	Marsch	**batakliği** *Tur.*	pantano	marais	pântano
river	Fluss	**batang** *Indon.*	río	rivière	rio
river	Fluss	**batha** *Ara.*	río	rivière	rio
marsh	Marsch	**bāṭlāq** *Per.*	pantano	marais	pântano
battlefield	Schlachtfeld	**battlefield** *Eng.*	campo de batalla	champ de bataille	campo de batalha
mountain	Berg	**batu** *Mal.*	montaña	montagne	montanha
bay	Bucht	**bay** *Eng.*	bahía	baie	baía
bayou	Altwasser	**bayou** *Fr., Eng.*	ensenada pantanosa	bayou	enseada pantanosa
beach	Strand	**beach** *Eng.*	playa	plage	praia
mountain	Berg	**bein, beinn** *Gae.*	montaña	montagne	montanha
snowcapped mountains	Schneegipfel	**belogorje** *Rus.*	nevados	montagnes neigeuses	picos nevados
mountain	Berg	**ben** *Gae.*	montaña	montagne	montanha
mountain, hill	Berg	**Berg** *Ger.*	montaña, colina	montagne, colline	montanha, colina
mountains	Berge	**berg** *Afk.*	montañas	montagnes	montanhas
hill(s), mountain(s)	Hügel, Berg(e)	**-berg** *Swe.*	colina(s), montaña(s)	colline(s), montagne(s)	colina(s), montanha(s)
mountains	Berge	**Berge** *Ger.*	montañas	montagnes	montanhas
mountains	Berge	**berge** *Afk.*	montañas	montagnes	montanhas
hills, mountains	Hügel, Berge	**-bergen** *Swe.*	colinas, montañas	collines, montagnes	colinas, montanhas
hill, mountain	Hügel, Berg	**-berget** *Swe.*	colina, montaña	colline, montagne	colina, montanha
upland	Bergland	**Bergland** *Ger.*	tierras altas	hautes terres	terras altas
battlefield	Schlachtfeld	**bfld., battlefield** *Eng.*	campo de batalla	champ de bataille	campo de batalha
mountain, hill	Berg	**Bg., Berg** *Ger.*	montaña, colina	montagne, colline	montanha, colina
bridge	Brücke	**bge., bridge** *Eng.*	puente	pont	ponte
bight	Bucht	**bight** *Eng.*	bahía	baie	baía, enseada
bill (point)	Landspitze	**bill** *Eng.*	punta	pointe	ponta
valley	Tal	**biq'at** *Heb.*	valle	vallée	vale
well	Brunnen	**bi'r** *Ara.*	pozo	puits	poço
lake	See	**birkat** *Ara.*	lago	lac	lago
mountains	Berge	**bjeshkët** *Alb.*	montañas	montagnes	montanhas
brook	Bach	**bk., brook** *Eng.*	arroyo	ruisseau	córrego, arroio
upland	Bergland	**blaenau** *Welsh*	tierras altas	hautes terres	terras altas
bluff(s)	Steilufer	**bluff(s)** *Eng.*	acantilado(s)	falaise(s)	falésia(s)
boulevard	Boulevard	**blvd., boulevard** *Fr., Eng.*	bulevar	boulevard	bulevar
mountain	Berg	**b'nom** *Viet.*	montaña	montagne	montanha
lake	See	**-bo** *Ch.*	lago	lac	lago
river mouth	Flussmündung	**boca** *Sp.*	boca	embouchure	foz
river mouth; pass	Flussmündung; Pass	**bocca** *It.*	boca; paso	embouchure; col	foz; passo
bay	Bucht	**bocht** *Du.*	bahía	baie	baía
bay	Bodden	**Bodden** *Ger.*	bahía	baie	baía
bog	Moor	**bog** *Eng.*	pantano	fondrière	pântano
strait	Meeresstrasse	**boğazı** *Tur.*	estrecho	détroit	estreito
range	Gebirge	**bogd** *Mong.*	sierra	chaîne	cordilheira
woods	Gehölz	**bois** *Fr.*	bosque	bois	bosque
enclosed basin	Becken	**bolsón** *Sp.*	bolsón	bassin fermée	bacia fechada
forest	Wald	**bory** *Pol.*	bosque	forêt	floresta
forest	Wald	**bosque** *Sp.*	bosque	forêt	floresta
boulevard	Boulevard	**boulevard** *Fr., Eng.*	boulevar	boulevard	bulevar
branch	Arm	**br., branch** *Eng.*	brazo	bras	braço
stream distributary	Flussarm	**braţul** *Rom.*	brazo de río	bras	braço de rio
breakwater	Wellenbrecher	**breakwater** *Eng.*	rompeolas	brise-lames	quebra-mar
glacier	Gletscher	**-breen** *Nor.*	glaciar	glacier	geleira
bridge	Brücke	**bridge** *Eng.*	puente	pont	ponte
brook	Bach	**brook** *Eng.*	arroyo	ruisseau	córrego
marsh	Bruch	**Bruch** *Ger.*	pantano	marais	pântano
bridge	Brücke	**Brücke** *Ger.*	puente	pont	ponte
bridge	Brücke	**brug** *Du.*	puente	pont	ponte
bay	Bucht	**Bucht** *Ger.*	bahía	baie	baía
bay	Bucht	**buchta** *Rus.*	bahía	baie	baía
mountain	Berg	**bufa** *Sp.*	bufa	montagne	montanha
bay	Bucht	**bugt** *Dan.*	bahía	baie	baía
lake	See	**buḥayrah** *Ara.*	lago	lac	lago
lake, lagoon	See, Lagune, Haff	**buḥayrat** *Ara.*	lago, laguna	lac, lagune	lago, laguna
mountain, hill	Berg, Hügel	**bukit** *Indon., Mal.*	montaña, colina	montagne, colline	montanha, colina
bay	Bucht	**-bukten** *Swe.*	bahía	baie	baía
mountain	Berg	**bulu** *Indon.*	montaña	montagne	montanha
castle	Burg	**Burg** *Ger.*	castillo	château	castelo
hill	Hügel	**burj** *Ara.*	colina	colline	colina
creek	Bach	**burn** *Ger.*	riachuelo	crique	riacho
cape	Kap	**burnu, burun** *Tur.*	cabo	cap	cabo
bay	Busen	**Busen** *Ger.*	bahía	baie	baía
butte(s)	Restberg(e)	**butte(s)** *Eng., Fr.*	butte(s)	butte(s)	colina, outeiro

C

ENGLISH	DEUTSCH	Map Form / Geographische Begriffe / Términos Geográficos / Termes Géographiques / Termos Geográficos	ESPAÑOL	FRANÇAIS	PORTUGUÊS
cape	Kap	**c., cabo** *Sp.* **cap** *Fr.* **cape** *Eng.*	cabo	cap	cabo
street	Strasse	**c., calle** *Sp.*	calle	rue	rua
peaks	Gipfel	**cabezas** *Sp.*	cabezas	cimes	picos
cape	Kap	**cabo** *Port., Sp.*	cabo	cap	cabo
waterfall	Wasserfall	**cachoeira** *Port.*	cascada	chute d'eau	cachoeira
street	Strasse	**calle** *Sp.*	calle	rue	rua
parkway	Ferienstrasse	**calzada** *Sp.*	calzada	allée de parc	alameda de parque
mosque	Moschee	**camii** *Tur.*	mezquita	mosquée	mesquita
road	Weg	**camino** *Sp.*	camino	route	rodovia
camp	Lager	**camp** *Eng., Fr.*	campo	camp	campo
plain	Ebene	**campo** *It.*	llanura	plaine	planície
brook; ravine	Bach; Tobel	**cañada** *Sp.*	cañada	ruisseau; ravin	ravina
canal	Kanal	**canal** *Eng.*	canal	canal	canal
canal, channel	Kanal	**canal** *Fr., Port., Sp.*	canal	canal	canal
canal, channel	Kanal	**canale** *It.*	canal	canal	canal
stream distributary	Flussarm	**caño** *Sp.*	caño	bras	braço de rio, igarapé
canyon	Cañon	**cañón** *Sp.*	cañón	canyon	canhão
canyon	Cañon	**canyon** *Eng.*	cañón	canyon	canhão
plateau	Hochebene	**cao nguyen** *Viet.*	meseta	plateau	planalto
cape	Kap	**cap** *Fr.*	cabo	cap	cabo
cape	Kap	**cape** *Eng.*	cabo	cap	cabo
capitol	Kapitol	**capitolio** *Sp.*	capitolio	capitole	capitólio
cape	Kap	**capo** *It.*	cabo	cap	cabo
captain	Kapitän	**capt., captain** *Eng.*	capitán	capitaine	capitão
highway	Strasse	**carretera** *Sp.*	carretera	route	rodovia
valley	Tal	**carse** *Gae.*	valle	vallée	vale
waterfall	Wasserfall	**cascada** *Sp.*	cascada	chute d'eau	queda d'água
waterfall	Wasserfall	**cascata** *It.*	cascada	chute d'eau	queda d'água
castle	Burg, Schloss	**castel, castello** *It.*	castillo	château	castelo
castle	Burg, Schloss	**castelo** *Port.*	castillo	château	castelo
castle	Burg, Schloss	**castillo** *Sp.*	castillo	château	castelo
castle	Burg, Schloss	**castle** *Eng.*	castillo	château	castelo
cataracts	Katarakten	**cataratas** *Port., Sp.*	cataratas	cataractes	cataratas
cathedral	Kathedrale	**catedral** *Sp.*	catedral	cathédrale	catedral
range	Gebirge	**catena** *Sp.*	catena	chaîne	cordilheira
cathedral	Kathedrale	**cathedral** *Eng.*	catedral	cathédrale	catedral
causeway	Dammweg	**causeway** *Eng.*	calzada	chaussée	calçada
upland	Bergland	**causse** *Fr.*	tierras altas	causse	terras altas
cave(s)	Höhle(n)	**cave(s)** *Eng.*	cueva(s)	caverne(s)	caverna(s)
cay	Klippe	**cay** *Eng.*	cayo	caye	baixio
cay(s)	Klippe(n)	**cayo(s)** *Sp.*	cayo(s)	cave(s)	baixio(s)
cemetery	Friedhof	**cementerio** *Sp.*	cementerio	cimetière	cemitério
cemetery	Friedhof	**cemetery** *Eng.*	cementerio	cimetière	cemitério
mountain(s), hill(s)	Berg(e), Hügel	**cerro(s)** *Sp.*	cerro(s)	montagne(s), colline(s)	montanha(s), colina(s)
range	Gebirge	**chaîne** *Fr.*	sierra	chaîne	cordilheira
channel	Kanal	**channel** *Eng.*	canal, estrecho	canal, détroit	canal, estreito
hills	Hügel	**chapada** *Port.*	colinas	collines	chapada
island	Insel	**char** *Ben.*	isla	île	ilha
castle	Burg, Schloss	**château** *Fr.*	castillo	château	castelo
island	Insel	**chau** *Ch.*	isla	île	ilha
road	Landstrasse	**chemin** *Fr.*	camino	chemin	rodovia
bay	Bucht	**chhàk** *Cbd.*	bahía	baie	baía
river	Fluss	**ch'i** *Ch.*	río	rivière	rio
lake	See	**-chi** *Ch.*	lago	lac	lago
cape	Kap	**chia** *Ch.*	cabo	cap	cabo
harbor	Hafen	**chiang** *Ch.*	puerto	port	porto
cape	Kap	**chiao** *Ch.*	cabo	cap	cabo
road	Landstrasse	**chin., chemin** *Fr.*	camino	chemin	rodovia
river	Fluss	**-ch'ŏn** *Kor.*	río	rivière	rio
reservoir	Stausse	**-chŏsuji** *Kor.*	embalse	réservoir	reservatório
intermittent lake, salt marsh	periodischer See, Salzmarsch	**chott** *Ara.*	lago intermitente, pantano salado	lac périodique, marais salé	lago intermitente, pântano salgado
range	Gebirge	**chr., chrebet** *Rus.*	sierra	chaîne	cordilheira
river	Fluss	**ch'uan** *Ch.*	río	rivière	rio
mountains	Berge	**chuŏr phnum** *Cbd.*	montañas	montagnes	montanhas
church	Kirche	**church** *Eng.*	iglesia	église	igreja
waterfalls	Wasserfälle	**chutes** *Fr.*	cascadas	chutes d'eau	quedas d'água
marsh	Marsch	**ciénaga** *Sp.*	ciénaga	marais	pântano
peak	Gipfel	**cima** *It., Sp.*	cima	cime	pico
peak	Gipfel	**cime** *Fr.*	cima	cime	pico
cemetery	Friedhof	**cimetière** *Fr.*	cementerio	cimetière	cemitério
city	Stadt	**città** *It.*	ciudad	ville	cidade
city	Stadt	**city** *Eng.*	ciudad	ville	cidade
city	Stadt	**ciudad** *Sp.*	ciudad	ville	cidade
claypan	Tonpfanne	**claypan** *Eng.*	capa de arcilla	couche argilleuse	camada de argila
cliff(s)	Kliff(e)	**cliff(s)** *Eng.*	risco(s)	falaise(s)	falésia(s)
mountain	Berg	**co** *Viet.*	montaña	montagne	montanha
mountain, hill	Berg, Hügel	**co., cerro** *Sp.*	cerro	montagne, colline	montanha, colina
coast	Küste	**coast** *Eng.*	costa	côte	costa
coast guard station	Küstenwacht-station	**coast guard station** *Eng.*	estación de los guardacostas	station des gardes de la côte	estação de guarda costeira
pass	Pass	**col** *Fr.*	paso	col	passo
college	Hochschule	**colegio** *Sp.*	colegio	collège	colégio
hill(s)	Hügel	**colina(s)** *Sp.*	colina(s)	colline(s)	colina(s)
college	Hochschule	**coll., college** *Eng.*	colegio	collège	colégio
hills	Hügel	**colli** *It.*	colinas	collines	colinas
hills	Hügel	**colline** *It.*	colinas	collines	colinas
hills	Hügel	**collines** *Fr.*	colinas	collines	colinas
common	Gemeindeland	**common** *Eng.*	campo común	commune	terra comum
islands	Inseln	**con** *Viet.*	islas	îles	ilhas
plain	Ebene	**conca** *It.*	llanura	plaine	planície
convent	Nonnenkloster	**convent** *Eng.*	convento	couvent	convento
convent	Nonnenkloster	**convento** *It., Port., Sp.*	convento	couvent	convento
range	Gebirge	**cord., cordillera** *Sp.*	cordillera	chaîne	cordilheira
mountain	Berg	**corno** *It.*	montaña	montagne	montanha
brook	Bach	**córrego** *Port.*	arroyo	ruisseau	córrego
coast	Küste	**costa** *Sp.*	costa	côte	costa
coast, hills	Küste, Hügel	**côte** *Fr.*	costa, colinas	côte	costa, colinas
hills	Hügel	**coteau** *Fr.*	colinas	coteau	colinas
coulee	breite Schlucht	**coulee** *Eng.*	rambla	coulée	barranco
coulee	breite Schlucht	**coulée** *Fr.*	rambla	coulée	barranco
county park	Park	**county park** *Eng.*	parque del condado	parc de comté	parque de condado
convent	Nonnenkloster	**couvent** *Fr.*	convento	couvent	convento
cove	kleine Bucht	**cove** *Eng.*	ensenada	anse	enseada
creek	Bach	**cr., creek** *Eng.*	riachuelo	crique	riacho
crag	Felsspitze	**crag** *Eng.*	despeñadero	pointe de rocher	despenhadeiro
crater	Krater	**crater** *Eng.*	cráter	cratère	cratera
crater	Krater	**cratère** *Fr.*	cráter	cratère	cratera
creek	Bach	**creek** *Eng.*	riachuelo	crique	riacho
peak	Gipfel	**croda** *It.*	pico	cime	pico
canal	Kanal	**csatorna** *Hung.*	canal	canal	canal
bay	Bucht	**cua** *Viet.*	bahía	baie	baía
hills, ridge	Hügel, Höhenrücken	**cuchilla** *Sp.*	cuchilla	collines, crête	coxilha
caves	Höhen	**cuevas** *Sp.*	cuevas	cavernes	cavernas
cove	kleine Bucht	**cul-de-sac** *Fr.*	ensenada	cul-de-sac	enseada
mountains	Berge	**culmea** *Rom.*	montañas	montagnes	montanhas
summit	Gipfel	**cumbre** *Sp.*	cumbre	sommet	cume

D

ENGLISH	DEUTSCH	Map Form / Geographische Begriffe / Términos Geográficos / Termes Géographiques / Termos Geográficos	ESPAÑOL	FRANÇAIS	PORTUGUÊS
mountain	Berg	**dağ, dağı** *Tur.*	montaña	montagne	montanha
mountains	Berge	**dāgh** *Per.*	montañas	montagnes	montanhas
mountains	Berge	**dağlar, dağları** *Tur.*	montañas	montagnes	montanhas
hill	Hügel	**ḍahr** *Ara.*	colina	colline	colina
plateau	Hochebene	**-dai, -daichi** *Jap.*	meseta	plateau	planalto

ENGLISH	DEUTSCH	Map Form / Geographische Begriffe / Términos Geográficos / Termes Géographiques / Termos Geográficos	ESPAÑOL	FRANÇAIS	PORTUGUÊS
mountain	Berg	**-dake** *Jap.*	montaña	montagne	montanha
valley	Tal	**-dal, -dalen** *Nor., Swe.*	valle	vallée	vale
dale	weites Tal	**dale** *Eng.*	valle ancho	vallée large	vale aberto
dam	Damm	**dam** *Eng.*	presa	barrage	represa
lake	See	**danau** *Indon.*	lago	lac	lago
island	Insel	**-dao** *Ch., Viet.*	isla	île	ilha
marsh	Marsch	**daqq** *Per.*	pantano	marais	pântano
lake	See	**daryācheh** *Per.*	lago	lac	lago
desert	Wüste	**dasht** *Per.*	desierto	désert	deserto
monastery	Kloster	**dayr** *Ara.*	monasterio	monastère	mosteiro
deep	Tiefe	**deep** *Eng.*	fosa marina	fossé marin	fossa submarina
delta	Delta	**delta** *Eng., Fr., Sp.*	delta	delta	delta
sea	Meer	**deniz, denizi,** *Tur.*	mar	mer	mar
monument	Denkmal	**Denkmal** *Ger.*	monumento	monument	monumento
pass	Pass	**deo** *Viet.*	paso	col	passo
depression	Senke	**depression** *Eng.*	depresión	dépression	depressão
river	Fluss	**deresi** *Tur.*	río	rivière	rio
desert	Wüste	**desert** *Eng.*	desierto	désert	deserto
desert	Wüste	**desierto** *Sp.*	desierto	désert	deserto
strait	Meeresstrasse	**détroit** *Fr.*	estrecho	détroit	estreito
escarpment	Landstufe	**dhar** *Ara.*	escarpa	escarpement	escarpa
canal	Kanal	**dhiórix** *Gr.*	canal	canal	canal
lake	See	**-dian** *Ch.*	lago	lac	lago
channel	Kanal	**diep** *Du.*	canal, estrecho	canal, détroit	canal, estreito
dike	Deich	**dijk** *Du.*	dique	digue	dique
district	Distrikt	**district** *Eng.*	distrito	district	distrito
district	Distrikt	**distrito** *Sp.*	distrito	district	distrito
ditch	Graben	**ditch** *Eng.*	acequia	fossé	fosso
peninsula	Halbinsel	**djazirah** *Indon.*	península	péninsule	península
mountain(s)	Berg(e)	**djebel** *Ara.*	montaña(s)	montagne(s)	montanha(s)
fjord	Fjord	**-djúp** *Ice.*	fiordo	fjord	fiorde
channel, sound	Kanal, Sund	**-djupet** *Swe.*	canal, sonda	canal, détroit	canal, estreito
zoo	Zoo	**djurpark** *Swe.*	parque zoológico	zoo	jardim zoológico
island	Insel	**-do** *Kor.*	isla	île	ilha
interfluve	Erhebung	**doāb** *Per.*	interfluvio	interfluve	interflúvio
dock	Dock	**dock** *Eng.*	muelle	quai	doca
mountain	Berg	**doi** *Thai*	montaña	montagne	montanha
valley	Tal	**dolina** *Rus.*	valle	vallée	vale
mountain	Berg	**dolok** *Indo.*	montaña	montagne	montanha
hills	Hügel	**dombrovidék** *Hung.*	colinas	collines	colinas
hills	Hügel	**dombvidék** *Hung.*	colinas	collines	colinas
peak	Gipfel	**dos** *Fr.*	pico	dos	pico
downs (hills)	Hügelland	**downs** *Eng.*	colinas	collines	terras baixas (colinas)
drive	Fahrweg	**dr., drive** *Eng.*	calzada	avenue	avenida
drain	Abzugsgraben	**drain** *Eng.*	desaguadero	drainage	escoadouro
draw	kleines Tal	**draw** *Eng.*	valle pequeño	ravine	bacia, vale
drive	Fahrweg	**drive** *Eng.*	calzada	avenue	avenida
dry lake	Trockensee	**dry lake** *Eng.*	lago seco	lac asséché	lago seco
dunes	Dünen	**dunes** *Eng., Fr.*	dunas	dunes	dunas
		E			
east	Ost	**e., east** *Eng.*	este	est	leste
school	Schule	**école** *Fr.*	escuela	école	escola
mountain	Berg	**-egga** *Nor.*	montaña	montagne	montanha
memorial	Ehrenmal	**Ehrenmal** *Ger.*	monumento	memorial	monumento
river	Fluss	**-elv, -elva** *Nor.*	río	rivière	rio
reservoir	Stausee	**embalse** *Sp.*	embalse	réservoir	reservatório
pier	Landungsbrücke	**embarcadero** *Sp.*	embarcadero	jetée	cais
valley	Tal	**'emeq** *Heb.*	valle	vallée	vale
monument	Denkmal	**emlékmű** *Hung.*	monumento	monument	monumento
spring	Quelle	**'en** *Heb.*	manantial	source	fonte, manancial
cove	kleine Bucht	**enseada** *Port.*	ensenada	anse	enseada
cove	kleine Bucht	**ensenada** *Sp.*	ensenada	anse	enseada
entrance	Einfahrt	**entrance** *Eng.*	entrada	entrée	entrada
forest	Wald	**erdő** *Hung.*	bosque	forêt	floresta
sand desert	Sandwüste	**erg** *Ara.*	desierto arenoso	désert de sable	deserto arenoso
escarpment	Landstufe	**escarpment** *Eng.*	escarpa	escarpement	escarpa
school	Schule	**escuela** *Sp.*	escuela	école	escola
highland	Hochland	**espigão** *Port.*	región montañosa	pays montagneux	espigão
station	Bahnhof, Stützpunkt	**est., estação** *Port.* **estación** *Sp.*	estación	station	estação
stadium	Stadion	**estadio** *Sp.*	estadio	stade	estádio
reservoir	Stausee	**estanque** *Sp.*	estanque	réservoir	reservatório
estuary	Trichtermündung	**estero** *Sp.*	estero	estuaire	estuário
road	Landstrasse	**estr., estrada** *Port.*	camino	route	estrada
strait	Meeresstrasse	**estrecho** *Sp.*	estrecho	détroit	estreito
estuary	Trichtermündung	**estuary** *Eng.*	estuario	estuaire	estuário
pond	Teich	**étang** *Fr.*	charca	étang	lagoa, açude
expressway	Autobahn	**expy., expressway** *Eng.*	autopista	autoroute	via expressa
island	Insel	**-ey** *Ice.*	isla	île	ilha
lake	See	**ežeras** *Lith.*	lago	lac	lago
lake	See	**ezers** *Latv.*	lago	lac	lago
		F			
faculty (school)	Fakultät	**faculté** *Fr.*	facultad	faculté	faculdade
fairground	Ausstellungsgelände	**fairground** *Eng.*	campo para ferias	champ de foire	terreno para feiras
cliff	Kliff	**falaise** *Fr.*	risco	falaise	falésia
waterfall	Wasserfall	**fall(s)** *Eng.*	cascada	chute d'eau	queda d'água
waterfall	Wasserfall	**Fall** *Ger.*	cascada	chute d'eau	queda d'água
waterfall	Wasserfall	**-fallet** *Swe.*	cascada	chute d'eau	queda d'água
river	Fluss	**far'** *Ara.*	río	rivière	rio
lighthouse	Leuchtturm	**faro** *Sp.*	faro	phare	farol
upland	Bergland	**farsh** *Ara.*	tierras altas	hautes terres	terras altas
fell (mountain, hill)	ödes Hügelland	**fell** *Eng.*	colina rocosa	colline rocheuse	colina rochosa
mountain	Berg	**-fell** *Ice.*	montaña	montagne	montanha
mountain	Berg	**-feng** *Ch.*	montaña	montagne	montanha
upland	Bergland	**fennsík** *Hung.*	tierras altas	hautes terres	terras altas
ferry	Fähre	**ferry** *Eng.*	balsadera	bac	balsa
lake	See	**fertő** *Hung.*	lago	lac	lago
fortress	Feste	**Feste** *Ger.*	fortaleza	fort	fortaleza
estuary, strait	Trichtermündung, Meeresstrasse	**firth** *Gae.*	estuario, estrecho	estuaire, détroit	estuário, estreito
mountain(s)	Berg(e)	**fjäll(en)** *Swe.*	montaña(s)	montagne(s)	montanha(s)
mountain	Berg	**fjället** *Swe.*	montaña	montagne	montanha
fjord	Fjord	**fjärden** *Swe.*	fiordo	fjord	fiorde
mountain	Berg	**-fjell, -fjellet** *Nor.*	montaña	montagne	montanha
mountain	Berg	**fjöll** *Ice.*	montaña	montagne	montanha
fjord	Fjord	**-fjord** *Nor.*	fiordo	fjord	fiorde
fjord, lake	Fjord, See	**-fjorden** *Nor., Swe.*	fiordo, lago	fjord, lac	fiorde, lago
fjord, bay	Fjord, Bucht	**fjördur** *Ice.*	fiordo, bahía	fjord, baie	fiorde, baía
fork	Arm	**fk., fork** *Eng.*	brazo	bras	braço de rio
flat	Flachland	**flat** *Eng.*	llano	plat	planície
river	Fluss	**-fljót** *Ice.*	río	rivière	rio
bay	Bucht	**-flói** *Ice.*	bahía	baie	baía
flood control basin	Hochwasserrückhaltebecken	**flood control basin** *Eng.*	cuenca para controlar la inundación	bassin de contrôle d'inondation	bacia de controle de inundações
airport	Flughafen	**Flughafen** *Ger.*	aeropuerto	aéroport	aeroporto
airport	Flugplatz	**Flugplatz** *Ger.*	aeropuerto	aéroport	aeroporto
airport	Flugplatz	**flygplats** *Swe.*	aeropuerto	aéroport	aeroporto
river mouth; pass	Flussmündung; Pass	**foce** *It.*	desembocadura; paso	embouchure; col	desembocadura; foz; passo

ENGLISH	DEUTSCH	Map Form / Geographische Begriffe / Términos Geográficos / Termes Géographiques / Termos Geográficos	ESPAÑOL	FRANÇAIS	PORTUGUÊS
canal	Kanal	**főcsatorna** *Hung.*	canal	canal	canal
glacier	Gletscher	**-fonn** *Nor.*	glaciar	glacier	geleira
spring	Quelle	**fontaine** *Fr.*	manantial	fontaine	fonte, manancial
pass	Pass	**forca** *It.*	paso	col	passo
inlet	Förde	**Förde** *Ger.*	abra	bras de mer	enseada
foreland	Vorland	**foreland** *Eng.*	promontorio	promontoire	promontório
forest	Wald	**forest** *Eng.*	bosque	forêt	floresta
forest reserve	Waldreservat	**forest reserve** *Eng.*	reserva de bosque	réserve forestière	reserva florestal
forest	Wald	**forêt** *Fr.*	bosque	forêt	floresta
waterfall	Wasserfall	**-forsen** *Swe.*	cascada	chute d'eau	queda d'água
forest	Forst	**Forst** *Ger.*	bosque	forêt	floresta
fort	Fort	**fort** *Eng., Fr.*	fuerte	fort	forte
waterfall	Wasserfall	**-foss** *Ice.*	cascada	chute d'eau	queda d'água
waterfall	Wasserfall	**-fossen** *Nor.*	cascada	chute d'eau	queda d'água
brook	Bach	**fosso** *It.*	arroyo	ruisseau	córrego
pass	Pass	**foum** *Ara.*	paso	col	passo
fracture zone	Bruchzone	**fracture zone** *Eng.*	zona de fractura	zone de faille	zona de fratura
freeway	Autobahn	**frwy., freeway** *Eng.*	autopista	autoroute	via expressa
fort	Fort	**ft., fort** *Eng., Fr.*	fuerte	fort	forte
stream distributary	Flussarm	**furo** *Port.*	brazo de río	bras	furo
		G			
mountain, hill	Berg, Hügel	**g., gora** *Rus.*	montaña, colina	montagne, colline	montanha, colina
mountain	Berg	**g., gunong** *Mal.* **gunung** *Indon.*	montaña	montagne	montanha
mountain	Berg	**-gai'sa** *Lapp.*	montaña	montagne	montanha
tunnel	Tunnel	**galleria** *It.*	túnel	tunnel	túnel
gallery	Galerie	**gallery** *Eng.*	galería	galerie	galeria
game farm	Wildfarm	**game farm** *Eng.*	criadero de caza	ferme de gibier	fazenda de caça
game park	Wildpark	**game park** *Eng.*	vedado de caza	parc à gibier	parque de caça
game refuge	Wildgehege	**game refuge** *Eng.*	refugio de caza	refuge de gibier	refúgio de caça
game reserve	Wildreservat	**game reserve** *Eng.*	vedado de caza	réserve à gibier	reserva de caça
game sanctuary	Wildschutzgebiet	**game sanctuary** *Eng.*	vedado de caza	réserve à gibier	santuário de caça
bay	Bucht	**-gang** *Ch.*	bahía	baie	baía
river	Fluss	**-gang** *Kor.*	río	rivière	rio
gap	Pass	**gap** *Eng.*	paso	col	passo
intermittent lake	periodischer See	**garaet** *Ara.*	lago intermitente	lac périodique	lago intermitente
garden	Garten	**gard., garden** *Eng.*	jardín	jardin	jardim
gardens	Gärten	**gardens** *Eng.*	jardines	jardins	jardins
mountain	Berg	**garet** *Ara.*	montaña	montagne	montanha
station	Bahnhof, Stützpunkt	**garı** *Tur.*	estación	station	estação
lake	See	**-gata** *Jap.*	lago	lac	lago
gate	Tor	**gate** *Eng.*	puerta	porte	portão
mountain torrent	Wildbach	**gave** *Fr.*	torrente	gave	torrente
range	Gebirge	**gebergte** *Du.*	sierra	chaîne	cordilheira
range	Gebirge	**Gebirge** *Ger.*	sierra	chaîne	cordilheira
pass	Pass	**geçidi** *Tur.*	paso	col	passo
oasis, well	Oase, Brunnen	**ghadir** *Ara.*	oasis, pozo	oasis, puits	oásis, poço
mountains	Berge	**ghar** *Pas.*	montañas	montagnes	montanhas
spring	Quelle	**ghayl** *Ara.*	manantial	source	manancial
bay	Bucht	**ghubbat** *Ara.*	bahía	baie	baía
dunes	Dünen	**ghurd** *Ara.*	dunas	dunes	dunas
island	Insel	**gili** *Indon.*	isla	île	ilha
peak	Gipfel	**Gipfel** *Ger.*	pico	cime	pico
hill	Hügel	**giva't** *Heb.*	colina	colline	colina
bay	Bucht	**gji** *Alb.*	bahía	baie	baía
glacier	Gletscher	**glacier** *Eng., Fr.*	glaciar	glacier	geleira
river	Fluss	**gol** *Mong.*	río	rivière	rio
lake	See	**göl** *Tur.*	lago	lac	lago
bald mountains	kahle Berge	**gol'cy** *Rus.*	montañas calvas	monts chauves	montanhas calvas
golf course	Golfplatz	**golf course** *Eng.*	campo de golf	champ de golf	campo de golfe
gulf	Golf	**golfe** *Fr.*	golfo	golfe	golfo
bay	Bucht	**golfete** *Sp.*	golfete	baie	baía
gulf	Golf	**golfo** *It., Sp.*	golfo	golfe	golfo
lake	See	**gölü** *Tur.*	lago	lac	lago
mountain, hill	Berg, Hügel	**gora** *Rus.*	montaña, colina	montagne, colline	montanha, colina
mountains	Berge	**gora** *S./C.*	montañas	montagnes	montanhas
mountain	Berg	**góra** *Pol.*	montaña	montagne	montanha
gorge	Schlucht	**gorge** *Eng., Fr.*	garganta	gorge	garganta
mountains, hills	Berge, Hügel	**gorje** *S./C.*	montañas, colinas	montagnes, collines	montanhas, colinas
ruins	Ruinen	**gorodišče** *Rus.*	ruinas	ruines	ruínas
mountains, hills	Berge, Hügel	**gory** *Rus.*	montañas, colinas	montagnes, collines	montanhas, colinas
mountains	Berge	**góry** *Pol.*	montañas	montagnes	montanhas
river	Fluss	**-gou** *Ch.*	río	rivière	rio
sinkhole	Schluckloch	**gouffre** *Fr.*	sumidero	gouffre	sumidouro
wadi	Wadi	**goulbin** *Hau.*	uadi	wadi	uádi
ditch	Graben	**Graben** *Ger.*	acequia	fossé	fosso
ridge	Höhenrücken	**gr'ada** *Rus.*	sierra	crête	cordilheira
mountain	Berg	**gradište** *Blg.*	montaña	montagne	montanha
ridges	Höhenrücken	**gr'ady** *Rus.*	sierras	crêtes	cordilheira
general	General	**gral., general** *Eng., Sp.*	general	général	geral
ridge	Grat	**Grat** *Ger.*	sierra	crête	cordilheira
grotto	Grotte	**grotta** *It.*	gruta	grotte	gruta
grotto	Grotte	**grotte** *Fr.*	gruta	grotte	gruta
group	Gruppe	**group** *Eng.*	grupo	groupe	grupo
island	Insel	**-grund** *Swe.*	isla	île	ilha
group	Gruppe	**grupo** *Sp.*	grupo	groupe	grupo
group	Gruppe	**gruppo** *It.*	grupo	groupe	grupo
pass	Pass	**-guan** *Ch.*	paso	col	passo
bay	Bucht	**guba** *Rus.*	bahía	baie	baía
mountain	Berg	**guelb** *Ara.*	montaña	montagne	montanha
gulch	Wildbachschlucht	**gulch** *Eng.*	quebrada	ravin	quebrada
gulf	Golf	**gulf** *Eng.*	golfo	golfe	golfo
mountain	Berg	**gunong** *Mal.*	montaña	montagne	montanha
mountain	Berg	**gunung** *Indon.*	montaña	montagne	montanha
islands	Inseln	**-guntō** *Jap.*	islas	îles	ilhas
		H			
upland	Bergland	**haḍabat** *Ara.*	tierras altas	hautes terres	terras altas
mountain	Berg	**hadjer** *Ara.*	montaña	montagne	montanha
lagoon	Haff	**Haff** *Ger.*	laguna	lagune	laguna
sea, lake	Meer, See	**-hai** *Ch.*	mar, lago	mer, lac	mar, lago
strait	Meeresstrasse	**-haixia** *Ch.*	estrecho	détroit	estreito
reef	Riff	**hakau** *Poly.*	arrecife	récif	recife
peninsula	Halbinsel	**Halbinsel** *Ger.*	península	péninsule	península
hall	Halle	**hall** *Eng., Fr.*	salón	hall	hall
peninsula	Halbinsel	**-halvøya** *Nor.*	península	péninsule	península
beach	Strand	**-hama** *Jap.*	playa	plage	praia
desert	Wüste	**hamada** *Ara.*	desierto	désert	deserto
plateau	Hochebene	**ḥammādat** *Ara.*	meseta	plateau	planalto
lake, marsh	See, Marsch	**hāmūn** *Per.*	lago, pantano	lac, marais	lago, pântano
point	Landspitze	**-hana** *Jap.*	punta	pointe	ponta
peninsula	Halbinsel	**-hantō** *Jap.*	península	péninsule	península
mountain, hill	Berg, Hügel	**har** *Heb.*	montaña, colina	montagne, colline	montanha, colina
harbor, harbour	Hafen	**harbor, harbour** *Eng.*	puerto	port	porto
mountains, hills	Berge, Hügel	**hare** *Heb.*	montañas, colinas	montagnes, collines	montanhas, colinas
ridge	Höhenrücken	**-harju** *Finn.*	sierra	crête	cordilheira
lava flow	Lavastrom	**ḥarrat** *Ara.*	corriente de lava	coulée de lave	corrente de lava
hills	Hügel	**hauteurs** *Fr.*	colinas	hauteurs	colinas

ENGLISH	DEUTSCH	Map Form / Geographische Begriffe / Términos Geográficos / Termes Géographiques / Termos Geográficos	ESPAÑOL	FRANÇAIS	PORTUGUÊS
sea, bay	Meer, Bucht	**-hav** *Swe.*	mar, bahía	mer, baie	mar, baía
harbor	Hafen	**havre** *Fr.*	puerto	havre	porto
oasis	Oase	**ḥawḍ** *Ara.*	oasis	oasis	oásis
lake	See	**hawr** *Ara.*	lago	lac	lago
harbor, harbour	Hafen	**hbr., harbor, harbour** *Eng.*	puerto	port	porto
headquarters	Hauptquartier	**hdqrs., headquarters** *Eng.*	cuartel general	guartier général	quartel-general
river	Fluss	**-he** *Ch.*	río	rivière	rio
head (headland)	Landspitze	**head** *Eng.*	promontorio	promontoire	promontório
heath	Heide	**heath** *Eng.*	matorral	lande	charneca
mountain(s)	Berg(e)	**hegy(ség)** *Hung.*	montaña(s)	montagne(s)	montanha(s)
heath	Heide	**Heide** *Ger.*	matorral	lande	charneca
plain	Ebene	**-heiya** *Jap.*	llanura	plaine	planície
river mouth	Flussmündung	**-hekou** *Ch.*	desembocadura	embouchure	desembocadura
hills	Hügel	**heuwells** *Afk.*	colinas	collines	colinas
highland	Hochland	**highland** *Eng.*	región montañosa	pays montagneux	terras altas
highway	Strasse	**highway** *Eng.*	carretera	route	rodovia
hill(s)	Hügel	**hill(s)** *Eng.*	colina(s)	colline(s)	colina(s)
race course	Rennbahn	**hipódromo** *Sp.*	hipódromo	hippodrome	hipódromo
race course	Rennbahn	**hippodrome** *Fr.*	hipódromo	hippodrome	hipódromo
historical	historisch	**hist., historical** *Eng.*	histórico	historique	histórico
historical park	historischer Park	**historical park** *Eng.*	parque histórico	parc historique	parque histórico
historic(al) site	historische Stätte	**historic(al) site** *Eng.*	sitio histórico	site historique	sítio histórico
river	Fluss	**hka** *Bur.*	río	rivière	rio
Her Majesty's Air Station (U.K.)	Luftwaffenstützpunkt (U.K.)	**H.M.A.S., Her Majesty's Air Station** *Eng.*	Real Estación Aeronáutica (U.K.)	Station Aérienne Royale (U.K.)	Estação Aérea Real (R.U.)
river	Fluss	**ho** *Ch.*	río	rivière	rio
reservoir	Stausse	**-ho** *Kor.*	embalse	réservoir	reservatório
mountain	Berg	**-hø** *Nor.*	montaña	montagne	montanha
plateau	Hochebene	**Hochebene** *Ger.*	meseta	plateau	planalto
forest	Hochwald	**Hochwald** *Ger.*	bosque	forêt	floresta
mountain	Berg	**-högarna** *Swe.*	montaña	montagne	montanha
height	Höhe	**Höhe** *Ger.*	altura	hauteur	elevação
cave(s)	Höhle(n)	**Höhle(n)** *Ger.*	cueva(s)	caverne(s)	caverna(s)
bay	Bucht	**hoi** *Ch.*	bahía	baie	baía
island	Insel	**-holm** *Dan.*	isla	île	ilha
hook	Haken	**hook** *Eng.*	gancho	crochet	cabo, promontório
mountain	Berg	**hora** *Czech., Slo.*	montaña	montagne	montanha
point; peak	Horn	**Horn** *Ger.*	punta; pico	pointe; cime	ponta; pico
ruin	Ruine	**ḥorva** *Heb.*	ruina	ruine	ruína
mountains	Berge	**hory** *Czech., Slo.*	montañas	montagnes	montanhas
hospital	Krankenhaus	**hospital** *Eng., Sp.*	hospital	hôpital	hospital
point	Landspitze	**houma** *Poly.*	punta	pointe	ponta
house	Haus	**house** *Eng.*	casa	maison	casa
island	Insel	**hsü** *Ch.*	isla	île	ilha
lake	See	**-hu** *Ch.*	lago	lac	lago
hill	Hügel	**Hügel** *Ger.*	colina	colline	colina
cape	Huk	**Huk** *Ger.*	cabo	cap	cabo
cape	Huk	**-huk** *Swe.*	cabo	cap	cabo
highway	Strasse	**hy., highway** *Eng.*	carretera	route	rodovia

I

island	Insel	**i., isla** *Sp.* **island** *Eng.*	isla	île	ilha
icefield	Eisdecke	**icefield** *Eng.*	helero	champ de glace	geleira
ice shelf	Schelfeis	**ice shelf** *Eng.*	corniza glacial	barrière de glace	banco de gelo
ice tongue	Eiszunge	**ice tongue** *Eng.*	lengua de glaciar	langue glaciaire	língua de geleira
dunes	Dünen	**idehan** *Ber.*	dunas	dunes	dunas
river	Fluss	**ig., igarapé** *Port.*	río	rivière	igarapé
church	Kirche	**iglesia** *Sp.*	iglesia	église	igreja
lake	See	**-ike** *Jap.*	lago	lac	lago
island(s)	Insel(n)	**île(s)** *Fr.*	isla(s)	île(s)	ilha(s)
islet(s)	kleine Insel(n)	**îlet(s)** *Fr.*	isleta(s)	îlet(s)	ilhota(s)
island(s)	Insel(n)	**ilha(s)** *Port.*	isla(s)	île(s)	ilha(s)
islet(s)	kleine Insel(n)	**ilhéu(s)** *Port.*	isleta(s)	îlot(s)	ilhéu(s)
hill, upland	Hügel, Bergland	**'ilw** *Ara.*	colina, tierras altas	colline, hautes terres	colina, terras altas
hill	Hügel	**'ilwat** *Ara.*	colina	colline	colina
lake	See	**in** *Bur.*	lago	lac	lago
Indian reservation	Indianerreservation	**Ind. res., Indian reservation, Indian reserve** *Eng.*	reserva de Indios	réserve Indienne	reserva indígena
inlet	Einfahrt	**inlet** *Eng.*	abra	bras de mer	enseada
island(s)	Insel(n)	**Insel(n)** *Ger.*	isla(s)	île(s)	ilha(s)
institute	Institut	**inst., institute** *Eng.*	instituto	institut	instituto
international	international	**int., international** *Eng.*	internacional	international	internacional
race course	Rennbahn	**ippodromo** *It.*	hipódromo	hippodrome	hipódromo
wadi	Wadi	**irhazer** *Ber.*	uadi	wadi	uádi
dunes	Dünen	**'irq** *Ara.*	dunas	dunes	dunas
islands	Inseln	**is., islands** *Eng.* **islas** *Sp.*	islas	îles	ilhas
island	Insel	**isla** *Sp.*	isla	île	ilha
island(s)	Insel(n)	**island(s)** *Eng.*	isla(s)	île(s)	ilha(s)
islands	Inseln	**islas** *Sp.*	islas	îles	ilhas
isle(s)	Insel(n)	**isle(s)** *Eng.*	isla(s)	île(s)	ilha(s)
islet(s)	kleine Insel(n)	**islet(s)** *Eng.*	isleta(s)	îlot(s)	ilhota(s)
islet	kleine Insel	**islote** *Sp.*	islote	îlot	ilhota
island	Insel	**isola** *It.*	isla	île	ilha
islands	Inseln	**isole** *It.*	islas	îles	ilhas
islet	kleine Insel	**isolotto** *It.*	isleta	îlot	ilhota
isthmus	Landenge	**isthme** *Fr.*	istmo	isthme	istmo
isthmus	Landenge	**isthmus** *Eng.*	istmo	isthme	istmo
isthmus	Landenge	**istmo** *Sp.*	istmo	isthme	istmo
island	Insel	**-iwa** *Jap.*	isla	île	ilha

J

mountain(s)	Berg(e)	**jabal** *Ara.*	montaña(s)	montagne(s)	montanha(s)
garden	Garten	**jardin** *Fr.*	jardín	jardin	jardim
garden	Garten	**jardín** *Sp.*	jardín	jardin	jardim
gardens	Gärten	**jardines** *Sp.*	jardines	jardins	jardins
lake	See	**järv** *Est.*	lago	lac	lago
lake	See	**-järvi** *Finn.*	lago	lac	lago
mountains	Berge	**jary** *Rus.*	montañas	montagnes	montanhas
cave	Höhle	**jaskyně** *Slo.*	cueva	caverne	caverna
lake	See	**-jaur** *Lapp.*	lago	lac	lago
islands	Inseln	**jazā'ir** *Ara.*	islas	îles	ilhas
island	Insel	**jazirat** *Ara.*	isla	île	ilha
island	Insel	**jazireh** *Per.*	isla	île	ilha
reservoir	Stausee	**jazovir** *Blg.*	embalse	réservoir	reservatório
mountain(s)	Berg(e)	**jbel** *Ara.*	montaña(s)	montagne(s)	montanha(s)
lake	See	**jezero** *S./C.*	lago	lac	lago
lake, lagoon	See, Lagune, Haff	**jezioro** *Pol.*	lago, laguna	lac, lagune	lago, laguna
river	Fluss	**-jiang** *Ch.*	río	rivière	rio
cape	Kap	**-jiao** *Ch.*	cabo	cap	cabo
mountains	Berge	**jibāl** *Ara.*	montañas	montagnes	montanhas
island	Insel	**-jima** *Jap.*	isla	île	ilha
saddle	Joch	**Joch** *Ger.*	paso	col	passo
river	Fluss	**-joki** *Finn.*	río	rivière	rio
glacier	Gletscher	**-jøkulen** *Nor.*	glaciar	glacier	geleira
glacier	Gletscher	**-jökull** *Ice.*	glaciar	glacier	geleira
gulf	Golf	**jūras līcis** *Latv.*	golfo	golfe	golfo
islands	Inseln	**juzur** *Ara.*	islas	îles	ilhas

K

ENGLISH	DEUTSCH	Map Form / Geographische Begriffe / Términos Geográficos / Termes Géographiques / Termos Geográficos	ESPAÑOL	FRANÇAIS	PORTUGUÊS
mountains	Berge	**kabīr** *Per.*	montañas	montagnes	montanhas
dunes	Dünen	**kahal** *Ara.*	dunas	dunes	dunas
sea	Meer	**-kai** *Jap.*	mar	mer	mar
strait	Meeresstrasse	**-kaikyō** *Jap.*	estrecho	détroit	estreito
mountain	Berg	**-kaise** *Lapp.*	montaña	montagne	montanha
navy installation	Anlage der Marine	**ka.j., kaijō-jieitai** *Jap.*	estación de la marina	installation navale	instalação naval
creek	Bach	**kali** *Indon.*	riachuelo	crique	riacho
mountain	Berg	**kalns** *Latv.*	montaña	montagne	montanha
ridge	Kamm	**Kamm** *Ger.*	sierra	crête	serra
canal	Kanal	**kanaal** *Du.*	canal	canal	canal
canal, channel	Kanal	**Kanal** *Ger.*	canal	canal	canal
canal, channel	Kanal	**kanal** *Rus., S./C., Swe.*	canal	canal	canal
canal, channel	Kanal	**kanał** *Pol.*	canal	canal	canal
canal, channel	Kanal	**Kanalen** *Swe.*	canal	canal	canal
canal, channel	Kanal	**kanava** *Finn.*	canal	canal	canal
pass	Pass	**kandao** *Pas.*	paso	col	passo
river	Fluss	**-kang** *Kor.*	río	rivière	rio
moor	Moor	**-kangas** *Finn.*	páramo	lande	charneca
national park	Nationalpark	**kansallis-puisto** *Finn.*	parque nacional	parc national	parque nacional
island	Insel	**kaôh** *Cbd.*	isla	île	ilha
cape	Kap	**Kap** *Ger.*	cabo	cap	cabo
gorge	Schlucht	**kapija** *S./C.*	garganta	gorge	garganta
cape	Kap	**-kapp** *Nor.*	cabo	cap	cabo
dunes	Dünen	**kathīb** *Ara.*	dunas	dunes	dunas
desert	Wüste	**kavīr** *Per.*	desierto	désert	deserto
mountain	Berg	**kawlat** *Ara.*	montaña	montagne	montanha
hill	Hügel	**kawm** *Ara.*	colina	colline	colina
mountain	Berg	**kediet** *Ara.*	montaña	montagne	montanha
lake	See	**kenohan** *Indon.*	lago	lac	lago
cape	Kap	**kep** *Alb.*	cabo	cap	cabo
islands	Inseln	**kepulauan** *Indon.*	islas	îles	ilhas
key(s), cay(s)	Klippe(n)	**key(s)** *Eng.*	cayo(s)	caye(s)	baixio(s)
intermittent lake	periodischer See	**khabrat** *Ara.*	lago intermitente	lac périodique	lago intermitente
gulf	Golf	**khalīj** *Ara.*	golfo	golfe	golfo
mountain	Berg	**khao** *Bur., Thai*	montaña	montagne	montanha
mountain	Berg	**khashm** *Ara.*	montaña	montagne	montanha
wadi	Wadi	**khatt** *Ara.*	uadi	wadi	uádi
wadi, river	Wadi, Fluss	**khawr** *Ara.*	uadi, río	wadi, rivière	uádi, rio
dam	Damm	**khazzān** *Ara.*	presa	barrage	represa
river, canal	Fluss, Kanal	**khlong** *Thai*	río, canal	rivière, canal	rio, canal
dunes	Dünen	**khubb** *Ara.*	dunas	dunes	dunas
kill (river, channel)	Fluss, Kanal	**kill** *Eng.*	río, canal	rivière, canal	rio, canal
cemetery	Friedhof	**kladb., kladbišče** *Rus.*	cementerio	cimetière	cemitério
cloister	Kloster	**klasztory** *Pol.*	claustro	cloître	claustro, convento
cloister, monastery	Kloster	**Kloster** *Ger.*	claustro, monasterio	cloître, monastère	claustro, mosteiro
knob	Kuppe	**knob** *Eng.*	protuberancia	bosse	cerro, colina
island	Insel	**ko** *Thai*	isla	île	ilha
lake, lagoon	See, Lagune, Haff	**-ko** *Jap.*	lago, laguna	lac, lagune	lago, laguna
harbor	Hafen	**-kō** *Jap.*	puerto	port	porto
highland	Hochland	**-kōchi** *Jap.*	región montañosa	pays montagneux	terras altas
mountain	Kogel	**Kogel** *Ger.*	montaña	montagne	montanha
plateau	Hochebene	**-kogen** *Jap.*	meseta	plateau	planalto
mountains	Berge	**koh** *Per.*	montañas	montagnes	montanhas
air force installation	Anlage der Luftwaffe	**ko.j., kōkū-jieitai** *Jap.*	estación aeronáutica	installation aérienne	instalação da força aérea
national park	Nationalpark	**-kokuritsu-kōen** *Jap.*	parque nacional	parc national	parque nacional
national park	Nationalpark	**-kokutei-kōen** *Jap.*	parque nacional	parc national	parque nacional
bay	Bucht	**kólpos** *Gr.*	bahía	baie	baía
bay	Bucht	**kong** *Ch.*	bahía	baie	baía
mountain	Berg	**kong** *Indon.*	montaña	montagne	montanha
peak	Kopf	**Kopf** *Ger.*	pico	cime	pico
bridge	Brücke	**köprüsü** *Tur.*	puente	pont	ponte
gulf, bay	Golf, Bucht	**körfezi** *Tur.*	golfo, bahía	golfe, baie	golfo, baía
spit	Landzunge	**kosa** *Rus.*	lengua de tierra	flèche	ponta de terra
rapids	Stromschnellen	**-koski** *Finn.*	rápidos	rapides	rápidos
pass	Pass	**kotal** *Per.*	paso	col	passo
basin	Becken	**kotlina** *Pol.*	cuenca	bassin	bacia
bay; pass	Bucht; Pass	**-kou** *Ch.*	bahía; paso	baie; col	baía; passo
mountains	Berge	**kras** *Slo.*	montañas	montagnes	montanhas
ridge	Höhenrücken	**kr'až** *Rus.*	sierra	crête	serra
escarpment	Landstufe	**kreb** *Ara.*	escarpa	escarpement	escarpa
fort	Fort	**krepost'** *Rus.*	fuerte	fort	forte
national park	Nationalpark	**krk., kokuritsu-kōen** *Jap.*	parque nacional	parc national	parque nacional
river	Fluss	**krueng** *Indon.*	río	rivière	rio
national park	Nationalpark	**ktk., kokutei-kōen** *Jap.*	parque nacional	parc national	parque nacional
river mouth	Flussmündung	**-ku** *Ch.*	desembocadura	embouchure	desembocadura
bay	Bucht	**kuala** *Mal.*	bahía	baie	baía
mountain(s)	Berg(e)	**kūh(ha)** *Per.*	montaña(s)	montagne(s)	montanha(s)
hill	Hügel	**-kulle** *Swe.*	colina	colline	colina
dome	Kuppe	**Kuppe** *Ger.*	domo	dôme	domo
strait	Meeresstrasse	**-kurkku** *Finn.*	estrecho	détroit	estreito
channel	Kanal	**kyle** *Gae.*	canal, estrecho	canal, détroit	canal, estreito
island	Insel	**kyun** *Bur.*	isla	île	ilha
hills	Hügel	**-kyūryū** *Jap.*	colinas	collines	colinas

L

lake	See	**l., lac** *Fr.* **lago** *It., Sp.* **lagoa** *Port.* **lake** *Eng.*	lago	lac	lago, lagoa
pass	Pass	**la** *Tib.*	paso	col	passo
province	Provinz	**lääni** *Finn.*	provincia	province	província
lake(s)	See(n)	**lac(s)** *Fr.*	lago(s)	lac(s)	lago(s)
lake	See	**lacul** *Rom.*	lago	lac	lago
river	Fluss	**lae** *Indon.*	río	rivière	rio
cape	Kap	**laem** *Thai*	cabo	cap	cabo
lagoon, lake	Lagune, Haff, See	**lag., laguna** *Sp.*	laguna	lagune, lac	laguna
lake	See	**lago** *It., Port., Sp.*	lago	lac	lago
lake, lagoon	See, Lagune, Haff	**lagoa** *Port.*	lago, laguna,	lac, lagune	lagoa
lagoon	Lagune, Haff	**lagoon** *Eng.*	laguna	lagune	laguna
lakes	Seen	**lagos** *Port., Sp.*	lagos	lacs	lagos
lagoon, lake	Lagune, Haff, See	**laguna** *Sp.*	laguna	lagune, lac	laguna, lago
lagoon	Lagune, Haff	**lagune** *Fr.*	laguna	lagune	laguna
bay	Bucht	**laht** *Est.*	bahía	baie	baía
gulf	Golf	**-lahti** *Finn.*	golfo	golfe	golfo
lake(s)	See(n)	**lake(s)** *Eng.*	lago(s)	lac(s)	lago(s)
county	Grafschaft	**län** *Swe.*	condado	comté	condado
lake	Lanke (See)	**Lanke** *Ger.*	lago	lac	lago
sea	Meer	**laut** *Indon.*	mar	mer	mar
lava flow	Lavastrom	**lava flow** *Eng.*	corriente de lava	coulée de lave	corrente de lava
hill, mountain	Hügel, Berg	**law** *Gae.*	colina, montaña	colline, montagne	colina montanha
mountains; forest	Berge; Wald	**les** *Czech*	montañas; bosque	montagnes; forêt	montanhas; floresta
forest	Wald	**les** *Rus.*	bosque	forêt	floresta
level (plain)	Niveau (Ebene)	**level** *Eng.*	nivel (llano)	niveau (plaine)	planície
islands	Inseln	**liehtao** *Ch.*	islas	îles	ilhas
lighthouse	Leuchtturm	**lighthouse** *Eng.*	faro	phare	farol
estuary	Trichtermündung	**liman** *Rus.*	estuario	estuaire	estuário

ENGLISH	DEUTSCH	Map Form / Geographische Begriffe / Términos Geográficos / Termes Géographiques / Termos Geográficos	ESPAÑOL	FRANÇAIS	PORTUGUÊS
bay	Bucht	**limanı** *Tur.*	bahía	baie	baía
lake	See	**límni** *Gr.*	lago	lac	lago
peak	Gipfel	**-ling** *Ch.*	pico	cime	pico
plain	Ebene	**llano** *Sp.*	llano	plaine	planície
plains	Ebenen	**llanos** *Sp.*	llanos	plaines	planícies
lake, inlet	See, Einfahrt	**loch** *Gae.*	lago, abra	lac, bras de mer	lago, angra
lock	Schleuse	**lock** *Eng.*	esclusa	écluse	eclusa
lock and dam	Damm mit Schleuse	**lock and dam** *Eng.*	presa y esclusa	écluse et barrage	represa e eclusa
gorge	Schlucht	**log** *Rus.*	garganta	gorge	garganta
mountain	Berg	**loi** *Bur.*	montaña	montagne	montanha
hills	Hügel	**lomas** *Sp.*	lomas	collines	colinas
lake	See	**lough** *Gae.*	lago	lac	lago
lowland	Tiefland	**lowland** *Eng.*	tierra baja	terrain bas	terras baixas
marsh	Luch (Bruch)	**Luch** *Ger.*	pantano	marais	pântano
airport	Flughafen	**luchthaven** *Du.*	aeropuerto	aéroport	aeroporto
island	Insel	**-luoto** *Finn.*	isla	île	ilha

M

ENGLISH	DEUTSCH	Map Form	ESPAÑOL	FRANÇAIS	PORTUGUÊS
mountains	Berge	**m., munţii** *Rom.*	montañas	montagnes	montanhas
island	Insel	**-maa** *Est.*	isla	île	ilha
river	Fluss	**mae** *Thai*	río	rivière	rio
strait	Meeresstrasse	**maḍīq** *Ara.*	estrecho	détroit	estreito
depression	Senke	**makhtesh** *Heb.*	depresión	dépression	depressão
bay	Bucht	**-man** *Kor.*	bahía	baie	baía
monastery	Kloster	**manastir** *S./C.*	monasterio	monastère	mosteiro
sea	Meer	**mar** *Sp.*	mar	mer	mar
marsh	Marsch	**marais** *Fr.*	pantano	marais	pântano
sea	Meer	**mare** *It.*	mar	mer	mar
Marine Corps Air Station	Flugstützpunkt des Marine-Corps	**Marine Corps Air Station** *Eng.*	estación aeronáutica de la infantería de marina	station aérienne des fusiliers marins	estação aérea de fuzileiros navais
Marine Corps Base	Marine-Corps-Stützpunkt	**Marine Corps Base** *Eng.*	base de la infantería de marina	base des fusiliers marins	base de fuzileiros navais
bay	Bucht	**marsā** *Ara.*	bahía	baie	baía
marsh	Marsch	**Marsch** *Ger.*	pantano	marais	pântano
marsh(es)	Marsch(en)	**marsh(es)** *Eng.*	pantano(s)	marais	pântano(s)
river mouth	Flussmündung	**maṣabb** *Ara.*	desembocadura	embouchure	desembocadura
canal	Kanal	**maṣrif** *Ara.*	canal	canal	canal
massif	Gebirgsmassiv	**massif** *Eng., Fr.*	macizo	massif	maciço
Marine Corps Air Station	Flugstützpunkt des Marine-Corps	**M.C.A.S., Marine Corps Air Station** *Eng.*	estación aeronáutica de la infantería de marina	station aérienne des fusiliers marins	estação aérea de fuzileiros navais
Marine Corps Base	Marine-Corps-Stützpunkt	**M.C.B., Marine Corps Base** *Eng.*	base de la infantería de marina	base des fusiliers marins	base de fuzileiros navais
meadow	Wiese	**meadow** *Eng.*	prado	prairie	pradaria
dunes	Dünen	**médanos** *Sp.*	médanos	dunes	dunas
sea, lake	Meer	**Meer** *Ger.*	mar, lago	mer, lac	mar, lago
sea, lake	Meer	**meer** *Afk., Du.*	mar, lago	mer, lac	mar, lago
hills	Hügel	**melkosopočnik** *Rus.*	colinas	collines	colinas
memorial	Gedenkstätte	**mem., memorial** *Eng., Fr.*	monumento	memorial	monumento
peninsula	Halbinsel	**menandjung** *Indon.*	península	péninsule	península
sea	Meer	**mer** *Fr.*	mar	mer	mar
mesa	Tafelberg	**mesa** *Sp.*	mesa	mesa	mesa
plateau	Hochebene	**meseta** *Sp.*	meseta	plateau	planalto
middle	Mittel-	**mid., middle** *Eng.*	medio	moyen	médio, central
spit	Landzunge	**mierzeja** *Pol.*	lengua de tierra	flèche	ponta de terra
bay	Bucht	**mifraẓ** *Heb.*	bahía	baie	baía
mines	Bergwerke	**mikhrot** *Heb.*	minas	mines	minas
military	militärisch	**mil., military** *Eng.*	militar	militaire	militar
harbor	Hafen	**-minato** *Jap.*	puerto	port	porto
mine	Bergwerk	**mine** *Eng., Fr.*	mina	mine	mina
mountain	Berg	**-mine** *Jap.*	montaña	montagne	montanha
cliff	Kliff	**minqār** *Ara.*	risco	falaise	falésia
cape	Kap	**-misaki** *Jap.*	cabo	cap	cabo
mission	Mission	**mission** *Eng., Fr.*	misión	mission	missão
monument	Denkmal	**mon., monument** *Eng. Fr.*	monumento	monument	monumento
monastery	Kloster	**monasterio** *Sp.*	monasterio	monastère	mosteiro
monastery	Kloster	**monastero** *It.*	monasterio	monastère	mosteiro
monastery	Kloster	**monastery** *Eng.*	monasterio	monastère	mosteiro
monastery	Kloster	**moní** *Gr.*	monasterio	monastère	mosteiro
mount	Berg	**mont** *Fr.*	monte	mont	monte
mountain	Berg	**montagna** *It.*	montaña	montagne	montanha
mountain(s)	Berg(e)	**montagne(s)** *Fr.*	montaña(s)	montagne(s)	montanha(s)
mountain(s)	Berg(e)	**montaña(s)** *Sp.*	montaña(s)	montagne(s)	montanha(s)
mount	Berg	**monte** *It., Port., Sp.*	monte	mont	monte
mountains	Berge	**montes** *Port., Sp.*	montes	monts	montes
mountains	Berge	**monti** *It.*	montes	monts	montes
mountains	Berge	**monts** *Fr.*	montes	monts	montes
monument	Denkmal	**monument** *Eng., Fr.*	monumento	monument	monumento
moor	Moor	**moor** *Eng.*	páramo	lande	pântano
moor	Moos	**Moos** *Ger.*	páramo	lande	pântano
sea	Meer	**more** *Rus.*	mar	mer	mar
mountain	Berg	**-mori** *Jap.*	montaña	montagne	montanha
mountain	Berg	**morne** *Fr.*	montaña	morne	montanha
hill, mountain	Hügel, Berg	**morro** *Port., Sp.*	morro	colline, montagne	morro
mosque	Moschee	**mosque** *Eng.*	mezquita	mosquée	mesquita
island, rock	Insel, Fels	**motu** *Poly.*	isla, roca	île, rocher	ilha, rochedo
island	Insel	**mouchão** *Port.*	isla	île	mouchão
mound	Erdhügel	**mound** *Eng.*	montículo	tertre	montículo
mount	Berg	**mount** *Eng.*	monte	mont	monte
mountain(s)	Berg(e)	**mountain(s)** *Eng.*	montaña(s)	montagne(s)	montanha(s)
mouth	Mündung	**mouth** *Eng.*	desembocadura	embouchure	desembocadura
mount	Berg	**mt., mount** *Eng.*	monte	mont	monte
mountain	Berg	**mtn., mountain** *Eng.*	montaña	montagne	montanha
mountains	Berge	**mts., mountains** *Eng.*	montañas	montagnes	montanhas
point	Landspitze	**mui** *Viet.*	punta	pointe	ponta
headland	Landspitze	**mull** *Gae.*	promontorio	promontoire	promontório
channel	Kanal	**mun** *Ch.*	canal,estrecho	canal, détroit	canal, estreito
depression	Senke	**munkhafaḍ** *Ara.*	depresión	dépression	depressão
mountain	Berg	**muntele** *Rom.*	montaña	montagne	montanha
mountains	Berge	**munţii** *Rom.*	montañas	montagnes	montanhas
museum	Museum	**museo** *It., Sp.*	museo	musée	museu
museum	Museum	**Museum** *Ger.*	museo	musée	museu
museum	Museum	**museum** *Eng.*	museo	musée	museu
museum	Museum	**múzeum** *Hung.*	museo	musée	museu
museum	Museum	**muzej** *Rus.*	museo	musée	museu
cape	Kap	**mys** *Rus.*	cabo	cap	cabo

N

ENGLISH	DEUTSCH	Map Form	ESPAÑOL	FRANÇAIS	PORTUGUÊS
north	Nord	**n., north** *Eng.*	norte	nord	norte
sea, gulf	Meer, Golf	**-nada** *Jap.*	mar, golfo	mer, golfe	mar, golfo
desert	Wüste	**nafūd** *Ara.*	desierto	désert	deserto
plateau, mountains	Hochebene, Berge	**nagorje** *Rus.*	meseta, montañas	plateau, montagnes	planalto, montanhas
river	Fluss	**nahr** *Ara.*	río	rivière	rio
sea	Meer	**-naikai** *Jap.*	mar	mer	mar
salt flat	Salzebene	**namakzār** *Per.*	salar	saline	salina
narrows	Meeresenge	**narrows** *Eng.*	angostura	goulet	estreito
peninsula	Halbinsel	**-näs** *Swe.*	península	péninsule	península
naval air station	Flugstützpunkt der Marine	**n.a.s., naval air station** *Eng.*	estación aeronáutica de la marina	station des forces aériennes navales	estação aérea da marinha

ENGLISH	DEUTSCH	Map Form / Geographische Begriffe / Términos Geográficos / Termes Géographiques / Termos Geográficos	ESPAÑOL	FRANÇAIS	PORTUGUÊS
National Aeronautics and Space Administration	Nationale Aeronautik- und Weltraum-Behörde	**N.A.S.A., National Aeronautics and Space Administration** *Eng.*	Administración Nacional Aeronáutica y Espacial	Administration Nationale de l'Espace et Aéronautique	Administração Nacional do Espaço e Aeronâutica
national park	Nationalpark	**nasjonal park** *Nor.*	parque nacional	parc national	parque nacional
national	national	**nat., national** *Eng., Fr.*	nacional	national	nacional
national battlefield site	Schlachtfeld	**national battlefield site** *Eng.*	campo de batalla nacional	champ de bataille national	campo de batalha nacional
national cemetery	National-friedhof	**national cemetery** *Eng.*	cementerio nacional	cimetière national	cemitério nacional
national forest	Wald in Gemeinbesitz	**national forest** *Eng.*	bosque nacional	forêt nationale	floresta nacional
national historical park	Park an historischer Stätte	**national historical park** *Eng.*	parque histórico nacional	parc historique national	parque histórico nacional
national historical site	historische Stätte	**national historical site** *Eng.*	lugar histórico nacional	site historique national	sítio histórico nacional
national laboratory	staatliche Forschungsanstalt	**national laboratory** *Eng.*	laboratorio nacional	laboratoire national	laboratório nacional
national memorial	nationale Gedenkstätte	**national memorial** *Eng.*	monumento nacional	memorial national	monumento nacional
national military park	Park bei einem Schlachtfeld	**national military park** *Eng.*	parque militar nacional	parc militaire national	parque militar nacional
national monument	Nationaldenkmal	**national monument** *Eng.*	monumento nacional	monument national	monumento nacional
national park	Nationalpark	**national park** *Eng.*	parque nacional	parc national	parque nacional
natioanal recreation area	Ausflugsgebiet	**national recreation area** *Eng.*	campo nacional de recreo	région de récréation nationale	área de lazer nacional
national seashore	öffentlicher Badestrand	**national seashore** *Eng.*	playa nacional	plage nationale	praia nacional
reserve	Naturpark	**Naturpark** *Ger.*	reserva natural	réserve naturelle	reserva natural
nature reserve	Naturschutzgebiet	**Naturschutzgebiet** *Ger.*	reserva natural	réserve naturelle	reserva natural
naval air station	Flugstützpunkt der Marine	**naval air station** *Eng.*	estación aeronáutica de la marina	station des forces aériennes navales	estação aérea da marinha
naval base	Flottenstützpunkt	**naval base** *Eng.*	base naval	base navale	base naval
naval station	Marinestation	**naval station** *Eng.*	estación naval	station navale	estação naval
naval base	Flottenstützpunkt	**n.b., naval base** *Eng.*	base naval	base navale	base naval
rock	Fels	**-ne** *Jap.*	roca	rocher	rochedo
neck	Landenge	**neck** *Eng.*	istmo	isthme	istmo
necropolis	Friedhof	**necrópolis** *Sp.*	necrópolis	nécropole	necrópole
cape	Kap	**neem** *Est.*	cabo	cap	cabo
peninsula, point	Halbinsel, Landspitze	**-nes** *Ice., Nor.*	península, punta	péninsule, pointe	península, ponta
promontory	Vorgebirge	**ness** *Gae.*	promontorio	promontoire	promontório
snowcapped mountain(s)	Schneegipfel	**nev(s)., nevado(s)** *Sp.*	nevado(s)	montagne(s) neigeuse(s)	pico(s) nevado(s)
mountain	Berg	**ngoc** *Viet.*	montaña	montagne	montanha
cape	Kap	**nina** *Est.*	cabo	cap	cabo
islands	Inseln	**nisoi** *Gr.*	islas	îles	ilhas
island	Insel	**nisos** *Gr.*	isla	île	ilha
lowland	Tiefland	**nizina** *Rus.*	tierra baja	terrain bas	terras baixas
lowland	Tiefland	**nižina** *Slo.*	tierra baja	terrain bas	terras baixas
lowland	Tiefland	**nizmennost'** *Rus.*	tierra baja	terrain bas	terras baixas
cape	Kap	**nos** *Blg.*	cabo	cap	cabo
naval station	Marinestation	**n.s., naval station** *Eng.*	estación naval	station navale	estação naval
nature reserve	Naturschutzgebiet	**Nsg., Naturschutzgebiet** *Ger.*	reserva natural	réserve naturelle	reserva natural
mountain	Berg	**nui** *Viet.*	montaña	montagne	montanha
lake	See	**-numa** *Jap.*	lago	lac	lago
mountains	Berge	**nuruu** *Mong.*	montañas	montagnes	montanhas
island	Insel	**nusa** *Indon.*	isla	île	ilha
lake	See	**nuur** *Mong.*	lago	lac	lago

O

ENGLISH	DEUTSCH	Map Form	ESPAÑOL	FRANÇAIS	PORTUGUÊS
bay	Bucht	**o** *Ch.*	bahía	baie	baía
island	Insel	**-ø** *Dan., Nor.*	isla	île	ilha
island	Insel	**-ö** *Swe.*	isla	île	ilha
island	Insel	**o., ostrov** *Rus.*	isla	île	ilha
islands	Inseln	**-öarna** *Swe.*	islas	îles	ilhas
oasis	Oase	**oasis** *Eng., Fr., Sp.*	oasis	oasis	oásis
observatory	Observatorium	**observatorio** *Sp.*	observatorio	observatoire	observatório
observatory	Observatorium	**observatory** *Eng.*	observatorio	observatoire	observatório
ocean	Ozean	**ocean** *Eng.*	océano	océan	oceano
island	Insel	**-ön** *Swe.*	isla	île	ilha
mountains	Berge	**óri** *Gr.*	montañas	montagnes	montanhas
bay	Bucht	**órmos** *Gr.*	bahía	baie	baía
mountain(s)	Berg(e)	**óros** *Gr.*	montaña(s)	montagne(s)	montanha(s)
island(s)	Insel(n)	**ostrov(a)** *Rus.*	isla(s)	île(s)	ilha(s)
island	Insel	**ostrovul** *Rom.*	isla	île	ilha
islands	Inseln	**otoci** *S./C.*	islas	îles	ilhas
island	Insel	**otok** *S./C.*	isla	île	ilha
wadi	Wadi	**ouadi** *Ara.*	uadi	wadi	uádi
wadi	Wadi	**oued** *Ara.*	uadi	wadi	uádi
outlet	Abfluss	**outlet** *Eng.*	desagüe	débouché	escoadouro
island	Insel	**-øy, -øya** *Nor.*	isla	île	ilha
lake	See	**oz., ozero** *Rus.*	lago	lac	lago
lakes	Seen	**ozera** *Rus.*	lagos	lacs	lagos

P

ENGLISH	DEUTSCH	Map Form	ESPAÑOL	FRANÇAIS	PORTUGUÊS
hills	Hügel	**pahorkatina** *Czech.*	colinas	collines	colinas
palace	Palast	**pal., palace** *Eng.*	palacio	palais	palácio
palace	Palast	**palacio** *Sp.*	palacio	palais	palácio
palace	Palast	**palais** *Fr.*	palacio	palais	palácio
palace	Palast	**palazzo** *It.*	palacio	palais	palácio
palace	Palast	**paleis** *Du.*	palacio	palais	palácio
railroad station	Bahnhof	**pályaudvar** *Hung.*	estación ferrocarril	gare	estação ferroviária
monument	Denkmal	**pam'atnik** *Rus.*	monumento	monument	monumento
plain	Ebene	**pampa** *Sp.*	pampa	plaine	pampa
basin	Becken	**pánev** *Czech*	cuenca	bassin	bacia
swamp	Sumpf	**pantanal** *Port., Sp.*	pantanal	marais	pantanal
marsh, swamp; reservoir	Marsch, Sumpf; Stausee	**pantano** *Sp.*	pantano	marais; réservoir	pântano
moor	Moor	**páramo** *Sp.*	páramo	lande	pântano
park	Park	**parc** *Fr.*	parque	parc	parque
national park	National park	**parc national** *Fr.*	parque nacional	parc national	parque nacional
park	Park	**parco** *It.*	parque	parc	parque
national park	Nationalpark	**parco nazionale** *It.*	parque nacional	parc national	parque nacional
provincial park	Naturpark	**parc provincial** *Fr.*	parque de la provincia	parc provincial	parque provincial
park	Park	**Park** *Ger.*	parque	parc	parque
park	Park	**park** *Eng.*	parque	parc	parque
national park	Nationalpark	**park narodowy** *Pol.*	parque nacional	parc national	parque nacional
parkway	Ferienstrasse	**parkway** *Eng.*	calzada	allée de parc	alameda de parque
park	Park	**parque** *Port., Sp.*	parque	parc	parque
national park	Nationalpark	**parq. nac., parque nacional** *Port., Sp.*	parque nacional	parc national	parque nacional
beach	Strand	**part** *Hung.*	playa	plage	praia
strait	Meeresstrasse	**pas** *Fr.*	estrecho	détroit	estreito
passage	Durchfahrt	**pasaje** *Sp.*	pasaje	passage	passagem
pass	Pass	**paso** *Sp.*	paso	col	passo
pass	Pass	**Pass** *Ger.*	paso	col	passo
pass	Pass	**pass** *Eng.*	paso	col	passo
passage	Durchfahrt	**passage** *Eng., Fr.*	pasaje	passage	passagem
passage	Durchfahrt	**passe** *Fr.*	pasaje	passe	passagem

ENGLISH	DEUTSCH	Map Form Geographische Begriffe Términos Geográficos Termes Géographiques Termos Geográficos	ESPAÑOL	FRANÇAIS	PORTUGUÊS
pass	Pass	**passo** *It.*	paso	col	passo
pass	Pass	**pasul** *Rom.*	paso	col	passo
creek	Bach	**patak** *Hung.*	riachuelo	crique	riacho
peak(s)	Gipfel	**peak(s)** *Eng.*	pico(s)	pic(s)	pico(s)
cave	Höhle	**pećina** *S./C.*	cueva	caverne	caverna
mountains	Berge	**peg., pegunungan** *Indon.*	montañas	montagnes	montanhas
sea	Meer	**pélagos** *Gr.*	mar	mer	mar
bay	Bucht	**pellg** *Alb.*	bahía	baie	baía
peninsula	Halbinsel	**pen., peninsula** *Eng.*	península	péninsule	península
peak; rock	Gipfel; Fels	**peña** *Sp.*	peña	pic; rocher	penha
peak; large rock	Gipfel; grosser Fels	**peñasco** *Sp.*	peñasco	pic; rocher	penhasco
basin	Becken	**-pendi** *Ch.*	cuenca	bassin	bacia
peninsula	Halbinsel	**peninsula** *Eng.*	península	péninsule	península
peninsula	Halbinsel	**península** *Sp.*	península	péninsule	península
peninsula	Halbinsel	**péninsule** *Fr.*	península	péninsule	península
rock	Fels	**peñón** *Sp.*	peñón	rocher	rochedo
pass	Pass	**pereval** *Rus.*	paso	col	passo
strait	Meeresstrasse	**pertuis** *Fr.*	estrecho	pertuis	estreito
sand desert	Sandwüste	**peski** *Rus.*	desierto arenoso	désert de sable	deserto arenoso
mountain	Berg	**phnum** *Cbd.*	montaña	montagne	montanha
mountain	Berg	**phou** *Lao.*	montaña	montagne	montanha
mountain	Berg	**phu** *Thai*	montaña	montagne	montanha
cape	Kap	**pi** *Ch.*	cabo	cap	cabo
plain	Ebene	**piano** *It.*	llanura	plaine	planicie
peak	Gipfel	**pic** *Fr.*	pico	pic	pico
peak	Gipfel	**picacho** *Sp.*	picacho	pic	pico
peak	Gipfel	**picco** *It.*	pico	pic	pico
peak(s)	Gipfel	**pico(s)** *Port., Sp.*	pico(s)	pic(s)	pico(s)
pier	Landungsbrücke	**pier** *Eng.*	embarcadero	jetée	cais
mountain	Berg	**-piggen** *Nor.*	montaña	montagne	montanha
peak	Gipfel	**pik** *Rus.*	pico	pic	pico
forest	Wald	**pinhal** *Port.*	bosque	forêt	pinhal
peak	Gipfel	**pique** *Fr.*	pico	pique	pico
pyramid	Pyramide	**pirámide** *Sp.*	pirámide	pyramide	pirâmide
peak(s)	Gipfel	**piton(s)** *Fr.*	pico(s)	piton(s)	pico(s)
peak	Gipfel	**piz, pizzo** *It.*	pico	pic	pico
peak	Gipfel	**pk., peak** *Eng.*	pico	pic	pico
parkway	Ferienstrasse	**pkwy., parkway** *Eng.*	calzada	allée de parc	avenida
plain	Ebene	**plain** *Eng.*	llanura	plaine	planície
plain	Ebene	**plaine** *Fr.*	llanura	plaine	planície
plains	Ebenen	**plains** *Eng.*	llanura	plaines	planícies
plateau	Hochebene	**planalto** *Port.*	meseta	plateau	planalto
planetarium	Planetarium	**planetario** *Sp.*	planetario	planétarium	planetário
planetarium	Planetarium	**planetarium** *Eng.*	planetario	planétarium	planetário
mountain, range	Berg, Gebirge	**planina** *S./C.*	montaña, sierra	montagne, chaîne	montanha, cordilheira
plateau	Hochebene	**plateau** *Eng., Fr.*	meseta	plateau	planalto
plateau	Hochebene	**plato** *Afk., Blg., Rus.*	meseta	plateau	planalto
beach	Strand	**playa** *Sp.*	playa	plage	praia
square	Platz	**plaza** *Sp.*	plaza	place	praça
plateau	Hochebene	**plošina** *Czech*	meseta	plateau	planalto
plateau	Hochebene	**ploskogorje** *Rus.*	meseta	plateau	planalto
pass	Pass	**poarta** *Rom.*	paso	col	passo
hill	Hügel	**poggio** *It.*	colina	colline	colina
mountains	Berge	**pohorie** *Slo.*	montañas	montanges	montanhas
point	Landspitze	**point** *Eng.*	punta	pointe	ponta
point	Landspitze	**pointe** *Fr.*	punta	pointe	ponta
island	Insel	**pol** *Du.*	isla	île	ilha
plain, basin	Ebene, Becken	**polje** *S./C.*	llanura, cuenca	plaine, bassin	planície, bacia
peninsula	Halbinsel	**poluostrov** *Rus.*	península	péninsule	península
peninsula	Halbinsel	**poluotok** *S./C.*	península	péninsule	península
pond	Teich	**pond** *Eng.*	charca	étang	lago
peak	Gipfel	**-pong** *Kor.*	pico	cime	pico
bridge	Brücke	**pont** *Fr.*	puente	pont	ponte
point	Landspitze	**ponta, pontal** *Port.*	punta	pointe	ponta, pontal
bridge	Brücke	**ponte** *Port.*	puente	pont	ponte
pool	Tümpel	**pool** *Eng.*	charco	étang	charco
rapids	Stromschnellen	**porog** *Rus.*	rápidos	rapides	rápidos
port	Hafen	**port** *Eng., Fr.*	puerto	port	porto
port	Hafen	**porto** *It.*	puerto	port	porto
strait	Meeresstrasse	**porthmós** *Gr.*	estrecho	détroit	estreito
provincial park	Naturpark	**p.p., provincial park** *Eng.*	parque de la provincia	parc provincial	parque provincial
beach	Strand	**praia** *Port.*	playa	plage	praia
reservoir	Stausee	**přehr., přehradová nádrž** *Czech*	embalse	réservoir	reservatório
reservoir, dam	Stausee, Damm	**presa** *Sp.*	presa	réservoir, barrage	represa
peninsula	Halbinsel	**presqu'île** *Fr.*	península	presqu'île	península
pass	Pass	**priesmyk** *Slo.*	paso	col	passo
reservoir	Stausee	**priehradová nádrž** *Slo.*	embalse	réservoir	reservatório
prison	Gefängnis	**prison** *Eng.*	prisión	prison	prisão
pass	Pass	**prohod** *Blg.*	paso	col	passo
strait	Meeresstrasse	**proliv** *Rus.*	estrecho	détroit	estreito
promontory	Vorgebirge	**promontorio** *It., Sp.*	promontorio	promontoire	promontório
promontory	Vorgebirge	**promontory** *Eng.*	promontorio	promontoire	promontório
provincial park	Naturpark	**prov. park, provincial park** *Eng.*	parque de la provincia	parc provincial	parque provincial
reservoir	Stausee	**prudy** *Rus.*	embalse	réservoir	reservatório
pass	Pass	**průsmyk** *Czech*	paso	col	passo
pass	Pass	**przełęcz** *Pol.*	paso	col	passo
cape	Kap	**przylądek** *Pol.*	cabo	cap	cabo
point	Landspitze	**pt., point** *Eng.*	punta	pointe	ponta
railroad station	Bahnhof	**pu., pályaudvar** *Hung.*	estación de ferrocarril	gare	estação ferroviária
port	Hafen	**puerto** *Sp.*	puerto	port	porto
peak	Gipfel	**puig** *Cat.*	pico	cime	pico
island	Insel	**pulau** *Indon., Mal.*	isla	île	ilha
islands	Inseln	**pulau-pulau** *Indon.*	islas	îles	ilhas
upland	Bergland	**puna** *Sp.*	puna	hautes terres	terras altas
point	Landspitze	**punt** *Du.*	punta	pointe	ponta
point, peak	Landspitze, Gipfel	**punta** *It., Sp.*	punta	pointe, cime	ponta
point	Landspitze	**puntilla** *Sp.*	puntilla	pointe	ponta pequena
peak	Gipfel	**puntjak** *Indon.*	pico	cime	pico
forest	Wald	**puszcza** *Pol.*	bosque	forêt	floresta
pyramid	Pyramide	**pyramid** *Eng.*	pirámide	pyramide	pirâmide

Q

ENGLISH	DEUTSCH	Map Form	ESPAÑOL	FRANÇAIS	PORTUGUÊS
salt flat	Salzebene	**qā'** *Ara.*	salar	saline	salina
pass	Pass	**qaf'** *Alb.*	paso	col	passo
canal	Kanal	**qanāt** *Ara.*	canal	canal	canal
hill	Hügel	**qārat** *Ara.*	colina	colline	colina
hills	Hügel	**qārāt** *Ara.*	colinas	collines	colinas
dunes	Dünen	**qawz** *Ara.*	dunas	dunes	dunas
creek	Bach	**qbda, quebrada** *Sp.*	quebrada	crique	arroio
mountain	Berg	**qolleh** *Per.*	montaña	montagne	montanha
canal	Kanal	**-qu** *Ch.*	canal	canal	canal
quarry	Steinbruch	**quarry** *Eng.*	cantera	carrière	pedreira
creek	Bach	**quebrada** *Sp.*	quebrada	crique	arroio
rapids	Stromschnellen	**quedas** *Port.*	rápidos	rapides	quedas
islands	Inseln	**-qundao** *Ch.*	islas	îles	ilhas
hill	Hügel	**qūr** *Ara.*	colina	colline	colina
mountain	Berg	**qurnat** *Ara.*	montaña	montagne	montanha

R

ENGLISH	DEUTSCH	Map Form	ESPAÑOL	FRANÇAIS	PORTUGUÊS
river	Fluss	**r., rio** *Port.* **rio** *Sp.* **river** *Eng.* **rivière** *Fr.*	río	rivière	rio
range	Gebirge	**ra., range** *Eng.*	sierra	chaîne	cordilheira
Royal Australian Air Force Station	Luftwaffenstützpunkt (Austl.)	**R.A.A.F.S., Royal Australian Air Station** *Eng.*	Real Estación Aeronáutica (Austl.)	Station Aérienne Royale (Austl.)	Real Estação da Força Aérea Australiana
race course	Rennbahn	**race course** *Eng.*	hipódromo	champ de course	hipódromo
race track	Rennbahn	**race track** *Eng.*	hipódromo	champ de course	hipódromo
raceway	Rennbahn	**raceway** *Eng.*	hipódromo	champ de course	hipódromo
river	Fluss	**rach** *Viet.*	río	rivière	rio
anchorage	Ankerplatz	**rada** *Sp.*	rada	ancrage	ancoradouro
cape	Kap	**rags** *Latv.*	cabo	cap	cabo
railroad	Eisenbahn	**railroad** *Eng.*	ferrocarril	chemin de fer	ferrovia
railway	Eisenbahn	**railway** *Eng.*	ferrocarril	chemin de fer	ferrovia
railway station	Bahnhof	**railway station** *Eng.*	estación de ferrocarril	gare	estação ferroviária
dunes	Dünen	**ramlat** *Ara.*	dunas	dunes	dunas
range(s)	Gebirge	**range(s)** *Eng.*	sierra(s)	chaîne(s)	cordilheira(s)
river	Fluss	**rão., ribeirão** *Port.*	río	rivière	rio, ribeirão
rapids	Stromschnellen	**rapides** *Fr.*	rápidos	rapides	rápidos
rapids	Stromschnellen	**rapids** *Eng.*	rápidos	rapides	rápidos
wadi	Wadi	**raqabat** *Ara.*	uadi	wadi	uádi
cape	Kap	**ras, ra's** *Ara.*	cabo	cap	cabo
cape	Kap	**rās** *Per.*	cabo	cap	cabo
ravine	Tobel	**ravine** *Eng.*	barranca	ravin	ravina
plain	Ebene	**ravnina** *Rus.*	llanura	plaine	planície
canal	Kanal	**rayyāḥ** *Ara.*	canal	canal	canal
flood plain	Überschwemmungsebene	**razlivy** *Rus.*	llanura de inundación	lit d'inondation	planície de inundação
road	Landstrasse	**rd., road** *Eng.*	camino	route	rodovia
reef	Riff	**récif** *Fr.*	arrecife	récif	recife
reefs	Riffe	**recifes** *Port.*	arrecifes	récifs	recifes
reefs	Riffe	**récifs** *Fr.*	arrecifes	récifs	recifes
reef(s)	Riff(e)	**reef(s)** *Eng.*	arrecife(s)	récif(s)	recife(s)
regional park	Regionalpark	**regional park** *Eng.*	parque regional	parc régional	parque regional
mountain	Berg	**-rei** *Jap.*	montaña	montagne	montanha
race course	Rennbahn	**Rennbahn** *Ger.*	hipódromo	champ de course	hipódromo
dam; reservoir	Damm; Stausee	**represa** *Port.*	presa; embalse	barrage; réservoir	represa
airport	Flughafen	**repülötér** *Hung.*	aeropuerto	aéroport	aeroporto
reservoir	Stausee	**res., reservoir** *Eng.*	embalse	réservoir	reservatório
reservation	Reservat	**reservation** *Eng.*	reservación	réservation	reserva
reservoir	Stausee	**reservatório** *Port.*	embalse	rèservoir	reservatório
reserve	Reservat	**reserve** *Eng.*	reserva	réserve	reserva
reserve	Reservat	**rèserve** *Fr.*	reserva	réserve	reserva
game reserve	Wildreservat	**rèserve de chasse** *Fr.*	vedado de caza	réserve de chasse	reserva de caça
reservoir	Stausee	**reservoir** *Eng.*	embalse	réservoir	reservatório
reservoir	Stausee	**réservoir** *Fr.*	embalse	réservoir	reservatório
islands	Inseln	**-retto** *Jap.*	islas	îles	ilhas
ria	Ria	**ría** *Sp.*	ría	ria	ria
creek	Bach	**riacho** *Port., Sp.*	riacho	crique	riacho
creek	Bach	**riachuelo** *Sp.*	riachuelo	crique	riacho
creek	Bach	**rib., ribeira** *Port.*	riachuelo	crique	ribeira
river	Fluss	**ribeirão** *Port.*	río	rivière	ribeirão
ridge	Höhenrücken	**ridge** *Eng.*	sierra	crête	serra
moor	Ried	**Ried** *Ger.*	páramo	lande	pântano
creek	Bach	**riera** *Sp.*	riera	crique	riacho
national museum	Reichsmuseum	**rijksmuseum** *Du.*	museo nacional	musée national	museu nacional
army installation	Anlage des Heeres	**rikujō-jieitai** *Jap.*	estación del ejército	installation militaire	instalação militar
river	Fluss	**rio** *Port.*	río	rivière	rio
river	Fluss	**río** *Sp.*	río	rivière	rio
river	Fluss	**riozinho** *Port.*	río	rivière	riozinho
rise (submarine)	Schwelle (untermeerische)	**rise** *Eng.*	elevación (submarina)	élévation (sous-marine)	elevação (submarina)
river	Fluss	**river** *Eng.*	río	rivière	rio
brook	Bach	**rivera** *Sp.*	rivera	ruisseau	córrego
coast	Küste	**riviera** *It.*	costa	côte	costa
river	Fluss	**rivière** *Fr.*	río	rivière	rio
army installation	Anlage des Heeres	**r.j., rikujō-jieitai** *Jap.*	estación del ejército	installation militaire	instalação do exército
road	Landstrasse	**road** *Eng.*	camino	route	rodovia
roads (anchorage)	Ankerplatz	**roads** *Eng.*	ancladero	ancrage	ancoradouro
rock	Fels	**roca** *Sp.*	roca	rocher	rochedo
rock, mountain	Fels, Berg	**rocca** *It.*	roca, montaña	rocher, montagne	rochedo, montanha
rock(s)	Fels(en)	**rock(s)** *Eng.*	roca(s)	rocher(s)	rochedo(s)
cape	Kap	**rt** *S./C.*	cabo	cap	cabo
brook	Bach	**rû** *Fr.*	arroyo	rû	córrego
mountains	Berge	**rudohorie** *Slo.*	montañas	montagnes	montanhas
brook	Bach	**ruisseau** *Fr.*	arroyo	ruisseau	córrego
mountain	Berg	**rujm** *Ara.*	montaña	montagne	montanha
run	Bach	**run** *Eng.*	arroyo	ruisseau	córrego

S

ENGLISH	DEUTSCH	Map Form	ESPAÑOL	FRANÇAIS	PORTUGUÊS
south	süd	**s., south** *Eng.*	sur	sud	sul
range	Gebirge	**sa., serra** *Port.*	sierra	chaîne	cordilheira
island	Insel	**saar** *Est.*	isla	île	ilha
savanna	Savanne	**sabana** *Sp.*	sabana	savane	savana
salt marsh; lagoon	Salzmarsch; Lagune, Haff	**sabkhat** *Ara.*	pantano salado; laguna	marais salé; lagune	pântano salgado; laguna
dam	Damm	**sadd** *Ara.*	presa	barrage	represa
wadi	Wadi	**saguia** *Ara.*	uadi	wadi	uádi
desert	Wüste	**ṣaḥrā'** *Ara.*	desierto	désert	deserto
cape	Kap	**-saki** *Jap.*	cabo	cap	cabo
salt flat	Salzebene	**salar** *Sp.*	salar	saline	salina
salt marsh, salt flat	Salzmarsch, Salzebene	**salina(s)** *Sp.*	salina(s)	marais salé, saline	salina(s)
salt marsh, salt flat	Salzmarsch, Salzebene	**salines** *Fr.*	pantano salado, salinas, salar	salines	pântano salgado, salinas
salt flat	Salzebene	**salt flat** *Eng.*	salar	saline	salina
salt lake	Salzsee	**salt lake** *Eng.*	lago salado	lac salé	lago salgado
salt marsh	Salzmarsch	**salt marsh** *Eng.*	pantano salado	marais salé	pântano salgado
waterfall	Wasserfall	**salto(s)** *Port., Sp.*	salto(s)	chute d'eau	salto(s)
reservoir	Stausee	**samudra** *Sin.*	embalse	réservoir	reservatório
range	Gebirge	**-sammyaku** *Jap.*	sierra	chaîne	cordilheira
mountain	Berg	**-san** *Jap., Kor.*	montaña	montagne	montanha
mountains	Berge	**-sanchi** *Jap.*	montañas	montagnes	montanhas
mountains	Berge	**-sanmaek** *Kor.*	montañas	montagnes	montanhas
shrine	Schrein	**santuario** *It., Sp.*	santuario	châsse	santuário
mountain	berg	**sar** *Pas.*	montaña	montagne	montanha
island	Insel	**sari** *Est.*	isla	île	ilha
desert	Wüste	**sarir** *Ara.*	desierto	désert	deserto
saddle	Sattel	**Sattel** *Ger.*	paso	col	passo
strait	Meeresstrasse	**šaurums** *Latv.*	estrecho	détroit	estreito
waterfall	Wasserfall	**saut** *Fr.*	cascada	saut	queda d'água
castle	Schloss	**Schloss** *Ger.*	castillo	château	castelo
gorge	Schlucht	**Schlucht** *Ger.*	garganta	gorge	garganta
school	Schule	**school** *Eng.*	escuela	école	escola
sea	Meer	**sea** *Eng.*	mar	mer	mar
seamount	untermeerische Kuppe	**seamount** *Eng.*	montaña submarina	montagne sous-marine	montanha submarina
sea scarp	Abbruch	**sea scarp** *Eng.*	cantil	escarpement sous-marine	escarpa submarina
dry lake	Trockensee	**sebjet** *Ara.*	lago seco	lac asséché	lago seco
salt flat	Salzebene	**sebkha** *Ara.*	salar	saline	salina
intermittent lake	periodischer See	**sebkra** *Ara.*	lago intermitente	lac périodique	lago intermitente
salt marsh	Salzmarsch	**sebkret** *Ara.*	pantano salado	marais salé	pântano salgado
airport	Flughafen	**sede-te'ufa** *Heb.*	aeropuerto	aéroport	aeroporto
saddle	Sattel	**sedlo** *Czech*	paso	col	passo
lake(s)	See(n)	**See(n)** *Ger.*	lago(s)	lac(s)	lago(s)

ENGLISH	DEUTSCH	Map Form / Geographische Begriffe / Términos Geográficos / Termes Géographiques / Termos Geográficos	ESPAÑOL	FRANÇAIS	PORTUGUÊS
strait	Meeresstrasse	**selat** *Indon.*	estrecho	détroit	estreito
peninsula	Halbsinel	**semenandjung** *Indon.*	península	péninsule	península
seminary	Seminar	**seminary** *Eng.*	seminario	séminaire	seminário
mountain	Berg	**-sen** *Jap.*	montaña	montagne	montanha
sound	Sund	**seno** *Sp.*	seno	détroit	estreito
range, mountain	Gebirge, Berg	**serra** *Port.*	sierra	chaîne, montagne	serra
ridge(s)	Höhenrücken	**serranía(s)** *Sp.*	serranía(s)	crête(s)	serrania(s)
rapids	Stromschnellen	**shallâl** *Ara.*	rápidos	rapides	rápidos
mountain(s); island	Berg(e); Insel	**-shan** *Ch.*	montaña(s); isla	montagne(s); île	montanha(s) ilha
pass	Pass	**-shankou** *Ch.*	paso	col	passo
mountains	Berge	**-shanling, -shanmai, -shanmo** *Ch.*	montañas	montagnes	montanhas
bay	Bucht	**sharm** *Ara.*	bahía	baie	baía
peninsula	Halbinsel	**shibh jazirat** *Ara.*	península	péninsule	península
island	Insel	**-shima** *Jap.*	isla	île	ilha
reef	Riff	**-shō** *Jap.*	arrecife	récif	recife
shoal(s)	Untiefe(n)	**shoal(s)** *Eng.*	bajo(s)	haut-fond(s)	baixio(s)
islands	Inseln	**-shotō** *Jap.*	islas	îles	ilhas
shrine	Schrein	**shrine** *Eng.*	santuario	châsse	santuário
river	Fluss	**-shui** *Ch.*	río	rivière	rio
reservoir	Stausee	**-shuiku** *Ch.*	embalse	réservoir	reservatório
strait	Meeresstrasse	**shuitao** *Ch.*	estrecho	détroit	estreito
temple	Tempel	**-si** *Ch.*	templo	temple	templo
range, ridge	Gebirge, Höhenrücken	**sierra** *Sp.*	sierra	chaîne, crête	serra
range	Gebirge	**silsilesi** *Tur.*	sierra	chaîne	cordilheira
rapids	Stromschnellen	**šivera** *Rus.*	rápidos	rapides	rápidos
lake	See	**-sjø** *Nor.*	lago	lac	lago
lakes	Seen	**-sjöarna** *Swe.*	lagos	lacs	lagos
lake	See	**-sjøen** *Nor.*	lago	lac	lago
lake, bay	See, Bucht	**-sjön** *Swe.*	lago, bahía	lac, baie	lago, baía
island	Insel	**-skär** *Swe.*	isla	île	ilha
forest	Wald	**-skog, -skogen** *Swe.*	basque	forêt	floresta
mountain	Berg	**slieve** *Gae.*	montaña	montagne	montanha
castle	Schloss	**slot** *Du.*	castillo	château	castelo
castle	Schloss	**slott** *Swe.*	castillo	château	castelo
slough	verlandende Wasserfläche	**slough** *Eng.*	pantano	fondrière	pântano, brejo
ridge	Höhenrücken	**snía., serranía** *Sp.*	serranía	crête	serrania
snowfield	Schneefeld	**snowfield** *Eng.*	ventisquero	champ de neige	campo de neve
lake	See	**-sø** *Dan.*	lago	lac	lago
sound	Sund	**sonda** *Sp.*	sonda	détroit	estreito
sound	Sund	**sound** *Eng.*	sonda	détroit	estreito
cave, tunnel	Höhle, Tunnel	**souterrain** *Fr.*	cueva, túnel	souterrain	caverna, túnel
state park	Naturpark	**s.p., state park** *Eng.*	parque provincial	parc régional	parque estadual
cave	Höhle	**špilja** *S./C.*	cueva	caverne	caverna
spit	Landzunge	**spit** *Eng.*	lengua de tierra	flèche	ponta de terra
peak	Spitze	**Spitze** *Ger.*	pico	cime	pico
spring	Quelle	**spr., spring** *Eng.*	manantial	source	fonte, manancial
square	Platz	**sq., square** *Eng.*	plaza	place	praça
range, ridge	Gebirge Höhenrücken	**srra., sierra** *Sp.*	sierra	chaîne, crête	serra
saint	Sankt	**st., saint** *Eng., Fr.*	san, santa, santo	saint	são, santa, santo
street	Strasse	**st., street** *Eng.*	calle	rue	rua
saint	Sankt	**sta., santa** *Port., Sp.*	santa	sainte	santa
station	Bahnhof, Stützpunkt	**sta., station** *Eng., Fr.*	estación	station	estação
stadium	Stadion	**stad., stadium** *Eng.*	estadio	stade	estádio
stadium	Stadion	**stadio** *It.*	estadio	stade	estádio
stadium	Stadion	**Stadion** *Ger.*	estadio	stade	estádio
stadium	Stadion	**stadion** *Rus.*	estadio	stade	estádio
stadium	Stadion	**stadium** *Eng.*	estadio	stade	estádio
state beach	öffentlicher Badestrand	**state beach** *Eng.*	playa provincial	plage régionale	praia estadual
state forest	Wald in Gemeinbesitz	**state forest** *Eng.*	bosque provincial	forêt régionale	floresta estadual
state historical park	Park an historischer Stätte	**state historical park** *Eng.*	parque histórico provincial	parc historique régional	parque histórico estadual
state park	Naturpark	**state park** *Eng.*	parque provincial	parc régional	parque estadual
state recreation area	Ausflugsgebiet	**state recreation area** *Eng.*	zona de recreo provincial	zone récréative regional	área de lazer estadual
station	Bahnhof, Stützpunkt	**station** *Eng., Fr.*	estación	station	estação
reservoir	Stausee	**Stausee** *Ger.*	embalse	réservoir	reservatório
station	Bahnhof, Stützpunkt	**stazione** *It.*	estación	station	estação
saint	Sankt	**ste., sainte** *Fr.*	santa	sainte	santa
mountains	Berge	**stěny** *Czech*	montañas	montagnes	montanhas
steppe	Steppe	**step'** *Rus.*	estepa	steppe	estepe
peak	Gipfel	**štít** *Slo.*	pico	cime	pico
saint	Sankt	**sto., santo** *Port., Sp.*	santo	saint	santo
strait(s)	Meeresstrasse	**strait(s)** *Eng.*	estrecho	détroit	estreito
stream	Strom	**stream eng.**	corriente de agua	cours d'eau	curso d'água
street	Strasse	**street** *Eng.*	calle	rue	rua
strait	Meeresstrasse	**stretto** *It.*	estrecho	détroit	estreito
stream	Strom	**Strom** *Ger.*	corriente de agua	cours d'eau	curso d'água
stream	Strom	**-ström, -strömmen** *Swe.*	corriente de agua	cours d'eau	curso d'água
river	Fluss	**-su** *Kor.*	río	rivière	rio
channel	Kanal	**-suidō** *Jap.*	canal, estrecho	canal, détroit	canal, estreito
sound	Sund	**Sund** *Ger.*	sonda	détroit	estreito
sound	Sund	**-sund** *Swe.*	sonda	détroit	estreito
river	Fluss	**suyu** *Tur.*	río	rivière	rio
swamp	Sumpf	**swamp** *Eng.*	pantano	marais	pântano
ridge	Höhenrücken	**syrt** *Tur.*	sierra	crête	serra
island	Insel	**sziget** *Hung.*	isla	île	ilha

T

ENGLISH	DEUTSCH	Map Form	ESPAÑOL	FRANÇAIS	PORTUGUÊS
tableland	Tafelland	**tableland** *Eng.*	mesa, altiplano	plateau	planalto
woods	Gehölz	**tailis** *Fr.*	bosque	taillis	bosque
reef	Riff	**taka** *Indon.*	arrecife	récif	recife
mountain	Berg	**-take** *Jap.*	montaña	montagne	montanha
waterfall	Wasserfall	**-taki** *Jap.*	cascada	chute d'eau	queda d'água
valley	Tal	**Tal** *Ger.*	valle	vallée	vale
mountain	Berg	**tall** *Ara.*	montaña	montagne	montanha
mountain, hill	Berg, Hügel	**tallat** *Ara.*	montaña, colina	montagne, colline	montanha, colina
hills	Hügel	**tallāt** *Ara.*	colinas	collines	colinas
dam	Talsperre	**Talsperre** *Ger.*	presa	barrage	represa
cape	Kap	**tandjung** *Indon.*	cabo	cap	cabo
point	Landspitze	**-tangar, -tangi** *Ice.*	punta	pointe	ponta
cape	Kap	**tanjong** *Mal.*	cabo	cap	cabo
island	Insel	**tao** *Ch.*	isla	île	ilha
hills	Hügel	**ţaraq** *Ara.*	colinas	collines	colinas
lake	See	**tasek** *Mal.*	lago	lac	lago
lake	See	**tasik** *Indon.*	lago	lac	lago
plateau	Hochebene	**tassili** *Ber.*	meseta	plateau	planalto
mountain	Berg	**taung** *Bur.*	montaña	montagne	montanha
range	Gebirge	**taungdan** *Bur.*	sierra	chaîne	cordilheira
theatre	Theater	**teatro** *It., Sp.*	teatro	théâtre	teatro
bay	Bucht	**teluk** *Indon.*	bahía	baie	baía
temple	Tempel	**temple** *Eng., Fr.*	templo	temple	templo
church	Kirche	**templom** *Hung.*	iglesia	église	igreja
desert	Wüste	**ténéré** *Ber.*	desierto	désert	deserto
peak, hill	Gipfel, Hügel	**tepe, tepesi** *Tur.*	pico, colina	cime, colline	pico, colina
territory	Territorium	**territory** *Eng.*	territorio	territoire	território
lagoon	Lagune, Haff	**thale** *Thai*	laguna	lagune	laguna
mountains	Berge	**thiu khao** *Thai*	montañas	montagnes	montanhas
mountain	Berg	**-tind, -tinderne** *Nor.*	montaña	montagne	montanha
ridge	Höhenrücken	**ţiwāl** *Ara.*	sierra	crête	serra
mountain	Berg	**-tjåkko, -tjåure** *Lapp.*	montaña	montagne	montanha
island	Insel	**-to** *Kor.*	isla	île	ilha
island	Insel	**-tō** *Jap.*	isla	île	ilha
lake	See	**tó** *Hung.*	lago	lac	lago
pass	Pass	**-tōge** *Jap.*	paso	col	passo
island	Insel	**tokong** *Mal.*	isla	île	ilha
lake	See	**tônlé** *Cbd.*	lago	lac	lago
mountain torrent	Wildbach	**torrente** *It., Sp.*	torrente	torrent	torrente
tower	Turm	**tower** *Eng.*	torre	tour	torre
turnpike	gebührenpflichtige Autobahn	**tpk., turnpike** *Eng.*	camino con peaje	grande route à péage	rodovia com pedágio
lake	See	**-träsk** *Swe.*	lago	lac	lago
trench	Tiefseegraben	**trench** *Eng.*	trinchera	tranchée	fossa submarina
trough	Tiefseegraben	**trough** *Eng.*	trinchera	tranchée	fossa submarina
volcano	Vulkan	**tulūl** *Ara.*	volcán	volcan	vulcão
tunnel	Tunnel	**túnel** *Sp.*	túnel	tunnel	túnel
tunnel	Tunnel	**tunnel** *Eng., Fr.*	túnel	tunnel	túnel
hill, mountain	Hügel, Berg	**-tunturi** *Finn.*	colina, montaña	colline, montagne	colina, montanha
island	Insel	**-tuo** *Ch.*	isla	île	ilha
canal	Kanal	**tur'at** *Ara.*	canal	canal	canal
turnpike	gebührenpflichtige Autobahn	**turnpike** *Eng.*	camino con peaje	grande route à péage	rodovia com pedágio

U-V

ENGLISH	DEUTSCH	Map Form	ESPAÑOL	FRANÇAIS	PORTUGUÊS
cape	Kap	**udjung** *Indon.*	cabo	cap	cabo
lagoon	Lagune, Haff	**-umi** *Jap.*	laguna	lagune	laguna
United Nations	Vereinte Nationen	**U.N., United Nations** *Eng.*	Naciones Unidas	Nations Unies	Nações Unidas
canal	Kanal	**-unga** *Jap.*	canal	canal	canal
university	Universität	**univ., universidad** *Sp.* **universidade** *Port.* **università** *It.* **university** *Eng.*	universidad	université	universidade
university	Universität	**Universität** *Ger.*	universidad	université	universidade
university	Universität	**université** *Fr.*	universidad	université	universidade
university	Universität	**universitet** *Rus.*	universidad	université	universidade
upland	Bergland	**upland** *Eng.*	tierras altas	hautes terres	terras altas
lake	See	**-ura** *Jap.*	lago	lac	lago
mountain(s)	Berg(e)	**uul** *Mong.*	montaña(s)	montagne(s)	montanha(s)
elevation(s)	Höhe(n)	**uval(y)** *Rus.*	altura(s)	élévation(s)	elevação(ões)
spring	Quelle	**'uyūn** *Ara.*	manantial	source	fonte, manancial
hill	Hügel	**-vaara** *Finn.*	colina	colline	colina
strait	Meeresstrasse	**väin** *Est.*	estrecho	détroit	estreito
valley	Tal	**val** *Fr., It.*	valle	val	vale
valley	Tal	**valle** *It., Sp.*	valle	vallée	vale
valley	Tal	**vallée** *Fr.*	valle	vallée	vale
waterfall	Wasserfall	**vallen** *Du.*	cascada	chute d'eau	queda d'água
valley	Tal	**valley** *Eng.*	valle	vallée	vale
valley	Tal	**vallon** *Fr.*	valle	vallon	vale
lake	See	**-vatn** *Ice., Nor.*	lago	lac	lago
lake	See	**-vatnet** *Nor.*	lago	lac	lago
lake	See	**-vattnett** *Swe.*	lago	lac	lago
reservoir	Stausee	**vdchr., vodochranilišče** *Rus.*	embalse	réservoir	reservatório
hills	Hügel	**-veden** *Swe.*	colinas	collines	colinas
upland	Bergland	**verch** *Rus.*	tierras altas	hautes terres	terras altas
lake	See	**-vesi** *Finn.*	lago	lac	lago
viaduct	Viadukt	**viaducto** *Sp.*	viaducto	viaduc	viaduto
plateau	Hochebene	**-vidda** *Nor.*	meseta	plateau	planalto
gulf	Golf	**-viken** *Swe.*	golfo	golfe	golfo
bay	Bucht	**vinh** *Viet.*	bahía	baie	baía
mountain	Berg	**virful** *Rom.*	montaña	montagne	montanha
airport	Flughafen	**vliegveld** *Du.*	aeropuerto	aéroport	aeroporto
channel	Kanal	**vliet** *Du.*	canal, estrecho	canal, détroit	canal, estreito
canal	Kanal	**vodnyj put'** *Rus.*	canal	canal	canal
reservoir	Stausee	**vodochranilišče** *Rus.*	embalse	réservoir	reservatório
railroad station	Bahnhof	**vokzal** *Rus.*	estación de ferrocarril	gare	estação ferroviária
volcano	Vulkan	**vol., volcán** *Sp.* **volcano** *Eng.*	volcán	volcan	vulcão
pass	Pass	**vorota** *Rus.*	paso	col	passo
upland	Bergland	**vozvyšennost'** *Rus.*	tierras altas	hautes terres	terras altas
mountain	Berg	**vrâh** *Blg.*	montaña	montagne	montanha
mountains	Berge	**vrchovina** *Czech, Slo.*	montañas	montagnes	montanhas
peak	Gipfel	**vrh** *S./C.*	pico	cime	pico
volcano	Vulkan	**vulkan** *Rus.*	volcán	volcan	vulcão
bay	Bucht	**vung** *Viet.*	bahía	baie	baía
mountain, hill	Berg, Hügel	**-vuori** *Finn.*	montaña, colina	montagne, colline	montanha, colina

W-Z

ENGLISH	DEUTSCH	Map Form	ESPAÑOL	FRANÇAIS	PORTUGUÊS
west	West	**w., west** *Eng.*	oeste	ouest	oeste
wadi	Wadi	**wādī** *Ara.*	uadi	wadi	uádi
oasis	Oase	**wāḥat, wāḥāt** *Ara.*	oasis	oasis	oásis
forest; mountains	Wald	**Wald** *Ger.*	bosque; montañas	forêt; montagnes	floresta; montanhas
bay	Bucht	**-wan** *Ch., Jap.*	bahía	baie	baía
wash	Wadi	**wash** *Eng.*	uadi	wadi	uádi
waterfalls	Wasserfälle	**Wasserfälle** *Ger.*	cascadas	chutes d'eau	quedas d'água
water (lake; river)	Wasser (See; Fluss)	**water** *Eng.*	agua (lago;rio)	eau (lac; rivière)	água (lago, rio)
waterway	Wasserstrasse	**waterway** *Eng.*	canal	canal	canal
pond	Weiher	**Weiher** *Ger.*	charca	étang	charco
well	Brunnen	**well** *Eng.*	pozo	puits	poço
bay	Wiek	**Wiek** *Ger.*	bahía	baie	baía
woods	Gehölz	**woods** *Eng.*	bosque	bois	bosque
water (lake; river)	Wasser (See; Fluss)	**wr., water** *Eng.*	agua (lago; rio)	eau (lac; rivière)	água (lago, rio)
river	Fluss	**-xi** *Ch.*	río	rivière	rio
strait	Meeresstrasse	**-xia** *Ch.*	estrecho	détroit	estreito
lake, sea	See, Meer	**yam** *Heb.*	lago, mar	lac, mer	lago, mar
mountain	Berg	**-yama** *Jap.*	montaña	montagne	montanha
sea, bay, lake	Meer, Bucht, See	**-yang** *Ch.*	mar, bahía, lago	mer, baie, lac	mar, baía, lago
peninsula	Halbinsel	**yarımadası** *Tur.*	península	péninsule	península
mountain	Berg	**yebel** *Ara.*	montaña	montagne	montanha
rock, island	Fels, Insel	**yen** *Ch.*	roca, isla	rocher, île	rochedo, ilha
mountains	Berge	**yoma** *Bur.*	montañas	montagnes	montanhas
island	Insel	**-yu** *Ch.*	isla	île	ilha
intermittent lake	periodischer See	**zahrez** *Ara.*	lago intermitente	lac périodique	lago intermitente
point	Landspitze	**-zaki** *Jap.*	punta	pointe	ponta
lagoon	Lagune, Haff	**zalew** *Pol.*	laguna	lagune	laguna
gulf, bay	Golf, Bucht	**zaliv** *Rus.*	golfo, bahía	golfe, baie	golfo, baía
reserve	Reservat	**zapov., zapovednik** *Rus.*	reserva	réserve	reserva
sea, lake	Meer, See	**zee** *Du.*	mar, lago	mer, lac	mar, lago
autonomous province	autonome Provinz	**zizhiqu** *Ch.*	provincia autónoma	province autonome	província autônoma
autonomous district	autonomer Distrikt	**zizhixian** *Ch.*	distrito autónomo	district autonome	distrito autônomo
zoo	Zoo	**zoo** *Eng.*	parque zoológico	zoo	jardim zoológico

THIS TABLE gives the area, population, population density, capital, and political status for every country in the world. The political units listed are categorized by political status in the last column of the table, as follows: A—independent countries; B—internally independent political entities which are under the protection of another country in matters of defense and foreign affairs; C—colonies and other dependent political units; and D—the major administrative subdivisions of Australia, Canada, China, the Soviet Union, the United Kingdom, and the United States. For comparison, the table also includes the continents and the world. For units categorized B, the names of protecting countries are specified in the political-status column. For units categorized C, the names of administering countries are given in parentheses in the first column.

The populations are estimates for January 1, 1988, made by Rand McNally & Company on the basis of official data, United Nations estimates, and other available information.

IN DIESER ÜBERSICHT sind Fläche, Bevölkerung, Bevölkerungsdichte, Hauptstadt und politischer Status für jedes Land der Erde aufgeführt. Die politischen Einheiten sind in der letzten Spalte der Tabelle nach ihrem politischen Status wie folgt gegliedert: A—souveräne Staaten; B—innenpolitisch unabhängige Länder unter der Protektion eines anderen Landes in Angelegenheiten der Aussenpolitik und Verteidigung; C—Kolonien oder anderweitig abhängige Gebiete; D—die wichtigsten Verwaltungseinheiten von Australien, Kanada, China, der Sowjetunion, dem Vereinigten Königreich und den Vereinigten Staaten. Für Vergleiche enthält die Übersicht auch Angabenüber die Kontinente und die Welt. Für die unter B eingestuften Einheiten ist der Name des Schutzstaates in der Spalte Politischer Status aufgeführt. Für die unter C eingestuften Gebiete steht der Name des die Verwaltung ausübenden Landes in Klammern in der ersten Spalte.

Die Bevölkerungsangaben sind Schätzungen zum 1. Januar 1988, die Rand McNally & Company auf der Grundlage amtlicher Zahlen, Schätzungen der Vereinten Nationen und anderer zugänglicher Informationen berechnet hat.

EL CUADRO ABAJO incluye la extensión, población y densidad de población, la capital y el estado político de todos los países del mundo. Las entidades políticas nombradas están clasificadas de acuerdo a su estado político en la última columna de la tabla, de esta manera: A—países independientes; B—entidades políticas internamente independientes las cuales se encuentran bajo la protección de otro país en cuanto a asuntos de defensa nacional y relaciones con el extranjero; C—colonias y otras entidades políticas dependientes; y D—las mayores subdivisiones administrativas de Australia, Canadá, China, la Unión Soviética, el Reino Unido, y los Estados Unidos. Para servir de medida comparativa, el cuadro también incluye los continentes y el mundo. Para las entidades de la clasificación B, los nombres de los países protectores están especificados en la columna de estado político. Para las unidades bajo la categoría C, los nombres de los países administradores se encuentran entre paréntesis en la primera columna.

Las poblaciones son los estimados de Rand McNally & Company, tomados el 1o. de Enero de 1988, en base a datos oficiales, estimados de las Naciones Unidas y varias otras informaciones disponibles.

CETTE TABLE donne, pour chaque pays du monde, les renseignements suivants: superficie, population, densité de population, capitale, statut politique. Les entités politiques sont classées, selon leur statut, dans la dernière colonne du tableau: A—pays indépendants; B—entités politiques indépendants intérieurement, mais qui se trouvent sous la protection d'un autre pays pour leur défense et leurs relations extérieures; C—colonies et autres entités politiques dépendantes; D—principales subdivisions administratives de l'Australie, du Canada, de la Chine, de l'U.R.S.S., du Royaume-Uni, des États-Unis. Pour permettre les comparaisons, la table comprend aussi les continents et le monde. Pour les entités politiques de la catégorie B, les noms des pays protecteurs sont spécifiés dans la colonne "statut politique". Pour celles de la catégorie C, les noms des pays administrateurs sont mis entre parenthèses dans la première colonne.

Les chiffres concernant la population sont des estimations au 1er janvier 1988, établies par Rand McNally & Company. d'après les sources officielles, les estimations des Nations Unies et autres informations disponibles.

A TABELA que se segue apresenta a área, a população, a densidade demográfica, a capital e o estatuto político de todos os países do mundo. As unidades políticas relacionadas na tabela estão classificadas de acordo com o respectivo estatuto político na última coluna, do seguinte modo: A—países independentes; B—unidades políticas internamente independentes mas que se encontram sob a proteção de outro país no tocante a assuntos de defesa nacional e negócios extrenos; C—colônias e outras unidades políticas dependentes; e D—subdivisões administrativas principais da Austrália, Canadá, China, União Soviética, Reino Unido e Estados Unidos. Para fins de comparabilidade, a tabela também inclui os continentes e o mundo. No tocante ás unidades classificadas em B, os nomes dos países protetores estão especificados na coluna relativa ao estatuto político. Para as unidades da categoria C, os nomes dos países administradores figuram entre parênteses na primeira coluna.

Os dados relativos à população são estimativas de Rand McNally & Company para 1 de janeiro de 1988, com base em dados oficiais, estimativas das Nações Unidas e outras informações disponíveis.

NAME / NAME / NOMBRE / NOM / NOME English / Englisch Inglés / Anglais / Inglês	Local / Einheimisch Local / Local / Local	AREA / FLÄCHE AREA / SUPERFICIE / ÁREA sq. km.	sq. mi.	POPULATION BEVÖLKERUNG POBLACIÓN POPULATION POPULAÇÃO	DENSITY PER BEVÖLKERUNGSDICHTE PRO / DENSIDAD POR DENSITÉ / DENSIDADE POR sq. km.	sq. mi.	CAPITAL HAUPSTADT CAPITAL CAPITALE CAPITAL	POLITICAL STATUS POLITISCHER STATUS ESTADO POLÍTICO STATUS POLITIQUE ESTATUTO POLÍTICO
†Afghanistan	Afghānestān	652,225	251,826	19,340,000	30	77	Kābol	A
Africa	. . .	30,300,000	11,700,000	615,300,000	20	53	. . .	. . .
Alabama, U.S.	Alabama	133,913	51,704	4,105,000	31	79	Montgomery	D
Alaska, U.S.	Alaska	1,530,693	591,004	565,000	0.4	1.0	Juneau	D
†Albania	Shqipëri	28,748	11,100	3,310,000	115	298	Tiranë	A
Alberta, Can.	Alberta	661,190	255,287	2,400,000	3.6	9.4	Edmonton	D
†Algeria	Algérie (French) / Djazaïr (Arabic)	2,381,741	919,595	23,820,000	10	26	El Djazaïr (Algiers)	A
American Samoa (U.S.)	American Samoa (English) / Amerika Samoa (Samoan)	199	77	39,000	196	506	Pago Pago	C
Andorra	Andorra	453	175	50,000	110	286	Andorra	B(Sp., Fr.)
†Angola	Angola	1,246,700	481,354	9,410,000	7.5	20	Luanda	A
Anguilla	Anguilla	91	35	6,900	76	197	The Valley	B(U.K.)
Anhwei, China	Anhui	140,000	54,054	53,290,000	381	986	Hefei	D
Antarctica	. . .	14,000,000	5,400,000	(1)	0	0	. . .	. . .
†Antigua and Barbuda	Antigua and Barbuda	443	171	83,000	187	485	St. John's	A
†Argentina	Argentina	2,780,092	1,073,400	31,730,000	11	30	Buenos Aires	A
Arizona, U.S.	Arizona	295,264	114,002	3,405,000	12	30	Phoenix	D
Arkansas, U.S.	Arkansas	137,764	53,191	2,405,000	17	45	Little Rock	D
Armenian S.S.R., U.S.S.R.	Arm'anskaja S.S.R.	29,800	11,506	3,445,000	116	299	Jerevan	D
Aruba	Aruba	193	75	65,000	337	867	Oranjestad	B(Neth.)
Asia	. . .	44,900,000	17,300,000	3,031,100,000	68	175	. . .	. . .
†Australia	Australia	7,682,300	2,966,155	16,330,000	2.1	5.5	Canberra	A
Australian Capital Territory, Austl.	Australian Capital Territory	2,400	927	270,000	113	291	Canberra	D
†Austria	Österreich	83,855	32,377	7,570,000	90	234	Wien (Vienna)	A
Azerbaijan S.S.R., U.S.S.R.	Azerbajdžanskaja S.S.R.	86,600	33,436	6,860,000	79	205	Baku	D
†Bahamas	Bahamas	13,939	5,382	245,000	18	46	Nassau	A
†Bahrain	Al-Baḥrayn	662	256	460,000	695	1,797	Al-Manāmah	A
†Bangladesh	Bangladesh	143,998	55,598	103,630,000	720	1,864	Dhaka (Dacca)	A
†Barbados	Barbados	430	166	256,000	595	1,542	Bridgetown	A
†Belgium	Belgique (French) / België (Flemish)	30,518	11,783	9,890,000	324	839	Bruxelles (Brussels)	A
†Belize	Belize	22,963	8,866	175,000	7.6	20	Belmopan	A
†Benin	Bénin	112,622	43,484	4,210,000	37	97	Porto-Novo and Cotonou	A
Bermuda (U.K.)	Bermuda	54	21	55,000	1,019	2,619	Hamilton	C
†Bhutan	Druk-Yul	46,500	17,954	1,490,000	32	83	Thimbu	B(India)
†Bolivia	Bolivia	1,098,581	424,165	6,725,000	6.1	16	Sucre and La Paz	A
Bophuthatswana(2)	Bophuthatswana	40,000	15,444	1,780,000	45	115	Mmabatho	B(S. Afr.)
†Botswana	Botswana	582,000	224,711	1,180,000	2.0	5.3	Gaborone	A
†Brazil	Brasil	8,511,965	3,286,488	143,360,000	17	44	Brasília	A
British Columbia, Can.	British Columbia (English) / Colombie-Britannique (French)	947,800	365,948	2,925,000	3.1	8.0	Victoria	D
British Indian Ocean Territory (U.K.)	British Indian Ocean Territory	60	23	(1)	0	0	. . .	C
†Brunei	Brunei	5,765	2,226	250,000	43	112	Bandar Seri Begawan	A
†Bulgaria	Bâlgarija	110,912	42,823	8,985,000	81	210	Sofija (Sofia)	A
†Burkina Faso	Burkina Faso	274,200	105,869	8,365,000	31	79	Ouagadougou	A
†Burma	Myanmā	676,577	261,228	38,670,000	57	148	Rangoon	A
†Burundi	Burundi	27,830	10,745	5,070,000	182	472	Bujumbura	A
†Byelorussian S.S.R., U.S.S.R.	Belorusskaja S.S.R.	207,600	80,155	10,210,000	49	127	Minsk	D
California, U.S.	California	411,041	158,704	27,835,000	68	175	Sacramento	D
†Cameroon	Cameroun (French) / Cameroon (English)	475,442	183,569	10,885,000	23	59	Yaoundé	A
†Canada	Canada	9,970,610	3,849,674	25,660,000	2.6	6.7	Ottawa	A
†Cape Verde	Cabo Verde	4,033	1,557	350,000	87	225	Praia	A
Cayman Islands (U.K.)	Cayman Islands	259	100	21,000	81	210	Georgetown	C
†Central African Republic	République centrafricaine	622,984	240,535	2,950,000	4.7	12	Bangui	A
†Chad	Tchad	1,284,000	495,755	5,415,000	4.2	11	N'Djamena	A
Chekiang, China	Zhejiang	102,000	39,382	41,615,000	408	1,057	Hangzhou	D
†Chile	Chile	756,626	292,135	12,555,000	17	43	Santiago	A
†China (excl. Taiwan)	Zhongguo	9,631,600	3,718,783	1,080,920,000	112	291	Beijing (Peking)	A
Christmas Island (Austl.)	Christmas Island	135	52	3,000	22	58	. . .	C
Ciskei(2)	Ciskei	5,386	2,080	790,000	147	380	Bisho	B(S. Afr.)
Cocos (Keeling) Islands (Austl.)	Cocos (Keeling) Islands	14	5.4	600	43	111	. . .	C
†Colombia	Colombia	1,141,748	440,831	29,890,000	26	68	Bogotá	A
Colorado, U.S.	Colorado	269,602	104,094	3,330,000	12	32	Denver	D
†Comoros	Comores (French) / Al-Qumur (Arabic)	2,171	838	430,000	198	513	Moroni	A
†Congo	Congo	342,000	132,047	2,050,000	6.0	16	Brazzaville	A
Connecticut, U.S.	Connecticut	12,999	5,019	3,245,000	250	647	Hartford	D
Cook Islands	Cook Islands	236	91	17,000	72	187	Avarua	B(N.Z.)
†Costa Rica	Costa Rica	51,100	19,730	2,675,000	52	136	San José	A
†Cuba	Cuba	110,861	42,804	10,400,000	94	243	La Habana (Havana)	A
†Cyprus	Kípros (Greek) / Kıbrıs (Turkish)	9,251	3,572	685,000	74	192	Levkosía (Nicosia)	A
†Czechoslovakia	Československo	127,905	49,384	16,055,000	126	325	Praha (Prague)	A
Delaware, U.S.	Delaware	5,297	2,045	640,000	121	313	Dover	D

NAME / NAME / NOMBRE / NOM / NOME English / Englisch Inglés / Anglais / Inglês	Local / Einheimisch Local / Local / Local	AREA / FLÄCHE AREA / SUPERFICIE / ÁREA sq. km.	sq. mi.	POPULATION BEVÖLKERUNG POBLACIÓN POPULATION POPULAÇÃO	DENSITY PER BEVÖLKERUNGSDICHTE PRO / DENSIDAD POR DENSITÉ / DENSIDADE POR sq. km.	sq. mi.	CAPITAL HAUPTSTADT CAPITAL CAPITALE CAPITAL	POLITICAL STATUS POLITISCHER STATUS ESTADO POLÍTICO STATUS POLITIQUE ESTATUTO POLÍTICO
†Denmark	Danmark	43,080	16,633	5,120,000	119	308	København	A
District of Columbia, U.S.	District of Columbia	179	69	620,000	3,464	8,986	Washington	D
†Djibouti	Djibouti	23,000	8,880	315,000	14	35	Djibouti	A
†Dominica	Dominica	752	290	90,000	120	310	Roseau	A
†Dominican Republic	República Dominicana	48,442	18,704	6,635,000	137	355	Santo Domingo	A
†Ecuador	Ecuador	283,561	109,484	10,065,000	35	92	Quito	A
†Egypt	Misr	1,001,450	386,662	51,320,000	51	133	Al-Qāhirah (Cairo)	A
†El Salvador	El Salvador	21,041	8,124	5,055,000	240	622	San Salvador	A
England, U.K.	England	130,439	50,363	47,585,000	365	945	London	D
†Equatorial Guinea	Guinea Ecuatorial	28,051	10,831	375,000	13	35	Malabo	A
Estonian S.S.R., U.S.S.R.	Estonskaja S.S.R.	45,100	17,413	1,565,000	35	90	Tallinn	D
†Ethiopia	Ityopiya	1,251,282	483,123	46,385,000	37	96	Adis Abeba	A
Europe	. . .	9,900,000	3,800,000	684,800,000	69	180	. . .	. . .
Faeroe Islands	Føroyar	1,399	540	47,000	34	87	Tórshavn	B(Den.)
Falkland Islands (excl. Dependencies) (U.K.)[3]	Falkland Islands (English) / Islas Malvinas (Spanish)	12,173	4,700	2,000	0.2	0.4	Stanley	C
†Fiji	Fiji	18,333	7,078	735,000	40	104	Suva	A
†Finland	Suomi (Finnish) / Finland (Swedish)	338,145	130,559	4,965,000	15	38	Helsinki (Helsingfors)	A
Florida, U.S.	Florida	151,949	58,668	12,060,000	79	206	Tallahassee	D
†France (excl. Overseas Departments)	France	547,026	211,208	55,730,000	102	264	Paris	A
French Guiana, Fr.	Guyane française	91,000	35,135	90,000	1.0	2.6	Cayenne	D
French Polynesia (Fr.)	Polynésie française	4,000	1,544	190,000	48	123	Papeete	C
Fukien, China	Fujian	123,000	47,491	27,995,000	228	589	Fuzhou	D
†Gabon	Gabon	267,667	103,347	1,415,000	5.3	14	Libreville	A
†Gambia	Gambia	11,295	4,361	800,000	71	183	Banjul	A
Georgia, U.S.	Georgia	152,587	58,914	6,260,000	41	106	Atlanta	D
Georgian S.S.R., U.S.S.R.	Gruzinskaja S.S.R.	69,700	26,911	5,350,000	77	199	Tbilisi	D
†German Democratic Republic	Deutsche Demokratische Republik	108,333	41,828	16,600,000	153	397	Berlin, Ost- (East Berlin)	A
†Germany, Federal Republic of	Bundesrepublik Deutschland	248,717	96,032	60,960,000	245	635	Bonn	A
†Ghana	Ghana	238,533	92,098	14,045,000	59	153	Accra	A
Gibraltar (U.K.)	Gibraltar	6.0	2.3	30,000	5,000	13,043	Gibraltar	C
†Greece	Ellás	131,944	50,944	10,010,000	76	196	Athínai (Athens)	A
Greenland	Kalaallit Nunaat (Eskimo) / Grønland (Danish)	2,175,600	840,004	55,000	0.0	0.1	Godthåb	B(Den.)
†Grenada	Grenada	344	133	90,000	262	677	St. George's	A
Guadeloupe (incl. Dependencies), Fr.	Guadeloupe	1,780	687	335,000	188	488	Basse-Terre	D
Guam (U.S.)	Guam	541	209	135,000	250	646	Agana	C
†Guatemala	Guatemala	108,889	42,042	8,550,000	79	203	Guatemala	A
Guernsey (incl. Dependencies) (U.K.)	Guernsey	78	30	80,000	1,026	2,667	St. Peter Port	C
†Guinea	Guinée	245,857	94,926	6,475,000	26	68	Conakry	A
†Guinea-Bissau	Guiné-Bissau	36,125	13,948	895,000	25	64	Bissau	A
†Guyana	Guyana	214,969	83,000	800,000	3.7	9.6	Georgetown	A
†Haiti	Haïti	27,750	10,714	5,470,000	197	511	Port-au-Prince	A
Hawaii, U.S.	Hawaii	16,765	6,473	1,085,000	65	168	Honolulu	D
Heilungkiang, China	Heilongjiang	460,000	177,607	34,155,000	74	192	Harbin	D
Honan, China	Henan	167,000	64,479	79,660,000	477	1,235	Zhengzhou	D
†Honduras	Honduras	112,088	43,277	4,845,000	43	112	Tegucigalpa	A
Hong Kong (U.K.)	Hong Kong	1,068	412	5,700,000	5,337	13,835	Hong Kong (Victoria)	C
Hopeh, China	Hebei	203,000	78,379	57,290,000	282	731	Shijiazhuang	D
Hunan, China	Hunan	211,000	81,468	58,050,000	275	713	Changsha	D
†Hungary	Magyarország	93,033	35,920	10,600,000	114	295	Budapest	A
Hupeh, China	Hubei	188,000	72,587	50,910,000	271	701	Wuhan	D
†Iceland	Ísland	103,000	39,769	245,000	2.4	6.2	Reykjavík	A
Idaho, U.S.	Idaho	216,435	83,566	1,045,000	4.8	13	Boise	D
Illinois, U.S.	Illinois	149,888	57,872	11,685,000	78	202	Springfield	D
†India (incl. partof Jammu and Kashmir)	India (English) / Bharat (Hindi)	3,203,975	1,237,062	789,120,000	246	638	New Delhi	A
Indiana, U.S.	Indiana	94,320	36,417	5,560,000	59	153	Indianapolis	D
†Indonesia	Indonesia	1,919,443	741,101	172,450,000	90	233	Jakarta	A
Inner Mongolia, China	Nei Monggol	1,200,000	463,323	20,755,000	17	45	Hohhot	D
Iowa, U.S.	Iowa	145,752	56,275	2,880,000	20	51	Des Moines	D
†Iran	Īrān	1,648,000	636,296	47,680,000	29	75	Tehrān	A
†Iraq	Al-'Irāq	438,317	169,235	16,745,000	38	99	Baghdād	A
†Ireland	Ireland (English) / Éire (Gaelic)	70,283	27,136	3,650,000	52	135	Dublin (Baile Átha Cliath)	A
Isle of Man	Isle of Man	572	221	65,000	114	294	Douglas	B(U.K.)
†Israel	Yisra'el (Hebrew) / Isrā'īl (Arabic)	20,325	7,848	4,315,000	212	550	Yerushalayim (Jerusalem)	A
Israeli Occupied Areas[4]	. . .	7,632	2,947	1,660,000	218	563	. . .	. . .
†Italy	Italia	301,268	116,320	57,390,000	190	493	Roma (Rome)	A
†Ivory Coast	Côte d'Ivoire	320,763	123,847	11,075,000	35	89	Abidjan and Yamoussoukro[5]	A
†Jamaica	Jamaica	10,991	4,244	2,330,000	212	549	Kingston	A
†Japan	Nihon	377,801	145,870	122,400,000	324	839	Tōkyō	A
Jersey (U.K.)	Jersey	116	45	55,000	474	1,222	St. Helier	C
†Jordan	Al-Urdunn	91,000	35,135	2,880,000	32	82	'Ammān	A
†Kampuchea (Cambodia)	Kâmpŭchéa Prâchéathipâtéyy	181,035	69,898	6,610,000	37	95	Phnum Pénh	A
Kansas, U.S.	Kansas	213,109	82,282	2,495,000	12	30	Topeka	D
Kansu, China	Gansu	390,000	150,580	21,080,000	54	140	Lanzhou	D
Kazakh S.S.R., U.S.S.R.	Kazachskaja S.S.R.	2,717,300	1,049,156	16,360,000	6.0	16	Alma-Ata	D
Kentucky, U.S.	Kentucky	104,672	40,414	3,770,000	36	93	Frankfort	D
†Kenya	Kenya	582,646	224,961	22,435,000	39	100	Nairobi	A
Kiangsi, China	Jiangxi	165,000	63,707	35,780,000	217	562	Nanchang	D
Kiangsu, China	Jiangsu	102,000	39,382	64,205,000	629	1,630	Nanjing (Nanking)	D
Kirghiz S.S.R., U.S.S.R.	Kirgizskaja S.S.R.	198,500	76,641	4,125,000	21	54	Frunze	D
Kiribati	Kiribati	726	280	65,000	90	232	Bairiki	A
Kirin, China	Jilin	187,000	72,201	23,780,000	127	329	Changchun	D
Korea, North	Chosŏn-minjujuŭi-inmīn-konghwaguk	120,538	46,540	21,185,000	176	455	P'yŏngyang	A
Korea, South	Taehan-min'guk	98,484	38,025	42,130,000	428	1,108	Sŏul (Seoul)	A
†Kuwait	Al-Kuwayt	17,818	6,880	1,935,000	109	281	Al-Kuwayt	A
Kwangsi Chuang, China	Guangxi Zhuangzu	237,000	91,506	39,995,000	169	437	Nanning	D
Kwangtung, China	Guangdong	231,000	89,190	64,640,000	280	725	Guangzhou (Canton)	D
Kweichow, China	Guizhou	174,000	67,182	30,700,000	176	457	Guiyang	D
†Laos	Lao	236,800	91,429	3,795,000	16	42	Viangchan (Vientiane)	A
Latvian S.S.R., U.S.S.R.	Latvijskaja S.S.R.	63,700	24,595	2,675,000	42	109	Rīga	D
†Lebanon	Al-Lubnān	10,400	4,015	2,755,000	265	686	Bayrūt (Beirut)	A
†Lesotho	Lesotho	30,355	11,720	1,635,000	54	140	Maseru	A
Liaoning, China	Liaoning	151,000	58,301	38,050,000	252	653	Shenyang (Mukden)	D
†Liberia	Liberia	111,369	43,000	2,415,000	22	56	Monrovia	A
†Libya	Lībiyā	1,759,540	679,362	4,050,000	2.3	6.0	Tarābulus (Tripoli)	A
Liechtenstein	Liechtenstein	160	62	29,000	181	468	Vaduz	A
Lithuanian S.S.R., U.S.S.R.	Litovskaja S.S.R.	65,200	25,174	3,670,000	56	146	Vilnius	D
Louisiana, U.S.	Louisiana	123,672	47,750	4,560,000	37	95	Baton Rouge	D
†Luxembourg	Luxembourg	2,586	998	370,000	143	371	Luxembourg	A
Macau (Port.)	Macau	17	6.6	415,000	24,412	62,879	Macau	C
†Madagascar	Madagasikara (Malagasy) / Madagascar (French)	587,041	226,658	10,660,000	18	47	Antananarivo	A
Maine, U.S.	Maine	86,156	33,265	1,190,000	14	36	Augusta	D
†Malawi	Malaŵi	118,484	45,747	7,620,000	64	167	Lilongwe	A
†Malaysia	Malaysia	330,228	127,502	16,640,000	50	131	Kuala Lumpur	A
†Maldives	Maldives	298	115	200,000	671	1,739	Male	A
†Mali	Mali	1,240,000	478,767	8,165,000	6.6	17	Bamako	A
†Malta	Malta	316	122	345,000	1,092	2,828	Valletta	A
Manitoba, Can.	Manitoba	649,950	250,947	1,085,000	1.7	4.3	Winnipeg	D
Marshall Islands (Trust Territory)	Marshall Islands	181	70	38,000	210	543	Majuro (island)	B(U.S.)
Martinique, Fr.	Martinique	1,100	425	330,000	300	776	Fort-de-France	D
Maryland, U.S.	Maryland	27,094	10,461	4,535,000	167	434	Annapolis	D

NAME / NAME / NOMBRE / NOM / NOME — English / Englisch / Inglés / Anglais / Inglês	Local / Einheimisch / Local / Local / Local	AREA / FLÄCHE / AREA / SUPERFICIE / ÁREA sq. km.	sq. mi.	POPULATION / BEVÖLKERUNG / POBLACIÓN / POPULATION / POPULAÇÃO	DENSITY PER / BEVÖLKERUNGSDICHTE PRO / DENSIDAD POR / DENSITÉ / DENSIDADE POR sq. km.	sq. mi.	CAPITAL / HAUPSTADT / CAPITAL / CAPITALE / CAPITAL	POLITICAL STATUS / POLITISCHER STATUS / ESTADO POLITICO / STATUS POLITIQUE / ESTATUTO POLITICO
Massachusetts, U.S.	Massachusetts	21,461	8,286	5,900,000	275	712	Boston	D
†Mauritania	Mauritanie (French) / Mūrītāniyā (Arabic)	1,030,700	397,956	1,745,000	1.7	4.4	Nouakchott	A
†Mauritius (incl. Dependencies)	Mauritius	2,040	788	1,035,000	507	1,313	Port Louis	A
Mayotte, (Fr.)(6)	Mayotte	373	144	60,000	161	417	Dzaoudzi and Mamoudzou(5)	C
†Mexico	México	1,972,547	761,605	83,040,000	42	109	Ciudad de México (Mexico City)	A
Michigan, U.S.	Michigan	251,506	97,107	9,230,000	37	95	Lansing	D
Micronesia, Federated States of (Trust Territory)	Federated States of Micronesia	702	271	101,000	144	373	Kolonia	B(U.S.)
Midway Islands (U.S.)	Midway Islands	5.2	2.0	500	96	250	. . .	C
Minnesota, U.S.	Minnesota	224,329	86,614	4,380,000	20	51	St. Paul	D
Mississippi, U.S.	Mississippi	123,519	47,691	2,690,000	22	56	Jackson	D
Missouri, U.S.	Missouri	180,514	69,697	5,200,000	29	75	Jefferson City	D
Moldavian S.S.R., U.S.S.R.	Moldavskaja S.S.R.	33,700	13,012	4,240,000	126	326	Kišin'ov (Kishinev)	D
Monaco	Monaco	1.9	0.7	29,000	15,263	41,429	Monaco	A
†Mongolia	Mongol Ard Uls	1,565,000	604,250	2,015,000	1.3	3.3	Ulaanbaatar (Ulan Bator)	A
Montana, U.S.	Montana	380,845	147,045	845,000	2.2	5.7	Helena	D
Montserrat (U.K.)	Montserrat	103	40	12,000	117	300	Plymouth	C
†Morocco (excl. Western Sahara)	Al-Magrib	446,550	172,414	24,445,000	55	142	Rabat	A
†Mozambique	Moçambique	799,379	308,642	14,595,000	18	47	Maputo	A
Namibia (excl. Walvis Bay)(S. Afr.)(7)	Namibia	823,144	317,818	1,225,000	1.5	3.9	Windhoek	C
Nauru	Nauru (English) / Naoero (Nauruan)	21	8.1	8,700	414	1,074	Yaren District	A
Nebraska, U.S.	Nebraska	200,336	77,350	1,625,000	8.1	21	Lincoln	D
†Nepal	Nepāl	147,181	56,827	17,900,000	122	315	Kathmandu	A
†Netherlands	Nederland	41,785	16,133	14,650,000	351	908	Amsterdam and 's-Gravenhage (The Hague)	A
Netherlands Antilles	Nederlandse Antillen	800	309	190,000	238	615	Willemstad	B(Neth.)
Nevada, U.S.	Nevada	286,354	110,562	985,000	3.4	8.9	Carson City	D
New Brunswick, Can.	New Brunswick (English) / Nouveau-Brunswick (French)	73,440	28,355	720,000	9.8	25	Fredericton	D
New Caledonia, Fr.	Nouvelle-Calédonie	19,079	7,366	155,000	8.1	21	Nouméa	D
Newfoundland, Can.	Newfoundland (English) / Terre-Neuve (French)	405,720	156,649	575,000	1.4	3.7	St. John's	D
New Hampshire, U.S.	New Hampshire	24,030	9,278	1,050,000	44	113	Concord	D
New Jersey, U.S.	New Jersey	20,168	7,787	7,750,000	384	995	Trenton	D
New Mexico, U.S.	New Mexico	314,927	121,594	1,515,000	4.8	12	Santa Fe	D
New South Wales, Austl.	New South Wales	801,600	309,500	5,670,000	7.1	18	Sydney	D
New York, U.S.	New York	136,588	52,737	18,000,000	132	341	Albany	D
†New Zealand	New Zealand	268,112	103,519	3,350,000	12	32	Wellington	A
†Nicaragua	Nicaragua	130,000	50,193	3,500,000	27	70	Managua	A
†Niger	Niger	1,267,000	489,191	7,045,000	5.6	14	Niamey	A
†Nigeria	Nigeria	923,768	356,669	110,240,000	119	309	Lagos and Abuja(5)	A
Ningsia Hui, China	Ningxia Huizu	66,000	25,483	4,325,000	66	170	Yinchuan	D
Niue	Niue	263	102	2,500	9.5	25	Alofi	B(N.Z.)
Norfolk Island (Austl.)	Norfolk Island	36	14	2,300	64	164	Kingston	C
North America	. . .	24,400,000	9,400,000	413,100,000	17	44	. . .	. . .
North Carolina, U.S.	North Carolina	136,412	52,669	6,470,000	47	123	Raleigh	D
North Dakota, U.S.	North Dakota	183,117	70,702	705,000	3.9	10	Bismarck	D
Northern Ireland, U.K.	Northern Ireland	14,122	5,453	1,575,000	112	289	Belfast	D
Northern Mariana Islands (Trust Territory)	Northern Mariana Islands	477	184	22,000	46	120	Saipan (island)	B(U.S.)
Northern Territory, Austl.	Northern Territory	1,346,200	519,771	150,000	0.1	0.3	Darwin	D
Northwest Territories, Can.	Northwest Territories (English) / Territoires du Nord-Ouest (French)	3,426,320	1,322,910	55,000	0.0	0.0	Yellowknife	D
†Norway (incl. Svalbard and Jan Mayen)	Norge	386,975	149,412	4,190,000	11	28	Oslo	A
Nova Scotia, Can.	Nova Scotia (English) / Nouvelle-Écosse (French)	55,490	21,425	885,000	16	41	Halifax	D
Oceania (incl. Australia)	. . .	8,500,000	3,300,000	25,500,000	3.0	7.7	. . .	. . .
Ohio, U.S.	Ohio	115,995	44,786	10,840,000	93	242	Columbus	D
Oklahoma, U.S.	Oklahoma	181,188	69,957	3,365,000	19	48	Oklahoma City	D
†Oman	'Umān	212,457	82,030	2,125,000	10	26	Masqaṭ (Muscat)	A
Ontario, Can.	Ontario	1,068,580	412,581	9,220,000	8.6	22	Toronto	D
Oregon, U.S.	Oregon	251,426	97,076	2,745,000	11	28	Salem	D
Pacific Islands, Trust Territory of the	Trust Territory of the Pacific Islands	1,857	717	175,000	94	244	Saipan (island)	B(U.S.)
†Pakistan (incl. part of Jammu and Kashmir)	Pākistān	879,902	339,732	105,720,000	120	311	Islāmābād	A
Palau (Trust Territory)	Palau (English) / Belau (Palauan)	497	192	14,000	28	73	Koror	B(U.S.)
†Panama	Panamá	77,082	29,762	2,300,000	30	77	Panamá	A
†Papua New Guinea	Papua New Guinea	462,840	178,704	3,510,000	7.6	20	Port Moresby	A
†Paraguay	Paraguay	406,752	157,048	3,955,000	9.7	25	Asunción	A
Peking, China	Beijing	16,800	6,487	9,945,000	592	1,533	Beijing (Peking)	D
Pennsylvania, U.S.	Pennsylvania	119,261	46,047	11,905,000	100	259	Harrisburg	D
†Peru	Perú	1,285,216	496,225	20,995,000	16	42	Lima	A
†Philippines	Pilipinas	300,000	115,831	57,410,000	191	496	Manila	A
Pitcairn (incl. Dependencies) (U.K.)	Pitcairn	49	19	60	1.2	3.2	Adamstown	C
†Poland	Polska	312,683	120,728	38,060,000	122	315	Warszawa (Warsaw)	A
†Portugal	Portugal	91,985	35,516	10,415,000	113	293	Lisboa (Lisbon)	A
Prince Edward Island, Can.	Prince Edward Island (English) / Île-du Prince-Édouard (French)	5,660	2,185	130,000	23	59	Charlottetown	D
Puerto Rico	Puerto Rico	9,104	3,515	3,325,000	365	946	San Juan	B(U.S.)
†Qatar	Qaṭar	11,000	4,247	320,000	29	75	Ad-Dawḥah (Doha)	A
Quebec, Can.	Québec	1,540,680	594,860	6,620,000	4.3	11	Québec	D
Queensland, Austl.	Queensland	1,727,200	666,876	2,655,000	1.5	4.0	Brisbane	D
Reunion, Fr.	Réunion	2,504	967	570,000	228	589	Saint-Denis	D
Rhode Island, U.S.	Rhode Island	3,139	1,212	990,000	315	817	Providence	D
†Romania	România	237,500	91,699	23,020,000	97	251	București (Bucharest)	A
Russian Soviet Federative Socialist Republic, U.S.S.R.	Rossijskaja S.F.S.R.	17,075,400	6,592,849	147,070,000	8.6	22	Moskva (Moscow)	D
†Rwanda	Rwanda	26,338	10,169	6,740,000	256	663	Kigali	A
†St. Christopher-Nevis	St. Christopher-Nevis	269	104	41,000	152	394	Basseterre	A
St. Helena (incl. Dependencies) (U.K.)	St. Helena	419	162	8,200	20	51	Jamestown	C
†St. Lucia	St. Lucia	616	238	140,000	227	588	Castries	A
St. Pierre and Miquelon (Fr.)	Saint-Pierre-et-Miquelon	242	93	6,200	26	67	Saint-Pierre	C
†St.Vincent and the Grenadines	St. Vincent and the Grenadines	388	150	115,000	296	767	Kingstown	A
San Marino	San Marino	61	24	23,000	377	958	San Marino	A
†Sao Tome and Principe	São Tomé e Príncipe	964	372	115,000	119	309	São Tomé	A
Saskatchewan, Can.	Saskatchewan	652,330	251,866	1,020,000	1.6	4.1	Regina	D
†Saudi Arabia	Al-'Arabīyah as-Su'ūdīyah	2,149,690	830,000	12,045,000	5.6	15	Ar-Riyāḍ (Riyadh)	A
Scotland, U.K.	Scotland	77,167	29,794	5,190,000	67	174	Edinburgh	D
†Senegal	Sénégal	196,722	75,955	6,690,000	34	88	Dakar	A
†Seychelles	Seychelles	453	175	65,000	143	371	Victoria	A
Shanghai, China	Shanghai	5,800	2,239	12,540,000	2,162	5,601	Shanghai	D
Shansi, China	Shanxi	157,000	60,618	27,130,000	173	448	Taiyuan	D
Shantung, China	Shandong	153,000	59,074	79,450,000	519	1,345	Jinan	D
Shensi, China	Shaanxi	196,000	75,676	31,020,000	158	410	Xi'an (Sian)	D
†Sierra Leone	Sierra Leone	72,325	27,925	3,885,000	54	139	Freetown	A
†Singapore	Singapore	620	239	2,650,000	4,274	11,088	Singapore	A
Sinkiang Uighur, China	Xinjiang Uygur	1,647,000	635,910	14,050,000	8.5	22	Ürümqi	D
†Solomon Islands	Solomon Islands	29,800	11,506	295,000	9.9	26	Honiara	A

NAME / NAME / NOMBRE / NOM / NOME — English / Englisch / Inglés / Anglais / Inglês	Local / Einheimisch / Local / Local / Local	AREA / FLÄCHE / AREA / SUPERFICIE / ÁREA sq. km.	sq. mi.	POPULATION / BEVÖLKERUNG / POBLACIÓN / POPULATION / POPULAÇÃO	DENSITY PER / BEVÖLKERUNGSDICHTE PRO / DENSIDAD POR / DENSITÉ / DENSIDADE POR sq. km.	sq. mi.	CAPITAL / HAUPSTADT / CAPITAL / CAPITALE / CAPITAL	POLITICAL STATUS / POLITISCHER STATUS / ESTADO POLITICO / STATUS POLITIQUE / ESTATUTO POLITICO
†Somalia	Somaliya	637,657	246,201	8,165,000	13	33	Muqdisho (Mogadishu)	A
†South Africa (incl. Walvis Bay)	South Africa (English) / Suid-Afrika (Afrikaans)	1,123,226	433,680	34,335,000	31	79	Pretoria, Cape Town, and Bloemfontein	A
South America	. . .	17,800,000	6,900,000	282,200,000	16	41	. . .	. . .
South Australia, Austl.	South Australia	984,000	379,925	1,400,000	1.4	3.7	Adelaide	D
South Carolina, U.S.	South Carolina	80,590	31,116	3,480,000	43	112	Columbia	D
South Dakota, U.S.	South Dakota	199,740	77,120	725,000	3.6	9.4	Pierre	D
South Georgia (incl. Dependencies) (Falk. Is.)	. . .	3,755	1,450	(1)	0	0	. . .	C
†Spain	España	504,750	194,885	39,690,000	79	204	Madrid	A
Spanish North Africa (Sp.)(8)	Plazas de Soberanía en el Norte de África	32	12	115,000	3,594	9,583	. . .	C
†Sri Lanka	Sri Lanka	64,652	24,962	16,550,000	256	663	Colombo and Sri Jayawardenapura(5)	A
†Sudan	As-Sūdān	2,505,813	967,500	24,235,000	9.7	25	Al-Kharṭūm (Khartoum)	A
†Suriname	Suriname	163,265	63,037	410,000	2.5	6.5	Paramaribo	A
†Swaziland	Swaziland	17,364	6,704	720,000	41	107	Mbabane	A
†Sweden	Sverige	440,945	170,250	8,380,000	19	49	Stockholm	A
Switzerland	Schweiz (German) / Suisse (French) / Svizzera (Italian)	41,293	15,943	6,515,000	158	409	Bern (Berne)	A
†Syria	As-Sūrīyah	185,180	71,498	11,155,000	60	156	Dimashq (Damascus)	A
Szechwan, China	Sichuan	569,000	219,692	105,280,000	185	479	Chengdu	D
Taiwan	T'aiwan	36,002	13,900	19,800,000	550	1,424	T'aipei	A
Tajik S.S.R., U.S.S.R.	Tajikskaja S.S.R.	143,100	55,251	4,755,000	33	86	Dušanbe	D
†Tanzania	Tanzania	945,087	364,900	23,610,000	25	65	Dar es Salaam and Dodoma(5)	A
Tasmania, Austl.	Tasmania	67,800	26,178	455,000	6.7	17	Hobart	D
Tennessee, U.S.	Tennessee	109,150	42,143	4,910,000	45	117	Nashville	D
Texas, U.S.	Texas	691,022	266,805	17,070,000	25	64	Austin	D
†Thailand	Prathet Thai	513,115	198,115	50,610,000	99	255	Krung Thep (Bangkok)	A
Tibet, China	Xizang	1,222,000	471,817	2,055,000	1.7	4.4	Lhasa	D
Tientsin, China	Tianjin	11,000	4,247	8,325,000	757	1,960	Tianjin (Tientsin)	D
†Togo	Togo	56,785	21,925	3,255,000	57	148	Lomé	A
Tokelau (N.Z.)	Tokelau	12	4.6	1,800	150	391	. . .	C
Tonga	Tonga	699	270	100,000	143	370	Nuku'alofa	A
Transkei(2)	Transkei	43,553	16,816	2,840,000	65	169	Umtata	B(S. Afr.)
†Trinidad and Tobago	Trinidad and Tobago	5,128	1,980	1,215,000	237	614	Port of Spain	A
Tsinghai, China	Qinghai	721,000	278,380	4,215,000	5.8	15	Xining	D
†Tunisia	Tunisie (French) / Tunis (Arabic)	163,610	63,170	7,660,000	47	121	Tunis	A
†Turkey	Türkiye	779,452	300,948	53,230,000	68	177	Ankara	A
Turkmen S.S.R., U.S.S.R.	Turkmenskaja S.S.R.	488,100	188,456	3,330,000	6.8	18	Aščhabad	D
Turks and Caicos Islands (U.K.)	Turks and Caicos Islands	430	166	9,100	21	55	Grand Turk	C
Tuvalu	Tuvalu	26	10	8,500	327	850	Funafuti	A
†Uganda	Uganda	241,139	93,104	16,045,000	67	172	Kampala	A
†Ukrainian S.S.R., U.S.S.R.	UkrainskajaS.S.R.	603,700	233,090	52,050,000	86	223	Kijev (Kiev)	D
†Union of Soviet Socialist Republics	Sojuz Sovetskich Socialističeskich Respublik	22,274,900	8,600,387	284,580,000	13	33	Moskva (Moscow)	A
†United Arab Emirates	Ittiḥād al-Imārāt al-'Arabīyah	83,600	32,278	1,385,000	17	43	Abū Ẓaby (Abu Dhabi)	A
†United Kingdom	United Kingdom	242,496	93,629	57,210,000	236	611	London	A
†United States	United States	9,529,202	3,679,245	245,650,000	26	67	Washington	A
†Uruguay	Uruguay	176,215	68,037	3,100,000	18	46	Montevideo	A
Utah, U.S.	Utah	219,895	84,902	1,710,000	7.8	20	Salt Lake City	D
Uzbek S.S.R., U.S.S.R.	Uzbekskaja S.S.R.	447,400	172,742	18,870,000	42	109	Taškent	D
†Vanuatu	Vanuatu	12,189	4,706	140,000	11	30	Port Vila	A
Vatican City	Città del Vaticano	0.4	0.2	700	1,750	3,500	Città del Vaticano (Vatican City)	A
Venda(2)	Venda	6,198	2,393	420,000	68	176	Thohoyandou	B(S. Afr.)
†Venezuela	Venezuela	912,050	352,145	18,510,000	20	53	Caracas	A
Vermont, U.S.	Vermont	24,900	9,614	550,000	22	57	Montpelier	D
Victoria, Austl.	Victoria	227,600	87,877	4,250,000	19	48	Melbourne	D
†Vietnam	Viet Nam	329,556	127,242	64,120,000	195	504	Ha-noi	A
Virginia, U.S.	Virginia	105,576	40,763	5,905,000	56	145	Richmond	D
Virgin Islands (U.S.)	Virgin Islands (U.S.)	344	133	120,000	349	902	Charlotte Amalie	C
Virgin Islands, British (U.K.)	British Virgin Islands	153	59	12,000	78	203	Road Town	C
Wake Island (U.S.)	Wake Island	7.8	3.0	300	38	100	. . .	C
Wales, U.K.	Wales	20,768	8,019	2,860,000	138	357	Cardiff	D
Wallis and Futuna (Fr.)	Wallis et Futuna	255	98	14,000	55	143	Mata-Utu	C
Washington, U.S.	Washington	176,479	68,139	4,540,000	26	67	Olympia	D
Western Australia, Austl.	Western Australia	2,525,500	975,101	1,480,000	0.6	1.5	Perth	D
Western Sahara	. . .	266,000	102,703	95,000	0.4	0.9	El Aaiún	. . .
†Western Samoa	Western Samoa (English) / Samoa i Sisifo (Samoan)	2,842	1,097	165,000	58	150	Apia	A
West Virginia, U.S.	West Virginia	62,771	24,236	1,935,000	31	80	Charleston	D
Wisconsin, U.S.	Wisconsin	171,491	66,213	4,850,000	28	73	Madison	D
Wyoming, U.S.	Wyoming	253,322	97,808	510,000	2.0	5.2	Cheyenne	D
†Yemen	Al-Yaman	195,000	75,290	9,775,000	50	130	Ṣan'ā'	A
†Yemen, People's Democratic Republic of	Jumhūrīyat al-Yaman ad-Dīmuqrāṭīyah ash-Sha'bīyah	336,869	130,066	2,475,000	7.3	19	'Adan (Aden)	A
†Yugoslavia	Jugoslavija	255,804	98,766	23,420,000	92	237	Beograd (Belgrade)	A
Yukon Territory, Can.	Yukon Territory	483,450	186,661	25,000	0.1	0.1	Whitehorse	D
Yunnan, China	Yunnan	436,000	168,341	35,240,000	81	209	Kunming	D
†Zaire	Zaïre	2,345,409	905,568	32,565,000	14	36	Kinshasa	A
†Zambia	Zambia	752,614	290,586	7,360,000	9.8	25	Lusaka	A
†Zimbabwe	Zimbabwe	390,759	150,873	8,570,000	22	57	Harare (Salisbury)	A
WORLD	. . .	149,800,000	57,800,000	5,052,000,000	34	87	. . .	. . .

† Member of the United Nations (1987).
. . . None, or not applicable.
(1) No permanent population.
(2) Bophuthatswana, Ciskei, Transkei and Venda are not recognized by the United Nations.
(3) Claimed by Argentina.
(4) Includes West Bank, Golan Heights and Gaza Strip.
(5) Future Capital.
(6) Claimed by Comoros.
(7) In October 1966 the United Nations terminated the South African mandate over Namibia, a decision which South Africa did not accept.
(8) Comprises Ceuta, Melilla, and several small islands.

† Mitglied der Vereinten Nationen (1987).
. . . Kein(e), oder nicht anwendbar.
(1) Bevölkerungszahl schwankend.
(2) Bophuthatswana, Ciskei, Transkei und Venda von Vereinten Nationen nicht anerkannt.
(3) Von Argentinien beansprucht.
(4) Westufer, Golan-Höhen und Gazastreifen einbegriffen.
(5) Zukünftige Hauptstadt.
(6) Von Komoren beansprucht.
(7) Im Oktober 1966 setzten die Vereinten Nationen dem Mandat Südafrikas über Namibia ein Ende; Südafrika erkannte diese Entscheidung nicht an.
(8) Umfasst Ceuta, Melilla und mehrere kleine Inseln.

† Miembro de las Naciones Unidas (1987).
. . . Ninguno, o no se aplica.
(1) Sin población permanente.
(2) Bophuthatswana, Ciskei, Transkei y Venda no reconocido por las Naciones Unidas.
(3) Reclamado por la Argentina.
(4) Incluye la ribera oeste, las alturas de Golán y la franja de Gaza.
(5) Capital futura.
(6) Reclamado por las Comores.
(7) En octubre de 1966, las Naciones Unidas terminaron el mandato asignado sobre Namibia, dicha decisión no fue aceptada por Sudáfrica.
(8) Comprende Ceuta, Melilla y various islas pequeñas.

† Membre des Nations Unies (1987).
. . . Pas d'information, ou pas applicable.
(1) Pas de population permanente.
(2) Bophuthatswana, Ciskei, Transkei et Venda non reconnaissent par les Nations Unies.
(3) Revendiqué par l'Argentine.
(4) Y compris Cisjordanie, hauteurs de Golan et la bande de Gaza.
(5) Capitale future.
(6) Revendiqué par les Comores.
(7) En octobre 1966, les Nations Unies ont mis fin au mandat de l'Afrique du Sud sur le Namibie; l'Afrique du Sud n'a pas accepté cetta décision.
(8) Inclus Ceuta, Melilla et plusieurs petites Îles.

† Membro das Nações Unidas (1987).
. . . Inexistente ou não aplicável.
(1) Sem população permanente.
(2) Bophuthatswana, Ciskei, Transkei e Venda não son reconhecido pelas Nações Unidas.
(3) Reivindicado pela Argentina.
(4) Incluindo a margem oeste, as colinas de Golan e a faixa de Gaza.
(5) Capital futuro.
(6) Reivindicado pelas Comores.
(7) Em outubro de 1966, as Nações Unidas terminaram o mandato da África do Sul sobre o Sudoeste Africano (Namíbia), decisão não acatada pela África do Sul.
(8) Compreende Ceuta, Melilla e várias ilhas pequenas.

THIS TABLE lists the major metropolitan areas of the world according to their estimated population on January 1, 1987. For convenience in reference, the areas are grouped by major region with the total for each region given. The number of areas by population classification is given in parentheses with each size group.

For ease of comparison, each metropolitan area has been defined by Rand McNally & Company according to consistent rules. A metropolitan area includes a central city, neighboring communities linked to it by continuous built-up areas, and more distant communities if the bulk of their population is supported by commuters to the central city. Some metropolitan areas have more than one central city; in such cases each central city is listed.

IN DIESER TABELLE sind die Hauptmetropolen der Welt verzeichnet, gemessen nach ihrer Bevölkerung, die nach dem Stand vom 1. Januar 1987 geschätzt wurde. Zur besseren Übersicht sind die Zonen nach grösseren Regionen gruppiert, wobei die Gesamtzahl für jede Region angegeben ist. Die Anzahl der Zonen ist nach Bevölkerung klassifiziert und in Klammern hinter denen nach Grössen sortierten Gruppen angegeben.

Zum einfacheren Vergleich ist jede Metropole von Rand McNally & Company nach übereinstimmenden Massstäben definiert worden. Eine Metropole schliesst eine zentrale Stadt mit benachbarten Gemeinden, die mit ihr durch ununterbrochen bebaute Gebiete verbunden sind ein, sowie weiter entfernte Gemeinden, wenn der grösste Teil ihrer Bevölkerung von den Pendlern unterhalten wird. Einige Metropolen haben mehr als eine zentrale Stadt; in solchen Fällen ist jede dieser zentralen Städte angeführt.

ESTA TABLA indica las principales áreas metropolitanas del mundo, de acuerdo con su población calculada al 1 de enero de 1987. Para facilitar las referencias, las áreas se han agrupado por regiones principales, indicándose el total para cada región. El número de áreas, clasificadas por población, se indica entre paréntesis en los grupos de cada tamaño.

Para facilitar las comparaciones, Rand McNally y Compañía ha definido cada área metropolitana de acuerdo con reglas consistentes. Un área metropolitana incluye una ciudad central, localidades vecinas vinculadas con ella mediante sectores construídos y contínuos, y localidades más distantes, si el grueso de su población lo constituye un núcleo que diariamente viaja a la ciudad central. Algunas áreas metropolitanas incluyen más de una ciudad central; en tales casos se indica cada una dichas ciudades.

CETTE TABLE contient la liste des aires métropolitaines les plus considérables dans le monde pour ce qui est du peuplement a la date du 1 er janvier 1987. Afin de faciliter la consultation, on a groupé les aires par grandes régions en indiquant la population totale pour chaque région, et, entre parenthèses, le nombre d'aires comprises dans celle-ci.

Afin de rendre plus faciles les comparaisons, Rand McNally & Co. a défini chaque aire métropolitaine selorègles cohérentes: une aire métropolitaine englobe une cité centrale ou métropole et l'environnement urbain continu qui s'y rattache; elle inclut également des agglomérations éloignées de la métropole lorsque la population de ces dernières est pour sa májorité constituée d'habitants se rendant quotidiennement dans la cité ou est situé le lieu de travail de ceux-ci. On trouvera quelques aires métropolitaines pourvues de plus d'une métropole. Dans ce cas, chaque métropole est mentionnée.

A TABELA que se segúe relaciona as principais áreas metropolitanas do mundo, de acordo com as respectivas populações, estimadas para 1 de janeiro de 1987. Para facilidade de referência, as áreas metropolitanas foram agrupadas dentro das regiões maiores, indicando-se, entre parênteses, os totais de cada região maior e o número de áreas metropolitanas, classificadas segundo a população, compreendidas em cada uma.

Para fins de comparabilidade, Rand McNally & Company definiu cada área metropolitana de acordo com regras uniformes. Uma área metropolitana inclui uma cidade central, as localidades vizinhas ligadas a ela por áreas construídas contínuas, e as localidades mais distantes, desde que a maior parte de suas respectivas populações dependa economicamente da cidade central e que para ela viaje diariamente. Algumas áreas metropolitanas incluem mais de uma cidade central; em tais casos, indicam-se ambas as cidades.

CLASSIFICATION KLASSIFIZIERT CLASIFICADAS CLASSIFICATION CLASSIFICAÇÃO	ANGLO-AMERICA ANGLO-AMERIKA AMÉRICA ANGLOSAJONA AMÉRIQUE ANGLO-SAXONNE AMÉRICA ANGLO-SAXÔNICA	LATIN AMERICA LATEIN-AMERIKA AMÉRICA LATINA AMÉRIQUE LATINE AMÉRICA LATINA	EUROPE EUROPA EUROPA EUROPE EUROPA	U.S.S.R. U.S.S.R. U.R.S.S. U.R.S.S. U.R.S.S.	WEST ASIA WESTASIEN ASIA OCCIDENTAL ASIE OCCIDENTALE ÁSIA OCIDENTAL	EAST ASIA OSTASIEN ASIA ORIENTAL ASIE ORIENTALE ÁSIA ORIENTAL	AFRICA-OCEANIA AFRIKA-OZEANIEN AFRICA-OCEANÍA AFRIQUE-OCÉANIE ÁFRICA-OCEANIA
OVER 15,000,000 (5)	New York	Ciudad de México (Mexico City) São Paulo				Ōsaka-Kōbe-Kyōto Tōkyō-Yokohama	
10,000,000-15,000,000 (8)	Los Angeles	Buenos Aires Rio de Janeiro	London	Moskva (Moscow)	Bombay Calcutta	Sŏul (Seoul)	
5,000,000-10,000,000 (19)	Chicago Philadelphia-Trenton-Wilmington San Francisco-Oakland-San Jose	Lima	Paris	Leningrad	Delhi-New Delhi İstanbul Karāchi Madras Tehrān	Beijing (Peking) Jakarta Krung Thep (Bangkok) Manila Shanghai Tianjin (Tientsin) T'aipei	Al-Qāhirah (Cairo)
3,000,000-5,000,000 (34)	Boston Dallas-Fort Worth Detroit-Windsor Houston Miami-Fort Lauderdale Toronto Washington	Belo Horizonte Bogotá Caracas Santiago	Athínai (Athens) Barcelona Berlin Essen-Dortmund-Duisburg (The Ruhr) Madrid Milano (Milan) Roma (Rome)		Baghdād Bangalore Dhaka (Dacca) Hyderābād, India Lahore	Nagoya Pusan Rangoon Shenyang (Mukden) Thanh-pho Ho Chi Minh (Sai-gon) Victoria (Hong Kong) Wuhan	Al-Iskandarīyah (Alexandria) Johannesburg Lagos Sydney
2,000,000-3,000,000 (47)	Atlanta Cleveland Minneapolis-St. Paul Montréal Pittsburgh St. Louis San Diego-Tijuana Seattle-Tacoma	Guadalajara La Habana (Havana) Medellín Monterrey Porto Alegre Recife Salvador	Birmingham Bruxelles (Brussels) Bucuresti (Bucharest) Budapest Hamburg Katowice-Bytom-Gliwice Lisboa (Lisbon) Manchester Napoli (Naples) Warszawa (Warsaw)	Baku Doneck-Makejevka Kijev (Kiev) Taškent	Ahmadābād Ankara Colombo Kānpur Pune (Poona)	Bandung Chongqing (Chungking) Guangzhou (Canton) Harbin Nanjing (Nanking) Singapore Surabaya Taegu	Cape Town Casablanca El Djazaïr (Algiers) Kinshasa Melbourne
1,500,000-2,000,000 (49)	Baltimore Denver Phoenix	Brasília Curitiba Fortaleza San Juan Santo Domingo	Amsterdam Beograd (Belgrade) Frankfurt am Main Glasgow Köln (Cologne) Leeds-Bradford München (Munich) Stuttgart Torino (Turin) Wien (Vienna)	Char'kov (Kharkov) Dnepropetrovsk Gor'kij (Gorkiy) Kujbyšev (Kuybyshev) Minsk Novosibirsk Sverdlovsk	Bayrūt (Beirut) Chittagong Dimashq (Damascus) İzmir Nāgpur Tel Aviv-Yafo	Changchun (Hsinking) Chengdu (Chengtu) Fukuoka Ha-noi Hiroshima-Kure Kaohsiung Kitakyūshū-Shimonoseki Kuala Lumpur Lüda (Dairen) (Dalian) Medan P'yongyang Sapporo Taiyuan Xi'an (Sian)	Abidjan Al-Kharṭūm (Khartoum)-Umm Durmān (Omdurman) Dakar Durban
1,000,000-1,500,000 (107)	Buffalo-Niagara Falls-Saint Catharines Cincinnati El Paso-Ciudad Juárez Hartford-New Britain Indianapolis Kansas City Milwaukee New Orleans Portland San Antonio Vancouver	Barranquilla Belém Cali Campinas Córdoba Goiânia Guatemala Guayaquil La Paz Maracaibo Montevideo Puebla Quito Rosario Santos	Antwerpen (Anvers) Dublin (Baile Átha Cliath) Düsseldorf Hannover København (Copenhagen) Lille-Roubaix Liverpool Łódź Lyon Mannheim Marseille Newcastle-Sunderland Nürnberg Porto Praha (Prague) Rotterdam Sofija (Sofia) Stockholm Valencia	Alma-Ata Čel'abinsk] (Chelyabinsk) Jerevan Kazan' Odessa Omsk Perm Rostov-na-Donu Saratov Tbilisi Ufa Volgograd	Al-Kuwayt 'Amman Ar-Riyad (Riyadh) Asansol Coimbatore Esfahān Faisalabad Halab (Aleppo) Indore Jaipur Jiddah Kābol Lucknow Madurai Mashhad Patna Rāwalpindi-Islāmābād Surat Vārānasi (Benares)	Anshan Changsha Fushun Guiyang (Kweiyang) Hangzhou (Hangchow) Jilin (Kirin) Jinan (Tsinan) Kunming Lanzhou (Lanchow) Nanchang Qingdao (Tsingtao) Qiqihar (Tsitsihar) Semarang Sendai Shijiazhuang Tangshan Ürümqui Zhengzhou (Chengchow)	Accra Adelaide Adis Abeba Brisbane Dar es Salaam Harare Ibadan Luanda Nairobi Perth Pretoria Ṭarābulus (Tripoli) Tunis
Total/Gesamtzahl Total/Total/Total (269)	34	36	48	25	42	57	27

ALL URBAN CENTERS of 50,000 or more population and many other important or well-known cities and towns are listed in the following table. The populations are from recent censuses (designated C) or official estimates (designated E) for the dates specified. For a few cities, only unofficial estimates are available (designated UE). For comparison, the total population of each country is also given. For each country, the date stated for the total population also applies to the cities, except those for which another date is specified.

Population estimates for 1988 for countries may be found in the World Information Table.

A population figure in parentheses and preceded by a star (★) is the population of a city's entire metropolitan area. To permit meaningful comparisons of metropolitan areas, these have been defined by Rand McNally according to consistent rules (see introduction to Metropolitan Areas Table), and in some cases may differ somewhat from the officially recognized metropolitan areas. Where a town is located within the metropolitan area of another city, that city's name is given in parentheses preceded by a star (★). The capital of a country is denoted by CAPITAL letters.

ALLE STÄDTISCHEN ZENTREN mit 50 000 oder mehr Einwohnern und zahlreiche andere bedeutende oder bekannte Städte sind in der folgenden Tabelle zusammengestellt. Die Bevölkerungszahlen stammen von neuesten Zählungen (mit C gekennzeichnet) oder amtlichen Schätzungen (E) zu den angegebenen Zeitpunkten. Für einige wenige Städte waren lediglich inoffizielle Schätzungen erhältlich (UE). Zu Vergleichszwecken ist ferner die Gesamtbevölkerung jedes Landes angegeben. Das Bezugsjahr für die Einwohnerzahl eines Landes betrifft auch die Städte mit Ausnahme jener, bei denen ein anderes Datum angegeben ist.

Schätzungen der Bevölkerungszahlen der Länder für 1988 finden sich in der Welt-Informationstabelle.

Bevölkerungszahlen in Klammern mit vorangestelltem Stern (★) beziehen sich auf die gesamte Stadtregion einer Stadt. Um sinnvolle Vergleiche von Stadtregionen zu ermöglichen, wurden diese von Rand McNally nach einheitlichen Regeln festgelegt (siehe Einleitung: Tabelle der Stadtregionen), weshalb sie in einigen Fällen etwas von der offiziellen Abgrenzung von Stadtregionen abweichen können. Ist eine Stadt in die Stadtregion einer anderen Grossstadt einbezogen, so wird der Name der Stadtregion mit vorangestelltem Stern (★) in Klammern aufgeführt. Die Hauptstadt eines Landes wird durch GROSSBUCHSTABEN hervorgehoben.

TODAS LOS CENTROS URBANOS de 50 000 habitantes o más y muchos otros de importancia así como bien conocidas ciudades y pueblos están incluídos en la tabla que se presenta a continuación. El número de habitantes indicados está tomado del censo más reciente (cifras identificadas con la letra C) o estimados oficiales (E) para las fechas especificadas. Para algunas ciudades, sólo existen informes no oficiales (UE). Para medida de comparación, la población total de cada país se encuentra incluída también.

Para permitir una comparación, se da la población total de cada país, referente al mismo año que se usa para las ciudades principles, excepto para aquellas en las que se especifica otra fecha. El número de habitantes para 1988 para los países, se encuentra en la Tabla de Información Mundial.

La segunda cifra para la población que aparece en paréntesis y está precedida por una estrella (★) constituye la población de un área metropolitana entera. Para permitir comparaciones validas de áreas metropolitanas, éstas fueron definidas por Rand McNally siguiendo las reglas establecidas para estos propósitos (véase la Introducción a la Tabla de las Areas Metropolitanas), y en algunas ocasiones pueden ser un poco distintas de las áreas metropolitanas oficialmente reconocidas. Cuando una población se encuentra dentro de los límites de un área metropolitana de otra ciudad, el nombre de ésta se da entre paréntesis precedido por una (★). La capital de un país se indica con letras MAYÚSCULAS.

TOUTES LES VILLES de plus de 50 000 habitants et des villes moins peuplées, mais cèlébres ou importantes, sont mentionnées dans la table ci-dessous. Les chiffres donnant la population proviennent de recensements récents (référence C), ou d'estimations officielles (référence E), aux dates indiquées. Pour quelques villes, on dispose seulement d'estimations non officielles (référence UE). La population totale de chaque pays est également donnée, ce qui permet des comparaisons. Dans chaque pays, la date des renseignements est identique pour les villes et le pays, sauf indication contraire.

On trouvera dans la table d'informations mondiales les estimations de la population en 1988 pour chaque pays.

Les chiffres entre parenthèses, précédés d'une étoile (★), indiquent la population de l'ensemble de la zone métropolitaine. Pour permettre d'établir des comparaisons significatives entre les zones métropolitaines, ces dernières ont été définies selon des critères uniformes par Rand McNally & Company (voir l'introduction à la table des zones métropolitaines). Parfois, les limites des zones métropolitaines ainsi définies diffèrent des limites officielles. Quand une ville fait partie de la zone métropolitaine d'une autre ville, le nom de celle-ci, précédé d'une étoile (★), est mis entre parenthèses. Le nom des capitales de pays est écrit en lettres MAJUSCULES.

TODOS OS CENTROS URBANOS de 50 000 habitantes e mais, bem como muitas outras cidades e vilas importantes ou muito conhecidas figuram na tabela que se apresenta em sequida. Os dados relativos à população referem-se a censos recentes (identificadas com a letra C), ou a estimativas oficiais (E) nas datas indicadas. Para algumas cidades só existem estimativas não oficiais (UE). Para fins de comparabilidade, apresenta-se também a população total de cada país.

Para cada país, a data de referência da população total aplica-se também às cidades exceto quando especificado em contrário. As estimativas da população dos países para 1988 encontra-se na *Tabela de informaçoes mundiais.*

Um dado de população apresentado entre parênteses e precedido por uma estrela (★), refere-se à população de toda a área metropolitana. Para fins de comparabilidade, as áreas metropolitanas foram definidas por Rand McNally segundo regras coerentes (ver a 'Introdução' à *Tabela das áreas metropolitanas),* e em certos casos podem ser um pouco diferentes das áreas metropolitanas oficialmente reconhecidas. Quando um centro urbano esta localizado dentro dos limites da área metropolitana de outro, seu nome figura entre parênteses precedido por uma estrela (★). A capital de um país é indicada por letras MAIÚSCULAS.

AFGHANISTAN / Afghānestān

1979 C	13,051,358
Herāt	140,323
Jalālābād	53,915
• KĀBOL	913,164
Mazār-e Sharīf	103,372
Qandahār	178,409
Qondūz	53,251

ALBANIA / Shqipëri

1983 E	2,841,300
Durrës	72,400
Elbasan	69,900
Korçë	57,100
Shkodër	71,200
• TIRANE	206,100
Vlorë	61,100

ALGERIA / Algérie / Djazaïr

1977 C	16,948,000
Aïn el Beïda (▲44,275)	42,578
Aïn Témouchent (▲41,987)	29,844
Annaba (Bône) (▲255,938)	222,607
Batna (▲112,095)	102,756
Béchar (▲72,790)	56,563
Bejaïa (Bougie) (▲89,530)	73,960
Beskra (▲90,471)	76,988
Bordj Bou Arreridj (▲65,007)	54,505
Boufarik (▲50,006)	33,561
Bou Saâda (▲50,104)	46,760
Douéra (1974E)	55,993
Ech Cheliff (Orléansville) (▲114,327)	80,500
El Boulaïda (▲160,893)	136,033
• EL DJAZAÏR (ALGIERS) (★1,724,705)	1,523,000
El Eulma (▲49,946)	41,564
El Wad (▲72,065)	47,173
Ghardaïa (▲70,508)	57,153
Ghilizane	55,450
Guelma (▲60,059)	56,106
Jijel (▲49,794)	35,065
Khemis (▲57,769)	37,252
Khenchla (▲50,297)	44,223
Laghouat (▲59,157)	40,156
Lemdiyya (▲72,251)	57,828
Mestghanem (▲101,639)	85,059
Mouaskar (▲62,301)	49,370
Qacentina (▲355,059)	344,454
Saïda (▲62,064)	55,855
Sidi bel Abbès (▲115,961)	112,988
Skikda (▲107,717)	91,395
Souq Ahras (▲60,059)	52,144
Stif (▲144,221)	129,754
Tbessa (▲67,194)	61,063
Tihert (▲62,915)	53,277
Tilimsen (▲109,408)	88,505
Tizi-Ouzou (▲73,120)	38,979
Touggourt (▲75,554)	42,519
Wahran (▲491,901)	409,788
Wargla (▲77,354)	42,098

AMERICAN SAMOA / Amerika Samoa

1980 C	32,279
• PAGO PAGO	3,075

ANDORRA

1982 C	38,051
• ANDORRA	14,928

ANGOLA

1982 E	8,140,000
Benguela (1974E)	60,000
Huambo (Nova Lisboa) (1974E)	65,000
Lobito (1974E)	120,000
• LUANDA	1,200,000

ANGUILLA

1974 C	6,519
• South Hill	774
THE VALLEY	760

ANTIGUA AND BARBUDA

1977 E	72,000
• SAINT JOHNS	24,359

ARGENTINA

1980 C	27,947,446
Almirante Brown (★Buenos Aires)	326,856
Avellaneda (★Buenos Aires)	330,654
Bahía Blanca	223,818
Berazategui (★Buenos Aires)	197,187
Berisso (★Buenos Aires)	64,255
• BUENOS AIRES (★10,700,000)	2,922,829
Campana (★Buenos Aires)	53,994
Caseros (Tres de Febrero) (★Buenos Aires)	343,004
Catamarca (★90,000)	77,931
Comodoro Rivadavia	96,865
Concordia	94,222
Córdoba (★1,070,000)	993,055
Corrientes	180,612
Esteban Echeverría (★Buenos Aires)	183,908
Florencio Varela (★Buenos Aires)	165,842
Formosa	93,603
General San Martín (★Buenos Aires)	384,306
General Sarmiento (San Miguel) (★Buenos Aires)	499,648
Godoy Cruz (★Mendoza)	141,553
Gualeguaychú	51,400
Junín	62,458
Lanús (★Buenos Aires)	465,691
La Plata (★Buenos Aires)	454,884
La Rioja	67,043
Las Heras (★Mendoza)	96,545
Lomas de Zamora (★Buenos Aires)	508,620
Mar del Plata	414,696
Melincué (★690,000)	118,427
Mendoza (★690,000)	118,427
Mercedes	50,992
Merlo (★Buenos Aires)	293,059
Moreno (★Buenos Aires)	188,524
Morón (★Buenos Aires)	596,769
Necochea	51,069
Neuquén	90,089
Olavarría	64,374
Paraná	161,638
Pergamino	68,612
Pilar (★Buenos Aires)	74,629
Posadas	143,889
Presidencia Roque Sáenz Peña	49,341
Punta Alta	56,620
Quilmes (★Buenos Aires)	445,662
Rafaela	53,273
Resistencia	220,104
Río Cuarto	110,254
Rosario (★1,045,000)	938,120
Salta	260,744
San Carlos de Bariloche	48,980
San Fernando (★Buenos Aires)	128,939
San Francisco (★58,536)	51,932
San Isidro (★Buenos Aires)	287,048
San Juan (★310,000)	117,731
San Justo (★Buenos Aires)	941,499
San Lorenzo (★Rosario)	78,983
San Luis	70,999
San Miguel de Tucumán (★525,000)	392,751
San Nicolás de los Arroyos	98,495
San Rafael	70,959
San Salvador de Jujuy	124,950
Santa Fe	291,966
Santiago del Estero (★200,000)	148,758
Tandil	79,429
Tigre (★Buenos Aires)	199,366
Trelew	52,372
Vicente López (★Buenos Aires)	289,815
Villa Krause (★San Juan)	66,506
Villa María	67,560
Villa Nueva (★Mendoza)	157,334
Zárate	67,143

ARUBA

1987 E	64,763
• ORANJESTAD	19,800

AUSTRALIA

1984 E	15,544,500
Adelaide (★983,200)	12,040
Albury (★57,440) (1981C)	53,214
Auburn (★Sydney)	46,900
Ballarat (★71,930) (1981C)	35,681
Bankstown (★Sydney)	153,600
Bendigo (★58,818) (1981C)	31,841
Blacktown (★Sydney)	192,200
Blue Mountains (★Sydney)	62,200
Box Hill (★Melbourne) (1981C)	47,579
Brisbane (★1,146,610)	734,750
Brisbane Water (★Sydney) (1981C)	71,984
Broadmeadows (★Melbourne) (1981C)	103,540
Brunswick (★Melbourne) (1981C)	44,464
Camberwell (★Melbourne) (1981C)	85,883
Campbelltown (★Sydney)	112,000
CANBERRA (★264,450)	243,450
Canning (★Perth)	60,940
Canterbury (★Sydney)	128,000
Caulfield (★Melbourne) (1981C)	69,922
Coburg (★Melbourne) (1981C)	55,035
Dandenong (★Melbourne) (1981C)	54,962
Darwin (★68,500) (1985E)	65,200
Doncaster (★Melbourne) (1981C)	90,660
Enfield (★Adelaide)	66,750
Essendon (★Melbourne) (1981C)	56,380
Fairfield (★Sydney)	143,500
Footscray (★Melbourne) (1981C)	49,756
Frankston (★Melbourne) (1981C)	78,808
Geelong (★137,173) (1981C)	14,471
Gosnells (★Perth)	59,150
Heidelberg (★Melbourne) (1981C)	64,757

▲ Population of an entire municipality, commune, or district, including rural area.
• Largest city in country.
★ Population or designation of the metropolitan area, including suburbs.
C Census. **E** Official estimate. **UE** Unofficial estimate.

▲ Bevölkerung eines ganzen städtischen Verwaltungsgebietes, eines Kommunalbezirkes oder eines Distrikts, einschliesslich ländlicher Gebiete.
• Grösste Stadt des Landes.
★ Bevölkerung oder Bezeichnung der Stadtregion einschliess lich Vororte.
C Volkszählung. **E** Offizielle Schätzung. **UE** Inoffizielle Schätzung.

▲ Población de un municipio, comuna o distrito entero, incluyendo sus áreas rurales.
• Ciudad más grande de un país.
★ Población o designación de un área metropolitana, incluyendo los suburbios.
C Censo. **E** Estimado oficial. **UE** Estimado no oficial.

▲ Population d'une municipalité, d'une commune ou d'un district, zone rurale incluse.
• Ville la plus peuplée du pays.
★ Population de l'agglomération (ou nom de la zone métropolitaine englobante).
C Recensement. **E** Estimation officielle. **UE** Estimation non officielle.

▲ População de um municipio, comuna ou distrito, inclusive as respectivas áreas rurais.
• Maior cidade de um país.
★ População ou indicação de uma área metropolitana.
C Censo. **E** Estimativa oficial. **UE** Estimativa não oficial.

Hobart (★168,359) (1981C)	47,920
Holroyd (★Sydney)	81,050
Hurstville (★Sydney)	66,000
Ipswich (★Brisbane)	73,680
Keilor (★Melbourne) (1981C)	81,762
Knox (★Melbourne) (1981C)	88,902
Kogarah (★Sydney)	47,450
Lake Macquarie (★Newcastle)	161,000
Launceston (★84,784) (1981C)	31,273
Leichhardt (★Sydney)	57,400
Liverpool (★Sydney)	94,700
Malvern (★Melbourne) (1981C)	43,211
Marion (★Adelaide)	70,910
Marrickville (★Sydney)	83,650
Melbourne (★2,722,817) (1981C)	63,388
Melville (★Perth)	66,510
Mitcham (★Adelaide)	61,950
Moorabbin (★Melbourne) (1981C)	97,810
Newcastle (★419,100)	138,800
Noarlunga (★Adelaide)	69,850
Northcote (★Melbourne) (1981C)	51,235
North Sydney (★Sydney)	49,600
Nunawading (★Melbourne) (1981C)	97,052
Oakleigh (★Melbourne) (1981C)	55,612
Parramatta (★Sydney)	131,800
Penrith (★Sydney)	131,000
Perth (★898,918)	82,600
Prahran (★Melbourne) (1981C)	45,018
Preston (★Melbourne) (1981C)	84,519
Randwick (★Sydney)	116,600
Rockdale (★Sydney)	84,650
Rockhampton (★56,520)	54,630
Ryde (★Sydney)	90,600
Saint Kilda (★Melbourne) (1981C)	49,366
Salisbury (★Adelaide)	92,270
Shoalhaven	56,600
Southport (★198,330)	116,540
Springvale (★Melbourne) (1981C)	80,186
Stirling (★Perth)	169,840
Sunshine (★Melbourne) (1981C)	94,419
• Sydney (★3,358,550)	79,400
Teatree Gully (★Adelaide)	73,500
Toowoomba	74,360
Townsville (★100,530)	82,140
Wagga Wagga	49,650
Waverley (★Sydney)	62,900
Waverley (★Melbourne) (1981C)	122,471
West Torrens (★Adelaide)	45,810
Willoughby (★Sydney)	52,950
Wollongong (★235,900)	176,500
Woodville (★Adelaide)	80,560
Woollahra (★Sydney)	53,150

AUSTRIA / Österreich

1981 C	7,555,338
Bruck an der Mur (★49,000)	15,068
Graz (★270,000)	243,166
Innsbruck (★150,000)	117,287
Klagenfurt (★97,000)	87,321
Leoben (★46,000)	31,989
Linz (★285,000)	199,910
Salzburg (★170,000)	139,426
Sankt Pölten	50,419
Steyr (★55,000)	38,942
Villach	52,692
Wels (★64,000)	51,060
• WIEN (VIENNA) (★1,875,000) (1982E)	1,524,510

BAHAMAS

1982 E	218,000
Freeport	25,000
• NASSAU	135,000

BAHRAIN / Al-Baḩrayn

1981 C	350,798
• AL-MANAMAH (★224,643)	108,684
Al-Muḩarraq (★Al-Manāmah)	46,061

BANGLADESH

1981 C	87,119,965
Barisāl	172,905
Begumganj	69,623
Bhairab Bāzār	63,563
Bogra	68,749
Brāhmanbāria	87,570
Chāndpur	85,656
Chittagong (★1,391,877)	980,000
Chuādānga	76,000
Comilla	184,132
• DHAKA (★3,430,312)	2,365,695
Dinājpur	96,718
Farīdpur	66,579
Gopālpur	31,725
Gulshan (★Dhaka)	215,444
Jamālpur	91,815
Jessore (★157,000)	148,927
Jhenida	47,953
Khulna	648,359
Kishorganj	52,302
Kurīgrām	47,641
Kushtia	74,892
Mādārīpur	63,917
Mīrpur (★Dhaka)	349,031
Mymensingh	190,991
Naogaon	52,975
Nārāyanganj (★Dhaka)	405,562
Narsingdi	76,841
Nawābganj	87,724
Noākhāli	59,065
Pābna	109,065
Patuākhāli	48,121
Rājshāhi (★171,600)	253,740
Rangpur	153,174
Saidpur	126,608
Sātkhira	52,156
Sherpur	48,214
Sirājganj	106,774
Sītākunda (★Chittagong)	237,520
Sylhet	168,371
Tangail	77,518
Tungi (★Dhaka)	94,580

BARBADOS

1980 C	248,983
• BRIDGETOWN (★115,000)	7,466

BELGIUM / België / Belgique

1983 E	9,858,017
Aalst (Alost) (★Bruxelles)	78,068
Anderlecht (★Bruxelles)	92,912
Antwerpen (★1,100,000)	490,524
Bastogne (▲11,567)	6,800
Brugge (Bruges) (★220,000)	118,218
• BRUXELLES (★2,395,000)	137,738
Charleroi (★490,000)	216,144
Etterbeek (★Bruxelles)	44,101
Forest (★Bruxelles)	50,260
Genk (★Hasselt)	61,808
Gent (★465,000)	236,540
Hasselt (★285,000)	65,437
Ixelles (★Bruxelles)	76,146
Kortrijk (Courtrai) (★201,000)	75,587
La Louvière (★148,000)	76,534
Leuven (Louvain) (★170,000)	85,068
Liège (Luik) (★755,000)	207,496
Mechelen (Malines) (★121,000)	77,010
Molenbeek-St.-Jean (★Bruxelles)	71,891
Mons (Bergen) (★245,000)	91,868
Mouscron (★Lille, France)	54,402
Namur (★145,000)	101,860
Oostende (Ostende) (★121,000)	69,129
Roeselare (Roulers)	51,649
Saint-Gilles (★Bruxelles)	44,193
Schaerbeek (★Bruxelles)	105,672
Seraing (★Liège)	63,001
Sint-Niklaas (Saint-Nicolas)	68,157
Spa	9,716
Tournai (Doornik) (▲67,379)	45,000
Uccle (★Bruxelles)	75,675
Verviers (★102,000)	54,294
Waterloo (★Bruxelles)	24,933
Woluwe-Saint-Lambert (Sint-Lambrechts-Woluwe) (★Bruxelles)	49,250

BELIZE

1980 C	145,353
• Belize City	39,771
BELMOPAN	2,935

BENIN / Bénin

1980 E	3,567,000
• Cotonou	215,000
PORTO-NOVO	123,000

BERMUDA

1985 E	56,000
• HAMILTON (★15,000)	1,676

BHUTAN / Druk-Yul

1977 E	1,232,000
• THIMBU	8,982

BOLIVIA

1985 E	6,429,226
Cochabamba	317,251
• LA PAZ	992,592
Oruro	178,393
Potosí	113,380
Santa Cruz	441,717
SUCRE	86,609
Tarija	60,621

BOPHUTHATSWANA

1982 E	1,347,000
• Ga-Rankuwa (1980C)	48,300
MMABATHO (★Mafikeng, S. Afr.) (1977E)	9,062

BOTSWANA

1982 E	973,000
Francistown	32,000
• GABORONE (1983E)	72,200

BRAZIL / Brasil

1980 C	119,002,706
Alagoinhas	76,331
Alegrete	54,746
Alvorada	90,339
Americana	121,743
Anápolis	160,571
Apucarana	63,678
Aracaju	287,934
Araçatuba	113,925
Araguari	73,307
Arapiraca	83,963
Araraquara	77,186
Araras	54,214
Araxá	51,311
Assis	57,184
Bagé	66,720
Barbacena	69,566
Barra do Piraí	51,191
Barra Mansa (★Volta Redonda)	123,335
Barretos	65,318
Bauru	180,093
Bayeux (★João Pessoa)	58,474
Belém (★1,000,000)	933,287
Belford Roxo (★Rio de Janeiro)	282,695
Belo Horizonte (★2,450,000)	1,780,855
Betim (★Belo Horizonte)	76,801
Blumenau	144,785
Botucatu	56,752
Bragança Paulista	60,976
BRASÍLIA	1,176,935
Cachoeira do Sul	59,977
Cachoeirinha (★Porto Alegre)	62,751
Cachoeiro de Itapemirim	85,024
Campina Grande	222,102
Campinas (★875,000)	566,627
Campo Grande	282,857
Campos	178,457
Campos Elyseos (★Rio de Janeiro)	162,997
Canoas (★Porto Alegre)	213,999
Carapicuíba (★São Paulo)	185,816
Cariacica (★Vitória)	57,702
Caruaru	137,502
Cascavel	100,329
Castanhal	51,729
Catanduva	64,755
Caucaia (★Fortaleza)	68,033
Cavaleiro (★Recife)	85,961
Caxias	56,668
Caxias do Sul	198,683
Chapecó	53,181
Coelho da Rocha (★Rio de Janeiro)	140,028
Colatina	61,120
Colombo (★Curitiba)	54,979
Conselheiro Lafaiete	66,229
Contagem (★Belo Horizonte)	111,545
Corumbá	66,077
Criciúma	74,018
Cruz Alta	53,659
Cruzeiro	55,182
Cubatão (★Santos)	78,303
Cuiabá	167,880
Curitiba (★1,300,000)	1,024,975
Diadema (★São Paulo)	228,660
Divinópolis	108,279
Dourados	76,783
Duque de Caxias (★Rio de Janeiro)	306,243
Embu (★São Paulo)	95,800
Esteio (★Porto Alegre)	50,208
Feira de Santana	227,004
Ferraz de Vasconcelos (★São Paulo)	54,810
Florianópolis (★240,000)	153,652
Fortaleza (★1,490,000)	1,307,611
Foz do Iguaçu	93,506
Franca	144,117
Garanhuns	64,823
Goiânia (★760,000)	702,858
Governador Valadares	173,624
Guaratinguetá	72,961
Guarujá (★Santos)	67,708
Guarulhos (★São Paulo)	426,693
Ijuí	52,520
Ilhéus	71,376
Imperatriz	111,705
Ipatinga (★200,000)	105,030
Ipiíba (★Rio de Janeiro)	98,069
Itabira	57,649
Itabuna	130,163
Itajaí	78,779
Itajubá	53,433
Itapecerica da Serra (★São Paulo)	52,346
Itapetininga	61,298
Itapevi (★São Paulo)	53,441
Itaquaquecetuba (★São Paulo)	73,064
Itaquari (★Vitória)	127,659
Itu	62,267
Ituiutaba	65,153
Itumbiara	56,573
Jaboatão (★Recife)	66,890
Jacareí	104,241
Jaú	59,561
Jequié	84,708
João Pessoa (★475,000)	290,247
Joinvile	216,986
Juàzeiro (★Petrolina)	60,811
Juàzeiro do Norte	125,191
Juiz de Fora	299,432
Jundiaí	221,888
Lajes	108,727
Limeira	137,809
Linhares	53,507
Londrina	257,899
Lorena	51,300
Luziânia	67,297
Macapá	88,930
Maceió	375,771
Manaus	611,763
Marília	103,815
Maringá	158,091
Mauá (★São Paulo)	205,740
Mesquita (★Rio de Janeiro)	125,314
Mogi das Cruzes (★São Paulo)	122,434
Mogi-Guaçu	65,421
Monjolo (★Rio de Janeiro)	96,165
Montes Claros	151,713
Mossoró	117,971
Muriaé	50,058
Muribeca dos Guararapes (★Recife)	137,903
Natal	376,446
Neves (★Rio de Janeiro)	138,130
Nilópolis (★Rio de Janeiro)	102,959
Niterói (★Rio de Janeiro)	382,736
Nova Friburgo	88,872
Nova Iguaçu (★Rio de Janeiro)	491,766
Novo Hamburgo (★Porto Alegre)	133,221
Olinda (★Recife)	266,751
Osasco (★São Paulo)	474,543
Ourinhos	52,671
Paranaguá	71,107
Paranavaí	52,593
Parnaíba	79,321
Parque Industrial (★Belo Horizonte)	166,626
Passo Fundo	103,064
Passos	56,956
Patos	58,705
Patos de Minas	59,849
Paulo Afonso	61,978
Pelotas	196,919
Petrolina (★175,000)	73,580
Petrópolis (★Rio de Janeiro)	150,249
Pindamonhangaba	51,147
Pinheirinho (★Curitiba)	41,248
Piracicaba	179,380
Poá (★São Paulo)	52,512
Poços de Caldas	81,440
Ponta Grossa	171,810
Porto Alegre (★2,225,000)	1,125,477
Porto Velho	101,162
Pouso Alegre	50,553
Praia Grande (★Santos)	54,038
Presidente Prudente	127,903
Queimados (★Rio de Janeiro)	94,303
Recife (★2,300,000)	1,203,899
Ribeirão Prêto	300,828
Rio Branco	87,449
Rio Claro	103,119
Rio de Janeiro (★8,975,000)	5,090,700
Rio Grande	130,149
Rondonópolis	52,315
Salvador (★1,725,000)	1,501,981
Santa Bárbara d'Oeste	71,880
Santa Cruz do Sul	52,096
Santa Maria	151,156
Santana do Livramento	58,072
Santarém	102,181
Santo André (★São Paulo)	549,556
Santo Ângelo	50,173
Santos (★900,000)	410,933
São Bernardo do Campo (★São Paulo)	381,097
São Caetano do Sul (★São Paulo)	163,082
São Carlos	109,167
São Gonçalo (★Rio de Janeiro)	221,591
São João del Rei	53,341
São João de Meriti (★Rio de Janeiro)	210,574
São José do Rio Prêto	172,127
São José dos Campos	268,034
São José dos Pinhais (★Curitiba)	55,332
São Leopoldo (★Porto Alegre)	94,868
São Lourenco da Mata (★Recife)	58,843
São Luís (★475,000)	182,258
• São Paulo (★12,525,000)	8,493,226
São Vicente (★Santos)	192,858
Sapucaia do Sul (★Porto Alegre)	78,849
Sete Lagoas	94,432
Sete Pontes (★Rio de Janeiro)	61,046
Sobral	69,208
Sorocaba	254,672
Suzano (★São Paulo)	95,167
Taboão da Serra (★São Paulo)	97,655
Taubaté	155,376
Teófilo Otoni	83,084
Teresina (★410,000)	339,042
Teresópolis	78,753
Timon (★Teresina)	55,266
Tubarão	64,508
Uberaba	180,228
Uberlândia	230,185
Uruguaiana	79,077
Varginha	57,774
Vicente de Carvalho (★Santos)	83,368
Vila Velha (★Vitória)	74,154
Vitória (★600,000)	165,090
Vitória da Conquista	125,516
Vitória de Santo Antão	62,870
Volta Redonda (★325,000)	180,126

BRUNEI

1981 C	191,765
• BANDAR SERI BEGAWAN	63,868
Seria	23,511

BULGARIA / Bâlgarija

1984 E	8,960,679
Blagoevgrad	70,000
Burgas	188,000
Dimitrovgrad	54,000
Gabrovo	84,000
Haskovo	91,000
Jambol	91,000
Kârdžali	60,000
Kazanlâk	62,000
Kjustendil	56,000
Lovеč	51,000
Mihajlovgrad	58,000
Pazardžik	81,000
Pernik	98,000
Pleven	144,000
Plovdiv	378,000
Razgrad	56,000
Ruse	185,000
Silistra	60,000
Sliven	104,000
• SOFIJA (★1,182,900)	1,102,000
Stara Zagora	152,000
Šumen	107,000
Tolbuhin	105,000
Varna	297,000
Veliko Târnovo	65,000
Vidin	64,000
Vraca	77,000

BURKINA FASO

1985 C	8,846,929
Bobo Dioulasso	231,162
Koudougou	51,670
• OUAGADOUGOU	442,223
Ouahigouya	38,604

BURMA / Myanmā

1983 C	35,313,905
Bassein	144,092
Henzada (1970E)	85,000
Insein (★Rangoon) (1973C)	143,625

▲ Population of an entire municipality, commune, or district, including rural area.
• Largest city in country.
★ Population or designation of the metropolitan area, including suburbs.
C Census. **E** Official estimate. **UE** Unofficial estimate.

▲ Bevölkerung eines ganzen städtischen Verwaltungsgebietes, eines Kommunalbezirkes oder eines Distrikts, einschliesslich ländlicher Gebiete.
• Grösste Stadt des Landes.
★ Bevölkerung oder Bezeichnung der Stadtregion einschliess lich Vororte.
C Volkszählung. **E** Offizielle Schätzung. **UE** Inoffizielle Schätzung.

Kanbe (★Rangoon) (1973C) 253,600
Mandalay 532,895
Monywa 106,873
Moulmein 219,991
Myingyan (1970E) 65,000
Pegu 150,447
Prome (Pyè) (1970E) 65,000
• RANGOON (★3,000,000) 2,458,712
Sittwe (Akyab) 107,607
Taunggyi 107,907
Tavoy (1970E) 53,000
Thingangyun (★Rangoon) (1973C) 141,210

BURUNDI

1983 E 4,523,513
• BUJUMBURA 229,980

CAMEROON / Cameroun

1984 E 9,542,400
Bafoussam 88,000
Bamenda 69,000
• Douala 841,000
Garoua 92,000
Kumba 64,000
Maroua 95,000
Ngaoundéré 58,000
Nkongsamba 101,000
YAOUNDE 561,000

CANADA

1981 C 24,343,181

CANADA: Alberta

1981 C 2,237,724
Calgary 592,743
Edmonton (★657,057) 532,246
Lethbridge 54,072
Medicine Hat (★49,645) 40,380
Red Deer 46,393

CANADA: British Columbia

1981 C 2,744,467
Burnaby (★Vancouver) 136,494
Kamloops (★64,997) 64,048
Kelowna (★77,468) 59,196
Nanaimo (★57,694) 47,069
Prince George 67,559
Richmond (★Vancouver) 96,154
Vancouver (★1,268,183) 414,281
Victoria (★233,481) 64,379

CANADA: Manitoba

1981 C 1,026,241
Winnipeg (★584,842) 564,473

CANADA: New Brunswick

1981 C 696,403
Fredericton (★64,439) 43,723
Moncton (★98,354) 54,743
Saint John (★114,048) 80,521

CANADA: Newfoundland

1981 C 567,681
Saint John's (★154,820) 83,770

CANADA: Northwest Territories

1981 C 45,741
Yellowknife 9,483

CANADA: Nova Scotia

1981 C 847,442
Dartmouth (★Halifax) 62,277
Halifax (★277,727) 114,594
Sydney (★87,489) 29,444

CANADA: Ontario

1981 C 8,625,107
Barrie (★61,271) 38,423
Brampton (★Toronto) 149,030
Brantford (★88,330) 74,315
Burlington (★Hamilton) 114,853
Cambridge (Galt) (★Kitchener) 77,183
Cornwall (★53,405) 46,144
East York (★Toronto) 101,974
Etobicoke (★Toronto) 298,713
Gloucester (★Ottawa) 72,859
Guelph (★78,456) 71,207
Hamilton (★542,095) 306,434
Kingston (★114,982) 52,616
Kitchener (★287,801) 139,734
London (★283,668) 254,280
Markham (★Toronto) 77,037
Mississauga (★Toronto) 315,056
Nepean (★Ottawa) 84,361
Niagara Falls (★Saint Catharines) 70,960
North Bay (★57,137) 51,268
North York (★Toronto) 559,521
Oakville (★Toronto) 75,773
Oshawa (★154,217) 117,519
OTTAWA (★717,978) 295,163
Peterborough (★85,701) 60,620
Saint Catharines (★304,353) 124,018
Sarnia (★83,951) 50,892
Sault Sainte Marie (★86,962) 82,697
Scarborough (★Toronto) 443,353
Sudbury (★149,923) 91,829
Thunder Bay (★121,379) 112,486
• Toronto (★2,998,947) 599,217
Waterloo (★Kitchener) 49,428
Windsor (★246,110) 192,083
York (★Toronto) 134,617

CANADA: Prince Edward Island

1981 C 122,506
Charlottetown (★44,999) 15,282

CANADA: Québec

1981 C 6,438,403
Beauport (★Québec) 60,447
Brossard (★Montréal) 52,232
Charlesbourg (★Québec) 68,326
Chicoutimi (★135,172) 60,064
Drummondville (★54,679) 27,374
Gatineau (★Ottawa) 74,988
Hull (★Ottawa) 56,225
Jonquière (★Chicoutimi) 60,354
La Salle (★Montréal) 76,299
Laval (★Montréal) 268,335
Longueuil (★Montréal) 124,320
Montréal (★2,828,349) 980,354
Montréal-Nord (★Montréal) 94,914
Québec (★576,075) 166,474
Sainte-Foy (★Québec) 68,883
Saint-Hubert (★Montréal) 60,573
Saint-Jean-sur-Richelieu (★60,710) 35,640
Saint-Laurent (★Montréal) 65,900
Saint-Léonard (★Montréal) 79,429
Shawinigan (★62,699) 23,011
Sherbrooke (★117,324) 74,075
Trois-Rivières (★111,453) 50,466
Verdun (★Montréal) 61,287

CANADA: Saskatchewan

1981 C 968,313
Regina (★164,313) 162,613
Saskatoon 154,210

CANADA: Yukon

1981 C 23,153
Whitehorse 14,814

CAPE VERDE / Cabo Verde

1980 C 296,093
Mindelo 36,265
• PRAIA 37,480

CAYMAN ISLANDS

1979 C 16,677
• GEORGETOWN 7,617

CENTRAL AFRICAN REPUBLIC / République centrafricaine

1982 E 2,395,000
• BANGUI 340,000
Bouar 48,000

CHAD / Tchad

1979 E 4,405,000
Abéché 54,000
Moundou 66,000
• N'DJAMENA 303,000
Sarh 65,000

CHILE

1982 C 11,329,736
Antofagasta 185,486
Apoquindo (★Santiago) (1970C) 90,722
Arica 139,320
Calama 81,684
Chillán 118,163
Concepción (★535,000) 267,891
Conchalí (★Santiago) (1970C) 246,046
Copiapó 69,045
Coquimbo 62,186
Coronel 65,918
Curicó 60,550
Iquique 110,153
La Cisterna (★Santiago) (1970C) 246,537
La Granja (★Santiago) (1970C) 163,882
La Serena 83,283
Linares 46,433
Lo Prado Arriba (★Santiago) (1970C) 112,548
Los Ángeles 70,529
Lota 47,133
Ñuñoa (★Santiago) (1970C) 280,733
Osorno 95,286
Ovalle 43,023
Providencia (★Santiago) (1970C) 85,678
Puente Alto (★Santiago) 109,239
Puerto Montt 84,410
Punta Arenas 95,332
Quilpué (★Valparaíso) 84,136
Quinta Normal (★Santiago) (1970C) 138,007
Rancagua 139,925
Renca (★Santiago) (1970C) 68,440
San Antonio 61,486
San Bernardo (★Santiago) 117,132
San Miguel (★Santiago) (1970C) 320,883
• SANTIAGO (★4,025,000) 425,924
Talca 128,544
Talcahuano (★Concepción) 202,368
Temuco 157,297
Valdivia 100,046
Vallenar 38,375
Valparaíso (★700,000) 265,355
Villa Alemana 55,766
Viña del Mar (★Valparaíso) 244,899

CHINA / Zhongguo

1982 C 1,008,175,288
Abagnar Qi 61,629
Acheng 95,148
Aihui (▲66,163) 60,000
Akesu 87,989
Anci (Langfang) (▲171,972) 75,000
Anda (Daqing) (▲764,046) 150,000
Anda 135,922
Ankang 97,318
Anqing (▲418,773) 160,000
Anqiu 59,374
Anshan (1985E) 1,280,000
Anshun (▲207,886) 100,000
Anyang (▲504,311) 250,000
Baicheng (▲266,420) 150,000
Baiquan 57,539
Baiyin (1975UE) 50,000
Baoding (▲502,407) 400,000
Baoji (▲338,754) 275,000
Baotou (▲1,063,600) (1984E) 866,200
Baoying 53,498
Bei'an 123,119
Beihai (▲168,442) 125,000
BEIJING (PEKING) (★6,450,000) (1985E) 5,860,000
Beipiao 131,829
Benxi (▲801,500) (1984E) 678,500
Bijie 113,977
Binxian 127,326
Boli 76,028
Bose 76,185
Boshan (1975UE) 100,000
Boxian 63,982
Boxing 57,554
Boyang 58,812
Bozhen 54,376
Butha Qi (Zalantun) 55,000
Cangshan (Bianzhuang) 79,334
Cangzhou (▲266,384) 120,000
Changchun (▲1,860,000) (1985E) 1,480,000
Changde (▲204,125) 175,000
Changge 67,002
Changqing 65,094
Changsha (1984E) 1,123,900
Changshou 54,832
Changshu 78,058
Changtu 51,920
Changyi 64,513
Changzhi (▲436,149) 300,000
Changzhou (Changchow) (▲500,740) 425,000
Chao'an (▲164,099) 130,000
Chaoxian 72,936
Chaoyang, Guangdong prov. 94,195
Chaoyang, Liaoning prov. (▲213,606) 125,000
Chengde (▲316,398) 150,000
Chengdu (Chengtu) (▲2,580,000) (1985E) 1,590,000
Chenghai 75,080
Chenxian (▲167,089) 85,000
Chifeng (▲297,929) 100,000
Chongqing (Chungking) (▲2,780,000) (1985E) 2,080,000
Chuxian 85,661
Chuxiong 52,596
Da'an 78,275
Dachangzhen (1975UE) 50,000
Dandong (▲537,745) 400,000
Dashiqiao 77,774
Dashitou 63,426
Datong 60,584
Datong (▲981,000) (1984E) 688,200
Dawa 164,928
Daxian (▲189,117) 100,000
Daxing (Huangcun) 55,110
Dehui 65,386
Dengfeng 49,746
Deqing 48,726
Deyang 86,696
Dezhou (▲260,724) 125,000
Didao (1975UE) 50,000
Dinghai 50,792
Dingxian 59,918
Dongguan 82,108
Donglong 58,557
Dongtai 70,875
Dukou (▲517,559) 200,000
Dunhua 118,770
Duyun 97,620
Echeng (▲124,255) 60,000
Enshi (▲98,712) 50,000
Erenhot 7,246
Ergun Zuoqi 56,050
Feixian 73,246
Fengcheng 66,412
Foshan (▲285,547) 200,000
Fujin 66,140
Fuling 93,652
Fulitun 56,318
Fushun (1985E) 1,240,000
Fuxian (Wafangdian) 130,881
Fuxin (▲653,200) (1984E) 551,300
Fuyang (▲169,893) 90,000
Fuyu, Heilongjiang prov. 53,490
Fuyu, Jilin prov. 106,514
Fuzhou, Fujian prov. (▲1,164,800) (1984E) 754,500
Fuzhou, Jiangxi prov. (▲161,512) 80,000
Gaixian 62,762
Ganhe 48,917
Gaomi 86,217
Gaoqing (Tianzhen) 70,411
Gaoyou 63,268
Gejiu (▲327,929) 250,000
Golmud (▲57,202) 40,000
Gongchangling 49,281
Gongxian 54,505
Guanghua (▲101,439) 50,000
Guangyuan 101,318
Guangzhou (Canton) (▲3,290,000) (1985E) 2,570,000
Guanxian, Shandong prov. 49,782
Guanxian, Sichuan prov. 65,891
Gucheng 57,781
Guilin (Kweilin) (▲429,988) 325,000
Guixian 58,016
Guiyang (▲1,352,700) (1984E) 871,000
Gushi 50,380
Haicheng 124,426
Haifeng 50,853
Haikou 266,302
Hailar (▲163,549) 90,000
Hailin 66,360
Hailong (Meihekou) 81,951
Hailun 88,986
Haimen 66,009
Haiyang (Dongcun) 77,098
Hami (▲94,878) 60,000
Handan (▲954,300) (1984E) 727,500
Hangu (1975UE) 100,000
Hangzhou (Hangchow) (1985E) 1,250,000
Hanzhong (▲396,795) 200,000
Harbin (1985E) 2,630,000
Hebi (▲351,869) 200,000
Hechi 63,958
Hechuan 63,119
Hefei (▲853,100) (1984E) 594,200
Hegang (▲576,159) 325,000
Helong 65,082
Hengshui (▲102,879) 50,000
Hengyang (▲527,105) 350,000
Heshan (▲101,694) 40,000
Heze (Caozhou) 141,174
Hohhot (▲778,000) (1984E) 542,800
Honghu 52,969
Hongjiang (▲67,283) 30,000
Horqin Youyi Qianqi (▲172,542) 100,000
Hotan 73,541
Houma (▲148,569) 60,000
Huadian 83,507
Huai'an 83,420
Huaibei (▲442,946) 150,000
Huaide 113,864
Huaihua (▲96,908) 50,000
Huainan (▲1,063,000) (1984E) 603,200
Huanan 51,080
Huanggang 65,961
Huangnihe 51,898
Huangshi (▲431,713) 200,000
Huangyan 50,262
Huanren 50,377
Huilai 58,771
Huinan (Chaoyang) 54,644
Huizhou (▲166,543) 100,000
Hulan 83,787
Hunjiang (▲681,290) 125,000
Huzhou (▲945,616) 135,000
Jiading 53,692
Jiamusi (Kiamusze) (▲529,830) 350,000
Ji'an (▲174,204) 115,000
Jiangling 85,813
Jiangmen (▲216,097) 175,000
Jiangyin 69,133
Jiangyou 78,762
Jian'ou 56,416
Jiaohe 49,021
Jiaojiang (▲154,559) 75,000
Jiaoxian 55,639
Jiaozuo (▲487,643) 350,000
Jiawang (1975UE) 50,000
Jiaxing (▲670,041) 175,000
Jiayuguan 81,378
Jiazi 91,976
Jidong 72,734
Jieshi 71,067
Jieyang 110,277
Jilin (Kirin) (▲1,114,100) (1984E) 882,700
Jimo 68,443
Jinan (Tsinan) (1985E) 1,430,000
Jinchang (Baijiazui) (▲111,477) 50,000
Jincheng 52,755
Jingdezhen (Kingtechen) (▲506,960) 400,000
Jingmen (▲112,738) 50,000
Jinhua (▲842,904) 125,000
Jining (▲156,800) 125,000
Jining (▲211,232) 150,000
Jining, Nei Monggol prov. (▲156,800) 125,000
Jining, Shandong prov. (▲211,232) 150,000
Jinshi 84,215
Jinxi 152,203
Jinxian 94,613
Jinzhou (Chinchou) (▲748,700) (1984E) 584,800
Jishou 49,225
Jishu 84,540
Jiujiang (▲364,687) 150,000
Jiutai 69,601
Jixi (▲798,900) (1984E) 626,300
Jixian 59,389
Juancheng 54,110
Junan (Shizilu) 90,222
Junxian 60,774
Juxian 51,666
Kaifeng (▲604,219) 450,000
Kaili 99,158
Kaiyuan (▲204,951) 100,000
Karamay (▲168,868) 90,000
Kashi (▲274,130) 150,000
Keshan 72,472
Korla (▲121,991) 50,000
Kunming (▲1,490,000) (1985E) 1,080,000
Kunshan 47,735
Kuytun (▲223,968) 75,000
Laiyang 52,387
Langxiang 70,731
Lanxi 49,337
Lanzhou (Lanchow) (▲1,350,000) (1985E) 1,060,000
Lechang 71,815
Leiyang (1980C) 77,044
Lengshuijiang (▲255,763) 150,000
Leshan (▲954,382) 150,000

▲ Población de un municipio, comuna o distrito entero, incluyendo sus áreas rurales.
• Ciudad más grande de un país.
★ Población o designación de un área metropolitana, incluyendo los suburbios.
C Censo. **E** Estimado oficial. **UE** Estimado no oficial.

▲ Population d'une municipalité, d'une commune ou d'un district, zone rurale incluse.
• Ville la plus peuplée du pays.
★ Population de l'agglomération (ou nom de la zone métropolitaine englobante).
C Recensement. **E** Estimation officielle. **UE** Estimation non officielle.

▲ População de um município, comuna ou distrito, inclusive as respectivas áreas rurais.
• Maior cidade de um país.
★ População ou indicação de uma área metropolitana.
C Censo. **E** Estimativa oficial. **UE** Estimativa não oficial.

Lhasa	105,897
Lianyungang (▲395,730)	275,000
Liaocheng	129,337
Liaoyang (▲448,807)	275,000
Liaoyuan (▲759,577)	300,000
Lihu	60,174
Liling	72,106
Linfen (▲190,626)	75,000
Linhai	66,699
Linhe	77,199
Linkou	55,444
Linqing	70,616
Linqu	84,196
Linru	51,744
Linxia	65,204
Lishi	51,316
Lishui	55,508
Liuhe	52,569
Liuzhou (▲585,387)	375,000
Liyujiang (1975UE)	50,000
Longjiang	78,403
Longyan (▲356,243)	75,000
Loudi (▲102,182)	50,000
Lu'an (▲145,597)	70,000
Lüda (Dairen) (▲1,630,000) (1985E)	1,380,000
Lufeng	86,688
Luohe (▲152,105)	90,000
Luoyang (Loyang) (▲1,023,900) (1984E)	624,000
Lushan	40,752
Lüshun (Port Arthur) (1975UE)	40,000
Luzhou (▲303,403)	250,000
Ma'anshan (▲350,513)	275,000
Manzhouli (▲107,875)	70,000
Maoming (▲409,744)	250,000
Meixian (▲109,647)	65,000
Mengyin	70,602
Mianyang, Hubei prov. (▲768,500)	52,525
Mianyang, Sichuan prov. (▲776,165)	100,000
Minhang (1975UE)	60,000
Minquan	52,591
Mishan	56,772
Mixian	64,776
Mudanjiang (▲580,982)	400,000
Muling	49,856
Muping	50,126
Nahe	60,211
N'aizishen	66,955
Nancha (1975UE)	50,000
Nanchang (1984E)	1,088,800
Nanchong	220,531
Nanjing (Nanking) (1985E)	2,250,000
Nanning (▲902,900) (1984E)	564,900
Nanpiao	67,274
Nanping (▲405,174)	100,000
Nantong (▲380,988)	300,000
Nanyang (▲271,872)	100,000
Neihuang	56,039
Neijiang (▲278,592)	225,000
Ning'an	57,888
Ningbo (▲468,232)	350,000
Ningyang	55,424
Nunjiang	74,647
Orogen Zizhiqi	52,142
Panshan	86,109
Panshi	63,015
Pingdingshan (▲475,950)	350,000
Pingliang	71,290
Pingxiang, Guangxi Zhuangzu prov. (▲78,300)	50,000
Pingxiang, Jiangxi prov. (▲1,224,762)	150,000
Pingyi	89,373
Pingyin	62,827
Puqi	63,197
Putuo	62,298
Qian Gorlos	72,307
Qingdao (Tsingtao) (1985E)	1,250,000
Qinggang	49,861
Qingjiang, Jiangsu prov. (▲246,617)	150,000
Qingjiang, Jiangxi prov.	49,377
Qingyuan	63,197
Qinhuangdao (▲403,701)	300,000
Qinzhou	51,452
Qiqihar (Tsitsihar) (▲1,246,000) (1984E)	955,200
Qitaihe (▲259,857)	125,000
Qixia	54,158
Qixian	53,041
Quanzhou (Chuanchou) (▲410,229)	175,000
Qujing	75,132
Quxian (▲971,787)	120,000
Raoping	60,177
Rizhao	78,489
Rongcheng	52,878
Rugao	50,780
Rui'an	57,261
Rushan (Xiacun)	65,903
Sanmenxia (▲140,410)	90,000
Sanming (▲204,307)	80,000
Shahe	83,870
• Shanghai (★9,300,000) (1985E)	6,980,000
Shangqiu (▲183,431)	150,000
Shangrao (▲136,924)	90,000
Shangshui	50,191
Shangzhi	56,186
Shanhetun	50,746
Shantou (Swatow) (▲722,805)	400,000
Shanwei	60,505
Shanxian	74,820
Shaoguan (▲344,892)	160,000
Shaowu	58,733
Shaoxing (▲1,107,176)	225,000
Shaoyang (▲399,257)	250,000
Shashi (▲243,792)	175,000
Shenxian	50,208

Shenyang (Mukden) (▲4,200,000) (1985E)	3,250,000
Shenzhen (▲113,616)	60,000
Shiguaigou (1975UE)	50,000
Shihezi (▲549,426)	75,000
Shijiazhuang (1984E)	1,127,800
Shiyan (▲301,420)	150,000
Shizuishan (▲304,228)	135,000
Shouguang	83,400
Shuangcheng	102,677
Shuangfeng	52,209
Shuangliao	73,874
Shuangyashan (▲397,525)	200,000
Shuicheng (▲2,089,552)	75,000
Shulan	52,924
Shuyang	52,247
Siping (▲344,390)	200,000
Sishui	82,990
Songjiang	68,052
Songjianghe	55,989
Suifenhe	19,842
Suihua	167,997
Suileng	66,643
Suining	90,632
Suixian (▲132,814)	60,000
Suqian	53,600
Suxian (▲193,253)	90,000
Suzhou (Soochow) (1984E)	695,500
Tai'an (▲1,274,770)	125,000
Tailai	58,541
Taiyuan (▲1,880,000) (1985E)	1,390,000
Taizhou (▲161,549)	150,000
Tancheng	61,857
Tangshan (▲1,366,100) (1984E)	921,100
Tao'an	72,021
Tengxian	61,404
Tianjin (Tientsin) (1985E)	5,380,000
Tianmen	52,066
Tianshui (▲186,460)	125,000
Tiefa (▲146,367)	60,000
Tieli	108,654
Tieling (▲210,754)	100,000
Tongchuan (▲377,710) (1980C)	200,000
Tonghua (▲354,843)	200,000
Tongliao (▲225,432)	80,000
Tongling (▲202,578)	100,000
Tongren	54,269
Tongxian	90,056
Tumen (▲93,197)	50,000
Ürümqi (▲1,147,300) (1984E)	947,000
Wangkui	62,638
Wangqing	66,055
Wanxian (▲269,757)	160,000
Weifang (▲371,993)	275,000
Weihai (▲210,415)	75,000
Weinan	88,492
Weishan (Xiazhen)	57,932
Weixian (Hanting)	50,180
Wendeng	57,189
Wenzhou (▲508,613)	325,000
Wuchang (1980C)	68,202
Wuchuan	61,348
Wuhai (▲219,616)	60,000
Wuhan (1985E)	3,400,000
Wuhu (▲456,222)	360,000
Wulian (Hongning)	51,718
Wusong	64,017
Wuwei (Liangzhou)	84,713
Wuxi (Wuhsi) (▲825,100) (1984E)	696,300
Wuzhou (1980C)	251,145
Xiaguan (▲119,877)	60,000
Xiamen (Amoy) (▲510,656)	350,000
Xi'an (Sian) (▲2,330,000) (1985E)	1,730,000
Xiangfan (▲316,007)	175,000
Xiangtan (▲482,953)	350,000
Xiangxiang	67,253
Xianyang (▲497,432)	200,000
Xiaogan (1980C)	69,479
Xiaoshan	61,332
Xichang	149,566
Xinghua	74,360
Xinglongzhen	52,961
Xingtai (▲335,804)	150,000
Xinhui	78,447
Xining (▲571,546)	400,000
Xinmin	48,028
Xintai	104,251
Xinwen (Suncun) (1975UE)	50,000
Xinxian	76,595
Xinxiang (▲508,609)	325,000
Xinyang (▲220,470)	125,000
Xinyu	70,604
Xiuyan	51,362
Xuancheng	62,805
Xuanhua (1975UE)	140,000
Xuanwei	70,081
Xuchang (▲227,678)	135,000
Xuguit Qi (Yakeshi)	114,164
Xuzhou (Süchow) (1984E)	806,400
Yaan	78,677
Yan'an (▲250,847)	150,000
Yancheng	150,030
Yangcheng	57,255
Yangjiang	88,527
Yangquan (▲466,563)	325,000
Yangzhou (▲304,959)	225,000
Yanji (▲175,957)	100,000
Yanji (Longjing)	59,970
Yanling	52,679
Yantai (Chefoo) (▲384,336)	200,000
Yanzhou	55,919
Yexian	54,086
Yi'an	60,633
Yibin (Ipin)	245,064
Yichuan, Henan prov.	58,914
Yichuan, Ningxia Huizu prov. (▲363,508)	200,000
Yichun (▲814,300) (1984E)	758,200
Yidu	78,040

Yilan	56,440
Yima (▲78,153)	50,000
Yinan (Jiehu)	67,803
Yinchuan (▲363,508)	200,000
Yingchengzi	66,844
Yingkou (▲419,640)	200,000
Yingtan (▲102,485)	50,000
Yining (▲225,024)	160,000
Yishan	54,148
Yishui	88,149
Yiyang (▲163,240)	125,000
Yiyuan (Nanma)	53,800
Yong'an	85,717
Yongchuan	69,940
Yuci (▲268,204)	120,000
Yueyang (▲980,945)	125,000
Yulin, Guangxi Zhuangzu prov.	99,082
Yulin, Shaanxi prov.	56,906
Yumen (Laojunmiao) (▲178,893)	150,000
Yuncheng, Shandong prov.	54,262
Yuncheng, Shansi prov.	82,158
Yunyang	54,903
Yushu	62,270
Yuxian	64,521
Yuyao	52,823
Zaozhuang (▲1,238,256)	150,000
Zhangjiakou (Kalgan) (▲605,911)	350,000
Zhangzhou (Longxi) (▲295,382)	160,000
Zhanjiang (▲867,062)	300,000
Zhao'an	50,979
Zhaodong	118,423
Zhaoqing (▲169,799)	100,000
Zhaotong (▲115,897)	60,000
Zhaoyuan	49,179
Zhaoyuan	56,389
Zhengzhou (Chengchow) (▲1,590,000) (1985E)	1,000,000
Zhenjiang (▲346,024)	250,000
Zhongshan (Shiqizhen)	98,307
Zhoucun (1975UE)	50,000
Zhoukouzhen (▲206,570)	150,000
Zhucheng	103,869
Zhuhai (▲133,211)	65,000
Zhumadian (▲141,973)	65,000
Zhuoxian	49,046
Zhuzhou (Chuchow) (▲385,660)	275,000
Zibo (▲2,280,500) (1984E)	762,500
Zigong (Tzukung) (▲875,339)	450,000
Ziyang	52,590
Zouping	49,274
Zouxian	90,333
Zunyi (▲341,959)	275,000

CISKEI

1981 E	645,000
BISHO (1970E)	4,800
• Mdantsane (★East London, S. Afr.) (1980C)	159,360

COLOMBIA

1985 C	26,525,670
Armenia	179,727
Barrancabermeja	139,708
Barranquilla (★1,125,000)	891,545
Bello (★Medellín)	198,183
• BOGOTÁ (★4,250,000)	3,967,988
Bucaramanga (★495,000)	342,169
Buenaventura	157,528
Buga	82,766
Cali (★1,400,000)	1,347,810
Cartagena	495,028
Cartago	92,231
Ciénaga	53,436
Cúcuta (★440,000)	355,828
Duitama	55,357
Envigado (★Medellín)	84,944
Florencia	66,025
Floridablanca (★Bucaramanga)	137,868
Girardot	65,281
Ibagué	265,598
Itagüí (★Medellín)	133,444
Magangué	49,450
Maicao	47,508
Malambo (★Barranquilla)	50,295
Manizales (★325,000)	275,220
Medellín (★2,070,000)	1,473,351
Montería	158,064
Neiva	179,609
Ocaña	51,922
Palmira	174,425
Pasto	196,800
Pereira (★390,000)	232,311
Popayán	140,839
Santa Marta	193,160
Sincelejo	118,559
Soacha (★Bogotá) (1981C)	99,953
Sogamoso	64,398
Soledad (★Barranquilla)	156,846
Tuluá	99,134
Tunja	87,334
Valledupar	140,481
Villavicencio	159,808
Zipaquirá	45,477

COMOROS / Al-Qumur / Comores

1980 C	346,992
• MORONI	20,112

CONGO

1984 C	1,912,429
• BRAZZAVILLE	595,102
Dolisie	49,458
Pointe-Noire	195,398

COOK ISLANDS

1981 C	17,753
• AVARUA	9,525

COSTA RICA

1984 C	2,416,809
Alajuela (▲34,556)	29,273
Desamparados (★San José)	43,352
Limón (▲52,602)	33,925
Puntarenas	29,224
• SAN JOSÉ (★670,000)	241,464

CUBA

1981 C	9,723,605
Bayamo	99,967
Camagüey	244,091
Cárdenas	59,352
Ciego de Avila	73,820
Cienfuegos	102,297
Guantánamo	166,558
Holguín	186,236
• LA HABANA (HAVANA) (★1,975,000)	1,914,466
Manzanillo	87,830
Matanzas	100,367
Palma Soriano	55,851
Pinar del Río	96,149
Sancti-Spíritus	71,430
Santa Clara	172,652
Santiago de Cuba	349,444
Victoria de las Tunas	84,735

CYPRUS / Kıbrıs / Kípros

1982 E	642,731
Ammókhostos (Famagusta) (1980E)	50,000
Lárnax (Larnaca) (★48,330)	35,823
Lemesós (Limassol) (★107,161)	74,782
• LEVKOSÍA (★149,071)	48,221

CZECHOSLOVAKIA / Československo

1986 E	15,520,839
Banská Bystrica	78,475
Bratislava	417,103
Brno	385,684
České Budějovice	94,451
Chomutov	58,445
Děčín	55,691
Frýdek-Místek (★Ostrava)	63,255
Gottwaldov	86,210
Havířov (★Ostrava)	91,873
Hradec Králové	99,571
Jihlava	53,429
Karlovy Vary (Carlsbad)	57,966
Karviná (★Ostrava)	75,377
Kladno (★87,000)	72,720
Košice	222,175
Liberec	100,917
Martin	62,328
Most	65,375
Nitra	85,276
Olomouc	106,086
Opava	62,237
Ostrava (★745,000)	327,791
Pardubice	94,206
Plzeň	175,244
• PRAHA (★1,270,000)	1,193,513
Přerov	51,294
Prešov	82,879
Prostějov	51,378
Teplice	54,592
Trenčín	54,986
Trnava	69,917
Ústí nad Labem (★106,000)	91,444
Žilina	91,703

DENMARK / Danmark

1985 E	5,111,108
Ålborg (▲154,750)	114,200
Århus (▲252,071)	194,900
Ballerup (★København)	46,872
Esbjerg (▲80,514)	71,000
Fredericia (▲45,879)	28,400
Frederiksberg (★København)	88,030
Gentofte (★København)	66,767
Gladsakse (★København)	62,470
Helsingør (Elsinore) (★København)	43,700
Horsens (▲54,461)	46,600
Hvidovre (★København)	50,350
• KØBENHAVN (★1,685,000)	478,615
Kolding (▲56,729)	41,700
Kongens Lyngby (★København)	50,225
Odense (▲171,468)	137,800
Randers	61,127
Rødovre (★København)	36,356
Rønne	15,343
Roskilde (★København)	39,500
Tårnby (★København)	40,400
Vejle (▲49,823)	43,700

DJIBOUTI

1976 E	226,000
• DJIBOUTI	120,000

DOMINICA

1984 E	77,000
• ROSEAU	9,348

DOMINICAN REPUBLIC / República Dominicana

1981 C	5,647,977
Barahona	49,334
La Romana	91,571
La Vega	52,432
San Cristóbal	58,520
San Francisco de Macorís	64,906
San Juan [de la Maguana]	49,764
San Pedro de Macorís	78,562
Santiago [de los Caballeros]	278,638
• SANTO DOMINGO	1,313,172

▲ Population of an entire municipality, commune, or district, including rural area.
• Largest city in country.
★ Population or designation of the metropolitan area, including suburbs.
C Census. **E** Official estimate. **UE** Unofficial estimate.

▲ Bevölkerung eines ganzen städtischen Verwaltungsgebietes, eines Kommunalbezirkes oder eines Distrikts, einschliesslich ländlicher Gebiete.
• Grösste Stadt des Landes.
★ Bevölkerung oder Bezeichnung der Stadtregion einschliess lich Vororte.
C Volkszählung. **E** Offizielle Schätzung. **UE** Inoffizielle Schätzung.

ECUADOR

1982 C	8,050,630
Alfaro (★Guayaquil)	49,660
Ambato	100,454
Cuenca	157,213
Esmeraldas	91,382
• Guayaquil (★1,255,000)	1,204,532
Ibarra	53,428
Loja	71,652
Machala	108,156
Manta	99,222
Milagro	77,010
Portoviejo	102,628
QUITO (★1,050,000)	890,355
Riobamba	75,455
Santo Domingo de los Colorados	69,235

EGYPT / Miṣr

1985 E	48,503,000
Al-Fayyūm	218,500
Al-Iskandarīyah (Alexandria) (★3,350,000)	2,821,000
Al-Ismā'īlīyah (★235,000)	191,700
Al-Jīzah (Giza) (★Al-Qāhirah)	1,608,400
Al-Maḥallah al-Kubrā	362,700
Al-Manṣūrah (★375,000)	328,700
Al-Minyā	191,800
• AL-QAHIRAH (CAIRO) (★9,300,000)	6,205,000
Al-Uqṣur (Luxor)	137,300
As-Suways (Suez)	254,000
Aswān	182,700
Asyūṭ	274,400
Az-Zaqāzīq	266,800
Banhā	115,500
Banī Suwayf	151,200
Bilbays (1966C)	58,070
Būlāq ad-Dakrūr (★Al-Qāhirah) (1966C)	75,130
Būr Sa'īd (Port Said)	374,000
Damanhūr	221,500
Dumyāṭ (Damietta)	118,100
Kafr ad-Dawwār (★Al-Iskandarīyah) (1983E)	160,554
Kafr ash-Shaykh (1966C)	51,544
Mallawī (1966C)	59,938
Minūf (1966C)	48,256
Mīt Ghamr (★82,000) (1966C)	43,665
Qalyūb (1966C)	49,303
Qinā	137,100
Sawhāj	131,300
Shibīn al-Kawm	129,600
Shubrā al-Khaymah (★Al-Qāhirah)	515,500
Ṭanṭā	364,700

EL SALVADOR

1983 E	4,949,000
Mejicanos (★San Salvador)	86,500
Nueva San Salvador	51,000
San Miguel	85,000
• SAN SALVADOR (★800,000)	445,100
Santa Ana	132,200
Villa Delgado (★San Salvador)	64,600

EQUATORIAL GUINEA / Guinea Ecuatorial

1983 C	300,000
• MALABO	30,710

ETHIOPIA / Ityopiya

1982 E	32,775,000
• ADIS ABEBA	1,408,068
Asmera	474,241
Bahir Dar	58,299
Debre Zeyit	57,251
Dese	83,288
Dire Dawa	91,629
Gonder	85,941
Harer	70,289
Jima	71,311
Mekele	52,332
Mitsiwa	36,839
Nazret	80,702

FAEROE ISLANDS / Føroyar

1985 E	45,464
• TÓRSHAVN	13,408

FALKLAND ISLANDS / Islas Malvinas

1980 C	1,813
• STANLEY	1,050

FIJI

1984 E	686,000
Lautoka (★37,000)	27,000
• SUVA (★150,000)	74,000

FINLAND / Suomi

1984 E	4,893,748
Espoo (Esbo) (★Helsinki)	152,929
• HELSINKI (HELSINGFORS) (★900,000)	484,263
Jyväskylä (★89,000)	64,834
Kotka	59,474
Kouvola (★55,000)	31,644
Kuopio	77,371
Lahti (★109,000)	94,347
Lappeenranta	53,966
Oulu (★112,000)	96,525
Pori	78,933
Tampere (★241,000)	168,150
Turku (Åbo) (★221,000)	162,282
Vaanta (Vanda) (★Helsinki)	141,991
Vaasa (Vasa)	54,497

FRANCE

1982 C	54,334,871
Aix-en-Provence	121,327
Ajaccio	54,089
Albi (★60,181)	45,947
Alès (★70,180)	43,268
Amiens (★154,498)	131,332
Angers (★195,859)	136,038
Angoulême (★103,552)	46,197
Annecy (★112,632)	49,965
Antibes (★Cannes)	62,859
Antony (★Paris)	54,610
Argenteuil (★Paris)	95,347
Arles (★52,547)	37,571
Armentières (★57,000)	24,834
Arras (★80,447)	41,736
Asnières [-sur-Seine] (★Paris)	71,077
Aubervilliers (★Paris)	67,719
Aulnay-sous-Bois (★Paris)	75,996
Avignon (★174,264)	89,132
Bastia (★50,596)	44,020
Bayonne (★127,477)	41,381
Beauvais	52,365
Belfort (★76,221)	51,206
Besançon (★120,772)	113,283
Béthune (★147,000)	25,508
Béziers (★81,347)	76,647
Blois (★61,049)	47,243
Bondy (★Paris)	44,301
Bordeaux (★640,012)	208,159
Boulogne-Billancourt (★Paris)	102,582
Boulogne-sur-Mer (★98,566)	47,653
Bourg-en-Bresse (★53,463)	41,098
Bourges (★92,202)	76,432
Brest (★201,145)	156,060
Brive-la-Gaillarde (★64,301)	51,511
Bruay-en-Artois (★110,000)	22,893
Caen (★183,526)	114,068
Calais (★100,823)	76,527
Cambrai (★49,581)	35,272
Cannes (★245,000)	72,259
Carcassonne	41,153
Castres	45,578
Châlons-sur-Marne (★63,061)	51,137
Chalon-sur-Saône (★78,064)	56,194
Chambéry (★96,163)	53,427
Champigny-sur-Marne (★Paris)	76,176
Charleville-Mézières (★67,694)	58,667
Chartres (★77,795)	37,119
Châteauroux (★66,851)	51,942
Châtellerault (★68,000)	35,838
Cherbourg (★85,485)	28,442
Cholet	55,524
Clamart (★Paris)	48,353
Clermont-Ferrand (★256,189)	147,361
Clichy (★Paris)	46,895
Cognac (★31,189)	20,660
Colmar (★82,468)	62,483
Colombes (★Paris)	78,777
Compiègne (★62,778)	40,384
Courbevoie (★Paris)	59,830
Creil (★82,505)	34,709
Créteil (★Paris)	71,693
Denain (★Valenciennes)	21,825
Dieppe (★41,812)	35,957
Dijon (★215,865)	140,942
Douai (★202,366)	42,576
Drancy (★Paris)	60,183
Dunkerque (★195,705)	73,120
Elbeuf (★51,083)	17,224
Épinal (★53,000)	37,818
Épinay-sur-Seine (★Paris)	50,314
Évreux (★54,654)	46,045
Fontainebleau (★40,000)	15,679
Fontenay-sous-Bois (★Paris)	52,627
Forbach (★66,000)	27,187
Fréjus (★60,289)	31,662
Gennevilliers (★Paris)	45,396
Grenoble (★392,021)	156,637
Hayange (★70,000)	17,848
Issy-les-Moulineaux (★Paris)	45,772
Ivry-sur-Seine (★Paris)	55,699
La Rochelle (★102,143)	75,840
La Seyne-sur-Mer (★Toulon)	57,659
Laval	50,360
Le Blanc-Mesnil (★Paris)	47,037
Le Havre (★254,595)	199,388
Le Mans (★191,080)	147,697
Lens (★327,383)	38,244
Le Puy (★42,382)	24,064
Levallois-Perret (★Paris)	53,500
Lille (★1,020,000)	168,424
Limoges (★171,689)	140,400
Longwy (★80,000)	17,338
Lorient (★104,025)	62,554
Lourdes	17,425
Lyon (★1,220,844)	413,095
Mâcon (★47,274)	38,404
Maisons-Alfort (★Paris)	51,065
Mantes-la-Jolie (★170,265)	43,564
Marseille (★1,110,511)	874,436
Maubeuge (★109,000)	36,061
Meaux (★55,797)	45,005
Melun (★82,479)	35,005
Menton (★35,000)	25,072
Mérignac (★Bordeaux)	51,306
Metz (★186,437)	114,232
Meudon (★Paris)	48,450
Montargis (★51,954)	16,110
Montbéliard (★128,194)	31,836
Montceau-les-Mines (★51,290)	26,925
Montluçon (★70,000)	49,912
Montpellier (★221,307)	197,231
Montreuil-sous-Bois (★Paris)	93,368
Moulins (★43,082)	25,159
Moyeuvre-Grande (★70,000)	10,287
Mulhouse (Mülhausen) (★220,613)	112,157
Nancy (★306,982)	96,317
Nanterre (★Paris)	88,578
Nantes (★468,857)	240,539
Neuilly-sur-Seine (★Paris)	64,170
Nevers (★59,274)	43,013
Nice (★449,496)	337,085
Nîmes (★132,343)	124,220
Niort (★61,959)	58,203
Noisy-le-Sec (★Paris)	36,880
Orléans (★220,478)	102,710
Orly (★Paris)	23,766
Pantin (★Paris)	43,553
• PARIS (★9,775,000) (1984E)	2,149,900
Pau (★131,265)	83,790
Périgueux (★59,716)	32,916
Perpignan (★137,915)	111,669
Pessac (★Bordeaux)	50,267
Poissy (★Paris)	36,389
Poitiers (★103,204)	79,350
Quimper	56,907
Reims (★199,388)	194,656
Rennes (★234,418)	117,234
Roanne (★81,786)	48,705
Rodez (★37,953)	24,368
Romans-sur-Isère (★47,083)	33,152
Roubaix (★Lille)	101,602
Rouen (★379,879)	101,945
Rueil-Malmaison (★Paris)	63,412
Saint-Brieuc (★83,900)	48,563
Saint-Chamond (★82,059)	40,267
Saint-Denis (★Paris)	90,829
Saint-Dizier	35,189
Saint-Étienne (★317,228)	204,955
Saint-Lô (★27,656)	23,212
Saint-Malo	46,347
Saint-Maur-des-Fossés (★Paris)	80,811
Saint-Nazaire (★130,271)	68,348
Saint-Ouen (★Paris)	43,606
Saint-Quentin (★71,887)	63,567
Sarcelles (★Paris)	53,630
Soissons (★47,305)	30,213
Strasbourg (★400,000)	248,712
Suresnes (★Paris)	35,187
Tarbes (★80,000)	51,422
Thionville (★138,034)	40,573
Toulon (★410,393)	179,423
Toulouse (★541,271)	347,995
Tourcoing (★Lille)	96,908
Tours (★262,786)	132,209
Troyes (★125,240)	63,581
Valence (★106,041)	66,356
Valenciennes (★349,505)	40,275
Vénissieux (★Lyon)	64,804
Verdun-sur-Meuse (★26,944)	21,516
Versailles (★Paris)	91,494
Vichy (★63,501)	30,527
Villefranche (★43,000)	28,881
Villejuif (★Paris)	52,448
Villeneuve-d'Ascq (★Lille)	59,527
Villeurbanne (★Lyon)	115,960
Vitry-sur-Seine (★Paris)	85,263
Wattrelos (★Lille)	44,626

FRENCH GUIANA / Guyane française

1982 C	72,012
• CAYENNE	38,093

FRENCH POLYNESIA / Polynésie française

1983 C	166,753
• PAPEETE (★80,000)	23,496

GABON

1985 E	1,312,000
Franceville	58,800
Lambaréné	49,500
• LIBREVILLE	235,700
Port Gentil	124,400

GAMBIA

1983 C	696,000
• BANJUL (★109,486)	44,536

GERMAN DEMOCRATIC REPUBLIC (EAST GERMANY) / Deutsche Demokratische Republik

1985 E	16,640,059
Altenburg	54,369
Bautzen	51,612
• BERLIN (OST) (★BERLIN)	1,215,586
Bitterfeld (★105,000)	20,961
Brandenburg	94,862
Cottbus	124,752
Dessau (★138,000)	103,569
Dresden (★640,000)	519,769
Eberswalde	54,239
Eisenach	50,559
Eisenhüttenstadt	48,810
Erfurt	216,046
Frankfurt an der Oder	85,593
Freiberg	49,945
Freital (★Dresden)	43,742
Gera	131,843
Görlitz	79,277
Gotha	57,591
Greifswald	65,275
Halberstadt	46,985
Halle (★475,000)	235,169
Halle-Neustadt (★Halle)	92,660
Hoyerswerda	69,670
Jena	107,401
Karl-Marx-Stadt (Chemnitz) (★460,000)	315,452
Leipzig (★690,000)	553,660
Magdeburg (★400,000)	288,965
Merseburg (★Halle)	47,415
Neubrandenburg	84,654
Nordhausen	47,385
Pirna	47,115
Plauen	77,570
Potsdam (★Berlin)	139,497
Riesa	49,428
Rostock	244,444
Schwedt	51,634
Schwerin	127,538
Stralsund	75,480
Suhl	54,392
Weimar	63,373
Wismar	57,465
Wittenberg	54,107
Zwickau (★162,000)	120,206

GERMANY, FEDERAL REPUBLIC OF (WEST GERMANY) / Bundesrepublik Deutschland

1986 E	61,020,474
Aachen (★535,000)	238,587
Aalen (★80,000)	63,195
Ahlen	52,405
Albstadt	45,870
Alsdorf (★Aachen)	45,896
Amberg	43,523
Arnsberg	74,970
Aschaffenburg (★145,000)	59,240
Augsburg (★405,000)	245,193
Baden-Baden	48,684
Bad Homburg (★Frankfurt am Main)	50,905
Bad Oeynhausen	43,207
Bad Salzuflen (★Herford)	50,819
Bamberg (★120,000)	69,920
Bayreuth (★90,000)	71,848
Berchtesgaden	8,099
Bergheim (★Köln)	54,061
Bergisch Gladbach (★Köln)	101,112
Bergkamen (★Essen)	47,747
Berlin (West) (★3,825,000)	1,860,084
Bielefeld (★515,000)	299,727
Bocholt	66,105
Bochum (★Essen)	382,041
BONN (★570,000)	290,769
Bottrop (★Essen)	112,487
Braunschweig (★330,000)	248,001
Bremen (★800,000)	526,377
Bremerhaven (★190,000)	133,521
Castrop-Rauxel (★Essen)	76,430
Celle	70,482
Cuxhaven	56,504
Dachau (★München)	32,682
Darmstadt (★305,000)	134,181
Delmenhorst (★Bremen)	70,546
Detmold	66,403
Dinslaken (★Essen)	61,032
Dormagen (★Köln)	57,293
Dorsten (★Essen)	72,945
Dortmund (★Essen)	572,094
Duisburg (★Essen)	518,260
Düren (★110,000)	84,272
Düsseldorf (★1,190,000)	561,686
Emden	49,686
Erlangen (★Nürnberg)	99,628
Eschweiler (★Aachen)	52,786
• Essen (★4,950,000)	619,991
Esslingen (★Stuttgart)	87,467
Euskirchen	45,309
Flensburg (★103,000)	86,779
Frankfurt am Main (★1,855,000)	595,348
Freiburg (★225,000)	184,230
Friedrichshafen	51,665
Fulda (★79,000)	54,780
Fürth (★Nürnberg)	97,331
Garbsen (★Hannover)	57,249
Garmisch-Partenkirchen	27,817
Gelsenkirchen (★Essen)	285,002
Giessen (★160,000)	71,104
Gladbeck (★Essen)	76,592
Göppingen (★155,000)	51,471
Goslar (★84,000)	49,636
Göttingen	133,394
Grevenbroich (★Düsseldorf)	57,049
Gummersbach	48,373
Gütersloh (★Bielefeld)	79,001
Hagen (★Essen)	206,408
Hamburg (★2,225,000)	1,579,884
Hameln (★72,000)	55,580
Hamm	166,379
Hanau (★Frankfurt am Main)	84,672
Hannover (★1,000,000)	508,298
Hattingen (★Essen)	55,051
Heidelberg (★Mannheim)	134,724
Heidenheim (★89,000)	47,584
Heilbronn (★230,000)	111,338
Herford (★120,000)	59,640
Herne (★Essen)	172,150
Herten (★Essen)	68,004
Hilden (★Düsseldorf)	53,413
Hildesheim (★140,000)	100,864
Hof	51,035
Hürth (★Köln)	50,741
Ingolstadt (★138,000)	91,836
Iserlohn	89,539
Kaiserslautern (★138,000)	97,664
Karlsruhe (★485,000)	268,211
Kassel (★360,000)	184,466
Kempten (Allgäu)	56,705
Kerpen (★Köln)	54,769
Kiel (★335,000)	245,682
Kleve	44,548
Koblenz (★180,000)	110,843
Köln (★1,760,000)	916,153
Konstanz	69,852
Krefeld (★Essen)	216,833
Landshut	56,779
Langenfeld (★Düsseldorf)	48,357
Leverkusen (★Köln)	155,077
Lippstadt	60,032
Lübeck (★260,000)	210,318
Lüdenscheid	73,292

▲ Población de un municipio, comuna o distrito entero, incluyendo sus áreas rurales.
• Ciudad más grande de un país.
★ Población o designación de un área metropolitana, incluyendo los suburbios.
C Censo. E Estimado oficial. UE Estimado no oficial.

▲ Population d'une municipalité, d'une commune ou d'un district, zone rurale incluse.
• Ville la plus peuplée du pays.
★ Population de l'agglomération (ou nom de la zone métropolitaine englobante).
C Recensement. E Estimation officielle. UE Estimation non officielle.

▲ População de um município, comuna ou distrito, inclusive as respectivas áreas rurais.
• Maior cidade de um país.
★ População ou indicação de uma área metropolitana.
C Censo. E Estimativa oficial. UE Estimativa não oficial.

Ludwigsburg (★Stuttgart)	76,973
Ludwigshafen (★Mannheim)	153,654
Lüneburg	59,645
Lünen (★Essen)	84,532
Mainz (★Wiesbaden)	188,571
Mannheim (★1,400,000)	294,984
Marburg	75,092
Marl (★Essen)	87,449
Meerbusch (★Düsseldorf)	49,037
Menden	52,082
Minden (★125,000)	75,511
Moers (★Essen)	97,760
Mönchengladbach (★410,000)	254,495
Mülheim an der Ruhr (★Essen)	171,948
München (Munich) (★1,955,000)	1,266,549
Münster	270,102
Neumünster	78,280
Neunkirchen/Saar (★135,000)	49,759
Neuss (★Düsseldorf)	143,512
Neustadt an der Weinstrasse	48,463
Neu-Ulm (★Ulm)	46,253
Neuwied (★150,000)	58,471
Norderstedt (★Hamburg)	67,232
Nordhorn	47,921
Nürnberg (★1,030,000)	465,255
Oberammergau	4,664
Oberhausen (★Essen)	222,664
Offenbach (★Frankfurt am Main)	107,090
Offenburg	50,207
Oldenburg	138,773
Osnabrück (★270,000)	153,202
Paderborn	109,606
Passau	52,523
Peine	45,707
Pforzheim (★220,000)	104,184
Pirmasens	46,526
Ratingen (★Düsseldorf)	88,718
Ravensburg (★75,000)	42,911
Recklinghausen (★Essen)	117,897
Regensburg (★205,000)	124,480
Remscheid (★Wuppertal)	121,204
Reutlingen (★160,000)	97,030
Rheine	70,662
Rosenheim	52,743
Rüsselsheim (★Wiesbaden)	57,579
Saarbrücken (★385,000)	186,229
Saarlouis (★115,000)	37,472
Salzgitter	105,958
Sankt Augustin (★Bonn)	50,624
Schwäbisch Gmünd	56,117
Schweinfurt (★110,000)	51,016
Siegburg (★170,000)	34,311
Siegen (★200,000)	107,421
Sindelfingen (★Stuttgart)	55,501
Solingen (★Wuppertal)	157,923
Stolberg (★Aachen)	56,435
Stuttgart (★1,925,000)	561,628
Trier (★125,000)	93,472
Troisdorf (★Siegburg)	60,981
Tübingen	75,825
Ulm (★210,000)	99,936
Unna (★Essen)	58,778
Velbert (★Essen)	88,403
Viersen (★Mönchengladbach)	78,489
Villingen-Schwenningen	76,303
Wesel	54,791
Wetzlar (★105,000)	50,063
Wiesbaden (★795,000)	266,623
Wilhelmshaven (★135,000)	95,570
Witten (★Essen)	102,259
Wolfenbüttel (★Braunschweig)	48,641
Wolfsburg	121,703
Worms (★Mannheim)	71,827
Wuppertal (★830,000)	376,579
Würzburg (★210,000)	127,997
Zweibrücken (★105,000)	33,018

GHANA

1984 C	12,205,574
• ACCRA (★1,250,000)	859,640
Ashiaman (★Accra)	49,427
Cape Coast	86,620
Koforidua	54,400
Kumasi (★600,000)	348,880
Obuasi	60,100
Sekondi (★175,352)	32,355
Sekondi-Takoradi (★220,000)	175,352
Tafo (★Kumasi)	50,432
Takoradi (★Sekondi)	61,527
Tamale (★168,091)	136,828
Tema (★Accra)	99,608
Teshie (★Accra)	62,954

GIBRALTAR

1985 E	29,000
• GIBRALTAR	29,000

GREECE / Ellás

1981 C	9,740,417
Aiyáleo (★Athínai)	81,906
Ampelókipoi (★Thessaloníki)	40,033
• ATHÍNAI (ATHENS) (★3,027,331)	885,737
Áyios Dhimítrios (★Athínai)	51,421
Ermoúpolis (★16,595)	13,876
Galátsion (★Athínai)	50,096
Ilioúpolis (★Athínai)	69,560
Ioánnina	44,829
Iráklion (★110,958)	102,398
Kalámai (★43,235)	42,075
Kalamariá (★Thessaloníki)	51,676
Kallithéa (★Athínai)	117,319
Kardhítsa	27,291
Kateríni (★39,895)	38,404
Kavála	56,375
Keratsínion (★Athínai)	74,179
Khalándrion (★Athínai)	54,320
Khalkís	44,867
Khaniá (★61,976)	47,451
Khíos (★29,742)	24,070
Koridhallós (★Athínai)	61,313
Kórinthos (Corinth)	22,658
Lárisa	102,048
Návplion	10,609
Néa Ionía (★Athínai)	59,202
Néa Liósia (★Athínai)	72,427
Neápolis (★Thessaloníki)	31,464
Néa Smírni (★Athínai)	67,408
Níkaia (★Athínai)	90,368
Palaión Fáliron (★Athínai)	53,273
Pátrai (★154,596)	142,163
Peristérion (★Athínai)	140,858
Piraiévs (Piraeus) (★Athínai)	196,389
Ródhos (Rhodes)	40,392
Spárti (Sparta) (★14,388)	12,975
Thessaloníki (Salonika) (★706,180)	406,413
Tríkala	40,857
Trípolis	21,311
Véroia	37,087
Víron (★Athínai)	57,880
Vólos (★107,407)	71,378
Zográfos (★Athínai)	84,548

GREENLAND / Grønland / Kalaallit Nunaat

1986 E	53,406
Egedesminde	3,200
• GODTHÅB	10,972

GRENADA

1979 E	110,100
• SAINT GEORGE'S (★25,000)	7,500

GUADELOUPE

1982 C	328,400
BASSE-TERRE (★26,600)	13,656
Les Abymes (★Pointe-à-Pitre)	56,165
• Pointe-à-Pitre (★83,000)	25,310

GUAM

1980 C	105,979
• AGANA (★44,000)	896

GUATEMALA

1981 C	6,054,227
Escuintla	36,931
• GUATEMALA (★1,100,000)	754,243
Quezaltenango	62,719

GUERNSEY

1986 C	55,482
• SAINT PETER PORT (★36,000)	16,085

GUINEA / Guinée

1980 E	4,830,000
• CONAKRY (1979E)	600,000
Kankan	229,000
Kindia (1979E)	80,000
Labé	253,000

GUINEA-BISSAU / Guiné-Bissau

1979 C	777,214
• BISSAU	109,486

GUYANA

1983 E	918,000
• GEORGETOWN (★188,000)	78,500

HAITI / Haïti

1982 C	5,053,791
Cap-Haïtien	64,406
Gonaïves	34,209
• PORT-AU-PRINCE (★760,000)	684,284

HONDURAS

1985 E	4,372,500
Choluteca	60,800
El Progreso	58,800
La Ceiba	65,400
San Pedro Sula	397,200
• TEGUCIGALPA	597,500

HONG KONG

1981 C	5,021,066
Kowloon (Jiulong) (★Victoria)	799,123
New Kowloon (Xinjiulong) (★Victoria)	1,651,064
Sha Tin (★Victoria)	109,471
Tsuen Wan (Quanwan) (★Victoria)	599,011
Tuen Mun (★Victoria)	89,901
• VICTORIA (★4,515,000)	1,183,621
Yuen Long	51,392

HUNGARY / Magyarország

1986 E	10,641,000
Békéscsaba (▲70,441)	61,200
• BUDAPEST (★2,540,000)	2,075,990
Debrecen	211,823
Dunaújváros	62,459
Eger	65,156
Érd (★Budapest)	45,928
Győr	129,116
Hódmezővásárhely (▲54,510)	45,600
Kaposvár	73,990
Kecskemét (▲102,889)	82,200
Miskolc	211,660
Nagykanizsa	55,336
Nyíregyháza (▲116,782)	90,500
Ózd	47,167
Pécs	177,104
Salgótarján	49,424
Sopron	56,500
Szeged	182,137
Székesfehérvár	111,478
Szolnok	80,461
Szombathely	86,013
Tatabánya	76,465
Vác	35,874
Veszprém	64,071
Zalaegerszeg	61,456

ICELAND / Ísland

1984 E	240,443
Akureyri	13,711
• REYKJAVÍK (★130,722)	88,745

INDIA / Bhārat

1981 C	685,184,692
Abohar	86,334
Achalpur	81,186
Ādilābād	53,482
Adītyapur (★Jamshedpur)	53,421
Ādoni	108,939
Agartala	132,186
Āgra (★747,318)	694,191
Ahmadābād (★2,400,000)	2,059,725
Ahmadnagar (★181,210)	143,937
Āīzawl	74,493
Ajmer	375,593
Akola	225,412
Akot	51,936
Alandur (★Madras)	97,449
Alīgarh	320,861
Alīpur Duār (★71,573)	45,324
Allāhābād (★650,070)	616,051
Alleppey	169,940
Alwar	145,795
Amalner	67,516
Ambāla (★233,110)	104,565
Ambāla Sadar (★Ambāla)	80,741
Ambarnāth (★Bombay)	96,347
Ambāsamudram (★52,591)	29,761
Ambattur (★Madras)	115,901
Āmbūr	66,042
Amrāvati	261,404
Amreli (★58,241)	56,598
Amritsar	594,844
Amroha	112,682
Anakāpalle	73,179
Ānand	83,936
Anantapur	119,531
Arcot (★94,363)	38,836
Arkonam	59,405
Arni	49,365
Arrah	125,111
Aruppukkottai	72,245
Asansol (★1,050,000)	183,375
Ashoknagar-Kalyangarh (★Hābra)	55,176
Āttūr	50,517
Aurangābād (★316,421)	284,607
Avadi (★Madras)	124,701
Azamgarh	66,523
Badagara	64,174
Bāgalkot	67,858
Bahraich	99,889
Baidyabāti (★Calcutta)	70,573
Bālāghāt (★53,183)	49,564
Balāngīr	54,943
Balasore	65,779
Ballarpur	61,398
Ballia	61,704
Bālly	147,735
Balrāmpur	46,058
Bālurghāt (★112,621)	104,646
Bal'y	54,859
Bānda	72,379
Bangalore (★2,950,000)	2,476,355
Bangaon	69,885
Bānkura	94,954
Bānsbāria (★Calcutta)	77,020
Bānswāra (★48,070)	46,749
Bāpatla	55,347
Baranagar (★Calcutta)	170,343
Bārāsat (★Calcutta)	66,504
Barauni	56,366
Baraut	46,292
Bareilly (★449,425)	386,734
Baripāda (★52,989)	40,314
Barmer	55,554
Baroda (★744,881)	734,473
Barrackpore (★Calcutta)	115,253
Bārsi	72,537
Basīrhāt	81,040
Basti	69,357
Batāla (★101,966)	87,135
Beāwar	89,998
Begusarai (★68,305)	56,633
Behāla (South Suburban) (★Calcutta)	378,765
Bela	49,932
Belgaum (★300,372)	274,430
Bellary	201,579
Berhampore (★102,311)	92,889
Berhampur	162,550
Bettiah	72,167
Betūl	46,293
Bhadrakh	60,600
Bhadrāvati (★130,606)	53,551
Bhadrāvati New Town (★Bhadrāvati)	77,055
Bhadreswar (★Calcutta)	58,858
Bhāgalpur	225,062
Bhandāra	56,025
Bharatpur	105,274
Bhatinda (★127,363)	124,453
Bhātpāra (★Calcutta)	260,761
Bhaunagar (★308,642)	307,121
Bhavāni (★80,472)	28,898
Bhilai (★490,214)	290,090
Bhīlwāra	122,625
Bhīmavaram	101,894
Bhind	74,515
Bhiwandi (★Bombay)	115,298
Bhiwāni	101,277
Bhopāl	671,018
Bhubaneswar	219,211
Bhuj (★70,211)	69,693
Bhusāwal (★132,142)	123,133
Bīdar	78,856
Bihār	151,343
Bījāpur	147,313
Bijnor	56,713
Bīkaner (★287,712)	253,174
Bilāspur (★187,104)	147,218
Bīr	80,287
Birlapur (★50,831)	20,470
Birnagar (★67,066)	14,581
Bishnupur	47,529
Bodhan	50,807
Bodināyakkanūr	59,168
Bokāro Steel City (★264,480)	224,099
Bombay (★9,950,000)	8,243,405
Botād	50,274
Brajrajnagar	54,033
Broach (★120,524)	110,070
Budaun	93,004
Budge Budge (★Calcutta)	66,424
Bulandshahr	103,436
Bulsār (★Bombay)	54,017
Būndi (★48,027)	47,736
Burdwān	167,364
Burhānpur	140,896
• Calcutta (★11,100,000)	3,305,006
Calicut (★546,058)	394,447
Cambay	68,791
Cannanore (★157,797)	60,904
Chākdaha	59,308
Chakradharpur (★44,532)	29,272
Chālisgaon	59,342
Champdāni (★Calcutta)	76,138
Chandannagar (★Calcutta)	101,925
Chandausi	66,970
Chandīgarh (★422,841)	373,789
Chandrapur	115,777
Changanācheri	51,955
Channapatna	50,725
Chāpra	111,564
Chhatarpur	51,959
Chhindwāra	75,178
Chidambaram (★62,543)	55,920
Chikmagalūr	60,582
Chilakalūrupet	61,645
Chīrāla	72,040
Chitradurga	74,580
Chittaranjan (★61,045)	50,748
Chittoor	86,230
Churu (★62,070)	61,811
Cochin (★685,836)	513,249
Coimbatore (★965,000)	704,514
Cooch Behār (★80,101)	62,127
Coonoor (★92,242)	44,750
Cuddalore	127,625
Cuddapah	103,125
Cumbum	50,340
Cuttack (★327,412)	269,950
Dabgram	76,402
Dabhoi	44,357
Daltonganj	51,952
Damoh (★76,758)	75,573
Dānāpur (★Patna)	58,684
Darbhanga	176,301
Darjeeling	57,603
Datia	49,386
Dāvangere	196,621
Dehra Dūn (★293,010)	211,416
Dehri	90,409
Delhi (★7,200,000)	4,884,234
Delhi Cantonment (★Delhi)	85,166
Deoband	51,270
Deoghar (★59,120)	52,904
Deolāli (★Nāsik)	77,666
Deolāli Cantonment (★Nāsik)	57,745
Deoria	55,720
Dewās	83,465
Dhamtari	55,797
Dhānbād (★825,000)	120,221
Dhār	48,870
Dharmapuri	51,223
Dharmavaram	50,969
Dhorāji (★77,716)	76,556
Dhrāngadhra	51,280
Dhubri (★45,580) (1971C)	36,503
Dhule	210,759
Dibrugarh (1971C)	80,348
Dindigul	164,103
Dohad (★82,256)	55,256
Dombivli (★Bombay)	103,222
Dum-Dum (★Calcutta)	33,604
Durg (★Bhilai)	114,637
Durgāpur	311,798
Elūru	168,154
English Bāzār	79,010
Erode (★275,999)	142,252
Etah	53,784
Etāwah	112,174
Faizābād (★143,167)	101,873
Farīdābād New Township (★Delhi)	330,864
Farrukhābād (★160,796)	145,793
Fatehpur	84,831
Fathpur, Rājasthān state	51,084
Fīrozābād	202,338
Fīrozpur (★105,840)	61,162
Gadag	117,368
Gandhidham (★61,489)	61,415
Gandhinagar	62,443
Gangāvathi	58,735
Garden Reach (★Calcutta)	191,107
Gārulia (★Calcutta)	57,061
Gauhāti (★200,377) (1971C)	123,783
Gaya	247,075
Ghāziābād (★287,170)	271,730
Ghāzīpur	60,725
Giridih	65,444
Godhra (★86,228)	85,784
Gonda	70,847

▲ Population of an entire municipality, commune, or district, including rural area.
• Largest city in country.
★ Population or designation of the metropolitan area, including suburbs.
C Census. **E** Official estimate. **UE** Unofficial estimate.

▲ Bevölkerung eines ganzen städtischen Verwaltungsgebietes, eines Kommunalbezirkes oder eines Distrikts, einschliesslich ländlicher Gebiete.
• Grösste Stadt des Landes.
★ Bevölkerung oder Bezeichnung der Stadtregion einschliess lich Vororte.
C Volkszählung. **E** Offizielle Schätzung. **UE** Inoffizielle Schätzung.

Gondal (★66,818)	66,096
Gondia	100,423
Gorakhpur (★307,501)	290,814
Gudivāda	80,198
Gudiyāttam (★80,674)	75,044
Gulbarga	221,325
Guna (★64,659)	60,255
Guntakal	84,599
Guntūr	367,699
Gurgaon (★100,877)	89,115
Guruvayur (★59,467)	17,858
Gwalior (★555,862)	539,015
Hābra (★129,610)	74,434
Hājīpur	62,520
Haldwāni	77,300
Hālisahar (★Calcutta)	95,579
Hānsi	50,365
Hanumāngarh	60,071
Hāpur	102,837
Hardoi	67,259
Hardwār (★145,946)	114,180
Harihar	52,334
Hassan	71,534
Hāthras	92,962
Hazāribāgh	80,155
Hindupur	55,901
Hinganghāt	59,075
Hisār (★137,369)	131,309
Hooghly-Chinsura (★Calcutta)	125,193
Hoshiārpur	85,648
Hospet (★115,351)	90,572
Howrah (★Calcutta)	744,429
Hubli-Dhārwār	527,108
Hyderābād (★2,750,000)	2,187,262
Ichalkaranji	133,751
Imphāl	156,622
Indore (★850,000)	829,327
Itārsi (★69,619)	62,499
Jabalpur (★757,303)	614,162
Jabalpur Cantonment (★Jabalpur)	61,026
Jadabpur (★Calcutta)	251,968
Jagādhri (★Yamunānagar)	43,102
Jagdalpur (★63,632)	51,286
Jagtiāl	53,213
Jaipur (★1,025,000)	977,165
Jālgaon	145,335
Jālna	122,276
Jalpaiguri	61,743
Jamālpur	78,356
Jammu (★223,361)	206,135
Jāmnagar (★317,362)	277,615
Jamshedpur (★669,580)	438,385
Jangaon	70,727
Jaora (★47,548)	47,129
Jaridih Bazar (★101,946)	46,477
Jaunpur	105,140
Jetpur (★63,074)	62,806
Jeypore	53,981
Jhānsi (★284,141)	246,172
Jharia (★Dhanbād)	57,496
Jhārsuguda	54,859
Jīnd	56,748
Jodhpur	506,345
Jorhāt (★70,674) (1971C)	30,247
Jullundur (★441,552)	408,186
Junāgadh (★120,416)	118,646
Kadaiyanallūr	60,306
Kadiri	52,774
Kaithal	58,385
Kākināda	226,409
Kālol (★Ahmadābād)	69,946
Kalyān (★Bombay)	136,052
Kāmārhāti (★Calcutta)	234,951
Kambam	50,340
Kāmthi (★Nāgpur)	67,364
Kānchipuram (★145,254)	130,926
Kānchrāpāra (★Calcutta)	88,798
Kānpur (★1,875,000)	1,481,789
Kānpur Cantonment (★Kānpur)	90,311
Kapūrthala	50,300
Karād	54,364
Kāraikkudi (★100,141)	66,993
Karīmnagar	86,125
Karnāl	132,107
Karūr (★93,810)	72,692
Kāsganj	61,402
Kashīpur	51,773
Katihār (★122,005)	104,781
Kātwa (★44,430)	32,890
Kāvali	48,119
Kayankulam	61,327
Kerkend (★Dhānbād)	75,186
Khadki (Kirkee) (★Pune)	80,797
Khadki Cantonment (★Pune)	80,835
Khāmgaon	61,992
Khammam	98,757
Khandwa	114,725
Khanna	53,761
Kharagpur (★232,575)	150,475
Kharagpur Railway Settlement (★Kharagpur)	82,100
Khargone	52,749
Khurja	67,119
Kishanganj	51,790
Kishangarh	62,032
Kolār	65,834
Kolār Gold Fields (★144,385)	77,679
Kolhāpur (★351,392)	340,625
Konnagar (★Calcutta)	51,211
Korba	83,387
Kota	358,241
Kot Kapūra	47,550
Kottagūdem	94,894
Kottayam	64,431
Kovilpatti	63,964
Krishnagiri	48,335
Krishnanagar	98,141
Kulti (★Asansol)	41,323
Kumbakonam (★141,794)	132,832
Kundla (★51,431)	49,740
Kurasia (★53,015)	12,963
Kurichi (★Coimbatore)	48,936
Kurnool	206,362
Lakhīmpur	61,003
Lalitpur	55,756
Lātūr	111,986
Lucknow (★1,060,000)	895,721
Lucknow Cantonment (★Lucknow)	59,614
Ludhiāna	607,052
Machilīpatnam (Bandar)	138,530
Madanapalle	54,938
Madgaon (Margao) (★64,858)	53,076
Madras (★4,475,000)	3,276,622
Madurai (★960,000)	820,891
Mahbūbnagar	87,503
Mahuva (★56,072)	53,625
Mainpuri	58,928
Mālegaon	245,883
Māler Kotla	65,756
Malkajgiri (★Hyderābād)	65,776
Mandasor	77,603
Mandya	100,285
Mangalore (★306,078)	172,252
Mango (★Jamshedpur)	67,284
Manjeri	53,959
Manmād	51,439
Mannārgudi	51,738
Mathura (★160,995)	147,493
Maunath Bhanjan	86,326
Māyūram	67,675
Meerut (★536,615)	417,395
Meerut Cantonment (★Meerut)	94,210
Mehsāna (★73,024)	72,872
Melappālaiyam (★Tirunelveli)	57,683
Mettuppālaiyam	59,537
Mhow (★76,037)	70,130
Midnapore	86,118
Miraj (★Sāngli)	105,455
Mirzāpur	127,787
Modinagar (★87,665)	78,243
Moga	80,272
Mokameh	51,047
Monghyr	129,260
Morādābād (★345,350)	330,051
Morena	69,864
Mormugão	69,684
Morvi	73,327
Motīhāri (★63,212)	57,911
Muktsar	50,941
Murwāra (★123,017)	77,862
Muzaffarnagar	171,816
Muzaffarpur	190,416
Mysore (★479,081)	441,754
Nabadwīp (★129,800)	109,108
Nadiād	142,689
Nāgappattinam (★90,650)	82,828
Nāgaur	48,005
Nāgda	56,602
Nāgercoil	171,648
Nagīna	50,405
Nāgpur (★1,302,066)	1,219,461
Naihāti (★Calcutta)	114,607
Najībābād	55,109
Nalgonda	62,458
Nānded	191,269
Nandurbār	65,394
Nandyāl	88,185
Nangi (★Calcutta)	54,035
Narasapur	46,033
Narasaraopet	67,032
Nāsik (★429,034)	262,428
Navsāri (★129,266)	106,793
Nawābganj (★62,216)	51,518
Neemuch (★68,853)	65,860
Nellore	237,065
NEW DELHI (★Delhi)	273,036
Neyveli (★98,866)	88,000
Nizāmābād	183,061
North Barrackpore (★Calcutta)	81,758
North Dum-Dum (★Calcutta)	96,418
Nowgong (1971C)	56,537
Ongole	85,302
Ootacamund	78,277
Orai	66,397
Outer Burnpur (★Asansol)	86,803
Pālakollu	46,146
Pālanpur	61,262
Pālayankottai (★Tirunelveli)	87,302
Pālghāt (★117,986)	111,245
Pāli	91,568
Pallavaram (★Madras)	83,901
Palni (★68,389)	64,444
Palwal	47,328
Panaji (Panjim) (★77,226)	43,165
Pānchur (★Calcutta)	51,223
Pandharpur	64,380
Pānihāti (★Calcutta)	205,718
Pānīpat	137,927
Panruti	43,042
Paramagudi	61,149
Parbhani	109,364
Parli	48,946
Pātan	79,196
Pathānkot	110,039
Patiāla (★206,254)	205,141
Patna (★1,025,000)	776,371
Pattukkottai	49,484
Periyakulam	44,310
Petlād	47,020
Phagwāra (★75,961)	72,499
Pīlībhīt	88,548
Pimpri-Chinchwad (★Pune)	220,966
Pollāchi (★114,971)	82,354
Pondicherry (★251,420)	162,636
Ponmalai (★Tiruchchirāppalli)	55,995
Ponnāni	43,226
Ponnūru Nidubrolu	50,206
Porbandar (★133,307)	115,182
Port Blair	49,634
Proddatūr	107,070
Pudukkottai	87,952
Pune (Poona) (★1,775,000)	1,203,351
Pune Cantonment (★Pune)	85,986
Puri	100,942
Purnea (★109,875)	91,144
Purūlia	73,904
Quilon (★167,598)	137,943
Rabkavi Banhatti	51,693
Rāe Bareli	89,697
Rāichūr	124,762
Raiganj (★66,705)	60,343
Raigarh (★69,791)	68,060
Raipur	338,245
Rājahmundry (★268,370)	203,358
Rājapālaiyam	101,640
Rajhara-Jharandalli	55,307
Rājkot	445,076
Rāj-Nāndgaon	86,367
Rājpur (★60,734)	43,985
Rājpura	58,645
Rāmanāthapuram	45,719
Rāmgarh (★65,268)	41,257
Rāmpur	204,610
Rānāghāt (★83,744)	58,356
Rānchī (★502,771)	489,626
Rānībennur	58,118
Rānīganj (★119,101)	48,702
Ratlām (★155,578)	142,319
Ratnāgiri	47,036
Raurkela (★322,610)	206,821
Raurkela Civil Township (★Raurkela)	96,000
Rewa	100,641
Rewāri	51,562
Rishra (★Calcutta)	81,001
Robertson Pet (★Kolār Gold Fields)	61,099
Rohtak	166,767
Roorkee (★79,076)	61,851
Sāgar (★207,479)	160,392
Sahāranpur	295,355
Saharsa	57,580
Sahijpur Bogha (★Ahmadābād)	65,327
Salem (★518,615)	361,394
Sambalpur (★162,214)	110,282
Sambhal	108,232
Sāngli (★268,988)	152,339
Sāntipur	82,980
Sardarnagar (★Ahmadābād)	50,128
Sardārshahr (★56,388)	55,473
Sasarām	73,457
Sātāra	83,336
Satna (★96,667)	90,476
Saunda (★99,990)	70,780
Sawai Mādhopur (★59,083)	28,139
Secunderābād Cantonment (★Hyderābād)	135,994
Sehore	52,190
Seoni	54,017
Serampore (★Calcutta)	127,304
Shahdol (★49,631)	44,342
Shāhjahānpur (★205,095)	185,396
Shāmli	51,850
Shikohābād	47,083
Shillong (★174,703)	109,244
Shimoga	151,783
Shivpuri	75,738
Sholāpur (★514,860)	511,103
Shrirampur	55,491
Sidhpur (★52,706)	51,953
Sīkar	102,970
Silchar (1971C)	52,596
Silīguri	154,378
Simla	70,604
Sindri (★Dhānbād)	70,645
Sirsa	89,068
Sītāpur	101,210
Sivakāsi (★83,072)	59,827
Siwān	51,284
Sonīpat	109,369
South Dum-Dum (★Calcutta)	230,266
Sri Gangānagar	123,692
Srīkākulam	68,145
Srikalahasti	51,306
Srīnagar (★606,002)	594,775
Srīrangam (★Tiruchchirāppalli)	64,241
Srīvilliputtūr	61,458
Sūjāngarh	55,546
Sultānpur	48,782
Surat (★913,806)	776,583
Surendranagar (★130,602)	89,619
Tādepallegūdem	62,574
Tādpatri	53,920
Tāmbaram (★Madras)	86,923
Tānda	54,474
Tanuku	53,618
Tellicherry (★98,704)	75,561
Tenāli	119,257
Tenkāsi	49,214
Thāna (★Bombay)	309,897
Thānesar	49,052
Thanjāvūr	184,015
Theni-Allinagaram	53,018
Tindivanam	56,520
Tinsukia (1971C)	54,911
Tiruchchirāppalli (★609,548)	362,045
Tiruchendūr (★68,884)	24,233
Tiruchengodu	53,941
Tirunelveli (★323,344)	128,850
Tirupati	115,292
Tiruppattūr	52,422
Tiruppur (★215,859)	165,223
Tiruvannāmalai	89,462
Tiruvottiyūr (★Madras)	134,014
Titāgarh (★Calcutta)	104,534
Tonk	77,653
Trichūr (★170,122)	77,923
Trivandrum (★520,125)	483,086
Tumkūr	108,670
Tuticorin (★250,677)	192,949
Udaipur	232,588
Udamalpet	54,852
Udgīr	50,564
Ujjain (★282,203)	278,454
Ulhāsnagar (★Bombay)	273,668
Unnāo	75,983
Upleta	54,907
Uttarpara-Kotrung (★Calcutta)	79,598
Valparai	115,452
Vāniyambādi (★75,042)	59,107
Vārānasi (Benares) (★925,000)	708,647
Vasai (Bassein) (★52,398)	34,940
Vellore (★274,041)	174,247
Verāval (★105,307)	85,048
Vidisha	65,521
Vijayawāda (★543,008)	454,577
Vikramasingapuram	49,319
Villupuram	77,091
Viramgām	48,275
Virudunagar	68,047
Vishākhapatnam (★603,630)	565,321
Visnagar	46,631
Vizianagaram	114,806
Warangal	335,150
Wardha	88,495
Yamunānagar (★160,424)	109,304
Yavatmāl	89,071
Yemmiganur	50,701

INDONESIA

1980 C	147,490,298
Ambon (▲208,898)	111,910
Balikpapan (▲280,675)	208,040
Banda Aceh (Kuturaja)	72,090
Bandung (★1,800,000)	1,462,637
Banjarmasin	381,286
Banyuwangi (1961C)	89,303
Bekasi (★Jakarta)	144,290
Bengkulu	64,783
Binjai	76,464
Blitar	78,503
Blora (1971C)	53,504
Bogor (★560,000)	247,409
Bojonegoro (1971C)	52,597
Bukittinggi	70,771
Cianjur	105,660
Cilacap	127,020
Cimahi (1971C)	72,367
Cirebon (★275,000)	223,776
Denpasar	159,230
Depok (★Jakarta)	126,690
Garut	145,620
Gorontalo	97,628
Gresik (1971C)	48,561
• JAKARTA (★7,000,000)	6,503,449
Jambi (▲230,373)	155,760
Jayapura (Sukarnapura) (1976E)	61,054
Jember	171,280
Jombang (1971C)	45,450
Kediri	221,830
Klaten	117,360
Krawang (1971C)	61,361
Kudus	154,480
Kupang (1971C)	52,698
Langsa (1971C)	55,016
Lumajang (1971C)	48,995
Madiun (★180,000)	150,562
Magelang (★160,000)	123,484
Malang	511,780
Manado	217,159
Martapura (1971C)	69,729
Mataram	210,490
Medan (★1,450,000)	1,378,955
Mojokerto	68,849
Padang (▲480,922)	296,680
Padangsidempuan (1971C)	49,090
Pakanbaru (1971C)	186,262
Palangkaraya	60,447
Palembang	787,187
Pangkalpinang	90,096
Parepare	86,450
Pasuruan (★125,000)	95,864
Pati (1971C)	46,037
Payakumbuh	78,836
Pekalongan (★260,000)	132,558
Pemalang (1971C)	77,672
Pematangsiantar	150,376
Ponorogo (1971C)	67,711
Pontianak	304,778
Probolinggo	100,296
Purwakarta (1971C)	49,703
Purwokerto	143,790
Purworejo (1971C)	52,956
Salatiga	85,849
Samarinda (▲264,718)	182,470
Semarang (★1,050,000)	1,026,671
Serang (1971C)	56,263
Sibolga	59,897
Situbondo (1971C)	55,348
Sukabumi (★225,000)	109,994
Surabaya (★2,150,000)	2,027,913
Surakarta (★550,000)	469,888
Tangerang (1971C)	50,893
Tanjungkarang (★375,000)	284,275
Tasikmalaya	192,270
Tebingtinggi	92,087
Tegal (★340,000)	131,728
Tulungagung (1971C)	68,899
Ujung Pandang (Makasar)	709,038
Watampone (1971C)	54,720
Yogyakarta (★480,000)	398,727

IRAN / Īrān

1982 E	40,777,000
Ābādān (1976C)	296,081
Āghā Jārī	64,000
Ahar	52,000
Ahvāz	471,000
Āmol	100,000

▲ Población de un municipio, comuna o distrito entero, incluyendo sus áreas rurales.
• Ciudad más grande de un país.
★ Población o designación de un área metropolitana, incluyendo los suburbios.
C Censo. **E** Estimado oficial. **UE** Estimado no oficial.

▲ Population d'une municipalité, d'une commune ou d'un district, zone rurale incluse.
• Ville la plus peuplée du pays.
★ Population de l'agglomération (ou nom de la zone métropolitaine englobante).
C Recensement. **E** Estimation officielle. **UE** Estimation non officielle.

▲ População de um município, comuna ou distrito, inclusive as respectivas áreas rurais.
• Maior cidade de um país.
★ População ou indicação de uma área metropolitana.
C Censo. **E** Estimativa oficial. **UE** Estimativa não oficial.

Andīmeshk	53,000
Arāk	210,000
Ardabīl	222,000
Bābol	96,000
Bakhtarān	532,000
Bandar-e ʻAbbās	175,000
Bandar-e Anzalī (Bandar-e Pahlavī)	83,000
Bandar-e Māh Shahr	88,000
Behbehān	84,000
Bīrjand	68,000
Bojnūrd	82,000
Borāzjān	53,000
Borūjerd	178,000
Būshehr	121,000
Dezfūl	141,000
Dow Rūd	52,000
Emāmshahr (Shāhrūd)	68,000
Eṣfahān	927,000
Eslāmābād-e Gharb	71,000
Eslamshahr (★Tehrān)	108,000
Fasā	67,000
Gonbad-e Qābūs	75,000
Gorgān	114,000
Hamadān	234,000
Īlām	75,000
Jahrom	68,000
Karaj (★Tehrān)	526,272
Kāshān	110,000
Kāzerūn	63,000
Kermān	239,000
Khomeynīshahr	98,000
Khorramābād	200,000
Khorramshahr (1976C)	146,709
Khvoy	103,000
Mahābād	63,000
Malāyer	84,000
Marāgheh	90,000
Marand	59,000
Marv Dasht	72,000
Mashhad	1,130,000
Masjed Soleymān	116,000
Mīāndowāb	52,000
Mīāneh	57,000
Najafābād	114,000
Neyshābūr	95,000
Orūmīyeh (Reẓā'īyeh)	263,000
Qā'emshahr	92,000
Qazvīn	244,000
Qom	424,000
Qomsheh	67,000
Qūchān	61,000
Rafsanjān	61,000
Rāmhormoz	53,000
Rasht	260,000
Sabzevār	108,000
Sanandaj	172,000
Saqqez	76,000
Sārī	125,000
Semnān	54,000
Shahr Kord	63,000
Shīrāz	800,000
Sīrjān	67,000
Tabrīz	852,000
• TEHRĀN (★6,400,000)	5,734,199
Torbat-e Ḥeydarīyeh	62,000
Varāmīn	51,000
Yazd	193,000
Zābol	58,000
Zāhedān	165,000
Zanjān	175,000
Zarrīn Shahr	69,000

IRAQ / Al ʻIrāq

1985 E	15,584,987
Ad-Dīwānīyah (1970E)	62,300
Al-ʻAmārah	131,758
Al-Baṣrah	616,700
Al-Ḥillah	215,249
Al-Mawṣil	570,926
An-Najaf	242,603
An-Nāṣirīyah	138,842
Ar-Ramādī	137,388
As-Sulaymānīyah	279,424
• BAGHDĀD (★4,000,000)	2,200,000
Baʻqūbah	114,516
Irbīl	333,903
Karbalā'	184,574
Kirkūk (1970E)	207,900

IRELAND / Éire

1981 C	3,443,405
Cork (★185,000)	136,344
• DUBLIN (BAILE ÁTHA CLIATH) (★1,140,000)	525,882
Dún Laoghaire (★Dublin)	54,496
Limerick (★82,000)	60,736
Waterford (★39,636)	38,473

ISLE OF MAN

1986 C	64,282
• DOUGLAS (★28,500)	20,368

ISRAEL / Isrā'īl / Yisra'el

1986 E	4,197,700
Ashdod	69,700
Ashqelon	55,100
Bat Yam (★Tel Aviv-Yafo)	131,200
Be'er Shevaʻ (Beersheba)	115,000
Bene Beraq (★Tel Aviv-Yafo)	102,400
Elat	20,400
Givʻatayim (★Tel Aviv-Yafo)	46,100
Ḥefa (★435,000)	224,600
Herzliyya (★Tel Aviv-Yafo)	67,100
Ḥolon (★Tel Aviv-Yafo)	138,800
Kefar Sava (★Tel Aviv-Yafo)	49,000
Naẓerat (Nazareth) (★73,000)	47,100
Netanya (★Tel Aviv-Yafo)	109,600
Petaḥ Tiqwa (★Tel Aviv-Yafo)	129,300
Ramat Gan (★Tel Aviv-Yafo)	116,000
Reḥovot (★Tel Aviv-Yafo)	70,300
Rishon leẒiyyon (★Tel Aviv-Yafo)	112,300
• Tel Aviv-Yafo (★1,650,000)	322,800
YERUSHALAYIM (★475,000)	457,700

ISRAELI OCCUPIED TERRITORIES

1983 E	1,280,727
Al-Quds (Jerusalem) (★Yerushalayim) (1976E)	90,000
Arīḥā (Jericho) (1967C)	6,829
Arīḥā (Jericho) (1967C)	6,829
Bayt Laḥm (Bethlehem) (1971E)	25,000
Bayt Laḥm (Bethlehem) (1971E)	25,000
• Ghazzah (1967C)	118,272
Khān Yūnis (1967C)	52,997
Nābulus (1971E)	64,000
Nābulus (1971E)	64,000
Rafaḥ (1967C)	49,812

ITALY / Italia

1981 C	56,243,935
Afragola (★Napoli)	57,564
Agrigento	51,931
Alessandria	100,518
Altamura	51,328
Ancona	106,421
Andria	83,319
Arezzo	91,535
Ascoli Piceno	54,193
Asti	76,950
Avellino	56,120
Aversa (★Napoli)	50,525
Bari (★450,000)	370,781
Barletta	83,719
Benevento (▲61,443)	51,900
Bergamo (★340,000)	121,846
Biella	53,572
Bitonto	49,616
Bologna (★530,000)	455,853
Bolzano	104,606
Brescia	206,460
Brindisi	88,947
Busto Arsizio (★Milano)	79,769
Cagliari (★300,000)	232,785
Caltanissetta (▲60,713)	54,000
Campobasso	48,291
Carpi (▲60,507)	52,400
Carrara (★Massa)	68,460
Caserta	66,754
Casoria (★Napoli)	68,355
Castellammare di Stabia (★Napoli)	70,317
Catania (★515,000)	378,521
Catanzaro	100,637
Cava de'Tirreni (★Salerno)	44,600
Cerignola (▲50,682)	44,700
Cesena (▲89,640)	67,600
Chieti	55,207
Cinisello Balsamo (★Milano)	80,323
Civitavecchia	45,836
Cologno Monzese (★Milano)	52,305
Como (★160,000)	95,183
Cosenza (★140,000)	105,806
Cremona	80,758
Crotone	58,281
Cuneo	55,385
Empoli	44,961
Ercolano (★Napoli)	57,495
Ferrara (▲150,265)	123,200
Firenze (★650,000)	453,293
Foggia	157,126
Foligno (▲52,484)	46,200
Forlì (▲109,815)	91,900
Gela	74,789
Genova (Genoa) (★830,000)	760,300
Grosseto (▲69,556)	61,500
Guidonia (★Roma)	50,990
Imola (▲60,010)	47,800
Imperia	41,838
L'Aquila	63,465
La Spezia (★188,000)	115,215
Latina (▲92,674)	81,000
Lecce	91,265
Lecco	51,349
Legnano (★Milano)	49,308
Livorno	175,371
Lucca	91,097
Manfredonia (▲52,674)	45,500
Mantova	60,932
Marsala (▲79,093)	46,300
Massa (★145,000)	65,726
Matera	51,000
Messina	255,890
Mestre (★Venezia)	197,952
• Milano (Milan) (★3,775,000)	1,634,638
Modena	179,933
Molfetta	65,951
Moncalieri (★Torino)	61,740
Monza (★Milano)	122,103
Napoli (Naples) (★2,765,000)	1,210,503
Nicastro (▲63,990)	30,700
Nocera Inferiore (▲47,698)	40,100
Novara	101,635
Padova (★270,000)	231,337
Palermo	699,691
Parma	176,750
Paternò	45,144
Pavia	85,056
Perugia	142,522
Pesaro	90,147
Pescara	131,345
Piacenza	108,177
Pisa	104,334
Pistoia (▲93,516)	83,600
Pordenone	51,369
Portici (★Napoli)	79,259
Potenza	65,388
Pozzuoli (★Napoli)	61,300
Prato (★202,000)	158,797
Ragusa (▲63,898)	53,000
Ravenna (▲137,597)	101,000
Reggio di Calabria	171,324
Reggio nell'Emilia	129,893
Rho (★Milano)	50,740
Rimini	126,949
Rivoli (★Torino)	49,146
ROMA (★3,115,000)	2,830,569
Rovigo	51,708
Salerno (★235,000)	157,243
San Benedetto del Tronto	44,464
San Giorgio a Cremano (★Napoli)	61,721
San Remo (▲60,787)	50,200
San Severo	54,273
Sassari	118,158
Savona (★115,000)	75,069
Scandicci (★Firenze)	53,974
Sesto Fiorentino (★Firenze)	44,869
Sesto San Giovanni (★Milano)	94,738
Siena	61,888
Siracusa	117,689
Taranto	242,774
Teramo (▲50,864)	40,300
Terni	111,401
Tivoli (★Roma)	50,969
Torino (★1,600,000)	1,103,520
Torre del Greco (★Napoli)	102,890
Trapani (▲71,430)	61,900
Trento	98,833
Treviso	87,069
Trieste (Triest)	251,380
Udine (★126,000)	101,264
Varese	90,285
Venezia (Venice) (★415,000)	92,400
Vercelli	51,975
Verona	261,208
Viareggio	58,136
Vicenza	113,931
Vigevano	65,228
Viterbo (▲57,830)	49,400
Vittoria	50,220

IVORY COAST / Côte d'Ivoire

1983 E	9,300,000
• ABIDJAN	1,500,000
Bouaké	275,000
Daloa	70,000
Korhogo	125,000
Man	55,000
YAMOUSSOUKRO	80,000

JAMAICA

1982 C	2,190,357
• KINGSTON (★740,000)	586,930
Montego Bay	70,265
Portmore (★Kingston)	66,976
Spanish Town (★Kingston)	89,097

JAPAN / Nihon

1985 C	121,047,196
Abiko (★Tōkyō)	111,661
Ageo (★Tōkyō)	178,589
Aizu-wakamatsu	118,144
Akashi (★Ōsaka)	263,365
Akishima (★Tōkyō)	97,544
Akita	296,381
Akō	52,376
Amagasaki (★Ōsaka)	509,115
Anan (▲60,752)	48,100
Anjō	133,061
Aomori	294,050
Arao (★Ōmuta)	62,570
Asahikawa	363,630
Asaka (★Tōkyō)	94,432
Ashikaga	167,656
Ashiya (★Ōsaka)	87,127
Atami	49,374
Atsugi (★Tōkyō)	175,596
Ayase (★Tōkyō)	71,146
Beppu	134,782
Bisai (★Nagoya)	56,234
Chiba (★Tōkyō)	788,920
Chichibu	61,013
Chigasaki (★Tōkyō)	185,029
Chikushino (★Fukuoka)	63,242
Chiryū (★Nagoya)	50,506
Chita (★Nagoya)	70,013
Chitose	73,610
Chōfu (★Tōkyō)	191,076
Chōshi (▲87,884)	77,900
Daitō (★Ōsaka)	122,440
Dazaifu (★Fukuoka)	57,737
Ebetsu (★Sapporo)	90,328
Ebina (★Tōkyō)	93,160
Fuchū (★Tōkyō)	201,972
Fuchū	47,751
Fuji (★370,000)	214,451
Fujieda (★Shizuoka)	111,987
Fujiidera (★Ōsaka)	65,257
Fujimi (★Tōkyō)	85,698
Fujinomiya (★Fuji)	112,642
Fujisawa (★Tōkyō)	328,387
Fuji-yoshida	54,796
Fukaya (▲89,123)	71,600
Fukuchiyama (▲65,995)	56,200
Fukui	250,261
Fukuoka (★1,750,000)	1,160,402
Fukushima	270,752
Fukuyama	360,264
Funabashi (★Tōkyō)	506,967
Fussa (★Tōkyō)	51,481
Gamagōri	85,580
Gifu	411,740
Ginowan	69,206
Gotemba	74,882
Gyōda	79,359
Habikino (★Ōsaka)	111,396
Hachinohe	241,428
Hachiōji (★Tōkyō)	426,650
Hadano (★Tōkyō)	141,806
Hagi	52,741
Hakodate	319,190
Hamada	51,070
Hamakita (▲77,227)	68,000
Hamamatsu	514,118
Hanamaki (▲69,885)	54,500
Handa (★Nagoya)	92,883
Hannō (★Tōkyō)	66,550
Hashima	59,760
Hatogaya (★Tōkyō)	55,424
Hatsukaichi (★Hiroshima)	52,020
Hekinan	63,778
Higashihiroshima (★Hiroshima)	84,718
Higashikurume (★Tōkyō)	110,079
Higashimatsuyama	70,425
Higashimurayama (★Tōkyō)	123,794
Higashiōsaka (★Ōsaka)	522,798
Higashiyamato (★Tōkyō)	69,879
Hikari (★Tokuyama)	49,245
Hikone	94,205
Himeji (★660,000)	452,916
Himi (▲62,110)	52,300
Hino (★Tōkyō)	156,006
Hirakata (★Ōsaka)	382,257
Hiratsuka (★Tōkyō)	229,976
Hirosaki (▲176,082)	134,800
Hiroshima (★1,575,000)	1,044,129
Hita (▲65,730)	57,900
Hitachi	206,075
Hōfu	118,074
Honjō (▲56,492)	49,200
Hōya (★Tōkyō)	91,563
Hyūga	59,159
Ibaraki (★Ōsaka)	250,468
Ichihara (★Tōkyō)	237,618
Ichikawa (★Tōkyō)	397,806
Ichinomiya (★Nagoya)	257,392
Ichinoseki (▲60,942)	49,200
Iida (▲92,402)	73,200
Iizuka (★110,000)	81,868
Ikeda (★Ōsaka)	101,682
Ikoma (★Ōsaka)	86,296
Imabari	125,116
Imari (▲62,044)	50,700
Ina (▲59,010)	48,600
Inagi (★Tōkyō)	50,749
Inazawa (★Nagoya)	83,200
Inuyama (★Nagoya)	68,723
Iruma (★Tōkyō)	118,603
Isahaya (▲88,374)	76,600
Ise (Uji-yamada)	105,455
Isehara (★Tōkyō)	77,765
Isesaki	112,458
Ishinomaki	122,674
Itami (★Ōsaka)	182,731
Itō	70,195
Iwaki (Taira) (1984C)	350,566
Iwakuni	111,831
Iwamizawa (▲81,665)	73,100
Iwata	80,811
Iwatsuki (★Tōkyō)	100,904
Izumi (★Sendai)	124,216
Izumi (★Ōsaka)	137,633
Izumi-ōtsu (★Ōsaka)	67,757
Izumi-sano (★Ōsaka)	91,563
Izumo (▲80,748)	68,000
Joetsu	130,659
Jōyō (★Ōsaka)	81,849
Kadoma (★Ōsaka)	140,545
Kaga	68,631
Kagoshima	530,496
Kainan (★Wakayama)	50,779
Kaizuka (★Ōsaka)	79,591
Kakamigahara	124,464
Kakegawa (▲68,723)	55,600
Kakogawa (★Ōsaka)	227,312
Kamagaya (★Tōkyō)	85,705
Kamaishi	60,005
Kamakura (★Tōkyō)	175,490
Kameoka (▲76,206)	66,500
Kamifukuoka (★Tōkyō)	57,641
Kanazawa	430,480
Kanoya (▲76,031)	60,200
Kanuma (▲88,079)	73,200
Karatsu (▲78,746)	70,100
Kariya (★Nagoya)	112,402
Kasai	52,107
Kasaoka (▲60,594)	53,500
Kashihara (★Ōsaka)	112,881
Kashiwa (★Tōkyō)	273,130
Kashiwara (★Ōsaka)	73,251
Kashiwazaki (▲86,020)	73,350
Kasuga (★Fukuoka)	75,554
Kasugai (★Nagoya)	256,991
Kasukabe (★Tōkyō)	171,889
Katano (★Ōsaka)	64,205
Katsuta	102,768
Kawachi-nagano (★Ōsaka)	91,261
Kawagoe (★Tōkyō)	285,435
Kawaguchi (★Tōkyō)	403,012
Kawanishi (★Ōsaka)	136,376
Kawasaki (★Tōkyō)	1,088,611
Kesennuma	68,139
Kimitsu (▲84,311)	71,900
Kiryū	131,268
Kisarazu	120,201
Kishiwada (★Ōsaka)	185,735
Kitakyūshū (★1,525,000)	1,056,400
Kitami	107,280
Kitamoto (★Tōkyō)	58,114
Kiyose (★Tōkyō)	65,067
Kōbe (★Ōsaka)	1,410,843
Kōchi	312,253
Kodaira (★Tōkyō)	158,673
Kōfu	202,405
Koga (★Tōkyō)	57,539
Koganei (★Tōkyō)	104,684
Kokubunji (★Tōkyō)	95,469
Komae (★Tōkyō)	73,646
Komaki (★Nagoya)	113,284
Komatsu	106,047
Kōnan (★Nagoya)	92,048

▲ Population of an entire municipality, commune, or district, including rural area.
• Largest city in country.
★ Population or designation of the metropolitan area, including suburbs.
C Census. **E** Official estimate. **UE** Unofficial estimate.

▲ Bevölkerung eines ganzen städtischen Verwaltungsgebietes, eines Kommunalbezirkes oder eines Distrikts, einschliesslich ländlicher Gebiete.
• Grösste Stadt des Landes.
★ Bevölkerung oder Bezeichnung der Stadtregion einschliess lich Vororte.
C Volkszählung. **E** Offizielle Schätzung. **UE** Inoffizielle Schätzung.

Kōnosu (★Tōkyō)	60,565
Kōriyama	301,672
Koshigaya (★Tōkyō)	253,483
Kudamatsu (★Tokuyama)	54,446
Kuki (★Tōkyō)	58,635
Kumagaya	143,496
Kumamoto	555,722
Kunitachi (★Tōkyō)	64,881
Kurashiki	413,644
Kure (★Hiroshima)	226,489
Kuroiso	49,742
Kurume	222,848
Kusatsu (★Ōsaka)	87,543
Kushiro	214,545
Kuwana (★Nagoya)	94,730
Kyōto (★Ōsaka)	1,479,125
Machida (★Tōkyō)	321,182
Maebashi	277,319
Maizuru	98,779
Marugame	74,273
Matsubara (★Ōsaka)	136,455
Matsudo (★Tōkyō)	427,479
Matsue	140,000
Matsumoto	197,348
Matsusaka (▲116,886)	104,200
Matsuyama	426,646
Mihara	85,975
Miki (★Ōsaka)	74,527
Minō (★Ōsaka)	114,770
Misato (★Tōkyō)	107,963
Mishima (★Numazu)	99,600
Mitaka (★Tōkyō)	166,175
Mito	228,987
Miyako	61,654
Miyakonojō (▲132,099)	107,600
Miyazaki	279,118
Mobara (▲76,931)	66,500
Moriguchi (★Ōsaka)	159,402
Morioka	235,469
Mukō (★Ōsaka)	52,216
Munakata	60,972
Muroran (★195,000)	136,209
Musashimurayama (★Tōkyō)	60,930
Musashino (★Tōkyō)	138,810
Mutsu	49,292
Nabari	56,474
Nagahama	55,532
Nagano	336,967
Nagaoka	183,756
Nagaokakyō (★Ōsaka)	75,242
Nagareyama (★Tōkyō)	124,682
Nagasaki	449,382
Nagoya (★4,800,000)	2,116,350
Naha	303,680
Nakama (★Kitakyūshū)	50,294
Nakatsu (▲66,258)	58,000
Nanao	50,581
Nara (★Ōsaka)	327,702
Narashino (★Tōkyō)	136,365
Narita	77,178
Naruto (▲64,330)	56,600
Naze	49,764
Neyagawa (★Ōsaka)	258,230
Niigata	475,633
Niihama	132,192
Niitsu (▲63,846)	55,600
Niiza (★Tōkyō)	129,284
Nishinomiya (★Ōsaka)	421,267
Nishio (▲91,930)	81,900
Nobeoka	136,381
Noboribetsu (★Muroran)	58,372
Noda (★Tōkyō)	105,937
Nōgata	64,479
Noshiro (▲59,167)	50,500
Numazu (★495,000)	210,484
Obihiro	162,930
Ōbu (★Nagoya)	66,696
Ōdate (▲71,794)	60,900
Odawara	185,947
Ōgaki	145,909
Ōita	390,105
Ōkawa	47,837
Okaya	61,750
Okayama	572,423
Okazaki	284,996
Okegawa (★Tōkyō)	61,499
Okinawa	101,205
Ōme (★Tōkyō)	110,830
Ōmi-hachiman (★Ōsaka)	63,794
Ōmiya (★Tōkyō)	373,015
Ōmura (▲69,472)	60,800
Ōmuta (★225,000)	159,423
Ōnojō (★Fukuoka)	69,431
Onomichi	100,642
Ōsaka (★16,450,000)	2,636,260
Ōta	133,670
Otaru (★Sapporo)	172,490
Ōtsu (★Ōsaka)	234,547
Owariashi (★Nagoya)	57,415
Oyama (▲134,242)	113,100
Sabae	61,452
Saga	168,254
Sagamihara (★Tōkyō)	482,778
Saijō (▲56,515)	50,400
Saiki	54,709
Sakado (★Tōkyō)	87,586
Sakai (★Ōsaka)	818,368
Sakaide	66,082
Sakata (▲101,392)	85,800
Saku (▲59,975)	48,400
Sakura (★Tōkyō)	109,000
Sakurai	59,011
Sanjō	86,325
Sano	80,753
Sapporo (★1,900,000)	1,542,979
Sasebo	250,635
Sayama (★Tōkyō)	144,366
Seki	64,148
Sendai, Kagoshima pref. (▲71,441)	57,800

▲ Población de un municipio, comuna o distrito entero, incluyendo sus áreas rurales.
• Ciudad más grande de un país.
★ Población o designación de un área metropolitana, incluyendo los suburbios.
C Censo. **E** Estimado oficial. **UE** Estimado no oficial.

Sendai, Miyagi pref. (★1,175,000)	700,248
Sennan (★Ōsaka)	60,062
Seto	124,625
Settsu (★Ōsaka)	86,332
Shibata (▲77,219)	62,800
Shijōnawate (★Ōsaka)	50,354
Shiki (★Tōkyō)	58,935
Shimada (▲72,388)	63,200
Shimizu (★Shizuoka)	242,166
Shimodate (▲63,957)	52,400
Shimonoseki (★Kitakyūshū)	269,167
Shiogama (★Sendai)	61,825
Shizuoka (★975,000)	468,362
Sōka (★Tōkyō)	194,204
Suita (★Ōsaka)	348,946
Suwa	52,330
Suzuka	164,937
Tachikawa (★Tōkyō)	146,531
Tagajō (★Sendai)	54,436
Tagawa	59,730
Tajimi (★Nagoya)	84,829
Takaishi (★Ōsaka)	66,974
Takamatsu	327,001
Takaoka (★220,000)	175,780
Takarazuka (★Ōsaka)	194,273
Takasago (★Ōsaka)	91,434
Takasaki	231,764
Takatsuki (★Ōsaka)	348,783
Takayama	65,033
Takefu	69,148
Tama (★Tōkyō)	122,131
Tamano	76,957
Tanabe (▲70,827)	59,800
Tanashi (★Tōkyō)	71,333
Tatebayashi (▲75,141)	65,500
Tenri (▲69,130)	59,700
Tochigi	86,289
Toda (★Tōkyō)	76,960
Tōkai (★Nagoya)	95,278
Toki	65,308
Tokoname (★Nagoya)	53,077
Tokorozawa (★Tōkyō)	275,165
Tokushima	257,886
Tokuyama (★250,000)	112,638
• TŌKYŌ (★27,700,000)	8,353,674
Tomakomai	158,058
Tondabayashi (★Ōsaka)	102,610
Toride (★Tōkyō)	78,609
Tosu	55,788
Tottori	137,060
Toyama	314,111
Toyoake (★Nagoya)	57,969
Toyohashi (▲322,142)	287,700
Toyokawa	107,430
Toyonaka (★Ōsaka)	413,219
Toyota	308,106
Tsu	150,692
Tsuchiura	120,175
Tsuruga	65,670
Tsuruoka (▲100,199)	87,900
Tsushima (★Nagoya)	58,728
Tsuyama (▲86,835)	77,000
Ube (★230,000)	174,854
Ueda (▲116,178)	102,300
Ueno (▲60,811)	51,800
Uji (★Ōsaka)	165,411
Uozu	49,824
Urasoe	81,612
Urawa (★Tōkyō)	377,233
Urayasu (★Tōkyō)	93,756
Usa (▲52,216)	39,500
Utsunomiya	405,384
Uwajima	71,379
Wakayama (★495,000)	401,357
Wakkanai	51,854
Wakō (★Tōkyō)	55,212
Warabi (★Tōkyō)	70,407
Yachiyo (★Tōkyō)	142,188
Yaizu (★Shizuoka)	108,557
Yamagata	245,159
Yamaguchi (▲124,213)	107,400
Yamato (★Tōkyō)	177,669
Yamato-kōriyama (★Ōsaka)	89,624
Yamato-takada (★Ōsaka)	65,223
Yao (★Ōsaka)	276,397
Yashio (★Tōkyō)	67,635
Yatsushiro (▲108,790)	88,700
Yawata (★Ōsaka)	72,338
Yokkaichi	263,003
Yokohama (★Tōkyō)	2,992,644
Yokosuka (★Tōkyō)	427,087
Yonago	131,794
Yonezawa (▲93,725)	82,800
Yono (★Tōkyō)	71,598
Yotsukaidō (★Tōkyō)	67,007
Yukuhashi (▲65,527)	58,900
Zama (★Tōkyō)	99,994
Zushi (★Tōkyō)	57,656

JERSEY

1981 C	72,970
• SAINT HELIER (★45,000)	24,941

JORDAN / Al Urdunn

1984 E	2,595,100
• 'AMMĀN (★1,250,000)	777,500
Ar Ruṣayfah (★'Ammān)	61,300
Az-Zarqā'	265,700
Irbid	136,200

KAMPUCHEA / Kâmpŭchéa Prâchéathĭpâtéyy

1981 E	5,756,141
• PHNUM PÉNH	400,000

KENYA

1984 E	19,536,000
Eldoret (1979C)	50,503

▲ Population d'une municipalité, d'une commune ou d'un district, zone rurale incluse.
• Ville la plus peuplée du pays.
★ Population de l'agglomération (ou nom de la zone métropolitaine englobante).
C Recensement. **E** Estimation officielle. **UE** Estimation non officielle.

Kisumu	167,100
Machakos	92,300
Meru (1979C)	72,049
Mombasa	425,600
• NAIROBI	1,103,600
Nakuru	101,700

KIRIBATI

1978 C	56,213
BAIRIKI	1,956
• Bikenibeu	3,971

KOREA, NORTH / Chosŏn-minjujuŭi-inmīn-konghwaguk

1981 E	18,317,000
Ch'ŏngjin	490,000
Haeju (1967E)	115,000
Hamhŭng (1970E)	150,000
Hŭngnam (1976E)	260,000
Kaesŏng (1976E)	240,000
Kimch'aek (Sŏngjin) (1967E)	265,000
Namp'o (1967E)	130,000
• P'YONGYANG (★1,600,000) (1980E)	1,283,000
Sinŭiju (1970E)	300,000
Songnim (1944C)	53,035
Wŏnsan (1970E)	350,000

KOREA, SOUTH / Taehan-min'guk

1983 E	39,951,000
Andong (▲111,152) (1982E)	93,000
Anyang (★Sŏul) (1982E)	274,093
Bucheon (★Sŏul)	340,000
Changwŏn (1982E)	130,862
Chech'on (▲96,343) (1982E)	66,700
Cheju (▲182,005) (1982E)	99,200
Chinhae (1982E)	122,864
Chinju	219,000
Ch'ŏnan (▲137,143) (1982E)	96,300
Ch'ŏngju	305,000
Chŏngŭp (▲66,009) (1980C)	45,200
Chŏnju (1982E)	294,549
Ch'unch'ŏn (1982E)	162,373
Ch'ungju (▲119,563) (1982E)	83,100
Ch'ungmu (1982E)	81,010
Inch'ŏn (★Sŏul) (1985C)	1,387,000
Iri (▲177,770) (1982E)	147,600
Kangnŭng (▲123,159) (1982E)	80,900
Kimch'ŏn (▲78,542) (1982E)	59,400
Kimhae (1982E)	72,741
Kumi (1982E)	118,593
Kŭmsŏng (1982E)	60,251
Kunsan (1982E)	175,700
Kwangju	843,000
Kwangmyŏng (★Sŏul) (1982E)	191,431
Kyŏngju (▲127,948) (1982E)	76,500
Masan	424,000
Mokp'o	228,000
Namwŏn (▲59,660) (1982E)	41,200
P'ohang (▲245,000)	200,500
Pusan (1985C)	3,517,000
P'yŏngt'aek (1980C)	60,842
Samch'ŏnp'o (▲72,741) (1982E)	43,700
Sangju (▲48,979) (1980C)	26,200
Sŏgwipo (1982E)	79,260
Sŏkch'o (1982E)	71,083
Songjŏng (▲50,800) (1980C)	32,300
Sŏngnam (★Sŏul)	417,000
Songtan (1982E)	64,470
• SŎUL (★13,400,000) (1985C)	9,646,000
Sunch'ŏn (▲116,323) (1982E)	78,100
Suwŏn (★Sŏul)	374,000
T'aebaek (1982E)	115,008
Taegu (1985C)	2,031,000
Taejŏn	800,000
Tongduchŏn (1982E)	67,763
Tonghae (1982E)	101,746
Ŭijŏngbu (★Sŏul) (1982E)	141,147
Ulsan (▲510,000)	345,700
Wŏnju (1982E)	143,546
Yŏngch'ŏn (1982E)	55,280
Yŏngju (▲84,769) (1982E)	60,800
Yŏsu (1982E)	172,681

KUWAIT / Al-Kuwayt

1985 C	1,697,301
Abraq Khīṭān (★Al-Kuwayt)	45,120
Al-Aḥmadī (★285,000)	26,899
Al-Farwānīyah (★Al-Kuwayt)	68,701
Al-Fuḥayḥīl (★Al-Aḥmadī)	50,081
Al-Jahrah (★Al-Kuwayt)	111,222
• AL-KUWAYT (★1,375,000)	44,335
As-Sālimīyah (★Al-Kuwayt)	153,359
Aṣ-Ṣulaybīyah (★Al-Kuwayt)	51,314
Hawallī (★Al-Kuwayt)	145,126
Qalīb ash-Shuyūkh (★Al-Kuwayt)	114,771
South Khīṭān (★Al-Kuwayt)	69,256
Subahiya (★Al-Aḥmadī)	60,787

LAOS / Lao

1981 E	3,811,000
Savannakhét (1973E)	50,691
• VIANGCHAN (VIENTIANE)	210,000

LEBANON / Al-Lubnān

1982 E	2,637,000
• BAYRŪT (★1,675,000)	509,000
Ṣaydā	105,000
Ṣūr (Tyre) (1970E)	12,500
Ṭarābulus (Tripoli)	198,000

LESOTHO

1976 C	1,213,960
• MASERU	14,686

▲ População de um municipio, comuna ou distrito, inclusive as respectivas áreas rurais.
• Maior cidade de um país.
★ População ou indicação de uma área metropolitana.
C Censo. **E** Estimativa oficial. **UE** Estimativa não oficial.

LIBERIA

1981 E	1,911,000
• MONROVIA	243,243

LIBYA / Lībiyā

1981 E	3,096,000
Al-Bayḍā (Beida)	96,300
Banghāzī	367,600
Misrātah	116,900
• ṬARABULUS (TRIPOLI)	858,500
Ṭubruq (Tobruk)	71,800

LIECHTENSTEIN

1985 E	27,076
• VADUZ	4,927

LUXEMBOURG

1981 C	364,606
Esch-sur-Alzette (★96,000)	25,142
• LUXEMBOURG (★112,000)	78,924

MACAU

1984 E	350,000
• MACAU	350,000

MADAGASCAR / Madagasikara

1982 E	9,230,000
• ANTANANARIVO	700,000
Antsirabe (▲91,000)	48,000
Antsiranana	100,000
Fianarantsoa	120,000
Mahajanga	85,000
Toamasina	100,000
Toliara	55,000

MALAWI / Malaŵi

1981 E	6,123,000
• Blantyre	229,000
LILONGWE	103,000

MALAYSIA

1980 C	13,486,433
Alor Setar	71,682
Batu Pahat	66,022
Butterworth (★George Town)	76,651
George Town (Pinang) (★525,000)	250,578
Ipoh	300,325
Johor Baharu (★Singapore)	249,880
Kelang	196,209
Keluang	51,778
Kota Baharu	170,559
Kota Kinabalu (Jesselton)	59,500
• KUALA LUMPUR (★1,250,000)	937,817
Kuala Terengganu	186,608
Kuantan	136,625
Kuching	74,229
Melaka (Malacca)	88,073
Miri	53,799
Muar (Bandar Maharani)	65,775
Petaling Jaya (★Kuala Lumpur)	218,331
Sandakan	73,144
Seremban	136,252
Sibu	86,860
Taiping	149,292
Telok Anson	49,711

MALDIVES

1985 C	181,453
• MALE	46,334

MALI

1980 E	6,982,000
• BAMAKO	502,000
Kayes	51,000
Mopti	63,000
Ségou	77,000
Sikasso	56,000
Tombouctou (Timbuktu) (1976C)	19,166

MALTA

1985 C	340,907
• VALLETTA (★215,000)	9,440

MARTINIQUE

1982 C	328,566
• FORT-DE-FRANCE (★116,017)	99,844

MAURITANIA / Mauritanie / Mūrītāniyā

1982 C	1,030,700
• NOUAKCHOTT	150,000

MAURITIUS

1984 E	1,023,934
Beau Bassin-Rose Hill (★Port Louis)	93,684
Curepipe (★Port Louis)	64,370
• PORT LOUIS (★415,000)	136,812
Quatre Bornes (★Port Louis)	65,699
Vacoas-Phoenix (★Port Louis)	55,456

MAYOTTE

1978 C	47,246
• DZAOUDZI (★6,979)	4,147

MEXICO / México

1980 C	67,395,826
Acapulco [de Juárez]	301,902
Aguascalientes	293,152
Apatzingán	55,522
Atlixco	53,207
Campeche	128,434
Cancún	33,273
Celaya	141,675

Chihuahua	385,603
Chilpancingo	67,498
Ciudad Chetumal	56,709
Ciudad del Carmen	72,489
• CIUDAD DE MÉXICO (★14,100,000)	8,831,079
Ciudad de Naucalpan de Juárez (★Ciudad de México)	723,723
Ciudad de Valles	65,609
Ciudad Guzmán	60,938
Ciudad Juárez (★El Paso, Tex., U.S.A.)	544,496
Ciudad Madero (★Tampico)	132,444
Ciudad Mante	70,647
Ciudad Obregón	165,572
Ciudad Victoria	140,161
Coatzacoalcos	127,170
Colima	86,044
Córdoba	99,972
Cuernavaca	192,770
Culiacán	304,826
Delicias	65,504
Durango	257,915
Ecatepec de Morelos (★Ciudad de México)	741,821
Ensenada	120,483
Fresnillo	56,066
Garza García (★Monterrey)	81,974
Gómez Palacio (★Torreón)	116,967
Guadalajara (★2,325,000)	1,626,152
Guadalupe (★Monterrey)	370,524
Guanajuato	48,981
Guaymas	54,826
Hermosillo	297,175
Heroica Nogales	65,603
Hidalgo del Parral	75,590
Iguala	66,005
Irapuato	170,138
Jalapa Enríquez	204,594
La Paz	91,453
La Piedad [Cavadas]	47,441
Las Choapas	35,807
León	593,002
Los Mochis	122,531
Matamoros (★Brownsville, Tex., U.S.A.)	188,745
Mazatlán	199,830
Mérida	400,142
Mexicali (★365,000)	341,559
Minatitlán	106,765
Monclova	115,786
Monterrey (★2,015,000)	1,090,009
Morelia	297,544
Navojoa	62,901
Netzahualcóyotl (★Ciudad de México)	1,341,230
Nuevo Laredo (★Laredo, Tex., U.S.A.)	201,731
Oaxaca [de Juárez]	154,223
Ocotlán	48,931
Orizaba (★215,000)	114,848
Pachuca	110,351
Piedras Negras	67,455
Poza Rica de Hidalgo	166,799
Puebla (★1,055,000)	835,759
Puerto Vallarta	38,645
Querétaro	215,976
Reynosa	194,693
Río Bravo	55,236
Salamanca	96,703
Saltillo	284,937
San Luis Potosí (★470,000)	362,371
San Luis Río Colorado	76,684
San Nicolás de los Garzas (★Monterrey)	280,696
Santa Catarina (★Monterrey)	87,673
Soledad Díez Gutiérrez (★San Luis Potosí)	49,173
Tampico (★435,000)	267,957
Tapachula	85,766
Tecomán	46,371
Tehuacán	79,547
Tepic	145,741
Tijuana (★San Diego, Calif., U.S.A.)	429,500
Tlalnepantla (★Ciudad de México)	778,173
Tlaquepaque (★Guadalajara)	133,500
Toluca [de Lerdo]	199,778
Torreón (★575,000)	328,086
Tulancingo	53,400
Tuxpan de Rodríguez Cano	56,037
Tuxtla Gutiérrez	131,096
Uruapan [del Progreso]	122,828
Veracruz (★385,000)	284,822
Villahermosa	158,216
Zacatecas	80,088
Zamora de Hidalgo	86,998
Zapopan (★Guadalajara)	345,390
Zitácuaro	47,520

MONACO

1982 C	27,063
• MONACO (★50,000)	27,063

MONGOLIA / Mongol Ard Uls

1985 E	1,866,300
Darchan	69,800
• ULAANBAATAR	488,200

MONTSERRAT

1980 C	11,606
• PLYMOUTH	1,568

MOROCCO / Al-Magreb

1982 C	20,419,555
Agadir	110,479
Beni-Mellal (1971C)	53,826
• Casablanca (Dar-el-Beida) (★2,250,000)	2,139,204
El-Jadida (Mazagan) (1971C)	55,501
Fès	448,823
Kenitra	188,194
Khouribga	127,181
Ksar-el-Kebir (1971C)	48,262
Larache (1971C)	45,710
Marrakech	439,728
Meknès	319,783
Mohammedia (Fedala)	105,120
Oujda	260,082
RABAT (★850,000)	518,616
Safi	197,309
Salé (★Rabat)	289,391
Tanger (Tangier)	266,346
Taza (1971C)	55,157
Tétouan	199,615

MOZAMBIQUE / Moçambique

1980 C	12,130,000
Beira	230,744
Chimoio	74,372
Inhambane	54,990
• MAPUTO (LOURENÇO MARQUES)	755,300
Nacala	80,426
Nampula	156,185
Quelimane	62,174

NAMIBIA

1984 E	1,507,000
• WINDHOEK	120,000

NAURU / Naoero

1984 E	8,000

NEPAL / Nepāl

1981 C	15,022,839
Bhaktapur	48,472
Birātnagar	93,544
• KATHMANDU (★320,000)	235,160
Lalitpur (★Kathmandu)	79,875

NETHERLANDS / Nederland

1984 E	14,394,600
Alkmaar (★120,000)	83,892
Almelo	62,941
Alphen aan den Rijn	54,560
Amersfoort (★130,000)	86,896
Amstelveen (★Amsterdam)	68,518
• AMSTERDAM (★1,825,000)	676,439
Apeldoorn	144,108
Arnhem (★290,746) (1982E)	128,598
Assen	46,745
Bergen op Zoom	45,568
Breda (★153,517)	118,662
Delft (★'s-Gravenhage)	86,733
Den Helder	63,826
Deventer	64,823
Dordrecht (★199,156)	107,475
Ede (▲86,816)	45,600
Eindhoven (★374,109)	192,854
Emmen (▲91,010)	36,100
Enschede (★248,200)	144,938
Geleen (★177,410)	34,828
Gouda	60,026
Groningen (★206,611)	167,866
Haarlem (★Amsterdam)	152,511
Haarlemmermeer (▲83,428)	11,400
Heerlen (★266,095)	93,283
Helmond	60,582
Hengelo (★Enschede)	76,855
Hilversum (★Amsterdam)	88,417
Hoorn	50,473
IJmuiden (★Amsterdam)	58,287
Kerkrade (★Heerlen)	53,231
Leeuwarden	85,435
Leiden (★176,360)	104,261
Maastricht (★157,329)	113,277
Nieuwegein	53,601
Nijmegen (★233,992)	147,102
Oss	50,086
Ridderkerk (★Rotterdam)	47,124
Rijswijk (★'s-Gravenhage)	49,790
Roosendaal	56,519
Rotterdam (★1,095,000)	555,349
Schiedam (★Rotterdam)	69,849
'S-GRAVENHAGE (THE HAGUE) (★775,000)	445,213
's-Hertogenbosch (★186,946)	89,059
Soest (★Armersfoort)	40,355
Spijkenisse (★Rotterdam)	54,381
Tilburg (★221,684)	154,094
Utrecht (★501,357)	230,414
Venlo (★87,000)	62,935
Vlaardingen (★Rotterdam)	76,466
Vlissingen (Flushing) (▲46,150)	26,500
Zaanstad (★Amsterdam)	128,413
Zeist (★Utrecht)	60,478
Zoetermeer (★'s-Gravenhage)	77,632
Zwolle	87,340

NETHERLANDS ANTILLES / Nederlandse Antillen

1984 E	178,744
• WILLEMSTAD (★130,000) (1981C)	31,883

NEW CALEDONIA / Nouvelle-Calédonie

1983 C	145,368
• NOUMEA (★83,000)	60,112

NEW ZEALAND

1985 E	3,265,300
• Auckland (★860,000)	143,600
Christchurch (★305,000)	161,700
Dunedin (★107,000)	74,500
Hamilton (★103,800)	96,700
Lower Hutt (★Wellington)	62,900
Manukau (★Auckland)	182,800
Napier (★112,700)	50,500
Palmerston North (★69,700)	62,700
Rotorua (★52,100)	39,200
Takapuna (★Auckland)	72,500
Tauranga (★60,300)	42,100
Waitemata (★Auckland)	99,000
WELLINGTON (★342,500)	133,200

NICARAGUA

1981 E	2,823,979
Chinandega	51,684
Granada	64,642
León	92,764
• MANAGUA	644,588
Masaya	54,708

NIGER

1983 E	5,772,000
Maradi	65,100
• NIAMEY	399,100
Zinder	82,800

NIGERIA

1982 E	89,117,500
Aba	210,700
Abakaliki	50,130
Abeokuta	301,000
Ado-Ekiti	253,300
Akure	114,400
Awka	78,360
Bauchi	60,730
Benin City	161,700
Bida (1963C)	55,007
Calabar	122,800
Deba (1963C)	60,679
Ede	216,400
Effon-Alaiye	107,900
Enugu	222,600
Epe	71,090
Gombe	76,000
Gusau	111,400
Ibadan	1,009,400
Ife	209,100
Igboho (1963C)	46,776
Ijebu-Igbo	110,300
Ikare	99,220
Ikerre	172,400
Ikire (1963C)	54,022
Ikirun (1963C)	79,516
Ikorodu (1963C)	81,024
Ikot Ekpene	61,280
Ila (1975E)	155,000
Ilawe-Ekiti (1963C)	80,833
Ilesha	266,700
Ilobu	140,100
Ilorin	335,400
Inisa (1963C)	52,482
Ise-Ekiti (1963C)	45,323
Iseyin	153,100
Iwo	255,100
Jos	145,400
Kaduna (1975E)	202,000
Kano	475,000
Katsina	145,500
Keffi	50,990
Kumo (1963C)	64,878
Lafia	86,320
Lafiagi	50,820
• LAGOS (★3,500,000)	1,404,000
Maiduguri	225,100
Makurdi	86,800
Minna	96,470
Mushin (★Lagos)	234,500
Nguru	69,520
Offa	138,800
Ogbomosho	514,400
Oka	100,900
Ondo	119,500
Onitsha	262,100
Oron	54,940
Oshogbo	336,000
Owerri	52,670
Owo (1963C)	89,693
Oyo	180,700
Port Harcourt	288,900
Sapele	98,110
Shagamu	82,600
Shaki	122,700
Shomolu (★Lagos)	104,100
Sokoto	144,300
Uyo	53,390
Warri	88,840
Zaria	267,300

NIUE

1979 E	3,578
• ALOFI	960

NORWAY / Norge

1983 E	4,122,707
Bergen (★239,000)	207,232
Drammen (★73,000)	50,605
Fredrikstad (★52,000)	27,618
Hammerfest	7,208
Kristiansand	61,834
Narvik	19,080
• OSLO (★720,000)	448,747
Skien (★77,981)	46,734
Stavanger (★132,000)	92,012
Tromsø	47,322
Trondheim	134,652

OMAN / 'Umān

1980 E	891,000
• MASQAṬ	30,000
Maṭrah (1971E)	14,000
• Ṣūr	30,000

PACIFIC ISLANDS, TRUST TERRITORY OF THE

1980 C	132,929
Garapan	2,063
Jarej-Uliga-Delap	8,583
Kolonia	5,549
Koror	6,222

PAKISTAN / Pākistān

1981 C	83,782,000
Abbottābād (★66,000)	32,000
Ahmadpur East	57,000
Bahāwalnagar	74,000
Bahāwalpur (★178,000)	150,000
Bannu (★43,000)	35,000
Campbellpore (★40,000)	26,000
Chārsadda	62,000
Chīchāwatni	50,000
Chiniot	106,000
Chishtiān Mandi	62,000
Daska	56,000
Dera Ghāzi Khān	103,000
Dera Ismāīl Khān (★68,000)	64,000
Drigh Road Cantonment (★Karāchi)	57,000
Faisalabad (Lyallpur)	1,092,000
Gojra	68,000
Gujrānwāla (★654,000)	597,000
Gujrānwāla Cantonment (★Gujrānwāla)	71,000
Gujrāt	154,000
Hāfizābād	83,000
Hyderābād (★833,000)	745,000
Hyderābād Cantonment (★Hyderābād)	50,000
ISLAMABAD (★RAWALPINDI)	201,000
Jacobābād	80,000
Jarānwāla	70,000
Jhang Sadar	195,000
Jhelum (★106,000)	92,000
Kamālia	61,000
Kāmoke	71,000
• Karāchi (★5,150,000)	4,776,000
Karāchi Cantonment (★Karāchi)	203,000
Kasūr	155,000
Khairpur	62,000
Khānewāl	89,000
Khānpur	71,000
Khāriān (★52,000)	16,000
Khushāb (★75,000)	56,000
Kohāt (★78,000)	55,000
Lahore (★2,975,000)	2,685,000
Lahore Cantonment (★Lahore)	237,000
Lārkāna	123,000
Leiah	52,000
Mandi Būrewāla	86,000
Mardān (★148,000)	142,000
Miānwāli	59,000
Mingāora	88,000
Mīrpur Khās	124,000
Multān (★730,000)	694,000
Muzaffargarh	53,000
Nawābshāh	102,000
Nowshera (★75,000)	39,000
Okāra (★154,000)	128,000
Pākpattan	70,000
Peshāwar (★575,000)	500,000
Peshāwar Cantonment (★Peshāwar)	55,000
Quetta (★285,000)	243,000
Rahīmyār Khān (★132,000)	119,000
Rāwalpindi (★1,040,000)	452,000
Rāwalpindi Cantonment (★Rāwalpindi)	354,000
Sādiqābad	64,000
Sāhiwāl (Montgomery)	152,000
Sargodha (★294,000)	235,000
Sargodha Cantonment (★Sargodha)	59,000
Shekhūpura	141,000
Shikārpur	88,000
Siālkot (★296,000)	252,000
Sukkur	193,000
Tando Ādam	63,000
Turbat	52,000
Vihāri	53,000
Wah	122,000
Wazīrābād	63,000

PANAMA / Panamá

1980 C	1,795,012
Balboa (★Panamá)	1,904
Colón (★88,000)	59,840
David	49,472
• PANAMÁ (★625,000)	389,172
San Miguelito (★Panamá)	156,611

PAPUA NEW GUINEA

1980 C	3,010,727
Lae	61,617
• PORT MORESBY	123,624
Rabaul	14,954

PARAGUAY

1982 C	3,026,165
• ASUNCIÓN (★700,000)	455,517
Fernando de la Mora (★Asunción)	66,810
Lambaré (★Asunción)	61,722
Puerto Presidente Stroessner	39,676
San Lorenzo (★Asunción)	74,632

PERU / Perú

1981 C	17,031,221
Arequipa (★446,942)	108,023
Ayacucho (★69,533)	57,432
Barranco (★Lima)	46,478
Barrio Obrero Industrial (★Lima)	404,856
Breña (★Lima)	112,398

▲ Population of an entire municipality, commune, or district, including rural area.
• Largest city in country.
★ Population or designation of the metropolitan area, including suburbs.
C Census. **E** Official estimate. **UE** Unofficial estimate.

▲ Bevölkerung eines ganzen städtischen Verwaltungsgebietes, eines Kommunalbezirkes oder eines Distrikts, einschliesslich ländlicher Gebiete.
• Grösste Stadt des Landes.
★ Bevölkerung oder Bezeichnung der Stadtregion einschliess lich Vororte.
C Volkszählung. **E** Offizielle Schätzung. **UE** Inoffizielle Schätzung.

Cajamarca	62,259
Callao (★Lima)	264,133
Cerro de Pasco (★66,373)	55,597
Chiclayo (★279,527)	213,095
Chimbote	223,341
Chorrillos (★Lima)	141,881
Chosica	65,139
Cuzco (★184,550)	89,563
Huacho	43,398
Huancayo (★164,954)	84,845
Huánuco	61,812
Ica	114,786
Iquitos	178,738
Jesús María (★Lima)	83,179
Juliaca	87,651
La Victoria (★Lima)	270,778
• LIMA (★4,608,010)	371,122
Lince (★Lima)	80,456
Magdalena Nueva (★Lima)	55,535
Miraflores (★Lima)	103,453
Pisco	55,604
Piura (★207,934)	144,609
Pucallpa	112,263
Pueblo Libre (★Lima)	83,985
Puno	67,397
Rímac (★Lima)	184,484
San Isidro (★Lima)	71,203
Sullana	89,037
Surco (★Lima)	146,636
Surquillo (★Lima)	134,158
Tacna	97,173
Talara	57,351
Trujillo (★354,301)	202,469
Tumbes	47,936
Vitarte (★Lima)	145,504

PHILIPPINES / Pilipinas

1980 C	48,098,460
Angeles	188,834
Antipolo (▲68,912)	60,000
Bacolod	262,415
Bacoor (★Manila)	90,364
Baguio	119,009
Baliuag	70,555
Biñan (★Manila)	83,684
Binangonan	80,989
Bislig (▲81,615)	40,000
Bocaue	49,693
Butuan (▲172,489)	69,600
Cagayan de Oro (▲227,312)	51,300
Cainta (★Manila)	59,025
Calamba (▲121,175)	41,400
Caloocan (★Manila)	467,816
Carmona (★Manila)	65,014
Cavite (★175,000)	87,666
Cebu (★600,000)	490,281
Cotabato (▲83,871)	61,600
Dagupan	98,344
Davao (▲610,375)	270,600
Dumaguete	83,411
General Santos (Dadiangas) (▲149,396)	58,900
Guagua	72,609
Iloilo	244,827
Isabela (Basilan) (▲49,891)	13,200
Jolo	52,429
Lapu-Lapu (Opon)	98,723
Las Piñas (★Manila)	136,514
Legazpi (▲99,766)	42,600
Lucena	107,880
Makati (★Manila)	372,631
Malabon (★Manila)	191,001
Malolos	95,699
Mandaluyong (★Manila)	205,366
Mandaue (★Cebu)	110,590
Mangaldan	50,434
• MANILA (★6,800,000)	1,630,485
Marawi	53,812
Marikina (★Manila)	211,613
Meycauayan (★Manila)	83,579
Muntinglupa (★Manila)	136,679
Naga	90,712
Navotas (★Manila)	126,146
Olongapo	156,430
Parañaque (★Manila)	208,552
Pasay (★Manila)	287,770
Pasig (★Manila)	268,570
Quezon City (★Manila)	1,165,865
San Fernando	110,891
San Juan del Monte (★Manila)	130,088
San Pablo (▲131,655)	48,000
San Pedro	74,556
Santa Cruz	60,620
Santa Rosa (★Manila)	64,325
Tacloban	102,523
Tagig (★Manila)	134,137
Valenzuela (★Manila)	212,363
Zamboanga (▲343,722)	69,600

PITCAIRN

1986 C	70
• ADAMSTOWN	64

POLAND / Polska

1984 E	37,063,000
Będzin (★Katowice)	77,100
Biała Podlaska	45,600
Białystok	245,400
Bielsko-Biała	174,100
Bydgoszcz	361,400
Bytom (Beuthen) (★Katowice)	239,200
Chełm	59,400
Chorzów (★Katowice)	144,200
Częstochowa	246,600
Dąbrowa Górnicza (★Katowice)	136,800
Dzierżoniów (Reichenbach) (★88,000)	37,900
Elbląg (Elbing)	117,000
Gdańsk (Danzig) (★890,000)	467,200
Gdynia (★Gdańsk)	243,100
Gliwice (Gleiwitz) (★Katowice)	212,500
Głogów	64,200
Gniezno	67,400
Gorzów Wielkopolski (Landsberg an der Warthe)	115,100
Grudziądz	93,900
Inowrocław	70,900
Jastrzębie-Zdrój	101,000
Jaworzno (★Katowice)	95,200
Jelenia Góra (Hirschberg)	90,400
Kalisz	103,500
• Katowice (★2,750,000)	363,300
Kędzierzyn Kozle	71,700
Kielce	200,500
Konin	74,400
Koszalin (Köslin)	99,500
Kraków (★820,000)	740,300
Legnica (Liegnitz)	97,700
Leszno	53,900
Łódź (★1,050,000)	849,400
Łomża	49,300
Lubin	72,500
Lublin (★380,000)	324,100
Mysłowice (★Katowice)	86,500
Nowy Sącz	69,700
Olsztyn (Allenstein)	147,100
Opole (Oppeln)	124,000
Ostrowiec Świętokrzyski	71,300
Ostrów Wielkopolski	67,100
Pabianice (★Łódź)	72,600
Piekary Śląskie (★Katowice)	67,800
Piła (Schneidemühl)	66,300
Piotrków Trybunalski	78,200
Płock	114,500
Poznań (★660,000)	574,100
Pruszków (★Warszawa)	52,600
Przemyśl	64,900
Puławy	49,300
Racibórz (Ratibor)	59,800
Radom	213,500
Ruda Śląska (★Katowice)	164,600
Rybnik	135,500
Rzeszów	138,000
Siedlce	62,900
Siemianowice Śląskie (★Katowice)	80,900
Słupsk (Stolp) (1983E)	90,600
Sopot (★Gdańsk)	51,500
Sosnowiec (★Katowice)	255,000
Stalowa Wola	62,900
Starachowice	54,300
Stargard Szczeciński (Stargard in Pommern)	64,600
Świdnica (Schweidnitz)	60,300
Świętochłowice (★Katowice)	61,000
Świnoujście (Swinemünde)	43,900
Szczecin (Stettin) (★440,000)	390,800
Tarnów	113,200
Tarnowskie Góry (★Katowice)	72,200
Tczew	57,500
Tomaszów Mazowiecki	66,100
Toruń	186,200
Tychy (★Katowice)	181,800
Wałbrzych (Waldenburg) (★205,000)	138,000
WARSZAWA (★2,175,000)	1,649,000
Włocławek	115,300
Wodzisław Śląski	107,700
Wrocław (Breslau)	636,000
Zabrze (Hindenburg) (★Katowice)	198,000
Zamość	54,800
Zawiercie	55,700
Zgierz (★Łódź)	54,900
Zielona Góra (Grünberg)	109,400
Żory	61,900

PORTUGAL

1981 C	9,833,014
Amadora (★Lisboa)	95,518
Barreiro (★Lisboa)	50,863
Braga	63,033
Coimbra	74,616
• LISBOA (★2,250,000)	807,167
Ponta Delgada	21,187
Porto (★1,225,000)	327,368
Setúbal	77,885
Vila Nova de Gaia (★Porto)	62,469

PUERTO RICO

1980 C	3,196,520
Arecibo (★160,336)	48,779
Bayamón (★San Juan)	185,087
Caguas (★San Juan)	87,214
Carolina (★San Juan)	147,835
Guaynabo (★San Juan)	65,075
Mayagüez (★200,464)	82,968
Ponce (★232,551)	161,739
• SAN JUAN (★1,775,260)	424,600

QATAR / Qaṭar

1983 E	281,000
• AD-DAWḤAH (DOHA)	190,000

REUNION / Réunion

1982 C	515,798
• SAINT-DENIS (▲109,072)	84,400

ROMANIA / România

1983 E	22,533,074
Alba-Iulia	59,369
Arad	183,774
Bacău	165,655
Baia-Mare	129,719
Bîrlad	66,476
Bistrița	67,311
Botoșani	94,536
Brăila	224,998
Brașov	331,240
• BUCUREȘTI (BUCHAREST) (★2,250,000)	1,995,156
Buzău	126,780
Călărași	63,005
Cluj-Napoca	301,244
Constanța	315,662
Craiova	260,422
Deva	75,161
Drobeta-Turnu-Severin	92,235
Focșani	77,391
Galați	285,077
Giurgiu	62,710
Hunedoara	87,001
Iași	305,598
Lugoj	51,763
Mediaș	70,933
Oradea	206,206
Petroșani (★74,000)	47,289
Piatra Neamț	102,584
Pitești	149,684
Ploiești (★300,000)	229,915
Reșița	101,902
Rîmnicu-Vîlcea	86,615
Roman	67,962
Satu-Mare	124,691
Sfîntu-Gheorghe	62,355
Sibiu	172,117
Slatina	68,525
Suceava	85,250
Timișoara	303,499
Tîrgoviște	82,034
Tîrgu-Jiu	81,488
Tîrgu-Mureș	154,506
Tulcea	79,290
Turda	59,695
Vaslui	57,571
Zalău	50,108

RWANDA

1983 E	5,762,000
• KIGALI	181,600

SAINT CHRISTOPHER-NEVIS

1980 C	44,404
• BASSETERRE	14,725
Charlestown	1,771

SAINT HELENA

1976 C	5,147
• JAMESTOWN	1,516

SAINT LUCIA

1984 C	134,006
• CASTRIES	50,798

SAINT PIERRE AND MIQUELON / Saint-Pierre-et-Miquelon

1982 C	6,041
• SAINT-PIERRE	5,371

SAINT VINCENT AND THE GRENADINES

1984 E	108,748
• KINGSTOWN (★27,948)	18,378

SAN MARINO

1980 E	21,537
• SAN MARINO	4,623

SAO TOME AND PRINCIPE / São Tomé e Príncipe

1970 C	73,631
• SÃO TOMÉ	17,380

SAUDI ARABIA / Al-ʿArabīyah as-Suʿūdīyah

1981 E	9,320,000
Abhā (1974C)	30,150
Ad-Dammām (1980E)	200,000
Al-Hufūf (1974C)	101,271
Al-Khubar (1974C)	48,817
Al-Madīnah (Medina) (1980E)	290,000
Al-Mubarraz (1974C)	54,325
AR-RIYĀD (RIYADH)	1,250,000
Aṭ-Ṭā'if (1980E)	300,000
Buraydah (1974C)	69,940
Ḥā'il (1974C)	40,502
• Jiddah	1,300,000
Khamīs Mushayt (1974C)	49,581
Makkah (Mecca) (1980E)	550,000
Najran (1974C)	47,501
Tabūk (1974C)	74,825

SENEGAL / Sénégal

1982 E	6,038,000
• DAKAR	1,341,000
Diourbel	64,913
Kaolack	125,776
Saint-Louis	107,072
Thiès	139,170
Ziguinchor	84,104

SEYCHELLES

1984 E	64,718
• VICTORIA	23,000

SIERRA LEONE

1979 C	3,381,000
• FREETOWN (★375,000)	300,000
Koindu (1974C)	75,800

SINGAPORE

1986 E	2,586,200
• SINGAPORE (★2,760,000)	2,586,200

SOLOMON ISLANDS

1978 E	212,868
• HONIARA	16,125

SOMALIA / Somaliya

1983 E	5,269,000
Berbera	65,000
Hargeysa	150,000
Kismaayo	70,000
Marka	100,000
• MUQDISHO	600,000

SOUTH AFRICA / Suid-Afrika

1980 C	24,208,140
Alexandra (★Johannesburg)	56,460
Atteridgeville-Saulsville (★Pretoria)	89,980
Bellville (★Cape Town)	65,720
Benoni (★Johannesburg)	68,500
Bloemfontein (★235,000)	102,600
Bloemfontein (black township) (★Bloemfontein)	91,020
Boksburg (★Johannesburg)	108,680
CAPE TOWN (KAAPSTAD) (★1,790,000)	859,940
Carletonville (★122,740)	100,220
Daveyton (★Johannesburg)	91,640
Durban (★1,550,000)	677,760
East London (Oos-Londen) (★320,000)	77,060
Edendale (★Pietermaritzburg)	47,560
Elsies River (★Cape Town)	75,240
Empumalanga (★Durban)	50,660
Evaton (★Vereeniging)	57,440
Galeshewe (★Kimberley)	70,540
Germiston (★Johannesburg)	113,000
Guguleto (★Cape Town)	74,760
• Johannesburg (★3,650,000)	703,980
Katlehong (★Johannesburg)	157,300
Kempton Park (★Johannesburg)	75,880
Kimberley (★145,000)	70,920
Klerksdorp (★205,000)	44,000
Krugersdorp (★Johannesburg)	70,040
Kwa Mashu (★Durban)	117,680
Kwa-Thema (★Johannesburg)	91,200
Kwazakele (★Port Elizabeth)	99,180
Ladysmith (★31,300)	21,880
Madadeni (★Newcastle)	60,940
Mafikeng (★16,000)	6,500
Mamelodi (★Pretoria)	144,000
New Brighton (★Port Elizabeth)	62,600
Newcastle (★155,000)	34,120
Oziweni (★Newcastle)	55,840
Paarl (★Cape Town)	59,140
Parow (★Cape Town)	68,760
Pietermaritzburg (★230,000)	126,300
Port Elizabeth (★690,000)	281,600
PRETORIA (★960,000)	435,100
Randburg (★Johannesburg)	65,840
Randfontein (★Johannesburg)	49,040
Roodepoort-Maraisburg (★Johannesburg)	129,700
Sandton (★Johannesburg)	70,540
Sebokeng (★Vereeniging)	165,080
Shapeville (★Vereeniging)	50,640
Soshanguve (★Pretoria)	63,220
Soweto (★Johannesburg)	868,580
Springs (★Johannesburg)	78,700
Tembisa (★Johannesburg)	195,080
Thabong (★Welkom)	49,520
Uitenhage (★Port Elizabeth)	49,840
Umlazi (★Durban)	190,120
Vanderbijlpark (★Vereeniging)	61,240
Vereeniging (★525,000)	60,680
Vosloosrus (★Johannesburg)	48,100
Walvisbaai (Walvis Bay) (★20,440)	11,600
Welkom (★215,000)	48,380
Westonaria (★Johannesburg)	54,560
Zwide (★Port Elizabeth)	81,580

SOVIET UNION (UNION OF SOVIET SOCIALIST REPUBLICS) / Sojuz Sovetskich Socialističeskich Respublik

1985 E	276,290,000
Abakan	147,000
Achtubinsk	52,000
Ačinsk	120,000
Akt'ubinsk	231,000
Alapajevsk	51,000
Alatyr' (1974E)	46,000
Aleksandrija	93,000
Aleksandrov	65,000
Aleksin	70,000
Alma-Ata (★1,130,000)	1,068,000
Almalyk	114,000
Al'metjevsk	123,000
Alytus	68,000
Amursk	51,000
Andižan	275,000
Andropov (Rybinsk)	251,000
Angarsk	256,000
Angren	122,000
Antracit (★Krasnyj Luč)	68,000
Anžero-Sudžensk	110,000
Apatity	76,000
Archangel'sk	408,000
Arkalyk	66,000
Armavir	168,000
Arsenjev	65,000
Art'om	72,000
Art'omovsk	91,000
Arzamas	105,000
Asbest	82,000

▲ Población de un municipio, comuna o distrito entero, incluyendo sus áreas rurales.
• Ciudad más grande de un país.
★ Población o designación de un área metropolitana, incluyendo los suburbios.
C Censo. **E** Estimado oficial. **UE** Estimado no oficial.

▲ Population d'une municipalité, d'une commune ou d'un district, zone rurale incluse.
• Ville la plus peuplée du pays.
★ Population de l'agglomération (ou nom de la zone métropolitaine englobante).
C Recensement. **E** Estimation officielle. **UE** Estimation non officielle.

▲ População de um municipio, comuna ou distrito, inclusive as respectivas áreas rurais.
• Maior cidade de um país.
★ População ou indicação de uma área metropolitana.
C Censo. **E** Estimativa oficial. **UE** Estimativa não oficial.

Aschabad	356,000
Astrachan'	493,000
Azov	79,000
Baku (★1,935,000)	1,104,000
Balakovo	180,000
Balašicha (★Moskva)	128,000
Balašov	97,000
Balchaš	82,000
Baranoviči	149,000
Barnaul (★635,000)	578,000
Batajsk (★Rostov-na-Donu)	96,000
Batumi	132,000
Bekabad	77,000
Belaja Cerkov'	181,000
Bel'cy	147,000
Belgorod	280,000
Belgorod-Dnestrovskij	52,000
Belogorsk	70,000
Beloreck	73,000
Belovo	117,000
Bendery	122,000
Berd'ansk	130,000
Berdičev	86,000
Berdsk (★Novosibirsk)	75,000
Berezniki	195,000
Bijsk	226,000
Birobidžan	78,000
Blagoveščensk	195,000
Bobrujsk	223,000
Bor (★Gor'kij)	64,000
Borisoglebsk	68,000
Borisov	132,000
Boroviči	63,000
Br'anka (★Stachanov)	64,000
Br'ansk	430,000
Bratsk	240,000
Brest	222,000
Brežnev (1984E)	414,000
Brovary (★Kijev)	67,000
Buchara	209,000
Bud'onnovsk	51,000
Bugul'ma	86,000
Buguruslan	53,000
Bujnaksk	51,000
Buzuluk	80,000
Čajkovskij	78,000
Čapajevsk	86,000
Čardžou	157,000
Čeboksary	389,000
Čechov	56,000
Čel'abinsk (★1,275,000)	1,096,000
Celinograd	262,000
Čeremchovo	73,000
Čerepovec	299,000
Čerkassy	273,000
Čerkessk	102,000
Černigov	278,000
Černogorsk	78,000
Černovcy	244,000
Červonograd	67,000
Chabarovsk	576,000
Charcyzsk (★Doneck)	66,000
Char'kov (★1,865,000)	1,554,000
Chasavjurt	73,000
Cherson	346,000
Chimki (★Moskva)	125,000
Chmel'nickij	217,000
Chodžejli	52,000
Cholmsk	50,000
Čimkent	369,000
Čirčik (★Taškent)	153,000
Čistopol'	65,000
Čita	336,000
Čusovoj	58,000
Daugavpils	124,000
Derbent	80,000
Dimitrov (★Krasnoarmejsk)	62,000
Dimitrovgrad	116,000
Dmitrov	63,000
Dneprodzeržinsk (★Dnepropetrovsk)	271,000
Dnepropetrovsk (★1,560,000)	1,153,000
Dolgoprudnyj (★Moskva)	69,000
Domodedovo (★Moskva)	50,000
Doneck (★2,185,000)	1,073,000
Drogobyč	74,000
Družkovka (★Kramatorsk)	69,000
Dubna	61,000
Dušanbe	552,000
Džalal-Abad	70,000
Džambul	303,000
Džankoj	50,000
Dzeržinsk (★Gor'kij)	274,000
Džezkazgan	102,000
Džizak	85,000
Ečmiadzin (★Jerevan)	51,000
Ekibastuz	119,000
Elektrostal'	148,000
Elista	81,000
Engel's (★Saratov)	177,000
Fastov	54,000
Feodosija	82,000
Fergana	195,000
Fr'azino (★Moskva)	50,000
Frunze	604,000
Gatčina (★Leningrad)	79,000
Georgijevsk	60,000
Georgiu-Dež	53,000
Glazov	94,000
Gomel'	465,000
Gori	61,000
Gor'kij (★1,965,000)	1,399,000
Gorlovka (★710,000)	342,000
Gorno-Altajsk (1974E)	39,000
Gr'azi (1974E)	42,000
Grodno	247,000
Groznyj	393,000
Gubkin	71,000
Gukovo	72,000
Gulistan (1975E)	39,000
Gurjev	145,000
Gus'-Chrustal'nyj	75,000
Iljičovsk (★Odessa)	50,000
Inta	56,000
Irbit	52,000
Irkutsk	597,000
Išim	64,000
Išimbaj	64,000
Iskitim	67,000
Ivano-Frankovsk	210,000
Ivanovo	474,000
Ivantejevka (★Moskva)	51,000
Izmail	89,000
Iz'um	62,000
Jakutsk	180,000
Jalta	86,000
Jangijul'	69,000
Jaroslavl'	626,000
Jefremov	57,000
Jegorjevsk	73,000
Jejsk	76,000
Jelec	116,000
Jelgava	70,000
Jenakijevo (★Gorlovka)	117,000
Jerevan (★1,240,000)	1,133,000
Jessentuki	83,000
Jevpatorija	103,000
Joškar-Ola	231,000
Jurga	89,000
Jūrmala (★Rīga)	60,000
Južno-Sachalinsk	158,000
Kalinin	438,000
Kaliningrad (Königsberg)	385,000
Kaliningrad (★Moskva)	143,000
Kaluga	297,000
Kaluš	65,000
Kamenec-Podol'skij	97,000
Kamensk-Šachtinskij	75,000
Kamensk-Ural'skij	200,000
Kamyšin	116,000
Kanaš	50,000
Kansk	105,000
Kara-Balta	53,000
Karaganda	617,000
Karši	133,000
Kaspijsk	58,000
Kattakurgan	60,000
Kaunas	405,000
Kazan' (★1,100,000)	1,047,000
Kemerovo	507,000
Kentau	58,000
Kerč'	168,000
Kijev (★2,740,000)	2,448,000
Kimry	60,000
Kinel' (1974E)	40,000
Kinešma	104,000
Kirov	411,000
Kirovabad	261,000
Kirovakan	165,000
Kirovo-Čepeck	85,000
Kirovograd	263,000
Kisel'ovsk (★Prokopjevsk)	126,000
Kišin'ov	624,000
Kislovodsk	108,000
Kizel (1974E)	42,000
Klaipėda (Memel)	195,000
Klimovsk (★Moskva)	56,000
Klin	94,000
Klincy	71,000
Kohtla-Järve	77,000
Kokand	166,000
Kokčetav	120,000
Kol'čugino (1974E)	43,000
Kolomna	156,000
Kolomyja	60,000
Kolpino (★Leningrad)	130,000
Kommunarsk (★Stachanov)	124,000
Komsomol'sk-Na-Amure	300,000
Konotop	90,000
Konstantinovka	114,000
Kopejsk (★Čel'abinsk)	100,000
Korkino (1981E)	63,000
Korosten' (1986E)	71,000
Korsakov (1974E)	40,000
Kostroma	269,000
Kotlas	68,000
Kovel'	63,000
Kovrov	153,000
Kramatorsk (★465,000)	192,000
Krasnoarmejsk (★170,000)	67,000
Krasnodar	609,000
Krasnodon	50,000
Krasnogorsk (★Moskva)	86,000
Krasnojarsk	872,000
Krasnokamensk	65,000
Krasnokamsk	57,000
Krasnoturjinsk	64,000
Krasnoufimsk (1974E)	40,000
Krasnoural'sk (1974E)	40,000
Krasnovodsk	57,000
Krasnyj Luč (★235,000)	111,000
Krasnyj Sulin (1974E)	43,000
Kremenčug	224,000
Krivoj Rog	684,000
Kropotkin	72,000
Krymsk (1983E)	50,000
Kstovo (★Gor'kij)	63,000
Kujbyšev (★1,480,000)	1,257,000
Kul'ab	66,000
Kumertau	59,000
Kungur	82,000
Kurgan	343,000
Kurgan-T'ube	51,000
Kursk	420,000
Kustanaj	199,000
Kutaisi	214,000
Kuzneck	97,000
Kyzyl	75,000
Kzyl-Orda	183,000
Labinsk	57,000
Leninabad	150,000
Leninakan	223,000
Leningrad (★5,650,000)	4,329,000
Leninogorsk, Tatarskaja A. S. S. R.	59,000
Leninogorsk, Vostočno-Kazachstanskaja oblast'	68,000
Leninsk-Kuzneckij	138,000
Lida	75,000
Liepāja	112,000
Lipeck	447,000
Lisičansk (★385,000)	122,000
Lobn'a (★Moskva)	58,000
Lozovaja	64,000
L'ubercy (★Moskva)	161,000
Lubny	57,000
Luck	172,000
L'vov	742,000
Lys'va	76,000
Lytkarino (★Moskva)	50,000
Machačkala	301,000
Magadan	142,000
Magnitogorsk	422,000
Majkop	140,000
Makejevka (★Doneck)	451,000
Marganec	54,000
Margilan	123,000
Mary	85,000
Melitopol'	170,000
Meždurečensk	101,000
Miass	160,000
Michajlovka	57,000
Mičurinsk	102,000
Mineral'nyje Vody	74,000
Mingečaur	74,000
Minsk (★1,525,000)	1,472,000
Minusinsk	69,000
Mogil'ov	343,000
Molodečno	84,000
Mončegorsk	61,000
Moršansk (1977E)	50,000
• MOSKVA (MOSCOW) (★12,650,000)	8,408,000
Mozyr'	93,000
Mukačevo	84,000
Murmansk	419,000
Murom	121,000
Mytišči (★Moskva)	151,000
Nachodka	150,000
Nal'čik	227,000
Namangan	275,000
Naro-Fominsk	58,000
Narva	79,000
Navoi	99,000
Nazarovo	60,000
Nebit-Dag	81,000
Neftejugansk	78,000
Neftekamsk	90,000
Ner'ungri	57,000
Nevinnomyssk	114,000
Nežin	79,000
Nikolajev	486,000
Nikol'skij	60,000
Nikopol'	155,000
Nižnekamsk	170,000
Nižnevartovsk	190,000
Nižnij Tagil	419,000
Noginsk	121,000
Nojabr'sk	60,000
Noril'sk	180,000
Novaja Kachovka	51,000
Novgorod	220,000
Novoaltajsk (★Barnaul)	50,000
Novočeboksarsk	103,000
Novočerkassk	186,000
Novodvinsk	50,000
Novograd-Volynskij	51,000
Novokujbyševsk (★Kujbyšev)	110,000
Novokuzneck	577,000
Novomoskovsk, Dnepropetrovsk oblast'	74,000
Novomoskovsk, Tula oblast' (★365,000)	147,000
Novopolock	84,000
Novorossijsk	175,000
Novošachtinsk	106,000
Novosibirsk (★1,545,000)	1,393,000
Novotroick	103,000
Novovolynsk	52,000
Novyj Urengoj	61,000
Nukus	139,000
Obninsk	91,000
Odessa (★1,190,000)	1,126,000
Odincovo (★Moskva)	116,000
Okt'abr'skij	102,000
Omsk (★1,130,000)	1,108,000
Ordžonikidze	303,000
Orechovo-Zujevo (★205,000)	136,000
Orenburg	519,000
Or'ol	328,000
Orša	119,000
Orsk	266,000
Oš	199,000
Osinniki	63,000
Panevėžys	116,000
Pärnu	53,000
Partizansk (1974E)	49,000
P'atigorsk	118,000
Pavlodar	315,000
Pavlograd	119,000
Pavlovo	71,000
Pavlovskij Posad	71,000
Pečora	62,000
Penza	527,000
Perm' (★1,125,000)	1,056,000
Pervomajsk	77,000
Pervoural'sk	136,000
Petrodvorec (★Leningrad)	77,000
Petropavlovsk	226,000
Petropavlovsk-Kamčatskij	245,000
Petrozavodsk	255,000
Pinsk	109,000
Podol'sk (★Moskva)	208,000
Polevskoj	69,000
Polock	79,000
Poltava	302,000
Poti (1977E)	54,000
Priluki	71,000
Prochladnyj	52,000
Prokopjevsk (★410,000)	274,000
Prževal'sk	60,000
Pskov	194,000
Puškin (★Leningrad)	91,000
Puškino	74,000
Ramenskoje (★Moskva)	85,000
R'azan'	494,000
Razdan	52,000
Rečica	69,000
Reutov (★Moskva)	66,000
Revda	65,000
Rīga (★970,000)	883,000
Romny	53,000
Roslavl'	60,000
Rossoš'	52,000
Rostov-na-Donu (★1,125,000)	986,000
Roven'ki	67,000
Rovno	221,000
Rubcovsk	165,000
Rubežnoje (★Lisičansk)	69,000
Rudnyj	116,000
Rustavi (★Tbilisi)	143,000
Ruzajevka	52,000
Rybnica	53,000
Ržev	70,000
Šachtinsk	59,000
Šacht'orsk (★Torez)	72,000
Šachty	221,000
Šadrinsk	86,000
Safonovo	55,000
Salavat	149,000
Sal'sk	61,000
Samarkand	371,000
Saran'	62,000
Saransk	307,000
Sarapul	110,000
Saratov (★1,145,000)	899,000
Ščekino	70,000
Ščelkovo (★Moskva)	106,000
Ščučinsk	52,000
Šeki (Nucha)	53,000
Semipalatinsk	317,000
Serov	102,000
Serpuchov	142,000
Sevastopol'	341,000
Ševčenko	147,000
Severodoneck (★Lisičansk)	124,000
Severodvinsk	230,000
Severomorsk	54,000
Šiauliai	134,000
Simferopol'	331,000
Slav'ansk (★Kramatorsk)	143,000
Slav'ansk-Na-Kubani	56,000
Sluck	53,000
Smela	71,000
Smolensk	331,000
Snežnoje (★Torez)	67,000
Soči	310,000
Sokol (1974E)	48,000
Soligorsk	85,000
Solikamsk	106,000
Solncevo (★Moskva) (1984E)	62,000
Solnečnogorsk (★Moskva)	52,000
Sosnovyj Bor	53,000
Šostka	85,000
Spassk-Dal'nij	58,000
Stachanov (★600,000)	110,000
Staryj Oskol	154,000
Stavropol'	293,000
Sterlitamak	240,000
Stryj	61,000
Stupino	73,000
Suchumi	126,000
Šuja	72,000
Sumgait (★Baku)	223,000
Sumy	256,000
Surgut	203,000
Sverdlovsk, Sverdlovsk oblast' (★1,540,000)	1,300,000
Sverdlovsk, Vorosilovgrad oblast'	81,000
Svetlogorsk	65,000
Svetlovodsk	53,000
Svobodnyj	77,000
Syktyvkar	213,000
Syzran'	173,000
Taganrog	289,000
Taldy-Kurgan	106,000
Tallinn	464,000
Tambov	296,000
Tartu	111,000
Tašauz	103,000
Taškent (★2,260,000)	2,030,000
Tbilisi (★1,335,000)	1,158,000
Temirtau	225,000
Termez	66,000
Ternopol'	182,000
Tichoreck	66,000
Tichvin	67,000
Tiraspol'	162,000
Tobol'sk	75,000
Tokmak	68,000
Toljatti	594,000
Tomsk	475,000
Torez (★285,000)	88,000
Toržok (1977E)	50,000
Troick	91,000
Tuapse	63,000
Tujmazy	51,000
Tula (★630,000)	532,000
Tulun	54,000
T'umen'	425,000
Turkestan	76,000
Tyndinskij	56,000
Uchta	100,000
Ufa (★1,080,000)	1,064,000
Uglič (1974E)	37,000

▲ Population of an entire municipality, commune, or district, including rural area.
• Largest city in country.
★ Population or designation of the metropolitan area, including suburbs.
C Census. **E** Official estimate. **UE** Unofficial estimate.

▲ Bevölkerung eines ganzen städtischen Verwaltungsgebietes, eines Kommunalbezirkes oder eines Distrikts, einschliesslich ländlicher Gebiete.
• Grösste Stadt des Landes.
★ Bevölkerung oder Bezeichnung der Stadtregion einschliess lich Vororte.
C Volkszählung. **E** Offizielle Schätzung. **UE** Inoffizielle Schätzung.

Ulan-Ude	335,000
Uljanovsk	544,000
Uman'	86,000
Ural'sk	192,000
Urgenč	116,000
Usolje-Sibirskoje	107,000
Ussurijsk	156,000
Ust'-Ilimsk	97,000
Ustinov	611,000
Ust'-Kamenogorsk	307,000
Ust'-Kut	56,000
Užgorod	107,000
Uzlovaja (★Novomoskovsk)	64,000
V'az'ma	55,000
Velikije Luki	110,000
Ventspils	51,000
Verchn'aja Salda	56,000
Vičuga	51,000
Vilnius	544,000
Vinnica	367,000
Vitebsk	335,000
Vladimir	331,000
Vladivostok	600,000
Volchov	50,000
Volgodonsk	165,000
Volgograd (Stalingrad) (★1,305,000)	974,000
Vologda	269,000
Vol'sk	66,000
Volžsk	58,000
Volžskij (★Volgograd)	245,000
Vorkuta	108,000
Voronež	850,000
Vorošilovgrad	497,000
Voskresensk	79,000
Votkinsk	99,000
Vyborg	80,000
Vyksa	59,000
Vyšnij Voločok	71,000
Zagorsk	112,000
Zaporožje	852,000
Ždanov	522,000
Zelenograd (★Moskva)	142,000
Železnodorožnyj (★Moskva)	86,000
Železnogorsk	77,000
Zel'onodol'sk	89,000
Žigulevsk (1977E)	50,000
Zima (1977E)	51,000
Žitomir	275,000
Zlatoust	204,000
Žoltyje Vody	59,000
Žukovskij	98,000
Zyr'anovsk	54,000

SPAIN / España

1984 E	38,872,389
Albacete	121,909
Alcalá de Henares (★Madrid)	146,994
Alcobendas (★Madrid)	66,249
Alcorcón (★Madrid)	144,478
Alcoy	67,431
Algeciras	92,474
Alicante	253,722
Almería	149,310
Avilés (★131,000)	89,992
Badajoz (▲116,790)	92,800
Badalona (★Barcelona)	229,281
Baracaldo (★Bilbao)	118,692
Barcelona (★4,040,000)	1,770,296
Bilbao (★985,000)	397,541
Burgos	155,849
Cáceres	69,734
Cádiz (★240,000)	160,839
Cartagena (▲174,195)	142,300
Castellón de la Plana	129,518
Cerdanyola de Vallés (★Barcelona)	52,337
Ciudad Real	53,546
Córdoba	291,370
Cornellá (★Barcelona)	90,270
Coslada (★Madrid)	60,297
Dos Hermanas	60,563
Elche (▲175,073)	144,600
Elda	55,322
El Ferrol del Caudillo (★129,000)	90,410
El Puerto de Santa María	59,844
Fuenlabrada (★Madrid)	107,283
Gerona	67,259
Getafe (★Madrid)	128,522
Gijón	262,395
Granada	256,191
Guadalajara	58,436
Hospitalet (★Barcelona)	288,290
Huelva	137,453
Irún	54,877
Jaén	102,262
Jerez de la Frontera (▲184,905)	138,700
La Coruña	240,463
La Línea	58,945
Las Palmas de Gran Canaria	377,353
Leganés (★Madrid)	168,984
León (★159,000)	133,658
Lérida (▲110,293)	87,800
Linares (▲58,149)	51,800
Logroño	113,576
Lugo (▲74,389)	62,300
• MADRID (★4,650,000)	3,200,234
Málaga	537,619
Manresa	66,951
Mataró	99,126
Móstoles (★Madrid)	164,304
Murcia (▲305,221)	200,300
Orense (▲98,649)	85,500
Oviedo	189,376
Palencia	74,311
Palma	311,197
Pamplona	181,668
Parla (★Madrid)	62,694
Ponferrada	56,710
Portugalete (★Bilbao)	59,307
Prat del Llobregat (★Barcelona)	63,433
Puertollano	51,845
Reus	82,354
Sabadell (★Barcelona)	189,775
Sagunto	57,380
Salamanca	159,336
San Baudilio de Llobregat (★Barcelona)	74,783
San Cristóbal de la Laguna (▲107,735) (1982E)	23,500
San Fernando (★Cádiz)	76,101
San Sebastián (★285,000)	178,906
Santa Coloma de Gramanet (★Barcelona)	140,274
Santa Cruz de Tenerife (1981C)	185,899
Santander	187,057
Santiago de Compostela (▲85,197)	62,300
Santurce-Antiguo (★Bilbao)	54,036
Segovia	53,005
Sevilla (★945,000)	672,435
Talavera de la Reina	67,216
Tarragona	113,075
Tarrasa (★Barcelona)	165,233
Toledo	57,778
Torrejón de Ardoz (★Madrid)	81,639
Torrente (★Valencia)	55,028
Valencia (★1,335,000)	785,273
Valladolid	331,404
Vigo	277,460
Vitoria	199,239
Zamora	61,151
Zaragoza	601,235

SPANISH NORTH AFRICA / Plazas de Soberanía en el Norte de África

1984 E	125,069
• Ceuta	68,822
Melilla	56,247

SRI LANKA

1983 E	15,416,000
Battaramulla (★Colombo) (1981C)	56,535
• COLOMBO (★1,975,000)	623,000
Dehiwala-Mount Lavinia (★Colombo)	181,000
Galle	88,000
Jaffna	128,000
Kandy	114,000
Kotte (★Colombo) (1982E)	102,000
Moratuwa (★Colombo) (1982E)	136,000
Negombo (1982E)	64,000

SUDAN / As-Sūdān

1983 C	20,564,364
Al-Fāshir (1973C)	51,932
• AL-KHARṬŪM (★1,350,000)	476,218
Al-Kharṭūm Baḥrī (★Al-Kharṭūm)	341,146
Al-Qaḍārif (1973C)	66,465
Al-Ubayyiḍ	140,000
53 Atbarah	73,000
Būr Sūdān (Port Sudan)	206,727
Jūbā (1973C)	56,737
Kassalā	143,000
Kūstī (1973C)	65,257
Nyala (1973C)	59,852
Umm Durmān (Omdurman) (★Al-Kharṭūm)	526,287
Wad Madanī	141,000
Wāw (1973C)	52,752

SURINAME

1980 C	354,860
• PARAMARIBO (★192,810)	67,905

SWAZILAND

1982 E	585,000
Manzini (★30,000)	14,000
• MBABANE	33,000

SWEDEN / Sverige

1984 E	8,342,621
Borås	99,945
Eskilstuna	88,664
Gävle (▲87,817)	67,300
Göteborg (★699,151)	424,085
Halmstad (▲76,971)	49,400
Helsingborg	104,689
Huddinge (★Stockholm)	69,581
Järfälla (★Stockholm)	55,776
Jönköping	107,031
Karlstad	74,324
Linköping	115,600
Luleå	66,811
Lund	81,199
Malmö (★305,000)	229,107
Mölndal (★Göteborg)	49,063
Nacka (★Stockholm)	59,009
Norrköping	118,451
Örebro	117,569
Österhaninge (★Stockholm)	33,000
Södertälje (★Stockholm)	79,429
Solna (★Stockholm)	48,828
• STOCKHOLM (★1,420,198)	653,455
Sundsvall (▲93,569)	50,600
Täby (★Stockholm)	52,771
Trollhättan	48,922
Tumba (★Stockholm)	65,927
Umeå (▲84,192)	54,900
Uppsala	152,579
Västerås	117,658
Växjö (▲66,173)	43,700

SWITZERLAND / Schweiz / Suisse / Svizzera

1985 E	6,455,900
Aarau (★51,300)	15,800
Arbon (★40,800)	12,400
Baden (★70,800)	14,000
Basel (Bâle) (★580,000)	176,200
BERN (BERNE) (★300,500)	140,600
Biel (Bienne) (★82,800)	52,600
Fribourg (Freiburg) (★55,800)	35,000
Genève (Geneva) (★435,000)	159,500
Lausanne (★256,400)	126,200
Locarno (★41,600)	14,300
Lugano (★93,000)	27,800
Luzern (★158,400)	61,000
Neuchâtel (★57,600)	32,700
Sankt Gallen (★114,000)	73,500
Schaffhausen (★53,300)	34,100
Thun (★66,000)	36,800
Vevey (★59,800)	15,400
Winterthur (★106,800)	84,600
Zug (★52,300)	21,300
• Zürich (★780,000)	354,500

SYRIA / As-Sūrīyah

1981 C	9,052,628
Al-Hasakah	73,426
Al-Lādhiqīyah (Latakia)	96,791
Al-Qāmishlī	92,990
Ar-Raqqah	87,138
Dar'ā	49,534
Dayr az-Zawr	92,091
• DIMASHQ (DAMASCUS) (★1,850,000) (1986E)	1,259,000
Dūmā (★Dimashq)	51,337
Halab (Aleppo) (★1,035,000)	985,413
Ḥamāh	177,208
Ḥimṣ	346,871
Idlib	51,682
Jaramānah (★Dimashq)	64,305
Ṭarṭūs	52,589

TAIWAN / T'aiwan

1982 E	18,457,923
Changhua (▲182,804) (1980C)	140,100
Chiai	252,376
Chilung	349,686
Chungho (★T'aipei) (1980C)	285,365
Chungli (1980C)	210,024
Chutung (1980C)	69,598
Fangshan (★Kaohsiung) (1980C)	222,817
Fengyüan (▲127,563) (1980C)	101,700
Hsichih (★T'aipei) (1980C)	70,031
Hsinchu	288,880
Hsinchuang (★T'aipei) (1980C)	182,623
Hsintien (★T'aipei) (1980C)	176,663
Hualien (1980C)	101,953
Ilan (▲81,751) (1980C)	70,900
Kangshan (1980C)	78,049
Kaohsiung (★1,675,000)	1,248,175
Lotung (1980C)	57,925
Lukang (1980C)	72,019
Miaoli (1980C)	81,500
Nant'ou (1980C)	84,038
P'ingchen (★T'aipei) (1980C)	98,054
P'ingtung (▲186,655) (1980C)	152,400
Sanchung (★T'aipei) (1980C)	350,383
Shulin (★T'aipei) (1980C)	75,700
Tach'i (1980C)	67,209
T'aichung	621,566
T'ainan	609,934
• T'AIPEI (★5,265,000)	2,327,641
T'aipeihsien (★T'aipei) (1980C)	414,556
T'aitung (▲110,352) (1980C)	79,100
Taoyüan (1980C)	182,884
T'oufen (1980C)	66,536
T'uch'eng (★T'aipei) (1980C)	34,834
Yangmei (1980C)	84,353
Yungho (★T'aipei) (1980C)	213,630

TANZANIA

1978 C	17,557,000
Arusha	55,000
• DAR ES SALAAM	757,346
Dodoma	46,000
Iringa	57,000
Kigoma	50,000
Mbeya	77,000
Morogoro	62,000
Moshi	52,000
Mtwara	49,000
Mwanza	111,000
Tabora	67,000
Tanga	103,000
Ujiji (1967C)	21,369
Zanzibar	110,669

THAILAND / Prathet Thai

1983 E	49,515,074
Chiang Mai	150,499
Chon Buri	46,792
Hat Yai	113,964
Khon Kaen	115,515
• KRUNG THEP (BANGKOK) (★5,900,000) (1984E)	5,174,682
Nakhon Ratchasima	190,762
Nakhon Sawan	95,128
Nakhon Si Thammarat	69,834
Phitsanulok	72,052
Phra Nakhon Si Ayutthaya	55,319
Sakon Nakhon	48,903
Samut Prakan (★Krung Thep)	65,155
Songkhla	79,725
Ubon Ratchathani	100,255
Udon Thani	82,483
Yala	55,947

TOGO

1981 C	2,702,945
• LOME	369,926

TOKELAU

1981 C	1,572

TONGA

1984 C	96,592
• NUKU'ALOFA	21,745

TRANSKEI

1982 E	2,400,000
• UMTATA (1978E)	30,000

TRINIDAD AND TOBAGO

1980 C	1,059,825
• PORT OF SPAIN (★425,000)	65,906
San Fernando	33,490

TUNISIA / Tunis / Tunisie

1975 C	5,588,209
Bardo (★Tunis)	49,367
Bizerte	62,856
El Kairouan	54,546
Sfax (★260,000)	171,297
Sousse	69,530
• TUNIS (★915,000)	550,404

TURKEY / Türkiye

1985 C	50,664,458
Adana	777,554
Adapazarı	152,291
Adıyaman	71,644
Afyon	87,033
Ağri	54,492
Akhisar	68,553
Aksaray	81,056
Amasya	53,431
ANKARA (★2,400,000)	2,235,035
Antakya (Antioch)	107,821
Antalya	261,114
Aydın	90,449
Bafra	53,482
Balıkesir	149,989
Bandırma	70,137
Batman	110,036
Bilecik	18,506
Bolu	50,288
Burdur	53,995
Bursa	612,510
Çanakkale	48,059
Ceyhan	72,624
Çorlu	59,107
Çorum	96,725
Denizli	169,130
Diyarbakır	305,940
Edirne	86,909
Elâzığ	182,296
Elbistan	47,756
Ereğli, Konya prov.	68,749
Ereğli, Zonguldak prov.	54,837
Erzincan	82,616
Erzurum	246,053
Eskişehir	366,765
Gaziantep	478,635
Gebze (★İzmit)	92,592
Gelibolu	16,715
Giresun	55,887
Gölcük	56,087
Gümüşhane	22,067
Hakkâri	20,754
İnegöl	54,659
İskenderun	152,096
Isparta	101,215
• İstanbul (★6,000,000)	5,475,982
İzmir (★1,600,000)	1,489,772
İzmit	233,338
Kadirli	47,609
Karabük	94,818
Karaman	64,735
Kars	69,293
Kastamonu	46,986
Kayseri	373,937
Kilis	59,876
Kırıkhan	52,780
Kırıkkale	208,018
Kırşehir	64,754
Konya	439,181
Kozan	50,324
Kütahya	118,773
Malatya	243,138
Manisa	127,012
Maraş	210,371
Mersin	314,350
Muş	42,159
Nazilli	77,627
Nevşehir	50,204
Niğde	49,068
Nizip	50,067
Ödemiş	47,475
Ordu	80,828
Osmaniye	103,824
Polatlı	52,737
Rize	50,221
Salihli	63,759
Samsun	240,674
Siirt	53,884
Sinop	23,148
Sivas	198,553
Siverek	48,333
Tarsus	146,502
Tatvan	51,906
Tekirdağ	63,215
Tokat	73,008
Trabzon	142,008

▲ Población de un municipio, comuna o distrito entero, incluyendo sus áreas rurales.
• Ciudad más grande de un país.
★ Población o designación de un área metropolitana, incluyendo los suburbios.
C Censo. E Estimado oficial. UE Estimado no oficial.

▲ Population d'une municipalité, d'une commune ou d'un district, zone rurale incluse.
• Ville la plus peuplée du pays.
★ Population de l'agglomération (ou nom de la zone métropolitaine englobante).
C Recensement. E Estimation officielle. UE Estimation non officielle.

▲ População de um municipio, comuna ou distrito, inclusive as respectivas áreas rurais.
• Maior cidade de um país.
★ População ou indicação de uma área metropolitana.
C Censo. E Estimativa oficial. UE Estimativa não oficial.

Turgutlu	65,740
Turhal	60,097
Urfa	194,969
Uşak	88,267
Van	110,653
Yalova	53,857
Yarımca	48,420
Zonguldak (★195,000)	117,879

TURKS AND CAICOS ISLANDS

1980 C	7,436
• GRAND TURK	3,146

TUVALU

1979 C	7,349
• FUNAFUTI	2,191

UGANDA

1982 E	14,121,000
Jinja	55,000
• KAMPALA	460,000

UNION OF SOVIET SOCIALIST REPUBLICS *see* SOVIET UNION

UNITED ARAB EMIRATES / Ittiḥād al-Imārāt al-ʿArabīyah

1980 C	980,000
• ABŪ ZABY	242,975
Al ʿAyn	101,663
Ash-Shāriqah	125,149
Dubayy	265,702

UNITED KINGDOM

1981 C	55,635,628

UNITED KINGDOM: England

1981 C	46,220,955
Accrington (★Blackburn)	36,459
Aldershot (★London)	53,665
Ashton-under-Lyne (★Manchester)	43,605
Aylesbury	51,999
Barnsley	76,783
Barrow-in-Furness	50,174
Basildon (★London)	94,800
Basingstoke	73,027
Bath	84,283
Bebington (★Liverpool)	62,618
Bedford	75,632
Beeston and Stapleford (★Nottingham)	64,785
Benfleet (★London)	50,783
Birkenhead (★Liverpool)	99,075
Birmingham (★2,675,000)	1,013,995
Blackburn (★221,900)	109,564
Blackpool (★280,000)	146,297
Blyth	35,101
Bognor Regis	50,323
Bolton (★Manchester)	143,960
Bootle	70,860
Bournemouth (★315,000)	142,829
Bracknell (★London)	52,257
Bradford (★Leeds)	293,336
Brentwood (★London)	51,212
Brighton (★420,000)	134,581
Bristol (★630,000)	413,861
Burnley (★160,000)	76,365
Burton upon Trent	59,040
Bury (★Manchester)	61,785
Bury Saint Edmunds	30,563
Camberley *see* Frimley and Camberley	
Cambridge	87,111
Cannock (★Birmingham)	54,503
Canterbury	34,546
Carlisle	72,206
Carlton (★Nottingham)	46,053
Chatham (★London)	65,835
Cheadle and Gatley (★Manchester)	59,478
Chelmsford (★London)	91,109
Cheltenham	87,188
Cheshunt (★London)	49,616
Chester	80,154
Chesterfield (★127,000)	73,352
Clacton-on-Sea	39,618
Colchester	87,476
Corby	48,704
Coventry (★645,000)	318,718
Crawley (★London)	80,113
Crewe	59,097
Crosby (★Liverpool)	54,103
Darlington	85,519
Dartford (★London)	62,032
Derby (★27,500)	218,026
Dewsbury (★Leeds)	49,612
Doncaster	74,727
Dover	33,461
Dudley (★Birmingham)	186,513
Dunstable (★Luton)	48,436
Durham	38,105
Eastbourne	86,715
Eastleigh (★Southampton)	58,585
Ellesmere Port (★Liverpool)	65,829
Epsom and Ewell (★London)	65,830
Esher / Molesey (★London)	46,688
Ewell *see* Epsom and Ewell	
Exeter	88,235
Fareham / Portchester (★Portsmouth)	55,563
Farnborough (★London)	48,063
Folkestone	42,949
Frimley and Camberley (★London)	45,108
Gateshead (★Newcastle)	91,429
Gillingham (★London)	92,531
Gloucester (★115,000)	106,526
Gosport (★Portsmouth)	69,664
Gravesend (★London)	53,450
Grays (★London)	45,881
Greasby / Moreton (★Liverpool)	56,410
Great Yarmouth	54,777
Grimsby (★145,000)	91,532
Guildford (★London)	61,509
Halesowen (★Birmingham)	57,533
Halifax	76,675
Harlow (★London)	79,150
Harrogate	63,637
Hartlepool (★Middlesbrough)	91,749
Hastings	74,979
Havant (★Portsmouth)	50,098
Hemel Hempstead (★London)	80,110
Hereford	48,277
Hertford (★London)	21,350
High Wycombe (▲156,800)	69,575
Hinckley (★Coventry)	35,510
Hove (★Brighton)	65,587
Huddersfield (▲377,400)	147,825
Huyton-with-Roby (★Liverpool)	62,011
Ipswich	129,661
Keighley (★Leeds)	49,188
Kidderminster	50,385
Kingston upon Hull (★350,000)	322,144
Kingswood (★Bristol)	54,736
Kirkby (★Liverpool)	52,825
Lancaster	43,902
Leeds (★1,540,000)	445,242
Leicester (★495,000)	324,394
Lincoln	79,980
Liverpool (★1,525,000)	538,809
• LONDON (★11,100,000)	6,851,400
Loughborough	44,895
Lowestoft	59,430
Luton (★220,000)	163,209
Macclesfield	47,525
Maidenhead (★London)	59,809
Maidstone	86,067
Manchester (★2,775,000)	437,612
Mansfield (★198,000)	71,325
Margate	53,137
Middlesbrough (★580,000)	158,516
Middleton (★Manchester)	51,373
Milton Keynes	36,886
Newcastle-under-Lyme (★Stoke-on-Trent)	73,208
Newcastle upon Tyne (★1,300,000)	199,064
Northampton	154,172
Norwich (★230,000)	169,814
Nottingham (★655,000)	273,300
Nuneaton (★Coventry)	60,337
Oldbury / Smethwick (★Birmingham)	153,268
Oldham (★Manchester)	107,095
Oxford (★230,000)	113,847
Penzance	18,501
Peterborough	113,404
Plymouth (★290,000)	238,583
Poole (★Bournemouth)	122,815
Portsmouth (★485,000)	174,218
Preston (★250,000)	166,675
Ramsgate	36,678
Reading (★200,000)	194,727
Redditch (★Birmingham)	61,639
Reigate / Redhill (★London)	48,241
Rochdale (★Manchester)	97,292
Rotherham (★Sheffield)	122,374
Royal Leamington Spa (★Coventry)	56,552
Royal Tunbridge Wells	57,699
Rugby	59,039
Runcorn (★Liverpool)	63,995
Saint Albans (★London)	76,709
Saint Helens	114,397
Sale (★Manchester)	57,872
Salford (★Manchester)	96,525
Salisbury	36,890
Scarborough	36,665
Scunthorpe	79,043
Sheffield (★710,000)	470,685
Shrewsbury	57,731
Slough (★London)	106,341
Solihull (★Birmingham)	93,940
Southampton (★415,000)	211,321
Southend-on-Sea (★London)	155,720
Southport (★Liverpool)	88,596
South Shields (★Newcastle)	86,488
Stafford	60,915
Staines (★London)	51,949
Stapleford *see* Beeston and Stapleford	
Stevenage	74,757
Stockport (★Manchester)	135,489
Stockton-on-Tees (★Middlesbrough)	86,699
Stoke-on-Trent (★440,000)	272,446
Stourbridge (★Birmingham)	55,136
Stratford-upon-Avon	20,941
Stretford (★Manchester)	47,522
Sunderland (★Newcastle)	195,064
Sutton Coldfield (★Birmingham)	102,572
Swindon	127,348
Tanworth	63,260
Taunton	47,793
Torquay (★112,400)	54,430
Wakefield (★Leeds)	74,764
Wallasey (★Liverpool)	62,465
Walsall (★Birmingham)	177,923
Walton and Weybridge (★London)	50,031
Warrington	81,366
Washington (★Newcastle)	48,856
Waterlooville (★Portsmouth)	57,296
Watford (★London)	109,503
West Bromwich (★Birmingham)	153,725
Weston-super-Mare	60,821
Weybridge *see* Walton and Weybridge	
Weymouth and Portland	38,384
Widnes	55,973
Wigan (★Manchester)	88,725
Woking (★London)	92,667
Wolverhampton (★Birmingham)	263,501
Worcester	75,466
Worthing (★Brighton)	90,687
York (★145,000)	123,126

UNITED KINGDOM: Northern Ireland

1981 C	1,488,077
Bangor (★Belfast) (1984E)	67,600
Belfast (★685,000) (1984E)	318,600
Castlereagh (★Belfast) (1984E)	59,400
Londonderry (★97,200) (1984E)	68,000
Lurgan (★63,000)	20,991
Newtownabbey (★Belfast) (1984E)	72,400

UNITED KINGDOM: Scotland

1981 C	5,035,315
Aberdeen	186,757
Ayr (★100,000)	48,493
Clydebank (★Glasgow)	51,832
Coatbridge	50,831
Cumbernauld (★Glasgow)	47,517
Dundee	172,294
Dunfermline (★125,817)	52,105
East Kilbride (★Glasgow)	70,454
Edinburgh (★630,000)	408,822
Falkirk (★148,171)	36,372
Glasgow (★1,800,000)	754,586
Greenock (★101,000)	58,436
Hamilton (★Glasgow)	51,666
Irvine (★94,000)	32,507
Kilmarnock (★84,000)	51,799
Kirkcaldy (★148,171)	46,356
Motherwell (★Glasgow)	30,616
Paisley (★Glasgow)	84,330
Perth	41,916
Stirling (★61,000)	36,640

UNITED KINGDOM: Wales

1981 C	2,790,462
Cardiff (★625,000)	262,313
Llanelli	45,336
Merthyr Tydfil	38,893
Neath (★ Swansea)	48,687
Newport (★310,000)	115,896
Pontypool (★Newport)	36,064
Port Talbot (★130,000)	40,078
Rhondda (★Cardiff)	70,980
Swansea (★275,000)	172,433
Wrexham	39,929

UNITED STATES

1980 C	226,549,248

UNITED STATES: Alabama

1980 C	3,894,046
Anniston (★102,900)	29,523
Auburn (★50,700)	28,471
Birmingham (★747,400)	286,799
Decatur (★76,700)	42,002
Dothan (★75,500)	48,750
Florence (★98,200)	37,029
Gadsden (★88,800)	47,565
Huntsville (★189,600)	142,513
Mobile (★361,900)	200,452
Montgomery (★225,000)	177,857
Tuscaloosa (★115,700)	75,211

UNITED STATES: Alaska

1980 C	401,851
Anchorage (★184,300)	174,431
Fairbanks (★39,900)	22,645
Juneau	19,528

UNITED STATES: Arizona

1980 C	2,718,425
Glendale (★Phoenix)	97,172
Mesa (★Phoenix)	152,453
Nogales (★81,400)	15,683
Phoenix (★1,482,400)	790,044
Scottsdale (★Phoenix)	88,622
Tempe (★Phoenix)	106,920
Tucson (★495,600)	336,503
Yuma (★58,100)	43,950

UNITED STATES: Arkansas

1980 C	2,286,357
Fayetteville (★87,000)	36,608
Fort Smith (★129,500)	71,626
Hot Springs National Park (★57,600)	36,228
Jonesboro (★43,700)	31,530
Little Rock (★382,000)	167,744
North Little Rock (★Little Rock)	64,388
Pine Bluff (★72,250)	56,636

UNITED STATES: California

1980 C	23,667,555
Alameda (★San Francisco)	63,852
Alhambra (★Los Angeles)	64,767
Anaheim (★Los Angeles)	219,494
Arden (★Sacramento)	52,000
Bakersfield (★245,100)	105,735
Baldwin Park (★Los Angeles)	50,554
Bellflower (★Los Angeles)	53,441
Berkeley (★San Francisco)	103,328
Buena Park (★Los Angeles)	64,165
Burbank (★Los Angeles)	84,625
Calexico (★365,000)	14,412
Carson (★Los Angeles)	81,221
Cerritos (★Los Angeles)	53,020
Chico (★57,300)	26,716
Chula Vista (★San Diego)	83,927
Citrus Heights (★Sacramento)	85,911
Compton (★Los Angeles)	81,230
Concord (★San Francisco)	103,763
Costa Mesa (★Los Angeles)	82,562
Cucamonga (★Los Angeles)	55,250
Daly City (★San Francisco)	78,427
Downey (★Los Angeles)	82,602
East Los Angeles (★Los Angeles)	110,017
El Cajon (★San Diego)	73,892
El Monte (★Los Angeles)	79,494
Escondido (★San Diego)	64,355
Eureka (★82,700)	24,153
Fairfield (★117,000)	58,099
Fountain Valley (★Los Angeles)	55,080
Fremont (★San Francisco)	131,945
Fresno (★389,500)	235,812
Fullerton (★Los Angeles)	102,246
Garden Grove (★Los Angeles)	123,307
Glendale (★Los Angeles)	139,060
Hawthorne (★Los Angeles)	56,437
Hayward (★San Francisco)	93,718
Hemet (★61,700)	24,438
Huntington Beach (★Los Angeles)	170,505
Inglewood (★Los Angeles)	94,162
Irvine (★Los Angeles)	62,134
Lakewood (★Los Angeles)	74,654
La Mesa (★San Diego)	50,308
Lancaster (★86,400)	48,027
Livermore (★San Francisco)	48,349
Lompoc (★43,400)	26,267
Long Beach (★Los Angeles)	361,355
Los Angeles (★9,763,600)	2,968,579
Lynwood (★Los Angeles)	48,409
Merced (★72,500)	36,499
Mission Viejo (★Los Angeles)	50,666
Modesto (★183,800)	106,963
Montebello (★Los Angeles)	52,929
Monterey (★127,900)	27,558
Monterey Park (★Los Angeles)	54,338
Mountain View (★San Francisco)	58,655
Napa (★71,500)	50,879
Newport Beach (★Los Angeles)	62,556
Norwalk (★Los Angeles)	84,901
Oakland (★San Francisco)	339,337
Oceanside (★129,100)	76,698
Ontario (★Los Angeles)	88,820
Orange (★Los Angeles)	91,450
Oxnard (★294,200)	108,195
Palm Springs (★80,900)	32,359
Palo Alto (★San Francisco)	55,225
Pasadena (★Los Angeles)	118,072
Pico Rivera (★Los Angeles)	53,387
Pomona (★Los Angeles)	92,742
Porterville (★46,300)	20,865
Redding (★96,300)	41,995
Redondo Beach (★Los Angeles)	57,102
Redwood City (★San Francisco)	54,951
Richmond (★San Francisco)	74,676
Riverside (★768,300)	170,591
Sacramento (★866,400)	275,741
Salinas (★109,400)	80,479
San Bernardino (★Riverside)	118,794
San Diego (★2,098,500)	875,538
San Francisco (★4,683,200)	678,974
San Jose (★San Francisco)	629,400
San Leandro (★San Francisco)	63,952
San Mateo (★San Francisco)	77,640
Santa Ana (★Los Angeles)	204,023
Santa Barbara (★170,300)	74,414
Santa Clara (★San Francisco)	87,700
Santa Cruz (★134,100)	41,483
Santa Maria (★67,500)	39,685
Santa Monica (★Los Angeles)	88,314
Santa Rosa (★153,300)	83,320
Simi Valley (★Los Angeles)	77,500
South Gate (★Los Angeles)	66,784
South San Francisco (★San Francisco)	49,393
Stockton (★213,000)	149,779
Sunnyvale (★San Francisco)	106,618
Thousand Oaks (★Los Angeles)	85,188
Torrance (★Los Angeles)	129,881
Vallejo (★San Francisco)	80,303
Ventura (San Buenaventura) (★Oxnard)	77,988
Visalia (★76,300)	49,729
Walnut Creek (★San Francisco)	56,125
Watsonville (★55,100)	23,662
West Covina (★Los Angeles)	80,292
Westminster (★Los Angeles)	71,133
Whittier (★Los Angeles)	68,558
Yuba City (★68,200)	18,736

UNITED STATES: Colorado

1980 C	2,889,735
Arvada (★Denver)	84,576
Aurora (★Denver)	158,588
Boulder (★165,200)	76,685
Colorado Springs (★301,500)	214,821
Denver (★1,405,300)	492,365
Fort Collins (★87,600)	65,092
Grand Junction (★74,300)	27,956
Greeley (★69,900)	53,006
Lakewood (★Denver)	113,808
Loveland (★42,000)	30,215
Pueblo (★117,000)	101,686
Westminster (★Denver)	50,211

UNITED STATES: Connecticut

1980 C	3,107,576
Bridgeport (★438,500)	142,546
Bristol (★Hartford)	57,370
Danbury (★New York)	60,470
East Hartford (★Hartford)	52,563
Fairfield (★Bridgeport)	54,849
Greenwich (★New York)	59,565
Hamden (★New Haven)	51,071
Hartford (★1,013,600)	136,392
Manchester (★Hartford)	49,761
Meriden (★New Haven)	57,118
Milford (★Bridgeport)	49,101
New Britain (★Hartford)	73,840
New Haven (★500,500)	126,101
New London (★250,800)	28,842
Norwalk (★New York)	77,767

▲ Population of an entire municipality, commune, or district, including rural area.
• Largest city in country.
★ Population or designation of the metropolitan area, including suburbs.
C Census. **E** Official estimate. **UE** Unofficial estimate.

▲ Bevölkerung eines ganzen städtischen Verwaltungsgebietes, eines Kommunalbezirkes oder eines Distrikts, einschliesslich ländlicher Gebiete.
• Grösste Stadt des Landes.
★ Bevölkerung oder Bezeichnung der Stadtregion einschliess lich Vororte.
C Volkszählung. **E** Offizielle Schätzung. **UE** Inoffizielle Schätzung.

Stamford (★New York) 102,466
Stratford (★Bridgeport) 50,541
Torrington (★54,300) 30,987
Waterbury (★205,000) 103,266
West Hartford (★Hartford) 61,301
West Haven (★New Haven) 53,184

UNITED STATES: Delaware

1980 C 594,317
Dover (★70,300) 23,507
Wilmington (★Philadelphia) 70,195

UNITED STATES: District of Columbia

1980 C 638,432
WASHINGTON (★3,221,400) 638,432

UNITED STATES: Florida

1980 C 9,747,117
Boca Raton (★Miami) 49,447
Clearwater (★Saint Petersburg) 85,528
Daytona Beach (★178,800) 54,176
De Land (★47,300) 15,354
Fort Lauderdale (★Miami) 153,279
Fort Myers (★163,200) 36,638
Fort Pierce (★83,300) 33,802
Fort Walton Beach (★88,900) 20,829
Gainesville (★123,100) 81,371
Hialeah (★Miami) 145,254
Hollywood (★Miami) 121,323
Jacksonville (★635,900) 540,920
Kendall (★Miami) 51,000
Lakeland (★138,900) 50,158
Largo (★Saint Petersburg) 58,977
Melbourne (★227,500) 46,536
Miami (★2,827,300) 346,865
Miami Beach (★Miami) 96,298
Naples (★66,600) 17,581
Ocala (★83,600) 37,170
Orlando (★619,300) 128,291
Panama City (★92,900) 33,346
Pensacola (★250,200) 57,619
Plantation (★Miami) 48,653
Pompano Beach (★Miami) 58,021
Saint Petersburg (★852,300) 238,647
Sarasota (★281,900) 48,868
Tallahassee (★136,900) 101,547
Tampa (★594,500) 271,598
Venice (★56,900) 12,153
West Palm Beach (★356,000) 63,305
Winter Haven (★85,300) 21,119

UNITED STATES: Georgia

1980 C 5,462,982
Albany (★105,200) 83,245
Athens (★102,500) 42,549
Atlanta (★1,962,500) 425,022
Augusta (★251,100) 47,532
Columbus (★233,400) 169,441
Macon (★227,400) 116,896
Rome (★74,200) 29,928
Savannah (★212,800) 141,651
Valdosta (★58,100) 37,596
Warner Robins (★Macon) 39,893

UNITED STATES: Hawaii

1980 C 964,691
Hilo (★43,200) 35,269
Honolulu (★762,600) 365,048

UNITED STATES: Idaho

1980 C 944,127
Boise (★164,200) 102,160
Idaho Falls (★66,200) 39,734
Lewiston (★43,600) 27,986
Nampa (★64,600) 25,112
Pocatello (★56,200) 46,340

UNITED STATES: Illinois

1980 C 11,427,414
Arlington Heights (★Chicago) 66,116
Aurora (★Chicago) 81,293
Bloomington (★85,300) 44,189
Champaign (★118,100) 58,267
Chicago (★7,717,100) 3,005,072
Cicero (★Chicago) 61,232
Danville (★72,900) 38,985
Decatur (★119,200) 93,896
De Kalb (★49,200) 33,157
Des Plaines (★Chicago) 55,374
East Saint Louis (★Saint Louis) 55,200
Elgin (★Chicago) 63,668
Evanston (★Chicago) 73,706
Galesburg (★43,500) 35,305
Joliet (★Chicago) 77,956
Kankakee (★83,300) 29,635
Mount Prospect (★Chicago) 52,634
Oak Lawn (★Chicago) 60,590
Oak Park (★Chicago) 54,887
Peoria (★319,700) 124,160
Quincy (★54,700) 42,554
Rockford (★280,700) 139,712
Schaumburg (★Chicago) 53,355
Skokie (★Chicago) 60,278
Springfield (★154,200) 100,054
Waukegan (★Chicago) 67,653

UNITED STATES: Indiana

1980 C 5,490,212
Anderson (★143,200) 64,695
Bloomington (★91,400) 52,044
Columbus (★64,700) 30,614
Elkhart (★138,500) 41,305
Evansville (★223,900) 130,496
Fort Wayne (★284,300) 172,349
Gary (★Chicago) 151,953
Hammond (★Chicago) 93,714
Indianapolis (★1,072,500) 700,807
Kokomo (★85,300) 47,808
Lafayette (★113,000) 43,011
Marion (★83,900) 35,874
Michigan City (★60,600) 36,850
Muncie (★130,600) 77,216
Richmond (★66,800) 41,349
South Bend (★279,500) 109,727
Terre Haute (★119,100) 61,125

UNITED STATES: Iowa

1980 C 2,913,808
Ames (★63,300) 45,775
Cedar Rapids (★153,200) 110,243
Clinton (★44,200) 32,828
Council Bluffs (★Omaha) 56,449
Davenport (★320,400) 103,264
Des Moines (★308,000) 191,003
Dubuque (★78,100) 62,321
Iowa City (★68,000) 50,508
Mason City (★40,600) 30,144
Sioux City (★101,600) 82,003
Waterloo (★129,700) 75,985

UNITED STATES: Kansas

1980 C 2,364,236
Hutchinson (★48,600) 40,284
Kansas City (★Kansas City, Mo.) 161,148
Lawrence (★54,200) 52,738
Manhattan (★42,000) 32,644
Overland Park (★Kansas City) 81,784
Salina (★42,200) 41,843
Topeka (★145,600) 118,690
Wichita (★372,200) 279,835

UNITED STATES: Kentucky

1980 C 3,660,330
Bowling Green (★52,700) 40,450
Covington (★Cincinnati) 49,567
Frankfort 25,973
Lexington (★255,600) 204,165
Louisville (★891,400) 298,694
Owensboro (★72,600) 54,450
Paducah (★69,700) 29,315

UNITED STATES: Louisiana

1980 C 4,206,098
Alexandria (★103,900) 51,565
Baton Rouge (★434,400) 238,876
Bossier City (★Shreveport) 50,817
Houma (★90,400) 32,602
Kenner (★New Orleans) 66,382
Lafayette (★164,800) 80,584
Lake Charles (★144,400) 75,226
Metairie (★New Orleans) 164,160
Monroe (★125,300) 57,597
New Iberia (★42,300) 32,766
New Orleans (★1,185,000) 557,927
Shreveport (★292,500) 205,820

UNITED STATES: Maine

1980 C 1,125,043
Augusta (★55,300) 21,819
Bangor (★83,500) 31,643
Lewiston (★84,700) 40,481
Portland (★193,800) 61,572

UNITED STATES: Maryland

1980 C 4,216,941
Annapolis (★67,900) 31,740
Baltimore (★1,960,400) 786,741
Bethesda (★Washington) 63,022
Columbia (★Washington) 52,518
Cumberland (★83,100) 25,933
Dundalk (★Baltimore) 71,293
Hagerstown (★127,000) 34,132
Salisbury (★62,600) 16,429
Silver Spring (★Washington) 64,100
Towson (★Baltimore) 51,083
Wheaton (★Washington) 48,600

UNITED STATES: Massachusetts

1980 C 5,737,093
Amherst (★41,800) 17,773
Boston (★3,971,700) 562,994
Brockton (★Boston) 95,172
Brookline (★Boston) 55,062
Cambridge (★Boston) 95,322
Chicopee (★Springfield) 55,112
Fall River (★157,200) 92,574
Fitchburg (★94,000) 39,580
Framingham (★Boston) 65,113
Lawrence (★Boston) 63,175
Lowell (★Boston) 92,418
Lynn (★Boston) 78,471
Malden (★Boston) 53,386
Medford (★Boston) 58,076
New Bedford (★166,700) 98,478
Newton (★Boston) 83,622
Northampton (★34,600) 29,286
Pittsfield (★83,500) 51,974
Quincy (★Boston) 84,743
Somerville (★Boston) 77,372
Springfield (★485,900) 152,319
Taunton (★53,100) 45,001
Waltham (★Boston) 58,200
Weymouth (★Boston) 55,601
Worcester (★402,900) 161,799

UNITED STATES: Michigan

1980 C 9,262,044
Ann Arbor (★Detroit) 107,969
Battle Creek (★102,600) 56,339
Benton Harbor (★102,200) 14,707
Clinton Township (★Detroit) 72,400
Dearborn (★Detroit) 90,660
Dearborn Heights (★Detroit) 67,706
Detroit (★4,691,900) 1,202,463
East Lansing (★Lansing) 51,392
Farmington Hills (★Detroit) 58,056
Flint (★521,200) 159,611
Grand Rapids (★503,800) 181,843
Holland (★75,800) 26,281
Jackson (★138,900) 39,739
Kalamazoo (★240,800) 79,722
Lansing (★352,600) 130,414
Livonia (★Detroit) 104,814
Monroe (★63,200) 23,531
Muskegon (★150,800) 40,823
Pontiac (★Detroit) 76,715
Port Huron (★164,700) 33,981
Redford Township (★Detroit) 58,441
Roseville (★Detroit) 54,311
Royal Oak (★Detroit) 70,893
Saginaw (★362,700) 77,508
Saint Clair Shores (★Detroit) 76,210
Sault Sainte Marie (★103,600) 14,448
Southfield (★Detroit) 75,568
Sterling Heights (★Detroit) 108,999
Taylor (★Detroit) 77,568
Troy (★Detroit) 67,102
Warren (★Detroit) 161,134
Westland (★Detroit) 84,603
Wyoming (★Grand Rapids) 59,616

UNITED STATES: Minnesota

1980 C 4,075,970
Bloomington (★Minneapolis) 81,831
Duluth (★145,800) 92,811
Mankato (★45,000) 28,646
Minneapolis (★2,012,400) 370,951
Rochester (★79,000) 57,890
Saint Cloud (★75,800) 42,566
Saint Paul (★Minneapolis) 270,230

UNITED STATES: Mississippi

1980 C 2,520,698
Biloxi (★196,900) 49,311
Columbus (★50,200) 27,503
Greenville (★51,700) 40,613
Gulfport (★Biloxi) 39,676
Hattiesburg (★66,400) 40,829
Jackson (★306,900) 202,895
Laurel (★47,200) 21,897
Meridian (★62,000) 46,577
Natchez (★47,600) 22,209
Pascagoula (★78,300) 29,318
Vicksburg (★47,000) 25,434

UNITED STATES: Missouri

1980 C 4,916,759
Cape Girardeau (★57,400) 34,361
Columbia (★81,800) 62,061
Florissant (★Saint Louis) 55,372
Independence (★Kansas City) 111,797
Jefferson City (★54,100) 33,619
Joplin (★76,100) 39,023
Kansas City (★1,272,400) 448,033
Saint Joseph (★87,300) 76,691
Saint Louis (★2,203,000) 452,801
Springfield (★192,600) 133,116

UNITED STATES: Montana

1980 C 786,690
Billings (★96,100) 66,842
Butte (★38,100) 37,205
Great Falls (★71,200) 56,725
Helena 23,938
Missoula (★64,900) 33,388

UNITED STATES: Nebraska

1980 C 1,569,825
Grand Island (★41,000) 33,180
Lincoln (★176,500) 171,932
Omaha (★538,600) 322,133

UNITED STATES: Nevada

1980 C 800,508
Carson City 32,022
Las Vegas (★453,800) 164,674
Reno (★176,200) 100,756

UNITED STATES: New Hampshire

1980 C 920,610
Concord (★59,800) 30,400
Manchester (★129,300) 90,936
Nashua (★Boston) 67,865
Portsmouth (★170,200) 26,254

UNITED STATES: New Jersey

1980 C 7,365,011
Atlantic City (★170,700) 40,199
Bayonne (★New York) 65,047
Bloomfield (★New York) 47,792
Brick Township (★New York) 53,629
Camden (★Philadelphia) 84,910
Cherry Hill (★Philadelphia) 68,785
Clifton (★New York) 74,388
East Orange (★New York) 77,878
Edison (★New York) 70,193
Elizabeth (★New York) 106,201
Irvington (★New York) 61,493
Jersey City 223,532
Middletown (★New York) 62,298
Newark (★New York) 329,248
Passaic (★New York) 52,463
Paterson (★New York) 137,970
Trenton (★Philadelphia) 92,124
Union (★New York) 50,184
Union City (★New York) 55,593
Vineland (★143,800) 53,753
Woodbridge (★New York) 90,074

UNITED STATES: New Mexico

1980 C 1,303,542
Albuquerque (★453,200) 332,336
Farmington (★45,200) 31,222
Las Cruces (★65,200) 45,086
Roswell (★45,000) 39,676
Santa Fe (★54,400) 49,299

UNITED STATES: New York

1980 C 17,558,165
Albany (★729,100) 101,727
Amherst (★Buffalo) 66,100
Auburn (★52,900) 32,548
Binghamton (★230,600) 55,860
Buffalo (★1,483,000) 357,870
Cheektowaga (★Buffalo) 92,145
Elmira (★90,800) 35,327
Glens Falls (★64,500) 15,897
Greece (★Rochester) 63,700
Hicksville (★New York) 43,245
Irondequoit (★Rochester) 57,648
Ithaca (★76,700) 28,732
Jamestown (★68,400) 35,775
Kingston (★88,000) 24,481
Levittown (★New York) 57,045
Lockport (★54,800) 24,844
Middletown (★72,700) 21,454
Mount Vernon (★New York) 66,713
Newburgh (★91,900) 23,438
New Rochelle (★New York) 70,794
• New York (★16,800,900) 7,071,639
Niagara Falls (★Buffalo) 71,384
Poughkeepsie (★191,700) 29,757
Rochester (★816,200) 241,741
Schenectady (★Albany) 67,972
Syracuse (★518,600) 170,105
Town of Tonawanda (★Buffalo) 72,795
Troy (★Albany) 56,638
Utica (★224,000) 75,632
West Seneca (★Buffalo) 51,210
Yonkers (★New York) 195,351

UNITED STATES: North Carolina

1980 C 5,880,965
Asheville (★159,900) 53,583
Burlington (★99,000) 37,266
Charlotte (★479,200) 315,473
Durham (★203,100) 100,538
Fayetteville (★236,200) 59,507
Gastonia (★125,400) 47,333
Goldsboro (★64,500) 34,705
Greensboro (★392,400) 155,642
Hickory (★81,600) 23,426
High Point (★Greensboro) 63,808
Jacksonville (★89,200) 22,586
Kannapolis (★103,100) 34,564
Raleigh (★282,800) 150,255
Rocky Mount (★67,400) 41,283
Salisbury (★61,500) 22,677
Wilmington (★109,700) 44,000
Winston-Salem (★278,400) 138,583

UNITED STATES: North Dakota

1980 C 652,717
Bismarck (★65,000) 44,485
Fargo (★108,800) 61,383
Grand Forks (★53,500) 43,765
Minot (★38,300) 32,843

UNITED STATES: Ohio

1980 C 10,797,603
Akron (★614,100) 237,177
Alliance (★50,700) 24,315
Ashtabula (★44,700) 23,449
Brunswick (★51,700) 28,104
Canton (★311,200) 93,077
Cincinnati (★1,480,100) 385,457
Cleveland (★2,218,400) 573,822
Cleveland Heights (★Cleveland) 56,438
Columbus (★963,600) 565,032
Dayton (★768,200) 193,536
East Liverpool (★51,700) 16,687
Elyria (★Cleveland) 57,538
Euclid (★Cleveland) 59,999
Hamilton (★Cincinnati) 63,189
Kettering (★Dayton) 61,186
Lakewood (★Cleveland) 61,963
Lancaster (★52,500) 34,953
Lima (★108,000) 47,827
Lorain (★Cleveland) 75,416
Mansfield (★112,700) 53,927
Marion (★57,300) 37,040
Middletown (★105,500) 43,719
Newark (★83,400) 41,200
Parma (★Cleveland) 92,548
Portsmouth (★69,100) 25,943
Sandusky (★61,900) 31,360
Springfield (★128,000) 72,563
Steubenville (★135,000) 26,400
Toledo (★595,500) 354,635
Warren (★Youngstown) 56,629
Youngstown (★499,600) 115,436
Zanesville (★69,700) 28,655

UNITED STATES: Oklahoma

1980 C 3,025,487
Enid (★54,300) 50,363
Lawton (★96,800) 80,054
Midwest City (★Oklahoma City) 49,559
Muskogee (★49,600) 40,011
Norman (★Oklahoma City) 68,020
Oklahoma City (★742,000) 403,484
Tulsa (★567,100) 360,919

▲ Población de un municipio, comuna o distrito entero, incluyendo sus áreas rurales.
• Ciudad más grande de un país.
★ Población o designación de un área metropolitana, incluyendo los suburbios.
C Censo. **E** Estimado oficial. **UE** Estimado no oficial.

▲ Population d'une municipalité, d'une commune ou d'un district, zone rurale incluse.
• Ville la plus peuplée du pays.
★ Population de l'agglomération (ou nom de la zone métropolitaine englobante).
C Recensement. **E** Estimation officielle. **UE** Estimation non officielle.

▲ População de um município, comuna ou distrito, inclusive as respectivas áreas rurais.
• Maior cidade de um país.
★ População ou indicação de uma área metropolitana.
C Censo. **E** Estimativa oficial. **UE** Estimativa não oficial.

UNITED STATES: Oregon

1980 C	2,633,156
Corvallis (★95,100)	40,960
Eugene (★218,100)	105,664
Medford (★117,600)	39,603
Portland (★1,227,200)	368,139
Salem (★175,300)	89,233

UNITED STATES: Pennsylvania

1980 C	11,864,751
Abington (★Philadelphia)	59,084
Allentown (★529,000)	103,758
Altoona (★128,900)	57,078
Bensalem (★Philadelphia)	52,368
Bethlehem (★Allentown)	70,419
Bristol (★Philadelphia)	58,773
Butler (★87,700)	17,026
Coatesville (★79,600)	10,698
Erie (★248,800)	119,123
Hanover (★56,000)	14,890
Harrisburg (★396,300)	53,264
Haverford (★Philadelphia)	52,371
Hazleton (★74,800)	27,318
Johnstown (★168,400)	35,496
Lancaster (★227,200)	54,725
Lebanon (★82,900)	25,711
Lower Merion Township (★Philadelphia)	59,629
New Castle (★76,400)	33,621
Oil City (★46,600)	13,881
Penn Hills (★Pittsburgh)	57,632
Philadelphia (★5,208,600)	1,688,210
Pittsburgh (★2,218,800)	423,959
Pottstown (★82,200)	22,729
Pottsville (★58,100)	18,195
Reading (★245,100)	78,686
Scranton (★492,700)	88,117
Sharon (★83,000)	19,057
State College (★82,100)	36,130
Uniontown (★60,100)	14,510
Upper Darby (★Philadelphia)	84,054
Washington (★69,100)	18,363
Wilkes-Barre (★Scranton)	51,551
Williamsport (★88,000)	33,401
York (★213,300)	44,619

UNITED STATES: Rhode Island

1980 C	947,154
Cranston (★Providence)	71,992
East Providence (★Providence)	50,980
Newport (★60,700)	29,259
Pawtucket (★Providence)	71,204
Providence (★921,800)	156,804
Warwick (★Providence)	87,123

UNITED STATES: South Carolina

1980 C	3,122,717
Anderson (★74,500)	27,546
Charleston (★352,000)	69,855
Columbia (★375,900)	101,229
Florence (★60,800)	29,842
Greenville (★328,500)	58,242
North Charleston (★Charleston)	62,504
Rock Hill (★76,900)	35,327
Spartanburg (★172,100)	43,826
Sumter (★77,400)	24,921

UNITED STATES: South Dakota

1980 C	690,768
Pierre	11,973
Rapid City (★58,100)	46,492
Sioux Falls (★92,200)	81,343

UNITED STATES: Tennessee

1980 C	4,591,120
Bristol (★81,500)	23,986
Chattanooga (★359,200)	169,728
Clarksville (★91,200)	54,777
Jackson (★60,500)	49,258
Johnson City (★125,500)	43,617
Kingsport (★116,600)	32,027
Knoxville (★490,000)	175,045
Memphis (★852,900)	646,174
Murfreesboro (★45,700)	32,845
Nashville (★633,900)	455,651

UNITED STATES: Texas

1980 C	14,227,574
Abilene (★103,600)	98,315
Amarillo (★153,300)	149,230
Arlington (★Dallas)	160,113
Austin (★430,200)	345,890
Baytown (★Houston)	56,923
Beaumont (★346,300)	118,102
Brownsville (★299,800)	84,997
Bryan (★86,600)	45,917
Corpus Christi (★272,000)	231,134
Dallas (★2,727,300)	904,078
Denton	48,063
El Paso (★1,037,700)	425,259
Fort Worth (★Dallas)	385,164
Freeport (★82,700)	13,444
Galveston (★144,700)	61,902
Garland (★Dallas)	138,857
Grand Prairie (★Dallas)	71,462
Harlingen (★88,200)	43,543
Houston (★2,755,100)	1,595,138
Irving (★Dallas)	109,943
Killeen (★119,500)	46,296
Laredo (★298,900)	91,449
Longview (★89,300)	62,762
Lubbock (★198,100)	173,979
Lufkin (★52,500)	28,562
McAllen (★207,600)	66,281
Mesquite (★Dallas)	67,053
Midland (★78,000)	70,525
Odessa (★112,200)	90,027
Pasadena (★Houston)	112,560
Plano (★Dallas)	72,331
Port Arthur (★Beaumont)	63,053
Richardson (★Dallas)	72,496
San Angelo (★77,300)	73,240
San Antonio (★968,200)	786,023
Sherman (★64,300)	30,413
Temple (★64,200)	42,354
Texarkana (★86,700)	31,271
Tyler (★97,500)	70,508
Victoria (★54,300)	50,695
Waco (★141,800)	101,261
Wichita Falls (★117,700)	94,201

UNITED STATES: Utah

1980 C	1,461,037
Logan (★50,300)	26,844
Ogden (★217,300)	64,407
Orem (★Provo)	52,399
Provo (★215,200)	74,108
Salt Lake City (★682,400)	163,034
Sandy (★Salt Lake City)	52,210
West Valley City (★Salt Lake City)	72,509

UNITED STATES: Vermont

1980 C	511,456
Burlington (★115,300)	37,712
Montpelier (★50,500)	8,241
Rutland (★49,800)	18,436

UNITED STATES: Virginia

1980 C	5,346,797
Alexandria (★Washington)	103,217
Arlington (★Washington)	152,599
Charlottesville (★75,000)	39,916
Chesapeake (★Norfolk)	114,486
Danville (★77,800)	45,642
Hampton (★Newport News)	122,617
Lynchburg (★119,500)	66,743
Martinsville (★70,200)	18,149
Newport News (★314,600)	144,903
Norfolk (★795,600)	266,979
Portsmouth (★Norfolk)	104,577
Richmond (★690,600)	219,214
Roanoke (★216,000)	100,220
Suffolk (★Norfolk)	47,621
Virginia Beach (★Norfolk)	262,199

UNITED STATES: Washington

1980 C	4,132,353
Bellevue (★Seattle)	73,903
Bellingham (★75,300)	45,794
Bremerton (★115,900)	36,208
Everett (★Seattle)	54,413
Lakes District (★Seattle)	54,533
Longview (★65,500)	31,052
Olympia (★97,400)	27,447
Pasco (★126,300)	18,425
Seattle (★2,077,100)	493,846
Spokane (★303,200)	171,300
Tacoma (★Seattle)	158,501
Yakima (★103,600)	49,826

UNITED STATES: West Virginia

1980 C	1,950,186
Beckley (★72,800)	20,492
Charleston (★236,300)	63,968
Clarksburg (★60,300)	22,371
Fairmont (★61,700)	23,863
Huntington (★273,900)	63,684
Morgantown (★71,500)	27,605
Parkersburg (★99,700)	39,946
Wheeling (★168,200)	43,070

UNITED STATES: Wisconsin

1980 C	4,705,642
Appleton (★167,600)	58,913
Beloit (★62,000)	35,207
Eau Claire (★88,100)	51,509
Fond du Lac (★50,700)	35,863
Green Bay (★161,300)	87,899
Janesville (★73,500)	51,071
Kenosha (★96,700)	77,685
La Crosse (★87,500)	48,347
Madison (★294,300)	170,616
Manitowoc (★59,400)	32,547
Milwaukee (★1,374,700)	636,297
Oshkosh (★67,600)	50,016
Racine (★136,300)	85,725
Sheboygan (★77,100)	48,085
Waukesha (★Milwaukee)	50,365
Wausau (★74,800)	32,426
Wauwatosa (★Milwaukee)	51,308
West Allis (★Milwaukee)	63,982

UNITED STATES: Wyoming

1980 C	469,557
Casper (★67,000)	51,016
Cheyenne (★61,900)	47,716

URUGUAY

1975 C	2,788,429
Las Piedras (★Montevideo)	53,331
Melo	38,487
Mercedes	34,512
Minas	35,225
• MONTEVIDEO (★1,450,000)	1,237,227
Paysandú	62,199
Rivera	48,780
Salto	73,897

VANUATU

1986 E	138,000
• PORT VILA (★18,000)	13,067

VATICAN CITY / Città del Vaticano

1982 E	736

VENDA

1985 E	459,819
Makwarela	3,712
• Shayandima	4,853
THOHOYANDOU	3,641

VENEZUELA

1981 C	14,515,885
Acarigua	80,200
Barcelona (1971C)	78,201
Barinas	90,000
Barquisimeto	504,000
Baruta (★Caracas)	180,100
Cabimas	183,000
Calabozo	51,000
• CARACAS (★3,600,000)	3,041,000
Carúpano	82,000
Catia La Mar (★Caracas) (1971C)	62,200
Chacao (★Caracas)	101,900
Ciudad Bolívar	151,000
Ciudad Guayana	212,000
Ciudad Ojeda (Lagunillas)	129,000
Coro	95,000
Cumaná	173,000
El Tigre	93,000
La Victoria	56,000
Los Dos Caminos (★Caracas) (1971C)	59,211
Los Teques (★Caracas)	96,400
Maiquetía (★Caracas) (1971C)	59,238
Maracaibo	929,000
Maracay	355,000
Maturín	181,000
Mérida	99,000
Petare (★Caracas)	334,800
Pozuelos	69,200
Puerto Cabello	94,000
Puerto la Cruz	81,800
Punto Fijo	123,000
San Cristóbal	280,000
San Felipe	56,000
Valencia	523,000
Valera	115,000

VIETNAM / Viet Nam

1979 C	52,741,766
Bien-hoa	190,086
Cam-pha (1971E)	90,000
Cam-ranh (1973E)	118,111
Can-tho	182,856
Da-lat (1973E)	105,072
Da-nang	318,655
Gia-dinh (1968E)	151,100
Hai-phong (▲1,279,067)	330,755
HA-NOI (★1,500,000)	819,913
Hon-gay	115,312
Hue	165,865
Long-xuyen	112,488
My-tho	101,496
Nam-dinh	161,180
Nha-trang	172,663
Phan-thiet (1967E)	58,300
Phu-vinh (1971E)	51,500
Qui-nhon	130,534
Rach-gia (1971E)	104,161
Thai-nguyen	138,023
Thanh-hoa	103,981
• Thanh-pho Ho Chi Minh (Sai-gon) (★3,100,000)	2,441,185
Vinh	154,040
Vung-tau (1971E)	108,436

VIRGIN ISLANDS, BRITISH

1980 C	12,034
• ROAD TOWN	2,479

VIRGIN ISLANDS OF THE UNITED STATES

1980 C	96,569
• CHARLOTTE AMALIE (★32,000)	11,842

WALLIS AND FUTUNA / Wallis et Futuna

1976 C	9,113
MATA-UTU	558
• Ono	624

WESTERN SAHARA

1974 E	108,000
• EL AAIÚN	20,000

WESTERN SAMOA / Samoa i Sisifo

1981 C	156,349
• APIA	33,170

YEMEN / Al-Yaman

1980 C	7,162,000
Al-Hudaydah	126,400
• ṢAN'Ā'	277,800
Ta'izz	119,600

YEMEN, PEOPLE'S DEMOCRATIC REPUBLIC OF / Jumhūrīyat al-Yaman ad-Dīmuqrāṭīyah ash-Sha'bīyah

1984 E	2,108,705
• 'ADAN (★318,000)	176,100
Al-Mukallā	58,000

YUGOSLAVIA / Jugoslavija

1981 C	22,427,595
Banja Luka (▲183,618)	104,000
• BEOGRAD (★1,400,000)	936,200
Bitola (▲137,835)	72,900
Kragujevac (▲164,823)	89,900
Ljubljana (▲305,211)	205,600
Maribor (▲185,699)	105,100
Niš (▲230,711)	151,600
Novi Sad (▲257,685)	170,800
Osijek (▲158,790)	103,600
Pančevo (★Beograd)	60,600
Priština (▲211,156)	96,100
Rijeka (▲193,044)	160,300
Sarajevo (▲448,500)	374,500
Skopje (▲506,547)	406,400
Split (▲235,922)	193,600
Subotica (▲154,611)	93,500
Titograd (▲132,290)	73,000
Tuzla (▲121,717)	61,100
Zagreb	768,700
Zenica (▲132,733)	60,500
Zrenjanin (▲139,300)	63,900

ZAIRE / Zaïre

1984 C	29,671,407
Bandundu	63,189
Beni	73,319
Boma	88,556
Bukavu	171,064
Bumba	46,823
Bunia	46,224
Butembo	78,633
Gandajika	60,263
Gemena	62,641
Goma	76,745
Ilebo (Port-Francqui)	48,831
Isiro	78,871
Kabinda	81,752
Kalemie (Albertville)	70,694
Kananga (Luluabourg)	290,898
Kikwit	146,784
Kindu	68,044
• KINSHASA (LÉOPOLDVILLE)	2,653,558
Kisangani (Stanleyville)	282,650
Kolwezi	201,382
Likasi (Jadotville)	194,465
Lisala	40,471
Lubumbashi (Élisabethville)	543,268
Matadi	144,742
Mbandaka (Coquilhatville)	125,263
Mbuji-Mayi (Bakwanga)	423,363
Mwene-Ditu	72,567
Tshikapa	105,484
Yangambi	53,726

ZAMBIA

1980 C	5,661,801
Chililabombwe (Bancroft) (★56,582)	25,900
Chingola	130,872
Kabwe (Broken Hill)	127,420
Kalulushi	53,383
Kitwe (★283,962)	207,500
Livingstone	61,296
Luanshya (★113,422)	61,600
• LUSAKA	535,830
Mufulira (★138,824)	77,100
Ndola	250,490

ZIMBABWE

1982 C	7,539,000
Bulawayo	413,814
Chitungwiza (★Harare)	172,556
Gweru	78,918
• HARARE (★890,000)	656,011
Mutare	69,621

▲ Population of an entire municipality, commune, or district, including rural area.
• Largest city in country.
★ Population or designation of the metropolitan area, including suburbs.
C Census. **E** Official estimate. **UE** Unofficial estimate.

▲ Bevölkerung eines ganzen städtischen Verwaltungsgebietes, eines Kommunalbezirkes oder eines Distrikts, einschliesslich ländlicher Gebiete.
• Grösste Stadt des Landes.
★ Bevölkerung oder Bezeichnung der Stadtregion einschliess lich Vororte.
C Volkszählung. **E** Offizielle Schätzung. **UE** Inoffizielle Schätzung.

The Index includes in a single alphabetical list some 160,000 names appearing on the maps. Each name is followed by a page reference to one or more maps and by the location of the feature on the map, in coordinates of latitude and longitude. If a page contains several maps, a lowercase letter identifies the particular map. The page reference for two-page maps is always to the left-hand page.

Most map features are indexed to the largest-scale map on which they appear. However, a feature usually is not indexed to a Metropolitan Area map if it is also shown on another map where it can be seen in a broader setting. Countries, mountain ranges, and other extensive features are generally indexed to the largest-scale map that shows them in their entirety.

The order in which index information is presented is shown in the English, German, Spanish, French, and Portuguese headings at the center of each two-page spread.

For example:

ENGLISH

Name	Page	Lat.°′	Long.°′

The features indexed are of three types: *point, areal,* and *linear.* For *point* features (for example, cities, mountain peaks, dams), latitude and longitude coordinates give the location of the point on the map. For *areal* features (countries, mountain ranges, etc.), the coordinates generally indicate the approximate center of the feature. For *linear* features (rivers, canals, aqueducts), the coordinates locate a terminating point—for example, the mouth of a river, or the point at which a feature reaches the map margin.

Name Forms Names in the Index, as on the maps, are generally in the local language and insofar as possible are spelled according to official practice. Diacritical marks are included, except that those used to indicate tone, as in Vietnamese, are usually not shown. Most features that extend beyond the boundaries of one country have no single official name, and these are usually named in English. Many English, German, Spanish, French, and Portuguese names, which may not be shown on the maps, appear in the Index as cross references. All cross references are indicated by the symbol →. A name that appears in a shortened version on the map due to space limitations is given in full in the Index, with the portion that is omitted on the map enclosed in brackets, for example, Acapulco [de Juárez].

Transliteration For names in languages not written in the Roman alphabet, the locally official transliteration system has been used where one exists. Thus, names in the Soviet Union and Bulgaria have been transliterated according to the systems adopted by the academies of science of these countries. Similarly, the transliteration for mainland Chinese names follows the Pinyin system, which has been officially adopted in mainland China. For languages with no one locally accepted transliteration system, notably Arabic, transliteration in general follows closely a system adopted by the United States Board on Geographic Names.

Alphabetization Names are alphabetized in the order of the letters of the English alphabet. Spanish *ll* and *ch*, for example, are not treated as distinct letters. Furthermore, diacritical marks are disregarded in alphabetization—German or Scandinavian *ä* or *ö* are treated as *a* or *o*.

The names of physical features may appear inverted, since they are always alphabetized under the proper, not the generic, part of the name, thus: "Gibraltar, Strait of ᵾ." Otherwise every entry, whether consisting of one word or more, is alphabetized as a single continuous entity. "Lakeland," for example, appears after "La Crosse" and before "La Salle." Names beginning with articles (Le Havre, Den Helder, Al-Qāhirah, As-Suways) are not inverted. Names beginning "Mc" are alphabetized as though spelled "Mac," and names beginning "St." and "Sainte" as though spelled "Saint."

In the case of identical names, towns are listed first, then political divisions, then physical features. Entries that are completely identical (including symbols, discussed below) are distinguished by abbreviations of their official country names and are sequenced alphabetically by country name. The many duplicate names in Canada, the United Kingdom, and the United States are further distinguished by abbreviations of the names of their primary subdivisions. (See list of abbreviations on pages 351-352).

Abbreviation and Capitalization Abbreviation and styling have been standardized for all languages. A period is used after every abbreviation even when this may not be the local practice. The abbreviation "St." is used only for "Saint." "Sankt" and other forms of the term are spelled out.

All names are written with an initial capital letter except for a few Dutch names, such as 's-Gravenhage. Capitalization of noninitial words in a name generally follows local practice.

Symbol The symbols that appear in the Index represent graphically the broad categories of the features named, for example, ʌ for mountain (Everest, Mount ʌ). An abbreviated key to the symbols, in the five Atlas languages, appears at the foot of each pair of Index pages. Superior numbers following some symbols in the Index indicate finer distinctions, for example, ʌ^1 for volcano (Fuji-san ʌ^1). A complete list of the symbols and superior numbers is given on page I•1.

Das Register umfasst in alphabetischer Anordnung etwa 160 000 in den Karten erscheinende Namen. Nach jedem Namen folgt die Seitenangabe zu einer oder mehreren Karten und die Lageangabe des Objektes in der Karte mit geographischer Länge und Breite. Enthält eine Seite mehrere Karten, so wird die betreffende Karte durch einen Kleinbuchstaben gekennzeichnet. Die Seitenangabe für Doppelseiten bezieht sich immer auf die linke Seite.

Die Verweise für die meisten Objekte in den Karten beziehen sich auf die Karte mit dem grössten Massstab. Normalerweise werden jedoch Verweise auf Objekte in den Karten der Stadtregionen nicht gegeben, wenn sie auf einer anderen Karte in grösserem Zusammenhang dargestellt sind. Die Lageangaben für Länder, Gebirgszüge und andere ausgedehnte Objekte beziehen sich allgemein auf die Karte grössten Massstabes, die sie in ihrer ganzen Ausdehnung zeigt.

Die Anordnung, in welcher die Lageangabe erfolgt, geht aus den englischen, deutschen, spanischen, französischen und portugiesischen Überschriften in der Mitte jeder Doppelseite hervor.

Zum Beispiel:

DEUTSCH

Name	Seite	Breite°′	Länge°′ E=Öst

Die aufgeführten Objekte gliedern sich in drei Gruppen: *punkt-, flächen-* und *linienförmige* Objekte. Bei *punktförmigen* Objekten (z.B. Städte, Berge, Dämme) beziehen sich die Angaben nach Länge und Breite auf die Signatur in der Karte. Bei *flächenhaften* Objekten (Länder, Gebirgszüge usw.) verweisen die Koordinaten im allgemeinen auf das ungefähre Zentrum des Objektes. Bei *linienhaften* Objekten (Flüsse, Kanäle, Wasserleitungen) beziehen sich die Koordinaten auf einen bestimmten Punkt, z.B. die Mündung eines Flusses oder den Punkt, an dem das Objekt den Kartenrand schneidet.

Namengebung Wie in den karten so sind auch im Register die Namen im allgemeinen in der örtlichen Namensform wiedergegeben und soweit als möglich in der amtlichen Schreibweise. Diakritische Zeichen wurden gesetzt; sie wurden nur dort weggelassen, wo sie, wie im Vietnamesischen, Tonhöhen kennzeichnen. Meist haben Objekte, die sich über die Grenzen eines Landes hinaus erstrecken, keinen einzelnen offiziellen Namen; normalerweise sind sie daher englisch beschriftet. Viele englische, deutsche, spanische, französische und portugiesische Namensformen, die nicht in den Karten enthalten sind, erscheinen im Register als Kreuzverweis. Alle Kreuzverweise werden durch das Symbol → gekennzeichnet. Namen, die aus Platzgründen in abgekürzter Form in der Karte erscheinen, werden im Register voll ausgeschrieben, wobei der auf der Karte weggelassene Teil in Klammern gesetzt ist, z.B. Acapulco [de Juárez].

Transkription Für die Transkription von Namen aus Sprachen, die nicht im lateinischen Alphabet geschrieben werden, wurde das offizielle Transkriptionssystem benutzt, sofern ein solches vorhanden ist. So wurden die Namen in der Sowjetunion und in Bulgarien nach dem von den wissenschaftlichen Akademien dieser Länder angewandten System transkribiert. Entsprechend wurden die Namen auf dem chinesischen Festland nach dem Pinyin-System übertragen, das offiziell in der Volksrepublik China eingeführt wurde. Bei Sprachen, für die ein allgemein anerkanntes Transkriptionssystem nicht vorliegt, vor allem für Arabisch, erfolgte die Transkription in enger Anlehnung an das vom United States Board on Geographic Names angewandte System.

Alphabetische Ordnung Die alphabetische Ordnung der Namen entspricht der Reihenfolge der Buchstaben im englischen Alphabet. So werden z.B. das spanische *ll* und *ch* nicht als besondere Buchstaben behandelt. Ferner wurden diakritische Zeichen beim Alphabetisieren nicht berücksichtigt, das deutsche oder skandinavische *ä* oder *ö* als *a* oder *o* behandelt.

Physische Objekte können umgestellt erscheinen, da sie immer nach dem Eigennamen und nicht nach dem Gattungsbegriff eingeordnet wurden, z.B. "Gibraltar, Strait of ᵾ". Ansonsten wurde jeder Eintrag, ob er aus einem Wort oder aus mehreren besteht, als eine einzige Einheit behandelt. So ist z.B. "Lakeland" nach "La Crosse," aber vor "La Salle" aufgeführt. Namen, die mit einem Artikel beginnen, wurden nicht umgestellt (Le Havre, Den Helder, Al-Qāhirah, As-Suways). Namen, die mit "Mc" beginnen, sind der Schreibweise "Mac" nach eingeordnet und Namen, die mit "St." und "Sainte" beginnen, entsprechend der Schreibweise "Saint".

Wo Namensgleichheit besteht, werden zunächst die Städte aufgeführt, dann politische Einheiten und schliesslich physische Objekte. Eintragungen, die vollkommen identisch sind (einschliesslich der weiter unten erläuterten Symbole), werden durch Hinzufügung der Abkürzung des offiziellen Ländernamens unterschieden und sind den Ländernamen nach alphabetisch geordnet. Die zahlreichen identischen Namen in Kanada, dem Vereinigten Königreich und den Vereinigten Staaten sind darüber hinaus noch durch Abkürzungen der obersten Verwaltungseinheit unterschieden. (Siehe Verzeichnis der Abkürzungen, Seite 351-352).

Abkürzungen und Grossschreibung Abkürzung und Schreibweise wurden für alle Sprachen vereinheitlicht. Nach jeder Abkürzung steht ein Punkt, auch wenn dies nicht der jeweiligen Gepflogenheit entspricht. Die Abkürzung "St." wird ausschliesslich für "Saint" gebraucht. "Sankt" und andere Formen dieses Begriffes werden ausgeschrieben.

Der erste Buchstabe eines Namens wird gross geschrieben, ausgenommen einige holländische Namen wie 's-Gravenhage. Die Grossschriebung der weiteren Worte eines zusammengesetzten Namens folgt im allgemeinen der landesüblichen Schreibweise.

Symbole Die im Register verwendeten Symbole veranschaulichen graphisch die zahlreichen Kategorien der benannten Objekte, z.B. ʌ = Berg (Everest, Mount ʌ). Eine Kurzgefasste Erläuterung der Symbole erscheint in jeder die fünf Sprachen des Atlas am Fusse jeder Doppelseite des Registers. Hochgestellte Ziffern hinter Symbolen im Register bezeichnen feinere Unterscheidungen, z.B. ʌ^1= Vulkan (Fuji-san ʌ^1). Eine vollständige Übersicht der Symbole und hochgestellten Ziffern findet sich auf Seite I•1.

El Índice contiene en una sola lista alfabética, alrededor de 160 000 nombres que aparecen en los mapas. Después de cada nombre está indicada la página o las páginas de referencia, en los cuales se encuentran los mismos, y las coordinadas de la latitud y la longitud del lugar del rasgo. Si una página contiene various mapas, letras minúsculas identifican el mapa correspondiente. Para mapas que ocupan dos páginas, la página de referencia siempre es la de la izquierda.

La mayoría de los nombres que figuran en el Índice, se efiere a los mapas en la escala más grande. Sin embargo, un nombre no se refiere en un mapa metropolitano si ya aparece en otro mapa, donde se muestra en un marco de mayor proporción. Los países, sierras y otros rasgos extensivos se refieren generalmente en el Índice en los mapas de escalas mayores en que se muestran completos.

El orden en que la información del Índice se presenta, aparece en un encabezamiento al centro de cada par de páginas, en inglés, alemán, español, francés y portugués.

Por ejemplo:

ESPAÑOL

Nombre	Página	Lat.°′	Long.°′ W=Oeste

Los rasgos anotados en el Índice son de tres tipos: *el punto, el área y la extensión linear.* Para rasgos que indican *el punto* (como por ejemplo, las ciudades, picos de montañas, presas), las coordinadas de latitud y longitud indican la posición exacta del punto sobre el mapa. Respecto a *las áreas* (como países, sierras, etc.), las coordinadas indican usualmente el centro aproximado del rasgo particular. En cuanto a *los rasgos lineares* (ríos, canales, acueductos) las coordinadas indican los puntos terminales, por ejemplo, la boca de un río, o el punto en que un rasgo físico alcanza el margen del mapa.

Las Formas de los Nombres Los nombres que aparecen en el Índice, así como también en los mapas, se dan en general en el idioma local, y en tanto que es posible siguen la ortografía oficialmente aceptada. Incluímos también marcas diacríticas, excepto las que se usan para indicar tono, como en la lengua vietnamita. A causa de que la mayoría de los rasgos que se extienden más allá de las fronteras de un país no tienen un solo nombre oficial, éstos se denominan usualmente en inglés. Muchos nombres, en inglés, alemán, español, francés y portugués, que pueden no figurar en el mapa, se dan como referencia de una página a otra en el Índice. Todas las referencias que pasan a otras páginas se indican con el símbolo →. Un nombre que aparece en el mapa en forma abreviada, debido a la limitación de espacio, en el Índice figura en su forma completa, poniendo entre paréntesis angulares la parte omitida en el mapa, por ejemplo Acapulco [de Juárez].

"Trasliteración" Para los nombres escritos en los idiomas que no usan el alfabeto latino, el sistema oficial de trasliteración ha sido utilizado donde localmente existe. Así, los nombres de la Unión Soviética y de Bulgaria se trasliteran conforme a los sistemas aceptados por las academias de las ciencias de sus respectivos países. De la misma manera, la trasliteración de los nombres en chino continental siguen el sistema Pinyin que ha sido oficialmente adoptado en este país. Para idiomas sin ningún sistema localmente aceptado de trasliteración, particularmente para el árabe, éstos se trasliteran usando por lo general un sistema adoptado por el United States Board on Geographic Names.

Alfabetización Los nombres se han ordenado de acuerdo con el alfabeto inglés. Las letras del alfabeto en español *ll* y *ch* por ejemplo, no se han considerado letras separadas. Además, los signos diacríticos no se toman en cuenta en la alfabetización—en alemán o escadinavo letras *ä* u *ö* se tratan como *a* u *o*.

Los nombres de los rasgos físicos algunas veces se invierten, ya que se ordenan alfabéticamente según la parte propia y no genérica del nombre. Así por ejemplo, en el caso del Estrecho de Gibraltar aparece: Gibraltar, Strait of ɥ. Por lo demás, cada renglón, sea una palabra o una frase, se alfabetiza como una unidad. Por ejemplo, "Lakeland" aparece después de "La Crosse" y antes de "La Salle". Los nombres que comienzan con artículos (Le Havre, Den Helder, Al-Qāhirah, As-Suways) no están invertidos. Nombres que empiezan con "Mc" se tratan como si fueran del grupo de "Mac", y los que comienzan con "St." y "Sainte" se incluyen con "Saint".

En los casos de nombres idénticos, las poblaciones aparecen primero, las divisiones políticas después y finalmente los rasgos físicos. En caso de ser completamente idénticos (incluyendo los símbolos, discutidos más abajo) se distinguen por medio de abreviaciones de los nombres oficiales de los países a que pertenecen y son puestos en orden alfabético, de acuerdo al nombre de cada país. Hay muchos nombres duplicados en Canadá, el Reino Unido y los Estados Unidos de América, y éstos se distinguen además, por sus subdivisiones primarias. (Vease abajo, la lista de abreviaciones en las páginas 351-352).

Abreviaciones y Mayúsculas Las abreviaciones y el uso de las mayúsculas se han hecho uniformes para todos los idiomas. Se usa un punto al final de la abreviación, aun cuando en algunos casos no sea ésta la práctica local. La abreviación "St." se usa sólo para "Saint". Las otras formas del mismo término, como "Sankt", se escriben completas.

La mayúscula se usa al comienzo de todos los nombres a excepción de algunos holandeses, como 's-Gravenhage. Las palabras que no son iniciales, se dan con mayúscula o minúscula, según la práctica local.

Símbolos Los símbolos que aparecen en el Índice representan gráficamente las grandes categorías de los rasgos que se han ido nombrando, por ejemplo, ʌ para montaña (Everest, Mount ʌ). Una clave abreviada para los símbolos aparece en los cinco idiomas del Atlas al pie de cada par de páginas del Índice. Los números que siguen más arriba del símbolo indican alguna diferencia más precisa, por ejemplo, ʌ[1] para un volcán (Fuji-san ʌ[1]). Una lista completa de símbolos y números superiores aparece en la página I•1.

L'index rassemble en une seule liste alphabétique, quelque 160 000 noms qui figurent sur les cartes. Chaque nom est suivi d'un renvoi à une ou plusieurs pages de cartes et de coordonnées géographiques qui permettent de localiser ce qu'il désigne. Si une page contient plusieurs cartes, une lettre minuscule permet d'identifier chaque carte. Pour les cartes en double page, la référence indiquée est toujours celle de la page de gauche.

En général, l'index renvoie aux cartes où l'information recherchée est reproduite à la plus grande échelle; cependant, les cartes de zones métropolitaines ne sont pas utilisées si le terme géographique figure sur une autre carte dans un contexte plus large. Pour les éléments de grande dimension comme les pays et les chaînes de montagnes, l'index renvoie généralement à la carte à grande échelle qui les représente en entier.

L'ordre des informations de l'index est rappelé en tête de chaque double page dans les cinq langues: anglais, allemand, espagnol, français et portugais.

Par exemple:

FRANÇAIS

Nom	Page	Lat.°′	Long.°′ W=Ouest

Les termes de l'index désignent des réalités géographiques de type *ponctuel*, *spatial* ou *linéaire*. Leur position est déterminée par les coordonnées géographiques du lieu quand les données sont de type *ponctuel* (villes, sommets, barrages, etc.), quand elles sont de type *spatial* (pays, chaînes de montagnes, etc.) par les coordonnées du centre approximatif de la zone considérée, et, quand elles sont du type *linéaire* (aqueducs, canaux, etc.) par les coordonnées soit d'un point terminal comme l'embouchure d'un cours d'eau, soit du point où les limites de la carte les interrompent.

Forme des Toponymes Les noms de l'index comme ceux des cartes sont généralement reproduits dans la langue locale et, dans la mesure du possible, selon leur orthographe officielle. Les signes diacritiques sont conservés, à l'exclusion de ceux qui servent à indiquer le ton, comme en vietnamien. La plupart des données géographiques qui s'étendent au-delà des frontières d'un pays sont nommées souvent en anglais, car elles n'ont pas de nom officiel unique. Beaucoup de noms anglais, allemands, espagnols, français et portugais, qui ne se trouvent pas sur les cartes, sont cités dans l'index sous forme de renvois. Tous les renvois sont signalés par le symbole (→). Un nom écrit sur la carte sous forme abrégée, par manque de place, figure en entier dans l'index; la partie omise est entre crochets, par exemple: Acapulco [de Juárez].

Transcription des Noms Pour les noms qui viennent de langues n'utilisant pas l'alphabet romain, le système local et officiel de transcription a été utilisé là où il existait. Ainsi, les noms russes et bulgares ont été transcrits selon les systèmes adoptés par les académies des sciences de ces pays. De même, pour la transcription des noms de la Chine continentale, on a employé le système Pinyin, officiellement adopté en Chine continentale. Pour les langues qui n'ont pas de système officiel de transcription en alphabet romain, notamment l'arabe, la transcription suit généralement de près le système adopté par le United States Board on Geographic Names (Comité américain pour les noms géographiques).

Ordre Alphabétique Les noms sont classés dans l'ordre de l'alphabet anglais. Les *ll* et *ch* espagnols, par exemple, ne sont pas traités comme des lettres séparées. De plus, on ne tient pas compte des signes diacritiques: le *ä* et le *ö* allemand ou scandinave correspondent au *a* et *o* sans tréma.

Les noms des données physiques peuvent se trouver inversés car ils sont toujours classés suivant le nom propre. Exemple: "Gibraltar, Strait of ɥ". Par ailleurs, les noms composés d'un ou plusieurs mots sont considérés comme une seule entité. Exemple: "Lakeland" est inscrit après "La Crosse" et avant "La Salle". Les noms qui commencent par un article (Le Havre, Den Helder, Al-Qāhirah, As-Suways) ne sont pas inversés. Les noms qui commencent par "Mc" sont classés comme s'ils s'écrivaient "Mac" et les noms qui commencent par "St." ou "Sainte" sont classés comme s'ils s'écrivaient "Saint".

Dans le cas de noms identiques, les villes sont inscrites d'abord, puis les divisions politiques, et ensuite les données physiques. Les noms qui sont tout à fait identiques (y compris les symboles qui s'y rapportent) se distinguent par leur pays d'origine, noté en abrégé dans l'ordre alphabétique. Les noms que l'on rencontre plusieurs fois, au Canada, au Royaume-Uni et aux Etats-Unis se distinguent grâce à l'abréviation de la première subdivision administrative de ce pays (voir la liste des abréviations de la page 351-352).

Abréviations et Majuscules L'usage des abréviations a été standardisé pour toutes les langues. Un point suit chaque abréviation, même quand ce n'est pas l'usage dans certaines langues. L'abréviation "St." sert uniquement pour le mot "Saint". "Sankt" et les autres formes du mot "Saint" sont écrites en entier.

Tous les noms commencent par une majuscule, sauf quelques noms des Pays-Bas comme 's-Gravenhage. Certains noms prennent une majuscule, même s'ils ne se trouvent pas au début du terme; on a adopté, en général, l'orthographe locale.

Symboles Les symboles utilisés dans l'index donnent une représentation graphique des réalités géographiques mentionnées. Par exemple, ʌ pour une montagne (Everest, Mount ʌ). Une explication abrégée des symboles dans les cinq langues de l'Atlas se trouve au bas de chaque double page de l'index. Les indices qui accompagnent certains symboles permettent une distinction plus précise. Par exemple, ʌ[1] pour volcan (Fujisan ʌ[1]). Une liste complète des symboles et indices est donnée à la page I•1.

O Índice contém, numa só lista alfabética, cerca de 160 000 nomes que figuram nos mapas. Segue-se a cada nome a referência a um ou mais mapas e a localização do acidente geográfico no mapa pelas respectivas coordenadas de latitude e longitude. A referência a mapas que ocupam duas páginas fica sempre na página da esquerda. A maior parte dos acidentes geográficos estão indexados no mapa em que aparecem em escala maior. No entanto, um acidente geográfico não é geralmente indexado num mapa de Área Metropolitana se também figura em outro mapa em que aparece em contexto mais amplo. Os países, cordilheiras e outros acidentes geográficos de maior extensão estão geralmente indexados no mapa em escala maior que os apresente em seu todo.

A ordem em que as informações são apresentadas no Índice figura no cabeçalho, a cada duas páginas, em inglês, alemão, espanhol, francês e PORTUGUÊS.

Por exemplo:

PORTUGUÊS

Nome	Página	Lat.°′	Long.°′ W=Oeste

Os acidentes indexados são de três tipos: *ponto*, *espacial* (área) e *linear* (extensão). Para acidentes que indicam *pontos* (como, por exemplo, cidades, picos de montanhas, represas), as coordenadas de latitude e longitude indicam a posição exata do ponto no mapa. No que se refere aos acidentes espaciais (como países, cordilheiras etc.), as coordenadas geralmente indicam o centro aproximado do acidente específico. Quanto aos *acidentes lineares* (rios, canais, aquedutos), as coordenadas localizam os pontos terminais, como, por exemplo, a foz de um rio, ou o ponto em que um acidente físico atinge a margem do mapa.

Formas dos nomes Os nomes que aparecem no Índice, assim como também nos mapas, são geralmente apresentados na língua local, e tanto quanto possível, seguem a ortografia oficial. Usam-se, também, os sinais diacríticos, exceto os que indicam tom, como na língua vietnamita. A maioria dos acidentes geográficos que se estendem além das fronteiras de um só país não possuem um nome oficial único; nesses casos, estão geralmente indicados em inglês. Muitos nomes em inglês, alemão, espanhol, português e francês podem não figurar nos mapas, mas aparecem no Índice como referências remissivas. Todas essas referências são indicadas pelo símbolo (→). Um nome que aparece no mapa em forma abreviada devido a limitações de espaço, figura no Índice em sua forma completa, com a parte omitida no mapa entre chaves (por exemplo, Acapulco [de Juárex]).

Transliteração Para os nomes escritos em línguas que não usam o alfabeto latino, foi utilizado o sistema oficial de transliteração, sempre que este existia. Assim, os nomes da União Soviética e da Bulgária foram transliterados de acordo com os sistemas adotados pelas academias de ciências desses países. Do mesmo modo, a transliteração dos nomes da China continental seguem o sistema Pinyin, que foi oficialmente adotado nesse país. Para as línguas que não possuem um sistema de transliteração adotado oficialmente, em especial o árabe, a transliteração geralmente segue de perto o sistema adotado pelo Conselho de Nomes Geográficos dos Estados Unidos (United States Board on Geographic Names).

Alfabetação Os nomes foram ordenados de acordo com o alfabeto inglês. Por exemplo, o espanhol *ll* e *ch* não foram considerados como letras separadas. Ademais, os sinais diacríticos não foram considerados na alfabetação. Por exemplo, em alemão ou escandinavo as letras *ä* ou *ö* foram tratradas como *a* ou *o*.

Os nomes dos acidentes físicos podem aparecer, às vezes, invertidos, já que foram sempre alfabetados pela parte específica e não genérica do nome, como, por exemplo, *Gibraltar, estreito de* ɥ. Por outro lado, cada entrada do Índice, quer constituída por uma só palavra ou mais de uma, foi alfabetada como uma unidade contínua. Por exemplo, "Lakeland" aparece depois de "La Grosse" e antes de "La Salle". Os nomes que começam por artigo (Le Havre, Den Helder, Al-Qāhirah, As-Suways) não são invertidos. Os nomes que começam por "Mc" são alfabetados como se fossem soletrados "Mac", e os que começam por "St." e "Sainte" como se fossem soletrados "Saint".

Nos casos de nomes idênticos, as cidades estão relacionadas em primeiro lugar; depois as divisões políticas e em seguida os acidentes físicos. As entradas completamente idênticas (inclusive símbolos, mencionados mais abaixo), distinguem-se pelas abreviaturas dos nomes oficiais dos países a que pertencem e são arrolados na ordem alfabética do nome do país. Os muitos nomes repetidos no Canadá, no Reino Unido e nos Estados Unidos, são ainda diferenciados pelas abreviaturas dos nomes das respectivas subdivisões primárias (Ver a lista de abreviaturas, das páginas 351-352).

Abreviações e uso de maiúsculas As abreviaturas e o estilo foram normalizados em todas as línguas. Usa-se um ponto depois de cada abreviatura, mesmo que não seja essa a prática local. A abreviatura "St." só é usada para "Saint". As outras formas do termo, tal como "Sankt", são escritas por extenso.

Todos os nomes são escritos com a inicial maiúscula exceto em alguns nomes holandeses, como 's-Gravenhage. O uso de maiúsculas em palavras não iniciais de um nome segue geralmente a prática local.

Símbolos Os símbolos que aparecem no Índice representam graficamente as grandes categorias dos acidentes indicados, por exemplo, ʌ para montanha (Everest, Mount ʌ). Uma chave abreviada dos símbolos nas cinco línguas do Atlas figura no pé de cada par de páginas do Índice. Os números altos que acompanham certos símbolos do Índice indicam diferenças mais precisas, como, por exemplo, ʌ[1] para vulcão (Fuji-san ʌ[1]). Uma lista completa de símbolos e números altos aparece à pág. I•1.

	LOCAL NAME	ENGLISH	DEUTSCH	ESPAÑOL	FRANÇAIS	PORTUGUÊS
Ab., Can.	Alberta	Alberta	Alberta	Alberta	Alberta	Alberta
Afg.	Afghānestān	Afghanistan	Afghanistan	Afganistán	Afghanistan	Afeganistão
Afr.	—	Africa	Afrika	Africa	Afrique	África
Ak., U.S.	Alaska	Alaska	Alaska	Alaska	Alaska	Alasca
Al., U.S.	Alabama	Alabama	Alabama	Alabama	Alabama	Alabama
Alg.	Algérie/ Djazaïr	Algeria	Algerien	Argelia	Algérie	Argélia
Am.Sam.	American Samoa/ Amerika Samoa	American Samoa	Amerikanisch-Samoa	Samoa Americana	Samoa américaines	Samoa Americana
And.	Andorra	Andorra	Andorra	Andorra	Andorre	Andorra
Ang.	Angola	Angola	Angola	Angola	Angola	Angola
Anguilla	Anguilla	Anguilla	Anguilla	Anguilla	Anguilla	Anguilla
Ant.	—	Antarctica	Antarktis	Antártida	Antarctique	Antártida
Antig.	Antigua and Barbuda	Antigua and Barbuda	Antigua und Barbuda	Antigua y Barbuda	Antigua-et -Barbuda	Antígua e Barbuda
Ar., U.S.	Arkansas	Arkansas	Arkansas	Arkansas	Arkansas	Arkansas
Arc. O.	—	Arctic Ocean	Nördliches Eismeer	Océano Artico	Océan Glacial arctique	Ártico, Oceano
Arg.	Argentina	Argentina	Argentinien	Argentina	Argentine	Argentina
Ar. Su.	Al-'Arabīyah as-Su'ūdīyah	Saudi Arabia	Saudi-Arabien	Arabia Saudita	Arabia saoudite	Arábia Saudita
Aruba	Aruba	Aruba	Aruba	Aruba	Aruba	Aruba
Asia	—	Asia	Asien	Asia	Asie	Ásia
Atl. O.	—	Atlantic Ocean	Atlantischer Ozean	Océano Atlántico	Océan Atlantique	Atlântico, Oceano
Austl.	Australia	Australia	Australien	Australia	Australie	Austrália
Az., U.S.	Arizona	Arizona	Arizona	Arizona	Arizona	Arizona
Ba.	Bahamas	Bahamas	Bahamas	Bahamas	Bahamas	Bahamas
Bahr.	Al-Baḥrayn	Bahrain	Bahrain	Bahrein	Bahreïn	Bahrein
Barb.	Barbados	Barbados	Barbados	Barbados	Barbade	Barbados
B.A.T.	British Antarctic Territory	British Antarctic Territory	Britisches Antarktis-Territorium	Territorio Antártico Británico	Territoires britanniques de l'Antarctique	Território Antártico Britânico
B.C., Can.	British Columbia	British Columbia	Britisch Kolumbien	Columbia Británica	Colombie britannique	Colúmbia Britânica
Bdi.	Burundi	Burundi	Burundi	Burundi	Burundi	Burundi
Bel.	Belgique/ België	Belgium	Belgien	Bélgica	Belgique	Bélgica
Belize	Belize	Belize	Belize	Belice	Belize	Belize
Bénin	Bénin	Benin	Benin	Benin	Bénin	Benin
Ber.	Bermuda	Bermuda	Bermuda	Bermudas	Bermudes	Bermudas
Ber. S.	—	Bering Sea	Beringmeer	Mar de Bering	Mer de Bering	Bering, Mar de
B.I.O.T.	British Indian Ocean Territory	British Indian Ocean Territory	Britisch-es Indischer Ozean-Territorium	Territorio Británico del Océano Indico	Territoire britannique de l'océan Indien	Território Britânico do Oceano Indico
Blg.	Bâlgarija	Bulgaria	Bulgarien	Bulgaria	Bulgarie	Bulgária
Bol.	Bolivia	Bolivia	Bolivien	Bolivia	Bolivie	Bolívia
Boph.	Bophuthat swana	Bophuthat-swana	Bophuthat-swana	Bophuthat-swana	Bophuthat-swana	Bophuthat-swana
Bngl.	Bangladesh	Bangladesh	Bangladesch	Bangladesh	Bangladesh	Bangladesh
Bots.	Botswana	Botswana	Botswana	Botswana	Botswana	Botsuana
Bra.	Brasil	Brazil	Brasilien	Brasil	Brésil	Brasil
B.R.D.	Bundesrepublik Deutschland	Federal Republic of Germany	Bundesrepublik Deutschland	República Federal de Alemania	République fédérale d' Allemagne	Alemanha, República Federal da
Bru.	Brunei	Brunei	Brunei	Brunei	Brunéi	Brunei
Br. Vir. Is.	British Virgin Islands	British Virgin Islands	Britischen Jungferninseln	Islas Vírgenes Británicas	Îles Vierges britanniques	Virgens Britânicas, Ilhas
Burkina	Burkina Faso	Burkina Faso	Burkina Faso	Burkina Faso	Burkina Faso	Burkina Faso
Ca., U.S.	California	California	Kalifornien	California	Californie	Califórnia
Cam.	Cameroun	Cameroon	Kamerun	Camerún	Cameroun	Camarão
Can.	Canada	Canada	Kanada	Canadá	Canada	Canadá
Carib. S.	—	Caribbean Sea	Karibisches Meer	Mar Caribe	Mer des Caraïbes	Caribe, Mar do
Cay. Is	Cayman Islands	Cayman Islands	Caiman-Inseln	Islas Caimán	Îles Caïmanes	Cayman, Ilhas
Centraf.	République centrafricaine	Central African Republic	Zentralafrikanische Republik	República Centroafricana	République centrafricaine	Centro-Africana, República
Česko.	Československo	Czechoslovakia	Tschechoslowakei	Checoslovaquia	Tchécoslovaquie	Tchecoslováquia
Chile	Chile	Chile	Chile	Chile	Chili	Chile
Christ. I.	Christmas Island	Christmas Island	Weihnachtsinsel	Isla Christmas	Île Christmas	Christmas, Ilha
Ciskei	Ciskei	Ciskei	Ciskei	Ciskei	Ciskei	Ciskei
C. Iv.	Côte d'Ivoire	Ivory Coast	Elfenbeinküste	Costa de Marfil	Côte d'Ivoire	Costa do Marfim
C.M.I.K.	Chosŏn-minjujuŭi-inmin-konghwaguk	North Korea	Nordkorea	Corea del Norte	Corée du Nord	Coréia do Norte
Co., U.S.	Colorado	Colorado	Colorado	Colorado	Colorado	Colorado
Cocos Is.	Cocos (Keeling) Islands	Cocos (Keeling) Islands	Cokos-Inseln	Islas Cocos (Keeling)	Îles des Cocos (Keeling)	Cocos (Keeling) Ihas
Col.	Colombia	Colombia	Kolumbien	Colombia	Colombie	Colômbia
Comores	Comores/ Al-Qumur	Comoros	Komoren	Comoras	Comores	Comores
Congo	Congo	Congo	Kongo	Congo	Congo	Congo
Cook Is.	Cook Islands	Cook Islands	Cook-Inseln	Islas Cook	Îles Cook	Cook, Ilhas
Ct., U.S.	Connecticut	Connecticut	Connecticut	Connecticut	Connecticut	Connecticut
C.R.	Costa Rica	Costa Rica	Costa Rica	Costa Rica	Costa Rica	Costa Rica
Cuba	Cuba	Cuba	Kuba	Cuba	Cuba	Cuba
C.V.	Cabo Verde	Cape Verde	Kap Verde	Cabo Verde	Cap-Vert	Cabo Verde
Dan.	Danmark	Denmark	Dänemark	Dinamarca	Danemark	Dinamarca
D.C., U.S.	District of Columbia	District of Columbia	District of Columbia	District of Columbia	District of Columbia	Distrito de Columbia
D.D.R.	Deutsche Demokratische Republik	German Democratic Republic	Deutsche Demokratische Republik	República Democrática Alemana	République démocratique allemande	Alemã, República Democrática
De., U.S.	Delaware	Delaware	Delaware	Delaware	Delaware	Delaware
Dji.	Djibouti	Djibouti	Djibouti	Djibouti	Djibouti	Djibout
D.Y.	Druk-Yul	Bhutan	Bhutan	Bhután	Bhoutan	Butã
Ec.	Ecuador	Ecuador	Ecuador	Ecuador	Équateur	Equador
Ellás	Ellás	Greece	Griechenland	Grecia	Grèce	Grécia
El Sal.	El Salvador	El Salvador	El Salvador	El Salvador	El Salvador	El Salvador
Eng., U.K.	England	England	England	Inglaterra	Angleterre	Inglaterra
Esp.	España	Spain	Spanien	España	Espagne	Espanha
Europe	—	Europe	Europa	Europa	Europe	Europa
Falk. Is.	Falkland Islands	Falkland Islands	Falkland-Inseln	Islas Malvinas	Îles Falkland	Falkland, Ilhas
Fiji	Fiji	Fiji	Fidschi	Fiji	Fidji	Fiji (Fidji)
Fl., U.S.	Florida	Florida	Florida	Florida	Floride	Flórida
Før.	Føroyar	Faeroe Islands	Färöer	Islas Feroe	Îles Féroé	Faeroe, Ilhas
Fr.	France	France	Frankreich	Francia	France	França
Ga., U.S.	Georgia	Georgia	Georgia	Georgia	Georgie	Geórgia
Gabon	Gabon	Gabon	Gabun	Gabón	Gabon	Gabão
Gam.	Gambia	Gambia	Gambia	Gambia	Gambie	Gâmbia
Ghana	Ghana	Ghana	Ghana	Ghana	Ghana	Gana
Gib.	Gibraltar	Gibraltar	Gibraltar	Gibraltar	Gibraltar	Gibraltar
Gren.	Grenada	Grenada	Grenada	Grenada	Grenade	Grenada
Guad.	Guadeloupe	Guadeloupe	Guadeloupe	Guadalupe	Guadeloupe	Guadalupe
Guam	Guam	Guam	Guam	Guam	Guam	Guam
Guat.	Guatemala	Guatemala	Guatemala	Guatemala	Guatemala	Guatemala
Guernsey	Guernsey	Guernsey	Guernsey	Guernesey	Guernesey	Guernsey
Gui.-B.	Guiné-Bissau	Guinea-Bissau	Guina-Bissau	Guinea-Bissau	Guinée-Bissau	Guiné-Bissau

	LOCAL NAME	ENGLISH	DEUTSCH	ESPAÑOL	FRANÇAIS	PORTUGUÊS
Gui. Ecu.	Guinea Ecuatorial	Equatorial Guinea	Äquatorial-guinea	Guinea Ecuatorial	Guinée équatoriale	Guiné Equatorial
Guinée	Guinée	Guinea	Guinea	Guinea	Guinée	Guiné
Guy.	Guyana	Guyana	Guyana	Guyana	Guyane	Guiana
Guy. Fr.	Guyane française	French Guiana	Französisch-Guayana	Guayana Francesa	Guyane française	Guiana Francesa
Haï.	Haïti	Haiti	Haiti	Haití	Haïti	Haiti
Hi., U.S.	Hawaii	Hawaii	Hawaii	Hawaii	Hawaii	Havaí
H.K.	Hong Kong	Hong Kong	Hongkong	Hong Kong	Hong-Kong	Hong Kong
Hond.	Honduras	Honduras	Honduras	Honduras	Honduras	Honduras
Ia., U.S.	Iowa	Iowa	Iowa	Iowa	Iowa	Iowa
Id., U.S.	Idaho	Idaho	Idaho	Idaho	Idaho	Idaho
I.I.A.	Ittiḥād al-Imārāt al-'Arabīyah	United Arab Emirates	Vereinigte Arabische Emirate	Emiratos Arabes Unidos	Émirats arabes unis	Emirados Árabes Unidos
Il., U.S.	Illinois	Illinois	Illinois	Illinois	Illinois	Illinois
In., U.S.	Indiana	Indiana	Indiana	Indiana	Indiana	Indiana
India	India/Bharat	India	Indien	India	Inde	Índia
Ind. O.	—	Indian Ocean	Indischer Ozean	Océano Indico	Océan Indien	Índico, Oceano
Indon.	Indonesia	Indonesia	Indonesien	Indonésia	Indonésie	Indonésia
I. of Man	Isle of Man	Isle of Man	Insel Man	Isla de Man	Île de Man	Man, Ilha de
Īrān	Īrān	Iran	Iran	Irán	Iran	Irã
'Irāq	Al-'Irāq	Iraq	Irak	Iraq	Iraq	Iraque
Ire.	Ireland/Éire	Ireland	Irland	Irlanda	Irlande	Irlanda
Ísland	Ísland	Iceland	Island	Islandia	Islande	Islândia
Isr. Occ.	—	Israeli Occupied Areas	Von Israel besetztes Gebiet	Áreas ocupadas por Israel	Territoires occupés par Israël	Áreas occupadas por Israel
It.	Italia	Italy	Italien	Italia	Italie	Itália
Ityo	Ityopiya	Ethiopia	Äthiopien	Etiopía	Éthiopie	Etiópia
Jam.	Jamaica	Jamaica	Jamaika	Jamaica	Jamaïque	Jamaica
Jersey	Jersey	Jersey	Jersey	Jersey	Jersey	Jersey
Jugo.	Jugoslavija	Yugoslavia	Jugoslawien	Yugoslavia	Yougoslavie	Iugoslávia
J.Y.D.S.	Jumhūrīyat al-Yaman ad-Dīmuqrāṭīyah ash-Sha'bīyah	People's Democratic Republic of Yemen	Demokratische Volksrepublik Jemen	República Popular Democrática del Yemen	République démocratique populaire du Yémen	Iêmen, República Popular Democrática do
Kal. Nun.	Kalaallit Nunaat/ Grønland	Greenland	Grönland	Groenlandia	Groenland	Groenlândia
Kam.	Kâmpŭchéa Prâchéathipâteyy	Kampuchea (Cambodia)	Kampuchea (Kambodscha)	Kampuchea (Camboya)	Kampuchea (Cambodge)	Kampuchea (Camboja)
Kenya	Kenya	Kenya	Kenia	Kenya	Kenya	Quênia
Kipros	Kipros/Kıbrıs	Cyprus	Zypern	Chipre	Chypre	Chipre
Kiribati	Kiribati	Kiribati	Kiribati	Kiribati	Kiribati	Kiribati
Ks., U.S.	Kansas	Kansas	Kansas	Kansas	Kansas	Kansas
Kuwayt	Al-Kuwayt	Kuwait	Kuwait	Kuwait	Koweït	Kuwait
Ky., U.S.	Kentucky	Kentucky	Kentucky	Kentucky	Kentucky	Kentucky
La., U.S.	Louisiana	Louisiana	Louisiana	Luisiana	Louisiane	Louisiana
Lao	Lao	Laos	Laos	Laos	Laos	Lao
Leso.	Lesotho	Lesotho	Lesotho	Lesotho	Lesotho	Lesoto
Liber.	Liberia	Liberia	Liberia	Liberia	Libéria	Libéria
Lībiyā	Lībiyā	Libya	Libyen	Libia	Libye	Líbia
Liech.	Liechtenstein	Liechtenstein	Liechtenstein	Liechtenstein	Liechtenstein	Liechtenstein
Lubnān	Al-Lubnān	Lebanon	Libanon	Líbano	Liban	Líbano
Lux.	Luxembourg	Luxembourg	Luxemburg	Luxemburgo	Luxembourg	Luxemburgo
Ma., U.S.	Massachusetts	Massachusetts	Massachusetts	Massachu-setts	Massachusetts	Massachusetts
Macau	Macau	Macau	Macau	Macao	Macao	Macau
Madag.	Madagasikara/ Madagascar	Madagascar	Madagaskar	Madagascar	Madagascar	Madagascar
Magreb	Al-Magreb	Morocco	Marokko	Marruecos	Maroc	Marrocos
Magy.	Magyarország	Hungary	Ungarn	Hungría	Hongrie	Hungria
Malaŵi	Malaŵi	Malawi	Malawi	Malawi	Malawi	Malaui
Malay.	Malaysia	Malaysia	Malaysia	Malasia	Malaisie	Malásia
Mald.	Maldives	Maldives	Malediven	Maldivas	Maldives	Maldivas
Mali	Mali	Mali	Mali	Malí	Mali	Mali
Malta	Malta	Malta	Malta	Malta	Malte	Malta
Mart.	Martinique	Martinique	Martinique	Martinica	Martinique	Martinica
Maur.	Mauritanie/ Mūrītāniyā	Mauritania	Mauretanien	Mauritania	Mauritanie	Mauritânia
Maus.	Mauritius	Mauritius	Mauritius	Mauricio	Maurice	Maurício
Mayotte	Mayotte	Mayotte	Mayotte	Mayotte	Mayotte	Mayotte
Mb., Can.	Manitoba	Manitoba	Manitoba	Manitoba	Manitoba	Manitoba
Md., U.S.	Maryland	Maryland	Maryland	Maryland	Maryland	Maryland
Me., U.S.	Maine	Maine	Maine	Maine	Maine	Maine
Medit. S.	—	Mediterranean Sea	Mittelmeer	Mar Mediterráneo	Méditerranée-Mer	Mediterrâneo, Mar
Méx.	México	Mexico	Mexiko	México	Mexique	México
Mi., U.S.	Michigan	Michigan	Michigan	Michigan	Michigan	Michigan
Mid. Is.	Midway Islands	Midway Islands	Midway-Inseln	Islas Midway	Îles Midway	Midway, Ilhas
Misr	Misr	Egypt	Ägypten	Egipto	Égypte	Egito
Mn., U.S.	Minnesota	Minnesota	Minnesota	Minnesota	Minnesota	Minnesota
Mo., U.S.	Missouri	Missouri	Missouri	Missouri	Missouri	Missouri
Moç.	Moçambique	Mozambique	Mosambik	Mozambique	Mozambique	Moçambique
Monaco	Monaco	Monaco	Monaco	Mónaco	Monaco	Mônaco
Mong.	Mongol Ard Uls	Mongolia	Mongolei	Mongolia	Mongolie	Mongólia
Monts.	Montserrat	Montserrat	Montserrat	Montserrat	Montserrat	Montserrat
Ms., U.S.	Mississippi	Mississippi	Mississippi	Misisipi	Mississippi	Mississippi
Mt., U.S.	Montana	Montana	Montana	Montana	Montana	Montana
Mya.	Myanma	Burma	Birma	Birmania	Birmanie	Birmânia
N.A.	—	North America	Nordamerika	América del Norte	Amérique du Nord	América do Norte
Namibia	Namibia	Namibia	Namibia	Namibia	Namibie	Namíbia
Nauru	Nauru/ Naoero	Nauru	Nauru	Nauru	Nauru	Nauru
N.B., Can.	New Brunswick	New Brunswick	Neubraun-schweig	Nueva Brunswick	Nouveau-Brunswick	Nova Brunswick
N.C., U.S.	North Carolina	North Carolina	Nord Karolina	Carolina del Norte	Caroline du Nord	Carolina do Norte
N. Cal.	Nouvelle Calédonie	New Caledonia	Neukaledonien	Nueva Caledonia	Nouvelle Calédonie	Nova Caledônia
N.D., U.S.	North Dakota	North Dakota	Nord Dakota	Dakota del Norte	Dakota du Nord	Dakota do Norte
Ne., U.S.	Nebraska	Nebraska	Nebraska	Nebraska	Nebraska	Nebraska
Ned.	Nederland	Netherlands	Niederlande	Países Bajos	Pays-Bas	Paises Baixos
Ned. Ant.	Nederlandse Antillen	Netherlands Antilles	Niederländische Antillen	Antillas Neerlandeses	Antilles néerlandaises	Antilhas Holandesas
Nepāl	Nepāl	Nepal	Nepal	Nepal	Népal	Nepal
Nf., Can	Newfoundland	Newfoundland	Neufundland	Terranova	Terre-Neuve	Terra Nova
N.H., U.S.	New Hampshire	New Hampshire	New Hampshire	Nuevo Hampshire	New Hampshire	Nova Hampshire
Nic.	Nicaragua	Nicaragua	Nicaragua	Nicaragua	Nicaragua	Nicárágua
Nig.	Nigeria	Nigeria	Nigeria	Nigeria	Nigéria	Nigéria
Niger	Niger	Niger	Niger	Niger	Niger	Niger
Nihon	Nihon	Japan	Japan	Japón	Japon	Japão
N. Ire., U.K.	Northern Ireland	Northern Ireland	Nordirland	Irlanda del Norte	Irlande du Nord	Irlanda do Norte
Niue	Niue	Niue	Niue	Niue	Nioué	Niue
N.J., U.S.	New Jersey	New Jersey	New Jersey	Nueva Jersey	New Jersey	Nova Jersey
N.M., U.S.	New Mexico	New Mexico	New Mexico	Nueva Mexico	Nouveau-Mexique	Nova México
Nor.	Norge	Norway	Norwegen	Noruega	Norvege	Noruega
Norf. I.	Norfolk Island	Norfolk Island	Norfolk-Insel	Isla Norfolk	Île Norfolk	Norfolk, Ilha

	LOCAL NAME	ENGLISH	DEUTSCH	ESPAÑOL	FRANÇAIS	PORTUGUÊS
N.S., Can.	Nova Scotia	Nova Scotia	Neu Schottland	Nueva Escocia	Nouvelle-Écosse	Nova Scotia
N.T., Can.	Northwest Territories	Northwest Territories	Nord-West Territorien	Territorios del Noroeste	Territoires du Nord-Ouest	Territórios do Noroeste
Nv., U.S.	Nevada	Nevada	Nevada	Nevada	Nevada	Nevada
N.Y., U.S.	New York	New York	New York	Nueva York	New York	Nova York
N.Z.	New Zealand	New Zealand	Neuseeland	Nueva Zelandia	Nouvelle-Zélande	Nova Zelândia
Oc.	—	Oceania	Ozeanien	Oceanía	Océanie	Oceania
Oh., U.S.	Ohio	Ohio	Ohio	Ohio	Ohio	Ohio
Ok., U.S.	Oklahoma	Oklahoma	Oklahoma	Oklahoma	Oklahoma	Oklahoma
On., Can.	Ontario	Ontario	Ontario	Ontario	Ontario	Ontário
Or., U.S.	Oregon	Oregon	Oregon	Oregón	Oregon	Oregon
Öst	Österreich	Austria	Österreich	Austria	Autriche	Austria
Pa., U.S.	Pennsylvania	Pennsylvania	Pennsylvanien	Pensilvania	Pennsylvanie	Pennsylvania
Pac., O.	—	Pacific Ocean	Pazifischer Ozean	Océano Pacífico	Océan Pacifique	Pacífico, Oceano
Pāk.	Pākistān	Pakistan	Pakistan	Pakistán	Pakistan	Paquistão
Pan.	Panamá	Panama	Panama	Panamá	Panama	Panamá
Pap. N. Gui.	Papua New Guinea	Papua New Guinea	Papua-Neuguinea	Papua Nueva Guinea	Papouasie-Nouvelle Guinée	Papua-Nova Guiné
Para.	Paraguay	Paraguay	Paraguay	Paraguay	Paraguay	Paraguai
P.E., Can.	Prince Edward Island	Prince Edward Island	Prinz Edward-Insel	Isla Príncipe Eduardo	Île-du-Prince Édouard	Príncipe Eduardo, Ilha do
Perú	Perú	Peru	Peru	Perú	Pérou	Peru
Pil.	Pilipinas	Philippines	Philippinen	Filipinas	Philippines	Filipinas
Pit.	Pitcairn	Pitcairn	Pitcairn	Pitcairn	Pitcairn	Pitcairni
Pol.	Polska	Poland	Polen	Polonia	Pologne	Polônia
Poly. fr.	Polynésie française	French Polynesia	Französisch-Polynesien	Polinesia Francesa	Polynésie fran çaise	Polinésia Francesa
Port.	Portugal	Portugal	Portugal	Portugal	Portugal	Portugal
P.Q., Can.	Québec	Quebec	Quebec	Quebec	Québec	Québec
P.R.	Puerto Rico	Puerto Rico	Puerto Rico	Puerto Rico	Porto Rico	Porto Rico
P.S.N.Á.	Plazas de Soberanía en el Norte de África	Spanish North Africa	Spanisch-Nordafrika	Plazas de Soberanía en el Norte de África	Afrique du Nord espagnole	África do Norte Espanhola
Qatar	Qaṭar	Qatar	Katar	Qatar	Qatar	Qatar
Rep. Dom.	República Dominicana	Dominican Republic	Dominikanische Republik	República Dominicana	République dominicaine	Dominicana, República
Réu.	Réunion	Reunion	Réunion	Reunión	Réunion	Reunião
R.I., U.S.	Rhode Island	Rhode Island	Rhode Island	Rhode Island	Rhode Island	Rhode Island
Rom.	România	Romania	Rumänien	Rumania	Roumanie	Romênia
Rw.	Rwanda	Rwanda	Ruanda	Rwanda	Rwanda	Ruanda
S.A.	—	South America	Südamerika	América del Sur	Amérique du Sud	América do Sul
S. Afr.	South Africa/Suid-Afrika	South Africa	Südafrika	Sudáfrica	Afrique du Sud	África do Sul
S.C., U.S.	South Carolina	South Carolina	Süd Karolina	Carolina del Sur	Caroline du Sud	Carolina do Sul
S. Ch. S.	—	South China Sea	Südchinesisches Meer	Mar de China Meridional	Mer de Chine Méridionale	China do Sul, Mar da
Schw.	Schweiz/Suisse/Svizzera	Switzerland	Schweiz	Suiza	Suisse	Suiça
Scot., U.K.	Scotland	Scotland	Schottland	Escocia	Écosse	Escócia
S.D., U.S.	South Dakota	South Dakota	Süd Dakota	Dakota del Sur	Dakota du Sud	Dakota do Sul
Sen.	Sénégal	Senegal	Senegal	Senegal	Sénégal	Senegal
Sey.	Seychelles	Seychelles	Seschellen	Seychelles	Seychelles	Seychelles
Shq.	Shqipëri	Albania	Albanien	Albania	Albanie	Albânia
Sing.	Singapore	Singapore	Singapur	Singapur	Singapour	Cingapura
Sk., Can.	Saskatchewan	Saskatchewan	Saskatchewan	Saskatchewan	Saskatchewan	Saskatchewan
S.L.	Sierra Leone	Sierra Leone	Sierra Leone	Sierra Leone	Sierra Leone	Sierra Leoa
S. Lan.	Sri Lanka	Sri Lanka	Sri Lanka	Sri Lanka	Sri Lanka	Sri Lanka
S. Mar.	San Marino	San Marino	San Marino	San Marino	Saint-Marin	San Marino
Sol. Is.	Solomon Islands	Solomon Islands	Salomonen	Islas Salomón	Îles Salomon	Salomão, Ilhas
Som.	Somaliya	Somalia	Somalia	Somalia	Somalie	Somália
S.S.S.R.	Sojuz Sovetskich Socialističeskich Respublik	Union of Soviet Socialist Republics	Union der Sozialistischen Sowjetrepubliken	Unión de Repúblicas Socialistas Soviéticas	Union des Républiques socialistes soviétiques	União das Repúblicas Socialistas Soviéticas
St. C.-N.	St. Christopher-Nevis	St. Christopher-Nevis	Sankt Christopher-Nevis	San Cristóbal-Nevis	Saint-Christophe-Nevis	São Cristóvão-Neves
St. Hel.	St. Helena	St. Helena	Sankt Helena	Santa Elena	Sainte-Hélène	Santa Helena
St. Luc.	St. Lucia	St. Lucia	Sankt Lucia	Santa Lucía	Sainte-Lucie	Santa Lúcia
S. Tom./P.	São Tomé e Príncipe	Sao Tome and Principe	São Tomé und Principe	São Tomé y Príncipe	Sao Tomé-et-Principe	São Tomé e Príncipe

	LOCAL NAME	ENGLISH	DEUTSCH	ESPAÑOL	FRANÇAIS	PORTUGUÊS
St. P./M.	St.-Pierre-et-Miquelon	St. Pierre and Miquelon	Saint-Pierre und Miquelon	San Pedro y Miquelón	Saint-Pierre-et-Miquelon	São Pedro e Miquelon
St. Vin.	St. Vincent and the Grenadines	St. Vincent and the Grenadines	Sankt Vincent und die Grenadinen	San Vicente y las Granadinas	Saint-Vincent-et-Grenadines	São Vicente e Granadinas
Süd.	As-Sūdān	Sudan	Sudan	Sudán	Soudan	Sudão
Suomi	Suomi/Finland	Finland	Finnland	Finlandia	Finlande	Finlândia
Sur.	Suriname	Suriname	Suriname	Suriname	Suriname	Suriname
Sūriy.	As-Sūriyah	Syria	Syrien	Siria	Syrie	Síria
Sve.	Sverige	Sweden	Schweden	Suecia	Suède	Suécia
Swaziland	Swaziland	Swasiland	Swazilandia	Swaziland	Suazilândia	
T.a.a.f.	Terres australes et antarctiques françaises	French Southern and Antarctic Territories	Französische Süd-und Antarktis-Gebiete	Tierras Australes y Antárticas Francesas	Terres australes et antarctiques françaises	Terras Austrais e Antárticas Francesas
Taehan	Taehan min'guk	South Korea	Sü]dkorea	Corea del Sur	Corée du Sud	Coréia do Sul
T'aiwan	T'aiwan	Taiwan	Taiwan	Taiwán	Taïwan	Taiwan (Formosa)
Tan.	Tanzania	Tanzania	Tansania	Tanzanía	Tanzanie	Tanzânia
Tchad	Tchad	Chad	Tschad	Chad	Tchad	Tchad
T./C. Is.	Turks and Caicos Islands	Turks and Caicos Islands	Turks und-Caicos-Inseln	Islas Turcas y Caicos	Îles Turques et Caïques	Turcas e Caicos, Ilhas
Thai	Prathet Thai	Thailand	Thailand	Tailandia	Thaïlande	Tailândia
Tn., U.S.	Tennessee	Tennessee	Tennessee	Tennessee	Tennessee	Tennessee
Togo	Togo	Togo	Togo	Togo	Togo	Togo
Tok.	Tokelau	Tokelau	Tokelau	Tokelau	Tokélaou	Tokelau
Tonga	Tonga	Tonga	Tonga	Tonga	Tonga	Tonga
Trans.	Transkei	Transkei	Transkei	Transkei	Transkei	Transkei
Trin.	Trinidad and Tobago	Trinidad and Tobago	Trinidad und Tobago	Trinidad y Tabago	Trinité-et-Tobago	Trinidad e Tobago
T.T.P.I.	Trust Territory of the Pacific Islands	Trust Territory of the Pacific Islands	Treuhandgebiet Pazifische Inseln	Territorio Fideicometido de las Islas Pacificas	Territorie sous tutelle îles du Pacifique	Pacífico, Ilhas do (Território sob Tutela)
Tun.	Tunisie/Tunis	Tunisia	Tunesien	Túnez	Tunisie	Tunísia
Tür.	Türkiye	Turkey	Türkei	Turquía	Turquie	Turquia
Tuvalu	Tuvalu	Tuvalu	Tuvalu	Tuvalu	Tuvalu	Tuvalu
Tx., U.S.	Texas	Texas	Texas	Texas	Texas	Texas
Ug.	Uganda	Uganda	Uganda	Uganda	Ouganda	Uganda
U.K.	United Kingdom	United Kingdom	Vereinigtes Königreich	Reino Unido	Royaume-Uni	Reino Unido
'Umān	'Umān	Oman	Oman	Omán	Oman	Omã
Ur.	Uruguay	Uruguay	Uruguay	Uruguay	Uruguay	Uruguai
Urd.	Al-Urdunn	Jordan	Jordanien	Jordania	Jordanie	Jordânia
U.S.	United States	United States	Vereinigte Staaten	Estados Unidos	États-Unis	Estados Unidos
Ut.,U.S.	Utah	Utah	Utah	Utah	Utah	Utah
Va., U.S.	Virginia	Virginia	Virginia	Virginia	Virginie	Virgínia
Vanuatu	Vanuatu	Vanuatu	Vanuatu	Vanuatu	Vanuatu	Vanuatu
Vat.	Cittá del Vaticano	Vatican City	Vatikanstadt	Ciudad del Vaticano	Cité du Vatican	Vaticano
Ven.	Venezuela	Venezuela	Venezuela	Venezuela	Venezuela	Venezuela
Venda	Venda	Venda	Venda	Venda	Venda	Venda
Viet.	Viet-nam	Vietnam	Vietnam	Viet-Nam	Viet Nam	Vietnam
Vir. Is., U.S.	Virgin Islands	Virgin Islands (U.S.)	Amerikanische Jungferninseln	Islas Vírgenes (americanas)	Îles Vierges (américaines)	Virgens Americanas, Ilhas
Vt., U.S.	Vermont	Vermont	Vermont	Vermont	Vermont	Vermont
Wa., U.S.	Washington	Washington	Washington	Washington	Washington	Washington
Wake I.	Wake Island	Wake Island	Wake	Isla Wake	Île de Wake	Wake
Wales, U.K.	Wales	Wales	Wales	Gales	Galles	Gales
Wal./F.	Wallis et Futuna	Wallis and Futuna	Wallis und Futuna	Wallis y Futuna	Wallis et Futuna	Wallis e Futuna
Wi., U.S.	Wisconsin	Wisconsin	Wisconsin	Wisconsin	Wisconsin	Wisconsin
W. Sah.	—	Western Sahara	Westliche Sahara	Sahara Occidentale	Sahara occidental	Saara Ocidental
W. Sam.	Western Samoa/Samoa i Sisifo	Western Samoa	Westsamoa	Samoa Occidental	Samoa-Occidental	Samoa Ocidental
W.V., U.S.	West Virginia	West Virginia	West Virginia	Virginia Occidental	Virginie Occidentale	Virgínia Ocidental
Wy., U.S.	Wyoming	Wyoming	Wyoming	Wyoming	Wyoming	Wyoming
Yaman	Al-Yaman	Yemen	Jemen	Yemen	Yémen	Iêmen
Yis.	Yisra'el/Isrā'īl	Israel	Israel	Israel	Israël	Israel
Yk., Can.	Yukon	Yukon	Yukon	Yukon	Yukon	Yukon
Zaïre	Zaïre	Zaire	Zaire	Zaire	Zaïre	Zaire
Zam.	Zambia	Zambia	Sambia	Zambia	Zambie	Zâmbia
Zhg.	Zhongguo	China	China	China	Chine	China
Zimb.	Zimbabwe	Zimbabwe	Simbabwe	Zimbabwe	Zimbabwe	Zimbabwe

Key to Index Symbols

The symbols below represent the categories into which the physical and cultural features are classified in the Index. Broad categories appear in **boldface** type. Symbols with superior numbers identify subcategories.

Schlüssel zu den Symbolen des Registers

Die folgenden Symbole veranschaulichen die Kategorien, nach denen physische und kulturgeographische Objekte im Register geordnet sind. Die Oberbegriffe sind in **Fettdruck** hervorgehoben. Symbole mit hochgestellten Nummern kennzeichnen Unterbegriffe.

Clave de los Símbolos del Índice

Los símbolos abajo representan las categorías dentro de las cuales están clasificados los rasgos físicos y culturales que están incluídos en el Índice. Las grandes categorías aparecen en **negrilla.** Los símbolos que tienen números en su parte superior identifican las subcategorías.

Signification des Symboles de l'Index

Les symboles ci-dessous représentent les catégories sous lesquelles les données physiques et culturelles sont classées dans l'index. Les symboles en caractères **gras** correspondent aux catégories principales. Ceux suivis d'un indice désignent les subdivisions d'une même catégorie.

Chave dos Símbolos do Índice

Os símbolos abaixo representam as categorias em que estão classificados os acidentes físicos e culturais no Índice. As grandes categorias aparecem em **negrito.** Os símbolos acompanhados de números altos identificam as subcategorias.

ENGLISH	DEUTSCH	ESPAÑOL	FRANÇAIS	PORTUGUÊS
∧ **Mountain**	∧ **Berg**	∧ **Montaña**	∧ **Montagne**	∧ **Montanha**
∧[1] Volcano	∧[1] Vulkan	∧[1] Volcán	∧[1] Volcan	∧[1] Vulcão
∧[2] Hill	∧[2] Hügel	∧[2] Colina	∧[2] Colline	∧[2] Colina
⩕ **Mountains**	⩕ **Berge**	⩕ **Montañas**	⩕ **Montagnes**	⩕ **Montanhas**
⩕[1] Plateau	⩕[1] Hochebene	⩕[1] Meseta	⩕[1] Plateau	⩕[1] Planalto
⩕[2] Hills	⩕[2] Hügel	⩕[2] Colinas	⩕[2] Collines	⩕[2] Colinas
)(**Pass**	)(**Pass**	)(**Paso**	)(**Col**	)(**Passo**
∨ **Valley, Canyon**	∨ **Tal, Cañon**	∨ **Valle, Cañón**	∨ **Vallée, Canyon**	∨ **Vale, Canhão**
≚ **Plain**	≚ **Ebene**	≚ **Llano**	≚ **Plaine**	≚ **Planície**
≚[1] Basin	≚[1] Becken	≚[1] Cuenca	≚[1] Bassin	≚[1] Bacia
≚[2] Delta	≚[2] Delta	≚[2] Delta	≚[2] Delta	≚[2] Delta
▸ **Cape**	▸ **Kap**	▸ **Cabo**	▸ **Cap**	▸ **Cabo**
▸[1] Peninsula	▸[1] Halbinsel	▸[1] Península	▸[1] Péninsule	▸[1] Península
▸[2] Spit, Sand Bar	▸[2] Landzunge, Sandbarre	▸[2] Lengua de Tierra, Bajo	▸[2] Flèche, Banc de sable	▸[2] Ponta de Terra, Banco de Areia
I **Island**	I **Insel**	I **Isla**	I **Île**	I **Ilha**
I[1] Atoll	I[1] Atoll	I[1] Atolón	I[1] Atoll	I[1] Atol
I[2] Rock	I[2] Fels	I[2] Roca	I[2] Rocher	I[2] Rochedo
II **Islands**	II **Inseln**	II **Islas**	II **Îles**	II **Ilhas**
II[1] Rocks	II[1] Felsen	II[1] Rocas	II[1] Rochers	II[1] Rochedos
⩡ **Other Topographic Features**	⩡ **Andere Topographische Objekte**	⩡ **Otros Elementos Topográficos**	⩡ **Autres données topographiques**	⩡ **Outros Acidentes Topográficos**
⩡[1] Continent	⩡[1] Erdteil	⩡[1] Continente	⩡[1] Continent	⩡[1] Continente
⩡[2] Coast, Beach	⩡[2] Küste, Strand	⩡[2] Costa, Playa	⩡[2] Côte, Plage	⩡[2] Costa, Praia
⩡[3] Isthmus	⩡[3] Landenge	⩡[3] Istmo	⩡[3] Isthme	⩡[3] Istmo
⩡[4] Cliff	⩡[4] Kliff	⩡[4] Risco	⩡[4] Falaise	⩡[4] Falésia
⩡[5] Cave, Caves	⩡[5] Höhle, Höhlen	⩡[5] Cueva, Cuevas	⩡[5] Caverne, Cavernes	⩡[5] Caverna, Cavernas
⩡[6] Crater	⩡[6] Krater	⩡[6] Cráter	⩡[6] Cratère	⩡[6] Cratera
⩡[7] Depression	⩡[7] Senke	⩡[7] Depresión	⩡[7] Dépression	⩡[7] Depressão
⩡[8] Dunes	⩡[8] Dünen	⩡[8] Dunas	⩡[8] Dunes	⩡[8] Dunas
⩡[9] Lava Flow	⩡[9] Lavastrom	⩡[9] Corriente de Lava	⩡[9] Coulée de lave	⩡[9] Corrente de Lava
≏ **River**	≏ **Fluss**	≏ **Río**	≏ **Rivière, Fleuve**	≏ **Rio**
≏[1] River Channel	≏[1] Flussarm	≏[1] Brazo de Río	≏[1] Bras de rivière	≏[1] Canal de Rio
≣ **Canal**	≣ **Kanal**	≣ **Canal**	≣ **Canal**	≣ **Canal**
≣[1] Aqueduct	≣[1] Aquädukt	≣[1] Acueducto	≣[1] Aqueduc	≣[1] Aqueduto
⅃ **Waterfall, Rapids**	⅃ **Wasserfall Stromschnellen**	⅃ **Cascada, Rápidos**	⅃ **Chute d'eau, Rapides**	⅃ **Quedas d'água, Rápidos**
ц **Strait**	ц **Meeresstrasse**	ц **Estrecho**	ц **Détroit**	ц **Estreito**
⊂ **Bay, Gulf**	⊂ **Bucht, Golf**	⊂ **Bahía, Golfo**	⊂ **Baie, Golfe**	⊂ **Baía, Golfo**
⊂[1] Estuary	⊂[1] Trichtermündung	⊂[1] Estuario	⊂[1] Estuaire	⊂[1] Estuário
⊂[2] Fjord	⊂[2] Fjord	⊂[2] Fiordo	⊂[2] Fjord	⊂[2] Fiorde
⊂[3] Bight	⊂[3] Bucht	⊂[3] Bahía	⊂[3] Baie	⊂[3] Enseada
⊜ **Lake, Lakes**	⊜ **See, Seen**	⊜ **Lago, Lagos**	⊜ **Lac, Lacs**	⊜ **Lago, Lagos**
⊜[1] Reservoir	⊜[1] Stausee	⊜[1] Embalse	⊜[1] Réservoir, Retenue	⊜[1] Reservatório
☰ **Swamp**	☰ **Sumpf**	☰ **Pantano**	☰ **Marais**	☰ **Pântano**
⍓ **Ice Features, Glacier**	⍓ **Eis- und Gletscherformen**	⍓ **Accidentes Glaciales, Glaciar**	⍓ **Formes glaciaires, Glacier**	⍓ **Acidentes Glaciares, Geleira**
⊤ **Other Hydrographic Features**	⊤ **Andere Hydrographische Objekte**	⊤ **Otros Elementos Hidrográficos**	⊤ **Autres données hydrographiques**	⊤ **Outros Acidentes Hidrográficos**
⊤[1] Ocean	⊤[1] Ozean	⊤[1] Océano	⊤[1] Océan	⊤[1] Oceano
⊤[2] Sea	⊤[2] Meer	⊤[2] Mar	⊤[2] Mer	⊤[2] Mar

ENGLISH	DEUTSCH	ESPAÑOL	FRANÇAIS	PORTUGUÊS
⊤ **Other Hydrographic Features**	⊤ **Andere Hydrographische Objekte**	⊤ **Otros Elementos Hidrográficos**	⊤ **Autres données hydrographiques**	⊤ **Outros Acidentes Hidrográficos**
⊤[3] Anchorage	⊤[3] Ankerplatz	⊤[3] Ancladero	⊤[3] Ancrage	⊤[3] Ancoradouro
⊤[4] Oasis, Well, Spring	⊤[4] Oase, Brunnen, Quelle	⊤[4] Oasis, Pozo, Manantial	⊤[4] Oasis, Puits, Source	⊤[4] Oásis, Poço, Fonte, Manancial
✢ **Submarine Features**	✢ **Untermeerische Objekte**	✢ **Accidentes Submarinos**	✢ **Formes de relief sous-marin**	✢ **Acidentes Submarinos**
✢[1] Depression	✢[1] Senke	✢[1] Depresión	✢[1] Dépression	✢[1] Depressão
✢[2] Reef, Shoal	✢[2] Riff, Untiefe	✢[2] Arrecife, Bajo	✢[2] Récif, Haut-fond	✢[2] Recife, Baixio
✢[3] Mountain, Mountains	✢[3] Berg, Berge	✢[3] Montaña, Montañas	✢[3] Montagne, Montagnes	✢[3] Montanha, Montanhas
✢[4] Slope, Shelf	✢[4] Abhang, Schelf	✢[4] Talud, Plataforma	✢[4] Talus, Plateau continental	✢[4] Talude, Plataforma
◻ **Political Unit**	◻ **Politische Einheit**	◻ **Unidad Política**	◻ **Entité politique**	◻ **Unidade Política**
◻[1] Independent Nation	◻[1] Unabhängiger Staat	◻[1] Nación Independiente	◻[1] État indépendant	◻[1] País Independente
◻[2] Dependency	◻[2] Abhängiges Gebiet	◻[2] Dependencia	◻[2] Dépendance	◻[2] Dependência
◻[3] State, Canton, Republic	◻[3] Land, Kanton, Republik	◻[3] Estado, Cantón, República	◻[3] État, Canton, République	◻[3] Estado, Cantão, República
◻[4] Province, Region, Oblast	◻[4] Provinz, Landschaft, Oblast	◻[4] Provincia, Región, Oblast	◻[4] Province, Région, Oblast	◻[4] Província, Região, Oblast
◻[5] Department, District, Prefecture	◻[5] Département, Distrikt, Präfektur	◻[5] Departamento, Distrito, Prefectura	◻[5] Département, District, Préfecture	◻[5] Departamento, Distrito, Prefeitura
◻[6] County	◻[6] Grafschaft	◻[6] Condado	◻[6] Comté	◻[6] Condado
◻[7] City, Municipality	◻[7] Stadt, Stadtkreis	◻[7] Ciudad, Municipalidad	◻[7] Ville, Municipalité	◻[7] Cidade, Municipalidade
◻[8] Miscellaneous	◻[8] Verschiedenes	◻[8] Misceláneo	◻[8] Divers	◻[8] Diversos
◻[9] Historical	◻[9] Historisch	◻[9] Histórico	◻[9] Historique	◻[9] Sítio Histórico
☋ **Cultural Institution**	☋ **Kulturelle Institution**	☋ **Institución Cultural**	☋ **Institution culturelle**	☋ **Instituição Cultural**
☋[1] Religious Institution	☋[1] Religiöse Institution	☋[1] Institución Religiosa	☋[1] Institution religieuse	☋[1] Instituição Religiosa
☋[2] Educational Institution	☋[2] Erziehungs-institution	☋[2] Institución Educacional	☋[2] Établissement d'éducation	☋[2] Estabelecimento de Ensino
☋[3] Scientific, Industrial Facility	☋[3] Wissenschaftliche, Industrielle Anlage	☋[3] Institución Científica o Industrial	☋[3] Établissement scientifique ou industriel	☋[3] Estabelecimento Científico ou Industrial
⊥ **Historical Site**	⊥ **Historische Stätte**	⊥ **Sitio Histórico**	⊥ **Site historique**	⊥ **Sítio Histórico**
♠ **Recreational Site**	♠ **Erholungs- und Ferienort**	♠ **Sitio de Recreo**	♠ **Centre de loisirs**	♠ **Área de Lazer**
⊠ **Airport**	⊠ **Flughafen**	⊠ **Aeropuerto**	⊠ **Aéroport**	⊠ **Aeroporto**
■ **Military Installation**	■ **Militäranlage**	■ **Instalación Militar**	■ **Installation militaire**	■ **Instalação Militar**
◆ **Miscellaneous**	◆ **Verschiedenes**	◆ **Misceláneo**	◆ **Divers**	◆ **Diversos**
◆[1] Region	◆[1] Region	◆[1] Región	◆[1] Région	◆[1] Região
◆[2] Desert	◆[2] Wüste	◆[2] Desierto	◆[2] Désert	◆[2] Deserto
◆[3] Forest, Moor	◆[3] Wald, Moor	◆[3] Bosque, Páramo	◆[3] Forêt, Lande	◆[3] Floresta, Pântano
◆[4] Reserve, Reservation	◆[4] Reservat	◆[4] Reserva, Reservación	◆[4] Réserve	◆[4] Reserva
◆[5] Transportation	◆[5] Verkehr	◆[5] Transporte	◆[5] Transport	◆[5] Transporte
◆[6] Dam	◆[6] Damm	◆[6] Presa	◆[6] Barrage	◆[6] Represa
◆[7] Mine, Quarry	◆[7] Bergwerk, Steinbruch	◆[7] Mina, Cantera	◆[7] Mine, Carrière	◆[7] Mina, Pedreira
◆[8] Neighborhood	◆[8] Nachbarschaft	◆[8] Barrio	◆[8] Quartier	◆[8] Arredores, Vizinhança
◆[9] Shopping Center	◆[9] Einkaufszentrum	◆[9] Mercado	◆[9] Centre commercial	◆[9] Shopping Center

A

ENGLISH — Name / Page / Lat.°′ / Long.°′

DEUTSCH — Name / Seite / Breite°′ / Länge°′ E = Ost

Symbols in the index entries represent the broad categories identified in the key at the right. Symbols with superior numbers (⋀[1]) identify subcategories (see complete key on page *I · 1*).

Kartensymbole in dem Registerverzeichnis stellen die rechts in Schlüssel erklärten Kategorien dar. Symbole mit hochgestellten Ziffern (⋀[1]) bezeichnen Unterabteilungen einer Kategorie (vgl. vollständiger Schlüssel auf Seite *I · 1*).

Los símbolos incluídos en el texto del índice representan las grandes categorias identificadas con la clave a la derecha. Los símbolos con numeros en su parte superior (⋀[1]) identifican las subcategorías (véase la clave completa en la página *I · 1*).

Les symboles de l'index représentent les catégories indiquées dans la légende à droite. Les symboles suivis d'un indice (⋀[1]) représentent des sous-catégories (voir légende complète à la page *I · 1*).

Os símbolos incluídos no texto do índice representam as grandes categorias identificadas com a chave à direita. Os símbolos com números em sua parte superior (⋀[1]) identificam as subcategorias (veja-se a chave completa à página *I · 1*).

∧ Mountain	Berg	Montaña	Montagne	Montanha
⋀ Mountains	Berge	Montañas	Montagnes	Montanhas
)(Pass	Pass	Paso	Col	Passo
V Valley, Canyon	Tal, Cañon	Valle, Cañón	Vallée, Canyon	Vale, Canhão
≚ Plain	Ebene	Llano	Plaine	Planície
≻ Cape	Kap	Cabo	Cap	Cabo
I Island	Insel	Isla	Île	Ilha
II Islands	Inseln	Islas	Îles	Ilhas
▴ Other Topographic Features	Andere Topographische Objekte	Otros Elementos Topográficos	Autres données topographiques	Outros acidentes topográficos

ESPAÑOL — Nombre | Página | Lat.°′ | Long.°′ W = Oeste
FRANÇAIS — Nom | Page | Lat.°′ | Long.°′ W = Ouest
PORTUGUÊS — Nome | Página | Lat.°′ | Long.°′ W = Oeste

Symbol	English	Deutsch	Español	Français	Português
≃	River	Fluss	Río	Rivière	Rio
≊	Canal	Kanal	Canal	Canal	Canal
∟	Waterfall, Rapids	Wasserfall, Stromschnellen	Cascada, Rápidos	Chute d'eau, Rapides	Cascata, Rápidos
ʊ	Strait	Meeresstrasse	Estrecho	Détroit	Estreito
ᴄ	Bay, Gulf	Bucht, Golf	Bahía, Golfo	Baie, Golfe	Baía, Golfo
⊜	Lake, Lakes	See, Seen	Lago, Lagos	Lac, Lacs	Lago, Lagos
≡	Swamp	Sumpf	Pantano	Marais	Pântano
⊓	Ice Features, Glacier	Eis- und Gletscherformen	Accidentes Glaciales	Formes glaciaires	Acidentes glaciares
╤	Other Hydrographic Features	Andere Hydrographische Objekte	Otros Elementos Hidrográficos	Autres données hydrographiques	Outros acidentes hidrográficos
✣	Submarine Features	Untermeerische Objekte	Accidentes Submarinos	Formes de relief sous-marin	Acidentes submarinos
□	Political Unit	Politische Einheit	Unidad Politica	Entité politique	Unidade política
ᴗ	Cultural Institution	Kulturelle Institution	Institución Cultural	Institution culturelle	Instituição cultural
⊥	Historical Site	Historische Stätte	Sitio Histórico	Site historique	Sitio histórico
♠	Recreational Site	Erholungs- und Ferienort	Sitio de Recreo	Centre de loisirs	Area de Lazer
⊠	Airport	Flughafen	Aeropuerto	Aéroport	Aeroporto
■	Military Installation	Militäranlage	Instalación Militar	Installation militaire	Instalação militar
◆	Miscellaneous	Verschiedenes	Misceláneo	Divers	Diversos

Name	Page	Lat.°′	Long.°′
Aksengir ≐	85	43.40 N	76.14 E
Aksenkino	80	53.59 N	53.06 E
Aksenovo	82	55.40 N	38.15 E
Aksentjevo	82	55.25 N	35.54 E
Akšij	86	47.37 N	55.56 E
Akšijrak, chrebet ⋏	85	41.20 N	74.15 E
Aksinjino, S.S.S.R.	82	55.44 N	36.59 E
Aksinjino, S.S.S.R.	82	56.02 N	38.12 E
Aks'onovo	88	58.51 N	101.43 E
Aks'onovo-Zilovskoje	88	53.04 N	117.32 E
Aksoran, gora ∧	86	48.27 N	75.32 E
Akstafa	84	41.08 N	45.28 E
Akstafa ≐	84	41.15 N	45.26 E
Aksu, S.S.S.R.	80	50.56 N	53.06 E
Aksu, S.S.S.R.	86	52.28 N	71.59 E
Aksu, S.S.S.R.	86	45.37 N	79.30 E
Aksu, Zhg.	90	41.10 N	80.20 E
Aksu ≐, S.S.S.R.	85	43.22 N	73.54 E
Aksu ≐, S.S.S.R.	86	46.20 N	78.15 E
Aksu ≐, Tür.	130	37.36 N	36.46 E
Aksuart, ozero ⊜	86	51.24 N	64.28 E
Aksuat, S.S.S.R.	86	51.32 N	64.34 E
Aksuat, S.S.S.R.	86	47.45 N	82.40 E
Aksuat, S.S.S.R.	86	48.16 N	83.50 E
Aksubajevo	80	54.52 N	50.50 E
Aksu-Džabaglinskij zapovednik ♦	85	42.20 N	70.35 E
Aksum	144	14.08 N	38.43 E
Aktal	85	41.25 N	75.03 E
Aktanyš	80	55.43 N	54.05 E
Aktas, S.S.S.R.	85	42.57 N	70.04 E
Aktaš, S.S.S.R.	85	41.38 N	69.44 E
Aktaš, S.S.S.R.	86	50.18 N	87.44 E
Aktas, S.S.S.R.	86	48.02 N	66.21 E
Aktas, S.S.S.R.	86	49.47 N	72.59 E
Aktas, S.S.S.R.	86	50.06 N	76.40 E
Aktaş Gölü ⊜	84	41.15 N	43.12 E
Aktasty	86	50.44 N	61.43 E
Aktau	86	50.16 N	73.02 E
Aktau, gora ∧	86	48.00 N	71.45 E
Aktepe	130	36.44 N	36.27 E
Akterek, S.S.S.R.	85	43.22 N	75.18 E
Akterek, S.S.S.R.	85	42.14 N	77.45 E
Akto	85	39.08 N	75.57 E
Aktobe	85	43.13 N	67.46 E
Aktogaj, S.S.S.R.	86	44.27 N	76.42 E
Aktogaj, S.S.S.R.	86	48.18 N	74.58 E
Aktogaj, S.S.S.R.	86	46.57 N	79.40 E
Aktubek	86	48.37 N	71.06 E
Akt'ubinsk	86	50.17 N	57.10 E
Akt'ubinskij	80	54.49 N	52.47 E
Aktumsyk	86	46.40 N	57.19 E
Akt'uz	85	42.54 N	76.07 E
Aku	150	6.42 N	7.20 E
Akūbū (Akobo) ≐	140	7.47 N	33.03 E
Akui ≐	96	34.06 N	134.33 E
Akula	152	2.22 N	20.11 E
Akuliči Pervyje	76	53.11 N	33.13 E
Akulovo, S.S.S.R.	82	55.31 N	36.42 E
Akulovo, S.S.S.R.	82	56.05 N	38.59 E
Akumadan	150	7.24 N	1.57 W
Akune	92	32.01 N	130.11 E
Akun Island I	180	54.12 N	165.35 W
Akure	150	7.15 N	5.12 E
Akureyri	24a	65.44 N	18.08 W
Akurli	272c	19.01 N	73.08 E
Akuša	84	42.17 N	47.21 E
Akuse	150	6.06 N	0.08 E
Akuseki-jima I	93b	29.27 N	129.37 E
Akutan	180	54.08 N	165.46 W
Akutan Island I	180	54.10 N	165.55 W
Akutan Pass ⋓	180	54.00 N	166.10 W
Akuticha	86	52.27 N	84.29 E
Akviran, Tür.	130	37.27 N	32.23 E
Akviran, Tür.	130	40.54 N	29.30 E
Akwanga	150	8.55 N	8.23 E
Akwatia	150	6.04 N	0.49 W
Akwawa ∧[2]	150	6.27 N	0.25 W
Akwaya	152	6.30 N	9.40 E
Akyab → Sittwe	110	20.09 N	92.54 E
Akyazı	130	40.41 N	30.37 E
Akyel	144	12.33 N	37.04 E
Akyr-T'ube	85	42.59 N	72.07 E
Akžajkyn, ozero ⊜	86	44.55 N	67.46 E
Akžal, S.S.S.R.	86	47.47 N	74.02 E
Akžal, S.S.S.R.	86	49.13 N	81.25 E
Akžar, S.S.S.R.	85	43.08 N	71.38 E
Akžar, S.S.S.R.	86	47.35 N	83.42 E
Akžaryk	86	48.34 N	75.30 E
Ål	26	60.38 N	8.34 E
Ala	64	45.45 N	11.00 E
Ala ≐	86	42.42 N	89.12 E
Alà, Monti di ⋏	71	40.40 N	9.14 E
Al-Abʿādīyah	142	31.22 N	31.07 E
Alabama	210	43.06 N	78.23 W
Alabama □[3], U.S.	178	32.50 N	87.00 W
Alabama □[3], U.S.	194	32.50 N	87.00 W
Alabama ≐	194	31.08 N	87.57 W
Alabama and Coushatta Indian Reservation ✦[4]	222	30.13 N	94.42 W
Alabaster	194	33.14 N	86.48 W
Alabat Island I	116	14.07 N	122.03 E
Al-ʿAbbāsah ash-Sharqīyah	142	30.32 N	31.43 E
Al-ʿAbbāsīyah	140	12.10 N	31.18 E
Al-ʿAbbāsīyah ✦[8]	273c	30.04 N	31.17 E
Alabino	82	55.31 N	37.01 E
Āl-ʿĀbis	144	18.04 N	43.10 E
Alabuga ≐	85	41.26 N	74.41 E
Ala-Buka	85	41.23 N	71.30 E
Alaca	130	40.10 N	34.51 E
Alacahan	130	39.07 N	37.37 E
Alaçalı	130	41.11 N	29.27 E
Alaçam	130	41.37 N	35.37 E
Alaçam Dağları ⋏	130	39.20 N	28.32 E
Alaçatı	130	38.16 N	26.23 E
Alachadzy	84	43.14 N	40.18 E
Alachua	192	29.47 N	82.29 W
Alacrán, Arrecife ✢[2]	232	22.24 N	89.42 W
Aladağ ∧, Tür.	84	40.11 N	42.49 E
Aladağ ∧, Tür.	130	37.44 N	35.09 E
Aladağlar ⋏	84	39.20 N	43.35 E
Ala Dağları ⋏	130	37.55 N	35.13 E
Al-ʿAdasīyah	132	32.40 N	35.37 E
Alà dei Sardi	71	40.39 N	9.20 E
Aladino	82	54.49 N	38.12 E
Aladinskij, porog ᒪ	86	58.24 N	95.29 E
Ala di Stura	62	45.19 N	7.19 E
Aladjino	82	56.21 N	37.04 E
Aladža-Džamija ⊛[1]	38	43.31 N	18.47 E
Aladža manastir ⊛[1]	38	43.17 N	28.01 E
Alafia ≐	220	27.52 N	82.23 W
Alafia, South Prong ≐	220	27.51 N	82.08 W
Alagbado	273a	6.41 N	3.18 E
Alagir	72	43.03 N	44.14 E
Alagna Valsesia	62	45.51 N	7.56 E
Alag nuur ⊜	102	45.09 N	94.28 E
Alagoa	256	22.10 S	44.38 W
Alagoa Grande	250	7.03 S	35.38 W
Alagoa Nova	250	7.04 S	35.46 W
Alagoas □[3]	250	9.00 S	36.00 W
Alagoinhas	255	12.07 S	38.26 W
Alagón	34	41.46 N	1.07 W
Alagón ≐	34	39.44 N	6.53 W
Alaguntan	273a	6.26 N	3.30 E
Alah ≐	116	6.53 N	124.33 E
Alahanpanjang	112	1.05 S	100.47 E
Alahärmä	26	63.14 N	22.51 E
Al-Ait	140	12.22 N	27.27 E
Al-ʿAjamīyīn	142	29.20 N	30.43 E
Alajärvi	26	63.00 N	23.49 E
Alajku	85	40.18 N	74.25 E
Alajõe	76	59.01 N	27.26 E
Alajskaja dolina V	85	39.30 N	73.00 E
Alajskij chrebet ⋏	85	39.45 N	72.00 E
Alajuela	236	10.01 N	84.13 W
Alajuela □[4]	236	10.30 N	84.30 W
Alajuela, Lago ⊜[1]	236	9.15 N	79.35 W
Ālājūjeh	84	38.57 N	46.41 E
Alakai Swamp ≡	229b	22.08 N	159.35 W
Alakamisy	157b	21.19 S	47.14 E
Alakanuk	180	62.41 N	164.37 W
Alakilise	130	39.56 N	38.38 E
Alaknanda ≐	124	30.08 N	78.36 E
Alakol', ozero ⊜	86	46.10 N	81.45 E
Al-ʿAkrīshah	142	31.08 N	30.09 E
Alak'ul'a	265a	59.44 N	29.56 E
Alakurtti	24	66.57 N	30.18 E
Al-ʿĀl	132	32.48 N	35.44 E
Alalakeiki Channel ⋓	229a	20.35 N	156.30 W
Al-ʿAlamayn	140	30.49 N	28.57 E
Al-ʿAlāqimah	142	30.37 N	31.38 E
Alalaú ≐	246	0.30 S	61.09 W
Al-ʿAmādīyah	128	37.06 N	43.29 E
Alamagan I	108	17.36 N	145.50 E
Al-ʿAmārah	128	31.50 N	47.09 E
Al-ʿAmār al-Kubrā	142	30.21 N	31.08 E
Alamata	144	12.25 N	39.33 E
Alamdānga	124	23.46 N	88.57 E
Alameda, Esp.	34	37.12 N	4.39 W
Alameda, Ca., U.S.	226	37.45 N	122.14 W
Alameda, N.M., U.S.	200	35.11 N	106.37 W
Alameda □[6]	226	37.35 N	121.55 W
Alameda, Estación ✦[5]	286e	33.27 S	70.41 W
Alameda Creek ≐	226	37.35 N	122.09 W
Alameda Naval Air Station ■	226	37.47 N	122.18 W
Alamedin	85	42.54 N	74.37 E
Alamein → Al-ʿAlamayn	140	30.49 N	28.57 E
Alamillo	200	31.02 N	110.35 W
Alaminos	116	16.10 N	119.59 E
Al-ʿĀmirīyah	142	31.01 N	29.48 E
ʿAlam Lek	128	37.02 N	65.57 E
Alamo, Méx.	234	20.55 N	97.41 W
Alamo, Ca., U.S.	226	37.51 N	122.02 W
Alamo, Ga., U.S.	192	32.08 N	82.46 W
Alamo, Mi., U.S.	216	42.22 N	85.43 W
Alamo, Nv., U.S.	204	37.21 N	115.09 W
Alamo, Tn., U.S.	194	35.47 N	89.07 W
Alamo ≐	204	33.14 N	115.39 W
Alamo Creek ≐	282	37.42 N	121.55 W
Alamo Creek, West Branch ≐	282	37.45 N	121.55 W
Alamogordo	200	32.53 N	105.57 W
Alamogordo Creek ≐	196	34.40 N	104.23 W
Alamo Heights	196	29.29 N	98.27 W
Alamo Indian Reservation ✦[4]	200	34.30 N	107.30 W
Alamo Lake ⊜[1]	200	34.20 N	113.30 W
Alamo Oaks	282	37.51 N	121.59 W
Alamor	246	4.02 S	80.02 W
Alamos, Méx.	196	26.25 N	100.25 W
Alamos, Méx.	232	27.01 N	108.56 W
Álamos, Río de los ≐	232	27.53 N	101.12 W
Alamosa	200	37.28 N	105.52 W
Alamosa ≐	200	37.22 N	105.46 W
Alamosa Creek ≐, N.M., U.S.	196	34.26 N	103.58 W
Alamosa Creek ≐, N.M., U.S.	200	33.20 N	107.21 W
Alamosa East	200	37.28 N	105.49 W
Álamos de San Felipe, Cerro ∧	232	30.41 N	112.35 W
Alampur, Bngl.	126	23.49 N	89.06 E
Alampur, India	272b	22.25 N	88.08 E
Alanäs	26	64.10 N	15.42 E
Al-ʿĀnāt	132	32.21 N	36.48 E
Al-Anbār □[4]	128	33.45 N	41.45 E
Aland	122	17.34 N	76.34 E
Aland ≐	54	53.02 N	11.34 E
Åland-Inseln → Ahvenanmaa II	26	60.15 N	20.00 E
Aland Sea ⊤[2]	26	60.00 N	19.30 E
Alandur	122	13.02 N	80.15 E
Alangalang	116	11.12 N	124.51 E
Alang-besar, Pulau I	114	2.12 N	100.39 E
Alanje	236	8.24 N	82.33 W
Alano di Piave	64	45.55 N	11.52 E
Alanson	190	45.26 N	84.47 W
Alanya	130	36.33 N	32.01 E
Al-ʿĀnz	132	32.23 N	36.38 E
Alaotra, Lac ⊜	157b	17.30 S	48.30 E
Alapaha	192	31.23 N	83.13 W
Alapaha ≐	192	30.26 N	83.06 W
Alapajevsk	86	57.52 N	61.42 E
Alaplı	130	41.11 N	31.24 E
Al-ʿAqabah	132	29.31 N	35.00 E
Al-ʿAqabah Landing Ground ⊠	132	29.32 N	34.59 E
ʿAlaqah, Jabal ∧	142	29.59 N	32.53 E
Alaquines	234	22.08 N	99.36 W
Al-ʿArabīyah as-Saʿūdīyah → Saudi Arabia □[1]	118	25.00 N	45.00 E
Al-Arak	130	34.38 N	38.35 E
Alarcón	34	39.33 N	2.05 W
Alarcón, Embalse de ⊜[1]	34	39.36 N	2.10 W
Al-ʿArīsh	132	31.08 N	33.48 E
Al-ʿArīsh Airfield ⊠	132	31.04 N	33.50 E
Al-ʿArmah ⋏[1]	128	25.30 N	46.30 E
Alarobia Vohiposa	157b	20.59 S	47.09 E
Alas	115b	8.32 S	117.00 E
Alas ≐, Indon.	114	3.05 N	97.55 E
Alaš ≐, S.S.S.R.	86	51.15 N	90.54 E
Alas, Selat ⋓	115b	8.40 S	116.40 E
Alasan	112	1.45 S	123.19 E
Alasdair, Sgurr ∧	46	57.12 N	6.14 W
Alaşehir	130	38.21 N	28.32 E
Alashanyouqi	102	40.02 N	103.33 E
Al-ʿAshārah	130	34.55 N	40.34 E
Al-Ashmūnayn	142	27.47 N	30.49 E
Al-ʿĀṣimah □[8]	132	31.45 N	36.30 E
Alasitan	120	37.01 N	76.59 E
Alaska	216	42.50 N	85.29 W
Alaska □[3]	180	65.00 N	153.00 W
Alaska, Gulf of ⊂	16	58.00 N	146.00 W
Alaska Peninsula ≻[1]	180	57.00 N	158.00 W
Alaska Range ⋏	180	62.30 N	150.00 W
Al-ʿAssāfīyah	128	28.21 N	39.08 E
Alassio	62	44.00 N	8.10 E
Alastaro	26	60.56 N	22.55 E
Alastuey	258	34.25 S	59.13 W
Al'at, S.S.S.R.	84	39.57 N	49.25 E
Alat, S.S.S.R.	128	39.26 N	63.48 E
Al-ʿAtāminah	142	27.20 N	30.50 E
Alatan'aola → Xin Barag Youqi	88	48.41 N	116.53 E
Al-Atārib	130	36.08 N	36.49 E
Al-Aṭāwilah	142	27.14 N	31.13 E
Al-ʿAṭf	142	29.39 N	31.16 E
Al-ʿAthāmīn ⋏	128	30.22 N	43.40 E
Al-ʿAtīqah	132	33.42 N	35.27 E
Alatna ≐	180	66.34 N	152.34 W
Alatri	66	41.43 N	13.21 E
Al-ʿAṭrūn	140	18.11 N	26.36 E
Alatyr'	80	54.51 N	46.36 E
Alatyr' ≐	80	54.52 N	46.36 E
Alausí	246	2.12 S	78.50 W
Alava □[4]	34	42.50 N	2.45 W
Alava, Cape ≻	224	48.10 N	124.43 W
Alaverdi	84	41.08 N	44.39 E
Alavieska	26	64.10 N	24.18 E
Alavus	26	62.35 N	23.37 E
Alaw ≐	44	53.18 N	4.32 W
Alaw, Llyn ⊜[1]	44	53.20 N	4.22 W
Alawa	150	10.20 N	6.39 E
Alāwalpur	123	31.26 N	75.39 E
Al-ʿAwjā'	142	30.58 N	30.32 E
Al-ʿAwsajīyah	128	26.49 N	41.41 E
ʿĀlayh	132	33.48 N	35.36 E
Al-ʿĀyn ⊤[4]	140	16.36 N	29.19 E
Alayor	34	39.56 N	4.08 E
Al-ʿAyyāsh ash-Sharqī	142	31.33 N	31.13 E
Al-ʿAyyāṭ	142	29.37 N	31.15 E
Alazani ≐	84	41.05 N	46.40 E
Alazeja ≐	74	70.51 N	153.34 E
Al-Azhar University ⊛[2]	273c	30.03 N	31.16 E
Al ʿAzīzah	142	31.11 N	31.57 E
Al-ʿAzīzīyah, Lībiyā	146	32.32 N	13.01 E
Al-ʿAzīzīyah, Miṣr	142	30.29 N	31.18 E
Al-ʿAzīzīyah, Miṣr	273c	29.52 N	31.15 E
Al-Azraq ✦[1]	132	31.52 N	36.50 E
Alb ≐	58	47.35 N	8.08 E
Alba, It.	62	44.42 N	8.02 E
Alba, Mi., U.S.	190	44.58 N	84.58 W
Alba, Pa., U.S.	210	41.42 N	76.50 W
Alba, Tx., U.S.	222	32.48 N	95.38 W
Alba □[6]	38	46.15 N	23.30 E
Alba, Foum de)(	148	20.27 N	3.36 W
Al-Bāb	130	36.22 N	37.31 E
Albacete	34	38.59 N	1.51 W
Albachten	52	51.55 N	7.31 E
Albacina	66	43.21 N	13.01 E
Al-Badʿ	128	28.25 N	35.00 E
Al-Badārī	140	26.59 N	31.25 E
Alba de Tormes	34	40.49 N	5.31 W
Al-Badrashayn	142	29.51 N	31.16 E
Ålbæk	26	57.36 N	10.25 E
Al-Bahnasā	142	28.32 N	30.39 E
Al-Baḥr al-Abyaḍ □[4]	140	13.15 N	32.25 E
Al-Baḥr al-Aḥmar □[4], Miṣr	142	28.45 N	32.00 E
Al-Baḥr al-Aḥmar □[4], Sūd.	140	20.00 N	35.15 E
Al-Baḥrayn → Bahrain □[1]	128	26.00 N	50.30 E
Albaida	34	38.51 N	0.31 W
Albairate	266b	45.25 N	8.56 E
Alba-Iulia	38	46.04 N	23.35 E
Al-Bajalāt	142	31.10 N	31.37 E
Al-Bājūr	142	30.26 N	31.02 E
Al-Bakātūsh	142	31.03 N	30.48 E
Al-Balāmūn	142	30.49 N	31.26 E
Al-Balāshūn	142	30.26 N	31.26 E
Al-Ballaḥ	142	30.46 N	32.19 E
Al-Ballāṣ	140	26.01 N	32.46 E
Al-Balqā' □[8]	132	31.50 N	35.40 E
Al-Bālūʿah ⊜	130	35.55 N	36.28 E
Al-Balyanā	140	26.14 N	32.00 E
Alban	32	43.54 N	2.28 E
Albanel, Lac ⊜	176	50.55 N	73.12 W
Albanella	68	40.30 N	15.08 E
Albani, Colli ⋏[2]	66	41.45 N	12.45 E
Albania (Shqipëri) □[1], Europe	22	41.00 N	20.00 E
Albania (Shqipëri) □[1], Europe	38	41.00 N	20.00 E
Albanie → Albania □[1]	38	41.00 N	20.00 E
Albanien → Albania □[1]	38	41.00 N	20.00 E
Albano, Lago ⊜	66	41.45 N	12.40 E
Albano, Monte ∧	66	43.50 N	10.58 E
Albano di Lucania	68	40.35 N	16.02 E
Albano Laziale	66	41.44 N	12.39 E
Albany, Austl.	162	35.02 S	117.53 E
Albany, N.Z.	172	36.43 S	174.42 E
Albany, Ca., U.S.	226	37.53 N	122.17 W
Albany, Ga., U.S.	192	31.34 N	84.09 W
Albany, Il., U.S.	190	41.47 N	90.13 W
Albany, In., U.S.	216	40.18 N	85.14 W
Albany, Ky., U.S.	194	36.41 N	85.08 W
Albany, Mn., U.S.	190	45.37 N	94.34 W
Albany, Mo., U.S.	194	40.14 N	94.19 W
Albany, N.Y., U.S.	210	42.39 N	73.45 W
Albany, Oh., U.S.	188	39.13 N	82.12 W
Albany, Or., U.S.	202	44.38 N	123.06 W
Albany, Tx., U.S.	196	32.43 N	99.17 W
Albany, Wi., U.S.	190	42.42 N	89.26 W
Albany □[6]	210	42.39 N	73.45 W
Albany ≐	176	52.17 N	81.31 W
Albany County Airport ⊠	210	42.45 N	73.48 W
Albany Creek	171a	27.21 S	152.58 E
Albany Park ✦[8]	278	41.58 N	87.43 W
Al-Barājīl	273c	30.04 N	31.09 E
Al-Barāmūn	142	31.07 N	31.26 E
Albardón	252	31.26 S	68.32 W
Albaredo d'Adige	64	45.19 N	11.16 E
Al-Bāriḥah	132	32.34 N	35.50 E
Al-Barnūjī	142	30.56 N	30.23 E
Albaron	62	43.37 N	4.28 E
Albaron ∧	62	45.20 N	7.07 E
Albarracín	34	40.25 N	1.26 W
Albarradas	234	16.50 N	96.15 W
Al-Barrah	128	24.55 N	45.52 E
Albarraque	266c	38.46 N	9.21 W
Al-Barshā	142	27.43 N	30.54 E
Al-Barun	140	11.44 N	33.30 E
Al-Basātīn ✦[8]	273c	29.59 N	31.16 E
Al-Baslaqūn	142	31.06 N	30.08 E
Al-Basqalūn	142	28.42 N	30.44 E
Al-Baṣrah (Basra)	128	30.30 N	47.47 E
Al-Baṣrah □[4]	128	30.20 N	47.35 E
Al-Batānūn	142	30.37 N	30.59 E
Al-Baṭḥā'	128	31.06 N	45.53 E
Al-Bāṭinah ✦[1]	128	23.45 N	57.20 E
Albatross Bay ⊂	164	12.45 S	141.43 E
Albatross Point ≻	172	38.06 S	174.41 E
Al-Batrūn	130	34.15 N	35.39 E
Al-Baṭrūnah	132	33.39 N	36.02 E
Al-Bauga	140	18.16 N	33.55 E
Al-Bawīṭī	140	28.21 N	28.52 E
Albay □[4]	116	13.00 N	123.40 E
Al-Bayahū	142	28.16 N	30.44 E
Al-Bayḍā (Beida), Lībiyā	146	28.22 N	18.55 E
Al-Bayḍā' (Beida), Lībiyā	146	32.46 N	21.43 E
Al-Bayḍā', Miṣr	142	31.10 N	30.05 E
Albay Gulf ⊂	116	13.10 N	124.00 E
Albazino	89	53.23 N	124.05 E
Albbruck	58	47.35 N	8.07 E
Albegna ≐	66	42.30 N	11.11 E
Albemarle	192	35.13 N	80.13 W
Albemarle and Chesapeake Canal ≍	208	36.43 N	76.15 W
Albemarle Sound ⋓	192	36.03 N	76.12 W
Albenga	62	44.03 N	8.13 E
Albens	62	45.47 N	5.57 E
Alberche ≐	34	39.58 N	4.46 W
Alberdi	252	26.10 S	58.09 W
Alberene	192	37.53 N	78.37 W
Alberga, Austl.	162	27.12 S	135.28 E
Ålberga, Sve.	40	58.44 N	16.34 E
Alberga Creek ≐	162	27.06 S	135.33 E
Albergaria-a-Velha	34	40.42 N	8.29 W
Alberhill	228	33.44 N	117.23 W
Alberique	34	39.07 N	0.31 W
Alberni Inlet ⊂	182	49.07 N	124.50 W
Alberobello	68	40.47 N	17.15 E
Alberona	68	41.26 N	15.07 E
Albero Sole ∧	70a	35.31 N	12.32 E
Albers	219	38.33 N	89.37 W
Alberschwende	58	47.27 N	9.49 E
Albersloh	52	51.52 N	7.43 E
Albert	50	50.00 N	2.39 E
Albert ≐	171a	27.42 S	153.15 E
Albert, Lake ⊜, Afr.	154	1.40 N	31.00 E
Albert, Lake ⊜, Austl.	166	35.38 S	139.17 E
Alberta	194	32.13 N	87.24 W
Alberta □[4], Can.	176	54.00 N	113.00 W
Alberta □[4], Can.	182	54.00 N	113.00 W
Alberta, Mount ∧	182	52.18 N	117.28 W
Albert Canyon	182	51.08 N	117.52 W
Albert City	198	42.46 N	94.56 W
Albert Edward, Mount ∧	164	8.23 S	147.24 E
Albert Edward Bay ⊂	176	69.32 N	103.00 W
Albert Falls	158	29.27 S	30.25 E
Albertfalva ✦[8]	264c	47.27 N	19.02 E
Alberti	252	35.02 S	60.16 W
Al'bertin	76	53.05 N	25.23 E
Albertina	256	22.12 S	46.37 W
Albertinia	158	34.13 S	21.36 E
Albertirsa	30	47.15 N	19.38 E
Albertkanaal ≍	56	50.39 N	5.37 E
Albert Lea	190	43.38 N	93.22 W
Albert Markham, Mount ∧	9	81.23 S	158.12 E
Albert Nile ≐	154	3.36 N	32.02 E
Alberto, Lago → Albert, Lake ⊜	154	1.40 N	31.00 E
Alberto Eduardo → Albert Edward, Mount ∧	164	8.23 S	147.24 E
Alberton, P.E., Can.	186	46.49 N	64.04 W
Alberton, S. Afr.	273d	26.16 S	28.08 E
Alberton, Mt., U.S.	202	47.00 N	114.29 W
Albert Park ♦	274b	37.51 S	144.57 E
Albert Peak ∧	182	51.02 N	117.51 W
Albertshof	264a	52.42 N	13.40 E
Albertson	276	40.46 N	73.38 W
Albertson Brook ≐	285	39.41 N	74.43 W
Albertson Brook, Blue Anchor Branch ≐	285	39.42 N	74.49 W
Albertson Brook, Pump Branch ≐	285	39.42 N	74.49 W
Albert Town	241q	18.17 N	77.33 W
Albertville, Fr.	62	45.41 N	6.23 E
Albertville, Al., U.S.	194	34.16 N	86.12 W
Albertville → Kalemie, Zaïre	154	5.56 S	29.12 E
Albestroff	56	48.56 N	6.51 E
Albettone	64	45.21 N	11.35 E
Albi	32	43.56 N	2.09 E
Albia, Ia., U.S.	190	41.01 N	92.48 W
Albia, N.Y., U.S.	210	42.43 N	73.39 W
Albiate	266b	45.39 N	9.15 E
Al-Bidʿ	128	28.25 N	35.04 E
Al Bidia	146	10.33 N	20.13 E
Albidona	68	39.55 N	16.28 E
Albignasego	64	45.21 N	11.52 E
Albin	198	41.25 N	104.05 W
Albina	250	5.30 N	54.03 W
Albina, Ponta ≻	152	15.51 S	11.44 E
Albinea	64	44.37 N	10.36 E
Albino	62	45.46 N	9.47 E
Albion, Austl.	274b	37.47 S	144.49 E
Albion, B.C., Can.	224	49.11 N	122.33 W
Albion, Ca., U.S.	204	39.13 N	123.46 W
Albion, Id., U.S.	202	42.24 N	113.34 W
Albion, Il., U.S.	194	38.22 N	88.03 W
Albion, In., U.S.	216	41.23 N	85.25 W
Albion, Ia., U.S.	190	42.06 N	92.59 W
Albion, Mi., U.S.	216	42.14 N	84.45 W
Albion, Ne., U.S.	198	41.41 N	98.00 W
Albion, N.J., U.S.	285	39.47 N	74.56 W
Albion, N.Y., U.S.	210	43.14 N	78.11 W
Albion, Pa., U.S.	214	41.53 N	80.22 W
Albion, R.I., U.S.	207	41.57 N	71.27 W
Albion, Wa., U.S.	202	46.47 N	117.14 W
Albion, Wi., U.S.	216	42.52 N	89.04 W
Albion Airstrip ⊠	285	39.46 N	74.58 W
Albion Park	170	34.34 S	150.47 E
Al-Biqāʿ □[4]	130	34.00 N	36.00 E
Al-Biqāʿ V	128	33.50 N	36.00 E
Al-Bi'r	128	28.50 N	36.19 E
Al-Bīrah	132	31.54 N	35.13 E
Al-Bi'r al-Jadīd	128	26.01 N	38.29 E
Al-Birīgāt	142	30.30 N	30.49 E
Al-Birk	144	18.13 N	41.33 E
Al-Birkah	146	24.54 N	10.11 E
Al-Birkah ⊤[4]	144	22.12 N	40.43 E
Albisola Marina	62	44.19 N	8.30 E
Albisola Superiore	62	44.20 N	8.31 E
Albizzate	62	45.43 N	8.44 E
Alblasserdam	52	51.52 N	4.40 E
Albo, Monte ∧	71	40.32 N	9.35 E
Albocácer	34	40.21 N	0.02 E
Albogas	266c	38.51 N	9.15 W
Alborán, Isla de I	34	35.58 N	3.02 W
Ålborg	26	57.03 N	9.56 E
Ålborg Bugt ⊂	26	56.45 N	10.30 E
Alborz, Reshteh-ye Kūhhā-ye ⋏	128	36.00 N	53.00 E
Albreda	182	52.38 N	119.09 W
Albright-Knox Art Gallery ⊛	284a	42.56 N	78.53 W
Albrighton	42	52.38 N	2.16 W
Albuch ⋏	56	48.15 N	9.50 E
Albuera	116	10.55 N	124.42 E
Albufeira	34	37.05 N	8.15 W
Ālbū Gharz, Sabkhat ⊜	130	34.45 N	41.15 E
Al-Buḥayrah □[4], Miṣr	142	30.59 N	30.12 E
Al-Buḥayrah □[4], Sūd.	140	7.30 N	29.30 E
Albula ≐	58	46.42 N	9.27 E
Al-Bunbah	146	32.24 N	23.08 E
Albuñol	34	36.47 N	3.12 W
Albuquerque, Bra.	248	19.23 S	57.26 W
Albuquerque, N.M., U.S.	200	35.05 N	106.39 W
Albuquerque, Cayos de II	236	12.10 N	81.50 W
Al-Buraymī	128	24.15 N	55.45 E
Alburg	206	44.58 N	73.18 W
Al-Burj	142	31.35 N	30.59 E
Al-Burjāyah	142	28.09 N	30.44 E
Alburno, Monte ∧	68	40.33 N	15.17 E
Alburquerque	34	39.13 N	7.00 W
Alburtis	208	40.31 N	75.36 W
Al-Burumbul	142	29.19 N	31.14 E
Albury, Austl.	166	36.05 S	146.55 E
Albury, N.Z.	172	44.14 S	170.52 E
Albury, Eng., U.K.	260	51.13 N	0.30 W
Albury Park ♦	260	51.13 N	0.29 W
Al-Buṣaylī	142	31.20 N	30.24 E
Al-Busayṭā' ≚	128	29.30 N	38.45 E
Al-Buṭānah ✦[1]	140	15.00 N	34.40 E
Al-Buṭaynah	132	32.57 N	36.42 E
Al-Buwayḍah	132	32.28 N	36.04 E
Al-Buzūn	144	15.35 N	50.55 E
Albuzzano	62	45.11 N	9.16 E
Alby, Fr.	62	45.49 N	6.01 E
Alby, Sve.	26	62.30 N	15.28 E
Alca	248	15.08 S	72.46 W
Alcabideche	266c	38.44 N	9.24 W
Alcácer do Sal	34	38.22 N	8.30 W
Alcains	34	39.55 N	7.27 W
Alcala	116	17.54 N	121.39 E
Alcalá de Guadaira	34	37.20 N	5.50 W
Alcalá de Henares	34	40.29 N	3.22 W
Alcalá la Real	34	37.28 N	3.56 W
Alcalde	200	36.05 N	106.03 W
Alcamo	70	37.59 N	12.58 E
Alčan ≐	89	46.38 N	134.22 E
Alcanadre ≐	34	41.37 N	0.12 E
Alcanar	34	40.33 N	0.29 E
Alcañices	34	41.42 N	6.21 W
Alcañiz	34	41.03 N	0.08 W
Alcântara, Bra.	250	2.24 S	44.24 W
Alcántara, Esp.	34	39.43 N	6.53 W
Alcantara, Pil.	116	12.16 N	122.03 E
Alcântara ✦[8]	266c	38.42 N	9.10 W
Alcantara ≐	70	37.49 N	15.16 E
Alcántara, Embalse de ⊜[1]	34	39.45 N	6.25 W
Alcantarilla	34	37.58 N	1.13 W
Alcantilado	255	16.23 S	53.31 W
Alcara li Fusi	70	38.01 N	14.42 E
Alcaraz	34	38.40 N	2.29 W
Alcarrache ≐	34	38.16 N	7.24 W
Alcatraz Island I	282	37.49 N	122.26 W
Alcaudete	34	37.36 N	4.05 W
Alcázar de San Juan	34	39.24 N	3.12 W
Alcazarquivir → Er-Rachidia	148	31.58 N	4.25 W
Alcester, Eng., U.K.	42	52.13 N	1.52 W
Alcester, S.D., U.S.	198	43.01 N	96.37 W
Alcester Island I	164	9.35 S	152.25 E
Alcihuatl	234	19.55 N	104.34 W
Alcira (Gigena), Arg.	252	32.45 S	64.20 W
Alcira, Esp.	34	39.09 N	0.26 W
Alcoa	192	35.47 N	83.58 W
Alcoa Center	279b	40.33 N	79.39 W
Alcoa Lake ⊜[1]	222	30.34 N	97.03 W
Alcobaça, Bra.	255	17.30 S	39.13 W
Alcobaça, Port.	34	39.33 N	8.59 W
Alcobendas	34	40.32 N	3.38 W
Alcochete	266c	38.45 N	8.58 W
Alcockspruit	158	27.55 S	30.01 E
Alcoitão	266c	38.44 N	9.24 W
Alcolea del Pinar	34	41.02 N	2.28 W
Alcolu	192	33.45 N	80.12 W
Alcomunga	234	18.25 N	97.02 W
Alconbury Brook ≐	42	52.19 N	0.12 W
Alconchel	34	38.31 N	7.04 W
Alcony	218	40.01 N	84.04 W
Alcorcón	266a	40.21 N	3.50 W
Alcorn	194	31.52 N	91.09 W
Alcorta	252	33.32 S	61.07 W
Alcoutim	34	37.28 N	7.28 W
Alcova Reservoir ⊜[1]	200	42.32 N	106.45 W
Alcove	210	42.28 N	73.55 W
Alcove Reservoir ⊜[1]	210	42.29 N	73.57 W
Alcovy ≐	192	33.26 N	83.50 W
Alcoy	34	38.42 N	0.28 W
Alcoy, Nevado ∧	248	11.17 S	76.30 W
Alcubierre	34	41.48 N	0.27 W
Alcudia	34	39.52 N	3.07 E
Alcudia, Bahía de ⊂	34	39.48 N	3.13 E
Alcyon Lake ⊜	285	39.44 N	75.08 W
Aldabra Island I	138	9.25 S	46.22 E
Aldama, Méx.	232	28.51 N	105.54 W
Aldama, Méx.	234	22.55 N	98.04 W
Aldama, Arroyo ≐	286b	23.05 N	82.15 W
Aldan, S.S.S.R.	74	58.37 N	125.24 E
Aldan, Pa., U.S.	285	39.55 N	75.17 W
Aldan ≐	74	63.28 N	129.35 E
Aldanskoje nagorje ⋏[1]	74	57.00 N	127.00 E
Aldbourne	42	51.31 N	1.37 W
Aldbrough	44	53.50 N	0.07 W
Aldbury	42	51.48 N	0.36 W
Alde ≐	42	52.03 N	1.28 E
Aldea Apeleg	254	44.41 S	70.51 W
Aldeburgh	42	52.09 N	1.35 E
Aldecoa ✦[8]	286b	23.07 N	82.24 W
Aldeia	256	23.30 S	46.51 W
Aldeia de Carapicuiba	287b	23.35 S	46.48 W
Aldeia de Paio Pires	266c	38.38 N	9.05 W
Aldeia Nova de Santo Bento	34	37.55 N	7.25 W
Aldeia Velha	256	22.47 S	42.55 W
Aldeinha	287b	23.45 S	46.53 W
Alden, Il., U.S.	216	42.27 N	88.31 W
Alden, Ia., U.S.	190	42.31 N	93.22 W
Alden, Mn., U.S.	190	43.40 N	93.34 W
Alden, N.Y., U.S.	210	42.54 N	78.29 W
Alden, Pa., U.S.	210	41.10 N	76.00 W
Alden Center	212	42.55 N	78.32 W
Aldenham	260	51.40 N	0.21 W
Aldenhoven	56	50.53 N	6.16 E
Aldenrade ✦[8]	263	51.31 N	6.44 E
Alder, Ben ∧	46	56.48 N	4.28 W
Alder Creek ≐	202	45.50 N	119.56 W
Aldergrove	224	49.04 N	122.28 W
Alder Lake ⊜[1]	224	46.45 N	122.15 W
Alderley	166	22.39 S	139.44 E
Alderley Edge	262	53.18 N	2.15 W
Aldermaston	42	51.23 N	1.09 W
Alderney I	43b	49.43 N	2.12 W
Alder Peak ∧	226	35.53 N	121.22 W
Aldersbach	60	48.36 N	13.05 E
Aldershot	42	51.15 N	0.47 W
Alderson	192	37.44 N	80.38 W
Alderton	224	47.10 N	122.14 W
Alderwood Manor	224	47.49 N	122.17 W
Aldine	222	29.54 N	95.24 W
Aldinga Bay ⊂	168b	35.20 S	138.25 E
Aldingen	58	48.05 N	8.41 E
Aldino	64	46.23 N	11.20 E
Aldo Bonzi	288	34.42 S	58.31 W
Aldridge	42	52.36 N	1.55 W
Aldwell, Lake ⊜[1]	224	48.05 N	123.34 W
Alechovščina	76	60.25 N	33.52 E
Aled ≐	44	53.14 N	3.34 W
Aledo, Il., U.S.	190	41.11 N	90.44 W
Aledo, Tx., U.S.	222	32.42 N	97.36 W
Alefa	144	11.57 N	36.52 E
Aleg	150	17.03 N	13.55 W
Alegranza, Isla I	148	29.23 N	13.30 W
Alegre	255	20.46 S	41.32 W
Alegre ≐	248	15.01 S	59.57 W
Alegres Mountain ∧	200	34.09 N	108.11 W
Alegrete	252	29.46 S	55.46 W
Alej ≐	86	52.52 N	83.36 E
Alejandría → Al-Iskandarīyah	142	31.12 N	29.54 E
Alejandro, Isla → Alexander Island I	9	71.00 S	70.00 W
Alejandro Roca	252	33.21 S	63.43 W
Alejandro Selkirk, Isla (Isla Más Afuera) I	244	33.45 S	80.46 W
Alejo Ledesma	252	33.37 S	62.37 W
Alejsk	86	52.28 N	82.45 E
Aleknagik	180	59.17 N	158.38 W
Aleknagik, Lake ⊜	180	59.20 N	158.45 W
Aleksandrija	78	48.40 N	33.07 E
Aleksandrijskaja	84	43.54 N	47.08 E
Aleksandrinka	83	47.47 N	37.41 E
Aleksandro-Kalinovo	83	48.25 N	37.40 E
Aleksandro-Nevskaja	84	43.55 N	46.35 E
Aleksandro-Nevskij	80	53.28 N	40.13 E
Aleksandropol'	83	49.42 N	38.50 E
Aleksandrov	82	56.24 N	38.43 E
Aleksandrov Gaj	80	50.09 N	48.34 E
Aleksandrovka, S.S.S.R.	78	47.42 N	31.16 E
Aleksandrovka, S.S.S.R.	78	46.32 N	35.29 E
Aleksandrovka, S.S.S.R.	78	46.47 N	39.01 E
Aleksandrovka, S.S.S.R.	78	48.43 N	36.55 E
Aleksandrovka, S.S.S.R.	78	48.57 N	32.14 E
Aleksandrovka, S.S.S.R.	80	50.47 N	52.59 E
Aleksandrovka, S.S.S.R.	80	52.36 N	50.37 E
Aleksandrovka, S.S.S.R.	83	47.55 N	37.35 E
Aleksandrovka, S.S.S.R.	83	48.05 N	37.27 E
Aleksandrovka, S.S.S.R.	83	47.26 N	39.13 E
Aleksandrovka, S.S.S.R.	85	43.27 N	77.20 E
Aleksandrovka, S.S.S.R.	86	56.32 N	90.47 E
Aleksandrovka, S.S.S.R.	86	53.07 N	69.50 E
Aleksandrovka, S.S.S.R.	86	52.43 N	54.17 E
Aleksandrovsk	83	48.35 N	39.12 E
Aleksandrovskaja, S.S.S.R.	265a	60.03 N	29.59 E
Aleksandrovskaja, S.S.S.R.	265a	59.44 N	30.21 E
Aleksandrovskij	78	51.03 N	36.44 E
Aleksandrovskij Šl'uz	86	59.26 N	89.20 E
Aleksandrovskij Zavod	88	50.55 N	117.57 E
Aleksandrovskoje, S.S.S.R.	84	44.42 N	43.00 E
Aleksandrovskoje, S.S.S.R.	86	56.44 N	85.23 E
Aleksandrovskoje, S.S.S.R.	86	60.26 N	77.50 E
Aleksandrovsk-Sachalinskij	89	50.54 N	142.10 E
Aleksandrów Kujawski	30	52.52 N	18.42 E
Aleksandrów Łódzki	30	51.49 N	19.19 E
Aleksaskino	80	50.57 N	47.42 E
Aleksejevka, S.S.S.R.	78	50.37 N	38.42 E
Aleksejevka, S.S.S.R.	78	47.14 N	36.32 E
Aleksejevka, S.S.S.R.	80	50.58 N	52.25 E
Aleksejevka, S.S.S.R.	80	52.35 N	51.17 E
Aleksejevka, S.S.S.R.	80	53.15 N	50.30 E
Aleksejevka, S.S.S.R.	80	53.02 N	42.46 E
Aleksejevka, S.S.S.R.	80	51.49 N	43.56 E
Aleksejevka, S.S.S.R.	80	52.18 N	48.01 E
Aleksejevka, S.S.S.R.	82	54.41 N	36.34 E
Aleksejevka, S.S.S.R.	83	47.38 N	38.49 E
Aleksejevka, S.S.S.R.	83	47.41 N	39.54 E
Aleksejevka, S.S.S.R.	83	49.25 N	38.46 E
Aleksejevka, S.S.S.R.	83	49.01 N	39.11 E
Aleksejevka, S.S.S.R.	86	52.30 N	79.33 E
Aleksejevka, S.S.S.R.	86	54.31 N	81.08 E
Aleksejevka, S.S.S.R.	86	55.22 N	72.03 E
Aleksejevka, S.S.S.R.	86	53.31 N	69.30 E
Aleksejevka, S.S.S.R.	86	51.59 N	70.59 E
Aleksejevka, S.S.S.R.	86	47.16 N	81.34 E
Aleksejevka, S.S.S.R.	86	48.25 N	85.40 E
Aleksejevo-Družkovka	83	48.34 N	37.36 E
Aleksejevo-Lozovskoje	78	49.24 N	40.39 E
Aleksejevo-Orlovka ✦[8]	83	48.04 N	38.25 E
Aleksejevo-Tuzlovka	83	47.50 N	39.24 E
Aleksejevsk	88	57.50 N	108.23 E
Aleksejevskaja	80	50.17 N	42.11 E
Aleksejevskoje	80	55.18 N	50.06 E
Aleksin	82	54.31 N	37.05 E
Aleksinac	38	43.32 N	21.43 E
Alella	266d	41.30 N	2.18 E
Alemana, República Democrática → German Democratic Republic □[1]	30	52.00 N	12.30 E
Alemania, Arg.	252	25.36 S	65.38 W
Alemania, Chile	252	25.10 S	69.55 W
Alemania, República Federal de → Germany, Federal Republic of □[1]	30	51.00 N	9.00 E
Alem Dağı ∧	267b	41.05 N	29.12 E
Alemdar	267b	41.03 N	29.14 E
Além Paraíba	256	21.52 S	42.41 W
Alençon	50	48.26 N	0.05 E
Alenquer	250	1.56 S	54.46 W
Alentejo □[9]	34	38.00 N	8.00 W
Alenuihaha Channel ⋓	229a	20.26 N	156.00 W
Alenz	130	37.51 N	41.36 E
Aléoutiennes, Îles → Aleutian Islands II	180	52.00 N	176.00 W
Alep → Ḥalab	130	36.12 N	37.10 E
Aleppo → Ḥalab	130	36.12 N	37.10 E
Alerces, Parque Nacional ♦	254	42.50 S	71.52 W
Aléria	36	42.05 N	9.30 E
Alert Bay	182	50.35 N	126.55 W
Alès, Fr.	62	44.08 N	4.05 E
Ales, It.	71	39.46 N	8.49 E
Aleșd	38	47.04 N	22.24 E
Alešino, S.S.S.R.	82	56.09 N	37.45 E
Alešino, S.S.S.R.	82	55.04 N	36.05 E
Aleški	80	51.38 N	41.46 E
Aleškovo	82	54.53 N	36.23 E
Alessandria	62	44.54 N	8.37 E
Alessandria □[4]	62	44.49 N	8.42 E
Alessandria del Carretto	68	39.57 N	16.23 E
Alessandria della Rocca	70	37.34 N	13.27 E
Alessano	68	39.53 N	18.20 E
Ålestrup	26	56.42 N	9.30 E
Ålesund	26	62.28 N	6.09 E
Aletschhorn ∧	58	46.28 N	8.00 E
Alëuten → Aleutian Islands II	180	52.00 N	176.00 W
Aleutianas, Islas → Aleutian Islands II	180	52.00 N	176.00 W
Aleutian Basin ✢[1]	16	57.00 N	177.00 E
Aleutian Islands II	180	52.00 N	176.00 W
Aleutian Range ⋏	180	59.00 N	155.00 W
Aleutian Trench ✢[1]	6	51.00 N	170.00 W
Aleutka	74	45.57 N	150.10 E
Alevina, mys ≻	74	58.50 N	151.20 E
Ale Water ≐	46	55.31 N	2.35 W
Alex	196	34.54 N	97.46 W
Alexander, Mb., Can.	184	49.50 N	100.17 W
Alexander, Il., U.S.	219	39.43 N	90.02 W
Alexander, N.Y., U.S.	210	42.54 N	78.16 W
Alexander, N.D., U.S.	198	47.50 N	103.38 W
Alexander ≐	132	32.24 N	34.52 E
Alexander, Cape ≻	175e	6.35 S	156.30 E
Alexander, Mount ∧, Austl.	162	22.39 S	115.32 E
Alexander, Mount ∧, Austl.	169	36.59 S	144.18 E
Alexander Archipelago II	180	56.30 N	134.00 W
Alexander Bay	156	28.40 S	16.30 E
Alexander City	194	32.56 N	85.57 W
Alexander Dam ⊜[1]	273d	26.13 S	28.25 E
Alexander Ditch ≍	279a	41.20 N	82.05 W
Alexander Hamilton Airport ⊠	241n	17.42 N	64.48 W
Alexander Indian Reserve ✦[4]	182	53.48 N	113.58 W
Alexander Island I	9	71.00 S	70.00 W
Alexander Nevsky Monastery ⊛[1]	265a	59.55 N	30.24 E
Alexandra, Austl.	169	37.12 S	145.43 E
Alexandra, N.Z.	172	45.15 S	169.24 E
Alexandra, S. Afr.	273d	26.06 S	28.05 E
Alexandra ≐	166	18.14 S	139.54 E
Alexandra Canal ≍	274a	33.56 S	151.10 E
Alexandra Falls ᒪ	176	60.29 N	116.18 W
Alexandra Park ♦	262	53.27 N	2.15 W
Alexandra Park Race Course ♦	260	51.36 N	0.08 W
Alexandretta → İskenderun	130	36.37 N	36.07 E
Alexandretta, Gulf of → İskenderun Körfezi ⊂	130	36.30 N	35.40 E
Alexandria, Austl.	166	19.05 S	136.40 E
Alexandria, Bra.	250	6.25 S	38.01 W
Alexandria, B.C., Can.	182	52.38 N	122.27 W
Alexandria, On., Can.	206	45.19 N	74.38 W

Symbols in the index entries represent the broad categories identified in the key at the right. Symbols with superior numbers (⋏[1]) identify subcategories (see complete key on page *I · 1).*

Kartensymbole in dem Registerverzeichnis stellen die rechts in Schlüssel erklärten Kategorien dar. Symbole mit hochgestellten Ziffern (⋏[1]) bezeichnen Unterabteilungen einer Kategorie (vgl. vollständiger Schlüssel auf Seite *I · 1).*

Los símbolos incluídos en el texto del índice representan las grandes categorias identificadas con la clave a la derecha. Los símbolos con numeros en su parte superior (⋏[1]) identifican las subcategorías (véase la clave completa en la página *I · 1).*

Les symboles de l'index représentent les catégories indiquées dans la légende à droite. Les symboles suivis d'un indice (⋏[1]) représentent des sous-catégories (voir légende complète à la page *I · 1).*

Os símbolos incluídos no texto do índice representam as grandes categorias identificadas com a chave à direita. Os símbolos com números em sua parte superior (⋏[1]) identificam as subcategorias (veja-se a chave completa à página *I · 1).*

∧ Mountain	Berg	Montaña	Montagne	Montanha
⋏ Mountains	Berge	Montañas	Montagnes	Montanhas
)(Pass	Pass	Paso	Col	Passo
V Valley, Canyon	Tal, Cañon	Valle, Cañón	Vallée, Canyon	Vale, Canhão
≚ Plain	Ebene	Llano	Plaine	Planície
≻ Cape	Kap	Cabo	Cap	Cabo
I Island	Insel	Isla	Île	Ilha
II Islands	Inseln	Islas	Îles	Ilhas
⩣ Other Topographic Features	Andere Topographische Objekte	Otros Elementos Topográficos	Autres données topographiques	Outros acidentes topográficos

ESPAÑOL: Nombre — Página — Lat.°′ — Long.°′ W = Oeste
FRANÇAIS: Nom — Page — Lat.°′ — Long.°′ W = Ouest
PORTUGUÊS: Nome — Página — Lat.°′ — Long.°′ W = Oeste

≃ River	Fluss	Río	Rivière	Rio		
≊ Canal	Kanal	Canal	Canal	Canal		
∟ Waterfall, Rapids	Wasserfall, Stromschnellen	Cascada, Rápidos	Chute d'eau, Rapides	Cascata, Rápidos		
ɥ Strait	Meeresstrasse	Estrecho	Détroit	Estreito		
c Bay, Gulf	Bucht, Golf	Bahía, Golfo	Baie, Golfe	Baía, Golfo		
⊜ Lake, Lakes	See, Seen	Lago, Lagos	Lac, Lacs	Lago, Lagos		
≡ Swamp	Sumpf	Pantano	Marais	Pântano		
⌂ Ice Features, Glacier	Eis- und Gletscherformen	Accidentes Glaciales	Formes glaciaires	Acidentes glaciares		
⫧ Other Hydrographic Features	Andere Hydrographische Objekte	Otros Elementos Hidrográficos	Autres données hydrographiques	Outros acidentes hidrográficos		
⊹ Submarine Features	Untermeerische Objekte	Accidentes Submarinos	Formes de relief sous-marin	Acidentes submarinos		
□ Political Unit	Politische Einheit	Unidad Politica	Entité politique	Unidade política		
ʊ Cultural Institution	Kulturelle Institution	Institución Cultural	Institution culturelle	Instituição cultural		
⊥ Historical Site	Historische Stätte	Sitio Histórico	Site historique	Sitio histórico		
♠ Recreational Site	Erholungs- und Ferienort	Sitio de Recreo	Centre de loisirs	Area de Lazer		
⊠ Airport	Flughafen	Aeropuerto	Aéroport	Aeroporto		
■ Military Installation	Militäranlage	Instalación Militar	Installation militaire	Instalação militar		
◆ Miscellaneous	Verschiedenes	Misceláneo	Divers	Diversos		

Symbols in the index entries represent the broad categories identified in the key at the right. Symbols with superior numbers (⋀[1]) identify subcategories (see complete key on page I · 1).

Kartensymbole in dem Registerverzeichnis stellen die rechts in Schlüssel erklärten Kategorien dar. Symbole mit hochgestellten Ziffern (⋀[1]) bezeichnen Unterabteilungen einer Kategorie (vgl. vollständiger Schlüssel auf Seite I · 1).

Los símbolos incluidos en el texto del índice representan las grandes categorías identificadas con la clave a la derecha. Los símbolos con numeros en su parte superior (⋀[1]) identifican las subcategorías (véase la clave completa en la página I · 1).

Les symboles de l'index représentent les catégories indiquées dans la légende à droite. Les symboles suivis d'un indice (⋀[1]) représentent des sous-catégories (voir légende complète à la page I · 1).

Os símbolos incluídos no texto do índice representam as grandes categorias identificadas com a chave à direita. Os símbolos com números em sua parte superior (⋀[1]) identificam as subcategorias (veja-se a chave completa à página I · 1).

∧ Mountain	Berg	Montaña	Montagne	Montanha
⋀ Mountains	Berge	Montañas	Montagnes	Montanhas
)(Pass	Pass	Paso	Col	Passo
V Valley, Canyon	Tal, Cañon	Valle, Cañón	Vallée, Canyon	Vale, Canhão
≐ Plain	Ebene	Llano	Plaine	Planície
> Cape	Kap	Cabo	Cap	Cabo
I Island	Insel	Isla	Île	Ilha
II Islands	Inseln	Islas	Îles	Ilhas
⊥ Other Topographic Features	Andere Topographische Objekte	Otros Elementos Topográficos	Autres données topographiques	Outros acidentes topográficos

ESPAÑOL / FRANÇAIS / PORTUGUÊS

Symbol	English	Deutsch	Español	Français	Português
≃	River	Fluss	Río	Rivière	Rio
≋	Canal	Kanal	Canal	Canal	Canal
L	Waterfall, Rapids	Wasserfall, Stromschnellen	Cascada, Rápidos	Chute d'eau, Rapides	Cascata, Rápidos
ʊ	Strait	Meeresstrasse	Estrecho	Détroit	Estreito
C	Bay, Gulf	Bucht, Golf	Bahía, Golfo	Baie, Golfe	Baía, Golfo
⊜	Lake, Lakes	See, Seen	Lago, Lagos	Lac, Lacs	Lago, Lagos
≡	Swamp	Sumpf	Pantano	Marais	Pântano
⊓	Ice Features, Glacier	Eis- und Gletscherformen	Accidentes Glaciales	Formes glaciaires	Acidentes glaciares
⊤	Other Hydrographic Features	Andere Hydrographische Objekte	Otros Elementos Hidrográficos	Autres données hydrographiques	Outros acidentes hidrográficos
✢	Submarine Features	Untermeerische Objekte	Accidentes Submarinos	Formes de relief sous-marin	Acidentes submarinos
□	Political Unit	Politische Einheit	Unidad Política	Entité politique	Unidade política
♥	Cultural Institution	Kulturelle Institution	Institución Cultural	Institution culturelle	Instituição cultural
⊥	Historical Site	Historische Stätte	Sitio Histórico	Site historique	Sitio histórico
♠	Recreational Site	Erholungs- und Ferienort	Sitio de Recreo	Centre de loisirs	Area de Lazer
⊠	Airport	Flughafen	Aeropuerto	Aéroport	Aeroporto
■	Military Installation	Militäranlage	Instalación Militar	Installation militaire	Instalação militar
◆	Miscellaneous	Verschiedenes	Misceláneo	Divers	Diversos

ENGLISH / DEUTSCH

Name	Page (Seite)	Lat.°′ (Breite°′)	Long.°′ (Länge°′ E = Ost)
An-Nafī	**128**	24.57 N	43.42 E
An-Nafūd ✦[2]	**128**	28.30 N	41.00 E
Annagassan	**48**	53.53 N	6.20 W
Annahütte	**54**	51.34 N	13.53 E
An-Najaf	**128**	31.59 N	44.20 E
An-Najaf □[4]	**128**	31.00 N	44.00 E
Annaka	**94**	36.19 N	138.54 E
An-Nakhl, Miṣr	**140**	29.55 N	33.45 E
An-Nakhl, Sūrīy.	**132**	33.00 N	36.07 E
Annalee ≃	**48**	54.03 N	7.24 W
Annalee Heights	**208**	38.51 N	77.10 W
Annalong	**48**	54.06 N	5.53 W
Anna Maria	**220**	27.31 N	82.44 W
Anna Maria Island I	**220**	27.30 N	82.43 W
An-Nāmir	**132**	32.47 N	36.13 E
Annamitique, Chaîne ⋏	**110**	17.00 N	106.00 E
Annan	**44**	54.59 N	3.16 W
Annan ≃	**44**	54.59 N	3.16 W
Annanberg	**164**	4.55 S	144.40 E
Annandale, Austl.	**166**	21.57 S	148.22 E
Annandale, Mn., U.S.	**190**	45.15 N	94.07 W
Annandale, N.J., U.S.	**210**	40.38 N	74.52 W
Annandale, Va., U.S.	**208**	38.49 N	77.11 W
Annandale V	**44**	55.10 N	3.25 W
Annandale-on-Hudson	**210**	42.01 N	73.54 W
Anna Plains	**162**	19.17 S	121.37 E
Anna Point ›	**174b**	0.30 S	166.56 E
Annapolis	**208**	38.58 N	76.29 W
Annapolis Basin ⊂	**186**	44.39 N	65.42 W
Annapolis Royal	**186**	44.45 N	65.31 W
Annapurna ʌ	**124**	28.34 N	83.50 E
An-Naqīrah ⊤[4]	**128**	27.53 N	48.15 E
An-Nāqūrah	**132**	33.07 N	35.08 E
Ann Arbor	**216**	42.16 N	83.43 W
Ann Arbor Municipal Airport ⊠	**281**	42.14 N	83.45 W
Anna Regina	**246**	7.16 N	58.30 W
Annaricken Brook ≃	**285**	40.03 N	74.42 W
An-Nāṣirīyah, ʿIrāq	**128**	31.02 N	46.16 E
An-Nāṣirīyah, Sūrīy.	**130**	33.52 N	36.49 E
Annaspan ⊜	**158**	28.33 S	25.47 E
An-Nawfalāb	**140**	15.52 N	32.32 E
An-Nawfalīyah	**146**	30.47 N	17.50 E
An-Nazlah	**132**	31.32 N	34.29 E
An-Nazlat	**142**	29.19 N	30.39 E
Annbank	**44**	55.28 N	4.30 W
Annean, Lake ⊜	**162**	26.54 S	118.14 E
Anne Arundel □[6]	**208**	38.59 N	76.30 W
Annebault	**50**	49.15 N	0.04 E
Annecy	**58**	45.54 N	6.07 E
Annecy, Lac d' ⊜	**58**	45.51 N	6.11 E
Annecy-le-Vieux	**58**	45.55 N	6.09 E
Annemasse	**58**	46.12 N	6.15 E
Annen ✦[8]	**263**	51.27 N	7.22 E
Annenkov Island I	**244**	54.29 S	37.05 W
Annenskij Most	**76**	60.45 N	37.10 E
Annenskoje	**86**	53.08 N	60.26 E
Anner ≃	**48**	52.22 N	7.39 W
Annet I	**42a**	49.54 N	6.21 W
Annet-sur-Marne	**261**	48.56 N	2.43 E
Annette	**182**	55.03 N	131.34 W
Annette Island I	**182**	55.10 N	131.28 W
Annevoie-Rouillon	**56**	50.21 N	4.50 E
Annezin	**50**	50.32 N	2.37 E
Annfield Plain	**44**	54.51 N	1.45 W
An-nhon	**110**	13.53 N	109.06 E
Anniangniang	**89**	51.33 N	125.49 E
Annicco	**62**	45.14 N	9.52 E
An-Nīl □[4]	**140**	19.00 N	33.00 E
An-Nīl al-Azraq □[4]	**140**	12.00 N	34.00 E
Anning	**102**	24.59 N	102.18 E
Anningdu	**102**	36.56 N	104.31 E
Anninger ʌ	**264b**	48.03 N	16.15 E
Annino	**265a**	59.46 N	30.03 E
Anninskije Mineral'nyje Vody	**89**	52.44 N	140.12 E
Annisquam	**283**	42.39 N	70.41 W
Annisquam ≃	**283**	42.39 N	70.41 W
Anniston	**194**	33.39 N	85.49 W
Annobón I	**138**	1.25 S	5.36 E
Annonay	**62**	45.14 N	4.40 E
Annopol	**30**	50.54 N	21.52 E
Anno-Rebrikovo	**83**	49.36 N	40.12 E
Annot	**62**	43.58 N	6.40 E
Annotto Bay	**241q**	18.16 N	76.46 W
Annsjön ⊜	**40**	58.48 N	15.26 E
An-Nubayrah	**142**	30.54 N	30.35 E
An-Nuhūd	**140**	12.42 N	28.26 E
An-Nuʿmān I	**128**	27.08 N	35.46 E
An-Nuwayrah	**142**	29.06 N	30.59 E
Annville, Ky., U.S.	**192**	37.19 N	83.58 W
Annville, Pa., U.S.	**208**	40.19 N	76.30 W
Annweiler am Trifels	**56**	49.12 N	7.58 E
Anō	**94**	34.46 N	136.27 E
Anoia	**68**	38.27 N	16.05 E
Anoka	**190**	45.11 N	93.23 W
Áno Liósia	**267c**	38.05 N	23.42 E
Año Nuevo Bay ⊂	**226**	37.07 N	122.19 W
Anopino	**80**	55.42 N	40.40 E
Anori, Bra.	**246**	3.47 S	61.38 W
Anorí, Col.	**246**	7.05 N	75.08 W
Anorotsangana	**157b**	13.56 S	47.55 E
Anosibe	**157b**	19.26 S	48.13 E
Anosyennes, Chaînes ⋏	**157b**	24.30 S	46.50 E
Anotaie ≃	**250**	3.29 N	52.04 W
Anpilogovo	**78**	51.47 N	36.01 E
Anping, Zhg.	**98**	38.16 N	115.30 E
Anping, Zhg.	**98**	34.01 N	115.07 E
Anping, Zhg.	**100**	26.33 N	113.22 E
Anping, Zhg.	**104**	41.11 N	123.26 E
Anping, Zhg.	**105**	39.43 N	116.53 E
Anpu	**102**	21.27 N	110.00 E
ʿAnqābīyah, Jabal al- ʌ[2]	**142**	30.01 N	31.37 E
Anqing	**100**	30.31 N	117.02 E
Anqiu	**98**	36.25 N	119.10 E
Anrath	**56**	51.17 N	6.28 E
Anren, Zhg.	**100**	28.04 N	119.20 E
Anren, Zhg.	**100**	26.42 N	113.16 E
Anrenzhen	**107**	30.31 N	103.38 E
Anröchte	**52**	51.33 N	8.19 E
Ans, Bel.	**56**	50.39 N	5.32 E
Ans, Dan.	**41**	56.19 N	9.36 E
Anṣāb	**128**	29.11 N	44.43 E
Ansager	**41**	55.42 N	8.45 E
Ansai	**102**	36.54 N	109.10 E
Anṣār	**132**	33.23 N	35.21 E
Ansbach	**56**	49.17 N	10.34 E
Anschan → Anshan	**104**	41.08 N	122.59 E
Anschlag	**263**	51.10 N	7.29 E
Anse	**58**	45.56 N	4.43 E
Anseba ≃	**144**	17.03 N	37.24 E
Anse-Bertrand	**241o**	16.29 N	61.31 W
Anse-d'Hainault	**238**	18.30 N	74.27 W
Anse La Raye	**241f**	13.57 N	61.03 W
Anselmo	**198**	41.37 N	99.51 W
Anseremme	**56**	50.15 N	4.54 E
Anserma	**246**	5.13 N	75.48 W
Ansfelden	**61**	48.13 N	14.17 E
Anshan	**104**	41.08 N	122.59 E
Anshun	**102**	26.15 N	105.56 E
Ansina	**252**	31.54 S	55.28 W
Ansley	**198**	41.17 N	99.22 W
Anson	**196**	32.45 N	99.53 W
Anson Bay ⊂, Austl.	**164**	13.20 S	130.06 E
Anson Bay ⊂, Norf. I.	**174c**	29.01 S	167.55 E
Anson Creek ≃	**212**	44.53 N	79.03 W
Ansŏng	**98**	37.02 N	127.16 E
Ansongo	**150**	15.40 N	0.30 E
Ansonia, Ct., U.S.	**207**	41.20 N	73.04 W
Ansonia, Oh., U.S.	**216**	40.12 N	84.38 W
Ansonville, N.C., U.S.	**192**	35.06 N	80.06 W
Ansonville, Pa., U.S.	**214**	40.51 N	78.34 W
Ansouis	**62**	43.44 N	5.28 E
Ansted	**188**	38.08 N	81.05 W
Anstey	**42**	52.40 N	1.11 W
Anstruther	**46**	56.13 N	2.42 W
Anstruther Lake ⊜	**212**	44.45 N	78.12 W
Ansudu	**164**	2.08 S	139.20 E
Ansus	**164**	1.44 S	135.49 E
Anta, Bra.	**256**	22.03 S	42.59 W
Anta, Perú	**248**	13.29 S	72.09 W
Anta, Cachoeira ∟	**255**	13.06 S	48.09 W
Anta, Cachoeira da ∟	**248**	7.29 S	61.51 W
Antabamba	**248**	14.19 S	72.55 W
Antakya (Antioch)	**130**	36.14 N	36.07 E
Antalaha	**157b**	14.53 S	50.16 E
Antalieptė	**76**	55.40 N	25.51 E
Antalovcy	**78**	48.38 N	22.31 E
Antalya	**130**	36.53 N	30.42 E
Antalya □[4]	**130**	37.00 N	31.00 E
Antalya, Gulf of → Antalya Körfezi ⊂	**130**	36.30 N	31.00 E
Antalya Körfezi ⊂	**130**	36.30 N	31.00 E
Antambohobe	**157b**	22.20 S	46.47 E
An-tan	**110**	15.26 N	108.39 E
Antanambao Manampotsy	**157b**	19.29 S	48.34 E
Antanambe	**157b**	16.26 S	49.52 E
Antananarivo	**157b**	18.55 S	47.31 E
Antananarivo □[4]	**157b**	19.00 S	47.00 E
Antanetibe	**157b**	18.27 S	46.42 E
Antanifotsy	**157b**	19.39 S	47.19 E
Antanimieva	**157b**	22.12 S	43.44 E
Antanimora	**157b**	24.49 S	45.40 E
Antar, Djebel ʌ	**148**	31.57 N	1.56 W
Antarctica ±[1]	**9**	87.00 S	60.00 E
Antarctic Peninsula ›[1]	**9**	69.30 S	65.00 W
Antarctique, Péninsule → Antarctic Peninsula ›[1]	**9**	69.30 S	65.00 W
Antarctiques territoires britanniques → British Antarctic Territory □[2]	**9**	60.00 S	45.00 W
Antarktis → Antarctica ±[1]	**9**	87.00 S	60.00 E
Antártica, Península → Antarctic Peninsula ›[1]	**9**	69.30 S	65.00 W
Antas	**250**	10.23 S	38.20 W
Antas, Ribeirão das ≃	**256**	21.47 S	46.36 W
Antas, Rio das ≃	**252**	29.04 S	51.21 W
An Teallach ʌ	**46**	57.48 N	5.14 W
Antechamber Bay ⊂	**168b**	35.48 S	138.05 E
Antegnate	**62**	45.29 N	9.47 E
Antela, Laguna de ⊜	**34**	42.07 N	7.41 W
Antelope Acres	**228**	34.44 N	118.19 W
Antelope Creek ≃, Nv., U.S.	**204**	40.00 N	117.24 W
Antelope Creek ≃, S.D., U.S.	**198**	45.19 N	102.27 W
Antelope Creek ≃, Wy., U.S.	**198**	43.29 N	105.23 W
Antelope Island I	**202**	40.57 N	112.12 W
Antelope Mine	**154**	21.02 S	28.27 E
Antelope Peak ʌ	**204**	41.19 N	114.58 W
Antelope Reservoir ⊜[1]	**202**	42.54 N	117.13 W
Antelope Valley V	**228**	34.45 N	118.20 W
Antelope Wash V	**204**	39.33 N	116.17 W
Antenor Navarro	**250**	6.44 S	38.27 W
Antequera, Bol.	**248**	18.29 S	66.53 W
Antequera, Esp.	**34**	37.01 N	4.33 W
Antequera, Para.	**252**	24.08 S	57.07 W
Antero Reservoir ⊜[1]	**200**	39.00 N	105.55 W
Anterselva, Lago d' ⊜	**64**	46.53 N	12.10 E
Anterselva di Sopra	**64**	46.52 N	12.08 E
Antes Fort	**210**	41.12 N	77.14 W
Antetikireja	**157b**	14.42 S	47.29 E
Antevamena	**157b**	21.02 S	44.08 E
Antey-Saint-André	**62**	45.48 N	7.36 E
Anthéor	**62**	43.26 N	6.53 E
Anthon	**198**	42.23 N	95.51 W
Anthony, Fl., U.S.	**192**	29.17 N	82.06 W
Anthony, Ks., U.S.	**198**	37.09 N	98.01 W
Anthony, N.M., U.S.	**200**	32.00 N	106.36 W
Anthony, R.I., U.S.	**207**	41.41 N	71.32 W
Anthony, Tx., U.S.	**200**	31.59 N	106.36 W
Anthony Chabot Regional Park ♠	**282**	37.45 N	122.06 W
Anthony Creek ≃	**188**	37.54 N	80.20 W
Anthony Lagoon	**162**	17.59 S	135.32 E
Anthony Peak ʌ	**204**	39.51 N	122.58 W
Anti-Atlas ⋏	**148**	30.00 N	8.30 W
Antibes	**62**	43.35 N	7.07 E
Antibes, Cap d' ›	**62**	43.32 N	7.07 E
Anticosti, Île d' I	**186**	49.30 N	63.00 W
Antiesen ≃	**60**	48.22 N	13.24 E
Antietam Creek, West Branch ≃	**208**	39.41 N	77.37 W
Antietam National Battlefield ♠	**188**	39.24 N	77.47 W
Antifer, Cap d' ›	**50**	49.41 N	0.10 E
Antignano	**66**	43.30 N	10.19 E
Antigo	**190**	45.08 N	89.09 W
Antigonish	**186**	45.35 N	61.55 W
Antigorio, Valle V	**58**	46.18 N	8.20 E
Antigua I	**240c**	17.03 N	61.48 W
Antigua and Barbuda □[1], N.A.	**230**	17.03 N	61.48 W
Antigua and Barbuda □[1], N.A.	**240c**	17.03 N	61.48 W
Antigua Guatemala	**236**	14.34 N	90.44 W
Antigues, Pointe d' ›	**241o**	16.26 N	61.33 W
Antiguo Morelos	**234**	22.33 N	99.05 W
Anti-Lebanon → Sharqī, Al-Jabal ash- ⋏	**132**	33.35 N	36.00 E
Antilla, Arg.	**252**	26.07 S	64.36 W
Antilla, Cuba	**240p**	20.50 N	75.45 W
Antillas, Archipiélago de las → West Indies II	**230**	19.00 N	70.00 W
Antillas Holandesas → Netherlands Antilles □[2]	**241s**	12.15 N	69.00 W
Antilles hollandaise → Netherlands Antilles □[2]	**241s**	12.15 N	69.00 W
Antilles néerlandaises → Netherlands Antilles □[2]	**241s**	12.15 N	69.00 W
Antillo	**70**	37.58 N	15.15 E
Antilyās	**132**	33.55 N	35.35 E
Antímano ✦[8]	**286c**	10.28 N	66.59 W
Antimari ≃	**248**	9.04 S	67.23 W
Antimony	**200**	38.07 N	111.59 W
Anting	**106**	31.18 N	121.09 E
Antioch → Antakya, Tür.	**130**	36.14 N	36.07 E
Antioch, Ca., U.S.	**226**	38.00 N	121.48 W
Antioch, Il., U.S.	**216**	42.28 N	88.05 W
Antioquia	**246**	6.33 N	75.50 W
Antioquia □[5]	**246**	7.00 N	75.30 W
Antipino, S.S.S.R.	**76**	55.55 N	33.16 E
Antipino, S.S.S.R.	**86**	57.49 N	66.34 E
Antipino, S.S.S.R.	**86**	59.01 N	55.10 E
Antipodes Islands II	**9**	49.40 S	178.47 E
Antipolo	**116**	14.35 N	121.10 E
Antipovka	**80**	49.50 N	45.20 E
Antiquarian Museum ʊ	**283**	42.27 N	71.20 W
Antique □[4]	**116**	11.00 N	121.45 E
Antisana ʌ[1]	**246**	0.30 S	78.08 W
Antler ≃	**184**	49.08 N	101.00 W
Antlers	**196**	34.13 N	95.37 W
Antoetra	**157b**	20.46 S	47.20 E
Antofagasta	**252**	23.39 S	70.24 W
Antofagasta □[4]	**252**	23.30 S	69.00 W
Antofagasta de la Sierra	**252**	26.04 S	67.25 W
Antofalla, Salar de ≚	**252**	25.44 S	67.45 W
Antofalla, Volcán ʌ[1]	**252**	25.34 S	67.55 W
Antoing	**50**	50.34 N	3.27 E
Antolana ʌ	**157b**	17.04 S	48.09 E
Antón, Pan.	**236**	8.24 N	80.16 W
Anton, Tx., U.S.	**196**	33.49 N	102.10 W
Anton Chico	**200**	35.12 N	105.08 W
Antongila, Helodrano ⊂	**157b**	15.45 S	49.50 E
Antonia	**219**	38.21 N	90.27 W
Antonibe	**157b**	15.07 S	47.24 E
Antonina	**252**	25.27 S	48.43 W
Antonina do Norte	**250**	6.43 S	39.58 W
Antoniny	**78**	49.49 N	26.52 E
Antonio Amaro	**232**	24.16 N	104.01 W
Antonio Carboni	**258**	35.12 S	59.20 W
Antônio Carlos	**256**	21.19 S	43.45 W
Antonio de Biedma	**254**	47.29 S	66.30 W
Antônio Diogo	**250**	4.18 S	38.45 W
Antonio Escobedo	**234**	20.46 N	103.57 W
Antônio João	**255**	23.15 S	55.31 W
Antônio Lemos	**250**	1.22 S	50.50 W
Antônio Prado	**252**	28.51 S	51.17 W
Antonito	**200**	37.05 N	106.00 W
Antón Lizardo, Punta de ›	**234**	19.03 N	95.58 W
Antonov	**78**	49.37 N	29.47 E
Antonovka, S.S.S.R.	**80**	54.55 N	49.30 E
Antonovka, S.S.S.R.	**86**	53.19 N	68.26 E
Antonovka, S.S.S.R.	**86**	45.38 N	80.15 E
Antonovo	**80**	49.23 N	51.47 E
Antony	**50**	48.45 N	2.18 E
Antopol'	**76**	52.12 N	24.47 E
Antou	**100**	26.07 N	118.11 E
Antracit	**83**	48.06 N	39.06 E
Antraigues	**62**	44.43 N	4.21 E
Antrain	**32**	48.27 N	1.29 W
Antratsit → Antracit	**83**	48.06 N	39.06 E
Antrift ≃	**56**	50.54 N	9.15 E
Antrim, N. Ire., U.K.	**48**	54.43 N	6.13 W
Antrim, Oh., U.S.	**214**	40.06 N	81.23 W
Antrim, Pa., U.S.	**210**	41.37 N	77.18 W
Antrodoco	**66**	42.25 N	13.05 E
Antronapiana	**58**	46.03 N	8.07 E
Antropovo, S.S.S.R.	**80**	58.26 N	43.00 E
Antropovo, S.S.S.R.	**82**	55.15 N	37.39 E
Antsakabary	**157b**	15.03 S	48.56 E
Antsalova	**157b**	18.40 S	44.37 E
Antsenavolo	**157b**	21.24 S	48.03 E
Antsiafabositra	**157b**	17.18 S	46.57 E
Antsirabe, Madag.	**157b**	14.00 S	49.59 E
Antsirabe, Madag.	**157b**	15.57 S	48.58 E
Antsirabe, Madag.	**157b**	19.51 S	47.02 E
Antsiranana	**157b**	12.16 S	49.17 E
Antsiranana □[4]	**157b**	13.30 S	49.10 E
Antsla	**76**	57.50 N	26.32 E
Antsohihy	**157b**	14.52 S	47.59 E
Anttis	**24**	67.16 N	22.52 E
Antu (Songjiang)	**98**	42.32 N	128.18 E
An-tuc (An-khe)	**110**	13.57 N	108.39 E
Antufash, Jazīrat I	**144**	15.45 N	42.22 E
Antulai, Gunong ʌ	**112**	4.40 N	116.21 E
Antun'	**89**	47.36 N	135.46 E
Antung → Dandong	**98**	40.08 N	124.20 E
Antuševo, S.S.S.R.	**76**	59.59 N	42.18 E
Antuševo, S.S.S.R.	**76**	59.54 N	37.40 E
Antwerp → Antwerpen, Bel.	**50**	51.13 N	4.25 E
Antwerp, N.Y., U.S.	**212**	44.11 N	75.36 W
Antwerp, Oh., U.S.	**216**	41.10 N	84.44 W
Antwerpen (Anvers)	**50**	51.13 N	4.25 E
Antwerpen □[4]	**56**	51.10 N	4.50 E
Antykan	**89**	54.55 N	135.12 E
Anua	**174u**	14.16 S	170.40 W
An Uaimh (Navan)	**48**	53.39 N	6.41 W
Anučino, S.S.S.R.	**80**	52.58 N	43.52 E
Anučino, S.S.S.R.	**89**	43.58 N	133.02 E
Anŭi	**98**	35.38 N	127.48 E
An'uj ≃	**89**	49.18 N	136.27 E
An'ujsk	**74**	68.18 N	161.38 E
An'ujskij chrebet ⋏, S.S.S.R.	**74**	67.30 N	166.00 E
Anujskij chrebet ⋏, S.S.S.R.	**86**	51.30 N	84.55 E
Anundshögen ⊥	**40**	59.25 N	16.32 E
Anūpgarh	**123**	29.11 N	73.13 E
Anūpshahr	**124**	28.22 N	78.16 E
Ānūr	**126**	22.55 N	87.39 E
Anuradhapura	**122**	8.21 N	80.23 E
Anvers → Antwerpen	**50**	51.13 N	4.25 E
Anversa degli Abruzzi	**66**	41.59 N	13.48 E
Anvers Island I	**9**	64.33 S	63.35 W
Anvik	**180**	62.40 N	160.12 W
Anvik ≃	**180**	62.39 N	160.14 W
Anvil Peak ʌ	**181a**	52.00 N	179.35 E
Anvil Range ⋏	**180**	62.30 N	133.50 W
Anvin	**50**	50.27 N	2.15 E
Anxi, Zhg.	**100**	25.06 N	118.12 E
Anxi, Zhg.	**100**	25.15 N	115.06 E
Anxi, Zhg.	**102**	40.32 N	95.51 E
Anxi, Zhg.	**106**	30.25 N	120.01 E
Anxian	**102**	31.40 N	104.32 E
Anxiang	**102**	29.23 N	112.09 E
Anxin (Xin'anzhen)	**105**	38.55 N	115.55 E
Anxing	**106**	31.24 N	119.06 E
Anxious Bay ⊂	**162**	33.25 S	134.35 E
Anyama	**150**	5.30 N	4.03 W
Anyang, Taehan	**98**	37.23 N	126.55 E
Anyang, Zhg.	**98**	36.06 N	114.21 E
Anyang ≃	**98**	36.01 N	114.46 E
Anyeke	**154**	2.24 N	32.31 E
A'nyêmaqên Shan ⋏	**102**	34.30 N	100.00 E
Anyer-kidul	**115a**	6.04 S	105.53 E
Anyi	**100**	28.50 N	115.31 E
Anykščiai	**76**	55.32 N	25.06 E
Anyox	**182**	55.25 N	129.49 W
Anysberg	**158**	33.31 S	20.46 E
Anyuan, Zhg.	**100**	26.36 N	116.38 E
Anyuan, Zhg.	**100**	27.37 N	113.54 E
Anyuan, Zhg.	**100**	25.08 N	115.28 E
Anyuanyi → Tianzhu	**102**	37.14 N	102.59 E
Anyue	**107**	30.06 N	105.21 E
Anza ≃	**58**	46.00 N	8.17 E
Anza-Borrego Desert State Park ♠	**204**	33.00 N	116.26 W
Anzac	**184**	56.27 N	111.02 W
Anzaldo	**248**	17.50 S	65.55 W
Anzano di Puglia	**68**	41.07 N	15.17 E
Anzbari ʌ	**123**	34.40 N	74.50 E
Anze	**102**	36.11 N	112.16 E
Anžero-Sudžensk	**86**	56.07 N	86.00 E
Anzhen	**106**	31.36 N	120.28 E
Anzhou	**105**	38.52 N	115.49 E
Anzhuang	**106**	31.04 N	121.01 E
Anzi, It.	**68**	40.31 N	15.55 E
Anzi, Zaïre	**152**	0.52 S	23.24 E
Anzicun	**105**	39.46 N	115.50 E
Anzin	**50**	50.22 N	3.30 E
Anzio	**66**	41.27 N	12.37 E
Anzoátegui □[3]	**246**	9.00 N	64.30 W
Anzob	**85**	39.10 N	68.48 E
Anzob, pereval ✕	**85**	39.07 N	68.52 E
Anzola dell'Emilia	**64**	44.33 N	11.11 E
Anzon ≃	**62**	45.45 N	3.57 E
Anžu, ostrova II	**74**	75.30 N	143.00 E
Aoba I	**175f**	15.25 S	167.50 E
Aoba / Maewo □[8]	**175f**	15.05 S	168.00 E
Aogaki	**96**	35.14 N	135.00 E
Aoga-shima I	**90**	32.28 N	139.46 E
Aohaibolihu	**104**	42.01 N	121.32 E
Aohandaba	**104**	42.05 N	121.59 E
Aohan Qi (Xinhui)	**98**	42.19 N	119.59 E
Aoíz	**34**	42.47 N	1.22 W
Aoji	**98**	42.31 N	130.23 E
Aojiang	**100**	27.37 N	120.33 E
Aojiao	**100**	23.37 N	117.26 E
Aola	**175e**	9.32 S	160.29 E
Aoliyingzi	**104**	42.14 N	121.58 E
Ao Luk	**110**	8.23 N	98.43 E
Aomar	**34**	36.30 N	3.47 E
Aomen → Macau	**100**	22.14 N	113.35 E
Aomori	**92**	40.49 N	140.45 E
Aonla	**124**	28.17 N	79.09 E
Aono-yama ʌ	**96**	34.27 N	131.48 E
Aóös (Vijosë) ≃	**38**	40.37 N	19.20 E
A'opo	**175a**	13.29 S	172.30 W
Aôral, Phnum ʌ	**110**	12.02 N	104.10 E
Aorangi Mountains ⋏	**172**	41.26 S	175.20 E
Aore I	**175f**	15.35 S	167.10 E
Aorere ≃	**172**	40.41 S	172.40 E
Aoshang	**100**	25.42 N	113.00 E
Ao-shima I, Nihon	**96**	33.44 N	132.29 E
Ao-shima I, Nihon	**96**	33.55 N	134.44 E
Aosta	**62**	45.44 N	7.20 E
Aosta □[4]	**58**	45.45 N	7.20 E
Aosta, Valle d' V	**62**	45.46 N	7.25 E
Aoste	**62**	45.35 N	5.36 E
Aotou	**100**	22.44 N	114.33 E
Aoudaghost ⊥	**150**	17.25 N	10.40 W
Aouderas	**150**	17.37 N	8.26 E
Aoudour, Oued ≃	**34**	35.02 N	5.02 W
Aouk, Bahr ≃	**146**	8.51 N	18.53 E
Aoukalé ≃	**146**	9.17 N	22.42 E
Aouk-Aoukalé, Réserve de Faune de l' ✦[4]	**146**	10.00 N	21.15 E
Aoukâr ✦[1]	**150**	18.00 N	9.30 W
Aoulime, Jebel ʌ	**148**	30.48 N	8.50 W
Aoumou	**175f**	21.24 S	165.50 E
Aourou	**150**	14.57 N	11.35 W
Aoya	**96**	35.31 N	133.59 E
Aoyama	**94**	34.40 N	136.11 E
Aoyama-tōge ✕	**94**	34.40 N	136.16 E
Aozi	**146**	21.04 N	18.41 E
Aozou	**146**	21.49 N	17.25 E
Apa ≃	**252**	22.06 S	58.00 W
Apache	**196**	34.53 N	98.21 W
Apache Junction	**200**	33.24 N	111.32 W
Apache Lake ⊜[1]	**200**	33.36 N	111.16 W
Apache Peak ʌ	**200**	31.49 N	110.25 W
Apalachee ≃	**192**	33.32 N	83.17 W
Apalachee Bay ⊂	**192**	30.00 N	84.13 W
Apalaches → Appalachian Mountains ⋏	**178**	41.00 N	77.00 W
Apalachicola	**192**	29.43 N	84.59 W
Apalachicola ≃	**192**	29.44 N	84.59 W
Apalachicola Bay ⊂	**192**	29.40 N	85.00 W
Apalachin	**210**	42.04 N	76.09 W
Apam, Ghana	**150**	5.17 N	0.44 W
Apam, Méx.	**234**	19.43 N	98.25 W
Apanás, Lago de ⊜[1]	**236**	13.11 N	85.59 W
Apango	**234**	17.44 N	99.20 W
Apapa ✦[8]	**273a**	6.27 N	3.22 E
Apapa Wharf ✦[5]	**273a**	6.23 N	3.23 E
Apaporis ≃	**246**	1.23 S	69.25 W
Aparados da Serra, Parque Nacional dos ♠	**252**	29.30 S	50.32 W
Aparan	**84**	40.36 N	44.23 E
Aparecida	**256**	22.50 S	45.14 W
Aparima ≃	**172**	46.20 S	168.01 E
Aparri	**116**	18.22 N	121.39 E
Apaseo el Grande	**234**	20.33 N	100.41 W
Apastovo	**80**	55.11 N	48.30 E
Apatin	**38**	45.40 N	18.59 E
Apatity	**24**	67.34 N	33.18 E
Apatzingán [de la Constitución]	**232**	19.05 N	102.21 W
Apaxtla de Castrejón	**234**	18.09 N	99.52 W
Ap-ba-tien	**269c**	10.44 N	106.36 E
Ap-binh-quoi	**269c**	10.48 N	106.36 E
Ap-binh-thanh	**110**	11.11 N	108.42 E
Apcheron, Péninsule de l' → Apšeronskij poluostrov ›[1]	**84**	40.30 N	50.00 E
Ape	**76**	57.32 N	26.40 E
Apeadero Funke	**258**	35.28 S	58.59 W
Apecchio	**66**	43.33 N	12.25 E
Ape Dale V	**42**	52.30 N	2.45 W
Apediá ≃	**248**	11.39 S	61.11 W
Apeganau Lake ⊜	**184**	55.35 N	99.35 W
Apelação	**266c**	38.49 N	9.08 W
Apeldoorn	**52**	52.13 N	5.58 E
Apeleg, Arroyo ≃	**254**	44.58 S	70.07 W
Apen	**52**	53.13 N	7.48 E
Apenes	**224**	49.16 N	124.41 W
Apeninos → Appennino ⋏	**36**	43.00 N	13.00 E
Apenninen → Appennino ⋏	**36**	43.00 N	13.00 E
Apennines → Appennino ⋏	**36**	43.00 N	13.00 E
Apennins → Appennino ⋏	**36**	43.00 N	13.00 E
Apensen	**52**	53.26 N	9.37 E
Apese ✦[8]	**273a**	6.25 N	3.25 E
Apetlon	**61**	47.45 N	16.50 E
Apeú	**250**	1.18 S	47.59 W
Apex	**192**	35.43 N	78.51 W
Apex Mountain ʌ	**180**	62.28 N	138.04 W
Api	**154**	3.40 N	25.26 E
Api ʌ	**124**	30.00 N	80.57 E
Api, Tanjung ›	**112**	0.48 S	121.39 E
Apía, Col.	**246**	5.05 N	75.58 W
Apia, W. Sam.	**175a**	13.50 S	171.44 W
Apiacá	**255**	21.08 S	41.34 W
Apiacá ≃	**250**	9.16 S	57.03 W
Apiacás, Serra dos ⋏[1]	**248**	10.15 S	57.15 W
Apiaí	**252**	24.31 S	48.50 W
Apiaú ≃	**246**	2.39 N	61.12 W
Apice	**68**	41.07 N	14.56 E
Apinajé	**250**	11.31 S	48.18 W
Apipilulco	**234**	18.11 N	99.41 W
Apisancho ≃	**248**	7.18 S	76.50 W
Apishapa ≃	**198**	38.08 N	103.57 W
Apiti	**172**	39.58 S	175.53 E
Apizaco	**234**	19.25 N	98.09 W
Apizolaya	**232**	24.50 N	102.15 W
Aplahoué	**150**	6.56 N	1.41 E
Aplao	**248**	16.05 S	72.31 W
Ap Lei Chau I	**271d**	22.15 N	114.09 E
Aplerbeck ✦[8]	**263**	51.29 N	7.33 E
Aplinskij, porog ∟	**88**	58.28 N	100.32 E
Apo	**234**	19.25 N	102.25 W
Apo, Mount ʌ	**116**	6.59 N	125.16 E
Apodi	**250**	5.39 S	37.48 W
Apodi ≃	**250**	4.56 S	37.10 W
Apo East Pass ⋓	**116**	12.40 N	120.40 E
Apolakkiá	**38**	36.06 N	27.50 E
Apolda	**54**	51.01 N	11.31 E
Apolima Strait ⋓	**175a**	13.50 S	172.10 W
Apolinario Saravia	**252**	24.25 S	64.02 W
Apollo	**214**	40.34 N	79.34 W
Apollo Bay	**166**	38.45 S	143.40 E
Apollo Beach	**220**	27.45 N	82.25 W
Apollonia ⊥	**146**	32.54 N	21.58 E
Apolo	**248**	14.43 S	68.31 W
Apón ≃	**246**	10.06 N	72.23 W
Aponguao ≃	**246**	4.48 N	61.36 W
Apopa	**236**	13.48 N	89.11 W
Apopka	**220**	28.40 N	81.30 W
Apopka, Lake ⊜	**220**	28.37 N	81.38 W
Apoquindo	**286e**	33.24 S	70.32 W
Aporá	**250**	11.39 S	38.05 W
Aporé	**255**	18.58 S	52.01 W
Aporé ≃	**255**	19.27 S	50.57 W
Apo Reef ⊹[2]	**116**	12.40 N	120.29 E
Aporema	**250**	1.14 N	50.49 W
Aporo	**234**	19.41 N	100.25 W
Apostle Islands II	**190**	46.50 N	90.30 W
Apostle Islands National Lakeshore ♠	**190**	46.55 N	91.00 W
Apóstoles	**252**	27.55 S	55.46 W
Apostólou Andréa, Akrotírion ›	**130**	35.42 N	34.35 E
Apostolovo	**78**	47.39 N	33.44 E
Apozolco	**234**	21.22 N	104.00 W
Appalachen → Appalachian Mountains ⋏	**178**	41.00 N	77.00 W
Appalaches, Monts → Appalachian Mountains ⋏	**178**	41.00 N	77.00 W
Appalachia	**192**	36.54 N	82.46 W
Appalachian Mountains ⋏	**178**	41.00 N	77.00 W
Äppelbo	**40**	60.30 N	14.00 E
Appelhülsen	**52**	51.54 N	7.25 E
Appen	**52**	53.40 N	9.44 E
Appennino (Apennines) ⋏	**36**	43.00 N	13.00 E
Appennino, Galleria dell' ✦[5]	**66**	44.10 N	11.10 E
Appennino Abruzzese ⋏	**66**	42.00 N	14.00 E
Appennino Calabrese ⋏	**68**	39.00 N	16.30 E
Appennino Campano ⋏	**66**	41.30 N	15.00 E
Appennino Ligure ⋏	**62**	44.30 N	9.00 E
Appennino Lucano ⋏	**68**	40.30 N	16.00 E
Appennino Tosco-Emiliano ⋏	**36**	44.00 N	11.30 E
Appennino Umbro-Marchigiano ⋏	**66**	43.00 N	13.00 E
Appenzell	**58**	47.20 N	9.25 E
Appenzell-Ausser Rhoden □[3]	**58**	47.22 N	9.28 E
Appenzell-Inner Rhoden □[3]	**58**	47.18 N	9.25 E
Appiano (Eppan)	**64**	46.28 N	11.15 E
Appiano Gentile	**62**	45.44 N	8.59 E
Appin	**170**	34.12 S	150.47 E
Appingedam	**52**	53.18 N	6.52 E
Apple ≃, U.S.	**190**	42.11 N	90.14 W
Apple ≃, Wi., U.S.	**190**	45.09 N	92.45 W
Appleby, S. Afr.	**158**	27.39 S	22.36 E
Appleby, Eng., U.K.	**44**	54.36 N	2.29 W
Appleby, Tx., U.S.	**222**	31.43 N	94.36 W
Apple Creek	**214**	40.45 N	81.50 W
Apple Creek ≃, Il., U.S.	**219**	39.22 N	90.37 W
Apple Creek ≃, Mo., U.S.	**194**	37.35 N	89.32 W
Apple Creek ≃, N.D., U.S.	**198**	46.40 N	100.46 W
Applecross	**46**	57.25 N	5.49 W
Appledore	**42**	51.03 N	4.10 W
Applegate	**226**	39.06 N	120.59 W
Applegate ≃	**202**	42.26 N	123.27 W
Apple Hill	**206**	45.13 N	74.46 W
Apple Orchard Mountain ʌ	**192**	37.31 N	79.31 W
Apples	**58**	46.34 N	6.25 E
Apple Springs	**222**	31.13 N	94.58 W
Appleton, Eng., U.K.	**262**	53.21 N	2.33 W
Appleton, Mn., U.S.	**198**	45.11 N	96.01 W
Appleton, Wa., U.S.	**224**	45.48 N	121.16 W
Appleton, Wi., U.S.	**190**	44.15 N	88.24 W
Appleton City	**194**	38.11 N	94.01 W
Apple Valley	**228**	34.30 N	117.11 W
Applewold	**214**	40.47 N	79.36 W
Appley Bridge	**262**	53.35 N	2.43 W
Appling	**192**	33.32 N	82.18 W
Appoigny	**50**	47.53 N	3.32 E
Appomattox	**192**	37.21 N	78.49 W
Appomattox ≃	**192**	37.18 N	77.18 W
Appomattox Court House National Historical Park ♠	**192**	37.23 N	78.48 W
Approuague ≃	**250**	4.38 N	51.58 W
Apra Harbor ⊂	**174p**	13.27 N	144.38 E
Aprelevka	**82**	55.33 N	37.04 E
Aprel'sk	**88**	58.10 N	114.34 E
Aprel'skij	**89**	53.30 N	126.16 E
Apremont	**58**	46.13 N	5.40 E
Apremont-la-Forêt	**56**	48.51 N	5.38 E
Aprica, Passo d' ✕	**64**	46.09 N	10.09 E
Apricena	**68**	41.47 N	15.27 E
Aprigliano	**68**	39.14 N	16.20 E
April ≃	**164**	4.18 S	142.26 E
Aprilia	**66**	41.36 N	12.39 E
Apscheron → Apšeronskij poluostrov ›[1]	**84**	40.30 N	50.00 E
Apšeronsk	**84**	44.28 N	39.44 E
Apšeronskij poluostrov ›[1]	**84**	40.30 N	50.00 E
Apshawa	**276**	41.01 N	74.22 W
Apsley	**212**	44.45 N	78.06 W
Apt	**62**	43.53 N	5.24 E
Aptakisic	**278**	42.12 N	87.56 W
Ap-talai	**110**	11.24 N	107.23 E
Ap-tan-hoa	**269c**	10.45 N	106.35 E
Ap-tan-my	**110**	11.43 N	108.49 E
Aptos	**226**	36.58 N	121.53 W
Apuane, Alpi ⋏	**64**	44.09 N	10.15 E
Apuaú ≃	**246**	2.32 S	60.48 W
Apucarana	**255**	23.33 S	51.29 W
Apuiarés	**250**	3.56 S	39.24 W
Apulia Station	**210**	42.49 N	76.05 W
Apure □[3]	**246**	7.10 N	68.50 W
Apure ≃	**246**	7.37 N	66.25 W
Apurímac □[5]	**248**	14.00 S	73.00 W
Apurímac ≃	**248**	11.48 S	74.03 W
Apurito	**246**	7.56 N	68.27 W
Āq ≃	**84**	38.59 N	45.27 E
Aqaba, Gulf of ⊂	**128**	29.00 N	34.40 E
Aqabah, Wādī al- V	**132**	30.14 N	33.53 E
Āqbolāgh	**84**	38.54 N	44.32 E
Āqcheh	**120**	36.56 N	66.11 E
ʿAqīq	**140**	18.14 N	38.12 E
ʿAqīq, Khalīj ⊂	**140**	18.20 N	38.10 E
ʿAqīq, Wādī al- V	**128**	24.17 N	40.10 E
Āq Koprūk	**120**	36.05 N	66.51 E
Aq Qalʿeh	**128**	37.01 N	54.30 E
ʿAqrabā	**132**	33.06 N	36.00 E
ʿAqrah	**128**	36.45 N	43.54 E
Aquarius Plateau ⋏[1]	**200**	38.05 N	111.40 W
Aquasco	**208**	38.35 N	76.43 W
Aquashicola	**210**	40.49 N	75.35 W
Aquashicola Creek ≃	**210**	40.47 N	75.37 W
Äquatorial-Guinea → Equatorial Guinea □[1]	**152**	2.00 N	9.00 E
Aquebogue	**207**	40.56 N	72.37 W
Aqueduct Race Track ♠	**276**	40.40 N	73.50 W
Aquia Creek ≃	**208**	38.23 N	77.18 W
Aquiaulne ≃	**50**	47.37 N	2.30 E
Aquibi, Cachoeira ∟	**250**	11.08 S	55.22 W
Aquidabã	**250**	10.17 S	37.02 W
Aquidabã ≃	**248**	20.58 S	57.50 W
Aquidabán ≃	**252**	23.11 S	57.32 W
Aquidauana	**248**	20.28 S	55.48 W
Aquidauana ≃	**248**	19.44 S	56.50 W
Aquila, Méx.	**234**	18.36 N	103.30 W
Aquila, Schw.	**58**	46.31 N	8.57 E
Aquileia	**64**	45.46 N	13.22 E
Aquiles Serdán	**232**	28.36 N	105.53 W
Aquilla, Oh., U.S.	**214**	41.34 N	81.09 W
Aquilla, Tx., U.S.	**222**	31.51 N	97.13 W
Aquilla Creek ≃	**222**	31.40 N	97.10 W
Aquilonia (S.M.)	**68**	41.00 N	15.29 E
Aquin	**238**	18.17 N	73.24 W
Aquincumi Múzeum ʊ	**264c**	47.34 N	19.03 E
Aquino	**66**	41.30 N	13.42 E
Aquio ≃	**246**	2.42 N	67.34 W
Ara ≃, Esp.	**34**	42.25 N	0.09 E
Ara ≃, Ire.	**48**	52.24 N	7.56 W
Ara ≃, Nihon	**92**	38.09 N	139.25 E
Ara ≃, Nihon	**94**	35.39 N	139.51 E
Arab	**194**	34.19 N	86.29 W
ʿArab, Baḥr al- ≃	**140**	9.02 N	29.28 E
ʿArab, Khalīj al- ⊂	**140**	30.55 N	29.05 E
Arab, Oued el V	**148**	34.41 N	6.31 E
Arab, Shatt al- ≃	**128**	29.57 N	48.34 E
ʿArab, Wādī al- V	**132**	32.35 N	35.35 E
ʿArabābād	**128**	33.02 N	57.41 E
ʿArabah, Wādī V	**142**	29.07 N	32.39 E
Araban	**130**	37.26 N	37.41 E
Arabatskaja strelka ›[2]	**78**	45.40 N	35.00 E
Arabatskij zaliv ⊂	**78**	45.20 N	35.30 E
Arabba	**64**	46.30 N	11.52 E
Arabelo	**246**	4.55 N	64.13 W
Arabi	**194**	29.57 N	90.00 W
Arabian Basin ⊹[1]	**12**	11.30 N	65.00 E
Arabian Desert → Sharqīyah, Aṣ-Ṣaḥrā' ash- ✦[2]	**140**	28.00 N	32.00 E
Arabian Peninsula ›[1]	**12**	25.00 N	45.00 E
Arabian Sea ⊤[2]	**118**	15.00 N	65.00 E
Arabia Saudita → Saudi Arabia □[1]	**118**	25.00 N	45.00 E
Arabie, Mer d' → Arabian Sea ⊤[2]	**118**	15.00 N	65.00 E
Arabie Saoudite → Saudi Arabia □[1]	**118**	25.00 N	45.00 E
Arabique, Péninsule → Arabian Peninsula ›[1]	**12**	25.00 N	45.00 E
Arabisches Meer → Arabian Sea ⊤[2]	**118**	15.00 N	65.00 E
Arab-Jengidža	**84**	39.29 N	44.58 E
ʿArab Muṭayr	**142**	27.16 N	31.14 E
Ara-Bure, porog ∟	**88**	53.00 N	100.12 E
Araç	**130**	41.15 N	33.21 E
Araçá ≃	**246**	0.25 S	62.55 W
Aracaju	**250**	10.55 S	37.04 W
Araçariguama	**256**	23.26 S	47.04 W
Aracataca	**246**	10.36 N	74.12 W
Aracati	**250**	4.34 S	37.46 W
Aracatiaçu, Açude ⊜[1]	**250**	3.56 S	39.59 W
Araçatuba	**255**	21.12 S	50.25 W
Araceli	**116**	10.33 N	119.59 E
Aracena	**34**	37.53 N	6.33 W
Arâches-les-Carroz	**58**	46.02 N	6.39 E
Arachino-seki ⊥	**94**	35.33 N	136.05 E
Araci	**250**	11.20 S	38.57 W
Aracides, Cape ›	**175e**	8.39 S	161.01 E
Aracitaba	**256**	21.20 S	43.23 W
Aracoiaba	**250**	4.23 S	38.49 W
Aracruz	**255**	19.49 S	40.16 W
Aracu ≃	**246**	4.20 S	59.15 W
Araçuaí	**255**	16.52 S	42.04 W
Araçuaí ≃	**255**	16.46 S	42.02 W
Arad, Rom.	**38**	46.11 N	21.20 E
ʿArad, Yis.	**132**	31.15 N	35.13 E
Arad □[6]	**38**	46.20 N	21.40 E
Arada, Hond.	**236**	14.48 N	88.18 W
Arada, Tchad	**146**	15.01 N	20.40 E
Aradeo	**68**	40.08 N	18.08 E
Aradhíppou	**130**	34.57 N	33.35 E
Arafali	**144**	15.05 N	39.45 E
Arafune-san ʌ	**94**	36.12 N	138.38 E
Arafura Sea ⊤[2]	**164**	9.00 S	133.00 E
Arafura Shelf ⊹[4]	**14**	10.00 S	137.00 E
Aragac, gora ʌ	**84**	40.32 N	44.14 E
Aragarças	**255**	15.55 S	52.15 W
Arago, Cape ›	**202**	43.18 N	124.25 W
Aragoiânia	**255**	16.57 S	49.30 W
Aragon	**192**	34.02 N	85.03 W
Aragón □[4]	**34**	41.30 N	0.30 W
Aragón ≃	**34**	42.13 N	1.44 W
Aragona	**70**	37.24 N	13.37 E
Aragua □[3]	**246**	10.00 N	67.10 W
Araguacema	**250**	8.50 S	49.34 W
Araguaçu	**255**	12.49 S	49.51 W
Aragua de Barcelona	**246**	9.28 N	64.49 W
Aragua de Maturín	**246**	9.58 N	63.29 W
Araguaia ≃	**242**	5.21 S	48.41 W
Araguaia, Braço Menor ≃	**250**	9.50 S	50.10 W
Araguaia, Parque Nacional do ♠	**250**	12.00 S	50.20 W
Araguaína	**250**	7.12 S	48.12 W
Araguainha	**255**	16.49 S	53.05 W
Araguao, Caño ≃[1]	**246**	9.15 N	60.50 W
Araguari	**255**	18.38 S	48.11 W
Araguari ≃, Bra.	**250**	1.15 N	49.55 W
Araguari ≃, Bra.	**255**	18.21 S	48.40 W
Araguatins	**250**	5.38 S	48.07 W
Aragvi ≃	**84**	41.50 N	44.43 E
ʿĀrah, Raʾs al- ›	**144**	12.36 N	43.56 E
Arai, Nihon	**94**	37.01 N	138.15 E
Arai, Nihon	**94**	34.41 N	137.34 E
Arāihāzār	**126**	23.47 N	90.40 E
Araioses	**250**	2.53 S	41.55 W
Ârak, Alg.	**148**	25.18 N	3.45 E
Arāk, Īrān	**128**	34.05 N	49.41 E
Araka	**154**	4.20 N	30.23 E
Arakamčečen, ostrov I	**180**	64.45 N	172.30 W
Arakan, porog ∟	**88**	57.35 N	96.36 E
Arakan Yoma ⋏	**110**	19.00 N	94.40 E
Arakawa, Nihon	**94**	35.57 N	139.02 E
Arakawa, Nihon	**174m**	26.39 N	128.15 E
Arakawa ✦[8]	**268**	35.47 N	139.47 E
Arakawa-dake ʌ	**94**	35.30 N	138.10 E
Arákhova	**38**	38.29 N	22.35 E
Árakhthos ≃	**38**	39.01 N	21.03 E
Araklı	**130**	40.57 N	40.03 E
Arakmeer, gora ʌ	**84**	42.38 N	46.49 E
Arakpur ✦[8]	**272a**	28.35 N	77.10 E
Araks (Aras) ≃	**84**	40.01 N	48.28 E
Aral, S.S.S.R.	**85**	42.32 N	72.40 E
Aral, S.S.S.R.	**85**	41.50 N	73.03 E
Araldy	**84**	44.18 N	50.24 E
Aral Sea → Aral'skoje more ⊤[2]	**86**	45.00 N	60.00 E
Aral'sk	**86**	46.48 N	61.40 E
Aral'skoje more (Aral Sea) ⊤[2]	**86**	45.00 N	60.00 E
Aralsor, ozero ⊜, S.S.S.R.	**80**	48.42 N	52.24 E
Aralsor, ozero ⊜, S.S.S.R.	**80**	49.05 N	48.12 E
Aralsul'fat	**86**	46.50 N	61.58 E
Aramá ≃	**250**	1.06 S	50.40 W
Aramac	**166**	22.59 S	145.14 E
Aramac ≃	**166**	23.02 S	144.31 E
Aramari	**255**	12.04 S	38.30 W
Arāmbāgh	**126**	22.53 N	87.47 E
Arambaza	**246**	2.04 S	73.06 W
Aramberri	**232**	24.06 N	99.49 W
Aramia ≃	**164**	7.45 S	142.20 E
Aramon	**62**	43.53 N	4.41 E
Arampampa	**248**	17.55 S	66.04 W
Aramtalla	**140**	6.47 N	29.13 E
Ārān	**128**	34.04 N	51.29 E
Arana	**258**	35.00 S	57.54 W
Arana, Sierra ⋏	**34**	37.20 N	3.30 W
Arancio, Lago ⊜	**70**	37.38 N	13.05 E
Aranda de Duero	**34**	41.41 N	3.41 W
Arandai	**164**	2.10 S	133.01 E
Arandas	**234**	20.42 N	102.21 W
Aranđelovac	**38**	44.18 N	20.35 E
Arandis	**156**	22.24 S	15.00 E
Aran Fawddwy ʌ	**42**	52.47 N	3.41 W
Arang	**120**	21.12 N	81.58 E
Ārāni, Bngl.	**126**	24.17 N	88.52 E
Arani, Bol.	**248**	17.34 S	65.46 W
Ārani, India	**122**	12.40 N	79.17 E
Aran Island I	**48**	54.58 N	8.33 W
Aran Islands II	**48**	53.07 N	9.43 W
Aranjuez	**34**	40.02 N	3.36 W
Aranos	**156**	24.09 S	19.09 E

Symbols in the index entries represent the broad categories identified in the key at the right. Symbols with superior numbers (⋏[1]) identify subcategories (see complete key on page *I · 1).*

Kartensymbole in dem Registerverzeichnis stellen die rechts in Schlüssel erklärten Kategorien dar. Symbole mit hochgestellten Ziffern (⋏[1]) bezeichnen Unterabteilungen einer Kategorie (vgl. vollständiger Schlüssel auf Seite *I · 1).*

Los símbolos incluidos en el texto del índice representan las grandes categorias identificadas con la clave a la derecha. Los símbolos con numeros en su parte superior (⋏[1]) identifican las subcategorías (véase la clave completa en la página *I · 1).*

Les symboles de l'index représentent les catégories indiquées dans la légende à droite. Les symboles suivis d'un indice (⋏[1]) représentent des sous-catégories (voir légende complète à la page *I · 1).*

Os símbolos incluídos no texto do índice representam as grandes categorias identificadas com a chave à direita. Os símbolos com números em sua parte superior (⋏[1]) identificam as subcategorias (veja-se a chave completa à página *I · 1).*

ʌ Mountain	Berg	Montaña	Montagne	Montanha
⋏ Mountains	Berge	Montañas	Montagnes	Montanhas
✕ Pass	Pass	Paso	Col	Passo
V Valley, Canyon	Tal, Cañon	Valle, Cañón	Vallée, Canyon	Vale, Canhão
≚ Plain	Ebene	Llano	Plaine	Planície
› Cape	Kap	Cabo	Cap	Cabo
I Island	Insel	Isla	Île	Ilha
II Islands	Inseln	Islas	Îles	Ilhas
✦ Other Topographic Features	Andere Topographische Objekte	Otros Elementos Topográficos	Autres données topographiques	Outros acidentes topográficos

ESPAÑOL

Nombre	Página	Lat.°′	Long.°′ W = Oeste
Aransas ≏	196	28.04 N	97.14 W
Aransas Pass	196	27.54 N	97.08 W
Arantāngi	122	10.10 N	78.59 E
Arantina	256	21.56 S	44.15 W
Aranyaprathet	110	13.41 N	102.30 E
Arany-hegyi-Patak ≏	264c	47.34 N	19.04 E
Arao	96	32.57 N	130.28 E
Araouane	150	18.54 N	3.33 W
Arapa, Laguna ⊜	248	15.10 S	70.01 W
Arapaho	196	35.34 N	98.57 W
Arapahoe	198	40.18 N	99.54 W
Arapaho National Recreation Area ♠	200	40.07 N	105.48 W
Arāpānja	272b	22.26 N	88.28 E
Arapawa Island I	172	41.11 S	174.19 E
Arapeí	256	22.41 S	44.27 W
Arapey	252	30.58 S	57.32 W
Arapey Chico ≏	252	30.57 S	57.30 W
Arapey Grande ≏	252	30.55 S	57.49 W
Arapiraca	250	9.45 S	36.39 W
Arapiri, Ilha I	250	2.04 S	54.56 W
Arápis	267c	37.59 N	23.32 E
Arapiuns ≏	250	2.18 S	55.00 W
Arapkir	130	39.03 N	38.30 E
Arapongas	255	23.23 S	51.27 W
Arapoti	255	24.08 S	49.50 W
Arapuni	172	38.04 S	175.39 E
Araquari	252	26.23 S	48.43 W
Araquil ≏	34	42.48 N	1.45 W
ʿArʿar	128	30.59 N	41.02 E
ʿArʿAr, Wādī V	128	31.23 N	42.26 E
Araranguá	252	28.56 S	49.29 W
Araraquara	255	21.47 S	48.10 W
Araras, Bra.	255	22.22 S	47.23 W
Araras, Bra.	256	22.49 S	46.36 W
Araras, Açude ⊜[1]	250	4.20 S	40.28 W
Araras, Ribeirão das ≏, Bra.	256	22.52 S	46.37 W
Araras, Ribeirão das ≏, Bra.	256	21.18 S	45.45 W
Ararat, Austl.	169	37.17 S	142.56 E
Ararat, S.S.S.R.	84	39.50 N	44.42 E
Ararat, Mount → Ağrı Dağı ∧	84	39.42 N	44.18 E
Arari	250	3.28 S	44.47 W
Arari, Lago ⊜	250	0.37 S	49.07 W
Arāria	124	26.08 N	87.24 E
Araripe	250	7.12 S	40.08 W
Araripe, Chapada do ⩘[1]	250	7.20 S	40.00 W
Araripina	250	7.33 S	40.34 W
Ararirá ≏	246	0.30 S	63.33 W
Arar Lugole	144	3.16 N	45.28 E
Araruama, Lagoa de ⊂	255	22.53 S	42.12 W
Araruna	250	6.32 S	35.44 W
Aras (Araks) ≏	84	40.01 N	48.28 E
ʿAras, Ḥawḍ al- ⊤[4]	142	30.51 N	32.32 E
Arashi-yama ∧[2]	270	35.01 N	135.40 E
Åråsviken ⊂	40	59.02 N	14.01 E
Arataú ≏	250	2.35 S	50.41 W
Ara Terra	144	6.38 N	40.57 E
Aratiba	252	27.24 S	52.19 W
Araticu ≏	250	1.55 S	49.51 W
Áratos	38	41.05 N	25.33 E
Aratuípe	255	13.05 S	39.00 W
Aratula	171a	27.59 S	152.32 E
Arau	114	6.26 N	100.16 E
Arauá	250	11.16 S	37.37 W
Arauá ≏, Bra.	246	4.06 S	63.36 W
Arauã ≏, Bra.	248	7.59 S	65.14 W
Arauá ≏, Bra.	248	5.40 S	60.48 W
Arauca	246	7.05 N	70.45 W
Arauca □[5]	246	6.40 N	71.00 W
Arauca ≏	246	7.24 N	66.35 W
Araucária	252	25.35 S	49.25 W
Arauco	252	37.15 S	73.19 W
Arauco, Golfo de ⊂	252	37.11 S	73.25 W
Araújo, Ilha do I	256	23.09 S	44.42 W
Araújos	255	19.56 S	45.04 W
Arauquita	246	7.02 N	71.25 W
Araure	246	9.34 N	69.13 W
Aravaca ◆[8]	266a	40.28 N	3.46 W
Aravaipa Creek ≏	200	32.50 N	110.43 W
Arāvalli Range ⩘	120	25.00 N	73.30 E
Aravan	85	40.32 N	72.30 E
Araviana ≏	34	41.41 N	2.07 W
Arawata ≏	172	44.00 S	168.41 E
Araxá	255	19.35 S	46.55 W
Araya	246	10.34 N	64.15 W
Araya, Punta de ≻	246	10.38 N	64.18 W
Arayat	116	15.10 N	120.46 E
Arba	144	9.01 N	40.23 E
Arba ≏	34	41.52 N	1.18 W
Arbagar	88	51.56 N	116.15 E
Ārbālia	126	22.41 N	88.47 E
Arba Minch	144	6.02 N	37.33 E
Arbatax	71	39.56 N	9.42 E
Arbaž	80	57.41 N	48.18 E
Arbedo	58	46.12 N	9.03 E
Arbel	132	32.49 N	35.29 E
Arbesbach	61	48.29 N	14.57 E
Arbia ≏	66	43.08 N	11.28 E
Arboga	40	59.24 N	15.50 E
Arbogaån ≏	40	59.26 N	16.04 E
Arbois	58	46.54 N	5.46 E
Arboledas	252	36.53 S	61.29 W
Arboletes	246	8.51 N	76.26 W
Arbon	58	47.31 N	9.26 E
Arbonne	50	48.25 N	2.34 E
Arborea	71	39.46 N	8.35 E
Arborea ◆[1]	71	39.50 N	8.50 E
Arborfield	184	53.06 N	103.39 W
Arborg	184	50.55 N	97.15 W
Arbrå	26	61.29 N	16.23 E
Arbroath	46	56.34 N	2.35 W
Arbu, Monte ∧	71	39.15 N	9.27 E
Arbuckle	226	39.01 N	122.03 W
Arbuckle, Lake ⊜	220	27.41 N	81.24 W
Arbuckle Creek ≏	220	27.26 N	81.17 W
Arbuckle Mountains ⩘	196	34.25 N	97.20 W
Arbuckles, Lake of the ⊜[1]	196	34.25 N	97.00 W
Arbury Hills	216	41.33 N	87.51 W
Arbus	71	39.32 N	8.36 E
Arbutus Lake ⊜	276	40.31 N	74.10 W
Arbuzinka	78	47.53 N	31.19 E
Arbuzovo	76	56.21 N	32.27 E
Arc ≏, Fr.	62	43.31 N	5.07 E
Arc ≏, Fr.	62	45.34 N	6.12 E
Arc, Bayou des ≏	194	35.00 N	91.30 W
Arcachon	32	44.37 N	1.12 W
Arcachon, Bassin d' ⊂	32	44.40 N	1.10 W
Arcadas	256	22.42 S	46.52 W
Arcade, It.	64	45.47 N	12.13 E
Arcade, Ca., U.S.	226	34.02 N	118.15 W
Arcade, N.Y., U.S.	210	42.32 N	78.25 W
Arcadia, Ca., U.S.	228	34.08 N	118.02 W
Arcadia, Fl., U.S.	220	27.12 N	81.51 W
Arcadia, In., U.S.	218	40.10 N	86.01 W
Arcadia, Ia., U.S.	198	42.01 N	95.02 W
Arcadia, Ks., U.S.	198	37.38 N	94.37 W
Arcadia, La., U.S.	194	32.32 N	92.55 W
Arcadia, Mi., U.S.	190	44.29 N	86.13 W
Arcadia, Mo., U.S.	194	37.35 N	90.37 W
Arcadia, Ne., U.S.	198	41.25 N	99.07 W
Arcadia, Oh., U.S.	216	41.06 N	83.31 W
Arcadia, Pa., U.S.	214	40.47 N	78.51 W
Arcadia, S.C., U.S.	192	34.57 N	81.59 W
Arcadia, Tx., U.S.	222	29.23 N	95.07 W
Arcadia, Wi., U.S.	190	44.15 N	91.30 W
Arcângelo	256	21.18 S	44.19 W
Arcanum	218	39.59 N	84.33 W
Arcas, Cayos II	232	20.12 N	91.58 W
Arcata	204	40.52 N	124.04 W
Arcatao	236	14.05 N	88.45 W
Arc de Triomphe ⊥	261	48.53 N	2.17 E
Arc Dome ∧	204	38.50 N	117.21 W
Arce	66	41.35 N	13.34 E
Arceburgo	256	21.22 S	46.56 W
Arčeda ≏	80	49.52 N	43.10 E

FRANÇAIS

Nom	Page	Lat.°′	Long.°′ W = Ouest
Arčedinsko-Donskije peski ◆[2]	80	49.33 N	43.15 E
Arcelia	234	18.17 N	100.16 W
Arcen	52	51.29 N	6.11 E
Arc-en-Barrois	58	47.57 N	5.00 E
Arces	50	48.05 N	3.36 E
Arc-et-Senans	58	47.02 N	5.46 E
Arcevia	66	43.30 N	12.56 E
Archambault, Lac ⊜	206	46.18 N	74.15 W
Archangaj □[8]	88	48.00 N	101.30 E
Archangel → Archangel'sk	24	64.34 N	40.32 E
Archangel'sk	24	64.34 N	40.32 E
Archangel'skaja	78	45.41 N	40.15 E
Archangel'skoje, S.S.S.R.	76	53.16 N	37.42 E
Archangel'skoje, S.S.S.R.	78	51.27 N	40.55 E
Archangel'skoje, S.S.S.R.	80	55.13 N	44.05 E
Archangel'skoje, S.S.S.R.	80	54.26 N	48.40 E
Archangel'skoje, S.S.S.R.	82	55.19 N	35.58 E
Archangel'skoje, S.S.S.R.	84	44.37 N	44.05 E
Archangel'skoje, S.S.S.R.	265b	55.47 N	37.18 E
Archara	89	49.27 N	130.07 E
Archara ≏	89	49.13 N	129.53 E
Archbald	210	41.29 N	75.32 W
Archbold	216	41.31 N	84.18 W
Archdale	192	35.54 N	79.58 W
Archer	192	29.31 N	82.31 W
Archer ≏	164	13.28 S	141.41 E
Archer, Lake ⊜	283	42.04 N	71.20 W
Archer, Mount ∧	166	23.20 S	150.34 E
Archer Bay ⊂	164	13.25 S	141.43 E
Archer Bend National Park ♠	164	13.30 S	142.20 E
Archer City	196	33.35 N	98.37 W
Archer's Post	154	0.39 N	37.41 E
Arches	58	48.07 N	6.32 E
Arches National Park ♠	200	38.42 N	109.45 W
Archi	66	42.05 N	14.23 E
Archiac	32	45.31 N	0.18 W
Archidona	34	37.05 N	4.23 W
Archipo-Osipovka	78	44.22 N	38.33 E
Archipovka	80	56.38 N	41.14 E
Archipovo	24	66.26 N	45.52 E
Archonskaja	84	43.07 N	44.30 E
Archshofen	56	49.27 N	10.04 E
Archville	276	41.07 N	73.52 W
Arci, Monte ∧	71	39.47 N	8.44 E
Arcidosso	66	42.52 N	11.33 E
Arcille	66	42.48 N	11.15 E
Arcinazzo Romano	66	41.48 N	13.12 E
Arcisate	62	45.54 N	8.52 E
Arcis-sur-Aube	50	48.32 N	4.08 E
Arciz	78	46.00 N	29.26 E
Arckaringa	162	27.56 S	134.45 E
Arckaringa Creek ≏	162	28.10 S	135.22 E
Arc-les-Gray	58	47.27 N	5.35 E
Arco, It.	64	45.55 N	10.53 E
Arco, Id., U.S.	202	43.38 N	113.17 W
Arco de Baúlhe	34	41.29 N	7.58 W
Arcola, Sk., Can.	184	49.37 N	102.30 W
Arcola, It.	64	44.07 N	9.54 E
Arcola, Il., U.S.	194	39.41 N	88.18 W
Arcola, In., U.S.	216	41.06 N	85.17 W
Arcola, Ms., U.S.	194	33.16 N	90.52 W
Arcola, Pa., U.S.	285	40.09 N	75.27 W
Arcola, Tx., U.S.	222	29.31 N	95.27 W
Arconate	266b	45.32 N	8.51 E
Arcore	266b	45.38 N	9.19 E
Arcos	255	20.17 S	45.32 W
Arcos de la Frontera	34	36.45 N	5.48 W
Arcot	122	12.54 N	79.20 E
Arcoverde	250	8.25 S	37.04 W
Arctic Bay	176	73.02 N	85.11 W
Arctic Ocean ⊤[1]	16	85.00 N	170.00 E
Arctic Red ≏	180	67.27 N	133.46 W
Arctic Red River	180	67.27 N	133.46 W
Arctic Village	180	68.08 N	145.19 W
Arctique, Océan Glacial → Arctic Ocean ⊤[1]	16	85.00 N	170.00 E
Arctowski ☉[3]	9	62.09 S	58.28 W
Arcturus	154	17.47 S	31.20 E
Arcueil	261	48.48 N	2.20 E
Arcuentu, Monte ∧	71	39.35 N	8.33 E
Arcy-sur-Cure	50	47.36 N	3.45 E
Ard, Loch ⊜	46	56.11 N	4.28 W
Arḍ, Ra's al- ≻	128	29.21 N	48.05 E
Arda ≏, Europe	38	41.39 N	26.29 E
Arda ≏, It.	64	45.02 N	10.02 E
Ardabīl	128	38.15 N	48.18 E
Ardagger	61	48.11 N	14.50 E
Ardagh	48	52.28 N	9.04 W
Ardahan	130	41.07 N	42.41 E
Ardakān, Īrān	128	30.16 N	52.01 E
Ardakān, Īrān	128	32.19 N	53.59 E
Ardal	128	31.59 N	50.39 E
Ardalanish, Rubh' ≻	46	56.17 N	6.18 W
Årdalsfjorden ⊂[2]	26	61.12 N	7.30 E
Årdalstangen	26	61.14 N	7.43 E
Ardanuç	130	41.08 N	42.04 E
Ardara, Ire.	48	54.46 N	8.25 W
Árdara, It.	71	40.37 N	8.48 E
Ardara, Pa., U.S.	279b	40.22 N	79.44 W
Ardarroch	46	57.25 N	5.38 W
Ardasa	130	40.35 N	39.18 E
Ardatov, S.S.S.R.	80	55.15 N	43.06 E
Ardatov, S.S.S.R.	80	54.51 N	46.13 E
Ardbeg	46	55.39 N	6.05 W
Ardcharnich	46	57.51 N	5.05 W
Ardea	66	41.36 N	12.33 E
Ardèche □[5]	62	44.40 N	4.20 E
Ardèche ≏	62	44.16 N	4.39 E
Ardee	48	53.52 N	6.33 W
Ardélik	146	12.26 N	21.25 E
Arden, Mb., Can.	184	50.17 N	99.14 W
Arden, Ca., U.S.	226	38.36 N	121.23 W
Arden, De., U.S.	208	39.48 N	75.29 W
Arden, Forest of ◆[3]	42	52.23 N	1.42 W
Arden, Mount ∧	166	32.09 S	137.59 E
Ardenay-sur-Mérize	50	48.00 N	0.25 E
Arden Mines	279b	40.12 N	80.17 W
Ardennes □[5]	50	49.40 N	4.40 E
Ardennes ◆[1]	56	50.10 N	5.45 E
Ardennes, Canal des ≊	50	49.26 N	4.02 E
Ardenno	58	46.10 N	9.39 E
Ardentinny	46	56.03 N	4.55 W
Ardenza	66	43.31 N	10.19 E
Arderin ∧[2]	48	53.02 N	7.40 W
Ardersier	46	57.34 N	4.02 W
Ardeşen	130	41.12 N	41.00 E
Ardestān	128	33.22 N	52.23 E
Ardey	263	51.28 N	7.43 E
Ardey ◆[8]	263	51.26 N	7.23 E
Ardeygebirge ⩘[2]	263	51.25 N	7.20 E
Ardez	58	46.46 N	10.11 E
Ardfern	46	56.10 N	5.32 W
Ardglass	48	54.16 N	5.37 W
Ardgroom	48	51.42 N	9.52 W
Ardila ≏	34	38.12 N	7.28 W
Ardill	184	49.53 N	105.49 W
Ardino	38	41.35 N	25.08 E
Ardlethan	166	34.21 S	146.54 E
Ardlui	46	56.18 N	4.43 W
Ardlussa	46	56.02 N	5.47 W
Ardmolich	46	56.49 N	5.41 W
Ardmore, Ire.	48	51.57 N	7.43 W
Ardmore, Al., U.S.	194	34.59 N	86.50 W
Ardmore, In., U.S.	216	41.41 N	86.19 W
Ardmore, Md., U.S.	284c	38.56 N	76.51 W
Ardmore, Ok., U.S.	196	34.10 N	97.08 W
Ardmore, Pa., U.S.	208	40.01 N	75.18 W
Ardmore Point ≻, Scot., U.K.	46	56.39 N	6.07 W

PORTUGUÊS

Nome	Página	Lat.°′	Long.°′ W = Oeste
Ardmore Point ≻, Scot., U.K.	46	55.42 N	6.01 W
Ardnamurchan ≻[1]	46	56.43 N	6.00 W
Ardnamurchan, Point of ≻	46	56.44 N	6.13 W
Ardnaree	48	54.06 N	9.08 W
Ardnave Point ≻	46	55.54 N	6.20 W
Ardoch	166	27.26 S	144.08 E
Ardon, Schw.	58	46.13 N	7.15 E
Ardon, S.S.S.R.	84	43.12 N	44.18 E
Ardon ≏	84	43.17 N	44.18 E
Ardon, Har ∧	132	30.38 N	34.57 E
Ardooie	50	50.59 N	3.12 E
Ardore	68	38.11 N	16.10 E
Ardoux ≏	50	47.42 N	1.35 E
Ardoz, Arroyo de ≏	266a	40.26 N	3.27 W
Ardres	50	50.51 N	1.59 E
Ardres ≏	50	49.18 N	3.40 E
Ardrishaig	46	56.01 N	5.27 W
Ardrossan, Austl.	168b	34.25 S	137.55 E
Ardrossan, Scot., U.K.	46	55.39 N	4.49 W
Ardsley, Eng., U.K.	44	53.32 N	1.28 W
Ardsley, N.Y., U.S.	276	41.00 N	73.50 W
Ardtalnaig	46	56.31 N	4.06 W
Arduan Island I	140	19.55 N	30.22 E
Ardusson ≏	50	48.30 N	3.32 E
Åre	26	63.24 N	13.04 E
Areado	256	21.21 S	46.09 W
Areal	256	22.14 S	43.07 W
Arèches	62	45.41 N	6.34 E
Arecibo	240m	18.28 N	66.43 W
Arecibo Observatory ☉[3]	240m	18.20 N	66.46 W
Areco ≏	258	33.56 S	59.16 W
Areeiro	266c	38.39 N	9.12 W
Arefjevo	86	57.01 N	90.40 E
Areguá	252	25.18 S	57.25 W
Areia, Bra.	250	6.58 S	35.42 W
Areia, Port.	266c	38.43 N	9.08 W
Areia, Ribeirão da ≏	255	16.07 S	45.52 W
Areia Branca, Bra.	250	4.56 S	37.07 W
Areia Branca, Bra.	256	22.48 S	46.51 W
Areia Branca, Bra.	287a	22.44 S	43.25 W
Areias	256	22.35 S	44.42 W
Arena	68	38.34 N	16.13 E
Arena, Point ≻	204	38.57 N	123.44 W
Arena, Punta ≻	232	23.33 N	109.28 W
Arena de la Ventana, Punta ≻	232	24.04 N	109.52 W
Arena Island I	116	9.14 N	120.46 E
Arenal, C.R.	236	10.29 N	84.53 W
Arenal, P.R.	240m	17.59 N	66.19 W
Arenal, Laguna de ⊜	236	10.32 N	84.56 W
Arenal, Punta del ≻	241r	10.03 N	61.56 W
Arenal, Volcán ∧[1]	236	10.28 N	84.44 W
Arenápolis	248	14.26 S	56.49 W
Arenas ≏	266d	41.26 N	2.00 E
Arenas, Punta ≻, Chile	248	21.39 S	70.10 W
Arenas, Punta ≻, P.R.	240m	18.07 N	65.35 W
Arenas, Punta de ≻	254	53.09 S	68.13 W
Arenas de San Pedro	34	40.12 N	5.05 W
Arendal	26	58.27 N	8.48 E
Arendonk	56	51.19 N	5.05 E
Arendsee	54	52.53 N	11.30 E
Arendsee ⊜	54	52.53 N	11.30 E
Arendtsville	208	39.55 N	77.18 W
Arenig Fawr ∧	42	52.55 N	3.45 W
Arenillas	246	3.33 S	80.04 W
Arenosa Creek ≏	196	28.52 N	96.44 W
Arenys de Mar	34	41.35 N	2.33 E
Arenzano	62	44.24 N	8.41 E
Arenzville	219	39.53 N	90.22 W
Arequipa	248	16.24 S	71.33 W
Arequipa □[5]	248	16.00 S	72.15 W
Arequito	252	33.09 S	61.28 W
Arero	144	4.45 N	38.49 E
Arês, Bra.	250	6.11 S	35.09 W
Arès, Fr.	32	44.46 N	1.08 W
Arese	266b	45.33 N	9.05 E
Aresing	60	48.32 N	11.18 E
Åreskutan ∧	26	63.26 N	13.06 E
Areuse ≏	58	46.56 N	6.53 E
Arévalo	34	41.04 N	4.43 W
Arezzo	66	43.25 N	11.53 E
Arezzo □[4]	66	43.32 N	11.50 E
Arfa', Jabal ∧	132	29.51 N	35.27 E
ʿArfā', Wādī al- V	132	30.16 N	36.34 E
Arga ≏	34	42.18 N	1.47 W
Argada	88	54.14 N	110.41 E
Argadargada	166	21.40 S	136.40 E
Argajaš	86	55.29 N	60.52 E
Argamasilla de Alba	34	39.07 N	3.06 W
Arganda	34	40.18 N	3.26 W
Argao	116	9.52 N	123.36 E
Arga-Sala ≏	74	68.30 N	112.12 E
Argedeb	144	6.10 N	41.10 E
Argegno	58	45.56 N	9.08 E
Argel → El Djazaïr	148	36.47 N	3.03 E
Argelès-Gazost	32	43.01 N	0.06 E
Argelès-sur-Mer	32	42.33 N	3.01 E
Argelia → Algeria □[1]	148	28.00 N	3.00 E
Argen ≏	58	47.35 N	9.33 E
Argens ≏	62	43.24 N	6.44 E
Argent	158	26.04 S	28.50 E
Argent, Côte d' ⛱[2]	32	43.30 N	1.30 W
Argenta, It.	66	44.37 N	11.50 E
Argenta, Il., U.S.	219	39.58 N	88.49 W
Argentan	32	48.45 N	0.01 W
Argentario, Monte ∧	66	42.24 N	11.09 E
Argentat	32	45.06 N	1.56 E
Argentera	62	44.24 N	6.57 E
Argentera ∧	62	44.10 N	7.18 E
Argenteuil	50	48.57 N	2.15 E
Argenteuil □[6]	206	45.45 N	74.30 W
Argentia	186	47.18 N	53.59 W
Argentiera	71	40.44 N	8.09 E
Argentière	58	45.59 N	6.56 E
Argentières	261	48.39 N	2.52 E
Argentina □[1]	244	34.00 S	64.00 W
Argentina ≏	62	43.50 N	7.51 E
Argentine	216	42.47 N	83.51 W
Argentine → Argentina □[1]	244	34.00 S	64.00 W
Argentine Basin ✦[1]	18	45.00 S	45.00 W
Argentinien → Argentina □[1]	244	34.00 S	64.00 W
Argentino, Hipódromo ♠	288	34.34 S	58.26 W
Argentino, Lago ⊜	254	50.13 S	72.25 W
Argentona	266d	41.33 N	2.24 E
Argentona, Riera ≏	266d	41.31 N	2.26 E
Argenton-Château	32	46.59 N	0.27 W
Argenton-sur-Creuse	32	46.35 N	1.31 E
Argent-sur-Sauldre	50	47.33 N	2.27 E
Argeș □[6]	38	45.00 N	24.45 E
Argeș ≏	38	44.04 N	26.37 E
Arghandāb ≏	128	31.27 N	64.23 E
Arghastān ≏	120	31.23 N	65.45 E
Argirita	256	21.37 S	42.50 W
Argıthanı	130	38.17 N	31.43 E
Argo	140	19.31 N	30.25 E
Ārgoal	126	21.58 N	87.38 E
Argo Island I	140	19.25 N	30.27 E
Argolikós Kólpos ⊂	38	37.33 N	22.45 E
Argonia	198	37.15 N	97.45 W
Argonne	190	45.39 N	88.52 W
Argonne ◆[1]	56	49.30 N	5.00 E
Argonne National Laboratory ☉[3]	216	41.43 N	87.58 W
Argopuro, Gunung ∧	115a	7.57 S	113.33 E
Árgos, Ellás	38	37.39 N	22.44 E
Argos, In., U.S.	216	41.14 N	86.15 W
Árgos Orestikón	38	40.28 N	21.16 E
Argostólion	38	38.10 N	20.30 E
Argoules	50	50.21 N	1.50 E
Argueil	50	49.32 N	1.31 E
Arguello, Point ≻	204	34.35 N	120.39 W
Argun	84	43.16 N	45.52 E
Argun' (Ergun) ≏, Asia	74	53.20 N	121.28 E
Argun ≏, S.S.S.R.	84	43.22 N	45.55 E
Argungu	150	12.45 N	4.31 E
Arguni, Teluk ⊂	164	3.06 S	133.42 E
Ārgur	272b	22.48 N	88.13 E
Argut	86	49.51 N	87.03 E
Argut ≏	86	50.16 N	86.43 E
Argyle, Mn., U.S.	198	48.19 N	96.49 W
Argyle, Mo., U.S.	219	38.18 N	92.02 W
Argyle, N.Y., U.S.	210	43.14 N	73.30 W
Argyle, Tx., U.S.	222	33.07 N	97.11 W
Argyle, Lake ⊜[1]	164	16.15 S	128.45 E
ʿArhāb, Wādī V	142	28.55 N	31.09 E
Århus	41	56.09 N	10.13 E
Århus □[6]	41	56.15 N	10.05 E
Århus Bugt ⊂	41	56.09 N	10.18 E
Aria	172	38.33 S	174.59 E
Aria ≏	164	5.45 S	149.15 E
Ariadnoje	89	45.08 N	134.25 E
Ariah	126	23.33 N	86.20 E
Ariake-kai ⊂	92	33.00 N	130.20 E
Ariāl Khān ≏	126	23.56 N	90.46 E
Ariāl Khān ≏[1]	126	22.38 N	90.32 E
Ariamácina, Lago di ⊜[1]	68	39.20 N	16.32 E
Ariamsvlei	156	28.07 S	19.49 E
Ariana	36	36.52 N	10.12 E
Ariano, Isola d' I	64	45.10 N	12.10 E
Ariano Irpino	68	41.09 N	15.05 E
Ariano nel Polesine	64	44.56 N	12.07 E
Ariari ≏	246	2.35 N	72.47 W
Arias	252	33.38 S	62.25 W
Arias, Arroyo de ≏	258	34.17 S	56.06 W
Arias, Cañada de ≏	258	34.39 S	58.59 W
Ariaú	250	3.11 S	57.14 W
Aribinda	150	14.14 N	0.52 W
Arica, Chile	248	18.29 S	70.20 W
Arica, Col.	246	2.08 S	71.47 W
Aricanduva, Ribeirão ≏	287b	23.32 S	46.33 W
Ariccia	66	41.43 N	12.40 E
Arichat	186	45.31 N	61.01 W
Arichuna	246	7.42 N	67.08 W
Arid, Cape ≻	162	34.00 S	123.09 E
Arida, Nig.	273a	6.34 N	3.16 E
Arida, Nihon	96	34.05 N	135.07 E
Arida ≏	96	34.05 N	135.06 E
Aridal, Sabkhat ⊜	148	26.12 N	14.05 W
Aridhaía	38	40.59 N	22.03 E
Ariège □[5]	32	43.00 N	1.30 E
Ariège ≏	32	43.31 N	1.25 E
Ariel	224	45.57 N	122.34 W
Arienzo	68	41.01 N	14.30 E
Arieș ≏	38	46.26 N	23.59 E
ʿArif, Har ∧	132	30.26 N	34.44 E
Ārifwāla	123	30.17 N	73.04 E
Ariguanabo, Laguna de ⊜	286b	22.56 N	82.33 W
Ariguaní ≏	246	9.35 N	73.46 W
Arīḥā (Jericho), Ghaz.	132	31.52 N	35.27 E
Arīḥā, Sūrīy.	130	35.48 N	35.36 E
Arīḥā, Urd.	132	31.25 N	35.47 E
Arikaree ≏	198	40.01 N	101.56 W
Arikaree, North Fork ≏	198	39.39 N	102.57 W
Arikawa	92	32.59 N	129.07 E
Arild	41	56.16 N	12.34 E
Arima	241r	10.38 N	61.17 W
Arima ◆[8]	270	34.48 N	135.15 E
Arima ≏	270	34.52 N	135.15 E
Arima-fuji ∧[2]	270	34.55 N	135.14 E
Arimine-dam ◆[6]	94	36.29 N	137.27 E
Arinagour	46	56.37 N	6.31 W
Aringay	116	16.26 N	120.21 E
Arino ◆[8]	270	34.50 N	135.14 E
Arinos ≏	248	10.25 S	58.20 W
Arinthod	58	46.23 N	5.34 E
Ario de Rosales	234	19.12 N	101.43 W
Ariogala	76	55.16 N	23.30 E
Aripeka	220	28.25 N	82.39 W
Ariporo ≏	246	6.03 N	69.54 W
Aripuanã	248	9.10 S	60.38 W
Aripuanã ≏	248	5.07 S	60.24 W
Ariquemes	248	9.56 S	63.04 W
Arisa ≏	246	7.32 N	64.00 W
Arisaig	46	56.51 N	5.51 W
Arisaig, Sound of ⊂	46	56.51 N	5.51 W
ʿArīsh, Wādī al- V	140	31.09 N	33.49 E
Arismendi	246	8.29 N	68.22 W
Arista, Méx.	234	15.56 N	93.48 W
Arista, Méx.	234	22.39 N	100.50 W
Aristazabal Island I	182	52.30 N	129.05 W
Aristes	210	40.49 N	76.20 W
Aristizábal, Cabo ≻	254	45.13 S	66.31 W
Aristovo	82	54.37 N	36.40 E
Aritao	116	16.18 N	121.02 E
Ariton	194	31.36 N	85.43 W
Aritzo	71	39.57 N	9.12 E
Arivonimamo	157b	19.01 S	47.15 E
Ariyalūr	122	11.08 N	79.05 E
Arizaro, Salar de ≡	252	24.42 S	67.45 W
Arizgoiti	34	43.13 N	2.54 W
Arizona	252	35.43 S	65.18 W
Arizona □[3], U.S.	178	34.00 N	112.00 W
Arizona □[3], U.S.	200	34.00 N	112.00 W
Arizpe	232	30.20 N	110.10 W
Arja	80	57.30 N	46.00 E
Årjäng	26	59.23 N	12.08 E
Arjasa	112	6.51 S	115.16 E
Arjawinangun	115a	6.39 S	108.24 E
Arjay	192	36.48 N	83.38 W
Arjeplog	24	66.00 N	17.58 E
Arjona, Col.	246	10.15 N	75.21 W
Arjona, Esp.	34	37.56 N	4.03 W
Arka	74	60.03 N	142.12 E
Arkabutla Lake ⊜[1]	194	34.45 N	90.06 W
Arkadak	80	51.58 N	43.28 E
Arkadelphia	194	34.07 N	93.03 W
Arkaig, Loch ⊜	46	56.58 N	5.08 W
Arkalyk	86	50.13 N	66.50 E
Arkansas □[3], U.S.	178	34.50 N	92.30 W
Arkansas □[3], U.S.	194	34.50 N	92.30 W
Arkansas ≏	178	33.48 N	91.04 W
Arkansas, Salt Fork ≏	196	36.36 N	97.03 W
Arkansas City, Ar., U.S.	194	33.36 N	91.12 W
Arkansas City, Ks., U.S.	198	37.03 N	97.02 W
Arkansas Post National Memorial ⊥	194	33.55 N	91.26 W
Arkanū, Jabal ∧	146	22.13 N	24.41 E
Arken-Ahon ∧	146	20.05 N	18.25 E
Arkhangélos	38	36.12 N	28.08 E
Arkhangel'sk → Archangel'sk	24	64.34 N	40.32 E
Arki	123	31.09 N	76.58 E
Árki I	38	37.22 N	26.45 E
Arkit	85	41.47 N	71.58 E
Arklow	48	52.48 N	6.09 W
Arkoma	194	35.21 N	94.26 W
Arkona, Kap ≻	54	54.41 N	13.26 E
Arkonam	122	13.06 N	79.40 E
Arkösund	26	58.30 N	16.56 E
Arkport	210	42.23 N	77.41 W
Arktičeskij, mys ≻	74	81.15 N	95.45 E
Arktičeskogo Instituta, ostrova II	74	75.20 N	81.55 E
Arkul'	80	57.17 N	50.03 E
Arkville	210	42.08 N	74.37 W
Arkwright	207	41.43 N	71.33 W
Ärla	40	59.17 N	16.40 E
Arlan	80	55.58 N	54.15 E
Arlanc	62	45.25 N	3.44 E
Arlanda flygplats ⊠	40	59.37 N	17.55 E
Arlanza ≏	34	42.06 N	4.09 W
Arlanzón ≏	34	42.03 N	4.17 W
Arlbergpass)(	64	47.08 N	10.12 E
Arlberg-Tunnel ◆[5]	58	47.08 N	10.12 E
Arlee	202	47.09 N	114.05 W
Arles	62	43.40 N	4.38 E
Arles à Port de Bouc, Canal d' ≊	62	43.40 N	4.37 E
Arlesey	42	52.01 N	0.14 W
Arlesheim	58	47.30 N	7.37 E
Arleta ◆[8]	280	34.15 N	118.26 W
Arleux	50	50.17 N	3.06 E
Arley	262	53.19 N	2.30 W
Arli	150	11.35 N	1.28 E
Arli, Parc National de l' ♠	150	11.35 N	1.30 E
Arlington, S. Afr.	158	28.06 S	27.54 E
Arlington, Ga., U.S.	192	31.26 N	84.43 W
Arlington, In., U.S.	218	39.38 N	85.34 W
Arlington, Ia., U.S.	190	42.44 N	91.40 W
Arlington, Ks., U.S.	198	37.53 N	98.10 W
Arlington, Ky., U.S.	194	36.47 N	89.00 W
Arlington, Ma., U.S.	207	42.24 N	71.09 W
Arlington, Mn., U.S.	190	44.36 N	94.04 W
Arlington, Ne., U.S.	198	41.27 N	96.21 W
Arlington, N.Y., U.S.	210	41.41 N	73.53 W
Arlington, Oh., U.S.	216	40.53 N	83.39 W
Arlington, Or., U.S.	202	45.43 N	120.11 W
Arlington, S.D., U.S.	198	44.21 N	97.07 W
Arlington, Tn., U.S.	194	35.18 N	89.40 W
Arlington, Tx., U.S.	222	32.44 N	97.06 W
Arlington, Vt., U.S.	210	43.04 N	73.09 W
Arlington, Va., U.S.	208	38.52 N	77.06 W
Arlington, Wa., U.S.	224	48.11 N	122.07 W
Arlington □[6]	284c	38.50 N	77.10 W
Arlington, Lake ⊜[1]	222	32.42 N	97.13 W
Arlington Heights, Il., U.S.	216	42.05 N	87.58 W
Arlington Heights, Ma., U.S.	283	42.25 N	71.11 W
Arlington Memorial Bridge ◆[5]	284c	38.53 N	77.03 W
Arlington Mill Reservoir ⊜[1]	283	42.48 N	71.13 W
Arlington National Cemetery ◆	284c	38.53 N	77.04 W
Arlit	150	19.00 N	7.38 E
Arlod	58	46.06 N	5.49 E
Arlon	56	49.41 N	5.49 E
Arlöv	41	55.39 N	13.05 E
Arltunga	162	23.26 S	134.41 E
Arl'uk	86	55.26 N	84.50 E
Arluno	62	45.30 N	8.56 E
Arly ≏	62	45.40 N	6.23 E
Arlyn Oaks	276	40.40 N	73.27 W
Arm ≏	184	50.46 N	105.00 W
Arma	198	37.32 N	94.42 W
Armação, Ponta da ≻	287a	22.53 S	43.08 W
Armada	214	42.50 N	82.53 W
Armadale, Austl.	168a	32.09 S	116.00 E
Armadale, On., Can.	275b	43.50 N	79.15 W
Armadale, S. Afr.	273d	26.17 S	27.57 E
Armadale, Scot., U.K.	46	55.54 N	3.42 W
Arma di Taggia	62	43.50 N	7.51 E
Armageddon → Tel Megiddo ⊥	132	32.35 N	35.11 E
Armagh, N. Ire., U.K.	48	54.21 N	6.39 W
Armagh, Pa., U.S.	214	40.27 N	79.02 W
Armagnac □[9]	32	43.45 N	0.10 E
Armah, Wādī V	144	18.15 N	51.00 E
Armainvilliers, Étang d' ⊜	261	48.45 N	2.44 E
Armainvilliers, Forêt d' ♠	261	48.45 N	2.45 E
Armance ≏	50	47.26 N	3.33 E
Armançon ≏, Fr.	50	47.57 N	3.30 E
Armançon ≏, Fr.	58	47.33 N	4.17 E
Arm'ansk	78	46.07 N	33.41 E
Arm'anskaja Sovetskaja Socialističeskaja Respublika □[3]	84	40.00 N	45.00 E
Armant	140	25.37 N	32.32 E
Armavir	72	45.00 N	41.08 E
Armazém	252	28.16 S	49.01 W
Armbrust	214	40.13 N	79.33 W
Armells Creek ≏	202	47.37 N	108.40 W
Armenia	246	4.31 N	75.41 W
Armenia → Arm'anskaja Sovetskaja Socialističeskaja Respublika □[3]	84	40.00 N	45.00 E
Armenia □[9]	84	40.30 N	43.30 E
Armeniș	38	45.12 N	22.19 E
Armenistís	38	37.36 N	26.08 E
Armeno	62	45.49 N	8.26 E
Armenonville-les-Gâtineaux	261	48.33 N	1.39 E
Armentières	50	50.41 N	2.53 E
Armento	68	40.18 N	16.04 E
Armería	234	18.56 N	103.58 W
Armería ≏	234	18.52 N	103.59 W
Armero	246	4.58 N	74.54 W
Armidale	166	30.31 S	151.39 E
Armijo	200	35.03 N	106.40 W
Armitage	42	52.44 N	1.53 W
Armit Lake ⊜	176	64.10 N	91.32 W
Armizonskoje	86	55.57 N	67.42 E
Armona	226	36.19 N	119.42 W
Armonk	276	41.07 N	73.42 W
Armor	210	42.44 N	78.48 W
Armori	122	20.28 N	79.59 E
Armour	198	43.19 N	98.20 W
Armoy	58	46.21 N	6.31 E
Armstrong, Arg.	252	32.47 S	61.36 W
Armstrong, B.C., Can.	182	50.27 N	119.12 W
Armstrong, Il., U.S.	216	40.18 N	87.53 W
Armstrong, Ia., U.S.	198	43.23 N	94.28 W
Armstrong, Mo., U.S.	194	39.16 N	92.42 W
Armstrong □[6]	214	40.49 N	79.32 W
Armstrong ≏	164	16.46 S	131.12 E
Armstrong, Mount ∧	180	63.12 N	133.16 W
Armstrong Station	176	50.18 N	89.02 W
Armthorpe	44	53.32 N	1.03 W
Ārmūr	122	18.48 N	78.17 E
Armutlu	130	40.31 N	28.50 E
Arnå ≏	41	54.57 N	8.53 E
Arnaccio	66	43.40 N	10.17 E
Arnaía	38	40.29 N	23.35 E
Arnarfjörður ⊂[2]	24a	65.45 N	23.40 W
Årnäs	40	58.41 N	13.35 E
Arnaud ≏	176	59.59 N	69.46 W
Arnaudville	194	30.24 N	91.56 W
Arnavad, gora ∧	85	38.33 N	71.31 E
Arnavutköy ≏	267b	41.13 N	29.12 E
Arnay-le-Duc	58	47.08 N	4.29 E
Arnaz	62	45.38 N	7.43 E
Arnborg	41	56.01 N	8.59 E
Arnbruck	60	49.08 N	13.00 E
Arncliffe	274a	33.56 S	151.09 E
Arneburg	54	52.40 N	12.00 E
Arnedo	34	42.13 N	2.06 W
Arneiro dos Marinheiros	266c	38.51 N	9.25 W
Arneiroz	250	6.20 S	40.08 W
Arnejevo	82	54.58 N	37.35 E
Arnemuiden	52	51.30 N	3.41 E
Årnes	26	60.09 N	11.28 E
Arnett	196	36.08 N	99.46 W
Arney ≏	48	54.16 N	7.37 W
Arnhem	52	51.59 N	5.55 E
Arnhem, Cape ≻	164	12.21 S	136.21 E
Arnhem Bay ⊂	164	12.20 S	136.12 E
Arnhem Land ◆[1]	164	13.10 S	134.30 E
Arnhem Land Aboriginal Reserve ◆[4]	164	13.10 S	134.30 E
Arni	64	44.04 N	10.15 E
Arnis	41	54.38 N	9.56 E
Árnissa	38	40.48 N	21.50 E
Arno I[1]	14	7.05 N	171.41 E
Arno ≏	66	43.41 N	10.17 E
Arno, Torrente ≏	266b	45.42 N	8.48 E
Arno Bay	166	33.54 S	136.34 E
Arnold, B.C., Can.	224	49.08 N	122.03 W
Arnold, Eng., U.K.	44	53.00 N	1.08 W
Arnold, Ca., U.S.	204	38.15 N	120.21 W
Arnold, Md., U.S.	208	39.01 N	76.30 W
Arnold, Mn., U.S.	190	46.52 N	92.05 W
Arnold, Mo., U.S.	219	38.25 N	90.22 W
Arnold, Ne., U.S.	198	41.25 N	100.11 W
Arnold, Pa., U.S.	214	40.34 N	79.46 W
Arnold ≏	164	15.19 S	134.06 E
Arnold Arboretum ♠	283	42.18 N	71.08 W
Arnold Mills	283	41.58 N	71.23 W
Arnold Mills Reservoir ⊜[1]	283	41.59 N	71.25 W
Arnolds Park	198	43.22 N	95.08 W
Arnoldstein	64	46.33 N	13.43 E
Arnon ≏	50	48.16 N	0.38 E
Arnos Vale Airfield ⊠	241h	13.09 N	61.13 W
Arnot	210	41.39 N	77.07 W
Arnouville-lès-Gonesse	261	49.00 N	2.25 E
Arnouville-lès-Mantes	261	48.55 N	1.44 E
Arnoya ≏	34	42.15 N	8.09 W
Arnprior	212	45.26 N	76.21 W
Arnsberg	56	51.24 N	8.03 E
Arnsberg □[5]	52	51.20 N	8.00 E
Arnschwang	60	49.16 N	12.49 E
Arnsdorf	54	51.05 N	13.59 E
Arnside	44	54.12 N	2.50 W
Arnstadt	54	50.50 N	10.57 E
Arnstein	56	49.58 N	9.58 E
Arnstorf	60	48.34 N	12.49 E
Arnum	41	55.15 N	8.59 E
Årø I	41	55.15 N	9.45 E
Aro ≏	246	8.01 N	64.11 W
Aroa	246	10.26 N	68.54 W
Aroa ≏	246	10.40 N	68.19 W
Aroa, Pointe ≻	174s	17.28 S	149.46 W
Aroab	156	26.47 S	19.40 E
Aroali	126	24.03 N	87.56 E
Arochukwu	150	5.23 N	7.55 E
Aroeiras	250	7.31 S	35.41 W
Ar'ofino	80	58.16 N	39.15 E
Arolla	58	46.02 N	7.29 E
Arolsen	56	51.23 N	9.01 E
Aroma	140	15.49 N	36.08 E
Aroma Park	216	41.04 N	87.48 W
Aromas	226	36.53 N	121.39 W
Aromaševo	86	56.52 N	68.39 E
Aron ≏	50	47.15 N	2.02 E
Arona, It.	62	45.46 N	8.34 E
Arona, Pap. N. Gui.	164	6.20 S	146.00 E
Arona, Pa., U.S.	279b	40.16 N	79.39 W
Aroostook ≏	186	46.48 N	67.45 W
Aropuk Lake ⊜	180	61.12 N	163.50 W
Arorae I	14	2.38 S	176.49 E
Arorangi	174k	21.13 S	159.49 W
Aroroy	116	12.31 N	123.24 E
Arosa	58	46.47 N	9.41 E
Arosa, Ría de ⊂[1]	34	42.28 N	8.57 W
Arosbaya	115a	6.56 S	112.51 E
Årøsund	41	55.16 N	9.45 E
Aro Usu, Tanjung ≻	164	8.20 S	130.45 E
Arowhana ∧	172	38.07 S	177.52 E
Arp	222	32.13 N	95.03 W
Arpa ≏	84	39.28 N	44.57 E
Arpaçay	84	40.52 N	43.20 E
Arpaçay (Achur'an) ≏	84	40.06 N	43.39 E
Arpačin	83	47.14 N	40.11 E
Arpaia	68	41.02 N	14.33 E
Arpajon	50	48.35 N	2.15 E
Ārpāra	126	23.23 N	89.23 E
Arpino	66	41.39 N	13.36 E
Arpoador, Ponta do ≻, Bra.	252	24.25 S	47.00 W
Arpoador, Ponta do ≻, Bra.	287a	22.59 S	43.12 W
Arquà Petrarca	64	45.16 N	11.43 E
Arquà Polesine	64	45.01 N	11.45 E
Arquata del Tronto	66	42.46 N	13.18 E
Arquata Scrivia	62	44.41 N	8.53 E
Arque	248	17.48 S	66.23 W
Arques	50	50.44 N	2.17 E
Arques-la-Bataille	50	49.53 N	1.08 E
Ar-Rabaḍ	128	23.11 N	39.32 E
Ar-Rabbah	132	31.16 N	35.44 E
Arracourt	58	48.44 N	6.32 E
Ar-Radīsīyah Baḥrī	140	24.57 N	32.53 E
Ar-Rafīd	132	32.57 N	35.53 E
Arraga	252	28.04 S	64.14 W
Arrah, C. Iv.	150	6.40 N	3.58 W
Arrah, India	124	25.34 N	84.40 E
Ar-Rahad	140	12.43 N	30.39 E
Ar-Raḥāminah	142	31.18 N	31.45 E
Ar-Raḥmānīyah	142	31.06 N	30.38 E
Arraial do Cabo	255	22.58 S	42.01 W
Arraias	255	12.56 S	46.57 W
Arraias ≏, Bra.	250	11.10 S	53.35 W
Arraias ≏, Bra.	255	12.28 S	47.18 W
Ar-Ramādī	128	33.25 N	43.17 E
Ar-Ramthā	132	32.34 N	36.00 E
Arran, Island of I	46	55.35 N	5.15 W
Ar-Rank	140	11.45 N	32.48 E
Arran Lake ⊜	212	44.29 N	81.16 W
Ar-Raqqah	130	35.56 N	39.01 E
Ar-Raqqah □[8]	130	36.00 N	39.00 E
Arras	50	50.17 N	2.47 E
Arras, Nuraghe ⊥	71	39.40 N	9.25 E
Ar-Rāshidah	140	25.35 N	28.56 E
Ar-Rass	128	25.52 N	43.28 E
Ar-Rastān	130	34.55 N	36.44 E
Arrats ≏	32	44.06 N	0.52 E
Ar-Rawḍah, Ar. Su.	128	26.05 N	40.37 E
Ar-Rawḍah, J.Y.D.S.	144	14.28 N	47.17 E
Ar-Rawḍah, Miṣr	142	27.48 N	30.52 E
Ar-Rawḍah, Miṣr	142	29.27 N	31.00 E
Ar-Rāwuk	144	15.45 N	48.54 E
Ar-Rayramūn	142	27.45 N	30.52 E
Ar-Rayyāḥ ar-Minūfīya ≊	142	30.20 N	31.00 E
Ar-Rayyāḥ at-Tawfīqī ≊	142	30.11 N	31.07 E
Arrecife	148	28.57 N	13.32 W
Arrecifes	252	34.03 S	60.07 W
Arrée, Montagnes d' ⩘	32	48.26 N	3.55 W
Arregui, Laguna ⊜	258	35.05 S	57.33 W
Arrentela	266c	38.38 N	9.06 W
Arresø ⊜	41	55.58 N	12.08 E
Arrey	200	32.50 N	107.19 W
Arriaga	234	16.14 N	93.54 W
Arriba	198	39.17 N	103.16 W
Arrild	41	55.09 N	8.58 E
Ar-Rimāh	128	25.34 N	47.09 E
Ar-Riyāḍ (Riyadh)	128	24.38 N	46.43 E
Arrochar	46	56.12 N	4.44 W
Arroio Grande	252	32.14 S	53.05 W
Arrojado ≏	255	13.24 S	44.20 W
Arronches	34	39.07 N	7.17 W
Arrone ≏, It.	66	41.52 N	12.11 E
Arrone ≏, It.	66	42.18 N	11.38 E
Arros ≏	32	43.40 N	0.02 W
Arroscia ≏	62	44.03 N	8.11 E
Arroux ≏	32	46.29 N	3.58 E
Arrow ≏, Eng., U.K.	42	52.12 N	2.43 W
Arrow ≏, Eng., U.K.	42	52.09 N	1.53 W
Arrow, Lough ⊜	48	54.04 N	8.21 W
Arrow Creek ≏	202	47.43 N	109.50 W
Arrowhead, Lake ⊜[1], Ca., U.S.	228	34.15 N	117.11 W
Arrowhead, Lake ⊜[1], Tx., U.S.	196	33.40 N	98.20 W
Arrowhead Peak ∧	228	34.13 N	117.16 W
Arrowhead Provincial Park ♠	212	45.24 N	79.13 W
Arrowhead Village	208	40.04 N	74.07 W
Arrow Lake ⊜	190	48.08 N	90.18 W
Arrowrock Reservoir ⊜[1]	202	43.36 N	115.51 W
Arrowsmith	216	40.27 N	88.38 W
Arrowsmith, Mount ∧, Austl.	166	30.09 S	141.50 E
Arrowsmith, Mount ∧, B.C., Can.	224	49.13 N	124.36 W

Symbol	English	Deutsch	Español	Français	Português
≏	River	Fluss	Río	Rivière	Rio
≊	Canal	Kanal	Canal	Canal	Canal
⌊	Waterfall, Rapids	Wasserfall, Stromschnellen	Cascada, Rápidos	Chute d'eau, Rapides	Cascata, Rápidos
⋈	Strait	Meeresstrasse	Estrecho	Détroit	Estreito
⊂	Bay, Gulf	Bucht, Golf	Bahía, Golfo	Baie, Golfe	Baía, Golfo
⊜	Lake, Lakes	See, Seen	Lago, Lagos	Lac, Lacs	Lago, Lagos
≡	Swamp	Sumpf	Pantano	Marais	Pântano
⊓	Ice Features, Glacier	Eis- und Gletscherformen	Accidentes Glaciales	Formes glaciaires	Acidentes glaciares
⊤	Other Hydrographic Features	Andere Hydrographische Objekte	Otros Elementos Hidrográficos	Autres données hydrographiques	Outros acidentes hidrográficos
✦	Submarine Features	Untermeerische Objekte	Accidentes Submarinos	Formes de relief sous-marin	Acidentes submarinos
□	Political Unit	Politische Einheit	Unidad Politica	Entité politique	Unidade política
☉	Cultural Institution	Kulturelle Institution	Institución Cultural	Institution culturelle	Instituição cultural
⊥	Historical Site	Historische Stätte	Sitio Histórico	Site historique	Sitio histórico
♠	Recreational Site	Erholungs- und Ferienort	Sitio de Recreo	Centre de loisirs	Area de Lazer
⊠	Airport	Flughafen	Aeropuerto	Aéroport	Aeroporto
■	Military Installation	Militäranlage	Instalación Militar	Installation militaire	Instalação militar
◆	Miscellaneous	Verschiedenes	Misceláneo	Divers	Diversos

Name	Page	Lat.°′	Long.°′
Arrowsmith, Mount ʌ, N.Z.	172	43.21 S	170.59 E
Arrowsmith Range ⋏	172	43.18 S	171.00 E
Arrowtown	172	44.56 S	168.50 E
Arrowwood	182	50.44 N	113.09 W
Arroyan, Arroyo ≃[1]	288	34.24 S	58.32 W
Arroyito	252	31.25 S	63.03 W
Arroyo	240m	17.58 N	66.04 W
Arroyo, Puerto c	240m	17.58 N	66.05 W
Arroyo de la Luz	34	39.29 N	6.35 W
Arroyo Frío	234	17.26 N	100.35 W
Arroyo Grande, Ca., U.S.	204	35.07 N	120.35 W
Arroyo Grande → Ismael Cortinas, Ur.	258	33.58 S	57.06 W
Arroyo Hondo	200	36.32 N	105.40 W
Arroyo Naranjo ◆[8]	286b	23.02 N	82.23 W
Arroyo Seco Park ♠	280	34.06 N	118.12 W
Arroyos y Esteros	252	25.04 S	57.06 W
Arrozal	256	22.37 S	44.03 W
Ar-Ruʿat	140	12.21 N	32.17 E
Ar-Rubʿal-Khālī ◆[2]	118	20.00 N	51.00 E
Ar-Rubayqī	142	30.10 N	31.46 E
Ar-Ruḥaybah	132	33.45 N	36.42 E
Ar-Rukhaymīyah ▾[4]	128	29.14 N	45.35 E
Ar-Rumaythah	128	31.32 N	45.12 E
Ar-Rummān	132	32.10 N	35.50 E
Ar-Ruqayyah ⊥	132	32.47 N	37.05 E
Ar-Ruṣāfah ⊥	130	35.37 N	38.45 E
Ar-Ruṣayriṣ	140	11.51 N	34.23 E
Ar-Rushaydah	132	32.40 N	36.50 E
Ar-Ruṭbah	128	33.02 N	40.17 E
Ar-Ru'ūs	142	29.21 N	31.04 E
Års	26	56.48 N	9.32 E
Aršan, S.S.S.R.	88	51.54 N	102.27 E
Aršan, S.S.S.R.	88	53.54 N	99.54 E
Aršan'-Zel'men'	80	47.36 N	44.36 E
Ārsāpota	272b	22.55 N	88.18 E
Arsbeck	56	51.08 N	6.12 E
Arsenal de Marinha ■	266c	38.39 N	9.09 W
Arsenal Football Club ♠	260	51.33 N	0.06 W
Arsenault Lake ⊜	184	55.06 N	108.30 W
Arsenjān	128	29.56 N	53.18 E
Arsenjev	89	44.10 N	133.15 E
Arsenjevka ≃	89	44.54 N	133.35 E
Arsenjevo	76	53.44 N	36.40 E
Ars-en-Ré	32	46.12 N	1.31 W
Arsi □[4]	144	8.00 N	39.40 E
Arsiè	64	45.59 N	11.45 E
Arsiero	64	45.48 N	11.21 E
Arsikere	122	13.20 N	76.15 E
Arsin	130	40.58 N	39.56 E
Aršincevo	78	45.17 N	36.25 E
Arsıyan Dağı ʌ	130	41.24 N	42.30 E
Arsk	80	56.06 N	49.54 E
Arslanbob	85	41.21 N	72.56 E
Ārslev	41	55.18 N	10.29 E
Arsoli	66	42.02 N	13.01 E
Ársos	130	34.50 N	32.46 E
Ars-sur-Formans	58	45.59 N	4.49 E
Ars-sur-Moselle	56	49.05 N	6.04 E
Årsta havsbad	40	59.05 N	18.10 E
Arsufhsa ≃	84	39.08 N	46.50 E
Årsunda	40	60.32 N	16.44 E
Arsuz	130	36.27 N	35.51 E
Art, Île I	175f	19.43 S	163.38 E
Árta, Ellás	38	39.09 N	20.59 E
Artá, Esp.	34	39.42 N	3.21 E
Artarmon	274a	33.49 S	151.11 E
Artašat	84	39.59 N	44.33 E
Arta Terme	64	46.28 N	13.01 E
Arteaga	234	18.28 N	102.25 W
Arteche	116	12.17 N	125.22 E
Artegna	64	46.14 N	13.09 E
Artemare	62	45.52 N	5.42 E
Artemisa	240p	22.49 N	82.46 W
Artemón	38	36.59 N	24.43 E
Artémou	150	15.31 N	12.16 W
Artemovsk → Art'omovsk	83	48.35 N	38.00 E
Artèn	64	46.00 N	11.50 E
Artenay	50	48.05 N	1.53 E
Artern	54	51.22 N	11.17 E
Artesia → Mosomane, Bots.	156	24.04 S	26.15 E
Artesia, Ca., U.S.	280	33.51 N	118.04 W
Artesia, Ms., U.S.	194	33.24 N	88.38 W
Artesia, N.M., U.S.	196	32.50 N	104.24 W
Artesia Lake ⊜	226	38.57 N	119.22 W
Artesian	198	44.00 N	97.55 W
Arth	58	47.04 N	8.31 E
Arthabaska	206	46.02 N	71.55 W
Arthabaska □[6]	206	46.05 N	72.00 W
Arthal	123	33.16 N	76.11 E
Arthala	272a	28.40 N	77.24 E
Arthies	261	49.06 N	1.48 E
Arthonnay	50	47.56 N	4.13 E
Arthur, On., Can.	212	43.50 N	80.32 W
Arthur, Il., U.S.	194	39.43 N	88.28 W
Arthur, Ne., U.S.	198	41.34 N	101.41 W
Arthur, N.D., U.S.	198	47.06 N	97.13 W
Arthur, Tn., U.S.	192	36.32 N	83.40 W
Arthur ≃, Austl.	166	41.03 S	144.40 E
Arthur ≃, Austl.	168a	33.31 S	116.50 E
Arthur, Lake ⊜[1]	214	40.57 N	80.05 W
Arthur Creek ≃	162	22.55 S	136.45 E
Arthur Kill ⋓	276	40.30 N	74.15 W
Arthur's Pass	172	42.57 S	171.34 E
Arthur's Pass)(	172	42.54 S	171.34 E
Arthur's Pass National Park ♠	172	42.50 S	171.40 E
Arthurs Seat ʌ[2]	169	38.21 S	144.57 E
Arthurs Town	238	24.38 N	75.42 W
Arthurton	168b	34.16 S	137.45 E
Arti	86	56.26 N	58.32 E
Artibonite ≃	238	19.15 N	72.47 W
Artico, Océano → Arctic Ocean ▾[1]	16	85.00 N	170.00 E
Artigas	252	30.24 S	56.28 W
Artigas ◆[8]	286c	10.30 N	66.56 W
Artigas, Casa de ⊥	258	34.39 S	56.03 W
Artik	84	40.37 N	43.59 E
Artilleros	258	34.22 S	57.34 W
Artilleros, Punta ›	258	34.28 S	57.32 W
Artillery Lake ⊜	176	63.09 N	107.52 W
Artlenburg	52	53.22 N	10.29 E
Artney, Glen V	46	56.20 N	4.04 W
Artois □[9]	50	50.30 N	2.30 E
Artois, Collines de l' ⋏[2]	50	50.25 N	2.10 E
Art'om	89	43.22 N	132.13 E
Art'om-Ostrov	84	40.28 N	50.20 E
Art'omovka, S.S.S.R.	78	49.46 N	35.04 E
Art'omovka, S.S.S.R.	83	48.29 N	37.23 E
Art'omovka, S.S.S.R.	83	47.53 N	38.38 E
Art'omovo	83	48.22 N	37.53 E
Art'omovsk, S.S.S.R.	83	48.27 N	38.42 E
Art'omovsk, S.S.S.R.	83	48.35 N	38.00 E
Art'omovsk, S.S.S.R.	86	54.21 N	93.26 E
Art'omovskij, S.S.S.R.	86	57.21 N	61.54 E
Art'omovskij, S.S.S.R.	88	58.12 N	114.45 E
Art'omovskij, S.S.S.R.	89	43.27 N	132.22 E
Artova	130	40.03 N	36.19 E
Artpark ♠	284a	43.10 N	79.03 W
Artuby ≃	62	43.44 N	6.22 E
Artur Nogueira	256	22.35 S	47.09 W
Arturo Segui ◆[8]	258	34.51 S	58.09 W
Artvin	130	41.11 N	41.49 E
Artvin □[4]	130	41.05 N	42.00 E
Artybaš	86	51.48 N	87.16 E
Artyk	74	64.12 N	145.06 E
Aru, Kepulauan II	164	6.00 S	134.30 E
Aru, Tanjung ›	112	2.10 S	116.34 E
Aru, Teluk c	114	4.09 N	98.12 E
Arua	154	3.01 N	30.55 E
Aruã ≃	250	2.39 S	55.38 W
Aruaddin	144	16.15 N	38.43 E
Aruanã	255	14.54 S	51.05 W
Aruângua (Luangwa) ≃	154	15.36 S	30.25 E
Aruba □[2]	241s	12.30 N	69.58 W
Aru Basin ✢[1]	14	5.00 S	134.00 E
Arucas	148	28.07 N	15.31 W
Arue	174s	17.32 S	149.32 W
Arufu	150	7.50 N	9.14 E
Arujá	256	23.24 S	46.20 W
Arujá □[7]	287b	23.24 S	46.20 W
Arumanduba	250	1.29 S	52.29 W
Arume	174m	26.36 N	128.07 E
Arume-wan c	174m	26.35 N	128.08 E
Arumuganeri	122	8.34 N	78.07 E
Arun ≃, Asia	124	26.49 N	87.09 E
Arun ≃, Eng., U.K.	42	50.48 N	0.33 W
Arunachal Pradesh □[8]	120	28.30 N	95.00 E
Arundel, P.Q., Can.	206	45.58 N	74.37 W
Arundel, Eng., U.K.	42	50.51 N	0.34 W
Arun Qi	89	48.07 N	123.28 E
Årup	41	55.23 N	10.04 E
Aruppukkottai	122	9.31 N	78.06 E
Arurandéua ≃	250	3.43 S	48.50 W
Arus, Tanjung ›	112	1.20 N	120.48 E
Arusha	154	3.22 S	36.41 E
Arusha □[4]	154	4.00 S	36.15 E
Arusha Chini	154	3.35 S	37.20 E
Arusha National Park ♠	154	3.17 S	36.56 E
Aruvi ≃	122	8.49 N	79.55 E
Aruwimi ≃	138	1.13 N	23.36 E
Arvada	200	39.48 N	105.05 W
Arvagh	48	53.55 N	7.34 W
Arvajcheer	90	46.15 N	102.48 E
Arve ≃	58	46.12 N	6.08 E
Arverne ◆[8]	276	40.35 N	73.48 W
Arves, Les Aiguilles d' ʌ	62	45.08 N	6.21 E
Arvi	120	20.59 N	78.14 E
Arvida	186	48.25 N	71.11 W
Arvidsjaur	24	65.35 N	19.07 E
Arvier	62	45.42 N	7.11 E
Arvieux	62	44.46 N	6.44 E
Arvika	26	59.39 N	12.36 E
Arvillard	62	45.27 N	6.07 E
Arvin	228	35.12 N	118.49 W
Arvo, Lago ⊜	68	39.14 N	16.29 E
Arvon, Mount ʌ	190	46.45 N	88.09 W
Arvonia	192	37.40 N	78.20 W
Àrvorezinha	252	28.53 S	52.10 W
Arwal	124	25.15 N	84.41 E
Arwala	112	7.41 S	126.49 E
Arxan	89	47.11 N	119.57 E
Aryamūn	142	31.11 N	30.54 E
Aryiroúpolis	267c	37.54 N	23.45 E
Arys → Orzysz, Pol.	30	53.49 N	21.56 E
Arys', S.S.S.R.	85	42.26 N	68.48 E
Arys' ≃	85	42.48 N	68.12 E
Arys, ozero ⊜	86	45.50 N	66.20 E
Arzachena	71	41.05 N	9.23 E
Arzamas	80	55.23 N	43.50 E
Arzana	71	39.55 N	9.31 E
Arzano	68	40.55 N	14.16 E
Arzberg	60	50.04 N	12.12 E
Arzew, Golfe d' c	34	35.50 N	0.10 W
Arzew, Salines d' ⊜	34	35.40 N	0.15 W
Arzfeld	56	50.05 N	6.16 E
Arzignano	64	45.31 N	11.20 E
Arziw	148	35.51 N	0.19 W
Arz Lubnān ◆[3]	130	34.14 N	36.03 E
Arzni	84	40.19 N	44.36 E
Arzo	164	2.56 S	140.47 E
Arzon ≃	62	45.11 N	3.54 E
Arzúa	34	42.56 N	8.09 W
As, Bel.	56	51.01 N	5.35 E
Aš, Česko.	54	50.10 N	12.10 E
Ås, Nor.	26	59.40 N	10.48 E
Asa, Nihon	96	34.33 N	132.26 E
Aša, S.S.S.R.	86	55.00 N	57.16 E
Asa ≃, Nihon	94	35.39 N	139.26 E
Asa ≃, Nihon	96	34.01 N	131.09 E
Asa ≃, Ven.	246	6.50 N	63.18 W
Asab	156	25.29 S	17.59 E
Asaba, Nig.	150	6.12 N	6.44 E
Asaba, Nihon	94	34.42 N	137.56 E
Asadābād, Afg.	120	34.52 N	71.09 E
Asadābād, Īrān	128	34.47 N	48.07 E
Asafo	150	6.11 N	0.28 W
Asaga Strait ⋓	174w	14.11 S	169.40 W
Asagaya ◆[8]	268	35.42 N	139.38 E
Aşağıçiğil	130	38.03 N	31.52 E
Aşağı Dağ ʌ	84	40.01 N	43.11 E
Aşağıhanik	130	37.43 N	39.59 E
Aşağı İhtik	130	39.38 N	38.49 E
Asagı Kuluşağı	130	38.39 N	38.39 E
Aşağılahan	130	38.50 N	39.59 E
Aşağı Mestikân	130	38.25 N	38.46 E
Ašagy-G'ojn'uk	84	41.18 N	47.00 E
Asahan	114	2.23 N	102.33 E
Asahan ≃	114	3.02 N	99.52 E
Asahi, Nihon	94	35.14 N	137.22 E
Asahi, Nihon	94	35.43 N	140.39 E
Asahi, Nihon	94	35.59 N	136.07 E
Asahi, Nihon	94	36.05 N	137.21 E
Asahi, Nihon	94	36.14 N	140.31 E
Asahi, Nihon	94	35.02 N	136.40 E
Asahi, Nihon	94	36.07 N	137.52 E
Asahi, Nihon	94	36.57 N	137.34 E
Asahi, Nihon	96	34.59 N	133.50 E
Asahi, Nihon	96	34.51 N	132.16 E
Asahi, Nihon	96	34.17 N	131.28 E
Asahi ◆[8], Nihon	268	35.29 N	139.33 E
Asahi ◆[8], Nihon	270	34.44 N	135.34 E
Asahi ≃	96	34.36 N	133.58 E
Asahi-dake ʌ, Nihon	92a	43.40 N	142.51 E
Asahi-dake ʌ, Nihon	94	37.14 N	139.21 E
Asahigawa → Asahikawa	92a	43.46 N	142.22 E
Asahi-gawa-daiichi-dam ◆[6]	96	34.53 N	133.22 E
Asahikawa	92a	43.46 N	142.22 E
Asahikawa-chūtonchi, Rikujō-Jieitai- ■	92a	43.49 N	142.25 E
Asahi-ko ⊜[1]	96	34.56 N	133.51 E
Asahi-sanchi ⋏	92	38.25 N	139.50 E
Ašt	85	40.41 N	70.20 E
Asaka	94	35.48 N	139.36 E
Asaka, Camp ■	268	35.47 N	139.36 E
Asakanskij Golec, gora ʌ	88	50.18 N	109.55 E
Asakawa	94	37.05 N	140.25 E
Asake ≃	94	35.00 N	136.41 E
Asako	96	35.14 N	134.48 E
Asakura	96	33.23 N	130.44 E
Asakusa ◆[8]	268	35.43 N	139.49 E
Asālafpur ◆[8]	272a	28.38 N	77.05 E
Asale	144	14.22 N	40.32 E
Asale, Lake ⊜	144	14.19 N	40.18 E
Asamankese	150	5.52 N	0.42 W
Asama-yama ʌ	94	36.24 N	138.31 E
Asanbani, India	126	22.43 N	86.20 E
Asanbāni, India	126	24.07 N	87.27 E
Asani	154	4.25 S	29.05 E
Asankrangwa	150	5.48 N	2.26 W
Asan-man c	98	36.56 N	126.51 E
Asansol, India	126	24.14 N	87.17 E
Asansol, India	126	23.41 N	86.59 E
Ašap	86	57.07 N	56.30 E
Ạsar	88	47.56 N	117.38 E
Åsarna	26	62.39 N	14.21 E
Asarum	26	56.12 N	14.50 E
Asashina	94	36.16 N	138.25 E
Āsāsuni	126	22.32 N	89.10 E
Asati	272b	22.29 N	88.14 E
Asa-yama ʌ	96	34.47 N	132.23 E
Asayita	144	11.33 N	41.30 E
Asbach	56	50.40 N	7.25 E
Asbeck	263	51.21 N	7.18 E
Asberg	263	51.26 N	6.40 E
Asbesberg ⋏	158	28.55 S	23.15 E
Asbest	86	57.00 N	61.30 E
Asbestos	206	45.46 N	71.57 W
Asbe Teferi	144	9.02 N	40.58 E
Åsbro	40	59.00 N	15.03 E
Asbury	210	40.41 N	75.00 W
Asbury Park	208	40.13 N	74.01 W
Ascea	68	40.08 N	15.11 E
Ascensión, Méx.	232	31.06 N	107.59 W
Ascensión, Méx.	232	24.20 N	99.55 W
Ascension I	10	7.57 S	14.22 W
Ascensión, Bahía de la c	232	19.40 N	87.30 W
Ascent	158	27.12 S	29.03 E
Aščerino	265b	55.36 N	37.46 E
Asch	58	47.57 N	10.49 E
Aščhabad	128	37.57 N	58.23 E
Aščhabad □[4], S.S.S.R.	128	38.30 N	58.30 E
Aščhabad □[4], S.S.S.R.	128	38.30 N	58.25 E
Aschach an der Donau	61	48.22 N	14.02 E
Aschaffenburg	56	49.59 N	9.09 E
Aschbach Markt	61	48.04 N	14.45 E
Ascheberg, B.R.D.	52	51.47 N	7.37 E
Ascheberg, B.R.D.	54	54.08 N	10.20 E
Aschendorf	52	53.04 N	7.22 E
Aschersleben	54	51.45 N	11.27 E
Asciano	66	43.14 N	11.33 E
Aščikol', ozero ⊜	86	45.05 N	67.15 E
Aščiozek ≃	80	49.12 N	48.06 E
Aščitastysor, ozero ⊜	86	49.19 N	63.59 E
Ascoli Piceno	66	42.51 N	13.34 E
Ascoli Piceno □[4]	66	43.01 N	13.34 E
Ascoli Satriano	68	41.12 N	15.34 E
Ascona	58	46.09 N	8.46 E
Ascope	248	7.43 S	79.07 W
Ascot, Austl.	171a	27.26 S	153.04 E
Ascot, Eng., U.K.	42	51.25 N	0.41 W
Ascot ≃	206	45.21 N	71.51 W
Ascotán	252	21.44 S	68.18 W
Ascros	62	43.55 N	7.01 E
Aščykol', ozero ⊜	85	43.32 N	70.35 E
Aščysu ≃	86	49.54 N	78.58 E
Aseb	144	13.00 N	42.45 E
Åseda	26	57.10 N	15.20 E
Asedjrad ⋏[1]	148	24.28 N	1.52 E
Asekejevo	80	53.36 N	52.49 E
Asela	144	7.59 N	39.08 E
Åsele	26	64.10 N	17.20 E
Asem ≃	115a	6.14 S	107.42 E
Asembagus	115a	7.45 S	114.14 E
Asembourg	56	49.43 N	6.02 E
Åsen	26	63.36 N	11.03 E
Asendabo	144	9.50 N	37.33 E
Asendorf	52	52.46 N	9.00 E
Asenovgrad	38	42.01 N	24.52 E
Åsensbruk	26	58.48 N	12.25 E
Aseri	76	59.27 N	26.52 E
Aṣfar, Jabal al- ʌ	132	32.12 N	36.54 E
Aṣfar al-Maḥaṭṭah	132	30.11 N	35.46 E
Asfordby	42	52.46 N	0.57 W
Aṣfūn al-Maṭāʿinah	140	25.23 N	32.32 E
Åsgårdstrand	26	59.21 N	10.28 E
Ash, Eng., U.K.	42	51.15 N	0.44 W
Ash, Eng., U.K.	42	51.17 N	1.16 E
Ash ≃	42	51.48 N	0.02 W
Åshammar	40	60.39 N	16.32 E
Ashanti □[4]	150	6.45 N	1.30 W
ʿAsharah, Wādī al- V	142	30.21 N	32.15 E
Asharoken	276	40.56 N	73.22 W
Ashaway	207	41.25 N	71.47 W
Ashbourne, Ire.	48	53.31 N	6.24 W
Ashbourne, Eng., U.K.	44	53.02 N	1.44 W
Ash Brook Swamp Reservation ♠	276	40.37 N	74.21 W
Ashburn, Ga., U.S.	192	31.42 N	83.39 W
Ashburn, Mo., U.S.	219	39.33 N	91.10 W
Ashburn, Va., U.S.	208	39.02 N	77.29 W
Ashburnham	207	42.38 N	71.54 W
Ashburton, Austl.	274b	37.52 S	145.05 E
Ashburton, N.Z.	172	43.55 S	171.45 E
Ashburton, Eng., U.K.	42	50.31 N	3.45 W
Ashburton ≃, Austl.	162	21.40 S	114.56 E
Ashburton ≃, N.Z.	172	44.04 S	171.48 E
Ashburton, North Branch ≃	172	43.54 S	171.44 E
Ashburton, South Branch ≃	172	43.44 S	171.32 E
Ashburton Downs	162	23.24 S	117.04 E
Ashby	207	42.40 N	71.49 W
Ashby, Lake ⊜	220	28.56 N	81.07 W
Ashby-de-la-Zouch	42	52.46 N	1.28 W
Ashchurch	42	52.00 N	2.07 W
Ash Creek ≃, Ca., U.S.	204	41.05 N	121.08 W
Ash Creek ≃, Ct., U.S.	276	41.08 N	73.14 W
Ashcroft	182	50.43 N	121.17 W
Ashdod, Ma., U.S.	283	42.04 N	70.45 W
Ashdod, Yis.	132	31.49 N	34.40 E
Ashdod ⊥	132	31.45 N	34.40 E
Ashdot Yaʿaqov	132	32.40 N	35.35 E
Ashdown	194	33.40 N	94.07 W
Ashdown Forest ◆[3]	42	51.04 N	0.03 E
Asheboro	192	35.42 N	79.48 W
Ashern	184	51.11 N	98.21 W
Asherton	196	28.26 N	99.45 W
Asheville	192	35.36 N	82.33 W
Ashewat	120	31.22 N	68.32 E
Asheweig ≃	176	54.17 N	87.12 W
Ashfield, Austl.	274a	33.53 S	151.08 E
Ashfield, Ma., U.S.	207	42.31 N	72.47 W
Ash Flat	194	36.13 N	91.36 W
Ashford, Austl.	166	29.20 S	151.06 E
Ashford, Eng., U.K.	42	51.08 N	0.53 E
Ashford, Eng., U.K.	260	51.26 N	0.27 W
Ashford, Al., U.S.	194	31.10 N	85.14 W
Ashford, Wa., U.S.	224	46.46 N	122.02 W
Ashford Airport ⊠	42	51.04 N	1.01 E
Ash Fork	200	35.13 N	112.28 W
Ash Grove	194	37.18 N	93.35 W
Ashhurst	172	40.18 S	175.45 E
Ashibe	92	33.48 N	129.46 E
Ashibetsu	92a	43.31 N	142.11 E
Ashida ≃	96	34.26 N	133.25 E
Ashikaga	94	36.20 N	139.27 E
Ashikagga-gakkō ⊥	94	36.22 N	139.30 E
Ashingdon	260	51.36 N	0.42 E
Ashington	44	55.12 N	1.35 W
Ashino-ko ⊜	94	35.13 N	139.00 E
Ashio	94	36.38 N	139.27 E
Ashio-sanchi ⋏	94	36.35 N	139.30 E
Ashippun	216	43.14 N	88.31 W
Ashippun ≃	216	43.10 N	88.33 W
Ashitaka-yama ʌ	94	35.12 N	138.49 E
Ashiya, Nihon	96	33.53 N	130.40 E
Ashiya, Nihon	96	34.43 N	135.17 E
Ashiya ≃	270	34.43 N	135.18 E
Ashiyasu	94	35.38 N	138.23 E
Ashiyoro	92a	43.15 N	143.30 E
Ashizuri-misaki ›	92	32.44 N	133.01 E
Ashizuri-Uwakai-kokuritsu-kōen ♠, Nihon	92	32.45 N	132.45 E
Ashizuri-Uwakai-kokuritsu-kōen ♠, Nihon	96	33.07 N	132.27 E
Ashkhabad → Aščhabad	128	37.57 N	58.23 E
Ashkum	216	40.53 N	87.57 W
Ashland, Al., U.S.	194	33.16 N	85.50 W
Ashland, Ca., U.S.	226	37.41 N	122.06 W
Ashland, Il., U.S.	219	39.53 N	90.00 W
Ashland, Ks., U.S.	198	37.11 N	99.45 W
Ashland, Ky., U.S.	188	38.28 N	82.38 W
Ashland, Me., U.S.	186	46.37 N	68.24 W
Ashland, Ma., U.S.	207	42.15 N	71.27 W
Ashland, Ms., U.S.	194	34.49 N	89.10 W
Ashland, Mo., U.S.	219	38.46 N	92.15 W
Ashland, Mt., U.S.	202	45.35 N	106.16 W
Ashland, Ne., U.S.	198	41.02 N	96.22 W
Ashland, N.H., U.S.	188	43.41 N	71.37 W
Ashland, N.J., U.S.	285	39.51 N	75.00 W
Ashland, N.Y., U.S.	210	42.18 N	74.20 W
Ashland, Oh., U.S.	214	40.52 N	82.19 W
Ashland, Or., U.S.	202	42.11 N	122.42 W
Ashland, Pa., U.S.	210	40.46 N	76.20 W
Ashland, Va., U.S.	208	37.45 N	77.28 W
Ashland, Wi., U.S.	190	46.35 N	90.53 W
Ashland □[6]	214	40.52 N	82.19 W
Ashland, Mount ʌ	202	42.05 N	122.43 W
Ashland City	194	36.16 N	87.03 W
Ashley, Austl.	166	29.19 S	149.49 E
Ashley, Eng., U.K.	262	53.21 N	2.20 W
Ashley, Il., U.S.	219	38.20 N	89.11 W
Ashley, In., U.S.	216	41.32 N	85.04 W
Ashley, Mi., U.S.	190	43.11 N	84.28 W
Ashley, Mo., U.S.	219	39.15 N	91.14 W
Ashley, N.D., U.S.	198	46.01 N	99.22 W
Ashley, Oh., U.S.	214	40.24 N	82.57 W
Ashley, Pa., U.S.	210	41.12 N	75.53 W
Ashley ≃	172	43.16 S	172.43 E
Ashley Creek ≃	200	40.21 N	109.22 W
Ashley Falls	207	42.03 N	73.20 W
Ashley Green	260	51.44 N	0.35 W
Ashmore	194	39.32 N	88.01 W
Ashmore Islands II	160	12.14 S	123.05 E
Ashmūn	142	30.18 N	30.58 E
Ashmura	132	33.03 N	35.39 E
Ashokan Reservoir ⊜[1]	210	41.58 N	74.10 W
Ashoknagar	120	24.34 N	77.43 E
Ashqelon	132	31.40 N	34.35 E
Ashridge Park ♠	260	51.48 N	0.34 W
Ash-Shabakah	128	30.49 N	43.39 E
Ash-Shabb ▾[4]	140	22.19 N	29.46 E
Ash-Shāgūr	132	31.50 N	35.39 E
Ash-Shā'ib ʌ[2]	142	29.50 N	30.56 E
Ash-Shajarah	132	32.39 N	35.56 E
Ash-Shallūfah	142	30.07 N	32.34 E
Ash-Shamāl □[4]	130	34.30 N	36.00 E
Ash-Shamālīyah □[4]	140	19.15 N	29.00 E
Ash-Shanāwīyah	142	29.08 N	31.08 E
Ash-Shaqrā'	128	25.15 N	45.15 E
Ash-Sharāh ◆[1]	132	30.20 N	35.30 E
Ash-Shāriqah	128	25.22 N	55.23 E
Ash-Sharmah	128	28.01 N	35.18 E
Ash-Sharqāṭ	128	35.27 N	43.16 E
Ash-Sharqīyah □[4]	142	30.48 N	31.48 E
Ash-Sharqīyah ◆[1]	128	27.00 N	49.00 E
Ash-Shaṭrah	128	31.25 N	46.10 E
Ash-Shawāshinah	142	29.22 N	30.36 E
Ash-Shawbak	132	30.32 N	35.34 E
Ash-Shaykh Faḍl	142	28.29 N	30.50 E
Ash-Shaykh ʿIbādah	142	27.48 N	30.52 E
Ash-Shaykh Miskīn	132	32.49 N	36.09 E
Ash-Shaykh Saʿd	132	32.50 N	36.02 E
Ash-Shaykh Timay	142	27.53 N	30.51 E
Ash-Shiḥr	144	14.44 N	49.35 E
Ash-Shīn	142	31.01 N	30.53 E
Ash-Shināfīyah	128	31.35 N	44.39 E
Ash-Shīyāḥ	132	33.51 N	35.30 E
Ash-Shufayyah	128	23.50 N	39.08 E
Ash-Shuhadā'	142	30.36 N	30.54 E
Ash-Shuqayq	144	17.43 N	42.01 E
Ash-Shurayf	128	25.43 N	39.14 E
Ash-Shurayk	140	18.48 N	33.34 E
Ash-Shuwayfāt	132	33.49 N	35.31 E
Ash-Shuwayr	132	33.55 N	35.43 E
Ash Slough ≃	226	37.02 N	120.32 W
Ashta, India	122	16.57 N	74.24 E
Ashta, India	124	23.01 N	76.43 E
Ashtabula	214	41.51 N	80.47 W
Ashtabula □[6]	214	41.44 N	80.46 W
Ashtabula ≃	214	41.55 N	80.47 W
Ashtabula, East Branch ≃	214	41.48 N	80.37 W
Ashtabula, Lake ⊜[1]	198	47.11 N	97.58 W
Ashtabula, West Branch ≃	214	41.48 N	80.37 W
Ashtead	260	51.19 N	0.18 W
Ashton, S. Afr.	158	33.50 S	20.05 E
Ashton, Eng., U.K.	262	53.13 N	2.45 W
Ashton, Id., U.S.	202	44.04 N	111.26 W
Ashton, Il., U.S.	190	41.51 N	89.13 W
Ashton, Ia., U.S.	198	43.18 N	95.47 W
Ashton, Md., U.S.	208	39.08 N	77.00 W
Ashton, Ne., U.S.	198	41.14 N	98.47 W
Ashton, R.I., U.S.	207	41.46 N	71.25 W
Ashton-in-Makerfield	262	53.29 N	2.39 W
Ashton-under-Lyne	262	53.29 N	2.06 W
Ashton upon Mersey	262	53.26 N	2.19 W
Ashuanipi Lake ⊜	176	52.35 N	66.10 W
Ashuelot ≃	188	42.46 N	72.29 W
Ashurst's Beacon ʌ[2]	262	53.34 N	2.45 W
Ashville, Al., U.S.	194	33.52 N	86.17 W
Ashville, N.Y., U.S.	214	42.06 N	79.23 W
Ashville, Oh., U.S.	218	39.42 N	82.57 W
Ashville, Pa., U.S.	214	40.34 N	78.33 W
Ashwater	42	50.44 N	4.16 W
Ashwaubenon	190	44.30 N	88.06 W
Ashworth Moor Reservoir ⊜[1]	262	53.38 N	2.16 W
Asi (Nahr al-ʿĀṣī) ≃	130	36.02 N	35.58 E
Asia ±[1]	4	50.00 N	100.00 E
Asia ±[1]	12	50.00 N	100.00 E
Asia, Kepulauan II	108	1.03 N	131.18 E
Asiago	64	45.52 N	11.30 E
Asia Menor → Asia Minor □[9]	22	39.00 N	32.00 E
Asia Minor □[9]	22	39.00 N	32.00 E
Asian Exhibition Area ♠	267d	35.47 N	51.24 E
Asid Gulf c	116	12.07 N	123.30 E
Asie → Asia ±[1]	12	50.00 N	100.00 E
Asie Mineure → Asia Minor □[9]	22	39.00 N	32.00 E
Asien → Asia ±[1]	12	50.00 N	100.00 E
Asikuma	150	5.35 N	1.00 W
Asilah	148	35.32 N	6.00 W
Asinara, Golfo dell' c	71	41.00 N	8.32 E
Asinara, Isola I	71	41.04 N	8.16 E
Asinaro ≃	70	36.53 N	15.08 E
Asino	86	57.00 N	86.09 E
Asipoquobah Lake ⊜	184	53.40 N	91.15 W
ʿAsīr ◆[1]	144	19.00 N	42.00 E
Ašitkovo	82	55.26 N	38.36 E
Aska	120	19.36 N	84.39 E
Aşkale	130	39.55 N	40.42 E
Askam in Furness	44	54.11 N	3.13 W
Askanija-Nova	78	46.27 N	33.52 E
Askanija-nova zapovednik ♠	78	46.37 N	33.54 E
Askarovo	86	53.21 N	58.30 E
Askeaton	48	52.36 N	8.58 W
Asker	26	59.50 N	10.26 E
Askern	44	53.37 N	1.09 W
Askersund	40	58.53 N	14.54 E
Askham	158	26.59 S	20.47 E
Askim	26	59.35 N	11.10 E
Askino	86	56.05 N	56.34 E
Askira	146	10.39 N	12.55 E
Askival ʌ	46	56.59 N	6.17 W
Askiz	86	53.08 N	90.32 E
Askja ʌ[1]	24a	65.00 N	16.48 W
Askø I	41	54.54 N	11.30 E
Äsköping	40	59.09 N	16.04 E
Askov	41	55.28 N	9.06 E
Askraal	158	34.09 S	20.52 E
Askrigg	44	54.19 N	2.04 W
Askvoll	26	61.21 N	5.04 E
Aslanapa	130	39.13 N	29.52 E
Aslan-Sara	84	39.02 N	48.16 E
Asleigh	284c	39.01 N	77.10 W
Åsljunga	41	56.19 N	13.22 E
Ašlyk	86	57.33 N	68.40 E
Ašlyk ≃	86	57.50 N	69.12 E
Asmaca	130	37.53 N	35.58 E
Āsmār	120	35.02 N	71.22 E
Asmara → Asmera	144	15.20 N	38.53 E
Asmera	144	15.20 N	38.53 E
Asmundtorp	41	55.53 N	12.56 E
Asnæs	41	55.49 N	11.31 E
Asnæs ›[1]	41	55.40 N	11.00 E
Asnebumskit Hill ʌ[2]	207	42.18 N	71.54 W
Åsnen ⊜	26	56.38 N	14.42 E
Asni	148	31.14 N	7.55 W
Asnières [-sur-Seine]	50	48.55 N	2.17 E
Asō, Nihon	94	35.59 N	140.29 E
Aso, Nihon	96	32.58 N	131.02 E
Aso ≃	66	43.06 N	13.51 E
Asoc	152	1.26 N	11.18 E
Aso-kokuritsu-kōen ♠	92	33.00 N	131.07 E
Asola	64	45.13 N	10.24 E
Asolo	64	45.48 N	11.54 E
Asomante	240m	18.23 N	66.36 W
Ason	273a	6.34 N	3.31 E
Asosa	144	10.03 N	34.32 E
Aso-san ʌ	92	32.53 N	131.06 E
Asoteriba, Jabal ʌ	140	21.51 N	36.30 E
Asotin	202	46.20 N	117.02 W
Asouf, Oued V	148	25.51 N	1.33 E
Asowsches Meer → Azovskoje more ▾[2]	78	46.00 N	36.00 E
Aspach	60	48.11 N	13.18 E
Aspach-le-Bas	58	47.46 N	7.09 E
Aspang Markt	61	47.33 N	16.06 E
Aspara ≃	85	43.17 N	73.28 E
Aspatria	44	54.46 N	3.20 W
Aspe	34	38.21 N	0.46 W
Aspe, Gave d' ≃	32	43.12 N	0.36 W
Aspen	200	39.11 N	106.49 W
Aspen Butte ʌ	202	42.19 N	122.05 W
Aspendale	274b	38.02 S	145.07 E
Aspendus ⊥	130	37.08 N	31.12 E
Aspen Hill	284c	39.04 N	77.04 W
Aspen Knolls	284c	39.05 N	77.05 W
Aspen Lake ⊜	202	42.18 N	122.00 W
Asperg	56	48.54 N	9.07 E
Aspermont	196	33.08 N	100.13 W
Aspern ◆[8]	264b	48.13 N	16.29 E
Aspers	208	39.59 N	77.13 W
Asperup	41	55.29 N	9.55 E
Aspid, Mount ʌ	180	53.30 N	167.33 W
Aspindza	84	41.36 N	43.15 E
Aspinwall → Colón, Pan.	236	9.22 N	79.54 W
Aspinwall, Pa., U.S.	279b	40.29 N	79.54 W
Aspiring, Mount ʌ	172	44.23 S	168.44 E
Aspö	40	59.29 N	17.02 E
Aspres-sur-Buëch	62	44.31 N	5.45 E
Aspromonte ⋏	68	38.10 N	15.55 E
Asprópirgos	267c	38.04 N	23.35 E
Aspull	262	53.34 N	2.35 W
Aspy Bay c	186	46.55 N	60.25 W
Asquins	50	47.29 N	3.45 E
Asquith, Austl.	274a	33.41 S	151.06 E
Asquith, Sk., Can.	184	52.08 N	107.13 W
Asralt chajrchan ʌ	88	48.29 N	107.24 E
Asrāni	123	29.31 N	72.07 E
Assa, Magreb	148	28.34 N	9.27 W
Assa, S.S.S.R.	85	43.02 N	71.10 E
Assa ≃, S.S.S.R.	84	43.13 N	45.25 E
Assa ≃, S.S.S.R.	85	43.55 N	70.25 E
As-Saʿata	140	13.37 N	29.59 E
Assab → Aseb	144	13.00 N	42.45 E
Assabet ≃	283	42.28 N	71.21 W
As-Sabkhah	130	35.48 N	39.15 E
Assad, Buḥayrat al- ⊜[1]	22	36.00 N	38.00 E
Aṣ-Ṣadārah	144	14.30 N	48.04 E
As-Saʿdīyah	128	34.11 N	45.07 E
Aṣ-Ṣaff	140	29.34 N	31.17 E
Aṣ-Ṣāfī	132	31.02 N	35.28 E
As-Safīrah	130	36.04 N	37.22 E
Aṣ-Ṣāfiyah	140	15.31 N	30.07 E
Assago	266b	45.24 N	9.08 E
Assaí	255	23.22 S	50.49 W
Aṣ-Ṣaʿīd □[9]	140	26.00 N	32.00 E
Assaikwatamo ≃	184	56.52 N	95.50 W
Assal, Lac ⊜	144	11.41 N	42.25 E
ʿAssāl al-Ward	132	33.52 N	36.24 E
As-Salamīyah	130	35.01 N	37.03 E
Aṣ-Ṣāliḥīyah	142	30.47 N	31.59 E
Aṣ-Ṣalīmah	144	14.02 N	45.46 E
As-Sallūm	140	31.34 N	25.09 E
As-Salmān	128	30.30 N	44.32 E
As-Salṭ	132	32.03 N	35.44 E
Assam □[3]	120	26.00 N	92.00 E
As-Samāwah	128	31.18 N	45.17 E
As-Samūʿ	132	31.24 N	35.04 E
Assam Valley V	124	26.30 N	90.30 E
ʿAssān	130	36.05 N	37.14 E
Aṣ-Ṣanāfīn Al-Qiblīyah	142	30.27 N	31.18 E
Aṣ-Ṣanamayn	132	33.05 N	36.10 E
As-Santah	142	30.45 N	31.08 E
Assaq, Oued V	148	25.41 N	14.40 W
Aṣ-Ṣaqlabīyah	130	35.22 N	36.23 E
Aṣ-Ṣarafand	132	33.27 N	35.18 E
Assaré	250	6.52 S	39.52 W
Aṣ-Ṣarīḥ	132	32.30 N	35.54 E
Aṣ-Ṣarīrīyah	142	28.20 N	30.45 E
Assateague Island I	208	38.05 N	75.10 W
Assateague Island National Seashore ♠	208	38.00 N	75.15 W
Assawoman Bay c	208	38.25 N	75.05 W
Assawoman Canal ≋	208	38.31 N	75.04 W
Assawompset Pond ⊜	207	41.50 N	70.55 W
Asse	50	50.55 N	4.12 E
Asse ≃	62	43.53 N	5.53 E
Assean Lake ⊜	184	56.13 N	96.30 W
Assebroek	50	51.12 N	3.16 E
Assekaifaf	148	27.08 N	8.50 E
Assel	52	53.41 N	9.25 E
Asseln ◆[8]	263	51.32 N	7.35 E
Assembleia Nacional, Palacio da ⊍	266c	38.43 N	9.09 W
Assemini	71	39.17 N	9.00 E
Assen	52	52.59 N	6.34 E
Assendelft	52	52.27 N	4.45 E
Assenede	50	51.14 N	3.45 E
Assens	41	55.16 N	9.55 E
Asserbo	41	56.01 N	12.01 E
Assergi	66	42.25 N	13.30 E
Asseria ⊥	36	44.02 N	15.39 E
Ássia	130	35.09 N	33.36 E
As-Sīb	128	23.41 N	58.11 E
As-Sidr	128	23.27 N	39.45 E
As-Sijn	132	32.47 N	36.28 E
As-Simākīyah	132	31.18 N	35.48 E
As-Sinbillāwayn	142	30.53 N	31.27 E
Assiniboia	184	49.38 N	105.59 W
Assiniboine ≃	184	49.53 N	97.08 W
Assiniboine, Mount ʌ	182	50.52 N	115.39 W
Assiniboine Indian Reserve ◆[4]	184	50.21 N	103.28 W
Assinika ≃	184	52.37 N	96.10 W
Assinippi	283	42.09 N	70.51 W
Assis	255	22.40 S	50.25 W
Assiscunk Creek ≃	208	40.05 N	74.51 W
Assisi	66	43.04 N	12.37 E
Asslar	56	50.35 N	8.28 E
Assling	60	48.00 N	12.00 E
Asso	62	45.52 N	9.16 E
Assodé ▾[4]	150	18.26 N	8.28 E
Assomada	150a	15.06 N	23.41 W
Assonet	207	41.47 N	71.04 W
Assoro	70	37.37 N	14.25 E
As-Subū' ⊥	140	22.45 N	32.34 E
As-Sūdān → Sudan □[1]	140	15.00 N	30.00 E
As-Sudd ◆[1]	140	8.00 N	31.00 E
As-Sufāl	144	14.06 N	48.42 E
Aṣ-Ṣufayyah	140	15.30 N	34.42 E
Aṣ-Ṣūfīyah	142	30.55 N	31.46 E
As-Sukhnah, Sūrīy.	130	34.52 N	38.52 E
As-Sukhnah, Urd.	132	32.08 N	36.04 E
As-Sulaymānīyah, Ar. Su.	128	24.09 N	47.19 E
As-Sulaymānīyah, ʿIrāq	128	35.33 N	45.26 E
As-Sulaymānīyah □[4]	128	35.30 N	45.25 E
As-Sulaymī	128	26.17 N	41.21 E
As-Sulayyil	144	20.27 N	45.34 E
As-Sulṭān	146	31.07 N	17.10 E
As-Sumayḥ	140	9.49 N	27.39 E
Aṣ-Ṣummān ◆[1]	128	25.00 N	47.00 E
As-Summāqīyāt	132	32.26 N	36.24 E
Assumption, Il., U.S.	219	39.31 N	89.02 W
Assumption, Oh., U.S.	216	41.40 N	83.54 W
Assumption Island I	138	9.45 S	46.30 E
Assunpink Creek ≃	285	40.13 N	74.46 W
As-Sūrīyah → Syria □[1]	128	35.00 N	38.00 E
As-Suʿūdīyah	142	29.33 N	31.14 E
Aṣ-Ṣuwār	130	35.30 N	40.39 E
As-Suwaydā'	132	32.42 N	36.34 E
As-Suwaydā' □[8]	132	32.45 N	36.45 E
As-Suways (Suez)	142	29.58 N	32.33 E
As-Suways □[4]	142	30.12 N	32.30 E
Assynt, Loch ⊜	46	58.11 N	5.06 W
Asta, Cima d' ʌ	64	46.10 N	11.36 E
Astachovo	83	47.52 N	39.37 E
Astaffort	32	44.04 N	0.40 E
Astakós	38	38.32 N	21.05 E
Āstāneh, Īrān	128	37.17 N	49.59 E
Āstāneh, Īrān	128	33.53 N	49.22 E
Āstārā, Īrān	128	38.26 N	48.52 E
Astara, S.S.S.R.	84	38.28 N	48.52 E
Aštarak	84	40.18 N	44.22 E
Astaškovo	82	55.32 N	38.38 E
Astatula	220	28.43 N	81.44 W
Asten, Ned.	52	51.24 N	5.45 E
Asten, Öst.	61	48.13 N	14.25 E
Asti	62	44.54 N	8.12 E
Asti □[4]	62	44.55 N	8.10 E
Astica	252	30.56 S	67.23 W
Astico ≃	64	45.37 N	11.37 E
Astillero	34	43.24 N	3.49 W
Astipálaia	38	36.30 N	26.30 E
Astipálaia I	38	36.35 N	26.25 E
Astley Bridge	262	53.36 N	2.26 W
Astley Green	262	53.29 N	2.27 W
Astley Hall ⊥	262	53.39 N	2.38 W
Astola Island I	128	25.07 N	63.51 E
Astolfo Dutra	256	21.19 S	42.52 W
Aston, Eng., U.K.	262	53.18 N	2.40 W
Aston, Pa., U.S.	285	39.52 N	75.26 W
Aston Clinton	42	51.48 N	0.44 W
Aston-on-Trent	42	52.52 N	1.23 W
Astor	123	35.22 N	74.51 E
Astor ≃	123	35.34 N	74.41 E
Astorga, Bra.	255	23.13 S	51.40 W
Astorga, Esp.	34	42.27 N	6.03 W
Astorga, Pil.	116	6.54 N	125.27 E
Astoria, Il., U.S.	219	40.13 N	90.21 W
Astoria, Or., U.S.	224	46.11 N	123.49 W
Astoria ◆[8]	276	40.46 N	73.55 W
Astoria Bridge ◆[5]	224	46.13 N	123.52 W
Astoria Column ⊥	224	46.11 N	123.50 W
Åstorp	41	56.08 N	12.57 E
Astove Island I	138	10.06 S	47.45 E
Astra	254	45.44 S	67.30 W
Astrachan'	80	46.21 N	48.03 E
Astrachanka	86	51.33 N	69.47 E
Astrachanskij	80	46.12 N	47.16 E
Astrachanskij zapovednik ◆[4]	80	46.00 N	48.32 E
Astrakhan → Astrachan'	80	46.21 N	48.03 E
Astrodome ♠	222	29.41 N	95.25 W
Astrolabe, Cape ›	175e	8.20 S	160.34 E
Astrolabe Bay c	164	5.20 S	145.50 E
Astrolabe Reefs ✢[2]	175f	19.48 S	165.37 E
Astudillo	34	42.12 N	4.18 W
Astura, Torre ⊥	66	41.24 N	12.46 E
Asturias	116	10.34 N	123.43 E
Asturias □[4]	34	43.20 N	6.00 W
Astwood Bank	42	52.15 N	1.56 W
Asubulak	86	49.31 N	83.03 E
Asuisui, Cape ›	175a	13.47 S	172.29 W
Asuka	96	34.28 N	135.50 E
Asuke	94	35.08 N	137.19 E
Asunción	252	25.16 S	57.40 W
Asunción, Bahía c	232	27.06 N	114.11 W
Asunción, Cerro de la ʌ	232	24.15 N	99.56 W
Asuncion Island I	108	19.40 N	145.24 E
Asunción Mita	236	14.20 N	89.43 W
Asunción Nochixtlán	234	17.28 N	97.14 W
Åsunden ⊜, Sve.	26	57.58 N	15.50 E
Åsunden ⊜, Sve.	26	57.44 N	13.22 E
Asunga, Wādī V	146	13.21 N	22.17 E
Asuni	71	39.52 N	8.56 E
ʿĀṣūr, Tall ʌ	132	31.59 N	35.17 E
Aşutka	130	39.09 N	38.37 E
Asuwa	94	36.01 N	136.16 E
Asuwa ≃	94	36.04 N	136.11 E
Aswad, Ar-Ra's al- ›	144	21.22 N	39.08 E
Aswān	140	24.05 N	32.53 E
Aswān High Dam → ʿĀli, As-Sadd al- ◆[6]	140	23.58 N	32.52 E
Aswatthaberia	272b	22.26 N	88.32 E
Asy ≃	85	43.31 N	78.20 E
Asyūṭ	142	27.11 N	31.11 E
Asyūṭ □[4]	142	27.20 N	30.50 E
Asyūṭī, Wādī al- V	142	27.11 N	31.16 E
Aszód	30	47.39 N	19.31 E
'Ata I, Tonga	14	22.20 S	176.12 W
Ata I, Tonga	174w	21.03 S	175.00 W
Atabaj	85	43.30 N	68.20 E
Atabapo ≃	246	4.03 N	67.42 W
Atabasca → Athabasca ≃	176	58.40 N	110.50 W
Atabasca, Lago → Athabasca, Lake ⊜	176	59.07 N	110.00 W
Atabey	130	37.57 N	30.39 E
Atacama □[4]	252	27.30 S	70.00 W
Atacama, Desierto de ◆[2]	18	24.30 S	69.15 W
Atacama, Puna de ⋏[1]	252	25.00 S	68.00 W
Atacama, Salar de ≚	252	23.30 S	68.15 W
Ataco	246	3.35 N	75.23 W
Atacora, Chaîne de l' ⋏	150	10.45 N	1.30 E
Atacuari ≃	246	3.47 S	70.44 W
Atafu I[1]	14	8.33 S	172.30 W
Atagaj	88	55.06 N	99.23 E
Atago-yama ʌ, Nihon	94	35.07 N	139.59 E
Atago-yama ʌ, Nihon	96	35.03 N	135.37 E
Ātāi ≃[1]	126	22.51 N	89.33 E
ʿAṭāʿiṭah, Jabal al- ʌ	132	30.40 N	35.39 E
Atakakup Indian Reserve ◆[4]	184	53.24 N	106.55 W
Atakano-seki ⊥	94	36.24 N	136.25 E
Ataki	78	48.25 N	27.47 E
Atakora □[5]	150	10.00 N	1.35 E
Atakora, Réserve d' ◆[4]	150	11.30 N	2.10 E
Atakpamé	150	7.32 N	1.08 E

Symbols in the index entries represent the broad categories identified in the key at the right. Symbols with superior numbers (⋏[1]) identify subcategories (see complete key on page *I · 1).*

Kartensymbole in dem Registerverzeichnis stellen die rechts in Schlüssel erklärten Kategorien dar. Symbole mit hochgestellten Ziffern (⋏[1]) bezeichnen Unterabteilungen einer Kategorie (vgl. vollständiger Schlüssel auf Seite *I · 1).*

Los símbolos incluídos en el texto del índice representan las grandes categorias identificadas con la clave a la derecha. Los símbolos con numeros en su parte superior (⋏[1]) identifican las subcategorías (véase la clave completa en la página *I · 1).*

Les symboles de l'index représentent les catégories indiquées dans la légende à droite. Les symboles suivis d'un indice (⋏[1]) représentent des sous-catégories (voir légende complète à la page *I · 1).*

Os símbolos incluídos no texto do índice representam as grandes categorias identificadas com a chave à direita. Os símbolos com números em sua parte superior (⋏[1]) identificam as subcategorias (veja-se a chave completa à página *I · 1).*

ʌ Mountain	Berg	Montaña	Montagne	Montanha
⋏ Mountains	Berge	Montañas	Montagnes	Montanhas
)(Pass	Pass	Paso	Col	Passo
V Valley, Canyon	Tal, Cañon	Valle, Cañón	Vallée, Canyon	Vale, Canhão
≚ Plain	Ebene	Llano	Plaine	Planície
› Cape	Kap	Cabo	Cap	Cabo
I Island	Insel	Isla	Île	Ilha
II Islands	Inseln	Islas	Îles	Ilhas
± Other Topographic Features	Andere Topographische Objekte	Otros Elementos Topográficos	Autres données topographiques	Outros acidentes topográficos

ESPAÑOL · FRANÇAIS · PORTUGUÊS

Nombre / Nom / Nome	Página / Page / Página	Lat.°′	Long.°′ W = Oeste / W = Ouest
Atalaia, Bra.	250	9.31 S	36.02 W
Atalaia, Port.	266c	38.42 N	8.55 W
Atalándi	38	38.39 N	23.00 E
Atalanka	88	54.50 N	103.05 E
Atalaya, Arg.	258	35.02 S	57.32 W
Atalaya, Pan.	236	8.03 N	80.56 W
Atalaya, Perú	248	10.44 S	73.45 W
Atalaya, Cerro ∧, Chile	254	52.45 S	72.42 W
Atalaya, Cerro ∧, Perú	248	12.38 S	71.56 W
Atalaya, Punta ≻	258	35.01 S	57.31 W
Atamanovka	88	51.56 N	113.37 E
Atamanovo	86	56.24 N	93.36 E
Atambua	112	9.07 S	124.54 E
Atami	94	35.05 N	139.04 E
Atapupu	112	9.00 S	124.51 E
ʿAtāq	144	14.33 N	46.48 E
ʿAtāqah, Jabal ⋏	142	29.58 N	32.20 E
Atâr	150	20.31 N	13.03 W
Ataram, ʿErg n- ◆[2]	148	23.46 N	1.44 E
Atarés, Castillo de ⊥	286b	23.08 N	82.21 W
Atāri	123	31.36 N	74.35 E
Atary	80	57.32 N	49.18 E
Atascadero	226	35.29 N	120.40 W
Atascosa ≃	196	28.26 N	98.12 W
At'aševo	80	54.36 N	46.06 E
Atasu	86	48.42 N	71.38 E
Atas uul ∧	102	43.18 N	96.36 E
Atata I	174w	21.03 S	175.15 W
Atatürk Heykeli ⊥	267b	41.00 N	28.59 E
Ataur	272a	28.43 N	77.24 E
Atbara (ʿAṭbarah) ≃	140	17.40 N	33.56 E
ʿAṭbarah	140	17.42 N	33.59 E
ʿAṭbarah (Atbara) ≃	140	17.40 N	33.56 E
Atbasar	86	51.48 N	68.20 E
At-Baši	85	41.10 N	75.48 E
Atbaši ≃	85	41.24 N	75.38 E
Atbaši, chrebet ⋏	85	40.55 N	75.40 E
Atchafalaya ≃	194	29.53 N	91.28 W
Atchafalaya Bay c	194	29.25 N	91.20 W
Atchison	198	39.33 N	95.07 W
Atco	208	39.46 N	74.53 W
Atebubu	150	7.45 N	0.59 W
Ateca	34	41.20 N	1.47 W
Atelchu ≃	255	12.05 S	53.46 W
Ateleta	66	41.51 N	14.12 E
Ateli	124	28.06 N	76.17 E
Atella	68	40.52 N	15.39 E
Atemajac de Brizuela	234	20.11 N	103.42 W
Atemajac del Valle	234	20.45 N	103.22 W
Atemar	80	54.11 N	45.24 E
Atemble	164	5.05 S	144.45 E
Atena Lucana	68	40.27 N	15.33 E
Atenango del Río	234	18.05 N	99.06 W
Atenas, C.R.	236	9.58 N	84.23 W
Atenas → Athínai, Ellás	38	37.58 N	23.43 E
Atencingo	234	18.30 N	98.36 W
Atenco □[7]	286a	19.34 N	99.00 W
Atengo ≃	234	21.50 N	104.43 W
Atenguillo	234	20.25 N	104.31 W
Atenguillo ≃	234	20.55 N	104.38 W
Atenquique	234	19.31 N	103.30 W
Atepcevo	82	55.20 N	36.46 E
Aterno ≃	66	42.11 N	13.51 E
Aterrado, Ribeirão do ≃	256	22.09 S	45.03 W
Atessa	66	42.04 N	14.27 E
Aṭfīḥ	142	29.24 N	31.15 E
Aṭfīḥī, Wādī al- ∨	142	29.23 N	31.16 E
Atghara	272b	22.37 N	88.27 E
Ātgharia	126	24.06 N	89.14 E
Atglen	208	39.57 N	75.58 W
Ath	50	50.38 N	3.47 E
Athabasca	182	54.43 N	113.17 W
Athabasca ≃	176	58.40 N	110.50 W
Athabasca, Lake ⊜	176	59.07 N	110.00 W
Athalmer	182	50.32 N	116.02 W
Athapapuskow Lake ⊜	184	54.33 N	101.40 W
Athārabānki ≃[1]	126	22.49 N	89.39 E
Athārān Hazāri	123	31.11 N	72.06 E
Athboy	48	53.37 N	6.55 W
Athea	48	52.28 N	9.17 W
Athen → Athínai	38	37.58 N	23.43 E
Athena	202	45.48 N	118.29 W
Athènes → Athínai	38	37.58 N	23.43 E
Athenry	48	53.18 N	8.45 W
Athens, On., Can.	212	44.38 N	75.57 W
Athens → Athínai, Ellás	38	37.58 N	23.43 E
Athens, Al., U.S.	194	34.48 N	86.58 W
Athens, Ga., U.S.	192	33.57 N	83.22 W
Athens, Il., U.S.	219	39.57 N	89.43 W
Athens, La., U.S.	194	32.39 N	93.01 W
Athens, Mi., U.S.	216	42.05 N	85.14 W
Athens, N.Y., U.S.	210	42.15 N	73.48 W
Athens, Oh., U.S.	188	39.19 N	82.06 W
Athens, Pa., U.S.	210	41.57 N	76.31 W
Athens, Tn., U.S.	192	35.26 N	84.35 W
Athens, Tx., U.S.	222	32.12 N	95.51 W
Athens, W.V., U.S.	192	37.25 N	81.00 W
Athens, Wi., U.S.	190	45.01 N	90.04 W
Athenstedt	54	51.56 N	10.55 E
Atherley	212	44.36 N	79.22 W
Atherstone	42	52.35 N	1.31 W
Atherton, Austl.	166	17.16 S	145.29 E
Atherton, Eng., U.K.	262	53.31 N	2.31 W
Atherton, Ca., U.S.	226	37.27 N	122.11 W
Athi ≃	154	2.59 S	38.31 E
Athiaínou	130	35.04 N	33.32 E
Athiémé	150	6.35 N	1.40 E
Athies-sous-Laon	50	49.34 N	3.41 E
Athínai (Athens), Ellás	38	37.58 N	23.43 E
Athínai (Athens), Ellás	267c	37.58 N	23.43 E
Athinisin Panepistimion ❦[2]	267c	37.59 N	23.44 E
Äthiopien → Ethiopia □[1]	144	9.00 N	39.00 E
Athi River	154	1.27 S	36.59 E
Athis-Mons	261	48.43 N	2.24 E
Athlat al-Bāshā ∧[2]	142	27.31 N	32.20 E
Athleague	48	53.34 N	8.15 W
Athlone	48	53.25 N	7.56 W
Athni	122	16.44 N	75.04 E
Athok	110	17.12 N	95.05 E
Athol, N.Z.	172	45.31 S	168.35 E
Athol, Ma., U.S.	207	42.35 N	72.13 W
Athol Bay c	212	43.53 N	77.15 W
Athol Island I	240b	25.05 N	77.16 W
Atholl, Forest of ◆[3]	46	56.50 N	4.00 W
Athol Springs	210	42.46 N	78.52 W
Áthos ∧	38	40.09 N	24.19 E
Ath-Thaʿlah	132	32.42 N	36.26 E
Ath-Thamad	140	29.41 N	34.18 E
Ath-Thanīyah	132	31.10 N	35.43 E
Athus	56	49.34 N	5.50 E
Athy	48	53.00 N	7.00 W
Ati	146	13.13 N	18.20 E
Atiak	154	3.15 N	32.07 E
Atibaia	256	23.07 S	46.33 W
Atibaia ≃	256	22.42 S	47.17 W
Atibainha, Reservatório ⊜[1]	256	23.10 S	46.20 W
Atico	248	16.14 S	73.39 W
Aticonipi, Lac ⊜	186	51.52 N	59.22 W
Atienza	34	41.12 N	2.52 W
Atigun Pass)(	180	68.08 N	149.29 W
Atik Lake ⊜	184	55.16 N	96.00 W
Atikokan	190	48.45 N	91.37 W
Atikonak Lake ⊜	176	52.40 N	64.30 W
Atil	200	30.50 N	111.35 W
Atimonan	116	14.00 N	121.55 E
Atina	66	41.37 N	13.48 E
Atiquizaya	236	13.58 N	89.46 W
Atirāmpattinam	122	10.21 N	79.24 E
Atışalan	267b	41.03 N	28.52 E
Atışmektebi	267b	40.55 N	29.11 E
Atitlán, Lago de ⊜	236	14.42 N	91.12 W
Atitlán, Volcán ∧[1]	236	14.35 N	91.11 W
Atiu I	14	20.02 S	158.07 W
Atka, S.S.S.R.	74	60.50 N	151.48 E
Atka, Ak., U.S.	180	52.12 N	174.12 W
Atka Island I	180	52.15 N	174.30 W
Atkaracalar	130	40.50 N	33.04 E
Atkarsk	80	51.52 N	45.00 E
Atkins	194	35.14 N	92.56 W
Atkinson, Il., U.S.	190	41.25 N	90.00 W
Atkinson, Ne., U.S.	198	42.31 N	98.58 W
Atkinson, N.H., U.S.	207	42.50 N	71.08 W
Atkinson, N.C., U.S.	192	34.31 N	78.10 W
Atkinson Island I	222	29.40 N	94.58 W
Atkinson Lake ⊜	184	55.59 N	94.48 W
Atkri	164	1.44 S	130.04 E
Atlacomulco de Fabela	234	19.48 N	99.53 W
Atlanta, Ga., U.S.	192	33.44 N	84.23 W
Atlanta, Il., U.S.	194	40.15 N	89.14 W
Atlanta, Mi., U.S.	190	45.00 N	84.08 W
Atlanta, Mo., U.S.	194	39.53 N	92.28 W
Atlanta, N.Y., U.S.	210	42.33 N	77.28 W
Atlanta, Oh., U.S.	218	39.34 N	83.11 W
Atlanta, Tx., U.S.	194	33.06 N	94.09 W
Atlantic, Ia., U.S.	198	41.24 N	95.00 W
Atlantic, N.C., U.S.	192	34.53 N	76.20 W
Atlantic, Pa., U.S.	214	41.30 N	80.21 W
Atlantic, Va., U.S.	208	37.54 N	75.30 W
Atlantic □[6]	208	39.27 N	74.44 W
Atlantic Beach, Fl., U.S.	192	30.20 N	81.23 W
Atlantic Beach, N.Y., U.S.	276	40.35 N	73.44 W
Atlantic City	208	39.21 N	74.25 W
Atlantic Highlands	208	40.24 N	74.02 W
Atlantic-Indian Basin ✢[1]	6	60.00 S	15.00 E
Atlantic-Indian Ridge ✢[3]	4	53.00 S	15.00 E
Atlántico □[5]	246	10.45 N	75.00 W
Atlántico, Océano → Atlantic Ocean ⊤[1]	8	5.00 S	25.00 W
Atlantic Ocean ⊤[1]	4	5.00 S	25.00 W
Atlantic Ocean ⊤[1]	8	5.00 S	25.00 W
Atlantic Peak ∧	200	42.37 N	109.00 W
Atlántida	252	34.46 S	55.45 W
Atlántida □[5]	236	15.40 N	87.00 W
Atlantique	276	40.39 N	73.10 W
Atlantique □[5]	150	6.35 N	2.15 E
Atlantique, Océan → Atlantic Ocean ⊤[1]	8	5.00 S	25.00 W
Atlantischer Ozean → Atlantic Ocean ⊤[1]	8	5.00 S	25.00 W
Atlas, Mi., U.S.	216	42.56 N	83.32 W
Atlas, Pa., U.S.	208	40.48 N	76.26 W
Atlasburg	214	40.20 N	80.23 W
Atlas Mountains ⋏	148	33.00 N	2.00 W
Atlasova, ostrov I	74	50.53 N	155.27 E
Atlasovo	92a	46.01 N	142.09 E
Atlas Saharien ⋏	148	33.25 N	1.20 E
Atlas Tellien ⋏	148	36.00 N	3.00 E
Atlin	180	59.35 N	133.42 W
Atlin Lake ⊜	180	59.20 N	133.45 W
ʿAtlit	132	32.41 N	34.56 E
Atlixco	234	18.54 N	98.26 W
Atmakūr	122	15.53 N	78.35 E
Atmanov Ugol	80	53.07 N	41.23 E
Atmis	80	53.28 N	43.57 E
Atmore	194	31.01 N	87.29 W
Ätna → Etna, Monte ∧[1]	70	37.46 N	15.00 E
Atna ≃	26	61.44 N	10.49 E
Atna Peak ∧	182	53.57 N	128.03 W
Atnarko ≃	182	52.22 N	126.04 W
Atnis	86	58.48 N	69.38 E
Atnosen	26	61.44 N	10.49 E
Atō	96	34.24 N	131.43 E
Atocha	248	20.56 S	66.14 W
Atocha, Estación de ◆[5]	266a	40.24 N	3.41 W
Atocongo	286d	12.08 S	76.56 W
Atocongo ⊥	286d	12.12 S	76.55 W
Atoka	196	34.23 N	96.07 W
Atotonilco	234	23.35 N	104.20 W
Atotonilco, Cerro ∧	196	26.08 N	104.43 W
Atotonilco, Lago de ⊜	234	20.22 N	103.39 W
Atotonilco de los Martínez	232	24.15 N	102.45 W
Atotonilco de Tula	234	20.00 N	99.13 W
Atotonilco el Alto	234	20.33 N	102.31 W
Atoui, Khaṭṭ ∨	150	20.04 N	15.59 W
Atoyac	234	20.01 N	103.32 W
Atoyac ≃, Méx.	234	17.05 N	100.29 W
Atoyac ≃, Méx.	234	18.10 N	98.31 W
Atoyac ≃, Méx.	234	16.30 N	97.31 W
Atoyac de Alvarez	234	17.12 N	100.26 W
Atpur	272b	22.50 N	88.23 E
Atrå	26	59.59 N	8.45 E
ʿAṭrah, Jabal ∧	132	29.40 N	35.34 E
Atrai ≃	124	24.29 N	89.03 E
Atrak (Atrek) ≃	128	37.28 N	53.57 E
Ätran ≃	26	56.53 N	12.30 E
Atrato ≃	246	8.17 N	76.58 W
Atrauli	124	28.02 N	78.17 E
Atrek (Atrak) ≃	128	37.28 N	53.57 E
Atri	66	42.35 N	13.58 E
Atripalda	68	40.55 N	14.50 E
Atrisco	200	34.59 N	106.41 W
Atrop	263	51.24 N	6.43 E
Atsion Lake ⊜	285	39.44 N	74.44 W
Atsugi	94	35.27 N	139.22 E
Atsugi-hikōjō ■	94	35.28 N	139.27 E
Atsumi, Nihon	92	38.37 N	139.35 E
Atsumi, Nihon	94	34.37 N	137.07 E
Atsumi-hantō ≻[1]	94	34.39 N	137.15 E
Atta	272a	28.34 N	77.20 E
At-Tabbīn	142	29.47 N	31.18 E
Aṭ-Ṭafīlah	132	30.50 N	35.36 E
At-Tahrīr □[4]	142	30.40 N	30.15 E
Aṭ-Ṭā'if	144	21.16 N	40.24 E
Attainville	261	49.03 N	2.21 E
At-Tāj	146	24.13 N	23.18 E
Aṭ-Ṭalibīyah	273c	30.00 N	31.11 E
At-Tall	132	33.36 N	36.18 E
Attalla	194	34.01 N	86.05 W
At-Tall al-Kabīr	142	30.34 N	31.47 E
At-Ta'mīm □[4]	128	35.25 N	44.20 E
At-Tamīmī	146	32.20 N	23.04 E
Attapu	110	14.48 N	106.50 E
Attar, Oued el ∨	148	33.27 N	5.26 E
At-Taṭālīyah	142	27.20 N	30.50 E
Attáviros ∧, Ellás	38	36.12 N	27.52 E
Attáviros ∧, Tür.	130	36.10 N	27.45 E
Attawapiskat	176	52.55 N	82.26 W
Attawapiskat ≃	176	52.57 N	82.18 W
Attawapiskat Lake ⊜	176	52.18 N	87.54 W
Attawaugan	207	41.52 N	71.52 W
Aṭ-Ṭawd	142	30.47 N	30.37 E
Aṭ-Ṭawīl ⋏	128	29.20 N	39.35 E
Aṭ-Ṭayrīyah	142	30.39 N	30.46 E
At-Taysīyah ≡	128	28.00 N	44.00 E
Aṭ-Ṭayyibah, Miṣr	142	28.16 N	30.39 E
Aṭ-Ṭayyibah, Sūrīy.	132	32.33 N	36.14 E
Aṭ-Ṭayyibah, Sūrīy.	132	32.48 N	36.46 E
Aṭ-Ṭayyibah, Urd.	132	32.33 N	35.43 E
Attel ≃	64	48.01 N	12.11 E
Attendorn	56	51.07 N	7.54 E
Attenhausen	58	47.59 N	10.20 E
Attenkirchen	60	48.30 N	11.46 E
Atterbury	219	40.04 N	89.55 W
Attersee	64	47.55 N	13.33 E
Attersee ⊜	64	47.52 N	13.33 E
Attert ≃	56	49.52 N	6.05 E
Attica, In., U.S.	216	40.17 N	87.14 W
Attica, Ks., U.S.	198	37.14 N	98.13 W
Attica, N.Y., U.S.	210	42.51 N	78.16 W
Attica, Oh., U.S.	214	41.03 N	82.53 W
Attichy	50	49.25 N	3.03 E
Attigliano	66	42.31 N	12.17 E
Attigny	56	49.29 N	4.35 E
Attikí □[5]	267c	38.00 N	23.40 E
Attikí □[9]	38	38.00 N	23.30 E
ʿAttīl	132	32.22 N	35.04 E
Attimis	64	46.11 N	13.16 E
Aṭ-Ṭīnah	142	31.03 N	32.18 E
Attingal	122	8.41 N	76.50 E
Attir	140	6.04 N	30.50 E
Attleboro	207	41.56 N	71.17 W
Attleborough	42	52.31 N	1.01 E
Attnang	60	48.01 N	13.43 E
Attock	123	33.54 N	72.15 E
Attow, Ben ∧	46	57.13 N	5.18 W
Attoyac ≃	194	31.29 N	94.18 W
Attu	181a	52.56 N	173.14 E
At-Tubah	144	12.40 N	43.30 E
Attu Island I	181a	52.55 N	173.00 E
Aṭ-Ṭunayb	132	31.48 N	35.57 E
Āttūr, India	122	11.36 N	78.37 E
Aṭ-Ṭūr, Miṣr	140	28.14 N	33.37 E
Aṭ-Ṭurayf	128	31.44 N	38.33 E
Aṭ-Ṭuwayshah	140	12.21 N	26.32 E
Aṭ-Ṭuwayyah	128	27.36 N	41.13 E
Attymon	48	53.19 N	8.35 W
Atucatiquini ≃	248	7.44 S	67.57 W
Atucha	258	33.58 S	59.18 W
Atuel ≃	252	36.17 S	66.50 W
Atuel, Bañados del ≡	252	36.30 S	66.55 W
Atuntaqui	246	0.20 N	78.13 W
Atuona	174y	9.48 S	139.02 W
At'urjevo	80	54.21 N	43.19 E
Atushi	85	39.43 N	76.08 E
Åtvidaberg	26	58.12 N	16.00 E
Atwater, Sk., Can.	184	50.47 N	102.10 W
Atwater, Ca., U.S.	226	37.20 N	120.36 W
Atwater, Il., U.S.	219	39.20 N	89.44 W
Atwater, Mn., U.S.	198	45.08 N	94.46 W
Atwater, Oh., U.S.	214	41.01 N	81.10 W
Atwood, On., Can.	212	43.40 N	81.01 W
Atwood, Ca., U.S.	280	33.52 N	117.50 W
Atwood, Il., U.S.	194	39.48 N	88.28 W
Atwood, In., U.S.	216	41.15 N	85.58 W
Atwood, Ks., U.S.	198	39.48 N	101.02 W
Atwood, Tn., U.S.	194	35.58 N	88.40 W
Atwood Lake ⊜[1]	214	40.33 N	81.13 W
Atzacán	234	18.54 N	97.05 W
Atzalpur	272a	28.43 N	77.21 E
Atzendorf	54	51.55 N	11.35 E
Atzgersdorf ◆[8]	264b	48.09 N	16.18 E
Au	58	47.19 N	9.59 E
Auagrām	126	23.31 N	87.41 E
Auaiá-Miçu ≃	250	10.51 S	53.08 W
Aua Island I	164	1.27 S	143.04 E
Aual Edo	144	4.14 N	40.37 E
Auari ≃	246	3.33 N	63.48 W
Auati Paraná ≃[1]	246	1.51 S	65.37 W
Auau Channel ʊ	229a	20.51 N	156.45 W
Aub	56	49.33 N	10.04 E
Aubá	112	9.02 S	125.22 E
Aubagne	62	43.17 N	5.34 E
Aubange	56	49.35 N	5.48 E
Aube □[5]	50	48.15 N	4.05 E
Aube ≃	50	48.34 N	3.43 E
Aubenas	62	44.37 N	4.23 E
Aubenton	50	49.50 N	4.12 E
Aubepierre	261	48.38 N	2.53 E
Aubergenville	261	48.58 N	1.51 E
Auberive	58	47.47 N	5.03 E
Auberry	226	37.04 N	119.29 W
Aubervilliers	50	48.55 N	2.23 E
Aubetin ≃	50	48.49 N	3.01 E
Aubette ≃	261	49.00 N	1.54 E
Aubigny-en-Artois	50	50.21 N	2.35 E
Aubigny-sur-Nère	50	47.29 N	2.26 E
Aubin	32	44.32 N	2.14 E
Aubinadong ≃	190	46.51 N	83.22 W
Aubonne	58	46.28 N	6.24 E
Auboué	56	49.13 N	5.59 E
Aubrac ⋏	32	44.40 N	3.00 E
Aubrey Cliffs ⩩[4]	200	35.45 N	113.00 W
Aubrey Lake ⊜[1]	190	46.54 N	83.11 W
Aubrives	56	50.06 N	4.46 E
Aubry Lake ⊜	180	67.23 N	126.30 W
Auburn, Austl.	168b	34.01 S	138.41 E
Auburn, Austl.	274a	33.51 S	151.02 E
Auburn, Al., U.S.	194	32.36 N	85.28 W
Auburn, Ca., U.S.	226	38.53 N	121.04 W
Auburn, Il., U.S.	219	39.35 N	89.44 W
Auburn, In., U.S.	216	41.22 N	85.03 W
Auburn, Ky., U.S.	194	37.02 N	86.54 W
Auburn, Me., U.S.	188	44.05 N	70.13 W
Auburn, Ma., U.S.	207	42.11 N	71.50 W
Auburn, Mi., U.S.	190	43.36 N	84.04 W
Auburn, Ne., U.S.	198	40.23 N	95.50 W
Auburn, N.J., U.S.	285	39.42 N	75.22 W
Auburn, N.Y., U.S.	210	42.55 N	76.33 W
Auburn, Pa., U.S.	208	40.35 N	76.05 W
Auburn, Wa., U.S.	224	47.18 N	122.13 W
Auburn ≃	166	25.38 S	151.12 E
Auburndale, Fl., U.S.	220	28.03 N	81.47 W
Auburndale, Ma., U.S.	283	42.21 N	71.22 W
Auburn Heights	216	42.38 N	83.13 W
Auburn Range ⋏	166	25.10 S	150.30 E
Auburn Ravine ∨	226	38.51 N	121.31 W
Auburn Southeast	210	42.54 N	76.32 W
Aubusson	32	45.57 N	2.11 E
Auby-sur-Semois	56	49.49 N	5.10 E
Auca Mahuida	252	37.53 S	68.31 W
Auca Mahuida, Cerro ∧	252	37.45 S	68.56 W
Aucará	248	14.15 S	74.05 W
Auce	76	56.28 N	22.53 E
Auch	32	43.39 N	0.35 E
Auchel	50	50.30 N	2.28 E
Auchenblae	46	56.54 N	2.26 W
Auchencairn	44	54.51 N	3.53 W
Auchi	150	7.02 N	6.14 E
Auchinleck	44	55.28 N	4.17 W
Auchterarder	46	56.18 N	3.43 W
Auchterderran	46	56.09 N	3.16 W
Auchtermuchty	46	56.17 N	3.15 W
Aucilla ≃	192	30.05 N	83.59 W
Auckland	172	36.52 S	174.46 E
Auckland Islands II	9	50.40 S	166.30 E
Auckland Park ◆[8]	273d	26.11 S	28.00 E
Auckland Park Race Course ♦	273d	26.11 S	28.00 E
Aude □[5]	32	43.05 N	2.30 E
Aude ≃	32	43.13 N	3.14 E
Audenge	32	44.41 N	1.00 W
Audenshaw	262	53.28 N	2.08 W
Audenshaw Reservoirs ⊜[1]	262	53.28 N	2.08 W
Auderghem	50	50.49 N	4.26 E
Audeux	58	47.16 N	5.53 E
Audierne	32	48.01 N	4.32 W
Audincourt	58	47.29 N	6.50 E
Audley	44	53.03 N	2.18 W
Audobon Park	285	39.54 N	75.05 W
Audo Range ⋏	144	6.30 N	41.30 E
Audrain □[6]	219	39.12 N	91.50 W
Audresselles	50	50.49 N	1.36 E
Audruicq	50	50.53 N	2.05 E
Audubon, Ia., U.S.	198	41.43 N	94.55 W
Audubon, N.J., U.S.	208	39.53 N	75.04 W
Audubon, Pa., U.S.	285	40.07 N	75.27 W
Audubon Lake ⊜[1]	198	47.35 N	101.10 W
Audubon Park	218	38.12 N	85.43 W
Audun-le-Roman	56	49.22 N	5.53 E
Aue	54	50.35 N	12.42 E
Aue ≃	52	53.05 N	8.04 E
Auer → Ora	64	46.21 N	11.18 E
Auerbach, B.R.D.	60	48.48 N	13.06 E
Auerbach, D.D.R.	54	50.41 N	12.54 E
Auerbach, D.D.R.	54	50.30 N	12.23 E
Auerbach in der Oberpfalz	60	49.42 N	11.38 E
Auersberg ∧	54	50.27 N	12.39 E
Auerswalde	54	50.54 N	12.55 E
Auezov	86	49.46 N	81.38 E
Auf dem Kreinberge	263	51.27 N	7.36 E
Auf dem Schnee ◆[8]	263	51.26 N	7.25 E
Auffargis	261	48.42 N	1.53 E
Auffay	50	49.43 N	1.06 E
Aufsess	60	49.54 N	11.13 E
Augarten ♦	264b	48.14 N	16.23 E
Augathella	166	25.48 S	146.35 E
Augher	48	54.26 N	7.09 W
Aughnacloy	48	54.25 N	6.58 W
Aughrim	48	52.51 N	6.17 W
Aughton, Eng., U.K.	44	53.22 N	1.18 W
Aughton, Eng., U.K.	262	53.32 N	2.56 W
Aughton Park	262	53.33 N	2.53 W
Aughwick Creek ≃	214	40.22 N	77.50 W
Auglaize □[6]	216	40.34 N	84.12 W
Auglaize ≃	216	41.17 N	84.21 W
Augrabies	158	28.37 S	20.20 E
Augrabies Falls National Park ♦	158	28.35 S	20.19 E
Augrabiesvalle ∟	158	28.35 S	20.19 E
Au Gres	190	44.02 N	83.41 W
Au Gres ≃	190	44.02 N	83.40 W
Au Gres, East Branch ≃	190	44.05 N	83.41 W
Augsburg	58	48.23 N	10.53 E
Augusta, Austl.	162	34.19 S	115.10 E
Augusta, It.	70	37.13 N	15.13 E
Augusta, Ar., U.S.	194	35.16 N	91.21 W
Augusta, Ga., U.S.	192	33.28 N	82.01 W
Augusta, Il., U.S.	194	40.13 N	90.57 W
Augusta, Ks., U.S.	198	37.41 N	97.58 W
Augusta, Ky., U.S.	218	38.46 N	84.00 W
Augusta, Me., U.S.	188	44.18 N	69.46 W
Augusta, Mi., U.S.	216	42.20 N	85.21 W
Augusta, Mo., U.S.	219	38.34 N	90.53 W
Augusta, Mt., U.S.	202	47.29 N	112.23 W
Augusta, N.J., U.S.	210	41.07 N	74.43 W
Augusta, Oh., U.S.	214	40.41 N	81.01 W
Augusta, Wi., U.S.	190	44.40 N	91.07 W
Augusta, Golfo di c	70	37.12 N	15.13 E
Augustdorf	52	51.53 N	8.43 E
Augustenborg	41	54.57 N	9.53 E
Augustine Island I	180	59.22 N	153.28 W
Augusto Severo	250	5.52 S	37.19 W
Augustów	30	53.51 N	22.59 E
Augustowski, Kanał ≅	76	53.54 N	23.26 E
Augustus, Mount ∧	162	24.20 S	116.50 E
Augustusburg	54	50.49 N	13.06 E
Augustus Downs	166	18.33 S	139.52 E
Augustus Island I	164	15.20 S	124.30 E
Auiia, Ribeirão ≃	255	12.09 S	53.20 W
Au in der Hallertau	60	48.33 N	11.45 E
Aujon ≃	58	48.09 N	4.48 E
Auki	175e	8.46 S	160.42 E
Aulander	192	36.13 N	77.06 W
Aulanko	26	61.02 N	24.27 E
Auld, Lake ⊜	162	22.32 S	123.44 E
Auldearn	46	57.34 N	3.49 W
Aulendorf	58	47.57 N	9.38 E
Aulestad	26	61.13 N	10.17 E
Auletta	68	40.34 N	15.25 E
Aulís ⊥	38	38.27 N	23.35 E
Aulla	64	44.12 N	9.58 E
Aulnay	32	46.01 N	0.21 W
Aulnay-sous-Bois	50	48.57 N	2.31 E
Aulnay-sur-Mauldre	261	48.56 N	1.51 E
Aulne ≃	32	48.17 N	4.16 W
Aulneau Peninsula ≻[1]	184	49.23 N	94.29 W
Aulnois-sur-Seille	56	48.52 N	6.19 E
Aulnoye-Aymeries	50	50.12 N	3.50 E
Ault, Fr.	50	50.06 N	1.27 E
Ault, Co., U.S.	200	40.34 N	104.43 W
Ault, Ky., U.S.	218	38.12 N	83.14 W
Aultbea	46	57.50 N	5.35 W
Aultman	214	40.34 N	79.16 W
Aultshire	216	40.13 N	85.19 W
Auma	54	50.42 N	11.54 E
Aumale	50	49.46 N	1.45 E
Auma Point ≻	164	7.55 S	145.25 E
Aumetz	56	49.25 N	5.56 E
Aumont-Aubrac	32	44.43 N	3.17 E
Aumühle	52	53.31 N	10.19 E
Auna	150	10.12 N	4.45 E
Auneau	50	48.27 N	1.46 E
Auneuil	50	49.22 N	2.00 E
Auning	26	56.26 N	10.23 E
Auno	146	11.50 N	12.53 E
Aunuu I	174u	14.17 S	170.33 W
Auob ≃	156	26.25 S	20.35 E
Auponhia	112	1.56 S	125.29 E
Aups	62	43.37 N	6.14 E
Aur, Pulau I	112	2.27 N	104.31 E
Aura	26	60.36 N	22.34 E
Aurach	56	49.15 N	10.25 E
Aurach ≃	56	49.34 N	10.59 E
Aurachmat	85	41.34 N	70.07 E
Auraiya	124	26.28 N	79.31 E
Aurangābād, India	122	19.53 N	75.20 E
Aurangābād, India	124	24.45 N	84.22 E
Auray	32	47.40 N	2.59 W
Aurdal	26	60.56 N	9.24 E
Aure	26	63.16 N	8.32 E
Aurelia	198	42.42 N	95.26 W
Aurelius	216	42.31 N	84.31 W
Aurès, Massif de l' ⋏	148	35.08 N	6.30 E
Auri, Kepulauan II	164	1.59 S	134.42 E
Aurich	52	53.28 N	7.29 E
Auriesville Shrine ❦[1]	210	42.54 N	74.19 W
Auriflama	255	20.41 S	50.34 W
Aurigny → Alderney I	43b	49.43 N	2.12 W
Aurilândia	255	16.44 S	50.28 W
Aurillac	32	44.56 N	2.26 E
Aurina, Valle ∨	64	47.00 N	12.00 E
Aurine, Alpi (Zillertaler Alpen) ⋏	64	47.00 N	11.55 E
Aurino ≃	64	46.48 N	11.55 E
Auriol	62	43.23 N	5.38 E
Aurisina	64	45.45 N	13.41 E
Aurizona	250	1.17 S	45.46 W
Aurlandsfjorden c[2]	26	61.05 N	7.02 E
Aurlandsvangen	26	60.54 N	7.11 E
Aurolzmünster	60	48.15 N	13.27 E
Auron	62	44.14 N	6.56 E
Auronzo di Cadore	64	46.33 N	12.26 E
Aurora, Bra.	250	6.57 S	38.58 W
Aurora, Bra.	287a	22.46 S	43.24 W
Aurora, On., Can.	212	44.00 N	79.28 W
Aurora, S. Afr.	158	32.42 S	18.29 E
Aurora, Co., U.S.	200	39.43 N	104.49 W
Aurora, Il., U.S.	216	41.45 N	88.19 W
Aurora, In., U.S.	218	39.03 N	84.54 W
Aurora, Me., U.S.	188	44.51 N	68.19 W
Aurora, Mn., U.S.	190	47.31 N	92.14 W
Aurora, Mo., U.S.	194	36.58 N	93.43 W
Aurora, Ne., U.S.	198	40.52 N	98.00 W
Aurora, N.Y., U.S.	210	42.45 N	76.42 W
Aurora, N.C., U.S.	192	35.18 N	76.47 W
Aurora, Oh., U.S.	214	41.19 N	81.20 W
Aurora, Or., U.S.	224	45.13 N	122.45 W
Aurora, Ut,. U.S.	200	38.55 N	111.56 W
Aurora, W.V., U.S.	188	39.19 N	79.33 W
Aurora ❦	265a	59.57 N	30.21 E
Aurora do Norte	255	12.43 S	46.24 W
Aurora Pond ⊜	279a	41.20 N	81.23 W
Auroux	62	44.45 N	3.44 E
Aursunden ⊜	26	62.40 N	11.40 E
Aurukun Mission	164	13.19 S	141.45 E
Aurunci, Monti ⋏	66	41.22 N	13.40 E
Aus	156	26.40 S	16.15 E
Ausable ≃, On., Can.	190	43.19 N	81.46 W
Au Sable ≃, Mi., U.S.	190	44.25 N	83.20 W
Au Sable, North Branch ≃	190	44.40 N	84.23 W
Au Sable, South Branch ≃	190	44.40 N	84.23 W
Au Sable Forks	188	44.26 N	73.40 W
Au Sable Point ≻	190	44.20 N	83.20 W
Auschwitz → Oświęcim	30	50.03 N	19.12 E
Ausevik ⊥	26	61.32 N	5.16 E
Auskerry I	46	59.02 N	2.34 W
Ausoni, Monti ⋏	66	41.25 N	13.20 E
Ausserferrera	58	46.33 N	9.26 E
Ausserfragant	64	46.56 N	13.06 E
Aussig → Ústí nad Labem	54	50.40 N	14.02 E
Aussois	62	45.14 N	6.45 E
Aust-Agder □[6]	26	58.50 N	8.00 E
Austerlitz → Slavkov u Brna	61	49.09 N	16.52 E
Austerlitz, Ned.	52	52.05 N	5.19 E
Austerlitz, N.Y., U.S.	210	42.19 N	73.28 W
Austerlitz ◆[5]	261	48.50 N	2.22 E
Austin, Bra.	287a	22.43 S	43.32 W
Austin, Mb., Can.	184	49.57 N	98.56 W
Austin, In., U.S.	218	38.45 N	85.48 W
Austin, Mn., U.S.	190	43.40 N	92.58 W
Austin, Nv., U.S.	204	39.29 N	117.04 W
Austin, Pa., U.S.	214	41.37 N	78.05 W
Austin, Tx., U.S.	222	30.16 N	97.44 W
Austin □[6]	222	29.53 N	96.15 W
Austin ◆[8]	278	41.54 N	87.45 W
Austin, Lake ⊜	162	27.40 S	118.00 E
Austin, Lake ⊜[1]	222	30.19 N	97.46 W
Austin Bayou ≃	222	29.07 N	95.18 W
Austinburg	214	41.46 N	80.51 W
Austin Channel ʊ	176	75.35 N	103.25 W
Austin Lake ⊜	216	42.11 N	85.33 W
Austinmer	170	34.18 S	150.56 E
Austin's Post	158	29.32 S	25.49 E
Austintown	214	41.06 N	80.45 W
Austinville	192	36.51 N	80.54 W
Austnes	26	62.38 N	6.16 E
Austonio	222	31.11 N	95.38 W
Austonley	262	53.34 N	1.50 W
Austral	274a	33.56 S	150.48 E
Australes, Îles II	14	23.00 S	150.00 W
Australia □[1]	160	25.00 S	135.00 E
Australia Mountain ∧	180	63.36 N	138.08 W
Australian-Antarctic Rise ✢[3]	9	50.00 S	130.00 E
Australian Capital Territory □[8]	171b	35.30 S	149.00 E
Australian War Memorial ⊥	171b	35.17 S	149.09 E
Australia Plains	168b	34.06 S	139.09 E
Australie → Australia □[1]	160	25.00 S	135.00 E
Australien → Australia □[1]	160	25.00 S	135.00 E
Australind	168a	33.16 S	115.44 E
Austral Seamounts ✢[3]	14	22.40 S	152.45 W
Austråt	26	63.43 N	9.45 E
Austria (Österreich) □[1], Europe	22	47.20 N	13.20 E
Austria (Österreich) □[1], Europe	30	47.20 N	13.20 E
Austvågøya I	24	68.20 N	14.36 E
Autazes	246	3.35 S	59.08 W
Auteuil, Fr.	50	49.21 N	2.05 E
Auteuil, Fr.	261	48.50 N	1.49 E
Autheuil	50	49.06 N	1.17 E
Authie ≃	50	50.21 N	1.38 E
Authon	62	44.14 N	6.08 E
Authon-du-Perche	50	48.12 N	0.55 E
Authon-la-Plaine	50	48.27 N	1.57 E
Auth Village	284c	38.49 N	76.55 W
Autlán de Navarro	234	19.46 N	104.22 W
Autore, Monte ∧	66	41.58 N	13.12 E
Autrey-lès-Gray	58	47.29 N	5.30 E
Autriche → Austria □[1]	30	47.20 N	13.20 E
Autumn Hill	284b	39.16 N	76.48 W
Autun	32	46.57 N	4.18 E
Auve	56	49.02 N	4.42 E
Auvergne	164	15.41 S	130.01 E
Auvergne □[9]	32	45.25 N	2.30 E
Auvernaux	261	48.32 N	2.30 E
Auvers-sur-Oise	50	49.04 N	2.10 E
Auvézère ≃	32	45.12 N	0.51 E
Aux Cayes → Les Cayes	238	18.12 N	73.45 W
Auxerre	50	47.48 N	3.34 E
Auxier	192	37.44 N	82.45 W
Auxi-le-Château	50	50.14 N	2.07 E
Auxon	50	48.06 N	3.55 E
Auxonne	58	47.12 N	5.23 E
Aux Sable Creek ≃	216	41.23 N	88.20 W
Auxvasse	219	39.01 N	91.53 W
Auxvasse Creek ≃	219	38.41 N	91.49 W
Auxy	58	46.57 N	4.24 E
Auyamita, Quebrada ≃	286c	10.30 N	66.46 W
Auyán Tepuy ∧	246	5.55 N	62.32 W
Auzances	32	46.02 N	2.30 E
Auzangate, Nevado ∧	248	13.48 S	71.14 W
Auzon ≃, Fr.	58	48.00 N	4.20 E
Auzon ≃, Fr.	62	44.02 N	4.54 E
Ava, Il., U.S.	194	37.53 N	89.29 W
Ava, Mo., U.S.	194	36.57 N	92.39 W
Avadchara	84	43.31 N	40.39 E
Avadh Plains ≡	124	26.20 N	82.00 E
Avai	255	22.08 S	49.22 W
Avakubi	154	1.20 N	27.34 E
Aval'	85	40.19 N	71.50 E
Aval, Falaise d' ⩩[4]	50	49.45 N	0.10 E
Avala ⊥	38	44.45 N	20.35 E
Avaldsnes	26	59.21 N	5.16 E
Avallon	50	47.29 N	3.54 E
Avaloirs, Les ∧[2]	32	48.28 N	0.07 W
Avalon, Ca., U.S.	228	33.20 N	118.19 W
Avalon, N.J., U.S.	208	39.06 N	74.43 W
Avalon, Pa., U.S.	214	40.30 N	80.04 W
Avalon, Tx., U.S.	222	32.12 N	96.48 W
Avalon, Wi., U.S.	216	42.38 N	88.52 W
Avalon Peninsula ≻[1]	186	47.30 N	53.30 W
Avana ≃	174k	21.14 S	159.43 W
Avanley	262	53.16 N	2.45 W
Avanos	130	38.43 N	34.51 E
Avant	196	36.29 N	96.03 W
Avaré	255	23.05 S	48.55 W
Avarskoje Kojsu ≃	84	42.47 N	46.48 E
Avarua	174k	21.12 S	159.46 W
Avarua Harbour c	174k	21.11 S	159.46 W
Avatanak Island I	180	54.03 N	165.19 W
Avatele	174v	19.06 S	169.55 W
Avatele Bay c	174v	19.05 S	169.56 W
Avatiu	174k	21.12 S	159.47 W
Avatiu Harbour c	174k	21.11 S	159.47 W
Avčala	84	41.48 N	44.48 E
ʿAvdat ⊥	132	30.48 N	34.46 E
Avdejevka	83	48.08 N	37.46 E
Avdotjino	83	47.55 N	37.51 E
Ave ≃	34	41.20 N	8.45 W
Avebury	42	51.27 N	1.51 W
Avebury Stone Circle ⊥	42	51.28 N	1.51 W
Avegbadje ∧	150	7.14 N	0.38 E
Aveiro, Bra.	250	3.15 S	55.10 W
Aveiro, Port.	34	40.38 N	8.39 W
Aveiro, Ria de ≃[1]	34	40.38 N	8.44 W
Āvej	128	35.34 N	49.13 E
Avelar	256	22.20 S	43.25 W
Avelengo	64	46.38 N	11.13 E
Aveley	260	51.30 N	0.16 E
Avelgem	50	50.46 N	3.26 E
Avella, It.	68	40.58 N	14.36 E
Avella, Pa., U.S.	214	40.16 N	80.27 W
Avellaneda, Arg.	252	29.07 S	59.40 W
Avellaneda, Arg.	258	34.39 S	58.23 W
Avellaneda □[5]	288	34.40 S	58.20 W
Avellaneda, Estacion ◆[5]	288	34.41 S	58.22 W
Avelle, Île I	275a	45.24 N	74.00 W
Avellino	68	40.54 N	14.47 E
Avellino □[4], It.	68	41.00 N	15.10 E
Avellino □[4], It.	68	40.57 N	15.00 E
Avenal	226	36.00 N	120.07 W
Avenal Creek ≃	226	35.47 N	120.04 W
Aven Armand ⩩[5]	32	44.15 N	3.22 E
Avenas	58	46.12 N	4.37 E
Avenches	58	46.53 N	7.02 E
Avenel	276	40.34 N	74.17 W
Aventureiro, Rio do ≃	256	21.52 S	42.39 W
Avenue	208	38.15 N	76.46 W
Avenwedde	52	51.55 N	8.27 E
Averbode	56	51.02 N	4.59 E
Averbode, Abbaye d' ❦[1]	56	51.02 N	4.59 E
Averill Lake ⊜	206	44.59 N	71.44 W
Averill Park	210	42.38 N	73.33 W
Avern ⊜	40	58.54 N	15.32 E
Avernakø I	41	55.01 N	10.17 E
Avernes	261	49.05 N	1.52 E
Avernes, Rû des ≃	261	49.04 N	2.51 E
Averøya I	26	63.01 N	7.34 E
Aversa	68	40.58 N	14.12 E
Avery, Ca., U.S.	226	38.13 N	120.22 W
Avery, Id., U.S.	202	47.15 N	115.48 W
Avery, Tx., U.S.	194	33.33 N	94.47 W
Avery Island	194	29.54 N	91.54 W
Aves, Isla de I	238	15.42 N	63.38 W
Aves, Islas de II	246	12.00 N	67.30 W
Avesnelles	50	50.07 N	3.57 E
Avesnes	32	50.07 N	3.56 E
Avesnes-le-Comte	50	50.17 N	2.32 E
Avesnes-lès-Aubert	50	50.12 N	3.23 E
Avesnes-sur-Helpe	50	50.07 N	3.56 E
Avesta	40	60.09 N	16.12 E
Aveto ≃	62	44.42 N	9.23 E
Avetrana	68	40.21 N	17.43 E
Aveyron □[5]	32	44.15 N	2.40 E
Aveyron ≃	32	44.05 N	1.16 E
Avezzano	66	42.02 N	13.25 E
Avgustovka	80	52.16 N	50.44 E
Aviano	64	46.04 N	12.36 E
Avich, Loch ⊜	46	56.16 N	5.20 W
Aviemore	46	57.12 N	3.50 W
Avigliana	62	45.05 N	7.23 E
Avigliano	68	40.44 N	15.44 E
Avignon	62	43.57 N	4.49 E
Ávila	34	40.39 N	4.42 W
Ávila, Sierra de ⋏	34	40.35 N	5.08 W
Avila Beach	226	35.10 N	120.43 W
Avilés	34	43.33 N	5.55 W
Avilla	216	41.22 N	85.14 W
Avilley	58	47.26 N	6.16 E
Avinger	222	32.54 N	94.33 W
Avinurme	76	58.59 N	26.51 E
Avio	64	45.44 N	10.56 E
Avion	50	50.24 N	2.50 E
Avioth	56	49.34 N	5.24 E
Avis	210	41.11 N	77.18 W
Avisio ≃	64	46.07 N	11.05 E
Avispa, Cerro ∧	246	1.16 N	65.51 W
Aviston	219	38.36 N	89.36 W
Aviz	34	39.03 N	7.53 W
Avize	50	48.58 N	4.01 E
Avlan Gölü ⊜	130	36.34 N	29.57 E
Avlum	41	56.16 N	8.48 E
Avnbøl	41	54.58 N	9.39 E
Avnik	130	39.50 N	41.59 E
Avoca, Austl.	169	37.05 S	143.28 E
Avoca, Ia., U.S.	198	41.28 N	95.20 W
Avoca, N.Y., U.S.	210	42.24 N	77.25 W
Avoca, Pa., U.S.	210	41.20 N	75.44 W
Avoca ≃, Austl.	166	35.42 S	143.44 E
Avoca ≃, Ire.	48	52.48 N	6.09 W
Avoca, Mount ∧	169	37.07 S	143.21 E
Avoca Beach	170	33.29 S	151.29 E
Avocado Heights	280	34.08 N	117.54 W
Avola, B.C., Can.	182	51.47 N	119.19 W
Avola, It.	70	36.54 N	15.08 E
Avon, Austl.	168b	34.17 S	138.20 E
Avon, Fr.	50	48.24 N	2.43 E
Avon, Ct., U.S.	207	41.48 N	72.49 W
Avon, Il., U.S.	190	40.39 N	90.26 W
Avon, Ma., U.S.	207	42.07 N	71.02 W
Avon, Mn., U.S.	190	45.36 N	94.27 W
Avon, Mt., U.S.	202	46.35 N	112.36 W
Avon, N.Y., U.S.	210	42.54 N	77.44 W
Avon, N.C., U.S.	192	35.21 N	75.30 W
Avon, Oh., U.S.	214	41.27 N	82.02 W
Avon, Pa., U.S.	208	40.22 N	76.23 W
Avon, S.D., U.S.	198	43.00 N	98.03 W
Avon □[6]	42	51.30 N	2.40 W
Avon ≃, Austl.	168a	31.40 S	116.07 E
Avon ≃, N.S., Can.	186	45.10 N	64.15 W
Avon ≃, On., Can.	212	43.18 N	81.11 W
Avon ≃, Eng., U.K.	42	51.30 N	2.43 W
Avon ≃, Eng., U.K.	42	50.17 N	3.52 W
Avon ≃, Eng., U.K.	42	50.43 N	1.46 W
Avon ≃, Eng., U.K.	42	52.25 N	1.31 W
Avon ≃, Eng., U.K.	42	51.59 N	2.10 W
Avon ≃, Scot., U.K.	46	56.01 N	3.40 W
Avon ≃, Scot., U.K.	46	57.25 N	3.23 W
Avon, Ben ∧	46	57.05 N	3.27 W
Avon, Rû d' ≃	261	48.39 N	2.46 E
Avon Basin c	279a	41.30 N	82.03 W
Avon by the Sea	208	40.11 N	74.00 W
Avondale, Az., U.S.	200	33.26 N	112.20 W
Avondale, Co., U.S.	198	38.14 N	104.21 W
Avondale, Md., U.S.	284c	38.56 N	76.59 W
Avondale, Oh., U.S.	214	39.47 N	84.08 W
Avondale Heights	274b	37.46 S	144.51 E
Avon Downs	166	20.05 S	137.30 E
Avondrust	158	34.21 S	21.51 E
Avon Lake	214	41.30 N	82.01 W
Avonlea	184	50.00 N	105.04 W
Avonmore, On., Can.	206	45.10 N	74.58 W
Avonmore, Pa., U.S.	214	40.31 N	79.27 W
Avonmore ≃	48	52.50 N	6.13 W
Avonmouth	42	51.31 N	2.42 W
Avon Park	220	27.35 N	81.30 W
Avon Reservoir ⊜[1]	170	34.24 S	150.40 E
Avontuur	158	33.44 S	23.11 E
Avon Water ≃	46	55.47 N	4.01 W
Avoudrey	58	47.08 N	6.26 E
Avrainville	261	48.34 N	2.15 E
Avranches	32	48.41 N	1.22 W
Avranlo	84	41.39 N	43.52 E
Avre ≃, Fr.	50	49.53 N	2.20 E
Avre ≃, Fr.	50	48.47 N	1.22 E
Avrieux	62	45.13 N	6.43 E
Avroult	50	50.38 N	2.09 E
Avtatkuul' ≃	180	64.06 N	178.10 E
Avtovo ◆[8]	265a	59.52 N	30.15 E
Avu Avu	175e	9.50 S	160.23 E
Awa, Nihon	96	34.04 N	134.12 E
Awa, Nihon	174m	26.36 N	127.56 E
Awaba	170	33.01 S	151.33 E
Aʿwaj, Nahr al- ≃	132	33.20 N	36.34 E
Awaji	96	34.35 N	135.01 E
Awaji-shima I	96	34.21 N	134.51 E
Awakino	172	38.39 S	174.38 E
ʿAwālī	128	26.05 N	50.33 E
Awang	115b	8.54 S	116.24 E
Awano	94	36.31 N	139.41 E
Awanui	172	35.03 S	173.15 E
Awara	94	36.13 N	136.12 E
Awarawar, Tanjung ≻	115a	6.45 S	111.56 E
Aware	144	8.15 N	44.10 E
Awarua Point ≻	172	44.15 S	168.03 E
Awasa	144	6.45 N	38.15 E
Awasa, Lake ⊜	144	7.05 N	38.25 E
Awasan Bay c	116	9.56 N	125.36 E
Awash	144	8.59 N	40.10 E
Awash ≃	144	11.45 N	41.05 E
Awa-shima I, Nihon	92	38.27 N	139.14 E
Awa-shima I, Nihon	96	34.16 N	133.38 E
Awash National Park ♦	144	9.05 N	40.00 E
Awaso	150	6.14 N	2.16 W
Awatere ≃	172	41.37 S	174.10 E
Awbārī	146	26.35 N	12.46 E
Awbārī, Ṣaḥrā' ⩩[8]	146	28.00 N	11.30 E
Awdheegle	144	1.59 N	44.50 E
Awe	150	8.09 N	9.07 E
Awe, Loch ⊜	46	56.15 N	5.17 W
Awegyun	110	12.44 N	98.44 E
Awgu	150	6.04 N	7.29 E
Awīn	267d	35.48 N	51.24 E
Awīsh al-Ḥajar	142	31.01 N	31.19 E
ʿAwjā', Wādī al- ∨	132	31.56 N	35.31 E
Awjilah	146	29.09 N	21.15 E
Awka	150	6.12 N	7.05 E
Awlād Mūsā	142	30.48 N	31.44 E

	English	Deutsch	Español	Français	Português
≃	River	Fluss	Río	Rivière	Rio
≅	Canal	Kanal	Canal	Canal	Canal
∟	Waterfall, Rapids	Wasserfall, Stromschnellen	Cascada, Rápidos	Chute d'eau, Rapides	Cascata, Rápidos
ʊ	Strait	Meeresstrasse	Estrecho	Détroit	Estreito
c	Bay, Gulf	Bucht, Golf	Bahía, Golfo	Baie, Golfe	Baía, Golfo
⊜	Lake, Lakes	See, Seen	Lago, Lagos	Lac, Lacs	Lago, Lagos
≡	Swamp	Sumpf	Pantano	Marais	Pântano
⊓	Ice Features, Glacier	Eis- und Gletscherformen	Accidentes Glaciales	Formes glaciaires	Acidentes glaciares
⊤	Other Hydrographic Features	Andere Hydrographische Objekte	Otros Elementos Hidrográficos	Autres données hydrographiques	Outros acidentes hidrográficos
✢	Submarine Features	Untermeerische Objekte	Accidentes Submarinos	Formes de relief sous-marin	Acidentes submarinos
□	Political Unit	Politische Einheit	Unidad Politica	Entité politique	Unidade política
❦	Cultural Institution	Kulturelle Institution	Institución Cultural	Institution culturelle	Institução cultural
⊥	Historical Site	Historische Stätte	Sitio Histórico	Site historique	Sitio histórico
♦	Recreational Site	Erholungs- und Ferienort	Sitio de Recreo	Centre de loisirs	Area de Lazer
⊠	Airport	Flughafen	Aeropuerto	Aéroport	Aeroporto
■	Military Installation	Militäranlage	Instalación Militar	Installation militaire	Instalação militar
◆	Miscellaneous	Verschiedenes	Misceláneo	Divers	Diversos

ENGLISH / DEUTSCH

Name	Page	Lat.°′	Long.°′
Awled Djellal	148	34.28 N	5.02 E
Awlef	148	26.58 N	1.05 E
Aworo Kit	140	10.59 N	32.38 E
Aworro	164	7.45 S	143.10 E
Awosting	276	41.09 N	74.20 W
Awsīm	273c	30.07 N	31.08 E
Awul	164	6.00 S	151.00 E
Awuna ≃	180	69.04 N	155.30 W
Awwal, Ash-Shallāl al- (First Cataract) ʟ	140	24.01 N	32.52 E
Axams	64	47.14 N	11.18 E
Axarfjörđur c	24a	66.15 N	16.45 W
Axat	32	42.48 N	2.14 E
Axbridge	42	51.18 N	2.49 W
Axe ≃, Eng., U.K.	42	51.19 N	2.59 W
Axe ≃, Eng., U.K.	42	50.42 N	3.03 W
Axe Creek ≃	169	36.46 S	144.30 E
Axedale	169	36.47 S	144.30 E
Axe Edge ⋏[2]	262	53.14 N	1.57 W
Axel	52	51.16 N	3.55 E
Axel Heiberg Island I	16	79.45 N	91.00 W
Axim	150	4.52 N	2.14 W
Axinim	246	4.02 S	59.22 W
Axiós (Vardar) ≃	38	40.35 N	22.50 E
Axis	194	30.55 N	88.01 W
Axixá	250	2.51 S	44.04 W
Ax-les-Thermes	32	42.43 N	1.50 E
Axminster	42	50.47 N	3.00 W
Axmouth	42	50.42 N	3.02 W
Axochiapan	234	18.30 N	98.46 W
Axtell, Ks., U.S.	198	39.52 N	96.15 W
Axtell, Ne., U.S.	198	40.28 N	99.07 W
Axtell, Tx., U.S.	222	31.39 N	96.58 W
Aÿ	50	49.03 N	4.00 E
Ayabaca	246	4.38 S	79.43 W
Ayabe	96	35.18 N	135.15 E
Ayachi, Ari n' ∧	148	32.29 N	4.57 W
Ayacucho, Arg.	252	37.09 S	58.29 W
Ayacucho, Bol.	248	17.51 S	63.20 W
Ayacucho, Perú	248	13.07 S	74.13 W
Ayacucho □[5]	248	14.00 S	74.00 W
Ayagekumuhu ◎	120	37.33 N	89.15 E
Ayamé	150	5.37 N	3.11 W
Ayamiken	152	2.07 N	10.01 E
Ayamonte	34	37.13 N	7.24 W
Āyān	272b	22.43 N	88.09 E
Ayancık	130	41.57 N	34.36 E
Ayangba	150	7.30 N	7.08 E
Ayapel	246	8.19 N	75.09 W
Ayarza, Laguna de ◎	236	14.25 N	90.08 W
Ayas, It.	62	45.50 N	7.41 E
Ayaş, Tür.	130	40.01 N	32.21 E
Ayase	94	35.26 N	139.26 E
Ayase ≃	268	35.45 N	139.49 E
Ayaviri	248	14.52 S	70.35 W
Ayaviri ≃	248	15.01 S	70.22 W
Ayazağa	267b	41.06 N	28.59 E
Āybak	120	36.16 N	68.01 E
Ayden	192	35.28 N	77.24 W
Aydere	128	38.24 N	56.45 E
Aydın	130	37.51 N	27.51 E
Aydın □[4]	130	37.45 N	28.00 E
Aydıncık	130	36.08 N	33.19 E
Aydın Dağları ⋏	130	38.00 N	28.00 E
Aydin Ula ∧	86	42.55 N	87.35 E
Aydos Dağı ∧	267b	40.56 N	29.15 E
Ayelu ∧	144	10.04 N	40.46 E
Ayer, Schw.	58	46.11 N	7.36 E
Ayer, Ma., U.S.	207	42.33 N	71.35 W
Ayer Baloi	114	1.35 N	103.20 E
Ayer Chawan, Pulau I	271c	1.17 N	103.42 E
Ayer Hitam, Malay.	114	1.55 N	103.11 E
Ayer Hitam, Malay.	114	2.56 N	102.24 E
Ayer Jerneh	114	4.24 N	103.24 E
Ayer Kuning Selatan	114	2.30 N	102.28 E
Ayer Merbau, Pulau I	271c	1.16 N	103.43 E
Ayers Cliff	206	45.10 N	72.03 W
Ayers Rock ∧	162	25.23 S	131.05 E
Ayersville	216	41.14 N	84.17 W
Ayía Marína	38	37.09 N	26.52 E
Ayía Paraskeví, Ellás	38	39.15 N	26.16 E
Ayía Paraskeví, Ellás	267c	38.01 N	23.50 E
Ayiássos	38	39.05 N	26.23 E
Ayía Varvára	267c	37.59 N	23.39 E
Ayina ≃	152	1.48 N	13.10 E
Ayınkâf	130	37.34 N	41.10 E
Áyioi Anáryiroi	267c	38.02 N	23.43 E
Áyion Óros ›[1]	38	40.15 N	24.15 E
Áyios Dhimítrios	267c	37.56 N	23.44 E
Áyios Evstrátios I	38	39.31 N	25.00 E
Áyios Ioánnis Réndis	267c	37.58 N	23.40 E
Áyios Kírikos	38	37.37 N	26.14 E
Áyios Nikólaos	38	35.11 N	25.42 E
Ayíou Nikoláou, Moní ɤ[1]	267c	37.53 N	23.27 E
Ayíou Órous, Kólpos c	38	40.12 N	24.03 E
Ayl	132	30.13 N	35.32 E
Aylesbury	42	51.50 N	0.50 W
Aylesford	260	51.18 N	0.29 E
Aylesham	42	51.13 N	1.13 E
Aylmer	188	45.26 N	75.50 W
Aylmer, Lake ◎	206	45.50 N	71.22 W
Aylmer, Mount ∧	182	51.19 N	115.26 W
Aylmer-East	212	45.26 N	75.50 W
Aylmer Lake ◎	176	64.05 N	108.30 W
Aylmer West	212	42.46 N	80.59 W
Aylsham, Sk., Can.	184	53.11 N	103.49 W
Aylsham, Eng., U.K.	42	52.49 N	1.15 E
ʿAyn al-ʿArab	130	36.54 N	38.21 E
ʿAyn Dār	128	25.59 N	49.23 E
ʿAyn Dīwār	130	37.17 N	42.11 E
Aynı	130	37.43 N	41.55 E
ʿAynīn ∓[4]	144	20.48 N	41.39 E
Aynor	192	33.59 N	79.11 W
ʿAynūnah	128	28.05 N	35.08 E
Ayo	248	15.41 S	72.16 W
Ayo Ayo	248	17.05 S	68.00 W
Ayod	140	8.07 N	31.26 E
Ayodhya	124	26.48 N	82.12 E
Ayo el Chico	234	20.32 N	102.21 W
Ayom	140	7.52 N	28.23 E
Ayoquezco	234	16.41 N	96.50 W
Ayora	34	39.04 N	1.03 W
Ayorou	150	14.44 N	0.55 E
Ayos	152	3.54 N	12.31 E
'Ayoûn el 'Atroûs	150	16.40 N	9.37 W
Ayr, Austl.	166	19.35 S	147.24 E
Ayr, On., Can.	212	43.17 N	80.27 W
Ayr, Scot., U.K.	44	55.28 N	4.38 W
Ayr ≃	44	55.29 N	4.28 W
ʿAyrah	132	32.37 N	36.32 E
Ayrancı	130	37.22 N	33.42 E
Ayre, Point of ›	44	54.26 N	4.22 W
Aysgarth	44	54.17 N	2.00 W
Aysha	144	10.46 N	42.37 E
ʿAytā al-Fakhkhār	132	33.38 N	35.54 E
ʿAytanīt	132	33.34 N	35.40 E
Ayton, Austl.	164	15.56 S	145.22 E
Ayton, On., Can.	212	44.03 N	80.56 W
Ayton, Eng., U.K.	44	54.14 N	0.29 W
Ayu, Kepulauan II	108	0.28 N	131.03 E
Ayulhai	102	44.36 N	115.36 E
Ayun ≃	110	13.24 N	108.28 E
Ayuñgon	116	9.51 N	123.08 E
Ayuquila ≃	234	19.23 N	103.51 W
Ayutla	234	20.07 N	104.22 W
Ayutla [de los Libres]	234	16.54 N	99.13 W
Ayvacık, Tür.	130	39.36 N	26.24 E
Ayvacık, Tür.	130	41.00 N	36.39 E
Ayvacık, Tür.	130	40.04 N	27.43 E
Ayvalı	130	38.44 N	37.38 E
Ayvalık	130	39.18 N	26.41 E
Aywaille	56	50.28 N	5.40 E
Azabarabān, Ra's ›	142	28.51 N	32.43 E
Azacualpa, Hond.	236	14.27 N	86.09 W
Azacualpa, Hond.	236	15.19 N	88.33 W
Azādpur ◆[8]	272a	28.43 N	77.11 E
Āzādshahr	128	37.07 N	55.16 E
Azai	94	35.26 N	136.18 E
Azaila	34	41.17 N	0.29 W
Azakpert	130	39.14 N	40.30 E
Azalea Park	220	28.32 N	81.18 W
Azama	174m	26.11 N	127.49 E
Azamatovo	80	53.18 N	53.28 E
Azambuja	34	39.04 N	8.52 W
Azamgarh	124	26.04 N	83.11 E
Azamgarh □[5]	124	26.00 N	83.00 E
Azamiga-dake ∧	96	34.20 N	131.47 E
Azángaro	248	14.55 S	70.13 W
Azángaro ≃	248	15.17 S	70.10 W
Azanka	86	58.02 N	64.48 E
Azao ∧	148	25.12 N	8.08 E
Azaouâd ◆[1]	150	19.00 N	3.00 W
Azaouagh, Vallée de l' V	150	15.30 N	3.18 E
Azapa, Quebrada de ≃	248	18.30 S	70.17 W
Azar V	150	16.02 N	4.04 E
Azara	150	8.21 N	9.12 E
Āzārbāijān-e Gharbī □[4]	84	38.00 N	45.00 E
Āzārbāijān-e Sharqī □[4]	84	38.00 N	47.00 E
Azare	150	11.40 N	10.11 E
Āẕar Shahr	128	37.45 N	45.59 E
Azas ≃	88	52.26 N	96.15 E
Azat, gora ∧[2]	86	46.55 N	69.00 E
Azay-le-Rideau	50	47.16 N	0.28 E
Azay-sur-Cher	50	47.21 N	0.51 E
Azay-sur-Indre	50	47.12 N	0.57 E
Aʿzāz	130	36.35 N	37.03 E
Azazga	148	36.44 N	4.22 E
Azcapotzalco □[7]	286a	19.28 N	99.12 W
Azcapotzalco ◆[8]	286a	19.28 N	99.12 W
Azcuénaga	258	34.23 S	59.21 W
Aždaak, gora ∧	84	40.13 N	44.56 E
Azdavay	130	41.39 N	33.18 E
Azeffâl ±[8]	148	21.00 N	14.45 W
Azeffoun	148	36.53 N	4.25 E
Azejevo	80	54.41 N	42.02 E
Azemmour	148	33.20 N	8.25 W
Azenhas do Mar	266c	38.50 N	9.28 W
Azennezal, 'Erg V	148	22.50 N	0.25 E
Azerbaijan → Azerbajdžanskaja Sovetskaja Socialističeskaja Respublika □[3]	84	40.30 N	47.30 E
Azerbajdžanskaja Sovetskaja Socialističeskaja Respublika □[3]	84	40.30 N	47.30 E
Azergues ≃	58	45.56 N	4.44 E
Azezo	144	12.35 N	37.28 E
Azgir	80	47.50 N	47.54 E
Azhikode	122	11.59 N	75.21 E
Azilal	148	31.58 N	6.34 W
Azilal □[4]	148	31.55 N	6.30 W
Azile	154	3.32 N	29.52 E
Azimganj	126	24.14 N	88.15 E
Azincourt	50	50.28 N	2.08 E
Azizbekov	84	39.40 N	45.30 E
Azle	222	32.53 N	97.32 W
Aznakajevo	80	54.53 N	53.04 E
Aznapuquio	286d	11.59 S	77.04 W
Azogues	246	2.44 S	78.50 W
Azoia	266c	38.46 N	9.29 W
Azor	132	32.01 N	34.48 E
Azores → Açores II	148a	38.30 N	28.00 W
Azores-Gibraltar Ridge ⊹[3]	10	37.00 N	16.00 W
Azores Plateau ⊹[3]	10	39.00 N	30.00 W
Azoum, Bahr (Wādī ʿAẓūm) V	146	10.53 N	20.15 E
Azov	83	47.07 N	39.25 E
Azov, Sea of → Azovskoje more ∓[2]	78	46.00 N	36.00 E
Azovo-Sivašskij zapovednik ◆[4]	78	46.08 N	35.08 E
Azovskij kanal ≍	83	47.07 N	39.27 E
Azovskoje	78	45.34 N	34.34 E
Azovskoje more (Sea of Azov) ∓[2]	78	46.00 N	36.00 E
Azoyú	234	16.43 N	98.44 W
Azpeitia	34	43.11 N	2.16 W
Azraq, Al-Bahr al- → Blue Nile ≃	140	15.38 N	32.31 E
Azraq, Bahr ≃	146	10.52 N	20.35 E
Azraq, Wādī al- V	140	10.33 N	28.40 E
Azrou	148	33.27 N	5.14 W
Aztalan State Park ♠	216	43.04 N	88.51 W
Aztec	200	36.49 N	107.59 W
Azteca, Estadio ♠	286a	19.18 N	99.09 W
Aztec Peak ∧	200	33.48 N	110.55 W
Aztec Ruins National Monument ♠	200	36.51 N	108.10 W
Azua	238	18.27 N	70.44 W
Azuaga	34	38.16 N	5.41 W
Azuay □[4]	246	3.00 S	79.00 W
Azucena	252	37.29 S	59.18 W
Azuchi	94	35.09 N	136.08 E
Azuchi-jō ⊥	94	35.10 N	136.08 E
Azuer ≃	34	39.08 N	3.36 W
Azuero, Península de ›[1]	246	7.40 N	80.35 W
Azuga	38	45.27 N	25.33 E
Azul	252	36.47 S	59.51 W
Azul, Cerro ∧, C.R.	236	9.54 N	85.14 W
Azul, Cerro ∧, Ec.	246a	0.54 S	91.21 W
Azul, Cerro ∧, Hond.	236	14.32 N	88.23 W
Azul, Serra ⋏[1]	248	14.50 S	54.50 W
Azul, Sierra ⋏	234	23.15 N	98.20 W
ʿAẓūm, Wādī (Bahr Azoum) V	146	10.53 N	20.15 E
Azuma, Nihon	94	36.33 N	138.54 E
Azuma, Nihon	94	35.56 N	140.28 E
Azuma, Nihon	94	36.36 N	138.20 E
Azuma, Nihon	94	36.31 N	139.19 E
Azumaya-san ∧	94	36.32 N	138.25 E
Azumazaka	270	34.26 N	135.39 E
Azumi	94	36.11 N	137.47 E
Azur, Côte D' ±[2]	62	43.30 N	7.00 E
Azurduy	248	19.59 S	64.29 W
Azure Clouds, Temple of the ɤ[1]	271a	40.00 N	116.11 E
Azure Lake ◎	182	52.23 N	120.00 W
Azusa	228	34.08 N	117.54 W
Azusa ≃	94	36.17 N	137.56 E
Ažu-Tajga, gora ∧	86	51.35 N	88.45 E
Az-Zabābidah	132	32.23 N	35.20 E
Az-Zāb al-Kabīr → Great Zab ≃	128	36.00 N	43.21 E
Az-Zāb aṣ-Ṣaghīr → Little Zab ≃	128	35.12 N	43.25 E
Az-Zabdānī	132	33.43 N	36.05 E
Aẓ-Ẓāhirīyah	132	31.25 N	34.58 E
Aẓ-Ẓahrān (Dhahran)	128	26.18 N	50.08 E
Az-Zamālik ◆[8]	273c	30.04 N	31.13 E
Azzanello	64	45.18 N	9.55 E
Az-Zankalūn	142	30.33 N	31.27 E
Azzano Decimo	64	45.53 N	12.43 E
Az-Zaqāzīq	142	30.35 N	31.31 E
Az-Zarbah	130	36.04 N	36.59 E
Az-Zarqā'	132	32.05 N	36.06 E
Az-Zawāmil	142	30.21 N	31.26 E
Az-Zāwiyah	146	32.45 N	12.44 E
Az-Zaydāb	140	17.26 N	33.53 E
Az-Zaydīyah	144	15.18 N	43.04 E
Az-Zaytīyah ◆[8]	142	29.58 N	32.31 E
Az-Zaytūn ◆[8]	273c	30.06 N	31.19 E
Azzel Matti, Sebkha ≌	148	25.55 N	0.56 E
Az-Zilfī	128	26.18 N	44.48 E
Az-Zrārīyah	132	33.21 N	35.20 E
Az-Zubayr	128	30.23 N	47.43 E
ʿAzzūn	132	32.11 N	35.03 E
Azzurra, Grotta (Blue Grotto) ±[5]	68	40.35 N	14.14 E
B			
Ba ≃, Viet.	110	13.02 N	109.03 E
Ba ≃, Zhg.	100	30.25 N	115.02 E
Ba ≃, Zhg.	102	31.03 N	107.08 E
Ba ≃, Zhg.	271a	39.57 N	116.38 E
Ba, Loch ◎	46	56.36 N	4.44 W
Baa	112	10.43 S	123.03 E
Baaba, Île I	175f	20.03 S	163.59 E
Baacagaan	102	45.35 N	99.27 E
Baad	58	47.19 N	10.07 E
Baah	112	10.28 S	121.59 E
Baak	263	51.25 N	7.10 E
Baal	56	51.02 N	6.17 E
Baao	116	13.27 N	123.22 E
Baar	58	47.12 N	8.32 E
Baar ◆[1]	58	48.00 N	8.30 E
Baarbach ≃	263	51.27 N	7.39 E
Baardheere	144	2.20 N	42.17 E
Baardskeerdersbos	158	34.34 S	19.35 E
Baargaal	144	11.17 N	51.04 E
Baarle-Hertog	56	51.27 N	4.56 E
Baarle-Nassau	52	51.27 N	4.53 E
Baarlo	52	51.20 N	6.05 E
Baarn	52	52.13 N	5.16 E
Baasrode	50	51.02 N	4.10 E
Baba	246	1.47 S	79.40 W
Baba ≃	152	6.25 N	17.07 E
Baba Burnu ›	130	39.29 N	26.04 E
Babaçulândia	250	7.13 S	47.46 W
Babadag, Rom.	38	44.54 N	28.43 E
Babadağ, Tür.	130	37.48 N	28.52 E
Babadag, gora ∧	84	41.02 N	48.19 E
Babaeski	130	41.26 N	27.06 E
Babahoyo	246	1.49 S	79.31 W
Babai (Sarju) ≃	124	27.42 N	81.16 E
Babailiqiao	100	32.26 N	118.57 E
Babajevo	76	59.23 N	35.56 E
Babajkovka	78	49.01 N	34.32 E
Babajurt	84	43.36 N	46.47 E
Babak	112	7.08 N	125.41 E
Babakin	162	32.07 S	118.01 E
Babana	150	10.26 N	3.50 E
Babanango	158	28.30 S	31.00 E
Babanka	78	48.43 N	30.26 E
Babanūsah	140	11.20 N	27.48 E
Babar, Kepulauan II	164	7.50 S	129.45 E
Babar, Pulau I	164	7.55 S	129.45 E
Bābarpur ◆[8]	272a	28.41 N	77.17 E
Babat, Indon.	112	2.45 S	103.38 E
Babat, Indon.	115a	7.06 S	112.10 E
Babatag, chrebet ⋏	85	38.15 N	68.20 E
Babati	154	4.13 S	35.45 E
Bābā Valī Ṣāḥeb	120	31.40 N	65.40 E
Babb	182	48.51 N	113.26 W
Babbacombe Bay c	42	50.30 N	3.25 W
Babb Creek ≃	210	41.33 N	77.23 W
Babbitt, Mn., U.S.	190	47.43 N	91.57 W
Babbitt, Nv., U.S.	204	38.32 N	118.38 W
Bʿabdā	132	33.50 N	35.32 E
Bʿabdāt	132	33.53 N	35.40 E
Babel, Mont de ∧	186	51.27 N	68.42 W
Babelijamun	164	2.04 S	137.43 E
Babelsberg ◆[8]	264a	52.24 N	13.05 E
Babelsberg, Schloss ⊥	264a	52.24 N	13.05 E
Babelthuap I	175b	7.30 N	134.36 E
Babenhausen, B.R.D.	56	49.57 N	8.56 E
Babenhausen, B.R.D.	58	48.09 N	10.15 E
Babenki	82	55.21 N	37.11 E
Babenkovo	83	49.15 N	37.21 E
Babeyru	154	1.52 N	27.27 E
Babi, Pulau I	114	2.05 N	96.39 E
Babia, Arroyo de la ≃	196	28.25 N	101.45 W
Babian ≃	102	22.58 N	101.44 E
Babiči	76	52.17 N	30.00 E
Bābil	142	30.41 N	31.00 E
Bābil □[4]	128	32.40 N	44.35 E
Babile	144	9.15 N	42.19 E
Babilônia	256	22.33 S	44.28 W
Babilônia ≃	255	17.10 S	53.05 W
Babimost	30	52.10 N	15.51 E
Babīna	124	25.15 N	78.28 E
Babina Greda	38	45.07 N	18.33 E
Babinda	166	17.20 S	145.55 E
Babine	182	55.19 N	126.37 W
Babine ≃	182	55.42 N	127.40 W
Babine Lake ◎	182	54.45 N	126.00 W
Babine Range ⋏	182	55.00 N	126.25 W
Babino, S.S.S.R.	76	56.44 N	34.17 E
Babino, S.S.S.R.	76	59.14 N	31.26 E
Babino, S.S.S.R.	76	59.50 N	40.49 E
Babino, S.S.S.R.	80	57.22 N	48.45 E
Babiogórski Park Narodowy ♠	30	49.35 N	19.30 E
Babo	164	2.33 S	133.25 E
Bābol	128	36.34 N	52.42 E
Bābol Sar	128	36.43 N	52.39 E
Babonã ≃	248	6.35 S	66.27 W
Baboon Point ›	158	32.19 S	18.20 E
Baboquivari Mountains ⋏	200	31.45 N	111.35 W
Baboquivari Peak ∧	200	31.46 N	111.35 W
Babor, Djebel ∧	34	36.30 N	5.28 E
Baborów	30	50.09 N	17.59 E
Babošino	82	54.13 N	37.08 E
Baboua	152	5.48 N	14.49 E
Babrongan Tower ∧[2]	162	18.36 S	123.33 E
Babson Park, Fl., U.S.	220	27.49 N	81.31 W
Babson Park, Ma., U.S.	283	42.18 N	71.23 W
Babson Reservoir ◎[1]	283	42.38 N	70.40 W
Babstovo	89	48.07 N	132.27 E
Bab-Taza	148	35.03 N	5.14 W
Bābu Bheri	272b	22.51 N	88.14 E
Bābūpur, India	126	24.01 N	87.10 E
Bābūpur, India	272a	28.30 N	76.59 E
Babura	150	12.46 N	9.01 E
Bābūsar Pass)(	123	35.09 N	74.03 E
Babuškin	88	51.41 N	105.54 E
Babuškin ◆[8]	265b	55.52 N	37.42 E
Babuyan	116	10.00 N	118.54 E
Babuyan Channel ʮ	116	18.44 N	121.40 E
Babuyan Island I	108	19.32 N	121.57 E
Babuyan Islands II	108	19.15 N	121.40 E
Baby	287a	22.42 S	43.23 W
Baby, Canal do ≍	287a	22.42 S	43.21 W
Babylon	210	40.41 N	73.19 W
Babylon ⊥	128	32.33 N	44.24 E
Babynino	76	54.23 N	35.43 E
Bača ≃	64	46.09 N	13.48 E
Bacaadweeyn	144	7.12 N	47.32 E
Bacaba, Igarapé ≃	246	3.35 S	68.45 W
Bacabal	250	4.14 S	44.47 W
Bacacay	116	13.18 N	123.47 E
Bacajá ≃	250	3.25 S	51.50 W
Bacajaí ≃	250	3.27 S	51.53 W
Bacalar, Laguna de ◎	232	18.43 N	88.22 W
Bacalhau, Canal do ≍	287a	23.03 S	43.35 W
Bacaligo	84	42.33 N	44.57 E
Bačalino	86	57.46 N	67.17 E
Bacan, Pulau I	164	0.35 S	127.30 E
Bacao	116	10.27 N	119.48 E
Bacarra	116	18.15 N	120.35 E
Bacatuba	250	5.40 S	43.42 W
Bacău	38	46.34 N	26.55 E
Bacău □[6]	38	46.30 N	26.45 E
Baccalieu Island I	186	48.08 N	52.48 W
Baccarat	58	48.27 N	6.45 E
Bacchiglione ≃	64	45.11 N	12.14 E
Bacchus Marsh	169	37.41 S	144.27 E
Baceno	58	46.16 N	8.19 E
Bacerac	232	30.18 N	108.50 W
Bacevići	76	53.24 N	29.14 E
Bac-giang	110	21.16 N	106.12 E
Bach	58	47.16 N	10.24 E
Bachagou	98	40.36 N	122.54 E
Bachaquero	246	9.56 N	71.08 W
Bacharach	56	50.04 N	7.46 E
Bacharden	128	38.26 N	57.25 E
Bachardok	128	38.46 N	58.30 E
Bachauan	116	12.28 N	122.06 E
Bachčisaraj	78	44.45 N	33.51 E
Bache	106	31.05 N	120.40 E
Bacheli	122	18.40 N	81.16 E
Bacheng	106	31.27 N	120.52 E
Bachi	100	24.48 N	115.49 E
Bachíniva	232	28.45 N	107.15 W
Bach-ma	110	16.12 N	107.52 E
Bachmač	78	51.13 N	32.46 E
Bachmetjevka	80	51.06 N	44.46 E
Bachmut ≃	83	48.56 N	38.03 E
Bachmutovka	83	48.52 N	39.03 E
Bachmutovo	76	56.22 N	34.03 E
Bacho	114	6.37 N	101.39 E
Bachok	114	6.04 N	102.24 E
Bacht	85	40.43 N	68.42 E
Bachta, S.S.S.R.	74	62.28 N	89.00 E
Bachta, S.S.S.R.	86	55.45 N	92.26 E
Bachtemir ≃	80	45.43 N	47.38 E
Bachten-Berg ∧[2]	264a	52.20 N	12.54 E
Bachty, S.S.S.R.	86	55.45 N	92.26 E
Bachty, S.S.S.R.	86	46.39 N	82.42 E
Bachu	90	39.50 N	78.20 E
Bachuma	144	6.48 N	35.53 E
Back ≃, N.T., Can.	176	67.15 N	95.15 W
Back ≃, Va., U.S.	208	37.06 N	76.17 W
Bačka ◆[1]	38	45.50 N	19.30 E
Bac-kan	110	22.08 N	105.50 E
Bačka Palanka	38	45.15 N	19.24 E
Bačka Topola	38	45.49 N	19.38 E
Back Bay ◆[8]	283	42.21 N	71.05 W
Back Bay c, India	272c	18.56 N	72.49 E
Back Bay c, Va., U.S.	208	36.35 N	75.57 W
Backberg	40	60.37 N	16.37 E
Backbone Ranges ⋏	180	63.30 N	129.00 W
Back Branch ≃	284c	38.50 N	76.48 W
Back Brook ≃	276	40.26 N	74.39 W
Back Channel ≃[1]	279b	40.30 N	80.05 W
Back Creek ≃	188	38.02 N	79.54 W
Backe	26	63.49 N	16.24 E
Bäckefors	26	58.48 N	12.10 E
Bäckehagen	40	60.39 N	15.34 E
Backford	262	53.15 N	2.54 W
Bäckhammar	40	59.10 N	14.11 E
Bački Petrovac	38	45.22 N	19.35 E
Backnang	56	48.56 N	9.25 E
Back River c	208	39.16 N	76.27 W
Back River Neck ›[1]	284b	39.18 N	76.26 W
Backstairs Passage ʮ	168b	35.42 S	138.05 E
Bac-lieu (Vinh-loi)	110	9.17 N	105.44 E
Bacliff	222	29.31 N	94.59 W
Bac-ninh	110	21.11 N	106.03 E
Baco, Mount ∧	116	12.49 N	121.10 E
Bacoachi	232	30.38 N	109.56 W
Bacoli	68	40.48 N	14.05 E
Bacolod	116	10.40 N	122.57 E
Bacon	116	13.03 N	124.03 E
Baconga ◆[8]	273b	4.18 S	15.16 E
Bacon Peak ∧	224	48.39 N	121.31 W
Bacons Run ≃	285	40.06 N	74.41 W
Baconton	192	31.22 N	84.09 W
Bacoor	116	14.28 N	120.56 E
Bacoor Bay c	269f	14.28 N	120.54 E
Bac-quang	110	22.29 N	104.52 E
Bacqueville-en-Caux	50	49.47 N	1.00 E
Bácsalmás	38	46.08 N	19.20 E
Bács-Kiskun □[6]	30	46.30 N	19.25 E
Bacton	42	52.52 N	1.28 E
Bacuag	116	9.37 N	125.38 E
Bacuit Bay c	116	11.07 N	119.23 E
Bácum	232	27.33 N	110.05 W
Bacungan	116	9.56 N	118.42 E
Bacup	262	53.43 N	2.12 W
Bacuranao ≃	286b	23.10 N	82.14 W
Bacuri, Cachoeira ʟ	250	5.29 S	54.18 W
Bacuri, Ilha do I	250	2.55 S	49.43 W
Bacurituba	250	2.43 S	44.43 W
Bačurka	24	68.32 N	56.57 E
Bacuyangan	116	9.39 N	122.27 E
Bād	128	33.41 N	52.01 E
Bad ≃, Mi., U.S.	190	43.18 N	84.06 W
Bad ≃, S.D., U.S.	198	44.22 N	100.22 W
Bad ≃, Wi., U.S.	190	46.38 N	90.40 W
Badʿ, Wādī V	142	29.41 N	32.20 E
Bada	88	51.23 N	109.54 E
Bad Abbach	60	48.56 N	12.03 E
Badagara	122	11.36 N	75.35 E
Badagri	150	6.27 N	2.55 E
Badagri □[8]	273a	6.27 N	3.18 E
Badagri Creek c	273a	6.25 N	3.18 E
Badahl	142	28.56 N	30.54 E
Bad Aibling	64	47.52 N	12.00 E
Badajia	100	33.57 N	120.17 E
Badajós ≃	246	3.15 S	63.02 W
Badajós, Lago ◎	246	3.15 S	62.47 W
Badajoz	34	38.53 N	6.58 W
Badakani	152	4.46 S	14.52 E
Badakhshan □[4]	120	36.45 N	72.00 E
Badal Khān Goth	120	26.31 N	67.06 E
Badalona	34	41.27 N	2.15 E
Badalucco	62	43.55 N	7.51 E
Badam	85	42.23 N	69.15 E
Bādāmi	122	15.55 N	75.41 E
Bādāmpahār	124	22.06 N	86.06 E
Badana, Lach V	144	0.50 S	42.04 E
Badanah	128	30.59 N	41.02 E
Badanga	146	11.36 N	17.26 E
Badanganj	126	22.54 N	87.33 E
Badaohao	104	41.47 N	121.57 E
Badaohe, Zhg.	98	40.24 N	118.42 E
Badaohe, Zhg.	98	40.02 N	122.17 E
Badarma	88	57.46 N	102.36 E
Badas	112	4.36 N	114.27 E
Badas, Kepulauan II	112	0.35 N	107.06 E
Badata, gora ∧	88	51.55 N	111.35 E
Bad Aussee	64	47.36 N	13.47 E
Bad Axe	190	43.48 N	83.00 W
Badaying	98	41.22 N	117.28 E
Badazhou	102	24.36 N	105.04 E
Bad Bentheim	52	52.19 N	7.10 E
Bad Bergzabern	56	49.07 N	8.00 E
Bad Berka	54	50.54 N	11.17 E
Bad Berleburg	52	51.03 N	8.23 E
Bad Berneck	60	50.03 N	11.40 E
Bad Bertrich	56	50.04 N	7.02 E
Bad Bibra	54	51.12 N	11.35 E
Bad Blankenburg	54	50.41 N	11.16 E
Bad Bramstedt	52	53.55 N	9.53 E
Bad Breisig	56	50.31 N	7.18 E
Bad Brückenau	56	50.18 N	9.47 E
Bad Buchau	58	48.03 N	9.36 E
Bad Camberg	56	50.18 N	8.16 E
Bad Creek ≃	216	41.25 N	83.57 W
Baddā	132	33.41 N	36.26 E
Badda Rogghie ∧	144	8.43 N	37.41 E
Baddeck	186	46.07 N	60.45 W
Bad Ditzenbach	56	48.35 N	9.41 E
Baddo ≃	120	28.13 N	64.50 E
Bad Doberan	54	54.06 N	11.53 E
Baddomalhi	123	31.59 N	74.40 E
Bad Dreibergen	52	53.12 N	8.01 E
Bad Driburg	52	51.44 N	9.01 E
Bad Düben	54	51.36 N	12.34 E
Bad Dürkheim	56	49.28 N	8.10 E
Bad Dürrenberg	54	51.18 N	12.04 E
Bad Dürrheim	58	48.01 N	8.32 E
Badé, Centraf.	152	6.41 N	17.07 E
Bade, Indon.	164	7.10 S	139.35 E
Badeggi	150	9.05 N	6.08 E
Badéguichéri	150	14.31 N	5.22 E
Bad Eilsen	52	52.14 N	9.06 E
Badel	54	52.44 N	11.19 E
Bad Elster	54	50.17 N	12.14 E
Bademli	130	37.02 N	32.41 E
Bad Ems	56	50.20 N	7.43 E
Baden, B.R.D.	52	53.00 N	9.04 E
Baden, On., Can.	212	43.24 N	80.39 W
Baden, Ityo.	144	17.00 N	38.00 E
Baden, Öst.	264b	48.00 N	16.14 E
Baden, Schw.	58	47.29 N	8.18 E
Baden, Pa., U.S.	214	40.38 N	80.13 W
Baden-Baden	56	48.46 N	8.14 E
Bad Endbach	56	50.45 N	8.32 E
Badenoch ◆[1]	46	56.57 N	4.19 W
Baden-Powell, Mount ∧	228	34.21 N	117.46 W
Badenweiler	58	47.48 N	7.40 E
Baden-Württemberg □[3]	30	48.30 N	9.00 E
Badenyon	46	57.15 N	3.05 W
Baderna	64	45.12 N	13.46 E
Badersleben	54	51.59 N	10.53 E
Bad Essen	52	52.19 N	8.20 E
Bad Feilnbach	64	47.46 N	12.00 E
Badfish Creek ≃	216	42.50 N	89.10 W
Bad Frankenhausen	54	51.21 N	11.06 E
Bad Freienwalde	54	52.47 N	14.01 E
Bad Friedrichshall	56	49.14 N	9.11 E
Bad Fusch	64	47.12 N	12.51 E
Bad Gandersheim	52	51.52 N	10.01 E
Badgastein	64	47.07 N	13.08 E
Badger, Nf., Can.	186	48.59 N	56.02 W
Badger, Mn., U.S.	198	48.46 N	96.00 W
Badger Creek ≃, Co., U.S.	198	40.17 N	103.42 W
Badger Creek ≃, Co., U.S.	200	38.28 N	105.52 W
Badger Creek ≃, Or., U.S.	224	45.16 N	121.11 W
Badger Pass)(	226	37.40 N	119.39 W
Badger's Mount	260	51.20 N	0.09 E
Badgery Creek ≃	274a	33.51 S	150.46 E
Badgery's Creek	274a	33.53 S	150.44 E
Bādghīsāt □[4]	128	35.00 N	63.45 E
Bad Gleichenberg	61	46.52 N	15.54 E
Bad Godesberg	56	50.41 N	7.10 E
Bad Goisern	64	47.38 N	13.37 E
Badgom	123	34.01 N	74.43 E
Bad Gottleuba	54	50.51 N	13.56 E
Bad Griesbach	58	48.27 N	8.14 E
Bad Grund	52	51.48 N	10.14 E
Bad Hall	61	48.02 N	14.13 E
Badhāna	123	31.28 N	74.37 E
Bad Harzburg	54	51.53 N	10.33 E
Bad Heilbrunn	64	47.45 N	11.28 E
Badhela ◆[8]	272a	28.38 N	77.04 E
Bad Helmstedt	54	52.14 N	11.03 E
Bad Hersfeld	56	50.52 N	9.42 E
Badhoevedorp	52	52.21 N	4.46 E
Bad Hofgastein	64	47.10 N	13.06 E
Bad Homburg vor der Höhe	56	50.13 N	8.37 E
Bad Honnef	56	50.39 N	7.13 E
Bad Hönningen	56	50.31 N	7.19 E
Badia (Abtei)	64	46.37 N	11.54 E
Badia, Val V	64	46.40 N	11.53 E
Badia Calavena	64	45.34 N	11.09 E
Badia Polesine	64	45.05 N	11.29 E
Badia Prataglia	66	43.47 N	11.52 E
Badia Tedalda	66	43.42 N	12.11 E
Badile Camuno, Pizzo ∧	58	46.01 N	10.25 E
Badīn	120	24.39 N	68.50 E
Bādinan	272b	22.54 N	88.14 E
Badinko ≃	150	13.42 N	9.35 W
Badin Lake ◎[1]	192	35.27 N	80.06 W
Badiraguato	232	25.22 N	107.31 W
Bad Ischl	64	47.43 N	13.37 E
Bad Kissingen	56	50.12 N	10.04 E
Bad Kleinen	54	53.46 N	11.28 E
Bad Kleinkirchheim	64	46.49 N	13.49 E
Bad Klosterlausnitz	54	50.55 N	11.52 E
Bad Kohlgrub	64	47.40 N	11.03 E
Bad König	56	49.45 N	9.01 E
Bad Königshofen im Grabfeld	56	50.18 N	10.29 E
Bad Kösen	54	51.08 N	11.43 E
Bad Köstritz	54	50.56 N	12.01 E
Bad Kreuznach	56	49.52 N	7.51 E
Bad Krozingen	58	47.55 N	7.43 E
Bādkulla	126	23.17 N	88.32 E
Bad Laasphe	56	50.56 N	8.24 E
Badlands ⋏[2], U.S.	198	46.45 N	103.30 W
Badlands ⋏[2], S.D., U.S.	198	43.30 N	102.20 W
Badlands National Park ♠	198	43.47 N	102.15 W
Bad Langensalza	56	51.06 N	10.38 E
Bad Lauchstädt	54	51.23 N	11.52 E
Bad Lausick	54	51.08 N	12.38 E
Bad Lauterberg [im Harz]	52	51.38 N	10.28 E
Bad Leonfelden	61	48.33 N	14.19 E
Bādli ◆[8]	272a	28.45 N	77.09 E
Bad Liebenstein	54	50.49 N	10.21 E
Bad Liebenwerda	54	51.31 N	13.23 E
Bad Liebenzell	56	48.46 N	8.44 E
Bad Lippspringe	52	51.46 N	8.49 E
Bad Meinberg	52	51.53 N	8.58 E
Bad Mergentheim	56	49.30 N	9.46 E
Badminton Stadium ♠	271c	1.18 N	103.53 E
Bad Mukran	54	54.26 N	13.35 E
Bad Münder	52	52.12 N	9.27 E
Bad Münster am Stein	56	49.49 N	7.51 E
Bad Münstereifel	56	50.33 N	6.46 E
Bad Muskau	54	51.32 N	14.43 E
Bad Nauheim	56	50.22 N	8.44 E
Bad Nenndorf	52	52.20 N	9.22 E
Badnera	122	20.52 N	77.44 E
Badner Lindkogel ∧	264b	48.01 N	16.11 E
Bad Neuenahr-Ahrweiler	56	50.33 N	7.08 E
Bad Neustadt an der Saale	56	50.19 N	10.13 E
Bad Niedernau	58	48.27 N	8.53 E
Bad Oeynhausen	52	52.12 N	8.48 E
Badogo	150	11.02 N	8.13 W
Badolato	68	38.34 N	16.31 E
Bad Oldesloe	52	53.48 N	10.22 E
Ba-don	110	17.45 N	106.27 E
Ba-dong, Viet.	110	9.40 N	106.34 E
Badong, Zhg.	102	31.02 N	110.20 E
Badonviller	58	48.30 N	6.54 E
Bad Orb	56	50.14 N	9.20 E
Badou, Togo	150	7.35 N	0.36 E
Badou, Zhg.	98	36.27 N	117.55 E
Badouling	100	32.10 N	117.36 E
Badoumbé	150	13.38 N	10.13 W
Bad Peterstal	58	48.26 N	8.12 E
Badplaas	158	25.57 S	30.35 E
Bad Polzin → Połczyn Zdrój	30	53.46 N	16.06 E
Bad Pyrmont	52	51.59 N	9.15 E
Badr	142	30.33 N	30.43 E
Bad Radkersburg	61	46.41 N	15.59 E
Bad Ragaz	58	47.00 N	9.30 E
Bādrāh	120	27.20 N	68.01 E
Badrao	120	34.46 N	69.40 E
Bad Rappenau	56	49.14 N	9.06 E
Bad Rehburg	52	52.26 N	9.13 E
Bad Reichenhall	64	47.43 N	12.52 E
Badr Ḥunayn	128	23.44 N	38.46 E
Badrīnāth	124	30.44 N	79.29 E
Bad Rippoldsau	58	48.26 N	8.19 E
Bad River Indian Reservation ◆[4]	190	46.33 N	90.40 W
Bad Rothenfelde	52	52.06 N	8.09 E
Bad Saarow-Pieskow	54	52.17 N	14.03 E
Bad Sachsa	54	51.36 N	10.32 E
Bad Säckingen	58	47.33 N	7.56 E
Bad Salzdetfurth	52	52.03 N	10.01 E
Bad Salzig	56	50.12 N	7.38 E
Bad Salzschlirf	56	50.37 N	9.29 E
Bad Salzuflen	52	52.05 N	8.44 E
Bad Salzungen	56	50.48 N	10.13 E
Bad Sankt Leonhard im Lavanttal	61	46.58 N	14.48 E
Bad Sassendorf	52	51.35 N	8.10 E
Bad Schandau	54	50.55 N	14.10 E
Bad Schmiedeberg	54	51.41 N	12.44 E
Bad Schwalbach	56	50.08 N	8.04 E
Bad Schwartau	54	53.55 N	10.40 E
Bad Segeberg	52	53.56 N	10.17 E
Bādshāhpur	124	25.47 N	82.49 E
Bad Soden	56	50.08 N	8.30 E
Bad Soden-Salmünster	56	50.17 N	9.22 E
Bad Sooden-Allendorf	56	51.16 N	9.58 E
Bad Steben	54	50.22 N	11.38 E
Bad Stuer	54	53.22 N	12.19 E
Bad Suderode	54	51.44 N	11.07 E
Bad Sulza	54	51.05 N	11.37 E
Bad Sülze	54	54.06 N	12.38 E
Bad Tatzmannsdorf	61	47.20 N	16.13 E
Bad Teinach	56	48.41 N	8.41 E
Bad Tennstedt	54	51.09 N	10.50 E
Bad Tölz	64	47.46 N	11.34 E
Badu, Bra.	287a	22.54 S	43.04 W
Badu, Zhg.	100	26.51 N	119.35 E
Badu, Zhg.	100	28.32 N	117.57 E
Badu, Zhg.	102	24.15 N	105.41 E
Badu Island I	164	10.07 S	142.08 E
Badulla	122	6.59 N	81.03 E
Badung, Selat ʮ	115b	8.40 S	115.22 E
Badupi	120	21.36 N	93.25 E
Bādura	126	22.16 N	90.21 E
Bad Urach	58	48.29 N	9.23 E
Bāduria	126	22.44 N	88.47 E
Badvel	122	14.45 N	79.03 E
Bad Vellach	61	46.26 N	14.33 E
Bad Vilbel	56	50.12 N	8.42 E
Bad Vöslau	61	47.57 N	16.16 E
Bad Waldsee	58	47.55 N	9.45 E
Bad Warmbrunn → Cieplice Śląskie-Zdrój	30	50.52 N	15.41 E
Badwater Creek ≃	202	43.17 N	108.08 W
Bad Westernkotten	52	51.38 N	8.21 E
Bad Wiessee	64	47.43 N	11.43 E
Bad Wildungen	56	51.07 N	9.07 E
Bad Wilsnack	54	52.57 N	11.57 E
Bad Wimpfen	56	49.14 N	9.09 E
Bad Windsheim	56	49.31 N	10.25 E
Bad Wörishofen	58	48.00 N	10.36 E
Bad Wurzach	58	47.54 N	9.54 E
Badžalskij chrebet ⋏	89	50.40 N	134.50 E
Bad Zwischenahn	52	53.11 N	8.00 E
Baediam	150	15.03 N	11.51 W
Bække	41	55.34 N	9.09 E
Baena	34	37.37 N	4.19 W
Baependi	256	21.57 S	44.53 W
Baependi ≃	256	21.52 S	45.04 W
Baer Field ⊠	216	40.59 N	85.11 W
Baerl	263	51.29 N	6.41 E
Baesweiler	56	50.54 N	6.11 E
Báez	240p	22.13 N	79.45 W
Baeza, Ec.	246	0.27 S	77.53 W
Baeza, Esp.	34	37.59 N	3.28 W
Baezaeko ≃	182	53.09 N	123.48 W
Bafa Gölü ◎	130	37.30 N	27.25 E
Bafang	152	5.09 N	10.11 E
Bafatá	150	12.10 N	14.40 W
Bafelé	150	10.09 N	10.08 W
Baffa	123	34.26 N	73.13 E
Baffin Basin ⊹[1]	16	73.15 N	67.00 W
Baffin Bay c, N.A.	16	73.00 N	66.00 W
Baffin Bay c, Tx., U.S.	196	27.15 N	97.33 W
Baffin Island I	176	68.00 N	70.00 W
Bafia	152	4.44 N	11.16 E
Bafilo	150	9.21 N	1.16 E
Bafing ≃, Afr.	150	13.49 N	10.50 W
Bafing ≃, Mali	150	12.27 N	7.07 W
Bafing Makana	150	12.33 N	10.15 W
Bafoulabé	150	13.48 N	10.50 W
Bafoussam	152	5.29 N	10.24 E
Bāfq	128	31.35 N	55.24 E
Bafra	130	41.34 N	35.56 E
Bafra Burnu ›	130	41.44 N	35.58 E
Bāft	128	29.14 N	56.38 E
Bafuku	154	4.15 N	27.54 E
Bafwabaka	154	2.07 N	27.40 E
Bafwabalinga	154	0.51 N	27.04 E
Bafwaboli	154	0.39 N	26.10 E
Bafwangbe	154	1.39 N	26.51 E
Bafwapada	154	0.56 N	26.57 E
Bafwasende	154	1.05 N	27.16 E
Bafwasomboli	154	1.27 N	27.01 E
Baga	126	22.26 N	90.28 E
Bagabag	116	16.37 N	121.15 E
Bagabag Island I	164	4.50 S	146.15 E
Baga-Burul	80	46.00 N	44.36 E
Bagac	116	14.36 N	120.23 E
Bagacay Point ›	116	8.58 N	124.48 E
Bagac Bay c	116	14.36 N	120.22 E
Bagaces	236	10.31 N	85.15 W
Baga Chentej nuruu ⋏	88	48.30 N	107.30 E
Bagage ∧	154	3.23 N	40.12 E
Bagagem ≃, Bra.	250	11.37 S	48.12 W
Bagagem ≃, Bra.	255	13.58 S	48.21 W
Bagaha	124	27.06 N	84.05 E
Bagahak, Gunong ∧	116	5.03 N	118.44 E
Bagajevskij	78	47.19 N	40.23 E
Bāgalkot	122	16.11 N	75.42 E
Bagamanoc	116	13.57 N	124.17 E
Bagamoyo	154	6.26 S	38.54 E
Bagan	86	54.06 N	77.40 E
Bagana	80	54.22 N	51.25 E
Bagana, Mount ∧	175e	6.09 S	155.12 E
Bagan Datoh	114	3.59 N	100.47 E
Bagañga	116	7.35 N	126.34 E
Bagan Serai	114	5.01 N	100.32 E
Bagansiapi-api	114	2.09 N	100.49 E
Bagansinembah	114	1.46 N	100.29 E
Bagansitukang	114	2.38 N	100.15 E
Baganza ≃	64	44.47 N	10.19 E
Bagara	85	40.55 N	68.26 E
Bağarası	130	37.42 N	27.33 E
Bagaroua	150	14.38 N	4.21 E
Bagasra	120	21.29 N	70.57 E
Bagata	152	3.44 S	17.57 E
Bāgātipāra	126	24.18 N	88.57 E
Bagawi	140	12.19 N	34.21 E
Bagband	52	53.21 N	7.36 E
Bagbe ≃	150	8.42 N	11.15 W
Bagbele	154	4.21 N	29.17 E
Bāgda	126	23.13 N	86.41 E
Bagdad → Baghdād, ʿIrāq	128	33.21 N	44.25 E
Bagdad, Az., U.S.	200	34.34 N	113.12 W
Bagdad, Fl., U.S.	194	30.35 N	87.01 W
Bagdad, Ky., U.S.	218	38.15 N	85.03 W
Bagdaha	126	23.13 N	88.53 E
Bagdanga	126	24.02 N	88.32 E
Bagdarin	88	54.26 N	113.36 E
Bagé	252	31.20 S	54.06 W
Bagehadu	120	35.25 N	84.50 E
Bâgé-le-Châtel	58	46.18 N	4.56 E
Bagenkop	41	54.45 N	10.41 E
Bagerovo	78	45.23 N	36.17 E
Bages et de Sigean, Étang de c	32	43.05 N	3.03 E
Bāgevādi	122	16.35 N	75.58 E
Baggao	116	17.56 N	121.46 E
Baggeryd	24	57.30 N	14.07 E
Baggetorp	40	59.01 N	16.04 E
Baggio ◆[8]	266b	45.27 N	9.06 E
Baggs	200	41.02 N	107.39 W
Baggy Point ›	42	51.09 N	4.16 W
Bāgh	123	33.59 N	73.47 E
Baghdād	128	33.21 N	44.25 E
Baghdād □[4]	128	33.30 N	44.30 E

Symbols in the index entries represent the broad categories identified in the key at the right. Symbols with superior numbers (⋏[1]) identify subcategories (see complete key on page *I · 1).*

Kartensymbole in dem Registerverzeichnis stellen die rechts in Schlüssel erklärten Kategorien dar. Symbole mit hochgestellten Ziffern (⋏[1]) bezeichnen Unterabteilungen einer Kategorie (vgl. vollständiger Schlüssel auf Seite *I · 1).*

Los símbolos incluídos en el texto del índice representan las grandes categorias identificadas con la clave a la derecha. Los símbolos con numeros en su parte superior (⋏[1]) identifican las subcategorías (véase la clave completa en la página *I · 1).*

Les symboles de l'index représentent les catégories indiquées dans la légende à droite. Les symboles suivis d'un indice (⋏[1]) représentent des sous-catégories (voir légende complète à la page *I · 1).*

Os símbolos incluídos no texto do índice representam as grandes categorias identificadas com a chave à direita. Os símbolos com números em sua parte superior (⋏[1]) identificam as subcategorias (veja-se a chave completa à página *I · 1).*

∧	Mountain	Berg	Montaña	Montagne	Montanha
⋏	Mountains	Berge	Montañas	Montagnes	Montanhas
)(	Pass	Pass	Paso	Col	Passo
V	Valley, Canyon	Tal, Cañon	Valle, Cañón	Vallée, Canyon	Vale, Canhão
≚	Plain	Ebene	Llano	Plaine	Planície
›	Cape	Kap	Cabo	Cap	Cabo
I	Island	Insel	Isla	Île	Ilha
II	Islands	Inseln	Islas	Îles	Ilhas
±	Other Topographic Features	Andere Topographische Objekte	Otros Elementos Topográficos	Autres données topographiques	Outros acidentes topográficos

Symbol	English	Deutsch	Español	Français	Português
≃	River	Fluss	Río	Rivière	Rio
≊	Canal	Kanal	Canal	Canal	Canal
⌊	Waterfall, Rapids	Wasserfall, Stromschnellen	Cascada, Rápidos	Chute d'eau, Rapides	Cascata, Rápidos
Ա	Strait	Meeresstrasse	Estrecho	Détroit	Estreito
⊂	Bay, Gulf	Bucht, Golf	Bahía, Golfo	Baie, Golfe	Baía, Golfo
⊜	Lake, Lakes	See, Seen	Lago, Lagos	Lac, Lacs	Lago, Lagos
≡	Swamp	Sumpf	Pantano	Marais	Pântano
⩎	Ice Features, Glacier	Eis- und Gletscherformen	Accidentes Glaciales	Formes glaciaires	Acidentes glaciares
⊤	Other Hydrographic Features	Andere Hydrographische Objekte	Otros Elementos Hidrográficos	Autres données hydrographiques	Outros acidentes hidrográficos
✣	Submarine Features	Untermeerische Objekte	Accidentes Submarinos	Formes de relief sous-marin	Acidentes submarinos
□	Political Unit	Politische Einheit	Unidad Politica	Entité politique	Unidade política
⚲	Cultural Institution	Kulturelle Institution	Institución Cultural	Institution culturelle	Instituição cultural
⊥	Historical Site	Historische Stätte	Sitio Histórico	Site historique	Sitio histórico
♠	Recreational Site	Erholungs- und Ferienort	Sitio de Recreo	Centre de loisirs	Area de Lazer
⊠	Airport	Flughafen	Aeropuerto	Aéroport	Aeroporto
■	Military Installation	Militäranlage	Instalación Militar	Installation militaire	Instalação militar
✤	Miscellaneous	Verschiedenes	Misceláneo	Divers	Diversos

Symbols in the index entries represent the broad categories identified in the key at the right. Symbols with superior numbers (ʌ1) identify subcategories (see complete key on page I · 1).

Kartensymbole in dem Registerverzeichnis stellen die rechts in Schlüssel erklärten Kategorien dar. Symbole mit hochgestellten Ziffern (ʌ1) bezeichnen Unterabteilungen einer Kategorie (vgl. vollständiger Schlüssel auf Seite I · 1).

Los símbolos incluídos en el texto del índice representan las grandes categorías identificadas con la clave a la derecha. Los símbolos con numeros en su parte superior (ʌ1) identifican las subcategorías (véase la clave completa en la página I · 1).

Les symboles de l'index représentent les catégories indiquées dans la légende à droite. Les symboles suivis d'un indice (ʌ1) représentent des sous-catégories (voir légende complète à la page I · 1).

Os símbolos incluídos no texto do índice representam as grandes categorias identificadas com a chave à direita. Os símbolos com números em sua parte superior (ʌ1) identificam as subcategorias (vejase a chave completa à página I · 1).

ʌ Mountain	Berg	Montaña	Montagne	Montanha
ʌ Mountains	Berge	Montañas	Montagnes	Montanhas
✕ Pass	Pass	Paso	Col	Passo
V Valley, Canyon	Tal, Cañon	Valle, Cañón	Vallée, Canyon	Vale, Canhão
≡ Plain	Ebene	Llano	Plaine	Planície
> Cape	Kap	Cabo	Cap	Cabo
I Island	Insel	Isla	Île	Ilha
II Islands	Inseln	Islas	Îles	Ilhas
⊥ Other Topographic Features	Andere Topographische Objekte	Otros Elementos Topográficos	Autres données topographiques	Outros acidentes topográficos

ESPAÑOL — Nombre / Página / Lat.°′ / Long.°′ W = Oeste
FRANÇAIS — Nom / Page / Lat.°′ / Long.°′ W = Ouest
PORTUGUÊS — Nome / Página / Lat.°′ / Long.°′ W = Oeste

Baojiagou 105 40.05 N 115.22 E
Baojiapu 104 40.51 N 122.14 E
Baojiatou 106 30.11 N 119.48 E
Baojiawazi 104 41.38 N 123.24 E
Baojing 102 28.43 N 109.25 E
Baokang → Horqin Zuoyi Zhongqi 89 44.07 N 123.18 E
Bao-lac 110 22.57 N 105.40 E
Baolin 107 30.24 N 105.02 E
Baolizhen 89 42.56 N 123.46 E
Bao-loc 110 11.32 N 107.48 E
Baolunyuan 102 32.22 N 105.40 E
Baomachang 107 29.58 N 104.12 E
Baon 116 6.47 N 126.05 E
Baonian 106 31.55 N 119.21 E
Baoning 102 23.31 N 106.24 E
Baoqing 89 46.21 N 132.14 E
Baoquan 98 36.16 N 119.04 E
Baoro 152 5.40 N 15.58 E
Baoshan, Zhg. 100 32.39 N 113.54 E
Baoshan, Zhg. 102 26.19 N 104.27 E
Baoshan, Zhg. 102 25.09 N 99.09 E
Baoshan, Zhg. 106 31.25 N 121.29 E
Baoting 110 18.42 N 109.45 E
Baotou (Paotow) 102 40.40 N 109.59 E
Baotun 104 42.29 N 122.52 E
Baoulé ≃, Afr. 150 12.36 N 6.34 W
Baoulé ≃, Mali 150 13.33 N 9.54 W
Baowei 102 22.39 N 106.50 E
Baoxikou 100 23.16 N 115.14 E
Baoxingchang 107 29.38 N 105.41 E
Baoxinji 100 32.35 N 115.00 E
Baoyi 100 32.13 N 116.42 E
Baoying 100 33.16 N 119.20 E
Baozhuchang 107 29.48 N 104.15 E
Baozidian 105 40.11 N 117.48 E
Bāp 120 27.23 N 72.21 E
Bapanling 104 40.58 N 123.08 E
Bāpatla 122 15.54 N 80.28 E
Bapaume 50 50.06 N 2.51 E
Bapchule 200 33.08 N 111.52 W
Bapsfontein 158 26.08 S 28.25 E
Baptiste Lake ⊜ 212 45.07 N 78.02 W
Baptistown 208 40.31 N 75.00 W
Bāqa el Gharbiyya 132 32.25 N 35.03 E
Baqar, Maṣrif Bahr al- ≋ 142 31.05 N 32.08 E
Baqar, Wādī al- V 146 27.49 N 18.37 E
Baqing 120 32.15 N 93.30 E
B'aqlīn 132 33.41 N 35.33 E
Ba'qūbah 128 33.45 N 44.38 E
Baquedano 252 23.20 S 69.51 W
Ba-queo 269c 10.48 N 106.38 E
Bar, Jugo. 38 42.05 N 19.05 E
Bar, S.S.S.R. 78 49.04 N 27.40 E
Bar, S.S.S.R. 88 51.17 N 107.33 E
Bar ≃ 56 49.42 N 4.50 E
Bāra, India 124 25.13 N 87.22 E
Bāra, India 272b 22.43 N 88.31 E
Bāra, India 272b 22.46 N 88.17 E
Bara, Nig. 146 10.22 N 10.44 E
Barawe 144 1.06 N 44.03 E
Barabai 112 2.35 S 115.23 E
Bāra Bāngurda 126 22.57 N 86.24 E
Bāra Banki 124 26.55 N 81.12 E
Bāra Banki □5 124 27.00 N 81.20 E
Barabanovo 82 54.43 N 38.10 E
Barābhūm 126 23.02 N 86.22 E
Barabinsk 86 55.21 N 78.21 E
Barabinskaja step' ≃ 86 55.00 N 79.00 E
Baraboo 190 43.28 N 89.44 W
Baraboo ≃ 190 43.29 N 89.26 W
Baraboulé 150 14.12 N 1.51 W
Baracaju ≃ 255 12.21 S 51.00 W
Baracchit 144 14.39 N 39.27 E
Barachois Pond Provincial Park ♦ 186 48.30 N 58.14 W
Baracoa, Cuba 240p 20.21 N 74.30 W
Baracoa, Hond. 236 15.43 N 87.52 W
Baradā ≃ 132 33.30 N 36.28 E
Baradero 258 33.48 S 59.30 W
Baradero ≃ 258 33.55 S 59.16 W
Baradili 71 39.43 N 8.54 E
Baradine 166 30.56 S 149.04 E
Bara Doāni 126 22.06 N 89.59 E
Baraga 190 46.46 N 88.29 W
Baragaon → Nālanda 124 25.07 N 85.25 E
Baragiano 68 40.41 N 15.35 E
Baragoi 154 1.47 N 36.47 E
Baraguá 240p 21.41 N 78.38 W
Baragwanath Aerodrome ⊠ 273d 26.15 S 27.59 E
Baragwanath Military Hospital ♦ 273d 26.16 S 27.56 E
Bārah 140 13.42 N 30.22 E
Barahanuddin 126 22.30 N 90.43 E
Barāigrām 126 24.19 N 89.10 E
Baraily 124 23.00 N 78.14 E
Bara Issa ≃ 150 16.09 N 3.28 W
Bara Jamda 124 22.09 N 85.23 E
Barajas, Aeropuerto ⊠ 266a 40.28 N 3.34 W
Barajas de Madrid ✦8 266a 40.28 N 3.35 E
Bara Jorda 126 23.10 N 86.50 E
Barak 130 36.51 N 37.59 E
Baraka 154 4.06 S 29.06 E
Baraka (Khawr Barakah) V 144 18.13 N 37.35 E
Barakah 140 10.58 N 27.59 E
Barakah, Khawr (Baraka) V 144 18.13 N 37.35 E
Barākar 126 24.07 N 86.14 E
Barākar ≃ 126 23.42 N 86.48 E
Bara Khunta 126 21.43 N 86.38 E
Barakī Barak 120 33.56 N 68.55 E
Barakkol'skij 86 52.12 N 67.49 E
Barākot 120 21.33 N 85.01 E
Barākpur 126 22.55 N 89.32 E
Barakula 166 26.26 S 150.31 E
Baral 272b 22.27 N 88.22 E
Baralaba 166 24.11 S 149.49 E
Barām 126 22.57 N 86.18 E
Baram ≃ 112 4.36 N 113.59 E
Baram, Tanjong ⟩ 112 4.35 N 113.59 E
Barama ≃ 246 7.40 N 59.15 W
Barāmāria 126 21.42 N 87.04 E
Bārāmati 122 18.09 N 74.35 E
Bārāmūla 123 34.12 N 74.21 E
Bārān, India 124 25.06 N 76.31 E
Baran', S.S.S.R. 76 54.30 N 28.40 E
Baran', S.S.S.R. 76 54.29 N 30.18 E
Baranagar 126 22.38 N 88.22 E
Baranakovo 86 58.08 N 82.58 E
Barancevo 82 55.04 N 37.38 E
Baranello 66 41.32 N 14.34 E
Barangbarang 112 6.24 S 120.28 E
Barangeon ≃ 57 47.12 N 2.10 E
Barani 150 13.10 N 3.53 W
Baraniki 80 46.31 N 41.50 E
Baranikovka 83 49.10 N 39.50 E
Baranoa 246 10.48 N 74.55 W
Barano d'Ischia 61 40.42 N 13.55 E
Baranof 180 57.05 N 134.50 W
Baranof Island I 180 57.00 N 135.00 W
Baranoviči 76 53.08 N 26.02 E
Baranovka 78 50.18 N 27.40 E
Baranovskoje 82 55.25 N 38.45 E
Barany, S.S.S.R. 76 57.23 N 28.07 E
Barany, S.S.S.R. 80 57.38 N 52.16 E
Baranya □6 30 46.05 N 18.15 E
Barão Ataliba Nogueira 256 22.24 S 46.45 W
Barão de Aquino 256 22.07 S 42.59 W
Barão de Cocais 255 19.56 S 43.28 W
Barão de Geraldo 256 22.49 S 47.06 W
Barão de Grajaú 250 6.45 S 43.01 W
Barão de Juparanã 256 22.21 S 43.41 W
Barão de Melgaço 248 16.13 S 55.58 W
Barão de Tromaí 250 1.29 S 45.36 W
Baraolt 38 46.05 N 25.36 E
Baraoltului, Munții ⩘ 38 46.05 N 25.45 E
Barapasi 164 2.07 S 137.00 E
Baraque de Fraiture ∧ 56 50.15 N 5.44 E
Baras 116 13.40 N 124.22 E
Barasāhi 126 21.43 N 86.44 E
Bārāsat, India 126 22.43 N 88.29 E
Bārāsat, India 272b 22.51 N 88.22 E
Baraševo 80 54.32 N 42.53 E
Baraši 78 50.43 N 28.01 E
Baraški 24 65.40 N 52.10 E
Barat, Lintasan ⵡ 115a 7.08 S 112.40 E
Baratā 266c 38.48 N 9.19 W
Baratang Island I 110 12.13 N 92.45 E
Barataria 194 29.43 N 90.07 W
Barataria Bay ⊂ 194 29.22 N 89.57 W
Barat Daya, Kepulauan II 108 7.25 S 128.00 E
Barate 112 9.54 S 123.38 E
Bar'atino, S.S.S.R. 76 54.19 N 34.31 E
Bar'atino, S.S.S.R. 82 54.43 N 36.49 E
Baratolia 126 22.25 N 86.37 E
Baratta 166 31.59 S 139.06 E
Baraula 272a 28.34 N 77.22 E
Baraúna ≃ 246 1.14 N 60.41 W
Baraut 124 29.06 N 77.16 E
Baraya 246 3.10 N 75.04 W
Barbacena 256 21.14 S 43.46 W
Barbacoas 246 1.41 N 78.09 W
Barbades → Barbados □1 241g 13.10 N 59.32 W
Barbadillo 286d 12.02 S 76.56 W
Barbadillo del Mercado 34 42.02 N 3.21 W
Barbadoes Island I 285 40.07 N 75.22 W
Barbados □1, N.A. 230 13.10 N 59.32 W
Barbados □1, N.A. 241g 13.10 N 59.32 W
Barbagia ✦1, It. 36 40.00 N 9.10 E
Barbagia ✦1, It. 71 39.55 N 9.12 E
Barbalha 250 7.19 S 39.17 W
Barbar 140 18.01 N 33.59 E
Bárbara 246 0.53 S 72.30 W
Barbarano Vicentino 64 45.24 N 11.32 E
Barbarasco 64 44.14 N 9.56 E
Barbareta, Isla I 236 16.26 N 86.09 W
Barbaros 130 40.54 N 27.27 E
Barbas, Cap ⟩ 148 22.18 N 16.41 W
Barbaši 76 57.42 N 28.24 E
Barbastro 34 42.02 N 0.08 E
Barbate ≃ 34 36.11 N 5.55 W
Barbate de Franco 34 36.12 N 5.55 W
Barbeau Peak ∧ 16 81.54 N 75.01 W
Barbentane 62 43.54 N 4.45 E
Barber Booth 262 53.22 N 1.50 W
Barberena 236 14.18 N 90.22 W
Barberena, Río de ≃ 234 22.34 N 97.52 W
Barberino di Mugello 66 44.00 N 11.15 E
Barberino Val d'Elsa 66 43.32 N 11.10 E
Barbers Point ⟩ 229c 21.18 N 158.07 W
Barbers Point Naval Air Station ■ 229c 21.19 N 158.04 W
Barberton, S. Afr. 156 25.48 S 31.03 E
Barberton, Oh., U.S. 214 41.00 N 81.36 W
Barbezieux 32 45.28 N 0.09 W
Bar Bigha 124 25.13 N 85.44 E
Barbil 124 22.06 N 85.20 E
Barbis 54 51.37 N 10.25 E
Barbizon 50 48.27 N 2.36 E
Barbosa, Col. 246 6.26 N 75.20 W
Barbosa, Col. 246 5.57 N 73.37 W
Barboursville 188 38.24 N 82.17 W
Barbourville 192 36.51 N 83.53 W
Barbuda I 238 17.38 N 61.48 W
Barbuise ≃ 50 48.33 N 3.35 E
Barby 54 51.58 N 11.53 E
Barčadiv 85 38.19 N 72.29 E
Barca Grande ≃ 258 34.09 S 58.23 W
Barcaldine 166 23.33 S 145.17 E
Barcarena 266c 38.44 N 9.17 W
Barcarena, Ribeira de ≃ 266c 38.42 N 9.27 W
Barcarrota 34 38.31 N 6.51 W
Barce → Al-Marj 146 32.30 N 20.54 E
Barcellona Pozzo di Gotto 70 38.09 N 15.13 E
Barcelona, Esp. 34 41.23 N 2.11 E
Barcelona, Esp. 266d 41.23 N 2.11 E
Barcelona, Méx. 232 26.12 N 103.25 W
Barcelona, Pil. 116 12.52 N 124.09 E
Barcelona, Ven. 246 10.08 N 64.42 W
Barcelona ✦8 266a 40.22 N 3.34 E
Barcelona, Aeropuerto Transoceánico de ⊠ 266d 41.18 N 2.05 E
Barcelona, Campo Fútbol Club ♦ 266d 41.23 N 2.08 E
Barcelona, Universidad de ᵾ2 266d 41.23 N 2.10 E
Barcelone → Barcelona 34 41.23 N 2.11 E
Barceloneta 240m 18.27 N 66.32 W
Barcelonnette 62 44.23 N 6.39 E
Barcelos, Bra. 246 0.58 S 62.57 W
Barcelos, Port. 34 41.32 N 8.37 W
Barchaticha 80 57.34 N 45.13 E
Barchyn ≃ 88 48.43 N 110.17 E
Barcillonnette 62 44.26 N 5.55 E
Barcin 30 52.52 N 17.57 E
Barcis 64 46.11 N 12.33 E
Barclay 208 39.08 N 75.51 W
Barclay Brook ≃ 276 40.19 N 74.22 W
Barcoo ≃ 166 25.30 S 142.50 E
Barcroft, Lake ⊜1 284c 38.51 N 77.09 W
Barcs 30 45.58 N 17.28 E
Barcy 261 49.01 N 2.53 E
Barczewo 30 53.50 N 20.42 E
Bard 62 45.36 N 7.45 E
Barda, S.S.S.R. 84 40.23 N 47.08 E
Barda, S.S.S.R. 86 56.54 N 55.38 E
Barda del Medio 252 38.43 S 68.10 W
Bardagué, Enneri V 146 22.06 N 16.28 E
Bardai, Süd. 140 12.43 N 21.53 E
Bardaï, Tchad 146 21.22 N 16.59 E
Bardawīl, Sabkhat al- ⊕ 140 31.10 N 33.10 E
Bardejov 30 49.18 N 21.16 E
Bárdenas Reales ⩘1 34 42.10 N 1.30 W
Bardeskan 128 35.12 N 57.58 E
Bardi 62 44.38 N 9.44 E
Bardīa 124 28.18 N 81.22 E
Bardīyah 140 31.46 N 25.06 E
Bardiz 130 40.26 N 42.20 E
Bardo 30 50.31 N 16.45 E
Bardo 36 36.50 N 10.06 E
Bardoc 162 30.20 S 121.17 E
Bardoli 120 21.07 N 73.07 E
Bardolino 64 45.33 N 10.43 E
Bardonecchia 62 45.05 N 6.42 E
Bardonia 276 41.07 N 74.00 W
Bardoux, Lac ⊜ 186 51.09 N 65.28 W
Bardowick 52 53.18 N 10.23 E
Bardsey Island I 42 52.45 N 4.45 W
Bardsey Sound ⵡ 42 52.47 N 4.48 W
Bardstown 194 37.48 N 85.28 W
Bardu 24 68.52 N 18.21 E
Bardufoss 24 69.04 N 18.30 E
Bardwell, Ky., U.S. 194 36.52 N 89.00 W
Bardwell, Tx., U.S. 222 32.16 N 96.42 W
Bardwell Lake ⊜1 222 32.16 N 96.39 W
Bare 144 4.42 N 42.47 E
Bareggio 266b 45.29 N 9.00 E
Barei, Wādī V 146 27.32 N 17.49 E
Bareilly 124 28.21 N 79.25 E
Barenburg 52 52.37 N 8.47 E
Barendrecht 52 51.51 N 4.32 E
Barengapāra 124 25.14 N 90.14 E
Bärenklau 54 51.49 N 14.25 E
Bärenstein, D.D.R. 54 50.30 N 13.02 E
Bärenstein, D.D.R. 54 50.46 N 13.47 E
Barentin 50 49.33 N 0.57 E
Barents Sea ▼2 12 74.00 N 36.00 E
Barents Trough ✦1 12 76.00 N 31.00 E
Barentu 144 15.04 N 37.37 E
Bareo 112 3.45 N 115.27 E
Baresville 208 39.48 N 76.57 W
Bareta 123 29.52 N 75.42 E
Barfleur 32 49.40 N 1.15 W
Barfleur, Pointe de ⟩ 32 49.42 N 1.16 W
Barga 64 44.04 N 10.29 E
Bargāchia, India 126 22.39 N 88.07 E
Bargāchia, India 272b 22.48 N 88.27 E
Bargagli 62 44.27 N 9.05 E
Bargaintown 208 39.22 N 74.35 W
Bargara 166 24.49 S 152.27 E
Bargarh 120 21.20 N 83.37 E
Bargas 34 39.56 N 4.03 W
Barge, It. 62 44.43 N 7.20 E
Barge, Ityo. 144 6.14 N 36.58 E
Barg-e Matāl 120 35.40 N 71.21 E
Bargemon 62 43.37 N 6.32 E
Bargen 58 47.48 N 8.37 E
Bargersville 218 39.31 N 86.10 W
Barghanak 128 33.56 N 62.26 E
Barghop 140 9.30 N 28.28 E
Bargo 170 34.18 S 150.35 E
Bargoed 42 51.43 N 3.15 W
Bargteheide 52 53.44 N 10.16 E
Bārguna 126 22.09 N 90.07 E
Barguzin 88 53.37 N 109.37 E
Barguzin ≃ 88 53.27 N 109.00 E
Barguzinskij chrebet ⩘ 88 54.30 N 110.20 E
Barguzinskij zapovednik ♦ 88 54.25 N 109.40 E
Bārh 124 25.29 N 85.43 E
Bar Harbor 188 44.23 N 68.12 W
Barharwa 124 24.52 N 87.47 E
Barhau 112 5.19 S 102.10 E
Barhi 124 24.18 N 85.25 E
Bar Hill 42 52.15 N 0.01 E
Barhiya 124 25.17 N 86.02 E
Bāri, India 124 23.03 N 78.05 E
Bāri, India 124 26.39 N 77.36 E
Bari, It. 68 41.07 N 16.52 E
Bari, Zaïre 152 3.19 N 19.23 E
Bari □4, It. 68 40.56 N 16.40 E
Bari □4, Som. 144 10.00 N 50.00 E
Bari ≃ 124 27.55 N 83.27 E
Baria ≃ 246 1.56 N 66.35 W
Baricella 64 44.39 N 11.32 E
Barichara 246 6.38 N 73.14 W
Barīdī, Ra's ⟩ 128 24.17 N 37.31 E
Bāri Doāb ⩘1 120 30.25 N 73.00 E
Barī Gāv 120 33.52 N 67.49 E
Barigazzo 64 44.16 N 10.39 E
Barigua, Salina de ≃ 241s 12.08 N 69.59 W
Barika 34 35.23 N 5.22 E
Barika, Oued ≃ 34 35.22 N 5.18 E
Barikiwa 154 9.28 S 37.54 E
Barīkowṭ 120 35.18 N 71.32 E
Barile 68 40.57 N 15.40 E
Barillas 236 15.48 N 91.18 W
Bariloche → San Carlos de Bariloche 254 41.09 S 71.18 W
Barilo-Krepinskaja 83 47.45 N 39.32 E
Barīm (Perim) I 144 12.40 N 43.25 E
Barima ≃ 246 8.33 N 60.25 W
Barin 84 39.13 N 44.28 E
Barinas, P.R. 240m 18.01 N 66.51 W
Barinas, Ven. 246 8.38 N 70.12 W
Barinas □3 246 8.10 N 69.50 W
Baring 224 47.46 N 121.29 W
Baring, Cape ⟩ 176 70.05 N 117.20 W
Baringa, Zaïre 152 6.17 S 16.55 E
Baringa, Zaïre 152 0.45 N 20.52 E
Baringo, Lake ⊜ 154 0.38 N 36.05 E
Båring Vig ⊂ 41 55.32 N 9.56 E
Barinitas 246 8.45 N 70.25 W
Baripāda 126 21.56 N 86.43 E
Bariri 255 22.04 S 48.44 W
Bāris 140 24.40 N 30.36 E
Barisacho 84 42.28 N 44.54 E
Bari Sādri 120 24.25 N 74.28 E
Barisāl 124 22.42 N 90.22 E
Barisan, Pegunungan ⩘ 112 3.00 S 102.15 E
Bari Sardo 71 39.50 N 9.38 E
Barisciano 66 42.19 N 13.35 E
Bariti Bil ⊜ 272b 22.48 N 88.26 E
Barito ≃ 112 3.32 S 114.29 E
Barjā 132 33.39 N 35.26 E
Barjac 62 44.18 N 4.21 E
Barjols 62 43.33 N 6.00 E
Barjora 126 23.26 N 87.17 E
Barjūj, Wādī V 146 25.57 N 13.12 E
Bark ≃ 216 42.55 N 88.50 W
Barka Kāna 124 23.37 N 85.29 E
Barkal 120 22.44 N 92.23 E
Barkam 102 31.50 N 102.40 E
Barkava 76 56.43 N 26.36 E
Barkelsby 41 54.30 N 9.50 E
Barken ⊜ 40 60.07 N 15.31 E
Barker, N.Y., U.S. 210 43.19 N 78.33 W
Barker, Ur. 258 34.16 S 57.27 W
Barker Point ⟩ 276 40.51 N 73.44 W
Barker Reservoir ⊜1 222 29.44 N 95.44 W
Barkers Brook ≃ 285 40.03 N 74.45 W
Barkerville 182 53.04 N 121.31 W
Barkerville Historic Park ♦ 182 53.04 N 121.30 W
Barkeyville 214 41.12 N 79.58 W
Barkhamsted Reservoir ⊜1 207 41.57 N 72.57 W
Barkhān 120 29.54 N 69.31 E
Barkhanpur 126 23.50 N 89.33 E
Barking ✦8 260 51.33 N 0.06 E
Barkingside ✦8 260 51.35 N 0.05 E
Barki Saraiya 124 24.10 N 85.53 E
Barkisland 262 53.41 N 1.55 W
Bark Lake ⊜, On., Can. 190 46.54 N 82.28 W
Bark Lake ⊜, On., Can. 212 45.27 N 77.51 W
Barkley, Lake ⊜1 194 36.40 N 87.55 W
Barkley Sound ⵡ 182 48.53 N 125.20 W
Barkly ≃ 169 37.32 S 146.32 E
Barkly, Mount ∧2 162 21.34 S 132.28 E
Barkly East 158 30.58 S 27.33 E
Barkly Tableland ⩘1 162 18.00 S 136.00 E
Barkly West 158 28.05 S 24.31 E
Barkol 102 43.35 N 93.01 E
Barksdale 196 29.44 N 100.02 W
Barkuhi 124 22.13 N 78.42 E
Barla 130 38.01 N 30.43 E
Bârlad → Bîrlad 38 46.14 N 27.40 E
Barlassina 266b 45.39 N 9.08 E
Barlaston 42 52.57 N 2.10 W
Barlby 44 53.48 N 1.03 W
Barleben 54 52.12 N 11.37 E
Bar-le-Duc 56 48.47 N 5.10 E
Barlee, Lake ⊜ 162 29.10 S 119.30 E
Barlee, Mount ∧2 162 24.37 S 128.06 E
Barlee Range ⩘ 162 23.35 S 115.50 E
Barles 62 44.16 N 6.16 E
Barletta 68 41.19 N 16.17 E
Barlin 50 50.27 N 2.37 E
Barlinek 30 52.59 N 15.13 E
Barling 194 35.19 N 94.18 W
Barlow 194 37.03 N 89.02 W
Barlow, Lake ⊜ 286a 42.41 N 83.19 W
Barluk 88 52.44 N 101.43 E
Barma 112 1.54 S 133.00 E
Barmancak, ozero ⊜ 86 52.08 N 61.29 E
Barmašovo 78 47.07 N 32.26 E
Barmedman 170 34.09 S 147.23 E
Barmen ✦8 263 51.17 N 7.13 E
Barmer 120 25.45 N 71.23 E
Barmer-Stausee ⊜1 263 51.14 N 7.16 E
Barmouth 42 52.43 N 4.03 W
Barmouth Bay ⊂ 42 52.42 N 4.08 W
Barmstedt 52 53.47 N 9.46 E
Barnaby Manor Oaks 284c 38.50 N 76.58 W
Barnagar 120 23.03 N 75.22 E
Barnāla 123 30.23 N 75.33 E
Barnard Castle 44 54.33 N 1.55 W
Barnasht 142 29.41 N 31.15 E
Bärnau 60 49.49 N 12.26 E
Barnaul 86 53.22 N 83.45 E
Bärnbach 61 47.05 N 15.06 E
Barn Bluff ∧ 166 41.43 S 145.56 E
Barneberg 54 52.08 N 11.03 E
Barnegat 208 39.45 N 74.13 W
Barnegat Bay ⊂ 208 39.52 N 74.07 W
Barnegat Light 208 39.45 N 74.06 W
Barne Inlet ⊂ 9 80.15 S 160.15 E
Barnes 214 41.40 N 79.01 W
Barnes ✦8 260 51.28 N 0.15 W
Barnesboro 214 40.39 N 78.46 W
Barnes Corners 212 43.49 N 75.49 W
Barnes Ice Cap ⊓ 176 70.00 N 73.15 W
Barnes Lake ⊜ 184 56.23 N 98.06 W
Barnes Sound ⵡ 220 25.14 N 80.23 W
Barnesville, Ga., U.S. 192 33.03 N 84.09 W
Barnesville, Mn., U.S. 198 46.39 N 96.25 W
Barnesville, Oh., U.S. 188 39.59 N 81.10 W
Barnet ✦8 260 51.40 N 0.13 W
Barnetby le Wold 44 53.35 N 0.25 W
Barnett 219 39.16 N 89.42 W
Barnetts 208 37.22 N 77.09 W
Barneveld, Ned. 52 52.08 N 5.35 E
Barneveld, N.Y., U.S. 210 43.16 N 75.12 W
Barneville-Carteret 32 49.23 N 1.47 W
Barnhart, Mo., U.S. 219 38.20 N 90.23 W
Barnhart, Tx., U.S. 196 31.08 N 101.10 W
Barnhill 214 40.27 N 81.21 W
Barnim ✦1 54 52.40 N 13.45 E
Barnoldswick 44 53.55 N 2.11 W
Barnówko 54 52.48 N 14.45 E
Barnsboro 285 39.46 N 75.09 W
Barnsdall 196 36.33 N 96.09 W
Barnsley 44 53.34 N 1.28 W
Barnstable 207 41.42 N 70.18 W
Barnstable □6 207 41.42 N 70.18 W
Barnstable Harbor ⊂ 207 41.43 N 70.18 W
Barnstaple 42 51.05 N 4.04 W
Barnstaple Bay ⊂ 42 51.05 N 4.20 W
Barnston 262 53.21 N 3.05 W
Barnstorf 52 52.42 N 8.30 E
Barnt Green 42 52.22 N 1.59 W
Barnton 262 53.16 N 2.33 W
Barntrup 52 51.59 N 9.06 E
Barnum Island 276 40.36 N 73.39 W
Barnwell, Ab., Can. 182 49.46 N 112.15 W
Barnwell, S.C., U.S. 192 33.14 N 81.21 W
Baro 150 8.37 N 6.25 E
Baro ≃ 144 8.26 N 33.13 E
Barobo 116 8.33 N 126.07 E
Baroda, India 122 22.18 N 73.12 E
Baroda, India 124 25.30 N 76.39 E
Baroda, Mi., U.S. 216 41.57 N 86.29 W
Baroe 158 33.13 S 24.33 E
Barometer ∧ 172 41.50 S 173.39 E
Baron Bluff ⟩4 241n 17.47 N 64.47 W
Baronissi 68 40.44 N 14.45 E
Barons 182 50.00 N 113.05 W
Barora Fa Island I 175e 7.30 S 158.20 E
Barora Ite Island I 175e 7.35 S 158.24 E
Barossa Reservoir ⊜1 168b 34.39 S 138.51 E
Barotac Nuevo 116 10.54 N 122.42 E
Barotac Viejo 116 11.03 N 122.51 E
Barouéli 150 13.04 N 6.50 W
Barpathār 120 26.17 N 93.53 E
Barpeta 120 26.19 N 91.00 E
Bar Point ⟩ 214 42.03 N 83.06 W
Barqah (Cyrenaica) □9 146 31.00 N 22.30 E
Barqah, Jabal al- ∧ 132 30.25 N 34.18 E
Barq al-'Izz 142 31.01 N 31.26 E
Barque Canada Reef ✦2 108 8.12 N 113.19 E
Barques, Pointe aux ⟩ 190 44.04 N 82.58 W
Barquisimeto 246 10.04 N 69.19 W
Barr 58 48.24 N 7.27 E
Barra, Bra. 250 11.05 S 43.10 W
Barra, Gam. 150 13.20 N 16.32 W
Barra I 46 56.58 N 7.29 W
Barra, Ponta da ⟩ 156 23.47 S 35.32 E
Barra, Sound of ⵡ 46 57.05 N 7.25 W
Barraba 166 30.22 S 150.36 E
Barracão 252 26.15 S 53.38 W
Barracão do Barreto 248 8.48 S 58.24 W
Barracas ✦8 288 34.38 S 58.22 W
Barrackpore 126 22.46 N 88.21 E
Barrackpore Airport ⊠ 272b 22.47 N 88.22 E
Barrackpore Cantonment 272b 22.46 N 88.22 E
Barrackville 188 39.30 N 80.10 W
Barracouta, Cape ⟩ 158 34.26 S 21.22 E
Barra da Estiva 255 13.38 S 41.19 W
Barra del Rio Grande 236 12.54 N 83.32 W
Barra de Santa Rosa 250 6.43 S 36.04 W
Barra de Santo Antônio 250 9.24 S 35.30 W
Barra de São Francisco 256 21.58 S 42.42 W
Barra do Bugres 248 15.05 S 57.11 W
Barra do Corda 250 5.30 S 45.15 W
Barra do Cuanza 152 9.09 S 13.00 E
Barra do Dande 152 8.28 S 13.22 E
Barra do Garças 255 15.53 S 52.15 W
Barra do Mendes 255 11.43 S 42.04 W
Barra do Piraí 256 22.28 S 43.49 W
Barra do Ribeiro 252 30.17 S 51.18 W
Barra dos Coqueiros 250 10.54 S 37.03 W
Barra Falsa, Ponta da ⟩ 156 22.55 S 35.37 E
Barrafranca 70 37.22 N 14.12 E
Barra Funda ✦8 287b 23.31 S 46.39 W
Barra Grande 250 9.02 S 43.11 W
Barra Head ⟩ 46 56.46 N 7.38 W
Barrali 71 39.28 N 9.06 E
Barra Mansa 256 22.32 S 44.11 W
Barranca, Perú 248 10.45 S 77.46 W
Barranca, Perú 248 4.50 S 76.42 W
Barrancabermeja 246 7.03 N 73.52 W
Barranca del Cobre, Parque Nacional ♦ 232 27.15 N 107.41 W
Barrancas, Chile 252 33.27 S 70.45 W
Barrancas, Col. 246 10.57 N 72.50 W
Barrancas, Ven. 246 8.46 N 70.06 W
Barrancas, Ven. 246 8.42 N 62.11 W
Barranco 286d 12.09 S 77.02 W
Barranco Azul 196 29.21 N 104.17 W
Barranco de Guadalupe 196 30.02 N 104.44 W
Barranco do Velho 34 37.14 N 7.56 W
Barrancos 34 38.08 N 6.59 W
Barrânia 256 21.33 S 46.32 W
Barranjoey Head ⟩ 170 33.34 S 151.20 E
Barranqueras 252 27.29 S 58.56 W
Barranquilla 246 10.59 N 74.48 W
Barranquitas 240m 18.11 N 66.18 W
Barra Ponta Gorda 236 11.31 N 83.48 W
Barras 250 4.15 S 42.18 W
Barrax 34 39.03 N 2.12 W
Barre, Ma., U.S. 207 42.25 N 72.06 W
Barre, Vt., U.S. 188 44.11 N 72.30 W
Barreal 252 31.38 S 69.28 W
Barre des Écrins ∧ 62 44.55 N 6.22 E
Barre Falls Dam ✦6 207 42.25 N 72.02 W
Barreiras 250 12.08 S 45.00 W
Barreirinha 250 2.47 S 57.03 W
Barreirinhas 250 2.45 S 42.50 W
Barreiro 266c 38.40 N 9.04 W
Barreiros 255 15.43 S 52.45 W
Barreiros 250 8.49 S 35.12 W
Barrême 62 43.57 N 6.22 E
Barren ≃ 194 37.11 N 86.37 W
Barren, Nosy II 157b 18.25 S 43.40 E
Barren Islands II 180 58.55 N 152.15 W
Barren River Lake ⊜1 194 36.45 N 86.02 W
Barren Run ≃ 279b 40.09 N 79.42 W
Barre Plains 207 42.22 N 72.06 W
Barret-le-Bas 62 44.16 N 5.44 E
Barretos 255 20.33 S 48.33 W
Barrett 222 29.53 N 95.04 W
Barrett, Mount ∧ 162 18.10 S 127.33 E
Barrhead, Ab., Can. 182 54.08 N 114.24 W
Barrhead, Scot., U.K. 46 55.48 N 4.24 W
Barrhill 44 55.07 N 4.46 W
Barriada Pomar Alto 266d 41.29 N 2.14 E
Barrie 212 44.24 N 79.40 W
Barriefield 212 44.14 N 76.28 W
Barrie Island I 190 45.55 N 82.40 W
Barrien 52 52.56 N 8.49 E
Barrier, Cape ⟩ 172 36.21 S 175.31 E
Barrier Bay ⊂ 9 67.45 S 81.10 E
Barrière 182 51.11 N 120.07 W
Barrier Range ⩘ 166 31.25 S 141.25 E
Barrier Reef ✦2 164 11.36 S 153.00 E
Barrigada 174p 13.28 N 144.48 E
Barrilla Draw V 196 31.21 N 103.23 W
Barr Ilyās 132 33.46 N 35.54 E
Barrington, N.S., Can. 186 43.34 N 65.34 W
Barrington, Il., U.S. 216 42.09 N 88.08 W
Barrington, N.J., U.S. 285 39.51 N 75.03 W
Barrington, R.I., U.S. 207 41.44 N 71.18 W
Barrington Hills 216 42.07 N 88.09 W
Barrington Lake ⊜ 184 56.55 N 100.15 W
Barrington Tops ∧ 166 32.00 S 151.28 E
Barrington Woods 278 42.09 N 88.04 W
Barringun 166 29.01 S 145.43 E
Barrinho 256 23.07 S 45.22 W
Barrio Azul ✦8 286b 23.04 N 82.23 W
Barrio Obrero Industrial 286d 12.04 S 77.04 W
Barrita Vieja 236 13.55 N 90.54 W
Barrīyat al-Uṣayfir 142 31.18 N 30.40 E
Barro, Bra. 250 7.11 S 38.47 W
Barro, Gui.-B. 150 12.24 N 15.30 W
Barro Alto 255 15.04 S 48.58 W
Barro Duro 250 2.52 S 42.17 W
Barrois □9 56 48.40 N 5.15 E
Barron 190 45.24 N 91.50 W
Barron Creek ≃ 282 37.27 N 122.05 W
Barron Lake 216 41.51 N 86.11 W
Barrouallie 241h 13.14 N 61.17 W
Barrow, Arg. 252 38.18 S 60.14 W
Barrow, Ak., U.S. 180 71.17 N 156.34 W
Barrow ≃ 48 52.15 N 7.00 W
Barrow, Point ⟩ 180 71.23 N 156.30 W
Barrow Bay ⊂ 212 44.58 N 81.13 W
Barrow Creek 162 21.33 S 133.53 E
Barrowford 44 53.52 N 2.13 W
Barrow-in-Furness 44 54.07 N 3.14 W
Barrow Island I 162 20.48 S 115.23 E
Barrow Range ⩘ 162 26.04 S 127.28 E
Barrows 184 52.49 N 101.27 W
Barrow Strait ⵡ 176 74.21 N 94.10 W
Barrowsville 207 41.56 N 71.12 W
Barrow upon Humber 44 53.41 N 0.23 W
Barry, Wales, U.K. 42 51.24 N 3.18 W
Barry, Il., U.S. 219 39.41 N 91.02 W
Barry, Tx., U.S. 222 32.06 N 96.38 W
Barry □6 216 42.35 N 85.18 W
Barrydale 158 33.55 S 20.43 E
Barrys Bay 212 45.29 N 77.41 W
Barrys Bay ⊂ 212 45.28 N 77.42 W
Barryton 190 43.45 N 85.08 W
Barrytown 210 42.00 N 73.56 W
Barryville 210 41.28 N 74.54 W
Barsakel'mes, ostrov I 86 45.40 N 59.58 E
Baršatas 86 48.13 N 78.21 E
Bårse 41 55.07 N 11.58 E
Bārsi 122 18.14 N 75.42 E
Baršin 86 49.45 N 69.36 E
Barsinghausen 52 52.18 N 9.27 E
Barskaun 85 42.10 N 77.37 E
Barssel 52 53.10 N 7.44 E
Barst 56 49.04 N 6.50 E
Barstow, Ca., U.S. 228 34.53 N 117.01 W
Barstow, Tx., U.S. 196 31.28 N 103.24 W
Barsuki 82 54.15 N 37.30 E
Bar-sur-Aube 58 48.14 N 4.43 E
Bar-sur-Seine 50 48.07 N 4.22 E
Bart 208 39.56 N 76.05 W
Bārta ≃ 76 56.21 N 21.03 E
Bartala 272b 22.33 N 88.16 E
Bartazuga, Jabal ∧ 140 21.44 N 33.33 E
Bartelso 219 38.32 N 89.28 W
Bartenheim 58 47.38 N 7.29 E
Bartenstein 56 49.21 N 9.53 E
Barter Island I 180 70.08 N 143.35 W
Barth 54 54.22 N 12.43 E
Barthe ≃ 54 54.22 N 12.41 E
Barthélemy, Deo ⩘ 110 19.26 N 104.06 E
Bartholomew □6 218 39.13 N 85.55 W
Bartholomew, Bayou ≃ 194 32.43 N 92.04 W
Bartibougou 150 12.52 N 0.48 E
Bartica 246 6.24 N 58.37 W
Bartın 130 41.38 N 32.21 E
Bartle Frere ∧ 166 17.23 S 145.49 E
Bartlesville 196 36.44 N 95.58 W
Bartlett, Il., U.S. 216 41.59 N 88.11 W
Bartlett, Ne., U.S. 198 41.53 N 98.33 W
Bartlett, N.H., U.S. 188 44.04 N 71.17 W
Bartlett, Tn., U.S. 194 35.12 N 89.52 W
Bartlett, Tx., U.S. 222 30.48 N 97.26 W
Bartlett Brook ≃ 283 42.42 N 71.13 W
Bartlett Cove 180 58.27 N 135.55 W
Bartlett Reservoir ⊜1 200 33.52 N 111.37 W
Bartletts Harbour 186 50.57 N 57.00 W
Bartley 198 40.14 N 100.18 W
Bartolomé Bavio → General Mansilla 258 35.05 S 57.45 W
Bartolomé de las Casas 252 25.24 S 59.34 W
Bartolomeu de Gusmão, Aeroporto ⊠ 256 22.56 S 43.43 W
Bartolomeu Dias 156 21.10 S 35.09 E
Barton, Austl. 162 30.31 S 132.39 E
Barton, N.Y., U.S. 210 42.03 N 76.27 W
Barton, Oh., U.S. 214 40.06 N 80.50 W
Barton, Vt., U.S. 188 44.44 N 72.10 W
Barton Aerodrome ⊠ 262 53.28 N 2.23 W
Barton Lake 216 42.06 N 85.35 W
Barton Lake ⊜ 184 52.00 N 94.06 W
Barton-le-Clay 42 51.57 N 0.25 W
Barton Mills 42 52.20 N 0.31 E
Barton Park ♦ 274a 33.57 S 151.09 E
Barton Run ≃ 285 39.53 N 74.51 W
Barton-under-Needwood 42 52.45 N 1.43 W
Barton-upon-Humber 44 53.41 N 0.27 W
Bartonville 190 40.39 N 89.39 W
Barton Water Swing Bridge ✦5 262 53.28 N 2.21 W
Bartoszyce 30 54.16 N 20.49 E
Bartow, Fl., U.S. 220 27.53 N 81.50 W
Bartow, Ga., U.S. 192 32.52 N 82.28 W
Baru, Kali ≃ 269e 6.10 S 106.51 E
Barú, Volcán ∧1 236 8.48 N 82.33 W
Barueri 256 23.31 S 46.53 W
Barugo 116 11.20 N 124.44 E
Bāruipāra 272b 22.46 N 88.14 E
Bāruipur 126 22.21 N 88.27 E
Bārūk, Jabal al- ∧ 132 33.43 N 35.45 E
Barumini 71 39.42 N 9.00 E
Barumun ≃ 114 2.30 N 100.09 E
Barun Bogd uul ∧ 90 44.57 N 100.15 E
Bāruni 124 25.29 N 85.59 E
Barun Su 102 42.27 N 111.01 E
Barun-Torej, ozero ⊜ 88 50.10 N 115.30 E
Barus 114 2.00 N 98.24 E
Baruta 286c 10.26 N 66.53 W
Baruth 54 52.03 N 13.30 E
Baruun Bajan-Ulaan 102 45.10 N 101.24 E
Baruun bogd uul ∧ 102 44.57 N 100.15 E
Baruun-Urt 90 46.42 N 113.15 E
Barva, Volcán ∧1 236 10.08 N 84.06 W
Barvas 46 58.22 N 6.32 W
Barvenkovo 78 48.54 N 37.02 E
Barver 52 52.37 N 8.35 E
Barvicha 265b 55.44 N 37.16 E
Barview 202 43.21 N 124.18 W
Barwa 126 23.51 N 86.26 E
Barwāh 120 22.16 N 76.03 E
Barwāla ✦8 272a 28.46 N 77.04 E
Bärwalde → Mieszkowice 30 52.46 N 14.30 E
Barwāni 120 22.02 N 74.54 E
Barwa Sāgar 124 25.23 N 78.44 E
Barwell 42 52.32 N 1.21 W
Barwice 30 53.45 N 16.22 E
Barwick 192 30.54 N 83.44 W
Barwidgee 162 27.02 S 120.54 E
Barwon ≃, Austl. 166 30.00 S 148.05 E
Barwon ≃, Austl. 169 38.13 S 144.25 E
Barybino, S.S.S.R. 82 55.16 N 37.54 E
Barybino, S.S.S.R. 82 54.56 N 37.47 E
Barycz ≃ 30 51.42 N 16.15 E
Barykino 83 49.17 N 38.24 E
Barykova, mys ⟩ 180 63.02 N 179.29 E
Barykovo 82 54.38 N 38.48 E
Barynino 82 55.47 N 36.21 E
Baryš 80 53.39 N 47.08 E
Baryš ≃ 80 54.35 N 46.48 E
Baryševka 78 50.22 N 31.19 E
Baryševo 86 54.58 N 83.11 E
Baryšniki 80 56.57 N 46.33 E
Barzah 132 33.34 N 36.19 E
Barzas 86 55.43 N 86.19 E
Barzio 58 45.57 N 9.27 E
Bas'a ≃ 76 53.46 N 31.01 E
Basacato del Este 152 3.37 N 8.54 E
Basai Dārāpur ✦8 272a 28.40 N 77.08 E
Bāsa'īdū 128 26.39 N 55.17 E
Basail, Arg. 252 27.52 S 59.18 W
Bāsāil, Bngl. 126 24.14 N 90.04 E
Basakin 80 48.11 N 42.18 E
Basāl 123 33.33 N 72.15 E
Basalt ≃ 166 19.38 S 145.52 E
Basalt Island I 271d 22.19 N 114.22 E
Basaluzzo 62 44.46 N 8.42 E
Basandīlah 142 31.12 N 31.26 E
Basankusu 152 1.14 N 19.48 E
Bašanta 80 46.05 N 41.56 E
Basanti 126 22.12 N 88.42 E
Basarabi 38 44.10 N 28.24 E
Basatongwulashan ∧ 120 33.05 N 91.30 E
Basavakalyān 122 17.52 N 76.57 E
Basavilbaso 252 32.22 S 58.53 W
Basbirin 130 37.19 N 41.38 E
Baščelakskij chrebet ⩘ 86 51.15 N 84.30 E
Baschi 66 42.40 N 12.13 E
Basco 108 20.27 N 121.58 E
Bascom 214 41.07 N 83.17 W
Bascuñán, Cabo ⟩ 252 28.51 S 71.30 W
Basdahl 52 53.26 N 8.59 E
Basdorf, B.R.D. 56 51.12 N 8.58 E
Basdorf, D.D.R. 54 52.44 N 13.26 E
Basekpio 154 4.44 N 24.40 E
Basel (Bâle) 58 47.33 N 7.35 E
Baselga di Pinè 64 46.08 N 11.14 E
Baselice 68 41.24 N 14.58 E
Basella 34 42.01 N 1.18 E
Basel-Land □3 58 47.30 N 7.50 E
Basel-Stadt □3 58 47.38 N 7.40 E
Basen ≃ 96 34.48 N 132.51 E
Bas-en-Basset 62 45.18 N 4.06 E
Basentello ≃ 68 40.40 N 16.23 E
Basento ≃ 68 40.21 N 16.50 E
Bașeu ≃ 38 47.44 N 27.15 E
Basey 116 11.17 N 125.04 E
Bashākerd, Kūhhā-ye ⩘ 128 26.42 N 59.00 E
Bashaw 182 52.35 N 112.58 W
Basher Kill ≃ 210 41.27 N 74.35 W
Bashgah Airfield ⊠ 267d 35.40 N 51.16 E
Bashi Channel ⵡ 108 22.00 N 121.00 E
Bashikejike 120 37.30 N 85.50 E
Bashiqiao 106 31.40 N 120.22 E
Bashtīl 273c 30.05 N 31.11 E
Basi, India 123 30.41 N 76.24 E
Basi, India 123 30.36 N 76.50 E
Basiad Bay ⊂ 116 14.16 N 122.19 E
Basiano 112 1.16 S 122.50 E
Basibasy 157b 22.10 S 43.40 E
Başıbüyük 267b 40.57 N 29.08 E
Basicò 70 38.04 N 15.04 E
Basid 85 38.07 N 72.09 E
Basilaki Island I 164 10.35 S 151.00 E
Basilan → Isabela 116 6.42 N 121.58 E
Basilan □4 116 6.35 N 121.55 E
Basilan Island I 116 6.34 N 122.03 E
Basilan Peak ∧ 116 6.33 N 122.04 E
Basilan Strait ⵡ 116 6.49 N 122.05 E
Basildon 260 51.35 N 0.25 E
Basildon □8 260 51.35 N 0.29 E
Basile 194 30.29 N 92.35 W
Basiliano 64 46.01 N 13.06 E
Basilicata □4 68 40.30 N 16.10 E
Basílio 252 31.53 S 53.01 W
Basiluzzo, Isola I 70 38.39 N 15.07 E
Basin, Mt., U.S. 202 46.16 N 112.15 W
Basin, Wy., U.S. 202 44.22 N 108.02 W
Bäsingen ⊜ 40 60.09 N 16.20 E
Basinger 220 27.24 N 81.01 W
Basingstoke 42 51.15 N 1.05 W
Basingstoke Canal ≍ 260 51.21 N 0.29 W
Basingwerk Abbey ᵾ1 262 53.17 N 3.12 W
Basin Lake ⊜ 184 52.38 N 105.18 W
Basīrhāt 126 22.40 N 88.53 E
Basīrpur 123 30.35 N 73.50 E
Basīt, Ra's al- ⟩ 130 35.51 N 35.48 E
Basiyingzi 104 42.05 N 121.37 E
Basjanovskij 86 58.19 N 60.44 E
Baška 36 44.58 N 14.46 E
Baskahegan Lake ⊜ 188 45.30 N 67.48 W
Baskakovka 76 54.36 N 34.19 E
Başkale 128 38.02 N 44.00 E
Baskatong, Réservoir ⊜1 190 46.48 N 75.50 W
Baškaus ≃ 86 51.09 N 87.43 E
Baškend 84 40.38 N 45.32 E
Basket Lake ⊜ 184 49.43 N 92.00 W
Basking Ridge 276 40.42 N 74.32 W
Baškino 82 55.18 N 36.41 E
Baškirskaja Avtonomnaja Sovetskaja Socialističeskaja Respublika □3 86 54.00 N 56.00 E
Baškirskij zapovednik ♦ 86 53.30 N 57.58 E
Başköy 84 39.53 N 44.32 E
Baskuduk 86 49.43 N 61.32 E
Baš-Kugandy 85 42.00 N 74.39 E
Baskunčak, ozero ⊜ 80 48.12 N 46.54 E
Baslow 44 53.15 N 1.38 W
Başmakcı 130 37.54 N 30.01 E
Bašmakovo 80 53.12 N 43.02 E
Basmat 122 19.19 N 77.10 E
Bäsna 40 60.32 N 15.12 E
Başnık 130 38.07 N 40.44 E
Bāsoda 124 23.51 N 77.56 E
Basoko 152 1.14 N 23.36 E
Basoko ≃ 273b 4.19 S 15.16 E
Basoli 123 32.30 N 75.49 E
Basom 210 43.04 N 78.24 W
Basongo 152 4.20 S 20.24 E
Basora, Punt ⟩ 241s 12.25 N 69.52 W

Symbol	English	Deutsch	Español	Français	Português
≃	River	Fluss	Río	Rivière	Rio
≍	Canal	Kanal	Canal	Canal	Canal
⊥	Waterfall, Rapids	Wasserfall, Stromschnellen	Cascada, Rápidos	Chute d'eau, Rapides	Cascata, Rápidos
ⵡ	Strait	Meeresstrasse	Estrecho	Détroit	Estreito
⊂	Bay, Gulf	Bucht, Golf	Bahía, Golfo	Baie, Golfe	Baía, Golfo
⊜	Lake, Lakes	See, Seen	Lago, Lagos	Lac, Lacs	Lago, Lagos
≋	Swamp	Sumpf	Pantano	Marais	Pântano
⊓	Ice Features, Glacier	Eis- und Gletscherformen	Accidentes Glaciales	Formes glaciaires	Acidentes glaciares
▼	Other Hydrographic Features	Andere Hydrographische Objekte	Otros Elementos Hidrográficos	Autres données hydrographiques	Outros acidentes hidrográficos
✦	Submarine Features	Untermeerische Objekte	Accidentes Submarinos	Formes de relief sous-marin	Acidentes submarinos
□	Political Unit	Politische Einheit	Unidad Politica	Entité politique	Unidade política
ᵾ	Cultural Institution	Kulturelle Institution	Institución Cultural	Institution culturelle	Instituição cultural
⊥	Historical Site	Historische Stätte	Sitio Histórico	Site historique	Sitio histórico
♦	Recreational Site	Erholungs- und Ferienort	Sitio de Recreo	Centre de loisirs	Area de Lazer
⊠	Airport	Flughafen	Aeropuerto	Aéroport	Aeroporto
■	Military Installation	Militäranlage	Instalación Militar	Installation militaire	Instalação militar
✦	Miscellaneous	Verschiedenes	Misceláneo	Divers	Diversos

Name	Page	Lat.°′	Long.°′
Basovizza	64	45.38 N	13.52 E
Başpınar	130	39.12 N	38.42 E
Basra → Al-Başrah	128	30.30 N	47.47 E
Bas-Rhin □[5]	32	48.35 N	7.40 E
Bass ≃	169	38.30 S	145.26 E
Bassano	182	50.47 N	112.28 W
Bassano del Grappa	64	45.46 N	11.44 E
Bassari	150	9.15 N	0.47 E
Bassas da India ✦[2]	138	21.25 S	39.42 E
Bass Creek ≃	216	42.37 N	89.04 W
Basse-Californie → Baja California ›[1]	232	28.00 N	113.30 W
Bassecourt	58	47.20 N	7.15 E
Bassein	110	16.47 N	94.44 E
Bassein ≃[1]	110	15.56 N	94.18 E
Basse-Kotto □[5]	152	5.00 N	21.30 E
Bassen	52	53.04 N	9.04 E
Bassenthwaite	44	54.41 N	3.12 W
Bassenthwaite Lake ⊜	44	54.38 N	3.13 W
Basse-Pointe	240e	14.52 N	61.07 W
Basses, Pointe des ›	241o	15.52 N	61.17 W
Basses-Alpes □[5]	62	44.10 N	6.00 E
Basse Santa Su	150	13.19 N	14.13 W
Basse-Terre, Guad.	241o	16.00 N	61.44 W
Basseterre, St. C.-N.	238	17.18 N	62.43 W
Basse Terre, Trin.	241r	10.08 N	61.18 W
Basse-Terre I	241o	16.10 N	61.40 W
Bassett, Ne., U.S.	198	42.35 N	99.32 W
Bassett, Va., U.S.	192	36.45 N	79.59 W
Bassett Creek ≃	194	31.25 N	87.56 W
Bassett Peak ∧	200	32.30 N	110.17 W
Bassfield	194	31.30 N	89.44 W
Bass Harbor	188	44.14 N	68.20 W
Bass Hill	274a	33.54 S	151.00 E
Bassignana	62	45.00 N	8.44 E
Bassikounou	150	15.52 N	5.57 W
Bassila	150	9.01 N	1.40 E
Bassin des Aghlabites ⊥	36	35.43 N	10.10 E
Bassingbourn	42	52.04 N	0.03 W
Bass Lake, Ca., U.S.	226	37.19 N	119.33 W
Bass Lake, In., U.S.	216	41.12 N	86.36 W
Bass Lake ⊜, On., Can.	212	44.49 N	76.08 W
Bass Lake ⊜, In., U.S.	216	41.13 N	86.36 W
Bass Lake ⊜[1]	226	37.19 N	119.34 W
Bass Point ›	170	34.36 S	150.54 E
Bass River	186	45.25 N	63.47 W
Bass Strait ʯ	166	39.20 S	145.30 E
Bassum	52	52.51 N	8.43 E
Basswood Lake ⊜, On., Can.	190	46.20 N	83.23 W
Basswood Lake ⊜, N.A.	190	48.06 N	91.40 W
Basta	126	21.41 N	87.03 E
Bästad	26	56.26 N	12.51 E
Basṭah	132	30.14 N	35.32 E
Bastak	128	27.14 N	54.22 E
Basṭām	128	36.29 N	55.04 E
Baštanka	78	47.24 N	32.25 E
Bastei ♠	54	50.58 N	14.04 E
Bastelica	36	42.00 N	9.02 E
Basti	124	26.48 N	82.43 E
Basti □[5]	124	27.00 N	82.50 E
Bastia, Fr.	32	42.42 N	9.27 E
Bastia, It.	66	43.04 N	12.33 E
Bastian	192	37.09 N	81.09 W
Bastiglia	64	44.43 N	11.00 E
Bastimentos	236	9.21 N	82.12 W
Bastimentos, Isla I	236	9.18 N	82.08 W
Bastogne	56	50.00 N	5.43 E
Bastrop, La., U.S.	194	32.46 N	91.54 W
Bastrop, Tx., U.S.	222	30.06 N	97.18 W
Bastrop □[6]	222	33.00 N	97.18 W
Bastrop, Lake ⊜[1]	222	30.09 N	97.18 W
Bastrop Bay ⊂	222	29.06 N	95.11 W
Bastrop State Park ♠	222	30.07 N	97.17 W
Bastuträsk	26	64.47 N	20.02 E
Basu, Pulau I	112	0.18 S	103.36 E
Basubāti	272b	22.47 N	88.12 E
Bāsudebpur, India	126	21.49 N	87.38 E
Bāsudebpur, India	272b	22.49 N	88.25 E
Basuo → Dongfang	110	19.05 N	108.39 E
Bāsūs	273c	30.08 N	31.13 E
Baswa	126	24.08 N	87.52 E
Basyūn	142	30.57 N	30.49 E
Bas-Zaïre □[4]	152	5.30 S	14.30 E
Bata	152	1.51 N	9.45 E
Bataan □[4]	116	14.40 N	120.25 E
Bataan, Mount ∧	116	14.31 N	120.28 E
Bataan Peninsula ›[1]	116	14.40 N	120.25 E
Batabanó	240p	22.43 N	82.17 W
Batabanó, Golfo de ⊂	240p	22.15 N	82.30 W
Batac	116	18.05 N	120.35 E
Batad	116	11.25 N	123.06 E
Batagaj	74	67.38 N	134.38 E
Batagaj-Alyta	74	67.48 N	130.25 E
Batag Island I	116	12.38 N	125.04 E
Batagol	88	52.22 N	100.45 E
Bataguaçu	255	21.42 S	52.22 W
Bataiporã	255	22.20 S	53.17 W
Batajsk	83	47.10 N	39.44 E
Batak	38	41.57 N	24.13 E
Batak, Jazovir ⊜[1]	38	41.59 N	24.11 E
Batakan	112	4.05 S	114.38 E
Batāla	123	31.48 N	75.12 E
Batalha, Bra.	250	9.41 S	37.08 W
Batalha, Bra.	250	4.01 S	42.05 W
Batalha, Port.	34	39.39 N	8.50 W
Bataly	86	52.52 N	62.00 E
Batam, Pulau I	112	1.05 N	104.03 E
Batama, S.S.S.R.	88	53.53 N	101.36 E
Batama, Zaïre	154	0.56 N	26.39 E
Batamaj	74	63.31 N	129.27 E
Batamšinskij	86	50.36 N	58.16 E
Batan, Pil.	116	11.35 N	122.30 E
Batan, Zhg.	98	34.10 N	120.04 E
Batanagar	126	22.31 N	88.15 E
Batang, Indon.	115a	6.55 S	109.45 E
Batang, Zhg.	102	30.02 N	99.02 E
Batangafo	152	7.18 N	18.18 E
Batangas	116	13.45 N	121.03 E
Batangas □[4]	116	13.50 N	121.00 E
Batangas Bay ⊂	116	13.43 N	121.00 E
Batangbatangdaya	115a	6.56 S	113.59 E
Batang Berjuntai	114	3.23 N	101.25 E
Batanghari ≃	112	1.16 S	104.05 E
Batang Kali	114	3.28 N	101.38 E
Batangtoru	114	1.29 N	99.03 E
Batan Island I, Pil.	108	20.26 N	121.58 E
Batan Island I, Pil.	116	13.15 N	124.00 E
Batan Islands II	108	20.30 N	121.50 E
Batanta, Pulau I	164	0.50 S	130.40 E
Batas ≃	287a	22.44 S	43.24 W
Batas Island I	116	11.10 N	119.36 E
Bátaszék	30	46.12 N	18.44 E
Batatais	255	20.53 S	47.37 W
Batatuba	256	23.04 S	46.25 W
Batavia, Arg.	252	34.47 S	65.41 W
Batavia, Il., U.S.	216	41.51 N	88.18 W
Batavia, Ia., U.S.	190	40.59 N	92.10 W
Batavia, Mi., U.S.	216	41.55 N	85.06 W
Batavia, N.Y., U.S.	210	42.59 N	78.11 W
Batavia, Oh., U.S.	218	39.04 N	84.10 W
Batawa	212	44.10 N	77.36 W
Batbatan Island I	116	11.28 N	121.55 E
Batcengel	88	47.47 N	101.58 E
Batchawana ≃	190	46.55 N	84.32 W
Batchawana Mountain ∧	190	47.04 N	84.24 W
Batchawanna Island I	190	46.53 N	84.30 W
Batchelor	164	13.04 S	131.01 E
Bătdâmbâng	110	13.06 N	103.12 E
Bate Bay ⊂	170	34.04 S	151.12 E
Bateckij	76	58.39 N	30.19 E
Bate Heath	262	53.19 N	2.28 W
Bateia	256	22.20 S	45.49 W
Batéké, Plateaux ∧∧[1]	152	3.30 S	15.45 E
Batemans Bay	166	35.43 S	150.11 E
Batenbrock ◆[8]	263	51.31 N	6.57 E
Batepito ≃	200	30.48 N	109.11 W
Bates, Mount ∧	174c	29.01 S	167.56 E
Batesburg	192	33.54 N	81.32 W
Bates Creek ≃	200	42.41 N	106.37 W
Bates Range ∧∧	162	27.25 S	121.13 E
Batesville, Ar., U.S.	194	35.46 N	91.38 W
Batesville, In., U.S.	218	39.18 N	85.13 W
Batesville, Ms., U.S.	194	34.18 N	89.56 W
Batesville, Tx., U.S.	196	28.57 N	99.37 W
Bath, N.B., Can.	186	46.31 N	67.36 W
Bath, On., Can.	212	44.11 N	76.47 W
Bath, Eng., U.K.	42	51.23 N	2.22 W
Bath, Il., U.S.	219	40.11 N	90.08 W
Bath, Me., U.S.	188	43.54 N	69.49 W
Bath, Mi., U.S.	216	42.49 N	84.26 W
Bath, N.Y., U.S.	210	42.20 N	77.19 W
Bath, Oh., U.S.	214	41.11 N	81.38 W
Bath, Pa., U.S.	208	40.43 N	75.23 W
Bath □[6]	218	38.14 N	83.48 W
Batha □[5]	146	14.00 N	19.00 E
Batha ≃	146	12.47 N	17.34 E
Bath Addition	285	40.06 N	74.52 W
Bathgate, Scot., U.K.	46	55.55 N	3.39 W
Bathgate, N.D., U.S.	198	48.52 N	97.28 W
Bathsheba	241g	13.13 N	59.31 W
Bathurst, Austl.	166	33.25 S	149.35 E
Bathurst, N.B., Can.	186	47.36 N	65.39 W
Bathurst → Banjul, Gam.	150	13.28 N	16.39 W
Bathurst, S. Afr.	158	33.30 S	26.50 E
Bathurst, Cape ›	176	70.35 N	128.00 W
Bathurst, Lake ⊜	170	35.04 S	149.44 E
Bathurst Inlet	176	66.50 N	108.01 W
Bathurst Inlet ⊂	176	68.10 N	108.50 W
Bathurst Island I, Austl.	164	11.37 S	130.23 E
Bathurst Island I, N.T., Can.	16	76.00 N	100.30 W
Bathurst Island Mission	164	11.45 S	130.38 E
Bati	144	11.10 N	40.02 E
Batia	150	10.54 N	1.29 E
Batiāgarh	124	24.07 N	79.21 E
Batié	150	9.53 N	2.55 W
Bāṭin, Wādī al- V	128	29.35 N	47.00 E
Batina	38	45.51 N	18.51 E
Batiquitos Lagoon ⊂	228	33.05 N	117.18 W
Batīr	132	31.16 N	35.42 E
Batırga	130	36.24 N	36.11 E
Batiscan ≃	206	46.31 N	72.15 W
Batiste Creek ≃	222	30.04 N	94.28 W
Batkanu	150	9.05 N	12.25 W
Batken	85	40.03 N	70.50 E
Batley	44	53.44 N	1.37 W
Batlow	171b	35.31 S	148.09 E
Batman	130	37.52 N	41.07 E
Batna	148	35.34 N	6.11 E
Batna □[5]	148	35.30 N	6.10 E
Batnorov	88	47.55 N	111.30 E
Batō, Nihon	94	36.44 N	140.10 E
Bato, Pil.	116	10.20 N	124.47 E
Ba-to, Viet.	110	14.46 N	108.44 E
Bato, Lake ⊜	116	13.19 N	123.21 E
Batoala	152	0.48 N	13.27 E
Batoche Rectory National Historic Site ⊥	184	52.41 N	106.02 W
Batoka	154	16.47 S	27.15 E
Baton Rouge	194	30.27 N	91.09 W
Batorampon Point ›	116	7.07 N	121.54 E
Batoti	123	33.06 N	75.19 E
Batouri	152	4.26 N	14.22 E
Batovi	255	15.53 S	53.24 W
Batpajsagyr, peski ◆[2]	80	47.20 N	48.40 E
Baṭrah	142	31.10 N	31.27 E
Ba-tri	110	10.02 N	106.36 E
Bātsawul	120	34.15 N	70.52 E
Batson	222	30.15 N	94.37 W
Batsto ≃	285	39.39 N	74.39 W
Batsto, Skit Branch ≃	285	39.46 N	74.41 W
Batsto State Historic Site ⊥	208	39.39 N	74.39 W
Bat Sûmber	88	48.29 N	106.42 E
Battaglia Terme	64	45.17 N	11.47 E
Battambang → Bătdâmbâng	110	13.06 N	103.12 E
Battenberg	56	51.01 N	8.38 E
Batten Kill ≃	188	43.06 N	73.35 W
Batterie, Pointe de la ›	240e	14.44 N	60.54 W
Bätterkinden	58	47.08 N	7.32 E
Battersea ◆[8]	260	51.28 N	0.10 W
Battersea Park ♠	260	51.29 N	0.09 W
Batticaloa	122	7.43 N	81.42 E
Battice	56	50.39 N	5.49 E
Battin	224	45.29 N	122.34 W
Battipaglia	68	40.37 N	14.58 E
Battle	42	50.55 N	0.29 E
Battle ≃	176	52.43 N	108.15 W
Battle Creek, Ia., U.S.	198	42.18 N	95.35 W
Battle Creek, Mi., U.S.	216	42.19 N	85.10 W
Battle Creek, Ne., U.S.	198	41.59 N	97.35 W
Battle Creek ≃, N.A.	202	48.36 N	109.11 W
Battle Creek ≃, Ca., U.S.	204	40.21 N	122.11 W
Battle Creek ≃, Id., U.S.	202	42.14 N	116.32 W
Battle Creek ≃, Mi., U.S.	216	42.19 N	85.12 W
Battle Creek ≃, Tx., U.S.	196	32.50 N	98.58 W
Battle Creek, North Fork ≃	204	40.26 N	122.00 W
Battle Creek, South Fork ≃	204	40.26 N	122.00 W
Battlefields	154	18.31 S	29.52 E
Battle Green ⊥	283	42.27 N	71.14 W
Battle Ground, In., U.S.	216	40.30 N	86.50 W
Battle Ground, Wa., U.S.	224	45.46 N	122.31 W
Battle Harbour	176	52.16 N	55.35 W
Battle Lake	198	46.16 N	95.42 W
Battlement Mesa ∧	200	39.20 N	108.00 W
Battlemount	158	26.57 S	23.46 E
Battle Mountain	204	40.38 N	116.56 W
Battle Mountain ∧	200	41.02 N	107.16 W
Battlesbridge	260	51.37 N	0.34 E
Battonya	30	46.17 N	21.01 E
Battuello	266b	45.27 N	8.56 E
Batu	115a	7.52 S	112.31 E
Batu ∧	144	6.55 N	39.46 E
Batu, Bukit ∧	112	2.16 N	113.43 E
Batu, Kepulauan II	110	0.18 S	98.28 E
Batuan	116	12.25 N	123.47 E
Batu Arang	114	3.19 N	101.28 E
Batuata, Pulau I	112	6.12 S	122.42 E
Batuata, Tanjung ›	115b	9.37 S	120.29 E
Batu-batu	112	4.09 S	119.52 E
Batu Berinchang, Gunong ∧	114	4.30 N	101.24 E
Batubetumpang	112	2.53 S	106.09 E
Batubrok, Bukit ∧	112	1.10 N	114.36 E
Batuc	232	29.15 N	109.44 W
Batu Caves	114	3.14 N	101.40 E
Batudaka, Pulau I	112	0.28 S	121.48 E
Batu Enam	114	2.35 N	102.43 E
Batu Gajah	114	4.28 N	101.03 E
Batui	112	1.17 S	122.33 E
Batui, Pegunungan ∧∧	112	1.15 S	122.10 E
Batuidu	112	10.38 S	123.25 E
Batukau, Bukit ∧	115b	8.20 S	115.05 E
Batukelau	112	0.48 N	115.01 E
Batu Laut	114	2.41 N	101.31 E
Batulicin	112	3.27 S	116.00 E
Batumata Point ›	164	10.17 S	148.57 E
Batumelinggang	114	3.50 N	98.25 E
Batumi	84	41.38 N	41.38 E
Batumundan	114	1.17 N	98.50 E
Batu Pahat (Bandar Penggaram)	114	1.51 N	102.56 E
Batupanjang	114	1.43 N	101.31 E
Batu Puteh, Gunong ∧	114	4.13 N	101.27 E
Batuputih	112	1.24 N	118.29 E
Baturaja	112	4.08 S	104.10 E
Batu Rakit	114	5.27 N	103.03 E
Baturetno	115a	7.59 S	110.56 E
Baturin	78	51.21 N	32.51 E
Baturino, S.S.S.R.	86	57.48 N	85.12 E
Baturino, S.S.S.R.	265b	55.35 N	37.31 E
Baturinskaja	78	45.47 N	39.22 E
Baturité	250	4.20 S	38.53 W
Baturotok	115b	8.42 S	117.10 E
Baturusa	112	2.02 S	106.07 E
Batusangkar	112	0.27 S	100.35 E
Batutinggi	112	1.55 S	113.19 E
Bat Yam	132	32.01 N	34.45 E
Batyrevo	80	55.04 N	47.38 E
Batyr-Mala, ozero ⊜	80	47.35 N	44.45 E
Bau	112	1.25 N	110.08 E
Baú, Igarapé do ≃	250	7.26 S	54.47 W
Bauang	116	16.31 N	120.20 E
Baubašata, gory ∧∧	85	41.20 N	72.45 E
Baubau	112	5.28 S	122.38 E
Bauchi	150	10.19 N	9.50 E
Bauchi □[3]	146	10.30 N	10.15 E
Baucina	70	37.55 N	13.32 E
Baud	32	47.52 N	3.01 W
Baudette	190	48.42 N	94.35 W
Baudh	120	20.50 N	84.19 E
Baudó ≃	246	4.57 N	77.22 W
Baudó, Serranía de ∧∧	246	6.00 N	77.05 W
Baudouin Stadium ♠	273b	4.20 S	15.20 E
Baudour	50	50.29 N	3.49 E
Bauernschaft	263	51.34 N	6.33 E
Bauerstown	279b	40.30 N	79.59 W
Baugo Creek ≃	216	41.40 N	86.04 W
Baukau ◆[8]	263	51.33 N	7.12 E
Baúl, Cerro ∧	234	17.38 N	100.19 W
Bauld, Cape ›	186	51.38 N	55.25 W
Baulkham Hills	274a	33.46 S	151.00 E
Baulmes	58	46.48 N	6.32 E
Bauma	58	47.23 N	8.53 E
Baumann, Pic ∧	150	6.52 N	0.46 E
Baumberg	263	51.07 N	6.54 E
Baume ≃	62	44.26 N	4.20 E
Baume-les-Dames	58	47.21 N	6.22 E
Baumholder	56	49.37 N	7.20 E
Baumschulenweg ◆[8]	264a	52.28 N	13.29 E
Baun	112	10.18 S	123.43 E
Baunach	56	49.59 N	10.50 E
Baunach ≃	56	49.59 N	10.51 E
Baunatal	56	51.16 N	9.25 E
Baunei	71	40.02 N	9.40 E
Baunt	88	55.16 N	113.08 E
Baunt, ozero ⊜	88	55.12 N	113.00 E
Bāuphal	126	22.25 N	90.33 E
Baure	150	12.50 N	8.45 E
Baures	248	13.35 S	63.35 W
Baures ≃	248	12.30 S	64.18 W
Bāuria	126	22.29 N	88.10 E
Bauru	255	22.19 S	49.04 W
Baús	255	18.19 S	53.10 W
Bausendorf	56	50.01 N	6.59 E
Bausenhagen	263	51.31 N	7.48 E
Bauska	76	56.24 N	24.14 E
Bauta	240p	22.59 N	82.33 W
Bauta □[7]	286b	22.59 N	82.33 W
Bautino	84	44.33 N	50.15 E
Bautzen	54	51.11 N	14.26 E
Bauxite	194	34.33 N	92.31 W
Bauya	150	8.11 N	12.34 W
Bavans	58	47.29 N	6.44 E
Bavari	62	44.26 N	9.01 E
Bavaria → Bayern □[3]	30	49.00 N	11.30 E
Bavarian Alps → Bayerische Alpen ∧∧	64	47.30 N	11.00 E
Bavay	50	50.18 N	3.47 E
Båven ⊜	40	59.01 N	16.56 E
Baveno	58	45.55 N	8.30 E
Bavilliers	58	47.37 N	6.50 E
Bavispe	232	30.24 N	108.50 W
Bavispe, Río de ≃	232	29.15 N	109.11 W
Bavleny	80	56.24 N	39.34 E
Bavly	80	54.25 N	53.17 E
Bavnhöj ∧[2]	41	55.55 N	10.07 E
Bavtugaj	84	43.11 N	46.49 E
Baw	110	23.19 N	95.50 E
Bāwal	124	28.05 N	76.35 E
Bawal, Pulau I	112	2.44 S	110.06 E
Bāwāli	272b	22.25 N	88.12 E
Bawang	115a	7.06 S	109.55 E
Baw Baw, Mount ∧	169	37.50 S	146.17 E
Baw Beese Lake ⊜	216	41.54 N	84.36 W
Bawdeswell	42	52.45 N	1.01 E
Bawdwin	110	23.06 N	97.18 E
Bawean, Pulau I	115a	5.46 S	112.40 E
Baweigang	106	31.57 N	120.14 E
Bawku	150	11.05 N	0.14 W
Bawlake	110	19.11 N	97.21 E
Bawmi	110	17.19 N	94.35 E
Bawtry	44	53.26 N	1.01 W
Baxdo	144	5.46 N	47.15 E
Baxenden	262	53.44 N	2.20 W
Baxian, Zhg.	105	39.06 N	116.23 E
Baxian (Yudongxi), Zhg.	107	29.23 N	106.32 E
Baxley	192	31.46 N	82.20 W
Baxter, Ia., U.S.	190	41.49 N	93.09 W
Baxter, Mn., U.S.	190	46.20 N	94.17 W
Baxter, Tn., U.S.	194	36.09 N	85.38 W
Baxter Estates	276	40.50 N	73.42 W
Baxter Springs	198	37.02 N	94.44 W
Baxter State Park ♠	188	46.00 N	68.58 W
Baxterville	194	31.05 N	89.35 W
Bay	194	35.44 N	90.33 W
Bay □[4]	144	2.30 N	43.30 E
Bay, Laguna de ⊜	116	14.23 N	121.15 E
Baya, Zaïre	152	4.57 N	19.43 E
Baya, Zaïre	154	11.52 S	27.27 E
Bayāḍah, Wādī al- V	146	26.08 N	18.35 E
Bayāḍ an-Naṣārā	142	29.04 N	31.08 E
Bayag	116	18.16 N	121.02 E
Bayala	158	27.47 S	32.08 E
Bay al-Kabīr, Wādī V	146	31.15 N	15.57 E
Bayambang	116	15.49 N	120.27 E
Bayamo	240p	20.23 N	76.39 W
Bayamo ≃	240p	20.34 N	76.44 W
Bayamón	240m	18.24 N	66.09 W
Bayan, Indon.	115b	8.16 S	116.26 E
Bayan, Zhg.	89	46.05 N	127.24 E
Bāyan, Band-e ∧∧	120	34.20 N	65.30 E
Bayāna	124	26.54 N	77.17 E
Bayanbayanan	269f	14.39 N	121.06 E
Bayanchagan	89	47.19 N	124.03 E
Bayang	116	7.48 N	124.12 E
Bayanga	152	2.53 N	16.19 E
Bayange	102	39.19 N	107.31 E
Bayan Har Shan ∧∧	102	33.48 N	98.10 E
Bayanheshuomiao	89	48.51 N	119.46 E
Bayanjie	89	49.36 N	124.37 E
Bayanluke	89	50.52 N	119.33 E
Bayannaobao	102	39.44 N	107.40 E
Bayano, Lago ⊜[1]	246	9.10 N	78.40 W
Bayan Obo	102	41.58 N	110.02 E
Bayan Tal	89	43.44 N	123.16 E
Bayard, Ia., U.S.	198	41.51 N	94.33 W
Bayard, Ne., U.S.	198	41.45 N	103.19 W
Bayard, N.M., U.S.	200	32.45 N	108.07 W
Bayard, Oh., U.S.	214	40.46 N	81.04 W
Bayard, W.V., U.S.	188	39.16 N	79.21 W
Bayard, Col)(	62	44.37 N	6.05 E
Bayard Cutting Arboretum State Park ♠	276	40.45 N	73.10 W
Bayat, Indon.	112	2.06 S	103.38 E
Bayat, Tür.	130	38.59 N	30.56 E
Bayat, Tür.	130	40.39 N	34.15 E
Bayawan	116	9.22 N	122.48 E
Bayawan ≃	116	9.22 N	122.48 E
Baybay	116	10.41 N	124.48 E
Bayberry	210	43.08 N	76.13 W
Bayble	46	58.12 N	6.13 W
Bayboro	192	35.08 N	76.46 W
Bay Bulls	186	47.19 N	52.49 W
Bayburt	130	40.16 N	40.15 E
Bay Center	224	46.37 N	123.57 W
Bay City, Mi., U.S.	190	43.35 N	83.53 W
Bay City, Or., U.S.	224	45.31 N	123.53 W
Bay City, Tx., U.S.	222	28.58 N	95.58 W
Bay Creek ≃, Il., U.S.	194	37.16 N	88.31 W
Bay Creek ≃, Il., U.S.	219	39.20 N	90.46 W
Baydā', Bi'r ⫪[4]	142	29.45 N	32.13 E
Bay de Verde	186	48.05 N	52.54 W
Baydhabo	144	3.07 N	43.39 E
Bay du Nord ≃	186	47.44 N	55.25 W
Baye, Cap ›	175f	20.57 S	165.25 E
Bayel	58	48.12 N	4.47 E
Bayerische Alpen ∧∧	64	47.30 N	11.00 E
Bayerisch Eisenstein	60	49.07 N	13.12 E
Bayerischer Wald ∧∧	60	49.00 N	12.40 E
Bayerischer Wald, Nationalpark ♠	60	48.56 N	13.28 E
Bayern □[3]	30	49.00 N	11.30 E
Bayeuen	114	4.36 N	97.53 E
Bayeux, Bra.	250	7.08 S	34.56 W
Bayeux, Fr.	32	49.16 N	0.42 W
Bay Farm Island I	282	37.43 N	122.14 W
Bayfield, Co., U.S.	200	37.13 N	107.35 W
Bayfield, Wi., U.S.	190	46.48 N	90.49 W
Bayfield, Île I	186	51.13 N	58.23 W
Bayford	260	51.46 N	0.06 W
'Bayh	132	33.44 N	35.31 E
Bayḥān al-Qaṣāb	144	14.48 N	45.43 E
Bay Harbor Islands	220	25.53 N	80.08 W
Bayhead, Scot., U.K.	46	57.33 N	7.24 W
Bay Head, N.J., U.S.	208	40.04 N	74.03 W
Bayiji	98	34.18 N	117.41 E
Bayındır	130	38.13 N	27.40 E
Bayingzi	104	41.28 N	120.46 E
Baykonur → Bajkonyr	86	47.50 N	66.03 E
Bay Kurt	85	39.58 N	75.33 E
Bay L'Argent	186	47.33 N	54.54 W
Bayley Point ›	164	16.56 S	139.02 E
Baylis	219	39.44 N	90.54 W
Bay Meadows Race Track ♠	282	37.32 N	122.18 W
Bay Minette	194	30.52 N	87.46 W
Baynūnah ◆[1]	128	23.50 N	52.45 E
Bayo	34	43.09 N	8.58 W
Bayombong	116	16.29 N	121.09 E
Bayon	58	48.29 N	6.19 E
Bayona	34	42.07 N	8.51 W
Bayonne, Fr.	32	43.29 N	1.29 W
Bayonne, N.J., U.S.	210	40.40 N	74.06 W
Bayonne ≃	206	46.05 N	73.10 W
Bayonne Bridge ◆[5]	276	40.38 N	74.09 W
Bayons	62	44.20 N	6.10 E
Bayou Bodcau Reservoir ⊜[1]	194	32.45 N	93.30 W
Bayou Cane	194	29.37 N	90.45 W
Bayou D'Arbonne Lake ⊜[1]	194	32.45 N	92.25 W
Bayou La Batre	194	30.24 N	88.14 W
Bayóvar	248	5.50 S	81.03 W
Bay Park	276	40.38 N	73.40 W
Bayport, Fl., U.S.	220	28.33 N	82.39 W
Bay Port, Mi., U.S.	190	43.50 N	83.22 W
Bayport, Mn., U.S.	190	45.01 N	92.46 W
Bayport, N.Y., U.S.	210	40.44 N	73.03 W
Bayraktar	84	39.41 N	42.08 E
Bayramiç	130	39.48 N	26.37 E
Bayramören	130	40.57 N	33.12 E
Bayreuth	60	49.57 N	11.35 E
Bay Ridge	208	38.56 N	76.27 W
Bay Ridge ◆[8]	276	40.37 N	74.02 W
Bay Ridge Channel ʯ	276	40.39 N	74.02 W
Bayrischzell	64	47.40 N	12.00 E
Bay Roberts	186	47.36 N	53.16 W
Bayrūt (Beirut)	130	33.53 N	35.30 E
Bayrūt □[4]	132	33.56 N	35.30 E
Bays, Lake of ⊜	212	45.15 N	79.04 W
Bay Saint Louis	194	30.18 N	89.19 W
Bay Shore	210	40.43 N	73.14 W
Bayshore Gardens	220	27.25 N	82.35 W
Bayside, On., Can.	212	44.07 N	77.30 W
Bayside, Ma., U.S.	283	42.18 N	70.53 W
Bayside, Wi., U.S.	216	43.10 N	87.54 W
Bayside ◆[8]	276	40.46 N	73.46 W
Bay Springs	194	31.58 N	89.17 W
Bay Springs Lake ⊜[1]	194	34.35 N	88.20 W
Bayston Hill	42	52.40 N	2.45 W
Bayswater	274b	37.51 S	145.16 E
Bayswater North	274b	37.49 S	145.17 E
Bayt ad-Dīn	132	33.42 N	35.35 E
Bayt ad-Din ⊥	132	33.41 N	35.34 E
Bayt al-Faqīh	144	14.32 N	43.20 E
Bayt Ḥānūm	132	31.32 N	34.33 E
Bayt Jālā	132	31.43 N	35.11 E
Bayt Jinn	132	33.19 N	35.53 E
Bayt Laḥm (Bethlehem)	132	31.43 N	35.12 E
Bayt Mirī	132	33.52 N	35.36 E
Baytown	222	29.44 N	94.58 W
Bayt Sāḥūr	132	31.42 N	35.13 E
Bayt Sīrā	132	31.53 N	35.03 E
Bayunglencir	112	2.03 S	103.41 E
Bayview, Austl.	274a	33.40 S	151.18 E
Bay View, N.Z.	172	39.25 S	176.53 E
Bay View, N.Y., U.S.	210	42.47 N	78.51 W
Bay View, Oh., U.S.	214	41.28 N	82.50 W
Bayview ◆[8]	282	37.44 N	122.23 W
Bay Village	214	41.29 N	81.55 W
Bayville, N.J., U.S.	208	39.54 N	74.09 W
Bayville, N.Y., U.S.	210	40.54 N	73.33 W
Baywood Park	226	35.20 N	120.50 W
Bayyāḍah, Ra's al- ›	132	33.10 N	35.10 E
Bayyā'īyah al-Kabīrah	130	35.42 N	37.09 E
Bayyūḍah ⫪[4]	140	17.32 N	32.07 E
Bayzo	150	13.52 N	4.45 E
Baza	34	37.29 N	2.46 W
Baza, Sierra de ∧∧	34	37.15 N	2.45 W
Bazai	100	24.32 N	114.10 E
Bazainville	261	48.48 N	1.40 E
Bazalija	78	49.43 N	26.27 E
Bazar	88	53.58 N	116.05 E
Bazarčaj	84	39.40 N	45.48 E
Bazard'uz'u, gora ∧	84	41.13 N	47.51 E
Bāzār-e Panjvā'ī	120	31.32 N	65.28 E
Bazargic → Tolbuhin	38	43.34 N	27.50 E
Bazar-Kurgan	85	41.02 N	72.45 E
Bazarnyje Mataki	80	54.56 N	49.56 E
Bazarnyj Karabulak	80	52.16 N	46.25 E
Bazarnyj Syzgan	80	53.45 N	46.46 E
Bazarovo	82	54.47 N	38.10 E
Bazaršolan	80	49.04 N	51.56 E
Bazartobe	80	49.23 N	51.50 E
Bazaruto, Ilha do I	156	21.40 S	35.28 E
Bazas	32	44.26 N	0.13 W
Bazavluk ≃	78	47.34 N	34.04 E
Bazdār	120	26.21 N	65.03 E
Bazeilles	56	49.40 N	4.59 E
Bazemont	261	48.56 N	1.52 E
Bazetta	214	41.20 N	80.47 W
Bazhong	102	31.51 N	106.39 E
Bazi	100	24.46 N	113.10 E
Baziège	32	43.27 N	1.37 E

ENGLISH Name	Page	Lat.°′	Long.°′
Bažigan	84	44.33 N	45.41 E
Bazine	198	38.26 N	99.41 W
Baziqiao	106	32.07 N	119.52 E
Bazkovskaja	80	49.36 N	41.43 E
Bazmān	128	27.49 N	60.12 E
Bazmān, Kūh-e ∧	128	28.04 N	60.01 E
Bazoches-les-Gallerandes	50	48.10 N	2.03 E
Bazoches-sur-Hoëne	50	48.33 N	0.28 E
Bazoj	86	55.45 N	83.22 E
Bazzano	64	44.30 N	11.05 E
Be ≃	110	11.06 N	106.58 E
Be, Nosy I	157b	13.20 S	48.15 E
Beach, Il., U.S.	216	42.26 N	87.50 W
Beach, N.D., U.S.	198	46.55 N	104.00 W
Beach, Tx., U.S.	222	30.20 N	95.29 W
Beach Channel ʯ	276	40.35 N	73.50 W
Beach City	214	40.39 N	81.34 W
Beach City Lake ⊜[1]	214	40.41 N	81.36 W
Beach Glen	276	40.56 N	74.29 W
Beach Haven, N.J., U.S.	208	39.33 N	74.14 W
Beach Haven, Pa., U.S.	210	41.04 N	76.11 W
Beach Haven Terrace	208	39.35 N	74.13 W
Beach Lake	210	41.36 N	75.09 W
Beach Lake ⊜	281	42.33 N	83.43 W
Beach Pond State Park ♠	207	41.35 N	71.45 W
Beachport	166	37.30 S	140.01 E
Beachville	212	43.05 N	80.49 W
Beachwood, N.J., U.S.	208	39.56 N	74.11 W
Beachwood, Oh., U.S.	214	41.27 N	81.30 W
Beachy Head ›	42	50.44 N	0.16 E
Beacon, Austl.	162	30.26 S	117.51 E
Beacon, N.Y., U.S.	210	41.30 N	73.58 W
Beacon Falls	207	41.26 N	73.03 W
Beacon Heights	284c	38.57 N	76.54 W
Beacon Hill, Austl.	274a	33.45 S	151.15 E
Beacon Hill, Wa., U.S.	224	46.08 N	122.57 W
Beacon Hill ∧[2], H.K.	271d	22.21 N	114.09 E
Beacon Hill ∧[2], Wales, U.K.	42	52.23 N	3.12 W
Beacon Rock State Park ♠	224	45.38 N	122.03 W
Beaconsfield, Austl.	166	41.12 S	146.48 E
Beaconsfield, Austl.	274b	38.03 S	145.22 E
Beaconsfield, P.Q., Can.	206	45.26 N	73.50 W
Beaconsfield, Eng., U.K.	260	51.37 N	0.39 W
Beaconsfield □[8]	260	51.34 N	0.35 W
Beadle Lake	216	42.18 N	85.12 W
Beagh, Slieve ∧[2]	48	54.21 N	7.12 W
Beagle, Canal ʯ	254	54.53 S	68.10 W
Beagle Bay Mission	162	16.58 S	122.40 E
Beagle Gulf ⊂	164	12.00 S	130.20 E
Beagle Reef ✦[2]	160	15.20 S	123.29 E
Bealanana	157b	14.33 S	48.44 E
Beale, Cape ›	182	48.44 N	125.20 W
Beale, Lake ⊜	122	19.45 N	73.44 E
Beale Air Force Base ■	226	39.08 N	121.20 W
Bealiba	169	36.48 S	143.33 E
Bealiba, Mount ∧[2]	169	36.49 S	143.38 E
Beallsville	214	40.04 N	80.01 W
Beals Creek ≃	196	32.10 N	100.51 W
Beam ≃	260	51.31 N	0.10 E
Beaminster	42	50.49 N	2.45 W
Bean	260	51.25 N	0.17 E
Beanblossom Creek ≃	194	39.20 N	86.39 W
Bean Creek ≃	216	41.35 N	84.19 W
Bear ≃, Sk., Can.	184	54.33 N	103.58 W
Bear ≃, U.S.	200	41.30 N	112.08 W
Bear ≃, Ca., U.S.	226	38.57 N	121.35 W
Bear, Mount ∧	180	61.17 N	141.09 W
Beara	164	7.30 S	144.50 E
Bear Bay ⊂	176	75.47 N	87.00 W
Bear Branch	218	38.55 N	85.05 W
Bear Brook ≃, On., Can.	212	45.25 N	75.10 W
Bear Brook ≃, N.J., U.S.	276	41.02 N	74.03 W
Bear Brook State Park ♠	188	43.05 N	71.26 W
Bear Butte ∧	198	44.28 N	103.26 W
Bear Canyon V	280	34.14 N	118.07 W
Bear Cove	182	50.44 N	127.27 W
Bear Creek	210	41.11 N	75.45 W
Bear Creek ≃, On., Can.	214	42.44 N	82.23 W
Bear Creek ≃, U.S.	194	34.46 N	88.05 W
Bear Creek ≃, U.S.	196	37.45 N	101.23 W
Bear Creek ≃, U.S.	216	41.17 N	83.57 W
Bear Creek ≃, Al., U.S.	194	33.11 N	88.05 W
Bear Creek ≃, Ca., U.S.	226	38.56 N	122.20 W
Bear Creek ≃, Ca., U.S.	226	38.02 N	121.18 W
Bear Creek ≃, Ca., U.S.	226	37.17 N	120.50 W
Bear Creek ≃, Ca., U.S.	228	34.10 N	117.01 W
Bear Creek ≃, Ca., U.S.	280	34.14 N	117.53 W
Bear Creek ≃, Co., U.S.	200	39.40 N	105.00 W
Bear Creek ≃, Il., U.S.	219	39.33 N	89.23 W
Bear Creek ≃, Il., U.S.	219	40.07 N	91.29 W
Bear Creek ≃, Md., U.S.	284b	39.13 N	76.30 W
Bear Creek ≃, Mo., U.S.	219	39.03 N	91.14 W
Bear Creek ≃, N.D., U.S.	198	46.10 N	98.06 W
Bear Creek ≃, Oh., U.S.	218	39.39 N	84.17 W
Bear Creek ≃, Or., U.S.	202	44.06 N	120.46 W
Bear Creek ≃, Or., U.S.	202	42.26 N	122.58 W
Bear Creek ≃, Pa., U.S.	214	41.23 N	78.50 W
Bear Creek ≃, Wy., U.S.	198	41.41 N	104.13 W
Bear Creek, South Fork ≃	219	40.09 N	91.18 W
Bear Creek, West Fork ≃	280	34.16 N	117.53 W
Bearden	194	33.43 N	92.36 W
Beardmore	176	49.36 N	87.57 W
Beardmore Glacier ⊓	9	83.45 S	171.00 E
Beardsley Lake ⊜[1]	226	38.13 N	120.03 W
Beardstown, Il., U.S.	219	40.01 N	90.25 W
Beardstown, In., U.S.	216	41.08 N	86.36 W
Beardy and Okemasis Indian Reserves ◆[4]	184	52.48 N	106.20 W
Bearfort Mountain ∧	276	41.09 N	74.23 W
Bear Head Creek ≃	194	30.18 N	93.35 W
Bear Head Lake ⊜	184	55.33 N	96.10 W
Bear Head Lake State Park ♠	190	47.49 N	92.04 W
Bearhead Mountain ∧	224	47.02 N	121.53 W
Bear Hill ∧[2], Ct., U.S.	207	41.39 N	73.24 W
Bear Hill ∧[2], N.Y., U.S.	210	41.18 N	74.00 W
Bear-in-the-Lodge Creek ≃	198	43.41 N	101.50 W
Bear Island I, Ant.	9	74.30 S	110.45 W
Bear Island I, Mb., Can.	184	54.53 N	98.04 W

DEUTSCH Name	Seite	Breite°′	Länge°′ E = Ost
Bear Island I, Ire.	48	51.40 N	9.48 W
Bear Island → Bjørnøya I	12	74.25 N	19.00 E
Bear Island I	284c	38.59 N	77.14 W
Bear Lake, B.C., Can.	182	56.11 N	126.51 W
Bear Lake, Pa., U.S.	214	42.00 N	79.30 W
Bear Lake ⊜, Ab., Can.	182	55.16 N	119.00 W
Bear Lake ⊜, B.C., Can.	182	56.06 N	126.45 W
Bear Lake ⊜, Mb., Can.	184	55.08 N	96.00 W
Bear Lake ⊜, On., Can.	212	45.26 N	79.35 W
Bear Lake ⊜, U.S.	200	42.00 N	111.20 W
Bear Mountain ∧, Ca., U.S.	228	35.12 N	118.38 W
Bear Mountain ∧, Ky., U.S.	192	37.32 N	84.16 W
Bear Mountain ∧, Or., U.S.	202	43.51 N	122.53 W
Bear Mountain ∧[2]	210	41.18 N	74.01 W
Bear Mountain State Park ♠	210	41.17 N	74.00 W
Béarn □[9]	32	43.20 N	0.45 W
Bear Pond ⊜	276	40.58 N	74.40 W
Bear River	186	44.34 N	65.39 W
Bear River Range ∧∧	200	41.50 N	111.30 W
Bear Run ≃	279b	40.33 N	80.04 W
Bearsden	46	55.56 N	4.20 W
Bears Paw Mountains ∧∧	202	48.15 N	109.30 W
Bearstead	260	51.16 N	0.35 E
Bearsville	210	42.02 N	74.09 W
Bear Swamp ≃	285	39.54 N	74.47 W
Bear Swamp ≡	285	39.53 N	74.45 W
Bear Swamp Brook ≃	276	41.04 N	74.13 W
Bear Swamp Lake ⊜	276	41.06 N	74.13 W
Beartooth Mountains ∧∧	202	45.00 N	109.30 W
Beartooth Pass)(	202	44.58 N	109.28 W
Bear Town	194	31.13 N	90.27 W
Beās	123	31.31 N	75.17 E
Beās ≃	123	31.10 N	74.59 E
Beasain	34	43.03 N	2.11 W
Beas de Segura	34	38.15 N	2.53 W
Beasley	222	29.30 N	95.55 W
Beasley Bay ⊂	208	37.51 N	75.44 W
Beason	219	40.09 N	89.12 W
Beata, Cabo ›	238	17.36 N	71.25 W
Beata, Isla I	238	17.35 N	71.31 W
Beatenberg	58	46.42 N	7.48 E
Beato ◆[8]	266c	38.44 N	9.06 W
Beaton	182	50.44 N	117.44 W
Beatrice, Al., U.S.	194	31.44 N	87.12 W
Beatrice, Ne., U.S.	198	40.16 N	96.44 W
Beatrice, Zimb.	154	18.15 S	30.55 E
Beatrice, Cape ›	164	14.15 S	136.59 E
Beattie	198	39.51 N	96.25 W
Beattock	44	55.18 N	3.28 W
Beatton ≃	176	56.10 N	120.25 W
Beatty, Nv., U.S.	204	36.54 N	116.45 W
Beatty, Oh., U.S.	218	39.53 N	83.50 W
Beatty Saugeen ≃	212	44.08 N	81.02 W
Beattyville	192	37.34 N	83.42 W
Beaubru	56	49.46 N	5.05 E
Beaucaire	62	43.48 N	4.38 E
Beauce ◆[1]	50	48.22 N	1.50 E
Beauceville	188	46.12 N	70.46 W
Beauchamp	261	49.01 N	2.12 E
Beauchamp Roding	260	51.46 N	0.18 E
Beauchêne, Lac ⊜	190	46.39 N	78.55 W
Beauchêne Island I	254	52.55 S	59.12 W
Beaucoup Creek ≃, Il., U.S.	194	37.47 N	89.17 W
Beaucoup Creek ≃, Il., U.S.	219	38.13 N	89.20 W
Beaucourt	58	47.29 N	6.55 E
Beaudesert	171a	27.59 S	153.00 E
Beaudette ≃	206	45.12 N	74.19 W
Beaudry, Lac ⊜	190	47.44 N	78.55 W
Beauduc, Pointe de ›	62	43.22 N	4.34 E
Beaufays	56	50.34 N	5.38 E
Beaufort, Austl.	169	37.26 S	143.23 E
Beaufort, Fr.	58	46.34 N	5.26 E
Beaufort, Fr.	62	45.43 N	6.35 E
Beaufort, Lux.	56	49.51 N	6.18 E
Beaufort, Malay.	112	5.20 N	115.45 E
Beaufort, Mo., U.S.	219	38.26 N	91.12 W
Beaufort, N.C., U.S.	192	34.43 N	76.39 W
Beaufort, S.C., U.S.	192	32.25 N	80.40 W
Beaufort ⊥	132	33.19 N	35.32 E
Beaufort, Cape ›	162	34.26 S	115.32 E
Beaufort, Massif de ∧∧[1]	62	45.44 N	6.35 E
Beaufort Island I	271d	22.11 N	114.15 E
Beaufort Marine Corps Air Station ■	192	32.30 N	80.44 W
Beaufort Sea ⫪[2]	16	73.00 N	140.00 W
Beaufort West	158	32.18 S	22.36 E
Beaugency	50	47.47 N	1.38 E
Beauharnois	206	45.19 N	73.52 W
Beauharnois □[6]	206	45.15 N	74.00 W
Beauharnois, Barrage de ◆[6]	275a	45.19 N	73.55 W
Beauharnois, Canal de ≅	206	45.19 N	73.54 W
Beaujeu	58	46.09 N	4.36 E
Beaujolais □[9]	32	46.05 N	4.10 E
Beaulieu	42	50.49 N	1.27 W
Beaulieu-lès-Loches	50	47.07 N	1.01 E
Beaulieu-sur-Mer	62	43.42 N	7.20 E
Beauly	46	57.29 N	4.29 W
Beauly ≃	46	57.28 N	4.28 W
Beauly Firth ⊂[1]	46	57.30 N	4.23 W
Beaumaris, Austl.	274b	37.59 S	145.02 E
Beaumaris, Wales, U.K.	44	53.16 N	4.05 W
Beaumaris Bay ⊂	274b	38.00 S	145.03 E
Beaumes-de-Venise	62	44.07 N	5.02 E
Beaumesnil	50	49.01 N	0.43 E
Beaumetz-lès-Loges	50	50.14 N	2.39 E
Beaumont, Bel.	50	50.14 N	4.14 E
Beaumont, Nf., Can.	186	49.37 N	55.41 W
Beaumont, Fr.	32	49.40 N	1.51 W
Beaumont, N.Z.	172	45.49 S	169.32 E
Beaumont, Ca., U.S.	228	33.55 N	116.58 W
Beaumont, Ms., U.S.	194	31.10 N	88.55 W
Beaumont, Tx., U.S.	194	30.05 N	94.06 W
Beaumont-du-Gâtinais	50	48.08 N	2.29 E
Beaumont-en-Argonne	56	49.32 N	5.03 E
Beaumont Hill ∧[2]	166	31.33 S	145.13 E
Beaumont-la-Ronce	50	47.34 N	0.40 E
Beaumont-le-Roger	50	49.05 N	0.47 E
Beaumont Place	222	29.50 N	95.14 W
Beaumont-sur-Oise	50	49.08 N	2.17 E
Beaumont-sur-Sarthe	50	48.13 N	0.08 E
Beaune	58	47.02 N	4.50 E
Beaune-la-Rolande	50	48.04 N	2.26 E
Beauport	206	46.52 N	71.11 W
Beaupré	186	47.03 N	70.54 W
Beaupréau	32	47.12 N	1.00 W
Beaupre Island I	212	44.26 N	76.19 W
Beaupré Lake ⊜	184	54.30 N	107.10 W
Beauraing	56	50.07 N	4.58 E
Beaurepaire	62	45.20 N	5.03 E
Beaurepaire-en-Bresse	58	46.40 N	5.23 E
Beaurières	62	44.35 N	5.33 E
Beaurivage	206	46.25 N	71.14 W
Beaurivage ≃	206	46.42 N	71.16 W
Beauséjour	184	50.04 N	96.33 W
Beausoleil	62	43.45 N	7.26 E
Beausoleil Island I	212	44.51 N	79.52 W
Beautor	50	49.39 N	3.20 E
Beauvais, Fr.	50	49.26 N	2.05 E

Symbols in the index entries represent the broad categories identified in the key at the right. Symbols with superior numbers (∧∧[1]) identify subcategories (see complete key on page *I · 1)*.

Kartensymbole in dem Registerverzeichnis stellen die rechts in Schlüssel erklärten Kategorien dar. Symbole mit hochgestellten Ziffern (∧∧[1]) bezeichnen Unterabteilungen einer Kategorie (vgl. vollständiger Schlüssel auf Seite *I · 1)*.

Los símbolos incluídos en el texto del índice representan las grandes categorias identificadas con la clave a la derecha. Los símbolos con numeros en su parte superior (∧∧[1]) identifican las subcategorías (véase la clave completa en la página *I · 1)*.

Les symboles de l'index représentent les catégories indiquées dans la légende à droite. Les symboles suivis d'un indice (∧∧[1]) représentent des sous-catégories (voir légende complète à la page *I · 1)*.

Os símbolos incluídos no texto do índice representam as grandes categorias identificadas com a chave à direita. Os símbolos com números em sua parte superior (∧∧[1]) identificam as subcategorias (veja-se a chave completa à página *I · 1)*.

Symbol	English	Deutsch	Español	Français	Português
∧	Mountain	Berg	Montaña	Montagne	Montanha
∧∧	Mountains	Berge	Montañas	Montagnes	Montanhas
)(	Pass	Pass	Paso	Col	Passo
V	Valley, Canyon	Tal, Cañon	Valle, Cañón	Vallée, Canyon	Vale, Canhão
≚	Plain	Ebene	Llano	Plaine	Planície
›	Cape	Kap	Cabo	Cap	Cabo
I	Island	Insel	Isla	Île	Ilha
II	Islands	Inseln	Islas	Îles	Ilhas
⊥	Other Topographic Features	Andere Topographische Objekte	Otros Elementos Topográficos	Autres données topographiques	Outros acidentes topográficos

ESPAÑOL · FRANÇAIS · PORTUGUÊS

Nombre / Nom / Nome	Página / Page	Lat.°′	Long.°′ W = Oeste / W = Ouest
Beauvais, Fr.	261	48.32 N	2.03 E
Beauvais Creek ≏	202	45.29 N	107.45 W
Beauvais-Tillé, Aéroport ⊠	50	49.28 N	2.07 E
Beauval, Sk., Can.	184	55.09 N	107.37 W
Beauval, Fr.	50	50.06 N	2.20 E
Beauvezer	62	44.09 N	6.36 E
Beauville	32	44.17 N	0.52 E
Beauvoir	261	48.39 N	2.52 E
Beauvoir-sur-Mer	32	46.55 N	2.02 W
Beauvoir-sur-Niort	32	46.11 N	0.28 W
Beaux Arts	224	47.35 N	122.11 W
Beaver, Ak., U.S.	180	66.22 N	147.24 W
Beaver, Ok., U.S.	196	36.48 N	100.31 W
Beaver, Or., U.S.	224	45.16 N	123.49 W
Beaver, Pa., U.S.	214	40.41 N	80.18 W
Beaver, Ut,. U.S.	200	38.16 N	112.38 W
Beaver, Wa., U.S.	224	48.03 N	124.19 W
Beaver, W.V., U.S.	192	37.44 N	81.08 W
Beaver □[6]	214	40.40 N	80.25 W
Beaver ≏, Can.	176	59.43 N	124.16 W
Beaver ≏, Can.	184	55.25 N	107.45 W
Beaver ≏, On., Can.	212	44.34 N	80.27 W
Beaver ≏, U.S.	196	36.35 N	99.30 W
Beaver ≏, N.Y., U.S.	188	43.54 N	75.30 W
Beaver ≏, Pa., U.S.	214	40.40 N	80.18 W
Beaver ≏, Ut,. U.S.	200	39.10 N	112.57 W
Beaver Brook	210	40.55 N	75.59 W
Beaver Brook ≏, U.S.	207	42.40 N	71.19 W
Beaver Brook ≏, Ma., U.S.	283	42.03 N	70.58 W
Beaver Brook ≏, Ma., U.S.	283	42.36 N	71.21 W
Beaver Brook ≏, Ma., U.S.	283	42.23 N	71.14 W
Beaver Brook ≏, N.J., U.S.	276	40.54 N	74.30 W
Beaver Brook ≏, N.J., U.S.	276	40.58 N	74.35 W
Beaver City	198	40.08 N	99.49 W
Beaver Creek, Yk., Can.	180	62.22 N	140.52 W
Beavercreek, Oh., U.S.	218	39.43 N	84.03 W
Beavercreek, Or., U.S.	224	45.17 N	122.32 W
Beaver Creek ≏, On., Can.	212	44.44 N	76.58 W
Beaver Creek ≏, On., Can.	212	44.30 N	77.42 W
Beaver Creek ≏, On., Can.	275b	43.51 N	79.20 W
Beaver Creek ≏, On., Can.	284a	42.58 N	79.01 W
Beaver Creek ≏, U.S.	198	47.20 N	103.39 W
Beaver Creek ≏, U.S.	198	40.04 N	99.20 W
Beaver Creek ≏, U.S.	198	43.25 N	103.59 W
Beaver Creek ≏, U.S.	216	40.58 N	87.49 W
Beaver Creek ≏, Ak., U.S.	180	66.15 N	147.32 W
Beaver Creek ≏, Ca., U.S.	226	38.12 N	120.19 W
Beaver Creek ≏, Co., U.S.	198	40.20 N	103.33 W
Beaver Creek ≏, Co., U.S.	198	38.22 N	104.58 W
Beaver Creek ≏, Il., U.S.	216	42.16 N	88.56 W
Beaver Creek ≏, Il., U.S.	219	38.33 N	89.30 W
Beaver Creek ≏, Ky., U.S.	218	38.31 N	84.11 W
Beaver Creek ≏, Md., U.S.	208	39.32 N	77.42 W
Beaver Creek ≏, Mo., U.S.	194	36.38 N	93.02 W
Beaver Creek ≏, Mt., U.S.	202	48.29 N	107.24 W
Beaver Creek ≏, Ne., U.S.	198	40.42 N	97.20 W
Beaver Creek ≏, Ne., U.S.	198	41.26 N	97.42 W
Beaver Creek ≏, N.J., U.S.	285	39.45 N	75.23 W
Beaver Creek ≏, N.Y., U.S.	212	44.36 N	75.22 W
Beaver Creek ≏, N.D., U.S.	198	46.15 N	100.29 W
Beaver Creek ≏, Oh., U.S.	216	41.25 N	83.51 W
Beaver Creek ≏, Oh., U.S.	216	40.34 N	84.45 W
Beaver Creek ≏, Oh., U.S.	218	39.57 N	83.46 W
Beaver Creek ≏, Ok., U.S.	196	34.00 N	97.57 W
Beaver Creek ≏, Or., U.S.	224	44.56 N	121.22 W
Beaver Creek ≏, Pa., U.S.	285	40.00 N	75.42 W
Beaver Creek ≏, Tx., U.S.	196	33.53 N	98.49 W
Beaver Creek ≏, Wy., U.S.	202	42.58 N	108.26 W
Beaver Creek State Park ♠	214	40.44 N	80.35 W
Beaver Crossing	198	40.46 N	97.16 W
Beaverdale	214	40.19 N	78.41 W
Beaver Dam, Ky., U.S.	194	37.24 N	86.52 W
Beaverdam, Oh., U.S.	216	40.50 N	83.59 W
Beaver Dam, Wi., U.S.	190	43.27 N	88.50 W
Beaverdam Brook ≏	276	40.26 N	74.28 W
Beaverdam Creek ≏, U.S.	284c	38.55 N	76.57 W
Beaverdam Creek ≏, Md., U.S.	284c	39.01 N	76.54 W
Beaverdam Creek ≏, N.J., U.S.	285	39.56 N	74.45 W
Beaver Dams	210	42.17 N	76.58 W
Beaver Dams Creek ≏	284a	43.06 N	79.11 W
Beaver Dam Wash V	200	36.54 N	114.55 W
Beaverdell	182	49.26 N	119.05 W
Beaver Falls, N.Y., U.S.	212	43.53 N	75.25 W
Beaver Falls, Pa., U.S.	214	40.45 N	80.19 W
Beaverhead ≏	202	45.31 N	112.21 W
Beaverhead Mountains ⋏	202	45.00 N	113.20 W
Beaverhill Lake ⊜, Ab., Can.	182	53.27 N	112.32 W
Beaver Hill Lake ⊜, Mb., Can.	184	54.16 N	94.53 W
Beaverhouse Lake ⊜	190	48.32 N	92.05 W
Beaver Island I	190	45.40 N	85.31 W
Beaver Island State Park ♠	210	42.58 N	78.57 W
Beaver Kill ≏	210	41.59 N	75.08 W
Beaver Lake	210	41.07 N	74.33 W
Beaver Lake ⊜, Ab., Can.	182	54.43 N	111.50 W
Beaver Lake ⊜, On., Can.	212	44.30 N	77.02 W
Beaver Lake ⊜, On., Can.	212	44.44 N	78.17 W
Beaver Lake ⊜, N.J., U.S.	276	41.05 N	74.33 W
Beaver Lake ⊜, N.Y., U.S.	276	40.53 N	73.34 W
Beaver Lake ⊜[1]	194	36.20 N	93.55 W
Beaver Lake Indian Reserve ✦[4]	182	54.39 N	111.54 W
Beaverlodge	182	55.13 N	119.26 W
Beaver Meadow	210	42.40 N	75.41 W
Beaver Meadows	210	40.55 N	75.54 W
Beaver Mountains ⋏	180	62.54 N	156.58 W
Beaver Run ≏, N.J., U.S.	276	41.11 N	74.36 W
Beaver Run ≏, Pa., U.S.	279b	40.34 N	79.33 W
Beaver Run ≏, Pa., U.S.	285	40.10 N	75.40 W
Beaver Run Reservoir ⊜[1]	214	40.29 N	79.33 W
Beavers Bend State Park ♠	194	34.08 N	94.42 W
Beaver Springs	208	40.45 N	77.13 W
Beaver Swamp Brook ≏	276	40.57 N	73.43 W
Beaverton, On., Can.	212	44.26 N	79.09 W
Beaverton, Mi., U.S.	190	43.52 N	84.29 W
Beaverton, Or., U.S.	224	45.29 N	122.48 W
Beaverton ≏	212	44.26 N	79.10 W
Beavertown	210	40.45 N	77.10 W
Beaverville	216	40.57 N	87.39 W
Beāwar	120	26.06 N	74.19 E
Beazley	252	33.45 S	66.39 W
Bebao	157b	17.22 S	44.33 E
Bebar ≏	114	3.07 N	103.27 E
Bebedouro	255	20.56 S	48.28 W
Bebeji	150	11.40 N	8.19 E
Bebek ✦[8]	267b	41.04 N	29.02 E
Bebekler	130	37.21 N	30.04 E
Bebelevo	82	54.32 N	36.30 E
Bebeli	130	36.41 N	35.27 E
Beberibe	250	4.11 S	38.08 W
Bebertal	54	52.15 N	11.18 E
Bebington	44	53.23 N	3.01 W
Béboto	146	8.16 N	16.56 E
Bebra	56	50.58 N	9.47 E
Becal	232	20.27 N	90.02 W
Bécancour	206	46.20 N	72.26 W
Bécancour ≏	206	46.22 N	72.27 W
Beccar ✦[8]	288	34.28 S	58.31 W
Beccaria	214	40.46 N	78.27 W
Beccles	42	52.28 N	1.34 E
Becconsall	262	53.42 N	2.50 W
Bečej	38	45.37 N	20.03 E
Beceni	38	45.23 N	26.46 E
Becerra Creek ≏	196	28.05 N	98.55 W
Becerreá	34	42.51 N	7.10 W
Becerro, Cayos II	236	15.57 N	83.17 W
Béchar	148	31.37 N	2.13 W
Béchar □[5]	148	29.00 N	3.00 W
Becharof Lake ⊜	180	58.00 N	156.30 W
Bechater	36	37.18 N	9.45 E
Bechem	150	7.05 N	2.02 W
Becher Bay ⊂	224	48.19 N	123.37 W
Becher Point ≻	168a	32.23 S	115.44 E
Bechet	38	43.46 N	23.58 E
Bechevin Bay ⊂	180	55.00 N	163.27 W
Bechhofen	56	49.09 N	10.33 E
Bechtelsville	208	40.22 N	75.38 W
Bechuanaland ✦[1]	158	27.10 S	22.10 E
Bechyně	30	49.18 N	14.29 E
Becke	263	51.24 N	7.47 E
Beckemeyer	219	38.36 N	89.26 W
Beckenham ✦[8]	260	51.24 N	0.02 W
Beckenried	58	46.58 N	8.29 E
Becket	207	42.19 N	73.05 W
Beckhausen ✦[8]	263	51.34 N	7.02 E
Beckingen	56	49.24 N	6.42 E
Beckinghausen ✦[8]	263	51.37 N	7.34 E
Beckington	42	51.16 N	2.18 W
Beck Lake ⊜	278	42.04 N	87.52 W
Beckler ≏	224	47.43 N	121.21 W
Beckley	188	37.46 N	81.11 W
Beck Pond ⊜	283	42.36 N	70.49 W
Becks Creek ≏	219	39.08 N	88.56 W
Beckum	52	51.45 N	8.02 E
Beckville	222	32.14 N	94.27 W
Beckwith Island I	212	44.52 N	80.08 W
Becky Peak ∧	204	39.58 N	114.36 W
Beclean	38	47.11 N	24.10 E
Bečov nad Teplou	54	50.02 N	12.19 E
Becsehely	61	46.27 N	16.48 E
Bedale	44	54.17 N	1.35 W
Bédarieux	32	43.37 N	3.09 E
Bédarrides	62	44.02 N	4.54 E
Bédaya	146	8.55 N	17.52 E
Bedburdyck	56	51.07 N	6.34 E
Bedburg, B.R.D.	56	50.59 N	6.35 E
Bedburg, B.R.D.	56	51.03 N	8.23 E
Bedburg-Hau	52	51.45 N	6.10 E
Beddgelert	44	53.01 N	4.06 W
Beddinge läge	41	55.21 N	13.29 E
Beddington ✦[8]	260	51.22 N	0.08 W
Beddome, Mount ∧	162	25.50 S	134.22 E
Beddouza, Ras ≻	148	32.34 N	9.19 W
Bedele	144	8.33 N	36.23 E
Beden Brook ≏	276	40.25 N	74.38 W
Bedeque Bay ⊂	186	46.22 N	63.53 W
Beder	41	56.04 N	10.13 E
Bederkesa	52	53.38 N	8.50 E
Bederwanak	144	9.34 N	44.23 E
Bedesa	144	8.54 N	40.47 E
Bedford, P.Q., Can.	206	45.07 N	72.59 W
Bedford, S. Afr.	158	32.41 S	26.05 E
Bedford, Eng., U.K.	42	52.08 N	0.29 W
Bedford, In., U.S.	218	38.51 N	86.29 W
Bedford, Ia., U.S.	198	40.40 N	94.43 W
Bedford, Ky., U.S.	218	38.35 N	85.19 W
Bedford, Ma., U.S.	207	42.29 N	71.16 W
Bedford, Mi., U.S.	216	42.23 N	85.13 W
Bedford, N.Y., U.S.	210	41.12 N	73.39 W
Bedford, Oh., U.S.	214	41.23 N	81.32 W
Bedford, Pa., U.S.	188	40.01 N	78.30 W
Bedford, Tx., U.S.	222	32.50 N	97.08 W
Bedford, Va., U.S.	192	37.20 N	79.31 W
Bedford □[6]	214	40.09 N	78.30 W
Bedford, Cape ≻	164	15.14 S	145.21 E
Bedfordale	168a	32.10 S	116.03 E
Bedford Harbour ⊂	162	33.35 S	120.35 E
Bedford Heights	279a	41.25 N	81.31 W
Bedford Hills	210	41.14 N	73.41 W
Bedford Island I	126	21.51 N	88.05 E
Bedford Level ☷	42	52.27 N	0.02 W
Bedford Park	278	41.46 N	87.49 W
Bedford Park ✦[8]	276	40.52 N	73.53 W
Bedfordshire □[6]	42	52.05 N	0.30 W
Bedford-Stuyvesant ✦[8]	276	40.41 N	73.55 W
Bedi, India	120	22.30 N	70.02 E
Bédi, Tchad	146	11.06 N	18.33 E
Bedias	222	30.46 N	95.57 W
Bedias Creek ≏	222	30.54 N	95.37 W
Bedinggong	112	2.42 S	106.13 E
Bédiondo	146	8.39 N	17.12 E
Bedirli	130	39.35 N	36.38 E
Bedlington	28	55.08 N	1.35 W
Bedlington ≏	44	55.10 N	1.34 W
Bedminster, N.J., U.S.	276	40.40 N	74.38 W
Bedminster, Pa., U.S.	208	40.26 N	75.11 W
Bedmond	260	51.43 N	0.25 W
Bednodemjanovsk	80	53.56 N	43.10 E
Bedoba	88	58.48 N	97.12 E
Bédoin	62	44.07 N	5.10 E
Bedok	271c	1.19 N	103.57 E
Bedong	114	5.44 N	100.31 E
Bedonia	62	44.30 N	9.38 E
Bedourie	166	24.21 S	139.28 E
Bedum	52	53.17 N	6.36 E
Bedwas	42	51.35 N	3.13 W
Bedworth	42	52.28 N	1.29 W
Beeac	169	38.12 S	143.38 E
Beebe, P.Q., Can.	206	45.01 N	72.09 W
Beebe, Ar., U.S.	194	35.04 N	91.52 W
Beech ≏	194	35.37 N	88.10 W
Beechal Creek ≏	166	27.24 S	145.13 E
Beech Bottom	214	40.13 N	80.39 W
Beech Brook ≏	276	41.08 N	74.18 W
Beech Creek	194	37.10 N	87.03 W
Beech Creek ≏	210	41.04 N	77.34 W
Beechcrest	214	41.05 N	81.20 W
Beecher, Il., U.S.	216	41.20 N	87.37 W
Beecher, Mi., U.S.	216	43.05 N	83.42 W
Beecher City	219	39.11 N	88.47 W
Beecher Falls	206	45.00 N	71.30 W
Beechey Head ≻	224	48.19 N	123.39 W
Beech Forest	169	38.38 S	143.34 E
Beech Fork ≏	194	37.46 N	85.41 W
Beech Grove	218	39.43 N	86.05 W
Beechmont	171a	28.07 S	153.11 E
Beechview ✦[8]	279b	40.25 N	80.02 W
Beechwood, Ky., U.S.	218	38.24 N	84.44 W
Beechwood, Ma., U.S.	283	42.12 N	70.49 W
Beechwood, Mi., U.S.	216	46.09 N	88.46 W
Beechworth	166	36.22 S	146.41 E
Beechy	184	50.51 N	107.25 W
Beeck ✦[8]	263	51.29 N	6.44 E
Beeckerwerth ✦[8]	263	51.29 N	6.41 E
Beecroft	274a	33.45 S	151.04 E
Beecroft Head ≻	170	35.01 S	150.51 E
Beecroft Peninsula ≻[1]	170	35.02 S	150.50 E
Beedenbostel	52	52.38 N	10.16 E
Beef Island I	240m	18.27 N	64.31 W
Beek, Ned.	52	51.51 N	5.54 E
Beek, Ned.	52	51.32 N	5.38 E
Beek, Ned.	56	50.56 N	5.49 E
Beela ≏	44	54.13 N	2.47 W
Beeleigh Abbey ⚜[1]	260	51.44 N	0.40 E
Beelen	52	51.55 N	8.07 E
Beelitz	54	52.14 N	12.58 E
Beemer	198	41.55 N	96.48 W
Beemster ✦[1]	52	52.35 N	4.55 E
Beendorf	54	52.14 N	11.05 E
Beenleigh	171a	27.43 S	153.12 E
Beerburrum	171a	26.58 S	152.58 E
Beerfelden	56	49.34 N	8.58 E
Bee Ridge	220	27.17 N	82.28 W
Beeringgnurding ∧	162	29.53 S	117.55 E
Be'er Menuḥa	132	30.19 N	35.08 E
Beernem	50	51.09 N	3.20 E
Be'er Ora	132	29.43 N	34.59 E
Beerse	56	51.19 N	4.52 E
Beersheba → Be'er Sheva'	132	31.14 N	34.47 E
Beersheba Springs	194	35.28 N	85.39 W
Be'er Sheva' (Beersheba)	132	31.14 N	34.47 E
Be'er Sheva', Naḥal V	132	31.11 N	34.35 E
Be'er Sheva', Sede-Te'ufa ⊠	132	31.16 N	34.43 E
Beerta	52	53.10 N	7.05 E
Be'er Toviyya	132	31.44 N	34.44 E
Beervlei Brak ≏	158	29.58 S	23.12 E
Beerwah	171a	26.51 S	152.58 E
Be'er Ya'agov	132	31.56 N	34.50 E
Beesenlaublingen	54	51.42 N	11.41 E
Beeskow	54	52.10 N	14.14 E
Beestekraal	156	25.23 S	27.38 E
Beesten	52	52.26 N	7.30 E
Beeston	42	52.56 N	1.12 W
Beet ≏	115a	6.16 S	107.15 E
Beethoven Peninsula ≻[1]	9	71.40 S	73.45 W
Beeton	212	44.05 N	79.47 W
Beetsterzwaag	52	53.03 N	6.05 E
Beetz, Lac ⊜	186	50.34 N	62.42 W
Beetzendorf	54	52.42 N	11.05 E
Beeville	196	28.24 N	97.44 W
Beevor, Mount ∧[2]	168b	34.56 S	139.02 E
Befale	152	0.28 N	20.58 E
Befandriana	157b	15.16 S	48.32 E
Befandriana Atsimo	157b	22.06 S	43.54 E
Befasy	157b	20.33 S	44.23 E
Befori	152	0.06 N	22.17 E
Befotaka, Madag.	157b	13.15 S	48.16 E
Befotaka, Madag.	157b	14.32 S	48.01 E
Befotaka, Madag.	157b	23.49 S	46.59 E
Befotaka, Madag.	157b	21.29 S	44.44 E
Befu ✦[8]	270	34.40 N	135.02 E
Beg, Lough ⊜	44	54.47 N	6.28 W
Bega	166	36.40 S	149.50 E
Bega (Begej) ≏	38	45.13 N	20.19 E
Begamganj	124	23.36 N	78.20 E
Begampur ✦[8]	272a	28.44 N	77.04 E
Begej (Bega) ≏	38	45.13 N	20.19 E
Beger	102	45.42 N	97.10 E
Beggars Point ≻	240c	17.10 N	61.48 W
Beggs	196	35.44 N	96.04 W
Begičevskij	76	53.47 N	38.15 E
Beginsel	158	26.57 S	20.39 E
Beglickaja, kosa ≻[2]	83	47.07 N	38.35 E
Begoml'	76	54.44 N	28.04 E
Begonias, Presa ⊜[1]	234	20.55 N	100.50 W
Begoro	150	6.23 N	0.23 W
Begovat → Bekabad	85	40.13 N	69.14 E
Begun'	78	51.24 N	28.17 E
Begunicy	76	59.35 N	29.19 E
Begusarai	124	25.25 N	86.08 E
Béhague, Pointe ≻	250	4.40 N	51.54 W
Behāla	126	22.31 N	88.19 E
Behbehān	128	30.35 N	50.14 E
Behm Canal ʮ	182	55.41 N	131.35 W
Beho	56	50.13 N	6.00 E
Béhoust	261	48.50 N	1.43 E
Behrāmpur	272a	28.38 N	77.24 E
Behren-lès-Forbach	56	49.10 N	6.57 E
Behring, Détroit de → Bering Strait ʮ	180	65.30 N	169.00 W
Behringen, B.R.D.	52	53.07 N	9.58 E
Behringen, D.D.R.	54	51.01 N	10.31 E
Behshahr	128	36.43 N	53.34 E
Beht, Oued ≏	148	34.25 N	6.26 W
Bei ≏	90	23.09 N	112.48 E
Bei'an	89	48.16 N	126.36 E
Beianhe	105	40.04 N	116.06 E
Beibaihua	105	38.57 N	114.51 E
Beibaozhen	106	31.33 N	121.38 E
Beibei	107	29.49 N	106.26 E
Beicai	106	31.12 N	121.34 E
Beicang	105	39.13 N	117.07 E
Beida → Al-Bayḍā'	146	32.46 N	21.43 E
Beida ≏	102	40.18 N	99.26 E
Beïda, Chott ⊜	34	35.56 N	5.49 E
Beidaihe	98	39.54 N	119.29 E
Beidaoqiao	86	44.12 N	89.38 E
Beidouzhen	107	30.02 N	104.26 E
Beidun	100	26.42 N	118.57 E
Beierfeld	54	50.33 N	12.47 E
Beiersdorf	264a	52.42 N	13.47 E
Beifangcun	105	40.20 N	116.42 E
Beifangzi	104	41.22 N	121.03 E
Beigang	100	29.20 N	113.41 E
Beighton	44	53.20 N	1.20 W
Beigi	144	9.20 N	34.29 E
Beiguan Dao I	100	27.10 N	120.32 E
Beiguo	106	31.47 N	120.33 E
Beihai	102	21.29 N	109.05 E
Bei Hai ⊜	271a	39.56 N	116.22 E
Beihedian	105	39.13 N	115.45 E
Beiheishang'gou	105	39.53 N	118.15 E
Beihuaidian	105	39.16 N	117.33 E
Beijialing	104	41.08 N	124.02 E
Beijiao	100	26.22 N	119.58 E
Beijiean	106	32.15 N	121.12 E
Beijijiazhuang	105	40.01 N	114.51 E
Beijing (Peking), Zhg.	105	39.55 N	116.25 E
Beijing (Peking), Zhg.	271a	39.55 N	116.25 E
Beijing Ji Chang (Capitol Airport) ⊠	105	40.03 N	116.35 E
Beijing Shi (Peking Shih) □[7]	98	40.15 N	116.30 E
Beiji Shan I	100	27.38 N	121.12 E
Beijuma ≏	105	39.30 N	115.56 E
Beikan	100	32.23 N	121.21 E
Beilen	52	52.52 N	6.31 E
Beilifang	104	41.59 N	121.57 E
Beiling	100	24.36 N	115.20 E
Beiliu	102	22.42 N	110.22 E
Beiliuwangshui	105	38.57 N	115.03 E
Beilizhen	110	19.10 N	108.43 E
Beilizigu	105	39.30 N	117.28 E
Beilngries	60	49.02 N	11.29 E
Beilong Shan I	100	27.40 N	120.58 E
Beilrode	54	51.35 N	13.03 E
Beilstein, B.R.D.	56	49.02 N	9.18 E
Beilstein, B.R.D.	56	50.36 N	8.14 E
Beilstein, B.R.D.	56	50.06 N	7.14 E
Beimaizhu	105	39.31 N	117.44 E
Beiminjiatun	104	42.38 N	122.43 E
Beimuzhen	107	29.31 N	105.05 E
Beinamar	146	8.40 N	15.23 E
Beine-Nauroy	50	49.15 N	4.13 E
Beinette	62	44.22 N	7.39 E
Beinwil	58	47.22 N	7.35 E
Beinwil am See	58	47.16 N	8.13 E
Beipa'a	164	8.30 S	146.35 E
Beipan ≏	102	25.05 N	106.00 E
Beipanxiaozhen	106	31.44 N	121.26 E
Beipiao	104	41.49 N	120.46 E
Beipo	102	21.14 N	109.53 E
Beiqi	98	40.27 N	122.20 E
Beiqiao	106	31.03 N	121.24 E
Beira	156	19.49 S	34.52 E
Beira Baixa □[9]	34	39.45 N	7.30 W
Beira Litoral □[9]	34	40.15 N	8.25 W
Beiru ≏	100	33.43 N	113.35 E
Beirut → Bayrūt	130	33.53 N	35.30 E
Beirut International Airport ⊠	132	33.49 N	35.30 E
Beisanjia	98	42.04 N	124.42 E
Beiseker	182	51.23 N	113.32 W
Beishakou	105	39.08 N	116.07 E
Beishan	102	24.28 N	108.35 E
Bei Shan ⋏	102	41.30 N	96.00 E
Beishangcun	105	39.28 N	116.58 E
Beishipian	105	40.43 N	116.55 E
Beishuangdong	105	40.32 N	117.24 E
Beishuiquan	98	40.05 N	114.40 E
Beisi	102	34.59 N	95.07 E
Beisu	98	38.13 N	114.46 E
Beitaitou	98	37.06 N	118.31 E
Beitang	105	39.07 N	117.42 E
Beitanshiqiao	106	31.05 N	121.38 E
Beitbridge	154	22.13 S	30.00 E
Beith	46	55.45 N	4.38 W
Beitstadfjorden ⊂[2]	26	63.53 N	11.00 E
Beiuș	38	46.40 N	22.21 E
Beiwei	106	32.05 N	121.12 E
Beiwenquan	107	29.51 N	106.24 E
Beiwu	105	40.04 N	116.48 E
Beiwudu	100	33.39 N	113.39 E
Beixiadai	106	32.12 N	120.08 E
Beixiejiadang	105	40.30 N	114.50 E
Beixili	89	51.47 N	125.45 E
Beixin'an	271a	39.55 N	116.08 E
Beixindian	105	39.44 N	116.44 E
Beixing	89	48.29 N	125.40 E
Beixinjing	106	31.13 N	121.22 E
Beixinliu	105	39.16 N	116.31 E
Beixinzhen	106	31.49 N	121.31 E
Beiyan	98	36.33 N	118.42 E
Beiyi ≏	105	39.19 N	115.39 E
Beiyin	106	31.07 N	120.47 E
Beiyindai	104	42.35 N	122.22 E
Beiyuan	105	40.01 N	116.24 E
Beizangzong	124	30.14 N	90.44 E
Beizhaijiawopeng	104	41.14 N	122.41 E
Beizhen, Zhg.	98	37.22 N	118.01 E
Beizhen (Gaoshanzi), Zhg.	104	41.36 N	121.47 E
Beizhouzhuang	106	31.52 N	120.24 E
Beizifu	98	42.09 N	120.29 E
Beja, Bra.	250	1.36 S	48.47 W
Beja, Port.	34	38.01 N	7.52 W
Beja, S.S.S.R.	86	53.03 N	90.54 E
Béja, Tun.	148	36.44 N	9.11 E
Beja □[5]	34	37.50 N	8.00 W
Béja □[8]	148	36.35 N	9.20 E
Bejaïa (Bougie)	148	36.45 N	5.05 E
Bejaïa □[5]	148	36.50 N	4.40 E
Bejaïa, Golfe de ⊂	34	36.45 N	5.25 E
Béjar	34	40.23 N	5.46 W
Bejestān	128	34.31 N	58.10 E
Beji ≏	120	29.47 N	67.58 E
Bejneu	86	45.15 N	55.07 E
Bejsug ≏	78	45.54 N	38.56 E
Bejsugskij liman ⊂	78	46.07 N	38.25 E
Bejtonovo	89	53.14 N	124.27 E
Bejucal	240p	22.56 N	82.23 W
Bejucal □[7]	286b	22.56 N	82.23 W
Bejuco	236	8.36 N	79.53 W
Bejuma	246	10.11 N	68.16 W
Bek ≏	152	2.29 N	15.15 E
Béka	146	9.04 N	12.53 E
Bekaa Valley → Al-Biqā' V	128	33.50 N	36.00 E
Bekabad	85	40.13 N	69.14 E
Bekancan	114	3.18 N	98.24 E
Bekasi	115a	6.14 S	106.59 E
Bekasi ≏	269e	6.10 S	107.02 E
Békásmegyer ✦[8]	264c	47.36 N	19.03 E
Bekasovo	82	55.26 N	36.49 E
Bekdaš	72	41.34 N	52.32 E
Békés	30	46.46 N	21.08 E
Békés □[6]	30	46.46 N	21.08 E
Békéscsaba	30	46.41 N	21.06 E
Beketovo	89	53.13 N	125.01 E
Bekilli	130	38.14 N	29.26 E
Bekily	157b	24.13 S	45.19 E
Bekirhan	130	38.10 N	41.19 E
Bekisopa	157b	21.40 S	45.54 E
Bekitro	157b	24.33 S	45.18 E
Bekkaria	36	35.22 N	8.15 E
Bekkersdal	273d	26.18 S	27.42 E
Bekkevoort	56	50.57 N	4.58 E
Beklemiševo, S.S.S.R.	80	53.52 N	47.25 E
Beklemiševo, S.S.S.R.	88	52.07 N	112.40 E
Bekodoka	157b	16.58 S	45.07 E
Bekoji	144	7.34 N	39.17 E
Bekok	114	2.18 N	103.08 E
Bekopaka	157b	19.09 S	44.48 E
Bekovo	80	52.28 N	43.43 E
Bektauata, gora ∧	86	47.30 N	74.50 E
Bektyševo	82	56.34 N	39.14 E
Bekwai	150	6.27 N	1.35 W
Bela, India	124	25.56 N	81.59 E
Bela, Pāk.	120	26.14 N	66.19 E
Bela, Zaïre	154	0.38 N	29.14 E
Bélabo	152	5.00 N	13.20 E
Belabolo	140	8.57 N	25.51 E
Bélâbre	32	46.33 N	1.09 E
Bela Crkva	38	44.54 N	21.26 E
Bela Cruz	250	3.03 S	40.11 W
Belaga	108	2.42 N	113.47 E
Bel'agaš	86	50.48 N	80.44 E
Bel-Air, Fr.	261	48.37 N	2.10 E
Bel Air, Md., U.S.	208	39.32 N	76.20 W
Bel Air, Va., U.S.	284c	38.52 N	77.10 W
Bel Air ✦[8]	280	34.05 N	118.27 W
Bélair, Île I	275a	45.37 N	73.48 W
Bel-Air, Morne ∧	241o	16.06 N	61.44 W
Bel Aire Estates	207	41.23 N	72.00 W
Belair Recreation Park ♠	168b	35.01 S	138.39 E
Belaja, S.S.S.R.	78	51.03 N	35.43 E
Belaja, S.S.S.R.	80	57.59 N	51.42 E
Belaja ≏, S.S.S.R.	78	45.04 N	39.23 E
Belaja ≏, S.S.S.R.	83	49.18 N	38.52 E
Belaja ≏, S.S.S.R.	83	48.35 N	39.10 E
Belaja ≏, S.S.S.R.	84	44.45 N	39.50 E
Belaja ≏, S.S.S.R.	86	55.54 N	53.33 E
Belaja ≏, S.S.S.R.	180	65.45 N	173.20 E
Belaja, gora ∧, S.S.S.R.	88	53.10 N	119.50 E
Belaja, gora ∧, S.S.S.R.	180	65.50 N	174.40 E
Belaja Ber'ozka	76	52.23 N	33.29 E
Belaja Cerkov'	78	49.49 N	30.07 E
Belaja Cholunica	86	58.50 N	50.48 E
Belaja Gora	76	58.31 N	31.45 E
Belaja Kalitva	78	48.11 N	40.46 E
Belaja Krinica, S.S.S.R.	78	47.21 N	33.10 E
Belaja Krinica, S.S.S.R.	78	50.38 N	29.29 E
Bel'ajevka, S.S.S.R.	78	46.29 N	30.12 E
Bel'ajevka, S.S.S.R.	86	51.24 N	56.26 E
Bel'ajevka, S.S.S.R.	86	57.28 N	55.28 E
Bel'ajevo	76	55.31 N	31.06 E
Belalcázar	34	38.34 N	5.10 W
Bel Alton	208	38.27 N	76.58 W
Belambanganumpu	112	4.54 S	105.03 E
Belampalli	122	19.02 N	79.30 E
Bělá nad Radbuzou	60	49.36 N	12.44 E
Belang	112	0.57 N	124.47 E
Bélanger ≏	184	53.26 N	97.40 W
Bel'aninovo	265b	55.57 N	37.39 E
Bel'anskij	80	47.45 N	41.33 E
Bela Palanka	38	43.13 N	22.19 E
Bělá pod Bezdězem	54	50.30 N	14.50 E
Belapurpāda	272c	19.01 N	73.02 E
Belas	266c	38.47 N	9.16 W
Belau (Palau) □[2], Oc.	14	5.00 N	137.00 E
Belavenona	157b	24.50 S	47.04 E
Bela Vista, Ang.	152	7.50 S	13.40 E
Bela Vista, Bra.	252	22.06 S	56.31 W
Bela Vista, Moç.	156	26.20 S	32.40 E
Bela Vista ✦[8]	287b	23.33 S	46.38 W
Bela Vista de Goiás	255	16.58 S	48.57 W
Bela Vista do Paraíso	255	23.00 S	51.12 W
Belawan	114	3.47 N	98.41 E
Belaya ∧	144	11.25 N	36.12 E
Belayan ≏	112	0.14 S	116.36 E
Belaya Tserkov' → Belaja Cerkov'	78	49.49 N	30.07 E
Belbo ≏	62	44.54 N	8.31 E
Belbubulo	140	9.57 N	34.04 E
Belbunia	126	23.17 N	87.09 E
Belcamp	208	39.28 N	76.14 W
Belcastro	68	39.02 N	16.47 E
Bełchatów	30	51.22 N	19.21 E
Belchen ∧	58	47.49 N	7.50 E
Belcher	194	32.44 N	93.49 W
Belcherāgh	120	35.50 N	65.14 E
Belcher Creek ≏	276	41.08 N	74.23 W
Belcher Islands II	176	56.20 N	79.30 W
Belchertown	207	42.16 N	72.24 W
Belchite	34	41.18 N	0.45 W
Bělčice	60	49.30 N	13.53 E
Belcoo	48	54.17 N	7.52 W
Belcourt	198	48.50 N	99.44 W
Bel'cy	78	47.46 N	27.56 E
Belda	126	22.05 N	87.21 E
Beldānga	126	23.56 N	88.15 E
Bel'd'ažki	76	52.39 N	35.42 E
Belding	216	43.05 N	85.13 W
Bele, ozero ⊜	86	54.39 N	90.12 E
Belebej	80	54.07 N	54.07 E
Belebelka	76	57.34 N	30.56 E
Belecke	52	51.29 N	8.20 E
Beled Weyne	144	4.45 N	45.12 E
Bélel, Cam.	152	7.03 N	14.26 E
Belel, Nig.	146	9.38 N	13.12 E
Belém, Bra.	250	1.27 S	48.29 W
Belém, Moç.	154	14.13 S	35.58 E
Belém ✦[8]	266c	38.42 N	9.12 W
Belém, Torre de ⊥	266c	38.42 N	9.13 W
Belém de São Francisco	250	8.46 S	38.58 W
Belén, Arg.	252	27.39 S	67.02 W
Belén, Chile	248	18.29 S	69.31 W
Belén, Col.	246	6.00 N	72.55 W
Belén, Col.	246	1.26 N	75.56 W
Belén, Nic.	236	11.30 N	85.53 W
Belén, Para.	252	23.30 S	57.06 W
Belen, Tür.	130	36.32 N	36.10 E
Belen, N.M., U.S.	200	34.39 N	106.46 W
Belén, Ur.	252	30.47 S	57.47 W
Belén ≏	252	28.00 S	66.52 W
Belén de Escobar	258	34.21 S	58.47 W
Belén del Refugio	234	21.31 N	102.25 W
Belene	38	43.39 N	25.07 E
Belenichino	78	50.56 N	36.37 E
Belen'kaja ≏	83	48.53 N	38.29 E
Belen'koje, S.S.S.R.	78	47.37 N	35.03 E
Belen'koje, S.S.S.R.	83	48.46 N	37.38 E
Belènzinho ✦[8]	287b	23.32 S	46.35 W
Bélep, Îles II	175f	19.45 S	163.40 E
Beles ≏	144	11.10 N	36.10 E
Belesar, Embalse de ⊜[1]	34	42.45 N	7.40 W
Belet Uen → Beled Weyne	144	4.45 N	45.12 E
Belews Lake ⊜[1]	192	36.17 N	80.03 W
Beleza, Ribeirão ≏	250	10.01 S	50.19 W
Belfair	224	47.27 N	122.49 W
Belfast, N.Z.	172	43.27 S	172.38 E
Belfast, S. Afr.	156	25.43 S	30.03 E
Belfast, N. Ire., U.K.	48	54.35 N	5.55 W
Belfast, Me., U.S.	188	44.25 N	69.00 W
Belfast, N.Y., U.S.	210	42.20 N	78.06 W
Belfast, Oh., U.S.	218	39.03 N	83.32 W
Belfast (Aldergrove) Airport ⊠	44	54.38 N	6.12 W
Belfast Lough ⊂	48	54.40 N	5.50 W
Belfeld	52	51.19 N	6.06 E
Belfield, Austl.	274a	33.54 S	151.05 E
Belfield, N.D., U.S.	198	46.53 N	103.11 W
Belfiore	64	45.23 N	11.12 E
Belford, Eng., U.K.	44	55.36 N	1.49 W
Belford, N.J., U.S.	276	40.25 N	74.05 W
Belford Roxo	256	22.46 S	43.24 W
Belfort	58	47.38 N	6.52 E
Belfort □[8]	58	47.38 N	6.55 E
Belforte del Chienti	66	43.10 N	13.14 E
Belfry, Ky., U.S.	192	37.37 N	82.16 W
Belfry, Mt., U.S.	202	45.08 N	109.00 W
Belgard → Białogard	30	54.01 N	16.00 E
Belgaum	122	15.52 N	74.31 E
Belgern	54	51.29 N	13.07 E
Bélgica → Belgium □[1]	30	50.50 N	4.00 E
Belgica Mountains ⋏	9	72.35 S	31.10 E
België → Belgium □[1]	30	50.50 N	4.00 E
Belgien → Belgium □[1]	30	50.50 N	4.00 E
Belgioioso	62	45.10 N	9.19 E
Belgique → Belgium □[1]	30	50.50 N	4.00 E
Belgium □[1], Europe	22	50.50 N	4.00 E
Belgium □[1], Europe	30	50.50 N	4.00 E
Belgodère	36	42.35 N	9.01 E
Belgorod	78	50.36 N	36.35 E
Belgorod-Dnestrovskij	78	46.12 N	30.20 E
Belgrad → Beograd	38	44.50 N	20.30 E
Belgrade → Beograd, Jugo.	38	44.50 N	20.30 E
Belgrade, Mn., U.S.	198	45.27 N	95.00 W
Belgrade, Mt., U.S.	202	45.46 N	111.10 W
Belgrade, Ne., U.S.	198	41.28 N	98.04 W
Belgrado → Beograd	38	44.50 N	20.30 E
Belgrad Ormanı ✦[3]	267b	41.10 N	28.55 E
Belgrano ✦[8]	288	34.34 S	58.28 W
Belgrano ≏	254	48.15 S	71.14 W
Belgrano, Lago ⊜	254	47.50 S	72.09 W
Belgrano II ⚜[3]	9	77.46 S	38.11 W
Belgrano III ⚜[3]	9	77.51 S	34.33 W
Belgrave	274b	37.55 S	145.21 E
Belhar	124	24.55 N	86.36 E
Belhaven	192	35.32 N	76.37 W
Belhus Park ♠	260	51.31 N	0.17 E
Beliābera	126	22.17 N	86.57 E
Beliātor	126	23.20 N	87.13 E
Belica, Jugo.	61	46.26 N	16.27 E
Belica, S.S.S.R.	78	51.07 N	35.34 E
Belice → Belize City	232	17.30 N	88.12 W
Belice → Belize □[1]	232	17.15 N	88.45 W
Belice ≏	70	37.35 N	12.52 E
Belichifor	140	6.33 N	33.16 E
Beliči	78	50.29 N	30.19 E
Belici ≏	70	37.31 N	13.50 E
Beličij, ostrov I	89	54.26 N	137.51 E
Belick	76	52.55 N	30.27 E
Belickoje	83	48.25 N	37.13 E
Beli Drim ≏	38	42.06 N	20.25 E
Beliki	78	49.15 N	34.16 E
Beliling, Gunung ∧	115b	8.37 S	119.59 E
Beli Manastir	38	45.46 N	18.36 E
Belin	32	44.30 N	0.47 W
Belinga	152	1.13 N	13.12 E
Belington	188	39.01 N	79.56 W
Belinskij	80	52.58 N	43.26 E
Belinyu	112	1.38 S	105.46 E
Belitung I	112	2.50 S	107.55 E
Belize □[1], N.A.	230	17.15 N	88.45 W
Belize □[1], N.A.	232	17.15 N	88.45 W
Belize ≏	232	17.32 N	88.14 W
Belize City	232	17.30 N	88.12 W
Belize Inlet ⊂	182	51.08 N	127.15 W
Belka	78	50.49 N	28.11 E
Belknap Crater ⚬[6]	202	44.17 N	121.50 W
Belkofski	180	55.05 N	162.02 W
Bel'kovo	82	56.15 N	38.48 E
Bel'kovskij, Ostrov I	74	75.32 N	135.44 E
Bell, Austl.	274b	37.45 S	145.00 E
Bell, Ciskei	158	33.15 S	27.23 E
Bell, Ca., U.S.	280	33.58 N	118.11 W
Bell □[6]	222	31.03 N	97.27 W
Bell ≏, P.Q., Can.	176	49.48 N	77.38 W
Bell ≏, Yk., Can.	180	67.17 N	137.46 W
Bella	68	40.45 N	15.32 E
Bella Bella	182	52.09 N	128.07 W
Bellac	32	46.07 N	1.02 E
Bellacaty, Pointe ≻	241o	16.25 N	61.24 W
Bella Coola	182	52.22 N	126.46 W
Bella Coola ≏	182	52.22 N	126.43 W
Bell Acres	279b	40.36 N	80.10 W
Bella Flor	248	11.09 S	67.49 W
Bellagio	58	45.59 N	9.15 E
Bellahy	48	53.58 N	8.48 W
Bellair	192	30.10 N	81.44 W
Bellaire, Mi., U.S.	190	44.58 N	85.12 W
Bellaire, Oh., U.S.	188	40.00 N	80.45 W
Bellaire, Tx., U.S.	222	29.42 N	95.27 W
Bella Isla, Estrecho de → Belle Isle, Strait of ʮ	176	51.35 N	56.30 W
Bella Lake ⊜	212	45.27 N	79.02 W
Bellambi	170	34.21 S	150.55 E
Bellamy, Al., U.S.	194	32.26 N	88.08 W
Bellamy, Va., U.S.	208	37.24 N	76.34 W
Bellano	58	46.03 N	9.18 E
Bellaria	66	44.09 N	12.28 E
Bellarine	169	38.08 S	144.37 E
Bellarine Peninsula ≻[1]	169	38.13 S	144.35 E
Bellariva	68	41.55 N	15.58 E
Bellary	122	15.09 N	76.56 E
Bellas Artes, Palacio de ⚜	286a	19.26 N	99.08 W
Bellata	166	29.55 S	149.47 E
Bella Tola ∧	58	46.15 N	7.39 E
Bella Unión	252	30.15 S	57.35 W
Bella Vista, Arg.	252	28.30 S	59.03 W
Bella Vista, Arg.	252	27.02 S	65.18 W
Bella Vista, Arg.	258	34.33 S	58.41 W
Bellavista, Chile	286e	33.31 S	70.37 W
Bella Vista, Para.	252	22.08 S	56.31 W
Bellavista, Perú	248	4.54 S	80.42 W
Bellavista, Perú	248	7.04 S	76.35 W
Bellavista, Perú	286d	12.04 S	77.08 W
Bellbird	170	32.51 S	151.21 E
Bellbrook, Austl.	166	30.49 S	152.31 E
Bellbrook, Oh., U.S.	218	39.38 N	84.04 W
Bell Brook ≏	168a	33.01 S	116.15 E
Bell Crags ∧[2]	44	55.03 N	2.22 W
Bell Creek ≏, Ca., U.S.	280	34.12 N	118.36 W
Bell Creek ≏, In., U.S.	218	40.09 N	85.27 W
Bellé, Sén.	150	14.25 N	12.18 W
Belle, Mo., U.S.	219	38.17 N	91.43 W
Belle, W.V., U.S.	188	38.13 N	81.32 W
Belle ≏, On., Can.	214	42.17 N	82.43 W
Belle ≏, Mi., U.S.	214	42.43 N	82.30 W
Belleair	220	27.55 N	82.48 W
Belleau	50	49.06 N	3.18 E
Belle Ayr Mountain ∧	210	42.07 N	74.29 W
Belle Bay ⊂	186	47.36 N	55.18 W
Belle Center	216	40.30 N	83.44 W
Belledonne, Chaîne de ⋏	62	45.18 N	6.08 E
Belle-Église	50	49.12 N	2.13 E
Belleek	48	54.28 N	8.06 W
Belle Farm Estates	208	39.23 N	76.45 W
Bellefontaine, Fr.	58	46.33 N	6.04 E
Bellefontaine, Fr.	261	49.06 N	2.28 E
Bellefontaine, Mart.	240e	14.40 N	61.10 W
Bellefontaine, Oh., U.S.	216	40.21 N	83.45 W
Bellefontaine Neighbors	219	38.44 N	90.13 W
Bellefonte, De., U.S.	208	39.45 N	75.30 W
Bellefonte, Md., U.S.	284c	38.47 N	76.52 W
Bellefonte, Pa., U.S.	214	40.54 N	77.46 W
Belle Fourche	198	44.40 N	103.51 W
Belle Fourche ≏	198	44.26 N	102.19 W
Belle Fourche Reservoir ⊜[1]	198	44.44 N	103.42 W
Bellegarde, Fr.	58	46.06 N	5.49 E
Bellegarde, Fr.	62	43.45 N	4.31 E
Bellegarde-du-Loiret	50	47.59 N	2.26 E
Bellegem	50	50.47 N	3.16 E
Belle Glade	220	26.41 N	80.40 W
Belle Glade Camp	220	26.40 N	80.41 W
Bellegrove	208	40.22 N	76.33 W
Belle Haven, Va., U.S.	208	37.33 N	75.49 W
Belle Haven, Va., U.S.	284c	38.47 N	77.04 W
Belleherbe	58	47.16 N	6.40 E
Belle Hôtesse ∧	241o	16.16 N	61.46 W
Belle-Île I	32	47.20 N	3.10 W
Belle Isle	220	28.27 N	81.21 W
Belle Isle I, Nf., Can.	176	51.55 N	55.20 W
Belle Isle I, Mi., U.S.	281	42.20 N	82.58 W
Belle Isle, Strait of ʮ	176	51.35 N	56.30 W
Belle Isle Park ♠	281	42.20 N	82.59 W
Bellelay	58	47.16 N	7.10 E
Bellême	50	48.22 N	0.34 E
Belle Mead	208	40.28 N	74.39 W
Bellemoor	285	39.43 N	75.35 W
Bellencombre	50	49.42 N	1.14 E
Belleoram	186	47.31 N	55.25 W
Belleplain	208	39.16 N	74.52 W
Belle-Plaine, Sk., Can.	184	50.24 N	105.09 W
Belle Plaine, Ia., U.S.	190	41.53 N	92.16 W
Belle Plaine, Ks., U.S.	198	37.23 N	97.16 W
Belle Plaine, Mn., U.S.	190	44.37 N	93.46 W
Belle Rive	219	38.14 N	88.45 W
Belle River	214	42.18 N	82.43 W
Bellerose	276	40.44 N	73.43 W
Bellerose ✦[8]	276	40.45 N	73.43 W
Bellerose Terrace	276	40.43 N	73.43 W
Belle Terre	276	40.58 N	73.04 W
Bellevaux-Ligneuville	56	50.24 N	6.00 E
Belle Vernon	214	40.07 N	79.52 W
Bellevesvre	58	46.50 N	5.22 E
Belleview, Fl., U.S.	192	29.03 N	82.03 W
Belleview, In., U.S.	218	38.53 N	85.23 W
Belle View, Va., U.S.	208	38.46 N	77.03 W
Belleville, On., Can.	212	44.10 N	77.23 W
Belleville, Fr.	56	48.49 N	6.06 E
Belleville, Il., U.S.	219	38.31 N	89.59 W
Belleville, In., U.S.	218	39.41 N	86.29 W
Belleville, Ks., U.S.	198	39.49 N	97.37 W

≏	River	Fluss	Río	Rivière	Rio
≅	Canal	Kanal	Canal	Canal	Canal
˪	Waterfall, Rapids	Wasserfall, Stromschnellen	Cascada, Rápidos	Chute d'eau, Rapides	Cascata, Rápidos
ʮ	Strait	Meeresstrasse	Estrecho	Détroit	Estreito
⊂	Bay, Gulf	Bucht, Golf	Bahía, Golfo	Baie, Golfe	Baía, Golfo
⊜	Lake, Lakes	See, Seen	Lago, Lagos	Lac, Lacs	Lago, Lagos
☷	Swamp	Sumpf	Pantano	Marais	Pântano
⍓	Ice Features, Glacier	Eis- und Gletscherformen	Accidentes Glaciales	Formes glaciaires	Acidentes glaciares
⍑	Other Hydrographic Features	Andere Hydrographische Objekte	Otros Elementos Hidrográficos	Autres données hydrographiques	Outros acidentes hidrográficos
✢	Submarine Features	Untermeerische Objekte	Accidentes Submarinos	Formes de relief sous-marin	Acidentes submarinos
□	Political Unit	Politische Einheit	Unidad Politica	Entité politique	Unidade política
⚜	Cultural Institution	Kulturelle Institution	Institución Cultural	Institution culturelle	Instituição cultural
⊥	Historical Site	Historische Stätte	Sitio Histórico	Site historique	Sitio histórico
♠	Recreational Site	Erholungs- und Ferienort	Sitio de Recreo	Centre de loisirs	Area de Lazer
⊠	Airport	Flughafen	Aeropuerto	Aéroport	Aeroporto
■	Military Installation	Militäranlage	Instalación Militar	Installation militaire	Instalação militar
✦	Miscellaneous	Verschiedenes	Misceláneo	Divers	Diversos

Belleville, Mi., U.S. 216 42.12 N 83.29 W
Belleville, N.J., U.S. 210 40.47 N 74.09 W
Belleville, N.Y., U.S. 212 43.47 N 76.07 W
Belleville, Pa., U.S. 214 40.36 N 77.43 W
Belleville, R.I., U.S. 207 41.33 N 71.28 W
Belleville, Wi., U.S. 216 42.51 N 89.32 W
Belleville Lake ⊜ 281 42.12 N 83.29 W
Belleville-sur-Meuse 56 49.11 N 5.23 E
Belleville-sur-Saône 58 46.06 N 4.45 E
Bellevue, Ab., Can. 182 49.35 N 114.22 W
Bellevue, Fr. 50 49.53 N 4.12 E
Bellevue, Id., U.S. 202 43.27 N 114.15 W
Bellevue, Ia., U.S. 190 42.15 N 90.25 W
Bellevue, Ky., U.S. 218 39.06 N 84.28 W
Bellevue, Md., U.S. 208 38.42 N 76.11 W
Bellevue, Mi., U.S. 216 42.26 N 85.01 W
Bellevue, Ne., U.S. 198 41.08 N 95.53 W
Bellevue, Oh., U.S. 214 41.16 N 82.50 W
Bellevue, Pa., U.S. 214 40.29 N 80.03 W
Bellevue, Tx., U.S. 196 33.38 N 98.01 W
Bellevue, Wa., U.S. 224 47.36 N 122.11 W
Bellevue ⊕[8] 273d 26.11 S 28.05 E
Belle Vue Zoological Gardens ♦ 262 53.28 N 2.11 W
Bell Ewart 212 44.16 N 79.33 W
Belley 62 45.46 N 5.41 E
Belleydoux 58 46.15 N 5.46 E
Belle Yella 150 7.22 N 10.00 W
Bellflower, Ca., U.S. 228 33.52 N 118.06 W
Bellflower, Il., U.S. 216 40.20 N 88.32 W
Bellflower, Mo., U.S. 219 39.00 N 91.21 W
Bell Gardens 228 33.57 N 118.09 W
Bellheim 56 49.11 N 8.16 E
Bell Hill ∧[2] 210 43.09 N 75.07 W
Bell Homestead ⊥ 212 43.04 N 80.18 W
Bellicourt 50 49.57 N 3.14 E
Bellingdon 260 51.44 N 0.38 W
Bellinge 41 55.20 N 10.20 E
Bellingen 166 30.27 S 152.54 E
Bellingham, Eng., U.K. 44 55.09 N 2.16 W
Bellingham, Ma., U.S. 207 42.05 N 71.28 W
Bellingham, Mn., U.S. 198 45.08 N 96.17 W
Bellingham, Wa., U.S. 224 48.45 N 122.29 W
Bellingham Bay C 224 48.45 N 122.35 W
Bellingshausen ⊌[3] 9 62.12 S 58.58 W
Bellingshausen Sea ⊤[2] 9 71.00 S 85.00 W
Bellingwolde 52 53.07 N 7.09 E
Bellinzago Novarese 62 45.34 N 8.38 E
Bellinzona 58 46.11 N 9.02 E
Bell Island I, Nf., Can. 186 47.36 N 52.58 W
Bell Island I, Nf., Can. 186 50.44 N 55.35 W
Bell Island Hot Springs 182 55.56 N 131.34 W
Bellmawr 208 39.52 N 75.05 W
Bellmead 222 31.35 N 97.06 W
Bellmore 276 40.40 N 73.31 W
Bell Mountain 228 34.35 N 117.15 W
Bellnhausen 56 50.42 N 8.43 E
Bello, Col. 246 6.20 N 75.33 W
Bello, Cuba 286b 23.07 N 82.24 W
Bello Horizonte → Belo Horizonte 255 19.55 S 43.56 W
Bellona 210 42.46 N 77.01 W
Bellona Plateau ✦[3] 14 20.30 S 158.30 E
Bellona Reefs ✦[2] 160 21.30 S 159.00 E
Bellone, Cap ≻ 157b 16.14 S 49.51 E
Bellosguardo 68 40.25 N 15.19 E
Bellot Strait ⊔ 176 71.58 N 94.45 W
Bellows Falls 188 43.08 N 72.26 W
Belloy-en-France 261 49.05 N 2.22 E
Bellpat 120 28.59 N 68.00 E
Bell Peninsula ≻[1] 176 63.50 N 82.00 W
Bell Point 279b 40.33 N 79.33 W
Bells, Tn., U.S. 194 35.43 N 89.05 W
Bells, Tx., U.S. 196 33.37 N 96.25 W
Bellsbank 44 55.18 N 4.23 W
Bells Bay C 212 45.30 N 77.51 W
Bells Corners 212 45.19 N 75.50 W
Bellshill 46 55.49 N 4.01 W
Bells Lake 285 39.44 N 75.02 W
Bells Lake ⊜ 285 39.45 N 75.04 W
Belltown, De., U.S. 208 38.44 N 75.10 W
Belltown, Il., U.S. 219 39.23 N 90.25 W
Belluno 64 46.09 N 12.13 E
Belluno □[4] 64 46.15 N 12.08 E
Bellvale 210 41.15 N 74.18 W
Bell Ville, Arg. 252 32.37 S 62.42 W
Bellville, S. Afr. 158 33.53 S 18.36 E
Bellville, Oh., U.S. 214 40.37 N 82.30 W
Bellville, Tx., U.S. 222 29.57 N 96.15 W
Bellwood, Il., U.S. 278 41.52 N 87.52 W
Bellwood, Ne., U.S. 198 41.20 N 97.14 W
Bellwood, Pa., U.S. 214 40.36 N 78.19 W
Bellwood, Lake ⊜ 212 43.46 N 80.20 W
Belly ≃ 182 49.46 N 113.02 W
Bellyk 86 54.32 N 91.17 E
Belm 52 52.18 N 8.08 E
Belmar, Md., U.S. 284b 39.21 N 76.32 W
Belmar, N.J., U.S. 208 40.10 N 74.01 W
Bélmez 34 38.16 N 5.12 W
Belmond 190 42.50 N 93.36 W
Belmont, Austl. 169 38.10 S 144.21 E
Belmont, Austl. 170 33.02 S 151.40 E
Belmont, Mb., Can. 184 49.24 N 99.27 W
Belmont, N.S., Can. 186 45.25 N 63.23 W
Belmont, On., Can. 212 42.53 N 81.05 W
Belmont, S. Afr. 158 29.28 S 24.22 E
Belmont, Eng., U.K. 262 53.38 N 2.30 W
Belmont, Ca., U.S. 226 37.31 N 122.16 W
Belmont, Ma., U.S. 283 42.23 N 71.10 W
Belmont, Mi., U.S. 216 43.05 N 85.37 W
Belmont, Ms., U.S. 194 34.30 N 88.12 W
Belmont, N.H., U.S. 188 43.26 N 71.28 W
Belmont, N.Y., U.S. 210 42.13 N 78.02 W
Belmont, Pa., U.S. 214 40.17 N 78.53 W
Belmont, S.C., U.S. 192 34.02 N 81.01 W
Belmont, Tx., U.S. 222 29.31 N 97.41 W
Belmont, Wi., U.S. 190 42.44 N 90.20 W
Belmont □[6] 214 40.05 N 80.54 W
Belmonte, Bra. 255 15.51 S 38.54 W
Belmonte, Esp. 34 43.17 N 6.14 W
Belmonte, Esp. 34 39.34 N 2.42 W
Belmonte, Port. 34 40.21 N 7.21 W
Belmonte Calabro 68 39.09 N 16.05 E
Belmonte Mezzagno 70 38.02 N 13.23 E
Belmont Harbor C 278 41.57 N 87.38 W
Belmont Lake ⊜, On., Can. 212 44.30 N 77.50 W
Belmont Lake ⊜, N.Y., U.S. 276 40.44 N 73.20 W
Belmont Lake State Park ♦ 276 40.43 N 73.20 W
Belmont Park 214 41.10 N 80.39 W
Belmont Park Race Track ♦ 276 40.43 N 73.43 W
Belmont Reservoir ⊜[1] 262 53.39 N 2.30 W
Belmont Slough ≃ 282 37.33 N 122.14 W
Belmopan 232 17.15 N 88.46 W
Belmore, Austl. 274a 33.55 S 151.05 E
Belmore, Oh., U.S. 216 41.09 N 83.56 W
Belmullet 48 54.14 N 10.00 W
Belmuri 272b 22.57 N 88.09 E
Belo 157b 19.42 S 44.33 E
BeŒil, Bel. 50 50.33 N 3.43 E
Beloeil, P.Q., Can. 206 45.34 N 73.12 W
Belœil, Château de ⊌ 50 50.35 N 3.44 E
Beloeil, Ruisseau ≃ 275a 45.39 N 73.12 W
Beloglazovo 86 56.05 N 72.40 E
Belogorje, S.S.S.R. 78 50.30 N 40.01 E
Belogorje, S.S.S.R. 78 50.01 N 26.25 E
Belogorka 80 50.42 N 53.27 E
Belogornoje 80 52.25 N 47.35 E
Belogorode 82 54.23 N 38.31 E
Belogorodka 78 50.00 N 26.39 E
Belogorovka 83 48.55 N 38.15 E
Belogorsk, S.S.S.R. 78 45.03 N 34.36 E
Belogorsk, S.S.S.R. 86 55.05 N 88.28 E
Belogorsk, S.S.S.R. 89 50.57 N 128.25 E
Belogorskij 86 49.27 N 83.10 E
Belogorskoje 80 53.35 N 48.12 E
Belogradčik 38 43.38 N 22.41 E
Beloguša 78 51.57 N 26.56 E
Beloha 157b 25.10 S 45.03 E
Belo Horizonte 255 19.55 S 43.56 W
Beloit, Ks., U.S. 198 39.27 N 98.06 W
Beloit, Oh., U.S. 214 40.55 N 80.59 W
Beloit, Wi., U.S. 216 42.30 N 89.01 W
Belo Jardim 250 8.20 S 36.26 W
Belojarsk 86 53.28 N 83.54 E
Belojarskij 86 56.45 N 61.24 E
Beloje, S.S.S.R. 80 58.23 N 39.24 E
Beloje, S.S.S.R. 83 48.31 N 39.04 E
Beloje, S.S.S.R. 86 48.55 N 82.58 E
Beloje, ozero ⊜ 76 60.11 N 37.37 E
Beloje more (White Sea) ⊤[2] 24 65.30 N 38.00 E
Belokamenskoje ⊕[8] 83 48.41 N 38.06 E
Belokany 84 41.43 N 46.26 E
Belokurakino 83 49.33 N 38.44 E
Belokuricha 86 51.59 N 84.59 E
Beloluck 83 49.41 N 39.02 E
Belomestnaja 76 52.24 N 37.37 E
Belomestnaja Dvojn'a 80 52.42 N 41.03 E
Belomorsk 24 64.32 N 34.48 E
Belomorsko-Baltijskij kanal ≋ 24 62.48 N 34.48 E
Belondo 152 0.16 S 19.31 E
Belonge 152 2.06 S 19.32 E
Belonia 124 23.15 N 91.27 E
Beloomut 76 54.57 N 39.20 E
Beloozersk 76 52.28 N 25.11 E
Belopolje 78 51.09 N 34.18 E
Belorado 34 42.25 N 3.11 W
Belorečensk 78 44.46 N 39.52 E
Beloreck 86 53.58 N 58.24 E
Belören 130 40.51 N 33.30 E
Belorusskaja gr'ada ∧ 76 53.40 N 27.00 E
Belorusskaja Sovetskaja Socialističeskaja Respublika □[3] 76 53.50 N 28.00 E
Beloščelje 24 64.52 N 46.56 E
Belo-sur-mer 157b 20.44 S 44.00 E
Belot, Lac ⊜ 180 66.55 N 126.18 W
Belousovka, S.S.S.R. 78 49.57 N 32.20 E
Belousovka, S.S.S.R. 86 50.08 N 82.33 E
Belousovo 82 55.05 N 36.40 E
Bel'ov 76 53.48 N 36.08 E
Belo Vale 255 20.25 S 44.01 W
Beloveжskaja Pušča, zapovednik ♦ 76 52.40 N 23.50 E
Belovo, S.S.S.R. 86 52.57 N 82.16 E
Belovo, S.S.S.R. 86 54.25 N 86.18 E
Belovodsk 83 49.12 N 39.35 E
Belovodskoje 85 42.50 N 74.06 E
Beloz'orje, S.S.S.R. 78 49.29 N 31.35 E
Beloz'orje, S.S.S.R. 78 49.18 N 31.54 E
Beloz'orka 78 46.37 N 32.27 E
Beloz'orsk 76 60.02 N 37.48 E
Beloz'orskoje 78 48.33 N 37.04 E
Belp 58 46.53 N 7.30 E
Belpāda 272c 19.02 N 73.03 E
Belpasso 70 37.35 N 14.58 E
Belper 42 53.01 N 1.29 W
Belpre 188 39.16 N 81.34 W
Belrose 274a 33.44 S 151.13 E
Belsano 214 40.31 N 78.52 W
Belsele 50 51.09 N 4.05 E
Bel'skaja Vol'a 78 51.27 N 25.49 E
Bel'skoje, S.S.S.R. 80 54.44 N 40.22 E
Bel'skoje, S.S.S.R. 86 57.49 N 92.09 E
Belson Run ≃ 279b 40.12 N 79.37 W
Belspring 192 37.11 N 80.36 W
Belt 202 47.23 N 110.55 W
Beltana 166 30.48 S 138.25 E
Belt Creek ≃ 202 47.36 N 111.02 W
Belted Range ⋌ 204 37.25 N 116.10 W
Belterra 250 2.38 S 54.57 W
Belthorn 262 53.43 N 2.26 W
Beltinci 61 46.36 N 16.15 E
Belton, Eng., U.K. 42 52.34 N 1.41 E
Belton, Eng., U.K. 44 53.33 N 0.49 W
Belton, Mo., U.S. 194 38.48 N 94.31 W
Belton, S.C., U.S. 192 34.31 N 82.29 W
Belton, Tx., U.S. 222 31.03 N 97.27 W
Belton Lake ⊜[1] 222 31.08 N 97.32 W
Beltra 48 54.13 N 8.37 W
Beltrán 252 27.50 S 64.04 W
Beltsville, Md., U.S. 208 39.02 N 76.54 W
Beltsville, Md., U.S. 284c 39.02 N 76.54 W
Bel'tsy → Bel'cy 78 47.46 N 27.56 E
Belturbet 48 54.06 N 7.28 W
Beltway Plaza ⊕[9] 284c 39.00 N 76.54 W
Bel'tyrskij 86 53.02 N 90.16 E
Beltzville Lake ⊜[1] 210 40.52 N 75.37 W
Beltzville State Park ♦ 210 40.52 N 75.36 W
Belucha, gora ∧ 86 49.48 N 86.40 E
Belucha, ozero ⊜ 80 49.20 N 46.05 E
Belugino 82 54.47 N 37.54 E
Belumut, Gunong ∧ 114 2.02 N 103.34 E
Belūr, India 122 13.10 N 75.52 E
Belur, India 272b 22.38 N 88.18 E
Beluran 112 5.54 N 117.33 E
Belur Math ⊌[1] 272b 22.38 N 88.22 E
Belušje 24 66.54 N 47.31 E
Belvedere, It. 64 45.44 N 13.23 E
Belvedere, Ca., U.S. 226 37.52 N 122.28 W
Belvedere, Va., U.S. 284c 38.50 N 77.10 W
Belvedere ⊕[8] 260 51.29 N 0.09 E
Belvedere ⊌ 264b 48.11 N 16.23 E
Belvedere di Spinello 68 39.12 N 16.53 E
Belvedere Homes 220 26.43 N 80.06 W
Belvedere Marittimo 68 39.37 N 15.52 E
Belvedere Ostrense 66 43.34 N 13.09 E
Belveren 130 37.39 N 37.34 E
Belvès 32 44.47 N 1.00 E
Belvidere, De., U.S. 208 39.43 N 75.37 W
Belvidere, Il., U.S. 216 42.15 N 88.50 W
Belvidere, N.J., U.S. 210 40.49 N 75.04 W
Belview 198 44.36 N 95.19 W
Belvis 266a 40.33 N 3.33 W
Belvís de la Jara 34 39.45 N 4.57 W
Belvoir ⊥ 132 32.36 N 35.31 E
Belvoir, Vale of V 42 52.57 N 0.53 W
Belyando ≃ 166 21.38 S 146.50 E
Belyj 76 55.50 N 32.56 E
Belyj, ostrov I 74 73.10 N 70.45 E
Belyje Berega 76 53.12 N 34.40 E
Belyje Kolodezi 82 54.55 N 38.42 E
Belyje Stolby 82 55.20 N 37.52 E
Belyje Vody 85 42.25 N 69.50 E
Belyj Gorodok 76 56.58 N 37.30 E
Belyj Jar, S.S.S.R. 80 53.57 N 48.58 E
Belyj Jar, S.S.S.R. 86 53.36 N 91.24 E
Belyj Jar, S.S.S.R. 86 58.26 N 85.01 E
Belyj Kalodez' 78 50.02 N 38.40 E
Belyj Kolodez' 78 50.12 N 37.08 E
Belyj Luch ≃ 80 57.43 N 43.42 E
Belyj Rast 82 56.08 N 37.26 E
Belyniči 76 53.59 N 29.42 E
Belynkoviči 76 53.15 N 32.08 E
Belz, Fr. 32 47.41 N 3.10 W
Belz, S.S.S.R. 78 50.23 N 24.01 E
Bełżec 30 50.24 N 23.26 E
Belzig 54 52.08 N 12.35 E
Belzoni 194 33.11 N 90.29 W
Bełżyce 30 51.11 N 22.18 E
Bem 219 38.15 N 91.28 W
Bemaraha, Plateau du ⋌[1] 157b 19.15 S 45.00 E
Bemarivo, Madag. 157b 16.56 S 44.21 E
Bemarivo, Madag. 157b 21.45 S 44.45 E
Bemarivo ≃, Madag. 157b 15.27 S 47.40 E
Bemarivo ≃, Madag. 157b 14.09 S 50.09 E
Bemavo 157b 21.37 S 45.24 E
Bemban 114 2.16 N 102.23 E
Bembe 152 7.02 S 14.18 E
Bembéréké 150 10.13 N 2.40 E
Bembézar ≃ 34 37.45 N 5.13 W
Bembezi ≃ 154 18.57 S 27.47 E
Bembou Sambayabé 150 10.55 N 13.44 W
Bembridge 42 50.41 N 1.05 W
Bement 194 39.55 N 88.34 W
Bemidji 190 47.28 N 94.52 W
Bemis 194 35.34 N 88.49 W
Bemmel 52 51.54 N 5.54 E
Bemolanga 157b 17.44 S 45.06 E
Bemposta 256 22.09 S 43.07 W
Bemus Point 214 42.09 N 79.23 W
Bemyž 80 56.08 N 51.44 E
Ben, Kinh ≋ 269c 10.43 N 106.37 E
Bena 150 11.18 N 5.55 E
Benaadir □[4] 144 2.07 N 45.24 E
Benāb 128 37.20 N 46.04 E
Benabarre 34 42.07 N 0.29 E
Bena-Dibele 152 4.07 S 22.50 E
Benagaria 126 24.11 N 87.37 E
Benagerie 166 31.25 S 140.24 E
Benahmed 148 33.07 N 7.17 W
Benain ≃ 112 9.39 S 124.59 E
Ben'akoni 76 54.15 N 25.22 E
Bena-Leka 152 5.08 S 22.10 E
Benalla 166 36.33 S 145.59 E
Benamejí 34 37.16 N 4.32 W
Benares → Vārānasi 124 25.20 N 83.00 E
Bénat, Cap ≻ 62 43.05 N 6.22 E
Benátky nad Jizerou 54 50.17 N 14.51 E
Bena-Tshadi 152 4.40 S 22.49 E
Benavente, Esp. 34 42.00 N 5.41 W
Benavente, Port. 34 38.59 N 8.48 W
Benavides 196 27.35 N 98.24 W
Benavidez 258 34.25 S 58.42 W
Ben Avon 279b 40.31 N 80.05 W
Ben Avon Heights 279b 40.31 N 80.04 W
Ben Badis 34 34.57 N 0.55 W
Benbane Head ≻ 48 55.15 N 6.28 W
Benbecula I 46 57.26 N 7.21 W
Ben Bolt 196 27.39 N 98.05 W
Benbonyathe Hill ∧ 166 30.24 S 139.11 E
Benbrook 222 32.40 N 97.27 W
Benbrook Lake ⊜[1] 222 32.38 N 97.27 W
Ben-cat 110 11.09 N 106.36 E
Bencha, Khao Phanom ∧ 110 8.17 N 98.56 E
Ben-Chicao, Col de)(34 36.12 N 2.45 E
Bencubbin 162 30.48 S 117.52 E
Benculuk 115a 8.26 S 114.13 E
Bend 202 44.03 N 121.18 W
Bendaja 150 7.10 N 11.15 W
Bende 150 5.36 N 7.39 E
Bendel □[3] 150 6.00 N 6.00 E
Bendela 152 3.18 S 17.36 E
Bendeleben, Mount ∧ 180 65.10 N 164.03 W
Bendemeer 166 30.53 S 151.10 E
Bender Beyla 144 9.29 N 50.49 E
Benderge ∧ 158 31.06 S 27.58 E
Bendersville 208 39.59 N 77.15 W
Bendery 78 46.48 N 29.29 E
Bendigo 169 36.46 S 144.17 E
Bendimahi ≃ 84 38.57 N 43.40 E
Bendo, Tanjung ≻ 115a 6.37 S 111.29 E
Bendorf 56 50.25 N 7.34 E
Bendugu 150 9.32 N 10.57 W
Bēne 76 56.29 N 23.04 E
Bene Beraq 132 32.05 N 34.50 E
Bene Berit 132 32.35 N 35.26 E
Benedict 208 38.30 N 76.40 W
Benediktenwand ⊥[4] 64 47.39 N 11.28 E
Beneditinos 250 5.27 S 42.22 W
Benedito Leite 250 7.13 S 44.34 W
Benemérita de San Cristóbal 238 18.25 N 70.06 W
Bénéna 150 13.07 N 4.22 W
Benenitra 157b 23.27 S 45.05 E
Benepú, Rada ⊤[3] 174z 27.10 S 109.25 W
Beneraird ∧[2] 44 55.04 N 4.57 W
Bene Re'em 132 31.46 N 34.47 E
Benešov 30 49.47 N 14.43 E
Benešov nad Ploučnicí 54 50.45 N 14.22 E
Bénestroff 56 48.55 N 6.45 E
Benetutti 71 40.27 N 9.10 E
Beneuvre 58 47.42 N 4.57 E
Bene Vagienna 62 44.33 N 7.50 E
Bénévent-l'Abbaye 32 46.07 N 1.38 E
Benevento 68 41.08 N 14.45 E
Benevento □[4] 68 41.15 N 14.17 E
Benezett 214 41.19 N 78.23 W
Benfeld 58 48.22 N 7.36 E
Benfica ⊕[8], Bra. 287a 22.53 S 43.15 W
Benfica ⊕[8], Port. 266c 38.45 N 9.12 W
Benfica, Estádio ♦ 266c 38.45 N 9.11 W
Bèng ≃, Lao 110 19.53 N 101.08 E
Beng ≃, Zhg. 98 35.05 N 118.24 E
Benga 154 13.19 S 34.16 E
Bengābād 126 24.18 N 86.21 E
Bengal, Bay of C 12 15.00 N 90.00 E
Bengala, Golfo del → Bengal, Bay of C 12 15.00 N 90.00 E
Bengalen, Golf von → Bengal, Bay of C 12 15.00 N 90.00 E
Bengamisa 154 0.57 N 25.10 E
Bengara 112 3.11 N 117.12 E
Ben Gardane 148 33.08 N 11.13 E
Bengasi → Banghāzī 146 32.07 N 20.04 E
Bengbis 152 3.27 N 12.27 E
Bengbu 100 32.58 N 117.24 E
Benger 168a 33.11 S 115.52 E
Benghazi → Banghāzī 146 32.07 N 20.04 E
Ben-giang 110 15.41 N 107.47 E
Bengkalis 114 1.28 N 102.07 E
Bengkalis, Pulau I 114 1.30 N 102.15 E
Bengkalis, Selat ⊔ 114 1.30 N 102.00 E
Bengkayang 112 0.50 N 109.29 E
Bengkoka ≃ 116 6.50 N 117.03 E
Bengkulu 112 3.48 S 102.16 E
Bengkulu □[4] 112 4.00 S 102.30 E
Bengo □[5] 152 8.30 S 13.20 E
Bengo ≃ 152 8.45 S 13.24 E
Bengo, Baía do C 152 8.43 S 13.21 E
Bengoi 164 3.01 S 130.12 E
Bengough 184 49.24 N 105.08 W
Bengtsfors 26 59.02 N 12.13 E
Benguela 152 12.35 S 13.25 E
Benguela □[5] 152 12.45 S 14.30 E
Benguerir 148 32.14 N 7.57 W
Benguet □[4] 116 16.30 N 120.40 E
Bengut, Cap ≻ 34 36.55 N 3.54 E
Benha → Banhā 142 30.28 N 31.11 E
Benham 192 36.57 N 82.56 W
Ben Hur 222 31.30 N 96.44 W
Beni, Nig. 146 10.27 N 10.24 E
Beni, Zaïre 154 0.30 N 29.28 E
Beni □[5] 248 14.00 S 65.30 W
Beni ≃ 248 10.23 S 65.24 W
Béni Abbas 148 30.08 N 2.10 W
Benicarló 34 40.25 N 0.26 E
Benicia 226 38.02 N 122.09 W
Benicia Capitol State Historic Park ♦ 282 38.03 N 122.09 W
Benicia State Recreation Area ♦ 282 38.05 N 122.13 W
Benicito ≃ 248 11.32 S 65.47 W
Benidorm 34 38.32 N 0.08 W
Beni-Mellal 148 32.22 N 6.29 W
Beni-Mellal □[4] 148 32.22 N 6.27 W
Benin (Bénin) □[1], Afr. 134 9.30 N 2.15 E
Benin (Bénin) □[1], Afr. 150 9.30 N 2.15 E
Benin ≃ 150 5.45 N 5.04 E
Benin, Bight of C[3] 150 5.30 N 3.00 E
Benin City 150 6.19 N 5.41 E
Benisa 34 38.34 N 0.03 E
Beni Saf 148 35.19 N 1.23 W
Benisheikh 146 11.49 N 12.29 E
Beni Suef → Banī Suwayf 142 29.05 N 31.05 E
Benito 184 51.55 N 101.31 W
Benito Juárez, Méx. 234 19.14 N 100.28 W
Benito Juárez, Méx. 234 17.50 N 92.32 W
Benito Juárez □[7] 286a 19.22 N 99.10 W
Benito Juárez, Parque Nacional ♦ 234 17.07 N 96.43 W
Benito Juárez, Presa ⊜[1] 234 16.27 N 95.30 W
Benit Point ≻ 116 9.54 N 125.17 E
Benjamim Constant 256 21.57 S 42.53 W
Benjamin 196 33.35 N 99.48 W
Benjamín, Isla I 254 44.40 S 74.08 W
Benjamín Aceval 252 24.58 S 57.34 W
Benjamin Constant 246 4.22 S 70.02 W
Benjamin Franklin Bridge ⊕[5] 285 39.57 N 75.08 W
Benjamín Hill 232 30.10 N 111.10 W
Benjamín Zorrilla 252 39.06 S 65.29 W
Benkelman 198 40.02 N 101.31 W
Benken 54 52.10 N 12.28 E
Benkovac 36 44.02 N 15.37 E
Benld 219 39.05 N 89.48 W
Benlidi 166 24.34 S 144.52 E
Benllech 44 53.19 N 4.13 W
Ben Lomond 226 37.05 N 122.05 W
Ben Mehidi 36 36.46 N 7.54 E
Benmore, Lake ⊜[1] 172 44.25 S 170.15 E
Benndale 194 30.52 N 88.48 W
Benndorf 54 51.34 N 11.29 E
Benneckenstein 54 51.40 N 10.45 E
Bennekom 52 52.00 N 5.40 E
Bennet 198 40.40 N 96.30 W
Bennett, Lake ⊜ 162 22.55 S 130.57 E
Bennetta, ostrov I 74 76.21 N 148.56 E
Bennett Lake ⊜, Can. 180 60.05 N 134.50 W
Bennett Lake ⊜, Mb., Can. 184 53.28 N 96.05 W
Bennett Lake ⊜, On., Can. 212 44.55 N 76.27 W
Bennett Pass)(224 45.18 N 121.39 W
Bennettsbridge 48 52.36 N 7.12 W
Bennetts Creek ≃ 210 42.16 N 77.35 W
Bennettsville 192 34.37 N 79.41 W
Bennettswood 274b 37.51 S 145.07 E
Bennigsen 52 52.14 N 9.40 E
Benninghofen ⊕[8] 263 51.29 N 7.31 E
Bennington, In., U.S. 218 38.52 N 85.08 W
Bennington, Ks., U.S. 198 39.01 N 97.35 W
Bennington, Vt., U.S. 210 42.52 N 73.11 W
Bennington □[6] 207 42.50 N 73.08 W
Bennington Battle Monument ⊥ 210 42.53 N 73.13 W
Benniu 106 31.52 N 119.48 E
Bennstedt 54 51.29 N 11.49 E
Beno 152 3.37 S 17.48 E
Benoa 115b 8.46 S 115.13 E
Ben Ohau Range ⋌ 172 44.00 S 170.00 E
Benoit 194 33.39 N 91.00 W
Benom, Gunong ∧ 114 3.49 N 102.04 E
Benoni 158 26.11 S 28.19 E
Benoni □[5] 273d 26.08 S 28.22 E
Benoni-Suid 273d 26.13 S 28.18 E
Bénoué (Benue) ≃ 134 7.48 N 6.46 E
Bénoué, Parc National de la ♦ 146 8.20 N 13.50 E
Benover 260 51.13 N 0.26 E
Bénoy 146 8.59 N 16.19 E
Benque Viejo 232 17.05 N 89.08 W
Benrad ⊕[8] 263 51.20 N 6.30 E
Benrath ⊕[8] 56 51.10 N 6.51 E
Benrath, Schloss ⊥ 263 51.10 N 6.52 E
Bensbach ≃ 164 9.08 S 141.00 E
Bensberg 56 50.58 N 7.09 E
Bensdorf 54 52.24 N 12.20 E
Ben Sekka, Rass ≻ 36 37.21 N 9.45 E
Bensenville 278 41.57 N 87.56 W
Bensersiel 52 53.40 N 7.34 E
Benshausen 54 50.38 N 10.35 E
Bensheim 56 49.41 N 8.37 E
Bensley 208 37.26 N 77.26 W
Ben-Slimane 148 33.41 N 7.10 W
Ben-Slimane □[4] 148 33.40 N 7.10 W
Ben Smih 36 36.23 N 7.31 E
Benson, Eng., U.K. 42 51.38 N 1.05 W
Benson, Az., U.S. 200 31.58 N 110.17 W
Benson, Md., U.S. 208 39.30 N 76.23 W
Benson, Mn., U.S. 198 45.18 N 95.35 W
Benson, N.C., U.S. 192 35.22 N 78.32 W
Bensonhurst ⊕[8] 276 40.35 N 73.59 W
Benson Point ≻ 174o 1.56 N 157.29 W
Bens Run ≃ 284b 39.19 N 76.48 W
Bent 128 26.17 N 59.31 E
Benta 114 4.01 N 101.58 E
Benteng (Salayar) 112 6.08 S 120.27 E
Bentheim, B.R.D. 52 52.17 N 7.10 E
Bentheim, Mi., U.S. 216 42.42 N 85.55 W
Ben-thuy 110 18.39 N 105.42 E
Bentiaba 152 14.15 S 12.21 E
Bentiaba ≃ 152 14.29 S 12.50 E
Bentinck Island I, Austl. 164 17.04 S 139.30 E
Bentinck Island I, Mya. 110 11.45 N 98.03 E
Bentiu 140 9.14 N 29.50 E
Bentleigh 274b 37.55 S 145.02 E
Bentley, Ab., Can. 182 52.28 N 114.04 W
Bentley, Eng., U.K. 44 53.33 N 1.09 W
Bentley College ⊌[2] 283 42.23 N 71.13 W
Bentleyville, Oh., U.S. 279a 41.25 N 81.26 W
Bentleyville, Pa., U.S. 214 40.07 N 80.00 W
Bento Gomes ≃ 248 16.40 S 57.12 W
Bento Gonçalves 252 29.10 S 51.31 W
Bentol 150 6.26 N 10.36 W
Benton, Ar., U.S. 194 34.33 N 92.35 W
Benton, Il., U.S. 194 37.59 N 88.55 W
Benton, In., U.S. 216 41.30 N 85.45 W
Benton, Ky., U.S. 194 36.51 N 88.21 W
Benton, La., U.S. 194 32.41 N 93.44 W
Benton, Ms., U.S. 194 32.49 N 90.15 W
Benton, Mo., U.S. 194 37.05 N 89.33 W
Benton, Oh., U.S. 214 40.36 N 81.51 W
Benton, Pa., U.S. 210 41.11 N 76.23 W
Benton, Tn., U.S. 192 35.10 N 84.39 W
Benton, Wi., U.S. 190 42.34 N 90.22 W
Benton □[6] 216 40.37 N 87.19 W
Benton City, Mo., U.S. 219 39.08 N 91.45 W
Benton City, Wa., U.S. 202 46.15 N 119.29 W
Bentong 114 3.32 N 101.55 E
Benton Harbor 216 42.07 N 86.26 W
Benton Heights 216 42.07 N 86.24 W
Bentonia 194 32.38 N 90.21 W
Benton Lake ⊜ 202 47.40 N 111.20 W
Benton Ridge 216 41.00 N 83.47 W
Bentonville, Ar., U.S. 194 36.22 N 94.12 W
Bentonville, In., U.S. 218 39.45 N 85.15 W
Bentonville, Oh., U.S. 218 38.45 N 83.37 W
Bent's Old Fort National Historic Site ⊥ 198 38.05 N 103.28 W
Benua, Pulau I 112 0.56 N 107.27 E
Benue □[3] 150 7.15 N 8.00 E
Benue (Bénoué) ≃ 134 7.48 N 6.46 E
Benut 114 1.38 N 103.16 E

ENGLISH — Name | Page | Lat.°′ | Long.°′

DEUTSCH — Name | Seite | Breite°′ | Länge°′ E = Ost

Benwee ∧ 48 53.35 N 9.31 W
Benwee Head ≻ 48 54.20 N 9.50 W
Ben Wheeler 222 32.27 N 95.42 W
Benxi (Xiaoshi), Zhg. 104 41.17 N 124.07 E
Benxi (Penhsi), Zhg. 104 41.18 N 123.45 E
Benza 152 6.16 S 12.57 E
Beograd (Belgrade) 38 44.50 N 20.30 E
Beohāri 124 24.03 N 81.23 E
Beonta 272b 22.31 N 88.31 E
Béoumi 150 7.40 N 5.34 W
Beowawe 204 40.35 N 116.28 W
Beppu 96 33.17 N 131.30 E
Beppu-wan C 96 33.18 N 131.35 E
Bequia I 241h 13.01 N 61.13 W
Bequimão 250 2.26 S 44.47 W
Bera, Bngl. 126 24.05 N 89.37 E
Bera, Bngl. 126 23.59 N 89.40 E
Bera, Tasek ⊜ 114 3.04 N 102.37 E
Berābāria 272b 22.52 N 88.34 E
Beraberi, India 272b 22.46 N 88.27 E
Berāberi, India 272b 22.51 N 88.12 E
Beraketa, Madag. 157b 24.11 S 45.42 E
Beraketa, Madag. 157b 23.07 S 44.25 E
Beramanja 157b 13.13 S 48.56 E
Bérandjoko 152 3.06 N 17.17 E
Berāsi 124 23.36 N 81.51 E
Berasia 124 23.38 N 77.26 E
Berat 38 40.42 N 19.57 E
Beratzhausen 60 49.06 N 11.48 E
Berau 58 47.42 N 8.15 E
Berau ≃ 112 2.10 N 117.42 E
Berau, Teluk C 164 2.30 S 132.30 E
Beravina 157b 18.10 S 45.14 E
Berazategui 258 34.46 S 58.13 W
Berazategui □[5] 288 34.50 S 58.10 W
Berbenno di Valtellina 64 46.10 N 9.44 E
Berbera 144 10.25 N 45.02 E
Berbérati 152 4.16 N 15.47 E
Berbería, Cabo ≻ 34 38.38 N 1.23 E
Berbice ≃ 246 6.17 N 57.32 W
Berceto 64 44.31 N 9.59 E
Berchem, Bel. 50 50.47 N 3.30 E
Berchem, Bel. 50 51.12 N 4.26 E
Berchidda 71 40.47 N 9.10 E
Berching 60 49.07 N 11.27 E
Berchtesgaden 64 47.38 N 13.01 E
Berchtesgaden, Nationalpark ♦ 64 47.30 N 13.00 E
Berchum 263 51.23 N 7.32 E
Berck 50 50.24 N 1.34 E
Berclair 196 28.32 N 97.36 W
Berčogur 86 48.25 N 58.44 E
Bercu 50 50.31 N 3.17 E
Berd 84 40.53 N 45.23 E
Berda ≃ 78 46.48 N 36.52 E
Berdaale 144 7.04 N 47.51 E
Berdale 144 4.56 N 45.02 E
Berd'ansk 78 46.45 N 36.49 E
Berd'anskaja kosa ≻[2] 78 46.42 N 36.48 E
Berd'anskij zaliv C 78 46.42 N 36.35 E
Berd'auš 86 55.09 N 59.09 E
Berdičev 78 49.54 N 28.36 E
Berdigest'ach 74 62.06 N 126.40 E
Berdniki 80 57.25 N 46.33 E
Berdorf 56 49.50 N 6.21 E
Berdsk 86 54.47 N 83.02 E
Berd'užje 86 55.48 N 68.19 E
Berdyansk → Berd'ansk 78 46.45 N 36.49 E
Bere, S.S.S.R. 128 39.47 N 58.06 E
Béré, Tchad 146 9.20 N 16.09 E
Berea, Ky., U.S. 192 37.34 N 84.17 W
Berea, Oh., U.S. 214 41.21 N 81.51 W
Berea, S.C., U.S. 192 34.53 N 82.27 W
Bere Alston 42 50.29 N 4.11 W
Beregajevo 86 57.10 N 87.32 E
Beregomet 78 48.12 N 25.21 E
Beregovo 78 48.13 N 22.39 E
Beregovoj 86 55.12 N 73.12 E
Bereguardo 62 45.15 N 9.01 E
Bereka ≃ 78 49.12 N 36.59 E
Bereketli 130 40.31 N 37.18 E
Bereku 154 4.27 S 35.44 E
Berekua 240d 15.14 N 61.19 W
Berekum 150 7.27 N 2.37 W
Bérem 152 7.33 N 13.55 E
Beren, liman ⊜ 80 46.52 N 44.55 E
Berenda Slough ≃ 226 37.00 N 120.29 W
Berendejevo 82 56.36 N 39.01 E
Berens ≃ 184 52.21 N 97.02 W
Berens Island I 184 52.18 N 97.17 W
Berens River 184 52.22 N 97.02 W
Bere Regis 42 50.46 N 2.14 W
Beresford, Austl. 166 29.14 S 136.40 E
Beresford, N.B., Can. 186 47.42 N 65.42 W
Beresford, S.D., U.S. 198 43.04 N 96.46 W
Beresina → Berezina ≃ 76 52.33 N 30.14 E
Berestečko 78 50.23 N 25.07 E
Berești 38 46.06 N 27.53 E
Beretău (Berettyó) ≃ 38 46.59 N 21.07 E
Berettyó (Beretău) ≃ 38 46.59 N 21.07 E
Berettyóújfalu 30 47.14 N 21.32 E
Berevo, Madag. 157b 17.14 S 44.17 E
Berevo, Madag. 157b 19.44 S 44.58 E
Berezajka 76 57.59 N 33.54 E
Berezan' 78 50.19 N 31.30 E
Berezanskaja 78 45.43 N 39.34 E
Berezanskij liman C[1] 78 46.43 N 31.30 E
Berežany 78 49.27 N 24.56 E
Berezdov 78 50.27 N 27.05 E
Berezina ≃, S.S.S.R. 76 52.33 N 30.14 E
Berezina ≃, S.S.S.R. 76 53.48 N 25.59 E
Berezino, S.S.S.R. 76 53.49 N 28.59 E
Berezino, S.S.S.R. 76 54.54 N 28.12 E
Berezino, S.S.S.R. 78 46.14 N 29.12 E
Berezino, S.S.S.R. 80 50.06 N 48.52 E
Berezinskij zapovednik ♦ 76 54.40 N 28.15 E
Berezna 78 51.34 N 31.47 E
Berezn'agi 78 49.59 N 41.06 E
Berezn'aki, S.S.S.R. 78 49.09 N 31.57 E
Berezn'aki, S.S.S.R. 78 49.51 N 33.01 E
Bereznegovatoje 78 47.20 N 32.49 E
Berežnica 78 51.27 N 26.27 E
Bereznik 24 62.51 N 42.40 E
Berezniki 86 59.24 N 56.46 E
Berford Lake ⊜ 212 44.48 N 81.11 W
Berg, B.R.D. 64 47.58 N 11.21 E
Berg, Lux. 56 49.49 N 6.05 E
Berg, Nor. 24 69.26 N 17.15 E
Berg, Öst. 64 46.45 N 13.09 E
Berga, D.D.R. 54 50.45 N 12.10 E
Berga, D.D.R. 54 51.27 N 11.00 E
Berga, Esp. 34 42.06 N 1.51 E
Berga, Sve. 40 59.21 N 16.26 E
Bergama 130 39.07 N 27.11 E
Bergambacht 52 51.56 N 4.46 E
Bergamo 62 45.41 N 9.43 E
Bergamo □[4] 64 45.50 N 9.48 E
Bergan Point ≻ 276 40.40 N 73.20 W
Bergantín 246 10.01 N 64.22 W
Bergantino 64 45.05 N 11.15 E
Bergbaumuseum ⊌ 263 51.29 N 7.13 E
Bergby 26 60.56 N 17.02 E
Berge, B.R.D. 52 52.37 N 7.44 E
Berge, B.R.D. 263 51.21 N 7.22 E
Berge, D.D.R. 54 53.15 N 11.50 E
Bergedorf ⊕[8] 52 53.29 N 10.13 E
Bergei ∧[2] 263 51.13 N 7.46 E
Bergeijk 52 51.19 N 5.22 E
Bergen → Mons, Bel. 50 50.27 N 3.56 E
Bergen, B.R.D. 52 52.48 N 9.58 E
Bergen, B.R.D. 54 52.53 N 10.58 E
Bergen, B.R.D. 64 47.48 N 12.35 E
Bergen, Ned. 52 52.40 N 4.41 E
Bergen, Nor. 26 60.23 N 5.20 E
Bergen, N.Y., U.S. 210 43.05 N 77.56 W
Bergen □[6] 210 40.53 N 74.03 W
Bergen aan Zee 52 52.38 N 4.37 E
Bergen [auf Rügen] 54 54.25 N 13.26 E
Bergen Basin C 276 40.39 N 73.49 W
Bergen-Belsen-Denkmal ⊥ 52 52.46 N 9.55 E
Berg en Dal 250 5.09 N 55.04 W
Bergenfield 210 40.55 N 73.59 W
Bergen Mall ⊕[9] 276 40.55 N 74.04 W
Bergen op Zoom 52 51.30 N 4.17 E
Berger 219 38.40 N 91.20 W
Bergerac 32 44.51 N 0.29 E
Bergères-lès-Vertus 50 48.53 N 4.00 E
Bergerhof 263 51.12 N 7.21 E
Bergfelde 54 52.40 N 13.19 E
Berggiesshübel 54 50.52 N 13.57 E
Berghausen, B.R.D. 263 51.18 N 7.17 E
Berghausen, B.R.D. 263 51.07 N 6.55 E
Bergheim, B.R.D. 56 50.55 N 6.38 E
Bergheim, Fr. 58 48.12 N 7.22 E
Bergheim, Öst. 64 47.50 N 13.02 E
Berghem 52 51.46 N 5.34 E
Berghofen ⊕[8] 263 51.29 N 7.32 E
Bergholtz 210 43.06 N 78.53 W
Bergholtz Creek ≃ 284a 43.05 N 78.57 W
Bergholz 214 40.31 N 80.53 W
Bergholz-Rehbrücke 54 52.20 N 13.05 E
Bergisch-Born 263 51.09 N 7.15 E
Bergisches Land ⊕[1] 56 51.00 N 7.10 E
Bergisch Gladbach 56 50.59 N 7.07 E
Bergkamen 52 51.38 N 7.38 E
Bergkvara 26 56.23 N 16.05 E
Bergland 190 46.35 N 89.34 W
Bergneustadt 56 51.01 N 7.39 E
Bergnicourt 50 49.25 N 4.15 E
Bergö I 26 62.58 N 21.11 E
Bergoo 188 38.29 N 80.18 W
Bergos 130 40.14 N 26.36 E
Bergplaas 158 33.54 S 22.40 E
Bergrheinfeld 56 50.00 N 10.10 E
Bergsäng 40 60.06 N 13.33 E
Bergsbrunna 40 59.49 N 17.43 E
Bergsche Maas ≃ 52 51.45 N 5.08 E
Bergshamra 40 59.38 N 18.37 E
Bergsjö 26 61.59 N 17.04 E
Bergslagen ⊕[1] 40 59.55 N 15.00 E
Bergstrom Air Force Base ■ 222 30.12 N 97.40 W
Bergtheim 56 49.54 N 10.04 E
Berguent 148 34.03 N 2.02 W
Bergues 50 50.58 N 2.26 E
Bergum 52 53.11 N 5.59 E
Bergün 58 46.38 N 9.45 E
Bergville 158 28.52 S 29.18 E
Bergvreten 40 60.31 N 16.26 E
Bergwitz 54 51.48 N 12.35 E
Berhala, Selat ⊔ 112 0.48 S 104.25 E
Berhampore 126 24.06 N 88.15 E
Berhampur 122 19.19 N 84.47 E
Beri 124 28.42 N 76.35 E
Berici, Monti ⋌ 64 45.26 N 11.31 E
Berih ≃ 271c 1.23 N 103.40 E
Berikul'skij 86 55.32 N 88.08 E
Beringa, ostrov I 74 55.00 N 165.15 E
Beringen 56 51.03 N 5.13 E
Bering Glacier ⊓ 180 60.15 N 143.30 W
Beringhausen 56 51.24 N 8.46 E
Beringil 140 12.10 N 25.41 E
Beringin 112 3.41 S 104.18 E
Beringovskij 180 63.03 N 179.19 E
Bering Sea ⊤[2] 16 60.00 N 175.00 W
Bering Strait ⊔ 180 65.30 N 169.00 W
Berinsfield 42 51.40 N 1.11 W
Berislav 78 46.51 N 33.26 E
Berisso 258 34.52 S 57.53 W
Berisso □[5] 288 34.55 S 57.53 W
Berja 34 36.51 N 2.57 W
Berkåk 26 62.50 N 10.00 E
Berkakit 74 56.34 N 124.48 E
Berkane 148 34.59 N 2.20 W
Berkel ≃ 52 52.09 N 6.12 E
Berkeley, Eng., U.K. 42 51.42 N 2.27 W
Berkeley, Ca., U.S. 226 37.52 N 122.16 W
Berkeley, Il., U.S. 278 41.53 N 87.54 W
Berkeley, Mo., U.S. 219 38.45 N 90.19 W
Berkeley, R.I., U.S. 207 41.55 N 71.25 W
Berkeley, Vale of V 42 51.43 N 2.25 W
Berkeley Heights 210 40.41 N 74.26 W
Berkeley Hills 279b 40.32 N 80.00 W
Berkeley Hills ⋌[2] 282 37.54 N 122.16 W
Berkeley Plantation ⊥ 208 37.19 N 77.10 W
Berkeley Springs 188 39.37 N 78.13 W
Berkhamsted 260 51.46 N 0.35 W
Berkheim 58 48.02 N 10.04 E
Berkley, Ma., U.S. 207 41.50 N 71.05 W
Berkley, Mi., U.S. 281 42.30 N 83.11 W
Berkner Island I 9 79.30 S 49.30 W
Berks □[6] 208 40.20 N 75.50 W
Berkshire, Ma., U.S. 207 42.30 N 73.11 W
Berkshire, N.Y., U.S. 210 42.18 N 76.11 W
Berkshire □[6], Eng., U.K. 42 51.30 N 1.20 W
Berkshire □[6], Ma., U.S. 207 42.27 N 73.15 W
Berkshire Downs ⋌[1] 42 51.33 N 1.24 W
Berkshire Hills ⋌[2] 207 42.20 N 73.10 W
Berlaar 56 51.07 N 4.39 E
Berlaimont 50 50.12 N 3.49 E
Berland ≃ 182 54.01 N 116.50 W
Berlanga de Duero 34 41.28 N 2.51 W
Berlenga I 34 39.25 N 9.30 W
Berlengas ≃ 250 5.39 S 42.19 W
Berlevåg 24 70.51 N 29.06 E
Berlicum 52 51.42 N 5.23 E
Berlikum 52 53.15 N 5.39 E
Berlin (West), B.R.D. 54 52.31 N 13.24 E
Berlin (West), B.R.D. 264a 52.31 N 13.24 E
Berlin (Ost), D.D.R. 54 52.30 N 13.25 E
Berlin (Ost), D.D.R. 264a 52.30 N 13.25 E
Berlin, S. Afr. 158 32.54 S 27.35 E
Berlin, Ct., U.S. 207 41.37 N 72.44 W
Berlin, Md., U.S. 208 38.19 N 75.13 W
Berlin, Ma., U.S. 207 42.22 N 71.38 W
Berlin, N.H., U.S. 188 44.28 N 71.11 W
Berlin, N.J., U.S. 208 39.47 N 74.55 W
Berlin, N.Y., U.S. 210 42.42 N 73.23 W
Berlin, Oh., U.S. 214 40.34 N 81.48 W
Berlin, Pa., U.S. 188 39.55 N 78.57 W
Berlin, Wi., U.S. 190 43.58 N 88.56 W
Berlin □[5] 264a 52.33 N 13.30 E
Berlin, Mount ∧ 9 76.03 S 135.52 W
Berlin Center 214 41.01 N 80.57 W
Berlinchen 54 53.13 N 12.34 E
Berliner Brücke ⊕[5] 263 51.27 N 6.47 E
Berliner Forst Düppel ⊕[3] 264a 52.25 N 13.08 E
Berliner Forst Düppel ♦ 264a 52.25 N 13.07 E
Berliner Forst Grunewald ♦ 264a 52.28 N 13.13 E
Berliner Mauer (Berlin Wall) ⊥ 264a 52.35 N 13.22 E
Berliner Stadtforst Spandau ♦ 264a 52.35 N 13.10 E
Berlinguet Inlet C 176 71.10 N 85.35 W
Berlin Heights 214 41.20 N 82.30 W
Berlin-Ichthyosaur State Park ♦ 204 38.51 N 117.35 W
Berlin Lake ⊜[1] 214 41.00 N 81.00 W
Berlin Mountain ∧ 210 42.42 N 73.17 W
Berlin Park ♦ 285 39.47 N 74.57 W
Berlin-Schönefeld, Flughafen ⊠ 54 52.23 N 13.31 E
Berlinsville 210 40.47 N 75.35 W
Berlin-Tegel, Flughafen ⊠ 54 52.34 N 13.18 E
Berlin-Tempelhof, Flughafen ⊠ 54 52.29 N 13.25 E
Bermagui 166 36.25 S 150.04 E
Bermamyt, gora ∧ 84 43.41 N 42.27 E
Bermejillo 232 25.53 N 103.37 W
Bermejo 252 31.37 S 67.39 W

Symbols in the index entries represent the broad categories identified in the key at the right. Symbols with superior numbers (⋌[1]) identify subcategories (see complete key on page *I · 1*).

Kartensymbole in dem Registerverzeichnis stellen die rechts in Schlüssel erklärten Kategorien dar. Symbole mit hochgestellten Ziffern (⋌[1]) bezeichnen Unterabteilungen einer Kategorie (vgl. vollständiger Schlüssel auf Seite *I · 1*).

Los símbolos incluídos en el texto del índice representan las grandes categorias identificadas con la clave a la derecha. Los símbolos con numeros en su parte superior (⋌[1]) identifican las subcategorías (véase la clave completa en la página *I · 1*).

Les symboles de l'index représentent les catégories indiquées dans la légende à droite. Les symboles suivis d'un indice (⋌[1]) représentent des sous-catégories (voir légende complète à la page *I · 1*).

Os símbolos incluídos no texto do índice representam as grandes categorias identificadas com a chave à direita. Os símbolos com números em sua parte superior (⋌[1]) identificam as subcategorias (veja-se a chave completa à página *I · 1*).

∧ Mountain	Berg	Montaña	Montagne	Montanha
⋌ Mountains	Berge	Montañas	Montagnes	Montanhas
)(Pass	Pass	Paso	Col	Passo
V Valley, Canyon	Tal, Cañon	Valle, Cañón	Vallée, Canyon	Vale, Canhão
≃ Plain	Ebene	Llano	Plaine	Planície
≻ Cape	Kap	Cabo	Cap	Cabo
I Island	Insel	Isla	Île	Ilha
II Islands	Inseln	Islas	Îles	Ilhas
⊥ Other Topographic Features	Andere Topographische Objekte	Otros Elementos Topográficos	Autres données topographiques	Outros acidentes topográficos

ESPAÑOL — FRANÇAIS — PORTUGUÊS

Nombre / Nom / Nome	Página / Page	Lat.°′	Long.°′ W = Oeste / Ouest
Bermejo ≃, Arg.	252	31.52 S	67.22 W
Bermejo ≃, S.A.	252	26.51 S	58.23 W
Bermejo, Paso de)(	252	32.50 S	70.05 W
Bermen, Lac ◎	176	53.35 N	68.55 W
Bermeo	34	43.26 N	2.43 W
Bermillo de Sayago	34	41.22 N	6.06 W
Bermo	124	23.47 N	85.57 E
Bermondsey ◆[8]	260	51.30 N	0.04 W
Bermuda □[2], N.A.	230	32.20 N	64.45 W
Bermuda □[2], N.A.	240a	32.20 N	64.45 W
Bermuda Rise ✢[3]	16	32.30 N	65.00 W
Bermudes → Bermuda □[2]	240a	32.20 N	64.45 W
Bermudian Creek ≃	208	40.01 N	76.55 W
Bern (Berne)	58	46.57 N	7.26 E
Bern (Berne) □[3]	58	46.55 N	7.35 E
Bern, Flughafen ⊠	58	46.55 N	7.30 E
Berna → Bern	58	46.57 N	7.26 E
Bernabéu, Estadio ♠	266a	40.27 N	3.41 W
Bernal ◆[8]	258	34.42 S	58.17 W
Bernalda	68	40.24 N	16.41 E
Bernalillo	200	35.18 N	106.33 W
Bernam ≃	114	3.48 N	100.57 E
Bernardston	207	42.40 N	72.33 W
Bernardsville	210	40.43 N	74.34 W
Bernasconi	252	37.54 S	63.43 W
Bernate	266b	45.29 N	8.49 E
Bernau am Chiemsee	64	47.48 N	12.22 E
Bernau bei Berlin	54	52.40 N	13.35 E
Bernaville	50	50.08 N	2.10 E
Bernay	50	49.06 N	0.36 E
Bernbeuren	58	47.44 N	10.46 E
Bernburg	54	51.48 N	11.44 E
Berndorf	61	47.57 N	16.08 E
Berne, B.R.D.	52	53.11 N	8.29 E
Berne → Bern, Schw.	58	46.57 N	7.26 E
Berne, In., U.S.	216	40.39 N	84.57 W
Berne, N.Y., U.S.	210	42.38 N	74.08 W
Berneburg	56	51.04 N	9.53 E
Berner Alpen ∧∧	58	46.30 N	7.30 E
Berneray I	46	57.43 N	7.12 W
Berneval-le-Grand	50	49.57 N	1.12 E
Berngardovka	265a	60.01 N	30.36 E
Bernhardina	158	27.53 S	28.40 E
Bernhards Bay	210	43.15 N	75.56 W
Bernhardsthal	61	48.41 N	16.52 E
Bernice	194	32.49 N	92.39 W
Bernie	194	36.40 N	89.58 W
Bernier Bay ⊂	176	71.00 N	87.30 W
Bernier Island I	162	24.52 S	113.08 E
Bernina ∧∧	58	46.22 N	9.50 E
Bernina, Passo del)(	58	46.24 N	10.03 E
Bernina, Piz ∧	58	46.21 N	9.51 E
Bernisdale	46	57.27 N	6.24 W
Bernkastel-Kues	56	49.55 N	7.04 E
Bernried	64	47.52 N	11.17 E
Bernsbach	54	50.34 N	12.46 E
Bernsdorf	54	51.22 N	14.04 E
Bernsfelden	56	49.34 N	9.53 E
Bernstadt, D.D.R.	54	51.03 N	14.50 E
Bernstadt → Bierutów, Pol.	30	51.08 N	17.32 E
Bernstein → Pełczyce	30	53.03 N	15.18 E
Bernville	208	40.26 N	76.07 W
Bero ≃	152	15.10 S	12.09 E
Beroga	114	2.56 N	101.55 E
Beroldingen ⊥	58	46.55 N	8.36 E
Berolzheim	56	49.28 N	9.32 E
Beromünster	58	47.12 N	8.11 E
Berón de Astrada	252	27.33 S	57.32 W
Beror Ḥayil	132	31.33 N	34.38 E
Beroroha	157b	21.41 S	45.10 E
Ber'ostovica	76	53.07 N	23.58 E
Beroun	30	49.58 N	14.04 E
Berounka ≃	30	50.00 N	14.24 E
Berovo	38	41.42 N	22.51 E
Berowra	170	33.37 S	151.09 E
Ber'oza, S.S.S.R.	76	52.32 N	24.59 E
Ber'oza, S.S.S.R.	78	51.44 N	33.52 E
Ber'ozno	78	51.00 N	26.45 E
Ber'ožnoje	76	59.55 N	39.17 E
Ber'ozovaja ≃	80	48.31 N	41.03 E
Ber'ozovaja Rudka	78	50.19 N	32.14 E
Ber'ozovka, S.S.S.R.	24	65.00 N	56.26 E
Ber'ozovka, S.S.S.R.	76	53.26 N	38.53 E
Ber'ozovka, S.S.S.R.	76	53.43 N	25.30 E
Ber'ozovka, S.S.S.R.	78	47.49 N	32.28 E
Ber'ozovka, S.S.S.R.	78	45.35 N	33.20 E
Ber'ozovka, S.S.S.R.	78	47.12 N	30.55 E
Ber'ozovka, S.S.S.R.	80	52.06 N	45.07 E
Ber'ozovka, S.S.S.R.	80	51.11 N	53.16 E
Ber'ozovka, S.S.S.R.	86	51.51 N	82.58 E
Ber'ozovka, S.S.S.R.	86	56.03 N	93.07 E
Ber'ozovka, S.S.S.R.	86	54.02 N	76.35 E
Ber'ozovka, S.S.S.R.	86	59.24 N	82.38 E
Ber'ozovka, S.S.S.R.	86	59.35 N	56.02 E
Ber'ozovka, S.S.S.R.	86	57.37 N	57.18 E
Ber'ozovka, S.S.S.R.	88	57.46 N	116.09 E
Ber'ozovka, S.S.S.R.	89	50.35 N	127.52 E
Ber'ozovka, S.S.S.R.	265a	59.56 N	30.49 E
Ber'ozovo, S.S.S.R.	74	63.56 N	65.02 E
Ber'ozovo, S.S.S.R.	78	51.35 N	27.20 E
Ber'ozovo, S.S.S.R.	80	51.56 N	48.28 E
Ber'ozovo, S.S.S.R.	82	54.03 N	36.24 E
Ber'ozovo, S.S.S.R.	82	54.19 N	38.17 E
Ber'ozovskaja	80	50.16 N	43.59 E
Ber'ozovskij	86	55.39 N	86.16 E
Ber'ozovskij R'adok	76	58.06 N	34.29 E
Ber'ozovskoje	86	55.50 N	89.36 E
Berra	64	44.59 N	11.58 E
Berras, Arroyo los ≃	288	34.34 S	58.40 W
Berre ≃	62	44.24 N	4.40 E
Berre, Étang de ⊂	62	43.27 N	5.08 E
Berrechid	148	33.17 N	7.35 W
Berre-des-Alpes	62	43.50 N	7.19 E
Berre-L'Étang	62	43.28 N	5.11 E
Ber Remad, Oued V	148	31.45 N	1.10 E
Berri	166	34.17 S	140.36 E
Berridale	171b	36.22 S	148.50 E
Berriedale	46	58.11 N	3.29 W
Berrien □[6]	216	41.59 N	86.30 W
Berrien Springs	216	41.56 N	86.20 W
Berrigan	166	35.40 S	145.49 E
Berrima	170	34.30 S	150.20 E
Berriozábal	234	16.48 N	93.16 W
Berriyyane	148	32.50 N	3.46 E
Berrouaghia	34	36.08 N	2.55 E
Berrugosa Point ›	116	10.23 N	125.33 E
Berry, Austl.	170	34.47 S	150.42 E
Berry, Al., U.S.	194	33.39 N	87.36 W
Berry, Ky., U.S.	218	38.31 N	84.23 W
Berry □[9]	50	47.20 N	2.10 E
Berry, Canal du ≊	50	47.17 N	1.25 E
Berry-au-Bac	50	49.24 N	3.54 E
Berry Creek ≃, Ab., Can.	182	50.50 N	111.36 W
Berry Creek ≃, Tx., U.S.	222	30.40 N	97.36 W
Berryessa, Lake ◎[1]	226	38.35 N	122.14 W
Berryessa Creek ≃	282	37.24 N	121.53 W
Berryessa Peak ∧	226	38.40 N	122.11 W
Berry Head ›	42	50.24 N	3.29 W
Berry Islands II	238	25.34 N	77.45 W
Berry Mountain ∧	208	40.31 N	77.02 W
Berrysburg	208	40.36 N	76.49 W
Berrys Creek ≃	276	40.47 N	74.05 W
Berryville	194	36.21 N	93.34 W
Beršad'	78	48.23 N	29.30 E
Berseba	156	26.00 S	17.46 E
Bersenbrück	52	52.33 N	7.56 E
Bersut	80	55.32 N	50.54 E
Berta ≃	84	41.09 N	41.53 E
Bertam	114	5.09 N	102.03 E
Berté, Lac ◎	186	50.48 N	68.30 W
Bertha	198	46.16 N	95.03 W
Berthåga	40	59.52 N	17.35 E
Berthelsdorf	54	51.05 N	14.13 E
Berthier □[6]	206	46.30 N	73.45 W
Berthierville	206	46.05 N	73.10 W
Berthold	198	48.18 N	101.44 W
Berthoud	200	40.18 N	105.04 W
Berthoud Pass)(	200	39.45 N	105.45 W
Bertincourt	50	50.05 N	2.59 E
Bertinoro	66	44.09 N	12.08 E
Bertioga	256	23.51 S	46.09 W
Bertioga, Enseada da ⊂	256	23.50 S	46.08 W
Bertkow	54	52.43 N	11.54 E
Bertlich	263	51.37 N	7.04 E
Bertogne	56	50.05 N	5.40 E
Bertolínia	250	7.38 S	43.57 W
Bertoua	152	4.35 N	13.41 E
Bertram	196	30.45 N	98.03 W
Bertrand, Mi., U.S.	216	41.46 N	86.15 W
Bertrand, Ne., U.S.	198	40.31 N	99.38 W
Bertrix	56	49.51 N	5.15 E
Bertry	50	50.05 N	3.27 E
Beru I	14	1.20 S	176.00 E
Beruas	114	4.30 N	100.47 E
Beruri	246	3.54 S	61.22 W
Berville	214	42.55 N	82.53 W
Berville-sur-Mer	50	49.26 N	0.22 E
Berwang	58	47.24 N	10.45 E
Berwick, Austl.	169	38.02 S	145.21 E
Berwick, N.S., Can.	186	45.03 N	64.44 W
Berwick, La., U.S.	194	29.41 N	91.13 W
Berwick, Me., U.S.	188	43.15 N	70.51 W
Berwick, Pa., U.S.	210	41.03 N	76.14 W
Berwick-upon-Tweed	44	55.46 N	2.00 W
Berwyn, Il., U.S.	216	41.51 N	87.47 W
Berwyn, Pa., U.S.	208	40.02 N	75.26 W
Berwyn ∧∧	42	52.53 N	3.24 W
Berwyn Heights	284c	38.59 N	76.54 W
Bērze ≃	76	56.41 N	23.37 E
Berzé-la-Ville	58	46.22 N	4.42 E
Berz-Macomb Airport ⊠	281	42.40 N	82.58 W
Bès ≃	62	44.08 N	6.14 E
Besalampy	157b	16.45 S	44.30 E
Besana in Brianza	62	45.42 N	9.17 E
Besançon	58	47.15 N	6.02 E
Besani	124	24.08 N	80.17 E
Besar, Gunong ∧, Malay.	114	5.10 N	101.18 E
Besar, Gunong ∧, Malay.	114	2.30 N	103.10 E
Besar, Gunung ∧	112	2.43 S	115.37 E
Besar, Pulau I	115b	8.28 S	122.22 E
Besar Hantu, Gunong ∧	114	3.12 N	102.02 E
Besaya ≃	34	43.21 N	4.04 W
Besbes	36	36.42 N	7.51 E
Besed' ≃	76	52.38 N	31.09 E
Besedino	78	51.42 N	36.28 E
Besedy	265b	55.37 N	37.47 E
Besenfeld	56	48.35 N	8.25 E
Bešenkoviči	76	55.03 N	29.27 E
Beserah	114	3.52 N	103.22 E
Besigheim	56	49.00 N	9.08 E
Besikama	112	9.36 S	124.57 E
Beşiktaş ◆[8]	267b	41.03 N	29.01 E
Beşiri	130	37.55 N	41.18 E
Besitang	114	4.02 N	98.12 E
Beškent	128	38.49 N	65.39 E
Beskid Mountains ∧∧	30	49.40 N	20.00 E
Beskra	148	34.51 N	5.44 E
Beskra □[5]	148	34.00 N	6.00 E
Beškube	85	39.50 N	68.18 E
Beskudnikovo ◆[8]	265b	55.52 N	37.34 E
Beslan	84	43.12 N	44.33 E
Beslenej	84	44.14 N	41.44 E
Besnard Lake ◎	184	55.24 N	106.05 W
Besni	130	37.41 N	37.52 E
Besor, Naḥal V	132	31.28 N	34.22 E
Besós ≃	266d	41.25 N	2.04 E
Besozzo	62	45.51 N	8.39 E
Besp'atovo	82	54.45 N	38.54 E
Beşpınar	130	41.09 N	35.14 E
Besputa ≃	82	54.50 N	37.58 E
Bessacarr	44	53.30 N	1.04 W
Bessancourt	261	49.02 N	2.13 E
Bessans	62	45.19 N	7.00 E
Bessarabia □[9]	78	47.00 N	28.30 E
Bessarabka, S.S.S.R.	78	46.20 N	28.58 E
Bessarabka, S.S.S.R.	86	53.37 N	73.17 E
Bessaz, gora ∧	85	43.49 N	68.40 E
Bessbrook	48	54.12 N	6.25 W
Besse, B.R.D.	56	51.13 N	9.23 E
Besse, Nig.	150	11.15 N	4.30 E
Bessèges	62	44.17 N	4.06 E
Bessemer, Al., U.S.	194	33.24 N	86.57 W
Bessemer, Mi., U.S.	190	46.28 N	90.03 W
Bessemer, Pa., U.S.	214	40.58 N	80.29 W
Bessemer City	192	35.17 N	81.17 W
Besser	41	55.52 N	10.39 E
Bessé-sur-Braye	50	47.50 N	0.45 E
Bessheim	26	61.31 N	8.51 E
Besshiyama	96	33.50 N	133.23 E
Bessho	270	34.27 N	135.31 E
Bessonovka	80	53.18 N	45.03 E
Best	52	51.31 N	5.24 E
Best'ach	74	61.52 N	129.55 E
Bestamak, S.S.S.R.	86	49.43 N	55.07 E
Bestamak, S.S.S.R.	86	49.13 N	78.21 E
Beštau, gora ∧	84	44.06 N	43.01 E
Besten	263	51.39 N	6.54 E
Bestensee	54	52.15 N	13.37 E
Bestfield	285	39.43 N	75.36 W
Bestobe	86	52.30 N	73.05 E
Beštor, gora ∧	85	42.03 N	70.50 E
Bestuževo	24	61.37 N	43.58 E
Bestwig	52	51.22 N	8.24 E
Besuki	115a	7.45 S	113.41 E
Besut ≃	114	5.48 N	102.35 E
Beswick Aboriginal Reserve ◆[4]	164	14.30 S	133.10 E
Betā	272b	22.55 N	88.14 E
Betafo	157b	19.50 S	46.51 E
Betāgi	126	22.25 N	90.11 E
Bet Alfa	132	32.31 N	35.26 E
Beta Main Canal ≊	226	36.34 N	120.11 W
Betamba	152	2.13 S	21.23 E
Betang Melaka	114	2.28 N	102.25 E
Betano	112	9.10 S	125.43 E
Betanzos, Bol.	248	19.34 S	65.27 W
Betanzos, Esp.	34	43.17 N	8.12 W
Betanzos, Ría de ⊂[1]	34	43.23 N	8.15 W
Betaré Oya	152	5.36 N	14.05 E
Betarsjön ◎	26	63.44 N	16.52 E
Bet Bet Creek ≃	169	36.52 S	143.52 E
Betbetti	140	15.06 N	24.12 E
Betchworth	260	51.14 N	0.16 W
Bet Dagan	132	32.00 N	34.50 E
Bete Hor	144	11.37 N	39.02 E
Betém	256	22.52 S	44.17 W
Bétera	34	39.35 N	0.27 W
Bétérou	150	9.12 N	2.16 E
Bet Guvrin	132	31.36 N	34.54 E
Bet Ha'arava	132	31.48 N	35.32 E
Bethal	158	26.27 S	29.28 E
Bethalto	219	38.54 N	90.02 W
Bethanien	156	26.32 S	17.11 E
Bethanien □[5]	156	26.30 S	17.00 E
Bethany, Ct., U.S.	207	41.25 N	72.59 W
Bethany, Il., U.S.	219	39.38 N	88.44 W
Bethany, Mo., U.S.	194	40.16 N	94.01 W
Bethany, N.Y., U.S.	210	42.55 N	78.08 W
Bethany, Ok., U.S.	196	35.31 N	97.37 W
Bethany, Pa., U.S.	210	41.37 N	75.21 W
Bethany, W.V., U.S.	214	40.12 N	80.33 W
Bethany Reservoir ◎[1]	226	37.47 N	121.37 W
Bet HaShitta	132	32.33 N	35.26 E
Bethel, Ak., U.S.	180	60.48 N	161.46 W
Bethel, Ct., U.S.	207	41.22 N	73.24 W
Bethel, De., U.S.	208	38.27 N	75.21 W
Bethel, Ky., U.S.	218	38.14 N	83.52 W
Bethel, Me., U.S.	188	44.24 N	70.47 W
Bethel, Mo., U.S.	219	39.52 N	92.01 W
Bethel, N.Y., U.S.	210	41.41 N	74.52 W
Bethel, N.C., U.S.	192	35.48 N	77.22 W
Bethel, Oh., U.S.	218	38.57 N	84.04 W
Bethel, Pa., U.S.	208	40.28 N	76.18 W
Bethel, Wa., U.S.	224	47.32 N	122.38 W
Bethel Acres	196	35.19 N	97.00 W
Bethel Island	226	38.01 N	121.39 W
Bethel Manor	208	37.06 N	76.25 W
Bethel Park	214	40.18 N	80.02 W
Bethelsdorp	158	33.52 S	25.34 E
Bethel Springs	194	35.14 N	88.36 W
Béthencourt-sur-Mer	50	50.05 N	1.30 E
Bethersden	42	51.08 N	0.48 E
Bethesda, Wales, U.K.	44	53.11 N	4.03 W
Bethesda, Md., U.S.	208	38.58 N	77.06 W
Bethesda, Oh., U.S.	188	40.00 N	81.04 W
Bethesdaweg	158	31.55 S	24.45 E
Bethford	284a	42.48 N	78.48 W
Bethgate	284b	39.18 N	76.51 W
Béthisy-Saint-Pierre	50	49.18 N	2.49 E
Bethlehem → Bayt Laḥm, Ghaz.	132	31.43 N	35.12 E
Bethlehem, S. Afr.	158	28.15 S	28.15 E
Bethlehem, S. Afr.	158	27.10 S	24.00 E
Bethlehem, Ct., U.S.	207	41.38 N	73.12 W
Bethlehem, In., U.S.	218	38.32 N	85.25 W
Bethlehem, Ky., U.S.	218	38.24 N	85.04 W
Bethlehem, Pa., U.S.	210	40.37 N	75.22 W
Bethlehem, W.V., U.S.	188	40.02 N	80.41 W
Bethlehem Center	210	42.40 N	73.42 W
Bethlehem Steel Corporation ⊛[3], Md., U.S.	284b	39.13 N	76.29 W
Bethlehem Steel Corporation (Lackawanna Plant) ⊛[3], N.Y., U.S.	284a	42.49 N	78.52 W
Bethnal Green ◆[8]	260	51.32 N	0.03 W
Bethoncourt	58	47.32 N	6.48 E
Bethpage	210	40.44 N	73.28 W
Bethpage State Park ♠	210	40.45 N	73.27 W
Bethulie	158	30.32 S	25.59 E
Bethune, Sk., Can.	184	50.43 N	105.08 W
Béthune, Fr.	50	50.32 N	2.38 E
Bethune, S.C., U.S.	192	34.24 N	80.20 W
Béthune ≃	50	49.53 N	1.09 E
Beticos, Sistemas ∧∧	34	37.00 N	4.00 W
Betijoque	246	9.23 N	70.44 W
Betil	126	24.14 N	89.43 E
Betio	174t	1.21 N	172.56 E
Betioky	157b	23.42 S	44.22 E
Betis ≃	114	4.53 N	101.48 E
Betlica	76	54.01 N	33.57 E
Bet Netofa, Biq'at ≡	132	32.49 N	35.19 E
Betnoti	126	21.44 N	86.51 E
Beton-Bazoches	50	48.42 N	3.15 E
Betong, Malay.	112	1.24 N	111.31 E
Betong, Thai	110	5.45 N	101.05 E
Betoota	166	25.42 S	140.44 E
Bétou	152	3.03 N	18.31 E
Betpak-Dala ◆[2]	86	46.00 N	70.00 E
Betroka	157b	23.16 S	46.06 E
Betsham	260	51.25 N	0.19 E
Bet Sh'ean	132	32.30 N	35.30 E
Bet She'arim, Ḥorbat ⊥	132	32.42 N	35.08 E
Bet Shemesh	132	31.45 N	35.00 E
Betsiamites	186	48.56 N	68.38 W
Betsiamites ≃	186	48.56 N	68.38 W
Betsiamites, Barrage ◆[6]	186	49.22 N	69.47 W
Betsiamites, Pointe de ›	186	48.55 N	68.37 W
Betsiamites, Réserve indienne de ◆[4]	186	49.05 N	68.37 W
Betsiboka ≃	157b	16.03 S	46.36 E
Betsie, Point ›	190	44.42 N	86.16 W
Betsioky	157b	21.31 S	44.28 E
Betsukai	92a	43.23 N	145.17 E
Betsy Layne	192	37.33 N	82.38 W
Betsy Ross Bridge ◆[5]	285	39.59 N	75.04 W
Bette ∧	146	22.00 N	19.12 E
Bettembourg	56	49.32 N	6.02 E
Bettendorf	190	41.31 N	90.30 W
Betterton	208	39.21 N	76.03 W
Bettiah	124	26.48 N	84.30 E
Bettie	222	32.48 N	94.58 W
Bettles Field	180	66.55 N	151.30 W
Bettola	62	44.47 N	9.36 E
Bettona	66	43.01 N	12.29 E
Bettrath ◆[8]	263	51.13 N	6.26 E
Bettsville	214	41.14 N	83.14 W
Bettyhill	46	58.32 N	4.14 W
Betty's Bay	158	34.22 S	18.52 E
Betūl	124	21.55 N	77.54 E
Betūl □[5]	124	22.00 N	78.00 E
Betumbe-Bongo	152	2.11 S	18.46 E
Betung, Indon.	112	1.52 S	103.16 E
Betung, Indon.	112	2.50 S	104.14 E
Betuwe ◆[1]	52	51.55 N	5.30 E
Betwa ≃	124	25.55 N	80.12 E
Betws-y-Coed	44	53.05 N	3.48 W
Betz	50	49.09 N	2.57 E
Betz ≃	50	48.09 N	2.45 E
Betzdorf	56	50.47 N	7.53 E
Betzenstein	60	49.41 N	11.25 E
Béu	152	6.14 S	15.28 E
Beucha	54	51.19 N	12.34 E
Beugneux	50	49.14 N	3.25 E
Beuil	62	44.06 N	6.59 E
Beulah, Austl.	166	35.56 S	142.26 E
Beulah, Co., U.S.	200	38.04 N	104.59 W
Beulah, Mi., U.S.	190	44.37 N	86.05 W
Beulah, Ms., U.S.	194	33.47 N	90.58 W
Beulah, N.D., U.S.	198	47.15 N	101.46 W
Beulah, Lake ◎	216	42.49 N	88.23 W
Beulah Beach	214	41.25 N	82.22 W
Beulah Reservoir ◎[1]	202	43.56 N	118.09 W
Beulaville	192	34.55 N	77.46 W
Beult ≃	260	51.14 N	0.25 E
Beure	58	47.12 N	6.00 E
Beureunun	114	5.18 N	95.59 E
Beuron	58	48.03 N	8.58 E
Beuthen → Bytom	30	50.22 N	18.54 E
Beuvron ≃, Fr.	50	47.28 N	3.31 E
Beuvron ≃, Fr.	50	47.29 N	1.15 E
Beuvronne ≃	261	48.56 N	2.44 E
Beuvry	50	50.31 N	2.41 E
Beuzeville	50	49.20 N	0.21 E
Bevagna	66	42.56 N	12.36 E
Bevensen	52	53.05 N	10.34 E
Bever ≃	52	52.01 N	7.46 E
Bevera ≃	62	43.49 N	7.34 E
Beveren	50	51.13 N	4.15 E
B. Everett Jordan Lake ◎[1]	192	35.45 N	79.00 W
Beverino	62	44.14 N	9.47 E
Beverley, Austl.	168a	32.06 S	116.56 E
Beverley, Eng., U.K.	44	53.52 N	0.26 W
Beverley Minster ⊛[1]	44	53.50 N	0.27 W
Beverley Springs	162	16.43 S	125.28 E
Beverlo	56	51.05 N	5.12 E
Beverly, Ma., U.S.	207	42.33 N	70.52 W
Beverly, N.J., U.S.	208	40.03 N	74.55 W
Beverly, Tx., U.S.	222	31.30 N	97.10 W
Beverly ◆[8]	278	41.43 N	87.41 W
Beverly Farms, Md., U.S.	284c	39.04 N	77.11 W
Beverly Farms, Ma., U.S.	283	42.34 N	70.49 W
Beverly Harbor ⊂	283	42.32 N	70.53 W
Beverly Hills, Austl.	274a	33.57 S	151.05 E
Beverly Hills, Ca., U.S.	228	34.04 N	118.23 W
Beverly Hills, Fl., U.S.	220	28.56 N	82.28 W
Beverly Hills, Mi., U.S.	216	42.31 N	83.13 W
Beverly Lake ◎	176	64.36 N	100.30 W
Beverly Municipal Airport ⊠	283	42.35 N	70.55 W
Beverly Run ≃	208	37.55 N	77.11 W
Beverly Shores	216	41.41 N	86.58 W
Bevern	52	51.51 N	9.29 E
Beverstausee ◎[1]	263	51.09 N	7.23 E
Beverstedt	52	53.26 N	8.49 E
Beverungen	52	51.39 N	9.22 E
Beverwijk	52	52.28 N	4.40 E
Bevier	194	39.45 N	92.34 W
Bevin, Lac ◎	206	45.57 N	74.35 W
Bevoalavo	157b	25.13 S	45.26 E
Bewani Mountains ∧∧	164	3.10 S	141.25 E
Bewār	124	27.13 N	79.18 E
Bewdley, On., Can.	212	44.05 N	78.19 W
Bewdley, Eng., U.K.	42	52.22 N	2.19 W
Bewl Bridge Reservoir ◎[1]	42	51.04 N	0.24 E
Bex	58	46.15 N	7.01 E
Bexhill on Sea	42	50.50 N	0.29 E
Bexley, Austl.	274a	33.57 S	151.08 E
Bexley, Oh., U.S.	218	39.58 N	82.56 W
Bexley ◆[8]	260	51.26 N	0.10 E
Beyazköy	130	41.21 N	27.42 E
Beybach ≃	56	50.13 N	7.23 E
Beyçayırı	130	40.15 N	26.55 E
Beyce	130	39.54 N	29.00 E
Beycuma	130	41.19 N	31.59 E
Bey Dağları ∧∧	130	36.40 N	30.15 E
Beydili	130	40.10 N	31.01 E
Beyenburg ◆[8]	263	51.15 N	7.18 E
Beykoz	130	41.08 N	29.05 E
Beykoz ◆[8]	267b	41.08 N	29.05 E
Beyla	150	8.41 N	8.37 W
Beylerbeyi ◆[8]	267b	41.03 N	29.03 E
Beylikahır	130	39.42 N	31.13 E
Beylul	144	13.10 N	42.26 E
Beynes	261	48.51 N	1.53 E
Beynes-Thiverval, Aérodrome de ⊠	261	48.51 N	1.54 E
Beyoğlu ◆[8]	267b	41.02 N	28.59 E
Beypazarı	130	40.10 N	31.56 E
Beypınarı	130	39.31 N	37.44 E
Beypore	122	11.11 N	75.49 E
Beyra	144	6.57 N	47.19 E
Beyrouth → Bayrūt	130	33.53 N	35.30 E
Beyşehir	130	37.41 N	31.43 E
Beyşehir Gölü ◎	130	37.40 N	31.30 E
Bezaha	157b	23.30 S	44.31 E
Bežanickaja vozvyšennost' ∧∧[1]	76	56.54 N	29.20 E
Bežanicy	76	56.58 N	29.53 E
Bezau	58	47.23 N	9.54 E
Bezavona ∧	157b	15.02 S	49.52 E
Bezdež	76	52.19 N	25.18 E
Bezděz ∧	54	50.32 N	14.43 E
Bezděz ⊥	54	50.32 N	14.46 E
Bèze	58	47.28 N	5.16 E
Bežeck	76	57.47 N	36.39 E
Bežeckij Verch ∧∧[1]	76	57.36 N	36.54 E
Bezenčuk	80	52.59 N	49.26 E
Bezerra ≃	255	13.16 S	47.31 W
Bezerros	250	8.14 S	35.45 W
Beẓet	132	33.05 N	35.08 E
Béziers	32	43.21 N	3.15 E
Bezmein	128	38.05 N	58.12 E
Bezmenšur	80	56.29 N	51.17 E
Bezons	261	48.56 N	2.13 E
Bežta	84	42.08 N	46.08 E
Bezwada → Vijayawāda	122	16.31 N	80.37 E
Bezym'anka	80	49.56 N	43.15 E
Bezym'annaja	80	51.20 N	46.26 E
Bezymennoje	83	47.06 N	37.56 E
Bezzecca	64	45.55 N	10.43 E
Bezzubovo	82	55.27 N	38.55 E
Bhabānipur, India	272b	22.57 N	88.27 E
Bhabānipur, India	272b	22.56 N	88.13 E
Bhābta	126	23.59 N	88.15 E
Bhabua	124	25.03 N	83.37 E
Bhadarwah	123	32.59 N	75.43 E
Bhadaur	123	30.29 N	75.19 E
Bhādgāon → Bhaktapur	124	27.42 N	85.27 E
Bhadohi	124	25.25 N	82.34 E
Bhādra	123	29.07 N	75.10 E
Bhadra ◎[1]	122	13.42 N	75.35 E
Bhadra ≃[1]	126	22.19 N	89.31 E
Bhadrāchalam	122	17.40 N	80.53 E
Bhadrakh	120	21.03 N	86.30 E
Bhadrāvati	122	13.52 N	75.43 E
Bhadreswar	126	22.50 N	88.21 E
Bhādua	272b	22.41 N	88.12 E
Bhāg	120	29.02 N	67.49 E
Bhagaiya	124	25.12 N	87.29 E
Bhāgalpur	124	25.15 N	87.00 E
Bhāgalpur □[5]	124	25.00 N	87.00 E
Bhāgirathi ≃, India	124	30.08 N	78.35 E
Bhāgīrathi ≃, India	126	23.25 N	88.23 E
Bhagirathpur	126	24.05 N	88.29 E
Bhagwānpur	126	22.07 N	87.45 E
Bhāi Pheru	123	31.12 N	73.57 E
Bhairab ≃[1]	126	22.51 N	89.34 E
Bhairab Bāzār	120	24.04 N	90.58 E
Bhairawa	124	27.31 N	83.24 E
Bhaironghāti	120	31.01 N	78.53 E
Bhaisa	122	19.06 N	77.58 E
Bhakkar	123	31.38 N	71.04 E
Bhākra Dam ◆[6]	123	31.24 N	76.30 E
Bhaktapur	124	27.42 N	85.27 E
Bhal	272c	19.11 N	73.08 E
Bhālki	122	18.02 N	77.13 E
Bhalswa ◆[8]	272a	28.44 N	77.10 E
Bhalwāl	123	32.16 N	72.54 E
Bhamo	110	24.16 N	97.14 E
Bhandāra	120	21.10 N	79.39 E
Bhandārdaha	272b	22.37 N	88.13 E
Bhandāria	126	22.29 N	90.04 E
Bhānder	124	25.44 N	78.45 E
Bhander Plateau ∧∧[1]	124	24.10 N	80.20 E
Bhāndup ◆[8]	272c	19.09 N	72.57 E
Bhānga	126	23.22 N	89.59 E
Bhāngar	126	22.31 N	88.37 E
Bhāngar Kāta Khāl ≃	272b	22.31 N	88.33 E
Bhānvad	120	21.56 N	69.47 E
Bhārat → India □[1]	118	20.00 N	77.00 E
Bharatpur, India	124	27.13 N	77.29 E
Bharatpur, India	126	23.53 N	88.05 E
Bharatpur □[5]	124	27.00 N	77.15 E
Bharthana	124	26.45 N	79.14 E
Bhātai	126	23.36 N	89.11 E
Bhātāpāra	120	21.44 N	81.56 E
Bhātār	126	23.25 N	87.54 E
Bhatewar	120	24.38 N	74.00 E
Bhatgaon → Bhaktapur	124	27.42 N	85.27 E
Bhātghar Lake ◎[1]	122	18.12 N	73.49 E
Bhātiāpāra Ghāt	124	23.13 N	89.42 E
Bhatinda	123	30.12 N	74.57 E
Bhatkal	122	13.58 N	74.34 E
Bhātpāra	126	22.52 N	88.24 E
Bhātpur	272b	22.43 N	88.25 E
Bhātsāla	126	22.33 N	90.30 E
Bhattapratāp	126	22.45 N	89.48 E
Bhattiprolu	122	16.06 N	80.47 E
Bhātua	272b	22.57 N	88.22 E
Bhaun	123	32.52 N	72.45 E
Bhaunagar	122	21.46 N	72.09 E
Bhaunja	272a	28.40 N	77.25 E
Bhavāni	122	11.27 N	77.41 E
Bhawānīgarh	124	30.16 N	76.02 E
Bhawāni Mandi	120	24.25 N	75.50 E
Bhawānipatna	122	19.54 N	83.10 E
Bhedia	126	23.36 N	87.42 E
Bheigeir, Beinn ∧[2]	46	55.44 N	6.05 W
Bhendkhal	272c	18.53 N	72.59 E
Bhera	123	32.29 N	72.55 E
Bheramara	126	24.02 N	88.58 E
Bheri ≃	124	28.44 N	81.16 E
Bheula, Beinn ∧	46	56.08 N	4.58 W
Bhīkampur	272a	28.45 N	77.27 E
Bhikangaon	120	21.52 N	75.57 E
Bhikna Thorī	124	27.21 N	84.37 E
Bhilai	120	21.13 N	81.26 E
Bhilainagar → Bhilai	120	21.13 N	81.26 E
Bhīlsa □[5]	124	24.00 N	77.50 E
Bhīlwāra	120	25.21 N	74.38 E
Bhīma ≃	122	16.24 N	77.18 E
Bhīmavaram	122	16.32 N	81.32 E
Bhimbar	123	32.59 N	74.04 E
Bhīmphedi	124	27.32 N	85.07 E
Bhīmpur, India	126	22.37 N	87.08 E
Bhimpur, India	272b	22.46 N	88.08 E
Bhind	124	26.34 N	78.48 E
Bhind □[5]	124	26.30 N	78.35 E
Bhinga	124	27.43 N	81.56 E
Bhīnmāl	120	25.00 N	72.15 E
Bhiwandi	122	19.18 N	73.04 E
Bhiwāni	124	28.47 N	76.08 E
Bhoāgāchi	272b	22.57 N	88.20 E
Bhojpur	124	27.10 N	87.03 E
Bhojudih	126	23.38 N	86.27 E
Bhokardan	122	20.16 N	75.46 E
Bhola	124	22.41 N	90.39 E
Bhola ≃[1]	126	22.04 N	89.49 E
Bhongaon	124	27.15 N	79.11 E
Bhongīr	122	17.31 N	78.53 E
Bhonrāsa	124	22.59 N	76.12 E
Bhopāl	124	23.16 N	77.24 E
Bhopar	272c	19.12 N	73.05 E
Bhopura	272a	28.42 N	77.20 E
Bhoutan → Bhutan □[1]	120	27.30 N	90.30 E
Bhowali	124	29.23 N	79.31 E
Bhuāpur	272a	28.43 N	77.26 E
Bhuban	120	20.53 N	85.50 E
Bhubaneswar	120	20.14 N	85.50 E
Bhucho	123	30.13 N	75.06 E
Bhuj	120	23.16 N	69.40 E
Bhunarheri	124	30.13 N	76.27 E
Bhunya	158	26.32 S	31.01 E
Bhusāwal	120	21.03 N	75.46 E
Bhūshana	126	23.24 N	89.40 E
Bhutali	272c	19.07 N	73.04 E
Bhutan (Druk-Yul) □[1], Asia	118	27.30 N	90.30 E
Bhutan (Druk-Yul) □[1], Asia	120	27.30 N	90.30 E
Bia ≃, Afr.	150	5.21 N	3.11 W
Biá ≃, Bra.	246	3.28 S	67.23 W
Bia, Phou ∧	110	18.59 N	103.09 E
Biābānak	128	32.11 N	64.11 E
Biabo ≃	248	6.58 S	76.23 W
Biacesa	64	45.56 N	10.47 E
Biache-Saint-Vaast	50	50.18 N	2.57 E
Biadene	64	45.47 N	12.04 E
Biafo Glacier ⊓	123	35.41 N	75.55 E
Biafra, Bight of ⊂[3]	134	4.00 N	8.00 E
Biak I	164	1.00 S	136.00 E
Biała	30	50.23 N	17.40 E
Biała ≃	30	50.03 N	20.55 E
Biała Piska	30	53.37 N	22.04 E
Biała Podlaska	30	52.02 N	23.06 E
Biała Podlaska □[4]	30	52.00 N	23.00 E
Biała Rawska	30	51.49 N	20.29 E
Białobrzegi	30	51.40 N	20.57 E
Białogard	30	54.01 N	16.00 E
Białowieski Park Narodowy ♠	30	52.40 N	23.50 E
Biały Bór	30	53.54 N	16.51 E
Białystok	30	53.09 N	23.09 E
Białystok □[4]	30	53.00 N	23.00 E
Bian ≃	164	8.07 S	139.56 E
Bian, Bidean nam ∧	46	56.38 N	5.02 W
Bianba	120	30.49 N	94.59 E
Biancavilla	70	37.38 N	14.52 E
Bianchi	68	39.06 N	16.24 E
Bianco	68	38.05 N	16.09 E
Bianco, Canale ≊	64	45.02 N	11.30 E
Bianco, Capo ›	70	37.23 N	13.16 E
Bianco, Monte (Mont Blanc) ∧	62	45.50 N	6.52 E
Bian'er	102	31.14 N	101.28 E
Bianga	152	4.51 N	20.25 E
Bian'gezhuang	105	39.28 N	115.53 E
Biankouma	150	7.44 N	7.37 W
Biankouma □[5]	150	7.45 N	7.30 W
Bianlinzhen	98	37.26 N	116.32 E
Bianminchang	107	29.41 N	105.04 E
Bianniulupucun	104	41.30 N	123.42 E
Bianquanwopu	104	41.21 N	120.48 E
Bianzè	62	45.18 N	8.07 E
Biaora	124	23.55 N	76.54 E
Biaro, Pulau I	112	2.05 N	125.20 E
Biarritz	32	43.29 N	1.34 W
Biasca	58	46.22 N	8.58 E
Bias Fortes	256	21.36 S	43.46 W
Biassono	62	45.37 N	9.16 E
Biaza	86	56.38 N	78.18 E
Bibā	142	28.55 N	30.59 E
Bibai	92a	43.19 N	141.52 E
Bibala	152	14.46 S	13.21 E
Bībān	142	30.47 N	30.40 E
Bibane, Bahiret el ⊂	148	33.16 N	11.19 E
Bibanga	152	6.15 S	23.56 E
Bibban, Khawr V	140	11.00 N	32.41 E
Bibb City	192	32.30 N	84.59 W
Bibbiano	64	44.40 N	10.28 E
Bibbiena	66	43.42 N	11.49 E
Bibbona	66	43.16 N	10.35 E
Bibémi	146	9.19 N	13.53 E
Biberach	58	48.20 N	8.02 E
Biberach an der Riss	58	48.06 N	9.47 E
Biberbach	56	48.31 N	10.48 E
Biberonne ≃	261	48.59 N	2.41 E
Bibert ≃	56	49.27 N	10.59 E
Bibey ≃	34	42.24 N	7.13 W
Bibiani	150	6.28 N	2.20 W
Bībi Chīni	126	22.28 N	90.12 E
Bībi Nāni	120	29.42 N	67.23 E
Bibione	64	45.38 N	13.00 E
Bibir'ovo	76	54.28 N	33.08 E
Biblián	246	2.42 S	78.52 W
Biblis	56	49.41 N	8.27 E
Bibo	102	29.02 N	99.20 E
Bic	186	48.22 N	68.42 W
Biča	86	57.53 N	70.37 E
Bicas	256	21.43 S	43.04 W
Bicas do Meio	256	22.31 S	45.21 W
Bicaz	38	46.54 N	26.05 E
Bicaz, Lacul ◎[1]	38	47.00 N	26.00 E
Biccari	68	41.24 N	15.11 E
Bicester	42	51.54 N	1.09 W
Bičevinka	76	59.44 N	37.40 E
Biche, Lac la ◎	182	54.50 N	112.03 W
Bichena	144	10.27 N	38.12 E
Bichhia	124	22.27 N	80.42 E
Bichl	64	47.43 N	11.24 E
Bichlbach	58	47.25 N	10.47 E
Bichota Canyon V	280	34.16 N	117.48 W
Biči ≃	89	52.10 N	139.50 E
Bičigt	88	47.06 N	95.05 E
Bickerstaffe	262	53.32 N	2.50 W
Bickerton, Cape ›	9	66.20 S	136.56 E
Bickerton Island I	164	13.45 S	136.12 E
Bickle Knob ∧	188	38.56 N	79.44 W
Bickley ◆[8]	260	51.24 N	0.03 E
Bicknacre, Eng., U.K.	42	51.41 N	0.35 E
Bicknacre, Eng., U.K.	260	51.42 N	0.35 E
Bicknell, In., U.S.	194	38.46 N	87.18 W
Bicknell, Ut., U.S.	200	38.20 N	111.32 W
Bicknor	260	51.18 N	0.40 E
Bicol ≃	116	13.44 N	123.07 E
Bicske	30	47.29 N	18.37 E
Bicudo ≃	255	18.04 S	44.33 W
Bičura	88	50.36 N	107.35 E
Bičurina	86	56.51 N	55.25 E
Bida, Nig.	146	12.20 N	13.25 E
Bida, Nig.	150	9.05 N	6.01 E
Bīdar	122	17.54 N	77.33 E
Bidde	144	0.58 N	42.37 E
Biddeford	188	43.29 N	70.27 W
Biddenden	42	51.07 N	0.39 E
Biddiyā	132	32.07 N	35.05 E
Biddulph	44	53.08 N	2.10 W
Bideford	42	51.01 N	4.13 W
Bidente ≃	66	44.24 N	12.12 E
Bidford-on-Avon	42	52.10 N	1.51 W
Bidhūna	124	26.49 N	79.31 E
Bidian	100	32.38 N	113.03 E
Bīdokht	128	34.21 N	58.46 E
Bidoni	71	40.07 N	8.56 E
Bidor	114	4.07 N	101.17 E
Bidston	262	53.24 N	3.05 W
Bidwell	188	38.55 N	82.17 W
Bidwell, Mount ∧	204	41.58 N	120.10 W
Bidya ≃[1]	126	21.56 N	88.42 E
Bidyādhari ≃	272b	22.23 N	88.35 E
Bidyādharpur	272b	22.50 N	88.24 E
Bidžan	89	47.58 N	131.58 E
Bidžan ≃	89	47.44 N	132.19 E
Bie	40	59.05 N	16.12 E
Bié □[5]	152	12.30 S	17.15 E
Biebelried	56	49.46 N	10.04 E
Bieber, B.R.D.	56	50.09 N	9.19 E
Bieber, Ca., U.S.	204	41.07 N	121.08 W
Biebrza ≃	30	53.13 N	22.25 E
Biecz	30	49.44 N	21.14 E
Biedenkopf	56	50.55 N	8.32 E
Biederitz	54	52.09 N	11.43 E
Biedermannsdorf	264b	48.05 N	16.21 E
Bieguzhuang	105	39.19 N	116.39 E
Biei	92a	43.35 N	142.28 E
Biel (Bienne)	58	47.10 N	7.12 E
Bielawa	30	50.41 N	16.38 E
Bielawski, Mount ∧	226	37.13 N	122.06 W
Bielefeld	52	52.01 N	8.31 E
Bieler Lake ◎	176	70.20 N	73.00 W
Bielersee ◎	58	47.05 N	7.10 E
Bielin	54	52.47 N	14.28 E
Biella	62	45.34 N	8.03 E
Bielsk	30	52.40 N	19.49 E
Bielsko-Biała	30	49.49 N	19.02 E
Bielsko-Biała □[4]	30	49.40 N	19.10 E
Bielsk Podlaski	30	52.47 N	23.12 E
Biemenhorst	52	51.49 N	6.36 E
Bienenbüttel	52	53.08 N	10.29 E
Bienfait	184	49.08 N	102.47 W
Bien-hoa	110	10.57 N	106.49 E
Bienne → Biel	58	47.10 N	7.12 E
Bienne ≃, Fr.	50	48.15 N	0.04 E
Bienne ≃, Fr.	58	46.20 N	5.38 E
Bienno	64	45.56 N	10.18 E
Bientina	66	43.42 N	10.37 E
Bienville	194	32.21 N	92.58 W
Bienville, Lac ◎	176	55.05 N	72.40 W
Biere, D.D.R.	54	51.58 N	11.39 E
Bière, Schw.	58	46.33 N	6.20 E
Bierné	28	47.49 N	0.32 W
Bieruń Stary	30	50.06 N	19.06 E
Bierutów	30	51.08 N	17.32 E
Bierwart	56	50.34 N	5.01 E
Biesbos ◆[1]	52	51.45 N	4.50 E
Biesdorf ◆[8]	264a	52.31 N	13.33 E
Biese ≃	54	52.45 N	11.37 E
Biesel ◆[8]	263	51.10 N	6.29 E
Biesenthal	54	52.46 N	13.37 E
Bieshan	105	39.58 N	117.29 E
Biesiesvlei	158	26.22 S	25.55 E
Biesles	58	48.05 N	5.18 E
Bieszczadzki Park Narodowy ♠	30	49.05 N	22.45 E
Bieteluobaoluosika	89	48.35 N	119.56 E
Bietigheim	56	48.54 N	8.14 E
Bietigheim-Bissingen	56	48.58 N	9.07 E
Bietschhorn ∧	58	46.24 N	7.51 E
Bièvre	56	49.56 N	5.01 E
Bièvre ≃	261	48.47 N	2.20 E
Bièvres	261	48.45 N	2.13 E
Biferno ≃	66	41.59 N	15.02 E
Bifoun	152	0.22 S	10.23 E
Bifuka	92a	44.29 N	142.21 E
Bifurcación	258	34.19 S	56.48 W
Big ≃, Austl.	169	37.18 S	146.02 E
Big ≃, N.T., Can.	176	72.30 N	125.14 W
Big ≃, Sk., Can.	184	53.50 N	107.02 W
Big ≃, Ak., U.S.	180	63.00 N	154.56 W
Big ≃, Mo., U.S.	219	38.28 N	90.37 W
Biga	130	40.13 N	27.14 E
Bigadiç	130	39.23 N	28.08 E
Big A Mountain ∧	192	37.03 N	82.02 W
Big Annemessex River ⊂	208	38.03 N	75.50 W
Big Antelope Creek ≃	202	42.28 N	117.13 W
Big Bald Mountain ∧, N.B., Can.	186	47.12 N	66.25 W
Big Bald Mountain ∧, Ga., U.S.	192	34.45 N	84.19 W
Big Baldy ∧	202	44.47 N	115.13 W
Big Baldy Mountain ∧	202	46.58 N	110.37 W
Big Bar Creek	182	51.12 N	122.06 W
Big Basin Redwoods State Park ♠	226	37.09 N	122.17 W
Big Bay	190	46.49 N	87.44 W
Big Bay ⊂, N.Z.	172	44.18 S	168.05 E
Big Bay ⊂, Vanuatu	175f	15.06 S	166.54 E
Big Bay De Noc ⊂	190	45.46 N	86.43 W
Big Bay Point ›	212	44.24 N	79.31 W
Big Bear City	228	34.15 N	116.50 W
Big Bear Lake	228	34.15 N	116.53 W
Big Bear Lake ◎	228	34.15 N	116.55 W
Big Beaver, Sk., Can.	184	49.08 N	105.10 W
Big Beaver, Pa., U.S.	214	40.50 N	80.20 W
Big Beaver Airport ⊠	281	42.33 N	83.06 W
Big Beaver Creek ≃, Mi., U.S.	281	42.32 N	83.01 W
Big Beaver Creek ≃, Oh., U.S.	218	39.01 N	83.03 W
Big Beaver Creek ≃, Wa., U.S.	224	48.40 N	121.08 W
Big Bell	162	27.21 S	117.40 E
Big Belt Mountains ∧∧	202	46.40 N	111.25 W
Big Bend, Swaz.	158	26.50 S	31.57 E
Big Bend, Wi., U.S.	216	42.52 N	88.12 W
Big Bend National Park ♠	196	29.12 N	103.12 W
Big Bend Reservoir ◎[1]	182	52.57 N	115.37 W
Big Black ≃	194	32.00 N	91.05 W
Big Blue ≃, U.S.	198	39.11 N	96.32 W
Big Blue ≃, In., U.S.	218	39.20 N	85.59 W
Big Blue, West Fork ≃	198	40.42 N	96.59 W
Big Bone Lick State Park ♠	218	38.53 N	84.45 W
Big Bonito Creek ≃	200	33.34 N	109.56 W
Big Brook ≃	276	40.19 N	74.10 W
Big Brushy Creek ≃, Tx., U.S.	222	32.32 N	96.20 W
Big Brushy Creek ≃, Tx., U.S.	222	29.12 N	96.55 W
Big Bureau Creek ≃	194	41.17 N	89.21 W
Bigbury Bay ⊂	42	50.16 N	3.48 W
Big Cabin Creek ≃	194	36.26 N	95.08 W
Big Canyon V	196	30.05 N	101.55 W

Symbol	English	Deutsch	Español	Français	Português
≃	River	Fluss	Río	Rivière	Rio
≊	Canal	Kanal	Canal	Canal	Canal
⌊	Waterfall, Rapids	Wasserfall, Stromschnellen	Cascada, Rápidos	Chute d'eau, Rapides	Cascata, Rápidos
)(	Strait	Meeresstrasse	Estrecho	Détroit	Estreito
⊂	Bay, Gulf	Bucht, Golf	Bahía, Golfo	Baie, Golfe	Baía, Golfo
◎	Lake, Lakes	See, Seen	Lago, Lagos	Lac, Lacs	Lago, Lagos
≡	Swamp	Sumpf	Pantano	Marais	Pântano
⊓	Ice Features, Glacier	Eis- und Gletscherformen	Accidentes Glaciales	Formes glaciaires	Acidentes glaciares
⊤	Other Hydrographic Features	Andere Hydrographische Objekte	Otros Elementos Hidrográficos	Autres données hydrographiques	Outros acidentes hidrográficos
✢	Submarine Features	Untermeerische Objekte	Accidentes Submarinos	Formes de relief sous-marin	Acidentes submarinos
□	Political Unit	Politische Einheit	Unidad Politica	Entité politique	Unidade política
⊛	Cultural Institution	Kulturelle Institution	Institución Cultural	Institution culturelle	Institução cultural
⊥	Historical Site	Historische Stätte	Sitio Histórico	Site historique	Sitio histórico
♠	Recreational Site	Erholungs- und Ferienort	Sitio de Recreo	Centre de loisirs	Area de Lazer
⊠	Airport	Flughafen	Aeropuerto	Aéroport	Aeroporto
■	Military Installation	Militäranlage	Instalación Militar	Installation militaire	Instalação militar
◆	Miscellaneous	Verschiedenes	Misceláneo	Divers	Diversos

Name	Page	Lat.°′	Long.°′
Big Carlos Pass ⊂	220	26.24 N	81.52 W
Big Cedar Lake ⊜	212	44.37 N	78.10 W
Big Chino Wash V	200	34.52 N	112.28 W
Big Clear Lake ⊜	212	44.43 N	76.55 W
Big Clifty	194	37.32 N	86.09 W
Big Coulee Creek ≃	202	46.17 N	108.56 W
Big Cow Creek ≃	194	30.34 N	93.44 W
Big Creek, B.C., Can.	182	51.44 N	123.03 W
Big Creek, Ca., U.S.	226	37.12 N	119.14 W
Big Creek ≃, B.C., Can.	182	51.40 N	122.50 W
Big Creek ≃, On., Can.	214	42.19 N	82.27 W
Big Creek ≃, On., Can.	214	42.36 N	80.27 W
Big Creek ≃, Ar., U.S.	194	34.21 N	91.03 W
Big Creek ≃, Ca., U.S.	226	37.12 N	119.19 W
Big Creek ≃, Ca., U.S.	226	36.53 N	119.15 W
Big Creek ≃, Id., U.S.	202	45.06 N	114.44 W
Big Creek ≃, Il., U.S.	219	39.07 N	88.52 W
Big Creek ≃, In., U.S.	216	40.38 N	86.46 W
Big Creek ≃, In., U.S.	218	38.48 N	85.39 W
Big Creek ≃, Ks., U.S.	198	38.47 N	98.55 W
Big Creek ≃, La., U.S.	194	32.10 N	91.53 W
Big Creek ≃, Mo., U.S.	194	40.02 N	94.07 W
Big Creek ≃, Mo., U.S.	219	38.52 N	90.50 W
Big Creek ≃, Oh., U.S.	279a	41.27 N	81.41 W
Big Creek ≃, Or., U.S.	224	46.11 N	123.35 W
Big Creek ≃, Tx., U.S.	222	29.22 N	95.34 W
Big Creek ≃, Tx., U.S.	222	31.09 N	96.52 W
Big Creek ≃, Wa., U.S.	224	47.15 N	121.10 W
Big Creek, East Fork ≃	194	40.16 N	94.03 W
Big Creek, West Fork ≃	194	40.16 N	94.03 W
Big Creek Parkway ♦	279a	41.24 N	81.45 W
Big Creek Peak ∧	202	44.28 N	113.32 W
Big Crow Island I	276	40.37 N	73.33 W
Big Cypress Creek ≃	222	33.00 N	94.51 W
Big Cypress Indian Reservation ◆[4]	220	26.14 N	80.49 W
Big Cypress National Preserve ♦	220	25.55 N	81.10 W
Big Cypress Swamp ⁝	220	26.10 N	81.38 W
Big Dalton Canyon V	280	34.10 N	117.48 W
Big Dalton Wash V	280	34.04 N	117.58 W
Big Darby Creek ≃	218	39.37 N	82.58 W
Big Delta	180	64.09 N	145.50 W
Big Desert ◆[2]	166	35.40 S	141.00 E
Big Diomede Island → Ratmanova, ostrov I	180	65.46 N	169.02 W
Big Ditch ≊	216	40.13 N	88.22 W
Big Dry Creek ≃	202	47.30 N	106.19 W
Big Eau Pleine ≃	190	44.48 N	90.00 W
Big Elk Creek ≃	208	39.35 N	75.52 W
Big Elkhart Creek ≃	222	31.22 N	95.41 W
Big Elm Creek ≃	222	30.53 N	96.56 W
Bigelow Bight ⊂[3]	188	43.15 N	70.30 W
Big Escambia Creek ≃	194	30.58 N	87.14 W
Big Falls	190	48.11 N	93.48 W
Big Flat	194	36.00 N	92.24 W
Big Flat Creek ≃	194	31.33 N	87.31 W
Big Flats	210	42.08 N	76.56 W
Bigfork, Mn., U.S.	190	47.44 N	93.39 W
Bigfork, Mt., U.S.	202	48.04 N	114.04 W
Big Fork ≃	190	48.31 N	93.43 W
Big Four Ditch ≊	216	40.27 N	88.10 W
Big Frog Mountain ∧	192	35.00 N	84.32 W
Biggar, Sk., Can.	184	52.04 N	108.00 W
Biggar, Scot., U.K.	46	55.38 N	3.32 W
Biggarsberg ⋏	158	28.12 S	29.48 E
Bigge	56	51.21 N	8.28 E
Bigge Island I	164	14.35 S	125.10 E
Biggers	194	36.19 N	90.48 W
Biggestausee ⊜[1]	56	51.05 N	7.55 E
Biggin Hill ◆[8]	42	51.18 N	0.04 E
Biggin Hill Aerodrome ⊠	260	51.19 N	0.03 E
Biggleswade	42	52.05 N	0.17 W
Biggs, Ca., U.S.	226	39.24 N	121.42 W
Biggs, Or., U.S.	224	45.40 N	120.50 W
Big Gull Lake ⊜	212	44.50 N	76.58 W
Big Gully Creek ≃	184	53.13 N	109.03 W
Bighāi ≃[1]	126	22.10 N	90.13 E
Big Hawk Lake ⊜	212	45.10 N	78.44 W
Bighead ≃	212	44.36 N	80.35 W
Big Hole ≃	202	45.34 N	112.20 W
Big Hole National Battlefield ⊥	202	45.35 N	113.35 W
Bighorn ≃	202	46.09 N	107.28 W
Bighorn Basin ≚[1]	202	44.15 N	108.10 W
Bighorn Canyon National Recreation Area ♦	202	45.00 N	108.15 W
Big Horn Lake ⊜[1]	202	45.06 N	108.08 W
Bighorn Mountains ⋏	202	44.00 N	107.30 W
Bight, Head of ›	162	31.30 S	131.10 E
Big Huckleberry Mountain ∧	224	45.51 N	121.47 W
Big Island	192	37.32 N	79.21 W
Big Island I, N.T., Can.	176	62.43 N	70.43 W
Big Island I, On., Can.	184	49.10 N	94.40 W
Big Island I, On., Can.	212	44.33 N	78.30 W
Big Knob ∧	192	36.40 N	82.31 W
Big Koniuji Island I	180	55.06 N	159.33 W
Big Lake, Ak., U.S.	180	61.33 N	149.52 W
Big Lake, Mn., U.S.	190	45.19 N	93.44 W
Big Lake, Tx., U.S.	196	31.11 N	101.27 W
Big Lake, Wa., U.S.	224	48.24 N	122.14 W
Big Lake ⊜, Me., U.S.	188	45.10 N	67.40 W
Big Lake ⊜, Wa., U.S.	224	48.23 N	122.12 W
Bigler	214	40.59 N	78.19 W
Biglerville	208	39.55 N	77.14 W
Big Lick Creek ≃	216	40.22 N	85.27 W
Big Lookout Mountain ∧	202	44.37 N	117.17 W
Big Lost ≃	202	43.50 N	112.44 W
Big Monon Ditch ≊	216	40.52 N	86.46 W
Big Mossy Point ›	184	53.41 N	97.57 W
Big Mountain ∧, B.C., Can.	180	56.53 N	131.31 W
Big Mountain ∧, Nv., U.S.	204	41.17 N	119.04 W
Big Mountain Creek ≃	182	55.04 N	118.39 W
Big Muddy ≃	194	37.35 N	89.31 W
Big Muddy, Casey Fork ≃	194	38.06 N	88.57 W
Big Muddy Creek ≃, Mt., U.S.	198	48.08 N	104.36 W
Big Muddy Creek ≃, N.D., U.S.	198	46.37 N	101.24 W
Big Muddy Lake ⊜	184	49.08 N	104.54 W
Big Muscamoot Bay ⊂	281	42.33 N	82.40 W
Bignasco	58	46.20 N	8.36 E
Big Nasty Creek ≃	198	45.41 N	102.51 W
Big Nemaha, North Fork ≃	198	40.04 N	95.43 W
Bignona	150	12.49 N	16.14 W
Big Oak Flat	226	37.49 N	120.16 W
Bigosovo	76	55.49 N	27.43 E
Bigot, Morne ∧[2]	240e	14.31 N	61.04 W
Big Otter ≃	192	37.07 N	79.23 W
Big Otter Creek ≃	212	42.38 N	80.48 W
Big Ox Creek ≃	218	38.44 N	85.52 W
Big Pine	204	37.09 N	118.17 W
Big Pine Creek ≃	216	40.18 N	87.15 W
Big Pine Key	220	24.40 N	81.21 W
Big Pine Key I	220	24.42 N	81.23 W
Big Pine Mountain ∧	204	34.42 N	119.39 W
Big Piney	200	42.32 N	110.06 W
Big Piney ≃	194	37.53 N	92.04 W
Big Piney Creek ≃	194	35.20 N	93.20 W
Big Pipe Creek ≃	208	39.36 N	77.17 W
Big Plain	218	39.50 N	83.17 W
Big Pocono State Park ♦	210	41.03 N	75.19 W
Bigpoint	194	30.35 N	88.28 W
Big Pond	210	41.53 N	76.43 W
Big Porcupine Creek ≃	202	46.16 N	106.43 W
Big Porcupine Lake ⊜	212	45.27 N	78.36 W
Big Prairie	214	40.40 N	82.06 W
Big Prairie Creek ≃	194	32.35 N	87.45 W
Big Quilcene ≃	224	47.49 N	122.52 W
Big Quill Lake ⊜	184	51.55 N	104.22 W
Big Raccoon Creek ≃	194	39.46 N	87.22 W
Big Rapids	190	43.41 N	85.29 W
Bigras, Île I	275a	45.31 N	73.51 W
Big Rib ≃	190	44.56 N	89.41 W
Big Rideau Lake ⊜	212	44.45 N	76.14 W
Big River	184	53.50 N	107.01 W
Big River Indian Reserve ◆[4]	184	53.33 N	107.10 W
Big Rock	216	41.46 N	88.33 W
Big Rock Creek ≃	216	41.38 N	88.32 W
Big Rocky Creek ≃	222	29.34 N	96.50 W
Big Run	214	40.58 N	78.52 W
Big Sable ≃	190	44.02 N	86.31 W
Big Sable Point ›	190	44.03 N	86.31 W
Big Salmon ≃	180	61.52 N	134.56 W
Big Salmon Range ⋏	180	61.10 N	133.45 W
Big Sand Lake ⊜	176	57.45 N	99.42 W
Big Sandy, Mt., U.S.	202	48.10 N	110.06 W
Big Sandy, Tn., U.S.	194	36.14 N	88.05 W
Big Sandy, Tx., U.S.	222	32.35 N	95.07 W
Big Sandy ≃, U.S.	188	38.25 N	82.36 W
Big Sandy ≃, Az., U.S.	200	34.19 N	113.31 W
Big Sandy ≃, Tn., U.S.	194	36.15 N	88.06 W
Big Sandy ≃, Wy., U.S.	202	41.51 N	109.47 W
Big Sandy Creek ≃, Ca., U.S.	226	35.47 N	120.43 W
Big Sandy Creek ≃, Co., U.S.	198	38.06 N	102.29 W
Big Sandy Creek ≃, Ga., U.S.	192	32.42 N	82.57 W
Big Sandy Creek ≃, Mt., U.S.	202	48.34 N	109.48 W
Big Sandy Creek ≃, Ne., U.S.	198	40.13 N	97.18 W
Big Sandy Creek ≃, Tx., U.S.	196	33.11 N	97.40 W
Big Sandy Creek ≃, Tx., U.S.	222	32.33 N	95.05 W
Big Sandy Creek ≃, Tx., U.S.	222	30.31 N	94.28 W
Big Sandy Lake ⊜, Sk., Can.	184	54.26 N	104.04 W
Big Sandy Lake ⊜, Mn., U.S.	190	46.45 N	93.17 W
Big Sandy Reservoir ⊜[1]	200	42.16 N	109.26 W
Big Satilla Creek ≃	192	31.27 N	82.03 W
Bigsby Island I	184	49.04 N	94.35 W
Big Sewickley Creek ≃	279b	40.35 N	80.13 W
Big Shawnee Creek ≃	216	40.15 N	87.18 W
Big Sheep Mountain ∧	202	47.03 N	105.43 W
Big Signal Peak ∧	204	39.31 N	123.06 W
Big Sinking Creek ≃	194	37.55 N	86.31 W
Big Sioux ≃	198	42.30 N	96.25 W
Big Sixmile Creek ≃	284a	43.02 N	79.01 W
Big Sky	202	45.17 N	111.17 W
Big Slough ≃	192	30.56 N	84.33 W
Big Smoky Valley V	204	38.30 N	117.15 W
Big Snowy Mountains ⋏	202	46.50 N	109.30 W
Big Southern Butte ∧	202	43.23 N	113.01 W
Big Spanish Channel ų	220	24.44 N	81.20 W
Bigspring, Mo., U.S.	219	38.38 N	91.28 W
Big Spring, Tx., U.S.	196	32.15 N	101.28 W
Big Springs	198	41.03 N	102.04 W
Big Spruce Knob ∧	188	38.16 N	80.12 W
Big Squaw Mountain ∧	188	45.30 N	69.45 W
Bigstick Lake ⊜	184	50.16 N	109.20 W
Bigstone ≃	184	55.55 N	94.36 W
Big Stone City	198	45.17 N	96.27 W
Big Stone Gap	192	36.52 N	82.44 W
Bigstone Lake ⊜, Mb., Can.	184	53.42 N	95.44 W
Big Stone Lake ⊜, U.S.	198	45.25 N	96.40 W
Big Sunflower ≃	194	32.40 N	90.40 W
Big Sur	226	36.16 N	121.48 W
Big Sur ≃	226	36.17 N	121.51 W
Big Sur ◆[1]	226	35.45 N	121.20 W
Big Swamp Creek ≃	194	32.19 N	86.49 W
Big Swan Creek ≃	194	35.46 N	87.24 W
Big Thicket National Preserve ♦	222	32.35 N	94.40 W
Big Thompson ≃	200	40.21 N	104.45 W
Big Timber	202	45.50 N	109.57 W
Big Timber Creek ≃	285	39.53 N	75.08 W
Big Timber Creek, North Branch ≃	285	39.50 N	75.05 W
Big Timber Creek, South Branch ≃	285	39.50 N	75.05 W
Big Torch Key I	220	24.43 N	81.26 W
Big Tree	210	42.46 N	78.49 W
Big Trout Lake ⊜, On., Can.	176	53.45 N	90.00 W
Big Trout Lake ⊜, On., Can.	212	44.56 N	78.56 W
Big Tujunga Canyon V	228	34.16 N	118.18 W
Big Tujunga Dam ◆[6]	280	34.18 N	118.12 W
Biguaçu	252	27.30 S	48.40 W
Big Valley	182	52.02 N	112.46 W
Bigwa	154	7.13 S	39.09 E
Big Walnut Creek ≃, In., U.S.	194	39.30 N	86.57 W
Big Walnut Creek ≃, Oh., U.S.	218	39.48 N	83.01 W
Big Warrambool ≃	166	30.05 S	147.33 E
Big Water	200	37.05 N	111.41 W
Big Wells	196	28.34 N	99.34 W
Big White Mountain ∧	182	49.42 N	118.58 W
Big Wills Creek ≃	194	33.59 N	86.00 W
Big Wood ≃	202	42.52 N	114.54 W
Bihać	36	44.49 N	15.52 E
Bīhar	124	25.11 N	85.31 E
Bihār □[3]	124	25.00 N	86.00 E
Biharamulo	154	2.38 S	31.20 E
Bihārīganj	124	25.44 N	86.59 E
Bihor □[6]	38	47.00 N	22.15 E
Bihoro	92a	43.49 N	144.07 E
Bihta	124	25.33 N	84.52 E
Bihu	100	28.21 N	119.48 E
Bija ≃	86	52.25 N	85.05 E
Bijagós, Arquipélago dos II	150	11.25 N	16.20 W
Bijainagar	120	25.56 N	74.38 E
Bijaipura	124	24.46 N	77.48 E
Bījāpur, India	122	18.48 N	80.49 E
Bījāpur, India	122	16.50 N	75.42 E
Bījār	128	35.52 N	47.36 E
Bijauri	124	28.06 N	82.20 E
Bijāwar	124	24.38 N	79.30 E
Bijbān Chāh	128	26.54 N	64.42 E
Bījbiāra	123	33.48 N	75.06 E
Bijeljina	38	44.45 N	19.13 E
Bijelo Polje	38	43.02 N	19.44 E
Bījenābād	128	27.55 N	58.03 E
Bijeypur	124	26.03 N	77.22 E
Bijiang	110	26.30 N	98.55 E
Bijia Shan ∧	105	40.17 N	116.50 E
Bijie	102	27.18 N	105.20 E
Bijlikol', ozero ⊜	85	43.03 N	70.41 E
Bijna	272b	22.55 N	88.27 E
Bijni	124	26.31 N	90.40 E
Bijnor	124	29.22 N	78.08 E
Bijnor □[5]	124	29.30 N	78.25 E
Bijōki	268	35.49 N	139.39 E
Bijou Creek ≃	198	40.17 N	103.52 W
Bijpur	126	22.56 N	88.26 E
Bijsk	86	52.34 N	85.15 E
Bijuk-Karasu ≃	78	45.27 N	34.47 E
Bijwāsan ◆[8]	272a	28.32 N	77.03 E
Bīkaner	120	28.01 N	73.18 E
Bīkaner □[5]	123	28.42 N	73.25 E
Bīkaner Canal ≊	123	30.08 N	73.57 E
Bikar I[1]	14	12.15 N	170.06 E
Bikbulovo	80	55.39 N	53.26 E
Bike	144	9.30 N	41.18 E
Bikeman Island I	174t	1.22 N	173.00 E
Bikenibeu	174t	1.21 N	173.07 E
Bikeqi	102	40.45 N	111.17 E
Bikeru	112	5.15 S	120.07 E
Bikfayyā	132	33.55 N	35.41 E
Bikié	152	3.06 S	13.52 E
Bikin	89	46.48 N	134.16 E
Bikin ≃	89	46.51 N	134.02 E
Bikini I[1]	14	11.35 N	165.23 E
Bikita	154	20.06 S	31.41 E
Bikl'an'	80	55.37 N	52.10 E
Bikoro	152	0.45 S	18.07 E
Bikuar, Parque Nacional do ♦	152	15.12 S	14.42 E
Bila ≃	114	2.30 N	100.08 E
Bilaa Point ›	116	9.49 N	125.26 E
Bilac	255	21.24 S	50.28 W
Bilād Zahrān ◆[1]	144	20.16 N	41.14 E
Bílá hora ⊥	54	50.10 N	14.10 E
Bilang, Teluk ⊂	112	1.15 N	121.25 E
Bilanga	150	12.32 N	0.02 E
Bilāra	120	26.10 N	73.42 E
Bilāri	124	28.38 N	78.48 E
Bil'arsk	80	54.58 N	50.22 E
Bilāsipāra	124	26.14 N	90.14 E
Bilāspur, India	123	31.20 N	76.45 E
Bilaspur, India	124	28.53 N	79.16 E
Bilāspur, India	124	22.05 N	82.09 E
Bilāspur □[5]	124	22.30 N	82.10 E
Bil'asuvar	84	39.24 N	48.24 E
Bilatan Island I	116	4.59 N	120.00 E
Bilato	112	0.32 N	122.38 E
Bilauktaung Range ⋏	110	13.00 N	99.00 E
Bilauri	124	28.41 N	80.21 E
Bilbao	34	43.15 N	2.58 W
Bilbays	142	30.25 N	31.34 E
Bilbays Military Base ■	142	30.24 N	31.36 E
Bilbilis ⊥	34	41.25 N	1.39 W
Bil'čir	88	51.02 N	110.34 E
Bileća	38	42.53 N	18.26 E
Bilecik	130	40.09 N	29.59 E
Bilecik □[4]	130	40.10 N	30.10 E
Biles Island I	285	40.10 N	74.45 W
Biłgoraj	30	50.34 N	22.43 E
Bilgrām	124	27.11 N	80.02 E
Bili	154	4.09 N	25.10 E
Bili ≃	136	4.09 N	22.29 E
Bilian	100	28.21 N	120.33 E
Bilican Dağları ⋏	130	38.58 N	42.10 E
Bilifyā	142	29.07 N	31.03 E
Bilimora	120	20.45 N	72.57 E
Bilin	110	17.14 N	97.15 E
Bilin ≃	110	17.05 N	97.08 E
Bílina	54	50.35 N	13.45 E
Bílina ≃	54	50.40 N	14.02 E
Bilioso ≃	68	40.39 N	16.24 E
Biliran Island I	116	11.35 N	124.28 E
Biliran Strait ų	116	11.30 N	124.28 E
Biliri	146	9.52 N	11.13 E
Biliu ≃	98	39.30 N	122.36 E
Bilk ◆[8]	263	51.12 N	6.47 E
Billabong Creek ≃	166	35.06 S	144.02 E
Billeberga	41	55.53 N	13.00 E
Billerbeck	52	51.59 N	7.17 E
Billerica	207	42.33 N	71.16 W
Billericay	260	51.38 N	0.25 E
Billesdon	42	52.37 N	0.55 W
Billesholm	41	56.03 N	13.00 E
Billiat	58	46.04 N	5.47 E
Billigheim	56	49.21 N	9.15 E
Billiluna	162	19.37 S	127.41 E
Billinge, Sve.	41	55.58 N	13.21 E
Billinge, Eng., U.K.	262	53.30 N	2.42 W
Billingen ⋏[2]	26	58.24 N	13.45 E
Billingham	44	54.36 N	1.17 W
Billings, Mo., U.S.	194	37.04 N	93.33 W
Billings, Mt., U.S.	202	45.46 N	108.30 W
Billings, Ok., U.S.	196	36.31 N	97.26 W
Billingsfors	26	58.59 N	12.15 E
Billings Heights	202	45.50 N	108.32 W
Billingshurst	42	51.01 N	0.28 W
Billmerich	263	51.30 N	7.47 E
Billolo ≃	273b	4.07 S	15.19 E
Billom	32	45.44 N	3.21 E
Billund	41	55.44 N	9.07 E
Bill Williams ≃	200	34.17 N	114.03 W
Bill Williams Mountain ∧	200	35.12 N	112.12 W
Billy Chinook, Lake ⊜[1]	202	44.33 N	121.20 W
Billy-Montigny	50	50.25 N	2.52 E
Bilma	146	18.41 N	12.56 E
Biloela	166	24.24 S	150.30 E
Bilo Gora ⋏	36	46.06 N	16.46 E
Biloxi	194	30.23 N	88.53 W
Biloxi ≃	194	30.26 N	89.00 W
Biloxi Creek ≃	222	31.05 N	94.37 W
Bilpa Morea Claypan ≚	166	25.00 S	140.00 E
Bilpin	170	33.30 S	150.31 E
Bilqās Qism Awwal	142	31.13 N	31.21 E
Bilsārā	126	23.05 N	88.10 E
Bilshausen	52	51.37 N	10.10 E
Bilsi	124	28.08 N	78.55 E
Bilston	42	52.34 N	2.04 W
Biltāj	142	31.00 N	30.59 E
Bilthoven	52	52.07 N	5.17 E
Biltine	146	14.32 N	20.55 E
Biltine □[5]	146	15.00 N	21.00 E
Biltmore Forest	192	35.32 N	82.31 W
Bilugyun Island I	110	16.24 N	97.32 E
Bilwaskarma	236	14.45 N	83.53 W
Bilzen	56	50.52 N	5.31 E
Bima	115b	8.28 S	118.43 E
Bimbān	140	24.26 N	32.53 E
Bimbe	152	11.49 S	15.49 E
Bimberi Peak ∧	171b	35.40 S	148.47 E
Bimbila	150	8.51 N	0.04 E
Bimbo	152	4.18 N	18.33 E
Bimbowrie	166	32.03 S	140.09 E
Bimé	273b	4.09 S	15.11 E
Bimini Islands II	192	25.42 N	79.15 W
Bin ≃	100	23.40 N	112.58 E
Bina	175e	8.55 S	160.46 E
Bīna-Etāwa	124	24.11 N	78.11 E
Binaiya, Gunung ∧	164	3.11 S	129.26 E
Binalbagan	116	10.12 N	122.50 E
Binalbagan ≃	116	10.12 N	122.51 E
Binalonan	116	16.03 N	120.36 E
Bin'an	89	45.50 N	127.45 E
Binanga	114	1.24 N	99.46 E
Binangonan	116	14.28 N	121.11 E
Binas	50	47.54 N	1.28 E
Binasco	62	45.20 N	9.06 E
Binau	56	49.22 N	9.04 E
Binboğadağı ∧	130	38.21 N	36.32 E
Binche	50	50.24 N	4.10 E
Binchuan	102	25.46 N	100.33 E
Bindal	24	65.06 N	12.30 E
Bindebango	166	27.45 S	147.24 E
Binder, Mong.	88	48.35 N	110.36 E
Binder, Tchad	146	9.58 N	14.28 E
Bindki	124	26.02 N	80.36 E
Bindlach	60	49.59 N	11.37 E
Bindloss	184	50.52 N	110.16 W
Bindo, Mount ∧	170	33.40 S	150.01 E
Bindow	264a	52.17 N	13.45 E
Bindura	154	17.19 S	31.20 E
Bine-El-Ouidane	148	32.07 N	6.26 W
Binéfar	34	41.51 N	0.18 E
Binford	198	47.33 N	98.20 W
Binga, Pil.	116	10.45 N	119.19 E
Binga, Zaïre	152	2.23 N	20.30 E
Binga, Monte ∧	156	19.45 S	33.04 E
Bingara	166	29.52 S	150.34 E
Bingaram Island I	122	10.56 N	72.17 E
Bingay Point ›	116	13.04 N	124.11 E
Bingcha	100	32.30 N	120.52 E
Bingen, B.R.D.	56	49.57 N	7.54 E
Bingen, Wa., U.S.	224	45.42 N	121.27 W
Binger	196	35.18 N	98.20 W
Bingerbrück	56	49.58 N	7.53 E
Bingerville	150	5.21 N	3.54 W
Bingfang	106	32.15 N	121.20 E
Bingham, Eng., U.K.	42	52.57 N	0.57 W
Bingham, Me., U.S.	188	45.03 N	69.52 W
Bingham ≃	168a	33.20 S	116.16 E
Bingham Creek ≃	224	47.09 N	123.24 W
Bingham Farms	281	42.32 N	83.16 W
Binghamton	210	42.05 N	75.55 W
Bin Ghashīr	146	32.41 N	13.11 E
Bin Ghunaymah, Jabal ⋏	146	25.00 N	15.30 E
Bingi	154	0.24 S	29.05 E
Bingley	44	53.51 N	1.50 W
Bingöl	130	38.53 N	40.29 E
Bingöl □[4]	130	39.00 N	40.40 E
Bingöl Dağları ⋏	130	39.20 N	41.20 E
Binhai (Dongkan)	100	34.03 N	119.51 E
Binh-ca	110	21.48 N	105.18 E
Binh-chanh	269c	10.40 N	106.34 E
Binh-gia	110	21.59 N	106.21 E
Binh-hung-hoa	269c	10.49 N	106.37 E
Binh-khe	110	13.57 N	108.51 E
Binh-kieu	110	15.35 N	108.04 E
Bin-Houyé	150	6.47 N	8.19 W
Binh-son	110	15.18 N	108.46 E
Binh-trung	269c	10.47 N	106.46 E
Binigsian Point ›	116	9.50 N	122.23 E
Bining	56	49.02 N	7.15 E
Binjai, Indon.	112	3.48 N	108.14 E
Binjai, Indon.	114	3.36 N	98.30 E
Binjohara	114	2.12 N	98.12 E
Binna Burra	171a	28.13 S	153.14 E
Binnah, Ras ›	144	11.08 N	51.10 E
Binnaway	166	31.33 S	149.23 E
Binnian, Slieve ∧	44	54.08 N	5.58 W
Binningen	58	47.32 N	7.34 E
Binodepur	126	23.26 N	89.30 E
Binongko, Pulau I	112	5.57 S	124.02 E
Binpur	126	22.36 N	86.55 E
Binscarth	184	50.37 N	101.16 W
Binsheim	263	51.31 N	6.42 E
Bintan, Pulau I	112	1.05 N	104.30 E
Bintang	150	13.10 N	16.08 W
Bintang, Gunong ∧	114	5.25 N	100.52 E
Bintauna	112	0.53 N	123.33 E
Bint Goda	140	13.17 N	31.33 E
Bintimani ∧	150	9.13 N	11.07 W
Bint Jubayl	132	33.07 N	35.26 E
Bintuhan	112	4.48 S	103.22 E
Bintulu	112	3.10 N	113.02 E
Bintuni, Teluk ⊂	164	2.20 S	133.30 E
Binxian, Zhg.	89	45.44 N	127.29 E
Binxian, Zhg.	98	37.28 N	117.56 E
Binxian, Zhg.	102	35.00 N	108.08 E
Binyamina	132	32.31 N	34.57 E
Binyang	102	23.18 N	108.46 E
Bin Yauri	150	10.47 N	4.50 E
Bin Yumayn, Ghayl ▾[4]	144	15.35 N	49.20 E
Binz	54	54.24 N	13.36 E
Binza	273b	4.21 S	15.14 E
Binza ◆[8]	273b	4.20 S	15.14 E
Binza ≃	273b	4.21 S	15.14 E
Bio Addo	144	8.18 N	49.48 E
Biobío □[4]	252	37.00 S	72.30 W
Biobío ≃	252	36.49 S	73.10 W
Biodi	154	3.19 N	28.35 E
Biograd	36	43.56 N	15.27 E
Bioko □[4]	152	3.30 N	8.40 E
Bioko I	152	3.30 N	8.40 E
Biola	226	36.48 N	120.00 W
Bionaz	62	45.52 N	7.25 E
Biondo	154	0.23 S	25.13 E
Biondo Monument ⊥	146	31.25 N	10.15 E
Biot	62	43.38 N	7.06 E
Bipindi	152	3.05 N	10.25 E
Bippus	216	40.56 N	85.37 W
Biqiao	106	31.02 N	119.02 E
Bīr	122	18.59 N	75.46 E
Bir, Ras ›	144	11.59 N	43.22 E
Bira, India	272b	22.47 N	88.34 E
Bira, S.S.S.R.	89	49.15 N	137.16 E
Bira, S.S.S.R.	89	49.02 N	132.30 E
Bira ≃	89	48.07 N	133.21 E
Birab	164	6.12 S	138.25 E
Bīraba	126	23.51 N	90.34 E
Birāk	146	27.32 N	14.16 E
Birakan	89	49.01 N	131.42 E
Bi'r ʿAlī	144	14.01 N	48.19 E
Bi'r al-Uzam	146	31.54 N	23.58 E
Birama, Ensenada de ⊂	240p	20.38 N	77.15 W
Birandža	89	54.35 N	136.18 E
Birao	146	10.17 N	22.47 E
Birati	272b	22.39 N	88.27 E
Birātnagar	124	26.29 N	87.17 E
Birava	154	2.21 S	28.54 E
Bīrbhūm □[5]	124	24.00 N	87.40 E
Bîrca	38	43.58 N	23.37 E
Bircao → Buur Gaabo	144	1.12 S	41.51 E
Birch	262	53.34 N	2.13 W
Birch ≃, Ab., Can.	176	58.30 N	112.15 W
Birch ≃, W.V., U.S.	188	38.35 N	80.53 W
Birch Bay	224	48.55 N	122.45 W
Birch Bay ⊂	224	48.53 N	122.47 W
Birch Bay State Park ♦	224	49.54 N	123.47 W
Birch Cliff ◆[8]	275b	43.41 N	79.17 W
Birch Creek ≃, Ak., U.S.	180	66.30 N	146.30 W
Birch Creek ≃, Id., U.S.	202	43.51 N	112.43 W
Birch Creek ≃, Mt., U.S.	202	48.26 N	112.15 W
Birch Creek ≃, Mt., U.S.	202	47.45 N	109.34 W
Birch Hill Dam ◆[6]	207	42.38 N	72.09 W
Birch Hills	184	52.59 N	105.25 W
Birchington	42	51.23 N	1.19 E
Birch Island	182	51.36 N	119.55 W
Birch Island I	184	52.25 N	99.55 W
Birch Lake ⊜, Ab., Can.	182	53.19 N	111.35 W
Birch Lake ⊜, On., Can.	184	51.24 N	92.20 W
Birch Lake ⊜, Sk., Can.	184	53.28 N	108.07 W
Birch Mountains ⋏[2]	176	57.30 N	112.30 W
Bir Chouhada	34	35.53 N	6.18 E
Birch Pond ⊜	283	42.28 N	71.00 W
Birch Reservoir ⊜[1]	196	36.31 N	96.12 W
Birch River	184	52.23 N	101.06 W
Birch Run	190	43.15 N	83.47 W
Birch Run ≃	285	40.09 N	75.37 W
Birchrunville	285	40.08 N	75.39 W
Birch Tree	194	36.59 N	91.29 W
Birch Vale	262	53.23 N	1.57 W
Birchwood, N.Z.	172	45.56 S	167.52 E
Birchwood, Eng., U.K.	44	53.13 N	0.36 W
Birchwood, Ak., U.S.	180	61.28 N	149.22 W
Birchwood, Wi., U.S.	190	45.39 N	91.33 W
Birchwood City	284c	38.49 N	76.59 W
Birchwood Park, De., U.S.	285	39.22 N	75.39 W
Birchwood Park, N.J., U.S.	208	40.06 N	74.09 W
Birchy Bay	186	49.21 N	54.44 W
Bird City	198	39.45 N	101.31 W
Bird Creek ≃	196	36.13 N	95.44 W
Bird Hills Wildflower Sanctuary ♦	169	38.23 S	144.11 E
Bird Island	198	44.46 N	94.53 W
Bird Island I, Falk. Is.	244	54.00 S	38.05 W
Bird Island I, S. Afr.	158	33.51 S	26.18 E
Bird Islet I	160	22.10 S	155.28 E
Bird River ⊂	284b	39.23 N	76.23 W
Birdsall	210	42.23 N	77.55 W
Birdsboro	208	40.15 N	75.48 W
Birds Landing	282	38.08 N	121.52 W
Birdsview	224	48.32 N	121.52 W
Birdsville	166	25.54 S	139.22 E
Birdtail Creek ≃	184	50.16 N	101.12 W
Birdum	164	15.39 S	133.13 E
Birdum Creek ≃	164	15.14 S	133.00 E
Birdwood	168b	34.49 S	138.57 E
Birecik	130	37.02 N	37.58 E
Bire Kpatua Game Reserve ◆[4]	154	5.12 N	27.36 E
Bir el Ater	148	34.44 N	8.03 E
Bir Enzaran	148	23.56 N	14.33 W
Bireuen	114	5.12 N	96.41 E
Bīrganj	124	27.00 N	84.52 E
Bir Ghbalou	34	36.16 N	3.35 E
Birgi	126	22.42 N	86.41 E
Birgi Vecchi	70	37.53 N	12.29 E
Biri	116	12.41 N	124.22 E
Birigui	255	21.18 S	50.19 W
Biri Island I	116	12.40 N	124.22 E
Birik	130	39.01 N	38.15 E
Birikčul'	86	53.20 N	89.56 E
Biril'ussy	86	57.07 N	90.32 E
Birimbāl	142	31.21 N	30.30 E
Birimbāl al-Qadīmah	142	31.10 N	31.44 E
Birimşe	130	38.03 N	38.32 E
Biritiba-Mirim	256	23.35 S	46.02 W
Bīrjand	128	32.53 N	59.13 E
Birkat as-Sab'	142	30.38 N	31.05 E
Birkat Ghiṭās	142	31.07 N	30.16 E
Birkdale	262	53.37 N	3.02 W
Birkeland	26	58.20 N	8.14 E
Birken	182	50.29 N	122.36 W
Birkenfeld, B.R.D.	56	48.52 N	8.38 E
Birkenfeld, B.R.D.	56	49.51 N	9.42 E
Birkenfeld, B.R.D.	56	49.39 N	7.10 E
Birkenfeld, Or., U.S.	224	45.59 N	123.20 W
Birkenhead	262	53.24 N	3.02 W
Birkenhead Park ♦	262	53.24 N	3.02 W
Birkenwerder bei Berlin	54	52.41 N	13.16 E
Birkerød	41	55.50 N	12.26 E
Birkesdorf	56	50.49 N	6.28 E
Birket Fatimé	146	12.54 N	19.05 E
Birkfeld	61	47.21 N	15.42 E
Birkholz	264a	52.38 N	13.34 E
Birkkarspitze ∧	64	47.25 N	11.25 E
Birk-Nack ›	41	54.48 N	9.55 E
Birksgate Range ⋏	162	27.10 S	129.45 E
Bîrlad	38	46.14 N	27.40 E
Bîrlad ≃	38	45.36 N	27.31 E
Birla Museum ᵾ	272b	22.32 N	88.22 E
Birlik, S.S.S.R.	80	47.28 N	50.32 E
Birlik, S.S.S.R.	86	44.05 N	73.31 E
Birling	260	51.19 N	0.25 E
Birling ∧[2]	274a	33.57 S	150.43 E
Birmā	142	30.51 N	30.54 E
Birmaj	84	39.46 N	47.56 E
Birmania → Burma □[1]	110	22.00 N	98.00 E
Birmanie → Burma □[1]	110	22.00 N	98.00 E
Birmingham, Eng., U.K.	42	52.30 N	1.50 W
Birmingham, Al., U.S.	194	33.31 N	86.48 W
Birmingham, Ia., U.S.	190	40.52 N	91.56 W
Birmingham, Mi., U.S.	216	42.32 N	83.12 W
Birmingham, N.J., U.S.	285	39.58 N	74.42 W
Birmingham, Oh., U.S.	214	41.20 N	82.21 W
Birmingham, Pa., U.S.	214	40.38 N	78.13 W
Birmingham Airport ⊠	42	52.27 N	1.45 W
Birmitrapur	124	22.24 N	84.46 E
Bîr Mogreïn (Fort-Trinquet)	148	25.14 N	11.35 W
Birnagar	126	23.14 N	88.33 E
Birnamwood	190	44.56 N	89.12 W
Bi'r Naṣīf	128	24.51 N	39.11 E
Birnbaum	64	46.41 N	12.54 E
Birni	150	10.00 N	1.31 E
Birnie I[1]	14	3.35 S	171.31 W
Birni Ngaouré	150	13.05 N	2.54 E
Birnin Gwari	150	11.01 N	6.48 E
Birnin Kebbi	150	12.32 N	4.12 E
Birni Nkonni	150	13.48 N	5.15 E
Birnin Kudu	150	11.27 N	9.30 E
Birobidžan	89	48.48 N	132.57 E
Birofel'd	89	48.26 N	132.47 E
Birome	222	31.49 N	96.58 W
Birqāsh	142	30.10 N	31.02 E
Birr	48	53.05 N	7.54 W
Birregurra	169	38.20 S	143.48 E
Birribi	164	9.31 S	147.27 E
Birrie ≃	166	29.43 S	146.37 E
Birrindudu	162	18.22 S	129.27 E
Birs ≃	58	47.22 N	7.22 E
Birsilpur	120	28.10 N	72.15 E
Birsk	86	55.25 N	55.32 E
Birstall	42	52.41 N	1.07 W
Birstein	56	50.21 N	9.19 E
Birštonas	76	54.37 N	24.02 E
Birten	263	51.38 N	6.29 E
Birtle	184	50.25 N	101.03 W
Birtley	44	54.54 N	1.34 W
Bir'učij	83	46.53 N	39.33 E
Bir'učij kosa ›[2]	78	46.08 N	35.05 E
Bir'učja ≃	83	47.23 N	39.07 E
Birufu	164	5.52 S	138.24 E
Bir'ukovo	83	47.57 N	39.44 E
Bir'ul'ka	88	53.52 N	106.21 E
Bir'ul'ovo ◆[8]	265b	55.35 N	37.40 E
Birungu, Parc des ♦	154	1.25 S	29.30 E
Birūr	122	13.37 N	75.58 E
Bir'usa	88	57.10 N	96.30 E
Bir'usa (Ona) ≃	88	57.43 N	95.24 E
Bir'usinsk	88	55.57 N	97.49 E
Biržai	76	56.12 N	24.45 E
Bîrzava ≃	38	45.16 N	20.49 E
Birżebbuġa	36	35.49 N	14.32 E
Bisa, Pulau I	164	1.15 S	127.28 E
Bisaccia	68	41.01 N	15.22 E
Bisacquino	70	37.42 N	13.15 E
Bisāi, India	126	22.10 N	86.24 E
Bisai, Nihon	94	35.16 N	136.44 E
Bīsalpur	124	28.18 N	79.48 E
Bisamberg	264b	48.20 N	16.22 E
Bisamberg ∧[2]	264b	48.19 N	16.22 E
Bisan-shotō II	96	34.24 N	133.50 E
Bisbee, Az., U.S.	200	31.26 N	109.55 W
Bisbee, N.D., U.S.	198	48.37 N	99.22 W
Biscarrosse	32	44.24 N	1.10 W
Biscarrosse et de Parentis, Lac de ⊂	32	44.20 N	1.10 W
Biscay, Bay of ⊂	32	44.00 N	4.00 W
Biscayne, Key I	220	25.42 N	80.10 W
Biscayne Bay ⊂	220	25.33 N	80.15 W
Biscayne National Park ♦	220	25.25 N	80.12 W
Bisceglie	68	41.14 N	16.31 E
Bischheim	58	48.37 N	7.45 E
Bischofsburg → Biskupiec	30	53.52 N	20.58 E
Bischofsgrün	60	50.03 N	11.47 E
Bischofsheim, B.R.D.	56	50.24 N	10.01 E
Bischofsheim, B.R.D.	56	49.59 N	8.22 E
Bischofshofen	64	47.25 N	13.13 E
Bischofstal → Ujazd	30	50.24 N	18.22 E
Bischofstein → Bisztynek	30	54.06 N	20.55 E
Bischofswerda	54	51.07 N	14.10 E
Bischofswiesen	64	47.39 N	12.57 E
Bischofszell	58	47.29 N	9.15 E
Bischwald, Étang de ⊜	56	49.00 N	6.42 E
Bischwiller	56	48.46 N	7.52 E
Biscoe, Ar., U.S.	194	34.49 N	91.24 W
Biscoe, N.C., U.S.	192	35.21 N	79.46 W
Biscoe Islands II	9	66.00 S	66.30 W
Biscotasi Lake ⊜	190	47.19 N	82.07 W
Biscucuy	246	9.22 N	69.59 W
Bise	174m	26.42 N	127.54 E
Bisei	96	34.41 N	133.33 E
Bisentina, Isola I	66	42.35 N	11.54 E
Bisenzio ≃	66	43.46 N	11.06 E
Biser	86	58.25 N	58.53 E
Biserovo	265b	55.47 N	38.07 E
Biserovskoje, ozero ⊜	265b	55.46 N	38.07 E
Bisert' ≃	86	56.39 N	57.55 E
Bise-zaki ›	174m	26.43 N	127.53 E
Bisha	144	15.28 N	37.34 E
Bīshah, Wādī V	144	21.24 N	43.26 E
Bishahari	126	23.10 N	89.01 E
Bishan	107	29.37 N	106.13 E
Bishanga	152	4.31 S	21.02 E
Bishaykhāli	126	23.28 N	89.09 E
Bishenpur	120	24.38 N	93.46 E
Bishkhāli ≃[1]	126	21.59 N	89.59 E
Bishnāh	123	32.37 N	74.52 E
Bishnupur, India	126	22.23 N	88.16 E
Bishnupur, India	126	23.05 N	87.19 E
Bishnupur, India	272b	22.37 N	88.31 E
Bisho	158	32.50 S	27.20 E
Bishop, Ca., U.S.	204	37.21 N	118.23 W
Bishop, Pa., U.S.	279b	40.19 N	80.12 W
Bishop, Tx., U.S.	196	27.35 N	97.47 W
Bishop Airport ⊠	216	42.58 N	83.44 W
Bishop Auckland	44	54.40 N	1.40 W
Bishop Rock I[2]	42a	49.52 N	6.27 W
Bishop's Castle	42	52.29 N	3.00 W
Bishop's Cleeve	42	51.57 N	2.04 W
Bishop's Falls	186	49.01 N	55.30 W
Bishops Frome	42	52.08 N	2.29 W
Bishops Head	208	38.16 N	76.04 W
Bishops Lydeard	42	51.04 N	3.12 W
Bishop's Stortford	42	51.53 N	0.09 E
Bishopsteignton	42	50.34 N	3.31 W
Bishopstoke	42	50.59 N	1.19 W
Bishopston	42	51.35 N	4.03 W
Bishop's Waltham	42	50.58 N	1.12 W
Bishopthorpe	44	53.55 N	1.06 W
Bishopton	206	45.35 N	71.35 W
Bishopville, Md., U.S.	208	38.26 N	75.11 W
Bishopville, S.C., U.S.	192	34.13 N	80.14 W
Bishrah, Maʿṭan ▾[4]	146	22.58 N	22.39 E
Bishrī, Jabal ⋏	130	35.26 N	39.32 E
Bisianumu	164	9.25 S	147.25 E
Bisignano	68	39.31 N	16.17 E
Bisina, Lake ⊜	154	1.38 N	33.56 E
Bisinadi Game Reserve ◆[4]	154	0.10 N	38.20 E
Bisingen	58	48.18 N	8.55 E
Biskamža	86	53.30 N	89.30 E
Biskaya, Golf von → Biscay, Bay of ⊂	32	44.00 N	4.00 W
Biskintā	132	33.57 N	35.48 E
Biškon' ≃	83	49.15 N	39.35 E
Biskupiec	30	53.52 N	20.58 E
Bisley, Eng., U.K.	42	51.45 N	2.08 W
Bisley, Eng., U.K.	260	51.20 N	0.38 W
Bislich	263	51.41 N	6.29 E
Bislig	116	8.13 N	126.19 E
Bislig Bay ⊂	116	8.14 N	126.22 E
Bismarck, Il., U.S.	216	40.16 N	87.37 W
Bismarck, Mo., U.S.	194	37.46 N	90.37 W
Bismarck, N.D., U.S.	198	46.48 N	100.47 W
Bismarck Archipelago II	164	5.00 S	150.00 E
Bismarck Range ⋏	164	5.30 S	144.45 E
Bismarck Sea ▾[2]	164	4.00 S	148.00 E
Bismark	54	52.39 N	11.32 E
Bismil	130	37.51 N	40.40 E
Bismo	26	61.53 N	8.16 E
Biso	154	1.46 N	31.25 E
Bison	198	45.31 N	102.27 W
Bison Peak ∧	200	39.14 N	105.30 W
Bispberg	40	60.22 N	15.47 E
Bispgården	26	63.02 N	16.37 E
Bispingen	52	53.05 N	10.00 E
Bisrakh	272a	28.34 N	77.26 E
Bisrāmpur	124	24.15 N	83.56 E
Bissa, Djebel ∧	34	36.26 N	1.28 E
Bissau	150	11.51 N	15.35 W
Bissaula	146	7.00 N	10.27 E
Bissegem	50	50.49 N	3.13 E
Bissendorf, B.R.D.	52	52.14 N	8.10 E
Bissendorf, B.R.D.	52	52.31 N	9.45 E
Bissett	184	51.02 N	95.40 W
Bissigh, Lach ≃	144	0.45 N	41.33 E
Bissikrima	150	10.51 N	10.56 W
Bissingen	56	48.43 N	10.37 E
Bissingheim ◆[8], B.R.D.	263	51.24 N	6.49 E
Bissingheim ◆[8], B.R.D.	263	51.21 N	7.31 E
Bissorã	150	12.14 N	15.31 W
Bistcho Lake ⊜	176	59.40 N	118.40 W
Bistineau, Lake ⊜[1]	194	32.25 N	93.22 W
Bistra ≃	38	45.29 N	22.11 E
Bistreț	38	43.54 N	23.30 E
Bistrica	61	46.33 N	16.16 E
Bistrița	38	47.08 N	24.30 E
Bistrița ≃	38	46.30 N	26.57 E
Bistrița-Năsăud □[6]	38	47.15 N	24.30 E
Biswān	124	27.30 N	81.00 E
Bisztynek	30	54.06 N	20.55 E
Bitadton	116	11.30 N	122.05 E
Bitam	152	2.05 N	11.29 E
Bitam, Oued ≃	34	35.15 N	5.11 E
Bitatolo ≃	273b	4.09 S	15.19 E
Bitburg	56	49.58 N	6.31 E
Bitca	265b	55.34 N	37.37 E
Bitca ≃	265b	55.34 N	37.37 E
Bitche	56	49.03 N	7.26 E
Bitchū	96	34.47 N	133.27 E
Bitéa, Ouadi V	146	13.11 N	20.10 E
Bitetto	68	41.02 N	16.45 E
Bithia ⊥	71	38.53 N	8.52 E
Bithlo	220	28.33 N	81.06 W
Bithynia □[9]	130	40.10 N	30.15 E
Bitia, Wādī V	140	17.34 N	32.15 E
Bitik	80	50.09 N	50.30 E
Bitkine	146	11.59 N	18.13 E

Symbols in the index entries represent the broad categories identified in the key at the right. Symbols with superior numbers (⋏[1]) identify subcategories (see complete key on page *I · 1).*

Kartensymbole in dem Registerverzeichnis stellen die rechts in Schlüssel erklärten Kategorien dar. Symbole mit hochgestellten Ziffern (⋏[1]) bezeichnen Unterabteilungen einer Kategorie (vgl. vollständiger Schlüssel auf Seite *I · 1).*

Los símbolos incluídos en el texto del índice representan las grandes categorias identificadas con la clave a la derecha. Los símbolos con numeros en su parte superior (⋏[1]) identifican las subcategorías (véase la clave completa en la página *I · 1).*

Les symboles de l'index représentent les catégories indiquées dans la légende à droite. Les symboles suivis d'un indice (⋏[1]) représentent des sous-catégories (voir légende complète à la page *I · 1).*

Os símbolos incluídos no texto do índice representam as grandes categorias identificadas com a chave à direita. Os símbolos com números em sua parte superior (⋏[1]) identificam as subcategorias (veja-se a chave completa à página *I · 1).*

∧ Mountain	Berg	Montaña	Montagne	Montanha
⋏ Mountains	Berge	Montañas	Montagnes	Montanhas
)(Pass	Pass	Paso	Col	Passo
V Valley, Canyon	Tal, Cañon	Valle, Cañón	Vallée, Canyon	Vale, Canhão
≚ Plain	Ebene	Llano	Plaine	Planície
› Cape	Kap	Cabo	Cap	Cabo
I Island	Insel	Isla	Île	Ilha
II Islands	Inseln	Islas	Îles	Ilhas
⊥ Other Topographic Features	Andere Topographische Objekte	Otros Elementos Topográficos	Autres données topographiques	Outros acidentes topográficos

ESPAÑOL · FRANÇAIS · PORTUGUÊS

Nombre / Nom / Nome	Página / Page	Lat.°′	Long.°′ W = Oeste / Ouest
Bitlis	130	38.22 N	42.06 E
Bitlis □[4]	130	38.30 N	42.10 E
Bitola	38	41.01 N	21.20 E
Bitolj → Bitola	38	41.01 N	21.20 E
Bitonto	68	41.06 N	16.42 E
Bitou	150	11.16 N	0.18 W
Bitra Island I	122	11.33 N	72.09 E
Bitritto	68	41.03 N	16.50 E
Bitschwiller-lès-Thann	58	47.50 N	7.05 E
Bitter Creek ≃, Ut,. U.S.	200	39.58 N	109.25 W
Bitter Creek ≃, Wy., U.S.	200	41.31 N	109.27 W
Bitterfeld	54	51.37 N	12.20 E
Bitterfontein	158	31.00 S	18.32 E
Bitter Lake ◎	184	50.08 N	109.48 W
Bittermark ✦[8]	263	51.27 N	7.28 E
Bitterness, Mount ∧	172	44.45 S	170.18 E
Bittern Lake ◎	184	53.55 N	105.50 W
Bitterroot ≃	202	46.52 N	114.06 W
Bitterroot, East Fork ≃	202	45.57 N	114.08 W
Bitterroot, West Fork ≃	202	45.57 N	114.08 W
Bitterroot Range ⋏	202	47.06 N	115.10 W
Bitterwater Creek ≃	226	35.41 N	119.58 W
Bitti	71	40.29 N	9.23 E
Bit'ug ≃	78	50.37 N	39.55 E
Bitung	112	1.27 N	125.11 E
Bitupitá	250	2.54 S	41.16 W
Bituruna	252	26.10 S	51.34 W
Biu	146	10.35 N	12.13 E
Bivalve	208	38.18 N	75.53 W
Bivins	194	33.01 N	94.12 W
Bivio	58	46.28 N	9.38 E
Bivona	70	37.37 N	13.26 E
Bivongi	68	38.28 N	16.27 E
Biwabik	190	47.31 N	92.20 W
Biwa-ko ◎	94	35.15 N	136.05 E
Biwa-ko-kokutei-kōen ♦	94	35.10 N	136.00 E
Biwa-ko-ōhashi ✦[5]	94	35.08 N	135.56 E
Bixby	196	35.56 N	95.52 W
Biyalā	142	31.10 N	31.13 E
Biyang	100	32.44 N	113.20 E
Biysk → Bijsk	86	52.34 N	85.15 E
Bi Yun Si (Temple of the Azure Clouds) ❦[1]	105	40.00 N	116.11 E
Biz'aki	80	55.56 N	52.28 E
Bizana	158	30.58 S	29.52 E
Biz'ar	86	57.31 N	56.09 E
Bizard, Île I	275a	45.29 N	73.54 W
Bižbul'ak	80	53.43 N	54.16 E
Bizcocho, Cuchilla del ⋏[2]	258	33.45 S	57.30 W
Bizen	96	34.44 N	134.09 E
Bizerte	148	37.17 N	9.52 E
Bizerte □[8]	148	37.10 N	9.50 E
Bizerte, Lac de ◎	36	37.12 N	9.52 E
Bjæverskov	41	55.27 N	12.02 E
Bjala	38	43.27 N	25.44 E
Bjala Slatina	38	43.28 N	23.56 E
Bjargtangar ≻	24a	65.31 N	24.32 W
Bjärnum	41	56.17 N	13.42 E
Bjärred	41	55.43 N	13.01 E
Bjärsjölagård	41	55.44 N	13.41 E
Bjästa	26	63.12 N	18.30 E
Bjelaja → Belaja ≃	72	55.54 N	53.33 E
Bjelovar	36	45.54 N	16.51 E
Bjernede	41	55.27 N	11.38 E
Bjerrelide ∧[2]	41	55.47 N	9.53 E
Bjerringbro	26	56.23 N	9.40 E
Björbo	40	60.28 N	14.42 E
Bjørkelangen	26	59.53 N	11.34 E
Björklinge	40	60.02 N	17.33 E
Björknäs	40	59.19 N	18.14 E
Björkö I	40	59.53 N	19.00 E
Björköby	26	63.21 N	21.19 E
Björköfjärden C	40	59.53 N	18.56 E
Björkvik	40	58.50 N	16.31 E
Björna	26	63.34 N	18.33 E
Bjørnafjorden C[2]	26	60.06 N	5.22 E
Björndammen	40	59.12 N	16.49 E
Björneborg → Pori, Suomi	26	61.29 N	21.47 E
Björneborg, Sve.	40	59.15 N	14.15 E
Bjornesfjorden ◎	26	60.10 N	7.41 E
Björnlunda	40	59.04 N	17.09 E
Bjørnøya (Bear Island) I	12	74.25 N	19.00 E
Bjurholm	26	63.56 N	19.13 E
Bjuv	41	56.05 N	12.54 E
Bkāsīn	132	33.34 N	35.35 E
Bla	150	12.57 N	5.46 W
Bla ≃	110	14.18 N	107.52 E
Blaby	42	52.34 N	1.09 W
Blace	38	43.17 N	21.18 E
Black (Lixianjiang) (Da) ≃, Asia	110	21.15 N	105.20 E
Black ≃, Mb., Can.	184	50.49 N	96.20 W
Black ≃, On., Can.	190	48.36 N	86.16 W
Black ≃, On., Can.	190	48.42 N	80.38 W
Black ≃, On., Can.	212	44.32 N	77.22 W
Black ≃, On., Can.	212	44.20 N	79.20 W
Black ≃, On., Can.	212	44.42 N	79.19 W
Black ≃, U.S.	194	35.38 N	91.19 W
Black ≃, Ak., U.S.	180	66.39 N	144.50 W
Black ≃, Az., U.S.	200	33.44 N	110.13 W
Black ≃, La., U.S.	194	31.16 N	91.50 W
Black ≃, Mi., U.S.	190	43.00 N	82.25 W
Black ≃, Mi., U.S.	190	45.39 N	84.29 W
Black ≃, Mi., U.S.	190	46.40 N	90.03 W
Black ≃, Mi., U.S.	214	43.00 N	82.25 W
Black ≃, N.M., U.S.	196	32.14 N	104.03 W
Black ≃, N.Y., U.S.	188	43.59 N	76.04 W
Black ≃, N.C., U.S.	192	34.35 N	78.16 W
Black ≃, Oh., U.S.	214	41.28 N	82.11 W
Black ≃, S.C., U.S.	192	33.24 N	79.15 W
Black ≃, Vt., U.S.	188	43.16 N	72.27 W
Black ≃, Vt., U.S.	188	44.55 N	72.13 W
Black ≃, Wa., U.S.	224	46.49 N	123.13 W
Black ≃, Wi., U.S.	190	43.57 N	91.22 W
Black, East Branch ≃	214	41.22 N	82.07 W
Black, East Fork ≃	190	44.26 N	90.42 W
Black, Middle Branch ≃	216	42.25 N	86.14 W
Black, South Branch ≃	216	42.25 N	86.15 W
Black, West Branch ≃	214	41.22 N	82.07 W
Blackadder Water ≃	46	55.46 N	2.15 W
Blackall	166	24.25 S	145.28 E
Black Bay C	190	48.40 N	88.30 W
Black Bay Peninsula ≻[1]	190	48.38 N	88.21 W
Black Bear Creek ≃	196	36.25 N	96.38 W
Black Bear Island Lake ◎	184	55.38 N	105.40 W
Blackberry Creek ≃	216	41.38 N	88.27 W
Blackberry Heights	216	41.45 N	88.23 W
Black Birch Lake ◎	184	56.54 N	107.45 W
Black Brook ≃, Ma., U.S.	283	41.59 N	71.03 W
Black Brook ≃, Ma., U.S.	283	42.38 N	71.21 W
Black Brook ≃, N.J., U.S.	276	40.42 N	74.31 W
Blackburn, Austl.	274b	37.49 S	145.09 E
Blackburn, Eng., U.K.	44	53.45 N	2.29 W
Blackburn, Scot., U.K.	46	55.52 N	3.38 W
Blackburn □[8]	262	53.42 N	2.28 W
Blackburn, Mount ∧	180	61.44 N	143.26 W
Blackbutt	171a	26.53 S	152.06 E
Black Butte ∧, Ca., U.S.	228	34.33 N	117.43 W
Black Butte ∧, Mt., U.S.	202	46.47 N	110.56 W
Black Butte ∧, Mt., U.S.	202	44.54 N	111.51 W
Black Butte Lake ◎[1]	204	39.45 N	122.20 W
Blackbutt Range ⋏	171a	27.00 S	152.00 E
Black Canyon of the Gunnison National Monument ♦	200	38.32 N	107.42 W
Blackcraig Hill ∧	44	55.20 N	4.08 W
Black Creek, B.C., Can.	182	49.50 N	125.08 W
Black Creek, On., Can.	284a	43.00 N	79.01 W
Black Creek, N.Y., U.S.	210	42.17 N	78.14 W
Black Creek ≃, On., Can.	214	42.43 N	82.21 W
Black Creek ≃, On., Can.	275b	43.41 N	79.32 W
Black Creek ≃, On., Can.	284a	42.59 N	79.01 W
Black Creek ≃, Az., U.S.	200	35.16 N	109.14 W
Black Creek ≃, Mi., U.S.	216	41.49 N	83.54 W
Black Creek ≃, Mi., U.S.	216	43.11 N	86.14 W
Black Creek ≃, Ms., U.S.	194	33.01 N	90.21 W
Black Creek ≃, Ms., U.S.	194	30.39 N	88.39 W
Black Creek ≃, Mo., U.S.	219	39.41 N	91.55 W
Black Creek ≃, N.Y., U.S.	210	43.19 N	75.04 W
Black Creek ≃, N.Y., U.S.	210	43.06 N	77.41 W
Black Creek ≃, N.Y., U.S.	284a	43.05 N	78.57 W
Black Creek ≃, N.Y., U.S.	284a	43.03 N	78.42 W
Black Creek ≃, Pa., U.S.	210	41.00 N	76.10 W
Black Creek ≃, S.C., U.S.	192	34.18 N	79.37 W
Black Creek Park ♦	275b	43.46 N	79.31 W
Black Creek Pioneer Village ⊥	275b	43.47 N	79.32 W
Black Cypress Creek ≃	222	32.53 N	94.26 W
Blackden Heath	262	53.14 N	2.20 W
Black Devon ≃	46	56.06 N	3.47 W
Black Diamond, Ab., Can.	182	50.42 N	114.14 W
Black Diamond, Wa., U.S.	224	47.18 N	122.00 W
Black Donald Lake ◎[1]	212	45.13 N	76.55 W
Black Down Hills ⋏[2]	42	50.57 N	3.09 W
Blackduck	190	47.43 N	94.32 W
Black Duck ≃	176	56.51 N	89.02 W
Black Eagle	202	47.31 N	111.16 W
Black Esk ≃	44	55.12 N	5.10 W
Blackfalds	182	52.23 N	113.47 W
Blackfeet Indian Reservation ✦[4]	202	48.40 N	113.00 W
Blackfellow Creek ≃	171a	27.34 S	152.14 E
Blackfoot, Id., U.S.	202	43.11 N	112.20 W
Blackfoot, Mt., U.S.	182	48.34 N	112.52 W
Blackfoot ≃, Id., U.S.	202	43.08 N	112.30 W
Blackfoot ≃, Mt., U.S.	202	46.52 N	113.53 W
Blackfoot, North Fork ≃	202	46.59 N	113.07 W
Blackfoot Indian Reserve ✦[4]	182	50.45 N	113.00 W
Blackfoot Reservoir ◎[1]	202	42.55 N	111.35 W
Blackford	46	56.15 N	3.46 W
Blackford □[6]	216	40.27 N	85.22 W
Black Forest → Schwarzwald ⋏	58	48.00 N	8.15 E
Blackhall Colliery	44	54.44 N	1.14 W
Blackhall Mountain ∧	200	41.02 N	106.41 W
Black Hameldon ∧[2]	262	53.44 N	2.08 W
Black Hawk	184	48.48 N	93.59 W
Black Hawk Creek ≃	190	42.30 N	92.21 W
Black Head ≻, Ire.	48	53.08 N	9.17 W
Black Head ≻, Eng., U.K.	42	50.01 N	5.06 W
Blackhead Bay C	186	48.34 N	53.15 W
Blackheath, Austl.	170	33.38 S	150.17 E
Blackheath, S. Afr.	273d	26.08 S	27.58 E
Blackheath, Eng., U.K.	260	51.12 N	0.31 W
Black Hill ∧[2], Eng., U.K.	262	53.20 N	2.01 W
Black Hill ∧[2], Eng., U.K.	262	53.33 N	1.53 W
Black Hills ⋏	198	44.00 N	104.00 W
Black Hills ⋏[2]	282	37.50 N	121.52 W
Blackhope Scar ∧	46	55.44 N	3.05 W
Black Horse, Oh., U.S.	214	41.09 N	81.18 W
Black Horse, Pa., U.S.	285	39.55 N	75.25 W
Black Horse, Pa., U.S.	285	40.06 N	75.19 W
Black Horse Creek ≃	285	40.05 N	75.43 W
Black Island I	184	51.10 N	96.30 W
Black Isle ≻[1]	46	57.35 N	4.15 W
Black Jack	219	38.47 N	90.16 W
Black Jack Mountain ∧	228	33.23 N	118.24 W
Black-Lake	206	46.03 N	71.21 W
Black Lake ◎, On., Can.	212	44.46 N	76.18 W
Black Lake ◎, Sk., Can.	176	59.10 N	105.20 W
Black Lake ◎, Mi., U.S.	190	45.28 N	84.15 W
Black Lake ◎, N.Y., U.S.	212	44.31 N	75.35 W
Black Lake ◎, Wa., U.S.	224	47.00 N	122.58 W
Black Lake Bayou ≃	194	32.01 N	93.09 W
Blacklegs Creek ≃	214	40.30 N	79.27 W
Blackley ✦[8]	262	53.31 N	2.13 W
Black Lick	214	40.28 N	79.11 W
Blacklick Creek ≃	214	40.28 N	79.13 W
Blacklick Creek, North Branch ≃	214	40.29 N	78.55 W
Blacklick Estates	218	39.54 N	83.22 W
Blacklog Mountain ∧	214	40.20 N	77.45 W
Blacklunans	46	56.44 N	3.22 W
Black Mesa ∧, U.S.	196	37.05 N	103.10 W
Black Mesa ∧, Az., U.S.	200	36.35 N	110.20 W
Blackmoor ⋏[1]	42	50.24 N	4.46 W
Blackmoorfoot Reservoir ◎[1]	262	53.37 N	1.51 W
Blackmoor Vale V	42	50.56 N	2.25 W
Blackmore	260	51.41 N	0.19 E
Blackmore, Mount ∧	202	45.27 N	111.01 W
Black Moshannon State Park ♦	214	40.54 N	78.03 W
Black Mountain	192	35.37 N	82.19 W
Black Mountain ∧, D.Y.	124	27.17 N	90.23 E
Black Mountain ∧, Wales, U.K.	42	51.52 N	3.46 W
Black Mountain ∧, U.S.	192	36.54 N	82.54 W
Black Mountain ∧, Az., U.S.	200	32.46 N	110.57 W
Black Mountain ∧, Ca., U.S.	226	35.24 N	120.21 W
Black Mountain ∧, Ca., U.S.	228	35.08 N	117.14 W
Black Mountain ∧, Ca., U.S.	282	37.19 N	122.09 W
Black Mountain ∧, Id., U.S.	202	46.53 N	115.33 W
Black Mountain ∧, Mt., U.S.	202	46.44 N	112.31 W
Black Mountain ∧, Or., U.S.	202	45.13 N	119.17 W
Black Mountain ∧, Wy., U.S.	202	44.45 N	107.22 W
Black Mountain ∧[2], Austl.	166	21.08 S	139.41 E
Black Mountain ∧[2], Ca., U.S.	228	32.59 N	117.07 W
Black Mountain ∧[2], Tx., U.S.	222	31.09 N	97.44 W
Black Mountains ⋏, Wales, U.K.	42	51.57 N	3.08 W
Black Mountains ⋏, Az., U.S.	200	35.30 N	114.30 W
Black Nossob ≃	156	23.05 S	18.45 E
Black Oak	216	41.33 N	87.23 W
Black Peak ∧	200	34.08 N	114.13 W
Black Pine Peak ∧	202	42.08 N	113.08 W
Black Pipe Creek ≃	198	43.47 N	101.14 W
Black Point	226	38.07 N	122.31 W
Black Point ≻, Austl.	168b	34.37 S	137.54 E
Black Point ≻, Austl.	170	34.47 S	150.50 E
Black Point ≻, Ak., U.S.	180	57.00 N	153.18 W
Blackpool	44	53.50 N	3.03 W
Blackpool □[8]	262	53.47 N	3.02 W
Blackpool (Squire's Gate) Airport ⊠	262	53.47 N	3.02 W
Blackpool Football Ground ♦	262	53.49 N	3.03 W
Blackpool Tower ❦	262	53.49 N	3.03 W
Black Range ⋏	200	33.20 N	107.50 W
Black River, Jam.	241q	18.01 N	77.51 W
Black River, N.Y., U.S.	212	44.00 N	75.47 W
Black River Bay C, Jam.	241q	18.00 N	77.51 W
Black River Bay C, N.Y., U.S.	212	43.58 N	76.07 W
Black River Falls	190	44.17 N	90.51 W
Black Rock, Austl.	274b	37.59 S	145.01 E
Black Rock, Ar., U.S.	194	36.06 N	91.05 W
Black Rock, Ma., U.S.	283	42.14 N	70.49 W
Black Rock I[2]	48	54.05 N	10.22 W
Black Rock II[1]	244	53.39 S	41.48 W
Black Rock Desert ✦[2]	204	41.10 N	119.00 W
Blackrod	262	53.35 N	2.35 W
Blacksburg, S.C., U.S.	192	35.07 N	81.30 W
Blacksburg, Va., U.S.	192	37.13 N	80.24 W
Blacks Creek ≃	285	40.08 N	74.43 W
Black Sea ⫪[2]	22	43.00 N	35.00 E
Blacks Fork ≃	200	41.24 N	109.38 W
Blacks Harbour	186	45.03 N	66.47 W
Blackshear	192	31.18 N	82.14 W
Blackshear, Lake ◎[1]	192	31.56 N	83.56 W
Blacksod Bay C	48	54.08 N	10.00 W
Black Springs, Austl.	170	33.52 S	149.42 E
Black Springs, Austl.	274b	37.46 S	145.19 E
Black Springs Hill ∧[2]	274b	37.46 S	145.19 E
Black Star Canyon V	280	33.47 N	117.39 W
Blackstone, Ma., U.S.	207	42.01 N	71.32 W
Blackstone, Va., U.S.	192	37.04 N	77.59 W
Blackstone ≃, Ab., Can.	182	52.50 N	116.07 W
Blackstone ≃, Yk., Can.	180	65.51 N	137.12 W
Blackstone Lake ◎	212	45.14 N	79.53 W
Black Sugarloaf Mountain ∧	166	31.20 S	151.33 E
Black Thunder Creek ≃	198	43.33 N	104.41 W
Blacktown	170	33.46 S	150.55 E
Blackville	192	33.21 N	81.16 W
Black Volta (Volta Noire) ≃	150	8.41 N	1.33 W
Blackwall Tunnel ✦[5]	260	51.30 N	0.01 E
Blackwalnut Point ≻	208	38.40 N	76.20 W
Black Warrior ≃	194	32.32 N	87.51 W
Blackwatch Hills	210	43.05 N	77.27 W
Blackwater, Austl.	166	23.35 S	148.53 E
Blackwater, Ire.	48	52.26 N	6.21 W
Blackwater ≃, Europe	44	54.31 N	6.34 W
Blackwater ≃, Ire.	48	51.51 N	7.50 W
Blackwater ≃, Ire.	48	53.39 N	6.43 W
Blackwater ≃, Eng., U.K.	260	51.45 N	1.00 E
Blackwater ≃, U.S.	194	30.36 N	87.02 W
Blackwater ≃, Md., U.S.	208	38.21 N	76.01 W
Blackwater ≃, Mo., U.S.	194	38.56 N	92.51 W
Blackwater ≃, Va., U.S.	208	36.33 N	76.55 W
Blackwater Creek ≃, Austl.	166	25.56 S	144.20 E
Black Water Creek ≃, Fl., U.S.	220	28.51 N	81.24 W
Blackwater Draw V	196	33.35 N	101.50 W
Blackwaterfoot	46	55.30 N	5.19 W
Blackwater Lake ◎	180	64.00 N	123.05 W
Blackwater Reservoir ◎[1]	46	56.41 N	4.46 W
Blackwater Sound ⊔	220	25.10 N	80.25 W
Blackwell, Ok., U.S.	196	36.48 N	97.16 W
Blackwell, Tx., U.S.	196	32.05 N	100.19 W
Blackwood, Austl.	168b	35.02 S	138.37 E
Blackwood, Austl.	169	37.29 S	144.19 E
Blackwood, N.J., U.S.	285	39.48 N	75.03 W
Blackwood ≃	162	34.19 S	115.11 E
Blackwood, Cape ≻	164	7.50 S	144.30 E
Blackwood Terrace	285	39.48 N	75.05 W
Bladel	52	51.23 N	5.13 E
Bladenboro	192	34.32 N	78.47 W
Bladensburg, Md., U.S.	284c	38.56 N	76.56 W
Bladensburg, Oh., U.S.	214	40.17 N	82.17 W
Blades	208	38.38 N	75.36 W
Bladgrond	158	28.52 S	19.57 E
Bladnoch ≃	44	54.51 N	4.25 W
Bladworth	184	51.18 N	106.09 W
Blaenau Ffestiniog	42	52.59 N	3.56 W
Blaenavon	42	51.48 N	3.05 W
Bláfell ∧	24a	64.32 N	19.53 W
Blagaj	36	43.15 N	17.50 E
Blagdon	42	51.20 N	2.43 W
Blagodarnoje	86	47.03 N	82.10 E
Blagodarnyj	72	45.06 N	43.27 E
Blagodatnoje, S.S.S.R.	78	51.32 N	34.54 E
Blagodatnoje, S.S.S.R.	83	47.42 N	37.25 E
Blagodatnoje, S.S.S.R.	83	47.53 N	38.29 E
Blagodatnoje, S.S.S.R.	86	51.18 N	72.49 E
Blagodatovka	80	52.14 N	50.27 E
Blagoevgrad	38	42.01 N	23.06 E
Blagoveščenka, S.S.S.R.	80	51.19 N	44.03 E
Blagoveščenka, S.S.S.R.	86	52.50 N	79.52 E
Blagoveščenka, S.S.S.R.	86	54.22 N	66.58 E
Blagoveščensk, S.S.S.R.	86	55.01 N	55.59 E
Blagoveščensk, S.S.S.R.	89	50.17 N	127.32 E
Blagoveščenskoje, S.S.S.R.	85	43.18 N	74.12 E
Blagoveščenskoje, S.S.S.R.	86	58.08 N	62.58 E
Blåhø ∧	26	62.45 N	9.19 E
Blåhøj	41	55.51 N	9.01 E
Blaichach	58	47.34 N	10.15 E
Blain, Fr.	32	47.29 N	1.46 W
Blain, Pa., U.S.	208	40.20 N	77.31 W
Blaina	42	51.46 N	3.10 W
Blain City	214	40.45 N	78.34 W
Blaine, Mn., U.S.	190	45.09 N	93.14 W
Blaine, Wa., U.S.	224	48.59 N	122.44 W
Blaine Creek ≃	188	38.11 N	82.37 W
Blaine Hill	279b	40.16 N	79.53 W
Blaine Lake	184	52.50 N	106.54 W
Blaineys	224	48.53 N	123.47 W
Blainville	206	45.40 N	73.52 W
Blainville-sur-l'Eau	58	48.33 N	6.24 E
Blair, On., Can.	212	43.23 N	80.23 W
Blair, Ne., U.S.	198	41.32 N	96.07 W
Blair, Ok., U.S.	196	34.46 N	99.20 W
Blair, Wi., U.S.	190	44.18 N	91.14 W
Blair □[6]	214	40.30 N	78.25 W
Blair Athol	166	22.42 S	147.33 E
Blair Atholl	46	56.46 N	3.51 W
Blairgowrie	46	56.36 N	3.21 W
Blairs Mills	214	40.17 N	77.43 W
Blairstown, Ia., U.S.	190	41.54 N	92.05 W
Blairstown, N.J., U.S.	210	40.59 N	74.57 W
Blairsville, Ga., U.S.	192	34.52 N	83.57 W
Blairsville, Pa., U.S.	214	40.25 N	79.15 W
Blaise ≃, Fr.	50	48.46 N	1.25 E
Blaise ≃, Fr.	58	48.38 N	4.43 E
Blaisy-Bas	58	47.22 N	4.44 E
Blaj	38	46.11 N	23.55 E
Blajkfjället ∧	26	64.33 N	16.12 E
Blakehurst	274a	33.59 S	151.07 E
Blakeley Canal ⌶	226	36.09 N	119.48 W
Blakely, Ga., U.S.	192	31.22 N	84.56 W
Blakely, Pa., U.S.	210	41.28 N	75.35 W
Blakely Island I	224	48.33 N	122.50 W
Blakeney, Eng., U.K.	42	52.58 N	1.00 E
Blakeney, Eng., U.K.	42	51.46 N	2.29 W
Blake Plateau ✢[4]	16	31.00 N	79.00 W
Blake Point ≻	190	48.12 N	88.25 W
Blake Ridge ✢[3]	16	29.00 N	73.30 W
Blakes	208	37.30 N	76.22 W
Blakesburg	190	40.57 N	92.38 W
Blakeslee, Oh., U.S.	216	41.31 N	84.44 W
Blakeslee, Pa., U.S.	210	41.06 N	75.36 W
Blalock Island I	202	45.53 N	119.41 W
Blâmont, Fr.	58	48.35 N	6.51 E
Blamont, Fr.	58	47.23 N	6.51 E
Blanc, Cap → Nouâdhibou, Râs ≻	148	20.46 N	17.03 W
Blanc, Cap ≻	36	37.20 N	9.51 E
Blanc, Mont ∧, P.Q., Can.	186	48.47 N	66.52 W
Blanc, Mont (Monte Bianco) ∧, Europe	62	45.50 N	6.52 E
Blanca	200	37.27 N	105.31 W
Blanca, Bahía C	252	38.55 S	62.10 W
Blanca, Isla I	248	9.06 S	78.38 W
Blanca, Laguna ◎	254	52.25 S	71.10 W
Blanca, Punta ≻	258	34.57 S	57.40 W
Blanca, Sierra ∧	200	31.15 N	105.26 W
Blanca Grande, Laguna ◎	252	38.26 S	63.55 W
Blanca Lake ◎	224	47.53 N	121.21 W
Blanca Peak ∧	200	37.35 N	105.29 W
Blanc du Cheilon, Mont ∧	58	45.59 N	7.25 E
Blanchard, Ok., U.S.	196	35.08 N	97.39 W
Blanchard, Pa., U.S.	210	41.04 N	77.36 W
Blanchard, Wa., U.S.	224	48.35 N	122.24 W
Blanchard ≃	216	41.02 N	84.18 W
Blanchardville	190	42.48 N	89.51 W
Blanche ≃, On., Can.	190	47.34 N	79.32 W
Blanche ≃, P.Q., Can.	206	46.40 N	72.08 W
Blanche, Cape ≻	162	33.01 S	134.09 E
Blanche, Dent ∧	58	46.03 N	7.36 E
Blanche, Lake ◎, Austl.	162	22.25 S	123.17 E
Blanche, Lake ◎, Austl.	166	29.15 S	139.39 E
Blanche, Mer → Beloje more ⫪[2]	24	65.30 N	38.00 E
Blanche Channel ⊔	175e	8.30 S	157.30 E
Blancheface	261	48.32 N	2.06 E
Blanchester	218	39.17 N	83.59 W
Blanchisseuse	241r	10.47 N	61.18 W
Blanco, S. Afr.	158	33.57 S	22.24 E
Blanco, Tx., U.S.	196	30.06 N	98.25 W
Blanco ≃, Arg.	252	30.12 S	69.05 W
Blanco ≃, Arg.	254	47.22 S	71.12 W
Blanco ≃, Bol.	248	13.09 S	63.46 W
Blanco ≃, Ec.	246	0.28 N	79.25 W
Blanco ≃, Perú	248	5.27 S	73.47 W
Blanco ≃, Tx., U.S.	196	29.51 N	97.55 W
Blanco, Cabo → Nouâdhibou, Râs ≻	148	20.46 N	17.03 W
Blanco, Cabo ≻	236	9.34 N	85.07 W
Blanco, Cañon V	200	35.20 N	105.05 W
Blanco, Cape ≻	202	42.50 N	124.34 W
Blanco, Lago ◎	254	54.03 S	69.00 W
Blanco, Mar → Beloje more ⫪[2]	24	65.30 N	38.00 E
Blanco, Monte → Blanc, Mont ∧	62	45.50 N	6.52 E
Blanco, Rio ≃	200	37.07 N	107.03 W
Blanco Creek ≃	196	28.19 N	97.19 W
Blanc-Sablon	186	51.25 N	57.07 W
Bland, Mo., U.S.	219	38.18 N	91.37 W
Bland, Va., U.S.	192	37.06 N	81.06 W
Blanda ≃	24a	65.39 N	20.18 W
Blandburg	214	40.41 N	78.24 W
Blandford	207	42.10 N	72.55 W
Blandford Forum	42	50.52 N	2.11 W
Blanding	200	37.37 N	109.28 W
Blandinsville	190	40.33 N	90.51 W
Blandon	208	40.26 N	75.53 W
Blandy	261	48.34 N	2.47 E
Blanes	34	41.41 N	2.48 E
Blangkejeren	114	3.59 N	97.20 E
Blangpidie	114	3.45 N	96.51 E
Blangy-le-Château	50	49.14 N	0.17 E
Blangy-sur-Bresle	50	49.56 N	1.38 E
Blanice ≃	61	49.05 N	14.03 E
Blankenberg	56	50.45 N	7.22 E
Blankenberge	50	51.19 N	3.08 E
Blankenburg	54	51.48 N	10.58 E
Blankenburg ✦[8]	264a	52.35 N	13.28 E
Blankenese ✦[8]	52	53.33 N	9.48 E
Blankenfelde	54	52.20 N	13.23 E
Blankenfelde ✦[8]	264a	52.37 N	13.23 E
Blankenhain	54	50.51 N	11.21 E
Blankenheim, B.R.D.	56	50.26 N	6.39 E
Blankenheim, D.D.R.	54	51.31 N	11.25 E
Blankensee	54	52.14 N	13.08 E
Blankenstein	263	51.24 N	7.14 E
Blanket	196	31.49 N	98.47 W
Blanquilla, Isla I	246	11.51 N	64.37 W
Blansko	30	49.22 N	16.39 E
Blanský Les ✦[3]	61	48.52 N	14.16 E
Blantyre	154	15.47 S	35.00 E
Blanzac	62	45.07 N	3.51 E
Blanzy	58	46.42 N	4.23 E
Blaricum	52	52.16 N	5.15 E
Blarney	48	51.56 N	8.34 W
Blarney Castle ⊥	48	51.56 N	8.34 W
Blasdell	210	42.47 N	78.49 W
Blasheim	52	52.18 N	8.34 E
Błaszki	30	51.39 N	18.27 E
Blatná	60	49.26 N	13.53 E
Blatnica	38	43.42 N	28.31 E
Blatten	58	46.25 N	7.50 E
Blatzheim	56	50.51 N	6.38 E
Blau ≃	58	48.23 N	9.49 E
Blaubeuren	58	48.24 N	9.47 E
Blauen ∧	58	47.47 N	7.42 E
Blauer Nil → Blue Nile ≃	140	15.38 N	32.31 E
Blaufelden	56	49.18 N	9.58 E
Blaustein	58	48.25 N	9.53 E
Blauvelt	276	41.03 N	73.57 W
Blauvelt State Park ♦	276	41.04 N	73.56 W
Blåvands Huk ≻	26	55.33 N	8.05 E
Blawenburg	276	40.24 N	74.42 W
Blawnox	279b	40.29 N	79.51 W
Blaxland	170	33.45 S	150.36 E
Blaxland Creek ≃	274a	33.48 S	150.46 E
Blaydon	44	54.58 N	1.42 W
Blaye-et-Sainte-Luce	32	45.08 N	0.39 W
Blayney	166	33.32 S	149.15 E
Blaze, Point ≻	164	12.56 S	130.12 E
Błażowa	30	49.54 N	22.05 E
Bleaker Island I	254	52.13 S	58.53 W
Bleaklow Head ∧	262	53.28 N	1.50 W
Blean	42	51.19 N	1.02 E
Bleckede	54	53.17 N	10.44 E
Bled	36	46.22 N	14.06 E
Bledsoe	196	33.38 N	103.01 W
Bleecker	210	43.07 N	74.22 W
Blefjell ∧	26	59.48 N	9.10 E
Blega	115a	7.08 S	113.03 E
Bleibach	58	48.07 N	8.01 E
Bleiberg ob Villach	64	46.37 N	13.41 E
Bleiburg	61	46.35 N	14.48 E
Bleicherode	54	51.26 N	10.34 E
Blekendorf	54	54.16 N	10.38 E
Blekinge □[9]	26	56.20 N	15.05 E
Blekinge Län □[6]	26	56.20 N	15.20 E
Blendecques	50	50.43 N	2.16 E
Bléneau	50	47.42 N	2.57 E
Blenheim, Austl.	171a	27.39 S	152.20 E
Blenheim, On., Can.	214	42.20 N	82.00 W
Blenheim, N.Z.	172	41.31 S	173.57 E
Blenheim, N.J., U.S.	285	39.48 N	75.05 W
Blenheim Palace ❦	42	51.47 N	1.21 W
Blenio, Val V	58	46.27 N	8.58 E
Blénod-lès-Pont-à-Mousson	56	48.53 N	6.03 E
Blénod-lès-Toul	58	48.36 N	5.50 E
Bléone ≃	62	44.03 N	6.00 E
Blérancourt	50	49.31 N	3.09 E
Bléré	50	47.20 N	1.00 E
Blerick	52	51.23 N	6.10 E
Blériot-Plage	50	50.57 N	1.50 E
Blesbokspruit ≃	273d	26.14 S	28.29 E
Blessing	222	28.52 N	96.13 W
Blessington	48	53.10 N	6.32 W
Bletchingley	260	51.14 N	0.06 W
Bletchley	42	52.00 N	0.46 W
Bletterans	58	46.45 N	5.27 E
Bleu → Chang ≃	90	31.48 N	121.10 E
Bleue, Mer ≋	212	45.24 N	75.30 W
Bleury	261	48.31 N	1.45 E
Bleus, Monts ⋏	154	1.30 N	30.30 E
Blevio	62	45.50 N	9.05 E
Blewett Falls Lake ◎[1]	192	35.03 N	79.54 W
Blexen	52	53.32 N	8.32 E
Blidö I	40	59.37 N	18.54 E
Blidworth	44	53.06 N	1.07 W
Bliedinghausen ✦[8]	263	51.09 N	7.12 E
Bliersheim	263	51.23 N	6.43 E
Blies ≃	56	49.07 N	7.04 E
Blieskastel	56	49.14 N	7.16 E
Bligh Sound ⊔	172	44.50 S	167.32 E
Bligh Water ⊔	175g	17.00 S	178.00 E
Bligny	50	49.11 N	3.52 E
Bligny-sur-Ouche	58	47.06 N	4.40 E
Blik, Mount ∧	116	6.58 N	124.15 E
Blind ≃	276	40.57 N	73.42 W
Blind Creek ≃	274b	37.54 S	145.12 E
Blindley Heath	260	51.12 N	0.04 W
Blind River	190	46.10 N	82.58 W
Blinman	166	31.06 S	138.41 E
Blinnenhorn ∧	58	46.26 N	8.19 E
Blinovskij	80	49.23 N	42.19 E
Bliss	210	42.34 N	78.15 W
Blissfield, Mi., U.S.	216	41.49 N	83.51 W
Blissfield, Oh., U.S.	214	40.24 N	81.58 W
Blitar	115a	8.06 S	112.09 E
Blithe ≃	42	52.45 N	1.50 W
Blithfield Reservoir ◎[1]	42	52.48 N	1.53 W
Blitta	150	8.19 N	0.59 E
Blizn'uki	78	48.52 N	36.33 E
Blocher	218	38.43 N	85.39 W
Block Dam ✦[6]	212	45.12 N	76.54 W
Block Island	207	41.10 N	71.33 W
Block Island I	207	41.11 N	71.35 W
Block Island Sound ⊔	207	41.10 N	71.45 W
Blockley	42	52.01 N	1.45 W
Blockton	198	40.36 N	94.28 W
Blodgett Mills	210	42.34 N	76.08 W
Bloed ≃	158	28.15 S	30.30 E
Bloedel	182	50.07 N	125.23 W
Bloedrivier, S. Afr.	158	28.06 S	30.33 E
Bloedrivier, S. Afr.	158	27.53 S	30.30 E
Bloekomspruit	158	26.45 S	28.21 E
Bloemendaal	52	52.24 N	4.37 E
Bloemfontein	158	29.12 S	26.07 E
Bloemhof	158	27.38 S	25.32 E
Bloemhofdam ◎[1]	158	27.40 S	25.40 E
Blois	50	47.35 N	1.20 E
Blokhus	26	57.15 N	9.35 E
Blokzijl	52	52.44 N	5.57 E
Blombacher Bach ✦[8]	263	51.15 N	7.14 E
Blombacka	40	59.37 N	13.47 E
Blomberg	52	51.56 N	9.05 E
Blomstermåla	26	56.59 N	16.20 E
Blonay	58	46.28 N	6.54 E
Blönduós	24a	65.39 N	20.15 W
Blongas	115b	8.53 S	116.02 E
Blonville-sur-Mer	50	49.19 N	0.02 E
Blood Indian Creek ≃	184	50.55 N	111.03 W
Blood Indian Reserve ✦[4]	182	49.30 N	113.10 W
Blood Mountain ∧	192	34.44 N	83.56 W
Blood River ⊥	158	28.20 S	30.35 E
Bloods Creek	162	26.28 S	135.17 E
Bloodsworth Island I	208	38.10 N	76.03 W
Bloodvein ≃	184	51.45 N	96.44 W
Bloody Foreland ≻	48	55.09 N	8.17 W
Bloomdale	216	41.10 N	83.33 W
Bloomer	190	45.06 N	91.29 W
Bloomfield, On., Can.	212	43.59 N	77.14 W
Bloomfield, Ct., U.S.	207	41.49 N	72.43 W
Bloomfield, In., U.S.	194	39.01 N	86.56 W
Bloomfield, Ia., U.S.	190	40.45 N	92.24 W
Bloomfield, Ky., U.S.	194	37.54 N	85.19 W
Bloomfield, Mo., U.S.	194	36.53 N	89.55 W
Bloomfield, Ne., U.S.	198	42.35 N	97.38 W
Bloomfield, N.J., U.S.	210	40.48 N	74.11 W
Bloomfield, N.M., U.S.	200	36.42 N	107.59 W
Bloomfield, Oh., U.S.	214	40.03 N	81.44 W
Bloomfield ✦[8]	279b	40.27 N	79.56 W
Bloomfield Glens	281	42.33 N	83.20 W
Bloomfield Highlands	281	42.36 N	83.16 W
Bloomfield Hills	216	42.35 N	83.14 W
Bloomfield Village	216	42.33 N	83.15 W
Bloomingburg, N.Y., U.S.	210	41.33 N	74.26 W
Bloomingburg, Oh., U.S.	218	39.36 N	83.23 W
Bloomingdale, Il., U.S.	216	41.57 N	88.04 W
Bloomingdale, Mi., U.S.	216	42.22 N	85.57 W
Bloomingdale, N.J., U.S.	210	41.00 N	74.19 W
Bloomingdale, Oh., U.S.	214	40.21 N	80.49 W
Blooming Glen	208	40.22 N	75.15 W
Blooming Grove, In., U.S.	218	39.30 N	85.04 W
Blooming Grove, N.Y., U.S.	210	41.25 N	74.11 W
Blooming Grove, Pa., U.S.	210	41.21 N	75.09 W
Blooming Grove, Tx., U.S.	222	32.06 N	96.43 W
Blooming Prairie	190	43.52 N	93.03 W
Bloomington, Ca., U.S.	228	34.04 N	117.23 W
Bloomington, Il., U.S.	216	40.29 N	88.59 W
Bloomington, In., U.S.	218	39.09 N	86.31 W
Bloomington, Mn., U.S.	190	44.50 N	93.17 W
Bloomington, N.Y., U.S.	210	41.53 N	74.03 W
Bloomington, Tx., U.S.	196	28.38 N	96.53 W
Bloomington, Wi., U.S.	190	42.53 N	90.55 W
Bloomington, Lake ◎[1]	216	40.37 N	88.55 W
Blooming Valley	214	41.40 N	80.03 W
Bloomsburg	210	41.00 N	76.27 W
Bloomsbury, Austl.	166	20.43 S	148.35 E
Bloomsbury, N.J., U.S.	210	40.39 N	75.05 W
Bloomsdale Gardens	285	40.07 N	74.52 W
Bloomville, N.Y., U.S.	210	42.20 N	74.48 W
Bloomville, Oh., U.S.	214	41.03 N	83.00 W
Blora	115a	6.57 S	111.25 E
Bloserville	208	40.12 N	77.24 W
Blossburg	210	41.40 N	77.03 W
Blossom	196	33.39 N	95.23 W
Blossom Hill	208	40.05 N	76.19 W
Blötberget	40	60.07 N	15.04 E
Blotzheim	58	47.36 N	7.29 E
Blouberg	156	23.08 S	28.56 E
Blouberg ∧	156	23.01 S	28.59 E
Bloubergstrand	158	33.47 S	18.28 E
Blouin, Lac ◎	190	48.10 N	77.44 W
Bloumet	148	23.27 N	6.06 E
Blountstown	192	30.26 N	85.02 W
Blountsville	194	34.04 N	86.35 W
Blountville	192	36.31 N	82.19 W
Blovice	60	49.35 N	13.33 E
Blovstrød	41	55.52 N	12.24 E
Blowering Reservoir ◎[1]	171b	35.30 S	148.15 E
Blowing Rock	192	36.08 N	81.40 W
Bloxham	42	52.02 N	1.22 W
Bloxom	208	37.49 N	75.37 W
Blšanka ≃	54	50.10 N	13.34 E
Blšany	54	50.10 N	13.29 E
Bludenz	58	47.09 N	9.49 E
Bludnaja ≃	88	51.24 N	110.39 E
Blue ≃, Az., U.S.	200	33.13 N	109.11 W
Blue ≃, Co., U.S.	200	40.03 N	106.24 W
Blue ≃, In., U.S.	216	41.07 N	85.30 W
Blue ≃, In., U.S.	218	38.11 N	86.19 W
Blue ≃, Ok., U.S.	196	33.53 N	95.56 W
Blue, Middle Fork ≃	218	38.33 N	86.07 W
Blue, South Fork ≃	218	38.26 N	86.11 W
Blue, West Fork ≃	218	38.33 N	86.07 W
Blue Anchor	285	39.41 N	74.52 W
Blue Anchor Brook ≃	285	39.42 N	74.49 W
Blue Ash	218	39.13 N	84.22 W
Blue Ball	218	39.29 N	84.21 W
Blue Bell	208	40.09 N	75.16 W
Bluebell Hill	260	51.20 N	0.30 E
Blue Bonnets, Champ de Course ♦	275a	45.29 N	73.39 W
Blue Brook ≃	276	40.40 N	74.25 W
Blue Buck Knob ∧[2]	194	36.57 N	92.07 W
Bluebush Swamp ≋	162	20.30 S	137.25 E
Blue Creek, Oh., U.S.	218	38.47 N	83.20 W
Blue Creek, Wa., U.S.	182	48.19 N	117.49 W
Blue Creek, Wa., U.S.	202	48.19 N	117.49 W
Blue Creek ≃, Ca., U.S.	226	38.28 N	120.22 W
Blue Creek ≃, Id., U.S.	202	42.02 N	116.08 W
Blue Creek ≃, Ne., U.S.	198	41.19 N	102.10 W
Blue Creek ≃, Oh., U.S.	216	41.07 N	84.26 W
Blue Creek ≃, Ut,. U.S.	200	41.31 N	112.24 W
Blue Cypress Lake ◎	220	27.44 N	80.45 W
Blue Earth	190	43.38 N	94.06 W
Blue Earth ≃	190	44.09 N	94.02 W
Bluefield, Va., U.S.	192	37.15 N	81.16 W
Bluefield, W.V., U.S.	192	37.16 N	81.13 W
Bluefields	236	12.00 N	83.45 W
Bluefields, Bahía de C	236	12.02 N	83.44 W
Bluefields Bay C	241q	18.10 N	78.03 W
Blue Grass Airport ⊠	218	38.02 N	84.36 W
Blue Grotto → Azzurra, Grotta ⫫[5]	68	40.35 N	14.14 E
Blue Hill, Me., U.S.	188	44.24 N	68.35 W
Blue Hill, Ne., U.S.	198	40.19 N	98.26 W
Blue Hill Bay C	188	44.15 N	68.30 W
Blue Hills	207	41.40 N	72.56 W
Blue Hills of Couteau ⋏[2]	186	47.59 N	57.43 W
Blue Hills Reservation ♦	283	42.13 N	71.05 W
Blue Island	216	41.39 N	87.40 W
Blue Jay	228	34.15 N	117.13 W
Bluejoint Lake ◎	202	42.35 N	119.40 W
Blue Knob ∧	214	40.17 N	78.34 W
Blue Knob State Park ♦	214	40.16 N	78.35 W
Blue Lagoon National Park ♦	154	15.30 S	27.25 E
Blue Licks Battlefield State Park ♦	218	38.26 N	84.00 W
Blue Marsh Lake ◎[1]	208	40.25 N	76.05 W
Blue Mesa Reservoir ◎[1]	200	38.27 N	107.10 W
Blue Mosque ❦[1]	273c	30.02 N	31.15 E
Blue Mound, Il., U.S.	219	39.42 N	89.07 W
Blue Mound, Ks., U.S.	198	38.05 N	95.00 W
Blue Mound, Tx., U.S.	222	32.51 N	97.19 W
Blue Mountain, Ms., U.S.	194	34.40 N	89.01 W
Blue Mountain, N.Y., U.S.	210	42.07 N	74.01 W
Blue Mountain ∧, N.B., Can.	186	47.49 N	66.19 W
Blue Mountain ∧, Nf., Can.	186	50.24 N	57.10 W
Blue Mountain ∧, Ar., U.S.	194	34.41 N	94.03 W
Blue Mountain ∧, Mt., U.S.	198	47.16 N	104.10 W
Blue Mountain ∧, N.H., U.S.	188	44.47 N	71.28 W
Blue Mountain ∧, Pa., U.S.	188	40.15 N	77.30 W
Blue Mountain ∧[2], On., Can.	190	48.15 N	80.07 W
Blue Mountain ∧[2], On., Can.	212	44.40 N	77.58 W
Blue Mountain Peak ∧	241q	18.03 N	76.35 W
Blue Mountains ⋏, Austl.	170	33.37 S	150.17 E
Blue Mountains ⋏, Jam.	241q	18.06 N	76.40 W
Blue Mountains ⋏, U.S.	202	45.30 N	118.15 W
Blue Mountains ⋏, Me., U.S.	188	44.50 N	70.35 W

Symbol	English	Deutsch	Español	Français	Português
≃	River	Fluss	Río	Rivière	Rio
⌶	Canal	Kanal	Canal	Canal	Canal
⌊	Waterfall, Rapids	Wasserfall, Stromschnellen	Cascada, Rápidos	Chute d'eau, Rapides	Cascata, Rápidos
⊔	Strait	Meeresstrasse	Estrecho	Détroit	Estreito
C	Bay, Gulf	Bucht, Golf	Bahía, Golfo	Baie, Golfe	Baía, Golfo
◎	Lake, Lakes	See, Seen	Lago, Lagos	Lac, Lacs	Lago, Lagos
≋	Swamp	Sumpf	Pantano	Marais	Pântano
⊼	Ice Features, Glacier	Eis- und Gletscherformen	Accidentes Glaciales	Formes glaciaires	Acidentes glaciares
⫪	Other Hydrographic Features	Andere Hydrographische Objekte	Otros Elementos Hidrográficos	Autres données hydrographiques	Outros acidentes hidrográficos
✢	Submarine Features	Untermeerische Objekte	Accidentes Submarinos	Formes de relief sous-marin	Acidentes submarinos
□	Political Unit	Politische Einheit	Unidad Politica	Entité politique	Unidade política
❦	Cultural Institution	Kulturelle Institution	Institución Cultural	Institution culturelle	Institução cultural
⊥	Historical Site	Historische Stätte	Sitio Histórico	Site historique	Sitio histórico
♦	Recreational Site	Erholungs- und Ferienort	Sitio de Recreo	Centre de loisirs	Area de Lazer
⊠	Airport	Flughafen	Aeropuerto	Aéroport	Aeroporto
■	Military Installation	Militäranlage	Instalación Militar	Installation militaire	Instalação militar
✦	Miscellaneous	Verschiedenes	Misceláneo	Divers	Diversos

Name	Page	Lat.°′	Long.°′
Blue Mountains National Park ♦	**170**	33.40 S	150.25 E
Blue Mud Bay ⊂	**164**	13.26 S	135.56 E
Blue Nile (Al-Baḥr al-Azraq) (Abay) ≃	**140**	15.38 N	32.31 E
Bluenose Lake ⊜	**180**	68.25 N	119.45 W
Blue Point	**276**	40.45 N	73.02 W
Blue Point ›	**276**	40.44 N	73.02 W
Blue Rapids	**198**	39.40 N	96.39 W
Blue Ridge, Ab., Can.	**182**	54.08 N	115.22 W
Blue Ridge, Ga., U.S.	**192**	34.51 N	84.19 W
Blue Ridge, Il., U.S.	**216**	40.17 N	88.29 W
Blue Ridge ⋏	**178**	37.00 N	82.00 W
Blue Ridge Summit	**208**	39.43 N	77.28 W
Blue River	**182**	52.05 N	119.17 W
Blue Rock Springs Park ♦	**282**	38.08 N	122.12 W
Bluesky	**182**	56.04 N	118.14 W
Blue Springs	**198**	40.08 N	96.39 W
Blue Stack Mountains ⋏	**48**	54.45 N	8.05 W
Bluestone ≃	**192**	37.34 N	80.59 W
Bluestone Dam ◆[6]	**192**	37.36 N	80.53 W
Bluestone Lake ⊜[1]	**192**	37.30 N	80.50 W
Bluestone State Park ♦	**192**	37.37 N	80.56 W
Bluewater	**200**	35.15 N	107.59 W
Blue Water Bridge ◆[5]	**214**	43.00 N	82.25 W
Bluff, N.Z.	**172**	46.36 S	168.20 E
Bluff, Ut,. U.S.	**200**	37.17 N	109.33 W
Bluff Cape ›	**110**	18.00 N	94.26 E
Bluff City, Il., U.S.	**219**	38.57 N	89.02 W
Bluff City, Tn., U.S.	**192**	36.28 N	82.15 W
Bluff Cove ⊂	**280**	33.48 N	118.24 W
Bluff Creek ≃, U.S.	**196**	36.58 N	97.26 W
Bluff Creek ≃, Ks., U.S.	**198**	37.02 N	99.29 W
Bluff Dale	**196**	32.21 N	98.01 W
Bluff Head ›	**271d**	22.11 N	114.12 E
Bluff Island I	**271d**	22.19 N	114.21 E
Bluff Knoll ∧	**162**	34.23 S	118.20 E
Bluff Park	**194**	33.24 N	86.51 W
Bluff Point ›	**162**	27.50 S	114.06 E
Bluffs	**219**	39.45 N	90.32 W
Bluff Springs	**219**	39.59 N	90.21 W
Bluffton, In., U.S.	**216**	40.44 N	85.10 W
Bluffton, Oh., U.S.	**216**	40.53 N	83.53 W
Bluffton, S.C., U.S.	**192**	32.14 N	80.51 W
Bluffy Lake ⊜	**184**	50.47 N	92.55 W
Bluford	**219**	38.20 N	88.45 W
Blum	**222**	32.09 N	97.24 W
Blumberg, B.R.D.	**58**	47.50 N	8.31 E
Blumberg, D.D.R.	**54**	52.36 N	13.37 E
Blumenau	**252**	26.56 S	49.03 W
Blumenhof	**184**	50.01 N	107.41 W
Blümlisalp ∧	**58**	46.30 N	7.47 E
Blunt	**198**	44.30 N	99.59 W
Blupblup Island I	**164**	3.30 S	144.37 E
Bly	**202**	42.23 N	121.02 W
Blying Sound ʮ	**180**	59.50 N	149.15 W
Blyth, Austl.	**168b**	33.51 S	138.29 E
Blyth, On., Can.	**190**	43.44 N	81.26 W
Blyth, Eng., U.K.	**44**	55.07 N	1.30 W
Blyth ≃, Austl.	**164**	12.04 S	134.35 E
Blyth ≃, Eng., U.K.	**42**	52.18 N	1.40 E
Blyth ≃, Eng., U.K.	**44**	55.08 N	1.31 W
Blyth Bridge	**46**	55.42 N	3.24 W
Blythe	**204**	33.36 N	114.35 W
Blythe ≃	**42**	52.31 N	1.42 W
Blythedale	**214**	40.15 N	79.48 W
Blytheswood	**214**	42.07 N	82.36 W
Blytheville	**194**	35.55 N	89.55 W
Blytheville Air Force Base ■	**194**	35.57 N	89.57 W
Blyth Range ⋏	**162**	26.50 S	129.00 E
Bnei Braq → Bene Beraq	**132**	32.05 N	34.50 E
Bø, Nor.	**24**	68.37 N	14.33 E
Bø, Nor.	**26**	59.25 N	9.04 E
Bo, S.L.	**150**	7.56 N	11.21 W
Boa	**154**	10.32 S	28.06 E
Boa Barrinha	**256**	23.18 S	47.10 W
Boac	**116**	13.27 N	121.50 E
Boaco	**236**	12.28 N	85.40 W
Boaco □[5]	**236**	12.30 N	85.30 W
Boadilla del Monte	**266a**	40.24 N	3.53 W
Boa Esperança, Bra.	**255**	21.05 S	45.34 W
Boa Esperança, Bra.	**256**	22.48 S	42.34 W
Boa Esperança, Represa ⊜[1]	**250**	6.50 S	44.00 W
Bo'ai	**102**	35.10 N	113.04 E
Boali	**152**	4.48 N	18.07 E
Boalia	**126**	23.35 N	88.57 E
Boalsburg	**214**	40.46 N	77.48 W
Boane	**156**	26.06 S	32.19 E
Boano, Pulau I	**164**	2.56 S	127.56 E
Boa Nova	**255**	14.22 S	40.10 W
Boara Pisani	**64**	45.08 N	11.47 E
Boara Polesine	**64**	45.07 N	11.48 E
Board Camp Mountain ∧	**204**	40.42 N	123.43 W
Boardman	**214**	41.01 N	80.39 W
Boardman ≃	**190**	44.46 N	85.38 W
Boarhills	**46**	56.19 N	2.42 W
Boario Terme	**64**	45.54 N	10.10 E
Boat Basin	**182**	49.29 N	126.25 W
Boat Channel ʮ	**212**	44.10 N	76.31 W
Boath	**46**	57.44 N	4.23 W
Boat Lake ⊜	**212**	44.44 N	81.13 W
Boatman	**166**	27.16 S	146.55 E
Boat of Garten	**46**	57.20 N	3.44 W
Boa Vereda	**256**	22.27 S	46.14 W
Boa Viagem	**250**	5.07 S	39.44 W
Boa Vida	**256**	22.18 S	42.47 W
Boa Vista, Bra.	**246**	2.49 N	60.40 W
Boa Vista, Bra.	**252**	26.17 S	48.50 W
Boa Vista I	**150a**	16.05 N	22.50 W
Boa Vista, Morro ∧[2]	**287a**	22.53 S	43.06 W
Boavita	**246**	6.20 N	72.35 W
Boawai	**115b**	8.46 S	121.10 E
Boayan Island I	**116**	10.34 N	119.09 E
Boaz	**194**	34.12 N	86.09 W
Boba	**115b**	8.57 S	121.04 E
Bobai	**102**	22.12 N	109.52 E
Bobbau	**54**	51.41 N	12.16 E
Bobbili	**122**	18.34 N	83.22 E
Bobbing	**260**	51.21 N	0.43 E
Bobbingworth	**260**	51.44 N	0.13 E
Bobbin Head	**274a**	33.39 S	151.08 E
Bobbio	**62**	44.46 N	9.23 E
Bobbio Pellice	**62**	44.48 N	7.07 E
Bobbys Run ≃	**285**	39.58 N	74.48 W
Bobcaygeon	**212**	44.33 N	78.33 W
Bobenheim-Roxheim	**56**	49.35 N	8.21 E
Bobigny	**50**	48.54 N	2.27 E
Böbingen, B.R.D.	**56**	48.49 N	9.54 E
Bobingen, B.R.D.	**58**	48.16 N	10.50 E
Bobitz	**54**	53.47 N	11.20 E
Bob Lake ⊜	**212**	44.55 N	78.47 W
Böblingen	**56**	48.41 N	9.01 E
Boblo Island Amusement Park ♦	**281**	42.06 N	83.07 W
Bobo Dioulasso	**150**	11.12 N	4.18 W
Boboiob, gora ∧	**85**	40.52 N	70.21 E
Bobolice	**30**	53.57 N	16.36 E
Bobonaza ≃	**246**	2.36 S	76.38 W
Bobonong	**156**	21.58 S	28.17 E
Bobotsari	**115a**	7.18 S	109.22 E
Bobr	**76**	54.20 N	29.16 E
Bóbr ≃, Pol.	**30**	52.04 N	15.04 E
Bobr ≃, S.S.S.R.	**76**	54.03 N	28.51 E
Bobrik ≃	**76**	52.08 N	26.46 E
Bobrikovo	**83**	47.56 N	39.13 E
Bobrinec	**78**	48.03 N	32.09 E
Bobrka	**78**	49.38 N	24.18 E
Bobrov	**78**	51.06 N	40.02 E
Bobrovica	**78**	50.44 N	31.22 E
Bobrujsk	**76**	53.09 N	29.14 E
Bobs Creek ≃	**219**	38.57 N	90.42 W
Bobs Lake ⊜	**212**	44.40 N	76.35 W
Bobtown	**188**	39.45 N	79.58 W
Bobuk	**140**	11.30 N	34.05 E
Bobures	**246**	9.15 N	71.11 W
Boby, Pic ∧	**157b**	22.12 S	46.55 E
Boca ◆[8]	**288**	34.38 S	58.21 W
Bôca, Cachoeira da ⌞	**250**	5.27 S	54.24 W
Boca Brava, Isla I	**236**	8.13 N	82.16 W
Boca Chica	**240m**	17.59 N	66.32 W
Boca Chica Key I	**220**	24.34 N	81.42 W
Bôca da Mata	**250**	9.41 S	36.11 W
Boca del Monte	**236**	8.21 N	82.07 W
Boca del Pozo	**246**	11.00 N	64.23 W
Boca del Río	**234**	19.06 N	96.06 W
Boca del Rosario	**258**	34.26 S	57.17 W
Boca de Quadra ʮ	**182**	55.08 N	130.50 W
Bôca do Acre	**248**	8.45 S	67.23 W
Bôca do Jari	**250**	1.07 S	51.58 W
Bocage, Cap ›	**175f**	21.12 S	165.35 E
Boca Grande	**220**	26.44 N	82.15 W
Boca Grande Channel ʮ	**220**	24.34 N	82.03 W
Boca Grande Key I	**220**	24.32 N	82.00 W
Bocaina ≃	**256**	22.40 S	45.00 W
Bocaina, Serra da ⋏	**256**	22.43 S	44.40 W
Bocaina de Minas	**256**	22.10 S	44.24 W
Bocaiúva	**255**	17.07 S	43.49 W
Bocanda	**150**	7.04 N	4.30 W
Bocanegra	**286d**	12.01 S	77.07 W
Bocaranga	**152**	6.59 N	15.39 E
Boca Raton	**220**	26.21 N	80.05 W
Boca Reservoir ⊜[1]	**226**	39.24 N	120.06 W
Bocas del Toro	**236**	9.20 N	82.15 W
Bocas del Toro □[4]	**236**	8.50 N	82.10 W
Bocas del Toro, Archipiélago de II	**236**	9.20 N	82.10 W
Bocay	**236**	14.19 N	85.10 W
Bocay ≃	**236**	14.20 N	85.10 W
Boccaleone	**66**	44.39 N	11.48 E
Boccea ◆[8]	**267a**	41.58 N	12.19 E
Bocchigliero	**68**	39.25 N	16.45 E
Boccon	**64**	45.19 N	11.39 E
Bocconi	**64**	44.01 N	11.46 E
Bočejkovo	**76**	55.01 N	29.09 E
Bochan	**88**	53.09 N	103.48 E
Bochil	**234**	16.59 N	92.55 W
Böch Möron	**86**	49.40 N	90.20 E
Bochnia	**30**	49.58 N	20.26 E
Bocholt, Bel.	**56**	51.10 N	5.35 E
Bocholt, B.R.D.	**52**	51.50 N	6.36 E
Bocholtz	**56**	50.49 N	6.00 E
Bochov	**54**	50.06 N	13.02 E
Bochum, B.R.D.	**56**	51.28 N	7.13 E
Bochum, B.R.D.	**263**	51.28 N	7.13 E
Bochum, S. Afr.	**156**	23.17 S	29.07 E
Bockel	**52**	53.12 N	9.17 E
Böckel ◆[8]	**263**	51.13 N	7.12 E
Bockenem	**52**	52.00 N	10.07 E
Bockhorn	**52**	53.23 N	8.01 E
Böckstein	**64**	47.05 N	13.07 E
Bockum	**263**	51.20 N	6.44 E
Bockum ◆[8]	**263**	51.21 N	6.38 E
Bockum-Hövel	**52**	51.42 N	7.46 E
Bocognano	**36**	42.05 N	9.03 E
Bocón, Caño ≃	**246**	3.42 N	67.53 W
Boconó	**246**	9.15 N	70.16 W
Bocq ≃	**56**	50.20 N	4.53 E
Boczów	**54**	52.19 N	14.58 E
Boda, Centraf.	**152**	4.19 N	17.28 E
Böda, Sve.	**26**	57.15 N	17.03 E
Boda, Sve.	**26**	61.01 N	15.13 E
Bodafors	**26**	57.30 N	14.42 E
Boda Glasbruk	**26**	56.44 N	15.40 E
Bodāi	**272b**	22.48 N	88.29 E
Bodajbo	**88**	57.51 N	114.10 E
Bodalangi	**152**	3.14 N	22.14 E
Bodalla	**166**	36.05 S	150.03 E
Bodallin	**162**	31.22 S	118.52 E
Bodåsgruvan	**40**	60.25 N	16.26 E
Bodcau Creek ≃	**194**	33.01 N	93.31 W
Boddam, Scot., U.K.	**46**	57.28 N	1.47 W
Boddam, Scot., U.K.	**46**	59.55 N	1.17 W
Boddington	**168a**	32.48 S	116.28 E
Bode	**198**	42.52 N	94.17 W
Bode ≃	**54**	52.01 N	11.12 E
Bodega Bay ⊂	**204**	38.15 N	123.00 W
Bodegraven	**52**	52.05 N	4.45 E
Bodélé ◆[1]	**146**	16.30 N	16.30 E
Bodelschwingh ◆[8]	**263**	51.33 N	7.22 E
Boden → Fleres, It.	**64**	46.58 N	11.21 E
Boden, Sve.	**26**	65.50 N	21.42 E
Bodenburg	**52**	52.01 N	10.01 E
Bodenfelde	**52**	51.38 N	9.33 E
Bodenheim	**56**	49.56 N	8.18 E
Bodenmais	**60**	49.04 N	13.06 E
Bodensee (Lake Constance) ⊜	**58**	47.35 N	9.25 E
Bodenteich	**54**	52.50 N	10.41 E
Bodenwerder	**52**	51.59 N	9.31 E
Bodenwies ∧	**61**	47.45 N	14.34 E
Bodenwöhr	**60**	49.16 N	12.19 E
Boderg, Lough ⊜	**48**	53.52 N	7.58 W
Bode Sadu	**150**	9.00 N	4.47 E
Bodhan	**122**	18.40 N	77.54 E
Bodiam	**42**	51.00 N	0.33 E
Bodināyakkanūr	**122**	10.01 N	77.21 E
Bodine, Mount ∧	**182**	55.37 N	125.49 W
Bodjoki	**152**	2.59 N	22.18 E
Bodjokola	**152**	3.54 N	20.17 E
Bodmin	**42**	50.29 N	4.43 W
Bodmin Moor ◆[3]	**42**	50.33 N	4.33 W
Bodø	**24**	67.17 N	14.23 E
Bodocó	**250**	7.47 S	39.55 W
Bodoquena, Serra da ⋏[1]	**248**	21.00 S	56.50 W
Bodoukpa	**152**	5.43 N	17.36 E
Bodri ≃	**115a**	6.52 S	110.10 E
Bodrog ≃	**38**	48.07 N	21.25 E
Bodrum	**130**	37.02 N	27.26 E
Bodstedt	**54**	54.22 N	12.37 E
Bo-duc (Bu-dop)	**110**	11.58 N	106.48 E
Bodzentyn	**30**	50.56 N	20.57 E
Boè, Piz ∧	**64**	46.31 N	11.48 E
Boëge	**58**	46.13 N	6.25 E
Boekelo	**52**	52.13 N	6.47 E
Boele ◆[8]	**263**	51.24 N	7.28 E
Boémbé	**152**	2.54 S	15.39 E
Boende	**152**	0.13 S	20.52 E
Bœng Lvea	**110**	12.36 N	105.34 E
Boeni	**157a**	12.55 S	45.06 E
Boën-sur-Lignon	**62**	45.44 N	3.59 E
Boeo, Capo ›	**70**	37.48 N	12.25 E
Boerboonfontein	**158**	33.43 S	20.32 E
Boerne	**196**	29.47 N	98.43 W
Boeslunde	**41**	55.18 N	11.17 E
Boesmanland □[5]	**156**	19.30 S	20.00 E
Boesmans ≃, S. Afr.	**158**	28.46 S	30.09 E
Boesmans ≃, S. Afr.	**158**	33.42 S	26.39 E
Boesmansriviermond	**158**	33.42 S	26.39 E
Boetsap	**158**	27.59 S	24.30 E
Boeuf ≃	**194**	31.52 N	91.47 W
Boeuf Creek ≃	**219**	38.36 N	91.09 W
Boffa	**150**	10.10 N	14.02 W
Boffalora	**266b**	45.28 N	8.50 E
Boffzen	**52**	51.45 N	9.23 E
Bofoku	**152**	0.57 S	20.53 E
Bofors	**40**	59.20 N	14.32 E
Bofosso	**150**	8.40 N	9.42 W
Bōfu → Hōfu	**96**	34.03 N	131.34 E
Boga	**154**	1.03 N	29.56 E
Bogachiel ≃	**224**	47.55 N	124.28 W
Bogadjim	**164**	5.25 S	145.45 E
Bogal, Lagh ≃	**154**	0.45 N	40.50 E
Bogale	**110**	16.17 N	95.24 E
Bogalusa	**194**	30.47 N	89.50 W
Bogan ≃	**166**	29.57 S	146.21 E
Bogandé	**150**	12.59 N	0.08 W
Bog and Vly Meadows ≡	**276**	40.56 N	74.19 W
Bogan Gate	**166**	33.07 S	147.48 E
Bogangolo	**152**	5.34 N	18.15 E
Bogantungan	**166**	23.39 S	147.18 E
Bogart, Mount ∧	**182**	50.55 N	115.14 W
Bogastow Brook ≃	**283**	42.12 N	71.22 W
Bogata	**196**	33.28 N	95.13 W
Bogataja Černeščina	**78**	48.59 N	35.35 E
Bogatiščevo-Jepišino	**82**	54.47 N	38.25 E
Bogatoje	**80**	53.04 N	51.24 E
Bogatyje Saby	**80**	56.01 N	50.27 E
Bogatynia	**54**	50.53 N	15.00 E
Bogatyr'	**80**	53.25 N	50.02 E
Bogatyrevo	**80**	50.22 N	48.46 E
Boğazkale	**130**	40.02 N	34.37 E
Boğazköy	**267b**	41.11 N	28.46 E
Boğazköy ≃	**267b**	41.10 N	28.49 E
Boğazlıyan	**130**	39.12 N	35.15 E
Bogbonga	**152**	1.35 N	19.25 E
Bogd	**102**	45.11 N	100.43 E
Bogdanovič	**86**	56.47 N	62.01 E
Bogdanovka, S.S.S.R.	**80**	52.42 N	50.46 E
Bogdanovka, S.S.S.R.	**80**	52.10 N	52.37 E
Bogdanovka, S.S.S.R.	**84**	41.18 N	43.35 E
Bogda Shan ⋏	**90**	43.30 N	89.45 E
Bogdo Ula ∧	**86**	43.50 N	88.20 E
Bogel	**56**	50.11 N	7.48 E
Bogembaj	**86**	52.29 N	72.20 E
Bogen	**60**	48.55 N	12.43 E
Bogense	**41**	55.34 N	10.06 E
Boger City	**192**	35.29 N	81.12 W
Boges	**56**	50.11 N	7.48 E
Bogess Creek ≃	**282**	37.18 N	122.19 W
Boget	**80**	49.40 N	47.59 E
Boggabilla	**166**	28.37 S	150.21 E
Boggabri	**166**	30.42 S	150.02 E
Boggeragh Mountains ⋏	**48**	52.03 N	8.55 W
Boggola, Mount ∧	**162**	23.48 S	117.40 E
Boggs Run ≃	**279b**	40.32 N	80.14 W
Boggstown	**218**	39.34 N	85.55 W
Boggy Creek ≃	**222**	31.07 N	95.46 W
Boggy Peak ∧	**240c**	17.03 N	61.51 W
Bogia	**164**	4.15 S	144.55 E
Bogie Lake ⊜	**281**	42.37 N	83.31 W
Bogilima	**152**	3.34 N	19.16 E
Boğlan	**130**	38.58 N	41.03 E
Bogliasco	**62**	44.23 N	9.04 E
Bognanco Fonti	**58**	46.07 N	8.12 E
Bognes	**24**	68.10 N	16.00 E
Bognor Regis	**42**	50.47 N	0.41 W
Bogny-sur-Meuse	**56**	49.51 N	4.46 E
Bogo, Cam.	**146**	10.44 N	14.36 E
Bogo, Pil.	**116**	11.03 N	124.00 E
Bogø I	**41**	54.56 N	12.04 E
Bogo Bay ⊂	**116**	11.05 N	124.01 E
Bogoduchov	**78**	50.10 N	35.30 E
Bogol Manyo	**144**	4.31 N	41.32 E
Bogol'ubovo, S.S.S.R.	**76**	55.32 N	32.57 E
Bogol'ubovo, S.S.S.R.	**80**	56.13 N	40.31 E
Bogomila	**38**	41.36 N	21.28 E
Bogong, Mount ∧	**166**	36.45 S	147.18 E
Bogong Peaks ⋏	**171b**	35.34 S	148.28 E
Bogor	**115a**	6.35 S	106.47 E
Bogoria, Lake ⊜	**154**	0.15 N	36.06 E
Bogoro	**154**	1.24 N	30.17 E
Bogorodčany	**78**	48.48 N	24.32 E
Bogorodick	**76**	53.46 N	38.08 E
Bogorodickoje	**80**	46.20 N	41.10 E
Bogorodičnoje	**83**	49.01 N	37.30 E
Bogorodsk, S.S.S.R.	**24**	62.16 N	52.28 E
Bogorodsk, S.S.S.R.	**80**	56.06 N	43.31 E
Bogorodskoje, S.S.S.R.	**80**	57.51 N	50.45 E
Bogorodskoje, S.S.S.R.	**80**	46.20 N	43.53 E
Bogorodskoje, S.S.S.R.	**82**	55.02 N	38.29 E
Bogorodskoje, S.S.S.R.	**82**	55.26 N	36.14 E
Bogorodskoje, S.S.S.R.	**89**	52.22 N	140.30 E
Bogorodskoje ◆[8]	**265b**	55.49 N	37.44 E
Bogoso	**150**	5.34 N	2.01 W
Bogosskij Chrebet ≃	**84**	42.15 N	46.05 E
Bogotá, Col.	**246**	4.36 N	74.05 W
Bogota, N.J., U.S.	**276**	40.52 N	74.01 W
Bogotol	**86**	56.12 N	89.33 E
Bogou	**150**	10.39 N	0.11 E
Bogovarovo	**24**	58.59 N	47.01 E
Bogra	**124**	24.51 N	89.22 E
Bograd	**86**	54.13 N	90.51 E
Bogrie Hill ∧[2]	**44**	55.08 N	3.55 W
Bogučany	**88**	58.23 N	97.29 E
Bogučar	**78**	49.57 N	40.33 E
Bogučar ≃	**78**	49.57 N	40.39 E
Bogué	**150**	16.35 N	14.16 W
Bogue Chitto	**194**	31.26 N	90.27 W
Bogue Chitto ≃	**194**	30.35 N	89.49 W
Bogue Chitto Creek ≃	**194**	32.10 N	87.14 W
Bogue Phalia ≃	**194**	33.15 N	90.44 W
Bogues Bay ⊂	**208**	37.52 N	75.29 W
Böğürtlen	**130**	37.10 N	38.04 E
Boguševsk	**76**	54.51 N	30.13 E
Boguslav	**78**	49.33 N	30.53 E
Bogustan	**85**	41.41 N	70.05 E
Bo Hai (Gulf of Chihli) ⊂	**98**	38.30 N	120.00 E
Bohai Haixia ʮ	**98**	38.15 N	121.00 E
Bohain-en-Vermandois	**50**	49.59 N	3.27 E
Bohai Wan ⊂	**98**	38.40 N	118.20 E
Bohan	**56**	49.52 N	4.53 E
Bohannon	**208**	37.24 N	76.22 W
Böheimkirchen	**61**	48.12 N	15.46 E
Bohemia	**210**	40.46 N	73.06 W
Bohemia → Čechy □[9]	**30**	49.50 N	14.00 E
Bohemia ≃	**208**	39.29 N	75.55 W
Bohemia Downs	**162**	18.53 S	126.14 E
Bohemian Forest ⋏	**30**	49.15 N	12.45 E
Bohetai	**104**	42.01 N	123.13 E
Bohicon	**150**	7.12 N	2.04 E
Bohin	**144**	11.44 N	51.15 E
Bohinjska Bistrica	**36**	46.17 N	13.57 E
Böhlen	**54**	51.12 N	12.23 E
Böhlitz-Ehrenberg ◆[8]	**54**	51.21 N	12.17 E
Böhme ≃	**52**	52.46 N	9.28 E
Böhmen → Čechy □[9]	**30**	49.50 N	14.00 E
Böhmenkirch	**56**	48.41 N	9.55 E
Böhmerwald → Bohemian Forest ⋏	**30**	49.15 N	12.45 E
Bohmte	**52**	52.22 N	8.19 E
Bohners Lake	**216**	42.37 N	88.17 W
Böhnsdorf ◆[8]	**264a**	52.24 N	13.33 E
Bohodou	**150**	9.46 N	9.04 W
Bohol	**144**	5.45 N	46.09 E
Bohol □[4]	**116**	9.50 N	124.10 E
Bohol I	**116**	9.50 N	124.10 E
Bohol Strait ʮ	**116**	9.45 N	123.40 E
Bohon	**116**	18.30 N	120.35 E
Bohongou	**150**	12.30 N	0.42 E
Bohorg	**152**	6.23 N	15.37 E
Bohorok	**114**	3.30 N	98.12 E
Bohsdorf	**54**	51.38 N	14.32 E
Bohuslän □[9]	**26**	58.15 N	11.50 E
Bohušovice nad Ohří	**54**	50.29 N	14.07 E
Bohutín	**60**	49.40 N	13.55 E
Boi	**150**	9.34 N	9.27 E
Boi, Ponta do ›	**256**	23.58 S	45.15 W
Boiaçu	**246**	0.27 S	61.46 W
Boiano	**66**	41.29 N	14.29 E
Boiceville	**210**	41.59 N	74.15 W
Boiestown	**186**	46.27 N	66.25 W
Boigu Island I	**164**	9.16 S	142.12 E
Boila	**154**	16.10 S	39.50 E
Boiling Springs, N.C., U.S.	**192**	35.30 N	81.37 W
Boiling Springs, Pa., U.S.	**208**	40.08 N	77.07 W
Boim	**250**	2.49 S	55.10 W
Boinville-en-Mantois	**261**	48.56 N	1.46 E
Boinvilliers	**261**	48.55 N	1.40 E
Boipeba, Ilha de I	**255**	13.39 S	38.55 W
Boiro	**34**	42.39 N	8.54 W
Bois, Lac des ⊜, N.T., Can.	**180**	66.40 N	125.15 W
Bois, Lac des → Woods, Lake of the ⊜, N.A.	**184**	49.15 N	94.45 W
Bois, Rio dos ≃	**255**	18.35 S	50.02 W
Bois Blanc Island I	**190**	45.45 N	84.28 W
Boisbriand	**275a**	45.37 N	73.51 W
Bois Brule ≃	**190**	46.45 N	91.37 W
Boischâtel	**206**	46.54 N	71.08 W
Bois-Colombes	**261**	48.55 N	2.16 E
Boisdale, Loch ⊂	**46**	57.08 N	7.19 W
Bois d'Arc Creek ≃	**196**	33.50 N	95.50 W
Bois-d'Arcy	**261**	48.48 N	2.01 E
Bois-des-Filion	**206**	45.40 N	73.45 W
Bois de Sioux ≃	**198**	46.16 N	96.36 W
Boise	**202**	43.36 N	116.12 W
Boise ≃	**202**	43.49 N	117.01 W
Boise, Middle Fork ≃	**202**	43.42 N	115.38 W
Boise, North Fork ≃	**202**	43.42 N	115.38 W
Boise, South Fork ≃	**202**	43.36 N	115.51 W
Boise City	**196**	36.43 N	102.30 W
Boisemont	**261**	49.01 N	2.00 E
Bois-Guillaume	**50**	49.28 N	1.08 E
Bois-le-Roi	**50**	48.28 N	2.42 E
Boissettes	**261**	48.31 N	2.37 E
Boissevain	**184**	49.14 N	100.03 W
Boissise-la-Bertrand	**261**	48.32 N	2.35 E
Boissy-l'Aillerie	**261**	49.05 N	2.02 E
Boissy-Saint-Léger	**50**	48.45 N	2.31 E
Boissy-sous-Saint-Yon	**261**	48.34 N	2.13 E
Boistfort Peak ∧	**224**	46.29 N	123.12 W
Boitzenburg	**54**	53.15 N	13.37 E
Boizenburg	**54**	53.22 N	10.43 E
Boja	**115a**	7.06 S	110.16 E
Bojadła	**30**	51.57 N	15.50 E
Bojarka	**78**	50.19 N	30.19 E
Bojarkino	**82**	54.57 N	38.31 E
Bojarsk	**88**	56.19 N	106.04 E
Bojayá ≃	**246**	6.35 N	76.54 W
Bojeador, Cape ›	**116**	18.30 N	120.34 E
Bojelebung	**116**	6.31 N	122.11 E
Bojevo	**78**	51.24 N	39.19 E
Boji Plain ≚	**154**	1.30 N	39.45 E
Bojizhang	**98**	41.49 N	117.46 E
Bojnūrd	**128**	37.28 N	57.19 E
Bojonegoro	**115a**	7.09 S	111.52 E
Boju	**150**	7.25 N	7.52 E
Boju Ega	**150**	7.24 N	8.04 E
B'ojuk-Kirs, gora ∧	**84**	39.41 N	46.44 E
Bojuru	**252**	31.38 S	51.26 W
Bokad	**272c**	18.53 N	72.58 E
Bokada	**152**	4.08 N	19.23 E
Bokal	**168a**	33.29 S	116.54 E
Bokala, Zaïre	**152**	3.07 S	17.02 E
Bokala, Zaïre	**152**	2.03 N	18.59 E
Bokalike	**120**	36.47 N	91.41 E
Bokani	**150**	9.26 N	5.13 E
Bokāro	**124**	23.51 N	86.02 E
Bokatola	**152**	0.38 S	18.46 E
Bokchito	**196**	34.01 N	96.08 W
Boké	**150**	10.56 N	14.18 W
Bokeelia	**220**	26.42 N	82.09 W
Bokel	**52**	53.23 N	8.46 E
Bokela	**152**	1.08 S	21.56 E
Bokes Creek ≃	**188**	40.19 N	83.10 W
Bokfontein	**158**	32.48 S	19.16 E
Bokhara	**158**	27.57 S	20.30 E
Bokhara ≃	**166**	29.55 S	146.42 E
Boki	**146**	8.48 N	13.32 E
Bokino	**80**	52.38 N	41.26 E
Bokkol ∧	**154**	1.50 N	37.02 E
Bok Koū	**110**	10.37 N	104.03 E
Böklund	**41**	54.36 N	9.34 E
Boknafjorden ⊂[2]	**26**	59.10 N	5.35 E
Boko, Congo	**152**	4.47 S	14.38 E
Boko, S.S.S.R.	**86**	49.05 N	81.38 E
Bokod	**116**	16.30 N	120.50 E
Bokode	**152**	3.58 N	19.29 E
Bokolako	**150**	13.36 N	12.33 W
Bokonbajevskoje	**85**	42.07 N	77.00 E
Bokondji	**152**	2.22 N	18.42 E
Bokondo	**152**	0.15 N	22.32 E
Bokong	**112**	9.58 S	124.04 E
Bokoro	**146**	12.23 N	17.03 E
Boko Songo	**152**	4.26 S	13.37 E
Bokota	**152**	0.51 S	22.18 E
Bokote	**152**	0.05 S	20.08 E
Bokovo-Antratsit → Antracit	**83**	48.06 N	39.06 E
Bokovo Platovo	**83**	48.07 N	39.01 E
Bokovskaja	**80**	49.15 N	41.49 E
Bokpunt ›	**158**	33.34 S	18.19 E
Bokpyin	**110**	11.16 N	98.46 E
Boksburg	**158**	26.12 S	28.14 E
Boksburg □[5]	**273d**	26.12 S	28.14 E
Boksburg-Noord	**273d**	26.12 S	28.15 E
Boksburg South	**273d**	26.14 S	28.15 E
Boksburg-West	**273d**	26.13 S	28.14 E
Boksitogorsk	**76**	59.28 N	33.51 E
Bokungu	**152**	0.41 S	22.19 E
Bol, Jugo.	**36**	43.16 N	16.40 E
Bol, Tchad	**146**	13.28 N	14.43 E
Bolaang Mongondow	**112**	0.56 N	124.10 E
Bolama, Gui.-B.	**150**	11.35 N	15.28 W
Bolama, Zaïre	**152**	1.57 N	22.58 E
Bolān ≃	**120**	28.38 N	67.42 E
Bolanda, Jabal ∧	**140**	7.44 N	25.28 E
Bol'andkiik ≃	**85**	39.11 N	72.17 E
Bolands	**240c**	17.02 N	61.53 W
Bolangum	**166**	36.46 S	142.53 E
Bolaños	**234**	21.41 N	103.47 W
Bolaños ≃	**234**	21.14 N	104.08 W
Bolaños de Calatrava	**34**	38.54 N	3.40 W
Bolay I	**152**	4.20 N	17.21 E
Bolayır	**130**	40.31 N	26.45 E
Bolbec	**50**	49.34 N	0.29 E
Bolčary	**86**	59.49 N	68.48 E
Bolchov	**76**	53.27 N	36.01 E
Bolchuny	**80**	47.59 N	46.25 E
Bolda ≃	**80**	46.10 N	48.14 E
Boldasevo	**80**	54.43 N	45.33 E
Boldekow	**54**	53.43 N	13.35 E
Bolderslev	**41**	54.59 N	9.18 E
Bold Heath	**262**	53.24 N	2.42 W
Boldon	**44**	54.57 N	1.27 W
Bol'džuan	**85**	38.19 N	69.40 E
Bole, Ghana	**150**	9.02 N	2.29 W
Bole, Zhg.	**86**	44.53 N	82.05 E
Bolechov	**78**	49.04 N	23.52 E
Boleko	**152**	1.31 S	19.53 E
Bolero	**154**	10.59 S	33.45 E
Boles	**194**	34.46 N	94.02 W
Bolesławiec	**30**	51.16 N	15.34 E
Boleszkowice	**30**	52.44 N	14.36 E
Boletice nad Labem	**54**	50.45 N	14.13 E
Boley	**196**	35.29 N	96.29 W
Bolgarčaj ≃	**84**	39.27 N	48.33 E
Bolgart	**162**	31.16 S	116.30 E
Bolgatanga	**150**	10.46 N	0.52 W
Bolgrad	**78**	45.41 N	28.36 E
Boli, Sūd.	**140**	6.01 N	28.43 E
Boli, Tchad	**146**	10.50 N	18.43 E
Boli, Zhg.	**89**	45.46 N	130.31 E
Bolia	**152**	1.36 S	18.23 E
Boliden	**26**	64.52 N	20.23 E
Boligee	**194**	32.45 N	88.01 W
Boligeqiu	**104**	42.14 N	121.40 E
Bolíkov	**61**	49.02 N	15.22 E
Bolinao	**116**	16.23 N	119.54 E
Bolinas	**226**	37.54 N	122.42 W

ENGLISH

Name	Page	Lat.°′	Long.°′
Boling	**222**	29.15 N	95.56 W
Bolingbrook	**216**	41.41 N	88.04 W
Bolinger Creek ≃	**282**	37.47 N	122.00 W
Bolingo	**152**	3.30 S	21.43 E
Bolishan	**89**	43.50 N	123.31 E
Bolivar, Austl.	**168b**	34.46 S	138.36 E
Bolívar, Col.	**246**	5.50 N	76.01 W
Bolívar, Col.	**246**	1.50 N	76.58 W
Bolívar, Col.	**246**	4.21 N	76.10 W
Bolívar, Perú	**248**	7.18 S	77.48 W
Bolivar, Mo., U.S.	**194**	37.36 N	93.24 W
Bolivar, N.Y., U.S.	**210**	42.04 N	78.10 W
Bolivar, Oh., U.S.	**214**	40.39 N	81.27 W
Bolivar, Pa., U.S.	**214**	40.23 N	79.09 W
Bolivar, Tn., U.S.	**194**	35.15 N	88.59 W
Bolívar □[3]	**246**	6.20 N	63.30 W
Bolívar □[4]	**246**	1.35 S	79.00 W
Bolívar □[5]	**246**	9.00 N	74.40 W
Bolívar, Cerro ∧	**246**	7.28 N	63.25 W
Bolívar, Pico ∧	**246**	8.30 N	71.02 W
Bolivar Peninsula ›[1]	**196**	29.27 N	94.39 W
Bolivar Run	**214**	41.59 N	78.39 W
Bolivia □[1], S.A.	**242**	17.00 S	65.00 W
Bolivia □[1], S.A.	**248**	17.00 S	65.00 W
Bolivie → Bolivia □[1]	**248**	17.00 S	65.00 W
Bolivien → Bolivia □[1]	**248**	17.00 S	65.00 W
Boljarovo	**38**	42.09 N	26.49 E
Boljoon	**116**	9.38 N	123.29 E
Bolkar Dağları ⋏	**130**	37.15 N	34.20 E
Bölkenbusch	**263**	51.21 N	7.06 E
Boll	**56**	48.38 N	9.37 E
Bolladello	**266b**	45.41 N	8.50 E
Bollate	**62**	45.33 N	9.07 E
Böllberg ∧[2]	**263**	51.23 N	7.19 E
Bollendorf	**56**	49.51 N	6.22 E
Bollène	**62**	44.17 N	4.45 E
Bollensdorf	**264a**	52.31 N	13.43 E
Bolles Canal ≋	**220**	26.38 N	80.34 W
Bolles Harbor	**216**	41.51 N	83.24 W
Bollin ≃	**262**	53.23 N	2.28 W
Bolling Air Force Base ■	**284c**	38.51 N	77.02 W
Bollington, Eng., U.K.	**262**	53.22 N	2.25 W
Bollington, Eng., U.K.	**262**	53.18 N	2.06 W
Bollmora	**40**	59.15 N	18.13 E
Bollnäs	**26**	61.21 N	16.25 E
Bollon	**166**	28.05 S	147.15 E
Bollstabruk	**26**	63.00 N	17.39 E
Bollstanäs	**40**	59.30 N	17.56 E
Bollullos par del Condado	**34**	37.20 N	6.32 W
Bollwerk	**263**	51.10 N	7.35 E
Bolmen ⊜	**26**	56.55 N	13.40 E
Bolnisi	**84**	41.28 N	44.33 E
Bolo	**144**	8.50 N	39.22 E
Bolobo	**152**	2.10 S	16.14 E
Bolochovo	**82**	54.05 N	37.50 E
Bologna	**64**	44.29 N	11.20 E
Bologna □[4]	**64**	44.28 N	11.26 E
Bologne, Fr.	**58**	48.12 N	5.08 E
Bologne → Bologna, It.	**64**	44.29 N	11.20 E
Bolognesi	**248**	6.35 S	73.10 W
Bolognetta	**70**	37.58 N	13.27 E
Bolognola	**66**	42.59 N	13.14 E
Bologoje	**76**	57.54 N	34.02 E
Bologovo	**76**	56.54 N	31.42 E
Bololo	**152**	3.50 S	21.08 E
Bolomba	**152**	0.29 N	19.12 E
Bolombo	**152**	3.59 S	21.22 E
Bolombo ≃	**152**	1.32 N	21.14 E
Bolon'	**89**	49.55 N	136.07 E
Bolon', ozero ⊜	**89**	49.51 N	136.22 E
Bolonchén de Rejón	**232**	20.00 N	89.49 W
Bolondo	**152**	0.27 N	20.01 E
Bolondrón	**240p**	22.46 N	81.27 W
Bolong ≃	**170**	34.15 S	149.36 E
Bolonia → Bologna	**64**	44.29 N	11.20 E
Bolótana	**71**	40.20 N	8.57 E
Bolotino	**78**	47.42 N	27.21 E
Bolotnoje	**86**	55.41 N	84.23 E
Boloto	**82**	54.10 N	36.20 E
Bolotovskoje	**86**	58.33 N	62.28 E
Bolovens, Plateau des ⋏[1]	**110**	15.20 N	106.20 E
Bolpur	**126**	23.40 N	87.43 E
Bol'šaja, S.S.S.R.	**76**	59.36 N	41.48 E
Bol'šaja, S.S.S.R.	**80**	45.59 N	42.42 E
Bol'šaja ≃	**80**	48.36 N	41.00 E
Bol'šaja Atn'a	**80**	56.15 N	49.27 E
Bol'šaja Balachn'a ≃	**74**	73.37 N	107.05 E
Bol'šaja Ber'ostovica	**76**	53.11 N	24.01 E
Bol'šaja Blagoveščenka	**78**	46.51 N	34.03 E
Bol'šaja Brembola	**82**	56.45 N	38.55 E
Bol'šaja Bukon'	**86**	48.53 N	82.43 E
Bol'šaja Čalykla ≃	**80**	51.51 N	49.34 E
Bol'šaja Černigovka	**80**	52.07 N	50.52 E
Bol'šaja Chalan'	**78**	50.56 N	37.26 E
Bol'šaja Cheta ≃	**74**	69.33 N	84.15 E
Bol'šaja Chobda ≃	**86**	50.56 N	54.34 E
Bol'šaja Chundala	**76**	60.04 N	34.18 E
Bol'šaja Čuja ≃	**88**	58.56 N	112.13 E
Bol'šaja Čurakovka	**86**	53.03 N	64.20 E
Bol'šaja Damba	**80**	46.57 N	51.47 E
Bol'šaja Dmitrijevka	**80**	51.21 N	45.15 E
Bol'šaja Dora	**76**	59.05 N	37.38 E
Bol'šaja Džalga	**80**	45.59 N	42.41 E
Bol'šaja Glušica	**80**	52.24 N	50.28 E
Bol'šaja Ižora	**76**	59.56 N	29.34 E
Bol'šaja Ižorka ≃	**265a**	59.48 N	30.36 E
Bol'šaja Kakša ≃	**80**	57.53 N	45.28 E
Bol'šaja Kamenka	**80**	53.39 N	50.31 E
Bol'šaja Kamenka ≃	**83**	48.22 N	40.04 E
Bol'šaja Kandala	**80**	54.32 N	49.22 E
Bol'šaja Kaskara	**86**	57.11 N	65.58 E
Bol'šaja Ket'	**86**	57.39 N	91.45 E
Bol'šaja Kinel' ≃	**80**	53.14 N	50.30 E
Bol'šaja Kirsanovka	**83**	47.40 N	38.54 E
Bol'šaja Kokšaga ≃	**80**	56.08 N	47.47 E
Bol'šaja Konkudera ≃	**88**	57.34 N	112.30 E
Bol'šaja Kugul'ta ≃	**80**	45.45 N	41.57 E
Bol'šaja Kuonamka ≃	**74**	70.45 N	113.24 E
Bol'šaja Laba ≃	**84**	44.16 N	40.53 E
Bol'šaja Lipovica	**80**	52.33 N	41.20 E
Bol'šaja Martynovka	**80**	47.17 N	41.40 E
Bol'šaja Mošanica	**76**	53.58 N	29.37 E
Bol'šaja Murta	**86**	56.55 N	93.07 E
Bol'šaja Neva ≃	**265a**	59.58 N	30.13 E
Bol'šaja Norja	**80**	56.41 N	52.43 E
Bol'šaja Ochta ◆[8]	**265a**	59.57 N	30.25 E
Bol'šaja Ol'šanka	**80**	51.32 N	44.17 E
Bol'šaja Orlovka	**80**	47.20 N	41.16 E
Bol'šaja Osinovaja ≃	**180**	66.30 N	174.00 E
Bol'šaja Pas'ma	**80**	58.38 N	43.53 E
Bol'šaja Rečka	**88**	51.57 N	104.44 E
Bol'šaja Ržaksa	**80**	52.08 N	42.13 E
Bol'šaja Sestra ≃	**82**	56.16 N	35.56 E
Bol'šaja Smedva ≃	**82**	54.50 N	38.34 E
Bol'šaja Sosnova	**80**	57.40 N	54.36 E
Bol'šaja Talovaja	**78**	46.58 N	40.37 E
Bol'šaja Tarel'	**88**	53.45 N	106.40 E
Bol'šaja Tavoložka	**80**	52.07 N	49.04 E
Bol'šaja Uča	**80**	56.37 N	52.05 E
Bol'šaja Usa	**86**	56.44 N	55.06 E
Bol'šaja Ussurka ≃	**89**	45.57 N	133.42 E
Bol'šaja Višera	**76**	58.55 N	32.08 E
Bol'šaja Vladimirovka	**86**	50.53 N	79.31 E
Bol'šaja Vys' ≃	**78**	48.45 N	30.54 E
Bolsa Knolls	**226**	36.44 N	121.38 W
Bol'šakovo, S.S.S.R.	**76**	54.53 N	21.40 E
Bol'šakovo, S.S.S.R.	**265b**	55.54 N	37.17 E
Bol'šečernigovka	**83**	48.57 N	39.25 E
Bol'šekrepinskaja	**83**	47.36 N	39.22 E
Bol'šelig	**24**	62.07 N	52.25 E
Bolsena	**66**	42.39 N	11.59 E
Bolsena, Lago di ⊜	**66**	42.36 N	11.56 E

DEUTSCH

Name	Seite	Breite°′	Länge°′ E = Ost
Bol'šenarymskoje	**86**	49.16 N	84.32 E
Bol'šerečje	**86**	56.06 N	74.38 E
Bol'šereck	**74**	52.25 N	156.24 E
Bol'šetroickoje	**78**	50.33 N	37.17 E
Bol'šeustjikinskoje	**86**	55.57 N	58.16 E
Bol'ševik, S.S.S.R.	**74**	62.44 N	147.30 E
Bol'ševik, S.S.S.R.	**76**	52.34 N	30.53 E
Bol'ševik, S.S.S.R.	**265a**	59.49 N	30.30 E
Bol'ševik, ostrov I	**74**	78.40 N	102.30 E
Bol'šezemel'skaja Tundra ◆[1]	**72**	67.30 N	56.00 E
Bolshoi Theatre ❦	**265b**	55.46 N	37.37 E
Bol'šije Algaši	**80**	55.22 N	46.29 E
Bol'šije Avt'uki	**78**	52.04 N	29.32 E
Bol'šije Belyniči	**82**	54.38 N	38.50 E
Bol'šije Berezniki	**80**	54.11 N	45.58 E
Bol'šije Gorki, S.S.S.R.	**82**	56.28 N	35.51 E
Bol'šije Gorki, S.S.S.R.	**265a**	59.42 N	29.51 E
Bol'šije Kajbicy	**80**	55.25 N	48.13 E
Bol'šije Kizi, ozero ⊜	**89**	51.38 N	140.20 E
Bol'šije Kl'uči	**80**	55.59 N	48.47 E
Bol'šije Kl'učišči	**80**	54.08 N	48.14 E
Bol'šije Liachvi ≃	**84**	41.58 N	44.06 E
Bol'šije Michalicyny	**80**	58.29 N	48.14 E
Bol'šije Ozerki	**80**	52.36 N	46.33 E
Bol'šije Pom'aly	**80**	56.42 N	46.40 E
Bol'šije Ručji	**82**	56.36 N	36.58 E
Bol'šije Saly	**83**	47.24 N	39.41 E
Bol'šije Tarchany	**80**	54.42 N	48.34 E
Bol'šije Ugli	**88**	57.47 N	112.51 E
Bol'šije Uki	**86**	56.57 N	72.37 E
Bol'šije Ždanovy	**80**	58.40 N	49.05 E
Bol'šoj	**80**	50.13 N	43.26 E
Bol'šoj An'uj ≃	**74**	68.30 N	160.49 E
Bol'šoj Ažbulat, ozero ⊜	**86**	53.17 N	77.25 E
Bol'šoj Balchan, chrebet ⋏	**128**	39.40 N	54.30 E
Bol'šoj Begičev, ostrov I	**74**	74.20 N	112.30 E
Bol'šoj Bogdo, gora ∧[2]	**80**	48.08 N	46.52 E
Bol'šoj Boktybaj, gora ∧	**86**	48.27 N	58.30 E
Bol'šoj Čeremšan ≃	**80**	54.11 N	49.39 E
Bol'šoj Civil' ≃	**80**	55.54 N	47.28 E
Bol'šoje, ozero ⊜	**265a**	60.04 N	30.39 E
Bol'šoje Aksu	**86**	43.20 N	79.35 E
Bol'šoje Aleksejevskoje	**82**	55.14 N	38.12 E
Bol'šoje Boldino	**80**	54.59 N	45.19 E
Bol'šoje Bun'kovo	**82**	55.51 N	38.37 E
Bol'šoje Goloustnoje	**88**	52.01 N	105.25 E
Bol'šoje Gorodišče, S.S.S.R.	**76**	57.17 N	30.31 E
Bol'šoje Gorodišče, S.S.S.R.	**78**	50.37 N	37.06 E
Bol'šoje Ignatovo	**80**	55.02 N	45.34 E
Bol'šoje Jarovoje, ozero ⊜	**86**	52.53 N	78.36 E
Bol'šoje Jašaltinskoje, ozero ⊜	**80**	46.17 N	42.27 E
Bol'šoje Kibejevo	**80**	56.55 N	47.05 E
Bol'šoje Korovino	**82**	54.30 N	39.02 E
Bol'šoje Manuškino	**265a**	59.53 N	30.49 E
Bol'šoje Michajlovskoje	**82**	56.47 N	38.04 E
Bol'šoje Mikuškino	**80**	53.56 N	51.42 E
Bol'šoje Muraškino	**80**	55.47 N	44.46 E
Bol'šoje Nagatkino	**80**	54.31 N	47.58 E
Bol'šoje Nurkejevo	**80**	55.22 N	52.40 E
Bol'šoje Nyrsy	**80**	55.44 N	50.19 E
Bol'šoje Ogar'ovo	**76**	53.33 N	37.43 E
Bol'šoje Pikino	**80**	56.25 N	44.22 E
Bol'šoje Polpino	**76**	53.14 N	34.30 E
Bol'šoje Ramenje	**76**	58.21 N	36.40 E
Bol'šoje Rybuškino	**80**	55.25 N	45.48 E
Bol'šoje Sazonovo	**80**	58.06 N	53.21 E
Bol'šoje Selo	**76**	57.43 N	38.56 E
Bol'šoje Šem'akino	**80**	55.03 N	48.38 E
Bol'šoje Soldatskoje	**78**	51.21 N	35.31 E
Bol'šoje Sudačje	**80**	50.49 N	44.05 E
Bol'šoje Topol'noje, ozero ⊜	**86**	53.20 N	78.00 E
Bol'šoje Uro	**88**	53.32 N	109.48 E
Bol'šoje Zagorje	**76**	57.51 N	28.57 E
Bol'šoje Žokovo	**82**	54.35 N	38.57 E
Bol'šoj Gašun ≃	**80**	47.22 N	42.43 E
Bol'šoj Ginaldag, gora ∧	**84**	40.20 N	45.57 E
Bol'šoj Golec, gora ∧	**88**	51.52 N	119.24 E
Bol'šoj Irgiz ≃	**80**	52.01 N	47.24 E
Bol'šoj Jenisej (Bij-Chem) ≃	**88**	51.43 N	94.26 E
Bol'šoj Jugan ≃	**86**	60.55 N	73.40 E
Bol'šoj Kamen'	**89**	43.06 N	132.21 E
Bol'šoj Kandarat'	**80**	54.25 N	47.00 E
Bol'šoj Kanym, gora ∧	**86**	54.13 N	88.20 E
Bol'šoj Karagaj	**86**	57.57 N	70.15 E
Bol'šoj Karaman ≃	**80**	51.40 N	46.38 E
Bol'šoj Kavkaz (Caucasus) ⋏	**84**	42.30 N	45.00 E
Bol'šoj Ketmen'	**86**	43.27 N	80.24 E
Bol'šoj Kujal'nik ≃	**78**	46.46 N	30.36 E
Bol'šoj Kujaš	**86**	55.50 N	61.06 E
Bol'šoj Kundyš ≃	**80**	56.32 N	47.23 E
Bol'šoj Kuvaj	**80**	54.37 N	47.05 E
Bol'šoj Kymynej, gora ∧	**180**	66.34 N	172.32 W
Bol'šoj L'achovskij, ostrov I	**74**	73.35 N	142.00 E
Bol'šoj Lug	**88**	52.07 N	104.10 E
Bol'šoj Matačynaj, gora ∧	**180**	66.28 N	179.25 W
Bol'šoj Melik	**80**	51.38 N	43.18 E
Bol'šoj Nesvetaj ≃	**83**	47.27 N	39.54 E
Bol'šoj Onguren	**88**	53.38 N	107.36 E
Bol'šoj Patom ≃	**88**	59.15 N	113.56 E
Bol'šoj Pit ≃	**86**	59.01 N	91.44 E
Bol'šoj Porog	**86**	52.35 N	92.18 E
Bol'šoj Šagan	**80**	50.57 N	51.08 E
Bol'šoj Sajan ⋏	**88**	52.00 N	99.30 E
Bol'šoj Salym ≃	**86**	60.55 N	70.25 E
Bol'šoj Šantar, ostrov I	**89**	55.00 N	137.42 E
Bol'šoj Šatan, gora ∧	**86**	53.41 N	57.36 E
Bol'šoj Simonogont	**265a**	59.50 N	29.49 E
Bol'šoj Sorokino	**86**	56.38 N	69.53 E
Bol'šoj Suchodol	**83**	48.25 N	39.53 E
Bol'šoj Sundyr'	**80**	56.07 N	46.46 E
Bol'šoj Tal'cy	**76**	59.13 N	33.00 E
Bol'šoj Tolkaj	**80**	53.30 N	51.57 E
Bol'šoj T'uters, ostrov I	**76**	59.51 N	27.13 E
Bol'šoj Uluj	**86**	56.39 N	90.36 E
Bol'šoj Uran ≃	**80**	52.24 N	53.15 E
Bol'šoj Uvat, ozero ⊜	**86**	57.35 N	70.30 E
Bol'šoj Uzen' ≃	**80**	48.50 N	49.40 E
Bol'šoj Uzigont	**265a**	59.48 N	29.53 E
Bol'šoj Vjass	**80**	53.48 N	45.30 E
Bol'šoj Vlasjevo	**89**	53.24 N	140.55 E
Bol'šoj Zelenčuk ≃	**84**	44.36 N	41.56 E
Bol'šovcy	**78**	49.12 N	24.44 E
Bolsover	**44**	53.14 N	1.18 W
Bolsward	**52**	53.03 N	5.31 E
Boltaña	**34**	42.27 N	0.04 E
Boltigen	**58**	46.38 N	7.24 E
Boltino	**265b**	55.58 N	37.41 E
Bolton, On., Can.	**212**	43.53 N	79.44 W
Bolton, Eng., U.K.	**262**	53.35 N	2.26 W
Bolton, Ct., U.S.	**207**	41.46 N	72.26 W
Bolton, Ms., U.S.	**194**	32.20 N	90.27 W
Bolton, N.C., U.S.	**192**	34.19 N	78.24 W
Bolton □[8]	**262**	53.34 N	2.28 W
Bolton Abbey	**44**	53.59 N	1.53 W
Bolton Abbey ❦[1]	**44**	53.59 N	1.54 W

Symbols in the index entries represent the broad categories identified in the key at the right. Symbols with superior numbers (⋏[1]) identify subcategories (see complete key on page *I · 1).*

Kartensymbole in dem Registerverzeichnis stellen die rechts in Schlüssel erklärten Kategorien dar. Symbole mit hochgestellten Ziffern (⋏[1]) bezeichnen Unterabteilungen einer Kategorie (vgl. vollständiger Schlüssel auf Seite *I · 1).*

Los símbolos incluídos en el texto del índice representan las grandes categorias identificadas con la clave a la derecha. Los símbolos con numeros en su parte superior (⋏[1]) identifican las subcategorías (véase la clave completa en la página *I · 1).*

Les symboles de l'index représentent les catégories indiquées dans la légende à droite. Les symboles suivis d'un indice (⋏[1]) représentent des sous-catégories (voir légende complète à la page *I · 1).*

Os símbolos incluídos no texto do índice representam as grandes categorias identificadas com a chave à direita. Os símbolos com números em sua parte superior (⋏[1]) identificam as subcategorias (veja-se a chave completa à página *I · 1).*

∧ Mountain	Berg	Montaña	Montagne	Montanha
⋏ Mountains	Berge	Montañas	Montagnes	Montanhas
)(Pass	Pass	Paso	Col	Passo
V Valley, Canyon	Tal, Cañon	Valle, Cañón	Vallée, Canyon	Vale, Canhão
≚ Plain	Ebene	Llano	Plaine	Planície
› Cape	Kap	Cabo	Cap	Cabo
I Island	Insel	Isla	Île	Ilha
II Islands	Inseln	Islas	Îles	Ilhas
♦ Other Topographic Features	Andere Topographische Objekte	Otros Elementos Topográficos	Autres données topographiques	Outros acidentes topográficos

ESPAÑOL

Nombre	Página	Lat.°′	Long.°′ W = Oeste
Bolton Bridge	44	53.58 N	1.57 W
Bolton Center	207	41.47 N	72.26 W
Bolton Creek ≃	212	44.58 N	76.23 W
Bolton Lake ⊜	184	54.16 N	95.47 W
Bolton-le-Sands	44	54.06 N	2.47 W
Bolton upon Dearne	44	53.31 N	1.19 W
Bolton Wanderers Football Ground ♠	262	53.34 N	2.25 W
Bolu	130	40.44 N	31.37 E
Bolu □[4]	130	40.40 N	31.30 E
Boluo, Zhg.	100	23.11 N	114.17 E
Boluo, Zhg.	100	24.27 N	113.03 E
Boluochi	98	41.24 N	119.56 E
Boluokeng	100	24.05 N	113.22 E
Bolus Head >	48	51.46 N	10.21 W
Bolva ≃	76	53.17 N	34.20 E
Bolvadin	130	38.42 N	31.04 E
Bolwarra	166	17.24 S	144.11 E
Bóly	30	45.58 N	18.32 E
Bolyčevo	82	55.46 N	35.43 E
Bolzaneto	62	44.27 N	8.54 E
Bolzano (Bozen)	64	46.31 N	11.22 E
Bolzano □[4]	64	46.43 N	11.30 E
Boma	152	5.51 S	13.03 E
Bomaderry	170	34.51 S	150.37 E
Bomal	56	50.23 N	5.32 E
Bomandjokou	152	0.34 N	14.23 E
Bomaneh	152	1.18 N	23.47 E
Bomarsund	26	60.13 N	20.15 E
Bomate	152	1.10 S	19.41 E
Bomba	66	42.02 N	14.22 E
Bombakabo	152	3.04 N	19.42 E
Bombala	166	36.54 S	149.14 E
Bombarral	34	39.16 N	9.09 W
Bombat	130	38.08 N	42.14 E
Bombay, India	122	18.58 N	72.50 E
Bombay, India	272c	18.58 N	72.50 E
Bombay, N.Y., U.S.	206	44.56 N	74.34 W
Bombay, University of ʊ[2]	272c	18.57 N	72.50 E
Bombay Harbour ᴄ	272c	18.57 N	72.53 E
Bomberai, Jazirah >[1]	164	3.00 S	133.00 E
Bombetoka, Baie de ᴄ	157b	15.50 S	46.17 E
Bombimba	152	0.31 N	19.24 E
Bombo	154	0.35 N	32.32 E
Bombo ≃	152	3.58 S	15.59 E
Bombo-Kasanji	152	5.54 S	21.51 E
Bomboma	152	2.25 N	18.54 E
Bombo-Makuka	152	5.26 S	16.19 E
Bombombwa	154	1.21 N	25.30 E
Bombon	261	48.34 N	2.52 E
Bomboyo	146	12.01 N	15.28 E
Bom Conselho	250	9.10 S	36.41 W
Bom Despacho	255	19.43 S	45.15 W
Bomei	100	22.57 N	115.46 E
Bömenzien	54	52.59 N	11.31 E
Bomhus	40	60.41 N	17.13 E
Bomili	154	1.40 N	27.01 E
Bom Jardim, Ilha do I	287a	23.02 S	43.35 W
Bom Jardim de Goiás	255	16.17 S	52.07 W
Bom Jardim de Minas	256	21.57 S	44.11 W
Bom Jesus, Ang.	152	9.09 S	13.34 E
Bom Jesus, Bra.	250	9.04 S	44.22 W
Bom Jesus da Gurguéia, Serra ⋏	250	9.00 S	43.00 W
Bom Jesus da Lapa	255	13.15 S	43.25 W
Bom Jesus da Terra Preta	256	23.15 S	46.36 W
Bom Jesus de Goiás	255	18.12 S	49.44 W
Bom Jesus dos Perdões	256	23.08 S	46.28 W
Bømlafjorden ᴄ[2]	26	59.39 N	5.20 E
Bomlitz	52	52.54 N	9.37 E
Bømlo I	26	59.46 N	5.12 E
Bommerholz	263	51.23 N	7.18 E
Bommern ◆[8]	263	51.25 N	7.20 E
Bomnak	89	54.46 N	128.51 E
Bomokandi ≃	154	3.39 N	26.08 E
Bomongiri	152	1.57 S	21.13 E
Bomongo	152	1.22 N	18.21 E
Bompata	150	6.38 N	1.04 W
Bompensiere	70	37.28 N	13.47 E
Bompietro	70	37.44 N	14.06 E
Bomputu	152	0.20 S	20.06 E
Bom Repouso	256	22.28 S	46.09 W
Bom Retiro, Bra.	252	27.48 S	49.31 W
Bom Retiro, Bra.	256	22.10 S	45.40 W
Bom Retiro ◆[8]	287b	23.32 S	46.38 W
Bom Retiro do Sul	252	29.37 S	51.56 W
Bom Sucesso, Bra.	248	15.43 S	56.07 W
Bom Sucesso, Bra.	255	23.42 S	51.45 W
Bom Sucesso, Bra.	256	22.52 S	45.33 W
Bom Sucesso, Bra.	287b	23.25 S	46.24 W
Bomu (Mbomou) ≃	136	4.08 N	22.26 E
Bon, Cap >	36	37.05 N	11.03 E
Bona	40	58.34 N	15.03 E
Boná, Isla I	236	8.34 N	79.36 W
Bona Bona Island I	164	10.30 S	149.50 E
Bon Accord	158	25.38 S	28.11 E
Bonaduz	58	46.49 N	9.25 E
Bonaero Park	273d	26.07 S	28.16 E
Bonai	114	1.16 N	100.52 E
Bonaigarh	120	21.50 N	84.57 E
Bonair, In., U.S.	278	41.31 N	87.22 W
Bon Air, Va., U.S.	208	37.31 N	77.33 W
Bon Aire	214	40.54 N	79.55 W
Bonaire I	241s	12.10 N	68.15 W
Bonampak ⊥	232	16.44 N	91.05 W
Bönan	40	60.44 N	17.18 E
Bonandolok	114	1.47 N	98.48 E
Bonanza, Nic.	236	14.01 N	84.35 W
Bonanza, Or., U.S.	202	42.11 N	121.24 W
Bonanza, Ut,. U.S.	200	40.01 N	109.10 W
Bonanza Peak ∧	224	48.14 N	120.52 W
Bonao	238	18.56 N	70.25 W
Bonaparte	190	40.41 N	91.48 W
Bonaparte ≃	182	50.46 N	121.17 W
Bonaparte, Lake ⊜	212	44.09 N	75.23 W
Bonaparte, Mount ∧	202	48.45 N	119.08 W
Bonaparte Archipelago II	160	14.17 S	125.18 E
Bonaparte Lake ⊜	182	51.16 N	120.35 W
Bonar Bridge	46	57.53 N	4.21 W
Bonarcado	71	40.04 N	8.38 E
Bonasila Dome ∧	180	62.19 N	160.30 W.
Bonasse	241r	10.05 N	61.52 W
Bonassola	62	44.11 N	9.35 E
Bonaventure	186	48.03 N	65.29 W
Bonaventure ≃	186	48.02 N	65.28 W
Bonaventure, Île I	186	48.30 N	64.10 W
Bonavista	186	48.39 N	53.07 W
Bonavista, Cape >	186	48.42 N	53.05 W
Bonavista Bay ᴄ	186	48.45 N	53.20 W
Bonawe	46	56.26 N	5.13 W
Bonawon	116	9.08 N	122.55 E
Bonbeach	274b	38.04 S	145.08 E
Bonboillon	58	47.20 N	5.42 E
Bon Bon	162	30.26 S	135.28 E
Bonbonon Point >	116	9.03 N	123.08 E
Bonchester Bridge	44	55.24 N	2.40 W
Boncourt	58	47.30 N	6.56 E
Bond	194	30.54 N	89.10 W
Bond □[6]	219	38.53 N	89.25 W
Bondari	80	52.57 N	42.04 E
Bondar'ov	83	49.22 N	39.10 E
Bondar'ovka	83	49.23 N	39.37 E
Bondeno	64	44.53 N	11.25 E
Bondi	274a	33.53 S	151.17 E
Bondo, Zaïre	152	1.22 S	23.53 E
Bondo, Zaïre	152	3.49 N	23.40 E
Bondoc Peninsula >[1]	116	13.30 N	122.30 E
Bondoc Point >	116	13.10 N	122.36 E
Bondorf	58	48.31 N	8.49 E
Bondoufle	261	48.37 N	2.23 E
Bondoukou	150	8.02 N	2.48 W
Bondoukou □[5]	150	8.00 N	3.30 W
Bondowoso	115a	7.55 S	113.49 E
Bondsville	207	42.12 N	72.20 W
Bonduel	190	44.44 N	88.26 W
Bondues	50	50.42 N	3.06 E

FRANÇAIS

Nom	Page	Lat.°′	Long.°′ W = Ouest
Bondy	261	48.54 N	2.28 E
Bondy, Forêt de ♠	261	48.55 N	2.35 E
Bône → Annaba, Alg.	148	36.54 N	7.46 E
Bone, Indon.	112	4.46 S	122.52 E
Bone, Indon.	112	5.09 S	122.37 E
Bone → Watampone, Indon.	112	4.32 S	120.20 E
Bone, Teluk ᴄ	112	4.00 S	120.40 E
Bonebone	112	2.36 S	120.33 E
Bon Echo Provincial Park ♠	212	44.52 N	77.15 W
Bonefro	66	41.42 N	14.56 E
Bone Island I	212	44.56 N	79.51 W
Bonelipu	112	4.50 S	123.11 E
Bonelohe	112	5.48 S	120.27 E
Bönen	52	51.36 N	7.44 E
Boneogeh	112	7.16 S	120.48 E
Bone Rate, Kepulauan II	112	7.00 S	121.00 E
Bone Rate, Pulau I	112	7.22 S	121.08 E
Bon Espérance, Cap de → Good Hope, Cape of >	158	34.24 S	18.30 E
Bo'ness	46	56.01 N	3.37 W
Bonesteel	198	43.04 N	98.56 W
Bonete, Cerro ∧	252	27.51 S	68.47 W
Bonete Chico, Cerro ∧	252	28.01 S	68.45 W
Bonětice	60	49.41 N	12.49 E
Bonfield	216	41.09 N	88.03 W
Bonfim	256	22.58 S	45.15 W
Bonfinópolis	255	16.38 S	48.58 W
Bonfol	58	47.29 N	7.09 E
Bong □[6]	150	7.00 N	9.30 W
Bonga	144	7.17 N	36.15 E
Bongabon	116	15.38 N	121.08 E
Bongabon ≃	116	12.40 N	121.33 E
Bongabong	116	12.45 N	121.29 E
Bongaigaon	124	26.28 N	90.34 E
Bongak	140	7.27 N	33.14 E
Bongandanga	152	1.30 N	21.03 E
Bongao Island I	116	5.01 N	119.46 E
Bongaree	171a	27.05 S	153.10 E
Bonggaw	116	5.02 N	119.46 E
Bongka	112	0.58 S	121.27 E
Bongka ≃	112	0.59 S	121.05 E
Bong-mieu	110	15.25 N	108.24 E
Bongo, Ang.	152	8.48 S	17.49 E
Bongo, Gabon	152	2.10 S	10.12 E
Bongo, Massif des ⋏	146	8.40 N	22.25 E
Bongo I	152	3.01 N	20.06 E
Bongo II	152	1.47 S	17.41 E
Bongo Island I	116	7.20 N	124.02 E
Bongolu	152	2.48 N	22.29 E
Bongon	112	6.35 N	116.52 E
Bongor	146	10.17 N	15.22 E
Bongou ≃	140	6.42 N	22.04 E
Bongouanou	150	6.39 N	4.12 W
Bongouanou □[5]	150	6.35 N	4.20 W
Bong Range ⋏	150	6.50 N	10.00 W
Bonham	196	33.34 N	96.10 W
Bonheiden	56	51.02 N	4.32 E
Bonhomme, Col du)(	58	48.10 N	7.06 E
Bonhomme, Morne ∧	238	19.05 N	72.18 W
Bonhomme Island I	219	38.42 N	90.36 W
Bonifacio, Fr.	36	41.23 N	9.10 E
Bonifacio, Pil.	116	8.03 N	123.37 E
Bonifacio, Strait of ʯ	36	41.20 N	9.15 E
Bonifacio Monument ⊥	269f	14.39 N	120.59 E
Bonifati	68	39.35 N	15.54 E
Bonifati, Capo >	68	39.35 N	15.52 E
Bonifay	194	30.47 N	85.40 W
Bonifica del Volturno ≚	68	41.01 N	14.00 E
Bonilla Island I	182	53.29 N	130.36 W
Bonin Islands → Ogasawara-guntō II	14	27.00 N	142.10 E
Bonita	194	32.55 N	91.40 W
Bonita, Point >	282	37.49 N	122.32 W
Bonita Springs	220	26.20 N	81.46 W
Bonito, Bra.	248	21.08 S	56.28 W
Bonito, Bra.	250	8.29 S	35.44 W
Bonito, It.	68	41.06 N	15.00 E
Bonito ≃, Bra.	255	16.31 S	51.23 W
Bonito ≃, Bra.	256	22.12 S	43.02 W
Bonito ≃, Bra.	256	22.09 S	43.40 W
Bonito, Pico ∧	236	15.38 N	86.55 W
Bonito, Rio ≃	200	33.23 N	105.16 W
Bonito de Santa Fé	250	7.19 S	38.31 W
Bonjol	112	0.01 S	100.13 E
Bonkoukou	150	14.01 N	3.13 E
Bon Meade	279b	40.33 N	80.14 W
Bonn	56	50.44 N	7.05 E
Bonnanaro	71	40.32 N	8.45 E
Bonndorf im Schwarzwald	58	47.49 N	8.20 E
Bonneauville	208	39.46 N	77.10 W
Bonne Bay (Woody Point)	186	49.30 N	57.56 W
Bonne Bay ᴄ	186	49.33 N	57.55 W
Bonnebosq	50	49.12 N	0.05 E
Bonnechere ≃	190	45.31 N	76.33 W
Bonneia	144	5.41 N	37.45 E
Bonnelles	261	48.37 N	2.02 E
Bonner	202	46.52 N	113.51 W
Bonners Ferry	202	48.41 N	116.18 W
Bonne-sur-Ménoge	58	46.10 N	6.20 E
Bonnet, Lac du ⊜	184	50.22 N	95.55 W
Bonnétable	50	48.11 N	0.26 E
Bonne Terre	194	37.55 N	90.33 W
Bonnet Plume ≃	180	65.55 N	134.58 W
Bonneuil-sur-Marne	261	48.46 N	2.29 E
Bonneval	50	48.11 N	1.24 E
Bonneval-sur-Arc	62	45.22 N	7.03 E
Bonnevaux	58	46.18 N	6.40 E
Bonneville, Fr.	58	46.05 N	6.25 E
Bonneville, Or., U.S.	224	45.38 N	121.57 W
Bonneville Dam ◆[6]	224	45.39 N	121.56 W
Bonneville Peak ∧	202	42.46 N	112.08 W
Bonneville Salt Flats ≚	200	40.45 N	113.52 W
Bonney, Lake ⊜	166	37.48 S	140.22 E
Bonney Lake	224	47.10 N	122.11 W
Bonnie Doone	192	35.05 N	78.57 W
Bonnières	50	49.02 N	1.35 E
Bonnie Rock	162	30.32 S	118.21 E
Bonnieux	62	43.49 N	5.18 E
Bonnievale	158	33.57 S	20.06 E
Bönninghardt	263	51.35 N	6.28 E
Bönninghardt ⋏[2]	263	51.34 N	6.27 E
Bonnots Mill	219	38.34 N	91.58 W
Bonny	150	4.27 N	7.10 E
Bonny ≃[1]	150	4.20 N	7.10 E
Bonnyrigg, Austl.	274a	33.54 S	150.54 E
Bonnyrigg, Scot., U.K.	46	55.52 N	3.08 W
Bonny-sur-Loire	50	47.34 N	2.50 E
Bonnyville	182	54.16 N	110.44 W
Bono, It.	71	40.25 N	9.02 E
Bono, Ar., U.S.	194	35.54 N	90.48 W
Bono, Oh., U.S.	214	41.38 N	83.16 W
Bonoi	164	1.51 S	137.48 E
Bonorva	71	40.25 N	8.46 E
Bonoua	150	5.16 N	3.36 W
Bonpas Creek ≃	194	38.16 N	87.59 W
Bonriki	174t	1.23 N	173.09 E
Bonriki Airport ⊠	174t	1.22 N	173.10 E
Bons	58	46.16 N	6.23 E
Bonsall	228	33.17 N	117.13 W
Bonsari	272c	19.04 N	73.02 E
Bon Secour	194	30.18 N	87.43 W
Bon-Secours, Bel.	50	50.30 N	3.36 E
Bonsecours, Fr.	50	49.26 N	1.08 E
Bonshaw	186	46.12 N	63.21 W
Bonsucesso ◆[8]	287a	22.52 S	43.15 W
Bontang	112	0.08 N	117.30 E
Bontberg ∧	158	32.21 S	21.04 E

PORTUGUÊS

Nome	Página	Lat.°′	Long.°′ W = Oeste
Bontebok National Park ♠	158	34.07 S	20.23 E
Bonthain	112	5.32 S	119.56 E
Bonthe	150	7.32 N	12.30 W
Bontoc	116	17.05 N	120.58 E
Bon Wier	194	30.44 N	93.39 W
Bonyhád	30	46.19 N	18.32 E
Boo, Kepulauan II	164	1.12 S	129.24 E
Booby Point >	284b	39.17 N	76.23 W
Boock	54	53.29 N	14.15 E
Boody	219	39.46 N	89.03 W
Boogardie	162	28.02 S	117.47 E
Booischot	56	51.03 N	4.46 E
Bookabie	162	31.50 S	132.41 E
Bookaloo	166	31.55 S	137.22 E
Book Cliffs ±[4]	200	39.20 N	109.00 W
Booke	152	2.33 S	22.00 E
Booker	196	36.27 N	100.32 W
Booker T. Washington National Monument ♠	192	37.01 N	79.45 W
Bookwalter	218	39.42 N	83.32 W
Boola	150	8.22 N	8.43 W
Boolaloo	162	22.35 S	115.51 E
Booleroo Centre	166	32.53 S	138.21 E
Booligal	166	33.52 S	144.53 E
Boologooro	162	24.21 S	114.02 E
Boom	50	51.05 N	4.22 E
Boomarra	166	19.33 S	140.20 E
Boomer	188	38.09 N	81.17 W
Boomi	166	28.44 S	149.35 E
Boomrivier	158	29.33 S	20.27 E
Boonah	171a	28.00 S	152.41 E
Böön cagaan nuur ⊜	102	45.35 N	99.09 E
Boone, Ia., U.S.	190	42.03 N	93.52 W
Boone, N.C., U.S.	192	36.13 N	81.40 W
Boone □[6], Il., U.S.	216	42.15 N	88.50 W
Boone □[6], In., U.S.	218	40.03 N	86.28 W
Boone □[6], Ky., U.S.	218	38.57 N	84.45 W
Boone □[6], Mo., U.S.	219	38.55 N	92.15 W
Boone ≃	190	42.19 N	93.56 W
Boone Draw V	196	33.51 N	103.42 W
Boone Grove	216	41.21 N	87.08 W
Boone Lake ⊜[1]	192	36.25 N	82.25 W
Boone Reservoir ⊜[1]	279b	40.15 N	80.08 W
Boones Mill	192	37.06 N	79.57 W
Booneville, Ar., U.S.	194	35.08 N	93.55 W
Booneville, Ky., U.S.	192	37.28 N	83.40 W
Booneville, Ms., U.S.	194	34.39 N	88.34 W
Boon Point >	240c	17.10 N	61.50 W
Boons	158	25.59 S	27.13 E
Boonsboro	208	39.30 N	77.39 W
Boonsville	222	33.04 N	97.52 W
Boonton	210	40.54 N	74.24 W
Boonton Reservoir ⊜[1]	276	40.53 N	74.25 W
Boonville, Ca., U.S.	204	39.00 N	123.21 W
Boonville, In., U.S.	194	38.02 N	87.16 W
Boonville, Mo., U.S.	194	38.58 N	92.44 W
Boonville, N.Y., U.S.	212	43.29 N	75.20 W
Boopi ≃	248	15.41 S	67.15 W
Boorama	144	9.56 N	43.11 E
Boorindal	166	30.21 S	146.08 E
Booroorban	166	34.56 S	144.46 E
Boorowa	166	34.26 S	148.43 E
Boorthanna	166	28.38 S	135.54 E
Boos	50	49.23 N	1.12 E
Boosaaso	144	11.17 N	49.11 E
Boossen	54	52.22 N	14.29 E
Boot	44	54.24 N	3.17 W
Bootahnie Indian Reserve ◆[4]	182	50.24 N	121.31 W
Booth	194	32.30 N	86.34 W
Booth, Lac ⊜	190	46.45 N	78.34 W
Boothbay Harbor	188	43.51 N	69.37 W
Boothby, Cape >	9	66.34 S	57.16 E
Booth Corner	285	39.51 N	75.29 W
Boothia, Gulf of ᴄ	176	71.00 N	91.00 W
Boothia Peninsula >[1]	176	70.30 N	95.00 W
Boothstown	262	53.30 N	2.25 W
Boothville	194	29.20 N	89.25 W
Booth Wood Reservoir ⊜[1]	262	53.38 N	1.58 W
Boothwyn	285	39.49 N	75.26 W
Bootle	262	53.28 N	3.00 W
Boot Reefs ✢[2]	164	10.00 S	144.40 E
Booué	152	0.06 S	11.56 E
Booysens ◆[8]	273d	26.14 S	28.01 E
Booze Creek ≃	284c	38.59 N	77.07 W
Bopeechee	166	29.36 S	137.23 E
Bopfingen	56	48.51 N	10.21 E
Bo Phloi	110	14.19 N	99.31 E
Bophuthatswana □[1], Afr.	138	26.00 S	25.35 E
Bophuthatswana □[1], Afr.	156	26.00 S	25.35 E
Boping	98	36.36 N	116.07 E
Boping Ling ⋏	100	25.00 N	117.00 E
Bopo	150	7.37 N	7.52 E
Bopolu	150	7.03 N	10.32 W
Boppard	56	50.14 N	7.35 E
Boqer, Har ∧	132	30.52 N	34.43 E
Boqueirão, Ilha do I	287a	22.46 S	43.09 W
Boqueirão, Serra do ⋏[2]	250	11.30 S	43.45 W
Boquerón	236	8.30 N	82.34 W
Boquerón □[5]	252	21.30 S	60.00 W
Boquerón, Bahía de ᴄ	240m	18.01 N	67.12 W
Boquerón, Túnel ◆[5]	286c	10.34 N	67.00 W
Boquet	279b	40.23 N	79.36 W
Boquilla, Presa de la ⊜[1]	232	27.30 N	105.30 W
Boquilla del Refugio	196	25.33 N	102.28 W
Boquillas del Carmen	232	29.17 N	102.53 W
Bor, Česko.	60	49.43 N	12.47 E
Bor, Jugo.	38	44.05 N	22.07 E
Bor, S.S.S.R.	24	63.00 N	42.38 E
Bor, S.S.S.R.	80	56.22 N	44.05 E
Bor, Süd.	140	6.12 N	31.33 E
Bor, Tür.	130	37.54 N	34.34 E
Bor, Lak ≃	154	1.18 N	40.40 E
Bora-Bora I	14	16.30 S	151.45 W
Borabu	110	16.02 N	103.07 E
Boraha, Nosy I	157b	16.50 S	49.55 E
Borah Peak ∧	202	44.08 N	113.48 W
Boraldaj ≃	85	42.33 N	69.07 E
Borale	144	9.10 N	42.35 E
Borambola	171b	35.12 S	147.41 E
Borang, Tanjung >	164	5.16 S	133.07 E
Boraré ≃	287b	23.46 S	46.39 W
Borås	26	57.43 N	12.55 E
Borāzjān	128	29.16 N	51.12 E
Borba, Bra.	246	4.24 S	59.35 W
Borba, Port.	34	38.48 N	7.27 W
Borbach ◆[8]	263	51.26 N	7.22 E
Borbeck ◆[8]	263	51.29 N	6.57 E
Borbera ≃	62	44.42 N	8.52 E
Borborema	255	21.37 S	49.04 W
Borca di Cadore	64	46.26 N	12.13 E
Borcea ≃	38	44.40 N	27.53 E
Borchen	52	51.39 N	8.44 E
Borculo, Ned.	52	52.07 N	6.31 E
Borculo, Mi., U.S.	216	42.53 N	86.01 W
Borda, Cape >	166	35.45 S	136.34 E
Borda da Mata, Bra.	256	22.37 S	47.01 W
Borda da Mata, Bra.	256	22.16 S	46.10 W
Bordeaux, Fr.	32	44.50 N	0.34 W
Bordeaux, S. Afr.	273d	26.06 S	28.01 E
Bordeaux ◆[8]	275a	45.33 N	73.41 W
Bordeaux Mountain ∧[2]	240m	18.20 N	64.44 W
Borden, Austl.	162	34.05 S	118.16 E
Borden, Sk., Can.	184	52.25 N	107.13 W
Borden, Eng., U.K.	260	51.20 N	0.42 E
Borden, In., U.S.	218	38.28 N	85.57 W
Borden, Canadian Forces Base ■	212	44.17 N	79.55 W
Borden Lake ⊜	190	47.50 N	83.18 W
Borden Peninsula >[1]	176	73.00 N	83.00 W
Bordentown	208	40.08 N	74.42 W
Border Mountains ⋏	164	3.40 S	141.05 E
Borders □[4]	46	55.37 N	3.15 W
Bordertown	166	36.19 S	140.47 E
Bordesholm	30	54.11 N	10.01 E
Borđeyri	24a	65.15 N	21.10 W
Bordighera	62	43.46 N	7.39 E
Bording	41	56.12 N	9.17 E
Bording Kirkeby	41	56.10 N	9.15 E
Bordino, Fiume di ≃	70	37.53 N	12.37 E
Bordj Bou Arreridj	148	36.04 N	4.46 E
Bordj Bounaama	34	35.51 N	1.36 E
Bordj Menaïel	148	36.44 N	3.43 E
Bordj Omar Idriss	148	28.09 N	6.43 E
Bordj Sidi Toui	148	32.44 N	11.22 E
Bordunskij	85	42.40 N	75.37 E
Bore, It.	62	44.43 N	9.47 E
Bore, Ityo.	144	4.40 N	37.40 E
Boré, Mali	150	15.08 N	3.29 W
Boreda	144	6.32 N	37.48 E
Boreham	260	51.46 N	0.33 E
Borehamwood	260	51.40 N	0.16 W
Borel Hill ∧	282	37.19 N	122.12 W
Borello, It.	64	41.55 N	14.18 E
Borello, It.	66	44.03 N	12.11 E
Borensberg	26	58.34 N	15.17 E
Boreray I	46	57.42 N	7.18 W
Boretto	64	44.54 N	10.33 E
Borgå (Porvoo)	26	60.24 N	25.40 E
Borgallo, Galleria del ◆[5]	62	44.25 N	9.53 E
Borgarnes	24a	64.35 N	21.53 W
Borgata Costiera	70	37.43 N	12.39 E
Børgefjell Nasjonalpark ♠	24	65.10 N	14.00 E
Borgentreich	52	51.34 N	9.14 E
Börger, B.R.D.	52	52.54 N	7.32 E
Borger, Ned.	52	52.55 N	6.46 E
Borger, Tx., U.S.	196	35.40 N	101.23 W
Borgerhout	50	51.13 N	4.26 E
Borgetto	70	38.03 N	13.08 E
Borggård	40	58.44 N	15.32 E
Borghetto	64	45.41 N	10.56 E
Borghetto di Vara	62	44.13 N	9.43 E
Borghetto Lodigiano	62	45.13 N	9.30 E
Borghetto Santo Spirito	62	44.06 N	8.14 E
Borgholm	26	56.53 N	16.39 E
Borghorst	52	52.07 N	7.23 E
Borgia	68	38.49 N	16.30 E
Borgio-Verezzi	62	44.10 N	8.18 E
Borgloon	56	50.48 N	5.20 E
Borg Mountain ∧	9	72.42 S	3.30 W
Borgne, Lake ᴄ	194	30.05 N	89.40 W
Borgnesse, Pointe >	240e	14.27 N	60.54 W
Borgo	64	46.03 N	11.27 E
Borgo alla Collina	66	43.45 N	11.43 E
Borgo a Mozzano	66	43.59 N	10.33 E
Borgo Cerreto	66	42.49 N	12.54 E
Borgo d'Ale	62	45.21 N	8.03 E
Borgoforte	64	45.03 N	10.45 E
Borgofranco d'Ivrea	62	45.30 N	7.51 E
Borgolavezzaro	62	45.19 N	8.42 E
Borgomanero	62	45.42 N	8.28 E
Borgomaro	62	43.58 N	7.56 E
Borgonovo Val Tidone	62	45.01 N	9.26 E
Borgo Pace	66	43.39 N	12.17 E
Borgoricco	64	45.32 N	11.58 E
Borgorose	66	42.11 N	13.13 E
Borgo San Dalmazzo	62	44.20 N	7.30 E
Borgo San Giacomo	64	45.21 N	9.58 E
Borgo San Lorenzo	66	43.57 N	11.23 E
Borgosatollo	64	45.28 N	10.14 E
Borgosesia	62	45.43 N	8.16 E
Borgo Ticino	266b	45.41 N	8.36 E
Borgo Tossignano	66	44.16 N	11.35 E
Borgou □[5]	150	10.30 N	2.50 E
Borgo Val di Taro	62	44.29 N	9.46 E
Borgo Vercelli	62	45.21 N	8.28 E
Borgsdorf	54	52.42 N	13.14 E
Borgu Game Reserve ◆[4]	150	10.15 N	4.10 E
Borgund ʊ[1]	26	61.03 N	7.49 E
Bori	150	4.42 N	7.21 E
Borig Delijn els ✢[2]	88	50.00 N	94.00 E
Borikhan	110	18.33 N	103.43 E
Borilovo	76	53.22 N	35.58 E
Borinage □[9]	50	50.30 N	4.00 E
Boring, Md., U.S.	208	39.31 N	76.49 W
Boring, Or., U.S.	224	45.25 N	122.22 W
Borinskoje	76	52.27 N	39.22 E
Borislav	78	49.16 N	23.27 E
Borisoglebsk	80	51.23 N	42.06 E
Borisoglebskij	80	57.16 N	39.09 E
Borisov, S.S.S.R.	76	54.15 N	28.30 E
Borisov, S.S.S.R.	78	50.11 N	26.31 E
Borisovka, S.S.S.R.	76	52.50 N	39.58 E
Borisovka, S.S.S.R.	78	50.36 N	36.01 E
Borisovo	82	55.25 N	36.03 E
Borisovo ◆[8]	265b	55.38 N	37.45 E
Borisovo-Sudskoje	76	59.54 N	36.01 E
Borisovskaja	76	60.12 N	39.48 E
Borispol'	78	50.21 N	30.57 E
Borja, Esp.	34	41.50 N	1.32 W
Borja, Perú	246	4.26 S	77.33 W
Borjas Blancas	34	41.31 N	0.52 E
Bork	52	51.40 N	7.30 E
Borkça	130	41.22 N	41.40 E
Borken, B.R.D.	52	51.51 N	6.51 E
Borken, B.R.D.	56	51.03 N	9.16 E
Borkenwirthe	52	51.53 N	6.50 E
Borki, S.S.S.R.	78	49.42 N	36.02 E
Borki, S.S.S.R.	86	59.08 N	82.15 E
Borkoldoj, chrebet ⋏	85	41.25 N	77.50 E
Børkop	41	55.39 N	9.39 E
Borkou ◆[1]	146	18.15 N	18.50 E
Borkou-Ennedi-Tibesti □[5]	146	18.15 N	18.50 E
Borkoviči	76	55.40 N	28.20 E
Borkum	52	53.35 N	6.40 E
Borkum I	52	53.35 N	6.41 E
Borland Manor	279b	40.15 N	80.09 W
Borlänge	40	60.29 N	15.25 E
Borle ◆[8]	272c	19.02 N	72.55 E
Borlu	130	38.44 N	28.27 E
Bormes-les-Mimosas	62	43.09 N	6.20 E
Bormida ≃	62	44.23 N	8.13 E
Bormida di Millesimo ≃	62	44.40 N	8.20 E
Bormida di Spigno ≃	62	44.40 N	8.20 E
Bormio	64	46.28 N	10.22 E
Born, D.D.R.	41	54.23 N	12.31 E
Born, D.D.R.	54	52.22 N	11.28 E
Born, D.D.R.	54	45.22 N	12.31 E
Borna, D.D.R.	54	51.19 N	13.11 E
Borna, D.D.R.	54	51.07 N	12.30 E
Borndiep ᴄ	52	53.25 N	5.35 E
Borne	52	52.18 N	6.45 E
Borne ≃	62	45.03 N	3.54 E
Borneo (Kalimantan) I	112	0.30 N	114.00 E
Bornheim	56	50.46 N	6.59 E
Bornholm I	26	55.10 N	15.00 E
Bornholte	52	51.52 N	8.29 E
Bornhöved	54	54.04 N	10.16 E
Börnicke, D.D.R.	54	52.41 N	12.56 E
Börnicke, D.D.R.	264a	52.40 N	13.38 E
Börnig ◆[8]	263	51.33 N	7.16 E
Bornim ◆[8]	264a	52.26 N	13.00 E
Borno	64	45.56 N	10.12 E
Bornos, Embalse de ⊜[1]	34	36.50 N	5.30 W
Bornova	130	38.27 N	27.14 E
Bornsdorf	54	51.46 N	13.41 E
Bornstedt ◆[8]	264a	52.25 N	13.02 E
Bornu □[3]	146	12.00 N	12.45 E
Boro ≃	140	8.52 N	26.11 E
Borobudur ⊥	115a	7.36 S	110.12 E
Borocay Island I	116	11.59 N	121.55 E
Borod'anka	78	50.39 N	29.56 E
Borodarou	150	10.59 N	2.53 E
Borodino, S.S.S.R.	78	46.18 N	29.13 E
Borodino, S.S.S.R.	82	55.32 N	35.50 E
Borodino, S.S.S.R.	82	56.53 N	37.00 E
Borodino, S.S.S.R.	88	55.55 N	94.55 E
Borodulicha	86	50.43 N	80.55 E
Borodulino	80	57.59 N	54.20 E
Borogoncy	74	62.42 N	131.08 E
Borohoro Shan ⋏	86	44.06 N	83.10 E
Boroko	112	0.55 N	123.16 E
Boroml'a	78	50.37 N	34.59 E
Boromo	150	11.45 N	2.56 W
Boron, Mali	150	14.01 N	7.30 W
Boron, Ca., U.S.	228	34.59 N	117.38 W
Boronga Islands II	110	19.58 N	93.06 E
Borongan	116	11.37 N	125.26 E
Boronia	274b	37.52 S	145.17 E
Boron'ki	76	53.09 N	32.08 E
Borore	71	40.13 N	8.48 E
Borotou	150	8.44 N	7.30 W
Boroughbridge	44	54.06 N	1.23 W
Borough Green	260	51.17 N	0.19 E
Borough Park ◆[8]	276	40.38 N	74.00 W
Borovaja, S.S.S.R.	78	50.12 N	30.07 E
Borovaja, S.S.S.R.	83	49.24 N	37.40 E
Borovaja ≃	83	48.58 N	38.24 E
Borovan	38	43.26 N	23.45 E
Borovany	61	48.54 N	14.39 E
Boroviči	76	58.24 N	33.55 E
Borovik ≃	83	49.11 N	38.33 E
Borovka ≃	80	52.54 N	52.00 E
Borovl'anka	86	52.38 N	84.29 E
Borovoj	24	59.55 N	51.38 E
Borovoje, S.S.S.R.	78	51.06 N	27.13 E
Borovoje, S.S.S.R.	86	53.04 N	70.19 E
Borovsk	82	55.12 N	36.30 E
Borovskaja	24	60.46 N	41.06 E
Borovskij	86	57.03 N	65.44 E
Borovskoj	86	53.48 N	64.12 E
Borovskoje, S.S.S.R.	83	48.51 N	38.34 E
Borovskoje, S.S.S.R.	86	52.39 N	82.08 E
Borovucha	76	55.36 N	28.37 E
Borovy	60	49.33 N	13.18 E
Borozdino	82	54.07 N	38.22 E
Borraan	144	10.14 N	48.44 E
Borrachudo ≃	255	18.12 S	45.16 W
Borrazópolis	255	23.56 S	51.36 W
Borrby	26	55.27 N	14.10 E
Borre	41	55.00 N	12.28 E
Borre ⊥	26	59.23 N	10.28 E
Borreby	41	55.14 N	11.19 E
Borriana	62	45.30 N	8.02 E
Borris	48	52.35 N	6.06 W
Borrisokane	48	52.59 N	8.07 W
Borrisoleigh	48	52.45 N	7.57 W
Borroloola	164	16.04 S	136.17 E
Borrowdale	44	54.31 N	3.10 W
Börry	52	52.01 N	9.27 E
Borș	38	47.07 N	21.49 E
Borșa, Rom.	38	46.56 N	23.40 E
Borșa, Rom.	38	47.39 N	24.40 E
Borsad	120	22.25 N	72.54 E
Borsano	266b	45.35 N	8.51 E
Borschemich	263	51.04 N	6.25 E
Borščov	78	48.48 N	26.03 E
Borščovo	82	56.30 N	36.51 E
Borščovočnyj chrebet ⋏	88	52.00 N	117.00 E
Borsdorf	54	51.21 N	12.32 E
Borskoje	80	53.02 N	51.43 E
Borsod-Abaúj-Zemplén □[6]	30	48.15 N	21.00 E
Börssum	54	52.04 N	10.35 E
Borstendorf	54	50.46 N	13.10 E
Bortala ≃	86	44.50 N	82.45 E
Borth, B.R.D.	52	51.36 N	6.33 E
Borth, Wales, U.K.	42	52.29 N	4.03 W
Borthwick Water ≃	44	55.24 N	2.50 W
Bortigali	71	40.17 N	8.50 E
Bortigiadas	71	40.53 N	9.02 E
Bort-les-Orgues, Fr.	32	45.24 N	2.30 E
Bort-les-Orgues, Fr.	32	43.49 N	2.53 E
Bortniči	78	50.22 N	30.41 E
Borto	88	53.35 N	111.53 E
Bortondale	285	39.54 N	79.24 W
Boru	164	10.14 S	148.50 E
Boruca	236	9.00 N	83.20 W
Borūjen	128	31.59 N	51.18 E
Borūjerd	128	33.54 N	48.46 E
Bor Ul Shan ⋏	102	41.20 N	98.55 E
Borve	46	56.58 N	7.32 W
Borz'a	88	50.24 N	116.31 E
Borz'a ≃	88	50.38 N	115.38 E
Borzna	78	51.15 N	32.25 E
Boržomi	84	41.50 N	43.21 E
Boržomskij zapovednik ♠	84	41.50 N	43.10 E
Borzonasca	62	44.25 N	9.23 E
Borzyszkowy	30	54.03 N	17.22 E
Bosa	71	40.18 N	8.30 E
Bosaga	86	47.55 N	72.58 E
Bosambi	152	2.24 N	22.39 E
Bosanska Dubica	36	45.11 N	16.49 E
Bosanska Gradiška	36	45.09 N	17.15 E
Bosanska Krupa	36	44.53 N	16.10 E
Bosanski Novi	36	45.03 N	16.23 E
Bosanski Petrovac	36	44.33 N	16.22 E
Bosanski Šamac	38	45.03 N	18.28 E
Bosansko Grahovo	36	44.11 N	16.22 E
Bősárkány	61	47.41 N	17.14 E
Bosau	54	54.06 N	10.25 E
Bosavi, Mount ∧	164	6.35 S	142.50 E
Boscastle	42	50.41 N	4.42 W
Bosco, It.	66	44.53 N	12.14 E
Bosco, It.	66	43.08 N	12.28 E
Boscobel	190	43.08 N	90.42 W
Bosco Chiesanuova	64	45.37 N	11.02 E
Bosco Marengo	62	44.49 N	8.41 E
Boscoreale	68	40.46 N	14.28 E
Bose	102	23.54 N	106.37 E
Bösel	52	53.00 N	7.58 E
Bosencheve, Parque Nacional ♠	234	19.36 N	100.15 W
Bosenge	152	1.18 N	22.19 E
Bósforo, Estrecho del → İstanbul Boğazı ʯ	130	41.06 N	29.04 E
Bosham	42	50.49 N	0.52 W
Boshan	98	36.29 N	117.50 E
Boshkung Lake ⊜	212	45.04 N	78.44 W
Boshoek	156	25.30 S	27.09 E
Boshof	158	28.34 S	25.04 E
Boshrūyeh	128	33.53 N	57.26 E
Bosilegrad	38	42.29 N	22.28 E
Bösingen	58	48.14 N	8.34 E
Bosjökloster	41	55.54 N	13.31 E
Boškajnar	85	38.13 N	68.51 E
Boskoop	52	52.04 N	4.35 E
Boskop	158	26.34 S	27.08 E
Boskop ∧	273d	26.05 S	27.57 E
Boskovice	30	49.29 N	16.40 E
Boskuil	158	27.23 S	25.51 E
Bosman	164	4.10 S	144.40 E
Bosna	272b	22.37 N	88.30 E
Bosna ≃	38	45.04 N	18.29 E
Bosna i Hercegovina □[3]	36	44.15 N	17.30 E
Bošn'akovo	89	49.38 N	142.10 E
Bosnik	164	1.10 S	136.14 E
Boso	272b	22.58 N	88.08 E
Bosobolo	152	4.11 N	19.54 E
Boso-Djafo	152	1.06 N	19.14 E
Bosogo	85	41.09 N	76.25 E
Bōsō-hantō >[1]	94	35.18 N	140.10 E
Bōsō-kyūryō ⋏[2]	268	35.08 N	139.56 E
Bososama	152	4.18 N	20.00 E
Bösperde	263	51.28 N	7.46 E
Bosphore, Détroit du → İstanbul Boğazı ʯ	130	41.06 N	29.04 E
Bosporus → İstanbul Boğazı ʯ	130	41.06 N	29.04 E
Bosque □[6]	222	31.55 N	97.35 W
Bosque, Paseo del ♠	288	34.55 S	57.56 W
Bosque Farms	200	34.53 N	106.40 W
Bosques	288	34.49 S	58.14 W
Bosques Petrificados, Monumento Natural ♠	254	47.39 S	68.07 W
Bosqueville	222	31.38 N	97.13 W
Bossangoa	152	6.29 N	17.27 E
Bossdorf	54	51.59 N	12.40 E
Bossé Bangou	150	13.21 N	1.18 E
Bossembélé	152	5.16 N	17.39 E
Bossentele	152	5.41 N	16.38 E
Bossert Estates	285	40.09 N	74.44 W
Bossier City	194	32.30 N	93.43 W
Bossley Bush Recreation Ground ♠	274a	33.52 S	150.54 E
Bossley Park	274a	33.52 S	150.54 E
Bosso	146	13.42 N	13.19 E
Bosso, Dallol V	150	12.25 N	2.50 E
Bossolasco	62	44.32 N	8.02 E
Bossut, Cape >	162	18.43 S	121.38 E
Bostān, Īrān	128	31.43 N	47.59 E
Bostān, Pāk.	120	30.26 N	67.02 E
Bostancı ◆[8]	267b	40.57 N	29.05 E
Bostandyk	80	49.38 N	48.54 E
Bosten Hu ⊜	90	42.00 N	87.00 E
Bostock Green	262	53.13 N	2.30 W
Boston, Pil.	116	7.52 N	126.22 E
Boston, Eng., U.K.	42	52.59 N	0.01 W
Boston, Ga., U.S.	192	30.47 N	83.47 W
Boston, In., U.S.	218	39.44 N	84.51 W
Boston, Ma., U.S.	207	42.21 N	71.03 W
Boston, Ma., U.S.	283	42.21 N	71.03 W
Boston, N.Y., U.S.	210	42.38 N	78.44 W
Boston, Pa., U.S.	279b	40.18 N	79.49 W
Boston Bar	182	49.52 N	121.26 W
Boston Bay ᴄ	283	42.22 N	70.54 W
Boston Brook ≃	283	42.37 N	71.00 W
Boston College ʊ[2]	283	42.20 N	71.10 W
Boston Common ♠	283	42.21 N	71.05 W
Boston Corners	210	42.03 N	73.31 W
Boston Creek ≃	212	43.02 N	79.56 W
Boston Harbor	224	47.08 N	122.54 W
Boston Harbor ᴄ	283	42.20 N	70.58 W
Boston Heights	214	41.15 N	81.30 W
Boston Mill	214	41.16 N	81.34 W
Boston Mountains ⋏	194	35.50 N	93.20 W
Boston Spa	44	53.54 N	1.21 W
Boston University ʊ[2]	283	42.21 N	71.07 W
Bosumtwi, Lake ⊜	150	6.30 N	1.25 W
Bosut ≃	38	44.57 N	19.22 E
Boswell, In., U.S.	216	40.31 N	87.22 W
Boswell, Ok., U.S.	196	34.01 N	95.52 W
Boswell, Pa., U.S.	214	40.09 N	79.01 W
Boswell Bay	180	60.24 N	146.08 W
Bosworth	194	39.28 N	93.20 W
Bosworth Airport ⊠	279a	41.26 N	82.00 W
Bosworth Field ⊥	42	52.36 N	1.25 W
Botād	120	22.10 N	71.40 E
Botafogo ◆[8]	287a	22.57 S	43.11 W
Botafogo, Enseada de ᴄ	287a	22.57 S	43.10 W
Botanic Gardens ♠	271c	1.19 N	103.48 E
Botany	274a	33.57 S	151.12 E
Botany Bay ◆[8]	260	51.41 N	0.07 W
Botany Bay ᴄ	170	33.59 S	151.12 E
Botejevo	78	46.41 N	35.52 E
Botelhos	256	21.39 S	46.24 W
Botera	152	11.37 S	14.17 E
Botersleegte	158	30.35 S	21.22 E
Botesdale	42	52.20 N	1.01 E
Boteti ≃	156	20.08 S	23.23 E
Botev ∧	38	42.43 N	24.55 E
Botevgrad	38	42.54 N	23.47 E
Botha's Hill	158	29.45 S	30.45 E
Bothaville	158	27.27 S	26.36 E
Bothell	224	47.45 N	122.12 W
Bothe-Napa Valley State Park ♠	226	38.32 N	122.32 W
Bothnia, Gulf of ᴄ	26	63.00 N	20.00 E
Bothwell, Austl.	166	42.23 S	147.00 E
Bothwell, On., Can.	214	42.38 N	81.52 W
Boticas	34	41.41 N	7.40 W
Botija, Isla I	258	33.52 S	59.02 W
Botkins	216	40.28 N	84.10 W
Botkul', ozero ⊜	80	48.46 N	46.40 E
Botkyrka	40	59.14 N	17.49 E
Botlich	84	42.39 N	46.14 E
Bot Makak	152	4.00 N	10.55 E
Botna ≃	78	46.45 N	29.34 E
Botnia, Golfo de → Bothnia, Gulf of ᴄ	26	63.00 N	20.00 E
Botola	152	1.17 S	18.13 E
Botolan	116	15.17 N	120.01 E
Botoșani	38	47.45 N	26.40 E
Botoșani □[6]	38	48.00 N	26.45 E
Botoșanița	38	47.53 N	26.07 E
Botou	150	12.40 N	2.03 E
Botovo	82	56.03 N	38.26 E
Bo-trach	110	17.35 N	106.32 E
Botrange ∧	56	50.30 N	6.08 E
Botricello	68	38.56 N	16.51 E
Botro	150	7.51 N	5.19 W
Botsford	210	41.21 N	73.15 W
Botswana □[1], Afr.	138	22.00 S	24.00 E
Botswana □[1], Afr.	156	22.00 S	24.00 E
Botte Donato, Monte ∧	68	39.17 N	16.26 E
Bottenhavet (Selkämeri) ᴄ	26	62.00 N	20.00 E
Bottenviken (Perämeri) ᴄ	26	65.00 N	23.00 E
Bottesford	42	52.56 N	0.48 W
Bottineau	198	48.49 N	100.26 W
Bottisham	42	52.13 N	0.16 E
Bottnischer Meerbusen → Bothnia, Gulf of ᴄ	26	63.00 N	20.00 E
Bottoms Reservoir ⊜[1]	262	53.28 N	1.58 W
Bottrop	52	51.31 N	6.55 E
Botucatu	255	22.52 S	48.26 W
Botwood	186	49.09 N	55.21 W
Boty	88	52.24 N	118.32 E
Bötzingen	58	48.04 N	7.44 E
Bötzow	54	52.39 N	13.08 E
Bötzsee ⊜	264a	52.34 N	13.50 E
Bouaflé, C. Iv.	150	6.59 N	5.45 W
Bouafle, Fr.	261	48.58 N	1.54 E
Bouaflé □[5]	150	6.50 N	5.45 W
Bou Ahmed	148	35.25 N	5.00 W
Bouaké	150	7.41 N	5.02 W
Bouaké □[5]	150	7.15 N	5.00 W
Bou Ali, Oued V	148	31.14 N	4.16 E
Bouânane	148	32.03 N	3.03 W
Bouandougou	150	8.13 N	5.40 W
Bouar	152	5.57 N	15.36 E
Bou Arada	36	36.20 N	9.38 E
Bou Areg, Sebkha ᴄ	34	35.10 N	2.45 W
Bouârfa	148	32.30 N	1.59 W
Bouaye	32	47.09 N	1.42 W
Boubandjidah, Parc National de ♠	146	8.45 N	14.45 E
Bou Bernous	148	27.18 N	2.59 W
Boubín ∧	60	48.59 N	13.51 E
Bouca	152	6.30 N	18.17 E
Bouchain	50	50.17 N	3.19 E
Bouchegouf	36	36.28 N	7.44 E
Boucher ≃	186	49.10 N	69.06 W
Boucher, Lac ⊜	186	51.07 N	59.35 W
Boucherville	206	45.36 N	73.27 W
Boucherville, Îles de II	275a	45.37 N	73.28 W
Bouches-du-Rhône □[5]	62	43.30 N	5.00 E
Bouchoir	50	49.45 N	2.41 E
Bouclans	58	47.14 N	6.15 E
Boucle du Baoulé, Parc National de la ♠	150	13.50 N	9.00 W
Boudjellil	34	36.20 N	4.21 E
Boudnib	148	31.57 N	4.38 W
Boudouaou	34	36.43 N	3.25 E

Symbol	English	Deutsch	Español	Français	Português
≃	River	Fluss	Río	Rivière	Rio
≚	Canal	Kanal	Canal	Canal	Canal
ʟ	Waterfall, Rapids	Wasserfall, Stromschnellen	Cascada, Rápidos	Chute d'eau, Rapides	Cascata, Rápidos
ʯ	Strait	Meeresstrasse	Estrecho	Détroit	Estreito
ᴄ	Bay, Gulf	Bucht, Golf	Bahía, Golfo	Baie, Golfe	Baía, Golfo
⊜	Lake, Lakes	See, Seen	Lago, Lagos	Lac, Lacs	Lago, Lagos
≡	Swamp	Sumpf	Pantano	Marais	Pântano
⍓	Ice Features, Glacier	Eis- und Gletscherformen	Accidentes Glaciales	Formes glaciaires	Acidentes glaciares
⫪	Other Hydrographic Features	Andere Hydrographische Objekte	Otros Elementos Hidrográficos	Autres données hydrographiques	Outros acidentes hidrográficos
✢	Submarine Features	Untermeerische Objekte	Accidentes Submarinos	Formes de relief sous-marin	Acidentes submarinos
□	Political Unit	Politische Einheit	Unidad Politica	Entité politique	Unidade política
ʊ	Cultural Institution	Kulturelle Institution	Institución Cultural	Institution culturelle	Institução cultural
⊥	Historical Site	Historische Stätte	Sitio Histórico	Site historique	Sitio histórico
♠	Recreational Site	Erholungs- und Ferienort	Sitio de Recreo	Centre de loisirs	Area de Lazer
⊠	Airport	Flughafen	Aeropuerto	Aéroport	Aeroporto
■	Military Installation	Militäranlage	Instalación Militar	Installation militaire	Instalação militar
◆	Miscellaneous	Verschiedenes	Misceláneo	Divers	Diversos

Name	Page	Lat.°′	Long.°′
Boudry	58	46.57 N	6.50 E
Boué	50	50.01 N	3.42 E
Bouenza □[5]	152	4.00 S	13.45 E
Boufarik	148	36.34 N	2.55 E
Bouffémont	261	49.03 N	2.18 E
Bou Ficha	36	36.18 N	10.29 E
Bougaa	34	36.20 N	5.05 E
Bougainville □[5]	175e	6.00 S	155.00 E
Bougainville I	175e	6.00 S	155.00 E
Bougainville, Cape ›	164	13.54 S	126.06 E
Bougainville, Détroit de ʉ	175f	15.50 S	167.10 E
Bougainville Reef ✦[2]	164	15.30 S	147.06 E
Bougainville Strait ʉ	175e	6.40 S	156.10 E
Bougar'oûn, Cap ›	34	37.06 N	6.28 E
Bough Beech Reservoir ⊜[1]	260	51.13 N	0.08 E
Boughton	44	53.12 N	1.00 W
Boughton Green	260	51.14 N	0.32 E
Boughton Malherbe	260	51.13 N	0.42 E
Boughton Place ⊍	260	51.13 N	0.32 E
Bougie → Bejaïa	148	36.45 N	5.05 E
Bougou	152	3.45 S	11.12 E
Bougouni	150	11.25 N	7.29 W
Bougouriba ≃	150	10.42 N	2.56 W
Bougzoul	34	35.42 N	2.51 E
Bou Hadjar	36	36.30 N	8.06 E
Bou Hajar	36	35.42 N	10.48 E
Bouillante	241o	16.06 N	61.45 W
Bouillon	56	49.48 N	5.04 E
Bouilly	50	48.12 N	4.00 E
Bouïra	148	36.23 N	3.54 E
Bouïra □[5]	148	36.00 N	4.00 E
Bouisy, Rû de ≃	261	48.34 N	2.45 E
Bou Izakarn	148	29.09 N	9.44 W
Boujad	148	32.48 N	6.26 W
Boujailles	58	46.53 N	6.05 E
Boujdour, Cap ›	148	26.08 N	14.30 W
Bouka ≃	150	11.00 N	10.50 W
Bou Kadir	148	36.04 N	1.07 E
Bou Khadra	36	35.45 N	8.02 E
Boukiéro	273b	4.12 S	15.18 E
Boukiéro, Mont ʌ[2]	273b	4.11 S	15.17 E
Boukombé	150	10.11 N	1.06 E
Boula Ibib	146	9.34 N	13.46 E
Boulaide	56	49.54 N	5.49 E
Boularderie Island I	186	46.15 N	60.30 W
Boulay-Moselle	56	49.11 N	6.30 E
Boulbon	62	43.52 N	4.41 E
Boulder, Austl.	162	30.47 S	121.29 E
Boulder, Co., U.S.	200	40.00 N	105.16 W
Boulder, Mt., U.S.	202	46.14 N	112.07 W
Boulder ≃	202	45.52 N	111.57 W
Boulder City	204	35.58 N	114.49 W
Boulder Creek	226	37.07 N	122.07 W
Boulder Creek ≃	200	37.47 N	111.22 W
Boulder Hill	216	41.41 N	88.25 W
Bouleaux, Lac des ⊜	275a	45.33 N	73.19 W
Bouli ≃	150	13.15 N	0.03 E
Boulia	166	22.54 S	139.54 E
Bouligny	56	49.17 N	5.45 E
Boullay-les-Troux	261	48.41 N	2.03 E
Boulmane	148	33.22 N	4.45 W
Boulmane □[4]	148	33.00 N	4.00 W
Boulogne ➜[8]	258	34.31 S	58.34 W
Boulogne, Bois de ♠	261	48.50 N	2.15 E
Boulogne-Billancourt	50	48.50 N	2.15 E
Boulogne-sur-Gesse	32	43.18 N	0.39 E
Boulogne-sur-Mer	50	50.43 N	1.37 E
Bouloire	50	47.58 N	0.33 E
Boulouli	150	15.34 N	9.21 W
Bouloupari	175f	21.52 S	166.04 E
Boulouris-sur-Mer	62	43.25 N	6.48 E
Boulsa	150	12.39 N	0.34 W
Boulsworth Hill ʌ	262	53.48 N	2.06 W
Bouly	150	15.19 N	11.48 W
Boumalne	148	31.32 N	5.27 W
Boumba ≃	152	2.02 N	15.12 E
Boumbé I ≃	152	4.04 N	15.23 E
Boumbé II ≃	152	4.08 N	15.08 E
Boumboum	150	15.01 N	1.42 W
Boûmdeïd	150	17.26 N	9.50 W
Bou Medfaa	34	36.22 N	2.28 E
Boumentana	152	6.59 N	16.56 E
Boumnyebe	152	3.52 N	10.49 E
Boumou	146	9.02 N	16.26 E
Bouna	150	9.16 N	3.00 W
Bouna □[5]	150	7.15 N	3.30 W
Boundary	180	64.04 N	141.06 W
Boundary Bay c	224	49.00 N	122.58 W
Boundary Peak ʌ	204	37.51 N	118.21 W
Boundary Ranges ⋏	180	59.00 N	134.00 W
Bound Brook	210	40.34 N	74.32 W
Bound Brook ≃, Ma., U.S.	283	42.13 N	70.47 W
Bound Brook ≃, N.J., U.S.	276	40.35 N	74.30 W
Boundiali	150	9.31 N	6.29 W
Boundiali □[5]	150	9.50 N	6.30 W
Boun Nua	110	21.38 N	101.54 E
Bountiful	200	40.53 N	111.52 W
Bounty Bay c	174e	25.04 S	130.05 W
Bounty Islands II	14	47.42 S	179.04 E
Bounty Trough ✦[1]	14	46.00 S	178.00 E
Bouqteb	148	34.02 N	0.05 E
Bouquet Reservoir ⊜[1]	228	34.35 N	118.24 W
Bouqueval	261	49.01 N	2.26 E
Boura	150	12.25 N	4.33 W
Bouradière	62	43.58 N	5.19 E
Bourail	175f	21.34 S	165.30 E
Bouray-sur-Juine	261	48.31 N	2.18 E
Bourbeuse ≃	194	38.24 N	90.53 W
Bourbeuse, Dry Fork ≃	194	38.16 N	91.26 W
Bourbon, In., U.S.	216	41.17 N	86.06 W
Bourbon, Mo., U.S.	194	38.09 N	91.14 W
Bourbon □[6]	218	38.14 N	84.14 W
Bourbon ≃	206	46.17 N	71.55 W
Bourbon-Lancy	32	46.38 N	3.46 E
Bourbonnais	216	41.08 N	87.52 W
Bourbonnais □[9]	32	46.20 N	3.00 E
Bourbonne-les-Bains	58	47.57 N	5.45 E
Bourbourg	50	50.57 N	2.12 E
Bourbre ≃	62	45.47 N	5.11 E
Bourdeaux	62	44.35 N	5.08 E
Bourdon, Île I	275a	45.43 N	73.29 W
Bourdon, Réservoir du ⊜[1]	50	47.36 N	3.07 E
Bourdonné	261	48.45 N	1.40 E
Bou Regreg, Oued ≃	148	34.03 N	6.50 W
Bourem	150	16.57 N	0.21 W
Bourg	194	29.33 N	90.36 W
Bourg-Achard	50	49.21 N	0.49 E
Bourganeuf	32	45.57 N	1.46 E
Bourg-Argental	62	45.18 N	4.33 E
Bourg-de-Péage	62	45.02 N	5.03 E
Bourg-en-Bresse	58	46.12 N	5.13 E
Bourges	32	47.05 N	2.24 E
Bourget	206	45.26 N	75.09 W
Bourget, Lac du ⊜	62	45.44 N	5.52 E
Bourg-la-Reine	261	48.47 N	2.19 E
Bourg-Lastic	32	45.39 N	2.33 E
Bourg-lés-Valence	62	44.57 N	4.53 E
Bourgneuf	261	48.36 N	2.00 E
Bourgneuf-en-Retz	32	47.02 N	1.57 W
Bourgogne	50	49.21 N	4.04 E
Bourgogne □[9]	32	47.00 N	4.30 E
Bourgogne, Canal de ≅	50	47.58 N	3.30 E
Bourgoin-Jallieu	62	45.35 N	5.17 E
Bourg-Saint-Andéol	62	44.22 N	4.39 E
Bourg-Saint-Maurice	62	45.37 N	6.46 E
Bourg-Saint-Pierre	58	45.57 N	7.12 E
Bourgtheroulde	50	49.18 N	0.53 E
Bourgueil	50	47.17 N	0.10 E
Bou Rjeïmât ∓[4]	150	19.04 N	15.08 W
Bourke	166	30.05 S	145.56 E
Bourmont	58	48.12 N	5.35 E
Bourne	42	52.46 N	0.23 W
Bourne ≃, Fr.	62	45.04 N	5.15 E
Bourne ≃, Eng., U.K.	42	51.02 N	1.47 W
Bournebridge	260	51.38 N	0.11 E
Bourne End	260	51.45 N	0.32 W
Bournemouth	42	50.43 N	1.54 W
Bourneville, Fr.	50	49.23 N	0.37 E
Bourneville, Oh., U.S.	218	39.17 N	83.09 W
Bourn Vincent Memorial Park ♠	48	52.01 N	9.30 W
Bouroum	150	13.37 N	0.39 W
Bourron-Marlotte	50	48.20 N	2.42 E
Bourscheid	56	49.55 N	6.04 E
Bourtange	52	53.00 N	7.11 E
Bourtanger Moor ➜[3]	52	53.00 N	7.15 E
Bourton-on-the-Water	42	51.53 N	1.45 W
Bourzanga	150	13.41 N	1.33 W
Bou Saâda	148	35.12 N	4.11 E
Bou Salem	36	36.36 N	8.59 E
Bousbecque	50	50.46 N	3.05 E
Bouse	200	33.55 N	114.00 W
Bou Sellam, Oued ≃	34	36.26 N	4.34 E
Bouse Wash V	200	34.02 N	114.20 W
Bou Smail	148	36.38 N	2.41 E
Boussac	32	46.21 N	2.13 E
Boussé, Burkina	150	12.39 N	1.53 W
Bousse, Fr.	56	49.17 N	6.12 E
Boussières	58	47.09 N	5.54 E
Bousso	146	10.29 N	16.43 E
Boussois	50	50.17 N	4.03 E
Boussouma	150	12.55 N	1.05 W
Boussu	50	50.26 N	3.48 E
Boussy-Saint-Antoine	261	48.41 N	2.32 E
Bout, Pointe du ›	240e	14.34 N	61.03 W
Bouteille, Lac de la ⊜	206	46.42 N	73.41 W
Bouteldja	36	36.47 N	8.12 E
Bou Temezguida ʌ	148	29.21 N	9.55 W
Boutilimit	150	17.33 N	14.42 W
Bouttencourt	50	49.56 N	1.38 E
Bouvard, Cape ›	168a	32.41 S	115.37 E
Bouvetøya I	9	54.26 S	3.24 E
Bouvier Bay c	281	42.39 N	82.38 W
Bouvières	62	44.30 N	5.13 E
Bouxières-aux-Dames	56	48.45 N	6.10 E
Bouxwiller	56	48.49 N	7.29 E
Bouyon	62	43.50 N	7.07 E
Bouza	150	14.25 N	6.02 E
Bou Zadjar	34	35.35 N	1.09 W
Bouzonville	56	49.18 N	6.32 E
Bov	41	54.50 N	9.23 E
Bova	68	38.00 N	15.56 E
Bøvågen	26	60.40 N	4.58 E
Bovalino Marina	68	38.10 N	16.11 E
Bova Marina	68	37.56 N	15.55 E
Bovard	279b	40.19 N	79.30 W
Bovec	36	46.20 N	13.33 E
Bovegno	64	45.48 N	10.16 E
Bovenden	52	51.35 N	9.55 E
Bovenkarspel	52	52.42 N	5.15 E
Bøverdal	26	61.43 N	8.21 E
Boves, Fr.	50	49.51 N	2.23 E
Boves, It.	62	44.19 N	7.33 E
Bovey	190	47.17 N	93.25 W
Bovey ≃	42	50.34 N	3.37 W
Bovey Tracey	42	50.36 N	3.40 W
Bovill	202	46.51 N	116.23 W
Boville Ernica	66	41.38 N	13.28 E
Bovina	196	34.31 N	102.53 W
Bovina Center	210	42.16 N	74.47 W
Bovingdon	260	51.44 N	0.32 W
Bövinghausen ➜[8]	263	51.31 N	7.19 E
Bovington Camp	42	50.42 N	2.14 W
Bovino	68	41.15 N	15.20 E
Bovisio Masciago	266b	45.37 N	9.09 E
Bovolenta	64	45.16 N	11.56 E
Bovolone	64	45.15 N	11.07 E
Bovril	252	31.21 S	59.26 W
Bovrup	41	54.59 N	9.36 E
Bow	224	48.33 N	122.23 W
Bow ≃, Austl.	162	16.32 S	128.39 E
Bow ≃, Ab., Can.	182	49.56 N	111.42 W
Bow ≃, Sk., Can.	184	54.56 N	105.13 W
Bo-Wadrif	158	32.26 S	20.07 E
Bowang	106	31.34 N	118.50 E
Bowbells	198	48.48 N	102.14 W
Bow Brook ≃	42	52.04 N	2.07 W
Bowburn	44	54.43 N	1.31 W
Bow Creek ≃	198	39.35 N	99.14 W
Bowden	182	51.55 N	114.02 W
Bowdle	198	45.27 N	99.39 W
Bowdoin, Lake ⊜	202	48.24 N	107.41 W
Bowdon, Eng., U.K.	262	53.23 N	2.22 W
Bowdon, Ga., U.S.	192	33.32 N	85.15 W
Bowdon, N.D., U.S.	198	47.28 N	99.42 W
Bowelling	168a	33.25 S	116.29 E
Bowen, Arg.	252	35.00 S	67.31 W
Bowen, Austl.	166	20.01 S	148.15 E
Bowen, Il., U.S.	194	40.56 N	91.04 W
Bowen ≃	166	20.24 S	147.21 E
Bowenfels	170	33.31 S	150.07 E
Bowen's Creek ≃	170	33.21 S	150.35 E
Bowers	208	39.15 N	75.36 W
Bowers Gifford	260	51.34 N	0.32 E
Bowers Mansion ⊥	226	39.17 N	119.50 W
Bowers Marshes ≡	260	51.33 N	0.32 E
Bowers Ridge ✦[3]	16	54.00 N	179.00 E
Bowerston	214	40.25 N	81.11 W
Bowersville	218	39.34 N	83.43 W
Bowgreave	44	53.52 N	2.45 W
Bowie, Az., U.S.	200	32.19 N	109.29 W
Bowie, Md., U.S.	208	39.00 N	76.46 W
Bowie, Tx., U.S.	196	33.33 N	97.50 W
Bowie Creek ≃	194	31.26 N	89.24 W
Bow Island	184	49.52 N	111.22 W
Bowkān	128	36.31 N	46.12 E
Bowland, Forest of ➜[3]	44	53.58 N	2.32 W
Bowles Creek ≃	222	32.02 N	94.59 W
Bowley Bar ›[2]	284b	39.18 N	76.23 W
Bowleys Quarters	284b	39.19 N	76.24 W
Bowling Green, Fl., U.S.	220	27.38 N	81.49 W
Bowling Green, Ky., U.S.	194	36.59 N	86.26 W
Bowling Green, Mo., U.S.	219	39.20 N	91.11 W
Bowling Green, Oh., U.S.	216	41.22 N	83.39 W
Bowling Green, Pa., U.S.	285	39.55 N	75.23 W
Bowling Green, Va., U.S.	208	38.02 N	77.20 W
Bowling Green, Cape ›	166	19.19 S	145.25 E
Bowman, Ca., U.S.	226	38.57 N	121.03 W
Bowman, Ga., U.S.	192	34.12 N	83.01 W
Bowman, N.D., U.S.	198	46.10 N	103.23 W
Bowman, S.C., U.S.	192	33.20 N	80.40 W
Bowman, Mount ʌ	182	51.10 N	121.55 W
Bowman Creek ≃, Pa., U.S.	210	41.31 N	75.58 W
Bowman Creek ≃, Wa., U.S.	224	45.50 N	121.03 W
Bowman-Haley Lake ⊜[1]	198	46.00 N	103.20 W
Bowman Island I	9	65.17 S	103.08 E
Bowman Lake ⊜[1]	226	39.27 N	120.38 W
Bowmans	168b	34.09 S	138.16 E
Bowmansdale	208	40.10 N	76.59 W
Bowmanstown	208	40.48 N	75.40 W
Bowmansville, N.Y., U.S.	212	42.56 N	78.41 W
Bowmansville, Pa., U.S.	208	40.10 N	76.04 W
Bowmanville	212	43.55 N	78.41 W
Bowmanville Creek ≃	212	43.53 N	78.40 W
Bowmont Water ≃	44	55.34 N	2.09 W
Bowmore	46	55.45 N	6.17 W
Bowness-on-Windermere	44	54.22 N	2.55 W
Bowokan, Kepulauan II	112	2.10 S	123.10 E
Bowral	170	34.28 S	150.25 E
Bowraville	166	30.39 S	152.51 E
Bowron ≃	182	54.04 N	121.48 W
Bowron Lake Provincial Park ♠	182	53.10 N	121.06 W
Bowsman	184	52.14 N	101.14 W
Bowwood	154	17.07 S	26.17 E
Box	42	51.26 N	2.15 W
Boxberg	56	49.29 N	9.38 E
Box Butte Creek ≃	198	42.28 N	102.37 W
Box Creek ≃, Tx., U.S.	222	31.33 N	95.43 W
Box Creek ≃, Tx., U.S.	222	31.35 N	95.10 W
Box Elder	202	48.19 N	110.00 W
Boxelder Creek ≃, U.S.	198	45.59 N	103.57 W
Boxelder Creek ≃, Co., U.S.	198	40.33 N	105.00 W
Box Elder Creek ≃, Co., U.S.	198	40.23 N	104.28 W
Box Elder Creek ≃, Mt., U.S.	202	46.57 N	108.04 W
Boxelder Creek ≃, S.D., U.S.	198	44.01 N	102.27 W
Boxey	186	47.25 N	55.34 W
Boxey Point ›	186	47.24 N	55.35 W
Boxford	207	42.39 N	70.59 W
Boxford State Forest ♠	283	42.39 N	71.02 W
Box Grove	275b	43.51 N	79.14 W
Box Hill	169	37.49 S	145.08 E
Boxholm	26	58.12 N	15.03 E
Boxian	100	33.53 N	115.45 E
Boxing	98	37.08 N	118.07 E
Boxley	260	51.18 N	0.33 E
Boxmeer	52	51.39 N	5.57 E
Boxmoor	260	51.45 N	0.29 W
Boxodoi	98	42.34 N	115.18 E
Boxtel	52	51.35 N	5.20 E
Boyabat	130	41.28 N	34.47 E
Boyabo	152	3.43 N	18.46 E
Boyacá □[5]	246	5.30 N	73.30 W
Boyacıköy ➜[8]	267b	41.06 N	29.02 E
Boyadel → Bojadła	30	51.57 N	15.50 E
Boyali	130	41.02 N	33.19 E
Boyalık	130	41.15 N	28.37 E
Boyang	100	28.59 N	116.40 E
Boyanup	168a	33.29 S	115.44 E
Boyasengese	152	3.29 N	20.33 E
Boyce	194	31.23 N	92.40 W
Boyceville	190	45.02 N	92.02 W
Boyd, Mn., U.S.	198	44.50 N	95.54 W
Boyd, Tx., U.S.	222	33.05 N	97.34 W
Boyd ≃	166	29.51 S	152.35 E
Boyd Glacier ⊓	9	77.14 S	145.25 W
Boyd's Cove	186	49.27 N	54.39 W
Boydton	192	36.40 N	78.23 W
Boyenge	152	0.25 N	18.51 E
Boyer ≃	198	41.28 N	95.55 W
Boyera	152	0.38 S	19.25 E
Boyer Ahmadī-e Kohkīlūyeh □[4]	128	30.40 N	50.42 E
Boyer Run ≃	279b	40.13 N	79.32 W
Boyers	214	41.06 N	79.54 W
Boyer's Creek ≃	284a	43.00 N	79.02 W
Boyertown	208	40.20 N	75.38 W
Boyes Hot Springs	226	38.19 N	122.29 W
Boykins	208	36.34 N	77.12 W
Boyle, Ab., Can.	182	54.35 N	112.49 W
Boyle, Ire.	48	53.58 N	8.18 W
Boyle, Ms., U.S.	194	33.42 N	90.50 W
Boyle Drain ≃	212	43.42 N	81.06 W
Boyle Heights ➜[8]	280	34.02 N	118.13 W
Boylston, Al., U.S.	194	32.26 N	86.17 W
Boylston, Ma., U.S.	207	42.23 N	71.42 W
Boyne	275b	43.29 N	79.50 W
Boyne ≃, Austl.	166	23.56 S	151.21 E
Boyne ≃, Mb., Can.	184	49.34 N	97.52 W
Boyne ≃, On., Can.	212	44.10 N	79.49 W
Boyne ≃, Ire.	48	53.43 N	6.15 W
Boyne Battlesite ⊥	48	53.42 N	6.23 W
Boyne City	190	45.12 N	85.00 W
Boyni Qara	120	36.19 N	66.53 E
Boynton	196	35.38 N	95.39 W
Boynton Beach	220	26.31 N	80.04 W
Boyo	152	5.43 N	21.33 E
Boyoali	115a	7.32 S	110.35 E
Boysen Reservoir ⊜[1]	202	43.19 N	108.11 W
Boysen State Park ♠	202	43.23 N	108.07 W
Boys Ranch	196	35.32 N	102.15 W
Boyuibe	248	20.25 S	63.17 W
Boyup Brook	162	33.50 S	116.24 E
Bozburun	130	36.41 N	28.04 E
Boz Burun ›	130	40.24 N	26.54 E
Boz Dağ ʌ, Tür.	130	37.18 N	29.12 E
Boz Dağ ʌ, Tür.	130	38.19 N	28.08 E
Boz Dağları ⋏	130	38.20 N	27.45 E
Bozdoğan	130	37.40 N	28.19 E
Bozel	62	45.27 N	6.39 E
Bozeman	202	45.40 N	111.02 W
Bozen → Bolzano	64	46.31 N	11.22 E
Bozene	152	2.56 N	19.12 E
Bozhen	98	38.07 N	116.32 E
Boží Dar	54	50.24 N	12.55 E
Bozkır	130	37.11 N	32.15 E
Bozkurt	130	37.49 N	29.37 E
Bozman	208	38.46 N	76.16 W
Bozoum	152	6.19 N	16.23 E
Bozovici	38	44.55 N	21.59 E
Bozšakol'	86	51.50 N	74.20 E
Bozum	52	53.05 N	5.42 E
Bozüyük	130	39.54 N	30.03 E
Bozyaka	130	37.08 N	31.12 E
Bozzolo	64	45.06 N	10.29 E
Bra	62	44.42 N	7.51 E
Braan ≃	46	56.33 N	3.35 W
Braås	26	57.04 N	15.03 E
Brabant □[4]	56	50.45 N	4.30 E
Brabante, Isla de → Brabant Island I	9	64.15 S	62.20 W
Brabant Island I	9	64.15 S	62.20 W
Brabant Lake ⊜	184	56.00 N	103.43 W
Brabrand	41	56.09 N	10.07 E
Brač, Otok I	36	43.20 N	16.40 E
Bracadale, Loch c	46	57.19 N	6.30 W
Bracciano	66	42.06 N	12.10 E
Bracciano, Lago di ⊜	66	42.07 N	12.14 E
Bracco, Passo del)(	62	44.15 N	9.34 E
Bracebridge	212	45.02 N	79.19 W
Bracebridge Heath	44	53.13 N	0.33 W
Braceville, Il., U.S.	216	41.14 N	88.16 W
Braceville, Oh., U.S.	214	41.14 N	80.58 W
Brachfield	222	32.03 N	94.39 W
Bracieux	50	47.33 N	1.33 E
Bracigliano	68	40.49 N	14.42 E
Bracigovo	38	42.01 N	24.22 E
Bräcke	26	62.43 N	15.27 E
Brackel ➜[8]	263	51.32 N	7.33 E
Bracken □[6]	218	38.40 N	84.06 W
Brackendale	182	49.46 N	123.09 W
Brackenheim	56	49.05 N	9.03 E
Brackenhurst	273d	26.19 S	28.06 E
Bracken Lake ⊜	184	53.37 N	99.50 W
Brackenridge	214	40.36 N	79.44 W
Brackett Field ⊠	280	34.05 N	117.47 W
Brackettville	196	29.18 N	100.25 W
Brački Kanal ʉ	36	43.24 N	16.40 E
Brackley	42	52.02 N	1.09 W
Bracknell	42	51.26 N	0.45 W
Bracktown	218	38.04 N	84.31 W
Brackwede	52	51.59 N	8.31 E
Braclav	78	48.50 N	28.55 E
Braco	46	56.15 N	3.53 W
Braço do Norte	252	28.17 S	49.11 W
Braço Grande, Igarapé ≃	250	3.43 S	48.49 W
Bracuí ≃	256	22.57 S	44.24 W
Brad	38	46.08 N	22.47 E
Bradano ≃	68	40.23 N	16.51 E
Bradbury	280	34.08 N	117.59 W
Bradbury Heights	284c	38.52 N	76.56 W
Braddock, N.J., U.S.	285	39.42 N	74.53 W
Braddock, Pa., U.S.	214	40.24 N	79.52 W
Braddock Acres	284c	38.49 N	77.10 W
Braddock Heights, Md., U.S.	208	39.25 N	77.30 W
Braddock Heights, N.Y., U.S.	210	43.19 N	77.42 W
Braddock Hills	279b	40.25 N	79.51 W
Braddock Point ›	210	43.19 N	77.43 W
Braddocks Millpond ⊜	285	39.49 N	74.51 W
Braden ≃	220	27.30 N	82.32 W
Bradenton	220	27.29 N	82.34 W
Bradenton Beach	220	27.28 N	82.42 W
Bradenville	214	40.19 N	79.20 W
Braderup	41	54.50 N	8.53 E
Bradford, On., Can.	212	44.07 N	79.34 W
Bradford, Eng., U.K.	44	53.48 N	1.45 W
Bradford, Ar., U.S.	194	35.25 N	91.27 W
Bradford, Il., U.S.	190	41.10 N	89.39 W
Bradford, N.Y., U.S.	210	42.22 N	77.07 W
Bradford, Oh., U.S.	218	40.08 N	84.26 W
Bradford, Pa., U.S.	214	41.57 N	78.38 W
Bradford, R.I., U.S.	207	41.23 N	71.44 W
Bradford, Tn., U.S.	194	36.04 N	88.48 W
Bradford, Vt., U.S.	188	43.59 N	72.09 W
Bradford □[6]	210	41.56 N	78.40 W
Bradford □[8]	262	53.47 N	1.52 W
Bradford Hills	285	40.01 N	75.39 W
Bradford Mountain ʌ	207	41.59 N	73.18 W
Bradford-on-Avon	42	51.20 N	2.15 W
Bradford Regional Airport ⊠	214	41.48 N	78.38 W
Bradfordwoods	214	40.38 N	80.05 W
Brading	42	50.41 N	1.09 W
Bradley, Ar., U.S.	194	33.05 N	93.39 W
Bradley, Ca., U.S.	226	35.51 N	120.47 W
Bradley, Fl., U.S.	220	27.48 N	81.59 W
Bradley, Il., U.S.	216	41.08 N	87.51 W
Bradley, Mi., U.S.	216	42.38 N	85.39 W
Bradley, S.D., U.S.	198	45.05 N	97.38 W
Bradley Beach	208	40.12 N	74.01 W
Bradley Farms	284c	39.00 N	77.11 W
Bradley Gardens	276	40.34 N	74.39 W
Bradley Institute	154	17.02 S	31.27 E
Bradley International Airport ⊠	207	41.55 N	72.40 W
Bradley Reefs ✦[2]	175e	6.52 S	160.48 E
Bradley Woods Reservation ♠	279a	41.25 N	81.58 W
Bradley W. Palmer State Park ♠	283	42.39 N	70.54 W
Bradner, B.C., Can.	224	49.06 N	122.25 W
Bradner, Oh., U.S.	214	41.19 N	83.26 W
Bradninch	42	50.50 N	3.25 W
Bradore-Bay	186	51.28 N	57.14 W
Bradshaw, Eng., U.K.	262	53.36 N	2.24 W
Bradshaw, Md., U.S.	208	39.25 N	76.22 W
Bradshaw, Ne., U.S.	198	40.53 N	97.44 W
Bradshaw, W.V., U.S.	192	37.21 N	81.47 W
Bradwell-on-Sea	42	51.44 N	0.54 E
Bradworthy	42	50.54 N	4.22 W
Brady, Mt., U.S.	202	48.02 N	111.50 W
Brady, Ne., U.S.	198	41.01 N	100.22 W
Brady, Tx., U.S.	196	31.08 N	99.20 W
Brady Creek ≃	196	31.07 N	98.59 W
Brady Lake	214	41.09 N	81.19 W
Brady Mountains ⋏[2]	196	31.20 N	99.40 W
Brae	46a	60.23 N	1.21 W
Brædstrup	41	55.58 N	9.37 E
Braemar	46	57.01 N	3.23 W
Braeside, Austl.	162	21.12 S	121.01 E
Braeside, Austl.	274b	37.59 S	145.07 E
Braeside, On., Can.	212	45.28 N	76.24 W
Braga	34	41.33 N	8.26 W
Bragado	252	35.08 S	60.30 W
Bragança, Bra.	250	1.03 S	46.46 W
Bragança, Port.	34	41.49 N	6.45 W
Bragança Paulista	256	22.57 S	46.34 W
Bragar	46	58.24 N	6.40 W
Bragin	78	51.47 N	30.14 E
Braginka ≃	78	51.22 N	30.24 E
Braginovka	78	48.29 N	36.21 E
Braham	190	45.43 N	93.10 W
Brahetrolleborg ⊥	41	55.09 N	10.22 E
Brahma Island I	220	27.52 N	81.15 W
Brāhmanbāria	120	23.59 N	91.07 E
Brāhmani ≃, India	120	20.39 N	86.46 E
Brāhmani ≃, India	126	24.09 N	88.01 E
Brahmapur	272b	22.28 N	88.22 E
Brahmaputra (Yaluzangbujiang) ≃	120	24.02 N	90.59 E
Brāhmaur	123	32.27 N	76.32 E
Braich y Pwll ›	42	52.48 N	4.36 W
Braidwood, Austl.	166	35.27 S	149.48 E
Braidwood, Il., U.S.	216	41.15 N	88.12 W
Braies (Prags)	64	46.42 N	12.08 E
Brăila	38	45.16 N	27.58 E
Brăila □[6]	38	45.00 N	27.40 E
Brăilei, Balta ≡	38	45.00 N	28.00 E
Brailov	78	49.06 N	28.09 E
Brain ≃	42	51.48 N	0.39 E
Brainard, Ne., U.S.	198	41.11 N	97.00 W
Brainard, N.Y., U.S.	210	42.30 N	73.31 W
Braine	50	49.20 N	3.32 E
Braine-l'Alleud	50	50.41 N	4.22 E
Braine-le-Château	50	50.41 N	4.16 E
Braine-le-Comte	50	50.36 N	4.08 E
Brainerd	190	46.21 N	94.12 W
Braint ≃	44	53.08 N	4.19 W
Braintree, Eng., U.K.	42	51.53 N	0.32 E
Braintree, Ma., U.S.	207	42.13 N	71.00 W
Braintree □[8]	260	51.47 N	0.36 E
Brak ≃, S. Afr.	158	29.35 S	22.55 E
Brak ≃, S. Afr.	158	31.32 S	21.33 E
Brake, B.R.D.	52	52.01 N	8.55 E
Brake, B.R.D.	52	53.19 N	8.28 E
Brake, B.R.D.	52	52.04 N	8.35 E
Brakel, Bel.	50	50.48 N	3.46 E
Brakel, B.R.D.	52	51.43 N	9.10 E
Brakna □[4]	150	17.30 N	13.30 W
Brakpan	158	26.14 S	28.22 E
Brakpan □[5]	273d	26.16 S	28.21 E
Brakpoort	158	31.20 S	23.22 E
Brakputs	158	29.29 S	18.24 E
Brakwater	156	22.24 S	17.06 E
Brålanda	26	58.34 N	12.22 E
Bralorne	182	50.47 N	122.49 W
Bramalea	212	43.44 N	79.43 W
Bramall Hall ⊥	262	53.23 N	2.09 W
Braman	196	36.55 N	97.20 W
Brambauer ➜[8]	263	51.35 N	7.27 E
Bramberg am Wildkogel	64	47.16 N	12.21 E
Bramble Bay c	171a	27.17 S	153.05 E
Bramble Cay I	164	9.08 S	143.52 E
Bramdrupdam	41	55.31 N	9.28 E
Bramey-Lenningsen	263	51.34 N	7.46 E
Bramfeld ➜[8]	52	53.37 N	10.04 E
Bramford	42	52.04 N	1.06 E
Bramhall	262	53.22 N	2.10 W
Bramhope	44	53.53 N	1.37 W
Bramley	260	51.12 N	0.34 W
Bramley ➜[8]	273d	26.08 S	28.05 E
Bramley Mountain ʌ	210	42.18 N	74.49 W
Bramming	41	55.28 N	8.42 E
Brampton, On., Can.	212	43.41 N	79.46 W
Brampton, Eng., U.K.	42	52.19 N	0.14 W
Brampton, Eng., U.K.	44	54.57 N	2.43 W
Brampton Airfield ⊠	275b	43.40 N	79.47 W
Bramsche	52	52.24 N	7.58 E
Bramsöfjärden ⊜	40	60.20 N	17.10 E
Bramstedt	52	53.22 N	8.41 E
Bran, Pasul)(	38	45.26 N	25.17 E
Brancaleone Marina	68	37.58 N	16.06 E
Brancaster	42	52.58 N	0.39 E
Brancaster Roads ∓[3]	42	53.05 N	0.45 W
Branch	186	46.53 N	53.57 W
Branch □[6]	216	41.55 N	85.03 W
Branch Brook Park ♠	276	40.46 N	74.10 W
Branch Dale	208	40.41 N	76.20 W
Branchport	210	42.36 N	77.09 W
Branchville, Ct., U.S.	207	41.16 N	73.26 W
Branchville, N.J., U.S.	210	41.08 N	74.45 W
Branchville, S.C., U.S.	192	33.15 N	80.48 W
Branchville, Va., U.S.	208	36.34 N	77.14 W
Branco	152	12.30 S	20.32 E
Branco ≃, Bra.	246	1.24 S	61.51 W
Branco ≃, Bra.	248	10.03 S	67.51 W
Branco ≃, Bra.	248	7.44 S	61.46 W
Branco ≃, Bra.	248	6.41 S	66.41 W
Branco ≃, Bra.	248	9.12 S	64.22 W
Branco ≃, Bra.	248	9.37 S	60.33 W
Branco ≃, Bra.	248	13.41 S	60.44 W
Branco ≃, Bra.	248	21.00 S	57.48 W
Branco ≃, Bra.	250	12.00 S	44.56 W
Branco ≃, Bra.	250	7.01 S	51.42 W
Branco ≃, Bra.	256	24.09 S	46.48 W
Branco, Ilhéu I	150a	16.39 N	24.41 W
Brand, B.R.D.	56	50.43 N	6.09 E
Brand, Öst.	58	47.06 N	9.44 E
Brandamore	208	40.03 N	75.50 W
Brandaris ʌ[2]	241s	12.17 N	68.24 W
Brandberg ʌ	156	21.10 S	14.33 E
Brandbu	26	60.28 N	10.30 E
Brande	41	55.57 N	9.07 E
Brandebourg → Brandenburg	54	52.24 N	12.32 E
Brandeis University ⊍[2]	283	42.22 N	71.16 W
Brandenberg	64	47.29 N	11.53 E
Brandenberg ʌ[2]	263	51.20 N	7.37 E
Brandenburg, D.D.R.	54	52.24 N	12.32 E
Brandenburg, Ky., U.S.	194	38.00 N	86.10 W
Brandenburg □[9]	54	52.00 N	13.30 E
Brandenburger Tor ⊥	264a	52.31 N	13.23 E
Brand-Erbisdorf	54	50.52 N	13.19 E
Brandfort	158	28.47 S	26.30 E
Br'andino	80	54.23 N	49.23 E
Brandis, D.D.R.	54	51.48 N	13.10 E
Brandis, D.D.R.	54	51.20 N	12.36 E
Brandizzo	62	45.11 N	7.51 E
Brandkop	158	31.13 S	19.13 E
Brandon, Mb., Can.	184	49.50 N	99.57 W
Brandon, Eng., U.K.	42	52.27 N	0.37 E
Brandon, Eng., U.K.	44	54.46 N	1.39 W
Brandon, Fl., U.S.	220	27.56 N	82.17 W
Brandon, Ms., U.S.	194	32.16 N	89.59 W
Brandon, S.D., U.S.	198	43.35 N	96.34 W
Brandon, Tx., U.S.	222	32.03 N	96.58 W
Brandon, Vt., U.S.	188	43.47 N	73.05 W
Brandon, Wi., U.S.	190	43.44 N	88.46 W
Brandon Bay c	48	52.15 N	10.05 W
Brandon Head ›	48	52.16 N	10.14 W
Brandon Mountain ʌ	48	52.14 N	10.15 W
Brandon Road Lock and Dam ➜[5]	278	41.30 N	88.06 W
Brandonville	210	40.52 N	76.10 W
Brand Park ♠	280	34.11 N	118.16 W
Brands Hatch Motor Race Circuit ♠	260	51.22 N	0.16 E
Brandsø I	41	55.21 N	9.43 E
Brandt	218	39.54 N	84.05 W
Brandvlei	158	30.25 S	20.30 E
Brandy Camp	214	41.19 N	78.41 W
Brandy Peak ʌ	202	42.36 N	123.53 W
Brandýsek	54	50.10 N	14.10 E
Brandýs nad Labem	54	50.10 N	14.41 E
Brandywine Battlefield ⊥	208	39.53 N	75.35 W
Brandywine Creek ≃, U.S.	285	39.44 N	75.32 W
Brandywine Creek ≃, In., U.S.	218	39.31 N	85.52 W
Brandywine Creek ≃, Oh., U.S.	279a	41.17 N	81.34 W
Brandywine Creek, East Branch ≃	208	39.55 N	75.39 W
Brandywine Creek, West Branch ≃	208	39.55 N	75.39 W
Brandywine Creek State Park ♠	285	39.48 N	75.35 W
Brandywine Park ♠	285	39.45 N	75.33 W
Brandywine Raceway ♠	285	39.50 N	75.32 W
Brandywine Springs Park ♠	285	39.45 N	75.38 W
Branford, Ct., U.S.	207	41.16 N	72.48 W
Branford, Fl., U.S.	192	29.57 N	82.55 W
Brani, Pulau I	271c	1.15 N	103.50 E
Braniewo	30	54.24 N	19.50 E
Branka, Česko.	60	49.50 N	12.33 E
Br'anka, S.S.S.R.	83	48.29 N	38.39 E
Br'anka, S.S.S.R.	86	59.08 N	93.27 E
Branlin ≃	50	47.51 N	3.06 E
Brannenburg	64	47.44 N	12.05 E
Branquinho ≃	248	5.45 S	71.27 W
Bransby	166	28.14 S	142.04 E
Bransfield Strait ʉ	9	63.00 S	59.00 W
Bransgore	42	50.47 N	1.44 W
Brańsk, Pol.	30	52.45 N	22.51 E
Br'ansk, S.S.S.R.	76	53.15 N	34.22 E
Br'ansk □[4], S.S.S.R.	76	53.00 N	34.00 E
Br'ansk □[4], S.S.S.R.	78	52.30 N	33.00 E
Br'anskaja Kosa, mys ›	84	44.22 N	47.00 E
Branson	194	36.38 N	93.13 W
Brant	210	42.35 N	79.01 W
Brant □[6]	212	43.10 N	80.20 W
Brant ≃	44	53.09 N	0.35 W
Br'anta ≃	89	54.27 N	127.42 E
Brantas ≃	115a	7.28 S	112.25 E
Brantford	212	43.08 N	80.16 W
Brantingham Lake ⊜	212	43.42 N	75.17 W
Brant Lake	188	43.40 N	73.45 W
Brantley	194	31.34 N	86.15 W
Brantôme	32	45.22 N	0.39 E
Brant Rock	283	42.05 N	70.38 W
Brantville	186	47.22 N	64.58 W
Branxholme	166	37.51 S	141.47 E
Branxton	170	32.39 S	151.22 E
Branzi	64	46.00 N	9.46 E
Brás ➜[8]	287b	23.32 S	46.36 W
Brás Cubas	256	23.32 S	46.13 W
Bras d'Or Lake ⊜	186	45.52 N	60.50 W
Brashear	222	33.07 N	95.44 W
Brasil → Brazil □[1]	242	10.00 S	55.00 W
Brasilândia ➜[8]	287b	23.28 S	46.41 W
Brasiléia	248	11.00 S	68.44 W
Brasília	255	15.47 S	47.55 W
Brasília, Lago de ⊜	255	15.48 S	47.50 W
Brasília, Parque Nacional de ♠	255	15.36 S	48.08 W
Brasília de Minas	255	16.12 S	44.26 W
Brasília Legal	250	3.49 S	55.36 W
Brasilien → Brazil □[1]	242	10.00 S	55.00 W
Braslav	76	55.38 N	27.02 E
Brașov	38	45.39 N	25.37 E
Brașov □[6]	38	45.45 N	25.15 E
Brass	150	4.19 N	6.14 E
Brass Castle	210	40.47 N	74.58 W
Brasschaat	50	51.17 N	4.27 E
Brassert	263	51.40 N	7.05 E
Brassey, Binjaran ⋏	112	4.54 N	117.30 E
Brassey, Mount ʌ	162	23.05 S	134.38 E
Brass Islands II	240m	18.24 N	64.58 W
Brassó → Brașov	38	45.39 N	25.37 E
Brasstown Bald ʌ	192	34.52 N	83.48 W
Brastad	26	58.23 N	11.29 E
Brasted	260	51.16 N	0.17 E
Brasted Chart	260	51.16 N	0.06 E
Břasy	60	49.50 N	13.35 E
Bratca	38	46.56 N	22.37 E
Bratcevo ➜[8]	265b	55.51 N	37.24 E
Bratejevo ➜[8]	265b	55.38 N	37.45 E
Bratenahl	279a	41.32 N	81.37 W
Brateș, Lacul ⊜	38	45.30 N	28.05 E
Bratislava	30	48.09 N	17.07 E
Bratol'ubovka	86	51.13 N	66.46 E
Bratsk	88	56.05 N	101.48 E
Bratskaja Kada	88	55.02 N	102.06 E
Bratskoje	78	47.52 N	31.34 E
Bratskoje vodochranilišče ⊜[1]	88	56.10 N	102.10 E
Brattfors	40	59.40 N	14.01 E
Brattleboro	207	42.51 N	72.33 W
Bratto	64	45.55 N	10.04 E
Brattvåg	26	62.36 N	6.27 E
Braubach	56	50.16 N	7.40 E
Braúnas	255	19.04 S	42.43 W
Braunau am Inn	60	48.15 N	13.02 E
Braunfels	56	50.31 N	8.23 E
Braunlage	54	51.44 N	10.37 E
Bräunlingen	58	47.55 N	8.26 E
Braunsbedra	54	51.15 N	11.49 E
Braunsberg → Braniewo	30	54.24 N	19.50 E
Braunschweig, B.R.D.	52	52.16 N	10.31 E
Braunschweig, S. Afr.	158	32.48 S	27.22 E
Braunschweig □[6]	54	52.10 N	10.30 E
Braunston	42	52.17 N	1.12 W
Braunton	42	51.07 N	4.10 W
Braunwald	58	46.56 N	9.00 E
Brava I	150a	14.52 N	24.43 W
Brava, Costa ≚[2]	34	41.45 N	3.04 E
Brava, Laguna ⊜	252	28.22 S	68.50 W
Brava, Punta ›	258	34.56 S	56.10 W
Brave	188	39.44 N	80.16 W
Bravića	78	47.22 N	28.26 E
Bråviken c	40	58.38 N	16.32 E
Bravo, Cerro ʌ, Bol.	248	17.40 S	64.35 W
Bravo, Cerro ʌ, Perú	248	5.32 S	79.15 W
Bravo del Norte (Rio Grande) ≃	178	25.55 N	97.09 W
Brawley	204	32.58 N	115.31 W
Brawley Peaks ⋏	204	38.15 N	118.55 W
Brawley Wash V	200	32.34 N	111.26 W
Bray, Bel.	50	50.26 N	4.06 E
Bray, Ire.	48	53.12 N	6.06 W
Bray ≃	42	50.59 N	3.53 W
Bray, Pays de ➜[1]	50	49.46 N	1.26 E
Braybrook	274b	37.47 S	144.51 E
Bray-Dunes	50	51.05 N	2.31 E
Braye ≃	50	47.45 N	0.42 E
Bray Head ›	48	51.53 N	10.26 W
Bray Island I	176	69.20 N	76.45 W
Braymer	194	39.35 N	93.47 W
Braysur-Seine	50	48.25 N	3.14 E
Bray-sur-Somme	50	49.56 N	2.43 E
Brayton	44	53.46 N	1.05 W
Brazeau ≃	182	52.55 N	115.15 W
Brazeau, Mount ʌ	182	52.33 N	117.21 W
Brazeau Dam ➜[6]	182	52.45 N	115.30 W
Brazen Head ›	158	31.43 S	29.25 E
Brazey-en-Plaine	58	47.08 N	5.13 E
Brazil	194	39.31 N	87.07 W
Brazil (Brasil) □[1]	242	10.00 S	55.00 W
Brazil Basin ✦[1]	8	15.00 S	25.00 W
Brazo Chico, Arroyo ≃	258	33.45 S	58.32 W
Brazo Largo, Arroyo ≃	258	33.47 S	58.36 W
Brazópolis	256	22.28 S	45.37 W
Brazoria	222	29.02 N	95.34 W
Brazoria □[6]	222	29.12 N	95.25 W
Brazoria Reservoir ⊜[1]	222	29.05 N	95.01 W
Brazos □[6]	222	30.40 N	96.18 W
Brazos ≃	196	28.53 N	95.23 W
Brazos, Clear Fork ≃	196	33.01 N	98.40 W
Brazos, Double Mountain Fork ≃	196	33.15 N	100.00 W
Brazos, Salt Fork ≃	196	33.15 N	100.00 W
Brazo Sur [del Rio Coig] ≃	254	51.32 S	70.04 W
Brazzaville, Congo	152	4.16 S	15.17 E
Brazzaville, Congo	273b	4.16 S	15.17 E
Brazzaville (Maya Maya) Airport ⊠	273b	4.15 S	15.15 E
Brčko	38	44.53 N	18.48 E
Brda ≃	30	53.07 N	18.08 E
Brdy ⋏	60	49.40 N	13.50 E
Bré → Bray	48	53.12 N	6.06 W
Brea	228	33.55 N	117.53 W
Brea, Punta ›	240m	17.56 N	66.55 W
Brea Canyon V	280	33.55 N	117.55 W
Brea Creek ≃	280	33.53 N	117.59 W
Breadalbane	166	23.49 S	139.35 E
Brea Dam ➜[6]	280	33.54 N	117.56 W
Breaden Bluff ʌ[2]	162	26.56 S	124.32 E
Breadysville	285	40.13 N	75.04 W
Breakenridge, Mount ʌ	182	49.43 N	121.56 W
Breakheart Reservation ♠	283	42.29 N	71.02 W
Breaksea Sound ʉ	172	45.35 S	166.40 E
Breaks Interstate Park ♠	192	37.17 N	82.18 W
Bream	42	51.45 N	2.34 W
Bream Bay c	172	35.55 S	174.30 E
Bream Head ›	172	35.51 S	174.35 E
Breamish ≃	44	55.31 N	1.56 W
Bream Tail ›	172	36.03 S	174.35 E
Brea Pozo	252	28.15 S	63.57 W
Breaston	44	52.54 N	1.19 W
Bréau	261	48.34 N	2.53 E
Breaux Bridge	194	30.16 N	91.53 W
Breaza	38	45.11 N	25.40 E
Brebes	115a	6.53 S	109.03 E
Brécey	32	48.44 N	1.10 W
Brechen	56	50.20 N	8.14 E
Brechfa	42	51.54 N	4.36 W
Brechin	46	56.44 N	2.40 W
Brecht	56	51.21 N	4.38 E
Brechten ➜[8]	263	51.35 N	7.28 E
Breckenridge, Co., U.S.	200	39.28 N	106.02 W
Breckenridge, Mi., U.S.	190	43.24 N	84.28 W
Breckenridge, Mn., U.S.	198	46.15 N	96.35 W
Breckenridge, Mo., U.S.	194	39.45 N	93.48 W
Breckenridge, Tx., U.S.	196	32.45 N	98.54 W
Breckerfeld	56	51.16 N	7.28 E
Breckland ➜[1]	42	52.28 N	0.37 E
Brecknock → Brecon	42	51.57 N	3.24 W
Brecknock, Península ›[1]	254	54.35 S	71.50 W
Brecksville	214	41.19 N	81.37 W
Břeclav	30	48.46 N	16.53 E
Brecon	42	51.57 N	3.24 W
Brecon Beacons ʌ	42	51.53 N	3.31 W
Brecon Beacons National Park ♠	42	51.52 N	3.25 W
Bred	41	55.22 N	10.07 E
Breda, Ned.	52	51.35 N	4.46 E
Breda, Ia., U.S.	198	42.10 N	94.58 W
Bredaryd	26	57.10 N	13.44 E
Bredasdorp	158	34.32 S	20.02 E
Bredbo	171b	35.57 S	149.10 E
Bredbo ≃	171b	35.58 S	149.08 E
Bredbury	262	53.25 N	2.06 W
Bredbyn	26	63.27 N	18.06 E
Breddin	54	52.52 N	12.13 E

Symbols in the index entries represent the broad categories identified in the key at the right. Symbols with superior numbers (⋏[1]) identify subcategories (see complete key on page *I · 1).*

Kartensymbole in dem Registerverzeichnis stellen die rechts in Schlüssel erklärten Kategorien dar. Symbole mit hochgestellten Ziffern (⋏[1]) bezeichnen Unterabteilungen einer Kategorie (vgl. vollständiger Schlüssel auf Seite *I · 1).*

Los símbolos incluídos en el texto del índice representan las grandes categorias identificadas con la clave a la derecha. Los símbolos con numeros en su parte superior (⋏[1]) identifican las subcategorías (véase la clave completa en la página *I · 1*).

Les symboles de l'index représentent le[…] indiquées dans la légende à droite. Les symboles suivis d'un indice (⋏[1]) représentent des sous-catégories (voir légende complète à la page *I · 1).*

Os símbolos incluídos no texto do índice representam as grandes categorias identificadas com a chave à direita. Os símbolos com números em sua parte superior (⋏[1]) identificam as subcategorias (veja-se a chave completa à página *I · 1).*

	English	Deutsch	Español	Français	Português
ʌ	Mountain	Berg	Montaña	Montagne	Montanha
⋏	Mountains	Berge	Montañas	Montagnes	Montanhas
)(	Pass	Pass	Paso	Col	Passo
V	Valley, Canyon	Tal, Cañon	Valle, Cañón	Vallée, Canyon	Vale, Canhão
≚	Plain	Ebene	Llano	Plaine	Planície
›	Cape	Kap	Cabo	Cap	Cabo
I	Island	Insel	Isla	Île	Ilha
II	Islands	Inseln	Islas	Îles	Ilhas
♠	Other Topographic Features	Andere Topographische Objekte	Otros Elementos Topográficos	Autres données topographiques	Outros acidentes topográficos

ESPAÑOL — FRANÇAIS — PORTUGUÊS

Nombre / Nom / Nome	Página / Page	Lat.°′	Long.°′ W = Oeste / W = Ouest
Brede Å ≃	41	55.09 N	8.42 E
Bredebro	41	55.03 N	8.49 E
Bredell	273d	26.05 S	28.17 E
Bredenbeck	52	52.15 N	9.37 E
Bredenbruch	263	51.21 N	7.45 E
Bredenbury	184	50.57 N	102.03 W
Bredene	50	51.14 N	2.58 E
Bredeney ◆[8]	263	51.24 N	6.59 E
Bredenscheid-Stüter	263	51.22 N	7.11 E
Bredereiche	54	53.08 N	13.14 E
Bredgar	260	51.18 N	0.42 E
Bredhurst	260	51.20 N	0.35 E
Bredon Hill ʌ[2]	42	52.06 N	2.03 W
Bredsjö	40	59.50 N	14.44 E
Bredsjön ⊜	40	60.13 N	13.55 E
Bredstedt	41	54.37 N	8.59 E
Bredsten	41	55.42 N	9.24 E
Bredy	86	52.26 N	60.21 E
Bree	56	51.08 N	5.36 E
Breë ≃	158	34.24 S	20.50 E
Breeches, Lac ⊜	206	45.54 N	71.28 W
Breedoge ≃	48	53.55 N	8.27 W
Breeds Pond ⊜	283	42.28 N	70.59 W
Breedsville	216	42.21 N	86.08 W
Breese	219	38.36 N	89.31 W
Breesport	210	42.10 N	76.44 W
Breeza Plains	164	14.50 S	144.07 E
Breezewood	279b	40.34 N	80.03 W
Breg ≃	58	47.57 N	8.31 E
Bregalnica ≃	38	41.43 N	22.09 E
Breganze	64	45.42 N	11.34 E
Bregenz	58	47.30 N	9.46 E
Bregenzer Wald ⋀	58	47.20 N	10.00 E
Bregninge, Dan.	41	55.41 N	11.19 E
Bregninge, Dan.	41	55.01 N	10.37 E
Bregovo	38	44.09 N	22.39 E
Breguzzo	64	46.00 N	10.42 E
Brégy	261	49.05 N	2.52 E
Bréhal	32	48.54 N	1.31 W
Brehna	54	51.33 N	12.12 E
Breiðafjörður ⊂	24a	65.15 N	23.15 W
Breidbach	158	32.54 S	27.27 E
Breid Bay ⊂	9	70.15 S	24.15 E
Breidenbach	56	49.08 N	7.25 E
Breidenstein	56	50.55 N	8.28 E
Breil-sur-Roya	62	43.56 N	7.30 E
Breinizer	214	40.24 N	79.16 W
Breisach	58	48.01 N	7.40 E
Breisgau □[9]	58	47.45 N	7.45 E
Breitenbrunn	54	50.29 N	12.46 E
Breitenfelde	52	53.36 N	10.38 E
Breitenfurt bei Wien	61	48.08 N	16.08 E
Breitengüssbach	56	49.58 N	10.53 E
Breitenlee ◆[8]	264b	48.15 N	16.30 E
Breitenstein	54	51.37 N	10.56 E
Breitenworbis	54	51.24 N	10.25 E
Breithorn ʌ	58	45.56 N	7.45 E
Breitlingsee ⊜	54	52.23 N	12.28 E
Breitscheid, B.R.D.	56	51.22 N	6.52 E
Breitscheid, B.R.D.	56	50.41 N	8.11 E
Breitsetten	61	48.12 N	16.42 E
Breitungen	54	50.45 N	10.20 E
Brejinho de Nazaré	250	11.01 S	48.34 W
Brejo	250	3.41 S	42.47 W
Brejo, Riacho do ≃	250	8.08 S	42.49 W
Brejo de São Felix	250	5.24 S	43.24 W
Brejões	255	13.06 S	39.48 W
Brejo Grande	250	10.26 S	36.28 W
Brejo Santo	250	7.29 S	39.00 W
Brejtovo	76	58.18 N	37.52 E
Brekken	26	62.39 N	11.53 E
Brekstad	26	63.41 N	9.41 E
Breloh	52	53.01 N	10.04 E
Bremangerlandet ɪ	26	61.51 N	5.02 E
Brembio	62	45.13 N	9.34 E
Brembo ≃	62	45.35 N	9.32 E
Brême → Bremen	52	53.04 N	8.49 E
Bremelau	58	48.20 N	9.32 E
Bremen, B.R.D.	52	53.04 N	8.49 E
Bremen, Ga., U.S.	192	33.43 N	85.08 W
Bremen, In., U.S.	216	41.26 N	86.08 W
Bremen, Oh., U.S.	188	39.42 N	82.25 W
Bremen □[3]	52	53.05 N	8.50 E
Bremen, Flughafen ⊠	52	53.03 N	8.46 E
Bremer ≃, Austl.	168b	35.23 S	139.02 E
Bremer ≃, Austl.	171a	27.39 S	152.45 E
Bremer Bay ⊂	162	34.23 S	119.25 E
Bremerhaven	52	53.33 N	8.34 E
Bremerton	224	47.34 N	122.37 W
Bremerton East	224	47.35 N	122.38 W
Bremervörde	52	53.29 N	9.08 E
Bremgarten	58	47.21 N	8.21 E
Bremke, B.R.D.	52	52.07 N	9.06 E
Bremke, B.R.D.	56	51.15 N	8.12 E
Bremke ◆[8]	263	51.23 N	7.41 E
Bremner ≃	190	48.41 N	85.31 W
Bremond	222	31.09 N	96.40 W
Brem River	182	50.26 N	124.39 W
Breña	286d	12.04 S	77.04 W
Brendel Lake ⊜	281	42.38 N	83.30 W
Brenderup	41	55.29 N	9.59 E
Brendlorenzen	56	50.20 N	10.13 E
Brendon Hills ⋀[2]	42	51.07 N	3.25 W
Brenes	34	37.33 N	5.52 W
Brenham	222	30.10 N	96.23 W
Brenig, Llyn ⊜[1]	44	53.05 N	3.32 W
Brenish	46	58.08 N	7.08 W
Brenish, Aird ›	46	58.08 N	7.08 W
Bren Mar Park	284c	38.48 N	77.09 W
Brenne ≃	50	47.38 N	4.16 E
Brennero (Brenner)	64	47.00 N	11.30 E
Brennero, Passo del → Brenner Pass)(	64	47.00 N	11.30 E
Brenner Pass)(	64	47.00 N	11.30 E
Breno, It.	64	45.57 N	10.18 E
Breno, Schw.	58	46.02 N	8.53 E
Brénod	58	46.04 N	5.36 E
Brent, Al., U.S.	194	32.56 N	87.09 W
Brent, Fl., U.S.	194	30.28 N	87.14 W
Brent ◆[8]	260	51.34 N	0.17 W
Brent ≃	260	51.28 N	0.18 W
Brenta ≃	64	45.11 N	12.18 E
Brenta, Gruppo di ⋀	64	46.11 N	10.54 E
Brentford ◆[8]	260	51.29 N	0.18 W
Brenthurst	273d	26.16 S	28.23 E
Brentino	64	45.40 N	10.55 E
Brentonico	64	45.49 N	10.57 E
Brent Reservoir ⊜[1]	260	51.35 N	0.15 W
Brentwood, Eng., U.K.	260	51.38 N	0.18 E
Brentwood, Ca., U.S.	226	37.55 N	121.41 W
Brentwood, Md., U.S.	208	38.56 N	76.57 W
Brentwood, N.Y., U.S.	210	40.46 N	73.14 W
Brentwood, Oh., U.S.	218	39.13 N	84.31 W
Brentwood, Pa., U.S.	214	40.22 N	79.58 W
Brentwood, Tn., U.S.	194	36.01 N	86.46 W
Brentwood □[8]	260	51.37 N	0.20 E
Brentwood Bay	224	48.35 N	123.28 W
Brentwood Estates	214	40.25 N	80.45 W
Brentwood Heights ◆[8]	280	34.04 N	118.30 W
Brentwood Lake	214	41.19 N	82.05 W
Brentwood Park	273d	26.08 S	28.18 E
Brenz ≃	56	48.34 N	10.24 E
Breo	62	44.23 N	7.49 E
Bréon, Ruisseu du ≃	261	48.40 N	2.49 E
Brera, Palazzo di ʊ	266b	45.28 N	9.11 E
Brereton Park	158	26.55 S	30.30 E
Brescello	64	44.54 N	10.31 E
Brescia	64	45.33 N	13.15 E
Brescia □[4]	64	45.38 N	10.18 E
Bresewitz	54	54.24 N	12.40 E
Brésil → Brazil □[1]	242	10.00 S	55.00 W
Breskens	52	51.24 N	3.34 E
Breslau, On., Can.	212	43.28 N	80.25 W
Breslau → Wrocław, Pol.	30	51.06 N	17.00 E
Breslau, Tx., U.S.	222	29.31 N	97.00 W
Bresle ≃	50	50.04 N	1.22 E
Bresles	50	49.25 N	2.15 E
Bresnahan, Mount ʌ	162	23.50 S	117.55 E
Bressanone (Brixen)	64	46.43 N	11.39 E
Bressay ɪ	46a	60.08 N	1.05 W
Bressay Sound ʉ	46a	60.07 N	1.09 W
Bresse ◆[1]	58	46.30 N	5.15 E
Bresso	266b	45.32 N	9.11 E
Bressuire	32	46.51 N	0.30 W
Brest, Blg.	38	43.38 N	24.35 E
Brest, Fr.	32	48.24 N	4.29 W
Brest, S.S.S.R.	76	52.06 N	23.42 E
Brestanica	36	45.59 N	15.29 E
Bretagne □[9]	32	48.00 N	3.00 W
Bretenoux	32	44.55 N	1.50 E
Breteuil	50	49.38 N	2.18 E
Breteuil-sur-Iton	50	48.50 N	0.55 E
Bréthencourt	261	48.30 N	1.55 E
Bretherton	262	53.41 N	2.48 W
Brétigny, Aérodrome de ⊠	261	48.35 N	2.20 E
Brétigny-sur-Orge	50	48.37 N	2.19 E
Bretnig	54	51.08 N	14.04 E
Breton	182	53.07 N	114.28 W
Bretón, Canal de ʉ	240p	21.10 N	79.30 W
Breton, Pertuis ʉ	32	46.25 N	1.20 W
Breton Bay ⊂	208	38.16 N	76.39 W
Breton Islands ɪɪ	194	29.28 N	89.11 W
Breton Sound ʉ	194	29.30 N	89.30 W
Breton Woods	208	40.02 N	74.06 W
Brett ≃	42	51.58 N	0.58 E
Brett, Cape ›	172	35.10 S	174.20 E
Bretten	56	49.02 N	8.42 E
Breu, Rio do ≃	246	3.29 S	66.20 W
Breueh, Pulau ɪ	110	5.41 N	95.05 E
Breuil-Bois-Robert	261	48.57 N	1.43 E
Breuil-Cervinia	58	45.56 N	7.38 E
Breuillet	261	48.34 N	2.10 E
Breuilpont	50	48.58 N	1.26 E
Breukelen	52	52.10 N	5.00 E
Breux	261	48.34 N	2.11 E
Brevard	192	35.14 N	82.44 W
Brevard □[6]	220	28.18 N	80.42 W
Brévenne ≃	62	45.51 N	4.40 E
Brevens bruk	40	59.01 N	15.35 E
Breves	250	1.40 S	50.29 W
Brevig Mission	180	65.20 N	166.29 W
Brevik, Nor.	26	59.04 N	9.42 E
Brevik, Sve.	40	59.21 N	18.12 E
Brevoort Island ɪ	176	63.30 N	64.20 W
Brewarrina	166	29.57 S	146.52 E
Brewer	188	44.47 N	68.45 W
Brewer Island ɪ	282	37.33 N	122.16 W
Brewersville	218	39.05 N	85.37 W
Brewerton	210	43.14 N	76.08 W
Brewerville	150	6.26 N	10.47 W
Brewongle	170	33.29 S	149.43 E
Brewood	42	52.41 N	2.10 W
Brewster, Ks., U.S.	198	39.22 N	101.22 W
Brewster, Ma., U.S.	207	41.45 N	70.05 W
Brewster, Mn., U.S.	198	43.41 N	95.28 W
Brewster, Ne., U.S.	198	41.56 N	99.51 W
Brewster, N.Y., U.S.	210	41.23 N	73.37 W
Brewster, Oh., U.S.	214	40.42 N	81.35 W
Brewster, Wa., U.S.	202	48.05 N	119.46 W
Brewster, Kap ›	16	70.19 N	22.05 W
Brewster, Lake ⊜	166	33.28 S	146.00 E
Brewster, Mount ʌ	172	44.04 S	169.27 E
Brewton	194	31.06 N	87.04 W
Breyten	158	26.16 S	30.00 E
Břežany	61	48.52 N	16.20 E
Brežice	36	45.54 N	15.36 E
Brézina	148	33.04 N	1.14 E
Brézins	62	45.21 N	5.19 E
Brežnev	80	55.42 N	52.19 E
Březnice	60	49.33 N	13.57 E
Breznik	38	42.44 N	22.54 E
Brezno, Česko.	30	48.50 N	19.39 E
Březno, Česko.	54	50.24 N	13.26 E
Brézolles	50	48.41 N	1.04 E
Březová	54	50.06 N	12.39 E
Březové Hory	60	49.41 N	13.58 E
Bria	152	6.32 N	21.59 E
Brian Boru Peak ʌ	182	55.05 N	127.35 W
Briançon	62	44.54 N	6.39 E
Brian Head ʌ	200	37.41 N	112.50 W
Brianza □[9]	62	45.40 N	9.10 E
Briar	222	33.00 N	97.34 W
Briarcliff Manor	210	41.08 N	73.49 W
Briar Creek	210	40.10 N	76.46 W
Briar Creek ≃	222	32.06 N	96.22 W
Briare	50	47.38 N	2.44 E
Briare, Canal de ≊	50	48.02 N	2.43 E
Briarres-sur-Essonne	50	48.14 N	2.25 E
Briarwood Beach	214	41.06 N	81.54 W
Briarwood Center ◆[9]	281	42.14 N	83.45 W
Briatico	68	38.43 N	16.02 E
Bribano	64	46.06 N	12.05 E
Bribie Island ɪ	171a	27.00 S	153.07 E
Bričany	78	48.22 N	27.04 E
Bricelyn	190	43.33 N	93.48 W
Brice Run ≃	284b	39.19 N	76.50 W
Brices Cross Roads National Battlefield Site ⊥	194	34.31 N	88.41 W
Briceville	192	36.10 N	84.11 W
Bricherasio	62	44.49 N	7.18 E
Bricht	263	51.41 N	6.51 E
Brickebacken	40	59.15 N	15.15 E
Brick Lake ⊜	220	28.10 N	81.12 W
Brick Township	208	40.04 N	74.08 W
Briçonnet, Lac ⊜	186	51.27 N	60.11 W
Bricquebec	32	49.28 N	1.38 W
Bridal Veil	224	45.33 N	122.10 W
Bridalveil Fall ʟ	226	37.43 N	119.39 W
Bride	44	54.22 N	4.22 W
Bride ≃	48	52.04 N	7.52 W
Bridesburg ◆[8]	285	40.00 N	75.04 W
Bridge	42	51.14 N	1.07 E
Bridge ≃	182	50.45 N	121.55 W
Bridge City	194	30.01 N	93.50 W
Bridge Creek ≃	224	48.26 N	120.52 W
Bridgehampton	207	40.56 N	72.18 W
Bridge Lake	182	51.29 N	120.43 W
Bridgend, Scot., U.K.	46	56.48 N	2.45 W
Bridgend, Scot., U.K.	46	55.48 N	6.16 W
Bridgend, Wales, U.K.	42	51.31 N	3.35 W
Bridgenorth	212	44.23 N	78.23 W
Bridge of Allan	46	56.09 N	3.57 W
Bridge of Gaur	46	56.41 N	4.27 W
Bridge of Orchy	46	56.30 N	4.46 W
Bridge of Weir	46	55.52 N	4.35 W
Bridgeport, On., Can.	212	43.29 N	80.29 W
Bridgeport, Al., U.S.	194	34.56 N	85.42 W
Bridgeport, Ca., U.S.	226	38.10 N	119.13 W
Bridgeport, Ct., U.S.	207	41.10 N	73.12 W
Bridgeport, Il., U.S.	194	38.42 N	87.45 W
Bridgeport, Mi., U.S.	190	43.21 N	83.52 W
Bridgeport, Ne., U.S.	198	41.39 N	103.05 W
Bridgeport, N.J., U.S.	285	39.48 N	75.20 W
Bridgeport, N.Y., U.S.	210	43.09 N	75.58 W
Bridgeport, Oh., U.S.	214	40.04 N	80.44 W
Bridgeport, Pa., U.S.	285	40.06 N	75.21 W
Bridgeport, Tx., U.S.	222	33.12 N	97.45 W
Bridgeport, Wa., U.S.	202	48.00 N	119.40 W
Bridgeport, W.V., U.S.	188	39.17 N	80.15 W
Bridgeport ◆[8]	278	41.51 N	87.39 W
Bridgeport, Lake ⊜[1]	222	33.13 N	97.48 W
Bridgeport, University of ʊ[2]	276	41.10 N	73.12 W
Bridgeport Airport ⊠	285	39.47 N	75.20 W
Bridgeport Harbor ⊂	276	41.10 N	73.11 W
Bridgeport Municipal Airport ⊠	276	41.10 N	73.08 W
Bridgeport Reservoir ⊜[1]	226	38.22 N	119.14 W
Bridger	202	45.17 N	108.54 W
Bridge River Indian Reserve ◆[4]	182	50.45 N	122.00 W
Bridger Peak ʌ	200	41.12 N	107.02 W
Bridges Point ›	174o	1.58 N	157.28 W
Bridgeton, Mo., U.S.	219	38.44 N	90.24 W
Bridgeton, N.J., U.S.	208	39.25 N	75.14 W
Bridgetown, Austl.	162	33.57 S	116.08 E
Bridgetown, Barb.	241g	13.06 N	59.37 W
Bridgetown, N.S., Can.	186	44.51 N	65.18 W
Bridgetown, Oh., U.S.	218	39.09 N	84.38 W
Bridge Trafford	262	53.14 N	2.49 W
Bridgeview	278	41.45 N	87.48 W
Bridgeville, De., U.S.	208	38.44 N	75.36 W
Bridgeville, Pa., U.S.	214	40.21 N	80.06 W
Bridgewater, Austl.	166	42.44 S	147.14 E
Bridgewater, N.S., Can.	186	44.23 N	64.31 W
Bridgewater, Ct., U.S.	210	41.32 N	73.22 W
Bridgewater, Me., U.S.	186	46.25 N	67.50 W
Bridgewater, Ma., U.S.	207	41.59 N	70.58 W
Bridgewater, N.Y., U.S.	210	42.58 N	75.15 W
Bridgewater, Pa., U.S.	285	40.05 N	74.55 W
Bridgewater, S.D., U.S.	198	43.33 N	97.30 W
Bridgewater, Va., U.S.	188	38.22 N	78.58 W
Bridgewater Canal ≊	262	53.20 N	2.45 W
Bridgewater State College ʊ[2]	283	41.59 N	70.58 W
Bridgman	216	41.57 N	86.33 W
Bridgnorth	42	52.33 N	2.25 W
Bridgton	188	44.03 N	70.42 W
Bridgwater	42	51.08 N	3.00 W
Bridgwater Bay ⊂	42	51.16 N	3.12 W
Bridlington	44	54.05 N	0.12 W
Bridlington Bay ⊂	44	54.04 N	0.08 W
Bridport	42	50.44 N	2.46 W
Brie ◆[1]	50	48.40 N	3.20 E
Briec	32	48.06 N	4.00 W
Brie-Comte-Robert	50	48.41 N	2.37 E
Brie Français ◆[1]	261	48.40 N	2.50 E
Brieg → Brzeg	30	50.52 N	17.27 E
Brielle, Ned.	52	51.54 N	4.10 E
Brielle, N.J., U.S.	208	40.06 N	74.03 W
Brienne-le-Château	58	48.24 N	4.32 E
Brienne-sur-Aisne	50	49.26 N	4.03 E
Brienno	58	45.55 N	9.07 E
Brienon-sur-Armançon	50	48.00 N	3.37 E
Brien Run ≃	284b	39.20 N	76.28 W
Brienz	58	46.46 N	8.03 E
Brienza	68	40.29 N	15.37 E
Brienzer Rothorn ʌ	58	46.48 N	8.04 E
Brienzersee ⊜	58	46.43 N	7.57 E
Brier Creek ≃	192	32.47 N	81.26 W
Brierfield	44	53.50 N	2.14 W
Brier Hill	212	44.32 N	75.40 W
Brier Island ɪ	186	44.16 N	66.22 W
Brierley Hill	42	52.29 N	2.07 W
Brier Mountain ʌ	210	41.37 N	77.02 W
Briese	264a	52.42 N	13.18 E
Briese ≃	264a	52.41 N	13.15 E
Brieselang	54	52.35 N	13.00 E
Briesen	54	52.20 N	14.16 E
Brieske	54	51.29 N	13.57 E
Brieskow-Finkenheerd	54	52.16 N	14.35 E
Briest	54	52.31 N	12.08 E
Briey	56	49.15 N	5.56 E
Brig	58	46.19 N	8.00 E
Brigach ≃	58	47.58 N	8.30 E
Brigantine	208	39.24 N	74.21 W
Brig Bay	186	51.04 N	56.55 W
Brigden	214	42.49 N	82.17 W
Brigg	44	53.34 N	0.30 W
Briggs	196	30.53 N	97.56 W
Brigham City	200	41.30 N	112.00 W
Brighouse	44	53.42 N	1.47 W
Brighstone	42	50.38 N	1.24 W
Bright	166	36.44 S	146.58 E
Brightlingsea	42	51.49 N	1.02 E
Brightmoor ◆[8]	281	42.24 N	83.14 W
Brighton, Austl.	168b	35.01 S	138.31 E
Brighton, Austl.	169	37.55 S	145.00 E
Brighton, On., Can.	212	44.02 N	77.44 W
Brighton, N.Z.	172	45.57 S	170.20 E
Brighton, Eng., U.K.	42	50.50 N	0.08 W
Brighton, Co., U.S.	200	39.59 N	104.49 W
Brighton, Fl., U.S.	220	27.14 N	81.06 W
Brighton, Il., U.S.	219	39.02 N	90.08 W
Brighton, Ia., U.S.	190	41.10 N	91.49 W
Brighton, Md., U.S.	284b	39.21 N	76.43 W
Brighton, Mi., U.S.	216	42.31 N	83.46 W
Brighton, N.Y., U.S.	210	43.08 N	77.33 W
Brighton ◆[8]	283	42.21 N	71.08 W
Brighton Downs	166	23.22 S	141.34 E
Brighton Indian Reservation ◆[4]	220	27.04 N	81.05 W
Brighton-Le-Sands	274a	33.58 S	151.09 E
Brighton Park ◆[8]	278	41.49 N	87.42 W
Brighton State Recreation Area ♦	216	42.30 N	83.48 W
Brightsand Lake ⊜	184	53.36 N	108.52 W
Brightwaters	276	40.43 N	73.16 W
Brightwood	224	45.23 N	122.01 W
Brightwood ◆[8]	284c	38.58 N	77.02 W
Brigittenau ◆[8]	264b	48.14 N	16.22 E
Brignoles	62	43.24 N	6.04 E
Brignoud	62	45.15 N	5.54 E
Brig o' Turk	46	56.13 N	4.22 W
Brigstock	42	52.27 N	0.36 W
Brigus	186	47.32 N	53.13 W
Brihuega	34	40.45 N	2.52 W
Briis-sous-Forges	261	48.38 N	2.07 E
Brijuni ɪ	64	44.55 N	13.46 E
Brikama	150	13.15 N	16.39 W
Brilhante ≃	255	21.58 S	54.18 W
Brill	42	51.49 N	1.03 W
Brilliant, B.C., Can.	182	49.19 N	117.38 W
Brilliant, Al., U.S.	194	34.01 N	87.45 W
Brilliant, Oh., U.S.	214	40.15 N	80.37 W
Brillion	190	44.10 N	88.03 W
Brilon	56	51.24 N	8.34 E
Brilyn Park	284c	38.54 N	77.10 W
Brimfield, Eng., U.K.	42	52.18 N	2.42 W
Brimfield, In., U.S.	216	41.27 N	85.24 W
Brimfield, Ma., U.S.	207	42.07 N	72.12 W
Brimfield, Oh., U.S.	214	41.06 N	81.21 W
Brimington	44	53.16 N	1.23 W
Brindabella	171b	35.23 S	148.45 E
Brindisi	68	40.38 N	17.56 E
Brindisi □[4]	68	40.35 N	17.40 E
Brindisi Montagna	68	40.37 N	15.57 E
Brindle	262	53.43 N	2.36 W
Brindley Heath	260	51.12 N	0.03 W
Bringelly	170	33.56 S	150.44 E
Bringelly Creek ≃	274a	33.58 S	150.38 E
Brinje	36	45.00 N	15.08 E
Brinkerton	279b	40.13 N	79.32 W
Brinkhaven	214	40.28 N	82.12 W
Brinkleigh	284b	39.18 N	76.50 W
Brinkley, Austl.	168b	35.14 S	139.13 E
Brinkley, Ar., U.S.	194	34.53 N	91.11 W
Brinkum	52	53.00 N	8.47 E
Brinkworth	166	33.42 S	138.24 E
Brinnon	224	47.40 N	122.53 W
Brinon-sur-Beuvron	50	47.17 N	3.30 E
Brins, Ābār al- ⊤[4]	142	30.29 N	30.05 E
Brinscall	262	53.41 N	2.34 W
Brinyan	46	59.07 N	2.59 W
Brion, Île ɪ	186	47.48 N	61.28 W
Brione	58	46.18 N	8.47 E
Briones Hills ⋀[2]	282	37.56 N	122.08 W
Briones Regional Park ♦	282	37.56 N	122.08 W
Briones Reservoir ⊜[1]	282	37.55 N	122.12 W
Brioni	64	44.55 N	13.46 E
Brionne	50	49.12 N	0.43 E
Brion-sur-Ource	58	47.55 N	4.39 E
Brioso ≃	255	20.21 S	52.05 W
Brioude	32	45.18 N	3.23 E
Briouze	32	48.42 N	0.22 W
Brisbane, Austl.	171a	27.28 S	153.02 E
Brisbane, Ca., U.S.	226	37.41 N	122.24 W
Brisbane ≃	171a	27.24 S	153.09 E
Brisbane, Mount ʌ	171a	27.05 S	152.32 E
Brisbane Ranges National Park ♦	169	37.52 S	144.14 E
Brisbane Water ⊂	170	33.28 S	151.20 E
Brisbane Water National Park ♦	170	33.30 S	151.15 E
Brisben	210	42.22 N	75.41 W
Brisbin	214	40.50 N	78.21 W
Briseñas de Matamoros	234	20.16 N	102.33 W
Brisighella	66	44.13 N	11.46 E
Brissac	62	43.52 N	3.42 E
Brissago	58	46.07 N	8.43 E
Bristol, Eng., U.K.	42	51.27 N	2.35 W
Bristol, Ct., U.S.	207	41.41 N	72.57 W
Bristol, Fl., U.S.	192	30.25 N	84.58 W
Bristol, Il., U.S.	216	41.39 N	88.27 W
Bristol, In., U.S.	216	41.43 N	85.49 W
Bristol, N.H., U.S.	188	43.35 N	71.44 W
Bristol, Pa., U.S.	208	40.06 N	74.51 W
Bristol, R.I., U.S.	207	41.40 N	71.16 W
Bristol, S.D., U.S.	198	45.20 N	97.44 W
Bristol, Tn., U.S.	192	36.35 N	82.11 W
Bristol, Vt., U.S.	188	44.08 N	73.04 W
Bristol, Va., U.S.	192	36.35 N	82.11 W
Bristol, Wi., U.S.	216	42.33 N	88.02 W
Bristol □[6], Ma., U.S.	207	41.54 N	71.06 W
Bristol □[6], R.I., U.S.	207	41.42 N	71.18 W
Bristol (Lulsgate) Airport ⊠	42	51.23 N	2.43 W
Bristol Bay ⊂	180	58.00 N	159.00 W
Bristol-Blake Reservation ♦	283	42.06 N	71.19 W
Bristol Center	210	42.49 N	77.23 W
Bristol Channel ʉ	42	51.20 N	4.00 W
Bristol Lake ⊜	204	34.28 N	115.41 W
Bristolville	214	41.23 N	80.52 W
Bristow	196	35.49 N	96.23 W
Bristow Island ɪ	164	9.08 S	143.14 E
Britânia	255	15.14 S	51.09 W
Británicas, Islas → British Isles ɪɪ	4	54.00 N	4.00 W
Britannia	275b	43.37 N	79.41 W
Britannia Beach	182	49.38 N	123.12 W
Britannia Range ⋀	9	80.00 S	158.00 E
Britische Jungfern-Inseln → British Virgin Islands □[2]	240m	18.30 N	64.30 W
Britisches Antarktis-Territorium → British Antarctic Territory □[2]	9	60.00 S	45.00 W
British Antarctic Territory □[2]	9	60.00 S	45.00 W
British Columbia □[4], Can.	176	54.00 N	125.00 W
British Columbia □[4], Can.	182	54.00 N	125.00 W
British Honduras → Belize □[1]	232	17.15 N	88.45 W
British Indian Ocean Territory □[2]	12	7.00 S	72.00 E
British Isles ɪɪ	4	54.00 N	4.00 W
British Mountains ⋀	180	69.00 N	140.20 W
British Museum ʊ	260	51.31 N	0.08 W
British Solomon Islands → Solomon Islands □[1]	175e	8.00 S	159.00 E
British Virgin Islands □[2], N.A.	230	18.30 N	64.30 W
British Virgin Islands □[2], N.A.	240m	18.30 N	64.30 W
Britland Edge Hill ʌ[2]	262	53.31 N	1.50 W
Briton Ferry	42	51.38 N	3.49 W
Brits	158	25.42 S	27.45 E
Britstown	158	30.37 S	23.30 E
Britt	190	43.05 N	93.48 W
Brittany → Bretagne □[9]	32	48.00 N	3.00 W
Brittas	48	53.14 N	6.27 W
Britten	158	27.42 S	25.17 E
Brittingham	196	25.45 N	103.24 W
Britton, Mi., U.S.	216	41.59 N	83.49 W
Britton, S.D., U.S.	198	45.47 N	97.45 W
Britton, Tx., U.S.	222	32.33 N	97.04 W
Britton, Mount ʌ[2]	162	26.31 S	134.43 E
Britz	54	52.53 N	13.49 E
Britz ◆[8]	264a	52.27 N	13.26 E
Brive-la-Gaillarde	32	45.10 N	1.32 E
Brives-Charensac	62	45.03 N	3.56 E
Briviesca	34	42.33 N	3.19 W
Brivio	62	45.44 N	9.27 E
Brixen im Thale	64	47.27 N	12.15 E
Brixham	42	50.24 N	3.30 W
Brixlegg	64	47.25 N	11.53 E
Brixton	166	23.32 S	144.57 E
Brixworth	42	52.20 N	0.54 W
Brlik	85	43.40 N	73.49 E
Brloh	61	48.56 N	14.13 E
Brno	30	49.12 N	16.37 E
Bro	40	59.31 N	17.38 E
Broa, Ensenada de la ⊂	240p	22.35 N	82.00 W
Broach	120	21.42 N	72.58 E
Broad ≃, U.S.	192	34.00 N	81.04 W
Broad ≃, Fl., U.S.	220	25.28 N	81.09 W
Broad ≃, Ga., U.S.	192	33.59 N	82.39 W
Broadalbin	210	43.03 N	74.11 W
Broad Arrow	162	30.20 S	121.27 E
Broad Axe	285	40.10 N	75.15 W
Broadback ≃	176	51.21 N	78.52 W
Broad Bay ⊂	46	58.15 N	6.15 W
Broadbottom	262	53.26 N	2.01 W
Broad Brook	207	41.54 N	72.32 W
Broad Chalke	42	51.02 N	1.57 W
Broad Clyst	42	50.46 N	3.26 W
Broad Creek ⊂	208	38.45 N	76.15 W
Broad Creek ≃	208	39.42 N	76.14 W
Broadford, Austl.	169	37.13 S	145.03 E
Broadford, Scot., U.K.	46	57.14 N	5.54 W
Broad Haven ⊂	48	54.18 N	9.55 W
Broadheath	262	53.24 N	2.21 W
Broadhurst Range ⋀	162	22.23 S	122.09 E
Broadkill ≃	208	38.47 N	75.10 W
Broad Law ʌ	46	55.30 N	3.22 W
Broadley Common	260	51.45 N	0.04 E
Broadmeadows	169	37.40 S	144.54 E
Broad Meadow Water ≃	44	53.28 N	6.12 W
Broadmoor	226	37.41 N	122.29 W
Broad Neck ›[1]	208	39.03 N	76.27 W
Broad Oak	42	50.57 N	0.36 E
Broad Pass)(	180	63.18 N	149.09 W
Broad Run ≃, Pa., U.S.	285	39.56 N	75.41 W
Broad Run ≃, Pa., U.S.	285	39.59 N	75.40 W
Broad Run ≃, Va., U.S.	208	38.41 N	77.29 W
Broad Sound ʉ, Austl.	166	22.10 S	149.45 E
Broad Sound ʉ, Ma., U.S.	283	42.25 N	70.58 W
Broad Sound Channel ʉ	166	22.05 S	150.20 E
Broadstairs	42	51.22 N	1.27 E
Broad Street	260	51.17 N	0.38 E
Broad Top	214	40.12 N	78.08 W
Broadus	198	45.26 N	105.24 W
Broadview, Sk., Can.	184	50.20 N	102.30 W
Broadview, Il., U.S.	216	41.51 N	87.51 W
Broadview, In., U.S.	218	39.10 N	87.33 W
Broadview Heights	214	41.18 N	81.41 W
Broadwater	198	41.35 N	102.51 W
Broadway, Eng., U.K.	42	52.02 N	1.51 W
Broadway, Oh., U.S.	214	40.20 N	83.24 W
Broadway, Va., U.S.	188	38.38 N	78.46 W
Broadwell	219	40.04 N	89.27 W
Broadwindsor	42	50.49 N	2.48 W
Broadwood	172	35.16 S	173.23 E
Broager	41	54.53 N	9.41 E
Brobo	150	7.43 N	4.42 W
Broby	26	56.15 N	14.05 E
Brobyværk	41	55.14 N	10.15 E
Broc	58	46.36 N	7.06 E
Brocēni	76	56.42 N	22.35 E
Brochel	46	57.26 N	6.01 W
Brochet	176	57.53 N	101.40 W
Brochet, Lac au ⊜	186	49.40 N	69.37 W
Brochterbeck	52	52.13 N	7.44 E
Brock	184	51.27 N	108.42 W
Brock ≃	44	53.52 N	2.47 W
Brock Creek ≃	285	40.15 N	74.50 W
Brocken ʌ	54	51.48 N	10.36 E
Brockenhurst	42	50.49 N	1.34 W
Brockenscheidt	263	51.38 N	7.25 E
Brockhagen	52	51.59 N	8.20 E
Brockham	260	51.14 N	0.17 W
Brockman ≃	168a	31.41 S	116.07 E
Brockman, Mount ʌ	162	22.28 S	117.18 E
Brock Monument ⊥	284a	43.09 N	79.04 W
Brockport, N.Y., U.S.	210	43.12 N	77.56 W
Brockport, Pa., U.S.	214	41.16 N	78.44 W
Brocks Beach	212	44.27 N	80.06 W
Brocks Creek	164	13.28 S	131.25 E
Brockton, Ma., U.S.	207	42.05 N	71.01 W
Brockton, Mt., U.S.	198	48.09 N	104.54 W
Brockton, Pa., U.S.	208	40.45 N	76.04 W
Brockton Reservoir ⊜[1]	283	42.07 N	71.03 W
Brock University ʊ[2]	284a	43.07 N	79.15 W
Brockville	212	44.35 N	75.41 W
Brockway	214	41.15 N	78.47 W
Brockworth	42	51.51 N	2.09 W
Brocoió, Ilha do ɪ	287a	22.45 S	43.07 W
Brocton	214	42.23 N	79.26 W
Brod, Česko.	60	49.51 N	12.45 E
Brod, Jugo.	38	41.31 N	21.12 E
Broddbo	40	59.59 N	16.28 E
Brodenbach	56	50.14 N	7.26 E
Broderick	226	38.35 N	121.30 W
Brodeur Peninsula ›[1]	176	73.00 N	88.00 W
Brodhead, Ky., U.S.	192	37.24 N	84.24 W
Brodhead, Wi., U.S.	190	42.37 N	89.22 W
Brodhead Creek ≃	210	40.59 N	75.08 W
Brodheadsville	210	40.55 N	75.24 W
Brodick	46	55.35 N	5.09 W
Brodnax	192	36.42 N	78.01 W
Brodnica	30	53.16 N	19.23 E
Brodokalmak	86	55.35 N	62.06 E
Brody, Pol.	30	51.45 N	14.45 E
Brody, S.S.S.R.	78	50.06 N	25.10 E
Broedersput	158	26.49 S	25.08 E
Broek [op Langendijk]	52	52.40 N	4.48 E
Brogan	202	44.14 N	117.30 W
Broglie	50	49.01 N	0.32 E
Brohlbach ≃	56	50.29 N	7.20 E
Broich ◆[8]	263	51.25 N	6.51 E
Broichweiden	56	50.49 N	6.09 E
Broitzem	52	52.14 N	10.29 E
Brok	30	52.43 N	21.52 E
Brok ʌ	123	34.32 N	76.35 E
Brokdorf	52	53.52 N	9.19 E
Broke	170	32.45 S	151.06 E
Broke Inlet ⊂	162	34.55 S	116.25 E
Broken ≃	169	36.41 S	146.00 E
Broken Arrow	196	36.03 N	95.47 W
Broken Back Range ⋀	170	32.47 S	151.13 E
Broken Bay ⊂	170	33.34 S	151.18 E
Broken Bow, Ne., U.S.	198	41.24 N	99.38 W
Broken Bow, Ok., U.S.	194	34.01 N	94.44 W
Broken Bow Lake ⊜[1]	194	34.10 N	94.40 W
Broken Cross, Eng., U.K.	262	53.15 N	2.29 W
Broken Cross, Eng., U.K.	262	53.15 N	2.10 W
Brokenhead ≃	184	50.25 N	96.40 W
Broken Hill, Austl.	166	31.57 S	141.27 E
Broken Hill → Kabwe, Zam.	154	14.27 S	28.27 E
Broken Ridge ✣[3]	12	31.30 S	95.00 E
Brokenstraw Creek ≃	214	41.51 N	79.09 W
Broken Sword Creek ≃	214	40.46 N	83.11 W
Brokopondo	250	5.04 N	54.58 W
Brokopondo □[5]	250	4.20 N	55.20 W
Brölbach ≃	56	50.47 N	7.18 E
Brolo	70	38.09 N	14.50 E
Bromberg → Bydgoszcz	30	53.08 N	18.00 E
Bromborough	262	53.19 N	2.59 W
Brome, B.R.D.	54	52.36 N	10.56 E
Brome, P.Q., Can.	206	45.12 N	72.34 W
Brome □[6]	206	45.10 N	72.30 W
Brome, Lac ⊜	206	45.15 N	72.30 W
Brome, Mont ʌ	206	45.17 N	72.38 W
Bromham	42	52.09 N	0.31 W
Bromley ◆[8]	260	51.24 N	0.02 E
Bromley Common ◆[8]	260	51.22 N	0.03 E
Bromley Plateau ✣[3]	18	32.00 S	35.00 W
Bromma ◆[8]	40	59.21 N	17.55 E
Bromma flygplats ⊠	40	59.21 N	17.55 E
Brommö ɪ	40	58.50 N	13.41 E
Bromo, Gunung ʌ	115a	7.57 S	112.57 E
Bromölla	26	56.04 N	14.28 E
Brompton, Eng., U.K.	44	54.22 N	1.25 W
Brompton, Eng., U.K.	260	51.23 N	0.33 E
Brompton, Lac ⊜	206	45.27 N	72.09 W
Bromptonville	206	45.28 N	71.57 W
Bromsgrove	42	52.20 N	2.03 W
Bromyard	42	52.11 N	2.30 W
Bron	62	45.44 N	4.55 E
Bron, Aéroport de ⊠	62	45.43 N	4.56 E
Brønderslev	26	57.16 N	9.58 E
Bronevskaja	24	61.43 N	39.10 E
Brong-Ahafo □[4]	150	7.45 N	1.30 W
Broni	62	45.04 N	9.16 E
Bronickaja Guta	78	50.56 N	27.19 E
Bronkhorstspruit	158	25.48 S	28.44 E
Bronkhorstspruitdam ⊜[1]	158	25.55 S	28.42 E
Bronkow	54	51.40 N	13.55 E
Bronllys	42	52.01 N	3.16 W
Bronlund Peak ʌ	176	57.26 N	126.38 W
Bronn	60	49.44 N	11.28 E
Bronnicy	82	55.25 N	38.16 E
Bronnikovo	86	58.32 N	68.25 E
Bronnoje	76	52.19 N	30.29 E
Brønnøysund	24	65.30 N	12.10 E
Bronnzell	56	50.31 N	9.41 E
Brøns	41	55.11 N	8.44 E
Bronson, Fl., U.S.	192	29.26 N	82.38 W
Bronson, Ks., U.S.	198	37.54 N	95.04 W
Bronson, Mi., U.S.	216	41.52 N	85.11 W
Bronson, Tx., U.S.	194	31.21 N	94.01 W
Bronson Lake ⊜	184	53.52 N	109.43 W
Bronte, It.	70	37.47 N	14.50 E
Bronte, Tx., U.S.	196	31.53 N	100.18 W
Bronte Creek ≃	212	43.23 N	79.43 W
Bronte Park	166	42.08 S	146.30 E
Bronwood	192	31.49 N	84.21 W
Bronx □[6]	210	40.49 N	73.56 W
Bronx ◆[8]	276	40.49 N	73.56 W
Bronx ≃	276	40.49 N	73.52 W
Bronx Park ♦	276	40.52 N	73.53 W
Bronxville	276	40.56 N	73.49 W
Bronx-Whitestone Bridge ◆[5]	276	40.48 N	73.50 W
Bronx Zoo ♦	276	40.51 N	73.53 W
Bronzolo (Branzoll)	64	46.24 N	11.19 E
Brooch, Lac ⊜	186	50.44 N	67.58 W
Broodsnyersplaas	158	26.03 S	29.29 E
Brook	216	40.51 N	87.21 W
Brookdale	226	37.06 N	122.06 W
Brooke	208	38.23 N	77.22 W
Brooke □[6]	214	40.18 N	80.33 W
Brookeborough	48	54.19 N	7.24 W
Brookeland	194	31.09 N	94.00 W
Brooker	192	29.53 N	82.19 W
Brooke's Point	116	8.47 N	117.50 E
Brookfield, N.S., Can.	186	45.15 N	63.17 W
Brookfield, Ct., U.S.	207	41.28 N	73.24 W
Brookfield, Il., U.S.	216	41.49 N	87.51 W
Brookfield, Ma., U.S.	207	42.12 N	72.06 W
Brookfield, Mi., U.S.	216	42.27 N	84.47 W
Brookfield, Mo., U.S.	194	39.47 N	93.04 W
Brookfield, N.Y., U.S.	210	42.48 N	75.19 W
Brookfield, Oh., U.S.	214	41.14 N	80.34 W
Brookfield, Wi., U.S.	216	43.03 N	88.06 W
Brookfield Center	207	41.27 N	73.23 W
Brookfield Zoo ♦	278	41.50 N	87.50 W
Brookford	192	35.42 N	81.20 W
Brookhaven, De., U.S.	285	39.42 N	75.41 W
Brookhaven, Ms., U.S.	194	31.34 N	90.26 W
Brookhaven, Pa., U.S.	285	39.52 N	75.22 W
Brookhaven Manor	278	41.44 N	87.58 W
Brookhaven National Laboratory ʊ[3]	207	40.54 N	72.52 W
Brookings, Or., U.S.	202	42.03 N	124.16 W
Brookings, S.D., U.S.	198	44.18 N	96.47 W
Brookland, Eng., U.K.	42	50.59 N	0.50 E
Brookland, Ar., U.S.	194	35.54 N	90.34 W
Brookland ◆[8]	284c	38.56 N	76.59 W
Brooklands	214	42.38 N	83.06 W
Brookland Terrace	285	39.44 N	75.37 W
Brooklandville	284b	39.25 N	76.40 W
Brooklawn	285	39.52 N	75.07 W
Brooklet	192	32.22 N	81.39 W
Brooklin	212	43.57 N	78.57 W
Brookline, Ma., U.S.	207	42.21 N	71.07 W
Brookline, N.H., U.S.	207	42.44 N	71.39 W
Brooklyn, N.S., Can.	186	44.03 N	64.42 W
Brooklyn, Ct., U.S.	207	41.47 N	71.57 W
Brooklyn, Il., U.S.	219	40.14 N	90.46 W
Brooklyn, In., U.S.	218	39.32 N	86.22 W
Brooklyn, Ia., U.S.	190	41.44 N	92.26 W
Brooklyn, Md., U.S.	284b	39.14 N	76.37 W
Brooklyn, Mi., U.S.	216	42.06 N	84.14 W
Brooklyn, Ms., U.S.	194	31.03 N	89.11 W
Brooklyn, Oh., U.S.	214	41.26 N	81.44 W
Brooklyn, Pa., U.S.	210	41.45 N	75.48 W
Brooklyn, Wa., U.S.	224	46.47 N	123.31 W
Brooklyn, Wi., U.S.	216	42.51 N	89.22 W
Brooklyn ◆[8], Md., U.S.	284b	39.14 N	76.36 W
Brooklyn ◆[8], N.Y., U.S.	210	40.42 N	74.00 W
Brooklyn Battery Tunnel ◆[5]	276	40.42 N	74.01 W
Brooklyn Bridge ◆[5]	276	40.42 N	74.00 W
Brooklyn Center	190	45.04 N	93.19 W
Brooklyn Heights	279a	41.24 N	81.40 W
Brooklyn Marine Park ♦	276	40.35 N	73.55 W
Brooklyn Museum ʊ	276	40.40 N	73.58 W
Brookmans Park	260	51.43 N	0.12 W
Brookmere	182	49.49 N	120.53 W
Brookmont	284c	38.57 N	77.07 W
Brookneal	192	37.03 N	78.56 W
Brook Park	214	41.23 N	81.48 W
Brookport	194	37.07 N	88.37 W
Brooks, Ab., Can.	182	50.35 N	111.53 W
Brooks, Ca., U.S.	226	38.45 N	122.09 W
Brooks, Me., U.S.	188	44.33 N	69.07 W
Brooks, Or., U.S.	224	45.02 N	122.57 W
Brooks, Mount ʌ	180	63.11 N	150.40 W
Brooks Air Force Base ■	196	29.21 N	98.25 W
Brooks Bay ⊂	182	50.13 N	127.55 W
Brooksburg	218	38.44 N	85.15 W
Brookshire	222	29.47 N	95.57 W
Brookside, De., U.S.	285	39.40 N	75.43 W
Brookside, N.J., U.S.	276	40.48 N	74.34 W
Brookside, Pa., U.S.	214	42.08 N	80.00 W
Brookside, Tx., U.S.	222	29.35 N	95.18 W
Brookside Park ♦	279a	41.27 N	81.43 W
Brooks Island ɪ	282	37.54 N	122.21 W
Brooks Mountain ʌ	180	65.33 N	167.09 W
Brooks Place	283	42.02 N	71.01 W
Brooks Range ⋀	180	68.00 N	154.00 W
Brookston	216	40.36 N	86.52 W
Brook Street	260	51.37 N	0.17 E
Brooksville, Fl., U.S.	220	28.33 N	82.23 W
Brooksville, Ky., U.S.	218	38.40 N	84.03 W
Brooksville, Ms., U.S.	194	33.14 N	88.34 W
Brookton	162	32.22 S	117.01 E
Brooktondale	210	42.23 N	76.24 W
Brookvale	274a	33.46 S	151.17 E
Brookview	210	42.32 N	73.43 W
Brookville, In., U.S.	218	39.25 N	85.00 W
Brookville, Ma., U.S.	207	42.07 N	71.00 W
Brookville, N.Y., U.S.	276	40.48 N	73.34 W
Brookville, Oh., U.S.	218	39.50 N	84.24 W
Brookville, Pa., U.S.	214	41.09 N	79.05 W
Brookville Lake ⊜[1]	218	39.30 N	85.00 W
Brookwood, Eng., U.K.	260	51.18 N	0.38 W
Brookwood, In., U.S.	278	40.30 N	87.22 W
Brooloo	166	26.29 S	152.42 E
Broom, Little Loch ⊂	46	57.54 N	5.22 W
Broom, Loch ⊂	46	57.52 N	5.08 W
Broomall	285	39.58 N	75.21 W
Broome	162	17.58 S	122.14 E
Broome □[6]	210	42.08 N	75.54 W
Broome County Airport ⊠	210	42.13 N	75.59 W
Broomes Island	208	38.25 N	76.32 W
Broomfield, Eng., U.K.	260	51.46 N	0.28 E
Broomfield, Eng., U.K.	260	51.14 N	0.38 E
Broomfield, Co., U.S.	200	39.55 N	105.05 W
Broons	32	48.19 N	2.16 W
Brooten	198	45.30 N	95.07 W
Brophy, Mount ʌ[2]	162	19.11 S	128.51 E
Brora	46	58.01 N	3.51 W
Brora ≃	46	58.01 N	3.52 W
Brørup	41	55.29 N	9.01 E
Broseley	42	52.37 N	2.29 W
Brosewere Bay ⊂	276	40.37 N	73.42 W
Brosna ≃	48	53.13 N	7.58 W
Brošnev-Osada	78	49.00 N	24.13 E
Brossac	32	45.20 N	0.03 W
Brossard	206	45.26 N	73.29 W
Brossasco	62	44.34 N	7.21 E
Brosso	62	45.30 N	7.48 E
Brotas de Macaúbas	255	12.00 S	42.38 W
Brothers Brook ≃	276	41.02 N	73.36 W
Brötjärna	40	60.30 N	15.01 E
Broto	34	42.36 N	0.06 W
Brotterode	54	50.49 N	10.26 E

Símbolo	English	Deutsch	Español	Français	Português
≃	River	Fluss	Río	Rivière	Rio
≊	Canal	Kanal	Canal	Canal	Canal
ʟ	Waterfall, Rapids	Wasserfall, Stromschnellen	Cascada, Rápidos	Chute d'eau, Rapides	Cascata, Rápidos
ʉ	Strait	Meeresstrasse	Estrecho	Détroit	Estreito
⊂	Bay, Gulf	Bucht, Golf	Bahía, Golfo	Baie, Golfe	Baía, Golfo
⊜	Lake, Lakes	See, Seen	Lago, Lagos	Lac, Lacs	Lago, Lagos
⊞	Swamp	Sumpf	Pantano	Marais	Pântano
⊓	Ice Features, Glacier	Eis- und Gletscherformen	Accidentes Glaciales	Formes glaciaires	Acidentes glaciares
⊤	Other Hydrographic Features	Andere Hydrographische Objekte	Otros Elementos Hidrográficos	Autres données hydrographiques	Outros acidentes hidrográficos
✣	Submarine Features	Untermeerische Objekte	Accidentes Submarinos	Formes de relief sous-marin	Acidentes submarinos
□	Political Unit	Politische Einheit	Unidad Politica	Entité politique	Unidade política
ʊ	Cultural Institution	Kulturelle Institution	Institución Cultural	Institution culturelle	Instituição cultural
⊥	Historical Site	Historische Stätte	Sitio Histórico	Site historique	Sitio histórico
♦	Recreational Site	Erholungs- und Ferienort	Sitio de Recreo	Centre de loisirs	Area de Lazer
⊠	Airport	Flughafen	Aeropuerto	Aéroport	Aeroporto
■	Military Installation	Militäranlage	Instalación Militar	Installation militaire	Instalação militar
◆	Miscellaneous	Verschiedenes	Misceláneo	Divers	Diversos

Symbols in the index entries represent the broad categories identified in the key at the right. Symbols with superior numbers (⋏[1]) identify subcategories (see complete key on page *I · 1*).

Kartensymbole in dem Registerverzeichnis stellen die rechts in Schlüssel erklärten Kategorien dar. Symbole mit hochgestellten Ziffern (⋏[1]) bezeichnen Unterabteilungen einer Kategorie (vgl. vollständiger Schlüssel auf Seite *I · 1*).

Los símbolos incluídos en el texto del índice representan las grandes categorias identificadas con la clave a la derecha. Los símbolos con numeros en su parte superior (⋏[1]) identifican las subcategorías (véase la clave completa en la página *I · 1*).

Les symboles de l'index représentent les catégories indiquées dans la légende à droite. Les symboles suivis d'un indice (⋏[1]) représentent des sous-catégories (voir légende complète à la page *I · 1*).

Os símbolos incluídos no texto do índice representam as grandes categorias identificadas com a chave à direita. Os símbolos com números em sua parte superior (⋏[1]) identificam as subcategorias (veja-se a chave completa à página *I · 1*).

∧ Mountain	Berg	Montaña	Montagne	Montanha
⋏ Mountains	Berge	Montañas	Montagnes	Montanhas
)(Pass	Pass	Paso	Col	Passo
V Valley, Canyon	Tal, Cañon	Valle, Cañón	Vallée, Canyon	Vale, Canhão
⊻ Plain	Ebene	Llano	Plaine	Planície
≻ Cape	Kap	Cabo	Cap	Cabo
I Island	Insel	Isla	Île	Ilha
II Islands	Inseln	Islas	Îles	Ilhas
⊥ Other Topographic Features	Andere Topographische Objekte	Otros Elementos Topográficos	Autres données topographiques	Outros acidentes topográficos

ESPAÑOL

Nombre	Página	Lat.°′	Long.°′ W = Oeste
Bukrino	82	54.48 N	36.14 E
Bukuka	88	51.11 N	116.39 E
Bukukun	88	49.27 N	111.08 E
Bukum, Pulau I	271c	1.14 N	103.47 E
Bukumbirwa	154	0.46 S	28.44 E
Bukum Kechil, Pulau I	271c	1.14 N	103.46 E
Bukunga	154	7.41 S	25.56 E
Bukuru	150	9.48 N	8.51 E
Bukuya	154	0.41 N	31.50 E
Būl, Kūh-e ∧	128	30.48 N	52.45 E
Bula	164	3.06 S	130.30 E
Bula ≃	80	55.12 N	48.23 E
Bula Atumba	152	8.40 S	14.48 E
Bulacan □[4]	116	15.00 N	121.05 E
Bulacaue Point ≻	116	11.36 N	123.09 E
Bülach	58	47.31 N	8.32 E
Bulajevo	86	54.54 N	70.26 E
Bulak	88	51.02 N	115.21 E
Bulaku ≃	164	8.06 S	139.12 E
Bulalacao	116	12.20 N	121.20 E
Bulalacao Island I	116	11.45 N	120.10 E
Bulalaqui Point ≻	116	11.17 N	124.03 E
Bulan, Pil.	116	12.40 N	123.52 E
Bulan, Pil.	116	6.44 N	124.47 E
Bulan, Ky., U.S.	192	37.18 N	83.09 W
Bulanaš	86	57.16 N	62.00 E
Bulancak	130	40.57 N	38.14 E
Bulandshahr	124	28.24 N	77.51 E
Bulandshahr □[5]	124	28.25 N	77.55 E
Bulanicha	86	52.48 N	84.57 E
Bulanık	130	39.05 N	42.15 E
Bulan Island I	116	6.08 N	121.50 E
Bulanovo	86	52.27 N	55.10 E
Būlāq	140	25.12 N	30.32 E
Būlāq ✦[8]	273c	30.04 N	31.14 E
Būlāq ad-Dakrūr	273c	30.02 N	31.11 E
Bulava	89	51.55 N	140.25 E
Bulavinovka	83	49.25 N	38.58 E
Bulawa, Gunung ∧	112	0.30 N	123.34 E
Bulawayo	154	20.09 S	28.36 E
Bulbjerg ∧[2]	26	57.09 N	9.02 E
Bulbul	130	36.46 N	36.49 E
Bulbul, Wādī ⋁	140	10.59 N	24.33 E
Bulcherry Island I	126	21.33 N	88.31 E
Buldan	130	38.03 N	28.51 E
Buldāna	122	20.32 N	76.11 E
Buldern	52	51.52 N	7.22 E
Buldibuyo	248	8.07 S	77.22 W
Buldir Island I	181a	52.21 N	175.54 E
Buldon	116	7.33 N	124.25 E
Buldurtinskij	80	50.05 N	53.11 E
Buldyrty ≃	80	49.48 N	52.34 E
Bulembu	158	25.56 S	31.06 E
Bulga	170	32.39 S	151.01 E
Bulgakovka	83	49.11 N	38.33 E
Bulgakovo	76	55.14 N	32.08 E
Bulgan, Mong.	86	46.53 N	91.05 E
Bulgan, Mong.	88	48.45 N	103.34 E
Bulgan, Mong.	102	44.05 N	103.32 E
Bulgan □[4]	88	49.00 N	103.30 E
Bulgaria (Bâlgarija) □[1], Europe	22	43.00 N	25.00 E
Bulgaria (Bâlgarija) □[1], Europe	38	43.00 N	25.00 E
Bulgarie → Bulgaria □[1]	38	43.00 N	25.00 E
Bulgarien → Bulgaria □[1]	38	43.00 N	25.00 E
Bulger	214	40.23 N	80.20 W
Bulgnéville	58	48.13 N	5.50 E
Bulgroo	166	25.48 S	143.59 E
Bulhale	144	5.20 N	46.29 E
Buliluyan	116	8.20 N	117.12 E
Buliluyan, Cape ≻	116	8.20 N	117.11 E
Bulim	271c	1.23 N	103.43 E
Bulimba	171a	27.25 S	153.04 E
Bulkeley	241g	13.07 N	59.32 W
Bulki	144	6.10 N	36.40 E
Bulkington	42	52.29 N	1.25 W
Bulkley ≃	182	55.13 N	127.40 W
Bulkley Ranges ⋏	182	54.30 N	127.30 W
Bull ≃	182	49.28 N	115.26 W
Bullabulling	162	31.01 S	120.32 E
Bullaque ≃	34	38.59 N	4.17 W
Bullara	162	22.40 S	114.03 E
Bullard	222	32.08 N	95.19 W
Bulla Regia ⊥	36	36.34 N	8.46 E
Bullas	34	38.03 N	1.40 W
Bullaxaar	144	10.23 N	44.25 E
Bullay	56	50.03 N	7.08 E
Bull Creek ≃, Nv., U.S.	204	38.43 N	115.34 W
Bull Creek ≃, N.Y., U.S.	284a	43.03 N	78.50 W
Bull Creek ≃, Oh., U.S.	214	40.42 N	80.32 W
Bull Creek ≃, S.D., U.S.	198	43.41 N	99.28 W
Bull Creek ≃, S.D., U.S.	198	45.40 N	103.18 W
Bull Creek ≃, Tx., U.S.	196	32.36 N	101.10 W
Bulldog	164	7.45 S	146.25 E
Bulle	58	46.37 N	7.04 E
Bullenbaai ᴄ	241s	12.11 N	69.04 W
Buller ≃	172	41.44 S	171.35 E
Buller, Mount ∧	169	37.09 S	146.26 E
Bullfinch	162	30.59 S	119.06 E
Bullfrog Creek ≃	200	37.19 N	110.44 W
Bull Harbour	182	50.54 N	127.55 W
Bullhead	198	45.45 N	101.04 W
Bullhead City	204	35.08 N	114.34 W
Bull Hide Creek ≃	222	31.23 N	97.01 W
Bull Hill ∧[2]	262	53.40 N	2.21 W
Bulli	170	34.20 S	150.55 E
Bullicame ♠	66	42.22 N	12.04 E
Büllingen	56	50.25 N	6.16 E
Bullioh	171b	36.12 S	147.20 E
Bullion	261	48.37 N	2.00 E
Bull Lake ⊜[1]	202	43.11 N	109.07 W
Bull Lake Creek ≃	202	43.14 N	109.02 W
Bull Mountain ∧	202	46.05 N	112.04 W
Bullock	192	36.30 N	78.33 W
Bullock Creek	166	17.43 S	144.31 E
Bullock Creek ≃	166	21.40 S	145.09 E
Bulloo ≃	166	28.43 S	142.30 E
Bulloo Downs	166	28.31 S	142.57 E
Bulloo Lake ⊜	166	28.43 S	142.25 E
Bulloo River Overflow ⊞	166	28.50 S	142.40 E
Bullpound Creek ≃	182	51.05 N	111.58 W
Bull Run ≃, Or., U.S.	224	45.26 N	122.15 W
Bull Run ≃, Va., U.S.	208	38.43 N	77.23 W
Bull Run Lake ⊜	224	45.27 N	121.50 W
Bull Run Reservoir Number 2 ⊜[1], Or., U.S.	224	45.28 N	122.10 W
Bull Run Reservoir Number 1 ⊜[1], Or., U.S.	224	45.30 N	122.04 W
Bullrun Rock ∧	202	44.21 N	118.17 W
Bulls	172	40.10 S	175.23 E
Bulls Bay ᴄ	192	32.59 N	79.33 W
Bullsbrook	168a	31.40 S	116.01 E
Bulls Gap	192	36.15 N	83.05 W
Bull Shoals	194	36.23 N	92.34 W
Bull Shoals Lake ⊜[1]	194	36.30 N	92.50 W
Bullskin Creek ≃	218	38.10 N	85.19 W
Bullville	210	41.33 N	74.22 W
Bully Creek ≃	202	43.58 N	117.15 W
Bully Hill	214	41.22 N	79.50 W
Bully-les-Mines	50	50.26 N	2.43 E
Bulmke-Hüllen ✦[8]	263	51.31 N	7.06 E
Bulnaj nuruu ⋏	88	49.05 N	98.30 E
Bulnes	252	36.44 S	72.18 W
Bulo Ghedudo	144	2.52 N	43.01 E
Bulok Gölü ⊜	130	38.32 N	32.55 E
Bulolo	164	7.10 S	146.40 E
Bulpham	260	51.33 N	0.22 E
Bulpitt	219	39.35 N	89.26 W
Bulsār	122	20.38 N	72.56 E
Bulstrode ≃	206	46.02 N	72.15 W
Bultei	71	40.27 N	9.03 E

FRANÇAIS

Nom	Page	Lat.°′	Long.°′ W = Ouest
Bultfontein	158	28.20 S	26.05 E
Buluan	116	6.44 N	124.47 E
Buluan ≃	116	6.47 N	124.47 E
Buluan, Lake ⊜	116	6.40 N	124.49 E
Buluduku	114	2.20 N	98.14 E
Bulugansk	88	52.24 N	110.23 E
Bulukumba	112	5.33 S	120.11 E
Bulukuto	152	0.12 S	21.42 E
Bululawang	115a	8.05 S	112.38 E
Bulungu, Zaïre	152	6.04 S	21.54 E
Bulungu, Zaïre	152	4.33 S	18.36 E
Buluntal	120	36.34 N	92.38 E
Bulupayung	114	1.38 N	99.11 E
Bulusan	116	12.45 N	124.08 E
Bulusan Volcano ∧	116	12.46 N	124.03 E
Bulwater	158	32.29 S	21.48 E
Bulwer	158	29.46 S	29.47 E
Bulyčevo	82	55.06 N	37.15 E
Bulyee	162	32.22 S	117.31 E
Bumba	152	2.11 N	22.28 E
Bumbah, Khalīj al- ᴄ	146	32.20 N	23.10 E
Bumbire Island I	154	1.40 S	31.53 E
Bumbles Green	260	51.44 N	0.02 E
Bumbo	152	6.55 S	19.16 E
Bumbu ≃	273b	4.23 S	15.18 E
Bumbulan	112	0.29 N	122.04 E
Bum Bum, Pulau I	112	4.27 N	118.40 E
Bumbuna	150	9.03 N	11.44 W
Bumbunga Lake ⊜	168b	33.54 S	138.11 E
Bumiayu	115a	7.15 S	109.00 E
Bumijawa	115a	7.10 S	109.07 E
Bumkin Island I	283	42.17 N	70.54 W
Bumping ≃	224	46.59 N	121.06 W
Bumping Lake ⊜	224	46.52 N	121.19 W
Bumpus, Mount ∧[2]	176	69.33 N	112.40 W
Bumtang ≃	124	26.56 N	90.51 E
Bumuhu ⊜	120	31.15 N	91.10 E
Buna, Kenya	154	2.47 N	39.31 E
Buna, Pap. N. Gui.	164	8.40 S	148.25 E
Buna, Tx., U.S.	194	30.26 N	93.58 W
Buna, Zaïre	152	3.15 S	18.59 E
Bunagāti	126	23.19 N	89.25 E
Bunai	164	2.11 S	147.14 E
Bunaj	85	38.26 N	71.32 E
Bun'atino	82	56.24 N	37.15 E
Bunavista	196	35.39 N	101.28 W
Bunawan	116	8.12 N	125.57 E
Bunazi	154	1.13 S	31.24 E
Bunbeg	48	55.03 N	8.18 W
Bunbury	168a	33.19 S	115.38 E
Bunceton	194	38.47 N	92.47 W
Bunclody	48	52.38 N	6.40 W
Buncrana	48	55.08 N	7.27 W
Bundaberg	166	24.52 S	152.21 E
Bundanoon	170	34.39 S	150.18 E
Bundarra	166	30.10 S	151.05 E
Bunde, B.R.D.	52	53.11 N	7.16 E
Bünde, B.R.D.	52	52.12 N	8.35 E
Bunde, Ned.	56	50.54 N	5.45 E
Bundeena	274a	34.05 S	151.09 E
Bundenthal	56	49.06 N	7.48 E
Bundesrepublik Deutschland → Germany, Federal Republic of □[1]	30	51.00 N	9.00 E
Bundey ≃	162	21.46 S	135.37 E
Bündheim	54	51.53 N	10.32 E
Būndi, India	120	25.27 N	75.39 E
Bundi, Pap. N. Gui.	164	5.40 S	145.15 E
Būndi □[5]	124	25.30 N	76.10 E
Bundick Creek ≃	194	30.36 N	92.57 W
Bundooma	162	24.54 S	134.16 E
Bundoora	274b	37.42 S	145.04 E
Bundoran	48	54.28 N	8.17 W
Būndu, India	124	23.11 N	85.35 E
Bundu, S. Afr.	158	29.45 S	22.02 E
Bunduqiyah	154	5.06 N	30.53 E
Bund'ur	86	57.32 N	82.01 E
Buner □[9]	123	34.35 N	72.35 E
Bunessan	46	56.19 N	6.14 W
Bunga	150	11.04 N	9.38 E
Bunga ≃	150	11.23 N	9.56 E
Bungamas	112	3.42 S	102.23 E
Bungay	42	52.28 N	1.26 E
Bungbulang	115a	7.27 S	107.35 E
Bunge	26	57.51 N	19.01 E
Bungegep	164	7.48 S	139.52 E
Bungendore	171b	35.15 S	149.27 E
Bunger Hills ⋏[2]	9	66.17 S	100.47 E
Bung Kan	110	18.23 N	103.37 E
Bungku	112	2.33 S	121.58 E
Bungo	152	7.26 S	15.23 E
Bungoma	154	0.34 N	34.34 E
Bungonia	170	34.51 S	149.57 E
Bungo-suidō ʯ	92	33.00 N	132.13 E
Bungo-takada	96	33.33 N	131.27 E
Bungsberg ∧[2]	54	54.12 N	10.43 E
Bungtlang	120	22.20 N	92.46 E
Bungu	154	7.38 S	39.03 E
Bunguran Selatan, Kepulauan II	112	2.45 N	109.00 E
Bunguran Utara, Kepulauan II	112	4.40 N	108.00 E
Buni ≃	115a	7.26 S	106.47 E
Bunia	154	1.34 N	30.15 E
Bunianga	152	3.34 S	20.06 E
Buninyong	169	37.39 S	143.53 E
Buninyong, Mount ∧	169	37.39 S	143.56 E
Bunji	123	35.40 N	74.36 E
Bunkeflo strand	41	55.33 N	12.57 E
Bunker	194	37.27 N	91.12 W
Bunker Group II	166	23.48 S	152.20 E
Bunker Hill, Il., U.S.	219	39.02 N	89.57 W
Bunker Hill, In., U.S.	216	40.40 N	86.06 W
Bunker Hill, Or., U.S.	202	43.21 N	124.12 W
Bunker Hill, Tx., U.S.	222	29.46 N	95.32 W
Bunker Hill ∧	204	39.15 N	117.08 W
Bunker Hill Monument ⊥	283	42.22 N	71.04 W
Bunkeya	154	10.07 S	27.17 E
Bunkie	194	30.57 N	92.10 W
Bunkyō ✦[8]	268	35.43 N	139.45 E
Bunnahowen	48	54.11 N	9.54 W
Bunnell	192	29.27 N	81.15 W
Bunnik	52	52.04 N	5.12 E
Bünningstedt	52	53.41 N	10.13 E
Buñol	34	39.25 N	0.47 W
Bunola	214	40.14 N	79.56 W
Bun Plains ⊞	154	0.44 N	40.42 E
Bunratty Castle ⊥	48	52.42 N	8.48 W
Bunschoten	52	52.14 N	5.22 E
Bunsuru ≃	150	13.21 N	6.23 E
Bunta	112	0.48 S	122.10 E
Buntine	162	29.59 S	116.34 E
Buntingford	42	51.57 N	0.01 W
Buntok	112	1.42 S	114.48 E
Bununu Dass	150	10.00 N	9.31 E
Bunut	112	0.46 N	112.30 E
Bunyambili	154	2.21 S	29.25 E
Bünyan	130	38.51 N	35.52 E
Bunyip	169	38.06 S	145.43 E
Bunyip ≃	169	38.13 S	145.27 E
Bunyrevo	82	54.34 N	37.09 E
Bunyu, Pulau I	112	3.30 N	117.50 E
Bunza	150	12.08 N	4.00 E
Buochs	58	46.58 N	8.22 E
Buol	112	1.10 N	121.26 E
Buolkalach	74	72.56 N	119.50 E
Buonalbergo	68	41.13 N	14.59 E
Buona Vista	271c	1.16 N	103.47 E
Buon-bu-n'jang	110	12.06 N	107.40 E
Buonconvento	66	43.08 N	11.29 E
Buon-mrong	110	12.48 N	108.28 E
Buon-ngo	110	12.30 N	108.28 E
Buon-thach-hom	110	12.17 N	108.48 E
Buon-ya-soup	110	13.05 N	107.52 E
Buor-Chaja, guba ᴄ	74	71.30 N	131.00 E
Buor-Chaja, mys ≻	74	71.56 N	132.40 E
Bupul	164	7.31 S	140.52 E
Buqay'āwīyah, Qā'al- ⊞	132	32.03 N	37.07 E
Buqayq	128	25.56 N	49.40 E

PORTUGUÊS

Nome	Página	Lat.°′	Long.°′ W = Oeste
Buqda Koosaar	144	4.31 N	44.49 E
Buqde Caqable	144	4.04 N	45.15 E
Buquim	250	11.09 S	37.37 W
Buquira ≃	256	23.10 S	45.54 W
Buquirivu ≃	287b	23.28 S	46.28 W
Buqūm, Ḥarrat al- ♟[9]	144	20.54 N	42.00 E
Bur	88	58.47 N	107.01 E
Bura, Kenya	154	3.30 S	38.18 E
Bura, Kenya	154	1.06 S	39.57 E
Bura Gaurānga ≃[1]	126	22.00 N	90.33 E
Burakin	162	30.31 S	117.10 E
Buraly	80	55.04 N	52.52 E
Buram	140	10.49 N	25.10 E
Buran	86	48.04 N	85.15 E
Burangulovo	86	53.26 N	58.23 E
Buranhém ≃	255	16.27 S	39.04 W
Burankol'	86	46.14 N	54.12 E
Burannoje	86	50.59 N	54.28 E
Burano ≃	66	43.37 N	12.40 E
Burao Kibir	144	8.42 N	45.29 E
Burāq	132	33.10 N	36.29 E
Burāri ✦[8]	272a	28.46 N	77.12 E
Buras	194	29.21 N	89.31 W
Buraševo	82	56.44 N	35.52 E
Burāthum	124	28.04 N	84.50 E
Bur'atskaja Avtonomnaja Sovetskaja Socialističeskaja Respublika □[3]	88	53.00 N	109.00 E
Burauen	116	10.58 N	124.53 E
Burayd, Bi'r ⫪[4]	142	29.08 N	32.07 E
Buraydah	128	26.20 N	43.59 E
Burayk	146	26.33 N	13.08 E
Buraykah	132	32.50 N	36.34 E
Burbach	56	50.45 N	8.05 E
Burbage, Eng., U.K.	42	51.20 N	1.40 W
Burbage, Eng., U.K.	262	53.15 N	1.56 W
Burbank, Ca., U.S.	226	37.19 N	121.55 W
Burbank, Ca., U.S.	228	34.10 N	118.18 W
Burbank, Il., U.S.	216	41.45 N	87.45 W
Burbank, Oh., U.S.	214	40.59 N	81.59 W
Burbank, Wa., U.S.	202	46.12 N	119.00 W
Burbank Studios ʊ[3]	280	34.09 N	118.21 W
Burbure	50	50.32 N	2.28 E
Burç	130	37.02 N	37.10 E
Burcei	71	39.21 N	9.21 E
Burcevo	82	55.02 N	38.09 E
Burcher	166	33.32 S	147.18 E
Burcin	62	45.26 N	5.26 E
Burco	144	9.31 N	45.34 E
Burda	124	25.50 N	77.35 E
Burdalyk	128	38.25 N	64.20 E
Burdekin ≃	166	19.39 S	147.30 E
Burdekin Falls ʟ	166	20.39 S	147.09 E
Burden	198	37.18 N	96.45 W
Burdeos → Bordeaux, Fr.	32	44.50 N	0.34 W
Burdeos, Pil.	116	14.51 N	121.58 E
Burdeos Bay ᴄ	116	14.44 N	122.06 E
Burdett, Ab., Can.	182	49.50 N	111.32 W
Burdett, Ks., U.S.	198	38.11 N	99.31 W
Burdett, N.Y., U.S.	210	42.25 N	76.50 W
Burdu □[4]	130	37.30 N	30.10 E
Burdul	272c	19.07 N	73.07 E
Burdur	130	37.43 N	30.17 E
Burdur Gölü ⊜	130	37.44 N	30.12 E
Burdwān	126	23.15 N	87.51 E
Burdwān □[5]	126	23.25 N	87.50 E
Burdwood Bank ✢[3]	18	54.15 S	59.00 W
Bure, Ityo.	144	8.15 N	35.09 E
Bure, Ityo.	144	10.47 N	37.06 E
Bure ≃	42	52.37 N	1.43 E
Bure, Pic de ∧	62	44.38 N	5.56 E
Bureå	26	64.37 N	21.12 E
Bureälven ≃	26	64.37 N	21.13 E
Bureg Changaj	88	48.14 N	103.57 E
Bureinskij chrebet ⋏	89	50.35 N	133.35 E
Bureja	89	49.52 N	129.48 E
Bureja ≃	89	49.25 N	129.35 E
Burekup	168a	33.19 S	115.49 E
Büren, B.R.D.	52	51.33 N	8.33 E
Büren, Mong.	88	47.13 N	95.54 E
Büren an der Aare	58	47.08 N	7.23 E
Büren Chaan	88	49.29 N	99.14 E
Bürengijn nuruu ⋏	88	49.15 N	104.30 E
Bures	261	48.57 N	1.58 E
Bures-sur-Yvette	261	48.42 N	2.10 E
Burey-en-Vaux	58	48.34 N	5.40 E
Burfjord	24	69.56 N	22.00 E
Burford, On., Can.	212	43.06 N	80.26 W
Burford, Eng., U.K.	42	51.49 N	1.38 W
Būr Fu'ād ✦[8]	142	31.15 N	32.19 E
Burg, B.R.D.	56	50.42 N	8.19 E
Burg, B.R.D.	263	51.08 N	7.09 E
Burg, D.D.R.	54	51.49 N	14.08 E
Burg, D.D.R.	54	52.16 N	11.51 E
Burg, Schloss ⊥	263	51.08 N	7.10 E
Burga	76	58.45 N	32.29 E
Burgas	38	42.30 N	27.28 E
Burgas □[4]	130	42.10 N	27.30 E
Burgaski zaliv ᴄ	38	42.30 N	27.33 E
Burgau	58	48.26 N	10.25 E
Burg [auf Fehmarn]	54	54.26 N	11.12 E
Burgaw	192	34.33 N	77.55 W
Burgaz ✦[8]	267b	40.53 N	29.03 E
Burgaz Adası I	267b	40.53 N	29.04 E
Burgbernheim	56	49.27 N	10.19 E
Burgdorf, B.R.D.	52	52.27 N	10.00 E
Burgdorf, Schw.	58	47.04 N	7.37 E
Burgebrach	56	49.50 N	10.44 E
Bürgel	54	50.56 N	11.45 E
Burgenland □[3]	61	47.30 N	16.20 E
Burgeo	186	47.37 N	57.37 W
Burgersdorp	158	31.00 S	26.20 E
Burger Township	273d	26.05 S	27.46 E
Burges, Mount ∧[2]	162	30.50 S	121.06 E
Burgess	208	37.53 N	76.21 W
Burgess Hill	42	50.57 N	0.07 W
Burgessville	212	43.01 N	80.39 W
Burgettstown	214	40.22 N	80.23 W
Burggrafenberg ∧[2]	263	51.13 N	7.07 E
Burghausen	60	48.09 N	12.49 E
Burghead	46	57.42 N	3.30 W
Burgheim	60	48.42 N	11.01 E
Burgh Heath	260	51.18 N	0.13 W
Burghill	214	41.22 N	80.34 W
Burgh le Marsh	44	53.09 N	0.15 E
Burghūth, Sabkhat al- ⊜	130	34.58 N	41.06 E
Burgin	194	37.45 N	84.46 W
Burgio	70	37.36 N	13.17 E
Burgjoss	56	50.12 N	9.29 E
Burgkirchen	60	48.12 N	13.06 E
Burgkunstadt	54	50.08 N	11.14 E
Bürglen, Schw.	58	46.53 N	8.40 E
Bürglen, Schw.	58	47.33 N	9.09 E
Burglengenfeld	60	49.13 N	12.03 E
Burgoon	214	41.16 N	83.15 W
Burgos, Esp.	34	42.21 N	3.42 W
Burgos, It.	71	40.23 N	8.59 E
Burgos, Méx.	232	24.57 N	98.47 W
Burgos, Pil.	116	16.04 N	119.52 E
Burgos, Pil.	116	15.30 N	120.24 E
Burgos □[4]	34	42.20 N	3.40 W
Burgsinn	56	50.09 N	9.38 E
Burgstädt	54	50.55 N	12.49 E
Burgstall, D.D.R.	54	52.24 N	11.41 E
Burgstall → Postal, It.	64	46.36 N	11.11 E
Burg Stargard	54	53.29 N	13.18 E
Burgsvik	26	57.03 N	18.16 E
Burgueño, Arroyo ≃	288	34.24 S	58.47 W
Burgund → Bourgogne □[9]	32	47.00 N	4.30 E
Burgundy → Bourgogne □[9]	32	47.00 N	4.30 E
Burgusio (Burgeis)	64	46.42 N	10.31 E
Burgwedel, B.R.D.	52	52.30 N	9.52 E
Burgwedel, B.R.D.	52	52.29 N	9.51 E
Burgwindheim	56	49.49 N	10.35 E
Burhābalang ≃	126	21.28 N	87.04 E
Burham	260	51.20 N	0.29 E

Burhan Budai Shan ⋏	102	36.00 N	96.00 E
Burhaniye, Tür.	130	37.57 N	28.45 E
Burhaniye, Tür.	130	39.30 N	26.58 E
Burhānpur	120	21.18 N	76.14 E
Burhar	124	23.13 N	81.32 E
Burhave	52	53.34 N	8.21 E
Burholme ✦[8]	285	40.03 N	75.05 W
Buri	255	23.48 S	48.35 W
Burias Island I	116	12.57 N	123.08 E
Burias Pass ʯ	116	13.00 N	123.15 E
Buribaj	86	51.57 N	58.11 E
Būr Ibrāhīm ✦[8]	142	29.57 N	32.34 E
Burica, Punta ≻	236	8.03 N	82.53 W
Burien	224	47.28 N	122.20 W
Buri Gandaki ≃	124	27.48 N	84.45 E
Burigi, Lake ⊜	154	2.05 S	31.15 E
Burila Mare	38	44.27 N	22.34 E
Burin	186	47.02 N	55.10 W
Burin Peninsula ≻[1]	186	47.00 N	55.40 W
Buriram	110	15.00 N	103.07 E
Burishwar ≃[1]	126	21.58 N	90.02 E
Buritama	255	21.03 S	50.08 W
Buriti, Bra.	250	3.55 S	42.57 W
Buriti, Bra.	255	16.27 S	53.27 W
Buriti ≃	248	12.50 S	58.28 W
Buriti Alegre	255	18.09 S	49.03 W
Buriti Bravo	250	5.50 S	43.50 W
Buriti Cortado	250	5.11 S	43.06 W
Buriticupu ≃	250	4.13 S	46.33 W
Buriti dos Lopes	250	3.10 S	41.52 W
Buritizal, Cachoeira do ʟ	250	0.17 N	54.40 W
Buritizeiro	255	17.21 S	44.58 W
Būriya	124	30.09 N	77.21 E
Burj al-'Arab	140	30.55 N	29.32 E
Burjasot	34	39.31 N	0.25 W
Burji	144	5.20 N	37.57 E
Burj Islām	130	35.41 N	35.48 E
Burj Mughayzil	142	31.27 N	30.23 E
Burj Ṣāfītā	130	34.49 N	36.07 E
Burkan ≃	85	41.43 N	76.46 E
Burkau	54	51.10 N	14.10 E
Burkburnett	196	34.05 N	98.34 W
Burke, S.D., U.S.	198	43.10 N	99.17 W
Burke, Tx., U.S.	222	31.14 N	94.46 W
Burke, Va., U.S.	284c	38.47 N	77.16 W
Burke ≃	166	23.12 S	139.33 E
Burke Channel ʯ	182	52.07 N	127.38 W
Burke Island I	9	73.15 S	104.35 W
Burke Lake County Park ♠	284c	38.45 N	77.18 W
Burke Lakefront Airport ⊠	279a	41.31 N	81.41 W
Burkesville	194	36.47 N	85.22 W
Burket	216	41.09 N	85.58 W
Burketown	166	17.43 S	139.34 E
Burkett Gardens	226	37.57 N	121.15 W
Burkettsville	216	40.21 N	84.39 W
Burkhardtsdorf	54	50.44 N	12.55 E
Burkina Faso □[1], Afr.	134	13.00 N	1.30 W
Burkina Faso □[1], Afr.	150	13.00 N	1.30 W
Burkit	80	47.03 N	50.42 E
Burksville	219	38.16 N	90.09 W
Burla	86	53.19 N	78.21 E
Burla ≃	86	53.20 N	78.02 E
Burladingen	58	48.17 N	9.07 E
Burleigh	208	39.02 N	74.51 W
Burleigh Falls	212	44.34 N	78.13 W
Burleigh Heads	171a	28.06 S	153.27 E
Burleson	222	32.32 N	97.19 W
Burleson □[6]	222	30.30 N	96.43 W
Burley, Id., U.S.	202	42.32 N	113.47 W
Burley, Wa., U.S.	224	47.25 N	122.37 W
Burley Griffin, Lake ⊜	171b	35.13 S	149.05 E
Burli, S.S.S.R.	80	51.25 N	52.44 E
Burli, S.S.S.R.	86	53.36 N	61.55 E
Burlingame, Ca., U.S.	226	37.35 N	122.21 W
Burlingame, Ks., U.S.	198	38.45 N	95.00 W
Burlingame State Park ♠	207	41.22 N	71.43 W
Burlington, Nf., Can.	186	49.45 N	56.02 W
Burlington, On., Can.	212	43.19 N	79.47 W
Burlington, Co., U.S.	198	39.18 N	102.16 W
Burlington, Ct., U.S.	207	41.46 N	72.57 W
Burlington, Il., U.S.	216	42.03 N	88.33 W
Burlington, In., U.S.	216	40.29 N	86.24 W
Burlington, Ia., U.S.	190	40.48 N	91.06 W
Burlington, Ks., U.S.	198	38.11 N	95.44 W
Burlington, Ky., U.S.	218	39.01 N	84.43 W
Burlington, Ma., U.S.	207	42.30 N	71.11 W
Burlington, Mi., U.S.	216	42.06 N	85.05 W
Burlington, N.J., U.S.	208	40.04 N	74.51 W
Burlington, N.C., U.S.	192	36.05 N	79.26 W
Burlington, N.D., U.S.	198	48.16 N	101.25 W
Burlington, Pa., U.S.	210	41.47 N	76.37 W
Burlington, Tx., U.S.	222	31.01 N	96.60 W
Burlington, Vt., U.S.	188	44.28 N	73.12 W
Burlington, Wa., U.S.	224	48.28 N	122.19 W
Burlington, Wi., U.S.	216	42.40 N	88.16 W
Burlington, Wy., U.S.	202	44.26 N	108.25 W
Burlington □[6]	208	39.50 N	74.47 W
Burlington Beach	216	41.30 N	87.03 W
Burlington County Airpark ⊠	285	39.56 N	74.50 W
Burlington Island I	285	40.05 N	74.51 W
Burlington Junction	194	40.26 N	95.03 W
Burlington Mall ✦[9]	283	42.29 N	71.13 W
Burlit	89	46.33 N	134.14 E
Burluk	80	50.34 N	44.33 E
Burma □[1]	110	22.00 N	98.00 E
Burmā, Tall ∧	132	30.38 N	35.50 E
Burmakino	80	57.27 N	40.20 E
Burn ≃	44	54.12 N	1.38 W
Burnaby	224	49.15 N	122.57 W
Burnaby Island I	182	52.24 N	131.20 W
Burnage	262	53.26 N	2.12 W
Burnas, ozero ⊜	78	45.52 N	30.08 E
Burnet	196	30.45 N	98.13 W
Burnett ≃	166	24.46 S	152.25 E
Burnett Bay ᴄ	176	73.53 N	124.00 W
Burnett Brook ≃	276	40.46 N	74.38 W
Burnett Heads	166	24.46 S	152.25 E
Burnettsville	216	40.46 N	86.36 W
Burney, Ca., U.S.	204	40.52 N	121.39 W
Burney, In., U.S.	218	39.19 N	85.38 W
Burnham, Eng., U.K.	260	51.33 N	0.39 W
Burnham, Il., U.S.	278	41.39 N	87.34 W
Burnham, Pa., U.S.	208	40.38 N	77.34 W
Burnham Beeches ✦[3]	260	51.34 N	0.38 W
Burnham Market	42	52.57 N	0.44 E
Burnham-on-Crouch	42	51.38 N	0.49 E
Burnham-on-Sea	42	51.15 N	3.00 W
Burnhamthorpe	275b	43.37 N	79.36 W
Burnhaven	46	57.29 N	1.47 W
Burnie	166	41.04 S	145.54 E
Burning Tree Estates	284c	39.01 N	77.12 W
Burnips	216	42.44 N	85.50 W
Burniston	44	54.19 N	0.26 W
Burnley	44	53.48 N	2.14 W
Burnley □[8]	262	53.46 N	2.15 W
Burnley Creek ≃	212	44.13 N	77.51 W
Burnley Football Ground ♠	262	53.48 N	2.14 W
Burnmouth	46	55.50 N	2.04 W
Burnoje	85	42.37 N	70.46 E
Burno-Okt'abr'skoje	85	42.42 N	70.49 E
Burnpur	126	23.40 N	86.57 E
Burns, Ks., U.S.	198	38.05 N	96.53 W
Burns, Or., U.S.	202	43.35 N	119.03 W
Burns, Tn., U.S.	194	36.03 N	87.18 W
Burns, Wy., U.S.	198	41.11 N	104.21 W
Burns Creek ≃	198	47.22 N	104.25 W

Burns Flat	196	35.20 N	99.10 W
Burns Harbor	216	41.37 N	87.10 W
Burnside, Austl.	168b	34.57 S	138.40 E
Burnside, Ky., U.S.	192	36.59 N	84.36 W
Burnside, Pa., U.S.	214	40.49 N	78.47 W
Burnside ≃	176	66.51 N	108.04 W
Burns Lake	182	54.14 N	125.46 W
Burnsville, Al., U.S.	194	32.28 N	86.53 W
Burnsville, Ms., U.S.	194	34.50 N	88.18 W
Burnsville, N.C., U.S.	192	35.55 N	82.18 W
Burnsville, W.V., U.S.	188	38.51 N	80.39 W
Burnt ≃, On., Can.	212	44.35 N	78.46 W
Burnt ≃, Or., U.S.	202	44.22 N	117.14 W
Burnt Cabins	214	40.05 N	77.54 W
Burnt Corn Creek ≃	194	31.06 N	87.04 W
Burnt Hills	210	42.54 N	73.53 W
Burnt Island, Nf., Can.	186	47.36 N	58.53 W
Burntisland, Scot., U.K.	46	56.03 N	3.15 W
Burnt Meadow Brook ≃	276	41.05 N	74.18 W
Burnt Mills, Lake ⊜	208	36.50 N	76.38 W
Burnt Mills Hills	284c	39.02 N	77.00 W
Burnt Mills Manor	284c	39.02 N	77.00 W
Burnt Mountain ∧	228	33.12 N	117.04 W
Burntop	158	26.49 S	30.54 E
Burnt Pine	174c	29.02 S	167.56 E
Burnt Pond ⊜	186	48.11 N	57.24 W
Burntwick Island I	260	51.25 N	0.41 E
Burntwood	42	52.41 N	1.56 W
Burntwood ≃	184	56.08 N	96.30 W
Burntwood Lake ⊜	184	55.29 N	100.07 W
Burnyj, porog ʟ	86	57.43 N	95.18 E
Buro	144	11.28 N	49.41 E
Buron	84	42.48 N	44.03 E
Buronzo	62	45.29 N	8.16 E
Burow	54	53.46 N	13.16 E
Burpengary	171a	27.10 S	152.57 E
Burpham	260	51.15 N	0.33 W
Burqin	86	47.43 N	86.53 E
Burqin ≃	86	47.40 N	86.55 E
Burra	166	33.40 S	138.56 E
Burra Burra Creek ≃	170	34.10 S	149.38 E
Burracoppin	162	31.23 S	118.29 E
Burra Creek ≃	168b	33.51 S	139.18 E
Burrage	283	42.02 N	70.51 W
Burrage Pond ⊜	283	42.01 N	70.52 W
Burragorang, Lake ⊜[1]	170	33.57 S	150.26 E
Burramurra	166	20.30 S	137.20 E
Burravoe	46a	60.32 N	1.28 W
Burrawang	170	34.36 S	150.31 E
Burray I	46	58.51 N	2.54 W
Burrel, Shq.	38	41.37 N	20.00 E
Burrel, Ca., U.S.	226	36.30 N	119.59 W
Burrendong Reservoir ⊜[1]	166	32.39 S	149.15 E
Burren Junction	166	30.06 S	148.58 E
Burriana	34	39.53 N	0.05 W
Burrill Lake ᴄ	170	35.23 S	150.27 E
Burrinjuck Reservoir ⊜[1]	166	35.00 S	148.45 E
Burro, Serranías del ⋏	196	29.10 N	102.05 W
Burr Oak, In., U.S.	216	41.15 N	86.25 W
Burr Oak, Ks., U.S.	198	39.51 N	98.18 W
Burr Oak, Mi., U.S.	216	41.50 N	85.19 W
Burroburro ≃	246	4.48 N	58.51 W
Burro Creek ≃	200	34.32 N	113.35 W
Burro Peak ∧	200	32.35 N	108.26 W
Burrowa, Mount ∧	171b	36.05 S	147.42 E
Burrow Head ≻	44	54.41 N	4.24 W
Burrowhill	260	51.21 N	0.36 W
Burrows	216	40.40 N	86.30 W
Burrows Island I	224	48.29 N	122.42 W
Burr Ridge	278	41.46 N	87.55 W
Burrs Mill Brook ≃	285	39.53 N	74.42 W
Burrton	198	38.01 N	97.40 W
Burrumbeet, Lake ⊜	169	37.30 S	143.39 E
Burrundie	164	13.32 S	131.42 E
Burruyacú	252	26.30 S	64.45 W
Burrwood	194	28.58 N	89.22 W
Burry Holms I	42	51.37 N	4.18 W
Burry Port	42	51.42 N	4.15 W
Bürs	58	47.09 N	9.48 E
Bursa	130	40.11 N	29.04 E
Bursa □[4]	130	40.10 N	29.00 E
Būr Safājah	140	26.44 N	33.56 E
Būr Sa'īd (Port Said)	142	31.16 N	32.18 E
Būr Sa'īd □[4]	142	30.36 N	32.15 E
Burscheid	56	51.05 N	7.06 E
Burscough	262	53.35 N	2.51 W
Burscough Bridge, Eng., U.K.	44	53.36 N	2.52 W
Burscough Bridge, Eng., U.K.	262	53.36 N	2.51 W
Bursey, Mount ∧	9	76.00 S	132.40 W
Bursol'	86	53.11 N	78.27 E
Bürstadt	56	49.38 N	8.27 E
Burstall	184	50.40 N	109.54 W
Burštyn	78	49.17 N	24.37 E
Būr Sūdān (Port Sudan)	140	19.37 N	37.14 E
Burt, Ia., U.S.	190	43.11 N	94.13 W
Burt, N.Y., U.S.	210	43.19 N	78.43 W
Būr Tawfīq ✦[8]	128	29.57 N	32.34 E
Burtenbach	58	48.20 N	10.26 E
Burt Lake ⊜	190	45.27 N	84.40 W
Burtnieku ezers ⊜	76	57.45 N	25.16 E
Burton, B.C., Can.	182	49.59 N	117.54 W
Burton, Eng., U.K.	42	50.44 N	1.45 W
Burton, Eng., U.K.	262	53.16 N	3.01 W
Burton, Il., U.S.	219	39.55 N	91.15 W
Burton, Mi., U.S.	216	43.01 N	84.16 W
Burton, Mi., U.S.	216	43.02 N	83.36 W
Burton, Oh., U.S.	214	41.28 N	81.08 W
Burton, Tx., U.S.	222	30.11 N	96.36 W
Burton, Wa., U.S.	224	47.23 N	122.27 W
Burton, Lake ⊜[1]	192	34.50 N	83.33 W
Burton Fleming	44	54.08 N	0.20 W
Burton Latimer	42	52.23 N	0.41 W
Burtons Bridge	216	42.17 N	88.14 W
Burton Seamount ✢[3]	14	32.00 S	171.45 W
Burtonsville	208	39.07 N	76.56 W
Burton upon Stather	44	53.39 N	0.41 W
Burton upon Trent	42	52.49 N	1.36 W
Burtonwood	262	53.26 N	2.39 W
Burtonwood Airfield ⊠	262	53.24 N	2.39 W
Burträsk	26	64.31 N	20.39 E
Burtundy	166	33.44 S	142.16 E
Burṭus	142	30.09 N	31.08 E
Burtville	162	28.47 S	122.39 E
Buru I	108	3.24 S	126.40 E
Buruanga	116	11.51 N	121.53 E
Burukan	89	53.02 N	136.03 E
Buruldaj	85	42.48 N	75.52 E
Burullus, Buḥayrat al- ⊜	142	31.30 N	30.50 E
Burūm	144	14.22 N	48.57 E
Burundaj	85	43.23 N	76.51 E
Burundi □[1], Afr.	138	3.15 S	30.00 E
Burundi □[1], Afr.	154	3.15 S	30.00 E
Burundučicha	80	58.21 N	46.07 E
Burun-Šibertuj, gora ∧, S.S.S.R.	74	49.42 N	109.59 E
Burun-Šibertuj, gora ∧, S.S.S.R.	88	49.43 N	109.59 E
Bururi	154	3.57 S	29.37 E
Burutu	150	5.21 N	5.31 E
Buruz Bāgān	126	23.03 N	89.00 E
Burwash	190	46.19 N	80.48 W
Burwash Landing	180	61.21 N	139.00 W
Burwell, Eng., U.K.	42	52.16 N	0.19 E
Burwell, Ne., U.S.	198	41.46 N	99.07 W
Burwell Bay ᴄ	208	37.04 N	76.38 W
Burwick	46	58.44 N	2.57 W
Burwood, Austl.	274a	33.53 S	151.06 E
Burwood, Austl.	274b	37.51 S	145.06 E
Bury, P.Q., Can.	206	45.28 N	71.30 W

Bury, Eng., U.K.	42	50.54 N	0.34 W
Bury, Eng., U.K.	262	53.36 N	2.17 W
Bury □[8]	262	53.35 N	2.19 W
Buryn'	78	51.13 N	33.49 E
Bury Saint Edmunds	42	52.15 N	0.43 E
Burzaco	258	34.49 S	58.24 W
Burzet	62	44.44 N	4.15 E
Burzil	123	34.52 N	75.07 E
Burzil Pass)(	123	34.54 N	75.06 E
Būṣ, Ghubbat al- ᴄ	142	29.36 N	32.22 E
Busa, Mount ∧	116	6.08 N	124.39 E
Busachi	71	40.02 N	8.54 E
Busalla	62	44.34 N	8.57 E
Busambra, Rocca ∧	70	37.51 N	13.24 E
Busan → Pusan	98	35.06 N	129.03 E
Busana	64	44.22 N	10.19 E
Busanga	152	0.51 S	22.04 E
Busanga Swamp ⊞	154	14.10 S	25.50 E
Busangu	154	8.32 S	25.31 E
Buṣayrah	130	35.09 N	40.26 E
Busby, Austl.	274a	33.54 S	150.53 E
Busby, Mt., U.S.	202	45.32 N	106.57 W
Busca	62	44.31 N	7.29 E
Buscate	266b	45.32 N	8.49 E
Buscbusc ≃	144	1.08 S	41.49 E
Buschberg ∧[2]	61	48.34 N	16.23 E
Busche	64	46.02 N	11.59 E
Busch Gardens ♠	280	34.13 N	118.28 W
Buschhausen ✦[8]	263	51.30 N	6.51 E
Busdorf	41	54.29 N	9.32 E
Buseck	56	50.36 N	8.47 E
Buseto Palizzolo	70	38.01 N	12.43 E
Būsh	142	29.09 N	31.08 E
Bush ≃, N. Ire., U.K.	44	55.13 N	6.32 W
Bush ≃, S.C., U.S.	192	34.08 N	81.36 W
Būshehr	128	28.59 N	50.50 E
Būshehr □[4]	128	28.50 N	51.20 E
Bushenyi	154	0.32 S	30.11 E
Bushey	260	51.39 N	0.22 W
Bushey Heath	260	51.38 N	0.20 W
Bushi	268	35.50 N	139.22 E
Bushimaie ≃	152	6.02 S	23.45 E
Bushiribana	241s	12.33 N	69.58 W
Bushkill	210	41.06 N	75.00 W
Bush Kill ≃	210	41.05 N	74.59 W
Bushkill Falls ʟ	210	41.09 N	75.01 W
Bushland	196	35.11 N	102.04 W
Bush Lot	246	6.12 N	57.16 W
Bushman Land □[9]	158	29.15 S	20.00 E
Bushmills	48	55.12 N	6.32 W
Bushnell, Fl., U.S.	220	28.39 N	82.06 W
Bushnell, Il., U.S.	190	40.33 N	90.30 W
Bush River ≃	208	39.21 N	76.14 W
Bushton	198	38.30 N	98.23 W
Bū Shubayrim, Wādī ⋁	146	27.07 N	19.30 E
Bushwick ✦[8]	276	40.42 N	73.55 W
Bushy Park	166	21.16 S	139.43 E
Bushy Park ♠	260	51.25 N	0.20 W
Bushy Run ≃	279b	40.20 N	79.40 W
Bushy Run Battlefield ⊥	279b	40.21 N	79.38 W
Busia	154	0.28 N	34.05 E
Busigny	50	50.02 N	3.28 E
Busing, Pulau I	271c	1.14 N	103.45 E
Businga	152	3.20 N	20.53 E
Büsingen	58	47.42 N	8.41 E
Busira ≃	152	0.15 S	18.59 E
Busjön ⊜, Sve.	40	60.06 N	13.28 E
Busjön ⊜, Sve.	40	60.31 N	13.58 E
Busk	78	49.58 N	24.37 E
Buskerud □[6]	26	60.25 N	9.12 E
Buskhyttan	40	58.40 N	16.56 E
Busko Zdrój	30	50.28 N	20.44 E
Buskul'	86	53.45 N	61.12 E
Busle	144	5.28 N	44.25 E
Busoga □[5]	154	0.40 N	33.30 E
Busovača	36	44.06 N	17.53 E
Buṣrā al-Ḥarīrī (Bosor)	132	32.50 N	36.20 E
Buṣrá ash-Shām	132	32.31 N	36.29 E
Bussana	62	43.49 N	7.51 E
Bussang	58	47.53 N	6.51 E
Bussang, Col de)(	58	47.54 N	6.54 E
Busse	89	51.16 N	126.58 E
Busselton	162	33.39 S	115.20 E
Busseri ≃	140	7.41 N	28.03 E
Busseto	64	44.59 N	10.02 E
Bussey	190	41.12 N	92.52 W
Bussières	62	45.50 N	4.16 E
Bussi sul Tirino	66	42.12 N	13.49 E
Busskoje	84	43.50 N	44.37 E
Bussolengo	64	45.28 N	10.51 E
Bussoleno	62	45.08 N	7.09 E
Bussum	52	52.16 N	5.10 E
Bussy-Rabutin, Château de ⊥	58	47.35 N	4.31 E
Bussy-Saint-Georges	261	48.51 N	2.42 E
Bustamante, Méx.	232	26.33 N	100.30 W
Bustamante, Méx.	234	23.26 N	99.47 W
Bustān, Wādī al- ⋁	142	28.24 N	30.49 E
Buštěhrad	54	50.09 N	14.10 E
Buşteni	38	45.25 N	25.32 E
Busti	214	42.02 N	79.17 W
Bustleton ✦[8]	285	40.05 N	75.02 W
Busto Arsizio	62	45.37 N	8.51 E
Busto Garolfo	62	45.33 N	8.53 E
Buston, S.S.S.R.	85	40.31 N	69.19 E
Buston, S.S.S.R.	128	40.04 N	64.49 E
Buštyna	78	48.04 N	23.27 E
Busu-Adula	152	2.05 N	21.40 E
Busuanga	116	12.10 N	119.55 E
Busuanga Island I	116	12.05 N	120.05 E
Busu-Djanoa	152	1.43 N	21.23 E
Bušuicha	76	59.02 N	40.26 E
Bušulej	88	52.45 N	117.13 E
Büsum	30	54.08 N	8.51 E
Busu-Melo	152	1.48 N	20.15 E
Bū Sunbul, Jabal ⋏[2]	146	23.10 N	22.21 E
Buta, S.S.S.R.	80	55.02 N	51.57 E
Buta, Zaïre	154	2.48 N	24.44 E
Butag	116	12.38 N	123.56 E
Butajira	144	8.07 N	38.22 E
Butan	38	43.39 N	23.45 E
Bután → Bhutan □[1]	120	27.30 N	90.30 E
Butand State Park ♠	226	37.13 N	122.20 W
Butantã ✦[8]	287b	23.34 S	46.43 W
Butantã, Instituto ʊ[3]	287b	23.34 S	46.43 W
Buta Ranquil	252	37.03 S	69.50 W
Butare	154	2.36 S	29.44 E
Butaritari I[1]	14	3.07 N	172.48 E
Butarque, Arroyo de ≃	266a	40.19 N	3.39 W
Butauanan Island I	116	14.07 N	123.17 E
Buṭayḥah	132	32.56 N	35.53 E
Butchart Gardens ♠	224	48.33 N	123.28 W
Butcher Island (Dia Deva) I	272c	18.58 N	72.54 E
Bute	168b	33.52 S	138.01 E
Bute, Island of I	46	55.50 N	5.06 W
Bute, Kyles of ʯ	46	55.53 N	5.13 W
Bute, Sound of ʯ	46	55.44 N	5.12 W
Büteelijn nuruu ⋏	88	50.00 N	104.50 E
Bute Giarti	144	4.33 N	37.45 E
Bute Inlet ᴄ	182	50.37 N	124.53 W
Butemba	154	1.09 N	31.36 E
Butembo	154	0.09 N	29.17 E
Butendorf ✦[8]	263	51.33 N	6.59 E
Butera	70	37.11 N	14.11 E
Butere	154	0.13 N	34.30 E
Bütgenbach	56	50.26 N	6.12 E
Butha Buthe	158	28.45 S	28.15 E
Butha Qi (Zalantun)	89	48.02 N	122.43 E
Buthidaung	110	20.52 N	92.32 E
Buthier ≃	62	45.44 N	7.22 E
Buthroton ⊥	38	39.46 N	20.00 E
Buti	66	43.44 N	10.35 E
Butiá	252	30.07 S	51.58 W
Butiaba	154	1.49 N	31.19 E
Butig Mountains ⋏	116	7.39 N	124.20 E
Butka	86	56.47 N	63.47 E
Butler, Al., U.S.	194	32.05 N	88.13 W

≃ River	Fluss	Río	Rivière	Rio	
≊ Canal	Kanal	Canal	Canal	Canal	
ʟ Waterfall, Rapids	Wasserfall, Stromschnellen	Cascada, Rápidos	Chute d'eau, Rapides	Cascata, Rápidos	
ʯ Strait	Meeresstrasse	Estrecho	Détroit	Estreito	
ᴄ Bay, Gulf	Bucht, Golf	Bahía, Golfo	Baie, Golfe	Baía, Golfo	
⊜ Lake, Lakes	See, Seen	Lago, Lagos	Lac, Lacs	Lago, Lagos	
⊞ Swamp	Sumpf	Pantano	Marais	Pântano	
⍓ Ice Features, Glacier	Eis- und Gletscherformen	Accidentes Glaciales	Formes glaciaires	Acidentes glaciares	
⫪ Other Hydrographic Features	Andere Hydrographische Objekte	Otros Elementos Hidrográficos	Autres données hydrographiques	Outros acidentes hidrográficos	

✢ Submarine Features	Untermeerische Objekte	Accidentes Submarinos	Formes de relief sous-marin	Acidentes submarinos
□ Political Unit	Politische Einheit	Unidad Politica	Entité politique	Unidade política
ʊ Cultural Institution	Kulturelle Institution	Institución Cultural	Institution culturelle	Instituição cultural
⊥ Historical Site	Historische Stätte	Sitio Histórico	Site historique	Sitio histórico
♠ Recreational Site	Erholungs- und Ferienort	Sitio de Recreo	Centre de loisirs	Area de Lazer
⊠ Airport	Flughafen	Aeropuerto	Aéroport	Aeroporto
■ Military Installation	Militäranlage	Instalación Militar	Installation militaire	Instalação militar
✦ Miscellaneous	Verschiedenes	Misceláneo	Divers	Diversos

Name	Page	Lat.°′	Long.°′
Butler, Ga., U.S.	192	32.33 N	84.14 W
Butler, Il., U.S.	219	39.12 N	89.32 W
Butler, In., U.S.	216	41.25 N	84.52 W
Butler, Ky., U.S.	218	38.47 N	84.22 W
Butler, Mo., U.S.	194	38.15 N	94.19 W
Butler, N.J., U.S.	210	41.00 N	74.20 W
Butler, Oh., U.S.	214	40.35 N	82.25 W
Butler, Ok., U.S.	196	35.38 N	99.11 W
Butler, Pa., U.S.	214	40.51 N	79.53 W
Butler, Tx., U.S.	222	30.19 N	97.18 W
Butler, Wi., U.S.	216	43.06 N	88.04 W
Butler □[6], Oh., U.S.	218	39.26 N	84.30 W
Butler □[6], Pa., U.S.	214	40.52 N	79.54 W
Butler, Lake ⊜	220	28.28 N	81.33 W
Butler Lake ⊜	278	42.17 N	87.58 W
Butler Point ›	207	41.40 N	70.43 W
Butler Reservoir ⊜[1]	276	40.59 N	74.23 W
Butlers Bridge	48	54.02 N	7.22 W
Butlerville	218	39.02 N	85.30 W
Butnau Lake ⊜	184	56.13 N	95.20 W
Butner	192	36.07 N	78.45 W
Buto	152	15.46 S	15.09 E
Butong	112	1.06 S	114.50 E
Bütow → Bytów	30	54.11 N	17.30 E
Butru	166	21.30 S	139.43 E
Butsha	154	0.57 N	29.13 E
Buttapietra	64	45.20 N	11.00 E
Butte, Mt., U.S.	202	46.00 N	112.32 W
Butte, Ne., U.S.	198	42.54 N	98.50 W
Butte □[6]	226	39.27 N	121.30 W
Butte City	226	39.28 N	121.59 W
Butte Creek ≃, Ca., U.S.	204	39.12 N	121.56 W
Butte Creek ≃, Or., U.S.	224	45.09 N	122.46 W
Butte du Lion ♠	50	50.40 N	4.24 E
Butte Falls	202	42.32 N	122.33 W
Buttelstedt	54	51.05 N	11.20 E
Butte Mountains ⋏	204	39.50 N	115.05 W
Butten	56	48.58 N	7.13 E
Butter Brook ≃	283	42.31 N	71.24 W
Butter Creek ≃	202	45.52 N	119.19 W
Butterfield, Il., U.S.	278	41.50 N	88.02 W
Butterfield, Mn., U.S.	198	43.57 N	94.47 W
Butterfield Creek ≃	278	41.33 N	87.37 W
Butterfield Lake ⊜	212	44.19 N	75.46 W
Butterley Reservoir ⊜[1]	262	53.35 N	1.56 W
Buttermere	44	54.33 N	3.17 W
Butternut	190	46.00 N	90.29 W
Butternut Creek ≃, N.Y., U.S.	210	42.25 N	75.22 W
Butternut Creek ≃, N.Y., U.S.	210	43.06 N	76.00 W
Butterwick	42	52.59 N	0.05 E
Butterworth, Malay.	114	5.25 N	100.24 E
Butterworth, Transkei	158	32.23 S	28.04 E
Buttevant	48	52.14 N	8.40 W
Büttgen	56	51.12 N	6.36 E
Buttlar	56	50.45 N	9.57 E
Buttle Lake ⊜	182	49.46 N	125.36 W
Button Islands II	176	60.35 N	64.45 W
Buttonville	275b	43.52 N	79.22 W
Buttonville Airfield ⊠	275b	43.52 N	79.23 W
Buttonwillow	226	35.24 N	119.28 W
Buttrio	64	46.01 N	13.20 E
Buttstädt	54	51.07 N	11.25 E
Butty Head ›	162	33.54 S	121.38 E
Buttzville	210	40.49 N	75.00 W
Butuan	116	8.57 N	125.33 E
Butuan Bay ⊂	116	9.06 N	125.20 E
Butuj	88	53.27 N	112.22 E
Bū Tumayyim, Wādī V	146	26.56 N	19.13 E
Butung, Pulau I	112	5.00 S	122.55 E
Buṭūris	142	31.00 N	30.15 E
Buturlino, S.S.S.R.	80	55.34 N	44.55 E
Buturlino, S.S.S.R.	82	54.55 N	37.29 E
Buturlinovka	78	50.50 N	40.36 E
Butwal	124	27.42 N	83.27 E
Butylicy	80	55.32 N	41.31 E
Butzbach	56	50.26 N	8.40 E
Bützfleth	52	53.39 N	9.28 E
Bützow	54	53.50 N	11.59 E
Bützsee ⊜	54	52.49 N	12.53 E
Butztown	208	40.39 N	75.22 W
Buuhoodle	144	8.15 N	46.20 E
Buulo Berde	144	3.51 N	45.34 E
Buur Gaabo	144	1.12 S	41.51 E
Buurgplaatz ∧	56	50.10 N	6.01 E
Buur Hakaba	144	2.47 N	44.05 E
Buur Haybe	144	3.57 N	45.07 E
Buwarah, Sabkhat al- ⊞	130	35.09 N	41.12 E
Buwayḍān	132	33.12 N	36.26 E
Buxar	124	25.35 N	83.59 E
Buxtehude	52	53.28 N	9.41 E
Buxton, Boph.	158	27.38 S	24.42 E
Buxton, Guy.	246	6.47 N	58.02 W
Buxton, Eng., U.K.	262	53.15 N	1.55 W
Buxton, N.C., U.S.	192	35.16 N	75.32 W
Buxton, N.D., U.S.	198	47.36 N	97.05 W
Buxton, Or., U.S.	224	45.41 N	123.11 W
Buxton, Mount ∧	182	51.35 N	127.55 W
Buxy	58	46.43 N	4.41 E
Buye	154	4.38 N	27.30 E
Buyiqiao	106	31.47 N	119.48 E
Buyo	150	6.16 N	7.03 W
Buyo, Barrage de ◆[6]	150	6.15 N	7.05 W
Buyuan ≃	102	21.51 N	101.13 E
Büyükada	130	40.52 N	29.07 E
Büyükarmudan	130	39.35 N	38.26 E
Büyükbakkal	267b	40.59 N	29.11 E
Büyükçekmece	130	41.01 N	28.34 E
Büyükdere ◆[8]	267b	41.09 N	29.02 E
Buyuk Doğanca	130	41.11 N	26.25 E
Büyükkale	130	38.01 N	27.34 E
Büyükkarıştıran	130	41.18 N	27.32 E
Büyükkemikli Burnu ›	130	40.18 N	26.14 E
Büyük Lâçin	130	40.47 N	34.54 E
Büyükmenderes ≃	130	37.27 N	27.11 E
Büyükzap → Great Zab ≃	128	36.00 N	43.21 E
Buyun Shan ∧	98	40.06 N	122.42 E
Buyun Uzun	128	39.13 N	63.19 E
Buzan ≃	80	46.18 N	49.06 E
Buzanaj, peski ◆[2]	80	47.30 N	49.50 E
Buzançais	32	46.53 N	1.25 E
Buzancy	56	49.25 N	4.57 E
Bužaninovo	82	56.23 N	38.18 E
Bužarovo	82	55.59 N	36.47 E
Buzău	38	45.09 N	26.49 E
Buzău □[6]	38	45.15 N	26.45 E
Buzău ≃	38	45.26 N	27.44 E
Buzăului, Munții ⋏	38	45.35 N	26.10 E
Buzen	96	33.37 N	131.08 E
Búzi ≃	156	19.50 S	34.43 E
Buziaș	38	45.39 N	21.36 E
Buziji	100	33.49 N	118.14 E
Buzinovka	80	48.32 N	43.53 E
Búzios, Ilha dos I	256	23.48 S	45.08 W
Búzios, Ponta dos ›	255	22.44 S	41.53 W
Buzlanovo	265b	55.46 N	37.13 E
Buzovna	84	40.31 N	50.04 E
Buzuluk, S.S.S.R.	80	52.47 N	52.15 E
Buzuluk, S.S.S.R.	86	51.55 N	66.16 E
Buzuluk ≃, S.S.S.R.	80	50.13 N	42.12 E
Buzuluk ≃, S.S.S.R.	80	52.47 N	52.16 E
Buzzards Bay	207	41.44 N	70.37 W
Buzzards Bay ⊂	207	41.33 N	70.47 W
Bwana Mkubwa	154	13.01 S	28.42 E
Bwasa	152	3.53 S	18.25 E
Bwendi	154	4.01 N	26.41 E
Bwlch	42	51.54 N	3.15 W
By	40	60.12 N	16.28 E
Byadgi	122	14.41 N	75.29 E
Byam Channel ʯ	176	75.20 N	105.20 W
Byam Martin Channel ʯ	176	75.45 N	104.00 W
Byam Martin Island I	176	75.15 N	104.00 W
Byberry Creek ≃	285	40.04 N	74.59 W
Byblos → Jubayl	130	34.07 N	35.39 E
Byček ≃	83	48.26 N	37.47 E
Bychawa	30	51.01 N	22.32 E
Bychov	76	53.32 N	30.12 E
Byčicha	76	55.41 N	29.58 E
Byčki, S.S.S.R.	76	54.15 N	34.39 E
Byčki, S.S.S.R.	80	53.38 N	40.54 E
Byculla ◆[8]	272c	18.58 N	72.49 E
Byczyna	30	51.07 N	18.11 E
Bydalen	26	63.06 N	13.47 E
Bydgoszcz	30	53.08 N	18.00 E
Bydgoszcz □[4]	30	53.15 N	18.00 E
Byelorussian Soviet Socialist Republic → Belorusskaja Sovetskaja Socialističeskaja Respublika □[3]	76	53.35 N	28.00 E
Byelorussian Station ◆[5]	265b	55.47 N	37.35 E
Byers, Pa., U.S.	285	40.05 N	75.41 W
Byers, Tx., U.S.	196	34.04 N	98.11 W
Byersdale	279b	40.37 N	80.13 W
Byers Run ≃	279b	40.24 N	79.42 W
Byesville	188	39.58 N	81.32 W
Byfang ◆[8]	263	51.24 N	7.06 E
Byfield, Eng., U.K.	42	52.11 N	1.14 W
Byfield, Ma., U.S.	207	42.45 N	70.56 W
Byfleet	260	51.20 N	0.29 W
Byford	168a	32.13 S	116.00 E
Byforde	284c	39.01 N	77.05 W
Bygdeå	26	64.04 N	20.51 E
Bygdeträsket ⊜	26	64.26 N	20.32 E
Bygdin	26	61.20 N	8.48 E
Bygdin ⊜	26	61.21 N	8.36 E
Bygi	80	57.13 N	53.44 E
Byglandsfjord	26	58.41 N	7.48 E
Byglandsfjorden ⊜	26	58.48 N	7.50 E
Byhalia	194	34.52 N	89.41 W
Byk ≃	78	46.55 N	29.28 E
Bykle	26	59.21 N	7.20 E
Bykov	89	47.21 N	142.32 E
Bykovec	78	47.13 N	28.27 E
Bykovka, S.S.S.R.	78	50.17 N	27.58 E
Bykovka, S.S.S.R.	82	55.29 N	37.40 E
Bykovo, S.S.S.R.	80	49.47 N	45.22 E
Bykovo, S.S.S.R.	82	54.01 N	37.54 E
Bykovo, S.S.S.R.	82	55.37 N	38.04 E
Bykovo Airport ⊠	265b	55.36 N	38.05 E
Bylas	200	33.08 N	110.07 W
Bylbasovka	83	48.51 N	37.30 E
Bylderup	41	54.57 N	9.07 E
Byley	262	53.13 N	2.25 W
Bylkyldak	86	48.38 N	75.16 E
Bylnice	30	49.04 N	18.01 E
Bylot Island I	176	73.13 N	78.34 W
Byng Inlet	190	45.46 N	80.33 W
Bynum, Mt., U.S.	182	47.58 N	112.18 W
Bynum, N.C., U.S.	192	35.46 N	79.08 W
Bynum, Tx., U.S.	222	31.58 N	97.00 W
Byōdōin Temple ʊ[1]	270	34.53 N	135.48 E
Byram ≃	276	40.59 N	73.39 W
Byramgore Reef ✦[2]	122	11.54 N	71.49 E
Byram Lake Reservoir ⊜[1]	276	41.10 N	73.41 W
Byrd, Lac ⊜	190	47.01 N	76.56 W
Byrd Glacier ⊓	9	80.15 S	160.20 E
Byrdstown	194	36.34 N	85.07 W
Byrka	88	50.39 N	118.31 E
Byrnedale	214	41.17 N	78.30 W
Byro	162	26.05 S	116.09 E
Byrock	166	30.40 S	146.24 E
Byron, Ca., U.S.	226	37.52 N	121.38 W
Byron, Ga., U.S.	192	32.39 N	83.45 W
Byron, Il., U.S.	190	42.07 N	89.15 W
Byron, Mi., U.S.	216	42.49 N	83.57 W
Byron, N.Y., U.S.	210	43.04 N	78.03 W
Byron, Wy., U.S.	202	44.47 N	108.30 W
Byron, Cape ›	166	28.39 S	153.38 E
Byron, Isla I	254	47.47 S	75.12 W
Byron Bay	166	28.39 S	153.37 E
Byron Center	216	42.49 N	85.42 W
Byrranga, gory ⋏	74	75.00 N	104.00 E
Byšice-Liblice	54	50.19 N	14.38 E
Bysjön ⊜	40	60.23 N	14.30 E
Byske	26	64.57 N	21.12 E
Byskeälven ≃	26	64.57 N	21.13 E
Bystraja ≃	80	47.58 N	41.00 E
Bystřany	54	50.38 N	13.51 E
Bystrica ≃	80	58.38 N	49.05 E
Bystřice	30	49.45 N	14.41 E
Bystřice pod Hostýnem	30	49.24 N	17.40 E
Bystrij Tanyp ≃	86	55.46 N	54.35 E
Bystrovka	85	42.47 N	75.43 E
Bystryj	86	57.50 N	73.58 E
Bystryj Istok	86	52.23 N	84.24 E
Bystrzyca Kłodzka	30	50.18 N	16.38 E
Bytantaj ≃	74	68.46 N	134.20 E
Bytča, Česko.	30	49.14 N	18.36 E
Bytča, S.S.S.R.	76	54.18 N	28.24 E
Byten'	76	52.54 N	25.29 E
Bytkov	78	48.38 N	24.26 E
Bytom (Beuthen)	30	50.22 N	18.54 E
Bytoš'	76	53.50 N	34.06 E
Bytów	30	54.11 N	17.30 E
Byumba	154	1.35 S	30.04 E
Byvalki	78	51.51 N	30.37 E
Byxelkrok	26	57.20 N	17.00 E
Bzyb' ≃	84	43.12 N	40.18 E
Bzybskij chrebet ⋏	84	41.18 N	40.41 E
C			
Ča ≃	110	18.46 N	105.47 E
Čaa-Chol'	86	51.32 N	92.23 E
Caacupé	252	25.23 S	57.09 W
Čaadajevka	80	53.09 N	45.56 E
Čaadajevo	80	55.40 N	42.02 E
Caaguazú	252	25.26 S	56.02 W
Caaguazú □[5]	252	25.00 S	55.45 W
Caála	152	12.51 S	15.33 E
Caamaño Sound ʯ	182	52.49 N	129.28 W
Caapiranga	246	3.18 S	61.13 W
Caapucú	252	26.13 S	57.12 W
Caazapá	252	26.09 S	56.24 W
Caazapá □[5]	252	26.10 S	56.00 W
Cabaçal ≃	248	16.00 S	57.42 W
Cabaceiras	250	7.30 S	36.17 W
Cabadbaran	116	9.10 N	125.38 E
Cabadiangan Plateau ⋏[1]	116	9.50 N	122.36 E
Cabagan	116	17.26 N	121.46 E
Cabaiguán	240p	22.05 N	79.30 W
Cabalete Island I	116	14.17 N	121.50 E
Cabalian	116	10.16 N	125.10 E
Cabaliana, Lago ⊜	246	3.20 S	60.50 W
Cabalian Bay ⊂	116	10.13 N	125.10 E
Cabalian Point ›	116	12.06 N	122.01 E
Caballería, Cabo de ›	34	40.05 N	4.05 E
Caballero Creek ≃	280	34.11 N	118.32 W
Caballito ◆[8]	288	34.37 S	58.27 W
Caballones, Cayo I	240p	20.52 N	79.00 W
Caballo Reservoir ⊜[1]	200	32.58 N	107.18 W
Caballos, Cerro de los ∧	234	23.04 N	102.55 W
Cabana	248	8.24 S	78.02 W
Cabanaconde	248	15.37 S	71.59 W
Cabañas	240p	22.58 N	82.55 W
Cabanatuan	116	15.29 N	120.58 E
Cabangan	116	15.10 N	120.03 E
Çabano	186	47.41 N	68.53 W
Čabanovka	83	49.02 N	38.46 E
Cabarruyan Island I	116	16.18 N	119.59 E
Cabaun Island I	116	12.34 N	124.30 E
Cabeceiras	255	15.48 S	46.59 W
Cabecera de Dupí	236	8.22 N	81.54 W
Cabeço de Montachique	266c	38.54 N	9.11 W
Cabedelo	250	6.58 S	34.50 W
Cabellera, Sierra de la ⋏	200	30.55 N	109.07 W
Cabery	216	41.00 N	88.12 W
Cabeza, Arrecife ✦[2]	234	19.04 N	95.51 W
Cabeza del Buey	34	38.43 N	5.13 W
Cabeza de Tigre	286c	10.28 N	66.46 W
Cabezas	248	18.46 S	63.24 W
Cabiao	116	15.15 N	120.51 E
Cabiate	266b	45.40 N	9.10 E
Cabildo, Arg.	252	38.29 S	61.54 W
Cabildo, Chile	252	32.26 S	71.05 W
Cabimas	246	10.23 N	71.28 W
Cabin Branch ≃, Md., U.S.	284b	39.13 N	76.35 W
Cabin Branch ≃, Md., U.S.	284c	38.51 N	76.48 W
Cabin Creek ≃	198	46.55 N	104.52 W
Cabinda	152	5.33 S	12.12 E
Cabinda □[5]	152	5.00 S	12.30 E
Cabinet Mountains ⋏	202	48.20 N	116.00 W
Cabingaan Island I	116	5.41 N	121.03 E
Cabin John	208	38.58 N	77.09 W
Cabin John Creek ≃	284b	38.58 N	77.09 W
Cabin John Creek Park ♠	284c	38.59 N	77.09 W
Cabin John Regional Park ♠	284c	39.02 N	77.09 W
Cabiri	152	8.52 S	13.39 E
Cabirülensar	130	37.00 N	38.59 E
Cable	190	46.12 N	91.17 W
Cable Airport ⊠	280	34.08 N	117.41 W
Cables	162	27.59 S	123.23 E
Cabo	250	8.17 S	35.02 W
Cabo Blanco	254	47.12 S	65.45 W
Cabo Delgado □[5]	154	12.35 S	39.00 E
Cabo Frio	255	22.53 S	42.01 W
Cabo Gracias a Dios	236	14.59 N	83.10 W
Cabo Ledo	152	9.39 S	13.17 E
Cabonga, Réservoir ⊜[1]	190	47.20 N	76.35 W
Cabool	194	37.07 N	92.06 W
Caboolture	166	27.05 S	152.57 E
Cabora Bassa	154	15.35 S	32.48 E
Cabora Bassa Dam ◆[6]	154	15.35 S	32.42 E
Cabo Raso	254	44.21 S	65.14 W
Cabo Rojo	240m	18.05 N	67.09 W
Cabot, Ar., U.S.	194	34.58 N	92.00 W
Cabot, Pa., U.S.	214	40.46 N	79.46 W
Cabot, Mount ∧	188	44.31 N	71.24 W
Cabot Head ›	212	45.14 N	81.17 W
Cabot Strait ʯ	186	47.20 N	59.30 W
Cabo Verde	256	21.28 S	46.24 W
Cabo Verde → Cape Verde □[1]	150a	16.00 N	24.00 W
Cabo Verde ≃	256	21.28 S	46.17 W
Cabo Verde, Ribeirão do ≃	256	21.20 S	44.32 W
Cabra	34	37.28 N	4.27 W
Cabra Island I	116	13.53 N	120.02 E
Cabral	238	18.15 N	71.13 W
Cabramatta	274a	33.54 S	150.56 E
Cabramatta Creek ≃	274a	33.54 S	150.57 E
Cabramurra	171b	35.58 S	148.23 E
Cabras	71	39.56 N	8.32 E
Cabras, Ribeirão das ≃	256	23.08 S	46.05 W
Cabras, Stagno di ⊜	71	39.57 N	8.29 E
Cabras Island I	174p	13.27 N	144.40 E
Cabrel	234	20.06 N	105.14 W
Cabrera I	34	39.09 N	2.56 E
Cabrera ≃, Col.	246	3.26 N	75.07 W
Cabrera ≃, Esp.	34	42.25 N	6.49 W
Cabrera, Sierra de la ⋏	34	42.12 N	6.40 W
Cabrera de Mataró	266d	41.32 N	2.24 E
Cabreúva	256	23.18 S	47.08 W
Cabri	184	50.37 N	108.28 W
Cabriel ≃	34	39.14 N	1.03 W
Cabrillo National Monument ♠	228	32.41 N	117.15 W
Cabrils	266d	41.32 N	2.22 E
Cabrobó	250	8.31 S	39.19 W
Cabruta	246	7.38 N	66.15 W
Cabucgayan	116	11.29 N	124.34 E
Cabuçu, Bra.	256	22.50 S	42.55 W
Cabuçu, Bra.	287a	22.47 S	43.32 W
Cabuçu, Bra.	287b	23.25 S	46.32 W
Cabuçu ≃, Bra.	287a	22.59 S	43.37 W
Cabuçu ≃, Bra.	287a	22.48 S	43.37 W
Cabuçu de Cima ≃	287b	23.31 S	46.33 W
Cabugao	116	17.48 N	120.27 E
Cabulauan Island I	116	11.23 N	120.06 E
Cabullones, Punta ›	240m	17.58 N	66.35 W
Cabulo	152	10.15 S	16.40 E
Cabure	246	11.08 N	69.38 W
Cabuta	152	9.50 S	14.48 E
Cabuya	236	9.36 N	85.06 W
Cabuyal	236	10.40 N	85.40 W
Cabuyaro	246	4.18 N	72.49 W
Caca	80	48.11 N	44.40 E
Caca, Laguna ⊜	286b	22.57 N	82.27 W
Caçador	252	26.47 S	51.00 W
Cacahoatán	236	14.59 N	92.10 W
Čačak	38	43.53 N	20.21 E
Cacaluta	234	20.03 N	104.52 W
Cacaoui, Lac ⊜	186	50.53 N	66.58 W
Caçapava	256	23.06 S	45.42 W
Caçapava do Sul	252	30.30 S	53.30 W
Caçapava Velha	256	23.07 S	45.39 W
Cacapon ≃	188	39.37 N	78.16 W
Cacapon State Park ♠	188	39.32 N	78.23 W
Cacas	130	38.23 N	41.17 E
Caccamo	70	37.56 N	13.40 E
Caccia, Capo ›	71	40.34 N	8.09 E
Caccuri	68	39.14 N	16.47 E
Čačenka ≃	265b	55.46 N	37.18 E
Cacequi	252	29.53 S	54.49 W
Cáceres, Bra.	248	16.04 S	57.41 W
Cáceres, Col.	246	7.35 N	75.20 W
Cáceres, Esp.	34	39.29 N	6.22 W
Cachan	261	48.48 N	2.20 E
Cachán ≃	234	18.11 N	103.08 W
Cacharí	252	36.24 S	59.32 W
Cache	196	34.37 N	98.37 W
Cache ≃, Ar., U.S.	194	34.42 N	91.20 W
Cache ≃, Il., U.S.	194	37.04 N	89.10 W
Caché, Lac ⊜	206	46.21 N	74.39 W
Cache Creek	182	50.48 N	121.19 W
Cache Creek ≃, Ca., U.S.	226	38.42 N	121.42 W
Cache Creek ≃, Ca., U.S.	228	35.06 N	117.58 W
Cache Creek, North Fork ≃	226	38.59 N	122.30 W
Cache la Poudre ≃	200	40.25 N	104.36 W
Cache la Poudre, North Fork ≃	198	40.54 N	105.22 W
Cache Mountain ∧	180	65.31 N	147.20 W
Cache Peak ∧, Ca., U.S.	228	35.13 N	118.15 W
Cache Peak ∧, Id., U.S.	202	42.11 N	113.40 W
Cache Slough ≃	226	38.11 N	121.40 W
Cacheu	150	12.16 N	16.10 W
Cacheu ⊂[1]	150	12.10 N	16.21 W
Cachí	252	25.06 S	66.11 W
Cachimbo	250	9.24 S	54.56 W
Cachimbo, Serra do ⋏	250	8.30 S	55.50 W
Cachimo	152	8.21 S	21.20 E
Cachingues	152	13.05 S	16.43 E
Cachir	88	48.06 N	98.52 E
Cáchira ≃	246	7.52 N	73.40 W
Cachkadzor	84	40.33 N	44.43 E
Cachoeira	255	12.36 S	38.58 W
Cachoeira, Reservatório ⊜[1]	256	23.03 S	46.15 W
Cachoeira, Ribeirão ≃	287b	23.38 S	46.43 W
Cachoeira, Rio da ≃	287a	23.00 S	43.18 W
Cachoeira Alta	255	18.48 S	50.58 W
Cachoeira de Goiás	255	16.44 S	50.38 W
Cachoeira de Minas	256	22.21 S	45.47 W
Cachoeira do Arari	250	1.01 S	48.58 W
Cachoeira do Sul	252	30.02 S	52.54 W
Cachoeira Paulista	256	22.40 S	45.01 W
Cachoeiras	287a	22.39 S	43.28 W
Cachoeiras de Macacu	256	22.28 S	42.39 W
Cachoeirinha	250	8.29 S	36.14 W
Cachoeiro de Itapemirim	255	20.51 S	41.06 W
Cachorros, Rio dos ≃	287a	22.52 S	43.34 W
Cachos, Punta ›	252	27.39 S	71.02 W
Çachos, Rio dos ≃	287b	23.36 S	46.26 W
Čachrov	60	49.16 N	13.18 E
Cachuela Esperanza	248	10.32 S	65.38 W
Cachuma, Lake ⊜[1]	204	34.35 N	119.55 W
Cacilhas	266c	38.41 N	9.09 W
Cacimbinhas	250	9.24 S	36.59 W
Cacine	150	11.08 N	14.57 W
Caciporé ≃	250	3.51 N	51.08 W
Caciporé, Cabo ›	250	3.55 N	51.07 W
Căciulați	38	44.38 N	26.10 E
Cacnipa Island I	116	10.30 N	119.04 E
Cacocum	240p	20.44 N	76.23 W
Cacólo	152	10.07 S	19.17 E
Caconda	152	13.43 S	15.06 E
Caconde	256	21.33 S	46.38 W
Cacra	248	12.48 S	75.48 W
Cactus	196	36.04 N	102.00 W
Cactus Flat ≚	204	37.45 N	116.45 W
Cactus Peak ∧	204	37.47 N	116.53 W
Caçu	255	18.37 S	51.04 W
Cacuaco	152	8.47 S	13.22 E
Cacula	152	14.29 S	14.10 E
Caculé	255	14.30 S	42.13 W
Caculuvar ≃	152	16.46 S	14.36 E
Caçumba, Ilha I	255	17.46 S	39.17 W
Cacuri	152	8.14 S	18.20 E
Cacuso	152	9.26 S	15.43 E
Çadale	144	2.45 N	46.19 E
Čadan	86	51.17 N	91.35 E
Cadaqués	34	42.17 N	3.17 E
Çadariri ≃	248	6.20 S	57.46 W
Čadca	30	49.26 N	18.48 E
Caddington	42	51.51 N	0.27 W
Caddo, Ok., U.S.	196	34.07 N	96.15 W
Caddo, Tx., U.S.	196	32.38 N	98.40 W
Caddo ≃	194	34.10 N	93.03 W
Caddo Creek ≃	196	34.14 N	96.59 W
Caddo Lake ⊜[1]	194	32.42 N	94.01 W
Caddo Mills	222	33.04 N	96.14 W
Caddo Peak ∧	222	32.29 N	97.24 W
Caddy Vista	216	42.50 N	87.54 W
Cadena, Arroyo de la ≃	196	26.17 N	104.00 W
Cadena, Cerro ∧	196	25.50 N	104.04 W
Cadena, Punta ›	240m	18.18 N	67.14 W
Cadenberge	52	53.46 N	9.04 E
Cadenet	62	43.44 N	5.22 E
Cadeo	62	44.58 N	9.48 E
Cader Bronwyn ∧	42	52.54 N	3.22 W
Cadereyta Jiménez	232	25.36 N	100.00 W
Cader Idris ∧	42	52.42 N	3.54 W
Cadibarrawirracanna, Lake ⊜	162	28.52 S	135.27 E
Cadig, Mount ∧	116	14.09 N	122.27 E
Cadillac, Sk., Can.	184	49.44 N	107.43 W
Cadillac, Fr.	32	44.38 N	0.19 W
Cadillac, Mi., U.S.	190	44.15 N	85.24 W
Cadipietra (Steinhaus)	64	46.59 N	11.59 E
Cadishead	262	53.25 N	2.26 W
Cadix → Cádiz	34	36.32 N	6.18 W
Cádiz, Esp.	34	36.32 N	6.18 W
Cadiz, Pil.	116	10.57 N	123.18 E
Cadiz, In., U.S.	218	39.57 N	85.30 W
Cadiz, Ky., U.S.	194	36.51 N	87.50 W
Cadiz, Oh., U.S.	214	40.16 N	80.59 W
Cádiz, Bahía de ⊂	34	36.32 N	6.16 W
Cádiz, Golfo de ⊂	34	36.50 N	7.10 W
Cadiz Lake ⊜	204	34.18 N	115.24 W
Cadlao Island I	116	11.13 N	119.21 E
Çadnam	42	50.55 N	1.35 W
Čadobec	88	58.40 N	98.51 E
Čadobec ≃	88	58.40 N	98.50 E
Cadogan	214	40.45 N	79.34 W
Cadomin	182	53.02 N	117.20 W
Cadoneghe	64	45.26 N	11.55 E
Cadore ◆[1]	64	46.30 N	12.20 E
Cadosia	210	41.58 N	75.16 W
Cadott	190	44.56 N	91.09 W
Cadoux	162	30.47 S	117.08 E
Cadure, Fosso delle ≃	267a	41.56 N	12.12 E
Caduruan Point ›	116	11.45 N	124.05 E
Cadwell	192	32.20 N	83.02 W
Cady Marsh Ditch ≍	278	41.33 N	87.29 W
Çady Mountain ∧[2]	224	48.33 N	123.07 W
Čadyr-Lunga	78	46.03 N	28.47 E
Cadzand	52	51.22 N	3.25 E
Caen	32	49.11 N	0.21 W
Caengo (Kwenge) ≃	152	4.50 S	18.42 E
Caerano di San Marco	64	45.47 N	12.00 E
Caere ⊥	66	42.02 N	12.07 E
Caergwrle	44	53.07 N	3.03 W
Caerleon	42	51.37 N	2.57 W
Caernarfon	44	53.08 N	4.16 W
Caernarfon Bay ⊂	44	53.05 N	4.30 W
Caernarfon Castle ⊥	44	53.08 N	4.16 W
Caerphilly	42	51.35 N	3.14 W
Caerphilly Castle ⊥	42	51.34 N	3.14 W
Caersws	42	52.31 N	3.25 W
Caesar Creek ≃	218	39.29 N	84.06 W
Caesar Creek, Anderson Fork ≃	218	39.33 N	83.58 W
Caesar Creek Lake ⊜[1]	218	39.30 N	84.00 W
Cæsarea → Qesari, Ḥorbat ⊥	132	32.30 N	34.53 E
Caetanópolis	255	19.18 S	44.24 W
Caeté	255	19.54 S	43.40 W
Caeté ≃	248	9.03 S	68.39 W
Caetité	255	14.04 S	42.29 W
Cafayate	252	26.05 S	65.58 W
Cafelândia do Leste Matogrossense	255	16.40 S	53.25 W
Cafima	152	16.39 S	16.27 E
Cafu	152	16.27 S	15.14 E
Cafuini ≃	246	1.17 N	57.11 W
Cafundó	256	22.31 S	46.25 W
Cagaan Chajrchan	88	49.25 N	94.15 E
Cagaan Gol	86	48.57 N	89.07 E
Cagaan Nuur, Mong.	86	49.32 N	89.42 E
Cagaannuur, Mong.	88	50.20 N	105.03 E
Cagaan-Ovoo	102	45.51 N	105.17 E
Cagaan Uul	88	49.28 N	98.30 E
Cagaan-Üür	88	50.32 N	101.30 E
Cágado ≃	256	22.02 S	43.09 W
Čagan ≃	80	51.12 N	51.20 E
Cagan-Aman	80	47.34 N	46.43 E
Cagan-Churtej, chrebet ⋏	88	51.32 N	110.00 E
Cagarras, Ilhas II	287a	23.02 S	43.12 W
Cagayan □[4]	116	18.00 N	121.50 E
Cagayan ≃	116	18.22 N	121.37 E
Cagayancillo	116	9.34 N	121.12 E
Cagayan de Oro	116	8.29 N	124.39 E
Cagayan de Sulu	116	7.01 N	118.30 E
Cagayan Island I	116	9.36 N	121.14 E
Cagayan Islands II	116	9.40 N	121.16 E
Cagayan Sulu Island I	116	7.01 N	118.30 E
Čagda	74	58.45 N	130.37 E
Cageri	84	42.39 N	42.45 E
Caggiano	68	40.34 N	15.29 E
Çağış	130	39.30 N	28.01 E
Çağlarca	130	39.05 N	39.10 E
Čagli	66	43.33 N	12.39 E
Cagliari	71	39.13 N	9.07 E
Cagliari □[4]	71	39.30 N	8.45 E
Cagliari, Golfo di ⊂	71	39.08 N	9.11 E
Cagliari, Stagno di ⊜	71	39.13 N	9.02 E
Čaglinka ≃	86	53.59 N	69.47 E
Cagnano Varano	68	41.49 N	15.47 E
Cagnes-sur-Mer	62	43.40 N	7.09 E
Čagoda	76	59.10 N	35.17 E
Čagoda ≃	76	59.05 N	35.18 E
Čagodošča ≃	76	58.57 N	36.35 E
Čagojan	89	52.08 N	128.15 E
Čagra ≃	80	52.37 N	48.15 E
Cağrankaya	84	40.47 N	40.33 E
Cagraray Island I	116	13.18 N	123.52 E
Cagua	246	10.11 N	67.27 W
Caguán ≃	246	0.08 S	74.18 W
Caguas	240m	18.14 N	66.02 W
Cagveri	84	41.48 N	43.29 E
Cagwait	116	8.55 N	126.18 E
Cahaba ≃	194	32.20 N	87.05 W
Cahabón	236	15.34 N	89.49 W
Cahabón ≃	236	15.25 N	89.36 W
Cahama	152	16.17 S	14.19 E
Caha Mountains ⋏	48	51.45 N	9.45 W
Caher	48	52.21 N	7.56 W
Caherdaniel	48	51.45 N	10.05 W
Cahersiveen	48	51.57 N	10.13 W
Cahokia	219	38.34 N	90.11 W
Cahokia Creek ≃	219	38.47 N	90.01 W
Cahokia Mounds State Park ♠	219	38.39 N	90.03 W
Cahoon Creek ≃	279a	41.29 N	81.55 W
Cahoon Park ♠	279a	41.29 N	81.56 W
Cahoonzie	210	41.26 N	74.43 W
Cahore Point ›	48	52.34 N	6.11 W
Cahors	32	44.27 N	1.26 E
Cahto Peak ∧	204	39.41 N	123.35 W
Cahuilla Indian Reservation ◆[4]	204	33.30 N	116.43 W
Cahuinari ≃	246	1.21 S	70.44 W
Cahuita, Punta ›	236	9.45 N	82.49 W
Caí ≃	252	29.56 S	51.16 W
Caia ≃	34	38.50 N	7.05 W
Caiabis, Serra dos ⋏[1]	248	11.30 S	56.30 W
Caianda	152	11.02 S	23.31 E
Caiapó ≃, Bra.	250	8.52 S	49.36 W
Caiapó ≃, Bra.	255	15.49 S	51.53 W
Caiapó, Serra do ⋏	255	17.00 S	52.00 W
Caiapônia	255	16.57 S	51.49 W
Caiazzo	68	41.11 N	14.22 E
Caibarién	240p	22.31 N	79.28 W
Cai-bau, Dao I	110	21.10 N	107.27 E
Caibiran	116	11.34 N	124.35 E
Caiçara, Bra.	250	6.36 S	35.29 W
Caiçara, Bra.	250	5.04 S	36.03 W
Caiçara, Bra.	255	15.34 S	50.12 W
Caicara, Ven.	246	7.37 N	66.10 W
Caiçara ≃	246	3.11 S	64.49 W
Caicara, Caño ≃	246	7.44 N	69.04 W
Caicara de Maturín	246	9.49 N	63.36 W
Caicedonia	246	4.20 N	75.50 W
Caicó	250	6.27 S	37.06 W
Caicos Islands II	238	21.56 N	71.58 W
Caicos Passage ʯ	238	22.00 N	72.30 W
Caieiras	256	23.22 S	46.44 W
Caieiras □[7]	287b	23.23 S	46.41 W
Caigou	100	33.16 N	114.32 E
Caihuaping	100	26.54 N	113.23 E
Caijiachang	107	29.44 N	106.29 E
Caijiagang	107	28.55 N	106.21 E
Caijialou	104	41.24 N	121.06 E
Caijiapo	102	34.17 N	107.39 E
Caijiazhuang	105	40.48 N	114.44 E
Caille	62	43.46 N	6.44 E
Cailloma	248	15.12 S	71.46 W
Caillou Bay ⊂	194	29.06 N	90.56 W
Caima Bay ⊂	116	13.42 N	122.48 E
Caimán, Islas → Cayman Islands □[2]	238	19.30 N	80.40 W
Caimanera	240p	19.59 N	75.09 W
Caïmanes → Cayman Islands □[2]	238	19.30 N	80.40 W
Caiman Point ›	116	15.55 N	119.46 E
Caimbambo	152	12.58 S	14.01 E
Cain ≃	42	52.46 N	3.08 W
Cain Creek ≃	198	44.17 N	98.10 W
Cainde	152	15.42 S	13.12 E
Caine ≃	248	18.23 S	65.21 W
Caino	64	45.38 N	10.18 E
Cains ≃	186	46.40 N	65.47 W
Cainsdorf	54	50.41 N	12.29 E
Cainsville	194	40.28 N	93.59 W
Cainta	269f	14.35 N	121.07 E
Cai-nuoc	110	8.56 N	105.01 E
Cairano	68	40.54 N	15.22 E
Cairari	250	2.33 S	49.07 W
Caird Coast ⊥[2]	9	76.00 S	24.30 W
Caire, Le → Al-Qāhirah	142	30.03 N	31.15 E
Cairnbrook	214	40.07 N	78.49 W
Cairn Curran Reservoir ⊜[1]	169	37.04 S	143.59 E
Cairndow	46	56.15 N	4.56 W
Cairngorm Mountains ⋏	46	57.04 N	3.50 W
Cairn Mountain ∧	180	61.10 N	155.20 W
Cairnryan	44	54.58 N	5.02 W
Cairns	166	16.55 S	145.46 E
Cairns Lake ⊜	184	51.42 N	94.30 W
Cairnsmore of Carsphairn ∧	44	55.15 N	4.12 W
Cairnsmore of Fleet ∧	44	54.59 N	4.20 W
Cairn Table ∧	44	55.29 N	4.02 W
Cairn Water ≃	44	55.07 N	3.45 W
Cairo → Al-Qāhirah, Mişr	142	30.03 N	31.15 E
Cairo, Ga., U.S.	192	30.52 N	84.12 W
Cairo, Il., U.S.	194	37.00 N	89.10 W
Cairo, Ne., U.S.	198	41.00 N	98.36 W
Cairo, N.Y., U.S.	210	42.17 N	73.59 W
Cairo, Oh., U.S.	216	40.49 N	84.05 W
Cairo, W.V., U.S.	188	39.12 N	81.09 W
Cairo (Almaza) Airport ⊠, Mişr	273c	30.06 N	31.22 E
Cairo (Imbābah) Airport ⊠, Mişr	273c	30.04 N	31.12 E
Cairo, University of ʊ[2]	273c	30.02 N	31.12 E
Cairoçu, Pico do ∧	256	23.18 S	44.36 W
Cairofa	152	14.05 S	12.54 E
Cairo International Airport ⊠	142	30.08 N	31.24 E
Cairo Main Station ◆[5]	273c	30.04 N	31.15 E
Cairo Montenotte	62	44.24 N	8.16 E
Cairu	255	13.30 S	39.03 W
Caister-on-Sea	42	52.39 N	1.44 E
Caistor	44	53.30 N	0.20 W
Caitingqiao	105	39.54 N	117.39 E
Caitou	152	14.28 S	13.06 E
Caiundo	152	15.46 S	17.28 E
Caivano	68	40.57 N	14.18 E
Caiwan	102	25.50 N	110.50 E
Caixi	100	25.15 N	116.28 E
Caiyu	105	39.39 N	116.37 E
Caiza	248	20.02 S	65.40 W
Caizhuang	98	34.17 N	114.08 E
Çaizi Hu ⊜	100	30.48 N	117.05 E
Čaja ≃, S.S.S.R.	86	58.08 N	82.57 E
Čaja ≃, S.S.S.R.	88	58.15 N	109.35 E
Cajabamba, Ec.	246	1.42 S	78.45 W
Cajabamba, Perú	248	7.37 S	78.03 W
Cajacay	248	10.10 S	77.26 W
Caja de Muertos, Isla I	240m	17.54 N	66.32 W
Cajamar	256	23.21 S	46.53 W
Cajamarca	248	7.10 S	78.31 W
Çajamarca □[5]	248	6.15 S	78.50 W
Čajan	85	43.02 N	69.23 E
Čajan ≃	85	42.52 N	68.56 E
Cajapió	250	2.58 S	44.48 W
Cajarc	32	44.29 N	1.50 E
Cajari	250	3.20 S	45.01 W
Cajari ≃	250	0.48 S	51.43 W
Çajatambo	248	10.29 S	77.02 W
Čajatyn, chrebet ⋏	89	52.25 N	138.25 E
Çajàzeiras	250	6.54 S	38.34 W
Čajek	85	41.56 N	74.30 E
Čajkovskij	80	56.47 N	54.09 E
Čajniče	38	43.33 N	19.04 E
Cajones ≃	234	17.45 N	95.55 W
Cajones, Cayos II	236	16.05 N	83.12 W
Cajon Mountain ∧	228	34.16 N	117.25 W
Cajon Pass)(	228	34.19 N	117.26 W
Cajon Summit)(	228	34.21 N	117.27 W
Caju ◆[8]	287a	22.53 S	43.13 W
Cajueiro	250	9.25 S	36.08 W
Cajuru	255	21.17 S	47.18 W
Caka	102	36.48 N	99.19 E
Çaka Yanhu ⊜	102	36.40 N	99.20 E
Čakčar, chrebet ⋏	85	38.35 N	67.28 E
Cakeni	152	17.48 S	19.27 E
Cakir	88	50.27 N	103.35 E
Çakıralan	130	41.10 N	35.47 E
Çakırgöl Dağı ∧	130	40.34 N	39.42 E
Çakmak	130	37.37 N	34.19 E
Çakmak Dağı ∧	130	39.46 N	42.12 E
Čakovec	61	46.23 N	16.26 E
Čakovice ◆[8]	54	50.08 N	14.31 E
Cakung ≃	269e	6.11 S	106.55 E
Çal	130	38.05 N	29.24 E
Čala, Transkei	158	31.30 S	27.37 E
Cala, Tür.	84	41.05 N	43.21 E
Cala, Embalse de ⊜[1]	34	37.50 N	6.00 W
Calabacillas	234	23.13 N	99.45 W
Calabanga	116	13.42 N	123.12 E
Calabar	150	4.57 N	8.19 E
Calabasas, Arroyo ≃	280	34.12 N	118.36 W
Calabazar ◆[8]	286b	23.01 N	82.22 W
Calabazas Creek ≃	282	37.25 N	121.58 W
Calabernardo	70	36.52 N	15.08 E
Calabogie	212	45.18 N	76.43 W
Calabogie Lake ⊜	212	45.16 N	76.45 W
Calabozo	246	8.56 N	67.26 W
Calabozo, Ensenada de ⊂	246	11.30 N	71.45 W
Calabria □[4]	68	39.00 N	16.30 E
Calabria, Parco Nazionale di ♠	68	38.09 N	15.54 E
Calabritto	68	40.47 N	15.13 E
Calabro ≃	70	37.53 N	14.11 E
Calabugdong Island I	116	11.06 N	119.41 E
Calaca	116	13.56 N	120.49 E
Calacuccia	36	42.20 N	9.03 E
Caladang, Mount ∧	116	14.49 N	121.21 E
Caladesi Island I	220	28.02 N	82.49 W
Caladesi Island State Park ♠	220	28.02 N	82.48 W
Cala d'Oliva	71	41.05 N	8.20 E
Calafat	38	43.59 N	22.56 E
Calafate	254	50.20 S	72.18 W
Calafquen, Lago ⊜	254	39.31 S	72.10 W
Calagnaan Island I	116	11.29 N	123.13 E
Cala Gonone	71	40.18 N	9.38 E
Calaguas Islands II	116	14.27 N	122.55 E
Calahorra	34	42.18 N	1.58 W
Calais, Fr.	50	50.57 N	1.50 E
Calais, Me., U.S.	188	45.11 N	67.16 W
Calais, Canal de ≍	50	50.57 N	1.51 E
Calais, Pas de (Strait of Dover) ʯ	50	51.00 N	1.30 E
Calala	152	12.59 S	23.30 E
Calalaste, Sierra de ⋏	252	25.30 S	67.30 W
Calalzo di Cadore	64	46.27 N	12.23 E
Calama, Bra.	248	8.03 S	62.53 W
Calama, Chile	252	22.28 S	68.56 W
Calamar, Col.	246	10.15 N	74.55 W
Calamar, Col.	246	1.58 N	72.41 W
Calamarca	248	16.55 S	68.09 W
Calamba, Pil.	116	14.13 N	121.10 E
Calamba, Pil.	116	8.35 N	123.39 E
Calamba, Pil.	116	10.11 N	123.17 E
Calamian Group II	116	12.00 N	120.00 E
Calamity Creek ≃	196	29.41 N	103.42 W
Calamocha	34	40.55 N	1.18 W
Calamonaci	70	37.31 N	13.17 E
Calamus ≃	198	41.48 N	99.09 W
Calañas	34	37.39 N	6.53 W
Calanca, Val V	58	46.22 N	9.07 E
Calanda	34	40.56 N	0.14 W
Calandagan Island I	116	10.39 N	120.15 E
Calang	114	4.38 N	95.34 E
Calangianus	71	40.56 N	9.11 E
Calanna	68	38.11 N	15.43 E
Calapan	116	13.25 N	121.10 E
Calape	116	9.54 N	123.52 E
Calapooia ≃	202	44.38 N	123.08 W
Calapooya Mountains ⋏	202	43.30 N	122.50 W
Călărași	38	44.11 N	27.20 E
Calarcá	246	4.31 N	75.38 W
Calascibetta	70	37.35 N	14.16 E
Calasetta	71	39.07 N	8.22 E
Calatabiano	70	37.49 N	15.14 E
Calatafimi	70	37.55 N	12.52 E
Calatagan	116	13.50 N	120.38 E
Calatayud	34	41.21 N	1.38 W
Calau	54	51.45 N	13.56 E
Calauag Bay ≃	116	14.02 N	122.13 E
Calavá, Capo ›	70	38.11 N	14.55 E
Calaveras □[6]	226	38.12 N	120.41 W
Calaveras ≃	226	37.58 N	121.22 W
Calaveras, North Fork ≃	226	38.12 N	120.43 W
Calaveras Big Trees State Park ♠	226	38.16 N	120.19 W
Calaveras Point ›	282	37.28 N	122.03 W
Calaveras Reservoir ⊜[1]	226	37.28 N	121.49 W
Calaveritas Creek ≃	226	38.10 N	120.40 W
Calavino	64	46.03 N	10.59 E
Calavite, Cape ›	116	13.27 N	120.18 E
Calavite, Mount ∧	116	13.29 N	120.24 E
Calavite Passage ʯ	116	13.36 N	120.25 E
Calavon ≃	62	43.51 N	5.00 E
Calawah ≃	224	47.56 N	124.27 W
Calawah, North Fork ≃	224	47.58 N	124.20 W
Calawah, South Fork ≃	224	47.58 N	124.20 W
Calayan	116	19.16 N	121.28 E
Çalayan Island I	116	19.20 N	121.27 E
Čalba	89	52.43 N	131.27 E
Calbayog	116	12.04 N	124.36 E
Calbe	54	51.54 N	11.46 E
Calbiga	116	11.38 N	125.01 E
Calbuco	254	41.46 S	73.08 W
Calca	248	13.20 S	71.57 W
Calçado ≃	256	22.05 S	43.04 W
Calcasieu ≃	194	30.05 N	93.20 W
Calcasieu Lake ⊜	194	29.50 N	93.17 W
Calceta	246	0.51 S	80.10 W
Calcha	248	21.06 S	67.31 W
Calchaquí	252	29.54 S	60.18 W
Calchaquí ≃	252	26.03 S	65.50 W
Calciano	68	40.35 N	16.11 E
Calcinaia	66	43.41 N	10.37 E
Calcinato	64	45.27 N	10.24 E
Calcio	62	45.30 N	9.50 E
Calcium	212	44.01 N	75.51 W
Calçoene	250	2.30 N	50.57 W
Calçoene ≃	250	2.30 N	50.50 W
Calcutta, India	126	22.32 N	88.22 E
Calcutta, India	272b	22.32 N	88.22 E
Calcutta, Oh., U.S.	214	40.40 N	80.34 W
Calcutta □[5]	126	22.30 N	88.30 E

Symbols in the index entries represent the broad categories identified in the key at the right. Symbols with superior numbers (⋏[1]) identify subcategories (see complete key on page *I · 1).*

Kartensymbole in dem Registerverzeichnis stellen die rechts in Schlüssel erklärten Kategorien dar. Symbole mit hochgestellten Ziffern (⋏[1]) bezeichnen Unterabteilungen einer Kategorie (vgl. vollständiger Schlüssel auf Seite *I · 1).*

Los símbolos incluídos en el texto del índice representan las grandes categorias identificadas con la clave a la derecha. Los símbolos con numeros en su parte superior (⋏[1]) identifican las subcategorías (véase la clave completa en la página *I · 1).*

Les symboles de l'index représentent les catégories indiquées dans la légende à droite. Les symboles suivis d'un indice (⋏[1]) représentent des sous-catégories (voir légende complète à la page *I · 1).*

Os símbolos incluídos no texto do índice representam as grandes categorias identificadas com a chave à direita. Os símbolos com números em sua parte superior (⋏[1]) identificam as subcategorias (veja-se a chave completa à página *I · 1).*

English	Deutsch	Español	Français	Português
∧ Mountain	Berg	Montaña	Montagne	Montanha
⋏ Mountains	Berge	Montañas	Montagnes	Montanhas
)(Pass	Pass	Paso	Col	Passo
V Valley, Canyon	Tal, Cañon	Valle, Cañón	Vallée, Canyon	Vale, Canhão
≚ Plain	Ebene	Llano	Plaine	Planície
› Cape	Kap	Cabo	Cap	Cabo
I Island	Insel	Isla	Île	Ilha
II Islands	Inseln	Islas	Îles	Ilhas
⊥ Other Topographic Features	Andere Topographische Objekte	Otros Elementos Topográficos	Autres données topographiques	Outros acidentes topográficos

ESPAÑOL

Nombre	Página	Lat.°′	Long.°′ W = Oeste
Calcutta, University of ⊍[2]	272b	22.35 N	88.22 E
Caldaro (Kaltern)	64	46.25 N	11.14 E
Caldarola	66	43.08 N	13.13 E
Caldas, Bra.	256	21.56 S	46.23 W
Caldas, Col.	246	6.05 N	75.38 W
Caldas □[5]	246	5.15 N	75.30 W
Caldas ≃	266d	41.31 N	2.13 E
Caldas da Rainha	34	39.24 N	9.08 W
Caldas de Reyes	34	42.36 N	8.38 W
Caldas Novas	255	17.45 S	48.38 W
Caldè	58	45.57 N	8.38 E
Caldecott Tunnel ⬥[5]	282	37.52 N	122.12 W
Caldeirão, Serra do ⋀	34	37.42 N	8.21 W
Calder ≃, Eng., U.K.	44	53.44 N	1.21 W
Calder ≃, Eng., U.K.	262	53.49 N	2.24 W
Calder, Loch ⊜	46	58.31 N	3.36 W
Caldera	252	27.04 S	70.50 W
Caldera de Taburiente, Parque Nacional de la ♠	148	28.48 N	17.52 W
Calder and Hebble Navigation Canal ≍	262	53.43 N	1.54 W
Calder Bridge	44	54.27 N	3.29 W
Calderbrook	262	53.39 N	2.05 W
Calderdale □[8]	262	53.44 N	2.00 W
Çaldere	130	40.49 N	37.01 E
Calderstones Park ♠	262	53.23 N	2.54 W
Caldes	64	46.22 N	10.56 E
Caldew ≃	44	54.54 N	2.56 W
Caldey Island I	42	51.38 N	4.41 W
Caldicot	42	51.36 N	2.45 W
Caldiero	64	45.22 N	11.11 E
Çaldıran	84	39.09 N	43.55 E
Caldonazzo	64	45.59 N	11.16 E
Caldonazzo, Lago di ⊜	64	46.01 N	11.15 E
Čaldonka	88	53.47 N	119.12 E
Caldwell, Id., U.S.	202	43.39 N	116.41 W
Caldwell, Ks., U.S.	198	37.01 N	97.36 W
Caldwell, N.J., U.S.	276	40.51 N	74.17 W
Caldwell, Oh., U.S.	188	39.44 N	81.31 W
Caldwell, Tx., U.S.	222	30.31 N	96.41 W
Caldwell □[6]	222	29.50 N	97.40 W
Caldwell Creek ≃	214	41.37 N	79.37 W
Caldwell-Wright Airport ⊠	276	40.53 N	74.17 W
Caldy	262	53.21 N	3.10 W
Cale ≃	42	50.59 N	2.20 W
Caledon, On., Can.	212	43.52 N	80.00 W
Caledon, S. Afr.	158	34.12 S	19.23 E
Caledon (Mohokare) ≃	158	30.31 S	26.05 E
Caledon East	212	43.52 N	79.52 W
Caledonia, Belize	232	18.14 N	88.29 W
Caledonia, N.S., Can.	186	44.22 N	65.02 W
Caledonia, On., Can.	212	43.04 N	79.56 W
Caledonia, Il., U.S.	216	42.22 N	88.53 W
Caledonia, Mi., U.S.	216	42.47 N	85.31 W
Caledonia, Mn., U.S.	190	43.38 N	91.29 W
Caledonia, Ms., U.S.	194	33.40 N	88.19 W
Caledonia, N.Y., U.S.	210	42.58 N	77.51 W
Caledonia, Oh., U.S.	214	40.38 N	82.58 W
Caledonia, Pa., U.S.	214	41.17 N	78.27 W
Caledonian Canal ≍	46	56.50 N	5.06 W
Caledonia State Park ♠	208	39.56 N	77.29 W
Calego	152	12.10 S	23.36 E
Calella	34	41.37 N	2.40 E
Calemba	152	16.04 S	15.44 E
Calen	166	20.54 S	148.46 E
Calendžicha	84	42.37 N	42.04 E
Calenzano	66	43.51 N	11.09 E
Calera, Al., U.S.	194	33.06 N	86.45 W
Calera, Ok., U.S.	196	33.56 N	96.25 W
Calera Creek ≃	282	37.27 N	121.54 W
Calera Víctor Rosales	234	22.57 N	102.42 W
Caleta, Punta ›	240p	20.04 N	74.18 W
Caleta Olivia	254	46.26 S	67.32 W
Caleufú	252	35.35 S	64.33 W
Calexico	204	32.40 N	115.29 W
Calf Island I	283	42.20 N	70.54 W
Calf Islands II	276	40.59 N	73.38 W
Calfkiller ≃	194	35.49 N	85.29 W
Calf of Man I	44	54.03 N	4.48 W
Calfpasture ≃	188	37.58 N	79.28 W
Calf Pasture Point ›	276	41.05 N	73.24 W
Çalgan	130	37.35 N	38.19 E
Calgary	182	51.03 N	114.05 W
Calhan	198	39.02 N	104.17 W
Calhariz ⬥[8]	266c	38.44 N	9.12 W
Calhoun, Al., U.S.	194	32.03 N	86.32 W
Calhoun, Ga., U.S.	192	34.30 N	84.57 W
Calhoun, Ky., U.S.	194	37.32 N	87.15 W
Calhoun, Mo., U.S.	194	38.28 N	93.37 W
Calhoun, Tn., U.S.	192	35.17 N	84.44 W
Calhoun □[6], Il., U.S.	219	39.09 N	90.37 W
Calhoun □[6], Mi., U.S.	216	42.14 N	85.00 W
Calhoun City	194	33.51 N	89.18 W
Calhoun Falls	192	34.05 N	82.35 W
Cali, Col.	246	3.27 N	76.31 W
Çalı, Tür.	130	40.10 N	28.54 E
Calian Point ›	116	6.07 N	125.42 E
Calicoan Island I	116	10.59 N	125.48 E
Calico Ghost Town ⊥	228	34.57 N	116.52 W
Calico Rock	194	36.07 N	92.08 W
Calicut	122	11.15 N	75.46 E
Caliente, Ca., U.S.	228	35.17 N	118.37 W
Caliente, Nv., U.S.	204	37.36 N	114.30 W
Caliente Creek ≃	228	35.17 N	118.48 W
Califon	210	40.43 N	74.50 W
California, Mo., U.S.	194	38.37 N	92.33 W
California, Pa., U.S.	214	40.03 N	79.53 W
California □[3], U.S.	178	37.30 N	119.30 W
California □[3], U.S.	204	37.30 N	119.30 W
California, Golfo de ⊂	232	28.00 N	112.00 W
California, University of ⊍[2]	282	37.52 N	122.15 W
California Aqueduct ≍[1]	204	33.52 N	117.12 W
California City	228	35.08 N	117.58 W
California Creek ≃	196	33.05 N	99.33 W
California Institute of Technology ⊍[2]	280	34.08 N	118.08 W
California Institution for Men ⊍	280	33.59 N	117.40 W
California Institution for Women ⊍	280	33.57 N	117.38 W
California-Los Angeles, University of (U.C.L.A.) ⊍[2]	280	34.04 N	118.26 W
California State Polytechnic University ⊍[2]	280	34.04 N	117.49 W
California State University (Northridge) ⊍[2], Ca., U.S.	280	34.14 N	118.32 W
California State University (Los Angeles) ⊍[2], Ca., U.S.	280	34.04 N	118.10 W
California State University (Dominguez Hills) ⊍[2], Ca., U.S.	280	33.52 N	118.17 W
California State University (Fullerton) ⊍[2], Ca., U.S.	280	33.53 N	117.53 W

FRANÇAIS

Nom	Page	Lat.°′	Long.°′ W = Ouest
California State University (Long Beach) ⊍[2], Ca., U.S.	280	33.47 N	118.06 W
California State University (Hayward) ⊍[2], Ca., U.S.	282	37.39 N	122.04 W
Calihualá	234	17.35 N	98.10 W
Calilegua	252	23.47 S	64.47 W
Călimănești	38	45.14 N	24.20 E
Călimani, Munții ⋀	38	47.07 N	25.03 E
Calimera	68	40.15 N	18.17 E
Calimere, Point ›	122	10.18 N	79.52 E
Calimesa	228	34.00 N	117.03 W
Calindó ≃	255	14.26 S	43.51 W
Calingasta	252	31.19 S	69.25 W
Calingiri	162	31.06 S	116.27 E
Calinog	116	11.07 N	122.32 E
Calintaan	116	12.35 N	120.56 E
Calion	194	33.19 N	92.32 W
Calipatria	204	33.07 N	115.30 W
Calispell Peak ∧	202	48.26 N	117.30 W
Calistoga	226	38.34 N	122.34 W
Calitri	68	40.54 N	15.27 E
Calitzdorp	158	33.33 S	21.42 E
Calixtlahuaca ⊥	234	19.20 N	99.42 W
Calizzano	62	44.14 N	8.07 E
Calka	84	41.37 N	44.05 E
Calkinskoje vodochranilišče ⊜[1]	84	41.38 N	44.03 E
Čalkojdy	85	40.44 N	73.39 E
Calla	226	37.46 N	121.11 W
Callabonna, Lake ⊜	166	29.45 S	140.04 E
Callabonna Creek ≃	166	29.38 S	140.08 E
Callac	32	48.24 N	3.26 W
Callaghan, Mount ∧	204	39.42 N	116.57 W
Callahan	192	30.33 N	81.49 W
Callahan, Mount ∧	200	39.26 N	108.07 W
Callahans	276	40.58 N	74.37 W
Callan	48	52.33 N	7.23 W
Callander, On., Can.	190	46.13 N	79.23 W
Callander, Scot., U.K.	46	56.15 N	4.14 W
Callang	116	17.02 N	121.38 E
Callanish	46	58.12 N	6.43 W
Callanmarca	248	12.52 S	74.38 W
Callanna	166	29.38 S	137.55 E
Callantsoog	52	52.49 N	4.41 E
Callao, Perú	248	12.04 S	77.09 W
Callao, Va., U.S.	208	37.58 N	76.33 W
Callao □[4]	286d	12.04 S	77.09 W
Callas	62	43.35 N	6.32 E
Callaway	198	41.17 N	99.55 W
Callaway □[6]	219	38.50 N	91.52 W
Callaway Gardens ♠	192	32.51 N	84.52 W
Calle	56	51.20 N	8.13 E
Callensburg	214	41.08 N	79.33 W
Callery	214	40.45 N	80.02 W
Call Hill ∧[2]	210	42.13 N	77.40 W
Calliano, It.	62	45.00 N	8.15 E
Calliano, It.	64	45.56 N	11.05 E
Calliaqua	241h	13.08 N	61.12 W
Callicoon	210	41.46 N	75.03 W
Callicoon Center	210	41.50 N	74.57 W
Calliham	196	28.29 N	98.21 W
Calling Lake	182	55.15 N	113.12 W
Calling Lake ⊜	182	55.13 N	113.15 W
Callington, Austl.	168b	35.07 S	139.02 E
Callington, Eng., U.K.	42	50.30 N	4.18 W
Calliope	166	24.00 S	151.12 E
Callosa de Ensarriá	34	38.39 N	0.07 W
Callosa de Segura	34	38.08 N	0.52 W
Calloway Canal ≍	226	35.24 N	119.01 W
Calmar, Ab., Can.	182	53.16 N	113.49 W
Calmar → Kalmar, Sve.	26	56.40 N	16.22 E
Calmar, Ia., U.S.	190	43.11 N	91.51 W
Călmățui ≃	38	44.50 N	27.50 E
Calmazzo	66	43.40 N	12.46 E
Calmbach	56	48.46 N	8.35 E
Çalm Lake ⊜	190	48.46 N	92.04 W
Čal'mny-Varre	24	67.10 N	37.33 E
Čalna	24	61.55 N	34.01 E
Calnalí	234	20.55 N	98.35 W
Calne	42	51.27 N	2.00 W
Calobre	236	8.19 N	80.51 W
Calola	152	16.30 S	17.51 E
Calolbon	116	13.36 N	124.06 E
Calólo	152	10.00 S	14.53 E
Calolziocorte	62	45.48 N	9.26 E
Calonne-Ricouart	50	50.29 N	2.29 E
Caloocan	269f	14.39 N	120.58 E
Caloosahatchee ≃	220	26.31 N	82.01 W
Caloosahatchee Canal ≍	220	26.46 N	81.27 W
Caloote	168b	34.58 S	139.16 E
Calore ≃, It.	68	40.31 N	15.01 E
Calore ≃, It.	68	41.11 N	14.28 E
Calotlán ≃	234	22.06 N	103.42 W
Caloundra	166	26.48 S	153.09 E
Caloveto	68	39.30 N	16.45 E
Calpan	234	19.06 N	98.27 W
Calpe	34	38.39 N	0.03 E
Çalpulalpan	234	19.35 N	98.35 W
Čalpy	80	55.05 N	53.06 E
Calshot	42	50.49 N	1.19 W
Calstock	42	50.30 N	4.12 W
Caltabellotta	70	37.34 N	13.13 E
Caltagirone	70	37.14 N	14.31 E
Caltagirone ≃	70	37.21 N	14.42 E
Caltanissetta	70	37.29 N	14.04 E
Caltanissetta □[4]	70	37.29 N	14.04 E
Caltavuturo	70	37.49 N	13.53 E
Çaltılıbük	130	39.57 N	28.36 E
Çaltra	48	53.26 N	8.25 W
Čaltyr'	83	47.17 N	39.30 E
Caluango	152	8.21 S	19.40 E
Calubian	116	11.27 N	124.26 E
Calucinga	152	11.18 S	16.12 E
Călugăreni	38	44.07 N	26.01 E
Caluire-et-Cuire	62	45.48 N	4.51 E
Calumbolaca	152	9.09 S	13.48 E
Calumet, Mi., U.S.	190	47.14 N	88.27 W
Calumet, Mn., U.S.	190	47.19 N	93.16 W
Calumet, Pa., U.S.	214	40.13 N	79.28 W
Calumet ≃	278	41.44 N	87.32 W
Calumet, Lake ⊜	216	41.41 N	87.35 W
Calumet City	216	41.36 N	87.31 W
Calumet Harbor ⊂	278	41.44 N	87.32 W
Calumet Park	278	41.39 N	87.39 W
Calumet Park ♠	278	41.43 N	87.32 W
Calumet Sag Channel ≍	278	41.42 N	87.57 W
Calunda	152	12.06 S	23.23 E
Caluquembe	152	13.47 S	14.44 E
Calusa Island I	116	9.37 N	121.01 E
Caluso	62	45.18 N	7.53 E
Caluula	144	11.58 N	50.45 E
Caluula, Raasiga ›	144	11.59 N	50.47 E
Caluya Island I	116	11.55 N	121.34 E
Calvados □[5]	32	49.10 N	0.30 W
Calvello	68	40.28 N	15.51 E
Calver	44	53.16 N	1.38 W
Calvera	68	40.09 N	16.09 E
Calvert, Al., U.S.	194	31.09 N	88.01 W
Calvert, Tx., U.S.	222	30.58 N	96.40 W
Calvert □[6]	208	38.33 N	76.35 W
Calvert ≃	164	16.17 S	137.44 E
Calvert, Lough ⊜	169	38.11 S	143.42 E
Calvert City	194	37.02 N	88.21 W
Calvert Hills	166	17.15 S	137.20 E
Calvert Island I	182	51.35 N	128.00 W
Calverton, Eng., U.K.	44	53.02 N	1.05 W
Calverton, Md., U.S.	284c	39.03 N	76.56 W
Calverton, N.Y., U.S.	207	40.55 N	72.45 W
Calvi	32	42.34 N	8.45 E
Calvi, Monte ∧	66	43.05 N	10.37 E
Calvi dell'Umbria	66	42.24 N	12.34 E
Calvillo	234	21.51 N	102.43 W
Calvin, Ok., U.S.	196	34.58 N	96.14 W
Calvin, Pa., U.S.	214	40.20 N	78.02 W

PORTUGUÊS

Nome	Página	Lat.°′	Long.°′ W = Oeste
Calvinia	158	31.25 S	19.45 E
Calvisano	64	45.20 N	10.20 E
Calvo, Monte ∧	68	41.44 N	15.46 E
Calvörde	54	52.23 N	11.17 E
Calw	56	48.43 N	8.44 E
Calwa	226	36.42 N	119.45 W
Calypso	192	35.09 N	78.06 W
Calzada	248	6.02 S	77.02 W
Cam ≃	42	52.21 N	0.15 E
Camabatela	152	8.11 S	15.22 E
Camaçari	255	12.41 S	38.18 W
Camachigama, Lac ⊜	190	47.50 N	76.19 W
Camacho, Bra.	256	22.20 S	47.13 W
Camacho, Méx.	232	24.25 N	102.18 W
Camacosni	236	14.57 N	85.08 W
Camacupa	152	12.03 S	17.30 E
Camaguán	246	8.06 N	67.36 W
Camagüey	240p	21.23 N	77.55 W
Camagüey □[4]	240p	21.30 N	78.00 W
Camagüey, Archipiélago de II	240p	22.18 N	78.00 W
Camaiore	64	43.56 N	10.18 E
Camaiú ≃	248	5.30 S	59.42 W
Camajuaní	240p	22.28 N	79.44 W
Camaldoli, Eremo di ⊍[1]	66	43.46 N	11.47 E
Camamu	255	13.57 S	39.07 W
Camaná	248	16.37 S	72.42 W
Camaná ≃	248	16.39 S	72.46 W
Camananaú ≃	246	1.51 S	61.14 W
Camanche	190	41.47 N	90.15 W
Camanche Reservoir ⊜[1]	226	38.13 N	120.58 W
Camandag Island I	116	11.59 N	124.25 E
Camanducaia	256	22.46 S	46.09 W
Camanducaia ≃, Bra.	256	22.39 S	46.58 W
Camanducaia ≃, Bra.	256	22.55 S	46.25 W
Camano Island I	224	48.10 N	122.30 W
Camaoi ≃	250	3.12 S	48.04 W
Camapuã	255	19.30 S	54.05 W
Camaquã	252	30.51 S	51.49 W
Camaquã ≃	252	31.17 S	51.47 W
Camará	246	3.55 S	62.44 W
Camarajibe	250	8.01 S	34.58 W
Camararé ≃	248	12.15 S	58.55 W
Camarat, Cap ›	62	43.12 N	6.41 E
Camarda	66	42.23 N	13.29 E
Çamardı	130	37.50 N	35.00 E
Camarès	32	43.49 N	2.53 E
Camargo	248	20.39 S	65.13 W
Camargue ⬥[1]	62	43.34 N	4.34 E
Camargue, Parc Naturel Regional de ♠	62	43.30 N	4.28 E
Camarillo	228	34.12 N	119.02 W
Camarillo Heights	228	34.14 N	119.02 W
Camarina ⊥	70	36.52 N	14.27 E
Camariñas	34	43.07 N	9.10 W
Camarines Norte □[4]	116	14.10 N	122.40 E
Camarines Sur □[4]	116	13.35 N	123.20 E
Camarón, Arroyo ≃	196	27.08 N	100.00 W
Camarón, Cabo ›	236	16.00 N	85.05 W
Camaronero, Laguna ⊂	234	23.00 N	106.07 W
Camarones	254	44.48 S	65.42 W
Camarones, Bahía ⊂	254	44.45 S	65.34 W
Camas, Esp.	34	37.24 N	6.02 W
Camas, Wa., U.S.	224	45.35 N	122.23 W
Camas Creek ≃, Id., U.S.	202	44.53 N	114.44 W
Camas Creek ≃, Id., U.S.	202	43.53 N	112.21 W
Camas Creek ≃, Id., U.S.	202	43.20 N	114.24 W
Camas Creek ≃, Or., U.S.	202	45.01 N	118.59 W
Camastra	70	37.15 N	13.47 E
Camatambo	152	6.30 S	15.18 E
Ca-mau → Quan-long	110	9.11 N	105.08 E
Camaxilo	152	8.21 S	18.56 E
Camba	112	4.54 S	119.50 E
Camba Cassai	152	9.40 S	19.18 E
Cambados	34	42.30 N	8.48 W
Cambaquara	256	23.54 S	45.27 W
Cambará	255	23.03 S	50.05 W
Çambar Dağı ∧	130	40.21 N	42.26 E
Cambay	120	22.18 N	72.37 E
Camberley	42	51.21 N	0.45 W
Camberwell	169	37.50 S	145.04 E
Camberwell ⬥[8]	260	51.28 N	0.05 W
Cambiano	62	44.58 N	7.47 E
Cambo	44	55.10 N	1.57 W
Cambo ≃	152	7.40 S	17.17 E
Cambodia → Kampuchea □[1]	110	13.00 N	105.00 E
Cambois	44	55.10 N	1.31 W
Cambonda, Serra ⋀	152	12.06 S	14.00 E
Camboon	166	25.03 S	150.26 E
Cambooya	171a	27.42 S	151.52 E
Camboriú	252	27.01 S	48.38 W
Camboriú, Ponta ›	252	25.10 S	47.55 W
Camborne	42	50.12 N	5.19 W
Cambra	210	41.11 N	76.18 W
Cambrai, Austl.	168b	34.39 S	139.17 E
Cambrai, Fr.	50	50.10 N	3.14 E
Cambremer	50	49.09 N	0.03 E
Cambria, Ca., U.S.	226	35.33 N	121.04 W
Cambria, In., U.S.	216	40.22 N	86.33 W
Cambria, Mi., U.S.	216	41.49 N	84.39 W
Cambria, Wi., U.S.	190	43.32 N	89.06 W
Cambria □[6]	214	40.29 N	79.16 W
Cambria Ice Field ⍓	182	55.55 N	129.30 W
Cambrian Mountains ⋀	42	52.35 N	3.35 W
Cambrian Park	226	37.15 N	121.55 W
Cambridge (Galt), On., Can.	212	43.22 N	80.19 W
Cambridge, N.Z.	172	37.53 S	175.28 E
Cambridge, Eng., U.K.	42	52.13 N	0.08 E
Cambridge, Id., U.S.	202	44.34 N	116.41 W
Cambridge, Il., U.S.	190	41.18 N	90.11 W
Cambridge, Ia., U.S.	190	41.53 N	93.31 W
Cambridge, Md., U.S.	208	38.33 N	76.04 W
Cambridge, Ma., U.S.	207	42.22 N	71.06 W
Cambridge, Mn., U.S.	190	45.34 N	93.13 W
Cambridge, Ne., U.S.	198	40.16 N	100.09 W
Cambridge, N.Y., U.S.	210	43.01 N	73.22 W
Cambridge, Oh., U.S.	188	40.02 N	81.35 W
Cambridge, Wi., U.S.	216	43.00 N	89.01 W
Cambridge Bay	176	69.03 N	105.05 W
Cambridge City	218	39.48 N	85.10 W
Cambridge Fiord ⊂[2]	176	71.20 N	74.44 W
Cambridge Gulf ⊂	164	14.55 S	128.15 E
Cambridge Park	274a	33.45 S	150.43 E
Cambridge Reservoir ⊜[1]	283	42.24 N	71.16 W
Cambridgeshire □[6]	42	52.20 N	0.05 E
Cambridge Springs	214	41.48 N	80.03 W
Cambrils	34	41.04 N	1.03 E
Cambuci	255	21.34 S	41.55 W
Cambuci ⬥[8]	287b	23.34 S	46.37 W
Cambuí	256	22.37 S	46.04 W
Cambulo	152	7.48 S	21.14 E
Cambundi-Catembo	152	10.09 S	17.31 E
Cambuquira	256	21.51 S	45.18 W
Cambural	286c	10.26 N	66.59 W
Camburg	54	51.03 N	11.42 E
Camburú ≃	256	23.41 S	45.28 W
Çamby	218	39.40 N	86.19 W
Čamčakly	128	37.56 N	63.06 E
Camden, Austl.	170	34.03 S	150.42 E
Camden, S. Afr.	158	26.38 S	30.07 E
Camden, Al., U.S.	194	31.59 N	87.17 W
Camden, Ar., U.S.	194	33.35 N	92.50 W
Camden, De., U.S.	208	39.06 N	75.32 W

Camden, Il., U.S.	219	40.09 N	90.46 W
Camden, In., U.S.	216	40.36 N	86.32 W
Camden, Me., U.S.	188	44.12 N	69.03 W
Camden, Mi., U.S.	216	41.45 N	84.45 W
Camden, Ms., U.S.	194	32.46 N	89.50 W
Camden, N.J., U.S.	208	39.55 N	75.07 W
Camden, N.Y., U.S.	210	43.20 N	75.44 W
Camden, N.C., U.S.	192	36.19 N	76.10 W
Camden, Oh., U.S.	218	39.37 N	84.38 W
Camden, S.C., U.S.	192	34.14 N	80.36 W
Camden, Tn., U.S.	194	36.03 N	88.05 W
Camden, Tx., U.S.	222	30.55 N	94.44 W
Camden □[6], N.J., U.S.	208	39.57 N	75.07 W
Camden □[6], N.C., U.S.	208	36.28 N	76.21 W
Camden ⬥[8]	260	51.33 N	0.10 W
Camden, Grupo II	254	54.40 S	71.58 W
Camden Aerodrome ⊠	274a	34.03 S	150.41 E
Camden Bay ⊂	180	70.00 N	145.00 W
Camden Hills State Park ♠	188	44.17 N	69.05 W
Camden Lake ⊜	212	44.25 N	76.52 W
Camden Station ⬥[5]	284b	39.17 N	76.37 W
Camdenton	194	38.00 N	92.44 W
Camedo	58	46.09 N	8.37 E
Cameia, Parque Nacional da ♠	152	11.45 S	21.20 E
Camel ≃	42	50.33 N	4.55 W
Camel, Mount ∧	169	36.45 S	144.43 E
Camelback Mountain ∧, Ak., U.S.	180	62.33 N	157.20 W
Camelback Mountain ∧, Pa., U.S.	210	41.03 N	75.21 W
Camelford	42	50.37 N	4.41 W
Camels Back ∧	172	36.58 S	175.35 E
Camels Hump ∧	188	44.19 N	72.53 W
Cameo Acres	282	37.51 N	121.58 W
Camerano	66	43.32 N	13.33 E
Cameri	62	45.30 N	8.39 E
Cameri, Aeroporto di ⊠	266b	45.32 N	8.40 E
Camerino	66	43.08 N	13.04 E
Cameron, Ca., U.S.	226	38.39 N	120.56 W
Cameron, La., U.S.	194	29.47 N	93.19 W
Cameron, Mo., U.S.	194	39.44 N	94.14 W
Cameron, N.Y., U.S.	210	42.12 N	77.24 W
Cameron, Pa., U.S.	214	41.27 N	78.10 W
Cameron, S.C., U.S.	192	33.33 N	80.42 W
Cameron, Tx., U.S.	222	30.51 N	96.58 W
Cameron, W.V., U.S.	188	39.49 N	80.34 W
Cameron, Wi., U.S.	190	45.24 N	91.44 W
Cameron □[6]	214	41.31 N	78.14 W
Cameron ≃	224	49.17 N	124.38 W
Cameron, Lac ⊜	206	46.06 N	74.50 W
Cameron Highlands	114	4.29 N	101.27 E
Cameron Hills ⋀[2]	176	59.48 N	118.00 W
Cameron Lake ⊜, B.C., Can.	224	49.17 N	124.37 W
Cameron Lake ⊜, On., Can.	212	44.34 N	78.45 W
Cameron Mills	210	42.11 N	77.22 W
Cameron Mountains ⋀	172	46.00 S	167.00 E
Cameron Run ≃	284c	38.48 N	77.04 W
Cameroon (Cameroun) □[1]	134	6.00 N	12.00 E
Cameroon Mountain ∧	152	4.12 N	9.11 E
Camerota	68	40.02 N	15.23 E
Cameroun → Cameroon □[1]	134	6.00 N	12.00 E
Camerún → Cameroon □[1]	134	6.00 N	12.00 E
Cametá	250	2.15 S	49.30 W
Camfield	164	17.09 S	131.21 E
Camiçi	130	40.40 N	37.00 E
Camiguin □[4]	116	9.15 N	124.40 E
Camiguin Island I, Pil.	116	18.56 N	121.55 E
Camiguin Island I, Pil.	116	9.11 N	124.42 E
Camiling	116	15.42 N	120.24 E
Camilla	192	31.13 N	84.12 W
Camillus	210	43.02 N	76.19 W
Camin	54	53.27 N	10.58 E
Camiña	248	19.18 S	69.26 W
Caminha	34	41.52 N	8.50 W
Camino	226	38.44 N	120.40 W
Camiranga	250	1.48 S	46.17 W
Camiri	248	20.03 S	63.31 W
Camisano Vicentino	64	45.31 N	11.43 E
Camissombo	152	8.10 S	20.39 E
Camiyanı	130	40.52 N	38.38 E
Camlad ≃	42	52.36 N	3.10 W
Çamlıbel	130	40.05 N	36.29 E
Çamlıca	130	40.46 N	26.39 E
Çamlıdere	130	40.30 N	32.29 E
Çam-lo	110	16.49 N	106.59 E
Čamlyk ≃	84	44.45 N	40.45 E
Cammal	210	41.24 N	77.28 W
Cammarata	70	37.38 N	13.38 E
Cammarta, Monte ∧	70	37.37 N	13.36 E
Cammin → Kamień Pomorski	30	53.58 N	14.46 E
Camoapa	236	12.23 N	85.31 W
Camocim	250	2.54 S	40.50 W
Camogli	62	44.21 N	9.09 E
Camonica, Val V	64	46.00 N	10.20 E
Camooweal	166	19.55 S	138.07 E
Camopi ≃	250	3.11 N	52.20 W
Camorim ≃	287a	22.59 S	43.25 W
Camorim, Represa do ⊜[1]	287a	22.58 S	43.27 W
Camorta Island I	110	8.08 N	93.30 E
Camote, Cerro ∧	286d	11.57 S	77.06 W
Camotes Islands II	116	10.40 N	124.24 E
Camotes Sea ⊤[2]	116	10.30 N	124.15 E
Camotlán ≃	234	22.01 N	104.15 W
Camowen ≃	48	54.36 N	7.18 W
Camp □[6]	222	33.00 N	94.58 W
Campagna	68	40.40 N	15.08 E
Campagna di Roma ⬥[1]	66	41.50 N	12.35 E
Campagna Lupia	64	45.21 N	12.06 E
Campagnano di Roma	66	42.08 N	12.23 E
Campagnatico	66	42.53 N	11.16 E
Campagne-lès-Hesdin	50	50.24 N	1.52 E
Campaign	194	35.46 N	85.37 W
Campamento	236	14.33 N	86.42 W
Campamento, Cerro ∧	286a	19.18 N	99.17 W
Campana, Arg.	258	34.10 S	58.57 W
Campana, It.	68	39.24 N	16.50 E
Campana, Isla I	254	48.20 S	75.15 W
Campanario	34	38.52 N	5.37 W
Campanario, Cerro de ∧	248	5.57 S	77.31 W
Campanella, Punta ›	68	40.34 N	14.19 E
Campanero, Cerro ∧	246	5.54 N	65.12 W
Campanha	256	21.50 S	45.24 W
Campania □[4]	68	40.55 N	14.50 E
Campania Island I	182	53.05 N	129.30 W
Camparada	266b	45.39 N	9.19 E
Campaspe ≃, Austl.	166	21.00 S	146.24 E
Campaspe ≃, Austl.	169	36.41 S	144.31 E
Campbell, S. Afr.	158	28.48 S	23.44 E
Campbell, Ca., U.S.	226	37.17 N	121.56 W
Campbell, Mn., U.S.	198	46.05 N	96.24 W
Campbell, Mo., U.S.	194	36.29 N	90.04 W
Campbell, Ne., U.S.	198	40.18 N	98.44 W
Campbell, N.Y., U.S.	210	42.13 N	77.11 W
Campbell, Oh., U.S.	214	41.04 N	80.35 W
Campbell, Tx., U.S.	222	33.09 N	95.57 W
Campbell □[6]	218	38.55 N	84.20 W
Campbell, Cape ›	172	41.44 S	174.17 E
Campbell Airport ⊠	279b	40.21 N	80.11 W
Campbellfield	274b	37.41 S	144.57 E
Campbellford	212	44.18 N	77.48 W
Campbell Hall	210	41.27 N	74.16 W

Campbell Hill ∧[2]	216	40.22 N	83.43 W
Campbell Island	182	52.10 N	128.09 W
Campbell Island I	9	52.30 S	169.05 E
Campbell Lake ⊜	182	50.01 N	125.27 W
Campbell Plateau ✤[3]	9	51.00 S	170.00 E
Campbellpore	123	33.46 N	72.22 E
Campbell Range ⋀	180	61.08 N	129.45 W
Campbell River	182	50.01 N	125.15 W
Campbells ≃	170	33.42 S	149.37 E
Campbell's Airport ⊠	278	42.20 N	88.04 W
Campbell's-Bay	188	45.44 N	76.36 W
Campbellsburg, In., U.S.	218	38.39 N	86.15 W
Campbellsburg, Ky., U.S.	218	38.31 N	85.12 W
Campbell Slough ≃	226	39.22 N	121.51 W
Campbellsport	190	43.35 N	88.16 W
Campbells River	170	33.54 S	149.37 E
Campbells Run ≃	279b	40.24 N	80.05 W
Campbellsville	194	37.20 N	85.20 W
Campbellton, N.B., Can.	186	48.00 N	66.40 W
Campbellton, Nf., Can.	186	49.17 N	54.56 W
Campbellton, P.E., Can.	186	46.47 N	64.18 W
Campbellton, Fl., U.S.	192	30.56 N	85.24 W
Campbell Town, Austl.	166	41.56 S	147.29 E
Campbelltown, Austl.	168b	34.53 S	138.40 E
Campbelltown, Austl.	170	34.04 S	150.49 E
Campbelltown, Pa., U.S.	208	40.17 N	76.35 W
Campbellville	212	43.29 N	79.59 W
Campbeltown	44	55.26 N	5.36 W
Camp Creek ≃, Ca., U.S.	226	38.38 N	120.40 W
Camp Creek ≃, Mo., U.S.	219	39.02 N	91.12 W
Camp Creek Lake ⊜[1]	222	31.03 N	96.19 W
Camp David ⊍	208	39.38 N	77.28 W
Camp de Frileuse ■	261	48.52 N	1.55 E
Camp de Satory ■	261	48.47 N	2.06 E
Camp Dix	218	38.29 N	83.17 W
Camp Douglas	190	43.55 N	90.16 W
Campeche	232	19.51 N	90.32 W
Campeche, Bahía de ⊂	232	20.00 N	94.00 W
Campeche Bank ✤[4]	16	22.00 N	90.00 W
Campechuela	240p	20.14 N	77.17 W
Campegine	64	44.45 N	10.32 E
Campello Monti	58	45.56 N	8.15 E
Camperdown, Austl.	169	38.14 S	143.09 E
Camperdown, S. Afr.	158	29.42 S	30.33 E
Camperville	184	51.59 N	100.09 W
Campestre, Bra.	256	21.16 S	42.56 W
Campestre, Bra.	256	21.43 S	46.15 W
Cam-pha	110	21.01 N	107.19 E
Camp Hill, Al., U.S.	194	32.48 N	85.39 W
Camp Hill, Pa., U.S.	208	40.14 N	76.55 W
Campi Bisenzio	66	43.49 N	11.08 E
Campidano ⬥[1]	71	39.30 N	8.47 E
Campiglia dei Fosci	66	43.27 N	11.03 E
Campiglia Marittima	66	43.03 N	10.37 E
Campillo de Llerena	34	38.30 N	5.50 W
Campillos	34	37.03 N	4.51 W
Campina ⬥[1]	34	37.45 N	4.45 W
Campina Grande	250	7.13 S	35.53 W
Campinas	256	22.54 S	47.05 W
Campina Verde	255	19.31 S	49.28 W
Campinho, Rio do ≃	287a	22.52 S	43.37 W
Campione del Garda	64	45.45 N	10.45 E
Campi Salentina	68	40.24 N	18.01 E
Campitello	64	46.28 N	11.44 E
Camp King	150	4.55 N	7.58 W
Camp Lake	216	42.32 N	88.09 W
Camp Lake ⊜	212	45.27 N	78.54 W
Camp Leger de Melun ■	261	48.34 N	2.34 E
Camp Lejeune Marine Corps Base ■	192	34.40 N	77.21 W
Campli	66	42.43 N	13.41 E
Camplong	112	10.02 S	123.55 E
Campo, Čam.	152	2.22 N	9.49 E
Campo, Moç.	156	17.44 S	36.21 E
Campo, Co., U.S.	198	37.06 N	102.34 W
Campo, Réserve de ⬥[4]	152	2.35 N	9.57 E
Campoalegre	246	2.41 N	75.20 W
Campo Alegre ≃	250	9.19 S	50.06 W
Campo Alegre de Goiás	255	17.39 S	47.45 W
Campobasso	66	41.34 N	14.39 E
Campobasso □[4]	66	41.38 N	14.35 E
Campobello di Licata	70	37.15 N	13.55 E
Campobello di Mazara	70	37.38 N	12.45 E
Campobello Island I	186	44.53 N	66.55 W
Campo Belo	255	20.53 S	45.16 W
Campo Blenio	58	46.34 N	8.56 E
Campo Catino	66	41.48 N	13.20 E
Campocologno	58	46.13 N	10.08 E
Campo Cumbica ■	287b	23.27 S	46.28 W
Campo da Bocaina	256	22.17 S	46.06 W
Campodarsego	64	45.30 N	11.54 E
Campo de Criptana	34	39.24 N	3.07 W
Campo de la Cruz	246	10.23 N	74.53 W
Campo de Marte ♠	286d	12.04 S	77.03 W
Campo de Marte ■	287b	23.30 S	46.37 W
Campo de Mayo ■	288	34.32 S	58.38 W
Campo di Giove	66	42.01 N	14.03 E
Campo di Trens (Trens)	64	46.52 N	11.29 E
Campo do Coelho	256	22.15 S	42.39 W
Campodolcino	58	46.24 N	9.21 E
Campo Erê	252	26.23 S	53.03 W
Campofelice di Fitalia	70	37.50 N	13.29 E
Campofelice di Roccella	70	37.59 N	13.53 E
Campofiorito	70	37.45 N	13.16 E
Campo Florido	255	19.47 S	48.35 W
Campoformido	64	46.01 N	13.09 E
Campo Formoso	250	10.31 S	40.20 W
Campofranco	70	37.30 N	13.43 E
Campogalliano	64	44.41 N	10.50 E
Campo Gallo	252	26.35 S	62.51 W
Campo Grande, Arg.	252	27.13 S	54.58 W
Campo Grande, Bra.	255	20.27 S	54.37 W
Campo Grande ⬥[8], Bra.	256	22.54 S	43.34 W
Campo Grande ⬥[8], Port.	266c	38.45 N	9.09 W
Campo Indian Reservation ⬥[4]	204	32.40 N	116.20 W
Cam Point ›	164	8.55 S	152.30 E
Campo Largo, Arg.	252	26.48 S	60.50 W
Campo Largo, Bra.	252	25.26 S	49.32 W
Campolaro	64	45.55 N	10.20 E
Campolasta (Astfeld)	64	46.40 N	11.22 E
Campolato, Capo ›	70	37.17 N	15.12 E
Campo Libertad ■	286b	23.05 N	82.26 W
Campolide	256	21.36 S	43.53 W
Campolieto	66	41.38 N	14.46 E
Campo Ligure	62	44.32 N	8.42 E
Campo Limpo	256	23.12 S	46.48 W
Campo Maior, Bra.	250	4.49 S	42.10 W
Campo Maior, Port.	34	39.01 N	7.04 W
Campomarino	66	41.57 N	15.02 E
Campo Militar Número Uno ■	286a	19.27 N	99.14 W
Campo Morado	234	17.35 N	100.05 W
Campomorone	62	44.30 N	8.53 E
Campo Mourão	255	24.03 S	52.22 W
Campo Nôvo	252	27.42 S	53.48 W
Campo Pequeno ♠	266c	38.44 N	9.08 W
Campo Quijano	252	24.55 S	65.39 W

Campora	68	40.19 N	15.17 E
Camporeale	70	37.54 N	13.06 E
Camporgiano	64	44.09 N	10.20 E
Camporredondo	248	6.07 S	78.21 W
Campos	255	21.45 S	41.18 W
Campos Altos	255	19.41 S	46.10 W
Camposampiero	64	45.34 N	11.56 E
Campo Santo, Arg.	252	24.40 S	65.06 W
Camposanto, It.	64	44.47 N	11.08 E
Campos Belos	255	13.03 S	46.53 W
Campos de Cunha	256	22.55 S	44.49 W
Campos do Jordão	256	22.44 S	45.35 W
Campos Elyseos	256	22.42 S	43.17 W
Campos Gerais	256	21.14 S	45.46 W
Campos Novos	252	27.24 S	51.12 W
Campos Sales	250	7.04 S	40.23 W
Campo Tencia, Pizzo ∧	58	46.26 N	8.43 E
Campotosto	66	42.33 N	13.22 E
Campotosto, Lago di ⊜	66	42.32 N	13.22 E
Campo Tures (Sand in Taufers)	64	46.55 N	11.57 E
Campovalano	66	42.44 N	13.40 E
Camp Parks Communications Annex ■	282	37.44 N	121.54 W
Camp Pendleton Marine Corps Base ■	228	33.19 N	117.18 W
Camp Point	219	40.02 N	91.04 W
Camp Ruby	222	30.42 N	94.45 W
Campsie	274a	33.55 S	151.06 E
Campsie Fells ⋀[2]	46	56.02 N	4.12 W
Camp Springs	208	38.48 N	76.54 W
Campti	194	31.53 N	93.07 W
Campton	192	37.44 N	83.32 W
Camptonville	226	39.27 N	121.03 W
Camptown	210	41.43 N	76.14 W
Campus	216	41.01 N	88.18 W
Campuya ≃	246	1.43 S	73.30 W
Camp Verde	200	34.33 N	111.51 W
Campville	210	42.06 N	76.09 W
Camp Wood	196	29.40 N	100.01 W
Cam-ranh	110	11.54 N	109.09 E
Camrose, Ab., Can.	182	53.01 N	112.50 W
Camrose, Wales, U.K.	42	51.51 N	5.01 W
Camsell ≃	176	65.40 N	118.07 W
Camu ≃	250	1.15 N	57.09 W
Camucia	66	43.16 N	11.58 E
Camucuio	152	14.12 S	13.20 E
Camurí Chiquito, Quebrada ≃	286c	10.37 N	66.52 W
Camuy	240m	18.29 N	66.51 W
Çam-xuyen	110	18.15 N	106.00 E
Çamyndy	85	41.37 N	74.20 E
Čamzinka	80	54.24 N	45.47 E
Çan, Tür.	130	39.09 N	40.13 E
Çan, Tür.	130	40.02 N	27.03 E
Çan ≃	260	51.48 N	0.25 E
Čaňa	30	48.37 N	21.18 E
Canaan, Ct., U.S.	207	42.01 N	73.19 W
Canaan, Fl., U.S.	220	28.48 N	81.14 W
Canaan, In., U.S.	218	38.52 N	85.25 W
Canaan, N.Y., U.S.	210	42.25 N	73.27 W
Canaan, Vt., U.S.	206	44.59 N	71.32 W
Canaan ≃	186	45.55 N	65.47 W
Canaan Lake ⊜	276	40.47 N	73.01 W
Canaan Valley State Park ♠	188	39.02 N	79.32 W
Cana Brava ≃, Bra.	255	13.11 S	48.11 W
Cana Brava ≃, Bra.	255	12.12 S	48.40 W
Cañacao Bay ⊂	269f	14.29 N	120.55 E
Canaçarí, Lago ⊜	250	2.57 S	58.15 W
Canachal	232	24.04 N	107.05 W
Canada □[1]	176	60.00 N	95.00 W
Canada Bay ⊂	186	50.43 N	56.10 W
Canada Dam ⬥[6]	126	24.10 N	87.10 E
Cañada de Caracheo	234	20.22 N	100.57 W
Cañada de Gómez	252	32.49 S	61.24 W
Cañada Honda	252	31.59 S	68.33 W
Canada Lake ⊜	210	43.10 N	74.32 W
Cañada Nieto	258	33.43 S	58.05 W
Canadarago Lake ⊜	210	42.48 N	75.01 W
Canada's Wonderland ♠	275b	43.51 N	79.33 W
Cañada Verde → Villa Huidobro	252	34.50 S	64.35 W
Canadaway Creek ≃	214	42.28 N	79.22 W
Canadensis	210	41.11 N	75.15 W
Canadian	196	35.54 N	100.22 W
Canadian ≃, U.S.	196	35.27 N	95.03 W
Canadian ≃, Co., U.S.	200	40.53 N	106.20 W
Canadian, Deep Fork ≃	196	35.28 N	95.50 W
Canadian Forces Base Trenton ■	212	44.07 N	77.33 W
Canadice Lake ⊜	210	42.43 N	77.34 W
Cañadón Seco	254	46.33 S	67.35 W
Canaguá ≃	246	7.57 N	69.36 W
Canaima	246	6.14 N	62.52 W
Canaima, Parque Nacional ♠	246	4.27 N	62.00 W
Canajoharie	210	42.54 N	74.34 W
Çanakkale	130	40.09 N	26.24 E
Çanakkale □[4]	130	40.10 N	26.45 E
Çanakkale Boğazı (Dardanelles) ⌵	130	40.15 N	26.25 E
Canal, Anse du ⊂	241o	16.23 N	61.30 W
Canal, Islas del → Channel Islands II	28	49.20 N	2.20 W
Canala	175f	21.32 S	165.57 E
Canale	62	44.48 N	8.00 E
Canale, Val V	64	46.29 N	13.30 E
Canale del Ferro ≃	64	46.21 N	13.07 E
Canalejas	234	19.57 N	99.39 W
Canal Flats	182	50.09 N	115.48 W
Canal Fulton	214	40.53 N	81.35 W
Canal Lake ⊜	212	44.34 N	79.03 W
Canal Lewisville	214	40.18 N	81.50 W
Canal Point	220	26.51 N	80.38 W
Canals	252	33.33 S	62.53 W
Canal Winchester	188	39.51 N	82.48 W
Canandaigua	210	42.52 N	77.20 W
Canandaigua Lake ⊜	210	42.49 N	77.16 W
Canandaigua Outlet ≃	210	43.04 N	77.00 W
Cananea	232	30.57 N	110.18 W
Cananéia	252	25.01 S	47.57 W
Cananguchal	246	0.51 N	75.47 W
Canan Station	214	40.28 N	78.26 W
Canapine, Forca)(	66	42.45 N	13.12 E
Canápolis	255	18.44 S	49.13 W
Canapville	50	49.19 N	0.08 E
Cañar	246	2.33 S	78.56 W
Cañar □[4]	246	2.30 S	79.00 W
Canard ≃	214	42.09 N	83.06 W
Canard, Lac au ⊜	206	45.48 N	71.31 W
Canarias, Islas (Canary Islands) II	148	28.00 N	15.30 W
Canaries	241f	13.55 N	61.04 W
Canaro	64	44.56 N	11.40 E
Canarreos, Archipiélago de los II	240p	21.50 N	82.30 W
Canarsie ⬥[8]	276	40.38 N	73.53 W
Canarsie Park ♠	276	40.38 N	73.53 W
Canarsie Pol I	276	40.37 N	73.52 W
Canary Basin ✤[1]	10	30.00 N	25.00 W
Canary Islands → Canarias, Islas II	148	28.00 N	15.30 W
Cañas	236	10.25 N	85.07 W
Cañas, Río de las ≃	234	22.29 N	105.36 W
Canaseraga	210	42.27 N	77.46 W
Canaseraga Creek ≃	210	42.45 N	77.50 W
Cañasgordas	246	6.45 N	76.01 W
Canastota	210	43.04 N	75.45 W
Canastra ≃	250	11.23 S	49.41 W
Canatlán	232	24.31 N	104.47 W

Symbol	English	Deutsch	Español	Français	Português
≃	River	Fluss	Río	Rivière	Rio
≍	Canal	Kanal	Canal	Canal	Canal
∟	Waterfall, Rapids	Wasserfall, Stromschnellen	Cascada, Rápidos	Chute d'eau, Rapides	Cascata, Rápidos
⌵	Strait	Meeresstrasse	Estrecho	Détroit	Estreito
⊂	Bay, Gulf	Bucht, Golf	Bahía, Golfo	Baie, Golfe	Baía, Golfo
⊜	Lake, Lakes	See, Seen	Lago, Lagos	Lac, Lacs	Lago, Lagos
≡	Swamp	Sumpf	Pantano	Marais	Pântano
⍓	Ice Features, Glacier	Eis- und Gletscherformen	Accidentes Glaciales	Formes glaciaires	Acidentes glaciares
⊤	Other Hydrographic Features	Andere Hydrographische Objekte	Otros Elementos Hidrográficos	Autres données hydrographiques	Outros acidentes hidrográficos
✤	Submarine Features	Untermeerische Objekte	Accidentes Submarinos	Formes de relief sous-marin	Acidentes submarinos
□	Political Unit	Politische Einheit	Unidad Politica	Entité politique	Unidade política
⊍	Cultural Institution	Kulturelle Institution	Institución Cultural	Institution culturelle	Instituição cultural
⊥	Historical Site	Historische Stätte	Sitio Histórico	Site historique	Sitio histórico
♠	Recreational Site	Erholungs- und Ferienort	Sitio de Recreo	Centre de loisirs	Area de Lazer
⊠	Airport	Flughafen	Aeropuerto	Aéroport	Aeroporto
■	Military Installation	Militäranlage	Instalación Militar	Installation militaire	Instalação militar
⬥	Miscellaneous	Verschiedenes	Misceláneo	Divers	Diversos

Symbols in the index entries represent the broad categories identified in the key at the right. Symbols with superior numbers (∧1) identify subcategories (see complete key on page I · 1).

Kartensymbole in dem Registerverzeichnis stellen die rechts in Schlüssel erklärten Kategorien dar. Symbole mit hochgestellten Ziffern (∧1) bezeichnen Unterabteilungen einer Kategorie (vgl. vollständiger Schlüssel auf Seite I · 1).

Los símbolos incluidos en el texto del índice representan las grandes categorías identificadas con la clave a la derecha. Los símbolos con numeros en su parte superior (∧1) identifican las subcategorías (véase la clave completa en la página I · 1).

Les symboles de l'index représentent les catégories indiquées dans la légende à droite. Les symboles suivis d'un indice (∧1) représentent des sous-catégories (voir légende complète à la page I · 1).

Os símbolos incluídos no texto do índice representam as grandes categorias identificadas com a chave à direita. Os símbolos com números em sua parte superior (∧1) identificam as subcategorias (veja-se a chave completa à página I · 1).

∧ Mountain	Berg	Montaña	Montagne	Montanha
∧ Mountains	Berge	Montañas	Montagnes	Montanhas
✕ Pass	Pass	Paso	Col	Passo
V Valley, Canyon	Tal, Cañon	Valle, Cañón	Vallée, Canyon	Vale, Canhão
≐ Plain	Ebene	Llano	Plaine	Planície
▸ Cape	Kap	Cabo	Cap	Cabo
I Island	Insel	Isla	Île	Ilha
II Islands	Inseln	Islas	Îles	Ilhas
± Other Topographic Features	Andere Topographische Objekte	Otros Elementos Topográficos	Autres données topographiques	Outros acidentes topográficos

Symbol	English	Deutsch	Español	Français	Português
≃	River	Fluss	Río	Rivière	Rio
⌶	Canal	Kanal	Canal	Canal	Canal
⌊	Waterfall, Rapids	Wasserfall, Stromschnellen	Cascada, Rápidos	Chute d'eau, Rapides	Cascata, Rápidos
⋓	Strait	Meeresstrasse	Estrecho	Détroit	Estreito
c	Bay, Gulf	Bucht, Golf	Bahía, Golfo	Baie, Golfe	Baía, Golfo
⊜	Lake, Lakes	See, Seen	Lago, Lagos	Lac, Lacs	Lago, Lagos
☷	Swamp	Sumpf	Pantano	Marais	Pântano
⌂	Ice Features, Glacier	Eis- und Gletscherformen	Accidentes Glaciales	Formes glaciaires	Acidentes glaciares
⊤	Other Hydrographic Features	Andere Hydrographische Objekte	Otros Elementos Hidrográficos	Autres données hydrographiques	Outros acidentes hidrográficos

Symbol	English	Deutsch	Español	Français	Português
✦	Submarine Features	Untermeerische Objekte	Accidentes Submarinos	Formes de relief sous-marin	Acidentes submarinos
□	Political Unit	Politische Einheit	Unidad Politica	Entité politique	Unidade política
♉	Cultural Institution	Kulturelle Institution	Institución Cultural	Institution culturelle	Instituição cultural
⊥	Historical Site	Historische Stätte	Sitio Histórico	Site historique	Sitio histórico
♠	Recreational Site	Erholungs- und Ferienort	Sitio de Recreo	Centre de loisirs	Area de Lazer
⊠	Airport	Flughafen	Aeropuerto	Aéroport	Aeroporto
■	Military Installation	Militäranlage	Instalación Militar	Installation militaire	Instalação militar
◆	Miscellaneous	Verschiedenes	Misceláneo	Divers	Diversos

Castel di Lucio 70 37.53 N 14.19 E
Castel di Iudica 70 37.30 N 14.38 E
Castel di Sangro 66 41.47 N 14.06 E
Castel di Tora 66 42.13 N 12.58 E
Castelfidardo 66 43.28 N 13.33 E
Castelfiorentino 66 43.36 N 10.58 E
Castelfondo 64 46.27 N 11.07 E
Castelforte 66 41.18 N 13.49 E
Castelfranco Emilia 64 44.37 N 11.03 E
Castelfranco in Miscano 68 41.18 N 15.05 E
Castelfranco Veneto 64 45.40 N 11.55 E
Castel Frentano 66 42.12 N 14.22 E
Castel Fusano ◆[8] 267a 41.44 N 12.19 E
Castel Gandolfo 66 41.45 N 12.39 E
Castel Giorgio 66 42.42 N 11.59 E
Castelgrande 68 40.47 N 15.26 E
Castelhanos, Baía de ⊂ 256 23.51 S 45.15 W
Castelhanos, Ponta dos ≻ 256 23.10 S 44.06 W
Casteljaloux 32 44.19 N 0.05 E
Castellabate 68 40.17 N 14.57 E
Castell'Alfero 62 44.59 N 8.13 E
Castellalto 66 42.40 N 13.49 E
Castellammare, Golfo di ⊂ 70 38.08 N 12.54 E
Castellammare del Golfo 70 38.01 N 12.53 E
Castellammare di Stabia 68 40.42 N 14.29 E
Castellamonte 62 45.23 N 7.42 E
Castellana, Grotte di ⊥[5] 68 40.53 N 17.07 E
Castellana Grotte 68 40.53 N 17.11 E
Castellana Sicula 70 37.47 N 14.02 E
Castellane 62 43.51 N 6.31 E
Castellaneta 68 40.37 N 16.57 E
Castellanza 62 45.37 N 8.54 E
Castellarano 64 44.30 N 10.44 E
Castell'Arquato 62 44.51 N 9.52 E
Castell'Azzara 66 42.46 N 11.42 E
Castellazzo Bormida 62 44.51 N 8.34 E
Castellbisbal 266d 41.29 N 1.59 E
Castelldefels 266d 41.17 N 1.59 E
Castelleone 62 45.18 N 9.46 E
Castelletto 266b 45.30 N 8.48 E
Castelletto di Brenzone 64 45.41 N 10.45 E
Castelli, Arg. 252 36.06 S 57.47 W
Castelli, It. 66 42.29 N 13.43 E
Castellina in Chianti 66 43.28 N 11.17 E
Castellina Marittima 66 43.25 N 10.35 E
Castelli Romani ◆[1] 267a 41.46 N 12.42 E
Castello, Monte ∧ 66 43.03 N 9.49 E
Castello d'Annone 62 44.53 N 8.19 E
Castello di Fiemme 64 46.17 N 11.26 E
Castello Lavazzo 64 46.17 N 12.18 E
Castellón □[4] 34 40.10 N 0.10 W
Castellón de la Plana 34 39.59 N 0.02 W
Castellote 34 40.48 N 0.19 W
Castello Tesino 64 46.04 N 11.38 E
Castellucchio 64 45.09 N 10.39 E
Castelluccio 68 40.00 N 15.58 E
Castell'Umberto 70 38.05 N 14.48 E
Castelluzzo 70 38.06 N 12.44 E
Castel Madama 66 41.58 N 12.52 E
Castel Maggiore 64 44.34 N 11.22 E
Castelmagno 62 44.24 N 7.13 E
Castelmassa 64 45.01 N 11.18 E
Castelmauro 66 41.50 N 14.43 E
Castelmezzano 68 40.32 N 16.03 E
Castelmoron-sur-Lot 32 44.24 N 0.30 E
Castelnaudary 32 43.19 N 1.57 E
Castelnau-Montratier 32 44.16 N 1.21 E
Castelnovo di Sotto 64 44.49 N 10.34 E
Castelnovo ne'Monti 64 44.26 N 10.24 E
Castelnuovo 64 45.26 N 10.47 E
Castelnuovo Berardenga 66 43.21 N 11.30 E
Castelnuovo dell'Abate 66 43.00 N 11.31 E
Castelnuovo della Daunia 68 41.35 N 15.07 E
Castelnuovo di Garfagnana 64 44.06 N 10.24 E
Castelnuovo di Porto 66 42.07 N 12.30 E
Castelnuovo di Val di Cecina 66 43.12 N 10.59 E
Castelnuovo Don Bosco 62 45.03 N 7.58 E
Castelnuovo Nigra 62 45.26 N 7.41 E
Castelnuovo Rangone 64 44.33 N 10.56 E
Castelnuovo Scrivia 62 44.59 N 8.53 E
Castelo 255 20.36 S 41.12 W
Castelo Branco 34 39.49 N 7.30 W
Castelo do Piauí 250 5.20 S 41.33 W
Castel Pagano 68 41.24 N 14.48 E
Castel Porziano ◆[8] 267a 41.44 N 12.24 E
Castelraimondo 66 43.12 N 13.04 E
Castel Romano ◆[8] 267a 41.44 N 12.27 E
Castel San Gimignano 66 43.24 N 11.00 E
Castel San Giorgio 68 40.47 N 14.42 E
Castel San Giovanni 62 45.04 N 9.26 E
Castel San Lorenzo 68 40.25 N 15.14 E
Castel San Pietro Terme 66 44.24 N 11.35 E
Castel Sant'Elia 66 42.15 N 12.22 E
Castelsaraceno 68 40.10 N 16.00 E
Castelsardo 71 40.55 N 8.43 E
Castelsarrasin 32 44.02 N 1.06 E
Castelsilano 68 39.16 N 16.46 E
Casteltermini 70 37.32 N 13.39 E
Castelvecchio Subequo 66 42.08 N 13.44 E
Castelvetere in Val Fortore 68 41.27 N 14.56 E
Castelvetrano 70 37.41 N 12.47 E
Castelvetro di Modena 64 44.30 N 10.57 E
Castelvetro Piacentino 64 45.05 N 9.59 E
Castel Viscardo 66 42.45 N 12.00 E
Castel Volturno, It. 66 44.13 N 11.37 E
Castel Volturno, It. 68 41.02 N 13.56 E
Castenaso 64 44.30 N 11.28 E
Castenedolo 64 45.28 N 10.18 E
Casterton 166 37.35 S 141.24 E
Castets 32 43.53 N 1.09 W
Castiglioncello 66 43.24 N 10.24 E
Castiglione Chiavarese 62 44.16 N 9.31 E
Castiglione d'Adda 62 45.13 N 9.41 E
Castiglione dei Pepoli 64 44.08 N 11.09 E
Castiglione del Lago 66 43.07 N 12.03 E
Castiglione della Pescaia 66 42.46 N 10.53 E
Castiglione delle Stiviere 64 45.23 N 10.29 E
Castiglione del Pepoli 66 44.08 N 11.09 E
Castiglione di Sicilia 70 37.53 N 15.07 E
Castiglione d'Orcia 66 43.00 N 11.37 E
Castiglione d'Ossola 58 46.03 N 8.13 E
Castiglione Messer Marino 66 41.52 N 14.27 E
Castiglione Olona 62 45.46 N 8.52 E
Castiglion Fibocchi 66 43.32 N 11.46 E
Castiglion Fiorentino 66 43.20 N 11.55 E
Castile 210 42.37 N 78.03 W
Castilho 255 20.52 S 51.29 W
Castilla 248 5.12 S 80.38 W
Castilla, Playa de ⊥[2] 34 37.00 N 6.33 W
Castilla-La Mancha □[4] 34 39.30 N 3.00 W
Castilla la Nueva □[9] 34 40.00 N 3.45 W
Castilla la Vieja □[9] 34 41.30 N 4.00 W
Castilla-León □[4] 34 41.30 N 5.00 W
Castillo 258 33.53 S 57.40 W
Castillo, Cerro ∧ 254 43.03 S 71.57 W
Castillo, Pampa del ≍ 254 45.58 S 68.24 W
Castillo de San Marcos National Monument ♦ 192 29.44 N 81.20 W
Castillo Incaico de Ingapirca ⊥ 246 2.34 S 78.50 W
Castillon-la-Bataille 32 44.51 N 0.03 W
Castillos 252 34.12 S 53.50 W
Castillos, Laguna de ◎ 252 34.20 S 53.54 W
Castillo Velasco 234 16.45 N 96.35 W
Castine 188 44.23 N 68.48 W
Castione della Presolana 64 45.54 N 10.04 E
Castions di Strada 64 45.54 N 13.11 E
Castle Acre 42 52.42 N 0.41 E
Castle Air Force Base ■ 226 37.22 N 120.34 W
Castlebar 48 53.52 N 9.17 W
Castlebay 46 56.57 N 7.28 W
Castlebellingham 48 53.54 N 6.23 W
Castleberry 194 31.17 N 87.01 W
Castleblayney 48 54.07 N 6.44 W
Castle Bruce 240d 15.26 N 61.16 W
Castle Cape ≻ 180 56.15 N 158.06 W
Castle Cary 42 51.06 N 2.31 W
Castlecliff 172 39.57 S 174.59 E
Castlecomer 48 52.48 N 7.12 W
Castleconnell 48 52.43 N 8.30 W
Castlecrag 274a 33.48 S 151.13 E
Castle Crags State Park ♦ 204 41.10 N 122.20 W
Castle Creek 210 42.14 N 75.55 W
Castle Creek ≃, Austl. 169 36.41 S 145.29 E
Castle Creek ≃, Id., U.S. 202 43.06 N 116.16 W
Castle Dale 200 39.23 N 110.27 W
Castledawson 44 54.47 N 6.33 W
Castlederg 48 54.42 N 7.36 W
Castledermot 48 52.55 N 6.50 W
Castle Dome Peak ∧ 200 33.05 N 114.08 W
Castle Donington 42 52.51 N 1.19 W
Castle Douglas 44 54.57 N 3.56 W
Castlefinn 48 54.47 N 7.35 W
Castleford 44 53.44 N 1.21 W
Castlegar 182 49.19 N 117.40 W
Castle Harbour ⊂ 240a 32.21 N 64.40 W
Castle Hill 274a 33.44 S 151.00 E
Castle Hills, De., U.S. 208 39.41 N 75.33 W
Castle Hills, Tx., U.S. 196 29.32 N 98.31 W
Castleisland 48 52.14 N 9.27 W
Castlemaine, Austl. 169 37.04 S 144.13 E
Castlemaine, Ire. 48 52.09 N 9.43 W
Castlemartyr 48 51.55 N 8.03 W
Castlemore 275b 43.47 N 79.41 W
Castle Mountain ∧, Ab., Can. 182 51.18 N 115.55 W
Castle Mountain ∧, Yk., Can. 180 64.32 N 135.25 W
Castle Mountain ∧, Ca., U.S. 226 35.56 N 120.20 W
Castle Neck ≻[1] 283 42.41 N 70.45 W
Castle Neck ≃ 283 42.40 N 70.44 W
Castle Park 228 32.36 N 117.04 W
Castle Peak ∧, Co., U.S. 200 39.01 N 106.52 W
Castle Peak ∧, Id., U.S. 202 44.02 N 114.35 W
Castle Peak ∧, Wa., U.S. 224 48.58 N 120.51 W
Castlepoint 172 40.54 S 176.13 E
Castle Point □[8] 260 51.33 N 0.35 E
Castlepollard 48 53.40 N 7.17 W
Castlerea 48 53.46 N 8.29 W
Castlereagh ≃ 166 30.12 S 147.32 E
Castle Rock, Co., U.S. 200 39.22 N 104.51 W
Castle Rock, Pa., U.S. 285 39.58 N 75.26 W
Castle Rock, Wa., U.S. 224 46.16 N 122.54 W
Castle Rock ∧, Or., U.S. 202 44.02 N 118.11 W
Castle Rock ∧, Va., U.S. 192 37.57 N 78.44 W
Castle Rock Butte ∧ 198 45.00 N 103.27 W
Castle Rock Lake ◎[1] 190 43.56 N 89.58 W
Castle Shannon 279b 40.21 N 80.01 W
Castleshaw Moor ◆[3] 262 53.36 N 2.00 W
Castleside 44 54.50 N 1.52 W
Castleton, Eng., U.K. 44 53.21 N 1.46 W
Castleton, Eng., U.K. 44 54.28 N 0.56 W
Castleton, Eng., U.K. 262 53.35 N 2.11 W
Castleton, In., U.S. 218 39.54 N 86.03 W
Castleton, Vt., U.S. 188 43.36 N 73.10 W
Castleton on Hudson 210 42.32 N 73.45 W
Castletown, I. of Man 44 54.04 N 4.40 W
Castletown, Scot., U.K. 46 58.35 N 3.23 W
Castletown Bearhaven (Castletown Bere) 48 51.39 N 9.55 W
Castletown Bere → Castletown Bearhaven 48 51.39 N 9.55 W
Castletown Geoghegan 48 53.26 N 7.38 W
Castletownroche 48 52.10 N 8.28 W
Castletownshend 48 51.32 N 9.11 W
Castlewellan 48 54.16 N 5.57 W
Castlewood, Ky., U.S. 218 38.04 N 84.27 W
Castlewood, S.D., U.S. 198 44.43 N 97.01 W
Castlewood, Va., U.S. 192 36.53 N 82.16 W
Častoje 82 54.11 N 37.47 E
Častooz'ornoje 86 55.34 N 67.53 E
Castor 182 52.13 N 111.53 W
Castor ≃, On., Can. 212 45.18 N 75.10 W
Castor ≃, Mo., U.S. 194 36.51 N 89.44 W
Castorano 66 42.54 N 13.43 E
Castor Creek ≃ 194 31.47 N 92.22 W
Castorland 212 43.53 N 75.30 W
Castra Vetera ⊥ 263 51.39 N 6.28 E
Castres 32 43.36 N 2.15 E
Castricum 52 52.33 N 4.39 E
Castries, Fr. 62 43.40 N 3.59 E
Castries, St. Luc. 241f 14.01 N 61.00 W
Castries, Port ⊂ 241f 14.01 N 61.01 W
Castro, Bra. 252 24.47 S 50.00 W
Castro, Chile 254 42.29 S 73.46 W
Castro, It. 64 45.48 N 10.04 E
Castro, Arroyo de ≃ 258 33.37 S 56.10 W
Castro, Punta ≻ 254 43.22 S 65.03 W
Castro Barros 252 30.35 S 65.44 W
Castrocaro Terme 66 44.10 N 11.57 E
Castrocielo 66 41.32 N 13.42 E
Castro Daire 34 40.54 N 7.56 W
Castro dei Volsci 66 41.30 N 13.24 E
Castro del Río 34 37.41 N 4.28 W
Castrofilippo 70 37.21 N 13.46 E
Castrojeriz 34 42.17 N 4.08 W
Castro Marim 34 37.13 N 7.26 W
Castronuño 34 41.23 N 5.16 W
Castronuovo di Sant'Andrea 68 40.11 N 16.11 E
Castronuovo di Sicilia 70 37.41 N 13.36 E
Castropignano 66 41.37 N 14.33 E
Castropol 34 43.32 N 7.02 W
Castrop-Rauxel 52 51.34 N 7.18 E
Castroreale 70 38.06 N 15.12 E
Castro-Urdiales 34 43.23 N 3.13 W
Castro Valley 226 37.41 N 122.05 W
Castro Verde 34 37.42 N 8.05 W
Castrovillari 68 39.49 N 16.13 E
Castroville, Ca., U.S. 226 36.45 N 121.45 W
Castroville, Tx., U.S. 196 29.21 N 98.52 W
Castrovirreyna 248 13.16 S 75.19 W
Castuera 34 38.43 N 5.33 W
Čast uul ∧ 86 48.40 N 90.45 E
Častyje 80 57.19 N 54.59 E
Casummit Lake 184 51.28 N 92.24 W
Casupá 252 34.07 S 55.39 W
Caswell Sound ʊ 172 45.00 S 167.10 E
Çat 130 39.40 N 41.00 E
Čat ≃ 184 51.07 N 91.25 W
Catabola 152 12.09 S 17.16 E
Catacamas 236 14.54 N 85.56 W
Catacaos 248 5.16 S 80.41 W
Catacocha 246 4.04 S 79.38 W
Cataguarino 256 21.18 S 42.43 W
Cataguases 256 21.24 S 42.41 W
Catahoula Lake ◎ 194 31.30 N 92.06 W
Çatak 128 38.01 N 43.07 E
Catalaban Island I 116 11.51 N 125.28 E
Çatalan 130 37.14 N 35.16 E
Catalão 255 18.10 S 47.57 W
Catalão, Ponta do ≻ 287a 22.51 S 43.13 W
Çatalca 130 41.09 N 28.27 E
Catalfaro ≃ 70 37.22 N 14.43 E
Catalina, Nf., Can. 186 48.31 N 53.05 W
Catalina, Chile 252 25.13 S 69.43 W
Catalina → Santa Catalina Island I 228 33.23 N 118.24 W
Catalina, Punta ≻ 254 52.32 S 68.47 W
Catalonia → Cataluña □[4] 34 42.00 N 2.00 E
Cataluña □[4] 34 41.40 N 1.30 E
Cataluña, Museo de Arte de ⚑ 266d 41.23 N 2.09 E
Catalzeytin 130 41.57 N 34.13 E
Catamarca □[4] 252 27.00 S 67.00 W
Catamare 286c 10.36 N 67.02 W
Catamayo 246 3.59 S 79.21 W
Catamayo ≃ 246 4.18 S 80.09 W
Catanauan 116 13.36 N 122.19 E
Catanduanes □[4] 116 13.47 N 124.16 E
Catanduanes Island I 116 13.45 N 124.15 E
Catanduva 255 21.08 S 48.58 W
Catane → Catania 70 37.30 N 15.06 E
Catania 70 37.30 N 15.06 E
Catania □[4] 70 37.23 N 14.40 E
Catania, Golfo di ⊂ 70 37.24 N 15.09 E
Catania, Piana di ≍ 70 37.25 N 14.51 E
Cataño 240m 18.27 N 66.07 W
Catanzaro 68 38.54 N 16.36 E
Catanzaro □[4] 68 38.54 N 16.36 E
Catanzaro Lido 68 38.49 N 16.36 E
Cataonia □[9] 130 38.00 N 35.00 E
Catára ≃ 152 13.34 S 12.35 E
Cataract Canyon V 200 36.03 N 112.35 W
Cataract Reservoir ◎[1] 170 34.16 S 150.48 E
Catarama 246 1.35 S 79.28 W
Cataraqui 212 44.16 N 76.32 W
Cataraqui ≃ 212 44.13 N 76.28 W
Cataricahua 248 18.14 S 66.49 W
Catarina 250 6.12 S 39.54 W
Catarman, Pil. 116 9.08 N 124.40 E
Catarman, Pil. 116 12.30 N 124.38 E
Catarroja 34 39.24 N 0.24 W
Catasauqua 208 40.39 N 75.29 W
Catastrophe, Cape ≻ 166 34.59 S 136.00 E
Catatumbo ≃ 246 9.22 N 71.45 W
Catawba 218 40.00 N 83.37 W
Catawba ≃ 192 34.36 N 80.54 W
Catawba Island 214 41.35 N 82.50 W
Catawissa, Mo., U.S. 219 38.25 N 90.47 W
Catawissa, Pa., U.S. 210 40.57 N 76.27 W
Catawissa Creek ≃ 210 40.57 N 76.28 W
Cataxa 154 15.58 S 33.12 E
Cat-ba, Dao I 110 20.50 N 107.00 E
Catbalogan 116 11.46 N 124.53 E
Catchabutan, Punta ≻ 236 15.50 N 86.32 W
Catchacoma Lake ◎ 212 44.45 N 78.20 W
Cateco Cangola 152 8.27 S 15.48 E
Cateel 116 7.48 N 126.27 E
Cateel ≃ 116 7.47 N 126.27 E
Cateel Bay ⊂ 116 7.54 N 126.25 E
Catemaco 234 18.25 N 95.07 W
Catemaco, Lago ◎ 234 18.25 N 95.05 W
Catembe 156 26.00 S 32.33 E
Catenanuova 70 37.34 N 14.41 E
Caterham 260 51.17 N 0.04 W
Catete 152 9.06 S 13.43 E
Catete ◆[8] 287a 22.55 S 43.10 W
Catete ≃ 250 6.04 S 54.09 W
Catfish Creek ≃, On., Can. 212 42.39 N 81.01 W
Catfish Creek ≃, N.Y., U.S. 212 43.31 N 76.19 W
Catfish Creek ≃, Tx., U.S. 222 31.47 N 95.56 W
Catford ◆[8] 260 51.27 N 0.01 W
Catharine Creek ≃ 210 42.21 N 76.51 W
Cathcart 158 32.18 S 27.09 E
Cathead Mountain ∧ 210 43.17 N 74.17 W
Cathedral City 204 33.46 N 116.27 W
Cathedral Gorge State Park ♦ 204 37.50 N 114.30 W
Cathedral Mountain ∧ 196 30.10 N 103.40 W
Cathedral of the Pines ⚑[1] 207 42.47 N 71.58 W
Cathedral Provincial Park ♦ 202 49.05 N 120.10 W
Cathedral Range ⋀ 226 37.47 N 119.21 W
Catherines Peak ∧ 241q 18.04 N 76.42 W
Catheys Valley 226 37.25 N 120.06 W
Cathlamet 224 46.12 N 123.22 W
Catholic University ⚑[2] 284c 38.56 N 77.00 W
Catia ◆[8] 286c 10.31 N 66.57 W
Catia La Mar 286c 10.36 N 67.02 W
Ca' Tiepolo 66 44.56 N 12.22 E
Catignano 66 42.21 N 13.57 E
Catingueira 250 7.08 S 37.37 W
Catingueiro 256 22.10 S 46.52 W
Catió 150 11.13 N 15.10 W
Catirina, Punta ≻ 71 40.29 N 9.32 E
Cat Island I, Ba. 238 24.27 N 75.30 W
Cat Island I, Ma., U.S. 283 42.31 N 70.49 W
Cat Island I, Ms., U.S. 194 30.13 N 89.06 W
Čatkal ≃ 85 41.38 N 70.01 E
Čatkal'skij chrebet ⋀ 85 41.40 N 71.05 E
Cat Lake ◎ 184 51.40 N 91.50 W
Catlettsburg 188 38.24 N 82.36 W
Catlin 194 40.03 N 87.42 W
Catlins ≃ 172 46.29 S 169.43 E
Catlodge 46 57.00 N 4.15 W
Catnip Mountain ∧ 204 41.52 N 119.23 W
Cato 210 43.10 N 76.34 W
Catoche, Cabo ≻ 232 21.35 N 87.05 W
Catoctin Creek ≃ 208 39.18 N 77.33 W
Catoctin Mountain ∧ 208 39.26 N 77.31 W
Cato Island I 166 23.15 S 155.32 E
Catolé do Rocha 250 6.21 S 37.45 W
Católica, Universidad ⚑[2], Chile 286e 33.27 S 70.39 W
Católica, Universidad ⚑[2], Perú 286d 12.04 S 77.05 W
Caton 44 54.04 N 2.43 W
Catonsville 208 39.16 N 76.43 W
Catonsville Manor 284b 39.18 N 76.44 W
Catoosa 196 36.11 N 95.44 W
Catorce 234 23.42 N 100.54 W
Catorce, Sierra de ⋀ 234 23.36 N 100.52 W
Catota 152 13.52 S 17.15 E
Catria, Monte ∧ 66 43.28 N 12.42 E
Catriló 252 36.26 S 63.24 W
Catrimani 246 0.27 N 61.41 W
Catrimani ≃ 246 0.28 N 61.44 W
Catrine 46 55.30 N 4.20 W
Cats, Mont des ∧[2] 50 50.47 N 2.40 E
Catshill 42 52.22 N 2.03 W
Catskill 210 42.13 N 73.51 W
Catskill Aqueduct ≃ 276 41.11 N 73.48 W
Catskill Creek ≃ 210 42.12 N 73.51 W
Catskill Game Farm ♦ 210 42.15 N 74.01 W
Catskill Mountains ⋀ 210 42.10 N 74.30 W
Catskill Park ♦ 210 42.00 N 74.30 W
Cat Spring 222 29.51 N 96.20 W
Catt, Mount ∧ 182 54.21 N 128.47 W
Cattai Creek ≃ 274a 33.40 S 150.56 E
Cattaraugus 210 42.19 N 78.52 W
Cattaraugus □[6] 214 42.15 N 78.45 W
Cattaraugus Creek ≃ 214 42.35 N 79.10 W
Cattaraugus Creek, South Branch ≃ 214 42.26 N 78.53 W
Cattaraugus Indian Reservation ◆[4] 210 42.33 N 78.56 W
Cattenom 56 49.25 N 6.15 E
Catterick 44 54.22 N 1.38 W
Catterick Garrison 44 54.22 N 1.43 W
Cattle Canyon V 280 34.14 N 117.46 W
Cattolica 66 43.58 N 12.44 E
Cattolica del Sacro Cuore, Università ⚑[2] 266b 45.27 N 9.11 E
Cattolica Eraclea 70 37.26 N 13.24 E
Catton 44 54.55 N 2.15 W
Catu 255 12.21 S 38.23 W
Catuala 152 16.29 S 19.03 E
Catuane 156 26.48 S 32.18 E
Catubig 116 12.24 N 125.03 E
Catubig ≃ 116 12.34 N 125.01 E
Catuçaba 256 23.15 S 45.12 W
Catumbela 152 12.25 S 13.34 E
Catumbela ≃ 152 12.27 S 13.29 E
Catur 154 13.45 S 35.30 E
Catus 32 44.34 N 1.20 E
Çatwick, Îles II 110 10.00 N 109.00 E
Čatyrk'ol', ozero ◎ 85 40.38 N 75.17 E
Čatyrtaš 85 40.55 N 76.26 E
Cau ≃ 110 21.07 N 106.18 E
Cau, Rach ≃ 269c 10.51 N 106.49 E
Cauaburi ≃ 246 0.17 S 65.56 W
Cauaxi ≃ 250 3.50 S 48.10 W
Cauayan, Pil. 116 16.56 N 121.46 E
Cauayan, Pil. 116 9.58 N 122.37 E
Caubvick, Mount (Mont d'Iberville) ∧ 176 58.53 N 63.43 W
Cauca □[5] 246 2.30 N 76.50 W
Cauca ≃ 246 8.54 N 74.28 W
Caucaia 250 3.42 S 38.39 W
Caucaia do Alto 256 23.41 S 47.02 W
Caucase, Monts du → Bol'šoj Kavkaz ⋀ 84 42.30 N 45.00 E
Caucasia 246 8.00 N 75.12 W
Caucaso → Bol'šoj Kavkaz ⋀ 84 42.30 N 45.00 E
Caucasus → Bol'šoj Kavkaz ⋀ 84 42.30 N 45.00 E
Caucete 252 31.39 S 68.17 W
Cauchari, Salar de ≍ 252 23.50 S 66.50 W
Cauchon Lake ◎ 184 55.25 N 96.30 W
Caudebec-en-Caux 50 49.32 N 0.44 E
Caudebec-lés-Elbeuf 50 49.17 N 1.02 E
Caudry 50 50.08 N 3.25 E
Caughdenoy 210 43.16 N 76.12 W
Caughnawaga 275a 45.25 N 73.41 W
Caughnawaga Indian Reserve ◆[4] 206 45.23 N 73.41 W
Cauitan, Mount ∧ 116 17.16 N 121.00 E
Cauit Point ≻, Pil. 116 9.18 N 126.12 E
Cauit Point ≻, Pil. 116 12.16 N 122.38 E
Cauldcleuch Head ∧ 44 55.18 N 2.51 W
Caulfield 169 37.53 S 145.03 E
Caulfield Racecourse ♦ 274b 37.53 S 145.02 E
Caulkerbush 44 54.54 N 3.40 W
Caulonia 68 38.23 N 16.25 E
Caumont-sur-Durance 62 43.54 N 4.57 E
Caumsett State Park ♦ 276 40.55 N 73.28 W
Çaúngula 152 8.25 S 18.40 E
Čaunskaja guba ⊂ 74 69.20 N 170.00 E
Cauquenes 252 35.58 S 72.21 W
Caura ≃ 246 7.38 N 64.53 W
Caurés ≃ 246 1.21 S 62.20 W
Caurimare ≃ 286c 10.28 N 66.48 W
Çausapscal 186 48.22 N 67.14 W
Čausovo 82 54.49 N 36.55 E
Çaussade 32 44.10 N 1.32 E
Čausy 76 53.48 N 30.58 E
Caution, Cape ≻ 182 51.10 N 127.47 W
Çauto ≃ 240p 20.33 N 77.14 W
Čauvaj 85 40.08 N 72.13 E
Cauvery ≃ 122 11.09 N 79.52 E
Cauvery Falls ⌊ 122 12.18 N 77.17 E
Caux, Pays de ◆[1] 50 49.40 N 0.40 E
Cava 256 22.41 S 43.26 W
Cava de' Tirreni 68 40.42 N 14.42 E
Cávado ≃ 34 41.32 N 8.48 W
Cavaglià 62 45.24 N 8.05 E
Cavaillon 62 43.50 N 5.02 E
Cavalaire-sur-Mer 62 43.10 N 6.32 E
Cavalcante 255 13.48 S 47.30 W
Cavalese 64 46.17 N 11.27 E
Cavalheiro 255 17.15 S 48.02 W
Cavalier 198 48.47 N 97.37 W
Cavalière 62 43.09 N 6.26 E
Cavalla (Cavally) ≃ 150 4.22 N 7.32 W
Cavallermaggiore 62 44.43 N 7.41 E
Cavalli Islands II 172 35.02 S 173.58 E
Cavallino, Litorale di ⊥[2] 64 45.27 N 12.30 E
Cavallo, Île I 71 41.21 N 9.16 E
Cavallo, Monte ∧ 64 46.08 N 12.30 E
Cavally (Cavalla) ≃ 150 4.22 N 7.32 W
Cavalos, Ribeirão dos ≃ 256 21.29 S 44.13 W
Cava Manara 62 45.08 N 9.07 E
Cavan 48 54.00 N 7.21 W
Cavan □[6] 48 53.55 N 7.30 W
Çavanaugh, Lake ◎ 224 48.23 N 122.00 W
Čavan'ga 24 66.06 N 37.47 E
Cavarzere 64 45.08 N 12.05 E
Cavaso del Tomba 64 45.51 N 11.52 E
Çavdır 130 37.09 N 29.42 E
Cave, It. 66 41.49 N 12.56 E
Cave, N.Z. 172 44.19 S 170.57 E
Cave City, Ar., U.S. 194 35.56 N 91.32 W
Cave City, Ky., U.S. 194 37.08 N 85.57 W
Cave Creek ≃ 200 33.34 N 112.07 W
Cave del Predil 64 46.26 N 13.34 E
Cavedine 64 45.59 N 10.59 E
Cave In Rock 194 37.29 N 88.10 W
Caveiras ≃ 252 27.35 S 50.56 W
Cavelo 152 17.33 S 19.21 E
Cavendish 166 37.31 S 142.02 E
Cavernago 62 45.38 N 9.46 E
Cavertitz 54 51.23 N 13.08 E
Cave Run Lake ◎[1] 188 38.03 N 83.30 W
Cave Spring 192 34.14 N 85.20 W
Cavettsville 279b 40.22 N 79.46 W
Cavezzo 64 44.50 N 11.02 E
Cavi 62 44.17 N 9.22 E
Caviana, Ilha I 250 0.10 N 50.10 W
Cavili Island I 116 9.17 N 120.50 E
Cavinzas, Isla I 286d 12.07 S 77.13 W
Cavite 116 14.29 N 120.55 E
Çavite □[4] 116 14.15 N 120.50 E
Čavka 84 41.44 N 41.45 E
Čavlisaj 85 41.08 N 69.44 E
Cavo, Monte ∧ 267a 41.45 N 12.42 E
Cavoli, Isola dei I 71 39.05 N 9.33 E
Cavonne ≃ 68 40.17 N 16.47 E

ENGLISH Name	Page	Lat.°′	Long.°′	DEUTSCH Name	Seite	Breite°′	Länge°′ E = Ost

Cavour 62 44.47 N 7.22 E
Cavour, Canale ≅ 62 45.11 N 7.54 E
Cavriago 64 44.42 N 10.31 E
Cavriana 64 45.21 N 10.36 E
Cavtat 38 42.35 N 18.13 E
Çavuş 130 37.36 N 31.56 E
Çavuşbaşı ≃ 267b 40.58 N 28.51 E
Çavuşçu Gölü ◎ 130 38.25 N 31.53 E
Çavuşlar 130 40.43 N 32.04 E
Čawatose, Lac ◎ 190 47.20 N 77.07 W
Cawayan 116 11.56 N 123.46 E
Cawdor 46 57.31 N 3.56 W
Cawker City 198 39.30 N 98.26 W
Cawnpore → Kānpur 124 26.28 N 80.21 E
Cawood, Eng., U.K. 44 53.50 N 1.07 W
Cawood, Ky., U.S. 192 36.47 N 83.13 W
Cawston, B.C., Can. 182 49.11 N 119.45 W
Cawston, Eng., U.K. 42 52.46 N 1.10 E
Cawthon 222 30.25 N 96.14 W
Caxambu 256 21.59 S 44.56 W
Caxias, Bra. 250 4.50 S 43.21 W
Caxias, Port. 266c 38.42 N 9.16 W
Caxias do Sul 252 29.10 S 51.11 W
Caxinas, Punta ≻ 236 16.01 N 86.02 W
Caxito 152 8.33 S 13.36 E
Caxiuana, Baía de ⊂ 250 1.45 S 51.20 W
Caxopa 152 11.52 S 20.52 E
Çay 130 38.35 N 31.02 E
Čayambe 246 0.03 N 78.08 W
Cayambe ∧[1] 246 0.02 N 77.59 W
Cayapoñga 116 5.48 N 125.33 E
Cayce 192 33.57 N 81.04 W
Çaycuma 130 41.25 N 32.05 E
Čaycuse 224 48.53 N 124.22 W
Caycuse ≃ 224 48.48 N 124.41 W
Cayenne 250 4.56 N 52.20 W
Cayenne □[8] 250 4.00 N 52.30 W
Cayes → Les Cayes 238 18.12 N 73.45 W
Cayeux-sur-Mer 50 50.11 N 1.29 E
Cayey 240m 18.07 N 66.10 W
Cayey, Sierra de ⋀ 240m 18.07 N 66.02 W
Çayırhan 130 40.06 N 31.37 E
Çayırlı 130 39.48 N 40.01 E
Çayırlıahmetçiler 130 40.58 N 31.27 E
Çayırşeyhi 130 39.18 N 35.40 E
Čaylus 32 44.14 N 1.46 E
Cayman Brac I 238 19.43 N 79.49 W
Cayman Islands □[2], N.A. 230 19.30 N 80.40 W
Cayman Islands □[2], N.A. 238 19.30 N 80.40 W
Cayman Trench ✦[1] 16 19.00 N 80.00 W
Cayna 248 10.11 S 76.20 W
Caynabo 144 8.57 N 46.26 E
Cay Point ≻ 240b 24.59 N 77.25 W
Cayra 130 40.41 N 39.06 E
Cayres 62 44.55 N 3.48 E
Cay Sal Bank ✦[2] 238 23.45 N 80.00 W
Cayucos 226 35.27 N 120.54 W
Cayuga, In., U.S. 194 39.56 N 87.27 W
Cayuga, N.Y., U.S. 210 42.55 N 76.44 W
Cayuga, N.D., U.S. 198 46.04 N 97.23 W
Cayuga, Tx., U.S. 222 31.57 N 95.57 W
Cayuga □[6] 210 42.56 N 76.34 W
Cayuga and Seneca Canal ≅ 210 42.56 N 76.44 W
Cayuga Creek ≃, N.Y., U.S. 210 42.52 N 78.47 W
Cayuga Creek ≃, N.Y., U.S. 284a 43.04 N 78.57 W
Cayuga Heights 210 42.27 N 76.29 W
Cayuga Lake ◎ 210 42.45 N 76.45 W
Cayuta 210 42.17 N 76.42 W
Cayuta Creek ≃ 210 41.59 N 76.30 W
Cazage 152 11.02 S 20.45 E
Cazalla de la Sierra 34 37.56 N 5.45 W
Căzănești 38 44.37 N 27.01 E
Cazaux et de Sanguinet, Lac de ⊂ 32 44.30 N 1.10 W
Cazenovia 210 42.55 N 75.51 W
Cazenovia Creek ≃ 210 42.52 N 78.50 W
Cazenovia Creek, East Branch ≃ 210 42.46 N 78.38 W
Cazenovia Creek, West Branch ≃ 210 42.46 N 78.39 W
Cazenovia Lake ◎ 210 42.57 N 75.53 W
Cazenovia Park ♦ 284a 42.51 N 78.48 W
Cazères 32 43.13 N 1.05 E
Cazhai 269b 31.12 N 121.34 E
Cazin 36 44.58 N 15.57 E
Çazis 58 46.43 N 9.25 E
Čazma 36 45.45 N 16.37 E
Cazombo 152 11.54 S 22.52 E
Cazones ≃ 234 20.44 N 97.12 W
Cazones, Golfo de ⊂ 240p 21.55 N 81.20 W
Cazorla, Esp. 34 37.55 N 3.00 W
Cazorla, Ven. 246 8.01 N 67.00 W
Cazula 154 15.25 S 33.40 E
Ccapi 248 13.52 S 72.05 W
Cchaltubo 84 42.20 N 42.35 E
Cchenisckali ≃ 84 42.07 N 42.18 E
Çchinvali 84 42.13 N 43.56 E
Čchorocku 84 42.32 N 42.07 E
Cchunkuri 84 42.23 N 42.34 E
Cea ≃ 34 42.00 N 5.36 W
Ceanannus Mór 48 53.44 N 6.53 W
Ceará → Fortaleza 250 3.43 S 38.30 W
Ceará □[3] 250 5.00 S 40.00 W
Ceará-Mirim 250 5.38 S 35.26 W
Ceará-Mirim ≃ 250 5.40 S 35.13 W
Ceatharlach → Carlow 48 52.50 N 6.55 W
Cébaco, Isla I 246 7.32 N 81.09 W
Ceballos, Méx. 232 26.32 N 104.09 W
Çeballos, Méx. 234 23.23 N 104.50 W
Čebarkul' 86 54.58 N 60.25 E
Çebeciköy 267b 41.07 N 28.52 E
Čeboksary 80 56.09 N 47.15 E
Cebolla Creek ≃ 200 38.29 N 107.13 W
Cebollar 252 29.06 S 66.33 W
Cebollatí 252 33.16 S 53.47 W
Cebollatí ≃ 252 33.09 S 53.38 W
Cebollita Peak ∧ 200 34.43 N 107.51 W
Céboruco, Volcán ∧[1] 234 21.09 N 104.30 W
Čebotovka, S.S.S.R. 83 48.42 N 39.51 E
Čebotovka, S.S.S.R. 83 48.41 N 40.00 E
Cebreros 34 40.27 N 4.28 W
Çebrikovo 78 47.09 N 30.06 E
Čebsara 76 59.12 N 38.50 E
Cebu 116 10.18 N 123.54 E
Cebu □[4] 116 10.20 N 123.45 E
Çebu I 116 10.20 N 123.45 E
Čeburgol' 78 45.34 N 38.07 E
Ceccano 66 41.34 N 13.20 E
Cecchignola ◆[8] 267a 41.49 N 12.29 E
Ceceda 196 26.04 N 103.25 W
Çeceli 130 39.43 N 33.52 E
Čečel'nik 78 48.14 N 29.21 E
Čečen', ostrov I 84 43.58 N 47.45 E
Čečeno-Ingušskaja Avtonomnaja Sovetskaja Socialističeskaja Respublika □[3] 84 43.15 N 45.40 E
Cecer Chaan → Ondörchaan 88 47.19 N 110.39 E
Cecerleg, Mong. 88 48.52 N 101.14 E
Cecerleg, Mong. 88 47.30 N 101.27 E
Çecerleg, Mong. 88 49.30 N 97.36 E
Čečersk 76 52.55 N 30.55 E
Čečeviči 76 53.31 N 29.51 E
Çecheng 105 39.06 N 116.48 E
Čechov, S.S.S.R. 82 55.09 N 37.27 E
Čechov, S.S.S.R. 89 47.28 N 141.59 E
Čechova, gora ∧ 89 47.03 N 142.50 E
Čechtice 30 49.37 N 15.03 E
Čechy □[9] 30 49.50 N 14.00 E
Cecil, Ga., U.S. 192 31.02 N 83.23 W
Cecil, Oh., U.S. 216 41.13 N 84.35 W
Cecil, Pa., U.S. 214 40.19 N 80.10 W
Cecil □[6] 208 39.36 N 75.50 W
Cecil Field Naval Air Station ■ 192 30.12 N 81.52 W
Cecilia 194 37.39 N 85.57 W
Cecilia, Mount ∧[2] 162 20.45 S 120.55 E
Cecil Park 274a 33.52 S 150.51 E
Cecil Plains 166 27.32 S 151.12 E
Cecil Rhodes, Mount ∧ 162 25.26 S 121.26 E
Cecilton 208 39.24 N 75.52 W
Cecina 66 43.19 N 10.31 E
Cecina ≃ 66 43.18 N 10.29 E
Çecita, Lago di ◎ 68 39.24 N 16.30 E
Čečuj ≃ 88 58.12 N 109.18 E
Čečujsk 88 58.05 N 108.42 E
Cedar ≃, U.S. 190 41.17 N 91.21 W
Cedar ≃, Mi., U.S. 190 45.25 N 87.21 W
Cedar ≃, Mi., U.S. 190 43.53 N 84.29 W
Cedar ≃, Ne., U.S. 198 41.22 N 97.57 W
Cedar ≃, N.Y., U.S. 188 43.51 N 74.11 W
Cedar ≃, Wa., U.S. 224 47.30 N 122.12 W
Cedar, Middle Branch ≃ 216 42.38 N 84.05 W
Cedar, West Branch ≃ 216 42.41 N 84.09 W
Cedar, West Fork ≃ 190 42.37 N 92.29 W
Cedar Bayou ≃ 222 29.41 N 94.56 W
Cedar Beach 284b 39.17 N 76.25 W
Cedar Bluff Reservoir ◎[1] 198 38.47 N 99.47 W
Cedar Bluffs 198 41.23 N 96.36 W
Cedar Breaks National Monument ♦ 200 37.29 N 112.53 W
Cedar Brook 208 39.42 N 74.54 W
Cedar Brook ≃, N.J., U.S. 276 40.19 N 74.33 W
Cedar Brook ≃, N.J., U.S. 276 40.23 N 74.23 W
Cedar Brook ≃, N.J., U.S. 285 39.40 N 74.43 W
Cedar Brook Park ♦ 275b 43.45 N 79.14 W
Cedarburg 190 43.17 N 87.59 W
Cedar City, Mo., U.S. 219 38.35 N 92.10 W
Cedar City, Ut,. U.S. 200 37.40 N 113.03 W
Cedar Creek 222 30.05 N 97.30 W
Cedar Creek ≃, Al., U.S. 194 32.13 N 87.06 W
Cedar Creek ≃, Az., U.S. 200 33.48 N 110.18 W
Cedar Creek ≃, Ct., U.S. 276 41.09 N 73.13 W
Cedar Creek ≃, De., U.S. 208 38.55 N 75.20 W
Cedar Creek ≃, Ga., U.S. 194 34.08 N 85.19 W
Cedar Creek ≃, Id., U.S. 202 42.24 N 114.49 W
Cedar Creek ≃, In., U.S. 216 41.12 N 85.02 W
Cedar Creek ≃, Ia., U.S. 190 40.58 N 91.40 W
Cedar Creek ≃, Ia., U.S. 198 42.24 N 94.59 W
Cedar Creek ≃, Ky., U.S. 218 38.25 N 84.53 W
Cedar Creek ≃, Mo., U.S. 219 38.38 N 92.13 W
Cedar Creek ≃, N.D., U.S. 198 46.07 N 101.18 W
Cedar Creek ≃, Oh., U.S. 214 41.38 N 83.17 W
Cedar Creek ≃, Pa., U.S. 279b 40.10 N 79.47 W
Cedar Creek ≃, Tx., U.S. 196 32.53 N 98.37 W
Cedar Creek ≃, Tx., U.S. 222 30.51 N 96.12 W
Cedar Creek ≃, Tx., U.S. 222 32.04 N 96.05 W
Cedar Creek ≃, Tx., U.S. 222 30.02 N 97.17 W
Cedar Creek ≃, Wa., U.S. 224 45.56 N 122.37 W
Cedar Creek Reservoir ◎[1] 222 32.20 N 96.10 W
Cedar Crest Manor 285 39.41 N 75.28 W
Cedaredge 200 38.54 N 107.55 W
Cedar Falls 190 42.31 N 92.26 W
Cedar Grove, On., Can. 275b 43.52 N 79.12 W
Cedar Grove, In., U.S. 218 39.21 N 84.56 W
Cedar Grove, N.J., U.S. 276 40.51 N 74.13 W
Cedar Grove, W.V., U.S. 188 38.13 N 81.25 W
Cedar Grove, Wi., U.S. 190 43.34 N 87.49 W
Cedar Grove Reservoir ◎[1] 276 40.52 N 74.13 W
Cedar Heights, Md., U.S. 284c 38.54 N 76.54 W
Cedar Heights, Pa., U.S. 285 40.05 N 75.17 W
Cedar Hill, Mo., U.S. 219 38.21 N 90.39 W
Cedar Hill, N.Y., U.S. 210 42.33 N 73.47 W
Cedar Hill, Tn., U.S. 194 36.33 N 86.59 W
Cedar Hill, Tx., U.S. 222 32.35 N 96.57 W
Cedar Hills 224 45.30 N 122.47 W
Cedar Hollow 285 40.04 N 75.31 W
Cedarhurst, Md., U.S. 208 39.07 N 76.41 W
Cedarhurst, N.Y., U.S. 276 40.37 N 73.43 W
Cedar Island I, Md., U.S. 208 37.56 N 75.52 W
Cedar Island I, N.Y., U.S. 276 40.38 N 73.21 W
Cedar Island I, Va., U.S. 208 37.39 N 75.36 W
Cedar Island Lake ◎ 281 42.38 N 83.28 W
Cedar Key 192 29.08 N 83.02 W
Cedar Knolls 276 40.49 N 74.26 W
Cedar Lake, In., U.S. 216 41.21 N 87.26 W
Cedar Lake, Tx., U.S. 222 28.54 N 95.35 W
Cedar Lake ◎, On., Can. 190 46.02 N 78.30 W
Cedar Lake ◎, In., U.S. 216 41.22 N 87.26 W
Cedar Lake ◎, N.J., U.S. 276 40.55 N 74.28 W
Cedar Lake ◎, Tx., U.S. 196 32.49 N 102.17 W
Cedar Lake ◎[1] 184 53.15 N 100.10 W
Cedar Lake Creek ≃ 222 28.50 N 95.35 W
Cedar Lane 222 28.54 N 95.38 W
Cedar Mill 224 45.32 N 122.51 W
Cedarmont 158 26.50 S 29.01 E
Cedar Mountain ∧ 204 41.36 N 120.16 W
Cedar Point 216 41.16 N 89.08 W
Cedar Point ≻, Ct., U.S. 276 41.06 N 73.22 W
Cedar Point ≻, Oh., U.S. 214 41.42 N 83.20 W
Cedar Point ≻, Oh., U.S. 214 41.30 N 82.41 W
Cedar Pond ◎ 276 41.07 N 74.06 W
Cedar Rapids, Ia., U.S. 190 41.59 N 91.40 W
Cedar Rapids, Ne., U.S. 198 41.34 N 98.09 W
Cedar Ridge 226 39.12 N 121.01 W
Cedar Run ≃ 208 38.41 N 77.29 W
Cedars 285 40.13 N 75.22 W
Cedars of Lebanon → Arz Lubnān ◆[3] 130 34.14 N 36.03 E

Symbols in the index entries represent the broad categories identified in the key at the right. Symbols with superior numbers (⋀[1]) identify subcategories (see complete key on page *I · 1).*

Kartensymbole in dem Registerverzeichnis stellen die rechts in Schlüssel erklärten Kategorien dar. Symbole mit hochgestellten Ziffern (⋀[1]) bezeichnen Unterabteilungen einer Kategorie (vgl. vollständiger Schlüssel auf Seite *I · 1).*

Los símbolos incluídos en el texto del índice representan las grandes categorias identificadas con la clave a la derecha. Los símbolos con numeros en su parte superior (⋀[1]) identifican las subcategorías (véase la clave completa en la página *I · 1).*

Les symboles de l'index représentent les catégories indiquées dans la légende à droite. Les symboles suivis d'un indice (⋀[1]) représentent des sous-catégories (voir légende complète à la page *I · 1).*

Os símbolos incluídos no texto do índice representam as grandes categorias identificadas com a chave à direita. Os símbolos com números em sua parte superior (⋀[1]) identificam as subcategorias (veja-se a chave completa à página *I · 1).*

∧ Mountain	Berg	Montaña	Montagne	Montanha
⋀ Mountains	Berge	Montañas	Montagnes	Montanhas
)(Pass	Pass	Paso	Col	Passo
V Valley, Canyon	Tal, Cañon	Valle, Cañón	Vallée, Canyon	Vale, Canhão
≍ Plain	Ebene	Llano	Plaine	Planicie
≻ Cape	Kap	Cabo	Cap	Cabo
I Island	Insel	Isla	Île	Ilha
II Islands	Inseln	Islas	Îles	Ilhas
⊥ Other Topographic Features	Andere Topographische Objekte	Otros Elementos Topográficos	Autres données topographiques	Outros acidentes topográficos

ESPAÑOL Nombre / FRANÇAIS Nom / PORTUGUÊS Nome	Página / Page	Lat.°′	Long.°′ W = Oeste / Ouest
Cedar Springs, On., Can.	214	42.17 N	82.02 W
Cedar Springs, Mi., U.S.	190	43.13 N	85.33 W
Cedar Swamp ⊞, Ma., U.S.	283	42.33 N	71.05 W
Cedar Swamp ⊞, N.J., U.S.	285	39.48 N	75.20 W
Cedartown	192	34.03 N	85.15 W
Cedarvale, B.C., Can.	182	55.01 N	128.20 W
Cedar Vale, Ks., U.S.	198	37.06 N	96.30 W
Cedarville, S. Afr.	158	30.23 S	29.03 E
Cedarville, Ca., U.S.	204	41.31 N	120.10 W
Cedarville, In., U.S.	216	41.12 N	85.01 W
Cedarville, Ma., U.S.	207	41.48 N	70.33 W
Cedarville, Mi., U.S.	190	46.00 N	84.22 W
Cedarville, N.J., U.S.	208	39.19 N	75.12 W
Cedarville, N.Y., U.S.	210	42.56 N	75.01 W
Cedarville, Oh., U.S.	218	39.44 N	83.48 W
Cedarville, Pa., U.S.	285	40.14 N	75.40 W
Cedarville Reservoir ⊜1	216	41.12 N	85.01 W
Cedar Wash V	200	35.53 N	111.25 W
Cedarwood Park	208	40.03 N	74.08 W
Cedegolo	64	46.05 N	10.21 E
Cedeira	34	43.39 N	8.03 W
Ceder	88	51.25 N	94.45 E
Cedillo, Embalse de ⊜1	34	39.40 N	7.25 W
Cedral	234	23.48 N	100.44 W
Cedrino ≃	71	40.23 N	9.44 E
Cedro	250	6.36 S	39.03 W
Cedrón ≃	34	39.48 N	3.33 W
Cedros, Hond.	236	14.35 N	87.08 W
Cedros, Méx.	232	24.41 N	101.47 W
Cedros, Isla I	232	28.12 N	115.15 W
Ceduna	162	32.07 S	133.40 E
Cedynia	30	52.50 N	14.14 E
Ceel	102	45.36 N	95.51 E
Ceelaayo	144	11.15 N	48.54 E
Ceel Afweyne	144	9.55 N	47.15 E
Ceel Berdaale	144	3.14 N	43.11 E
Ceel Berde	144	4.50 N	43.39 E
Ceel Buur	144	4.40 N	46.37 E
Ceel Dhaab	144	8.56 N	46.30 E
Ceel Dheere, Som.	144	3.51 N	47.12 E
Ceeldheere, Som.	144	5.22 N	46.11 E
Ceel Doofaar	144	10.38 N	49.02 E
Ceel Waaq	144	2.44 N	41.01 E
Ceel Xamurre	144	7.13 N	48.54 E
Ceemadle	144	5.14 N	46.56 E
Ceepeecee	182	49.52 N	126.43 W
Ceerigaabo	144	10.37 N	47.22 E
Cefalà Diana	70	37.54 N	13.28 E
Cefalonia → Kefallinía I	38	38.15 N	20.35 E
Cefalù	70	38.02 N	14.01 E
Cefni ≃	44	53.12 N	4.23 W
Cefn-mawr	42	52.58 N	3.04 W
Ceg	144	8.58 N	45.20 E
Cega ≃	34	41.33 N	4.46 W
Čeganly	80	53.54 N	53.34 E
Čegdomyn	89	51.07 N	133.05 E
Čegem ≃	84	43.38 N	43.48 E
Čegem Pervyj	84	43.34 N	43.35 E
Čegitun'	180	66.34 N	171.06 W
Cegléd	30	47.10 N	19.48 E
Ceglie Messapico	68	40.39 N	17.31 E
Cehegín	34	38.06 N	1.48 W
Ceheng	102	25.10 N	105.48 E
Cehnice	60	49.12 N	14.02 E
Cehu-Silvaniei	38	47.25 N	23.11 E
Ceiba	240m	18.16 N	65.39 W
Ceiba ≃	240p	21.38 N	78.52 W
Ceibo, Arroyo ≃	258	33.57 S	58.27 W
Ceilán → Sri Lanka □1	122	7.00 N	81.00 E
Čeil'dag	84	40.17 N	49.18 E
Ceiriog ≃	42	52.57 N	3.02 W
Ceirw ≃	42	52.59 N	3.27 W
Čejč	61	48.57 N	16.57 E
Čekalin	82	54.06 N	36.15 E
Čekan	80	54.51 N	53.34 E
Čekanovskij	88	56.13 N	101.25 E
Çekerek ≃	130	40.34 N	35.46 E
Čekmaguš	86	55.08 N	54.40 E
Çekmeköy	267b	41.03 N	29.10 E
Čekšino	76	59.39 N	40.33 E
Čekujevo	24	63.34 N	38.56 E
Čekunda	89	50.48 N	132.10 E
Čel'abinsk	86	55.10 N	61.24 E
Čelákovice	54	50.10 N	14.46 E
Celâlli	130	39.42 N	37.26 E
Celano	66	42.05 N	13.33 E
Celanova	34	42.09 N	7.58 W
Celaya	234	20.31 N	100.49 W
Čelbas ≃	78	46.06 N	38.59 E
Čelbasskaja	78	45.59 N	39.22 E
Celbridge	48	53.20 N	6.33 W
Cele	120	37.00 N	80.47 E
Celebes → Sulawesi I	112	2.00 S	121.00 E
Celebes Basin ✦1	14	4.00 N	122.00 E
Celebes Sea ₸2	112	3.00 N	122.00 E
Çeleblier	130	41.26 N	32.57 E
Čeleken	128	39.26 N	53.07 E
Celendín	248	6.52 S	78.09 W
Celenza sul Trigno	66	41.52 N	14.35 E
Celenza Valfortore	68	41.34 N	14.58 E
Celerina	58	46.31 N	9.51 E
Celeryville	214	41.02 N	82.45 W
Celeste	196	33.18 N	96.12 W
Celestún	232	20.52 N	90.24 W
Celica	246	4.07 S	79.59 W
Celico	68	39.19 N	16.20 E
Çelikhân	130	38.02 N	38.15 E
Celina, S.S.S.R.	80	46.32 N	41.02 E
Celina, Oh., U.S.	216	40.32 N	84.34 W
Celina, Tn., U.S.	194	36.33 N	85.30 W
Celina, Tx., U.S.	196	33.19 N	96.47 W
Celinnoje, S.S.S.R.	86	53.04 N	85.40 E
Celinnoje, S.S.S.R.	86	54.31 N	63.39 E
Celinnyj	80	46.40 N	44.32 E
Celinograd	86	51.10 N	71.30 E
Celinogradskaja □4	86	51.00 N	71.00 E
Celje	36	46.14 N	15.16 E
Čelkar	86	47.50 N	59.36 E
Cellar Head ≻	46	58.26 N	6.10 W
Celldömölk	30	47.16 N	17.09 E
Celle	52	52.37 N	10.05 E
Celle, Ruisseau la ≃	261	48.35 N	2.01 E
Celle Ligure	62	44.20 N	8.33 E
Celles	56	50.14 N	5.01 E
Celles-sur-Plaine	58	48.28 N	6.57 E
Cellettes	50	47.32 N	1.23 E
Cellina ≃	64	46.02 N	12.47 E
Cellino Attanasio	66	42.35 N	13.52 E
Cellino San Marco	68	40.28 N	17.58 E
Čelmozero	24	64.18 N	31.48 E
Čelno-Veršiny	80	54.26 N	51.06 E
Čelobitjevo	265b	55.55 N	37.40 E
Celone ≃	68	41.36 N	15.41 E
Celorico da Beira	34	40.38 N	7.23 W
Celoron	214	42.06 N	79.17 W
Celtic Sea ₸2	28	51.00 N	6.30 W
Celtic Shelf ✦4	10	49.15 N	7.00 W
Çeltik	130	41.11 N	32.19 E
Çeltikçi, Tür.	130	40.20 N	32.28 E
Çeltikçi, Tür.	130	37.32 N	30.29 E
Čel'uš	86	51.32 N	87.46 E
Čel'uskin, mys ≻	74	77.45 N	104.20 E
Čel'uskincev park ♠	265a	60.01 N	30.19 E
Cemaes Head ≻	42	52.07 N	4.44 W
Čemal	86	51.25 N	86.01 E
Čembilej	80	55.19 N	45.43 E
Cembra	64	46.10 N	11.13 E
Cembra, Val di V	64	46.10 N	11.13 E
Cement	196	34.55 N	98.08 W
Cement City	216	42.04 N	84.19 W
Cementon, N.Y., U.S.	210	42.09 N	73.55 W
Cementon, Pa., U.S.	208	40.41 N	75.30 W
Čemer	78	51.07 N	31.13 E
Čemerisy	78	51.42 N	30.24 E
Čemerno	36	43.11 N	18.37 E
Čemerno ⅹ	38	43.14 N	18.37 E
Čemerovcy	78	49.01 N	26.21 E
Cemesskaja buchta c	78	44.40 N	37.50 E
Cemilbey	130	40.21 N	35.04 E
Çemişgezek	130	39.04 N	38.55 E
Cemmaes	42	52.37 N	3.42 W
Čemolgan	85	43.23 N	76.37 E
Cempi, Teluk c	115b	8.44 S	118.25 E
Čenča	88	55.57 N	110.59 E
Cencenighe	64	46.21 N	11.58 E
Čenchermandal	88	47.37 N	109.05 E
Čency	82	56.03 N	36.01 E
Cenderawasih, Teluk c	164	2.30 S	135.20 E
Cendras	62	44.09 N	4.04 E
Cene	62	45.47 N	9.49 E
Cenepa ≃	246	4.35 S	78.12 W
Ceneri, Monte ⅹ	58	46.08 N	8.55 E
Čengel	86	48.56 N	89.10 E
Čengel'dy, S.S.S.R.	85	41.51 N	68.59 E
Čengel'dy, S.S.S.R.	85	43.59 N	77.26 E
Çengelköy ✦8	267b	41.03 N	29.03 E
Cengles, Croda di ∧	64	46.34 N	10.38 E
Ceno ≃	36	44.41 N	10.05 E
Cenovo	38	43.32 N	25.39 E
Cenrana	112	3.18 S	118.50 E
Censeau	58	46.49 N	6.04 E
Centallo	62	44.30 N	7.35 E
Centenario	252	38.48 S	68.08 W
Centenário do Sul	255	22.48 S	51.37 W
Centennial Lake ⊜	285	39.50 N	74.51 W
Centennial Lake ⊜1	212	45.10 N	72.05 W
Centennial Mountains ∧	202	44.35 N	111.55 W
Centennial Park ♠, Austl.	274a	33.54 S	151.14 E
Centennial Park ♠, On., Can.	275b	43.39 N	79.35 W
Centennial Wash V	200	33.14 N	112.46 W
Centeno	66	42.48 N	11.49 E
Center, Co., U.S.	200	37.45 N	106.06 W
Center, In., U.S.	216	40.26 N	86.04 W
Center, Mo., U.S.	219	39.30 N	91.31 W
Center, Ne., U.S.	198	42.36 N	97.52 W
Center, N.D., U.S.	198	47.06 N	101.17 W
Center, Tx., U.S.	194	31.47 N	94.10 W
Centerbrook	207	41.21 N	72.24 W
Center Brunswick	210	42.45 N	73.37 W
Centerburg	214	40.18 N	82.41 W
Center City	190	45.23 N	92.48 W
Center Cross	208	37.48 N	76.46 W
Centereach	210	40.51 N	73.06 W
Centerfield	218	38.21 N	83.24 W
Center Hill	220	28.38 N	81.59 W
Center Hill Lake ⊜1	194	36.00 N	85.45 W
Center Line	214	42.29 N	83.01 W
Center Moriches	208	40.48 N	72.47 W
Center Mountain ∧	202	45.06 N	115.13 W
Center Point, Al., U.S.	194	33.37 N	86.41 W
Center Point, Ia., U.S.	190	42.11 N	91.47 W
Center Point, Tx., U.S.	196	29.57 N	99.02 W
Centerport, N.Y., U.S.	210	40.54 N	73.22 W
Centerport, Pa., U.S.	208	40.29 N	76.01 W
Center Square, N.J., U.S.	285	39.46 N	75.23 W
Center Square, Pa., U.S.	208	40.10 N	75.18 W
Centerton, In., U.S.	218	39.30 N	86.23 W
Centerton, N.J., U.S.	285	39.31 N	75.10 W
Center Valley	208	40.32 N	75.24 W
Centerville, De., U.S.	285	39.49 N	75.37 W
Centerville, In., U.S.	218	39.49 N	84.59 W
Centerville, Ia., U.S.	190	40.43 N	92.52 W
Centerville, Ma., U.S.	207	41.38 N	70.20 W
Centerville, Mo., U.S.	194	37.26 N	90.57 W
Centerville, N.Y., U.S.	210	42.29 N	78.15 W
Centerville, Oh., U.S.	218	39.37 N	84.09 W
Centerville, Pa., U.S.	188	40.02 N	79.58 W
Centerville, S.D., U.S.	198	43.07 N	96.57 W
Centerville, Tn., U.S.	194	35.46 N	87.28 W
Centerville, Tx., U.S.	222	31.15 N	95.58 W
Centerville, Ut., U.S.	200	40.55 N	111.52 W
Centerville, Wa., U.S.	224	45.45 N	120.54 W
Centinela	196	28.47 N	100.34 W
Cento	64	44.43 N	11.17 E
Centocelle ✦8	267a	41.53 N	12.34 E
Cento Croci, Passo di ⅹ	62	44.25 N	9.37 E
Centola	68	40.04 N	15.19 E
Central, Bra.	250	11.08 S	42.08 W
Central, Ak., U.S.	180	65.34 N	144.48 W
Central, Az., U.S.	200	32.52 N	109.47 W
Central, N.M., U.S.	200	32.46 N	108.09 W
Central, S.C., U.S.	192	34.43 N	82.46 W
Central, Tx., U.S.	222	31.26 N	94.49 W
Central □4, Ghana	150	5.30 N	1.00 W
Central □4, Kenya	154	0.45 S	37.00 E
Central □4, Malawi	154	13.00 S	34.00 E
Central □4, Sol.Is.	175e	9.10 S	159.50 E
Central □4, Scot., U.K.	46	56.05 N	4.20 W
Central □4, Zam.	154	14.30 S	29.00 E
Central □5, Bots.	156	21.30 S	26.00 E
Central □5, Pap. N. Gui.	164	9.00 S	147.00 E
Central □5, Para.	252	25.30 S	57.30 W
Central □5, Ug.	154	0.10 N	32.00 E
Central, Cordillera ∧, Col.	246	5.00 N	75.00 W
Central, Cordillera ∧, C.R.	236	10.10 N	84.05 W
Central, Cordillera ∧, Perú	248	8.00 S	77.00 W
Central, Cordillera ∧, Pil.	116	17.20 N	120.57 E
Central, Cordillera ∧, P.R.	240m	18.10 N	66.35 W
Central, Macizo → Central, Massif ∧	32	45.00 N	3.10 E
Central, Massif ∧	32	45.00 N	3.10 E
Central, Planalto ∧1	242	18.00 S	47.00 W
Central, Sistema ∧	34	40.30 N	5.00 W
Central African Republic □1	136	7.00 N	21.00 E
Central Aguirre	240m	17.57 N	66.13 W
Central Australia Aboriginal Reserve ✦4	162	24.00 S	128.15 E
Central Barren	218	38.22 N	86.06 W
Central Brāhui Range ∧	120	29.20 N	66.55 E
Central Bridge	210	42.42 N	74.20 W
Central Butte	184	50.47 N	106.30 W
Central City, Il., U.S.	219	38.32 N	89.07 W
Central City, Ia., U.S.	190	42.12 N	91.31 W
Central City, Ky., U.S.	194	37.17 N	87.07 W
Central City, Ne., U.S.	198	41.07 N	98.00 W
Central City, Pa., U.S.	214	40.06 N	78.48 W
Central Division □5	175g	18.05 S	178.30 E
Central Falls	207	41.53 N	71.23 W
Central Heights	200	33.24 N	110.48 W
Central Highlands	279b	40.16 N	79.50 W
Centralia, Il., U.S.	219	38.31 N	89.08 W
Centralia, Ks., U.S.	198	39.43 N	96.07 W
Centralia, Mo., U.S.	219	39.12 N	92.08 W
Centralia, Tx., U.S.	222	31.16 N	95.02 W
Centralia, Wa., U.S.	224	46.42 N	122.57 W
Centralia, Lake ⊜	219	38.32 N	88.59 W
Centralia Draw V	196	31.27 N	101.16 W
Centralia Reservoir ⊜1	219	38.32 N	89.08 W
Centralina	255	18.34 S	49.13 W
Central Intelligence Agency ♦	284c	38.57 N	77.09 W
Central Internacional, Aeropuerto ✈	286a	19.26 N	99.04 W
Central Island I	154	3.30 N	36.03 E
Central Islip	210	40.47 N	73.12 W
Central Kalahari Game Reserve ✦4	156	22.15 S	23.45 E
Central Lake	190	45.04 N	85.15 W
Central Makrān Range ∧	128	26.40 N	64.30 E
Central Mount Stuart ∧	162	21.54 S	133.27 E
Central Mount Wedge ∧	162	22.51 S	131.50 E
Central'no-Bokovskoj ✦8	83	48.11 N	39.03 E
Central'nolesnoj Zapovednik ✦4	76	56.32 N	32.50 E
Central Nyack	276	41.06 N	73.57 W
Central'nyj, S.S.S.R.	76	53.41 N	39.38 E
Central'nyj, S.S.S.R.	86	55.12 N	87.40 E
Central'nyj, S.S.S.R.	86	58.45 N	84.28 E
Central'nyj, S.S.S.R.	86	57.41 N	80.57 E
Central'nyj, S.S.S.R.	265b	55.53 N	37.52 E
Central'nyje Karakumy ✦2	128	39.00 N	60.00 E
Central'nyj park imeni Gor'kogo ♠	265b	55.44 N	37.36 E
Central Pacific Basin ✦1	14	5.00 N	175.00 W
Central Park, N.J., U.S.	276	40.26 N	74.18 W
Central Park, Wa., U.S.	224	46.58 N	123.41 W
Central Park ♠	276	40.47 N	73.58 W
Central Point	202	42.22 N	122.54 W
Central Railroad Station ✦5	272c	18.58 N	72.50 E
Central Range ∧, Leso.	158	29.35 S	28.35 E
Central Range ∧, Pap. N. Gui.	164	5.00 S	142.30 E
Central Square	210	43.17 N	76.08 W
Central Utah Canal ≅	200	39.35 N	112.12 W
Central Valley, Ca., U.S.	204	40.40 N	122.22 W
Central Valley, N.Y., U.S.	210	41.19 N	74.07 W
Central Village	207	41.43 N	71.54 W
Centre	194	34.09 N	85.40 W
Centre □5	150	12.00 N	1.10 W
Centre □6	210	40.55 N	77.44 W
Centre, Canal du ≅	32	46.27 N	4.07 E
Centre Atomique de Marcoule ♦3	62	44.08 N	4.42 E
Centre City	285	39.46 N	75.10 W
Centre d'Énergie de Pierrelatte ♦3	62	44.21 N	4.44 E
Centre d'Études ♦3	261	48.33 N	2.21 E
Centre-Est □5	150	11.35 N	0.30 W
Centre Hall	214	40.50 N	77.41 W
Centre Island	276	40.54 N	73.32 W
Centre Island I	172	46.28 S	167.51 E
Centre Island Park ♠	275b	43.37 N	79.23 W
Centre Lake ⊜	212	44.36 N	75.51 W
Centre-Nord □5	150	13.30 N	1.00 W
Centre-Ouest □5	150	12.00 N	2.25 W
Centre Peak ∧	182	55.41 N	126.26 W
Centre-Sud □4	152	4.10 N	12.00 E
Centreville, Al., U.S.	194	32.56 N	87.08 W
Centreville, Il., U.S.	219	38.35 N	90.07 W
Centreville, Ky., U.S.	218	38.13 N	84.24 W
Centreville, Md., U.S.	208	39.02 N	76.04 W
Centreville, Mi., U.S.	216	41.55 N	85.31 W
Centreville, Ms., U.S.	194	31.05 N	91.04 W
Centreville, Va., U.S.	208	38.50 N	77.26 W
Centro Puntas	240m	18.22 N	67.16 W
Centro Río Mayo	254	45.35 S	71.06 W
Centro Simón Bolívar ✦9	286c	10.30 N	66.55 W
Centuripe	70	37.37 N	14.44 E
Century, Fl., U.S.	194	30.58 N	87.15 W
Century, W.V., U.S.	188	39.05 N	80.11 W
Century City ✦8	280	34.03 N	118.26 W
Century III Mall ✦9	279b	40.21 N	79.57 W
Century Village	220	26.42 N	80.05 W
Cenxi	102	22.59 N	111.00 E
Čepca ≃	80	57.54 N	53.25 E
Čepca ≃	80	58.36 N	50.04 E
Čepeckij	80	58.29 N	51.12 E
Čepel'	78	49.19 N	36.55 E
Čepelare	38	41.44 N	24.41 E
Čepel'ovo	82	55.11 N	37.30 E
Čepovan	64	46.03 N	13.47 E
Cepoy	50	48.03 N	2.44 E
Ceprano	66	41.33 N	13.31 E
Čepřovice	60	49.10 N	13.59 E
Ceptia	152	12.56 S	17.35 E
Cepu	115a	7.09 S	111.35 E
Ceraiona	64	45.35 N	10.50 E
Ceram → Seram I	164	3.00 S	129.00 E
Cerami	70	37.49 N	14.30 E
Cerami ≃	70	37.42 N	14.29 E
Ceram Sea → Seram, Laut ₸2	108	2.30 S	128.00 E
Cerano, It.	62	45.25 N	8.47 E
Cerano, Méx.	234	20.07 N	101.23 W
Ceraso	68	40.11 N	15.15 E
Cerbicale, Îles II	71	41.34 N	9.24 E
Čerčany	60	49.51 N	14.43 E
Cerchiara di Calabria	68	39.51 N	16.23 E
Čerchov ∧	60	49.23 N	12.47 E
Cercié	58	46.07 N	4.40 E
Cerco, Alto do ∧	256	22.38 S	45.22 W
Cercola	66	40.51 N	14.21 E
Cerda	70	37.54 N	13.49 E
Čerdakly	80	54.23 N	48.51 E
Cerdas	248	20.48 S	66.29 W
Cerdeña, Isla de → Sardegna I	71	40.00 N	9.00 E
Čerdojak	86	48.48 N	84.00 E
Cerdon, Fr.	50	47.38 N	2.22 E
Cerdon, Fr.	58	46.05 N	5.28 E
Čerdyn'	24	60.23 N	56.24 E
Cère ≃	32	44.55 N	1.53 E
Cerea	64	45.12 N	11.13 E
Cereal	184	51.25 N	110.48 W
Cereales	252	36.49 S	63.51 W
Čerecha ≃	76	57.46 N	28.21 E
Cereglio	64	44.18 N	11.04 E
Čereja	76	54.37 N	29.17 E
Čerek ≃	84	43.42 N	44.03 E
Čeremchovo	88	53.09 N	103.05 E
Čeremisinovo	78	51.54 N	37.15 E
Čeremoš ≃	78	48.23 N	25.37 E
Čeremšan, S.S.S.R.	80	55.15 N	48.07 E
Čeremšan, S.S.S.R.	80	54.40 N	51.30 E
Čeremšanka, S.S.S.R.	86	59.10 N	76.51 E
Čeremšanka, S.S.S.R.	86	56.07 N	60.19 E
Čeremšany	89	44.42 N	135.43 E
Cerenti	112	0.30 S	101.52 E
Čerepanovka	80	57.07 N	54.10 E
Čerepanovo	86	54.13 N	83.22 E
Čerepaška, ostrov I	83	47.11 N	38.59 E
Čerepet'	82	54.07 N	36.23 E
Čerepkovo ✦8	265b	55.46 N	37.23 E
Čerepovec	76	59.08 N	37.54 E
Ceres, Arg.	252	29.53 S	61.57 W
Ceres, Bra.	255	15.17 S	49.35 W
Ceres, It.	62	45.19 N	7.23 E
Ceres, S. Afr.	158	33.21 S	19.18 E
Ceres, Ca., U.S.	226	37.35 N	120.57 W
Ceres, N.Y., U.S.	210	42.00 N	78.16 W
Ceresco, Mi., U.S.	216	42.16 N	85.04 W
Ceresco, Ne., U.S.	198	41.03 N	96.38 W
Ceresole Reale	62	45.26 N	7.15 E
Céreste	62	43.51 N	5.35 E
Céret	32	42.29 N	2.45 E
Cereté	246	8.53 N	75.48 W
Čerevkovka	78	48.50 N	37.40 E
Čerevkovka ✦8	83	48.50 N	37.40 E
Čerevkovo	24	61.46 N	45.12 E
Cereweh	115b	8.52 S	116.51 E
Cerf Island I	138	9.32 S	50.59 E
Čerga	86	51.35 N	85.38 E
Cergy	261	49.02 N	2.04 E
Ceri ≃	42	52.03 N	4.29 W
Ceriale	62	44.06 N	8.14 E
Ceriana	62	43.53 N	7.46 E
Ceriano	266b	45.38 N	9.05 E
Cerignola	68	41.16 N	15.54 E
Čerikov	76	53.34 N	31.23 E
Cérilly	32	46.37 N	2.49 E
Cerisano	68	39.16 N	16.11 E
Cerisiers	50	48.08 N	3.29 E
Čerkašina	88	58.37 N	108.30 E
Čerkasovo	82	54.33 N	36.48 E
Čerkasskoje, S.S.S.R.	78	48.44 N	35.22 E
Čerkasskoje, S.S.S.R.	80	52.26 N	47.13 E
Čerkasskoje, S.S.S.R.	83	48.50 N	37.23 E
Čerkassy, S.S.S.R.	76	52.41 N	38.43 E
Čerkassy, S.S.S.R.	78	49.26 N	32.04 E
Çerkeş	130	40.50 N	32.54 E
Čerkesovskij	80	50.41 N	42.34 E
Čerkessk	84	44.14 N	42.04 E
Çerkezköy	130	41.17 N	28.00 E
Čerkizovo, S.S.S.R.	82	55.12 N	38.45 E
Čerkizovo, S.S.S.R.	265b	55.57 N	37.22 E
Čerkizovo, S.S.S.R.	265b	55.58 N	37.48 E
Cerknica	36	45.48 N	14.22 E
Čerkovišče	76	55.54 N	30.51 E
Čerlak	86	54.09 N	74.48 E
Čerlakskij	86	53.47 N	74.31 E
Cermei	38	46.33 N	21.51 E
Čermen	84	43.11 N	44.42 E
Cermignano	66	42.35 N	13.47 E
Çermik	130	38.09 N	39.27 E
Čermoz	86	58.53 N	56.08 E
Čern'	76	53.27 N	36.55 E
Cerna, Jugo.	38	45.11 N	18.42 E
Cerna, Rom.	38	45.04 N	28.18 E
Čern'achov	78	50.27 N	28.39 E
Čern'achovsk (Insterburg)	76	54.38 N	21.49 E
Černá hora ∧	60	48.58 N	13.48 E
Čern'ajevo	89	52.45 N	126.00 E
Černak	85	43.24 N	68.02 E
Čern'anka	78	50.55 N	37.49 E
Cernăuţi → Černovcy	78	48.18 N	25.56 E
Černava	76	53.37 N	39.09 E
Černavčicy	76	52.13 N	23.44 E
Černavka, S.S.S.R.	80	52.18 N	47.14 E
Černavka, S.S.S.R.	80	52.11 N	42.25 E
Cernavodă	38	44.21 N	28.01 E
Černá v Pošumaví	61	48.44 N	14.07 E
Cernay	58	47.49 N	7.10 E
Cernay-la-Ville	50	48.40 N	1.58 E
Cerne Abbas	42	50.49 N	2.29 W
Černeckoje	82	55.15 N	37.20 E
Cernei, Munţii ∧	38	45.02 N	22.31 E
Černelica	78	48.48 N	25.26 E
Černevcy	78	48.33 N	28.09 E
Černigov	78	51.30 N	31.18 E
Černigov □4	76	52.13 N	32.45 E
Černigovka, S.S.S.R.	78	47.13 N	36.14 E
Černigovka, S.S.S.R.	86	50.28 N	71.27 E
Černigovka, S.S.S.R.	89	49.37 N	129.57 E
Černigovka, S.S.S.R.	89	44.21 N	132.33 E
Černigovskaja	78	44.41 N	39.40 E
Černi vrâh ∧	38	42.34 N	23.17 E
Černobaj	78	49.41 N	32.19 E
Cernobbio	62	45.50 N	9.04 E
Černobyl'	78	51.16 N	30.14 E
Černogolovka	82	56.00 N	38.22 E
Černogorsk	86	53.49 N	91.18 E
Černokol'skaja	86	56.42 N	72.49 E
Černomorskij zapovednik ✦4	78	46.10 N	32.00 E
Černorečenskoje	85	43.00 N	74.55 E
Černorečje	84	43.15 N	45.41 E
Černošín	60	49.49 N	12.53 E
Černovcy	78	48.18 N	25.56 E
Čerňovice	60	49.49 N	13.06 E
Černovka, S.S.S.R.	86	56.47 N	76.28 E
Černovka, S.S.S.R.	89	51.43 N	128.12 E
Čern'ovo, S.S.S.R.	76	58.39 N	28.14 E
Čern'ovo, S.S.S.R.	82	54.43 N	38.36 E
Čern'ovo, S.S.S.R.	265b	55.50 N	37.18 E
Černovskije Kopi	88	52.00 N	113.15 E
Černovskoje, S.S.S.R.	80	58.42 N	47.23 E
Černovskoje, S.S.S.R.	80	57.29 N	54.36 E
Černucha	80	55.36 N	43.46 E
Černuchi	78	50.16 N	32.57 E
Černuchino	83	48.19 N	38.30 E
Cernusco sul Naviglio	62	45.31 N	9.19 E
Černuška, S.S.S.R.	86	56.29 N	56.03 E
Černuška, S.S.S.R.	88	52.58 N	101.55 E
Cerny-en-Laonnois	50	49.27 N	3.40 E
Černyševsk	88	52.35 N	117.00 E
Černyševskij	74	63.00 N	112.15 E
Černyškovskij	80	48.27 N	42.14 E
Černyšova, gr'ada ∧	24	66.30 N	59.00 E
Čer'omuchova	80	54.57 N	51.09 E
Čer'omuški ✦8	265b	55.41 N	37.35 E
Cerralvo	232	26.06 N	99.37 W
Cerralvo, Isla I	232	24.15 N	109.55 W
Cerreto, Passo del ⅹ	64	44.18 N	10.13 E
Cerreto d'Esi	66	43.19 N	12.59 E
Cerreto Guidi	66	43.45 N	10.53 E
Cerreto Sannita	68	41.17 N	14.33 E
Cerrigydrudion	44	53.02 N	3.33 W
Cërrik	38	41.02 N	19.57 E
Cerrillos, Arg.	252	24.54 S	65.29 W
Cerrillos, N.M., U.S.	200	35.26 N	106.07 W
Cerrina	62	45.07 N	8.13 E
Cerritos, Méx.	234	22.26 N	100.17 W
Cerritos, Ca., U.S.	280	33.52 N	118.05 W
Cerro	58	45.54 N	8.36 E
Cerro, Forca di ⅹ	66	42.45 N	12.47 E
Cerro Azul, Arg.	252	27.38 S	55.29 W
Cêrro Azul, Bra.	252	24.50 S	49.15 W
Cerro Azul, Méx.	234	21.12 N	97.44 W
Cerro Azul, Perú	248	13.02 S	76.30 W
Cerro Chato	252	33.06 S	55.08 W
Cerro Colorado	252	33.52 S	55.33 W
Cêrro Corá	250	6.03 S	36.21 W
Cerro de Garnica, Parque Nacional ♠	234	19.35 N	100.47 W
Cerro de las Campanas, Parque Nacional ♠	234	20.40 N	100.30 W
Cerro de las Mesas ⊥	234	18.47 N	96.05 W
Cerro de los Angeles ♦1	266a	40.19 N	3.41 W
Cerro de Pasco	248	10.41 S	76.16 W
Cerro Gordo	219	39.53 N	88.43 W
Cerro Grande ≃	286c	10.37 N	66.49 W
Cêrro Largo	252	28.09 S	54.45 W
Cerro Moreno	252	23.28 S	70.25 W
Cerrón, Cerro ∧	246	10.19 N	70.39 W
Cerrón Grande, Embalse ⊜1	236	14.00 N	89.00 W
Cerro Prieto	204	32.27 N	115.17 W
Cerros Colorados, Embalse ⊜1	252	38.35 S	68.40 W
Cerro Vera	252	33.11 S	57.28 W
Čerskij	74	68.45 N	161.45 E
Čerskogo, chrebet ∧, S.S.S.R.	74	65.00 N	144.00 E
Čerskogo, chrebet ∧, S.S.S.R.	88	52.00 N	114.00 E
Čerskogo, gora ∧	88	55.05 N	108.40 E
Cersosimo	68	40.03 N	16.21 E
Certaldo	66	43.33 N	11.02 E
Čertanovka ≃	265b	55.38 N	37.47 E
Čertanovo ✦8	265b	55.38 N	37.37 E
Čertkovo	83	49.23 N	40.10 E
Čertolino	76	56.12 N	33.54 E
Čertomlyk	78	47.37 N	34.09 E
Certosa (Karthaus)	64	46.42 N	10.54 E
Certosa di Pavia	62	45.15 N	9.09 E
Čerusti	76	55.33 N	40.01 E
Červ'anka	88	57.41 N	99.33 E
Cervantes	116	16.59 N	120.44 E
Cervarezza	64	44.23 N	10.20 E
Cervaro	66	41.29 N	13.54 E
Cervaro ≃	68	41.30 N	15.52 E
Cervati, Monte ∧	68	40.17 N	15.29 E
Cervelló	266d	41.24 N	1.57 E
Cervello, Cozzo ∧	68	39.24 N	16.05 E
Cervelló, Riera de ≃	266d	41.24 N	2.01 E
Červen'	76	53.42 N	28.26 E
Červen Brjag	38	43.16 N	24.06 E
Červený Kostelec	30	50.29 N	16.06 E
Cervera	34	41.40 N	1.17 E
Cervera del Río Alhama	34	42.01 N	1.57 W
Cervera de Pisuerga	34	42.52 N	4.30 W
Cerveteri	66	42.00 N	12.06 E
Cervi, Monte dei ∧	70	37.53 N	13.58 E
Cervia	66	44.15 N	12.22 E
Cervialto, Monte ∧	68	40.47 N	15.08 E
Cervignano del Friuli	64	45.49 N	13.20 E
Cervin, Mont → Matterhorn ∧	58	45.59 N	7.43 E
Cervinara	68	41.01 N	14.37 E
Cervino (Matterhorn) ∧	58	45.59 N	7.43 E
Cervione	36	42.20 N	9.31 E
Červl'onnaja	84	43.30 N	45.54 E
Cervo, Esp.	34	43.40 N	7.25 W
Cervo, It.	62	43.55 N	8.07 E
Cervo ≃	62	45.22 N	8.24 E
Cervo, Capo ≻	62	43.55 N	8.08 E
Cervo, Rio do ≃, Bra.	256	21.12 S	45.10 W
Cervo, Rio do ≃, Bra.	256	22.07 S	45.49 W
Cervo, Serra do ∧	256	22.06 S	46.07 W
Červonaja Kamenka	78	48.38 N	33.26 E
Červonoarmejsk, S.S.S.R.	78	50.08 N	25.16 E
Červonoarmejsk, S.S.S.R.	78	50.28 N	28.14 E
Červonoarmejskoje, S.S.S.R.	78	45.47 N	28.44 E
Červonoarmejskoje, S.S.S.R.	78	47.57 N	35.27 E
Červonograd	78	50.24 N	24.14 E
Červonogranitnoje	78	50.34 N	28.33 E
Červonoje, S.S.S.R.	78	51.46 N	34.04 E
Červonoje, S.S.S.R.	78	49.57 N	28.53 E
Červonoje, ozero ⊜	76	52.24 N	27.57 E
Červonopartizansk	83	48.04 N	39.50 E
Červonyj Donec	78	49.29 N	36.34 E
Cesana Torinese	62	44.57 N	6.47 E
Cesano, It.	66	43.45 N	13.10 E
Cesano, It.	66	42.07 N	12.21 E
Cesano ≃	66	43.45 N	13.10 E
Cesano Boscone	266b	45.27 N	9.06 E
Cesano Maderno	62	45.38 N	9.08 E
Cesar □5	246	9.20 N	73.30 W
César ≃	246	9.00 N	73.58 W
Cesaró	70	37.50 N	14.43 E
Cesate	266b	45.36 N	9.05 E
Cesena	66	44.08 N	12.15 E
Cesenatico	66	44.12 N	12.24 E
Cesi, Poggio ∧	267a	42.02 N	12.44 E
Cesiomaggiore	64	46.05 N	11.59 E
Cēsis	76	57.18 N	25.15 E
Česká Kamenice	54	50.47 N	14.26 E
Česká Kublice	60	49.22 N	12.52 E
Česká Lípa	54	50.42 N	14.32 E
Česká Socialistická Republika □3	30	49.40 N	15.10 E
Česká Třebová	30	49.54 N	16.27 E
České Budějovice	61	48.59 N	14.28 E
České středohoří ∧	54	50.35 N	14.09 E
Českomoravská vrchovina ∧1	30	49.20 N	15.30 E
Československo → Czechoslovakia □1	30	49.30 N	17.00 E
Český Brod	54	50.02 N	14.58 E
Český Krumlov	61	48.49 N	14.19 E
Česma	86	53.50 N	60.40 E
Çeşme	130	38.18 N	26.19 E
Céspedes	240p	21.35 N	78.17 W
Cessalto	64	45.42 N	12.36 E
Češskaja guba c	24	67.30 N	46.30 E
Cessnock	170	32.50 S	151.21 E
Cesson	261	48.34 N	2.36 E
Cestos ≃	150	5.40 N	9.10 W
Cesvaine	76	56.58 N	26.19 E
Čet' ≃	86	56.51 N	86.48 E
Cetara	68	40.39 N	14.42 E
Cetate	38	44.06 N	23.03 E
Cetatea Albă → Belgorod-Dnestrovskij	78	46.12 N	30.20 E
Četbulak	85	41.17 N	73.58 E
Cetian	100	25.44 N	116.22 E
Cetina ≃	36	43.26 N	16.42 E
Cetinje	38	42.23 N	18.55 E
Çetinkaya	130	39.15 N	37.38 E
Cetona	66	42.58 N	11.54 E
Cetona, Monte ∧	66	42.56 N	11.52 E
Cetraro	68	39.31 N	15.56 E
Cetronia	208	40.35 N	75.31 W
Četyrboki	78	50.02 N	27.01 E
Céüse, Montagne de ∧	62	44.31 N	5.57 E
Ceuta	34	35.53 N	5.19 W
Ceva	62	44.23 N	8.02 E
Cevedale, Monte (Zufallspitze) ∧	64	46.27 N	10.37 E
Cevennen → Cévennes ✦1	32	44.00 N	3.30 E
Cévennes ✦1	32	44.00 N	3.30 E
Cévennes, Parc National des ♠	32	44.15 N	3.40 E
Cevins	62	45.35 N	6.28 E
Cevio	58	46.19 N	8.36 E
Cevizli	130	37.12 N	31.45 E
Cevizlik	84	40.48 N	39.38 E
Ceyhan	130	37.04 N	35.47 E
Ceyhan ≃	130	36.45 N	35.42 E
Ceylânpınar	130	36.51 N	40.02 E
Ceylon, Sk., Can.	184	49.28 N	104.36 W
Ceylon, Mn., U.S.	198	43.32 N	94.37 W
Ceylon → Sri Lanka □1	122	7.00 N	81.00 E
Ceyzériat	58	46.10 N	5.19 E
Cèze ≃	62	44.06 N	4.42 E
Chaam, Ned.	52	51.31 N	4.52 E
Cha-am, Thai	110	12.48 N	99.58 E
Chaanling	100	29.39 N	113.49 E
Chaatl Island I	182	53.00 N	132.25 W
Chabanais	32	45.52 N	0.43 E
Chabang Tiga	114	5.19 N	103.08 E
Chabaricha	24	65.50 N	52.16 E
Chabařovice	54	50.40 N	13.56 E
Chabarovo	72	69.39 N	60.24 E
Chabarovsk	89	48.27 N	135.06 E
Chabarovsk □4	89	54.00 N	136.00 E
Chabarowsk → Chabarovsk	89	48.27 N	135.06 E
Chabary	86	53.37 N	79.33 E
Chabás	252	33.15 S	61.22 W
Chabeuil	62	44.54 N	5.01 E
Chabez	84	44.02 N	41.47 E
Chābi	124	22.49 N	80.41 E
Chabjuwardoo Bay c	162	22.57 S	113.48 E
Chablais ✦1	58	46.18 N	6.39 E
Chablis	50	47.49 N	3.48 E
Chabogongba	120	31.47 N	81.14 E
Chaboje	265a	59.53 N	30.46 E
Chabot, Lake ⊜, Ca., U.S.	282	38.08 N	122.14 W
Chabot, Lake ⊜, Ca., U.S.	282	37.43 N	122.07 W
Chabris	50	47.15 N	1.39 E
Chabuchaer	86	43.42 N	81.04 E
Chabu-Rabot, pereval ⅹ	85	38.40 N	70.43 E
Chacabuco	252	34.38 S	60.29 W
Chacaito, Quebrada ≃	286c	10.29 N	66.52 W
Chacaltianguis	234	18.20 N	95.50 W
Chacanilla	248	6.13 S	77.51 W
Chacao	286c	10.30 N	66.51 W
Chácara	256	21.41 S	43.13 W
Chacarão, Cachoeira do ⌊	250	6.32 S	58.12 W
Chacarilla	286d	12.02 S	77.01 W
Chacarita, Cementerio de la ✦	288	34.33 S	58.28 W
Chacayán	248	10.24 S	76.25 W
Chachani, Nevado ∧	248	16.12 S	71.33 W
Chachapoyas, Perú	242	6.13 S	77.51 W
Chachapoyas, Perú	248	6.13 S	77.51 W
Chachas	248	15.30 S	72.16 W
Chachoengsao	110	13.42 N	101.05 E
Chāchora	124	24.10 N	76.59 E
Chāchro	120	25.07 N	70.15 E
Chachu	120	33.16 N	81.41 E
Chačinčaj ≃	84	40.13 N	47.18 E
Chačmas	84	41.28 N	48.48 E
Chaco □4	252	26.25 S	60.30 W
Chaco □5	248	20.00 S	60.30 W
Chaco ≃	200	36.46 N	108.39 W
Chaco Austral ✦1	252	26.30 S	61.30 W
Chaco Boreal ✦1	252	23.00 S	60.00 W
Chaco Central ✦1	252	25.00 S	59.45 W
Chaco Culture National Historical Park ♠	200	36.06 N	108.00 W
Chaco Mesa ∧	200	35.47 N	107.35 W
Chacón, Arroyo ≃	288	34.53 S	58.39 W
Chacon, Cape ≻	182	54.42 N	132.00 W
Chacra Cerro	286d	11.55 S	77.04 W
Chacra Ríos, Coliseo ♠	286d	12.03 S	77.04 W
Chacuaco Creek ≃	196	37.34 N	103.38 W
Chad (Tchad) □1, Afr.	136	15.00 N	19.00 E
Chad (Tchad) □1, Afr.	146	15.00 N	19.00 E
Chad, Lake (Lac Tchad) ⊜	146	13.20 N	14.00 E
Chada-Bulak	88	50.38 N	116.18 E
Chadbourn	192	34.19 N	78.49 W
Chadderton	262	53.33 N	2.08 W
Chadds Ford	285	39.52 N	75.35 W
Chādegān	128	32.46 N	50.39 E
Chadian, Zhg.	102	26.48 N	105.48 E
Chadian, Zhg.	105	39.14 N	117.45 E
Chadian, Zhg.	107	30.14 N	105.56 E
Chadianzi	107	30.31 N	104.22 E
Chadiza	154	14.05 S	32.28 E
Chadron	198	42.49 N	103.00 W
Chadstone	274b	37.53 S	145.05 E
Chadwell Saint Mary	260	51.29 N	0.22 E
Chadwick	190	42.01 N	89.53 W
Chadwick Manor	284b	39.19 N	76.46 W
Chadwick Pond ⊜	283	42.44 N	71.05 W
Chadwicks	210	43.01 N	75.16 W
Chadyžensk	78	44.25 N	39.33 E
Chadžalmachi	84	42.26 N	47.13 E
Chadžibejskij liman ⊜	78	46.39 N	30.33 E
Chae Hom	110	18.43 N	99.35 E
Chaem ≃	110	18.11 N	98.38 E
Chaersen	89	46.19 N	121.54 E
Chaeryŏng	98	38.24 N	125.36 E
Chafarinas, Islas II	34	35.11 N	2.26 W
Chafe	150	11.56 N	6.55 E
Chaffee	194	37.10 N	89.39 W
Chaffins	207	42.21 N	71.51 W
Chafurray	246	3.10 N	73.14 W
Chāgai	128	29.18 N	64.42 E
Chāgai Hills ∧2	128	29.30 N	64.15 E
Chagandianlisu	102	41.47 N	103.29 E
Chagang Do □4	98	40.50 N	126.30 E
Chaghcharān	120	34.32 N	65.15 E
Chagny	58	46.55 N	4.45 E
Chagos Archipelago II	12	6.00 S	72.00 E
Chagos-Laccadive Plateau ✦3	12	3.00 N	73.00 E
Chagrin ≃	214	41.40 N	81.27 W
Chagrin, Aurora Branch ≃	279a	41.25 N	81.25 W
Chagrin Falls	214	41.26 N	81.24 W
Chagrin Falls Park	214	41.21 N	81.32 W
Chagrin Valley Parkway ♠	279a	41.26 N	81.25 W
Chaguanas	241r	10.31 N	61.25 W
Chaguaramas	246	9.20 N	66.16 W
Chaguaya	248	21.49 S	64.50 W
Chahaignes	50	47.44 N	0.31 E
Chāhak	128	33.17 N	58.54 E
Chahal	236	15.45 N	89.34 W
Chahancheluo	98	41.39 N	114.22 E
Chahanwusu → Dulan	102	36.16 N	98.28 E
Chahār Bāgh, Afg.	120	35.58 N	69.38 E
Chahār Bāgh, Afg.	128	37.00 N	65.14 E
Chahār Borjak	128	30.17 N	62.03 E
Chahār Deh-ye Ghowrband	120	34.59 N	68.44 E
Chahār Mahāl-e Bakhtīārī □4	128	32.00 N	51.00 E
Chahayang	89	48.24 N	124.15 E
Chahe, Zhg.	100	33.16 N	119.02 E
Chahe, Zhg.	102	33.48 N	97.22 E
Chahe, Zhg.	105	39.50 N	115.21 E
Chāh Gheybī, Hāmūn-e ⊞	128	28.06 N	60.50 E
Chahuamiao	100	33.00 N	115.56 E
Chahuites	234	16.17 N	94.11 W
Chai ≃	104	42.20 N	123.52 E
Chai Badan	110	15.04 N	101.05 E
Chaibāsā	124	22.34 N	85.49 E
Chaigou	98	36.15 N	119.36 E
Chaihe	89	44.47 N	129.42 E
Chaijiawan	100	29.10 N	113.06 E
Chaillé-les-Marais	32	46.24 N	1.01 W
Chailley	50	48.05 N	3.42 E
Chailly-en-Bière	50	48.28 N	2.35 E
Chainat	110	15.11 N	100.08 E
Chainhurst	260	51.12 N	0.29 E
Chain O'Lakes State Park ♠, Il., U.S.	216	42.27 N	88.11 W
Chain O'Lakes State Park ♠, In., U.S.	216	41.20 N	85.26 W
Chainpur	124	23.08 N	84.15 E
Chaipudyrskaja guba c	24	68.30 N	59.30 E
Chaiqiao	100	29.51 N	121.56 E
Chairel, Laguna de c	234	22.17 N	97.50 W
Chaishudian	105	40.46 N	116.30 E
Chaiši	84	42.57 N	42.12 E
Chait	85	39.11 N	70.53 E
Chaital	126	22.31 N	88.47 E
Chaitén	254	42.55 S	72.43 W
Chaiwopu	86	43.33 N	87.59 E
Chaiya	110	9.23 N	99.14 E
Chaiyaphum	110	15.48 N	102.02 E
Chajarí	252	30.46 S	57.59 W

≃	River	Fluss	Río	Rivière	Rio
≅	Canal	Kanal	Canal	Canal	Canal
⌊	Waterfall, Rapids	Wasserfall, Stromschnellen	Cascada, Rápidos	Chute d'eau, Rapides	Cascata, Rápidos
ⅹ	Strait	Meerestrasse	Estrecho	Détroit	Estreito
c	Bay, Gulf	Bucht, Golf	Bahía, Golfo	Baie, Golfe	Baía, Golfo
⊜	Lake, Lakes	See, Seen	Lago, Lagos	Lac, Lacs	Lago, Lagos
⊞	Swamp	Sumpf	Pantano	Marais	Pântano
⊠	Ice Features, Glacier	Eis- und Gletscherformen	Accidentes Glaciales	Formes glaciaires	Acidentes glaciares
₸	Other Hydrographic Features	Andere Hydrographische Objekte	Otros Elementos Hidrográficos	Autres données hydrographiques	Outros acidentes hidrográficos
✦	Submarine Features	Untermeerische Objekte	Accidentes Submarinos	Formes de relief sous-marin	Acidentes submarinos
□	Political Unit	Politische Einheit	Unidad Politica	Entité politique	Unidade política
♦	Cultural Institution	Kulturelle Institution	Institución Cultural	Institution culturelle	Instituição cultural
⊥	Historical Site	Historische Stätte	Sitio Histórico	Site historique	Sitio histórico
♠	Recreational Site	Erholungs- und Ferienort	Sitio de Recreo	Centre de loisirs	Área de Lazer
✈	Airport	Flughafen	Aeropuerto	Aéroport	Aeroporto
■	Military Installation	Militäranlage	Instalación Militar	Installation militaire	Instalação militar
✦	Miscellaneous	Verschiedenes	Misceláneo	Divers	Diversos

Name	Page	Lat.°′	Long.°′
Chajdarken	85	39.57 N	71.21 E
Chajia	107	29.37 N	104.27 E
Chajian	100	32.40 N	118.46 E
Chajianling	98	39.14 N	114.36 E
Chajiaqiao	100	34.00 N	120.07 E
Chajrchan	88	48.35 N	101.56 E
Chajrchandulaan	102	45.57 N	102.03 E
Chajul	236	15.30 N	91.02 W
Chaka	154	4.49 N	31.14 E
Chakachamna Lake ⊜	180	61.13 N	152.35 W
Chakaer	120	36.32 N	80.43 E
Chakāltor	126	23.14 N	86.22 E
Chak Amru	123	32.22 N	75.11 E
Chakari	154	18.05 S	29.51 E
Chakaria	120	21.45 N	92.05 E
Chakarnaba	146	14.13 N	20.51 E
Chakasskaja Avtonomnaja Oblast' □[8]	86	53.00 N	90.00 E
Chākdaha, India	126	23.05 N	88.31 E
Chakdaha, India	272b	22.20 N	88.20 E
Chake Chake	154	5.15 S	39.46 E
Chakhānsūr	128	31.10 N	62.04 E
Chākia	124	26.25 N	85.03 E
Chak Jhumra	123	31.34 N	73.11 E
Chakkarat	110	15.00 N	102.16 E
Chakou, Zhg.	98	38.03 N	113.36 E
Chakou, Zhg.	105	38.53 N	116.41 E
Chakradharpur	124	22.42 N	85.38 E
Chakrāta	120	30.42 N	77.51 E
Chākulia	126	22.29 N	86.43 E
Chakwadām	102	27.29 N	98.31 E
Chakwāl	123	32.56 N	72.52 E
Chal	272c	19.06 N	73.08 E
Chala	248	15.52 S	74.16 W
Chalabesa	154	11.22 S	31.01 E
Chalais	32	45.16 N	0.02 E
Chalamont	58	46.00 N	5.10 E
Chalampé	58	47.49 N	7.33 E
Chalan Kanoa	174n	15.08 N	145.43 E
Chalatenango	236	14.03 N	88.56 W
Chalaua	154	16.06 S	39.11 E
Chalaux ≃	50	47.23 N	3.54 E
Chalaxung	102	34.10 N	97.44 E
Chalbi Desert ◆[2]	154	3.00 N	37.20 E
Chalcatongo de Hidalgo	234	17.02 N	97.35 W
Chalchgol	88	48.11 N	114.54 E
Chalchihuites	234	23.29 N	103.53 W
Chalchis Terara ∧	144	9.08 N	36.44 E
Chalchuapa	236	13.59 N	89.41 W
Chalchyn ≃	88	47.55 N	117.47 E
Chalcis → Khalkís	38	38.28 N	23.36 E
Chalco [de Díaz Covarrubias]	234	19.16 N	98.54 W
Chaldan	84	40.43 N	47.15 E
Chaldon	260	51.17 N	0.07 W
Chaleine	261	48.36 N	1.43 E
Chalengkou	120	37.57 N	93.40 E
Châlette-sur-Loing	50	48.01 N	2.44 E
Chaleur Bay ⊂	186	48.00 N	65.45 W
Chalfant	279b	40.25 N	79.52 W
Chalfant Run ≃	279b	40.25 N	79.48 W
Chalfont	208	40.17 N	75.13 W
Chalfont Common	260	51.38 N	0.33 W
Chalfonte	285	39.49 N	75.32 W
Chalfont Saint Giles	260	51.38 N	0.34 W
Chalfont Saint Peter	260	51.37 N	0.33 W
Chalford	42	51.45 N	2.09 W
Chalhuanca	248	14.17 S	73.15 W
Chalifert	261	48.53 N	2.46 E
Chalihuey	234	22.43 N	104.04 W
Chalilovo	86	51.24 N	58.04 E
Chalindrey	58	47.48 N	5.26 E
Chaling	100	26.47 N	113.33 E
Chālisgaon	122	20.28 N	75.01 E
Chalisi	102	32.55 N	102.04 E
Chaliun	88	48.50 N	103.59 E
Chalk	260	51.26 N	0.25 E
Chalkabad	86	42.42 N	59.43 E
Chalk Draw V	196	29.36 N	103.15 W
Chalk River	190	46.01 N	77.27 W
Chalkyitsik	180	66.39 N	143.43 W
Challakere	122	14.19 N	76.39 E
Challans	32	46.51 N	1.53 W
Challapata	248	18.54 S	66.47 W
Challenge	226	39.29 N	121.13 W
Challenger, Mount ∧	224	48.50 N	121.20 W
Challenger Deep ◆[1]	14	11.21 N	142.12 E
Challes-les-Eaux	62	45.33 N	5.59 E
Challis	202	44.30 N	114.13 W
Challviri, Salar de ≚	248	22.32 S	67.34 W
Chal'mer-Ju	24	67.58 N	64.50 E
Chalmers	216	40.39 N	86.52 W
Chalmette	194	29.56 N	89.57 W
Chalone Creek ≃	226	36.21 N	121.14 W
Chalonnes-sur-Loire	32	47.21 N	0.46 W
Châlons-sur-Marne	50	48.57 N	4.22 E
Chalon-sur-Saône	58	46.47 N	4.51 E
Chalosse ◆[1]	32	43.45 N	0.30 W
Chalt	123	36.15 N	74.20 E
Chaltel, Cerro (Monte Fitzroy) ∧	254	49.17 S	73.05 W
Chalturin	80	58.33 N	48.50 E
Chalturino	78	49.31 N	35.17 E
Chaluhe	89	43.43 N	126.00 E
Chaluolehu ⊜	120	34.00 N	81.45 E
Châlus, Fr.	32	45.39 N	0.59 E
Chālūs, Īrān	128	36.38 N	51.26 E
Cham, B.R.D.	60	49.13 N	12.41 E
Cham, Schw.	58	47.11 N	8.28 E
Chama, Perú	286d	12.08 S	77.00 W
Chama, N.M., U.S.	200	36.54 N	106.34 W
Chama ≃	246	9.03 N	71.40 W
Chama, Rio ≃	200	36.03 N	106.05 W
Chamah, Gunong ∧	114	5.13 N	101.33 E
Chamaicó	252	35.03 S	64.58 W
Chamal, Sierra ⋏	234	22.45 N	99.15 W
Chamama	154	12.55 S	33.43 E
Chamamat'urt	84	43.36 N	46.30 E
Chaman	120	30.55 N	66.27 E
Chamangonge	152	11.16 S	20.24 E
Chamao, Khao ∧	110	12.57 N	101.45 E
Chamarande	261	48.31 N	2.13 E
Chamar-Daban, chrebet ⋏	88	51.15 N	105.00 E
Chāmārpāra	272b	22.35 N	88.08 E
Chamaya ≃	248	5.44 S	78.39 W
Chamb ≃	60	49.13 N	12.42 E
Chamba, India	123	32.34 N	76.08 E
Chamba, Moç.	154	12.07 S	36.57 E
Chamba, Tan.	154	11.35 S	36.58 E
Chambal ≃	124	26.30 N	79.15 E
Chambaran, Plateau de ⋏[1]	62	45.15 N	5.15 E
Chambas	240p	22.12 N	78.55 W
Chambas ≃	240p	22.24 N	78.54 W
Chamberlain, Sk., Can.	184	50.50 N	105.34 W
Chamberlain, S.D., U.S.	198	43.48 N	99.19 W
Chamberlain ≃	164	15.08 S	128.06 E
Chamberlain Lake ⊜	186	46.17 N	69.20 W
Chamberlin, Mount ∧	180	69.16 N	144.55 W
Chamberry, Ruisseau ≃	275a	45.20 N	73.58 W
Chambers, Az., U.S.	200	35.11 N	109.25 W
Chambers, Ne., U.S.	198	42.12 N	98.44 W
Chambers, N.Y., U.S.	210	42.16 N	76.57 W
Chambers □[6]	222	29.42 N	94.40 W
Chambers Brook ≃	276	40.35 N	74.41 W
Chambersburg, Il., U.S.	219	39.49 N	90.39 W
Chambersburg, In., U.S.	218	38.31 N	86.24 W
Chambersburg, Pa., U.S.	208	39.56 N	77.39 W
Chambers Corner	285	40.01 N	74.44 W
Chambers Creek ≃	222	31.58 N	96.10 W
Chambers Creek, North Fork ≃	222	32.16 N	96.58 W
Chambers Creek, South Fork ≃	222	32.16 N	96.58 W
Chambers Island I	190	45.11 N	87.21 W
Chambéry	62	45.34 N	5.56 E
Chambeshi ≃	154	11.21 S	30.37 E
Chambi, Jebel ∧	148	35.11 N	8.42 E
Chambira ≃, Perú	246	4.28 S	74.50 W
Chambira ≃, Perú	246	3.55 S	73.45 W
Chamblee	192	33.53 N	84.17 W
Chambley-Bussières	56	49.03 N	5.54 E
Chambly, P.Q., Can.	275a	45.27 N	73.17 W
Chambly, Fr.	50	49.10 N	2.15 E
Chambly □[6]	206	45.30 N	73.20 W
Chambly, Bassin de ⊜	206	45.27 N	73.17 W
Chambly, Canal de ≍	275a	45.25 N	73.15 W
Chambois	50	48.48 N	0.07 E
Chambon-sur-Dolore	62	45.30 N	3.37 E
Chambon-sur-Voueize	32	46.11 N	2.25 E
Chambord, Château de ⊥	50	47.37 N	1.31 E
Chambourcy	261	48.54 N	2.03 E
Chambri Lake ⊜	164	4.16 S	143.08 E
Chambry	261	49.00 N	2.54 E
Chamburi Kalāt	128	26.09 N	64.43 E
Chamdo → Qamdo	102	31.11 N	97.15 E
Chame	236	8.35 N	79.53 W
Chame, Punta ›	236	8.39 N	79.42 W
Chamela	234	19.32 N	105.05 W
Chamela, Bahía ⊂	234	19.33 N	105.07 W
Chamelecón	236	15.24 N	88.01 W
Chamelecón ≃	236	15.51 N	87.49 W
Chamical	252	30.21 S	66.19 W
Chamizo	258	34.10 S	56.41 W
Chamizo, Arroyo ≃	258	34.15 S	56.44 W
Chamkanī	120	33.48 N	69.49 E
Chamlia ≃	124	29.38 N	80.24 E
Chamo, Lake ⊜	144	5.50 N	37.33 E
Chamois, It.	62	45.50 N	7.37 E
Chamois, Mo., U.S.	219	38.40 N	91.46 W
Chamojie	89	49.25 N	124.45 E
Chamoli	124	30.24 N	79.21 E
Chamoli □[5]	124	30.30 N	79.30 E
Chamonix-Mont-Blanc	58	45.55 N	6.52 E
Chamousset	62	45.33 N	6.12 E
Chamoux-sur-Gelon	62	45.32 N	6.13 E
Chāmpa	124	22.03 N	82.39 E
Champādānga	126	22.50 N	87.58 E
Champagne, Yk., Can.	180	60.47 N	136.29 W
Champagne, Fr.	62	45.16 N	4.48 E
Champagne □[9]	32	49.00 N	4.30 E
Champagne Castle ∧	158	29.06 S	29.20 E
Champagne-en-Valromay	58	45.54 N	5.41 E
Champagner-Berge ∧[2]	264a	52.31 N	13.05 E
Champagne-sur-Seine	50	48.24 N	2.48 E
Champagney	58	47.42 N	6.41 E
Champagnole	58	46.45 N	5.55 E
Champagny	62	45.27 N	6.42 E
Chāmpāhāti	126	22.23 N	88.29 E
Champaign	194	40.06 N	88.14 W
Champaign □[6], Il., U.S.	216	40.07 N	88.12 W
Champaign □[6], Oh., U.S.	218	40.07 N	83.45 W
Champapur	126	24.02 N	86.31 E
Champaquí, Cerro ∧	252	31.59 S	64.56 W
Champaran □[5]	124	26.50 N	84.40 E
Champasak	110	14.53 N	105.52 E
Champāwat	124	29.20 N	80.06 E
Champcueil	261	48.31 N	2.27 E
Champdāni	126	22.48 N	88.21 E
Champdeniers	32	46.29 N	0.24 W
Champdepraz	62	45.41 N	7.39 E
Champdeuil	261	48.37 N	2.44 E
Champdor	58	46.01 N	5.36 E
Champdoré, Lac ⊜	176	55.55 N	65.49 W
Champeaux	50	48.35 N	2.48 E
Champeix	32	45.36 N	3.08 E
Champerico	236	14.18 N	91.55 W
Champéry	58	46.10 N	6.52 E
Champex	58	46.02 N	7.07 E
Champier	62	45.27 N	5.17 E
Champigneulles	56	48.44 N	6.10 E
Champigny-sur-Marne	261	48.49 N	2.31 E
Champion, Ab., Can.	182	50.14 N	113.09 W
Champion, Mi., U.S.	190	46.30 N	87.57 W
Champion, Oh., U.S.	214	41.17 N	80.51 W
Champion, Pa., U.S.	214	40.05 N	79.21 W
Champions	222	29.59 N	95.31 W
Champlain	206	44.59 N	73.26 W
Champlain □[6]	206	46.45 N	72.35 W
Champlain ≃	206	46.27 N	72.17 W
Champlain, Lake ⊜	188	44.45 N	73.15 W
Champlain, Pont ◆[5]	206	45.28 N	73.32 W
Champlain Canal ≍	210	43.20 N	73.34 W
Champlan	261	48.43 N	2.16 E
Champlin Creek ≃	276	40.43 N	73.12 W
Champlitte-et-le-Prélot	58	47.37 N	5.31 E
Champlon	56	50.07 N	5.28 E
Champoluc	62	45.50 N	7.44 E
Champotón	232	19.21 N	90.43 W
Champrond-en-Gâtine	50	48.24 N	1.05 E
Champs	50	47.44 N	3.36 E
Champs-sur-Marne	261	48.51 N	2.36 E
Chāmpua	124	22.05 N	85.40 E
Champvans	58	47.06 N	5.26 E
Chāmrāil	272b	22.38 N	88.18 E
Chāmrājnagar Rāmasamudram	122	11.55 N	76.57 E
Chamrousse	62	45.08 N	5.52 E
Chamsara ≃	88	52.42 N	95.46 E
Chamusca	34	39.21 N	8.29 W
Chamza Chakimzada	85	40.26 N	71.30 E
Chana	110	6.55 N	100.44 E
Chanabadskij	85	40.49 N	72.58 E
Chanakyapuri □[9]	272a	28.36 N	77.11 E
Chānanwāla	123	30.22 N	73.57 E
Chañar	252	30.32 S	65.58 W
Chañaral	252	26.21 S	70.37 W
Chañaral, Isla I	252	29.02 S	71.35 W
Chanārān	128	36.39 N	59.06 E
Chanas	62	45.18 N	4.49 E
Chānasma	120	23.43 N	72.07 E
Chanbogd	102	43.12 N	107.10 E
Chancay	248	11.35 S	77.16 W
Chancay ≃	248	11.37 S	77.15 W
Chance	208	38.10 N	75.56 W
Chanceaux	58	47.31 N	4.42 E
Chanceaux-sur-Choisille	50	47.28 N	0.42 E
Chanch	88	51.30 N	100.40 E
Chan Chan ⊥	248	8.06 S	79.05 W
Chanchelulla Peak ∧	204	40.28 N	122.59 W
Chanchiang → Zhanjiang	102	21.12 N	110.23 E
Chanchöchij uul ⋏	88	49.30 N	94.30 E
Chanchongor	102	43.50 N	104.25 E
Chanco	252	35.44 S	72.32 W
Chancy	58	46.08 N	6.00 E
Chanda → Chandrapur, India	122	19.57 N	79.18 E
Chanda, S.S.S.R.	88	55.00 N	107.14 E
Chanda ≃	88	55.00 N	107.14 E
Chāndābila	126	22.05 N	87.00 E
Chandagajty	86	50.44 N	92.03 E
Chandalar	180	67.30 N	148.30 W
Chandalar ≃	180	66.36 N	145.48 W
Chandalar, East Fork ≃	180	67.05 N	147.16 W
Chandalar, Middle Fork ≃	180	67.10 N	148.19 W
Chandalar, North Fork ≃	180	67.10 N	148.19 W
Chandan Chauki	124	28.33 N	80.47 E
Chandankiāri	126	23.34 N	86.22 E
Chandannagar	126	22.51 N	88.21 E
Chandanpratap	126	23.33 N	89.24 E
Chandapāra	126	22.46 N	90.16 E
Chandar	126	23.54 N	89.58 E
Chandausi	124	28.27 N	78.46 E
Chāndbāli	120	20.47 N	86.46 E
Chandeleur Islands II	194	29.48 N	88.51 W
Chandeleur Sound ų	194	29.55 N	89.10 W
Chanderi	124	24.43 N	78.08 E
Chandernagore → Chandannagar	126	22.51 N	88.21 E
Chandīgarh	123	30.44 N	76.55 E
Chandīgarh □[3]	123	30.45 N	76.45 E
Chāndil	124	22.58 N	86.03 E
Chandīpur	126	23.59 N	89.01 E
Chanditala	272b	22.41 N	88.16 E
Chandla	124	25.05 N	80.12 E
Chandler, P.Q., Can.	186	48.21 N	64.41 W
Chandler, Az., U.S.	200	33.18 N	111.50 W
Chandler, In., U.S.	194	38.02 N	87.22 W
Chandler, Ok., U.S.	196	35.42 N	96.52 W
Chandler, Tx., U.S.	222	32.18 N	95.29 W
Chandler ≃	180	69.27 N	151.30 W
Chandler, Mount ∧[2]	162	27.00 S	133.20 E
Chandler Lake ⊜	180	68.15 N	152.43 W
Chandler Park ♠	281	42.24 N	82.58 W
Chandler's Cross	260	51.40 N	0.27 W
Chandler's Ford	42	50.59 N	1.23 W
Chandlers Valley	214	41.56 N	79.18 W
Chandlerville	219	40.02 N	90.09 W
Chandless ≃	248	9.08 S	69.51 W
Chāndor Hills ⋏[2]	122	20.30 N	74.00 E
Chandos Lake ⊜	212	44.49 N	78.00 W
Chāndpara	126	22.58 N	88.47 E
Chāndpur, Bngl.	120	22.08 N	91.55 E
Chāndpur, Bngl.	124	23.13 N	90.39 E
Chāndpur, India	124	29.09 N	78.16 E
Chāndpur ◆[8]	272a	28.45 N	77.01 E
Chāndra	126	22.28 N	87.09 E
Chandra Dighalia	126	23.04 N	89.46 E
Chandrakona	126	22.44 N	87.31 E
Chandrakona Road	126	22.44 N	87.21 E
Chandrapur	122	19.57 N	79.18 E
Chāndvad	122	20.20 N	74.15 E
Chandyga	74	62.40 N	135.36 E
Chanfang	105	39.56 N	115.55 E
Chang (Yangtze) ≃, Zhg.	90	31.48 N	121.10 E
Chang ≃, Zhg.	100	26.53 N	119.41 E
Chang ≃, Zhg.	100	28.59 N	116.42 E
Chang, Ko I	110	12.05 N	102.20 E
Changa	84	44.27 N	50.36 E
Changācha	126	23.16 N	89.01 E
Changaj	88	47.52 N	99.28 E
Changajn nuruu ⋏	90	47.30 N	100.00 E
Changal	88	49.19 N	104.24 E
Changalane	156	26.17 S	32.11 E
Changan → Xi'an, Zhg.	102	34.15 N	108.52 E
Chang'an, Zhg.	102	26.00 N	109.34 E
Changanācheri	122	9.28 N	76.33 E
Changane ≃	156	24.43 S	33.32 E
Chang'anzhen	106	30.28 N	120.27 E
Changara	154	16.54 S	33.14 E
Changarul'skij chrebet ⋏	88	51.10 N	103.00 E
Changbai	98	41.26 N	128.11 E
Changbai Shan ⋏	98	41.40 N	128.00 E
Changbu	100	23.48 N	115.26 E
Changcaocun	105	39.49 N	115.47 E
Changchaoling	106	31.00 N	119.40 E
Changcheng, Zhg.	100	31.49 N	116.54 E
Changcheng, Zhg.	110	19.24 N	108.42 E
Chang Cheng (Great Wall) ⊥	98	40.30 N	116.30 E
Chang Chenmo ≃	120	34.17 N	78.19 E
Changchiak'ou → Zhangjiakou	105	40.50 N	114.53 E
Ch'angchih → Changzhi	102	36.11 N	113.08 E
Changchou → Zhangzhou	100	24.33 N	117.39 E
Changchow → Changzhou	106	31.47 N	119.57 E
Changchun	89	43.53 N	125.19 E
Changchunling	89	45.22 N	125.28 E
Changdan	98	37.56 N	126.45 E
Changdang Hu ⊜	106	31.35 N	119.35 E
Changdao (Sihou)	98	37.56 N	120.42 E
Changde	102	29.02 N	111.41 E
Changdian	105	40.01 N	116.32 E
Ch'angdo	98	38.30 N	127.40 E
Ch'ang-dong	98	39.03 N	126.34 E
Change Islands	186	49.40 N	54.25 W
Changeon ≃	50	47.16 N	0.05 E
Changfeng	100	32.27 N	117.09 E
Changgang	100	24.38 N	113.05 E
Changgangzi	104	41.26 N	122.41 E
Changge	100	34.15 N	113.50 E
Changgi-ap ›	98	36.05 N	129.34 E
Changgi-li	271b	37.35 N	126.44 E
Changgi-ri	271b	37.38 N	126.41 E
Changgou	105	39.34 N	115.53 E
Changgouyu	105	39.44 N	115.52 E
Changguandian	100	32.58 N	115.16 E
Changguowei	100	29.15 N	121.56 E
Changgye-ri	98	34.33 N	126.49 E
Changgyong Palace ⊕	271b	37.36 N	127.00 E
Changhai	98	39.18 N	122.35 E
Chang-hai → Shanghai	106	31.14 N	121.28 E
Changhang	98	36.01 N	126.40 E
Changhe	106	30.11 N	120.11 E
Changhowŏn	98	37.08 N	127.39 E
Chang Hu ⊜	100	30.15 N	112.35 E
Changhua, T'aiwan	100	24.05 N	120.32 E
Changhua, Zhg.	100	30.11 N	119.13 E
Changhŭng	98	34.41 N	126.52 E
Changhŭng-ni	98	40.24 N	128.19 E
Changi	271c	1.23 N	103.59 E
Changi, Tanjong ›	271c	1.23 N	104.00 E
Changi Airport ⊠	271c	1.22 N	103.59 E
Changi Prison ⊕	271c	1.22 N	103.58 E
Changji	86	44.01 N	87.19 E
Changjiang, Zhg.	100	25.19 N	113.56 E
Changjiang, Zhg.	110	19.17 N	109.02 E
Changjiangbu	100	30.52 N	113.43 E
Changjiapuzi	104	40.51 N	123.43 E
Changjiazhuang	105	40.35 N	115.24 E
Changjie	100	29.16 N	121.40 E
Changjing	106	31.45 N	120.29 E
Changjin-gang ≃	98	41.24 N	127.45 E
Changjin-ŭp	98	40.23 N	127.15 E
Changkai	100	28.04 N	116.18 E
Changkalajier	85	40.09 N	76.59 E
Changkeng	106	30.19 N	121.57 E
Changkiakow → Zhangjiakou	105	40.50 N	114.53 E
Changlapod Pass)(	124	30.08 N	87.06 E
Changle, Zhg.	98	36.42 N	118.49 E
Changle, Zhg.	100	29.25 N	120.37 E
Changle, Zhg.	100	26.00 N	119.31 E
Changlejie	100	28.52 N	113.19 E
Changleqiao	106	30.21 N	119.51 E
Changlezhen	106	31.56 N	121.15 E
Changli, Zhg.	98	36.57 N	119.45 E
Changli, Zhg.	98	39.43 N	119.11 E
Changling	89	44.15 N	123.58 E
Changlingfeng	105	40.11 N	118.24 E
Changlingji	100	32.30 N	114.54 E
Changlingzi, Zhg.	98	39.47 N	122.43 E
Changlingzi, Zhg.	98	39.33 N	121.19 E
Changlinhe	100	31.40 N	117.29 E
Changlun	114	6.26 N	100.26 E
Changmong-ni	98	34.58 N	128.41 E
Changning, Zhg.	102	26.19 N	112.21 E
Changning, Zhg.	102	24.55 N	99.35 E
Changning (Anningqiao), Zhg.	102	28.21 N	104.53 E
Changning, Zhg.	105	39.59 N	114.55 E
Ch'angnyŏng	98	35.33 N	128.29 E
Changnyŏn-ni	98	38.37 N	125.16 E
Changokurt	72	61.58 N	64.18 E
Ch'angpin	100	23.19 N	121.27 E
Changping	105	40.14 N	116.14 E
Changputong	102	28.05 N	98.29 E
Ch'angp'yŏng-dong	98	41.27 N	127.31 E
Changqiao, Zhg.	100	24.15 N	117.39 E
Changqiao, Zhg.	100	26.49 N	118.50 E
Changqing	98	36.34 N	116.43 E
Changsa	102	19.51 N	110.53 E
Changsan-got ›	98	38.08 N	124.39 E
Changsha, Zhg.	100	28.12 N	112.58 E
Changsha, Zhg.	100	24.13 N	116.07 E
Changshaba Shuiku ⊜[1]	107	29.42 N	104.40 E
Changshageng	107	30.00 N	104.35 E
Changshan, Zhg.	98	36.54 N	117.50 E
Changshan, Zhg.	100	28.55 N	118.30 E
Changshan, Zhg.	107	29.30 N	104.13 E
Changshan ≃	100	28.57 N	118.50 E
Changshan Qundao II	98	39.00 N	122.45 E
Changsheng	100	26.16 N	116.01 E
Changshengqiao	107	29.31 N	106.39 E
Changshitai	104	42.33 N	120.43 E
Changshitou	102	35.03 N	99.11 E
Changshou	102	29.51 N	107.06 E
Changshoudian	100	31.26 N	112.35 E
Changshoujie	100	28.44 N	113.57 E
Changshu	106	31.39 N	120.45 E
Changshui	102	34.21 N	111.29 E
Changsŏng	98	35.20 N	126.49 E
Changsŏng-ni	98	40.58 N	127.04 E
Changsu	98	35.40 N	127.32 E
Changtai, Zhg.	100	24.40 N	117.46 E
Changtai, Zhg.	100	28.34 N	118.37 E
Changtai, Zhg.	104	41.34 N	122.00 E
Changtancun	104	41.33 N	123.02 E
Ch'angte → Changde	102	29.02 N	111.41 E
Changteh → Anyang	98	36.06 N	114.21 E
Changting, Zhg.	89	44.32 N	128.47 E
Changting, Zhg.	100	25.52 N	116.20 E
Changtumiao	102	43.30 N	114.34 E
Changuinola ≃	236	9.28 N	82.27 W
Changwu, Zhg.	89	46.00 N	125.36 E
Changwu, Zhg.	102	35.09 N	107.42 E
Changxindianzhen	105	39.49 N	116.12 E
Changxing	106	31.01 N	119.54 E
Changxing Dao I, Zhg.	98	39.34 N	121.23 E
Changxing Dao I, Zhg.	106	31.24 N	121.42 E
Changxingdian, Zhg.	104	41.27 N	121.44 E
Changxingdian, Zhg.	104	41.33 N	123.23 E
Changxingzhen	104	41.40 N	122.14 E
Changxuanling	100	31.08 N	114.20 E
Changyi	98	36.51 N	119.23 E
Changyŏn	98	38.15 N	125.06 E
Changyuan	98	35.13 N	114.39 E
Changyukou	105	40.46 N	115.08 E
Changzhi	102	36.11 N	113.08 E
Changzhou (Changchow)	106	31.47 N	119.57 E
Chanhanga	152	16.04 S	14.07 E
Chanh-hung	269c	10.44 N	106.41 E
Chani	88	57.05 N	120.58 E
Chani ≃	88	57.02 N	120.59 E
Chanino	76	54.13 N	36.37 E
Chanka, ozero (Xingkai Hu) ⊜	89	45.00 N	132.24 E
Chankiang → Zhanjiang	102	21.12 N	110.23 E
Chankou	102	35.52 N	104.27 E
Chanlar	84	40.34 N	46.20 E
Channagiri	122	14.02 N	75.56 E
Channahon	216	41.26 N	88.14 W
Channapatna	122	12.39 N	77.13 E
Channel Country ◆[1]	166	24.45 S	141.00 E
Channel Islands II, Europe	28	49.20 N	2.20 W
Channel Islands II, Ca., U.S.	204	33.30 N	119.15 W
Channel Islands National Park ♠	204	33.28 N	119.02 W
Channel Lake	216	42.29 N	88.08 W
Channel North Basin ⊂	174h	2.49 S	171.43 W
Channel-Port-aux-Basques	186	47.34 N	59.09 W
Channelview	222	29.46 N	95.06 W
Channing, Mi., U.S.	190	46.08 N	88.05 W
Channing, Tx., U.S.	196	35.41 N	102.20 W
Chantada	34	42.37 N	7.46 W
Chantajskoje, ozero ⊜	74	68.20 N	91.00 E
Chantajskoje vodochranilišče ⊜[1]	72	68.00 N	88.00 E
Chantang	100	33.41 N	117.37 E
Chantau	86	44.13 N	73.51 E
Chanteloup	261	48.51 N	2.44 E
Chanteloup-les-Vignes	261	48.59 N	2.02 E
Chantengo, Laguna ⊂	234	16.37 N	99.07 W
Chanthaburi	110	12.36 N	102.09 E
Chantilly	50	49.12 N	2.28 E
Chantonnay	32	46.41 N	1.03 W
Chantraine	58	48.10 N	6.26 E
Chantrans	58	47.03 N	6.09 E
Chantrey Inlet ⊂	176	67.48 N	96.20 W
Chanty-Mansijsk	74	61.00 N	69.06 E
Chanty-Mansijskij Nacional'nyj Okrug □[8]	86	60.15 N	70.45 E
Chanujn ≃	88	49.22 N	102.22 E
Chanumla	110	8.19 N	93.05 E
Chanute	198	37.40 N	95.27 W
Chanute Air Force Base ■	216	40.18 N	88.09 W
Chanuwāla	123	32.44 N	73.08 E
Chanžonkovo	83	48.06 N	38.06 E
Chao ≃	105	40.36 N	117.08 E
Chao, Isla I	248	8.45 S	78.47 W
Chao'an	100	23.41 N	116.38 E
Chaobai ≃	105	39.48 N	117.08 E
Chaobai Xinhe ≃	105	39.37 N	117.26 E
Chaocheng	98	36.05 N	115.35 E
Ch'aochou	100	22.33 N	120.32 E
Ch'aochou → Chao'an	100	23.41 N	116.38 E
Chao Hu ⊜	100	31.31 N	117.33 E
Chaomidian	105	39.04 N	117.01 E
Chao Phraya ≃	110	13.32 N	100.36 E
Chaor ≃	89	46.48 N	123.37 E
Chaoshui, Zhg.	89	49.44 N	127.21 E
Chaoshui, Zhg.	98	37.42 N	120.55 E
Chaouen	148	35.10 N	5.16 W
Chaouen □[4]	148	35.15 N	5.00 W
Chaource	50	48.04 N	4.08 E
Chaoxian	100	31.36 N	117.52 E
Chaoyang, Zhg.	89	44.34 N	126.20 E
Chaoyang, Zhg.	100	23.17 N	116.37 E
Chaoyang, Zhg.	104	41.35 N	120.28 E
Chaoyangchuan	98	42.54 N	129.21 E
Chaoyangcun	89	50.02 N	124.16 E
Chaoyanggou	104	42.07 N	121.04 E
Chaoyangpo	89	43.37 N	124.42 E
Chaoyangshan	89	43.02 N	125.40 E
Chaozhuang	98	34.18 N	114.56 E
Chapa	110	22.21 N	103.50 E
Chapada dos Guimarães	248	15.26 S	55.45 W
Chapadinha	250	3.44 S	43.21 W
Chapala	234	20.18 N	103.12 W
Chapala, Lago de ⊜	234	20.15 N	103.00 W
Chaparé ≃	248	15.58 S	64.42 W
Chapareillan	62	45.28 N	5.58 E
Chāparmukh	120	26.12 N	92.32 E
Chaparra	240p	21.10 N	76.29 W
Chaparra, Bahía de ⊂	240p	21.13 N	76.31 W
Chaparral	246	3.43 N	75.28 W
Chapčeranga	88	49.42 N	112.24 E
Chapeauroux	62	44.50 N	3.44 E
Chapecó	252	27.06 S	52.36 W
Chapel-en-le-Frith	262	53.20 N	1.54 W
Chapelfell Top ∧	44	54.41 N	2.13 W
Chapelhall	46	55.50 N	3.56 W
Chapel Hill, De., U.S.	285	39.42 N	75.44 W
Chapel Hill, N.C., U.S.	192	35.54 N	79.03 W
Chapel Hill, Tn., U.S.	194	35.37 N	86.41 W
Chapel Hill Channel ų	276	40.32 N	74.02 W
Chapelle Creek ≃	198	44.16 N	99.55 W
Chapellerie	261	49.02 N	2.26 E
Chapel Oaks	284c	38.54 N	76.55 W
Chapel Point ›	42	50.16 N	4.46 W
Chapel Saint Leonards	44	53.13 N	0.19 E
Chapelton	241q	18.05 N	77.16 W
Chapeltown, Eng., U.K.	44	53.28 N	1.28 W
Chapeltown, Eng., U.K.	262	53.38 N	2.24 W
Chapet	261	48.58 N	1.56 E
Chapéu, Ribeirão do ≃	256	23.14 S	45.18 W
Chapicuy	252	31.39 S	57.54 W
Chapimarca	248	13.58 S	73.04 W
Chapin	219	39.46 N	90.24 W
Chapin, Lake ⊜	216	41.56 N	86.21 W
Chaplain, Lake ⊜[1]	224	47.57 N	121.51 W
Chapleau	190	47.50 N	83.24 W
Chapleau ≃	190	48.29 N	82.57 W
Chapleau, Lac ⊜	206	46.14 N	74.57 W
Chaplin, Sk., Can.	184	50.28 N	106.40 W
Chaplin, Ct., U.S.	207	41.47 N	72.07 W
Chaplin ≃	194	37.50 N	85.11 W
Chaplin Lake ⊜	184	50.18 N	106.35 W
Chapman, Ks., U.S.	198	38.58 N	97.01 W
Chapman, Ne., U.S.	198	41.01 N	98.09 W
Chapman, Pa., U.S.	208	40.46 N	75.24 W
Chapman, Cape ›	176	69.12 N	88.59 W
Chapman, Mount ∧	182	51.50 N	118.20 W
Chapman College ⊕[2]	280	33.47 N	117.51 W
Chapman Creek ≃	198	38.58 N	97.00 W
Chapman Lake ⊜	184	56.58 N	98.12 W
Chapman's (Okwa) ≃	156	22.30 S	23.00 E
Chapmanville	188	37.58 N	82.01 W
Chapman Woods	280	34.08 N	118.05 W
Chapo	196	29.17 N	104.20 W
Chaponval	261	49.04 N	2.09 E
Chappaqua	210	41.09 N	73.45 W
Chappell	198	41.05 N	102.28 W
Chappell Hill	222	30.09 N	96.16 W
Chāpra, India	124	25.46 N	84.45 E
Chāpra, India	126	23.32 N	88.33 E
Chapry	83	47.14 N	39.31 E
Chaptico Bay ⊂	208	38.21 N	76.49 W
Chapultepec, Méx.	204	31.50 N	116.38 W
Chapultepec, Méx.	204	32.22 N	115.05 W
Chapultepec ∧	234	23.27 N	103.04 W
Chapultepec, Bosque de ♠	286a	19.25 N	99.12 W
Chapultepec, Castillo de ⊥	286a	19.25 N	99.11 W
Chá Pungana	152	13.44 S	18.39 E
Chaqui	248	19.36 S	65.32 W
Chaquiago	252	27.32 S	66.21 W
Char ≃	42	50.44 N	2.53 W
Char ⍑[4]	148	21.31 N	12.51 W
Charaa ≃	88	49.38 N	105.49 E
Charabali	80	47.24 N	47.16 E
Chara-Chužar	88	52.30 N	99.39 E
Charadai	252	27.38 S	59.54 W
Charagua	248	19.48 S	63.13 W
Charagun	88	51.36 N	111.05 E
Char-Ajrag	102	45.49 N	109.17 E
Charal	88	51.58 N	96.39 E
Charalá	246	6.17 N	73.10 W
Charām	128	30.45 N	50.44 E
Charaña	248	17.36 S	69.28 W
Charanor	88	50.05 N	116.40 E
Charanpur	126	23.45 N	87.02 E
Charapán	234	19.41 N	102.06 W
Charapucu, Ilha I	250	0.18 S	50.48 W
Charata	252	27.13 S	61.12 W
Charauz	88	52.16 N	106.17 E
Charavines-les-Bains	62	45.26 N	5.31 E
Charazani → Amarete	248	15.14 S	68.58 W
Charazargaj	88	52.57 N	104.41 E
Charbala	74	64.07 N	120.19 E
Char Bansi	126	22.59 N	90.43 E
Charbatovo	88	53.46 N	106.00 E
Charbon	170	32.54 S	149.58 E
Charcana	248	15.15 S	73.04 W
Charcas	234	23.08 N	101.07 W
Charco Azul, Bahía de ⊂	236	8.15 N	82.45 W
Charco Hondo	240m	18.25 N	66.43 W
Charcos de Figueroa	232	27.45 N	102.11 W
Charcos de Risa	232	26.15 N	103.10 W
Charcot Island I	9	69.45 S	75.15 W
Charcyzsk	83	48.02 N	38.09 E
Chard	42	50.53 N	2.58 W
Chardon	214	41.36 N	81.08 W
Charduār	120	26.52 N	92.46 E
Chardzhou → Čardžou	128	39.06 N	63.34 E
Charef, Oued V	148	34.07 N	2.05 W
Charente □[5]	32	45.40 N	0.10 E
Charente ≃	32	45.57 N	1.05 W
Charente-Maritime □[5]	32	45.30 N	0.45 W
Charenton-du-Cher	32	46.44 N	2.38 E
Charenton-le-Pont	261	48.49 N	2.25 E
Charentonne ≃	50	49.07 N	0.44 E
Charest ≃	206	46.36 N	72.14 W
Chārghāt	126	24.17 N	88.45 E
Char Hāim	126	23.04 N	90.38 E
Chari ≃	146	12.58 N	14.31 E
Chariāl Canal ≍	272b	22.28 N	88.11 E
Chari-Baguirmi □[5]	146	11.30 N	16.30 E
Charik	88	54.15 N	101.39 E
Chārīkār	120	35.01 N	69.11 E
Charing	42	51.13 N	0.48 E
Charing Cross	214	42.20 N	82.06 W
Charino, S.S.S.R.	76	59.57 N	43.44 E
Charino, S.S.S.R.	82	54.33 N	37.52 E
Charistvala	84	42.26 N	43.02 E
Chariton	190	41.00 N	93.18 W
Chariton ≃	194	39.19 N	92.57 W
Chariton, Mussel Fork ≃	194	39.24 N	92.55 W
Charitonovo, S.S.S.R.	24	61.27 N	47.28 E
Charitonovo, S.S.S.R.	82	56.52 N	36.44 E
Charity	246	7.24 N	58.36 W
Charkhāri	124	25.24 N	79.45 E
Charkhi Dādri	124	28.37 N	76.16 E
Char'kin	80	48.46 N	51.49 E
Charkop ◆[8]	272c	19.13 N	72.49 E
Char'kov (Kharkov)	78	50.00 N	36.15 E
Char'kov □[4]	83	49.42 N	37.10 E
Charkow → Char'kov	78	50.00 N	36.15 E
Char Lākhpur	126	24.04 N	90.40 E
Char Lālmohan	126	22.13 N	90.42 E
Charland, Lac ⊜	206	46.52 N	74.11 W
Charlbury	42	51.53 N	1.29 W
Charl Cilliers	158	26.39 S	29.12 E
Charlemagne	206	45.43 N	73.29 W
Charlemont	207	42.37 N	72.52 W
Charleroi, Bel.	50	50.25 N	4.26 E
Charleroi, Pa., U.S.	214	40.08 N	79.53 W
Charleroi à Bruxelles, Canal de ≍	50	50.51 N	4.19 E
Charles □[6]	208	38.32 N	76.59 W
Charles ≃	207	42.22 N	71.03 W
Charles, Cape ›	208	37.08 N	75.58 W
Charles, Lake ⊜	278	42.15 N	87.58 W
Charles, Peak ∧	162	32.52 S	121.11 E
Charlesbourg	206	46.51 N	71.16 W
Charles Branch ≃	284c	38.47 N	76.48 W
Charles City, Ia., U.S.	190	43.03 N	92.40 W
Charles City, Va., U.S.	208	37.20 N	77.04 W
Charles City □[6]	208	37.20 N	77.02 W
Charles de Gaulle, Aéroport ⊠	50	49.01 N	2.33 E
Charles Island I	176	62.40 N	74.15 W
Charles Lee Tilden Regional Park ♠	282	37.54 N	122.15 W
Charles Mill Lake ⊜[1]	214	40.45 N	82.22 W
Charles Mound ∧[2]	190	42.30 N	90.14 W
Charles Point ›	164	12.23 S	130.36 E
Charles Sound ų	172	45.02 S	167.04 E
Charleston, Austl.	168b	34.55 S	138.54 E
Charleston, N.Z.	172	41.54 S	171.26 E
Charleston, Ar., U.S.	194	35.17 N	94.02 W
Charleston, Il., U.S.	194	39.29 N	88.10 W
Charleston, Ms., U.S.	194	34.00 N	90.03 W
Charleston, Mo., U.S.	194	36.55 N	89.21 W
Charleston, S.C., U.S.	192	32.46 N	79.55 W
Charleston, W.V., U.S.	188	38.20 N	81.37 W
Charleston Air Force Base ■	192	32.55 N	80.03 W
Charleston Lake ⊜	212	44.32 N	76.00 W
Charleston Peak ∧	204	36.16 N	115.42 W
Charlestown, Austl.	170	32.58 S	151.42 E
Charlestown, Ire.	48	53.57 N	8.49 W
Charlestown, St. C.-N.	238	17.08 N	62.37 W
Charlestown, S. Afr.	158	27.30 S	29.55 E
Charlestown, In., U.S.	218	38.27 N	85.40 W
Charlestown, Md., U.S.	208	39.34 N	75.58 W
Charlestown, N.H., U.S.	188	43.14 N	72.25 W
Charlestown, Pa., U.S.	285	40.06 N	75.33 W
Charlestown, R.I., U.S.	207	41.22 N	71.38 W
Charles Town, W.V., U.S.	188	39.17 N	77.51 W
Charlestown ◆[8]	283	42.23 N	71.04 W
Charlesworth	262	53.26 N	1.59 W
Charleville	166	26.24 S	146.15 E
Charleville → Ráth Luirc	48	52.21 N	8.41 W
Charleville-Mézières	56	49.46 N	4.43 E
Charlevoix	190	45.19 N	85.15 W
Charlevoix, Lake ⊜	190	45.15 N	85.08 W
Charley ≃	180	65.20 N	142.49 W
Charlie Bluff	216	42.50 N	88.58 W
Charlie Creek ≃	220	27.21 N	81.49 W
Charlie Lake	182	56.16 N	120.57 W
Charlieu	32	46.10 N	4.10 E
Charlotte, Mi., U.S.	216	42.33 N	84.50 W
Charlotte, N.C., U.S.	192	35.13 N	80.50 W
Charlotte, Tn., U.S.	194	36.10 N	87.20 W
Charlotte, Tx., U.S.	196	28.51 N	98.42 W
Charlotte □[6]	220	26.54 N	81.58 W
Charlotte Amalie	240m	18.21 N	64.56 W
Charlotte Court House	192	37.03 N	78.39 W
Charlotte Creek ≃	210	42.27 N	75.01 W
Charlotte Harbor	220	26.57 N	82.04 W
Charlotte Harbor ⊂	220	26.45 N	82.12 W
Charlotte Lake ⊜	182	52.11 N	125.20 W
Charlottenberg	26	59.53 N	12.17 E
Charlottenburg	250	5.51 N	54.46 W
Charlottenburg ◆[8]	264a	52.31 N	13.16 E
Charlottenburg, Schloss ⊥	264a	52.31 N	13.14 E
Charlottesburg Reservoir ⊜[1]	276	41.02 N	74.26 W
Charlottesville, In., U.S.	218	39.47 N	85.36 W
Charlottesville, Va., U.S.	192	38.01 N	78.28 W
Charlottetown, P.E., Can.	186	46.14 N	63.08 W
Charlotte Town (Gouyave), Gren.	241k	12.10 N	61.44 W
Charlotteville	210	42.33 N	74.40 W
Charlovka	24	68.47 N	37.15 E
Charlton, Austl.	166	36.16 S	143.21 E
Charlton, Ma., U.S.	207	42.08 N	71.58 W
Charlton ◆[8]	260	51.29 N	0.02 E
Charlton City	207	42.08 N	71.59 W
Charlton Island I	176	52.00 N	79.30 W
Charlton Kings	42	51.53 N	2.03 W
Charlu	24	61.48 N	30.52 E
Charly-sur-Marne	50	48.58 N	3.17 E
Charm	214	40.30 N	81.47 W
Charmentray	261	48.57 N	2.47 E
Charmes	58	48.22 N	6.17 E
Charmes-sur-Rhône	62	44.52 N	4.50 E
Charmey	58	46.38 N	7.10 E
Charminster	42	50.43 N	2.28 W
Charmois-l'Orgueilleux	58	48.06 N	6.16 E
Charmont-en-Beauce	50	48.14 N	2.06 E
Charmouth	42	50.45 N	2.55 W
Charnay-lès-Mâcon	58	46.18 N	4.47 E
Charneca	266c	38.44 N	9.27 W
Charneca ◆[8]	266c	38.47 N	9.08 W
Charnley ≃	164	16.25 S	124.57 E
Charnock Richard	262	53.38 N	2.41 W
Char nuur ⊜, Mong.	88	48.06 N	93.12 E
Char nuur ⊜, Mong.	88	48.20 N	96.05 E
Charnwood Forest ◆[3]	42	52.43 N	1.15 W
Charny, P.Q., Can.	206	46.43 N	71.16 W
Charny, Fr.	50	47.53 N	3.06 E
Charny, Fr.	261	48.58 N	2.46 E
Charny-sur-Meuse	56	49.12 N	5.22 E
Charo	234	19.45 N	101.03 W
Charolles	32	46.26 N	4.17 E
Charouine	148	29.01 N	0.16 W
Charovsk	76	59.59 N	40.11 E
Charpi ≃	89	49.40 N	136.10 E
Charquemont	58	47.13 N	6.49 E
Charred Oak Estates	284c	39.00 N	77.10 W
Charrette Creek ≃	219	38.37 N	91.03 W
Charron Lake ⊜	184	52.45 N	95.15 W
Charroux	32	46.09 N	0.24 E
Chars	50	49.10 N	1.56 E
Chārsadda	123	34.09 N	71.44 E
Charter Oak, Ca., U.S.	280	34.06 N	117.52 W
Charter Oak, Ia., U.S.	198	42.04 N	95.35 W
Charters Towers	166	20.05 S	146.16 E
Charterwood	279b	40.33 N	80.00 W
Chartiers Creek ≃	214	40.28 N	80.03 W
Chartiers Run ≃, Pa., U.S.	279b	40.36 N	79.43 W
Chartiers Run ≃, Pa., U.S.	279b	40.15 N	80.12 W
Chartley	207	41.56 N	71.13 W
Chartres	50	48.27 N	1.30 E
Chartrettes	50	48.29 N	2.42 E
Chartridge	260	51.44 N	0.39 W
Chart Sutton	260	51.13 N	0.35 E
Chartwell ⊥	260	51.14 N	0.05 E
Char Us nuur ⊜	90	48.00 N	92.10 E
Charutajuvom	24	66.49 N	59.30 E

Symbols in the index entries represent the broad categories identified in the key at the right. Symbols with superior numbers (⋏[1]) identify subcategories (see complete key on page *I · 1).*

Kartensymbole in dem Registerverzeichnis stellen die rechts in Schlüssel erklärten Kategorien dar. Symbole mit hochgestellten Ziffern (⋏[1]) bezeichnen Unterabteilungen einer Kategorie (vgl. vollständiger Schlüssel auf Seite *I · 1).*

Los símbolos incluídos en el texto del índice representan las grandes categorias identificadas con la clave a la derecha. Los símbolos con numeros en su parte superior (⋏[1]) identifican las subcategorías (véase la clave completa en la página *I · 1).*

Les symboles de l'index représentent les catégories indiquées dans la légende à droite. Les symboles suivis d'un indice (⋏[1]) représentent des sous-catégories (voir légende complète à la page *I · 1).*

Os símbolos incluídos no texto do índice representam as grandes categorias identificadas com a chave à direita. Os símbolos com números em sua parte superior (⋏[1]) identificam as subcategorías (veja-se a chave completa à página *I · 1).*

∧ Mountain	Berg	Montaña	Montagne	Montanha
⋏ Mountains	Berge	Montañas	Montagnes	Montanhas
)(Pass	Pass	Paso	Col	Passo
V Valley, Canyon	Tal, Cañon	Valle, Cañón	Vallée, Canyon	Vale, Canhão
≚ Plain	Ebene	Llano	Plaine	Planície
› Cape	Kap	Cabo	Cap	Cabo
I Island	Insel	Isla	Île	Ilha
II Islands	Inseln	Islas	Îles	Ilhas
◆ Other Topographic Features	Andere Topographische Objekte	Otros Elementos Topográficos	Autres données topographiques	Outros acidentes topográficos

ESPAÑOL

Nombre	Página	Lat. °′	Long. °′ W = Oeste
Chãs	126	23.38 N	86.10 E
Chasav'urt	84	43.15 N	46.37 E
Chascomús	258	35.34 S	58.01 W
Chascomús, Laguna ⊜	258	35.36 S	58.01 W
Chašdala	85	39.42 N	67.07 E
Chase, B.C., Can.	182	50.49 N	119.41 W
Chase, Ak., U.S.	180	62.27 N	150.07 W
Chase, Ks., U.S.	198	38.21 N	98.20 W
Chase, Md., U.S.	208	39.21 N	76.22 W
Chase, Mount ∧	188	46.07 N	68.29 W
Chase Brook ≃	283	42.48 N	71.27 W
Chase City	192	36.47 N	78.27 W
Chase Field Naval Air Station ■	196	28.21 N	97.40 W
Chasefu	154	11.55 S	33.08 E
Chase Lake	212	43.46 N	75.19 W
Chase River	224	49.08 N	123.55 W
Chasicó	254	40.18 S	68.58 W
Chasidaba	104	42.19 N	121.19 E
Chaska	190	44.47 N	93.36 W
Chaslands Mistake ›	172	46.38 S	169.22 E
Chasŏng	98	41.27 N	126.37 E
Chasŏngganggu	98	41.34 N	126.36 E
Chassahowitzka	220	28.43 N	82.34 W
Chassahowitzka Bay c	220	28.41 N	82.40 W
Chassahowitzka Swamp ≡	220	28.38 N	82.37 W
Chasseron, Mont ∧	58	46.51 N	6.33 E
Chasse-sur-Rhône	62	45.34 N	4.49 E
Chassezac ≃	62	44.26 N	4.19 E
Chašuri	84	42.00 N	43.36 E
Chasurta	88	52.17 N	108.52 E
Chasuta	248	6.35 S	76.11 W
Chãt	128	37.59 N	55.16 E
Chatanbulag	102	43.09 N	109.08 E
Chatanga	74	71.58 N	102.30 E
Chatanga ≃	74	72.55 N	106.00 E
Chatangskij zaliv c	74	73.30 N	109.00 E
Chatanika	180	65.07 N	147.31 W
Chatanika ≃	180	65.04 N	149.18 W
Château-Arnoux	62	44.06 N	6.00 E
Chateaubelair	241h	13.17 N	61.15 W
Chateaubelair Bay c	241h	13.17 N	61.15 W
Châteaubriant	32	47.43 N	1.23 W
Château-Chinon	32	47.04 N	3.56 E
Château d'Oex	58	46.28 N	7.08 E
Château-du-Loir	50	47.42 N	0.25 E
Châteaudun	50	48.05 N	1.20 E
Châteaufort	261	48.44 N	2.06 E
Chateaugay	206	44.55 N	74.04 W
Château-Gontier	32	47.50 N	0.42 W
Châteauguay	206	45.23 N	73.45 W
Châteauguay □[6]	206	45.15 N	73.45 W
Châteauguay ≃	188	45.24 N	73.45 W
Châteauguay-Centre	206	45.21 N	73.45 W
Châteauguay Heights	275a	45.23 N	73.44 W
Château-Landon	50	48.09 N	2.42 E
Château-la-Vallière	50	47.33 N	0.19 E
Châteaulin	32	48.12 N	4.05 W
Châteaumeillant	32	46.34 N	2.12 E
Châteauneuf	62	43.23 N	5.10 E
Châteauneuf-de-Randon	62	44.39 N	3.40 E
Châteauneuf-du-Pape	62	44.03 N	4.50 E
Châteauneuf-du-Rhône	62	44.29 N	4.43 E
Châteauneuf-en-Thymerais	50	48.35 N	1.15 E
Châteauneuf-sur-Charente	32	45.36 N	0.03 W
Châteauneuf-sur-Loire	50	47.52 N	2.14 E
Châteauneuf-sur-Sarthe	32	47.41 N	0.30 W
Châteauneuf-Val-de-Bargis	50	47.17 N	3.14 E
Château-Porcien	50	49.32 N	4.15 E
Château-Queyras	62	44.45 N	6.47 E
Châteauredon	62	44.01 N	6.13 E
Châteaurenard, Fr.	50	47.56 N	2.56 E
Châteaurenard, Fr.	62	43.53 N	4.51 E
Château-Renault	50	47.35 N	0.55 E
Château-Richer	186	46.58 N	71.01 W
Châteauroux	32	46.49 N	1.42 E
Château-Salins	56	48.49 N	6.30 E
Château-Thierry	50	49.03 N	3.24 E
Châteauvillain	58	48.02 N	4.55 E
Châtel	58	46.17 N	6.50 E
Châtel-Censoir	50	47.31 N	3.38 E
Châtelet	50	50.24 N	4.31 E
Châtelineau	56	50.25 N	4.31 E
Châtellerault	32	46.49 N	0.33 E
Châtel-Saint-Denis	58	46.32 N	6.54 E
Châtel-sur-Moselle	58	48.18 N	6.24 E
Châtelus-Malvaleix	32	46.18 N	2.01 E
Châtenay-en-France	261	49.04 N	2.27 E
Châtenay-Malabry	261	48.46 N	2.17 E
Châtenois, Fr.	58	48.18 N	5.50 E
Châtenois, Fr.	58	48.16 N	7.24 E
Châtenois-les-Forges	58	47.34 N	6.51 E
Chatfield, Mn., U.S.	190	43.50 N	92.11 W
Chatfield, Oh., U.S.	214	40.57 N	82.56 W
Chatgal	88	50.26 N	100.09 E
Chatham, N.B., Can.	186	47.02 N	65.28 W
Chatham, On., Can.	214	42.24 N	82.11 W
Chatham, Eng., U.K.	42	51.23 N	0.32 E
Chatham, Il., U.S.	219	39.40 N	89.42 W
Chatham, La., U.S.	194	32.18 N	92.27 W
Chatham, Ma., U.S.	207	41.40 N	69.57 W
Chatham, N.J., U.S.	210	40.44 N	74.23 W
Chatham, N.Y., U.S.	210	42.21 N	73.35 W
Chatham, Oh., U.S.	214	41.06 N	82.01 W
Chatham, Pa., U.S.	208	39.51 N	75.49 W
Chatham, Va., U.S.	192	36.49 N	79.23 W
Chatham ◆[8]	278	41.45 N	87.37 W
Chatham ≃	220	25.42 N	81.17 W
Chatham, Isla I	254	50.40 S	74.20 W
Chatham Head	186	47.00 N	65.33 W
Chatham Islands II	14	43.55 S	176.30 W
Chatham Rise ✦[3]	14	43.30 S	178.00 W
Chatham Sound ⩀	182	54.32 N	130.35 W
Chatham Strait ⩀	180	57.30 N	134.45 W
Chatian	100	27.54 N	118.58 E
Châtillon, Fr.	261	48.48 N	2.17 E
Châtillon, It.	62	45.45 N	7.37 E
Châtillon-Coligny	50	47.50 N	2.51 E
Châtillon-en-Bazois	32	47.03 N	3.40 E
Châtillon-en-Diois	62	44.41 N	5.28 E
Châtillon-la-Borde	261	48.33 N	2.49 E
Châtillon-sur-Chalaronne	58	46.07 N	4.58 E
Châtillon-sur-Indre	32	46.59 N	1.11 E
Châtillon-sur-Loire	50	47.35 N	2.45 E
Châtillon-sur-Marne	50	49.06 N	3.45 E
Châtillon-sur-Seine	58	47.51 N	4.33 E
Chating	106	31.21 N	119.25 E
Chãtmohar	126	24.13 N	89.15 E
Chat Moss ◆[3]	262	53.27 N	2.27 W
Chato, Cerro ∧	254	42.29 S	72.01 W
Chatom	194	31.27 N	88.15 W
Chatonville	261	48.33 N	1.52 E
Chatou	261	48.54 N	2.09 E
Chatpur ◆[8]	272b	22.36 N	88.22 E
Chatra, India	124	24.13 N	84.52 E
Chatra, India	272b	22.46 N	88.20 E
Chatrapur	122	19.21 N	84.59 E
Châtres	261	48.43 N	2.49 E
Chats, Lac des ⊜	212	45.28 N	76.23 W
Chatsquot Mountain ∧	182	53.08 N	127.30 W
Chãtsu	120	26.36 N	75.57 E
Chatswood	274a	33.48 S	151.12 E
Chatsworth, Austl.	166	21.58 S	140.19 E
Chatsworth, On., Can.	212	44.27 N	80.54 W
Chatsworth, Ga., U.S.	192	34.45 N	84.46 W
Chatsworth, Il., U.S.	216	40.45 N	88.17 W
Chatsworth, N.J., U.S.	208	39.49 N	74.32 W

FRANÇAIS

Nom	Page	Lat. °′	Long. °′ W = Ouest
Chatsworth, Zimb.	154	19.38 S	31.13 E
Chatsworth ◆[8]	280	34.15 N	118.36 W
Chatsworth Reservoir ⊜[1]	228	34.14 N	118.37 W
Chattahoochee	192	30.42 N	84.50 W
Chattahoochee ≃	192	30.52 N	84.57 W
Chattanooga, Oh., U.S.	216	40.38 N	84.47 W
Chattanooga, Tn., U.S.	194	35.02 N	85.18 W
Chattaroy	192	37.42 N	82.16 W
Chattenden	260	51.25 N	0.32 E
Chatteris	42	52.27 N	0.03 E
Châttillon-de-Michaille	58	46.08 N	5.47 E
Chattolanee	284b	39.24 N	76.45 W
Chatton	44	55.33 N	1.55 W
Chatun'	82	55.00 N	37.50 E
Chaturat	110	15.34 N	101.51 E
Chatwood	208	39.58 N	75.35 W
Chatyrka	74	62.03 N	175.15 E
Chaubaria	126	22.59 N	88.40 E
Chaubourg, Mount ∧[2]	241f	14.02 N	60.57 W
Chauconin	261	48.58 N	2.51 E
Chaudes-Aigues	32	44.51 N	3.00 E
Chaudfontaine	56	50.35 N	5.38 E
Chaudière ≃	186	46.45 N	71.17 W
Chauekuktuli, Lake ⊜	180	60.03 N	158.45 W
Chauffayer	62	44.45 N	6.01 E
Chaugãcha	126	23.16 N	89.01 E
Chauk	110	20.54 N	94.50 E
Chaukhandi	272a	28.37 N	77.24 E
Chaullay	248	12.57 S	72.39 W
Chaulnes	50	49.49 N	2.48 E
Chaumergy	58	46.51 N	5.29 E
Chaumes-en-Brie	261	48.40 N	2.51 E
Chaumont, Fr.	58	48.07 N	5.08 E
Chaumont, N.Y., U.S.	212	44.04 N	76.07 W
Chaumont ≃	212	44.04 N	76.08 W
Chaumont, Rû de ≃	261	48.31 N	2.40 E
Chaumont Bay c	212	44.02 N	76.13 W
Chaumont-en-Vexin	50	49.16 N	1.53 E
Chaumont-Porcien	50	49.39 N	4.15 E
Chaumont-sur-Aire	56	48.56 N	5.15 E
Chaumont-sur-Loire	50	47.29 N	1.11 E
Chaumont-sur-Tharonne	50	47.37 N	1.54 E
Chaumua	272b	22.39 N	88.33 E
Chaumuhãni	124	22.56 N	91.07 E
Chauncey	188	39.23 N	82.07 W
Chaŭn-do I	98	34.53 N	126.03 E
Chaungwabyin	110	13.41 N	98.22 E
Chaungzon	110	16.22 N	97.32 E
Chauny	50	49.37 N	3.13 E
Chaupãran	124	24.23 N	85.15 E
Chau-phu	110	10.42 N	105.07 E
Chaussin	58	46.58 N	5.25 E
Chausu-yama ∧	94	35.14 N	137.39 E
Chausuyama-kofun ⊥	94	36.25 N	139.50 E
Chautãra	124	27.46 N	85.42 E
Chautauqua	214	42.12 N	79.28 W
Chautauqua □[6]	214	42.15 N	79.30 W
Chautauqua Creek ≃	214	42.20 N	79.36 W
Chautauqua Lake ⊜	214	42.12 N	79.27 W
Chauvigny	32	46.34 N	0.39 E
Chauvin, Ab., Can.	184	52.42 N	110.07 W
Chauvin, La., U.S.	194	29.26 N	90.35 W
Chauvirey-le-Châtel	58	47.47 N	5.45 E
Chauvry	261	49.03 N	2.16 E
Chavakkad	122	10.32 N	76.06 E
Chaval	250	3.02 S	41.15 W
Chavanges	58	48.31 N	4.34 E
Chavannes, Lac ⊜	190	46.51 N	77.10 W
Chavarría, Arg.	252	28.57 S	58.35 W
Chavarría, Perú	286d	12.01 S	77.05 W
Chavast	85	40.13 N	68.50 E
Chavenay	261	48.51 N	1.59 E
Chavenay-Villepreux, Aérodrome de ⊠	261	48.51 N	1.58 E
Chavertovo	82	54.17 N	39.12 E
Chaves, Bra.	250	0.10 S	49.55 W
Chaves, Port.	34	41.44 N	7.28 W
Chaves, Ribeirão dos ≃	256	21.24 S	44.29 W
Chaville	261	48.48 N	2.10 E
Chaviña	248	14.59 S	73.50 W
Chavinda	234	20.01 N	102.27 W
Cháviva	246	4.22 N	72.20 W
Chavki	82	54.20 N	38.13 E
Chavornay	58	46.43 N	6.34 E
Chavuma	152	13.05 S	22.40 E
Chawa'nanake	120	31.36 N	89.41 E
Chawang	110	8.25 N	99.30 E
Chawinda	123	32.21 N	74.42 E
Chay ≃	110	21.39 N	105.12 E
Chayanta	248	18.27 S	66.30 W
Chayuan, Zhg.	100	29.20 N	121.34 E
Chayuan, Zhg.	100	27.40 N	112.57 E
Chayue	106	30.49 N	119.21 E
Chazay-d'Azergues	62	45.53 N	4.37 E
Chazelles-sur-Lyon	62	45.38 N	4.23 E
Chazratišoch, chrebet ⋏	85	38.30 N	70.15 E
Chazumba	234	18.12 N	97.40 W
Chazy	188	44.53 N	73.26 W
Chbar ≃	110	13.19 N	107.05 E
Cheadle, Eng., U.K.	42	52.59 N	1.59 W
Cheadle, Eng., U.K.	262	53.24 N	2.13 W
Cheadle Hulme	262	53.22 N	2.12 W
Cheaha Mountain ∧	194	33.30 N	85.47 W
Cheakamus Indian Reserve ◆[4]	182	49.48 N	123.11 W
Cheam ◆[8]	260	51.21 N	0.13 W
Cheam View	224	49.15 N	121.41 W
Cheapside	222	29.17 N	97.24 W
Cheat ≃	188	39.45 N	79.54 W
Cheat, Shavers Fork ≃	188	39.06 N	79.33 W
Cheb	54	50.01 N	12.25 E
Chebacco Lake ⊜	283	42.37 N	70.48 W
Chebanse	216	41.00 N	87.54 W
Chebba	148	35.14 N	10.02 E
Chebeigou	89	43.28 N	127.04 E
Chebogue Point ›	186	43.45 N	66.07 W
Cheboksary → Čeboksary	80	56.09 N	47.15 E
Cheboygan	190	45.38 N	84.28 W
Chech, Erg ◆[2]	148	25.00 N	2.15 W
Ch'ech'eng	100	22.05 N	120.42 E
Chech'on	98	37.08 N	128.12 E
Chęciny	30	50.48 N	20.28 E
Checleset Bay c	182	50.03 N	127.40 W
Checoslovaquia → Czechoslovakia □[1]	30	49.30 N	17.00 E
Checotah	196	35.28 N	95.31 W
Chedabucto Bay c	186	45.23 N	61.10 W
Chedaoyu	105	40.22 N	117.57 E
Cheddar	42	51.17 N	2.46 W
Cheddleton	44	53.04 N	2.02 W
Cheduba Island I	110	18.48 N	93.38 E
Cheduba Strait ⩀	110	18.56 N	93.45 E
Chedun	100	24.09 N	117.19 E
Chée ≃	56	48.45 N	4.39 E
Cheektowaga	210	42.55 N	78.46 W
Cheepie	166	26.39 S	145.01 E
Cheesequake	276	40.25 N	74.17 W
Cheesequake Creek ≃	276	40.28 N	74.16 W
Cheesequake State Park ♠	276	40.26 N	74.16 W
Cheetham Hill ◆[8]	262	53.31 N	2.15 W
Chefang, Zhg.	104	41.35 N	121.26 E
Chefang, Zhg.	106	31.15 N	120.45 E
Chef-Boutonne	32	46.07 N	0.04 W
Chefoo → Yantai	98	37.33 N	121.20 E
Chefornak	180	60.13 N	164.12 W
Chefumage ≃	152	12.15 S	22.19 E
Chefuzwe	156	17.38 S	24.30 E

PORTUGUÊS

Nome	Página	Lat. °′	Long. °′ W = Oeste
Chegar Perah	114	4.25 N	101.56 E
Chegga ⊤[4]	148	25.30 N	5.46 W
Chegutu	154	18.10 S	30.14 E
Chehalis	224	46.39 N	122.57 W
Chehalis ≃	224	46.57 N	123.50 W
Chehalis, South Fork ≃	224	46.40 N	123.15 W
Chehalis Indian Reservation ◆[4]	224	46.49 N	123.13 W
Chehe	102	25.00 N	107.38 E
Chehel Dokhtarãn	128	35.06 N	62.19 E
Cheheqiao	105	40.21 N	118.16 E
Cheil, Ras el ›	144	7.44 N	49.50 E
Cheine	54	52.52 N	11.04 E
Cheiron, Cime du ∧	62	43.49 N	6.58 E
Chejiatun	104	41.57 N	123.01 E
Chejiawopeng	104	42.29 N	123.07 E
Cheju	90	33.31 N	126.32 E
Cheju-do I	90	33.20 N	126.30 E
Chekiang → Zhejiang □[4]	100	29.00 N	120.00 E
Chek Jawa, Tanjong ›	271c	1.24 N	104.00 E
Chek Kang	271d	22.26 N	114.21 E
Chela, Serra da ∧	152	16.00 S	13.10 E
Chelan	202	47.50 N	120.00 W
Chelan □[6]	224	47.56 N	120.52 W
Chelan, Lake ⊜	202	48.05 N	120.30 W
Chelas ◆[8]	266c	38.45 N	9.07 W
Cheleiros	266c	38.53 N	9.20 W
Cheleiros, Ribeira de ≃	266c	38.54 N	9.22 W
Chelelektu	144	6.00 N	38.09 E
Chelford	262	53.16 N	2.16 W
Chelforó	252	39.04 S	66.32 W
Chelghoum el Aïd	148	36.10 N	6.10 E
Chéliff, Oued ≃	148	36.01 N	0.07 E
Chelīk-e Yãs Khãn	120	37.05 N	66.14 E
Chellaston	42	52.53 N	1.27 W
Chelles	50	48.53 N	2.36 E
Chelles-le-Pin, Aérodrome de ⊠	261	48.55 N	2.35 E
Chełm	30	51.10 N	23.28 E
Chełm □[4]	30	51.20 N	23.20 E
Chelmer ≃	260	51.48 N	0.40 E
Chelmer and Blackwater Navigation ≋	260	51.44 N	0.43 E
Chełmno	30	53.22 N	18.26 E
Chelmorton	262	53.13 N	1.50 W
Chelmsford, On., Can.	190	46.35 N	81.12 W
Chelmsford, Eng., U.K.	260	51.44 N	0.28 E
Chelmsford, Ma., U.S.	207	42.35 N	71.21 W
Chelmsford □[8]	260	51.44 N	0.30 E
Chelmsford Dam ⊜[1]	158	28.02 S	29.52 E
Chełmża	30	53.12 N	18.37 E
Chelsea, Austl.	169	38.03 S	145.07 E
Chelsea, Ia., U.S.	190	41.55 N	92.23 W
Chelsea, Ma., U.S.	207	42.23 N	71.02 W
Chelsea, Mi., U.S.	216	42.19 N	84.01 W
Chelsea, Ok., U.S.	196	36.32 N	95.25 W
Chelsea, Pa., U.S.	285	39.52 N	75.28 W
Chelsea, Vt., U.S.	188	43.59 N	72.26 W
Chelsea Estates	208	39.41 N	75.36 W
Chelsea Park	224	47.28 N	122.21 W
Chelsfield ◆[8]	260	51.21 N	0.08 E
Cheltenham, Austl.	274a	33.46 S	151.05 E
Cheltenham, Austl.	274b	37.58 S	145.03 E
Cheltenham, Eng., U.K.	42	51.54 N	2.04 W
Cheltenham, Md., U.S.	208	38.44 N	76.49 W
Cheltenham, Pa., U.S.	208	40.03 N	75.05 W
Chel'ul'ja	26	61.44 N	30.41 E
Chelva	34	39.45 N	0.59 W
Chelvand	128	38.18 N	48.50 E
Chelyabinsk → Čel'abinsk	86	55.10 N	61.24 E
Chelyãma	126	23.37 N	86.33 E
Chelyan	188	38.11 N	81.29 W
Chelyuskintsy Ice Tongue ⊓	9	66.20 S	82.00 E
Chemaïa	148	32.05 N	8.37 W
Chemainus	224	48.55 N	123.43 W
Chemainus ⊜	224	48.53 N	123.41 W
Chemaogang	106	31.33 N	121.52 E
Chemax	232	20.39 N	87.56 W
Chemba	154	17.08 S	34.52 E
Chembūr ◆[8]	272c	19.04 N	72.54 E
Chemchâm, Sebkhet ⊜	148	21.05 N	12.05 W
Chemčik ≃	86	51.47 N	92.00 E
Chemehuevi Indian Reservation ◆[4]	204	34.30 N	114.23 W
Chemillé	32	47.13 N	0.44 W
Chemin	58	46.59 N	5.19 E
Cheminis, Colline ∧[2]	190	48.08 N	79.31 W
Chemnitz → Karl-Marx-Stadt	54	50.50 N	12.55 E
Chemnitz ≃	54	50.59 N	12.47 E
Chemor	114	4.43 N	101.07 E
Chemulpo → Inch'ŏn	98	37.28 N	126.38 E
Chemult	202	43.13 N	121.46 W
Chemung, Il., U.S.	216	42.25 N	88.40 W
Chemung, N.Y., U.S.	210	42.01 N	76.37 W
Chemung □[6]	210	42.06 N	76.49 W
Chemung ≃	210	41.55 N	76.31 W
Chemung County Airport ⊠	210	42.10 N	76.53 W
Chemung Lake ⊜	212	44.25 N	78.22 W
Chena, Cerro de ∧	286e	33.36 N	70.45 W
Chenãb ≃	123	29.23 N	71.02 E
Chenachane	148	26.00 N	4.15 W
Chenail Ecarté ≃[1]	214	42.28 N	82.29 W
Chenango □[6]	210	42.32 N	75.31 W
Chenango ≃	210	42.05 N	75.55 W
Chenango Bridge	210	42.10 N	75.51 W
Chenango Forks	210	42.14 N	75.50 W
Chenango Valley State Park ♠	210	42.14 N	75.50 W
Chenaut	258	34.15 S	59.13 W
Chen Barag Qi	89	49.21 N	119.31 E
Chenbofang	98	37.27 N	115.18 E
Chencai	100	29.37 N	120.22 E
Chenchiang → Zhenjiang	106	32.13 N	119.26 E
Chencun	100	22.58 N	113.13 E
Chendai	100	23.48 N	117.24 E
Chendauli ◆[8]	272c	19.07 N	72.54 E
Chenderiang	114	4.16 N	101.14 E
Chenderoh, Tasek ⊜	114	4.58 N	100.57 E
Chêne, Rivière du ≃, P.Q., Can.	206	46.34 N	72.00 W
Chêne, Rivière du ≃, P.Q., Can.	206	45.33 N	73.54 W
Chenele	152	12.54 S	23.54 E
Chenequa	216	43.06 N	88.23 W
Chénéville	206	45.53 N	75.03 W
Cheney, Ks., U.S.	198	37.37 N	97.46 W
Cheney, Wa., U.S.	202	47.29 N	117.34 W
Cheney Reservoir ⊜[1]	198	37.45 N	97.50 W
Cheneys Point	214	42.08 N	79.24 W
Cheneyville	194	31.00 N	92.17 W
Chenfang	100	28.01 N	117.32 E
Cheng'an	98	36.27 N	114.41 E
Chengannur	122	9.20 N	76.38 E
Chengbu	102	26.18 N	110.13 E
Chengchow → Zhengzhou	102	34.48 N	113.39 E
Chengde, Zhg.	105	40.58 N	117.53 E
Chengde (Xiabancheng), Zhg.	105	40.47 N	118.08 E
Chengdu (Chengtu)	107	30.39 N	104.04 E
Chengele	120	28.47 N	96.16 E
Chenggang	100	26.32 N	115.26 E
Chenggu	102	33.10 N	107.22 E
Chenghai	100	23.30 N	116.46 E
Cheng Hu ⊜	106	31.13 N	120.49 E
Chenghuang	102	22.32 N	109.39 E
Chengjia	100	24.50 N	112.50 E
Chengjiahe	100	32.18 N	112.27 E
Chengjiang	102	24.45 N	102.54 E
Chengjiangzhen	107	29.52 N	106.23 E
Chengjiazhen	107	29.24 N	104.36 E
Chengkou	102	31.54 N	108.41 E
Chenglingji	100	29.26 N	113.09 E
Chenglong	100	24.51 N	114.41 E
Chengmai	110	19.48 N	110.02 E
Chengmao	106	31.10 N	120.53 E
Chengpu	100	25.46 N	118.48 E
Chengqian	98	35.21 N	117.21 E
Chengqianwei	100	28.09 N	116.13 E
Chengshan Jiao ›	98	37.24 N	122.42 E
Chengteh → Chengde	105	40.58 N	117.53 E
Chengtu → Chengdu	107	30.39 N	104.04 E
Ch'engtzuliao	269d	25.06 N	121.27 E
Chengwu	98	34.58 N	115.52 E
Chengxian	102	33.43 N	105.41 E
Chengxi Hu ⊜	100	32.24 N	116.15 E
Chengyang, Zhg.	98	36.18 N	120.22 E
Chengyang, Zhg.	100	29.59 N	119.44 E
Chengzi, Zhg.	98	41.57 N	117.16 E
Chengzi, Zhg.	105	39.58 N	116.02 E
Chengzitan	98	39.30 N	122.30 E
Ch'enhsien → Chenxian	100	25.48 N	112.59 E
Chen Hu ⊜	100	30.29 N	113.22 E
Chenies	260	51.41 N	0.32 W
Chenil, Lac ⊜	186	51.51 N	59.41 W
Cheniménil	58	48.08 N	6.36 E
Chenji	100	33.50 N	119.11 E
Chenjiachang, Zhg.	107	29.35 N	104.52 E
Chenjiachang, Zhg.	107	30.04 N	105.15 E
Chenjiagang	98	34.25 N	119.49 E
Chenjiahe	102	29.28 N	109.59 E
Chenjiaji	100	30.42 N	114.21 E
Chenjiapang	106	31.14 N	119.42 E
Chenjiapu	105	40.31 N	115.37 E
Chenjiaqiao	106	31.27 N	121.16 E
Chenjiatun, Zhg.	104	42.20 N	124.06 E
Chenjiatun, Zhg.	104	40.57 N	121.01 E
Chenjiawan	106	31.02 N	120.35 E
Chenjiaxiang	100	31.29 N	113.45 E
Chenjiazhen	106	31.30 N	121.48 E
Chenjiazui	105	39.17 N	116.59 E
Chenkeng	100	25.06 N	116.15 E
Chenlingjiao	106	30.23 N	118.47 E
Chenliu	98	34.43 N	114.31 E
Chenlong	269b	31.17 N	121.25 E
Chennevières	261	49.00 N	2.07 E
Chennevières-lès-Lovres	261	49.03 N	2.33 E
Chenoa	216	40.44 N	88.43 W
Chenonceaux	50	47.20 N	1.04 E
Chenonceaux, Château de ⊥	50	47.20 N	1.04 E
Chenôve	58	47.17 N	5.00 E
Chenoweth	224	45.37 N	121.13 W
Chenqiao	98	34.58 N	114.32 E
Chenquingqiao	89	49.08 N	127.16 E
Chenshanzhuang	105	39.43 N	117.30 E
Chenshichang	107	29.17 N	106.00 E
Chens-sur-Léman	58	46.20 N	6.16 E
Chentang	102	23.54 N	110.39 E
Chentejn nuruu ⋏	88	48.30 N	108.30 E
Chentij	88	48.05 N	109.45 E
Chentij □[4]	88	48.00 N	110.30 E
Chenxi	102	27.51 N	109.59 E
Chenxian	100	25.48 N	112.59 E
Chenxiangtun	104	41.36 N	123.30 E
Chenyang, Zhg.	100	33.47 N	120.10 E
Chenyang → Shenyang, Zhg.	104	41.48 N	123.27 E
Cheonan → Ch'ŏnan	98	36.48 N	127.09 E
Cheongju → Ch'ŏngju	98	36.39 N	127.31 E
Chepachet	207	41.54 N	71.40 W
Chepaúa	152	12.58 S	22.43 E
Chepén	248	7.13 S	79.27 W
Chépénéhé	175f	20.47 S	167.09 E
Chepes	252	31.21 S	66.36 W
Chepkotet ∧	154	1.15 N	35.26 E
Chepo	246	9.10 N	79.06 W
Chepstow	42	51.39 N	2.41 W
Cheptainville	261	48.33 N	2.16 E
Cher □[5]	32	47.05 N	2.30 E
Cher ≃	32	47.21 N	0.29 E
Cheradi, Isole II	68	40.27 N	17.10 E
Cherain	56	50.11 N	5.52 E
Cherán	234	19.41 N	101.57 W
Chéran ≃	62	45.53 N	5.56 E
Cheranchi	150	12.40 N	7.42 E
Cherangany Hills ⋏[2]	154	1.15 N	35.27 E
Cherasco	62	44.39 N	7.51 E
Cherãt	123	33.49 N	71.53 E
Cheraw	192	34.41 N	79.53 W
Cheraw State Park ♠	192	34.36 N	79.55 W
Cherbaniani Reef ✦[2]	122	12.18 N	71.53 E
Cherbourg	32	49.39 N	1.39 W
Cherchell	148	36.36 N	2.12 E
Cheremkhovo → Čeremchovo	88	53.09 N	103.05 E
Chérence	261	49.05 N	1.41 E
Chereponi	150	10.09 N	0.17 E
Cherepovets → Čerepovec	76	59.08 N	37.54 E
Chergui, Chott ech ⊜	148	34.21 N	0.30 E
Chergui, Île I	148	34.44 N	11.14 E
Chergui, Zahrez ⊜	148	35.12 N	3.32 E
Cheribon → Cirebon	115a	6.44 S	108.34 E
Cherio ≃	64	45.46 N	9.55 E
Cherita, Sebkhet ⊜	36	35.21 N	10.19 E
Cheriton	208	37.17 N	75.58 W
Cheriyam Island I	122	10.09 N	73.40 E
Cherkassy → Čerkassy	78	49.26 N	32.04 E
Cherkessk → Čerkessk	84	44.14 N	42.04 E
Cherlen → Kerulen ≃	90	48.48 N	117.00 E
Chermside	171a	27.23 S	153.02 E
Chernigov → Černigov	78	51.30 N	31.18 E
Chernobyl → Černobyl'	78	51.16 N	30.14 E
Chernofski	180	53.24 N	167.33 W
Chernogorsk → Černogorsk	86	53.49 N	91.18 E
Chernovtsy → Černovcy	78	48.18 N	25.56 E
Chero ≃	62	44.58 N	9.51 E
Cherokee, Al., U.S.	194	34.45 N	87.58 W
Cherokee, Ia., U.S.	198	42.44 N	95.33 W
Cherokee, Ks., U.S.	198	37.20 N	94.48 W
Cherokee, Ok., U.S.	196	36.45 N	98.21 W
Cherokee, Tx., U.S.	196	30.59 N	98.43 W
Cherokee □[6]	222	31.48 N	95.10 W
Cherokee, Lake ⊜[1]	222	32.21 N	94.39 W
Cherokee Canal ≋	226	39.18 N	121.55 W
Cherokee Lake ⊜[1]	192	36.16 N	83.20 W
Cherokee Point ›	192	26.16 N	77.03 W
Cherokee Ranch	208	40.25 N	75.55 W
Cherokees, Lake O' The ⊜[1]	194	36.39 N	94.49 W
Cherokee Sound	238	26.17 N	77.04 W
Cherokee Village	194	36.17 N	91.30 W
Chéroy	50	48.12 N	3.00 E
Cherpuči	89	53.01 N	138.52 E
Cherquenco	252	38.41 S	72.00 W
Cherrabun	162	18.29 S	125.19 E
Cherrapunji	120	25.18 N	91.42 E
Cherry Brook ≃, Ma., U.S.	283	42.23 N	71.17 W
Cherry Brook ≃, N.J., U.S.	276	41.01 N	74.00 W
Cherry City	279b	40.29 N	79.58 W
Cherry Creek, B.C., Can.	224	49.17 N	124.47 W
Cherry Creek, N.Y., U.S.	214	42.17 N	79.06 W
Cherry Creek ≃, Az., U.S.	200	33.41 N	110.49 W
Cherry Creek ≃, Ca., U.S.	226	37.53 N	119.58 W
Cherry Creek ≃, Co., U.S.	198	39.45 N	105.01 W
Cherry Creek ≃, Mt., U.S.	198	46.48 N	105.15 W
Cherry Creek ≃, N.D., U.S.	198	47.41 N	103.02 W
Cherry Creek ≃, S.D., U.S.	198	44.36 N	101.30 W
Cherry Creek ≃, Tx., U.S.	196	31.13 N	103.34 W
Cherry Creek, East Fork ≃	226	38.06 N	119.47 W
Cherry Creek, West Fork ≃	226	38.04 N	119.54 W
Cherry Fork	218	38.53 N	83.37 W
Cherry Grove, N.Y., U.S.	210	40.39 N	73.06 W
Cherry Grove, Or., U.S.	224	45.26 N	123.14 W
Cherry Hill, Il., U.S.	278	41.32 N	88.02 W
Cherry Hill, N.J., U.S.	208	39.56 N	75.01 W
Cherry Hill ◆[8]	284b	39.15 N	76.38 W
Cherry Hill Mall ◆[9]	285	39.56 N	75.02 W
Cherry Island I	285	39.43 N	75.31 W
Cherry Lake ⊜[1]	226	38.00 N	119.54 W
Cherryland	226	37.41 N	122.06 W
Cherry Lane	279b	40.34 N	79.33 W
Cherryplain	210	42.38 N	73.22 W
Cherry Point Marine Corps Air Station ■	192	34.54 N	76.54 W
Cherryvale	198	37.16 N	95.33 W
Cherry Valley, Ar., U.S.	194	35.24 N	90.45 W
Cherry Valley, Ca., U.S.	228	33.57 N	116.53 W
Cherry Valley, Il., U.S.	216	42.14 N	88.56 W
Cherry Valley, Ma., U.S.	207	42.14 N	71.52 W
Cherry Valley, N.Y., U.S.	210	42.47 N	74.45 W
Cherry Valley, Pa., U.S.	214	41.10 N	79.48 W
Cherry Valley Creek ≃	210	42.35 N	74.56 W
Cherryville, N.C., U.S.	192	35.22 N	81.22 W
Cherryville, Pa., U.S.	208	40.45 N	75.33 W
Cherrywood	275b	43.52 N	79.08 W
Cherson	78	46.38 N	32.35 E
Chersonesskij, mys ›	78	44.35 N	33.23 E
Chertsey	260	51.24 N	0.30 W
Cherwell ≃	42	51.44 N	1.15 W
Chesaco Park	284b	39.19 N	76.30 W
Chesaning	190	43.11 N	84.06 W
Chesapeake	208	36.49 N	76.16 W
Chesapeake and Delaware Canal ≋	208	39.32 N	75.51 W
Chesapeake and Ohio Canal National Historical Park ♠	208	39.03 N	77.16 W
Chesapeake Bay c	208	38.40 N	76.25 W
Chesapeake Bay Bridge-Tunnel ◆[5]	208	37.00 N	76.02 W
Chesapeake Beach	208	38.41 N	76.32 W
Chesapeake City	208	39.31 N	75.48 W
Chesaw	182	48.56 N	119.03 W
Chesdin, Lake ⊜[1]	208	37.15 N	77.33 W
Cheseaux	58	46.35 N	6.36 E
Chesham	260	51.43 N	0.38 W
Chesham Bois	260	51.41 N	0.37 W
Cheshire, Ct., U.S.	207	41.29 N	72.54 W
Cheshire, Ma., U.S.	207	42.33 N	73.09 W
Cheshire, N.Y., U.S.	210	42.49 N	77.20 W
Cheshire □[6], Eng., U.K.	44	53.23 N	2.30 W
Cheshire □[6], N.H., U.S.	207	42.50 N	72.15 W
Cheshire Plain ≡	44	53.17 N	2.40 W
Cheshire Reservoir ⊜[1]	207	42.32 N	73.11 W
Chesht-e Sharīf	128	34.21 N	63.44 E
Cheshunt	260	51.43 N	0.02 W
Chesil Beach ⩡[2]	42	50.38 N	2.33 W
Chesilhurst	285	39.43 N	74.52 W
Cheslatta Lake ⊜	182	53.44 N	125.18 W
Chesley	212	44.17 N	81.05 W
Chesnee	192	35.08 N	81.51 W
Chess ≃	260	51.38 N	0.27 W
Chessington ◆[8]	260	51.21 N	0.18 W
Chessy	261	48.53 N	2.46 E
Chest Creek ≃	214	40.53 N	78.44 W
Chester, Eng., U.K.	262	53.12 N	2.54 W
Chester, Ca., U.S.	204	40.18 N	121.13 W
Chester, Ct., U.S.	207	41.24 N	72.27 W
Chester, Il., U.S.	194	37.54 N	89.49 W
Chester, Md., U.S.	208	38.58 N	76.17 W
Chester, Ma., U.S.	207	42.16 N	72.58 W
Chester, Mt., U.S.	202	48.30 N	110.58 W
Chester, Ne., U.S.	198	40.00 N	97.37 W
Chester, N.J., U.S.	210	40.47 N	74.41 W
Chester, Ok., U.S.	196	36.12 N	98.55 W
Chester, Pa., U.S.	208	39.50 N	75.21 W
Chester, S.C., U.S.	192	34.42 N	81.12 W
Chester, Tx., U.S.	222	30.55 N	94.36 W
Chester, Vt., U.S.	188	43.15 N	72.35 W
Chester, Va., U.S.	208	37.21 N	77.26 W
Chester, W.V., U.S.	214	40.36 N	80.33 W
Chester □[6]	208	39.58 N	75.36 W
Chester □[8]	262	53.16 N	2.52 W
Chester ≃	208	39.00 N	76.10 W
Chester Basin	186	44.34 N	64.19 W
Chesterbrook	284c	38.55 N	77.09 W
Chester Brook ≃	283	42.23 N	71.14 W
Chesterbrook Woods	284c	38.56 N	77.08 W
Chester Creek ≃	208	39.50 N	75.22 W
Chester Creek, East Branch ≃	285	39.56 N	75.32 W
Chester Creek, West Branch ≃	285	39.54 N	75.27 W
Chesterfield, Eng., U.K.	44	53.15 N	1.25 W
Chesterfield, Ct., U.S.	207	41.24 N	72.11 W
Chesterfield, Il., U.S.	219	39.15 N	90.04 W
Chesterfield, In., U.S.	218	40.06 N	85.35 W
Chesterfield, Ma., U.S.	207	42.23 N	72.50 W
Chesterfield, S.C., U.S.	192	34.44 N	80.05 W
Chesterfield, Va., U.S.	192	37.22 N	77.30 W
Chesterfield □[6]	208	37.20 N	77.25 W
Chesterfield, Île I	157b	16.20 S	43.58 E
Chesterfield, Îles II	160	19.30 S	158.00 E
Chesterfield Inlet	176	63.21 N	90.42 W
Chesterfield Inlet c	176	63.25 N	90.45 W
Chester Heights	285	39.53 N	75.28 W
Chester Hill, Austl.	274a	33.53 S	151.00 E
Chesterhill, Oh., U.S.	188	39.29 N	81.51 W
Chester Hill, Pa., U.S.	214	40.53 N	78.14 W
Chester Island I	285	39.50 N	75.21 W
Chesterland	214	41.31 N	81.21 W
Chester-le-Street	44	54.52 N	1.34 W
Chester Morse Lake ⊜[1]	224	47.23 N	121.42 W
Chester Springs	285	40.06 N	75.37 W
Chesterton	216	41.36 N	87.03 W
Chesterton Range ⋏	166	25.30 S	147.27 E
Chestertown	208	39.12 N	76.04 W
Chesterville, On., Can.	212	45.06 N	75.14 W
Chesterville, Oh., U.S.	214	40.29 N	82.41 W
Chestnut	219	40.03 N	89.11 W
Chestnut Hill, Ma., U.S.	283	42.20 N	71.10 W
Chestnut Hill, Pa., U.S.	210	40.04 N	75.12 W
Chestnut Hill ◆[8]	285	40.04 N	75.13 W
Chestnut Hill ∧[2]	285	40.13 N	75.45 W
Chestnut Hill Estates	285	39.41 N	75.42 W
Chestnut Hill Reservoir ⊜[1]	283	42.20 N	71.10 W
Chestnut Ridge ∧	214	40.09 N	79.24 W
Chestnut Ridge Park ♠	284a	42.43 N	78.46 W
Chest Peak ∧	172	43.06 S	172.01 E
Chesu	120	30.31 N	82.37 E
Chesuncook Lake ⊜	188	46.00 N	69.20 W
Cheswick	214	40.32 N	79.47 W
Cheswold	208	39.13 N	75.35 W
Chet ≃	42	52.33 N	1.32 E
Cheta ≃	74	71.54 N	102.06 E
Chetaibi	36	37.04 N	7.23 E
Chetco ≃	202	42.03 N	124.16 W
Chetek	190	45.18 N	91.39 W
Chéticamp	186	46.38 N	61.01 W
Chet Iter, Oued V	148	21.39 N	2.30 E
Chetlat Island I	122	11.42 N	72.42 E
Chetopa	198	37.02 N	95.05 W
Chetput	122	12.28 N	79.21 E
Chetumal Bay c	232	18.20 N	88.05 W
Chetwynd	182	55.42 N	121.40 W
Cheung Chau I	271d	22.12 N	114.01 E
Cheung Shue Tan	271d	22.26 N	114.12 E
Chevak	180	61.39 N	165.17 W
Cheval-Blanc, Montagne du ⋏	62	44.07 N	6.26 E
Cheval Blanc, Pointe du ›	238	19.41 N	73.27 W
Chevannes	261	48.32 N	2.27 E
Chevelon Creek ≃	200	34.57 N	110.31 W
Chevening	260	51.18 N	0.08 E
Chevenoz	58	46.20 N	6.39 E
Cheverly	284c	38.55 N	76.54 W
Cheverny	50	47.30 N	1.28 E
Chevillon	58	48.32 N	5.08 E
Chevilly-Larue	261	48.46 N	2.21 E
Chevington Drift	44	55.17 N	1.36 W
Cheviot, N.Z.	172	42.49 S	173.16 E
Cheviot, Oh., U.S.	218	39.09 N	84.36 W
Cheviot Hills ⋏[2]	44	55.22 N	2.22 W
Chevreuse	50	48.42 N	2.03 E
Chèvreville	261	49.07 N	2.51 E
Chevril, Lac du ⊜	62	45.29 N	6.56 E
Chevry-Cossigny	261	48.43 N	2.40 E
Chevy Chase	284c	38.58 N	77.04 W
Chevy Chase Heights	214	40.36 N	79.08 W
Chevy Chase View	284c	39.01 N	77.05 W
Chewaucan ≃	202	42.30 N	120.18 W
Chew Bahir (Lake Stefanie) ⊜	144	4.40 N	36.50 E
Chewelah	202	48.16 N	117.42 W
Chew Magna	42	51.22 N	2.35 W
Chew Reservoir ⊜[1]	262	53.31 N	1.56 W
Chews Landing	285	39.50 N	75.04 W
Chewton, Austl.	169	37.05 S	144.16 E
Chewton, Pa., U.S.	214	40.53 N	80.20 W
Chexbres	58	46.29 N	6.47 E
Cheyenne, Ok., U.S.	196	35.36 N	99.40 W
Cheyenne, Wy., U.S.	200	41.08 N	104.49 W
Cheyenne ≃	198	44.40 N	101.15 W
Cheyenne, Dry Fork ≃	198	43.25 N	105.23 W
Cheyenne River Indian Reservation ◆[4]	198	45.00 N	100.40 W
Cheyenne Wells	198	38.49 N	102.21 W
Cheyne Bay c	162	34.35 S	118.50 E
Cheyne Point ›	162	33.58 S	122.34 E
Cheyney	285	39.56 N	75.31 W
Cheyney University of Pennsylvania ⊍[2]	285	39.56 N	75.32 W
Chezhen	98	37.54 N	117.37 E
Chhab	123	33.14 N	71.54 E
Chhabra	124	24.40 N	76.50 E
Chhachhrauli	124	30.15 N	77.22 E
Chhajãrsi	272a	28.38 N	77.23 E
Chhalera Bãngar	272a	28.33 N	77.20 E
Chhanka	126	23.59 N	89.55 E
Chhãtak	120	25.02 N	91.40 E
Chhatarpur, India	124	24.23 N	84.11 E
Chhatarpur, India	124	24.55 N	79.36 E
Chhatarpur □[5]	124	24.55 N	79.35 E
Chhãtna	126	23.18 N	86.58 E
Chhattīsgarh ≡	122	21.15 N	82.00 E
Chhay Arêng ≃	110	11.31 N	103.25 E
Chhêb Kândal	110	13.45 N	105.24 E
Chheharta	123	31.38 N	74.48 E
Chhibrãmau	124	27.09 N	79.31 E
Chhinãmor	272b	22.48 N	88.18 E
Chhindwãra	124	22.04 N	78.56 E
Chhindwãra □[5]	124	22.00 N	78.50 E
Chhiruti	126	24.01 N	88.11 E
Chhitauni	124	27.09 N	83.58 E
Chhlong ≃	110	12.15 N	105.58 E
Chhota Bãisdia	126	22.00 N	90.27 E
Chhota-Chhindwãra	124	23.03 N	79.29 E
Chhota Udepur	120	22.19 N	74.01 E
Chhukha Dzong	124	27.09 N	89.36 E
Chi ≃, Thai	110	15.11 N	104.43 E
Chi ≃, Zhg.	100	32.51 N	117.59 E
Chía	246	4.52 N	74.04 W
Chiador	256	22.01 S	43.03 W
Chiador, Cachoeira do ʟ	256	22.03 S	43.02 W
Chiahsien	100	23.05 N	120.35 E
Chiahsing → Jiaxing	106	30.46 N	120.45 E
Chiai	100	23.29 N	120.27 E
Chialamberto	62	45.22 N	7.21 E
Chiali	100	23.10 N	120.10 E
Chiambala ≃	152	16.22 S	11.49 E
Chiampo	64	45.33 N	11.17 E
Chiampo ≃	64	45.20 N	11.16 E
Chiamussu → Jiamusi	89	46.50 N	130.21 E
Chian → Ji'an	100	27.07 N	114.58 E
Chiana, Val di V	66	43.15 N	11.50 E
Chianciano Terme	66	43.03 N	11.50 E
Chiang Dao	110	19.22 N	98.58 E
Chiange	152	15.45 S	13.48 E
Chiang Kham	110	19.32 N	100.18 E
Chiang Khan	110	17.52 N	101.36 E
Chiang Khian	110	19.37 N	100.00 E
Chiang Mai	110	18.47 N	98.59 E
Chiangmen → Jiangmen	100	22.35 N	113.05 E
Chiang Rai	110	19.54 N	99.50 E
Chiang Saen	110	20.16 N	100.05 E
Chiangtu → Yangzhou	100	32.24 N	119.26 E
Chiangyin → Jiangyin	106	31.55 N	120.16 E
Chiani ≃	66	42.52 N	12.14 E
Chianni	66	43.29 N	10.38 E
Chianti □[4]	66	43.22 N	11.23 E
Chianti ⋏[1]	66	43.25 N	11.20 E
Chianti, Monti del ⋏	66	43.32 N	11.25 E
Chiaohsi	100	24.49 N	121.46 E
Chiaohsien → Jiaoxian	98	36.18 N	119.58 E
Chiaopan	100	24.50 N	121.21 E
Chiaotso → Jiaozuo	102	35.15 N	113.13 E
Chiao-Tung Normal University ⊍[2]	269b	31.14 N	121.24 E
Chiapa	248	19.32 S	69.13 W

Symbol	English	Deutsch	Español	Français	Português
≃	River	Fluss	Río	Rivière	Rio
≋	Canal	Kanal	Canal	Canal	Canal
ʟ	Waterfall, Rapids	Wasserfall, Stromschnellen	Cascada, Rápidos	Chute d'eau, Rapides	Cascata, Rápidos
⩀	Strait	Meeresstrasse	Estrecho	Détroit	Estreito
c	Bay, Gulf	Bucht, Golf	Bahía, Golfo	Baie, Golfe	Baía, Golfo
⊜	Lake, Lakes	See, Seen	Lago, Lagos	Lac, Lacs	Lago, Lagos
≡	Swamp	Sumpf	Pantano	Marais	Pântano
✻	Ice Features, Glacier	Eis- und Gletscherformen	Accidentes Glaciales	Formes glaciaires	Acidentes glaciares
⊤	Other Hydrographic Features	Andere Hydrographische Objekte	Otros Elementos Hidrográficos	Autres données hydrographiques	Outros acidentes hidrográficos
✦	Submarine Features	Untermeerische Objekte	Accidentes Submarinos	Formes de relief sous-marin	Acidentes submarinos
□	Political Unit	Politische Einheit	Unidad Politica	Entité politique	Unidade política
⊍	Cultural Institution	Kulturelle Institution	Institución Cultural	Institution culturelle	Instituição cultural
⊥	Historical Site	Historische Stätte	Sitio Histórico	Site historique	Sitio histórico
♠	Recreational Site	Erholungs- und Ferienort	Sitio de Recreo	Centre de loisirs	Area de Lazer
⊠	Airport	Flughafen	Aeropuerto	Aéroport	Aeroporto
■	Military Installation	Militäranlage	Instalación Militar	Installation militaire	Instalação militar
◆	Miscellaneous	Verschiedenes	Misceláneo	Divers	Diversos

ENGLISH Name Page Lat.°' Long.°' / DEUTSCH Name Seite Breite°' Länge°' E = Ost

Chiapa de Corzo 234 16.42 N 93.00 W
Chiapaot'ai 100 24.11 N 121.00 E
Chiapas □3 232 16.30 N 92.30 W
Chiaramonte Gulfi 70 37.02 N 14.42 E
Chiaramonti 71 40.45 N 8.49 E
Chiaravalle 66 43.36 N 13.19 E
Chiaravalle Centrale 68 38.41 N 16.25 E
Chiareggio 64 46.19 N 9.47 E
Chiari 62 45.32 N 9.56 E
Chiaromonte 68 40.07 N 16.13 E
Chiasso 58 45.50 N 9.01 E
Chiautla de Tapia 234 18.17 N 98.36 W
Chiautzingo 234 19.12 N 98.28 W
Chiavari 62 44.19 N 9.19 E
Chiavenna 58 46.19 N 9.24 E
Chiawelo 273d 26.17 S 27.52 E
Chiba 94 35.36 N 140.07 E
Chiba □5 94 35.30 N 140.20 E
Chibabava 156 20.19 S 33.39 E
Chiba-kō c 268 35.35 N 140.06 E
Chibakou 100 29.36 N 113.01 E
Chibango 152 13.38 S 21.56 E
Chiba University ʊ2 268 35.38 N 140.06 E
Chibemba 152 15.45 S 14.05 E
Chibi 154 20.19 S 30.30 E
Chibia 152 15.11 S 13.41 E
Chibouet ≏ 206 45.47 N 72.52 W
Chibougamau 176 49.55 N 74.22 W
Chibuto 156 24.44 S 33.33 E
Chibuzhangchuhu ⊜ 120 33.25 N 90.15 E
Chibwe 154 14.12 S 28.31 E
Chica, Laguna ⊜ 234 20.06 N 96.40 W
Chicago, Il., U.S. 216 41.51 N 87.39 W
Chicago, Il., U.S. 278 41.51 N 87.39 W
Chicago, North Branch ≏ 216 41.53 N 87.38 W
Chicago, North Branch, West Fork ≏ 278 42.03 N 87.54 W
Chicago, South Branch ≏ 278 41.53 N 87.38 W
Chicago, University of ʊ2 278 41.47 N 87.36 W
Chicago Botanic Garden ♦ 278 42.09 N 87.47 W
Chicago Harbor c 278 41.53 N 87.37 W
Chicago Heights 216 41.30 N 87.38 W
Chicago-Hinsdale Airport ⊠ 278 41.46 N 87.56 W
Chicago Lawn ✈8 278 41.47 N 87.41 W
Chicago-Midway Airport ⊠ 216 41.47 N 87.45 W
Chicago-O'Hare International Airport ⊠ 278 41.59 N 87.54 W
Chicago Park 226 39.09 N 120.58 W
Chicago Portage National Historic Site ⊥ 278 41.48 N 87.49 W
Chicago Ridge 216 41.42 N 87.46 W
Chicago Sanitary and Ship Canal ≅ 216 41.32 N 88.05 W
Chicago Stadium ♦ 278 41.53 N 87.40 W
Chicama ≏ 248 7.56 S 79.17 W
Chicamacomico ≏ 208 38.26 N 75.59 W
Chicamba, Barragem de ✈6 156 19.08 S 33.00 E
Chicapa ≏ 152 6.26 S 20.47 E
Chic-Chocs, Monts ⋏ 186 48.55 N 66.00 W
Chichagof Island I 180 57.30 N 135.30 W
Chichas, Cordillera de ⋏ 248 20.30 S 66.30 W
Chichāwatni 123 30.32 N 72.42 E
Chiché ≏ 250 8.15 S 53.30 W
Chicheng 98 40.54 N 115.46 E
Chichén Itzá 232 20.40 N 88.34 W
Chichén Itzá ⊥ 232 20.40 N 88.35 W
Chichester, Eng., U.K. 42 50.50 N 0.48 W
Chichester, N.Y., U.S. 210 42.06 N 74.19 W
Chichester Range ⋏ 162 22.00 S 118.50 E
Chichester Range National Park ♦ 162 21.25 S 117.20 E
Chichi 100 23.50 N 120.47 E
Chichibu 94 35.59 N 139.05 E
Chichibu-Tama-kokuritsu-kōen ♦ 94 35.52 N 139.00 E
Chichica 236 8.22 N 81.40 W
Chichicastenango 236 14.56 N 91.07 W
Chichigalpa 236 12.34 N 87.02 W
Chichigapa 234 17.47 N 94.25 W
Ch'ich'ihaerh → Qiqihar 89 47.19 N 123.55 E
Chichihualco 234 17.41 N 99.39 W
Chichijima-rettō II 14 27.06 N 142.12 E
Chichimilá 232 20.37 N 88.13 W
Chichiriviche 246 10.56 N 68.16 W
Chicholi 124 22.01 N 77.40 E
Chichra 126 22.19 N 86.53 E
Chicicatiapa ≏ 234 18.18 N 96.19 W
Chickahominy ≏ 208 37.14 N 76.53 W
Chickaloon 180 61.48 N 148.28 W
Chickamauga 192 34.52 N 85.17 W
Chickamauga Lake ⊜1 192 35.22 N 85.02 W
Chickamin ≏ 182 55.47 N 130.58 W
Chickasaw, Al., U.S. 194 30.45 N 88.04 W
Chickasaw, Oh., U.S. 216 40.26 N 84.30 W
Chickasaw Bogue ≏ 194 32.17 N 87.55 W
Chickasawhatchie Creek ≏ 192 31.19 N 84.29 W
Chickasawhay ≏ 194 31.00 N 88.45 W
Chickasaw National Recreation Area ♦ 196 34.25 N 96.59 W
Chickasha 196 35.03 N 97.56 W
Chicken 180 64.04 N 141.56 W
Chicken Brook ≏ 283 42.08 N 71.25 W
Chickerell 42 50.37 N 2.30 W
Chickies Creek ≏ 208 40.03 N 76.32 W
Chiclana de la Frontera 34 36.25 N 6.08 W
Chiclayo 248 6.46 S 79.51 W
Chico, Ca., U.S. 204 39.43 N 121.50 W
Chico, Tx., U.S. 196 33.17 N 97.47 W
Chico, Wa., U.S. 224 47.36 N 122.42 W
Chico ≏, Arg. 254 43.48 S 66.25 W
Chico ≏, Arg. 254 42.25 S 70.30 W
Chico ≏, Arg. 254 49.56 S 68.32 W
Chico ≏, Pan. 236 8.20 N 80.28 W
Chico ≏, Pil. 116 17.58 N 121.36 E
Chico ≏, S.A. 254 51.40 S 69.09 W
Chico, Arroyo ≏ 286b 23.02 N 82.17 W
Chicoasen, Presa ⊜1 234 16.55 N 93.05 W
Chicobi, Lac ⊜ 190 48.53 N 78.30 W
Chico Creek ≏ 198 38.15 N 104.20 W
Chicolete Creek ≏ 222 29.05 N 96.49 W
Chicomba 152 14.09 S 14.57 E
Chicomo 156 24.31 S 34.17 E
Chicomuselo 232 15.46 N 92.16 W
Chiconautla, Cerro ⋏ 286a 19.39 N 98.58 W
Chicono 154 12.56 S 35.43 E
Chicontepec 234 20.58 N 98.10 W
Chicopee, Ga., U.S. 192 34.15 N 83.50 W
Chicopee, Ma., U.S. 207 42.08 N 72.36 W
Chicopee ≏ 207 42.09 N 72.37 W
Chicora 214 40.56 N 79.44 W
Chicorato 232 26.02 N 107.54 W
Chicot, Lake ⊜ 194 33.20 N 91.14 W
Chicot, Rivière du ≏ 275a 45.35 N 73.51 W
Chicot State Park ♦ 194 30.47 N 92.19 W
Chicoutimi 186 48.26 N 71.04 W
Chicoutimi ≏ 186 48.26 N 71.05 W
Chicoutimi, Réserve ♦ 186 48.30 N 70.15 W
Chicualoque 234 20.23 N 97.39 W
Chicuma 152 13.23 S 14.51 E
Chicxulub 232 21.08 N 89.31 W
Chidambaram 122 11.24 N 79.42 E
Chiddingfold 42 51.06 N 0.37 W
Chiddingstone Causeway 260 51.12 N 0.10 E
Chidenguele 156 24.54 S 34.13 E
Chidlow 168a 31.52 S 116.14 E
Chi-do I 98 35.04 N 126.13 E
Chidu 120 31.50 N 94.30 E
Chief 222 32.33 N 96.10 W
Chief Justice William Cushing Memorial State Park ♦ 283 42.10 N 70.45 W
Chiefland 192 29.28 N 82.51 W
Chiefs Point ≻ 212 44.42 N 81.18 W
Chief's Point Indian Reserve ✈4 212 44.41 N 81.17 W
Chiehyang → Jieyang 100 23.35 N 116.21 E
Chiemgauer Alpen ⋏ 64 47.40 N 12.30 E
Chiemsee ⊜ 64 47.54 N 12.29 E
Chien, Bayou de ≏ 194 36.35 N 89.11 W
Chienes (Kiens) 64 46.48 N 11.50 E
Chiengi 154 8.39 S 29.10 E
Chiengo 152 13.20 S 21.55 E
Chiens, Rivière aux ≏ 275a 45.39 N 73.46 W
Chienti ≏ 66 43.18 N 13.45 E
Chieri 62 45.01 N 7.49 E
Chiers ≏ 56 49.39 N 5.00 E
Chiesa in Valmalenco 64 46.16 N 9.51 E
Chiese ≏ 64 45.08 N 10.25 E
Chieti 66 42.21 N 14.10 E
Chieti □4 66 42.07 N 14.21 E
Chietla 234 18.31 N 98.35 W
Chieuti 68 41.51 N 15.10 E
Chieveley 42 51.27 N 1.19 W
Chièvres 50 50.35 N 3.48 E
Chifeng (Ulanhad) 98 42.18 N 119.00 E
Chigasaki 94 35.19 N 139.24 E
Chiginagak, Mount ⋀ 180 57.08 N 156.59 W
Chigmit Mountains ⋏ 180 60.00 N 153.00 W
Chignahuapan 234 19.50 N 98.02 W
Chignall Saint James 260 51.46 N 0.25 E
Chignall Smealy 260 51.47 N 0.25 E
Chignecto, Cape ≻ 186 45.20 N 64.57 W
Chignecto Bay c 186 45.35 N 64.45 W
Chignik 180 56.18 N 158.23 W
Chignik Bay c 180 56.22 N 158.15 W
Chignik Lagoon 180 56.21 N 158.31 W
Chignik Lake 180 56.15 N 158.45 W
Chignolo Po 62 45.09 N 9.29 E
Chigombe ≏ 156 23.26 S 33.19 E
Chigorodó 246 7.41 N 76.42 W
Chigu 100 27.34 N 114.40 E
Chigubo 156 22.50 S 33.34 E
Chigwell 260 51.38 N 0.05 E
Chigwell Row 260 51.37 N 0.07 E
Chigyŏng 98 39.51 N 127.26 E
Chihaya-akasaka 270 34.24 N 135.38 E
Chihaya Castle ⊥ 270 34.25 N 135.40 E
Chihe 100 32.32 N 117.58 E
Ch'ihfeng → Chifeng 98 42.18 N 119.00 E
Chihli, Gulf of → Bo Hai c 98 38.30 N 120.00 E
Chihpen 100 22.42 N 121.02 E
Ch'ihshang 100 23.07 N 121.12 E
Chihsi → Jixi 89 45.17 N 130.59 E
Ch'ihsing Shan ⋏, T'aiwan 100 25.10 N 121.33 E
Ch'ihsing Shan ⋏, T'aiwan 269d 25.10 N 121.33 E
Ch'ihsing Yen I 100 21.46 N 120.49 E
Chihtungtsun 100 22.44 N 120.14 E
Chihu 100 24.07 N 117.51 E
Chihuahua 232 28.38 N 106.05 W
Chihuahua □3 232 28.30 N 106.00 W
Chihuahuan Desert ✈2 16 35.00 N 106.00 W
Chii-san ⋀ 98 35.20 N 127.44 E
Chii-san Kukrip Kongwŏn ♦ 98 35.20 N 127.39 E
Chiitola 26 61.16 N 29.38 E
Chikaskia ≏ 196 36.37 N 97.15 W
Chik Ballāpur 122 13.28 N 77.44 E
Chikhli 122 20.21 N 76.15 E
Chikindzonot 232 20.20 N 88.29 W
Chikmagalūr 122 13.19 N 75.47 E
Chiknai ≏ 126 24.06 N 89.17 E
Chiknāyakanhalli 122 13.26 N 76.37 E
Chikoa 154 13.24 S 32.07 E
Chikodi 122 16.26 N 74.36 E
Chikou 100 30.44 N 117.32 E
Chikrēng ≏ 110 12.51 N 104.14 E
Ch'ik'u 100 23.08 N 120.07 E
Chikugo 96 33.12 N 130.30 E
Chikugo ≏ 92 33.09 N 130.21 E
Chikujō-kichi, Kōkū-jieitai- ■ 96 33.41 N 131.03 E
Chikuma ≏ 94 36.59 N 138.35 E
Chikuminuk Lake ⊜ 180 60.14 N 159.00 W
Chikura 94 34.57 N 139.57 E
Chikusa 96 35.09 N 134.26 E
Chikusa ≏ 96 34.44 N 134.22 E
Chikushino 96 33.29 N 130.31 E
Chikwawa 154 16.03 S 34.48 E
Chi-kyaw 110 20.17 N 93.54 E
Chikyu-misaki ≻ 92a 42.18 N 141.00 E
Chila, Ang. 152 12.04 S 14.29 E
Chila, Méx. 234 18.55 N 102.28 W
Chilacachapa 234 18.17 N 99.43 W
Chilakalūrupet 122 16.05 N 80.10 E
Chilako ≏ 182 53.54 N 122.59 W
Chilam 123 35.03 N 75.07 E
Chilanga 154 15.34 S 28.17 E
Chilanko Forks 182 52.06 N 124.10 W
Chilapa de Alvarez 234 17.36 N 99.10 W
Chilapa de Díaz 234 17.31 N 97.41 W
Chilās 123 35.26 N 74.05 E
Chilaw 122 7.34 N 79.47 E
Chilca 248 12.32 S 76.44 W
Chilca, Cordillera de ⋏ 248 15.30 S 71.50 W
Chilca, Punta ≻ 248 12.27 S 76.48 W
Chilchota 234 19.51 N 102.08 W
Chilcotin ≏ 182 51.45 N 122.24 W
Chilcott Island I 166 16.58 S 149.58 E
Childers 166 25.14 S 152.17 E
Childersburg 194 33.16 N 86.21 W
Childer Thornton 262 53.17 N 2.57 W
Childress 196 34.25 N 100.12 W
Childs 210 41.34 N 75.32 W
Chile □1 244 30.00 S 71.00 W
Chile, Hipódromo ♦ 286e 33.24 S 70.41 W
Chile, Universidad de ʊ2 286e 33.27 S 70.40 W
Chile Basin ✈1 18 33.00 S 80.00 W
Chile Chico 254 46.33 S 71.44 W
Chilecito, Arg. 252 29.10 S 67.30 W
Chilecito, Arg. 252 33.53 S 69.03 W
Chilengue, Serra do ⋏ 152 13.10 S 15.18 E
Chileno, Arroyo ≏, Ur. 258 33.55 S 58.08 W
Chileno, Arroyo ≏, Ur. 288 34.22 S 57.54 W
Chile Rise ✈3 18 40.00 S 90.00 W
Chilete 248 7.14 S 78.51 W
Chilham 42 51.15 N 0.57 E
Chilhowie 192 36.47 N 81.40 W
Chili 216 40.52 N 86.02 W
Chili → Chile □1 244 30.00 S 71.00 W
Chili ≏ 248 16.23 S 71.46 W
Chili, Ouadi V 146 16.44 N 20.53 E
Chilia, Braţul ≏1 78 45.18 N 29.40 E
Chili Center 210 43.05 N 77.44 W
Chililabombwe (Bancroft) 154 12.18 S 27.43 E
Chilin → Jilin 89 43.51 N 126.33 E
Chilingchang 107 28.58 N 105.31 E
Chilivani 71 40.36 N 8.56 E
Chilka Lake ⊜ 122 19.45 N 85.25 E
Chilkat Pass ⋊ 180 59.43 N 136.35 W
Chilko ≏ 182 52.08 N 123.30 W
Chilko Lake ⊜ 182 51.20 N 124.05 W
Chilko Lake Indian Reserve ✈4 182 51.25 N 124.07 W
Chillagoe 166 17.09 S 144.32 E
Chillán 252 36.36 S 72.07 W
Chillar 252 37.18 S 59.59 W
Chilla Saroda ✈8 272a 28.36 N 77.18 E
Chillicothe, Il., U.S. 190 40.55 N 89.29 W
Chillicothe, Mo., U.S. 194 39.47 N 93.33 W
Chillicothe, Oh., U.S. 218 39.19 N 82.58 W
Chillicothe, Tx., U.S. 196 34.15 N 99.30 W
Chilliwack 224 49.10 N 121.57 W
Chilliwack ≏ 224 49.05 N 121.57 W
Chilliwack Lake ⊜ 224 49.03 N 121.25 W
Chillón 286d 11.55 S 77.05 W
Chillón ≏ 248 11.57 S 77.09 W
Chillon, Château de ⊥ 58 46.25 N 6.56 E
Chillum 284c 38.58 N 76.59 W
Chilly 84 39.25 N 49.05 E
Chilly-Mazarin 261 48.42 N 2.19 E
Chilmāri 124 25.33 N 89.43 E
Chilmark 207 41.20 N 70.44 W
Chilo 218 38.48 N 84.08 W
Chiloane, Ilha I 156 20.40 S 34.55 E
Chiloé, Isla de I 254 42.30 S 73.55 W
Chilok 88 51.21 N 110.28 E
Chilok ≏ 88 51.19 N 106.59 E
Chilōn 232 17.14 N 92.25 W
Chilonga 154 12.03 S 31.21 E
Chilongo 152 13.55 S 16.35 E
Chiloquin 202 42.34 N 121.51 W
Chilovo 76 57.46 N 29.23 E
Chilpancingo [de los Bravos] 234 17.33 N 99.30 W
Chilpi 124 22.15 N 81.33 E
Chilston Park ♦ 260 51.12 N 0.42 E
Chiltern □8 260 51.40 N 0.37 W
Chiltern Hills ⋏2 42 51.42 N 0.48 W
Chilton, Eng., U.K. 44 54.39 N 1.33 W
Chilton, Tx., U.S. 222 31.16 N 97.03 W
Chilton, Wi., U.S. 190 44.01 N 88.09 W
Chiluage 152 9.30 S 21.47 E
Chilubula Mission 154 10.09 S 31.00 E
Chilumba 154 10.28 S 34.12 E
Chilung 100 25.08 N 121.44 E
Chilung 269d 25.07 N 121.27 E
Chilung Kang c 269d 25.09 N 121.45 E
Chilung Shih □7 269d 25.08 N 121.45 E
Chiluvya 154 12.18 S 34.01 E
Chilwa, Lake ⊜ 154 15.12 S 35.50 E
Chilwell 169 38.10 S 144.21 E
Chimaco 152 15.12 S 21.56 E
Chimacum 224 48.00 N 122.46 W
Chimacum Creek ≏ 224 48.03 N 122.45 W
Chimakela 152 15.24 S 16.58 E
Chimalhuacán □7 286a 19.24 N 99.00 W
Chimaltenango 236 14.40 N 90.49 W
Chimaltenango □5 236 14.40 N 90.55 W
Chimaltitán 234 21.46 N 103.50 W
Chimán 246 8.42 N 78.37 W
Chimanimani National Park ♦ 154 19.48 S 33.56 E
Chimay 50 50.03 N 4.19 E
Chimbarongo 252 34.42 S 71.03 W
Chimbas 252 31.29 S 68.32 W
Chimborazo □4 246 2.00 S 78.48 W
Chimborazo ⋀1 246 1.28 S 78.48 W
Chimbote 248 9.05 S 78.36 W
Chimbu □5 164 6.05 S 145.00 E
Chimbua 152 16.32 S 15.08 E
Ch'imei Yü I 100 23.13 N 119.26 E
Chimichagua 246 9.15 N 73.49 W
Chimkent → Čimkent 85 42.18 N 69.36 E
Chimki 82 55.54 N 37.26 E
Chimki-Chovrino ✈8 265b 55.51 N 37.30 E
Chimkinskoje vodochranilišče ⊜1 265b 55.51 N 37.28 E
Chimney Reservoir ⊜1 204 41.25 N 117.10 W
Chimney Rock National Historic Site ♦ 198 41.39 N 103.20 W
Chimoio 156 19.08 S 33.29 E
Chimon Island I 276 41.04 N 73.23 W
Chimpay 252 39.10 S 66.09 W
Chimpembe 154 9.31 S 29.33 E
Chimpiro ≏ 154 17.32 S 35.29 E
Chin □8 110 22.00 N 93.30 E
China, Méx. 232 25.42 N 99.14 W
Chinā, Nihon 174m 26.24 N 127.46 E
China (Zhongguo) □1 90 35.00 N 105.00 E
China, Tanjong ≻ 271c 1.14 N 103.51 E
Chinácota 246 7.37 N 72.36 W
China Grove 192 35.34 N 80.34 W
China Lake ⊜ 204 35.46 N 117.39 W
China Lake Naval Weapons Center ■ 204 35.35 N 117.10 W
Chinameca 236 13.30 N 88.21 W
China Meridional, Mar de → South China Sea ⊤2 108 10.00 N 113.00 E
Chinan, Taehan 98 35.48 N 127.25 E
Chinan → Jinan, Zhg. 98 36.40 N 116.57 E
Chinandega 236 12.37 N 87.09 W
Chinandega □5 236 12.45 N 87.05 W
China Spring 222 31.39 N 97.18 W
Chinati Peak ⋀ 196 29.57 N 104.29 W
Chinatown ✈8 282 37.48 N 122.26 W
Chinchaga ≏ 176 58.50 N 118.20 W
Chincheros 248 13.27 S 73.44 W
Chinchiang → Quanzhou 100 24.54 N 118.35 E
Chinchilla, Austl. 166 26.45 S 150.38 E
Chinchilla, Pa., U.S. 210 41.28 N 75.41 W
Chinchiná 246 4.58 N 75.36 W
Chincholi 272c 19.10 N 73.08 E
Chinchón, Esp. 34 40.08 N 3.25 W
Chinch'ŏn, Taehan 98 36.52 N 127.26 E
Chinchorro, Banco ✈4 232 18.35 N 87.22 W
Chinchou → Jinzhou 104 41.07 N 121.08 E
Chincilla de Monte Aragón 34 38.55 N 1.43 W
Chincolco 252 32.13 S 70.50 W
Chincoteague 208 37.55 N 75.22 W
Chincoteague Bay c 208 38.06 N 75.15 W
Chincoteague Inlet c 208 37.53 N 75.25 W
Chinde 156 18.37 S 36.24 E
Chindo 98 34.28 N 126.15 E
Chin-do I 98 34.25 N 126.15 E
Chindong 98 35.07 N 128.29 E
Chindwin ≏ 110 21.26 N 95.15 E
Chine (la République populaire de) → China □1, Asia 90 35.00 N 105.00 E
Chine (nationaliste) → Taiwan □1, Asia 100 23.30 N 121.00 E
Chinen 174m 26.09 N 127.49 E
Chineni 123 33.02 N 75.17 E
Chine Orientale, Mer de → East China Sea ⊤2 90 30.00 N 126.00 E
Chinese Camp 226 37.52 N 120.26 W
Chinese Cemetery ✈ 269f 14.38 N 120.59 E
Chinese University ʊ2 271d 22.26 N 114.12 E
Chingamba 152 15.49 S 18.20 E
Chingansk 89 49.07 N 131.11 E
Chingarora Creek ≏ 276 40.27 N 74.12 W
Ch'ingchiang → Qingjiang 100 33.35 N 119.02 E
Chingford ✈8 260 51.38 N 0.01 E
Chingleput 122 12.42 N 79.59 E
Chingmei ✈8 269d 24.59 N 121.32 E
Chingola 154 12.32 S 27.52 E
Chingoni 157a 12.48 S 45.08 E
Chingoroi 152 13.37 S 14.01 E
Chingshih → Jinshi 102 29.39 N 111.52 E
Ch'ingtao → Qingdao 98 36.06 N 120.19 E
Chingtechen → Jingdezhen 100 29.16 N 117.11 E
Ch'ingt'ung 269d 25.02 N 121.43 E
Chinguar 152 12.36 S 16.20 E
Chinguetti 150 20.27 N 12.22 W
Chingune 156 20.38 S 34.55 E
Chinhae 98 35.09 N 128.40 E
Chinhae-man c 98 35.01 N 128.34 E
Chin Hills ⋏2 108 22.30 N 93.30 E
Chinhoyi 154 17.22 S 30.12 E
Chinhsien → Jinxian 98 39.04 N 121.40 E
Chinhua → Jinhua 100 29.07 N 119.39 E
Ch'inhuangtao → Qinhuangdao 98 39.56 N 119.36 E
Chīnī 120 31.32 N 78.15 E
Chiniak, Cape ≻ 180 57.36 N 152.08 W
Chining → Jining, Zhg. 98 35.25 N 116.36 E
Chining → Jining, Zhg. 102 40.57 N 113.02 E
Chiniot 123 31.43 N 72.59 E
Chinit ≏ 110 12.55 N 105.35 E
Chinitna Point ≻ 180 59.43 N 153.02 W
Chinitos 232 25.01 N 107.54 W
Chiniziua 156 19.00 S 35.09 E
Chinjan 120 30.34 N 67.58 E
Chinju 98 35.11 N 128.05 E
Chinkiang → Zhenjiang 106 32.13 N 119.26 E
Chinko ≏ 136 4.50 N 23.53 E
Chinkuashih 100 25.07 N 121.51 E
Chin Lakes ⊜ 182 49.37 N 112.13 W
Chinle 200 36.09 N 109.33 W
Chinle Creek ≏ 200 37.12 N 109.43 W
Chinle Wash V 200 36.54 N 109.45 W
Chinley 262 53.20 N 1.56 W
Chinley Churn ⋀2 262 53.21 N 1.57 W
Chinmen 100 24.27 N 118.21 E
Chinmen Tao I 100 24.27 N 118.23 E
Chinnampo → Namp'o 98 38.45 N 125.23 E
Chinnor 42 51.43 N 0.56 W
Chino, Nihon 94 35.59 N 138.09 E
Chino, Ca., U.S. 228 34.00 N 117.41 W
Chino Airport ⊠ 280 33.59 N 117.38 W
Chino Creek ≏ 280 33.53 N 117.38 W
Chino Hills ⋏2 280 33.56 N 117.45 W
Chinon 50 47.10 N 0.15 E
Chinook, Ab., Can. 184 51.27 N 110.56 W
Chinook, Mt., U.S. 202 48.35 N 109.13 W
Chinook, Wa., U.S. 224 46.16 N 123.56 W
Chinook Cove 182 51.14 N 120.10 W
Chino Valley 200 34.45 N 112.27 W
Chinowths Corner 226 35.20 N 119.11 W
Chinpāi 126 23.50 N 87.28 E
Chinquapin 192 34.49 N 77.49 W
Chinsali 154 10.34 S 32.03 E
Chinshan 100 25.13 N 121.38 E
Chinshui 100 24.36 N 120.53 E
Chintāmani 122 13.24 N 78.04 E
Chintembwe 154 13.25 S 33.59 E
Chintheche 154 11.52 S 34.09 E
Chinú 246 9.06 N 75.24 W
Chinunje 154 11.19 S 37.19 E
Chinwangtao → Qinhuangdao 98 39.56 N 119.36 E
Chio 56 49.44 N 5.20 E
Chinyama Litapi 152 13.31 S 22.21 E
Chioco 154 16.25 S 32.50 E
Chioggia 64 45.13 N 12.17 E
Chiomonte 62 45.07 N 6.59 E
Chios → Khíos 38 38.22 N 26.08 E
Chios → Khíos I 38 38.22 N 26.00 E
Chipao 248 14.15 S 73.57 W
Chipata (Fort Jameson) 154 13.39 S 32.40 E
Chipehua, Bahía c 234 16.03 N 95.23 W
Chipei Tao I 100 23.45 N 119.37 E
Chipera 154 15.28 S 32.30 E
Chiperone ⋀ 154 16.28 S 35.12 E
Chipili 154 10.44 S 29.04 E
Chiping 98 36.37 N 116.16 E
Chipinge 154 20.12 S 32.38 E
Chip Lake ⊜ 182 53.40 N 115.20 W
Chipley 194 30.46 N 85.32 W
Chiplūn 122 17.32 N 73.31 E
Chipman 186 46.11 N 65.53 W
Chipogolo 154 6.52 S 36.02 E
Chipoka 154 14.00 S 34.31 E
Chipola ≏ 192 30.01 N 85.05 W
Chippawa ✈8 284a 43.04 N 79.03 W
Chippawa Channel ≏1 284a 43.04 N 79.01 W
Chippego Lake ⊜ 212 44.34 N 76.49 W
Chippenham 42 51.28 N 2.07 W
Chipperfield 260 51.42 N 0.29 W
Chippewa ≏, Mi., U.S. 190 43.35 N 84.17 W
Chippewa ≏, Mn., U.S. 198 44.56 N 95.44 W
Chippewa ≏, Wi., U.S. 190 44.25 N 92.10 W
Chippewa, East Branch ≏ 198 45.20 N 95.36 W
Chippewa, East Fork ≏ 190 45.53 N 91.05 W
Chippewa, Lake ⊜ 190 45.56 N 91.13 W
Chippewa Bay c 212 44.27 N 75.47 W
Chippewa Creek ≏ 212 44.27 N 75.46 W
Chippewa Falls 190 44.56 N 91.23 W
Chippewa Lake 214 41.04 N 81.54 W
Chippewanuck Creek ≏ 216 41.07 N 86.12 W
Chipping Campden 42 52.03 N 1.46 W
Chipping Norton 42 51.56 N 1.32 W
Chipping Ongar 260 51.43 N 0.15 E
Chipping Sodbury 42 51.33 N 2.24 W
Chippis 58 46.17 N 7.33 E
Chippokes Plantation State Park ♦ 208 37.08 N 76.44 W
Chipps Island I 282 38.03 N 121.55 W
Chipre → Cyprus □1 130 35.00 N 33.00 E
Chipstead, Eng., U.K. 260 51.17 N 0.09 E
Chipstead, Eng., U.K. 260 51.18 N 0.10 W
Chipuriro 154 16.39 S 30.42 E
Chiquelequele 152 16.40 S 19.06 E
Chiquián 248 10.09 S 77.11 W
Chiquihuitlán de Juárez 234 17.59 N 96.48 W
Chiquimula 236 14.48 N 89.33 W
Chiquimula □5 236 14.40 N 89.25 W
Chiquimulilla 236 14.05 N 90.23 W
Chiquinata, Bahía c 248 20.20 S 70.10 W
Chiquinquirá 246 5.37 N 73.50 W
Chiquintirca 248 13.09 S 73.41 W
Chiquita 152 8.38 S 17.05 E
Chiquito Creek ≏ 226 37.20 N 119.20 W
Chira ≏ 246 4.54 S 81.08 W
Chira, Isla I 236 10.06 N 85.09 W
Chirad 272c 19.09 N 73.07 E
Chiradzulu 154 15.42 S 35.10 E
Chirāgh Delhi ✈8 272a 28.32 N 77.14 E
Chirāla 122 15.49 N 80.21 E
Chiramba 154 16.55 S 34.39 E
Chirape 156 21.18 S 33.33 E
Chirāwa 120 28.15 N 75.38 E
Chirchik → Čirčik 85 41.29 N 69.35 E
Chire (Shire) ≏ 154 17.42 S 35.19 E
Chiredzi 154 21.03 S 31.45 E
Chireno 194 31.30 N 94.21 W
Chirens 62 45.25 N 5.33 E
Chirfa 146 20.57 N 12.21 E
Chirgaon 124 25.35 N 78.49 E
Chiricahua Mountains ⋏ 200 31.50 N 109.15 W
Chiricahua National Monument ♦ 200 32.02 N 109.19 W
Chiricahua Peak ⋀ 200 31.52 N 109.20 W
Chiriguaná 246 9.22 N 73.36 W
Chirikof Island I 180 55.50 N 155.35 W
Chirilagua 236 13.13 N 88.08 W
Chirinos 248 5.16 S 78.52 W
Chiriquí 236 8.24 N 82.19 W
Chiriquí □4 236 8.30 N 82.00 W
Chiriquí ≏ 236 8.30 N 82.26 W
Chiriquí, Golfo de c 246 8.00 N 82.20 W
Chiriquí, Laguna de c 236 9.03 N 82.00 W
Chiriquí Grande 236 8.57 N 82.07 W
Chiriquí Viejo ≏ 236 8.20 N 82.41 W
Chirk 42 52.56 N 3.03 W
Chirki 126 24.03 N 86.09 E
Chirle 272c 18.56 N 73.02 E
Chirmiri Colliery 124 23.12 N 82.21 E
Chirnside 46 55.48 N 2.13 W
Chiromo 154 16.33 S 35.08 E
Chirovo 76 58.56 N 33.24 E
Chirripó ≏ 236 10.41 N 83.41 W
Chirripó, Cerro ⋀ 236 9.29 N 83.30 W
Chirsa 84 41.31 N 46.06 E
Chirundu 154 15.59 S 28.54 E
Chirvosti 265a 59.57 N 30.37 E
Chiryū 94 35.00 N 137.02 E
Chisago City 190 45.22 N 92.53 W
Chisamba 154 14.58 S 28.23 E
Chisana 180 62.09 N 142.10 W
Chisapani 124 27.34 N 85.08 E
Chisasibi 176 53.50 N 79.00 W
Chiscas 246 6.33 N 72.29 W
Chisec 236 15.49 N 90.17 W
Chiseldon 42 51.31 N 1.44 W
Chisenga 154 9.56 S 33.26 E
Chisep'o 98 34.50 N 128.42 E
Ch'ishan 100 22.53 N 120.28 E
Chishanji 98 36.56 N 122.23 E
Chishi 100 27.42 N 117.58 E
Chishisi 100 25.32 N 113.11 E
Chisholm, Al., U.S. 194 32.25 N 86.15 W
Chisholm, Me., U.S. 188 44.28 N 70.12 W
Chisholm, Mn., U.S. 190 47.29 N 92.53 W
Chisholm, Tx., U.S. 222 32.51 N 96.22 W
Chisholm Mills 182 54.55 N 114.08 W
Chishtiān Mandi 123 29.48 N 72.52 E
Chishui 102 28.29 N 105.38 E
Chishui ≏, Zhg. 102 28.53 N 105.48 E
Chishui ≏, Zhg. 107 28.49 N 105.50 E
Chishuihe 102 27.50 N 105.32 E
Chišig-Öndör 88 48.19 N 103.25 E
Chisimaio → Kismaayo 144 0.22 N 42.32 E
Chișinău → Kišin'ov 78 47.00 N 28.50 E
Chișineu-Criș 38 46.31 N 21.31 E
Chislaviči 76 54.11 N 32.10 E
Chislehurst ✈8 260 51.25 N 0.04 E
Chislenghien (Gellingen) 50 50.39 N 3.52 E
Chisone ≏ 62 44.49 N 7.25 E
Chisone, Valle del V 62 45.01 N 7.07 E
Chisos Mountains ⋏ 196 29.15 N 103.20 W
Chisseaux 50 47.20 N 1.05 E
Chissengue 152 9.14 S 20.42 E
Chissilo 152 13.34 S 16.30 E
Chist'akovo → Torez 83 48.01 N 38.37 E
Chistochina 180 62.34 N 144.40 W
Chistopol → Čistopol' 80 55.21 N 50.37 E
Chistyakovo → Torez 83 48.01 N 38.37 E
Chiswellgreen 260 51.44 N 0.22 W
Chiswick ✈8 260 51.29 N 0.16 W
Chita, Col. 246 6.11 N 72.28 W
Chita, Nihon 94 35.00 N 136.51 E
Chita → Čita 88 52.03 N 113.30 E
Chitado 152 17.20 S 13.54 E
Chitagá 246 7.09 N 72.40 W
Chita-hantō ≻1 94 34.50 N 136.53 E
Chitambo 154 12.55 S 30.39 E
Chitanda ≏ 152 16.01 S 15.12 E
Chitāpur 122 17.07 N 77.05 E
Chitarda 126 21.50 N 86.57 E
Chitata 152 13.47 S 15.43 E
Chitato 152 7.20 S 20.47 E
Chita-wan c 94 34.47 N 136.58 E
Chitek ≏ 184 54.06 N 108.16 W
Chitek Lake ⊜, Mb., Can. 184 52.26 N 99.25 W
Chitek Lake ⊜, Sk., Can. 184 53.44 N 107.47 W
Chitembo 152 13.34 S 16.40 E
Chitina 180 61.31 N 144.27 W
Chitina ≏ 180 61.30 N 144.28 W
Chitipa 154 9.43 S 33.16 E
Chitokoloki 152 13.50 S 23.13 E
Chitorgarh 120 24.53 N 74.38 E
Chitose 92a 42.49 N 141.39 E
Chitose-chūtonchi, Rikujō-jieitai- ■ 92a 42.46 N 141.40 E
Chitou Shan I 100 27.40 N 120.50 E
Chitra ≏1 126 22.53 N 89.40 E
Chitradurga 122 14.14 N 76.24 E
Chitrakūt Dham 124 25.11 N 80.52 E
Chitrāl 123 35.51 N 71.47 E
Chitra Lada Palace ♦ 269a 13.46 N 100.32 E
Chitrasāli 272b 22.52 N 88.09 E
Chitrāvati ≏ 122 14.48 N 78.14 E
Chitré 236 7.58 N 80.26 W
Chittagong 120 22.20 N 91.50 E
Chittaranjan 126 23.52 N 86.52 E
Chittenango 210 43.02 N 75.52 W
Chittenango Creek ≏ 210 43.11 N 76.00 W
Chittenango Falls 210 42.58 N 75.50 W
Chittering 162 31.29 S 116.06 E
Chittoor 122 13.12 N 79.07 E
Chittūr 122 10.42 N 76.45 E
Chitu, Ityo. 144 8.36 N 37.59 E
Ch'itu, T'aiwan 269d 25.06 N 121.43 E
Chitungwiza 154 17.45 S 31.16 E
Chiuchiang → Jiujiang 100 29.44 N 115.59 E
Chiuchiu 252 22.21 S 68.39 W
Chiuduno 62 45.40 N 9.51 E
Chiumbe 152 12.29 S 16.08 E
Chiúme 152 15.03 S 21.14 E
Chiuppano 64 45.46 N 11.28 E
Chiuro 64 46.10 N 9.59 E
Chiusa (Klausen) 64 46.38 N 11.34 E
Chiusa di Pesio 62 44.19 N 7.40 E
Chiusa di San Michele 62 45.06 N 7.19 E
Chiusaforte 64 46.24 N 13.18 E
Chiusa Sclafani 70 37.41 N 13.16 E
Chiusella ≏ 62 45.17 N 7.52 E
Chiusi 66 43.01 N 11.57 E
Chiusi, Lago di ⊜ 66 43.03 N 11.58 E
Chiúta 154 15.34 S 33.17 E
Chiuta, Lake ⊜ 154 14.55 S 35.50 E
Chiv 84 41.46 N 47.54 E
Chiva, Esp. 34 39.28 N 0.43 W
Chiva, S.S.S.R. 85 41.24 N 60.22 E
Chivacoa 246 10.10 N 68.54 W
Chivapuri ≏ 246 6.25 N 66.23 W
Chivasso 62 45.11 N 7.53 E
Chivato, Punta ≻ 232 27.05 N 111.59 W
Chivay 248 15.40 S 71.35 W
Chivhu 154 19.01 S 30.53 E
Chivilcoy 252 34.53 S 60.01 W
Chivirira Falls ∟ 154 21.14 S 32.20 E
Chiwanda 154 11.22 S 34.54 E
Chiwawa ≏ 224 47.47 N 120.40 W
Chixi 100 28.22 N 116.22 E
Chixoy ≏ 236 16.03 N 90.27 W
Chiyoda, Nihon 94 36.12 N 139.26 E
Chiyoda, Nihon 94 36.11 N 140.14 E
Chiyoda, Nihon 96 34.41 N 132.32 E
Chiyoda ✈8 268 35.41 N 139.44 E
Chizarira National Park ♦ 154 17.45 S 28.00 E
Chizhen 100 31.55 N 118.12 E
Chizidian 100 32.22 N 115.11 E
Chizu 96 35.16 N 134.14 E
Chjargas 88 49.32 N 93.48 E
Chjargas nuur ⊜ 88 49.12 N 93.24 E
Chkalov → Orenburg 86 51.54 N 55.06 E
Chlebnikovo, S.S.S.R. 80 56.38 N 49.56 E
Chlebnikovo, S.S.S.R. 265b 55.58 N 37.31 E
Chlebodarnyj 80 46.41 N 40.50 E
Chlebodarovka 83 47.29 N 37.23 E
Chlevnoje 76 52.12 N 39.05 E
Chloride 200 35.24 N 114.11 W
Chlum 60 48.52 N 13.55 E
Chlum ⋀ 61 48.42 N 14.04 E
Chmelevicy 80 57.45 N 46.26 E
Chmelevo 82 56.09 N 39.08 E
Chmelevoje 78 48.34 N 31.24 E
Chmelita 76 55.25 N 33.53 E
Chmel'nickij 78 49.25 N 27.00 E
Chmel'nik 78 49.33 N 27.57 E
Chmel'niki, S.S.S.R. 82 56.52 N 38.13 E
Chmel'niki, S.S.S.R. 82 56.53 N 38.39 E
Chmielnik 30 50.37 N 20.46 E
Chmost' ≏ 76 54.45 N 32.34 E
Choa Chu Kang 271c 1.22 N 103.41 E
Choāli 272b 22.24 N 88.24 E
Choâm Khsant 110 14.13 N 104.56 E
Choapa ≏ 252 31.38 S 71.34 W
Choapan 234 17.20 N 95.57 W
Choba 154 2.26 N 38.03 E
Chobe □5 156 18.30 S 25.00 E
Chobe ≏ 156 17.50 S 25.05 E
Chobeju 24 64.53 N 60.10 E
Chobe National Park ♦ 156 18.45 S 24.15 E
Chobham 260 51.21 N 0.36 W
Chobham Common ♦ 260 51.23 N 0.37 W
Chobi 84 42.21 N 41.53 E
Chocamán 234 18.59 N 97.01 W
Choccolocco Creek ≏ 194 33.33 N 86.11 W
Choceň 30 50.00 N 16.13 E
Chocenice 60 49.33 N 13.31 E
Chochis, Cerro ⋀ 248 18.04 S 60.03 W
Choch'iwŏn 98 36.37 N 127.18 E
Chochloma 80 56.58 N 43.54 E
Chöchmor't 88 47.21 N 94.33 E
Chochol'skij 78 51.34 N 38.45 E
Cho-chu 110 21.54 N 105.39 E
Chocianów 30 51.25 N 15.55 E
Chociwel 30 53.28 N 15.19 E
Chocó □5 246 6.00 N 77.00 W
Chocolate Bay c 222 29.11 N 95.09 W
Chocolate Bayou ≏ 222 29.13 N 95.13 W
Chocolate Mountains ⋏ 204 33.20 N 115.15 W
Chocontá 246 5.09 N 73.41 W
Chocope 248 7.47 S 79.13 W
Choctawhatchee, East Fork ≏ 194 31.21 N 85.33 W
Choctawhatchee, West Fork ≏ 194 31.21 N 85.33 W
Choctawhatchee Bay c 194 30.25 N 86.21 W
Choctaw Lake ⊜1 218 39.58 N 83.29 W
Chodarus 88 52.36 N 99.19 E
Chodavaram 122 17.50 N 82.57 E
Chodecz 30 52.24 N 19.01 E
Ch'o-do I, C.M.I.K. 98 38.32 N 124.50 E
Ch'o-do I, Taehan 98 34.14 N 127.15 E
Chodoi 114 2.50 N 101.27 E
Chodorov 78 49.24 N 24.17 E
Chodosy 76 53.56 N 31.29 E
Chodov 54 50.11 N 12.43 E
Chodovaja Griva 80 57.08 N 50.16 E
Chodovaricha 24 68.57 N 53.40 E
Chodz' ≏ 84 44.43 N 40.45 E
Chodžaimetk 85 39.37 N 69.14 E
Chodžakala 128 38.43 N 56.20 E
Chodžejli 72 42.48 N 59.25 E
Chodzież 30 52.59 N 16.56 E
Choele-Choel 252 39.16 S 65.41 W
Chofombo 154 14.35 S 31.50 E
Chōfu 94 35.39 N 139.33 E
Chofu Airport ⊠ 268 35.40 N 139.32 E
Chogo Lungma Glacier ⊓ 123 35.52 N 75.19 E
Chogot 88 53.15 N 105.52 E
Chohtan 120 25.29 N 71.04 E
Choiceland 184 53.27 N 104.25 W
Choichuff, Laga ≏ 154 1.34 N 39.24 E
Choisel 261 48.41 N 2.01 E
Choiseul 241f 13.47 N 61.03 W
Choiseul I 175e 7.05 S 157.00 E
Choiseul Sound Ʋ 254 51.57 S 58.35 W
Choisy 58 45.59 N 6.03 E
Choisy-le-Roi 261 48.46 N 2.25 E
Choix 232 26.43 N 108.17 W
Chojna 30 52.58 N 14.28 E
Chojnice 30 53.42 N 17.34 E
Chojniki 78 51.53 N 29.56 E
Chojnów 30 51.17 N 15.56 E
Chōkai-san ⋀ 92 39.06 N 140.03 E
Choke ≏ 144 10.45 N 37.35 E
Choke Canyon Lake ⊜1 196 28.30 N 98.20 W
Chokio 198 45.34 N 96.10 W
Chokoloskee 220 25.48 N 81.21 W
Chokwé 156 24.32 S 32.59 E
Cholame 226 35.43 N 120.17 W
Cholame Creek ≏ 226 35.39 N 120.22 W
Cholame Hills ⋏2 226 35.45 N 120.30 W
Cholbon 88 51.53 N 116.15 E
Cholodarkipčak 85 39.51 N 68.52 E
Cholet 32 47.04 N 0.53 W
Cholila 254 42.31 S 71.27 W
Chŏlla Namdo □4 98 34.45 N 127.00 E
Chŏlla Pukto □4 98 35.45 N 127.15 E
Cholm 76 57.09 N 31.11 E
Cholmec 76 56.21 N 33.21 E
Cholmeč', S.S.S.R. 78 52.09 N 30.37 E
Cholmogorovka 86 44.25 N 78.31 E
Cholmogorskaja 24 63.49 N 40.39 E
Cholmogory 24 64.15 N 41.40 E
Cholmsk 89 47.03 N 142.03 E
Cholmskij 78 44.52 N 38.24 E
Cholmy, S.S.S.R. 78 51.52 N 32.40 E
Cholmy, S.S.S.R. 82 56.56 N 38.33 E
Cholm-Žirkovskij 76 55.31 N 33.29 E
Cholodnaja Balka 83 48.02 N 38.04 E
Choloj ≏ 88 53.12 N 112.47 E
Choloma 236 15.34 N 87.56 W
Cho-lon ✈8 269c 10.46 N 106.40 E
Chŏlŏnbuir 88 47.55 N 112.57 E
Cholopeniči 76 54.31 N 28.58 E
Ch'olsan 98 39.46 N 124.40 E
Cholsey 42 51.34 N 1.10 W
Choltobino 82 54.11 N 38.28 E
Choltoson 88 50.20 N 103.20 E
Choluj, S.S.S.R. 80 56.34 N 41.53 E
Choluj, S.S.S.R. 80 56.04 N 42.08 E
Cholula [de Rivadabia] 234 19.04 N 98.18 W
Choluteca 236 13.18 N 87.12 W
Choluteca □5 236 13.20 N 87.10 W
Choluteca ≏ 236 13.07 N 87.19 W

Symbols in the index entries represent the broad categories identified in the key at the right. Symbols with superior numbers (⋏1) identify subcategories (see complete key on page I · 1).

Kartensymbole in dem Registerverzeichnis stellen die rechts in Schlüssel erklärten Kategorien dar. Symbole mit hochgestellten Ziffern (⋏1) bezeichnen Unterabteilungen einer Kategorie (vgl. vollständiger Schlüssel auf Seite I · 1).

Los símbolos incluidos en el texto del índice representan las grandes categorías identificadas con la clave a la derecha. Los símbolos con números en su parte superior (⋏1) identifican las subcategorías (véase la clave completa en la página I · 1).

Les symboles de l'index représentent les catégories indiquées dans la légende à droite. Les symboles suivis d'un indice (⋏1) représentent des sous-catégories (voir légende complète à la page I · 1).

Os símbolos incluídos no texto do índice representam as grandes categorias identificadas com a chave à direita. Os símbolos com números em sua parte superior (⋏1) identificam as subcategorias (veja-se a chave completa à página I · 1).

⋀ Mountain	Berg	Montaña	Montagne	Montanha
⋏ Mountains	Berge	Montañas	Montagnes	Montanhas
⋊ Pass	Pass	Paso	Col	Passo
V Valley, Canyon	Tal, Cañon	Valle, Cañón	Vallée, Canyon	Vale, Canhão
≃ Plain	Ebene	Llano	Plaine	Planície
≻ Cape	Kap	Cabo	Cap	Cabo
I Island	Insel	Isla	Île	Ilha
II Islands	Inseln	Islas	Îles	Ilhas
⊥ Other Topographic Features	Andere Topographische Objekte	Otros Elementos Topográficos	Autres données topographiques	Outros acidentes topográficos

ESPAÑOL

Nombre	Página	Lat.°′	Long.°′ W = Oeste
Choma	**154**	16.48 S	26.59 E
Chomedey ◆[8]	**275a**	45.32 N	73.44 W
Chomen Swamp ≋	**144**	9.25 N	37.20 E
Chomérac	**62**	44.42 N	4.39 E
Chomičev	**80**	48.11 N	45.01 E
Chomiomo ∧	**124**	28.01 N	88.31 E
Cho-moi, Viet.	**110**	10.33 N	105.24 E
Cho-moi, Viet.	**269c**	10.51 N	106.38 E
Chomo Lhāri ∧	**124**	27.50 N	89.15 E
Chom Thong	**110**	18.25 N	98.41 E
Chomu	**120**	27.10 N	75.44 E
Chomutec	**78**	50.06 N	33.44 E
Chomutov	**54**	50.28 N	13.26 E
Chomutovka	**78**	51.56 N	34.33 E
Chomutovka ≏	**54**	50.11 N	13.37 E
Chomutovo, S.S.S.R.	**76**	52.51 N	37.27 E
Chomutovo, S.S.S.R.	**88**	52.28 N	104.25 E
Chomutovskaja	**83**	47.03 N	40.04 E
Chomutovskaja Step', zapovednik ♦	**83**	47.17 N	38.11 E
Chōnan, Nihon	**94**	35.24 N	140.14 E
Ch'ŏnan, Taehan	**98**	36.48 N	127.09 E
Chon'atino	**82**	55.11 N	38.07 E
Chon Buri	**110**	13.22 N	100.59 E
Chonchi	**254**	42.38 S	73.47 W
Choncholoj	**88**	51.08 N	108.14 E
Chon Daen	**110**	16.11 N	100.51 E
Chone	**246**	0.41 S	80.06 W
Chone ≏	**246**	0.35 S	80.25 W
Chong'an	**100**	27.45 N	118.02 E
Ch'ŏngch'ŏn-gang ≏	**98**	39.35 N	125.28 E
Ch'ŏngdan	**98**	37.58 N	125.56 E
Chongde	**106**	30.32 N	120.26 E
Ch'ŏngdo	**98**	35.38 N	128.43 E
Chonggu	**106**	31.12 N	121.10 E
Ch'ŏngha	**98**	36.13 N	129.20 E
Ch'onghak-ni	**271b**	37.43 N	127.05 E
Chonghe	**89**	44.43 N	127.45 E
Ch'ŏngjin	**98**	41.47 N	129.50 E
Chŏngju, C.M.I.K.	**98**	39.41 N	125.13 E
Ch'ŏngju, Taehan	**98**	36.39 N	127.31 E
Chŏng Kal	**110**	13.57 N	103.35 E
Chongkanzhen	**107**	30.09 N	105.37 E
Chongli (Xiwanzi)	**98**	40.54 N	115.16 E
Chongming	**106**	31.37 N	121.24 E
Chongming Dao I	**106**	31.36 N	121.33 E
Chongoene	**156**	25.00 S	33.47 E
Chongor	**102**	45.59 N	112.45 E
Chongos Bajo	**248**	12.07 S	75.16 W
Chongoyape	**248**	6.39 S	79.24 W
Chong Pang	**271c**	1.26 N	103.50 E
Chŏngp'yŏng-chŏsuji ⊜[1]	**98**	37.40 N	127.30 E
Chongqing, Zhg.	**107**	30.39 N	103.41 E
Chongqing (Chungking), Zhg.	**107**	29.34 N	106.35 E
Chongren, Zhg.	**100**	29.37 N	120.43 E
Chongren, Zhg.	**100**	27.46 N	116.01 E
Chongru	**100**	27.01 N	120.10 E
Ch'ŏngsan	**98**	36.22 N	127.46 E
Ch'ŏngsan-do I	**98**	34.11 N	126.54 E
Chongshi	**100**	25.24 N	115.28 E
Chŏngsŏn	**98**	37.22 N	128.38 E
Ch'ŏngsong	**98**	41.47 N	129.48 E
Chŏngŭp	**98**	35.36 N	126.51 E
Chongwe ≏	**154**	15.43 S	29.20 E
Chongwu	**100**	24.53 N	118.55 E
Chongxi	**98**	42.07 N	128.59 E
Chongxin	**102**	35.13 N	107.29 E
Ch'ŏngyang, Taehan	**98**	36.27 N	126.48 E
Chongyang, Zhg.	**100**	29.33 N	114.00 E
Chongyang ≏	**100**	27.18 N	118.08 E
Chongyi	**100**	25.44 N	114.18 E
Chongzuo	**102**	22.21 N	107.26 E
Chŏnju	**98**	35.49 N	127.08 E
Chonkham	**120**	27.48 N	96.02 E
Ch'ŏnma	**98**	40.03 N	125.01 E
Chonos, Archipiélago de los II	**254**	45.00 S	74.00 W
Ch'ŏnsu-ri	**98**	41.43 N	128.45 E
Chontaleña, Cordillera ⩘	**236**	11.50 N	84.50 W
Chontales □[5]	**236**	12.05 N	85.10 W
Chon-thanh	**110**	11.24 N	106.36 E
Chŏnŭi	**98**	36.42 N	127.11 E
Chonuu	**74**	66.27 N	143.06 E
Chonzie, Ben ∧	**46**	56.27 N	3.59 W
Cho Oyu ∧	**124**	28.06 N	86.39 E
Chopan	**124**	24.31 N	83.02 E
Chopda	**120**	21.15 N	75.18 E
Chopim ≏	**252**	25.35 S	53.05 W
Chopinzinho	**252**	25.51 S	52.30 W
Chop'or ≏	**80**	49.36 N	42.19 E
Chop'orskij zapovednik ◆[4]	**80**	51.15 N	41.48 E
Choptank ≏	**208**	38.38 N	76.13 W
Chopwell	**44**	54.55 N	1.49 W
Chor	**89**	47.53 N	134.58 E
Chor ≏	**89**	47.48 N	134.43 E
Chora Saādatpur	**272a**	28.36 N	77.21 E
Chordil sar'dag ⩘	**88**	50.50 N	99.40 E
Chorejver	**24**	67.25 N	58.03 E
Chorges	**62**	44.33 N	6.17 E
Chori	**84**	41.37 N	45.59 E
Chorin ⊥	**54**	52.54 N	13.52 E
Chorina ≏	**83**	49.23 N	38.13 E
Chorinsk	**88**	52.10 N	109.46 E
Chorley	**262**	53.39 N	2.39 W
Chorley □[8]	**262**	53.38 N	2.38 W
Chorleywood	**260**	51.39 N	0.31 W
Chorlovo	**82**	55.20 N	38.49 E
Chorlton-cum-Hardy ◆[8]	**262**	53.27 N	2.17 W
Choro ≏	**248**	16.25 S	64.35 W
Chorog	**120**	37.31 N	71.33 E
Chorol, S.S.S.R.	**78**	49.47 N	33.17 E
Chorol', S.S.S.R.	**89**	44.25 N	132.04 E
Chorol ≏	**78**	49.28 N	33.47 E
Chorolque, Cerro ∧	**248**	20.56 S	66.01 W
Choros, Isla I	**252**	29.16 S	71.33 W
Chorošovo	**82**	55.08 N	38.47 E
Chorošovo ◆[8]	**265b**	55.47 N	37.28 E
Chorostkov	**78**	49.13 N	25.55 E
Choroszcz	**30**	53.09 N	22.59 E
Chorreras, Cerro ∧	**232**	26.02 N	106.21 W
Chorrillos	**286d**	12.10 S	77.02 W
Chorrochó	**250**	8.59 S	39.06 W
Chorro Creek ≏	**226**	35.20 N	120.50 W
Chort'ak, gora ∧	**88**	53.15 N	110.45 E
Ch'ŏrwŏn	**98**	38.16 N	127.12 E
Chorzele	**30**	53.16 N	20.55 E
Ch'osan	**98**	40.50 N	125.47 E
Chosanch'am	**98**	40.22 N	126.11 E
Chosedachard	**24**	67.02 N	59.22 E
Chosen	**220**	26.42 N	80.41 W
Chošeutovo	**80**	47.02 N	47.50 E
Chōshi	**94**	35.44 N	140.50 E
Choshi-ōhashi ◆[5]	**94**	35.44 N	140.50 E
Chōshi-zuka-kofun ⊥	**94**	34.42 N	137.50 E
Choshui ≏	**100**	24.03 N	120.24 E
Chosica	**248**	11.54 S	76.42 W
Chos Malal	**252**	37.23 S	70.16 W
Chosŏn Minjujuŭi In'min Konghwaguk → Korea, North □[1]	**98**	40.00 N	127.00 E
Chosrech	**84**	41.59 N	47.18 E
Chosta	**84**	43.33 N	39.53 E
Choszczno	**30**	53.10 N	15.26 E
Chota	**248**	6.33 S	78.39 W
Chotanāgpur Plateau ⩘[1]	**124**	23.30 N	84.30 E
Chotča ≏	**82**	56.54 N	37.35 E
Choteau	**202**	47.48 N	112.10 W
Choteau Creek ≏	**198**	42.51 N	98.09 W
Chotěboř	**30**	49.43 N	15.40 E
Choten'	**78**	51.07 N	34.46 E
Chotěšov, Česko.	**60**	49.39 N	13.12 E
Chotešov, S.S.S.R.	**78**	51.43 N	24.47 E

FRANÇAIS

Nom	Page	Lat.°′	Long.°′ W = Ouest
Chotila	**120**	22.25 N	71.11 E
Chotilovo	**76**	57.44 N	34.05 E
Chotimsk	**76**	53.26 N	32.35 E
Chotin	**78**	48.29 N	26.30 E
Chotisino	**82**	54.24 N	36.33 E
Chot'kovo, S.S.S.R.	**76**	53.46 N	35.14 E
Chot'kovo, S.S.S.R.	**76**	52.56 N	35.23 E
Chot'kovo, S.S.S.R.	**82**	56.15 N	38.00 E
Chotla, Cerro de ∧	**234**	17.55 N	101.31 W
Chotovn'a	**76**	53.17 N	30.32 E
Chotuš'	**82**	54.32 N	37.44 E
Chotynec	**76**	53.08 N	35.24 E
Chotyniči	**76**	52.38 N	26.18 E
Chouchiak'ou → Shangshui	**100**	33.33 N	114.34 E
Chouk'ou → Shangshui	**100**	33.33 N	114.34 E
Choûm	**148**	21.18 N	13.01 W
Chouteau	**196**	36.11 N	95.20 W
Chovaling	**85**	38.21 N	69.58 E
Chovd, Mong.	**86**	48.08 N	91.23 E
Chovd, Mong.	**86**	48.01 N	91.38 E
Chovd, Mong.	**86**	49.16 N	90.55 E
Chovd, Mong.	**102**	44.42 N	102.24 E
Chovd □[4]	**86**	48.00 N	91.30 E
Chovd ≏	**90**	48.06 N	92.11 E
Chövsgöl	**102**	43.36 N	109.39 E
Chövsgöl □[4]	**88**	50.00 N	100.00 E
Chövsgöl nuur ⊜	**88**	51.00 N	100.30 E
Chovu-Aksy	**88**	51.11 N	93.53 E
Chowan ≏	**192**	36.00 N	76.40 W
Chowchilla	**226**	37.07 N	120.15 W
Chowchilla ≏	**226**	37.07 N	120.32 W
Chowchilla, East Fork ≏	**226**	37.20 N	119.50 W
Chowchilla, West Fork ≏	**226**	37.20 N	119.50 W
Chown, Mount ∧	**182**	53.24 N	119.22 W
Ch'owŏn-ni	**98**	39.40 N	127.17 E
Choya	**252**	28.30 S	64.52 W
Choyak-to I	**98**	34.22 N	126.54 E
Chozapini, Ozero ⊜	**84**	41.15 N	43.12 E
Chrapun'	**78**	51.42 N	27.29 E
Chr'aščevka	**80**	53.48 N	49.06 E
Chrást	**60**	49.48 N	13.29 E
Chrebtovo	**82**	56.35 N	38.16 E
Chrenovoje	**80**	51.07 N	40.17 E
Chreščatij	**83**	49.37 N	39.42 E
Chřibská	**54**	50.50 N	14.29 E
Chříč	**60**	49.57 N	13.39 E
Chriesman	**222**	30.36 N	96.46 W
Chrisman	**194**	39.48 N	87.40 W
Chrissiesmeer	**158**	26.16 S	30.13 E
Chrissiesmeer ⊜	**158**	26.19 S	30.13 E
Christanshåb	**176**	68.50 N	51.12 W
Christburg → Dzierzgoń	**30**	53.56 N	19.21 E
Christchurch, N.Z.	**172**	43.32 S	172.38 E
Christchurch, Eng., U.K.	**42**	50.44 N	1.45 W
Christ Church Cathedral ᵾ[1]	**273a**	6.27 N	3.23 E
Christian □[6]	**219**	39.33 N	89.18 W
Christian ≏	**180**	66.36 N	145.49 W
Christian, Cape >	**176**	70.31 N	68.18 W
Christian, Point >	**174e**	25.04 S	130.07 W
Christiana, Jam.	**241q**	18.10 N	77.29 W
Christiana, S. Afr.	**158**	27.52 S	25.08 E
Christiana, De., U.S.	**285**	39.39 N	75.39 W
Christiana, Pa., U.S.	**208**	39.57 N	75.59 W
Christiana Creek ≏	**216**	41.41 N	85.59 W
Christianburg	**218**	38.17 N	85.06 W
Christian Channel ⲩ	**212**	44.47 N	80.08 W
Christian Island I	**212**	44.50 N	80.13 W
Christian Island Indian Reserve ◆[4]	**212**	44.50 N	80.10 W
Christiansburg, Oh., U.S.	**218**	40.03 N	84.01 W
Christiansburg, Va., U.S.	**192**	37.07 N	80.24 W
Christiansfeld	**41**	55.21 N	9.29 E
Christiansø I	**26**	55.19 N	15.12 E
Christian Sound ⲩ	**180**	55.56 N	134.40 W
Christiansted	**241n**	17.45 N	64.42 W
Christie, Mount ∧	**180**	63.01 N	129.40 W
Christie, Mount ∧[2]	**216**	42.53 N	83.20 W
Christie Bay ⊂	**176**	62.32 N	111.10 W
Christie Lake ⊜, Mb., Can.	**184**	56.54 N	96.56 W
Christie Lake ⊜, On., Can.	**212**	44.48 N	76.26 W
Christina ≏, Ab., Can.	**184**	56.40 N	111.03 W
Christina ≏, De., U.S.	**285**	39.43 N	75.31 W
Christina Lake ⊜, Ab., Can.	**182**	55.38 N	110.55 W
Christina Lake ⊜, B.C., Can.	**182**	49.05 N	118.14 W
Christinovka	**78**	48.49 N	29.58 E
Christišče	**83**	48.55 N	37.30 E
Christmas	**220**	28.32 N	81.01 W
Christmas Bay ⊂	**222**	29.03 N	95.11 W
Christmas Creek	**162**	18.53 S	125.55 E
Christmas Creek ≏	**162**	18.29 S	125.23 E
Christmas Island □[2], Oc.	**108**	10.30 S	105.40 E
Christmas Island □[2], Oc.	**112**	10.30 S	105.40 E
Christmas Island → Kiritimati I[1]	**174o**	1.52 N	157.20 W
Christmas Mountain ∧	**180**	64.34 N	160.34 W
Christmas Ridge ✦[3]	**14**	5.00 N	160.00 W
Christoforovka	**78**	47.59 N	33.05 E
Christoforovo	**24**	60.53 N	47.13 E
Christ of the Andes → Cristo Redentor ⊥	**252**	32.50 S	70.05 W
Christoph Columbus-Spitze → Cristóbal Colón, Pico ∧	**246**	10.50 N	73.41 W
Christopher	**194**	37.58 N	89.03 W
Christopher Lake ⊜	**162**	24.49 S	127.42 E
Christoval	**196**	31.12 N	100.30 W
Chroma ≏	**74**	71.36 N	144.49 E
Chromtau	**86**	50.17 N	58.27 E
Chrudim	**30**	49.57 N	15.48 E
Chrustal'nyj	**89**	44.24 N	135.06 E
Chrzanów	**30**	50.09 N	19.24 E
Chu ≏, Asia	**110**	19.53 N	105.45 E
Chu ≏, Zhg.	**100**	32.08 N	118.43 E
Chu ≏, Zhg.	**106**	32.15 N	119.03 E
Chuādānga	**124**	23.38 N	88.51 E
Chualar	**226**	36.34 N	121.31 W
Chuanbu	**106**	31.17 N	119.49 E
Chuanchang ≍	**100**	33.46 N	119.51 E
Chuanergu	**105**	39.20 N	117.43 E
Chuan'gang	**106**	31.57 N	121.04 E
Chuangjiapuzi	**104**	40.50 N	124.06 E
Chuanliao	**100**	28.17 N	120.13 E
Chuansha	**106**	31.12 N	121.42 E
Chuanshan	**100**	29.53 N	121.57 E
Chuanxindian	**104**	41.25 N	120.30 E
Chuanyao Gang ⊂	**106**	32.12 N	121.25 E
Chuathbaluk	**180**	61.40 N	159.15 W
Chubbuck	**202**	42.55 N	112.27 W
Chūbu-Sangaku-kokuritsu-kōen ♦	**94**	36.30 N	137.41 E
Chubut □[4]	**254**	44.00 S	69.00 W
Chubut ≏	**254**	43.20 S	65.03 W
Ch'üchiang → Shaoguan	**100**	24.50 N	113.37 E
Chuchi Lake ⊜	**182**	55.10 N	124.33 W
Chuchou → Zhuzhou	**100**	27.50 N	113.09 E
Chuchra	**78**	50.13 N	34.49 E
Chu Chua	**182**	51.21 N	120.10 W
Chuchuwayha Indian Reserve ◆[4]	**182**	49.21 N	120.06 W
Chuckatuck	**208**	36.52 N	76.35 W
Chučni	**84**	41.57 N	47.55 E
Chucuito	**248**	15.53 S	69.53 W
Chucun	**100**	33.04 N	116.32 E

PORTUGUÊS

Nome	Página	Lat.°′	Long.°′ W = Oeste
Chucunaque ≏	**246**	8.09 N	77.44 W
Chudan ≏	**88**	52.08 N	109.40 E
Chudanskij chrebet ⩘	**88**	52.00 N	110.00 E
Chudat	**84**	41.38 N	48.42 E
Chudeč	**60**	49.58 N	13.05 E
Chudleigh	**42**	50.36 N	3.38 W
Chudojelan'	**88**	54.42 N	99.37 E
Chudzirt	**86**	47.05 N	91.10 E
Chuen Lung	**271d**	22.24 N	114.06 E
Chugach Islands II	**180**	59.06 N	151.42 W
Chugach Mountains ⩘	**180**	61.00 N	145.00 W
Chuginadak Island I	**180**	52.49 N	169.50 W
Chūgoku-sanchi ⩘	**96**	34.58 N	132.57 E
Chugwater	**200**	41.45 N	104.49 W
Chugwater Creek ≏	**198**	42.07 N	104.51 W
Chugyn-ri	**271b**	37.39 N	126.50 E
Chūhar Kāna	**123**	31.45 N	73.48 E
Chuhe	**100**	34.03 N	113.35 E
Chuhuichupa	**232**	29.38 N	108.22 W
Chuí	**252**	33.41 S	53.27 W
Chuius Mountain ∧	**182**	54.51 N	124.30 W
Chukai	**114**	4.15 N	103.25 E
Chukchi Sea ⍑[2]	**16**	69.00 N	171.00 W
Chukehu ⊜	**120**	31.40 N	88.00 E
Chukou	**100**	25.44 N	113.22 E
Chulakeaganhe ≏	**120**	36.35 N	92.20 E
Chulalongkorn University ᵾ[2]	**269a**	13.44 N	100.33 E
Chula Vista	**228**	32.38 N	117.05 W
Chuld	**102**	45.04 N	105.35 E
Chulga ≏	**24**	64.20 N	61.00 E
Chullora	**274a**	33.54 S	151.04 E
Chulmleigh	**42**	50.55 N	3.52 W
Chulo	**84**	41.41 N	42.18 E
Chulp'o	**98**	35.37 N	126.40 E
Chulucanas	**248**	5.06 S	80.10 W
Chulumani	**248**	16.24 S	67.31 W
Chuluota	**220**	28.38 N	81.10 W
Chuma	**248**	15.24 S	68.56 W
Chumaerhe ≏	**120**	34.39 N	95.00 E
Chumalag	**84**	43.14 N	44.28 E
Chumbicha	**252**	28.52 S	66.14 W
Chummi, ozero ⊜	**89**	50.18 N	137.17 E
Chum Phae	**110**	16.32 N	102.06 E
Chumphon	**110**	10.30 N	99.10 E
Chumphon Buri	**110**	15.21 N	103.24 E
Chumpi	**248**	15.06 S	73.46 W
Chum Saeng	**110**	15.54 N	100.19 E
Chumunjin	**98**	37.54 N	128.49 E
Chunal	**262**	53.25 N	1.57 W
Chunan, T'aiwan	**100**	24.41 N	120.52 E
Chun'an, Zhg.	**100**	29.35 N	118.58 E
Chunār	**124**	25.08 N	82.54 E
Chuncheon → Ch'unch'ŏn	**98**	37.52 N	127.43 E
Chunchi, Ec.	**246**	2.17 S	78.55 W
Chunchi, Zhg.	**100**	27.22 N	119.20 E
Ch'unch'ŏn	**98**	37.52 N	127.43 E
Chunchula	**194**	30.55 N	88.12 W
Chūnd	**123**	31.26 N	72.16 E
Chung-ang University ᵾ[2]	**271b**	37.30 N	126.58 E
Chungari ≏	**89**	50.04 N	136.55 E
Ch'ungch'ŏng Namdo □[4]	**98**	36.30 N	127.00 E
Ch'ungch'ŏng Pukdo □[4]	**98**	36.45 N	128.00 E
Chunggang-ni	**98**	40.52 N	127.20 E
Chung Hau	**271d**	22.16 N	114.00 E
Chungho	**269d**	25.00 N	121.30 E
Chung Hsing Bridge ◆[5]	**269d**	25.03 N	121.29 E
Chunghwa	**98**	38.52 N	125.47 E
Ch'ungju	**98**	36.58 N	127.58 E
Chungking → Chongqing	**107**	29.34 N	106.35 E
Chungli	**100**	24.57 N	121.13 E
Chungliao	**100**	22.41 N	121.28 E
Ch'ungmu	**98**	34.51 N	128.25 E
Chungp'u	**100**	23.25 N	120.31 E
Chungp'yŏngjang	**98**	41.11 N	128.03 E
Chungsam-ni	**98**	38.34 N	127.09 E
Chŭngsan	**98**	39.06 N	125.22 E
Chŭngsanha-ri ◆[8]	**271b**	37.35 N	126.54 E
Chungshan → Zhongshan	**100**	22.31 N	113.22 E
Chungshan Bridge ◆[5]	**269d**	25.05 N	121.31 E
Chunguj ≏	**88**	48.51 N	93.32 E
Chungyang Shanmo ⩘	**100**	23.30 N	121.00 E
Chunheji	**100**	32.12 N	115.22 E
Chunhua, Zhg.	**102**	34.50 N	108.31 E
Chunhua, Zhg.	**106**	31.56 N	118.56 E
Chunhuás	**232**	19.12 N	88.55 W
Chūniān	**123**	30.58 N	73.59 E
Chuntuquí	**232**	17.31 N	90.09 W
Chünüj ≏	**88**	48.48 N	102.00 E
Chunya	**154**	8.32 S	33.25 E
Ch'unyang, Taehan	**98**	36.56 N	128.54 E
Chunyang, Zhg.	**89**	43.43 N	129.28 E
Chunzach	**84**	42.33 N	46.43 E
Chunze	**124**	29.51 N	88.41 E
Chūō	**96**	35.00 N	133.58 E
Chūō ◆[8], Nihon	**268**	35.40 N	139.47 E
Chūō ◆[8], Nihon	**270**	34.42 N	135.11 E
Chuŏr Phnum Krâvanh ⩘	**110**	12.00 N	103.15 E
Chuosijia	**102**	31.53 N	101.59 E
Chupaca	**248**	12.04 S	75.19 W
Chupadera Arroyo ∨	**200**	33.47 N	106.37 W
Chupadero, Cerro ∧	**200**	31.01 N	111.37 W
Chupaderos	**234**	23.50 N	102.20 W
Chupara Point >	**241r**	10.48 N	61.22 W
Chuquibamba	**248**	15.50 S	72.39 W
Chuquibambilla	**248**	14.07 S	72.43 W
Chuquicamata	**252**	22.19 S	68.56 W
Chuquisaca □[5]	**248**	20.00 S	64.20 W
Chuquitanta	**286d**	11.58 S	77.06 W
Chur	**58**	46.51 N	9.32 E
Churach ≏	**88**	48.37 N	110.42 E
Churachandpur	**120**	24.20 N	93.40 E
Churāmankāti	**126**	23.14 N	89.09 E
Churcampa	**248**	12.42 S	74.24 W
Church	**262**	53.45 N	2.24 W
Churchdown	**42**	51.53 N	2.10 W
Church Hill, Md., U.S.	**208**	39.08 N	75.59 W
Church Hill, Tn., U.S.	**192**	36.31 N	82.42 W
Churchill, Mb., Can.	**176**	58.46 N	94.10 W
Churchill, Oh., U.S.	**214**	41.09 N	80.39 W
Churchill, Pa., U.S.	**279b**	40.27 N	79.51 W
Churchill, Va., U.S.	**284c**	38.54 N	77.10 W
Churchill ≏, Can.	**176**	58.47 N	94.12 W
Churchill ≏, Nf., Can.	**176**	53.30 N	60.10 W
Churchill, Cape >	**176**	58.46 N	93.12 W
Churchill, Mount ∧, B.C., Can.	**182**	49.58 N	123.51 W
Churchill, Mount ∧, Ak., U.S.	**180**	61.25 N	141.43 W
Churchill Downs ♦	**218**	38.12 N	85.46 W
Churchill Falls ∟	**176**	53.35 N	64.27 W
Churchill Lake ⊜	**184**	55.55 N	108.20 W
Churchill National Park ♦	**169**	37.58 S	145.17 E
Church Point	**194**	30.24 N	92.12 W
Church Rock	**200**	35.32 N	108.35 W
Church Street	**260**	51.26 N	0.28 E
Church Stretton	**42**	52.32 N	2.49 W
Churchton	**208**	38.48 N	76.32 W
Churchtown, Eng., U.K.	**262**	53.40 N	2.58 W
Churchtown, Pa., U.S.	**208**	40.08 N	75.58 W
Church View	**208**	37.41 N	76.41 W
Churchville, On., Can.	**275b**	43.38 N	79.45 W
Churchville, Md., U.S.	**208**	39.33 N	76.14 W

Churchville, N.Y., U.S.	**210**	43.06 N	77.53 W
Churchville, Pa., U.S.	**285**	40.11 N	75.01 W
Churdan	**198**	42.09 N	94.28 W
Churen Himāl ∧	**124**	28.44 N	83.12 E
Churfirsten ⩘	**58**	47.08 N	9.17 E
Churia Range ⩘	**124**	27.40 N	83.40 E
Churintzio	**234**	20.09 N	102.04 W
Chürmen	**102**	43.20 N	104.05 E
Churmuli	**89**	51.00 N	136.50 E
Churn ≏	**42**	51.38 N	1.53 W
Churn Creek ≏	**182**	51.30 N	122.17 W
Churnet ≏	**42**	52.55 N	1.50 W
Churni ≏[1]	**126**	23.28 N	88.44 E
Chursdorf	**54**	50.46 N	12.15 E
Churu	**120**	28.18 N	74.57 E
Churu □[5]	**123**	28.45 N	74.50 E
Churubusco, In., U.S.	**216**	41.13 N	85.19 W
Churubusco, N.Y., U.S.	**206**	44.57 N	73.56 W
Churuguara	**246**	10.49 N	69.32 W
Churumuco	**234**	18.37 N	101.38 W
Churwalden	**58**	46.47 N	9.33 E
Chušenga	**88**	51.27 N	110.55 E
Chushālgarh	**123**	33.30 N	71.54 E
Chushan	**100**	23.45 N	120.40 E
Chushul	**120**	33.36 N	78.39 E
Chuska Mountains ⩘	**200**	36.15 N	108.50 W
Chuska Peak ∧	**200**	35.53 N	108.50 W
Chusovoy → Čusovoj	**86**	58.17 N	57.49 E
Chust	**78**	48.10 N	23.18 E
Chusuut uul ∧	**88**	47.45 N	105.45 E
Chūta	**174m**	26.32 N	127.58 E
Chutag	**88**	49.23 N	102.43 E
Chutag Uul	**102**	43.23 N	110.13 E
Chute-à-Blondeau	**206**	45.35 N	74.29 W
Chute-Panet	**206**	46.51 N	71.51 W
Chutorskoj	**80**	46.52 N	42.59 E
Chutu ≏	**89**	49.27 N	140.02 E
Chutung	**100**	24.44 N	121.05 E
Chuŭl	**98**	41.33 N	129.34 E
Chuwang	**98**	36.02 N	114.52 E
Chuwang-san Kukrip Kongwŏn ♦	**98**	36.26 N	129.10 E
Chuwei	**269d**	25.08 N	121.27 E
Chuxian	**100**	32.19 N	118.17 E
Chuxiong	**102**	25.02 N	101.30 E
Chuy	**252**	33.41 S	53.27 W
Chuzenji-ko ⊜	**94**	36.44 N	139.29 E
Chuzhai	**100**	33.22 N	113.37 E
Chužir	**88**	53.11 N	107.20 E
Chūzu	**94**	35.06 N	136.00 E
Chvalynsk	**80**	52.30 N	48.07 E
Chvančkara	**84**	42.34 N	43.01 E
Chvastoviči	**76**	53.28 N	35.06 E
Chvatovka	**80**	52.21 N	46.34 E
Chvojnaja	**76**	58.54 N	34.32 E
Chvorost'anka	**80**	52.36 N	48.59 E
Chvostovo	**92a**	46.08 N	142.14 E
Chwefru ≏	**42**	52.09 N	3.25 W
Ch'wiya-ri	**98**	38.03 N	125.32 E
Chypre → Cyprus □[1]	**130**	35.00 N	33.00 E
Chyrov	**78**	49.33 N	22.49 E
Ci ≏, Zhg.	**98**	38.19 N	115.23 E
Ci ≏, Zhg.	**100**	33.27 N	115.31 E
Ciago	**64**	46.12 N	12.46 E
Ciagola, Monte ∧	**68**	39.54 N	15.53 E
Ciales	**240m**	18.20 N	66.28 W
Ciamis	**115a**	7.20 S	108.21 E
Ciampino	**66**	41.48 N	12.36 E
Ciampino, Aeroporto di ⊠	**267a**	41.48 N	12.36 E
Cianciana	**70**	37.31 N	13.26 E
Ciandur	**115a**	6.24 S	105.59 E
Cianjur	**115a**	6.49 S	107.08 E
Ciano d'Enza	**64**	44.36 N	10.24 E
Cianorte	**255**	23.37 S	52.37 W
Çians, Gorges du ∨	**62**	43.57 N	6.59 E
Čiatura	**84**	42.17 N	43.17 E
Ciavolo	**70**	37.46 N	12.33 E
Ciawi, Indon.	**115a**	7.10 S	108.09 E
Ciawi, Indon.	**115a**	6.40 S	106.50 E
Ciawigebang	**115a**	6.58 S	108.34 E
Ciba	**107**	29.07 N	105.55 E
Cibadak	**115a**	6.53 S	106.46 E
Çibaliung	**115a**	6.46 S	105.51 E
Čibargata	**85**	41.08 N	69.48 E
Cibatu	**115a**	7.06 S	107.59 E
Cibeber	**115a**	6.56 S	107.07 E
Cibecue	**200**	34.02 N	110.29 W
Cibiana	**64**	46.23 N	12.17 E
Çibinong	**115a**	6.27 S	106.51 E
Čibisovka	**78**	50.47 N	40.05 E
Čibižek	**86**	54.27 N	93.40 E
Cibolo Creek ≏, Tx., U.S.	**196**	28.57 N	97.53 W
Cibolo Creek ≏, Tx., U.S.	**196**	29.34 N	104.24 W
Cibolo Creek ≏, Tx., U.S.	**196**	28.27 N	98.54 W
Cibuta	**200**	31.04 N	110.54 W
Cicagna	**62**	44.25 N	9.14 E
Cicala	**68**	39.01 N	16.29 E
Çicalengka	**115a**	6.59 S	107.50 E
Ćićarija ⩘	**36**	45.30 N	13.54 E
Čičatka	**89**	54.03 N	121.18 E
Cicciano	**68**	40.58 N	14.32 E
Cicero, Il., U.S.	**216**	41.50 N	87.45 W
Cicero, In., U.S.	**218**	40.07 N	86.00 W
Cicero, N.Y., U.S.	**210**	43.10 N	76.07 W
Cicero Creek ≏	**194**	40.01 N	86.01 W
Cícero Dantas	**250**	10.36 S	38.23 W
Čichačovo, S.S.S.R.	**76**	57.17 N	29.54 E
Čichačovo, S.S.S.R.	**89**	51.50 N	141.07 E
Čichareši	**84**	42.48 N	43.03 E
Ciche, Sgurr na ∧	**46**	57.01 N	5.27 W
Çicheng	**100**	30.00 N	121.22 E
Čičikleja ≏	**78**	47.23 N	31.34 E
Čičkajul ≏	**86**	57.34 N	85.44 E
Cicladas, Islas de la → Kikládhes II	**38**	37.30 N	25.00 E
Cicolano ◆[1]	**66**	42.12 N	13.12 E
Cicurug	**115a**	6.47 S	106.47 E
Cidacos ≏	**34**	42.19 N	1.55 W
Cidade, Rio da ≏	**256**	22.25 S	43.09 W
Cidade Universitária ᵾ[2], Bra.	**287a**	22.52 S	43.14 W
Cidade Universitária ᵾ[2], Bra.	**287b**	23.33 S	46.43 W
Cide	**130**	41.54 N	33.00 E
Cidra	**240m**	18.11 N	66.10 W
Cidra, Lago de ⊜[1]	**240m**	18.12 N	66.08 W
Ciechanów	**30**	52.53 N	20.38 E
Ciechanów □[4]	**30**	53.00 N	20.20 E
Ciechanowiec	**30**	52.42 N	22.31 E
Ciechocinek	**30**	52.52 N	18.49 E
Ciego de Avila	**240p**	21.51 N	78.46 W
Ciego de Avila □[4]	**240p**	22.00 N	78.40 W
Ciempozuelos	**34**	40.10 N	3.37 W
Ciénaga	**246**	11.01 N	74.15 W
Ciénaga de Oro	**246**	8.53 N	75.37 W
Ciénega de Flores	**196**	25.57 N	100.11 W
Cienfuegos	**240p**	22.09 N	80.27 W
Cienfuegos □[4]	**240p**	22.10 N	80.25 W
Cienfuegos, Bahía de ⊂	**240p**	22.07 N	80.29 W
Čierna [nad Tisou]	**30**	48.25 N	22.05 E
Čierny Balog	**30**	48.45 N	19.40 E
Cíes, Islas II	**34**	42.13 N	8.54 W
Cieszanów	**30**	50.16 N	23.08 E
Cieszyn	**30**	49.45 N	18.38 E
Cieza	**34**	38.14 N	1.25 W
Çiftalan	**267b**	41.15 N	28.54 E
Çiftehan	**130**	37.31 N	34.46 E
Çifteler	**130**	39.22 N	31.03 E
Çiftlik, Tür.	**130**	40.08 N	39.27 E
Çiftlik, Tür.	**130**	38.11 N	34.30 E
Cifuentes, Cuba	**240p**	22.39 N	80.03 W
Cifuentes, Esp.	**34**	40.47 N	2.37 W
Čiganak, S.S.S.R.	**80**	51.47 N	43.18 E
Čiganak, S.S.S.R.	**86**	45.06 N	73.58 E
Čiganaki	**80**	47.57 N	43.05 E
Čigirin	**78**	49.04 N	32.40 E
Čigliano	**62**	45.18 N	8.01 E
Čigorak	**80**	51.26 N	42.09 E
Cigou	**100**	33.51 N	113.35 E
Cigüela ≏	**34**	39.08 N	3.44 W
Cihangir	**130**	40.03 N	29.07 E
Cihara	**115a**	6.52 S	106.06 E
Cihuatlán	**234**	19.14 N	104.35 W
Čiili	**86**	44.10 N	66.45 E
Cijara, Embalse de ⊜[1]	**34**	39.18 N	4.52 W
Čijen	**85**	43.08 N	75.55 E
Çijiawu	**105**	39.48 N	115.59 E
Čijirčik, pereval)(	**85**	40.15 N	73.20 E
Čijli ≏	**85**	40.17 N	72.38 E
Çijulang	**115a**	7.44 S	108.27 E
Čik	**86**	55.01 N	82.27 E
Cikajang	**115a**	7.22 S	107.47 E
Cikalong-kulon	**115a**	6.42 S	107.12 E
Çikampek	**115a**	6.24 S	107.27 E
Čikan	**88**	54.54 N	105.39 E
Cikarang	**115a**	6.15 S	107.09 E
Çikatomas	**115a**	7.37 S	108.15 E
Čikišl'ar	**128**	37.34 N	53.55 E
Čikoj	**88**	50.16 N	106.54 E
Čikoj ≏	**88**	51.02 N	106.39 E
Čikola	**84**	43.12 N	43.55 E
Cikou	**100**	29.42 N	114.46 E
Cıksı	**130**	38.30 N	40.55 E
Cilacap	**115a**	7.44 S	109.00 E
Çilader	**130**	41.02 N	37.06 E
Čilamaya	**115a**	6.15 S	107.35 E
Cilavegna	**62**	45.19 N	8.44 E
Çıldır	**84**	41.08 N	43.07 E
Çıldır Gölü ⊜	**84**	41.04 N	43.15 E
Čiledug	**115a**	6.54 S	108.44 E
Çilegon	**115a**	6.01 S	106.03 E
Čilekovo	**80**	47.50 N	43.30 E
Cilento ⩘	**68**	40.17 N	15.19 E
Çilento ◆[1]	**36**	40.15 N	15.10 E
Čil'gazi	**85**	40.10 N	70.39 E
Cili	**102**	29.17 N	111.00 E
Çilicia □[9]	**130**	36.40 N	34.20 E
Çilik, S.S.S.R.	**85**	43.36 N	78.15 E
Çilik, S.S.S.R.	**86**	51.07 N	54.07 E
Čilik ≏	**85**	43.05 N	78.28 E
Cililin	**115a**	6.56 S	107.26 E
Cilimus	**115a**	6.52 S	108.29 E
Cilincing ◆[8]	**269e**	6.06 S	106.56 E
Cill Airne → Killarney	**48**	52.03 N	9.30 W
Cill Chainnigh → Kilkenny	**48**	52.39 N	7.15 W
Cilleruelo de Bezana	**34**	42.58 N	3.51 W
Cil'ma ≏	**24**	65.27 N	52.06 E
Cimabanche (Schluderbach)	**64**	46.37 N	12.11 E
Cima Gogna	**64**	46.31 N	12.28 E
Cimahi	**115a**	6.53 S	107.32 E
Cimalaka	**115a**	6.49 S	107.56 E
Cimalmotto	**58**	46.17 N	8.29 E
Cimarron, Ks., U.S.	**198**	37.48 N	100.20 W
Cimarron, N.M., U.S.	**200**	36.30 N	104.54 W
Cimarron ≏, U.S.	**196**	36.10 N	96.17 W
Cimarron ≏, N.M., U.S.	**196**	36.20 N	104.31 W
Cimarron, North Fork ≏	**196**	37.25 N	101.13 W
Čimbaj	**86**	42.57 N	59.47 E
Čimčinej, gora ∧[2]	**180**	63.37 N	178.04 E
Cimetière, Pointe du >	**241o**	15.58 N	61.19 W
Cimini, Monti ⩘	**66**	42.20 N	12.10 E
Ciminna	**70**	37.54 N	13.34 E
Çimino, Monte ∧	**66**	42.24 N	12.12 E
Čimion	**85**	40.16 N	71.31 E
Čimišlija	**78**	46.32 N	28.44 E
Çimitile	**68**	40.56 N	14.31 E
Čimkent	**85**	42.18 N	69.36 E
Čimkent □[4]	**85**	42.30 N	68.00 E
Čimkorgon	**85**	42.50 N	75.30 E
Cimla ≏	**80**	48.01 N	42.24 E
Ciml'ansk	**80**	47.38 N	42.04 E
Ciml'anskoje vodochranilišče ⊜[1]	**80**	48.00 N	43.00 E
Cimolais	**64**	46.17 N	12.26 E
Cimone, Monte ∧	**64**	44.12 N	10.42 E
Cîmpeni	**38**	46.22 N	23.03 E
Cîmpia Turzii	**38**	46.33 N	23.54 E
Cîmpina	**38**	45.08 N	25.44 E
Cimpu	**112**	3.25 S	120.22 E
Cîmpulung	**38**	45.16 N	25.03 E
Cîmpulung Moldovenesc	**38**	47.31 N	25.34 E
Čimtarga, gora ∧	**85**	39.12 N	68.10 E
Čina ≏	**88**	54.20 N	112.24 E
Çina, Tanjung >	**112**	5.56 S	104.45 E
Čınabad	**85**	40.52 N	71.58 E
Činadijevo	**78**	48.30 N	22.50 E
Cinandali	**84**	41.53 N	45.34 E
Çınar	**130**	37.44 N	40.25 E
Çınarcık	**130**	40.39 N	29.06 E
Çinaruco ≏	**246**	6.41 N	67.07 W
Čınaz	**85**	40.56 N	68.45 E
Cinca ≏	**34**	41.26 N	0.21 E
Cincar ∧	**36**	43.54 N	17.04 E
Cincinnati, Ia., U.S.	**190**	40.37 N	92.55 W
Cincinnati, Oh., U.S.	**218**	39.09 N	84.27 W
Cincinnatus	**210**	42.32 N	75.53 W
Cinco, Canal Numero ≍	**252**	37.35 S	57.20 W
Cinco Balas, Cayos II	**240p**	21.06 N	79.20 W
Cinco de Mayo	**196**	25.46 N	104.19 W
Cinco Palos, Sierra ⩘	**234**	22.40 N	99.36 W
Cinco Pinos	**236**	13.14 N	86.52 W
Cinco Saltos	**252**	38.49 S	68.04 W
Cinderella	**273d**	26.15 S	28.16 E
Cinderella Dam ⊜[1]	**273d**	26.15 S	28.14 E
Cinderford	**42**	51.50 N	2.29 W
Cinder Island I	**276**	40.36 N	73.36 W
Çine	**130**	37.36 N	28.04 E
Činebar	**224**	46.36 N	122.32 W
Cinema	**182**	53.14 N	122.27 W
Ciney	**56**	50.18 N	5.06 E
Cingaly	**86**	60.13 N	69.45 E
Çingife	**130**	37.20 N	37.33 E
Čingis	**86**	54.08 N	81.41 E
Čingistaj	**86**	49.13 N	85.55 E
Cingoli	**66**	43.22 N	13.13 E
Cinigiano	**66**	42.53 N	11.24 E
Çinisello Balsamo	**62**	45.33 N	9.13 E
Činiševcy	**78**	47.42 N	28.52 E
Çinisi	**70**	38.09 N	13.06 E
Činja-Voryk	**24**	63.13 N	52.38 E
Cinkota ◆[8]	**264c**	47.31 N	19.14 E
Cinnaminson	**285**	40.00 N	74.59 W
Cínovec	**54**	50.43 N	13.45 E
Cinq, Lac des ⊜	**206**	46.51 N	72.59 W
Cinq Doigts, Lac ⊜	**206**	46.36 N	74.32 W
Cinquefrondi	**68**	38.25 N	16.06 E
Cinquemiglia, Piano delle ≚	**66**	41.50 N	14.00 E
Cinqueterre □[9]	**62**	44.10 N	9.45 E
Cintalapa ≏	**234**	16.41 N	93.36 W
Cintalapa de Figueroa	**234**	16.44 N	93.43 W
Cinto, Monte ∧	**36**	42.23 N	8.56 E
Cinto Euganeo	**64**	45.16 N	11.40 E
Cintra → Sintra	**34**	38.48 N	9.23 W
Cintra, Golfe de ⊂	**148**	23.00 N	16.20 W
Cinzas, Rio das ≏	**252**	22.56 S	50.32 W
Ciocănești	**38**	44.12 N	27.04 E
Ciociaria ◆[1]	**66**	41.45 N	13.15 E
Çiomas	**115a**	6.12 S	106.01 E
Čiovo, Otok I	**36**	43.30 N	16.20 E
Cipa ≏	**88**	55.23 N	115.55 E
Ciparay	**115a**	7.03 S	107.43 E
Cipatujah	**115a**	7.45 S	108.00 E
Cipikan	**88**	54.55 N	113.21 E
Cipikan ≏	**88**	55.14 N	113.05 E
Cipó	**250**	11.06 S	38.31 W
Cipó ≏	**255**	18.40 S	43.59 W
Cipolândia	**255**	20.08 S	55.24 W
Cipolletti	**252**	38.56 S	67.59 W
Çiqikou	**107**	29.35 N	106.26 E
Čir	**80**	48.29 N	43.10 E
Čir ≏	**80**	48.35 N	42.51 E
Çiraadhame	**144**	10.30 N	49.22 E
Čirachčaj ≏	**84**	41.40 N	48.11 E
Čiragidzor	**84**	40.27 N	46.19 E
Ciranjang	**115a**	6.49 S	107.14 E
Circeo, Monte ∧	**66**	41.14 N	13.03 E
Circeo, Parco Nazionale del ♦	**66**	41.17 N	13.05 E
Čirčik	**85**	41.29 N	69.35 E
Čirčik ≏	**85**	40.54 N	68.41 E
Çırçır	**130**	40.04 N	36.48 E
Circle, Ak., U.S.	**180**	65.50 N	144.04 W
Circle, Mt., U.S.	**202**	47.20 N	105.35 W
Circle Hot Springs	**180**	65.28 N	144.39 W
Circleville, N.Y., U.S.	**210**	41.31 N	75.23 W
Circleville, Oh., U.S.	**218**	39.36 N	82.56 W
Circleville, Pa., U.S.	**279b**	40.20 N	79.44 W
Circleville, Ut., U.S.	**200**	38.10 N	112.16 W
Circleville Mountain ∧	**200**	38.12 N	112.24 W
Circular Reef ✦[2]	**164**	3.25 S	147.47 E
Circus World ♦	**220**	28.14 N	81.38 W
Cirebon	**115a**	6.44 S	108.34 E
Cireglio	**66**	43.59 N	10.51 E
Ciremay, Gunung ∧	**115a**	6.54 S	108.24 E
Cirencester	**42**	51.44 N	1.59 W
Çirey-sur-Vezouze	**58**	48.35 N	6.57 E
Čirgalandy	**88**	50.36 N	97.20 E
Ciriè	**62**	45.14 N	7.36 E
Çirigliano	**68**	40.24 N	16.10 E
Čirikovo	**82**	55.23 N	37.14 E
Ciriquiri ≏	**248**	8.05 S	65.18 W
Cirk, gora ∧	**180**	64.33 N	175.25 E
Cîrlibaba	**38**	47.35 N	25.07 E
Cirò	**68**	39.23 N	17.04 E
Çirò Marina	**68**	39.22 N	17.08 E
Čirpan	**38**	42.12 N	25.20 E
Ciruas	**115a**	6.06 S	106.13 E
Cisa, Passo della)(	**64**	44.28 N	9.55 E
Cisano	**64**	45.32 N	10.43 E
Cisarua	**115a**	6.40 S	106.59 E
Cisco, Il., U.S.	**219**	40.01 N	88.43 W
Cisco, Tx., U.S.	**196**	32.23 N	98.58 W
Cishan	**98**	36.37 N	114.07 E
Cishangang	**106**	30.55 N	119.31 E
Ciskei □[1], Afr.	**138**	32.50 S	27.00 E
Ciskei □[1], Afr.	**158**	32.50 S	27.00 E
Cislago	**62**	45.39 N	8.58 E
Cisliano	**266b**	45.27 N	8.59 E
Çismar	**54**	54.11 N	10.59 E
Čismena	**82**	56.02 N	36.13 E
Cismon ≏	**64**	46.55 N	11.43 E
Çismon del Grappa	**64**	45.55 N	11.44 E
Čišmy	**86**	54.35 N	55.20 E
Cisnădie	**38**	45.43 N	24.09 E
Cisne	**194**	38.31 N	88.26 W
Cisneros	**246**	6.33 N	75.04 W
Cisnes ≏	**254**	44.45 S	72.42 W
Cisolok	**115a**	6.57 S	106.26 E
Cison di Valmarino	**64**	45.58 N	12.10 E
Cispus ≏	**224**	46.25 N	122.10 W
Cisse ≏	**50**	47.25 N	0.47 E
Çissna Park	**216**	40.33 N	87.53 W
Čistá, Česko.	**54**	50.06 N	12.44 E
Čistá, Česko.	**60**	50.02 N	13.35 E
Cisterna di Latina	**66**	41.35 N	12.49 E
Cisternino	**68**	40.44 N	17.25 E
Cistern Point >	**238**	23.43 N	77.35 W
Çistierna	**34**	42.48 N	5.07 W
Čistoje	**80**	56.32 N	43.02 E
Čistooz'ornoje	**86**	54.43 N	76.33 E
Čistopol'	**80**	55.21 N	50.37 E
Čistopolje, S.S.S.R.	**83**	47.31 N	39.27 E
Čistopolje, S.S.S.R.	**86**	52.34 N	67.15 E
Čistovodovka	**83**	49.24 N	37.20 E
Čita	**88**	52.03 N	113.30 E
Čita □[4]	**88**	52.00 N	117.00 E
Čita ≏	**88**	52.00 N	113.30 E
Citac, Nevado ∧	**248**	12.50 S	75.15 W
Citaré ≏	**250**	1.11 N	54.41 W
Citeli-Ckaro	**84**	41.28 N	46.07 E
Cité Universitaire ᵾ[2]	**261**	48.49 N	2.20 E
Citlaltépetl, Volcán (Pico de Orizaba) ∧[1]	**234**	19.01 N	97.16 W
Citra	**192**	29.24 N	82.06 W
Citronelle	**194**	31.05 N	88.13 W
Citrus □[6]	**220**	28.52 N	82.28 W
Citrusdal	**158**	32.36 S	19.00 E
Citrus Heights	**226**	38.42 N	121.16 W
Citrus Springs	**220**	29.00 N	82.27 W
Citrus Tower ᵾ	**220**	28.33 N	81.44 W
Cittadella	**64**	45.39 N	11.47 E
Città della Pieve	**66**	42.57 N	12.00 E
Città del Vaticano → Vatican City □[1]	**66**	41.54 N	12.27 E
Città di Castello	**66**	43.27 N	12.14 E
Cittaducale	**66**	42.23 N	12.57 E
Cittanova	**68**	38.21 N	16.05 E
Cittareale	**66**	42.37 N	13.10 E
Città Sant'Angelo	**66**	42.31 N	14.03 E
Città Universitaria ᵾ[2]	**267a**	41.55 N	12.31 E
City Beach	**168a**	31.56 S	115.45 E
City Bell ◆[8]	**258**	34.52 S	58.05 W
City Island ◆[8]	**276**	40.51 N	73.47 W
City Mills	**283**	42.06 N	71.21 W
City of Hope National Medical Center ᵾ	**280**	34.08 N	117.58 W
City Of Industry	**280**	34.01 N	117.57 W
City of London ◆[8]	**260**	51.31 N	0.05 W
City of Sunrise	**220**	26.08 N	80.14 W
City of Westminster ◆[8]	**260**	51.30 N	0.09 W
City Point	**220**	28.24 N	80.45 W
City University of New York Brooklyn College ᵾ[2]	**276**	40.38 N	73.57 W
City University of New York City College ᵾ[2]	**276**	40.49 N	73.57 W
City University of New York Queens College ᵾ[2]	**276**	40.44 N	73.49 W
City University of New York York College ᵾ[2]	**276**	40.42 N	73.48 W
Ciucaș ∧	**38**	45.31 N	25.55 E
Ciudad	**234**	23.44 N	105.42 W
Ciudad Acuña	**232**	29.18 N	100.55 W
Ciudad Altamirano	**234**	18.20 N	100.40 W
Ciudad Anáhuac	**232**	27.14 N	100.09 W
Ciudad Barrios	**236**	13.46 N	88.16 W
Ciudad Bolívar	**246**	8.08 N	63.33 W
Ciudad Bolivia	**246**	8.21 N	70.34 W
Ciudad Camargo, Méx.	**232**	27.40 N	105.10 W
Ciudad Camargo, Méx.	**232**	26.19 N	98.50 W
Ciudad Chetumal	**232**	18.30 N	88.18 W
Ciudad Darío	**236**	12.43 N	86.08 W
Ciudad de Guayana → Ciudad Guayana	**246**	8.22 N	62.40 W
Ciudad de la Habana □[4]	**240p**	23.08 N	82.22 W
Ciudad del Cabo → Cape Town	**158**	33.55 S	18.22 E
Ciudad del Carmen	**232**	18.38 N	91.50 W
Ciudad del Maíz	**234**	22.24 N	99.36 W
Ciudad de los Deportes ♦	**286a**	19.23 N	99.11 W
Ciudad del Vaticano → Vatican City □[1]	**66**	41.54 N	12.27 E

≏ River	Fluss	Río	Rivière	Rio
≍ Canal	Kanal	Canal	Canal	Canal
∟ Waterfall, Rapids	Wasserfall, Stromschnellen	Cascada, Rápidos	Chute d'eau, Rapides	Cascata, Rápidos
ⲩ Strait	Meeresstrasse	Estrecho	Détroit	Estreito
⊂ Bay, Gulf	Bucht, Golf	Bahía, Golfo	Baie, Golfe	Baía, Golfo
⊜ Lake, Lakes	See, Seen	Lago, Lagos	Lac, Lacs	Lago, Lagos
≋ Swamp	Sumpf	Pantano	Marais	Pântano
⍓ Ice Features, Glacier	Eis- und Gletscherformen	Accidentes Glaciales	Formes glaciaires	Acidentes glaciares
⍑ Other Hydrographic Features	Andere Hydrographische Objekte	Otros Elementos Hidrográficos	Autres données hydrographiques	Outros acidentes hidrográficos

✦ Submarine Features	Untermeerische Objekte	Accidentes Submarinos	Formes de relief sous-marin	Acidentes submarinos
□ Political Unit	Politische Einheit	Unidad Politica	Entité politique	Unidade política
ᵾ Cultural Institution	Kulturelle Institution	Institución Cultural	Institution culturelle	Instituição cultural
⊥ Historical Site	Historische Stätte	Sitio Histórico	Site historique	Sitio histórico
♦ Recreational Site	Erholungs- und Ferienort	Sitio de Recreo	Centre de loisirs	Area de Lazer
⊠ Airport	Flughafen	Aeropuerto	Aéroport	Aeroporto
■ Military Installation	Militäranlage	Instalación Militar	Installation militaire	Instalação militar
◆ Miscellaneous	Verschiedenes	Misceláneo	Divers	Diversos

Name	Page	Lat.°′	Long.°′
Ciudad de México (Mexico City), Méx.	234	19.24 N	99.09 W
Ciudad de México (Mexico City), Méx.	286a	19.24 N	99.09 W
Ciudad de Naucalpan de Juárez	286a	19.28 N	99.14 W
Ciudad de Nutrias	246	8.05 N	69.18 W
Ciudad Deportiva ♠, Cuba	286b	23.07 N	82.22 W
Ciudad Deportiva ♠, Méx.	286a	19.24 N	99.06 W
Ciudad de Valles	234	21.59 N	99.01 W
Ciudad de Villaldama	232	26.30 N	100.26 W
Ciudadela	34	40.02 N	3.50 E
Ciudadela, Parque de la ♠	266d	41.23 N	2.11 E
Ciudad General Belgrano	288	34.43 S	58.32 W
Ciudad Guayana	246	8.22 N	62.40 W
Ciudad Guerrero	232	28.33 N	107.30 W
Ciudad Guzmán	234	19.41 N	103.29 W
Ciudad Hidalgo, Méx.	234	19.41 N	100.34 W
Ciudad Hidalgo, Méx.	236	14.41 N	92.09 W
Ciudad Ixtepec	234	16.34 N	95.06 W
Ciudad Jiménez	232	27.08 N	104.55 W
Ciudad Juárez	232	31.44 N	106.29 W
Ciudad Lerdo	196	25.32 N	103.32 W
Ciudad Lineal ◆[8]	266a	40.27 N	3.40 W
Ciudad López Mateos	286a	19.33 N	99.15 W
Ciudad Madero	234	22.16 N	97.50 W
Ciudad Mante	234	22.44 N	98.57 W
Ciudad Manuel Doblado	234	20.44 N	101.56 W
Ciudad Melchor Múzquiz	232	27.53 N	101.31 W
Ciudad Mendoza	234	18.48 N	97.11 W
Ciudad Mier	232	26.26 N	99.09 W
Ciudad Miguel Alemán	232	26.23 N	99.01 W
Ciudad Morelos	232	32.38 N	114.52 W
Ciudad Obregón	232	27.29 N	109.56 W
Ciudad Ocampo	234	22.50 N	99.20 W
Ciudad Ojeda (Lagunillas)	246	10.12 N	71.19 W
Ciudad Piar	246	7.27 N	63.19 W
Ciudad Real	34	38.59 N	3.56 W
Ciudad Rodrigo	34	40.36 N	6.32 W
Ciudad Sahagún	234	19.47 N	98.33 W
Ciudad Santos	234	21.36 N	98.58 W
Ciudad Serdán	234	18.59 N	97.27 W
Ciudad Tecún Umán	236	14.40 N	92.09 W
Ciudad Trujillo → Santo Domingo	238	18.28 N	69.54 W
Ciudad Universitaria ◆[8]	266a	40.27 N	3.44 W
Ciudad Universitaria ʊ[2], Esp.	266a	40.27 N	3.43 W
Ciudad Universitaria ʊ[2], Méx.	286a	19.20 N	99.11 W
Ciudad Universitaria ʊ[2], Ven.	286c	10.29 N	66.53 W
Ciudad Victoria, Méx.	204	32.20 N	115.06 W
Ciudad Victoria, Méx.	234	23.44 N	99.08 W
Ciudad Vieja	236	14.31 N	90.46 W
Ciuma	152	13.14 S	15.40 E
Ciurana ≃	34	41.08 N	0.39 E
Civa Burnu ›	130	41.22 N	36.35 E
Civate	62	45.50 N	9.21 E
Civenna	58	45.56 N	9.16 E
Civetta, Monte ʌ	64	46.23 N	12.03 E
Civezzano	64	46.05 N	11.11 E
Cividale del Friuli	64	46.06 N	13.25 E
Cividate	62	45.33 N	9.50 E
Cividate Camuno	64	45.57 N	10.17 E
Civil' ≃, S.S.S.R.	80	56.08 N	47.35 E
Civil' ≃, S.S.S.R.	80	56.05 N	47.37 E
Civil'sk	80	55.53 N	47.29 E
Civita	68	39.49 N	16.18 E
Civitacampomarano	66	41.47 N	14.41 E
Civita Castellana	66	42.17 N	12.25 E
Civita di Bagno	66	42.18 N	13.26 E
Civitanova Alta	66	43.19 N	13.40 E
Civitanova del Sannio	66	41.40 N	14.24 E
Civitanova Marche	66	43.18 N	13.44 E
Civitaquana	66	42.19 N	13.54 E
Civitavecchia	66	42.06 N	11.48 E
Civitella del Tronto	66	42.46 N	13.40 E
Civitella di Romagna	66	44.00 N	11.56 E
Civitella in Val di Chiana	66	43.25 N	11.43 E
Civitella Marittima	66	43.00 N	11.17 E
Civitella Roveto	66	41.54 N	13.25 E
Civray	32	46.09 N	0.18 E
Çivril	130	38.18 N	29.45 E
Ciwidey	115a	7.06 S	107.27 E
Cixerri ≃	71	39.17 N	8.59 E
Cixi	100	30.11 N	121.15 E
Cixian	98	36.22 N	114.23 E
Çiyutuo	104	41.31 N	122.53 E
Čiža	24	67.06 N	44.19 E
Čižapka ≃	86	59.01 N	79.36 E
Čiža Vtoraja	80	50.52 N	49.40 E
Cize	58	46.12 N	5.26 E
Čizhuping	107	29.11 N	103.36 E
Čižinskije razlivy ≡	80	50.25 N	49.40 E
Cizre	130	37.20 N	42.12 E
C.J. Strike Reservoir ⊜[1]	202	42.57 N	115.53 W
Čkalov → Orenburg	86	51.54 N	55.06 E
Čkalovo, S.S.S.R.	78	46.28 N	34.11 E
Čkalovo, S.S.S.R.	86	53.38 N	70.24 E
Čkalovsk, S.S.S.R.	80	56.46 N	43.16 E
Čkalovsk, S.S.S.R.	85	41.15 N	68.00 E
Čkalovsk, S.S.S.R.	85	40.13 N	69.50 E
Čkalovskij	265b	55.54 N	38.04 E
Ç K Creek ≃	202	47.36 N	108.29 W
Čkyně	60	49.07 N	13.49 E
Čľa, ozero ⊜	89	53.27 N	140.53 E
Clachan	46	55.45 N	5.34 W
Clackamas	224	45.24 N	122.34 W
Clackamas □[6]	224	45.10 N	122.16 W
Clackamas ≃	224	45.22 N	122.36 W
Clackamas, Oak Grove Fork ≃	224	45.05 N	122.03 W
Clackamas Heights	224	45.23 N	122.34 W
Clackline	168a	31.43 S	116.31 E
Clackmannan	46	56.06 N	3.46 W
Clacton-on-Sea	42	51.48 N	1.09 E
Cladich	46	56.21 N	5.05 W
Claerwen ≃	42	52.44 N	3.37 W
Claerwen Reservoir ⊜[1]	42	52.17 N	3.43 W
Claflin	198	38.31 N	98.32 W
Claiborne	194	31.32 N	87.31 W
Clain ≃	32	46.47 N	0.32 E
Claire, Lake ⊜	176	58.35 N	112.05 W
Claire, Pointe ›	275a	45.25 N	73.50 W
Clairefontaine-en-Yvelines	50	48.37 N	1.55 E
Clair Engle Lake ⊜[1]	204	40.52 N	122.43 W
Claireville	275b	43.45 N	79.38 W
Claireville Reservoir ⊜[1]	275b	43.45 N	79.39 W
Clairis ≃	50	48.07 N	2.45 E
Clairmarais	50	50.46 N	2.18 E
Clairmont	182	55.16 N	118.47 W
Clairton	214	40.17 N	79.52 W
Clairvaux-les-Lacs	58	46.34 N	5.45 E
Claix	62	45.07 N	5.40 E
Clallam □[6]	224	48.10 N	123.49 W
Clallam Bay	224	48.15 N	124.15 W
Clam ≃, Mi., U.S.	190	44.05 N	85.00 W
Clam ≃, Wi., U.S.	190	45.57 N	92.33 W
Clam, North Fork ≃	190	45.46 N	92.18 W
Clamart	261	48.48 N	2.16 E
Clamecy	50	47.27 N	3.31 E
Clam Gulch	180	60.15 N	151.22 W
Clam Lake ⊜	184	55.19 N	105.43 W
Clampton	162	29.56 S	119.06 E
Clan Alpine Mountains ⋀	204	39.40 N	117.55 W
Clandonald	182	53.34 N	110.44 W
Clandon Park ♠	260	51.15 N	0.30 W
Clandulla	170	32.55 S	149.57 E
Clane	48	53.18 N	6.41 W
Clans	62	44.00 N	7.09 E
Clanton	194	32.50 N	86.37 W
Clanwilliam	158	32.11 S	18.54 E
Claonaig	46	55.46 N	5.22 W
Clapham	42	52.09 N	0.29 W
Clapier, Mont ʌ	62	44.07 N	7.25 E
Clapperton Island I	190	46.02 N	82.13 W
Clapp Farm	214	41.24 N	79.32 W
Clàr, Loch nan ⊜	46	58.17 N	4.08 W
Clara, Arg.	252	31.50 S	58.49 W
Clara, Ire.	48	53.20 N	7.36 W
Clara, Ms., U.S.	194	31.34 N	88.41 W
Clara ≃	166	18.30 S	141.18 E
Clara City	198	44.57 N	95.21 W
Clara Island I	110	10.54 N	97.55 E
Claraville	166	18.40 S	141.43 E
Claraz	252	37.54 S	59.17 W
Clare, Austl.	166	33.25 S	143.55 E
Clare, Austl.	168b	33.50 S	138.36 E
Clare, Eng., U.K.	42	52.05 N	0.35 E
Clare, Mi., U.S.	190	43.49 N	84.46 W
Clare □[6]	48	52.50 N	9.00 W
Clare ≃, On., Can.	212	44.28 N	77.17 W
Clare ≃, Ire.	48	53.20 N	9.03 W
Clarecastle	48	52.49 N	8.57 W
Claregalway	48	53.21 N	8.57 W
Clare Island I	48	53.48 N	10.00 W
Claremont, On., Can.	212	43.58 N	79.07 W
Claremont, Eng., U.K.	260	51.21 N	0.22 W
Claremont, Ca., U.S.	228	34.05 N	117.43 W
Claremont, N.H., U.S.	188	43.22 N	72.20 W
Claremont, S.D., U.S.	198	45.40 N	98.00 W
Claremont, Va., U.S.	208	37.13 N	76.57 W
Claremont ʌ	204	39.53 N	120.57 W
Claremore	196	36.18 N	95.36 W
Claremorris	48	53.44 N	9.00 W
Clarence, N.Z.	172	42.10 S	173.56 E
Clarence, Il., U.S.	216	40.28 N	87.58 W
Clarence, Ia., U.S.	190	41.53 N	91.03 W
Clarence, Mo., U.S.	219	39.44 N	92.15 W
Clarence, N.Y., U.S.	210	42.59 N	78.35 W
Clarence, Pa., U.S.	214	41.03 N	77.56 W
Clarence ≃, Austl.	166	29.25 S	153.22 E
Clarence ≃, N.Z.	172	42.10 S	173.57 E
Clarence, Isla I	254	54.10 S	71.50 W
Clarence, Port c	180	65.15 N	166.40 W
Clarence Cannon Dam ◆[6]	219	39.31 N	91.39 W
Clarence Center	210	43.00 N	78.35 W
Clarence Creek	206	45.30 N	75.13 W
Clarence Fahnestock Memorial State Park ♠	210	41.26 N	73.50 W
Clarence Island I	9	61.09 S	54.06 W
Clarence J. Brown Reservoir ⊜[1]	218	39.58 N	83.44 W
Clarence Strait ʉ, Austl.	164	12.00 S	131.00 E
Clarence Strait ʉ, Ak., U.S.	180	55.25 N	132.00 W
Clarence Town, Austl.	170	32.35 S	151.47 E
Clarence Town, Ba.	238	23.06 N	74.59 W
Clarenceville, P.Q., Can.	206	45.04 N	73.15 W
Clarenceville, Mi., U.S.	281	42.27 N	83.19 W
Clarendon, Austl.	168b	35.07 S	138.38 E
Clarendon, Ar., U.S.	194	34.41 N	91.18 W
Clarendon, N.Y., U.S.	210	43.11 N	78.04 W
Clarendon, Pa., U.S.	214	41.46 N	79.05 W
Clarendon, Tx., U.S.	196	34.56 N	100.53 W
Clarendon Hills	278	41.47 N	87.57 W
Clarens	158	28.30 S	28.29 E
Clarenville	186	48.10 N	53.58 W
Claresholm	182	50.02 N	113.35 W
Claret	62	43.52 N	3.54 E
Clarholz	52	51.54 N	8.11 E
Claridge	214	40.21 N	79.37 W
Clarie Coast ⊥[2]	9	66.30 S	133.00 E
Clarin	116	9.58 N	124.01 E
Clarinda	198	40.44 N	95.02 W
Clarines	246	9.56 N	65.10 W
Clarington	214	41.20 N	79.07 W
Clarion, Ia., U.S.	190	42.43 N	93.43 W
Clarion, Pa., U.S.	214	41.12 N	79.23 W
Clarion □[6]	214	41.13 N	79.24 W
Clarion ≃	214	41.07 N	79.41 W
Clarión, Isla I	232	18.22 N	114.44 W
Clarion, West Branch ≃	214	41.29 N	78.41 W
Clarion Fracture Zone ⊥	16	18.00 N	122.00 W
Clarissa	198	46.07 N	94.56 W
Clark, N.J., U.S.	276	40.38 N	74.18 W
Clark, Oh., U.S.	214	40.27 N	81.54 W
Clark, S.D., U.S.	198	44.52 N	97.43 W
Clark, Tx., U.S.	222	30.23 N	94.46 W
Clark □[6], In., U.S.	218	38.17 N	85.44 W
Clark □[6], Oh., U.S.	218	39.56 N	83.49 W
Clark □[6], Wa., U.S.	224	45.48 N	122.31 W
Clark, Lake ⊜	180	60.15 N	154.15 W
Clark, Mount ʌ	180	64.25 N	124.12 W
Clark, Point ›	190	44.04 N	81.45 W
Clark Air Base (U.S.) ■	116	15.11 N	120.32 E
Clark Branch ≃	285	39.43 N	74.45 W
Clark Canyon Reservoir ⊜[1]	202	44.58 N	112.51 W
Clark Creek ≃	208	40.22 N	76.58 W
Clarkdale	200	34.46 N	112.03 W
Clarke ≃	166	19.12 S	145.30 E
Clarke City	186	50.12 N	66.38 W
Clarke Island I	166	40.33 S	148.10 E
Clarke Lake ⊜	184	54.25 N	106.51 W
Clarke Range ⋀	166	20.50 S	148.33 E
Clarke River	166	19.13 S	145.27 E
Clarkesville	192	34.36 N	83.31 W
Clarkfield	198	44.47 N	95.48 W
Clark Fork	202	48.08 N	116.10 W
Clark Fork ≃	202	48.09 N	116.15 W
Clark Hill	218	38.18 N	83.12 W
Clarklake	216	42.04 N	84.21 W
Clark Lake ⊜	216	42.07 N	84.19 W
Clark Mills	210	43.06 N	75.22 W
Clark Mountain ʌ, Ca., U.S.	204	35.32 N	115.35 W
Clark Mountain ʌ, Wa., U.S.	224	48.03 N	120.57 W
Clarks, La., U.S.	194	32.01 N	92.08 W
Clarks, Ne., U.S.	198	41.12 N	97.50 W
Clarks ≃	194	37.03 N	88.33 W
Clarks, West Fork ≃	194	36.59 N	88.31 W
Clarksboro	285	39.47 N	75.13 W
Clarksburg, On., Can.	212	44.43 N	80.27 W
Clarksburg, Ca., U.S.	226	38.25 N	121.32 W
Clarksburg, Il., U.S.	219	39.20 N	88.44 W
Clarksburg, In., U.S.	218	39.26 N	85.20 W
Clarksburg, Md., U.S.	208	39.14 N	77.16 W
Clarksburg, N.J., U.S.	208	40.11 N	74.26 W
Clarksburg, Oh., U.S.	218	39.30 N	83.09 W
Clarksburg, W.V., U.S.	188	39.16 N	80.20 W
Clarksburg State Park ♠	207	42.43 N	73.06 W
Clarks Creek ≃, Ks., U.S.	198	39.05 N	96.42 W
Clarks Creek ≃, Ky., U.S.	218	38.40 N	84.44 W
Clarksdale	194	34.12 N	90.34 W
Clarks Green	210	41.30 N	75.42 W
Clark's Harbour	186	43.26 N	65.38 W
Clarks Hill	216	40.14 N	86.43 W
Clarks Hill Lake ⊜[1]	192	33.50 N	82.20 W
Clarks Island I	283	42.01 N	70.38 W
Clarks Mills	214	41.24 N	80.11 W
Clarkson, On., Can.	275b	43.31 N	79.37 W
Clarkson, Ky., U.S.	194	37.29 N	86.13 W
Clarkson, Ne., U.S.	198	41.43 N	97.07 W
Clarkson, N.Y., U.S.	210	43.14 N	77.56 W
Clarks Point	180	58.51 N	158.30 W
Clarks Summit	210	41.29 N	75.42 W
Clarkston, Mi., U.S.	216	42.44 N	83.25 W
Clarkston, Wa., U.S.	202	46.24 N	117.02 W
Clark's Town	241q	18.25 N	77.34 W
Clarksville, Ar., U.S.	194	35.28 N	93.27 W
Clarksville, De., U.S.	208	38.32 N	75.08 W
Clarksville, In., U.S.	218	38.15 N	85.47 W
Clarksville, Ia., U.S.	190	42.47 N	92.40 W
Clarksville, Md., U.S.	208	39.12 N	76.56 W
Clarksville, Mi., U.S.	216	42.50 N	85.14 W
Clarksville, Mo., U.S.	219	39.22 N	90.54 W
Clarksville, N.Y., U.S.	210	42.35 N	73.58 W
Clarksville, Oh., U.S.	218	39.24 N	83.58 W
Clarksville, Tn., U.S.	194	36.31 N	87.21 W
Clarksville, Tx., U.S.	196	33.36 N	95.03 W
Clarksville, Va., U.S.	192	36.37 N	78.33 W
Clarksville City	222	32.32 N	94.34 W
Clarkton, Mo., U.S.	194	36.27 N	89.58 W
Clarkton, N.C., U.S.	192	34.29 N	78.39 W
Claro ≃, Bra.	255	15.28 S	51.43 W
Claro ≃, Bra.	255	19.06 S	47.52 W
Claro ≃, Bra.	255	19.08 S	50.40 W
Claro, Arroyo ≃	288	34.25 S	58.41 W
Claro, Ribeirão ≃	287b	23.40 S	46.17 W
Clary	50	50.05 N	3.24 E
Claryville	210	41.55 N	74.34 W
Clashmore	48	52.00 N	7.48 W
Clatskanie	224	46.06 N	123.12 W
Clatskanie ≃	224	46.08 N	123.14 W
Clatsop □[6]	224	46.01 N	123.41 W
Clatsop Spit ›[2]	224	46.13 N	124.01 W
Clatteringshaws Lake ⊜	44	55.05 N	4.17 W
Claude	196	35.07 N	101.22 W
Claudy	44	54.54 N	7.09 W
Claughton	44	54.06 N	2.40 W
Claussnitz	54	50.56 N	12.53 E
Clausthal-Zellerfeld	52	51.48 N	10.20 E
Claver	116	9.35 N	125.44 E
Claverack	210	42.13 N	73.44 W
Claveria, Pil.	116	18.37 N	121.05 E
Claveria, Pil.	116	8.38 N	124.55 E
Clavet	184	52.00 N	106.23 W
Clavey ≃	226	37.52 N	120.07 W
Clawit, Mount ʌ	116	16.58 N	120.58 E
Clawson, Mi., U.S.	281	42.32 N	83.08 W
Clawson, Tx., U.S.	222	31.24 N	94.47 W
Claxton	192	32.09 N	81.54 W
Clay, Ky., U.S.	194	37.28 N	87.49 W
Clay, Tx., U.S.	222	30.23 N	96.21 W
Clay, W.V., U.S.	188	38.27 N	81.05 W
Clay □[6]	219	38.45 N	88.40 W
Claybank Creek ≃	194	31.10 N	85.44 W
Clay Center, Ks., U.S.	198	39.22 N	97.07 W
Clay Center, Ne., U.S.	198	40.31 N	98.03 W
Clay Center, Oh., U.S.	214	41.33 N	83.21 W
Clay City, Il., U.S.	194	38.41 N	88.21 W
Clay City, In., U.S.	194	39.16 N	87.06 W
Clay City, Ky., U.S.	192	37.51 N	83.55 W
Clay Creek ≃	198	38.06 N	102.31 W
Clay Cross	44	53.10 N	1.24 W
Claydon	42	52.06 N	1.07 E
Claye-Souilly	50	48.57 N	2.42 E
Claygate	260	51.22 N	0.20 W
Claygate Cross	260	51.16 N	0.19 E
Clayhole Wash V	200	36.59 N	113.17 W
Clayhurst	182	56.15 N	120.01 W
Claymont	208	39.48 N	75.27 W
Clayoquot Sound ʉ	182	49.11 N	126.08 W
Claypole	288	34.48 S	58.20 W
Claypool, Az., U.S.	200	33.24 N	110.50 W
Claypool, In., U.S.	216	41.07 N	85.52 W
Claysburg	214	40.17 N	78.27 W
Clay Springs	200	34.21 N	110.18 W
Claysville	214	40.07 N	80.24 W
Clayton, Austl.	274b	37.56 S	145.07 E
Clayton, Eng., U.K.	262	53.47 N	1.52 W
Clayton, Al., U.S.	194	31.52 N	85.26 W
Clayton, Ca., U.S.	282	37.57 N	121.56 W
Clayton, De., U.S.	208	39.17 N	75.38 W
Clayton, Ga., U.S.	192	34.52 N	83.24 W
Clayton, Il., U.S.	219	40.01 N	90.57 W
Clayton, In., U.S.	218	39.41 N	86.31 W
Clayton, La., U.S.	194	31.43 N	91.32 W
Clayton, Mi., U.S.	216	41.52 N	84.14 W
Clayton, Mo., U.S.	219	38.38 N	90.19 W
Clayton, N.J., U.S.	208	39.39 N	75.05 W
Clayton, N.M., U.S.	196	36.27 N	103.11 W
Clayton, N.Y., U.S.	212	44.14 N	76.05 W
Clayton, N.C., U.S.	192	35.39 N	78.27 W
Clayton, Ok., U.S.	196	34.35 N	95.21 W
Clayton, Tx., U.S.	222	32.06 N	94.28 W
Clayton, Wa., U.S.	182	48.00 N	117.33 W
Clayton □[6]	166	29.06 S	138.05 E
Claytonia	214	41.00 N	79.58 W
Clayton-le-Moors	262	53.47 N	2.23 W
Clayton-le-Woods	262	53.41 N	2.38 W
Clayton Park ♠	285	39.52 N	75.29 W
Clayton Valley V	282	37.58 N	121.58 W
Claytonville	216	40.34 N	87.49 W
Clay Village	218	38.11 N	85.07 W
Clayville	210	42.59 N	75.15 W
Clear ≃	182	56.11 N	119.42 W
Clear, Cape ›, Ire.	48	51.24 N	9.30 W
Clear, Cape ›, Ak., U.S.	180	59.48 N	147.54 W
Clear, Lake ⊜	212	45.26 N	77.12 W
Clear, Mount ʌ	171b	35.52 S	149.04 E
Clear Boggy Creek ≃	196	34.03 N	95.47 W
Clearbrook, B.C., Can.	224	49.08 N	122.26 W
Clearbrook, Mn., U.S.	198	47.41 N	95.25 W
Clear Creek	218	39.07 N	86.32 W
Clear Creek ≃, Al., U.S.	194	34.00 N	87.19 W
Clear Creek ≃, Az., U.S.	200	34.59 N	110.38 W
Clear Creek ≃, Ca., U.S.	204	40.31 N	122.22 W
Clear Creek ≃, Ca., U.S.	280	34.17 N	118.12 W
Clear Creek ≃, Ca., U.S.	282	37.20 N	122.21 W
Clear Creek ≃, Ky., U.S.	218	38.10 N	85.17 W
Clear Creek ≃, Mo., U.S.	194	38.00 N	93.56 W
Clear Creek ≃, Mt., U.S.	202	48.46 N	109.25 W
Clear Creek ≃, Ne., U.S.	198	41.08 N	99.06 W
Clear Creek ≃, Oh., U.S.	218	39.33 N	84.20 W
Clear Creek ≃, Or., U.S.	224	45.23 N	122.29 W
Clear Creek ≃, Or., U.S.	224	45.09 N	121.31 W
Clear Creek ≃, Tn., U.S.	192	36.05 N	84.42 W
Clear Creek ≃, Tx., U.S.	196	33.16 N	97.03 W
Clear Creek ≃, Tx., U.S.	222	29.33 N	95.05 W
Clear Creek ≃, Tx., U.S.	222	29.09 N	97.23 W
Clear Creek ≃, Wa., U.S.	224	46.07 N	122.00 W
Clear Creek ≃, Wy., U.S.	202	44.53 N	106.04 W
Clear Creek State Park ♠	214	41.20 N	79.05 W
Clearfield, Ia., U.S.	198	40.48 N	94.28 W
Clearfield, Ky., U.S.	218	38.09 N	83.25 W
Clearfield, Pa., U.S.	214	41.01 N	78.26 W
Clearfield, Ut,. U.S.	200	41.06 N	112.01 W
Clearfield □[6]	214	41.02 N	78.27 W
Clearfield Creek ≃	214	41.02 N	78.24 W
Clear Fork Reservoir ⊜[1]	214	40.42 N	82.38 W
Clearing ◆[8]	278	41.47 N	87.47 W
Clear Island I	48	51.26 N	9.30 W
Clearlake, Ca., U.S.	226	38.57 N	122.38 W
Clear Lake, Ia., U.S.	190	43.08 N	93.22 W
Clear Lake, S.D., U.S.	198	44.44 N	96.40 W
Clearlake, Wa., U.S.	224	48.28 N	122.14 W
Clear Lake, Wi., U.S.	190	45.15 N	92.16 W
Clear Lake ⊜, Mb., Can.	184	50.42 N	100.00 W
Clear Lake ⊜, On., Can.	212	45.14 N	79.57 W
Clear Lake ⊜, On., Can.	212	44.30 N	78.13 W
Clear Lake ⊜, On., Can.	212	44.59 N	79.33 W
Clear Lake ⊜, In., U.S.	216	41.44 N	84.50 W
Clear Lake ⊜[1], Ca., U.S.	204	39.02 N	122.50 W
Clear Lake ⊜[1], La., U.S.	194	31.55 N	93.05 W
Clearlake Oaks	226	39.07 N	122.40 W
Clearlake Park	226	38.58 N	122.39 W
Clear Lake Reservoir ⊜[1]	204	41.52 N	121.08 W
Clear Lake Shores	222	29.33 N	95.02 W
Clearmont	202	44.38 N	106.22 W
Clear Run	214	41.08 N	78.45 W
Clear Site	180	64.19 N	149.11 W
Clearview, Oh., U.S.	214	41.25 N	82.10 W
Clearview, Wa., U.S.	224	47.45 N	122.06 W
Clearview, W.V., U.S.	214	40.09 N	80.41 W
Clearview Estates	279b	40.34 N	80.16 W
Clearwater, B.C., Can.	182	51.38 N	120.02 W
Clearwater, Mb., Can.	184	49.08 N	99.01 W
Clearwater, Fl., U.S.	220	27.57 N	82.48 W
Clearwater, Ks., U.S.	198	37.30 N	97.30 W
Clearwater, Ne., U.S.	198	42.10 N	98.11 W
Clearwater, S.C., U.S.	192	33.29 N	81.53 W
Clearwater, Wa., U.S.	224	47.34 N	124.17 W
Clearwater ≃, Can.	184	56.44 N	111.23 W
Clearwater ≃, Ab., Can.	182	52.23 N	114.50 W
Clearwater ≃, B.C., Can.	182	51.42 N	120.00 W
Clearwater ≃, Id., U.S.	202	46.25 N	117.02 W
Clearwater ≃, Mn., U.S.	198	47.54 N	96.16 W
Clearwater ≃, Mt., U.S.	202	46.58 N	113.23 W
Clearwater ≃, Wa., U.S.	224	47.33 N	124.21 W
Clearwater, Middle Fork ≃	202	46.09 N	115.59 W
Clearwater, North Fork ≃	202	46.30 N	116.19 W
Clearwater, South Fork ≃	202	46.09 N	115.59 W
Clear Water Bay c	271d	22.17 N	114.18 E
Clearwater Beach Island I	220	27.59 N	82.49 W
Clearwater Lake ⊜, B.C., Can.	182	52.15 N	120.13 W
Clearwater Lake ⊜, Mb., Can.	184	54.05 N	101.00 W
Clearwater Lake Provincial Park ♠	184	54.03 N	101.10 W
Clearwater Mountains ⋀	202	46.00 N	115.30 W
Cleator Moor	44	54.31 N	3.30 W
Clebit	196	34.21 N	94.52 W
Cleburne	222	32.20 N	97.23 W
Cleckheaton	44	53.43 N	1.43 W
Clee Hills ⋀[2]	42	52.25 N	2.35 W
Cle Elum	224	47.11 N	120.56 W
Cle Elum ≃	224	47.11 N	121.01 W
Cle Elum Lake ⊜[1]	224	47.18 N	121.06 W
Cleethorpes	44	53.34 N	0.02 W
Cleeve Cloud ʌ[2]	42	51.34 N	2.00 W
Clefmont	58	48.06 N	5.31 E
Cleggan	48	53.33 N	10.09 W
Cleland Heights	285	39.44 N	75.34 W
Clelles	62	44.50 N	5.37 E
Clementon	285	39.48 N	74.59 W
Clementsport	186	44.40 N	65.37 W
Clemson	192	34.41 N	82.50 W
Clemville	222	29.00 N	96.08 W
Clendenin	188	38.29 N	81.20 W
Clendening Lake ⊜[1]	214	40.16 N	81.13 W
Clenze	54	52.56 N	10.58 E
Cleobury Mortimer	42	52.23 N	2.29 W
Cleona	208	40.20 N	76.28 W
Cléon-d'Andran	62	44.37 N	4.56 E
Cleopatra Needle ʌ	116	10.07 N	118.58 E
Clères	50	49.36 N	1.07 E
Clerke Rocks II[1]	244	55.01 S	34.41 W
Clermont, Austl.	166	22.49 S	147.39 E
Clermont, P.Q., Can.	186	47.41 N	70.14 W
Clermont, Fr.	50	49.23 N	2.24 E
Clermont, Fl., U.S.	220	28.32 N	81.46 W
Clermont, N.J., U.S.	285	39.59 N	74.48 W
Clermont, Pa., U.S.	214	41.41 N	78.29 W
Clermont □[6]	218	39.05 N	84.11 W
Clermont-en-Argonne	56	49.06 N	5.04 E
Clermont-Ferrand	32	45.47 N	3.05 E
Clermont State Park ♠	210	42.05 N	73.55 W
Clerval	58	47.24 N	6.30 E
Clervaux	56	50.04 N	6.01 E
Cléry-Saint-André	50	47.49 N	1.45 E
Cles	64	46.22 N	11.02 E
Cleve	166	33.42 S	136.30 E
Clevedon	42	51.27 N	2.51 W
Cleveland, Austl.	171a	27.32 S	153.17 E
Cleveland, Al., U.S.	194	33.59 N	86.34 W
Cleveland, Fl., U.S.	220	26.57 N	82.00 W
Cleveland, Ga., U.S.	192	34.35 N	83.45 W
Cleveland, Ms., U.S.	194	33.44 N	90.43 W
Cleveland, N.Y., U.S.	210	43.14 N	75.53 W
Cleveland, N.C., U.S.	192	35.43 N	80.40 W
Cleveland, Oh., U.S.	214	41.29 N	81.41 W
Cleveland, Oh., U.S.	279a	41.29 N	81.41 W
Cleveland, Ok., U.S.	196	36.18 N	96.27 W
Cleveland, Tn., U.S.	194	35.09 N	84.52 W
Cleveland, Tx., U.S.	222	30.20 N	95.05 W
Cleveland, Va., U.S.	192	36.56 N	82.09 W
Cleveland □[6]	44	54.35 N	1.15 W
Cleveland, Cape ›	166	19.11 S	147.01 E
Cleveland, Mount ʌ, Austl.	166	41.25 S	145.23 E
Cleveland, Mount ʌ, Mt., U.S.	202	48.56 N	113.51 W
Cleveland Heights	214	41.31 N	81.33 W
Cleveland Hills ⋀[2]	44	54.23 N	1.05 W
Cleveland-Hopkins International Airport ⊠	279a	41.25 N	81.51 W
Clevelândia	252	26.24 S	52.21 W
Clevelândia do Norte	250	3.49 N	51.52 W
Cleveland Museum of Art ʊ	279a	41.31 N	81.37 W
Cleveland National Forest ♠	280	33.47 N	117.38 W
Cleveland Park ◆[8]	284c	38.56 N	77.04 W
Cleveland Peninsula ›[1]	182	55.45 N	132.00 W
Cleveland Pond ⊜	283	42.07 N	70.58 W
Cleveland State University ʊ[2]	279a	41.30 N	81.40 W
Cleveland Zoo ♠	279a	41.27 N	81.43 W
Cleveleys	44	53.53 N	3.03 W
Cleversburg	208	40.02 N	77.28 W
Cleves → Kleve, B.R.D.	52	51.48 N	6.09 E
Cleves, Oh., U.S.	218	39.10 N	84.45 W
Clew Bay c	48	53.50 N	9.50 W
Clewer	158	25.55 S	29.07 E
Clewiston	220	26.45 N	80.56 W
Cley next the Sea	42	52.58 N	1.03 E
Clichy	50	48.54 N	2.18 E
Clichy-sous-Bois	261	48.55 N	2.33 E
Clifden	48	53.29 N	10.01 W
Clifden Bay c	48	53.28 N	10.05 W
Cliffdale Creek ≃	166	16.56 S	138.48 E
Cliffdell	224	46.44 N	120.42 W
Cliffe	260	51.28 N	0.30 E
Cliffe Marshes ≡	260	51.28 N	0.30 E
Cliffe Woods	260	51.26 N	0.30 E
Clifford, On., Can.	212	43.58 N	80.58 W
Clifford, S. Afr.	158	31.04 S	27.28 E
Clifford, In., U.S.	218	39.16 N	85.52 W
Clifford, Pa., U.S.	210	41.39 N	75.36 W
Clifford Park ♠	274b	37.43 S	145.16 E
Cliffside	210	42.31 N	74.59 W
Cliffside Park	276	40.58 N	73.57 W
Cliffwood	276	40.26 N	74.14 W
Cliffwood Beach	276	40.26 N	74.13 W
Clifton, Austl.	171a	27.56 S	151.54 E
Clifton, Eng., U.K.	262	53.46 N	2.49 W
Clifton, Az., U.S.	200	33.03 N	109.17 W
Clifton, Il., U.S.	216	40.56 N	87.56 W
Clifton, Ks., U.S.	198	39.34 N	97.16 W
Clifton, N.J., U.S.	210	40.51 N	74.09 W
Clifton, N.Y., U.S.	210	43.03 N	77.49 W
Clifton, Or., U.S.	224	46.12 N	123.27 W
Clifton, Tn., U.S.	194	35.23 N	87.59 W
Clifton, Tx., U.S.	222	31.46 N	97.34 W
Clifton, Lake ⊜	168a	32.49 S	115.41 E
Clifton Court Forebay ⊜[1]	226	37.50 N	121.35 W
Clifton Forge	192	37.48 N	79.49 W
Clifton Gorge V	42	51.28 N	2.37 W
Clifton Heights, N.Y., U.S.	284a	42.44 N	78.56 W
Clifton Heights, Pa., U.S.	285	39.55 N	75.17 W
Clifton Hills	166	26.52 S	138.50 E
Clifton Knolls	210	42.52 N	73.46 W
Clifton Park ♠	284b	39.19 N	76.35 W
Clifton Point ›	240b	25.01 N	77.34 W
Clifton Springs	210	42.57 N	77.08 W
Clifty, Mount ʌ	224	47.07 N	121.10 W
Clifty Creek ≃	218	39.09 N	85.54 W
Clifty Falls State Park ♠	218	38.45 N	85.26 W
Clignon ≃	50	49.07 N	3.04 E
Climax, Sk., Can.	184	49.13 N	108.23 W
Climax, Co., U.S.	200	39.22 N	106.10 W
Climax, Ga., U.S.	192	30.52 N	84.25 W
Climax, Mi., U.S.	216	42.14 N	85.20 W
Climax, Pa., U.S.	214	40.59 N	79.23 W
Clinch ≃	192	35.53 N	84.29 W
Clinchco	192	37.09 N	82.21 W
Clingen	54	51.14 N	10.55 E
Clingmans Dome ʌ	192	35.35 N	83.30 W
Clinton, B.C., Can.	182	51.05 N	121.35 W
Clinton, On., Can.	190	43.37 N	81.32 W
Clinton, N.Z.	172	46.12 S	169.22 E
Clinton, Al., U.S.	194	32.55 N	88.00 W
Clinton, Ar., U.S.	194	35.35 N	92.27 W
Clinton, Ct., U.S.	207	41.16 N	72.31 W
Clinton, Il., U.S.	219	40.09 N	88.57 W
Clinton, In., U.S.	194	39.39 N	87.23 W
Clinton, Ia., U.S.	190	41.50 N	90.11 W
Clinton, Ky., U.S.	194	36.40 N	88.59 W
Clinton, La., U.S.	194	30.51 N	91.00 W
Clinton, Me., U.S.	188	44.38 N	69.30 W
Clinton, Md., U.S.	208	38.45 N	76.53 W
Clinton, Ma., U.S.	207	42.25 N	71.41 W
Clinton, Mi., U.S.	216	42.04 N	83.58 W
Clinton, Mn., U.S.	198	45.27 N	96.26 W
Clinton, Ms., U.S.	194	32.20 N	90.19 W
Clinton, Mo., U.S.	194	38.22 N	93.46 W
Clinton, N.J., U.S.	210	40.38 N	74.54 W
Clinton, N.Y., U.S.	210	43.02 N	75.22 W
Clinton, N.C., U.S.	192	34.59 N	78.19 W
Clinton, Oh., U.S.	214	40.56 N	81.42 W
Clinton, Ok., U.S.	196	35.30 N	98.58 W
Clinton, Pa., U.S.	214	40.29 N	80.18 W
Clinton, S.C., U.S.	192	34.28 N	81.52 W
Clinton, Tn., U.S.	192	36.06 N	84.07 W
Clinton, Tx., U.S.	222	33.06 N	96.14 W
Clinton, Wa., U.S.	224	47.58 N	122.21 W
Clinton, Wi., U.S.	216	42.33 N	88.51 W
Clinton □[6], Il., U.S.	219	38.37 N	89.22 W
Clinton □[6], In., U.S.	216	40.17 N	86.31 W
Clinton □[6], Mi., U.S.	216	42.56 N	84.36 W
Clinton □[6], N.Y., U.S.	206	44.57 N	73.42 W
Clinton □[6], Oh., U.S.	218	39.27 N	83.50 W
Clinton □[6], Pa., U.S.	210	41.08 N	71.26 W
Clinton ≃	214	42.36 N	82.48 W
Clinton, Cape ›	166	22.32 S	150.47 E
Clinton, Lake ⊜[1]	194	40.10 N	88.50 W
Clinton, Middle Branch ≃	281	42.36 N	82.54 W
Clinton, North Branch ≃	214	42.36 N	82.54 W
Clinton-Colden Lake ⊜	176	63.58 N	107.27 W
Clintondale	210	41.01 N	77.29 W
Clinton Lake ⊜[1]	198	38.55 N	95.25 W
Clinton Park	210	42.36 N	73.43 W
Clinton Reservoir ⊜[1]	276	41.05 N	74.27 W
Clinton Township	214	42.33 N	82.53 W
Clintonville, Mi., U.S.	281	42.43 N	83.22 W
Clintonville, Pa., U.S.	214	41.12 N	79.53 W
Clintonville, Wi., U.S.	190	44.37 N	88.45 W
Clintwood	192	37.09 N	82.27 W
Clio, Al., U.S.	194	31.42 N	85.36 W
Clio, Mi., U.S.	190	43.10 N	83.44 W
Clio, S.C., U.S.	192	34.34 N	79.32 W
Clipperton I[1]	230	10.17 N	109.13 W
Clipperton Fracture Zone ⊥	16	10.00 N	115.00 W
Clisham ʌ	46	57.57 N	6.49 W
Clisson	32	47.05 N	1.17 W
Clitheroe	44	53.53 N	2.23 W
Clitunno ≃	66	42.56 N	12.37 E
Clive, Austl.	166	22.46 S	149.18 E
Clive, N.Z.	172	39.35 S	176.55 E
Cliza	248	17.36 S	65.56 W
Cloates, Point ›	162	22.43 S	113.40 E
Clock Face	262	53.25 N	2.43 W
Clocolan	158	29.00 S	27.30 E
Clodomira	252	27.35 S	64.08 W
Cloe	214	40.56 N	78.56 W
Cloete	196	27.55 N	101.10 W
Cloghan, Ire.	48	53.13 N	7.53 W
Cloghan, Ire.	48	54.51 N	7.56 W
Cloghane	48	52.13 N	10.12 W
Clogheen	48	52.16 N	8.00 W
Clogher	48	54.25 N	7.12 W
Clogher Head ›	48	53.48 N	6.12 W
Cloghjordan	48	52.57 N	8.02 W
Clonakilty	48	51.37 N	8.54 W
Clonakilty Bay c	48	51.35 N	8.50 W
Cloncurry	166	20.42 S	140.30 E
Cloncurry ≃	166	18.37 S	140.40 E
Clondalkin	48	53.19 N	6.24 W
Clonee	48	53.25 N	6.26 W
Clones	48	54.11 N	7.15 W
Clonfert	48	53.14 N	8.05 W
Clonmacnois ⊥	48	53.20 N	7.59 W
Clonmany	48	55.14 N	7.25 W
Clonmel	48	52.21 N	7.42 W
Clonroche	48	52.27 N	6.43 W
Clontarf	274a	33.48 S	151.16 E
Cloone	48	53.57 N	7.46 W
Clo-oose, B.C., Can.	224	48.40 N	124.49 W
Cloppenburg	52	52.50 N	8.02 E
Cloquallum Creek ≃	224	46.58 N	123.24 W
Cloquet	190	46.43 N	92.27 W
Cloquet ≃	190	46.52 N	92.35 W
Clorinda	252	25.17 S	57.43 W
Closter	276	40.58 N	73.57 W
Cloudcroft	200	32.57 N	105.44 W
Cloud Peak ʌ, Ak., U.S.	180	68.24 N	148.26 W
Cloud Peak ʌ, Wy., U.S.	202	44.25 N	107.10 W
Cloudy Bay c	172	41.27 S	174.10 E
Cloudy Mountain ʌ	180	63.11 N	156.05 W
Clough	48	54.18 N	5.50 W
Clough Foot	262	53.43 N	2.08 W
Clova	46	56.50 N	3.06 W
Clova, Glen V	46	56.49 N	3.04 W
Clove Lakes Park ♠	276	40.37 N	74.07 W
Clovelly, Austl.	274a	33.55 S	151.16 E
Clovelly, Eng., U.K.	42	51.00 N	4.24 W
Clover	192	35.06 N	81.13 W
Clover Bank	210	42.45 N	78.53 W
Clover Creek ≃, Id., U.S.	202	42.34 N	115.38 W
Clover Creek ≃, Id., U.S.	202	43.00 N	115.11 W
Cloverdale, B.C., Can.	224	49.06 N	122.44 W
Cloverdale, Al., U.S.	194	34.56 N	87.46 W
Cloverdale, Ca., U.S.	204	38.48 N	123.00 W
Cloverdale, Il., U.S.	278	41.56 N	88.07 W
Cloverdale, In., U.S.	194	39.30 N	86.47 W
Cloverdale, Ky., U.S.	218	38.10 N	84.53 W
Cloverdale, Mi., U.S.	216	42.32 N	85.23 W
Cloverdale, Oh., U.S.	216	41.01 N	84.18 W
Cloverdale, Or., U.S.	224	45.12 N	123.53 W
Cloverdale Mall ◆[9]	275b	43.38 N	79.34 W
Cloverdene	273d	26.09 S	28.22 E
Cloverleaf	222	29.46 N	95.10 W
Clover Pass	182	55.28 N	131.47 W
Cloverport	194	37.50 N	86.37 W
Cloverville	216	43.11 N	86.10 W
Clovis, Ca., U.S.	226	36.49 N	119.42 W
Clovis, N.M., U.S.	196	34.24 N	103.12 W
Clowbridge Reservoir ⊜[1]	262	53.45 N	2.16 W
Clowne	44	53.18 N	1.16 W
Cloyes-sur-le-Loir	50	48.00 N	1.14 E
Cloyne	48	51.51 N	8.08 W
Cluain Meala → Clonmel	48	52.21 N	7.42 W
Cluanie, Loch ⊜	46	57.07 N	5.05 W
Cluj-Napoca	38	46.47 N	23.36 E
Cluj-Napoca □[6]	38	46.45 N	23.45 E
Clun	42	52.26 N	3.00 W
Clun ≃	42	52.22 N	2.53 W
Clune	214	40.34 N	79.18 W
Clunes	169	37.18 S	143.47 E
Clun Forest ◆[3]	42	52.28 N	3.07 W
Clunie Water ≃	46	57.00 N	3.24 W
Cluny, Austl.	166	24.31 S	139.35 E
Cluny, Fr.	58	46.26 N	4.39 E
Cluses	58	46.04 N	6.36 E
Clusone	64	45.53 N	9.57 E
Clute	222	29.01 N	95.23 W
Clutha ≃	172	46.21 S	169.48 E
Clwyd □[6]	44	53.05 N	3.20 W
Clwyd ≃	44	53.20 N	3.30 W
Clwyd, Vale of V	44	53.12 N	3.24 W
Clwydian Range ⋀	44	53.10 N	3.20 W
Clydach	42	51.43 N	3.50 W
Clyde, Ab., Can.	182	54.09 N	113.39 W
Clyde, N.Z.	172	45.11 S	169.19 E
Clyde, Ca., U.S.	226	38.02 N	122.02 W
Clyde, Ks., U.S.	198	39.35 N	97.23 W
Clyde, Mi., U.S.	281	42.41 N	83.37 W
Clyde, N.Y., U.S.	210	43.05 N	76.52 W
Clyde, N.C., U.S.	192	35.32 N	82.54 W
Clyde, Oh., U.S.	214	41.18 N	82.58 W
Clyde, Tx., U.S.	196	32.24 N	99.30 W
Clyde ≃, Austl.	170	35.23 S	150.15 E
Clyde ≃, N.S., Can.	186	43.35 N	65.25 W
Clyde ≃, On., Can.	212	44.58 N	76.22 W
Clyde ≃, Dom.	240d	15.33 N	61.18 W
Clyde ≃, Scot., U.K.	46	55.56 N	4.29 W
Clyde ≃, N.Y., U.S.	210	43.04 N	77.00 W
Clyde ≃, Vt., U.S.	188	44.56 N	72.12 W
Clyde, Firth of c[1]	46	55.42 N	5.00 W
Clydebank	46	55.54 N	4.24 W
Clydegale Lake ⊜	212	45.25 N	78.23 W
Clyde Lake ⊜	182	55.18 N	111.28 W
Clyde No.3	214	39.59 N	80.03 W
Clyde Park	202	45.53 N	110.36 W
Clyde Potts Reservoir ⊜[1]	276	40.48 N	74.35 W
Clyde River	176	70.25 N	68.30 W
Clydesdale	158	26.54 S	27.55 E
Clydesdale V	46	55.42 N	3.50 W
Clymer, N.Y., U.S.	214	42.01 N	79.37 W
Clymer, Pa., U.S.	214	40.40 N	79.00 W
Clynnog-fawr	44	53.01 N	4.23 W
Clywedog ≃	42	52.27 N	3.32 W
Ćmielów	30	50.53 N	21.31 E
Cna ≃, S.S.S.R.	76	52.10 N	27.03 E
Cna ≃, S.S.S.R.	76	57.33 N	34.36 E
Cna ≃, S.S.S.R.	80	54.32 N	42.05 E
Cna ≃, S.S.S.R.	82	55.03 N	39.09 E
Côa ≃	34	41.05 N	7.06 W
Coacalco □[7]	286a	19.37 N	99.06 W
Coacalco de Berriozábal	286a	19.37 N	9.05 W
Coachella	204	33.40 N	116.10 W
Coachella Canal ≅	204	33.34 N	116.00 W
Coachford	48	51.53 N	8.48 W
Coacoyole	232	24.31 N	106.34 W
Coacuilco	234	21.07 N	98.35 W
Coahoma	196	32.18 N	101.18 W
Coahuayana	234	18.44 N	103.41 W
Coahuayana, Río de ≃	234	18.41 N	103.45 W
Coahuayutla de Guerrero	234	18.19 N	101.49 W
Coahuila	200	32.12 N	114.59 W
Coahuila □[3]	232	27.20 N	102.00 W
Coal ≃	180	59.39 N	126.57 W
Coalbrook	158	26.51 S	27.53 E
Coalbrookdale	42	52.38 N	2.30 W
Coalburg	214	41.11 N	80.36 W
Coalburn	46	55.36 N	3.54 W
Coal City	216	41.17 N	88.17 W
Coalcomán de Matamoros	234	18.47 N	103.09 W
Coal Creek	180	65.22 N	143.10 W
Coal Creek ≃, Co., U.S.	198	40.30 N	104.26 W
Coal Creek ≃, In., U.S.	194	39.57 N	87.25 W
Coal Creek ≃, Wa., U.S.	202	47.19 N	118.36 W
Coal Creek Flat	172	45.29 S	169.18 E
Coaldale, Ab., Can.	182	49.43 N	112.37 W
Coaldale, Pa., U.S.	210	40.49 N	75.54 W
Coal Fire Creek ≃	194	33.15 N	88.18 W
Coal Fork	188	38.19 N	81.32 W
Coalgate, N.Z.	172	43.29 S	171.58 E

Symbols in the index entries represent the broad categories identified in the key at the right. Symbols with superior numbers (⋀[1]) identify subcategories (see complete key on page I · 1).

Kartensymbole in dem Registerverzeichnis stellen die rechts in Schlüssel erklärten Kategorien dar. Symbole mit hochgestellten Ziffern (⋀[1]) bezeichnen Unterabteilungen einer Kategorie (vgl. vollständiger Schlüssel auf Seite I · 1).

Los símbolos incluidos en el texto del índice representan las grandes categorías identificadas con la clave a la derecha. Los símbolos con números en su parte superior (⋀[1]) identifican las subcategorías (véase la clave completa en la página I · 1).

Les symboles de l'index représentent les catégories indiquées dans la légende à droite. Les symboles suivis d'un indice (⋀[1]) représentent des sous-catégories (voir légende complète à la page I · 1).

Os símbolos incluídos no texto do índice representam as grandes categorias identificadas com a chave à direita. Os símbolos com números em sua parte superior (⋀[1]) identificam as subcategorias (veja-se a chave completa à página I · 1).

ʌ Mountain	Berg	Montaña	Montagne	Montanha
⋀ Mountains	Berge	Montañas	Montagnes	Montanhas
)(Pass	Pass	Paso	Col	Passo
V Valley, Canyon	Tal, Cañon	Valle, Cañón	Vallée, Canyon	Vale, Canhão
⊻ Plain	Ebene	Llano	Plaine	Planície
› Cape	Kap	Cabo	Cap	Cabo
I Island	Insel	Isla	Île	Ilha
II Islands	Inseln	Islas	Îles	Ilhas
⊥ Other Topographic Features	Andere Topographische Objekte	Otros Elementos Topográficos	Autres données topographiques	Outros acidentes topográficos

ESPAÑOL: Nombre | Página | Lat.°′ | Long.°′ W = Oeste
FRANÇAIS: Nom | Page | Lat.°′ | Long.°′ W = Ouest
PORTUGUÊS: Nome | Página | Lat.°′ | Long.°′ W = Oeste

Coalgate, Ok., U.S. 196 34.32 N 96.13 W
Coal Grove 188 38.30 N 82.38 W
Coal Harbour 182 50.36 N 127.35 W
Coal Hill 194 35.26 N 93.40 W
Coal Hill Park ♦ 271a 39.56 N 116.23 E
Coalhurst 182 49.45 N 112.56 W
Coalinga 226 36.08 N 120.21 W
Coalisland 48 54.33 N 6.42 W
Coal Island I 172 46.07 S 166.38 E
Coalmont 182 49.31 N 120.41 W
Coalpit Heath 42 51.32 N 2.28 W
Coalport 214 40.44 N 78.32 W
Coal River 180 59.45 N 126.55 W
Coal Run ≃ 279b 40.21 N 80.07 W
Coalspur 182 53.11 N 117.01 W
Coalton 219 39.17 N 89.19 W
Coaltown 214 41.02 N 80.20 W
Coal Valley ∨ 204 38.00 N 115.05 W
Coalville, S. Afr. 158 26.01 S 29.10 E
Coalville, Eng., U.K. 42 52.44 N 1.20 W
Coalville, Ut., U.S. 200 40.55 N 111.23 W
Coamo 240m 18.05 N 66.22 W
Coamo, Lago ⊜1 240m 18.01 N 66.23 W
Coapilla 234 17.08 N 93.10 W
Coaraci 255 14.38 S 39.32 W
Coari 246 4.05 S 63.08 W
Coari ≃ 246 4.30 S 63.33 W
Coari, Lago de ⊜ 246 4.15 S 63.22 W
Coarsegold 226 37.16 N 119.42 W
Coast □4 154 3.00 S 39.30 E
Coast Mountains ∧ 176 55.00 N 129.00 W
Coast Ranges ∧ 178 41.00 N 123.30 W
Coatán ≃ 236 14.48 N 92.31 W
Coatbridge 46 55.52 N 4.01 W
Coatepec 234 19.27 N 96.58 W
Coatepec de Harinas 234 18.54 N 99.43 W
Coatepeque 236 14.42 N 91.52 W
Coatepeque, Lago de ⊜ 236 13.52 N 89.33 W
Coatepetl, Cerro ∧ 234 18.25 N 97.35 W
Coates Creek ≃ 212 44.24 N 79.54 W
Coatesville 208 39.58 N 75.49 W
Coaticook 206 45.08 N 71.48 W
Coaticook ≃ 206 45.20 N 71.53 W
Coatsburg 219 40.02 N 91.10 W
Coats Island I 176 62.30 N 83.00 W
Coats Land ✦1 9 77.00 S 28.00 W
Coatzacoalcos 234 18.09 N 94.25 W
Coatzacoalcos ≃ 234 18.10 N 94.27 W
Coatzacoalcos, Bahía ⊂ 234 18.10 N 94.27 W
Coatzintla 234 20.29 N 97.27 W
Coayllo 248 12.44 S 76.28 W
Coazze 62 45.03 N 7.18 E
Cobá ⊥ 232 20.36 N 87.35 W
Cobadin 38 44.04 N 28.13 E
Coballo Cocha 246 3.54 S 70.32 W
Cobalt, On., Can. 190 47.24 N 79.41 W
Cobalt, Ct., U.S. 207 41.33 N 72.33 W
Cobán 236 15.29 N 90.19 W
Čobanlar 130 38.41 N 30.47 E
Cobar 166 31.30 S 145.49 E
Cobargo 166 36.23 S 149.53 E
Cobb 226 38.49 N 122.43 W
Cobb Creek ≃ 196 35.05 N 98.25 W
Cobberas, Mount ∧ 166 36.52 S 148.10 E
Cobbetts Pond ⊜ 283 42.48 N 71.17 W
Cobbin's Brook ≃ 260 51.41 N 0.01 W
Cobb Island 208 38.16 N 76.51 W
Cobb Island I, Md., U.S. 208 38.16 N 76.51 W
Cobb Island I, Va., U.S. 208 37.20 N 75.44 W
Cobbitty 274a 34.01 S 150.41 E
Cobbitty ∧2 274a 33.59 S 150.42 E
Cobble Hill 224 48.41 N 123.36 W
Cobble Mountain Reservoir ⊜1 207 42.08 N 72.55 W
Cobblestone Mountain ∧ 228 34.37 N 118.52 W
Cobb Neck ➤1 208 38.20 N 76.55 W
Cobbs Creek ≃ 285 39.54 N 75.15 W
Cobbs Creek Park ♦ 285 39.58 N 75.16 W
Cobb Seamount ✦3 16 46.46 N 130.49 W
Cobden, Austl. 169 38.20 S 143.05 E
Cobden, On., Can. 190 45.38 N 76.53 W
Cobden, Il., U.S. 194 37.31 N 89.15 W
Cobeña 266a 40.34 N 3.30 W
Cobequid Bay ⊂ 186 45.21 N 63.45 W
Cobequid Mountains ∧ 186 45.31 N 64.05 W
Cobh 48 51.51 N 8.17 W
Cobham, Eng., U.K. 260 51.23 N 0.24 E
Cobham, Eng., U.K. 260 51.20 N 0.25 W
Cobham ≃ 184 53.15 N 93.58 W
Cobham Hall ⊥ 260 51.23 N 0.25 E
Cobija, Bol. 248 11.02 S 68.44 W
Cobija, Chile 252 22.33 S 70.16 W
Coblenz → Koblenz 56 50.21 N 7.35 E
Cobleskill 210 42.40 N 74.29 W
Cobleskill Creek ≃ 210 42.43 N 74.20 W
Coboconk 212 44.39 N 78.48 W
Cobo Hall ⌖ 281 42.19 N 83.03 W
Coboglo, gora ∧ 84 42.50 N 46.23 E
Čoboto, Cerro ∧ 200 31.29 N 112.05 W
Čoboty 265b 55.39 N 37.21 E
Cobourg 212 43.58 N 78.10 W
Cobourg Peninsula ➤1 164 11.20 S 132.15 E
Cobourg Peninsula National Park ♦ 164 11.25 S 132.15 E
Cobquecura 252 36.08 S 72.47 W
Cobram 166 35.55 S 145.39 E
Cobras, Ilha das I 287a 22.54 S 43.10 W
Cobre ≃ 236 8.01 N 81.18 W
Cobué 154 12.04 S 34.50 E
Coburg, Austl. 169 37.45 S 144.58 E
Coburg, B.R.D. 56 50.15 N 10.58 E
Coburg Island I 176 76.00 N 79.25 W
Coburn 210 40.52 N 77.28 W
Coburn Mountain ∧ 188 45.28 N 70.06 W
Coca ≃ 246 0.29 S 76.58 W
Coca, Pizzo di ∧ 64 46.04 N 10.01 E
Coca, Punta ➤ 236 12.28 N 83.30 W
Cocachacra 248 17.06 S 71.46 W
Cocais ∧ 256 21.51 S 42.53 W
Cocais, Ribeirão dos ≃ 256 21.59 S 47.15 W
Cocal 250 3.28 S 41.34 W
Cocalico Creek ≃ 208 40.07 N 76.14 W
Coccaglio 62 45.34 N 9.58 E
Cocconato 62 45.05 N 8.02 E
Cocentaina 34 38.45 N 0.26 W
Cochabamba 248 17.24 S 66.09 W
Cochabamba □5 248 17.30 S 65.40 W
Cochagual 252 31.54 S 68.23 W
Cochatauri 84 42.01 N 42.15 E
Cochato ≃ 283 42.10 N 71.01 W
Coche, Isla I 246 10.45 N 63.55 W
Cochem 56 50.11 N 7.09 E
Cochesett 283 42.01 N 71.02 W
Cochetopa Creek ≃ 200 38.31 N 106.47 W
Cochichewick, Lake ⊜ 283 42.42 N 71.06 W
Cochin 122 9.58 N 76.14 E
Cochinos, Bahía de (Bay of Pigs) ⊂ 240p 22.07 N 81.10 W
Cochinos, Cayos II 236 15.57 N 86.33 W
Cochise Head ∧ 200 32.03 N 109.18 W
Cochiti Indian Reservation ✦4 200 35.37 N 106.20 W
Cochituate 207 42.19 N 71.21 W
Cochituate, Lake ⊜ 283 42.17 N 71.22 W
Cochituate State Park ♦ 207 42.20 N 71.22 W
Cochran 192 32.23 N 83.21 W
Cochrane, Ab., Can. 182 51.11 N 114.28 W
Cochrane, On., Can. 176 49.04 N 81.01 W
Cochrane, Wi., U.S. 190 44.13 N 91.50 W
Cochrane ≃ 176 57.52 N 101.38 W
Cochrane, Lago (Lago Pueyrredón) ⊜ 254 47.20 S 72.00 W
Cochranton 214 41.31 N 80.02 W
Cochranville 208 39.53 N 75.55 W
Cochstedt 54 51.53 N 11.24 E
Cockatoo-Inseln → Buccaneer Archipelago II 160 16.17 S 123.20 E
Cock Bridge 46 57.09 N 3.14 W
Cockburn 166 32.05 S 141.00 E
Cockburn, Canal ⊍ 254 54.20 S 71.30 W
Cockburn, Cape ➤ 164 11.20 S 132.52 E
Cockburn, Mount ∧ 162 22.46 S 130.36 E
Cockburn Island I 190 45.55 N 83.22 W
Cockburn Sound ⊍ 168a 32.12 S 115.42 E
Cockburnspath 46 55.56 N 2.21 W
Cock Clarks 260 51.42 N 0.37 E
Cockenoe Island I 276 41.05 N 73.21 W
Cockenzie 46 55.58 N 2.58 W
Cockerham 44 53.59 N 2.50 W
Cockermouth 44 54.40 N 3.21 W
Cockeysville 208 39.28 N 76.38 W
Cockfield 44 54.37 N 1.48 W
Cockfosters ✦8 260 51.39 N 0.09 W
Cockpit Country ✦1 241q 18.18 N 77.43 W
Cockrell Hill 222 32.44 N 96.53 W
Cockroach Island I 240m 18.24 N 65.04 W
Cockscomb Point ➤ 174u 14.14 S 170.40 W
Coclé □4 236 8.30 N 80.15 W
Coclé del Norte ≃ 236 9.05 N 80.35 W
Coclois 50 48.28 N 4.20 E
Coco ≃ 236 15.00 N 83.10 W
Coco, Cayo I 240p 22.30 N 78.28 W
Coco, Isla del I 230 5.32 N 87.04 W
Côco, Rio do ≃ 250 9.27 S 50.02 W
Cocoa 220 28.23 N 80.44 W
Cocoa Beach 220 28.19 N 80.36 W
Cocobeach 152 0.59 N 9.36 E
Coco Channel ⊍ 110 13.45 N 93.00 E
Cococi 250 6.25 S 40.30 W
Cocodrie Lake ⊜1 194 30.58 N 92.25 W
Coco Islands II 110 14.05 N 93.18 E
Coconino Plateau ∧1 200 35.50 N 112.30 W
Cocorocuma, Cayos ✦2 236 15.45 N 83.00 W
Côcos 255 14.10 S 44.33 W
Cocos (Keeling) Islands □2 14 12.10 S 96.55 E
Cocos Bay ⊂ 241r 10.27 N 61.00 W
Cocos Island I 174p 13.14 N 144.39 E
Cocos Lagoon ⊂ 174p 13.14 N 144.38 E
Cocos Ridge ✦3 16 5.30 N 86.00 W
Cocotá ✦8 287a 22.49 S 43.11 W
Cocotitlán 234 19.14 N 98.52 W
Cocuiza ≃ 246 10.59 N 71.17 W
Cocula, Méx. 234 18.14 N 99.40 W
Cocula, Méx. 234 20.23 N 103.50 W
Cod ≃ 44 54.10 N 1.22 W
Cod, Cape ➤1 207 41.42 N 70.15 W
Codăeşti 38 46.52 N 27.46 E
Codajás 246 3.50 S 62.05 W
Codaruina 71 40.56 N 8.49 E
Coddenham 42 52.09 N 1.07 E
Codera, Cabo ➤ 246 10.35 N 66.05 W
Coderre 184 50.10 N 106.23 W
Coderre, Ruisseau ≃ 275a 45.43 N 73.19 W
Codesa 182 55.45 N 118.04 W
Codfish Island I 172 46.47 S 167.38 E
Codigoro 66 44.49 N 12.08 E
Cod Island I 176 57.45 N 61.50 W
Codlea 38 45.42 N 25.27 E
Codnor 42 53.03 N 1.23 W
Codó 250 4.29 S 43.53 W
Codogno 62 45.09 N 9.42 E
Codorus 208 39.48 N 76.52 W
Codorus Creek ≃ 208 40.03 N 76.38 W
Codorus State Park ♦ 208 39.48 N 76.54 W
Codòzinho 250 4.46 S 44.10 W
Codpa 248 18.50 S 69.44 W
Codro 86 50.50 N 88.34 E
Codroipo 64 45.58 N 12.59 E
Codrongianos 71 40.39 N 8.41 E
Codroy 186 47.53 N 59.24 W
Codroy Pond ⊜ 186 48.04 N 58.52 W
Codru-Moma, Munţii ∧ 38 46.30 N 22.20 E
Codsall 42 52.38 N 2.12 W
Cody, Ne., U.S. 198 42.56 N 101.14 W
Cody, Wy., U.S. 202 44.31 N 109.03 W
Coeburn 192 36.56 N 82.27 W
Coelemu 252 36.29 S 72.42 W
Coelho da Rocha 256 22.47 S 43.23 W
Coelho Neto 250 4.15 S 43.00 W
Coemba 152 12.08 S 18.05 E
Coen 164 13.56 S 143.12 E
Coen ≃, Austl. 164 13.56 S 142.02 E
Coën ≃, C.R. 236 9.34 N 82.58 W
Coeneo [de la Libertad] 234 19.49 N 101.35 W
Coeroeni ≃ 250 3.21 N 57.31 W
Coesfeld 52 51.56 N 7.10 E
Coetivy Island I 138 7.08 S 56.16 E
Coeur d'Alene 202 47.40 N 116.46 W
Coeur d'Alene ≃ 202 47.28 N 116.48 W
Coeur d'Alene Indian Reservation ✦4 202 47.18 N 116.45 W
Coeur d'Alene Lake ⊜ 202 47.32 N 116.48 W
Coeur d'Alene Mountains ∧ 202 47.50 N 116.05 W
Coevorden 52 52.40 N 6.45 E
Coeymans 210 42.28 N 73.48 W
Coffeen 219 39.05 N 89.24 W
Coffeen Lake ⊜1 219 39.03 N 89.20 W
Coffeeville 194 33.58 N 89.40 W
Coffeyville 198 37.02 N 95.36 W
Coffin Bay ⊂ 162 34.27 S 135.19 E
Coffin Bay Peninsula ➤1 162 34.32 S 135.15 E
Coffs Harbour 166 30.18 S 153.08 E
Cofimvaba 158 32.00 S 27.35 E
Cofradía 236 15.24 N 88.09 W
Cofre de Perote, Cerro (Nauhcampatépetl) ∧ 234 19.29 N 97.08 W
Cofre de Perote, Parque Nacional ♦ 234 19.32 N 97.10 W
Cofrentes 34 39.14 N 1.04 W
Coggeshall 42 51.52 N 0.41 E
Coggiola 62 45.41 N 8.11 E
Coggon 190 42.16 N 91.31 W
Coghinas ≃ 71 40.56 N 8.48 E
Coghinas, Lago del ⊜1 71 40.45 N 9.02 E
Coglians, Monte (Hohe Warte) ∧ 64 46.37 N 12.53 E
Cogliate 266b 45.39 N 9.05 E
Cognac 32 45.42 N 0.20 W
Cogne 62 45.37 N 7.21 E
Cognin 62 45.34 N 5.54 E
Cogo 152 1.05 N 9.42 E
Cogoleto 62 44.23 N 8.39 E
Cogolin 62 43.15 N 6.32 E
Cogollo del Cengio 64 45.47 N 11.25 E
Cogolludo 34 40.57 N 3.05 W
Cogolo 64 46.21 N 10.41 E
Cograjskoje vodochranilišče ⊜1 80 45.30 N 44.25 E
Cogswell 198 46.06 N 97.46 W
Cogswell Reservoir ⊜1 280 34.14 N 117.58 W
Cogt 102 45.25 N 96.01 E
Cogtoandman' 102 45.50 N 104.28 E
Cogton Bay ⊂ 116 9.51 N 124.33 E
Cogt-Ovoo 102 44.25 N 105.20 E
Cogun 130 39.20 N 34.08 E
Cohansey ≃ 208 39.21 N 75.22 W
Cohasset 207 42.14 N 70.48 W
Cohasset Harbor ⊂ 283 42.15 N 70.47 W
Cohenga ≃ 248 10.17 S 73.57 W
Cohoctah 216 42.46 N 83.57 W
Cohocton 210 42.30 N 77.30 W
Cohocton ≃ 210 42.09 N 77.05 W
Cohoe 180 60.23 N 151.18 W
Cohoes 210 42.46 N 73.42 W
Cohoni 248 16.44 S 67.51 W
Cohoon, Lake ⊜1 208 36.45 N 76.38 W
Cohuna 166 35.49 S 144.13 E
Coiba, Isla de I 246 7.27 N 81.45 W
Coig ≃ 254 50.58 S 69.11 W
Coigeach, Rubha ➤ 46 58.06 N 5.26 W
Coignières 261 48.45 N 1.55 E
Coihaique 254 45.34 S 72.04 W
Coils Creek ≃ 204 39.32 N 116.16 W
Coimbatore 122 11.00 N 76.58 E
Coimbra, Bra. 248 19.55 S 57.47 W
Coimbra, Bra. 255 20.52 S 42.48 W
Coimbra, Port. 34 40.12 N 8.25 W
Coín, Esp. 34 36.40 N 4.45 W
Coin, Ia., U.S. 198 40.39 N 95.13 W
Coina ≃ 266c 38.38 N 9.03 W
Coipasa, Lago ⊜ 248 19.12 S 68.07 W
Coipasa, Salar de ≃ 248 19.26 S 68.09 W
Coire → Chur 58 46.51 N 9.32 E
Coire, Loch ⊜ 46 58.13 N 4.21 W
Coixtlahuaca 234 17.43 N 97.19 W
Čojbalsan, Mong. 88 48.25 N 114.52 E
Čojbalsan, Mong. 88 48.04 N 114.30 E
Čojbalsan uul ∧ 88 47.49 N 107.00 E
Cojedes 246 9.37 N 68.55 W
Cojedes □3 246 9.20 N 68.20 W
Cojimar ✦8 286b 23.10 N 82.18 W
Cojimar ≃ 286b 23.10 N 82.17 W
Cojudo Blanco, Cerro ∧ 254 47.05 S 69.20 W
Cojumatlán de Régules 234 20.07 N 102.50 W
Cojutepeque 236 13.43 N 88.56 W
Čokak 130 37.45 N 36.19 E
Cokato 190 45.04 N 94.11 W
Cokeburg 214 40.06 N 80.04 W
Coker 273a 6.29 N 3.20 E
Cokeville 200 42.04 N 110.57 W
Čoktal 85 42.36 N 76.44 E
Čokurdach 74 70.38 N 147.55 E
Colāba ✦8 272c 18.54 N 72.48 E
Colāba Point ➤ 272c 18.53 N 72.48 E
Colac 169 38.20 S 143.35 E
Colac, Lake ⊜ 169 38.18 S 143.35 E
Čolakli 130 38.22 N 38.33 E
Colalao del Valle 252 26.22 S 65.57 W
Colán Conhué 254 43.16 S 69.01 W
Colapsin Point ➤ 116 6.38 N 125.26 E
Colares, Bra. 250 0.56 S 48.17 W
Colares, Port. 34 38.48 N 9.27 W
Colares, Ribeira de ≃ 266c 38.49 N 9.28 W
Colatina 255 19.32 S 40.37 W
Colbe 56 50.51 N 8.48 E
Colbeck, Cape ➤ 9 77.06 S 157.48 W
Colberry Park 281 42.36 N 83.16 W
Colbert 196 33.51 N 96.30 W
Colbinabbin 166 36.35 S 144.49 E
Colbitz 54 52.19 N 11.36 E
Colbitz-Letzlinger Heide ✦3 54 52.27 N 11.35 E
Colborne, On., Can. 212 42.51 N 80.19 W
Colborne, On., Can. 212 44.00 N 77.53 W
Colbún 252 35.42 S 71.25 W
Colburn, Eng., U.K. 44 54.23 N 1.41 W
Colburn, In., U.S. 216 40.31 N 86.42 W
Colby, Ks., U.S. 198 39.23 N 101.03 W
Colby, Wi., U.S. 190 44.54 N 90.18 W
Colca 248 12.18 S 75.13 W
Colca ≃ 248 15.51 S 72.26 W
Colcamar 248 6.16 S 77.55 W
Colcapirhua 248 17.25 S 66.15 W
Colchester, On., Can. 214 41.59 N 82.56 W
Colchester, Eng., U.K. 42 51.54 N 0.54 E
Colchester, Ct., U.S. 207 41.34 N 72.19 W
Colchester, Il., U.S. 190 40.25 N 90.47 W
Coldbackie 46 58.31 N 4.23 W
Cold Bay 180 55.11 N 162.30 W
Cold Bay ⊂ 180 55.13 N 162.33 W
Coldblow ✦8 260 51.26 N 0.10 E
Cold Brook 210 43.15 N 75.03 W
Cold Creek ≃ 212 44.12 N 77.36 W
Colden 210 42.39 N 78.41 W
Cold Fell ∧ 44 54.54 N 2.36 W
Cold Harbor Battlefield ⊥ 208 37.36 N 77.20 W
Coldingham 46 55.53 N 2.10 W
Colditz 54 51.07 N 12.48 E
Cold Lake 184 54.27 N 110.10 W
Cold Lake ⊜ 184 54.33 N 110.05 W
Cold Lake, Canadian Forces Base ■ 184 54.25 N 110.17 W
Cold Lake Indian Reserve ✦4 184 54.33 N 110.10 W
Cold Norton 260 51.40 N 0.40 E
Coldrerio 64 45.38 N 10.50 E
Cold Spring, Ky., U.S. 218 39.01 N 84.26 W
Cold Spring, Mn., U.S. 190 45.27 N 94.25 W
Cold Spring, N.J., U.S. 208 38.58 N 74.55 W
Cold Spring, N.Y., U.S. 210 41.25 N 73.57 W
Coldspring, Tx., U.S. 222 30.36 N 95.08 W
Cold Spring Harbor 276 40.52 N 73.27 W
Cold Spring Harbor ⊂ 276 40.53 N 73.28 W
Coldsprings, On., Can. 212 44.17 N 78.18 W
Cold Springs, N.Y., U.S. 210 43.08 N 76.15 W
Cold Spring Terrace 276 40.50 N 73.26 W
Coldstream, Austl. 169 37.44 S 145.23 E
Coldstream, Scot., U.K. 46 55.39 N 2.15 W
Cold Stream ≃ 226 39.35 N 120.22 W
Coldwater, On., Can. 212 44.42 N 79.40 W
Coldwater, Ks., U.S. 198 37.16 N 99.19 W
Coldwater, Mi., U.S. 216 41.56 N 85.00 W
Coldwater, Ms., U.S. 194 34.41 N 89.58 W
Coldwater, Oh., U.S. 216 40.28 N 84.37 W
Coldwater ≃, On., Can. 212 44.44 N 79.39 W
Coldwater ≃, Mi., U.S. 216 42.04 N 85.08 W
Coldwater ≃, Ms., U.S. 194 34.11 N 90.13 W
Coldwater Canyon ∨ 280 34.14 N 117.44 W
Coldwater Creek ≃ 196 36.40 N 101.08 W
Coldwater Indian Reserve ✦4 182 50.04 N 120.48 W
Coldwater Lake ⊜ 216 41.49 N 84.58 W
Cole □6 219 38.30 N 92.13 W
Cole ≃ 152 9.07 S 15.50 E
Cole ≃, Eng., U.K. 42 52.28 N 1.44 W
Cole ≃, Eng., U.K. 42 51.42 N 1.42 W
Colebrook, N.H., U.S. 188 44.53 N 71.29 W
Colebrook, Oh., U.S. 214 41.32 N 80.46 W
Colebrook River Lake ⊜1 207 42.03 N 73.04 W
Cole Camp 194 38.27 N 93.12 W
Coledale 170 34.17 S 150.57 E
Coleford, Eng., U.K. 42 51.48 N 2.36 W
Coleford, Eng., U.K. 42 51.14 N 2.27 W
Colégio, Morro do ∧ 287b 23.38 S 46.21 W
Coleman, Ab., Can. 182 49.38 N 114.30 W
Coleman, Fl., U.S. 220 28.47 N 82.04 W
Coleman, Md., U.S. 208 39.20 N 76.05 W
Coleman, Mi., U.S. 190 43.45 N 84.35 W
Coleman, Tx., U.S. 196 31.49 N 99.25 W
Coleman, Wi., U.S. 190 45.03 N 88.02 W
Coleman ≃ 164 15.06 S 141.38 E
Coleman, Lake ⊜1 196 32.02 N 99.30 W
Colembert 50 50.45 N 1.50 E
Colen Lakes ⊜ 184 54.33 N 95.25 W
Colenso 158 28.50 S 29.42 E
Colerain 214 40.07 N 80.49 W
Coleraine, Austl. 166 37.36 S 141.42 E
Coleraine, N. Ire., U.K. 48 55.08 N 6.40 W
Coleraine, Mn., U.S. 190 47.17 N 93.25 W
Coleridge 198 42.30 N 97.12 W
Coleridge, Lake ⊜ 172 43.17 S 171.30 E
Coles 194 31.16 N 91.01 W
Coles, Punta ➤ 248 17.42 S 71.23 W
Colesberg 158 30.45 S 25.05 E
Coles Brook ≃ 276 40.55 N 74.02 W
Coleshill, Eng., U.K. 42 52.30 N 1.42 W
Coleshill, Eng., U.K. 260 51.39 N 0.38 W
Coles Point 208 38.09 N 76.38 W
Colesville, Md., U.S. 284c 39.05 N 77.00 W
Colesville, N.J., U.S. 210 41.15 N 74.39 W
Coleto Creek ≃ 196 28.41 N 97.01 W
Coleville, Sk., Can. 184 51.43 N 109.16 W
Coleville, Ca., U.S. 226 38.33 N 119.30 W
Colfax, Ca., U.S. 226 39.06 N 120.57 W
Colfax, Il., U.S. 216 40.34 N 88.36 W
Colfax, In., U.S. 194 40.11 N 86.40 W
Colfax, Ia., U.S. 190 41.40 N 93.14 W
Colfax, La., U.S. 194 31.31 N 92.42 W
Colfax, Wa., U.S. 202 46.52 N 117.21 W
Colfax, Wi., U.S. 190 44.59 N 91.43 W
Colfiorito 66 43.02 N 12.55 E
Colgate 216 43.12 N 88.12 W
Colgate Creek ≃ 284b 39.15 N 76.32 W
Colgong 124 25.16 N 87.13 E
Colgrave Sound ⊍ 46 60.37 N 0.58 W
Colhué Huapi, Lago ⊜ 254 45.30 S 68.48 W
Coliban ≃ 169 36.56 S 144.33 E
Colibris, Pointe des ➤, Guad. 241o 16.17 N 61.06 W
Colibris, Pointe des ➤, Guad. 241o 16.15 N 61.11 W
Colico 58 46.08 N 9.22 E
Coligny, Fr. 58 46.23 N 5.21 E
Coligny, S. Afr. 158 26.17 S 26.15 E
Colijnsplaat 52 51.46 N 3.51 E
Colima, Méx. 200 32.25 N 115.05 W
Colima, Méx. 234 19.14 N 103.43 W
Colima □3 234 19.10 N 104.00 W
Colima, Nevado de ∧ 234 19.33 N 103.38 W
Colimes ≃ 246 1.32 S 80.00 W
Colin ≃ 50 47.08 N 2.32 E
Colina 252 33.12 S 70.41 W
Colinas, Bra. 250 6.02 S 44.14 W
Colinas, Bra. 255 14.12 S 48.03 W
Colinet 186 47.13 N 53.33 W
Colinton, Austl. 171b 35.51 S 149.09 E
Colinton, Ab., Can. 182 54.37 N 113.15 W
Coll I 46 56.38 N 6.34 W
Colla 258 34.04 S 57.21 W
Colla, Arroyo ≃ 258 34.19 S 57.20 W
Collagna 64 44.21 N 10.16 E
Collalbo (Klobenstein) 64 46.32 N 11.28 E
Collalto Sabino 66 42.08 N 13.02 E
Collamer 210 43.06 N 76.04 W
Collarenebri 166 29.33 S 148.35 E
Collarmele 66 42.03 N 13.38 E
Collaroy 274a 33.44 S 151.18 E
Collazzone 66 42.54 N 12.26 E
Collbran 200 39.14 N 107.57 W
Collecchio 64 44.45 N 10.13 E
Collecorvino 66 42.27 N 14.01 E
Colle di Tora 66 42.13 N 12.57 E
Colle di Val d'Elsa 66 43.25 N 11.07 E
Colleen Bawn 154 21.00 S 29.13 E
Colleferro 66 41.44 N 12.59 E
College 180 64.51 N 147.47 W
College City 226 39.00 N 122.00 W
College Corner 218 39.30 N 84.36 W
Collegedale 194 35.04 N 85.03 W
College Meadows 218 39.56 N 86.07 W
College Park, Ga., U.S. 192 33.39 N 84.26 W
College Park, Md., U.S. 208 38.58 N 76.56 W
College Park Airport ⊠ 284c 38.58 N 76.55 W
College Place 202 46.02 N 118.23 W
College Point ✦8 276 40.47 N 73.51 W
College Station, Ar., U.S. 194 34.43 N 92.13 W
College Station, Tx., U.S. 222 30.37 N 96.20 W
Collegeville, In., U.S. 216 40.54 N 87.09 W
Collegeville, Pa., U.S. 208 40.11 N 75.27 W
Collégien 261 48.50 N 2.40 E
Collegno 62 45.05 N 7.34 E
Colle Isarco (Gossensass) 64 46.56 N 11.26 E
Collepardo 66 41.46 N 13.22 E
Collepasso 68 40.04 N 18.10 E
Collepietro 66 42.13 N 13.46 E
Collerina 166 29.41 S 146.38 E
Collesalvetti 66 43.35 N 10.28 E
Colle Sannita 68 41.22 N 14.50 E
Collesano 70 37.55 N 13.56 E
Colletorto 66 41.40 N 14.58 E
Colleymount 182 54.01 N 126.09 W
Colleyville 222 32.52 N 97.09 W
Colliano 68 40.43 N 15.17 E
Colli a Volturno 66 41.36 N 14.06 E
Colli del Tronto 66 42.52 N 13.44 E
Colli di Monte Bove 66 42.06 N 13.09 E
Collie 168a 33.21 S 116.09 E
Collie ≃ 168a 33.18 S 115.44 E
Collie East ≃ 168a 33.18 S 116.10 E
Collier □6 220 26.10 N 81.22 W
Collier Bay ⊂ 160 16.10 S 124.15 E
Collier Bridge ✦5 220 26.57 N 82.04 W
Collier City 220 26.14 N 80.09 W
Collier Law ∧2 44 54.46 N 1.58 W
Collier Range ∧ 162 24.43 S 119.12 E
Collier Range National Park ♦ 162 24.40 S 119.15 E
Collier Row ✦8 260 51.36 N 0.10 E
Colliers 214 40.22 N 80.32 W
Collier-Seminole State Park ♦ 220 25.59 N 81.36 W
Colliersville 210 42.29 N 74.59 W
Collierville 194 35.02 N 89.39 W
Collie South ≃ 168a 33.18 S 116.10 E
Collieston 46 57.21 N 1.56 W
Colliford Reservoir ⊜1 42 50.32 N 4.33 W
Colligan ≃ 48 52.06 N 7.38 W
Collin □6 222 33.07 N 96.35 W
Collina, Passo della)(66 44.01 N 10.56 E
Collingbourne Kingston 42 51.18 N 1.13 W
Collingdale 208 39.54 N 75.16 W
Collingham 44 53.54 N 1.24 W
Collingswood 285 39.55 N 75.04 W
Collingwood, Austl. 274b 37.48 S 145.00 E
Collingwood, On., Can. 212 44.29 N 80.13 W
Collingwood, N.Z. 172 40.40 S 172.41 E
Collingwood Bay ⊂ 164 9.20 S 149.30 E
Collins, Ga., U.S. 192 32.10 N 82.06 W
Collins, Ia., U.S. 190 41.54 N 93.18 W
Collins, Ms., U.S. 194 31.38 N 89.33 W
Collins, N.Y., U.S. 210 42.30 N 78.55 W
Collins, Oh., U.S. 214 41.16 N 82.30 W
Collins ≃ 194 35.48 N 85.37 W
Collins, Mount ∧2 190 47.51 N 80.59 W
Collins Bay 212 44.15 N 76.36 W
Collinsburg 214 40.13 N 79.46 W
Collins Center 210 42.30 N 78.51 W
Collins Lake ⊜ 212 44.22 N 76.27 W
Collins Park 208 39.41 N 75.33 W
Collinston 194 32.41 N 91.52 W
Collinsville, Austl. 166 20.34 S 147.51 E
Collinsville, Al., U.S. 194 34.15 N 85.51 W
Collinsville, Ca., U.S. 282 38.05 N 121.51 W
Collinsville, Ct., U.S. 207 41.48 N 72.55 W
Collinsville, Il., U.S. 219 38.40 N 89.59 W
Collinsville, Ms., U.S. 194 32.29 N 88.50 W
Collinsville, N.J., U.S. 276 40.49 N 74.28 W
Collinsville, Ok., U.S. 196 36.21 N 95.50 W
Collinsville, Tx., U.S. 196 33.32 N 96.54 W
Collinwood 194 35.10 N 87.44 W
Collio 64 45.48 N 10.20 E
Collipulli 252 37.57 S 72.26 W
Collique Alto 286d 11.55 S 77.03 W
Collister 202 43.38 N 116.15 W
Collobrières 62 43.14 N 6.18 E
Collombey 58 46.16 N 6.57 E
Collomsville 210 41.09 N 77.09 W
Collon 48 53.47 N 6.29 W
Collonges 58 46.08 N 5.54 E
Collooney 48 54.11 N 8.29 W
Colma 226 37.41 N 122.28 W
Colma Creek ≃ 282 37.38 N 122.23 W
Colman 198 43.58 N 96.48 W
Colmar 58 48.05 N 7.22 E
Colmar Manor 284c 38.55 N 76.56 W
Colmars 62 44.11 N 6.38 E
Colmenar 34 36.54 N 4.20 W
Colmenar de Oreja 34 40.06 N 3.23 W
Colmenar Viejo 34 40.40 N 3.46 W
Colmeneros 234 18.06 N 101.40 W
Colmesneil 194 30.54 N 94.25 W
Colmnitz 54 50.54 N 13.31 E
Colmonell 44 55.08 N 4.55 W
Coln ≃ 42 51.42 N 1.42 W
Colnbrook 260 51.29 N 0.31 W
Colne 44 53.52 N 2.09 W
Colne ≃, Eng., U.K. 42 51.48 N 1.01 E
Colne ≃, Eng., U.K. 260 51.26 N 0.30 W
Colney Heath 260 51.44 N 0.15 W
Colney Street 260 51.42 N 0.20 W
Colo 190 42.01 N 93.18 W
Colo ≃ 170 33.26 S 150.53 E
Colobraro 68 40.11 N 16.25 E
Cologna Veneta 64 45.18 N 11.23 E
Cologne → Köln, B.R.D. 56 50.56 N 6.59 E
Cologne, Mn., U.S. 190 44.46 N 93.46 W
Cologne, N.J., U.S. 208 39.30 N 74.36 W
Cologno al Serio 62 45.37 N 9.42 E
Cologno Monzese 266b 45.32 N 9.17 E
Cololo, Nevado ∧ 248 14.53 S 69.06 W
Coloma, Ca., U.S. 226 38.48 N 120.53 W
Coloma, Mi., U.S. 216 42.11 N 86.18 W
Coloma, Wi., U.S. 190 44.02 N 89.31 W
Coloma, Ensenada de la ⊂ 240p 22.13 N 83.34 W
Colomb-Béchar → Béchar 148 31.37 N 2.13 W
Colombes 50 48.55 N 2.15 E
Colombey-les-Belles 58 48.32 N 5.54 E
Colombey-les-Deux-Eglises 58 48.13 N 4.53 E
Colômbia, Bra. 255 20.30 S 48.37 W
Colombia, Col. 246 3.24 N 74.49 W
Colombia, Méx. 196 27.42 N 99.45 W
Colombia □1, S.A. 242 4.00 N 72.00 W
Colombia □1, S.A. 246 4.00 N 72.00 W
Colombian Basin ✦1 16 13.00 N 76.00 W
Colombie → Colombia □1 246 4.00 N 72.00 W
Colombie-Britannique → British Columbia □4 182 54.00 N 125.00 W
Colombier 58 46.58 N 6.52 E
Colombo, Bra. 252 25.17 S 49.14 W
Colombo, S. Lan. 122 6.56 N 79.51 E
Colome 198 43.15 N 99.42 W
Colomiers 32 43.37 N 1.20 E
Colón, Arg. 252 33.53 S 61.07 W
Colón, Arg. 252 32.13 S 58.08 W
Colón, Cuba 240p 22.43 N 80.54 W
Colón, Pan. 236 9.22 N 79.54 W
Colon, Mi., U.S. 216 41.57 N 85.19 W
Colón, Ur. 252 33.53 S 54.43 W
Colón, Ur. 258 34.48 S 56.14 W
Colón □4 236 9.00 N 80.20 W
Colón □5 236 15.40 N 85.30 W
Colón, Archipiélago de (Galapagos Islands) II 246a 0.30 S 90.30 W
Colón, Cementerio ✦ 286b 23.08 N 82.23 W
Colón, Isla I 236 9.24 N 82.17 W
Colón, Montañas de ∧ 236 14.55 N 84.45 W
Colón, Teatro ♦ 288 34.36 S 58.23 W
Colona 162 31.38 S 132.05 E
Colonard-Corubert 50 48.25 N 0.39 E
Colonarie ≃ 241h 13.14 N 61.06 W
Colonel Danforth Park ♦ 275b 43.47 N 79.10 W
Colonelganj 124 27.08 N 81.42 E
Coloneşti 38 46.34 N 27.18 E
Colonet 204 31.05 N 116.10 W
Colonet, Cabo ➤ 204 30.58 N 116.19 W
Colongulac, Lake ⊜ 169 38.10 S 143.11 E
Colonia → Köln, B.R.D. 56 50.56 N 6.59 E
Colonia, T.T.P.I. 174q 9.31 N 138.08 E
Colonia, N.J., U.S. 210 40.34 N 74.18 W
Colonia □5 258 34.10 S 57.30 W
Colônia ≃ 255 15.11 S 39.45 W
Colonia, Aeropuerto ⊠ 258 34.28 S 57.49 W
Colonia, Cuchilla de la ∧2 258 34.15 S 57.35 W
Colonia Agrícola de Turén 246 9.15 N 69.05 W
Colonia Alvear 252 35.00 S 67.40 W
Colonia Caroya 252 31.02 S 64.05 W
Colonia Cristóbal Obregón 234 16.20 N 93.30 W
Colonia del Sacramento 258 34.28 S 57.51 W
Colonia Dora 252 28.36 S 62.57 W
Colonia Elisa 252 26.56 S 59.32 W
Colonia Guadalupe 204 32.04 N 116.37 W
Colonia Hogar Ricardo Gutiérrez 288 34.51 S 58.51 W
Colonia José Mármol 252 26.59 S 60.44 W
Colonial Acres 208 39.31 N 76.20 W
Colonia Las Heras 254 46.33 S 68.57 W
Colonia Lavalleja 252 31.06 S 57.01 W
Colonial Beach 208 38.15 N 76.57 W
Colonial Crest 208 40.20 N 76.50 W
Colônia Leopoldina 250 8.57 S 35.39 W
Colonial Heights, Il., U.S. 278 41.05 N 88.01 W
Colonial Heights, Va., U.S. 208 37.14 N 77.24 W
Colonial Manor 285 39.51 N 75.09 W
Colonial National Historical Park ♦ 208 37.12 N 76.45 W
Colonial Park 208 40.18 N 76.48 W
Colonial Village, N.Y., U.S. 210 43.08 N 78.58 W
Colonial Village, Pa., U.S. 285 40.04 N 75.24 W
Colonial Village Airport ⊠ 284a 43.08 N 78.58 W
Colonial Williamsburg ⊥ 208 37.16 N 76.42 W
Colonia Morelos 200 30.50 N 109.10 W
Colonia Nicolich 258 34.50 S 56.02 W
Colonia Progreso, Méx. 204 32.35 N 115.37 W
Colonia Progreso, Méx. 234 23.48 N 103.18 W
Colonia Providencia 240m 17.59 N 66.00 W
Colonias Unidas 252 26.42 S 59.38 W
Colonia Valdense 258 34.20 S 57.14 W
Colonia Villafañe 252 26.12 S 59.05 W
Colonie 210 42.43 N 73.50 W
Colon Koret 152 0.34 N 23.28 E
Colonna 267a 41.50 N 12.45 E
Colonna, Capo ➤ 68 39.02 N 17.11 E
Colonnata 64 44.05 N 10.10 E
Colón Ridge ✦3 18 2.00 N 96.00 W
Colonsay 184 51.59 N 105.53 W
Colonsay I 46 56.04 N 6.13 W
Colony 198 38.04 N 95.21 W
Colora 208 39.40 N 76.06 W
Colorada, Laguna ≋ 254 44.50 S 68.15 W
Colorada, Punta ➤ 288 34.45 S 58.06 W
Coloradas, Lomas ∧2 254 43.24 S 67.24 W
Colorado, C.R. 236 10.46 N 83.35 W
Colorado, Hond. 236 15.47 N 87.19 W
Colorado, Ak., U.S. 180 63.09 N 149.26 W
Colorado □6 222 29.40 N 96.30 W
Colorado □3 178 39.00 N 105.30 W
Colorado ≃, Arg. 244 39.50 S 62.08 W
Colorado ≃, Bra. 248 13.03 S 62.20 W
Colorado ≃, N.A. 200 31.54 N 114.57 W
Colorado ≃, Tx., U.S. 196 28.36 N 95.58 W
Colorado ≅ 286a 19.24 N 98.59 W
Colorado, Cerro ∧, Arg. 254 45.02 S 69.38 W
Colorado, Cerro ∧, Chile 286e 33.24 S 70.45 W
Colorado, Cerro ∧, Méx. 232 31.31 N 115.31 W
Colorado, Cerro ∧, Perú 286d 12.07 S 76.55 W
Colorado, Williams Fork ≃ 200 40.03 N 106.11 W
Colorado City, Az., U.S. 200 36.59 N 112.58 W
Colorado City, Co., U.S. 200 37.56 N 104.50 W
Colorado City, Tx., U.S. 196 32.23 N 100.51 W
Colorado de Abajo 196 26.28 N 99.54 W
Colorado National Monument ♦ 200 39.04 N 108.25 W
Colorado Plateau ∧1 200 36.30 N 108.00 W
Colorado River Aqueduct ≅1 204 33.50 N 117.23 W
Colorado River Indian Reservation ✦4 200 34.00 N 114.25 W
Colorados, Archipiélago de los II 240p 22.36 N 84.20 W
Colorado Springs 200 38.50 N 104.49 W
Colorines 234 19.07 N 100.12 W
Colorno 64 44.56 N 10.23 E
Colosimi 68 39.07 N 16.24 E
Colosseo ⊥ 267a 41.54 N 12.29 E
Colotepec ≃ 234 15.47 N 97.03 W
Colotlán 234 22.06 N 103.16 W
Colotlipa 234 17.25 N 99.09 W
Colo Vale 170 34.24 S 150.29 E
Čolpon 85 42.12 N 75.28 E
Čolpon-Ata 85 42.40 N 77.06 E
Colpoys Bay ⊂ 212 44.47 N 81.05 W
Colquechaca 248 18.40 S 66.01 W
Colquencha 248 17.00 S 68.17 W
Colquiri 248 17.25 S 67.08 W
Colquitt 192 31.10 N 84.44 W
Colsterworth 42 52.48 N 0.37 W
Colstrip 202 45.53 N 106.37 W
Colt 194 35.07 N 90.48 W
Colta 248 15.10 S 73.18 W
Coltauco 252 34.18 S 71.06 W
Coltishall 42 52.44 N 1.22 E
Colton, Austl. 162 33.29 S 134.56 E
Colton, Ca., U.S. 228 34.04 N 117.18 W
Colton, Oh., U.S. 216 41.28 N 83.57 W
Colton, Or., U.S. 224 45.10 N 122.26 W
Colton, S.D., U.S. 198 43.47 N 96.55 W
Coltons Point 208 38.13 N 76.45 W
Colts Neck 208 40.17 N 74.10 W
Coltsville Center 214 41.05 N 80.34 W
Columbia, Al., U.S. 192 31.17 N 85.06 W
Columbia, Ca., U.S. 226 38.02 N 120.24 W
Columbia, Ct., U.S. 207 41.42 N 72.18 W
Columbia, Il., U.S. 219 38.26 N 90.12 W
Columbia, In., U.S. 218 39.35 N 85.12 W
Columbia, Ky., U.S. 194 37.06 N 85.18 W
Columbia, La., U.S. 194 32.06 N 92.04 W
Columbia, Md., U.S. 208 39.14 N 76.50 W
Columbia, Ms., U.S. 194 31.15 N 89.50 W
Columbia, Mo., U.S. 219 38.57 N 92.20 W
Columbia, N.J., U.S. 210 40.55 N 75.05 W
Columbia, N.C., U.S. 192 35.55 N 76.15 W
Columbia, Pa., U.S. 208 40.02 N 76.30 W
Columbia, S.C., U.S. 192 34.00 N 81.02 W
Columbia, Tn., U.S. 194 35.36 N 87.02 W
Columbia □6, N.Y., U.S. 210 42.15 N 73.47 W
Columbia □6, Or., U.S. 224 45.57 N 123.03 W
Columbia □6, Pa., U.S. 210 41.00 N 76.28 W
Columbia ≃ 176 46.15 N 124.05 W
Columbia, Cape ➤ 16 83.08 N 70.35 W
Columbia, Lake ⊜1 216 42.05 N 84.18 W
Columbia, Mount ∧ 182 52.09 N 117.25 W
Columbia Airport ⊠ 279a 41.19 N 81.58 W
Columbia Basin ≚1 202 46.45 N 119.05 W
Columbia Center 279a 41.19 N 81.56 W
Columbia City, In., U.S. 216 41.09 N 85.29 W
Columbia City, Or., U.S. 224 45.53 N 122.48 W
Columbia Cross Roads 210 41.50 N 76.48 W
Columbia Falls, Me., U.S. 188 44.39 N 67.43 W
Columbia Falls, Mt., U.S. 202 48.22 N 114.10 W
Columbia Heights 224 46.09 N 122.58 W
Columbia Hills 284b 39.15 N 76.50 W
Columbia Icefield ⊓ 182 52.10 N 117.30 W
Columbia Lake ⊜ 182 50.15 N 115.57 W
Columbia Lake Indian Reserve ✦4 182 50.25 N 115.57 W
Columbia Mountains ∧ 182 52.00 N 119.00 W
Columbiana, Al., U.S. 194 33.10 N 86.36 W
Columbiana, Oh., U.S. 214 40.53 N 80.41 W
Columbiana □6 214 40.47 N 80.46 W
Columbia Plateau ∧1 202 44.00 N 117.30 W
Columbia Regional Airport ⊠ 219 38.50 N 92.13 W
Columbia Road Reservoir ⊜1 198 45.45 N 98.15 W
Columbia State Historical Park ♦ 226 38.02 N 120.25 W
Columbia Station 214 41.20 N 81.57 W
Columbia University ✦2 276 40.48 N 73.58 W
Columbiaville, Mi., U.S. 190 43.09 N 83.24 W
Columbiaville, N.Y., U.S. 210 42.19 N 73.45 W
Columbine, Cape ➤ 158 32.47 S 17.52 E
Columbretes, Islas II 34 39.52 N 0.40 E
Columbus, Ga., U.S. 192 32.29 N 84.59 W
Columbus, In., U.S. 218 39.12 N 85.55 W
Columbus, Ks., U.S. 198 37.10 N 94.50 W
Columbus, Ms., U.S. 194 33.29 N 88.25 W
Columbus, Mt., U.S. 202 45.38 N 109.15 W
Columbus, Ne., U.S. 198 41.25 N 97.22 W
Columbus, N.J., U.S. 208 40.04 N 74.43 W
Columbus, N.M., U.S. 200 31.49 N 107.38 W
Columbus, N.C., U.S. 192 35.15 N 82.11 W
Columbus, N.D., U.S. 198 48.54 N 102.46 W
Columbus, Oh., U.S. 214 39.57 N 82.59 W
Columbus, Pa., U.S. 214 41.56 N 79.35 W
Columbus, Tx., U.S. 222 29.42 N 96.32 W
Columbus, Wi., U.S. 190 43.20 N 89.00 W

Symbol	English	Deutsch	Español	Français	Português
≃	River	Fluss	Rio	Rivière	Rio
⌇	Canal	Kanal	Canal	Canal	Canal
⌇	Waterfall, Rapids	Wasserfall, Stromschnellen	Cascada, Rápidos	Chute d'eau, Rapides	Cascata, Rápidos
⊍	Strait	Meeresstrasse	Estrecho	Détroit	Estreito
⊂	Bay, Gulf	Bucht, Golf	Bahía, Golfo	Baie, Golfe	Baía, Golfo
⊜	Lake, Lakes	See, Seen	Lago, Lagos	Lac, Lacs	Lago, Lagos
≋	Swamp	Sumpf	Pantano	Marais	Pântano
⊓	Ice Features, Glacier	Eis- und Gletscherformen	Accidentes Glaciales	Formes glaciaires	Acidentes glaciares
⌖	Other Hydrographic Features	Andere Hydrographische Objekte	Otros Elementos Hidrográficos	Autres données hydrographiques	Outros acidentes hidrográficos
✦	Submarine Features	Untermeerische Objekte	Accidentes Submarinos	Formes de relief sous-marin	Acidentes submarinos
□	Political Unit	Politische Einheit	Unidad Política	Entité politique	Unidade política
✦	Cultural Institution	Kulturelle Institution	Institución Cultural	Institution culturelle	Instituição cultural
⊥	Historical Site	Historische Stätte	Sitio Histórico	Site historique	Sitio histórico
♦	Recreational Site	Erholungs- und Ferienort	Sitio de Recreo	Centre de loisirs	Area de Lazer
⊠	Airport	Flughafen	Aeropuerto	Aéroport	Aeroporto
■	Military Installation	Militäranlage	Instalación Militar	Installation militaire	Instalação militar
✦	Miscellaneous	Verschiedenes	Misceláneo	Divers	Diversos

Name	Page	Lat.°′	Long.°′
Columbus Air Force Base ■	194	33.38 N	88.26 W
Columbus Grove	216	40.55 N	84.03 W
Columbus Junction	190	41.16 N	91.21 W
Columbus Lake ⊜¹	194	33.35 N	88.30 W
Columbus Park ♦	278	41.53 N	87.47 W
Columbus Point ≻, Ba.	238	24.08 N	75.16 W
Columbus Point ≻, Trin.	241r	11.08 N	60.48 W
Columbus Salt Marsh ≚	204	38.04 N	117.58 W
Coluna	255	18.14 S	42.50 W
Colusa	226	39.12 N	122.00 W
Colusa □⁶	226	39.13 N	122.01 W
Colusa Trough ≖	226	39.02 N	121.59 W
Colver	214	40.32 N	78.47 W
Colville, N.Z.	172	36.38 S	175.28 E
Colville, Wa., U.S.	202	48.32 N	117.54 W
Colville ≐, Ak., U.S.	180	70.25 N	150.30 W
Colville ≐, Wa., U.S.	202	48.37 N	118.05 W
Colville, Cape ≻	172	36.28 S	175.21 E
Colville Channel ʯ	172	36.23 S	175.24 E
Colville Indian Reservation ◆⁴	202	48.15 N	119.00 W
Colville Lake ⊜	180	67.10 N	126.00 W
Colvin Run	284c	38.58 N	77.18 W
Colwell	44	55.04 N	2.04 W
Colwood	224	48.26 N	123.29 W
Colwyn	285	39.55 N	75.15 W
Colwyn Bay	44	53.18 N	3.43 W
Colyton, Austl.	274a	33.47 S	150.48 E
Colyton, Eng., U.K.	42	50.44 N	3.04 W
Comacchio	66	44.42 N	12.11 E
Comacchio, Valli di ⊂	66	44.38 N	12.06 E
Comal	115a	6.55 S	109.31 E
Comala	234	19.19 N	103.45 W
Comalapa, Guat.	236	14.44 N	90.53 W
Comalapa, Nic.	236	12.17 N	85.31 W
Comalcalco	234	18.16 N	93.13 W
Comales	232	26.10 N	98.56 W
Comalito, Cerro ∧	234	20.30 N	104.36 W
Comallo	254	40.40 S	63.30 W
Comallo, Arroyo ≐	254	40.29 S	70.12 W
Coman, Mount ∧	9	74.02 S	65.04 W
Comana	38	43.54 N	28.19 E
Comanche, Ok., U.S.	196	34.22 N	97.57 W
Comanche, Tx., U.S.	196	31.53 N	98.36 W
Comanche Creek ≐, Co., U.S.	198	39.53 N	104.19 W
Comanche Creek ≐, Tx., U.S.	196	31.06 N	102.24 W
Comandante Fontana	252	25.20 S	59.41 W
Comandante Leal	252	30.53 S	65.47 W
Comandante Luis Piedrabuena	254	49.59 S	68.54 W
Comandante Nicanor Otamendi	252	38.07 S	57.51 W
Comănești	38	46.25 N	26.26 E
Comanja de Corona	234	21.19 N	101.42 W
Comarapa	248	17.54 S	64.29 W
Comar Gambon	144	3.10 N	45.47 E
Comas, Perú	248	11.46 S	75.02 W
Comas, Perú	286d	11.57 S	77.04 W
Comayagua	236	14.25 N	87.37 W
Comayagua □⁵	236	14.30 N	87.40 W
Comayagua, Montañas de ⩘	236	14.23 N	87.26 W
Combahee ≐	192	32.30 N	80.31 W
Combarbalá	252	31.11 S	71.02 W
Combeaufontaine	58	47.43 N	5.53 E
Combe Martin	42	51.13 N	4.02 W
Comber, On., Can.	214	42.14 N	82.33 W
Comber, N. Ire., U.K.	48	54.33 N	5.45 W
Comberbach	262	53.17 N	2.32 W
Combermere Bay ⊂	110	19.37 N	93.34 E
Comberton	42	52.11 N	0.02 E
Combe Seamount ✦³	14	12.32 S	177.35 W
Combie, Lake ⊜¹	226	39.01 N	121.02 W
Comblain-au-Pont	56	50.28 N	5.35 E
Combles	50	50.01 N	2.52 E
Combloux	62	45.54 N	6.39 E
Combourg	32	48.25 N	1.45 W
Comboyne	166	31.36 S	152.29 E
Comboyuro Point ≻	171a	27.04 S	153.24 E
Combres	50	48.19 N	1.04 E
Combronde	32	45.59 N	3.05 E
Combs	262	53.18 N	1.57 W
Combs-la-Ville	50	48.40 N	2.34 E
Combs Reservoir ⊜¹	262	53.19 N	1.57 W
Comburg ◈¹	56	49.06 N	9.44 E
Comb Wash V	200	37.13 N	109.42 W
Come by Chance	186	47.51 N	53.58 W
Comeglians	64	46.31 N	12.52 E
Comelico Superiore	64	46.35 N	12.30 E
Comendador Gomes	255	19.41 S	49.05 W
Comer	192	34.03 N	83.07 W
Comercinho	255	16.19 S	41.47 W
Comerío	240m	18.13 N	66.14 W
Comet	166	23.37 S	148.33 E
Comet ≐	166	23.34 S	148.32 E
Cometela	156	21.51 S	34.29 E
Comfort, N.C., U.S.	192	35.00 N	77.30 W
Comfort, Tx., U.S.	196	29.58 N	98.54 W
Comfort, Cape ≻	176	65.08 N	83.21 W
Comfort, Point ≻	276	40.27 N	74.08 W
Comfrey	198	44.06 N	94.54 W
Comilla	124	23.27 N	91.12 E
Comines	50	50.46 N	3.01 E
Comino, Capo ≻	71	40.32 N	9.49 E
Comiskey Park ♦	278	41.50 N	87.38 W
Comiso	70	36.56 N	14.36 E
Comitán [de Domínguez]	232	16.15 N	92.08 W
Comitini	70	37.24 N	13.39 E
Comloșu Mare	38	45.54 N	20.38 E
Commack	210	40.50 N	73.17 W
Commagene □⁹	130	37.50 N	38.00 E
Commencement Bay ⊂	224	47.17 N	122.28 W
Commentry	32	46.17 N	2.44 E
Commerce, Ga., U.S.	192	34.12 N	83.27 W
Commerce, Mi., U.S.	216	42.34 N	83.30 W
Commerce, Ok., U.S.	196	36.56 N	94.52 W
Commerce, Tx., U.S.	196	33.14 N	95.53 W
Commerce City	198	39.49 N	104.56 W
Commerciale Luigi Bocconi, Università ◈²	266b	45.26 N	9.11 E
Commercial Point	218	39.46 N	83.04 W
Commercy	56	48.45 N	5.35 E
Commewijne □⁵	250	5.30 N	55.00 W
Comminges ◆¹	32	43.15 N	0.45 E
Committee Bay ⊂	176	68.30 N	86.30 W
Commodore	214	40.43 N	78.57 W
Commodore Barry Bridge ◆⁵	285	39.49 N	75.22 W
Commondale	158	27.20 S	30.56 E
Common Edge	262	53.47 N	3.02 W
Commonwealth Bay ⊂	9	66.54 S	142.40 E
Commonwealth Range ⩘	9	84.15 S	172.20 E
Commoron Creek ≐	166	28.22 S	150.08 E
Community Center	228	34.16 N	118.44 W
Como, Austl.	274a	34.00 S	151.04 E
Como, It.	62	45.47 N	9.05 E
Como, Ms., U.S.	194	34.30 N	89.56 W
Como, N.C., U.S.	208	36.30 N	77.00 W
Como, Tx., U.S.	222	33.03 N	95.28 W
Como, Wi., U.S.	216	42.37 N	88.28 W
Como □¹	58	45.59 N	9.13 E
Como ≐	58	45.48 N	9.05 E
Como, Lago di ⊜	58	46.00 N	9.20 E
Como, Lake ⊜	216	42.36 N	88.29 W
Como, Mount ∧	226	39.02 N	119.28 W
Comodoro Py	252	35.19 S	60.31 W
Comodoro Rivadavia	254	45.52 S	67.30 W
Como Lake ⊜	190	47.55 N	83.30 W
Comologno	58	46.12 N	8.34 E
Comondú	232	26.03 N	111.46 W
Comonfort	234	20.43 N	100.46 W
Comoras → Comoros □¹	157a	12.10 S	44.15 E
Comores → Comoros □¹	157a	12.10 S	44.15 E
Comores, Archipel des II	157a	12.10 S	44.15 E
Comorin, Cape ≻	122	8.06 N	77.33 E
Comoros (Comores) □¹, Afr.	138	12.10 S	44.15 E
Comoros (Comores) □¹, Afr.	157a	12.10 S	44.15 E
Comox	182	49.40 N	124.55 W
Comox, Canadian Forces Base ■	182	49.43 N	124.54 W
Companhia Siderúrgica Nacional ◈³	256	22.31 S	44.07 W
Compans	261	49.00 N	2.40 E
Compatsch	58	46.58 N	10.25 E
Compiègne	50	49.25 N	2.50 E
Compo Cove ⊂	276	41.07 N	73.21 W
Compostela, Méx.	234	21.15 N	104.53 W
Compostela, Pil.	116	7.40 N	126.02 E
Comprida, Ilha I, Bra.	252	24.50 S	47.42 W
Comprida, Ilha I, Bra.	287a	23.02 S	43.12 W
Comps-sur-Artuby	62	43.43 N	6.30 E
Compstall	262	53.25 N	2.03 W
Compton, Eng., U.K.	260	51.13 N	0.38 W
Compton, Ca., U.S.	228	33.53 N	118.13 W
Compton, Il., U.S.	216	41.42 N	89.05 W
Compton □⁶	206	45.20 N	71.25 W
Compton Airport ⊠	280	33.53 N	118.15 W
Compton Creek ≐, Ca., U.S.	280	33.50 N	118.12 W
Compton Creek ≐, N.J., U.S.	276	40.26 N	74.05 W
Comptonville	273d	26.17 S	27.58 E
Comrie	46	56.22 N	4.00 W
Comstock, Mi., U.S.	216	42.17 N	85.30 W
Comstock, Ne., U.S.	198	41.33 N	99.15 W
Comstock, Tx., U.S.	196	29.41 N	101.11 W
Comstock Park	216	43.02 N	85.40 W
Comunanza	66	42.57 N	13.25 E
Con ≐, S.S.S.R.	76	52.54 N	36.00 E
Çon ≐, Viet.	110	19.04 N	105.00 E
Čona ≐, S.S.S.R.	74	62.54 N	111.06 E
Cona ≐, Scot., U.K.	46	56.46 N	5.14 W
Conakry	150	9.31 N	13.43 W
Conambo ≐	246	2.07 S	76.03 W
Conanicut Island I	207	41.32 N	71.21 W
Cona Niyeo	254	41.53 S	67.00 W
Conara Junction	166	41.50 S	147.26 E
Conasauga ≐	192	34.33 N	84.55 W
Conaskonk Point ≻	276	40.27 N	74.11 W
Conca ≐	66	43.58 N	12.43 E
Concarán	252	32.34 S	65.15 W
Concarneau	32	47.52 N	3.55 W
Conceição, Bra.	248	7.24 S	58.05 W
Conceição, Bra.	250	7.33 S	38.31 W
Conceição, Moç.	156	18.45 S	36.10 E
Conceição ≐	250	12.24 S	46.57 W
Conceição, Cachoeira ⌊	248	9.34 S	64.22 W
Conceição, Ilha da I	287a	22.52 S	43.07 W
Conceição da Aparecida	255	21.06 S	46.12 W
Conceição da Barra	255	18.35 S	39.45 W
Conceição da Ibitipoca	256	21.43 S	43.55 W
Conceição da Pedra	256	22.09 S	45.27 W
Conceição das Alagoas	255	19.55 S	48.23 W
Conceição de Ipanema	255	19.55 S	41.41 W
Conceição de Jacareí	256	23.02 S	44.09 W
Conceição do Almeida	255	12.48 S	39.12 W
Conceição do Araguaia	250	8.15 S	49.17 W
Conceição do Canindé	250	7.54 S	41.34 W
Conceição do Coité	250	11.33 S	39.16 W
Conceição do Formoso	256	21.25 S	43.21 W
Conceição do Mato Dentro	255	19.01 S	43.25 W
Conceição do Maú	246	3.35 N	59.53 W
Conceição do Norte	255	12.13 S	47.18 W
Conceição do Rio Verde	256	21.53 S	45.05 W
Conceição dos Ouros	256	22.25 S	45.47 W
Concepción, Arg.	252	28.23 S	57.53 W
Concepción, Arg.	252	27.20 S	65.35 W
Concepción, Bol.	248	11.29 S	66.31 W
Concepción, Bol.	248	16.15 S	62.04 W
Concepción, Chile	252	36.50 S	73.03 W
Concepción, Col.	246	6.46 N	72.42 W
Concepción, Guat.	236	15.37 N	91.41 W
Concepción, Para.	252	23.25 S	57.17 W
Concepción, Perú	248	11.55 S	75.17 W
Concepcion, Pil.	116	11.13 N	123.06 E
Concepcion, Pil.	116	10.42 N	123.03 E
Concepcion, Pil.	116	12.24 N	122.06 E
Concepcion, Pil.	116	15.19 N	120.39 E
Concepción □⁵	252	23.00 S	57.00 W
Concepción, Bahía ⊂	232	26.39 N	111.48 W
Concepción, Estrecho del ʯ	254	50.30 S	74.55 W
Concepción, Laguna ⊜	248	17.29 S	61.25 W
Concepción, Río de la ≐	232	30.32 N	113.02 W
Concepción, Volcán ∧¹	236	11.34 N	85.37 W
Concepcion Bay ⊂	116	11.15 N	123.07 E
Concepción de Ataco	236	13.52 N	89.51 W
Concepción de Buenos Aires	234	19.58 N	103.16 W
Concepción de la Sierra	252	27.59 S	55.31 W
Concepción de la Vega	238	19.13 N	70.31 W
Concepcíon del Oro	232	24.38 N	101.25 W
Concepción del Uruguay	252	32.29 S	58.14 W
Concepción Quezaltepeque	236	14.06 N	88.58 W
Conception, Point ≻	204	34.27 N	120.27 W
Conception Bay ⊂, Nf., Can.	186	47.45 N	53.00 W
Conception Bay ⊂, Namibia	156	23.53 S	14.28 E
Concession	154	17.22 S	30.57 E
Conchagua	236	13.19 N	87.52 W
Conchagua, Volcán de ∧¹	236	13.14 N	87.46 W
Conchal	256	22.20 S	47.10 W
Conchal, Ribeirão do ≐	256	22.20 S	47.10 W
Conchalí	286e	33.24 S	70.39 W
Conchas ≐	196	35.23 N	104.18 W
Conchas Dam	196	35.22 N	104.11 W
Conchas Lake ⊜¹	196	35.25 N	104.14 W
Conche	186	50.53 N	55.54 W
Conches-en-Ouche	50	48.58 N	0.56 E
Conchi	252	22.02 S	68.38 W
Conchillas	258	34.15 S	58.04 W
Conchitas, Arroyo ≐	258	34.45 S	58.09 W
Concho	200	34.28 N	109.36 W
Concho ≐	196	31.34 N	99.43 W
Conchos ≐, Méx.	232	29.35 N	104.25 W
Conchos ≐, Méx.	232	25.07 N	98.32 W
Concise	58	46.51 N	6.43 E
Conco	64	45.48 N	11.36 E
Concón	252	32.55 S	71.31 W
Concononongon Point ≻	116	12.14 N	120.13 E
Conconully	182	48.33 N	119.44 W
Concord, Austl.	274a	33.52 S	151.06 E
Concord, On., Can.	275b	43.48 N	79.29 W
Concord, Ca., U.S.	226	37.58 N	122.01 W
Concord, Ga., U.S.	192	33.05 N	84.26 W
Concord, Il., U.S.	219	39.49 N	90.22 W
Concord, Ky., U.S.	218	38.41 N	83.29 W
Concord, Ma., U.S.	207	42.27 N	71.20 W
Concord, Mi., U.S.	216	42.10 N	84.38 W
Concord, Mo., U.S.	219	38.31 N	90.23 W
Concord, N.H., U.S.	188	43.12 N	71.32 W
Concord, N.C., U.S.	192	35.24 N	80.34 W
Concord, Pa., U.S.	214	40.15 N	77.42 W
Concord, Tx., U.S.	222	31.16 N	96.09 W
Concord ≐	283	42.39 N	71.18 W
Concord Battleground ⊥	283	42.28 N	71.21 W
Concordia, Arg.	252	31.24 S	58.02 W
Concórdia, Bra.	246	4.35 S	66.35 W
Concórdia, Bra.	252	27.14 S	52.01 W
Concordia, Méx.	232	25.47 N	103.07 W
Concordia, Méx.	234	23.17 N	106.04 W
Concordia, Perú	246	4.30 S	74.55 W
Concordia, Ks., U.S.	198	39.34 N	97.39 W
Concordia, Mo., U.S.	194	38.59 N	93.34 W
Concordia Gardens	216	41.09 N	85.08 W
Concordia Sagittaria ⊥	64	45.45 N	12.51 E
Concordia sulla Secchia	64	44.55 N	10.59 E
Concord Naval Weapons Station ■	282	38.03 N	122.02 W
Concordville	285	39.53 N	75.31 W
Concord West	274a	33.51 S	151.05 E
Concorezzo	62	45.35 N	9.20 E
Concrete	224	48.32 N	121.44 W
Con-cuong	110	19.02 N	104.54 E
Conda	152	11.06 S	14.20 E
Condamine	166	26.56 S	150.08 E
Condamine ≐	166	27.07 S	149.48 E
Condat-en-Féniers	32	45.21 N	2.46 E
Condé, Ang.	152	10.50 S	14.37 E
Conde, Bra.	255	11.49 S	37.37 W
Condé, Fr.	32	48.51 N	0.33 W
Conde, S.D., U.S.	198	45.09 N	98.05 W
Condécourt	261	49.02 N	1.57 E
Condé-en-Brie	50	49.00 N	3.33 E
Condega	236	13.21 N	86.24 W
Condeixa	250	0.54 S	48.36 W
Conderilla Señor	286d	12.02 S	77.05 W
Condé-sur-l'Escaut	50	50.27 N	3.35 E
Condè-sur-Vesgre	261	48.45 N	1.40 E
Condeúba	255	14.53 S	41.59 W
Condino	64	45.53 N	10.36 E
Condobolin	166	33.05 S	147.09 E
Condom	32	43.58 N	0.22 E
Condon	202	45.14 N	120.11 W
Condoto	246	5.06 N	76.37 W
Condove	62	45.07 N	7.18 E
Condrieu	62	45.27 N	4.46 E
Condroz □⁹	56	50.25 N	5.00 E
Cone	196	33.48 N	101.23 W
Conecuh ≐	194	30.58 N	87.14 W
Conegliano	64	45.53 N	12.18 E
Conejos	200	37.05 N	106.01 W
Conejos ≐	200	37.18 N	105.44 W
Conemaugh	214	40.24 N	78.52 W
Conemaugh ≐	214	40.28 N	79.27 W
Conemaugh River Lake ⊜¹	214	40.28 N	79.17 W
Cone Mountain ∧	180	66.12 N	156.03 W
Conero, Monte ∧	66	43.33 N	13.36 E
Conestoga	208	39.57 N	76.21 W
Conestoga Creek ≐	208	39.56 N	76.23 W
Conestogo	212	43.32 N	80.30 W
Conestogo ≐	212	43.32 N	80.29 W
Conestogo Lake ⊜	212	43.44 N	80.44 W
Conesus	210	42.43 N	77.41 W
Conesus Lake ⊜	210	42.47 N	77.43 W
Conesville	214	40.11 N	81.53 W
Conewago Creek ≐	208	40.07 N	76.42 W
Conewago Lake ⊜	208	40.06 N	76.52 W
Conewango Creek ≐	214	41.50 N	79.09 W
Coney Island ◆⁸	276	40.34 N	74.00 W
Confederation Lake ⊜	184	51.05 N	92.44 W
Configni	66	42.25 N	12.38 E
Conflans-en-Jarnisy	56	49.10 N	5.51 E
Conflans-Sainte-Honorine	50	48.59 N	2.06 E
Conflenti	68	39.04 N	16.17 E
Conflict Group II	164	10.45 S	151.45 E
Confluence	188	39.48 N	79.21 W
Confolens	32	46.01 N	0.41 E
Confraternidad, Parque ♦	286d	12.09 S	77.02 W
Confusion Bay ⊂	186	49.58 N	55.47 W
Confuso ≐	252	25.09 S	57.34 W
Cong	48	53.32 N	9.19 W
Congamond	207	42.01 N	72.46 W
Congaree ≐	192	33.45 N	80.37 W
Congelin	168a	32.50 S	116.54 E
Congers	210	41.09 N	73.56 W
Congers Lake ⊜	276	41.09 N	73.57 W
Cong Hoa Stadium ♦	269c	10.45 N	106.40 E
Conghua	100	23.32 N	113.32 E
Congjiang	102	25.41 N	108.47 E
Congleton	44	53.10 N	2.13 W
Congo	250	7.48 S	36.40 W
Congo □¹, Afr.	138	1.00 S	15.00 E
Congo □¹, Afr.	152	1.00 S	15.00 E
Congo (Zaire) (Zaïre) ≐	138	6.04 S	12.24 E
Congo, Democratic Republic of the → Zaire □¹	138	4.00 S	25.00 E
Congo, République démocratique du → Zaire □¹	138	4.00 S	25.00 E
Congo, république du → Congo □¹	152	1.00 S	15.00 E
Congo, Serra do ⩘	152	6.30 S	13.43 E
Congo Basin ≚¹	10	0.00	20.00 E
Congonhal	256	22.09 S	46.02 W
Congonhas, Aeroporto de ⊠	256	23.38 S	46.38 W
Congonhinhas	255	23.33 S	50.33 W
Congost ≐	266d	41.33 N	2.15 E
Congregación Cuauhtémoc	234	22.38 N	98.08 W
Congregación Ignacio Zaragoza	234	23.15 N	98.50 W
Congresbury	42	51.23 N	2.48 W
Congress, Sk., Can.	184	49.46 N	106.00 W
Congress, Oh., U.S.	214	40.55 N	82.03 W
Conie ≐	50	48.06 N	1.30 E
Conigli, Isola dei I	70a	35.30 N	12.33 E
Coningsby	44	53.07 N	0.10 W
Conisbrough	44	53.29 N	1.13 W
Coniston, On., Can.	190	46.29 N	80.51 W
Coniston, Eng., U.K.	44	54.22 N	3.05 W
Coniston Water ⊜	44	54.20 N	3.04 W
Conitaca	232	24.10 N	106.43 W
Conjeeveram → Kānchipuram	122	12.50 N	79.43 E
Conjola	170	35.13 S	150.27 E
Çonjola, Lake ⊂	170	35.16 S	150.27 E
Čon-Kemin ≐	85	42.42 N	75.54 E
Conklin, Ab., Can.	182	55.38 N	111.05 W
Conklin, N.Y., U.S.	210	42.02 N	75.48 W
Conklingville Dam ◆⁶	210	43.17 N	74.02 W
Conklin Point ≻	276	40.41 N	73.17 W
Conkouati	152	4.00 S	11.13 E
Conliège	58	46.39 N	5.36 E
Conlin, Lake ⊜	220	28.14 N	81.07 W
Çonlu	130	40.13 N	28.06 E
Conn, Lough ⊜	48	54.04 N	9.20 W
Connah's Quay	44	53.13 N	3.03 W
Connaught □⁹	48	53.45 N	9.00 W
Connaughton	285	40.05 N	75.19 W
Connaughton, Mount ∧²	162	22.42 S	122.40 E
Connaught Place ♦	272a	28.38 N	77.12 E
Connaux	62	44.05 N	4.36 E
Conneaut	214	41.56 N	80.33 W
Conneaut Creek ≐	214	41.58 N	80.33 W
Conneaut Lake	214	41.36 N	80.19 W
Conneaut Lake ⊜	214	41.37 N	80.18 W
Conneaut Outlet ≐	214	41.33 N	80.06 W
Conneautville	214	41.45 N	80.22 W
Connecticut □³, U.S.	178	41.45 N	72.45 W
Connecticut □³, U.S.	207	41.45 N	72.45 W
Connecticut ≐	188	41.17 N	72.21 W
Connell	202	46.39 N	118.51 W
Connell, Mount ∧	182	49.18 N	115.38 W
Connellsville	188	40.01 N	79.35 W
Connelly	210	41.55 N	73.59 W
Connel Park	44	55.23 N	4.12 W
Connemara	166	24.13 S	142.17 E
Connemara ◆¹	48	53.25 N	9.45 W
Conner	116	17.48 N	121.19 E
Connerré	50	48.03 N	0.30 E
Connersville, Fl., U.S.	220	27.54 N	81.47 W
Connersville, In., U.S.	218	39.38 N	85.08 W
Connetquot ≐	276	40.43 N	73.08 W
Connetquot Brook ≐	276	40.45 N	73.09 W
Connetquot River State Park ♦	210	40.46 N	73.09 W
Connewarre, Lake ⊜	169	38.14 S	144.27 E
Conn Island I	284c	39.00 N	77.16 W
Conn Lake ⊜	176	70.34 N	73.30 W
Connoquenessing	214	40.49 N	80.59 W
Connoquenessing Creek ≐	214	40.51 N	80.19 W
Connors Range ⩘	166	21.40 S	149.10 E
Conodoguinet Creek ≐	208	40.17 N	76.55 W
Conon ≐	46	57.34 N	6.26 W
Cononaco ≐	246	1.32 S	75.35 W
Cononbridge	46	57.34 N	4.26 W
Conorochite ≐	246	2.41 N	67.29 W
Conotton Creek ≐	214	40.34 N	81.23 W
Conover	192	35.42 N	81.13 W
Conowingo	208	39.40 N	76.09 W
Conowingo ◆⁶	208	39.33 N	76.04 W
Conowingo Creek ≐	208	39.41 N	76.12 W
Conowingo Dam ◆⁶	208	39.39 N	76.10 W
Conquest	184	51.32 N	107.17 W
Conquista	255	19.56 S	47.33 W
Conquista, Ribeirão da ≐	256	21.17 S	43.51 W
Conrad, Ia., U.S.	190	42.13 N	92.52 W
Conrad, Mt., U.S.	202	48.10 N	111.56 W
Conrado	256	22.32 S	43.33 W
Conroe	222	30.18 N	95.27 W
Conroe, Lake ⊜¹	222	30.25 N	95.37 W
Çonsandolo	66	44.39 N	11.46 E
Čon-Saryoj	85	42.37 N	76.53 E
Conscience Bay ⊂	276	40.57 N	73.07 W
Consdorf	56	49.46 N	6.20 E
Consecon	212	44.00 N	77.31 W
Conselheiro Lafaiete	255	20.40 S	43.48 W
Conselheiro Paulino	256	22.13 S	42.31 W
Conselheiro Pena	255	19.10 S	41.30 W
Conselice	66	44.31 N	11.49 E
Conselve	64	45.14 N	11.52 E
Conservatória	256	22.18 S	43.57 W
Consett	44	54.51 N	1.49 W
Conshohocken	208	40.04 N	75.18 W
Consolação	256	22.33 S	45.55 W
Consolação ◆⁸	287b	23.33 S	46.39 W
Consolación del Norte	240p	22.45 N	83.33 W
Consolación del Sur	240p	22.30 N	83.31 W
Consolidated Main Reef Mines ◆⁷	273d	26.11 S	27.56 E
Con Son II	110	8.43 N	106.36 E
Consort	184	52.01 N	110.46 W
Constable	206	44.56 N	74.18 W
Constableville	212	43.34 N	75.25 W
Constance → Konstanz	58	47.40 N	9.10 E
Constance, Lake → Bodensee ⊜	58	47.35 N	9.25 E
Constance Lake ⊜	212	45.25 N	75.58 W
Constanța	38	44.11 N	28.39 E
Constanța □⁶	38	44.20 N	28.20 E
Constant Creek ≐	212	45.17 N	76.46 W
Constantia	210	43.14 N	76.00 W
Constantina	34	37.52 N	5.37 W
Constantine → Qacentina	148	36.22 N	6.37 E
Constantine	216	41.50 N	85.40 W
Constantine, Cape ≻	180	58.25 N	158.50 W
Constantinople → İstanbul	130	41.01 N	28.58 E
Constant Lake ⊜	212	45.24 N	77.00 W
Constânzia	34	39.28 N	8.20 W
Constitución, Chile	252	35.20 S	72.25 W
Constitución, Ur.	252	31.05 S	57.50 W
Constitución ◆⁸	288	34.37 S	58.23 W
Constitución de 1857, Parque Nacional ♦	204	32.05 N	115.55 W
Constitution, Mount ∧	224	48.40 N	122.50 W
Consuegra	34	39.28 N	3.36 W
Consul	184	49.21 N	109.30 W
Consuma	66	43.47 N	11.35 E
Consuma, Passo della)(	66	43.47 N	11.36 E
Contai	126	21.47 N	87.45 E
Contamana	248	7.15 S	74.54 W
Contarina	64	45.00 N	12.13 E
Contas, Rio de ≐	255	14.17 S	39.01 W
Contee	208	39.05 N	76.52 W
Contendas do Sincorá	255	13.45 S	41.02 W
Contentnea Creek ≐	192	35.21 N	77.23 W
Contes	62	43.49 N	7.19 E
Contessa Entellina	70	37.44 N	13.11 E
Contigliano	66	42.24 N	12.46 E
Continental	216	41.06 N	84.15 W
Continental Peak ∧	200	42.16 N	108.43 W
Contoocook Lake ⊜	207	42.47 N	72.01 W
Contraalmirante Cordero	252	38.44 S	68.10 W
Contra Costa □⁶	226	37.55 N	121.55 W
Contra Costa Canal ≖	282	38.02 N	121.58 W
Contra Loma Reservoir ⊜¹	282	37.58 N	121.49 W
Contramaestre	240p	20.18 N	76.15 W
Contramaestre ≐	240p	20.31 N	76.18 W
Contratación	246	6.18 N	73.29 W
Contrecoeur	206	45.51 N	73.14 W
Contre Island ≻¹	276	40.54 N	73.32 W
Contreras □⁷	286a	19.16 N	99.16 W
Contreras, Embalse de ⊜¹	34	39.32 N	1.30 W
Contres	50	47.25 N	1.26 E
Contrexéville	58	48.11 N	5.54 E
Contrisson	56	48.48 N	4.57 E
Controller Bay ⊂	180	60.07 N	144.15 W
Contumazá	248	7.22 S	78.49 W
Contursi	68	40.39 N	15.14 E
Contwoyto Lake ⊜	176	65.42 N	110.50 W
Conty	50	49.44 N	2.09 E
Contz-les-Bains	56	49.27 N	6.21 E
Convención	246	8.28 N	73.21 W
Convent	194	30.01 N	90.49 W
Convento	236	9.21 N	83.30 W
Convent Station	276	40.47 N	74.26 W
Conversano	68	40.58 N	17.08 E
Converse	216	40.34 N	85.52 W
Converse Lake ⊜	276	41.08 N	73.39 W
Converse Pond Brook ≐	276	41.03 N	73.40 W
Convoy	216	40.55 N	84.42 W
Conway, P.E., Can.	186	46.40 N	63.59 W
Conway, S. Afr.	158	31.43 S	25.16 E
Conway, Ar., U.S.	194	35.05 N	92.26 W
Conway, Fl., U.S.	220	28.30 N	81.19 W
Conway, Ma., U.S.	207	42.30 N	72.42 W
Conway, Mo., U.S.	194	37.30 N	92.49 W
Conway, N.H., U.S.	188	43.58 N	71.07 W
Conway, N.C., U.S.	192	36.26 N	77.13 W
Conway, Pa., U.S.	214	40.39 N	80.14 W
Conway, S.C., U.S.	192	33.50 N	79.02 W
Conway, Wa., U.S.	224	48.21 N	122.21 W
Conway, Cape ≻	166	20.32 S	148.56 E
Conway, Lake ⊜	162	28.17 S	135.35 E
Conway, Lake ⊜¹	194	35.00 N	92.25 W
Conway, Mount ∧	162	23.45 S	133.25 E
Conway Springs	198	37.23 N	97.38 W
Conwy	44	53.17 N	3.50 W
Conwy ≐	44	53.17 N	3.50 W
Conwy, Vale of V	44	53.12 N	3.48 W
Conwy Bay ⊂	44	53.18 N	3.55 W
Conyers	192	33.40 N	84.01 W
Conyngham	210	40.59 N	76.03 W
Coo	56	50.24 N	5.52 E
Coober Pedy	162	29.01 S	134.43 E
Cooch Behār	124	26.19 N	89.26 E
Cooch Behār □⁵	124	26.20 N	89.20 E
Coogee, Austl.	168a	32.07 S	115.46 E
Coogee, Austl.	274a	33.55 S	151.16 E
Coogee Bay ⊂	274a	33.55 S	151.16 E
Coogoon ≐	166	27.19 S	148.50 E
Cook, Austl.	162	30.37 S	130.25 E
Cook, In., U.S.	216	41.22 N	87.26 W
Cook, Mn., U.S.	190	47.51 N	92.41 W
Cook, Ne., U.S.	198	40.30 N	96.09 W
Cook, Wa., U.S.	224	45.43 N	121.40 W
Cook □⁶	216	41.53 N	87.45 W
Cook, Bahía ⊂	254	55.10 S	70.10 W
Cook, Baie de ⊂	174s	17.29 S	149.49 W
Cook, Cape ≻	182	50.08 N	127.55 W
Cook, Mount ∧	172	43.36 S	170.10 E
Cook, Point ≻	274b	37.55 S	144.48 E
Cook, Récif de ✦²	175f	19.25 S	163.50 E
Cookardinia	171b	35.34 S	147.14 E
Cook Bay ⊂	212	44.15 N	79.30 W
Cookbundoon ≐	170	34.28 S	150.04 E
Cook Creek ≐	224	47.17 N	124.05 W
Cooke, Mount ∧	168a	32.25 S	116.18 E
Cookernup	168a	33.00 S	115.54 E
Cookes Peak ∧	200	32.32 N	107.44 W
Cookeville	194	36.09 N	85.30 W
Cook Forest State Park ♦	214	41.22 N	79.12 W
Cookham	42	51.34 N	0.43 W
Cookhouse	158	32.45 S	25.49 E
Cook Ice Shelf ⊓	9	68.40 S	152.30 E
Cooking Lake ⊜	182	53.25 N	113.02 W
Cook Inlet ⊂	180	60.30 N	152.00 W
Cook-Inseln → Cook Islands □²	14	20.00 S	158.00 W
Cook Island I	174o	1.57 N	157.28 W
Cook Islands □²	14	20.00 S	158.00 W
Cooks ≐	274a	33.56 S	151.10 E
Cooksburg	214	41.20 N	79.12 W
Cooks Falls	210	41.57 N	74.59 W
Cook's Harbour	186	51.36 N	55.52 W
Cookshire	206	45.25 N	71.38 W
Cooksmill Green	260	51.44 N	0.22 E
Cooks Mills	284a	43.00 N	79.11 W
Cookstown, On., Can.	212	44.11 N	79.42 W
Cookstown, N. Ire., U.K.	48	54.39 N	6.45 W
Cook Strait ʯ	172	41.15 S	174.30 E
Cooksville, Il., U.S.	216	40.33 N	88.43 W
Cooksville, Md., U.S.	208	39.19 N	77.01 W
Cooksville, Wi., U.S.	216	42.50 N	89.14 W
Cooksville Creek ≐	275b	43.34 N	79.34 W
Cooktown	164	15.28 S	145.15 E
Cookville	222	33.11 N	94.51 W
Coolabah	166	31.02 S	146.43 E
Cooladdi	166	26.39 S	145.28 E
Coolah	166	31.50 S	149.42 E
Coolamon	166	34.49 S	147.12 E
Coolaney	48	54.11 N	8.29 W
Coolangatta	171a	28.10 S	153.32 E
Coolawanyah	162	21.47 S	117.48 E
Coole ≐	50	48.56 N	4.21 E
Cooleemee	192	35.48 N	80.33 W
Cooley Lake ⊜	281	42.37 N	83.27 W
Coolgardie	162	30.57 S	121.10 E
Coolidge, Az., U.S.	200	32.58 N	111.31 W
Coolidge, Ga., U.S.	192	31.00 N	83.51 W
Coolidge, Tx., U.S.	222	31.45 N	96.38 W
Coolidge, Mount ∧	198	43.44 N	103.29 W
Coolidge Dam ◆⁶	200	33.00 N	110.20 W
Coolidge Field ⊠	240c	17.09 N	61.47 W
Coolidge Point ≻	283	42.34 N	70.44 W
Coolin	202	48.28 N	116.50 W
Cooling	260	51.27 N	0.32 E
Cooloongup, Lake ⊜	168a	32.18 S	115.47 E
Coolspring	214	41.02 N	79.05 W
Coolumburra, Mount ∧	170	35.01 S	150.10 E
Coolup	168a	32.44 S	115.53 E
Cooma	171b	36.14 S	149.08 E
Cooma Creek ≐	171b	36.07 S	149.11 E
Coombe Cottage ⊥	274b	37.43 S	145.23 E
Coomberdale	162	30.28 S	116.02 E
Coomera	171a	27.52 S	153.19 E
Coomera ≐	171a	27.53 S	153.24 E
Coominya	171a	27.23 S	152.30 E
Coonabarabran	166	31.16 S	149.17 E
Coonalpyn	166	35.42 S	139.51 E
Coonamble	166	30.57 S	148.23 E
Coonana	162	31.01 S	123.07 E
Coon Creek ≐, Ca., U.S.	226	38.51 N	121.34 W
Coon Creek ≐, Il., U.S.	216	42.15 N	88.48 W
Coon Creek ≐, Tx., U.S.	222	31.59 N	95.52 W
Coon Creek Lake ⊜¹	222	32.04 N	95.52 W
Coondambo	166	31.04 S	135.52 E
Coondapoor	122	13.38 N	74.42 E
Coongan ≐	162	20.53 S	119.47 E
Coongoola	166	27.39 S	145.54 E
Coonoor	122	11.21 N	76.49 E
Coon Rapids, Ia., U.S.	198	41.52 N	94.41 W
Coon Rapids, Mn., U.S.	190	45.10 N	93.19 W
Coontown	276	40.37 N	74.31 W
Coon Valley	190	43.42 N	91.00 W
Cooper	196	33.22 N	95.41 W
Cooper ≐, N.J., U.S.	285	39.57 N	75.07 W
Cooper ≐, Wa., U.S.	224	47.23 N	121.23 W
Cooper, Mount ∧, Austl.	162	26.11 S	127.56 E
Cooper, Mount ∧, B.C., Can.	182	50.11 N	117.12 W
Cooper, North Branch ≐	285	39.55 N	75.02 W
Cooper Center	216	42.23 N	85.37 W
Cooper Creek ≐	166	28.29 S	137.46 E
Cooper Island I	240m	18.22 N	64.30 W
Cooper Landing	180	60.29 N	149.51 W
Cooper Mountain ∧	180	60.23 N	149.51 W
Cooper River Parkway ♦	285	39.55 N	75.03 W
Cooper Road	194	32.26 N	93.48 W
Coopers	194	32.46 N	86.33 W
Coopersale Common	260	51.42 N	0.08 E
Coopersburg	208	40.30 N	75.23 W
Coopers Plains, Austl.	171a	27.34 S	153.02 E
Coopers Plains, N.Y., U.S.	210	42.11 N	77.08 W
Cooperstown, N.Y., U.S.	210	42.42 N	74.55 W
Cooperstown, N.D., U.S.	198	47.26 N	98.07 W
Cooperstown, Pa., U.S.	214	41.30 N	79.52 W
Cooperstown, Pa., U.S.	214	40.43 N	79.57 W
Coopersville	216	43.03 N	85.56 W
Coorabie	162	31.54 S	132.18 E
Cooranbong	170	33.04 S	151.27 E
Coorong National Park ♦	168b	35.40 S	139.05 E
Coorow	162	29.53 S	116.01 E
Cooroy	166	26.25 S	152.55 E
Coorparoo	171a	27.30 S	153.03 E
Coos □⁶	206	45.04 N	71.20 W
Coosa ≐	194	32.30 N	86.16 W
Coosawhatchie ≐	192	32.32 N	80.52 W
Coos Bay	202	43.22 N	124.12 W
Coos Bay ⊂	202	43.23 N	124.16 W
Cootamundra	166	34.39 S	148.02 E
Cootehill	48	54.04 N	7.05 W
Cooyar	171a	26.59 S	151.50 E
Cooyar Creek ≐	171a	27.24 S	152.03 E
Çooyar Mountain ∧	171a	26.57 S	151.47 E
Čop	78	48.26 N	22.10 E
Copacabana, Arg.	252	28.12 S	67.29 W
Copacabana, Bol.	248	16.10 S	69.05 W
Copacabana ◆⁸	287a	22.58 S	43.11 W
Copacabana, Forte de ⊥	287a	22.59 S	43.11 W
Copainalá	234	17.05 N	93.12 W
Copake	210	42.06 N	73.33 W
Copake Falls	210	42.07 N	73.31 W
Copala	234	16.37 N	98.58 W
Copalillo	234	18.02 N	99.07 W
Copalis ≐	224	47.07 N	124.13 W
Copalis Beach	224	47.06 N	124.10 W
Copalita ≐	234	15.46 N	96.03 W
Copalquín	232	25.29 N	107.00 W
Copán, Hond.	236	14.50 N	89.09 W
Copan, Ok., U.S.	196	36.53 N	95.55 W
Copán □⁵	236	14.50 N	89.00 W
Copán ⊥	236	14.50 N	89.09 W
Copanatoyac	234	17.15 N	98.45 W
Copándaro de Galeana	234	19.53 N	101.13 W
Copan Lake ⊜¹	196	36.55 N	95.56 W
Copano Bay ⊂	196	28.05 N	97.05 W
Copatana	246	2.48 S	67.04 W
Cope	198	39.39 N	102.51 W
Copeá, Paraná ≐¹	246	3.52 S	63.20 W
Copeau ≐	184	52.45 N	103.00 W
Copeland	220	25.57 N	81.21 W
Copeland Island I	44	54.41 N	5.32 W
Copenhagen → København, Dan.	41	55.40 N	12.35 E
Copenhagen, N.Y., U.S.	212	43.53 N	75.40 W
Copenhague → København	41	55.40 N	12.35 E
Copenhaver	284c	39.04 N	77.11 W
Copertino	68	40.16 N	18.03 E
Copetonas	252	38.43 S	60.27 W
Copeville	222	33.05 N	96.25 W
Copiague	210	40.40 N	73.24 W
Copiague Neck ≻¹	276	40.40 N	73.22 W
Copiapó	252	27.22 S	70.20 W
Copiapó ≐	252	27.19 S	70.56 W
Copinsay I	46	58.54 N	2.40 W
Coplay	208	40.40 N	75.29 W
Copley, Austl.	166	30.32 S	138.25 E
Copley, Oh., U.S.	214	41.06 N	81.39 W
Copmanthorpe	44	53.55 N	1.08 W
Copoas, Mount ∧	116	10.48 N	119.17 E
Copolo	152	10.22 S	14.07 E
Çoporito	246	8.56 N	62.00 W
Čopoviči	78	50.49 N	27.58 E
Copparo	64	44.54 N	11.49 E
Coppell	222	32.57 N	97.01 W
Coppename ≐	250	5.48 N	55.55 W
Coppenbrügge	52	52.07 N	9.32 E
Copper ≐	180	60.30 N	144.50 W
Copperas Cove	196	31.07 N	97.54 W
Copperas Mountain ∧	276	41.02 N	74.28 W
Copperbelt □⁴	154	13.00 S	28.00 E
Copper Butte ∧	202	48.42 N	118.28 W
Copper Center	180	61.58 N	145.19 W
Copper Cliff	190	46.28 N	81.04 W
Copper Creek ≐	192	36.40 N	82.45 W
Copper Harbor	190	47.27 N	87.53 W
Coppermine	176	67.50 N	115.05 W
Coppermine ≐	176	67.49 N	115.04 W
Copper Mine Point ≻, Br. Vir. Is.	240m	18.26 N	64.25 W
Coppermine Point ≻, On., Can.	190	46.59 N	84.47 W
Copper Mountain	182	49.20 N	120.33 W
Copper Mountain ∧, Ak., U.S.	182	55.14 N	132.36 W
Copper Mountain ∧, Wy., U.S.	200	43.27 N	107.57 W
Copperopolis	226	37.59 N	120.38 W
Coppet	58	46.19 N	6.12 E
Coppin State College ◈²	284b	39.19 N	76.40 W
Copplestone	42	50.49 N	3.45 W
Coppull	262	53.37 N	2.40 W
Copster Green	262	53.48 N	2.30 W
Coptic Museum ◈	273c	30.00 N	31.13 E
Copton Creek ≐	182	54.16 N	119.15 W
Copton Point ≻	116	10.00 N	123.22 E
Coqueiro Grande, Serra do ∧	256	21.40 S	42.55 W
Coquet ≐	44	55.22 N	1.37 W
Coquet Dale V	44	55.16 N	1.50 W
Coquí	240m	17.59 N	66.14 W
Coquilhatville → Mbandaka	152	0.04 N	18.16 E
Coquille	202	43.10 N	124.11 W
Coquille ≐	202	43.07 N	124.26 W
Coquille, East Fork ≐	202	43.06 N	124.04 W
Coquille, Middle Fork ≐	202	43.05 N	124.09 W
Coquille, South Fork ≐	202	43.02 N	124.07 W
Coquimatlán	234	19.12 N	103.48 W
Coquimbo	252	29.58 S	71.21 W
Coquimbo □⁴	252	30.45 S	71.00 W
Coquina Key I	220	27.44 N	82.38 W
Corabia	38	43.46 N	24.30 E
Coração de Jesus	255	16.42 S	44.22 W
Coração de Maria	255	12.14 S	38.45 W
Corace ≐	68	38.49 N	16.37 E
Coracora	248	15.02 S	73.47 W
Corail, Mer de → Coral Sea ▿²	14	20.00 S	158.00 E
Çorak Gölü ⊜	130	37.40 N	29.46 E
Čoral	214	40.29 N	79.10 W
Coralaque ≐	248	16.26 S	70.45 W
Coral Bay ⊂, Pil.	116	8.25 N	117.20 E
Coral Bay ⊂, Vir. Is., U.S.	240m	18.20 N	64.41 W
Coral Gables	220	25.43 N	80.16 W
Coral Harbour	176	64.08 N	83.10 W
Coral Hills	284c	38.52 N	76.55 W
Coral Sea ▿²	14	20.00 S	158.00 E
Coral Sea Basin ✦¹	14	14.00 S	152.00 E
Coral Sea Islands Territory □⁸	166	18.30 S	152.00 E
Coral Springs	220	26.16 N	80.13 W
Coralville	190	41.40 N	91.34 W
Coralville Lake ⊜¹	190	41.47 N	91.48 W
Coram, Mt., U.S.	202	48.25 N	114.02 W
Coram, N.Y., U.S.	210	40.52 N	73.00 W
Corangamite, Lake ⊜	169	38.10 S	143.25 E
Corantijn (Corentyne) ≐	250	5.55 N	57.05 W
Coraopolis	214	40.31 N	80.10 W

Symbols in the index entries represent the broad categories identified in the key at the right. Symbols with superior numbers (⩘¹) identify subcategories (see complete key on page *I* · 1).

Kartensymbole in dem Registerverzeichnis stellen die rechts in Schlüssel erklärten Kategorien dar. Symbole mit hochgestellten Ziffern (⩘¹) bezeichnen Unterabteilungen einer Kategorie (vgl. vollständiger Schlüssel auf Seite *I* · 1).

Los símbolos incluídos en el texto del índice representan las grandes categorías identificadas con la clave a la derecha. Los símbolos con numeros en su parte superior (⩘¹) identifican las subcategorías (véase la clave completa en la página *I* · 1).

Les symboles de l'index représentent les catégories indiquées dans la légende à droite. Les symboles suivis d'un indice (⩘¹) représentent des sous-catégories (voir légende complète à la page *I* · 1).

Os símbolos incluídos no texto do índice representam as grandes categorias identificadas com a chave à direita. Os símbolos com números em sua parte superior (⩘¹) identificam as subcategorias (veja-se a chave completa à página *I* · 1).

English	Deutsch	Español	Français	Português
∧ Mountain	Berg	Montaña	Montagne	Montanha
⩘ Mountains	Berge	Montañas	Montagnes	Montanhas
)(Pass	Pass	Paso	Col	Passo
V Valley, Canyon	Tal, Cañon	Valle, Cañón	Vallée, Canyon	Vale, Canhão
≚ Plain	Ebene	Llano	Plaine	Planicie
≻ Cape	Kap	Cabo	Cap	Cabo
I Island	Insel	Isla	Île	Ilha
II Islands	Inseln	Islas	Îles	Ilhas
⊥ Other Topographic Features	Andere Topographische Objekte	Otros Elementos Topográficos	Autres données topographiques	Outros acidentes topográficos

ESPAÑOL Nombre / FRANÇAIS Nom / PORTUGUÊS Nome	Página / Page	Lat.°′	Long.°′ W = Oeste / W = Ouest
Coraopolis Heights	279b	40.29 N	80.10 W
Corato	68	41.09 N	16.25 E
Corbara, Lago di ⊜[1]	66	42.43 N	12.15 E
Corbeil-Essonnes	50	48.36 N	2.29 E
Corbenay	58	47.54 N	6.20 E
Corbeny	50	49.28 N	3.49 E
Corbeolona	62	45.10 N	9.22 E
Corbera, Riera de ≃	266d	41.27 N	1.59 E
Corberon	58	47.01 N	4.59 E
Corbeta Uruguay ♉[3]	9	59.27 S	27.15 W
Corbett	210	42.03 N	75.02 W
Corbetta	62	45.28 N	8.55 E
Corbettsville	210	42.01 N	75.48 W
Corbie	50	49.55 N	2.30 E
Corbiere Point ≻	43b	49.11 N	2.15 W
Corbières ⋏	32	42.55 N	2.38 E
Corbigny	50	47.15 N	3.40 E
Corbin	192	36.56 N	84.05 W
Corbion	56	49.48 N	5.00 E
Corbola	64	45.00 N	12.05 E
Corbones ≃	34	37.36 N	5.39 W
Corbridge	44	54.58 N	2.01 W
Corbu	38	44.29 N	24.43 E
Corby	42	52.29 N	0.40 W
Corcaigh → Cork	48	51.54 N	8.28 W
Córcega	240m	18.19 N	67.15 W
Córcega, Isla de → Corse I	36	42.00 N	9.00 E
Corciano	66	43.08 N	12.17 E
Corcieux	58	48.10 N	6.53 E
Corcolle ◆[8]	267a	41.55 N	12.46 E
Corcoran	226	36.05 N	119.33 W
Corcovado ∧	287a	22.57 S	43.13 W
Corcovado, Golfo ⊂	254	43.30 S	73.30 W
Corcovado, Volcán ∧[1]	254	43.12 S	72.48 W
Corcubión	34	42.57 N	9.11 W
Cordâ ≃	250	6.26 S	48.17 W
Cordeaux Reservoir ⊜[1]	170	34.22 S	150.45 E
Cordeiro	255	22.02 S	42.22 W
Cordele, Ga., U.S.	192	31.57 N	83.46 W
Cordele, Tx., U.S.	222	29.08 N	96.38 W
Cordell	196	35.17 N	98.59 W
Cordell Hull Reservoir ⊜[1]	194	36.25 N	85.40 W
Cordenons	64	45.59 N	12.42 E
Corder	194	39.05 N	93.38 W
Cordes	32	44.04 N	1.57 E
Cordignano	64	45.57 N	12.25 E
Cordillera □[5]	252	25.15 S	57.00 W
Cordillo Downs	166	26.43 S	140.38 E
Cordisburgo	255	19.07 S	44.21 W
Córdoba, Arg.	252	31.24 S	64.11 W
Córdoba, Esp.	34	37.53 N	4.46 W
Córdoba, Méx.	234	18.53 N	96.56 W
Córdoba □[4]	252	32.00 S	64.00 W
Córdoba □[5]	246	8.20 N	75.40 W
Córdoba, Península ≻[1]	254	53.20 S	72.50 W
Cordon	116	16.40 N	121.28 E
Cordova → Córdoba, Esp.	34	37.53 N	4.46 W
Córdova, Perú	248	14.04 S	75.03 W
Cordova, Al., U.S.	194	33.45 N	87.11 W
Cordova, Ak., U.S.	180	60.33 N	145.46 W
Cordova, Il., U.S.	190	41.41 N	90.19 W
Cordova, Md., U.S.	208	38.52 N	75.59 W
Cordova Bay ⊂	182	54.55 N	132.35 W
Cordova Lake ⊜	212	44.35 N	77.49 W
Cordova Peak ∧	180	60.51 N	145.16 W
Corea, Estrecho de → Korea Strait Ψ	90	34.00 N	129.00 E
Corea del Norte → Korea, North □[1]	98	40.00 N	127.00 E
Corea del Sur → Korea, South □[1]	98	36.30 N	128.00 E
Coreaú	250	3.33 S	40.39 W
Coreaú ≃	250	2.54 S	40.50 W
Core Creek ≃	285	40.11 N	74.55 W
Corée, Détroit de → Korea Strait Ψ	90	34.00 N	129.00 E
Coree, Mount ∧	171b	35.18 S	148.48 E
Corée du Nord → Korea, North □[1]	98	40.00 N	127.00 E
Corée du Sud → Korea, South □[1]	98	36.30 N	128.00 E
Coreglia Antelminelli	64	44.04 N	10.31 E
Coreinbob	171b	35.13 S	147.38 E
Coremas	250	7.01 S	37.58 W
Corentyne (Corantijn) ≃	250	5.55 N	57.05 W
Corerepe	232	25.40 N	108.40 W
Corese Terra	66	42.10 N	12.42 E
Corey Lake ⊜	216	41.55 N	85.45 W
Corfe Castle	42	50.38 N	2.04 W
Corfield	166	21.43 S	143.22 E
Corfu → Kérkira, Ellás	38	39.36 N	19.56 E
Corfu, N.Y., U.S.	210	42.57 N	78.24 W
Corfu → Kérkira I	38	39.40 N	19.42 E
Corhanwarrabul Creek ≃	274b	37.55 S	145.12 E
Cori	66	41.39 N	12.55 E
Coria	34	39.59 N	6.32 W
Coria del Río	34	37.16 N	6.03 W
Coriaí ≃	250	3.18 S	52.04 W
Coribe	255	13.50 S	44.28 W
Coricudgy, Mount ∧	170	32.50 S	150.22 E
Corigliano Calabro	68	39.36 N	16.31 E
Corigliano d'Otranto	68	40.09 N	18.15 E
Corinaldo	66	43.39 N	13.03 E
Corinda	166	17.53 S	138.35 E
Corinne, Pa., U.S.	285	39.54 N	75.40 W
Corinne, Ut,. U.S.	200	41.33 N	112.06 W
Corinne, W.V., U.S.	192	37.34 N	81.21 W
Corinth → Kórinthos, Ellás	38	37.56 N	22.56 E
Corinth, Ky., U.S.	218	38.29 N	84.33 W
Corinth, Ms., U.S.	194	34.56 N	88.31 W
Corinth, N.Y., U.S.	210	43.14 N	73.49 W
Corinth, Gulf of → Korinthiakós Kólpos ⊂	38	38.19 N	22.04 E
Corinth Canal → Korínthou, Dhiórix ≊	38	37.57 N	22.56 E
Corinto, Bra.	255	18.21 S	44.27 W
Corinto, El Sal.	236	13.49 N	87.58 W
Corinto, Nic.	236	12.29 N	87.10 W
Corio	169	38.04 S	144.23 E
Corio Bay ⊂	169	38.07 S	144.24 E
Coripata	248	16.18 S	67.36 W
Corire	248	16.14 S	72.28 W
Coris	248	9.50 S	77.45 W
Corisco, Isla de I	152	0.53 N	9.20 E
Corixao ≃	248	18.22 S	57.23 W
Cork (Corcaigh)	48	51.54 N	8.28 W
Cork □[6]	48	52.00 N	8.30 W
Cork Airport ⊠	48	51.51 N	8.29 W
Cork Harbour ⊂	48	51.45 N	8.15 W
Corkscrew	220	26.28 N	81.33 W
Corkscrew Swamp ≡	220	26.25 N	81.34 W
Čorku	85	39.58 N	70.33 E
Corlay	32	48.19 N	3.03 W
Corleone	70	37.49 N	13.18 E
Corleto Perticara	68	40.23 N	16.03 E
Çorlu	130	41.09 N	27.48 E
Cormainville	50	48.08 N	1.36 E
Cormano	266b	45.33 N	9.10 E
Cormatin	58	46.33 N	4.41 E
Cormeilles	50	49.15 N	0.23 E
Cormeilles-en-Parisis	50	48.59 N	2.12 E
Cormery	50	47.16 N	0.51 E
Cormons	64	45.58 N	13.28 E
Cormoran Reef ✢[2]	175b	7.50 N	134.32 E
Cormorant	184	54.14 N	100.35 W
Cormorant Lake ⊜	184	54.13 N	100.47 W
Çorna	64	45.53 N	10.10 E
Čornaja, S.S.S.R.	24	68.35 N	56.30 E
Čornaja, S.S.S.R.	78	47.37 N	29.20 E
Čornaja, S.S.S.R.	82	55.45 N	38.04 E
Čornaja ≃, S.S.S.R.	265a	59.47 N	30.10 E
Čornaja ≃, S.S.S.R.	265a	59.50 N	30.00 E
Čornaja ≃, S.S.S.R.	265a	60.01 N	30.10 E
Čornaja ≃, S.S.S.R.	265a	59.55 N	30.59 E
Čornaja ≃, S.S.S.R.	265b	55.41 N	37.58 E
Čornaja Cholunica	86	58.51 N	51.42 E
Čornaja Gr'az', S.S.S.R.	82	54.31 N	35.52 E
Čornaja Gr'az', S.S.S.R.	82	54.58 N	36.48 E
Čornaja Gr'az', S.S.S.R.	265b	55.58 N	37.19 E
Čornaja Rečka	265a	59.56 N	30.58 E
Čornaja rečka ≃, S.S.S.R.	265a	59.46 N	30.45 E
Čornaja rečka ≃, S.S.S.R.	265a	59.55 N	30.22 E
Čornaja Sloboda	24	60.48 N	37.46 E
Cornaredo	266b	45.30 N	9.02 E
Cornas	62	44.58 N	4.51 E
Cornedo Vicentino	64	45.37 N	11.20 E
Cornelia, S. Afr.	158	27.13 S	28.52 E
Cornelia, Ga., U.S.	192	34.30 N	83.31 W
Cornélio Procópio	255	23.08 S	50.39 W
Cornelius, N.C., U.S.	192	35.29 N	80.51 W
Cornelius, Or., U.S.	224	45.31 N	123.03 W
Cornelius Grinnell Bay ⊂	176	63.20 N	64.50 W
Cornell, Il., U.S.	216	41.00 N	88.44 W
Cornell, Wi., U.S.	190	45.10 N	91.08 W
Cornellá	266d	41.21 N	2.05 E
Corner Brook	186	48.57 N	57.57 W
Corner Inlet ⊂	169	38.43 S	146.20 E
Corner Store	285	40.07 N	75.30 W
Cornersville	194	35.21 N	86.50 W
Cornes, Lac des ⊜	206	46.43 N	75.09 W
Cornforth	44	54.42 N	1.31 W
Cornhill	46	57.36 N	2.42 W
Cornholme	262	53.44 N	2.08 W
Cornia ≃	66	42.57 N	10.33 E
Corniglia	62	44.07 N	9.42 E
Corniglio	64	44.28 N	10.05 E
Corning, Ar., U.S.	194	36.24 N	90.34 W
Corning, Ca., U.S.	204	39.55 N	122.10 W
Corning, Ia., U.S.	198	40.59 N	94.44 W
Corning, Ks., U.S.	198	39.39 N	96.01 W
Corning, N.Y., U.S.	210	42.08 N	77.03 W
Corning, Oh., U.S.	188	39.36 N	82.05 W
Cornish	188	43.48 N	70.48 W
Cornish, Mount ∧	162	20.13 S	126.28 E
Cornland	219	39.56 N	89.24 W
Çorno ≃	66	42.49 N	12.55 E
Čornobajevka	78	46.42 N	32.32 E
Çorno Grande ∧	66	42.28 N	13.34 E
Čornoje, S.S.S.R.	80	57.32 N	46.25 E
Čornoje, S.S.S.R.	86	51.44 N	77.34 E
Čornolesskoje	84	44.42 N	43.42 E
Čornomorskij	78	44.51 N	38.29 E
Čornomorskoje, S.S.S.R.	78	45.30 N	32.42 E
Čornomorskoje, S.S.S.R.	78	45.03 N	35.58 E
Čornoreck	86	52.45 N	76.40 E
Cornuda	64	45.50 N	12.00 E
Cornwall, On., Can.	206	45.02 N	74.44 W
Cornwall, N.Y., U.S.	210	41.26 N	74.01 W
Cornwall, Pa., U.S.	208	40.16 N	76.24 W
Cornwall □[6]	42	50.30 N	4.40 W
Cornwall Bridge	207	41.49 N	73.22 W
Cornwallis Island I	176	75.15 N	94.30 W
Cornwall on Hudson	210	41.27 N	74.00 W
Cornwell	220	27.23 N	81.05 W
Çornwells Heights	285	40.04 N	74.56 W
Čornyj Jar	80	48.04 N	46.08 E
Čornyj Mys, S.S.S.R.	24	68.20 N	38.37 E
Čornyj Mys, S.S.S.R.	86	55.33 N	80.04 E
Čornyj Ostrov	78	49.32 N	26.46 E
Čornyj Otrog	86	51.55 N	55.59 E
Čornyj Tašlyk ≃	78	48.11 N	30.51 E
Corny Point	166	34.55 S	137.03 E
Coro	246	11.25 N	69.41 W
Coro, Golfete de ⊂	241s	11.30 N	69.55 W
Coroaci	255	18.35 S	42.17 W
Coroa Grande	256	22.54 S	43.52 W
Coroatá	250	4.08 S	44.08 W
Çoroca ≃	152	15.43 S	11.55 E
Čoroch (Çoruh) ≃	130	41.36 N	41.35 E
Corocoro	248	17.12 S	68.29 W
Corocoro Island I	246	8.30 N	60.10 W
Coroico	248	16.10 S	67.44 W
Coroico ≃	248	15.27 S	67.50 W
Coromandel, Bra.	255	18.28 S	47.13 W
Coromandel, N.Z.	172	36.46 S	175.30 E
Coromandel Coast ⏏[2]	122	13.30 N	80.30 E
Coromandel Peninsula ≻[1]	172	36.50 S	175.35 E
Coromandel Range ⋏	172	37.00 S	175.40 E
Coron	116	12.00 N	120.12 E
Corona, Ca., U.S.	228	33.52 N	117.33 W
Corona, N.M., U.S.	200	34.15 N	105.36 W
Corona ◆[8]	276	40.45 N	73.52 W
Coronación, Golfo de la → Coronation Gulf ⊂	176	68.25 N	110.00 W
Coronación, Isla de la → Coronation Island I	9	60.37 S	45.30 W
Corona del Mar ◆[8]	228	33.36 N	117.52 W
Coronado, Méx.	234	22.55 N	100.56 W
Coronado, Ca., U.S.	228	32.41 N	117.10 W
Coronado, Bahía de ⊂	236	9.00 N	83.50 W
Coronado National Memorial ♠	200	31.10 N	110.29 W
Coronado Naval Amphibious Base ■	228	32.40 N	117.10 W
Coronados, Golfo de los ⊂	254	41.40 S	74.00 W
Coronation	182	52.05 N	111.27 W
Coronation Gardens ♠	275b	43.41 N	79.29 W
Coronation Gulf ⊂	176	68.25 N	110.00 W
Coronation Island I, B.A.T.	9	60.37 S	45.30 W
Coronation Island I, Ak., U.S.	180	55.52 N	134.15 W
Coronation Park ♠	273d	26.06 S	27.47 E
Coron Bay ⊂	116	11.54 N	120.08 E
Coronda	252	31.58 S	60.55 W
Coronel	252	37.01 S	73.08 W
Coronel Bogado	252	27.11 S	56.18 W
Coronel Brandsen	258	35.10 S	58.14 W
Coronel Dorrego	252	38.42 S	61.17 W
Coronel Du Graty	252	27.40 S	60.56 W
Coronel Eugenio del Busto	252	38.57 S	64.15 W
Coronel Fabriciano	255	19.31 S	42.38 W
Coronel Moldes, Arg.	252	33.38 S	64.36 W
Coronel Moldes, Arg.	252	25.16 S	65.29 W
Coronel Murta	255	16.37 S	42.11 W
Coronel Oviedo	252	25.25 S	56.27 W
Coronel Pacheco	256	21.35 S	43.16 W
Coronel Ponce	255	15.34 S	55.01 W
Coronel Pringles	252	37.58 S	61.22 W
Coronel Suárez	252	37.28 S	61.55 W
Coronel Vidal	252	37.27 S	57.43 W
Coronel Vivida	252	25.58 S	52.34 W
Corongo	248	8.35 S	77.55 W
Corongoros	234	19.17 N	102.48 W
Coronie □[5]	250	5.50 N	56.20 W
Coron Island I	116	11.55 N	120.14 E
Coronita	228	33.52 N	117.36 W
Coropuna, Nevado ∧	248	15.31 S	72.42 W
Çorovodë	38	40.30 N	20.13 E
Corowa	166	36.02 S	146.23 E
Corozal, Belize	232	18.24 N	88.24 W
Corozal, Col.	246	9.19 N	75.18 W
Corozal, Hond.	236	15.48 N	86.43 W
Corozal, P.R.	240m	18.21 N	66.17 W
Corps	62	44.49 N	5.57 E
Corpus	252	27.07 S	55.31 W
Corpus Christi	196	27.48 N	97.23 W
Corpus Christi, Lake ⊜[1]	196	28.10 N	97.53 W
Corpus Christi Bay ⊂	196	27.48 N	97.20 W
Corpus Christi Naval Air Station ■	196	27.42 N	97.16 W
Corque	248	18.21 S	67.42 W
Corquín	236	14.34 N	88.52 W
Corral	254	39.52 S	73.26 W
Corral de Almaguer	34	39.46 N	3.11 W
Corral de Bustos	252	33.17 S	62.12 W
Corralillo	240p	22.59 N	80.35 W
Corralito	252	32.03 S	64.12 W
Corralito, Arroyo del ≃	258	33.39 S	58.03 W
Corralito, Cuchilla del ⋏[2]	258	33.40 S	57.44 W
Corralitos, Méx.	196	26.57 N	104.39 W
Corralitos, Ca., U.S.	226	36.59 N	121.48 W
Corran	46	56.43 N	5.14 W
Corraun Peninsula ≻[1]	48	53.54 N	9.53 W
Correas, Arroyo ≃	288	34.24 S	58.32 W
Correboi, Arcu)(	71	40.05 N	9.21 E
Correctionville	198	42.28 N	95.47 W
Corredor	287b	23.27 S	46.19 W
Correggio	64	44.46 N	10.47 E
Corregidor Island I	116	14.23 N	120.35 E
Córrego do Bom Jesus	256	22.38 S	46.02 W
Córrego do Ouro, Bra.	255	16.18 S	50.32 W
Córrego do Ouro, Bra.	256	21.22 S	45.47 W
Córrego Rico	255	15.14 S	47.48 W
Correia de Almeida	256	21.17 S	43.38 W
Corrente	250	10.27 S	45.10 W
Corrente ≃, Bra.	250	4.18 S	42.11 W
Corrente ≃, Bra.	255	19.19 S	50.50 W
Corrente ≃, Bra.	255	13.08 S	43.28 W
Correntes	250	9.08 S	36.19 W
Correntes ≃	255	17.38 S	55.08 W
Correntes, Cabo das ≻	156	24.11 S	35.34 E
Correntezas	256	22.30 S	42.31 W
Correnti, Isola delle I	70	36.38 N	15.05 E
Correntina	255	13.20 S	44.39 W
Corrèze □[5]	32	45.20 N	1.50 E
Correzzana	266b	45.40 N	9.18 E
Corrib, Lough ⊜	48	53.26 N	9.14 W
Corridonia	66	43.15 N	13.30 E
Corrientes	252	27.28 S	58.50 W
Corrientes □[4]	252	29.00 S	58.00 W
Corrientes ≃, Arg.	252	30.21 S	59.33 W
Corrientes ≃, S.A.	246	3.43 S	74.35 W
Corrientes, Cabo ≻, Arg.	252	38.01 S	57.32 W
Corrientes, Cabo ≻, Col.	246	5.30 N	77.34 W
Corrientes, Cabo ≻, Cuba	240p	21.45 N	84.31 W
Corrientes, Cabo ≻, Méx.	234	20.25 N	105.42 W
Corrientes, Ensenada de ⊂	240p	21.51 N	84.36 W
Corrigan	222	30.59 N	94.49 W
Corrigin	162	32.21 S	117.52 E
Corrimal	170	34.22 S	150.54 E
Corringham	260	51.31 N	0.28 E
Corrofin	48	52.56 N	9.03 W
Corroios	266c	38.38 N	9.09 W
Corropoli	66	42.49 N	13.50 E
Corrumpa Creek ≃	196	36.36 N	102.52 W
Corry	214	41.55 N	79.38 W
Corryong	171b	36.12 S	147.54 E
Corryong Creek ≃	171b	36.06 S	147.59 E
Corryvreckan, Gulf of Ψ	46	56.09 N	5.44 W
Corsano	68	39.53 N	18.22 E
Corse (Corsica) I	36	42.00 N	9.00 E
Corse, Cap ≻	62	43.00 N	9.25 E
Corse-du-Sud □[5]	36	41.50 N	9.00 E
Corserine ∧	44	55.09 N	4.22 W
Corsham	42	51.26 N	2.11 W
Corsica, Pa., U.S.	214	41.10 N	79.12 W
Corsica, S.D., U.S.	198	43.25 N	98.24 W
Corsica → Corse I	36	42.00 N	9.00 E
Corsicana	222	32.05 N	96.28 W
Corsica River ⊂	208	39.05 N	76.08 W
Corsico	62	45.26 N	9.07 E
Corsock	44	55.04 N	3.57 W
Corson Inlet ⊂	208	39.12 N	74.39 W
Cortaccia (Kurtatsch)	64	46.19 N	11.13 E
Cortachy	46	56.43 N	2.58 W
Cort Adelaer, Kap ≻	176	62.00 N	42.00 W
Cortaderas	252	32.30 S	65.00 W
Cortado, Rio do ≃	287a	23.00 S	43.25 W
Cortale	68	38.50 N	16.25 E
Cortazar	234	20.29 N	100.56 W
Corte	36	42.18 N	9.08 E
Corte Alto	254	40.57 S	73.10 W
Cortegana	34	37.55 N	6.49 W
Corte Madera	226	37.55 N	122.31 W
Corte Madera Creek ≃	282	37.23 N	122.14 W
Cortemaggiore	64	44.59 N	9.56 E
Cortemilia	62	44.35 N	8.12 E
Corteno Golgi	64	46.10 N	10.15 E
Cortes	116	9.17 N	126.11 E
Cortés □[5]	236	15.30 N	88.00 W
Cortes ♉	266a	40.25 N	3.41 W
Cortés, Ensenada de ⊂	240p	22.05 N	83.52 W
Cortez, Co., U.S.	200	37.20 N	108.35 W
Cortez, Fl., U.S.	220	27.28 N	82.41 W
Cortez, Sea of → California, Golfo de ⊂	232	28.00 N	112.00 W
Cortez Mountains ⋏	204	40.20 N	116.20 W
Cortina Creek ≃	226	39.06 N	122.02 W
Cortina d'Ampezzo	64	46.32 N	12.08 E
Çortines	258	34.34 S	59.13 W
Čortkov	78	49.01 N	25.48 E
Cortland, Il., U.S.	216	41.55 N	88.41 W
Cortland, In., U.S.	218	38.58 N	85.58 W
Cortland, Ne., U.S.	198	40.30 N	96.42 W
Cortland, N.Y., U.S.	210	42.36 N	76.10 W
Cortland, Oh., U.S.	214	41.19 N	80.43 W
Cortland □[6]	210	42.36 N	76.11 W
Corton	42	52.32 N	1.44 E
Cortona	66	43.16 N	11.59 E
Çorubal (Koliba) ≃	150	11.57 N	15.06 W
Čoruch-Dajron	85	40.24 N	69.40 E
Coruche	34	38.57 N	8.31 W
Çoruh (Čoroch) ≃	130	41.36 N	41.35 E
Çorum, Tür.	130	39.14 N	28.27 E
Çorum, Tür.	130	40.33 N	34.58 E
Çorum □[4]	130	40.30 N	34.40 E
Corumbá	248	19.01 S	57.39 W
Corumbá ≃	255	18.19 S	48.55 W
Corumbá de Goiás	255	15.55 S	48.48 W
Corumbaíba	255	18.09 S	48.34 W
Corumbataí ≃	252	23.55 S	51.57 W
Corumbaú, Ponta de ≻	255	16.53 S	39.06 W
Corumbiara Antigo ≃	248	13.13 S	62.06 W
Corumo ≃	246	6.49 N	60.52 W
Corund	38	46.28 N	25.11 E
Corunna, On., Can.	214	42.53 N	82.26 W
Corunna → La Coruña, Esp.	34	43.22 N	8.23 W
Corunna, In., U.S.	216	41.26 N	85.08 W
Corunna, Mi., U.S.	216	42.58 N	84.07 W
Corunna Downs	162	21.28 S	119.51 E
Coruripe	250	10.08 S	36.10 W
Corvallis, Mt., U.S.	202	46.18 N	114.06 W
Corvallis, Or., U.S.	202	44.33 N	123.15 W
Corvara in Badia	64	46.33 N	11.52 E
Corve ≃	42	52.22 N	2.43 W
Corve Dale V	42	52.30 N	2.40 W
Corvey, Kloster ♉[1]	52	51.46 N	9.25 E
Corviale ◆[8]	267a	41.52 N	12.25 E
Corvo I	148a	39.42 N	31.06 W
Corwen	42	52.59 N	3.22 W
Corwin, Cape ≻	180	59.54 N	165.41 W
Corwith	190	42.59 N	93.57 W
Corydon, In., U.S.	218	38.12 N	86.07 W
Corydon, Ia., U.S.	190	40.45 N	93.19 W
Corydon, Ky., U.S.	194	37.44 N	87.42 W
Coryell	222	31.33 N	97.37 W
Coryell □[6]	222	31.25 N	97.40 W
Coryell Creek ≃	222	31.23 N	97.35 W
Coryton	260	51.31 N	0.31 E
Coryville	214	41.53 N	78.24 W
Corzu	38	44.28 N	23.10 E
Corzuela	252	26.57 S	60.58 W
Cos → Kos I	38	36.50 N	27.10 E
Cosa (Ansedonia) ⊥	66	42.25 N	11.18 E
Cosamaloapan [de Carpio]	232	18.22 N	95.48 W
Cosapa	248	18.11 S	68.40 W
Coscile ≃	68	39.42 N	16.28 E
Cos Cob	276	41.02 N	73.36 W
Cos Cob Harbor ⊂	276	41.01 N	73.36 W
Coscomatepec [de Bravo]	234	19.04 N	97.02 W
Cosel → Koźle	30	50.20 N	18.08 E
Coseley	42	52.33 N	2.06 W
Cosenza	68	39.17 N	16.15 E
Cosenza □[4]	68	39.28 N	16.25 E
Cosgrove's Creek ≃	274a	33.50 S	150.46 E
Coshocton	214	40.16 N	81.51 W
Coshocton □[6]	214	40.16 N	81.51 W
Cosigüina, Punta ≻	236	12.54 N	87.41 W
Cosigüina, Volcán ∧[1]	236	12.59 N	87.34 W
Coslada	266a	40.26 N	3.34 W
Cosmo ◆[8]	256	22.54 S	43.37 W
Cosmoledo Island I	138	9.43 S	47.35 E
Cosmópolis, Bra.	256	22.38 S	47.12 W
Cosmopolis, Wa., U.S.	224	46.57 N	123.46 W
Cosmorama	255	20.28 S	49.47 W
Cosmos	198	44.56 N	94.41 W
Cosmos ◆[8]	287a	22.55 S	44.37 W
Cosne-Cours-sur-Loire	50	47.24 N	2.55 E
Cosoleacaque	234	18.00 N	94.37 W
Cospán	248	7.26 S	78.33 W
Cosquín	252	31.15 S	64.29 W
Cossato	62	45.34 N	8.10 E
Cossatot ≃	194	33.48 N	94.09 W
Cossayuna	210	43.11 N	73.26 W
Cossayuna Lake ⊜	210	43.12 N	73.25 W
Cossebaude	54	51.05 N	13.38 E
Cossé-le-Vivien	28	47.57 N	0.55 W
Cossoine	71	40.27 N	8.43 E
Cosson ≃	50	47.30 N	1.15 E
Cossonay	58	46.37 N	6.31 E
Cost	222	29.26 N	97.32 W
Costa, Cayo I	220	26.41 N	82.15 W
Costa, Sierra de la → Coast Ranges ⋏	178	41.00 N	123.30 W
Costacciaro	66	43.21 N	12.42 E
Costa de Caparica	266c	38.38 N	9.14 W
Costa del Marfil → Ivory Coast □[1]	150	8.00 N	5.00 W
Costa de San José	258	33.51 S	56.53 W
Costa di Rovigo	64	45.03 N	11.42 E
Costa Mesa	228	33.38 N	117.55 W
Costanera, Cadena → Coast Mountains ⋏	176	55.00 N	129.00 W
Costanero, Canal de ≊	288	34.28 S	58.28 W
Costa Rica	232	28.55 N	111.36 W
Costa Rica □[1], N.A.	230	10.00 N	84.00 W
Costa Rica □[1], N.A.	236	10.00 N	84.00 W
Costaros	62	44.54 N	3.50 E
Costas	256	22.39 S	45.56 W
Costello	214	41.36 N	78.03 W
Costelloe	48	53.17 N	9.32 W
Costermansville → Bukavu	154	2.30 S	28.52 E
Costessey	42	52.40 N	1.11 E
Costești	38	44.40 N	24.53 E
Costiera, Catena ⋏	68	39.20 N	16.05 E
Costigan Lake ⊜	184	56.56 N	105.55 W
Costigliole d'Asti	62	44.47 N	8.11 E
Costigliole Saluzzo	62	44.34 N	7.29 E
Costilla	200	36.58 N	105.31 W
Costilla Creek ≃	200	36.59 N	105.43 W
Cosumnes ≃	226	38.16 N	121.26 W
Cosumnes, Middle Fork ≃	226	38.33 N	120.51 W
Cosumnes, North Fork ≃	226	38.33 N	120.51 W
Cosumnes, South Fork ≃	226	38.33 N	120.49 W
Coswig, D.D.R.	54	51.07 N	13.34 E
Coswig, D.D.R.	54	51.53 N	12.26 E
Cotabambas	248	13.45 S	72.21 W
Cotabato	116	7.13 N	124.15 E
Cotacajes ≃	248	16.00 S	67.01 W
Cotagaita	248	20.50 S	65.41 W
Cotagaita ≃	248	21.01 S	65.23 W
Cotahuasi	248	15.12 S	72.56 W
Cotão ∧[2]	266c	38.45 N	9.18 W
Co Ta-roun ∧	110	17.17 N	106.17 E
Cotati	226	38.20 N	122.42 W
Cotaxtla ≃	234	19.02 N	96.08 W
Coteau-Landing	206	45.15 N	74.13 W
Coteau-Station	206	45.17 N	74.14 W
Coteaux	238	18.12 N	74.02 W
Côte d'Ivoire → Ivory Coast □[1]	150	8.00 N	5.00 W
Côte-d'Or □[5]	50	47.30 N	4.50 E
Cotegipe	255	12.02 S	44.15 W
Cote Indian Reserve ◆[4]	184	51.38 N	101.53 W
Cotentin ≻[1]	32	49.30 N	1.30 W
Côte-Saint-Luc	275a	45.28 N	73.40 W
Côtes-du-Nord □[5]	32	48.25 N	2.40 W
Côte Visitation ◆[8]	275a	45.33 N	73.36 W
Cotherstone	166	22.37 S	148.14 E
Cothi ≃	42	51.52 N	4.10 W
Coti ≃	248	8.36 S	65.33 W
Cotia	256	23.37 S	46.56 W
Cotia □[7]	287b	23.38 S	46.56 W
Cotia ≃	256	23.31 S	46.51 W
Cotia, Represa de ⊜[1]	287b	23.44 S	46.57 W
Cotignac	62	43.32 N	6.09 E
Cotignola	66	44.23 N	11.56 E
Cotija de la Paz	234	19.49 N	102.43 W
Cotingo ≃	246	3.55 N	60.30 W
Cotis, Laguna ⊜	258	35.11 S	59.16 W
Cotmeana ≃	38	44.24 N	24.45 E
Cotoca	248	17.49 S	63.03 W
Cotonou	150	6.21 N	2.26 E
Cotopaxi □[4]	246	0.55 S	78.55 W
Cotopaxi ∧[1]	246	0.40 S	78.26 W
Cotorra, Isla I	241r	10.02 N	62.16 W
Cotovêlo, Cachoeira do ʟ	248	7.08 S	58.43 W
Cotronei	68	39.09 N	16.47 E
Cotswold Hills ⋏[2]	42	51.45 N	2.10 W
Cottage Grove, In., U.S.	218	39.36 N	84.52 W
Cottage Grove, Or., U.S.	202	43.47 N	123.03 W
Cottage Grove, Wi., U.S.	216	43.05 N	89.12 W
Cottage Hills	219	38.55 N	90.04 W
Cottageville	192	32.56 N	80.28 W
Cottam, On., Can.	214	42.08 N	82.45 W
Cottam, Eng., U.K.	262	53.47 N	2.46 W
Cottanello	66	42.24 N	12.41 E
Cottbus	54	51.45 N	14.19 E
Cottbus □[5]	54	51.45 N	14.00 E
Cottekill	210	41.51 N	74.06 W
Cottel Island I	186	48.51 N	53.42 W
Cottenham	42	52.18 N	0.09 E
Cotter	194	36.16 N	92.32 W
Cotter ≃	171b	35.19 S	148.57 E
Cottesloe	168a	31.59 S	115.45 E
Cottiennes, Alpes (Alpi Cozie) ⋏	62	44.45 N	7.00 E
Cottingham	44	53.47 N	0.24 W
Cottleville	219	38.44 N	90.39 W
Cottondale, Al., U.S.	194	33.11 N	87.27 W
Cottondale, Fl., U.S.	192	30.47 N	85.22 W
Cotton Lake ⊜, Mb., Can.	184	55.05 N	96.50 W
Cotton Lake ⊜, Tx., U.S.	222	29.48 N	94.48 W
Cotton Plant	194	35.00 N	91.15 W
Cottonport	194	30.59 N	92.03 W
Cotton Valley	194	32.49 N	93.25 W
Cottonwood, Az., U.S.	200	34.44 N	112.00 W
Cottonwood, Ca., U.S.	204	40.23 N	122.16 W
Cottonwood, Id., U.S.	202	46.02 N	116.20 W
Cottonwood, Mn., U.S.	198	44.36 N	95.40 W
Cottonwood ≃, Ks., U.S.	198	38.23 N	96.03 W
Cottonwood ≃, Mn., U.S.	198	44.17 N	94.25 W
Cottonwood Creek ≃, Ca., U.S.	226	36.27 N	119.20 W
Cottonwood Creek ≃, Ca., U.S.	226	36.52 N	120.12 W
Cottonwood Creek ≃, Mt., U.S.	202	48.33 N	107.45 W
Cottonwood Creek ≃, N.D., U.S.	198	46.16 N	98.15 W
Cottonwood Creek ≃, Ok., U.S.	196	35.54 N	97.27 W
Cottonwood Creek ≃, Or., U.S.	202	43.53 N	117.43 W
Cottonwood Creek ≃, Tx., U.S.	196	31.23 N	103.46 W
Cottonwood Creek ≃, Tx., U.S.	196	32.48 N	100.21 W
Cottonwood Creek ≃, Ut,. U.S.	200	39.09 N	110.55 W
Cottonwood Creek ≃, Wy., U.S.	202	43.51 N	108.09 W
Cottonwood Creek, Middle Fork ≃	204	40.23 N	122.20 W
Cottonwood Creek, South Fork ≃	204	40.23 N	122.20 W
Cottonwood Falls	198	38.22 N	96.32 W
Cottonwood Wash V, Az., U.S.	200	36.19 N	113.59 W
Cottonwood Wash V, Az., U.S.	200	35.00 N	110.39 W
Cotubandê	287a	22.51 S	43.01 W
Cotuhé ≃	246	2.53 S	69.44 W
Cotuí	238	19.03 N	70.09 W
Cotuit	207	41.37 N	70.26 W
Cotulla	196	28.26 N	99.14 W
Cotunduba, Ilha de I	287a	22.58 S	43.09 W
Coubert	261	48.40 N	2.42 E
Coubre, Pointe de la ≻	32	45.41 N	1.13 W
Coubron	261	48.55 N	2.35 E
Couches-les-Mines	58	46.52 N	4.34 E
Couchiching, Lake ⊜	212	44.40 N	79.23 W
Coucouron	62	44.48 N	3.58 E
Coucy-le-Château-Auffrique	50	49.31 N	3.19 E
Coudekerque-Branche	50	51.02 N	2.24 E
Coudersport	214	41.46 N	78.01 W
Coudres, Île aux I	186	47.24 N	70.23 W
Couesnon ≃	32	48.37 N	1.31 W
Cougar	224	46.03 N	122.17 W
Cougar Reservoir ⊜[1]	202	44.06 N	122.12 W
Couhé	32	46.18 N	0.11 E
Couillet	50	50.23 N	4.27 E
Couilly-Pont-aux-Dames	261	48.53 N	2.52 E
Coulanges-la-Vineuse	50	47.42 N	3.35 E
Coulanges-sur-Yonne	50	47.31 N	3.32 E
Coulee City	202	47.36 N	119.17 W
Coulee Dam	202	47.57 N	118.58 W
Coulee Dam National Recreation Area ♠	202	48.10 N	118.15 W
Coulihaut	240d	15.30 N	61.29 W
Coulman Island I	9	73.27 S	169.40 E
Coulmier-le-Sec	58	47.45 N	4.29 E
Coulogne	50	50.55 N	1.53 E
Coulomby	50	50.42 N	2.00 E
Coulommiers	50	48.49 N	3.05 E
Coulon ≃	62	43.51 N	5.00 E
Coulonge ≃	190	45.51 N	76.46 W
Coulonge Est ≃	190	46.06 N	76.44 W
Coulsdon ◆[8]	260	51.19 N	0.08 W
Coulta	166	34.23 S	135.29 E
Coulters	279b	40.18 N	79.48 W
Coulterville, Ca., U.S.	226	37.42 N	120.11 W
Coulterville, Il., U.S.	194	38.11 N	89.36 W
Counce	194	35.02 N	88.16 W
Council	202	44.44 N	116.26 W
Council Bluffs	198	41.15 N	95.51 W
Council Grove	198	38.39 N	96.29 W
Council Grove Lake ⊜[1]	198	38.42 N	96.31 W
Coundon	44	54.40 N	1.39 W
Countegany	171b	36.11 S	149.27 E
Countesthorpe	42	52.33 N	1.08 W
Country Campus	222	30.49 N	95.26 W
Country Club Estates	220	28.03 N	81.57 W
Country Club Hills	278	41.34 N	87.43 W
Country Club View	284c	38.49 N	77.19 W
Country Hills	279b	40.19 N	79.42 W
Country Homes	202	47.44 N	117.24 W
Country Ridge Estates	276	41.02 N	73.41 W
Countryside	278	41.46 N	87.52 W
Countryside Lake ⊜	278	42.15 N	88.03 W
Countryside Manor	278	42.18 N	87.56 W
Coupar Angus	46	56.33 N	3.17 W
Coupeville	224	48.13 N	122.41 W
Coupland	222	30.28 N	97.24 W
Coupon	214	40.32 N	78.31 W
Coupvray	261	48.54 N	2.48 E
Courbevoie	50	48.54 N	2.15 E
Courbons	62	44.06 N	6.12 E
Courçay	50	47.15 N	0.52 E
Courcelle	261	48.42 N	2.06 E
Courcelles, Bel.	50	50.28 N	4.22 E
Courcelles, Fr.	261	49.07 N	2.18 E
Courcelles-Chaussy	56	49.07 N	6.24 E
Courcelles-sur-Nied	56	49.04 N	6.18 E
Courchevel	62	45.25 N	6.38 E
Cour-Cheverny	50	47.30 N	1.27 E
Courcibo ≃	250	4.53 N	53.00 W
Courçon	32	46.15 N	0.49 W
Courcouronnes	261	48.37 N	2.24 E
Courdimanche	261	49.02 N	2.00 E
Cour-et-Buis	62	45.26 N	5.00 E
Courgent	261	48.54 N	1.40 E
Courland → Kurzeme □[9]	76	56.50 N	22.30 E
Courmayeur	62	45.47 N	6.58 E
Couronne, Cap ≻	62	43.19 N	5.03 E
Couronnement, Île du → Coronation Island I	9	60.37 S	45.30 W
Courpière	62	45.45 N	3.33 E
Courquetaine	261	48.41 N	2.45 E
Course Brook ≃	283	42.17 N	71.22 W
Courseulles	28	49.20 N	0.27 W
Courson-les-Carrières	50	47.36 N	3.30 E
Court	58	47.14 N	7.20 E
Courtacon	50	48.42 N	3.17 E
Courtalain	50	48.05 N	1.09 E
Courtenay, B.C., Can.	182	49.41 N	125.00 W
Courtenay, Fr.	50	48.02 N	3.03 E
Courthézon	62	44.05 N	4.53 E
Courtice	212	43.55 N	78.46 W
Courtisols	56	48.59 N	4.31 E
Courtland, On., Can.	212	42.51 N	80.38 W
Courtland, Al., U.S.	194	34.40 N	87.18 W
Courtland, Ca., U.S.	226	38.20 N	121.34 W
Courtland, Va., U.S.	208	36.42 N	77.04 W
Courtleigh	284b	39.22 N	76.46 W
Courtmacsherry	48	51.38 N	8.43 W
Courtmacsherry Bay ⊂	48	51.35 N	8.40 W
Courtney, Pa., U.S.	279b	40.13 N	79.58 W
Courtney, Tx., U.S.	222	30.16 N	96.04 W
Courtney Creek ≃	196	31.16 N	102.50 W
Courtomer, Fr.	50	48.38 N	0.22 E
Courtomer, Fr.	261	48.39 N	2.54 E
Courtown	48	52.38 N	6.13 W
Courtrai → Kortrijk	50	50.50 N	3.16 E
Courtright	214	42.49 N	82.28 W
Courtry, Fr.	261	48.55 N	2.36 E
Courtry, Fr.	261	48.33 N	2.46 E
Court-Saint-Étienne	50	50.39 N	4.34 E
Courville-sur-Eure	50	48.27 N	1.15 E
Coushatta	194	32.00 N	93.20 W
Cousin ≃	50	47.15 N	4.04 E
Cousiño, Parque ♠	286e	33.28 S	70.40 W
Cousolre	50	50.15 N	4.09 E
Coussegrey	50	47.57 N	4.01 E
Coussey	58	48.25 N	5.41 E
Coustellet	62	43.53 N	5.11 E
Coutances	32	49.03 N	1.26 W
Coutevroult	261	48.52 N	2.51 E
Couto de Magalhães ≃	255	13.37 S	53.09 W
Couto Magalhães	250	8.17 S	49.16 W
Coutras	32	45.02 N	0.08 W
Coutts	182	49.00 N	111.57 W
Couture, Lac ⊜	176	60.07 N	75.20 W
Couture-sur-Loir	50	47.45 N	0.41 E
Couves, Ilha das I	256	23.25 S	44.52 W
Couvet	58	46.56 N	6.38 E
Couvin	50	50.03 N	4.29 E
Cova da Piedade	266c	38.40 N	9.10 W
Covane	156	21.22 S	33.56 E
Covasna	38	45.51 N	26.11 E
Covasna □[6]	38	46.00 N	26.00 E
Cove, Scot., U.K.	46	57.51 N	5.42 W
Cove, Or., U.S.	202	45.17 N	117.48 W
Cove Bay	46	57.06 N	2.04 W
Covedale	218	39.07 N	84.36 W
Cove Harbor ⊂	276	41.03 N	73.30 W
Cove Island I	190	45.17 N	81.44 W
Covelo, Ang.	152	12.06 S	13.55 E
Covelo, Ca., U.S.	204	39.47 N	123.14 W
Cove Neck	276	40.53 N	73.31 W
Cove Neck ≻[1]	276	40.53 N	73.30 W
Coventry, Eng., U.K.	42	52.25 N	1.30 W
Coventry, Ct., U.S.	207	41.46 N	72.18 W
Coventry, De., U.S.	285	39.40 N	75.38 W
Coventry, R.I., U.S.	207	41.41 N	71.34 W
Coventry Cathedral ♉[1]	42	52.25 N	1.30 W
Coventryville	285	40.10 N	75.41 W
Cove Palisades State Park ♠	202	44.34 N	121.15 W
Cove Point	208	38.22 N	76.23 W
Cove Point ≻	208	38.23 N	76.23 W
Cover ≃	44	54.17 N	1.46 W
Covered Wells	200	31.48 N	111.59 W
Covert	216	42.17 N	86.15 W
Covigliaio	66	44.08 N	11.18 E
Covilhã	34	40.17 N	7.30 W
Covina	228	34.05 N	117.53 W
Covington, Ga., U.S.	192	33.35 N	83.51 W
Covington, In., U.S.	194	40.08 N	87.23 W
Covington, Ky., U.S.	218	39.05 N	84.30 W
Covington, La., U.S.	194	30.28 N	90.06 W
Covington, Oh., U.S.	218	40.07 N	84.21 W
Covington, Ok., U.S.	196	36.18 N	97.35 W
Covington, Pa., U.S.	210	41.45 N	77.05 W
Covington, Tn., U.S.	194	35.33 N	89.38 W
Covington, Tx., U.S.	222	32.11 N	97.16 W
Covington, Va., U.S.	192	37.47 N	79.59 W
Covões	266c	38.50 N	9.20 W
Covunco, Arroyo ≃	252	38.29 S	69.32 W
Cow ≃	190	47.23 N	83.59 W
Cowal ◆[1]	46	56.05 N	5.08 W
Cowal, Lake ⊜	166	33.35 S	147.25 E
Cowan, Ky., U.S.	218	38.24 N	83.54 W
Cowan, Tn., U.S.	194	35.09 N	86.00 W
Cowan, Lake ⊜	162	31.50 S	121.50 E
Cowan Creek ≃	274a	33.40 S	151.10 E
Cowanesque	210	41.56 N	77.30 W
Cowanesque ≃	210	42.00 N	77.07 W
Cowan Heights	280	33.47 N	117.47 W
Cowan Lake ⊜, Sk., Can.	184	54.00 N	107.15 W
Cowan Lake ⊜, Oh., U.S.	218	39.23 N	83.54 W
Cowan Lake State Park ♠	218	39.23 N	83.53 W
Cowansburg	279b	40.15 N	79.46 W
Cowanshannock Creek ≃	214	40.51 N	79.30 W
Cowansville, P.Q., Can.	206	45.12 N	72.45 W
Cowansville, Pa., U.S.	214	40.53 N	79.36 W
Cowaramup	162	33.52 S	115.05 E
Coward	192	33.58 N	79.44 W
Coward Springs	166	29.24 S	136.49 E
Cowarie	166	27.43 S	138.20 E
Cow Bayou ≃	222	31.19 N	97.00 W
Cowbridge	42	51.28 N	3.27 W
Cowburn Tunnel ◆[5]	262	53.21 N	1.52 W
Cow Canyon V	280	34.01 N	120.06 W
Cowcowing Lakes ⊜	162	31.01 S	117.18 E
Cow Creek ≃, Ks., U.S.	198	38.02 N	97.56 W
Cow Creek ≃, Mt., U.S.	202	47.47 N	108.56 W
Cow Creek ≃, Ok., U.S.	196	34.10 N	98.00 W
Cow Creek ≃, Or., U.S.	202	42.57 N	123.20 W
Cow Creek ≃, Wa., U.S.	202	46.45 N	118.09 W
Cowden, Il., U.S.	219	39.15 N	88.52 W
Cowden, Pa., U.S.	279b	40.19 N	80.13 W
Cowdenbeath	46	56.07 N	3.21 W
Coweeman ≃	224	46.06 N	122.52 W
Cowell	166	33.41 S	136.55 E
Cowen	188	38.24 N	80.33 W
Cowen, Mount ∧	202	45.23 N	110.29 W
Cowes, Austl.	169	38.27 S	145.14 E
Cowes, Eng., U.K.	42	50.45 N	1.18 W
Cowessess Indian Reserve ◆[4]	184	50.31 N	102.42 W
Coweta	196	35.57 N	95.39 W
Cow Green Reservoir ⊜[1]	44	54.40 N	2.18 W
Cow Gulch ≃	202	46.02 N	107.52 W
Cow Head	186	49.55 N	57.48 W
Cowhouse Creek ≃	222	31.10 N	97.35 W
Cowichan ≃	224	48.46 N	123.38 W
Cowichan Bay	224	48.44 N	123.40 W
Cowichan Lake ⊜	224	48.54 N	124.20 W

Symbol	English	Deutsch	Español	Français	Português
≃	River	Fluss	Río	Rivière	Rio
≊	Canal	Kanal	Canal	Canal	Canal
ʟ	Waterfall, Rapids	Wasserfall, Stromschnellen	Cascada, Rápidos	Chute d'eau, Rapides	Cascata, Rápidos
Ψ	Strait	Meeresstrasse	Estrecho	Détroit	Estreito
⊂	Bay, Gulf	Bucht, Golf	Bahía, Golfo	Baie, Golfe	Baía, Golfo
⊜	Lake, Lakes	See, Seen	Lago, Lagos	Lac, Lacs	Lago, Lagos
≡	Swamp	Sumpf	Pantano	Marais	Pântano
⊓	Ice Features, Glacier	Eis- und Gletscherformen	Accidentes Glaciales	Formes glaciaires	Acidentes glaciares
⊤	Other Hydrographic Features	Andere Hydrographische Objekte	Otros Elementos Hidrográficos	Autres données hydrographiques	Outros acidentes hidrográficos
✢	Submarine Features	Untermeerische Objekte	Accidentes Submarinos	Formes de relief sous-marin	Acidentes submarinos
□	Political Unit	Politische Einheit	Unidad Politica	Entité politique	Unidade política
♉	Cultural Institution	Kulturelle Institution	Institución Cultural	Institution culturelle	Institução cultural
⊥	Historical Site	Historische Stätte	Sitio Histórico	Site historique	Sitio histórico
♠	Recreational Site	Erholungs- und Ferienort	Sitio de Recreo	Centre de loisirs	Area de Lazer
⊠	Airport	Flughafen	Aeropuerto	Aéroport	Aeroporto
■	Military Installation	Militäranlage	Instalación Militar	Installation militaire	Instalação militar
◆	Miscellaneous	Verschiedenes	Misceláneo	Divers	Diversos

Name	Page	Lat.°′	Long.°′
Cowiche Creek, North Fork ≃	224	46.38 N	120.41 W
Cowiche Creek, South Fork ≃	224	46.38 N	120.41 W
Cowie Water ≃	46	56.58 N	2.12 W
Cowles Dam ⊜[1]	273d	26.13 S	28.28 E
Cowlesville	210	42.51 N	78.28 W
Cowley, Austl.	166	26.54 S	144.49 E
Cowley, Ab., Can.	182	49.34 N	114.05 W
Cowley, Eng., U.K.	42	51.43 N	1.12 W
Cowley, Wy., U.S.	202	44.53 N	108.28 W
Cowley ◆[8]	260	51.32 N	0.29 W
Cowlitz □[6]	224	46.07 N	122.43 W
Cowlitz ≃	224	46.05 N	122.53 W
Cowm Reservoir ⊜[1]	262	53.40 N	2.11 W
Cow Palace ♥	282	37.42 N	122.25 W
Cowpasture ≃	188	37.48 N	79.45 W
Cowpens	192	35.01 N	81.48 W
Cowpens National Battlefield ♠	192	35.06 N	81.46 W
Cowra	166	33.50 S	148.41 E
Cox ≃	164	15.19 S	135.25 E
Cox, Mount ∧[2]	162	24.55 S	125.36 E
Coxá ≃	255	14.16 S	44.11 W
Cox Creek ≃	212	43.35 N	80.29 W
Coxheath	42	51.14 N	0.29 E
Coxim	255	18.30 S	54.45 W
Coxim ≃	255	18.34 S	54.46 W
Coxipi, Lac ⊜	186	51.33 N	58.25 W
Coxipó da Ponte	248	15.38 S	56.04 W
Coxquihui	234	20.11 N	97.35 W
Coxs ≃	170	33.57 S	150.25 E
Coxsackie	210	42.21 N	73.48 W
Cox's Bāzār	120	21.26 N	91.59 E
Cox's Cove	186	49.07 N	58.05 W
Coyaguaima, Cerro ∧	252	22.55 S	66.35 W
Coyah	150	9.43 N	13.23 W
Coyame	232	29.28 N	105.06 W
Coyanosa Draw ∨	196	31.18 N	103.06 W
Coya Sur	252	22.25 S	69.38 W
Coyle, Water of ≃	44	55.28 N	4.32 W
Coyoacán □[7]	286a	19.19 N	99.11 W
Coyoacán ◆[8]	286a	19.20 N	99.10 W
Coyote	226	37.13 N	121.44 W
Coyote ≃	232	30.48 N	112.35 W
Coyote Creek ≃, Ca., U.S.	204	33.13 N	116.13 W
Coyote Creek ≃, Ca., U.S.	226	37.28 N	122.03 W
Coyote Creek ≃, Ca., U.S.	280	33.47 N	118.05 W
Coyote Creek, East Fork ≃	226	37.10 N	121.30 W
Coyote Creek, Middle Fork ≃	226	37.10 N	121.30 W
Coyote Hills ⋏[2]	282	37.33 N	122.05 W
Coyote Hills Regional Park ♠	282	37.33 N	122.06 W
Coyote Lake ⊜	204	35.04 N	116.45 W
Coyote Lake ⊜[1]	226	37.06 N	121.32 W
Coyotepec	234	19.46 N	99.12 W
Coyote Point ›	282	37.35 N	122.19 W
Coyote Wash ∨, Az., U.S.	200	32.40 N	114.08 W
Coyote Wash ∨, N.M., U.S.	200	36.11 N	108.33 W
Coy Pond ⊜	283	42.36 N	70.49 W
Coyuca de Benítez	234	17.02 N	100.04 W
Coyuca de Catalán	234	18.20 N	100.39 W
Coyutla	234	20.15 N	97.39 W
Cozad	198	40.51 N	99.59 W
Cozes	32	45.35 N	0.50 W
Cozie, Alpi (Alpes Cottiennes) ⋏	62	44.45 N	7.00 E
Cozoyoapan	234	16.46 N	98.15 W
Cozumel	232	20.31 N	86.55 W
Cozumel, Isla de I	232	20.25 N	86.55 W
Cozy Lake	276	41.01 N	74.30 W
Crab Alley Bay ⊂	208	38.55 N	76.17 W
Crab Creek ≃	202	46.49 N	119.55 W
Crab Hill	241g	13.19 N	59.38 W
Crab Meadow ≡	276	40.55 N	73.20 W
Crab Orchard, Ky., U.S.	192	37.27 N	84.30 W
Crab Orchard, Tn., U.S.	192	35.54 N	84.52 W
Crab Orchard Lake ⊜[1]	194	37.43 N	89.05 W
Crabtree	214	40.21 N	79.28 W
Crabtree Creek ≃	279b	40.21 N	79.30 W
Crabtree Mills	206	45.58 N	73.28 W
Craches	261	48.34 N	1.49 E
Crackenback ≃	171b	36.21 S	148.36 E
Craco	68	40.23 N	16.26 E
Cracovie → Kraków	30	50.03 N	19.58 E
Cradle Mountain-Lake Saint Clair National Park ♠	166	42.00 S	146.00 E
Cradock, Austl.	166	32.04 S	138.30 E
Cradock, S. Afr.	158	32.08 S	25.36 E
Cradock Channel ⋓	172	36.11 S	175.15 E
Crafers-Bridgewater	168b	35.01 S	138.47 E
Crafton	214	40.26 N	80.03 W
Crafts Creek ≃	285	40.07 N	74.46 W
Cragg Vale	262	53.42 N	2.00 W
Cragsmoor	210	41.40 N	74.23 W
Crai	42	51.55 N	3.36 W
Craig, B.C., Can.	224	49.18 N	124.15 W
Craig, Ak., U.S.	182	55.29 N	133.09 W
Craig, Co., U.S.	200	40.30 N	107.32 W
Craig, Mo., U.S.	194	40.11 N	95.22 W
Craig, Ne., U.S.	198	41.47 N	96.21 W
Craig, Point ∧	162	26.51 S	126.19 E
Craigavon	48	54.27 N	6.24 W
Craig Beach	214	41.07 N	81.01 W
Craig Creek ≃	192	37.39 N	79.49 W
Craigellachie	182	50.59 N	118.43 W
Craighall ◆[8]	273d	26.07 S	28.02 E
Craighall Park ◆[8]	273d	26.08 S	28.01 E
Craighouse	46	55.51 N	5.57 W
Craigmont	202	46.14 N	116.27 W
Craigmyle	182	51.40 N	112.15 W
Craignish Point ›	46	56.07 N	5.37 W
Craignure	46	56.28 N	5.42 W
Craigsville, Pa., U.S.	214	40.51 N	79.39 W
Craigsville, Va., U.S.	192	38.04 N	79.23 W
Craigville	216	40.47 N	85.06 W
Craik	184	51.03 N	105.49 W
Crail	46	56.16 N	2.38 W
Crailsheim	56	49.08 N	10.04 E
Craiova	38	44.19 N	23.48 E
Crake ≃	44	54.14 N	3.03 W
Craley	208	39.57 N	76.31 W
Cramant	50	48.59 N	3.59 E
Cramlington	44	55.05 N	1.36 W
Cranage	262	53.12 N	2.22 W
Cranberry	214	41.21 N	79.43 W
Cranberry Brook ≃	283	42.11 N	71.01 W
Cranberry Creek	210	43.09 N	74.14 W
Cranberry Island I	212	44.44 N	81.18 W
Cranberry Lake	210	40.57 N	74.44 W
Cranberry Lake ⊜, On., Can.	212	44.26 N	76.19 W
Cranberry Lake ⊜, On., Can.	212	44.47 N	75.50 W
Cranberry Lake ⊜, N.Y., U.S.	188	44.10 N	74.50 W
Cranberry Lake ⊜, Wa., U.S.	224	47.17 N	123.05 W
Cranberry Mountain ∧	182	50.42 N	118.12 W
Cranberry Pond ⊜	276	41.08 N	74.12 W
Cranberry Portage	184	54.35 N	101.23 W
Cranborne Chase ◆[3]	42	50.55 N	2.05 W
Cranbourne	169	38.06 S	145.17 E
Cranbrook, Austl.	162	34.18 S	117.32 E
Cranbrook, B.C., Can.	182	49.31 N	115.46 W
Cranbrook, Eng., U.K.	42	51.06 N	0.33 E
Cranbrook Academy of Art ♥	281	42.34 N	83.14 W
Cranbury	276	40.18 N	74.30 W
Cranbury Brook ≃	276	40.19 N	74.37 W
Crandall	222	32.37 N	96.27 W
Crandon	190	45.34 N	88.54 W
Crandon Lakes	210	41.07 N	74.50 W
Crane, Az., U.S.	204	32.42 N	114.40 W
Crane, In., U.S.	194	38.53 N	86.54 W
Crane, Mo., U.S.	194	36.54 N	93.34 W
Crane, Tx., U.S.	196	31.23 N	102.20 W
Crane Beach ±[2]	283	42.41 N	70.46 W
Cranebrook	274a	33.43 S	150.42 E
Crane Creek ≃	190	43.01 N	91.58 W
Crane Lake ⊜, On., Can.	212	45.13 N	79.57 W
Crane Lake ⊜, Sk., Can.	184	50.06 N	109.06 W
Crane Mountain ∧	202	42.04 N	120.13 W
Crane Neck Point ›	210	40.58 N	73.10 W
Crane River Indian Reserve ◆[4]	184	51.30 N	99.14 W
Cranesville	214	41.54 N	80.21 W
Cranfield	42	52.05 N	0.35 W
Cranfills Gap	222	31.46 N	97.50 W
Cranford	210	40.39 N	74.19 W
Crange ◆[8]	263	51.32 N	7.11 E
Cran-Gévrier	58	45.54 N	6.06 E
Crank	262	53.29 N	2.45 W
Cranleigh	42	51.09 N	0.30 W
Crans	58	46.19 N	7.28 E
Cranston	207	41.46 N	71.26 W
Cranston Heights	285	39.38 N	75.38 W
Craolândia	250	7.57 S	47.15 W
Craon	32	47.51 N	0.57 W
Craonne	50	49.26 N	3.47 E
Craponne, Fr.	62	45.44 N	4.43 E
Craponne, Fr.	62	45.20 N	3.51 E
Craponne, Canal de ≊	62	43.40 N	4.39 E
Crary Mountains ⋏	9	76.48 S	117.40 W
Craryville	210	42.11 N	73.35 W
Crasna, Rom.	38	45.36 N	26.08 E
Crasna, Rom.	38	46.31 N	27.51 E
Crasna (Kraszna) ≃	38	48.09 N	22.20 E
Crassier	58	46.22 N	6.11 E
Crater Lake ⊜, St. Vin.	241h	13.20 N	61.11 W
Crater Lake ⊜, Or., U.S.	202	42.56 N	122.06 W
Crater Lake National Park ♠	202	42.49 N	122.08 W
Crater Mount ∧	164	6.30 S	145.10 E
Crater Point ›	164	5.22 S	152.09 E
Craters of the Moon National Monument ♠	202	43.20 N	113.35 W
Crateús	250	5.10 S	40.40 W
Crathie	46	57.02 N	3.12 W
Crati ⋏	68	39.43 N	16.31 E
Crato	250	7.14 S	39.23 W
Crau ◆[1]	62	43.36 N	4.50 E
Crauford, Cape ›	176	73.43 N	84.50 W
Craughwell	48	53.13 N	8.43 W
Cravant	50	47.41 N	3.41 E
Cravari ≃	248	12.06 S	58.03 W
Cravat	219	38.25 N	89.06 W
Craven	184	50.39 N	104.50 W
Craven Arms	42	52.26 N	2.50 W
Cravensville	171b	36.24 S	147.34 E
Cravo Norte	246	6.18 N	70.12 W
Cravo Norte ≃	246	6.18 N	70.12 W
Cravo Sur ≃	246	4.42 N	71.36 W
Crawfish ≃	216	43.00 N	88.49 W
Crawford, Scot., U.K.	44	55.28 N	3.40 W
Crawford, Co., U.S.	200	38.42 N	107.36 W
Crawford, Ms., U.S.	194	33.18 N	88.36 W
Crawford, Ne., U.S.	198	42.40 N	103.24 W
Crawford, Tx., U.S.	222	31.32 N	97.27 W
Crawford □[6], In., U.S.	218	38.20 N	86.28 W
Crawford □[6], Oh., U.S.	214	40.48 N	82.58 W
Crawford □[6], Pa., U.S.	214	41.39 N	80.10 W
Crawford Bay	182	49.42 N	116.48 W
Crawford Countryside	278	41.32 N	87.43 W
Crawford Notch State Park ♠	188	44.13 N	71.25 W
Crawfordsville, Ar., U.S.	194	35.13 N	90.19 W
Crawfordsville, In., U.S.	194	40.02 N	86.52 W
Crawfordville, Fl., U.S.	192	30.10 N	84.22 W
Crawfordville, Ga., U.S.	192	33.33 N	82.53 W
Crawinkel	54	50.47 N	10.47 E
Crawley	42	51.07 N	0.12 W
Crawshawbooth	262	53.43 N	2.17 W
Crayford ◆[8]	260	51.27 N	0.11 E
Crays Hill	260	51.36 N	0.28 E
Crazy Mountains ⋏	202	46.08 N	110.20 W
Crazy Peak ∧	202	46.01 N	110.16 W
Crazy Woman Creek ≃	202	44.29 N	106.08 W
Creagan	46	56.33 N	5.17 W
Creagorry	46	57.26 N	7.19 W
Creal Springs	194	37.37 N	88.50 W
Creamery	285	40.13 N	75.25 W
Crean Lake ⊜	184	54.05 N	106.10 W
Crêches-sur-Saône	58	46.15 N	4.47 E
Crécy, Forêt de ♠	261	48.48 N	2.53 E
Crécy-en-Brie	50	48.51 N	2.55 E
Crécy-en-Ponthieu	50	50.15 N	1.53 E
Crécy-sur-Serre	50	49.42 N	3.37 E
Credenhill	42	52.06 N	2.48 W
Credit ≃	212	43.33 N	79.35 W
Crediton	42	50.47 N	3.39 W
Cree ≃, Sk., Can.	176	59.00 N	105.47 W
Cree ≃, Scot., U.K.	44	54.52 N	4.20 W
Creede	200	37.50 N	106.55 W
Creedmoor	192	36.07 N	78.41 W
Creedmore	222	30.12 N	97.43 W
Creek Brook ≃	283	42.47 N	71.08 W
Creek Locks	210	41.52 N	74.03 W
Creekmouth ◆[8]	260	51.31 N	0.06 E
Creekside	214	40.40 N	79.11 W
Creekwood	278	41.39 N	87.59 W
Creel	232	27.45 N	107.38 W
Cree Lake ⊜	176	57.30 N	106.30 W
Creemore	212	44.19 N	80.06 W
Creetown	44	54.54 N	4.23 W
Cregganbaun	48	53.42 N	9.51 W
Creglingen	56	49.28 N	10.01 E
Crégy-lès-Meaux	261	48.58 N	2.52 E
Créhange	56	49.03 N	6.35 E
Creighton, Sk., Can.	184	54.45 N	101.54 W
Creighton, S. Afr.	158	30.01 S	29.51 E
Creighton, Ne., U.S.	198	42.28 N	97.54 W
Creighton, Pa., U.S.	214	40.35 N	79.46 W
Creighton Creek ≃	169	36.43 S	145.22 E
Creighton Mine	190	46.28 N	81.11 W
Creil, Fr.	50	49.16 N	2.29 E
Creil, Ned.	52	52.45 N	5.40 E
Crema	62	45.22 N	9.41 E
Cremia	58	46.05 N	9.16 E
Crémieu	62	45.43 N	5.15 E
Cremlingen	54	52.15 N	10.39 E
Cremona, Ab., Can.	182	51.33 N	114.29 W
Cremona, It.	64	45.07 N	10.02 E
Cremona □[4]	64	45.12 N	10.00 E
Crenshaw, Ms., U.S.	194	34.30 N	90.12 W
Crenshaw, Pa., U.S.	214	41.15 N	78.46 W
Crep Nudo ∧	64	46.13 N	12.24 E
Crepori ≃	250	5.42 S	57.08 W
Crépy-en-Laonnois	50	49.36 N	3.31 E
Crépy-en-Valois	50	49.14 N	2.54 E
Créquy	50	50.29 N	2.03 E
Creran, Loch ⊜	46	56.31 N	5.20 W
Cres	36	44.58 N	14.25 E
Cres, Otok I	36	44.50 N	14.25 E
Cresaptown	188	39.35 N	78.50 W
Crescent, N.Y., U.S.	210	42.49 N	73.43 W
Crescent, Ok., U.S.	196	35.57 N	97.35 W
Crescent, Or., U.S.	202	43.27 N	121.41 W
Crescent, Lake ⊜	224	48.05 N	123.50 W
Crescent Beach, B.C., Can.	224	49.04 N	122.53 W
Crescent Beach, Fl., U.S.	220	27.15 N	82.32 W
Crescent City, Ca., U.S.	204	41.45 N	124.12 W
Crescent City, Fl., U.S.	192	29.25 N	81.30 W
Crescent City, Il., U.S.	216	40.46 N	87.51 W
Crescent Ditch ≊	226	36.29 N	120.07 W
Crescent Heights, N.J., U.S.	285	39.58 N	74.43 W
Crescent Heights, Tx., U.S.	222	32.11 N	95.56 W
Crescentino	62	45.11 N	8.06 E
Crescent Lake ⊜, Fl., U.S.	192	29.28 N	81.30 W
Crescent Lake ⊜, Or., U.S.	202	43.29 N	121.59 W
Crescent Lake Estates	281	42.38 N	83.25 W
Crescent Spur	182	53.35 N	120.41 W
Crescentville ◆[8]	285	40.02 N	75.05 W
Crescenzago ◆[8]	266b	45.30 N	9.15 E
Cresco, Ia., U.S.	190	43.22 N	92.06 W
Cresco, Pa., U.S.	210	41.09 N	75.17 W
Crespano del Grappa	64	45.49 N	11.50 E
Crespian	62	43.53 N	4.06 E
Crespières	261	48.53 N	1.55 E
Crespin	50	50.25 N	3.39 E
Crespino	64	44.59 N	11.53 E
Crespo	252	32.02 S	60.19 W
Cressbrook Creek ≃	171a	27.05 S	152.27 E
Cressely	261	48.43 N	2.05 E
Cressey	226	37.25 N	120.40 W
Cresskill	276	40.56 N	73.57 W
Cresskill Brook ≃	276	40.57 N	73.58 W
Cresson, Pa., U.S.	214	40.27 N	78.35 W
Cresson, Tx., U.S.	222	32.32 N	97.37 W
Cressona	208	40.37 N	76.11 W
Cressy	169	38.02 S	143.38 E
Crest	62	44.44 N	5.02 E
Cresta	58	46.28 N	9.31 E
Crested Butte	200	38.52 N	106.59 W
Cresthaven	220	26.03 N	80.08 W
Crest Hill	216	41.33 N	88.05 W
Crestline, Ca., U.S.	228	34.14 N	117.17 W
Crestline, Oh., U.S.	214	40.47 N	82.44 W
Creston, B.C., Can.	182	49.06 N	116.31 W
Creston, Nf., Can.	186	47.09 N	55.11 W
Creston, Ca., U.S.	226	35.31 N	120.31 W
Creston, Il., U.S.	216	41.56 N	88.58 W
Creston, Ia., U.S.	198	41.03 N	94.21 W
Creston, Oh., U.S.	214	40.59 N	81.53 W
Crestone Peak ∧	200	37.58 N	105.36 W
Crestview, Fl., U.S.	194	30.45 N	86.34 W
Crestview, Wi., U.S.	216	42.49 N	87.49 W
Crestview Heights	210	42.05 N	76.07 W
Crestwood, Il., U.S.	278	41.39 N	87.45 W
Crestwood, Ky., U.S.	218	38.19 N	85.28 W
Crestwood, Mo., U.S.	219	38.33 N	90.22 W
Crestwood Hills	192	35.56 N	84.05 W
Creswell, Eng., U.K.	44	53.16 N	1.12 W
Creswell, Or., U.S.	202	43.55 N	123.01 W
Creswell Bay ⊂	176	72.35 N	93.25 W
Creswell Creek ≃	162	18.10 S	135.11 E
Creswell Downs	162	17.57 S	135.55 E
Creswick	169	37.26 S	143.54 E
Creta, Isla de → Kríti I	38	35.29 N	24.42 E
Crete, Il., U.S.	216	41.27 N	87.38 W
Crete, Ne., U.S.	198	40.37 N	96.57 W
Crete → Kríti I	38	35.29 N	24.42 E
Crete, Sea of → Kritikón Pélagos ⊤[2]	38	35.46 N	23.54 E
Créteil	50	48.48 N	2.28 E
Crétéville	36	36.40 N	10.20 E
Cretin, Cape ›	164	6.40 S	147.52 E
Creus, Cabo de ›	34	42.19 N	3.19 E
Creuse □[5]	32	46.05 N	2.00 E
Creuse ≃	32	47.00 N	0.34 E
Creussen	60	49.51 N	11.37 E
Creutzwald	56	49.12 N	6.41 E
Creuzburg	56	51.03 N	10.15 E
Crevacuore	62	45.41 N	8.15 E
Crevalcore	64	44.43 N	11.09 E
Creve Coeur, Il., U.S.	190	40.38 N	89.35 W
Creve Coeur, Mo., U.S.	219	38.39 N	90.25 W
Crèvecœur-en-Auge	50	49.07 N	0.01 E
Crèvecœur-en-Brie	261	48.45 N	2.55 E
Crèvecœur-le-Grand	50	49.36 N	2.05 E
Crevillente	34	38.15 N	0.48 W
Crevoladossola	58	46.09 N	8.18 E
Crewe, Eng., U.K.	44	53.05 N	2.27 W
Crewe, Va., U.S.	192	37.10 N	78.07 W
Crewkerne	42	50.53 N	2.48 W
Crews Lake ⊜	220	28.23 N	82.31 W
Crewsville	220	27.16 N	81.36 W
Crianlarich	46	56.23 N	4.36 W
Crib Point	169	38.22 S	145.12 E
Cricamola ≃	236	8.59 N	81.54 W
Criccieth	42	52.55 N	4.14 W
Crichi	68	38.57 N	16.38 E
Criciúma	252	28.40 S	49.23 W
Crick	42	52.21 N	1.07 W
Cricket	192	36.10 N	81.11 W
Crickhowell	42	51.53 N	3.07 W
Cricklade	42	51.39 N	1.51 W
Cridersville	216	40.39 N	84.09 W
Crieff	46	56.23 N	3.52 W
Criel-sur-Mer	50	50.01 N	1.19 E
Criffell ∧	44	54.57 N	3.38 W
Crikvenica	36	45.11 N	14.42 E
Crillon, Mount ∧	180	58.40 N	137.10 W
Crimea → Krymskij poluostrov ›[1]	78	45.00 N	34.00 E
Crimmitschau	54	50.49 N	12.23 E
Crimond	46	57.36 N	1.54 W
Crinan	46	56.05 N	5.35 W
Crîngeni	38	44.01 N	24.47 E
Cringila	170	34.28 S	150.53 E
Cripple Creek	200	38.44 N	105.10 W
Criquetot l'Esneval	50	49.39 N	0.16 E
Crirninoso, Monte ∧	256	21.32 S	43.25 W
Crisenoy	261	48.36 N	2.45 E
Crisfield	208	37.59 N	75.51 W
Crisólia	256	22.15 S	46.25 W
Crisóstomo, Ribeirão ≃	250	10.19 S	50.26 W
Crispiano	68	40.36 N	17.14 E
Criss Creek	182	51.03 N	120.44 W
Crissiumal	252	27.30 S	54.07 W
Cristal, Monts de ⋏	152	0.30 N	10.30 E
Cristal, Sierra del ⋏	240p	20.33 N	75.31 W
Cristalândia	250	10.36 S	49.11 W
Cristalina	255	16.45 S	47.36 W
Cristalino ≃	255	12.38 S	50.40 W
Cristallo ∧	64	46.34 N	12.12 E
Cristianópolis	255	17.13 S	48.45 W
Cristina	256	22.13 S	45.16 W
Cristinápolis	250	11.29 S	37.46 W
Cristino Castro	250	8.49 S	44.13 W
Cristóbal	236	9.21 N	79.55 W
Cristóbal, Punta de ›	240p	22.12 N	81.51 W
Cristóbal Colón, Pico ∧	246	10.50 N	73.41 W
Cristoforo Colombo, Aeroporto di ⊠	62	44.25 N	8.49 E
Cristo Redentor ⊥	252	32.50 S	70.05 W
Cristo Redentor, Estatua do ♥[1]	287a	22.57 S	43.13 W
Cristuru-Secuiesc	38	46.17 N	25.02 E
Crișu Alb ≃	38	46.42 N	21.17 E
Crișu Negru ≃	38	46.42 N	21.16 E
Crișu Repede (Sebes Körös) ≃	38	46.55 N	20.59 E
Crittenden	218	38.46 N	84.36 W
Crivitz, D.D.R.	54	53.35 N	11.38 E
Crivitz, Wi., U.S.	190	45.13 N	88.00 W
Crixalândia	255	15.18 S	47.15 W
Crixás	255	14.27 S	49.58 W
Crixás ≃	250	11.02 S	48.34 W
Crixás Açu ≃	255	13.19 S	50.36 W
Crixás Mirim ≃	255	13.30 S	50.30 W
Črna	61	46.28 N	14.51 E
Crna ≃	38	41.35 N	21.59 E
Crna Gora □[3]	38	42.30 N	19.18 E
Črni vrh ∧	61	46.29 N	15.14 E
Črnomelj	36	45.34 N	15.11 E
Croachy	46	57.19 N	4.14 W
Croagh Patrick ∧	48	53.46 N	9.40 W
Croajingolong National Park ♠	166	37.40 S	149.30 E
Croal ≃	262	53.33 N	2.23 W
Croatia → Hrvatska □[3]	36	45.10 N	15.30 E
Croce dello Scrivano, Passo)(	68	40.34 N	15.50 E
Croce Domini, Passo di)(	64	45.54 N	10.24 E
Crocefieschi	62	44.35 N	9.01 E
Crocetta del Montello	64	45.50 N	12.02 E
Crocheron	208	38.14 N	76.03 W
Crockenhill	260	51.23 N	0.10 E
Crocker	194	37.56 N	92.15 W
Crocker, Banjaran ⋏	112	5.40 N	116.14 E
Crockery Creek ≃	216	43.02 N	86.05 W
Crocketford	44	55.02 N	3.50 W
Crockett, Ca., U.S.	226	38.03 N	122.12 W
Crockett, Tx., U.S.	222	31.19 N	95.27 W
Crockham Hill	260	51.14 N	0.04 E
Crocus Hill → The Valley	238	18.13 N	63.04 W
Croft	262	53.26 N	2.33 W
Crofton, B.C., Can.	224	48.52 N	123.38 W
Crofton, Ky., U.S.	194	37.02 N	87.29 W
Crofton, Md., U.S.	208	39.00 N	76.41 W
Crofton, Ne., U.S.	198	42.43 N	97.29 W
Croft State Park ♠	192	34.49 N	81.52 W
Croggan	46	56.22 N	5.42 W
Croghan	212	43.53 N	75.23 W
Croglin	44	54.49 N	2.39 W
Croick	46	57.53 N	4.35 W
Croil Islands II	206	44.58 N	74.58 W
Croisette, Cap ›	62	43.13 N	5.20 E
Croisilles	50	50.12 N	2.53 E
Croissy-Beaubourg	261	48.50 N	2.40 E
Croissy-sur-Seine	261	48.53 N	2.09 E
Croix	50	50.40 N	3.09 E
Croix, Lac à la ⊜	186	51.16 N	70.13 W
Croix, Lac la ⊜	190	48.21 N	92.05 W
Croker, Cape ›, Austl.	164	10.58 S	132.35 E
Croker, Cape ›, On., Can.	212	44.58 N	80.59 W
Croker Island I	164	11.12 S	132.32 E
Crolles	62	45.17 N	5.53 E
Cromarty	46	57.40 N	4.02 W
Cromarty Firth ⊂[1]	46	57.41 N	4.07 W
Cromby	285	40.09 N	75.32 W
Cromer, Austl.	274a	33.44 S	151.17 E
Cromer, Eng., U.K.	42	52.56 N	1.18 E
Cromford	44	53.06 N	1.34 W
Cromínia	255	17.17 S	49.21 W
Cromore	46	58.09 N	6.29 W
Crompton Point ›	240d	15.35 N	61.19 W
Cromwell, N.Z.	172	45.03 S	169.12 E
Cromwell, Al., U.S.	194	32.13 N	88.16 W
Cromwell, Ct., U.S.	207	41.35 N	72.38 W
Cromwell, In., U.S.	216	41.24 N	85.36 W
Cromwell Park ♠	279a	41.28 N	82.08 W
Cronadun	172	42.02 S	171.52 E
Cronenberg ◆[8]	263	51.12 N	7.08 E
Cronin, Mount ∧	182	54.54 N	126.52 W
Cronton	262	53.23 N	2.46 W
Cronulla	170	34.03 S	151.09 E
Cronulla Beach ±[2]	274a	34.02 S	151.11 E
Croob, Slieve ∧[2]	44	54.20 N	5.58 W
Crook, Eng., U.K.	44	54.43 N	1.44 W
Crook, Co., U.S.	198	40.51 N	102.48 W
Crooked ≃, B.C., Can.	182	54.50 N	122.54 W
Crooked ≃, Mo., U.S.	194	39.13 N	93.49 W
Crooked ≃, Or., U.S.	202	44.34 N	121.16 W
Crooked Creek	180	61.52 N	158.08 W
Crooked Creek ≃, U.S.	196	36.57 N	100.06 W
Crooked Creek ≃, Ar., U.S.	194	36.14 N	92.29 W
Crooked Creek ≃, Il., U.S.	219	38.30 N	89.25 W
Crooked Creek ≃, In., U.S.	216	40.45 N	86.30 W
Crooked Creek ≃, Mo., U.S.	219	39.34 N	91.55 W
Crooked Creek ≃, Pa., U.S.	210	41.55 N	77.08 W
Crooked Creek ≃, Pa., U.S.	214	40.45 N	79.33 W
Crooked Creek Lake ⊜[1]	214	40.42 N	79.30 W
Crooked Island I	238	22.45 N	74.13 W
Crooked Island Passage ⋓	238	22.55 N	74.35 W
Crooked Lake, In., U.S.	216	41.41 N	85.02 W
Crooked Lake, Mi., U.S.	216	42.29 N	85.25 W
Crooked Lake ⊜, Nf., Can.	186	48.24 N	56.17 W
Crooked Lake ⊜, Sk., Can.	184	50.36 N	102.45 W
Crooked Lake ⊜, N.A.	190	48.13 N	91.50 W
Crooked Lake ⊜, Fl., U.S.	220	27.48 N	81.35 W
Crooked Lake ⊜, In., U.S.	216	41.40 N	85.03 W
Crooked River	184	52.51 N	103.44 W
Crookes Point ›	276	40.32 N	74.08 W
Crookham	279b	40.12 N	79.59 W
Crookston	198	47.46 N	96.36 W
Crookstown	48	51.50 N	8.50 W
Crooksville	188	39.46 N	82.05 W
Crookwell	166	34.28 S	149.28 E
Croom	48	52.31 N	8.42 W
Cropalati	68	39.31 N	16.43 E
Cropani	68	38.58 N	16.47 E
Cropper	218	38.18 N	85.06 W
Crosby, Eng., U.K.	262	53.30 N	3.02 W
Crosby, Mn., U.S.	190	46.28 N	93.57 W
Crosby, Ms., U.S.	194	31.17 N	91.03 W
Crosby, N.D., U.S.	198	48.54 N	103.17 W
Crosby, Pa., U.S.	214	41.45 N	78.24 W
Crosby, Tx., U.S.	222	29.55 N	95.04 W
Crosby, Mount ∧	202	43.53 N	109.20 W
Crosby Lake ⊜	212	44.45 N	76.26 W
Crosbyton	196	33.39 N	101.14 W
Crosia	68	39.34 N	16.46 E
Crosne	261	48.43 N	2.28 E
Cross ≃	152	4.42 N	8.21 E
Cross Banks II	283	42.43 N	70.49 W
Cross Bay ⊂	184	53.15 N	99.25 W
Cross Bay Bridge ◆[5]	276	40.35 N	73.49 W
Crossbost	46	58.08 N	6.23 W
Cross City	192	29.38 N	83.07 W
Cross County Center ◆[9]	276	40.56 N	73.51 W
Cross Creek ≃, Ca., U.S.	226	36.08 N	119.38 W
Cross Creek ≃, Oh., U.S.	214	40.18 N	80.36 W
Crossen, D.D.R.	54	50.45 N	12.29 E
Crossen → Krosno Odrzańskie, Pol.	30	52.04 N	15.05 E
Crossens	262	53.41 N	2.57 W
Crossett	194	33.07 N	91.57 W
Cross Fell ∧	44	54.42 N	2.29 W
Crossfield	182	51.26 N	114.02 W
Crossgar	48	54.24 N	5.45 W
Cross Hands	42	51.48 N	4.04 W
Crosshaven	48	51.48 N	8.17 W
Crosshill	44	55.19 N	4.39 W
Crossinsee ⊜	264a	52.22 N	13.41 E
Cross Island I	272c	18.57 N	72.51 E
Cross Keys	285	39.42 N	75.01 W
Cross Keys Airfield ⊠	285	39.42 N	75.02 W
Cross Lake	184	54.37 N	97.47 W
Cross Lake ⊜, Mb., Can.	184	54.45 N	97.30 W
Cross Lake ⊜, On., Can.	190	46.53 N	79.57 W
Cross Lake ⊜, N.Y., U.S.	210	43.08 N	76.29 W
Crossley, Mount ∧	172	42.50 S	172.04 E
Crossmaglen	48	54.05 N	6.37 W
Crossman	168a	32.47 S	116.36 E
Crossman ≃	168a	32.47 S	116.32 E
Crossman Peak ∧	200	34.32 N	114.07 W
Crossmolina	48	54.06 N	9.20 W
Cross Plains, In., U.S.	218	38.57 N	85.12 W
Cross Plains, Tx., U.S.	196	32.08 N	99.11 W
Cross Plains, Wi., U.S.	190	43.06 N	89.39 W
Cross River □[3]	150	5.50 N	8.30 E
Cross Roads	222	32.03 N	95.58 W
Cross Sound ⋓	180	58.10 N	136.30 W
Crossville, Il., U.S.	194	38.09 N	88.03 W
Crossville, Tn., U.S.	194	35.56 N	85.01 W
Crosswicks	285	40.09 N	74.38 W
Crosswicks Creek ≃	208	40.09 N	74.43 W
Crostolo ≃	64	44.55 N	10.38 E
Croston, Eng., U.K.	44	53.39 N	2.46 W
Croston, Eng., U.K.	262	53.40 N	2.46 W
Croswell	190	43.16 N	82.37 W
Crotch Lake ⊜	212	44.55 N	76.48 W
Crotenay	58	46.45 N	5.49 E
Crothersville	218	38.48 N	85.50 W
Croton	214	40.14 N	82.41 W
Crotona Park ♠	276	40.50 N	73.54 W
Croton Creek ≃	196	33.18 N	100.25 W
Crotone	68	39.05 N	17.07 E
Croton Falls	210	41.21 N	73.40 W
Croton-on-Hudson	210	41.12 N	73.53 W
Croton Point ›	276	41.10 N	73.54 W
Crottendorf	54	50.30 N	12.56 E
Crouch ≃	42	51.37 N	0.57 E
Croult ≃	261	48.57 N	2.25 E
Crouse Run ≃	279b	40.35 N	79.58 W
Crouy	50	49.24 N	3.22 E
Crow ≃	190	45.15 N	93.31 W
Crow, North Fork ≃	190	45.05 N	93.45 W
Crow, South Fork ≃	190	45.05 N	93.45 W
Crow Agency	202	45.36 N	107.27 W
Crowborough	42	51.03 N	0.09 E
Crow Creek ≃, U.S.	198	40.23 N	104.29 W
Crow Creek ≃, Ca., U.S.	282	37.42 N	122.03 W
Crow Creek ≃, Il., U.S.	194	40.56 N	89.27 W
Crow Creek ≃, Mt., U.S.	198	45.45 N	105.06 W
Crow Creek ≃, Mt., U.S.	202	46.11 N	111.29 W
Crow Creek ≃, S.D., U.S.	198	43.57 N	99.15 W
Crow Creek ≃, Wy., U.S.	202	43.19 N	109.09 W
Crow Creek Indian Reservation ◆[4]	198	44.11 N	99.30 W
Crowder, Ms., U.S.	194	34.10 N	90.08 W
Crowder, Ok., U.S.	196	35.07 N	95.40 W
Crowduck Lake ⊜	184	50.08 N	95.15 W
Crowdy Head ›	166	31.50 S	152.45 E
Crowe ≃	212	44.22 N	77.46 W
Crowe Lake ⊜	212	44.29 N	77.46 W
Crowell	196	33.59 N	99.43 W
Crowfoot, Mount ∧	172	45.33 S	167.03 E
Crow Hill ∧[2]	262	53.42 N	1.58 W
Crowhurst	260	51.12 N	0.01 W
Crow Indian Reservation ◆[4]	202	45.27 N	108.00 W
Crow Lake	184	49.12 N	93.57 W
Crow Lake ⊜	212	44.43 N	76.37 W
Crowland	42	52.41 N	0.11 W
Crowl Creek ≃	166	31.58 S	144.53 E
Crowle	44	53.37 N	0.49 W
Crowley, Ca., U.S.	226	36.21 N	119.17 W
Crowley, La., U.S.	194	30.12 N	92.22 W
Crowley, Tx., U.S.	222	32.34 N	97.21 W
Crowley, Lake ⊜[1]	204	37.37 N	118.44 W
Crowleys Ridge ∧	194	35.45 N	90.45 W
Crowlin Islands II	46	57.20 N	5.44 W
Crown	214	41.23 N	79.16 W
Crown Hill	212	44.26 N	79.39 W
Crown Island I	164	5.05 S	146.55 E
Crown Memorial Beach ♠	282	37.46 N	122.16 W
Crown Mines ◆[7]	273d	26.13 S	28.00 E
Crown Mountain ∧	240m	18.21 N	64.58 W
Crown Point, In., U.S.	216	41.25 N	87.21 W
Crownpoint, N.M., U.S.	200	35.40 N	108.09 W
Crown Point, N.Y., U.S.	188	43.57 N	73.26 W
Crown Point State Park ♠	224	45.32 N	122.15 W
Crown Prince Frederik Island I	176	70.02 N	86.50 W
Crown Village	276	40.40 N	73.27 W
Crow Peak ∧	202	46.18 N	111.54 W
Crow Rock Creek ≃	202	47.06 N	106.15 W
Crows Fork Creek ≃	219	38.47 N	91.52 W
Crows Landing	226	37.24 N	121.04 W
Crow's Nest, Austl.	171a	27.16 S	152.03 E
Crows Nest, Austl.	274a	33.50 S	151.12 E
Crowsnest, Ab., Can.	182	49.38 N	114.41 W
Crowsnest Pass	182	49.36 N	114.26 W
Crowsnest Pass)(	182	49.39 N	114.45 W
Crows Nest Peak ∧	198	44.03 N	103.58 W
Crowthorne	42	51.23 N	0.49 W
Crowton	262	53.16 N	2.38 W
Crow Wing ≃	198	46.19 N	94.20 W
Croxley Green	260	51.39 N	0.27 W
Croxteth Park ♠	262	53.26 N	2.53 W
Croy	46	57.31 N	4.02 W
Croyde	42	51.07 N	4.13 W
Croydon, Austl.	166	18.12 S	142.14 E
Croydon, Austl.	169	37.48 S	145.17 E
Croydon, Austl.	274a	33.53 S	151.07 E
Croydon, Pa., U.S.	208	40.05 N	74.54 W
Croydon ◆[8]	260	51.23 N	0.06 W
Croydon Park	274a	33.54 S	151.07 E
Croydon Peak ∧	188	43.28 N	72.13 W
Croydon Station	182	53.05 N	119.44 W
Crozet	192	38.04 N	78.42 W
Crozet, Îles II	6	46.00 S	52.00 E
Crozet Basin ⊹[1]	6	39.00 S	60.00 E
Crozon	32	48.15 N	4.29 W
Cruachan, Ben ∧	46	56.25 N	5.08 W
Cruas	62	44.39 N	4.46 E
Crucea	38	44.32 N	28.14 E
Crucero	248	14.21 S	70.00 W
Crucero, Cerro ∧	234	21.41 N	104.25 W
Cruces, Cuba	240p	22.21 N	80.16 W
Cruces, Méx.	232	29.26 N	107.24 W
Crucilândia	255	20.23 S	44.21 W
Crucoli	68	39.25 N	17.00 E
Cruden Bay	46	57.25 N	1.50 W
Crudgington	42	52.46 N	2.33 W
Crudine Creek ≃	170	33.05 S	149.40 E
Cruger	194	33.19 N	90.13 W
Cruillas	232	24.45 N	98.31 W
Crum Creek ≃	285	39.51 N	75.19 W
Crumhorn Mountain ∧	210	42.33 N	74.55 W
Crumlin, On., Can.	212	43.01 N	81.09 W
Crumlin, N. Ire., U.K.	48	54.37 N	6.14 W
Crum Lynne	285	39.52 N	75.20 W
Crummock Water ⊜	44	54.34 N	3.18 W
Crump Lake ⊜	202	42.17 N	119.50 W
Crumpton	208	39.14 N	75.55 W
Crumstown	216	41.38 N	86.25 W
Crupet	56	50.21 N	4.48 E
Cruseilles	58	46.02 N	6.07 E
Cruser Brook ≃	276	40.27 N	74.39 W
Crusheen	48	52.58 N	8.53 W
Crusnes	56	49.26 N	5.55 E
Crusnes ≃	56	49.27 N	5.36 E
Cruz, Arroyo de la ≃, Ca., U.S.	226	35.42 N	121.09 W
Cruz, Arroyo de la ≃, Ur.	258	34.00 S	56.08 W
Cruz, Cabo ›	240p	19.51 N	77.44 W
Cruz, Cañada de la ≃	258	34.09 S	58.58 W
Cruz, Cayo I	240p	22.15 N	77.49 W
Cruz, Pico de la ∧	148	28.44 N	17.52 W
Cruz Alta, Arg.	252	33.01 S	61.49 W
Cruz Alta, Bra.	252	28.39 S	53.36 W
Cruz Bay	240m	18.20 N	64.48 W
Cruz das Almas	256	22.44 S	46.51 W
Cruz de Elorza	234	23.49 N	100.29 W
Cruz del Eje	252	30.44 S	64.48 W
Cruz Descoberta	256	22.45 S	46.48 W
Cruzeiro	256	22.34 S	44.58 W
Cruzeiro do Oeste	255	23.46 S	53.04 W
Cruzeiro do Sul	248	7.38 S	72.36 W
Cruzeta	250	6.25 S	36.47 W
Cruz Grande, Chile	252	29.25 S	71.18 W
Cruz Grande, Méx.	234	16.44 N	99.08 W
Cruzília	256	21.50 S	44.48 W
Cruz Machado	252	26.01 S	51.21 W
Cruzy-le-Châtel	50	47.51 N	4.12 E
Crvenka	38	45.39 N	19.28 E
Crymmych	42	51.59 N	4.40 W
Crynant	42	51.43 N	3.45 W
Crysler	188	45.13 N	75.09 W
Crystal, Mn., U.S.	190	45.01 N	93.21 W
Crystal, N.D., U.S.	198	48.35 N	97.40 W
Crystal ≃	200	39.25 N	107.14 W
Crystal Bay	226	39.13 N	120.00 W
Crystal Bay ⊂	220	28.55 N	82.43 W
Crystal Beach, On., Can.	284a	42.52 N	79.04 W
Crystal Beach, Fl., U.S.	220	28.05 N	82.46 W
Crystal Beach, Tx., U.S.	222	29.27 N	94.38 W
Crystal Brook	166	33.21 S	138.13 E
Crystal Cave ±[5]	208	40.32 N	75.51 W
Crystal City, Mb., Can.	184	49.09 N	98.56 W
Crystal City, Mo., U.S.	219	38.13 N	90.22 W
Crystal City, Tx., U.S.	196	28.40 N	99.49 W
Crystal Creek ≃	278	41.58 N	87.51 W
Crystal Creek National Park ♠	166	18.55 S	146.20 E
Crystal Falls	190	46.05 N	88.20 W
Crystal Gardens	216	42.14 N	88.23 W
Crystal Lake, Il., U.S.	216	42.14 N	88.18 W
Crystal Lake, N.Y., U.S.	210	42.31 N	74.12 W
Crystal Lake, N.Y., U.S.	210	42.28 N	78.20 W
Crystal Lake ⊜, On., Can.	212	44.45 N	78.30 W
Crystal Lake ⊜, Ma., U.S.	283	42.29 N	71.05 W
Crystal Lake ⊜, Ma., U.S.	283	42.48 N	71.09 W
Crystal Lake ⊜, Mi., U.S.	190	44.40 N	86.10 W
Crystal Lake ⊜, N.J., U.S.	276	41.02 N	74.15 W
Crystal Lakes	218	39.52 N	84.04 W
Crystal Lawns	216	41.34 N	88.09 W
Crystal Manor	216	42.14 N	88.17 W
Crystal Palace Stadium and Motor Race Track ♠	260	51.25 N	0.04 W
Crystal River	192	28.54 N	82.35 W
Crystal Spring Lake ⊜	285	39.43 N	75.01 W
Crystal Springs, Fl., U.S.	220	28.10 N	82.09 W
Crystal Springs, Ms., U.S.	194	31.59 N	90.21 W
Crystal Springs Dam ◆[6]	282	37.32 N	122.22 W
Crystal Vista	216	42.14 N	88.24 W
Csepel ◆[8]	264c	47.24 N	19.14 E
Csepel-sziget I	30	47.15 N	18.57 E
Csepreg	61	47.24 N	16.43 E
Cserhát ⋏	30	47.55 N	19.30 E
Cserta ≃	61	46.35 N	16.36 E
Csesznek ⊥	30	47.16 N	17.53 E
Csesztreg	61	46.43 N	16.31 E
Csobánka	264c	47.38 N	18.58 E
Csomád	264c	47.40 N	19.15 E
Csömödér	61	46.37 N	16.39 E
Csömör	264c	47.33 N	19.14 E
Csömöri-patak ≃	264c	47.36 N	19.07 E
Csongrád	30	46.43 N	20.09 E
Csongrád □[6]	30	46.25 N	20.15 E
Csorna	30	47.37 N	17.16 E
Csurgó	30	46.16 N	17.06 E
Ču	85	43.36 N	73.45 E
Ču ≃	86	45.00 N	67.44 E
Cúa	246	10.10 N	66.54 W
Cuacnopalan	234	18.49 N	97.30 W
Cuácua ≃	154	17.54 S	36.48 E
Cua Cung-hau ≃[1]	110	9.46 N	106.34 E
Cuadro Nacional	252	34.37 S	68.17 W
Cuajimalpa □[7]	286a	19.21 N	99.17 W
Cuajimalpa ◆[8]	286a	19.21 N	99.18 W
Cuajinicuilapa	234	16.28 N	98.25 W
Cuajone	248	17.00 S	70.43 W
Cuále	152	8.06 S	16.03 E
Cua-lo	110	18.49 N	105.43 E
Cuamato	152	17.05 S	15.09 E
Cuamba	154	14.49 S	36.33 E
Cuambog	116	7.20 N	125.52 E
Cuanavale ≃	152	15.07 S	19.14 E
Cuando	152	16.32 S	22.07 E
Cuando (Kwando) ≃	152	18.27 S	23.32 E
Cuando Cubango □[5]	152	16.00 S	20.00 E
Cuangar	152	17.36 S	18.39 E
Cuango, Ang.	152	14.30 S	18.59 E
Cuango, Ang.	152	9.10 S	17.58 E
Cuango, Ang.	152	6.17 S	16.41 E
Cuango (Kwango) ≃	152	3.14 S	17.23 E
Cuanza ≃	152	9.19 S	13.08 E
Cuanza Norte □[5]	152	8.50 S	14.30 E
Cuanza Sul □[5]	152	10.50 S	14.50 E
Cuao ≃	246	4.55 N	67.40 W
Cuapiaxtla	234	19.18 N	97.46 W
Cua-rao	110	19.16 N	104.27 E
Cuaró	252	30.37 S	56.54 W
Cuartillo, Arroyo ≃	258	33.45 S	59.06 W
Cuarto ≃	252	33.25 S	63.02 W
Cuary ≃	246	1.30 N	68.11 W
Cua Song-bay-hap ⊂	110	8.46 N	104.52 E
Cuatir ≃	152	17.01 S	18.09 E
Cuatro Caminos	286b	22.54 N	82.23 W

Symbols in the index entries represent the broad categories identified in the key at the right. Symbols with superior numbers (⋏[1]) identify subcategories (see complete key on page *I · 1).*

Kartensymbole in dem Registerverzeichnis stellen die rechts in Schlüssel erklärten Kategorien dar. Symbole mit hochgestellten Ziffern (⋏[1]) bezeichnen Unterabteilungen einer Kategorie (vgl. vollständiger Schlüssel auf Seite *I · 1).*

Los símbolos incluídos en el texto del índice representan las grandes categorias identificadas con la clave a la derecha. Los símbolos con numeros en su parte superior (⋏[1]) identifican las subcategorías (véase la clave completa en la página *I · 1).*

Les symboles de l'index représentent les catégories indiquées dans la légende à droite. Les symboles suivis d'un indice (⋏[1]) représentent des sous-catégories (voir légende complète à la page *I · 1).*

Os símbolos incluídos no texto do índice representam as grandes categorias identificadas com a chave à direita. Os símbolos com números em sua parte superior (⋏[1]) identificam as subcategorias (veja-se a chave completa à página *I · 1).*

English	Deutsch	Español	Français	Português
∧ Mountain	Berg	Montaña	Montagne	Montanha
⋏ Mountains	Berge	Montañas	Montagnes	Montanhas
)(Pass	Pass	Paso	Col	Passo
∨ Valley, Canyon	Tal, Cañon	Valle, Cañón	Vallée, Canyon	Vale, Canhão
≚ Plain	Ebene	Llano	Plaine	Planície
› Cape	Kap	Cabo	Cap	Cabo
I Island	Insel	Isla	Île	Ilha
II Islands	Inseln	Islas	Îles	Ilhas
± Other Topographic Features	Andere Topographische Objekte	Otros Elementos Topográficos	Autres données topographiques	Outros acidentes topográficos

ESPAÑOL — Nombre / Página / Lat.°′ / Long.°′ W = Oeste
FRANÇAIS — Nom / Page / Lat.°′ / Long.°′ W = Ouest
PORTUGUÊS — Nome / Página / Lat.°′ / Long.°′ W = Oeste

Cuatro Ciénegas [de Carranza] 196 26.59 N 102.05 W
Cuatro Islands II 116 10.31 N 124.39 E
Cuauhtémoc, Méx. 232 28.25 N 106.52 W
Cuauhtémoc, Méx. 234 19.20 N 103.36 W
Cuautémoc □[7] 286a 19.26 N 99.09 W
Cuautepec [de Hinojosa] 234 20.02 N 98.18 W
Cuautepec el Alto ◆[8] 286a 19.34 N 99.08 W
Cuautitlán 234 19.26 N 104.23 W
Cuautitlán □[7] 286a 19.39 N 99.13 W
Cuautitlán ≃ 286a 19.41 N 99.13 W
Cuautitlán [de Romero Rubio] 234 19.40 N 99.11 W
Cuautla 234 20.11 N 104.21 W
Cuautla Morelos 234 18.48 N 98.57 W
Cuautzin, Cerro ∧ 286a 19.09 N 99.06 W
Cuba, Port. 34 38.10 N 7.53 W
Cuba, Al., U.S. 194 32.25 N 88.22 W
Cuba, Il., U.S. 190 40.29 N 90.11 W
Cuba, Ks., U.S. 198 39.48 N 97.27 W
Cuba, Mo., U.S. 194 38.03 N 91.24 W
Cuba, N.M., U.S. 200 36.01 N 106.57 W
Cuba, N.Y., U.S. 210 42.13 N 78.16 W
Cuba □[1], N.A. 230 21.30 N 80.00 W
Cuba □[1], N.A. 240p 21.30 N 80.00 W
Cubabi, Cerro ∧ 200 31.42 N 112.46 W
Cubadak 112 0.19 N 100.00 E
Cubagua, Isla I 246 10.48 N 64.10 W
Cuba Island I 276 40.38 N 73.32 W
Cubal 152 13.02 S 14.19 E
Cubal ≃, Ang. 152 15.22 S 12.39 E
Cubal ≃, Ang. 152 12.42 S 13.56 E
Cubal ≃, Ang. 152 11.19 S 13.48 E
Cuba Lake ⊜ 210 42.15 N 78.18 W
Cubanea 254 41.02 S 70.16 W
Cubango (Okavango) ≃ 138 18.50 S 22.25 E
Cubangui ≃ 152 14.22 S 19.58 E
Čubaricha 86 57.37 N 68.22 E
Čubarovo 82 55.12 N 36.56 E
Cubatão 256 23.53 S 46.25 W
Cubatão, Serra de ≜[4] 256 23.52 S 46.28 W
Cubati 250 6.51 S 36.21 W
Cub Hills ⋏[2] 184 54.20 N 104.30 W
Cubia ≃ 152 16.01 S 21.50 E
Čublas 24 64.44 N 45.00 E
Cub Run ≃ 208 38.48 N 77.28 W
Çubuk 130 40.15 N 33.02 E
Çubuklu ◆[8] 267b 41.06 N 29.04 E
Cuc ≃ 250 1.22 N 53.33 W
Cucamonga 228 34.06 N 117.35 W
Cucamonga Creek ≃ 280 33.57 N 117.37 W
Cucamonga Peak ∧ 228 34.14 N 117.36 W
Cuccaro Vetere 68 40.09 N 15.18 E
Cucco, Monte ∧ 66 43.22 N 12.45 E
Čučeviči 76 52.35 N 26.52 E
Cuchara, Río de la ≃ 234 16.37 N 97.41 W
Cucharas 234 22.52 N 105.19 W
Cucharas ≃ 198 37.55 N 104.32 W
Cuchi 152 14.36 S 16.58 E
Cuchi ≃ 152 15.28 S 17.21 E
Cuchibi ≃ 152 15.00 S 20.45 E
Cuchilla Alta, Cerro ∧ 236 15.10 N 88.12 W
Cuchilla Áquila, Cerro ∧ 234 21.27 N 101.03 W
Cuchillo-Có 252 38.20 S 64.37 W
Cuchillo Negro Creek ≃ 200 33.08 N 107.14 W
Cuchivero ≃ 246 7.40 N 65.57 W
Čuchloma 76 58.45 N 42.41 E
Čuchlomskoje, ozero ⊜ 76 58.46 N 42.35 E
Cuchumatanes, Sierra de los ⋏ 236 15.35 N 91.25 W
Cuckels Brook ≃ 276 40.33 N 74.33 W
Cuckfield 42 51.00 N 0.09 W
Cuckney 44 53.15 N 1.08 W
Cuckold Point ≻ 284b 39.14 N 76.24 W
Čučkovo, S.S.S.R. 76 59.36 N 41.14 E
Čučkovo, S.S.S.R. 80 54.17 N 41.26 E
Cucuí 246 1.12 N 66.50 W
Čučuleny 78 47.02 N 28.22 E
Cucumbi 152 10.17 S 19.05 E
Cucuron 62 43.47 N 5.26 E
Cucurpe 232 30.20 N 110.43 W
Cúcuta 246 7.54 N 72.31 W
Cudachar 84 42.21 N 47.11 E
Cudahy, Ca., U.S. 280 33.57 N 118.11 W
Cudahy, Wi., U.S. 216 42.57 N 87.51 W
Cuddalore 122 11.45 N 79.45 E
Cuddapah 122 14.28 N 78.49 E
Cuddeback Lake ⊜ 228 35.18 N 117.28 W
Cuddebackville 210 41.28 N 74.36 W
Cuddia ≃ 70 37.53 N 12.37 E
Cuddington, Eng., U.K. 44 53.14 N 2.36 W
Cuddington, Eng., U.K. 262 53.14 N 2.36 W
Cuddle Lake ⊜ 184 55.25 N 95.47 W
Cuddy 279b 40.21 N 80.09 W
Cuddy Mountain ∧ 202 44.46 N 116.47 W
Cudgegong 170 32.48 S 149.49 E
Cudgegong ≃ 170 32.37 S 149.43 E
Cudgewa 171b 36.12 S 147.46 E
Cudgewa Creek ≃ 171b 36.03 S 147.55 E
Cudham ◆[8] 260 51.19 N 0.05 E
Cudia Park ♠ 275b 43.43 N 79.13 W
Čudin 76 52.44 N 26.59 E
Cudjoe Key I 220 24.40 N 81.30 W
Čudnov 78 50.04 N 28.06 E
Čudovo 76 59.07 N 31.41 E
Čudskoje ozero (Peipsi järv) ⊜ 76 58.45 N 27.30 E
Cudworth, Sk., Can. 184 52.30 N 105.45 W
Cudworth, Eng., U.K. 44 53.35 N 1.25 W
Cue 162 27.25 S 117.54 E
Cuebe ≃ 152 15.48 S 17.30 E
Cueio ≃, Ang. 152 15.27 S 21.21 E
Cueio ≃, Ang. 152 16.17 S 17.46 E
Cuelei ≃ 152 15.33 S 17.21 E
Cuéllar 34 41.24 N 4.19 W
Cuenca, Ec. 246 2.53 S 78.59 W
Cuenca, Esp. 34 40.04 N 2.08 W
Cuencamé [de Ceniceros] 232 24.53 N 103.42 W
Cuerámaro 234 20.37 N 101.43 W
Cuernavaca 234 18.55 N 99.15 W
Cuero 222 29.05 N 97.17 W
Cuers 62 43.14 N 6.04 E
Cuervo, Laguna del ⊜ 232 29.17 N 105.57 W
Cuervos 204 32.38 N 114.52 W
Cuesmes 50 50.26 N 3.55 E
Cuesta Pass)(226 35.21 N 120.38 W
Cueto 240p 20.39 N 75.56 W
Cuetzala del Progreso 234 18.07 N 99.50 W
Cuetzalan del Progreso 234 20.02 N 97.31 W
Cuevas del Almanzora 34 37.18 N 1.53 W
Cuevo 248 20.27 S 63.32 W
Čufarovo 80 54.06 N 47.19 E
Cuffley 260 51.47 N 0.07 W
Cufra → Al-Kufrah ⊤[4] 146 24.20 N 23.15 E
Cufré 258 34.12 S 57.06 W
Cufré, Arroyo ≃ 258 34.27 S 57.09 W
Cufré, Cuchilla ⋏[2] 258 34.20 S 57.10 W
Cuggiono 62 45.31 N 8.49 E
Cugir 38 45.50 N 23.22 E
Cuglieri 71 40.11 N 8.34 E
Cugo ≃ 152 7.18 S 16.39 E
Čugujev 78 49.50 N 36.41 E
Čugujevka 89 44.08 N 133.53 E
Čugunaš 86 52.52 N 87.46 E
Čuguš, gora ∧ 84 43.47 N 40.16 E
Cuiabá 248 15.35 S 56.05 W
Cuiabá ≃ 248 17.05 S 56.36 W
Cuiari 246 1.30 N 68.11 W
Cuichapa 234 17.59 N 94.15 W
Cuieiras ≃ 246 2.50 S 60.31 W
Cuigezhuang, Zhg. 105 40.02 N 117.54 E
Cuigezhuang, Zhg. 105 40.01 N 116.28 E
Cuihuangkou 105 39.32 N 117.11 E
Cuijiatun 104 40.57 N 121.09 E
Cuijiazhuang 104 40.57 N 122.44 E
Cuilapa 236 14.17 N 90.18 W
Cuilcagh ∧ 48 54.10 N 7.48 W
Cuilco 236 15.24 N 91.58 W
Cuilco (San Miguel) ≃ 236 15.56 N 92.10 W
Ču-Ilijskije gory ⋏ 85 43.52 N 75.00 E
Cuillin Hills ⋏[2] 46 57.15 N 6.15 W
Cuilo (Kwilu) ≃, Afr. 152 3.22 S 17.22 E
Cuilo ≃, Afr. 152 5.52 S 16.35 E
Cuilo Futa 152 6.25 S 15.44 E
Cuimba 152 6.08 S 14.38 E
Cuio 152 12.58 S 12.58 E
Cuiqiao 98 34.12 N 114.36 E
Cuiseaux 58 46.30 N 5.24 E
Cuisery 58 46.33 N 5.00 E
Cuisy 261 49.01 N 2.46 E
Cuité 250 6.29 S 36.09 W
Cuitláhuac 234 18.49 N 96.43 W
Cuíto ≃ 152 18.01 S 20.48 E
Cuíto-Cuanavale 152 15.10 S 19.10 E
Cuitzeo, Lago de ⊜ 234 19.55 N 101.05 W
Cuitzeo del Porvenir 234 19.59 N 101.09 W
Cuitzmala 234 19.23 N 104.59 W
Cuiuni ≃ 246 0.45 S 63.07 W
Cuivre ≃ 219 38.56 N 90.42 W
Cuivre, North Fork ≃ 219 39.02 N 90.59 W
Cuivre, West Fork ≃ 219 39.02 N 90.59 W
Cuivre River State Park ♠ 219 39.02 N 90.57 W
Čuja 88 59.12 N 112.25 E
Čuja ≃, S.S.S.R. 86 50.24 N 86.39 E
Čuja ≃, S.S.S.R. 88 59.17 N 112.24 E
Cují 286c 10.28 N 67.02 W
Çukas 112 0.25 S 104.18 E
Čukčagirskoje ozero ⊜ 89 52.00 N 136.36 E
Čukotskij, mys ≻ 180 64.14 N 173.10 W
Čukotskij poluostrov ≻[1] 180 66.00 N 175.00 W
Çukurca 128 37.15 N 43.37 E
Čukurčak 85 41.47 N 71.07 E
Cukurino 83 48.05 N 37.18 E
Culaba 116 11.40 N 124.32 E
Čulak-Kurgan 85 43.46 N 69.12 E
Culaman 116 5.58 N 125.40 E
Cu-lao Ong-con I 269c 10.45 N 106.50 E
Cu-lao Thu I 110 10.33 N 108.57 E
Culari ≃ 250 1.27 N 53.42 W
Culasi, Pil. 116 11.26 N 122.03 E
Culasi, Pil. 116 10.43 N 125.43 E
Culasian 116 8.51 N 117.29 E
Culasi Point ≻ 116 11.37 N 122.42 E
Culbertson, Mt., U.S. 198 48.08 N 104.30 W
Culbertson, Ne., U.S. 198 40.13 N 100.50 W
Culbertson Run ≃ 285 40.03 N 75.45 W
Culbin 168a 33.10 S 116.50 E
Culcairn 166 35.40 S 147.03 E
Culcheth 262 53.27 N 2.32 W
Culdaff 48 55.18 N 7.11 W
Culdaff Bay ⊂ 48 55.17 N 7.10 W
Culebra, Isla de I 240m 18.19 N 65.17 W
Culebra, Laguna de la ⊜ 234 22.28 N 98.20 W
Culebra, Sierra de la ⋏ 34 41.54 N 6.20 W
Culebra Peak ∧ 200 37.07 N 105.11 W
Culebrinos ≃ 240m 18.24 N 67.11 W
Culebrita, Isla I 240m 18.19 N 65.14 W
Culebro, Arroyo del ≃ 266a 40.19 N 3.34 W
Culemborg 52 51.56 N 5.13 E
Culgoa ≃ 166 29.56 S 146.20 E
Culham Inlet ⊂ 162 33.55 S 120.04 E
Culiacán 232 24.48 N 107.24 W
Culiacán ≃ 232 24.31 N 107.41 W
Culiacán, Cerro ∧ 234 20.20 N 100.58 W
Culiacancito 232 24.50 N 107.32 W
Culion 116 11.53 N 120.01 E
Culion Island I 116 11.50 N 119.55 E
Cúllar de Baza 34 37.35 N 2.34 W
Cull Creek ≃ 282 37.42 N 122.03 W
Cullen, Scot., U.K. 46 57.41 N 2.49 W
Cullen, La., U.S. 194 32.58 N 93.27 W
Cullen Bullen 170 33.18 S 150.01 E
Cullen Point ≻ 164 11.57 S 141.54 E
Culleoka, Tn., U.S. 194 35.28 N 86.58 W
Culleoka, Tx., U.S. 222 33.08 N 96.29 W
Cullera 34 39.10 N 0.15 W
Cullicudden 46 57.39 N 4.13 W
Cullin, Lough ⊜ 48 53.57 N 9.12 W
Cullinan 158 25.40 S 28.31 E
Cullman 194 34.10 N 86.50 W
Culloden Battlesite ⊥ 46 57.28 N 4.05 W
Cullom 216 40.53 N 88.16 W
Cullompton 42 50.52 N 3.24 W
Cullowhee 192 35.18 N 83.10 W
Cully 58 46.29 N 6.44 E
Cullybackey 48 54.53 N 6.21 W
Culm ≃ 42 50.46 N 3.31 W
Čul'man 74 56.52 N 124.52 E
Cülmen 130 37.19 N 38.48 E
Culmore 284c 38.51 N 77.08 W
Culoz 62 45.51 N 5.47 E
Culpeper 188 38.28 N 77.59 W
Culpina 248 20.50 S 64.58 W
Culrain 46 57.55 N 4.24 W
Cults 46 57.07 N 2.10 W
Cultus Lake 224 49.04 N 121.58 W
Cultus Lake ⊜ 224 49.03 N 121.58 W
Cultus Lake Provincial Park ♠ 224 49.03 N 121.58 W
Culú Culú, Arroyo ≃ 258 35.19 S 58.57 W
Culú Culú, Laguna ⊜ 258 35.20 S 58.59 W
Culuene ≃ 255 12.56 S 52.51 W
Çulukidze 84 42.20 N 42.25 E
Čuluunchoroot 88 49.41 N 114.15 E
Čuluut 102 45.48 N 107.05 E
Čuluutyn ≃ 88 49.11 N 100.41 E
Culvain ∧ 46 56.56 N 5.17 W
Culver, In., U.S. 216 41.13 N 86.25 W
Culver, Or., U.S. 202 44.31 N 121.12 W
Culver, Point ≻ 162 32.54 S 124.43 E
Culver City 228 34.01 N 118.23 W
Culverden 172 42.46 S 172.51 E
Culvers Lake 210 41.10 N 74.48 W
Culverstone Green 260 51.20 N 0.21 E
Čulym 86 55.06 N 80.58 E
Čulym ≃, S.S.S.R. 86 57.43 N 83.51 E
Čulym ≃, S.S.S.R. 86 54.38 N 78.16 E
Čulyšman ≃ 86 51.20 N 87.45 E
Čum 24 67.06 N 63.07 E
Cuma 152 12.52 S 15.05 E
Cuma (Cumae) ⊥ 68 40.50 N 14.06 E
Čumakovo 86 55.41 N 79.02 E
Cumalı 130 36.42 N 27.27 E
Cuman' 78 50.49 N 25.53 E
Cumaná 246 10.28 N 64.10 W
Cumanacoa 246 10.15 N 63.55 W
Cumanayagua 240p 22.09 N 80.12 W
Cumaovası 130 38.15 N 27.09 E
Cumare, Cerro ∧[2] 246 0.28 N 73.52 W
Cumari 255 18.16 S 48.11 W
Cumbal 246 0.54 N 77.47 W
Cumbal, Nevado de ∧ 246 0.57 N 77.52 W
Cumbe 250 10.21 S 37.14 W
Cumbee 220 28.04 N 81.55 W
Cumberland, B.C., Can. 182 49.37 N 125.01 W
Cumberland, Ia., U.S. 198 41.16 N 94.52 W
Cumberland, Ky., U.S. 192 36.58 N 82.59 W
Cumberland, Md., U.S. 188 39.39 N 78.45 W
Cumberland, Va., U.S. 192 37.29 N 78.14 W
Cumberland, Wa., U.S. 224 47.16 N 121.55 W
Cumberland, Wi., U.S. 190 45.31 N 92.01 W
Cumberland □[6], N.J., U.S. 208 39.26 N 75.14 W
Cumberland □[6], Pa., U.S. 208 40.12 N 77.12 W
Cumberland ≃ 178 37.09 N 88.25 W
Cumberland, Lake ⊜[1] 194 36.57 N 84.55 W
Cumberland, South Fork ≃ 192 36.58 N 84.36 W
Cumberland Bay ⊂ 241h 13.16 N 61.17 W
Cumberland City 194 36.23 N 87.38 W
Cumberland Falls State Resort Park ♠ 192 36.50 N 84.20 W
Cumberland Gap)(192 36.36 N 83.41 W
Cumberland Gap National Historical Park ♠ 192 36.36 N 83.40 W
Cumberland Hill 207 41.58 N 71.27 W
Cumberland House 184 53.58 N 102.16 W
Cumberland Indian Reserve ◆[4] 184 53.04 N 104.50 W
Cumberland Island National Seashore ♠ 192 30.50 N 81.27 W
Cumberland Islands II 166 20.40 S 149.09 E
Cumberland Lake ⊜ 184 54.02 N 102.17 W
Cumberland Peninsula ≻[1] 176 66.50 N 64.00 W
Cumberland Plateau ⋏[1] 192 36.20 N 84.30 W
Cumberland Sound ʊ 176 65.10 N 65.30 W
Cumbernauld 46 55.58 N 3.59 W
Cumborah 166 29.44 S 147.46 E
Cumbres de Monterrey, Parque Nacional ♠ 232 25.31 N 100.18 W
Cumbria □[6] 44 54.30 N 3.00 W
Cumbrian Mountains ⋏ 44 54.30 N 3.05 W
Čumbur-Kosa 83 46.57 N 38.53 E
Cumby 222 33.08 N 95.50 W
Cumeral Nuevo 200 30.54 N 110.51 W
Cumiana 62 44.59 N 7.22 E
Čumikan 89 54.42 N 135.19 E
Cuminá → Paru de Oeste ≃ 250 1.30 S 56.00 W
Cuminapanema ≃ 250 1.09 S 54.54 W
Cuminestown 46 57.32 N 2.20 W
Cumming 192 34.12 N 84.08 W
Cummings Mountain ∧ 228 35.03 N 118.34 W
Cummington 207 42.27 N 72.53 W
Cummins 166 34.16 S 135.44 E
Cummins, Mount ∧ 182 52.03 N 118.15 W
Cummins Creek ≃ 222 29.43 N 96.31 W
Cummins Range ⋏ 162 19.05 S 127.10 E
Cumnock 44 55.27 N 4.16 W
Cumnor 42 51.44 N 1.20 W
Cumpas 232 30.02 N 109.48 W
Çumra 130 37.34 N 32.48 E
Cumshewa Inlet ⊂ 182 53.03 N 131.45 W
Cumuripa 232 28.08 N 109.53 W
Cumwhinton 44 54.52 N 2.51 W
Čumyš ≃ 86 53.31 N 83.10 E
Čun'a ≃, S.S.S.R. 74 61.36 N 96.30 E
Čuna ≃, S.S.S.R. 88 57.47 N 95.26 E
Cunani 250 2.52 N 51.06 W
Cunauaru ≃ 246 3.10 S 63.01 W
Cunaviche 246 7.22 N 67.25 W
Cunco 252 38.55 S 72.02 W
Cuncumén 252 31.53 S 70.38 W
Cundeelee Aboriginal Reserve ◆[4] 162 30.30 S 123.25 E
Cunderdin 162 31.39 S 117.15 E
Cundinamarca □[5] 246 5.00 N 74.00 W
Čundža 86 43.32 N 79.28 E
Cunene □[5] 152 16.30 S 15.30 E
Cunene (Kunene) ≃ 152 17.20 S 11.50 E
Cuneo 62 44.23 N 7.32 E
Cuneo □[4] 62 44.31 N 7.34 E
Cunewalde 54 51.06 N 14.30 E
Cuney 222 32.02 N 95.25 W
Çungüş 130 38.13 N 39.17 E
Cunha 256 23.05 S 44.58 W
Cunhambebe 256 23.00 S 44.20 W
Cunha Porã 252 26.54 S 53.09 W
Cunhinga 152 12.11 S 16.47 E
Cunhinga ≃ 152 10.38 S 16.48 E
Cunhuã, Igarapé ≃ 248 5.46 S 64.36 W
Cunlhat 62 45.38 N 3.35 E
Cunliffe 168b 34.05 S 137.45 E
Cunnamulla 166 28.04 S 145.41 E
Cunningham, Austl. 171a 28.09 S 151.51 E
Cunningham, Ks., U.S. 198 37.38 N 98.25 W
Cunningham, Lake ⊜ 240b 25.04 N 77.26 W
Cunninghame □[9] 46 55.40 N 4.30 W
Cunningham Falls State Park ♠ 208 39.35 N 77.27 W
Cunningham Park ♠, Ma., U.S. 283 42.15 N 71.03 W
Cunningham Park ♠, N.Y., U.S. 276 40.44 N 73.46 W
Cunninghams Gap National Park ♠ 171a 28.01 S 152.22 E
Čunojar 88 57.27 N 97.18 E
Cunqian 100 28.30 N 115.10 E
Čunskij, S.S.S.R. 88 56.05 N 99.41 E
Čunskij, S.S.S.R. 88 57.26 N 97.31 E
Cuntan 107 29.37 N 106.36 E
Cunucunuma ≃ 246 3.13 N 65.58 W
Čuny 76 59.39 N 36.04 E
Cuokkaraš'ša ∧ 24 69.57 N 24.32 E
Cuorgnè 62 45.23 N 7.39 E
Čupa 24 66.16 N 33.00 E
Čupachovka 78 50.23 N 34.36 E
Čupalejka 80 55.11 N 42.33 E
Cupar, Sk., Can. 184 50.57 N 104.12 W
Cupar, Scot., U.K. 46 56.19 N 3.01 W
Cupecê, Ribeirão ≃ 287b 23.37 S 46.42 W
Cupello 66 42.04 N 14.40 E
Cuperly 50 49.04 N 4.26 E
Cupertino 226 37.19 N 122.01 W
Cupica, Golfo de ⊂ 246 6.35 N 77.25 W
Cupins 255 19.51 S 51.03 W
Cupra Marittima 66 43.01 N 13.51 E
Cupramontana 66 43.27 N 13.07 E
Ćuprija 38 43.56 N 21.23 E
Čuprovo 24 64.14 N 46.36 E
Cupsaw Lake ⊜ 276 41.07 N 74.15 W
Cuqiao 107 30.36 N 103.59 E
Cuquema ≃ 152 12.03 S 17.40 E
Cuquenán ≃ 246 4.45 N 61.30 W
Cuquío 234 20.55 N 103.02 W
Čur 80 57.07 N 52.58 E
Curaçá 250 8.59 S 39.54 W
Curaçao I 241s 12.11 N 69.00 W
Curacautín 252 38.26 S 71.53 W
Curacaví 252 33.24 S 71.09 W
Čuračiki 80 55.44 N 47.26 E
Curacó ≃ 252 38.49 S 64.57 W
Curaglia 58 46.41 N 8.51 E
Curahuara 248 17.40 S 68.02 W
Curanilahue 252 37.28 S 73.21 W
Curanipe 252 35.50 S 72.38 W
Curanja ≃ 248 9.58 S 70.58 W
Čurapča 74 62.00 N 132.24 E
Curapi ≃ 250 1.25 N 53.49 W
Curaray ≃ 246 2.20 S 74.05 W
Čurbek 85 39.59 N 69.56 E
Curcani 38 44.12 N 26.35 E
Curcubăta ∧ 38 46.27 N 22.42 E
Curdies ≃ 169 38.30 S 142.55 E
Cure ≃ 50 47.40 N 3.41 E
Curecanti National Recreation Area ♠ 200 38.24 N 107.25 W
Curepipe 157c 20.19 S 57.31 E
Curepto 252 35.05 S 72.01 W
Curequetê ≃ 248 8.20 S 65.40 W
Curiapo 246 8.33 N 61.00 W
Curib 84 42.14 N 46.49 E
Curicó 252 34.59 S 71.14 W
Curicuriari ≃ 246 0.14 S 66.48 W
Curicuriari, Serra ∧[2] 246 0.20 S 66.50 W
Curières, Lac ⊜ 206 46.41 N 74.51 W
Curimatá 250 10.02 S 44.17 W
Curimeo 234 20.01 N 101.42 W
Curinga 68 38.49 N 16.19 E
Curious, Mount ∧ 162 27.28 S 114.20 E
Curisevo ≃ 255 12.14 S 53.17 W
Curitiba 252 25.25 S 49.15 W
Curitibanos 252 27.18 S 50.36 W
Curiuaú ≃ 246 1.51 S 61.14 W
Curiúva 255 24.02 S 50.27 W
Curl Curl 274a 33.46 S 151.18 E
Curlew 182 48.53 N 118.35 W
Curlewis 166 31.07 S 150.16 E
Curnamona 166 31.39 S 139.32 E
Curoca Norte 152 16.18 S 12.58 E
Curone ≃ 62 45.03 N 8.54 E
Curon Venosta (Graun) 64 46.49 N 10.32 E
Čurovići 78 52.10 N 32.01 E
Currais Novos 250 6.15 S 36.31 W
Curralinho 250 1.48 S 49.47 W
Curramulka 168b 34.42 S 137.42 E
Curran 219 39.44 N 89.46 W
Currant Creek ≃, Co., U.S. 200 38.29 N 105.24 W
Currant Creek ≃, Mt., U.S. 202 46.22 N 108.39 W
Currant Mountain ∧ 204 38.55 N 115.25 W
Currarong 170 35.01 S 150.49 E
Currency Creek 168b 35.28 S 138.46 E
Current ≃, On., Can. 190 48.27 N 89.11 W
Current ≃, U.S. 194 36.16 N 90.57 W
Current Islands II 192 25.22 N 76.49 W
Currie, Austl. 166 39.56 S 143.52 E
Currie, Scot., U.K. 46 55.54 N 3.20 W
Currie, Mn., U.S. 198 44.04 N 95.39 W
Currituck 192 36.26 N 76.00 W
Currituck □[6] 208 36.28 N 76.03 W
Currituck Seamount ✤[3] 14 30.00 S 173.30 W
Currituck Sound ʊ 192 36.20 N 75.52 W
Curry 180 62.37 N 150.01 W
Curry, Lake ⊜[1] 226 38.22 N 122.08 W
Curry Rivel 42 51.02 N 2.52 W
Curryville, Mo., U.S. 219 39.20 N 91.20 W
Curryville, Pa., U.S. 214 40.17 N 78.20 W
Cursi 68 40.09 N 18.18 E
Curslack ◆[8] 52 53.27 N 10.13 E
Curtarolo 64 45.31 N 11.50 E
Curtea-de-Argeș 38 45.08 N 24.41 E
Curtice 214 41.29 N 82.49 W
Curtina 252 32.09 S 56.07 W
Curtin Springs 162 25.20 S 131.45 E
Curtis, Esp. 34 43.07 N 8.03 W
Curtis, Ar., U.S. 194 33.59 N 93.06 W
Curtis, Ne., U.S. 198 40.37 N 100.30 W
Curtis, Port ⊤[3] 166 24.00 S 151.30 E
Curtis Bay ⊂ 284b 39.13 N 76.35 W
Curtis Channel ʊ 166 23.30 S 151.45 E
Curtis Creek ⊂ 284b 39.12 N 76.35 W
Curtis Island I, Austl. 166 23.38 S 151.09 E
Curtis Island I, N.Z. 14 30.30 S 178.34 W
Curtis Lake ⊜ 176 66.38 N 89.02 W
Curtisville 214 40.38 N 79.51 W
Curu ≃ 250 3.22 S 39.04 W
Curuá ≃, Bra. 250 5.23 S 54.22 W
Curuá ≃, Bra. 250 1.55 S 55.07 W
Curuá ≃, Bra. 255 13.51 S 51.38 W
Curuá, Ilha I 250 0.48 N 50.10 W
Curuá do Sul ≃ 250 2.39 S 54.10 W
Curuaés ≃ 250 7.30 S 54.45 W
Curuan 116 7.13 N 122.14 E
Curuá Una ≃ 250 2.24 S 54.05 W
Curubandé 236 10.43 N 85.26 W
Curuçá 250 0.43 S 47.50 W
Curuçá ◆[8] 287b 23.30 S 46.25 W
Curuçá ≃ 246 4.27 S 71.23 W
Curuçambaba 250 2.08 S 49.18 W
Curug, Indon. 115a 6.15 S 106.33 E
Čurug, Jugo. 38 45.29 N 20.04 E
Curuguaty 252 24.31 S 55.42 W
Curumo 286c 10.27 N 66.52 W
Curumu 250 1.01 S 51.03 W
Curunga 152 12.51 S 21.12 E
Curup 112 3.28 S 102.32 E
Curupá 250 9.54 S 45.54 W
Curupayty, Riacho ≃ 248 22.03 S 58.00 W
C'urupinsk 78 46.37 N 32.43 E
Curupira, Sierra de ⋏ 246 1.25 N 64.30 W
Cururu ≃, Bra. 248 7.12 S 58.03 W
Cururu ≃, Bra. 250 0.39 S 50.11 W
Cururu-Açu ≃ 250 8.58 S 57.13 W
Cururupu 250 1.50 S 44.52 W
Curutu ≃ 246 5.05 N 63.28 W
Curuzú Cuatiá 252 29.47 S 58.03 W
Curva Grande 250 2.37 S 45.27 W
Curvelo 255 18.45 S 44.25 W
Curwensville 214 40.58 N 78.31 W
Curwensville Lake ⊜[1] 214 40.55 N 78.37 W
Curwensville State Park ♠ 214 40.55 N 78.34 W
Cusago 266b 45.27 N 9.02 E
Cusano Milanino 62 45.33 N 9.11 E
Cusano Mutri 68 41.20 N 14.30 E
Cusapin 236 9.11 N 81.54 W
Cusco → Cuzco 248 13.31 S 71.59 W
Cuscuzeiro, Pico do ∧ 256 23.18 S 44.47 W
Cushabatay ≃ 248 7.09 S 75.08 W
Cushendall 48 55.06 N 6.04 W
Cushendun 48 55.07 N 6.03 W
Cushina ≃ 48 53.11 N 7.05 W
Cushing, Ok., U.S. 196 35.59 N 96.46 W
Cushing, Tx., U.S. 222 31.43 N 94.50 W
Cushing Memorial State Park ♠ 283 42.10 N 70.45 W
Cushman 194 35.52 N 91.45 W
Cushman, Lake ⊜[1] 224 47.28 N 123.14 W
Cusiana ≃ 246 4.33 N 71.51 W
Cusick 202 48.20 N 117.17 W
Cusihuiriáchic 232 28.14 N 106.50 W
Cusna, Monte ∧ 64 44.17 N 10.23 E
Čusovaja ≃ 86 58.13 N 56.22 E
Čusovoj 86 58.17 N 57.49 E
Cusset 32 46.08 N 3.28 E
Cusseta 192 32.18 N 84.46 W
Cussewago Creek ≃ 214 41.38 N 80.11 W
Cussey-sur-l'Ognon 58 47.20 N 5.56 E
Cusso ≃ 152 14.16 S 15.36 E
Cust, N.Z. 172 43.19 S 172.22 E
Čust, S.S.S.R. 85 41.00 N 71.15 E
Custar 216 41.17 N 83.51 W
Custer, Mi., U.S. 190 43.57 N 86.13 W
Custer, Mt., U.S. 202 46.07 N 107.33 W
Custer, Ok., U.S. 196 35.40 N 98.53 W
Custer, S.D., U.S. 198 43.46 N 103.35 W
Custer, Wa., U.S. 224 48.55 N 122.38 W
Custer Battlefield National Monument ♠ 202 45.32 N 107.20 W
Custer City 214 41.54 N 78.39 W
Custer Creek ≃ 198 46.42 N 105.29 W
Custer State Park ♠ 198 43.43 N 103.23 W
Custines 56 48.48 N 6.09 E
Custódia 250 8.07 S 37.39 W
Custonaci 70 38.04 N 12.41 E
Cut and Shoot 222 30.19 N 95.25 W
Cutato ≃ 152 10.33 S 16.48 E
Cut Bank 202 48.37 N 112.19 W
Cutbank ≃ 182 54.44 N 118.31 W
Cut Bank Creek ≃, N.A. 198 48.35 N 100.52 W
Cut Bank Creek ≃, Mt., U.S. 202 48.29 N 112.14 W
Cut Beaver Lake ⊜ 184 53.47 N 102.38 W
Čutejevo 80 55.16 N 47.47 E
Cutervo 248 6.22 S 78.51 W
Cuthand Creek ≃ 194 33.23 N 94.57 W
Cuthbert 192 31.46 N 84.47 W
Cut Knife 184 52.44 N 109.01 W
Cutler, Ca., U.S. 226 36.31 N 119.17 W
Cutler, Me., U.S. 188 44.39 N 67.12 W
Cutler Ridge 220 25.34 N 80.20 W
Cutlerville 216 42.50 N 85.39 W
Čutovo 78 49.43 N 35.10 E
Cutral-Có 252 38.56 S 69.14 W
Cutro 68 39.02 N 16.59 E
Cutrofiano 68 40.07 N 18.12 E
Cuttack 120 20.30 N 85.50 E
Cuttyhunk Island I 207 41.25 N 70.56 W
Čutyr' 80 57.24 N 53.17 E
Cutzamalá ≃ 234 18.22 N 100.39 W
Cutzamala de Pinzón 234 18.28 N 100.34 W
Cutzio 234 18.39 N 100.54 W
Čuvašskaja Avtonomnaja Sovetskaja Socialističeskaja Respublika □[3] 80 55.30 N 47.00 E
Cuvette □[5] 152 0.30 S 16.00 E
Cuvier, Cape ≻ 162 24.05 S 113.22 E
Cuvilly 50 49.33 N 2.42 E
Cuvo ≃ 152 10.50 S 13.47 E
Cuxhaven 52 53.52 N 8.42 E
Cuxton 260 51.22 N 0.27 E
Cuyabá → Cuiabá 248 15.35 S 56.05 W
Cuyaguateje ≃ 240p 22.05 N 83.58 W
Cuyahoga □[6] 214 41.30 N 81.41 W
Cuyahoga ≃ 214 41.30 N 81.42 W
Cuyahoga County Airport ⊠ 279a 41.34 N 81.29 W
Cuyahoga Falls 214 41.08 N 81.29 W
Cuyahoga Heights 279a 41.26 N 81.39 W
Cuyahoga Valley National Recreation Area ♠ 214 41.20 N 81.35 W
Cuyama ≃ 204 34.54 N 120.18 W
Cuyamaca Peak ∧ 204 32.57 N 116.36 W
Cuyamaca Rancho State Park ♠ 204 32.58 N 116.32 W
Cuyamel 236 15.38 N 88.12 W
Cuyapo 116 15.46 N 120.40 E
Cuyk 52 51.44 N 5.52 E
Cuyler 210 42.44 N 75.57 W
Cuylerville 210 42.47 N 77.52 W
Cuyo 116 10.51 N 121.00 E
Cuyo East Pass ʊ 116 11.00 N 121.28 E
Cuyo Island I 116 10.51 N 121.02 E
Cuyo Islands II 116 11.04 N 120.57 E
Cuyo West Pass ʊ 116 11.00 N 120.30 E
Cuyubini ≃ 246 8.20 N 60.20 W
Cuyuni ≃ 246 6.23 N 58.41 W
Cuyutlán, Laguna de ⊂ 234 19.00 N 104.10 W
Cuzco 248 13.31 S 71.59 W
Cuzco □[5] 248 12.30 S 72.30 W
Čuzik ≃ 86 58.03 N 80.37 E
Cuzna ≃ 34 38.04 N 4.41 W
Cuzzago 58 46.00 N 8.22 E
Cvetkovo 78 49.11 N 31.33 E
Cvetnogorsk 86 54.14 N 90.27 E
Cvetnoje 78 48.57 N 32.29 E
Cvikov 54 50.48 N 14.40 E
Cwmbran 42 51.39 N 3.00 W
Cyangugu 154 2.29 S 28.54 E
Cybinka 30 52.12 N 14.48 E
Cybulev 78 49.06 N 29.50 E
Cyclades → Kikládhes II 38 37.30 N 25.00 E
Cyclone 214 41.50 N 78.35 W
Cygnet 216 41.14 N 83.38 W
Cygnet Bay ⊂ 162 16.35 S 123.05 E
Cygnet Lake ⊜ 184 56.47 N 94.54 W
Cygnet River 168b 35.42 S 137.31 E
Cylburn Park ♠ 284b 39.21 N 76.39 W
Cynin ≃ 42 51.48 N 4.29 W
Cynthiana, Ky., U.S. 218 38.23 N 84.17 W
Cynthiana, Oh., U.S. 218 39.10 N 83.21 W
Cynwyl Elfed 42 51.55 N 4.22 W
Cypern → Cyprus □[1] 130 35.00 N 33.00 E
Cypress, Ca., U.S. 280 33.49 N 118.02 W
Cypress, La., U.S. 194 31.36 N 93.02 W
Cypress, Tx., U.S. 222 29.58 N 95.42 W
Cypress Bayou ≃ 194 35.03 N 91.42 W
Cypress Creek ≃, Fl., U.S. 220 28.05 N 82.24 W
Cypress Creek ≃, Tx., U.S. 194 30.19 N 93.45 W
Cypress Creek ≃, Tx., U.S. 222 30.02 N 95.19 W
Cypress Gardens ♠ 220 28.00 N 81.42 W
Cypress Hills ⋏[2] 184 49.40 N 109.30 W
Cypress Hills Provincial Park ♠, Ab., Can. 184 49.39 N 110.10 W
Cypress Hills Provincial Park ♠, Sk., Can. 184 49.39 N 109.30 W
Cypress Island I 224 48.35 N 122.42 W
Cypress Lake ⊜, Sk., Can. 184 49.28 N 109.29 W
Cypress Lake ⊜, Fl., U.S. 220 28.05 N 81.19 W
Cypress Point ≻ 226 36.35 N 121.59 W
Cypress Quarters 220 27.15 N 80.48 W
Cypress River 184 49.34 N 99.05 W
Cypress Swamp ≃ 208 37.02 N 76.53 W
Cypress Swamp ≡ 208 38.30 N 75.17 W
Cyprus □[1], Asia 22 35.00 N 33.00 E
Cyprus □[1], Asia 130 35.00 N 33.00 E
Cyrenaica → Barqah □[9] 146 31.00 N 22.30 E
Cyrene 219 39.17 N 91.06 W
Cyrene ⊥ 146 32.49 N 21.52 E
Cyril 196 34.53 N 98.12 W
Cyrildene ◆[8] 273d 26.11 S 28.06 E
Cyrus Field Bay ⊂ 176 62.50 N 64.55 W
Cysoing 50 50.34 N 3.13 E
Cythera → Kíthira I 38 36.20 N 22.58 E
Czaplinek 30 53.34 N 16.14 E
Czarna Białostocka 30 53.19 N 23.16 E
Czarna Woda 30 53.51 N 18.06 E
Czarne 30 53.42 N 16.57 E
Czarnków 30 52.55 N 16.34 E
Czechoslovakia (Československo) □[1], Europe 22 49.30 N 17.00 E
Czechoslovakia (Československo) □[1], Europe 30 49.30 N 17.00 E
Czempiń 30 52.10 N 16.47 E
Czerniejewo 30 52.26 N 17.30 E
Czernowitz → Černovcy 78 48.18 N 25.56 E
Czersk 30 53.48 N 18.00 E
Czerwieńsk 30 52.01 N 15.25 E
Częstochowa 30 50.49 N 19.06 E
Częstochowa □[4] 30 50.40 N 19.15 E
Człopa 30 53.06 N 16.08 E
Człuchów 30 53.41 N 17.21 E
Czudec 30 49.57 N 21.50 E

D

Da → Black ≃, Asia 110 21.15 N 105.20 E
Da ≃, Zhg. 100 28.10 N 120.14 E
Daaden 56 50.44 N 7.58 E
Da'an, Zhg. 89 45.28 N 124.18 E
Da'an, Zhg. 100 23.05 N 115.37 E
Da'an, Zhg. 107 29.23 N 106.01 E
Daan, Zhg. 110 23.19 N 110.34 E
Daanbantayan 116 11.14 N 124.00 E
Daba 104 42.06 N 122.00 E
Ḍabāb, Jabal aḍ- ∧ 132 31.02 N 35.38 E
Dabagou 104 42.27 N 122.00 E
Ḍab'ah, Ra's aḍ- ≻ 140 31.05 N 28.26 E
Dabai 150 11.31 N 5.11 E
Dabaizhuang 105 39.27 N 117.23 E
Dabajuro 246 11.02 N 70.40 W
Dabakala 150 8.22 N 4.26 W
Dabakala □[5] 150 8.20 N 4.25 W
Dabali 104 41.51 N 120.37 E
Daba Ling ∧ 100 24.28 N 113.17 E
Dabancheng 86 43.21 N 88.19 E
Dabangdian 100 31.37 N 113.41 E
Dabaojiagangzi 104 42.09 N 123.33 E
Dabaozhuang 105 40.18 N 116.58 E
Dabaozi 105 40.11 N 115.10 E
Daba Shan ⋏ 102 31.55 N 109.05 E
Dabasi 107 28.55 N 105.09 E
Dabat 144 12.58 N 37.48 E
Dabayingzi 104 42.11 N 121.35 E
Dabbūrīya 132 32.41 N 35.22 E
Dabegabis 158 28.07 S 18.36 E
Dabeiba 246 7.01 N 76.16 W
Dabeiwa 105 40.48 N 117.31 E
Dabeiyingzi 104 42.05 N 122.08 E
Dabendorf 54 52.14 N 13.26 E
Daber → Dobra 30 53.35 N 15.18 E
Daberas 156 25.38 S 18.29 E
Daberg ◆[8] 263 51.40 N 7.47 E
Dabhoi 120 22.11 N 73.26 E
Dābhol 122 17.36 N 73.10 E
Ḍab'ī, Wādī aḍ- ∨ 132 31.42 N 36.42 E
Dąbie 30 52.06 N 18.49 E
Dąbie ◆[8] 54 53.24 N 14.40 E
Dąbie, Jezioro ⊜ 54 53.27 N 14.40 E
Dabie Shan ⋏ 100 31.00 N 115.40 E
Dabilda 146 12.46 N 14.34 E
Ḍablān 130 34.52 N 40.34 E
Ďáblice ◆[8] 54 50.08 N 14.29 E
Dabnou 150 14.09 N 5.22 E
Dabo 58 48.39 N 7.14 E
Dabob Bay ⊂ 224 47.47 N 122.50 W
Dabobeizhuang 105 39.18 N 117.59 E
Dabola 150 10.45 N 11.07 W
Dabong 114 5.23 N 102.01 E
Daborow 144 6.21 N 48.43 E
Dabou 150 5.19 N 4.23 W
Daboya 150 9.32 N 1.23 W
Dabra 124 25.54 N 78.20 E
Dābri ◆[8] 272a 28.37 N 77.05 E
Dąbrowa Białostocka 30 53.39 N 23.20 E
Dąbrowa Tarnowska 30 50.11 N 21.00 E
Dabsan Hu ⊜ 102 36.58 N 94.55 E
Dabu, Zhg. 100 23.52 N 116.54 E
Dabu, Zhg. 100 24.20 N 114.35 E
Dabu, Zhg. 100 24.19 N 116.43 E
Dabus ≃ 144 10.48 N 35.10 E
Dabusutu-Ula, gora ∧ 86 50.44 N 92.40 E
Dacaitun 104 41.38 N 121.18 E
Dacangzigou 104 40.59 N 121.01 E
Dacaocun 105 40.34 N 117.07 E
Dacca → Dhaka 126 23.43 N 90.25 E
Dachakou 100 29.38 N 118.18 E
Dachang, Zhg. 105 39.53 N 116.59 E
Dachang, Zhg. 106 32.12 N 118.45 E
Dachang, Zhg. 106 31.18 N 121.25 E
Dachang Airport ⊠ 269b 31.18 N 121.25 E
Dachangshan Dao I 98 39.10 N 122.34 E
Dachau 60 48.15 N 11.27 E
Dachauer Moos ≡ 60 48.12 N 11.25 E
Dacheng 100 28.34 N 115.31 E
Dachengji 100 33.52 N 119.26 E
Dachenjiabao 106 32.11 N 120.22 E
Dachen Shan I 106 30.21 N 121.52 E
Dachixu 100 25.10 N 116.46 E
Dachongyu 105 40.23 N 117.41 E
Dachsberg ∧[2] 263 51.30 N 6.30 E
Dachsteinhöhlen ≜[5] 64 47.32 N 13.43 E
Dačice 61 49.05 N 15.26 E
Dačnoje ◆[8] 265a 59.50 N 30.16 E
Dacoma 196 36.39 N 98.33 W
Dacorum □[8] 260 51.45 N 0.30 W
Dacun, Zhg. 102 27.55 N 101.08 E
Dacun, Zhg. 106 31.12 N 119.40 E
Dadal 88 49.01 N 111.37 E
Dadanawa 246 2.50 N 59.30 W
Dadaolizhuang 105 39.59 N 116.59 E
Dadaotun 104 41.46 N 122.13 E
Dadar ◆[8] 272c 19.01 N 72.50 E
Daday 130 41.28 N 33.28 E
Dadayungou 104 41.23 N 123.25 E
Daddys Creek ≃ 192 36.05 N 84.47 W
Dade □[6] 220 25.33 N 80.32 W
Dade Battlefield Historic Memorial ⊥ 220 28.38 N 82.09 W
Dade City 220 28.21 N 82.11 W
Dadès, Oued ≃ 148 30.55 N 6.47 W
Dadeville 194 32.49 N 85.45 W
Dādhar 120 29.28 N 67.39 E
Dadian 100 33.36 N 117.16 E
Dadiangas → General Santos 116 6.07 N 125.11 E
Dadianzi 104 42.11 N 124.02 E
Dadingjiawopu 104 41.13 N 122.16 E
D'adino 88 55.44 N 105.45 E
Dadiya 146 9.37 N 11.26 E
Dadle 144 5.20 N 46.58 E
Ḍadnah 128 25.33 N 56.21 E
Dadon 124 27.57 N 78.28 E
Dadonggejiang 105 39.51 N 116.48 E
Dadongzhou 104 41.44 N 124.00 E
Dadou ≃ 32 43.44 N 1.49 E
Dādpur, India 272b 22.42 N 88.33 E
Dādpur, India 272b 22.54 N 88.31 E
Dādra and Nagar Haveli □[8] 122 20.05 N 73.00 E
Dādri 124 28.34 N 77.33 E
Dādu 120 26.44 N 67.47 E
Dadu ≃ 102 29.33 N 103.45 E
Dadugang 102 22.23 N 100.55 E
Dadukou, Zhg. 100 25.44 N 119.05 E
Dadukou, Zhg. 107 28.45 N 105.13 E
Dadukou, Zhg. 107 29.28 N 106.29 E
Daegu → Taegu 98 35.52 N 128.35 E
Daejeon → Taejŏn 98 36.20 N 127.26 E
Daerhanwangfu 89 44.19 N 122.15 E
Da'erhao 98 41.45 N 116.01 E
Daet 116 14.05 N 122.55 E
Daf' 146 28.03 N 19.57 E
Dafan, Zhg. 100 29.41 N 114.40 E
Dafan, Zhg. 104 42.38 N 122.11 E
Dafang 102 27.04 N 105.31 E
Dafangshen, Zhg. 104 42.25 N 123.14 E
Dafangshen, Zhg. 104 42.34 N 123.28 E
Dafangshen, Zhg. 104 42.36 N 123.04 E
Dafanhe 104 42.13 N 123.43 E
Dafanpuzi 104 41.37 N 122.50 E
Dafeng 100 33.12 N 120.30 E
Dafna 132 33.14 N 35.38 E
Dafoe 184 51.46 N 104.32 W
Dafoe ≃ 184 55.55 N 94.48 W
Dafoe Lake ⊜ 184 55.43 N 96.15 W
Da Fo Si (Great Buddha Temple) ☉[1] 106 30.16 N 120.09 E
Dafoutuo 105 40.24 N 115.58 E
Dafu 100 29.55 N 118.35 E
Dafu ≃ 100 30.52 N 113.32 E
Dāfūr al-Janūbīyah □[4] 140 11.45 N 25.25 E
Dagā ≃ 110 16.56 N 94.45 E
Daga Medo 144 7.59 N 43.01 E
Dagana 150 16.31 N 15.30 W

Symbol	English	Deutsch	Español	Français	Português
≃	River	Fluss	Río	Rivière	Rio
≊	Canal	Kanal	Canal	Canal	Canal
∟	Waterfall, Rapids	Wasserfall, Stromschnellen	Cascada, Rápidos	Chute d'eau, Rapides	Cascata, Rápidos
ʊ	Strait	Meeresstrasse	Estrecho	Détroit	Estreito
⊂	Bay, Gulf	Bucht, Golf	Bahía, Golfo	Baie, Golfe	Baía, Golfo
⊜	Lake, Lakes	See, Seen	Lago, Lagos	Lac, Lacs	Lago, Lagos
≡	Swamp	Sumpf	Pantano	Marais	Pântano
⊓	Ice Features, Glacier	Eis- und Gletscherformen	Accidentes Glaciales	Formes glaciaires	Acidentes glaciares
⊤	Other Hydrographic Features	Andere Hydrographische Objekte	Otros Elementos Hidrográficos	Autres données hydrographiques	Outros acidentes hidrográficos
✤	Submarine Features	Untermeerische Objekte	Accidentes Submarinos	Formes de relief sous-marin	Acidentes submarinos
□	Political Unit	Politische Einheit	Unidad Politica	Entité politique	Unidade política
☉	Cultural Institution	Kulturelle Institution	Institución Cultural	Institution culturelle	Institução cultural
⊥	Historical Site	Historische Stätte	Sitio Histórico	Site historique	Sitio histórico
♠	Recreational Site	Erholungs- und Ferienort	Sitio de Recreo	Centre de loisirs	Area de Lazer
⊠	Airport	Flughafen	Aeropuerto	Aéroport	Aeroporto
■	Military Installation	Militäranlage	Instalación Militar	Installation militaire	Instalação militar
◆	Miscellaneous	Verschiedenes	Misceláneo	Divers	Diversos

ENGLISH / DEUTSCH

Name	Page (Seite)	Lat.°′ (Breite°′)	Long.°′ (Länge°′ E = Ost)
Dagang, Zhg.	100	33.12 N	120.07 E
Dagang, Zhg.	100	22.49 N	113.23 E
Dagang, Zhg.	106	32.12 N	119.39 E
Dagangtou	100	28.18 N	119.44 E
Daganwangzhai	104	40.49 N	122.33 E
Daganzo de Arriba	266a	40.33 N	3.27 W
Dagaokan	104	40.46 N	122.22 E
Dagaolifangcun	104	41.10 N	122.28 E
Dagaolitun	104	42.26 N	123.53 E
Dagaoyang	106	30.35 N	120.26 E
Daga Post	140	9.12 N	33.58 E
Dagash	140	19.22 N	33.24 E
Dagcanglhamo	102	34.02 N	102.30 E
Dagda	76	56.06 N	27.32 E
Dageløkke	41	55.04 N	10.53 E
Dagenham ◆8	260	51.32 N	0.10 E
Dagestanskaja Avtonomnaja Sovetskaja Socialističeskaja Respublika □3	84	43.00 N	47.00 E
Dagestanskije Ogni	84	42.07 N	48.12 E
Daggafontein	273d	26.18 S	28.28 E
Daggafontein Mines ◆7	273d	26.18 S	28.29 E
Daggett	228	34.51 N	116.53 W
Dagg Sound ⊔	172	45.23 S	166.46 E
Daghfalī	140	19.17 N	32.30 E
Dağkızılca	130	38.18 N	27.24 E
Dagmersellen	58	47.13 N	7.59 E
Dagö → Hiiumaa I	76	58.52 N	22.40 E
Dagomys	84	43.40 N	39.41 E
Dagongtun	89	42.48 N	121.58 E
Dagoretti	154	1.18 S	36.46 E
Dagsboro	208	38.32 N	75.14 W
Dagshai	123	30.53 N	77.03 E
Dagu	105	38.59 N	117.41 E
Dagu ≐	98	36.15 N	120.06 E
Dagua, Col.	246	3.40 N	76.41 W
Dagua, Pap. N. Gui.	164	3.25 S	143.20 E
Daguan, Zhg.	100	31.14 N	117.01 E
Daguan, Zhg.	102	27.44 N	104.16 E
Daguan Hu ⊜	100	30.00 N	116.24 E
Daguao	240m	18.14 N	65.41 W
Dagufen'gou	105	40.41 N	116.20 E
D'aguilar, Cape ≻	271d	22.14 N	114.15 E
D'Aguilar, Mount ∧	171a	27.19 S	152.47 E
D'Aguilar Range ⋀	171a	27.10 S	152.45 E
Dagujia	98	42.22 N	124.52 E
Dagujiazi	104	42.20 N	123.20 E
Da Guokui Shan ∧	89	45.17 N	129.30 E
Dagupan	116	16.03 N	120.20 E
Dagushan	104	41.03 N	123.02 E
Dagus Mines	214	41.21 N	78.36 W
Dagutang	100	29.38 N	116.06 E
Dagwin	110	18.04 N	97.41 E
Dahabān	144	21.55 N	39.04 E
Dahalac National Park ♠	144	15.40 N	40.05 E
Dahanchang	105	39.29 N	117.05 E
Dahaneh-ye Ghowrī	120	35.54 N	68.30 E
Dahaneh-ye Kāshār	120	35.09 N	66.14 E
Dahan-e Qowmghī	120	34.28 N	66.31 E
Dahantun	104	42.10 N	122.41 E
Dahasah, Wādī V	142	28.08 N	31.00 E
Daḥdāḥ, Tall ∧2	132	32.36 N	36.03 E
Dahe	106	31.42 N	120.37 E
Dahebei	105	39.10 N	117.39 E
Daheiding Shan ∧	89	47.58 N	129.07 E
Daheiyugou	104	41.21 N	121.55 E
Dahekou	106	32.16 N	119.05 E
Dahengdu	100	29.03 N	121.30 E
Dahengin Dao I	100	22.06 N	113.30 E
Daheqiao	100	29.25 N	115.16 E
Dahijuri	126	22.31 N	86.59 E
Da Hinggan Ling ⋀	90	49.00 N	122.00 E
Dahīrpur ◆8	272a	28.43 N	77.12 E
Dahl	56	51.18 N	7.31 E
Dahl ◆8	263	51.11 N	6.26 E
Dahlak Archipelago II	144	15.45 N	40.30 E
Dahle	263	51.18 N	7.45 E
Dahlem	56	50.23 N	6.33 E
Dahlem ◆8	264a	52.28 N	13.17 E
Dahlem, Museum ♥	264a	52.27 N	13.18 E
Dahlen	54	51.22 N	12.59 E
Dahlenburg	54	53.11 N	10.44 E
Dahlerau	263	51.13 N	7.19 E
Dahlewitz	54	52.19 N	13.26 E
Dahlgren, Il., U.S.	194	38.12 N	88.41 W
Dahlgren, Va., U.S.	208	38.19 N	77.03 W
Dahlhausen	54	53.03 N	12.20 E
Dahlia	154	18.35 S	27.08 E
Dahlonega	192	34.31 N	83.59 W
Dahlonega Plateau ⋀1	192	34.10 N	84.20 W
Dahlwitz	264a	52.30 N	13.38 E
Dahlwitz-Hoppegarten	54	52.30 N	13.38 E
Dahmani	36	35.57 N	8.50 E
Dahmarū	142	28.41 N	30.49 E
Dahme, B.R.D.	54	54.13 N	11.04 E
Dahme, D.D.R.	54	51.52 N	13.25 E
Dahme ≐	54	52.25 N	13.35 E
Dahn	56	49.09 N	7.47 E
Dahomey → Benin □1	150	9.30 N	2.15 E
Dahong	106	31.53 N	121.17 E
Dahongmen	105	39.50 N	116.25 E
Dahongqi	104	41.52 N	122.36 E
Dahong Shan ⋀	100	31.30 N	113.00 E
Dahongtaizi	104	41.41 N	121.23 E
Dahoucun	105	38.51 N	115.37 E
Dahra	146	29.34 N	17.50 E
Dahra ⋀	34	36.25 N	1.00 E
Dähre	54	52.48 N	10.54 E
Dahsah, Wādī ad- V	142	27.19 N	31.26 E
Dahshūr	142	29.45 N	31.14 E
Dahu, Zhg.	100	26.22 N	119.06 E
Dahu, Zhg.	100	26.04 N	117.19 E
Dahua	102	23.44 N	107.59 E
Dahuan	100	22.33 N	113.29 E
Dahuangdi	104	42.08 N	122.27 E
Dahuangji	98	35.06 N	115.15 E
Dahuangpu	105	39.26 N	117.16 E
Dahuangshanpu	104	41.16 N	121.23 E
Dahuashan	105	40.17 N	117.04 E
Dahuasi	107	30.05 N	104.08 E
Dahujiang	100	26.10 N	114.57 E
Dahūk	128	36.52 N	43.00 E
Dahūk □4	128	37.00 N	43.00 E
Dahuni	164	10.31 S	149.55 E
Dahuofang Shuiku ⊜1	98	41.55 N	124.15 E
Dahushan	104	41.37 N	122.09 E
Dahy, Nafūd ad- ◆2	118	22.20 N	45.35 E
Dai I	175e	7.57 S	160.37 E
Dai ≐	100	26.14 N	119.40 E
Dai, Pulau I	164	7.33 S	129.41 E
Daia	38	44.00 N	25.59 E
Daian	94	35.05 N	136.33 E
Daibagnyahāti	126	22.33 N	89.52 E
Daibosatsu-rei ∧	94	35.45 N	138.51 E
Daibu, Zhg.	100	32.19 N	117.12 E
Daibu, Zhg.	106	31.18 N	119.30 E
Daibutsu ♥1	94	35.19 N	139.32 E
Daiei	96	35.29 N	133.45 E
Daifang	100	27.32 N	115.41 E
Daigo	94	36.46 N	140.21 E
Daigo ◆8	270	34.57 N	135.50 E
Daiguantun	105	39.57 N	117.50 E
Dai Hai ⊜	102	40.31 N	112.43 E
Daihaiyingzi	104	42.30 N	121.26 E
Daiji	100	33.48 N	115.03 E
Daijiagou	107	30.00 N	106.33 E
Daijiayao	100	32.56 N	120.19 E
Daikanbō ∧	96	33.00 N	131.04 E
Daik-u	110	17.47 N	96.40 E
Dā'īl	132	32.45 N	36.08 E
Dailekh	124	28.50 N	81.44 E
Dailing	89	47.01 N	129.02 E
Dailly	44	55.16 N	4.43 W
Daimanji-san ∧	92	36.15 N	133.19 E
Daimiel	34	39.04 N	3.37 W
Daimon, Nihon	94	36.44 N	137.03 E
Daimon, Nihon	268	35.53 N	139.44 E
Daimuken-zan ∧	94	35.15 N	138.10 E
Dainan	100	32.43 N	120.06 E
Daingean	48	53.18 N	7.17 W
Daingerfield	222	33.01 N	94.43 W
Dainhāt	126	23.37 N	88.04 E
Dainichiga-take ∧	94	36.00 N	136.50 E
Dainkog	102	32.31 N	97.59 E
Daintree	164	16.15 S	145.19 E
Daintree River National Park ♠	164	16.15 S	145.10 E
Daiō-zaki ≻	92	34.17 N	136.54 E
Dāira Dīn Panāh	123	30.34 N	70.56 E
Dairago	266b	45.34 N	8.52 E
Daireaux	252	36.36 S	61.45 W
Dairen → Lüda	98	38.53 N	121.35 E
Dairsie	46	56.20 N	2.56 W
Dairy	46	55.43 N	4.43 W
Dairy City → Cypress	280	33.50 N	118.01 W
Dairy Creek, East Fork ≐	224	45.34 N	123.09 W
Dairy Creek, West Fork ≐	224	45.34 N	123.09 W
Dairyland → La Palma, Ca., U.S.	280	33.51 N	118.02 W
Dairyland, N.Y., U.S.	210	41.45 N	74.33 W
Dairyland Reservoir ⊜1	190	45.30 N	91.00 W
Dairy Valley → Cerritos	280	33.51 N	118.05 W
Dai-sen ∧	96	35.22 N	133.33 E
Daisen-oki-kokuritsu-kōen ♠	96	35.20 N	133.35 E
Daisen-zan ∧	96	34.07 N	133.56 E
Daisetsu-zan-kokuritsu-kōen ♠	92a	43.30 N	142.57 E
Daisetta	222	30.06 N	94.38 W
Daishan	100	30.14 N	122.12 E
Daishin	94	37.12 N	140.15 E
Daishōji ≐	94	36.18 N	136.15 E
Daisizhen	107	29.14 N	105.09 E
Daitō, Nihon	96	34.42 N	135.38 E
Daitō, Nihon	96	35.19 N	132.58 E
Daiwa, Nihon	96	34.32 N	132.57 E
Daiwa, Nihon	96	34.57 N	132.39 E
Daixi	106	30.40 N	120.01 E
Daixian	102	39.08 N	113.01 E
Daixiqiao	106	31.36 N	120.04 E
Daiya ≐	94	36.45 N	139.46 E
Daiyun Shan ⋀	100	25.46 N	118.16 E
Dajabón	238	19.33 N	71.42 W
Dājal	120	29.33 N	70.23 E
Da'jānīyah, Jabal ad- ∧	132	30.34 N	35.43 E
Dajarra	166	21.41 S	139.31 E
Dajian Shan ∧	102	26.42 N	103.34 E
Dajidian	105	38.50 N	115.26 E
Dajindian	100	34.24 N	112.58 E
Dajing, Zhg.	100	28.24 N	121.07 E
Dajing, Zhg.	100	28.59 N	113.19 E
Dajin Shan II	106	30.41 N	121.26 E
Dajishan	100	24.38 N	114.26 E
Dajitai	104	42.20 N	121.11 E
Dajiuba	120	36.50 N	89.35 E
Daji Yang ⊔	100	30.54 N	122.18 E
Daju	105	39.12 N	115.31 E
Da Juh	102	36.40 N	94.04 E
Dak ⊜	128	32.48 N	61.14 E
Daka ≐	150	8.19 N	0.13 W
Dakangpu	104	41.32 N	121.06 E
Dakanzi	104	40.52 N	122.53 E
Dakar	150	14.40 N	17.26 W
Dakar □4	150	14.45 N	17.25 W
Dākātia ≐1	126	22.57 N	90.42 E
Dakecihu ⊜	120	31.55 N	87.35 E
Dakeng	100	26.18 N	115.32 E
Dakengkou	100	24.33 N	113.37 E
Daketa ≐	144	7.16 N	42.13 E
Dak-gle	110	15.11 N	107.48 E
Dakhal, Bi'r ad- ⊤4	142	28.40 N	32.24 E
Dakhal, Wādī ad- V	142	28.49 N	32.45 E
Dākhilah, Al-Wāḥāt ad- ⊤4	140	25.30 N	29.05 E
Dakhla	148	23.43 N	15.57 W
Dakhlet Nouâdhibou □4	148	20.40 N	16.00 W
Dakingari	150	11.37 N	4.01 E
Dakka → Dhaka	124	23.43 N	90.25 E
Dākoānk	110	7.02 N	93.43 E
Dakongcheng	105	39.30 N	117.09 E
Dakongwan	104	40.51 N	122.19 E
Dakoro	150	14.31 N	6.46 E
Dakota City, Ia., U.S.	190	42.43 N	94.12 W
Dakota City, Ne., U.S.	198	42.24 N	96.25 W
Dakou	100	34.27 N	112.44 E
Dakoutun	105	39.35 N	117.14 E
Đakovica	38	42.23 N	20.25 E
Đakovo	38	45.19 N	18.25 E
Dakshingram	126	24.03 N	87.48 E
Dak-to	110	14.42 N	107.51 E
Dakumu	89	48.51 N	124.18 E
Dakunlun	98	36.34 N	117.52 E
Dákura, Laguna c	236	14.24 N	83.15 W
Dakwa	154	4.00 N	26.26 E
Dakwah, Tall ad- ∧2	132	33.25 N	36.56 E
Dala, Ang.	152	11.03 S	20.17 E
Dala, Ang.	152	8.05 S	15.50 E
Dala, Sol.Is.	175e	8.35 S	160.40 E
Dalaas	58	47.07 N	10.00 E
Dalaba	150	10.42 N	12.15 W
Dalabani	150	10.28 N	9.27 W
Dala Cachibo	152	10.28 S	14.39 E
Dalad Qi	102	40.28 N	110.02 E
Dala-Floda	40	60.31 N	14.47 E
Dalaguete	116	9.46 N	123.32 E
Dalahan (Shiqizhan)	89	52.06 N	125.46 E
Dala-Husby	40	60.21 N	16.00 E
Dala-Järna	26	60.33 N	14.21 E
Dalajchöl	86	47.59 N	90.47 E
Dalaji	89	51.38 N	120.06 E
Dalälven ≐	40	60.38 N	17.27 E
Dalama	130	37.47 N	28.04 E
Dalaman ≐	130	36.40 N	28.45 E
Dalāmī	140	11.52 N	30.28 E
Dalan	100	23.19 N	114.47 E
Dalan Dzadgad	102	43.37 N	104.29 E
Dalandžargalan	102	45.55 N	109.05 E
Dalane ◆1	26	58.35 N	6.20 E
Dalang	100	22.57 N	113.56 E
Dalantuozi	104	41.28 N	122.47 E
Dalao	150	11.29 N	13.40 W
Dalarna □9	26	61.01 N	14.04 E
Dalarö	40	59.08 N	18.24 E
Dalat, Malay.	112	2.44 N	111.56 E
Da-lat, Viet.	110	11.56 N	108.25 E
Dalavakasır	130	37.14 N	41.45 E
Dalayaozi	105	40.49 N	117.41 E
Dalbana ≐	250	4.48 S	57.27 W
Dālbandin	128	28.53 N	64.25 E
Dalbeattie	44	54.56 N	3.49 W
D'Albertis Dome ∧	164	5.00 S	142.05 E
Dalbosjön c	26	58.45 N	12.48 E
Dalby, Austl.	166	27.11 S	151.16 E
Dalby, Sve.	41	55.40 N	13.20 E
Dalby Söderskogs Nationalpark ♠	41	55.43 N	13.17 E
Dalcahue	254	42.23 S	73.40 W
Dalch ≐	42	50.52 N	3.47 W
Dale, Nor.	26	60.35 N	5.49 E
Dale, Nor.	26	61.22 N	5.25 E
Dale, Wales, U.K.	42	51.43 N	5.11 W
Dale, In., U.S.	194	38.10 N	86.59 W
Dale, Pa., U.S.	214	40.18 N	78.54 W
Dale, Tx., U.S.	222	29.56 N	97.34 W
Dale ≐	168a	32.10 S	116.49 E
Dale, Mount ∧	168a	32.08 S	116.18 E
Dale Bridge	168a	32.05 S	116.49 E
Dalecarlia → Dalarna □9	26	61.01 N	14.04 E
Dale City	208	38.38 N	77.18 W
Dale Hollow Lake ⊜1	192	36.36 N	85.19 W
Dale Lake ⊜	204	34.08 N	115.42 W
Dalen	26	59.27 N	8.00 E
Dalengtu	98	41.11 N	113.45 E
Dalešice, údolní nádrž ⊜1	61	49.09 N	16.05 E
Daleside	158	26.30 S	28.04 E
Dale South ≐	168a	32.16 S	116.47 E
Dalesville	206	45.42 N	74.24 W
Dalesville ≐	206	45.40 N	74.24 W
Daleszyce	30	50.48 N	20.48 E
Dalet	110	19.59 N	93.51 E
Daleville, Al., U.S.	194	31.18 N	85.42 W
Daleville, In., U.S.	218	40.07 N	85.33 W
Daleville, Pa., U.S.	210	41.18 N	75.31 W
Dalfsen	52	52.30 N	6.16 E
Dalgaranga	162	27.46 S	117.02 E
Dalgaranger ∧	162	27.51 S	117.06 E
Dalgety	171b	36.30 S	148.50 E
Dalgety Bay	46	56.02 N	3.20 W
Dalgety Brook ≐	162	25.07 S	115.47 E
Dalgety Downs	162	25.17 S	116.15 E
Dalgomai	124	26.06 N	90.47 E
Dalhalvaig	46	58.28 N	3.54 W
Dalhart	196	36.03 N	102.30 W
Dalhausen	52	51.37 N	9.17 E
Dalhousie, N.B., Can.	186	48.04 N	66.23 W
Dalhousie, India	123	32.32 N	75.59 E
Dalhousie, Cape ≻	180	70.14 N	129.42 W
Dalhousie Island I	126	21.35 N	88.45 E
Dalhousie Lake ⊜	212	44.58 N	76.35 W
Dalhousie Square ♠	272b	22.33 N	88.22 E
Dali, Zhg.	102	34.47 N	109.57 E
Dali, Zhg.	102	25.38 N	100.09 E
Dalian Dao I	100	25.40 N	119.42 E
Daliangdi	98	41.54 N	115.45 E
Daliang Shan ⋀	102	28.00 N	103.00 E
Dalianhe	104	40.57 N	123.15 E
Daliankeng	105	40.54 N	117.45 E
Dalian Wan c	98	38.57 N	121.45 E
Dalianwukou	106	30.17 N	119.00 E
Daliao ≐	104	40.42 N	122.08 E
Dalías	34	36.49 N	2.52 W
Dalikou	100	26.52 N	118.00 E
Dalin, Zhg.	89	43.43 N	122.45 E
Dalin, Zhg.	107	30.17 N	104.07 E
Daling	104	41.27 N	121.15 E
Daling ≐	98	40.56 N	121.43 E
Dalingbeigou	104	40.42 N	123.08 E
Dalipe Point ≻	116	10.46 N	121.55 E
Daliushugou	104	40.46 N	122.14 E
Daliutai	104	41.25 N	121.55 E
Daliutun	104	42.14 N	122.46 E
Daliuzhen	105	38.51 N	116.19 E
Daliuzhuang	100	33.04 N	114.03 E
Dāliyat el Karmel	132	32.42 N	35.03 E
Daliyya	132	32.35 N	35.04 E
Dalizi	98	41.45 N	126.49 E
Dalj	38	45.29 N	18.59 E
Daljā'	142	27.39 N	30.42 E
Dalkarlsberg	40	59.26 N	14.51 E
Dalkeith	46	55.54 N	3.04 W
Dālkola	124	25.52 N	87.51 E
Dall, Mount ∧	180	62.35 N	152.18 W
Dāllah, 'Ayn ⊤4	140	27.19 N	27.20 E
Dallardsville	222	30.38 N	94.38 W
Dallas, Scot., U.K.	46	57.33 N	3.28 W
Dallas, Al., U.S.	194	33.50 N	86.39 W
Dallas, Ga., U.S.	192	33.55 N	84.50 W
Dallas, N.C., U.S.	192	35.18 N	81.10 W
Dallas, Or., U.S.	202	44.55 N	123.18 W
Dallas, Pa., U.S.	210	41.20 N	75.57 W
Dallas, Tx., U.S.	222	32.46 N	96.47 W
Dallas, Wi., U.S.	190	45.15 N	91.48 W
Dallas □6	222	32.17 N	96.47 W
Dallas Center	190	41.41 N	93.57 W
Dallas City	190	40.38 N	91.10 W
Dallas-Fort Worth Regional Airport ⊠	222	32.54 N	97.01 W
Dallas Naval Air Station ■	222	32.44 N	96.59 W
Dallastown	208	39.53 N	76.38 W
Dallgow	54	52.32 N	13.05 E
Dalli Rajhāra	122	20.35 N	81.04 E
Dall Island I	182	54.50 N	132.55 W
Dall Lake ⊜	180	60.18 N	163.35 W
Dalmā' I	128	24.30 N	52.20 E
Dalmacija □9	36	43.00 N	17.00 E
Dalmacio Vélez Sarsfield	252	32.36 S	63.35 W
Dalmally	46	56.24 N	4.58 W
Dal'mamedli	84	40.42 N	46.34 E
Dalmatia	208	40.39 N	76.54 W
Dalmatia → Dalmacija □9	36	43.00 N	17.00 E
Dalmatovo	86	56.16 N	62.56 E
Dalmau	124	26.04 N	81.02 E
Dalmellington	44	55.19 N	4.24 W
Dalmeny	184	52.20 N	106.46 W
Dalmine	62	45.39 N	9.36 E
Dalmose	41	55.18 N	11.26 E
Dal'n'aja	89	45.56 N	142.04 E
Dal'n'aja Muja	88	54.21 N	103.37 E
Dalnaspidal	46	56.50 N	4.14 W
Dal'negorsk	89	44.35 N	135.35 E
Dal'neje-Konstantinovo	80	55.49 N	44.06 E
Dal'nerečensk	89	45.55 N	133.43 E
Dal'ne-Rusanovo	82	54.15 N	36.45 E
Dal'nik	78	46.28 N	30.34 E
Daloa	150	6.53 N	6.27 W
Daloa □5	150	7.00 N	6.45 W
Dalong	120	28.54 N	90.33 E
Dalongchang	105	39.50 N	116.06 E
Dalonghua	105	39.18 N	115.18 E
Dalongtian	100	24.14 N	115.44 E
Dalovice	54	50.11 N	12.55 E
Dalqū	140	20.07 N	30.37 E
Dalroy	182	51.07 N	113.39 W
Dalry, Scot., U.K.	44	55.07 N	4.10 W
Dalry, Scot., U.K.	46	55.43 N	4.44 W
Dalrymple	44	55.23 N	4.35 W
Dalrymple, Mount ∧	166	21.02 S	148.38 E
Dalrymple Creek ≐	171a	27.59 S	151.46 E
Dalrymple Lake ⊜	212	44.38 N	79.07 W
Dalsbruk (Taalintehdas)	26	60.02 N	22.31 E
Dalsingh Sarai	124	25.40 N	85.50 E
Dalsingpara	124	26.47 N	89.22 E
Dalsjöfors	26	57.43 N	13.05 E
Dalsland □9	26	58.30 N	12.50 E
Dals-Långed	26	58.55 N	12.18 E
Dal'stroja	180	68.19 N	177.39 W
Dalton, S. Afr.	158	29.20 S	30.40 E
Dalton, Eng., U.K.	262	53.34 N	2.46 W
Dalton, Ga., U.S.	192	34.47 N	84.58 W
Dalton, Ma., U.S.	207	42.28 N	73.10 W
Dalton, Ne., U.S.	198	41.24 N	102.58 W
Dalton, N.Y., U.S.	210	42.32 N	77.57 W
Dalton, Oh., U.S.	214	40.47 N	81.41 W
Dalton, Pa., U.S.	210	41.32 N	75.44 W
Dalton City	219	39.43 N	88.48 W
Daltonganj	124	24.02 N	84.04 E
Dalton Gardens	202	47.43 N	116.46 W
Dalton Iceberg Tongue ⍓	9	66.15 S	121.30 E
Dalton-in-Furness	44	54.09 N	3.11 W
Dalu	104	41.27 N	123.19 E
Dalubeikou	105	38.59 N	117.12 E
Daludalu	114	1.05 N	100.15 E
Dalu Dao I	98	39.44 N	123.45 E
Daluis, Gorges de V	62	44.04 N	6.49 E
Dalum, B.R.D.	52	52.35 N	7.14 E
Dalum, Dan.	41	55.22 N	10.22 E
Daluojiazhuang	106	32.09 N	120.08 E
Daluotaozi	104	41.17 N	122.52 E
Daluoxi	100	25.14 N	118.36 E
Daluping	100	26.11 N	114.30 E
Dalupiri Island I, Pil.	116	19.05 N	121.14 E
Dalupiri Island I, Pil.	116	12.25 N	124.16 E
Daluxi	100	24.28 N	117.01 E
Dalview	273d	26.15 S	28.21 E
Dalvík	24a	65.59 N	18.32 W
Dalwallinu	162	30.17 S	116.40 E
Dalwhinnie	46	56.56 N	4.14 W
Dalworthington Gardens	222	32.42 N	97.10 W
Daly ≐	164	13.20 S	130.19 E
Daly Bay c	176	64.00 N	89.40 W
Daly City	226	37.43 N	122.31 W
Daly Lake ⊜	184	56.33 N	105.40 W
Daly Point ≻	212	44.53 N	80.14 W
Daly River	164	13.45 S	130.50 E
Daly River Aboriginal Reserve ◆4	164	14.20 S	130.00 E
Daly Waters	164	16.15 S	133.22 E
Dāmā, Sūrīy.	132	32.57 N	36.25 E
Dama, Zhg.	100	32.03 N	118.02 E
Damagum	146	11.41 N	11.20 E
Damān	122	20.25 N	72.51 E
Damān □8	122	20.10 N	73.00 E
Damanhār Shubra	273c	30.07 N	31.14 E
Damanhūr	142	31.02 N	30.28 E
Damanling	105	40.36 N	115.08 E
Damaopu	104	41.16 N	121.07 E
Damar	130	41.15 N	41.34 E
Damar, Pulau I, Indon.	164	1.00 S	128.24 E
Damar, Pulau I, Indon.	164	7.09 S	128.40 E
Damara	152	4.58 N	18.42 E
Damaraja	115a	6.55 S	108.05 E
Damaraland □5	156	21.00 S	14.20 E
Damaraland □9	156	22.34 S	17.06 E
Damāṣ, Miṣr	142	30.48 N	31.20 E
Damas → Dimashq, Sūrīy.	132	33.30 N	36.18 E
Damasco → Dimashq	132	33.30 N	36.18 E
Damascus → Dimashq, Sūrīy.	132	33.30 N	36.18 E
Damascus, Ar., U.S.	194	35.22 N	92.24 W
Damascus, Ga., U.S.	192	34.33 N	84.56 W
Damascus, Md., U.S.	208	39.17 N	77.12 W
Damascus, Oh., U.S.	214	40.54 N	80.58 W
Damascus, Pa., U.S.	210	41.42 N	75.04 W
Damascus, Va., U.S.	192	36.38 N	81.47 W
Damascus International Airport ⊠	132	33.29 N	36.13 E
Damaskus → Dimashq	132	33.30 N	36.18 E
Damāṭ	142	30.57 N	30.57 E
Damaturu	146	11.45 N	11.58 E
Damāvand	128	35.43 N	52.04 E
Damāvand, Qolleh-ye ∧	128	35.56 N	52.08 E
Damba	152	6.41 S	15.08 E
Dambach-la-Ville	58	48.20 N	7.26 E
Dambarta	150	12.26 N	8.31 E
Dambeck	54	52.48 N	11.09 E
Dambuki	89	54.21 N	127.38 E
Dam-doi	110	8.50 N	105.15 E
Damelevières	58	48.33 N	6.23 E
Damen Dao I	100	27.58 N	121.06 E
Damengjialazi	104	41.04 N	120.53 E
Damengzhuang	105	39.32 N	116.59 E
Damergou ◆1	150	15.00 N	8.55 E
Damerham	42	50.57 N	1.52 W
Dämeritzsee ⊜	264a	52.25 N	13.45 E
Damery	50	49.04 N	3.53 E
Dames Quarter	208	38.11 N	75.53 W
Dam Gamad	140	13.17 N	27.28 E
Dāmghān	128	39.09 N	54.22 E
Damianópolis	255	14.33 S	46.10 W
Damianzhen	107	30.36 N	104.10 E
Damiao, Zhg.	98	42.26 N	118.22 E
Damiao, Zhg.	98	34.20 N	117.23 E
Damiao, Zhg.	102	37.18 N	104.39 E
Damiao, Zhg.	104	42.33 N	122.18 E
Damiaochang	107	29.39 N	106.05 E
Damiaogou	104	41.06 N	123.52 E
Damiaojiang	106	31.00 N	120.28 E
Damiaoshang	105	39.56 N	115.12 E
Dămienești	38	46.44 N	26.59 E
Damietta → Dumyāṭ	142	31.25 N	31.48 E
Damietta Branch → Dumyāṭ, Far' ≐	142	31.32 N	31.51 E
Damietta Mouth → Dumyāṭ, Maṣabb ≐1	142	31.32 N	31.51 E
Damin	100	28.56 N	120.29 E
Daming	98	36.19 N	115.06 E
Damingzhen	104	42.34 N	123.36 E
Damintun	104	41.52 N	122.56 E
Dāmiyā	132	32.06 N	35.33 E
Damm	263	51.40 N	6.48 E
Dammai Island I	116	5.47 N	120.25 E
Dammarie	50	48.21 N	1.30 E
Dammarie-lès-Lys	50	48.31 N	2.39 E
Dammartin-en-Goële	50	49.03 N	2.41 E
Dammartin-en-Serve	50	48.54 N	1.37 E
Dammastock ∧	58	46.39 N	8.25 E
Damme, Bel.	50	51.15 N	3.17 E
Damme, B.R.D.	52	52.30 N	8.08 E
Damme, D.D.R.	54	53.17 N	14.01 E
Dammer Berge ⋀2	52	52.32 N	8.10 E
Dāmodar ≐	124	22.17 N	88.05 E
Dāmodar Main Canal ⌅	126	23.01 N	87.53 E
Damoh, India	118	23.50 N	79.27 E
Damoh, India	124	23.50 N	79.27 E
Damoh □5	124	24.00 N	79.30 E
Damon	222	29.17 N	95.45 W
Damongo	150	9.05 N	1.49 W
Damotapāda	272c	19.03 N	73.04 E
Damous	34	36.33 N	1.42 E
Damozhuang	105	39.53 N	115.40 E
Dampar, Tasek ⊜	114	3.02 N	102.43 E
Dampelas → Sabang	112	0.11 N	119.51 E
Dampier	162	20.39 S	116.45 E
Dampier, Cape ≻	164	6.02 S	151.02 E
Dampier, Selat ⊔	164	0.40 S	130.40 E
Dampier Archipelago II	162	20.35 S	116.35 E
Dampier Land ≻1	162	17.30 S	122.55 E
Dampierre, Fr.	50	48.42 N	1.59 E
Dampierre, Fr.	58	47.09 N	5.45 E
Dampierre, Château de ⊥	261	48.42 N	1.59 E
Dampierre-en-Burly	50	47.46 N	2.31 E
Dampierre-sur-Linotte	58	47.31 N	6.14 E
Dampierre-sur-Salon	58	47.33 N	5.41 E
Dampier Strait ⊔	164	5.36 S	148.12 E
Dampit	115a	8.13 S	112.45 E
Dampmart	261	48.53 N	2.44 E
Damprichard	58	47.15 N	6.53 E
Dâmrei, Chuŏr Phnum ⋀	110	11.00 N	104.05 E
Damují ≐	240p	22.11 N	80.33 W
Damüls	58	47.17 N	9.53 E
Dāmurhuda	126	23.36 N	88.47 E
Damutougou	98	42.28 N	118.56 E
Damville	50	48.52 N	1.04 E
Damvillers	56	49.20 N	5.24 E
Dan	132	33.14 N	35.39 E
Dan ≐, U.S.	192	36.42 N	78.45 W
Dan ≐, Zhg.	102	33.02 N	111.20 E
Dana, Cam.	146	10.14 N	15.18 E
Dana, In., U.S.	194	39.48 N	87.29 W
Dana, Mount ∧	226	37.54 N	119.13 W
Dana, Pulau I	112	10.50 S	121.16 E
Danahu	102	42.28 N	93.32 E
Danai	112	0.29 N	103.26 E
Danajon Bank ✣4	116	10.16 N	124.17 E
Danakil → Denakil ◆1	144	13.00 N	41.00 E
Danakil National Park ♠	144	10.50 N	40.45 E
Danané	150	7.16 N	8.09 W
Danané □5	150	7.00 N	8.10 W
Da-nang	110	16.04 N	108.13 E
Danan'gou	105	40.32 N	117.49 E
Danao, Pil.	116	10.32 N	124.02 E
Danao, Pil.	116	12.29 N	122.39 E
Dana Point	228	33.29 N	117.44 W
Dana Point ≻	228	33.28 N	117.43 W
Dānāpur	124	25.38 N	85.03 E
Danba	102	31.00 N	101.50 E
Danboro	208	40.21 N	75.08 W
Danbury, Eng., U.K.	260	51.44 N	0.33 E
Danbury, Ct., U.S.	207	41.23 N	73.27 W
Danbury, Ia., U.S.	198	42.14 N	95.43 W
Danbury, Ne., U.S.	198	40.02 N	100.24 W
Danbury, N.C., U.S.	192	36.24 N	80.12 W
Danbury, Tx., U.S.	222	29.14 N	95.21 W
Danby Lake ⊜	204	34.14 N	115.07 W
Dancheng	100	33.39 N	115.11 E
Danchengji	100	33.47 N	116.17 E
Dancug	144	10.58 N	49.04 E
Daṇḍ	120	31.37 N	65.41 E
Dandaragan	162	30.40 S	115.42 E
Dande ≐	152	8.28 S	13.21 E
Dandeldhura	124	29.18 N	80.35 E
Dandeli	122	15.15 N	74.37 E
Dandenong	169	37.59 S	145.12 E
Dandenong, Mount ∧	274b	37.50 S	145.21 E
Dandenong Creek ≐	274b	38.01 S	145.05 E
Danderyd	40	59.25 N	18.01 E
Dandīl	142	29.10 N	31.02 E
Dandong	98	40.08 N	124.20 E
Dandot	123	32.39 N	72.58 E
Dandridge	192	36.00 N	83.24 W
Dan Dume	150	11.27 N	7.10 E
Dane □6	216	43.04 N	89.15 W
Dane ≐	44	53.15 N	2.31 W
Dane County Regional Airport-Truax Field ⊠	216	43.08 N	89.20 W
Dänemark → Denmark □1	26	56.00 N	10.00 E
Dänemark-Strasse → Denmark Strait ⊔	10	67.00 N	25.00 W
Danevang	222	29.03 N	96.13 W
Danewitz	264a	52.44 N	13.40 E
Danfeng	102	33.40 N	110.17 E
Danfengzhen	102	24.50 N	103.56 E
Danforth, Il., U.S.	216	40.49 N	87.59 W
Danforth, Me., U.S.	188	45.39 N	67.52 W
Danforth Hills ⋀	200	40.15 N	108.00 W
Dang ≐	102	40.30 N	94.42 E
Dānga, Bngl.	126	23.54 N	90.36 E
Dānga, India	272b	22.47 N	88.28 E
Danga ≐	271c	1.27 N	103.43 E
Dangādiha	126	21.30 N	86.19 E
Dangan Liedao II	100	22.00 N	114.14 E
Dangara, S.S.S.R.	85	38.06 N	69.22 E
Dangara, S.S.S.R.	85	40.35 N	70.54 E
Dangba	98	40.46 N	118.32 E
Dangchang	102	34.03 N	104.23 E
Dangcheng	98	38.46 N	114.34 E
Dange, Ang.	152	7.56 S	15.02 E
Dange, Ang.	152	8.09 S	14.46 E
Dange, Nig.	150	12.52 N	5.21 E
Dange-lá-Menha	152	9.32 S	14.39 E
Danger, Point ≻	171a	28.10 S	153.33 E
Danger Point ≻	158	34.40 S	19.17 E
Danghe Nanshan ⋀	102	38.53 N	96.11 E
Danghui	105	40.03 N	117.04 E
Dangila	144	11.16 N	36.50 E
Dangkou	106	31.32 N	120.34 E
Dango	140	10.00 N	24.45 E
Dan Gora	150	11.30 N	8.09 E
Dangshan	98	34.26 N	116.21 E
Dangtu	100	31.34 N	118.30 E
Dan Gulbi	150	11.38 N	6.16 E
Dangxiong	120	30.31 N	91.08 E
Dangyang	102	30.50 N	111.38 E
Dangyu	105	40.00 N	118.01 E
Dani	150	13.43 N	0.10 W
Dania	220	26.03 N	80.08 W
Daniel	200	42.51 N	110.04 W
Daniel, Mount ∧	224	47.34 N	121.11 W
Daniel Boone Home ⊥	219	38.39 N	90.52 W
Daniel Boone Homestead State Historic Site ⊥	208	40.21 N	75.49 W
Daniel-Johnson, Barrage ◆6	186	50.39 N	68.44 W
Daniels	284b	39.26 N	77.03 W
Daniel's Harbour	186	50.14 N	57.35 W
Danielskuil	158	28.11 S	23.33 E
Danielson	207	41.48 N	71.53 W
Daniels Pass)(	200	40.18 N	111.15 W
Daniels Run ≐	284c	38.51 N	77.17 W
Danielsville, Ga., U.S.	192	34.07 N	83.13 W
Danielsville, Pa., U.S.	208	40.48 N	75.32 W
Danilov	80	58.12 N	40.12 E
Danilovka, S.S.S.R.	80	52.33 N	45.23 E
Danilovka, S.S.S.R.	80	50.21 N	44.06 E
Danilovka, S.S.S.R.	86	52.23 N	70.39 E
Danilovo	82	55.40 N	38.46 E
Danilovskaja vozvyšennost' ⋀1	80	58.12 N	40.16 E
Danilovskoje	82	56.48 N	35.45 E
Daning, Zhg.	102	24.39 N	111.51 E
Daning, Zhg.	102	36.33 N	110.38 E
Daningbashi	85	38.45 N	75.04 E
Dänisch Nienhof	54	54.28 N	10.07 E
Daniupucun	104	41.23 N	122.37 E
Danja	150	11.21 N	7.31 E
Danjiangkou Shuiku ⊜1	102	32.37 N	111.30 E
Danjo-guntō II	92	32.02 N	128.23 E
Danjoutin	58	47.37 N	6.52 E
Ḍank	128	23.33 N	56.17 E
Dankama	150	13.20 N	7.44 E
Dankersen	52	52.17 N	8.58 E
Danki	82	54.55 N	37.34 E
Dankov	76	53.15 N	39.08 E
Dankova, Pik ∧	85	41.05 N	77.38 E
Danleng, Zhg.	102	29.18 N	103.10 E
Danleng, Zhg.	102	29.58 N	103.31 E
Danleng, Zhg.	107	30.01 N	103.30 E
Danlí	236	14.00 N	86.35 W
Danmark → Denmark □1	26	56.00 N	10.00 E
Dannebrog	198	41.07 N	98.32 W
Dannemare	41	54.45 N	11.12 E
Dannemarie	58	47.38 N	7.08 E
Dannemora, Sve.	40	60.11 N	17.49 E
Dannemora, N.Y., U.S.	188	44.43 N	73.43 W
Dannenberg	54	53.06 N	11.05 E
Dannenreich	264a	52.19 N	13.45 E
Dannenwalde	54	53.04 N	13.11 E
Dannevirke	172	40.12 S	176.07 E
Dannewerk	41	54.29 N	9.31 E
Dannhauser	158	28.04 S	30.04 E
Dano	150	11.09 N	3.04 W
Danompari	112	0.09 N	115.02 E
Dañoso, Cabo ≻	254	48.50 S	67.13 W
Dan Ryan Woods ♠	278	41.45 N	87.39 W
Dan Sai	110	17.17 N	101.09 E
Danshan	107	30.06 N	104.54 E
Danshui	100	22.49 N	114.27 E
Dansville, Mi., U.S.	216	42.34 N	84.18 W
Dansville, N.Y., U.S.	210	42.33 N	77.41 W
Dāntan	126	21.57 N	87.16 E
Dante	192	36.58 N	82.17 W
Dantewāra	122	18.54 N	81.21 E
Dantuzhen	106	32.12 N	119.31 E
Danube ≐	22	45.20 N	29.40 E
Danube, Mouths of the ≐1	38	45.10 N	29.50 E
Danubio → Danube ≐	22	45.20 N	29.40 E
Danubyu	110	17.15 N	95.35 E
Danvers, Il., U.S.	190	40.31 N	89.10 W
Danvers, Ma., U.S.	207	42.34 N	70.55 W
Danvers ≐	283	42.32 N	70.53 W
Danville, P.Q., Can.	206	45.47 N	72.01 W
Danville, Ar., U.S.	194	35.03 N	93.23 W
Danville, Ca., U.S.	226	37.49 N	121.59 W
Danville, Ga., U.S.	192	32.36 N	83.14 W
Danville, Il., U.S.	194	40.07 N	87.37 W
Danville, In., U.S.	218	39.45 N	86.31 W
Danville, Ky., U.S.	194	37.42 N	84.46 W
Danville, Mo., U.S.	219	38.54 N	91.32 W
Danville, Oh., U.S.	214	40.26 N	82.15 W
Danville, Pa., U.S.	210	40.57 N	76.36 W
Danville, Vt., U.S.	188	44.25 N	72.07 W
Danville, Va., U.S.	192	36.35 N	79.23 W
Danville, Wa., U.S.	182	48.59 N	118.30 W
Danxian (Nada)	110	19.35 N	109.17 E
Danyang, Zhg.	100	26.22 N	119.30 E
Danyang, Zhg.	106	32.00 N	119.35 E
Danzig → Gdańsk	30	54.23 N	18.40 E
Dao	116	10.31 N	121.57 E
Dâo ≐, Port.	34	40.20 N	8.11 W
Dao ≐, Zhg.	100	30.44 N	114.39 E
Daocheng	102	29.06 N	100.38 E
Daodemiao	89	43.41 N	120.19 E
Daodi	105	39.32 N	118.11 E
Daoguanhe	100	30.54 N	114.57 E
Daohu	100	29.42 N	117.29 E
Daolazui	105	40.06 N	115.06 E
Daoliban	104	41.52 N	121.37 E
Daolin	100	27.59 N	112.42 E
Daolinggang	98	34.02 N	114.34 E
Daoliupu	107	30.12 N	105.09 E
Daomaguan	98	39.07 N	114.38 E
Daosa	124	26.53 N	76.20 E
Daoshiwu	106	30.18 N	118.57 E
Daoshuqiao	106	31.51 N	119.41 E
Daotiandi	89	48.53 N	130.03 E
Dao Timmi	146	20.32 N	13.33 E
Daotou	98	37.14 N	120.20 E
Daoukro	150	7.03 N	3.58 W
Daoulas	32	48.22 N	4.15 W
Daoura, Oued V	148	28.15 N	3.30 W
Daoxian	102	25.35 N	111.27 E
Daozhen	102	28.42 N	107.56 E
Daozi	89	45.00 N	123.43 E
Dapa	116	9.46 N	126.03 E
Dapango	150	10.52 N	0.12 E
Dapanzhuang	98	37.20 N	115.28 E
Dapaozi	89	45.27 N	122.07 E
Dapchi	146	12.28 N	11.32 E
Dapdap	116	14.14 N	122.15 E
Dapeng	100	22.34 N	114.29 E
Daphne	194	30.36 N	87.54 W
Dapiak, Mount ∧	116	8.15 N	123.28 E
Daping, Zhg.	100	23.11 N	115.49 E
Daping, Zhg.	100	24.24 N	115.58 E
Dapingshan	102	25.30 N	109.39 E
Dapishi	100	26.30 N	112.54 E
Dapitan	116	8.39 N	123.25 E
Dapitan ≐	116	8.38 N	123.25 E
Dapitan Bay c	116	8.40 N	123.23 E
Dapto	170	34.30 S	150.47 E
Dapu, Zhg.	98	40.34 N	124.12 E
Dapu, Zhg.	100	23.16 N	113.32 E
Dapu, Zhg.	106	31.19 N	119.56 E
Dapujie	100	27.01 N	112.46 E
Da Qaidam	102	37.53 N	95.07 E
Da Qaidam Hu ⊜	102	37.50 N	95.00 E
Daqian	106	30.55 N	120.11 E
Daqiangmen	106	31.29 N	120.27 E
Daqiangzi	104	42.21 N	120.29 E
Daqiao, Zhg.	100	29.39 N	121.26 E
Daqiao, Zhg.	100	26.38 N	118.54 E
Daqiao, Zhg.	100	28.11 N	114.16 E
Daqiao, Zhg.	100	32.21 N	119.41 E
Daqiao, Zhg.	100	24.56 N	113.09 E
Daqiao, Zhg.	106	30.59 N	121.14 E
Daqiao, Zhg.	107	28.52 N	105.40 E
Daqiaojie	106	30.46 N	119.14 E
Daqiaokou	100	27.06 N	113.38 E
Daqiaotou	106	30.47 N	120.52 E
Daqiaozhai	102	25.21 N	106.15 E
Daqing	98	39.13 N	118.51 E
Daqing ≐	105	39.04 N	116.55 E
Daqinggou, Zhg.	98	41.16 N	114.10 E
Daqinggou, Zhg.	98	41.12 N	125.07 E
Daqing Shan ∧, Zhg.	89	45.35 N	127.51 E
Daqing Shan ∧, Zhg.	104	42.03 N	123.45 E
Daqing Shan ∧, Zhg.	104	41.47 N	121.15 E
Daqiu	100	25.24 N	119.39 E
Daqqāq	140	12.56 N	26.58 E
Daquan	102	41.21 N	95.17 E
Daquanshan	98	40.14 N	113.47 E
Daquantou	105	39.31 N	114.46 E
Daquanyan	104	42.37 N	123.32 E
Dāqūf	142	28.24 N	30.38 E
Daqu Shan I	100	30.27 N	122.20 E
Dara, Sén.	150	15.21 N	15.29 W
Dar'ā, Sūrīy.	132	32.37 N	36.06 E
Dar'ā □8	132	33.00 N	36.10 E
Dārāb	128	28.45 N	54.34 E
Dārāban	120	31.44 N	70.20 E
Darabani	38	48.11 N	26.35 E
Darāfisah	140	13.23 N	31.59 E
Daraga	116	11.54 N	123.52 E
Daragodleh	144	10.10 N	44.51 E
Daraina	157b	13.12 S	49.40 E
Darājīl	142	30.39 N	30.52 E
Darakeh	267d	35.48 N	51.23 E
Darakht-e Yahyá	120	31.50 N	68.08 E
Daram Island I	116	11.38 N	124.47 E
Dārān	128	32.59 N	50.24 E
Daraoli ◆8	272c	19.11 N	72.48 E
Darap	112	1.13 S	112.03 E
Dār as-Salām	273c	29.59 N	31.13 E
Darasun	88	51.40 N	114.00 E
Daraut-Kurgan	85	39.33 N	72.13 E
Darave	272c	19.02 N	73.01 E
Darāw	140	24.25 N	32.56 E
Darawah	142	30.13 N	31.06 E
Dārayyā	132	33.27 N	36.15 E
Darazo	146	11.00 N	10.24 E
Darb Al-Ḥājj	142	30.10 N	31.33 E
Darb al-Ḥajj, Jabal ∧	132	30.05 N	35.26 E
Darband, Īrān	267d	35.49 N	51.26 E
Darband, Pāk.	123	34.20 N	72.52 E
Darbāsīyah	130	37.04 N	40.39 E
Darbaza	85	41.35 N	69.02 E
Darbėnai	76	56.01 N	21.15 E
Dar-Beni-Kriche-Bahri	34	35.30 N	5.20 W
Darbhanga	124	26.10 N	85.54 E
Darbhanga □5	124	26.00 N	86.00 E
Darbod (Taikang)	89	46.52 N	124.27 E
D'Arbonne, Bayou ≐	194	32.34 N	92.09 W
Darburruk	144	9.44 N	44.31 E
Darby, Mt., U.S.	202	46.01 N	114.10 W
Darby, Pa., U.S.	208	39.55 N	75.15 W
Darby, Cape ≻	180	64.20 N	162.22 W
Darby Creek ≐	285	39.52 N	75.18 W
Darbydale	218	39.51 N	83.11 W
Darčeli	84	42.27 N	41.42 E
Darchan	88	49.29 N	105.55 E
D'Archiac, Mount ∧	172	43.28 S	170.35 E
D'Arcy	182	50.33 N	122.29 W
D'Arcy Island I	224	48.34 N	123.17 W
Darda	38	45.37 N	18.41 E
Dardadine	168a	33.14 S	116.50 E
Dardanelle, Ar., U.S.	194	35.13 N	93.09 W
Dardanelle, Ca., U.S.	226	38.20 N	119.50 W
Dardanelle Lake ⊜1	194	35.25 N	93.20 W
Dardanelles → Çanakkale Boğazı ⊔	130	40.15 N	26.25 E
Dardanup	168a	33.24 S	115.45 E
Dardara	34	35.08 N	5.15 W

Symbols in the index entries represent the broad categories identified in the key at the right. Symbols with superior numbers (⋀1) identify subcategories (see complete key on page *I · 1).*

Kartensymbole in dem Registerverzeichnis stellen die rechts in Schlüssel erklärten Kategorien dar. Symbole mit hochgestellten Ziffern (⋀1) bezeichnen Unterabteilungen einer Kategorie (vgl. vollständiger Schlüssel auf Seite *I · 1).*

Los símbolos incluídos en el texto del índice representan las grandes categorias identificadas con la clave a la derecha. Los símbolos con numeros en su parte superior (⋀1) identifican las subcategorías (véase la clave completa en la página *I · 1).*

Les symboles de l'index représentent les catégories indiquées dans la légende à droite. Les symboles suivis d'un indice (⋀1) représentent des sous-catégories (voir légende complète à la page *I · 1).*

Os símbolos incluídos no texto do índice representam as grandes categorias identificadas com a chave à direita. Os símbolos com números em sua parte superior (⋀1) identificam as subcategorias (veja-se a chave completa à página *I · 1).*

∧ Mountain	Berg	Montaña	Montagne	Montanha
⋀ Mountains	Berge	Montañas	Montagnes	Montanhas
)(Pass	Pass	Paso	Col	Passo
V Valley, Canyon	Tal, Cañon	Valle, Cañón	Vallée, Canyon	Vale, Canhão
≚ Plain	Ebene	Llano	Plaine	Planície
≻ Cape	Kap	Cabo	Cap	Cabo
I Island	Insel	Isla	Île	Ilha
II Islands	Inseln	Islas	Îles	Ilhas
⊥ Other Topographic Features	Andere Topographische Objekte	Otros Elementos Topográficos	Autres données topographiques	Outros acidentes topográficos

ESPAÑOL — Nombre | Página | Lat.°′ | Long.°′ W = Oeste
FRANÇAIS — Nom | Page | Lat.°′ | Long.°′ W = Ouest
PORTUGUÊS — Nome | Página | Lat.°′ | Long.°′ W = Oeste

Nombre / Nom / Nome	Página / Page	Lat.°′	Long.°′
Dardenelles Cone ∧	226	38.25 N	119.53 W
Dardenne Creek ≃	219	38.52 N	90.32 W
Dardesheim	54	51.59 N	10.49 E
Dardistān □9	123	35.30 N	74.00 E
Dare	208	37.10 N	76.26 W
Darebin Creek ≃	274b	37.47 S	145.02 E
Dareda	154	4.13 S	35.33 E
Dar-el-Beida → Casablanca	148	33.39 N	7.35 W
Darende	130	38.34 N	37.30 E
Darent ≃	260	51.28 N	0.13 E
Daresbury	262	53.21 N	2.38 W
Dar es Salaam	154	6.48 S	39.17 E
Dar-Es-Salaam □4	154	6.30 S	39.25 E
Daressalam → Dar es Salaam	154	6.48 S	39.17 E
Darfeld	52	52.01 N	7.16 E
Darfo	64	45.53 N	10.11 E
Dārfūr ash-Shamālīyah □4	140	16.00 N	25.25 E
Dargai	123	34.11 N	71.53 E
Dargan-Ata	72	40.29 N	62.10 E
Dargaville	172	35.56 S	173.53 E
Dargol	150	13.55 N	1.15 E
Dargol ≃	150	13.53 N	1.33 E
Dargun	54	53.54 N	12.51 E
Darhan Muminggan Lianheqi	102	41.50 N	110.27 E
Dari	140	5.48 N	30.21 E
Dāriāpur	126	23.36 N	89.27 E
Darıca	130	40.45 N	29.23 E
Darie Hills ⋏	144	8.21 N	47.16 E
Darién, Col.	246	3.56 N	76.31 W
Darien, Ct., U.S.	207	41.04 N	73.28 W
Darien, Ga., U.S.	192	31.22 N	81.26 W
Darien, N.Y., U.S.	210	42.54 N	78.21 W
Darien, Wi., U.S.	216	42.36 N	88.42 W
Darién, Serranía del ⋏	246	8.20 N	77.22 W
Darien Center	210	42.54 N	78.23 W
Darien Lakes State Park ♠	210	42.55 N	78.25 W
Dariense, Cordillera ⋏	236	12.55 N	85.30 W
Dariganga	102	45.18 N	113.52 E
Darigayos Point >	116	16.50 N	120.20 E
Dariv	88	46.57 N	93.38 E
Darjeeling	124	27.02 N	88.16 E
Darjeeling □5	124	26.50 N	88.20 E
Darjevka	83	47.42 N	39.41 E
Darjinskij	86	49.04 N	72.56 E
Darjinskoje	80	51.20 N	51.44 E
Darkan	168a	33.20 S	116.44 E
Darke □6	218	40.06 N	84.38 W
Darke Peak	166	33.28 S	136.12 E
Darkhāna	123	30.39 N	72.11 E
Darkhazīneh	128	31.54 N	48.59 E
Dark Head >	241h	13.17 N	61.16 W
Darkin ≃	168a	32.00 S	116.14 E
Darkūsh	130	35.59 N	36.23 E
Darlag	102	33.48 N	99.52 E
Darlaston	42	52.34 N	2.02 W
Darley Woods	285	39.49 N	75.28 W
Darling, S. Afr.	158	33.23 S	18.23 E
Darling, Ms., U.S.	194	34.21 N	90.16 W
Darling ≃	166	34.07 S	141.55 E
Darling, Lake ⊜1	198	48.35 N	101.40 W
Darling Downs ◆1	166	27.30 S	150.30 E
Darlingford	184	49.12 N	98.22 W
Darling Range ⋏	162	31.25 S	116.00 E
Darlington, Austl.	168a	31.55 S	116.05 E
Darlington, Austl.	169	38.00 S	143.03 E
Darlington, Eng., U.K.	44	54.31 N	1.34 W
Darlington, Md., U.S.	208	39.38 N	76.12 W
Darlington, Pa., U.S.	214	40.49 N	80.26 W
Darlington, Pa., U.S.	285	39.54 N	75.28 W
Darlington, S.C., U.S.	192	34.17 N	79.52 W
Darlington, Wi., U.S.	190	42.40 N	90.07 W
Darlington Brook ≃	276	41.05 N	74.11 W
Darlington Corners	285	39.55 N	75.34 W
Darlington Range ⋏	171a	27.50 S	153.15 E
Darlot, Lake ⊜	162	27.48 S	121.35 E
Darłowo	30	54.26 N	16.23 E
Darmstadt	56	49.53 N	8.40 E
Darmstadt □5	56	49.45 N	8.40 E
Darnah	146	32.46 N	22.39 E
Darnall	158	29.23 S	31.18 E
Darnétal	50	49.27 N	1.09 E
Darney	58	48.05 N	6.03 E
Darnick	166	32.51 S	143.37 E
Darnley, Cape >	9	67.43 S	69.30 E
Darnley Bay c	176	69.35 N	123.30 W
Daroca	34	41.07 N	1.25 W
Darodih	126	23.14 N	86.27 E
Daror	144	8.14 N	44.42 E
Dar-Ould-Zidouh	148	32.22 N	6.49 W
Darou Mousti	150	15.03 N	16.03 W
Darovoje	82	54.34 N	38.22 E
Darr ≃	166	23.39 S	143.50 E
Darra	171a	27.34 S	152.58 E
Darragh	279b	40.16 N	79.41 W
Darrah, Mount ∧	182	49.28 N	114.35 W
Darrang □5	124	25.30 N	89.30 E
Darregueira	252	37.42 S	63.10 W
Darreh Gaz	128	37.27 N	59.07 E
Darrington	224	48.15 N	121.36 W
Darrouzett	196	36.27 N	100.20 W
Darryl Gardens	284b	39.25 N	76.25 W
Dārsana	126	23.32 N	88.52 E
Darscheid	56	50.12 N	6.53 E
Darss >1	54	54.25 N	12.31 E
Darsser Ort >	54	54.29 N	12.31 E
Dart ≃	42	50.20 N	3.33 W
Dart, Cape >	9	73.06 S	126.20 W
Dār Ta'izzah	130	36.17 N	36.51 E
Dartford	260	51.27 N	0.14 E
Dartford □8	260	51.26 N	0.15 E
Dartford Tunnel ◆5	260	51.28 N	0.16 E
Dartmoor	166	37.55 S	141.17 E
Dartmoor ◆3	42	50.35 N	4.00 W
Dartmoor National Park ♠	42	50.37 N	3.52 W
Dartmouth, N.S., Can.	186	44.40 N	63.34 W
Dartmouth, Eng., U.K.	42	50.21 N	3.35 W
Dartmouth ≃	186	48.53 N	64.34 W
Dartmouth, Lake ⊜	166	26.04 S	145.18 E
Dartmouth Woods	285	39.50 N	75.31 W
Darton	44	53.36 N	1.32 W
Dartuch, Cabo >	34	39.56 N	3.48 E
Daru, Pap. N. Gui.	164	9.04 S	143.21 E
Daru, S.L.	150	7.59 N	10.50 W
Daruvar	36	45.36 N	17.13 E
Darvaza	128	40.11 N	58.24 E
Darvāzahgêy	120	31.48 N	67.44 E
Darvazskij chrebet ⋏	85	38.30 N	71.15 E
Darvel	46	55.37 N	4.18 W
Darvel, Teluk c	112	4.50 N	118.30 E
Darvinskij Zapovednik ◆4	76	58.50 N	37.40 E
Darwen	262	53.42 N	2.28 W
Darwen ≃	262	53.45 N	2.41 W
Darwendale	154	17.43 S	30.33 E
Dārwha	122	20.19 N	77.46 E
Darwin, Arg.	254	39.12 S	65.46 W
Darwin, Austl.	164	12.28 S	130.50 E
Darwin, Bahía c	254	45.27 S	74.40 W
Darwin, Cordillera ⋏	254	54.40 S	70.00 W
Darwin, Isla I	246a	1.39 N	92.00 W
Darwin, Volcán ∧1	246a	0.10 S	91.18 W
Darwin River	164	12.49 S	130.58 E
Daryābād	124	26.53 N	81.33 E
Darya Khān	123	31.48 N	71.06 E
Daryāpur	120	20.56 N	77.20 E
Darz Āb	120	35.58 N	65.22 E
Darzo	64	45.51 N	10.33 E
Dār Zubi	140	13.07 N	23.40 E
Dās	123	35.05 N	75.05 E
Dās I	128	25.09 N	52.53 E
Dasāda	120	23.19 N	71.50 E
Dasanjiazi	104	42.31 N	122.54 E
Dašava	78	49.16 N	24.01 E
Daš Balbar	88	49.31 N	114.21 E
Dasburg	56	50.03 N	6.07 E
Dase → Dese	144	11.05 N	39.41 E
Dašev	78	49.00 N	29.26 E
Dasha ≃	98	38.20 N	115.22 E
Dashafa	105	39.19 N	116.19 E
Dashalitu	104	42.31 N	122.30 E
Dashan	98	38.02 N	117.39 E
Dashankou	105	40.17 N	115.49 E
Dashanpu	107	29.25 N	104.49 E
Dashaping	100	29.24 N	113.51 E
Dashengfenchang	106	31.53 N	121.34 E
Dashengpu	104	41.13 N	121.02 E
Dashentang	105	39.13 N	117.56 E
Dashetai	102	40.58 N	109.19 E
Dashi	107	30.39 N	105.37 E
Dashi ≃	105	39.35 N	116.05 E
Dashields Dam ◆6	214	40.33 N	80.12 W
Dashiqiao, Zhg.	100	33.57 N	113.53 E
Dashiqiao, Zhg.	104	41.52 N	123.17 E
Dashiqiao, Zhg.	107	30.07 N	106.12 E
Dashiqiao, Zhg.	107	30.28 N	106.29 E
Dashitou, Zhg.	89	43.19 N	128.28 E
Dashitou, Zhg.	102	42.49 N	95.19 E
Dashizhai	89	46.16 N	121.25 E
Dashlūṭ	142	27.34 N	30.42 E
Dash Point	224	47.19 N	122.26 W
Dasht ≃	128	25.10 N	61.40 E
Dasht-e Āzādegān (Sūsangerd)	128	31.34 N	48.11 E
Dashtīārī ≃	128	25.09 N	61.32 E
Dashu	106	31.13 N	120.56 E
Dashun	100	28.06 N	119.52 E
Dashutang	102	23.00 N	103.55 E
Dashuwan	105	40.37 N	117.19 E
Dasi (Huangfansi)	102	38.15 N	100.22 E
Dasiji	100	33.48 N	115.55 E
Dašinčilen	88	47.51 N	104.03 E
Dasing	60	48.23 N	11.03 E
Dasizhan	89	45.53 N	130.24 E
Daska	123	32.20 N	74.21 E
Daškesan	84	40.30 N	46.04 E
Daskop	158	33.44 S	22.43 E
Daškovka	76	53.44 N	30.13 E
Dasmina	126	22.17 N	90.35 E
Dasol	116	15.59 N	119.52 E
Dasol Bay c	116	15.53 N	119.51 E
Daspalla	120	20.21 N	84.51 E
Dassalan Island I	116	6.45 N	121.28 E
Dassel, B.R.D.	52	51.48 N	9.41 E
Dassel, Mn., U.S.	190	45.04 N	94.18 W
Dasseneiland I	158	33.26 S	18.04 E
Dasserat, Lac ⊜	190	48.16 N	79.25 W
Dassiefontein	158	31.35 S	24.25 E
Dassow	54	53.50 N	10.59 E
Dasswang	60	49.09 N	11.40 E
Dastakert	84	39.23 N	46.02 E
Dastgardān	128	34.19 N	56.51 E
Daštidžum	85	38.01 N	70.12 E
Daštioburdon	85	39.24 N	69.04 E
Dastjerd	128	34.33 N	50.15 E
Dāsuria	126	24.07 N	89.08 E
Dasūya	123	31.49 N	75.38 E
Datachang	107	28.55 N	104.21 E
Datagenoyang	112	2.03 N	115.10 E
Datai	105	39.58 N	115.54 E
Dataizi	104	41.17 N	121.46 E
Datan, Zhg.	98	41.35 N	116.00 E
Datan, Zhg.	98	39.31 N	122.11 E
Datang, Zhg.	100	24.47 N	113.43 E
Datang, Zhg.	100	25.17 N	114.56 E
Datang, Zhg.	102	22.23 N	108.23 E
Datang, Zhg.	102	24.11 N	109.00 E
Datça	130	36.45 N	27.40 E
Datchet	260	51.29 N	0.34 W
Datchet Reservoir ⊜1	260	51.29 N	0.33 W
Date	92a	42.27 N	140.51 E
Date Creek ≃	200	34.13 N	113.29 W
Datia	124	25.40 N	78.28 E
Datia □5	124	25.50 N	78.30 E
Datian, Zhg.	100	25.42 N	117.49 E
Datian, Zhg.	100	24.06 N	116.19 E
Datian Ding ∧	102	22.17 N	111.13 E
Datianwei	100	25.54 N	115.10 E
Dativli	272c	19.11 N	73.03 E
D'at'kovo	76	53.36 N	34.20 E
D'atloviči	76	52.20 N	26.50 E
D'atlovo, S.S.S.R.	76	53.28 N	25.24 E
D'atlovo, S.S.S.R.	82	56.14 N	36.16 E
Datong, Zhg.	89	46.03 N	124.50 E
Datong, Zhg.	100	30.48 N	117.45 E
Datong, Zhg.	100	32.50 N	118.52 E
Datong, Zhg.	102	37.03 N	101.45 E
Datong, Zhg.	102	40.05 N	113.18 E
Datong ≃	102	36.20 N	102.55 E
Datong Shan ⋏	102	38.00 N	99.30 E
Datongzhen	106	32.12 N	121.19 E
Datoushan	98	41.50 N	117.08 E
Dātra	272b	22.58 N	88.16 E
Datta	89	49.18 N	140.22 E
Dattapāra	126	23.01 N	90.53 E
Dattapukur	126	22.45 N	88.33 E
Dattapulia	126	23.14 N	88.43 E
Datteln	52	51.40 N	7.23 E
Datteln-Hamm-Kanal ≅	263	51.39 N	7.21 E
Dattilo	70	37.58 N	12.39 E
Datu, Tanjung >	112	2.06 N	109.39 E
Datuan	106	30.58 N	121.44 E
Datumakuta	112	2.32 N	117.51 E
Datun, Zhg.	89	43.49 N	125.12 E
Datun, Zhg.	98	40.37 N	119.57 E
Datun, Zhg.	104	40.59 N	122.55 E
Datuopu	100	28.03 N	112.58 E
Datu Piang	116	7.01 N	124.30 E
Daua (Dawa) ≃	144	4.11 N	42.06 E
Daudkāndi	126	23.32 N	90.43 E
Dāūd Khel	123	32.53 N	71.34 E
Daudnagar	124	25.02 N	84.24 E
Daugai	76	54.22 N	24.20 E
Daugård	41	55.44 N	9.43 E
Daugava (Zapadnaja Dvina) ≃	76	57.04 N	24.03 E
Daugavpils	76	55.53 N	26.32 E
Dauin	116	9.12 N	123.16 E
Daulatābād (Shirin Tagāo), Afg.	120	36.26 N	64.55 E
Daulatabad, India	126	24.08 N	88.22 E
Daulatkhan	126	22.38 N	90.49 E
Daulatpur, Bngl.	126	24.00 N	88.52 E
Daulatpur, Bngl.	126	22.53 N	89.31 E
Daulatpur (Ramchandrapur), Bngl.	126	23.58 N	89.50 E
Daulatpur, India	272b	22.26 N	88.18 E
Daulatpur, Pāk.	120	26.30 N	67.58 E
Daulatpur ◆8	272a	28.44 N	77.06 E
Daule, Ec.	246	0.24 N	80.00 W
Daule, Ec.	246	1.50 S	79.56 W
Daule, India	272c	19.10 N	73.03 E
Daule ≃	246	2.10 S	79.52 W
Daultāla	123	33.12 N	73.09 E
Daulton Creek ≃	226	37.04 N	119.59 W
Daun	56	50.11 N	6.50 E
Daund	122	18.28 N	74.36 E
Daung Kyun I	110	12.14 N	98.05 E
Daunia, Monti della ⋏	68	41.27 N	15.06 E
Dauphin, Mb., Can.	184	51.09 N	100.03 W
Dauphin, Pa., U.S.	208	40.22 N	76.55 W
Dauphin □6	208	40.15 N	76.52 W
Dauphin ≃	184	51.58 N	98.04 W
Dauphiné □9	62	44.50 N	6.00 E
Dauphin Island	194	30.15 N	88.07 W
Dauphin Island I	194	30.14 N	88.12 W
Dauphin Lake ⊜	184	51.17 N	99.48 W
Daura	150	13.02 N	8.21 E
Daurija	88	49.56 N	116.52 E
Daurskoje	86	55.14 N	92.05 E
Dausenau	56	50.20 N	7.45 E
D'Auteuil, Lac ⊜	186	50.38 N	61.17 W
Dautphetal	56	50.51 N	8.32 E
Dāvangere	122	14.28 N	75.55 E
Davant	194	29.37 N	89.51 W
Davao	116	7.04 N	125.36 E
Davao □4	116	7.40 N	125.50 E
Davao ≃	116	7.04 N	125.37 E
Davao del Sur □4	116	6.50 N	125.20 E
Davao Gulf c	116	6.40 N	125.55 E
Davao Oriental □4	116	7.30 N	126.30 E
Dāvar Panāh	128	27.21 N	62.21 E
Dāvarzan	128	36.23 N	56.50 E
Davegoriale	144	8.45 N	44.50 E
Davel	158	26.24 S	29.40 E
Daveluyville	206	46.12 N	72.08 W
Davenda	88	53.33 N	119.18 E
Davenham	262	53.14 N	2.31 W
Davenport, Ca., U.S.	226	37.00 N	122.11 W
Davenport, Fl., U.S.	220	28.09 N	81.36 W
Davenport, Ia., U.S.	190	41.31 N	90.34 W
Davenport, Ne., U.S.	198	40.18 N	97.48 W
Davenport, N.Y., U.S.	210	42.28 N	74.51 W
Davenport, Ok., U.S.	196	35.42 N	96.45 W
Davenport, Wa., U.S.	202	47.39 N	118.08 W
Davenport, Mount ∧	162	22.23 S	130.51 E
Davenport Downs	166	24.08 S	141.07 E
Davenport Range ⋏	162	20.47 S	134.48 E
Daventry	42	52.16 N	1.09 W
Davey, Port c	166	43.19 S	145.55 E
Daveyton	273d	26.09 S	28.25 E
David	236	8.26 N	82.26 W
David City	198	41.15 N	97.07 W
David-Gorodok	78	52.03 N	27.14 E
Davido-Nikol'skoje	83	48.30 N	39.50 E
David Point >	241k	12.14 N	61.39 W
Davids Island I	276	40.53 N	73.46 W
Davidson, Sk., Can.	184	51.16 N	105.59 W
Davidson, N.C., U.S.	192	35.29 N	80.50 W
Davidson, Ok., U.S.	196	34.14 N	99.04 W
Davidson Creek ≃	222	30.21 N	96.27 W
Davidson Heights	214	40.35 N	80.15 W
Davidson Lake ⊜	184	53.47 N	99.37 W
Davidson Mountains ⋏	180	68.45 N	142.10 W
Davidson Park ♠	274a	33.45 S	151.12 E
Davidsville	214	40.14 N	78.56 W
Davie	220	26.03 N	80.13 W
Davies, Mount ∧	162	26.14 S	129.16 E
Davignab	158	27.32 S	19.48 E
Davila	116	18.29 N	120.35 E
Davilla	222	30.47 N	97.17 W
Davington	44	55.18 N	3.12 W
Davin Lake ⊜	184	56.50 N	103.40 W
Davinópolis	255	15.58 S	50.08 W
Daviot	46	57.25 N	4.08 W
Davis, Ca., U.S.	226	38.32 N	121.44 W
Davis, N.C., U.S.	192	34.47 N	76.27 W
Davis, Ok., U.S.	196	34.30 N	97.07 W
Davis, W.V., U.S.	188	39.07 N	79.27 W
Davis ≃	162	21.42 S	121.05 E
Davis ʋ3	9	68.35 S	77.58 E
Davis, Mount ∧	188	39.47 N	79.10 W
Davis Bay c	9	66.08 S	134.05 E
Davisboro	192	32.58 N	82.36 W
Davisburg	216	42.45 N	83.33 W
Davis City	190	40.38 N	93.48 W
Davis Cove	186	47.40 N	54.18 W
Davis Creek ≃, Mi., U.S.	281	42.27 N	83.43 W
Davis Creek ≃, Mo., U.S.	219	39.12 N	91.53 W
Davis Dam	200	35.10 N	114.33 W
Davis Dam ◆6	200	35.11 N	114.21 W
Davis Island I	279b	40.29 N	80.05 W
Davis Lake ⊜	278	42.16 N	88.05 W
Davis-Monthan Air Force Base ■	200	32.11 N	110.53 W
Davis Mountains ⋏	196	30.35 N	104.00 W
Davison	216	43.02 N	83.31 W
Davis Park	210	40.42 N	72.59 W
Davis Point >	282	38.03 N	122.15 W
Davis Sea ⍑2	9	66.00 S	92.00 E
Davis Strait ⟗	176	67.00 N	57.00 W
Davlekanovo	86	54.13 N	55.03 E
Davo ≃	150	5.00 N	6.08 W
Davoli	68	38.39 N	16.29 E
Davos	58	46.48 N	9.50 E
Davron	261	48.52 N	1.57 E
Davst	86	50.36 N	92.28 E
Davulga	130	38.58 N	31.23 E
Davutlar	130	37.43 N	27.17 E
Davy	192	37.28 N	81.39 W
Davydkovo, S.S.S.R.	82	56.17 N	36.49 E
Davydkovo, S.S.S.R.	265b	55.35 N	37.12 E
Davydov, gora ∧	88	52.34 N	107.25 E
Davydov Brod	78	47.14 N	33.12 E
Davydovka	78	51.10 N	39.25 E
Davydovo	82	55.37 N	38.52 E
Davydovskoje	82	55.52 N	36.48 E
Davyhulme	262	53.27 N	2.22 W
Dawa, Zhg.	104	41.00 N	122.03 E
Dawa, Zhg.	104	41.54 N	123.32 E
Dawa (Daua) ≃	144	4.11 N	42.06 E
Dawaki	150	12.06 N	8.20 E
Dawan	102	23.52 N	109.29 E
Dawang	98	36.58 N	118.31 E
Dawangcun	106	30.45 N	118.59 E
Dawangdian	105	39.04 N	115.26 E
Dawangdong	105	38.53 N	116.21 E
Dawangjia Dao I	98	39.27 N	123.07 E
Dawangsangou	104	41.43 N	121.36 E
Dawangzhai	269b	31.22 N	121.25 E
Dawangzhuang, Zhg.	105	39.23 N	116.28 E
Dawangzhuang, Zhg.	105	38.59 N	115.56 E
Dawāsir, Wādī ad- V	144	20.24 N	46.29 E
Dawatun	104	41.05 N	121.01 E
Daweizhuang	105	39.34 N	116.53 E
Daweizigou	104	42.38 N	123.09 E
Dawen ≃	98	35.38 N	116.24 E
Dawenkou	98	35.59 N	117.07 E
Dawera, Pulau I	164	7.44 S	130.00 E
Dawes Park ♠	278	42.03 N	87.40 W
Dawlan	110	16.44 N	98.01 E
Dawlish	42	50.35 N	3.28 W
Dawn	208	37.50 N	77.22 W
Dawna Range ⋏	110	16.50 N	98.15 E
Dawqah	144	19.36 N	40.54 E
Dawrah	140	12.22 N	24.19 E
Daws Heath	260	51.34 N	0.37 E
Dawson, Yk., Can.	180	64.04 N	139.25 W
Dawson, Ga., U.S.	192	31.46 N	84.26 W
Dawson, Il., U.S.	219	39.51 N	89.28 W
Dawson, Mn., U.S.	198	44.55 N	96.03 W
Dawson, Ne., U.S.	198	40.07 N	95.49 W
Dawson, Tx., U.S.	222	31.53 N	96.42 W
Dawson ≃	166	23.38 S	149.46 E
Dawson, Isla I	254	53.55 S	70.45 W
Dawson, Mount ∧	182	51.09 N	117.25 W
Dawson Bay c	184	52.55 N	100.50 W
Dawson Creek	182	55.46 N	120.14 W
Dawson Inlet c	176	61.50 N	93.25 W
Dawson-Lambton Glacier ⩩	9	76.15 S	27.30 W
Dawson Range ⋏, Austl.	166	24.20 S	149.45 E
Dawson Range ⋏, Yk., Can.	180	62.40 N	139.00 W
Dawson Ridge	214	40.42 N	80.22 W
Dawson Springs	194	37.10 N	87.41 W
Dawsonville	192	34.25 N	84.07 W
Dawu, Zhg.	100	31.34 N	114.06 E
Dawu, Zhg.	102	31.07 N	101.08 E
Dawudapu	104	41.36 N	123.03 E
Dawuji	271a	39.51 N	116.30 E
Dawujiawopeng	104	41.55 N	122.29 E
Dawujiazi	104	42.16 N	121.52 E
Dawulaba	104	42.13 N	122.23 E
Dawulah	104	41.56 N	121.05 E
Dax	32	43.43 N	1.03 W
Daxian	102	31.18 N	107.30 E
Daxin, Zhg.	100	33.54 N	118.30 E
Daxin, Zhg.	102	22.50 N	107.26 E
Daxing, Zhg.	98	39.44 N	116.20 E
Daxing (Huangcun), Zhg.	105	39.44 N	116.20 E
Daxing, Zhg.	106	31.50 N	121.40 E
Daxingchang	107	30.17 N	103.26 E
Daxingcun	106	31.45 N	121.40 E
Daxingzhai	102	23.13 N	102.21 E
Daxinji	100	34.03 N	119.28 E
Daxinzhuang, Zhg.	105	40.23 N	116.44 E
Daxinzhuang, Zhg.	105	39.26 N	118.20 E
Daxiyang	106	30.21 N	121.58 E
Daxu, Zhg.	100	29.32 N	121.52 E
Daxu, Zhg.	102	25.09 N	110.21 E
Daxue Shan ⋏	102	30.10 N	101.50 E
Daxujia	98	34.18 N	117.34 E
Dayakou	102	22.46 N	100.18 E
Dayanchi	102	27.41 N	101.55 E
Dayang, Zhg.	98	36.04 N	116.31 E
Dayang, Zhg.	100	25.56 N	118.48 E
Dayang ≃	98	39.54 N	123.40 E
Dayangcha	98	42.04 N	126.43 E
Dayanggou	104	41.14 N	123.51 E
Dayang Shan I	106	30.35 N	122.00 E
Dayangshu	89	49.45 N	124.35 E
Dayaniguas, Ensenada de c	240p	22.20 N	83.15 W
Dayao, Zhg.	100	27.59 N	113.42 E
Dayao, Zhg.	102	25.43 N	101.13 E
Dayaoshan	102	24.05 N	110.17 E
Daya Wan c	100	22.37 N	114.40 E
Dayboro	171a	27.11 S	152.50 E
Daye	100	30.06 N	114.57 E
Dayghar	272c	19.09 N	73.03 E
Day Heights	218	39.11 N	84.14 W
Dayi	107	30.37 N	103.31 E
Dayiji	100	32.32 N	119.14 E
Daying, Zhg.	98	39.53 N	123.07 E
Daying, Zhg.	98	39.19 N	113.46 E
Daying, Zhg.	98	34.27 N	113.59 E
Daying, Zhg.	98	37.19 N	115.43 E
Daying, Zhg.	100	33.59 N	112.51 E
Daying, Zhg.	105	39.05 N	116.06 E
Daying (Taping) ≃	102	24.17 N	97.14 E
Dayingzi, Zhg.	98	41.19 N	118.19 E
Dayingzi, Zhg.	98	41.28 N	120.21 E
Dayingzi, Zhg.	104	41.08 N	122.50 E
Dayiqiao	106	31.44 N	120.45 E
Day Island	224	47.15 N	122.33 W
Day Lake ⊜	224	48.23 N	121.58 W
Daylesford	169	37.21 S	144.09 E
Daymán ≃	252	31.30 S	58.02 W
Daym Zubayr	140	7.43 N	26.13 E
Dayong, Zhg.	100	22.28 N	113.16 E
Dayong, Zhg.	102	29.06 N	110.29 E
Dayou	98	34.12 N	119.52 E
Dayr, Jabal ad- ∧	140	12.27 N	30.42 E
Dayr Abū Sa'īd	132	32.30 N	35.41 E
Dayr al-'Ashā'ir	132	33.32 N	36.01 E
Dayr al-Balaḥ	132	31.25 N	34.21 E
Dayr al-Ghuṣūn	132	32.21 N	35.05 E
Dayr 'Alī	132	33.17 N	36.18 E
Dayr 'Allā	132	32.12 N	35.37 E
Dayr 'Aṭīyah	130	34.06 N	36.46 E
Dayr az-Zawr	130	35.20 N	40.09 E
Dayr az-Zawr □8	130	35.30 N	39.00 E
Dayr Dibwān	132	31.55 N	35.16 E
Dayr Ḥāfir	130	36.09 N	37.42 E
Dayrīk	130	37.10 N	42.08 E
Dayr Jabal Aṭ-Ṭayr	142	28.17 N	30.45 E
Dayr Mawās	142	27.38 N	30.51 E
Dayr Qānūn	132	33.36 N	36.08 E
Dayr Sharaf	132	32.15 N	35.11 E
Dayrūṭ, Miṣr	142	27.33 N	30.49 E
Dayrūṭ, Miṣr	142	31.13 N	30.30 E
Dayrūṭ ash-Sharīf	142	27.35 N	30.49 E
Days Island I	284b	39.24 N	76.22 W
Daysland	182	52.52 N	112.15 W
Day Star Indian Reserve ◆4	184	51.43 N	104.14 W
Dayton, Il., U.S.	216	41.23 N	88.47 W
Dayton, In., U.S.	216	40.22 N	86.46 W
Dayton, Ia., U.S.	190	42.15 N	94.04 W
Dayton, Ky., U.S.	218	39.06 N	84.28 W
Dayton, Mi., U.S.	216	41.48 N	86.26 W
Dayton, Nv., U.S.	226	39.14 N	119.35 W
Dayton, N.J., U.S.	276	40.22 N	74.30 W
Dayton, N.Y., U.S.	210	42.25 N	78.58 W
Dayton, Oh., U.S.	218	39.45 N	84.11 W
Dayton, Or., U.S.	224	45.13 N	123.04 W
Dayton, Pa., U.S.	214	40.52 N	79.14 W
Dayton, Tn., U.S.	194	35.29 N	85.00 W
Dayton, Tx., U.S.	222	30.02 N	94.53 W
Dayton, Va., U.S.	188	38.24 N	78.56 W
Dayton, Wa., U.S.	202	46.19 N	117.58 W
Dayton, Wy., U.S.	202	44.52 N	107.15 W
Daytona Beach	192	29.12 N	81.01 W
Dayton Municipal Airport ⊠	218	39.54 N	84.13 W
Dayu, Indon.	112	1.59 S	115.04 E
Dayu, Zhg.	100	25.24 N	114.22 E
Dayuba	107	29.15 N	103.34 E
Dayu Ling ⋏	100	25.20 N	114.16 E
Da Yunhe (Grand Canal) ≅	90	32.12 N	119.31 E
Dayu Shan I, Zhg.	100	26.57 N	120.21 E
Dayu Shan I, Zhg.	106	30.19 N	121.58 E
Dayushupu	104	41.32 N	121.24 E
Dayville, Ct., U.S.	207	41.50 N	71.53 W
Dayville, Or., U.S.	202	44.28 N	119.32 W
Dazaifu ⊥	96	33.31 N	130.31 E
Dazaoliyingzi	104	42.07 N	121.20 E
Dazaomiao	106	32.06 N	121.29 E
Dazhang ≃	100	25.56 N	119.12 E
Dazhangzi	98	40.38 N	118.07 E
Dazhaotai	104	41.14 N	123.03 E
Dazhengjiatun	98	39.37 N	122.52 E
Dazhengzhuangzi	105	39.16 N	116.46 E
Dazhi	100	34.29 N	113.17 E
Dazhiba	102	27.09 N	99.52 E
Dazhifang	104	41.21 N	123.12 E
Dazhou	100	28.53 N	118.58 E
Dazhu	102	30.48 N	107.12 E
Dazhuangke	105	40.32 N	115.42 E
Dazhubao	107	28.59 N	103.38 E
Dazhuyuan	100	23.43 N	115.57 E
Dazifangshen	104	42.27 N	124.12 E
Daziling	104	41.21 N	121.26 E
Daziying	104	41.42 N	123.36 E
Dazkırı	130	37.55 N	29.52 E
Dazu	107	29.43 N	105.42 E
Dazui	100	30.16 N	114.02 E
De Aar	158	30.39 S	24.00 E
Dead ≃, Me., U.S.	188	45.20 N	69.58 W
Dead ≃, Mi., U.S.	190	46.34 N	87.24 W
Dead ≃, N.J., U.S.	276	40.39 N	74.31 W
Deadhorse	180	70.11 N	148.27 W
Dead Horse Point State Park ♠	200	38.28 N	109.44 W
Deadman ≃	182	50.45 N	120.55 W
Deadman Brook ≃	276	41.08 N	73.22 W
Deadman Creek ≃, Austl.	274a	33.58 S	151.00 E
Deadman Creek ≃, Ca., U.S.	226	37.12 N	120.42 W
Deadman Hill ∧	162	23.48 S	119.25 E
Deadmans Cay	238	23.14 N	75.14 W
Deadman's Creek Indian Reserve ◆4	182	50.49 N	121.00 W
Dead Run ≃	284c	38.57 N	77.11 W
Dead Sea (Al-Baḥr al-Mayyit) (Yam HaMelaḥ) ⊜	132	31.30 N	35.30 E
Deadwood	198	44.22 N	103.43 W
Deadwood ≃	202	44.05 N	115.40 W
Deagan Island I	116	12.15 N	123.51 E
Deakin	162	30.46 S	128.58 E
Deakin, Mount ∧2	162	17.38 S	130.48 E
Deakin Bay c	9	68.23 S	150.10 E
Deal, Eng., U.K.	42	51.14 N	1.24 E
Deal, N.J., U.S.	208	40.15 N	74.00 W
Deale	208	38.46 N	76.33 W
Dealesville	158	28.40 S	25.37 E
Deal Island	208	38.09 N	75.56 W
Deal Island I	208	38.09 N	75.56 W
Deam Lake ⊜1	218	38.28 N	85.51 W
De'an	100	29.20 N	115.46 E
Dean ≃, B.C., Can.	182	52.50 N	126.57 W
Dean ≃, Eng., U.K.	44	53.20 N	2.14 W
Dean, Forest of ◆3	42	51.48 N	2.30 W
Dean Channel ⟗	182	52.33 N	127.13 W
Deane	262	53.34 N	2.28 W
Deán Funes	252	30.26 S	64.21 W
Dean Row	262	53.20 N	2.11 W
Deans	276	40.24 N	74.30 W
Deansboro	210	43.00 N	75.26 W
Deans Dundas Bay c	176	72.15 N	118.25 W
Deanville	222	30.26 N	96.46 W
Dearborn	216	42.18 N	83.10 W
Dearborn □6	218	39.06 N	84.51 W
Dearborn ≃	202	47.07 N	111.55 W
Dearborn Heights, Il., U.S.	278	41.43 N	87.48 W
Dearborn Heights, Mi., U.S.	216	42.20 N	83.16 W
Dearg, Beinn ∧	46	57.47 N	4.56 W
Dearham	44	54.42 N	3.26 W
Dearne ≃	44	53.30 N	1.16 W
Dear Reservoir ⊜1	44	55.20 N	3.37 W
Dease ≃	180	59.54 N	128.30 W
Dease Arm c	180	66.52 N	119.37 W
Dease Lake ⊜	180	58.35 N	130.02 W
Dease Strait ⟗	176	68.40 N	108.00 W
Death Valley	204	36.18 N	116.25 W
Death Valley V	204	36.30 N	117.00 W
Death Valley National Monument ♠	204	36.30 N	117.00 W
Deatsville	194	32.36 N	86.23 W
Deauville	50	49.22 N	0.04 E
Deba	146	10.20 N	11.54 E
Debagrām	126	23.41 N	88.18 E
Debal'cevo	83	48.20 N	38.24 E
Debānāndapur	272b	22.56 N	88.22 E
Debao	102	23.21 N	106.31 E
Debar	38	41.31 N	20.30 E
De Bary	220	28.52 N	81.18 W
Debauch Mountain ∧	180	64.31 N	159.52 W
Débé	241r	10.12 N	61.27 W
Debed ≃	84	41.22 N	44.58 E
Deben ≃	42	51.58 N	1.24 E
Debenham	42	52.13 N	1.11 E
De Beque	200	39.20 N	108.12 W
De Berry	194	32.18 N	94.10 W
Debesy	80	57.39 N	53.49 E
Debhāta	124	22.33 N	88.58 E
Dębica	30	50.04 N	21.24 E
De Bilt	52	52.06 N	5.10 E
Debipur	126	24.14 N	88.38 E
Debīr Char	126	22.24 N	90.41 E
Dęblin	30	51.35 N	21.50 E
Dębno	30	52.45 N	14.40 E
Débo, Lac ⊜	150	15.18 N	4.09 W
Deborah, Mount ∧	180	63.38 N	147.15 W
Deborah West, Lake ⊜	162	30.45 S	119.07 E
Deboyne Islands II	164	10.45 S	152.25 E
Debra	126	22.24 N	87.33 E
Debra Sina	144	9.51 N	39.50 E
Debre Birhan	144	9.40 N	39.33 E
Debrecen	30	47.32 N	21.38 E
Debre Markos	144	10.20 N	37.45 E
Debre May	144	11.19 N	37.30 E
Debre Tabor	144	11.50 N	38.05 E
Debre Zebit	144	11.50 N	38.40 E
Debre Zeyit	144	8.45 N	38.59 E
Debrzno	30	53.33 N	17.14 E
Debstedt	52	53.37 N	8.38 E
Decatur, Al., U.S.	194	34.36 N	86.59 W
Decatur, Ga., U.S.	192	33.46 N	84.17 W
Decatur, Il., U.S.	219	39.50 N	88.57 W
Decatur, In., U.S.	216	40.50 N	84.56 W
Decatur, Mi., U.S.	216	42.06 N	85.58 W
Decatur, Ms., U.S.	194	32.26 N	89.06 W
Decatur, Ne., U.S.	198	42.00 N	96.14 W
Decatur, Oh., U.S.	218	38.49 N	83.42 W
Decatur, Tn., U.S.	192	35.30 N	84.47 W
Decatur, Tx., U.S.	222	33.14 N	97.35 W
Decatur □6	218	39.20 N	85.29 W
Decatur, Lake ⊜1	219	39.51 N	88.52 W
Decatur Island I	224	48.31 N	122.50 W
Decatur Municipal Airport ⊠	219	39.50 N	88.52 W
Decaturville	194	35.35 N	88.07 W
Decazeville	32	44.34 N	2.15 E
Deccan ⋏1	122	17.00 N	78.00 E
Decelles, Réservoir ⊜1	190	47.42 N	78.08 W
Deception ≃	156	21.04 S	24.25 E
Deception, Mount ∧	224	47.49 N	123.14 W
Deception Bay c	171a	27.07 S	153.05 E
Deception Island I	9	62.57 S	60.38 W
Deception Lake ⊜	184	56.33 N	104.15 W
Deception Pass ≅	224	48.24 N	122.38 W
Deception Pass State Park ♠	224	48.24 N	122.39 W
Dechang	102	27.24 N	102.10 E
Dechêne, Lac ⊜	186	51.15 N	67.51 W
Dechenhöhle ⩶5	263	51.22 N	7.39 E
Decherd	194	35.12 N	86.04 W
Dechu	120	26.47 N	72.20 E
Déchy	50	50.21 N	3.07 E
Decimomannu	71	39.19 N	8.58 E
Decimoputzu	71	39.20 N	8.55 E
Děčín	54	50.48 N	14.13 E
Děčínské stěny ⋏	54	50.50 N	14.12 E
Decize	32	46.50 N	3.27 E
Decker Lake	182	54.17 N	125.50 W
Decker Lake ⊜1	222	30.18 N	97.36 W
Deckers Point	214	40.46 N	78.59 W
Deckerville	190	43.31 N	82.44 W
De Cocksdorp	52	53.08 N	4.52 E
Decollatura	68	39.03 N	16.21 E
Decorah	190	43.18 N	91.47 W
Decs	30	46.17 N	18.46 E
Deda	38	46.57 N	24.53 E
Dedaye	110	16.24 N	95.53 E
Deddington	42	51.59 N	1.19 W
Dededo	174p	13.31 N	144.49 E
Dedegöl Dağı ∧	130	37.39 N	31.17 E
Dedeköy	130	37.58 N	29.36 E
Dedeleben	54	52.03 N	10.25 E
Dedeli	84	39.11 N	43.05 E
Dedelow	54	53.22 N	13.48 E
Dedemsvaart	52	52.36 N	6.28 E
Dedenevo	82	56.15 N	37.31 E
Deder	144	9.22 N	41.26 E
Dedesdorf	52	53.27 N	8.30 E
Dedham	207	42.14 N	71.10 W
Dediāpāda	120	21.38 N	73.35 E
Dedilovskije Vyselki	82	54.20 N	38.03 E
Dedinovo	82	55.03 N	39.07 E
Dedo, Cerro ∧	254	44.49 S	71.52 W
Dedo de Deus ∧	256	22.30 S	43.03 W
De Doorns	158	33.28 S	19.41 E
Dédougou	150	12.28 N	3.28 W
Dedoviči	76	57.32 N	29.56 E
Dedovsk	82	55.52 N	37.07 E
Dedu	89	48.31 N	126.14 E
Deduru ≃	122	7.36 N	79.48 E
Dedza	154	14.22 S	34.20 E
Dee ≃, Ire.	48	53.52 N	6.21 W
Dee ≃, U.K.	44	53.20 N	3.12 W
Dee ≃, Eng., U.K.	44	54.18 N	2.32 W
Dee ≃, Scot., U.K.	44	54.50 N	4.03 W
Dee ≃, Scot., U.K.	46	57.09 N	2.07 W
Dee, Loch ⊜	44	55.05 N	4.24 W
Deedsville	216	40.55 N	86.06 W
De Efteling ♠	52	51.39 N	5.02 E
Deeg	124	27.28 N	77.20 E
Deelfontein	158	30.59 S	23.48 E
Deelpan	158	26.19 S	25.36 E
Deenwood	192	31.14 N	82.23 W
Deep ≃, In., U.S.	216	41.34 N	87.17 W
Deep ≃, N.C., U.S.	192	35.36 N	79.03 W
Deepavaal Brook ≃	276	40.53 N	74.16 W
Deep Bay c	184	56.25 N	103.00 W
Deep Brook ≃, Ma., U.S.	283	42.38 N	71.22 W
Deep Brook ≃, N.J., U.S.	276	40.58 N	74.09 W
Deep Creek ≃, Austl.	169	37.24 S	144.54 E
Deep Creek ≃, U.S.	200	41.44 N	113.00 W
Deep Creek ≃, Ca., U.S.	228	34.20 N	117.14 W
Deep Creek ≃, De., U.S.	208	38.38 N	75.37 W
Deep Creek ≃, Id., U.S.	202	42.15 N	116.40 W
Deep Creek ≃, Md., U.S.	284b	39.17 N	76.28 W
Deep Creek ≃, Tx., U.S.	196	32.45 N	99.10 W
Deep Creek ≃, Tx., U.S.	196	32.31 N	100.55 W
Deep Creek ≃, Ut., U.S.	200	40.10 N	113.50 W
Deep Creek Indian Reserve ◆4	182	52.16 N	122.07 W
Deeping Fen ≋	42	52.44 N	0.13 W
Deep Red Creek ≃	196	34.17 N	98.39 W
Deep River, On., Can.	190	46.06 N	77.30 W
Deep River, Ct., U.S.	207	41.23 N	72.26 W
Deep River, Ia., U.S.	190	41.34 N	92.22 W
Deep River, Wa., U.S.	224	46.21 N	123.41 W
Deep Run ≃, Md., U.S.	284b	39.13 N	76.42 W
Deep Run ≃, Md., U.S.	284b	39.25 N	76.40 W
Deep Run ≃, N.J., U.S.	276	40.26 N	74.22 W
Deep Run ≃, N.J., U.S.	285	39.44 N	74.41 W
Deepwater, Austl.	166	29.27 S	151.51 E
Deepwater, Mo., U.S.	194	38.15 N	93.46 W
Deep Water, N.J., U.S.	208	39.41 N	75.29 W
Deep Well	162	24.25 S	134.05 E
Deer ≃, N.Y., U.S.	188	44.55 N	74.43 W
Deer ≃, N.Y., U.S.	212	43.56 N	75.34 W
Deer Creek, In., U.S.	216	40.37 N	86.23 W
Deer Creek, Mn., U.S.	198	46.23 N	95.19 W
Deer Creek ≃, U.S.	208	39.37 N	76.09 W
Deer Creek ≃, Ca., U.S.	204	39.56 N	122.04 W
Deer Creek ≃, Ca., U.S.	226	39.13 N	121.17 W
Deer Creek ≃, Ca., U.S.	226	35.56 N	119.28 W
Deer Creek ≃, Ca., U.S.	226	38.22 N	121.21 W
Deer Creek ≃, Ca., U.S.	282	37.24 N	122.09 W
Deer Creek ≃, Il., U.S.	278	41.32 N	87.37 W
Deer Creek ≃, In., U.S.	216	40.34 N	86.41 W
Deer Creek ≃, Ks., U.S.	198	39.40 N	99.06 W
Deer Creek ≃, Ms., U.S.	194	32.33 N	90.47 W
Deer Creek ≃, Ne., U.S.	198	40.28 N	100.00 W
Deer Creek ≃, Oh., U.S.	218	39.27 N	83.00 W
Deer Creek ≃, Ok., U.S.	196	35.38 N	98.28 W
Deer Creek ≃, Or., U.S.	224	45.08 N	123.15 W
Deer Creek ≃, Pa., U.S.	279b	40.32 N	79.51 W
Deer Creek ≃, Wa., U.S.	224	48.16 N	121.55 W
Deer Creek ≃, Wy., U.S.	200	42.52 N	105.52 W
Deer Creek ≃, Wy., U.S.	202	43.09 N	107.42 W
Deer Creek Indian Reservation ◆4	190	47.50 N	93.25 W
Deer Creek Lake ⊜1	218	39.40 N	83.15 W
Deerfield, Il., U.S.	216	42.10 N	87.50 W
Deerfield, In., U.S.	216	40.17 N	84.59 W
Deerfield, Ks., U.S.	198	37.58 N	101.07 W
Deerfield, Ma., U.S.	207	42.32 N	72.36 W
Deerfield, Mi., U.S.	216	41.53 N	83.46 W
Deerfield, Oh., U.S.	214	41.01 N	81.03 W
Deerfield, Wi., U.S.	216	43.03 N	89.04 W
Deerfield ≃	207	42.35 N	72.35 W
Deerfield Beach	220	26.19 N	80.06 W
Deerfield Manor	278	42.10 N	87.55 W
Deerfield Street	208	39.31 N	75.14 W
Deer Grove ♠	278	42.09 N	88.04 W
Deer Harbor	224	48.37 N	123.00 W
Deering	180	66.05 N	162.43 W
Deering, Mount ∧2	162	24.53 S	129.04 E
Deer Island >1	283	42.21 N	70.58 W
Deer Island I, N.B., Can.	186	45.00 N	66.57 W
Deer Island I, Ak., U.S.	180	54.53 N	162.25 W
Deer Island I, Or., U.S.	224	45.58 N	122.50 W
Deer Isle	188	44.13 N	68.40 W
Deer Lake, Nf., Can.	186	49.10 N	57.26 W
Deer Lake, Pa., U.S.	208	40.37 N	76.03 W
Deer Lake ⊜, Nf., Can.	186	49.07 N	57.35 W
Deer Lake ⊜, On., Can.	184	52.40 N	94.30 W
Deer Lakes Regional Park ♠	279b	40.38 N	79.49 W
Deerlijk	50	50.51 N	3.21 E
Deer Lodge	202	46.23 N	112.44 W
Deer Mountain ∧	188	45.01 N	70.56 W
Deer Park, Austl.	274b	37.47 S	144.47 E
Deer Park, Al., U.S.	194	31.13 N	88.19 W
Deer Park, Ca., U.S.	226	38.32 N	122.28 W
Deer Park, Il., U.S.	278	42.09 N	88.04 W
Deer Park, N.Y., U.S.	210	40.45 N	73.19 W
Deer Park, Oh., U.S.	218	39.12 N	84.23 W
Deer Park, Tx., U.S.	222	29.42 N	95.07 W
Deer Park, Wa., U.S.	202	47.57 N	117.28 W
Deer Park Airport ⊠	276	40.46 N	73.19 W
Deerpass Bay c	180	65.56 N	122.25 W
Deer Pond ⊜, Nf., Can.	186	48.30 N	54.45 W
Deer Pond ⊜, N.J., U.S.	276	40.57 N	74.24 W
Deer River, Mn., U.S.	190	47.19 N	93.47 W
Deer River, N.Y., U.S.	212	43.56 N	75.36 W
Deer Sound ⟗	46	58.58 N	2.48 W
Deersville	214	40.19 N	81.11 W
Deer Trail	198	39.36 N	104.02 W
Deerwood	190	46.28 N	93.53 W
Deesa	120	24.15 N	72.10 E
Dee Why	170	33.45 S	151.17 E
Dee Why Head >	274a	33.46 S	151.19 E
Dee Why Lagoon c	274a	33.45 S	151.18 E
Deex Nugaaleed V	144	7.58 N	49.51 E
Defengzhuang	98	41.02 N	113.16 E
Defereggen V	64	46.55 N	12.25 E
Defereggen Alpen ⋏	64	46.52 N	12.20 E
Deferiet	212	44.02 N	75.41 W
Defiance, Ia., U.S.	198	41.49 N	95.20 W
Defiance, Oh., U.S.	216	41.17 N	84.21 W
Defiance, Pa., U.S.	214	40.10 N	78.14 W
Defiance □6	216	41.19 N	84.30 W
Defiance, Mount ∧	224	45.38 N	121.43 W
Defiance Plateau ⋏1	200	36.00 N	109.15 W
De Forest	190	43.14 N	89.20 W
De Forest Lake ⊜	276	41.08 N	73.58 W

Symbol	English	Deutsch	Español	Français	Português
≃	River	Fluss	Río	Rivière	Rio
≅	Canal	Kanal	Canal	Canal	Canal
⌊	Waterfall, Rapids	Wasserfall, Stromschnellen	Cascada, Rápidos	Chute d'eau, Rapides	Cascata, Rápidos
⟗	Strait	Meeresstrasse	Estrecho	Détroit	Estreito
c	Bay, Gulf	Bucht, Golf	Bahía, Golfo	Baie, Golfe	Baía, Golfo
⊜	Lake, Lakes	See, Seen	Lago, Lagos	Lac, Lacs	Lago, Lagos
≋	Swamp	Sumpf	Pantano	Marais	Pântano
⩩	Ice Features, Glacier	Eis- und Gletscherformen	Accidentes Glaciales	Formes glaciaires	Acidentes glaciares
⍑	Other Hydrographic Features	Andere Hydrographische Objekte	Otros Elementos Hidrográficos	Autres données hydrographiques	Outros acidentes hidrográficos
⬥	Submarine Features	Untermeerische Objekte	Accidentes Submarinos	Formes de relief sous-marin	Acidentes submarinos
□	Political Unit	Politische Einheit	Unidad Politica	Entité politique	Unidade política
ʋ	Cultural Institution	Kulturelle Institution	Institución Cultural	Institution culturelle	Instituição cultural
⊥	Historical Site	Historische Stätte	Sitio Histórico	Site historique	Sitio histórico
♠	Recreational Site	Erholungs- und Ferienort	Sitio de Recreo	Centre de loisirs	Area de Lazer
⊠	Airport	Flughafen	Aeropuerto	Aéroport	Aeroporto
■	Military Installation	Militäranlage	Instalación Militar	Installation militaire	Instalação militar
◆	Miscellaneous	Verschiedenes	Misceláneo	Divers	Diversos

Name	Page	Lat.°′	Long.°′
De Funiak Springs	194	30.43 N	86.06 W
Deganga	126	22.40 N	88.39 E
Deganwy	44	53.18 N	3.47 W
Deganya	132	32.42 N	35.35 E
Dega Werabe	144	8.08 N	45.22 E
Dêgê	102	31.50 N	98.40 E
Degeberga	26	55.50 N	14.05 E
Degeh Bur	144	8.13 N	43.34 E
Dégelis (Sainte-Rose-du-Dégelis)	186	47.33 N	68.39 W
Degema	150	4.45 N	6.47 E
Degerby	26	60.02 N	20.23 E
Degeres	85	43.14 N	75.49 E
Degerfors	40	59.14 N	14.26 E
Degerhamn	26	56.21 N	16.24 E
Degerndorf	64	47.44 N	12.06 E
Deggendorf	60	48.51 N	12.59 E
Deggingen	56	48.36 N	9.43 E
Degh ≃	123	31.36 N	74.09 E
Değirmendere	130	38.07 N	27.09 E
Deglunden ⊜	40	60.05 N	13.49 E
Dego	62	44.27 N	8.19 E
Degollado	234	20.28 N	102.09 W
Degoma	144	12.28 N	37.37 E
Degong	114	4.05 N	101.08 E
De Graafschap ⟡[1]	52	52.00 N	6.30 E
De Graff	216	40.18 N	83.54 W
De Gray Lake ⊜[1]	194	34.15 N	93.15 W
De Grey	162	20.10 S	119.12 E
De Grey ≃	162	20.12 S	119.11 E
Degt'ari	78	50.35 N	32.45 E
Degt'arka ≃	265a	59.57 N	30.52 E
Degt'arsk	86	56.42 N	60.06 E
Degunino ⟡[8]	265b	55.52 N	37.33 E
De Haan	50	51.16 N	3.02 E
Dehalak Deset I	144	15.40 N	40.05 E
Deharda	126	21.40 N	87.25 E
De Hart Reservoir ⊜[1]	208	40.28 N	76.45 W
Deh Bālā	123	34.04 N	70.29 E
Deh Bārez	128	27.26 N	57.12 E
Deh Bīd	128	30.38 N	53.13 E
Dehdez	128	31.43 N	50.17 E
Dehej	120	21.42 N	72.35 E
Dehgolān	128	35.17 N	47.25 E
Dehibat	148	32.01 N	10.42 E
Dehiwala-Mount Lavinia	122	6.51 N	79.52 E
Deh Kord	128	33.49 N	48.53 E
Dehlorān	128	32.41 N	47.16 E
De Hoek	158	32.57 S	18.46 E
De Hoge Veluwe, Nationale Park ♦	52	52.02 N	5.55 E
Dehpehk I	174r	6.57 N	158.18 E
Dehra Dūn	124	30.19 N	78.02 E
Dehra Dūn □[5]	124	30.20 N	78.00 E
Dehri	124	24.52 N	84.11 E
Dehrn	56	50.25 N	8.05 E
Deh Salm	128	31.12 N	59.19 E
Dehu	122	18.35 N	73.51 E
Dehua	100	25.32 N	118.15 E
Dehuang	98	35.12 N	114.25 E
Dehui	89	44.34 N	125.43 E
Deidesheim	56	49.24 N	8.11 E
Deilbach ≃	263	51.23 N	7.05 E
Deilinghofen	56	51.22 N	7.47 E
Dein	164	5.30 S	146.10 E
Deining	60	49.13 N	11.32 E
Deinze	50	50.59 N	3.32 E
Deir el Asad	132	32.56 N	35.16 E
Deister ⩕	52	52.15 N	9.30 E
Deiva Marina	62	44.13 N	9.30 E
Dej	38	47.09 N	23.52 E
Deje	40	59.36 N	13.28 E
Dejima	94	36.05 N	140.20 E
Dejnau	128	39.15 N	63.11 E
De Jongs, Tanjong ›	164	6.56 S	138.32 E
Deka ≃	154	18.04 S	26.42 E
De Kalb, Il., U.S.	216	41.55 N	88.45 W
De Kalb, Ms., U.S.	194	32.46 N	88.39 W
De Kalb, Tx., U.S.	194	33.30 N	94.36 W
De Kalb □[6], Il., U.S.	216	41.59 N	88.41 W
De Kalb □[6], In., U.S.	216	41.22 N	85.04 W
De Kalb Junction	212	44.30 N	75.16 W
Dekan, Hochland von → Deccan ⩕[1]	122	17.00 N	78.00 E
De-Kastri	89	51.28 N	140.47 E
Dekehtik I	174r	7.00 N	158.12 E
Dekemhare	144	15.05 N	39.02 E
Dekese	152	3.27 S	21.24 E
Deke Sokehs I	174r	6.59 N	158.11 E
Dekhgila Military Base ■	142	31.08 N	29.48 E
Dekina	150	7.39 N	7.02 E
Dékoa	152	6.19 N	19.04 E
De Koog	52	53.05 N	4.45 E
De Krim	52	52.38 N	6.38 E
De La Blanche, Lac ⊜	186	50.05 N	69.29 W
Delabole	42	50.37 N	4.42 W
Delafield	216	43.03 N	88.24 W
Del Aire	280	33.55 N	118.21 W
Delamere, Austl.	164	15.45 S	131.33 E
Delamere, Austl.	168b	35.35 S	138.11 E
Delamere, Eng., U.K.	262	53.13 N	2.39 W
Delamere Forest ⟡[3]	262	53.14 N	2.38 W
Delami Mayal, Jabal ∧	140	11.38 N	30.23 E
Del Amo Fashion Center ⟡[9]	280	33.50 N	118.21 W
De Lancey, N.Y., U.S.	210	42.12 N	74.58 W
De Lancey, Pa., U.S.	214	40.59 N	78.58 W
Delanco	208	40.03 N	74.57 W
De Land	220	29.01 N	81.18 W
Delanggu	115a	7.37 S	110.41 E
Delano, Ca., U.S.	226	35.46 N	119.14 W
Delano, Mn., U.S.	190	45.02 N	93.47 W
Delano, Pa., U.S.	210	40.50 N	76.04 W
Delano Peak ∧	200	38.22 N	112.23 W
Delanson	210	42.44 N	74.11 W
Delaport Point ›	240b	25.05 N	77.27 W
Delapu	120	31.35 N	90.35 E
Delārām	128	32.11 N	63.25 E
Delareyville	158	26.44 S	25.29 E
Delarof Islands II	181a	51.30 N	178.45 W
Delaronde Lake ⊜	184	54.05 N	107.05 W
Del'atiči	76	53.47 N	25.59 E
Del'atin	78	48.32 N	24.37 E
Delatite ≃	169	37.10 S	146.00 E
Delavan, Il., U.S.	194	40.22 N	89.32 W
Delavan, Wi., U.S.	216	42.37 N	88.38 W
Delavan Lake	216	42.35 N	88.37 W
Delavan Lake ⊜	216	42.37 N	88.38 W
Delaware, On., Can.	214	42.55 N	81.25 W
Delaware, N.J., U.S.	210	40.53 N	75.03 W
Delaware, Oh., U.S.	214	40.17 N	83.04 W
Delaware, Ok., U.S.	196	36.46 N	95.38 W
Delaware □[6], In., U.S.	216	40.18 N	85.23 W
Delaware □[6], N.Y., U.S.	210	42.17 N	74.55 W
Delaware □[6], Oh., U.S.	214	40.18 N	83.04 W
Delaware □[6], Pa., U.S.	208	39.55 N	75.23 W
Delaware □[3], U.S.	178	39.10 N	75.30 W
Delaware □[3], U.S.	208	39.10 N	75.30 W
Delaware ≃, U.S.	188	39.20 N	75.25 W
Delaware ≃, U.S.	196	32.02 N	104.01 W
Delaware ≃, Ks., U.S.	198	39.03 N	95.24 W
Delaware, East Branch ≃	210	41.55 N	75.17 W
Delaware, University of ♁[2]	285	39.41 N	75.45 W
Delaware, West Branch ≃	210	41.56 N	75.17 W
Delaware and Raritan Canal ≋	208	40.29 N	74.26 W
Delaware Aqueduct ≋[1]	210	42.05 N	74.54 W
Delaware Bay c	208	39.05 N	75.15 W
Delaware City	208	39.34 N	75.35 W
Delaware Lake ⊜[1]	214	40.20 N	83.00 W
Delaware Memorial Bridge ⟡[5]	285	40.07 N	74.50 W
Delaware Memorial Bridges ⟡[5]	208	39.41 N	75.31 W
Delaware Mountains ⩕	196	31.35 N	104.40 W
Delaware Museum of Natural History ♁	285	39.47 N	75.36 W
Delaware Park	210	40.43 N	75.11 W
Delaware Park ♦	284a	42.56 N	78.52 W
Delaware Park Race Track ♦	285	39.42 N	75.40 W
Delaware Seashore State Park ♦	208	38.38 N	75.04 W
Delaware State Park ♦	214	40.23 N	83.04 W
Delaware Water Gap	210	40.59 N	75.09 W
Delaware Water Gap National Recreation Area ♦	210	41.08 N	74.55 W
Delbrück	52	51.46 N	8.33 E
Delburne	182	52.12 N	113.14 W
Delcambre	194	29.57 N	91.59 W
Del Campillo	252	34.22 S	64.29 W
Del Carril	258	35.31 S	59.30 W
Del City	196	35.26 N	97.26 W
Delcommune, Lac ⊜[1]	154	10.45 S	25.45 E
Del Dios	228	33.04 N	117.08 W
Delegate	166	37.03 S	148.58 E
Délembé	146	9.53 N	22.37 E
Delémont	58	47.22 N	7.21 E
De Leon	196	32.06 N	98.32 W
De Leon Springs	192	29.07 N	81.21 W
de Lesquin, Aéroport ⊠	50	50.35 N	3.07 E
Delet ⋓	26	60.15 N	20.35 E
Delevan	210	42.29 N	78.28 W
Delfim Moreira	256	22.30 S	45.17 W
Delfinópolis	255	20.20 S	46.51 W
Delft	52	52.00 N	4.21 E
Delft Island I	122	9.30 N	79.42 E
Delfzijl	52	53.19 N	6.46 E
Delgada, Punta ›	254	42.46 S	63.38 W
Delgado, Cabo ›	154	10.40 S	40.35 E
Del Gallego	116	13.56 N	122.36 E
Delgany	48	53.08 N	6.05 W
Delger ≃	88	49.17 N	100.40 E
Delger chaan uul ∧	88	50.00 N	106.22 E
Delgerchangaj	102	45.15 N	104.50 E
Delgerchet	102	45.52 N	110.26 E
Delgercogt	102	46.08 N	106.23 E
Delgerech	102	45.48 N	111.12 E
Del Haven	208	39.03 N	74.56 W
Delhi, On., Can.	212	42.51 N	80.30 W
Delhi, India	124	28.40 N	77.13 E
Delhi, India	272a	28.40 N	77.13 E
Delhi, Ca., U.S.	226	37.26 N	120.46 W
Delhi, Il., U.S.	219	39.03 N	90.15 W
Delhi, Ia., U.S.	190	42.25 N	91.19 W
Delhi, La., U.S.	194	32.27 N	91.29 W
Delhi, N.Y., U.S.	210	42.16 N	74.54 W
Delhi □[3]	123	28.37 N	77.10 E
Delhi, University of ♁[2]	272a	28.42 N	77.13 E
Delhi Cantonment	272a	28.36 N	77.08 E
Delhi Hills	218	39.05 N	84.36 W
Delhi Railroad Station ⟡[5]	272a	28.40 N	77.13 E
Delhi Tail Distributary ≋	272a	28.41 N	77.10 E
Deli, Pulau I	115a	7.00 S	105.32 E
Delia, Ab., Can.	182	51.38 N	112.23 W
Delia, It.	70	37.21 N	13.55 E
Delia ≃	70	37.19 N	13.58 E
Delianuova	68	38.14 N	15.55 E
Deliblato	38	44.50 N	21.03 E
Delice	130	39.58 N	34.02 E
Delice ≃	130	40.28 N	34.10 E
Delices	240d	15.17 N	61.16 W
Deliceto	68	41.13 N	15.23 E
Delicias, Cuba	240p	21.11 N	76.34 W
Delicias, Méx.	232	28.13 N	105.28 W
De Lier	52	51.57 N	4.15 E
Delight	194	34.01 N	93.30 W
Delightful	214	41.18 N	80.57 W
Deliiilyas	130	39.20 N	36.48 E
Delījān	128	33.59 N	50.40 E
Delıklıkaya ›	130	41.12 N	30.20 E
Deliktaş	130	39.21 N	37.13 E
Delingde	74	70.08 N	114.00 E
Delingha	102	37.14 N	97.11 E
Dēliņkalns ∧[2]	76	57.30 N	26.58 E
Déli Pályaudvar ⟡[5]	264c	47.30 N	19.01 E
Delisle	184	51.55 N	107.08 W
Delisle ≃	206	45.17 N	74.11 W
Delitua	114	3.30 N	98.41 E
Delitzsch	54	51.31 N	12.20 E
Delkern	228	35.21 N	119.01 W
Dell	46	58.30 N	6.20 W
Dellach	64	46.40 N	13.05 E
Dell City	200	31.56 N	105.12 W
Delle	58	47.30 N	7.00 E
Dellenbaugh, Mount ∧	200	36.07 N	113.32 W
Dellensjöarna ⊜	26	61.54 N	16.41 E
Delles	148	36.55 N	3.55 E
Delligsen	52	51.57 N	9.48 E
Dello	64	45.25 N	10.04 E
Dell Rapids	198	43.50 N	96.43 W
Dellroy	214	40.33 N	81.11 W
Dellwig	263	51.29 N	7.41 E
Dellwig ⟡[8]	263	51.29 N	6.56 E
Dellwood	219	38.44 N	90.17 W
Dellwood Highlands	278	41.34 N	88.03 W
Del Mar, Ca., U.S.	228	32.57 N	117.15 W
Delmar, De., U.S.	208	38.27 N	75.34 W
Delmar, Ia., U.S.	190	42.00 N	90.36 W
Delmar, Md., U.S.	208	38.27 N	75.34 W
Delmar, N.Y., U.S.	210	42.37 N	73.49 W
Del Mar Hills	196	27.37 N	99.26 W
Delmarva Peninsula ›[1]	208	38.30 N	75.30 W
Del Mar Woods	278	42.12 N	87.51 W
Delmas, Sk., Can.	184	52.55 N	108.36 W
Delmas, S. Afr.	158	26.08 S	28.43 E
Delmas □[5]	273d	26.10 S	28.33 E
Delme	56	48.53 N	6.24 E
Delme ≃	52	53.05 N	8.40 E
Delmenhorst	52	53.03 N	8.38 E
Delmiro Gouveia	250	9.23 S	37.59 W
Delmont, N.J., U.S.	208	39.12 N	74.57 W
Delmont, Pa., U.S.	214	40.25 N	79.34 W
Delmont, S.D., U.S.	198	43.16 N	98.09 W
Del Monte Heights	226	36.36 N	121.50 W
Del Monte Park	226	36.36 N	121.56 W
Delnice	36	45.24 N	14.48 E
Del Norte	200	37.40 N	106.21 W
Del Norte Coast Redwood State Park ♦	204	41.38 N	124.05 W
De-Longa, ostrova II	74	76.30 N	153.00 E
De Long Mountains ⩕	180	68.20 N	162.00 W
De-Long-Strasse → Longa, proliv ⋓	74	70.20 N	178.00 E
Deloraine, Austl.	166	41.31 S	146.39 E
Deloraine, Mb., Can.	184	49.12 N	100.29 W
Delorme, Lac ⊜	176	54.31 N	69.52 W
Deloro	212	44.31 N	77.37 W
Delos → Dhílos ⊥	38	37.26 N	25.16 E
Delph, Eng., U.K.	44	53.34 N	2.01 W
Delph, Eng., U.K.	262	53.34 N	2.01 W
Delphi	216	40.35 N	86.40 W
Delphi → Dhelfoí ⊥	38	38.30 N	22.29 E
Delphi Falls	210	42.53 N	75.55 W
Delphos, Ks., U.S.	198	39.16 N	97.46 W
Delphos, Oh., U.S.	216	40.50 N	84.20 W
Delph Reservoir ⊜[1]	262	53.38 N	2.27 W
Delportshoop	158	28.22 S	24.20 E
Del Puerto Creek ≃	226	37.32 N	121.07 W
Delran	285	40.01 N	74.57 W
Delrath	263	51.08 N	6.47 E
Delray ⟡[8]	281	42.18 N	83.08 W
Delray Beach	220	26.27 N	80.04 W
Del Rey	226	36.40 N	119.36 W
Del Rey Oaks	226	36.36 N	121.50 W
Del Rio, Fl., U.S.	220	28.03 N	82.26 W
Del Rio, Tx., U.S.	196	29.21 N	100.53 W
Del Rosa	228	34.08 N	117.15 W
Delsbo	26	61.48 N	16.35 E
Delson	206	45.22 N	73.33 W
Delstern ⟡[8]	263	51.20 N	7.31 E
Delta, On., Can.	212	44.37 N	76.08 W
Delta, Méx.	200	32.22 N	115.12 W
Delta, Co., U.S.	200	38.44 N	108.04 W
Delta, Mo., U.S.	194	37.11 N	89.44 W
Delta, Oh., U.S.	216	41.34 N	84.00 W
Delta, Pa., U.S.	208	39.43 N	76.19 W
Delta, Ut,. U.S.	200	39.21 N	112.34 W
Delta □[9]	194	33.30 N	90.45 W
Delta ≃	180	64.09 N	146.18 W
Delta Amacuro □[8]	246	8.30 N	61.30 W
Delta Barrage ⟡[6]	142	30.11 N	31.07 E
Delta Beach	184	50.11 N	98.19 W
Delta City	194	33.04 N	90.47 W
Delta Downs	166	17.00 S	141.18 E
Delta Junction	180	64.02 N	145.41 W
Delta Mendota Canal ≋	226	37.49 N	121.34 W
Delta Peak ∧	180	56.39 N	129.34 W
Delta Reservoir ⊜[1]	210	43.17 N	75.26 W
Deltaville	208	37.33 N	76.20 W
Delton	216	42.29 N	85.24 W
Deltona	220	28.54 N	81.15 W
Delungra	166	29.39 S	150.50 E
Del'un-Uranskij chrebet ⩕	88	56.30 N	114.00 E
Delüün	86	47.42 N	90.59 E
De Luz Creek ≃	228	33.22 N	117.19 W
Del Valle	222	30.12 N	97.40 W
Del Valle, Lake ⊜[1]	226	37.35 N	121.43 W
Del Verme Falls ↳	144	5.27 N	40.17 E
Delvin	48	53.36 N	7.05 W
Delvinë	38	39.57 N	20.06 E
Del Viso	258	34.27 S	58.48 W
Delyn □[8]	262	53.16 N	3.11 W
Demak	115a	6.53 S	110.38 E
Demaki	80	58.26 N	51.43 E
Dem'ansk	76	57.38 N	32.28 E
Demarcation Point ›	180	69.40 N	141.15 W
Demarest	276	40.57 N	73.57 W
Demarest Brook ≃	276	40.57 N	73.58 W
Demavend, Mount → Damāvand, Qolleh-ye ∧	128	35.56 N	52.08 E
Demba	152	5.30 S	22.16 E
Demba Chio	152	9.41 S	13.41 E
Dembecha	144	10.35 N	37.30 E
Dembéni	157a	11.50 S	43.24 E
Dembi	144	8.05 N	36.27 E
Dembia, Centraf.	154	5.07 N	24.25 E
Dembia, Zaïre	154	3.31 N	25.50 E
Dembi Dolo	144	8.32 N	34.48 E
Dembo	152	3.56 S	12.35 E
Dême ≃	50	47.43 N	0.29 E
Demer ≃	56	50.58 N	4.42 E
Demerara ≃	246	6.48 N	58.10 W
Demerthin	54	52.58 N	12.17 E
Demidov	76	55.16 N	31.31 E
Demidovka	78	50.25 N	25.20 E
Demidovo	76	59.17 N	38.17 E
Deming, N.M., U.S.	200	32.16 N	107.45 W
Deming, Wa., U.S.	224	48.49 N	122.12 W
Demini ≃	246	0.46 S	62.56 W
Demirci	130	39.03 N	28.40 E
Demircidere	130	37.33 N	27.50 E
Demir Kapija V	38	41.24 N	22.15 E
Demirköy	130	41.49 N	27.45 E
Demirtaş	130	40.16 N	29.06 E
Demitz-Thumitz	54	51.09 N	14.14 E
Demjanka ≃	86	59.34 N	69.20 E
Demjanovo	24	60.22 N	47.03 E
Demjanskoje	86	59.36 N	69.18 E
Demjas	80	51.13 N	49.08 E
Demmeltrath ⟡[8]	263	51.11 N	7.03 E
Demmin	54	53.54 N	13.02 E
Demmitt	182	55.26 N	119.54 W
Demnate	148	31.44 N	6.59 W
Democracy, Monument of ⊥	269a	13.45 N	100.30 E
Democrat Point ›	276	40.37 N	73.18 W
Demoiselles, Grotte des ⊥[5]	62	43.55 N	3.45 E
Demone, Val ⟡[1]	70	37.58 N	14.35 E
Demonte	62	44.19 N	7.17 E
De Montigny, Lac ⊜	190	48.08 N	77.54 W
Demopolis	194	32.31 N	87.50 W
Demorest	192	34.33 N	83.32 W
De Mossville	218	38.48 N	84.25 W
Demotte	216	41.12 N	87.12 W
Dempo, Gunung ∧	112	4.02 S	103.09 E
Dempster, Point ›	162	33.39 S	123.52 E
Demsa	146	9.32 N	13.14 E
Demta	164	2.20 S	140.08 E
Demurino	78	48.10 N	36.29 E
De Naauwte	158	30.08 S	21.42 E
Denain	50	50.20 N	3.23 E
Denair	226	37.32 N	120.47 W
Denakil ⟡[1]	144	13.00 N	41.00 E
Denali	180	63.11 N	147.28 W
Denali National Park	180	63.44 N	148.54 W
Denali National Park ♦	180	63.15 N	150.30 W
Denan	144	6.30 N	43.30 E
Denare Beach	184	54.40 N	102.05 W
Denau	85	38.16 N	67.54 E
Denbigh, On., Can.	212	45.08 N	77.16 W
Denbigh, Wales, U.K.	44	53.11 N	3.25 W
Denbigh, Cape ›	180	64.23 N	161.31 W
Den Burg	52	53.03 N	4.48 E
Denby Dale	44	53.35 N	1.38 W
Den Chai	110	17.59 N	100.04 E
Dendang	112	3.05 S	107.54 E
Dender (Dendre) ≃	50	51.02 N	4.06 E
Denderleeuw	50	50.53 N	4.04 E
Dendermonde	50	51.02 N	4.07 E
Dendre (Dender) ≃	50	51.02 N	4.06 E
Dendron, S. Afr.	156	23.25 S	29.11 E
Dendron, Va., U.S.	208	37.02 N	76.56 W
Dendy Park ♦	274b	37.56 S	145.00 E
Deneba	144	9.50 N	39.09 E
Denekamp	52	52.23 N	7.00 E
Denenchōfu ⟡[8]	268	35.35 N	139.41 E
Deneysville	158	26.53 S	28.06 E
Denežnikovo, S.S.S.R.	82	55.26 N	38.07 E
Denežnikovo, S.S.S.R.	83	49.02 N	38.57 E
Dengcheng	100	33.41 N	114.27 E
Deng Deng	152	5.12 N	13.31 E
Denge	154	3.34 N	28.14 E
Denge Marsh ⩶	42	50.57 N	0.55 E
Dengfeng	100	34.29 N	113.04 E
Denggongchang	107	30.24 N	103.49 E
Dengguanzhen	107	29.10 N	104.56 E
Dengkou	102	40.20 N	106.59 E
Denglongshu	98	41.20 N	115.15 E
Dengmingsi	98	37.53 N	116.42 E
Dêngqên	102	31.32 N	95.27 E
Dengshahe	98	39.13 N	122.04 E
Dengta	100	24.01 N	114.49 E
Denguiro	152	5.38 N	23.02 E
Dengxian	102	32.42 N	112.01 E
Dengyoufang	98	41.34 N	114.32 E
Den Haag → 's-Gravenhage	52	52.06 N	4.18 E
Denham, Austl.	162	25.55 S	113.32 E
Denham, Eng., U.K.	260	51.34 N	0.30 W
Denham, In., U.S.	216	41.09 N	86.43 W
Denham, Mount ∧	241q	18.13 N	77.32 W
Denham Aerodrome ⊠	260	51.36 N	0.31 W
Denham Island I	166	16.43 S	139.09 E
Denham Place ♁	260	51.34 N	0.30 W
Denham Range ⩕	166	21.55 S	147.46 E
Denham Sound ⋓	162	25.40 S	113.15 E
Denham Springs	194	30.29 N	90.57 W
Den Helder	52	52.54 N	4.45 E
Denholme	262	53.48 N	1.54 W
Denia	34	38.51 N	0.07 E
Denial Bay	162	32.06 S	133.32 E
Dénié	150	11.14 N	7.29 W
Deniliquin	166	35.32 S	144.58 E
Deniskoviči, S.S.S.R.	76	52.19 N	31.43 E
Deniskoviči, S.S.S.R.	76	52.44 N	26.41 E
Denison, Ia., U.S.	198	42.01 N	95.21 W
Denison, Tx., U.S.	196	33.45 N	96.32 W
Denison, Mount ∧	180	58.25 N	154.27 W
Denison Dam ⟡[6]	196	33.50 N	96.34 W
Denisovka	24	66.14 N	55.20 E
Denisōvo	82	54.28 N	37.51 E
Denisy	261	48.33 N	1.56 E
Denizli	130	37.46 N	29.06 E
Denizli □[4]	130	37.40 N	29.15 E
Denkanikota	122	12.32 N	77.48 E
Denkendorf	60	48.56 N	11.27 E
Denkingen	58	47.53 N	9.19 E
Denklingen, B.R.D.	56	50.55 N	7.39 E
Denklingen, B.R.D.	58	47.55 N	10.51 E
Den'kovo	82	56.01 N	36.21 E
Denman Glacier ◸	9	66.45 S	99.25 E
Denmark, Austl.	162	34.57 S	117.21 E
Denmark, S.C., U.S.	192	33.19 N	81.08 W
Denmark, Wi., U.S.	190	44.20 N	87.49 W
Denmark (Danmark) □[1], Europe	22	56.00 N	10.00 E
Denmark (Danmark) □[1], Europe	26	56.00 N	10.00 E
Denmark, Lake ⊜	276	40.58 N	74.31 W
Denmark Bay c	176	70.33 N	103.20 W
Denmark Strait ⋓	10	67.00 N	25.00 W
Denmead	42	50.54 N	1.04 W
Dennemont	261	49.01 N	1.42 E
Dennery	241f	13.55 N	60.54 W
Dennis	207	41.44 N	70.11 W
Dennis Head ›	46	59.23 N	2.23 W
Dennison	214	40.23 N	81.20 W
Dennis Port	207	41.39 N	70.07 W
Denniston	172	41.44 S	171.48 E
Denniston Creek ≃	282	37.30 N	122.28 W
Dennisville	208	39.11 N	74.49 W
Denny	46	56.02 N	3.55 W
Den Oever	52	52.56 N	5.02 E
Denouval	261	48.58 N	2.03 E
Denpasar	115b	8.39 S	115.13 E
Denshaw	262	53.35 N	2.02 W
Dent Ditch ≋	279a	41.18 N	82.08 W
Denton, Eng., U.K.	262	53.27 N	2.07 W
Denton, Md., U.S.	208	38.53 N	75.49 W
Denton, Mi., U.S.	281	42.20 N	83.03 W
Denton, Mt., U.S.	202	47.19 N	109.56 W
Denton, N.C., U.S.	192	35.38 N	80.06 W
Denton, Tx., U.S.	222	33.12 N	97.07 W
Denton □[6]	222	33.07 N	97.10 W
Denton Creek ≃	196	32.58 N	96.57 W
Dentonia Park ♦	275b	43.42 N	79.17 W
D'Entrecasteaux, Point ›	162	34.50 S	116.00 E
D'Entrecasteaux Islands II	164	9.30 S	150.40 E
Dents du Midi ⩕	58	46.10 N	6.56 E
Denver, Co., U.S.	200	39.44 N	104.59 W
Denver, In., U.S.	216	40.51 N	86.04 W
Denver, Ia., U.S.	190	42.40 N	92.20 W
Denver, Pa., U.S.	208	40.13 N	76.08 W
Denver City	196	32.57 N	102.49 W
Denville	210	40.53 N	74.28 W
Denzlingen	58	48.04 N	7.52 E
Deoband	124	29.42 N	77.41 E
Deocha	126	24.03 N	87.35 E
Deodoro ⟡[8]	287a	22.51 S	43.23 W
Deogarh, India	120	25.32 N	73.54 E
Deogarh, India	122	21.32 N	84.44 E
Deogarh, India	124	24.33 N	78.15 E
Deogarh ∧	124	23.32 N	82.16 E
Deogarh Hills ⩕[2]	124	23.35 N	82.30 E
Deoghar	124	24.29 N	86.42 E
Deogsu Palace ♁	271b	37.35 N	126.58 E
Deolāli	122	19.57 N	73.50 E
Deoli, India	120	25.45 N	75.23 E
Deoli, India	126	22.03 N	86.49 E
Deoli ⟡[8]	272a	28.30 N	77.14 E
Deopāra	126	22.55 N	90.15 E
Deori	124	23.08 N	78.41 E
Deoria	124	26.31 N	83.47 E
Deoria □[5]	124	26.50 N	83.50 E
Deori Khās	124	23.24 N	79.01 E
Deosai Mountains ⩕	123	35.20 N	75.12 E
Deosil	124	23.42 N	82.15 E
Dep ≃	89	52.54 N	127.45 E
Depāl	126	21.44 N	87.33 E
De Panne	50	51.06 N	2.35 E
Depāra	272b	22.53 N	88.34 E
Departure Bay	224	49.12 N	123.58 W
DePaul University ♁[2]	278	41.56 N	87.39 W
Depauville	212	44.08 N	76.04 W
Depauw	218	38.20 N	86.13 W
De Peel ⩶	52	51.25 N	6.00 E
De Pere	190	44.26 N	88.03 W
Depew, N.Y., U.S.	210	42.54 N	78.41 W
Depew, Ok., U.S.	196	35.48 N	96.30 W
Deping	98	37.28 N	116.57 E
De Pinte	50	51.00 N	3.39 E
Depoe Bay	202	44.48 N	124.03 W
Depok	115a	6.24 S	106.50 E
Deport	196	33.32 N	95.19 W
Deposit	210	42.03 N	75.25 W
Depósito	246	3.12 N	60.35 W
Deptford	285	39.50 N	75.07 W
Deptford ⟡[8]	260	51.28 N	0.02 W
Deptford Mall ⟡[9]	285	39.50 N	75.06 W
Deptford Terrace	285	39.48 N	75.09 W
Depuch Island I	162	20.38 S	117.43 E
Depue	190	41.19 N	89.18 W
Deputy	218	38.48 N	85.39 W
Dêqên	102	28.38 N	98.52 E
Deqing, Zhg.	102	23.09 N	111.45 E
Deqing, Zhg.	106	30.33 N	120.05 E
De Queen	194	34.02 N	94.20 W
De Quincy	194	30.27 N	93.25 W
Dera, Lach (Lak Dera) V	144	0.35 N	41.50 E
Dera Bugti	120	29.02 N	69.09 E
Derac	238	19.39 N	71.49 W
Dera Ghāzi Khān	123	30.03 N	70.38 E
Dera Gopipur	123	31.54 N	76.13 E
Dera Ismāīl Khān	123	31.50 N	70.54 E
Dera Nānak	123	32.02 N	75.01 E
Dera Nawāb	123	29.06 N	71.16 E
Dera-patak ≃	264c	47.39 N	19.05 E
Derāwar Fort	123	28.46 N	71.20 E
Deražn'a	78	49.16 N	27.26 E
Derbent	84	42.03 N	48.18 E
Derbesiye	130	37.06 N	40.40 E
Derbeškinskij	80	55.52 N	53.30 E
Derbetovka	80	45.48 N	43.05 E
Der Bodden ⋓	54	54.16 N	13.12 E
Derby, Austl.	162	17.18 S	123.38 E
Derby, Austl.	166	41.09 S	147.47 E
Derby, S. Afr.	158	25.55 S	27.02 E
Derby, Eng., U.K.	42	52.55 N	1.29 W
Derby, Ct., U.S.	207	41.19 N	73.05 W
Derby, Ks., U.S.	198	37.32 N	97.16 W
Derby, Me., U.S.	188	45.14 N	68.58 W
Derby, N.Y., U.S.	210	42.40 N	78.58 W
Derby, Oh., U.S.	218	39.46 N	83.12 W
Derby, Vt., U.S.	206	44.57 N	72.08 W
Derby Acres	226	35.15 N	119.35 W
Derby Line	206	45.00 N	72.05 W
Derbyshire □[6]	44	53.00 N	1.33 W
Der-Chantecoq, Lac du ⊜[1]	58	48.35 N	4.46 E
Derdepoort	156	24.42 S	26.20 E
Derecho ≃	246	2.38 S	69.54 W
Derečin	76	53.15 N	24.55 E
Derecske	30	47.21 N	21.34 E
Dereishaklı	130	41.03 N	39.08 E
Dereköy, Tür.	130	39.16 N	27.19 E
Dereköy, Tür.	130	40.08 N	37.47 E
Dereköy, Tür.	130	41.56 N	27.21 E
Dereli	130	40.45 N	38.27 E
Derenburg	54	51.52 N	10.54 E
Derendorf ⟡[8]	263	51.15 N	6.48 E
Derenwu	105	39.40 N	116.46 E
Dereseki	267b	41.08 N	29.08 E
Derev'anka	24	61.34 N	34.27 E
Derewa ≃	164	2.48 S	136.10 E
Derg ≃	48	54.44 N	7.25 W
Derg, Lough ⊜, Ire.	48	53.00 N	8.20 W
Derg, Lough ⊜, Ire.	48	54.36 N	7.53 W
Dergači, S.S.S.R.	78	50.07 N	36.07 E
Dergači, S.S.S.R.	80	51.14 N	48.46 E
Dergaon	120	26.42 N	93.58 E
Der Grabow c	54	54.23 N	12.50 E
De Ridder	194	30.50 N	93.17 W
De Rijp	52	52.34 N	4.50 E
Derik	130	37.22 N	40.17 E
Derinkuyu	130	38.23 N	34.45 E
Der Kanal → English Channel ⋓	28	50.20 N	1.00 W
Derkul	80	51.16 N	51.18 E
Derkul ≃	83	48.35 N	39.41 E
Dermbach	56	50.43 N	10.06 E
Dermott	194	33.31 N	91.26 W
Dermulo	64	46.20 N	11.04 E
Derne	263	51.35 N	7.41 E
Derne ⟡[8]	263	51.34 N	7.31 E
Dernieres, Isles II	194	29.02 N	90.47 W
Dernoviči	78	51.36 N	29.43 E
Deroche	224	49.11 N	122.04 W
Dero Eri	144	9.01 N	46.43 E
Dêrong	102	28.47 N	99.14 E
Déroute, Passage de la ⋓	32	49.25 N	2.00 W
Derrame	196	26.19 N	104.23 W
Derravaragh, Lough ⊜	48	53.40 N	7.24 W
Derre	154	16.56 S	36.11 E
Derrick City	214	41.58 N	78.34 W
Derrinallum	169	37.57 S	143.13 E
Derry → Londonderry, N. Ire., U.K.	48	55.00 N	7.19 W
Derry, N.H., U.S.	188	42.52 N	71.19 W
Derry, Pa., U.S.	214	40.20 N	79.18 W
Derrybrien	48	53.04 N	8.36 W
Derrykeevan	48	55.08 N	6.29 W
Derryveagh Mountains ⩕	48	55.00 N	8.05 W
Derry West	275b	43.39 N	79.42 W
Der Sārāi ⟡[8]	272a	28.33 N	77.11 E
Dersau	54	54.07 N	10.20 E
Dersingham	42	52.51 N	0.30 E
Derudeb	140	17.32 N	36.06 E
De Rust	158	33.30 S	22.32 E
Deruta	66	42.59 N	12.25 E
De Ruyter	210	42.45 N	75.53 W
DeRuyter Reservoir ⊜[1]	210	42.49 N	75.53 W
Der'uzino	82	56.18 N	38.16 E
Derval	32	47.40 N	1.40 W
Derventa	38	44.58 N	17.55 E
Derwent	182	53.39 N	110.58 W
Derwent ≃, Austl.	166	43.03 S	147.22 E
Derwent ≃, Eng., U.K.	44	53.45 N	0.57 W
Derwent ≃, Eng., U.K.	44	54.57 N	1.41 W
Derwent ≃, Eng., U.K.	44	54.38 N	3.34 W
Derwent ≃, Eng., U.K.	44	52.53 N	1.17 W
Derwent Bridge	166	42.08 S	146.13 E
Derwent Reservoir ⊜[1]	44	54.50 N	2.00 W
Derwent Water ⊜	44	54.34 N	3.08 W
Deržavino	80	53.13 N	52.22 E
Deržavinsk	86	51.03 N	66.19 E
Desaguadero ≃, Arg.	252	34.13 S	66.47 W
Desaguadero ≃, Bol.	248	18.24 S	67.05 W
Deşt	130	39.10 N	39.49 E
Des Allemands	194	29.49 N	90.28 W
Désappointement, Îles du II	14	14.10 S	141.20 W
Des Arc	194	34.58 N	91.29 W
Desborough	42	52.27 N	0.49 W
Descabezado Grande, Volcán ∧[1]	252	35.36 S	70.45 W
Descanso, Bra.	252	26.50 S	53.35 W
Descanso, Ca., U.S.	204	32.51 N	116.37 W
Descanso, Punta ›	204	32.16 N	117.03 W
Descanso Gardens ♦	280	34.12 N	118.13 W
Descartes	32	46.58 N	0.42 E
Deschaillons	206	46.32 N	72.07 W
Deschambault	206	46.39 N	71.56 W
Deschambault Lake	184	54.55 N	103.22 W
Deschambault Lake ⊜	184	54.40 N	103.35 W
Descharme Lake ⊜	184	57.05 N	109.13 W
Deschênes	212	45.23 N	75.48 W
Deschênes, Lac ⊜	212	45.22 N	75.51 W
Deschutes ≃, Or., U.S.	202	45.38 N	120.54 W
Deschutes ≃, Wa., U.S.	224	47.02 N	122.54 W
Descoberto	256	21.27 S	42.58 W
Descoberto, Serra do ∧	256	21.24 S	42.57 W
Dese	144	11.05 N	39.41 E
Deseado ≃	254	47.45 S	65.54 W
Deseado, Cabo ›	254	52.44 S	74.44 W
Desembarco de los 33 Orientales, Monumento ⊥	258	33.48 S	58.25 W
Desengaño, Punta ›	254	49.15 S	67.37 W
Desenzano del Garda	64	45.28 N	10.32 E
Deseret Peak ∧	200	40.28 N	112.38 W
Deseronto	212	44.12 N	77.03 W
Désert ≃	190	46.23 N	75.58 W
Désert, Lac ⊜	190	46.35 N	76.19 W
Desertas, Ilhas II	148	32.30 N	16.30 W
Desert Creek ≃	226	38.48 N	119.19 W
Desert Hot Springs	204	33.57 N	116.30 W
Desert Lake ⊜, On., Can.	212	44.32 N	76.35 W
Desert Lake ⊜, Nv., U.S.	204	36.58 N	115.05 W
Desert Mountains ⩕	226	39.16 N	119.00 W
Desert Peak ∧	200	41.11 N	113.22 W
Desert Valley V	204	41.15 N	118.20 W
Desert View Highlands	228	34.37 N	118.13 W
Desfogue del Lago, Canal de ≋	286a	19.26 N	99.03 W
Desford	42	52.39 N	1.17 W
Desha	194	35.44 N	91.40 W
Deshaies	241o	16.18 N	61.48 W
Desheng	102	24.45 N	108.28 E
Deshengchang	107	29.06 N	105.25 E
Deshengpo	102	26.58 N	103.59 E
Deshengtai	104	42.14 N	123.45 E
Deshengyingzi	104	41.44 N	123.14 E
Deshler, Ne., U.S.	198	40.08 N	97.43 W
Deshler, Oh., U.S.	216	41.12 N	83.53 W
Deshnoke	120	27.48 N	73.21 E
Deshon Manor	214	40.52 N	79.57 W
Deshu	128	30.26 N	63.19 E
Deshun	106	31.58 N	120.29 E
Desiderio Tello	252	31.13 S	66.19 W
Desio	62	45.37 N	9.13 E
Des Lacs ≃	198	48.17 N	101.25 W
Deslinde, Arroyo ≃	258	33.44 S	58.52 W

Name	Seite	Breite°′	Länge°′ E = Ost
Desloge	194	37.52 N	90.31 W
Desmarais	182	55.56 N	113.49 W
De Smet	198	44.23 N	97.33 W
De Smet, Lake ⊜[1]	202	44.29 N	106.45 W
Des Moines, Ia., U.S.	190	41.36 N	93.36 W
Des Moines, N.M., U.S.	196	36.45 N	103.50 W
Des Moines, Wa., U.S.	224	47.24 N	122.19 W
Des Moines ≃	178	40.22 N	91.26 W
Des Moines, East Fork ≃	198	42.41 N	94.12 W
Desmoronado, Cerro ∧	234	20.21 N	104.59 W
Dešná, Česko.	61	48.58 N	15.33 E
Desna, S.S.S.R.	78	50.56 N	30.46 E
Desna ≃, S.S.S.R.	78	50.33 N	30.32 E
Desna ≃, S.S.S.R.	82	55.26 N	37.30 E
Desolación, Isla I	254	53.00 S	74.10 W
Désolation, Cap de la → Disappointment, Cape ›	244	54.53 S	36.07 W
Desolation Point ›	116	10.28 N	125.39 E
Desor, Mount ∧[2]	190	47.58 N	89.01 W
De Soto, Il., U.S.	194	37.49 N	89.13 W
De Soto, In., U.S.	216	40.15 N	85.17 W
De Soto, Mo., U.S.	194	38.08 N	90.33 W
De Soto, Tx., U.S.	222	32.35 N	96.51 W
De Soto □[6]	220	27.11 N	81.48 W
De Soto City	220	27.26 N	81.24 W
De Soto National Memorial ⊥	220	27.31 N	82.40 W
De Soto State Park ♦	194	34.28 N	85.36 W
Despatch	158	33.46 S	25.30 E
Despeñaperros, Desfiladero de)(	34	38.24 N	3.30 W
Des Plaines	216	42.02 N	87.53 W
Des Plaines ≃	216	41.24 N	88.16 W
Despotovac	38	44.05 N	21.33 E
Despujols	116	12.31 N	122.01 E
Desroches, Île I	138	5.41 S	53.41 E
Desruisseaux	241f	13.47 N	60.56 W
Dessau	54	51.50 N	12.14 E
Dessel	56	51.14 N	5.07 E
Destacado Island I	116	12.16 N	124.06 E
De Steeg	52	52.02 N	6.04 E
Destek	130	40.51 N	36.12 E
Destelbergen	50	51.03 N	3.48 E
Destêrro	250	7.17 S	37.06 W
Destin	194	30.23 N	86.29 W
Destruction, Mount ∧[2]	162	24.35 S	127.59 E
Destruction Bay	180	61.15 N	138.48 W
Destruction Island I	224	47.40 N	124.30 W
Desulo	71	40.01 N	9.14 E
Desvres	50	50.40 N	1.50 E
Deta	38	45.24 N	21.13 E
Detčino	82	54.49 N	36.19 E
Dete	154	18.38 S	26.50 E
Dethlingen	52	52.57 N	10.07 E
Detling	260	51.18 N	0.34 E
Detmold	52	51.56 N	8.52 E
Detmold □[6]	52	51.48 N	8.00 E
Detour, Point ›	190	45.36 N	86.37 W
De Tour Village	190	46.00 N	83.54 W
Detrital Wash V	200	36.02 N	114.28 W
Detroit, Il., U.S.	219	39.37 N	90.40 W
Detroit, Mi., U.S.	216	42.20 N	83.03 W
Detroit, Mi., U.S.	281	42.20 N	83.03 W
Detroit, Or., U.S.	202	44.44 N	122.08 W
Detroit, Tx., U.S.	196	33.40 N	95.16 W
Detroit ≃	214	42.06 N	83.08 W
Detroit, University of ♁[2]	281	42.25 N	83.08 W
Detroit Beach	216	41.55 N	83.20 W
Detroit City Airport ⊠	281	42.25 N	83.01 W
Detroit Institute of Arts ♁	281	42.22 N	83.04 W
Detroit Lake ⊜[1]	202	44.42 N	122.10 W
Detroit Lakes	198	46.48 N	95.50 W
Detroit Metropolitan-Wayne County Airport ⊠	281	42.13 N	83.22 W
Detroit Race Course ♦	281	42.23 N	83.19 W
Detroit-Windsor Tunnel ⟡[5]	281	42.20 N	83.02 W
Detroit Zoological Park ♦	281	42.29 N	83.09 W
Detskosel'skij	265a	59.44 N	30.28 E
Dettelbach	56	49.48 N	10.09 E
Dettifoss ↳	24a	65.50 N	16.20 W
Dettingen an der Erms	56	48.32 N	9.20 E
Dettwiller	56	48.45 N	7.28 E
Det Udom	110	14.54 N	105.05 E
Detva	30	48.31 N	19.28 E
Deua National Park ♦	166	36.00 S	149.45 E
Deuben	54	51.06 N	12.04 E
Deuels Corners	284a	42.45 N	78.45 W
Deuil-la-Barre	261	48.59 N	2.20 E
Deūlgaon Rāja	122	20.01 N	76.02 E
Deulpur	272b	22.36 N	88.10 E
Deulti	126	22.26 N	87.56 E
Deurne, Bel.	50	51.13 N	4.28 E
Deurne, Ned.	52	51.28 N	5.47 E
Deusen ⟡[8]	263	51.33 N	7.26 E
Deutsche Bucht c	30	54.30 N	7.30 E
Deutsche Demokratische Republik → German Democratic Republic □[1]	30	52.00 N	12.30 E
Deutsch Eylau → Iława	30	53.37 N	19.33 E
Deutschfeistritz	61	47.11 N	15.20 E
Deutschkreutz	61	47.36 N	16.38 E
Deutsch Krone → Wałcz	30	53.17 N	16.28 E
Deutschlandsberg	61	46.49 N	15.13 E
Deutsch-Neudorf	54	50.38 N	13.27 E
Deutsch Wagram	61	48.18 N	16.34 E
Deutsch Wusterhausen	264a	52.18 N	13.35 E
Deutzen	54	51.06 N	12.26 E
Deux-Montagnes	206	45.32 N	73.53 W
Deux-Montagnes □[6]	206	45.35 N	74.05 W
Deux Montagnes, Lac des ⊜	206	45.28 N	73.59 W
Deux-Sèvres □[5]	32	46.30 N	0.20 W
Deva	38	45.53 N	22.55 E
Devakottai	122	9.57 N	78.49 E
De Valls Bluff	194	34.47 N	91.27 W
Devaprayāg	124	30.09 N	78.37 E
Dev'atern'a	80	56.12 N	53.24 E
Dev'atiny	24	60.56 N	36.46 E
Devault	285	40.05 N	75.32 W
Dévaványa	30	47.02 N	20.58 E
Devecikonağı	130	39.55 N	28.34 E
Devecser	30	47.06 N	17.26 E
Deve Dağı ∧	130	40.34 N	41.21 E
Develi	130	38.23 N	35.30 E
Deventer	52	52.15 N	6.10 E
Deveron ≃	46	57.40 N	2.31 W
Devers	222	30.02 N	94.36 W
Devers Canal, West Branch ≋	222	29.57 N	94.46 W
Deversoir Military Base ■	142	30.25 N	32.20 E
Devès, Monts du ⩕	32	45.00 N	3.45 E
Devgad Bāria	120	22.42 N	73.54 E
De View, Bayou ≃	194	34.48 N	91.18 W
Devīkot	120	26.42 N	71.12 E
Devil Lake ⊜	212	44.35 N	76.27 W
Deville	56	49.53 N	4.42 E
Déville-lès-Rouen	50	49.28 N	1.02 E
Devil Peak ∧	226	37.32 N	119.44 W

Symbols in the index entries represent the broad categories identified in the key at the right. Symbols with superior numbers (⩕[1]) identify subcategories (see complete key on page *I · 1).*

Kartensymbole in dem Registerverzeichnis stellen die rechts in Schlüssel erklärten Kategorien dar. Symbole mit hochgestellten Ziffern (⩕[1]) bezeichnen Unterabteilungen einer Kategorie (vgl. vollständiger Schlüssel auf Seite *I · 1).*

Los símbolos incluídos en el texto del índice representan las grandes categorias identificadas con la clave a la derecha. Los símbolos con numeros en su parte superior (⩕[1]) identifican las subcategorías (véase la clave completa en la página *I · 1).*

Les symboles de l'index représentent les catégories indiquées dans la légende à droite. Les symboles suivis d'un indice (⩕[1]) représentent des sous-catégories (voir légende complète à la page *I · 1).*

Os símbolos incluídos no texto do índice representam as grandes categorias identificadas com a chave à direita. Os símbolos com números em sua parte superior (⩕[1]) identificam as subcategorias (veja-se a chave completa à página *I · 1).*

∧ Mountain	Berg	Montaña	Montagne	Montanha
⩕ Mountains	Berge	Montañas	Montagnes	Montanhas
)(Pass	Pass	Paso	Col	Passo
V Valley, Canyon	Tal, Cañon	Valle, Cañón	Vallée, Canyon	Vale, Canhão
≚ Plain	Ebene	Llano	Plaine	Planície
› Cape	Kap	Cabo	Cap	Cabo
I Island	Insel	Isla	Île	Ilha
II Islands	Inseln	Islas	Îles	Ilhas
⊥ Other Topographic Features	Andere Topographische Objekte	Otros Elementos Topográficos	Autres données topographiques	Outros acidentes topográficos

Devil River Peak ∧ 172 40.58 S 172.39 E
Devils ≃ 196 29.39 N 100.58 W
Devil's Bridge 42 52.23 N 3.51 W
Devils Brook ≃ 276 40.20 N 74.37 W
Devils Canyon V 280 34.16 N 117.58 W
Devil's Den State Park ♦ 194 35.46 N 94.16 W
Devils Hole Rapids ᒪ 284a 43.08 N 79.03 W
Devils Hopyard State Park ♦ 207 41.28 N 72.22 W
Devil's Island → Diable, Île du I 250 5.17 N 52.35 W
Devils Lake 198 48.06 N 98.51 W
Devils Lake ⊜, Mi., U.S. 216 41.58 N 84.17 W
Devils Lake ⊜, N.D., U.S. 198 48.01 N 98.52 W
Devils Lake State Park ♦ 190 43.24 N 89.44 W
Devils Paw ∧ 180 58.44 N 133.50 W
Devils Postpile National Monument ♦ 226 37.37 N 119.05 W
Devils Tower ∧ 198 44.31 N 104.57 W
Devils Tower National Monument ♦ 198 44.31 N 104.57 W
Devil's Water ≃ 44 54.58 N 2.02 W
Devin 38 41.45 N 24.24 E
Devine, B.C., Can. 182 50.32 N 122.30 W
Devine, Tx., U.S. 196 29.08 N 98.54 W
Devizes 42 51.22 N 1.59 W
Devladovo 78 48.07 N 33.45 E
De Voe Lake ⊜ 276 40.23 N 74.23 W
Devoll ≃ 38 40.49 N 19.51 E
Dévoluy ⊼ 62 44.39 N 5.53 E
Devon, Ab., Can. 182 53.22 N 113.44 W
Devon, S. Afr. 158 26.21 S 28.48 E
Devon, Pa., U.S. 285 40.02 N 75.25 W
Devon □[6] 42 50.45 N 3.50 W
Devon ≃, Eng., U.K. 42 53.04 N 0.43 W
Devon ≃, Scot., U.K. 46 56.07 N 3.51 W
Devon Island I 16 75.00 N 87.00 W
Devonport, Austl. 166 41.11 S 146.21 E
Devonport, N.Z. 172 36.49 S 174.48 E
Devonport, Eng., U.K. 42 50.22 N 4.10 W
Devonshire 285 39.49 N 75.32 W
Devonshire Plaza ✦[9] 281 42.17 N 83.00 W
Devore 228 34.13 N 117.25 W
Devoto 252 31.24 S 62.19 W
Devrek 130 41.13 N 31.57 E
Devrekâni 130 41.36 N 33.51 E
Devres ≃ 130 41.06 N 34.25 E
Devure ≃ 154 20.00 S 32.20 E
Dewa, Ujung ⋗ 114 2.55 N 95.48 E
Dewakang-lompo, Pulau I 112 5.24 S 118.25 E
Dewar 196 35.27 N 95.56 W
Dewart 210 41.07 N 76.53 W
Dewart Lake ⊜ 216 41.22 N 85.47 W
Dewās 120 22.58 N 76.04 E
Dewas □[5] 124 22.30 N 76.30 E
Dewa-sanchi ⊼[2] 92 39.05 N 140.10 E
Dewdney 224 49.10 N 122.12 W
Dewetsdorp 158 29.33 S 26.34 E
Dewey, P.R. 240m 18.18 N 65.18 W
Dewey, Il., U.S. 216 40.19 N 88.17 W
Dewey, Ok., U.S. 196 36.47 N 95.56 W
Dewey, Wa., U.S. 224 48.25 N 122.37 W
Dewey Beach 208 38.41 N 75.04 W
Deweyville 194 30.18 N 93.45 W
De Witt, Ar., U.S. 194 34.17 N 91.20 W
Dewitt, Il., U.S. 219 40.11 N 88.47 W
De Witt, Ia., U.S. 190 41.49 N 90.32 W
De Witt, Mi., U.S. 216 42.50 N 84.34 W
De Witt, Ne., U.S. 198 40.23 N 96.55 W
De Witt, N.Y., U.S. 210 43.02 N 76.03 W
De Witt □[6], Il., U.S. 216 40.12 N 88.55 W
De Witt □[6], Tx., U.S. 222 29.07 N 97.20 W
Dewittville 214 42.14 N 79.27 W
Dewsbury 44 53.42 N 1.37 W
Dexing 100 28.54 N 117.36 E
Dexingjie 98 39.54 N 122.50 E
Dexter, Me., U.S. 188 45.01 N 69.17 W
Dexter, Mi., U.S. 216 42.20 N 83.53 W
Dexter, Mo., U.S. 194 36.47 N 89.57 W
Dexter, N.M., U.S. 196 33.11 N 104.22 W
Dexter, N.Y., U.S. 212 44.00 N 76.02 W
Dexterity Fiord c[2] 176 71.11 N 73.03 W
Deyang 102 31.14 N 104.22 E
Dey-Dey, Lake ⊜ 162 29.12 S 131.04 E
Deyhūk 128 33.17 N 57.30 E
Deyyer 128 27.50 N 51.55 E
Dez ≃ 128 31.39 N 48.52 E
Dezfūl 128 32.23 N 48.24 E
Dez Gerd 128 30.45 N 51.57 E
Dezhou 98 37.27 N 116.18 E
Dežneva, mys ⋗ 180 66.06 N 169.45 W
Dezong 120 32.09 N 90.20 E
Dezzo di Scalve 64 45.59 N 10.05 E
Dgāmcha, Sebkhet te-n- ⊜ 150 18.45 N 15.48 W
Dhabān Singh 124 31.44 N 73.34 E
Dhāding 124 27.52 N 84.55 E
Dhādkā 126 22.47 N 86.30 E
Dhāfna ∧ 267c 38.07 N 23.38 E
Dháfni 38 37.48 N 22.01 E
Dhafníon, Moní ✿[1] 267c 38.01 N 23.38 E
Dhahab 140 28.29 N 34.32 E
Dhahran → Az-Zahrān 128 26.18 N 50.08 E
Dhaka (Dacca), Bngl. 126 23.43 N 90.25 E
Dhāka, India 124 26.41 N 85.10 E
Dhākauli 124 24.45 N 77.51 E
Dhakuria Lake ⊜ 272b 22.31 N 88.22 E
Dhaleswari ≃ 126 23.32 N 90.34 E
Dhāli 130 35.01 N 33.25 E
Dhamār 144 14.46 N 44.23 E
Dhampur 124 29.19 N 78.31 E
Dhāmrai 126 23.55 N 90.13 E
Dhamtari 122 20.41 N 81.34 E
Dhāmura 126 22.53 N 90.12 E
Dhanaula 123 30.17 N 75.35 E
Dhanaura 124 28.58 N 78.15 E
Dhānbād 126 23.48 N 86.27 E
Dhānbād □[5] 124 23.47 N 86.26 E
Dhandhuka 120 22.22 N 71.59 E
Dhanera 120 24.31 N 72.02 E
Dhaneswargāti 126 23.25 N 89.20 E
Dhangarhi 124 28.41 N 80.36 E
Dhaniākhāli 126 22.58 N 88.06 E
D'Hanis 196 29.20 N 99.17 W
Dhankuta 124 26.59 N 87.20 E
Dhansar 272c 19.07 N 73.05 E
Dhanushkodi 122 9.11 N 79.24 E
Dhānyahānā 272b 22.48 N 88.11 E
Dhār 120 22.36 N 75.18 E
Dharampur 122 20.32 N 73.11 E
Dharān Bāzār 124 26.49 N 87.17 E
Dharangaon 120 21.01 N 75.16 E
Dhārāpuram 122 10.44 N 77.31 E
Dhāri 120 21.20 N 71.01 E
Dhāriwāl 123 31.57 N 75.19 E
Dharmābād 122 18.54 N 77.51 E
Dharmapuri 122 12.08 N 78.10 E
Dharmavaram 122 14.26 N 77.43 E
Dharmjaygarh 124 22.28 N 83.13 E
Dharmkot 123 30.57 N 75.14 E
Dharmsāla 123 32.13 N 76.19 E
Dhārni 120 21.33 N 76.53 E
Dharoor, Tog V 144 10.10 N 50.00 E
Dharug National Park ♦ 170 33.25 S 151.05 E
Dhārwār 122 15.28 N 75.01 E
Dhasān ≃ 124 25.48 N 79.24 E
Dhātrigrām 126 23.15 N 88.20 E
Dhaulāgiri ∧ 124 28.42 N 83.30 E
Dhebar Lake ⊜ 120 24.16 N 74.00 E
Dhelfoi ⊥ 38 38.30 N 22.29 E
Dhenkānāl 120 20.40 N 85.36 E
Dherínia 130 35.03 N 33.57 E
Dhërmiu ✿[1] 38 40.08 N 19.42 E
Dherue, Loch an ⊜ 46 58.25 N 4.27 W
Dheskáti 38 39.55 N 21.49 E
Dheune ≃ 58 46.54 N 5.00 E
Dhiavolítsion 38 37.18 N 21.58 E
Dhībān 132 31.30 N 35.47 E
Dhidhimótikhon 38 41.21 N 26.30 E
Dhiinsoor 144 2.24 N 42.59 E
Dhī Qār □[4] 128 31.00 N 46.15 E
Dhikti ∧ 38 35.08 N 25.22 E
Dhilos ⊥ 38 37.26 N 25.16 E
Dhimitsána 38 37.37 N 22.03 E
Dhiónisos 267c 38.06 N 23.53 E
Dhirārsām 126 23.57 N 90.25 E
Dhirwah, Wādī adh- V 132 31.18 N 36.56 E
Dhodhekánisos (Dodecanese) II 38 36.30 N 27.00 E
Dhodhóni ⊥ 38 39.34 N 20.47 E
Dhokra 272b 22.40 N 88.34 E
Dholka 120 22.43 N 72.28 E
Dholpur 124 26.42 N 77.54 E
Dhomhnull, Sgurr ∧ 46 56.45 N 5.27 W
Dhone 122 15.25 N 77.53 E
Dhopākholai 126 23.08 N 89.10 E
Dhorāji 120 21.44 N 70.27 E
Dhosha 126 22.15 N 88.33 E
Dhowa 126 24.03 N 86.54 E
Dhoxáton 38 41.05 N 24.14 E
Dhrāngadhra 120 22.59 N 71.28 E
Dhrapetsóna 267c 37.57 N 23.37 E
Dhrol 120 22.34 N 70.25 E
Dhron ≃ 56 49.52 N 6.54 E
Dhubāb 144 12.56 N 43.25 E
Dhubri 124 26.01 N 89.59 E
Dhudiāl 123 33.04 N 72.58 E
Dhulāgarh 272b 22.35 N 88.11 E
Dhulāsār 126 21.52 N 90.14 E
Dhule 120 20.54 N 74.47 E
Dhulia → Dhule 120 20.54 N 74.47 E
Dhuliān 124 24.41 N 87.58 E
Dhulikhel 124 27.37 N 85.33 E
Dhūlsīrās ✦[8] 272a 28.33 N 77.02 E
Dhūnn 56 51.06 N 7.16 E
Dhünn-Stausee ⊜[1] 263 51.05 N 7.16 E
Dhupgāri 124 26.36 N 89.01 E
Dhurbo 144 11.37 N 50.20 E
Dhūri 124 30.22 N 75.52 E
Dhutumkhar ≃ 272c 18.54 N 73.00 E
Dhuudo 144 9.20 N 50.12 E
Dhuudo V 144 9.14 N 50.39 E
Dhuusa Mareeb 144 5.31 N 46.24 E
Dia I 38 35.27 N 25.13 E
Diabaig 46 57.34 N 5.40 W
Diabakania 150 10.38 N 10.58 W
Diable, Île du (Devil's Island) I 250 5.17 N 52.35 W
Diable, Lac du ⊜ 206 46.31 N 74.20 W
Diable, Morne au ∧ 240d 15.37 N 61.27 W
Diable, Pointe du ⋗ 240e 14.47 N 60.54 W
Diable, Rivière du ≃ 206 46.03 N 74.38 W
Diablo, Ca., U.S. 226 37.50 N 121.58 W
Diablo, Wa., U.S. 224 48.43 N 121.09 W
Diablo, Canyon V 200 35.18 N 110.59 W
Diablo, Isla del → Diable, Île du I 250 5.17 N 52.35 W
Diablo, Mount ∧ 226 37.53 N 121.55 W
Diablo, Sierra del ⊼ 196 27.20 N 104.05 W
Diablo Lake ⊜[1] 224 48.43 N 121.08 W
Diablo Plateau ⊼[1] 200 31.30 N 105.30 W
Diablo Range ⊼ 226 37.00 N 121.20 W
Diablotin, Morne ∧ 240d 15.30 N 61.24 W
Diabo 150 7.47 N 5.11 W
Diaca 154 11.30 S 39.59 E
Diadema 256 23.42 S 46.37 W
Diadema □[7] 287b 23.42 S 46.36 W
Diadema Argentina 254 45.46 S 67.40 W
Diafarabé 150 14.09 N 5.01 W
Diagonal 198 40.48 N 94.20 W
Diaka ≃[1] 150 15.13 N 4.14 W
Dialakoto 150 13.19 N 13.18 W
Dialassagou 150 13.45 N 3.37 W
Diamant, Pointe du ⋗ 240e 14.27 N 61.03 W
Diamante, Arg. 252 32.04 S 60.39 W
Diamante, It. 68 39.41 N 15.49 E
Diamante ≃ 252 34.31 S 66.56 W
Diamante, Punta del ⋗ 234 16.47 N 99.52 W
Diamante de Ubá 256 21.12 S 42.55 W
Diamantina 255 18.15 S 43.36 W
Diamantina ≃ 166 26.45 S 139.10 E
Diamantina Fracture Zone ✦ 14 36.00 S 105.00 E
Diamantina Lakes 166 23.46 S 141.09 E
Diamantino 248 14.25 S 56.27 W
Diamantino ≃ 255 16.08 S 52.28 W
Diamond, Il., U.S. 216 41.17 N 88.15 W
Diamond, Mo., U.S. 194 37.00 N 94.19 W
Diamond, Oh., U.S. 214 41.06 N 81.01 W
Diamond Bar 228 34.01 N 117.48 W
Diamond Brook ≃ 276 40.56 N 74.08 W
Diamond Creek 274b 37.41 S 145.09 E
Diamond Creek ≃ 169 37.44 S 145.09 E
Diamond Harbour 126 22.12 N 88.12 E
Diamond Head ⋗[6] 229c 21.16 N 157.49 W
Diamond Hill 207 41.59 N 71.24 W
Diamond Hill Reservoir ⊜[1] 283 42.00 N 71.24 W
Diamond Hill State Park ♦ 283 42.00 N 71.26 W
Diamond Islets II 166 17.25 S 150.58 E
Diamond Lake 216 42.15 N 88.00 W
Diamond Lake ⊜, On., Can. 212 45.04 N 78.02 W
Diamond Lake ⊜, Il., U.S. 278 42.15 N 88.00 W
Diamond Lake ⊜, Mi., U.S. 216 41.54 N 85.59 W
Diamond Lake ⊜, Or., U.S. 202 43.10 N 122.09 W
Diamond Peak ∧, Id., U.S. 202 44.09 N 113.05 W
Diamond Peak ∧, Or., U.S. 202 43.33 N 122.09 W
Diamond Peak ∧, Wa., U.S. 202 46.07 N 117.32 W
Diamond Springs 226 38.41 N 120.48 W
Diamondville 200 41.46 N 110.32 W
Diana 222 32.43 N 94.45 W
Diana Bay c 176 60.50 N 69.50 W
Dianalund 41 55.32 N 11.30 E
Dianbai 102 21.30 N 111.01 E
Dian Chi ⊜ 102 24.50 N 102.42 E
Diancun 105 39.55 N 116.14 E
Dianfangba 102 32.54 N 103.35 E
Diangounté Kamara 150 14.33 N 9.31 W
Dianhu 100 33.58 N 119.38 E
Dianji 98 36.32 N 120.27 E
Dianjiang 102 30.21 N 107.23 E
Diano, Vallo di V 68 40.21 N 15.36 E
Diano Marina 62 43.54 N 8.05 E
Dianópolis 250 11.38 S 46.50 W
Dianqianhe 100 30.44 N 116.02 E
Dianra 150 8.45 N 6.14 W
Dianshang 106 31.10 N 118.51 E
Dianshan Hu ⊜ 106 31.08 N 120.55 E
Diantou 100 27.18 N 120.11 E
Dianzi 104 41.37 N 122.05 E
Diaobingshan 104 42.28 N 123.33 E
Diao'ecun 105 40.43 N 115.49 E
Diaohetou 105 39.17 N 116.43 E
Diaopu 100 32.22 N 119.54 E
Diaoshuilouzi 104 40.59 N 122.22 E
Diaotai 100 29.40 N 119.19 E
Diaowo 105 39.30 N 116.04 E
Diapaga 150 12.04 N 1.47 E
Diapangou 150 12.07 N 0.11 E
Diaphilo, Puntan ⋗ 174n 15.00 N 145.35 E
Dias 256 22.28 S 45.34 W
Diascund Creek Reservoir ⊜[1] 208 37.27 N 76.54 W
Diavolo, Mount ∧ 110 12.42 N 92.55 E
Diaz 110 10.07 N 5.28 W
Diaz 194 35.38 N 91.15 W
Diaz Point ⋗ 156 26.38 S 15.05 E
Dibai 124 28.13 N 78.15 E
Dibang ≃ 120 27.50 N 95.32 E
Dibay → Dubayy 128 25.18 N 55.18 E
Dibaya 152 6.30 S 22.57 E
Dibbīn 132 32.26 N 36.34 E
Dibble Iceberg Tongue ⌂ 9 65.40 S 135.10 E
Dibeng 158 27.35 S 22.54 E
D'Iberville 194 30.25 N 88.53 W
Dibete 156 23.45 S 26.26 E
Dibi 144 4.13 N 41.56 E
Dibo 144 6.31 N 41.52 E
Diboll 222 31.11 N 94.46 W
Dibrugarh 120 27.29 N 94.54 E
Dibs 140 12.34 N 24.14 E
Dibs, Bi'r ⊤[4] 140 22.12 N 29.32 E
Dichāon Kalān ✦[8] 272a 28.39 N 76.59 E
Dick, Mount ∧[2] 168a 31.35 S 116.42 E
Dickelsbach ≃ 263 51.24 N 6.45 E
Dickens 196 33.37 N 100.50 W
Dickerson 208 39.13 N 77.25 W
Dickey ≃ 224 47.55 N 124.37 W
Dickey Lake ⊜, On., Can. 212 44.47 N 77.44 W
Dickey Lake ⊜, Wa., U.S. 224 48.06 N 124.31 W
Dickinson, N.D., U.S. 198 46.52 N 102.47 W
Dickinson, Pa., U.S. 208 40.07 N 77.20 W
Dickinson, Tx., U.S. 222 29.27 N 95.03 W
Dickinson Bayou ≃ 222 29.28 N 94.58 W
Dickinson Island I 281 42.37 N 82.38 W
Dickins Seamount ✦[3] 16 54.30 N 137.00 W
Dicks 158 27.43 S 30.10 E
Dickson, Ok., U.S. 196 34.11 N 96.59 W
Dickson, Tn., U.S. 194 36.04 N 87.23 W
Dickson City 210 41.28 N 75.36 W
Dicle → Tigris ≃ 128 31.00 N 47.25 E
Dicomano 66 43.53 N 11.31 E
Diculom 116 7.54 N 122.14 E
Dicun 100 33.46 N 117.32 E
Didam 52 51.56 N 6.08 E
Didao 89 45.22 N 130.51 E
Didbiran 89 51.58 N 139.20 E
Didcot 42 51.37 N 1.15 W
Didesa ≃ 144 9.56 N 35.45 E
Didiéni 150 13.53 N 8.06 W
Didimbo 152 17.30 S 21.45 E
Didinga Hills ⊼ 154 4.20 N 33.35 E
Didsbury 182 51.40 N 114.08 W
Didsbury ✦[8] 262 53.25 N 2.14 W
Diduyon ≃ 116 16.36 N 121.42 E
Dīdwāna 120 27.24 N 74.34 E
Didy 157b 18.07 S 48.32 E
Didyma ⊥ 130 37.25 N 27.15 E
Die 62 44.45 N 5.22 E
Die Aue ✦[1] 263 51.40 N 6.35 E
Die Berg ∧ 156 25.12 S 30.09 E
Die Boss 158 31.59 S 19.44 E
Diébougou 150 10.58 N 3.15 W
Dieburg 56 49.54 N 8.50 E
Diecicho de Julio 252 33.41 S 53.33 W
Dieciocho de Marzo 232 25.38 N 97.50 W
Diecke 150 7.21 N 8.58 W
Diedenhofen → Thionville 56 49.22 N 6.10 E
Diedersdorf 264a 52.20 N 13.21 E
Die Erpe ≃ 264a 52.27 N 13.38 E
Diefenbaker, Lake ⊜[1] 184 51.00 N 106.55 W
Diego de Almagro 252 26.23 S 70.03 W
Diego de Almagro, Isla I 254 51.25 S 75.10 W
Diego de Ocampo, Pico ∧ 238 19.35 N 70.45 W
Diego Garcia I 12 7.20 S 72.25 E
Diego Gaynor 258 34.17 S 59.14 W
Diego Ramírez, Islas II 244 56.30 S 68.44 W
Die Haard ✦[1] 263 51.41 N 7.15 E
Diekirch 56 49.53 N 6.10 E
Diekseе ⊜ 54 54.10 N 10.30 E
Dielingen 52 52.26 N 8.20 E
Dielsdorf 58 47.29 N 8.27 E
Diéma 150 14.32 N 9.12 W
Diemansputs 158 29.54 S 21.33 E
Diemberg 150 12.28 N 16.47 W
Diemel ≃ 52 51.39 N 9.27 E
Diemel-Talsperre ✦[6] 56 51.22 N 8.42 E
Diemen 52 52.20 N 4.58 E
Diemuchuoke 120 32.42 N 79.29 E
Dien-bien-phu 110 21.23 N 103.01 E
Diepenau 52 52.25 N 8.44 E
Diepenbeek 56 50.54 N 5.24 E
Diepenheim 52 52.12 N 6.33 E
Diepensee 264a 52.22 N 13.31 E
Diepenveen 52 52.18 N 6.08 E
Diepholz 52 52.35 N 8.21 E
Diepoldsau 58 47.23 N 9.38 E
Dieppe, N.B., Can. 186 46.06 N 64.45 W
Dieppe, Fr. 50 49.56 N 1.05 E
Dierbao 98 40.20 N 114.32 E
Dierdorf 56 50.33 N 7.39 E
Dieren 52 52.03 N 6.06 E
Dierhagen 54 54.18 N 12.21 E
Dierks 194 34.07 N 94.00 W
Diersbach 60 48.25 N 13.34 E
Diersfordt 263 51.42 N 6.33 E
Di'er Songhua ≃ 89 45.26 N 124.39 E
Diesdorf 52 52.45 N 10.52 E
Dieskau 54 51.26 N 12.02 E
Diessem ✦[8] 263 51.20 N 6.35 E
Diessen 52 47.56 N 11.06 E
Diessenhofen 58 47.41 N 8.45 E
Diest 56 50.59 N 5.03 E
Dietenheim 58 48.12 N 10.04 E
Dietersburg 60 48.30 N 12.55 E
Dietersdorf 56 50.13 N 10.49 E
Dietfurt 58 48.57 N 10.56 E
Dietfurt an der Altmühl 60 49.02 N 11.35 E
Dietikon 58 47.24 N 8.24 E
Dietmannsried 58 47.49 N 10.17 E
Dietrich 202 42.54 N 114.15 W
Dietzenbach 56 50.01 N 8.47 E
Dietzhölztal 56 50.51 N 8.27 E
Dieue-sur-Meuse 56 49.04 N 5.25 E
Dieulefit 62 44.31 N 5.04 E
Dieulouard 56 48.51 N 6.04 E
Dieuze 56 48.49 N 6.43 E
Dievenіškės 76 54.12 N 25.37 E
Dievenow → Dziwnów 30 54.03 N 14.45 E
Diever 52 52.52 N 6.19 E
Die Ville ⊼[2] 56 50.40 N 6.55 E
Die Wurzen (Koren) ✕ 64 46.31 N 13.45 E
Diez 56 50.22 N 8.01 E
Diez de Octubre 232 24.44 N 104.39 W
Dif 144 0.59 N 40.57 E
Difang 98 35.23 N 117.52 E
Diffa 146 13.19 N 12.37 E
Diffa □[5] 146 16.00 N 13.30 E
Differdange 56 49.31 N 5.52 E
Difficult Run ≃ 284c 38.58 N 77.14 W
Diffun 116 16.34 N 121.33 E
Difuri I 122 5.44 N 73.08 E
Dīg 118 27.28 N 77.20 E
Digambarpur 126 21.51 N 88.26 E
Digba 154 4.24 N 25.47 E
Digboi 120 27.23 N 95.38 E
Digby 186 44.37 N 65.46 W
Digby Neck ⋗[1] 186 44.30 N 66.10 W
Dige 98 34.22 N 114.28 E
Digerberget ∧[2] 40 60.35 N 13.25 E
Digges Islands II 176 62.35 N 78.00 W
Diggle 262 53.34 N 1.59 W
Dighalia 126 23.07 N 89.39 E
Dighīpāra 126 21.58 N 88.17 E
Dighode 272c 18.54 N 73.02 E
Dighra 272b 22.47 N 88.32 E
Dighton, Ks., U.S. 198 38.28 N 100.28 W
Dighton, Ma., U.S. 207 41.48 N 71.07 W
Di Giorgio 228 35.15 N 118.51 W
Digin 132 18.33 N 77.36 E
Digmoor 262 53.32 N 2.45 W
Dignagar 126 23.27 N 87.41 E
Dignano 64 46.05 N 12.56 E
Digne 62 44.06 N 6.14 E
Digoin 32 46.29 N 3.59 E
Digomi 84 41.47 N 44.44 E
Digong 104 42.11 N 122.03 E
Digor 84 40.23 N 43.24 E
Digora 84 43.10 N 44.09 E
Digos 116 6.45 N 125.20 E
Digra 272b 22.50 N 88.20 E
Digras 122 20.07 N 77.43 E
Digri 120 25.10 N 69.07 E
Digui 152 5.28 N 20.50 E
Digul ≃ 164 7.07 S 138.42 E
Dih 130 37.46 N 42.11 E
Dihaer 86 42.35 N 89.49 E
Dihun 144 7.18 N 42.42 E
Diirmentobe 86 45.44 N 63.37 E
Dijag 24 65.48 N 57.39 E
Dijlah → Tigris ≃ 128 31.00 N 47.25 E
Dijlah, Wādī V 142 29.58 N 31.18 E
Dijle (Dyle) ≃ 56 50.53 N 4.42 E
Dijohan Point ⋗ 116 16.19 N 122.14 E
Dijon 58 47.19 N 5.01 E
Dik 146 9.58 N 17.31 E
Dikaja 76 59.15 N 39.30 E
Dikala 154 4.41 N 31.23 E
Dikan'ka 78 49.49 N 34.32 E
Dikbıyık 130 41.13 N 36.38 E
Dike 190 42.27 N 92.37 W
Dikhil 144 11.06 N 42.22 E
Dikili 130 39.04 N 26.53 E
Dikirnis 142 31.05 N 31.35 E
Dikli 76 57.35 N 25.06 E
Diklosmta, gora ∧ 84 42.29 N 45.47 E
Dikmen 130 39.53 N 32.50 E
Dikodougou 150 9.04 N 5.46 W
Diksmuide (Dixmude) 50 51.02 N 2.52 E
Dikson 74 73.30 N 80.35 E
Dikwa 146 12.02 N 13.56 E
Dila 144 6.21 N 38.17 E
Dilbeek 50 50.51 N 4.16 E
Dile Point ⋗ 116 17.34 N 120.20 E
Dilerpur 272b 22.51 N 88.10 E
Dili 112 8.33 S 125.35 E
Dilia V 146 16.53 N 11.00 E
Diligent Strait 및 110 12.11 N 92.57 E
Dilian 110 11.35 N 108.04 E
Dilijan 84 40.45 N 44.52 E
Diližanskij zapovednik ♦ 84 40.40 N 45.00 E
Dill ≃ 56 50.33 N 8.29 E
Dill City 196 35.16 N 99.08 W
Dillenburg 56 50.44 N 8.17 E
Diller 198 40.06 N 96.56 W
Dilley, Or., U.S. 224 45.29 N 123.07 W
Dilley, Tx., U.S. 196 28.40 N 99.10 W
Dilling 140 12.03 N 29.39 E
Dillingen 56 49.21 N 6.44 E
Dillingen an der Donau 56 48.34 N 10.29 E
Dillingham 180 59.02 N 158.29 W
Dillon, Co., U.S. 200 39.37 N 106.02 W
Dillon, Mt., U.S. 202 45.12 N 112.38 W
Dillon, S.C., U.S. 192 34.24 N 79.22 W
Dillon ≃ 184 55.56 N 108.57 W
Dillon Cone ∧ 172 42.16 S 173.13 E
Dillon Lake ⊜ 184 55.45 N 109.30 W
Dillon Lake ⊜[1] 188 40.02 N 82.10 W
Dillon Mountain ∧ 200 33.51 N 108.48 W
Dillon Reservoir ⊜[1] 200 39.35 N 106.02 W
Dillon State Park ♦ 188 40.03 N 82.08 W
Dillonvale 214 40.11 N 80.46 W
Dillsboro 218 39.01 N 85.03 W
Dillsburg 208 40.06 N 77.02 W
Dilltown 214 40.29 N 79.00 W
Dillwyn 192 37.32 N 78.27 W
Dilly 150 15.01 N 7.40 W
Dilolo 152 10.42 S 22.20 E
Dilsen 56 51.02 N 5.44 E
Dilworth 198 46.52 N 96.42 W
Dilworthtown 285 39.54 N 75.34 W
Dima, Ang. 152 15.27 S 20.10 E
Dima, Indon. 114 1.20 N 97.20 E
Dimāpur 120 25.54 N 93.44 E
Dimas 234 23.43 N 106.47 W
Dimashq (Damascus) 132 33.30 N 36.18 E
Dimashq □[4] 132 33.30 N 37.00 E
Dimass, Rass ⋗ 36 35.37 N 11.03 E
Dimataling 116 7.32 N 123.22 E
Dimbelenge 152 5.33 S 23.07 E
Dimbokro 150 6.39 N 4.42 W
Dimbokro □[5] 150 6.45 N 4.15 W
Dimboola 166 36.27 S 142.02 E
Dîmboviţa □[6] 38 45.00 N 25.30 E
Dîmboviţa ≃ 38 44.14 N 26.27 E
Dimbulah 166 17.09 S 145.07 E
Dime Box 222 30.21 N 96.50 W
Dimetoka 130 40.16 N 27.17 E
Dimitrov 83 48.15 N 37.18 E
Dimitrovgrad, Blg. 38 42.03 N 25.36 E
Dimitrovgrad, Jugo. 38 43.01 N 22.47 E
Dimitrovgrad, S.S.S.R. 80 54.14 N 49.39 E
Dimitrovo → Pernik, Blg. 38 42.36 N 23.02 E
Dimitrovo, S.S.S.R. 78 48.36 N 33.01 E
Dimitrovskoje 85 40.16 N 44.54 E
Dimlang ∧ 146 8.24 N 11.47 E
Dimmitt 196 34.33 N 102.18 W
Dimo 154 5.19 N 29.10 E
Dimock 210 41.45 N 75.32 W
Dimona 132 31.04 N 35.02 E
Dimondale 216 42.38 N 84.38 W
Dinach 144 9.15 N 50.37 E
Dinagat 116 9.59 N 125.35 E
Dinagat Island I 116 10.12 N 125.35 E
Dinagat Sound 및 116 9.59 N 125.40 E
Dinahican Point ⋗ 116 14.42 N 121.44 E
Dinājpur 124 25.38 N 88.38 E
Dinalupihan 116 14.52 N 120.28 E
Dinamarca → Denmark □[1] 26 56.00 N 10.00 E
Dinamarca, Estrecho de → Denmark Strait 및 10 67.00 N 25.00 W
Dinami 68 38.31 N 16.09 E
Dinamita 196 25.43 N 103.38 W
Dinamo 80 50.15 N 41.38 E
Dinan 32 48.27 N 2.02 W
Dīnānagar 123 32.09 N 75.28 E
Dinant 56 50.16 N 4.55 E
Dinar 130 38.04 N 30.10 E
Dinara ∧ 36 43.50 N 16.35 E
Dinard 32 48.38 N 2.04 W
Dinaric Alps → Dinara ⊼ 36 43.50 N 16.35 E
Dinarische Alpen → Dinara ⊼ 36 43.50 N 16.35 E
Dinas, Pil. 116 7.38 N 123.20 E
Dinas, Wales, U.K. 42 51.00 N 4.54 W
Dinas Head ⋗ 42 52.02 N 4.54 W
Dinas Powys 42 51.26 N 3.14 W
Dindanko 150 14.08 N 9.30 W
Dindar, Nahr ad- (Dinder) ≃ 140 14.06 N 33.40 E
Dindārpur ✦[8] 272a 28.36 N 76.59 E
Dinde 152 14.12 S 13.44 E
Dinder (Nahr ad-Dindar) ≃ 140 14.06 N 33.40 E
Dinder National Park ♦ 140 12.40 N 35.20 E
Dindi ≃ 122 16.21 N 79.13 E
Dindigul 122 10.21 N 77.57 E
Dindima 150 10.18 N 10.12 E
Dindori 124 22.57 N 81.05 E
Dineksaray 130 37.23 N 32.37 E
Dinga, Pāk. 120 25.26 N 67.10 E
Dinga, Pāk. 123 32.38 N 73.43 E
Dinga, Zaïre 152 5.19 S 16.34 E
Dingalan Bay c 116 15.18 N 121.25 E
Dingan 110 19.44 N 110.21 E
Dingba 154 3.24 N 27.55 E
Dingbian 102 37.40 N 107.41 E
Dingbianji 102 36.37 N 108.41 E
Dingcheng 106 31.18 N 119.10 E
Dingden 52 51.46 N 6.37 E
Dinge 152 4.58 S 12.22 E
Dingelsdorf 58 47.44 N 9.09 E
Dingelstädt 54 51.18 N 10.19 E
Dingelstedt 54 51.58 N 10.58 E
Dingeryu 105 39.37 N 114.55 E
Dingfeng 106 31.20 N 121.45 E
Dinggou 100 32.34 N 119.39 E
Dinghai 100 30.02 N 122.06 E
Dingila 154 3.39 N 26.22 E
Dingjia 107 29.24 N 106.09 E
Dingjiagou 104 40.40 N 122.35 E
Dingjiandian 100 32.06 N 120.52 E
Dingjiasuo 100 32.32 N 120.40 E
Dingjiazhuang 106 32.11 N 120.16 E
Dingjie 124 28.29 N 88.06 E
Dingkouzhen 102 39.55 N 106.40 E
Dingla 124 27.21 N 87.08 E
Dingle 48 52.08 N 10.15 W
Dingle ✦[8] 262 53.23 N 2.57 W
Dingle Bay c 48 52.05 N 10.15 W
Dingley 274b 37.58 S 145.07 E
Dinglingen 58 48.20 N 7.50 E
Dingman Creek ≃ 212 42.55 N 81.25 W
Dingmans Ferry 210 41.14 N 74.53 W
Dingnan 100 24.48 N 114.59 E
Dingnan ≃ 100 24.28 N 115.26 E
Dingo 166 23.39 S 149.20 E
Dingolfing 60 48.38 N 12.31 E
Dingras 116 18.06 N 120.42 E
Dingri 120 28.35 N 86.38 E
Dingshuzhen 106 31.17 N 119.50 E
Dingtao 98 35.04 N 115.34 E
Dingtuna 40 59.34 N 16.22 E
Dinguira 150 14.11 N 11.16 W
Dinguiraye 150 11.18 N 10.43 W
Dingwall, N.S., Can. 186 46.54 N 60.28 W
Dingwall, Scot., U.K. 46 57.35 N 4.29 W
Dingxi 102 35.33 N 104.32 E
Dingxian 98 38.32 N 114.59 E
Dingxiang 102 38.30 N 113.00 E
Dingxiao 102 25.13 N 105.07 E
Dingxing 105 39.17 N 115.46 E
Dingyan 100 32.23 N 120.45 E
Dingyuan 100 32.32 N 117.40 E
Dingzhouying 105 40.20 N 115.43 E
Dingzichang 107 28.54 N 106.08 E
Dingzi Gang c 98 36.37 N 120.50 E
Dinh, Mui ⋗ 110 11.22 N 109.01 E
Dinhāta 124 26.08 N 89.28 E
Dinh-ca 110 21.45 N 106.05 E
Dinh-lap 110 21.33 N 107.06 E
Dinin ≃ 48 52.43 N 7.18 W
Dinkel ≃ 52 52.30 N 6.58 E
Dinkelsbühl 56 49.04 N 10.19 E
Dinkelscherben 58 48.21 N 10.35 E
Dinkey Creek ≃ 226 36.54 N 119.07 W
Dinklage 52 52.40 N 8.07 E
Dinnebito Wash V 200 35.29 N 111.14 W
Dinner Point ⋗ 220 28.28 N 82.41 W
Dinnet 46 57.03 N 2.54 W
Dinnington 44 53.22 N 1.12 W
Dinokwe 156 23.24 S 26.40 E
Dinorwic 184 49.41 N 92.30 W
Dinorwic Lake ⊜ 184 49.37 N 92.33 W
Dinosaur 200 40.14 N 109.00 W
Dinosaur Lake ⊜[1] 182 55.57 N 122.07 W
Dinosaur National Monument ♦ 200 40.32 N 108.58 W
Dinosaur Provincial Park ♦ 182 50.45 N 111.30 W
Dinskaja 78 45.13 N 39.14 E
Dinslaken 52 51.34 N 6.44 E
Dinslaken ✦[8] 263 51.36 N 6.43 E
Dinslakener Bruch 263 51.35 N 6.43 E
Dinslaken-Schwarze Heide, Flughafen ⊠ 263 51.37 N 6.51 E
Dinsmore 184 51.20 N 107.26 W
Dintel ≃ 52 51.39 N 4.22 E
Dinteloord 52 51.37 N 4.22 E
Dinuba 226 36.32 N 119.23 W
Dinwiddie, S. Afr. 273d 26.16 S 28.10 E
Dinwiddie, Va., U.S. 208 37.04 N 77.35 W
Dinwiddie □[6] 208 37.10 N 77.20 W
Dinxperlo 52 51.52 N 6.29 E
Diö 56 56.38 N 14.13 E
Diobo 152 2.16 N 20.29 E
Diodār 120 24.06 N 71.47 E
Dioïla 150 12.29 N 6.44 W
Diois ⊼[9] 62 44.40 N 5.20 E
Diomede 180 65.47 N 169.00 W
Dion ≃ 150 10.12 N 8.39 W
Dionisio 255 19.49 S 42.45 W
Dionísio Cerqueira 252 26.15 S 53.38 W
Dionne, Lac ⊜ 186 49.26 N 67.55 W
Dions 62 43.56 N 4.19 E
Diorama 255 16.21 S 51.14 W
Dios 175e 5.33 S 154.58 E
Diósd 264c 47.25 N 18.57 E
Diouloulou 150 13.03 N 16.34 W
Dioumanténé 150 10.32 N 5.55 W
Dioundiou 150 12.37 N 3.33 E
Diounganі 150 14.19 N 2.44 W
Dioura 150 14.50 N 5.15 W
Diourbel 150 14.40 N 16.15 W
Diourbel □[4] 150 14.40 N 16.00 W
Dipaculao 116 15.51 N 121.32 E
Dipai 100 23.50 N 114.06 E
Dīpālpur 123 30.40 N 73.39 E
Dipignano 68 39.15 N 16.15 E
Dipilo, Pizzo ∧ 66 37.57 N 13.59 E
Diplo 120 24.28 N 69.35 E
Dipolog 116 8.35 N 123.20 E
Dippoldiswalde 54 50.54 N 13.40 E
Dipton 172 45.54 S 168.22 E
Dipu 106 30.38 N 119.41 E
Diqiyingzi 104 42.11 N 121.29 E
Dique Florentino Ameghino 254 43.40 S 66.25 W
Dīr 123 35.12 N 71.53 E
Dira, Djebel ∧ 34 36.05 N 3.38 E
Diré 150 16.16 N 3.24 W
Direction, Cape ⋗ 164 12.51 S 143.32 E
Dire Dawa 144 9.37 N 41.52 E
Direkli 130 39.43 N 36.40 E
Diriamba 236 11.51 N 86.14 W
Dirico 152 17.58 S 20.47 E
Dirillo, Lago ⊜ 70 37.08 N 14.42 E
Dirimo 236 11.52 N 86.03 W
Diriyah 146 30.09 N 10.26 W
Dirk Hartog Island I 162 25.48 S 113.00 E
Dirkiesdorp 158 27.10 S 30.25 E
Dirkou 146 19.01 N 12.53 E
Dirkshorn 52 52.45 N 4.45 E
Dirksland 52 51.44 N 4.06 E
Dirmaich 60 48.27 N 12.30 E
Dirmstein 140 13.37 N 26.06 E
Dirranbandi 166 28.35 S 148.14 E
Dirri 144 4.01 N 46.43 E
Dirs 144 18.32 N 42.05 E
Dirschau → Tczew 30 54.06 N 18.47 E
Dirty Devil ≃ 200 37.53 N 110.24 W
Disah 140 12.02 N 34.19 E
Disappointment, Cape ⋗, Falk. Is. 244 54.53 S 36.07 W
Disappointment, Cape ⋗, Wa., U.S. 224 46.18 N 124.03 W
Disappointment, Lake ⊜ 162 23.30 S 122.50 E
Disappointment, Mount ∧ 169 37.25 S 145.18 E
Disappointment Creek ≃ 200 38.01 N 108.51 W
Disaster Bay c 166 37.17 S 150.00 E
Disautel 182 48.22 N 119.14 W
Disbrow Drain ⌂ 281 42.06 N 83.27 W
Disco 214 42.41 N 83.02 W
Discovery 273d 26.10 S 27.54 E
Discovery Bay c, Austl. 166 38.12 S 141.07 E
Discovery Bay c, H.K. 271d 22.18 N 114.01 E
Discovery Bay c, Wa., U.S. 224 48.05 N 122.50 W
Discovery Island I 224 48.25 N 123.15 W
Discovery Passage 및 182 50.00 N 125.15 W
Discovery Tablemount ✦[3] 8 42.00 S 0.10 E
Disentis 58 46.43 N 8.51 E
Dishāshah 142 28.59 N 30.51 E
Dishergarh 126 23.41 N 86.50 E
Dishman 202 47.39 N 117.16 W
Dishnā 140 26.07 N 32.28 E
Dishna ≃ 180 63.37 N 157.18 W
Disīdi 130 38.47 N 39.00 E
Disihao 100 28.01 N 117.06 E
Disko 216 41.00 N 85.57 W
Disko I 176 69.50 N 53.30 W
Disko Bugt c 176 69.15 N 52.00 W
Disley 262 53.21 N 2.02 W
Disley Tunnel ✦[5] 262 53.22 N 2.03 W
Dismal ≃ 198 41.50 N 100.05 W
Dismal Lakes ⊜ 176 67.26 N 117.07 W
Dismal Swamp Canal ⌂ 208 36.45 N 76.20 W
Disna 76 55.33 N 28.10 E
Disna ≃ 76 55.34 N 28.12 E
Disney 196 36.28 N 95.00 W
Disneyland ♦ 228 33.48 N 117.55 W
Disneyworld ♦ 220 28.27 N 81.28 W
Diso 68 40.00 N 18.23 E
Dispur 120 26.08 N 91.47 E
Disputanta 208 37.07 N 77.13 W
Disraeli 206 45.54 N 71.21 W
Diss 42 52.23 N 1.07 E
Dissen 52 52.07 N 8.12 E
Dissimieux, Lac ⊜ 186 49.51 N 69.48 W
Distant 214 40.58 N 79.21 W
Disteghil Sār ∧ 123 36.19 N 75.12 E
Distelн 263 51.36 N 7.09 E
Distington 44 54.36 N 3.32 W
District Heights 284c 38.51 N 76.53 W
District of Columbia □[3] 208 38.54 N 77.01 W
Distrito Especial □[5] 246 4.15 N 74.15 W
Distrito Federal □[5], Arg. 258 34.36 S 58.26 W
Distrito Federal □[5], Bra. 255 15.45 S 47.45 W
Distrito Federal □[5], Méx. 234 19.15 N 99.10 W
Distrito Federal □[5], Ven. 246 10.30 N 66.55 W
Distroff 56 49.20 N 6.16 E
Disūq 142 31.08 N 30.39 E
Ditfurt 54 51.50 N 11.11 E
Dithmarschen ✦[1] 30 54.05 N 9.00 E
Dit Island I 116 11.15 N 120.56 E
Dittaino ≃ 70 37.25 N 15.00 E
Ditton, Eng., U.K. 260 51.18 N 0.27 E
Ditton, Eng., U.K. 262 53.22 N 2.45 W
Ditton ≃ 206 45.23 N 71.12 W
Ditton Priors 42 52.30 N 2.35 W
Ditzingen 56 48.49 N 9.03 E
Ditzum 52 53.18 N 7.16 E
Diu 120 20.42 N 70.59 E
Diuata Mountains ⊼ 116 9.10 N 125.47 E
Diuata Point ⋗ 116 9.05 N 125.12 E
Dīva 272c 19.09 N 72.59 E
Divalá 236 8.25 N 82.43 W
Divāndarreh 128 35.55 N 47.02 E
Divčice 61 49.06 N 14.19 E
Dive 272c 19.11 N 73.02 E
Divejevo 80 55.03 N 43.15 E
Divenié 152 2.41 S 12.05 E
Divenskaja 76 59.12 N 30.01 E
Diveria ≃ 58 46.09 N 8.19 E
Divernon 219 39.33 N 89.39 W
Dives ≃ 32 49.19 N 0.05 W
Diviči 84 41.12 N 48.59 E
Dividing Creek 208 39.16 N 75.06 W
Dividing Creek ≃ 208 38.05 N 75.32 W
Dividing Ridge ∧ 219 39.07 N 90.39 W
Divignano 266b 45.40 N 8.36 E
Divilacan Bay c 116 17.25 N 122.19 E
Divin 78 51.58 N 24.35 E
Divine Corners 210 41.48 N 74.40 W
Divinhe 156 20.40 S 34.49 E
Divino 255 20.37 S 42.09 W
Divinolândia 256 21.40 S 46.45 W
Divinópolis 255 20.09 S 44.54 W
Divion 50 50.28 N 2.30 E
Divis ∧[2] 44 54.37 N 6.01 W
Divisa Nova 256 21.31 S 46.12 W
Divisões, Serra das ⊼[2] 255 17.00 S 51.00 W
Divisor, Serra do (Cordillera Ultraoriental) ⊼[1] 248 8.20 S 73.30 W
Divizija 78 45.57 N 29.59 E
Divnogorsk 86 55.58 N 92.22 E
Divnoje 80 45.55 N 43.21 E
Divo 150 5.50 N 5.22 W
Divo □[5] 150 5.30 N 5.20 W
Divonne-les-Bains 58 46.22 N 6.08 E
Divriği 130 39.23 N 38.07 E
Dīwāl Qol 120 34.19 N 67.54 E
Dix, Il., U.S. 219 38.27 N 88.56 W
Dix, Ne., U.S. 198 41.14 N 103.29 W
Dix ≃ 192 37.49 N 84.43 W
Dix, Lac des ⊜ 58 46.03 N 7.24 E
Dixboro 216 42.19 N 83.39 W
Dixfield 188 44.32 N 70.27 W
Dix Hills 276 40.49 N 73.20 W
Dixie 275b 43.36 N 79.36 W
Dixie Valley V 204 39.50 N 117.55 W
Dix Milles, Lac ⊜ 190 46.46 N 77.45 W
Dixmoor 278 41.38 N 87.40 W
Dixmude → Diksmuide 50 51.02 N 2.52 E
Dixon, Ca., U.S. 226 38.19 N 121.49 W
Dixon, Il., U.S. 190 41.50 N 89.28 W
Dixon, Ky., U.S. 194 37.31 N 87.41 W
Dixon, Mo., U.S. 194 37.59 N 92.05 W
Dixon, N.M., U.S. 200 36.11 N 105.53 W
Dixon, Oh., U.S. 216 40.57 N 84.48 W
Dixon Entrance 및 182 54.25 N 132.30 W
Dixons Mills 194 32.04 N 87.47 W
Dixons Pond ⊜ 276 40.53 N 74.21 W
Dixonville 214 40.42 N 79.00 W
Dixville 206 45.04 N 71.46 W
Diyā al-Kawm 142 30.38 N 31.05 E
Diyadin 84 39.33 N 43.41 E
Diyālā □[4] 128 34.00 N 45.00 E
Diyālā (Sīrvān) ≃ 128 33.14 N 44.31 E
Diyanga 152 1.29 S 11.52 E
Diyarbakır 130 37.55 N 40.14 E
Diyarbakır □[4] 130 38.00 N 40.15 E
Diyarb Najm 142 30.45 N 31.26 E
Diyu al-Wusta 142 30.54 N 31.33 E
Dizangsi 102 23.00 N 106.20 E
Dizhou 102 23.00 N 106.20 E
Dizy 56 49.04 N 3.58 E
Dizzard Point ⋗ 42 50.45 N 4.38 W
Dja ≃ 152 2.02 N 15.12 E
Dja, Réserve du ✦[4] 152 3.05 N 13.00 E
Djabalpur → Jabalpur 124 23.10 N 79.57 E
Djabir 152 0.32 N 24.05 E
Djadié ≃ 152 0.46 N 12.58 E
Djado 146 21.01 N 12.18 E
Djado, Plateau du ⊼[1] 146 21.45 N 12.50 E

≃ River	Fluss	Río	Rivière	Rio	
⌂ Canal	Kanal	Canal	Canal	Canal	
ᒪ Waterfall, Rapids	Wasserfall, Stromschnellen	Cascada, Rápidos	Chute d'eau, Rapides	Cascata, Rápidos	
및 Strait	Meeresstrasse	Estrecho	Détroit	Estreito	
c Bay, Gulf	Bucht, Golf	Bahía, Golfo	Baie, Golfe	Baía, Golfo	
⊜ Lake, Lakes	See, Seen	Lago, Lagos	Lac, Lacs	Lago, Lagos	
⊞ Swamp	Sumpf	Pantano	Marais	Pântano	
⌂ Ice Features, Glacier	Eis- und Gletscherformen	Accidentes Glaciales	Formes glaciaires	Acidentes glaciares	
⊤ Other Hydrographic Features	Andere Hydrographische Objekte	Otros Elementos Hidrográficos	Autres données hydrographiques	Outros acidentes hidrográficos	

✦ Submarine Features	Untermeerische Objekte	Accidentes Submarinos	Formes de relief sous-marin	Acidentes submarinos	
□ Political Unit	Politische Einheit	Unidad Política	Entité politique	Unidade política	
✿ Cultural Institution	Kulturelle Institution	Institución Cultural	Institution culturelle	Instituição cultural	
⊥ Historical Site	Historische Stätte	Sitio Histórico	Site historique	Sitio histórico	
♦ Recreational Site	Erholungs- und Ferienort	Sitio de Recreo	Centre de loisirs	Area de Lazer	
⊠ Airport	Flughafen	Aeropuerto	Aéroport	Aeroporto	
■ Military Installation	Militäranlage	Instalación Militar	Installation militaire	Instalação militar	
✦ Miscellaneous	Verschiedenes	Misceláneo	Divers	Diversos	

Djaipur
→ Jaipur 120 26.55 N 75.49 E
Djakarta
→ Jakarta 269e 6.10 S 106.48 E
Djakonovo 82 54.34 N 38.20 E
Djakovka 80 50.43 N 46.46 E
Djakovo 83 47.57 N 39.09 E
Djakovo ✦[8] 265b 55.39 N 37.40 E
Djamâa 148 33.32 N 6.00 E
Djamba, Ang. 152 16.46 S 13.59 E
Djamba, Zaïre 152 9.49 S 22.07 E
Djambala 152 2.33 S 14.45 E
Djamschedpur
→ Jamshedpur 126 22.48 N 86.11 E
Djanet 148 24.34 N 9.29 E
Djaouro Mbali 152 5.52 N 13.29 E
Djaret, Oued V 148 26.32 N 1.30 E
Djaul Island I 164 2.56 S 150.55 E
Djebobo ∧ 150 8.20 N 0.35 E
Djébrène 146 11.14 N 19.01 E
Djédaa 146 13.31 N 18.34 E
Djedda
→ Jiddah 144 21.30 N 39.12 E
Djedi, Oued V 148 34.28 N 6.05 E
Djéké Djéké 146 8.25 N 18.12 E
Djelo-Binza 273b 4.23 S 15.16 E
Djema 140 6.03 N 25.19 E
Djember
→ Jember, Indon. 115a 8.10 S 113.42 E
Djember, Tchad 146 10.25 N 17.50 E
Djemila ⊥ 34 36.25 N 5.44 E
Djénné 150 13.54 N 4.33 W
Djenoun, Garet el ∧ 148 25.05 N 5.25 E
Djérem ≃ 152 5.20 N 13.24 E
Djibasso 150 13.07 N 4.10 W
Djibo 150 14.06 N 1.38 W
Djibouti 144 11.36 N 43.09 E
Djibouti □[1], Afr. 136 11.30 N 43.00 E
Djibouti □[1], Afr. 144 11.30 N 43.00 E
Djibrouïa 150 13.13 N 11.14 W
Djiri 273b 4.08 S 15.19 E
Djiri ≃ 273b 4.11 S 15.20 E
Djohong 152 6.50 N 14.42 E
Djokjakarta
→ Yogyakarta 115a 7.48 S 110.22 E
Djokoumatombi 152 0.47 N 15.22 E
Djokupunda 152 5.27 S 20.58 E
Djolu 152 0.37 N 22.21 E
Djombo 152 1.21 N 20.22 E
Djoua ≃ 152 1.13 N 13.12 E
Djouari ≃ 273b 4.13 S 15.08 E
Djoubissi 152 6.12 N 20.45 E
Djoué ≃ 273b 4.19 S 15.14 E
Djougou 150 9.42 N 1.40 E
Djoum 152 2.40 N 12.40 E
Djouna 146 10.27 N 20.04 E
Djourab, Erg du ⊥[8] 146 16.40 N 18.50 E
Djugu 154 1.55 N 30.30 E
Djúpivogur 24a 64.40 N 14.10 W
Djura 40 60.37 N 15.00 E
Djurås 40 60.33 N 15.08 E
Djurmo 40 60.33 N 15.10 E
Djurö 40 59.19 N 18.41 E
Djurö I 26 58.52 N 13.28 E
Djursholm 40 59.24 N 18.05 E
Dlouhá Ves 60 49.12 N 13.31 E
Dmanisi 84 41.22 N 44.12 E
Dmitr'ašovka 76 52.09 N 39.04 E
Dmitrija Lapteva, proliv ꞩ 74 73.00 N 142.00 E
Dmitrijevka, S.S.S.R. 76 52.53 N 40.47 E
Dmitrijevka, S.S.S.R. 78 50.56 N 32.58 E
Dmitrijevka, S.S.S.R. 83 48.55 N 39.10 E
Dmitrijevka, S.S.S.R. 83 47.56 N 38.56 E
Dmitrijevka, S.S.S.R. 85 43.30 N 77.02 E
Dmitrijevka, S.S.S.R. 86 55.10 N 75.36 E
Dmitrijev-L'govskij 78 52.08 N 35.05 E
Dmitrijevskij 86 49.08 N 57.50 E
Dmitrijevskoje, S.S.S.R. 80 45.48 N 41.54 E
Dmitrijevskoje, S.S.S.R. 82 54.40 N 37.38 E
Dmitrijev Usad, S.S.S.R. 76 54.08 N 43.08 E
Dmitrijev Usad, S.S.S.R. 80 54.14 N 43.18 E
Dmitrijevy Gory 80 55.12 N 41.47 E
Dmitrov 82 56.21 N 37.31 E
Dmitrovcy 82 55.16 N 38.55 E
Dmitroviči 76 53.59 N 29.06 E
Dmitrovka, S.S.S.R. 78 48.48 N 32.44 E
Dmitrovka, S.S.S.R. 78 45.29 N 35.04 E
Dmitrovka, S.S.S.R. 78 46.51 N 36.35 E
Dmitrovskij Pogost 76 55.19 N 39.49 E
Dmitrovsk-Orlovskij 76 52.30 N 35.09 E
Dmuchajlovka 78 49.03 N 34.46 E
Dnepr ≃ 78 46.30 N 32.18 E
Dnepr'any 78 46.44 N 33.16 E
Dneprodzeržinsk 78 48.30 N 34.37 E
Dneprodzeržinskoje vodochranilšče ⊜[1] 78 48.45 N 34.00 E
Dnepropetrovsk 78 48.27 N 34.59 E
Dneprovka 78 47.26 N 34.38 E
Dneprovskij liman ⊂[1] 78 46.35 N 31.55 E
Dneprovsko-Bugskij kanal ≅ 78 52.03 N 25.35 E
Dneprovskoje 76 55.40 N 33.55 E
Dnestr ≃ 78 46.18 N 30.17 E
Dnestrovskij liman ⊜ 78 46.15 N 30.17 E
Dnieper
→ Dnepr ≃ 78 46.30 N 32.18 E
Dniepropetrovsk
→ Dnepropetrovsk 78 48.27 N 34.59 E
Dniester
→ Dnestr ≃ 78 46.18 N 30.17 E
Dno 76 57.50 N 29.59 E
Do, Lac ⊜ 150 15.54 N 2.45 W
Doa 154 16.44 S 34.32 E
Do Āb-e Mīkh-e Zarrīn 120 35.16 N 68.00 E
Doaktown 186 46.33 N 66.08 W
Doangdoangan-besar, Pulau I 112 5.24 S 117.55 E
Doany 157b 14.22 S 49.31 E
Doba 146 8.39 N 16.51 E
Dobane 140 6.24 N 24.42 E
Dobbertin 54 53.37 N 12.04 E
Dobbiaco (Toblach) 64 46.44 N 12.14 E
Dobbin 222 30.22 N 95.46 W
Dobbins 226 39.22 N 121.12 W
Dobbins Air Force Base ■ 192 33.54 N 84.31 W
Dobbs Ferry 210 41.00 N 73.52 W
Dobbyn 166 19.48 S 140.00 E
Dobczyce 30 49.54 N 20.06 E
Dobel 56 48.48 N 8.29 E
Dobele 76 56.37 N 23.16 E
Döbeln 54 51.07 N 13.07 E
Doberai, Jazirah (Vogelkop) ≻[1] 164 1.30 S 132.30 E
Döberitz 264a 52.33 N 13.03 E
Doberlug-Kirchhain 54 51.38 N 13.34 E
Döbern 54 51.37 N 14.36 E
Dobiegniew 30 52.59 N 15.47 E
Döbling ✦[8] 264b 48.15 N 16.22 E
Dobo 164 5.46 S 134.13 E
Doboj 38 44.44 N 18.06 E
Dobra, Pol. 30 51.54 N 18.37 E
Dobra, Pol. 30 53.35 N 15.18 E
Dobra ≃ 36 45.33 N 15.31 E
Dobr'anka, S.S.S.R. 78 52.04 N 31.11 E
Dobr'anka, S.S.S.R. 86 58.27 N 56.24 E
Dobr'ankka 78 48.21 N 30.54 E
Dobřany 60 49.40 N 13.18 E
Dobra Stausee ⊜[1] 61 48.35 N 15.20 E
Dobre Miasto 30 53.59 N 20.25 E
Döbriach 64 46.47 N 13.39 E
Dobrich
→ Tolbuhin 38 43.34 N 27.50 E
Dobrinka, S.S.S.R. 80 52.09 N 40.29 E
Dobrinka, S.S.S.R. 80 48.49 N 42.58 E
Dobrinka, S.S.S.R. 80 50.49 N 41.51 E
Dobříš 30 49.47 N 14.11 E
Dobritz 54 52.01 N 12.13 E
Dobrodzień 30 50.44 N 18.27 E
Dobroje, S.S.S.R. 76 57.06 N 32.02 E
Dobroje, S.S.S.R. 76 52.52 N 39.48 E
Dobroměřice 54 50.23 N 13.46 E
Dobromil' 78 49.34 N 22.47 E
Dobropolje 78 48.28 N 37.05 E
Dobroslavka 76 52.24 N 26.15 E
Dobroteasa 38 44.47 N 24.23 E
Dobrotvor 78 50.14 N 24.22 E
Dobroveličkovka 78 48.23 N 31.11 E
Dobrovolje 78 48.41 N 36.37 E
Dobrovol'sk 76 54.46 N 22.31 E
Dobrudžansko plato ⩘[1] 38 43.32 N 27.50 E
Dobruja ✦[1] 38 44.00 N 28.00 E
Dobruš 76 52.25 N 31.19 E
Dobruška 30 50.17 N 16.10 E
Dobryn' 78 51.46 N 29.12 E
Dobrzany 30 53.22 N 15.25 E
Dobrzyń nad Wisłą 30 52.38 N 19.20 E
Dobšiná 30 48.49 N 20.23 E
Dobson 192 36.23 N 80.43 W
Doce ≃, Bra. 255 19.37 S 39.49 W
Doce ≃, Bra. 255 18.28 S 51.05 W
Doce de Octubre 196 25.38 N 97.47 W
Doce Leguas, Cayos de las II 240p 20.55 N 79.05 W
Dochart ≃ 46 56.28 N 4.20 W
Döčin ≃ 88 49.39 N 114.48 E
Docking 42 52.55 N 0.38 E
Dock Junction 192 31.11 N 81.31 W
Dockton 224 47.22 N 122.27 W
Dockweiler 56 50.15 N 6.46 E
Dockweiler Beach State Park ♦ 280 33.55 N 118.26 W
Doctor Arroyo 234 23.40 N 100.11 W
Doctor Cecilio Báez 252 25.03 S 56.19 W
Doctor Coss 196 25.55 N 99.11 W
Doctor Edmund A. Babler Memorial State Park ♦ 219 38.36 N 90.43 W
Doctor González 232 25.52 N 99.57 W
Doctor Hicks Range ⩘ 162 28.40 S 124.20 E
Doctor Pedro P. Peña 252 22.26 S 62.22 W
Doctors Creek ≃ 208 40.11 N 74.41 W
Doda 123 33.08 N 75.34 E
Doda Betta ∧ 122 11.24 N 76.44 E
Dod Ballāpur 122 13.18 N 77.32 E
Doddinghurst, Eng., U.K. 42 51.40 N 0.18 E
Doddinghurst, Eng., U.K. 260 51.40 N 0.18 E
Doddridge 194 33.05 N 93.54 W
Dodds Island I 219 38.35 N 91.59 W
Doddsville 194 33.39 N 90.31 W
Dodecanese
→ Dhodhekánisos II 38 36.30 N 27.00 E
Dodéo 152 7.29 N 12.04 E
Dodge, Ne., U.S. 198 41.43 N 96.52 W
Dodge, Tx., U.S. 222 30.45 N 95.24 W
Dodge □[6] 216 43.14 N 88.40 W
Dodge Brothers State Park Number 4 ♦, Mi., U.S. 281 42.37 N 83.22 W
Dodge Brothers State Park Number 8 ♦, Mi., U.S. 281 42.36 N 83.01 W
Dodge Center 190 44.01 N 92.51 W
Dodge City 198 37.45 N 100.01 W
Dodge Park 284c 38.56 N 76.53 W
Dodger Stadium ♦ 280 34.04 N 118.14 W
Dodgeville 190 42.57 N 90.07 W
Dodman Point ≻ 42 50.13 N 4.48 W
Dodo Goei 140 5.57 N 29.26 E
Dodola 144 7.02 N 39.07 E
Dodoma 154 6.11 S 35.45 E
Dodoma □[4] 154 6.00 S 36.00 E
Dodori ≃ 154 1.52 S 41.02 E
Dodsland 184 51.48 N 108.49 W
Dodson, La., U.S. 194 32.04 N 92.39 W
Dodson, Mt., U.S. 202 48.23 N 108.14 W
Dodson, Tx., U.S. 196 34.46 N 100.02 W
Dodson Peninsula ≻[1] 9 75.46 S 62.50 W
Dodurga 130 39.48 N 29.55 E
Doe Lake ⊜ 212 45.32 N 79.25 W
Doe River 182 56.00 N 120.05 W
Doerun 192 31.19 N 83.55 W
Doesburg 52 52.01 N 6.09 E
Doetinchem 52 51.58 N 6.17 E
Dog ≃ 190 48.51 N 89.37 W
Dogāchia 272b 22.58 N 88.31 E
Dogadda 124 29.48 N 78.37 E
Dōga-mori ∧ 96 33.09 N 132.53 E
Doğanbey, Tür. 130 37.37 N 27.11 E
Doğanbey, Tür. 130 38.04 N 26.53 E
Doğanbey, Tür. 130 37.48 N 31.54 E
Doğançay 130 40.37 N 30.20 E
Doganella 66 41.34 N 12.56 E
Doğanhisar 130 38.09 N 31.41 E
Doğanşehir 130 38.06 N 37.53 E
Dog Creek 182 51.35 N 122.15 W
Dog Creek ≃, B.C., Can. 182 51.35 N 122.17 W
Dog Creek ≃, Mt., U.S. 202 47.44 N 109.36 W
Dog Creek ≃, Oh., U.S. 216 41.03 N 84.23 W
Dog Ear Creek ≃ 198 43.42 N 99.59 W
Dog Island I 192 29.48 N 84.35 W
Dog Islands II 240m 18.29 N 64.28 W
Dog Lake ⊜, Mb., Can. 184 51.02 N 98.30 W
Dog Lake ⊜, On., Can. 190 48.46 N 89.32 W
Dog Lake ⊜, On., Can. 190 48.18 N 84.10 W
Dog Lake ⊜, On., Can. 212 44.27 N 76.20 W
Dogliani 62 44.32 N 7.56 E
Dogna 64 46.27 N 13.19 E
Dōgo I 92 36.15 N 133.16 E
Dogondoutchi 150 13.38 N 4.02 E
Dōgo-yama ∧ 96 35.04 N 133.14 E
Dogpound Creek ≃ 182 51.50 N 114.24 W
Dogs, Isle of I 260 51.29 N 0.01 W
D'ogtevo, S.S.S.R. 78 49.10 N 40.39 E
D'ogtevo, S.S.S.R. 80 49.11 N 40.39 E
Doğubayazıt 84 39.32 N 44.08 E
Doguéraoua 150 13.58 N 5.35 E
Dogura 164 10.05 S 150.05 E
Doha
→ Ad-Dawḥah 128 25.17 N 51.32 E
Dohad 120 22.50 N 74.16 E
Dohār 126 23.35 N 90.09 E
Dohhi 124 24.32 N 84.54 E
Dohna 54 50.57 N 13.51 E
Dohrgaul 263 51.06 N 7.27 E
Dohrīghāt 124 26.16 N 83.31 E
Doi 96 33.57 N 133.26 E
Doi, Kinh ≅ 269c 10.43 N 106.37 E
Doiran, Lake ⊜ 38 41.13 N 22.44 E
Dois de Novembro, Cachoeira ᒪ 248 8.52 S 62.16 W
Dois Irmãos 250 9.16 S 49.05 W
Dois Irmãos, Pico ∧ 287a 22.59 S 43.14 W
Dois Riachos 250 9.23 S 37.05 W
Dōjō 268 35.51 N 139.37 E
Dōjō ✦[8] 270 34.52 N 135.14 E
Doka, Indon. 164 6.39 S 134.15 E
Doka, Sūd. 140 13.31 N 35.46 E
Doki ≃ 96 34.18 N 133.48 E
Dokka 26 60.50 N 10.05 E
Dokkum 52 53.19 N 6.00 E
Dokmetepe 130 40.19 N 36.18 E
Dokri 120 27.23 N 68.06 E
Dokšicy 76 54.54 N 27.46 E
Dokská pahorkatina ⩘[2] 54 50.30 N 14.45 E
Doksy 54 50.35 N 14.38 E
Dokučajevsk 83 47.44 N 37.40 E
Dol'a, S.S.S.R. 83 47.53 N 37.41 E
Dola, Oh., U.S. 216 40.47 N 83.42 W
Dolak ≃ 164 8.20 S 138.30 E
Doland 198 44.53 N 98.06 W
Dolany 60 49.27 N 13.15 E
Dolavon 254 43.18 S 65.42 W
Dolaybaköy 267b 40.54 N 29.15 E
Dolbeau 176 48.53 N 72.14 W
Dolberg 52 51.42 N 7.55 E
Dolceacqua 62 43.51 N 7.37 E
Dolcedorme, Serra ∧ 68 39.53 N 16.13 E
Dol-de-Bretagne 32 48.33 N 1.45 W
Dole 58 47.06 N 5.30 E
Dolega 236 8.34 N 82.25 W
Dolen 222 30.26 N 94.54 W
Dolgaja 86 55.49 N 64.15 E
Dolgaja, kosa ≻[2] 78 46.43 N 37.41 E
Dolgarrog 44 53.11 N 3.51 W
Dolgelin 54 52.29 N 14.24 E
Dolgellau 42 52.44 N 3.53 W
Dolgen'koje 83 49.01 N 37.19 E
Dolgeville 210 43.06 N 74.46 W
Dolgij, ostrov I 24 69.15 N 59.04 E
Dolgij Most 88 56.45 N 96.48 E
Dolginovo 76 54.39 N 27.29 E
Dolgoi Island I 180 55.10 N 161.45 W
Dolgoje 78 52.04 N 37.34 E
Dolgoprudnyj 82 55.56 N 37.31 E
Dolgorukovo 76 52.19 N 38.21 E
Dolgoščelje 24 66.03 N 43.24 E
Dolianova 71 39.22 N 9.10 E
Dolina, S.S.S.R. 78 48.58 N 24.01 E
Dolina, S.S.S.R. 83 48.59 N 37.27 E
Dolinnyj 80 51.16 N 52.11 E
Dolinovskoje 83 48.36 N 38.33 E
Dolinsk 89 47.21 N 142.48 E
Dolinskaja 78 48.07 N 32.44 E
Dolisie 152 4.12 S 12.41 E
Dolj □[6] 38 44.15 N 23.45 E
Döllach 64 46.58 N 12.54 E
Dollar 46 56.09 N 3.40 W
Dollard ⊂ 52 53.17 N 7.10 E
Dollard-des-Ormeaux 206 45.29 N 73.49 W
Dollar Law ∧ 46 55.33 N 3.17 W
Döllbach 56 50.26 N 9.44 E
Dolle 54 52.25 N 11.37 E
Dollern 52 53.32 N 9.32 E
Dollerup 41 54.46 N 9.40 E
Döllnitz 54 51.24 N 12.01 E
Dollnstein 60 48.52 N 11.04 E
Döllstädt 54 51.05 N 10.49 E
Dolmabahçe Sarayı ʋ 267b 41.02 N 29.00 E
Dolmatovka 78 46.13 N 32.26 E
Dolmatovskij 80 57.29 N 42.18 E
Dolni Dâbnik 38 43.24 N 24.26 E
Dolní Dvořiště 61 48.39 N 14.27 E
Dolní Jiřetín 54 50.35 N 13.33 E
Dolni Lom 38 43.31 N 22.47 E
Dolni Žandov 60 50.02 N 12.34 E
Dolný Kubín 30 49.12 N 19.17 E
Dolo 64 45.25 N 12.05 E
Dolohmwar ∧ 174r 6.52 N 158.14 E
Dolokmerawan 114 3.10 N 99.08 E
Dolokparibuan 114 3.01 N 98.39 E
Dolomites
→ Dolomiti ⩘ 64 46.25 N 11.50 E
Dolomiti (Dolomiten) ⩘ 64 46.25 N 11.50 E
Dolon' 86 50.40 N 79.18 E
Dolon ≃ 62 45.18 N 4.46 E
Dolon, pereval)(85 41.52 N 75.45 E
Dolores, Arg. 252 36.20 S 57.40 W
Dolores, Col. 246 3.33 N 74.54 W
Dolores, Esp. 34 38.08 N 0.46 W
Dolores, Guat. 232 16.31 N 89.25 W
Dolores, Méx. 196 26.20 N 101.29 W
Dolores, Méx. 232 28.53 N 108.27 W
Dolores, Co., U.S. 200 37.28 N 108.30 W
Dolores, Ur. 252 33.33 S 58.13 W
Dolores, Ven. 246 8.18 N 69.34 W
Dolores ≃, Pil. 116 12.02 N 125.29 E
Dolores ≃, U.S. 200 38.49 N 109.17 W
Dolores, Mission ʋ[1] 282 37.46 N 122.26 W
Dolores Hidalgo 234 21.10 N 100.56 W
Dolphin, Cape ≻ 254 51.15 S 58.57 W
Dolphin and Union Strait ꞩ 176 69.05 N 114.45 W
Dolphin Head ∧ 241q 18.22 N 78.10 W
Dölsach 64 46.49 N 12.51 E
Dolsk 30 52.00 N 17.03 E
Dol'skoje 82 54.47 N 36.26 E
Dolton, Eng., U.K. 42 50.53 N 4.01 W
Dolton, Il., U.S. 216 41.38 N 87.36 W
Dolwyddelan 42 53.03 N 3.53 W
Dolžak 78 48.41 N 26.32 E
Dolžanskaja, S.S.S.R. 78 46.37 N 37.48 E
Dolžanskaja, S.S.S.R. 83 48.03 N 39.39 E
Dolžicy, S.S.S.R. 76 58.00 N 29.51 E
Dolžicy, S.S.S.R. 76 58.31 N 29.08 E
Dolžik 78 50.13 N 35.55 E
Dom ∧, Indon. 164 2.40 S 136.53 E
Dom ∧, Schw. 58 46.06 N 7.50 E
D'oma ≃ 86 54.42 N 55.57 E
Domacha 76 52.28 N 34.58 E
Domačovo 78 51.44 N 23.37 E
Domadare 144 1.50 N 41.13 E
Domaine, Pointe du ≻ 275a 45.23 N 73.54 W
Domanevka 78 47.37 N 30.58 E
Domaniç 130 39.48 N 29.37 E
Domaniči 76 53.02 N 33.25 E
Domanico 68 39.13 N 16.12 E
Dom Aquino 255 15.48 S 54.53 W
Domar, Enneri V 146 18.11 N 18.04 E
Domariāganj 124 27.13 N 82.40 E
Domart-en-Ponthieu 50 50.04 N 2.07 E
Domasi 154 15.18 S 35.20 E
Domaška 80 53.00 N 50.47 E
Domaso 58 46.09 N 9.19 E
Domat/Ems 58 46.50 N 9.28 E
Domažlice 60 49.27 N 12.56 E
Dombaj 84 43.17 N 41.37 E
Dombaj-Ul'gen, gora ∧ 84 43.14 N 41.41 E
Dombarovskij 86 50.46 N 59.32 E
Dombås 26 62.05 N 9.08 E
Dombasle-sur-Meurthe 58 48.38 N 6.21 E
Dombe 156 19.59 S 33.25 E
Dombe Grande 152 12.58 S 13.11 E
Dombes ✦[1] 58 46.00 N 5.03 E
Dombóvár 30 46.23 N 18.08 E
Dombrád 30 48.14 N 21.56 E
Dombresson 58 47.04 N 6.58 E
Domburg 52 51.34 N 3.30 E
Dom Cavati 255 19.23 S 42.06 W
Dôme, Puy de ∧ 32 45.47 N 2.58 E
Dome Creek 182 53.44 N 121.01 W
Domegge di Cadore 64 46.27 N 12.25 E
Domène 62 45.12 N 5.50 E
Dome Peak ∧, Pil. 116 5.37 N 125.20 E
Dome Peak ∧, Wa., U.S. 224 48.18 N 121.02 W
Domett 172 42.51 S 173.13 E
Domèvre-en-Haye 56 48.49 N 5.55 E
Domeyko 252 28.57 S 70.54 W
Domeyko, Cordillera ⩘ 252 24.30 S 69.00 W
Domfront 32 48.36 N 0.39 W
Domiciano Ribeiro 255 16.56 S 47.46 W
Dominal, Parc ♦ 62 44.52 N 6.32 E
Domíngo M. Irala 252 25.54 S 54.43 W
Domingos Martins 255 20.22 S 40.40 W
Dominguez 280 33.50 N 118.13 W
Dominguez Channel ꞩ 280 38.47 N 118.15 W
Dominguez Hills ⩘[2] 280 33.52 N 118.14 W
Dominica □[1], N.A. 230 15.30 N 61.20 W
Dominica □[1], N.A. 240d 15.30 N 61.20 W
Dominica Channel ꞩ 238 15.10 N 61.15 W
Dominicain (république)
→ Dominican Republic □[1] 238 19.00 N 70.40 W
Dominical 236 9.13 N 83.51 W
Dominicana, República
→ Dominican Republic □[1] 238 19.00 N 70.40 W
Dominican Republic (República Dominicana) □[1], N.A. 230 19.00 N 70.40 W
Dominican Republic (República Dominicana) □[1], N.A. 238 19.00 N 70.40 W
Dominikanische Republik
→ Dominican Republic □[1] 238 19.00 N 70.40 W
Dominion 186 46.13 N 60.01 W
Dominion, Cape ≻ 176 66.13 N 74.28 W
Dominion Astrophysical Observatory ʋ[3] 224 48.31 N 123.25 W
Dominion City 184 49.08 N 97.09 W
Dominique
→ Dominica □[1] 240d 15.30 N 61.20 W
Domiongo 152 4.37 S 21.15 E
Domitilla, Catacombe di ⊥ 267a 41.52 N 12.31 E
Dömitz 54 53.08 N 11.14 E
Dom Joaquim 255 18.57 S 43.16 W
Domleschg V 58 46.44 N 9.28 E
Dommartin-lès-Toul 58 48.40 N 5.54 E
Dommartin-Varimont 56 48.58 N 4.46 E
Dommary-Baroncourt 56 49.17 N 5.42 E
Dommel ≃ 52 51.40 N 5.20 E
Dommitzsch 54 51.38 N 12.53 E
Domnarvet 40 60.30 N 15.27 E
Domnești 38 44.25 N 25.56 E
Domnino 82 54.10 N 38.11 E
Dom Noi ≃ 110 15.17 N 105.28 E
Domo 144 7.54 N 46.52 E
Domodedovo 82 55.26 N 37.46 E
Domodossola 58 46.07 N 8.17 E
Domohani 124 26.35 N 88.48 E
Domoni 157a 12.15 S 44.32 E
Domont 261 49.02 N 2.20 E
Dompaire 58 48.13 N 6.13 E
Dom Pedrito 252 30.59 S 54.40 W
Dom Pedro 250 4.29 S 44.27 W
Dom Pedro II, Estação ✦[5] 287a 23.54 S 43.12 W
Dompu 115b 8.32 S 118.28 E
Domremy 184 52.47 N 105.44 W
Domrémy-la-Pucelle 58 48.27 N 5.41 E
Domselaar 258 35.04 S 58.18 W
Dom Silvério 255 20.09 S 42.58 W
Domsjö 26 63.15 N 18.43 E
Domus de Maria 71 38.57 N 8.52 E
Domusnovas 71 39.19 N 8.39 E
Domuyo, Volcán ∧[1] 252 36.38 S 70.26 W
Domvast 50 50.12 N 1.55 E
Dom Viçoso 256 22.13 S 45.09 W
Dom Yai ≃ 110 15.18 N 105.10 E
Domžale 36 46.08 N 14.36 E
Don ≃, On., Can. 212 43.39 N 79.21 W
Don ≃, India 122 16.17 N 76.27 E
Don ≃, Lao 110 15.07 N 105.48 E
Don ≃, S.S.S.R. 72 47.04 N 39.18 E
Don ≃, Eng., U.K. 44 53.39 N 0.59 W
Don ≃, Eng., U.K. 262 53.47 N 2.14 W
Don ≃, Scot., U.K. 46 57.08 N 2.05 W
Don, East Branch ≃, On., Can. 212 43.42 N 79.20 W
Don, East Branch ≃, On., Can. 275b 43.43 N 79.20 W
Don, West Branch ≃ 275b 43.43 N 79.20 W
Dona Ana, Moç. 154 17.25 S 35.07 E
Dona Ana, N.M., U.S. 200 32.23 N 106.48 W
Donada 64 45.02 N 12.12 E
Donadeu 252 26.43 S 62.44 W
Dona Eusébia 256 21.18 S 42.48 W
Donaghadee 48 54.39 N 5.33 W
Donaghmore 48 54.32 N 6.49 W
Donahoe Creek ≃ 222 30.49 N 97.12 W
Donald 166 36.22 S 143.00 E
Donalda 182 52.35 N 112.34 W
Donaldson, Ar., U.S. 194 34.14 N 92.55 W
Donaldson, In., U.S. 216 41.22 N 86.27 W
Donaldson, Pa., U.S. 208 40.38 N 76.24 W
Donaldson Crossroads 279b 40.16 N 80.07 W
Donaldson Dam ⊜[1] 273d 26.17 S 27.41 E
Donaldsonville 194 30.06 N 90.59 W
Donalsonville 192 31.02 N 84.52 W
Donard, Slieve ∧ 48 54.11 N 5.55 W
Donau
→ Danube ≃ 22 45.20 N 29.40 E
Donaueschingen 58 47.57 N 8.29 E
Donaufeld ✦[8] 264b 48.15 N 16.25 E
Donau Kanal ≅ 264b 48.10 N 16.30 E
Donaumoos ≡, B.R.D. 58 48.30 N 10.15 E
Donaumoos ≡, B.R.D. 60 48.40 N 11.15 E
Donaupark ♦ 264b 48.14 N 16.25 E
Donauried ✦[1] 56 48.35 N 10.40 E
Donaustadt ✦[8] 264b 48.13 N 16.30 E
Donaustauf 60 49.02 N 12.13 E
Donauturm ʋ 264b 48.14 N 16.25 E
Donauwörth 56 48.43 N 10.46 E
Don Benito 34 38.57 N 5.52 W
Dönberg 263 51.18 N 7.10 E
Don Bosco ✦[8] 258 34.42 S 58.18 W
Doncaster, Austl. 274b 37.47 S 145.08 E
Doncaster, On., Can. 275b 43.48 N 79.25 W
Doncaster, Eng., U.K. 44 53.32 N 1.07 W
Doncaster ≃ 206 45.58 N 74.06 W
Doncaster East 274b 37.47 S 145.10 E
Doncaster Indian Reserve ✦[4] 206 46.09 N 74.07 W
Donchery 56 49.42 N 4.52 E
Doncovka 83 49.35 N 39.16 E
Dondaicha 120 21.20 N 74.34 E
Dondo, Ang. 152 9.38 S 14.25 E
Dondo, Moç. 156 19.36 S 34.44 E
Dondo, Teluk ⊂ 112 0.55 N 120.30 E
Dondra Head ≻ 122 5.55 N 80.35 E
Don-duong 110 11.51 N 108.35 E
Dond'ušany 78 48.15 N 27.37 E
Doneck, S.S.S.R. 83 48.21 N 40.02 E
Doneck, S.S.S.R. 83 48.00 N 37.48 E
Doneck □[4] 83 48.00 N 37.30 E
Doneckij kr'až ∧ 83 48.15 N 38.45 E
Donegal, Ire. 48 54.39 N 8.07 W
Donegal, S. Afr. 158 26.10 S 23.58 E
Donegal, Pa., U.S. 214 40.07 N 79.23 W
Donegal □[6] 48 54.50 N 8.00 W
Donegal Bay ⊂ 48 54.30 N 8.30 W
Doneraile, Ire. 48 52.13 N 8.35 W
Doneraile, S.C., U.S. 192 34.19 N 79.53 W
Donetsk
→ Doneck 83 48.00 N 37.48 E
Dong ≃, Zhg. 100 23.42 N 117.13 E
Dong ≃, Zhg. 100 23.06 N 114.00 E
Dong ≃, Zhg. 100 25.00 N 118.27 E
Dong ≃, Zhg. 102 42.10 N 101.00 E
Donga ≃ 146 8.19 N 9.58 E
Dongan
→ Mishan, Zhg. 89 45.33 N 131.52 E
Dong'an, Zhg. 89 47.20 N 134.10 E
Dong'an, Zhg. 100 33.24 N 114.24 E

ENGLISH Name	Page	Lat.°′	Long.°′

Dong'an, Zhg. 102 26.17 N 111.07 E
Dong'an, Zhg. 106 30.30 N 118.48 E
Dong'an, Zhg. 106 31.35 N 119.44 E
Dongao 100 29.12 N 121.25 E
Dongara 162 29.15 S 114.56 E
Dongargarh 120 21.12 N 80.44 E
Dongba, Zhg. 105 39.58 N 116.32 E
Dongba, Zhg. 106 31.18 N 119.03 E
Dongbahe 105 39.58 N 116.27 E
Dongbaimiao 105 40.34 N 116.05 E
Dongbei 100 27.15 N 116.06 E
Dongbeicha 98 41.43 N 127.23 E
Dongbeijipo 98 36.06 N 117.08 E
Dongbulizhadamu 120 34.27 N 93.12 E
Dongchan 107 30.20 N 105.20 E
Dongchang 106 31.52 N 121.38 E
Dongchangjie 106 32.04 N 119.18 E
Dongcheng 100 28.56 N 121.16 E
Dongchong 100 26.35 N 119.52 E
Dongchuan 102 26.10 N 103.01 E
Dongcun 106 30.57 N 121.46 E
Dongdaoan 98 38.21 N 117.12 E
Dong Dian ≡ 105 39.03 N 116.35 E
Dongduluo 105 39.04 N 115.15 E
Dong'e (Tongcheng) 98 36.14 N 116.16 E
Dongen 52 51.37 N 4.56 E
Dong'ezhen 98 36.11 N 116.16 E
Dongfang (Basuo) 110 19.05 N 108.39 E
Dongfeng, Zhg. 98 42.40 N 125.28 E
Dongfeng, Zhg. 100 27.20 N 118.53 E
Dongfengtai 105 39.34 N 117.45 E
Donggala 112 0.40 S 119.44 E
Donggang 100 22.58 N 115.57 E
Donggangzi 89 45.53 N 129.49 E
Donggi 112 1.33 S 122.15 E
Donggi Cona ⊜ 102 37.10 N 96.55 E
Donggong Shan ⩘ 100 27.36 N 119.26 E
Donggongsuo 106 32.07 N 121.25 E
Donggou, Zhg. 98 39.54 N 124.09 E
Donggou, Zhg. 100 33.38 N 119.40 E
Donggou, Zhg. 106 32.17 N 118.59 E
Donggu 100 26.46 N 115.22 E
Dongguan, Zhg. 100 27.49 N 116.25 E
Dongguan, Zhg. 100 23.03 N 113.46 E
Dongguan, Zhg. 106 30.22 N 119.28 E
Dongguan, Zhg. 107 30.47 N 106.16 E
Dongguang 98 37.53 N 116.30 E
Dongguanpu 106 31.13 N 120.43 E
Dongguanyingzi 104 41.55 N 120.38 E
Donggugang 105 39.10 N 116.49 E
Dong-hai, Viet. 110 12.34 N 109.14 E
Donghai (Niushan), Zhg. 98 34.30 N 118.47 E
Dong Hai
→ East China Sea ⊤[2] 90 30.00 N 126.00 E
Donghai Dao I 102 21.02 N 110.25 E
Dongheng ≅ 106 31.54 N 120.17 E
Donghezhen 106 31.08 N 120.17 E
Dong-hoi 110 17.29 N 106.36 E
Donghu 100 26.28 N 113.07 E
Donghu ⊜ 120 32.10 N 84.40 E
Donghuanggou 104 40.43 N 123.29 E
Dongi 112 2.02 S 121.28 E
Dongio 58 46.27 N 8.58 E
Dongjia 98 37.18 N 118.24 E
Dongjiangkou 102 33.37 N 108.49 E
Dongjie 100 25.53 N 116.22 E
Dongjielang 100 31.03 N 115.57 E
Dongjingcheng 89 44.07 N 129.09 E
Dongjingji 98 40.02 N 114.01 E
Dongjingling 104 41.18 N 123.15 E
Dongjiu 120 29.58 N 94.53 E
Dongkaihecheng 104 41.04 N 122.38 E
Dongkalang 112 0.10 N 120.06 E
Dongkeng, Zhg. 100 27.48 N 119.42 E
Dongkeng, Zhg. 100 24.59 N 114.54 E
Dong-khe 110 22.26 N 106.27 E
Dongkou 98 35.29 N 115.20 E
Donglan 102 24.40 N 107.18 E
Donglaohuyu 104 42.28 N 124.17 E
Donglaojunpu 104 41.24 N 121.22 E
Dongli 102 20.50 N 110.20 E
Dongliang 104 42.00 N 121.25 E
Dongliangjia 105 40.52 N 118.17 E
Donglidian 98 36.02 N 118.23 E
Donglinchang 107 29.39 N 104.07 E
Dongling 104 41.50 N 123.35 E
Dongliu, Zhg. 100 30.14 N 116.53 E
Dongliu, Zhg. 106 32.06 N 118.58 E
Dongliujiazi 104 42.21 N 122.44 E
Donglizhuang 105 39.21 N 116.47 E
Donglong 100 23.36 N 116.50 E
Donglucun 89 49.28 N 128.50 E
Dongmen 100 28.29 N 114.02 E
Dongming 98 35.18 N 115.08 E
Dong-nai ≃ 110 10.45 N 106.46 E
Dongnangou 104 41.25 N 122.02 E
Dongning 89 44.04 N 131.07 E
Dongo, Ang. 152 14.36 S 15.48 E
Dongo, It. 58 46.07 N 9.17 E
Dongo, Zaïre 152 2.43 N 18.24 E
Dongobe 152 4.37 N 23.12 E
Dongobesh 154 4.04 S 35.23 E
Dongola
→ Dunqulah 140 19.10 N 30.29 E
Dongon Point ≻ 116 12.44 N 120.48 E
Dongou 152 2.02 N 18.04 E
Dongping, Zhg. 98 35.55 N 116.18 E
Dongping, Zhg. 100 27.24 N 118.39 E
Dongping, Zhg. 102 21.43 N 112.15 E
Dongping Hu ⊜ 98 36.00 N 116.12 E
Dongpu 100 30.03 N 120.34 E
Dongqian 106 30.52 N 120.23 E
Dongqiao 100 31.12 N 112.48 E
Dongqing 106 31.49 N 120.03 E
Dongqingduizi 104 41.02 N 122.08 E
Dongsanjiazi 104 41.54 N 122.48 E
Dongsanlintang 106 31.09 N 121.31 E
Dongsanpu 100 33.38 N 117.09 E
Dongsha ≃ 104 41.07 N 121.50 E
Dongshaer 120 28.41 N 89.09 E
Dongshajiao 100 30.19 N 122.09 E
Dongshan, Zhg. 100 23.42 N 117.24 E
Dongshan, Zhg. 102 19.50 N 110.14 E
Dongshan, Zhg. 106 31.04 N 120.24 E
Dongshan Dao I 100 23.40 N 117.25 E
Dongshanqiao 106 31.52 N 118.46 E
Dongshe 106 32.07 N 121.12 E
Dongsheng 102 39.49 N 109.59 E
Dongsheshanzi 104 42.15 N 123.09 E
Dongshi, Zhg. 100 24.42 N 118.27 E
Dongshi, Zhg. 100 24.43 N 115.59 E
Dongshi, Zhg. 271a 39.49 N 116.34 E
Dongshuiyan 105 39.15 N 115.23 E
Dongtai 100 32.51 N 120.20 E
Dongtai Hu ⊂ 106 31.05 N 120.30 E
Dongtaipingzhen 89 45.18 N 122.05 E
Dongtangou 105 39.23 N 118.22 E
Dongtianmu Shan ∧ 106 30.22 N 119.31 E
Dongtiao ≃ 106 30.51 N 120.06 E
Dongting 98 38.29 N 115.08 E
Dongtinghu 106 30.53 N 119.30 E
Dongting Hu ⊜ 102 29.20 N 112.54 E
Dongtingxi 102 28.34 N 110.36 E
Dongtou 100 27.50 N 121.09 E
Dongtou Shan I 100 27.50 N 121.08 E
Dong-trieu 110 21.05 N 106.31 E
Dongtuhulu 104 41.55 N 121.33 E
Dongtuoshanzi 104 42.10 N 123.08 E
Dongtuozi 104 41.17 N 121.53 E
Dong-van 110 23.16 N 105.22 E
Dongwangfu 89 44.47 N 120.53 E
Dongwangzhuang 106 32.16 N 120.32 E
Dongwe ≃ 152 13.58 S 23.53 E
Dongwuquan 105 39.20 N 115.43 E
Dongxi, Zhg. 100 28.35 N 120.02 E
Dongxi, Zhg. 102 28.47 N 106.39 E
Dongxi, Zhg. 107 28.46 N 106.39 E
Dongxi, Zhg. 107 30.24 N 104.33 E
Dongxia 106 31.11 N 119.05 E
Dongxiagaogao 104 42.36 N 122.30 E
Dongxiang 100 28.13 N 116.35 E

DEUTSCH Name	Seite	Breite°′	Länge°′ E = Ost

Dongxiang Dao I 100 25.36 N 119.48 E
Dongxing 89 46.23 N 127.52 E
Dongxingchang, Zhg. 107 29.16 N 103.55 E
Dongxingchang, Zhg. 107 29.36 N 105.04 E
Dongxinghe 105 39.46 N 114.49 E
Dongxinpu 104 41.00 N 123.18 E
Dongxinzhen 106 31.57 N 121.42 E
Dongyang, Zhg. 89 48.03 N 124.17 E
Dongyang, Zhg. 100 29.16 N 120.14 E
Dongyangqiao 106 30.52 N 120.34 E
Dongyao 98 35.56 N 113.58 E
Dongyian 105 39.22 N 115.46 E
Dongyin ≃ 105 39.09 N 117.43 E
Dongyou 100 27.10 N 118.37 E
Dongyuemiao 106 31.36 N 119.14 E
Dongyuezhen 107 30.24 N 103.32 E
Dongzhang 100 25.44 N 119.17 E
Dongzhaocun 105 40.02 N 116.46 E
Dongzhaozhuang 105 39.57 N 118.24 E
Dongzhenbeng 106 30.59 N 121.01 E
Dongzhi 100 30.07 N 116.59 E
Dongzhizhuang 105 40.25 N 116.50 E
Dongzhuangpu 105 40.34 N 115.42 E
Dongziya 105 38.50 N 116.44 E
Donie 222 31.29 N 96.13 W
Doninga 150 10.37 N 1.26 W
Donington 42 52.55 N 0.12 W
Doniphan, Mo., U.S. 194 36.37 N 90.49 W
Doniphan, Ne., U.S. 198 40.46 N 98.22 W
Don Islands II 116 11.05 N 123.38 E
Donja Stubica 36 45.59 N 15.58 E
Donjek ≃ 180 62.35 N 140.00 W
Donjezk
→ Doneck 83 48.00 N 37.48 E
Donji Vakuf 36 44.09 N 17.25 E
Donk 52 51.33 N 5.37 E
Donkerpoort 158 30.32 S 25.30 E
Donkey Creek ≃ 198 44.12 N 104.58 W
Donkey Town 260 51.20 N 0.39 W
Don Martín 196 27.32 N 100.37 W
Don Matías 246 6.30 N 75.22 W
Don Mills ✦[8] 275b 43.44 N 79.20 W
Don Mills Centre ✦[9] 275b 43.44 N 79.21 W
Don Muang Airport ⊠ 269a 13.56 N 100.37 E
Donna 196 26.10 N 98.03 W
Donna, Punta sa ∧ 71 40.35 N 9.25 E
Donna Buang, Mount ∧ 169 37.43 S 145.40 E
Donnacona 206 46.40 N 71.47 W
Donnalucata 70 36.45 N 14.38 E
Donnaz 62 45.36 N 7.46 E
Donnell Lake ⊜[1] 226 38.20 N 119.56 W
Donnellson 219 39.02 N 89.29 W
Donnelly, Ab., Can. 182 55.44 N 117.06 W
Donnelly, Ak., U.S. 180 63.41 N 145.53 W
Donnelly, Id., U.S. 202 44.43 N 116.04 W
Donnellys Crossing 172 35.43 S 173.37 E
Donnemarie-Dontilly 50 48.29 N 3.08 E
Donner 194 29.41 N 90.56 W
Donner Lake ⊜[1] 226 39.20 N 120.16 W
Donner Memorial State Park ♦ 226 39.18 N 120.16 W
Donner Pass)(226 39.19 N 120.20 W
Donnersberg ∧ 56 50.23 N 8.32 E
Donner und Blitzen ≃ 202 43.17 N 118.49 W
Donnybrook, Austl. 162 33.35 S 115.49 E
Donnybrook, S. Afr. 158 30.00 S 29.48 E
Donora 214 40.10 N 79.51 W
Donors Hills 166 18.42 S 140.33 E
Donoughmore 48 51.57 N 8.45 W
Donovan 216 40.53 N 87.37 W
Don Pedro Reservoir ⊜[1] 226 37.43 N 120.23 W
Don Peninsula ≻[1] 182 52.30 N 128.10 W
Donque 152 15.28 S 14.06 E
Donskaja gr'ada ⩘[2] 80 49.30 N 42.00 E
Donskoj, S.S.S.R. 76 53.58 N 38.20 E
Donskoj, S.S.S.R. 83 48.49 N 40.06 E
Donskoj, S.S.S.R. 83 47.25 N 40.14 E
Donskoje, S.S.S.R. 76 52.37 N 39.00 E
Donskoje, S.S.S.R. 80 45.21 N 41.59 E
Donskoje, S.S.S.R. 83 47.31 N 37.33 E
Donskoje belogorje ⩘[1] 78 50.30 N 39.45 E
Donsol 116 12.54 N 123.36 E
Don Torcuato 288 34.30 S 58.38 W
Don Torcuato, Aeródromo ⊠ 288 34.30 S 58.36 W
Donuzlav, ozero ⊜ 78 45.23 N 33.05 E
Donyztau ⩘ 86 46.25 N 57.00 E
Donzdorf 56 48.41 N 9.48 E
Donzère 62 44.27 N 4.43 E
Donzy 50 47.22 N 3.08 E
Dooagh 48 53.59 N 10.09 W
Dood nuur ⊜ 88 51.20 N 99.20 E
Doogort 48 54.01 N 10.01 W
Doolow 144 4.10 N 42.05 E
Doomadgee Aboriginal Reserve ✦[4] 166 17.43 S 138.36 E
Doomadgee Mission 166 17.56 S 138.49 E
Doon, On., Can. 212 43.23 N 80.26 W
Doon, Ia., U.S. 198 43.16 N 96.13 W
Doon ≃ 44 55.26 N 4.38 W
Doon, Loch ⊜ 44 55.15 N 4.22 W
Doonbeg 48 52.44 N 9.32 W
Doonbeg ≃ 48 52.44 N 9.34 W
Doondi 166 28.15 S 148.28 E
Doonerak, Mount ∧ 180 67.56 N 150.37 W
Doongalla Forest Reserve ♦ 274b 37.51 S 145.20 E
Doonside 274a 33.46 S 150.52 E
Dooralong 170 33.12 S 151.22 E
Doorn 52 52.03 N 5.21 E
Doorndam 158 28.03 S 21.03 E
Doornik
→ Tournai 50 50.36 N 3.23 E
Door Peninsula ≻[1] 190 44.55 N 87.20 W
Dopping Brook ≃ 283 42.12 N 71.23 W
Dor 132 32.37 N 34.55 E
Dora 194 33.43 N 87.05 W
Dora, Lake ⊜, Austl. 162 22.05 S 122.55 E
Dora, Lake ⊜, Fl., U.S. 220 29.00 N 81.37 W
Dora Baltea ≃ 62 45.11 N 8.05 E
Dora di Rhêmes ≃ 62 45.42 N 7.11 E
Dorado 240m 18.28 N 66.15 W
Doraha 123 30.49 N 76.01 E
Dorāh Ān)(123 36.07 N 71.15 E
Dorain, Beinn ∧ 46 56.30 N 4.42 W
Dorândia 256 22.27 S 43.57 W
Dora Riparia ≃ 62 45.05 N 7.44 E
Doraville 192 33.53 N 84.17 W
Dorback Burn ≃ 46 57.31 N 3.40 W
Dorcheat, Bayou ≃ 194 32.30 N 93.21 W
Dorchester, N.B., Can. 186 45.54 N 64.31 W
Dorchester, On., Can. 212 42.59 N 81.04 W
Dorchester, Eng., U.K. 42 50.43 N 2.26 W
Dorchester, Eng., U.K. 42 51.39 N 1.10 W
Dorchester, Il., U.S. 219 39.05 N 89.53 W
Dorchester, Ne., U.S. 198 40.38 N 97.06 W
Dorchester, N.J., U.S. 208 39.16 N 74.58 W
Dorchester, Wi., U.S. 190 45.00 N 90.20 W
Dorchester □[6] 208 38.34 N 76.04 W
Dorchester ✦[8] 283 42.17 N 71.04 W
Dorchester, Cape ≻ 176 65.29 N 77.30 W
Dorchester Bay ⊂ 283 42.19 N 71.02 W
Dorchester Crossing 186 46.10 N 64.34 W
Dorchester Estates 284c 38.47 N 76.55 W
Dorchester Heights National Historic Site ⊥ 283 42.20 N 71.03 W
Dorchheim 56 50.30 N 8.04 E
Dordabis 156 22.52 S 17.38 E

Symbols in the index entries represent the broad categories identified in the key at the right. Symbols with superior numbers (⩘[1]) identify subcategories (see complete key on page *I · 1).*

Kartensymbole in dem Registerverzeichnis stellen die rechts in Schlüssel erklärten Kategorien dar. Symbole mit hochgestellten Ziffern (⩘[1]) bezeichnen Unterabteilungen einer Kategorie (vgl. vollständiger Schlüssel auf Seite *I · 1).*

Los símbolos incluídos en el texto del índice representan las grandes categorias identificadas con la clave a la derecha. Los símbolos con numeros en su parte superior (⩘[1]) identifican las subcategorías (véase la clave completa en la página *I · 1).*

Les symboles de l'index représentent les catégories indiquées dans la légende à droite. Les symboles suivis d'un indice (⩘[1]) représentent des sous-catégories (voir légende complète à la page *I · 1).*

Os símbolos incluídos no texto do índice representam as grandes categorias identificadas com a chave à direita. Os símbolos com números em sua parte superior (⩘[1]) identificam as subcategorias (veja-se a chave completa à página *I · 1).*

∧ Mountain	Berg	Montaña	Montagne	Montanha
⩘ Mountains	Berge	Montañas	Montagnes	Montanhas
)(Pass	Pass	Paso	Col	Passo
V Valley, Canyon	Tal, Cañon	Valle, Cañón	Vallée, Canyon	Vale, Canhão
≚ Plain	Ebene	Llano	Plaine	Planície
≻ Cape	Kap	Cabo	Cap	Cabo
I Island	Insel	Isla	Île	Ilha
II Islands	Inseln	Islas	Îles	Ilhas
⊥ Other Topographic Features	Andere Topographische Objekte	Otros Elementos Topográficos	Autres données topographiques	Outros acidentes topográficos

ESPAÑOL Nombre / FRANÇAIS Nom / PORTUGUÊS Nome	Página / Page	Lat.°′	Long.°′ W = Oeste / W = Ouest
Dordives	50	48.09 N	2.46 E
Dordogne □[5]	32	45.10 N	0.45 E
Dordogne ≏	32	45.02 N	0.35 W
Dordon	42	52.36 N	1.37 W
Dordrecht, Ned.	52	51.49 N	4.40 E
Dordrecht, S. Afr.	158	31.20 S	27.03 E
Doré ≏, Sk., Can.	184	54.56 N	107.45 W
Dore ≏, Fr.	62	45.50 N	3.35 E
Dore ≏, Eng., U.K.	42	51.57 N	2.52 W
Dore, Monts ⋏	32	45.30 N	2.45 E
Doreissou	146	10.33 N	15.08 E
Doré Lake	184	54.38 N	107.24 W
Doré Lake ⊜	184	54.46 N	107.17 W
Dorena	202	43.43 N	122.51 W
Dörentrup	52	52.03 N	8.59 E
Dores	46	57.22 N	4.15 W
Dores do Indaiá	255	19.27 S	45.36 W
Dores do Paraibuna	256	21.31 S	43.39 W
Dorfen	60	48.17 N	12.08 E
Dorfgastein	64	47.15 N	13.06 E
Dorfmark	52	52.54 N	9.46 E
Dorgali	71	40.17 N	9.35 E
Dörgön nuur ⊜	88	47.40 N	93.30 E
Doring ≏	158	31.54 S	18.39 E
Doringbaai	158	31.48 S	18.15 E
Doringkop ∧	273d	26.15 S	27.50 E
Dorino	82	56.28 N	36.09 E
Dorion-Vaudreuil	206	45.23 N	74.01 W
Dorje Lāpka ∧	124	28.11 N	85.47 E
Dorking	260	51.14 N	0.20 W
Dorloo	210	42.43 N	74.37 W
Dormaa Ahenkro	150	7.17 N	2.53 W
Dormagen	56	51.05 N	6.50 E
Dormans	50	49.04 N	3.38 E
Dormidontovka	89	47.45 N	134.57 E
Dormont	279b	40.23 N	80.02 W
Dornach	58	47.29 N	7.37 E
Dornap	263	51.15 N	7.04 E
Dornbach ◆[8]	264b	48.14 N	16.18 E
Dornbirn	58	47.25 N	9.44 E
Dornburg	56	50.30 N	8.07 E
Dorndorf, D.D.R.	54	51.00 N	11.40 E
Dorndorf, D.D.R.	56	50.50 N	10.05 E
Dornecy	50	47.26 N	3.35 E
Dorney	260	51.30 N	0.40 W
Dornhan	58	48.21 N	8.30 E
Dornie	46	57.17 N	5.31 W
Dorno	62	45.09 N	8.57 E
Dornoch	46	57.52 N	4.02 W
Dornoch Firth ⊂[1]	46	57.53 N	4.00 W
Dornod □[4]	88	48.00 N	115.00 E
Dornogov' □[4]	102	44.30 N	110.00 E
Dornsife	208	40.45 N	76.47 W
Dornstadt	58	48.28 N	9.56 E
Dornstetten	58	48.28 N	8.30 E
Dornumersiel	52	53.40 N	7.28 E
Doro, Indon.	115a	7.02 S	109.41 E
Doro, Mali	150	16.09 N	0.51 W
Dorochovo	82	55.33 N	36.23 E
Dorog	30	47.43 N	18.44 E
Dorogobuž	76	54.55 N	33.18 E
Dorohoi	38	47.57 N	26.24 E
Dorokempo	115b	8.33 S	118.15 E
Doromata	115b	8.46 S	118.13 E
Doromo	154	3.49 N	26.17 E
Dorošata	80	57.21 N	51.08 E
Dorošicha	82	56.52 N	35.50 E
Dorotea	26	64.16 N	16.24 E
Dorothy	208	39.24 N	74.49 W
Dorothy, Lake ⊜	224	47.34 N	121.22 W
Dorotockeys Run ≏	276	40.59 N	73.58 W
Dorpat → Tartu	76	58.23 N	26.43 E
Dörpen	52	52.57 N	7.20 E
Dorr	216	42.43 N	85.43 W
Dorrance	198	38.50 N	98.35 W
Dorre Island I	162	25.09 S	113.07 E
Dorrigo	166	30.21 S	152.43 E
Dorris	204	41.58 N	121.55 W
Dorsale ⋏	36	36.00 N	9.50 E
Dorset, Oh., U.S.	214	41.41 N	80.40 W
Dorset, Vt., U.S.	210	43.15 N	73.05 W
Dorset □[6]	42	50.47 N	2.20 W
Dorset Peak ∧	188	43.19 N	73.02 W
Dorsey Run ≏	284b	39.11 N	76.48 W
Dorseyville	279b	40.35 N	79.53 W
Dorsten	52	51.39 N	6.58 E
Dorstfeld ◆[8]	263	51.31 N	7.25 E
Dort → Dordrecht	52	51.49 N	4.40 E
Dortan	58	46.19 N	5.40 E
Dortmund, B.R.D.	52	51.31 N	7.28 E
Dortmund, B.R.D.	263	51.31 N	7.28 E
Dortmund-Ems-Kanal ≋	52	51.32 N	7.27 E
Dortmunder Rieselfelder ◆[1]	263	51.39 N	7.25 E
Dortmund-Wickede, Flughafen ⊠	263	51.32 N	7.35 E
Dorton	192	37.16 N	82.34 W
Dörtyol	130	36.52 N	36.12 E
Dorum	52	53.41 N	8.34 E
Doruma	154	4.44 N	27.42 E
Dorval	206	45.27 N	73.44 W
Dorval, Île I	275a	45.26 N	73.45 W
Dorval Gardens Centre ◆[9]	275a	45.27 N	73.44 W
Dörverden	52	52.51 N	9.13 E
Dörvöldžin	88	48.08 N	93.58 E
Dörzbach	56	49.23 N	9.42 E
Dos, Canal Numero ≋	252	36.21 S	56.54 W
Dosara	150	12.32 N	6.09 E
Dos Arroyos	234	17.02 N	99.40 W
Dosatuj	88	50.23 N	118.38 E
Dos Bahías, Cabo ≻	254	44.55 S	65.32 W
Dos Bocas	240m	18.20 N	66.40 W
Dos Bocas, Lago ⊜[1]	240m	18.19 N	66.40 W
Doščatoje	80	55.23 N	42.07 E
Dosewallips ≏	224	47.42 N	122.53 W
Doshan Tappeh Airfield ⊠	267d	35.42 N	51.28 E
Dos Hermanas	34	37.17 N	5.55 W
Dos Hermanas, Islas II	258	34.05 S	58.17 W
Dōshi	94	35.32 N	139.02 E
Dōshi ≏	94	35.36 N	139.14 E
Doshisha University ⊍[2]	270	35.02 N	135.46 E
Dosi	164	5.56 S	134.34 E
Dösjebro	41	55.49 N	13.01 E
Do-son	110	20.42 N	106.47 E
Dosoris Island ≻[1]	276	40.53 N	73.38 W
Dosoris Pond ⊜	276	40.54 N	73.38 W
Dos Palos	226	36.59 N	120.37 W
Dos Reyes, Punta ≻	252	24.33 S	70.35 W
Dosse ≏	54	53.13 N	12.20 E
Dosséo, Bahr ≏	146	9.01 N	19.38 E
Dossin Great Lakes Museum ⊍	281	42.20 N	82.59 W
Dosso	150	13.03 N	3.12 E
Dosso □[5]	150	13.00 N	3.00 E
Dossor	80	47.32 N	53.01 E
Doster	216	42.27 N	85.33 W
Doswell	208	37.51 N	77.27 W
Dothan	194	31.13 N	85.23 W
Doting Cove	186	49.27 N	53.57 W
Dot Lake	180	63.40 N	144.04 W
Dotnuva	76	55.21 N	23.54 E
Dotson	222	32.01 N	94.31 W
Döttingen	58	47.34 N	8.16 E
Doty	224	46.38 N	123.16 W
Dou ≏	105	39.13 N	118.03 E
Douai	50	50.22 N	3.04 E
Douala	152	4.03 N	9.42 E
Douala-Edéa, Réserve de ◆[4]	152	4.30 S	9.50 E
Douarnenez	32	48.06 N	4.20 W
Doubabougou	150	14.13 N	7.59 W
Double, Lac ⊜	186	50.46 N	70.23 W
Double, Pointe ≻	241o	16.20 N	61.00 W
Double Bayou	222	29.41 N	94.39 W
Double Cone ∧	172	45.04 S	168.48 E
Double Island Point ≻	166	25.56 S	153.11 E
Double Mountain ∧	228	35.02 N	118.29 W
Double Point ≻	166	17.39 S	146.09 E
Double Springs	194	34.08 N	87.24 W
Doubletop Peak ∧	200	43.21 N	110.17 W
Doubs	58	46.56 N	6.21 E
Doubs □[5], Fr.	58	47.10 N	6.25 E
Doubs □[5], Fr.	58	47.10 N	6.15 E
Doubs ≏	58	46.54 N	5.02 E
Doubs, Saut de ⌞	58	47.05 N	6.43 E
Doubtful Sound ⋓	172	45.17 S	166.51 E
Doubtless Bay ⊂	172	34.55 S	173.25 E
Douchy	50	47.57 N	3.03 E
Douchy-les-Mines	50	50.18 N	3.23 E
Doudeville	50	49.43 N	0.48 E
Doudian	105	39.39 N	116.03 E
Doué ≏[1]	150	16.38 N	15.02 W
Douentza	150	15.00 N	2.57 W
Dougga ⊥	36	36.25 N	9.13 E
Doughboy	170	35.15 S	149.39 E
Doughboy Bay ⊂	172	47.02 S	167.41 E
Douglas, Mb., Can.	184	49.53 N	99.42 W
Douglas, On., Can.	212	45.31 N	76.56 W
Douglas, I. of Man	44	54.09 N	4.28 W
Douglas, S. Afr.	158	29.04 S	23.46 E
Douglas, Scot., U.K.	46	55.33 N	3.51 W
Douglas, Ak., U.S.	180	58.16 N	134.22 W
Douglas, Az., U.S.	200	31.20 N	109.32 W
Douglas, Ga., U.S.	192	31.30 N	82.51 W
Douglas, Mi., U.S.	216	42.38 N	86.12 W
Douglas, N.D., U.S.	198	47.51 N	101.30 W
Douglas, Wy., U.S.	200	42.45 N	105.22 W
Douglas □[6]	226	38.55 N	119.39 W
Douglas ≏	262	53.43 N	2.50 W
Douglas, Cape ≻	180	58.52 N	153.18 W
Douglas, Mount ∧	180	58.52 N	153.31 W
Douglas, Mount ∧[2]	162	28.39 S	123.53 E
Douglas Aircraft Company ⊍[3]	280	33.50 N	118.09 W
Douglas Channel ⋓	182	53.30 N	129.12 W
Douglas Creek ≏	200	40.06 N	108.46 W
Douglas Lake	182	50.10 N	120.12 W
Douglas Lake ⊜[1]	192	36.00 N	83.22 W
Douglas Lake Indian Reserve ◆[4]	182	50.10 N	120.49 W
Douglas Park	170	34.11 S	150.43 E
Douglas Park ♠	278	41.52 N	87.42 W
Douglass, Ks., U.S.	198	37.31 N	97.01 W
Douglass, Tx., U.S.	222	31.40 N	94.53 W
Douglass Run ≏	279b	40.15 N	79.48 W
Douglassville	208	40.15 N	75.44 W
Douglasville	192	33.45 N	84.44 W
Douglas Water ≏	46	55.38 N	3.46 W
Dougouzi, Zhg.	89	49.57 N	127.01 E
Dougouzi, Zhg.	104	41.16 N	122.34 E
Douhutun	98	42.06 N	124.50 E
Douigny	152	3.11 S	10.45 E
Doujiapu	104	41.05 N	122.12 E
Doujiazhuang	105	40.22 N	116.59 E
Doukkane, Djebel ∧	36	35.23 N	8.00 E
Doulaincourt	58	48.19 N	5.12 E
Doulevant-le-Château	58	48.23 N	4.55 E
Doullens	50	50.09 N	2.21 E
Doumanaba	150	11.40 N	5.56 W
Doumanga	152	2.41 S	12.40 E
Doumba Bélo	152	5.05 N	14.18 E
Doumdégué	152	7.29 N	18.58 E
Doumé, Cam.	152	5.32 N	12.19 E
Doumé, Cam.	152	4.14 N	13.27 E
Doumé ≏	152	4.06 N	14.34 E
Doumen, Zhg.	100	22.12 N	113.16 E
Doumen, Zhg.	105	39.18 N	115.53 E
Douna	150	14.39 N	1.44 W
Doune	46	56.12 N	4.05 W
Doune Castle ⊥	46	56.11 N	4.03 W
Dounguila	152	2.53 S	11.58 E
Doupov	54	50.10 N	13.08 E
Doupovské hory ⋏	54	50.13 N	13.08 E
Dour	50	50.24 N	3.47 E
Doura	150	13.14 N	5.55 W
Dourada, Serra ⋏	255	16.05 S	50.15 W
Dourada, Serra ⋏[1]	255	13.10 S	48.45 W
Douradinho	256	21.45 S	45.46 W
Dourado ≏, Bra.	255	21.22 S	49.41 W
Dourado ≏, Bra.	256	21.43 S	45.44 W
Dourados	255	22.13 S	54.48 W
Dourados ≏	255	21.58 S	54.18 W
Dourbali	146	11.49 N	15.52 E
Dourdan	50	48.32 N	2.01 E
Dourdou ≏	32	44.00 N	2.41 E
Dourges	50	50.26 N	2.59 E
Dourkoulé	146	14.27 N	22.13 E
Douro (Duero) ≏	34	41.08 N	8.40 W
Doushanhe	100	31.38 N	114.42 E
Dousman	216	43.00 N	88.28 W
Douthat State Park ♠	192	37.55 N	79.50 W
Douvaine	58	46.19 N	6.18 E
Douvres → Dover	42	51.08 N	1.19 E
Douvres, Falaises de ⊥[4]	273b	4.06 S	15.25 E
Douvrin	50	50.31 N	2.50 E
Doux ≏	62	45.04 N	4.50 E
Douy-la-Ramée	261	49.04 N	2.53 E
Douyu	98	37.53 N	114.30 E
Douz	148	33.28 N	9.01 E
Douze ≏	32	43.54 N	0.30 W
Douzhangzhuang	105	39.23 N	116.55 E
Douzishan	107	29.04 N	104.57 E
Douziyu	105	40.18 N	117.19 E
Douzy	56	49.40 N	5.03 E
Dovadola	66	44.07 N	11.53 E
Dovbyš	78	50.22 N	27.59 E
Dove ≏, Eng., U.K.	44	52.50 N	1.35 W
Dove ≏, Eng., U.K.	44	54.12 N	0.54 W
Dove Creek	200	37.45 N	108.54 W
Dove Creek ≏, Tx., U.S.	196	31.20 N	100.36 W
Dove Creek ≏, Ut,. U.S.	200	41.37 N	113.15 W
Dove Holes	262	53.18 N	1.53 W
Dove Holes Tunnel ◆[5]	262	53.18 N	1.53 W
Dover, Austl.	166	43.19 S	147.01 E
Dover, S. Afr.	158	27.02 S	27.46 E
Dover, Eng., U.K.	42	51.08 N	1.19 E
Dover, Ar., U.S.	194	35.24 N	93.06 W
Dover, De., U.S.	208	39.09 N	75.31 W
Dover, Fl., U.S.	220	27.59 N	82.13 W
Dover, Id., U.S.	202	48.15 N	116.36 W
Dover, Ky., U.S.	218	38.45 N	83.52 W
Dover, Ma., U.S.	283	42.14 N	71.17 W
Dover, N.H., U.S.	188	43.11 N	70.52 W
Dover, N.J., U.S.	210	40.53 N	74.34 W
Dover, N.C., U.S.	192	35.12 N	77.26 W
Dover, Oh., U.S.	214	40.31 N	81.28 W
Dover, Ok., U.S.	196	35.58 N	97.54 W
Dover, Pa., U.S.	208	40.00 N	76.51 W
Dover, Tn., U.S.	194	36.29 N	87.50 W
Dover, Point ≻	162	32.32 S	125.32 E
Dover, Strait of (Pas de Calais) ⋓	50	51.00 N	1.30 E
Dover Air Force Base ■	208	39.08 N	75.28 W
Dover-Foxcroft	188	45.11 N	69.13 W
Dover Heights	274a	33.53 S	151.17 E
Dover Hills	276	40.52 N	74.33 W
Dover Plains	210	41.44 N	73.35 W
Dovers Hills ⋏[2]	162	23.10 S	128.45 E
Dove Stone Reservoir ⊜[1]	262	53.32 N	1.58 W
Doveton	274b	38.00 S	145.14 E
Dovey Valley V	42	52.35 N	3.50 W
Dovol'noje	86	54.30 N	79.40 E
Dovre	26	61.59 N	9.15 E
Dovrefjell ⋏	26	62.06 N	9.25 E
Dovsk	76	53.09 N	30.28 E
Dowa	154	13.40 S	33.58 E
Dowagiac	216	41.59 N	86.06 W
Dowagiac ≏	216	41.51 N	86.16 W
Dowagiac Creek ≏	216	41.49 N	86.10 W
Dowally	46	56.36 N	3.37 W
Dow City	198	41.55 N	95.29 W
Dowden Terrace	284c	38.50 N	77.08 W
Dowell	208	38.20 N	76.27 W
Dowerin	162	31.12 S	117.02 E
Dowi, Tanjung ≻	114	1.31 N	97.25 E
Dowker, Île I	275a	45.24 N	73.54 W
Dowlatābād, Afg.	120	36.59 N	66.50 E
Dowlatābād, Afg.	120	36.26 N	64.55 E
Dowlatābād, Īrān	128	28.18 N	56.40 E
Dowlatābād, Īrān	267d	35.37 N	51.27 E
Dowlat Yār	120	34.33 N	65.47 E
Dowling Lake ⊜	182	51.44 N	112.00 W
Downderry	42	50.22 N	4.22 W
Downe ◆[8]	260	51.20 N	0.03 E
Down East	285	40.03 N	75.32 W
Downers Grove	216	41.48 N	88.00 W
Downey, Ca., U.S.	228	33.56 N	118.07 W
Downey, Id., U.S.	202	42.25 N	112.07 W
Downey, Il., U.S.	278	42.18 N	87.51 W
Downey Creek ≏	224	48.16 N	121.14 W
Downham, Eng., U.K.	42	52.26 N	0.15 E
Downham, Eng., U.K.	260	51.38 N	0.30 E
Downham Market	42	52.36 N	0.23 E
Down House ⊥	260	51.20 N	0.03 E
Downieville	226	39.33 N	120.49 W
Downing	194	40.29 N	92.22 W
Downingtown	208	40.00 N	75.42 W
Downingtown Airport ⊠	285	39.59 N	75.45 W
Downpatrick	48	54.20 N	5.43 W
Downpatrick Head ≻	48	54.20 N	9.20 W
Downs, Il., U.S.	216	40.24 N	88.52 W
Downs, Ks., U.S.	198	39.30 N	98.32 W
Downs Mountain ∧	200	43.18 N	109.40 W
Downsview Dells Park ♠	275b	43.44 N	79.30 W
Downsville	210	42.04 N	74.59 W
Downsville Dam ◆[6]	210	42.05 N	74.58 W
Downton	42	51.00 N	1.44 W
Downton, Mount ∧	182	52.42 N	124.51 W
Downton Lake ⊜	182	50.51 N	123.00 W
Downwind Acres Airfield ⊠	281	42.09 N	83.34 W
Dow Rūd	128	33.28 N	49.04 E
Dows	190	42.39 N	93.30 W
Dowsārī	128	28.25 N	57.59 E
Dowshī	120	35.37 N	68.41 E
Doygaab	144	0.59 N	43.32 E
Doyle	204	40.01 N	120.06 W
Doyles	186	47.50 N	59.12 W
Doylesburg	214	40.13 N	77.42 W
Doylestown, Oh., U.S.	214	40.58 N	81.41 W
Doylestown, Pa., U.S.	208	40.18 N	75.07 W
Doyline	194	32.32 N	93.25 W
Dōzan ≏	96	33.58 N	133.47 E
Dōzen II	92	36.05 N	133.05 E
Dozier	194	31.29 N	86.21 W
Dozois, Réservoir ⊜[1]	190	47.30 N	77.05 W
Dozza	66	44.22 N	11.37 E
Drâa, Cap ≻	148	28.44 N	11.08 W
Dra'a, Hamada du ◆[2]	148	29.00 N	6.45 W
Drâa, Oued V	148	28.43 N	11.09 W
Draa el Mizan	34	36.32 N	3.50 E
Drabble → José Enrique Rodó	258	33.41 S	57.34 W
Drabenderhöhe	56	50.57 N	7.27 E
Drabov	78	49.58 N	32.08 E
Drac ≏	62	45.13 N	5.41 E
Dracena	255	21.32 S	51.29 W
Drachenfels ⊥	56	50.40 N	7.12 E
Drachten	52	53.06 N	6.05 E
Dracut	207	42.40 N	71.18 W
Dragalina	38	44.26 N	27.20 E
Drăgănești-Olt	38	44.10 N	24.32 E
Drăgănești-Vlașca	38	44.06 N	25.36 E
Drăgășani	38	44.40 N	24.16 E
Drag Lake ⊜	212	45.05 N	78.24 W
Dragone ≏	64	44.23 N	10.37 E
Dragonera, Isla I	34	39.35 N	2.19 E
Dragoni	68	41.16 N	14.18 E
Dragonja ≏	64	45.28 N	13.37 E
Dragons Mouth ⋓	241r	10.45 N	61.46 W
Dragon Swamp ≏	208	37.33 N	76.34 W
Dragoon	200	32.01 N	110.02 W
Dragør	41	55.36 N	12.41 E
Draguignan	62	43.32 N	6.28 E
Drain	202	43.39 N	123.19 W
Drake, Mo., U.S.	219	38.28 N	91.28 W
Drake, N.D., U.S.	198	47.55 N	100.22 W
Drakenburg	52	52.41 N	9.13 E
Drakensberg ⋏	156	27.00 S	30.00 E
Drake Passage ⋓	18	58.00 S	70.00 W
Drake Peak ∧	202	42.19 N	120.07 W
Drakesboro	194	37.13 N	87.02 W
Drakes Branch	192	36.59 N	78.36 W
Drakes Brook ≏	276	40.49 N	74.43 W
Drake Well Museum ⊍	214	41.36 N	79.39 W
Drakino	82	54.52 N	37.17 E
Dráma	38	41.09 N	24.08 E
Dramburg → Drawsko Pomorskie	30	53.32 N	15.48 E
Drammen	26	59.44 N	10.15 E
Drancy	50	48.56 N	2.27 E
Dranda	84	42.53 N	41.09 E
Drang ≏	110	13.19 N	107.21 E
Drangajökull ⊓	24a	66.11 N	22.15 W
Drangstedt	52	53.36 N	8.44 E
Dranov, Ostrovul I	38	44.52 N	29.15 E
Dransfeld	52	51.30 N	9.45 E
Dranske	54	54.38 N	13.14 E
Drap	62	43.45 N	7.19 E
Draper, N.C., U.S.	192	36.31 N	79.41 W
Draper, Ut,. U.S.	200	40.31 N	111.51 W
Draperstown	48	54.48 N	6.47 W
Drās	123	34.27 N	75.46 E
Drās ≏	123	34.37 N	75.59 E
Drau (Drava) (Dráva) ≏	36	45.33 N	18.55 E
Drava (Drau) (Dráva) ≏	36	45.33 N	18.55 E
Draveil	50	48.41 N	2.25 E
Dravinja ≏	36	46.22 N	15.57 E
Dravograd	61	46.35 N	15.02 E
Dravosburg	279b	40.21 N	79.51 W
Drawno	30	53.13 N	15.45 E
Drawsko Pomorskie	30	53.32 N	15.48 E
Drayton, On., Can.	212	43.46 N	80.40 W
Drayton, Eng., U.K.	42	51.38 N	1.18 W
Drayton, N.D., U.S.	198	48.34 N	97.10 W
Drayton, S.C., U.S.	192	34.58 N	81.54 W
Drayton Plains	216	42.41 N	83.22 W
Drayton Valley	182	53.13 N	114.59 W
Draženov	60	49.28 N	12.52 E
Drean	36	36.41 N	7.46 E
Drebkau	54	51.39 N	14.13 E
Dreieich	56	50.01 N	8.41 E
Dreifelder Weiher ⊜	56	50.36 N	7.49 E
Dreihausen	56	50.43 N	8.50 E
Dreiherrnspitze (Picco dei Tre Signori) ∧	64	47.04 N	12.15 E
Dreikikir	164	3.35 S	142.45 E
Drejø I	41	54.58 N	10.25 E
Dremsel, Mount ∧	164	2.10 S	146.55 E
Drena	64	45.58 N	10.56 E
Drenovec	38	43.42 N	22.59 E
Drensteinfurt	52	51.48 N	7.44 E
Drenthe □[4]	52	52.45 N	6.30 E
Dresde → Dresden	54	51.03 N	13.44 E
Dresden, On., Can.	214	42.35 N	82.11 W
Dresden, D.D.R.	54	51.03 N	13.44 E
Dresden, N.Y., U.S.	210	42.41 N	76.58 W
Dresden, Oh., U.S.	214	40.07 N	82.00 W
Dresden, Tn., U.S.	194	36.17 N	88.42 W
Dresden □[5]	54	51.10 N	14.00 E
Dresher	285	40.08 N	75.10 W
Dretun	76	55.41 N	29.13 E
Dreux	50	48.44 N	1.22 E
Drevenack	263	51.40 N	6.45 E
Drew	194	33.48 N	90.31 W
Drewer	263	51.40 N	7.07 E
Drewitz, D.D.R.	54	52.22 N	13.07 E
Drewitz, D.D.R.	54	52.12 N	12.10 E
Drewitz ◆[8]	264a	52.22 N	13.08 E
Drewryville	208	36.42 N	77.18 W
Drews Reservoir ⊜[1]	202	42.10 N	120.40 W
Drew University ⊍[2]	276	40.46 N	74.25 W
Drexel	218	39.44 N	84.17 W
Drexel Gardens	218	39.44 N	86.15 W
Drexel Hill	285	39.56 N	75.17 W
Drexel University ⊍[2]	285	39.57 N	75.11 W
Drezdenko	30	52.51 N	15.50 E
Drezna	82	55.44 N	38.51 E
Dribin	76	54.08 N	31.06 E
Driebergen	52	52.03 N	5.16 E
Drienov	30	48.53 N	21.17 E
Driesen → Drezdenko	30	52.51 N	15.50 E
Driffield	44	54.00 N	0.27 W
Drifton	210	41.00 N	75.54 W
Driftpile ≏	182	55.23 N	115.40 W
Drift Pile River Indian Reserve ◆[4]	182	55.18 N	115.45 W
Driftwood, B.C., Can.	182	55.49 N	126.25 W
Driftwood, Pa., U.S.	214	41.20 N	78.08 W
Driftwood ≏, B.C., Can.	182	55.43 N	126.15 W
Driftwood ≏, In., U.S.	218	39.12 N	85.56 W
Driftwood Creek ≏	198	40.11 N	100.39 W
Driggs	202	43.43 N	111.06 W
Drimnin	46	56.36 N	6.00 W
Drimoleague	48	51.38 N	9.14 W
Drin ≏	38	41.45 N	19.34 E
Drina ≏	38	44.53 N	19.21 E
Dringenberg	52	51.40 N	9.02 E
Drinit, Pellg i ⊂	38	41.45 N	19.28 E
Driorejo	115a	7.21 S	112.37 E
Driscoll	196	27.40 N	97.45 W
Driskill Mountain ∧[2]	194	32.25 N	92.54 W
Drissa ≏	76	55.47 N	27.55 E
Drisv'aty, ozero ⊜	76	55.38 N	26.35 E
Driver	208	36.49 N	76.30 W
Drizzle Lake ⊜	212	45.20 N	78.10 W
Drjanovo	38	42.58 N	25.27 E
Drnholec	61	48.52 N	16.29 E
Drniš	36	43.51 N	16.09 E
Dro	64	45.58 N	10.54 E
Drøbak	26	59.39 N	10.39 E
Drobeta-Turnu-Severin	38	44.38 N	22.39 E
Drobylevo	82	55.44 N	35.53 E
Drobyš'ovo, S.S.S.R.	83	49.02 N	37.44 E
Drobyšovo, S.S.S.R.	86	53.58 N	74.40 E
Drochtersen	52	53.42 N	9.23 E
Drocourt	261	49.03 N	1.46 E
Droë Harts ≏	158	27.35 S	24.41 E
Drogheda (Droichead Átha)	48	53.43 N	6.21 W
Drogičin	76	52.11 N	25.09 E
Drogobyč	78	49.21 N	23.30 E
Drohiczyn	30	52.24 N	22.41 E
Drohobycz → Drogobyč	78	49.21 N	23.30 E
Droichead Átha → Drogheda	48	53.43 N	6.21 W
Droichead Nua	48	53.11 N	6.48 W
Droitwich	42	52.16 N	2.09 W
Drokija	78	48.03 N	27.48 E
Drolshagen	56	51.01 N	7.46 E
Dromahair	48	54.14 N	8.19 W
Dromana	169	38.21 S	144.58 E
Dromara	44	54.23 N	6.01 W
Dromcolliher	48	52.20 N	8.54 W
Drôme □[5]	62	44.35 N	5.10 E
Drôme ≏	62	44.46 N	4.46 E
Drömling ◆[1]	54	52.29 N	11.04 E
Dromod	48	53.51 N	7.55 W
Dromore	48	54.25 N	6.09 W
Dromore West	48	54.15 N	8.53 W
Dronero	62	44.28 N	7.22 E
Dronfield	44	53.19 N	1.27 W
Drongan	44	55.26 N	4.27 W
Drongen	50	51.03 N	3.40 E
Dronne ≏	32	45.02 N	0.09 W
Dronninglund	26	57.09 N	10.18 E
Dronrijp	52	53.11 N	5.38 E
Dröschede	263	51.22 N	7.39 E
Drosendorf Stadt	61	48.52 N	15.37 E
Drosiá	267c	38.07 N	23.52 E
Drösing	61	48.32 N	16.54 E
Droskovo	76	52.31 N	37.05 E
Drossen → Ośno	30	52.28 N	14.50 E
Drottningholms slott ⊥	40	59.19 N	17.53 E
Droué	50	48.02 N	1.05 E
Droue-sur-Drouette	261	48.36 N	1.42 E
Drouette ≏	261	48.37 N	1.37 E
Drouin	169	38.08 S	145.51 E
Drov'anaja	88	51.35 N	113.02 E
Droylsden	262	53.29 N	2.10 W
Droyssig	54	51.02 N	12.01 E
Dr. Petru Groza	38	46.32 N	22.28 E
Druid Hill Park ♠	284b	39.19 N	76.39 W
Druja	76	55.47 N	27.27 E
Druk-Yul → Bhutan □[1]	120	27.30 N	90.30 E
Drulingen	56	48.52 N	7.11 E
Drum, Mount ∧	180	62.07 N	144.35 W
Drumbeg	46	58.14 N	5.12 W
Drumbo	212	43.14 N	80.33 W
Drumcliff	48	54.20 N	8.30 W
Drumheller	182	51.28 N	112.42 W
Drumlish	48	53.48 N	7.46 W
Drummond, N.Z.	172	46.09 S	168.09 E
Drummond, Mt., U.S.	202	46.40 N	113.08 W
Drummond, Wi., U.S.	190	46.20 N	91.15 W
Drummond □[6]	206	45.50 N	72.20 W
Drummond, Lake ⊜	208	36.36 N	76.28 W
Drummond Island I	190	46.00 N	83.40 W
Drummond Range ⋏	166	23.30 S	147.15 E
Drummondville	206	45.53 N	72.29 W
Drummore	44	54.42 N	4.54 W
Drummoyne	274a	33.51 S	151.09 E
Drumquin	48	54.37 N	7.30 W
Drumright	196	35.59 N	96.36 W
Drumshanbo	48	54.02 N	8.02 W
Drunen	52	51.42 N	5.08 E
Drusenheim	56	48.46 N	7.57 E
Druskininkai	76	54.01 N	23.58 E
Drut' ≏	76	53.03 N	30.42 E
Druten	52	51.54 N	5.36 E
Druyes-les-Belles-Fontaines	50	47.33 N	3.25 E
Družba, S.S.S.R.	78	52.03 N	33.56 E
Družba, S.S.S.R.	86	45.15 N	82.26 E
Družba, S.S.S.R.	265b	55.53 N	37.45 E
Družina	74	68.14 N	145.18 E
Družkovka	83	48.37 N	37.33 E
Družnaja Gorka	76	59.17 N	30.08 E
Drvar	36	44.22 N	16.24 E
Drwęca ≏	30	53.00 N	18.42 E
Dry ≏	164	14.54 S	132.24 E
Dry Arm ⊂	202	47.45 N	106.20 W
Dry Bay ⊂	180	59.08 N	138.25 W
Dryberry Lake ⊜	184	49.33 N	93.53 W
Dryburgh Abbey ⊍[1]	46	55.34 N	2.40 W
Dry Cimarron ≏	196	36.54 N	102.59 W
Dry Creek ≏, Ca., U.S.	204	38.35 N	122.51 W
Dry Creek ≏, Ca., U.S.	226	37.27 N	120.37 W
Dry Creek ≏, Ca., U.S.	226	38.39 N	121.28 W
Dry Creek ≏, Ca., U.S.	226	38.22 N	122.18 W
Dry Creek ≏, Ca., U.S.	226	38.58 N	121.32 W
Dry Creek ≏, Ca., U.S.	226	39.13 N	121.25 W
Dry Creek ≏, Ca., U.S.	226	38.14 N	121.24 W
Dry Creek ≏, Ca., U.S.	226	36.58 N	120.13 W
Dry Creek ≏, Ca., U.S.	226	36.47 N	119.46 W
Dry Creek ≏, Ca., U.S.	282	37.22 N	122.23 W
Dry Creek ≏, Or., U.S.	202	43.34 N	117.21 W
Dry Creek ≏, Or., U.S.	224	45.30 N	121.03 W
Dry Creek ≏, Tx., U.S.	222	32.46 N	95.28 W
Dry Creek ≏, Wy., U.S.	202	43.13 N	108.54 W
Dry Creek ≏, Wy., U.S.	202	44.30 N	108.03 W
Dry Creek Mountain ∧	204	41.22 N	116.22 W
Dryden, On., Can.	184	49.47 N	92.50 W
Dryden, N.Y., U.S.	210	42.29 N	76.17 W
Dryden, Wa., U.S.	224	47.32 N	120.33 W
Dry Devils ≏, Tx., U.S.	196	29.47 N	100.59 W
Dry Devils ≏, Tx., U.S.	196	30.20 N	100.57 W
Dryfe Water ≏	44	55.08 N	3.26 W
Dry Fork ≏	194	37.58 N	91.31 W
Dry Frio ≏	196	29.17 N	99.39 W
Drygalski Island I	9	65.45 S	92.30 E
Dry Lake ⊜	198	48.15 N	98.58 W
Drymen	46	56.04 N	4.27 W
Dry Prong	194	31.34 N	92.31 W
Dry Ridge	218	38.40 N	84.35 W
Dry Run	214	40.10 N	77.45 W
Drysdale	169	38.11 S	144.34 E
Drysdale ≏	164	13.59 S	126.51 E
Drysdale River National Park ♠	164	15.00 S	127.00 E
Dry Tortugas II	220	24.38 N	82.55 W
Drzewica	30	51.27 N	20.28 E
Drzewice	54	52.38 N	14.38 E
Dschang	152	5.27 N	10.04 E
Dschidda → Jiddah	144	21.30 N	39.12 E
Dschuba → Jubba ≏	144	0.15 S	42.38 E
Du	150	10.30 N	0.59 W
Du ≏	102	32.48 N	110.38 E
Dua ≏	152	3.20 N	20.53 E
Duabo	150	5.40 N	8.05 W
Duāigaon	126	24.14 N	90.51 E
Duala → Douala	152	4.03 N	9.42 E
Dualchi	71	40.13 N	8.54 E
Du'an	102	24.06 N	108.10 E
Duancun	105	38.52 N	115.56 E
Duane L. Bliss State Park ♠	226	38.59 N	120.06 W
Duanesburg	210	42.46 N	74.08 W
Duanjialing	105	39.59 N	117.09 E
Duaringa	166	23.43 S	149.40 E
Duarte	228	34.08 N	117.58 W
Duarte, Pico ∧	238	19.02 N	70.59 W
Duartina	255	22.24 S	49.25 W
Duas Barras	256	22.02 S	42.32 W
Duayaw Nkwanta	150	7.10 N	2.06 W
Dubā, Ar. Su.	128	27.21 N	35.40 E
Dubá, Česko.	54	50.34 N	14.33 E
Dubach	194	32.41 N	92.39 W
Dubai → Dubayy	128	25.18 N	55.18 E
Dubawnt ≏	176	64.33 N	100.06 W
Dubawnt Lake ⊜	176	63.08 N	101.30 W
Dubayy	128	25.18 N	55.18 E
Dubbeldam	52	51.47 N	4.42 E
Dubbo	166	32.15 S	148.36 E
Dubbo Hill ∧	171b	35.25 S	148.36 E
Dube ≏	150	5.45 N	8.00 W
Dubele	154	2.54 N	29.33 E
Dübendorf	58	47.25 N	8.38 E
Dübener Heide ◆[3]	54	51.40 N	12.40 E
Dubenskij	86	51.27 N	56.38 E
Dubh Artach II[1]	46	56.08 N	6.40 W
Dubí	54	50.42 N	13.45 E
Dubi Bheri	272b	22.53 N	88.17 E
Dubica	36	45.11 N	16.48 E
Dubie	154	8.33 S	28.32 E
Dubinino	82	56.09 N	37.01 E
Dubino	58	46.09 N	9.27 E
Dubjazy	80	56.08 N	49.13 E
Dubki, S.S.S.R.	265a	60.00 N	30.00 E
Dubki, S.S.S.R.	265b	55.41 N	37.14 E
Dublin, Austl.	168b	34.27 S	138.21 E
Dublin, On., Can.	212	43.31 N	81.17 W
Dublin (Baile Átha Cliath), Ire.	48	53.20 N	6.15 W
Dublin, Ca., U.S.	226	37.42 N	121.56 W
Dublin, Ga., U.S.	192	32.32 N	82.54 W
Dublin, In., U.S.	218	39.48 N	85.12 W
Dublin, Md., U.S.	208	39.39 N	76.16 W
Dublin, Oh., U.S.	214	40.06 N	83.07 W
Dublin, Pa., U.S.	208	40.22 N	75.12 W
Dublin, Tx., U.S.	196	32.05 N	98.20 W
Dublin, Va., U.S.	192	37.06 N	80.41 W
Dublin □[6]	48	53.20 N	6.15 W
Dublin (Collinstown) Airport ⊠	44	53.26 N	6.15 W
Dublin Bay ⊂	48	53.20 N	6.06 W
Dublin-Belgard □[6]	48	53.15 N	6.20 W
Dublin Canyon V	282	37.42 N	121.59 W
Dublin-Fingal □[6]	48	53.30 N	6.15 W
Dublon I	175c	7.23 N	151.53 E
Dubna, S.S.S.R.	82	54.09 N	36.58 E
Dubna, S.S.S.R.	82	56.44 N	37.10 E
Dubna ≏, S.S.S.R.	76	56.22 N	26.10 E
Dubna ≏, S.S.S.R.	82	56.47 N	37.15 E
Dubňany	30	48.55 N	17.06 E
Dubnevo	82	55.06 N	38.08 E
Dubnica nad Váhom	30	48.58 N	18.09 E
Dubno	78	50.26 N	25.44 E
Dubois, Id., U.S.	202	44.10 N	112.13 W
Dubois, Il., U.S.	219	38.13 N	89.13 W
Dubois, In., U.S.	194	38.26 N	86.48 W
Du Bois, Ne., U.S.	198	40.02 N	96.02 W
Du Bois, Pa., U.S.	214	41.07 N	78.45 W
Dubois, Wy., U.S.	200	43.32 N	109.37 W
Du Bois Reservoir ⊜[1]	214	41.06 N	78.38 W
Duboistown	210	41.13 N	77.02 W
Dub'onki	80	54.27 N	46.18 E
Dubossarskoje vodochranilišče ⊜[1]	78	47.35 N	29.00 E
Dubossary	78	47.16 N	29.08 E
Dubovaja Rošča	76	53.11 N	36.04 E
Dubov'azovka	78	51.08 N	33.22 E
Dubovići	78	51.38 N	33.35 E
Dubovka, S.S.S.R.	78	51.26 N	41.25 E
Dubovka, S.S.S.R.	80	49.03 N	44.50 E
Dubovoje	76	53.08 N	40.05 E
Dubovskij	80	56.21 N	46.48 E
Dubovskoje	80	47.25 N	42.46 E
Dubovyj Ovrag	80	48.20 N	44.37 E
Dubovyj Umet	80	52.59 N	50.17 E
Duboweitun	89	50.42 N	120.14 E
Dubra	126	23.32 N	86.31 E
Dubrājpur	126	23.48 N	87.23 E
Dubréka	150	9.48 N	13.31 W
Dubrova, S.S.S.R.	76	52.25 N	29.58 E
Dubrova, S.S.S.R.	78	51.47 N	28.13 E
Dubrova, S.S.S.R.	80	56.59 N	54.33 E
Dubrova, S.S.S.R.	80	57.42 N	55.01 E
Dubrovica	78	51.34 N	26.34 E
Dubroviči	80	54.39 N	39.56 E
Dubrovicy	82	56.46 N	39.10 E
Dubrovino	86	55.28 N	83.17 E
Dubrovka, S.S.S.R.	76	53.42 N	33.30 E
Dubrovka, S.S.S.R.	76	59.51 N	30.56 E
Dubrovka, S.S.S.R.	76	59.13 N	36.13 E
Dubrovka, S.S.S.R.	82	54.44 N	36.21 E
Dubrovka, S.S.S.R.	83	47.54 N	39.02 E
Dubrovki	80	53.49 N	43.19 E
Dubrovnik	38	42.38 N	18.07 E
Dubrovno	76	54.35 N	30.41 E
Dubrovnoje, S.S.S.R.	86	57.58 N	69.25 E
Dubrovnoje, S.S.S.R.	86	54.49 N	68.06 E
Dubrovo	76	59.51 N	33.34 E
Dubrovskoje	88	58.45 N	111.10 E
Dubunskaja	86	43.46 N	80.13 E
Dubuque	190	42.30 N	90.39 W
Dubysa ≏	76	55.05 N	23.26 E
Duchana	85	38.02 N	68.13 E
Duchang	100	29.15 N	116.13 E
Duchcov	54	50.37 N	13.45 E
Ducherow	54	53.46 N	13.46 E
Duchesne	200	40.09 N	110.24 W
Duchesne ≏	200	40.05 N	109.41 W
Duchess	166	21.22 S	139.52 E
Duchovnickoje	80	52.28 N	48.15 E
Duchovščina	76	55.12 N	32.25 E
Duck ≏, Austl.	274a	33.50 S	151.02 E
Duck ≏, Tn., U.S.	194	36.02 N	87.52 W
Duckabush ≏	224	47.38 N	122.56 W
Duck Bay	184	52.10 N	100.09 W
Duck Creek ≏, On., Can.	281	42.18 N	82.41 W
Duck Creek ≏, Ca., U.S.	226	37.55 N	121.16 W
Duck Creek ≏, In., U.S.	218	40.08 N	85.57 W
Duck Creek ≏, Nv., U.S.	204	40.06 N	114.43 W
Duck Creek ≏, N.D., U.S.	198	46.03 N	102.14 W
Duck Creek ≏, Tx., U.S.	196	33.14 N	100.42 W
Duck Creek ≏, Tx., U.S.	222	32.48 N	96.31 W
Duck Creek ≏, Tx., U.S.	222	31.06 N	96.17 W
Duck Creek ≏, Wi., U.S.	190	44.33 N	88.02 W
Duck Hill	194	33.37 N	89.42 W
Duck Island Harbor ⊂	276	40.55 N	73.23 W
Duck Key I	220	24.46 N	80.56 W
Duck Lake, Sk., Can.	184	52.47 N	106.13 W
Duck Lake, Mi., U.S.	216	42.24 N	84.47 W
Duck Lake ⊜, Mb., Can.	184	54.52 N	98.11 W
Duck Lake ⊜, Mi., U.S.	216	42.23 N	84.47 W
Duck Lake ⊜, Mi., U.S.	281	42.40 N	83.35 W
Duck Mountain ∧	184	51.35 N	101.00 W
Duck Mountain Provincial Park ♠, Mb., Can.	184	51.36 N	100.55 W
Duck Mountain Provincial Park ♠, Sk., Can.	184	51.38 N	101.53 W
Duck Valley Indian Reservation ◆[4]	204	42.00 N	116.10 W
Duckwall Mountain ∧	226	37.58 N	120.07 W
Duclair	50	49.29 N	0.53 E
Ducos	240e	14.34 N	60.58 W
Du Couedic, Cape ≻	166	36.04 S	136.42 E
Ducun	106	31.07 N	120.27 E
Duda ≏	246	2.33 N	74.02 W
Dudačkino	76	59.57 N	32.53 E
Dudčany	78	47.12 N	33.46 E
Duddington	42	52.36 N	0.32 W
Duddon ≏	44	54.15 N	3.13 W
Dudelange	56	49.28 N	6.05 E
Dudergofka ≏	265a	59.52 N	30.12 E
Duderstadt	52	51.31 N	10.16 E
Dūdhi	124	24.13 N	83.15 E
Dudh Kosi ≏	124	27.08 N	86.26 E
Dudhnai	124	25.59 N	90.44 E
Dudinka	74	69.25 N	86.15 E
Dudkin	78	47.53 N	40.32 E
Dudley, Eng., U.K.	42	52.30 N	2.05 W
Dudley, Eng., U.K.	44	55.03 N	1.35 W
Dudley, Ma., U.S.	207	42.02 N	71.55 W
Dudley, Pa., U.S.	214	40.12 N	78.10 W
Dudley Pond ⊜	283	42.20 N	71.22 W
Dudleyville	200	32.58 N	110.47 W
Dudna ≏	122	19.07 N	76.54 E
Dudorovskij	76	53.40 N	35.22 E
Dudullu	267b	41.02 N	29.09 E
Dudweiler	56	49.17 N	7.02 E
Dudzele	50	51.17 N	3.14 E
Due	89	50.50 N	142.06 E
Duékoué	150	6.45 N	7.21 W
Dueré	250	11.20 S	49.17 W
Duerji	89	45.39 N	121.49 E
Duerna ≏	34	42.19 N	5.54 W
Duero (Douro) ≏	34	41.08 N	8.40 W
Dueville	64	45.38 N	11.32 E
Due West	192	34.20 N	82.23 W
Dufault, Lac ⊜	190	48.19 N	79.00 W
Duff Dunbar	123	32.15 N	77.12 E
Duffel	50	51.06 N	4.31 E
Dufferin □[6]	212	44.05 N	80.15 W
Duffer Peak ∧	204	41.40 N	118.44 W
Duffield, Austl.	162	25.50 S	134.40 E
Duffield, Eng., U.K.	42	52.58 N	1.29 W
Duffins Creek ≏	212	43.49 N	79.02 W
Dufftown	46	57.26 N	3.08 W
Dufourspitze ∧	58	45.55 N	7.52 E
Dufresne ≏	206	46.16 N	73.59 W
Dufur	224	45.27 N	121.07 W
Duga Resa	36	45.27 N	15.30 E
Duga-Zapadnaja, mys ≻	74	59.09 N	145.59 E
Dugdemona ≏	194	31.47 N	92.22 W
Dugede	120	30.54 N	90.48 E
Dugger	194	39.04 N	87.16 W
Dugino	83	47.09 N	39.27 E
Dugi Otok I	36	44.00 N	15.04 E
Dugna	82	54.25 N	36.51 E
Dugny	261	48.57 N	2.25 E
Dugny-sur-Meuse	56	49.06 N	5.23 E
Dug Pond ⊜	283	42.17 N	71.22 W
Du Gué ≏	176	57.21 N	70.45 W
Dugui Qarag	102	39.38 N	108.40 E
Duğur	130	41.31 N	42.42 E
Dugway Proving Ground ■	200	40.10 N	113.15 W
Duhernal Lake ⊜	276	40.24 N	74.22 W
Duhi	140	7.07 N	28.45 E
Duhnen	52	53.53 N	8.38 E
Duhu	100	22.04 N	112.56 E
Duich, Loch ⊂	46	57.14 N	5.30 W
Duida, Cerro ∧	246	3.25 N	65.40 W
Duifken Point ≻	164	12.33 S	141.38 E
Duilongdeqing	124	29.56 N	90.42 E
Duingen	52	52.00 N	9.42 E
Duingt	62	45.50 N	6.12 E
Duino	64	45.46 N	13.36 E
Duirinish	46	57.19 N	5.41 W
Duisburg, B.R.D.	56	51.25 N	6.46 E
Duisburg, B.R.D.	263	51.25 N	6.46 E
Duissern ◆[8]	263	51.26 N	6.47 E
Duitama	246	5.50 N	73.02 W
Duiveland I	52	51.38 N	4.00 E
Duiwelskloof	156	23.42 S	30.06 E
Duji, Zhg.	98	34.11 N	115.48 E
Duji, Zhg.	98	37.44 N	116.50 E
Dujiahang	106	31.03 N	121.29 E
Dujuuma	144	1.15 N	42.34 E
Dukambiya	144	14.47 N	37.28 E
Dukana ⊤[4]	154	3.59 N	37.16 E
Dukazi	120	30.54 N	92.52 E
Duke	196	34.39 N	99.34 W

	English	Deutsch	Español	Français	Português
≏	River	Fluss	Río	Rivière	Rio
≋	Canal	Kanal	Canal	Canal	Canal
⌞	Waterfall, Rapids	Wasserfall, Stromschnellen	Cascada, Rápidos	Chute d'eau, Rapides	Cascata, Rápidos
⋓	Strait	Meeresstrasse	Estrecho	Détroit	Estreito
⊂	Bay, Gulf	Bucht, Golf	Bahía, Golfo	Baie, Golfe	Baía, Golfo
⊜	Lake, Lakes	See, Seen	Lago, Lagos	Lac, Lacs	Lago, Lagos
⁙	Swamp	Sumpf	Pantano	Marais	Pântano
⊓	Ice Features, Glacier	Eis- und Gletscherformen	Accidentes Glaciales	Formes glaciaires	Acidentes glaciares
⊤	Other Hydrographic Features	Andere Hydrographische Objekte	Otros Elementos Hidrográficos	Autres données hydrographiques	Outros acidentes hidrográficos
✧	Submarine Features	Untermeerische Objekte	Accidentes Submarinos	Formes de relief sous-marin	Acidentes submarinos
□	Political Unit	Politische Einheit	Unidad Politica	Entité politique	Unidade política
⊍	Cultural Institution	Kulturelle Institution	Institución Cultural	Institution culturelle	Institução cultural
⊥	Historical Site	Historische Stätte	Sitio Histórico	Site historique	Sitio histórico
♠	Recreational Site	Erholungs- und Ferienort	Sitio de Recreo	Centre de loisirs	Area de Lazer
⊠	Airport	Flughafen	Aeropuerto	Aéroport	Aeroporto
■	Military Installation	Militäranlage	Instalación Militar	Installation militaire	Instalação militar
◆	Miscellaneous	Verschiedenes	Misceláneo	Divers	Diversos

Duke Center 214 41.57 N 78.28 W
Duke Island I 182 54.56 N 131.20 W
Duke of York Bay c 176 65.25 N 84.50 W
Duke of York Island I 164 4.10 S 152.26 E
Dukes □6 207 41.23 N 70.31 W
Dukes Brook ≃ 276 40.33 N 74.37 W
Duk Fadiat 140 7.45 N 31.25 E
Duk Faiwil 140 7.30 N 31.29 E
Dukhān 128 25.25 N 50.48 E
Dukhmays 142 31.07 N 31.04 E
Duki 120 30.09 N 68.34 E
Dukinfield 262 53.29 N 2.05 W
Dukla 30 49.34 N 21.41 E
Dukla Pass)(30 49.25 N 21.43 E
Dukou 102 26.40 N 101.39 E
Dūkštas 76 55.32 N 26.20 E
Duku, Nig. 146 10.49 N 10.46 E
Duku, Nig. 150 11.10 N 4.55 E
Dula 152 4.41 N 20.22 E
Dūlāb 267d 35.37 N 51.27 E
Dulag 116 10.57 N 125.02 E
Dulāi 124 23.57 N 89.31 E
Dulais ≃ 42 51.41 N 3.47 W
Dulan (Chahanwusu) 102 36.16 N 98.28 E
Dul'apino 80 57.15 N 40.49 E
Dulas ≃, Wales, U.K. 42 52.36 N 3.50 W
Dulas ≃, Wales, U.K. 42 52.16 N 3.22 W
Dulas Bay c 44 53.23 N 4.15 W
Dulata 86 43.26 N 80.50 E
Dulayb, Khawr V 140 11.45 N 32.47 E
Dulaym 146 25.58 N 14.03 E
Dulce 200 36.56 N 106.59 W
Dulce ≃ 252 30.31 S 62.32 W
Dulce, Arroyo ≃ 258 35.28 S 57.41 W
Dulce, Bahía c 234 16.33 N 98.50 W
Dulce, Golfo c 236 8.32 N 83.14 W
Dulce Grande 234 22.59 N 102.14 W
Dulce Nombre de Culmí 236 15.09 N 85.37 W
Dul'durga 88 50.41 N 113.36 E
Duleek 48 53.39 N 6.25 W
Dulgalach ≃ 74 67.44 N 133.12 E
Dulin 98 38.22 N 116.43 E
Duliu, Zhg. 105 39.13 N 116.16 E
Duliu, Zhg. 105 39.01 N 116.54 E
Duliu Jianhe ≃ 105 38.51 N 117.20 E
Duljo Point > 116 9.35 N 123.43 E
Dulkaninna 166 29.01 S 138.27 E
Dülken 56 51.15 N 6.20 E
Dulles International Airport ⊠ 208 38.58 N 77.28 W
Dullstroom 156 25.27 S 30.07 E
Dülmen 52 51.51 N 7.16 E
Dulnain Bridge 46 57.16 N 3.41 W
Dulnan ≃ 46 57.18 N 3.40 W
Dulovka 76 57.32 N 28.20 E
Dulovo 38 43.49 N 27.09 E
Dulq Maghār 130 36.22 N 38.39 E
D'ul'tydag, gora ʌ 84 41.58 N 46.56 E
Dulung ≃ 126 22.08 N 87.05 E
Dulunguin Point > 116 7.45 N 122.05 E
Duluth, Ga., U.S. 192 34.00 N 84.08 W
Duluth, Mn., U.S. 190 46.45 N 92.07 W
Dulverton 42 51.03 N 3.33 W
Dulwich ➛8 260 51.26 N 0.05 W
Duma, Bots. 156 18.45 S 22.46 E
Dūmā, Lubnān 130 34.12 N 35.50 E
Dūmā, Sūrīy. 132 33.35 N 36.24 E
Duma, Zaïre 154 4.57 N 27.19 E
Dumaguete 116 9.18 N 123.18 E
Dumai 114 1.41 N 101.27 E
Dumalag 116 11.18 N 122.37 E
Dumalinao 116 7.49 N 123.23 E
Dumali Point > 116 13.07 N 121.33 E
Dumanjug 116 10.04 N 123.26 E
Dumanlıdağ ʌ 84 40.30 N 43.26 E
Dumanquilas Bay c 116 7.34 N 123.04 E
Dumaran Channel ꟾ 116 10.25 N 119.45 E
Dumaran Island I 116 10.33 N 119.51 E
Dumaresq ≃ 166 28.40 S 150.28 E
Dumaring 112 1.36 N 118.12 E
Dumas, Ar., U.S. 194 33.53 N 91.29 W
Dumas, Tx., U.S. 196 35.51 N 101.58 W
Dumayr 132 33.38 N 36.40 E
Dumbarton 46 55.57 N 4.35 W
Dumbarton Bridge ➛5 282 37.31 N 122.07 W
Dumbarton Point > 282 37.30 N 122.06 W
Ďumbier ʌ 30 48.57 N 19.37 E
Dumbleyung 162 33.19 S 117.44 E
Dumbo 152 14.06 S 17.24 E
Dumboa 146 11.10 N 12.45 E
Dumbrăveni 38 46.14 N 24.35 E
Dum-Dum 126 22.35 N 88.24 E
Dum-Dum International Airport ⊠ 126 22.38 N 88.25 E
Dume, Point > 228 34.00 N 118.48 W
Dumei 100 24.47 N 117.21 E
Dümeli 130 40.32 N 33.31 E
Dumfries, Scot., U.K. 44 55.04 N 3.37 W
Dumfries, Va., U.S. 208 38.34 N 77.19 W
Dumfries and Galloway □4 44 55.00 N 4.00 W
Duminiči 76 53.55 N 35.06 E
Dumjor 272b 22.38 N 88.13 E
Dumka 126 24.16 N 87.15 E
Dumlupınar 130 38.52 N 30.00 E
Dummar 132 33.32 N 36.14 E
Dümmer ⊜ 52 52.31 N 8.19 E
Dummer Range ⋏ 162 20.11 S 125.59 E
Dumoga-kecil 112 0.31 N 123.55 E
Dumoine ≃ 190 46.13 N 77.51 W
Dumoine, Lac ⊜ 190 46.53 N 77.54 W
Dumont, Ia., U.S. 190 42.45 N 92.58 W
Dumont, N.J., U.S. 210 40.56 N 73.59 W
Dumont, Lac ⊜ 190 46.04 N 76.27 W
Dumont d'Urville ʊ3 9 66.35 S 140.00 E
Dümpelfeld 56 50.27 N 6.56 E
Dümpten ➛8 263 51.27 N 6.54 E
Dumpu 164 5.50 S 145.45 E
Dumra 124 26.34 N 85.31 E
Dumraon 124 25.33 N 84.09 E
Dumria 126 22.47 N 89.26 E
Dumuriā 126 22.11 N 86.20 E
Dumyāṭ (Damietta) 142 31.25 N 31.48 E
Dumyāṭ □4 142 31.20 N 31.45 E
Dumyāṭ, Far' (Damietta Branch) ≃ 142 31.32 N 31.51 E
Dumyāṭ, Maṣabb (Damietta Mouth) ≃1 142 31.32 N 31.51 E
Dün ʌ 54 51.21 N 10.30 E
Duna → Danube ≃ 22 45.20 N 29.40 E
Dünaburg → Daugavpils 76 55.53 N 26.32 E
Dunaff Head > 48 55.17 N 7.33 W
Dunaföldvár 30 46.48 N 18.55 E
Dunaharaszti 30 47.21 N 19.05 E
Dunaj, S.S.S.R. 89 42.52 N 132.22 E
Dunaj, S.S.S.R. 265a 59.58 N 30.56 E
Dunaj → Danube ≃ 22 45.20 N 29.40 E
Dunaj, ostrova II 74 73.52 N 124.29 E
Dunajec ≃ 30 50.14 N 20.44 E
Dunajevcy 78 48.54 N 26.51 E
Dunajevo 88 52.05 N 117.02 E
Dunajská Streda 30 48.01 N 17.35 E
Dunakeszi 30 47.38 N 19.08 E
Dunany Point > 44 53.52 N 6.14 W
Dunărea → Danube ≃ 22 45.20 N 29.40 E
Dunărea Veche ≃ 38 45.17 N 28.02 E
Duna-Tisza-csatorna ≅ 264c 47.21 N 19.05 E
Dunaújváros 30 46.58 N 18.57 E
Dunav → Danube ≃ 22 45.20 N 29.40 E
Dunavățu-de-Sus 38 44.59 N 29.13 E
Duna-Völgyi-főcsatorna ≅ 30 46.12 N 18.56 E
Dunback 172 45.23 S 170.38 E
Dunbar, Scot., U.K. 46 56.00 N 2.31 W
Dunbar, W.V., U.S. 188 38.21 N 81.44 W
Dunbarton 275b 43.49 N 79.06 W
Dunbeath 46 58.15 N 3.25 W
Dunblane, Sk., Can. 184 51.11 N 106.52 W
Dunblane, Scot., U.K. 46 56.12 N 3.59 W
Dunboyne 48 53.24 N 6.28 W
Duncan, B.C., Can. 224 48.47 N 123.42 W
Duncan, Az., U.S. 200 32.43 N 109.06 W
Duncan, Ms., U.S. 194 34.02 N 90.44 W
Duncan, Ok., U.S. 196 34.30 N 97.57 W
Duncan ≃ 182 50.11 N 116.57 W
Duncan Lake ⊜1 182 50.20 N 117.00 W
Duncannon 208 40.23 N 77.01 W
Duncan Passage ꟾ 110 11.00 N 92.30 E
Duncans 241q 18.28 N 77.32 W
Duncansby Head > 46 58.39 N 3.02 W
Duncan's Creek ≃ 274a 33.53 S 150.39 E
Duncansville 214 40.25 N 78.26 W
Duncanville 222 32.39 N 96.54 W
Dunchurch 42 52.20 N 1.16 W
Duncormick 48 52.14 N 6.39 W
Dundaga 76 57.31 N 22.21 E
Dundāhera 272a 28.38 N 77.26 E
Dundalk, On., Can. 212 44.10 N 80.24 W
Dundalk (Dún Dealgan), Ire. 48 54.01 N 6.25 W
Dundalk, Md., U.S. 208 39.15 N 76.31 W
Dundalk Bay c 48 53.57 N 6.17 W
Dundas, Austl. 274a 33.48 S 151.02 E
Dundas, On., Can. 212 43.16 N 79.58 W
Dundas, Mn., U.S. 190 44.25 N 93.12 W
Dundas, Cape > 212 44.57 N 81.07 W
Dundas, Lake ⊜ 162 32.35 S 121.50 E
Dundas Island I 182 54.33 N 130.55 W
Dundas Peninsula >1 176 74.50 N 111.30 W
Dundas Strait ꟾ 164 11.20 S 131.35 E
Dún Dealgan → Dundalk 48 54.01 N 6.25 W
Dundee, S. Afr. 158 28.12 S 30.16 E
Dundee, Scot., U.K. 46 56.28 N 3.00 W
Dundee, Fl., U.S. 220 28.01 N 81.37 W
Dundee, Il., U.S. 216 42.06 N 88.17 W
Dundee, Mi., U.S. 216 41.57 N 83.39 W
Dundee, Ms., U.S. 194 34.31 N 90.27 W
Dundee, N.Y., U.S. 210 42.31 N 76.58 W
Dundee, Oh., U.S. 214 40.35 N 81.37 W
Dundee, Or., U.S. 224 45.16 N 123.00 W
Dundee Creek c 284b 39.21 N 76.22 W
Dundgov' □4 102 45.30 N 106.30 E
Dundīṭ 142 30.41 N 31.18 E
Dundonald 46 55.34 N 4.35 W
Dundoo 166 27.39 S 144.39 E
Dundrum, Ire. 48 53.17 N 6.15 W
Dundrum, N. Ire., U.K. 48 54.16 N 5.51 W
Dundrum Bay c 48 54.13 N 5.45 W
Dundurn 184 51.49 N 106.30 W
Dundwa Range ⋏ 124 27.45 N 82.30 E
Duneaton Water ≃ 46 55.32 N 3.42 W
Dunedin, N.Z. 172 45.52 S 170.30 E
Dunedin, Fl., U.S. 220 28.01 N 82.46 W
Dunedoo 166 32.01 S 149.24 E
Duneland Beach 216 41.35 N 86.50 W
Dunellen 276 40.35 N 74.28 W
Dunewood 276 40.38 N 73.11 W
Dunfanaghy 48 55.11 N 7.59 W
Dunfermline 46 56.04 N 3.29 W
Du Ngae, Khao ʌ 110 15.10 N 98.47 E
Dungannon, N. Ire., U.K. 48 54.31 N 6.46 W
Dungannon, Va., U.S. 192 36.49 N 82.28 W
Dūngarpur 120 23.50 N 73.43 E
Dungarvan 48 52.05 N 7.37 W
Dungarvan Harbour c 48 52.10 N 7.35 W
Dungas 150 13.04 N 9.20 E
Dungau ➛1 60 48.50 N 12.40 E
Dungeness > 42 50.55 N 0.58 E
Dungeness ≃ 224 48.08 N 123.06 W
Dungeness, Punta > 254 52.23 S 68.25 W
Dungeness Bay c 224 48.10 N 123.07 W
Dungeness Spit >2 224 48.10 N 123.09 W
Dungiven 48 54.55 N 6.55 W
Dunglow 48 54.57 N 8.22 W
Dungo, Lagoa do ⊜ 152 17.20 S 18.58 E
Dungog 166 32.24 S 151.46 E
Dungu 154 3.37 N 28.34 E
Dungu ≃ 154 3.37 N 28.34 E
Dungun ≃ 114 4.47 N 103.23 E
Dunham 206 45.08 N 72.48 W
Dunham Lake ⊜ 281 42.39 N 83.41 W
Dunham-on-the-Hill 262 53.15 N 2.47 W
Dunham Park ♦ 262 53.23 N 2.24 W
Dunham Town 262 53.23 N 2.24 W
Dunheved, Austl. 274a 33.45 S 150.47 E
Dunheved → Launceston, Eng., U.K. 42 50.38 N 4.21 W
Dunholme 44 53.18 N 0.28 W
Dunhou 100 27.02 N 114.58 E
Dunhua 89 43.21 N 128.13 E
Dunhuang 102 40.12 N 94.41 E
Dunières 62 45.13 N 4.20 E
Dunilovo, S.S.S.R. 76 57.46 N 38.55 E
Dunilovo, S.S.S.R. 80 57.00 N 41.27 E
Dunkeld 46 56.34 N 3.35 W
Dunkeld ➛8 273d 26.09 S 28.03 E
Dunkellin ≃ 48 53.12 N 8.54 W
Dunkelsteinerwald ➛3 61 48.15 N 15.29 E
Dunkern ⊜ 40 59.09 N 16.52 E
Dunker Pond ⊜ 276 41.05 N 74.28 W
Dunkerque 50 51.03 N 2.22 E
Dunkerrin 48 52.55 N 7.55 W
Dunkery Hill ʌ2 42 51.11 N 3.35 W
Dunkineely 48 54.38 N 8.23 W
Dunkinsville 218 38.51 N 83.30 W
Dunkirk → Dunkerque, Fr. 50 51.03 N 2.22 E
Dunkirk, Eng., U.K. 42 51.17 N 0.59 E
Dunkirk, In., U.S. 216 40.22 N 85.12 W
Dunkirk, N.Y., U.S. 214 42.28 N 79.20 W
Dunkirk, Oh., U.S. 216 40.47 N 83.38 W
Dunk's Green 260 51.15 N 0.19 E
Dunkuj 140 12.50 N 32.49 E
Dunkwa, Ghana 150 5.58 N 1.46 W
Dunkwa, Ghana 150 5.22 N 1.12 W
Dún Laoghaire 48 53.17 N 6.08 W
Dun Laoghaire-Rathdown □6 48 53.15 N 6.10 W
Dunlap, In., U.S. 216 41.38 N 85.55 W
Dunlap, Ia., U.S. 198 41.51 N 95.36 W
Dunlap, Tn., U.S. 194 35.22 N 85.23 W
Dunlap Acres 228 34.03 N 117.06 W
Dunlavin 48 53.02 N 6.41 W
Dunleary → Dún Laoghaire 48 53.17 N 6.08 W
Dunleer 48 53.50 N 6.24 W
Dunleith 285 39.42 N 75.33 W
Dun-le-Palestel 32 46.18 N 1.40 E
Dunlo 214 40.17 N 78.43 W
Dunlop 46 55.43 N 4.32 W
Dunloy 48 55.01 N 6.25 W
Dunmanus Bay c 48 51.35 N 9.45 W
Dunmanway 48 51.43 N 9.06 W
Dunmarra 164 16.42 S 133.25 E
Dunmore, Ire. 48 53.36 N 8.46 W
Dunmore, Pa., U.S. 210 41.25 N 75.37 W
Dunmore Cave ≗5 48 52.44 N 7.15 W
Dunmore East 48 52.09 N 7.00 W
Dunmore Town 238 25.30 N 76.39 W
Dunmurry 48 54.33 N 6.01 W
Dunn 192 35.18 N 78.36 W
Dunnamanagh 48 54.52 N 7.18 W
Dünnbach ≃ 56 50.10 N 7.18 E
Dunnellon 220 29.02 N 82.27 W
Dunnet 46 58.31 N 3.20 W
Dunnet Bay c 46 58.37 N 3.24 W
Dunnet Head > 46 58.40 N 3.24 W
Dunnigan 226 38.53 N 121.58 W
Dunning 198 41.49 N 100.06 W
Dunning Creek ≃ 214 40.02 N 78.28 W
Dunnington 44 53.57 N 0.59 W
Dunningtown 279b 40.25 N 79.35 W
Dunn Loring 284c 38.53 N 77.14 W
Dunn Loring Woods 284c 38.52 N 77.14 W
Dunnockshaw 262 53.45 N 2.17 W
Dunnottar Castle ⊥ 46 56.57 N 2.11 W
Dunns Bridge 216 41.13 N 86.59 W
Dunnville 212 42.54 N 79.36 W
Dunolly 169 36.52 S 143.44 E
Dunoon 46 55.57 N 4.56 W
Dunqul ⊤4 140 23.26 N 31.37 E
Dunqulah 140 19.10 N 30.29 E
Dunqulah al-Qadīmah 140 18.13 N 30.45 E
Dunqunāb 140 21.06 N 37.05 E
Dunqunāb, Khalīj c 140 21.05 N 37.08 E
Dunrea 184 49.25 N 99.44 W
Dun Rig ʌ 46 55.34 N 3.10 W
Duns 46 55.47 N 2.20 W
Dunsandel 172 43.40 S 172.11 E
Dunseith 198 48.48 N 100.03 W
Dunsford 42 50.41 N 3.40 W
Dunsmuir 204 41.13 N 122.16 W
Dunstable, Eng., U.K. 42 51.53 N 0.32 W
Dunstable, Ma., U.S. 207 42.40 N 71.29 W
Dunstaffnage Castle ⊥ 46 56.26 N 5.32 W
Dunstan Mountains ⋏ 172 44.57 S 169.32 E
Dunster, B.C., Can. 182 53.08 N 119.50 W
Dunster, Eng., U.K. 42 51.12 N 3.27 W
Dun-sur-Auron 32 46.53 N 2.34 E
Dun-sur-Meuse 56 49.23 N 5.11 E
Duntelchaig, Loch ⊜ 46 57.20 N 4.18 W
Dunton Green 260 51.18 N 0.11 E
Dunton Wayletts 260 51.35 N 0.24 E
Duntou 100 29.21 N 119.46 E
Duntroon 172 44.52 S 170.41 E
Duntroon Royal Military College ■ 171b 35.18 S 149.12 E
Dunvegan, S. Afr. 273d 26.09 S 28.09 E
Dunvegan, Scot., U.K. 46 57.26 N 6.35 W
Dunvegan, Loch c 46 57.28 N 6.40 W
Dunvegan Castle ⊥ 46 57.26 N 6.35 W
Dunvegan Head > 46 57.31 N 6.43 W
Dunville 186 47.16 N 53.54 W
Dunwich 171a 27.31 S 153.23 E
Dunyāpur 123 29.48 N 71.44 E
Duobukur ≃ 89 49.56 N 125.12 E
Duogu'nao 102 31.32 N 103.14 E
Duojundian 105 39.22 N 117.31 E
Duolun (Dolonnur) 98 42.15 N 116.18 E
Duolundabohuer 120 33.25 N 93.54 E
Duomaer 120 34.15 N 79.45 E
Duomo ʊ1 266b 45.27 N 9.11 E
Duomula 120 34.07 N 82.30 E
Duong-dong 110 10.13 N 103.58 E
Duopatela 120 28.28 N 88.14 E
Duoyuezhen 107 30.11 N 103.42 E
Duozhu 100 22.59 N 114.43 E
Duozhuang 98 35.35 N 118.12 E
Du Page □6 216 41.52 N 88.06 W
Du Page ≃ 216 41.25 N 88.14 W
Du Page, East Branch ≃ 278 41.42 N 88.09 W
Dupang Ling ⋏ 102 25.32 N 111.11 E
Duparquet, Lac ⊜ 190 48.28 N 79.16 W
Dupax 116 16.17 N 121.05 E
Duping 102 27.11 N 108.20 E
Dupl'atka 80 51.07 N 42.20 E
Dupli 82 54.21 N 36.54 E
Dupo 219 38.31 N 90.13 W
Dupont, In., U.S. 218 38.53 N 85.31 W
Dupont, Oh., U.S. 216 41.03 N 84.18 W
Dupont, Pa., U.S. 210 41.19 N 75.44 W
Du Pont, Wa., U.S. 224 47.05 N 122.37 W
Dupont Research Center ʊ3 285 39.46 N 75.34 W
Dupree 198 45.02 N 101.36 W
Duque Bacelar 250 4.09 S 42.57 W
Duque de Caxias 256 22.47 S 43.18 W
Duque de Caxias □7 287a 22.45 S 43.16 W
Duque de York, Isla I 254 50.40 S 75.20 W
Duquesne 214 40.22 N 79.51 W
Duquesne University ʊ2 279b 40.26 N 79.59 W
DuQuoin 194 37.59 N 89.15 W
Dūrā 132 31.30 N 35.02 E
Durack ≃ 164 15.33 S 127.52 E
Durack Range ⋏ 160 17.00 S 128.00 E
Durağan 130 41.25 N 35.04 E
Durak 130 39.42 N 28.17 E
Durak Dağı ʌ 84 39.46 N 43.45 E
Dural 170 33.41 S 151.02 E
Duran 200 34.28 N 105.23 W
Durance ≃ 62 43.55 N 4.44 E
Durand, Il., U.S. 190 42.26 N 89.19 W
Durand, Mi., U.S. 216 42.54 N 83.59 W
Durand, Wi., U.S. 190 44.37 N 91.57 W
Durand Reef ✣2 175f 22.03 S 168.39 E
Durango, Esp. 34 43.10 N 2.37 W
Durango, Méx. 234 24.02 N 104.40 W
Durango, Co., U.S. 200 37.16 N 107.52 W
Durango □3 232 24.50 N 104.50 W
Duranillin 168a 33.31 S 116.48 E
Durant, Ia., U.S. 190 41.35 N 90.54 W
Durant, Ms., U.S. 194 33.04 N 89.51 W
Durant, Ok., U.S. 196 33.59 N 96.22 W
Duras 32 44.41 N 0.11 E
Duraton ≃ 34 41.37 N 4.07 W
Duraur V 144 10.33 N 49.07 E
Durazno 252 33.22 S 56.31 W
Durazno, Arroyo ≃ 258 34.41 S 58.52 W
Durazzo → Durrës 38 41.19 N 19.26 E
Durbādānga 126 22.57 N 89.15 E
Durban 158 29.55 S 30.56 E
Durban Roodepoort Deep Gold Mines ➛7 273d 26.10 S 27.51 E
Durbanville 158 33.50 S 18.39 E
Durbe 76 56.35 N 21.21 E
D'urbel'džin 85 41.16 N 74.57 E
Durbet-Daba, pereval)(86 49.37 N 89.25 E
Durbin 188 38.32 N 79.49 W
Durbuy 56 50.21 N 5.28 E
Durchholz 263 51.23 N 7.17 E
Durdent ≃ 50 49.51 N 0.36 E
Đurđevac 36 46.03 N 17.04 E
Durdur V 144 10.34 N 43.58 E
Dureji 120 25.53 N 67.18 E
Düren 56 50.48 N 6.28 E
Durg 120 21.11 N 81.17 E
Durg □5 124 22.00 N 81.10 E
Durgāpur 126 23.29 N 87.20 E
Durham, On., Can. 212 44.10 N 80.49 W
Durham, Eng., U.K. 44 54.47 N 1.34 W
Durham, Ca., U.S. 204 39.38 N 121.47 W
Durham, Ct., U.S. 207 41.28 N 72.40 W
Durham, Mo., U.S. 219 39.58 N 91.40 W
Durham, N.H., U.S. 188 43.08 N 70.55 W
Durham, N.C., U.S. 192 35.59 N 78.53 W
Durham, Or., U.S. 224 45.25 N 122.46 W
Durham □6, On., Can. 212 43.56 N 78.53 W
Durham □6, Eng., U.K. 44 54.45 N 1.45 W
Durham Cathedral ʊ1 44 54.46 N 1.36 W
Durham Downs 166 27.05 S 141.54 E
Durham Heights ʌ 176 71.08 N 122.56 W
Durham Pond ⊜ 276 41.00 N 74.27 W
Durhamville 210 43.07 N 75.40 W
Durian ≃ 115a 6.01 S 106.24 E
Durian, Selat ꟾ 114 0.42 N 103.42 E
Duriansebatang 112 0.47 S 109.56 E
Durian Tipus 114 3.07 N 102.13 E
D'urinskije razlivy ≋ 80 50.25 N 50.20 E
Durlabhpur 272b 22.47 N 88.29 E
Durlach ➛8 56 49.00 N 8.28 E
Durleşty 78 47.02 N 28.45 E
Durmersheim 56 48.56 N 8.16 E
Durmitor ʌ 38 43.08 N 19.01 E
Durness 46 58.33 N 4.45 W
Durness, Kyle of c 46 58.34 N 4.49 W
Durneva, ostrova II 80 45.25 N 52.50 E
Durnikino 80 51.39 N 42.49 E
Dürnkrut 61 48.28 N 16.51 E
Dürnstein ⊥ 61 48.24 N 15.32 E
Duro ʌ 144 5.31 N 37.12 E
Durón 34 40.38 N 2.43 W
Duross Heights 285 39.40 N 75.37 W
Dürre Liesing ≃ 264b 48.08 N 16.16 E
Durrell 186 49.40 N 54.44 W
Dürrenboden 58 46.57 N 8.50 E
Durrës 38 41.19 N 19.26 E
Durrie 166 25.38 S 140.16 E
Durrington 42 51.13 N 1.45 W
Dürröhrsdorf 54 51.01 N 14.00 E
Durrow 48 52.50 N 7.22 W
Durrus 48 51.36 N 9.31 W
Dursey Head > 48 51.35 N 10.14 W
Dursey Island I 48 51.36 N 10.12 W
Dursley 42 51.42 N 2.21 W
Dursunbey 130 39.35 N 28.38 E
D'urt'uli 86 55.29 N 54.52 E
Duru 154 4.14 N 28.45 E
Dūruḥ 128 32.17 N 60.30 E
Durunkah 142 27.08 N 31.10 E
Durūz, Jabal ad- ⋏ 132 32.40 N 36.44 E
D'Urville Island I 172 40.50 S 173.52 E
Duryea 210 41.20 N 75.44 W
Dury Voe c 46a 60.20 N 1.08 W
Dušak 128 37.13 N 60.02 E
Dušanbe 85 38.35 N 68.48 E
Dušanbe □4 85 38.40 N 69.40 E
Dušekan 74 60.39 N 109.03 E
Dušeti 84 42.06 N 44.42 E
Dusetos 76 55.45 N 25.51 E
Dushan, Zhg. 100 31.36 N 116.14 E
Dushan, Zhg. 102 25.53 N 107.30 E
Du Shan ʌ 98 40.30 N 118.45 E
Dushanbe → Dušanbe 85 38.35 N 68.48 E
Dushan Hu ⊜ 98 35.06 N 116.52 E
Dushantou 106 30.46 N 119.47 E
Dushanzi 86 44.20 N 84.51 E
Dusheng 98 38.23 N 116.33 E
Dushichang 107 29.10 N 106.31 E
Dushikou 98 41.17 N 115.38 E
Dushore 210 41.31 N 76.24 W
Düshorn 52 52.49 N 9.37 E
Dushu 100 33.21 N 113.09 E
Dushu Hu ⊜ 106 31.17 N 120.42 E
Dusios ežeras ⊜ 76 54.18 N 23.42 E
Dusky Sound ꟾ 172 45.47 S 166.28 E
Dušocha, gora ʌ 85 39.10 N 70.01 E
Duson 194 30.14 N 92.11 W
Dušonovo 82 56.04 N 38.18 E
Düssel 263 51.16 N 7.03 E
Düsselbach ≃ 263 51.13 N 6.45 E
Düsseldorf, B.R.D. 56 51.12 N 6.47 E
Düsseldorf, B.R.D. 263 51.12 N 6.47 E
Düsseldorf □5 52 51.15 N 7.00 E
Düsseldorf, Flughafen ⊠ 56 51.17 N 6.47 E
Düsseldorf, Universität ʊ2 263 51.12 N 6.48 E
Düsseldorf-Mettmann □8 263 51.16 N 6.58 E
Dusslingen 58 48.27 N 9.03 E
Dussnang 58 47.26 N 8.58 E
Dustin 196 35.16 N 96.01 W
Dutaliutexingsishan ⋏ 120 34.15 N 87.00 E
Dutch Creek ≃, B.C., Can. 182 50.20 N 115.52 W
Dutch Creek ≃, Ar., U.S. 194 35.03 N 93.24 W
Dutchess □6 210 41.42 N 73.56 W
Dutch Harbor 180 53.53 N 166.32 W
Dutch John 200 40.55 N 109.23 W
Dutchman Creek ≃ 226 37.11 N 120.28 W
Dutianjie 102 24.38 N 101.31 E
Dutlwe 156 23.55 S 23.47 E
Dutoitspiek ʌ 158 33.46 S 19.12 E
Dutou, Zhg. 100 22.54 N 115.12 E
Dutou, Zhg. 106 31.19 N 120.54 E
Dutovlje 64 45.46 N 13.50 E
Dutovo 24 63.47 N 56.35 E
Dutsen Wai 150 10.50 N 8.12 E
Dutton, On., Can. 214 42.39 N 81.30 W
Dutton, Eng., U.K. 262 53.19 N 2.38 W
Dutton, Mi., U.S. 216 42.50 N 85.35 W
Dutton, Mt., U.S. 202 47.50 N 111.42 W
Dutton ≃ 166 20.45 S 143.12 E
Dutton, Mount ʌ, Ak., U.S. 180 55.10 N 162.15 W
Dutton, Mount ʌ, Ut., U.S. 200 38.01 N 112.13 W
Dutun 105 39.46 N 117.02 E
Dutzow 219 38.37 N 90.59 W
Duut 86 47.30 N 91.40 E
Duval, Lac ⊜ 190 46.19 N 76.55 W
Duvall 224 47.44 N 121.59 W
Duvan 86 55.42 N 57.54 E
Duvanka ≃ 83 49.35 N 38.10 E
Duved 26 63.24 N 12.52 E
Duvernay ➛8 275a 45.35 N 73.40 W
Duvno 36 43.43 N 17.14 E
Duwamish 224 47.32 N 122.19 W
Duwaydār, Bi'r ad- ⊤4 142 30.55 N 32.31 E
Duxbury 207 42.02 N 70.40 W
Duxbury Bay c 207 42.02 N 70.39 W
Duxbury Beach ≗2 283 42.03 N 70.38 W
Duxun 100 23.55 N 117.37 E
Duyagan Point > 116 12.36 N 121.33 E
Duyun 102 26.12 N 107.31 E
Düzce 130 40.50 N 31.10 E
Duze 100 29.07 N 118.56 E
Dve Mogili 38 43.36 N 25.52 E
Dvina Occidental → Zapadnaja Dvina ≃ 76 57.04 N 24.03 E
Dvina Setentrional → Severnaja Dvina ≃ 24 64.32 N 40.30 E
Dvinje, ozero ⊜ 76 56.08 N 31.12 E
Dvinsk → Daugavpils 76 55.53 N 26.32 E
Dvinskaja guba c 24 65.00 N 39.45 E
Dvojnovskij 80 51.03 N 42.27 E
Dvorcy 82 54.37 N 36.00 E
Dvorec 88 58.23 N 99.56 E
Dvoriši 76 58.12 N 35.13 E
Dvornikovo 82 55.30 N 38.38 E
Dvuch Cirkov, gora ʌ 74 67.35 N 168.07 E
Dvugorbaja, gora ʌ 180 68.30 N 179.20 E
Dvulučnoje 78 50.02 N 38.02 E
Dvurečnaja 78 49.52 N 37.40 E
Dvůr Králové [nad Labem] 30 50.26 N 15.48 E
Dwangwa ≃ 154 12.33 S 34.12 E
Dwarbasini 272b 22.59 N 88.14 E
Dwārka 120 22.14 N 68.58 E
Dwārka ≃ 126 23.44 N 88.11 E
Dwārkeswar ≃ 126 23.06 N 87.21 E
Dwarli 272c 19.12 N 73.08 E
Dwars Kill ≃ 276 40.58 N 73.58 W
Dwellingup 168a 32.43 S 116.02 E
D.W. Field Park ♦ 283 42.06 N 71.03 W
Dwight 216 41.05 N 88.25 W
Dwight D. Eisenhower Lock ➛5 206 45.00 N 74.45 W

ENGLISH

Name	Page	Lat.°′	Long.°′

Dwina-Bucht → Dvinskaja guba c 24 65.00 N 39.45 E
Dwingeloo 52 52.50 N 6.21 E
Dworshak Reservoir ⊜1 202 46.40 N 116.00 W
Dwyfor ≃ 42 52.55 N 4.17 W
Dwyka 158 33.02 S 21.30 E
Dwyka ≃ 158 33.18 S 21.39 E
Dybbøl 41 54.55 N 9.45 E
Dyberry Creek ≃ 210 41.35 N 75.15 W
Dyce 46 57.12 N 2.11 W
Dyche Stadium ♦ 278 42.04 N 87.41 W
Dychtau, gora ʌ 84 43.03 N 43.08 E
Dyck, Schloss ⊥ 263 51.09 N 6.34 E
Dyer, In., U.S. 216 41.29 N 87.31 W
Dyer, Tn., U.S. 194 36.04 N 88.59 W
Dyer, Cape > 176 66.37 N 61.18 W
Dyer Bay c 212 45.10 N 81.18 W
Dyer Island I 158 34.41 S 19.25 E
Dyero 150 12.50 N 6.30 W
Dyersburg 194 36.02 N 89.23 W
Dyersville 190 42.29 N 91.07 W
Dyess Air Force Base ■ 196 32.25 N 99.51 W
Dyfed □6 42 52.00 N 4.30 W
Dyfi ≃ 42 52.32 N 4.03 W
Dyje (Thaya) ≃ 61 48.37 N 16.56 E
Dyke 46 57.36 N 3.41 W
Dyke Ackland Bay c 164 9.00 S 148.45 E
Dyken Pond ⊜ 210 42.43 N 73.26 W
Dykes Pond ⊜ 283 42.36 N 70.44 W
Dyle (Dijle) ≃ 56 51.04 N 4.25 E
Dyleň ʌ 60 49.58 N 12.30 E
Dylym 84 43.04 N 46.38 E
Dymchurch 42 51.02 N 1.00 E
Dyment 184 49.37 N 92.19 W
Dymer 78 50.47 N 30.18 E
Dymock 42 51.59 N 2.26 W
Dynamo Stadium ♦ 265b 55.48 N 37.34 E
Dynów 30 49.49 N 22.14 E
Dyreborg 41 55.04 N 10.13 E
Dyrnesvågen 26 63.26 N 7.51 E
Dyrotz 264a 52.33 N 12.58 E
Dysart, Sk., Can. 184 50.56 N 104.02 W
Dysart, Scot., U.K. 46 56.08 N 3.08 W
Dysart, Ia., U.S. 190 42.10 N 92.18 W
Dysart, Pa., U.S. 214 40.36 N 78.31 W
Dýšina 60 49.46 N 13.29 E
Dysnų ežeras ⊜ 76 55.29 N 26.20 E
Dysselsdorp 158 33.34 S 22.28 E
Dysynni ≃ 42 52.36 N 4.05 W
Dzaamar 88 48.10 N 104.50 E
Dzaamaryn uul ʌ 88 48.10 N 104.30 E
Džabžur 84 40.54 N 43.58 E
Dzachuj 102 44.59 N 96.37 E
Džagdy, chrebet ⋏ 89 53.40 N 131.00 E
Džalagaš 86 45.05 N 64.40 E
Džalal-Abad 85 40.56 N 73.00 E
Džalinda 89 53.29 N 123.54 E
Džamantau, gory ⋏ 85 40.55 N 74.40 E
Džamašuj 85 40.52 N 71.28 E
Džambejty 80 50.16 N 52.35 E
Džambul, S.S.S.R. 80 47.34 N 50.12 E
Džambul, S.S.S.R. 85 42.54 N 71.22 E
Džambul, S.S.S.R. 86 47.12 N 71.42 E
Džambul □4 86 44.00 N 72.00 E
Džambul, gora ʌ 86 44.46 N 73.08 E
Džanga 128 40.00 N 53.03 E
Džangi-Džol 85 41.36 N 72.08 E
Džankoj 78 45.43 N 34.24 E
Džansugurov 86 45.24 N 79.29 E
Džanybek 80 49.25 N 46.51 E
Dzaoudzi 157a 12.47 S 45.17 E
Džardžan 74 68.43 N 124.02 E
Džargalant → Chovd, Mong. 86 48.01 N 91.39 E
Džargalant, Mong. 88 48.40 N 100.43 E
Džargalant, Mong. 88 46.57 N 115.15 E
Džargalant, Mong. 88 48.33 N 99.20 E
Džargaltchaan 88 47.28 N 109.30 E
Džarylgačkij, ostrov I 78 46.02 N 32.55 E
Džarylgačskij zaliv c 78 46.05 N 32.50 E
Dzaudzhikau → Ordžonikidze 84 43.03 N 44.40 E
Džaur 89 50.02 N 138.30 E
Džava 84 42.24 N 43.54 E
Dzavchan 88 48.48 N 93.07 E
Dzavchan □4 88 48.00 N 96.00 E
Dzavchan ≃ 88 48.54 N 93.23 E
Dzavchan Mandal 88 48.19 N 95.07 E
Džavchlant → Uliastaj 88 47.45 N 96.49 E
Džazator 86 49.45 N 87.23 E
Džbán ʌ 54 50.12 N 13.45 E
Džebel 128 39.38 N 54.14 E
Džebrail 84 39.23 N 47.02 E
Dzegamčaj ≃ 84 41.00 N 45.59 E
Dzelter ≃ 88 50.30 N 105.06 E
Dzemul 232 21.12 N 89.18 W
Dzeng 152 3.45 N 12.00 E
Dženretlen, mys > 180 67.07 N 173.45 W
Džergetal 85 41.30 N 75.47 E
Džermuk 84 39.51 N 45.41 E
Dzerzhinsk → Dzeržinsk 80 56.15 N 43.24 E
Dzeržinsk, S.S.S.R. 76 53.41 N 27.08 E
Dzeržinsk, S.S.S.R. 78 50.09 N 27.56 E
Dzeržinsk, S.S.S.R. 80 56.15 N 43.24 E
Dzeržinsk, S.S.S.R. 83 48.26 N 37.50 E
Dzeržinskaja, gora ʌ2 76 53.51 N 27.03 E
Dzeržinskij, S.S.S.R. 78 48.02 N 39.26 E
Dzeržinskij, S.S.S.R. 82 55.38 N 37.50 E
Dzeržinskij ➛8 83 48.02 N 39.26 E
Dzeržinskoje, S.S.S.R. 86 56.49 N 95.18 E
Dzeržinskoje, S.S.S.R. 86 45.50 N 81.07 E
Džetim, chrebet ⋏ 85 41.35 N 77.05 E
Džetygara 86 52.11 N 61.12 E
Džetyoguz 85 42.27 N 78.14 E
Džetyoguzskij zapovednik ♦ 85 42.15 N 78.20 E
Džetysaj 85 40.47 N 68.16 E
Džezdy 86 48.04 N 67.05 E
Džezkazgan, S.S.S.R. 86 47.53 N 67.27 E
Džezkazgan, S.S.S.R. 86 47.47 N 67.46 E
Džezkazgan □4 86 47.20 N 69.00 E
Dzhalilabad 84 39.14 N 48.31 E
Dzhambul → Džambul 85 42.54 N 71.22 E
Działdowo 30 53.15 N 20.10 E
Działoszyce 30 50.22 N 20.21 E
Dzibalchén 232 19.31 N 89.45 W
Dzibilchaltun ⊥ 232 21.05 N 89.36 W
Džida ≃ 88 50.37 N 106.14 E
Džidinskij chrebet ⋏ 88 50.10 N 102.00 E
Dzierzgoń 30 53.56 N 19.21 E
Dzierżoniów (Reichenbach) 30 50.44 N 16.39 E
Dzilam González 232 21.17 N 88.56 W
Džilav 85 39.19 N 67.45 E
Džilga 85 41.43 N 69.01 E
Džinst 102 45.24 N 100.35 E
Dzioua 148 33.14 N 5.14 E
Džirgatal' 85 39.13 N 71.12 E
Dzitás 232 20.51 N 88.31 W
Dzitbalché 232 20.19 N 90.03 W
Dziwna ≃1 54 54.01 N 14.44 E
Dziwnów 30 54.03 N 14.45 E
Džizak 85 40.06 N 67.50 E
Džizak □4 85 40.35 N 67.40 E
Dzodze 150 6.14 N 1.00 E
Džubga 78 44.20 N 38.43 E
Džugdžur, chrebet ⋏ 74 58.00 N 136.00 E
Džūkste 76 56.47 N 23.15 E
Džul'fa 84 38.58 N 45.38 E
Džumabazar 85 39.31 N 67.13 E
Džumgoltau, chrebet ⋏ 85 42.18 N 74.32 E

DEUTSCH

Name	Seite	Breite°′	Länge°′ E = Ost

Dzungarian Basin → Junggar Pendi ≚1 86 45.00 N 88.00 E
Dzungarian Gate (Džungarskije vorota))(86 45.25 N 82.25 E
Džungarskij Alatau, chrebet ⋏ 86 45.00 N 81.00 E
Džungarskije vorota → Dzungarian Gate)(86 45.25 N 82.25 E
Džurak-Sal ≃ 80 47.18 N 43.36 E
Dzürch 88 48.55 N 100.10 E
Džurin 78 48.41 N 28.18 E
Džurun 86 49.15 N 57.37 E
Džusaly 86 45.28 N 64.05 E
Dzüün Changaj 88 49.17 N 95.14 E
Džüün Charaa 88 48.52 N 106.28 E
Dzüün Gov 88 49.55 N 93.47 E
Dzuunmod 88 47.45 N 106.55 E
Džvari 84 42.43 N 42.04 E
Dzygovka 78 48.22 N 28.19 E

E

Eads 198 38.28 N 102.46 W
Eagar 200 34.06 N 109.17 W
Eagle, Ak., U.S. 180 64.46 N 141.16 W
Eagle, Co., U.S. 200 39.39 N 106.49 W
Eagle, N.Y., U.S. 210 42.33 N 78.18 W
Eagle, Wi., U.S. 216 42.52 N 88.28 W
Eagle ≃, Nf., Can. 176 53.35 N 57.25 W
Eagle ≃, Yk., Can. 180 67.20 N 137.10 W
Eagle ≃, Co., U.S. 200 39.39 N 107.04 W
Eagle, Mount ʌ 241n 17.46 N 64.49 W
Eagle Bay 182 50.56 N 119.12 W
Eagle Bend 198 46.09 N 95.02 W
Eagle Bridge 210 42.57 N 73.24 W
Eagle Butte 198 45.00 N 101.14 W
Eagle Chief Creek ≃ 196 36.22 N 98.27 W
Eagle Creek 224 45.21 N 122.21 W
Eagle Creek ≃, Sk., Can. 184 52.22 N 107.24 W
Eagle Creek ≃, Az., U.S. 200 32.58 N 109.25 W
Eagle Creek ≃, In., U.S. 218 39.43 N 86.12 W
Eagle Creek ≃, Ky., U.S. 218 38.36 N 85.04 W
Eagle Creek ≃, Mt., U.S. 202 48.12 N 111.11 W
Eagle Creek ≃, N.M., U.S. 196 32.47 N 104.20 W
Eagle Creek ≃, Oh., U.S. 214 41.18 N 80.53 W
Eagle Creek ≃, Oh., U.S. 218 38.43 N 83.51 W
Eagle Creek ≃, Or., U.S. 202 44.45 N 117.10 W
Eagle Creek ≃, Or., U.S. 224 45.21 N 122.23 W
Eagle Creek, East Fork ≃ 218 38.47 N 83.43 W
Eagle Creek, West Fork ≃ 218 38.47 N 83.43 W
Eagle Creek Reservoir ⊜1 218 39.50 N 86.18 W
Eagledale 224 47.37 N 122.32 W
Eagle Farm Airport ⊠ 171a 27.27 S 153.11 E
Eagle Grove 190 42.39 N 93.54 W
Eagle Harbor 210 43.15 N 78.15 W
Eaglehawk 169 36.43 S 144.15 E
Eagle Hill ≃ 283 42.42 N 70.49 W
Eagle Key I 220 25.09 N 80.36 W
Eagle Lake, Fl., U.S. 220 27.59 N 81.45 W
Eagle Lake, Me., U.S. 186 47.02 N 68.35 W
Eagle Lake, Mi., U.S. 216 41.48 N 86.02 W
Eagle Lake, Tx., U.S. 222 29.35 N 96.20 W
Eagle Lake ⊜, B.C., Can. 182 51.55 N 124.25 W
Eagle Lake ⊜, On., Can. 184 50.39 N 94.54 W
Eagle Lake ⊜, On., Can. 184 49.42 N 93.13 W
Eagle Lake ⊜, On., Can. 212 44.41 N 76.43 W
Eagle Lake ⊜, On., Can. 212 45.08 N 78.29 W
Eagle Lake ⊜, Ca., U.S. 204 40.39 N 120.44 W
Eagle Lake ⊜, Me., U.S. 186 46.20 N 69.20 W
Eagle Lake ⊜, Mi., U.S. 216 41.48 N 86.02 W
Eagle Lake ⊜, Tx., U.S. 222 29.34 N 96.21 W
Eagle Lake ⊜, Wi., U.S. 216 42.42 N 88.07 W
Eagle Mountain, Ca., U.S. 204 33.49 N 115.27 W
Eagle Mountain, Tx., U.S. 222 32.52 N 97.30 W
Eagle Mountain ʌ 202 46.20 N 115.07 W
Eagle Mountain ʌ2 190 47.54 N 90.33 W
Eagle Mountain Lake ⊜1 222 32.55 N 97.30 W
Eagle Nest Butte ʌ 198 43.27 N 101.39 W
Eagle Nest Lake ⊜ 222 29.13 N 95.37 W
Eagle Pass 196 28.42 N 100.29 W
Eagle Peak ʌ, Ca., U.S. 204 41.17 N 120.12 W
Eagle Peak ʌ, Ca., U.S. 228 35.15 N 118.28 W
Eagle Peak ʌ, Ca., U.S. 282 37.54 N 121.54 W
Eagle River, Mi., U.S. 190 47.24 N 88.18 W
Eagle River, Wi., U.S. 190 45.55 N 89.14 W
Eagle Rock 192 37.38 N 79.48 W
Eagle Rock ➛8 280 34.09 N 118.12 W
Eagle Rock Reservation ♦ 276 40.49 N 74.14 W
Eaglesfield 44 55.03 N 3.12 W
Eaglesham, Ab., Can. 182 55.47 N 117.53 W
Eaglesham, Scot., U.K. 46 55.44 N 4.18 W
Eagles Mere 210 41.25 N 76.35 W
Eagleton Village 192 35.46 N 83.56 W
Eagletown 194 34.02 N 94.34 W
Eagle Village 180 64.47 N 141.07 W
Eagleville, Ct., U.S. 207 41.47 N 72.16 W
Eagleville, Pa., U.S. 285 40.10 N 75.24 W
Eagleville, Wi., U.S. 216 42.52 N 88.26 W
Ealing ➛8 260 51.31 N 0.20 W
Eamont ≃ 44 54.40 N 2.39 W
Earaheedy 162 25.34 S 121.39 E
Earby 44 53.56 N 2.08 W
Earcroft 262 53.43 N 2.29 W
Eardisley 42 52.08 N 2.59 W
Eardley Lake ⊜ 184 52.32 N 96.05 W
Ear Falls 184 50.38 N 93.13 W
Earle 194 35.16 N 90.28 W
Earlestown 262 53.27 N 2.39 W
Earl Grey 184 50.56 N 104.45 W
Earlham 194 41.29 N 94.07 W
Earlimart 226 35.53 N 119.16 W
Earlington 194 37.16 N 87.30 W
Earlish 46 57.34 N 6.23 W
Earl Park 216 40.40 N 87.24 W
Earl Rowe Provincial Park ♦ 212 44.10 N 79.54 W
Earls Barton 42 52.15 N 0.45 W
Earls Colne 42 51.56 N 0.42 E
Earl Shilton 42 52.35 N 1.20 W
Earl Soham 42 52.14 N 1.16 E
Earlston 46 55.39 N 2.40 W

Symbols in the index entries represent the broad categories identified in the key at the right. Symbols with superior numbers (⋏1) identify subcategories (see complete key on page I · 1).

Kartensymbole in dem Registerverzeichnis stellen die rechts in Schlüssel erklärten Kategorien dar. Symbole mit hochgestellten Ziffern (⋏1) bezeichnen Unterabteilungen einer Kategorie (vgl. vollständiger Schlüssel auf Seite I · 1).

Los símbolos incluídos en el texto del índice representan las grandes categorias identificadas con la clave a la derecha. Los símbolos con numeros en su parte superior (⋏1) identifican las subcategorías (véase la clave completa en la página I · 1).

Les symboles de l'index représentent les catégories indiquées dans la légende à droite. Les symboles suivis d'un indice (⋏1) représentent des sous-catégories (voir légende complète à la page I · 1).

Os símbolos incluídos no texto do índice representam as grandes categorias identificadas com a chave à direita. Os símbolos com números em sua parte superior (⋏1) identificam as subcategorias (veja-se a chave completa à página I · 1).

ʌ	Mountain	Berg	Montaña	Montagne	Montanha
⋏	Mountains	Berge	Montañas	Montagnes	Montanhas
)(	Pass	Pass	Paso	Col	Passo
V	Valley, Canyon	Tal, Cañon	Valle, Cañón	Vallée, Canyon	Vale, Canhão
≚	Plain	Ebene	Llano	Plaine	Planície
>	Cape	Kap	Cabo	Cap	Cabo
I	Island	Insel	Isla	Île	Ilha
II	Islands	Inseln	Islas	Îles	Ilhas
≗	Other Topographic Features	Andere Topographische Objekte	Otros Elementos Topográficos	Autres données topographiques	Outros acidentes topográficos

ESPAÑOL — Nombre | Página | Lat.°′ | Long.°′ W = Oeste
FRANÇAIS — Nom | Page | Lat.°′ | Long.°′ W = Ouest
PORTUGUÊS — Nome | Página | Lat.°′ | Long.°′ W = Oeste

Nombre	Página	Lat.°′	Long.°′ W = Oeste
Earlton	210	42.21 N	73.54 W
Earlville, Il., U.S.	216	41.35 N	88.55 W
Earlville, N.Y., U.S.	210	42.44 N	75.33 W
Earlville, Pa., U.S.	208	40.19 N	75.44 W
Earlwood	274a	33.56 S	151.08 E
Early, Ia., U.S.	198	42.27 N	95.09 W
Early, Tx., U.S.	196	31.45 N	98.54 W
Early Winters Creek ≃	224	48.35 N	120.35 W
Earn ≃	46	56.21 N	3.19 W
Earn, Loch ⊜	46	56.23 N	4.14 W
Earnslaw, Mount ∧	172	44.37 S	168.24 E
Earth	196	34.14 N	102.24 W
Eas	175f	16.22 S	168.12 E
Easington	44	54.47 N	1.19 W
Easingwold	44	54.07 N	1.11 W
Easky	48	54.18 N	8.58 W
Easley	192	34.49 N	82.36 W
East ≃, On., Can.	190	45.20 N	79.17 W
East ≃, Co., U.S.	200	38.40 N	106.51 W
East ≃, N.Y., U.S.	276	40.48 N	73.48 W
East Acton	283	42.28 N	71.24 W
East Allen ≃	44	54.55 N	2.19 W
East Alliance	214	40.55 N	81.04 W
East Alligator ≃	164	12.08 S	132.42 E
East Alton	219	38.52 N	90.06 W
East Amherst	210	43.01 N	78.42 W
East-Angus	206	45.29 N	71.40 W
East Arlington	210	43.03 N	73.08 W
East Atlantic Beach	276	40.35 N	73.43 W
East Aurora	210	42.46 N	78.36 W
East Avon	210	42.55 N	77.42 W
East Baines ≃	164	15.38 S	129.58 E
East Bangor	210	40.52 N	75.11 W
East Barming	260	51.16 N	0.28 E
East Barnet ◆ 8	260	51.38 N	0.09 W
East Basin c	279a	41.32 N	81.40 W
East Bay c, Fl., U.S.	194	30.05 N	85.32 W
East Bay c, N.Y., U.S.	210	40.38 N	73.32 W
East Bay c, Tx., U.S.	222	29.30 N	94.35 W
East Bedfont ◆ 8	260	51.27 N	0.26 W
East Bend	192	36.12 N	80.30 W
East Berbice-Corentyne □ 5	246	4.00 N	58.15 W
East Berkshire	206	44.56 N	72.42 W
East-Berlin → Berlin (Ost), D.D.R.	264a	52.30 N	13.25 E
East Berlin, Ct., U.S.	207	41.37 N	72.42 W
East Berlin, N.J., U.S.	285	39.48 N	74.55 W
East Berlin, Pa., U.S.	208	39.56 N	76.58 W
East Bernard	222	29.32 N	96.04 W
East Bernstadt	192	37.11 N	84.07 W
East Berwick	210	41.03 N	76.13 W
East Bethany	210	42.56 N	78.06 W
East Bhāgīrath Plain ⩩	126	23.30 N	88.30 E
East Bijou Creek ≃	198	39.51 N	104.08 W
East Billerica	283	42.34 N	71.14 W
East Blackstone	207	42.02 N	71.31 W
East Bloomfield	210	42.54 N	77.26 W
East Boston ◆ 8	283	42.23 N	71.02 W
Eastbourne, N.Z.	172	41.18 S	174.54 E
Eastbourne, Eng., U.K.	42	50.46 N	0.17 E
East Brady	214	40.59 N	79.36 W
East Braintree	184	49.37 N	95.38 W
East Branch	210	41.59 N	75.08 W
East Branch Lake ⊜ 1	214	41.35 N	78.35 W
East Brewster	207	41.46 N	70.03 W
East Brewton	194	31.05 N	87.03 W
East Bridgewater	207	42.02 N	70.58 W
East Brimfield Lake ⊜ 1	207	42.06 N	72.10 W
East Brookfield	207	42.13 N	72.02 W
East Brooklyn	207	41.47 N	71.53 W
East Brother I	271d	22.20 N	113.58 E
East Brunswick	208	40.25 N	74.23 W
East Bucas Island I	116	9.43 N	126.02 E
East Burwood	274b	37.51 S	145.09 E
Eastbury	260	51.37 N	0.25 W
East Butler	214	40.53 N	79.51 W
East Cache Creek ≃	196	34.08 N	98.16 W
East Caicos I	238	21.41 N	71.30 W
East Calder	46	55.54 N	3.27 W
East Canaan	207	42.00 N	73.17 W
East Canada Creek ≃	210	43.00 N	74.45 W
East Canton	214	40.47 N	81.17 W
East Cape >, N.Z.	172	37.41 S	178.33 E
East Cape >, Ak., U.S.	181a	51.21 N	179.29 E
East Cape >, Fl., U.S.	220	25.07 N	81.05 W
East Carancahua Creek ≃	222	28.51 N	96.19 W
East Carbon	200	39.32 N	110.24 W
East Carlisle	214	41.19 N	82.05 W
East Caroline Basin ✢ 1	14	4.00 N	146.45 E
East Castor ≃	212	45.16 N	75.17 W
East Catfish Creek ≃	212	42.47 N	81.04 W
East Channel ≃ 1	180	69.20 N	134.00 W
East Chatham	210	42.25 N	73.32 W
East Chelmsford	207	42.36 N	71.18 W
Eastchester	210	40.57 N	73.49 W
Eastchester Bay c	276	40.51 N	73.48 W
East Chicago	216	41.38 N	87.27 W
East Chicago Heights	278	41.30 N	87.35 W
East China Sea ⫪ 2	90	30.00 N	126.00 E
Eastchurch	42	51.25 N	0.52 E
East Clandon	260	51.15 N	0.29 W
East Claridon	214	41.32 N	81.07 W
East Cleddau ≃	42	51.46 N	4.52 W
East Cleveland	214	41.31 N	81.34 W
East Coast Bays	172	36.45 S	174.46 E
East Concord	210	42.33 N	78.38 W
Eastcote ◆ 8	260	51.35 N	0.24 W
East Cote Blanche Bay c	194	29.35 N	91.40 W
East Coulee	182	51.20 N	112.29 W
East Creek ≃	276	40.27 N	74.09 W
East Cross Creek ≃	212	44.17 N	78.44 W
East Dean	42	50.45 N	0.12 E
East Delaware Aqueduct ≅ 1	210	41.52 N	74.31 W
East Demerara-West Coast Berbice □ 5	246	6.20 N	58.00 W
East Dennis	207	41.44 N	70.09 W
East Dereham	42	52.41 N	0.56 E
East Detroit	214	42.28 N	82.57 W
East Dismal Swamp ⩩	192	35.45 N	76.35 W
East Ditch ≅	276	40.56 N	74.19 W
East Douglas	207	42.04 N	71.42 W
East Dublin	192	32.32 N	82.52 W
East Dubuque	190	42.29 N	90.38 W
East Dundee	216	42.06 N	88.16 W
East Durham	210	42.22 N	74.06 W
East Ely	204	39.15 N	114.53 W
Eastend, Sk., Can.	184	49.31 N	108.48 W
East End, Vir. Is., U.S.	240m	18.21 N	64.40 W
East End Point >	240b	25.03 N	77.16 W
East Enterprise	218	38.52 N	84.59 W
Easter Island → Pascua, Isla de I	174z	27.07 S	109.22 W
Easterly	222	31.06 N	96.23 W
Eastern □ 4, Ghana	150	6.30 N	0.30 W
Eastern □ 4, Kenya	154	0.05 N	38.00 E
Eastern □ 4, S.L.	150	8.15 N	11.00 W
Eastern □ 4, Zam.	154	13.00 S	32.15 E
Eastern □ 5	154	1.25 N	33.50 E
Eastern Bay c	208	38.51 N	76.19 W
Eastern Channel → Tsushima-kaikyō ʊ	92	34.00 N	129.00 E
Eastern Cherokee Indian Reservation ◆ 4	192	35.25 N	83.24 W
Eastern Cove c	168b	35.46 S	137.50 E
Eastern Creek ≃, Austl.	166	20.10 S	141.08 E
Eastern Creek ≃, Austl.	274a	33.39 S	150.51 E
Eastern Division □ 5	175g	19.00 S	180.00 E
Eastern Fields ✢ 2	164	10.20 S	145.45 E
Eastern Ghāts ⋏	122	14.00 N	78.50 E
Eastern Highlands □ 5	164	6.30 S	145.15 E
Eastern Island I	174g	28.12 N	177.20 W
Eastern Isles II	42a	49.57 N	6.15 W
Eastern Michigan University ⱴ 2	281	42.15 N	83.37 W
Eastern Neck Island I	208	39.02 N	76.13 W
Eastern Point >	283	42.35 N	70.40 W
Eastern Samar □ 4	116	12.00 N	125.00 E
Eastern Sayans → Vostočnyj Sajan ⋏	88	53.00 N	97.00 E
Eastern Shore ◆ 1	208	38.40 N	75.50 W
Eastern Yamuna Canal ≅	272a	28.40 N	77.15 E
East Falkland I	254	51.55 S	59.00 W
East Falls ◆ 8	285	40.01 N	75.11 W
East Falmouth	207	41.34 N	70.33 W
East Farleigh	260	51.15 N	0.29 E
East Farmingdale	276	40.44 N	73.26 W
East Faxon	210	41.15 N	76.58 W
East Fayetteville	192	35.05 N	78.51 W
Eastfield	44	54.14 N	0.24 W
East Flat Rock	192	35.16 N	82.25 W
Eastford	207	41.54 N	72.04 W
East Foxboro	283	42.03 N	71.12 W
East Freedom	214	40.21 N	78.26 W
East Freetown	207	41.46 N	70.57 W
East Frisian Islands → Ostfriesische Inseln II	52	53.44 N	7.25 E
East Gaffney	192	35.04 N	81.37 W
East Gallatin ≃	202	45.53 N	111.20 W
Eastgate	224	47.34 N	122.09 W
East Germany → German Democratic Republic □ 1	30	52.00 N	12.30 E
East Ghor Canal → Ghawr ash-Sharqīyah, Qanāt al- ≅	132	32.41 N	35.38 E
East Glacier Park	202	48.26 N	113.13 W
East Glenville	210	42.53 N	73.55 W
East Granby	207	41.56 N	72.43 W
East Grand Forks	198	47.55 N	97.01 W
East Grand Rapids	216	42.56 N	85.36 W
East Greenbush	210	42.35 N	73.42 W
East Greenville, Oh., U.S.	214	40.48 N	81.36 W
East Greenville, Pa., U.S.	208	40.24 N	75.30 W
East Greenwich, N.Y., U.S.	210	43.09 N	73.24 W
East Greenwich, R.I., U.S.	207	41.39 N	71.27 W
East Grinstead	42	51.08 N	0.01 W
East Gwillimbury	212	44.08 N	79.25 W
East Haddam	207	41.27 N	72.27 W
East Half Hollow Hills	276	40.57 N	72.11 W
Eastham, Eng., U.K.	262	53.19 N	2.58 W
Eastham, Ma., U.S.	207	41.49 N	69.58 W
East Ham ◆ 8	260	51.32 N	0.03 E
East Hampton, Ct., U.S.	207	41.34 N	72.30 W
Easthampton, Ma., U.S.	207	42.16 N	72.40 W
East Hampton, N.Y., U.S.	207	40.57 N	72.11 W
East Hanningfield	260	51.41 N	0.34 E
East Hanover	276	40.48 N	74.22 W
East Harbor State Park ♠	214	41.32 N	82.49 W
East Harling	42	52.26 N	0.55 E
East Hartford	207	41.46 N	72.36 W
East Hartland	207	41.59 N	72.54 W
East Harwich	207	41.43 N	70.02 W
East Haven	207	41.16 N	72.52 W
East Hazel Crest	278	41.35 N	87.39 W
East Helena	202	46.35 N	111.54 W
East Hemet	228	33.45 N	116.57 W
East Herkimer	210	43.02 N	74.58 W
East Hertfordshire □ 8	260	51.46 N	0.02 W
East Hickory	214	41.35 N	79.24 W
East Highland Park	208	37.36 N	77.25 W
East Hills, Austl.	274a	33.58 S	150.59 E
East Hills, N.Y., U.S.	276	40.47 N	73.37 W
East Hoathly	42	50.55 N	0.10 E
East Horsley	42	51.15 N	0.26 W
East Humber ≃	212	43.47 N	79.35 W
East Huntington	276	40.52 N	73.24 W
East Ilsley	42	51.32 N	1.17 W
East Irvington	276	41.03 N	73.51 W
East Island > 1	276	40.54 N	73.38 W
East Islip	276	40.43 N	73.11 W
East Jewett	210	42.14 N	74.09 W
East Jordan	190	45.09 N	85.07 W
East Keansburg	276	40.26 N	74.07 W
East Kelowna	182	49.51 N	119.25 W
East Kilbride	46	55.46 N	4.10 W
East Killingly	207	41.50 N	71.49 W
East Kingston	210	41.57 N	73.58 W
Eastlake, Mi., U.S.	190	44.15 N	86.18 W
Eastlake, Oh., U.S.	214	41.39 N	81.27 W
East Lake ⊜, On., Can.	184	53.42 N	93.10 W
East Lake ⊜, On., Can.	212	43.55 N	77.12 W
East Lake ⊜, N.J., U.S.	276	40.58 N	74.21 W
East Lake Tohopekaliga ⊜	220	28.18 N	81.17 W
East Lamma Channel ʊ	271d	22.14 N	114.09 E
Eastland	196	32.24 N	98.49 W
Eastland Center ◆ 9	281	42.27 N	82.56 W
Eastland Shopping Plaza ◆ 9	279b	40.22 N	79.50 W
East Lansdowne	285	39.56 N	75.16 W
East Lansing	216	42.44 N	84.29 W
East Laurinburg	192	34.46 N	79.26 W
East Leake	42	52.49 N	1.10 W
Eastleigh	42	50.58 N	1.22 W
East Lewistown	214	40.57 N	80.42 W
East Liberty	216	40.19 N	83.34 W
East Liberty ◆ 8	279b	40.27 N	79.55 W
East Licking Creek ≃	208	40.32 N	77.24 W
East Lindfield	274a	33.46 S	151.11 E
East Linton	46	55.59 N	2.39 W
East Liverpool	214	40.37 N	80.34 W
East Loch Roag c	46	58.14 N	6.48 W
East Loch Tarbert c	46	57.52 N	6.45 W
East London (Oos-Londen)	158	33.00 S	27.55 E
East Longmeadow	207	42.03 N	72.30 W
East Looe	42	50.22 N	4.27 W
East Los Angeles	228	34.01 N	118.10 W
East Lyme	207	41.22 N	72.13 W
East Lynn	216	40.28 N	87.48 W
East Lynn Lake ⊜ 1	188	38.05 N	82.20 W
Eastmain	176	52.15 N	78.30 W
Eastmain ≃	176	52.15 N	78.35 W
Eastmain-Opinaca, Réservoir ⊜ 1	176	52.25 N	76.35 W
East Malling	260	51.17 N	0.26 E
Eastman, P.Q., Can.	206	45.18 N	72.19 W
Eastman, Ga., U.S.	192	32.11 N	83.10 W
Eastman Lake ⊜ 1	226	37.14 N	119.58 W
East Mansfield	283	42.01 N	71.10 W
East Mariana Basin ✢ 1	14	12.00 N	153.00 E
East Marin Island I	282	37.58 N	122.27 W
East Markham	44	53.15 N	0.54 W
East McKeesport	279b	40.23 N	79.48 W
East Meadow	210	40.43 N	73.33 W
East Meadow ≃	283	42.47 N	71.02 W
East Meadow Brook ≃	276	40.39 N	73.34 W
East Meadowview	216	41.08 N	87.52 W
East Mecca	214	41.24 N	80.45 W
East Meredith	210	42.25 N	74.53 W
East Midlands Airport ⊠	42	52.50 N	1.20 W
East Millbury	207	42.13 N	71.44 W
East Mill Creek ≃	222	29.55 N	96.17 W
East Millinocket	188	45.37 N	68.34 W
East Millstone	276	40.30 N	74.35 W
East Missoula	202	46.52 N	113.58 W
East Molesey	260	51.24 N	0.21 W
East Moline	190	41.30 N	90.26 W
East Monongahela	279b	40.12 N	79.55 W
East Mountain	222	32.35 N	94.51 W
East Mustang Creek ≃	222	29.03 N	96.27 W
East Naples	220	26.06 N	81.44 W
East Nassau	210	42.30 N	73.30 W
East Newark	276	40.48 N	73.59 W
East New Britain □ 5	164	6.00 S	152.00 E
East New Market	208	38.35 N	75.55 W
East New York ◆ 8	276	40.40 N	73.53 W
East Nimār □ 5	124	22.00 N	76.30 E
East Nishnabotna ≃	198	40.39 N	95.37 W
East Nodaway ≃	194	40.38 N	95.01 W
East Norriton	208	40.09 N	75.18 W
East Northfield	207	42.43 N	72.27 W
East Northport	210	40.52 N	73.19 W
East Norwich	210	40.50 N	73.32 W
East Novaya Zemlya Trough ✢ 1	12	73.30 N	61.00 E
East Olympia	224	46.58 N	122.50 W
Easton, Eng., U.K.	42	50.32 N	2.26 W
Easton, Ca., U.S.	226	36.39 N	119.47 W
Easton, Ct., U.S.	207	41.15 N	73.17 W
Easton, Il., U.S.	219	40.14 N	89.50 W
Easton, Md., U.S.	208	38.46 N	76.04 W
Easton, Ma., U.S.	283	42.02 N	71.06 W
Easton, Pa., U.S.	208	40.41 N	75.13 W
Easton, Tx., U.S.	222	32.23 N	94.35 W
Easton, Wa., U.S.	224	47.14 N	121.10 W
Eastondale	283	42.02 N	71.04 W
Easton Reservoir ⊜ 1	207	41.16 N	73.16 W
East Orange	210	40.46 N	74.12 W
East Orleans	207	41.47 N	69.58 W
East Otto	210	42.23 N	78.45 W
Eastover	192	33.52 N	80.41 W
East Pacific Rise ✢ 3	6	20.00 S	115.00 W
East Pakistan → Bangladesh □ 1	118	24.00 N	90.00 E
East Palatka	192	29.39 N	81.35 W
East Palestine	214	40.50 N	80.32 W
East Palo Alto	226	37.28 N	122.08 W
East Park Reservoir ⊜ 1	226	39.21 N	122.30 W
East Parkrose	224	45.33 N	122.32 W
East Peak ∧	116	11.13 N	119.29 E
East Peckham	260	51.15 N	0.23 E
East Pecos	200	35.34 N	105.39 W
East Pembroke, Ma., U.S.	283	42.05 N	70.46 W
East Pembroke, N.Y., U.S.	210	42.59 N	78.18 W
East Peoria	190	40.39 N	89.34 W
East Pepperell	207	42.39 N	71.34 W
East Petersburg	208	40.06 N	76.21 W
East Pharsalia	210	42.34 N	75.43 W
East Pine	182	55.43 N	121.13 W
East Pines	284c	38.57 N	76.55 W
East Pittsburgh	279b	40.23 N	79.50 W
Eastpoint, Fl., U.S.	192	29.44 N	84.52 W
East Point, Ga., U.S.	192	33.40 N	84.26 W
East Point >, P.E., Can.	186	46.27 N	61.58 W
East Point >, Ma., U.S.	207	42.25 N	70.54 W
East Point >, Vir. Is., U.S.	241n	17.45 N	64.34 W
Eastpoint ◆ 9	284b	39.18 N	76.31 W
Eastport, Nf., Can.	186	48.39 N	53.45 W
Eastport, Id., U.S.	202	49.00 N	116.10 W
Eastport, Me., U.S.	188	44.54 N	66.59 W
Eastport, N.Y., U.S.	207	40.49 N	72.44 W
East Porterville	204	36.04 N	118.56 W
East Potomac Park ♠	284c	38.52 N	77.01 W
East Prairie	194	36.46 N	89.23 W
East Prairie ≃	182	55.34 N	116.25 W
East Prospect	208	39.58 N	76.31 W
East Providence	207	41.48 N	71.22 W
East Pryor Mountain ∧	202	45.11 N	108.20 W
East Quogue	207	40.51 N	72.35 W
East Rājasthān Uplands ⋏ 1	124	26.40 N	76.35 E
East Randolph	210	42.10 N	78.56 W
East Retford	44	53.19 N	0.56 W
East Richmond	226	37.57 N	122.19 W
Eastridge Center ◆ 9	282	37.20 N	121.49 W
East Rigaud ≃	206	45.27 N	74.22 W
Eastriggs	44	54.59 N	3.10 W
East River c	208	37.24 N	76.21 W
East Rochester, N.Y., U.S.	210	43.06 N	77.29 W
East Rochester, Oh., U.S.	214	40.45 N	81.02 W
East Rockaway	276	40.38 N	73.40 W
East Rockingham	192	34.55 N	79.45 W
East Rockwood	216	42.03 N	83.13 W
East Rosebud Creek ≃	202	45.29 N	109.27 W
East Rudolf National Park ♠	154	3.55 N	36.20 E
East Rutherford	276	40.50 N	74.05 W
Eastry	42	51.15 N	1.18 E
East Saint Louis	219	38.38 N	90.09 W
East Salem	208	40.37 N	77.14 W
East Salt Creek ≃	200	39.13 N	108.54 W
East Sandwich	207	41.44 N	70.27 W
East Sandy Creek ≃	214	41.22 N	79.51 W
East Schodack	210	42.34 N	73.38 W
East Scotia Basin ✢ 1	9	57.00 S	35.00 W
East Sepik □ 5	164	4.00 S	143.30 E
East Setauket	210	40.57 N	73.06 W
East Shoal Lake ⊜	184	50.23 N	97.37 W
East Siberian Sea → Vostočno-Sibirskoje more ⫪ 2	12	74.00 N	166.00 E
East Side	210	41.04 N	75.46 W
Eastside Bypass ≅	226	37.05 N	120.28 W
East Side Canal ≅, Ca., U.S.	226	37.21 N	120.55 W
East Side Canal ≅, Ca., U.S.	226	35.33 N	119.33 W
East Sister Island I	166	39.39 S	148.00 E
East Sixteen Mile Creek ≃	275b	43.28 N	79.48 W
East Smethport	214	41.49 N	78.26 W
East Smithfield	210	41.52 N	76.38 W
East Sooke	224	48.22 N	123.43 W
Eastsound	224	48.41 N	122.54 W
East Sound ʊ	224	48.39 N	122.53 W
East Sparta	214	40.40 N	81.21 W
East Spencer	192	35.40 N	80.25 W
East Springbrook	284c	39.04 N	77.00 W
East Springfield, Oh., U.S.	214	40.27 N	80.52 W
East Springfield, Pa., U.S.	214	41.57 N	80.28 W
East Stony Creek ≃	210	43.15 N	74.12 W
East Stour ≃	42	51.08 N	0.53 E
East Stroudsburg	210	40.59 N	75.10 W
East Sudbury	283	42.24 N	71.24 W
East Syracuse	210	43.04 N	76.05 W
East Tawas	190	44.16 N	83.29 W
East Templeton	207	42.33 N	72.02 W
East Texas	210	40.33 N	75.33 W
East Thompson	207	42.00 N	71.48 W
East Tilbury	260	51.28 N	0.26 E
East Troy	216	42.47 N	88.24 W
East Tustin	280	33.46 N	117.49 W
Eastvale	214	40.46 N	80.19 W
East Vandergrift	214	40.36 N	79.34 W
Eastview	218	40.19 N	80.38 W
Eastville	208	37.21 N	75.56 W
East Walker ≃	204	38.53 N	119.10 W
East Walpole	207	42.09 N	71.12 W
East Wareham	207	41.45 N	70.40 W
East Washington	214	40.10 N	80.14 W
East Waterford	208	40.22 N	77.36 W
East Wemyss	46	56.09 N	3.04 W
East Wenatchee	202	47.24 N	120.17 W
East Wenonah	285	39.47 N	75.08 W
East White Plains	276	41.03 N	73.47 W
Eastwick ◆ 8	285	39.55 N	75.14 W
East Wickham ◆ 8	260	51.28 N	0.07 E
East Williamson	210	43.14 N	77.09 W
East Williston	276	40.46 N	73.38 W
East Wilmington	192	34.13 N	77.53 W
East Wittering	42	50.41 N	0.53 W
Eastwood, Austl.	274a	33.48 S	151.05 E
Eastwood, Eng., U.K.	44	53.01 N	1.18 W
Eastwood, Eng., U.K.	260	51.34 N	0.40 E
Eastwood, Eng., U.K.	262	53.43 N	2.03 W
Eastwood, Mi., U.S.	216	42.18 N	85.33 W
Eastwood, Pa., U.S.	279b	40.17 N	79.31 W
East Worcester	210	42.37 N	74.40 W
East Yegua Creek ≃	222	30.19 N	96.45 W
East Yellow Creek ≃	194	39.38 N	93.04 W
East York, On., Can.	212	43.41 N	79.20 W
East York, Pa., U.S.	208	39.58 N	76.43 W
Eaton, Austl.	168a	33.19 S	115.43 E
Eaton, Co., U.S.	200	40.31 N	104.42 W
Eaton, In., U.S.	216	40.20 N	85.21 W
Eaton, N.Y., U.S.	210	42.51 N	75.37 W
Eaton, Oh., U.S.	218	39.44 N	84.38 W
Eaton ≃	206	45.28 N	71.39 W
Eaton Estates	214	41.19 N	82.01 W
Eatonia	184	51.13 N	109.23 W
Eaton Nord ≃	206	45.24 N	71.35 W
Eaton Park	220	28.00 N	81.54 W
Eaton Rapids	216	42.30 N	84.39 W
Eatons Neck	276	40.56 N	73.24 W
Eatons Neck > 1	276	40.57 N	73.23 W
Eatons Neck Point >	210	40.57 N	73.24 W
Eaton Socon	42	52.13 N	0.18 W
Eatonton	192	33.19 N	83.23 W
Eatontown	208	40.17 N	74.03 W
Eatonville	224	46.52 N	122.15 W
Eaton Wash V	280	34.04 N	118.03 W
Eaton Wash Dam ◆ 6	280	34.10 N	118.06 W
Eau ≃	44	53.31 N	0.44 W
Eaubonne	261	49.00 N	2.17 E
Eau Claire, Mi., U.S.	216	41.59 N	86.17 W
Eau Claire, Pa., U.S.	214	41.08 N	79.48 W
Eau Claire, Wi., U.S.	190	44.48 N	91.29 W
Eau Claire ≃, Wi., U.S.	190	44.49 N	91.31 W
Eau Claire ≃, Wi., U.S.	190	44.55 N	89.37 W
Eau Claire, Lac à l' ⊜, P.Q., Can.	176	56.10 N	74.25 W
Eau Claire, Lac à l' ⊜, P.Q., Can.	206	46.33 N	73.04 W
Eau d'Heure ≃	56	50.18 N	4.24 E
Eau Galle ≃	190	44.37 N	92.00 W
Eau Gallie	220	28.08 N	80.38 W
Eaulne ≃	50	49.54 N	1.07 E
Eauripik I 1	108	6.42 N	143.03 E
Eauripik Rise ✢ 3	14	3.00 N	142.00 E
Eauze	32	43.52 N	0.06 E
Ebabaka	152	2.30 S	18.19 E
Eban	150	9.44 N	4.56 E
Ebanga	152	12.44 S	14.44 E
Ebangalakata	152	0.29 S	21.29 E
Ebano	234	22.13 N	98.22 W
Ebb and Flow Indian Reserve ◆ 4	184	51.05 N	99.05 W
Ebb and Flow Lake ⊜	184	51.05 N	98.56 W
Ebbegebirge ⋏	56	51.08 N	7.46 E
Ebbegebirge, Naturpark ♠	263	51.06 N	7.45 E
Ebben Creek ≃	283	42.38 N	70.45 W
Ebberup	41	55.15 N	9.59 E
Ebbetts Pass)(	226	38.33 N	119.48 W
Ebbs	64	47.38 N	12.13 E
Ebbw ≃	42	51.33 N	2.59 W
Ebbw Vale	42	51.47 N	3.12 W
Ebebiyín	152	2.09 N	11.20 E
Ebeji (El Beïd) ≃	146	12.32 N	14.11 E
Ebejty, ozero ⊜	86	54.38 N	71.44 E
Ebeleben	54	51.17 N	10.43 E
Ebeltoft	41	56.12 N	10.41 E
Ebeltoft Vig c	41	56.10 N	10.36 E
Ebenau	64	47.47 N	13.11 E
Ebendorf	54	52.11 N	11.34 E
Ebene Reichenau	64	46.51 N	13.54 E
Ebenezer	275b	43.46 N	79.40 W
Ebenezer Ridge ∧	218	39.06 N	84.55 W
Eben Junction	190	46.21 N	86.58 W
Ebensburg	214	40.29 N	78.43 W
Ebensee	64	47.48 N	13.46 E
Ebensfeld	56	50.04 N	10.58 E
Eberbach	56	49.28 N	8.59 E
Ebergassing	264b	48.03 N	16.31 E
Eber Gölü ⊜	130	38.38 N	31.12 E
Ebergötzen	52	51.34 N	10.06 E
Ebermannstadt	60	49.43 N	11.13 E
Ebern	56	50.05 N	10.47 E
Eberndorf	61	46.35 N	14.38 E
Ebersbach, B.R.D.	56	48.43 N	9.31 E
Ebersbach, D.D.R.	54	51.00 N	14.35 E
Ebersberg	60	48.05 N	11.58 E
Eberschwang	60	48.09 N	13.34 E
Ebersdorf	52	53.31 N	9.03 E
Ebersdorf bei Coburg	56	50.13 N	11.04 E
Eberstein	61	46.48 N	14.34 E
Eberswalde	54	52.50 N	13.49 E
Ebetsu	92a	43.07 N	141.34 E
Ebian	102	29.10 N	103.20 E
Ebina	94	35.26 N	139.25 E
Ebingen	58	48.13 N	9.01 E
Ebino	92	32.03 N	130.50 E
Ebinur Hu ⊜	86	44.55 N	82.55 E
Ebi-Sekigahara-Yōrō-kokutei-kōen ♠	94	35.30 N	136.30 E
Ebnat	58	47.15 N	9.08 E
Ebo	152	11.02 S	14.41 E
Ebola ≃	152	3.20 N	20.57 E
Eboli	68	40.37 N	15.04 E
Ebolowa	152	2.54 N	11.09 E
Ebon I 1	14	4.35 N	168.44 E
Ebonda	152	2.12 N	22.21 E
Ebony	156	22.05 S	15.15 E
Eboshi-yama ∧	96	35.04 N	133.04 E
Eboué Stadium ♠	273b	4.17 S	15.18 E
Ebrach	56	49.50 N	10.29 E
Ebreichsdorf	61	47.58 N	16.24 E
Ébrié, Lagune c	150	5.14 N	4.26 W
Ebro ≃	34	40.43 N	0.54 E
Ebro, Delta del ⩩ 2	34	40.43 N	0.54 E
Ebro, Embalse del ⊜ 1	34	43.00 N	3.58 W
Ebstorf	52	53.01 N	10.25 E
Ebute-Ikorodu	273a	6.37 N	3.30 E
Ebute-Metta ◆ 8	273a	6.29 N	3.23 E
Ecatepec □ 7	286a	19.36 N	99.04 W
Ecatepec de Morelos	286a	19.35 N	99.04 W
Écaussinnes-d'Enghen	50	50.34 N	4.10 E
Ecclefechan	44	55.03 N	3.17 W
Eccles, Eng., U.K.	260	51.19 N	0.29 E
Eccles, Eng., U.K.	262	53.29 N	2.21 W
Eccles, W.V., U.S.	192	37.46 N	81.15 W
Eccleshall	42	52.52 N	2.15 W
Eccleston, Eng., U.K.	44	53.38 N	2.43 W
Eccleston, Eng., U.K.	262	53.39 N	2.44 W
Eccleston, Eng., U.K.	262	53.27 N	2.47 W
Eccleston, Md., U.S.	284b	39.24 N	76.44 W
Eceabat	130	40.11 N	26.21 E
Echabi	89	53.30 N	142.59 E
Echague	116	16.42 N	121.40 E
Echallens	58	46.38 N	6.38 E
Echaporã	255	22.26 S	50.12 W
Echarcon	261	48.34 N	2.24 E
Échauffour	50	48.44 N	0.23 E
Ech Cheliff (Orléansville)	148	36.10 N	1.20 E
Ech Cheliff □ 5	148	36.20 N	1.50 E
Echeconnee Creek ≃	192	32.39 N	83.36 W
Echelon Mall ◆ 9	285	39.51 N	75.00 W
Echeng	100	30.24 N	114.51 E
Échenoz-la-Méline	58	47.36 N	6.08 E
Echi ≃	94	35.13 N	136.07 E
Echigawa	94	35.10 N	136.12 E
Echigo-sammyaku ⋏	92	37.50 N	139.50 E
Echimamish ≃	184	54.20 N	97.27 W
Eching	60	48.18 N	11.37 E
Echizen	94	35.54 N	136.00 E
Echizen-Kaga-kaigan-kokutei-kōen ♠	94	36.08 N	136.05 E
Echizen-misaki >	94	35.59 N	135.57 E
Echo	198	44.37 N	95.25 W
Echo Bay	176	66.05 N	118.02 W
Echo Bay c	276	40.54 N	73.46 W
Echoing ≃	184	55.51 N	92.05 W
Echoing Lake ⊜	184	54.31 N	92.15 W
Echo Lake ⊜, Il., U.S.	278	42.13 N	88.05 W
Echo Lake ⊜, N.J., U.S.	276	41.04 N	74.25 W
Echo Summit ∧	226	38.50 N	120.02 W
Echouani, Lac ⊜	190	47.46 N	75.42 W
Echt, Ned.	52	51.06 N	5.52 E
Echt, Scot., U.K.	46	57.08 N	2.26 W
Echternach	56	49.48 N	6.26 E
Echternacherbrück	56	49.49 N	6.25 E
Echuca	166	36.08 S	144.46 E
Echunga	168b	35.07 S	138.48 E
Écija	34	37.32 N	5.05 W
Ecilda Paullier	258	34.22 S	57.04 W
Eck, Loch ⊜	46	56.05 N	5.00 W
Eckartsberga	54	51.07 N	11.34 E
Eckbolsheim	58	48.35 N	7.41 E
Eckernförde	41	54.28 N	9.50 E
Eckernförder Bucht c	41	54.30 N	10.02 E
Eckerö I	26	60.14 N	19.35 E
Eckington	44	53.19 N	1.21 W
Eckley	210	40.59 N	75.51 W
Eckville	182	52.21 N	114.22 W
Eckwarderhörne	52	53.31 N	8.14 E
Eclectic	194	32.38 N	86.02 W
Ecleto	222	29.03 N	97.45 W
Ecleto Creek ≃	196	28.52 N	97.45 W
Eclipse Sound ʊ	176	72.38 N	79.00 W
Ečmiadzin	84	40.10 N	44.18 E
Ecola State Park ♠	224	45.57 N	123.58 W
Ècole ≃	261	48.32 N	2.33 E
Écommoy	50	47.50 N	0.16 E
Econfina ≃	192	30.02 N	83.55 W
Econlockhatchee ≃	220	28.42 N	81.02 W
Economy, In., U.S.	218	39.58 N	85.05 W
Economy, Pa., U.S.	214	40.39 N	80.14 W
Economy Park ♠	279b	40.37 N	80.12 W
Écorce, Lac de l' ⊜ 1	190	47.05 N	76.24 W
Écorces, Lac des ⊜	206	46.00 N	74.32 W
Ecorse	216	42.14 N	83.08 W
Ecorse ≃	281	42.14 N	83.09 W
Ecorse, South Branch ≃	281	42.14 N	83.09 W
Écos	50	49.10 N	1.39 E
Écosse → Scotland □ 8	28	57.00 N	4.00 W
Écouen	50	49.01 N	2.23 E
Écouen, Château d' ⊥	261	49.01 N	2.23 E
Écouis	50	49.19 N	1.26 E
Ecoute, Rû d' ≃	261	48.39 N	2.26 E
Ecquevilly	261	48.57 N	1.55 E
Écrins, Barre des ∧	62	44.55 N	6.22 E
Écrins, Massif des ⋏ 1	62	44.55 N	6.20 E
Écrins, Parc National des ♠	62	44.50 N	6.15 E
Écrosnes	261	48.33 N	1.44 E
Ecru	194	34.21 N	89.01 W
Ecser	264c	47.27 N	19.20 E
Ecstall ≃	182	54.09 N	129.56 W
Ecuador □ 1, S.A.	242	2.00 S	77.30 W
Ecuador □ 1, S.A.	246	2.00 S	77.30 W
Ecuandureo	234	20.10 N	102.11 W
Écueillé	32	47.05 N	1.21 E
Écuisses	58	46.45 N	4.32 E
Ecum Secum	186	44.58 N	62.08 W
Écury-sur-Coole	50	48.54 N	4.20 E
Ed, Ityo.	144	13.52 N	41.40 E
Ed, Sve.	26	58.55 N	11.55 E
Eda ◆ 8	268	35.34 N	139.34 E
Edah	162	28.17 S	117.10 E
Edam, Sk., Can.	184	53.12 N	108.46 W
Edam, Ned.	52	52.31 N	5.03 E
Eday I	46	59.11 N	2.47 W
Edderton	46	57.50 N	4.10 W
Eddington Gardens	285	40.06 N	74.57 W
Eddleston	46	55.43 N	3.13 W
Eddrachillis Bay c	46	58.18 N	5.15 W
Eddy	222	31.18 N	97.15 W
Eddystone	208	39.51 N	75.20 W
Eddystone Point >	166	41.00 S	148.21 E
Eddystone Rocks II 1	42	50.12 N	4.15 W
Eddyville, Ia., U.S.	190	41.09 N	92.38 W
Eddyville, Ky., U.S.	194	37.05 N	88.04 W
Eddyville, N.Y., U.S.	210	41.54 N	74.02 W
Ede, Ned.	52	52.03 N	5.40 E
Ede, Nig.	150	7.44 N	4.27 E
Edéa	152	3.48 N	10.08 E
Edebäck	40	60.04 N	13.33 E
Edebo	40	60.01 N	18.34 E
Edegem	52	51.09 N	4.27 E
Edehon Lake ⊜	176	60.25 N	97.15 W
Edéia	255	17.18 S	49.55 W
Edelény	30	48.18 N	20.44 E
Edelsfeld	60	49.34 N	11.42 E
Edelshausen	60	48.37 N	11.17 E
Edelweiss	273d	26.16 S	28.28 E
Edelweiss Spitze ∧	64	47.07 N	12.50 E
Edemissen	52	52.23 N	10.16 E
Eden, Austl.	166	37.04 S	149.54 E
Éden, Bra.	287a	22.48 S	43.24 W
Eden, N. Ire., U.K.	48	54.44 N	5.47 W
Eden, Mi., U.S.	216	42.32 N	84.26 W
Eden, Ms., U.S.	194	32.59 N	90.19 W
Eden, N.Y., U.S.	210	42.39 N	78.53 W
Eden, Tx., U.S.	196	31.12 N	99.50 W
Eden, Wy., U.S.	200	42.03 N	109.26 W
Eden ≃, Eng., U.K.	42	51.10 N	0.11 E
Eden ≃, Eng., U.K.	44	54.57 N	3.01 W
Eden ≃, Scot., U.K.	46	56.22 N	2.50 W
Eden ≃, Wales, U.K.	42	52.48 N	3.53 W
Edenbridge	260	51.12 N	0.04 E
Edenburg	158	29.45 S	25.56 E
Eden Canyon V	282	37.42 N	122.01 W
Edendale, N.Z.	172	46.19 S	168.47 E
Edendale, S. Afr.	158	29.39 S	30.18 E
Edendale, S. Afr.	273d	26.09 S	28.09 E
Edenderry	48	53.20 N	7.03 W
Edenfield	262	53.40 N	2.18 W
Eden Hill ∧ 2	207	41.20 N	73.19 W
Edenkoben	56	49.17 N	8.07 E
Eden Lake ⊜	184	56.38 N	100.15 W
Eden Mills	212	43.35 N	80.09 W
Eden Park ◆ 8	260	51.23 N	0.02 W
Edenside V	44	54.40 N	2.35 W
Edenton	192	36.03 N	76.36 W
Edenvale	273d	26.08 S	28.09 E
Eden Valley, Austl.	168b	34.39 S	139.06 E
Eden Valley, Mn., U.S.	190	45.19 N	94.32 W
Edenville	158	27.37 S	27.34 E
Edeowie	166	31.27 S	138.27 E
Eder ≃	56	51.13 N	9.27 E
Ederkopf ∧	56	50.56 N	8.12 E
Ederny	48	54.32 N	7.39 W
Edersee ⊜ 1	56	51.11 N	9.00 E
Eder-Talsperre ◆ 6	56	51.11 N	9.02 E
Edesheim	56	49.16 N	8.08 E
Edessa → Édhessa	38	40.48 N	22.03 E
Edewecht	52	53.07 N	8.02 E
Edfu → Idfū	140	24.58 N	32.52 E
Edgar, Ne., U.S.	198	40.22 N	97.58 W
Edgar, Wi., U.S.	190	44.55 N	89.57 W
Edgard	194	30.03 N	90.34 W
Edgar Ranges ⋏	162	18.43 S	123.25 E
Edgars Creek ≃	274b	37.44 S	144.58 E
Edgartown	207	41.23 N	70.30 W
Edgartown Harbor c	207	41.24 N	70.30 W
Edgecliff	222	32.39 N	97.22 W
Edgecumbe	172	37.59 S	176.50 E
Edgefield	192	33.47 N	81.55 W
Edge Hill ◆ 8	262	53.24 N	2.57 W
Edge Hill ∧ 2	42	52.08 N	1.27 W
Edgeley, On., Can.	275b	43.48 N	79.31 W
Edgeley, N.D., U.S.	198	46.21 N	98.42 W
Edgely	285	40.07 N	74.50 W
Edgemere	208	39.14 N	76.26 W
Edgemont, Ca., U.S.	228	33.53 N	117.18 W
Edgemont, Pa., U.S.	285	39.57 N	75.27 W
Edgemont, S.D., U.S.	198	43.18 N	103.49 W
Edgemont Park	216	42.44 N	84.36 W
Edgemoor	285	39.45 N	75.30 W
Edge Mountain ∧	180	58.12 N	152.06 W
Edgeøya I	12	77.45 N	22.30 E
Edgeroi	166	30.07 S	149.48 E
Edgerton, Ab., Can.	184	52.45 N	110.27 W
Edgerton, In., U.S.	216	41.05 N	84.49 W
Edgerton, Mn., U.S.	198	43.52 N	96.07 W
Edgerton, Oh., U.S.	216	41.26 N	84.44 W
Edgerton, Wi., U.S.	216	42.50 N	89.04 W
Edgerton, Wy., U.S.	200	43.24 N	106.14 W
Edgewater, Al., U.S.	194	33.31 N	86.57 W
Edgewater, Fl., U.S.	220	28.59 N	80.54 W
Edgewater, N.J., U.S.	276	40.50 N	73.58 W
Edgewater Park	285	40.04 N	74.54 W
Edgewater Park ♠	279a	41.29 N	81.43 W
Edgewater Point >	276	40.55 N	73.44 W
Edgewood, B.C., Can.	182	49.47 N	118.08 W
Edgewood, Fl., U.S.	220	28.29 N	81.22 W
Edgewood, Il., U.S.	219	38.55 N	88.40 W
Edgewood, In., U.S.	218	40.06 N	85.44 W
Edgewood, Ia., U.S.	190	42.38 N	91.24 W
Edgewood, Md., U.S.	208	39.25 N	76.17 W
Edgewood, Oh., U.S.	214	41.52 N	80.46 W
Edgewood, Pa., U.S.	279b	40.25 N	79.52 W
Edgewood, Tx., U.S.	222	32.42 N	95.53 W
Edgeworth	214	40.33 N	80.11 W
Edgeworthstown → Mostrim	48	53.42 N	7.36 W
Edgware ◆ 8	260	51.37 N	0.17 W
Edgworth	262	53.39 N	2.24 W
Édhessa	38	40.48 N	22.03 E
Edievale	172	45.48 S	169.22 E
Ediger	56	50.06 N	7.09 E
Edimbourg → Edinburgh	46	55.57 N	3.13 W
Edimburgo → Edinburgh	46	55.57 N	3.13 W
Edina, Liber.	150	6.01 N	10.10 W
Edina, Mn., U.S.	190	44.53 N	93.20 W
Edina, Mo., U.S.	219	40.10 N	92.10 W
Edinboro	214	41.52 N	80.07 W
Edinboro Lake ⊜	214	41.53 N	80.08 W
Edinburg, Il., U.S.	219	39.39 N	89.23 W
Edinburg, In., U.S.	218	39.21 N	85.58 W
Edinburg, Ms., U.S.	194	32.47 N	89.20 W
Edinburg, N.Y., U.S.	210	43.13 N	74.07 W
Edinburg, N.D., U.S.	198	48.29 N	97.51 W
Edinburg, Oh., U.S.	214	41.06 N	81.09 W
Edinburg, Tx., U.S.	196	26.18 N	98.09 W
Edinburg, Va., U.S.	188	38.49 N	78.33 W
Edinburgh	46	55.57 N	3.13 W
Edinburgh (Turnhouse) Airport ⊠	46	55.57 N	3.21 W
Edinburgh Castle ⊥	46	55.56 N	3.14 W
Edinburgh Channel ʊ	236	14.45 N	82.40 W
Edinburgh Mountain ∧	224	48.38 N	124.24 W
Edinburgh Reef ✢ 2	236	14.50 N	82.39 W
Edincik	130	40.20 N	27.51 E
Edingen → Enghien	50	50.42 N	4.02 E
Edirne	130	41.40 N	26.34 E
Edirne □ 4	130	41.20 N	26.40 E
Edison, Ga., U.S.	192	31.33 N	84.44 W
Edison, N.J., U.S.	210	40.27 N	74.18 W
Edison, Oh., U.S.	214	40.33 N	82.51 W
Edison, Pa., U.S.	208	40.17 N	75.07 W
Edison Bridge ◆ 5	214	41.27 N	82.49 W
Edison National Historic Site ⊥	276	40.47 N	74.14 W
Edison Park ◆ 8	278	42.01 N	87.49 W
Edisseja	84	44.03 N	44.33 E
Edisto ≃	192	32.39 N	80.24 W
Edisto, North Fork ≃	192	33.16 N	80.53 W
Edisto, South Fork ≃	192	33.16 N	80.53 W
Edisto Island I	192	32.35 N	80.20 W
Edith	170	33.48 S	149.55 E
Edith, Mount ∧	202	46.26 N	111.11 W
Edithburgh	168b	35.06 S	137.44 E
Edith Cavell, Mount ∧	182	52.40 N	118.03 W
Edith River	164	14.11 S	132.02 E
Edithvale	274b	38.02 S	145.07 E
Edith Weston	42	52.37 N	0.37 W
Edjejou, Oued i-n- V	148	22.46 N	4.05 E
Edjeleh	148	27.38 N	9.50 E
Edjerir ≃	150	18.06 N	0.50 E
Edjudina	162	29.48 S	122.23 E
Edmeston	210	42.41 N	75.14 W
Edmond	196	35.39 N	97.28 W
Edmondbyers	44	54.51 N	1.58 W
Edmonds	224	47.48 N	122.22 W
Edmondson Heights	284b	39.18 N	76.43 W
Edmonston	284c	38.57 N	76.56 W
Edmonton, Austl.	166	17.01 S	145.45 E
Edmonton, Ab., Can.	182	53.33 N	113.28 W
Edmonton, Ky., U.S.	194	36.58 N	85.36 W
Edmonton ◆ 8	260	51.37 N	0.04 W
Edmore, Mi., U.S.	190	43.24 N	85.02 W
Edmore, N.D., U.S.	198	48.24 N	98.27 W
Edmund	162	23.46 S	116.02 E
Edmund Lake ⊜	184	54.45 N	93.15 W
Edmundson Acres	228	35.14 N	118.49 W
Edmundston	186	47.22 N	68.20 W
Edna, Ks., U.S.	198	37.03 N	95.21 W
Edna, Pa., U.S.	279b	40.19 N	79.39 W
Edna, Tx., U.S.	222	28.58 N	96.38 W
Edna Bay	180	55.57 N	133.40 W
Ednor	208	39.09 N	76.59 W
Edo ≃	94	35.37 N	139.53 E
Edogawa ◆ 8	268	35.42 N	139.52 E
Edolo	64	46.11 N	10.20 E
Edom	222	32.22 N	95.37 W

Symbol	English	Deutsch	Español	Français	Português
≃	River	Fluss	Río	Rivière	Rio
≅	Canal	Kanal	Canal	Canal	Canal
∟	Waterfall, Rapids	Wasserfall, Stromschnellen	Cascada, Rápidos	Chute d'eau, Rapides	Cascata, Rápidos
ʊ	Strait	Meeresstrasse	Estrecho	Détroit	Estreito
c	Bay, Gulf	Bucht, Golf	Bahía, Golfo	Baie, Golfe	Baía, Golfo
⊜	Lake, Lakes	See, Seen	Lago, Lagos	Lac, Lacs	Lago, Lagos
⩩	Swamp	Sumpf	Pantano	Marais	Pântano
⍓	Ice Features, Glacier	Eis- und Gletscherformen	Accidentes Glaciales	Formes glaciaires	Acidentes glaciares
⫪	Other Hydrographic Features	Andere Hydrographische Objekte	Otros Elementos Hidrográficos	Autres données hydrographiques	Outros acidentes hidrográficos
✢	Submarine Features	Untermeerische Objekte	Accidentes Submarinos	Formes de relief sous-marin	Acidentes submarinos
□	Political Unit	Politische Einheit	Unidad Política	Entité politique	Unidade política
ⱴ	Cultural Institution	Kulturelle Institution	Institución Cultural	Institution culturelle	Instituição cultural
⊥	Historical Site	Historische Stätte	Sitio Histórico	Site historique	Sítio histórico
♠	Recreational Site	Erholungs- und Ferienort	Sitio de Recreo	Centre de loisirs	Area de Lazer
⊠	Airport	Flughafen	Aeropuerto	Aéroport	Aeroporto
■	Military Installation	Militäranlage	Instalación Militar	Installation militaire	Instalação militar
◆	Miscellaneous	Verschiedenes	Misceláneo	Divers	Diversos

ENGLISH: Name · Page · Lat.°′ · Long.°′ — DEUTSCH: Name · Seite · Breite°′ · Länge°′ E = Ost

Name	Page	Lat.°′	Long.°′
Edon	216	41.33 N	84.46 W
Edosaki	94	35.57 N	140.19 E
Edremit	130	39.35 N	27.01 E
Edremit Körfezi ⊂	130	39.30 N	26.45 E
Edrengijn nuruu ⋏	102	44.15 N	97.45 E
Edsall Park	284c	38.48 N	77.11 W
Edsbro	40	59.54 N	18.29 E
Edsbruk	26	58.02 N	16.28 E
Edsbyn	26	61.23 N	15.49 E
Edsgatan	40	59.26 N	13.33 E
Edson	182	53.35 N	116.26 W
Edson Butte ∧	202	42.52 N	124.20 W
Eduardo Castex	252	35.54 S	64.18 W
Eduardo VII, Península → Edward VII Peninsula ›[1]	9	77.40 S	155.00 W
Eduni, Mount ∧	180	64.15 N	128.04 W
Edward ≃, Austl.	164	14.44 S	141.35 E
Edward ≃, Austl.	166	35.33 S	144.58 E
Edward, Lake ⊜	154	0.25 S	29.30 E
Edward, Mount ∧	162	23.22 S	131.55 E
Edwardes Park ♠	274b	37.43 S	145.00 E
Edward Island I	190	48.24 N	88.36 W
Edwards, Ca., U.S.	228	34.54 N	117.53 W
Edwards, Ms., U.S.	194	32.19 N	90.36 W
Edwards, N.Y., U.S.	212	44.19 N	75.15 W
Edwards ≃	190	41.09 N	90.59 W
Edwards Air Force Base ■	228	34.54 N	117.52 W
Edwards Airport ⊠	276	40.45 N	73.03 W
Edwardsburg	216	41.47 N	86.04 W
Edwards Butte ∧	224	45.23 N	123.41 W
Edwards Creek	166	28.21 S	135.51 E
Edwards Gardens ♠	275b	43.44 N	79.22 W
Edwards Plateau ⋏[1]	196	31.20 N	101.00 W
Edwards Point ›	169	38.13 S	144.42 E
Edwards Run ≃	285	39.48 N	75.12 W
Edwardsville, Il., U.S.	219	38.48 N	89.57 W
Edwardsville, In., U.S.	218	38.16 N	85.55 W
Edwardsville, Pa., U.S.	210	41.16 N	75.55 W
Edward VIII Bay ⊂	9	66.50 S	57.00 E
Edward VII Peninsula ›[1]	9	77.40 S	155.00 W
Edwinstowe	44	53.12 N	1.04 W
Edzell	46	56.48 N	2.39 W
Edziza, Mount ∧	180	57.40 N	130.36 W
Eede	52	51.15 N	3.28 E
Eefde	52	52.10 N	6.14 E
Eek	180	60.12 N	162.15 W
Eek ≃	180	60.12 N	162.15 W
Eeklo	50	51.11 N	3.34 E
Eel ≃, Ca., U.S.	204	40.40 N	124.20 W
Eel ≃, In., U.S.	194	39.07 N	86.57 W
Eel ≃, In., U.S.	216	40.45 N	86.22 W
Eel, Middle Fork ≃	204	39.42 N	123.21 W
Eel, North Fork ≃	204	39.57 N	123.26 W
Eel, South Fork ≃	204	40.22 N	123.55 W
Eel Bay ⊂	212	44.19 N	76.02 W
Eelde	52	53.07 N	6.35 E
Eels Creek ≃	212	44.35 N	78.03 W
Eels Lake ⊜	212	44.54 N	78.08 W
Eemskanaal ≋	52	53.15 N	6.45 E
Eerbeek	52	52.07 N	6.04 E
Eersel	52	51.22 N	5.19 E
Eexta	52	53.10 N	6.59 E
Efate □[8]	175f	17.45 S	168.20 E
Éfaté I	175f	17.40 S	168.25 E
Eferding	61	48.18 N	14.02 E
Effigy Mounds National Monument ♠	190	43.06 N	91.13 W
Effingham, Eng., U.K.	260	51.16 N	0.24 W
Effingham, Il., U.S.	194	39.07 N	88.32 W
Effingham, Ks., U.S.	198	39.31 N	95.24 W
Effingham □[6]	219	39.07 N	88.33 W
Effingham Lake ⊜	212	44.59 N	77.22 W
Effort	210	40.56 N	75.26 W
Efiduasi	150	6.51 N	1.24 W
Efkere	130	38.47 N	35.40 E
Eforie Nord	38	44.06 N	28.38 E
Eforie Sud	38	44.03 N	28.38 E
Efrikemer ≋[1]	267b	41.03 N	28.58 E
Efringen-Kirchen	58	47.49 N	7.35 E
Ega ≃	34	42.19 N	1.55 W
Egadi, Isole II	70	37.58 N	12.16 E
Egan	222	32.28 N	97.17 W
Egaña	252	36.59 S	59.06 W
Egan Range ⋏	204	39.10 N	114.55 W
Eganville	190	45.32 N	77.06 W
Egau ≃	58	48.36 N	10.34 E
Egba □[8]	273a	6.41 N	3.23 E
Egbe, Nig.	150	8.16 N	5.31 E
Egbe, Nig.	273a	6.33 N	3.17 E
Egbunda	154	2.44 N	27.12 E
Egedesminde	176	68.42 N	52.45 W
Égée, Mer → Aegean Sea ▿[2]	38	38.30 N	25.00 E
Egegik	180	58.13 N	157.22 W
Egeln	54	51.56 N	11.25 E
Egeo, Mar → Aegean Sea ▿[2]	38	38.30 N	25.00 E
Eger → Cheb, Česko.	54	50.01 N	12.25 E
Eger, Magy.	30	47.54 N	20.23 E
Eger ≃, B.R.D.	56	48.50 N	10.37 E
Eger (Ohře) ≃, Europe	54	50.32 N	14.08 E
Egeria Mountain ∧	182	53.55 N	130.22 W
Egernsund	41	54.54 N	9.37 E
Egerpohl	263	51.07 N	7.27 E
Egersund	26	58.27 N	6.00 E
Egerton	262	53.38 N	2.26 W
Egerton, Mount ∧	9	80.50 S	158.50 E
Egeskov ⊥	41	55.10 N	10.30 E
Egestorf	52	53.11 N	10.04 E
Egestorf [am Süntel]	52	52.17 N	9.31 E
Egg	58	47.26 N	9.54 E
Egg Creek ≃	198	48.22 N	100.47 W
Egge ⋏	52	51.40 N	8.55 E
Eggebek	41	54.37 N	9.22 E
Eggelsberg	60	48.05 N	13.00 E
Eggenberg, Schloss ⊥	61	47.05 N	15.25 E
Eggenburg	61	48.39 N	15.50 E
Eggenfelden	60	48.25 N	12.46 E
Eggenstein-Leopoldshafen	56	49.04 N	8.23 E
Eggerscheid	263	51.19 N	6.53 E
Eggersdorf	54	52.32 N	13.49 E
Eggesin	54	53.41 N	14.05 E
Egg Harbor City	208	39.31 N	74.38 W
Egg Island Point ›	208	39.11 N	75.08 W
Egg Lagoon	166	39.39 S	143.58 E
Egg Lake ⊜, Mb., Can.	184	54.21 N	101.26 W
Egg Lake ⊜, Sk., Can.	184	55.05 N	105.30 W
Egglestone Abbey ♁[1]	44	54.32 N	1.54 W
Egglham	60	48.32 N	13.04 E
Egglkofen	60	48.24 N	12.27 E
Eggmühl	60	48.51 N	12.11 E
Egham	260	51.26 N	0.34 W
Egherta	144	2.04 N	43.11 E
Éghezée	56	50.36 N	4.54 E
Egijn ≃	88	49.24 N	103.36 E
Eğil	130	38.15 N	40.05 E
Egilsay I	46	59.09 N	2.56 W
Egilsstaðir	24a	65.16 N	14.18 W
Eging	60	48.43 N	13.16 E
Egipto → Egypt □[1]	140	27.00 N	30.00 E
Égletons	32	45.24 N	2.03 E
Eglin Air Force Base ■	194	30.29 N	86.30 W
Eglinton	48	55.02 N	7.11 W
Eglisau	58	47.34 N	8.32 E
Egloskerry	42	50.39 N	4.27 W
Égly	261	48.35 N	2.13 E
Egmond aan Zee	52	52.36 N	4.37 E
Egmond-Binnen	52	52.35 N	4.39 E
Egmont, Cape ›	172	39.17 S	173.45 E
Egmont, Mount ∧	172	39.18 S	174.04 E
Egmont Bay ⊂	186	46.35 N	64.12 W
Egmont Channel)(	220	27.36 N	82.45 W
Egmont Key I	220	27.35 N	82.46 W
Egmont National Park ♠	172	39.15 S	174.05 E
Egna (Neumarkt)	64	46.19 N	11.16 E
Egnach	58	47.33 N	9.23 E
Egnazia ⊥	68	40.53 N	17.24 E
Egoryevsk → Jegorjevsk	82	55.23 N	39.02 E
Egota ◈[8]	268	35.43 N	139.40 E
Egra	126	21.54 N	87.32 E
Egremont, Ab., Can.	182	54.02 N	113.08 W
Egremont, Eng., U.K.	44	54.29 N	3.33 W
Eğret	130	38.57 N	30.18 E
Égreville	50	48.10 N	2.52 E
Eğridir	130	37.52 N	30.51 E
Eğridir Gölü ⊜	130	38.02 N	30.53 E
Eğriköy	130	38.44 N	27.21 E
Egrisskij chrebet ⋏	84	42.49 N	42.24 E
Egton	44	54.26 N	0.45 W
Egtved	41	55.37 N	9.18 E
Éguas, Rio das ≃	255	13.26 S	44.14 W
Éguilles	62	43.34 N	5.22 E
Eguisheim	58	48.03 N	7.18 E
Egum Atoll I[1]	164	9.25 S	151.55 E
Egvekinot	180	66.19 N	179.10 W
Egyházasrádóc	61	47.05 N	16.37 E
Egypt, Ma., U.S.	207	42.12 N	70.45 W
Egypt, Pa., U.S.	208	40.41 N	75.32 W
Egypt, Tx., U.S.	222	29.24 N	96.14 W
Egypt (Mişr) □[1], Afr.	136	27.00 N	30.00 E
Egypt (Mişr) □[1], Afr.	140	27.00 N	30.00 E
Egypt, Lake of ⊜[1]	194	37.35 N	88.55 W
Égypte → Egypt □[1]	140	27.00 N	30.00 E
Egyptian Museum ♁	273c	30.03 N	31.14 E
Eha-Amufu	150	6.40 N	7.46 E
Ehekirchen	60	48.38 N	11.06 E
Ehen ≃	44	54.25 N	3.30 W
Ehime □[5]	96	33.40 N	132.50 E
Ehingen	58	48.17 N	9.43 E
Ehingen ◈[8]	263	51.22 N	6.42 E
Ehle ≃	54	52.12 N	11.44 E
Ehmen	54	52.24 N	10.41 E
Ehra-Lessien	54	52.34 N	10.46 E
Ehrang	56	49.49 N	6.41 E
Ehrenberg	200	33.36 N	114.31 W
Ehrenberg Range ⋏	162	23.18 S	130.20 E
Ehrenbreitstein, Feste ⊥	56	50.21 N	7.37 E
Ehrenburg ⊥	56	50.12 N	7.27 E
Ehrenfeld	214	40.22 N	78.46 W
Ehrenfriedersdorf	54	50.38 N	12.58 E
Ehrenhausen	61	46.43 N	15.35 E
Ehreshoven	56	50.58 N	7.20 E
Ehrhardt	192	33.05 N	81.00 W
Ehrhorn	52	53.10 N	9.53 E
Ehringhausen	263	51.11 N	7.33 E
Ehringhausen ◈[8]	263	51.09 N	7.11 E
Ehrwald	58	47.24 N	10.55 E
Ehwa Women's University ♁[2]	271b	37.34 N	126.56 E
Ei	92	31.12 N	130.30 E
Éibar	34	43.11 N	2.28 W
Eibau	54	50.58 N	14.40 E
Eibelstadt	56	49.43 N	10.00 E
Eibenstock	54	50.29 N	12.35 E
Eibergen	52	52.06 N	6.39 E
Eibiswald	61	46.41 N	15.15 E
Eibsee ⊜	64	47.27 N	10.58 E
Eicha	54	50.21 N	10.34 E
Eich-Berg ∧[2]	264a	52.39 N	13.50 E
Eiche, D.D.R.	264a	52.34 N	13.36 E
Eiche, D.D.R.	264a	52.25 N	12.58 E
Eichenbarleben	54	52.10 N	11.24 E
Eichenbrandt	264a	52.38 N	13.51 E
Eichendorf	60	48.38 N	12.51 E
Eichgraben	61	48.10 N	15.59 E
Eichlinghofen ◈[8]	263	51.29 N	7.24 E
Eichsfeld ◈[1]	56	51.25 N	10.20 E
Eichstädt	264a	52.42 N	13.07 E
Eichstätt	60	48.54 N	11.12 E
Eichstetten	58	48.05 N	7.44 E
Eichtersheim	56	49.14 N	8.46 E
Eichwalde	54	52.22 N	13.37 E
Eickelborn	52	51.39 N	8.13 E
Eicken ◈[8]	263	51.13 N	6.26 E
Eickerend	263	51.13 N	6.34 E
Eickerkopf ∧[2]	263	51.21 N	7.42 E
Eicklingen	52	52.33 N	10.10 E
Eide	26	62.55 N	7.26 E
Eidelstedt ◈[8]	52	53.36 N	9.53 E
Eider ≃	41	54.19 N	8.58 E
Eiderstedt ›[1]	41	54.22 N	8.50 E
Eidfjord	26	60.28 N	7.05 E
Eidsvåg, Nor.	26	60.27 N	5.21 E
Eidsvåg, Nor.	26	62.47 N	8.03 E
Eidsvold	166	25.22 S	151.07 E
Eidsvoll	26	60.19 N	11.14 E
Eifa	56	50.58 N	8.34 E
Eifel ⋏	56	50.15 N	6.45 E
Eiffel, Tour ⊥	261	48.51 N	2.18 E
Eiffel Flats	154	18.15 S	29.59 E
Eifgenbach ≃	263	51.05 N	7.09 E
Eigen ◈[8]	263	51.33 N	6.57 E
Eigenji	94	35.04 N	136.18 E
Eigenrieden	54	51.11 N	10.22 E
Eiger ∧	58	46.35 N	8.00 E
Eigg I	46	56.54 N	6.10 W
Eigg, Sound of)(	46	56.51 N	6.13 W
Eighe, Carn ∧	46	57.17 N	5.07 W
Eight Degree Channel)(	122	8.00 N	73.00 E
Eighteenmile Creek ≃, N.Y., U.S.	210	42.43 N	78.58 W
Eighteenmile Creek ≃, N.Y., U.S.	210	43.21 N	78.43 W
Eight Mile Creek ≃, On., Can.	284a	43.14 N	79.11 W
Eightmile Creek ≃, In., U.S.	216	40.57 N	85.22 W
Eightmile Creek ≃, Or., U.S.	224	45.36 N	121.05 W
Eights Coast ≗[2]	9	73.30 S	93.00 W
Eighty Four	279b	40.11 N	80.08 W
Eighty Mile Beach ≗[2]	162	19.45 S	121.00 E
Eiheiji	94	36.05 N	136.20 E
Eijerlandsche Gat ⊂	52	53.12 N	4.50 E
Eijsden	56	50.47 N	5.43 E
Eikeren ⊜	26	59.38 N	9.58 E
Eikesdalsvatnet ⊜	26	62.34 N	8.11 E
Eildon	169	37.14 S	145.56 E
Eildon, Lake ⊜[1]	169	37.11 S	145.55 E
Eilean Gowan Island I	212	45.02 N	79.25 W
Eileen	216	41.17 N	88.15 W
Eilenburg	54	51.27 N	12.37 E
Eil Malk I	175b	7.09 N	134.22 E
Eilpe ◈[8]	263	51.21 N	7.29 E
Eilsleben	54	52.09 N	11.13 E
Eimbeckhausen	52	52.14 N	9.25 E
Eimke	52	52.58 N	10.19 E
Eina	26	60.38 N	10.36 E
Einasleigh	166	18.31 S	144.05 E
Einasleigh ≃	166	17.30 S	142.17 E
Einbeck	52	51.49 N	9.52 E
Eindhoven	52	51.26 N	5.28 E
Eine	50	50.52 N	3.37 E
Einme	110	16.54 N	95.11 E
Einöd	56	49.16 N	7.19 E
Einödriegel ∧	60	48.56 N	13.02 E
Einruhr	56	50.35 N	6.22 E
Einsiedel	54	50.46 N	12.58 E
Einsiedeln	58	47.08 N	8.45 E
Einville-au-Jard	58	48.39 N	6.30 E
Eirauli	272c	19.10 N	72.59 E
Éire → Ireland □[1]	48	53.00 N	8.00 W
Eiru ≃	248	6.42 S	69.52 W
Eirunepé	248	6.40 S	69.52 W
Eisbach ≃	56	49.38 N	8.22 E
Eisch ≃	56	49.45 N	6.07 E
Eiseb ≃	156	20.33 S	20.59 E
Eisenach	54	50.59 N	10.19 E
Eisenberg, B.R.D.	56	49.38 N	8.05 E
Eisenberg, D.D.R.	54	50.58 N	11.53 E
Eisenberg ∧[2]	61	47.12 N	16.24 E
Eisenerz	61	47.33 N	14.53 E
Eisenerzer Alpen ⋏	61	47.28 N	14.45 E
Eisenhower Center ♁	198	38.54 N	97.12 W
Eisenhower Memorial Park ♠	276	40.44 N	73.34 W
Eisenhüttenstadt	54	52.10 N	14.39 E
Eisenkappel	61	46.29 N	14.35 E
Eisenschmitt	56	50.03 N	6.43 E
Eisenstadt	61	47.51 N	16.32 E
Eisfeld	54	50.26 N	10.54 E
Eisgarn	61	48.54 N	15.06 E
Eishken	46	58.01 N	6.32 W
Eishort, Loch ⊂	46	57.10 N	5.59 W
Eišiškės	76	54.10 N	25.00 E
Eisk → Jejsk	78	46.42 N	38.16 E
Eisleben	54	51.31 N	11.32 E
Eislingen	56	48.42 N	9.42 E
Eisriesenwelt ≗[5]	64	47.32 N	13.10 E
Eita	174t	1.21 N	173.05 E
Eithon ≃	42	52.12 N	3.27 W
Eitorf	56	50.46 N	7.26 E
Ejasi → Eyasi, Lake ⊜	154	3.40 S	35.05 E
Ejby, Dan.	41	55.30 N	12.07 E
Ejby, Dan.	41	55.26 N	9.57 E
Ejea de los Caballeros	34	42.08 N	1.08 W
Ejeda	157b	24.20 S	44.31 E
Ejido	246	8.33 N	71.14 W
Ejigbo	273a	6.33 N	3.18 E
Ejin Horo Qi	102	39.27 N	109.40 E
Ejin Qi	102	41.50 N	100.50 E
Ejstrup	41	55.59 N	9.17 E
Ejura	150	7.23 N	1.22 W
Ejutla de Crespo	234	16.34 N	96.44 W
Ekalaka	198	45.53 N	104.33 W
Ekáli	267c	38.07 N	23.50 E
Ekanga	152	2.23 S	23.14 E
Ekas	115b	8.53 S	116.27 E
Ekaterinburg → Sverdlovsk	86	56.51 N	60.36 E
Ekaterinodar → Krasnodar	78	45.02 N	39.00 E
Ekaterinoslav → Dnepropetrovsk	78	48.27 N	34.59 E
Ekeby	41	56.00 N	12.58 E
Ekenäs (Taamisaari)	26	59.58 N	23.26 E
Ekenässjön	26	57.30 N	15.00 E
Ekerö I	40	59.18 N	17.43 E
Eket, Nig.	150	4.39 N	7.56 E
Eket, Sve.	41	56.15 N	13.11 E
Eketahuna	172	40.39 S	175.42 E
Ekhínos	38	41.17 N	24.59 E
Ekiatapskij chrebet ⋏	74	68.30 N	179.00 E
Ekibastuz	86	51.42 N	75.22 E
Ekimčan	89	53.04 N	132.58 E
Ekitykskij chrebet ⋏	180	67.45 N	179.00 E
Eko → Lagos	150	6.27 N	3.24 E
Ekoli	152	0.23 S	24.16 E
Ekoln ⊜	40	59.45 N	17.37 E
Ekolsund	40	59.37 N	17.22 E
Ekolsundsviken ⊂	40	59.35 N	17.24 E
Ekombe	152	1.16 N	21.36 E
Ekonda	74	65.47 N	105.17 E
Ekoungounou	152	0.33 S	15.38 E
Ekovamou	152	0.07 N	16.31 E
Ekpoma	150	6.46 N	6.08 E
Eksāra	272b	22.38 N	88.17 E
Eksel	56	51.09 N	5.23 E
Eksere	130	36.48 N	32.01 E
Eksjö	26	57.40 N	14.57 E
Ekuk	180	58.49 N	158.34 W
Ekuku	152	0.42 S	21.38 E
Ekuta	152	2.59 N	18.42 E
Ekwan ≃	176	53.14 N	82.13 W
Ekwata	152	0.13 S	9.18 E
Ekwendeni	154	11.23 S	33.50 E
Ekwok	180	59.22 N	157.30 W
El- → Ad-, Al-, An-, Ar-, As-, Ash-, At-, Az-			
Ela	110	19.37 N	96.13 E
El Aaiún (La'youn)	148	27.09 N	13.12 W
El Abiadh Sidi Cheikh	148	32.56 N	0.42 E
El 'Açâba □[4]	150	16.10 N	11.30 W
El 'Açâba ⋏[1]	150	16.00 N	12.00 W
El-Adde	144	2.35 N	46.09 E
El Adeb Larache	148	27.22 N	8.52 E
El Adelanto	236	14.10 N	89.50 W
El Affroun	34	36.30 N	2.38 E
El Agreb	148	30.48 N	5.30 E
El Aguacate	286c	10.28 N	66.59 W
El Aguilar	252	23.12 S	65.42 W
Elaía	38	39.35 N	20.20 E
Elaine	194	34.18 N	90.51 W
El Alamein → Al-'Alamayn	140	30.49 N	28.57 E
El Álamo, Méx.	196	27.32 N	100.52 W
El Álamo, Méx.	196	26.29 N	99.46 W
El Álamo, Méx.	204	31.34 N	116.02 W
El Alia	36	37.10 N	10.03 E
El Alto, Chile	286e	33.30 S	70.43 W
El Alto, Perú	246	4.18 S	81.07 W
Elam	285	39.51 N	75.32 W
Elamanchili	122	17.33 N	82.52 E
El Amparo de Apure	246	7.06 N	70.45 W
Elan ≃	38	46.07 N	28.04 E
Elancourt	261	48.47 N	1.58 E
Elands ≃, S. Afr.	156	25.10 S	29.10 E
Elands ≃, S. Afr.	158	25.31 S	26.39 E
Elandsbaai	158	32.19 S	18.21 E
Elandsfontein	273d	26.10 S	28.12 E
Elandsvlei	158	32.19 S	19.33 E
El Angel	246	0.37 N	77.56 W
Elanora Heights	274a	33.42 S	151.17 E
El Aouinet	36	35.52 N	7.54 E
El Arahal	34	37.16 N	5.33 W
El Arba	34	36.37 N	3.13 E
El Arco	232	28.00 N	113.25 W
El Arenal	234	20.47 N	103.42 W
El Aricha	148	34.09 N	1.10 W
El Aroussa	36	36.22 N	9.28 E
El Arrabal Torrelletas	266d	41.21 N	1.57 E
El Arrayán	286e	33.21 S	70.28 W
Elassón	38	39.54 N	22.11 E
Elat	132	29.33 N	34.57 E
Elat, Gulf of → Aqaba, Gulf of ⊂	128	29.00 N	34.40 E
Elat, Sede Te'Ufa ⊠	132	29.34 N	34.55 E
El Avagi	144	3.36 N	46.57 E
El Avila, Cerro ∧	286c	10.33 N	66.52 W
El Ávila, Parque Nacional ♠	246	10.35 N	66.48 W
El Avión	232	24.08 N	106.59 W
Elâzığ	130	38.41 N	39.14 E
Elâzığ □[4]	130	38.35 N	39.30 E
El Azúcar, Presa de ⊜[1]	196	26.10 N	99.00 W
El Azul, Sierra ⋏	234	23.25 N	100.30 W
Elba, Al., U.S.	194	31.24 N	86.04 W
Elba, Mi., U.S.	216	43.02 N	83.26 W
Elba, N.Y., U.S.	210	43.04 N	78.11 W
Elba → Elbe ≃	30	53.50 N	9.00 E
Elba, Isola d' I	66	42.46 N	10.17 E
El'ban	89	50.06 N	136.31 E
El Banco	246	9.00 N	73.58 W
El Barco de Avila	34	40.21 N	5.31 W
El Barco de Valdeorras	34	42.25 N	6.59 W
El Barreal	200	31.17 N	107.10 W
El Barril	234	23.02 N	102.08 W
El Barrio	234	16.48 N	95.15 W
Elbasan	38	41.06 N	20.05 E
Elbaşı	130	38.41 N	35.59 E
El Baúl	246	8.57 N	68.17 W
Elbe	224	46.45 N	121.49 W
Elbe (Labe) ≃	30	53.50 N	9.00 E
Elbe, Île d' → Elba, Isola di I	66	42.46 N	10.17 E
Elbe-Havel-Kanal ≋	54	52.24 N	12.23 E
El Beïd (Ebeji) ≃	146	12.32 N	14.11 E
El-Beida → Al-Bayḍā'	146	32.46 N	21.43 E
Elbe-Lübeck-Kanal ≋	54	53.50 N	10.36 E
Elberfeld ◈[8]	263	51.16 N	7.08 E
Elbert	198	39.13 N	104.32 W
Elbert, Mount ∧	200	39.07 N	106.27 W
Elberta	190	44.37 N	86.13 W
Elberton	192	34.06 N	82.52 W
Elbeuf	50	49.17 N	1.00 E
Elbeyli	130	36.41 N	37.26 E
El Beyyadh	148	33.40 N	1.01 E
Elbing → Elbląg	30	54.10 N	19.25 E
Elbingerode	54	51.45 N	10.46 E
Elbistan	130	38.13 N	37.12 E
Elbląg (Elbing)	30	54.10 N	19.25 E
Elbląg □[4]	30	54.00 N	19.30 E
El Bluff	236	11.59 N	83.40 W
El Bolsón	254	41.58 S	71.31 W
El Bonillo	34	38.57 N	2.32 W
El Bordo	246	2.06 N	76.58 W
El-Borj	34	35.43 N	5.40 W
El-Borouj	148	32.30 N	7.10 W
El Bosque	234	17.04 N	92.44 W
El Bosque, Aeropuerto ⊠	286e	33.34 S	70.42 W
El Boulaïda	148	36.28 N	2.50 E
El Boulaïda □[5]	148	36.20 N	2.20 E
Elbow	184	51.07 N	106.35 W
Elbow ≃	182	51.03 N	114.02 W
Elbow Cay I	238	23.57 N	80.29 W
Elbow Lake	198	45.59 N	95.58 W
Elbow Lake ⊜	184	54.50 N	100.53 W
Elbridge	210	43.02 N	76.27 W
El'brus, gora (Mount Elbrus) ∧	84	43.21 N	42.26 E
Elbrus, Mount → El'brus, gora ∧	84	43.21 N	42.26 E
El'brusskij	84	43.38 N	42.10 E
Elbsandsteingebirge ⋏	54	50.50 N	14.20 E
Elburg	52	52.26 N	5.50 E
El Burgo de Osma	34	41.35 N	3.04 W
Elburn	216	41.53 N	88.28 W
Elburz Mountains → Alborz, Reshteh-ye Kūhhā-ye ⋏	128	36.00 N	53.00 E
El'buzd	83	46.53 N	39.41 E
El'buzd ≃	83	46.53 N	39.43 E
El Caburé	252	26.01 S	62.22 W
El Cajon	228	32.47 N	116.57 W
El Callao	246	7.21 N	61.49 W
El Calvario	246	4.22 N	73.40 W
El Calvario ◈[8]	286b	23.05 N	82.20 W
El Calverio	246	8.59 N	67.00 W
El Campamento	240m	18.22 N	66.28 W
El Campamento ◈[8]	266a	40.24 N	3.46 W
El Campo	222	29.11 N	96.16 W
El Capitan ∧, Ca., U.S.	226	37.43 N	119.38 W
El Capitan ∧, Mt., U.S.	202	46.01 N	114.23 W
El Capomo	234	21.17 N	105.13 W
El Caribe	286c	10.37 N	66.50 W
El Carmen, Arg.	252	24.23 S	65.16 W
El Carmen, Bol.	248	18.49 S	58.33 W
El Carmen, Chile	286e	33.21 S	70.43 W
El Carmen, Col.	246	8.30 N	73.27 W
El Carmen, Méx.	234	15.35 N	93.05 W
El Carmen, Méx.	234	19.19 N	97.40 W
El Carmen, Perú	248	13.30 S	76.04 W
El Carmen, Ven.	286c	10.24 N	67.01 W
El Carmen, Ven.	286c	10.24 N	66.50 W
El Carmen, Canal ≋	286e	33.18 S	70.41 W
El Carmen de Bolívar	246	9.43 N	75.08 W
El Carricito	232	28.24 N	103.23 W
El Carril	252	25.05 S	65.28 W
El Carrizal	234	23.00 N	97.50 W
El Carrizo	232	29.58 N	105.16 W
El Casco	196	25.34 N	104.35 W
El Castillo	236	11.01 N	84.24 W
El Cedral	236	16.26 N	90.03 W
El Cedrito	232	29.11 N	101.59 W
El Cenajo, Embalse de ⊜[1]	34	38.25 N	2.00 W
El Centinela	204	32.38 N	115.40 W
El Centinela, Cerro ∧	234	19.13 N	104.17 W
El Centro	204	32.47 N	115.33 W
El Cerrito, Col.	246	3.42 N	76.19 W
El Cerrito, Ca., U.S.	226	37.54 N	122.18 W
El Cerrito, Ca., U.S.	228	37.54 N	122.18 W
El Cerro, Bol.	248	17.31 S	61.34 W
El Cerro, Ur.	258	34.00 S	58.15 W
El Cerro Del Aripo ∧	241r	10.43 N	61.15 W
El Chamal	234	23.56 N	97.54 W
El Chante	234	19.41 N	104.10 W
El Charco Largo	232	24.10 N	97.58 W
Elche	34	38.15 N	0.42 W
Elche de la Sierra	34	38.27 N	2.03 W
El Chimborazo, Cerro ∧	236	13.05 N	85.58 W
El'chkakvun ≃	180	68.42 N	171.00 E
Elcho	190	45.26 N	89.11 W
Elcho Island I	164	11.55 S	135.45 E
El Cholar	252	37.25 S	70.39 W
El Chorrillo	252	33.18 S	66.16 W
El Ciprés	204	31.50 N	116.38 W
El Coacoyul	234	17.37 N	101.26 W
El Cobre	240p	20.03 N	75.57 W
El Cocuy	246	6.25 N	72.27 W
El Cojo	286c	10.37 N	66.53 W
El Cojo, Quebrada ≃	286c	10.37 N	66.53 W
El Colorado	252	26.18 S	59.22 W
El Colorado, Canal de ≋	286e	33.34 S	70.32 W
El Cóndor, Cerro ∧	252	26.38 S	68.22 W
El Congo	236	13.54 N	89.30 W
El Consuelo	232	31.02 N	111.53 W
El Corazón	246	1.12 S	79.06 W
El Corcovado	254	43.32 S	71.36 W
El Corozo	286c	10.35 N	66.58 W
El Corpus	236	13.16 N	87.03 W
El Corte de Madera Creek ≃	282	37.19 N	122.20 W
El Cortijo	286e	33.22 S	70.42 W
El Coto	240m	18.28 N	66.44 W
El Cotorro ◈[8]	286b	23.03 N	82.16 W
El Coyote	200	30.50 N	112.40 W
El Coyote, Laguna ⊜	196	27.14 N	103.18 W
El Cozón	232	31.18 N	112.29 W
El Cristo	240p	20.07 N	75.45 W
El Cubo → Casigua	246	8.46 N	72.30 W
El Cuco	236	13.10 N	88.07 W
El Cuidado	234	22.20 N	103.07 W
El Cuy	254	39.56 S	68.20 W
Elda	34	38.29 N	0.47 W
Eldagsen	52	52.10 N	9.40 E
El Dambahaddo	144	3.17 N	46.40 E
El Dátil	232	30.07 N	112.15 W
Elde ≃	54	53.14 N	11.27 E
Eldekanal ≋	54	53.24 N	11.36 E
Eldena, D.D.R.	54	53.13 N	11.25 E
Eldena, D.D.R.	54	54.05 N	13.26 E
El Depósito	234	17.44 N	94.23 W
El Der V	144	8.49 N	47.28 E
El Dere	144	5.07 N	43.10 E
Elder Island I	276	40.38 N	73.23 W
Elder Mills	275b	43.49 N	79.38 W
Eldersville	214	40.21 N	80.29 W
Elderton	214	40.42 N	79.21 W
El Descanso	204	32.12 N	116.55 W
El Desemboque, Méx.	232	29.30 N	112.27 W
El Desemboque, Méx.	232	30.30 N	112.59 W
Eldforsen	40	60.26 N	14.13 E
El'dikan	74	60.48 N	135.11 E
Eldingen	52	52.41 N	10.21 E
Eld Inlet ⊂	224	47.04 N	123.01 W
El Diviso	246	1.22 N	78.14 W
El Djazaïr (Algiers)	148	36.47 N	3.03 E
El Djazaïr □[5]	148	36.50 N	3.00 E
El Djelfa	148	34.40 N	3.15 E
El Djelfa □[5]	148	35.20 N	3.50 E
Eldon, Ia., U.S.	190	40.55 N	92.13 W
Eldon, Mo., U.S.	194	38.20 N	92.34 W
Eldon Hazlet State Park ♠	219	38.39 N	89.22 W
Eldora, Ia., U.S.	190	42.21 N	93.05 W
Eldora, Pa., U.S.	279b	40.10 N	79.53 W
Eldorado, Arg.	252	26.24 S	54.38 W
Eldorado, Bra.	252	24.32 S	48.06 W
El Dorado, Méx.	232	24.17 N	107.21 W
El Dorado, Ar., U.S.	194	33.12 N	92.39 W
El Dorado, Ca., U.S.	226	38.41 N	120.51 W
Eldorado, Il., U.S.	194	37.48 N	88.26 W
El Dorado, Ks., U.S.	198	37.49 N	96.51 W
Eldorado, Oh., U.S.	218	39.54 N	84.40 W
Eldorado, Ok., U.S.	196	34.28 N	99.38 W
Eldorado, Tx., U.S.	196	30.51 N	100.36 W
El Dorado, Ven.	246	6.44 N	61.38 W
El Dorado □[6]	226	38.43 N	120.48 W
Eldorado Hills	226	38.37 N	120.27 W
Eldoradopark	273d	26.18 S	27.53 E
El Dorado Park ♠	280	33.49 N	118.05 W
Eldorado Peak ∧	224	48.32 N	121.08 W
El Dorado Springs	194	37.52 N	94.01 W
Eldoret	154	0.31 N	35.17 E
Eldred, Il., U.S.	219	39.17 N	90.33 W
Eldred, N.Y., U.S.	210	41.32 N	74.53 W
Eldred, Pa., U.S.	214	41.57 N	78.23 W
Eldridge	190	41.39 N	90.35 W
Eldridge, Mount ∧	180	64.46 N	141.48 W
Eldridges Hill	285	39.40 N	75.18 W
El Dudu	144	2.37 N	41.46 E
Eleanor	188	38.32 N	81.55 W
Eleanor, Lake ⊜[1]	226	37.59 N	119.51 W
Eleasar	158	26.40 S	26.53 E
Electra	196	34.01 N	98.55 W
Electric City	202	47.56 N	119.02 W
Eleele	229b	21.55 N	159.35 W
Elefante, Isla del → Elephant Island I	9	61.10 S	55.14 W
Elefantes, Fiordo ⊂[2]	254	46.10 S	73.41 W
Elefantes, Rio dos (Olifants) ≃	156	24.10 S	32.40 E
Elegest ≃	88	51.32 N	94.05 E
El Eglab ◈[2]	148	26.25 N	5.00 W
Elei, Wādī V	140	22.04 N	34.27 E
Eleja	76	56.26 N	23.42 E
Elektrogorsk	82	55.53 N	38.47 E
Elektrostal'	82	55.47 N	38.28 E
Elektrougli	82	55.43 N	38.13 E
Elektrozavod	80	52.34 N	54.01 E
Elele	150	5.07 N	6.48 E
Elemi	130	41.04 N	35.30 E
Elena	38	42.56 N	25.53 E
El Encantado	286c	10.27 N	66.47 W
El Encanto, Col.	246	1.37 S	73.14 W
El Encanto, Guat.	232	17.17 N	89.34 W
Elend	54	51.44 N	10.41 E
Elepete	273a	6.41 N	3.28 E
Elephant, Mount ∧[2]	169	37.58 S	143.12 E
Elephanta Caves ≗[5]	272c	18.58 N	72.56 E
Elephanta Island (Ghārāpuri) I	272c	18.57 N	72.55 E
Elephant Butte Lake State Park ♠	200	33.11 N	107.14 W
Elephant Butte Reservoir ⊜[1]	200	33.19 N	107.10 W
Elephant Island I	9	61.10 S	55.14 W
Elephant Lake ⊜	212	45.08 N	78.07 W
Elephant Mountain ∧	188	44.46 N	70.46 W
Elesbão Veloso	250	6.13 S	42.08 W
Eleşkirt	130	39.48 N	42.42 E
El Éstor	236	15.32 N	89.21 W
El Estribo	234	22.26 N	99.17 W
Elets → Jelec	76	52.37 N	38.30 E
El Eulma	148	36.08 N	5.40 E
Eleusis → Elevsís	38	38.02 N	23.32 E
Eleutério	256	22.19 S	46.43 W
Eleutero ≃	70	38.06 N	13.29 E
Eleuthera I	238	25.10 N	76.14 W
Eleuthera Point ›	238	24.40 N	76.11 W
Eleva	190	44.34 N	91.28 W
Eleven Point ≃	194	36.09 N	91.05 W
Elevsínos, Kólpos ⊂	267c	38.02 N	23.34 E
Elevsís	38	38.02 N	23.32 E
Elevtheroúpolis	38	40.55 N	24.16 E
El Fahs	36	36.22 N	9.55 E
El Faro, It.	71	40.36 N	8.13 E
El Faro, P.R.	240m	18.00 N	66.47 W
Elfenbeinküste → Ivory Coast □[1]	150	8.00 N	5.00 W
El Ferrol del Caudillo	34	43.29 N	8.14 W
Elfers	220	28.13 N	82.43 W
Elfgen	263	51.05 N	6.32 E
Elfin Cove	180	58.12 N	136.20 W
Elfrida	200	31.41 N	109.41 W
Elfros	184	51.43 N	103.52 W
El Fud	144	7.20 N	42.50 E
El Fuerte	232	26.25 N	108.39 W
El Galpón	252	25.23 S	64.38 W
Elgershausen	56	51.16 N	9.22 E
El Ghazawet	148	35.06 N	1.51 W
Elgin, Austl.	168a	33.31 S	115.37 E
Elgin, On., Can.	212	44.36 N	76.13 W
Elgin, Scot., U.K.	46	57.39 N	3.20 W
Elgin, Il., U.S.	216	42.02 N	88.16 W
Elgin, Ia., U.S.	190	42.57 N	91.37 W
Elgin, Mn., U.S.	190	44.07 N	92.15 W
Elgin, Ne., U.S.	198	41.59 N	98.05 W
Elgin, N.D., U.S.	198	46.24 N	101.50 W
Elgin, Oh., U.S.	216	40.44 N	84.28 W
Elgin, Ok., U.S.	196	34.46 N	98.17 W
Elgin, Or., U.S.	202	45.33 N	117.54 W
Elgin, Pa., U.S.	214	41.54 N	79.45 W
Elgin, Tx., U.S.	222	30.20 N	97.22 W
Elgin □[6]	214	42.42 N	81.15 W
Elgin, Lake ⊜	206	45.45 N	71.20 W
El Gogorrón, Parque Nacional ♠	234	21.48 N	100.48 W
Elgol	46	57.09 N	6.06 W
El Golfete ⊜	236	15.44 N	88.53 W
El Golfo de Santa Clara	232	31.42 N	114.30 W
El Goloso ◈[8]	266a	40.33 N	3.42 W
Elgon, Mount ∧	154	1.08 N	34.33 E
Elgoras, gora ∧	24	68.06 N	31.30 E
El Granada	226	37.30 N	122.28 W
El Grara	148	32.46 N	4.34 E
El Grove	34	42.30 N	8.52 W
El Grullo	234	19.48 N	104.13 W
El Guaje	232	27.52 N	103.18 W
El Guamo	246	10.02 N	74.59 W
El Guanábano	286c	10.24 N	67.01 W
El Guapo	246	10.09 N	65.58 W
El Guarapo	286c	10.36 N	66.58 W
El Guayabo	246	8.37 N	72.20 W
El'gygytgyn, ozero ⊜	180	67.30 N	172.00 E
El Hadjar	36	36.48 N	7.45 E
Elham	42	51.10 N	1.07 E
El Ḥammâmi ◈[1]	148	23.03 N	11.30 W
El Hank ≗[4]	148	24.30 N	7.00 W
El Haouaria	36	37.03 N	11.02 E
El Hatillo	286c	10.26 N	66.49 W
El Hatillo, Quebrada ≃	286c	10.27 N	66.47 W
El Havre → Le Havre	50	49.30 N	0.08 E
El Higo	234	21.46 N	98.28 W
Elhovo	38	42.10 N	26.34 E
El Huecú	252	37.37 S	70.36 W
Eliase	164	8.21 S	130.47 E
Elías Piña	238	18.53 N	71.42 W
Elías Romero	258	34.46 S	58.52 W
Eliasville	196	32.57 N	98.46 W
Elida, N.M., U.S.	196	33.56 N	103.39 W
Elida, Oh., U.S.	216	40.47 N	84.12 W
El Idrissia	148	34.30 N	2.37 E
Elila	154	2.43 S	25.53 E
Elila ≃	154	2.45 S	25.53 E
Elim, Namibia	156	17.48 S	15.31 E
Elim, S. Afr.	158	34.35 S	19.45 E
Elim, Ak., U.S.	180	64.37 N	162.15 W
Elimsport	210	41.08 N	77.02 W
Elingampangu	152	2.03 S	24.02 E
Elin Pelin	38	42.40 N	23.36 E
Eliot	188	43.09 N	70.48 W
Elipa	152	0.53 S	24.34 E
Elisabeth-Sophien-Koog	41	54.30 N	8.53 E
Élisabethville	261	48.58 N	1.51 E
Élisabethville → Lubumbashi	154	11.40 S	27.28 E
Elisenvaara	24	61.25 N	29.46 E
Eliseu Martins	250	8.13 S	43.42 W
Elista	80	46.16 N	44.14 E
Elizabeth, Austl.	168b	34.43 S	138.40 E
Elizabeth, Co., U.S.	200	39.21 N	104.35 W
Elizabeth, Il., U.S.	190	42.19 N	90.13 W
Elizabeth, La., U.S.	194	30.52 N	92.47 W
Elizabeth, N.J., U.S.	210	40.39 N	74.12 W
Elizabeth, Pa., U.S.	214	40.16 N	79.53 W
Elizabeth, W.V., U.S.	188	39.03 N	81.23 W
Elizabeth ≃, N.J., U.S.	276	40.38 N	74.12 W
Elizabeth ≃, Va., U.S.	208	36.54 N	76.20 W
Elizabeth, Cape ›	224	47.22 N	124.22 W
Elizabeth, Lake ⊜[1]	282	37.33 N	121.58 W
Elizabeth, West Branch ≃	276	40.42 N	74.14 W
Elizabeth Bay ⊂	156	27.04 S	15.11 E
Elizabeth City	192	36.18 N	76.13 W
Elizabeth Creek ≃	222	33.02 N	97.14 W
Elizabeth Islands II	207	41.27 N	70.47 W
Elizabeth Lake ⊜	281	42.38 N	83.23 W
Elizabeth Lake Estates	281	42.38 N	83.22 W
Elizabeth Park ♠	281	42.07 N	83.11 W
Elizabeth Reef I[1]	160	29.56 S	159.04 E
Elizabethton	192	36.20 N	82.12 W
Elizabethtown, Il., U.S.	194	37.26 N	88.18 W
Elizabethtown, In., U.S.	218	39.08 N	85.48 W
Elizabethtown, Ky., U.S.	194	37.41 N	85.51 W
Elizabethtown, N.Y., U.S.	188	44.12 N	73.35 W
Elizabethtown, N.C., U.S.	192	34.37 N	78.36 W
Elizabethtown, Pa., U.S.	208	40.09 N	76.36 W
Elizabethville	208	40.32 N	76.48 W
Eliza Howell Park ♠	281	42.24 N	83.16 W
Elizaville, In., U.S.	218	40.08 N	86.24 W
Elizaville, N.Y., U.S.	210	42.03 N	73.48 W
El-Jadida (Mazagan)	148	33.16 N	8.30 W
El-Jadida □[4]	148	33.00 N	8.40 W
El Jaralito	232	26.07 N	104.10 W
El Jebel	200	39.23 N	107.05 W
El-Jebha	34	35.13 N	4.38 W
El Jem	148	35.18 N	10.43 E
El Jícaro	236	13.43 N	86.08 W
El Jícaro ≃	236	13.31 N	86.00 W
El Jobean	220	26.58 N	82.13 W
Ełk	30	53.50 N	22.22 E
Elk □[6]	214	41.26 N	78.43 W
Elk ≃, Ab., Can.	182	52.55 N	115.40 W
Elk ≃, B.C., Can.	182	49.10 N	115.14 W
Ełk ≃, Pol.	30	53.31 N	22.47 E
Elk ≃, U.S.	194	34.46 N	87.16 W
Elk ≃, Co., U.S.	200	40.29 N	106.58 W
Elk ≃, Ks., U.S.	198	37.15 N	95.41 W
Elk ≃, Mn., U.S.	190	45.18 N	93.34 W
Elk ≃, Mo., U.S.	194	36.38 N	94.38 W
Elk ≃, W.V., U.S.	188	38.21 N	81.38 W
Elk ≃, Wi., U.S.	190	45.42 N	90.37 W
Elkader	190	42.51 N	91.24 W
El Kantara	148	33.41 N	10.55 E
El-Karafab	140	18.10 N	31.36 E
Elk Bayou ≃	226	36.06 N	119.24 W
Elk City	196	35.24 N	99.24 W
Elk City Lake ⊜[1]	198	37.15 N	95.55 W
Elk Creek	204	39.36 N	122.32 W
Elk Creek ≃, Ok., U.S.	196	34.48 N	99.09 W
Elk Creek ≃, Or., U.S.	202	43.38 N	123.34 W
Elk Creek ≃, Pa., U.S.	214	42.01 N	80.22 W
Elk Creek ≃, S.D., U.S.	198	44.15 N	102.22 W
Elk Creek ≃, Wa., U.S.	224	46.38 N	123.17 W
Elkedra ≃	162	21.08 S	136.22 E
El Kef	148	36.11 N	8.43 E
El Kef □[8]	148	36.00 N	9.00 E
El-Kelâa-Des-Srarhna	148	32.02 N	7.23 W
El-Kelâa-Des-Srarhna □[4]	148	32.05 N	7.30 W
El Kere	144	5.51 N	42.06 E
El Kerma	34	35.36 N	0.35 W
Elk Grove	226	38.24 N	121.22 W
Elk Grove Village	278	42.00 N	87.58 W
Elkhart, Il., U.S.	219	40.01 N	89.29 W
Elkhart, In., U.S.	216	41.40 N	85.58 W
Elkhart, Ks., U.S.	198	37.00 N	101.53 W
Elkhart, Tx., U.S.	222	31.38 N	95.35 W
Elkhart □[6]	216	41.35 N	85.50 W
Elkhart ≃	216	41.41 N	85.58 W
Elkhart Lake	190	43.50 N	88.01 W
El Khaṭṭ ≗[4]	148	22.40 N	10.05 W
Elkhead Creek ≃	200	40.31 N	107.26 W
Elkhead Mountains ⋏	200	40.50 N	107.05 W
Elk Hills ⋏[2]	226	35.15 N	119.25 W
El Khnâchîch ≗[4]	148	21.50 N	3.45 W
Elkhorn, Mb., Can.	184	49.58 N	101.14 W
Elk Horn, Ia., U.S.	198	41.35 N	95.03 W
Elkhorn, Wi., U.S.	216	42.40 N	88.32 W
Elkhorn ≃	198	41.07 N	96.19 W
Elkhorn City	192	37.18 N	82.21 W
Elkhorn Creek ≃, Ky., U.S.	218	38.19 N	84.52 W
Elkhorn Creek ≃, Mo., U.S.	219	39.05 N	91.20 W
Elkhorn Mountain ∧	182	49.48 N	125.50 W
Elki	128	37.34 N	43.10 E
Elkin	192	36.14 N	80.50 W
Elkins	188	38.55 N	79.50 W
Elkins Park	208	40.04 N	75.07 W
Elk Island I	184	50.45 N	96.32 W
Elk Island National Park ♠	182	53.37 N	112.45 W
Elkland	210	41.59 N	77.18 W
Elk Mills	208	39.39 N	75.49 W
Elk Mountain	200	41.41 N	106.24 W
Elk Mountain ∧, Wa., U.S.	224	46.08 N	122.28 W
Elk Mountain ∧, Wy., U.S.	200	41.38 N	106.32 W

Symbols in the index entries represent the broad categories identified in the key at the right. Symbols with superior numbers (⋏[1]) identify subcategories (see complete key on page *I · 1)*.

Kartensymbole in dem Registerverzeichnis stellen die rechts in Schlüssel erklärten Kategorien dar. Symbole mit hochgestellten Ziffern (⋏[1]) bezeichnen Unterabteilungen einer Kategorie (vgl. vollständiger Schlüssel auf Seite *I · 1)*.

Los símbolos incluídos en el texto del índice representan las grandes categorias identificadas con la clave a la derecha. Los símbolos con numeros en su parte superior (⋏[1]) identifican las subcategorías (véase la clave completa en la página *I · 1)*.

Les symboles de l'index représentent les catégories indiquées dans la légende à droite. Les symboles suivis d'un indice (⋏[1]) représentent des sous-catégories (voir légende complète à la page *I · 1)*.

Os símbolos incluídos no texto do índice representam as grandes categorias identificadas com a chave à direita. Os símbolos com números em sua parte superior (⋏[1]) identificam as subcategorias (veja-se a chave completa à página *I · 1)*.

∧ Mountain	Berg	Montaña	Montagne	Montanha
⋏ Mountains	Berge	Montañas	Montagnes	Montanhas
)(Pass	Pass	Paso	Col	Passo
V Valley, Canyon	Tal, Cañon	Valle, Cañón	Vallée, Canyon	Vale, Canhão
≚ Plain	Ebene	Llano	Plaine	Planície
› Cape	Kap	Cabo	Cap	Cabo
I Island	Insel	Isla	Île	Ilha
II Islands	Inseln	Islas	Îles	Ilhas
≗ Other Topographic Features	Andere Topographische Objekte	Otros Elementos Topográficos	Autres données topographiques	Outros acidentes topográficos

ESPAÑOL / FRANÇAIS / PORTUGUÊS

Nombre / Nom / Nome	Página / Page / Página	Lat.°′	Long.°′ W = Oeste / W = Ouest / W = Oeste
Elk Neck ≻[1]	208	39.35 N	75.55 W
Elk Neck State Park ♦	208	39.30 N	75.58 W
Elko, B.C., Can.	182	49.18 N	115.07 W
Elko, Nv., U.S.	204	40.49 N	115.45 W
El Kouif	36	35.29 N	8.19 E
Elk Peak ∧	202	46.27 N	110.46 W
Elk Plain	224	47.04 N	122.24 W
Elk Point, Ab., Can.	182	53.54 N	110.54 W
Elk Point, S.D., U.S.	198	42.41 N	96.41 W
Elk Rapids	190	44.53 N	85.24 W
El Krib	36	36.19 N	9.09 E
Elkridge	284b	39.12 N	76.42 W
Elk River, Id., U.S.	202	46.47 N	116.10 W
Elk River, Mn., U.S.	190	45.18 N	93.35 W
Elk River c	208	39.31 N	75.55 W
El Kseur	34	36.46 N	4.49 E
Elk State Park ♦	214	41.38 N	78.34 W
Elkton, Ky., U.S.	194	36.48 N	87.09 W
Elkton, Md., U.S.	208	39.36 N	75.50 W
Elkton, Mi., U.S.	190	43.49 N	83.10 W
Elkton, Oh., U.S.	214	40.46 N	80.42 W
Elkton, S.D., U.S.	198	44.14 N	96.28 W
Elkton, Va., U.S.	188	38.24 N	78.37 W
El Kure	144	5.41 N	42.21 E
Elkville	194	37.54 N	89.14 W
Ell, Lake ◎	162	29.13 S	127.46 E
Ellamar	180	60.54 N	146.42 W
Elland	262	53.41 N	1.50 W
Ellard Lake ◎	184	54.33 N	91.55 W
Ellás → Greece □[1]	38	39.00 N	22.00 E
Ellavalla	162	25.05 S	114.22 E
Ellaville	192	32.14 N	84.18 W
Ellefeld	54	50.29 N	12.23 E
Ellef Ringnes Island I	16	78.30 N	104.00 W
El Leh	144	3.48 N	39.48 E
Elleker	162	35.00 S	117.43 E
Ellemandsbjerg ∧[2]	41	56.07 N	10.32 E
Ellen ≃	44	54.43 N	3.30 W
Ellen, Mount ∧	200	38.07 N	110.49 W
Ellen Brook ≃	168a	31.48 S	116.00 E
Ellendale, Austl.	162	17.56 S	124.48 E
Ellendale, De., U.S.	208	38.48 N	75.25 W
Ellendale, Mn., U.S.	190	43.52 N	93.18 W
Ellendale, N.D., U.S.	198	46.00 N	98.31 W
Ellensburg	202	46.59 N	120.32 W
Ellenton, Fl., U.S.	220	27.31 N	82.31 W
Ellenton, Ga., U.S.	192	31.10 N	83.35 W
Ellenville	210	41.43 N	74.23 W
Eller ◆[8]	263	51.12 N	6.51 E
Ellerbe	192	35.04 N	79.46 W
Ellero ≃	62	44.27 N	7.54 E
Ellerspring ∧[2]	56	49.55 N	7.37 E
Ellès	36	35.57 N	9.06 E
Ellesmere	42	52.54 N	2.54 W
Ellesmere, Lake c	172	43.48 S	172.25 E
Ellesmere Island I	16	81.00 N	80.00 W
Ellesmere Park	262	53.29 N	2.20 W
Ellesmere Port	262	53.17 N	2.54 W
Ellesmere Port □[8]	262	53.18 N	2.47 W
Ellettsville	194	39.14 N	86.37 W
Ellewoutsdijk	52	51.24 N	3.49 E
Ellezelles	50	50.44 N	3.41 E
Ellice ≃	176	68.02 N	103.26 W
Ellice Islands → Tuvalu □[1]	14	8.00 S	178.00 E
Ellichpur → Achalpur	120	21.16 N	77.31 E
Ellicott City	208	39.16 N	76.47 W
Ellicott Creek ≃	210	43.01 N	78.53 W
Ellicott Creek Park ♦	284a	43.01 N	78.50 W
Ellicottville	210	42.16 N	78.40 W
Ellijay	192	34.41 N	84.28 W
El Limón, Méx.	234	18.05 N	101.59 W
El Limón, Méx.	234	19.49 N	104.11 W
El Limoncito	286c	10.29 N	66.47 W
El Limón de Talleaché	232	24.16 N	107.04 W
Ellingen	56	49.04 N	10.58 E
Ellinger	222	29.50 N	96.44 W
Ellinghorst ◆[8]	263	51.34 N	6.57 E
Ellington, Eng., U.K.	44	55.13 N	1.34 W
Ellington, Ct., U.S.	207	41.54 N	72.28 W
Ellington, Mo., U.S.	194	37.14 N	90.58 W
Ellington, N.Y., U.S.	214	42.13 N	79.07 W
Ellinikón	267c	37.53 N	23.44 E
Ellinikón, Aerolimín ⊠	267c	37.54 N	23.44 E
Ellinwood	198	38.21 N	98.34 W
Elliot	158	31.18 S	27.50 E
Elliot, Mount ∧	166	19.29 S	146.58 E
Elliotdale	158	31.55 S	28.38 E
Elliotganj	126	23.31 N	90.52 E
Elliot Lake	190	46.23 N	82.39 W
Elliot Lake ◎	184	52.55 N	95.20 W
Elliott, Austl.	162	17.33 S	133.32 E
Elliott, Il., U.S.	216	40.28 N	88.16 W
Elliott, Ia., U.S.	198	41.09 N	95.10 W
Elliott, Ms., U.S.	194	33.36 N	89.45 W
Elliott □[6]	218	38.13 N	83.10 W
Elliott, Mount ∧	162	20.29 S	126.37 E
Elliott Bay c	224	47.36 N	122.22 W
Elliott Key I	220	25.27 N	80.11 W
Elliottville	218	38.11 N	83.16 W
Ellis	198	38.56 N	99.33 W
Ellis □[6]	222	32.20 N	96.48 W
Ellisburg	212	43.44 N	76.08 W
Ellis Island I	276	40.42 N	74.02 W
Ellis Mountain ∧	224	48.10 N	124.19 W
Ellison Creek Reservoir ◎[1]	222	32.56 N	94.43 W
Ellisport	224	47.25 N	122.26 W
Ellisras	156	23.40 S	27.46 E
Elliston, Austl.	162	33.39 S	134.55 E
Elliston, Nf., Can.	186	48.38 N	53.03 W
Elliston, Mt., U.S.	202	46.33 N	112.25 W
Ellisville, Ms., U.S.	194	31.36 N	89.11 W
Ellisville, Mo., U.S.	219	38.35 N	90.35 W
Ellmau	64	47.31 N	12.18 E
Ellmauer Halt ∧	64	47.34 N	12.18 E
Ellon	46	57.22 N	2.05 W
Ellora	122	20.01 N	75.10 E
Ellore → Elūru	122	16.42 N	81.06 E
Elloree	192	33.31 N	80.34 W
Ellport	214	40.51 N	80.15 W
Ellrich	54	51.35 N	10.40 E
Ellsworth, Il., U.S.	216	40.27 N	88.43 W
Ellsworth, Ks., U.S.	198	38.43 N	98.13 W
Ellsworth, Me., U.S.	188	44.32 N	68.25 W
Ellsworth, Mi., U.S.	190	45.09 N	85.14 W
Ellsworth, Mn., U.S.	198	43.31 N	96.01 W
Ellsworth, Oh., U.S.	214	41.01 N	80.52 W
Ellsworth, Pa., U.S.	214	40.06 N	80.01 W
Ellsworth, Wa., U.S.	224	45.37 N	122.36 W
Ellsworth, Wi., U.S.	190	44.43 N	92.29 W
Ellsworth Air Force Base ■	198	44.08 N	103.05 W
Ellsworth Land ◆[1]	9	75.30 S	80.00 W
Ellsworth Mountains ⩓	9	79.00 S	85.00 W
El Lucero	196	25.53 N	103.25 W
Ellwangen	56	48.57 N	10.07 E
Ellwanger Berge ⩓[2]	56	49.00 N	10.15 E
Ellwood City	214	40.51 N	80.17 W
Elm, B.R.D.	52	53.31 N	9.12 E
Elm, Schw.	58	46.55 N	9.11 E
Elm, Eng., U.K.	42	52.38 N	0.10 E
Elm ∧	64	47.40 N	13.57 E
Elm ⩓[2]	54	52.09 N	10.53 E
Elm ≃, U.S.	198	45.36 N	98.19 W
Elm ≃, Il., U.S.	194	38.24 N	88.14 W
Elm ≃, N.D., U.S.	198	47.15 N	96.50 W
Elma, Ia., U.S.	190	43.14 N	92.26 W
Elma, N.Y., U.S.	210	42.51 N	78.38 W
Elma, Wa., U.S.	224	47.00 N	123.24 W
El Macero	226	38.33 N	121.41 W
El Machorro, Punta ≻	200	31.03 N	114.51 W
Elmadağ (Küçükyozgat)	130	39.55 N	33.15 E
Elma Dağı ∧	130	39.49 N	33.00 E
El Mahia ◆[1]	148	22.30 N	2.30 W
El Maitén	254	42.03 S	71.10 W
El Malah	34	35.24 N	1.05 W
Elmalı	130	36.44 N	29.56 E
El Manchón	236	14.23 N	92.02 W
El Maneadero	232	31.45 N	116.35 W
El Manteco	246	7.27 N	62.32 W
El Marsa el Kebir	148	35.45 N	0.43 W
Elmas	71	39.16 N	9.03 E
Elmas, Aeroporto di ⊠	71	39.14 N	9.03 E
Elmas Burnu ≻	267b	41.13 N	29.13 E
Elmaton	222	28.53 N	96.09 W
El Mayoco	254	42.39 S	70.59 W
Elmbridge □[8]	260	51.22 N	0.23 W
Elm Brook ≃	283	42.29 N	71.16 W
Elm City	192	35.48 N	77.51 W
Elm Creek, Mb., Can.	184	49.41 N	98.00 W
Elm Creek, Ne., U.S.	198	40.43 N	99.22 W
Elm Creek ≃, Mn., U.S.	198	43.45 N	94.11 W
Elm Creek ≃, S.D., U.S.	198	44.21 N	102.42 W
Elm Creek ≃, Tx., U.S.	196	32.40 N	99.41 W
Elm Creek ≃, Tx., U.S.	196	33.12 N	98.50 W
Elm Creek ≃, Tx., U.S.	196	28.54 N	100.12 W
Elm Creek ≃, Tx., U.S.	222	29.15 N	97.32 W
El Meco	234	22.35 N	99.20 W
El Médano	232	24.25 N	111.30 W
El Melón, Sierra ⩓	234	23.56 N	99.39 W
Elmen	58	47.20 N	10.32 E
El Menia	148	30.30 N	2.50 E
Elmer	208	39.35 N	75.10 W
El Mghayyar	148	33.55 N	5.58 E
Elm Grove	216	43.02 N	88.04 W
Elmhurst, Austl.	169	37.11 S	143.15 E
Elmhurst, Il., U.S.	216	41.53 N	87.56 W
Elmhurst, Pa., U.S.	210	41.22 N	75.32 W
Elmhurst ◆[8]	276	40.44 N	73.53 W
El Mijao	286c	10.23 N	66.48 W
El Milagro	252	31.01 S	65.59 W
El Miliyya	148	36.48 N	6.14 E
El Mimbre	196	25.40 N	102.20 W
Elmina	150	5.05 N	1.21 W
El Minao	240m	18.22 N	66.05 W
Elmira, On., Can.	212	43.36 N	80.33 W
Elmira, P.E., Can.	186	46.27 N	62.04 W
Elmira, Ca., U.S.	226	38.21 N	121.55 W
Elmira, N.Y., U.S.	210	42.05 N	76.48 W
El Mirage	200	33.36 N	112.19 W
El Mirage Lake ◎	228	34.38 N	117.35 W
Elmira Heights	210	42.07 N	76.49 W
Elm Mott	222	31.40 N	97.06 W
Elmo, Mt., U.S.	182	47.49 N	114.20 W
Elmo, Tx., U.S.	222	32.43 N	96.10 W
El Mohammadia	148	35.33 N	0.03 E
El Molinillo	34	39.28 N	4.13 W
El Molinito	286a	19.27 N	99.15 W
Elmont, N.Y., U.S.	276	40.42 N	73.42 W
Elmont, Va., U.S.	208	37.42 N	77.29 W
El Monte, Chile	252	33.41 S	71.01 W
El Monte, Ca., U.S.	228	34.04 N	118.01 W
El Monte Airport ⊠	280	34.06 N	118.02 W
Elmora	214	40.36 N	78.45 W
El Moral	196	28.51 N	100.39 W
Elmore, Austl.	166	36.30 S	144.37 E
Elmore, Mn., U.S.	190	43.30 N	94.05 W
Elmore, Oh., U.S.	214	41.28 N	83.17 W
Elmore City	196	34.37 N	97.23 W
El Morro ⊥	240m	18.28 N	66.07 W
El Morro National Monument ♦	200	35.05 N	108.22 W
Elm Point ≻	276	40.49 N	73.46 W
Elmpt	56	51.13 N	6.10 E
El Mreiti ⊤[4]	148	23.29 N	7.52 W
El Mreyyé ◆[1]	150	19.30 N	7.00 W
Elmschenhagen ◆[8]	54	54.18 N	10.12 E
Elmsdale	186	44.58 N	63.30 W
Elmsford	210	41.03 N	73.49 W
Elmshorn	52	53.45 N	9.39 E
Elm Springs	194	36.12 N	94.14 W
Elmsta	26	59.58 N	18.48 E
Elmstein	56	49.21 N	7.56 E
Elmswell	42	52.15 N	0.53 E
El Mulato	196	29.22 N	104.10 W
Elmvale	212	44.35 N	79.52 W
Elmville	218	38.20 N	84.46 W
Elmwood, On., Can.	212	44.14 N	81.03 W
Elmwood, Il., U.S.	190	40.46 N	89.57 W
Elmwood, Md., U.S.	284b	39.21 N	76.32 W
Elmwood, Ma., U.S.	283	42.00 N	70.57 W
Elmwood, Ne., U.S.	198	40.50 N	96.17 W
Elmwood, Wi., U.S.	190	44.46 N	92.08 W
Elmwood ◆[8]	285	39.56 N	75.14 W
Elmwood Park, Il., U.S.	216	41.55 N	87.48 W
Elmwood Park, N.J., U.S.	276	40.54 N	74.07 W
Elmwood Park, Wi., U.S.	216	42.41 N	87.50 W
Elmwood Park ♦	285	40.08 N	75.21 W
El Naranjo, Arg.	252	25.44 S	64.59 W
El Naranjo, Méx.	234	22.30 N	98.38 W
Elne	32	42.36 N	2.58 E
El Negralejo	266a	40.24 N	3.31 W
El Negrito	236	15.16 N	87.41 W
El Nevado, Cerro ∧	252	35.35 S	68.30 W
El Nido, Pil.	116	11.11 N	119.23 E
El Nido, Ca., U.S.	226	37.08 N	120.29 W
El Nihuil	252	35.02 S	68.40 W
El Niybo	144	4.32 N	39.59 E
Elnora, Ab., Can.	182	51.59 N	113.12 W
Elnora, In., U.S.	194	38.52 N	87.05 W
El Oasis	286c	10.35 N	66.59 W
El-Obeid → Al-Ubayyiḍ	140	13.11 N	30.13 E
Elobey, Islas II	152	0.59 N	9.30 E
Elogbatindi	152	3.27 N	10.08 E
Eloida, Lake ◎	212	44.40 N	75.58 W
Elói Mendes	256	21.37 S	45.34 W
Eloise	220	27.59 N	81.44 W
Elora, On., Can.	212	43.41 N	80.26 W
Elora, Tn., U.S.	194	35.00 N	86.21 W
El Oro □[4]	246	3.30 S	79.50 W
Elortondo	252	33.42 S	61.37 W
Elorza	246	7.03 N	69.31 W
El Oso	246	4.59 N	65.25 W
El Otro Lado	286c	10.24 N	66.49 W
Eloy	200	32.45 N	111.33 W
Éloyes	58	48.06 N	6.37 E
El Pacayal	232	15.37 N	92.02 W
El Palmar, Bol.	248	21.54 S	63.39 W
El Palmar, Ven.	246	7.58 N	61.53 W
El Palmar, Ven.	286c	10.38 N	66.52 W
El Palomar	288	34.36 S	58.36 W
El Palomar, Base Aérea Militar ■	288	34.37 S	58.37 W
El Palqui	252	30.45 S	70.59 W
El Pantanoso, Arroyo ≃	288	34.47 S	58.40 W
El Pao, Ven.	246	8.01 N	62.38 W
El Pao, Ven.	246	9.38 N	68.08 W
El Paradero	246	10.38 N	69.32 W
El Paraíso, Hond.	236	13.51 N	86.34 W
El Paraíso, Méx.	234	17.25 N	100.15 W
El Paraíso □[5]	236	14.10 N	86.30 W
El Pardo ◆[8]	266a	40.31 N	3.47 W
El Pardo, Embalse de ◎[1]	266a	40.33 N	3.48 W
El Pardo, Monte de ⩓[2]	266a	40.33 N	3.48 W
El Paso, Il., U.S.	216	40.44 N	89.00 W
El Paso, Tx., U.S.	200	31.45 N	106.29 W
El Paso Creek ≃	228	35.02 N	118.51 W
El Paso de Robles → Paso Robles	226	35.38 N	120.41 W
El Paso Peaks ⩓	204	35.28 N	117.43 W
El Pato	246	2.50 N	74.48 W
El Paují	286c	10.26 N	66.49 W
El Pedregal ◆[8]	286c	10.30 N	66.51 W
El Peñuelo	232	24.34 N	100.46 W
El Peral	286e	33.35 S	70.34 W
El Perú	246	7.19 N	61.49 W
El Pescado, Arroyo ≃	258	34.54 S	57.47 W
Elphin	48	53.51 N	8.12 W
Elphinstone	184	50.33 N	100.19 W
El Picacho, Cerro ∧	234	20.40 N	100.43 W
El Pilar	246	10.32 N	63.09 W
El Pinar, Parque Nacional ♦	286c	10.29 N	66.56 W
El Piñón	246	10.24 N	74.50 W
El Pintado	252	24.38 S	61.27 W
El Piojo, Arroyo ≃	288	34.50 S	58.45 W
El Piquete	252	24.13 S	64.39 W
El Placer	234	23.33 N	106.10 W
El Plantío ◆[8]	266a	40.28 N	3.49 W
El Platanillo	234	18.28 N	101.52 W
El Plomo	200	31.15 N	112.04 W
El Polvorín	240m	18.26 N	66.17 W
El Porcal	266a	40.18 N	3.32 W
El Portal, Ca., U.S.	226	37.40 N	119.46 W
El Portal, Fl., U.S.	220	25.51 N	80.11 W
El Porvenir, Méx.	196	27.33 N	104.57 W
El Porvenir, Méx.	204	32.05 N	116.38 W
El Porvenir, Méx.	232	31.15 N	105.51 W
El Porvenir, Méx.	234	15.44 N	93.22 W
El Potosí	232	24.51 N	100.19 W
El Potosí, Parque Nacional ♦	234	22.00 N	99.58 W
El Potrero	196	26.23 N	100.27 W
El Potro, Cerro ∧	252	28.24 S	69.39 W
El Progreso, Ec.	246a	0.54 S	89.33 W
El Progreso, Guat.	236	14.51 N	90.04 W
El Progreso, Guat.	236	14.21 N	89.51 W
El Progreso, Hond.	236	15.21 N	87.49 W
El Progreso □[5]	236	14.50 N	90.00 W
El Puente del Arzobispo	34	39.48 N	5.10 W
El Puerto de Santa María	34	36.36 N	6.13 W
El Puesto	252	27.57 S	67.38 W
El Qala	148	36.50 N	8.30 E
El Qoll	148	37.00 N	6.34 E
El Quebrachal	252	25.17 S	64.04 W
El Quelite	234	23.32 N	106.28 W
Elquera Bushland ♦	274a	33.42 S	150.04 E
Elqui ≃	252	29.54 S	71.17 W
Elrama	214	40.15 N	79.55 W
El Ranchito	234	18.40 N	103.41 W
El Rastro	246	9.03 N	67.27 W
El Real de Santa María	246	8.08 N	77.43 W
El Recreo ◆[8]	286c	10.30 N	66.53 W
El Remolino, Méx.	196	28.44 N	101.07 W
El Remolino, Méx.	234	17.39 N	94.13 W
El Reno	196	35.31 N	97.57 W
El Rio	228	34.13 N	119.10 W
El Rito	200	36.20 N	106.11 W
El Rito ≃	200	36.12 N	106.14 W
El Roba	154	3.57 N	40.01 E
El Roble	234	23.32 N	106.14 W
Elrose	184	51.13 N	108.01 W
Elroy	190	43.44 N	90.16 W
El Rucio	234	23.23 N	102.05 W
Elsa, Yk., Can.	180	63.55 N	135.28 W
Elsa, Tx., U.S.	196	26.17 N	97.59 W
Elsa ≃	66	43.43 N	10.52 E
Elsah	219	38.57 N	90.22 W
El Sahuaro	200	31.05 N	112.55 W
El Salado	252	26.25 S	70.19 W
El Salto, Chile	286e	33.23 S	70.38 W
El Salto, Méx.	234	23.47 N	105.22 W
El Salto, Méx.	234	20.32 N	103.11 W
El Salvador	116	8.34 N	124.32 E
El Salvador □[1], N.A.	230	13.50 N	88.55 W
El Salvador □[1], N.A.	236	13.50 N	88.55 W
El Samán de Apure	246	7.55 N	68.44 W
El Santo	240p	22.42 N	79.41 W
Elsass → Alsace □[9]	32	48.30 N	7.30 E
El Sauce	236	12.53 N	86.32 W
El Sauce, Laguna ◎	258	35.20 S	58.16 W
El Sauz	232	29.02 N	106.16 W
El Sauzal	232	31.54 N	116.41 W
Elsberry	219	39.10 N	90.46 W
Elsbethen	64	47.45 N	13.05 E
Elsburg	273d	26.15 S	28.12 E
Elsdorf, B.R.D.	52	53.14 N	9.20 E
Elsdorf, B.R.D.	56	50.54 N	6.34 E
El Seco, Laguna ◎	258	35.31 S	58.42 W
El Segundo	228	33.55 N	118.24 W
Elsen	52	51.44 N	8.39 E
Elsenham	42	51.55 N	0.14 E
Elsenz ≃	56	49.24 N	8.48 E
Elsey	263	51.22 N	7.34 E
Elsfleth	52	53.14 N	8.28 E
El Siasgo, Arroyo ≃	258	35.33 S	58.33 W
Elsie, Mi., U.S.	216	43.05 N	84.23 W
Elsie, Or., U.S.	224	45.52 N	123.35 W
Elsinore → Helsingør, Dan.	41	56.02 N	12.37 E
Elsinore, Ut,. U.S.	200	38.40 N	112.08 W
Elsinore, Lake ◎[1]	228	33.39 N	117.21 W
El Sitio	286c	10.28 N	66.46 W
Elsmere, De., U.S.	208	39.44 N	75.35 W
Elsmere, Ky., U.S.	218	39.00 N	84.36 W
Elsmere, N.Y., U.S.	210	42.37 N	73.49 W
El Sobrante	226	37.58 N	122.17 W
El Socorro	246	8.59 N	65.44 W
El Sombrero	246	9.23 N	67.03 W
Elspark	273d	26.16 S	28.14 E
Elspeet	52	52.17 N	5.46 E
Elst	52	51.55 N	5.50 E
Elstal	54	52.32 N	12.59 E
Elstead	42	51.11 N	0.43 W
Elster	54	51.50 N	12.49 E
Elsterberg	54	50.36 N	12.10 E
Elstergebirge ⩓	54	50.15 N	12.20 E
Elsterwerda	54	51.28 N	13.31 E
Elston, In., U.S.	216	40.22 N	86.55 W
Elston, Mo., U.S.	219	38.37 N	92.19 W
Elstra	54	51.13 N	14.08 E
Elstree	42	51.39 N	0.16 W
Elstree Aerodrome ⊠	260	51.39 N	0.19 W
El Sueco	232	29.54 N	106.24 W
El Tajín ⊥	234	20.27 N	97.23 W
El Tala	252	26.07 S	65.17 W
El Talar	258	34.27 S	58.39 W
El Tamarindo	236	13.11 N	87.54 W
El Tambo	246	1.26 N	77.23 W
El Tanque	196	26.28 N	99.38 W
El Tapextle	234	23.52 N	105.33 W
El Tarf	36	36.45 N	8.20 E
Elten	52	51.52 N	6.10 E
El Tepozteco, Parque Nacional ♦	234	19.00 N	99.00 W
El Terrero	234	18.58 N	102.28 W
Eltham, Austl.	169	37.44 S	145.09 E
Eltham, N.Z.	172	39.26 S	174.18 E
Eltham ◆[8]	260	51.27 N	0.04 E
Eltham Palace ʊ	260	51.27 N	0.03 E
El Tigre, Col.	246	2.28 N	68.15 W
El Tigre, Ven.	246	8.55 N	64.15 W
El Tigre, Isla I	236	13.16 N	87.38 W
El Tigrito → San José de Guanipa	246	8.54 N	64.09 W
El Timbiriche	234	18.38 N	101.31 W
El Tisey, Cerro ∧	236	12.59 N	86.22 W
Eltmann	56	49.58 N	10.40 E
El Tocuyo	246	9.47 N	69.48 W
El Tofo	252	29.27 S	71.15 W
El'ton, S.S.S.R.	80	49.08 N	46.50 E
Elton, Eng., U.K.	262	53.16 N	2.49 W
Elton, La., U.S.	194	30.28 N	92.41 W
Elton, Pa., U.S.	214	40.17 N	78.48 W
El'ton, ozero ◎	80	49.16 N	46.35 E
El Toreo ♦	286a	19.27 N	99.13 W
El Toro	228	33.37 N	117.41 W
El Toro ∧	240m	18.16 N	65.49 W
El Toro I	234	21.26 N	97.31 W
El Toro Marine Corps Air Station ■	228	33.41 N	117.44 W
El Tranco, Embalse de ◎[1]	34	38.10 N	2.45 W
El Tránsito, Chile	252	28.52 S	70.17 W
El Tránsito, El Sal.	236	13.22 N	88.21 W
El Trapiche	246	3.03 N	77.33 W
El Trébol	252	32.12 S	61.42 W
El Triunfo, Hond.	236	15.46 N	87.26 W
El Triunfo, Hond.	236	13.06 N	87.00 W
El Triunfo, Méx.	232	23.47 N	110.08 W
El Tuito	234	20.19 N	105.22 W
El Tunal	252	24.48 S	65.45 W
El Turbio	254	51.41 S	72.05 W
Eltville	56	50.02 N	8.07 E
Eltz, Burg ⊥	56	50.12 N	7.20 E
El-Uarre	144	3.41 N	45.20 E
Elura → Ellora	122	20.01 N	75.10 E
Elūru	122	16.42 N	81.06 E
Elva	76	58.13 N	26.25 E
El Valle	236	8.36 N	80.08 W
El Valle ◆[8]	286c	10.27 N	66.55 W
Elvas	34	38.53 N	7.10 W
Elvas ≃	256	21.12 S	44.08 W
Elven	32	47.44 N	2.35 W
El Venado, Isla I	236	11.57 N	83.44 W
El Verano	226	38.18 N	122.29 W
El Verde	234	23.21 N	106.09 W
Elverdissen	52	52.05 N	8.38 E
Elverlingsen	263	51.17 N	7.42 E
Elverta	226	38.43 N	121.28 W
Elverum	26	60.53 N	11.34 E
El Viejo	236	12.40 N	87.10 W
El Vigía	246	8.38 N	71.39 W
El Vigía, Cerro ∧	234	21.19 N	104.03 W
Elvins	194	37.50 N	90.31 W
Elvira	258	35.14 S	59.29 W
Elvo ≃	62	45.23 N	8.21 E
El Volcán, Arg.	252	33.15 S	66.12 W
El Volcán, Chile	252	33.49 S	70.11 W
El Wad	148	33.20 N	6.58 E
El Wak	154	2.49 N	40.56 E
El Wanza	148	35.57 N	8.04 E
Elwell, Lake ◎[1]	202	48.22 N	111.17 W
Elwha ≃	224	48.10 N	123.35 W
Elwood, Austl.	274b	37.53 S	144.59 E
Elwood, Il., U.S.	216	41.24 N	88.07 W
Elwood, In., U.S.	216	40.16 N	85.50 W
Elwood, Ks., U.S.	198	39.45 N	94.52 W
Elwood, Ne., U.S.	198	40.35 N	99.51 W
Elwood, N.J., U.S.	208	39.35 N	74.43 W
Elwood, N.Y., U.S.	207	40.50 N	73.20 W
Elwood Park, Fl., U.S.	220	27.28 N	82.30 W
Elwood Park, Pa., U.S.	279b	40.10 N	80.17 W
Elwy ≃	44	53.16 N	3.26 W
Elwyn	285	39.54 N	75.24 W
Elxleben	54	51.02 N	10.56 E
Ely, Eng., U.K.	42	52.24 N	0.16 E
Ely, Mn., U.S.	190	47.54 N	91.52 W
Ely, Mo., U.S.	219	39.41 N	91.39 W
Ely, Nv., U.S.	204	39.14 N	114.53 W
Ely, Isle of ◆[1]	42	52.24 N	0.10 E
El Yagual	246	7.29 N	68.25 W
Ely Cathedral ʊ[1]	42	52.24 N	0.16 E
Elyria	214	41.22 N	82.06 W
Elyria Airport ⊠	279a	41.20 N	82.06 W
Elysburg	210	40.51 N	76.33 W
Elysian Park ♦	280	34.05 N	118.14 W
El Yunque ∧	240m	18.19 N	65.48 W
Elywood Park ♦	279a	41.23 N	82.06 W
Elz	56	50.25 N	8.02 E
Elz ≃	58	48.21 N	7.45 E
Elzach	58	48.10 N	8.04 E
El Zamural	286c	10.27 N	67.00 W
El Zapotal	234	15.27 N	93.10 W
El Zapotán	234	18.41 N	103.39 W
El Zapote de Calabacillas	232	25.42 N	106.32 W
Elzbach ≃	56	50.12 N	7.22 E
Elze, B.R.D.	52	52.35 N	9.44 E
Elze, B.R.D.	52	52.07 N	9.44 E
El Zig-Zag	286c	10.33 N	66.58 W
Émaé I	175f	17.04 S	168.24 E
Emajõgi ≃	76	58.26 N	27.15 E
Emali	154	2.05 S	37.38 E
Emalı Bendi ◆[6]	267b	41.04 N	29.06 E
Emāmshahr (Shāhrūd)	128	36.25 N	55.01 E
Emån ≃	26	57.08 N	16.30 E
Émancé	261	48.35 N	1.44 E
Emas, Parque Nacional das ♦	255	18.08 S	52.48 W
Emba	86	48.50 N	58.08 E
Emba ≃	80	46.38 N	53.14 E
Embarcación	252	23.13 S	64.06 W
Embarras ≃, Ab., Can.	182	53.27 N	116.37 W
Embarras ≃, Il., U.S.	194	38.39 N	87.37 W
Embarras, North Fork ≃	194	38.55 N	87.59 W
Embarrass	190	44.39 N	88.42 W
Embarrass ≃, Mn., U.S.	190	47.24 N	92.25 W
Embarrass ≃, Wi., U.S.	190	44.23 N	88.45 W
Embetsu	92a	44.44 N	141.47 E
Embid	34	40.58 N	1.43 W
Embira ≃	248	7.19 S	70.15 W
Embleton	44	55.30 N	1.37 W
Embo	46	57.54 N	3.59 W
Emboabas	256	21.18 S	44.08 W
Embondo	152	0.15 N	19.38 E
Embrach	58	47.30 N	8.36 E
Embreeville, Pa., U.S.	285	39.56 N	75.44 W
Embreeville, Tn., U.S.	192	36.10 N	82.27 W
Embro	212	43.09 N	80.54 W
Embrun, On., Can.	212	45.16 N	75.17 W
Embrun, Fr.	62	44.34 N	6.30 E
Embry	50	50.29 N	1.58 E
Embsay	44	53.58 N	1.59 W
Embu, Bra.	256	23.39 S	46.51 W
Embu, Kenya	154	0.32 S	37.27 E
Embu □[7]	287b	23.40 S	46.50 W
Embu-Guaçu	256	23.49 S	46.48 W
Embu-Guacu □[7]	287b	23.48 S	46.48 W
Embu-Mirim ≃	287b	23.39 S	46.51 W
Emden, B.R.D.	52	53.22 N	7.12 E
Emden, Il., U.S.	194	40.18 N	89.29 W
Emden, Mo., U.S.	219	39.48 N	91.52 W
Emei	107	29.36 N	103.31 E
Emeigh	214	40.42 N	78.47 W
Emel' (Emin) ≃	86	46.20 N	81.46 E
Emelle	194	32.43 N	88.18 W
Emerado	198	47.55 N	97.21 W
Émerainville	261	48.49 N	2.37 E
Emerald, Austl.	166	23.32 S	148.10 E
Emerald, Austl.	169	37.56 S	145.26 E
Emerald Bay State Park ♦	226	38.57 N	120.05 W
Emerald Lake	226	37.28 N	122.16 W
Emero ≃	248	13.19 S	67.17 W
Emerson, Mb., Can.	184	49.00 N	97.12 W
Emerson, Ar., U.S.	194	33.05 N	93.11 W
Emerson, Ga., U.S.	192	34.07 N	84.45 W
Emerson, Ia., U.S.	198	41.01 N	95.24 W
Emerson, Mo., U.S.	219	39.53 N	91.42 W
Emerson, Ne., U.S.	198	42.17 N	96.44 W
Emerson, N.J., U.S.	276	40.58 N	74.01 W
Emery, S.D., U.S.	198	43.36 N	97.37 W
Emery, Ut,. U.S.	200	38.55 N	111.14 W
Emeryville, On., Can.	214	42.18 N	82.45 W
Emeryville, Ca., U.S.	226	37.50 N	122.17 W
Emet	130	39.20 N	29.15 E
Emgayet	146	29.04 N	12.58 E
Emhouse	222	32.09 N	96.35 W
Emi	88	50.36 N	97.49 E
Emigrant Gap	226	39.17 N	120.40 W
Emigrant Gap)(	226	39.18 N	120.40 W
Emigsville	208	40.01 N	76.44 W
Emiliano Zapata, Méx.	232	17.45 N	91.46 W
Emiliano Zapata, Méx.	234	16.10 N	94.01 W
Emilia-Romagna □[4]	66	44.35 N	11.00 E
Emílio de Carvalho	152	5.55 S	12.57 E
Emily Provincial Park ♦	212	44.21 N	78.31 W
Emin	86	46.32 N	83.39 E
Emin (Emel') ≃	86	46.20 N	81.46 E
Eminābād	123	32.02 N	74.16 E
Emine, nos ≻	38	42.42 N	27.51 E
Eminence, Ky., U.S.	218	38.22 N	85.10 W
Eminence, Mo., U.S.	194	37.09 N	91.21 W
Emira Island I	164	1.40 S	150.00 E
Emiralem	130	38.36 N	27.09 E
Emiratos Arabes Unidos → United Arab Emirates □[1]	128	24.00 N	54.00 E
Emirdağ	130	39.01 N	31.10 E
Emir Dağları ⩓	130	38.50 N	31.15 E
Emirhan	130	39.42 N	37.46 E
Emir Pasha Gulf c	154	2.32 S	31.52 E
Emissi, Tarso ∧	146	21.13 N	18.32 E
Emita	166	40.00 S	147.54 E
Emlembe ∧	158	25.57 S	31.11 E
Emlenton	214	41.11 N	79.43 W
Emlichheim	52	52.36 N	6.50 E
Emmaån ≃	40	58.44 N	15.35 E
Emmaboda	26	56.38 N	15.32 E
Emmaste	76	58.42 N	22.36 E
Emmaus, S.S.S.R.	82	56.47 N	36.07 E
Emmaus, Pa., U.S.	208	40.32 N	75.29 W
Emmaville	166	29.26 S	151.36 E
Emme ≃	58	47.13 N	7.34 E
Emmeline Lake ◎	184	55.00 N	106.22 W
Emmeloord	52	52.43 N	5.45 E
Emmen	52	52.47 N	6.54 E
Emmenbrücke	58	47.04 N	8.17 E
Emmendingen	58	48.07 N	7.50 E
Emmental V	58	46.56 N	7.45 E
Emmer ≃	52	52.03 N	9.23 E
Emmer-Compascuum	52	52.48 N	7.02 E
Emmer-Erfscheidenveen	52	52.48 N	7.01 E
Emmerich	52	51.50 N	6.15 E
Emmerstedt	54	52.15 N	10.58 E
Emmerthal	52	52.03 N	9.23 E
Emmet, Austl.	166	24.40 S	144.28 E
Emmet, Ar., U.S.	194	33.43 N	93.28 W
Emmetsburg	198	43.06 N	94.40 W
Emmett, Id., U.S.	202	43.52 N	116.29 W
Emmett, Mi., U.S.	214	42.59 N	82.45 W
Emmiganūru	122	15.44 N	77.29 E
Emmitsburg	208	39.42 N	77.20 W
Emmonak	180	62.46 N	164.30 W
Emneth	42	52.38 N	0.11 E
Emo	190	48.38 N	93.50 W
Emőd	30	47.56 N	20.49 E
Emory	222	32.52 N	95.46 W
Emory ≃	192	35.56 N	84.29 W
Emory Peak ∧	196	29.13 N	103.17 W
Empalme	232	27.58 N	110.51 W
Empalme Escobedo	234	20.41 N	100.44 W
Empalme Purísima	234	23.55 N	105.05 W
Empalme San Vicente	258	34.58 S	58.22 W
Empangeni	158	28.50 S	31.48 E
Empedrado, Arg.	252	27.57 S	58.48 W
Empedrado, Chile	252	35.36 S	72.17 W
Emperor Jimmu, Tomb Of ⊥	270	34.29 N	135.47 E
Emperor Nintoku, Tomb of ⊥	270	34.34 N	135.29 E
Emperor Range ⩓	175e	5.45 S	154.55 E
Emperor Seamounts ✦[3]	6	42.00 N	170.00 E
Emperor Tenchi, Tomb of ⊥	270	34.59 N	135.48 E
Empfingen	58	48.24 N	8.42 E
Empire, Ca., U.S.	226	37.38 N	120.54 W
Empire, La., U.S.	194	29.23 N	89.35 W
Empire, Nv., U.S.	204	40.34 N	119.20 W
Empire, Oh., U.S.	214	40.30 N	80.37 W
Empoli	66	43.43 N	10.57 E
Emporia, Ks., U.S.	198	38.24 N	96.10 W
Emporia, Va., U.S.	208	36.41 N	77.32 W
Emporium	214	41.30 N	78.14 W
Empress	184	50.57 N	110.00 W
Empress Augusta Bay c	175e	6.25 S	155.05 E
Emptinne	56	50.19 N	5.07 E
Ems ≃	52	53.30 N	7.00 E
Emscher ≃	263	51.34 N	6.42 E
Emscher Bruch ◆[1]	263	51.34 N	7.09 E
Emsdetten	52	52.10 N	7.31 E
Ems-Jade-Kanal ≅	52	53.19 N	7.10 E
Emskirchen	56	49.33 N	10.43 E
Emsland ◆[1]	52	52.50 N	7.20 E
Emst ◆[8]	263	51.21 N	7.30 E
Emstek	52	52.50 N	8.09 E
Emsworth, Eng., U.K.	42	50.51 N	0.56 W
Emsworth, Pa., U.S.	214	40.30 N	80.05 W
Emu	89	43.45 N	128.10 E
Emu, Mount ∧[2]	169	37.35 S	143.27 E
Emu Creek ≃	171a	26.56 S	152.19 E
Emu Downs	168b	33.54 S	138.59 E
Emukae	92	33.18 N	129.38 E
Emu Park	166	23.15 S	150.50 E
Emu Plains	274a	33.45 S	150.41 E
Emur ≃	89	53.24 N	124.00 E
Emuren	273a	6.40 N	3.31 E
Emyvale	48	54.20 N	6.59 W
En (Inn) ≃, Europe	32	48.35 N	13.28 E
En ≃, Zhg.	100	27.12 N	115.08 E
Ena	94	35.27 N	137.25 E
Enana	156	17.29 S	16.19 E
Enånger	26	61.32 N	17.00 E
Enaratoli	164	3.55 S	136.21 E
Enard Bay c	46	58.05 N	5.20 W
Ena-san ∧	94	35.26 N	137.36 E
Ena-san Tunnel ◆[5]	94	35.30 N	137.40 E
Enbacka	40	60.25 N	15.36 E
Enborne ≃	42	51.24 N	1.06 W
Encampment	200	41.12 N	106.47 W
Encampment ≃	200	41.18 N	106.43 W
Encantado	252	29.15 S	51.53 W
Encantado ◆[8]	287a	22.54 S	43.18 W
Encanto, Cape ≻	116	15.44 N	121.37 E
Encarnação ◆[8]	266c	38.47 N	9.06 W
Encarnación	252	27.20 S	55.54 W
Encarnación de Díaz	234	21.31 N	102.14 W
Encha	98	37.25 N	115.42 E
Enchenberg	56	49.01 N	7.20 E
Enchi	150	5.49 N	2.49 W
Enchilayas	200	30.50 N	112.50 W
Enchovas, Enseada das c	256	23.57 S	45.18 W
Enciastraia, Monte ∧	62	44.22 N	6.53 E
Encinal	196	28.02 N	99.21 W
Encinitas	228	33.02 N	117.17 W
Encino, N.M., U.S.	200	34.39 N	105.27 W
Encino, Tx., U.S.	196	26.57 N	98.08 W
Encino ◆[8]	280	34.09 N	118.30 W
Encino Reservoir ◎[1]	280	34.05 N	118.31 W
Encontrados	246	9.03 N	72.14 W
Encounter Bay c	168b	35.35 S	138.44 E
Encrucijada, Cuba	240p	22.37 N	79.52 W
Encrucijada, Méx.	234	18.18 N	93.29 W
Encruzilhada	255	15.31 S	40.54 W
Encruzilhada do Sul	252	30.32 S	52.31 W
Encs	30	48.20 N	21.08 E
Endako	182	54.05 N	125.02 W
Endako ≃	182	54.05 N	124.55 W
Endau ≃	114	2.39 N	103.38 E
Ende	115b	8.50 S	121.39 E
Ende, Pulau I	115b	8.53 S	121.32 E
Ende, Teluk c	115b	8.52 S	121.30 E
Endeavor, Pa., U.S.	214	41.35 N	79.23 W
Endeavor, Wi., U.S.	190	43.42 N	89.27 W
Endeavour	184	52.08 N	102.40 W
Endeavour Strait ʮ	164	10.50 S	142.15 E
Endelave I	41	55.46 N	10.17 E
Enderbury I[1]	14	3.08 S	171.05 W
Enderby, B.C., Can.	182	50.33 N	119.08 W
Enderby, Eng., U.K.	42	52.36 N	1.12 W
Enderby Land ◆[1]	9	67.30 S	53.00 E
Enderlin	198	46.37 N	97.36 W
Endicott, N.Y., U.S.	210	42.05 N	76.02 W
Endicott, Wa., U.S.	202	46.55 N	117.40 W
Endicott Mountains ⩓	180	67.50 N	152.00 W
Endimari ≃	248	8.46 S	66.07 W
Endine	64	45.46 N	9.59 E
Endine Gaiano	64	45.48 N	9.59 E
Endingen	58	48.09 N	7.42 E
Endja, Oued ≃	34	36.31 N	6.15 E
Endō	268	35.23 N	139.27 E
Endola	156	17.37 S	15.50 E
ʿEn Dor	132	32.39 N	35.25 E
Endorf in Oberbayern	64	47.54 N	12.18 E
Endre ≃	62	43.28 N	6.36 E
Endrick ∧	170	35.12 S	150.12 E
Endrick ≃	170	35.01 S	150.03 E
Endwell	210	42.06 N	76.01 W
Ene ≃	248	11.09 S	74.19 W
Eneabba	162	29.50 S	115.20 E
Enemonzo	64	46.25 N	12.53 E
Enewetak I[1]	14	11.30 N	162.15 E
Enez	130	40.44 N	26.04 E
Enfer, Pointe d' ≻	240e	14.24 N	60.52 W
Enfida	36	36.07 N	10.23 E
Enfield, Austl.	168b	34.53 S	138.35 E
Enfield, Austl.	274a	33.53 S	151.06 E
Enfield, N.Z.	172	45.03 S	170.52 E
Enfield, Ct., U.S.	207	41.58 N	72.35 W
Enfield, N.H., U.S.	188	43.38 N	72.08 W
Enfield, N.C., U.S.	192	36.10 N	77.40 W
Enfield, Va., U.S.	208	37.43 N	77.12 W
Enfield ◆[8]	260	51.40 N	0.05 W
Engadine	170	34.04 S	151.01 E
Engaño, Cabo ≻	238	18.37 N	68.20 W
Engaru	92a	44.03 N	143.31 E
Engažimo	88	57.51 N	114.56 E
Engcobo	158	31.37 S	28.00 E
ʿEn Gedi	132	31.27 N	35.23 E
Engelberg	58	46.49 N	8.25 E
Engelhard	192	35.30 N	75.59 W
Engelhartszell	60	48.31 N	13.44 E
Engel's	80	51.30 N	46.07 E
Engelsdorf	54	51.20 N	12.29 E
Engelskirchen	56	50.59 N	7.24 E
Engelsmanplaat I	52	53.28 N	6.02 E
Engel's'ovo	83	48.22 N	39.23 E
Engen, B.R.D.	58	47.51 N	8.46 E
Engen, B.C., Can.	182	54.02 N	124.18 W
Engenheiro Passos	256	22.30 S	44.41 W
Engenheiro Paulo de Frontin	256	22.33 S	43.41 W
Engenho	248	15.10 S	56.25 W
Engenho, Ilha do I	287a	22.50 S	43.07 W
Engenho de Dentro ◆[8]	287a	22.54 S	43.18 W
Engenho do Mato	287a	22.52 S	43.01 W
Engenho Nôvo	256	21.49 S	43.00 W
Engenho Nôvo ◆[8]	287a	22.55 S	43.17 W
Enger	52	52.08 N	8.34 E
Engestofte	41	54.46 N	11.34 E
Engesvang	41	56.10 N	9.21 E
ʿEn Gev	132	32.47 N	35.38 E
Enggano, Pulau I	112	5.24 S	102.16 E
Enghershatu ∧	144	16.40 N	38.20 E
Enghien (Edingen)	50	50.42 N	4.02 E
Enghien-les-Bains	261	48.58 N	2.19 E
Enghien-Moisselles, Aéroport d' ⊠	261	49.02 N	2.21 E
Engiadina Bassa V	58	46.50 N	10.20 E
Engis	56	50.35 N	5.25 E
Engizek Dağı ∧	130	37.50 N	37.10 E
Engjan	26	63.09 N	8.32 E
England	194	34.32 N	91.58 W
England □[8]	28	52.30 N	1.30 W
England Air Force Base ■	194	31.20 N	92.33 W
Englebright Lake ◎[1]	226	39.15 N	121.15 W
Englee	186	50.44 N	56.06 W
Englefield, Cape ≻	176	69.51 N	85.39 W
Englefield Green	260	51.26 N	0.35 W
Englefontaine	50	50.11 N	3.39 E
Englehart	190	47.49 N	79.52 W
Englehart ≃	190	47.51 N	79.50 W
Engleside	208	38.43 N	77.05 W
Englewood, B.C., Can.	182	50.33 N	126.53 W
Englewood, Co., U.S.	200	39.38 N	104.59 W
Englewood, Fl., U.S.	220	26.57 N	82.21 W
Englewood, In., U.S.	218	38.50 N	86.31 W
Englewood, Ks., U.S.	198	37.02 N	99.58 W
Englewood, N.J., U.S.	210	40.53 N	73.58 W
Englewood, Oh., U.S.	218	39.52 N	84.18 W
Englewood, Tn., U.S.	192	35.25 N	84.29 W
Englewood ◆[8]	278	41.47 N	87.39 W
Englewood Cliffs	276	40.53 N	73.57 W
Englewood Dam ◆[6]	218	39.52 N	84.17 W
English, In., U.S.	218	38.20 N	86.27 W
English, Ky., U.S.	218	38.37 N	85.08 W
English ≃, On., Can.	176	50.12 N	95.00 W
English (Rivière des Anglais) ≃, N.A.	206	45.13 N	73.50 W
English ≃, Ia., U.S.	190	41.29 N	91.30 W
English Bay	180	59.22 N	151.55 W
English Bāzār	124	25.00 N	88.09 E
English Center	210	41.26 N	77.17 W
English Channel (La Manche) ʮ	28	50.20 N	1.00 W
English Coast ⫠[2]	9	73.45 S	73.00 W
English Harbour West	186	47.28 N	55.29 W
Englishman ≃	224	49.22 N	124.18 W
Englishtown	208	40.17 N	74.21 W
Engong	152	0.36 N	10.06 E
Engter	52	52.23 N	8.04 E
Enguera	34	38.59 N	0.41 W
Engum	41	55.44 N	9.40 E
Engure	76	57.10 N	23.13 E
Engures ezers ◎	76	57.16 N	23.06 E
Engwilen	58	47.37 N	9.05 E
ʿEn Ḥarod	132	32.33 N	35.23 E
ʿEn HaShofet	132	32.35 N	35.06 E
Enid	196	36.23 N	97.52 W
Enid Lake ◎[1]	194	34.10 N	89.50 W
Enilda	182	55.25 N	116.18 W
Eningen unter Achalm	58	48.29 N	9.16 E
Eniwa	92a	42.45 N	141.33 E
Eniwetok → Enewetak I[1]	14	11.30 N	162.15 E
eNjesuthi ∧	158	29.09 S	29.23 E
Enka	192	35.32 N	82.39 W
Enkenbach	56	49.29 N	7.54 E
Enkhuizen	52	52.42 N	5.17 E
Enkirch	56	49.59 N	7.07 E
Enköping	40	59.38 N	17.04 E
Enle	102	24.00 N	101.07 E
Enmedio	196	29.04 N	103.29 W
Enmelen	180	65.01 N	175.54 W
Enmore	246	6.46 N	57.59 W
Enna	70	37.34 N	14.16 E
Enna □[4]	70	37.35 N	14.26 E
Ennadai Lake ◎	176	60.53 N	101.15 W
Enné, Ouadi V	146	14.24 N	18.45 E
Ennedi ⩓[1]	146	17.15 N	22.00 E
Ennell, Lough ◎	48	53.28 N	7.24 W
Ennenda	58	47.01 N	9.05 E
Ennepe ≃	263	51.22 N	7.27 E
Ennepe-Ruhr-Kreis □[8]	263	51.21 N	7.15 E
Ennepestausee ◎[1]	263	51.14 N	7.25 E
Ennepetal	56	51.18 N	7.22 E
Ennerdale Water ◎	44	54.31 N	3.23 W
Ennery	261	49.05 N	2.06 E

≃ River	Fluss	Río	Rivière	Rio
≅ Canal	Kanal	Canal	Canal	Canal
L Waterfall, Rapids	Wasserfall, Stromschnellen	Cascada, Rápidos	Chute d'eau, Rapides	Cascata, Rápidos
ʮ Strait	Meeresstrasse	Estrecho	Détroit	Estreito
c Bay, Gulf	Bucht, Golf	Bahía, Golfo	Baie, Golfe	Baía, Golfo
◎ Lake, Lakes	See, Seen	Lago, Lagos	Lac, Lacs	Lago, Lagos
≡ Swamp	Sumpf	Pantano	Marais	Pântano
⍓ Ice Features, Glacier	Eis- und Gletscherformen	Accidentes Glaciales	Formes glaciaires	Acidentes glaciares
⊤ Other Hydrographic Features	Andere Hydrographische Objekte	Otros Elementos Hidrográficos	Autres données hydrographiques	Outros acidentes hidrográficos

✦ Submarine Features	Untermeerische Objekte	Accidentes Submarinos	Formes de relief sous-marin	Acidentes submarinos
□ Political Unit	Politische Einheit	Unidad Politica	Entité politique	Unidade política
ʊ Cultural Institution	Kulturelle Institution	Institución Cultural	Institution culturelle	Institução cultural
⊥ Historical Site	Historische Stätte	Sitio Histórico	Site historique	Sitio histórico
♦ Recreational Site	Erholungs- und Ferienort	Sitio de Recreo	Centre de loisirs	Area de Lazer
⊠ Airport	Flughafen	Aeropuerto	Aéroport	Aeroporto
■ Military Installation	Militäranlage	Instalación Militar	Installation militaire	Instalação militar
◆ Miscellaneous	Verschiedenes	Misceláneo	Divers	Diversos

'En Netafim 132 29.35 N 34.53 E
Enngonia 166 29.19 S 145.51 E
Enniger 52 51.50 N 7.56 E
Ennigerloh 52 51.50 N 8.02 E
Ennigloh 52 52.12 N 8.34 E
Ennis, Ire. 48 52.50 N 8.59 W
Ennis, Mt., U.S. 202 45.20 N 111.43 W
Ennis, Tx., U.S. 222 32.19 N 96.37 W
Enniscorthy 48 52.30 N 6.34 W
Enniskillen 48 54.21 N 7.38 W
Ennis Lake ◎[1] 202 45.26 N 111.41 W
Ennistimon 48 52.57 N 9.15 W
Enns 61 48.13 N 14.29 E
Enns ≃ 30 48.14 N 14.32 E
Ennstaler Alpen ⋏ 61 47.37 N 14.35 E
Eno 26 62.48 N 30.09 E
Enø I 41 55.10 N 11.40 E
Eno ≃ 96 34.53 N 132.41 E
Enochs 196 33.52 N 102.46 W
Enoggera Army Base ■ 171a 27.25 S 152.58 E
Enola 208 40.17 N 76.56 W
Enon 218 39.53 N 83.56 W
Enontekiö 24 68.23 N 23.38 E
Enon Valley 214 40.51 N 80.28 W
Enoree ≃ 192 34.26 N 81.25 W
Enosburg Falls 188 44.54 N 72.48 W
Eno-shima I 94 35.18 N 139.29 E
Enping 102 22.11 N 112.17 E
Enrekang 112 3.34 S 119.47 E
Enrile 116 17.34 N 121.42 E
Enrique Fynn 258 34.50 S 59.08 W
Enrique Urien 252 27.34 S 60.32 W
Enriquillo 238 17.54 N 71.14 W
Enriquillo, Lago ◎ 238 18.27 N 71.39 W
Ens 52 52.38 N 5.50 E
Ensay 166 37.23 S 147.50 E
Ensay I 46 57.46 N 7.05 W
Enschede 52 52.12 N 6.53 E
Ensdorf 60 49.21 N 11.56 E
Enseada 256 23.29 S 45.05 W
Ensenada, Arg. 258 34.51 S 57.55 W
Ensenada, Méx. 232 31.52 N 116.37 W
Ensenada, P.R. 240m 17.58 N 66.56 W
Ensenada □[5] 288 34.50 S 58.00 W
Enshi 102 30.17 N 109.19 E
Enshū-nada ⊤[2] 92 34.27 N 137.38 E
Ensisheim 58 47.52 N 7.21 E
Enstaberga 40 58.45 N 16.51 E
Entebbe 154 0.04 N 32.28 E
Entenbühl ∧ 60 49.46 N 12.24 E
Enter 52 52.18 N 6.34 E
Enterprise, Guy. 246 6.56 N 58.24 W
Enterprise, Al., U.S. 194 31.18 N 85.51 W
Enterprise, Ca., U.S. 204 39.32 N 121.22 W
Enterprise, Ks., U.S. 198 38.54 N 97.07 W
Enterprise, Ms., U.S. 194 32.10 N 88.49 W
Enterprise, Or., U.S. 202 45.25 N 117.16 W
Enterprise, Ut,. U.S. 200 37.34 N 113.43 W
Entiat ≃ 202 47.40 N 120.14 W
Entiat, Lake ◎ 202 47.40 N 120.12 W
Entiat Mountains ⋏ 224 48.00 N 120.42 W
Entinas, Punta ≻ 34 36.41 N 2.46 W
Entlebuch 58 47.00 N 8.04 E
Entlebuch V 58 46.58 N 8.00 E
Entracque 62 44.14 N 7.24 E
Entraigues-sur-Sorgue 62 44.00 N 4.55 E
Entrains-sur-Nohain 50 47.27 N 3.15 E
Entrance, Cape ≻ 164 2.21 S 150.12 E
Entraunes 62 44.11 N 6.45 E
Entraygues 32 44.39 N 2.34 E
Entrechaux 62 44.13 N 5.08 E
Entrée, Île d' I 186 47.17 N 61.42 W
Entremont-le-Vieux 62 45.26 N 5.53 E
Entrepeñas, Embalse de ◎[1] 34 40.34 N 2.42 W
Entre Ríos, Bol. 248 21.32 S 64.12 W
Entre Rios, Bra. 255 11.56 S 38.05 W
Entre Ríos □[4] 252 32.00 S 59.00 W
Entre Ríos, Cordillera ⋏ 236 14.19 N 85.26 W
Entre Rios de Minas 255 20.41 S 44.04 W
Entrevaux 62 43.57 N 6.49 E
Entrèves 62 45.49 N 6.57 E
Entriken 214 40.20 N 78.12 W
Entroncamento 34 39.28 N 8.28 W
Entupido 256 22.30 S 44.51 W
Entwistle 182 53.36 N 115.00 W
Enu, Pulau I 164 7.05 S 134.30 E
Enugu 150 6.27 N 7.27 E
Enumclaw 224 47.12 N 121.59 W
Enurmino 180 66.57 N 171.49 W
Envalira, Port d')(34 42.35 N 1.45 E
Envermeu 50 49.54 N 1.16 E
Envies, Rivière des ≃ 206 46.37 N 72.24 W
Envigado 246 6.10 N 75.35 W
Envira 248 7.18 S 70.13 W
'En Yahav 132 30.38 N 35.11 E
Enyamba 154 3.40 S 24.58 E
Enyang 102 31.48 N 106.31 E
Enyellé 152 2.49 N 18.06 E
Enys, Mount ∧ 172 43.14 S 171.38 E
Enz ≃ 56 49.01 N 9.07 E
Enza ≃ 64 44.54 N 10.31 E
Enzan 94 35.42 N 138.44 E
Enzbach ≃ 56 49.54 N 6.25 E
Enzenkirchen 60 48.23 N 13.39 E
Enzesfeld 61 47.55 N 16.10 E
Enzklösterle 56 48.40 N 8.28 E
Eo ≃ 34 43.28 N 7.03 W
Eolia 219 39.14 N 91.00 W
Eolie o Lipari, Isole II 70 38.30 N 14.50 E
Epanomí 38 40.26 N 22.56 E
Épars, Bois de l' ♦ 261 48.45 N 1.45 E
Epazote, Cerro ∧ 232 24.35 N 105.07 W
Epe, B.R.D. 52 52.11 N 7.02 E
Epe, Ned. 52 52.21 N 6.00 E
Epe, Nig. 150 6.37 N 3.59 E
Epecuén, Lago ◎ 252 37.10 S 62.54 W
Épéhy 50 50.02 N 3.10 E
Epéna 152 1.22 N 17.29 E
Épernay 50 49.03 N 3.57 E
Épernon 50 48.37 N 1.41 E
Épernon, Les Taillis d' ♦ 261 48.40 N 1.45 E
Epes 194 32.41 N 88.07 W
Ephesus ⊥ 130 37.55 N 27.17 E
Ephraim 200 39.21 N 111.35 W
Ephrata, Pa., U.S. 208 40.10 N 76.10 W
Ephrata, Wa., U.S. 202 47.19 N 119.33 W
Ephrata Cloister ⊥ 208 40.12 N 76.09 W
Ephratah 210 43.00 N 74.32 W
Epi □[8] 175f 16.42 S 168.15 E
Épi I 175f 16.43 S 168.15 E
Épiais-lès-Louvres 261 49.02 N 2.33 E
Épila 34 41.36 N 1.17 W
Épinac-Les-Mines 58 46.59 N 4.31 E
Épinal 58 48.11 N 6.27 E
Épinay-sous-Sénart 261 48.42 N 2.31 E
Épinay-sur-Orge 261 48.40 N 2.20 E
Épinay-sur-Seine 261 48.57 N 2.19 E
Episcopia 68 40.04 N 16.06 E
Episkopí 130 34.40 N 32.54 E
Epo 164 8.40 S 146.30 E
Époisses 50 47.30 N 4.10 E
Epokiro 156 21.41 S 19.08 E
Epomeo, Monte ∧ 68 40.44 N 13.54 E
Épône 261 48.57 N 1.49 E
Eport, Loch c 46 57.33 N 7.11 W
Eppalock, Lake ◎[1] 169 36.52 S 144.31 E
Eppelborn 56 49.24 N 6.58 E
Eppendorf ◆[8] 263 51.27 N 7.11 E
Eppenhausen ◆[8] 263 51.21 N 7.31 E
Eppeville 50 49.44 N 3.03 E
Epping, Austl. 169 37.39 S 145.02 E
Epping, Austl. 274a 33.46 S 151.05 E
Epping, Eng., U.K. 260 51.43 N 0.07 E
Epping, N.H., U.S. 188 43.02 N 71.04 W
Eppingen 56 49.08 N 8.54 E
Epping Forest □[8] 260 51.43 N 0.10 E
Epping Forest ◆[3] 260 51.40 N 0.03 E
Epping Green, Eng., U.K. 260 51.44 N 0.05 E
Epping Green, Eng., U.K. 260 51.45 N 0.07 W
Epping Upland 260 51.43 N 0.06 E
Epsom 260 51.20 N 0.16 W
Epsom and Ewell □[8] 260 51.20 N 0.16 W
Epsom Downs Race Course ♦ 260 51.19 N 0.15 W
Epte ≃ 50 49.04 N 1.37 E
Épuisay 50 47.54 N 0.56 E
Epukiro ≃ 156 20.45 S 21.05 E
Epupa Falls L 152 16.55 S 13.10 E
Epuyén 254 42.14 S 71.21 W
Epworth 44 53.32 N 0.49 W
Eqlīd 128 30.55 N 52.39 E
Equality 194 37.44 N 88.20 W
Équateur □[4] 152 1.00 N 20.30 E
Équateur → Ecuador □[1] 246 2.00 S 77.30 W
Equatorial Guinea (Guinea Ecuatorial) □[1] 152 2.00 N 9.00 E
Équihen-Plage 50 50.41 N 1.34 E
Equimina ≃ 152 13.11 S 12.47 E
Equinox Mountain ∧ 210 43.10 N 73.08 W
Equinunk 210 41.51 N 75.14 W
Equi Terme 64 44.09 N 10.10 E
Era ≃, It. 66 43.40 N 10.38 E
Era ≃, Pap. N. Gui. 164 7.35 S 144.41 E
Erac Creek ≃ 166 26.56 S 145.48 E
Eraclea 64 45.35 N 12.40 E
Eraclea ⊥ 68 40.13 N 16.40 E
Eraclea Minoa ⊥ 70 37.23 N 13.17 E
Eradu 162 28.41 S 115.02 E
Éragny 261 49.01 N 2.06 E
Eramosa ≃ 212 43.32 N 80.14 W
Eran Bay c 116 9.06 N 117.43 E
Eranga 152 1.52 S 18.56 E
Erangal ◆[8] 272c 19.10 N 72.47 E
Erap 164 6.35 S 146.40 E
Erath 194 29.57 N 92.02 W
Erave 164 6.40 S 143.50 E
Erave ≃ 164 6.40 S 143.55 E
Erba 62 45.48 N 9.15 E
Erba, Jabal ∧, Sūd. 140 19.04 N 36.46 E
Erba, Jabal ∧, Sūd. 140 20.45 N 36.50 E
Erbaa 130 40.42 N 36.36 E
Erbach, B.R.D. 56 49.40 N 8.59 E
Erbach, B.R.D. 58 48.20 N 9.53 E
Erbendorf 60 49.50 N 12.03 E
Erbeskopf ∧ 56 49.44 N 7.05 E
Erchie 68 40.26 N 17.44 E
Erciş 84 39.02 N 43.22 E
Erciyeş Dağı ∧ 130 38.32 N 35.28 E
Ercolano 68 40.48 N 14.21 E
Ercolano (Herculaneum) ⊥ 68 40.46 N 14.20 E
Érd 30 47.23 N 18.56 E
Erdao ≃, Zhg. 98 42.39 N 127.35 E
Erdao ≃, Zhg. 104 42.16 N 122.20 E
Erdao Bai ≃ 98 42.34 N 128.08 E
Erdaobaihe 98 42.22 N 128.07 E
Erdaofang, Zhg. 104 41.54 N 123.57 E
Erdaofang, Zhg. 104 41.37 N 122.34 E
Erdaofangshen 104 42.09 N 123.17 E
Erdaogangzi, Zhg. 104 41.57 N 122.09 E
Erdaogangzi, Zhg. 104 42.04 N 123.06 E
Erdaohe 89 43.37 N 127.35 E
Erdaohezi, Zhg. 89 45.07 N 127.16 E
Erdaohezi, Zhg. 89 45.08 N 129.39 E
Erdaojingzi 104 41.49 N 122.20 E
Erdaoliangzi, Zhg. 98 40.50 N 119.04 E
Erdaoliangzi, Zhg. 105 40.31 N 118.03 E
Erdaowan 89 47.58 N 124.33 E
Erdek 130 40.24 N 27.48 E
Erdemli 130 36.37 N 34.18 E
Erdene, Mong. 88 47.48 N 107.55 E
Erdene, Mong. 102 44.15 N 111.14 E
Erdene, Mong. 102 45.08 N 97.45 E
Erdene Bulgan 88 50.07 N 101.35 E
Erdene-Büren 86 48.26 N 91.27 E
Erdenedalaj 102 46.02 N 104.55 E
Erdene Mandal 88 48.30 N 101.21 E
Erdenheim 285 40.05 N 75.12 W
Erdevik 38 45.07 N 19.25 E
Erdiao 106 32.12 N 121.12 E
Erding 60 48.18 N 11.54 E
Erdinger Moos ≡ 60 48.22 N 11.52 E
Erdnijevskij 80 46.52 N 46.17 E
Erebato ≃ 246 5.54 N 64.16 W
Erebus, Mount ∧ 9 77.32 S 167.09 E
Erechim 252 27.38 S 52.17 W
Ereğli, Tür. 130 37.31 N 34.04 E
Ereğli, Tür. 130 41.17 N 31.25 E
Eregun 273a 6.36 N 3.22 E
Erei, Monti ⋏ 70 37.27 N 14.19 E
Eremita 256 21.35 S 45.04 W
Erenas 116 12.25 N 124.19 E
Erenhot 102 43.46 N 112.05 E
Erenköy 130 40.58 N 38.08 E
Erenköy ◆[8] 267b 40.58 N 29.04 E
Erepecu, Lago do ◎ 250 1.20 S 56.35 W
Eresma ≃ 34 41.26 N 4.45 W
Eressós 38 39.18 N 25.51 E
Erétria 38 38.24 N 23.48 E
Erez 132 31.34 N 34.34 E
Érezée 56 50.18 N 5.33 E
Erfa ≃ 56 49.40 N 9.23 E
Erfde 41 54.19 N 9.19 E
Erfenisdam ◎[1] 158 28.33 S 26.50 E
Erfoud 148 31.28 N 4.10 W
Erft ≃ 56 51.11 N 6.44 E
Erftstadt 56 50.48 N 6.46 E
Erfurt 54 50.58 N 11.01 E
Erfurt □[5] 54 51.10 N 10.45 E
Ergak-Targak-Tajga, chrebet ⋏ 88 53.25 N 95.30 E
Ergani 130 38.17 N 39.46 E
Ergene ≃ 130 41.01 N 26.22 E
Ergenzingen 58 48.29 N 8.48 E
Erges (Erjas) ≃ 34 39.40 N 7.01 W
Ērgļi 76 56.54 N 25.38 E
Ergolding 60 48.35 N 12.10 E
Ergoldsbach 60 48.41 N 12.12 E
Ergste 56 51.25 N 7.34 E
Erguig, Bahr ≃ 146 11.22 N 15.24 E
Ergun (Argun') ≃ 74 53.20 N 121.28 E
Ergun Youqi 89 50.14 N 120.10 E
Ergun Zuoqi 89 50.47 N 121.31 E
Erguvejem ≃ 180 65.20 N 176.00 W
Er Hai ◎ 102 25.48 N 100.11 E
Erhlin 100 23.54 N 120.22 E
Erhshui 100 23.49 N 120.36 E
Erhulai 98 41.23 N 125.08 E
Eria ≃ 34 42.03 N 5.44 W
Erial 208 39.46 N 75.00 W
Eriba 140 16.37 N 36.04 E
Eriboll 46 58.28 N 4.41 W
Eriboll, Loch c 46 58.31 N 4.41 W
Erica, Austl. 169 37.59 S 146.22 E
Erica, Ned. 52 52.43 N 6.55 E
Erice 70 38.02 N 12.35 E
Ericeira 34 38.59 N 9.25 W
Erichsen Lake ◎ 176 70.38 N 80.21 W
Erichshagen 52 52.40 N 9.14 E
Ericht, Loch ◎ 46 56.48 N 4.24 W
Erick 196 35.12 N 99.51 W
Erickson, B.C., Can. 182 49.05 N 116.28 W
Erickson, Mb., Can. 184 50.30 N 99.55 W
Ericson 198 41.46 N 98.40 W
Erie, Co., U.S. 200 40.03 N 105.03 W
Erie, Il., U.S. 190 41.39 N 90.04 W
Erie, Ks., U.S. 198 37.34 N 95.14 W
Erie, Mi., U.S. 216 41.47 N 83.29 W
Erie, Pa., U.S. 214 42.07 N 80.05 W
Erie □[6], N.Y., U.S. 210 42.54 N 78.53 W
Erie □[6], Oh., U.S. 214 41.27 N 82.42 W
Erie □[6], Pa., U.S. 214 42.08 N 80.04 W
Erie, Lake ◎ 214 42.15 N 81.00 W
Erieau 214 42.16 N 81.56 W
Erie Basin c 276 40.40 N 74.01 W
Erie Beach, On., Can. 214 42.16 N 82.00 W
Erie Beach, On., Can. 284a 42.53 N 78.57 W
Erie Canal → New York State Barge Canal ≊ 210 43.05 N 78.43 W
Erie County Fairgrounds ♦ 284a 42.45 N 78.49 W
Erie International Airport ⊠ 214 42.05 N 80.11 W
Eriksberg ⊥ 40 58.56 N 16.22 E
Eriksdale 184 50.52 N 98.06 W
Erímanthos ∧ 38 37.59 N 21.51 E
Erimo 92a 42.01 N 143.09 E
Erimo-misaki ≻ 92a 41.55 N 143.15 E
Erin, On., Can. 212 43.45 N 80.07 W
Erin, N.Y., U.S. 210 42.11 N 76.40 W
Erin, Tn., U.S. 194 36.19 N 87.41 W
Erindale 275b 43.32 N 79.39 W
Ering 60 48.18 N 13.09 E
Eriskay I 46 57.04 N 7.18 W
Erisort, Loch c 46 58.07 N 6.24 W
Eriswil 58 47.05 N 7.51 E
Erith ◆[8] 260 51.29 N 0.10 E
Erithraí 38 38.13 N 23.19 E
Eritrea □[9] 144 15.20 N 39.00 E
Erivan → Jerevan 84 40.11 N 44.30 E
Erjas (Erges) ≃ 34 39.40 N 7.01 W
Erjiazhen 106 32.02 N 121.13 E
Erkelenz 56 51.05 N 6.19 E
Erken ◎ 40 59.51 N 18.34 E
Erken-Jurt 84 44.27 N 41.54 E
Erkheim 58 48.02 N 10.20 E
Erkilet 130 38.49 N 35.27 E
Erkina ≃ 48 52.51 N 7.23 W
Erkner 54 52.25 N 13.45 E
Erkner, Forst ◆[3] 264a 52.22 N 13.47 E
Erkowit 140 18.46 N 37.07 E
Erkrath 56 51.13 N 6.55 E
Erl 64 47.41 N 12.11 E
Erlach, Öst. 61 47.43 N 16.13 E
Erlach, Schw. 58 47.03 N 7.06 E
Erlands Point 224 47.36 N 122.42 W
Erlangen 60 49.36 N 11.01 E
Erlanger 218 39.01 N 84.36 W
Erlanghe 100 30.19 N 116.04 E
Erlangmiao 100 33.46 N 112.23 E
Erlau ≃ 60 48.34 N 13.36 E
Erlauf ≃ 61 48.12 N 15.11 E
Erlbach 54 50.18 N 12.22 E
Erldunda 162 25.14 S 133.12 E
Erle ◆[8] 263 51.33 N 7.05 E
Erli 62 44.08 N 8.06 E
Erling 106 31.53 N 119.36 E
Erling, Lake ◎[1] 194 33.05 N 93.35 W
Erlistoun 162 28.20 S 122.08 E
Erlongshan, Zhg. 89 47.20 N 132.28 E
Erlongshan, Zhg. 89 50.04 N 126.47 E
Erlongshantun 89 48.28 N 126.31 E
Erlsbach 64 46.55 N 12.15 E
Erma 208 38.58 N 74.54 W
Ermana, chrebet ⋏ 88 50.00 N 113.30 E
Ermatingen 58 47.41 N 9.06 E
Erme ≃ 42 50.18 N 3.56 W
Ermelik 130 39.42 N 39.02 E
Ermelindo Matarazo ◆[8] 287b 23.29 S 46.29 W
Ermelo, Ned. 52 52.17 N 5.37 E
Ermelo, S. Afr. 158 26.34 S 29.58 E
Ermenak 130 36.38 N 32.54 E
Ermendegou 104 42.02 N 121.56 E
Ermenonville 50 49.08 N 2.42 E
Ermidas 34 38.00 N 8.23 W
Ermil Post 140 13.37 N 27.36 E
Ermineskin Indian Reserve ◆[4] 182 52.52 N 113.30 W
Ermington 274a 33.48 S 151.04 E
Ermita de los Correa 234 22.54 N 103.01 W
Ermont 50 48.59 N 2.16 E
Ermoúpolis 38 37.26 N 24.56 E
Ermsleben 54 51.44 N 11.21 E
Ernaballa Mission 162 26.17 S 132.07 E
Ernākulam 122 9.59 N 76.17 E
Erndtebrück 56 50.59 N 8.15 E
Erne ≃ 48 54.30 N 8.16 W
Erne, Lower Lough ◎ 48 54.26 N 7.46 W
Erne, Upper Lough ◎ 48 54.14 N 7.32 W
Ernée 32 48.18 N 0.56 W
Ernest 214 40.41 N 79.10 W
Ernestina 258 35.16 S 59.34 W
Ernest Sound ʯ 182 55.52 N 132.10 W
Ernici, Monti ⋏ 66 41.48 N 13.22 E
Ernstbrunn 61 48.32 N 16.22 E
Ernst-Thälman, Pioneerpark ♦ 264a 52.28 N 13.33 E
Ernst-Thälmann-Stadion ♦ 264a 52.23 N 13.05 E
Erode 122 11.21 N 77.44 E
Eromanga 166 26.40 S 143.16 E
Erongo 156 21.44 S 15.53 E
Erongo ⋏ 156 21.45 S 15.37 E
Erota 144 16.14 N 37.55 E
Erp 56 50.46 N 6.43 E
Erpuzi 105 40.29 N 115.33 E
Erquelinnes 50 50.18 N 4.07 E
Err, Piz d' ∧ 58 46.33 N 9.41 E
Errabiddy 162 25.28 S 117.07 E
Er-Rachidia 148 31.58 N 4.25 W
Er-Rachidia □[4] 148 31.15 N 4.05 W
Erramala Range ⋏ 122 15.30 N 78.10 E
Errego 154 16.02 S 37.14 E
Errer ≃ 144 7.32 N 42.05 E
Er-Riad → Ar-Riyāḍ 128 24.38 N 46.43 E
Errigal Mountain ∧ 48 55.02 N 8.07 W
Errington 224 49.17 N 124.22 W
Erris Head ≻ 48 54.19 N 10.00 W
Errochty, Loch ◎ 46 56.45 N 4.12 W
Errogie 46 57.16 N 4.22 W
Errol Heights 224 45.28 N 122.36 W
Erromango I 175f 18.45 S 169.05 E
Ersekë 38 40.20 N 20.41 E
Ershijiazi 104 41.17 N 120.32 E
Ershilipu 105 40.07 N 117.24 E
Ershiqizhan 89 53.23 N 123.16 E
Ershiwuzhan 89 53.22 N 123.55 E
Erskine 198 47.40 N 96.00 W
Erskine, Lake ◎ 276 41.06 N 74.15 W
Erskine Inlet c 176 76.15 N 102.20 W
Erskine Park 274a 33.49 S 150.47 E
Erstein 58 48.26 N 7.40 E
Erste Wiener Hochquellenleitung ≊[1] 61 48.10 N 16.17 E
Erstfeld 58 46.49 N 8.39 E
Ertai, Zhg. 86 46.07 N 90.06 E
Ertai, Zhg. 86 44.14 N 80.52 E
Ertaizi, Zhg. 104 42.35 N 124.00 E
Ertaizi, Zhg. 104 40.47 N 120.54 E
Ertaizi, Zhg. 104 41.52 N 121.56 E
Ertaizi, Zhg. 104 42.05 N 123.35 E
Ertil' 78 51.51 N 40.49 E
Ertingen 58 48.06 N 9.28 E
Ertix (Irtyš) ≃ 74 61.04 N 68.52 E
Erto 64 46.16 N 12.22 E
Ertra □[4] 144 15.20 N 39.00 E
Ertuğrul 130 39.34 N 27.43 E
Ertvelde 50 51.11 N 3.45 E
Erua 172 39.14 S 175.24 E
Eruar 126 23.28 N 87.52 E
Erudina 166 31.28 S 139.23 E
Erundu 156 20.36 S 16.25 E
Erunkan 273a 6.37 N 3.24 E
Erva, Ponta da ≻ 266c 38.50 N 8.58 W
Erval 252 32.02 S 53.24 W
Ervalla 40 59.22 N 15.15 E
Erving 207 42.36 N 72.23 W
Ervy-le-Châtel 50 48.02 N 3.55 E
Erwin, N.C., U.S. 192 35.19 N 78.40 W
Erwin, Tn., U.S. 192 36.08 N 82.25 W
Erwitte 52 51.37 N 8.20 E
Erwood 184 52.50 N 102.10 W
Erxleben 54 52.13 N 11.14 E
Érythrée → Eritrea □[9] 144 15.20 N 39.00 E
Eryuan 102 26.06 N 99.55 E
Erzaohang 106 31.05 N 121.49 E
Erzberg ◆[7] 61 47.32 N 14.54 E
Erzgebirge (Krušné hory) ⋏ 54 50.30 N 13.10 E
Erzhan 89 43.58 N 128.44 E
Erzhuang 105 39.24 N 117.22 E
Erzin 88 50.15 N 95.10 E
Erzincan 130 39.44 N 39.29 E
Erzincan □[4] 130 39.40 N 39.30 E
Erzingen 58 47.39 N 8.25 E
Erzurum 130 39.55 N 41.17 E
Erzurum □[4] 130 40.00 N 41.30 E
Esa-Ala 164 9.44 S 150.49 E
Esambo 152 3.40 S 23.24 E
Esan-misaki ≻ 92a 41.49 N 141.11 E
Esashi, Nihon 92 41.52 N 140.07 E
Esashi, Nihon 92 39.12 N 141.09 E
Esashi, Nihon 92a 44.56 N 142.35 E
Esbiye 130 40.57 N 38.44 E
Esbjerg 26 55.28 N 8.27 E
Esbly 261 48.54 N 2.49 E
Esbo → Espoo 26 60.13 N 24.40 E
Esborn 263 51.23 N 7.20 E
Esca ≃ 34 42.37 N 1.03 W
Escada 250 8.22 S 35.14 W
Escalada 258 34.10 S 59.07 W
Escalante, Pil. 116 10.50 N 123.33 E
Escalante, Ut,. U.S. 200 37.46 N 111.36 W
Escalante ≃, Ut,. U.S. 200 37.17 N 110.53 W
Escalante ≃, Ven. 246 9.15 N 71.50 W
Escalante Desert ◆[2] 200 37.50 N 113.30 W
Escalaplano 71 39.37 N 9.21 E
Escalón, Méx. 232 26.45 N 104.20 W
Escalon, Ca., U.S. 226 37.47 N 120.59 W
Escalona 34 40.10 N 4.24 W
Escambia ≃ 194 30.32 N 87.11 W
Escanaba 190 45.44 N 87.04 W
Escanaba ≃ 190 45.47 N 87.04 W
Escandón, Puerto de)(34 40.17 N 1.00 W
Escárcega de Matamoros 232 18.37 N 90.43 W
Escarpada Point ≻ 116 18.31 N 122.13 E
Escarpado Peak ∧ 116 8.36 N 117.22 E
Escarpment 284a 43.10 N 79.00 W
Escatawpa ≃ 194 30.25 N 88.35 W
Escaudain 50 50.20 N 3.21 E
Escaut (Schelde) ≃ 50 51.22 N 4.15 E
Esch ≃ 56 48.54 N 6.04 E
Eschach 58 47.44 N 9.36 E
Eschau 58 48.29 N 7.43 E
Eschebrügge 52 52.37 N 6.46 E
Eschede 52 52.44 N 10.14 E
Eschen 58 47.13 N 9.31 E
Eschenau 60 49.34 N 11.12 E
Eschenbach 60 49.45 N 11.49 E
Eschenburg 56 50.49 N 8.20 E
Eschenlohe 64 47.36 N 11.11 E
Eschershausen 52 51.56 N 9.38 E
Eschlkam 60 49.18 N 12.55 E
Escholzmatt 58 46.55 N 7.56 E
Eschscholtz Bay c 180 66.18 N 161.25 W
Esch-sur-Alzette 56 49.30 N 5.59 E
Esch-sur-Sûre 56 49.55 N 5.55 E
Eschwege 56 51.11 N 10.04 E
Eschweiler 56 50.49 N 6.16 E
Esclave, Grand Lac de l' → Great Slave Lake ◎ 176 61.30 N 114.00 W
Esclavo, Gran Lago del → Great Slave Lake ◎ 176 61.30 N 114.00 W
Escobal 236 9.09 N 79.58 W
Escobar □[5] 288 34.23 S 58.46 W
Escobar, Arroyo ≃ 288 34.21 S 58.44 W
Escobedo 196 27.13 N 101.21 W
Escocesa, Bahía c 238 19.25 N 69.45 W
Escoheag 207 41.36 N 71.45 W
Escondido 228 33.07 N 117.05 W
Escondido ≃, Méx. 196 28.39 N 100.34 W
Escondido ≃, Nic. 236 12.04 N 83.45 W
Escondido Creek ≃ 228 33.01 N 117.15 W
Escorial → San Lorenzo de El Escorial 34 40.35 N 4.09 W
Escoutay ≃ 62 44.29 N 4.42 E
Escravos ≃[1] 150 5.35 N 5.10 E
Escrick 44 53.53 N 1.02 W
Escuadrón 201 ◆[8] 286a 19.22 N 99.06 W
Escudero, Arroyo ≃ 258 34.20 S 57.05 W
Escudo de Veraguas, Isla I 236 9.06 N 81.33 W
Escuinapa [de Hidalgo] 234 22.51 N 105.48 W
Escuintla, Guat. 236 14.18 N 90.47 W
Escuintla, Méx. 232 15.20 N 92.38 W
Escuintla □[5] 236 14.10 N 91.00 W
Escuminac, Point ≻ 186 47.04 N 64.46 W
Escurial, Serra do ∧ 250 10.04 S 41.05 W
Esebi 154 2.57 N 30.39 E
Eséka 152 3.39 N 10.46 E
Esenler 267b 41.02 N 28.51 E
Esenli 130 40.41 N 37.24 E
Esens 52 53.39 N 7.37 E
Ésera ≃ 34 42.06 N 0.15 E
Esesi 130 39.49 N 39.19 E
Eşfahān (Isfahan) 128 32.40 N 51.38 E
Eşfahān □[4] 128 33.00 N 52.00 E
Esgueva ≃ 34 41.40 N 4.43 W
Eshan 102 24.11 N 102.22 E
Esher ◆[8] 260 51.23 N 0.22 W
Eshkāshem 123 36.42 N 71.34 E
Eshowe 158 28.58 S 31.29 E
Esh-Sham → Dimashq 132 33.30 N 36.18 E
Eshta'ol 132 31.47 N 35.00 E
Esh Winning 44 54.47 N 1.43 W
Esiama 150 4.56 N 2.21 W
Esigodini 154 20.18 S 28.56 E
Esine 64 45.55 N 10.15 E
Esino ≃ 66 43.39 N 13.22 E
Esira 157b 24.20 S 46.42 E
Esirgâh 130 39.48 N 38.52 E
Esk 171a 27.15 S 152.25 E
Esk ≃, N.Z. 172 43.06 S 171.57 E
Esk ≃, U.K. 44 54.58 N 3.04 W
Esk ≃, Eng., U.K. 44 54.29 N 0.37 W
Esk ≃, Eng., U.K. 44 54.21 N 3.23 W
Esk ≃, Scot., U.K. 46 55.57 N 3.03 W
Eskdale, N.Z. 172 39.24 S 176.50 E
Eskdale, W.V., U.S. 188 38.05 N 81.26 W
Eskdale V 44 55.10 N 3.00 W
Eske, Lough ◎ 48 54.41 N 8.03 W
Eski Dzhumaya → Târgovište 38 43.15 N 26.34 E
Eskifjörđur 24a 65.04 N 13.59 W
Eskiikan 85 43.12 N 68.31 E
Eskiköy 130 36.36 N 30.34 E
Eskilstrup 41 54.51 N 11.54 E
Eskilstuna 40 59.22 N 16.30 E
Eski Malatya 130 38.26 N 38.23 E
Eskimo Lakes ◎ 180 69.15 N 132.17 W
Eskimo Point 176 61.07 N 94.03 W
Eskipazar 130 40.58 N 32.33 E
Eskişehir 130 39.46 N 30.32 E
Eskişehir □[4] 130 39.35 N 31.10 E
Eskridge 198 38.51 N 96.06 W
Esla ≃ 34 41.29 N 6.03 W
Eslāmābād-e Gharb 128 34.06 N 46.31 E
Eslām Qal'eh 128 34.40 N 61.04 E
Eslarn 60 49.35 N 12.32 E

ENGLISH Name	Page	Lat.°′	Long.°′	DEUTSCH Name	Seite	Breite°′	Länge°′ E = Ost

Eslohe 56 51.15 N 8.09 E
Eslöv 41 55.50 N 13.20 E
Esmā'īlābād 128 28.48 N 56.39 E
Eşme 130 38.24 N 28.59 E
Esmeralda, Austl. 166 18.50 S 142.34 E
Esmeralda, Cuba 240p 21.51 N 78.07 W
Esmeralda, Méx. 196 25.40 N 103.30 W
Esmeralda, Isla I 254 48.57 S 75.25 W
Esmeraldas 246 0.59 N 79.42 W
Esmeraldas □[4] 246 0.40 N 79.30 W
Esmeraldas ≃ 246 0.58 N 79.38 W
Esmirna → İzmir 130 38.25 N 27.09 E
Esmond, N.D., U.S. 198 48.02 N 99.45 W
Esmond, R.I., U.S. 207 41.52 N 71.29 W
Esnagi Lake ◎ 190 48.38 N 84.32 W
Esneux 56 50.32 N 5.34 E
Esong 152 2.09 N 10.58 E
Esopus Creek ≃ 210 42.04 N 73.56 W
Espada, Punta ≻ 246 12.05 N 71.07 W
Espagne → Spain □[1] 34 40.00 N 4.00 W
Espalion 32 44.31 N 2.46 E
Espaly-Saint-Marcel 62 45.03 N 3.52 E
España → Spain □[1] 34 40.00 N 4.00 W
Espanola, On., Can. 190 46.15 N 81.46 W
Espanola, N.M., U.S. 200 35.59 N 106.04 W
Española, Isla I 246a 1.25 S 89.42 W
Esparta 236 9.59 N 84.40 W
Esparto 226 38.41 N 122.00 W
Espasingen 58 47.49 N 9.00 E
Espe, Dan. 41 55.12 N 10.25 E
Espe, S.S.S.R. 85 43.52 N 74.10 E
Espejo 34 37.41 N 4.33 W
Espejo, Canal de ≊ 286e 33.32 S 70.43 W
Espelkamp 52 52.25 N 8.36 E
Espenberg, Cape ≻ 180 66.33 N 163.36 W
Espenhain 54 51.11 N 12.29 E
Espera, Arroyo ≃[1] 288 34.24 S 58.36 W
Espera Feliz 255 20.39 S 41.55 W
Esperança, Bra. 246 4.24 S 69.52 W
Esperança, Bra. 250 7.01 S 35.51 W
Esperance, Austl. 162 33.51 S 121.53 E
Esperance, N.Y., U.S. 210 42.46 N 74.15 W
Esperance Bay c 162 33.51 S 121.53 E
Esperantina 250 3.54 S 42.14 W
Esperantinópolis 250 4.53 S 44.53 W
Esperanza, Arg. 252 31.27 S 60.56 W
Esperanza, Méx. 232 27.35 N 109.56 W
Esperanza, Méx. 234 18.52 N 97.24 W
Esperanza, Pil. 116 8.43 N 125.36 E
Esperanza, Pil. 116 11.44 N 124.03 E
Esperanza, P.R. 240m 18.06 N 65.28 W
Esperanza, S. Afr. 158 30.21 S 30.40 E
Esperanza ʋ[3] 9 63.24 S 56.59 W
Esperanza Inlet c 182 49.48 N 126.50 W
Espergærde 41 56.00 N 12.34 E
Esperia 66 41.23 N 13.41 E
Esperito, Arroyo ≃[1] 288 34.23 S 58.36 W
Espevær 26 59.36 N 5.10 E
Espichel, Cabo ≻ 34 38.25 N 9.13 W
Espinal, Col. 246 4.09 N 74.53 W
Espinal, Méx. 234 16.29 N 95.03 W
Espinar 248 14.47 S 71.29 W
Espinazo 196 26.16 N 101.06 W
Espinazo, Sierra del → Espinhaço, Serra do ⋏ 255 17.30 S 43.30 W
Espinazo del Diablo, Sierra ⋏ 234 23.55 N 106.00 W
Espingarda ≃ 250 10.03 S 47.13 W
Espinhaço, Serra do ⋏ 255 17.30 S 43.30 W
Espinho 34 41.00 N 8.39 W
Espinillo 252 24.58 S 58.34 W
Espinillo, Arroyo ≃ 258 34.59 S 57.36 W
Espinillo, Punta ≻ 258 34.50 S 56.26 W
Espino 246 8.34 N 66.01 W
Espinosa 255 14.56 S 42.50 W
Espinos de Judio 234 19.52 N 104.35 W
Espírito Santo → Vila Velha 250 3.13 N 51.13 W
Espírito Santo □[3] 255 19.30 S 40.30 W
Espírito Santo do Dourado 256 22.03 S 45.58 W
Espiritu Santo I 175f 15.15 S 166.50 E
Espíritu Santo, Bahía del c 232 19.20 N 87.35 W
Espíritu Santo, Isla del I 232 24.30 N 110.22 W
Espita 232 21.01 N 88.19 W
Esplanada 255 11.47 S 37.57 W
Esplugas 266d 41.22 N 2.05 E
Espoir, Bay d' c 186 47.50 N 55.51 W
Espoo (Esbo) 26 60.13 N 24.40 E
Esposende 34 41.32 N 8.47 W
Esposizione Universale di Roma ♦ 267a 41.50 N 12.28 E
Espumoso 252 28.44 S 52.51 W
Espungabera 156 20.29 S 32.48 E
Espy 210 41.00 N 76.24 W
Espyville Station 214 41.36 N 80.29 W
Esquatzel Coulee V 202 46.17 N 119.07 W
Esquel 254 42.54 S 71.19 W
Esquimalt 224 48.26 N 123.24 W
Esquina 252 30.01 S 59.32 W
Esquina Negra 258 35.02 S 58.03 W
Esquipulas, Guat. 236 14.34 N 89.21 W
Esquipulas, Nic. 236 12.40 N 85.47 W
Esquiú 252 29.23 S 65.17 W
Esrum Sø ◎ 41 56.00 N 12.24 E
Essa ≃ 76 54.53 N 28.40 E
Essaoui Mellene, Oued V 148 27.26 N 6.40 E
Essaouira (Mogador) 148 31.30 N 9.47 W
Essaouira □[4] 148 31.25 N 9.30 W
Essarts 261 48.30 N 1.46 E
Essé 152 4.05 N 11.53 E
Esse ≃ 66 43.16 N 11.54 E
Esseg → Osijek 38 45.33 N 18.41 E
Es-Sekhira 148 34.17 N 10.06 E
Essel ◆[8] 263 51.37 N 7.15 E
Essen, Bel. 50 51.28 N 4.28 E
Essen, B.R.D. 52 52.43 N 7.57 E
Essen, B.R.D. 56 51.28 N 7.01 E
Essen, B.R.D. 263 51.28 N 7.01 E
Essenbach 60 48.37 N 12.13 E
Essenberg 263 51.26 N 6.42 E
Essendon, Austl. 169 37.46 S 144.55 E
Essendon, Eng., U.K. 260 51.46 N 0.09 W
Essendon, Mount ∧ 162 24.59 S 120.28 E
Essendon Airport ⊠ 169 37.43 S 144.53 E
Essen-Mülheim, Flughafen ⊠ 263 51.24 N 6.58 E
Essentuki → Jessentuki 84 44.03 N 42.51 E
Essequibo ≃ 246 6.59 N 58.23 W
Es Sers 36 36.04 N 9.02 E
Essex, On., Can. 214 42.10 N 82.49 W
Essex, Ct., U.S. 207 41.21 N 72.23 W
Essex, Il., U.S. 216 41.11 N 88.11 W
Essex, Ia., U.S. 198 40.50 N 95.18 W
Essex, Md., U.S. 208 39.18 N 76.28 W
Essex, Ma., U.S. 207 42.37 N 70.47 W
Essex, Mo., U.S. 194 36.48 N 89.51 W
Essex, Mt., U.S. 182 48.16 N 113.36 W
Essex □[6], On., Can. 214 42.10 N 82.50 W
Essex □[6], Eng., U.K. 42 51.48 N 0.40 E
Essex □[6], Ma., U.S. 207 42.40 N 70.55 W
Essex □[6], N.J., U.S. 210 40.48 N 74.12 W
Essex □[6], Vt., U.S. 206 44.57 N 71.43 W
Essex □[6], Va., U.S. 208 37.55 N 76.55 W
Essex ≃ 283 42.39 N 70.46 W
Essex Bay c 283 42.39 N 70.44 W
Essex Fells 276 40.49 N 74.17 W
Essex Junction 188 44.29 N 73.06 W
Essex Skypark ⊠ 284b 39.18 N 76.28 W
Essexville 190 43.36 N 83.50 W
Essing 60 48.56 N 11.47 E
Essington 285 39.52 N 75.18 W
Essling ◆[8] 264b 48.13 N 16.32 E
Esslingen 56 48.45 N 9.16 E
Es Smala es Souassi 36 35.21 N 10.33 E
Esson Lake ◎ 212 45.02 N 78.16 W
Essonne □[5] 50 48.36 N 2.20 E
Essonne ≃ 50 48.37 N 2.29 E
Essoyes 58 48.04 N 4.32 E
Es-Suki 140 13.20 N 33.54 E
Essvik 26 62.19 N 17.24 E
Est □[4] 152 4.00 N 14.00 E
Est □[5] 150 12.00 N 1.00 E
Est ◆[5] 261 48.53 N 2.22 E
Est, Canal de l' ≊ 58 48.45 N 5.35 E
Est, Cap ≻ 157b 15.16 S 50.29 E
Est, Île de l' I 186 47.37 N 61.26 W
Est, Pointe de l' ≻ 186 49.08 N 61.41 W
Estacada 224 45.17 N 122.19 W
Estaca de Bares, Punta de la ≻ 34 43.46 N 7.42 W
Estacado, Llano ≚ 196 33.30 N 102.40 W
Estado, Parque do ♦ 287b 23.39 S 46.37 W
Estados, Isla de los (Staten Island) I 254 54.47 S 64.15 W
Estados Unidos → United States □[1] 178 38.00 N 97.00 W
Eşţahbānāt 128 29.08 N 54.04 E
Estaires 50 50.38 N 2.43 E
Estambul → İstanbul 130 41.01 N 28.58 E
Estância, Bra. 250 11.16 S 37.26 W
Estancia, Pil. 116 11.28 N 123.09 E
Estancia, S. Afr. 158 26.17 S 29.52 E
Estancia, N.M., U.S. 200 34.45 N 106.03 W
Estancia de los López 234 20.53 N 104.31 W
Estandarte 250 1.26 S 45.32 W
Estanislao del Campo 252 25.03 S 60.06 W
Estanzuelas 236 13.38 N 88.30 W
Estarreja 34 40.45 N 8.34 W
Estats, Pique d' ∧ 34 42.40 N 1.24 E
Estavayer-le-Lac 58 46.51 N 6.50 E
Estcourt 158 29.01 S 29.52 E
Este 64 45.14 N 11.39 E
Este ≃ 52 53.32 N 9.47 E
Este, Parque Nacional del ♦ 286c 10.30 N 66.50 W
Este, Punta ≻ 240m 18.08 N 65.16 W
Esteban Echeverría 258 34.50 S 58.28 W
Esteban Echeverría □[5] 288 34.51 S 58.32 W
Estefanía, Lago → Stefanie, Lake ◎ 144 4.40 N 36.50 E
Esteio 252 29.51 S 51.10 W
Estelí 236 13.05 N 86.23 W
Estelí □[5] 236 13.10 N 86.20 W
Estella 34 42.40 N 2.02 W
Estelline, S.D., U.S. 198 44.34 N 96.54 W
Estelline, Tx., U.S. 196 34.33 N 100.26 W
Estell Manor 208 39.24 N 74.44 W
Estèng 62 44.14 N 6.45 E
Estepa 34 37.18 N 4.54 W
Estepas de Kirguises → Kirgizskij chrebet ⋏ 85 42.30 N 74.00 E
Estepona 34 36.26 N 5.08 W
Ester 180 64.51 N 148.01 W
Esterel ⋏ 62 43.30 N 6.50 E
Esterhazy 184 50.40 N 102.08 W
Esterhazy, Schloss ⊥ 61 47.51 N 16.32 E
Estérias, Cap ≻ 152 0.37 N 9.20 E
Esternay 50 48.44 N 3.34 E
Estero 220 26.26 N 81.49 W
Estero Bay c, Ca., U.S. 226 35.24 N 120.53 W
Estero Bay c, Fl., U.S. 220 26.25 N 81.52 W
Estero Island I 220 26.26 N 81.56 W
Estéron ≃ 62 43.49 N 7.11 E
Esteros 252 26.37 S 63.39 W
Esterwegen 52 52.59 N 7.38 E
Estes Park 200 40.22 N 105.31 W
Este Sudeste, Cayos del II 236 12.26 N 81.27 W
Estevan 184 49.08 N 102.59 W
Estevan Group II 182 53.05 N 129.40 W
Estevan Point 182 49.23 N 126.33 W
Esther Island I 180 60.50 N 148.05 W
Estherville 198 43.24 N 94.49 W
Estí ≃ 236 8.28 N 82.16 W
Estill 192 32.45 N 81.14 W
Estissac 50 48.16 N 3.49 E
Estiva 256 22.28 S 46.02 W
Estiva, Ribeirão da ≃ 287b 23.44 S 46.23 W
Estling, Lake ◎ 276 40.53 N 74.30 W
Estocolmo → Stockholm 40 59.20 N 18.03 E
Eston, Sk., Can. 184 51.10 N 108.46 W
Eston, Eng., U.K. 44 54.34 N 1.07 W
Estonia → Estonskaja Sovetskaja Socialističeskaja Respublika □[3] 76 59.00 N 26.00 E
Estonskaja Sovetskaja Socialističeskaja Respublika □[3] 76 59.00 N 26.00 E
Estoril 266c 38.42 N 9.23 W
Estrasburgo → Strasbourg 58 48.35 N 7.45 E
Estrées-Saint-Denis 50 49.26 N 2.39 E
Estrêla 252 29.29 S 51.58 W
Estrela ∧ 34 40.19 N 7.37 W
Estrêla ≃ 287a 22.43 S 43.13 W
Estrela, Serra da ⋏ 34 40.20 N 7.38 W
Estrêla do Indaiá 255 19.31 S 45.47 W
Estrêla do Leste 255 16.17 S 53.34 W
Estrêla do Norte 255 13.49 S 49.04 W
Estrêla do Sul 255 18.46 S 47.42 W
Estrella ≃ 226 35.45 N 120.41 W
Estrella, Cerro de la ∧ 286a 19.20 N 99.05 W
Estrella, Punta ≻ 232 30.55 N 114.43 W
Estremadura □[9] 34 39.15 N 9.10 W
Estremoz 34 38.51 N 7.35 W
Estrondo, Serra do ⋏[1] 250 9.00 S 48.45 W
Estuaire □[4] 152 0.15 N 10.00 E
Estuary 184 50.56 N 109.46 W
Esumba, Île I 152 2.00 N 21.12 E
Eszék → Osijek 38 45.33 N 18.41 E
Esztergom 30 47.48 N 18.45 E
Étables 32 48.38 N 2.50 W
Etadunna 166 28.43 S 138.38 E
Etah, India 124 27.38 N 78.40 E
Etah, Kal. Nun. 16 78.19 N 72.38 W
Etah □[5] 124 27.40 N 78.50 E
Étain 56 49.13 N 5.38 E
Etajima 96 34.15 N 132.30 E
Eta-jima I 96 34.15 N 132.28 E
Étalle 56 49.41 N 5.36 E
Étamaniou ≃ 186 50.17 N 59.58 W
Étampes 50 48.26 N 2.09 E
Etamunbanie, Lake ◎ 166 26.15 S 139.44 E
Étaples 50 50.31 N 1.39 E
États-Unis → United States □[1] 178 38.00 N 97.00 W
Etāwah, India 124 25.32 N 76.22 E
Etāwah, India 124 26.46 N 79.02 E
Etāwah □[5] 124 26.40 N 79.20 E
Etchemin ≃ 186 46.46 N 71.14 W
Etchojoa 232 26.55 N 109.38 W
Etchoropo 232 26.41 N 109.40 W

Symbols in the index entries represent the broad categories identified in the key at the right. Symbols with superior numbers (⋏[1]) identify subcategories (see complete key on page *I · 1).*

Kartensymbole in dem Registerverzeichnis stellen die rechts in Schlüssel erklärten Kategorien dar. Symbole mit hochgestellten Ziffern (⋏[1]) bezeichnen Unterabteilungen einer Kategorie (vgl. vollständiger Schlüssel auf Seite *I · 1).*

Los símbolos incluídos en el texto del índice representan las grandes categorias identificadas con la clave a la derecha. Los símbolos con numeros en su parte superior (⋏[1]) identifican las subcategorías (véase la clave completa en la página *I · 1).*

Les symboles de l'index représentent les catégories indiquées dans la légende à droite. Les symboles suivis d'un indice (⋏[1]) représentent des sous-catégories (voir légende complète à la page *I · 1).*

Os símbolos incluídos no texto do índice representam as grandes categorias identificadas com a chave à direita. Os símbolos com números em sua parte superior (⋏[1]) identificam as subcategorias (veja-se a chave completa à página *I · 1).*

	English	Deutsch	Español	Français	Português
∧	Mountain	Berg	Montaña	Montagne	Montanha
⋏	Mountains	Berge	Montañas	Montagnes	Montanhas
)(	Pass	Pass	Paso	Col	Passo
V	Valley, Canyon	Tal, Cañon	Valle, Cañón	Vallée, Canyon	Vale, Canhão
≚	Plain	Ebene	Llano	Plaine	Planície
≻	Cape	Kap	Cabo	Cap	Cabo
I	Island	Insel	Isla	Île	Ilha
II	Islands	Inseln	Islas	Îles	Ilhas
♦	Other Topographic Features	Andere Topographische Objekte	Otros Elementos Topográficos	Autres données topographiques	Outros acidentes topográficos

ESPAÑOL — Nombre · Página · Lat.°′ · Long.°′ W = Oeste
FRANÇAIS — Nom · Page · Lat.°′ · Long.°′ W = Ouest
PORTUGUÊS — Nome · Página · Lat.°′ · Long.°′ W = Oeste

Symbol	English	Deutsch	Español	Français	Português
≃	River	Fluss	Río	Rivière	Rio
≊	Canal	Kanal	Canal	Canal	Canal
ʟ	Waterfall, Rapids	Wasserfall, Stromschnellen	Cascada, Rápidos	Chute d'eau, Rapides	Cascata, Rápidos
ʉ	Strait	Meeresstrasse	Estrecho	Détroit	Estreito
ϲ	Bay, Gulf	Bucht, Golf	Bahía, Golfo	Baie, Golfe	Baía, Golfo
⊜	Lake, Lakes	See, Seen	Lago, Lagos	Lac, Lacs	Lago, Lagos
⁞	Swamp	Sumpf	Pantano	Marais	Pântano
⊓	Ice Features, Glacier	Eis- und Gletscherformen	Accidentes Glaciales	Formes glaciaires	Acidentes glaciares
⫟	Other Hydrographic Features	Andere Hydrographische Objekte	Otros Elementos Hidrográficos	Autres données hydrographiques	Outros acidentes hidrográficos
✢	Submarine Features	Untermeerische Objekte	Accidentes Submarinos	Formes de relief sous-marin	Acidentes submarinos
▫	Political Unit	Politische Einheit	Unidad Politica	Entité politique	Unidade política
☋	Cultural Institution	Kulturelle Institution	Institución Cultural	Institution culturelle	Instituição cultural
⊥	Historical Site	Historische Stätte	Sitio Histórico	Site historique	Sitio histórico
♠	Recreational Site	Erholungs- und Ferienort	Sitio de Recreo	Centre de loisirs	Area de Lazer
⊠	Airport	Flughafen	Aeropuerto	Aéroport	Aeroporto
■	Military Installation	Militäranlage	Instalación Militar	Installation militaire	Instalação militar
⬥	Miscellaneous	Verschiedenes	Misceláneo	Divers	Diversos

Name	Page	Lat.°′	Long.°′
Fan ≃	**104**	42.16 N	123.40 E
Fana	**150**	12.47 N	6.57 W
Fanaco, Lago ⊜	**70**	37.39 N	13.33 E
Fanad Head ›	**48**	55.16 N	7.38 W
Fanado ≃	**255**	17.10 S	42.40 W
Fanambana	**157b**	13.34 S	50.00 E
Fanan I	**175c**	7.11 N	151.59 E
Fanano	**64**	44.12 N	10.47 E
Fanārah	**142**	30.17 N	32.21 E
Fanchang	**100**	31.07 N	118.12 E
Fanch'eng → Xiangfan	**102**	32.03 N	112.01 E
Fancher, Il., U.S.	**219**	39.16 N	88.47 W
Fancher, N.Y., U.S.	**210**	43.15 N	66.06 W
Fanchuan	**100**	32.40 N	119.42 E
Fancy	**241h**	13.22 N	61.11 W
Fancy Creek ≃	**198**	39.28 N	96.45 W
Fancy Prairie	**219**	39.59 N	89.36 W
Fandriana	**157b**	20.14 S	47.23 E
Fane ≃	**48**	53.57 N	6.22 W
Fanepura	**123**	31.29 N	72.54 E
Faneroménis, Moní ʊ[1]	**267c**	37.59 N	23.26 E
Fang	**110**	19.55 N	99.13 E
Fangaga ∧	**144**	17.30 N	38.01 E
Fangak	**140**	9.04 N	30.53 E
Fangbian	**106**	31.42 N	119.06 E
Fangcheng, Zhg.	**100**	33.16 N	112.59 E
Fangcheng, Zhg.	**102**	21.49 N	108.22 E
Fangcheng, Zhg.	**105**	39.16 N	115.28 E
Fangcun, Zhg.	**100**	29.04 N	118.36 E
Fangcun, Zhg.	**100**	26.50 N	118.15 E
Fangdao	**100**	27.01 N	118.06 E
Fängersee ⊜	**264a**	52.35 N	13.50 E
Fangguan	**105**	39.20 N	115.58 E
Fangji	**100**	31.54 N	115.35 E
Fangjiachang	**107**	30.05 N	104.16 E
Fangjiazhuang	**106**	30.45 N	119.53 E
Fangliao	**100**	22.22 N	120.35 E
Fangmutun	**98**	42.34 N	124.34 E
Fangniu	**102**	27.40 N	100.25 E
Fangshan, T'aiwan	**100**	22.16 N	120.39 E
Fangshan, Zhg.	**98**	39.42 N	115.58 E
Fang Shan ∧	**106**	31.40 N	119.16 E
Fang Shan ∧[2]	**106**	31.29 N	119.09 E
Fangshanzhen	**104**	41.54 N	122.05 E
Fangshen	**104**	42.02 N	124.04 E
Fangshengpu	**107**	30.20 N	104.54 E
Fangsi	**98**	36.56 N	116.29 E
Fangtai	**106**	31.19 N	121.12 E
Fangxi	**100**	28.23 N	114.38 E
Fangxian	**102**	32.02 N	110.45 E
Fangxianzhen	**106**	32.00 N	119.44 E
Fangzheng	**89**	45.50 N	128.50 E
Fangzi	**98**	36.36 N	119.07 E
Fanhões	**266c**	38.53 N	9.09 W
Fanipol'	**76**	53.45 N	27.20 E
Fanjakana	**157b**	21.10 S	46.53 E
Fanjiadai	**106**	32.04 N	120.15 E
Fanjiadian	**104**	41.41 N	121.50 E
Fanjiatun	**89**	43.43 N	125.06 E
Fanjiazhuang	**105**	39.12 N	117.20 E
Fannaråken ∧	**26**	61.31 N	7.55 E
Fannettsburg	**214**	40.04 N	77.50 W
Fannich, Loch ⊜	**46**	57.38 N	5.00 W
Fannrem	**26**	63.16 N	9.50 E
Fanny, Mount ∧	**202**	45.20 N	117.41 W
Fanny Bay	**182**	49.30 N	124.50 W
Fano	**66**	43.50 N	13.01 E
Fanø I	**26**	55.25 N	8.25 E
Fanqiao	**100**	28.48 N	121.10 E
Fans, Col des)(	**62**	44.56 N	4.47 E
Fanshan, Zhg.	**100**	27.21 N	120.24 E
Fanshan, Zhg.	**105**	40.13 N	115.25 E
Fanshang	**106**	31.40 N	120.01 E
Fanshawe Lake ⊜	**212**	43.05 N	81.10 W
Fansher Creek ≃	**214**	42.37 N	82.01 W
Fanshui	**100**	33.07 N	119.25 E
Fan-si-pan ∧	**110**	22.15 N	103.46 E
Fantasy Island ♦	**284a**	43.02 N	78.58 W
Fanthyttan	**40**	59.40 N	15.06 E
Fanwood	**276**	40.38 N	74.23 W
Fanxian	**98**	35.57 N	115.38 E
Fanzhen	**98**	36.14 N	117.21 E
Faoileann, Bàgh nam ⊂	**46**	56.23 N	7.17 W
Faqīrah, Wādī V	**142**	28.52 N	30.57 E
Faqqūʻah	**132**	32.30 N	35.24 E
Fāqūs	**142**	30.44 N	31.48 E
Farab	**85**	39.14 N	67.28 E
Faraday ʊ[3]	**9**	65.15 S	64.16 W
Faraday, Mount ∧	**172**	42.02 S	171.34 E
Faradje	**154**	3.44 N	29.43 E
Faradofay	**157b**	25.02 S	47.00 E
Farafangana	**157b**	22.49 S	47.50 E
Farāfirah, Al-Wāḥat al- ⊤[4]	**140**	27.15 N	28.10 E
Farāh	**128**	32.22 N	62.07 E
Farāh □[4]	**128**	33.00 N	62.30 E
Farāh ≃	**128**	31.29 N	61.24 E
Faraḥābād	**267d**	35.42 N	51.30 E
Farahalana	**157b**	14.26 S	50.10 E
Farā'id, Jabal al- ∧	**140**	23.31 N	35.20 E
Fara in Sabina	**66**	42.12 N	12.43 E
Farallon de Medinilla I	**108**	16.01 N	146.04 E
Farallon de Pajaros I	**108**	20.32 N	144.54 E
Farallon Islands II	**204**	37.43 N	123.03 W
Faramana	**150**	12.03 N	4.40 W
Faranah	**150**	10.02 N	10.44 W
Fara Novarese	**62**	45.33 N	8.27 E
Farasān, Jazā'ir II	**144**	16.48 N	41.54 E
Farasān al-Kabīr I	**144**	16.42 N	42.00 E
Faratsiho	**157b**	19.24 S	46.57 E
Faraulep I[1]	**108**	8.36 N	144.33 E
Farazād	**267d**	35.47 N	51.21 E
Farber	**219**	39.16 N	91.34 W
Farbovano	**78**	50.09 N	31.51 E
Farcăul ∧	**38**	47.56 N	24.27 E
Farchant	**64**	47.32 N	11.06 E
Farcy	**261**	48.31 N	2.37 E
Fardes ≃	**34**	37.35 N	3.00 W
Fare ≃	**50**	47.39 N	0.14 E
Fareara, Pointe ›	**174s**	17.52 S	149.39 W
Far Eastern University ʊ[2]	**269f**	14.36 N	120.59 E
Fareham	**42**	50.51 N	1.10 W
Fårevejle	**41**	55.48 N	11.27 E
Farewell	**180**	62.31 N	153.53 W
Farewell, Cape ›	**172**	40.30 S	172.41 E
Farewell Spit ›[2]	**172**	40.31 S	172.52 E
Färgelanda	**26**	58.34 N	11.59 E
Fargniers	**50**	49.39 N	3.19 E
Fargo	**198**	46.52 N	96.47 W
Far Hills	**276**	40.41 N	74.38 W
Faria ≃	**287a**	22.53 S	43.15 W
Fāriʻah, Wādī al- V	**132**	32.06 N	35.31 E
Faribault	**190**	44.17 N	93.16 W
Faribault, Lac ⊜	**176**	59.00 N	72.00 W
Farīdābād	**124**	28.26 N	77.19 E
Farīdganj	**126**	23.08 N	90.45 E
Farīdkot	**123**	30.40 N	74.45 E
Farīdnagar	**124**	28.46 N	77.37 E
Farīdpur, Bngl.	**126**	24.10 N	89.26 E
Farīdpur, Bngl.	**126**	23.36 N	89.50 E
Farīdpur, India	**124**	28.13 N	79.33 E
Farīdpur Station	**126**	24.10 N	89.10 E
Farié Haoussa	**150**	13.48 N	1.38 E
Fārigh, Wādī al- V	**146**	29.59 N	19.25 E
Färila	**26**	61.48 N	15.51 E
Farilhões II	**34**	39.28 N	9.34 W
Farim	**150**	12.27 N	15.17 W
Farīmān	**128**	35.43 N	59.53 E
Farina	**219**	38.50 N	88.46 W
Faringdon	**42**	51.40 N	1.35 W
Farington	**262**	53.43 N	2.42 W
Farinha ≃	**250**	6.51 S	47.30 W
Farini d'Olmo	**62**	44.43 N	9.34 E
Fariš	**85**	40.35 N	66.52 E
Fariske	**130**	36.37 N	32.38 E
Fāriskūr	**142**	31.20 N	31.43 E
Farit, Amba ∧	**144**	10.56 N	38.58 E
Färjestaden	**26**	56.39 N	16.27 E
Farkwa	**154**	5.24 S	35.36 E
Farleigh	**260**	51.19 N	0.02 W
Farley	**190**	42.26 N	91.00 W
Farley Green	**260**	51.12 N	0.29 W
Farmahīn	**128**	34.30 N	49.41 E
Farmer City	**216**	40.14 N	88.38 W
Farmers Branch	**222**	32.55 N	96.53 W
Farmersburg	**194**	39.14 N	87.22 W
Farmers Fork	**208**	38.02 N	76.45 W
Farmer's Museum ʊ	**210**	42.42 N	74.57 W
Farmers Retreat	**218**	38.58 N	85.06 W
Farmersville, Ca., U.S.	**226**	36.17 N	119.12 W
Farmersville, Il., U.S.	**219**	39.26 N	89.39 W
Farmersville, Pa., U.S.	**208**	40.08 N	76.10 W
Farmersville, Tx., U.S.	**222**	33.09 N	96.21 W
Farmersville Station	**210**	42.26 N	78.22 W
Farmerville	**194**	32.46 N	92.24 W
Farmingdale, N.J., U.S.	**208**	40.11 N	74.10 W
Farmingdale, N.Y., U.S.	**276**	40.43 N	73.26 W
Farmington, Ca., U.S.	**226**	37.56 N	120.59 W
Farmington, Ct., U.S.	**207**	41.43 N	72.49 W
Farmington, De., U.S.	**208**	38.52 N	75.34 W
Farmington, Il., U.S.	**190**	40.41 N	90.00 W
Farmington, Ia., U.S.	**190**	40.38 N	91.44 W
Farmington, Me., U.S.	**188**	44.40 N	70.09 W
Farmington, Mi., U.S.	**216**	42.27 N	83.22 W
Farmington, Mn., U.S.	**190**	44.38 N	93.08 W
Farmington, Mo., U.S.	**194**	37.47 N	90.25 W
Farmington, Mt., U.S.	**182**	47.54 N	112.11 W
Farmington, N.H., U.S.	**188**	43.23 N	71.03 W
Farmington, N.M., U.S.	**200**	36.43 N	108.13 W
Farmington, Ut,. U.S.	**200**	40.58 N	111.53 W
Farmington ≃	**207**	41.51 N	72.38 W
Farmington, West Branch ≃	**207**	41.52 N	72.57 W
Farmington Flood Control Basin ⊜[1]	**226**	37.55 N	120.55 W
Farmington Hills	**281**	42.28 N	83.23 W
Farmingville	**210**	40.49 N	73.01 W
Farmland	**218**	40.11 N	85.07 W
Far Mountain ∧	**182**	52.46 N	125.17 W
Farm Pond ⊜, Ma., U.S.	**283**	42.17 N	71.26 W
Farm Pond ⊜, Ma., U.S.	**283**	42.14 N	71.21 W
Farmville, N.C., U.S.	**192**	35.35 N	77.35 W
Farmville, Va., U.S.	**192**	37.18 N	78.23 W
Färna	**40**	59.47 N	15.51 E
Farnam	**198**	40.42 N	100.12 W
Farnawā	**142**	30.59 N	30.39 E
Farnborough	**42**	51.17 N	0.46 W
Farnborough -◆-[8]	**260**	51.21 N	0.04 E
Farncombe	**260**	51.12 N	0.36 W
Farndon	**44**	53.05 N	0.51 W
Färnebofjärden ⊜	**40**	60.14 N	16.47 E
Farne Islands II	**44**	55.38 N	1.38 W
Farnham, P.Q., Can.	**206**	45.17 N	72.59 W
Farnham, Eng., U.K.	**42**	51.13 N	0.49 W
Farnham, N.Y., U.S.	**214**	42.36 N	79.05 W
Farnham, Va., U.S.	**208**	37.53 N	76.37 W
Farnham, Mount ∧	**182**	50.29 N	116.30 W
Farnham Common	**260**	51.33 N	0.37 W
Farnham Royal	**260**	51.32 N	0.37 W
Farnhamville	**198**	42.16 N	94.24 W
Farningham	**260**	51.23 N	0.13 E
Farnroda	**54**	50.56 N	10.23 E
Farnworth	**262**	53.33 N	2.24 W
Faro, Bra.	**250**	2.11 S	56.44 W
Faro, Port.	**34**	37.01 N	7.56 W
Faro □[5]	**34**	37.15 N	8.00 W
Faro ≃	**146**	9.21 N	12.55 E
Faro, Punta ›	**246**	11.07 N	74.51 W
Faro, Punta del ›	**70**	38.16 N	15.39 E
Faro, Réserve du -◆-[4]	**146**	8.10 N	12.35 E
Färöer → Faeroe Islands □[2]	**22**	62.00 N	7.00 W
Fårön I	**26**	57.56 N	19.08 E
Fårösund	**26**	57.52 N	19.03 E
Farquhar, Cape ›	**162**	23.37 S	113.37 E
Farquhar Group II	**138**	10.10 S	51.10 E
Farr	**46**	57.21 N	4.12 W
Farra d'Isonzo	**64**	45.56 N	12.31 E
Farragut	**198**	40.43 N	95.28 W
Farragut State Recreation Area ♦	**202**	47.55 N	116.35 W
Farrandsville	**210**	41.10 N	77.31 W
Farrar ≃	**46**	57.24 N	4.50 W
Farrar Pond ⊜	**283**	42.25 N	71.21 W
Farrars Creek ≃	**166**	25.35 S	140.43 E
Farrāshband	**128**	28.53 N	52.06 E
Farrell	**214**	41.12 N	80.29 W
Farrell Flat	**168b**	33.50 S	138.47 E
Farrer Park ♦	**271c**	1.19 N	103.51 E
Farrington Lake ⊜	**276**	40.26 N	74.28 W
Farrington Lake Heights	**276**	40.26 N	74.27 W
Far Rockaway -◆-[8]	**276**	40.36 N	73.45 W
Farrukhābād	**124**	27.24 N	79.34 E
Farrukhābād □[5]	**124**	27.15 N	79.35 E
Farrukhnagar, India	**124**	28.27 N	76.49 E
Farrukhnagar, India	**272a**	28.43 N	77.23 E
Fārs □[4]	**128**	29.00 N	53.00 E
Fársala	**38**	39.18 N	22.23 E
Farschviller	**56**	49.06 N	6.54 E
Fārsī	**128**	33.47 N	63.15 E
Farsīs	**142**	30.40 N	31.14 E
Farsø	**26**	56.47 N	9.21 E
Farsta	**40**	59.14 N	18.04 E
Farsund	**26**	58.05 N	6.48 E
Fartak, Ra's ›	**118**	15.38 N	52.15 E
Fartura, Rio da ≃	**256**	21.37 S	46.55 W
Farukolu I	**122**	6.12 N	73.16 E
Farum	**41**	55.48 N	12.22 E
Fårvang	**41**	56.16 N	9.44 E
Farvel, Kap ›	**176**	59.45 N	44.00 W
Farwell, Mi., U.S.	**190**	43.50 N	84.52 W
Farwell, Tx., U.S.	**196**	30.15 N	103.15 W
Fāryāb □[4]	**128**	36.00 N	65.00 E
Fasā	**128**	28.56 N	53.42 E
Fasano	**68**	40.50 N	17.22 E
Faščovka	**83**	48.16 N	38.37 E
Fashkhah, ʻAyn ⊤[4]	**132**	31.43 N	35.27 E
Fåsjön ⊜	**40**	59.36 N	14.58 E
Fasmund ›[1]	**41**	54.32 N	13.35 E
Fassa	**150**	13.26 N	8.15 W
Fassberg	**52**	52.54 N	10.10 E
Fasterholt	**41**	56.01 N	9.07 E
Fastnet Rock I[2]	**48**	51.24 N	9.35 W
Fastov	**78**	50.06 N	29.55 E
Fastoveckaja	**78**	45.56 N	40.09 E
Fatagar, Tanjung ›	**164**	2.46 S	131.57 E
Fataki	**154**	4.46 S	28.11 E
Fatala ≃	**150**	10.13 N	14.00 W
Fat Deer Key I	**220**	24.44 N	81.00 W
Fate	**222**	32.56 N	96.23 W
Fatehābād, India	**123**	29.31 N	75.27 E
Fatehābād, India	**124**	27.01 N	78.19 E
Fatehgarh, India	**124**	27.22 N	79.38 E
Fatehgarh, India	**124**	24.48 N	76.58 E
Fatehgarh Chūriān	**123**	31.52 N	74.58 E
Fatehjang	**123**	33.34 N	72.39 E
Fatehpur, India	**120**	27.59 N	74.57 E
Fatehpur, India	**124**	25.56 N	80.48 E
Fatehpur, India	**124**	27.10 N	81.13 E
Fatehpur, India	**126**	22.17 N	88.14 E
Fatehpur, India	**126**	24.05 N	87.44 E
Fatehpur, Pāk.	**123**	31.09 N	71.13 E
Fatehpur □[5]	**124**	25.50 N	81.00 E
Fatehpur Sīkri	**124**	27.06 N	77.40 E
Fathai	**140**	8.05 N	31.48 E
Fatigue, Mount ∧	**169**	38.34 S	146.18 E
Fatikli	**130**	36.08 N	36.12 E
Fatima, Arg.	**258**	34.26 S	59.00 W
Fátima, Bra.	**248**	16.11 S	54.58 W
Fátima, Port.	**34**	39.37 N	8.39 W
Fāṭimah, Wādī V	**144**	21.27 N	39.09 E
Fatoto	**150**	13.26 N	13.52 W
Fat'ož	**78**	52.07 N	35.52 E
Fatsa	**130**	41.02 N	37.31 E
Fatshan → Foshan	**100**	23.03 N	113.09 E
Fat Tong Point ›	**271d**	22.16 N	114.15 E
Fatu-Berlio	**112**	8.56 S	125.52 E
Fatulla	**126**	23.38 N	90.29 E
Fatumu	**174w**	21.13 S	175.07 W
Fatunda	**152**	4.08 S	17.13 E
Fatwā	**124**	25.31 N	85.19 E
Fauabu	**175e**	8.34 S	160.43 E
Faucigny	**58**	46.07 N	6.22 E
Faucille, Col de la)(	**58**	46.22 N	6.02 E
Faucilles, Monts ⋏	**58**	48.07 N	6.16 E
Faucogney	**58**	47.51 N	6.34 E
Faucon-de-Barcelonnette	**62**	44.24 N	6.41 E
Fauglia	**66**	43.34 N	10.31 E
Fauldhouse	**46**	55.50 N	3.37 W
Faulkton	**198**	45.02 N	99.07 W
Faulquemont	**56**	49.03 N	6.36 E
Fauquembergues	**50**	50.36 N	2.05 E
Fauquier	**182**	49.53 N	118.05 W
Fauquier □[6]	**208**	38.35 N	77.35 W
Făurei	**38**	45.06 N	27.14 E
Faure Island I	**162**	25.51 S	113.52 E
Fauresmith	**158**	29.42 S	25.21 E
Fauro Island I	**175e**	6.55 S	156.04 E
Fauske	**24**	67.15 N	15.24 E
Faust	**182**	55.19 N	115.38 W
Faustovo	**82**	55.26 N	38.29 E
Fauville-en-Caux	**50**	49.39 N	0.35 E
Fauvillers	**56**	49.51 N	5.40 E
Faux-Cap	**157b**	25.33 S	45.32 E
Fåvang	**26**	61.27 N	10.11 E
Favara	**70**	37.19 N	13.39 E
Faverges	**62**	45.45 N	6.18 E
Faverney	**58**	47.46 N	6.06 E
Faversham	**42**	51.20 N	0.53 E
Favières	**261**	48.46 N	2.47 E
Favignana	**70**	37.56 N	12.20 E
Favignana, Isola I	**70**	37.56 N	12.19 E
Favoriten -◆-[8]	**264b**	48.11 N	16.23 E
Favourable Lake ⊜	**184**	52.53 N	93.56 W
Favrieux	**261**	48.57 N	1.39 E
Fawcett	**182**	54.32 N	114.05 W
Fawcett Lake ⊜	**182**	55.19 N	113.57 W
Fawkham Green	**260**	51.22 N	0.17 E
Fawkner	**274b**	37.43 S	144.58 E
Fawkner Park ♦	**274b**	37.50 S	144.59 E
Fawley	**42**	50.49 N	1.20 W
Fawn ≃, On., Can.	**176**	55.22 N	88.20 W
Fawn ≃, U.S.	**216**	41.51 N	85.40 W
Fawn Grove	**208**	39.44 N	76.27 W
Fawnie Nose ∧	**182**	53.16 N	125.08 W
Fawnie Range ⋏	**182**	53.10 N	125.00 W
Fawsett Farms	**284c**	38.59 N	77.14 W
Faxaflói ⊂	**24a**	64.25 N	23.00 W
Faxälven ≃	**26**	63.13 N	17.13 E
Faxinal	**255**	23.59 S	51.22 W
Faxinal do Soturno	**252**	29.37 S	53.26 W
Faxon	**210**	41.15 N	76.58 W
Faya	**146**	17.55 N	19.07 E
Fayd	**128**	27.07 N	42.27 E
Fayence	**62**	43.37 N	6.41 E
Fayerweather Island I	**276**	41.08 N	73.13 W
Fayette, Al., U.S.	**194**	33.41 N	87.49 W
Fayette, Ia., U.S.	**190**	42.50 N	91.48 W
Fayette, Ms., U.S.	**194**	31.42 N	91.03 W
Fayette, Mo., U.S.	**194**	39.08 N	92.41 W
Fayette, N.Y., U.S.	**210**	42.49 N	76.49 W
Fayette, Oh., U.S.	**216**	41.40 N	84.19 W
Fayette □[6], Il., U.S.	**219**	38.58 N	89.06 W
Fayette □[6], In., U.S.	**218**	39.39 N	85.08 W
Fayette □[6], Ky., U.S.	**218**	38.07 N	84.30 W
Fayette □[6], Oh., U.S.	**218**	39.32 N	83.26 W
Fayette □[6], Pa., U.S.	**214**	40.05 N	79.39 W
Fayette □[6], Tx., U.S.	**222**	29.50 N	96.57 W
Fayette, Lake ⊜[1]	**222**	29.56 N	96.44 W
Fayette City	**214**	40.06 N	79.50 W
Fayetteville, Ar., U.S.	**194**	36.03 N	94.09 W
Fayetteville, Ga., U.S.	**192**	33.26 N	84.27 W
Fayetteville, Il., U.S.	**219**	38.22 N	89.48 W
Fayetteville, N.Y., U.S.	**210**	43.02 N	76.00 W
Fayetteville, N.C., U.S.	**192**	35.03 N	78.52 W
Fayetteville, Oh., U.S.	**218**	39.11 N	83.55 W
Fayetteville, Pa., U.S.	**208**	39.54 N	77.33 W
Fayetteville, Tn., U.S.	**194**	35.09 N	86.34 W
Fayetteville, Tx., U.S.	**222**	29.54 N	96.41 W
Fayetteville, W.V., U.S.	**188**	38.03 N	81.06 W
Faylakah I	**128**	29.25 N	48.22 E
Fayl-Billot	**58**	47.47 N	5.36 E
Fayrā	**144**	13.17 N	43.25 E
Fay-sur-Lignon	**62**	44.59 N	4.14 E
Fayville	**207**	42.17 N	71.30 W
Fayyum → Al-Fayyūm	**142**	29.19 N	30.50 E
Fažana	**64**	44.55 N	13.49 E
Fazao	**150**	8.42 N	0.46 E
Fazao, Parc National du ♦	**150**	8.40 N	0.42 E
Fazeley	**42**	52.37 N	1.42 W
Fazenda de Cima	**248**	15.56 S	56.37 W
Fazenda Libongo	**152**	8.24 S	13.24 E
Fazenda Nova	**255**	16.11 S	50.48 W
Fāzilka	**123**	30.24 N	74.02 E
Fāzilpur	**120**	29.18 N	70.27 E
Fazzān (Fezzan) □[9]	**146**	26.00 N	14.00 E
Fdérik	**148**	22.41 N	12.43 W
Feale ≃	**48**	52.28 N	9.40 W
Fear, Cape ›	**192**	33.50 N	77.58 W
Fearnhead	**262**	53.25 N	2.33 W
Feasterville	**208**	40.08 N	75.00 W
Feather ≃	**204**	38.47 N	121.36 W
Feather, Middle Fork ≃	**204**	39.34 N	121.26 W
Feather, North Fork ≃	**204**	39.34 N	121.28 W
Feather, North Fork, East Branch ≃	**204**	40.01 N	121.13 W
Feather, South Fork ≃	**204**	39.33 N	121.28 W
Featherbed Top ∧	**262**	53.26 N	1.52 W
Featherly Regional Park ♦	**280**	33.52 N	117.42 W
Featherston	**172**	41.07 S	175.20 E
Featherstone, Eng., U.K.	**44**	53.41 N	1.21 W
Featherstone, Zimb.	**154**	18.42 S	30.49 E
Feathertop, Mount ∧	**166**	36.54 S	147.08 E
Fécamp	**50**	49.45 N	0.22 E
Fedala → Mohammedia	**148**	33.44 N	7.24 W
Fedderwardergroden	**52**	53.35 N	8.05 E
Feddet ›[1]	**41**	55.09 N	12.07 E
Federación	**252**	31.00 S	57.54 W
Federal, Arg.	**252**	30.57 S	58.48 W
Federal, Pa., U.S.	**279b**	40.23 N	80.09 W
Federal Capital Territory (Suleja) □[3]	**150**	9.00 N	7.15 E
Federalsburg	**208**	38.41 N	75.46 W
Federal Territory □[8]	**273a**	6.29 N	3.25 E
Federal Way	**224**	47.19 N	122.18 W
Federation Forest State Park ♦	**224**	47.09 N	121.40 W
Federsee ⊜	**58**	48.05 N	9.38 E
Fedeshk	**128**	32.45 N	58.50 E
Fedje	**26**	60.47 N	4.42 E
Fedons Camp ∧	**241k**	12.07 N	61.42 W
Fedorino	**82**	55.08 N	36.06 E
Fedosejevka	**80**	46.53 N	44.00 E
Fedosejevskaja	**24**	62.07 N	40.42 E
Fedosicha	**86**	54.47 N	81.54 E
Fedosjino	**82**	55.08 N	38.30 E
Fedotovo	**82**	55.41 N	39.12 E
Feeagh, Lough ⊜	**48**	53.55 N	9.36 W
Feeding Hills	**207**	42.04 N	72.40 W
Feehanville	**278**	42.05 N	87.54 W
Feerfeer	**144**	8.30 N	47.55 E
Feesburg	**218**	38.52 N	83.58 W
Fefan I	**175c**	7.21 N	151.51 E
Fehérgyarmat	**30**	47.58 N	22.32 E
Fehmarn I	**54**	54.28 N	11.08 E
Fehmarn Belt (Femer Bælt) ⋓	**41**	54.35 N	11.15 E
Fehmarnsund ⋓	**54**	54.24 N	11.07 E
Fehrbellin	**54**	52.49 N	12.46 E
Fehring	**61**	46.56 N	16.01 E
Feia, Lagoa ⊂	**255**	22.00 S	41.20 W
Feicheng	**98**	36.15 N	116.46 E
Feichten	**58**	47.02 N	10.44 E
Feidong	**100**	31.52 N	117.29 E
Feignies	**50**	50.18 N	3.55 E
Feigumfossen ⌊	**26**	61.23 N	7.26 E
Feiheji	**100**	33.36 N	115.36 E
Fei Huang ≃	**100**	33.35 N	119.02 E
Feijó	**248**	8.09 S	70.21 W
Feiketu	**89**	45.46 N	127.09 E
Feilding	**172**	40.13 S	175.34 E
Feiler ∧	**58**	47.07 N	10.52 E
Feiliqiao	**106**	31.05 N	119.05 E
Feilitzsch	**54**	50.22 N	11.56 E
Feilong, Zhg.	**107**	30.25 N	106.20 E
Feilong, Zhg.	**107**	30.36 N	105.54 E
Feilongguan	**107**	28.57 N	105.05 E
Feiluan	**100**	26.35 N	119.35 E
Feio ≃	**255**	21.03 S	51.47 W
Feira	**154**	15.37 S	30.25 E
Feira de Santana	**255**	12.15 S	38.57 W
Feistritz ≃	**61**	47.01 N	16.08 E
Feistritz an der Gail	**64**	46.34 N	13.36 E
Feistritzer Spitze ∧	**61**	46.31 N	14.45 E
Feixi	**100**	31.42 N	117.10 E
Feixian	**98**	35.18 N	117.57 E
Feixiang	**98**	36.34 N	114.49 E
Feiyun ≃	**100**	27.48 N	120.36 E
Fejaj, Chott ≡	**148**	33.55 N	9.10 E
Fejér □[6]	**30**	47.10 N	18.35 E
Fejø I	**41**	54.57 N	11.26 E
Feklistova, ostrov I	**89**	55.02 N	136.55 E
Felâhiye	**130**	39.06 N	35.35 E
Felanitx	**34**	39.28 N	3.08 E
Felbertauren-Tunnel -◆-[5]	**64**	47.08 N	12.31 E
Felda	**220**	26.33 N	81.26 W
Felda ≃, B.R.D.	**56**	50.42 N	9.03 E
Felda ≃, D.D.R.	**56**	50.51 N	10.05 E
Feldafing	**64**	47.57 N	11.17 E
Feldaist ≃	**61**	48.19 N	14.34 E
Feld am See	**64**	46.47 N	13.45 E
Feldbach	**61**	46.57 N	15.54 E
Feldberg, B.R.D.	**58**	47.51 N	8.02 E
Feldberg, D.D.R.	**54**	53.20 N	13.26 E
Feldberg ∧	**58**	47.52 N	8.00 E
Felderbach ≃	**263**	51.22 N	7.08 E
Feldhausen	**263**	51.37 N	6.59 E
Feldis	**58**	46.48 N	9.26 E
Feldkirch	**58**	47.14 N	9.36 E
Feldkirchen an der Donau	**61**	48.21 N	14.03 E
Feldkirchen bei Graz	**61**	47.01 N	15.27 E
Feldkirchen in Kärnten	**61**	46.43 N	14.05 E
Feldmark	**263**	51.41 N	6.38 E
Feldstetten	**58**	48.28 N	9.37 E
Felhit	**144**	16.43 N	38.02 E
Feliciano	**240m**	18.28 N	67.08 W
Feliciano, Arroyo ≃	**252**	31.06 S	59.54 W
Felicity	**218**	38.50 N	84.05 W
Felino	**64**	44.42 N	10.15 E
Felipe Carrillo Puerto	**232**	19.35 N	88.03 W
Felix, Cape ›	**176**	69.54 N	97.50 W
Felix, Rio ≃	**196**	33.08 N	104.19 W
Felixburg	**154**	19.29 S	30.51 E
Felixdorf	**61**	47.53 N	16.15 E
Félix Gómez	**232**	29.50 N	111.30 W
Felixlândia	**255**	18.47 S	44.55 W
Felixstowe	**42**	51.58 N	1.20 E
Felixton	**158**	28.50 S	31.53 E
Félix U. Gómez	**232**	30.35 N	105.50 W
Felizzano	**62**	44.54 N	8.26 E
Fella ≃	**64**	46.21 N	13.07 E
Fellbach	**56**	48.48 N	9.15 E
Felletin	**32**	45.53 N	2.10 E
Felling	**44**	54.57 N	1.33 W
Fellingsbro	**40**	59.26 N	15.35 E
Fellows	**226**	35.11 N	119.32 W
Fellows Creek ≃	**281**	42.17 N	83.26 W
Fellowship	**285**	39.55 N	74.58 W
Fellsburg	**214**	40.11 N	79.49 W
Fellsmere	**220**	27.46 N	80.36 W
Fellwick	**285**	40.08 N	75.11 W
Felpham	**42**	50.47 N	0.39 W
Felsberg	**56**	51.08 N	9.25 E
Felsenmeer, Naturschutzgebiet ♦	**263**	51.25 N	7.45 E
Felső-Válicka ≃	**61**	46.52 N	16.53 E
Felszabadulási Emlékmű ⊥	**264c**	47.29 N	19.03 E
Feltham -◆-[8]	**260**	51.27 N	0.24 W
Felt Lake ⊜	**282**	37.23 N	122.11 W
Felton, Ca., U.S.	**226**	37.03 N	122.04 W
Felton, De., U.S.	**208**	39.00 N	75.34 W
Felton, Pa., U.S.	**208**	39.51 N	76.34 W
Feltre	**64**	46.01 N	11.54 E
Felts Mills	**212**	44.01 N	75.46 W
Feltwell	**42**	52.29 N	0.32 E
Fêmeas, Rio das ≃	**255**	12.27 S	45.12 W
Femer Bælt (Fehmarn Belt) ⋓	**41**	54.35 N	11.15 E
Femme Osage Creek ≃	**219**	38.39 N	90.44 W
Femmøller	**41**	56.14 N	10.35 E
Femø I	**41**	54.58 N	11.33 E
Femunden ⊜	**26**	62.12 N	11.52 E
Femundsenden	**26**	61.55 N	11.55 E
Femundsmarka Nasjonalpark ♦	**26**	62.20 N	12.07 E
Fen ≃	**102**	35.36 N	110.42 E
Fena Valley Reservoir ⊜[1]	**174p**	13.21 N	144.42 E
Fendaozi	**104**	41.35 N	120.51 E
Fenelon Falls	**212**	44.32 N	78.45 W
Fenelton	**214**	40.52 N	79.44 W
Fener -◆-[8]	**267b**	41.02 N	28.56 E
Fenerbahçe Stadyumu ♦	**267b**	40.59 N	29.02 E
Fener Burnu ›	**130**	41.07 N	39.25 E
Fener Tepesi ∧[2]	**267b**	41.09 N	28.47 E
Fenestrelle	**62**	45.02 N	7.03 E
Fénétrange	**56**	48.51 N	7.01 E
Feng ≃	**105**	39.25 N	116.57 E
Fengcheng, Zhg.	**98**	40.27 N	124.02 E
Fengcheng, Zhg.	**100**	28.10 N	115.46 E
Fengcheng, Zhg.	**102**	38.32 N	101.50 E
Fengcheng, Zhg.	**106**	30.55 N	121.38 E
Fengdengwu	**105**	39.42 N	117.55 E
Fengdian	**107**	30.41 N	104.51 E
Fengdu	**102**	29.58 N	107.41 E
Fengfeng	**98**	36.28 N	114.14 E
Fenggang, Zhg.	**100**	28.34 N	116.34 E
Fenggang, Zhg.	**102**	27.58 N	107.47 E
Fenggaopu	**107**	29.24 N	105.41 E
Fenghua	**100**	29.40 N	121.24 E
Fenghuang, Zhg.	**100**	23.58 N	116.44 E
Fenghuang, Zhg.	**102**	24.25 N	107.17 E
Fenghuang, Zhg.	**102**	27.58 N	109.19 E
Fenghuang, Zhg.	**106**	31.21 N	121.44 E
Fenghuangchang	**107**	29.44 N	106.19 E
Fenghuang Shan ∧	**107**	28.54 N	106.35 E
Fenghuanjing	**100**	31.11 N	117.49 E
Fenghui	**100**	29.56 N	120.58 E
Fengjia, Zhg.	**98**	37.03 N	121.42 E
Fengjia, Zhg.	**104**	42.35 N	122.30 E
Fengjiabao	**102**	36.12 N	104.49 E
Fengjiakou	**98**	38.11 N	116.44 E
Fengjianjiao	**106**	30.41 N	120.51 E
Fengjiatun	**104**	41.14 N	122.00 E
Fengjiawopeng	**104**	42.19 N	123.40 E
Fengjiaxiang	**106**	30.56 N	121.06 E
Fengjie	**102**	31.03 N	109.31 E
Fengjing	**106**	30.53 N	121.01 E
Fengkou	**100**	30.05 N	113.18 E
Fengle, Zhg.	**89**	45.47 N	125.26 E
Fengle, Zhg.	**100**	27.13 N	118.11 E
Fenglezhen	**98**	36.14 N	114.18 E
Fengliang	**100**	23.59 N	116.14 E
Fenglin, T'aiwan	**100**	23.45 N	121.26 E
Fenglin, Zhg.	**100**	28.19 N	120.46 E
Fengling Guan)(	**100**	28.14 N	118.29 E
Fenglingtou	**100**	28.26 N	117.50 E
Fengman	**89**	43.46 N	126.41 E
Fengnan (Xugezhuang)	**105**	39.34 N	118.06 E
Fengning (Dagezhen)	**98**	41.12 N	116.32 E
Fengpin	**100**	23.36 N	121.31 E
Fengpingzi	**102**	32.46 N	105.12 E
Fengqiao, Zhg.	**100**	29.46 N	120.26 E
Fengqiao, Zhg.	**106**	31.19 N	120.33 E
Fengqing	**102**	24.46 N	99.52 E
Fengqiu	**98**	35.05 N	114.25 E
Fengrun	**105**	39.50 N	118.07 E
Fengshan, Zhg.	**89**	46.22 N	128.30 E
Fengshan, Zhg.	**98**	41.14 N	117.05 E
Fengshan, Zhg.	**102**	22.01 N	109.59 E
Fengshi	**100**	24.42 N	116.34 E
Fengshun	**100**	23.48 N	116.11 E
Fengtai, Zhg.	**100**	32.44 N	116.43 E
Fengtai, Zhg.	**105**	39.51 N	116.16 E
Fengtian, Zhg.	**100**	27.24 N	114.43 E
Fengtian, Zhg.	**100**	25.46 N	115.30 E
Fengtien → Shenyang	**104**	41.48 N	123.27 E
Fengting	**100**	25.16 N	118.54 E
Fengwan	**100**	24.48 N	113.50 E
Fengxi	**102**	31.48 N	109.50 E
Fengxian, Zhg.	**98**	34.42 N	116.34 E
Fengxian, Zhg.	**102**	33.57 N	106.44 E
Fengxian, Zhg.	**106**	30.55 N	121.27 E
Fengxiang	**102**	34.29 N	107.29 E
Fengxin	**100**	28.43 N	115.23 E
Fengyang, Zhg.	**100**	32.52 N	117.34 E
Fengyang, Zhg.	**100**	24.49 N	117.53 E
Fengyi	**102**	31.44 N	103.53 E
Fengyu	**100**	26.31 N	119.18 E
Fengyüan	**100**	24.15 N	120.43 E
Fengzhen	**102**	40.24 N	113.09 E
Fengzhou	**100**	25.41 N	113.52 E
Fengzhuangtou	**106**	31.00 N	118.39 E
Fenholloway ≃	**192**	29.59 N	83.47 W
Fen Hu ⊜	**106**	31.00 N	120.47 E
Feni	**124**	23.00 N	91.24 E
Fenicia Moncata ⊥	**70**	37.33 N	14.57 E
Feni Islands II	**14**	4.05 S	153.42 E
Fenimore Pass ⋓	**180**	52.00 N	175.35 W
Fenino	**265b**	55.44 N	37.57 E
Fenis	**62**	45.44 N	7.29 E
Feniscowles	**262**	53.43 N	2.32 W
Fenjie	**106**	32.17 N	120.20 E
Fennimore	**190**	42.59 N	90.39 W
Fennville	**216**	42.35 N	86.06 W
Fenny Compton	**42**	52.09 N	1.20 W
Fenny Stratford	**42**	52.00 N	0.43 W
Feno, Capo di ›, Fr.	**36**	41.57 N	8.36 E
Feno, Capo di ›, Fr.	**71**	41.23 N	9.06 E
Fenoarivo, Madag.	**157b**	18.26 S	46.34 E
Fenoarivo, Madag.	**157b**	21.43 S	46.24 E
Fenoarivo, Madag.	**157b**	20.52 S	46.53 E
Fenoarivo Atsinanana	**157b**	17.22 S	49.25 E
Fensfjorden ⊂[2]	**26**	60.51 N	4.50 E
Fenshui	**104**	40.41 N	122.32 E
Fenshui ≃	**100**	29.49 N	119.41 E
Fenshui'ao	**100**	25.20 N	114.43 E
Fenshuidunshen	**106**	31.30 N	120.01 E
Fenshuiling, Zhg.	**107**	28.51 N	105.35 E
Fenshuiling, Zhg.	**107**	30.20 N	105.15 E
Fenshuipu	**107**	30.05 N	104.05 E
Fenshuizhen	**107**	29.44 N	103.55 E
Fenshuizui	**100**	30.35 N	113.38 E
Fensmark	**41**	55.17 N	11.49 E
Fenstanton	**42**	52.18 N	0.04 W
Fenton, Mi., U.S.	**216**	42.47 N	83.42 W
Fenton, Mo., U.S.	**219**	38.32 N	90.22 W
Fenton, Lake ⊜	**216**	42.50 N	83.43 W
Fentou	**105**	38.53 N	116.32 E
Fentress	**222**	29.45 N	97.47 W
Fenway Park ♦	**283**	42.21 N	71.06 W
Fenwick	**188**	38.13 N	80.34 W
Fenwick Island ›[1]	**208**	38.25 N	75.03 W
Fenyang	**102**	37.17 N	111.48 E
Fenyi	**100**	27.47 N	114.42 E
Feodosija	**78**	45.02 N	35.23 E
Feodosijskij zaliv ⊂	**78**	45.05 N	35.35 E
Fépin	**56**	50.01 N	4.44 E
Fer, Cap de ›	**148**	37.05 N	7.10 E
Ferbane	**48**	53.15 N	7.49 W
Ferbitz	**264a**	52.30 N	13.01 E
Ferch	**264a**	52.19 N	12.56 E
Fercher Berge ∧[2]	**264a**	52.19 N	12.57 E
Ferchland	**54**	52.26 N	12.00 E
Ferdig	**182**	48.45 N	111.46 W
Ferdinand	**194**	38.13 N	86.51 W
Ferdinandshof	**54**	53.39 N	13.53 E
Ferdows	**128**	34.00 N	58.09 E
Fère-Champenoise	**50**	48.45 N	3.59 E
Fère-en-Tardenois	**50**	49.12 N	3.31 E
Ferencváros -◆-[8]	**264c**	47.28 N	19.06 E
Ferentillo	**66**	42.37 N	12.47 E
Ferentino	**66**	41.42 N	13.15 E
Fergana	**85**	40.23 N	71.46 E
Fergana □[4]	**85**	40.30 N	71.20 E
Ferganskaja dolina V	**85**	40.50 N	71.30 E
Ferganskij chrebet ⋏	**85**	41.00 N	74.00 E
Fergus	**212**	43.42 N	80.22 W
Fergus Falls	**198**	46.16 N	96.04 W
Ferguson, Austl.	**168a**	33.26 S	115.51 E
Ferguson, B.C., Can.	**182**	50.41 N	117.28 W
Ferguson, Ky., U.S.	**192**	37.04 N	84.36 W
Ferguson, Mo., U.S.	**219**	38.44 N	90.18 W
Ferguson ≃	**168a**	33.21 S	115.40 E
Fergusonville	**285**	40.07 N	74.54 W
Fergusson Island I	**164**	9.30 S	150.40 E
Fériana	**148**	34.57 N	8.34 E
Ferihegyi Repülőtér ⊠	**264c**	47.26 N	19.15 E
Ferkéssédougou	**150**	9.36 N	5.12 W
Ferkéssédougou □[5]	**150**	9.30 N	4.50 W
Ferla	**70**	37.07 N	14.56 E
Ferlach	**61**	46.31 N	14.18 E
Ferleiten	**64**	47.10 N	12.49 E
Ferlo -◆-[1]	**150**	0.15 N	0.14 W
Ferlo, Vallée du V	**150**	15.42 N	15.30 W
Fermiers, Île aux I	**275a**	45.40 N	73.27 W
Fermignano	**66**	43.40 N	12.39 E
Fermin, Point ›	**228**	33.42 N	118.18 W
Fermi National Accelerator Laboratory ʊ[3]	**216**	41.50 N	88.15 W
Fermo	**66**	43.09 N	13.43 E
Fermont	**176**	52.47 N	67.05 W
Fermoselle	**34**	41.19 N	6.23 W
Fermoy	**48**	52.08 N	8.16 W
Fernandes Belo	**250**	1.07 S	46.19 W
Fernández	**252**	27.55 S	63.54 W
Fernández Leal	**200**	30.51 N	108.17 W
Fernandina, Isla I	**246a**	0.25 S	91.30 W
Fernandina Beach	**192**	30.40 N	81.27 W
Fernando de la Mora	**252**	25.19 S	57.36 W
Fernando de Noronha □[3]	**250**	3.51 S	32.25 W
Fernando de Noronha, Ilha I	**250**	3.51 S	32.25 W
Fernandópolis	**255**	20.16 S	50.14 W
Fernando Póo → Bioko I	**152**	3.30 N	8.40 E
Fernán-Núñez	**34**	37.40 N	4.43 W
Fernão Veloso, Baía de ⊂	**154**	14.20 S	40.45 E
Ferndale, S. Afr.	**273d**	26.05 S	27.59 E
Ferndale, Ca., U.S.	**204**	40.34 N	124.15 W
Ferndale, Fl., U.S.	**220**	28.37 N	81.42 W
Ferndale, Md., U.S.	**208**	39.10 N	76.38 W
Ferndale, Mi., U.S.	**216**	42.27 N	83.08 W
Ferndale, N.Y., U.S.	**210**	41.46 N	74.44 W
Ferndale, Pa., U.S.	**214**	40.17 N	78.54 W
Ferndale, Wa., U.S.	**202**	48.50 N	122.35 W
Ferndale Lake ⊜	**222**	32.57 N	95.05 W
Ferndown	**42**	50.48 N	1.55 W
Ferney-Voltaire	**58**	46.15 N	6.07 E
Fern Glen	**210**	40.57 N	76.10 W
Fernhatten ⋏[2]	**41**	56.15 N	10.48 E
Fernhill Heath	**42**	52.14 N	2.12 W
Fernie	**182**	49.30 N	115.03 W
Fernilee	**262**	53.18 N	1.58 W
Fernilee Reservoir ⊜[1]	**262**	53.17 N	1.59 W
Fernley	**204**	39.36 N	119.15 W
Ferno	**62**	45.37 N	8.45 E
Fernow, Mount ∧	**224**	47.45 N	121.14 W
Fern Park	**220**	28.41 N	81.20 W
Fernpass)(	**58**	47.22 N	10.50 E
Fern Ridge Lake ⊜[1]	**202**	44.05 N	123.18 W
Ferns	**48**	52.35 N	6.31 W
Ferntree Gully National Park ♦	**169**	37.53 S	145.19 E
Fernvale	**171a**	27.27 S	152.39 E
Fernway, Il., U.S.	**278**	41.36 N	87.50 W
Fernway, Pa., U.S.	**214**	40.41 N	80.07 W
Fernwood, Id., U.S.	**202**	47.06 N	116.23 W
Fernwood, N.Y., U.S.	**210**	43.16 N	73.40 W
Fernwood, Pa., U.S.	**285**	39.57 N	75.15 W
Ferny Creek	**274b**	37.53 S	145.21 E
Feroé, Islas → Faeroe Islands □[2]	**22**	62.00 N	7.00 W
Feroës → Faeroe Islands □[2]	**22**	62.00 N	7.00 W
Ferokh	**122**	11.11 N	75.51 E
Feroleto Antico	**68**	38.58 N	16.23 E
Feroleto della Chiesa	**68**	38.28 N	16.04 E
Ferolle Point ›	**186**	51.05 N	57.07 W
Ferozepore → Fīrozpur	**123**	30.55 N	74.36 E
Férrai	**130**	40.54 N	26.10 E
Ferrandina	**68**	40.29 N	16.28 E
Ferrara	**64**	44.50 N	11.35 E
Ferrara □[4]	**64**	44.48 N	11.50 E
Ferrat, Cap ›	**34**	35.54 N	0.23 W
Ferrato, Capo ›	**71**	39.18 N	9.38 E
Ferraz de Vasconcelos	**256**	23.32 S	46.22 W
Ferraz de Vasconcelos □[7]	**287b**	23.33 S	46.21 W
Ferrazzano	**66**	41.32 N	14.40 E
Ferré, Cap ›	**240e**	14.28 N	60.49 W
Ferreira, Ang.	**152**	12.53 S	22.48 E
Ferreira, S. Afr.	**158**	29.13 S	26.10 E
Ferreira, Riacho ≃	**250**	10.06 S	42.13 W
Ferreira do Alentejo	**34**	38.03 N	8.07 W
Ferreira Gomes	**250**	0.48 N	51.08 W
Ferreiros	**256**	22.25 S	43.34 W
Ferrell	**285**	39.41 N	75.12 W
Ferrell's Bridge Dam -◆-[6]	**222**	32.45 N	94.30 W
Ferreñafe	**248**	6.38 S	79.45 W
Ferrera Erbognone	**62**	45.07 N	8.52 E
Ferret	**58**	45.55 N	7.06 E
Ferret, Cap ›	**32**	44.37 N	1.15 W
Ferreyra	**252**	31.28 S	64.08 W
Ferriday	**194**	31.37 N	91.33 W
Ferriere	**62**	44.38 N	9.30 E
Ferrière-la-Grande	**50**	50.15 N	4.00 E
Ferrières	**50**	48.05 N	2.47 E
Ferrières-en-Brie	**50**	48.49 N	2.43 E
Ferris	**222**	32.32 N	96.39 W
Ferritslev	**41**	55.18 N	10.36 E
Ferro ≃	**255**	12.27 S	54.31 W
Ferrol → El Ferrol del Caudillo	**34**	43.29 N	8.14 W
Ferrol, Península de ›[1]	**248**	9.10 S	78.37 W
Ferron	**200**	39.05 N	111.08 W
Ferron Creek ≃	**200**	39.09 N	110.55 W
Ferros	**255**	19.14 S	43.02 W
Ferru, Monte ∧	**71**	39.44 N	9.38 E
Ferruzzano	**68**	38.02 N	16.05 E
Ferry, Pointe ›	**241o**	16.17 N	61.49 W
Ferryhill	**44**	54.41 N	1.33 W
Ferryland	**186**	47.02 N	52.53 W
Ferry Point Park ♦	**276**	40.49 N	73.50 W
Ferrysburg	**216**	43.05 N	86.13 W
Ferry Village	**284a**	43.58 N	78.57 W
Ferryville → Menzel Bourguiba	**148**	37.10 N	9.48 E
Feršampenuaz	**86**	53.32 N	59.51 E
Fertile	**198**	47.32 N	96.16 W
Fertilia, Aeroporto di ⊠	**71**	40.37 N	8.15 E
Fertő (Neusiedler See) ⊜	**61**	47.50 N	16.45 E
Fertőd ⊥	**61**	47.37 N	16.53 E
Fertőrákos	**61**	47.43 N	16.39 E
Fertőújlak	**61**	47.40 N	16.51 E
Ferulargiu, Monte ∧	**71**	40.31 N	9.34 E
Ferzikovo	**82**	54.32 N	36.45 E
Fès	**148**	34.05 N	4.57 W
Fès □[4]	**148**	33.55 N	4.57 W
Feshi	**152**	6.07 S	18.10 E
Feshie ≃	**46**	57.08 N	3.55 W
Fessenden	**198**	47.38 N	99.37 W
Festenberg → Twardogóra	**30**	51.22 N	17.28 E
Festus	**219**	38.13 N	90.23 W
Fetcham	**260**	51.17 N	0.22 W
Fet Dom, Tanjung ›	**164**	1.53 S	129.43 E
Fété Bowé	**150**	14.56 N	13.30 W
Fetești	**38**	44.23 N	27.50 E
Fethaland, Point of ›	**46a**	60.38 N	1.18 W
Fethard	**48**	52.27 N	7.41 W
Fethiye	**130**	36.37 N	29.07 E
Fethiye Körfezi ⊂	**130**	36.40 N	29.00 E
Fetisovo	**72**	42.46 N	52.38 E
Fetlar I	**46a**	60.37 N	0.52 W
Fetsund	**26**	59.56 N	11.10 E
Fetterangus	**46**	57.33 N	2.01 W
Fettercairn	**46**	56.51 N	2.34 W
Feucherolles	**261**	48.52 N	1.58 E
Feucht	**60**	49.22 N	11.13 E
Feuchtwangen	**56**	49.10 N	10.20 E
Feudingen	**56**	50.56 N	8.19 E
Feuerland → Tierra del Fuego, Isla Grande de I	**254**	54.00 S	69.00 W
Feuet	**146**	24.57 N	10.04 E
Feuilles, Baie aux ⊂	**176**	58.55 N	69.20 W
Feuilles, Rivière aux ≃	**176**	58.47 N	70.04 W
Feuquières-en-Vimeu	**50**	50.04 N	1.36 E
Feura Bush	**210**	42.35 N	73.53 W
Feurs	**62**	45.45 N	4.14 E

Symbols in the index entries represent the broad categories identified in the key at the right. Symbols with superior numbers (⋏[1]) identify subcategories (see complete key on page *I · 1*).

Kartensymbole in dem Registerverzeichnis stellen die rechts in Schlüssel erklärten Kategorien dar. Symbole mit hochgestellten Ziffern (⋏[1]) bezeichnen Unterabteilungen einer Kategorie (vgl. vollständiger Schlüssel auf Seite *I · 1*).

Los símbolos incluídos en el texto del índice representan las grandes categorias identificadas con la clave a la derecha. Los símbolos con numeros en su parte superior (⋏[1]) identifican las subcategorías (véase la clave completa en la página *I · 1*).

Les symboles de l'index représentent les catégories indiquées dans la légende à droite. Les symboles suivis d'un indice (⋏[1]) représentent des sous-catégories (voir légende complète à la page *I · 1*).

Os símbolos incluídos no texto do índice representam as grandes categorias identificadas com a chave à direita. Os símbolos com números em sua parte superior (⋏[1]) identificam as subcategorias (veja-se a chave completa à página *I · 1*).

∧	Mountain	Berg	Montaña	Montagne	Montanha
⋏	Mountains	Berge	Montañas	Montagnes	Montanhas
)(	Pass	Pass	Paso	Col	Passo
V	Valley, Canyon	Tal, Cañon	Valle, Cañón	Vallée, Canyon	Vale, Canhão
≚	Plain	Ebene	Llano	Plaine	Planície
›	Cape	Kap	Cabo	Cap	Cabo
I	Island	Insel	Isla	Île	Ilha
II	Islands	Inseln	Islas	Îles	Ilhas
♦	Other Topographic Features	Andere Topographische Objekte	Otros Elementos Topográficos	Autres données topographiques	Outros acidentes topográficos

Nombre / Nom / Nome	Página / Page	Lat.°′	Long.°′ W = Oeste / Ouest
Fevik	26	58.23 N	8.42 E
Fevzipaşa	130	37.07 N	36.37 E
Féy	56	49.02 N	6.06 E
Feyzābād, Afg.	120	37.06 N	70.34 E
Feyzābād, Īrān	128	35.01 N	58.46 E
Feyzin	62	45.40 N	4.51 E
Fez → Fès	148	34.05 N	4.57 W
Fezzan → Fazzān □9	146	26.00 N	14.00 E
Ffestiniog	42	52.58 N	3.55 W
Fforest Fawr ✦1	42	51.52 N	3.36 W
F. Gilbert Hills State Forest ♠	283	42.03 N	71.17 W
Fiambalá	252	27.41 S	67.38 W
Fiamignano	66	42.16 N	13.07 E
Fian	150	10.23 N	2.29 W
Fianarantsoa	157b	21.26 S	47.05 E
Fianarantsoa □4	157b	22.00 S	47.00 E
Fianga	146	9.55 N	15.09 E
Fiano	62	45.13 N	7.31 E
Fiantsonana	157b	19.09 S	46.12 E
Fiastra, Abbazia di v1	66	43.13 N	13.25 E
Fiavè	64	46.00 N	10.50 E
Ficarazzi	70	38.05 N	13.28 E
Ficarolo	64	44.57 N	11.26 E
Ficarra	70	38.06 N	14.50 E
Fiche	144	9.52 N	38.46 E
Fichtelberg	60	50.01 N	11.51 E
Fichtelberg ʌ	54	50.26 N	12.57 E
Fichtelgebirge ⩘	30	50.00 N	11.55 E
Fichtenau	264a	52.27 N	13.42 E
Ficksburg	158	28.57 S	27.50 E
Ficulle	66	42.50 N	12.04 E
Ficuzza ≐	70	37.00 N	14.20 E
Fidalgo ≐	250	7.28 S	42.32 W
Fidalgo Island I	224	48.25 N	122.35 W
Fiddlers Hamlet	260	51.41 N	0.08 E
Fiddletown	226	38.30 N	120.46 W
Fiddyment Creek ≐	278	41.36 N	88.03 W
Fidelity	219	39.09 N	90.10 W
Fidenza	64	44.52 N	10.03 E
Fidimīn	142	29.23 N	30.46 E
Fiditi	150	7.45 N	3.53 E
Fidji → Fiji □1	175g	18.00 S	178.00 E
Fidler Lake ◎	184	57.11 N	96.57 W
Fidschi → Fiji □1	175g	18.00 S	178.00 E
Fiè (Völs)	64	46.31 N	11.30 E
Fieberbrunn	64	47.29 N	12.33 E
Field	182	51.24 N	116.29 W
Fieldale	192	36.42 N	79.56 W
Field Museum v	278	41.53 N	87.37 W
Fieldon	219	39.07 N	90.30 W
Fieldsboro	285	40.08 N	74.43 W
Fieldstone	276	40.44 N	74.33 W
Fiemme, Val di V	64	46.24 N	11.25 E
Fiener Bruch ⊞	54	52.19 N	12.10 E
Fienvillers	50	50.07 N	2.14 E
Fier	38	40.43 N	19.34 E
Fier ≐	58	45.56 N	5.50 E
Fiera Campionaria ♠	266b	45.28 N	9.09 E
Fiera di Primiero	64	46.10 N	11.49 E
Fierenana	157b	18.29 S	48.24 E
Fiery Creek ≐, Austl.	166	18.23 S	139.52 E
Fiery Creek ≐, Austl.	169	37.44 S	142.56 E
Fiesch	58	46.20 N	8.10 E
Fiesole	66	43.48 N	11.17 E
Fiesso d'Artico	64	45.24 N	12.02 E
Fiesso Umbertiano	64	44.56 N	11.36 E
Fife	224	47.14 N	122.22 W
Fife □4	46	56.13 N	3.02 W
Fife Lake, Sk., Can.	184	49.12 N	105.43 W
Fife Lake, Mi., U.S.	190	44.34 N	85.21 W
Fife Lake ◎	184	49.14 N	105.53 W
Fife Ness ≻	46	56.17 N	2.36 W
Fifield	190	45.52 N	90.25 W
Fifteenmile Creek ≐, Or., U.S.	224	45.37 N	121.07 W
Fifteenmile Creek ≐, Wy., U.S.	202	44.01 N	108.01 W
Fifth Cataract → Khāmis, Ash-Shallāl al- ∟	140	18.23 N	33.47 E
Fifth Depot Lake ◎	212	44.36 N	76.52 W
Figeac	32	44.37 N	2.02 E
Figeholm	26	57.22 N	16.33 E
Fig Garden	226	36.48 N	119.47 W
Fighting Island I	281	42.13 N	83.07 W
Figline Valdarno	66	43.37 N	11.28 E
Figtree	154	20.24 S	28.21 E
Figueira → Governador Valadares, Bra.	255	18.51 S	41.56 W
Figueira, Bra.	287a	22.42 S	43.27 W
Figueira, Cachoeira ∟	250	9.49 S	58.13 W
Figueira da Foz	34	40.09 N	8.52 W
Figueras	34	42.16 N	2.58 E
Figuig	148	32.10 N	1.15 W
Figuig □4	148	32.40 N	2.15 W
Fihaonana	157b	18.35 S	47.12 E
Fiherenana ≐	157b	23.19 S	43.37 E
Fiji □1, Oc.	14	18.00 S	178.00 E
Fiji □1, Oc.	175g	18.00 S	178.00 E
Fiji Islands II	14	18.00 S	178.00 E
Fijnaart	52	51.37 N	4.31 E
Fik	144	8.10 N	42.18 E
Fika	146	11.17 N	11.18 E
Fiktūriyā, Bi'r ⊤4	142	30.24 N	30.36 E
Filabusi	154	20.34 S	29.20 E
Filadélfia, Bra.	250	7.21 S	47.30 W
Filadelfia, C.R.	236	10.26 N	85.34 W
Filadelfia, It.	68	38.48 N	16.18 E
Filadelfia → Philadelphia, Pa., U.S.	208	39.57 N	75.07 W
Fil'akovo	30	48.17 N	19.51 E
Filandari	68	38.37 N	16.02 E
Filatova Gora	76	57.40 N	28.10 E
Filchner Ice Shelf ⊓	9	79.00 S	40.00 W
Filderstadt	56	48.41 N	9.13 E
File Lake ◎	184	54.53 N	100.20 W
Filettino	66	41.53 N	13.19 E
Filey	44	54.12 N	0.17 W
Filey Bay ⊂	44	54.12 N	0.16 W
Fili ✦8	265b	55.45 N	37.31 E
Filí ⊥	38	38.10 N	23.40 E
Filiano	68	40.49 N	15.42 E
Filiași	38	44.33 N	23.31 E
Filiatrá	38	37.10 N	21.35 E
Filicudi, Isola I	70	38.34 N	14.34 E
Filimonovo	86	56.12 N	95.28 E
Filingué	150	14.21 N	3.19 E
Filipinas → Philippines □1	116	13.00 N	122.00 E
Filipinas, Mar de → Philippine Sea ⊤2	14	20.00 N	135.00 E
Filipino Cemetery and Memorial ✦	269f	14.31 N	121.02 E
Filippoi ⊥	38	41.00 N	24.16 E
Filippovka	80	53.59 N	49.46 E
Filippovo	80	58.18 N	50.30 E
Filippovskoje, S.S.S.R.	82	56.06 N	38.37 E
Filippovskoje, S.S.S.R.	82	56.48 N	39.07 E
Filipstad	40	59.43 N	14.10 E
Filisola	234	17.50 N	94.19 W
Fillmore, Sk., Can.	184	49.50 N	103.25 W
Fillmore, Ca., U.S.	228	34.23 N	118.55 W
Fillmore, Il., U.S.	219	39.07 N	89.17 W
Fillmore, N.Y., U.S.	210	42.27 N	78.06 W
Fillmore, Ut., U.S.	200	38.58 N	112.19 W
Fillmore Glen State Park ♠	210	42.42 N	76.20 W
Filogaso	68	38.41 N	16.14 E
Filomeno Mata	234	20.12 N	97.42 W
Filonovskaja	80	50.34 N	42.46 E
Filottrano	66	43.26 N	13.21 E
Fils ≐	56	48.42 N	9.25 E
Filskov	41	55.48 N	9.02 E
Filton	42	51.31 N	2.35 W
Filtu	144	5.07 N	40.39 E
Filzbach	58	47.07 N	9.08 E
Fimi ≐	152	3.01 S	16.58 E
Fina, Réserve de ✦4	150	12.50 N	8.30 W
Finale Emilia	64	44.50 N	11.17 E
Finale Ligure	62	44.10 N	8.20 E
Finarwa	144	13.06 N	39.01 E
Finca El Rey, Parque Nacional ♠	252	25.00 S	64.40 W
Fincastle	192	37.29 N	79.52 W
Finch	206	45.11 N	75.07 W
Fincham	42	52.37 N	0.30 E
Finchley ✦8	260	51.36 N	0.10 W
Finderne	276	40.34 N	74.35 W
Findhorn	46	57.39 N	3.36 W
Findhorn ≐	46	57.38 N	3.38 W
Findlay, Il., U.S.	219	39.31 N	88.45 W
Findlay, Oh., U.S.	216	41.02 N	83.39 W
Findlay, Mount ʌ	182	50.04 N	116.28 W
Findley Lake	214	42.07 N	79.44 W
Findley Lake ◎	214	42.06 N	79.43 W
Findochty	46	57.41 N	2.54 W
Fine Arts, Museum of v	283	42.20 N	71.06 W
Finedon	42	52.20 N	0.39 W
Finejevo	82	56.02 N	38.53 E
Finesville	210	40.36 N	75.10 W
Fingal, Austl.	166	41.39 S	147.58 E
Fingal, On., Can.	214	42.43 N	81.19 W
Fingal, N.D., U.S.	198	46.45 N	97.47 W
Finger Lake ◎	184	53.09 N	93.30 W
Fingoè	154	15.12 S	31.50 E
Finike	130	36.18 N	30.09 E
Finike Körfezi ⊂	130	36.17 N	30.16 E
Finisk ≐	48	52.07 N	7.50 W
Finistère □5	32	48.20 N	4.00 W
Finisterre	196	25.59 N	103.15 W
Finisterre → Land's End ≻	42	50.03 N	5.44 W
Finisterre, Cabo de ≻	34	42.53 N	9.16 W
Finisterre Range ⩘	164	5.50 S	146.05 E
Finja	41	56.10 N	13.41 E
Finjasjön ◎	41	56.08 N	13.42 E
Finke	162	25.34 S	134.35 E
Finke ≐	162	26.20 S	136.00 E
Finke, Mount ʌ2	162	30.55 S	134.02 E
Finke Gorge National Park ♠	162	23.15 S	132.50 E
Finkenkrug	264a	52.34 N	13.03 E
Finkenwerder ✦8	52	53.31 N	9.52 E
Finksburg	208	39.29 N	76.53 W
Finland (Suomi) □1, Europe	22	64.00 N	26.00 E
Finland (Suomi) □1, Europe	24	64.00 N	26.00 E
Finland, Gulf of (Suomenlahti) (Finskij Zaliv) ⊂	26	60.00 N	27.00 E
Finlande → Finland □1	24	64.00 N	26.00 E
Finlandia → Finland □1	24	64.00 N	26.00 E
Finlandia, Golfo de → Finland, Gulf of ⊂	26	60.00 N	27.00 E
Finland Station ✦5	265a	59.57 N	30.22 E
Finlas, Loch ◎	44	55.15 N	4.25 W
Finlay ≐	176	56.54 N	124.57 W
Finley, Austl.	166	35.39 S	145.35 E
Finley, N.D., U.S.	198	47.30 N	97.50 W
Finley Creek ≐	194	36.58 N	93.22 W
Finleyville, Pa., U.S.	214	40.09 N	78.11 W
Finleyville, Pa., U.S.	214	40.15 N	80.00 W
Finleyville Airport ⊠	279b	40.15 N	80.01 W
Finmoore	182	53.59 N	123.37 W
Finn ≐	48	54.50 N	7.29 W
Finne ✦1	54	51.13 N	11.19 E
Finnegan	182	51.07 N	112.04 W
Finnentrop	56	51.09 N	7.58 E
Finnerödja	40	58.56 N	14.26 E
Finney Creek ≐	224	48.31 N	121.51 W
Finnhamn	40	59.28 N	18.50 E
Finnigan, Mount ʌ	164	15.49 S	145.17 E
Finnis, Cape ≻	162	33.38 S	134.51 E
Finnischer Meerbusen → Finland, Gulf of ⊂	26	60.00 N	27.00 E
Finniss	168b	35.24 S	138.49 E
Finniss ≐	168b	35.30 S	138.53 E
Finnland → Finland □1	24	64.00 N	26.00 E
Finnmark □6	24	70.00 N	25.00 E
Finn Mountain ʌ	180	60.37 N	157.11 W
Finno ʌ2	154	3.27 N	41.32 E
Finnskogen ✦3	26	60.40 N	12.40 E
Finnsnes	24	69.14 N	17.59 E
Finocchio ✦8	267a	41.53 N	12.41 E
Finow	54	52.50 N	13.43 E
Finowfurt	54	52.51 N	13.41 E
Finowkanal ≋	54	52.51 N	13.24 E
Fins, Fr.	50	50.02 N	3.03 E
Fins, ʿUmān	128	22.56 N	59.13 E
Finsbury	273d	26.13 S	27.39 E
Finschhafen	164	6.35 S	147.50 E
Finse	26	60.36 N	7.30 E
Finskij zaliv → Finland, Gulf of ⊂	26	60.00 N	27.00 E
Finspång	40	58.43 N	15.47 E
Finsta	40	59.44 N	18.30 E
Finsteraarhorn ʌ	58	46.32 N	8.08 E
Finsterwalde	54	51.38 N	13.42 E
Finsterwolde	52	53.12 N	7.04 E
Fintel	52	53.10 N	9.40 E
Fintona	48	54.30 N	7.19 W
Fintown	48	54.52 N	8.08 W
Finvoy	48	55.00 N	6.30 W
Fionn Loch ◎	46	57.46 N	5.29 W
Fiora ≐	66	42.20 N	11.34 E
Fiorano Modenese	64	44.32 N	10.49 E
Fiordland National Park ♠	172	45.30 S	167.20 E
Fiorenzuola d'Arda	62	44.56 N	9.55 E
Fiorenzuola di Focara	66	43.57 N	12.48 E
Fiorito ✦8	288	34.42 S	58.27 W
Fīq	132	32.47 N	35.42 E
Fırat → Euphrates ≐	128	31.00 N	47.25 E
Firavitoba	246	5.40 N	73.00 W
Fircrest	224	47.14 N	122.30 W
Fire ≐	190	48.52 N	83.21 W
Firebaugh	226	36.51 N	120.27 W
Firebrick	218	38.41 N	83.03 W
Fire Island I	210	40.42 N	73.00 W
Fire Island Inlet ⊂	276	40.38 N	73.16 W
Fire Island National Seashore ♠	188	40.38 N	73.08 W
Fire Island Pines	276	40.40 N	73.04 W
Fire Islands II	276	40.40 N	73.11 W
Firenze (Florence)	66	43.46 N	11.15 E
Firenze □4	66	43.50 N	11.20 E
Firenzuola	66	44.07 N	11.23 E
Firesteel Creek ≐	198	43.43 N	97.58 W
Firgrove	262	53.37 N	2.08 W
Firmat	252	33.27 S	61.29 W
Firminópolis	255	16.40 S	50.19 W
Firminy	62	45.23 N	4.18 E
Firmo	68	39.43 N	16.10 E
Firovo	76	57.29 N	33.40 E
Fīrozābād	124	27.09 N	78.25 E
Fīrozpur	123	30.55 N	74.36 E
Firozpur Jhirka	124	27.48 N	76.57 E
Firsanovka	265b	55.57 N	37.15 E
Firsovo	88	52.20 N	118.06 E
First Broad ≐	192	35.11 N	81.37 W
First Cataract → Awwal, Ash-Shallāl al- ∟	140	24.01 N	32.52 E
First Cliff ⊥4	283	42.12 N	70.43 W
First Connecticut Lake ◎	206	45.05 N	71.15 W
First Han-gang Bridge ✦5	271b	37.32 N	126.56 E
First Herring Brook ≐	283	42.11 N	70.45 W
First King	162	31.49 S	124.21 E
First Watchung Mountain ʌ	276	40.55 N	74.10 W
Firth	198	40.31 N	96.36 W
Firth ≐	180	69.32 N	139.22 W
Fir'uza	128	37.56 N	58.04 E
Fīrūzābād	128	28.50 N	52.36 E
Fīrūz Bahram	267d	35.38 N	51.15 E
Fīrūz Kūh	128	35.45 N	52.47 E
Fischa ≐	264b	48.04 N	16.35 E
Fischamend	61	48.07 N	16.37 E
Fischbach, B.R.D.	56	49.44 N	7.23 E
Fischbach, B.R.D.	60	49.25 N	11.12 E
Fischbachau	64	47.43 N	11.57 E
Fischbacher Alpen ⩘	61	47.28 N	15.30 E
Fischbeck, B.R.D.	52	52.09 N	9.17 E
Fischbeck, D.D.R.	54	52.32 N	12.01 E
Fischeln ✦8	263	51.18 N	6.35 E
Fischen	58	47.28 N	10.16 E
Fischhausen → Primorsk	76	54.44 N	20.01 E
Fischland ⊥2	54	54.22 N	12.25 E
Fish ≐, Austl.	170	33.29 S	149.37 E
Fish (Vis) ≐, Namibia	156	28.07 S	17.45 E
Fish ≐, Al., U.S.	194	30.25 N	87.50 W
Fish ≐, Me., U.S.	186	47.15 N	68.36 W
Fishbourne	42	50.44 N	1.12 W
Fish Brook ≐, Ma., U.S.	283	42.38 N	70.58 W
Fish Brook ≐, Ma., U.S.	283	42.42 N	71.13 W
Fish Camp	226	37.29 N	119.38 W
Fish Canyon V	280	34.11 N	117.55 W
Fish Creek ≐, On., Can.	212	43.13 N	81.13 W
Fish Creek ≐, U.S.	216	41.28 N	84.45 W
Fish Creek ≐, Mi., U.S.	190	43.04 N	84.51 W
Fish Creek ≐, Mt., U.S.	202	46.17 N	109.13 W
Fish Creek ≐, N.Y., U.S.	212	43.12 N	75.43 W
Fish Creek ≐, Or., U.S.	224	45.09 N	122.09 W
Fish Creek, East Branch ≐	212	43.16 N	75.38 W
Fish Creek, West Branch ≐	212	43.16 N	75.38 W
Fish Creek Mountain ʌ	224	45.05 N	122.08 W
Fisheating Creek ≐	220	26.57 N	81.07 W
Fisher, Austl.	162	30.33 S	130.58 E
Fisher, Ar., U.S.	194	35.29 N	90.58 W
Fisher, Il., U.S.	216	40.18 N	88.21 W
Fisher, La., U.S.	194	31.29 N	93.27 W
Fisher, Pa., U.S.	214	41.16 N	79.15 W
Fisher ≐, Mb., Can.	184	51.26 N	97.18 W
Fisher ≐, Mt., U.S.	202	48.22 N	115.19 W
Fisher Bay ⊂, Mb., Can.	184	51.30 N	97.16 W
Fisher Bay ⊂, Mi., U.S.	281	42.36 N	82.39 W
Fisher Branch	184	51.05 N	97.37 W
Fisher Channel ✕	182	52.10 N	127.42 W
Fisher Glacier ⊓	9	73.15 S	66.00 E
Fisher Heights	279b	40.10 N	79.54 W
Fishermans Island I	208	37.06 N	75.58 W
Fisherman's Wharf ✦	282	37.48 N	122.25 W
Fishermens Bend Airfield ⊠	274b	37.50 S	144.55 E
Fisher Peak ʌ	192	36.33 N	80.50 W
Fisher River Indian Reserve ✦4	184	51.26 N	97.20 W
Fishers, In., U.S.	218	39.57 N	86.00 W
Fishers, N.Y., U.S.	210	43.00 N	77.28 W
Fishers Island I	207	41.16 N	72.02 W
Fishers Peak ʌ	196	37.06 N	104.28 W
Fisher Strait ✕	176	63.15 N	83.00 W
Fishertown	214	40.08 N	78.35 W
Fisherville	275b	43.47 N	79.28 W
Fishguard	42	51.59 N	4.59 W
Fishhook	219	39.48 N	90.53 W
Fish House	210	43.08 N	74.08 W
Fishing Bay ⊂	208	38.18 N	76.01 W
Fishing Creek	208	38.20 N	76.14 W
Fishing Creek ≐, Ky., U.S.	192	37.06 N	84.41 W
Fishing Creek ≐, N.C., U.S.	192	35.57 N	77.31 W
Fishing Creek ≐, Pa., U.S.	210	40.58 N	76.28 W
Fishing Creek ≐, Pa., U.S.	210	41.07 N	77.29 W
Fishing Creek ≐, S.C., U.S.	192	34.36 N	80.54 W
Fishing Islands II	212	44.45 N	81.20 W
Fishing Lake ◎, Mb., Can.	184	52.07 N	95.25 W
Fishing Lake ◎, Sk., Can.	184	51.50 N	103.32 W
Fishkill	210	41.32 N	73.53 W
Fishkill Creek ≐	210	41.29 N	73.59 W
Fish Lake	216	41.34 N	86.33 W
Fish Lake ◎, On., Can.	282	44.06 N	77.11 W
Fish Lake ◎, Mi., U.S.	216	42.03 N	85.52 W
Fish Lake ◎, Wa., U.S.	224	47.50 N	120.42 W
Fishmoor Reservoir ◎1	262	53.44 N	2.28 W
Fish Point ≻	214	41.43 N	82.40 W
Fishpool	262	53.35 N	2.17 W
Fish River	166	17.55 S	137.45 E
Fishs Eddy	210	41.58 N	75.10 W
Fisk	194	36.46 N	90.12 W
Fiskárdhon	38	38.27 N	20.35 E
Fiskdale	207	42.06 N	72.06 W
Fiskebäckskil	26	58.15 N	11.27 E
Fismes	50	49.18 N	3.41 E
Fišt, gora ʌ	84	43.58 N	39.54 E
Fitchburg, Ma., U.S.	207	42.35 N	71.48 W
Fitchburg, Wi., U.S.	216	42.57 N	89.28 W
Fitchville, Ct., U.S.	207	41.33 N	72.09 W
Fitchville, Oh., U.S.	214	41.06 N	82.29 W
Fitful Head ≻	46a	59.54 N	1.23 W
Fitiuta	174w	14.13 S	169.27 W
Fito, Mount ʌ	175a	13.55 S	171.44 W
Fitri, Lac ◎	146	12.50 N	17.28 E
Fittja	40	59.15 N	17.52 E
Fittleworth	42	50.58 N	0.35 W
Fitzgerald	192	31.42 N	83.15 W
Fitzgerald River National Park ♠	162	34.00 S	119.30 E
Fitz Henry	279b	40.10 N	79.45 W
Fitz Hugh Sound ✕	182	51.40 N	127.57 W
Fitzmaurice ≐	164	14.50 S	129.44 E
Fitz Roy, Arg.	254	47.02 S	67.15 W
Fitzroy, Austl.	274b	37.48 S	144.59 E
Fitzroy ≐, Austl.	162	17.31 S	123.35 E
Fitzroy ≐, Austl.	166	23.32 S	150.52 E
Fitzroy, Monte (Cerro Chaltel) ʌ	254	49.17 S	73.05 W
Fitzroy Crossing	162	18.11 S	125.35 E
Fitzwilliam	207	42.46 N	72.08 W
Fitzwilliam Island I	190	45.30 N	81.45 W
Fiuggi	66	41.48 N	13.13 E
Fiumalbo	64	44.11 N	10.39 E
Fiume → Rijeka	36	45.20 N	14.27 E
Fiumedinisi	70	38.02 N	15.23 E
Fiumefreddo Bruzio	68	39.14 N	16.04 E
Fiumefreddo di Sicilia	70	37.47 N	15.12 E
Fiumesino	66	43.38 N	13.22 E
Fiume Veneto	64	45.56 N	12.44 E
Fiumicino	66	41.46 N	12.14 E
Fiumicino ✦8	66	41.46 N	12.14 E
Five Corners	283	42.01 N	71.07 W
Five Cowrie Creek ≐1	273a	6.27 N	3.27 E
Five Dock	274a	33.52 S	151.08 E
Five Forks	284c	38.47 N	77.16 W
Five Islands	186	45.25 N	64.02 W
Five Islands Harbour ⊂	240c	17.06 N	61.54 W
Fivemile ≐	276	41.03 N	73.27 W
Fivemile Creek ≐, N.Y., U.S.	210	42.22 N	77.22 W
Fivemile Creek ≐, Or., U.S.	224	45.36 N	121.05 W
Fivemile Creek ≐, Wy., U.S.	202	43.14 N	108.12 W
Fivemile Point	210	42.06 N	75.48 W
Fivemiletown	48	54.23 N	7.18 W
Five Penny Borve	46	58.25 N	6.25 W
Five Points, Ca., U.S.	226	36.26 N	120.06 W
Five Points, In., U.S.	218	39.35 N	86.20 W
Five Points, N.M., U.S.	200	35.03 N	106.39 W
Five Points, Oh., U.S.	218	39.41 N	83.12 W
Five Points, Pa., U.S.	214	40.34 N	80.15 W
Five Points, Pa., U.S.	285	39.50 N	75.42 W
Fivizzano	64	44.14 N	10.08 E
Fiwila Mission	154	13.58 S	29.36 E
Fixin	58	47.15 N	4.58 E
Fix-Saint-Geneys	62	45.08 N	3.40 E
Fizi	154	4.18 S	28.57 E
Fizuli	84	39.37 N	47.08 E
Fjællebroen	41	55.03 N	10.24 E
Fjærlandsfjorden ⊂2	26	61.17 N	6.40 E
Fjällåsen	24	67.29 N	20.10 E
Fjällbacka	26	58.36 N	11.17 E
Fjällsjöälven ≐	26	63.29 N	16.50 E
Fjärdhundra	40	59.47 N	16.56 E
Fjärdhundra □9	40	59.47 N	16.55 E
Fjenneslev	41	55.26 N	11.40 E
Fjerritslev	26	57.05 N	9.16 E
Fjugesta	40	59.10 N	14.52 E
Fkih-Ben-Salah	148	32.32 N	6.40 W
Flackta	40	59.23 N	16.27 E
Fladnitz im Raabtal	61	46.59 N	15.47 E
Fladså ≐	41	55.19 N	8.54 E
Fladungen	56	50.31 N	10.08 E
Flag Creek ≐	278	41.43 N	87.55 W
Flagler	198	39.17 N	103.04 W
Flagler Beach	192	29.28 N	81.07 W
Flagstaff, Transkei	158	31.05 S	29.29 E
Flagstaff, Az., U.S.	200	35.11 N	111.39 W
Flagstaff Lake ◎1	188	45.10 N	70.15 W
Flagtown	276	40.31 N	74.41 W
Flaken-See ◎	264a	52.25 N	13.46 E
Flåm	26	60.50 N	7.07 E
Flambeau ≐	190	45.18 N	91.15 W
Flambeau, South Fork ≐	190	45.39 N	90.48 W
Flamborough, On., Can.	212	43.20 N	79.53 W
Flamborough, Eng., U.K.	44	54.06 N	0.07 W
Flamborough Head ≻	44	54.07 N	0.04 W
Fläming ✦1	54	52.00 N	12.30 E
Flaming Gorge National Recreation Area ♠	200	41.30 N	109.30 W
Flaming Gorge Reservoir ◎1	200	41.15 N	109.30 W
Flamingo	220	25.09 N	80.56 W
Flamingo, Teluk ⊂	164	5.33 S	138.00 E
Flanagan	216	40.52 N	88.51 W
Flanagan ≐	184	52.50 N	93.28 W
Flanagan Passage ✕	240m	18.18 N	64.39 W
Flanders, On., Can.	190	48.44 N	92.05 W
Flanders, N.J., U.S.	276	40.50 N	74.41 W
Flanders, N.Y., U.S.	207	40.49 N	72.36 W
Flanders (Flandre) (Vlaanderen) □9	50	51.00 N	3.00 E
Flanders Airport ⊠	276	40.50 N	74.41 W
Flandes	246	4.18 N	74.49 W
Flandorf	264b	48.21 N	16.23 E
Flandre → Flanders □9	50	51.00 N	3.00 E
Flandreau	198	44.02 N	96.35 W
Flannan Islands II	46	58.18 N	7.36 W
Flåren ◎	26	57.02 N	14.06 E
Flasher	198	46.27 N	101.13 W
Fläsjön ◎	26	64.06 N	15.51 E
Flat, Ak., U.S.	180	62.27 N	158.01 W
Flat, Tx., U.S.	222	31.19 N	97.38 W
Flat ≐, N.T., Can.	180	61.33 N	125.18 W
Flat ≐, Mi., U.S.	190	42.56 N	85.20 W
Flat ≐, N.C., U.S.	192	36.05 N	78.49 W
Flat Bay	186	48.24 N	58.36 W
Flat Branch ≐	219	39.33 N	89.16 W
Flatbush ✦8	276	40.39 N	73.56 W
Flat Creek ≐, Ky., U.S.	218	38.17 N	83.48 W
Flat Creek ≐, Mo., U.S.	194	36.45 N	93.31 W
Flat Creek ≐, Mt., U.S.	202	47.43 N	109.50 W
Flat Creek ≐, N.J., U.S.	276	40.27 N	74.10 W
Flat Creek Reservoir ◎1	222	31.12 N	95.45 W
Flatey	24a	65.19 N	23.07 W
Flateyri	24a	65.59 N	23.42 W
Flathead ≐	202	47.22 N	114.47 W
Flathead, Middle Fork ≐	202	48.28 N	114.04 W
Flathead, North Fork ≐	202	48.28 N	114.04 W
Flathead, South Fork ≐	202	48.23 N	114.04 W
Flathead Indian Reservation ✦4	202	47.30 N	114.25 W
Flathead Lake ◎	202	47.52 N	114.08 W
Flat Holm I	42	51.23 N	3.08 W
Flat Lake ◎	182	54.59 N	112.55 W
Flat Lick	192	36.49 N	83.46 W
Flatonia	222	29.41 N	97.06 W
Flatow, D.D.R.	264a	52.44 N	12.57 E
Flatow → Złotów, Pol.	30	53.22 N	17.02 E
Flat River, P.E., Can.	186	46.01 N	62.52 W
Flat River, Mo., U.S.	194	37.51 N	90.31 W
Flat River Reservoir ◎1	207	41.42 N	71.37 W
Flat Rock, Al., U.S.	194	34.46 N	85.42 W
Flat Rock, Il., U.S.	194	38.54 N	87.40 W
Flat Rock, In., U.S.	218	39.22 N	85.50 W
Flat Rock, Mi., U.S.	216	42.05 N	83.17 W
Flat Rock, Oh., U.S.	214	41.14 N	82.51 W
Flatrock ≐	218	39.12 N	85.56 W
Flatrock Creek ≐	216	41.10 N	84.27 W
Flatrock Lake ◎	184	55.37 N	100.47 W
Flatruet ⩘2	26	62.45 N	12.50 E
Flats	222	32.50 N	95.53 W
Flattery, Cape ≻, Austl.	164	14.58 S	145.21 E
Flattery, Cape ≻, Wa., U.S.	224	48.23 N	124.43 W
Flatts	240a	32.19 N	64.44 W
Flatwillow Creek ≐	202	46.56 N	107.55 W
Flatwood	194	32.27 N	86.15 W
Flatwoods	188	38.31 N	82.43 W
Flaugherty Run ≐	279b	40.33 N	80.13 W
Flaunden	260	51.42 N	0.32 W
Flavigny-sur-Moselle	58	48.34 N	6.11 E
Flavigny-sur-Ozerain	58	47.30 N	4.32 E
Flavy-le-Martel	50	49.43 N	3.12 E
Flawil	58	47.24 N	9.12 E
Flaxcombe	184	51.29 N	109.36 W
Flaxman Island I	180	70.13 N	146.00 W
Flax Pond ◎, Ma., U.S.	283	42.29 N	70.57 W
Flax Pond ◎, N.Y., U.S.	276	40.58 N	73.08 W
Flaxton	198	48.53 N	102.23 W
Flaxville	198	48.48 N	105.10 W
Flechas Point ≻	116	10.22 N	119.34 E
Flechtingen	54	52.20 N	11.14 E
Fleckeby	41	54.29 N	9.41 E
Flecken Zechlin	54	53.09 N	12.46 E
Fleesensee ◎	54	53.30 N	12.29 E
Fleet	42	51.16 N	0.50 W
Fleet ≐	46	57.57 N	4.05 W
Fleets Bay ⊂	208	37.40 N	76.19 W
Fleetville	210	41.36 N	75.43 W
Fleetwing Estates	285	40.07 N	74.51 W
Fleetwood, Eng., U.K.	44	53.56 N	3.01 W
Fleetwood, Pa., U.S.	208	40.27 N	75.49 W
Flehe ✦8	263	51.12 N	6.47 E
Flehingen	56	49.05 N	8.46 E
Fleischmanns	210	42.09 N	74.31 W
Fleischman Village	284c	38.51 N	76.57 W
Flekkefjord	26	58.17 N	6.41 E
Fleming, Co., U.S.	198	40.40 N	102.50 W
Fleming, Pa., U.S.	214	40.55 N	77.52 W
Fleming □6	218	38.21 N	83.42 W
Fleming Creek ≐, On., Can.	214	42.38 N	81.47 W
Fleming Creek ≐, Ky., U.S.	218	38.22 N	83.57 W
Fleming Creek ≐, Mi., U.S.	281	42.16 N	83.40 W
Fleming-Neon	192	37.11 N	82.42 W
Flemingsburg	218	38.25 N	83.44 W
Flemington, N.J., U.S.	210	40.30 N	74.51 W
Flemington, Pa., U.S.	210	41.07 N	77.28 W
Flemington Racecourse ♠	274b	37.47 S	144.55 E
Flemish Cap ⊹4	16	47.00 N	45.00 W
Flemsdorf	54	53.02 N	14.10 E
Flen	40	59.04 N	16.35 E
Flensburg	41	54.47 N	9.26 E
Flensburger Förde ⊂	41	54.49 N	9.45 E
Fleres (Boden)	64	46.58 N	11.21 E
Flers	32	48.45 N	0.34 W
Flers-sur-Noye	50	49.44 N	2.15 E
Flesherton	212	44.16 N	80.33 W
Flesko, Tanjung ≻	112	0.29 N	124.30 E
Fletcher, On., Can.	214	42.18 N	82.18 W
Fletcher, N.C., U.S.	192	35.25 N	82.30 W
Fletcher, Oh., U.S.	218	40.08 N	84.06 W
Fletcher, Ok., U.S.	196	34.49 N	98.14 W
Fletcher Islands II	9	72.40 S	94.10 W
Fletcher Moss Museum v	262	53.25 N	2.14 W
Fletchers Pond ◎1	190	44.58 N	83.52 W
Fletchers Creek ≐	275b	43.38 N	79.42 W
Fleurance	32	43.50 N	0.40 E
Fleur-de-Lys	186	50.07 N	56.08 W
Fleurier	58	46.54 N	6.35 E
Fleurieu Peninsula ≻1	168b	35.30 S	138.30 E
Fleurus	56	50.29 N	4.33 E
Fleurville	58	46.27 N	4.53 E
Fleury-les-Aubrais	50	47.56 N	1.55 E
Fleury-Mérogis	261	48.38 N	2.22 E
Fleury-sur-Andelle	50	49.22 N	1.22 E
Fleuth ≐	263	51.32 N	6.26 E
Fleuve □4	150	16.00 N	14.30 W
Flevoland □4	52	52.30 N	5.30 E
Flexanville	261	48.51 N	1.44 E
Flexenpass ✕	58	47.09 N	10.10 E
Fley ✦8	263	51.23 N	7.30 E
Flieden	56	50.25 N	9.33 E
Flierich	263	51.35 N	7.48 E
Flight Locks ✦3	284a	43.08 N	79.12 W
Flimby	44	54.41 N	3.31 W
Flims	58	46.50 N	9.17 E
Flinders ≐	166	17.36 S	140.36 E
Flinders Bay ⊂	162	34.23 S	115.19 E
Flinders Chase National Park ♠	166	36.00 S	136.45 E
Flinders Island I, Austl.	162	33.44 S	134.31 E
Flinders Island I, Austl.	166	40.00 S	148.00 E
Flinders Peak ʌ	171a	27.49 S	152.49 E
Flinders Peak ʌ2	169	37.51 S	144.24 E
Flinders Range ⩘	160	31.25 S	138.45 E
Flinders Ranges National Park ♠	166	31.20 S	138.45 E
Flinders Reefs ⊹2	166	17.37 S	148.31 E
Flinders Street Station ✦5	274b	37.49 S	144.58 E
Flinesjön ◎	40	60.23 N	16.06 E
Flines-lèz-Râches	50	50.25 N	3.11 E
Flin Flon	184	54.46 N	101.53 W
Flingern ✦8	263	51.14 N	6.49 E
Flins-sur-Seine	261	48.58 N	1.52 E
Flint, Wales, U.K.	44	53.15 N	3.07 W
Flint, Mi., U.S.	216	43.00 N	83.41 W
Flint, Tx., U.S.	222	32.12 N	95.21 W
Flint I	14	11.26 S	151.48 W
Flint ≐, U.S.	194	34.30 N	86.31 W
Flint ≐, Ga., U.S.	192	30.52 N	84.38 W
Flint ≐, Mi., U.S.	190	43.21 N	84.03 W
Flint, South Branch ≐	216	43.10 N	83.23 W
Flint Castle ⊥	262	53.16 N	3.07 W
Flint Creek ≐, Al., U.S.	194	34.30 N	86.57 W
Flint Creek ≐, Mt., U.S.	202	46.39 N	113.08 W
Flint Creek ≐, N.Y., U.S.	210	42.57 N	77.03 W
Flint Creek Range ⩘	202	46.20 N	113.05 W
Flinthill	219	38.53 N	90.52 W
Flint Hills ⩘2	198	37.50 N	96.40 W
Flint Lake ◎, N.T., Can.	176	69.10 N	74.20 W
Flint Lake ◎, In., U.S.	216	41.31 N	87.03 W
Flinton, Austl.	166	27.54 S	149.34 E
Flinton, Pa., U.S.	214	40.43 N	78.31 W
Flint Peak ʌ	280	34.10 N	118.12 W
Flint Pond ◎	283	42.40 N	71.26 W
Flintrännan ✕	41	55.34 N	12.50 E
Flintridge	228	34.11 N	118.11 W
Flintville	194	35.03 N	86.25 W
Flipper Point ≻	174a	19.18 N	166.35 E
Flippin	194	36.16 N	92.35 W
Flirey	56	48.53 N	5.50 E
Flirsch	58	47.09 N	10.24 E
Flisa	26	60.34 N	12.06 E
Flitwick	42	52.00 N	0.29 W
Flixecourt	50	50.01 N	2.05 E
Flize	56	49.42 N	4.46 E
Flobecq (Vloesberg)	50	50.44 N	3.44 E
Floby	26	58.08 N	13.20 E
Floda, Sve.	26	57.48 N	12.22 E
Floda, Sve.	40	59.04 N	16.21 E
Flodden	44	55.38 N	2.10 W
Flodden Field Battlesite ⊥	44	55.38 N	2.13 W
Flogny	50	47.57 N	3.52 E
Flöha	54	50.51 N	13.04 E
Flöha ≐	54	50.51 N	13.04 E
Floing	56	49.43 N	4.56 E
Flomaton	194	31.00 N	87.15 W
Flomborn	56	49.41 N	8.08 E
Flomot	196	34.14 N	100.59 W
Floodwood	190	46.55 N	92.55 W
Flora, Il., U.S.	194	38.40 N	88.29 W
Flora, In., U.S.	216	40.32 N	86.31 W
Flora, Ms., U.S.	194	32.32 N	90.18 W
Florac	32	44.19 N	3.36 E
Florala	194	31.00 N	86.19 W
Floral City	220	28.45 N	82.17 W
Floral Park, Mt., U.S.	202	45.57 N	112.26 W
Floral Park, N.Y., U.S.	210	40.43 N	73.42 W
Florange	56	49.20 N	6.07 E
Florânia	250	6.08 S	36.49 W
Flora Vista	200	36.47 N	108.04 W
Flore, Piton ʌ	241f	13.58 N	60.57 W
Floreffe	56	50.26 N	4.45 E
Florence → Firenze, It.	66	43.46 N	11.15 E
Florence, Al., U.S.	194	34.47 N	87.40 W
Florence, Az., U.S.	200	33.02 N	111.23 W
Florence, Ca., U.S.	228	33.58 N	118.14 W
Florence, Co., U.S.	200	38.23 N	105.07 W
Florence, Ks., U.S.	198	38.14 N	96.55 W
Florence, Ky., U.S.	218	38.59 N	84.37 W
Florence, N.J., U.S.	285	40.07 N	74.49 W
Florence, Or., U.S.	202	43.58 N	124.05 W
Florence, Pa., U.S.	214	40.26 N	80.26 W
Florence, S.C., U.S.	192	34.11 N	79.45 W
Florence, Tx., U.S.	222	30.51 N	97.48 W
Florence, Wi., U.S.	190	45.55 N	88.15 W
Florencia, Col.	246	1.36 N	75.36 W
Florencia → Firenze, It.	66	43.46 N	11.15 E
Florencio Sánchez	258	33.53 S	57.24 W
Florencio Varela	258	34.49 S	58.17 W
Florencio Varela □5	288	34.52 S	58.15 W
Florennes	56	50.15 N	4.37 E
Florentia	273d	26.16 S	28.08 E
Florentino Ameghino, Embalse ◎1	254	43.55 S	66.20 W
Florenville	56	49.42 N	5.18 E
Florenz → Firenze	66	43.46 N	11.15 E
Flores, Bra.	250	7.51 S	37.59 W
Flores, Perú	286d	12.01 S	77.01 W
Flores □5	258	33.48 S	56.50 W
Flores ✦8	288	34.38 S	58.28 W
Flores I, Indon.	115b	8.30 S	121.00 E
Flores I, Port.	148a	39.26 N	31.13 W
Flores, Cachoeira das ∟	255	14.19 S	53.32 W
Flores, Laut (Flores Sea) ⊤2	112	8.00 S	120.00 E
Flores, Rio das ≐	256	22.05 S	43.34 W
Flores, Selat ✕	115b	8.25 S	122.55 E
Flores Chica, Laguna ◎	258	35.30 S	59.01 W
Flores da Cunha	252	29.02 S	51.11 W
Flôres de Goiás	255	14.34 S	47.04 W
Flores Grande, Laguna ◎	258	35.34 S	59.02 W
Flores Island I	182	49.20 N	126.10 W
Flores Sea → Flores, Laut ⊤2	112	8.00 S	120.00 E
Floresta, Bra.	250	8.36 S	38.34 W
Floresta, It.	70	37.59 N	14.55 E
Floresta ✦8	288	34.38 S	58.29 W
Floresta Azul	255	14.51 S	39.41 W
Florestina	255	18.29 S	48.01 W
Florešty	78	47.53 N	28.17 E
Floresville	196	29.08 N	98.09 W
Florham Park	210	40.47 N	74.23 W
Floriano, Bra.	250	6.47 S	43.01 W
Floriano, Bra.	256	22.27 S	44.18 W
Floriano Peixoto, Bra.	248	9.03 S	67.24 W
Floriano Peixoto, Bra.	250	9.32 S	35.36 W
Florianópolis	252	27.35 S	48.34 W
Florida, Col.	246	3.21 N	76.15 W
Florida, Cuba	240p	21.32 N	78.14 W
Florida, Hond.	236	15.01 N	88.50 W
Florida, Perú	248	5.50 S	77.55 W
Florida, P.R.	240m	18.22 N	66.34 W
Florida, P.R.	240m	18.14 N	65.47 W
Florida, S. Afr.	273d	26.11 S	27.55 E
Florida, In., U.S.	218	40.10 N	85.42 W
Florida, N.Y., U.S.	210	41.19 N	74.21 W
Florida, Oh., U.S.	216	41.20 N	84.12 W
Florida, Ur.	258	34.06 S	56.13 W
Florida □5	258	34.00 S	56.15 W
Florida ✦8	288	34.31 S	58.30 W
Florida □3, U.S.	178	28.00 N	82.00 W
Florida □3, U.S.	192	28.00 N	82.00 W
Florida ≐	200	37.03 N	107.52 W
Florida, Cape ≻	220	25.40 N	80.09 W
Florida, Cerro la ʌ	234	23.13 N	99.15 W
Florida, Straits of ✕	238	25.00 N	79.45 W
Florida Bay ⊂	220	25.00 N	80.45 W
Floridablanca	246	7.04 N	73.06 W
Florida Caverns State Park ♠	192	30.50 N	85.18 W
Florida City	220	25.26 N	80.28 W
Florida Islands II	175e	9.00 S	160.10 E
Florida Keys II	220	24.45 N	81.00 W
Florida Lake ◎1	273d	26.11 S	27.54 E
Florida Ridge	220	27.35 N	80.23 W
Floridia	70	37.05 N	15.09 E
Florido ≐	232	27.43 N	105.10 W
Floridsdorf ✦8	264b	48.16 N	16.24 E
Floridsdorfer Brücke ✦5	264b	48.14 N	16.23 E
Florien	194	31.26 N	93.27 W
Florin	226	38.29 N	121.24 W
Flórina	38	40.47 N	21.24 E
Florisbad	158	28.46 S	26.06 E
Florissant	219	38.47 N	90.19 W
Florissant Fossil Beds National Monument ♠	200	38.54 N	105.16 W
Floriston	226	39.24 N	120.01 W
Florø	26	61.36 N	5.00 E
Flörsheim	56	50.01 N	8.26 E
Florvåg	26	60.25 N	5.14 E
Flosaille	62	45.39 N	5.18 E
Floss	60	49.44 N	12.17 E
Flossach ≐, B.R.D.	58	48.24 N	10.25 E
Flossach ≐, B.R.D.	64	48.13 N	10.30 E
Flossenbürg	60	49.44 N	12.21 E
Flossmoor	216	41.32 N	87.41 W
Flotantes, Jardínes ♠	286a	19.16 N	99.06 W
Flöthbach ≐	263	51.17 N	6.26 E
Flotta I	46	58.50 N	3.07 W
Flotte, Cap de ≻	175f	21.10 S	167.25 E
Flotten Lake ◎	184	54.38 N	108.30 W
Flourtown	285	40.06 N	75.12 W
Flowerfield	278	41.52 N	88.02 W
Flower Hill	276	40.48 N	73.40 W
Flower Mound	222	33.02 N	97.04 W
Flower's Cove	186	51.18 N	56.44 W
Flowery Branch	192	34.11 N	83.55 W
Floyd, N.M., U.S.	196	34.13 N	103.35 W
Floyd, Tx., U.S.	222	33.09 N	96.15 W
Floyd, Va., U.S.	192	36.54 N	80.19 W
Floyd □6	218	38.18 N	85.49 W
Floyd ≐	198	42.30 N	96.23 W
Floydada	196	33.59 N	101.20 W
Floyds Fork ≐	218	38.00 N	85.41 W
Fluchthorn ʌ	58	46.53 N	10.13 E
Flüela Pass ✕	58	46.45 N	9.57 E
Flüelen	58	46.54 N	8.37 E
Fluessen ◎	52	52.57 N	5.30 E
Flughafen Wien-Schwechat ⊠	61	48.07 N	16.33 E
Flühli	58	46.53 N	8.01 E
Flumen ≐	34	41.43 N	0.09 W
Flumendosa ≐	71	39.26 N	9.37 E
Flumendosa, Lago Alto del ◎1	71	39.56 N	9.26 E
Flumeri	68	41.05 N	15.09 E
Flumet	62	45.49 N	6.31 E
Fluminimaggiore	71	39.26 N	8.30 E
Flums	58	47.05 N	9.20 E
Fluren	263	51.41 N	6.33 E
Flushing → Vlissingen, Ned.	52	51.26 N	3.35 E
Flushing, Mi., U.S.	216	43.03 N	83.51 W
Flushing, Oh., U.S.	214	40.08 N	81.03 W
Flushing ✦8	276	40.45 N	73.49 W
Flushing Airport ⊠	276	40.47 N	73.50 W
Flushing Bay ⊂	276	40.46 N	73.51 W
Flushing Meadow-Corona Park ♠	276	40.45 N	73.51 W
Fluvanna, N.Y., U.S.	214	42.07 N	79.16 W
Fluvanna, Tx., U.S.	196	32.53 N	101.09 W
Fly	34	42.12 N	3.07 E
Fly ≐	164	8.30 S	143.41 E
Fly Creek	210	42.43 N	74.59 W

Symbol	English	Deutsch	Español	Français	Português
≐	River	Fluss	Río	Rivière	Rio
≋	Canal	Kanal	Canal	Canal	Canal
∟	Waterfall, Rapids	Wasserfall, Stromschnellen	Cascada, Rápidos	Chute d'eau, Rapides	Cascata, Rápidos
✕	Strait	Meeresstrasse	Estrecho	Détroit	Estreito
⊂	Bay, Gulf	Bucht, Golf	Bahía, Golfo	Baie, Golfe	Baía, Golfo
◎	Lake, Lakes	See, Seen	Lago, Lagos	Lac, Lacs	Lago, Lagos
⊞	Swamp	Sumpf	Pantano	Marais	Pântano
⊓	Ice Features, Glacier	Eis- und Gletscherformen	Accidentes Glaciales	Formes glaciaires	Acidentes glaciares
⊤	Other Hydrographic Features	Andere Hydrographische Objekte	Otros Elementos Hidrográficos	Autres données hydrographiques	Outros acidentes hidrográficos

Symbol	English	Deutsch	Español	Français	Português
⊹	Submarine Features	Untermeerische Objekte	Accidentes Submarinos	Formes de relief sous-marin	Acidentes submarinos
□	Political Unit	Politische Einheit	Unidad Política	Entité politique	Unidade política
v	Cultural Institution	Kulturelle Institution	Institución Cultural	Institution culturelle	Instituição cultural
⊥	Historical Site	Historische Stätte	Sitio Histórico	Site historique	Sitio histórico
♠	Recreational Site	Erholungs- und Ferienort	Sitio de Recreo	Centre de loisirs	Area de Lazer
⊠	Airport	Flughafen	Aeropuerto	Aéroport	Aeroporto
■	Military Installation	Militäranlage	Instalación Militar	Installation militaire	Instalação militar
✦	Miscellaneous	Verschiedenes	Misceláneo	Divers	Diversos

Name	Page	Lat.°′	Long.°′
Fly Creek ≃	202	45.59 N	107.59 W
Flyinge	41	55.45 N	13.21 E
Flying Fish Cove	112	10.25 S	105.43 E
Flynn	222	31.09 N	96.08 W
Foam Lake	184	51.39 N	103.33 W
Fobbing	260	51.32 N	0.29 E
Fobello	62	45.53 N	8.10 E
Foča, Jugo.	38	43.31 N	18.46 E
Foça, Tür.	130	38.39 N	26.46 E
Focene ◆[8]	267a	41.48 N	12.14 E
Fochabers	46	57.37 N	3.05 W
Fochville	158	26.30 S	27.30 E
Fockbek	41	54.18 N	9.36 E
Focșani	38	45.41 N	27.11 E
Fodda, Oued ≃	34	35.14 N	1.28 E
Fodé	152	5.29 N	23.18 E
Fodécontea	150	10.50 N	14.22 W
Foding Shan ∧	102	27.08 N	108.02 E
F'odorovka, S.S.S.R.	78	47.33 N	36.33 E
F'odorovka, S.S.S.R.	78	49.23 N	35.07 E
F'odorovka, S.S.S.R.	80	51.09 N	51.59 E
F'odorovka, S.S.S.R.	80	53.28 N	49.38 E
F'odorovka, S.S.S.R.	80	52.21 N	52.55 E
F'odorovka, S.S.S.R.	82	56.15 N	37.14 E
F'odorovka, S.S.S.R.	83	47.20 N	38.23 E
F'odorovka, S.S.S.R.	86	56.05 N	78.49 E
F'odorovka, S.S.S.R.	86	53.38 N	62.42 E
F'odorovka, S.S.S.R.	86	53.22 N	76.18 E
F'odorovka, S.S.S.R.	86	53.11 N	55.11 E
F'odorovskoje, S.S.S.R.	82	56.44 N	36.58 E
F'odorovskoje, S.S.S.R.	82	56.08 N	38.04 E
F'odorovskoje, S.S.S.R.	82	56.07 N	38.52 E
Foëcy	50	47.10 N	2.10 E
Foelsche ≃	164	16.03 S	136.50 E
Foeni	38	45.30 N	20.53 E
Fogang (Shijiao)	100	23.52 N	113.32 E
Fogdön ≻[1]	40	59.25 N	16.52 E
Fogelevo	85	42.03 N	69.32 E
Fogelsville	208	40.35 N	75.38 W
Foggaret el Arab	148	27.03 N	2.59 E
Foggaret ez Zoua	148	27.20 N	3.00 E
Foggia	68	41.27 N	15.34 E
Foggia □[4]	68	41.30 N	15.30 E
Foggy Island Bay ⊂	180	70.15 N	147.30 W
Foglia ≃	66	43.55 N	12.54 E
Foglianise	68	41.10 N	14.40 E
Fogliano, Lago di ⊂	66	41.24 N	12.54 E
Foglizzo	62	45.16 N	7.49 E
Fogo	186	49.43 N	54.17 W
Fogo I	150a	14.55 N	24.25 W
Fogo, Cape ≻	186	49.39 N	54.00 W
Fogo Island I	186	49.40 N	54.13 W
Fogolawa	150	12.19 N	8.41 E
Fogueteiro	266c	38.37 N	9.07 W
Fohnsdorf	61	47.13 N	14.41 E
Föhr I	30	54.43 N	8.30 E
Foia ∧	34	37.19 N	8.36 W
Foiano della Chiana	66	43.15 N	11.49 E
Foiano di Val Fortore	68	41.21 N	14.59 E
Foins, Lac aux ⊜	190	47.05 N	78.11 W
Foivre ≃	56	49.30 N	4.32 E
Foix	32	42.58 N	1.36 E
Foix □[9]	32	43.00 N	1.40 E
Fojnica	36	43.58 N	17.54 E
Foki	80	56.42 N	54.21 E
Fokino	76	53.27 N	34.24 E
Fokku	150	11.40 N	4.31 E
Folakara	157b	18.20 S	45.02 E
Folamasi	104	41.56 N	121.27 E
Folarskardhuten ∧	26	60.37 N	7.45 E
Folcroft	208	39.53 N	75.17 W
Folda ⊂[2]	24	67.36 N	14.50 E
Foldingbro	41	55.26 N	9.01 E
Folembray	50	49.33 N	3.17 E
Foley, Al., U.S.	194	30.24 N	87.41 W
Foley, Mn., U.S.	190	45.39 N	93.54 W
Foley, Mo., U.S.	219	39.02 N	90.44 W
Foleyet	190	48.15 N	82.27 W
Foley Island I	176	68.35 N	75.10 W
Folgaria	64	45.55 N	11.10 E
Folgefonni ⊓	26	60.00 N	6.20 E
Folger Hill ∧[2]	207	41.17 N	70.01 W
Foligno	66	42.57 N	12.42 E
Folk	219	38.26 N	92.06 W
Folkärna	40	60.09 N	16.19 E
Folkestone	42	51.05 N	1.11 E
Folkingham	42	52.54 N	0.24 W
Folkston	192	30.49 N	82.00 W
Folkwangmuseum ʋ	263	51.27 N	7.00 E
Follafoss	26	63.59 N	11.06 E
Follainville-Dennemont	261	49.01 N	1.43 E
Follansbee	214	40.19 N	80.35 W
Folldal	26	62.08 N	10.03 E
Folle Anse, Pointe de ≻	241o	15.57 N	61.20 W
Follebu	26	61.14 N	10.17 E
Follets Island I	222	29.02 N	95.10 W
Follett	196	36.26 N	100.08 W
Follina	64	45.57 N	12.07 E
Föllinge	26	63.40 N	14.37 E
Follonica	66	42.55 N	10.45 E
Follonica, Golfo di ⊂	66	42.54 N	10.43 E
Folly Branch ≃	284b	38.56 N	76.49 W
Folmhusen	52	53.10 N	7.28 E
Folschviller	56	49.04 N	6.41 E
Folsom, Ca., U.S.	226	38.40 N	121.10 W
Folsom, N.J., U.S.	208	39.36 N	74.50 W
Folsom, Pa., U.S.	285	39.53 N	75.19 W
Folsom Lake ⊜[1]	226	38.43 N	121.08 W
Folsom Lake State Recreation Area ♠	226	38.46 N	121.06 W
Fomboni	157a	12.16 S	43.45 E
Fomento, Cuba	240p	22.06 N	79.43 W
Fomento, Ur.	258	34.26 S	57.14 W
Fomin	80	46.58 N	43.38 E
Fominiči	76	54.07 N	34.41 E
Fominki	80	55.57 N	42.22 E
Fominskaja	24	61.17 N	48.40 E
Fominskoje, S.S.S.R.	24	59.43 N	42.05 E
Fominskoje, S.S.S.R.	76	58.59 N	39.06 E
Fomkino	80	54.25 N	50.30 E
Foncine-le-Bas	58	46.38 N	6.03 E
Fonda, Ia., U.S.	198	42.34 N	94.50 W
Fonda, N.Y., U.S.	210	42.57 N	74.22 W
Fondachelli	70	37.58 N	15.11 E
Fond d'Or Bay ⊂	241f	13.56 N	60.54 W
Fond du Lac, Sk., Can.	176	59.19 N	107.10 W
Fond du Lac, Wi., U.S.	190	43.46 N	88.26 W
Fond du Lac ≃	176	59.17 N	106.00 W
Fond du Lac Indian Reservation ◆[4]	190	46.45 N	92.37 W
Fondi	66	41.21 N	13.25 E
Fondi, Lago di ⊂	66	41.19 N	13.20 E
Fondo	64	46.26 N	11.08 E
Fondouk el Aouareb	36	35.34 N	9.46 E
Fongfong	140	12.56 N	23.14 E
Fonni	71	40.07 N	9.15 E
Fonsagrada	34	43.08 N	7.04 W
Fonseca	246	10.54 N	72.51 W
Fonseca, Golfo de ⊂	236	13.10 N	87.40 W
Fons-Outre-Gardon	62	43.54 N	4.11 E
Font ≃	44	55.10 N	1.44 W
Fontaine, Fr.	58	47.40 N	7.00 E
Fontaine, Fr.	62	45.11 N	5.40 E
Fontainebleau, Fr.	50	48.24 N	2.42 E
Fontainebleau, S. Afr.	273d	26.07 S	27.59 E
Fontaine-Française	58	47.31 N	5.22 E
Fontaine-le-Dun	50	49.49 N	0.51 E
Fontaine-lès-Dijon	58	47.21 N	5.01 E
Fontaine-lès-Grès	50	48.25 N	3.54 E
Fontaine-lès-Luxeuil	58	47.51 N	6.20 E
Fontaines	58	46.51 N	4.46 E
Fontaines-sur-Saône	62	45.50 N	4.51 E
Fontan	62	44.00 N	7.33 E
Fontana, Arg.	252	27.25 S	59.02 W
Fontana, Ca., U.S.	228	34.05 N	117.26 W
Fontana, Wi., U.S.	216	42.33 N	88.34 W
Fontana, Lago ⊜	254	44.56 S	71.30 W
Fontanafredda	64	45.58 N	12.34 E
Fontana Lake ⊜[1]	192	35.26 N	83.38 W
Fontanarosa	68	41.01 N	15.01 E
Fontanarossa, Aeroporto di ⊠	70	37.29 N	15.03 E
Fontanelas	266c	38.51 N	9.26 W
Fontanelice	66	44.15 N	11.33 E
Fontanella	64	45.27 N	9.48 E
Fontanellato	64	44.53 N	10.10 E
Fontanelle	198	41.17 N	94.33 W
Fontanetto Po	62	45.12 N	8.11 E
Fontanigorda	62	44.33 N	9.19 E
Fontarabie, Lac ⊜	186	51.10 N	66.25 W
Fontas ≃	176	58.20 N	121.50 W
Fonte, Bra.	287b	23.25 S	46.21 W
Fonte, It.	64	45.47 N	11.53 E
Fonte, It.	66	41.46 N	13.13 E
Fonte Avellana, Monastero di ʋ[1]	66	43.29 N	12.45 E
Fonte Blanda	66	42.34 N	11.10 E
Fonte Boa	246	2.32 S	66.01 W
Fonte Colombo, Convento di ʋ[1]	66	42.23 N	12.50 E
Fontenay, Abbaye de ʋ[1]	50	47.39 N	4.24 E
Fontenay-aux-Roses	261	48.47 N	2.17 E
Fontenay-en-Parisis	261	49.03 N	2.27 E
Fontenay-le-Comte	32	46.28 N	0.48 W
Fontenay-le-Fleury	261	48.49 N	2.03 E
Fontenay-lès-Briis	261	48.37 N	2.09 E
Fontenay-le-Vicomte	261	48.33 N	2.24 E
Fontenay-Saint-Père	261	49.02 N	1.45 E
Fontenay-sous-Bois	261	48.51 N	2.29 E
Fontenay-Trésigny	50	48.42 N	2.52 E
Fonteneau, Lac ⊜	186	51.55 N	61.30 W
Fontenelle	186	48.53 N	64.33 W
Fontenelle Creek ≃	200	42.05 N	110.08 W
Fontenelle Reservoir ⊜[1]	200	42.05 N	110.06 W
Fontespina	66	43.17 N	13.45 E
Fontevivo	64	44.51 N	10.10 E
Font Hill Manor	284b	39.17 N	76.52 W
Fontibón	246	4.40 N	74.09 W
Fonti del Clitunno ⫪[4]	66	42.49 N	12.46 E
Fontoy	56	49.21 N	6.00 E
Fontur ≻	24a	66.23 N	14.30 W
Fontvieille	62	43.43 N	4.43 E
Fonyód	30	46.44 N	17.34 E
Fonzaso	64	46.01 N	11.48 E
Foochow → Fuzhou	100	26.06 N	119.17 E
Foot Creek ≃	198	45.26 N	98.29 W
Foothill Farms	226	38.40 N	121.20 W
Foothills	182	53.04 N	116.48 W
Footprint Lake ⊜	184	55.47 N	98.53 W
Footscray	169	37.48 S	144.54 E
Footville	216	42.40 N	89.12 W
Foping	102	33.21 N	107.59 E
Foppolo	64	46.03 N	9.45 E
Fora, Ponta de ≻	287a	22.57 S	43.07 W
Foraker, Mount ∧	180	62.56 N	151.26 W
Forari	175f	17.39 S	168.32 E
Forbach, B.R.D.	56	48.41 N	8.21 E
Forbach, Fr.	56	49.11 N	6.54 E
Forbes	166	33.23 S	148.01 E
Forbes, Lac ⊜	206	46.31 N	74.12 W
Forbes, Mount ∧	182	51.52 N	116.56 W
Forbes Field ♠	279b	40.27 N	79.57 W
Forbesganj	124	26.18 N	87.15 E
Forbes Reef	158	26.10 S	31.05 E
Forbes Road	214	40.21 N	79.32 W
Forbestown	226	39.31 N	121.16 W
Forcados	150	5.22 N	5.24 E
Forcados ≃[1]	150	5.25 N	5.19 E
Forcalquier	62	43.58 N	5.47 E
Force	214	41.15 N	78.30 W
Forchheim, B.R.D.	60	49.43 N	11.04 E
Forchheim, D.D.R.	54	50.43 N	13.16 E
Forclaz, Col de la)(	58	46.04 N	7.00 E
Ford, Scot., U.K.	46	56.10 N	5.26 W
Ford, Ks., U.S.	198	37.38 N	99.45 W
Ford □[6]	216	40.27 N	88.06 W
Ford ≃	190	45.40 N	87.09 W
Ford, Cape ≻	164	13.26 S	129.52 E
Ford City, Ca., U.S.	226	35.09 N	119.27 W
Ford City, Pa., U.S.	214	40.46 N	79.31 W
Ford City ◆[9]	278	41.46 N	87.44 W
Ford Cliff	214	40.45 N	79.32 W
Ford Dam ◆[6]	281	42.13 N	83.33 W
Ford Dry Lake ⊜	204	33.38 N	115.00 W
Førde, Nor.	26	59.36 N	5.29 E
Førde, Nor.	26	61.27 N	5.52 E
Førdefjorden ⊂[2]	26	61.28 N	5.39 E
Forden	42	52.36 N	3.08 W
Förderstedt	54	51.54 N	11.38 E
Fordham University ʋ[2]	276	40.51 N	73.53 W
Fordingbridge	42	50.56 N	1.47 W
Ford Lake ⊜	281	42.13 N	83.36 W
Ford Mansion ⊥	276	40.48 N	74.28 W
Ford Motor Company (River Rouge Plant) ʋ[3]	281	42.18 N	83.10 W
Ford Museum ʋ	281	42.18 N	83.14 W
Fordongianus	71	39.59 N	8.48 E
Ford Ranges ⋏	9	77.00 S	145.00 W
Fords	276	40.31 N	74.18 W
Fords Bridge	166	29.45 S	145.26 E
Fordsburg ◆[8]	273d	26.13 S	28.02 E
Fords Prairie	224	46.44 N	122.59 W
Fordsville	194	37.38 N	86.43 W
Fordville	198	48.13 N	97.47 W
Fordyce	194	33.48 N	92.24 W
Fordyce Lake ⊜[1]	226	39.23 N	120.28 W
Foré	150	13.08 N	10.42 W
Forécariah	150	9.26 N	13.06 W
Forel, Mont ∧	176	67.00 N	37.00 W
Foreland Point ≻	42	51.16 N	3.47 W
Foreman	194	33.43 N	94.23 W
Foremost	184	49.29 N	111.25 W
Forenza	68	40.51 N	15.51 E
Forepaugh Airport ⊠	279a	41.21 N	81.30 W
Foresman	216	40.52 N	87.18 W
Forest, Bel.	50	50.48 N	4.19 E
Forest, On., Can.	190	43.06 N	82.00 W
Forest, In., U.S.	216	40.22 N	86.19 W
Forest, Ms., U.S.	194	32.21 N	89.28 W
Forest, Oh., U.S.	216	40.48 N	83.30 W
Forest □[6]	214	41.29 N	79.27 W
Forest, Middle Branch ≃	198	48.13 N	97.48 W
Forest Acres	192	34.01 N	80.59 W
Forestburg	182	52.35 N	112.04 W
Forest City, Ia., U.S.	190	43.15 N	93.38 W
Forest City, N.C., U.S.	192	35.20 N	81.51 W
Forest City, Pa., U.S.	210	41.39 N	75.28 W
Forest Creek ≃	226	38.23 N	120.28 W
Forest Gate ◆[8]	260	51.33 N	0.02 E
Forest Glade	222	31.39 N	96.31 W
Forest Grove, B.C., Can.	182	51.46 N	121.06 W
Forest Grove, Or., U.S.	224	45.31 N	123.06 W
Forest Grove, Pa., U.S.	279b	40.18 N	75.04 W
Forest Heights	284c	38.49 N	77.00 W
Forest Hill, Austl.	171a	27.35 S	152.22 E
Forest Hill, Austl.	171b	35.09 S	147.27 E
Forest Hill, Austl.	274b	37.50 S	145.11 E
Foresthill, Ca., U.S.	226	39.01 N	120.49 W
Forest Hill, Md., U.S.	208	39.35 N	76.23 W
Forest Hill, Tx., U.S.	222	32.40 N	97.16 W
Forest Hill ◆[8]	275b	43.42 N	79.24 W
Forest Hill Park ♠	279a	41.31 N	81.35 W
Forest Hill Parkway ♠	279a	41.33 N	81.36 W
Forest Hills	279b	40.25 N	79.51 W
Forest Hills ◆[8]	276	40.42 N	73.51 W
Forest Home	194	31.52 N	86.50 W
Forestier Peninsula ≻[1]	166	42.57 S	147.55 E
Forest Knolls	284c	39.02 N	77.01 W
Forest Lake, Il., U.S.	216	42.13 N	88.03 W
Forest Lake, Mn., U.S.	190	45.16 N	92.59 W
Forest Lake ⊜, Il., U.S.	278	42.13 N	88.03 W
Forest Lake ⊜, Ma., U.S.	283	42.43 N	71.15 W
Forest Lawn Memorial Park ◆	280	34.09 N	118.19 W
Forest Manor	284c	38.50 N	76.53 W
Forest Park, Ga., U.S.	192	33.37 N	84.22 W
Forest Park, Il., U.S.	278	41.52 N	87.48 W
Forest Park, Oh., U.S.	218	39.16 N	84.34 W
Forest Park ◆[8]	284b	39.19 N	76.41 W
Forest Park ♠	276	40.42 N	73.51 W
Forest River	278	42.05 N	87.54 W
Forest Row	42	51.06 N	0.02 E
Forest View	278	41.49 N	87.47 W
Forestville, Austl.	274a	33.46 S	151.13 E
Forestville, P.Q., Can.	186	48.45 N	69.06 W
Forestville, Md., U.S.	284c	38.50 N	76.52 W
Forestville, N.Y., U.S.	214	42.28 N	79.10 W
Forestville, Pa., U.S.	214	41.06 N	80.00 W
Forestville, Wi., U.S.	190	44.41 N	87.28 W
Forêt l'Orient, Lac de la ⊜[1], Fr.	50	48.17 N	4.20 E
Forêt l'Orient, Lac de la ⊜[1], Fr.	58	48.17 N	4.20 E
Forêt-Noire → Schwarzwald ⋏	58	48.00 N	8.15 E
Forez, Monts du ⋏	32	45.35 N	3.48 E
Forfar	46	56.38 N	2.54 W
Forfry	261	49.03 N	2.51 E
Forgan	196	36.54 N	100.32 W
Forgaria	64	46.13 N	12.58 E
Forge Acres	284b	39.25 N	76.27 W
Forge Heights	284b	39.25 N	76.25 W
Forges-les-Bains	261	48.38 N	2.06 E
Forges-les-Eaux	50	49.37 N	1.33 E
Forget, Pointe ≻	275a	45.27 N	73.58 W
Forge Village	207	42.34 N	71.29 W
Forggensee ⊜	58	47.36 N	10.44 E
Forillon, Parc National de ♠	186	48.55 N	64.12 W
Forino	68	40.52 N	14.44 E
Foristell	219	38.49 N	90.57 W
Fork	208	39.28 N	76.27 W
Forked Creek ≃	216	41.19 N	88.09 W
Forked Deer ≃	194	35.56 N	89.35 W
Forked Deer, Middle Fork ≃	194	36.01 N	89.13 W
Forked Deer, North Fork ≃	194	36.00 N	89.26 W
Forked Deer, South Fork ≃	194	36.00 N	89.26 W
Forked River	208	39.50 N	74.11 W
Forks	224	47.57 N	124.23 W
Forkston	210	41.31 N	76.07 W
Forksville	210	41.29 N	76.36 W
Forleti, Arroyo ≃	288	34.35 S	58.41 W
Forlì	66	44.13 N	12.03 E
Forlì □[4]	64	44.05 N	12.02 E
Forlimpopoli	66	44.11 N	12.07 E
Forman	198	46.06 N	97.38 W
Formazza	58	46.22 N	8.26 E
Formby	262	53.34 N	3.05 W
Formby Hills ⋏[2]	262	53.34 N	3.06 W
Formby Point ≻	262	53.33 N	3.06 W
Formentera I	34	38.42 N	1.28 E
Formentor, Cabo de ≻	34	39.58 N	3.12 E
Formerie	50	49.39 N	1.44 E
Formia	66	41.15 N	13.37 E
Formiga	255	20.27 S	45.25 W
Formiga ≃	256	22.18 S	42.52 W
Formigine	64	44.34 N	10.51 E
Formignana	64	44.50 N	11.51 E
Formosa, Arg.	252	26.11 S	58.11 W
Formosa, Bra.	255	15.32 S	47.20 W
Formosa □[4]	252	25.00 S	60.00 W
Formosa → Taiwan □[1]	100	23.30 N	121.00 E
Formosa, Ilha I	150	11.29 N	15.58 W
Formosa, Serra ⋏[1]	250	12.00 S	55.00 W
Formosa Strait → Taiwan Strait ⋓	100	24.00 N	119.00 E
Formoso ≃, Bra.	250	10.34 S	49.56 W
Formoso ≃, Bra.	255	17.25 S	44.57 W
Formoso ≃, Bra.	255	13.26 S	44.14 W
Formoso ≃, Bra.	255	18.25 S	52.28 W
Formoso ≃, Bra.	256	21.20 S	43.10 W
Forncelle	66	43.55 N	11.06 E
Fornelli	71	41.00 N	8.14 E
Forney	222	32.44 N	96.28 W
Forni Avoltri •	64	46.35 N	12.46 E
Forni di sopra	64	46.25 N	12.35 E
Forni di sotto	64	46.23 N	12.40 E
Forni di Val d'Astico	64	45.51 N	11.22 E
Forno	64	46.21 N	11.37 E
Forno Alpi Graie	62	45.22 N	7.13 E
Forno di Zoldo	64	46.21 N	12.11 E
Fornosovo	76	59.35 N	30.35 E
Fornovo di Taro	64	44.42 N	10.06 E
Foro Romano ⊥	267a	41.54 N	12.29 E
Føroyar → Faeroe Islands □[2]	22	62.00 N	7.00 W
Forpost	86	56.47 N	72.10 E
Forres, Arg.	252	27.53 S	63.58 W
Forres, Scot., U.K.	46	57.37 N	3.38 W
Forrest, Austl.	162	30.51 S	128.06 E
Forrest, Austl.	169	38.31 S	143.43 E
Forrest, Il., U.S.	216	40.45 N	88.24 W
Forrest ≃	164	15.18 S	128.04 E
Forrest, Mount ∧	162	24.48 S	127.45 E
Forrestal Research Center ʋ[3]	276	40.21 N	74.37 W
Forrest City	194	35.00 N	90.47 W
Forrester Island I	182	54.48 N	133.32 W
Forrest Lakes ⊜	162	29.12 S	128.46 E
Forreston, Il., U.S.	190	42.07 N	89.34 W
Forreston, Tx., U.S.	222	32.16 N	96.52 W
Forrest River Aboriginal Reserve ◆[4]	164	15.00 S	127.40 E
Fors	40	60.13 N	16.18 E
Forsan	196	32.07 N	101.22 W
Forsayth	166	18.35 S	143.36 E
Forsbacka	40	60.37 N	16.53 E
Forsby	26	60.30 N	25.56 E
Forserum	26	57.42 N	14.28 E
Forshaga	40	59.32 N	13.28 E
Forsmark	40	60.22 N	18.09 E
Forssa	26	60.49 N	23.38 E
Forst	54	51.44 N	14.39 E
Förste	52	51.44 N	10.10 E
Forster	166	32.11 S	152.31 E
Forstwald ◆[8]	263	51.18 N	6.30 E
Forsyth, Ga., U.S.	192	33.02 N	83.56 W
Forsyth, Il., U.S.	219	39.56 N	88.57 W
Forsyth, Mo., U.S.	194	36.41 N	93.07 W
Forsyth, Mt., U.S.	202	46.15 N	106.40 W
Forsyth Island I	164	16.50 S	139.06 E
Forsyth Range ⋏	166	22.45 S	143.15 E
Fort ◆[8]	272c	18.56 N	72.50 E
Fort Abbās	123	29.12 N	72.52 E
Fort Adams	194	31.05 N	91.32 W
Fort Albany	176	52.15 N	81.37 W
Fort Alexander Indian Reserve ◆[4]	184	50.27 N	96.15 W
Fortaleza	250	3.43 S	38.30 W
Fortaleza ≃	248	10.40 S	77.52 W
Fortaleza de Santa Teresa ♠	252	33.59 S	53.32 W
Fortaleza do Ituxi	248	7.29 S	66.20 W
Fortaleza dos Nogueiras	250	6.54 S	46.09 W
Fort Allen ■	240m	18.01 N	66.30 W
Fort Amherst National Historic Park ♠	186	46.12 N	63.09 W
Fort Ancient State Memorial ⊥	218	39.24 N	84.06 W
Fort Anne National Historic Park ♠	186	44.44 N	65.26 W
Fort Apache Indian Reservation ◆[4]	200	34.01 N	110.28 W
Fort-Archambault → Sarh	146	9.09 N	18.23 E
Fort Assiniboine	182	54.20 N	114.46 W
Fort Atkinson	216	42.55 N	88.50 W
Fort Augusta ⊥	210	40.53 N	76.46 W
Fort Augustus	46	57.09 N	4.41 W
Fort Baker ■	282	37.50 N	122.29 W
Fort Battleford National Historic Park ♠	184	52.42 N	108.15 W
Fort Bayard → Zhanjiang	102	21.12 N	110.23 E
Fort Beaufort	158	32.46 S	26.40 E
Fort Beauséjour National Historic Park ♠	186	45.51 N	64.18 W
Fort Belknap Agency	202	48.28 N	108.45 W
Fort Belknap Indian Reservation ◆[4]	202	48.16 N	108.38 W
Fort Belvoir ■	208	38.44 N	77.10 W
Fort Bend □[6]	222	29.32 N	95.47 W
Fort Benjamin Harrison ■	218	39.52 N	86.01 W
Fort Benning ■	192	32.22 N	84.50 W
Fort Benton	202	47.49 N	110.40 W
Fort Berthold Indian Reservation ◆[4]	198	47.40 N	102.25 W
Fort Bidwell	204	41.51 N	120.09 W
Fort Bliss ■	200	32.15 N	106.00 W
Fort Bowie National Historic Site ⊥	200	32.09 N	109.24 W
Fort Bragg	204	39.26 N	123.48 W
Fort Bragg ■	192	35.09 N	78.59 W
Fort Branch	194	38.15 N	87.34 W
Fort Bridger	200	41.19 N	110.23 W
Fort Calhoun	198	41.27 N	96.01 W
Fort Campbell ■	194	36.39 N	87.29 W
Fort Canby State Park ♠	224	46.17 N	124.04 W
Fort Canning ■	271c	1.18 N	103.51 E
Fort-Carnot	157b	21.53 S	47.28 E
Fort Caroline National Memorial ⊥	192	30.20 N	81.30 W
Fort Carson ■	200	38.44 N	104.48 W
Fort Casey Historical State Park ♠	224	48.10 N	122.40 W
Fort Chambly National Historic Park ♠	206	45.27 N	73.17 W
Fort Chipewyan	176	58.42 N	111.08 W
Fort Churchill Historic State Monument ⊥	226	39.18 N	119.17 W
Fort Clatsop National Memorial ⊥	224	46.08 N	123.54 W
Fort Cobb	196	35.05 N	98.26 W
Fort Cobb Reservoir ⊜[1]	196	35.12 N	98.29 W
Fort Collins	200	40.35 N	105.05 W
Fort Columbia Historical State Park ♠	224	46.15 N	123.56 W
Fort Constantine	166	20.28 S	140.37 E
Fort-Coulonge	188	45.51 N	76.44 W
Fort Covington	206	44.59 N	74.29 W
Fort Custer State Recreation Area ♠	216	42.18 N	85.20 W
Fort Davis, Al., U.S.	194	32.14 N	85.42 W
Fort Davis, Tx., U.S.	196	30.35 N	103.53 W
Fort Davis National Historic Site ⊥	196	30.33 N	103.53 W
Fort de Douaumont ⊥	56	49.13 N	5.25 E
Fort Defiance	200	35.44 N	109.04 W
Fort-de-France	240e	14.36 N	61.05 W
Fort-de-France, Baie de ⊂	240e	14.34 N	61.04 W
Fort-de-France-Lamentin, Aérodrome de ⊠	240e	14.35 N	61.00 W
Fort Deposit	194	31.59 N	86.34 W
Fort Detrick ■	208	39.27 N	77.26 W
Fort de Vaux ⊥	56	49.12 N	5.28 E
Fort Devens ■	207	42.32 N	71.37 W
Fort Dix ■	208	40.00 N	74.33 W
Fort Dodge	190	42.29 N	94.10 W
Fort Donelson National Military Park ♠	194	36.26 N	87.49 W
Fort Duchesne	200	40.17 N	109.51 W
Fort Dupont Park ♠	284c	38.53 N	76.57 W
Forte, Monte ∧	71	40.43 N	8.15 E
Forteau	186	51.28 N	56.58 W
Forte dei Marmi	64	43.57 N	10.10 E
Forte de Magoito	266c	38.52 N	9.27 W
Fort Edward	210	43.16 N	73.35 W
Forte República	152	7.45 S	16.23 E
Fort Erie	212	42.54 N	78.56 W
Fort Erie Race Track ♠	284a	42.55 N	78.56 W
Fortescue ≃	162	21.00 S	116.06 E
Fort Eustis ■	208	37.09 N	76.35 W
Fortevoit	46	56.20 N	3.32 W
Fortezza (Franzensfeste)	64	46.47 N	11.37 E
Fort Fairfield	186	46.46 N	67.50 W
Fort Fitzgerald	176	59.53 N	111.37 W
Fort Foote Village	284c	38.46 N	77.01 W
Fort-Foureau	146	12.05 N	15.02 E
Fort Frances	190	48.36 N	93.24 W
Fort Franklin	180	65.11 N	123.46 W
Fort Fraser	182	54.04 N	124.33 W
Fort Frederica National Monument ♠	192	31.12 N	81.26 W
Fort Gaines	192	31.36 N	85.02 W
Fort Garland	200	37.25 N	105.26 W
Fort Gay	188	38.06 N	82.35 W
Fort George ⊥	284a	43.15 N	79.04 W
Fort George G. Meade ■	208	39.05 N	76.50 W
Fort Gibson	196	35.47 N	95.15 W
Fort Gibson Lake ⊜[1]	196	36.00 N	95.18 W
Fort Good Hope	180	66.15 N	128.38 W
Fort Gordon ■	192	33.25 N	82.11 W
Fort-Gourand → Fdérik	148	22.41 N	12.43 W
Fort Green	220	27.36 N	81.56 W
Forth	46	55.47 N	3.41 W
Forth ≃	46	56.03 N	3.44 W
Forth, Carse of V	46	56.08 N	4.05 W
Forth, Firth of ⊂	46	56.10 N	2.45 W
Förtha	56	50.56 N	10.14 E
Fort Hall	202	43.02 N	112.26 W
Fort Hall Indian Reservation ◆[4]	202	43.10 N	112.10 W
Fort Hamilton ■	276	40.37 N	74.02 W
Forth Bridge ◆[5]	46	56.00 N	3.25 W
Fort Hertz → Putao	102	27.21 N	97.24 E
Fort Hill → Chitipa	154	9.43 S	33.16 E
Fort Hill ■	188	38.04 N	77.19 W
Fort Hill State Memorial ⊥	218	39.07 N	83.25 W
Fort Hood ■	222	31.08 N	97.46 W
Fort Howard	208	39.12 N	76.27 W
Fort Huachuca ■	200	31.33 N	110.20 W
Fort Hunter	210	42.57 N	74.17 W
Fort Hunter Liggett ■	226	35.55 N	121.15 W
Fortierville	206	46.29 N	72.02 W
Fortin, Lac ⊜	186	50.50 N	67.46 W
Fortín Ayacucho	248	19.58 S	59.47 W
Fortín Coroneles Sanchez	248	19.20 S	59.58 W
Fortín de las Flores	234	18.54 N	97.00 W
Fortine	182	48.45 N	114.54 W
Fortín Florida	248	20.45 S	59.17 W
Fortín Garrapatal	248	21.27 S	61.30 W
Fortín Teniente Montanía	252	22.04 S	59.57 W
Fortín Uno	252	38.51 S	65.17 W
Fort Jackson ■	192	34.01 N	80.57 W
Fort Jameson → Chipata	154	13.39 S	32.40 E
Fort Jefferson National Monument ♠	220	24.37 N	82.54 W
Fort Jennings	216	40.54 N	84.17 W
Fort Jeudy, Point of ≻	241k	12.00 N	61.42 W
Fort Johnson	210	42.57 N	74.14 W
Fort Johnston → Mangochi	154	14.28 S	35.16 E
Fort Jones	204	41.36 N	122.50 W
Fort Kent	186	47.15 N	68.35 W
Fort Klamath	202	42.42 N	121.59 W
Fort Knox ■	194	37.54 N	85.57 W
Fort-Lamy → N'Djamena	146	12.07 N	15.03 E
Fort Langley	224	49.10 N	122.35 W
Fort Langley National Historic Park ♠	224	49.10 N	122.35 W
Fort Laramie	200	42.12 N	104.31 W
Fort Laramie National Historic Site ♠	198	42.09 N	104.41 W
Fort Larned National Historic Site ⊥	198	38.10 N	99.12 W
Fort Lauderdale	220	26.07 N	80.08 W
Fort Lauderdale-Hollywood International Airport ⊠	220	26.04 N	80.09 W
Fort Laurens State Memorial ⊥	214	40.38 N	81.27 W
Fort Leavenworth ■	198	39.21 N	94.55 W
Fort Le Boeuf ⊥	214	41.56 N	79.59 W
Fort Lee	210	40.51 N	73.58 W
Fort Lee ■	208	37.14 N	77.20 W
Fort Lennox National Historic Park ♠	206	45.06 N	73.16 W
Fort Leonard Wood ■	194	37.45 N	92.07 W
Fort Lewis ■	224	47.05 N	122.37 W
Fort Liard	176	60.15 N	123.28 W
Fort Lincoln State Park ♠	198	46.45 N	100.52 W
Fort Littleton	214	40.04 N	77.58 W
Fort Loramie	216	40.21 N	84.22 W
Fort Loudoun Lake ⊜[1]	192	35.45 N	84.10 W
Fort Lupton	200	40.05 N	104.48 W
Fort Lyon Canal ≊	198	38.11 N	102.31 W
Fort Macleod	182	49.43 N	113.25 W
Fort Madison	190	40.37 N	91.18 W
Fort-Mahon-Plage	50	50.21 N	1.34 E
Fort Malden National Historic Park ♠	281	42.06 N	83.07 W
Fort Matanzas National Monument ♠	192	29.40 N	81.18 W
Fort McClellan ■	194	33.43 N	85.47 W
Fort McDermitt Indian Reservation ◆[4]	202	42.00 N	117.32 W
Fort McDowell Indian Reservation ◆[4]	200	33.38 N	111.41 W
Fort McHenry National Monument and Historic Shrine ♠	208	39.16 N	76.35 W
Fort Mckinley	218	39.47 N	84.15 W
Fort McMurray	184	56.44 N	111.23 W
Fort McNair ■	284c	38.52 N	77.04 W
Fort McPherson	180	67.27 N	134.53 W
Fort Meade	220	27.45 N	81.48 W
Fort Mill	192	35.00 N	80.56 W
Fort Miller	210	43.10 N	73.35 W
Fort Mitchell, Al., U.S.	192	32.21 N	85.01 W
Fort Mitchell, Ky., U.S.	218	39.03 N	84.32 W
Fort Mojave Indian Reservation ◆[4]	200	34.55 N	114.35 W
Fort Monmouth ■	208	40.19 N	74.02 W
Fort Monroe ■	208	37.00 N	76.18 W
Fort Montgomery	210	41.20 N	73.59 W
Fort Morgan	198	40.15 N	103.47 W
Fort Myer ■	284c	38.53 N	77.05 W
Fort Myers	220	26.38 N	81.52 W
Fort Myers Beach	220	26.27 N	81.56 W
Fort Myers Shores	220	26.43 N	81.45 W
Fort Myers Villas	220	26.34 N	81.52 W
Fort Necessity National Battlefield ⊥	188	39.47 N	79.39 W
Fort Neck ≻[1]	276	40.39 N	73.28 W
Fort Nelson	176	58.49 N	122.43 W
Fort Nelson ≃	176	59.30 N	124.00 W
Fort Niagara Beach	284a	43.16 N	79.03 W
Fort Niagara State Park ♠, N.Y., U.S.	210	43.16 N	79.03 W
Fort Niagara State Park ♠, N.Y., U.S.	284a	43.16 N	79.03 W
Fort Nonsense ⊥	276	40.48 N	74.29 W
Fort Norman	180	64.54 N	125.34 W
Fort Nottingham	158	29.25 S	29.55 E
Fort Ogden	220	27.05 N	81.57 W
Fort Ord ■	226	36.40 N	121.48 W
Fortore ≃	68	41.55 N	15.17 E
Fort Parker State Park ♠	222	31.36 N	96.33 W
Fort Payne	194	34.26 N	85.43 W
Fort Peck	202	48.00 N	106.26 W
Fort Peck Dam ◆[6]	202	47.52 N	106.38 W
Fort Peck Indian Reservation ◆[4]	202	48.22 N	105.40 W
Fort Peck Lake ⊜[1]	202	47.45 N	106.50 W
Fort Pierce	220	27.26 N	80.19 W
Fort Pierce Inlet ⊂	220	27.28 N	80.18 W
Fort Pierre	198	44.21 N	100.22 W
Fort Pitt Tunnels ◆[5]	279b	40.25 N	80.00 W
Fort Plain	210	42.55 N	74.37 W
Fort Point National Historical Site ⊥	282	37.48 N	122.28 W
Fort Polk ■	194	31.04 N	93.11 W
Fort Portal	154	0.40 N	30.17 E
Fort Providence	176	61.21 N	117.39 W
Fort Pulaski National Monument ⊥	192	32.01 N	80.59 W
Fort Qu'Appelle	184	50.46 N	103.48 W
Fort Raleigh National Historic Site ⊥	192	35.55 N	75.40 W
Fort Randall Dam ◆[6]	198	42.48 N	98.35 W
Fort Recovery	216	40.24 N	84.46 W
Fort Resolution	176	61.10 N	113.40 W
Fortress Mountain ∧	202	44.20 N	109.47 W
Fortress of Louisbourg National Historic Park ♠	186	45.56 N	59.57 W
Fort Riley ■	198	39.04 N	96.47 W
Fort Ritchie ■	208	39.43 N	77.30 W
Fort Rixon	154	20.01 S	29.18 E
Fort Robinson State Park ♠	198	42.41 N	103.30 W
Fort Rodd Hill National Historic Park ♠	224	48.26 N	123.28 W
Fortrose, N.Z.	172	46.34 S	168.48 E
Fortrose, Scot., U.K.	46	57.34 N	4.09 W
Fort Rosebery → Mansa	154	11.12 S	28.53 E
Fort Rucker ■	194	31.20 N	85.42 W
Fort-Rupert	176	51.30 N	78.45 W
Fort Saint James	182	54.26 N	124.15 W
Fort Saint John	182	56.15 N	120.51 W
Fort Salonga	276	40.55 N	73.18 W
Fort Sam Houston ■	196	29.27 N	98.27 W
Fort Sandeman	120	31.20 N	69.27 E
Fort Saskatchewan	182	53.43 N	113.13 W
Fort Scott	198	37.50 N	94.42 W
Fort Şeneca	214	41.13 N	83.10 W
Fort-Ševčenko	84	44.31 N	50.16 E
Fort Severn	176	56.00 N	87.38 W
Fort Shawnee	216	40.41 N	84.08 W
Fort Sheridan ■	216	42.13 N	87.48 W
Fort Sill ■	196	34.40 N	98.25 W
Fort Simcoe Historical State Park ♠	224	46.21 N	120.50 W
Fort Simpson	176	61.52 N	121.23 W
Fort Sisseton State Park ♠	198	45.39 N	97.32 W
Fort Smith, N.T., Can.	176	60.00 N	111.53 W
Fort Smith, Ar., U.S.	194	35.23 N	94.23 W
Fort Steele	182	49.37 N	115.38 W
Fort Stevens State Park ♠	224	46.10 N	124.00 W
Fort Stewart ■	192	31.52 N	81.37 W
Fort Stockton	196	30.53 N	102.52 W
Fort Sumner	196	34.28 N	104.14 W
Fort Sumter National Monument ♠	192	32.44 N	79.46 W
Fort Supply	196	36.34 N	99.34 W
Fort Tejon State Historical Park ♠	228	34.52 N	118.53 W
Fort Thomas, Az., U.S.	200	33.02 N	109.57 W
Fort Thomas, Ky., U.S.	218	39.04 N	84.26 W
Fort Thompson	198	44.04 N	99.26 W
Fort Tilden ■	276	40.33 N	73.53 W
Fort Totten	198	47.58 N	98.59 W
Fort Totten Indian Reservation ◆[4]	198	47.53 N	98.50 W
Fort Totten Park ♠	284c	38.57 N	77.00 W
Fort Towson	196	34.01 N	95.15 W
Fort-Trinquet → Bîr Mogreïn	148	25.14 N	11.35 W
Fortuna, Arg.	252	35.07 S	65.23 W
Fortuna, Ca., U.S.	204	40.35 N	124.09 W
Fortuna, Río de la ≃	248	16.36 S	58.46 W
Fortuna Ledge (Marshall)	180	61.53 N	162.05 W
Fortune	186	47.04 N	55.50 W
Fortune Bay ⊂	186	47.25 N	55.25 W
Fortune Ditch ≊	279a	41.20 N	82.03 W
Fortune Harbour	186	49.31 N	55.15 W
Fortuneswell	42	50.34 N	2.27 W
Fort Union National Monument ♠	200	35.55 N	105.01 W
Fort Union Trading Post National Historical Site ⊥	198	48.00 N	104.03 W
Fort Valley	192	32.33 N	83.53 W
Fort Vancouver National Historic Site ⊥	224	45.38 N	122.37 W
Fort Vermilion	176	58.24 N	116.00 W
Fortville	218	39.55 N	85.50 W
Fort Wadsworth ■	276	40.36 N	74.04 W
Fort Walton Beach	194	30.24 N	86.37 W
Fort Washakie	200	43.00 N	108.52 W
Fort Washington	208	40.08 N	75.12 W
Fort Washington Forest	208	38.43 N	76.59 W
Fort Washington State Park ♠	285	40.07 N	75.14 W
Fort Wayne	216	41.07 N	85.07 W
Fort Wayne Military Museum ʋ	281	42.18 N	83.06 W
Fort Wellington	246	6.24 N	57.36 W
Fort Wellington National Historic Park ♠	212	44.44 N	75.31 W
Fort White	192	29.55 N	82.42 W
Fort William → Thunder Bay, On., Can.	190	48.23 N	89.15 W
Fort William, Scot., U.K.	46	56.49 N	5.07 W
Fort William ⊥	272b	22.33 N	88.20 E
Fort Worth	222	32.43 N	97.19 W
Fort Yates	198	46.05 N	100.37 W
Forty Foot Drain ≊	42	52.28 N	0.05 W
Forty Fort	210	41.16 N	75.52 W
Fortymile ≃	180	64.26 N	140.32 W
Fort Yukon	180	66.34 N	145.17 W
Fort Yuma Indian Reservation ◆[4]	204	32.48 N	114.34 W
Forum ♠, P.Q., Can.	275a	45.29 N	73.35 W
Forum ♠, Ca., U.S.	280	33.57 N	118.20 W
Forūr, Jazīreh-ye I	128	26.17 N	54.32 E
Forza d'Agrò	70	37.55 N	15.20 E
Foscagno, Passo di)(	64	46.30 N	10.08 E
Fosdinovo	64	44.08 N	10.01 E
Fosforescénte, Bahía ⊂	240m	17.59 N	67.01 W
Fosforitnyj	82	55.19 N	38.54 E
Foshan	100	23.03 N	113.09 E
Fosna ≻[1]	24	64.00 N	10.30 E
Fosnavåg	26	62.21 N	5.39 E
Foso	150	5.42 N	1.17 W
Foss	46	56.41 N	3.58 W
Foss ≃, Eng., U.K.	44	53.57 N	1.06 W
Foss ≃, Wa., U.S.	224	47.43 N	121.18 W
Fossacesia	66	42.15 N	14.29 E
Fossacesia Marina	66	42.15 N	14.30 E
Fossa Eugeniana ≊	263	51.33 N	6.36 E
Fossano	62	44.33 N	7.43 E
Fossanova, Abbazia di ʋ[1]	66	41.29 N	13.13 E
Fossato, Colle di)(	66	43.19 N	12.47 E
Fossato di Vico	66	43.18 N	12.46 E
Fossé	56	49.27 N	5.00 E
Fosse-Martin	261	49.05 N	2.54 E
Fosses	261	49.06 N	2.29 E
Fosses-la-Ville	56	50.24 N	4.42 E
Fossil	202	44.59 N	120.12 W
Fossil Butte National Monument ♠	202	41.50 N	110.40 W
Fossil Downs	162	18.08 S	125.38 E
Fossil Lake ⊜	202	43.18 N	120.15 W
Fossombrone	66	43.41 N	12.48 E
Fosston	198	47.34 N	95.45 W
Fos-sur-Mer	62	43.26 N	4.57 E
Foster, Austl.	169	38.39 S	146.12 E
Foster, Ky., U.S.	218	38.47 N	84.12 W
Foster, R.I., U.S.	207	41.51 N	71.45 W
Foster ≃	184	55.47 N	105.49 W
Foster, Mount ∧	180	59.48 N	135.29 W
Foster Brook	214	41.59 N	78.37 W

Symbols in the index entries represent the broad categories identified in the key at the right. Symbols with superior numbers (⋏[1]) identify subcategories (see complete key on page *I · 1*).

Kartensymbole in dem Registerverzeichnis stellen die rechts in Schlüssel erklärten Kategorien dar. Symbole mit hochgestellten Ziffern (⋏[1]) bezeichnen Unterabteilungen einer Kategorie (vgl. vollständiger Schlüssel auf Seite *I · 1*).

Los símbolos incluídos en el texto del índice representan las grandes categorías identificadas con la clave a la derecha. Los símbolos con numeros en su parte superior (⋏[1]) identifican las subcategorías (véase la clave completa en la página *I · 1*).

Les symboles de l'index représentent les catégories indiquées dans la légende à droite. Les symboles suivis d'un indice (⋏[1]) représentent des sous-catégories (voir légende complète à la page *I · 1*).

Os símbolos incluídos no texto do índice representam as grandes categorias identificadas com a chave à direita. Os símbolos com números em sua parte superior (⋏[1]) identificam as subcategorias (veja-se a chave completa à página *I · 1*).

∧ Mountain	Berg	Montaña	Montagne	Montanha
⋏ Mountains	Berge	Montañas	Montagnes	Montanhas
)(Pass	Pass	Paso	Col	Passo
V Valley, Canyon	Tal, Cañon	Valle, Cañón	Vallée, Canyon	Vale, Canhão
≝ Plain	Ebene	Llano	Plaine	Planície
≻ Cape	Kap	Cabo	Cap	Cabo
I Island	Insel	Isla	Île	Ilha
II Islands	Inseln	Islas	Îles	Ilhas
◆ Other Topographic Features	Andere Topographische Objekte	Otros Elementos Topográficos	Autres données topographiques	Outros acidentes topográficos

ESPAÑOL — Nombre | Página | Lat.°′ | Long.°′ W = Oeste

FRANÇAIS — Nom | Page | Lat.°′ | Long.°′ W = Ouest

PORTUGUÊS — Nome | Página | Lat.°′ | Long.°′ W = Oeste

Foster City	226	37.33 N	122.16 W
Foster Creek ≃	198	44.34 N	98.12 W
Fosterdale	210	41.42 N	74.58 W
Foster Joseph Sayers Reservoir ⊜[1]	214	41.02 N	77.40 W
Foster Park	228	34.21 N	119.18 W
Fosters	194	33.05 N	87.41 W
Fosters Pond ⊜	283	42.37 N	71.08 W
Foster Street	260	51.46 N	0.09 E
Foster Village	229c	21.21 N	157.55 W
Fostoria	214	41.09 N	83.25 W
Fót	264c	47.37 N	19.12 E
Fotadrevo	157b	24.03 S	45.01 E
Fotan	100	24.12 N	117.53 E
Fothergill	44	54.42 N	3.30 W
Fóti-Somlyó ∧[2]	264c	47.38 N	19.13 E
Foucarmont	50	49.51 N	1.34 E
Fou-Chouen → Fushun	104	41.52 N	123.53 E
Fouesnant	32	47.54 N	4.01 W
Foug	56	48.41 N	5.47 E
Fougamou	152	1.13 S	10.36 E
Fougères	32	48.21 N	1.12 W
Fougères-sur-Bièvre	50	47.27 N	1.21 E
Fougerolles	58	47.53 N	6.24 E
Fouhsin → Fuxin	104	42.03 N	121.46 E
Fouju	261	48.35 N	2.47 E
Fouke	194	33.16 N	93.53 W
Foula I	46a	60.08 N	2.05 W
Foulain	58	48.02 N	5.13 E
Foulalaba	150	10.41 N	7.22 W
Foula Mori	150	12.10 N	13.51 W
Foulatari	146	13.41 N	12.03 E
Foul Bay ⊂	140	23.30 N	35.39 E
Fouling → Fuling	102	29.42 N	107.21 E
Foulness ≃	44	53.47 N	0.43 W
Foulness Island I	42	51.36 N	0.55 E
Foulness Point ›	42	51.38 N	0.57 E
Foulpointe	157b	17.41 S	49.31 E
Foulsham	42	52.48 N	1.01 E
Foulwind, Cape ›	172	41.45 S	171.28 E
Foumban	152	5.43 N	10.55 E
Foumbot	152	5.30 N	10.38 E
Foumbouni	157a	11.50 S	43.30 E
Foum-El-Hisn	148	28.59 N	8.55 W
Foum-Zguid	148	30.04 N	6.54 W
Foundiougne	150	14.08 N	16.28 W
Fountain, Co., U.S.	198	38.40 N	104.42 W
Fountain, Fl., U.S.	192	30.09 N	85.38 W
Fountain □[6]	216	40.17 N	87.13 W
Fountain City, In., U.S.	218	39.57 N	84.55 W
Fountain City, Wi., U.S.	190	44.07 N	91.43 W
Fountain Creek ≃, Co., U.S.	198	38.15 N	104.35 W
Fountain Creek ≃, Il., U.S.	219	38.20 N	90.22 W
Fountain Green	200	39.37 N	111.38 W
Fountain Hill	208	40.36 N	75.23 W
Fountain Inn	192	34.41 N	82.11 W
Fountain Park	216	41.50 N	84.32 W
Fountain Peak ∧	204	34.57 N	115.32 W
Fountain Place	194	30.31 N	91.09 W
Fountains Abbey ʋ[1]	44	54.07 N	1.34 W
Fountains Creek ≃	208	36.33 N	77.21 W
Fountaintown	218	39.41 N	85.46 W
Fountain Valley	228	33.42 N	117.57 W
Fourche LaFave ≃	194	34.58 N	92.35 W
Fourche Maline ≃	194	34.55 N	94.55 W
Fourchu	186	45.43 N	60.15 W
Four Corners	202	44.55 N	122.58 W
Four Elms	260	51.13 N	0.06 E
Four Hole Swamp ≃	192	33.03 N	80.24 W
Fouriesburg	158	28.38 S	28.14 E
Fourmies	50	50.00 N	4.03 E
Four Mile Creek ≃, On., Can.	284a	43.15 N	79.08 W
Fourmile Creek ≃, N.Y., U.S.	284a	43.17 N	79.00 W
Four Mile Creek ≃, Oh., U.S.	218	39.26 N	84.32 W
Four Mile Creek State Park ♠	284a	43.16 N	79.00 W
Fourmile Draw V	196	32.40 N	104.18 W
Four Mile Lake ⊜	212	44.40 N	78.44 W
Four Mile Run ≃	284c	38.50 N	77.02 W
Four Mountains, Islands of II	180	52.50 N	170.00 W
Fournaise, Piton de la ∧	157c	21.14 S	55.43 E
Fourneau, Pointe à ›	275a	45.22 N	73.51 W
Fourneaux, Fr.	50	47.53 N	1.48 E
Fourneaux, Fr.	62	45.11 N	6.39 E
Fournier, Lac ⊜	186	51.33 N	65.25 W
Fournière, Lac ⊜	190	48.04 N	78.03 W
Foúrnoi I	130	37.34 N	26.30 E
Four Oaks	192	35.26 N	78.25 W
Fourqueux	261	48.53 N	2.04 E
Fours	32	46.49 N	3.43 E
Fourteenmile Creek ≃	218	38.26 N	85.37 W
Fourth Cataract → Rābiʿ, Ash-Shallāl ar- ᒐ	140	18.47 N	32.03 E
Fourth Cliff ±[4]	283	42.09 N	70.42 W
Four Towns	281	42.37 N	83.25 W
Fous, Pointe des ›	240d	15.12 N	61.20 W
Foussard ≃	50	48.16 N	1.17 E
Fouta Djalon ◆[1]	150	11.30 N	12.30 W
Fou-Tcheou → Fuzhou	100	26.06 N	119.17 E
Fouyang → Fuyang	100	32.54 N	115.49 E
Fouzon ≃	50	47.16 N	1.27 E
Foveaux Strait ʉ	172	46.35 S	168.00 E
Foveran	46	57.18 N	2.02 W
Fowey	42	50.20 N	4.38 W
Fowler, Ca., U.S.	226	36.37 N	119.40 W
Fowler, Co., U.S.	198	38.07 N	104.01 W
Fowler, In., U.S.	216	40.37 N	87.19 W
Fowler, Ks., U.S.	198	37.23 N	100.11 W
Fowler, Mi., U.S.	216	43.00 N	84.44 W
Fowler, Oh., U.S.	214	41.19 N	80.40 W
Fowler, Lake ⊜	168b	35.06 S	137.37 E
Fowler, Point ›	162	32.02 S	132.29 E
Fowler Creek ≃	281	42.17 N	83.30 W
Fowlers Bay	162	31.59 S	132.27 E
Fowlerton	196	28.28 N	98.48 W
Fowlerville	216	42.39 N	84.04 W
Fowliang → Jingdezhen	100	29.16 N	117.11 E
Fowman	128	37.13 N	49.19 E
Fox	180	64.51 N	147.46 W
Fox ≃, Mb., Can.	184	56.03 N	93.18 W
Fox ≃, U.S.	194	40.18 N	91.30 W
Fox ≃, U.S.	216	41.21 N	88.50 W
Fox ≃, Il., U.S.	194	38.32 N	88.08 W
Fox ≃, Wi., U.S.	190	44.32 N	88.01 W
Fox, Cape ›	182	54.47 N	130.51 W
Foxboro, On., Can.	212	44.15 N	77.26 W
Foxboro, Ma., U.S.	207	42.03 N	71.15 W
Foxboro Raceway ♠	283	42.06 N	71.16 W
Fox Brook ≃	276	41.03 N	74.13 W
Foxburg	214	41.09 N	79.41 W
Fox Chapel	279b	40.30 N	79.55 W
Fox Chase ◆[8]	285	40.04 N	75.05 W
Fox Chase Manor	285	40.05 N	75.06 W
Fox Creek ≃, Ky., U.S.	218	38.16 N	83.41 W
Fox Creek ≃, N.Y., U.S.	210	42.41 N	74.18 W
Foxe Basin ⊂	176	68.25 N	77.00 W
Foxe-Becken → Foxe Basin ⊂	176	68.25 N	77.00 W
Foxe Channel ʉ	176	64.30 N	80.00 W
Foxen ⊜	26	59.23 N	11.52 E
Foxe Peninsula ›[1]	176	65.00 N	76.00 W
Foxford	48	53.58 N	9.08 W
Fox Glacier	172	43.28 S	170.00 E
Foxhall	284c	39.04 N	77.03 W
Fox Harbour	186	47.19 N	53.55 W
Fox Hills	284c	39.02 N	77.11 W
Foxhole	42	50.21 N	4.52 W
Foxholes	44	54.08 N	0.28 W
Fox Hollow Lake ⊜	276	41.02 N	74.40 W
Fox Island I, On., Can.	212	44.28 N	78.24 W
Fox Island I, Wa., U.S.	224	47.16 N	122.37 W
Fox Islands II	180	53.30 N	168.00 W
Fox Lake, Il., U.S.	216	42.23 N	88.11 W
Fox Lake, Wi., U.S.	190	43.33 N	88.54 W
Fox Lake ⊜	216	42.25 N	88.09 W
Fox Mountain ∧	180	61.55 N	133.22 W
Foxpark	200	41.05 N	106.09 W
Fox Point	216	43.09 N	87.54 W
Fox Point ›	276	40.54 N	73.35 W
Fox River Estates	216	41.58 N	88.20 W
Fox River Grove	216	42.12 N	88.12 W
Foxton	172	40.28 S	175.18 E
Foxton Beach	172	40.28 S	175.13 E
Foxvale	283	42.02 N	71.14 W
Fox Valley, Austl.	274a	33.45 S	151.06 E
Fox Valley, Sk., Can.	184	50.29 N	109.28 W
Foxwells	208	37.38 N	76.18 W
Foxwist Green	262	53.12 N	2.34 W
Foxworth	194	31.14 N	89.52 W
Foyedong	98	40.41 N	119.12 E
Foyers	46	57.14 N	4.29 W
Foyle ≃	48	54.59 N	7.18 W
Foyle, Lough ⊂	48	55.06 N	7.08 W
Foynes	48	52.37 N	9.06 W
Foza	64	45.54 N	11.38 E
Foz do Cunene	152	17.16 S	11.50 E
Foz do Iguaçu	252	25.33 S	54.35 W
Foz do Jordão	248	9.23 S	71.56 W
Foz Giraldo	34	40.00 N	7.43 W
Foziling	100	31.20 N	116.17 E
Frabosa Soprana	62	44.17 N	7.48 E
Fracción del Refugio	234	21.57 N	100.02 W
Frackville	208	40.47 N	76.13 W
Fraction Run ≃	278	41.34 N	88.04 W
Fraga, Arg.	252	33.30 S	65.48 W
Fraga, Esp.	34	41.31 N	0.21 E
Fragagnano	68	40.26 N	17.28 E
Fragneto Monforte	68	41.15 N	14.46 E
Fragoso, Cayo I	240p	22.44 N	79.30 W
Fragrant Hills Park ♠	271a	39.59 N	116.11 E
Fragua, Sierra de la ⋏	196	26.41 N	102.13 W
Fraile Muerto	252	32.31 S	54.32 W
Fraïn, Chott el ⊜	34	35.57 N	5.38 E
Fraire	50	50.16 N	4.30 E
Fraisans	58	47.09 N	5.46 E
Fraisse	62	45.23 N	4.15 E
Fraize	58	48.11 N	7.00 E
Fram	61	46.27 N	15.38 E
Frameries	50	50.24 N	3.54 E
Framingham	207	42.16 N	71.25 W
Framingham State College ʋ[2]	283	42.18 N	71.26 W
Framlingham	42	52.13 N	1.21 E
Frammersbach	56	50.04 N	9.28 E
Framnes Mountains ⋏	9	67.50 S	62.35 E
Frampol	30	50.41 N	22.40 E
Frampton Cotterell	42	51.32 N	2.29 W
Frampton on Severn	42	51.46 N	2.22 W
França, Bra.	250	11.34 S	40.36 W
Franca, Bra.	255	20.32 S	47.24 W
Français, Récif des ✣[2]	175f	19.40 S	163.20 E
Francavilla al Mare	66	42.25 N	14.17 E
Francavilla Angitola	68	38.46 N	16.16 E
Francavilla d'Ete	66	43.11 N	13.32 E
Francavilla di Sicilia	70	37.54 N	15.08 E
Francavilla Fontana	68	40.31 N	17.35 E
Francavilla in Sinni	68	40.05 N	16.12 E
Francavilla Marittima	68	39.49 N	16.23 E
France □[1], Europe	22	46.00 N	2.00 E
France □[1], Europe	32	46.00 N	2.00 E
Frances ≃	180	60.12 N	129.02 W
Francés, Cabo ›	240p	21.54 N	84.02 W
Francés, Punta ›	240p	21.38 N	83.12 W
Frances Creek	164	13.35 S	131.52 E
Francês dos Carvalhos	256	22.05 S	44.29 W
Frances Lake ⊜	180	61.25 N	129.30 W
Francés Viejo, Cabo ›	238	19.39 N	69.55 W
Francesville	216	40.59 N	86.52 W
Franceville	152	1.38 S	13.35 E
Francfort-sur-Main → Frankfurt am Main	56	50.07 N	8.40 E
Franche-Comté □[9]	58	47.00 N	6.00 E
Franchère, Lac ⊜	206	46.47 N	74.58 W
Franches-Montagnes ⋏	58	47.12 N	7.00 E
Francia	252	32.33 S	56.37 W
Francia → France □[1]	32	46.00 N	2.00 E
Francia, Estación de ◆[5]	266d	41.23 N	2.11 E
Francia, Peña de ∧	34	42.35 N	8.02 W
Francis	184	50.05 N	103.55 W
Francis, Lake ⊜	206	45.02 N	71.20 W
Francisca, Punta ›	232	21.34 N	87.21 W
Francis Case, Lake ⊜[1]	198	43.15 N	99.00 W
Francisco A. Berra	258	35.23 S	58.51 W
Francisco Alvarez	258	34.38 S	58.52 W
Francisco Beltrão	252	26.05 S	53.04 W
Francisco González Villarreal	232	25.22 N	97.53 W
Francisco I. Madero, Méx.	232	25.45 N	103.21 W
Francisco I. Madero, Méx.	232	24.32 N	104.22 W
Francisco I. Madero, Méx.	234	16.50 N	93.50 W
Francisco I. Madero, Méx.	234	21.36 N	104.49 W
Francisco José, Tierra → Zeml'a Franca-Iosifa II	12	81.00 N	55.00 E
Francisco Morato	256	23.16 S	46.45 W
Francisco Morazán □[5]	236	14.15 N	87.15 W
Francisco Perito Moreno, Parque Nacional ♠	254	47.50 S	72.08 W
Francisco Primo Verdad	234	21.48 N	101.55 W
Francisco Sá	255	16.28 S	43.30 W
Francisco Zarco	204	32.06 N	116.30 W
Francis E. Warren Air Force Base ■	198	41.09 N	104.52 W
Francistown	156	21.11 S	27.32 E
Francitas	222	28.52 N	96.20 W
Franco da Rocha	256	23.20 S	46.43 W
Francofonte	70	37.14 N	14.53 E
François	186	47.35 N	56.45 W
François, Lacs à ⊜	186	51.40 N	65.49 W
François-Joseph, Îles du → Zeml'a Franca-Iosifa II	12	81.00 N	55.00 E
François Lake	182	54.04 N	125.44 W
François Lake ⊜	182	54.00 N	125.40 W
Francolise	68	41.11 N	14.03 E
Franconia Notch State Park ♠	188	44.06 N	71.43 W
Franconville	261	48.59 N	2.14 E
Francs Peak ∧	202	43.58 N	109.20 W
Francueil	50	47.19 N	1.05 E
Franeker	52	53.11 N	5.32 E
Frangy	58	46.01 N	5.56 E
Frank	279b	40.16 N	79.48 W
Frank and Poet Drain ≅	281	42.06 N	83.12 W
Frankby	262	53.22 N	3.08 W
Frankel City	196	32.23 N	102.47 W
Franken □[9]	30	50.00 N	10.00 E
Frankenau	56	51.05 N	8.56 E
Frankenbach	56	50.40 N	8.34 E
Frankenberg	54	50.54 N	13.01 E
Frankenberg-Eder	56	51.03 N	8.48 E
Frankenburg	60	48.05 N	13.30 E
Frankenheim	56	50.32 N	10.04 E
Frankenhöhe ⋏	56	49.15 N	10.15 E
Frankenmarkt	64	47.59 N	13.25 E
Frankenmuth	190	43.19 N	83.44 W
Frankenstein	56	49.26 N	7.58 E
Frankenstein → Ząbkowice Śląskie	30	50.36 N	16.53 E
Frankenthal	56	49.32 N	8.21 E
Frankenwald ⋏	54	50.18 N	11.36 E
Frankfield	241q	18.09 N	77.22 W
Frankford, On., Can.	212	44.12 N	77.36 W
Frankford, De., U.S.	208	38.31 N	75.14 W
Frankford, Mo., U.S.	219	39.29 N	91.19 W
Frankford ◆[8]	285	40.01 N	75.05 W
Frankford Arsenal ■	285	40.00 N	75.04 W
Frankfort, S. Afr.	158	32.44 S	27.28 E
Frankfort, S. Afr.	158	27.17 S	28.30 E
Frankfort, Il., U.S.	216	41.29 N	87.50 W
Frankfort, In., U.S.	216	40.16 N	86.30 W
Frankfort, Ks., U.S.	198	39.42 N	96.25 W
Frankfort, Ky., U.S.	218	38.12 N	84.52 W
Frankfort, Mi., U.S.	190	44.38 N	86.14 W
Frankfort, N.Y., U.S.	210	43.02 N	75.04 W
Frankfort, Oh., U.S.	218	39.24 N	83.10 W
Frankfort, S.D., U.S.	198	44.52 N	98.18 W
Frankfort Springs	214	40.30 N	80.25 W
Frankfurt □[5]	54	52.30 N	14.00 E
Frankfurt am Main	56	50.07 N	8.40 E
Frankfurt am Main, Flughafen ⊠	56	50.02 N	8.33 E
Frankfurt an der Oder	54	52.20 N	14.33 E
Frank G. Bonelli Regional County Park ♠	280	34.05 N	117.49 W
Frank Hann National Park ♠	162	32.50 S	120.25 E
Fränkische Alb ⋏[2]	60	49.20 N	11.30 E
Fränkische Rezat ≃	56	49.11 N	11.01 E
Fränkische Saale ≃	56	50.03 N	9.42 E
Fränkische Schweiz ◆[1]	60	49.45 N	11.25 E
Frank Key I	220	25.07 N	80.54 W
Frankland ≃	162	34.58 S	116.49 E
Frankleben	54	51.18 N	11.56 E
Franklin, S. Afr.	158	30.18 S	29.30 E
Franklin, Az., U.S.	200	32.40 N	109.04 W
Franklin, Ga., U.S.	192	33.16 N	85.05 W
Franklin, Id., U.S.	202	42.00 N	111.48 W
Franklin, Il., U.S.	219	39.37 N	90.03 W
Franklin, In., U.S.	218	39.28 N	86.03 W
Franklin, Ky., U.S.	194	36.43 N	86.34 W
Franklin, La., U.S.	194	29.47 N	91.30 W
Franklin, Me., U.S.	188	44.35 N	68.13 W
Franklin, Ma., U.S.	207	42.05 N	71.23 W
Franklin, Mi., U.S.	281	42.31 N	83.18 W
Franklin, Mn., U.S.	198	44.31 N	94.52 W
Franklin, Ne., U.S.	198	40.05 N	98.57 W
Franklin, N.H., U.S.	188	43.26 N	71.38 W
Franklin, N.J., U.S.	210	41.07 N	74.34 W
Franklin, N.Y., U.S.	210	42.20 N	75.09 W
Franklin, N.C., U.S.	192	35.10 N	83.22 W
Franklin, Oh., U.S.	218	39.33 N	84.18 W
Franklin, Pa., U.S.	214	41.24 N	79.50 W
Franklin, Tn., U.S.	194	35.55 N	86.52 W
Franklin, Tx., U.S.	222	31.01 N	96.29 W
Franklin, Vt., U.S.	206	44.58 N	72.55 W
Franklin, Va., U.S.	208	36.40 N	76.55 W
Franklin, W.V., U.S.	188	38.39 N	79.20 W
Franklin, Wi., U.S.	216	42.54 N	88.03 W
Franklin □[5]	176	72.00 N	100.00 W
Franklin □[6], In., U.S.	218	39.25 N	85.01 W
Franklin □[6], Ky., U.S.	218	38.14 N	84.52 W
Franklin □[6], Ma., U.S.	207	42.36 N	72.36 W
Franklin □[6], Mo., U.S.	219	38.25 N	91.03 W
Franklin □[6], N.Y., U.S.	206	44.57 N	74.18 W
Franklin □[6], Oh., U.S.	218	39.57 N	83.00 W
Franklin □[6], Pa., U.S.	208	39.56 N	77.40 W
Franklin □[6], Tx., U.S.	222	33.07 N	95.13 W
Franklin □[6], Vt., U.S.	206	44.57 N	72.52 W
Franklin, Mount ∧	171b	35.29 S	148.47 E
Franklin, Point ›	180	70.54 N	158.48 W
Franklin Bay ⊂	176	69.45 N	126.00 W
Franklin Canyon Reservoir ⊜[1]	280	34.06 N	118.25 W
Franklin Delano Roosevelt, Parque Nacional ♠	258	34.52 S	56.03 W
Franklin Delano Roosevelt National Historic Site ⊥	210	41.46 N	73.56 W
Franklin Delano Roosevelt Park ♠	285	39.54 N	75.11 W
Franklin D. Roosevelt Lake ⊜[1]	202	48.20 N	118.10 W
Franklin Farms	279b	40.10 N	80.16 W
Franklin Grove	190	41.50 N	89.18 W
Franklin Harbor ⊂	166	33.42 S	136.56 E
Franklin Institute ʋ	285	39.57 N	75.11 W
Franklin Island I	212	45.24 N	80.20 W
Franklin Lake ⊜, N.T., Can.	176	66.56 N	96.03 W
Franklin Lake ⊜, Nv., U.S.	204	40.24 N	115.12 W
Franklin Lake ⊜, N.J., U.S.	276	40.59 N	74.13 W
Franklin Lakes	276	41.01 N	74.12 W
Franklin Mountains ⋏, N.T., Can.	180	63.00 N	123.50 W
Franklin Mountains ⋏, N.Z.	172	44.55 S	167.45 E
Franklin Park, Il., U.S.	216	41.56 N	87.51 W
Franklin Park, Md., U.S.	284c	39.03 N	77.06 W
Franklin Park, N.J., U.S.	276	40.26 N	74.32 W
Franklin Park, N.Y., U.S.	210	43.05 N	76.05 W
Franklin Park, Pa., U.S.	279b	40.35 N	80.06 W
Franklin Park, Va., U.S.	284c	38.55 N	77.09 W
Franklin Park ♠	283	42.18 N	71.06 W
Franklin Pond ⊜	276	41.06 N	74.35 W
Franklin Ridge ∧	282	38.00 N	122.10 W
Franklin River	224	49.06 N	124.49 W
Franklin Roosevelt Park ◆[8]	273d	26.09 S	27.59 E
Franklin Springs	210	43.02 N	75.24 W
Franklin Square	210	40.42 N	73.40 W
Franklin State Forest ♠	283	42.04 N	71.26 W
Franklin Strait ʉ	176	72.00 N	96.00 W
Franklinton, La., U.S.	194	30.50 N	90.09 W
Franklinton, N.C., U.S.	192	36.06 N	78.27 W
Franklintown	208	40.05 N	77.02 W
Franklinville, N.J., U.S.	208	39.37 N	75.04 W
Franklinville, N.Y., U.S.	210	42.20 N	78.27 W
Frankreich → France □[1]	32	46.00 N	2.00 E
Frankston, Austl.	169	38.08 S	145.07 E
Frankston, Tx., U.S.	222	32.03 N	95.30 W
Franksville	216	42.45 N	87.54 W
Frankton	216	40.13 N	85.46 W
Frankville	194	31.38 N	88.08 W
Frånö	26	62.54 N	17.50 E
Fr'anovo	82	56.08 N	38.27 E
Franschhoek	158	33.55 S	19.09 E
Fransfontein	156	20.12 S	15.01 E
Fränsta	26	62.30 N	16.09 E
Františkovy Lázně	54	50.04 N	12.21 E
Franvillers	50	49.58 N	2.30 E
Franzburg	54	54.11 N	12.52 E
Franzensburg ⊥	264b	48.04 N	16.22 E
Franzensfeste → Fortezza	64	46.47 N	11.37 E
Franz Josef Glacier	172	43.24 S	170.11 E
Franz Josef Land → Zeml'a Franca-Iosifa II	12	81.00 N	55.00 E
Franz-Josefs-Bahnhof ◆[5]	264b	48.13 N	16.21 E
Franz-Josefs-Höhe ♠	64	47.04 N	12.45 E
Französische Süd- und Antarktis-Gebiete → French Southern and Antarctic Territories □[2]	6	49.30 S	69.30 E
Französisch-Polynesien → French Polynesia □[2]	14	15.00 S	140.00 W
Frasca, Capo della ›	71	39.46 N	8.27 E
Frascati	66	41.48 N	12.41 E
Frascineto	68	39.50 N	16.16 E
Frasdorf	64	47.48 N	12.16 E
Fraser, Co., U.S.	200	39.56 N	105.49 W
Fraser, Mi., U.S.	281	42.32 N	82.56 W
Fraser ≃, B.C., Can.	182	49.09 N	123.12 W
Fraser ≃, Nf., Can.	176	56.35 N	61.55 W
Fraser ≃, Co., U.S.	200	40.06 N	105.58 W
Fraser, Mount ∧	162	25.39 S	118.23 E
Fraserburg	158	31.55 S	21.30 E
Fraserburgh	46	57.42 N	2.00 W
Fraser Island I	166	25.15 S	153.10 E
Fraser Lake	182	54.04 N	124.51 W
Fraser Lake ⊜	182	54.05 N	124.35 W
Fraser Mills	224	49.14 N	122.52 W
Fraser National Park ♠	169	37.10 S	145.50 E
Fraser Plateau ⋏[1]	182	52.00 N	123.00 W
Fraser Range	162	32.03 S	122.48 E
Frasertown	172	38.58 S	177.24 E
Frasne	58	46.51 N	6.10 E
Frasnes-lez-Anvaing	50	50.40 N	3.36 E
Frassine ≃	64	45.18 N	11.37 E
Frassinoro	64	44.18 N	10.34 E
Frati, Monte dei ∧	66	43.40 N	12.10 E
Fratres	61	48.59 N	15.21 E
Frattamaggiore	68	40.57 N	14.16 E
Frattócchie	267a	41.46 N	12.37 E
Frauenburg → Frombork	30	54.22 N	19.41 E
Frauenfeld	58	47.34 N	8.54 E
Frauenkirchen	61	47.50 N	16.56 E
Frauenstein	54	50.48 N	13.32 E
Frauental an der Lassnitz	61	46.48 N	15.14 E
Frauenwald	54	50.35 N	10.51 E
Fray Bentos	252	33.08 S	58.18 W
Fray Luis Beltrán	252	39.19 S	65.46 W
Fray Marcos	252	34.11 S	55.44 W
Frazee	198	46.43 N	95.42 W
Frazer, Mt., U.S.	202	48.03 N	106.02 W
Frazer, Pa., U.S.	208	40.02 N	75.33 W
Frazeysburg	214	40.07 N	82.07 W
Frazier Mountain ∧	228	34.47 N	118.58 W
Frazier Park	228	34.49 N	118.56 W
Fr'azino	82	55.58 N	38.04 E
Frazzanò	70	38.04 N	14.44 E
Frecheiras	250	2.51 S	42.05 W
Frecheirinha	250	3.46 S	40.48 W
Frechen	56	50.54 N	6.49 E
Frechilla	34	42.08 N	4.50 W
Freckenhorst	52	51.55 N	7.58 E
Freckleton	262	53.45 N	2.52 W
Freddo ≃	70	38.01 N	12.54 E
Fredeburg	56	51.11 N	8.18 E
Freden	52	51.56 N	9.54 E
Fredensborg	41	55.58 N	12.24 E
Fredensborg Slot ⊥	41	55.58 N	12.23 E
Frederic	190	45.39 N	92.28 W
Frederica	208	39.00 N	75.27 W
Fredericia	41	55.35 N	9.46 E
Frederick, Il., U.S.	219	40.04 N	90.26 W
Frederick, Md., U.S.	208	39.24 N	77.24 W
Frederick, Ok., U.S.	196	34.23 N	99.01 W
Frederick, S.D., U.S.	198	45.49 N	98.30 W
Frederick □[6]	208	39.25 N	77.25 W
Frederick Hills ⋏[2]	164	12.41 S	136.00 E
Frederick House ≃	190	49.06 N	81.10 W
Frederick House Lake ⊜	190	48.40 N	80.55 W
Frederick Island I	162	34.04 S	122.00 E
Frederick Reef ✣[2]	166	20.58 S	154.23 E
Fredericksburg, In., U.S.	218	38.26 N	86.11 W
Fredericksburg, Ia., U.S.	190	42.57 N	92.11 W
Fredericksburg, Oh., U.S.	214	40.40 N	81.52 W
Fredericksburg, Pa., U.S.	214	40.27 N	76.26 W
Fredericksburg, Tx., U.S.	196	30.16 N	98.52 W
Fredericksburg, Va., U.S.	208	38.18 N	77.27 W
Fredericksburg Battlefield ⊥	208	38.17 N	77.28 W
Frederick Sound ʉ	180	57.00 N	133.00 W
Fredericktown, Mo., U.S.	194	37.33 N	90.17 W
Fredericktown, Oh., U.S.	214	40.28 N	82.32 W
Frederico Westphalen	252	27.22 S	53.24 W
Fredericton	186	45.58 N	66.39 W
Fredericton Junction	186	45.40 N	66.37 W
Frederik Hendrik-Eiland → Yos Sudarsa, Pulau I	164	7.50 S	138.30 E
Frederiksberg, Dan.	41	55.25 N	11.34 E
Frederiksberg, Dan.	41	55.41 N	12.32 E
Frederiksborg □[6]	41	55.56 N	12.18 E
Frederiksborg Slot ⊥	41	55.56 N	12.19 E
Frederikshåb	176	62.00 N	49.43 W
Frederikshavn	26	57.26 N	10.32 E
Frederikssund	41	55.50 N	12.04 E
Frederiksted	241n	17.43 N	64.53 W
Frederiksværk	41	55.58 N	12.02 E
Frederik Willem IV Vallen ᒐ	250	3.28 N	57.37 W
Fredersdorf bei Berlin	54	52.31 N	13.44 E
Fredonia, Col.	246	5.55 N	75.41 W
Fredonia, Az., U.S.	200	36.03 N	112.08 W
Fredonia, Ks., U.S.	198	37.32 N	95.49 W
Fredonia, N.Y., U.S.	214	42.26 N	79.19 W
Fredonia, N.D., U.S.	198	46.19 N	99.05 W
Fredonia, Pa., U.S.	214	41.20 N	80.14 W
Fredrika	26	64.05 N	18.24 E
Fredriksberg	40	60.08 N	14.23 E
Fredrikstad	26	59.13 N	10.57 E
Freeburg, Il., U.S.	219	38.25 N	89.54 W
Freeburg, Mo., U.S.	219	38.18 N	91.55 W
Freeburg, Pa., U.S.	208	40.46 N	76.57 W
Freedom, Ca., U.S.	226	36.56 N	121.46 W
Freedom, Pa., U.S.	214	40.40 N	80.14 W
Freehold, N.J., U.S.	208	40.15 N	74.16 W
Freehold, N.Y., U.S.	210	42.22 N	74.03 W
Freeland, Mi., U.S.	190	43.31 N	84.07 W
Freeland, Pa., U.S.	210	41.01 N	75.53 W
Freeland, Wa., U.S.	224	48.01 N	122.32 W
Freeland Park	216	40.37 N	87.30 W
Freeling, Mount ∧	162	22.35 S	133.06 E
Freel Peak ∧	226	38.52 N	119.54 W
Freels, Cape ›, Nf., Can.	186	49.15 N	53.28 W
Freels, Cape ›, Nf., Can.	186	46.37 N	53.33 W
Freeman	198	43.21 N	97.26 W
Freeman ≃	182	54.20 N	114.47 W
Freeman, Lake ⊜	216	40.42 N	86.45 W
Freemansburg	210	40.37 N	75.20 W
Freemount	48	52.16 N	8.53 W
Freeport, Ba.	238	26.30 N	78.45 W
Freeport, N.S., Can.	186	44.17 N	66.19 W
Freeport, On., Can.	212	43.25 N	80.25 W
Freeport, Fl., U.S.	194	30.29 N	86.08 W
Freeport, Il., U.S.	190	42.17 N	89.37 W
Freeport, Me., U.S.	188	43.51 N	70.06 W
Freeport, Mi., U.S.	216	42.45 N	85.18 W
Freeport, N.Y., U.S.	210	40.39 N	73.35 W
Freeport, Oh., U.S.	214	40.12 N	81.15 W
Freeport, Pa., U.S.	210	40.40 N	79.41 W
Freeport, Tx., U.S.	222	28.57 N	95.21 W
Freer	196	27.52 N	98.37 W
Freest	54	54.08 N	13.43 E
Freeston	222	31.32 N	96.15 W
Freestone	171a	28.08 S	152.08 E
Freestone □[6]	222	31.44 N	96.10 W
Freetown, Antig.	240c	17.03 N	61.42 W
Freetown, S.L.	150	8.30 N	13.15 W
Freetown, In., U.S.	218	38.58 N	86.07 W
Freetown, N.Y., U.S.	207	40.58 N	72.11 W
Freeville	210	42.30 N	76.20 W
Freewood Acres	208	40.10 N	74.15 W
Freezeout Lake ⊜	202	47.40 N	112.03 W
Fregenal de la Sierra	34	38.10 N	6.39 W
Fregene ◆[8]	66	41.51 N	12.12 E
Freiberg	54	50.54 N	13.20 E
Freiberger Mulde ≃	54	51.10 N	12.48 E
Freiburg → Świebodzice	30	50.52 N	16.19 E
Freiburg → Fribourg	58	46.48 N	7.09 E
Freiburg □[5]	58	48.00 N	8.25 E
Freiburg an der Elbe	52	53.49 N	9.17 E
Freiburger Mulde ≃	54	51.10 N	12.48 E
Freiburg im Breisgau	58	47.59 N	7.51 E
Freienbach	58	47.12 N	8.45 E
Freienhufen	54	51.35 N	13.58 E
Freienwalde in Pommern → Chociwel	30	53.28 N	15.19 E
Freie Universität ʋ[2]	264a	52.26 N	13.16 E
Freigericht	56	50.08 N	9.07 E
Freihung	60	49.37 N	11.55 E
Freiland	61	47.58 N	15.34 E
Freilassing	64	47.50 N	12.59 E
Freilingen	56	50.33 N	7.50 E
Freinberg	60	48.34 N	13.31 E
Freinsheim	56	49.30 N	8.13 E
Freirina	252	28.30 S	71.06 W
Freisen	56	49.33 N	7.14 E
Freisenbruch ◆[8]	263	51.27 N	7.06 E
Freising	60	48.23 N	11.44 E
Freistadt, Öst.	61	48.31 N	14.31 E
Freistadt → Kożuchów, Pol.	30	51.45 N	15.35 E
Freital	54	51.00 N	13.39 E
Freiwaldau → Gozdnica	30	51.26 N	15.06 E
Freiwalde	54	51.58 N	13.44 E
Freixial	266c	38.54 N	9.09 W
Fréjus	62	43.26 N	6.44 E
Fréjus, Tunnel du ◆[5]	62	45.08 N	6.40 E
Frémainville	261	49.04 N	1.52 E
Fremantle	168a	32.03 S	115.45 E
Fremdingen	56	48.58 N	10.27 E
Fremington	42	51.04 N	4.07 W
Fremont, Ca., U.S.	226	37.32 N	121.59 W
Fremont, In., U.S.	216	41.43 N	84.55 W
Fremont, Ia., U.S.	190	41.12 N	92.26 W
Fremont, Mi., U.S.	190	43.28 N	85.56 W
Fremont, Ne., U.S.	198	41.26 N	96.29 W
Fremont, N.C., U.S.	192	35.32 N	77.58 W
Fremont, Oh., U.S.	214	41.21 N	83.07 W
Fremont, Wi., U.S.	190	44.15 N	88.51 W
Fremont ≃	200	38.24 N	110.42 W
Fremont Canyon V	280	33.48 N	117.42 W
Fremont Island I	200	41.09 N	112.20 W
Fremont Lake ⊜	202	42.57 N	109.49 W
Fremont Peak ∧, Ca., U.S.	226	36.46 N	121.30 W
Fremont Peak ∧, Ca., U.S.	228	35.12 N	117.27 W
Fremont Valley V	228	35.10 N	118.00 W
French ≃	190	45.56 N	80.54 W
French Broad ≃	192	35.57 N	83.51 W
Frenchburg	192	37.57 N	83.37 W
French Camp	226	37.53 N	121.16 W
Frenchcap Cay I	240m	18.14 N	64.51 W
French Creek ≃, Mb., Can.	184	57.02 N	92.12 W
French Creek ≃, U.S.	214	41.25 N	79.50 W
French Creek ≃, Oh., U.S.	279a	41.27 N	82.07 W
French Creek ≃, Pa., U.S.	208	40.08 N	75.31 W
French Creek ≃, S.D., U.S.	198	43.38 N	102.55 W
French Creek, South Branch ≃, Pa., U.S.	214	41.54 N	79.54 W
French Creek, South Branch ≃, Pa., U.S.	285	40.10 N	75.42 W
French Creek, West Branch ≃	214	41.58 N	79.52 W
French Creek State Park ♠	208	40.13 N	75.47 W
French Frigate Shoals ✣[2]	14	23.45 N	166.10 W
French Guiana (Guyane français) □[2], S.A.	242	4.00 N	53.00 W
French Guiana (Guyane français) □[2], S.A.	250	4.00 N	53.00 W
French Island I	169	38.21 S	145.21 E
French Lick	194	38.32 N	86.37 W
Frenchman (Frenchman Creek) ≃	202	48.24 N	107.05 W
Frenchman Bay ⊂	188	44.25 N	68.10 W
Frenchman Butte	184	53.35 N	109.38 W
Frenchman Creek (Frenchman) ≃, N.A.	202	48.24 N	107.05 W
Frenchman Creek ≃, U.S.	198	40.13 N	100.50 W
Frenchman Lake ⊜	204	36.48 N	116.56 W
Frenchman Point ›	212	44.35 N	81.18 W
Frenchman's Bay ⊂	275b	43.49 N	79.05 W
Frenchmans Cap ∧	166	42.16 S	145.50 E
Frenchman's Creek ≃, On., Can.	284a	42.56 N	78.56 W
Frenchmans Creek ≃, Ca., U.S.	282	37.29 N	122.27 W
French Meadows Reservoir ⊜[1]	226	39.07 N	120.25 W
Frenchpark	48	53.52 N	8.26 W
French Pass	172	40.56 S	173.50 E
French Polynesia □[2]	14	15.00 S	140.00 W
Frenchs Forest	274a	33.45 S	151.14 E
French Southern and Antarctic Territories □[2]	6	49.30 S	69.30 E
French Stream ≃	283	42.07 N	70.53 W
Frenchtown	210	40.31 N	75.03 W
Frenda	148	35.02 N	1.01 E
Freneuse	261	49.03 N	1.36 E
Frensdorferhaar	52	52.25 N	7.03 E
Frenštát pod Radhoštěm	30	49.33 N	18.14 E
Frentani, Monti dei ⋏	66	41.54 N	14.37 E
Frépillon	261	49.03 N	2.12 E
Frere	158	28.52 S	29.47 E
Freren	52	52.29 N	7.32 E
Fresco	150	5.05 N	5.34 W
Fresco ≃	250	6.39 S	51.59 W
Freshfield	262	53.34 N	3.04 W
Freshfield, Mount ∧	182	51.44 N	116.57 W
Freshford	48	52.43 N	7.24 W
Fresh Meadows ◆[8]	276	40.44 N	73.48 W
Fresh Pond ⊜, Ma., U.S.	283	42.23 N	71.09 W
Fresh Pond ⊜, N.Y., U.S.	276	40.55 N	73.18 W
Freshwater	42	50.40 N	1.30 W
Freshwater Creek ≃	226	39.12 N	122.04 W
Fresia	254	41.09 S	73.27 W
Fresnes	261	48.45 N	2.19 E
Fresne-Saint-Mamès	58	47.33 N	5.52 E
Fresnes-en-Woëvre	56	49.08 N	5.39 E
Fresnes-sur-Escaut	50	50.26 N	3.35 E
Fresnes-sur-Marne	261	48.56 N	2.45 E
Fresnillo	234	23.10 N	102.53 W
Fresno, Col.	246	5.09 N	75.01 W
Fresno, Ca., U.S.	226	36.44 N	119.46 W
Fresno, Oh., U.S.	214	40.20 N	81.44 W
Fresno, Tx., U.S.	222	29.32 N	95.27 W
Fresno □[6]	226	36.38 N	119.45 W
Fresno ≃	226	37.05 N	120.33 W
Fresno, Lewis Fork ≃	226	37.20 N	119.39 W
Fresno, Portillo del)(	34	42.38 N	3.46 W
Fresno Air Terminal ⊠	226	36.46 N	119.43 W
Fresno Reservoir ⊜[1]	202	48.41 N	109.57 W
Fresno Slough ≃	226	36.47 N	120.22 W
Fresnoy-Folny	50	49.53 N	1.26 E
Fresnoy-le-Grand	50	49.57 N	3.25 E
Fressenneville	50	50.04 N	1.34 E
Fressin	50	50.27 N	2.03 E
Freswick	46	58.35 N	3.05 W
Fréteval	50	47.53 N	1.13 E
Frétigney-et-Velloreille	58	47.29 N	5.56 E
Fretin	50	50.33 N	3.08 E
Frettes	58	47.41 N	5.34 E
Freu, Cabo del ›	34	39.45 N	3.27 E
Freudenberg, B.R.D.	56	49.44 N	9.19 E
Freudenberg, B.R.D.	56	50.54 N	7.52 E
Freudenberg, D.D.R.	264a	52.42 N	13.49 E
Freudenstadt	58	48.28 N	8.25 E
Frévent	50	50.16 N	2.17 E
Frew ≃	162	20.00 S	135.38 E
Frewash ≃	42	52.53 N	1.14 W
Frewena	162	19.25 S	135.25 E
Frewsburg	214	42.03 N	79.09 W
Freyburg	54	51.13 N	11.46 E
Freycinet, Cape ›	162	34.06 S	114.59 E
Freycinet Estuary ⊂[1]	162	26.25 S	113.45 E
Freycinet National Park ♠	166	42.10 S	148.20 E
Freycinet Peninsula ›[1]	166	42.13 S	148.18 E
Freyenstein	54	53.17 N	12.20 E
Freyming-Merlebach	56	49.09 N	6.48 E
Freyre	252	31.10 S	62.06 W
Freystadt	60	49.12 N	11.20 E
Freyung	60	48.48 N	13.33 E
Fria	150	10.05 N	13.32 W
Fria, Cape ›	152	18.30 S	12.01 E
Friant	226	36.59 N	119.42 W
Friant Dam ◆[6]	226	37.00 N	119.43 W
Friant-Kern Canal ≅	226	35.22 N	119.06 W
Friars Point	194	34.22 N	90.38 W
Frías, Arg.	252	28.39 S	65.09 W
Frías, Perú	248	4.52 S	79.57 W
Fribourg (Freiburg)	58	46.48 N	7.09 E
Fribourg (Freiburg) □[3]	58	46.45 N	7.05 E
Frick	58	47.31 N	8.01 E
Frick Park ♠	279b	40.26 N	79.54 W
Friday	222	31.07 N	95.15 W
Friday Harbor	224	48.32 N	123.00 W
Fridaythorpe	44	54.01 N	0.40 W
Fridingen an der Donau	58	48.01 N	8.56 E
Fridley	190	45.05 N	93.15 W
Fridolfing	60	48.00 N	12.49 E
Fridtjof Nansen, Mount ∧	9	85.21 S	167.33 W
Friedberg, B.R.D.	56	50.20 N	8.45 E
Friedberg, B.R.D.	58	48.21 N	10.58 E
Friedberg, Öst.	61	47.27 N	16.03 E
Friedeberg in der Neumark → Strzelce Krajeńskie	30	52.53 N	15.32 E
Friedeburg [Saale]	54	51.37 N	11.44 E
Friedenau ◆[8]	264a	52.28 N	13.20 E
Friedens	214	40.03 N	79.00 W
Friedensburg	208	40.36 N	76.14 W
Friedersdorf, D.D.R.	54	52.17 N	13.47 E
Friedersdorf, D.D.R.	54	51.01 N	14.34 E
Friedersdorf, D.D.R.	54	51.39 N	12.21 E
Friedesheim	158	27.55 S	26.43 E
Friedland, B.R.D.	56	51.25 N	9.55 E
Friedland, D.D.R.	54	53.40 N	13.33 E
Friedland, D.D.R.	54	52.06 N	14.16 E
Friedland → Mieroszów, Pol.	30	50.41 N	16.10 E
Friedrich-Ebert-Brücke ◆[5]	263	51.28 N	6.43 E
Friedrich Krupp-Aktiengesellschaft ʋ[3]	263	51.28 N	7.00 E
Friedrichroda	54	50.52 N	10.34 E
Friedrichsbrunn	54	51.41 N	11.02 E
Friedrichsdorf	56	50.15 N	8.38 E
Friedrichsfeld	263	51.38 N	6.39 E
Friedrichsfelde ◆[8]	264a	52.31 N	13.31 E
Friedrichshafen	58	47.39 N	9.28 E
Friedrichshagen ◆[8]	264a	52.27 N	13.38 E
Friedrichshof	264a	52.19 N	13.46 E
Friedrichsort ◆[8]	54	54.24 N	10.11 E
Friedrichsruh, Schloss ⊥	52	53.32 N	10.20 E
Friedrichsruhe	54	53.31 N	11.45 E
Friedrichstadt	41	54.22 N	9.05 E
Friedrichsthal, B.R.D.	56	49.19 N	7.06 E
Friedrichsthal, D.D.R.	54	52.48 N	13.16 E
Friedrichstrasse, Bahnhof ◆[5]	264a	52.31 N	13.24 E
Friedrichswalde	54	53.02 N	13.42 E
Frielas	266c	38.49 N	9.09 W
Frielendorf	56	50.58 N	9.19 E
Friemersheim	263	51.23 N	6.42 E
Friend, Ne., U.S.	198	40.39 N	97.17 W
Friend, Or., U.S.	224	45.21 N	121.16 W
Friends Colony ◆[8]	272a	28.34 N	77.16 E
Friendship, N.Y., U.S.	210	42.12 N	78.08 W
Friendship, Tn., U.S.	194	35.54 N	89.14 W
Friendship, Wi., U.S.	190	43.58 N	89.49 W
Friendship Creek ≃	285	39.55 N	74.43 W
Friendship Shoal ✣[2]	112	5.58 N	112.31 E
Friends Meeting House State Memorial ⊥	214	40.09 N	80.47 W
Friendswood	222	29.31 N	95.12 W
Friern Barnet ◆[8]	260	51.37 N	0.10 W
Fries	192	36.42 N	80.58 W
Friesach	61	46.57 N	14.24 E
Friesack	54	52.44 N	12.34 E
Friesenheim	58	48.22 N	7.53 E
Friesenhofen	58	47.45 N	10.04 E
Friesenried	58	47.52 N	10.31 E
Friesland □[4]	52	53.03 N	5.45 E
Friesland □[9]	30	53.00 N	5.40 E
Fries Mills	285	39.39 N	75.03 W
Friesoythe	52	53.01 N	7.51 E
Frigate Point ›	174g	28.11 N	177.24 W
Frigento	68	41.01 N	15.06 E
Frignano	68	41.00 N	14.10 E
Frignano ◆[1]	64	44.20 N	10.51 E
Friguia	150	12.03 N	10.56 W
Friitala	26	61.26 N	21.52 E

≃	River	Fluss	Río	Rivière	Rio
≅	Canal	Kanal	Canal	Canal	Canal
ᒐ	Waterfall, Rapids	Wasserfall, Stromschnellen	Cascada, Rápidos	Chute d'eau, Rapides	Cascata, Rápidos
ʉ	Strait	Meeresstrasse	Estrecho	Détroit	Estreito
⊂	Bay, Gulf	Bucht, Golf	Bahía, Golfo	Baie, Golfe	Baía, Golfo
⊜	Lake, Lakes	See, Seen	Lago, Lagos	Lac, Lacs	Lago, Lagos
≋	Swamp	Sumpf	Pantano	Marais	Pântano
⌂	Ice Features, Glacier	Eis- und Gletscherformen	Accidentes Glaciales	Formes glaciaires	Acidentes glaciares
⊤	Other Hydrographic Features	Andere Hydrographische Objekte	Otros Elementos Hidrográficos	Autres données hydrographiques	Outros acidentes hidrográficos

✣	Submarine Features	Untermeerische Objekte	Accidentes Submarinos	Formes de relief sous-marin	Acidentes submarinos
□	Political Unit	Politische Einheit	Unidad Politica	Entité politique	Unidade política
ʋ	Cultural Institution	Kulturelle Institution	Institución Cultural	Institution culturelle	Institução cultural
⊥	Historical Site	Historische Stätte	Sitio Histórico	Site historique	Sitio histórico
♠	Recreational Site	Erholungs- und Ferienort	Sitio de Recreo	Centre de loisirs	Area de Lazer
⊠	Airport	Flughafen	Aeropuerto	Aéroport	Aeroporto
■	Military Installation	Militäranlage	Instalación Militar	Installation militaire	Instalação militar
◆	Miscellaneous	Verschiedenes	Misceláneo	Divers	Diversos

Name	Page	Lat.°′	Long.°′
Frillendorf ◆[8]	**263**	51.28 N	7.05 E
Frindsbury	**260**	51.24 N	0.30 E
Frinsted	**260**	51.17 N	0.43 E
Frinton-on-Sea	**42**	51.50 N	1.14 E
Frintrop ◆[8]	**263**	51.29 N	6.55 E
Frío ≃, N.A.	**236**	11.08 N	84.46 W
Frio ≃, Tx., U.S.	**196**	28.30 N	98.10 W
Frio, Cabo ≻	**255**	22.53 S	42.00 W
Friockheim	**46**	56.38 N	2.38 W
Frio Draw V	**196**	34.50 N	102.19 W
Friona	**196**	34.38 N	102.43 W
Frisa, Loch ⊜	**46**	56.34 N	6.05 W
Frisange	**56**	49.32 N	6.12 E
Frisches Haff → Vislinskij Zaliv c	**30**	54.27 N	19.40 E
Frisco, Pa., U.S.	**214**	40.51 N	80.16 W
Frisco, Tx., U.S.	**222**	33.09 N	96.49 W
Frisco City	**194**	31.26 N	87.24 W
Frisco Creek ≃	**196**	36.34 N	101.23 W
Frisian Islands II	**30**	53.35 N	6.40 E
Fristad	**26**	57.50 N	13.01 E
Fritch	**196**	35.38 N	101.36 W
Fritsla	**26**	57.33 N	12.47 E
Fritzlar	**56**	51.08 N	9.16 E
Friuli □[9]	**64**	46.00 N	13.00 E
Friuli-Venezia Giulia □[4]	**64**	46.00 N	13.00 E
Friza, proliv ʮ	**74**	45.30 N	149.10 E
Frizington	**44**	54.32 N	3.30 W
Frobisher	**184**	49.12 N	102.26 W
Frobisher Bay	**176**	63.44 N	68.28 W
Frobisher Bay c	**176**	62.30 N	66.00 W
Frobisher Lake ⊜	**184**	56.25 N	108.20 W
Frodsham	**262**	53.18 N	2.44 W
Frog Lake ⊜	**184**	53.55 N	110.18 W
Frohavet ʮ	**26**	63.52 N	9.26 E
Frohburg	**54**	51.03 N	12.33 E
Frohlinde ◆[8]	**263**	51.32 N	7.21 E
Frohnau ◆[8]	**264a**	52.38 N	13.18 E
Frohnhausen	**263**	51.29 N	7.48 E
Frohnhausen ◆[8]	**263**	51.27 N	6.58 E
Frohnleiten	**61**	47.16 N	15.20 E
Frohse	**54**	52.02 N	11.43 E
Froid	**198**	48.20 N	104.30 W
Froid, Lac ⊜	**206**	46.40 N	74.32 W
Froid, Ruisseau ≃	**206**	46.23 N	74.46 W
Froidmont-Cohartille	**50**	49.41 N	3.42 E
Froidos	**56**	49.03 N	5.07 E
Froissy	**50**	49.34 N	2.13 E
Froitzheim	**56**	50.42 N	6.34 E
Frolišči, S.S.S.R.	**80**	56.25 N	42.39 E
Frolišči, S.S.S.R.	**82**	56.18 N	39.13 E
Frolovo	**80**	49.47 N	43.39 E
Froman Run ≃	**279b**	40.12 N	80.00 W
Fromberg	**202**	45.23 N	108.54 W
Frombork	**30**	54.22 N	19.41 E
Frome	**42**	51.14 N	2.20 W
Frome ≃, Austl.	**166**	29.06 S	137.52 E
Frome ≃, Eng., U.K.	**42**	52.03 N	2.38 W
Frome ≃, Eng., U.K.	**42**	50.41 N	2.04 W
Frome, Lake ⊜	**166**	30.48 S	139.48 E
Frome Downs	**166**	31.13 S	139.46 E
Fromelennes	**56**	50.08 N	4.52 E
Fromentières	**50**	48.54 N	3.43 E
Frömern	**263**	51.30 N	7.44 E
Frommern	**58**	48.15 N	8.52 E
Fröndenberg	**56**	51.28 N	7.46 E
Frönsberg	**263**	51.21 N	7.46 E
Fronteiras	**250**	7.05 S	40.37 W
Frontenac, Fl., U.S.	**220**	28.27 N	80.46 W
Frontenac, Ks., U.S.	**198**	37.27 N	94.41 W
Frontenac □[6], On., Can.	**212**	44.40 N	76.45 W
Frontenac □[6], P.Q., Can.	**206**	45.42 N	71.15 W
Frontenard	**58**	46.55 N	5.10 E
Frontenex-Villard-Rosset	**62**	45.38 N	6.19 E
Frontera	**234**	18.32 N	92.38 W
Frontera, Punta ≻	**234**	18.36 N	92.42 W
Fronteras	**200**	30.56 N	109.31 W
Frontier, Sk., Can.	**184**	49.12 N	108.34 W
Frontier, Mi., U.S.	**216**	41.47 N	84.36 W
Frontier, Wy., U.S.	**200**	41.48 N	110.32 W
Frontignan	**62**	43.27 N	3.45 E
Frontino	**246**	6.46 N	76.08 W
Frontino, Páramo ∧	**246**	6.28 N	76.04 W
Frontón, Isla I	**286d**	12.07 S	77.11 W
Front Range ⩘, Leso.	**158**	29.05 S	28.20 E
Front Range ⩘, Co., U.S.	**200**	39.45 N	105.45 W
Front Royal	**188**	38.55 N	78.11 W
Frose	**54**	51.48 N	11.23 E
Frosinone	**66**	41.38 N	13.19 E
Frosinone □[4]	**66**	41.37 N	13.27 E
Frosna ≻[1]	**26**	63.45 N	10.25 E
Frosolone	**66**	41.36 N	14.27 E
Frösön	**26**	63.11 N	14.32 E
Frost	**222**	32.05 N	96.48 W
Frostavallen	**41**	55.58 N	13.30 E
Frostburg	**188**	39.39 N	78.55 W
Frost Creek ≃	**276**	40.54 N	73.37 W
Frostproof	**220**	27.44 N	81.31 W
Frotheim	**52**	52.21 N	8.40 E
Frouard	**56**	48.46 N	6.08 E
Frövi	**40**	59.28 N	15.22 E
Frøya I	**24**	63.43 N	8.42 E
Fruges	**50**	50.31 N	2.08 E
Fruita	**200**	39.09 N	108.43 W
Fruitdale, Al., U.S.	**194**	31.20 N	88.24 W
Fruitdale, Or., U.S.	**202**	42.24 N	123.20 W
Fruithurst	**194**	33.43 N	85.26 W
Fruitland, Id., U.S.	**202**	44.00 N	116.54 W
Fruitland, Md., U.S.	**208**	38.19 N	75.37 W
Fruitland Park	**220**	28.51 N	81.54 W
Fruitport	**216**	43.07 N	86.09 W
Fruitvale, B.C., Can.	**182**	49.07 N	117.33 W
Fruitvale, Tx., U.S.	**222**	32.41 N	95.48 W
Fruitvale, Wa., U.S.	**202**	46.37 N	120.33 W
Fruitville	**192**	27.19 N	82.27 W
Frumușița	**38**	45.40 N	28.04 E
Frunze, S.S.S.R.	**78**	46.16 N	34.52 E
Frunze, S.S.S.R.	**83**	48.40 N	38.45 E
Frunze, S.S.S.R.	**85**	40.07 N	71.44 E
Frunze, S.S.S.R.	**85**	42.54 N	74.36 E
Frunze □[4]	**85**	42.30 N	74.00 E
Frunzovka	**78**	47.20 N	29.44 E
Frutal	**255**	20.02 S	48.55 W
Frutigen	**58**	46.35 N	7.39 E
Frutillar	**254**	41.07 S	73.03 W
Fryburg	**214**	41.21 N	79.26 W
Frýdek-Místek	**30**	49.41 N	18.22 E
Frýdlant	**30**	50.56 N	15.05 E
Frye	**279b**	40.11 N	79.56 W
Fryeburg	**188**	44.00 N	70.58 W
Fryerning	**260**	51.41 N	0.22 E
Fryingpan ≃	**200**	39.22 N	107.02 W
Fu ≃, Zhg.	**100**	29.52 N	115.28 E
Fu ≃, Zhg.	**100**	28.36 N	116.04 E
Fu ≃, Zhg.	**102**	29.59 N	106.16 E
Fua'amotu	**174w**	21.16 S	175.08 W
Fua'amotu International Airport ⊠	**174w**	21.17 S	175.08 W
Fu'an, Zhg.	**100**	27.08 N	119.40 E
Fu'an, Zhg.	**100**	32.41 N	120.41 E
Fuanjie	**100**	25.29 N	117.53 E
Fubao	**107**	28.47 N	106.05 E
Fubine	**62**	44.58 N	8.26 E
Fucecchio	**66**	43.44 N	10.48 E
Fuchang	**100**	30.06 N	113.08 E
Fucheng	**98**	37.52 N	116.07 E
Fuchikou	**100**	29.51 N	115.27 E
Fuchow → Fuzhou	**100**	28.01 N	116.20 E
Fuchs-Berg ∧[2]	**264a**	52.27 N	13.51 E
Fuchskaute ∧	**56**	50.27 N	7.52 E
Füchtorf	**52**	52.03 N	8.02 E
Fuchū, Nihon	**94**	35.40 N	139.29 E
Fuchū, Nihon	**94**	36.39 N	137.10 E
Fuchū, Nihon	**96**	34.34 N	133.14 E
Fuchū, Nihon	**96**	34.24 N	132.30 E
Fuchun ≃	**106**	30.10 N	120.09 E
Fucine	**64**	46.18 N	10.44 E
Fucino, Conca del ≚	**66**	42.01 N	13.31 E
Fudan University ⊻[2]	**269b**	31.17 N	121.29 E
Fuday I	**46**	57.03 N	7.23 W
Fuding	**100**	27.21 N	120.12 E
Fudu ≃	**107**	29.52 N	106.10 E
Fuefuki ≃	**94**	35.33 N	138.28 E
Fuelbeckestausee ⊜[1]	**263**	51.15 N	7.40 E
Fuencaliente	**34**	38.24 N	4.18 W
Fuencarral ◆[8]	**266a**	40.30 N	3.41 W
Fuenlabrada	**266a**	40.17 N	3.48 W
Fuensalida	**34**	40.03 N	4.12 W
Fuensanta, Embalse de ⊜[1]	**34**	38.23 N	2.13 W
Fuente	**196**	28.40 N	100.32 W
Fuente de Cantos	**34**	38.15 N	6.18 W
Fuente de Oro	**246**	3.28 N	73.37 W
Fuenteobejuna	**34**	38.16 N	5.25 W
Fuentesaúco	**34**	41.14 N	5.30 W
Fuentes de Ebro	**34**	41.31 N	0.38 W
Fuerli	**105**	39.40 N	116.41 E
Fuerte ≃	**232**	25.54 N	109.22 W
Fuerte Olimpo	**248**	21.02 S	57.54 W
Fuerteventura I	**148**	28.20 N	14.00 W
Fuerza, Castillo de la ⊥	**286b**	23.09 N	82.21 W
Fufeng	**102**	34.20 N	107.51 E
Fuga Island I	**116**	18.52 N	121.22 E
Fugama, Wādī V	**140**	14.43 N	24.36 E
Fügen	**64**	47.21 N	11.51 E
Fuglebjerg	**41**	55.18 N	11.34 E
Fugløysund ʮ	**24**	70.12 N	20.20 E
Fugong	**102**	27.09 N	98.52 E
Fugou	**98**	34.04 N	114.24 E
Fuhai	**86**	47.06 N	87.23 E
Fuhe	**100**	23.22 N	113.37 E
Fuhlenbrock ◆[8]	**263**	51.32 N	6.54 E
Fuhrberg	**52**	52.34 N	9.50 E
Fuhse ≃	**52**	52.37 N	10.03 E
Fuhsien → Fuxian	**98**	39.37 N	122.01 E
Fuhu	**100**	29.11 N	118.04 E
Fuji, Nihon	**94**	35.09 N	138.39 E
Fuji, Zhg.	**98**	34.24 N	114.48 E
Fuji, Zhg.	**107**	29.09 N	105.23 E
Fuji ≃	**94**	35.07 N	138.39 E
Fuji, Mount → Fuji-san ∧[1]	**94**	35.22 N	138.44 E
Fujiafeng	**105**	39.11 N	117.32 E
Fujian (Fukien) □[4]	**100**	26.00 N	118.00 E
Fujiatun	**104**	41.42 N	123.44 E
Fujiawopu	**104**	40.58 N	122.14 E
Fujiazhen	**107**	29.57 N	104.18 E
Fujiazhuangcun	**104**	41.15 N	122.20 E
Fujie	**106**	31.09 N	119.27 E
Fujieda	**94**	34.52 N	138.16 E
Fuji-Hakone-Izu-kokuritsu-kōen ♠	**94**	35.21 N	138.44 E
Fujiidera	**96**	34.34 N	135.36 E
Fujikawa	**94**	35.08 N	138.37 E
Fujikubo	**268**	35.50 N	139.32 E
Fujimi, Nihon	**94**	36.27 N	139.05 E
Fujimi, Nihon	**94**	35.55 N	138.15 E
Fujimi, Nihon	**94**	35.51 N	139.33 E
Fujin	**89**	47.14 N	132.00 E
Fujino	**94**	35.37 N	139.10 E
Fujinomiya	**94**	35.12 N	138.38 E
Fujioka, Nihon	**94**	35.12 N	137.12 E
Fujioka, Nihon	**94**	36.15 N	139.05 E
Fujioka, Nihon	**94**	36.15 N	139.39 E
Fuji-san ∧[1]	**94**	35.22 N	138.44 E
Fujisawa	**94**	35.21 N	139.29 E
Fujishiro	**94**	35.55 N	140.07 E
Fujiwara, Nihon	**94**	35.09 N	136.30 E
Fujiwara, Nihon	**94**	36.51 N	139.44 E
Fujiwara-dam ◆[6]	**94**	36.49 N	139.02 E
Fujiyama → Fuji-san ∧[1]	**94**	35.22 N	138.44 E
Fuji-yoshida	**94**	35.29 N	138.48 E
Fukagawa	**92a**	43.43 N	142.03 E
Fukagawa ◆[8]	**268**	35.40 N	139.48 E
Fukami	**268**	35.28 N	139.28 E
Fukane I	**174w**	21.05 S	175.02 W
Fukang	**86**	44.10 N	87.59 E
Fukasaka-tunnel ◆[5]	**94**	35.35 N	136.10 E
Fuka Shan ∧	**89**	47.55 N	120.53 E
Fukaya	**94**	36.12 N	139.17 E
Fukiage	**94**	36.06 N	139.27 E
Fukiai ◆[8]	**270**	34.42 N	135.12 E
Fukien → Fujian □[4]	**100**	26.00 N	118.00 E
Fukou, Zhg.	**100**	25.45 N	118.28 E
Fukou, Zhg.	**100**	26.28 N	117.40 E
Fukube	**96**	35.33 N	134.18 E
Fukuchiyama	**96**	35.18 N	135.07 E
Fukude	**94**	34.40 N	137.53 E
Fukue	**92**	32.41 N	128.50 E
Fukuei Chiao ≻	**100**	25.18 N	121.32 E
Fukue-jima I	**92**	32.40 N	128.45 E
Fukui, Nihon	**94**	36.04 N	136.13 E
Fukui, Nihon	**270**	34.51 N	135.34 E
Fukui □[5]	**92**	36.00 N	136.15 E
Fukuma	**96**	33.46 N	130.28 E
Fukumitsu	**94**	36.33 N	136.52 E
Fukuno	**94**	36.35 N	136.55 E
Fukuoka, Nihon	**94**	35.34 N	137.27 E
Fukuoka, Nihon	**94**	36.42 N	136.56 E
Fukuoka, Nihon	**96**	33.35 N	130.24 E
Fukuoka □[5]	**96**	33.45 N	130.30 E
Fukuoka-chūtonchi, Rikujō-jieitai- ■	**96**	33.32 N	130.28 E
Fukuroda-no-taki ∟	**94**	36.46 N	140.25 E
Fukuroi	**94**	34.45 N	137.55 E
Fukushima, Nihon	**92**	37.45 N	140.28 E
Fukushima, Nihon	**92a**	41.29 N	140.15 E
Fukushima □[5]	**94**	37.08 N	140.00 E
Fukushima ◆[8]	**270**	34.42 N	135.29 E
Fukusumi	**270**	34.37 N	135.56 E
Fukutani ◆[8]	**270**	34.43 N	135.02 E
Fukuyama	**96**	34.29 N	133.22 E
Fukuzaki	**96**	34.57 N	134.45 E
Fulacunda	**150**	11.44 N	15.03 W
Fūlādī, Kūh-e ∧	**120**	34.38 N	67.32 E
Fūlād Maḥalleh	**128**	36.02 N	53.44 E
Fulanga Island I	**175g**	19.08 S	178.34 W
Fulanga Passage ʮ	**175g**	19.00 S	178.40 W
Fulbourn	**42**	52.11 N	0.13 E
Fulda, B.R.D.	**56**	50.33 N	9.41 E
Fulda, Mn., U.S.	**198**	43.52 N	95.36 W
Fulda ≃	**30**	51.25 N	9.39 E
Fuldatal	**56**	51.22 N	9.31 E
Fuldera	**58**	46.37 N	10.22 E
Fule	**102**	25.27 N	104.19 E
Fulerum ◆[8]	**263**	51.26 N	6.57 E
Fulford Harbour	**224**	48.46 N	123.27 W
Fulgatore	**70**	37.57 N	12.42 E
Fulham ◆[8]	**260**	51.29 N	0.12 W
Fuli	**100**	23.11 N	121.14 E
Fuliji	**100**	33.46 N	116.58 E
Fuling	**102**	29.42 N	107.21 E
Fulitun	**89**	46.42 N	131.10 E
Fullarton ≃	**166**	20.15 S	141.10 E
Fullen ⊜	**40**	60.31 N	16.09 E
Fuller Springs	**222**	31.18 N	94.41 W
Fullerton, Ca., U.S.	**228**	33.52 N	117.55 W
Fullerton, Ky., U.S.	**218**	38.43 N	82.58 W
Fullerton, Md., U.S.	**284b**	39.22 N	76.31 W
Fullerton, Ne., U.S.	**198**	41.21 N	97.58 W
Fullerton, Pa., U.S.	**208**	40.38 N	75.28 W
Fullerton Municipal Airport ⊠	**280**	33.52 N	117.59 W
Fullerton Point ≻	**240c**	17.06 N	61.54 W
Fulmer	**260**	51.33 N	0.34 W
Fulong	**102**	22.57 N	107.41 E
Fulongchang	**107**	30.03 N	103.38 E
Fulongquan	**89**	44.22 N	124.36 E
Fulpmes	**64**	47.10 N	11.21 E
Fulshear	**222**	29.41 N	95.54 W
Fulton, Al., U.S.	**194**	31.47 N	87.43 W
Fulton, Ar., U.S.	**194**	33.36 N	93.48 W
Fulton, Il., U.S.	**190**	41.52 N	90.09 W
Fulton, In., U.S.	**216**	40.56 N	86.15 W
Fulton, Ks., U.S.	**198**	38.00 N	94.43 W
Fulton, Ky., U.S.	**194**	36.30 N	88.52 W
Fulton, Md., U.S.	**208**	39.09 N	76.55 W
Fulton, Mi., U.S.	**216**	47.17 N	88.21 W
Fulton, Ms., U.S.	**194**	34.16 N	88.24 W
Fulton, Mo., U.S.	**219**	38.50 N	91.56 W
Fulton, N.Y., U.S.	**210**	43.19 N	76.25 W
Fulton, Oh., U.S.	**214**	40.27 N	82.49 W
Fulton, Tx., U.S.	**196**	28.04 N	97.02 W
Fulton □[6], Il., U.S.	**219**	40.13 N	90.17 W
Fulton □[6], In., U.S.	**216**	41.04 N	86.13 W
Fulton □[6], N.Y., U.S.	**210**	43.00 N	74.22 W
Fulton □[6], Oh., U.S.	**216**	41.33 N	84.09 W
Fulton □[6], Pa., U.S.	**214**	40.06 N	78.04 W
Fulton ≃	**182**	54.48 N	126.07 W
Fultondale	**194**	33.36 N	86.47 W
Fultonham	**210**	42.31 N	75.03 W
Fultonville	**210**	42.57 N	74.22 W
Fuluchang	**107**	29.38 N	106.08 E
Fulufjället ∧	**26**	61.33 N	12.43 E
Fuluzhen	**107**	29.18 N	103.40 E
Fulwood	**262**	53.47 N	2.41 W
Fumaça	**256**	22.17 S	44.19 W
Fumahashi	**94**	36.42 N	137.19 E
Fumane	**156**	24.29 S	33.58 E
Fumay	**56**	49.59 N	4.42 E
Fumel	**32**	44.29 N	0.57 E
Fumin, Zhg.	**102**	25.16 N	102.26 E
Fumin, Zhg.	**106**	31.54 N	121.10 E
Fumintun	**98**	42.29 N	126.22 E
Fuminzhen	**106**	31.37 N	121.39 E
Funa ≃	**273b**	4.23 S	15.19 E
Funabashi	**94**	35.42 N	139.59 E
Funafuti I	**14**	8.31 S	179.13 E
Funagawa → Oga	**92**	39.53 N	139.51 E
Funakuyā	**175d**	24.30 N	124.17 E
Funan	**100**	32.39 N	115.32 E
Funan Gaba	**144**	4.25 N	37.57 E
Funaoka	**96**	35.23 N	134.14 E
Funasaka	**270**	34.48 N	135.17 E
Funäsdalen	**26**	62.32 N	12.33 E
Funchal	**148**	32.38 N	16.54 W
Funchal □[5]	**148**	32.40 N	16.55 W
Fundación	**246**	10.31 N	74.11 W
Fundão, Bra.	**255**	19.55 S	40.24 W
Fundão, Port.	**34**	40.08 N	7.30 W
Fundão, Ilha do I	**287a**	22.51 S	43.14 W
Funde	**272c**	18.54 N	72.58 E
Fundición de Avalos	**232**	28.35 N	106.00 W
Fundo ≃	**250**	10.12 S	44.39 W
Fundo, Arroio ≃	**287a**	22.58 S	43.22 W
Fundo, Córrego ≃	**287b**	23.46 S	46.47 W
Fundy, Bay of c	**186**	45.00 N	66.00 W
Fundy National Park ♠	**186**	45.38 N	65.00 W
Fünfkirchen → Pécs	**30**	46.05 N	18.13 E
Funhalouro	**156**	23.03 S	34.25 E
Funil, Ribeirão do ≃	**256**	22.02 S	43.46 W
Funil, Rio do ≃	**256**	22.58 S	44.34 W
Funing, Zhg.	**98**	39.54 N	119.14 E
Funing, Zhg.	**100**	33.47 N	119.48 E
Funing, Zhg.	**102**	23.33 N	105.35 E
Funiuchang	**107**	29.03 N	106.33 E
Funiu Shan ⩘	**100**	33.40 N	112.30 E
Funk Island I	**186**	49.46 N	53.10 W
Funks Creek ≃	**226**	39.19 N	122.11 W
Funkturm ⊻	**264a**	52.31 N	13.16 E
Funne ≃	**263**	51.42 N	7.36 E
Funnel Creek ≃	**166**	22.18 S	148.57 E
Funnel Hill ∧[2]	**272c**	18.54 N	73.07 E
Funo	**96**	34.53 N	132.47 E
Funshinagh, Lough ⊜	**48**	53.31 N	8.07 W
Funsi	**150**	10.17 N	1.58 W
Funtana Coberta ⊥	**71**	39.34 N	9.21 E
Funtua	**150**	11.31 N	7.17 E
Fuorn, Pass dal (Ofenpass))(	**58**	46.37 N	10.15 E
Fuping	**102**	34.47 N	109.07 E
Fuqiao	**106**	31.36 N	121.12 E
Fuqikou	**100**	29.44 N	117.48 E
Fuqing	**100**	25.44 N	119.22 E
Fuquay-Varina	**192**	35.35 N	78.48 W
Füramoos	**58**	48.00 N	9.53 E
Furancungo	**154**	14.55 S	33.35 E
Furano	**92a**	43.21 N	142.24 E
Furci Siculo	**70**	37.57 N	15.23 E
Furculești	**38**	43.52 N	25.09 E
Fures	**62**	45.19 N	5.30 E
Fūrg	**128**	28.18 N	55.13 E
Furkapass)(	**58**	46.34 N	8.25 E
Furka-Tunnel ◆[5]	**58**	46.33 N	8.26 E
Furlong	**208**	40.18 N	75.05 W
Furmanov	**80**	57.15 N	41.07 E
Furmanovka	**86**	44.17 N	72.57 E
Furmanovo	**80**	49.42 N	49.28 E
Furn, Wādī al- V	**142**	30.13 N	31.40 E
Furnace	**46**	56.09 N	5.10 W
Furnace Brook ≃	**283**	42.06 N	70.43 W
Furnace Creek ≃	**284b**	39.11 N	76.35 W
Furnace Pond ⊜	**283**	42.03 N	70.49 W
Furnari	**70**	38.07 N	15.08 E
Furnas, Reprêsa de ⊜[1]	**255**	20.45 S	46.00 W
Furn ash-Shubbāk	**132**	33.52 N	35.31 E
Furneaux Group II	**166**	40.10 S	148.05 E
Furnes → Veurne	**50**	51.04 N	2.40 E
Furness Abbey ⊻[1]	**44**	54.07 N	3.12 W
Furness Fells ⩘[2]	**44**	54.18 N	3.07 W
Furong Shan ∧	**100**	27.30 N	115.52 E
Furqlus	**130**	34.36 N	37.05 E
Fürstenau, B.R.D.	**52**	51.50 N	9.19 E
Fürstenau, B.R.D.	**52**	52.31 N	7.40 E
Fürstenberg, B.R.D.	**52**	51.44 N	9.24 E
Fürstenberg, D.D.R.	**54**	52.09 N	14.40 E
Fürstenberg/Havel	**54**	53.11 N	13.08 E
Fürstenfeld	**61**	47.03 N	16.05 E
Fürstenfeldbruck	**60**	48.10 N	11.15 E
Fürstenfelde → Boleszkowice	**30**	52.44 N	14.36 E
Fürstenhagen	**56**	51.12 N	9.41 E
Fürstenstein	**60**	48.43 N	13.20 E
Fürstenwalde	**54**	52.21 N	14.04 E
Fürstenwerder	**54**	53.24 N	13.34 E
Fürstenzell	**60**	48.32 N	13.19 E
Furtei	**71**	39.34 N	8.57 E
Fürth, B.R.D.	**56**	49.28 N	10.59 E
Fürth, B.R.D.	**56**	49.39 N	8.47 E
Furth im Wald	**60**	49.18 N	12.51 E
Furtwangen	**58**	48.03 N	8.12 E
Furuba ≃	**256**	23.21 S	44.57 W
Furubō-san ∧[2]	**270**	34.53 N	135.19 E
Furudal	**26**	61.10 N	15.08 E
Furudono	**94**	37.05 N	140.34 E
Furukawa, Nihon	**92**	38.34 N	140.58 E
Furukawa, Nihon	**94**	36.14 N	137.11 E
Furulund	**41**	55.46 N	13.04 E
Furusund	**40**	59.40 N	18.55 E
Furu-tone ≃	**94**	35.48 N	139.51 E
Furuvik	**40**	60.39 N	17.20 E
Furuyakami	**268**	35.55 N	139.32 E
Fürwiggestausee ⊜[1]	**263**	51.09 N	7.41 E
Fury and Hecla Strait ʮ	**176**	69.56 N	84.00 W
Fusagasugá	**246**	4.21 N	74.22 W
Fusain ≃	**50**	48.09 N	2.45 E
Fusan → Pusan	**98**	35.06 N	129.03 E
Fuscaldo	**68**	39.25 N	16.02 E
Fusch	**64**	47.13 N	12.49 E
Fuschl am See	**64**	47.48 N	13.18 E
Fuschun → Fushun	**104**	41.52 N	123.53 E
Fuse → Higashiōsaka, Nihon	**96**	34.39 N	135.35 E
Fuse, Nihon	**268**	35.53 N	140.00 E
Fushan, Zhg.	**98**	37.29 N	121.16 E
Fushan, Zhg.	**102**	35.58 N	111.51 E
Fushan, Zhg.	**106**	31.49 N	120.46 E
Fushimi ◆[8]	**270**	34.55 N	135.46 E
Fushino ≃	**96**	34.03 N	131.24 E
Fushuigang	**100**	31.21 N	113.40 E
Fushun (Funan), Zhg.	**104**	41.52 N	123.53 E
Fushun, Zhg.	**107**	29.11 N	105.00 E
Fushuncheng	**104**	41.53 N	123.51 E
Fusignano	**66**	44.28 N	11.57 E
Fusilier	**184**	51.51 N	109.46 W
Fusin → Fuxin	**104**	42.03 N	121.46 E
Fusine in Valromana	**64**	46.30 N	13.39 E
Fusio	**58**	46.27 N	8.40 E
Fusō	**94**	35.21 N	136.55 E
Fusong	**98**	42.18 N	127.20 E
Fussa	**94**	35.45 N	139.20 E
Füssen	**64**	47.34 N	10.42 E
Fuste, Picacho del ∧	**196**	27.35 N	102.47 W
Fusui	**102**	22.32 N	107.56 E
Futa, Passo della)(	**66**	44.05 N	11.17 E
Futaba	**94**	35.41 N	138.30 E
Futago-san ∧	**96**	33.35 N	131.36 E
Futamata → Tenryū	**94**	34.52 N	137.49 E
Futamatagawa ◆[8]	**268**	35.28 N	139.33 E
Futami, Nihon	**94**	34.30 N	136.47 E
Futami, Nihon	**96**	33.41 N	132.38 E
Futang, Zhg.	**102**	24.26 N	112.09 E
Futang, Zhg.	**106**	30.40 N	119.35 E
Futaoi-jima I	**96**	34.06 N	130.47 E
Futatabi-yama ∧	**270**	34.43 N	135.11 E
Futatsubashi ◆[8]	**268**	35.28 N	139.30 E
Futatsu-ne I[2]	**174f**	24.46 N	141.18 E
Fu Tau Pun Chau I	**271d**	22.21 N	114.22 E
Futian	**100**	27.26 N	114.56 E
Futianhe	**100**	31.30 N	115.05 E
Futianpu	**100**	27.22 N	112.47 E
Futjāni ≃	**126**	24.06 N	90.09 E
Futschou → Fuzhou	**100**	26.06 N	119.17 E
Futtsu, Nihon	**94**	35.19 N	139.49 E
Futtsu, Nihon	**94**	35.13 N	139.52 E
Futtsu-misaki ≻	**268**	35.19 N	139.46 E
Futun ≃	**100**	26.51 N	117.46 E
Futuna I	**175f**	19.32 S	170.14 E
Futuna, Île I	**14**	14.15 S	178.09 W
Futuyu	**105**	39.18 N	114.50 E
Fuveau	**62**	43.27 N	5.34 E
Fuwah	**142**	31.12 N	30.33 E
Fuwen	**86**	47.13 N	89.39 E
Fuxi, Zhg.	**100**	27.14 N	119.50 E
Fuxi, Zhg.	**100**	25.14 N	113.52 E
Fuxi ≃	**107**	29.09 N	104.57 E
Fuxian (Wafangdian), Zhg.	**98**	39.37 N	122.01 E
Fuxian, Zhg.	**102**	36.02 N	109.13 E
Fuxian Hu ⊜	**102**	24.30 N	102.55 E
Fuxin, Zhg.	**104**	42.08 N	121.45 E
Fuxin, Zhg.	**104**	42.03 N	121.46 E
Fuxing, Zhg.	**107**	30.27 N	106.04 E
Fuxing, Zhg.	**107**	30.24 N	104.53 E
Fuxing, Zhg.	**107**	29.54 N	105.43 E
Fuxingchang	**107**	29.40 N	105.13 E
Fuxing Dao I	**269b**	31.17 N	121.23 E
Fuxinghao	**104**	42.35 N	120.32 E
Fuyang, Zhg.	**100**	32.54 N	115.49 E
Fuyang, Zhg.	**100**	30.03 N	119.57 E
Fuyang, Zhg.	**100**	23.36 N	116.37 E
Fuyang ≃	**98**	38.14 N	116.05 E
Fuyouertuo Shan ∧	**89**	45.52 N	119.48 E
Fuyu, Zhg.	**89**	47.49 N	124.27 E
Fuyu, Zhg.	**89**	45.10 N	124.50 E
Fuyuan, Zhg.	**89**	48.21 N	134.18 E
Fuyuan, Zhg.	**102**	25.39 N	104.12 E
Fuzhai	**100**	29.32 N	120.02 E
Fuzhong	**102**	24.28 N	111.22 E
Fuzhou, Zhg.	**100**	28.01 N	116.20 E
Fuzhou (Foochow), Zhg.	**100**	26.06 N	119.17 E
Fuzhoucheng	**98**	39.45 N	121.47 E
Fuzhuang	**98**	34.57 N	118.17 E
Fuzhuangyi	**98**	38.02 N	116.08 E
Fyfield	**260**	51.45 N	0.16 E
Fylde □[8]	**262**	53.46 N	2.53 W
Fylde ≻[1]	**262**	53.47 N	2.56 W
Fylland ≻[1]	**41**	56.00 N	9.15 E
Fyn □[6]	**41**	55.20 N	10.25 E
Fyn I	**41**	55.20 N	10.30 E
Fyne, Loch c	**46**	56.00 N	5.24 E
Fyns Hoved ≻	**41**	55.37 N	10.36 E
Fyresvatn ⊜	**26**	59.06 N	8.12 E
Fyrisån ≃	**40**	59.47 N	17.39 E
Fysingen ⊜	**40**	59.34 N	17.55 E
Fyvie	**46**	57.25 N	2.23 W
Fzâra, Gara'et ⊜	**36**	36.47 N	7.30 E
G			
Ga	**150**	9.47 N	2.30 W
Gaaden	**264b**	48.03 N	16.12 E
Gaalkacyo	**144**	6.47 N	47.26 E
Gaanderen	**52**	51.56 N	6.21 E
Gabah	**144**	8.08 N	50.02 E
Gabai	**146**	11.05 N	11.39 E
Gabaldon	**116**	15.28 N	121.19 E
Gabare	**38**	43.19 N	23.55 E
Gabarus	**186**	45.50 N	60.09 W
Gabarus Bay c	**186**	45.51 N	60.07 W
Gabas ≃	**32**	43.46 N	0.42 W
Gabbs	**204**	38.52 N	117.55 W
Gabby Heights	**214**	40.09 N	80.15 W
Gabela	**152**	10.48 S	14.20 E
Gaberones → Gaborone	**156**	24.45 S	25.55 E
Gabès	**148**	33.53 N	10.07 E
Gabès □[8]	**148**	33.15 N	9.00 E
Gabès, Golfe de c	**148**	34.00 N	10.25 E
Gabia	**152**	4.34 S	17.07 E
Gabiarra	**255**	16.15 S	39.41 W
Gabicce Mare	**66**	43.58 N	12.46 E
Gabii ⊥	**267a**	41.54 N	12.43 E
Gabil	**146**	11.09 N	18.12 E
Gabilan Creek ≃	**226**	36.41 N	121.38 W
Gabilan Range ⩘	**226**	36.30 N	121.15 W
Gąbin	**30**	52.25 N	19.44 E
Gabir	**140**	8.35 N	24.40 E
Gable Mountain ∧	**182**	54.30 N	121.40 W
Gablenz	**54**	51.41 N	14.31 E
Gablingen	**58**	48.27 N	10.49 E
Gablitz	**61**	48.14 N	16.09 E
Gablonz → Jablonec nad Nisou	**30**	50.44 N	15.10 E
Gabon □[1], Afr.	**138**	1.00 S	11.45 E
Gabon □[1], Afr.	**152**	1.00 S	11.45 E
Gabon, Estuaire du c[1]	**152**	0.25 N	9.20 E
Gaborone	**156**	24.45 S	25.55 E
Gabras	**140**	10.16 N	26.14 E
Gabria	**64**	45.52 N	13.34 E
Gabriel	**250**	11.14 S	41.53 W
Gabriel Strait ʮ	**176**	61.45 N	65.30 W
Gabriel y Galan, Embalse de ⊜[1]	**34**	40.15 N	6.15 W
Gabriel Zamora	**234**	19.05 N	102.05 W
Gābrīk	**128**	25.44 N	58.28 E
Gabriola	**224**	49.12 N	123.50 W
Gabriola Island I	**224**	49.10 N	123.47 W
Gabrovo	**38**	42.52 N	25.19 E
Gabun → Gabon □[1]	**152**	1.00 S	11.45 E
Gaby	**62**	45.43 N	7.53 E
Gacé	**50**	48.48 N	0.18 E
Gachetá	**246**	4.49 N	73.36 W
Gachpar	**174q**	9.33 N	138.10 E
Gachsārān	**128**	30.12 N	50.47 E
Gackle	**198**	46.37 N	99.08 W
Gacko	**38**	43.10 N	18.32 E
Gad'ač	**78**	50.22 N	34.00 E
Gadag	**122**	15.25 N	75.37 E
Gadamai	**140**	17.09 N	36.06 E
Gādarwāra	**124**	22.55 N	78.47 E
Gadbjerg	**41**	55.46 N	9.20 E
Gäddede	**26**	64.30 N	14.09 E
Gadderbaum	**52**	52.00 N	8.31 E
Gade ≃	**260**	51.38 N	0.28 W
Gadebusch	**54**	53.42 N	11.07 E
Gadein	**140**	8.11 N	28.44 E
Gadera ≃	**64**	46.47 N	11.54 E
Gadevang	**41**	55.58 N	12.18 E
Gadilovići	**76**	53.05 N	30.16 E
Gadis ≃	**114**	1.03 N	98.55 E
Gadmen	**58**	46.44 N	8.21 E
Gado Bravo, Ilha do I	**250**	10.54 S	42.52 W
Gádor	**34**	36.57 N	2.29 W
Gádor, Sierra de ⩘	**34**	36.54 N	2.47 W
Gadra	**120**	25.40 N	70.37 E
Gadrut	**84**	39.32 N	47.02 E
Gadsden, Al., U.S.	**194**	34.00 N	86.00 W
Gadsden, Az., U.S.	**200**	32.33 N	114.47 W
Gadwāl	**122**	16.14 N	77.48 E
Gadzi	**152**	4.47 N	16.42 E
Gaer (Geeryasha)	**120**	31.44 N	80.21 E
Gaerwen	**44**	53.13 N	4.16 W
Găești	**38**	44.43 N	25.19 E
Gaeta	**66**	41.12 N	13.35 E
Gaeta, Golfo di c	**66**	41.06 N	13.30 E
Gaferut I	**108**	9.14 N	145.23 E
Gaffney	**192**	35.04 N	81.39 W
Gafour	**36**	36.18 N	9.19 E
Gafsa	**148**	34.25 N	8.48 E
Gafsa □[8]	**148**	34.15 N	8.25 E
Gafurov	**85**	40.14 N	69.44 E
Gag, Pulau I	**164**	0.27 S	129.52 E
Gagal	**146**	9.01 N	15.08 E
Gagarawa	**150**	12.25 N	9.32 E
Gagarin	**76**	55.33 N	35.00 E
Gage	**196**	36.18 N	99.45 W
Gagere ≃	**150**	13.21 N	6.23 E
Gages Lake	**278**	42.21 N	87.59 W
Gages Lake ⊜	**278**	42.21 N	88.00 W
Gagetown	**186**	45.47 N	66.09 W
Gagetown, Canadian Forces Base ■	**186**	45.43 N	66.15 W
Gaggenau	**56**	48.48 N	8.19 E
Gaggi	**70**	37.51 N	15.13 E
Gaggiano	**62**	45.24 N	9.02 E
Gaghamni	**140**	11.41 N	28.19 E
Gagil Tamil I	**174q**	9.32 N	138.10 E
Gagino	**80**	55.14 N	45.02 E
Gagliano Castelferrato	**70**	37.43 N	14.32 E
Gagliano del Capo	**68**	39.50 N	18.22 E
Gagnef	**40**	60.35 N	15.04 E
Gagnia	**152**	1.28 S	16.02 E
Gagnoa	**150**	6.08 N	5.56 W
Gagnoa □[5]	**150**	6.00 N	5.55 W
Gagnon	**176**	51.53 N	68.10 W
Gagnon, Lac ⊜	**206**	46.07 N	75.07 W
Gagny	**261**	48.53 N	2.32 E
Gagra	**84**	43.20 N	40.15 E
Gagret	**123**	31.40 N	76.04 E
Gahanna	**218**	40.01 N	82.52 W
Gahlen	**52**	51.40 N	6.52 E
Gahmen ◆[8]	**263**	51.36 N	7.32 E
Gaiarine	**64**	45.52 N	12.29 E
Gaibānda	**124**	25.19 N	89.33 E
Gaichtpass)(	**58**	47.27 N	10.37 E
Gaigalava	**76**	56.40 N	27.18 E
Gaighāta	**126**	22.56 N	88.44 E
Gaijiatun	**104**	40.50 N	122.37 E
Gail	**196**	32.46 N	101.27 W
Gail ≃	**64**	46.36 N	13.53 E
Gailberg Sattel)(	**64**	46.43 N	12.58 E
Gail Creek ≃	**222**	31.07 N	95.23 W
Gaildorf	**56**	49.00 N	9.46 E
Gaillac	**32**	43.54 N	1.55 E
Gaillard, Château ⊥	**50**	48.09 N	1.54 E
Gaillard, Lac ⊜	**186**	50.06 N	68.47 W
Gaillard, Lake ⊜	**207**	41.21 N	72.46 W
Gaillefontaine	**50**	49.39 N	1.37 E
Gaillimh → Galway	**48**	53.16 N	9.03 W
Gaillon, Fr.	**50**	49.10 N	1.20 E
Gaillon, Fr.	**261**	49.02 N	1.54 E
Gailtaler Alpen ⩘	**64**	46.42 N	13.00 E
Gaima	**164**	8.20 S	142.55 E
Gaimán	**254**	43.17 S	65.29 W
Gaimersheim	**60**	48.49 N	11.22 E
Gaines, Mi., U.S.	**216**	42.52 N	83.54 W
Gaines, Pa., U.S.	**210**	41.45 N	77.34 W
Gainesboro	**194**	36.21 N	85.39 W
Gainesville, Fl., U.S.	**192**	29.39 N	82.19 W
Gainesville, Ga., U.S.	**192**	34.17 N	83.49 W
Gainesville, Mo., U.S.	**194**	36.36 N	92.25 W
Gainesville, N.Y., U.S.	**210**	42.38 N	78.08 W
Gainesville, Tx., U.S.	**196**	33.37 N	97.07 W
Gainford	**44**	54.32 N	1.44 W
Gainsborough, Sk., Can.	**184**	49.10 N	101.26 W
Gainsborough, Eng., U.K.	**44**	53.24 N	0.46 W
Gainsborough Creek ≃	**184**	49.10 N	101.02 W
Gaiole in Chianti	**66**	43.28 N	11.26 E
Gairdner ≃	**162**	34.17 S	119.28 E
Gairdner, Lake ⊜	**162**	31.35 S	136.00 E
Gairloch	**46**	57.42 N	5.40 W
Gairloch, Loch c	**46**	57.44 N	5.44 W
Gairn ≃	**46**	57.03 N	3.05 W
Gais, It.	**64**	46.50 N	11.57 E
Gais, Schw.	**58**	47.22 N	9.27 E
Gaisberg ∧	**64**	47.48 N	13.07 E
Gaisbeuren	**58**	47.54 N	9.43 E
Gaital, Cerro ∧	**236**	8.37 N	80.07 W
Gaither	**208**	39.21 N	76.59 W
Gaithersburg	**208**	39.08 N	77.12 W
Gaixian	**98**	40.24 N	122.22 E
Gaiziņa kalns ∧[2]	**76**	56.52 N	25.57 E
Gaj, Jugo.	**36**	45.29 N	17.02 E
Gaj, S.S.S.R.	**86**	51.27 N	58.27 E
Gajā	**272b**	22.52 N	88.10 E
Gajčur ≃	**78**	47.57 N	36.11 E
Gajendragarh	**122**	15.44 N	75.59 E
Gajiram	**146**	12.30 N	13.12 E
Gajny	**24**	60.15 N	54.15 E
Gājol	**124**	25.13 N	88.12 E
Gajsin	**78**	48.48 N	29.24 E
Gaj Singhpur	**123**	29.40 N	73.27 E
Gajuapara ≃	**250**	4.17 S	47.25 W
Gajutino	**76**	58.42 N	38.32 E
Gajvoron	**78**	48.22 N	29.52 E
Gakarosa ∧	**158**	27.54 S	23.33 E
Gakona	**180**	62.18 N	145.18 W
Gākuch	**123**	36.10 N	73.45 E
Gakugsa	**24**	61.34 N	36.26 E
Gal, Punta de ≻	**34**	39.10 N	1.05 E
Gāla	**126**	24.18 N	89.54 E
Galaassija	**128**	39.52 N	64.27 E
Galāchipa	**126**	22.10 N	90.25 E
Galahad	**182**	52.31 N	111.56 W
Galamares	**266c**	38.48 N	9.25 W
Galán, Cerro ∧	**252**	25.55 S	66.52 W
Galana ≃	**154**	3.09 S	40.08 E
Galangue	**152**	13.48 S	16.09 E
Galanovo	**80**	56.09 N	54.07 E
Galanta	**30**	48.12 N	17.43 E
Galápagos □[4]	**246a**	0.30 S	90.30 W
Galapagos Islands → Colón, Archipiélago de II	**246a**	0.30 S	90.30 W
Galaroza	**34**	37.55 N	6.42 W
Galas ≃	**114**	5.31 N	102.12 E
Galashiels	**46**	55.37 N	2.49 W
Galata ◆[8]	**267b**	41.01 N	28.58 E
Galata Köprüsü ◆[5]	**267b**	41.00 N	28.57 E
Galata Kulesi ⊻	**267b**	41.01 N	28.58 E
Galatea	**172**	38.25 S	176.45 E
Galați	**38**	45.26 N	28.03 E
Galați □[6]	**38**	45.45 N	27.45 E
Galatia	**194**	37.50 N	88.36 W
Galatia □[9]	**130**	39.30 N	32.40 E
Galatina	**68**	40.10 N	18.10 E
Galatone	**68**	40.09 N	18.04 E
Galatro	**68**	38.28 N	16.06 E
Galátsion	**267c**	38.01 N	23.45 E
Galatz → Galați	**38**	45.26 N	28.03 E
Galaure ≃	**62**	45.11 N	4.49 E
Gala Water ≃	**46**	55.37 N	2.48 W
Galax	**192**	36.39 N	80.55 W
Galaxídhion	**38**	38.22 N	22.23 E
Galbyn gov' ◆[2]	**102**	42.30 N	107.00 E
Galdhøpiggen ∧	**26**	61.37 N	8.17 E
Gale, Lac ⊜	**190**	46.46 N	76.51 W
Galeairy Lake ⊜	**212**	45.29 N	78.17 W
Galeana, Méx.	**232**	30.07 N	107.38 W
Galeana, Méx.	**232**	24.50 N	100.04 W
Galeão, Aeroporto do ⊠	**256**	22.50 S	43.15 W
Galeata	**66**	44.00 N	11.55 E
Galegu	**140**	12.36 N	35.02 E
Galeh Dār	**128**	27.38 N	52.42 E
Galela	**108**	1.50 N	127.50 E
Galena, Austl.	**162**	27.50 S	114.41 E
Galena, Ak., U.S.	**180**	64.44 N	156.57 W
Galena, Il., U.S.	**190**	42.25 N	90.25 W
Galena, In., U.S.	**218**	38.21 N	85.56 W
Galena, Ks., U.S.	**198**	37.04 N	94.38 W
Galena, Md., U.S.	**208**	39.20 N	75.52 W
Galena, Mo., U.S.	**194**	36.48 N	93.27 W
Galena, Oh., U.S.	**214**	40.12 N	82.52 W
Galena Park	**222**	29.43 N	95.13 W
Galenbecker See ⊜	**54**	53.38 N	13.43 E
Galeota Point ≻	**241r**	10.08 N	60.59 W
Galera ≃	**248**	14.25 S	60.07 W
Galera, Punta ≻, Chile	**254**	39.59 S	73.43 W
Galera, Punta ≻, Ec.	**246**	0.49 N	80.03 W
Galera Point ≻	**241r**	10.49 N	60.55 W
Galeria ⊥	**267a**	42.02 N	12.18 E
Galeria, Fosso la ≃	**267a**	41.48 N	12.21 E
Galesburg, Il., U.S.	**190**	40.56 N	90.22 W
Galesburg, Mi., U.S.	**216**	42.17 N	85.25 W
Gales Creek	**224**	45.35 N	123.12 W
Gales Creek ≃	**224**	45.29 N	123.06 W
Gales Ferry	**207**	41.25 N	72.04 W
Gales Point ≻	**283**	42.33 N	70.47 W
Galesville, Md., U.S.	**208**	38.50 N	76.32 W
Galesville, Wi., U.S.	**190**	44.04 N	91.20 W
Galeton	**214**	41.43 N	77.38 W
Galeville	**210**	43.05 N	76.10 W
Galgasc	**144**	0.11 N	41.38 E
Galgate	**44**	54.00 N	2.47 W
Galguduud □[4]	**144**	5.00 N	46.30 E
Galheirão ≃	**255**	12.23 S	45.05 W
Galheiros	**255**	13.18 S	46.25 W
Gali	**84**	42.38 N	41.44 E
Gali, Torrente de ≃	**266d**	41.28 N	2.00 E
Galiano	**224**	48.52 N	123.21 W
Galiano Island I	**224**	48.56 N	123.29 W
Galibier, Col du)(	**62**	45.04 N	6.24 E
Galič, S.S.S.R.	**78**	49.08 N	24.43 E
Galič, S.S.S.R.	**80**	58.23 N	42.21 E
Galicia □[4]	**34**	42.45 N	8.00 W
Galicia □[9]	**22**	49.00 N	22.00 E
Galičskaja vozvyšennost' ⩘[2]	**24**	58.25 N	42.20 E
Galičskoje, ozero ⊜	**80**	58.24 N	42.18 E
Galien	**216**	41.47 N	86.29 W
Galien ≃	**216**	41.48 N	86.45 W
Galilee	**207**	41.22 N	71.30 W
Galilee → HaGalil □[9]	**132**	32.54 N	35.20 E
Galilee, Lake ⊜	**166**	22.21 S	145.48 E
Galilee, Sea of → Kinneret, Yam ⊜	**132**	32.48 N	35.35 E
Galiléia	**255**	19.00 S	41.33 W
Galim	**152**	7.06 N	12.29 E
Galina Point ≻	**241q**	18.24 N	76.53 W
Galindo Creek ≃	**282**	37.58 N	122.02 W
Galion	**214**	40.44 N	82.47 W
Galion, Baie du c	**240e**	14.44 N	60.57 W
Galion, Rivière du ≃	**240e**	14.44 N	60.57 W
Galis	**115a**	7.08 S	113.33 E
Galisteo Creek ≃	**200**	35.31 N	106.22 W
Galite, Canal de la ʮ	**36**	37.20 N	9.00 E
Galiuro Mountains ⩘	**200**	32.40 N	110.20 W
Galižana	**64**	44.56 N	13.52 E
Galka'yo	**144**	6.47 N	47.26 E
Galkhausen	**263**	51.05 N	6.58 E
Galkino, S.S.S.R.	**82**	54.46 N	35.49 E
Galkino, S.S.S.R.	**86**	55.36 N	62.55 E
Galkino, S.S.S.R.	**86**	52.14 N	78.20 E
Gall'aaral	**85**	40.02 N	67.35 E
Gallan Head ≻	**46**	58.14 N	7.03 W
Gallarate	**62**	45.40 N	8.47 E
Gallardon	**50**	48.32 N	1.42 E
Gallatin, Mo., U.S.	**194**	39.54 N	93.57 W
Gallatin, Pa., U.S.	**279b**	40.12 N	79.53 W
Gallatin, Tn., U.S.	**194**	36.23 N	86.26 W
Gallatin, Tx., U.S.	**222**	31.54 N	95.09 W
Gallatin □[6]	**218**	38.45 N	84.51 W
Gallatin ≃	**202**	45.56 N	111.29 W
Gallatin Range ⩘	**202**	45.15 N	111.05 W
Galle	**122**	6.02 N	80.13 E
Gállego ≃	**34**	41.39 N	0.51 W
Gallegos ≃	**254**	51.36 S	68.59 W
Galles → Wales □[8]	**28**	52.30 N	3.30 W
Galleyend	**260**	51.42 N	0.29 E
Galley Head ≻	**48**	51.30 N	8.57 W
Galleywood	**260**	51.42 N	0.28 E
Galliano	**194**	29.26 N	90.17 W
Galliate	**62**	45.29 N	8.42 E
Gallicano	**64**	44.04 N	10.26 E
Gallicano nel Lazio	**267a**	41.52 N	12.49 E
Gallicchio	**68**	40.17 N	16.08 E
Gallico	**68**	38.10 N	15.41 E
Galliera Veneta	**64**	45.39 N	11.49 E
Gallinara I	**62**	44.02 N	8.14 E
Gallinas ≃	**196**	35.10 N	104.55 W
Gallinas, Punta ≻	**246**	12.28 N	71.40 W
Gallinas Creek ≃	**282**	38.01 N	122.30 W
Gallinas Peak ∧	**200**	34.13 N	105.45 W
Gallio	**64**	45.53 N	11.33 E
Gallipoli, Austl.	**166**	19.10 S	137.55 E
Gallipoli, It.	**68**	40.03 N	17.58 E
Gallipoli → Gelibolu, Tür.	**130**	40.24 N	26.40 E
Gallipoli Peninsula → Gelibolu Yarımadası ≻[1]	**130**	40.20 N	26.30 E
Gallipolis	**188**	38.48 N	82.12 W
Gallitzin	**214**	40.28 N	78.33 W
Gallivaggio	**58**	46.21 N	9.21 E
Gällivare	**24**	67.07 N	20.45 E
Gallneukirchen	**61**	48.21 N	14.25 E
Gällö	**26**	62.55 N	15.14 E
Gallo, Capo ≻	**70**	38.13 N	13.19 E
Gallo, Lago del ⊜[1]	**64**	46.07 N	10.10 E
Gallo, Lago di ⊜[1]	**58**	46.37 N	10.10 E
Gallo, Laguna ⊜	**258**	35.30 S	58.28 W
Gallo Arroyo V	**200**	33.55 N	105.00 W
Galloo Island I	**212**	43.54 N	76.25 W
Galloupes Point ≻	**283**	42.28 N	70.53 W
Galloway □[9]	**44**	55.00 N	4.25 W
Galloway, Mull of ≻	**44**	54.38 N	4.50 W
Galloway Creek ≃, Md., U.S.	**284b**	39.18 N	76.23 W
Galloway Creek ≃, Mi., U.S.	**281**	42.39 N	83.12 W
Galluis	**261**	48.48 N	1.48 E
Gallup	**200**	35.31 N	108.44 W
Gallupville	**210**	42.40 N	74.14 W
Gallur	**34**	41.52 N	1.19 W
Gallura ◆[1]	**71**	41.00 N	9.13 E
Gally, Rû de ≃	**261**	48.53 N	1.53 E
Gälnan ʮ	**40**	59.31 N	18.45 E
Gålö I	**40**	59.05 N	18.17 E
Galop Island I	**212**	44.46 N	75.24 W

Symbols in the index entries represent the broad categories identified in the key at the right. Symbols with superior numbers (⩘[1]) identify subcategories (see complete key on page *I · 1)*.

Kartensymbole in dem Registerverzeichnis stellen die rechts in Schlüssel erklärten Kategorien dar. Symbole mit hochgestellten Ziffern (⩘[1]) bezeichnen Unterabteilungen einer Kategorie (vgl. vollständiger Schlüssel auf Seite *I · 1)*.

Los símbolos incluídos en el texto del índice representan las grandes categorias identificadas con la clave a la derecha. Los símbolos con numeros en su parte superior (⩘[1]) identifican las subcategorías (véase la clave completa en la página *I · 1)*.

Les symboles de l'index représentent les catégories indiquées dans la légende à droite. Les symboles suivis d'un indice (⩘[1]) représentent des sous-catégories (voir légende complète à la page *I · 1)*.

Os símbolos incluídos no texto do índice representam as grandes categorias identificadas com a chave à direita. Os símbolos com números em sua parte superior (⩘[1]) identificam as subcategorias (veja-se a chave completa à página *I · 1)*.

	English	Deutsch	Español	Français	Português
∧	Mountain	Berg	Montaña	Montagne	Montanha
⩘	Mountains	Berge	Montañas	Montagnes	Montanhas
)(	Pass	Pass	Paso	Col	Passo
V	Valley, Canyon	Tal, Cañon	Valle, Cañón	Vallée, Canyon	Vale, Canhão
≚	Plain	Ebene	Llano	Plaine	Planície
≻	Cape	Kap	Cabo	Cap	Cabo
I	Island	Insel	Isla	Île	Ilha
II	Islands	Inseln	Islas	Îles	Ilhas
≗	Other Topographic Features	Andere Topographische Objekte	Otros Elementos Topográficos	Autres données topographiques	Outros acidentes topográficos

ESPAÑOL · FRANÇAIS · PORTUGUÊS

Nombre / Nom / Nome	Página / Page	Lat.°′	Long.°′ W = Oeste / W = Ouest
Galoppo, Ippodromo del ♠	266b	45.28 N	9.07 E
Galougo	150	13.50 N	11.04 W
Galsi	126	23.20 N	87.42 E
Galston	46	55.36 N	4.24 W
Galt, Mong.	88	48.46 N	99.53 E
Galt, Ca., U.S.	226	38.15 N	121.17 W
Gal Tardo	144	3.34 N	45.58 E
Galtat Zemmour	148	25.15 N	12.20 W
Galtelli	71	40.23 N	9.37 E
Galten	41	56.09 N	9.55 E
Galten c	40	59.27 N	16.09 E
Galtür	58	46.58 N	10.11 E
Galtymore Mountains ∧	48	52.22 N	8.10 W
Galty Mountains ⋏	48	52.25 N	8.10 W
Galūgāh-e Āsīyeh	128	34.01 N	59.55 E
Galugur	114	2.34 N	99.39 E
Galula	154	8.36 S	33.02 E
Galuut	88	48.33 N	113.12 E
Galva, Il., U.S.	190	41.10 N	90.02 W
Galva, Ia., U.S.	198	42.30 N	95.25 W
Galva, Ks., U.S.	198	38.22 N	97.32 W
Galvarino	252	38.24 S	72.47 W
Galveston, In., U.S.	216	40.34 N	86.11 W
Galveston, Tx., U.S.	222	29.17 N	94.47 W
Galveston □[6]	222	29.20 N	94.53 W
Galveston Bay c	222	29.36 N	94.57 W
Galveston Island I	222	29.13 N	94.55 W
Gálvez	252	32.02 S	61.13 W
Galvin, Austl.	274b	37.51 S	144.49 E
Galvin, Wa., U.S.	224	46.44 N	123.01 W
Galway (Gaillimh), Ire.	48	53.16 N	9.03 W
Galway, N.Y., U.S.	210	43.01 N	74.02 W
Galway □[6]	48	53.20 N	9.00 W
Galway Bay c	48	53.10 N	9.15 W
Galway Borough □[6]	48	53.17 N	9.03 W
Gam ≃	110	21.55 N	105.12 E
Gam, Pulau I	164	0.27 S	130.36 E
Gama, Isla I	254	40.29 S	62.12 W
Gamaches	50	49.59 N	1.33 E
Gamagōri	94	34.50 N	137.14 E
Gamalejevka	80	52.16 N	53.26 E
Gamaliel	194	36.38 N	85.47 W
Gaman	130	41.10 N	36.20 E
Ga-Mankoeng	156	23.57 S	29.42 E
Gamare, Lake ⊜	144	11.30 N	41.40 E
Gamarra	246	8.20 N	73.45 W
Gamawa	146	12.08 N	10.32 E
Gamay	116	12.23 N	125.18 E
Gamay Bay c	116	12.21 N	125.21 E
Gambach	56	50.28 N	8.44 E
Gambaga	150	10.32 N	0.26 W
Gambais	261	48.46 N	1.40 E
Gambaiseuil	261	48.45 N	1.44 E
Gambang	114	3.43 N	103.06 E
Gambara, It.	64	45.15 N	10.18 E
Gámbara, Méx.	234	18.55 N	102.05 W
Gambarie	68	38.10 N	15.50 E
Gambassi	66	43.32 N	10.57 E
Gambatesa	66	41.30 N	14.54 E
Gambela	144	8.18 N	34.37 E
Gambell	180	63.46 N	171.46 W
Gambellara	64	45.28 N	11.20 E
Gamber	208	39.27 N	76.56 W
Gambia □[1], Afr.	134	13.30 N	15.30 W
Gambia □[1], Afr.	150	13.30 N	15.30 W
Gambia (Gambie) ≃	150	13.28 N	16.34 W
Gambi Atrash	140	10.03 N	33.47 E
Gambie → Gambia □[1]	150	13.30 N	15.30 W
Gambie (Gambia) ≃	150	13.28 N	16.34 W
Gambier	214	40.22 N	82.23 W
Gambier, Îles II	6	21.20 S	136.30 W
Gamble Mansion State Historic Site ⊥	220	27.32 N	82.32 W
Gambo, Nf., Can.	186	48.46 N	54.14 W
Gambo, Centraf.	152	4.39 N	22.16 E
Gamboa	236	9.07 N	79.42 W
Gamboli	120	29.50 N	68.26 E
Gambolò	62	45.15 N	8.51 E
Gamboma	152	1.53 S	15.51 E
Gamboula	152	4.08 N	15.09 E
Gambrill State Park ♠	208	39.30 N	77.30 W
Gamchab ≃	156	28.15 S	17.26 E
Gamé	150	6.44 N	1.11 E
Game Creek ≃	285	39.41 N	75.28 W
Gamen-See ⊜	264a	52.40 N	13.51 E
Gaming	61	47.56 N	15.06 E
Gamka ≃	158	33.18 S	21.39 E
Gamlakarleby → Kokkola	26	63.50 N	23.07 E
Gamla Uppsala	40	59.54 N	17.38 E
Gamleby	26	57.54 N	16.24 E
Gamlitz	61	46.43 N	15.33 E
Gammel Estrup ⊥	26	56.26 N	10.21 E
Gammelstad ʊ[1]	26	65.38 N	22.01 E
Gammertingen	58	48.15 N	9.13 E
Gammon ≃	184	51.07 N	95.09 W
Gammon, Point ≻	207	41.36 N	70.16 W
Gamō, Nihon	94	35.03 N	136.11 E
Gamō, Nihon	268	35.52 N	139.48 E
Gamoep	158	29.55 S	18.25 E
Ga-Mogara ≃	158	27.07 S	22.57 E
Gamo Gofa □[4]	144	5.45 N	37.00 E
Gamon	150	13.20 N	12.55 W
Gamova, mys ≻	89	42.35 N	131.12 E
Gamph, Slieve ⋏	48	54.05 N	9.00 W
Gampoko	273b	4.16 S	15.10 E
Gampola	122	7.10 N	80.34 E
Gampongbatak	114	4.48 N	97.39 E
Gampoui	273b	4.08 S	15.22 E
Gams	58	47.12 N	9.28 E
Gamsfeld ∧	64	47.37 N	13.29 E
Gamtoos ≃	158	33.58 S	25.01 E
Gamud ∧	144	4.05 N	38.03 E
G'amyš, gora ∧	84	40.18 N	46.23 E
Gan ≃, Zhg.	89	49.12 N	125.14 E
Gan ≃, Zhg.	100	29.12 N	116.00 E
Ganado, Az., U.S.	200	35.42 N	109.32 W
Ganado, Tx., U.S.	222	29.02 N	96.31 W
Ganano ≃	116	16.45 N	121.44 E
Gananoque	212	44.20 N	76.10 W
Gananoque ≃	212	44.19 N	76.09 W
Gananoque Lake ⊜	212	44.27 N	76.09 W
Ganaraska ≃	212	43.57 N	78.18 W
Ganargua Creek ≃	210	43.04 N	77.00 W
Ganassi	116	7.49 N	124.06 E
Gancevīči	76	52.45 N	26.26 E
Ganchangba	107	28.52 N	103.41 E
Ganči	85	39.58 N	69.08 E
Gand → Gent	50	51.03 N	3.43 E
Ganda, Ang.	152	13.02 S	14.40 E
Ganda, Zaïre	152	4.05 N	23.32 E
Gandadiwata, Bulu ∧	112	2.42 S	119.27 E
Gandajika	152	6.45 S	23.57 E
Gandak (Nārāyani) ≃	124	25.39 N	85.13 E
Gandara	258	35.26 S	58.06 W
Gāndarbal	123	34.14 N	74.47 E
Ganda Singhwāla	123	31.02 N	74.31 E
Gandāva	120	28.37 N	67.29 E
Gandavaroyi Falls ∟	154	17.17 S	29.07 E
Gānde	126	24.10 N	86.26 E
Gander	186	48.57 N	54.37 W
Gander ≃	186	49.15 N	54.30 W
Gander Bay	186	49.18 N	54.29 W
Gander Bay c	186	49.25 N	54.28 W
Ganderkesee	52	53.02 N	8.32 E
Gander Lake ⊜	186	48.55 N	54.40 W
Gandesa	34	41.03 N	0.26 E
Gandevi	120	20.49 N	72.59 E
Gāndhi Sāgar ⊜[1]	120	24.18 N	75.21 E
Gandi	150	12.55 N	5.49 E
Gandi, Wādī V	140	11.23 N	24.31 E
Gandía	34	38.58 N	0.11 W
Gandino	62	45.49 N	9.54 E
Gando	152	12.30 S	17.25 E
Gandole	146	8.26 N	11.34 E
Gandou	152	2.24 N	17.27 E
Gandrange	56	49.16 N	6.08 E
Gandria	58	46.01 N	9.00 E
Gandu	255	13.45 S	39.30 W
Gandy Bridge ⬥[5]	220	27.53 N	82.34 W
G'andžačaj ≃	84	40.54 N	46.28 E
Gandzha → Kirovabad	84	40.40 N	46.22 E
Ganfang	100	28.40 N	114.51 E
Ganfosi	107	29.36 N	104.03 E
Ganga → Ganges ≃	124	23.22 N	90.32 E
Gangādharpur	272b	22.36 N	88.11 E
Gangafani	150	14.23 N	2.24 W
Gangājalghāti	126	23.25 N	87.07 E
Gangala-Na-Bodio	154	3.41 N	29.08 E
Gangalingolo	273b	4.20 S	15.09 E
Gan Gan	254	42.30 S	68.16 W
Ganganagar → Sri Gangānagar	123	29.55 N	73.53 E
Gangāpur, India	120	25.13 N	74.16 E
Gangāpur, India	122	19.41 N	75.01 E
Gangāpur, India	124	26.29 N	76.43 E
Gangara, Niger	150	14.36 N	8.30 E
Gangara, Niger	150	13.33 N	7.14 E
Gāngārāmpur	124	25.24 N	88.31 E
Ganga Sāgar	126	21.38 N	88.05 E
Gangaw	110	22.11 N	94.07 E
Gangāwati	122	15.26 N	76.32 E
Gangaw Range ⋏	110	24.50 N	96.40 E
Ganga-Yamuna Doāb ⋏[1]	124	26.40 N	79.30 E
Gangcheng	98	35.52 N	116.52 E
Gangdaba, Tchabal ∧	152	7.44 N	12.45 E
Gangdhār	120	23.57 N	75.37 E
Gangdisê Shan ⋏	120	31.00 N	82.00 E
Gangdisishan ∧	120	31.29 N	80.45 E
Gangelt	56	50.59 N	5.59 E
Ganges, B.C., Can.	224	48.51 N	123.30 W
Ganges, Fr.	62	43.56 N	3.42 E
Ganges (Ganga) (Padma) ≃	124	23.22 N	90.32 E
Ganges, Mouths of the ≃[1]	120	22.00 N	89.00 E
Ganges Delta ≚[2]	124	23.00 N	89.00 E
Ganghu	120	32.05 N	86.45 E
Gangi	70	37.49 N	14.13 E
Gangkofen	60	48.26 N	12.34 E
Gangkou, Zhg.	100	29.45 N	115.44 E
Gangkou, Zhg.	100	29.21 N	117.58 E
Gangkou, Zhg.	100	22.38 N	113.22 E
Gangkou, Zhg.	100	22.36 N	114.54 E
Gangkou, Zhg.	100	29.12 N	113.19 E
Gangkou, Zhg.	106	30.44 N	118.54 E
Gangkouzhen	106	31.45 N	120.40 E
Ganglasishan ⋏	120	31.00 N	82.50 E
Gang Mills	210	42.08 N	77.06 W
Gāngnāpur	126	23.09 N	88.38 E
Gangneung → Kangnŭng	98	37.45 N	128.54 E
Gango ≃	152	9.48 S	15.40 E
Gangoa	102	37.15 N	100.28 E
Gangoh	124	29.46 N	77.15 E
Gangotri	120	30.56 N	79.02 E
Gangou	98	40.30 N	119.27 E
Gangoumen	98	41.40 N	116.35 E
Gangouyi	102	36.01 N	105.03 E
Gangqiao	107	30.13 N	105.22 E
Gang Ranch	182	51.33 N	122.20 W
Gangshangji	100	28.06 N	116.30 E
Gangtok	124	27.20 N	88.37 E
Gangtou	98	38.04 N	113.56 E
Gangtouli	106	31.42 N	119.02 E
Gangu	102	34.45 N	105.20 E
Gangwa, Zaïre	152	3.30 S	20.55 E
Gangwa, Zhg.	105	39.48 N	116.10 E
Gangwei	100	24.20 N	118.01 E
Ganhezi	86	44.08 N	88.32 E
Ganhu	102	44.33 N	94.09 E
Gani	164	0.47 S	128.13 E
Ganišob	85	39.03 N	70.47 E
Ganj Dundwara	124	27.44 N	78.57 E
Ganjiang	107	29.42 N	103.38 E
Ganlanshan ∧	124	29.54 N	90.02 E
Ganlu	106	31.32 N	120.35 E
Ganluchang	107	29.54 N	104.47 E
Ganluo	102	29.03 N	102.59 E
Gannahoek	158	26.44 S	24.08 E
Gannan	89	47.54 N	123.30 E
Gannano, Lago di ⊜	68	40.19 N	16.26 E
Gannapan	158	30.23 S	22.12 E
Gannat	32	46.06 N	3.12 E
Gannett Peak ∧	200	43.11 N	109.39 W
Gannovka	83	48.33 N	38.35 E
Gannvalley	198	44.02 N	98.59 W
Ganos Dağı ∧	130	40.47 N	27.16 E
Ganpingsi	102	35.13 N	102.30 E
Ganpu	106	30.24 N	120.53 E
Ganquan	102	36.25 N	109.16 E
Gansbaai	158	34.35 S	19.22 E
Gänsbrunnen	58	47.16 N	7.28 E
Gansen	120	37.25 N	92.15 E
Gänserndorf	61	48.20 N	16.43 E
Gansevoort	210	43.12 N	73.39 W
Ganso Azul	248	8.51 S	74.44 W
Ganspan	158	27.57 S	24.47 E
Gansu (Kansu) □[4]	102	37.00 N	103.00 E
Ganta	150	7.15 N	8.59 W
Gantan	100	29.37 N	119.34 E
Gantang, Zhg.	100	26.56 N	119.40 E
Gantang, Zhg.	102	22.58 N	109.00 E
Gantao ≃	98	38.01 N	114.07 E
Gante → Gent	50	51.03 N	3.43 E
Gantheaume, Cape ≻	166	36.05 S	137.27 E
Gantheaume Bay c	162	27.44 S	114.07 E
Gantheaume Point ≻	162	17.59 S	122.10 E
Gantiadi	84	43.24 N	40.06 E
Gantian	100	27.30 N	113.10 E
Gantt	194	31.24 N	86.29 W
Gantung	112	2.58 S	108.09 E
Gantung, Mount ∧	116	8.57 N	117.48 E
Ganu Mór ∧	46	58.25 N	4.53 W
Gan'uškino	80	46.36 N	49.16 E
Ganwo	150	11.13 N	4.42 E
Ganxi, Zhg.	100	28.08 N	118.06 E
Ganxi, Zhg.	102	29.02 N	109.32 E
Ganyanchi	102	36.39 N	105.18 E
Ganyesa	158	26.35 S	24.10 E
Ganyu (Qing Kou)	98	34.52 N	119.10 E
Ganzê	102	31.40 N	100.01 E
Ganzhenyi	100	30.33 N	113.21 E
Ganzhou, Zhg.	100	25.54 N	114.55 E
Ganzhou, Zhg.	100	28.49 N	115.25 E
Ganzhou → Zhangye, Zhg.	102	38.56 N	100.27 E
Ganzhuermiao	88	48.24 N	118.08 E
Ganzlin	54	53.23 N	12.15 E
Gao	150	16.16 N	0.03 W
Gao □[4]	150	18.00 N	1.30 E
Gao'an	100	28.25 N	115.22 E
Gaobaita	271a	39.53 N	116.30 E
Gaobei	100	26.37 N	114.38 E
Gaobeidian	271a	39.54 N	116.33 E
Gaobu	100	27.48 N	117.01 E
Gaochang	107	28.49 N	104.24 E
Gaocheng, Zhg.	98	38.04 N	114.49 E
Gaocheng, Zhg.	100	31.57 N	113.25 E
Gaocheng, Zhg.	106	31.28 N	119.48 E
Gaochengzhai	104	41.24 N	123.43 E
Gaochun	106	31.20 N	118.52 E
Gaocun	98	37.05 N	122.12 E
Gaodianzi	102	30.40 N	110.01 E
Gao Feng ∧	106	30.34 N	118.40 E
Gaogongmiao	100	33.25 N	115.53 E
Gaogou	100	34.03 N	119.15 E
Gaohe	100	22.47 N	112.57 E
Gaohebu	100	30.44 N	116.50 E
Gaoil, Sliabh ∧	46	55.55 N	5.28 W
Gaojiabu	102	38.30 N	110.11 E
Gaojiadi	98	41.33 N	114.58 E
Gaojiadian	98	42.40 N	124.28 E
Gaojian	100	29.04 N	121.14 E
Gaojiapuzi	104	41.22 N	123.36 E
Gaojiaqiao	106	30.43 N	120.38 E
Gaojiatun	104	41.06 N	121.19 E
Gaojiawopeng	104	41.28 N	122.10 E
Gaojiawopu	104	41.50 N	122.47 E
Gaojiazhai	269b	31.23 N	121.33 E
Gaojiazhen	102	30.05 N	107.51 E
Gaokan	104	40.46 N	122.23 E
Gaokeng	100	27.40 N	113.58 E
Gaolan	102	36.25 N	103.56 E
Gaolan Dao I	100	21.55 N	113.15 E
Gaolao	104	41.54 N	120.59 E
Gaoli	105	39.17 N	115.38 E
Gaoliang	107	29.45 N	105.15 E
Gaoliban	104	41.39 N	121.58 E
Gaolifangshen	104	42.27 N	123.21 E
Gaolimen	98	40.22 N	124.02 E
Gaoling	105	40.32 N	117.01 E
Gaolinying	105	39.06 N	115.38 E
Gaoliying	105	40.10 N	116.29 E
Gaoliyingzi	104	41.56 N	124.17 E
Gaolong	100	26.56 N	113.45 E
Gaolou	105	39.59 N	116.50 E
Gaolouchang, Zhg.	107	29.51 N	104.41 E
Gaolouchang, Zhg.	107	30.03 N	105.58 E
Gaoluo	98	37.27 N	113.55 E
Gaomi	98	36.23 N	119.44 E
Gaona	252	25.12 S	64.05 W
Gaopi	100	24.14 N	116.39 E
Gaoping, Zhg.	102	35.48 N	112.52 E
Gaoping, Zhg.	107	30.28 N	105.45 E
Gaopingba	107	30.47 N	106.06 E
Gaoqiao, Zhg.	100	30.08 N	119.56 E
Gaoqiao, Zhg.	100	26.36 N	117.46 E
Gaoqiao, Zhg.	102	28.06 N	106.36 E
Gaoqiao, Zhg.	106	32.14 N	119.38 E
Gaoqiao, Zhg.	106	31.21 N	121.34 E
Gaoqiaomen	106	32.01 N	118.51 E
Gaoqiaozhen	104	40.55 N	121.00 E
Gaoqing (Tianzhen)	98	37.11 N	117.47 E
Gaoqipu	104	41.32 N	121.40 E
Gaosha	100	26.27 N	117.56 E
Gaoshaling	105	38.51 N	117.36 E
Gaoshan, Zhg.	100	25.29 N	119.34 E
Gaoshan, Zhg.	107	29.26 N	104.28 E
Gaoshanbao	105	40.40 N	117.29 E
Gaoshangbao	98	39.11 N	118.30 E
Gaoshanpu	102	27.10 N	105.14 E
Gaoshantai	104	42.22 N	122.28 E
Gaoshanzi	104	41.34 N	122.02 E
Gaoshengchang	107	29.59 N	105.31 E
Gaoshengzhen	104	41.20 N	122.12 E
Gaoshi	107	29.36 N	104.44 E
Gaoshikan	107	29.12 N	105.04 E
Gaosichang	107	30.17 N	104.52 E
Gaotai	102	39.20 N	99.58 E
Gaotaishan	104	42.02 N	122.52 E
Gaotan, Zhg.	100	30.23 N	117.23 E
Gaotan, Zhg.	100	23.12 N	115.22 E
Gaotan, Zhg.	102	32.22 N	108.36 E
Gaotang	98	36.54 N	116.14 E
Gaotangji	100	32.24 N	116.01 E
Gaotingsi	100	26.05 N	112.53 E
Gaotuozi	104	41.08 N	122.40 E
Gaoua	150	10.20 N	3.11 W
Gaoual	150	11.45 N	13.12 W
Gaoxian	102	28.20 N	104.38 E
Gaoxingru	100	26.28 N	115.14 E
Gaoxinji	98	34.11 N	115.33 E
Gaoya	98	36.22 N	118.49 E
Gaoyang	98	34.30 N	114.40 E
Gaoyapu	107	29.14 N	106.19 E
Gaoyi	98	37.36 N	114.36 E
Gaoyou, Zhg.	100	32.47 N	119.27 E
Gaoyou, Zhg.	100	28.25 N	115.31 E
Gaoyou Hu ⊜	100	32.50 N	119.20 E
Gaozhangjia	102	36.06 N	107.18 E
Gaozhou	102	21.55 N	110.50 E
Gaozi	106	32.11 N	119.18 E
Gaoziba	107	29.01 N	106.00 E
Gaozuo	100	33.57 N	118.03 E
Gap, Fr.	62	44.34 N	6.05 E
Gap, Pa., U.S.	208	39.59 N	76.01 W
Gapālnagar	272b	22.49 N	88.08 E
Gapan	116	15.19 N	120.57 E
Gapeau ≃	62	43.07 N	6.11 E
Gapern ⊜	40	59.31 N	13.40 E
Gara, Lough ⊜	48	53.55 N	8.25 W
Garacad	144	6.57 N	49.19 E
Garachiné	246	8.04 N	78.22 W
Garachiné, Punta ≻	246	8.06 N	78.25 W
Garadag	144	9.26 N	46.52 E
Gārādāha	126	24.14 N	89.34 E
Garagoa	246	5.05 N	73.21 W
Garaguso	68	40.33 N	16.14 E
Garah	166	29.04 S	149.38 E
Garai ≃[1]	126	23.32 N	89.31 E
Garaina	164	7.50 S	147.10 E
Garamba ≃	154	3.53 N	29.12 E
Garamba, Parc National de la ♠	154	4.10 N	29.30 E
Gara Muleta ∧	144	9.17 N	41.47 E
Garānberia	272b	22.24 N	88.34 E
Garancières	261	48.49 N	1.46 E
Garango	150	11.48 N	0.34 W
Garanhuns	250	8.54 S	36.29 W
Garapan	174n	15.12 N	145.43 E
Garautha	124	25.34 N	79.18 E
Garba	146	9.12 N	20.30 E
Garbagna	266b	45.23 N	8.39 E
Garbagnate Milanese	266b	45.35 N	9.05 E
Garbahaarey	144	3.19 N	42.13 E
Garbatella ⬥[8]	267a	41.52 N	12.29 E
Garba Tula	154	0.32 N	38.31 E
Garber	196	36.26 N	97.35 W
Garberville	204	40.06 N	123.47 W
Garbokaraj	88	54.09 N	99.52 E
Garboldisham	42	52.24 N	0.56 E
Garbsen	52	52.25 N	9.34 E
Garça	255	22.14 S	49.37 W
Garças, Rio das ≃	255	15.54 S	52.16 W
Garcevo	76	52.45 N	32.59 E
Garches	261	48.51 N	2.11 E
Garching	60	48.15 N	11.39 E
Garching an der Alz	60	48.08 N	12.34 E
Garchitorena	116	13.52 N	123.40 E
García	232	29.59 N	108.20 W
García, Laguna ⊜	288	34.58 S	58.09 W
García de la Cadena	234	21.09 N	103.28 W
García de Sola, Embalse de ⊜[1]	34	39.15 N	5.05 W
Garcia Hernandez	116	9.37 N	124.18 E
Garcias	255	20.34 S	52.13 W
Garcitas Creek ≃	222	28.51 N	96.46 W
Gard □[5]	62	44.00 N	4.00 E
Gard ≃	62	43.51 N	4.37 E
Gard, Pont du ⬥[5]	62	43.56 N	4.36 E
Garda	64	45.34 N	10.42 E
Garda, Lago di ⊜	64	45.40 N	10.41 E
Gardabani	84	41.28 N	45.06 E
Gardanne	62	43.27 N	5.28 E
Garde, Lac la ⊜	190	46.46 N	78.14 W
Gardelegen	54	52.31 N	11.23 E
Garden ≃	190	46.32 N	84.09 W
Gardena	228	33.53 N	118.18 W
Gardena, Val V	64	46.35 N	11.35 E
Garden Acres	226	37.58 N	121.13 W
Garden City, Ga., U.S.	192	32.06 N	81.09 W
Garden City, Ks., U.S.	198	37.58 N	100.52 W
Garden City, Mi., U.S.	216	42.19 N	83.19 W
Garden City, Mo., U.S.	194	38.33 N	94.11 W
Garden City, N.Y., U.S.	210	40.43 N	73.38 W
Garden City, Tx., U.S.	196	31.52 N	101.29 W
Garden City → Qasr al-Dubārā ⬥[8]	273c	30.02 N	31.14 E
Garden City Park	276	40.44 N	73.39 W
Garden City Raceway ♠	284a	43.09 N	79.11 W
Gardendale	194	33.39 N	86.48 W
Garden Farms	226	35.24 N	120.07 W
Garden Gate Village	282	37.20 N	122.02 W
Garden Grove, Ca., U.S.	228	33.46 N	117.56 W
Garden Grove, Ia., U.S.	190	40.50 N	93.36 W
Garden Home	224	45.27 N	122.45 W
Garden Island I, Austl.	168a	32.13 S	115.41 E
Garden Island I, Mi., U.S.	190	45.49 N	85.30 W
Garden Lakes	192	34.17 N	85.16 W
Garden Peninsula ≻[1]	190	45.45 N	86.35 W
Garden Plain	198	37.39 N	97.41 W
Garden Prairie	216	42.15 N	88.44 W
Garden Reach	126	22.33 N	88.17 E
Gardenside	218	38.03 N	84.33 W
Garden State Arts Center ʊ	276	40.24 N	74.11 W
Garden State Plaza ⬥[9]	276	40.55 N	74.05 W
Gardenton	184	49.05 N	96.40 W
Garden Valley	226	38.51 N	120.51 W
Garden View	210	41.16 N	77.03 W
Gardenville	208	40.22 N	75.07 W
Gardermoen	26	60.13 N	11.06 E
Gardey	252	37.17 S	59.21 W
Gardēz	120	33.37 N	69.07 E
Gardinas → Grodno	76	53.41 N	23.50 E
Gardiner, Me., U.S.	188	44.13 N	69.46 W
Gardiner, Mt., U.S.	202	45.01 N	110.42 W
Gardiner, N.Y., U.S.	210	41.41 N	74.09 W
Gardiner, Or., U.S.	202	43.43 N	124.06 W
Gardiner, Wa., U.S.	224	48.03 N	122.55 W
Gardiner Dam ⬥[6]	184	51.17 N	106.51 W
Gardiner Range ⋏	162	23.50 S	131.46 E
Gardiners Bay c	207	41.08 N	72.10 W
Gardiners Creek ≃	274b	37.50 S	145.02 E
Gardiners Island I	207	41.05 N	72.07 W
Garding	41	54.20 N	8.46 E
Gardner, Il., U.S.	216	41.11 N	88.18 W
Gardner, Ks., U.S.	198	38.48 N	94.55 W
Gardner, Ma., U.S.	207	42.34 N	71.59 W
Gardner Canal c	182	53.28 N	128.15 W
Gardner Lake ⊜	207	41.31 N	72.13 W
Gardner Pinnacles II[1]	14	25.00 N	167.55 W
Gardnersville	218	38.46 N	84.30 W
Gardnertown	210	41.32 N	74.04 W
Gardnerville	226	38.56 N	119.44 W
Gardno	54	53.15 N	14.38 E
Gardolo	64	46.07 N	11.05 E
Gardon d'Alès ≃	62	44.02 N	4.08 E
Gardon d'Anduze ≃	62	44.02 N	4.08 E
Gardone Riviera	64	45.37 N	10.34 E
Gardone Val Trompia	64	45.41 N	10.11 E
Gårdsjö	40	58.52 N	14.19 E
Gårdskär	40	60.37 N	17.35 E
Gardunha, Serra da ⋏	34	40.05 N	7.31 W
Gare Loch c	46	56.01 N	4.48 W
Garelochhead	46	56.05 N	4.50 W
Gareloi Island I	181a	51.47 N	178.48 W
Garenfeld	263	51.24 N	7.31 E
Gare Simon	273b	4.15 S	15.11 E
Garešnica	36	45.35 N	16.56 E
Garessio	62	44.12 N	8.02 E
Garet, Mont ∧[1]	175f	14.16 S	167.30 E
Garfield, Ks., U.S.	198	38.04 N	99.14 W
Garfield, N.J., U.S.	210	40.52 N	74.06 W
Garfield, N.M., U.S.	200	32.45 N	107.15 W
Garfield, Wa., U.S.	202	47.00 N	117.08 W
Garfield Heights	214	41.25 N	81.36 W
Garfield Mountain ∧	202	44.31 N	112.37 W
Garfield Park	285	39.42 N	75.33 W
Garfield Park ♠, Il., U.S.	278	41.53 N	87.43 W
Garfield Park ♠, Oh., U.S.	279a	41.26 N	81.36 W
Garfield Peak ∧	200	42.47 N	107.18 W
Garforth	44	53.48 N	1.22 W
Garga	88	54.26 N	110.33 E
Gargaliánoi	38	37.04 N	21.39 E
Gargano, Promontorio del ≻	68	41.50 N	16.00 E
Gargano, Testa del ≻	68	41.49 N	16.12 E
Gargantua, Cape ≻	190	47.36 N	85.02 W
Garga Sarali	152	5.11 N	14.00 E
Gargazzone (Gargazon)	64	46.35 N	11.12 E
Gargellen	58	46.58 N	9.56 E
Gargenville	261	49.00 N	1.49 E
Garges-lès-Gonesse	261	48.58 N	2.25 E
Gargnano	64	45.41 N	10.40 E
Gargouna	150	15.56 N	0.13 E
Gargrave	44	53.59 N	2.06 W
Gargždai	76	55.43 N	21.24 E
Garhākota	124	23.46 N	79.09 E
Garhbeta	126	22.51 N	87.19 E
Garhdīwāla	123	31.44 N	75.45 E
Garhi Jasaya	272a	28.46 N	77.16 E
Garhi Katiya	272a	28.45 N	77.16 E
Garhi Khairo	120	28.04 N	67.59 E
Garhi Malehra	124	25.02 N	79.40 E
Garhmuktesar	124	28.48 N	78.06 E
Garhshankar	123	31.13 N	76.08 E
Garhwal □[5]	124	30.00 N	78.50 E
Gari	86	59.26 N	62.21 E
Garibaldi, Bra.	252	29.15 S	51.32 W
Garibaldi, B.C., Can.	182	49.58 N	123.09 W
Garibaldi, Or., U.S.	224	45.34 N	123.55 W
Garibaldi, Casa di ⊥	71	41.13 N	9.27 E
Garibaldi, Mount ∧	182	49.51 N	123.01 W
Garibaldi Provincial Park ♠	182	50.00 N	122.50 W
Garies	158	30.30 S	18.00 E
Garigliano ≃	68	41.13 N	13.45 E
Gariglione, Monte ∧	68	39.09 N	16.41 E
Garín	258	34.26 S	58.44 W
Garín, Arroyo ≃	288	34.23 S	58.43 W
Garinin	46	58.21 N	6.50 W
Garin Regional Park ♠	282	37.38 N	122.03 W
Garipçe Burnu ≻	267b	41.13 N	29.07 E
Garissa	154	0.28 S	39.38 E
Garita Palmera	236	13.44 N	90.05 W
Gariya	272b	22.28 N	88.23 E
Gārji	272b	22.51 N	88.19 E
Garkida	146	10.25 N	12.36 E
Garko	150	11.38 N	8.48 E
Garland, Al., U.S.	194	31.33 N	86.49 W
Garland, Md., U.S.	284b	39.11 N	76.39 W
Garland, Pa., U.S.	214	41.49 N	79.27 W
Garland, Tx., U.S.	222	32.54 N	96.38 W
Garland, Ut., U.S.	200	41.44 N	112.09 W
Garland Park ♠	275b	43.44 N	79.35 W
Garland Peak ∧	224	48.01 N	120.43 W
Garlasco	62	45.12 N	8.55 E
Garlate	62	45.49 N	9.23 E
Garlate, Lago di ⊜	58	45.49 N	9.24 E
Garliava	76	54.49 N	23.52 E
Garlieston	44	54.48 N	4.22 W
Garlin	32	43.34 N	0.15 W
Garm	85	39.02 N	70.22 E
Garm Āb	120	32.14 N	65.01 E
Garmal	144	8.35 N	50.19 E
Gärmersdorf	60	49.26 N	11.54 E
Garmisch-Partenkirchen	64	47.29 N	11.05 E
Garmouth	46	57.40 N	3.07 W
Garmsar	128	35.20 N	52.13 E
Garnavillo	190	42.52 N	91.14 W
Garne	261	48.41 N	1.58 E
Garner, Ia., U.S.	190	43.06 N	93.36 W
Garner, N.C., U.S.	192	35.42 N	78.36 W
Garnet Range ⋏	202	46.45 N	113.15 W
Garnett	198	38.16 N	95.14 W
Garni Habibullāh Khan	123	34.24 N	73.23 E
Garnijskij zapovednik ♠	84	40.00 N	44.55 E
Garnish	186	47.14 N	55.22 W
Garnock ≃	46	55.38 N	4.42 W
Garnpung, Lake ⊜	166	33.30 S	143.12 E
Garona → Garonne ≃	32	45.02 N	0.36 W
Garonne ≃	32	45.02 N	0.36 W
Garoowe	144	8.24 N	48.29 E
Garou, Lac ⊜	150	16.04 N	2.45 W
Garoua, Cam.	146	9.18 N	13.24 E
Garoua, Niger	146	13.53 N	13.11 E
Garoua Boulaï	152	5.53 N	14.33 E
Garove Island I	164	4.40 S	149.30 E
Garpenberg	40	60.19 N	16.12 E
Garphyttan	40	59.19 N	14.56 E
Garphyttans Nationalpark ♠	40	59.17 N	14.51 E
Garraf, Costa de ⊤[2]	266d	41.16 N	2.02 E
Garrattsville	210	42.39 N	75.10 W
Garrel	52	52.57 N	8.01 E
Garret Mountain Reservation ♠	276	40.54 N	74.11 W
Garretson	198	43.43 N	96.30 W
Garrett, In., U.S.	216	41.20 N	85.08 W
Garrett, Ky., U.S.	192	37.28 N	82.49 W
Garrett Creek ≃	222	32.57 N	95.44 W
Garrett Park	208	39.02 N	77.05 W
Garrett Park Estates	284c	39.02 N	77.06 W
Garrettsville	214	41.17 N	81.06 W
Garrison, N. Ire., U.K.	48	54.25 N	8.05 W
Garrison, Ky., U.S.	218	38.36 N	83.10 W
Garrison, Md., U.S.	208	39.24 N	76.45 W
Garrison, Mt., U.S.	202	46.31 N	112.48 W
Garrison, N.Y., U.S.	210	41.23 N	73.56 W
Garrison, N.D., U.S.	198	47.39 N	101.24 W
Garrison, Tx., U.S.	222	31.49 N	94.30 W
Garrison Dam ⬥[6]	198	47.22 N	101.25 W
Garron Point ≻	48	55.03 N	5.57 W
Garros	46	57.37 N	6.11 W
Garrovillas	34	39.43 N	6.33 W
Garry ≃	46	56.43 N	3.47 W
Garry, Loch ⊜	206	45.15 N	74.43 W
Garry Bay c	176	68.55 N	85.05 W
Garry Lake ⊜	176	66.00 N	100.00 W
Gars am Kamp	61	48.36 N	15.40 E
Garsdale Head	44	54.19 N	2.20 W
Garsen	154	2.16 S	40.07 E
Garskolk	158	30.41 S	22.02 E
Gårslev	41	55.38 N	9.43 E
Garson	190	46.34 N	80.52 W
Garson Lake ⊜	184	56.19 N	110.02 W
Garstang	44	53.55 N	2.47 W
Garstedt	52	53.41 N	9.58 E
Garsten	61	48.01 N	14.24 E
Garston	260	51.41 N	0.23 W
Garston ⬥[8]	262	53.21 N	2.53 W
Garswood	262	53.29 N	2.40 W
Gartempe ≃	32	46.48 N	0.50 E
Gartenstadt ⬥[8]	263	51.30 N	7.26 E
Garthby Station (Beaulac)	206	45.50 N	71.23 W
Gartow	54	53.02 N	11.29 E
Gartrop-Bühl	263	51.40 N	6.49 E
Gartz	54	53.12 N	14.23 E
Garu	150	10.51 N	0.11 W
Garub	156	26.33 S	16.00 E
Garubhāsa	124	26.33 N	90.22 E
Gārulia	126	22.49 N	88.22 E
Garut	115a	7.13 S	107.54 E
Garve	46	57.37 N	4.42 W
Garvellachs II	46	56.14 N	5.47 W
Garvey Reservoir ⊜[1]	280	34.13 N	118.07 W
Garvie Mountains ⋏	172	45.30 S	168.50 E
Garwa	124	24.11 N	83.49 E
Garwin	190	42.05 N	92.40 W
Garwolin	30	51.54 N	21.37 E
Garwood, N.J., U.S.	276	40.39 N	74.19 W
Garwood, Tx., U.S.	222	29.27 N	96.24 W
Gary, In., U.S.	216	41.35 N	87.20 W
Gary, S.D., U.S.	198	44.47 N	96.27 W
Gary, Tx., U.S.	194	32.07 N	94.22 W
Gary, W.V., U.S.	192	37.21 N	81.33 W
Gary Harbor c	278	41.38 N	87.20 W
Garyi	102	30.54 N	98.56 E
Gary Municipal Airport ⊠	278	41.37 N	87.25 W
Garysburg	208	36.27 N	77.33 W
Garz	54	54.19 N	13.20 E
Garza	252	28.09 S	63.32 W
Garza Ayala	196	26.29 N	100.02 W
Garza García	196	25.40 N	100.24 W
Garzas Creek ≃	226	37.13 N	120.57 W
Garzeno	58	46.08 N	9.15 E
Garzón, Col.	246	2.12 N	75.38 W
Garzón, Ur.	252	34.36 S	54.33 W
Gas	261	48.34 N	1.40 E
Gasan	116	13.19 N	121.51 E
Gasan-Kuli	128	37.27 N	53.59 E
Gas City	216	40.29 N	85.36 W
Gascogne □[9]	32	44.00 N	0.05 E
Gascogne, Golfe de → Biscay, Bay of c	32	44.00 N	4.00 W
Gasconade	219	38.40 N	91.33 W
Gasconade □[6]	219	38.27 N	91.30 W
Gasconade ≃	194	38.40 N	91.33 W
Gasconade, Osage Fork ≃	194	37.45 N	92.26 W
Gascoyne ≃	162	24.52 S	113.37 E
Gascoyne, Mount ∧	162	24.58 S	116.38 E
Gascoyne Junction	162	25.03 S	115.12 E
Gash (Nahr al-Qāsh) ≃	140	16.48 N	35.51 E
Gashaka	146	7.21 N	11.27 E
Gasherbrum I ∧	123	35.43 N	76.43 E
Gashua	146	12.54 N	11.00 E
Gasline	284a	42.53 N	79.11 W
Gasny	50	49.05 N	1.36 E
Gaspar	252	26.56 S	48.58 W
Gaspard Creek ≃	182	51.34 N	122.17 W
Gasparilla Island I	220	26.46 N	82.16 W
Gasparilla Sound ⊔	220	26.48 N	82.15 W
Gaspé	186	48.50 N	64.29 W
Gaspé, Baie de c	186	48.46 N	64.17 W
Gaspé, Cap ≻	186	48.45 N	64.10 W
Gaspé Peninsula → Gaspésie, Péninsule de la ≻[1]	186	48.30 N	65.00 W
Gaspereau Lake ⊜	186	44.57 N	64.34 W
Gasperina	68	38.44 N	16.30 E
Gaspésie, Parc Provincial de la ♠	186	48.55 N	66.00 W
Gaspésie, Péninsule de la ≻[1]	186	48.30 N	65.00 W
Gaspoltshofen	60	48.08 N	13.46 E
Gasport	210	43.11 N	78.34 W
Gaspra	78	44.27 N	34.07 E
Gassan	150	12.49 N	3.12 W
Gas-san ∧	92	38.32 N	140.01 E
Gassaway	188	38.40 N	80.46 W
Gasselte	52	52.57 N	6.46 E
Gassen → Jasień	30	51.46 N	15.01 E
Gassin	62	43.13 N	6.35 E
Gassino Torinese	62	45.08 N	7.49 E
Gassol	146	8.32 N	10.28 E
Gastein → Badgastein	64	47.07 N	13.08 E
Gasteiner Tal V	64	47.11 N	13.06 E
Gastello	89	49.07 N	142.58 E
Gaston, In., U.S.	216	40.18 N	85.30 W
Gaston, N.C., U.S.	192	36.30 N	77.38 W
Gaston, Or., U.S.	224	45.26 N	123.08 W
Gaston, Lake ⊜[1]	192	36.35 N	78.00 W
Gastonia, N.C., U.S.	192	35.15 N	81.11 W
Gastonia, Tx., U.S.	222	32.37 N	96.24 W
Gastonville	279b	40.15 N	79.59 W
Gastoúni	38	37.51 N	21.16 E
Gastre	254	42.17 S	69.14 W
Gästrikland □[9]	40	60.30 N	16.27 E
Gat	132	31.37 N	34.47 E
Gata, Cabo de ≻	34	36.43 N	2.12 W
Gata, Sierra de ⋏	34	40.14 N	6.45 W
Gătaia	38	45.26 N	21.26 E
Gátas, Akrotírion ≻	130	34.34 N	33.02 E
Gatčina	76	59.34 N	30.08 E
Gate	196	36.51 N	100.03 W
Gateacre ⬥[8]	262	53.23 N	2.51 W
Gate City	192	36.38 N	82.34 W
Gatehouse of Fleet	44	54.53 N	4.11 W
Gatersleben	54	51.49 N	11.17 E
Gates, N.Y., U.S.	210	43.09 N	77.41 W
Gates, N.C., U.S.	208	36.30 N	76.46 W
Gates □[6]	208	36.28 N	76.43 W
Gateshead	44	54.58 N	1.37 W
Gateshead Island I	176	70.22 N	100.27 W
Gates Mills	279a	41.31 N	81.24 W
Gates of the Arctic National Park ♠	180	67.45 N	153.30 W
Gatesville, N.C., U.S.	192	36.24 N	76.45 W
Gatesville, Tx., U.S.	222	31.26 N	97.44 W
Gateway	200	38.40 N	108.58 W
Gateway Arch ʊ	219	38.37 N	90.12 W
Gateway National Recreation Area ♠	276	40.34 N	74.16 W
Gateway of India ⊥	272c	18.55 N	72.50 E
Gaths Mine	154	20.00 S	30.31 E
Gathurst	262	53.34 N	2.42 W
Gatié Loumo	150	15.28 N	4.37 W
Gâtine, Hauteurs de ⋏[2]	32	46.40 N	0.50 W
Gatineau	212	45.29 N	75.38 W
Gatineau □[6]	212	45.25 N	75.45 W
Gatineau ≃	176	45.27 N	75.40 W
Gatineau, Parc de la ♠	188	45.30 N	76.05 W
Gatley	262	53.23 N	2.14 W
Gatlinburg	192	35.42 N	83.30 W
Gato, Arroyo del ≃, Arg.	288	34.55 S	58.37 W
Gato, Arroyo del ≃, Arg.	288	34.51 S	57.56 W
Ga'ton	132	33.00 N	35.13 E
Gato Negro	286c	10.33 N	66.57 W
Gatow ⬥[8]	264a	52.29 N	13.11 E
Gatow, Flugplatz ⊠	264a	52.28 N	13.08 E
Gattendorf	61	48.01 N	16.59 E
Gattières	62	43.46 N	7.11 E
Gattinara	62	45.37 N	8.22 E
Gatton	171a	27.33 S	152.17 E
Gattorna	62	44.26 N	9.11 E
Gatún, Lago ⊜[1]	236	9.12 N	79.55 W
Gatun Locks ⬥[5]	236	9.16 N	79.55 W
Gatvand	128	32.15 N	48.50 E
Gau-Algesheim	56	49.57 N	8.01 E
Gauchy	50	49.49 N	3.16 E
Gaucín	34	36.31 N	5.19 W
Gauer Lake ⊜	184	57.00 N	97.50 W
Gauguin, Musée ʊ	174s	17.45 S	149.23 W
Gauhāti	120	26.10 N	91.45 E
Gauja ≃	76	57.09 N	24.16 E
Gaujiena	76	57.30 N	26.40 E
Gaukler Point ≻	281	42.27 N	82.52 W
Gaula ≃	26	63.21 N	10.14 E
Gauley ≃	188	38.10 N	81.12 W
Gauley Bridge	188	38.10 N	81.11 W
Gaultois	186	47.36 N	55.54 W
Gaunless ≃	44	54.40 N	1.41 W
Gau-Odernheim	56	49.47 N	8.11 E
Gaura Barhaj	124	26.17 N	83.44 E
Gaurain-Ramecroix	50	50.35 N	3.29 E
Gaurama	252	27.34 S	52.03 W
Gaurambha	126	22.39 N	89.34 E
Gaurela	124	22.45 N	81.54 E
Gaurhāti	126	22.46 N	87.48 E
Gauribaradia	126	23.45 N	89.52 E
Gauribidanūr	122	13.37 N	77.31 E
Gauri Phanta	124	28.41 N	80.33 E
Gauripur	124	26.05 N	89.58 E
Gauri Sankar ∧	124	27.57 N	86.21 E
Gaurnadi	126	22.58 N	90.14 E
Gause	222	30.47 N	96.43 W
Gausta ∧	26	59.50 N	8.35 E
Gauthiot, Chutes ∟	146	9.43 N	14.34 E
Gauting	60	48.04 N	11.23 E
Gavá	34	41.18 N	2.01 E
Gāvanpāda	272c	18.57 N	73.01 E
Gavardo	64	45.35 N	10.26 E
Gávdhos I	38	34.50 N	24.06 E
Gávea ⬥[8]	287a	22.58 S	43.14 W
Gávea, Hipódromo da ♠	287a	22.58 S	43.13 W
Gavel-Långsjön ⊜	40	59.50 N	18.18 E
Gavello	64	45.01 N	11.55 E
Gavet	62	45.04 N	5.52 E
Gavi	62	44.41 N	8.49 E
Gavia, Arroyo de la ≃	266a	40.21 N	3.40 W
Gavião ≃	255	14.06 S	41.01 W
Gavião, Pico do ∧	256	21.37 S	44.50 W
Gavilán	286c	10.24 N	66.51 W
Gavinana	66	44.05 N	10.45 E
Gavins Point Dam ⬥[6]	198	42.48 N	97.40 W
Gaviões	256	22.34 S	42.33 W
Gavirate	62	45.50 N	8.43 E
Gavja ≃	76	53.49 N	25.35 E
Gāvkhūnī, Bātlāq-e ≡	128	32.06 N	52.52 E
Gāv Koshī	128	28.38 N	57.12 E
Gävle	40	60.40 N	17.10 E
Gävleborgs Län □[6]	26	61.30 N	16.15 E
Gävlebukten c	40	60.42 N	17.20 E
Gavnø	41	55.11 N	11.44 E
Gavoi	71	40.10 N	9.12 E
Gavorrano	66	42.55 N	10.54 E
Gavrilov-Jam	80	57.18 N	39.51 E
Gavrilovka	83	48.37 N	37.31 E
Gavrilovka Vtoraja	80	52.53 N	42.46 E
Gavrilov Posad	80	56.33 N	40.07 E
Gávrion	38	37.52 N	24.46 E
Gavry	76	56.55 N	27.53 E
Gawachab	156	27.03 S	17.50 E
Gawān	124	24.37 N	85.55 E
Gaweinstal	61	48.28 N	16.35 E
Gāwīlgarh Hills ⋏[2]	122	21.20 N	77.00 E
Gawler	168b	34.37 S	138.44 E
Gawler ≃	168b	34.41 S	138.27 E
Gawler Ranges ⋏	162	32.30 S	136.00 E
Gawso	150	6.48 N	2.31 W
Gawsworth	262	53.13 N	2.10 W
Gawthorpe Hall ⊥	262	53.48 N	2.18 W
Gaxun Nur (Juyanhai) ⊜	102	42.22 N	100.34 E
Gaya, India	124	24.47 N	85.00 E
Gaya, Niger	150	11.53 N	3.27 E
Gaya, Nig.	150	11.53 N	9.02 E
Gaya □[5]	124	24.50 N	84.50 E
Gay City State Park ♠	207	41.42 N	72.28 W
Gayéri	150	12.39 N	0.29 E
Gay Head	207	41.20 N	70.48 W
Gay Hill	222	30.16 N	96.30 W
Gaylord, Mi., U.S.	190	45.01 N	84.40 W
Gaylord, Mn., U.S.	190	44.33 N	94.13 W
Gaylordsville	207	41.38 N	73.29 W
Gayndah	166	25.37 S	151.36 E
Gays Mills	190	43.19 N	90.50 W
Gayton, Eng., U.K.	42	52.45 N	0.34 E
Gayton, Eng., U.K.	262	53.19 N	3.06 W
Gayt on Sands ✣[4]	262	53.17 N	3.07 W
Gaza → Ghazzah	128	31.30 N	34.28 E
Gaza □[5]	156	23.30 S	32.45 E
Gazalkent	85	41.33 N	69.47 E
Gazaoua	150	13.32 N	7.55 E
Gaza Strip □[9]	132	31.25 N	34.20 E
Gazelle Channel ⊔	164	2.50 S	150.55 E
Gazelle Peninsula ≻[1]	164	4.40 S	152.00 E
Gazeran	261	48.38 N	1.46 E
Gazeran, Bois de ♠	261	48.40 N	1.45 E
Gazi, Kenya	154	4.25 S	39.30 E
Gazi, Zaïre	154	1.04 N	24.31 E
Gaziantep	130	37.05 N	37.22 E
Gaziantep □[4]	130	37.00 N	37.20 E
Gazimur ≃	88	52.57 N	120.22 E
Gazimurskij Zavod	88	51.33 N	118.22 E
Gazipaşa	130	36.17 N	32.20 E

≃	River	Fluss	Río	Rivière	Rio	✣	Submarine Features	Untermeerische Objekte	Accidentes Submarinos	Formes de relief sous-marin	Acidentes submarinos
≊	Canal	Kanal	Canal	Canal	Canal	□	Political Unit	Politische Einheit	Unidad Politica	Entité politique	Unidade política
∟	Waterfall, Rapids	Wasserfall, Stromschnellen	Cascada, Rápidos	Chute d'eau, Rapides	Cascata, Rápidos	ʊ	Cultural Institution	Kulturelle Institution	Institución Cultural	Institution culturelle	Institução cultural
⊔	Strait	Meeresstrasse	Estrecho	Détroit	Estreito	⊥	Historical Site	Historische Stätte	Sitio Histórico	Site historique	Sitio histórico
c	Bay, Gulf	Bucht, Golf	Bahía, Golfo	Baie, Golfe	Baía, Golfo	♠	Recreational Site	Erholungs- und Ferienort	Sitio de Recreo	Centre de loisirs	Area de Lazer
⊜	Lake, Lakes	See, Seen	Lago, Lagos	Lac, Lacs	Lago, Lagos	⊠	Airport	Flughafen	Aeropuerto	Aéroport	Aeroporto
≡	Swamp	Sumpf	Pantano	Marais	Pântano	■	Military Installation	Militäranlage	Instalación Militar	Installation militaire	Instalação militar
⊓	Ice Features, Glacier	Eis- und Gletscherformen	Accidentes Glaciales	Formes glaciaires	Acidentes glaciares	⬥	Miscellaneous	Verschiedenes	Misceláneo	Divers	Diversos
⊤	Other Hydrographic Features	Andere Hydrographische Objekte	Otros Elementos Hidrográficos	Autres données hydrographiques	Outros acidentes hidrográficos						

Name	Page	Lat.°′	Long.°′
Gāzīpura	126	22.46 N	90.43 E
Gazira Sporting Club ♠	273c	30.04 N	31.13 E
Gaznau	85	40.10 N	71.02 E
Gazoldo degli Ippoliti	64	45.12 N	10.35 E
Gazos Creek ≃	226	37.10 N	122.22 W
Gazzada	62	45.47 N	8.51 E
Gazzaniga	62	45.48 N	9.50 E
Gazzuolo	64	45.04 N	10.35 E
Gbangbatok	150	7.48 N	12.23 W
Gbanhala ≃	150	10.14 N	8.38 W
Gbaoui Bodanga	152	5.33 N	16.45 E
Gbarnga	150	7.00 N	9.29 W
Gbogbo	273a	6.36 N	3.31 E
Gboko	150	7.20 N	8.57 E
Gbon	150	9.50 N	6.27 W
Gbwado	152	3.54 N	20.46 E
Gcoverega	156	19.08 S	24.15 E
Gdańsk (Danzig)	30	54.23 N	18.40 E
Gdańsk □[4]	30	54.15 N	18.25 E
Gdansk, Gulf of c	30	54.40 N	19.15 E
Gden'	78	51.20 N	30.25 E
Gdov	76	58.44 N	27.48 E
Gdyel	34	35.48 N	0.26 W
Gdynia	30	54.32 N	18.33 E
Gearhart	224	46.01 N	123.54 W
Gearhart Mountain ʌ	202	42.30 N	120.53 W
Gearhartville	214	40.53 N	78.15 W
Geary, N.B., Can.	186	45.46 N	66.29 W
Geary, Ok., U.S.	196	35.43 N	98.22 W
Geauga □[6]	214	41.35 N	81.12 W
Geauga Lake Park ♠	279a	41.21 N	81.23 W
Geba ≃	150	11.46 N	15.36 W
Gebaberg ʌ	56	50.36 N	10.16 E
Gebe, Pulau I	164	0.05 S	129.20 E
Gebeit Mine	140	21.03 N	36.19 E
Gebeler	130	39.26 N	29.00 E
Gebeme	130	40.38 N	37.48 E
Gebenbach	60	49.32 N	11.53 E
Gebesee	54	51.07 N	10.56 E
Gebi	84	42.46 N	43.30 E
Gebilu	144	10.35 N	41.28 E
Gebra	54	51.24 N	10.35 E
Gebweiler → Guebwiller	58	47.55 N	7.12 E
Gebze	130	40.48 N	29.25 E
Gecha	144	7.31 N	35.22 E
Gechang	106	31.05 N	119.27 E
Gecun	106	32.10 N	119.37 E
Geddes, Mi., U.S.	281	42.16 N	83.40 W
Geddes, S.D., U.S.	198	43.15 N	98.41 W
Gede, Gunung ʌ	115a	6.47 S	106.59 E
Gedera	132	31.49 N	34.46 E
Gedern	56	50.25 N	9.12 E
Gedian	100	30.32 N	114.38 E
Gedi National Monument ♠	154	3.19 S	40.03 E
Gedinne	56	49.59 N	4.56 E
Gediz	130	39.02 N	29.25 E
Gediz ≃	130	38.35 N	26.48 E
Gedlegube	144	6.52 N	45.02 E
Gedo	144	8.58 N	37.27 E
Gedo □[4]	144	3.00 N	42.00 E
Gedongdalem	112	5.04 S	105.25 E
Gedongtataan	115a	5.23 S	105.05 E
Gedser	41	54.35 N	11.57 E
Gedser Odde ›	41	54.34 N	11.59 E
Geduld	273d	26.15 S	28.25 E
Gedun	100	27.39 N	118.26 E
Geebung	171a	27.22 S	153.03 E
Gee Cross	262	53.26 N	2.04 W
Geehi	171b	36.24 S	148.11 E
Geehi ≃	171b	36.11 S	148.02 E
Geel	56	51.10 N	5.00 E
Geelong	169	38.08 S	144.21 E
Geelong West	169	38.08 S	144.20 E
Geelvink Channel ɥ	162	28.30 S	114.10 E
Geer ≃	56	50.51 N	5.42 E
Geeste ≃	52	53.32 N	8.35 E
Geesthacht	52	53.26 N	10.22 E
Geeveston	166	43.10 S	146.55 E
Gefell	54	50.26 N	11.52 E
Gefle → Gävle	40	60.40 N	17.10 E
Gefrees	54	50.06 N	11.44 E
Gegang	100	30.04 N	117.38 E
Gegečkori	84	42.25 N	42.22 E
Gegenmiao	89	45.58 N	122.15 E
Gegong	100	30.05 N	117.11 E
Gegou	98	35.24 N	118.32 E
Gegu	105	38.59 N	117.30 E
Gehackte Berge ⋏[2]	264a	52.41 N	13.30 E
Gehlenburg → Biała Piska	30	53.37 N	22.04 E
Gehrden	52	52.18 N	9.36 E
Gehren	54	50.39 N	10.59 E
Gehu	100	27.46 N	119.16 E
Ge Hu ◎	106	31.36 N	119.51 E
Gehua	164	10.20 S	150.25 E
Geidam	146	12.57 N	11.57 E
Geiger	194	32.52 N	88.18 W
Geigertown	208	40.13 N	75.50 W
Geihoku	96	34.44 N	132.17 E
Geikie ≃	176	57.45 N	103.52 W
Geilenkirchen	56	50.57 N	6.07 E
Geilo	26	60.31 N	8.12 E
Geinō	94	34.48 N	136.25 E
Geiranger	26	62.06 N	7.12 E
Geisa	56	50.43 N	9.57 E
Geisberg ʌ	60	49.53 N	11.03 E
Geisecke	263	51.27 N	7.37 E
Geisei	96	33.31 N	133.49 E
Geiselhöring	60	48.50 N	12.23 E
Geisenfeld	60	48.41 N	11.37 E
Geisenhausen	60	48.28 N	12.15 E
Geisenheim	56	49.59 N	7.58 E
Geisingen	58	47.55 N	8.38 E
Geislingen an der Steige	56	48.36 N	9.50 E
Geismar	52	51.31 N	9.57 E
Geispolsheim	58	48.31 N	7.39 E
Geisstein ʌ	64	47.20 N	12.30 E
Geistenbeck ◆[8]	263	51.09 N	6.27 E
Geistown	214	40.17 N	78.52 W
Geist Reservoir ◎[1], In., U.S.	218	39.56 N	85.56 W
Geist Reservoir ◎[1], Pa., U.S.	285	39.57 N	75.24 W
Geisweid	56	50.55 N	8.01 E
Geita	154	2.52 S	32.10 E
Geithain	54	51.03 N	12.41 E
Geiyō-shotō II	96	34.10 N	132.45 E
Gejah	272a	28.31 N	77.23 E
Gejiatun	98	40.27 N	119.55 E
Gejiu (Kokiu)	102	23.22 N	103.06 E
Geka, mys ›	180	64.26 N	178.10 E
Gel, Meydān-e ≚	128	29.04 N	54.50 E
Gela	70	37.04 N	14.15 E
Gela ≃	70	37.03 N	14.15 E
Gela, Golfo di c	70	37.03 N	14.10 E
Geladi	144	6.57 N	46.25 E
Gelai ʌ[1]	154	2.33 S	36.05 E
Gelan	102	30.03 N	107.04 E
Gelang, Tanjong ›	114	3.58 N	103.26 E
Gelaochang	107	29.36 N	103.39 E
Gelasa, Selat ɥ	112	2.40 S	107.15 E
Gelber Fluss → Huang ≃	90	37.32 N	118.19 E
Gelbes Meer → Yellow Sea ⫧[2]	90	36.00 N	123.00 E
Gelderland □[4]	52	52.10 N	5.50 E
Geldermalsen	52	51.53 N	5.17 E
Geldern	52	51.31 N	6.20 E
Geldern □[8]	263	51.25 N	6.27 E
Geldrop	52	51.25 N	5.33 E
Geleen	56	50.58 N	5.52 E
Gelegra	130	40.01 N	31.50 E
Gelemso	144	8.48 N	40.35 E
Gelenau	54	50.42 N	12.58 E
Gelenbe	130	39.10 N	27.50 E
Gelendost	130	38.07 N	31.01 E
Gelendžik	78	44.33 N	38.06 E
Gelfingen	58	47.13 N	8.16 E
Gelgaudiškis	76	55.05 N	23.00 E
Gelib → Jilib	144	0.29 N	42.46 E
Gelibolu	130	40.24 N	26.40 E
Gelibolu Yarımadası (Gallipoli Peninsula) ›[1]	130	40.20 N	26.30 E
Gelidonya Burnu ›	130	36.13 N	30.25 E
Gelinden	56	50.46 N	5.15 E
Gélise ≃	32	44.11 N	0.17 E
Geliting	115b	8.39 S	122.18 E
Geliting, Teluk c	115b	8.36 S	122.17 E
Gellénháza	61	46.46 N	16.47 E
Gellenstrom ɥ	54	54.28 N	13.03 E
Gellep-Stratum ◆[8]	263	51.20 N	6.41 E
Gellibrand	169	38.32 S	143.32 E
Gellibrand ≃	169	38.41 S	143.09 E
Gellibrand, Point ›	274b	37.52 S	144.54 E
Gellingen → Ghislenghien	50	50.39 N	3.52 E
Gellinsoor	144	6.26 N	46.42 E
Gel'm'azov	78	49.49 N	31.49 E
Gelnhausen	56	50.11 N	9.11 E
Gelså ≃	41	55.19 N	8.54 E
Gelsdorf	56	50.35 N	7.02 E
Gelsenkirchen	52	51.31 N	7.07 E
Gelsenkirchen-Horst, Galopprennbahn ♠	263	51.32 N	7.02 E
Gelsted	41	55.24 N	9.59 E
Gelt ≃	44	54.56 N	2.47 W
Geltendorf	60	48.07 N	11.01 E
Gelterkinden	58	47.28 N	7.51 E
Gelting	41	54.45 N	9.53 E
Geltow	54	52.22 N	12.58 E
Geltsa	144	6.14 N	37.05 E
Geluji	98	37.08 N	121.50 E
Geluksburg	158	28.30 S	29.33 E
Geluwe	50	50.48 N	3.04 E
Gelveri	130	38.17 N	34.23 E
Gemas	114	2.35 N	102.37 E
Gembloux	56	50.34 N	4.41 E
Gembrook	169	37.57 S	145.33 E
Gemen	52	51.51 N	6.52 E
Gemena	152	3.15 N	19.46 E
Gemengchi ◎	120	31.15 N	89.15 E
Gémenos	62	43.18 N	5.38 E
Gemerek	130	39.11 N	36.05 E
Gemert	52	51.34 N	5.40 E
Gemla	26	56.52 N	14.38 E
Gemlik	130	40.26 N	29.09 E
Gemlik Körfezi c	130	40.25 N	28.55 E
Gemolong	115a	7.24 S	110.50 E
Gemona del Friuli	64	46.16 N	13.09 E
Gemonio	62	45.53 N	8.40 E
Gemsbok National Park ♠	156	25.15 S	21.10 E
Gemünd	56	50.34 N	6.30 E
Gemünden, B.R.D.	56	50.03 N	9.41 E
Gemünden, B.R.D.	56	50.58 N	8.58 E
Gemünden, B.R.D.	56	49.54 N	7.28 E
Gemuzhakechi ◎	120	33.47 N	85.30 E
Gen ≃	89	50.16 N	119.22 E
Genadendal	158	34.02 S	19.33 E
Genaibashi	268	35.21 N	140.04 E
Genale (Jubba) ≃	144	0.15 S	42.38 E
Genappe	50	50.36 N	4.27 E
Genarp	41	55.36 N	13.23 E
Genazzano	66	41.50 N	12.58 E
Genç	130	38.46 N	40.35 E
Gençay	32	46.23 N	0.24 E
Gencek	130	37.27 N	31.33 E
Gencsapáti	61	47.17 N	16.36 E
Gending	115a	7.48 S	113.18 E
Gendrey	58	47.12 N	5.41 E
Gendringen	52	51.52 N	6.22 E
Gendt	52	51.53 N	5.59 E
Genegantslet Creek ≃	210	42.18 N	75.48 W
Genemuiden	52	52.37 N	6.07 E
General ≃	236	8.59 N	83.11 W
General Acha	252	37.23 S	64.36 W
General Alvear, Arg.	252	36.03 S	60.01 W
General Alvear, Arg.	252	34.58 S	67.42 W
General Aquino	252	24.26 S	56.42 W
General Arenales	252	34.18 S	61.18 W
General Belgrano	252	35.46 S	58.30 W
General Bernardo O'Higgins ʋ[3]	9	63.19 S	57.54 W
General Bravo	232	25.48 N	99.10 W
General Butler State Resort Park ♠	218	38.40 N	85.10 W
General Cabrera	252	32.48 S	63.52 W
General Câmara	252	29.54 S	51.46 W
General Campos	252	31.32 S	58.24 W
General Carneiro	255	15.42 S	52.45 W
General Carrera, Lago (Lago Buenos Aires) ◎	254	46.35 S	72.00 W
General Cepeda	232	25.23 N	101.27 W
General Conesa, Arg.	252	36.30 S	57.20 W
General Conesa, Arg.	254	40.06 S	64.26 W
General Daniel Cerri	252	38.42 S	62.24 W
General del Sur, Cementerio ◆	286c	10.28 N	66.55 W
General Elizardo Aquino	252	26.53 S	56.17 W
General Enrique Martínez	252	33.12 S	53.48 W
General Enrique Mosconi	252	22.36 S	63.49 W
General Escobedo, Méx.	196	25.49 N	100.20 W
General Escobedo, Méx.	232	25.30 N	105.15 W
General Eugenio A. Garay, Para.	248	20.31 S	62.08 W
General Eugenio A. Garay, Para.	252	25.55 S	56.11 W
General Galarza	252	32.43 S	59.24 W
General Güemes	252	24.40 S	65.03 W
General Guido	252	36.40 S	57.46 W
General Gutiérrez	252	32.57 S	68.48 W
General Hornos	258	34.53 S	58.56 W
General Island I	116	9.25 N	126.00 E
General José de San Martín	252	26.33 S	59.21 W
General Juan Madariaga	252	37.00 S	57.09 W
General La Madrid	252	37.16 S	61.17 W
General Las Heras	258	34.56 S	58.57 W
General Las Heras □[5]	288	34.56 S	58.51 W
General Lavalle	252	36.24 S	56.58 W
General Levalle	252	34.01 S	63.56 W
General Lorenzo Vintter	254	40.44 S	64.29 W
General Luna	116	9.47 N	126.09 E
General MacArthur (Pambuhan Sur)	116	11.15 N	125.32 E
General Mansilla (Bartolomé Bavio)	258	35.05 S	57.45 W
General Manuel Belgrano, Cerro ʌ	252	29.01 S	67.49 W
General Mitchell Field ⊠	216	42.57 N	87.54 W
General Motors Corporation (Pontiac Division) ʋ[3]	281	42.49 N	83.17 W
General Motors Proving Grounds ʋ[3]	281	42.35 N	83.41 W
General Motors Technical Center ʋ[3]	281	42.31 N	83.02 W
General'nyj ≃	265a	60.00 N	30.32 E
General O'Brien	252	34.54 S	60.45 W
General Pacheco	288	34.28 S	58.38 W
General Panfilo Natera	234	22.40 N	102.06 W
General Paz, Arg.	252	27.45 S	57.37 W
General Paz, Arg.	258	35.31 S	58.19 W
General Pico	252	35.40 S	63.44 W
General Pinedo	252	27.19 S	61.17 W
General Pinto	252	34.46 S	61.53 W
General Pizarro	252	24.13 S	64.01 W
General Plaza (Limón)	246	2.58 S	78.25 W
General Roca	252	39.02 S	67.35 W
General Rodríguez	258	34.36 S	58.57 W
General Rojo	252	33.28 S	60.17 W
General Saavedra	248	17.15 S	63.10 W
General Sampaio	250	4.02 S	39.29 W
General San Martín, Arg.	252	37.59 S	63.34 W
General San Martín, Arg.	258	34.34 S	58.32 W
General San Martín □[5]	288	34.34 S	58.34 W
General Santos (Dadiangas)	116	6.07 N	125.11 E
General Sarmiento	258	34.33 S	58.43 W
General Sarmiento □[5]	288	34.32 S	58.43 W
General'skoje	83	47.28 N	39.35 E
General Terán	232	25.16 N	99.41 W
General Tinio	116	15.21 N	121.03 E
General Toševo	38	43.42 N	28.02 E
General Treviño	196	26.14 N	99.29 W
General Urquiza ◆[8]	288	34.34 S	58.29 W
General Vargas	252	29.42 S	54.40 W
General Viamonte (Los Toldos)	252	35.01 S	61.01 W
General Villegas	252	35.02 S	63.01 W
General Vintter, Lago (Lago Palena) ◎	254	43.55 S	71.40 W
General Warren Village	285	40.02 N	75.32 W
General Zuazua	196	25.54 N	100.07 W
Gênes → Genova	62	44.25 N	8.57 E
Genesee, Id., U.S.	202	46.33 N	116.55 W
Genesee, Pa., U.S.	214	41.59 N	77.52 W
Genesee, Wi., U.S.	216	42.58 N	88.21 W
Genesee □[6], Mi., U.S.	216	42.56 N	83.41 W
Genesee □[6], N.Y., U.S.	210	43.00 N	78.11 W
Genesee ≃	210	43.16 N	77.36 W
Geneseo, Il., U.S.	190	41.26 N	90.09 W
Geneseo, Ks., U.S.	198	38.30 N	98.09 W
Geneseo, N.Y., U.S.	210	42.47 N	77.49 W
Geneva → Genève, Schw.	58	46.12 N	6.09 E
Geneva, S. Afr.	158	27.50 S	27.08 E
Geneva, Al., U.S.	194	31.01 N	85.51 W
Geneva, Fl., U.S.	220	28.44 N	81.07 W
Geneva, Il., U.S.	216	41.53 N	88.18 W
Geneva, In., U.S.	216	40.35 N	84.57 W
Geneva, Ne., U.S.	198	40.31 N	97.35 W
Geneva, N.Y., U.S.	210	42.52 N	77.00 W
Geneva, Oh., U.S.	214	41.48 N	80.56 W
Geneva, Pa., U.S.	214	41.35 N	80.14 W
Geneva, Wa., U.S.	224	48.45 N	122.24 W
Geneva, Lake (Lac Léman) (Lac de Gèneve) ◎, Europe	58	46.25 N	6.30 E
Geneva, Lake ◎, Wi., U.S.	216	42.34 N	88.30 W
Geneva-on-the-Lake	214	41.52 N	80.57 W
Genève (Geneva)	58	46.12 N	6.09 E
Genève □[3]	58	46.15 N	6.10 E
Genève, Lac de → Geneva, Lake ◎	58	46.25 N	6.30 E
Genève-Cointrin, Aéroport ⊠	58	46.14 N	6.06 E
Genevois ◆[1]	58	46.03 N	6.14 E
Genévriers, Île des I	186	51.15 N	58.26 W
Genf → Genève	58	46.12 N	6.09 E
Genga	66	43.26 N	12.56 E
Gengenbach	58	48.24 N	8.01 E
Genghis Khan, Wall of ⊥, Asia	88	49.00 N	115.00 E
Genghis Khan, Wall of ⊥, Mong.	88	49.00 N	116.00 E
Gengji	100	33.47 N	112.47 E
Gengma	102	23.34 N	99.06 E
Gengputou	106	31.12 N	119.55 E
Gengzhuang	104	40.59 N	122.42 E
Geničesk	78	46.11 N	34.48 E
Génicourt	261	49.05 N	2.04 E
Génicourt-sur-Meuse	56	49.02 N	5.26 E
Genil ≃	34	37.42 N	5.19 W
Génissiat	58	46.03 N	5.47 E
Genk	56	50.58 N	5.30 E
Genkai	96	33.51 N	130.30 E
Genkai-kokutei-kōen ♠	96	33.54 N	130.31 E
Genkai-nada ⫧[2]	92	34.00 N	130.00 E
Genkanyj, chrebet ⋏	180	66.15 N	172.20 W
Genlis	58	47.14 N	5.13 E
Gennach ≃	58	48.10 N	10.43 E
Gennargentu, Monti del ⋏	71	40.01 N	9.19 E
Gennebreck	263	51.19 N	7.12 E
Gennep	52	51.42 N	5.58 E
Genner	41	55.07 N	9.26 E
Gennes	32	47.20 N	0.14 W
Gennevilliers	261	48.56 N	2.18 E
Genoa, Austl.	166	37.29 S	149.35 E
Genoa → Genova, It.	62	44.25 N	8.57 E
Genoa, Il., U.S.	216	42.05 N	88.41 W
Genoa, Ne., U.S.	198	41.26 N	97.43 W
Genoa, Nv., U.S.	226	39.00 N	119.50 W
Genoa, N.Y., U.S.	210	42.40 N	76.32 W
Genoa, Oh., U.S.	214	41.31 N	83.21 W
Genoa, Wi., U.S.	190	43.34 N	91.13 W
Genoa, Arroyo ≃	254	44.58 S	70.06 W
Genoa City	216	42.29 N	88.19 W
Genoa Peak ʌ	226	39.03 N	119.53 W
Genola	62	44.35 N	7.39 E
Génolhac	62	44.21 N	3.57 E
Genova (Genoa)	62	44.25 N	8.57 E
Genova □[4]	62	44.30 N	9.04 E
Genova, Golfo di c	62	44.10 N	8.55 E
Genova, Val V	64	46.11 N	10.40 E
Genovesa, Isla I	246a	0.20 N	89.58 W
Genrijetty, ostrov I	74	77.06 N	156.30 E
Gensan → Wŏnsan	98	39.09 N	127.25 E
Gens de Terre ≃	190	46.53 N	76.00 W
Genshagen	264a	52.19 N	13.19 E
Genshagener Heide ◆[3]	264a	52.20 N	13.18 E
Genshiryoku-kenkyūsho ʋ[3]	94	36.27 N	140.36 E
Gensingen	56	49.53 N	7.55 E
Gensungen	56	51.08 N	9.26 E
Gent (Gand)	50	51.03 N	3.43 E
Gentbrugge	50	51.03 N	3.45 E
Gent-Brugge, Kanaal ≍	50	51.03 N	3.43 E
Genteng	115a	8.22 S	114.09 E
Genteng, Gili I	115a	7.12 S	113.54 E
Genteng, Tanjung ›	115a	7.23 S	106.24 E
Genthin	54	52.24 N	12.09 E
Gentilly	261	48.49 N	2.21 E
Gentilly ≃	206	46.24 N	72.21 W
Genting	114	3.42 N	98.10 E
Gentio do Ouro	250	11.25 S	42.30 W
Gentioux	32	45.47 N	1.59 E
Gentofte	41	55.45 N	12.33 E
Gentry	194	36.16 N	94.29 W
Gentry, Lake ◎	220	28.08 N	81.15 W
Genua → Genova	62	44.25 N	8.57 E
Genuang	114	2.29 N	102.53 E
Genval	50	50.43 N	4.29 E
Genyem	164	2.46 S	140.12 E
Genzano di Lucania	68	40.51 N	16.02 E
Genzano di Roma	66	41.42 N	12.41 E
Geographe Bay c	162	33.35 S	115.15 E
Geographe Channel ɥ	162	24.40 S	113.20 E
Geokčaj	84	40.39 N	47.44 E
Geokčaj ≃	84	40.39 N	47.45 E
Geok-Tepe	128	38.09 N	57.58 E
Geonkhāli	126	22.12 N	88.03 E
George, S. Afr.	158	33.58 S	22.24 E
George, Ia., U.S.	198	43.20 N	96.00 W
George, Tx., U.S.	222	30.59 N	96.07 W
George ≃, Austl.	162	20.50 S	117.28 E
George ≃, P.Q., Can.	176	58.49 N	66.10 W
George, Cape ›	186	45.53 N	61.53 W
George, Lake ◎, Austl.	162	22.37 S	123.38 E
George, Lake ◎, Austl.	166	35.05 S	149.25 E
George, Lake ◎, N.A.	190	46.28 N	84.10 W
George, Lake ◎, Ug.	154	0.02 N	30.12 E
George, Lake ◎, U.S.	216	41.45 N	85.00 W
George, Lake ◎, Fl., U.S.	192	29.17 N	81.36 W
George, Lake ◎, In., U.S.	216	41.40 N	87.30 W
George, Lake ◎, N.Y., U.S.	188	43.35 N	73.35 W
George Air Force Base ■	228	34.35 N	117.22 W
George B. Stevenson Dam ◆[6]	214	41.25 N	78.01 W
George Gill Range ⋏	162	24.15 S	131.36 E
George H. Crosby Manitou State Park ♠	190	47.29 N	91.10 W
George Island I	254	52.19 S	59.45 W
George Mason University ʋ[2]	284c	38.50 N	77.17 W
Georgensgmünd	56	49.11 N	11.00 E
Georgenthal	54	50.49 N	10.40 E
Georges ≃	170	33.57 S	150.58 E
Georges Bank ✣[4]	16	41.15 N	67.30 W
Georges Hall	274a	33.55 S	150.59 E
Georges Island I	283	42.19 N	70.56 W
George Sound ɥ	172	44.50 S	167.23 E
Georges River Bridge ◆[5]	274a	34.00 S	151.07 E
Georges Run	214	40.21 N	80.37 W
Georges Run ≃	279b	40.23 N	80.06 W
Georgetown, Austl.	166	18.18 S	143.33 E
George Town, Austl.	166	41.06 S	146.50 E
Georgetown → Halton Hills	190	43.37 N	79.56 W
Georgetown, P.E., Can.	186	46.11 N	62.32 W
Georgetown, Cay. Is.	238	19.18 N	81.23 W
Georgetown, Gam.	150	13.30 N	14.47 W
Georgetown, Guy.	18	6.48 N	58.10 W
Georgetown, Guy.	246	6.48 N	58.10 W
George Town (Pinang), Malay.	114	5.25 N	100.20 E
Georgetown, St. Vin.	241h	13.16 N	61.08 W
Georgetown, Ca., U.S.	226	38.54 N	120.50 W
Georgetown, Co., U.S.	200	39.42 N	105.41 W
Georgetown, Ct., U.S.	207	41.15 N	73.26 W
Georgetown, De., U.S.	208	38.41 N	75.23 W
Georgetown, Fl., U.S.	192	29.23 N	81.38 W
Georgetown, Ga., U.S.	192	31.53 N	85.06 W
Georgetown, Id., U.S.	202	42.29 N	111.22 W
Georgetown, Il., U.S.	194	39.58 N	87.38 W
Georgetown, In., U.S.	218	38.17 N	85.58 W
Georgetown, Ky., U.S.	218	38.12 N	84.33 W
Georgetown, Ma., U.S.	207	42.43 N	70.59 W
Georgetown, Ms., U.S.	194	31.52 N	90.09 W
Georgetown, N.J., U.S.	285	40.04 N	74.39 W
Georgetown, N.Y., U.S.	210	42.46 N	75.44 W
Georgetown, Oh., U.S.	218	38.51 N	83.54 W
Georgetown, Pa., U.S.	214	40.39 N	80.30 W
Georgetown, S.C., U.S.	192	33.22 N	79.17 W
Georgetown, Tx., U.S.	222	30.37 N	97.40 W
Georgetown ◆[8]	284c	38.54 N	77.03 W
Georgetown, Lake ◎[1]	222	30.40 N	97.45 W
Georgetown Lake ◎	202	46.11 N	113.17 W
Georgetown Rowley State Forest ♠	283	42.42 N	70.58 W
Georgetown University ʋ[2]	284c	38.54 N	77.04 W
George V Coast ±[2]	9	68.30 S	147.30 E
George VI Sound ɥ	9	71.00 S	68.00 W
George Washington Birthplace National Monument ♠	208	38.11 N	76.56 W
George Washington Bridge ◆[5]	276	40.51 N	73.57 W
George Washington Carver National Monument ♠	194	37.00 N	94.19 W
George West	196	28.19 N	98.07 W
Georgia → Gruzinskaja Sovetskaja Socialističeskaja Respublika □[3]	84	42.00 N	44.00 E
Georgia □[3], U.S.	178	32.50 N	83.15 W
Georgia □[3], U.S.	192	32.50 N	83.15 W
Georgia, Strait of ɥ	182	49.20 N	124.00 W
Georgia del Sur, Isla de → South Georgia I	244	54.15 S	36.45 W
Georgia Heights	278	41.32 N	87.20 W
Georgiana	194	31.38 N	86.44 W
Georgian Bay c	190	45.15 N	80.50 W
Georgian Bay Islands National Park ♠	190	44.54 N	79.52 W
Géorgie du Sud → South Georgia I	244	54.15 S	36.45 W
Georgijevka, S.S.S.R.	80	53.18 N	51.01 E
Georgijevka, S.S.S.R.	83	48.26 N	39.17 E
Georgijevka, S.S.S.R.	85	42.11 N	70.00 E
Georgijevka, S.S.S.R.	85	43.03 N	74.43 E
Georgijevka, S.S.S.R.	86	49.19 N	81.35 E
Georgijevsk	84	44.09 N	43.28 E
Georgina ≃	166	23.30 S	139.47 E
Georgina Island I	212	44.23 N	79.17 W
Georgina Island Indian Reserve ◆[4]	212	44.22 N	79.19 W
Georgiu-Dež (Liski)	78	50.59 N	39.30 E
Georgsmarienhütte	52	52.12 N	8.02 E
Georg von Neumayer ʋ[3]	9	70.37 S	8.22 W
Gera	54	50.52 N	12.04 E
Gera □[5]	54	50.45 N	11.45 E
Gera ≃	54	51.08 N	10.56 E
Geraardsbergen	50	50.46 N	3.52 E
Geraberg	54	50.43 N	10.50 E
Gerabronn	56	49.15 N	9.55 E
Gerace	68	38.16 N	16.13 E
Geraci Siculo	70	37.51 N	14.09 E
Gerais, Chapada dos ⋏[1]	255	17.40 S	45.20 W
Gerais, Serra dos ʌ	256	21.54 S	44.06 W
Geral, Serra ±[4], Bra.	250	11.15 S	46.30 W
Geral, Serra ±[4], Bra.	252	26.30 S	50.30 W
Gerald	219	38.23 N	91.19 W
Geral de Goiás, Serra ±[4]	242	13.00 S	46.15 W
Geraldine, N.Z.	172	44.05 S	171.14 E
Geraldine, Mt., U.S.	202	47.36 N	110.15 W
Geraldton, Austl.	162	28.46 S	114.36 E
Geraldton, On., Can.	176	49.44 N	86.57 W
Gerard, Lake ◎	276	41.06 N	74.33 W
Gerard, Mount ʌ	162	27.13 S	122.41 E
Gérardmer	58	48.04 N	6.53 E
Geras	61	48.48 N	15.40 E
Gerasa ⊥	132	32.17 N	35.53 E
Gerasdorf	61	48.18 N	16.28 E
Gerasimovka	86	58.37 N	71.53 E
Gerber	204	40.03 N	122.08 W
Gerber Reservoir ◎[1]	202	42.12 N	121.06 W
Gerbéviller	58	48.30 N	6.31 E
Gerblingerode	52	51.29 N	10.15 E
Gerbstedt	54	51.38 N	11.37 E
Gerca	78	48.09 N	26.16 E
Gerchsheim	56	49.42 N	9.47 E
Gercüş	130	37.34 N	41.23 E
Gerdau	158	26.28 S	26.06 E
Gerdine, Mount ʌ	180	61.35 N	152.26 W
Gerdview	273d	26.10 S	28.11 E
Gère ≃	62	45.32 N	4.54 E
Gerede	130	40.48 N	32.12 E
Gerenzano	266b	45.38 N	9.00 E
Gereshk	120	31.48 N	64.34 E
Geretsried	64	47.51 N	11.28 E
Gérgal	34	37.07 N	2.33 W
Gerge'bil	84	42.31 N	47.05 E
Gerger	130	38.02 N	39.02 E
Geria Nij	126	23.56 N	86.55 E
Gerik	114	5.25 N	101.08 E
Gering	198	41.49 N	103.39 W
Geringswalde	54	51.04 N	12.54 E
Geriş	130	36.58 N	31.44 E
Gerlachovský štít ʌ	30	49.12 N	20.08 E
Gerlafingen	58	47.10 N	7.34 E
Gerli ◆[8]	288	34.41 S	58.23 W
Gerlingen	56	48.48 N	9.03 E
Gerlos	64	47.14 N	12.02 E
Gerlospass)(	64	47.14 N	12.08 E
Gerlova Hut'	60	49.10 N	13.17 E
Germa (Jarmah) ⊥	146	26.33 N	13.04 E
Germagnano	62	45.15 N	7.28 E
Germain, Grand lac ◎	186	51.12 N	66.41 W
Germán	232	25.10 N	97.54 W
German Democratic Republic (Deutsche Demokratische Republik) □[1], Europe	22	52.00 N	12.30 E
German Democratic Republic (Deutsche Demokratische Republik) □[1], Europe	30	52.00 N	12.30 E
Germania	214	41.39 N	77.40 W
Germano	214	40.25 N	80.57 W
Germanoviči	76	55.25 N	27.44 E
Germansen, Mount ʌ	182	55.37 N	124.50 W
Germansen Lake ◎	182	55.41 N	124.53 W
Germansen Landing	182	55.47 N	124.43 W
Germansville	208	40.42 N	75.42 W
Germantown, Il., U.S.	219	38.33 N	89.32 W
Germantown, Ky., U.S.	218	38.39 N	83.57 W
Germantown, N.Y., U.S.	210	42.08 N	73.54 W
Germantown, Oh., U.S.	218	39.37 N	84.22 W
Germantown, Tn., U.S.	194	35.05 N	89.48 W
Germantown, Wi., U.S.	216	43.13 N	88.06 W
Germantown ◆[8]	285	40.03 N	75.11 W
Germantown Dam ◆[6]	218	39.38 N	84.24 W
Germany, Federal Republic of (Bundesrepublik Deutschland) □[1], Europe	22	51.00 N	9.00 E
Germany, Federal Republic of (Bundesrepublik Deutschland) □[1], Europe	30	51.00 N	9.00 E
Germany Flats ≚	276	41.05 N	74.39 W
Germay	58	48.25 N	5.21 E
Germencik	130	37.51 N	27.37 E
Germendorf	54	52.45 N	13.10 E
Germering, B.R.D.	60	48.08 N	11.22 E
Germering, B.R.D.	64	48.08 N	11.22 E
Germersheim	56	49.13 N	8.22 E
Germfask	190	46.14 N	85.55 W
Germī	128	39.01 N	48.03 E
Germili	130	39.06 N	38.49 E
Germiston	158	26.13 S	28.11 E
Germiston □[5]	273d	26.15 S	28.10 E
Germiston South	273d	26.15 S	28.10 E
Germiter	130	38.28 N	37.36 E
Gernrode	54	51.43 N	11.08 E
Gernsbach	56	48.46 N	8.19 E
Gernsheim	56	49.44 N	8.29 E
Gero	94	35.48 N	137.14 E
Geroda	56	50.17 N	9.53 E
Gerola Alta	58	46.03 N	9.32 E
Geroldsgrün	54	50.20 N	11.35 E
Geroldstein	56	50.06 N	7.56 E
Gerolsbach	60	48.30 N	11.22 E
Gerolstein	56	50.13 N	6.40 E
Gerolzhofen	56	49.54 N	10.21 E
Gerona, Esp.	34	41.59 N	2.49 E
Gerona, Pil.	116	15.36 N	120.36 E
Geronimo	196	34.28 N	98.22 W
Gerpinnes	50	50.20 N	4.31 E
Gerrards Cross	260	51.35 N	0.34 W
Gerrei ◆[1]	71	39.28 N	9.17 E
Gerresheim ◆[8]	263	51.14 N	6.52 E
Gerringong	170	34.45 S	150.50 E
Gerry	214	42.12 N	79.15 W
Gers □[5]	32	43.40 N	0.30 E
Gers ≃	32	44.09 N	0.39 E
Gersau	58	47.00 N	8.32 E
Gersdorf	54	50.45 N	12.42 E
Gersfeld	56	50.27 N	9.55 E
Gershøj	41	55.43 N	11.59 E
Gersprenz ≃	56	49.59 N	9.04 E
Gerstetten	56	48.37 N	10.01 E
Gersthofen	58	48.25 N	10.53 E
Gerstungen	56	50.58 N	10.04 E
Gertak Sanggul, Tanjong ›	114	5.15 N	100.11 E
Gerthe ◆[8]	263	51.31 N	7.17 E
Gerufa	156	19.17 S	26.02 E
Gervais	224	45.06 N	122.53 W
Gerwisch	54	52.10 N	11.44 E
Gerza	142	29.26 N	31.11 E
Gerze	130	41.48 N	35.12 E
Gerzen	60	48.31 N	12.25 E
Gerzensee	58	46.51 N	7.33 E
Gescher	52	51.57 N	6.59 E
Geschriebenstein (Írottkő) ʌ	61	47.21 N	16.26 E
Geschwenda	54	50.44 N	10.49 E
Gesees	60	49.54 N	11.32 E
Geseke	52	51.38 N	8.31 E
Geser	164	3.53 S	130.54 E
Gesher HaZiw	132	33.02 N	35.06 E
Gesi	115a	7.20 S	111.01 E
Gesoa	164	8.25 S	143.35 E
Gespunsart	56	49.49 N	4.50 E
Gessertshausen	58	48.20 N	10.44 E
Gesso ≃	62	44.24 N	7.33 E
Gessopalena	66	42.03 N	14.16 E
Gesten	41	55.31 N	9.12 E
Gesualdo	68	41.00 N	15.04 E
Geta	26	60.23 N	19.50 E
Getafe	34	40.18 N	3.43 W
Getafe, Aeropuerto ⊠	266a	40.18 N	3.43 W
Gete ≃	56	50.57 N	5.07 E
Gethaoli	272c	19.08 N	73.01 E
Geti	154	1.13 N	30.12 E
Getinge	26	56.49 N	12.44 E
Gettorf	41	54.24 N	9.58 E
Gettysburg, Oh., U.S.	218	40.06 N	84.29 W
Gettysburg, Pa., U.S.	208	39.49 N	77.13 W
Gettysburg, S.D., U.S.	198	45.00 N	99.57 W
Gettysburg National Military Park ♠	208	39.49 N	77.15 W
Getulândia	256	22.40 S	44.06 W
Getulina	255	21.49 S	49.55 W
Getulio	116	10.45 N	122.40 E
Getúlio Vargas	252	27.50 S	52.16 W
Getz Ice Shelf ⊓	9	75.00 S	129.00 W
Getzville	210	43.01 N	78.46 W
Geudubang	114	4.54 N	97.23 E
Geumpang	114	4.48 N	96.09 E
Geureudong, Gunung ʌ	114	4.48 N	96.48 E
Gevān	128	26.03 N	57.17 E
Gevaş	128	38.16 N	43.07 E
Gevelsberg	56	51.19 N	7.20 E
Gevgelija	38	41.08 N	22.30 E
Gévora ≃	34	38.53 N	6.57 W
Gevrey-Chambertin	58	47.14 N	4.57 E
Gewane	144	10.10 N	40.39 E
Geweke ◆[8]	263	51.22 N	7.25 E
Gex	58	46.20 N	6.04 E
Geyer	54	50.37 N	12.55 E
Geyer Ditch ≍	216	41.36 N	86.25 W
Geyikli	130	39.48 N	26.12 E
Geysdorp	158	26.32 S	25.18 E
Geyser	202	47.15 N	110.29 W
Geyserville	204	38.42 N	122.54 W
Geyshtasar, Kūh-e ʌ	84	38.51 N	47.14 E
Geyuan	100	28.31 N	117.44 E
Geyve	130	40.30 N	30.18 E
Gézenti	146	21.41 N	18.18 E
Gezer	132	31.52 N	34.55 E
Gez Gölü ◎	130	38.35 N	33.06 E
Gezihu ◎	120	38.10 N	90.42 E
Gföhl	61	48.31 N	15.30 E
Ghabāghib	132	33.10 N	36.13 E
Ghābat al-ʿArab	140	9.02 N	29.29 E
Ghadaf, Wādī al- V	132	31.46 N	36.50 E
Ghadāmis	146	30.08 N	9.30 E
Ghaddūwah	146	26.26 N	14.18 E
Ghafe	272c	19.05 N	73.07 E
Ghaggar ≃	123	29.30 N	74.53 E
Ghaghar Reservoir ◎[1]	124	24.38 N	83.11 E
Ghāghra ≃	124	25.47 N	84.37 E
Ghāgra	124	23.17 N	84.33 E
Ghairatganj	124	23.24 N	78.13 E
Ghakhar	123	32.18 N	74.09 E
Ghallah, Wādī al- V	140	10.25 N	27.32 E
Ghammāzah al-Kubrā	142	29.43 N	31.18 E
Ghamrīn	142	30.30 N	30.55 E
Ghana □[1], Afr.	134	8.00 N	1.00 W
Ghana □[1], Afr.	150	8.00 N	1.00 W
Ghansoli	272c	19.08 N	72.59 E
Ghanzi	156	21.38 S	21.45 E
Ghanzi □[5]	156	22.00 S	23.00 E
Ghārāpuri	272c	18.54 N	72.56 E
Gharaunda	124	29.33 N	76.58 E
Gharbah, Wādī V	142	29.40 N	31.58 E
Gharbi, Chott ◎	148	33.50 N	1.30 W
Gharbi, Oued el V	148	31.50 N	0.51 E
Gharbīyah, Aṣ-Ṣaḥrā' al- (Western Desert) ◆[2]	140	27.00 N	27.00 E
Ghardaïa	148	32.31 N	3.37 E
Ghardimaou	36	36.26 N	8.27 E
Gharghoda	124	22.10 N	83.21 E
Gharībwāl	123	32.41 N	73.10 E
Gharīfah	132	33.38 N	35.33 E
Gharig	140	10.47 N	27.33 E
Ghārīyat al-Gharbīyah	132	32.41 N	36.13 E
Ghārīyat ash-Sharqīyah	132	32.40 N	36.16 E
Gharo	120	24.44 N	67.35 E
Gharrāf, Shaṭṭ al- ≃	128	32.30 N	45.48 E
Gharroli ◆[8]	272a	28.37 N	77.20 E
Gharsa, Chott el ◎	148	34.06 N	7.50 E
Gharw, Jazīrat I	142	31.21 N	30.06 E
Gharyān	146	32.10 N	13.01 E
Ghaṣm	132	32.33 N	36.22 E
Ghāt	146	24.58 N	10.11 E
Ghātākhān	126	23.02 N	90.26 E
Ghātāl	126	22.40 N	87.43 E
Ghatampur	272b	22.54 N	88.10 E
Ghatere, Mount ʌ	175e	7.49 S	158.54 E
Ghātkopar ◆[8]	272c	19.05 N	72.54 E
Ghātprabha ≃	122	16.20 N	75.48 E
Ghātsīla	126	22.36 N	86.29 E
Ghats Occidentales → Western Ghāts ⋏	122	14.00 N	75.00 E
Ghats Orientales → Eastern Ghāts ⋏	122	14.00 N	78.50 E
Għawdex I	36	36.03 N	14.15 E
Ghawr ash-Sharqīyah, Qanāt al- ≍	132	32.41 N	35.38 E
Ghaylah ʌ[1]	132	33.11 N	37.05 E
Ghayl Bā Wazīr	144	14.48 N	49.21 E
Ghayth, Wādī V	132	30.59 N	36.00 E
Ghazāl, Baḥr al- ≃	140	9.31 N	30.25 E
Ghazal, Bahr el V	146	13.01 N	15.28 E
Ghazālat al-Khīs	142	30.34 N	31.34 E
Ghāziābād	123	28.40 N	77.26 E
Ghāzīpur, India	124	25.35 N	83.34 E
Ghazipur, India	272b	22.36 N	88.34 E
Ghāzīpur □[5]	124	25.40 N	83.20 E
Ghāzipur ◆[8]	272a	28.38 N	77.19 E
Ghazīr	130	34.01 N	35.40 E
Ghazlūna	120	31.24 N	67.49 E
Ghaznī	120	33.33 N	68.26 E
Ghaznī □[4]	120	33.00 N	68.00 E
Ghaznī ≃	120	32.35 N	67.58 E
Ghazni Khel	123	32.33 N	70.44 E
Ghazzah (Gaza), Ghaz.	132	31.30 N	34.28 E
Ghazzah, Lubnān	132	33.40 N	35.49 E
Gheā ≃	272b	22.52 N	88.19 E
Ghedi	64	45.24 N	10.16 E
Ghemme	62	45.37 N	8.25 E
Ghennes Heights	279b	40.09 N	79.56 W
Ghent → Gent, Bel.	50	51.03 N	3.43 E
Ghent, Ky., U.S.	218	38.44 N	85.03 W
Ghent, N.Y., U.S.	210	42.19 N	73.36 W
Ghent, Oh., U.S.	214	41.09 N	81.38 W
Gheora ◆[8]	272a	28.42 N	77.01 E
Gheorghe Gheorghiu-Dej	38	46.14 N	26.44 E

Symbols in the index entries represent the broad categories identified in the key at the right. Symbols with superior numbers (⋏[1]) identify subcategories (see complete key on page *I · 1)*.

Kartensymbole in dem Registerverzeichnis stellen die rechts in Schlüssel erklärten Kategorien dar. Symbole mit hochgestellten Ziffern (⋏[1]) bezeichnen Unterabteilungen einer Kategorie (vgl. vollständiger Schlüssel auf Seite *I · 1)*.

Los símbolos incluídos en el texto del índice representan las grandes categorias identificadas con la clave a la derecha. Los símbolos con numeros en su parte superior (⋏[1]) identifican las subcategorías (véase la clave completa en la página *I · 1)*.

Les symboles de l'index représentent les catégories indiquées dans la légende à droite. Les symboles suivis d'un indice (⋏[1]) représentent des sous-catégories (voir légende complète à la page *I · 1)*.

Os símbolos incluídos no texto do índice representam as grandes categorias identificadas com a chave à direita. Os símbolos com números em sua parte superior (⋏[1]) identificam as subcategorias (veja-se a chave completa à página *I · 1)*.

ʌ Mountain	Berg	Montaña	Montagne	Montanha
⋏ Mountains	Berge	Montañas	Montagnes	Montanhas
)(Pass	Pass	Paso	Col	Passo
V Valley, Canyon	Tal, Cañon	Valle, Cañón	Vallée, Canyon	Vale, Canhão
≚ Plain	Ebene	Llano	Plaine	Planície
› Cape	Kap	Cabo	Cap	Cabo
I Island	Insel	Isla	Île	Ilha
II Islands	Inseln	Islas	Îles	Ilhas
◆ Other Topographic Features	Andere Topographische Objekte	Otros Elementos Topográficos	Autres données topographiques	Outros acidentes topográficos

ESPAÑOL / FRANÇAIS / PORTUGUÊS

Nombre / Nom / Nome	Página / Page / Página	Lat.°′	Long.°′ W = Oeste / W = Ouest / W = Oeste
Gheorgheni	38	46.43 N	25.36 E
Gherla	38	47.02 N	23.55 E
Ghesar	272c	19.09 N	73.05 E
Ghigo	62	44.53 N	7.03 E
Ghilarza	71	40.07 N	8.50 E
Ghilizane	148	35.44 N	0.30 E
Ghīn, Tall ∧	132	32.39 N	36.43 E
Ghior	126	23.54 N	89.53 E
Ghislenghien	50	50.39 N	3.52 E
Ghisonaccia	36	42.00 N	9.25 E
Ghizar ≃	123	36.15 N	73.25 E
Ghizunabeana Islands II	175e	7.31 S	158.42 E
Ghlin	50	50.28 N	3.53 E
Ghlò, Beinn a ∧	46	56.50 N	3.43 W
Gholson	222	31.43 N	97.12 W
Ghonda ◆[8]	272a	28.41 N	77.16 E
Ghondi ◆[8]	272a	28.42 N	77.16 E
Ghorāsahan	124	26.50 N	85.08 E
Ghorāsāl	126	23.56 N	90.38 E
Ghoshpur, Bngl.	126	23.27 N	89.39 E
Ghoshpur, India	272b	22.23 N	88.29 E
Ghotki	120	28.01 N	69.19 E
Ghowr □[4]	128	34.00 N	65.00 E
Ghubaysh	140	12.09 N	27.21 E
Ghudāf, Wādī al- ∨	128	32.56 N	43.30 E
Ghulayfiqah	144	14.27 N	43.02 E
Ghunthur	130	34.23 N	37.09 E
Ghurāb, Jabal ∧[2]	142	28.58 N	31.16 E
Ghurayrah	144	18.37 N	42.41 E
Ghūrīān	128	34.21 N	61.30 E
Ghushuri	272b	22.37 N	88.22 E
Ghuwaybah, Wādī ∨	142	29.36 N	32.20 E
Ghuwayr, ʿAyn al- ⍑[4]	132	31.37 N	35.25 E
Ghuzzayil, Sabkhat ◎	146	29.50 N	19.35 E
Gia-dinh	110	10.48 N	106.42 E
Giaginskaja	78	44.53 N	40.05 E
Giang ≃	110	17.40 N	106.30 E
Giannutri, Isola di I	66	42.15 N	11.06 E
Giano, Monte ∧	66	42.25 N	13.06 E
Giano dell'Umbria	66	42.50 N	12.35 E
Giant City State Park ♠	194	37.39 N	89.12 W
Giant Mountain ∧	188	44.10 N	73.44 W
Giant's Castle ∧	158	29.21 S	29.27 E
Giant's Castle Game Reserve ◆[4]	158	29.16 S	29.30 E
Giant's Causeway ♠	44	55.14 N	6.30 W
Giants Neck	207	41.18 N	72.13 W
Giants Tomb Island I	212	44.55 N	80.00 W
Gianyar	115b	8.32 S	115.20 E
Gia-rai	110	9.14 N	105.28 E
Giardinello	70	38.05 N	13.09 E
Giardinetto	68	41.19 N	15.24 E
Giardini	70	37.50 N	15.17 E
Giarratana	70	37.03 N	14.48 E
Giarre	70	37.43 N	15.11 E
Giaveno	62	45.02 N	7.21 E
Giazza	64	45.39 N	11.07 E
Giba	71	39.04 N	8.38 E
Gibara	240p	21.07 N	76.08 W
Gibbon, Mn., U.S.	190	44.32 N	94.31 W
Gibbon, Ne., U.S.	198	40.44 N	98.50 W
Gibbons	182	53.50 N	113.20 W
Gibbonsville	202	45.33 N	113.55 W
Gibb River	164	15.39 S	126.38 E
Gibbs, Mount ∧	162	32.55 S	120.00 E
Gibbsboro	285	39.50 N	74.58 W
Gibbstown	208	39.49 N	75.17 W
Gibellina	70	37.47 N	12.58 E
Gibeon	156	25.09 S	17.43 E
Gibilmanna, Santuario di ⅴ[1]	70	37.59 N	14.02 E
Gibraleón	34	37.23 N	6.58 W
Gibraltar, Gib.	34	36.08 N	5.21 W
Gibraltar, Mi., U.S.	216	42.06 N	83.12 W
Gibraltar, Pa., U.S.	208	40.17 N	75.52 W
Gibraltar □[2], Europe	22	36.08 N	5.21 W
Gibraltar □[2], Europe	34	36.08 N	5.21 W
Gibraltar, Strait of (Estrecho de Gibraltar) ⋓	34	35.57 N	5.36 W
Gibraltar Point ≻, On., Can.	275b	43.36 N	79.23 W
Gibraltar Point ≻, Eng., U.K.	44	53.05 N	0.19 E
Gibsland	194	32.32 N	93.03 W
Gibson, Austl.	162	33.39 S	121.48 E
Gibson, Ga., U.S.	192	33.14 N	82.35 W
Gibson, N.Y., U.S.	210	42.08 N	76.59 W
Gibson, Pa., U.S.	210	41.44 N	75.38 W
Gibson ≃	212	44.58 N	79.51 W
Gibson, Lake ◎[1]	284a	43.06 N	79.14 W
Gibsonburg	214	41.23 N	83.19 W
Gibson City	216	40.27 N	88.22 W
Gibson Desert ◆[2]	162	24.30 S	126.00 E
Gibson Hill ∧[2]	214	41.51 N	80.10 W
Gibsonia, Fl., U.S.	220	28.06 N	81.58 W
Gibsonia, Pa., U.S.	214	40.38 N	79.59 W
Gibson Indian Reserve ◆[4]	212	45.01 N	79.44 W
Gibson Island I	208	39.05 N	76.26 W
Gibsons	182	49.24 N	123.30 W
Gibsonton	220	27.51 N	82.22 W
Gidajevo	24	59.57 N	52.22 E
Gidami	144	9.58 N	34.37 E
Gidda	144	9.34 N	35.23 E
Giddalūr	122	15.21 N	78.55 E
Giddarbāha	123	30.12 N	74.40 E
Giddings	222	30.10 N	96.56 W
Gideälven ≃	26	63.20 N	19.08 E
Gidea Park ◆[8]	260	51.35 N	0.12 E
Gideåvallen	26	63.29 N	18.58 E
Gideon	194	36.27 N	89.55 W
Gidgee	162	27.16 S	119.22 E
Gidgi, Lake ◎	162	29.16 S	126.03 E
Gidhni	126	22.29 N	86.51 E
Gidole	144	5.38 N	37.30 E
Gidrotorf	80	56.28 N	43.33 E
Gidžaki, gora ∧	84	40.25 N	49.01 E
Giebelstadt	56	49.39 N	9.56 E
Gieboldehausen	52	51.36 N	10.13 E
Giedraičiai	76	55.05 N	25.15 E
Gielow	54	53.42 N	12.44 E
Gielsdorf	264a	52.36 N	13.52 E
Gien	50	47.42 N	2.38 E
Giengen	56	48.37 N	10.14 E
Giens	62	43.02 N	6.08 E
Gier ≃	62	45.35 N	4.46 E
Gierath	263	51.07 N	6.33 E
Gierle	56	51.16 N	4.51 E
Giesebitz → Izbica	30	54.42 N	17.26 E
Gieselwerder	52	51.36 N	9.33 E
Giesenkirchen ◆[8]	263	51.09 N	6.30 E
Giesing ◆[8]	64	48.06 N	11.35 E
Giessbachfälle ∟	58	46.42 N	8.03 E
Giessen	56	50.35 N	8.40 E
Giessen □[5]	56	50.40 N	8.40 E
Gieten	52	53.00 N	6.46 E
Giethoorn	52	52.43 N	6.05 E
Gièvres	50	47.16 N	1.40 E
Giez	62	45.45 N	6.15 E
Giffone	68	38.27 N	16.10 E
Giffoni Valle Piana	68	40.44 N	14.56 E
Gifford, Scot., U.K.	46	55.54 N	2.45 W
Gifford, Fl., U.S.	220	27.40 N	80.24 W
Gifford, Il., U.S.	216	40.18 N	88.01 W
Gifford, In., U.S.	216	41.06 N	87.01 W
Gifford, Pa., U.S.	214	41.51 N	78.36 W
Gifford ≃	176	70.21 N	83.05 W
Gifford Creek	162	24.05 S	116.11 E
Gifford Pinchot State Park ♠	208	40.04 N	76.53 W
Giffre ≃	58	46.05 N	6.30 E
Gifhorn	52	52.29 N	10.33 E
Giflitz	56	51.09 N	9.07 E
Gif-sur-Yvette	261	48.42 N	2.08 E
Gifu	94	35.25 N	136.45 E
Gifu □[5]	94	35.45 N	137.00 E
Gigant	80	46.30 N	41.20 E
Giganta, Cerro ∧	232	26.07 N	111.36 W
Giganta, Sierra de la ⛰	232	25.30 N	111.15 W
Gigante	246	2.23 N	75.33 W
Gigante Islands II	116	11.36 N	123.20 E
Gigen	38	43.42 N	24.29 E
Gigena → Alcira	252	32.45 S	64.20 W
Giggleswick	44	54.04 N	2.17 W
Gigha, Sound of ⋓	46	55.41 N	5.42 W
Gigha Island I	46	55.41 N	5.46 W
Gig Harbor	224	47.19 N	122.34 W
Giglio, Isola del I	66	42.21 N	10.54 E
Giglio Castello	66	42.22 N	10.54 E
Gigliola	66	44.51 N	12.14 E
Giglio Porto	66	42.22 N	10.55 E
Gigmoto	116	13.47 N	124.23 E
Gignod	62	45.46 N	7.17 E
Gihu → Gifu	94	35.25 N	136.45 E
Gijón	34	43.32 N	5.40 W
Gikongoro	154	2.29 S	29.34 E
Gila ≃	200	32.43 N	114.33 W
Gila, Middle Fork ≃	200	33.14 N	108.14 W
Gila Bend	200	32.56 N	112.42 W
Gila Bend Indian Reservation ◆[4]	200	33.00 N	112.46 W
Gila Bend Mountains ⛰	200	33.10 N	113.10 W
Gila Cliff Dwellings National Monument ♠	200	33.02 N	108.16 W
Gila Mountains ⛰	200	33.05 N	109.50 W
Gīlān □[4]	128	37.15 N	49.30 E
Gīlān-e Gharb	128	34.08 N	45.55 E
Gila River Indian Reservation ◆[4]	200	33.12 N	112.00 W
Gilātala	126	22.36 N	89.41 E
Gilberdyke	44	53.45 N	0.44 W
Gilbert, La., U.S.	194	32.02 N	91.39 W
Gilbert, Mn., U.S.	190	47.29 N	92.27 W
Gilbert ≃, Austl.	166	16.35 S	141.15 E
Gilbert ≃, Austl.	168b	34.22 S	138.40 E
Gilbert, Mount ∧	182	50.51 N	124.20 W
Gilbert Airport ⊠	279a	41.22 N	81.58 W
Gilbert Island I	219	39.35 N	91.11 W
Gilbert Islands → Kiribati □[1]	14	5.00 S	170.00 W
Gilbert Islands II	14	0.30 S	174.00 E
Gilbert Lake ◎	281	42.34 N	83.17 W
Gilbert Lake State Park ♠	210	42.36 N	75.08 W
Gilberton	210	40.48 N	76.13 W
Gilbertown	194	31.52 N	88.19 W
Gilbert Peak ∧	224	46.30 N	121.25 W
Gilbert Plains	184	51.09 N	100.29 W
Gilbert River	166	18.09 S	142.52 E
Gilberts	216	42.06 N	88.23 W
Gilbert Seamount ✣[3]	16	52.50 N	150.10 W
Gilbertsville, N.Y., U.S.	210	42.28 N	75.19 W
Gilbertsville, Pa., U.S.	208	40.19 N	75.37 W
Gilbertville	207	42.18 N	72.12 W
Gilbjerg Hoved ≻	41	56.08 N	12.17 E
Gilboa	216	41.01 N	83.55 W
Gilboaʿ, Hare ⛰[2]	132	32.30 N	35.23 E
Gilbués	250	9.50 S	45.21 W
Gilching	60	48.07 N	11.17 E
Gildehaus	52	52.18 N	7.06 E
Gildford	202	48.34 N	110.17 W
Gilead	216	41.48 N	85.09 W
Giles, Arroyo de ≃	258	34.20 S	59.23 W
Giles Creek ≃	162	17.25 S	130.50 E
Giles Meteorological Station ⅴ[3]	162	25.02 S	128.18 E
Giles Point ≻	168b	35.03 S	137.45 E
Gilette	62	43.51 N	7.10 E
Gilford	48	54.23 N	6.22 W
Gilford Island I	182	50.45 N	126.25 W
Gilford Park	208	39.58 N	74.08 W
Gilgai	162	31.15 S	119.56 E
Gilgandra	166	31.42 S	148.39 E
Gilgil	154	0.30 S	36.19 E
Gil Gil Creek ≃	166	29.10 S	148.51 E
Gilgit	123	35.55 N	74.18 E
Gilgit □[8]	123	36.15 N	74.45 E
Gilgit ≃	123	35.44 N	74.38 E
Gilgit Wazārat □[8]	123	35.10 N	74.50 E
Gilgo Island I	276	40.38 N	73.25 W
Gilgo State Park ♠	276	40.38 N	73.22 W
Gilima	154	3.55 N	28.22 E
Gilimanuk	115a	8.10 S	114.26 E
Gilirang	112	3.55 S	120.09 E
Gil Island I	182	53.13 N	129.15 W
Gill, Lough ◎	48	54.16 N	8.24 W
Gillam	184	56.21 N	94.43 W
Gilleland Creek ≃	222	30.13 N	97.32 W
Gilleleje	41	56.07 N	12.19 E
Gillen, Lake ◎	162	26.11 S	124.38 E
Gilles, Lake ◎	166	32.50 S	136.45 E
Gillespie	219	39.07 N	89.49 W
Gillespie Point ≻	172	43.24 S	169.50 E
Gillett, Ar., U.S.	194	34.07 N	91.22 W
Gillett, Pa., U.S.	210	41.57 N	76.48 W
Gillett, Wi., U.S.	190	44.53 N	88.18 W
Gillette, N.J., U.S.	276	40.41 N	74.28 W
Gillette, Wy., U.S.	198	44.17 N	105.30 W
Gillette Castle State Park ♠	207	41.26 N	72.25 W
Gillian, Lake ◎	176	69.32 N	75.23 W
Gillingham, Eng., U.K.	42	51.02 N	2.17 W
Gillingham, Eng., U.K.	260	51.24 N	0.33 E
Gillingham □[8]	260	51.22 N	0.35 E
Gills Rock	190	45.17 N	87.01 W
Gilman, Ct., U.S.	207	41.34 N	72.11 W
Gilman, Il., U.S.	216	40.46 N	87.59 W
Gilman, Ia., U.S.	190	41.52 N	92.47 W
Gilman, Wi., U.S.	190	45.10 N	90.48 W
Gilman Hot Springs	228	33.50 N	116.59 W
Gilman Lake	285	39.41 N	75.11 W
Gilmer, Il., U.S.	278	42.14 N	88.02 W
Gilmer, Tx., U.S.	222	32.43 N	94.56 W
Gilmer Park	216	41.36 N	86.15 W
Gilmore	171b	35.20 S	148.11 E
Gilmore City	198	42.44 N	94.27 W
Gilmore Creek ≃	171b	35.18 S	148.13 E
Gilo ≃	144	8.10 N	33.15 E
Gilroy	226	37.00 N	121.34 W
Gilserberg	56	50.57 N	9.04 E
Gilsizer Slough ≃	226	38.58 N	121.44 W
Gilston Park ♠	260	51.48 N	0.04 E
Giltner	198	40.46 N	98.09 W
Gil'uj ≃	89	53.58 N	127.30 E
Giluwe, Mount ∧	164	6.05 S	143.50 E
Gilwern	42	51.51 N	3.06 W
Gilze	52	51.33 N	4.57 E
Gimån ≃	26	62.28 N	16.20 E
Gimbi	144	9.10 N	35.42 E
Gimcheon → Kimch'ŏn	98	36.07 N	128.05 E
Gimie, Mount ∧	241f	13.52 N	61.01 W
Gimigliano	68	38.58 N	16.32 E
Gimlet	218	38.13 N	83.09 W
Gimli	184	50.38 N	96.59 W
Gimo	40	60.11 N	18.11 E
Gimoly	24	63.03 N	32.19 E
Gimone ≃	32	44.00 N	1.06 E
Gimont	32	43.38 N	0.53 E
Gimpu	112	1.36 S	120.02 E
Ginderich	263	51.39 N	6.32 E
Ginebra → Genève	58	46.12 N	6.09 E
Gineste, Col de la)(	62	43.15 N	5.27 E
Gingell	216	42.43 N	83.17 W
Gingera, Mount ∧	171b	35.35 S	148.47 E
Ginger Hill	279b	40.12 N	80.00 W
Ginger Island I	240m	18.24 N	64.28 W
Gingin, Austl.	162	31.21 S	115.42 E
Gin Gin, Austl.	166	25.00 S	151.58 E
Gingindlovu	158	29.02 S	31.30 E
Gingoog	116	8.50 N	125.07 E
Gingoog Bay ⊂	116	8.59 N	125.05 E
Gingst	54	54.27 N	13.16 E
Ginir	144	7.07 N	40.46 E
Ginkakuji Temple ⅴ[1]	270	35.03 N	135.47 E
Ginkgo State Park ♠	202	46.59 N	120.01 W
Ginnosar	132	32.51 N	35.31 E
Ginosa	68	40.35 N	16.46 E
Ginostra	70	38.47 N	15.11 E
Ginowan	174m	26.17 N	127.46 E
Ginoza	174m	26.28 N	127.57 E
Ginter	214	40.46 N	78.23 W
Ginza ◆[8]	268	35.40 N	139.47 E
Ginzo de Limia	34	42.03 N	7.43 W
Gioi	68	40.17 N	15.13 E
Gioia, Golfo di ⊂	68	38.30 N	15.45 E
Gioia dei Marsi	66	41.57 N	13.42 E
Gioia del Colle	68	40.48 N	16.56 E
Gioia Tauro	68	38.26 N	15.54 E
Gioia Vecchio	66	41.54 N	13.44 E
Gioiosa Ionica	68	38.20 N	16.18 E
Gioiosa Marea	70	38.10 N	14.54 E
Giornico	58	46.24 N	8.52 E
Giovi, Passo dei)(	62	44.33 N	8.57 E
Giovinazzo	68	41.11 N	16.40 E
Giporlos	116	11.07 N	125.27 E
Gipping ≃	42	52.04 N	1.10 E
Gipsy	214	40.48 N	78.53 W
Giraglia, Île de la I	62	43.02 N	9.24 E
Giralia	162	22.41 S	114.21 E
Giraltovce	30	49.07 N	21.31 E
Girard, Il., U.S.	219	39.26 N	89.46 W
Girard, Ks., U.S.	198	37.30 N	94.50 W
Girard, Mi., U.S.	216	42.02 N	85.00 W
Girard, Oh., U.S.	214	41.09 N	80.42 W
Girard, Pa., U.S.	214	42.00 N	80.19 W
Girard, Tx., U.S.	196	33.22 N	100.40 W
Girardot	246	4.18 N	74.48 W
Girardville	208	40.47 N	76.17 W
Giraud, Pointe ≻	240d	15.19 N	61.15 W
Giraul ≃	152	15.04 S	12.08 E
Giraumont	56	49.10 N	5.55 E
Girbovu	38	44.44 N	23.21 E
Gird Gwalior □[5]	124	26.00 N	78.00 E
Girdletree	208	38.05 N	75.23 W
Giresun	130	40.55 N	38.24 E
Giresun □[4]	130	40.30 N	38.30 E
Girgarre	166	36.24 S	144.59 E
Girgaum ◆[8]	272c	18.57 N	72.48 E
Girgenti → Agrigento	70	37.18 N	13.35 E
Girgir, Cape ≻	164	3.50 S	144.34 E
Gīr Hills ⛰[2]	120	21.18 N	71.00 E
Giri ≃	152	0.28 N	17.59 E
Giridih	126	24.11 N	86.18 E
Girifalco	68	38.49 N	16.25 E
Girilambone	166	31.15 S	146.54 E
Girimira	130	37.07 N	41.26 E
Girna ≃	122	21.08 N	75.19 E
Giro, Nig.	150	11.06 N	4.46 E
Giro, Zaïre	154	3.08 N	29.15 E
Giromagny	58	47.45 N	6.50 E
Girón, Ec.	246	3.10 S	79.08 W
Giron, Fr.	58	46.14 N	5.46 E
Gironde □[5]	32	44.45 N	0.35 W
Gironde ⊂[1]	32	45.20 N	0.45 W
Gironville-sous-les-Côtes	56	48.48 N	5.40 E
Girou ≃	32	43.46 N	1.23 E
Girouxville	182	55.45 N	117.20 W
Girton	42	52.14 N	0.05 E
Girtys Run ≃	279b	40.28 N	79.58 W
Giru	166	19.31 S	147.06 E
Giruá	252	28.02 S	54.21 W
Girvan	44	55.15 N	4.51 W
Girvan, Water of ≃	44	55.15 N	4.51 W
Girvas	24	62.30 N	33.40 E
Girwa ≃	124	28.15 N	81.05 E
Gisborne, Austl.	169	37.29 S	144.35 E
Gisborne, N.Z.	172	38.40 S	178.01 E
Gisborne Lake ◎	186	47.48 N	54.50 W
Giscome	182	54.04 N	122.22 W
Gisenyi	154	1.42 S	29.15 E
Gishyita	154	2.11 S	29.18 E
Gislaved	26	57.18 N	13.32 E
Gislev	41	55.13 N	10.37 E
Gislinge	41	55.44 N	11.33 E
Gislövs läge	41	55.21 N	13.14 E
Gisors	50	49.17 N	1.47 E
Gissar	85	38.33 N	68.35 E
Gissarskij chrebet ⛰	85	39.00 N	68.40 E
Gisselfeld	41	55.18 N	11.59 E
Gissi	66	42.01 N	14.33 E
Gisslarbo	40	59.38 N	15.49 E
Gistel	50	51.10 N	2.57 E
Giswil	58	46.50 N	8.11 E
Gitambo	154	4.21 N	24.45 E
Gitarama	154	2.07 S	29.45 E
Gitega	154	3.26 S	29.56 E
Gittelde	52	51.48 N	10.10 E
Giuba, Isole II	144	0.45 S	42.19 E
Giudicarie, Valli ∨	64	45.58 N	10.45 E
Giugliano in Campania	68	40.56 N	14.12 E
Giuliana	70	37.40 N	13.14 E
Giulianova	66	42.45 N	13.57 E
Giulie, Alpi → Julian Alps ⛰	36	46.00 N	14.00 E
Giumbo → Jumboo	144	0.15 S	42.38 E
Giurgiu	38	43.53 N	25.57 E
Giussano	62	45.42 N	9.14 E
Givʿatayim	132	32.04 N	34.48 E
Givʿat Brenner	132	31.52 N	34.48 E
Give	41	55.51 N	9.15 E
Giverny	50	49.04 N	1.32 E
Givet	56	50.08 N	4.50 E
Givors	62	45.35 N	4.46 E
Givrine, Col de la)(	58	46.27 N	6.05 E
Givry	58	46.47 N	4.45 E
Givry-en-Argonne	56	48.57 N	4.53 E
Givry Island I	175c	7.07 N	151.53 E
Giyon	144	8.30 N	38.00 E
Giza → Al-Jīzah	142	30.01 N	31.13 E
Gīzāb	120	33.23 N	66.16 E
Giždvan	128	40.06 N	64.41 E
Gizen	140	10.49 N	34.48 E
Gizeux	50	47.24 N	0.12 E
Gižiga	74	62.03 N	160.30 E
Gižiginskaja guba ⊂	74	61.30 N	158.00 E
Gizo	175e	8.06 S	156.51 E
Gizo Island I	175e	8.04 S	156.48 E
Giżycko	30	54.03 N	21.47 E
Gizzeria	68	38.59 N	16.12 E
Gjedved	41	55.56 N	9.51 E
Gjern	41	56.14 N	9.45 E
Gjirokastër	38	40.05 N	20.10 E
Gjoa Haven	176	68.38 N	95.57 W
Gjøvik	26	60.48 N	10.42 E
Gjuesevo	38	42.14 N	22.28 E
Gjuhëzës, Kep i ≻	38	40.25 N	19.18 E
Glace Bay	186	46.12 N	59.57 W
Glacier, B.C., Can.	182	51.16 N	117.31 W
Glacier, Wa., U.S.	224	48.53 N	121.56 W
Glacier Bay ⊂	180	58.40 N	136.00 W
Glacier Bay National Park ♠	180	58.45 N	136.30 W
Glacier Hills	276	40.51 N	74.28 W
Glacier National Park ♠, B.C., Can.	182	51.15 N	117.35 W
Glacier National Park ♠, Mt., U.S.	202	48.35 N	113.40 W
Glacier Peak ∧	224	48.07 N	121.07 W
Glad'	76	59.07 N	32.06 E
Gl'ad'anskoje	86	54.54 N	65.06 E
Gladbach → Mönchengladbach	56	51.12 N	6.28 E
Gladbeck	52	51.34 N	6.59 E
Gladbrook	190	42.11 N	92.42 W
Gladden	279b	40.21 N	80.11 W
Gladden Heights	279b	40.22 N	80.15 W
Glade Creek ≃	202	45.54 N	119.42 W
Gladenbach	56	50.46 N	8.34 E
Glades □[6]	220	26.59 N	81.12 W
Glade Spring	192	36.47 N	81.46 W
Gladesville	274a	33.50 S	151.08 E
Gladewater	222	32.32 N	94.56 W
Gladewater, Lake ◎[1]	222	32.35 N	94.57 W
Gladkovka	78	46.23 N	32.36 E
Gladsakse	41	55.44 N	12.29 E
Gladstone, Austl.	166	23.51 S	151.16 E
Gladstone, Austl.	166	33.17 S	138.22 E
Gladstone, Mb., Can.	184	50.13 N	98.57 W
Gladstone, Mi., U.S.	190	45.51 N	87.01 W
Gladstone, Mo., U.S.	194	39.12 N	94.33 W
Gladstone, N.J., U.S.	210	40.43 N	74.39 W
Gladstone, Or., U.S.	224	45.22 N	122.35 W
Gladstone Brook ≃	276	40.43 N	74.40 W
Gladwin	190	43.58 N	84.29 W
Gladwyne	285	40.02 N	75.17 W
Gladys Lake ◎	180	59.55 N	132.55 W
Glænø I	41	55.12 N	11.28 E
Glafsfjorden ◎	26	59.34 N	12.37 E
Gláma ∧	24a	65.47 N	23.00 W
Glåma ≃	26	59.12 N	10.57 E
Glamis	46	56.36 N	3.00 W
Glamis Castle ⊥	46	56.37 N	3.00 W
Glamoč	36	44.03 N	16.51 E
Glamor Lake ◎	212	44.58 N	78.23 W
Glamsbjerg	41	55.16 N	10.07 E
Glan	116	5.49 N	125.10 E
Glan ◎	40	58.37 N	15.58 E
Glan ≃, B.R.D.	56	49.47 N	7.43 E
Glan ≃, Öst.	61	46.36 N	14.25 E
Glan ≃, Pil.	116	5.50 N	125.12 E
Glanamman	42	51.48 N	3.54 W
Gland	58	46.26 N	6.16 E
Gland ≃	50	49.55 N	4.05 E
Glandon, Col du)(	62	45.14 N	6.11 E
Glandorf, B.R.D.	52	52.05 N	7.59 E
Glandorf, Oh., U.S.	216	41.01 N	84.04 W
Glâne ≃	58	46.47 N	7.08 E
Glanegg	61	46.44 N	14.11 E
Glanerbrug	52	52.13 N	6.58 E
Glanmire	48	51.55 N	8.24 W
Glanshammar	40	59.19 N	15.24 E
Glanum ⊥	62	43.49 N	4.47 E
Glan-y-Don	262	53.19 N	3.15 W
Glaris → Glarus	58	47.02 N	9.04 E
Glarner Alpen ⛰	58	46.55 N	9.00 E
Glärnisch ⛰	58	47.00 N	9.00 E
Glarus	58	47.02 N	9.04 E
Glarus □[3]	58	47.00 N	9.03 E
Glascarnoch, Loch ◎	46	57.40 N	4.50 W
Glasco, Ks., U.S.	198	39.21 N	97.50 W
Glasco, N.Y., U.S.	210	42.02 N	73.56 W
Glasgow, Scot., U.K.	46	55.53 N	4.15 W
Glasgow, Il., U.S.	219	39.33 N	90.29 W
Glasgow, Ky., U.S.	194	36.59 N	85.54 W
Glasgow, Mo., U.S.	194	39.13 N	92.50 W
Glasgow, Mt., U.S.	202	48.11 N	106.38 W
Glasgow, Pa., U.S.	214	40.42 N	78.27 W
Glasgow, Va., U.S.	192	37.38 N	79.27 W
Glasgow (Abbotsinch) Airport ⊠	46	55.52 N	4.26 W
Glashütte, B.R.D.	52	53.41 N	10.02 E
Glashütte, D.D.R.	54	50.51 N	13.47 E
Glashütte ◆[8]	263	51.13 N	6.52 E
Glaslyn	184	53.21 N	108.22 W
Glaslyn ≃	42	52.56 N	4.06 W
Glas Maol ∧	46	56.52 N	3.22 W
Glasow	54	52.20 N	13.28 E
Glass, Loch ◎	46	57.43 N	4.30 W
Glassan	48	53.28 N	7.52 W
Glassboro	208	39.42 N	75.06 W
Glassboro State College ⅴ[2]	285	39.42 N	75.07 W
Glass House Mountains	171a	26.53 S	152.58 E
Glassmanor	284c	38.49 N	76.59 W
Glass Mountains ⛰	196	30.25 N	103.15 W
Glassport	214	40.19 N	79.53 W
Glastonbury, Eng., U.K.	42	51.06 N	2.43 W
Glastonbury, Ct., U.S.	207	41.42 N	72.36 W
Glatt ≃	58	47.34 N	8.28 E
Glatten	58	48.26 N	8.31 E
Glattfelden	58	47.33 N	8.30 E
Glatz → Kłodzko	30	50.27 N	16.39 E
Glaubitz	54	51.19 N	13.22 E
Glauchau	54	50.49 N	12.32 E
Glaven ≃	42	52.58 N	1.03 E
Glaze Brook ≃	262	53.25 N	2.27 W
Glazebury	262	53.28 N	2.30 W
Glaževo	76	59.41 N	32.05 E
Glazok	80	53.06 N	40.42 E
Glazov	80	58.09 N	52.40 E
Glazovo, S.S.S.R.	82	54.57 N	37.22 E
Glazovo, S.S.S.R.	82	54.47 N	37.34 E
Glazovo, S.S.S.R.	82	55.38 N	35.46 E
Glazunovka	76	52.30 N	36.19 E
Glazunovskaja	80	49.50 N	42.51 E
Gleason	194	36.12 N	88.36 W
Glebovka	78	46.38 N	39.59 E
Glebovo, S.S.S.R.	82	56.54 N	37.43 E
Glebovo, S.S.S.R.	82	56.39 N	38.42 E
Gleed	224	46.40 N	120.37 W
Glehn	263	51.10 N	6.35 E
Gleichen	182	50.52 N	113.03 W
Gleidingen	52	52.16 N	9.50 E
Gleinalpe ⛰	61	47.15 N	15.03 E
Gleisdorf	61	47.06 N	15.44 E
Gleiwitz → Gliwice	30	50.17 N	18.40 E
Glejbjerg	41	55.33 N	8.50 E
Glemsford	42	52.06 N	0.41 E
Glen ≃, Ire.	48	54.38 N	8.40 W
Glen ≃, Eng., U.K.	42	52.51 N	0.06 W
Glen Acres	285	39.58 N	75.34 W
Glen Afton	172	37.37 S	175.02 E
Glen Alice	170	33.02 S	150.13 E
Glen Allen	208	37.39 N	77.30 W
Glen Alpine	192	35.43 N	81.46 W
Glenamaddy	48	53.37 N	8.35 W
Glenamoy	48	54.14 N	9.42 W
Glenarchy	275b	43.29 N	79.46 W
Glenarden	208	38.56 N	76.52 W
Glenarm, N. Ire., U.K.	48	54.58 N	5.57 W
Glen Arm, Md., U.S.	284b	39.27 N	76.30 W
Glen Ashton Farms	285	40.06 N	74.55 W
Glen Aubrey	210	42.15 N	76.01 W
Glenavon, Sk., Can.	184	50.10 N	103.10 W
Glen Avon, S. Afr.	158	31.43 S	26.12 E
Glen Avon, Ca., U.S.	228	34.01 N	117.29 W
Glenavy, N.Z.	172	44.55 S	171.06 E
Glenavy, N. Ire., U.K.	48	54.36 N	6.13 W
Glenbeigh	48	52.02 N	9.58 W
Glenboro	184	49.32 N	99.15 W
Glenbrook	170	33.46 S	150.37 E
Glenbrook Heights	226	39.15 N	121.02 W
Glenburn, N.D., U.S.	198	48.30 N	101.13 W
Glenburn, Pa., U.S.	210	41.31 N	75.44 W
Glen Burnie	208	39.09 N	76.37 W
Glen Burnie Park	208	39.09 N	76.38 W
Glen Campbell	214	40.49 N	78.50 W
Glen Canyon ∨	200	37.10 N	110.50 W
Glen Canyon Dam ◆[6]	200	36.48 N	111.13 W
Glen Canyon National Recreation Area ♠	200	37.00 N	111.20 W
Glen Carbon	219	38.44 N	89.58 W
Glencoe, Austl.	166	37.42 S	140.37 E
Glencoe, On., Can.	214	42.45 N	81.43 W
Glencoe, S. Afr.	158	28.12 S	30.07 E
Glencoe, Al., U.S.	194	33.57 N	85.55 W
Glencoe, Il., U.S.	216	42.08 N	87.45 W
Glencoe, Ky., U.S.	218	38.42 N	84.49 W
Glencoe, Md., U.S.	208	39.32 N	76.38 W
Glencoe, Mn., U.S.	190	44.46 N	94.09 W
Glencolumbkille	48	54.43 N	8.45 W
Glencoul, Loch ⊂	46	58.14 N	4.58 W
Glencova	154	19.59 S	31.26 E
Glen Cove	210	40.51 N	73.38 W
Glendale, Az., U.S.	200	33.32 N	112.11 W
Glendale, Ca., U.S.	228	34.08 N	118.15 W
Glendale, Ma., U.S.	207	42.17 N	73.20 W
Glendale, Ms., U.S.	194	31.21 N	89.18 W
Glendale, Mo., U.S.	219	38.35 N	90.22 W
Glendale, Or., U.S.	202	42.44 N	123.25 W
Glendale, R.I., U.S.	207	41.58 N	71.37 W
Glendale, Tx., U.S.	222	31.01 N	95.18 W
Glendale, Ut,. U.S.	200	37.19 N	112.35 W
Glendale, Wi., U.S.	216	43.08 N	87.56 W
Glendale, Zimb.	154	17.21 S	31.04 E
Glendale Heights, Il., U.S.	278	41.54 N	88.04 W
Glendale Heights, Md., U.S.	284c	38.59 N	76.49 W
Glendale Lake ◎	214	40.41 N	78.32 W
Glendalough ⊥	48	53.01 N	6.26 W
Glen Davis	170	33.08 S	150.17 E
Glendive	198	47.06 N	104.42 W
Glendo	200	42.30 N	105.01 W
Glendoe Forest ◆[3]	46	57.06 N	4.37 W
Glendon, Ab., Can.	182	54.15 N	111.10 W
Glendon, Pa., U.S.	208	40.40 N	75.14 W
Glendora, Ca., U.S.	228	34.08 N	117.51 W
Glendora, N.J., U.S.	285	39.50 N	75.04 W
Glendo Reservoir ◎[1]	198	42.31 N	104.58 W
Glendo State Park ♠	198	42.33 N	104.58 W
Glendowan	48	54.58 N	7.57 W
Glen Eagle, Austl.	168a	32.17 S	116.11 E
Gleneagle, Austl.	171a	27.57 S	152.59 E
Glen Echo	284c	38.58 N	77.08 W
Glen Echo Amusement Park ♠	284c	38.58 N	77.08 W
Glen Echo Heights	284c	38.58 N	77.08 W
Gleneden Beach	202	44.53 N	124.02 W
Glen Elder	198	39.29 N	98.18 W
Glenelg, Austl.	168b	34.59 S	138.31 E
Glenelg, Scot., U.K.	46	57.13 N	5.38 W
Glenelg ≃	166	38.03 S	141.00 E
Glen Ellen	226	38.22 N	122.31 W
Glenelly ≃	48	54.44 N	7.18 W
Glen Ellyn	278	41.52 N	88.04 W
Glen Ellyn Countryside	278	41.55 N	88.04 W
Glenfarg	46	56.16 N	3.24 W
Glenfarne	48	54.17 N	7.59 W
Glenfield, Austl.	274a	33.58 S	150.54 E
Glenfield, Eng., U.K.	42	52.39 N	1.12 W
Glenfield, N.Y., U.S.	212	43.43 N	75.24 W
Glenfield, Pa., U.S.	279b	40.31 N	80.08 W
Glenfinnan	46	56.52 N	5.27 W
Glen Flora	222	29.21 N	96.12 W
Glen Florrie	162	22.55 S	115.59 E
Glenford	210	42.00 N	74.07 W
Glen Forest	168a	31.54 S	116.06 E
Glengallan Creek ≃	171a	28.09 S	151.53 E
Glen Gardner	210	40.41 N	74.56 W
Glengarriff	48	51.45 N	9.33 W
Glengarry Range ⛰	162	26.13 S	118.59 E
Glengyle	166	24.48 S	139.37 E
Glenham	210	41.31 N	73.55 W
Glenhaven	274a	33.42 S	151.00 E
Glen Head	276	40.50 N	73.37 W
Glen Hills	208	39.04 N	77.12 W
Glenhope	172	41.39 S	172.39 E
Glenhuntly	274b	37.54 S	145.03 E
Glen Innes	166	29.44 S	151.44 E
Glen Island I	276	40.53 N	73.47 W
Glen Lake	224	48.26 N	123.31 W
Glenluce	44	54.53 N	4.49 W
Glenluce Abbey ⅴ[1]	44	54.53 N	4.50 W
Glen Lyon	210	41.10 N	76.04 W
Glen Miller	212	44.08 N	77.35 W
Glen Mills	285	39.55 N	75.30 W
Glenmont, N.Y., U.S.	210	42.36 N	73.46 W
Glenmont, Oh., U.S.	214	40.31 N	82.06 W
Glenmoor	214	40.40 N	80.37 W
Glenmoore, Pa., U.S.	208	40.05 N	75.46 W
Glen Moore, Pa., U.S.	208	40.03 N	76.18 W
Glenmora	194	30.58 N	92.35 W
Glenmore	284b	39.11 N	76.36 W
Glenmorgan	166	27.15 S	149.41 E
Glenn, Ca., U.S.	226	39.31 N	122.01 W
Glenn, Mi., U.S.	216	42.31 N	86.13 W
Glenn □[6]	226	39.29 N	122.18 W
Glennallen	180	62.07 N	145.33 W
Glenn-Colusa Canal ≚	226	39.07 N	122.08 W
Glenn Dale	284c	38.59 N	76.49 W
Glenns Creek ≃	218	38.09 N	84.52 W
Glenns Ferry	202	42.57 N	115.18 W
Glenn Shoals, Lake ◎[1]	219	39.13 N	89.28 W
Glennville	192	31.56 N	81.55 W
Glen Oak	278	41.53 N	88.02 W
Glenolden	285	39.54 N	75.17 W
Glenoma	224	46.30 N	122.09 W
Glenorchy	172	44.51 S	168.23 E
Glenore Grove	171a	27.32 S	152.24 E
Glenorie	170	33.33 S	151.00 E
Glenormiston	166	22.55 S	138.48 E
Glen Park	212	44.00 N	75.57 W
Glenreagh	166	30.03 S	152.59 E
Glen Richey	214	40.57 N	78.29 W
Glen Riddle	285	39.54 N	75.26 W
Glenridge, Ma., U.S.	283	42.14 N	71.19 W
Glen Ridge, N.J., U.S.	276	40.48 N	74.12 W
Glen Robertson	206	45.21 N	74.30 W
Glen Rock, N.J., U.S.	276	40.57 N	74.08 W
Glen Rock, Pa., U.S.	208	39.47 N	76.43 W
Glenrock, Wy., U.S.	200	42.52 N	105.52 W
Glen Rose	222	32.14 N	97.45 W
Glen Ross	212	44.16 N	77.36 W
Glenrothes	46	56.12 N	3.10 W
Glenroy, Austl.	162	21.46 S	114.49 E
Glenroy, Austl.	162	17.22 S	126.06 E
Glenroy, Austl.	274b	37.42 S	144.55 E
Glenroy ≃	172	42.00 S	172.20 E
Glens Falls	210	43.18 N	73.38 W
Glenshaw	214	40.31 N	79.58 W
Glenshee ∨	46	56.48 N	3.30 W
Glenside, S. Afr.	158	29.25 S	30.47 E
Glenside, N.J., U.S.	208	39.40 N	75.29 W
Glenside, Pa., U.S.	208	40.06 N	75.09 W
Glen Spey	210	41.29 N	74.49 W
Glen Stewart Park ♠	275b	43.41 N	79.18 W
Glenties	48	54.47 N	8.17 W
Glen Ullin	198	46.48 N	101.49 W
Glenview	216	42.04 N	87.47 W
Glenview Countryside	278	42.04 N	87.50 W
Glenview Naval Air Station ■	216	42.05 N	87.50 W
Glenville, Ire.	48	52.03 N	8.26 W
Glenville, Mn., U.S.	190	43.34 N	93.16 W
Glenville, N.Y., U.S.	276	41.04 N	73.50 W
Glenville, W.V., U.S.	188	38.56 N	80.50 W
Glenvista	273d	26.17 S	28.13 E
Glen Waverley	274b	37.53 S	145.10 E
Glen White	192	37.43 N	81.16 W
Glen Wild	210	41.29 N	74.49 W
Glen Wild Lake ◎	276	41.02 N	74.20 W
Glenwillard	214	40.34 N	80.13 W
Glen Williams	212	43.40 N	79.55 W
Glenwillow	214	41.22 N	81.28 W
Glenwood, Ab., Can.	182	49.22 N	113.31 W
Glenwood, Nf., Can.	186	48.59 N	54.52 W
Glenwood, Al., U.S.	194	31.39 N	86.10 W
Glenwood, Ar., U.S.	194	34.19 N	93.33 W
Glenwood, Ga., U.S.	192	32.10 N	82.40 W
Glenwood, Il., U.S.	278	41.32 N	87.36 W
Glenwood, In., U.S.	218	39.37 N	85.18 W
Glenwood, Ia., U.S.	198	41.02 N	95.44 W
Glenwood, Mn., U.S.	198	45.39 N	95.23 W
Glenwood, N.J., U.S.	210	41.15 N	74.29 W
Glenwood, N.M., U.S.	200	33.19 N	108.52 W
Glenwood, N.Y., U.S.	210	42.37 N	78.39 W
Glenwood, Or., U.S.	224	45.38 N	123.16 W
Glenwood, Tx., U.S.	222	32.39 N	94.51 W
Glenwood, Ut,. U.S.	200	38.45 N	111.59 W
Glenwood, Va., U.S.	192	36.35 N	79.21 W
Glenwood, Wa., U.S.	224	46.01 N	121.17 W
Glenwood City	190	45.03 N	92.10 W
Glenwood Landing	276	40.50 N	73.39 W
Glenwood Park	284c	38.58 N	76.50 W
Glenwood Springs	200	39.33 N	107.19 W
Gleschendorf	54	54.02 N	10.40 E
Glesien	54	51.27 N	12.13 E
Gletsch	58	46.34 N	8.22 E
Glew	258	34.53 S	58.23 W
Glidden, Ia., U.S.	198	42.03 N	94.43 W
Glidden, Tx., U.S.	222	29.42 N	96.35 W
Glidden, Wi., U.S.	190	46.08 N	90.34 W
Glide	202	43.18 N	123.06 W
Gliener Berg ∧[2]	264a	52.42 N	13.00 E
Glienicke, D.D.R.	54	52.13 N	14.05 E
Glienicke, D.D.R.	54	52.37 N	13.19 E
Glífa	38	38.57 N	22.58 E
Glifádha	267c	37.52 N	23.45 E
Glimåkra	26	56.18 N	14.08 E
Glimmingehus	26	55.30 N	14.13 E
Glin	48	52.34 N	9.17 W
Glina	36	45.20 N	16.06 E
Glina ≃	36	45.26 N	16.07 E
Glin'any	78	49.49 N	24.30 E
Glinde	52	53.32 N	10.13 E
Glindow	54	52.21 N	12.54 E
Glindowsee ◎	264a	52.21 N	12.56 E
Glinka	76	54.39 N	32.52 E
Glinkovo	85	42.55 N	69.40 E
Glittertinden ∧	26	61.39 N	8.33 E
Gliwice (Gleiwitz)	30	50.17 N	18.40 E
G. L. Martin State Airport ⊠	284b	39.20 N	76.25 W
Globe, Az., U.S.	200	33.23 N	110.47 W
Globe, Ky., U.S.	218	38.17 N	83.14 W
Globino	78	49.23 N	33.17 E
Glod'any	78	47.47 N	27.31 E
Glodeanu-Siliştea	38	44.50 N	26.48 E
Glodok ◆[8]	269e	6.08 S	106.48 E
Glogau → Głogów	30	51.40 N	16.05 E
Gloggnitz	61	47.40 N	15.57 E
Glogn ≃	58	46.46 N	9.12 E
Głogów, Pol.	30	51.40 N	16.05 E
Głogów, Pol.	30	50.10 N	21.58 E
Głogówek	30	50.22 N	17.51 E
Glommersträsk	26	65.16 N	19.38 E
Glonn	64	47.59 N	11.52 E
Glonn ≃	60	48.26 N	11.36 E
Glorenza (Glurns)	64	46.40 N	10.33 E
Glória	250	9.11 S	38.18 W
Gloria, Bahía de la ⊂	240p	21.50 N	77.40 W
Glória de Dourados	255	22.21 S	54.13 W
Gloria Glens Park	214	41.03 N	81.54 W
Glorieta	200	35.34 N	105.46 W
Glorieuses, Îles II	138	11.30 S	47.20 E
Glörstausee ◎[1]	263	51.14 N	7.29 E
Glos-la-Ferrière	50	48.51 N	0.36 E
Glossop	262	53.27 N	1.57 W
Glossopteris, Mount ∧	9	84.44 S	113.51 W
Gloster	194	31.11 N	91.01 W
Glostrup	41	55.40 N	12.24 E
Glotovka	80	53.57 N	46.42 E
Glotovo	24	63.30 N	49.23 E
Gloucester, Austl.	166	31.59 S	151.58 E
Gloucester, On., Can.	212	45.22 N	75.35 W
Gloucester, Eng., U.K.	42	51.53 N	2.14 W
Gloucester, Ma., U.S.	207	42.36 N	70.39 W
Gloucester, Va., U.S.	208	37.24 N	76.31 W
Gloucester □[6], N.J., U.S.	208	39.50 N	75.10 W
Gloucester □[6], Va., U.S.	208	37.25 N	76.30 W
Gloucester, Cape ≻	164	5.27 S	148.25 E
Gloucester, Vale of ∨	42	51.55 N	2.10 W
Gloucester City	285	39.53 N	75.07 W
Gloucester Fisherman ⊥	283	42.36 N	70.40 W
Gloucester Harbor ⊂	207	42.36 N	70.40 W
Gloucester Island I	166	20.01 S	148.27 E
Gloucester Point	208	37.15 N	76.29 W
Gloucester Pool ◎	212	44.51 N	79.43 W
Gloucestershire □[6]	42	51.47 N	2.15 W
Glouster	188	39.30 N	82.05 W
Glover-Archbold Park ♠	284c	38.55 N	77.05 W
Glover Creek ≃	194	34.02 N	94.56 W
Glover Island I	186	48.44 N	57.45 W
Glovers Reef ✣[2]	232	16.49 N	87.48 W
Gloversville	210	43.03 N	74.20 W
Glovertown	186	48.41 N	54.02 W
Glowe	54	54.35 N	13.28 E
Glöwen	54	52.55 N	12.05 E
Głowno	30	51.58 N	19.44 E
Głubczyce	30	50.13 N	17.49 E
Glubokij, S.S.S.R.	78	48.31 N	40.19 E
Glubokij, S.S.S.R.	80	47.01 N	42.47 E
Glubokij, S.S.S.R.	89	52.53 N	129.44 E
Glubokoje, S.S.S.R.	76	55.08 N	27.41 E
Glubokoje, S.S.S.R.	82	54.32 N	38.32 E
Glubokoje, S.S.S.R.	86	50.06 N	82.19 E
Głuchołazy	30	50.20 N	17.22 E
Gluchov	78	51.41 N	33.53 E
Gluchovo	265b	55.46 N	37.16 E
Glückauf-Kampfbahn ♠	263	51.32 N	7.05 E
Glücksburg	41	54.50 N	9.33 E
Glückstadt, B.R.D.	52	53.47 N	9.25 E
Gluckstadt, S. Afr.	158	27.57 S	31.02 E
Glucomanka, gora ∧	89	45.10 N	135.48 E
Glud	41	55.49 N	10.00 E
Glumslöv	41	55.56 N	12.48 E
Glumsø	41	55.21 N	11.42 E
Gluša	76	53.05 N	28.52 E
Glusburn	44	53.54 N	1.59 W
Glusk	76	52.54 N	28.41 E
Gluškeviči	78	51.34 N	27.47 E
Gluškovo	78	51.22 N	34.38 E
Glybokaja	78	48.07 N	25.56 E
Glyde ≃, Austl.	164	12.15 S	135.03 E
Glyde ≃, Ire.	48	53.52 N	6.21 W
Glyder Fawr ∧	42	53.06 N	4.01 W
Glyme ≃	42	51.49 N	1.22 W
Glyndebourne	50	50.52 N	0.04 E
Glyndon, Md., U.S.	208	39.28 N	76.48 W
Glyndon, Mn., U.S.	198	46.52 N	96.34 W
Glyngøre	26	56.46 N	8.52 E
Glyn-Neath	42	51.46 N	3.38 W
Gmelinka	80	50.24 N	46.54 E
Gmünd, Öst.	61	48.47 N	15.00 E
Gmünd, Öst.	64	46.54 N	13.32 E
Gmund am Tegernsee	64	47.45 N	11.44 E
Gmunden	64	47.55 N	13.48 E
Gnadenhutten	214	40.21 N	81.26 W
Gnadenhutten Monument ⊥	214	40.21 N	81.25 W
Gnalta	166	31.03 S	142.20 E
Gnaraloo	162	23.51 S	113.31 E
Gnarp	26	62.03 N	17.16 E
Gnarpurt, Lake ◎	169	38.03 S	143.24 E
Gnarrenburg	52	53.22 N	9.00 E
Gnaw Bone	218	39.12 N	86.09 W
Gnesen → Gniezno	30	52.31 N	17.37 E
Gnesta	40	59.03 N	17.18 E
Gnezdovo	76	54.47 N	31.47 E

≃ River	Fluss	Río	Rivière	Rio	
≚ Canal	Kanal	Canal	Canal	Canal	
∟ Waterfall, Rapids	Wasserfall, Stromschnellen	Cascada, Rápidos	Chute d'eau, Rapides	Cascata, Rápidos	
⋓ Strait	Meeresstrasse	Estrecho	Détroit	Estreito	
⊂ Bay, Gulf	Bucht, Golf	Bahía, Golfo	Baie, Golfe	Baía, Golfo	
◎ Lake, Lakes	See, Seen	Lago, Lagos	Lac, Lacs	Lago, Lagos	
≡ Swamp	Sumpf	Pantano	Marais	Pântano	
⍓ Ice Features, Glacier	Eis- und Gletscherformen	Accidentes Glaciales	Formes glaciaires	Acidentes glaciares	
⍑ Other Hydrographic Features	Andere Hydrographische Objekte	Otros Elementos Hidrográficos	Autres données hydrographiques	Outros acidentes hidrográficos	

✣ Submarine Features	Untermeerische Objekte	Accidentes Submarinos	Formes de relief sous-marin	Acidentes submarinos
□ Political Unit	Politische Einheit	Unidad Politica	Entité politique	Unidade política
ⅴ Cultural Institution	Kulturelle Institution	Institución Cultural	Institution culturelle	Institução cultural
⊥ Historical Site	Historische Stätte	Sitio Histórico	Site historique	Sitio histórico
♠ Recreational Site	Erholungs- und Ferienort	Sitio de Recreo	Centre de loisirs	Area de Lazer
⊠ Airport	Flughafen	Aeropuerto	Aéroport	Aeroporto
■ Military Installation	Militäranlage	Instalación Militar	Installation militaire	Instalação militar
◆ Miscellaneous	Verschiedenes	Misceláneo	Divers	Diversos

ENGLISH

Name	Page	Lat.°′	Long.°′
Gniben >	41	56.01 N	11.18 E
Gniew	30	53.51 N	18.49 E
Gniewkowo	30	52.54 N	18.25 E
Gniezno	30	52.31 N	17.37 E
Gnilaja Lipa ≃	78	49.07 N	24.44 E
Gnilec	76	52.22 N	36.01 E
Gniloj Jelanec ≃	78	47.20 N	31.44 E
Gniloj Tikič ≃	78	48.47 N	30.53 E
Gnivan'	78	49.06 N	28.20 E
Gnjilane	38	42.28 N	21.29 E
Gnoien	54	53.58 N	12.42 E
Gnosall	42	52.47 N	2.15 W
Gnosjö	26	57.22 N	13.44 E
Gnowangerup	162	33.56 S	117.59 E
Gō ≃	96	35.02 N	132.13 E
Goa	116	13.42 N	123.29 E
Goa □[8]	122	14.20 N	74.00 E
Goageb	156	26.44 S	17.15 E
Goalen Head >	166	36.40 S	150.05 E
Goāliar ≃	126	24.07 N	90.18 E
Goālpāra	124	26.11 N	90.37 E
Goāltor	126	22.43 N	87.10 E
Goalundo Ghāt	126	23.43 N	89.46 E
Goan	150	13.14 N	5.09 W
Goascorán	236	13.36 N	87.45 W
Goascorán ≃	236	13.25 N	87.48 W
Goat Fell ∧	46	55.38 N	5.12 W
Goathland	44	54.23 N	0.44 W
Goat Island I	284a	43.05 N	79.04 W
Goat Mountain ∧	202	47.21 N	113.21 W
Goat Peak ∧	224	46.56 N	121.16 W
Goba, Ityo.	144	7.02 N	40.00 E
Goba, Moç.	156	26.12 S	32.08 E
Gobabis	156	22.30 S	18.58 E
Gobabis □[5]	156	22.30 S	19.00 E
Gobai ≃	126	23.37 N	86.28 E
Gobardānga	126	22.53 N	88.45 E
Göbel	130	40.00 N	28.09 E
Gobernador Andonaegui	258	34.10 S	59.19 W
Gobernador Costa	254	44.04 S	70.35 W
Gobernador Gregores	254	48.46 S	70.15 W
Gobernador Ingeniero Valentín Virasoro	252	28.03 S	56.02 W
Gobernador Juan E. Martínez	252	28.55 S	58.56 W
Gobernador Monteverde	288	34.48 S	58.16 W
Gobernador Racedo	252	31.34 S	60.04 W
Gobernador Udaondo	258	35.18 S	58.36 W
Gobi ◆[2]	102	43.00 N	105.00 E
Gobindapur, India	126	23.16 N	87.58 E
Gobindapur, India	272b	22.23 N	88.25 E
Gobindapur, India	272b	22.55 N	88.12 E
Gobindgarh	123	30.41 N	76.18 E
Gobindpur	126	23.50 N	86.31 E
Göblberg ∧	60	48.06 N	13.32 E
Gobles	216	42.21 N	85.52 W
Gobō	96	33.53 N	135.10 E
Gobowen	42	52.53 N	3.02 W
Gobra	126	23.45 N	89.12 E
Gobur	154	4.20 N	31.04 E
Gobustan	84	40.06 N	49.24 E
Gobza ≃	76	55.16 N	31.31 E
Göçbeyli	130	39.13 N	27.25 E
Goceano, Catena del ⋏	71	40.28 N	9.02 E
Goce Delčev	38	41.34 N	23.44 E
Goch	52	51.41 N	6.10 E
Gochas	156	24.55 S	18.55 E
Gochsheim	56	50.01 N	10.16 E
Go-cong	269c	10.50 N	106.50 E
Göcsej ⋏[2]	61	46.43 N	16.42 E
Goðafoss ∟	24a	65.40 N	17.30 W
Godāgāri	124	24.28 N	88.20 E
Godalming	42	51.11 N	0.37 W
Godalo	144	4.28 N	43.24 E
Godar	128	28.10 N	63.14 E
Godāvari ≃	122	17.00 N	81.45 E
Godāvari, Mouths of the ≃[1]	122	16.25 N	82.00 E
Godbout	186	49.19 N	67.37 W
Godbout ≃	186	49.19 N	67.36 W
Godda	124	24.50 N	87.13 E
Goddard	218	38.22 N	83.37 W
Goddard Space Flight Center ⊌	284c	39.00 N	76.52 W
Godeffroy	210	41.27 N	74.37 W
Godega di Sant'Urbano	64	45.56 N	12.24 E
Godegård	40	58.44 N	15.09 E
Godelheim	52	51.44 N	9.22 E
Gödene	130	36.34 N	30.21 E
Godere	144	5.05 N	43.50 E
Goderich	190	43.45 N	81.43 W
Goderville	50	49.39 N	0.22 E
Godfrey	219	38.57 N	90.11 W
Godhavn	176	69.15 N	53.33 W
Godhra	120	22.45 N	73.38 E
Godinlabe	144	5.54 N	46.38 E
Godinne	56	50.21 N	4.52 E
Godley	222	32.27 N	97.32 W
Godmanchester	42	52.19 N	0.11 W
Godo, Indon.	115b	8.33 S	118.40 E
Gōdo, Nihon	94	35.25 N	136.36 E
Gōdo, Nihon	268	35.51 N	139.44 E
Gödöllő	264c	47.36 N	19.22 E
Gödöllői Dombvidék ⋏[2]	264c	47.37 N	19.16 E
Godong	115a	7.02 S	110.46 E
Godoy Cruz	252	32.55 S	68.50 W
Godramstein	56	49.12 N	8.05 E
Godrano	70	37.54 N	13.26 E
Gods ≃	184	56.22 N	92.51 W
Godshill	42	50.38 N	1.14 W
Godshorn	52	52.26 N	9.43 E
Gods Lake	184	54.40 N	94.09 W
Gods Lake ⊜	184	54.40 N	94.20 W
Gods Mercy, Bay of ⊂	176	63.30 N	86.10 W
Godstone	260	51.15 N	0.04 W
Godthåb	176	64.11 N	51.44 W
Goduncovo	82	56.29 N	39.02 E
Godwin Austen → K2 ∧	123	35.53 N	76.30 E
Goéland, Lac au ⊜	176	49.47 N	76.48 W
Goélands, Lac aux ⊜	176	55.27 N	64.17 W
Goeree I	52	51.50 N	3.55 E
Goes	52	51.30 N	3.54 E
Goetzenbruck	56	48.59 N	7.23 E
Goff, Som.	144	2.39 N	41.00 E
Goff, Ks., U.S.	198	39.39 N	95.55 W
Goff Creek ≃	196	36.43 N	101.29 W
Goffle Brook ≃	276	40.56 N	74.08 W
Goff's Oak	260	51.43 N	0.05 W
Goffstown	188	43.01 N	71.36 W
Gogama	190	47.40 N	81.43 W
Gogebic, Lake ⊜	190	46.30 N	89.35 W
Gogebic Range ⋏[2]	190	46.30 N	90.10 W
Göggingen	58	48.20 N	10.52 E
Gogha	120	21.41 N	72.17 E
Gogland, ostrov I	76	60.04 N	27.00 E
Goglio	58	46.18 N	8.16 E
Gogoi	156	20.17 S	33.08 E
Gogolevo	78	49.56 N	33.48 E
Gogonou	150	10.50 N	2.50 E
Gogo-shima I	96	33.54 N	132.41 E
Gogrial	140	8.32 N	28.07 E
Gohad	124	26.26 N	78.27 E
Gohāla	126	23.15 N	89.59 E
Gohāla ≃	126	24.08 N	89.35 E
Gohāna	124	29.08 N	76.42 E
Gohfeld	52	52.12 N	8.45 E
Gohitafla	150	7.30 N	5.53 W
Göhl	54	54.17 N	10.56 E
Gohoku	96	33.39 N	133.21 E
Go Home Lake ⊜	212	45.00 N	79.51 W
Gohpur	120	26.53 N	93.38 E
Gohr	263	51.06 N	6.43 E
Göhrde	54	53.08 N	10.52 E
Göhren	54	54.20 N	13.44 E
Goiana, Bra.	250	7.33 S	34.59 W
Goianá, Bra.	256	21.32 S	43.12 W
Goianápolis	255	16.30 S	49.01 W
Goiandira	255	18.08 S	48.06 W
Goianésia	255	15.18 S	49.07 W
Goiânia	255	16.40 S	49.16 W
Goianinha	250	6.16 S	35.12 W
Goianira	255	16.30 S	49.26 W
Goianorte	250	8.35 S	48.56 W
Goiás	255	15.56 S	50.08 W
Goiás □[3]	255	15.00 S	49.00 W
Goiatuba	255	18.01 S	49.22 W
Goichran	120	31.04 N	78.07 E
Goil, Loch ⊂	46	56.08 N	4.52 W
Goio-Erê	252	24.12 S	53.01 W
Goio-Erê ≃	252	24.14 S	53.21 W
Goirle	52	51.32 N	5.04 E
Góis, Bra.	256	22.33 S	46.18 W
Góis, Port.	34	40.09 N	8.07 W
Goito	64	45.15 N	10.40 E
Gojam □[4]	144	11.00 N	37.00 E
Gojeb ≃	144	7.20 N	37.21 E
Gojō	96	34.21 N	135.42 E
Gojōme	92	39.56 N	140.07 E
Gojra	123	31.09 N	72.41 E
Gojtchskij, pereval)(	84	44.18 N	39.18 E
Gokāk	122	16.10 N	74.50 E
Gokarna	126	24.03 N	88.07 E
Gokase ≃	92	32.35 N	131.42 E
Gökçe	130	40.11 N	25.55 E
Gökçeada I	130	40.10 N	25.50 E
Gökçen	130	38.07 N	27.53 E
Gökdere, Tür.	130	38.44 N	40.13 E
Gökdere, Tür.	130	40.29 N	36.47 E
Gōkōmutsumi	268	35.48 N	139.59 E
Göksholm	40	59.16 N	15.33 E
Göksu ≃, Tür.	84	39.19 N	42.17 E
Göksu ≃, Tür.	130	36.20 N	34.05 E
Göksu ≃, Tür.	130	37.37 N	35.35 E
Göksu Deresi ≃	267b	41.06 N	29.03 E
Göksun	130	38.03 N	36.30 E
Göktepe	130	37.15 N	28.36 E
Gök Tepe ∧	130	36.53 N	29.17 E
Gokwe	154	18.07 S	28.58 E
Gol	26	60.42 N	8.57 E
Gol, Khawr V	140	6.55 N	30.16 E
Golabāri	272b	22.36 N	88.20 E
Golāghāt	120	26.31 N	93.58 E
Gola Gokaran Nath	124	28.05 N	80.28 E
Gola Island I	48	55.05 N	8.22 W
Golaja Pristan'	78	46.31 N	32.31 E
Gołańcz	30	52.57 N	17.18 E
Golan Heights ⊥[4]	132	32.55 N	35.42 E
Golāshkerd	128	27.59 N	57.16 E
Golbaf	128	29.51 N	57.44 E
Gölbası, Tür.	130	37.50 N	37.40 E
Gölbaşı, Tür.	130	39.48 N	32.49 E
Golborne	262	53.29 N	2.36 W
Golcar	262	53.39 N	1.51 W
Gol'čicha	74	71.43 N	83.36 E
Golconda, Il., U.S.	194	37.22 N	88.29 W
Golconda, Nv., U.S.	204	40.57 N	117.29 W
Gölcuk, Tür.	130	39.18 N	27.59 E
Gölcük, Tür.	130	40.44 N	29.48 E
Golczewo	54	53.49 N	14.59 E
Gołdap	30	54.19 N	22.19 E
Goldau	58	47.03 N	8.33 E
Gold Bar	224	47.51 N	121.41 W
Gold Beach	202	42.24 N	124.25 W
Goldbeck	54	52.43 N	11.52 E
Goldberg, D.D.R.	54	53.35 N	12.05 E
Goldberg → Złotoryja, Pol.	30	51.08 N	15.55 E
Goldberger See ⊜	54	53.36 N	12.07 E
Goldbergtunnel ◆[5]	263	51.01 N	7.28 E
Goldbey	58	48.12 N	6.26 E
Goldboro	186	45.11 N	61.39 W
Gold Bridge	182	50.51 N	122.50 W
Gold Coast → Southport	171a	27.58 S	153.25 E
Gold Coast ⊥[2]	150	5.20 N	0.45 W
Gold Creek	180	62.46 N	149.41 W
Gold Creek ≃	182	49.04 N	115.12 W
Golden, B.C., Can.	182	51.18 N	116.58 W
Golden, Ire.	48	52.29 N	7.58 W
Golden, Co., U.S.	200	39.45 N	105.13 W
Golden, Il., U.S.	219	40.07 N	91.01 W
Golden Bay ⊂	172	40.40 S	172.50 E
Golden Beach	220	25.57 N	80.07 W
Golden Brook ≃	283	42.44 N	71.19 W
Golden City	194	37.23 N	94.05 W
Goldendale	224	45.49 N	120.49 W
Golden Ears Provincial Park ♠	182	49.30 N	122.25 W
Goldene Aue V	54	51.25 N	11.00 E
Golden Gate	220	26.09 N	81.43 W
Golden Gate ⋓	226	37.49 N	122.29 W
Golden Gate Bridge ◆[5]	282	37.49 N	122.28 W
Golden Gate Fields Race Track ♠	282	37.53 N	122.19 W
Golden Gate Highlands National Park ♠	158	28.30 S	28.40 E
Golden Gate National Recreation Area ♠	282	37.49 N	122.31 W
Golden Gate Park ♠	282	37.46 N	122.28 W
Golden Green	260	51.12 N	0.21 E
Golden Hill Creek ≃	210	43.22 N	78.28 W
Golden Hinde ∧	182	49.40 N	125.45 W
Golden Horn → Haliç ⊂	267b	41.02 N	28.58 E
Golden Lake ⊜	190	45.35 N	77.20 W
Golden Meadow	194	29.22 N	90.15 W
Golden Prairie	184	50.14 N	109.38 W
Golden Ring Mall ◆[9]	284b	39.20 N	76.29 W
Golden Rock	122	10.48 N	78.44 E
Goldenrod	220	28.37 N	81.18 W
Golden Spike National Historic Site ♠	202	41.38 N	112.35 W
Goldenstedt	52	52.48 N	8.25 E
Golden Valley V	42	52.00 N	2.56 W
Golders Green ◆[8]	260	51.35 N	0.12 W
Goldfield, Ia., U.S.	190	42.44 N	93.55 W
Goldfield, Nv., U.S.	204	37.42 N	117.14 W
Gold Lake ⊜	212	44.43 N	78.17 W
Goldlauter	54	50.38 N	10.44 E
Gold Mountain ∧	204	37.15 N	117.18 W
Goldney	258	34.37 S	59.18 W
Goldonna	194	32.01 N	92.54 W
Goldpan Peak ∧	180	61.12 N	153.22 W
Gold River	182	49.41 N	126.08 W
Gold Rock	184	49.27 N	92.43 W
Gold Run	226	39.10 N	120.52 W
Goldsand Lake ⊜	184	57.02 N	101.08 W
Goldsboro, Md., U.S.	208	39.02 N	75.47 W
Goldsboro, N.C., U.S.	192	35.23 N	77.59 W
Goldsmith, In., U.S.	216	40.17 N	86.08 W
Goldsmith, Tx., U.S.	196	31.58 N	102.36 W
Goldsmith, Lake ⊜	169	37.32 S	143.21 E
Goldston	192	35.35 N	79.19 W
Goldstone Lake ⊜	228	35.22 N	116.54 W
Goldstream Provincial Park ♠	224	48.29 N	123.33 W
Goldsworthy	162	20.20 S	119.30 E
Goldsworthy, Mount ∧[2]	162	20.21 S	119.32 E
Goldthwaite	196	31.26 N	98.34 W
Golec, gora ∧	88	58.39 N	94.10 E
Goleen	48	51.28 N	9.43 W
Golela	158	27.20 S	31.55 E
Goleniów	30	53.36 N	14.50 E
Goleta	204	34.26 N	119.49 W
Goleta, Cerro ∧	234	18.38 N	100.04 W
Golf, Fl., U.S.	220	26.31 N	80.06 W
Golf, Il., U.S.	278	42.03 N	87.48 W
Golfcrest	216	41.57 N	83.22 W
Golfe-Juan	62	43.34 N	7.05 E
Golfito	236	8.38 N	83.11 W
Golf Manor	285	39.42 N	75.28 W
Golf Mill ◆[9]	278	42.03 N	87.50 W
Golfo Aranci	71	40.59 N	9.38 E
Golfside	281	42.15 N	83.41 W
Golf View	208	39.43 N	75.28 W
Golfview Hills	278	41.47 N	87.56 W
Goliad	196	28.40 N	97.23 W
Goliad □[6]	222	28.52 N	97.22 W
Golicyno, S.S.S.R.	80	53.38 N	44.07 E
Golicyno, S.S.S.R.	80	55.58 N	40.26 E
Golicyno, S.S.S.R.	82	55.37 N	36.59 E
Golina	30	52.16 N	18.05 E
Golin Baixing	89	44.53 N	121.58 E
Golinda	222	31.25 N	97.05 W
Goljama Kamčija ≃	38	43.03 N	27.29 E
Goljam Perelik ∧	38	41.36 N	24.34 E
Goljanovo ◆[8]	265b	55.49 N	37.48 E
Goljevo	265b	55.48 N	37.19 E
Gölköy	130	40.42 N	37.38 E
Gollach ≃	56	49.31 N	10.00 E
Göllersbach ≃	61	48.22 N	16.11 E
Göllet	130	40.45 N	42.18 E
Golling an der Salzach	64	47.36 N	13.10 E
Gollnow → Goleniów	30	53.36 N	14.50 E
Golm	264a	52.24 N	12.57 E
Gölmarmara	130	38.42 N	27.56 E
Golmberg ∧[2]	54	52.01 N	13.21 E
Gol'movskij	83	48.25 N	38.05 E
Golmud	102	36.22 N	94.55 E
Golmud ≃	102	36.54 N	95.11 E
Golo ≃	32	42.31 N	9.32 E
Goloby	78	51.06 N	24.59 E
Golodnaja Guba, ozero ⊜	24	67.52 N	52.48 E
Gologory ⋏	78	49.45 N	24.35 E
Golo Island I	116	13.40 N	120.22 E
Golok (Kolok) ≃	114	6.15 N	102.05 E
Golongoso	146	9.00 N	19.09 E
Golovačovka	85	42.52 N	71.13 E
Golovanevsk	78	48.23 N	30.28 E
Golovanovo	80	54.55 N	40.27 E
Golovčin	76	54.04 N	29.55 E
Golovčino	78	50.32 N	35.47 E
Golovin	180	64.33 N	163.02 W
Golovinka	84	43.48 N	39.28 E
Golovino, S.S.S.R.	76	55.58 N	40.26 E
Golovino, S.S.S.R.	82	56.01 N	39.11 E
Golovinščino	80	53.18 N	43.59 E
Golovinskaja	88	53.26 N	102.43 E
Golovnino	82	54.23 N	36.10 E
Golovno	78	51.21 N	24.04 E
Golovskoje	88	55.30 N	105.32 E
Golpara □[5]	124	26.25 N	89.25 E
Golpāyegān	128	33.27 N	50.18 E
Gölpazarı	130	40.15 N	30.19 E
Golra	123	33.42 N	72.58 E
Golrān	128	35.06 N	61.41 E
Gols	61	47.54 N	16.55 E
Gol'šany	76	54.15 N	26.01 E
Gölsdorf	54	51.59 N	12.39 E
Golspie, Austl.	170	34.17 S	149.40 E
Golspie, Scot., U.K.	46	57.58 N	3.58 W
Golssen	54	51.58 N	13.36 E
Gol't'ajevo	82	55.13 N	36.02 E
Gol't'avino	88	58.26 N	98.27 E
Golub-Dobrzyń	30	53.08 N	19.02 E
Golubi	76	59.28 N	41.39 E
Golubinskij	80	48.52 N	43.34 E
Golubovka, S.S.S.R.	78	48.53 N	35.19 E
Golubovka, S.S.S.R.	86	53.09 N	74.12 E
Golubovka ◆[8]	83	48.38 N	38.39 E
Golumet'	88	53.03 N	102.21 E
Golungo Alto	152	9.08 S	14.46 E
Golva	198	46.44 N	103.59 W
Gölveren	130	37.48 N	33.52 E
Golweyn	144	1.40 N	44.35 E
Golynki	76	54.52 N	31.23 E
Golyšmanovo, S.S.S.R.	86	56.28 N	68.38 E
Golyšmanovo, S.S.S.R.	86	56.23 N	68.23 E
Golzheim ◆[8]	263	51.15 N	6.46 E
Golzow, D.D.R.	54	52.34 N	14.29 E
Golzow, D.D.R.	54	52.16 N	12.36 E
Goma	154	1.41 S	29.14 E
Gomadan-zan ∧	96	34.03 N	135.34 E
Gomagoi	64	46.35 N	10.32 E
Gomaringen	58	48.27 N	9.05 E
Gomas, Sierra de ⋏	196	26.23 N	100.32 W
Gomati ≃	124	25.32 N	83.10 E
Gomati Plain ≍	124	26.30 N	81.10 E
Goma Tsétsé	273b	4.14 S	15.08 E
Gombari	154	2.43 N	29.04 E
Gombe, Nig.	146	10.19 N	11.02 E
Gombe, Zaïre	152	0.42 S	17.35 E
Gombe Stream National Park ♠	154	4.30 S	29.42 E
Gombi	146	10.10 N	12.45 E
Gomboro	150	13.29 N	2.46 W
Gomel'	76	52.25 N	31.00 E
Gomel' □[4]	78	52.00 N	29.00 E
Gömele	130	40.02 N	30.34 E
Gomer	216	40.51 N	84.11 W
Gomera I	148	28.06 N	17.08 W
Gometra I	46	56.29 N	6.17 W
Gometz-la-Ville	261	48.40 N	2.08 E
Gometz-le-Châtel	261	48.41 N	2.08 E
Gomez	220	27.06 N	80.09 W
Gómez Farías, Méx.	232	29.18 N	107.40 W
Gómez Farías, Méx.	234	19.47 N	103.29 W
Gómez Palacio	232	25.34 N	103.30 W
Gómez Plata	246	6.41 N	75.12 W
Gomīshān	128	37.04 N	54.06 E
Gommécourt	261	49.05 N	1.36 E
Gommern	54	52.04 N	11.50 E
Gomogomo	164	6.46 S	134.42 E
Gomoh	126	23.52 N	86.10 E
Gompa	123	35.02 N	77.20 E
Goms V	58	46.27 N	8.15 E
Gomshall	260	51.13 N	0.27 W
Gomumu, Pulau I	164	1.49 S	127.38 E
Gona	164	8.37 S	148.17 E
Gonābād	128	34.20 N	58.42 E
Gonaïves	238	19.27 N	72.41 W
Gonaka	152	2.56 S	13.14 E
Gonam	88	57.21 N	131.12 E
Gonam ≃	74	57.21 N	131.14 E
Gonarezhou National Park ♠	154	21.30 S	32.00 E
Gonars	64	45.53 N	13.13 E
Gonäs	40	60.09 N	15.06 E
Gonâve, Golfe de la ⊂	238	19.00 N	73.30 W
Gonâve, Île de la I	238	18.51 N	73.03 W
Gonbad-e Qābūs	128	37.17 N	55.17 E
Gonçalves	256	22.40 S	45.51 W
Gonçalves Dias	250	4.57 S	44.14 W
Gončarovka	78	50.32 N	39.28 E
Goncelin	62	45.20 N	5.59 E
Gonda	124	27.08 N	81.56 E
Gonda □[5]	124	27.00 N	82.00 E
Gondal	120	21.58 N	70.48 E
Gondang	115a	7.24 S	111.06 E
Gondar → Gonder	144	12.40 N	37.30 E
Gonder	144	12.40 N	37.30 E
Gonder □[4]	144	13.10 N	37.00 E
Gondey	146	9.07 N	19.19 E
Gondia	120	21.27 N	80.12 E
Gondola	156	19.10 S	33.40 E
Gondomar	34	41.09 N	8.32 W
Gondrecourt-le-Château	58	48.31 N	5.30 E
Gondreville	58	48.42 N	5.58 E
Gondrexange, Étang de ⊜	58	48.42 N	6.54 E
Gönen, Tür.	130	40.06 N	27.39 E
Gönen, Yis.	132	33.08 N	35.39 E
Gonesse	50	48.59 N	2.27 E
Gonfaron	62	43.19 N	6.17 E
Gong ≃	100	26.00 N	115.22 E
Gong'an	102	30.02 N	112.04 E
Gonganbao	86	44.59 N	86.18 E
Gonganpucun	104	41.19 N	123.27 E
Gongbuchang	105	40.17 N	116.15 E
Gongchangling	104	41.06 N	123.30 E
Gongcheng	102	24.49 N	110.46 E
Gongchenqiao	106	30.20 N	120.08 E
Gongchuan, Zhg.	100	26.06 N	117.24 E
Gongchuan, Zhg.	102	23.40 N	107.50 E
Gongcun	105	39.28 N	116.10 E
Gongdaoqiao	100	32.36 N	119.22 E
Gongdian	100	28.06 N	116.56 E
Gongen-yama ∧	94	35.40 N	139.01 E
Gongfang	100	27.36 N	115.34 E
Gongga Shan (Minya Konka) ∧	102	29.35 N	101.51 E
Gongge	120	29.17 N	90.46 E
Gonggeershan ∧	120	38.37 N	75.20 E
Gonghe	102	36.20 N	100.48 E
Gonghui	98	41.12 N	114.37 E
Gongjialu	106	31.17 N	121.40 E
Gongjiatun	104	40.55 N	120.37 E
Gongjiazhai	104	41.57 N	124.01 E
Gongjing	107	29.21 N	104.43 E
Gongjingying	105	39.12 N	116.11 E
Gongkou	98	35.38 N	119.47 E
Gongli	98	35.55 N	117.24 E
Gongling	100	26.18 N	119.40 E
Gongliu	86	43.30 N	82.15 E
Gonglu Shan ∧	106	30.39 N	119.18 E
Gongo	146	9.00 N	18.56 E
Gongogi	255	14.19 S	39.29 W
Gongola □[3]	146	9.00 N	11.40 E
Gongola ≃	146	9.30 N	12.04 E
Gongoué	152	0.32 S	9.12 E
Gongo-Yembe	152	1.58 S	18.40 E
Gongpengzi	89	45.09 N	125.39 E
Gongping	100	23.05 N	115.24 E
Gongpingxu	100	26.12 N	112.51 E
Gongshan	102	25.50 N	103.13 E
Gongshiya	120	31.25 N	84.37 E
Gongsizhen	106	31.41 N	121.48 E
Gongtangtou	106	31.48 N	118.42 E
Gongxi	100	27.38 N	115.52 E
Gongxian	102	34.48 N	113.03 E
Gongyefu	98	42.16 N	118.32 E
Gongyemiao	89	43.40 N	121.06 E
Gongyingzi	98	40.54 N	119.41 E
Gongzhutun	104	42.10 N	123.00 E
Gongzui	107	29.19 N	103.28 E
Goni, It.	71	39.34 N	9.17 E
Goñi, Ur.	252	33.31 S	56.24 W
Goniądz	30	53.30 N	22.45 E
Goniānamandi	123	30.19 N	74.54 E
Gonini ≃	250	4.10 N	54.24 W
Goniri	146	11.30 N	12.20 E
Gonjo	102	30.43 N	98.19 E
Gonnesa	71	39.16 N	8.28 E
Gonnesa, Golfo di ⊂	71	39.17 N	8.23 E
Gonnosfanadiga	71	39.29 N	8.39 E
Gonnostramatza	71	39.41 N	8.50 E
Gonochovo	86	52.57 N	81.20 E
Gōnoura	92	33.45 N	129.41 E
Gonubie Mouth	158	32.57 S	28.01 E
Gonža	89	53.36 N	125.19 E
Gonzaga, It.	64	44.57 N	10.49 E
Gonzaga, Pil.	116	18.16 N	122.00 E
Gonzales, Ca., U.S.	226	36.30 N	121.26 W
Gonzales, La., U.S.	194	30.14 N	90.55 W
Gonzales, Tx., U.S.	222	29.30 N	97.27 W
Gonzales □[6]	222	29.28 N	97.30 W
González	258	34.14 S	56.52 W
González, Riacho ≃	252	22.48 S	57.54 W
González Catán	258	34.46 S	58.39 W
González Chaves	252	38.02 S	60.06 W
González Moreno	252	35.33 S	63.22 W
González Ortega	204	32.40 N	115.23 W
González Risos	258	34.52 S	59.13 W
Gonzanamá	246	4.15 S	79.27 W
Goobarragandra ≃	171b	35.20 S	148.15 E
Goochland	192	37.41 N	77.53 W
Good Easter	260	51.47 N	0.21 E
Goodells	214	42.59 N	82.40 W
Goode Mountain ∧	224	48.29 N	120.55 W
Goodenough, Mount ∧	180	67.56 N	135.31 W
Goodenough Bay ⊂	164	9.55 S	150.00 E
Goodenough Island I	164	9.20 S	150.15 E
Gooderham	212	44.54 N	78.23 W
Goodeve	184	51.04 N	103.10 W
Goodfellow Air Force Base ■	196	31.26 N	100.25 W
Good Hope, S. Afr.	158	31.51 S	21.55 E
Good Hope, Oh., U.S.	218	39.26 N	83.21 W
Good Hope, Cape of (Kaap die Gooie Hoop) >	158	34.24 S	18.30 E
Goodhope Bay ⊂	180	66.10 N	163.45 W
Good Hope Mountain ∧	182	51.09 N	124.10 W
Goodhouse	158	28.57 S	18.13 E
Goodhue	190	44.24 N	92.37 W
Gooding	202	42.56 N	114.42 W
Goodison	214	42.44 N	83.10 W
Goodland, Fl., U.S.	220	25.55 N	81.38 W
Goodland, In., U.S.	216	40.45 N	87.17 W
Goodland, Ks., U.S.	198	39.21 N	101.42 W
Goodlands	184	49.05 N	100.35 W
Goodlow Park	222	32.07 N	96.14 W
Goodman, Ms., U.S.	194	32.58 N	89.54 W
Goodman, Wi., U.S.	190	45.37 N	88.21 W
Goodman Bay ⊂	240b	25.05 N	77.24 W
Goodna	171a	27.37 S	152.54 E
Goodnews Bay	180	59.07 N	161.35 W
Goodnight	200	38.14 N	104.43 W
Goodooga	166	29.07 S	147.27 E
Goodradigbee ≃	170	35.08 S	148.41 E
Goodrich, Mi., U.S.	216	42.55 N	83.30 W
Goodrich, N.D., U.S.	198	47.28 N	100.07 W
Goodrich, Tx., U.S.	222	30.36 N	94.57 W
Good Spirit Lake ⊜	184	51.34 N	102.40 W
Good Spirit Lake Provincial Park ♠	184	51.36 N	102.45 W
Good Thunder	190	44.00 N	94.03 W
Goodview	190	44.03 N	91.41 W
Goodville	208	40.08 N	76.00 W
Goodwater	194	33.03 N	86.03 W
Goodwell	196	36.35 N	101.38 W
Goodwick	42	52.00 N	5.00 W
Goodwin, Lake ⊜	224	48.08 N	122.18 W
Goodwives ≃	276	41.04 N	73.28 W
Goodwood	212	44.02 N	79.12 W
Goodyear	200	33.26 N	112.21 W
Goof, Webi ≃	144	1.10 N	43.43 E
Gooie Hoop, Kaap die → Good Hope, Cape of >	158	34.24 S	18.30 E
Goole	44	53.42 N	0.52 W
Goolgowi	166	33.59 S	145.42 E
Goolwa	168b	35.31 S	138.47 E
Goomalling	162	31.19 S	116.49 E
Goombalie	166	29.59 S	145.24 E
Goombungee	171a	27.18 S	151.51 E
Goomburra	171a	28.03 S	152.07 E
Goonda	156	19.51 S	34.00 E
Goondiwindi	166	28.32 S	150.19 E
Goongarrie	162	30.03 S	121.09 E
Goonyella	166	21.45 S	147.55 E
Goor	52	52.14 N	6.35 E
Goose ≃, Ab., Can.	182	54.58 N	117.11 W
Goose ≃, N.D., U.S.	198	47.28 N	96.52 W
Goose Bay → Happy Valley-Goose Bay	176	53.20 N	60.25 W
Goose Bay ⊂	281	42.35 N	82.41 W
Gooseberry Creek ≃	202	43.55 N	108.04 W
Goose Creek	192	32.58 N	80.01 W
Goose Creek ≃, U.S.	202	42.33 N	113.46 W
Goose Creek ≃, Ne., U.S.	198	42.02 N	100.03 W
Goose Creek ≃, N.Y., U.S.	214	42.06 N	79.22 W
Goose Creek ≃, Va., U.S.	208	39.06 N	77.29 W
Goose Island I	182	51.55 N	128.25 W
Goose Lake ⊜, Mb., Can.	184	54.26 N	101.30 W
Goose Lake ⊜, On., Can.	184	51.46 N	93.00 W
Goose Lake ⊜, On., Can.	212	44.25 N	78.52 W
Goose Lake ⊜, On., Can.	214	42.31 N	82.31 W
Goose Lake ⊜, Sk., Can.	184	51.45 N	107.23 W
Goose Lake ⊜, U.S.	204	41.57 N	120.25 W
Goose Lake Canal ≋	226	35.50 N	119.37 W
Goose Lake Prairie State Park ♠	216	41.21 N	88.18 W
Gooseprairie	224	46.54 N	121.15 W
Goostrey	262	53.13 N	2.20 W
Gooty	122	15.07 N	77.38 E
Gopālganj, Bngl.	124	23.01 N	89.50 E
Gopālganj, India	124	26.28 N	84.26 E
Gopālnagar, India	126	23.03 N	88.45 E
Gopālnagar, India	272b	22.50 N	88.14 E
Gopālpur, Bngl.	126	24.12 N	89.01 E
Gopālpur, India	272b	22.38 N	88.27 E
Gopeng	114	4.28 N	101.10 E
Göpfritz an der Wild	61	48.43 N	15.24 E
Gopīballabhpur	126	22.13 N	86.54 E
Gopichettipālaiyam	122	11.28 N	77.27 E
Gopinagar	272b	22.50 N	88.07 E
Goppenstein	58	46.22 N	7.45 E
Göppingen	56	48.42 N	9.40 E
Goqên	102	29.15 N	96.59 E
Gor	123	35.32 N	74.31 E
Góra, Pol.	30	51.40 N	16.33 E
Gora, S.S.S.R.	76	60.02 N	41.43 E
Gor'ačegorsk	86	55.24 N	88.55 E
Gor'ačij Kl'uč	84	44.37 N	39.07 E
Gor'ačinsk	88	52.59 N	108.18 E
Goradit	144	11.25 N	38.25 E
Goradiz	84	39.27 N	47.20 E
Góra Kalwaria	30	51.59 N	21.12 E
Gorakhpur	124	26.45 N	83.22 E
Gorakhpur □[5]	124	27.00 N	83.30 E
Gor'any	76	55.25 N	29.02 E
Goras	124	25.32 N	76.56 E
Goražde	38	43.40 N	18.56 E
Gorbačevo Michajlovka	83	47.50 N	38.00 E
Gorbatov	80	56.08 N	43.04 E
Gorbatovka	80	56.15 N	43.45 E
Gorbica	88	53.06 N	119.13 E
Gorboviči	76	53.49 N	30.41 E
Gorčucha	80	57.43 N	43.43 E
Gorda, Punta >, Chile	248	19.18 S	70.18 W
Gorda, Punta >, Cuba	240p	22.24 N	82.10 W
Gorda, Punta >, Méx.	234	19.14 N	96.11 W
Gorda, Punta >, Nic.	236	11.26 N	83.48 W
Gorda, Punta >, Nic.	236	14.21 N	83.12 W
Gordejevka	76	52.59 N	31.58 E
Gordes, Fr.	62	43.54 N	5.12 E
Gördes, Tür.	130	38.54 N	28.18 E
Gordil	146	9.44 N	21.35 E
Gørding	41	55.29 N	8.48 E
Gordium ⊥	130	39.41 N	32.01 E
Gordo	194	33.19 N	87.54 W
Gordo, Cerro ∧	234	20.46 N	102.35 W
Gordola	58	46.11 N	8.52 E
Gordon, Scot., U.K.	46	55.41 N	2.34 W
Gordon, Ga., U.S.	192	32.52 N	83.19 W
Gordon, Ne., U.S.	198	42.48 N	102.12 W
Gordon, Oh., U.S.	218	39.56 N	84.31 W
Gordon, Pa., U.S.	208	40.45 N	76.21 W
Gordon, Wi., U.S.	190	46.14 N	91.47 W
Gordon ≃	224	48.35 N	124.24 W
Gordon, Isla I	254	54.58 S	69.35 W
Gordon, Lake ⊜[1]	166	42.42 S	146.12 E
Gordon Creek ≃	198	42.49 N	100.40 W
Gordon Downs	162	18.44 S	128.35 E
Gordon Heights	207	40.51 N	72.58 W
Gordon Horne Peak ∧	182	51.46 N	118.50 W
Gordon Indian Reserve ◆[4]	184	51.16 N	104.16 W
Gordon Lake ⊜, Ab., Can.	184	56.30 N	110.25 W
Gordon Lake ⊜, Sk., Can.	184	55.50 N	106.26 W
Gordon Lakes	276	41.03 N	74.22 W
Gordon Pass ⊂	220	26.06 N	81.48 W
Gordon River	224	48.47 N	124.21 W
Gordon's Bay	158	34.10 S	18.52 E
Gordonsville	188	38.08 N	78.11 W
Gordonton	172	37.40 S	175.18 E
Gordonvale	166	17.05 S	145.47 E
Gordonville	220	27.57 N	81.49 W
Gore, Austl.	166	28.17 S	151.29 E
Gore, N.S., Can.	186	45.07 N	63.43 W
Gore, Ityo.	144	8.08 N	35.33 E
Gore, N.Z.	172	46.06 S	168.58 E
Goré, Tchad	146	7.53 N	16.40 E
Gore Bay	190	45.55 N	82.28 W
Gorebridge	46	55.51 N	3.02 W
Goreda	164	3.39 S	134.58 E
Goree	196	33.28 N	99.31 W
Gore Hill	274a	33.49 S	151.11 E
Görele	130	41.02 N	39.00 E
Gorelki	82	54.15 N	37.37 E
Goreloje	80	52.57 N	41.28 E
Gorelovo	265a	59.47 N	30.08 E
Gorelovo Airport ◆	265a	59.47 N	30.05 E
Gorelyj ≃	265a	59.58 N	30.28 E
Göreme	130	38.26 N	34.54 E
Gore Mountain ∧	188	44.55 N	71.48 W
Gorenki	265b	55.48 N	37.55 E
Gore Point >, Austl.	166	17.38 S	139.56 E
Gore Point >, Ak., U.S.	180	59.12 N	151.00 W
Gore Range ⋏	200	40.00 N	106.30 W
Goretovka ◆	265b	55.56 N	37.20 E
Gorey, Ire.	48	52.40 N	6.18 W
Gorey, Jersey	43b	49.12 N	2.02 W
[illegible]			
Gorgān	128	36.50 N	54.29 E
Gorgān ≃	128	36.59 N	54.04 E
Gorgany ⋏	78	48.30 N	24.00 E
Gorge Lake ⊜[1]	224	48.42 N	121.13 W
Görgeshausen	56	50.24 N	7.56 E
Gorgoglione	68	40.23 N	16.09 E
Gorgol □[4]	150	16.00 N	13.00 W
Gorgol el Abiod ≃	150	16.04 N	12.58 W
Gorgol el Akhḍar ≃	150	16.13 N	12.58 W
Gorgona, Isla I	246	2.59 N	78.12 W
Gorgonzola	62	45.32 N	9.24 E
Gorgor	248	10.35 S	77.02 W
Gorgora	144	12.13 N	37.16 E
Gorgoram	146	12.40 N	11.43 E
Gorgova	38	45.11 N	29.10 E
Gorham, Me., U.S.	188	43.40 N	70.26 W
Gorham, N.H., U.S.	188	44.23 N	71.10 W
Gorham, N.Y., U.S.	210	42.47 N	77.07 W
Gorhambury House ♠	260	51.47 N	0.24 W
Gori	84	41.58 N	44.07 E
Goria	272b	22.24 N	88.29 E
Gorica → Gorizia	64	45.57 N	13.38 E
Goričan	61	46.23 N	16.41 E
Goricy	76	57.09 N	36.44 E
Gorinchem	52	51.50 N	5.00 E
Goring	42	51.32 N	1.09 W
Goring-by-Sea	42	50.49 N	0.25 W
Goring Gap V	42	51.32 N	1.08 W

DEUTSCH

Name	Seite	Breite°′	Länge°′ E = Ost
Goris	84	39.31 N	46.23 E
Göritz	54	53.24 N	13.54 E
Göritzhain	54	50.58 N	12.47 E
Gorizia	64	45.57 N	13.38 E
Gorizia □[4]	64	45.55 N	13.30 E
Gorj □[6]	38	45.00 N	23.20 E
Gorjani	38	45.24 N	18.21 E
Gor'kaja Balka	84	44.17 N	43.59 E
Gor'kaja balka V	84	44.38 N	45.00 E
Görke	54	53.51 N	13.38 E
Gorki, S.S.S.R.	76	54.17 N	30.59 E
Gorki → Gor'kij, S.S.S.R.	80	56.20 N	44.00 E
Gorki, S.S.S.R.	80	57.38 N	45.05 E
Gorki, S.S.S.R.	82	56.54 N	38.51 E
Gorki, S.S.S.R.	82	54.18 N	36.08 E
Gorki, S.S.S.R.	82	55.32 N	37.45 E
Gorki, S.S.S.R.	265b	55.57 N	37.55 E
Gor'kij (Gorky)	80	56.20 N	44.00 E
Gorki Park → Centralnyj park imeni Gor'kogo ♠	265b	55.44 N	37.36 E
Gorki Vtoryje	265b	55.44 N	37.11 E
Gor'kiy → Gor'kij	80	56.20 N	44.00 E
Gor'koje, ozero ⊜	86	52.30 N	81.20 E
Gor'kovskoje	86	55.22 N	74.24 E
Gor'kovskoje vodochranilišče ⊜[1]	80	57.00 N	43.10 E
Gorky → Gor'kij	80	56.20 N	44.00 E
Gorlago	62	45.40 N	9.49 E
Gorla Maggiore	266b	45.40 N	8.53 E
Gorla Minore	266b	45.39 N	8.54 E
Gorleston on Sea	42	52.36 N	1.43 E
Gørlev	41	55.32 N	11.14 E
Gorlice	30	49.40 N	21.10 E
Görlitz	54	51.09 N	14.59 E
Gorlosen	54	53.11 N	11.27 E
Gorlovka, S.S.S.R.	83	48.18 N	38.03 E
Gorlovka, S.S.S.R.	84	41.14 N	43.42 E
Gorlovo	76	53.50 N	39.02 E
Gorm, Loch ⊜	46	55.48 N	6.25 W
Gorman, Ca., U.S.	228	34.48 N	118.51 W
Gorman, Tx., U.S.	196	32.12 N	98.40 W
Gorman Creek ≃	228	34.38 N	118.45 W
Görmin	54	53.59 N	13.16 E
Gorn'ackij, S.S.S.R.	24	67.32 N	64.03 E
Gorn'ackij, S.S.S.R.	78	48.17 N	40.55 E
Gorn'ackoje	78	47.42 N	34.08 E
Gorna Dzhumaya → Blagoevgrad	38	42.01 N	23.06 E
Gornaja Prolejka	80	49.24 N	44.59 E
Gorn'ak, S.S.S.R.	76	53.36 N	39.29 E
Gorn'ak, S.S.S.R.	78	50.20 N	24.10 E
Gorn'ak, S.S.S.R.	83	48.04 N	37.24 E
Gorn'ak, S.S.S.R.	86	51.00 N	81.29 E
Gornalunga ≃	70	37.24 N	15.03 E
Gorna Orjahovica	38	43.07 N	25.41 E
Gornergrat ♠	58	45.59 N	7.47 E
Gornja Radgona	61	46.41 N	16.00 E
Gornji Grad	36	46.18 N	14.49 E
Gornji Milanovac	38	44.01 N	20.27 E
Gornji Vakuf	36	43.56 N	17.35 E
Gorno-Altajsk	86	51.58 N	85.58 E
Gorno-Altajskaja Avtonomnaja Oblast' □[8]	86	51.00 N	86.00 E
Gorno-Badachšanskaja Avtonomnaja Oblast' □[4]	85	38.30 N	73.00 E
Gornoje	86	48.29 N	85.00 E
Gorno-Lesnoj zapovednik ♠	85	41.10 N	69.55 E
Gornopravdinsk	86	60.07 N	69.54 E
Gornostajevka	78	47.01 N	33.44 E
Gorno-Vod'anoje	80	49.16 N	44.56 E
Gornovodnoje	89	43.42 N	134.44 E
Gornozavodsk, S.S.S.R.	86	58.20 N	58.32 E
Gornozavodsk, S.S.S.R.	89	46.34 N	141.49 E
Gornyj, S.S.S.R.	80	51.46 N	48.34 E
Gornyj, S.S.S.R.	89	50.48 N	136.29 E
Gornyj, S.S.S.R.	89	44.57 N	133.59 E
Gornyj Balyklej	80	49.34 N	45.04 E
Gornyje Kl'uči	89	45.12 N	133.31 E
Gornyj Tikič ≃	78	48.47 N	30.53 E
Goro, Ityo.	144	6.56 N	40.32 E
Goro, N. Cal.	175f	22.16 S	167.02 E
Gorochan ∧	144	9.22 N	37.04 E
Gorochov	78	50.30 N	24.45 E
Gorochovatka	83	49.21 N	37.31 E
Gorochovec	80	56.12 N	42.40 E
Gorochovje	76	56.31 N	30.29 E
Gorodec, S.S.S.R.	76	58.32 N	29.47 E
Gorodec, S.S.S.R.	76	52.12 N	24.40 E
Gorodec, S.S.S.R.	76	52.58 N	30.21 E
Gorodec, S.S.S.R.	76	53.33 N	30.02 E
Gorodec, S.S.S.R.	78	51.17 N	26.19 E
Gorodec, S.S.S.R.	80	56.38 N	43.30 E
Gorodeja	76	53.19 N	26.32 E
Gorodenka	38	48.41 N	25.29 E
Gorodišče, S.S.S.R.	76	53.44 N	29.48 E
Gorodišče, S.S.S.R.	76	59.38 N	32.08 E
Gorodišče, S.S.S.R.	76	53.19 N	26.00 E
Gorodišče, S.S.S.R.	78	51.09 N	38.04 E
Gorodišče, S.S.S.R.	78	49.17 N	31.27 E
Gorodišče, S.S.S.R.	80	53.17 N	45.42 E
Gorodišče, S.S.S.R.	80	48.48 N	44.29 E
Gorodišče, S.S.S.R.	82	54.53 N	38.13 E
Gorodišče, S.S.S.R.	82	56.47 N	38.52 E
Gorodišče, S.S.S.R.	83	48.19 N	38.39 E
Gorodišče, S.S.S.R.	83	49.03 N	39.38 E
Gorodišči	82	55.52 N	39.05 E
Gorodkovka	78	48.23 N	28.42 E
Gorodn'a, S.S.S.R.	78	51.53 N	31.36 E
Gorodn'a, S.S.S.R.	82	54.57 N	38.49 E
Gorodn'a, S.S.S.R.	82	56.43 N	36.19 E
Gorodn'a ≃	265b	55.48 N	37.46 E
Gorodnica	78	50.48 N	27.20 E
Gorodno	76	57.32 N	29.35 E
Gorodok, S.S.S.R.	76	55.28 N	29.59 E
Gorodok, S.S.S.R.	78	49.10 N	26.34 E
Gorodok, S.S.S.R.	78	49.47 N	23.39 E
Gorod'onka	78	48.41 N	25.29 E
Goroka	164	6.05 S	145.25 E
Gorokan	170	33.16 S	151.30 E
Gorom-Gorom	150	14.26 N	0.14 W
Gorong, Pulau I	164	3.59 S	131.25 E
Gorongosa, Parque Nacional da ♠	156	18.45 S	34.15 E
Gorongosa, Serra da ∧	154	18.30 S	34.03 E
Gorongose ≃	156	20.30 S	34.40 E
Gorontalo	112	0.33 N	123.03 E
Goronyo	150	13.26 N	5.39 E
Goroubi ≃	150	12.54 N	2.23 E
Gorouol ≃	150	14.42 N	0.53 E
Górowo Iławeckie	30	54.17 N	20.30 E
Gorple Reservoirs ⊜[1]	262	53.47 N	2.06 W
Gorran ⊜	40	59.43 N	17.32 E
Gorredijk	52	53.00 N	6.03 E
Gorron	50	48.25 N	0.49 W
Görsdorf	54	51.34 N	13.14 E
Goršečnoje	78	51.32 N	38.02 E
Gorsedd	262	53.17 N	3.16 W
Gorseinon	42	51.40 N	4.02 W
Gorskaja	265a	60.03 N	29.59 E
Gorskoje	83	48.46 N	38.41 E
Gorškovo	82	54.26 N	37.59 E
Gorst	224	47.32 N	122.42 W
Gort	48	53.04 N	8.50 W
Gortahork	48	55.08 N	8.09 W
Gorton ◆[8]	262	53.27 N	2.10 W
Görtschitz ≃	61	46.45 N	14.32 E
Görukle	130	40.14 N	28.50 E
Gorul ∧	38	45.48 N	26.25 E
Gorumna Island I	48	53.15 N	9.40 W
Gor'un ≃	89	50.45 N	137.50 E

Symbols in the index entries represent the broad categories identified in the key at the right. Symbols with superior numbers (⋏[1]) identify subcategories (see complete key on page *I* · *1*).

Kartensymbole in dem Registerverzeichnis stellen die rechts in Schlüssel erklärten Kategorien dar. Symbole mit hochgestellten Ziffern (⋏[1]) bezeichnen Unterabteilungen einer Kategorie (vgl. vollständiger Schlüssel auf Seite *I* · *1*).

Los símbolos incluídos en el texto del índice representan las grandes categorías identificadas con la clave a la derecha. Los símbolos con numeros en su parte superior (⋏[1]) identifican las subcategorías (véase la clave completa en la página *I* · *1*).

Les symboles de l'index représentent les catégories indiquées dans la légende à droite. Les symboles suivis d'un indice (⋏[1]) représentent des sous-catégories (voir légende complète à la page *I* · *1*).

Os símbolos incluídos no texto do índice representam as grandes categorias identificadas com a chave à direita. Os símbolos com números em sua parte superior (⋏[1]) identificam as subcategorias (veja-se a chave completa à página *I* · *1*).

∧ Mountain	Berg	Montaña	Montagne	Montanha
⋏ Mountains	Berge	Montañas	Montagnes	Montanhas
)(Pass	Pass	Paso	Col	Passo
V Valley, Canyon	Tal, Cañon	Valle, Cañón	Vallée, Canyon	Vale, Canhão
≍ Plain	Ebene	Llano	Plaine	Planície
> Cape	Kap	Cabo	Cap	Cabo
I Island	Insel	Isla	Île	Ilha
II Islands	Inseln	Islas	Îles	Ilhas
⊥ Other Topographic Features	Andere Topographische Objekte	Otros Elementos Topográficos	Autres données topographiques	Outros acidentes topográficos

ESPAÑOL

Nombre	Página	Lat.°′	Long.°′ W = Oeste
Gorutuba ≃	255	14.57 S	43.33 W
Görwihl	58	47.39 N	8.04 E
Gory, S.S.S.R.	76	54.16 N	31.13 E
Gory, S.S.S.R.	80	48.38 N	51.46 E
Goryn' ≃	78	52.08 N	27.17 E
Görz → Gorizia	64	45.57 N	13.38 E
Gorzano, Monte ∧	66	42.37 N	13.24 E
Gorze	56	49.03 N	6.00 E
Görzig	54	51.40 N	12.00 E
Görzke	54	52.10 N	12.22 E
Górzno	30	53.13 N	19.38 E
Gorzów Śląski	30	51.02 N	18.24 E
Gorzów Wielkopolski (Landsberg an der Warthe)	30	52.44 N	15.15 E
Gorzów Wielkopolski □[4]	30	52.45 N	15.20 E
Górzyca	54	52.29 N	14.40 E
Gosāba	126	22.10 N	88.48 E
Gosainthan ∧	120	28.22 N	85.50 E
Gosairhāt	126	23.05 N	90.26 E
Gosaldo	64	46.13 N	11.58 E
Gosau	64	47.34 N	13.31 E
Gosauseen ⊜	64	47.32 N	13.31 E
Gosberton	42	52.51 N	0.09 W
Gošča	78	50.36 N	26.41 E
Göschenen	58	46.40 N	8.35 E
Goschen Strait ʊ	164	10.09 S	150.56 E
Gose	96	34.27 N	135.44 E
Gosen, D.D.R.	264a	52.24 N	13.43 E
Gosen, Nihon	92	37.44 N	139.11 E
Gosford	170	33.26 S	151.21 E
Gosforth, Eng., U.K.	44	55.01 N	1.37 W
Gosforth, Eng., U.K.	44	54.26 N	3.27 W
Gosforth Park ♠	273d	26.14 S	28.10 E
Gosforth Park Race Course ♠	273d	26.14 S	28.08 E
Goshabi	140	17.58 N	31.06 E
Goshen, N.S., Can.	186	45.23 N	61.59 W
Goshen, Ca., U.S.	226	36.21 N	119.25 W
Goshen, Ct., U.S.	207	41.49 N	73.13 W
Goshen, In., U.S.	216	41.34 N	85.50 W
Goshen, Ma., U.S.	207	42.26 N	72.48 W
Goshen, N.J., U.S.	208	39.08 N	74.51 W
Goshen, N.Y., U.S.	210	41.24 N	74.19 W
Goshen, Oh., U.S.	218	39.14 N	84.10 W
Goshiki	96	34.24 N	134.47 E
Goshogawara	92	40.48 N	140.27 E
Goshute Indian Reservation ◆[4]	200	39.53 N	114.08 W
Goshute Lake ⊜	204	40.08 N	114.38 W
Goshute Valley V	204	40.40 N	114.30 W
Goslar	52	51.54 N	10.25 E
Gosnells	168a	32.04 S	116.00 E
Gospić	36	44.33 N	15.23 E
Gosport, Eng., U.K.	42	50.48 N	1.08 W
Gosport, In., U.S.	194	39.21 N	86.40 W
Gossa	54	51.40 N	12.26 E
Gossas	150	14.30 N	16.04 W
Gossau	58	47.25 N	9.15 E
Gosse ◆[8]	263	51.08 N	7.01 E
Gosselies	56	50.28 N	4.25 E
Gössenheim	56	50.01 N	9.46 E
Gossensass → Colle Isarco	64	46.56 N	11.26 E
Gosser Hill	279b	40.37 N	79.37 W
Gossi	150	15.49 N	1.17 W
Gossinga	140	8.39 N	25.59 E
Gössnitz	54	50.53 N	12.26 E
Gossolengo	62	44.59 N	9.37 E
Gössweinstein	60	49.46 N	11.20 E
Gostagajevskaja	78	45.01 N	37.30 E
Gostilovo	82	55.18 N	38.36 E
Gostiščevo	78	50.47 N	36.39 E
Gostivar	38	41.47 N	20.54 E
Göstling an der Ybbs	61	47.48 N	14.55 E
Gostyń	30	51.53 N	17.00 E
Gostynin	30	52.26 N	19.29 E
Gosudarev Bajrak	83	48.21 N	38.08 E
Göta älv ≃	26	57.42 N	11.52 E
Göta kanal ≋	40	58.50 N	13.58 E
Gotchen Creek ≃	224	46.00 N	121.30 W
Got Creek ≃	284a	43.03 N	78.42 W
Gotebo	196	35.04 N	98.52 W
Göteborg (Gothenburg)	26	57.43 N	11.58 E
Göteborgs Och Bohus län □[6]	26	58.30 N	11.30 E
Gotel Mountains ⋏	152	6.55 N	11.15 E
Gotemba	94	35.18 N	138.56 E
Götene	26	58.32 N	13.29 E
Gotešty	78	46.09 N	28.10 E
Gotha, D.D.R.	54	50.57 N	10.41 E
Gotha, Fl., U.S.	220	28.32 N	81.31 W
Gothem	26	57.35 N	18.43 E
Gothenburg → Göteborg, Sve.	26	57.43 N	11.58 E
Gothenburg, Ne., U.S.	198	40.55 N	100.09 W
Gothèye	150	13.52 N	1.34 E
Gotland I	26	57.30 N	18.33 E
Gotlands Län □[6]	26	57.30 N	18.30 E
Gotoputovo	86	56.46 N	70.10 E
Gotō-rettō II	92	32.50 N	129.00 E
Gotska Sandön I	26	58.23 N	19.16 E
Gōtsu	96	35.00 N	132.14 E
Gottenheim	58	48.03 N	7.44 E
Götterswickerhamm	263	51.35 N	6.40 E
Gottesbrücke	264a	52.25 N	13.49 E
Gotthard Tunnel ◆[5]	58	46.35 N	8.35 E
Göttin	264a	52.27 N	12.54 E
Göttingen, B.R.D.	52	51.32 N	9.55 E
Göttingen, B.R.D.	56	50.52 N	8.46 E
Göttin See ⊜	264a	52.28 N	12.54 E
Gottmadingen	58	47.44 N	8.47 E
Gottolengo	64	45.17 N	10.16 E
Gottorf, Schloss ⊥	41	54.30 N	9.32 E
Gottsbüren	52	51.35 N	9.30 E
Gottvaterkapelle ♁[1]	60	49.42 N	11.41 E
Gottwaldov	30	49.13 N	17.41 E
Gotval'd	78	49.40 N	36.19 E
Götzendorf	264b	48.01 N	16.35 E
Götzis	58	47.20 N	9.38 E
Gouarec	32	48.13 N	3.11 W
Goubangzi	104	41.22 N	121.46 E
Goubone	146	20.43 N	17.08 E
Gouda, Ned.	52	52.01 N	4.43 E
Gouda, S. Afr.	158	33.19 S	19.04 E
Goudet	62	44.53 N	3.55 E
Goudge	252	34.40 S	68.08 W
Goudhurst	42	51.07 N	0.28 E
Goudiry	150	14.11 N	12.43 W
Goudoumaria	146	13.42 N	11.10 E
Goudswaard	52	51.47 N	4.16 E
Gouéké	150	8.02 N	8.43 W
Goûfi, Djebel el ∧	34	36.57 N	6.27 E
Gougezhuang	105	38.53 N	116.11 E
Gough Island I	10	40.20 S	10.00 W
Gough Lake ⊜	182	52.02 N	112.28 W
Gouin, Réservoir ⊜[1]	176	48.38 N	74.54 W
Goujiaozhen	107	30.36 N	106.33 E
Goukou	89	48.39 N	122.06 E
Goulais ≃	190	46.43 N	84.27 W
Goulburn	170	34.45 S	149.43 E
Goulburn ≃	169	36.41 S	145.12 E
Goulburn Islands II	164	11.33 S	133.26 E
Goulburn Weir ⊜[1]	169	36.45 S	145.08 E
Gould	194	33.59 N	91.33 W
Gould City	190	46.05 N	85.41 W
Gould Park	214	40.04 N	82.53 W
Goulds	220	25.33 N	80.22 W
Gouldsboro	210	41.44 N	75.28 W
Gouldsboro State Park ♠	210	41.13 N	75.28 W
Goulet Lake ⊜	184	55.23 N	96.18 W
Goulia	150	10.01 N	7.11 W
Goulicun	106	31.40 N	120.00 E
Goulimime	148	28.56 N	10.04 W
Goulimine □[4]	148	28.30 N	9.45 W
Goulmima	148	31.02 N	5.00 W
Goumbati ∧[2]	150	13.08 N	12.06 W
Goumbou	150	14.59 N	7.27 W

FRANÇAIS

Nom	Page	Lat.°′	Long.°′ W = Ouest
Gouménissa	38	40.57 N	22.27 E
Goumois	58	47.16 N	6.57 E
Gouna	146	8.32 N	13.34 E
Gounda ≃	146	9.25 N	20.57 E
Goundam	150	16.25 N	3.40 W
Goundi	146	9.22 N	17.22 E
Gounou-Gaya	146	9.38 N	15.31 E
Gouougang, Mount ∧	170	33.53 S	150.07 E
Goupillières	261	48.53 N	1.46 E
Gouraya	34	36.34 N	1.55 E
Gourbassi	150	13.24 N	11.38 W
Gourbeyre	241o	16.00 N	61.42 W
Gourcy	150	13.13 N	2.21 W
Gourdhead Run ≃	279b	40.33 N	79.57 W
Gourdon, Fr.	32	44.44 N	1.23 E
Gourdon, Fr.	62	43.43 N	6.59 E
Gouré	150	13.58 N	10.18 E
Gouri, Ruins of ⊥	124	24.53 N	88.07 E
Gourin	32	48.08 N	3.36 W
Gouripur	124	24.46 N	90.34 E
Gourits ≃	158	34.21 S	21.52 E
Gourlay Lake ⊜	190	48.52 N	84.54 W
Gourma Rharous	150	16.53 N	1.55 W
Gournay-en-Bray	50	49.29 N	1.44 E
Gournay-sur-Marne	261	48.52 N	2.34 E
Gouro	146	19.33 N	19.33 E
Gourock	46	55.58 N	4.49 W
Goussainville	50	49.01 N	2.28 E
Goussonville	261	48.55 N	1.46 E
Goutou	105	39.49 N	117.11 E
Gouvêa	255	18.27 S	43.44 W
Gouveia	266c	38.50 N	9.26 W
Gouverneur	212	44.20 N	75.27 W
Gouyadong	100	25.10 N	112.55 E
Gov'altaj □[4]	102	45.30 N	96.00 E
Govan	184	51.18 N	105.00 W
Go-vap	269c	10.49 N	106.41 E
Govardhan	124	27.30 N	77.28 E
Gove	198	38.57 N	100.29 W
Govea ≃	286b	22.56 N	82.30 W
Govena, mys >	74	59.48 N	166.06 E
Govenlock	184	49.15 N	109.48 W
Gove Peninsula >[1]	164	12.20 S	136.50 E
Goverla, gora ∧	78	48.10 N	24.32 E
Governador, Ilha do I	287a	22.48 S	43.12 W
Governador Portela	256	22.29 S	43.30 W
Governador Valadares	255	18.51 S	41.56 W
Government Camp	224	45.18 N	121.45 W
Governor Bond Lake ⊜[1]	219	38.56 N	89.23 W
Governor Dodge State Park ♠	190	43.00 N	90.07 W
Governor Generoso	116	6.39 N	126.05 E
Governor Head >	170	35.07 S	150.46 E
Governor Nice Memorial Bridge ◆[5]	208	38.22 N	77.00 W
Governor Printz Park ♠	285	39.52 N	75.18 W
Governors Harbour	238	25.10 N	76.14 W
Governors Island I	276	40.41 N	74.01 W
Govind Balabh Pant Sāgar ⊜[1]	124	24.05 N	82.50 E
Govindgarh	124	24.23 N	81.18 E
Govind Sāgar ⊜[1]	123	31.20 N	76.45 E
Gov'-Ugtaal	102	46.04 N	107.30 E
Gowan ≃	184	55.49 N	94.08 W
Gowanda	210	42.27 N	78.56 W
Gowan Range ⋏	166	25.00 S	145.00 E
Gowen City	208	40.45 N	76.32 W
Gower	194	39.36 N	94.35 W
Gower >[1]	42	51.36 N	4.10 W
Gowerton	42	51.39 N	4.01 W
Gowienica ≃	54	53.40 N	14.38 E
Gowmal (Gumal) ≃	120	31.56 N	70.22 E
Gowmal Kalay	120	32.29 N	68.55 E
Gowna, Lough ⊜	48	53.51 N	7.34 W
Gowrie	198	42.16 N	94.17 W
Gowy ≃	262	53.17 N	2.51 W
Goya	252	29.08 S	59.16 W
Goyania → Goiânia	255	16.40 S	49.16 W
Goyatz	54	52.01 N	14.09 E
Goyave	241o	16.08 N	61.34 W
Goyaves, Grande Rivière à ≃	241o	16.18 N	61.37 W
Goyaves, Îlets à II	241o	16.10 N	61.48 W
Goyder ≃	164	12.38 S	135.11 E
Goyder Creek ≃	162	25.39 S	134.47 E
Goyelle, Lac ⊜	186	50.47 N	60.45 W
Goyeneche	258	35.20 S	58.43 W
Goyer, Île I	275a	45.29 N	73.17 W
Goyerkāta	124	26.42 N	89.02 E
Göykazi	130	36.14 N	29.59 E
Göynücek	130	40.24 N	35.32 E
Göynük	130	40.24 N	30.47 E
Göynük ≃	84	38.55 N	40.34 E
Goyt ≃	262	53.24 N	2.09 W
Goz-Beïda	146	12.13 N	21.25 E
Gozdnica	30	51.26 N	15.06 E
Gozdowice	54	52.45 N	14.18 E
Gozen-yama	94	36.32 N	140.20 E
Gözne	130	36.59 N	34.34 E
Gozo → Għawdex I	36	36.03 N	14.15 E
Göz Tepe ∧[2]	267b	41.06 N	29.06 E
Gozzano	62	45.45 N	8.26 E
Graaff-Reinet	158	32.14 S	24.32 E
Graafwater	158	32.00 S	18.37 E
Graauw	52	51.20 N	4.05 E
Grabc'ovo	82	54.34 N	36.22 E
Graben-Neudorf	56	49.09 N	8.29 E
Grabenstätt	64	47.51 N	12.32 E
Grabill	216	41.12 N	84.58 W
Grabo	150	4.55 N	7.30 W
Grabouw	158	34.09 S	19.02 E
Grabovaja Balka, les ♠	83	48.09 N	38.37 E
Grabovo	86	53.07 N	74.52 E
Grabow	54	53.16 N	11.34 E
Grabowiec	30	50.50 N	23.33 E
Grabów nad Prosną	30	51.31 N	18.06 E
Gračac	36	44.18 N	15.51 E
Gračanica	38	44.42 N	18.19 E
Gračanica, Manastir ♁[1]	38	42.36 N	21.09 E
Graçay	50	47.08 N	1.51 E
Grace	202	42.34 N	111.43 W
Gracefield	188	46.06 N	76.03 W
Graceham	208	39.36 N	77.22 W
Graceton	214	40.30 N	79.10 W
Graceville, Fl., U.S.	192	30.57 N	85.31 W
Graceville, Mn., U.S.	198	45.34 N	96.26 W
Gračevka	82	55.06 N	36.49 E
Grächen	58	46.12 N	7.50 E
Grachovo	80	56.04 N	51.58 E
Grači	80	49.49 N	43.33 E
Gracia ◆[8]	266d	41.23 N	2.09 E
Gracias	236	14.35 N	88.35 W
Gracias a Dios □[5]	236	15.10 N	84.20 W
Gracias a Dios, Cabo >	236	15.00 N	83.10 W
Gračiki ≃	83	48.30 N	39.52 E
Graciosa I	148a	39.04 N	28.00 W
Graciosa, Isla I	148	29.15 N	13.30 W
Gračov	80	49.26 N	41.32 E
Gračovka, S.S.S.R.	80	52.07 N	40.01 E
Gračovka, S.S.S.R.	80	52.57 N	52.52 E
Gračov Kust	80	51.59 N	49.50 E
Gradačac	38	44.53 N	18.26 E
Gradara	66	43.57 N	12.46 E
Gradaús	250	7.43 S	51.11 W
Gradaús, Serra dos ⋏[1]	250	8.00 S	50.45 W
Gr'adcy	76	56.24 N	31.55 E
Gräddö	40	59.46 N	19.02 E
Gradisca d'Isonzo	64	45.53 N	13.30 E
Gradižsk	78	49.13 N	33.07 E
Grado, Esp.	34	43.23 N	6.04 W
Grado, It.	64	45.40 N	13.23 E
Grado, Laguna di c	64	45.43 N	13.20 E

PORTUGUÊS

Nome	Página	Lat.°′	Long.°′ W = Oeste
Gradoli	66	42.39 N	11.51 E
Grady, Ar., U.S.	194	34.04 N	91.42 W
Grady, N.M., U.S.	196	34.49 N	103.19 W
Gradyville	285	39.57 N	75.28 W
Graemsay I	46	58.56 N	3.17 W
Græsted	41	56.04 N	12.17 E
Graettinger	198	43.14 N	94.45 W
Gräfelfing	60	48.07 N	11.25 E
Grafenau	60	48.52 N	13.25 E
Gräfenberg	60	49.39 N	11.15 E
Grafenberg ◆[8]	263	51.14 N	6.50 E
Gräfenhainichen	54	51.44 N	12.27 E
Gräfenroda	54	50.45 N	10.48 E
Gräfenthal	54	50.31 N	11.18 E
Gräfentonna	54	51.05 N	10.44 E
Grafenwöhr	60	49.43 N	11.54 E
Graffignano	66	42.34 N	12.12 E
Grafham Water ⊜	42	52.17 N	0.20 W
Gräfinau-Angstedt	54	50.42 N	11.01 E
Grafing bei München	60	48.02 N	11.59 E
Gråfjell ∧	26	60.16 N	9.29 E
Graford	196	32.56 N	98.14 W
Gräfrath ◆[8]	263	51.13 N	7.04 E
Grafschaft Bentheim □[9]	52	52.30 N	7.00 E
Grafton, Austl.	166	29.41 S	152.56 E
Grafton, On., Can.	212	44.00 N	78.01 W
Grafton, Il., U.S.	219	38.58 N	90.25 W
Grafton, Ma., U.S.	207	42.12 N	71.41 W
Grafton, N.Y., U.S.	210	42.46 N	73.27 W
Grafton, N.D., U.S.	198	48.24 N	97.24 W
Grafton, Oh., U.S.	214	41.16 N	82.03 W
Grafton, W.V., U.S.	188	39.20 N	80.01 W
Grafton, Wi., U.S.	190	43.19 N	87.57 W
Grafton, Cape >	164	16.52 S	145.55 E
Grafton Lakes State Park ♠	210	42.48 N	73.28 W
Grafty Green	260	51.12 N	0.41 E
Graglia	62	45.33 N	7.59 E
Gragnano	68	40.41 N	14.31 E
Gragnano Trebbiense	62	45.01 N	9.34 E
Graham, Ca., U.S.	280	34.15 N	118.31 W
Graham, N.C., U.S.	192	36.04 N	79.24 W
Graham, Tx., U.S.	196	33.06 N	98.35 W
Graham, Wa., U.S.	224	47.03 N	122.17 W
Graham, Mount ∧	200	32.42 N	109.52 W
Graham Cave State Park ♠	219	38.55 N	91.32 W
Graham Creek ≃	218	38.49 N	85.39 W
Graham Island I	182	53.40 N	132.30 W
Graham Lake ⊜, On., Can.	212	44.34 N	75.53 W
Graham Lake ⊜, Me., U.S.	188	44.40 N	68.25 W
Graham Land ◆[1]	9	66.00 S	63.30 W
Graham Memorial Park ♠	284b	39.25 N	76.30 W
Graham Moore, Cape >	176	72.52 N	76.04 W
Graham Moore Bay c	176	75.26 N	101.25 W
Grahamstad → Grahamstown	158	33.19 S	26.31 E
Grahamstown	158	33.19 S	26.31 E
Grahamsville	210	41.51 N	74.33 W
Grahn	218	38.17 N	83.04 W
Graie, Alpi (Alpes Grées) ⋏	62	45.30 N	7.10 E
Graiguenamanagh	48	52.32 N	6.57 W
Grain	260	51.28 N	0.43 E
Grain, Isle of I	42	51.27 N	0.41 E
Grain Coast ⩟[2]	150	5.00 N	9.00 W
Grainfield	198	39.06 N	100.27 W
Grajagan	115a	8.35 S	114.13 E
Grajagan, Teluk c	115a	8.40 S	114.18 E
Grajaú	250	5.49 S	46.08 W
Grajaú ≃	250	3.41 S	44.48 W
Grajewo	30	53.39 N	22.27 E
Grajvoron	78	50.28 N	35.39 E
Gram	41	55.17 N	9.04 E
Gramacho	287a	22.44 S	43.18 W
Gramada	38	43.50 N	22.39 E
Gramado	252	29.24 S	50.54 W
Gramalote	246	7.53 N	72.48 W
Gramastetten	61	48.23 N	14.12 E
Gramat	32	44.47 N	1.43 E
Gramatneusiedl	264b	48.02 N	16.29 E
Grambling	194	32.31 N	92.42 W
Gramilla	252	27.18 S	64.37 W
Gramínea	256	22.10 S	46.38 W
Graminha, Reprêsa da ⊜[1]	256	21.40 S	46.35 W
Grammer	218	39.09 N	85.43 W
Grammichele	70	37.13 N	14.38 E
Grammont → Geraardsbergen	50	50.46 N	3.52 E
Gramoteino	86	54.31 N	86.22 E
Grampian	214	40.57 N	78.36 W
Grampian □[4]	46	57.15 N	2.45 W
Grampian Mountains ⋏	46	56.55 N	4.00 W
Gramschatz	56	49.56 N	9.58 E
Gramsh	38	40.52 N	20.11 E
Gramzow	54	53.12 N	14.00 E
Gran → Esztergom	30	47.48 N	18.45 E
Grana ≃	62	44.25 N	7.27 E
Granaatboskolk	158	30.02 S	19.51 E
Granada, Col.	246	3.34 N	73.45 W
Granada, Esp.	34	37.13 N	3.41 W
Granada, Nic.	236	11.56 N	85.57 W
Granada, Pil.	116	10.40 N	123.02 E
Granada, Co., U.S.	198	38.03 N	102.18 W
Granada, Mn., U.S.	190	43.41 N	94.20 W
Granada □[5]	236	11.50 N	86.00 W
Granada → Grenada □[1]	241k	12.07 N	61.40 W
Granada Hills ◆[8]	280	34.16 N	118.31 W
Granadella	34	41.21 N	0.40 E
Granado	286d	12.04 S	76.57 W
Granaglione	66	44.07 N	10.58 E
Gran Altiplanicie Central ⋏[1]	254	48.55 S	69.25 W
Granard	48	53.47 N	7.30 W
Granarolo dell'Emilia	64	44.33 N	11.27 E
Granatello	70	37.53 N	12.32 E
Gran Bahía Australiana → Great Australian Bight c[3]	162	35.00 S	135.00 E
Gran Bajo de San Julián V	254	49.30 S	68.30 W
Gran Barrera de Arrecifes → Great Barrier Reef ✢[2]	160	18.00 S	145.50 E
Granbergsdal	40	59.24 N	14.35 E
Granbury	222	32.26 N	97.47 W
Granbury, Lake ⊜[1]	222	32.25 N	97.45 W
Granby, P.Q., Can.	206	45.24 N	72.44 W
Granby, Co., U.S.	200	40.05 N	105.56 W
Granby, Ct., U.S.	207	41.57 N	72.47 W
Granby, Ma., U.S.	207	42.15 N	72.31 W
Granby, Mo., U.S.	194	36.55 N	94.15 W
Granby ≃	182	49.03 N	118.25 W
Granby, Lake ⊜[1]	200	40.09 N	105.50 W
Gran Canal del Desagüe ≋	286a	19.29 N	99.05 W
Gran Canaria I	148	28.00 N	15.36 W
Grancey-le-Château	58	47.40 N	5.02 E
Gran Chaco ≚	18	23.00 S	60.00 W
Grand	58	48.23 N	5.29 E
Grand ≃, On., Can.	212	42.51 N	79.34 W
Grand ≃, U.S.	194	39.23 N	93.06 W
Grand ≃, Mi., U.S.	216	43.04 N	86.15 W
Grand ≃, Oh., U.S.	214	41.46 N	81.17 W
Grand ≃, S.D., U.S.	198	45.40 N	100.32 W
Grand ≃, Wi., U.S.	190	43.45 N	89.16 W
Grand, East Fork ≃	194	40.12 N	94.21 W
Grand, Lac ⊜	190	47.10 N	76.57 W
Grand, North Fork ≃	198	45.47 N	102.16 W
Grand, South Fork ≃	198	45.43 N	102.17 W
Grandas	34	43.13 N	6.52 W
Grandas de Salime, Embalse de ⊜[1]	34	43.10 N	6.45 W
Grand Bahama I	238	26.38 N	78.25 W
Grand Ballon ∧	58	47.55 N	7.08 E
Grand Bank	186	47.06 N	55.46 W
Grand Banks of Newfoundland ✢[4]	16	45.00 N	53.00 W
Grand Bassa □[6]	150	6.00 N	9.30 W
Grand-Bassam	150	5.12 N	3.44 W
Grand Bay, N.B., Can.	186	45.18 N	66.12 W
Grand Bay, Al., U.S.	194	30.28 N	88.20 W
Grand Bay c	240d	15.14 N	61.19 W
Grand Beach	184	50.35 N	96.40 W
Grand Bend	190	43.15 N	81.45 W
Grand Béréby	150	4.38 N	6.55 W
Grand Blanc	216	42.55 N	83.37 W
Grand-Bourg	241o	15.53 N	61.19 W
Grand Bruit	186	47.41 N	58.13 W
Grand Caille Point >	241f	13.52 N	61.05 W
Grand Calumet ≃	278	41.38 N	87.34 W
Grand Calumet, Île du I	190	45.44 N	76.41 W
Grand Canal ≋	48	53.21 N	6.14 W
Grand Canal → Da Yunhe ≋	90	32.12 N	119.31 E
Grand Cane	194	32.05 N	93.48 W
Grand Cañon du Verdon ♠	62	43.47 N	6.27 E
Grand Canyon	200	36.03 N	112.08 W
Grand Canyon V	200	36.10 N	112.45 W
Grand Canyon National Park ♠	200	36.15 N	112.58 W
Grand Canyon of Pennsylvania ♠	210	41.43 N	77.28 W
Grand Cape Mount □[6]	150	7.00 N	11.00 W
Grand Cayman I	238	19.20 N	81.15 W
Grand Central Terminal ◆[5]	276	40.45 N	73.59 W
Grand Centre	184	54.25 N	110.13 W
Grand Cess	150	4.36 N	8.10 W
Grandchamp, Fr.	58	47.43 N	5.27 E
Grandchamp, Fr.	261	48.43 N	1.37 E
Grand-Charmont	58	47.32 N	6.50 E
Grand Chenier	194	29.46 N	92.58 W
Grand Combin ∧	58	45.56 N	7.18 E
Grand Coulee	202	47.56 N	119.00 W
Grand Coulee V	202	47.45 N	119.15 W
Grand Coulee Dam ◆[6]	202	47.57 N	118.59 W
Grand-Couronne	50	49.21 N	1.00 E
Grand Cul-de-Sac Marin c	241o	16.20 N	61.35 W
Grande ≃, Arg.	252	36.52 S	69.45 W
Grande ≃, Arg.	252	24.12 S	64.42 W
Grande ≃, Bol.	248	15.51 S	64.39 W
Grande ≃, Bra.	242	11.05 S	43.09 W
Grande ≃, Bra.	255	20.06 S	51.04 W
Grande ≃, Bra.	287a	22.55 S	43.25 W
Grande ≃, Bra.	287b	23.45 S	46.22 W
Grande ≃, Chile	252	30.35 S	71.11 W
Grande ≃, Esp.	34	39.07 N	0.44 W
Grande ≃, It.	70	37.55 N	13.13 E
Grande ≃, Méx.	234	17.13 N	100.55 W
Grande ≃, Méx.	234	17.43 N	96.56 W
Grande ≃, Méx.	234	16.47 N	95.52 W
Grande ≃, Pan.	236	8.18 N	80.24 W
Grande ≃, Perú	248	14.59 S	75.29 W
Grande ≃, S.A.	254	53.48 S	67.40 W
Grande, Arroyo ≃, Arg.	258	34.37 S	59.25 W
Grande, Arroyo ≃, Arg.	288	34.45 S	58.08 W
Grande, Arroyo ≃, Méx.	234	23.55 N	98.44 W
Grande, Arroyo ≃, Ur.	252	33.08 S	57.09 W
Grande, Arroyo ≃, Ur.	258	33.37 S	57.09 W
Grande, Bahía c[3]	254	50.45 S	68.45 W
Grande, Boca c	220	26.43 N	82.16 W
Grande, Boca ≃[1]	246	8.38 N	60.30 W
Grande, Cañada ≃, Arg.	258	35.15 S	59.23 W
Grande, Cañada ≃, Arg.	258	35.19 S	57.48 W
Grande, Cayo I	240p	20.59 N	79.09 W
Grande, Cerro ∧, Méx.	234	21.45 N	103.05 W
Grande, Cerro ∧, Méx.	234	20.30 N	103.02 W
Grande, Cerro ∧, Méx.	234	20.43 N	101.12 W
Grande, Cerro ∧, Méx.	234	23.39 N	100.51 W
Grande, Corixa (Curiche Grande) ≡	248	17.10 S	58.20 W
Grande, Cuchilla ∧	252	33.15 S	55.07 W
Grande, Curiche (Corixa Grande) ≡	248	17.10 S	58.20 W
Grande, Igarapé ≃	250	3.37 S	48.53 W
Grande, Ilha I, Bra.	252	23.45 S	54.03 W
Grande, Ilha I, Bra.	256	23.09 S	44.14 W
Grande, Isola I	70	37.53 N	12.26 E
Grande, Lago ⊜, Arg.	254	47.44 S	68.04 W
Grande, Lago ⊜, Bra.	250	2.16 S	54.17 W
Grande, Laguna c	286b	23.05 N	82.30 W
Grande, Laguna ⊜	258	34.14 S	58.53 W
Grande, Mare (Taranto) c	68	40.27 N	17.12 E
Grande, Naviglio ≋	266b	45.35 N	8.42 E
Grande, Ponta >	255	16.22 S	39.01 W
Grande, Praia ⩟[2]	256	24.05 S	46.30 W
Grande, Punta >	252	25.06 S	70.30 W
Grande, Ribeirão ≃	256	22.11 S	43.19 W
Grande, Rio (Bravo del Norte) ≃	178	25.55 N	97.09 W
Grande, Salina ≡	68	40.26 N	17.18 E
Grande, Serra ⋏	250	6.00 S	40.52 W
Grande, Serra → Geral, Serra ⩟[4]	250	11.15 S	46.30 W
Grande, Sierra ⋏	196	29.40 N	104.55 W
Grande, Volcán ∧[1]	234	20.06 N	101.38 W
Grande-Anse, N.B., Can.	186	47.48 N	65.11 W
Grande Anse, Guad.	241o	16.18 N	61.04 W
Grande Anse, La c	275a	45.23 N	73.53 W
Grande Anse Bay c	241k	12.02 N	61.45 W
Grande Baie, La c	275a	45.29 N	74.00 W
Grande Casse, Pointe de la ∧	62	45.24 N	6.50 E
Grande Cayemite I	238	18.37 N	73.45 W
Grande Chartreuse, Couvent de la ♁[1]	62	45.22 N	5.50 E
Grande da Botija, Ilha I	246	3.58 S	62.53 W
Grande de Añasco ≃	240m	18.16 N	67.11 W
Grande de Arecibo ≃	240m	18.29 N	66.42 W
Grande de Jutaí, Ilha I	250	3.15 S	49.37 W
Grande de Lipez ≃	248	20.47 S	67.14 W
Grande de Loíza ≃	240m	18.27 N	65.53 W
Grande de Manacapuru, Lago ⊜	246	3.04 S	61.25 W
Grande de Manatí ≃	240m	18.29 N	66.32 W
Grande de Matagalpa ≃	236	12.54 N	83.32 W
Grande de Santa Marta, Ciénaga c	246	10.50 N	74.25 W
Grande de Santiago ≃	234	21.36 N	105.26 W
Grande de Tarija ≃	248	22.53 S	64.21 W
Grande de Térraba ≃	236	9.03 N	83.40 W
Grande do Curuaí, Lago ⊜	250	2.15 S	55.20 W
Grande do Gurupá, Ilha I	250	1.00 S	51.30 W
Grande do Tapará, Ilha I	250	2.14 S	54.39 W
Grande Île de Criques I	273b	4.20 S	15.25 E
Grande Inferior, Cuchilla ⋏[2]	258	33.50 S	56.27 W
Grand-Entrée	186	47.33 N	61.34 W
Grande Pointe >	241o	15.58 N	61.38 W
Grande-Prairie	182	55.10 N	118.48 W
Grand Erg de Bilma ◆[2]	146	18.30 N	14.00 E
Grand Erg Occidental ◆[2]	148	30.30 N	0.30 E
Grand Erg Oriental ◆[2]	148	30.30 N	7.00 E
Grande-Rivière	186	48.24 N	64.30 W
Grande Rivière, La ≃	176	53.50 N	79.00 W
Grande Ronde ≃	202	46.05 N	116.59 W
Grandes, Salinas ≚, Arg.	252	30.05 S	65.05 W
Grandes, Salinas ≚, Arg.	252	23.43 S	66.00 W
Grandes Antillas, Islas → Greater Antilles II	238	20.00 N	74.00 W
Grandes Antilles, Îles → Greater Antilles II	238	20.00 N	74.00 W
Grande Sassière, Aiguille de la ∧	62	45.30 N	7.00 E
Grande Sauldre ≃	50	47.22 N	1.55 E
Gran Desierto de Arena → Great Sandy Desert ◆[2]	162	21.30 S	125.00 E
Gran Desierto Victoria → Great Victoria Desert ◆[2]	162	28.30 S	127.45 E
Grandes-Piles	206	46.41 N	72.44 W
Grande-Synthe	50	51.01 N	2.19 E
Grand-Étang	186	46.33 N	61.02 W
Grande-Terre I	241o	16.20 N	61.25 W
Grande Vigie, Pointe de la >	241o	16.31 N	61.28 W
Grand Eyvia ≃	62	45.42 N	7.14 E
Grand Falls, N.B., Can.	186	47.03 N	67.44 W
Grand Falls, Nf., Can.	186	48.56 N	55.40 W
Grandfalls, Tx., U.S.	196	31.20 N	102.51 W
Grandfather Mountain ∧	192	36.07 N	81.48 W
Grandfield	196	34.13 N	98.41 W
Grand Forks, B.C., Can.	182	49.02 N	118.27 W
Grand Forks, N.D., U.S.	198	47.55 N	97.01 W
Grand Forks Air Force Base ■	198	47.57 N	97.25 W
Grand-Fort-Philippe	50	51.00 N	2.06 E
Grand-Fougeray	32	47.44 N	1.44 W
Grand-Gallargues	62	43.43 N	4.10 E
Grand Gedeh □[6]	150	6.00 N	8.00 W
Grand Gorge	210	42.21 N	74.29 W
Grand-Halleux	56	50.19 N	5.54 E
Grand Haven	216	43.03 N	86.13 W
Grand Haven State Park ♠	216	43.02 N	86.13 W
Grand Hers ≃	32	43.47 N	1.20 E
Grandiči	76	53.43 N	23.49 E
Grandin, Lac ⊜	176	63.59 N	119.00 W
Grandioznyj, pik ∧	88	53.50 N	96.11 E
Grand Island, Fl., U.S.	220	28.53 N	81.44 W
Grand Island, Ne., U.S.	198	40.55 N	98.20 W
Grand Island, N.Y., U.S.	212	43.01 N	78.58 W
Grand Island I, On., Can.	212	44.34 N	78.50 W
Grand Island I, Mi., U.S.	190	46.30 N	86.40 W
Grand Island I, N.Y., U.S.	210	43.02 N	78.58 W
Grand Isle	194	29.14 N	89.59 W
Grand Isle □[6]	206	44.57 N	73.17 W
Grand Junction, Co., U.S.	200	39.03 N	108.33 W
Grand Junction, Ia., U.S.	198	42.01 N	94.14 W
Grand Junction, Mi., U.S.	216	42.24 N	86.04 W
Grand Junction, Tn., U.S.	194	35.02 N	89.11 W
Grand Lac Salé → Great Salt Lake ⊜	200	41.10 N	112.30 W
Grand lac Victoria ⊜	190	47.31 N	77.30 W
Grand-Lahou	150	5.08 N	5.01 W
Grand Lake	200	40.15 N	105.49 W
Grand Lake ⊜, N.B., Can.	186	45.55 N	66.05 W
Grand Lake ⊜, Nf., Can.	186	49.00 N	57.25 W
Grand Lake ⊜, N.A.	186	45.43 N	67.50 W
Grand Lake ⊜, La., U.S.	194	29.55 N	91.25 W
Grand Lake ⊜, La., U.S.	194	29.55 N	92.47 W
Grand Lake ⊜, Mi., U.S.	190	45.18 N	83.30 W
Grand Lake ⊜, Oh., U.S.	216	40.30 N	84.32 W
Grand Lake Saint Marys State Park ♠	216	40.33 N	84.27 W
Grand Ledge	216	42.45 N	84.44 W
Grand Lieu, Lac de ⊜	32	47.06 N	1.40 W
Grand'Maison, Barrage de ◆[6]	62	45.12 N	6.07 E
Grand Manan Channel ʊ	186	44.45 N	66.52 W
Grand Manan Island I	186	44.40 N	66.50 W
Grand Marais, Mi., U.S.	190	46.40 N	85.59 W
Grand Marais, Mn., U.S.	190	47.45 N	90.20 W
Grand Meadow	190	43.42 N	92.34 W
Grand-Mère	206	46.37 N	72.41 W
Grand Mesa ∧	200	39.00 N	108.00 W
Grandmesnil, Lac ⊜	186	51.19 N	67.33 W
Grand Morin ≃	50	48.54 N	2.50 E
Grand Muveran ∧	58	46.14 N	7.08 E
Grandola, It.	58	46.02 N	9.13 E
Grândola, Port.	34	38.10 N	8.34 W
Grand Pabos, Rivière du ≃	186	48.21 N	64.43 W
Grand Palace ♁	269a	13.45 N	100.30 E
Grand Passage ʊ	175f	18.45 S	163.10 E
Grand-Popo	150	6.17 N	1.50 E
Grand Portage	190	47.57 N	89.41 W
Grand Portage Indian Reservation ◆[4]	190	47.55 N	89.45 W
Grand Portage National Monument ♠	190	48.02 N	89.38 W
Grand Prairie	222	32.44 N	96.59 W
Grandpré	56	49.20 N	4.52 E
Grand Pré National Historic Park ♠	186	45.08 N	64.18 W
Grand Prix Airport ⊠	281	42.33 N	83.11 W
Grand Rapids, Mb., Can.	184	53.08 N	99.20 W
Grand Rapids, Mi., U.S.	216	42.58 N	85.40 W
Grand Rapids, Mn., U.S.	190	47.14 N	93.31 W
Grand Rapids, Oh., U.S.	216	41.24 N	83.51 W
Grand Rhône ≃	62	43.20 N	4.50 E
Grand Ridge	216	41.14 N	88.50 W
Grandrieu, Bel.	50	50.12 N	4.10 E
Grandrieu, Fr.	62	44.47 N	3.38 E
Grand River	214	41.44 N	81.17 W
Grand' Rivière	240e	14.52 N	61.11 W
Grand Ronde	224	45.03 N	123.36 W
Grand Roy	241k	12.08 N	61.45 W
Grand Ruisseau, Le ≃	275a	45.39 N	73.12 W
Grand-Saint-Bernard, Col du)(	58	45.50 N	7.10 E
Grand-Saint-Bernard, Tunnel du ◆[5]	58	45.51 N	7.11 E
Grand Saline	222	32.40 N	95.42 W
Grand Saline Creek ≃	222	32.41 N	95.36 W
Grandson	58	46.49 N	6.38 E
Grand Terrace	228	34.02 N	117.18 W
Grand Teton ∧	202	43.44 N	110.48 W
Grand Teton National Park ♠	202	43.30 N	110.45 W
Grand Tower	194	37.37 N	89.29 W
Grand Traverse Bay c	190	45.02 N	85.30 W
Grand Traverse Bay, East Arm c	190	44.52 N	85.28 W
Grand Traverse Bay, West Arm c	190	44.52 N	85.35 W
Grandtully	46	56.39 N	3.46 W
Grand Turk	238	21.28 N	71.08 W
Grand Union Canal ≋	260	51.30 N	0.02 W
Grand Valley, On., Can.	212	43.54 N	80.19 W
Grand Valley, Pa., U.S.	214	41.43 N	79.32 W
Grandview, Mb., Can.	184	51.10 N	100.42 W
Grandview, Il., U.S.	219	42.06 N	89.50 W
Grandview, Mo., U.S.	194	38.53 N	94.31 W
Grandview, Pa., U.S.	279b	40.10 N	79.52 W
Grandview, Tx., U.S.	222	32.16 N	97.11 W
Grandview, Wa., U.S.	202	46.15 N	119.54 W
Grand View, Wi., U.S.	190	46.22 N	91.06 W
Grandview Beach	216	41.50 N	83.24 W
Grandview Heights, Oh., U.S.	218	39.58 N	83.02 W
Grandview Heights, Pa., U.S.	208	40.03 N	76.17 W
Grandview Homes	216	40.44 N	84.04 W
Grand View-on-Hudson	276	41.44 N	73.55 W
Grandvillars	58	47.33 N	6.58 E
Grandville	216	42.54 N	85.45 W
Grandvilliers	50	49.40 N	1.56 E
Grand Wash Cliffs ⩟[4]	200	35.40 N	113.50 W
Grand Winterberg ∧	56	48.59 N	7.37 E
Grandyle Village	210	43.00 N	78.57 W
Grâne	62	44.44 N	4.55 E
Grañén	34	41.56 N	0.22 W
Graneros	252	34.04 S	70.44 W
Granetalsperre ◆[6]	52	51.48 N	10.27 E
Graney, Lough ⊜	48	52.59 N	8.40 W
Grangärde	40	60.16 N	14.59 E
Grange, Austl.	168b	34.54 S	138.30 E
Grange, Eng., U.K.	262	53.23 N	3.09 W
Grange, Bois de la ♠	261	48.45 N	2.30 E
Grange-Bléneau, Château de la ⊥	50	48.41 N	2.55 E
Grange Hill	260	51.37 N	0.05 E
Grangemouth	46	56.02 N	3.45 W
Grängen ⊜	40	59.45 N	14.47 E
Grangent, Lac de ⊜[1]	62	45.25 N	4.15 E
Grange-over-Sands	44	54.12 N	2.55 W
Granger, Tx., U.S.	222	30.43 N	97.26 W
Granger, Wa., U.S.	202	46.20 N	120.11 W
Granger, Wy., U.S.	200	41.35 N	109.58 W
Granger Draw V	196	30.20 N	100.57 W
Granger Lake ⊜[1]	222	30.42 N	97.22 W
Granges → Grenchen	58	47.11 N	7.24 E
Grängesberg	40	60.05 N	14.59 E
Granges-sur-Vologne	58	48.09 N	6.47 E
Grangeville, Id., U.S.	202	45.55 N	116.07 W
Grangeville, Pa., U.S.	208	39.47 N	76.58 W
Grangousier Hill ∧[2]	190	47.35 N	84.56 W
Gran Guardia	252	25.52 S	58.53 W
Granite, Md., U.S.	284b	39.21 N	76.51 W
Granite, Ok., U.S.	196	34.57 N	99.22 W
Granite City	219	38.42 N	90.08 W
Granite Creek ≃	224	48.43 N	120.55 W
Granite Dome ∧	226	38.13 N	119.44 W
Granite Downs	162	26.57 S	133.30 E
Granite Falls, Mn., U.S.	198	44.48 N	95.32 W
Granite Falls, N.C., U.S.	192	35.47 N	81.25 W
Granite Falls, Wa., U.S.	224	48.05 N	121.58 W
Granite Lake ⊜[1]	186	48.08 N	57.05 W
Granite Mountain ∧, Austl.	171b	35.44 S	148.13 E
Granite Mountain ∧, Ak., U.S.	180	65.26 N	161.14 W
Granite Mountain ∧, Ak., U.S.	182	55.30 N	132.35 W
Granite Mountains ⋏	202	42.35 N	107.30 W
Granite Pass)(	202	44.38 N	107.30 W
Granite Peak	162	25.38 S	121.21 E
Granite Peak ∧, Mt., U.S.	202	45.10 N	109.48 W
Granite Peak ∧, Mt., U.S.	202	45.34 N	112.02 W
Granite Peak ∧, Nv., U.S.	204	41.40 N	117.35 W
Granite Peak ∧, Nv., U.S.	204	40.48 N	119.25 W
Granite Range ⋏	204	41.00 N	119.35 W
Graniteville, Ma., U.S.	207	42.35 N	71.27 W
Graniteville, S.C., U.S.	192	33.33 N	81.48 W
Graniteville, Vt., U.S.	188	44.09 N	72.29 W
Graniti	70	37.53 N	15.14 E
Granitnoje	83	47.27 N	37.52 E
Granito	250	7.43 S	39.36 W
Granitogorsk	85	42.44 N	73.27 E
Granitola, Capo >	70	37.34 N	12.41 E
Granitola Torretta	70	37.34 N	12.40 E
Granity	172	41.38 S	171.51 E
Granitzenbach ≃	61	47.11 N	14.46 E
Granja, Bra.	250	3.06 S	40.50 W
Granja, Port.	266c	38.51 N	9.06 W
Gran Khingan → Da Hinggan Ling ⋏	90	49.00 N	122.00 E
Granki	76	54.51 N	31.27 E
Grankulla (Kauniainen)	26	60.13 N	24.45 E
Gran Lago Salado → Great Salt Lake ⊜	200	41.10 N	112.30 W
Gran Laguna Salada ⊜	254	44.24 S	67.23 W
Granma □[4]	240p	21.20 N	76.50 W
Gränna	26	58.01 N	14.28 E
Grannoch, Loch ≃	44	55.00 N	4.17 W
Granollers	34	41.37 N	2.18 E
Granön	26	64.15 N	19.19 E
Granov	78	48.52 N	29.34 E
Gran Pajonal ⋏	248	10.45 S	74.30 W
Gran Paradiso ∧	62	45.32 N	7.16 E
Gran Paradiso, Parco Nazionale del ♠	62	45.34 N	7.18 E
Gran Piedra ∧	240p	20.01 N	75.38 W
Gran Pilastro (Hochfeiler) ∧	64	46.58 N	11.44 E
Gran Rio ≃	250	4.01 N	55.31 W

≃ River	Fluss	Río	Rivière	Rio
≋ Canal	Kanal	Canal	Canal	Canal
ʟ Waterfall, Rapids	Wasserfall, Stromschnellen	Cascada, Rápidos	Chute d'eau, Rapides	Cascata, Rápidos
ʊ Strait	Meeresstrasse	Estrecho	Détroit	Estreito
c Bay, Gulf	Bucht, Golf	Bahía, Golfo	Baie, Golfe	Baía, Golfo
⊜ Lake, Lakes	See, Seen	Lago, Lagos	Lac, Lacs	Lago, Lagos
≡ Swamp	Sumpf	Pantano	Marais	Pântano
⊓ Ice Features, Glacier	Eis- und Gletscherformen	Accidentes Glaciales	Formes glaciaires	Acidentes glaciares
‡ Other Hydrographic Features	Andere Hydrographische Objekte	Otros Elementos Hidrográficos	Autres données hydrographiques	Outros acidentes hidrográficos

✢ Submarine Features	Untermeerische Objekte	Accidentes Submarinos	Formes de relief sous-marin	Acidentes submarinos
□ Political Unit	Politische Einheit	Unidad Politica	Entité politique	Unidade política
♁ Cultural Institution	Kulturelle Institution	Institución Cultural	Institution culturelle	Instituição cultural
⊥ Historical Site	Historische Stätte	Sitio Histórico	Site historique	Sitio histórico
♠ Recreational Site	Erholungs- und Ferienort	Sitio de Recreo	Centre de loisirs	Area de Lazer
⊠ Airport	Flughafen	Aeropuerto	Aéroport	Aeroporto
■ Military Installation	Militäranlage	Instalación Militar	Installation militaire	Instalação militar
◆ Miscellaneous	Verschiedenes	Misceláneo	Divers	Diversos

Gran Sasso d'Italia ⋏ 66 42.27 N 13.42 E
Gransee 54 53.00 N 13.09 E
Grant, Fl., U.S. 220 27.55 N 80.31 W
Grant, Mi., U.S. 190 43.20 N 85.48 W
Grant, Ne., U.S. 198 40.50 N 101.43 W
Grant □[6], In., U.S. 216 40.33 N 85.40 W
Grant □[6], Ky., U.S. 218 38.39 N 84.39 W
Grant ≃ 190 42.40 N 90.45 W
Grant, Lake ⊜ 218 39.00 N 83.53 W
Grant, Mount ʌ 204 38.34 N 118.48 W
Grant, Point ≻ 169 38.31 S 145.07 E
Granta ≃ 42 52.10 N 0.06 E
Grant Birthplace ⊥ 218 38.54 N 84.14 W
Grant City 194 40.29 N 94.24 W
Grantham, Austl. 171a 27.34 S 152.12 E
Grantham, Eng., U.K. 42 52.55 N 0.39 W
Grantham, Pa., U.S. 208 40.09 N 77.00 W
Grant-Kohrs Ranch National Historic Site ⊥ 202 46.25 N 112.40 W
Grant Lake ⊜[1] 226 37.50 N 119.07 W
Grant Mills 283 41.57 N 71.26 W
Granton 46 55.59 N 3.14 W
Grantorto 64 45.36 N 11.43 E
Grantown on Spey 46 57.20 N 3.58 W
Grant Park 216 41.14 N 87.39 W
Grant Park ♦ 278 41.52 N 87.37 W
Grant Point ≻ 176 68.19 N 98.53 W
Grant Range ⋏ 204 38.25 N 115.30 W
Grants 200 35.09 N 107.50 W
Grantsburg, In., U.S. 218 38.17 N 86.28 W
Grantsburg, Wi., U.S. 190 45.46 N 92.40 W
Grantshouse 46 55.53 N 2.19 W
Grants Pass 202 42.26 N 123.19 W
Grants Patch 162 30.27 S 121.07 E
Grant-Suttie Bay c 176 69.47 N 77.15 W
Grantsville, Ut., U.S. 200 40.36 N 112.27 W
Grantsville, W.V., U.S. 188 38.55 N 81.05 W
Grantville, Ga., U.S. 192 33.14 N 84.50 W
Grantville, Pa., U.S. 208 40.23 N 76.39 W
Granum 182 49.52 N 113.30 W
Granville, Austl. 274a 33.50 S 151.01 E
Granville, Fr. 32 48.50 N 1.36 W
Granville, Il., U.S. 190 41.15 N 89.13 W
Granville, Ma., U.S. 207 42.04 N 72.51 W
Granville, Mo., U.S. 219 39.34 N 92.06 W
Granville, N.Y., U.S. 188 43.24 N 73.15 W
Granville, N.D., U.S. 198 48.16 N 100.50 W
Granville, Oh., U.S. 214 40.04 N 82.31 W
Granville, Pa., U.S. 208 40.33 N 77.38 W
Granville, W.V., U.S. 188 39.38 N 79.59 W
Granville Lake ⊜ 184 56.18 N 100.30 W
Granvin 26 60.33 N 6.43 E
Granzin, D.D.R. 54 53.25 N 12.53 E
Granzin, D.D.R. 54 53.30 N 11.56 E
Grão Mogol 255 16.34 S 42.54 W
Grão Mongol, Ribeirão ≃ 256 21.46 S 43.40 W
Grape Creek ≃ 200 38.26 N 105.16 W
Grape Island I 283 42.16 N 70.55 W
Grapeland 222 31.29 N 95.28 W
Grapeview 224 47.19 N 122.50 W
Grapeville 214 40.19 N 79.36 W
Grapevine 222 32.56 N 97.04 W
Grapevine Lake ⊜[1] 222 32.59 N 97.06 W
Grapevine Peak ʌ 204 36.57 N 117.09 W
Grappa, Monte ʌ 64 45.52 N 11.48 E
Grappenhall 262 53.22 N 2.32 W
Grarem 34 36.31 N 6.19 E
Gras, Lac de ⊜ 176 64.30 N 110.30 W
Grasbult 158 30.52 S 21.47 E
Grasdorf 52 52.06 N 10.09 E
Graskop 156 24.58 S 30.49 E
Grasleben 54 52.18 N 11.01 E
Grasmere, S. Afr. 158 26.26 S 27.52 E
Grasmere, Eng., U.K. 44 54.28 N 3.02 W
Grasmere Lake ⊜ 276 40.36 N 74.05 W
Gräsö 40 60.21 N 18.28 E
Gräsö I 40 60.24 N 18.25 E
Grasonville 208 38.57 N 76.12 W
Grass ≃, Mb., Can. 184 56.03 N 96.33 W
Grass ≃, N.Y., U.S. 188 44.59 N 74.46 W
Grass, North Branch ≃ 188 44.25 N 75.06 W
Grass, South Branch ≃ 188 44.22 N 75.05 W
Grassano 68 40.38 N 16.18 E
Grassau 64 47.47 N 12.27 E
Grass Creek 202 43.56 N 108.39 W
Grass Creek ≃ 202 43.52 N 108.22 W
Grasscroft 262 53.32 N 2.02 W
Grasse 62 43.40 N 6.55 E
Grassendale ◆[8] 262 53.21 N 2.54 W
Grassflat 214 41.00 N 78.07 W
Grass Hassock Channel ⊔ 276 40.36 N 73.48 W
Grasshopper Creek ≃ 202 45.06 N 112.47 W
Grassington 44 54.04 N 4.59 W
Grass Island I 276 40.39 N 73.18 W
Grässjön ⊜ 40 59.52 N 13.43 E
Grass Lake 216 42.15 N 84.13 W
Grass Lake ⊜ 216 42.27 N 88.10 W
Grass Patch 162 33.14 S 121.43 E
Grass Range 202 47.01 N 108.48 W
Grassridge Dam ⊜[1] 158 31.45 S 25.29 E
Grass River Provincial Park ♦ 184 54.40 N 100.50 W
Grass Valley, Austl. 168a 31.38 S 116.48 E
Grass Valley, Ca., U.S. 226 39.13 N 121.03 W
Grass Valley, Or., U.S. 224 45.21 N 120.47 W
Grassy 166 40.03 S 144.04 E
Grassy ≃ 190 48.22 N 81.27 W
Grassy Bay c 276 40.38 N 73.48 W
Grassy Brook ≃ 284a 43.03 N 79.07 W
Grassy Creek ≃, In., U.S. 216 40.55 N 86.30 W
Grassy Creek ≃, Mo., U.S. 219 39.54 N 91.37 W
Grassy Hill ʌ 271d 22.25 N 114.09 E
Grassy Island I 276 41.04 N 73.23 W
Grassy Island Lake ⊜ 184 51.50 N 110.20 W
Grassy Key I 220 24.46 N 80.57 W
Grassy Lake 182 49.49 N 111.43 W
Grassy Lake ⊜ 220 27.13 N 81.20 W
Grassy Plains 182 53.57 N 125.54 W
Grassy Sprain Reservoir ⊜[1] 276 40.58 N 73.51 W
Gråsten 41 54.55 N 9.36 E
Grästorp 26 58.20 N 12.40 E
Graterford 285 40.13 N 75.27 W
Graterford State Correctional Institution ◆ 285 40.14 N 75.26 W
Grates Point ≻ 186 48.10 N 52.57 W
Gratis 218 39.38 N 84.31 W
Gratitunon 115a 7.43 S 113.00 E
Gratkorn 61 47.08 N 15.21 E
Gratwein 61 47.07 N 15.19 E
Gratz, Ky., U.S. 218 38.28 N 84.57 W
Gratz, Pa., U.S. 208 40.37 N 76.43 W
Gratztown 279b 40.14 N 79.47 W
Graubünden (Grischun) □[3] 58 46.45 N 9.30 E
Graudenz → Grudziądz 30 53.29 N 18.45 E
Graue Hörner ʌ 58 46.57 N 9.23 E
Graukogel ʌ 64 47.06 N 13.10 E
Graulhet 32 43.46 N 2.00 E
Graulinster 56 49.45 N 6.18 E
Graun → Curon Venosta 64 46.49 N 10.32 E
Graupa 54 51.00 N 13.54 E
Gravatá 250 8.12 S 35.34 W
Gravatá ≃ 255 16.53 S 42.10 W
Grave 52 51.45 N 5.44 E
Grave Creek ≃ 202 42.39 N 123.35 W
Gravedona 58 46.09 N 9.18 E
Gravelbourg 184 49.53 N 106.34 W
Gravelines 50 50.59 N 2.07 E
Gravellona-Toce 58 45.55 N 8.26 E
Gravell Point ≻ 176 67.10 N 76.43 W
Gravelly Bay c 284a 42.52 N 79.15 W
Gravelly Brook ≃ 276 40.25 N 74.13 W
Gravelly Pond ⊜ 283 42.36 N 70.48 W
Gravelotte, Fr. 56 49.07 N 6.01 E
Gravelotte, S. Afr. 156 23.56 S 30.34 E
Gravenhurst 212 44.55 N 79.22 W
Grävenwiesbach 56 50.23 N 8.27 E
Grave Peak ʌ 202 46.24 N 114.44 W
Gravesend, Austl. 166 29.35 S 150.19 E
Gravesend, Eng., U.K. 260 51.27 N 0.24 E
Gravesend Bay c 276 40.36 N 74.01 W
Gravesham □[8] 260 51.25 N 0.24 E
Gravette 194 36.25 N 94.27 W
Gravigny 50 49.03 N 1.10 E
Gravina 70 37.34 N 15.03 E
Gravina di Matera ≃ 68 40.37 N 16.49 E
Gravina in Puglia 68 40.49 N 16.25 E
Gravina Island I 182 55.17 N 131.45 W
Gray, Fr. 58 47.27 N 5.35 E
Gray, Ga., U.S. 192 33.00 N 83.32 W
Gray, Ky., U.S. 192 36.56 N 84.00 W
Gray, Pa., U.S. 214 40.08 N 79.05 W
Grayback Mountain ʌ, Ak., U.S. 180 57.08 N 153.54 W
Grayback Mountain ʌ, Or., U.S. 202 42.07 N 123.18 W
Grayland 224 46.48 N 124.05 W
Grayling, Ak., U.S. 180 62.57 N 160.03 W
Grayling, Mi., U.S. 190 44.39 N 84.42 W
Graylyn Crest 285 39.48 N 75.31 W
Grays, Eng., U.K. 42 51.29 N 0.20 E
Grays, Eng., U.K. 260 51.29 N 0.20 E
Grays ≃ 224 46.18 N 123.41 W
Grays Harbor □[6] 224 47.09 N 123.45 W
Grays Harbor c 224 46.56 N 124.05 W
Grayshott 42 51.11 N 0.45 W
Grayslake 216 42.21 N 88.03 W
Grays Lake ⊜ 278 42.21 N 88.03 W
Grays Lake ⊜ 202 43.04 N 111.26 W
Grays Lake Outlet ≃ 202 43.22 N 111.46 W
Grayson, Sk., Can. 184 50.44 N 102.40 W
Grayson, Al., U.S. 194 34.16 N 87.19 W
Grayson, Ca., U.S. 226 37.33 N 121.10 W
Grayson, Ky., U.S. 218 38.19 N 82.56 W
Grayson, La., U.S. 194 32.02 N 92.06 W
Grayson Lake ⊜[1] 218 38.13 N 83.00 W
Grayson Lake State Park ♦ 218 38.13 N 83.02 W
Grays Peak ʌ 200 39.37 N 105.45 W
Grays Point 274a 34.04 S 151.05 E
Grays River 224 46.21 N 123.36 W
Gray Summit 219 38.29 N 90.49 W
Graysville 194 35.26 N 85.05 W
Graytown 214 41.33 N 83.16 W
Grayville 194 37.57 N 88.00 W
Gray Wolf ≃ 224 47.55 N 123.07 W
Graz 61 47.05 N 15.27 E
Grazalema 34 36.46 N 5.22 W
Graždanka ◆[8] 265a 60.00 N 30.24 E
Gr'azeva ≃ 265b 55.51 N 37.08 E
Gr'azi 80 52.29 N 39.57 E
Grazierville 214 40.40 N 78.16 W
Gr'aznoje 82 54.02 N 39.07 E
Gr'aznovo, S.S.S.R. 82 54.18 N 36.49 E
Gr'aznovo, S.S.S.R. 265b 55.57 N 37.34 E
Gr'aznyj Irtek 80 51.56 N 53.11 E
Gr'azovec 76 58.53 N 40.14 E
Grdelica 38 42.54 N 22.04 E
Greåker 26 59.16 N 11.02 E
Greasby 262 53.23 N 3.07 W
Great ≃ 241k 12.08 N 61.36 W
Great Abaco I 238 26.28 N 77.05 W
Great Adventure ♦ 208 40.09 N 74.27 W
Great America ♦ 282 37.24 N 121.59 W
Great Amwell 260 51.48 N 0.01 W
Great Artesian Basin ≚[1] 166 25.00 S 143.00 E
Great Australian Bight c[3] 162 35.00 S 130.00 E
Great Ayton 44 54.30 N 1.08 W
Great Bacolet Point ≻ 241k 12.04 N 61.37 W
Great Baddow 260 51.43 N 0.29 E
Great Bahama Bank ◆[4] 238 23.15 N 78.00 W
Great Barrier Island I 172 36.10 S 175.25 E
Great Barrier Reef ◆[2] 160 18.00 S 145.50 E
Great Barrier Reef Marine Park ♦ 218 23.35 S 152.30 E
Great Barrington 207 42.11 N 73.21 W
Great Barrow 262 53.12 N 2.48 W
Great Basin ≚[1] 178 40.00 N 117.00 W
Great Bay c 208 39.30 N 74.23 W
Great Bear ≃ 180 64.54 N 125.35 W
Great Bear Lake ⊜ 176 66.00 N 120.00 W
Great Beaver Lake ⊜ 182 54.25 N 123.45 W
Great Bend, Ks., U.S. 198 38.21 N 98.45 W
Great Bend, N.Y., U.S. 212 44.02 N 75.43 W
Great Bend, Pa., U.S. 210 41.58 N 75.44 W
Great Bernera I 46 58.13 N 6.49 W
Great Bitter Lake → Murrah al-Kubrā, Al-Buhayrah al- ⊜ 142 30.20 N 32.23 E
Great Blasket Island I 48 52.05 N 10.32 W
Great Blue Hill ʌ[2] 207 42.13 N 71.07 W
Great Bookham 260 51.16 N 0.22 W
Great Braxted 260 51.48 N 0.42 E
Great Brewster Island I 283 42.20 N 70.53 W
Great Britain I 22 54.00 N 2.00 W
Great Brook ≃ 276 40.42 N 74.31 W
Great Buddha ◆[1] 268 35.19 N 139.32 E
Great Budworth 262 53.18 N 2.30 W
Great Burnt Lake ⊜ 186 48.20 N 56.13 W
Great Burso Bank ◆[4] 262 53.29 N 3.06 W
Great Burstead 260 51.36 N 0.25 E
Great Camanoe I 240m 18.29 N 64.32 W
Great Captain Island I 276 40.59 N 73.38 W
Great Central 182 49.19 N 124.59 W
Great Central Lake ⊜ 182 49.27 N 125.12 W
Great Channel ⊔ 110 6.25 N 94.20 E
Great Chazy ≃ 188 44.56 N 73.23 W
Great Clifton 44 54.31 N 3.29 W
Great Coco Island I 110 14.05 N 93.24 E
Great Coharie Creek ≃ 192 34.50 N 78.22 W
Great Cove c 276 40.43 N 74.12 W
Great Crosby 262 53.29 N 3.01 W
Great Crossing 218 38.08 N 84.38 W
Great Cumbrae Island I 46 55.46 N 4.55 W
Great Dismal Swamp ⋕ 192 36.30 N 76.30 W
Great Ditch ≚ 276 40.24 N 74.31 W
Great Divide Basin ≚[1] 202 42.00 N 108.10 W
Great Dividing Range ⋏ 160 25.00 S 147.00 E
Great Driffield 44 54.00 N 0.27 W
Great Duck Island I 190 45.40 N 82.58 W
Great Dunmow 42 51.53 N 0.22 E
Great Eau ≃ 44 53.25 N 0.13 E
Great Egg Harbor ≃ 208 39.18 N 74.40 W
Great Egg Harbor Bay c 208 39.18 N 74.37 W
Great Egg Harbor Inlet c 208 39.20 N 74.20 W
Greater Antilles II 238 20.00 N 74.00 W
Greater Bombay □[5] 272c 19.08 N 72.51 E
Greater Buffalo International Airport ⋈ 210 42.56 N 78.44 W
Greater Cincinnati Airport ⋈ 218 39.03 N 84.40 W
Greater Khingan Range → Da Hinggan Ling ⋏ 90 49.00 N 122.00 E
Greater London □[6] 260 51.30 N 0.10 W
Greater Manchester □[6] 44 53.30 N 2.20 W
Greater Pittsburgh International Airport ⋈ 214 40.29 N 80.14 W
Greater Sunda Islands II 108 2.00 S 110.00 E
Greater Wilmington Airport ⋈ 208 39.41 N 75.36 W
Greater Wollongong → Wollongong 170 34.25 S 150.54 E
Great Escape ♦ 210 43.22 N 73.42 W
Great Exuma I 238 23.32 N 75.50 W
Great Falls, Mb., Can. 184 50.27 N 96.02 W
Great Falls, Mt., U.S. 202 47.30 N 111.17 W
Great Falls, S.C., U.S. 192 34.34 N 80.54 W
Great Falls, Va., U.S. 284c 39.00 N 77.17 W
Great Falls ⌞ 284c 39.00 N 77.16 W
Great Falls Park ♦ 284c 39.00 N 77.15 W
Great Fish Point ≻ 158 33.30 S 27.10 E
Great Gable ʌ 44 54.28 N 3.12 W
Great Gaddesden 260 51.47 N 0.30 W
Great Grimsby → Grimsby 44 53.35 N 0.05 W
Great Guana Cay I 238 24.00 N 76.20 W
Great Hameldon ʌ[2] 262 53.45 N 2.19 W
Great Harwood 262 53.48 N 2.24 W
Great Haywood 42 52.48 N 2.00 W
Greathead Bay c 241h 13.08 N 61.14 W
Great Himalaya Range ⋏ 120 29.00 N 83.00 E
Greathouse Peak ʌ 202 46.46 N 109.21 W
Great Inagua I 238 21.05 N 73.18 W
Great Indian Desert (Thar Desert) ◆[2] 120 27.00 N 71.00 E
Great Island I, Ire. 48 51.52 N 8.17 W
Great Island I, N.Y., U.S. 276 40.38 N 73.30 W
Great Island I, N.Y., U.S. 276 41.05 N 73.44 W
Great Karroo (Groot Karroo) ⋏[1] 158 32.25 S 22.40 E
Great Kills ◆[8] 276 40.33 N 74.10 W
Great Kills Harbor c 276 40.32 N 74.08 W
Great Kills Park ♦ 276 40.33 N 74.08 W
Great La Cloche Island I 190 46.01 N 81.52 W
Great Lake ⊜ 166 41.52 S 146.45 E
Great Lakes Naval Training Center ■ 216 42.18 N 87.50 W
Great Lakes Steel Works ◆[3] 281 42.15 N 83.08 W
Great Machipongo Inlet c 208 37.22 N 75.43 W
Great Malvern 42 52.07 N 2.19 W
Great Marsh ⋕ 208 36.32 N 75.57 W
Great Marton 262 53.48 N 3.02 W
Great Massingham 44 52.46 N 0.40 E
Great Meadows 210 40.52 N 74.54 W
Great Meadows National Wildlife Refuge ◆[4] 283 42.29 N 71.20 W
Great Mercury Island I 172 36.37 S 175.48 E
Great Meteor Tablemount ◆[3] 18 30.00 N 28.30 W
Great Miami ≃ 188 39.06 N 84.49 W
Great Mills 208 38.14 N 76.30 W
Great Misery Island I 283 42.33 N 70.48 W
Great Missenden 42 51.43 N 0.43 W
Great Mis Tor ʌ 42 50.34 N 4.01 W
Great Mosque ◆[1] 146 32.46 N 22.40 E
Great Namaqualand ◆[9] 156 25.00 S 17.00 E
Great Neck 276 40.48 N 73.43 W
Great Neck ≻[1], Ma., U.S. 283 42.42 N 70.48 W
Great Neck ≻[1], N.Y., U.S. 276 40.50 N 73.45 W
Great Neck Estates 276 40.47 N 73.44 W
Great Nicobar I 110 7.00 N 93.50 E
Great North East Channel ⊔ 164 9.30 S 143.25 E
Great Notch Reservoir ⊜[1] 276 40.53 N 74.12 W
Great Ormes Head ≻ 44 53.21 N 3.52 W
Great Ouse ≃ 42 52.47 N 0.22 E
Great Oxney Green 260 51.44 N 0.25 E
Great Palm Island I 166 18.43 S 146.37 E
Great Parndon 260 51.45 N 0.05 E
Great Patchogue Lake ⊜ 276 40.46 N 73.01 W
Great Peconic Bay c 207 40.56 N 72.30 W
Great Pee Dee ≃ 192 33.21 N 79.16 W
Great Piece Meadows ⋕ 276 40.54 N 74.19 W
Great Plain of the Koukdjuak ≚ 176 66.00 N 73.00 W
Great Plains ≚ 16 42.00 N 100.00 W
Great Point ≻ 207 41.23 N 70.03 W
Great Pubnico Lake ⊜ 186 43.42 N 65.43 W
Great Quittacas Pond ⊜ 207 41.48 N 70.54 W
Great River 276 40.45 N 73.10 W
Great Ruaha ≃ 154 7.56 S 37.52 E
Great Sacandaga Lake ⊜ 210 43.08 N 74.10 W
Great Saint Bernard Pass → Grand-Saint-Bernard, Col du)(58 45.50 N 7.10 E
Great Sale Cay I 192 27.00 N 78.12 W
Great Salt Lake ⊜ 200 41.10 N 112.30 W
Great Salt Lake Desert ◆[2] 200 40.40 N 113.30 W
Great Salt Plains Lake ⊜[1] 196 36.44 N 98.12 W
Great Sand Dunes National Monument ◆ 200 37.43 N 105.36 W
Great Sand Hills ◆[2] 184 50.35 N 109.05 W
Great Sandy Desert ◆[2] 162 21.30 S 125.00 E
Great Sankey, Eng., U.K. 44 53.23 N 2.37 W
Great Sankey, Eng., U.K. 262 53.23 N 2.39 W
Great Santa Cruz Island I 116 6.52 N 122.03 E
Great Scarcies (Kolenté) ≃ 150 8.55 N 13.08 W
Great Sea Reef ◆[2] 175g 16.15 S 179.00 E
Great Seneca Creek ≃ 208 39.08 N 77.20 W
Great Shelford 42 52.09 N 0.09 E
Great Sitkin Island I 180 52.03 N 176.07 W
Great Slave Lake ⊜ 176 61.30 N 114.00 W
Great Smoky Mountains ⋏ 192 35.35 N 83.30 W
Great Smoky Mountains National Park ♦ 192 35.39 N 83.30 W
Great Sound ⊔, Ber. 240a 32.17 N 64.51 W
Great Sound ⊔, N.J., U.S. 208 39.06 N 74.47 W
Great South Bay c 210 40.40 N 73.17 W
Great Stour ≃ 42 51.19 N 1.15 E
Great Sutton 262 53.17 N 2.56 W
Great Swamp National Wildlife Refuge ◆[4] 276 40.43 N 74.28 W
Great Tenasserim ≃ 110 12.24 N 98.37 E
Great Thatch Island I 240m 18.23 N 64.43 W
Great Tobago I 240m 18.27 N 64.48 W
Great Torrington 42 50.57 N 4.08 W
Great Totham 260 51.47 N 0.43 E
Great Usutu (Maputo) (Lusutfu) ≃ 158 26.11 S 32.42 E
Great Valley 210 42.13 N 78.38 W
Great Victoria Desert ◆[2] 162 28.30 S 127.45 E
Great Wall → Chang Cheng ⊥ 98 40.30 N 116.30 E
Great Waltham 260 51.48 N 0.28 E
Great Warley 260 51.35 N 0.17 E
Great Whernside ʌ 44 54.09 N 1.59 W
Great Wicomico ≃ 208 37.48 N 76.18 W
Great Wyrley 42 52.41 N 2.01 W
Great Yarmouth 42 52.37 N 1.44 E
Great Zab (Büyükzap) (Az-Zāb al-Kabīr) ≃ 128 36.00 N 43.21 E
Great Zimbabwe Ruins National Park ♦ 154 20.17 S 30.57 E
Grebbestad 26 58.42 N 11.15 E
Grebenhain 56 50.29 N 9.19 E
Grebenka 78 50.07 N 32.25 E
Grebenstein 56 51.26 N 9.24 E
Grebnevo 265b 55.58 N 38.05 E
Greb'onki 78 49.57 N 30.12 E
Gréboun ʌ 150 20.00 N 8.35 E
Grèce → Greece □[1] 38 39.00 N 22.00 E
Grecia 236 10.05 N 84.18 W
Grecia → Greece □[1] 38 39.00 N 22.00 E
Grečiškino 83 48.52 N 38.54 E
Grecken ⊜ 40 59.35 N 14.44 E
Greco 252 32.48 S 57.03 W
Greco ◆[8] 266b 45.30 N 9.13 E
Greco, Monte ʌ 66 41.48 N 14.00 E
Greco Island I 282 37.31 N 122.11 W
Greding 60 49.03 N 11.21 E
Gredos, Sierra de ⋏ 34 40.18 N 5.05 W
Gredstedbro 41 55.24 N 8.45 E
Greece 210 43.12 N 77.41 W
Greece (Ellás) □[1], Europe 22 39.00 N 22.00 E
Greece (Ellás) □[1], Europe 38 39.00 N 22.00 E
Greeley, Co., U.S. 200 40.25 N 104.42 W
Greeley, Ks., U.S. 198 38.19 N 95.26 W
Greeley, Ne., U.S. 198 41.33 N 98.32 W
Greeley, Pa., U.S. 210 41.25 N 75.00 W
Greeleyville 192 33.34 N 79.59 W
Green □[6] 216 42.48 N 89.25 W
Green ≃, N.B., Can. 186 47.18 N 68.09 W
Green ≃, U.S. 200 38.11 N 109.53 W
Green ≃, U.S. 207 42.35 N 72.36 W
Green ≃, U.S. 207 42.10 N 73.22 W
Green ≃, Il., U.S. 190 41.28 N 90.23 W
Green ≃, Il., U.S. 216 41.46 N 89.10 W
Green ≃, Ky., U.S. 194 37.55 N 87.30 W
Green ≃, N.D., U.S. 198 46.52 N 102.35 W
Green ≃, Wa., U.S. 224 47.33 N 122.20 W
Green ≃, Wa., U.S. 224 46.20 N 122.34 W
Greenacres, Ca., U.S. 226 35.23 N 119.07 W
Green Acres, De., U.S. 285 39.47 N 75.30 W
Greenacres, Wa., U.S. 202 47.39 N 117.06 W
Green Acres ◆[9] 276 40.40 N 73.43 W
Greenacres City 220 26.37 N 80.07 W
Greenbackville 208 38.00 N 75.23 W
Greenbank 224 48.06 N 122.34 W
Green Bay 190 44.31 N 88.01 W
Green Bay c, Nf., Can. 186 49.43 N 55.58 W
Green Bay c, On., Can. 212 44.38 N 76.36 W
Green Bay c, U.S. 190 45.00 N 87.30 W
Greenbelt 284c 39.00 N 76.53 W
Greenbelt Park ♦ 284c 38.59 N 76.54 W
Greenbo Lake ⊜ 218 38.29 N 82.54 W
Greenbo Lake State Resort Park ♦ 218 38.29 N 82.54 W
Greenbooth Reservoir ⊜[1] 262 53.38 N 2.13 W
Greenbrae 226 37.57 N 122.31 W
Greenbrier, Ar., U.S. 194 35.14 N 92.23 W
Green Brier, Tn., U.S. 194 36.25 N 86.48 W
Greenbrier ≃ 192 37.39 N 80.53 W
Greenbrier State Park ♦ 208 39.33 N 77.38 W
Green Brook 276 40.36 N 74.27 W
Green Brook ≃ 276 40.33 N 74.32 W
Greenbrook 194 30.51 N 90.40 W
Greenbush, Ma., U.S. 207 42.11 N 70.45 W
Greenbush, Mn., U.S. 198 48.42 N 96.10 W
Greenbush, Va., U.S. 208 37.45 N 75.41 W
Greenbushes 162 33.51 S 116.03 E
Green Camp 214 40.31 N 83.12 W
Green Cape ≻ 166 37.15 S 150.03 E
Greencastle, Ire. 48 55.12 N 6.59 W
Greencastle, In., U.S. 194 39.38 N 86.51 W
Greencastle, Pa., U.S. 188 39.47 N 77.43 W
Green City 194 40.16 N 92.57 W
Green Cove Springs 192 29.59 N 81.40 W
Green Creek 208 39.02 N 74.54 W
Green Creek ≃, Oh., U.S. 214 41.26 N 83.01 W
Green Creek ≃, Pa., U.S. 285 39.53 N 75.28 W
Greencrest Park 214 41.23 N 80.24 W
Greendale, Austl. 274a 33.55 S 150.39 E
Greendale, In., U.S. 218 39.06 N 84.51 W
Greendale, Wi., U.S. 216 42.56 N 87.59 W
Greene, B.R.D. 52 51.52 N 9.56 E
Greene, Ia., U.S. 190 42.53 N 92.48 W
Greene, N.Y., U.S. 210 42.19 N 75.46 W
Greene, R.I., U.S. 207 41.41 N 71.44 W
Greene □[6], Il., U.S. 219 39.18 N 90.24 W
Greene □[6], N.Y., U.S. 210 42.13 N 73.52 W
Greene □[6], Oh., U.S. 218 39.41 N 83.56 W
Greeneville 192 36.06 N 82.42 W
Greenfield, Eng., U.K. 262 53.32 N 2.01 W
Greenfield, Wales, U.K. 44 53.18 N 3.13 W
Greenfield, Ca., U.S. 226 36.19 N 121.14 W
Greenfield, Il., U.S. 219 39.20 N 90.12 W
Greenfield, In., U.S. 218 39.47 N 85.46 W
Greenfield, Ia., U.S. 198 41.18 N 94.27 W
Greenfield, Ma., U.S. 207 42.35 N 72.36 W
Greenfield, Mo., U.S. 194 37.24 N 93.50 W
Greenfield, Oh., U.S. 218 39.21 N 83.22 W
Greenfield, Tn., U.S. 194 36.09 N 88.48 W
Greenfield, Wi., U.S. 216 42.58 N 88.02 W
Greenfield-Park, P.Q., Can. 275a 45.29 N 73.29 W
Greenfield Park, N.Y., U.S. 210 41.44 N 74.29 W
Greenfields Village 285 75.10 N 39.49 W
Greenfield Village ⊥ 281 42.18 N 83.14 W
Greenford ◆[8] 260 51.32 N 0.21 W
Green Forest 194 36.20 N 93.26 W
Green Harbor 207 42.04 N 70.39 W
Green Harbor ≃ 283 42.05 N 70.39 W
Green Head ≻ 162 30.05 S 114.58 E
Green Hill 285 39.59 N 75.36 W
Greenhill ◆[8] 260 51.35 N 0.20 W
Greenhills, S. Afr. 273d 26.10 S 27.40 E
Greenhills, Oh., U.S. 218 39.16 N 84.31 W
Greenhithe 260 51.27 N 0.17 E
Greenhorn Creek ≃ 198 38.08 N 104.38 W
Greenhurst 214 42.07 N 79.19 W
Green Hut Park 276 40.50 N 74.39 W
Green Island, N.Z. 172 45.54 S 170.26 E
Greenisland, N. Ire., U.K. 48 54.42 N 5.52 W
Green Island, N.Y., U.S. 210 42.44 N 73.41 W
Green Island I 241k 12.14 N 61.35 W
Green Island Bay c 116 10.12 N 119.22 E
Green Islands II 14 4.30 S 154.10 E
Green Knoll 276 40.36 N 74.36 W
Green Lake, Sk., Can. 184 54.17 N 107.47 W
Green Lake, Wi., U.S. 190 43.50 N 88.57 W
Green Lake ⊜, B.C., Can. 182 51.26 N 121.15 W
Green Lake ⊜, Sk., Can. 184 54.10 N 107.43 W
Green Lake ⊜, Mi., U.S. 281 42.36 N 83.25 W
Green Lake ⊜, N.Y., U.S. 284a 42.45 N 78.45 W
Green Lake ⊜, Wi., U.S. 190 43.41 N 88.57 W
Green Lakes State Park ♦ 212 43.03 N 75.58 W
Greenlal (Saint-Grégoire-de-Greenlay) 206 45.34 N 72.01 W
Greenland, Ar., U.S. 194 35.59 N 94.10 W
Greenland, Mi., U.S. 190 46.46 N 89.06 W
Greenland (Kalaallit Nunaat) □[2] 16 70.00 N 40.00 W
Greenland Basin ◆[1] 16 73.30 N 5.00 W
Greenland-Iceland Rise ◆[3] 10 67.00 N 27.00 W
Greenlands 158 27.07 S 27.40 E
Greenland Sea ◆[2] 16 77.00 N 1.00 W
Green Lane 208 40.20 N 75.28 W
Green Lane Reservoir ⊜[1] 208 40.22 N 75.29 W
Greenlaw 46 55.43 N 2.28 W
Greenlawn 276 40.52 N 73.21 W
Greenlawn Park 285 40.07 N 74.51 W
Greenleaf 198 39.43 N 96.58 W
Green Lookout Mountain ʌ 224 45.52 N 122.08 W
Green Manorville 207 42.00 N 72.32 W
Green Meadows 284c 38.58 N 76.57 W
Greenmount, Austl. 168a 31.54 S 116.03 E
Greenmount, Austl. 171a 27.47 S 151.54 E
Greenmount, Eng., U.K. 262 53.37 N 2.20 W
Greenmount, Md., U.S. 208 39.37 N 76.51 W
Green Mountains ⋏ 188 43.45 N 72.45 W
Green Oak Lake ⊜ 281 42.27 N 83.43 W
Green Oaks 278 42.18 N 87.55 W
Greenock, Austl. 168b 34.27 S 138.55 E
Greenock, Scot., U.K. 46 55.57 N 4.45 W
Greenock, Pa., U.S. 279b 40.19 N 79.48 W
Greenodd 44 54.14 N 3.04 W
Greenore Point ≻ 48 52.15 N 6.18 W
Greenough 162 28.57 S 114.44 E
Greenough ≃ 162 28.51 S 114.38 E
Greenough, Mount ʌ 180 69.10 N 141.35 W
Green Park 208 40.23 N 77.19 W
Green Peter Lake ⊜[1] 202 44.28 N 122.30 W
Green Point ≻ 276 40.43 N 73.06 W
Green Pond, Al., U.S. 194 33.13 N 87.07 W
Green Pond, N.J., U.S. 276 41.01 N 74.29 W
Green Pond ⊜ 276 41.00 N 74.30 W
Green Pond Brook ≃ 276 40.53 N 74.34 W
Greenport 207 41.06 N 72.21 W
Green Ridge 285 39.51 N 75.25 W
Green River, Pap. N. Gui. 164 3.55 S 141.10 E
Green River, Ut., U.S. 200 38.59 N 110.09 W
Green River, Wy., U.S. 200 41.31 N 109.27 W
Green River Lake ⊜[1] 194 37.15 N 85.15 W
Greensboro, Al., U.S. 194 32.42 N 87.35 W
Greensboro, Fl., U.S. 192 30.34 N 84.44 W
Greensboro, Ga., U.S. 192 33.34 N 83.10 W
Greensboro, Md., U.S. 208 38.58 N 75.48 W
Greensboro, N.C., U.S. 192 36.04 N 79.47 W
Greensborough 274b 37.42 S 145.06 E
Greensburg, In., U.S. 218 39.20 N 85.29 W
Greensburg, Ks., U.S. 198 37.36 N 99.17 W
Greensburg, Ky., U.S. 194 37.15 N 85.29 W
Greensburg, Oh., U.S. 214 40.56 N 81.28 W
Greensburg, Pa., U.S. 214 40.18 N 79.32 W
Greens Farms 276 41.07 N 73.19 W
Greens Fork 218 39.53 N 85.02 W
Greenside ◆[8] 273d 26.09 S 28.01 E
Greens Lake c 222 29.16 N 94.59 W
Greens Peak ʌ 200 34.07 N 109.35 W
Greenspond 186 49.04 N 53.34 W
Green Springs 214 41.15 N 83.03 W
Greenstead 260 51.42 N 0.14 E
Greenstone 208 39.45 N 77.27 W
Greenstone Point ≻ 46 57.55 N 5.38 W
Green Street 260 51.40 N 0.16 W
Green Street Green ◆[8] 260 51.21 N 0.04 E
Greensville □[6] 208 36.40 N 77.30 W
Green Swamp ⋕, Fl., U.S. 220 28.20 N 81.48 W
Green Swamp ⋕, N.C., U.S. 192 34.10 N 78.20 W
Greentown, In., U.S. 216 40.28 N 85.58 W
Greentown, Oh., U.S. 214 40.56 N 81.28 W
Greentown, Pa., U.S. 210 41.19 N 75.18 W
Green Tree 279b 40.24 N 80.02 W
Greenup, Il., U.S. 194 39.14 N 88.09 W
Greenup, Ky., U.S. 218 38.34 N 82.49 W
Greenup □[6] 218 38.33 N 83.00 W
Greenup Dam ◆[6] 218 38.39 N 82.52 W
Greenvale, Austl. 166 18.59 S 145.07 E
Greenvale, N.Y., U.S. 276 40.49 N 73.38 W
Green Valley, On., Can. 206 45.16 N 74.36 W
Green Valley, Az., U.S. 200 31.52 N 110.59 W
Green Valley, Il., U.S. 190 40.24 N 89.38 W
Green Valley Creek ≃ 226 38.13 N 122.08 W
Greenview 219 40.04 N 89.44 W
Green Village, N.J., U.S. 276 40.44 N 74.27 W
Greenvillage, Pa., U.S. 208 40.00 N 77.36 W
Greenville, Liber. 150 5.01 N 9.03 W
Greenville, Al., U.S. 194 31.49 N 86.37 W
Greenville, Ca., U.S. 204 40.08 N 120.57 W
Greenville, Fl., U.S. 192 30.28 N 83.37 W
Greenville, Ga., U.S. 192 33.01 N 84.42 W
Greenville, Il., U.S. 219 38.53 N 89.24 W
Greenville, In., U.S. 218 38.22 N 85.59 W
Greenville, Ky., U.S. 194 37.12 N 87.10 W
Greenville, Me., U.S. 188 45.28 N 69.35 W
Greenville, Mi., U.S. 190 43.10 N 85.15 W
Greenville, Ms., U.S. 194 33.24 N 91.03 W
Greenville, Mo., U.S. 194 37.08 N 90.27 W
Greenville, N.H., U.S. 207 42.46 N 71.48 W
Greenville, N.Y., U.S. 210 40.59 N 73.49 W
Greenville, N.Y., U.S. 276 40.59 N 73.49 W
Greenville, N.C., U.S. 192 35.36 N 77.22 W
Greenville, Oh., U.S. 218 40.06 N 84.37 W
Greenville, Pa., U.S. 214 41.24 N 80.23 W
Greenville, R.I., U.S. 207 41.52 N 71.33 W
Greenville, S.C., U.S. 192 34.51 N 82.23 W
Greenville, Tx., U.S. 222 33.08 N 96.06 W
Greenville Creek ≃ 218 40.07 N 84.22 W
Greenville Place 285 39.46 N 75.36 W
Greenwater ≃ 224 47.09 N 121.39 W
Greenwater Lake ⊜ 190 48.34 N 90.26 W
Greenwater Lake Provincial Park ♦ 184 52.33 N 103.33 W
Greenwell Point 170 34.55 S 150.44 E
Greenwich, Austl. 274a 33.50 S 151.11 E
Greenwich, Ct., U.S. 207 41.01 N 73.37 W
Greenwich, N.J., U.S. 208 39.23 N 75.20 W
Greenwich, N.Y., U.S. 210 43.05 N 73.29 W
Greenwich, Oh., U.S. 214 41.01 N 82.30 W
Greenwich ◆[8] 260 51.28 N 0.02 E
Greenwich Cove c 276 41.01 N 73.35 W
Greenwich Creek ≃ 276 41.02 N 73.37 W
Greenwich Observatory ◆[3] 260 51.28 N 0.00
Greenwich Point ≻ 276 41.00 N 73.34 W
Greenwich Village ◆[8] 276 40.44 N 74.00 W
Greenwood, B.C., Can. 182 49.05 N 118.41 W
Greenwood, Ar., U.S. 194 35.12 N 94.15 W
Greenwood, Ca., U.S. 226 38.54 N 120.55 W
Greenwood, De., U.S. 208 38.48 N 75.35 W
Greenwood, In., U.S. 218 39.36 N 86.06 W
Greenwood, Ma., U.S. 283 42.29 N 71.04 W
Greenwood, Ms., U.S. 194 33.30 N 90.10 W
Greenwood, Ne., U.S. 198 40.57 N 96.26 W
Greenwood, N.Y., U.S. 210 42.08 N 77.38 W
Greenwood, Pa., U.S. 214 40.32 N 78.21 W
Greenwood, S.C., U.S. 192 34.11 N 82.09 W
Greenwood, Wi., U.S. 190 44.46 N 90.35 W
Greenwood, Lake ⊜[1] 192 34.15 N 82.02 W
Greenwood Cemetery ◆ 276 40.39 N 73.59 W
Greenwood Lake 210 41.13 N 74.17 W
Greenwood Lake ⊜, U.S. 210 41.11 N 74.19 W
Greenwood Lake ⊜, Ma., U.S. 283 42.00 N 71.17 W
Greenwood Race Track ♦ 275b 43.40 N 79.19 W
Greer, Oh., U.S. 214 40.31 N 82.13 W
Greer, S.C., U.S. 192 34.56 N 82.13 W
Greers Ferry Lake ⊜[1] 194 35.30 N 92.10 W
Greerton 172 37.43 S 176.08 E
Grées, Alpes (Alpi Graie) ⋏ 62 45.30 N 7.10 E
Greeson, Lake ⊜[1] 194 34.10 N 93.45 W
Greetland 262 53.41 N 1.52 W
Greetsiel 52 53.30 N 7.05 E
Greffiers 261 48.37 N 1.51 E
Grefrath, B.R.D. 56 51.20 N 6.20 E
Grefrath, B.R.D. 263 51.11 N 6.38 E
Gregadoo 171b 35.14 S 147.27 E
Gregbe 150 6.48 N 6.43 W
Gregg 279b 40.24 N 80.10 W
Gregg □[6] 222 32.30 N 94.50 W
Greggio 62 45.27 N 8.23 E
Greg Greg 171b 36.03 S 148.02 E
Gregoire Lake Indian Reserve ◆[4] 184 56.28 N 111.10 W
Gregório ≃ 248 6.50 S 70.46 W
Gregory, Mi., U.S. 216 42.27 N 84.05 W
Gregory, S.D., U.S. 198 43.13 N 99.25 W
Gregory, Tx., U.S. 196 27.55 N 97.17 W
Gregory ≃ 166 17.53 S 139.17 E
Gregory, Lake ⊜, Austl. 162 25.38 S 119.58 E
Gregory, Lake ⊜, Austl. 166 28.55 S 139.00 E
Gregory, Port c[3] 162 28.10 S 114.14 E
Gregory Range ⋏ 166 19.00 S 143.05 E
Grégy-sur-Yerre 261 48.40 N 2.37 E
Greifenberg → Gryfice 30 53.56 N 15.12 E
Greifenburg 64 46.45 N 13.11 E
Greifendorf 54 51.01 N 13.06 E
Greifenhagen → Gryfino 30 53.12 N 14.30 E
Greifensee 58 47.22 N 8.41 E
Greifensee ⊜ 58 47.21 N 8.41 E
Greifenstein 264b 48.21 N 16.25 E
Greiffenberg 54 53.05 N 13.58 E
Greifswald 54 54.05 N 13.23 E
Greifswalder Bodden c 54 54.15 N 13.35 E
Greifswalder Oie I 54 54.14 N 13.55 E
Greim ʌ 61 47.15 N 14.09 E
Grein 61 48.14 N 14.51 E
Greiz 54 50.39 N 12.12 E
Grejdernoje 80 46.53 N 45.01 E
Grejsdal 41 55.45 N 9.32 E
Grekov 80 47.24 N 43.41 E
Grekovo 83 48.54 N 40.14 E
Grem'ačevo 82 54.14 N 45.35 E
Grem'ačij 88 57.01 N 108.12 E
Grem'ačinsk, S.S.S.R. 86 58.34 N 57.51 E
Grem'ačinsk, S.S.S.R. 88 52.48 N 107.57 E
Grem'ačje 78 51.39 N 38.21 E
Gremersdorf 54 54.20 N 10.55 E
Gremicha 24 68.03 N 39.27 E
Grenå 26 56.25 N 10.53 E
Grenada 194 33.46 N 89.48 W
Grenada □[1], N.A. 230 12.07 N 61.40 W
Grenada □[1], N.A. 241k 12.07 N 61.40 W
Grenada Lake ⊜[1] 194 33.50 N 89.40 W
Grenade → Grenada □[1] 241k 12.07 N 61.40 W
Grenadier Island I 212 44.03 N 76.22 W
Grenadier Pond ⊜ 275b 43.38 N 79.28 W
Grenadine Islands II 238 12.40 N 61.15 W
Grenagh 48 52.00 N 8.37 W
Grenay 50 50.27 N 2.44 E
Grenchen 58 47.11 N 7.24 E
Grenell 212 44.16 N 76.04 W
Grenen ≻[2], Dan. 26 57.44 N 10.40 E
Grenen ≻[2], Dan. 26 57.44 N 10.40 E
Grenfell, Austl. 166 33.54 S 148.10 E
Grenfell, Sk., Can. 184 50.25 N 102.56 W
Grenloch 285 39.47 N 75.03 W

Symbols in the index entries represent the broad categories identified in the key at the right. Symbols with superior numbers (⋏[1]) identify subcategories (see complete key on page I · 1).

Kartensymbole in dem Registerverzeichnis stellen die rechts in Schlüssel erklärten Kategorien dar. Symbole mit hochgestellten Ziffern (⋏[1]) bezeichnen Unterabteilungen einer Kategorie (vgl. vollständiger Schlüssel auf Seite I · 1).

Los símbolos incluidos en el texto del índice representan las grandes categorías identificadas con la clave a la derecha. Los símbolos con números en su parte superior (⋏[1]) identifican las subcategorías (véase la clave completa en la página I · 1).

Les symboles de l'index représentent les catégories indiquées dans la légende à droite. Les symboles suivis d'un indice (⋏[1]) représentent des sous-catégories (voir légende complète à la page I · 1).

Os símbolos incluídos no texto do índice representam as grandes categorias identificadas com a chave à direita. Os símbolos com números em sua parte superior (⋏[1]) identificam as subcategorias (veja-se a chave completa à página I · 1).

ʌ Mountain	Berg	Montaña	Montagne	Montanha
⋏ Mountains	Berge	Montañas	Montagnes	Montanhas
)(Pass	Pass	Paso	Col	Passo
∨ Valley, Canyon	Tal, Cañon	Valle, Cañón	Vallée, Canyon	Vale, Canhão
≚ Plain	Ebene	Llano	Plaine	Planície
≻ Cape	Kap	Cabo	Cap	Cabo
I Island	Insel	Isla	Île	Ilha
II Islands	Inseln	Islas	Îles	Ilhas
⊥ Other Topographic Features	Andere Topographische Objekte	Otros Elementos Topográficos	Autres données topographiques	Outros acidentes topográficos

ESPAÑOL — Nombre · Página · Lat.°′ · Long.°′ W = Oeste
FRANÇAIS — Nom · Page · Lat.°′ · Long.°′ W = Ouest
PORTUGUÊS — Nome · Página · Lat.°′ · Long.°′ W = Oeste

Grenoble 62 45.10 N 5.43 E
Grenola 198 37.20 N 96.27 W
Grenora 198 48.37 N 103.56 W
Grenville, P.Q., Can. 206 45.37 N 74.36 W
Grenville, Gren. 241k 12.07 N 61.37 W
Grenville, Cape › 164 11.58 S 143.14 E
Grenville Bay 206 45.38 N 74.36 W
Grenville Bay ⊂ 241k 12.07 N 61.36 W
Grenville Channel ᴜ 182 53.40 N 129.40 W
Grenzaa ≃ 52 52.39 N 6.45 E
Grenz-Berg ∧² 264a 52.27 N 13.44 E
Grenzlandring ♦ 56 51.11 N 6.17 E
Gréolières 62 43.48 N 6.57 E
Gréoux-les-Bains 62 43.45 N 5.53 E
Greppin 54 51.39 N 12.18 E
Gresenhorst 54 54.09 N 12.26 E
Gresham 224 45.29 N 122.25 W
Gresham Park 192 33.42 N 84.19 W
Gresik, Indon. 112 2.18 S 103.57 E
Gresik, Indon. 115a 7.09 S 112.38 E
Gressåmoen Nasjonalpark ♦ 26 64.15 N 13.08 E
Gresse-en-Vercors 62 44.54 N 5.34 E
Gressey 261 48.50 N 1.37 E
Gressitt 208 37.29 N 76.43 W
Gressk 76 53.10 N 27.29 E
Gressoney, Val di ∨ 62 45.47 N 7.49 E
Gressoney-la-Trinité 62 45.50 N 7.49 E
Gressoney-Saint-Jean 62 45.47 N 7.49 E
Gressy 261 48.58 N 2.41 E
Gresten 61 48.00 N 15.02 E
Grésy-sur-Aix 62 45.43 N 5.57 E
Grésy-sur-Isère 62 45.36 N 6.15 E
Greta 170 32.41 S 151.24 E
Greta ≃, Eng., U.K. 44 54.32 N 1.53 W
Greta ≃, Eng., U.K. 44 54.36 N 3.10 W
Greta ≃, Eng., U.K. 44 54.09 N 2.36 W
Gretna, Mb., Can. 184 49.02 N 97.35 W
Gretna, Scot., U.K. 44 54.59 N 3.04 W
Gretna, La., U.S. 194 29.54 N 90.03 W
Gretna, Va., U.S. 192 36.57 N 79.21 W
Gretz-Armainvilliers 50 48.44 N 2.44 E
Greussen 54 51.14 N 10.57 E
Greve, Dan. 41 55.36 N 12.15 E
Greve, It. 66 43.35 N 11.19 E
Greve ≃ 66 43.46 N 11.13 E
Grevel ✦⁸ 263 51.34 N 7.33 E
Grevelingen ᴜ 52 51.45 N 4.00 E
Grevelingendam ✦⁵ 52 51.40 N 4.10 E
Greven 52 52.05 N 7.36 E
Grevená 38 40.05 N 21.25 E
Grevenbroich 56 51.05 N 6.35 E
Grevenbroich □⁸ 263 51.08 N 6.38 E
Greven-Granzin 54 53.29 N 10.48 E
Grevenmacher 56 49.42 N 6.20 E
Grevesmühlen 54 53.51 N 11.10 E
Greve Strand 41 55.35 N 12.14 E
Greville Bay ⊂ 186 45.22 N 64.38 W
Grevinge 41 55.48 N 11.34 E
Grey □⁶ 212 44.20 N 80.45 W
Grey ≃, Nf., Can. 186 47.38 N 57.05 W
Grey ≃, N.Z. 172 42.27 S 171.12 E
Grey, Cape › 164 13.00 S 136.40 E
Grey, Point ›, Austl. 169 38.34 S 143.59 E
Grey, Point ›, B.C., Can. 224 49.16 N 123.16 W
Greyabbey 48 54.32 N 5.33 W
Greybull 202 44.29 N 108.03 W
Greybull ≃ 202 44.28 N 108.03 W
Grey Eagle 190 45.49 N 94.44 W
Grey Islands ıı 186 50.50 N 55.37 W
Greylingstad 158 26.44 S 28.45 E
Greylock, Mount ∧ 207 42.38 N 73.10 W
Greymouth 172 42.28 S 171.12 E
Grey Range ∧ 166 27.00 S 143.35 E
Grey River 186 47.35 N 57.06 W
Greys ≃ 202 43.10 N 111.00 W
Greystanes 274a 33.49 S 150.55 E
Greystoke 44 54.40 N 2.52 W
Greystones 48 53.09 N 6.04 W
Greyton 158 34.04 S 19.38 E
Greytown, N.Z. 172 41.05 S 175.27 E
Greytown → San Juan del Norte, Nic. 236 10.55 N 83.42 W
Greytown, S. Afr. 158 29.07 S 30.30 E
Grez-Doiceau 56 50.44 N 4.42 E
Grez-sur-Loing 50 48.19 N 2.42 E
Grezzana 64 45.31 N 11.01 E
Gribanovskij 80 51.27 N 41.58 E
Gribb Bank ✦⁴ 9 61.30 S 88.00 E
Gribbel Island ı 182 53.25 N 129.00 W
Gribbin Head › 42 50.19 N 4.40 W
Gribingui □⁵ 152 7.00 N 19.15 E
Gribingui ≃ 146 8.33 N 19.05 E
Gribingui-Bamingui, Réserve de Faune du ✦⁴ 146 8.00 N 19.10 E
Gribovka 82 54.19 N 38.27 E
Gricev 78 49.58 N 27.14 E
Gridley, Ca., U.S. 226 39.21 N 121.41 W
Gridley, Il., U.S. 216 40.44 N 88.52 W
Griebnitz See ◎ 264a 52.24 N 13.06 E
Griechenland → Greece □¹ 38 39.00 N 22.00 E
Griekwastad 158 28.49 S 23.15 E
Grier City 210 40.50 N 76.04 W
Gries am Brenner 64 47.03 N 11.29 E
Griesbach im Rottal 60 48.28 N 13.11 E
Griesen 64 47.29 N 10.56 E
Griesheim 56 49.50 N 8.34 E
Gries im Sellrain 64 47.12 N 11.09 E
Grieskirchen 60 48.14 N 13.50 E
Griessen 52 52.00 N 9.12 E
Griesspitzen ∧ 64 47.22 N 10.58 E
Griffen 61 46.42 N 14.44 E
Griffin, Sk., Can. 184 49.40 N 103.26 W
Griffin, Ga., U.S. 192 33.14 N 84.15 W
Griffin, Lake ◎ 220 28.52 N 81.51 W
Griffin Bay ⊂ 224 48.30 N 122.58 W
Griffiss Air Force Base ■ 210 43.14 N 75.26 W
Griffith, Austl. 166 34.17 S 146.03 E
Griffith, In., U.S. 216 41.31 N 87.25 W
Griffith Airport ⊗ 278 41.31 N 87.23 W
Griffith Island ı, N.T., Can. 176 74.35 N 95.30 W
Griffith Island ı, On., Can. 212 44.51 N 80.54 W
Griffith Park ♦ 280 34.09 N 118.17 W
Grifton 192 35.22 N 77.26 W
Griggs Drain ≡ 281 42.11 N 83.26 W
Griggs Reservoir ◎¹ 214 40.03 N 83.06 W
Griggstown 276 40.26 N 74.36 W
Griggsville 219 39.42 N 90.43 W
Grignan 62 44.25 N 4.54 E
Grignano 64 45.42 N 13.43 E
Grignasco 62 45.41 N 8.20 E
Grigno 64 46.01 N 11.38 E
Grignols 32 44.23 N 0.03 W
Grignon 261 48.51 N 1.57 E
Grigny 62 45.37 N 4.47 E
Grigoriopol' 78 47.10 N 29.18 E
Grigorjevka, S.S.S.R. 78 46.17 N 33.44 E
Grigorjevka, S.S.S.R. 83 47.27 N 38.23 E
Grigorjevka, S.S.S.R. 85 42.43 N 77.30 E
Grigorjevskoje, S.S.S.R. 82 54.49 N 37.59 E
Grigorjevskoje, S.S.S.R. 82 54.48 N 39.15 E
Grigorovka, S.S.S.R. 78 51.03 N 32.51 E
Grigorovka, S.S.S.R. 78 50.05 N 30.39 E
Grigorovka, S.S.S.R. 82 54.38 N 36.20 E
Grigorovo 82 56.42 N 37.35 E
Grigorovskoje 82 54.17 N 36.21 E
Grijalva ≃ 232 18.36 N 92.39 W
Grijpskerk 52 53.15 N 6.18 E
Grillbach ≃ 263 51.11 N 6.44 E
Grillby 40 59.37 N 17.15 E
Grillenburg 54 50.57 N 13.31 E
Grim, Cape › 166 40.41 S 144.41 E
Grima 152 3.59 N 17.06 E
Grimajlov 78 49.20 N 26.01 E
Grimaldi 68 39.08 N 16.14 E
Grimari 152 5.44 N 20.03 E
Grimaud 62 43.16 N 6.31 E
Grimbergen 50 50.56 N 4.23 E
Grimeford Village 262 53.36 N 2.34 W
Grimes 226 39.04 N 121.54 W
Grimes □⁶ 222 30.35 N 96.00 W
Grimlinghausen ✦⁸ 263 51.10 N 6.44 E
Grimma 54 51.14 N 12.43 E
Grimmen 54 54.07 N 13.02 E
Grimmenstein 61 47.38 N 16.06 E
Grimmialp 58 46.34 N 7.29 E
Grimmitzsee ◎ 54 52.58 N 13.47 E
Grimsargh 262 53.48 N 2.38 W
Grimsby, On., Can. 212 43.12 N 79.34 W
Grimsby, Eng., U.K. 44 53.35 N 0.05 W
Grimselpass)(58 46.34 N 8.21 E
Grimselsee ◎ 58 46.34 N 8.18 E
Grimsey ı 24a 66.34 N 18.00 W
Grimshaw 182 56.11 N 117.36 W
Grimsstaðir 24a 65.40 N 16.01 W
Grimstad 26 58.20 N 8.36 E
Grimstead 208 37.30 N 76.18 W
Grin'ava 78 47.59 N 24.49 E
Grindavík 24a 63.52 N 22.27 W
Grindelwald 58 46.37 N 8.02 E
Grindsted 41 55.45 N 8.56 E
Grindstone Island → Cap-aux-Meules 186 47.23 N 61.52 W
Grindstone Island ı 212 44.16 N 76.07 W
Grinnell 190 41.44 N 92.43 W
Grinnell, Lake ◎ 276 41.06 N 74.38 W
Grinnell Peninsula ›¹ 176 76.40 N 95.00 W
Grin'ovo 76 52.35 N 33.04 E
Grintavec ∧ 61 46.21 N 14.32 E
Grinzing ✦⁸ 264b 48.15 N 16.21 E
Grip 26 63.14 N 7.37 E
Gripsholms slott ⊥ 40 59.15 N 17.13 E
Gripsholmsviken ⊂ 40 59.17 N 17.20 E
Griqualand East □⁹ 158 30.30 S 29.00 E
Griqualand West □⁹ 158 28.20 S 23.30 E
Grisdale 224 47.22 N 123.37 W
Grisee → Gresik 115a 7.09 S 112.38 E
Grišino 82 56.13 N 37.40 E
Griškovcy 78 49.56 N 28.36 E
Gris-Nez, Cap › 50 50.52 N 1.35 E
Grisolia 68 39.43 N 15.51 E
Grisons → Graubünden □³ 58 46.45 N 9.30 E
Grisslehamn 40 60.06 N 18.50 E
Grissom Air Force Base ■ 216 40.40 N 86.08 W
Gristow 54 54.10 N 13.20 E
Griswold, Mb., Can. 184 49.45 N 100.25 W
Griswold, Ia., U.S. 198 41.14 N 95.08 W
Griswold Creek ≃ 279a 41.27 N 81.23 W
Griswoldville 207 42.39 N 72.42 W
Grisy-Suisnes 261 48.41 N 2.40 E
Grivai' Pamia 152 7.03 N 19.26 E
Grivenskaja 78 45.38 N 38.09 E
Grizzana 64 44.15 N 11.09 E
Grizzly Bay ⊂ 226 38.07 N 122.01 W
Grizzly Bear Mountain ∧ 176 65.22 N 121.00 W
Grizzly Bear's Head and Lean Man Indian Reserve ✦⁴ 184 52.33 N 108.16 W
Grizzly Creek ≃ 282 37.52 N 122.06 W
Grizzly Flats 226 38.38 N 120.31 W
Grizzly Island ı 282 38.08 N 121.58 W
Grizzly Mountain ∧, Id., U.S. 202 47.43 N 116.06 W
Grizzly Mountain ∧, Or., U.S. 202 44.26 N 120.57 W
Grizzly Mountain ∧, Wa., U.S. 202 48.25 N 118.30 W
Grizzly Slough ≃ 282 38.06 N 121.53 W
Grmeč ∧ 68 44.40 N 16.30 E
Groais Island ı 186 50.57 N 55.35 W
Grobbendonk 56 51.12 N 4.43 E
Gröben 264a 52.17 N 13.10 E
Gröbener-See ◎ 264a 52.17 N 13.11 E
Gröbenzell 60 48.11 N 11.22 E
Grobiņa 76 56.33 N 21.10 E
Groblersdal 156 25.15 S 29.25 E
Groblershoop 158 28.55 S 20.59 E
Gröbming 64 47.26 N 13.54 E
Grobogan 115a 7.01 S 110.55 E
Gröbzig 54 51.41 N 11.52 E
Grodekovo 85 42.49 N 71.29 E
Grödig 64 47.44 N 13.02 E
Gröditsch 54 52.03 N 13.59 E
Gröditz 54 51.24 N 13.27 E
Grodków 30 50.43 N 17.22 E
Grodno 76 53.41 N 23.50 E
Grodno □⁴ 76 54.00 N 25.30 E
Grodovka 83 48.15 N 37.23 E
Grodz'anka 76 53.33 N 28.45 E
Grodzisk Mazowiecki 30 52.07 N 20.37 E
Grodzisk [Wielkopolski] 30 52.14 N 16.22 E
Groede 52 51.23 N 3.30 E
Groen ≃, S. Afr. 158 30.40 S 23.17 E
Groen ≃, S. Afr. 158 29.00 S 22.10 E
Groenland → Greenland □² 16 70.00 N 40.00 W
Groenlandia → Greenland □² 16 70.00 N 40.00 W
Groenlo 52 52.03 N 6.38 E
Groenvlei 158 27.27 S 30.13 E
Groesbeck, Oh., U.S. 218 39.13 N 84.35 W
Groesbeck, Tx., U.S. 222 31.31 N 96.32 W
Groesbeek 52 51.47 N 5.55 E
Grofa, gora ∧ 78 48.37 N 23.56 E
Grogol, Kali ≃ 269e 6.10 S 106.47 E
Grogol-hilir ✦⁸ 269e 6.13 S 106.47 E
Grohnde 52 52.01 N 9.25 E
Groitzsch 54 51.09 N 12.16 E
Groix 32 47.38 N 3.28 W
Groix, Île de ı 32 47.38 N 3.27 W
Grójec 30 51.52 N 20.52 E
Grokgak 115a 8.11 S 114.47 E
Grolley 58 46.50 N 7.05 E
Grombalia 148 36.36 N 10.30 E
Grömitz 54 54.09 N 10.58 E
Gromo 64 45.58 N 9.56 E
Gromokleja ≃ 78 47.21 N 32.14 E
Gromoslavka 80 48.12 N 43.37 E
Gromovka 78 46.19 N 34.06 E
Gronau, B.R.D. 52 52.13 N 7.02 E
Gronau, B.R.D. 52 52.05 N 9.46 E
Grondines (Saint-Charles-des-Grondines) 206 46.36 N 72.03 W
Grondneus 158 28.06 S 20.48 E
Grone 52 51.32 N 9.53 E
Grönenbach 58 47.52 N 10.13 E
Grong 24 64.28 N 12.18 E
Grongemouth 44 56.01 N 3.44 W
Gröningen, D.D.R. 54 51.56 N 11.12 E
Groningen, Ned. 52 53.13 N 6.33 E
Groningen, Sur. 250 5.48 N 55.28 W
Groningen □⁴ 52 53.15 N 6.45 E
Grønland → Greenland □² 16 70.00 N 40.00 W
Gronlid 184 53.06 N 104.28 W
Grønsund ᴜ 41 54.53 N 12.08 E
Grönwohld 52 53.39 N 10.21 E
Groom 196 35.12 N 101.06 W
Groom Lake ◎ 204 37.15 N 115.48 W
Groot ≃, S. Afr. 158 33.54 S 21.39 E
Groot ≃, S. Afr. 158 33.45 S 24.36 E
Groot-Berg ≃ 158 32.47 S 18.08 E
Groot-Brakrivier 158 34.01 S 21.46 E
Grootdraaidam ◎¹ 158 26.56 S 29.20 E
Grootebroek 52 52.43 N 5.13 E
Groote Eylandt ı 164 14.00 S 136.40 E
Grootfontein 156 19.32 S 18.05 E
Groot Karasberge ∧ 158 27.20 S 18.40 E
Groot Karoo → Great Karroo ∧¹ 158 32.25 S 22.40 E
Groot-Kei ≃ 158 32.41 S 28.22 E
Groot Laagte ≃ 156 20.37 S 21.37 E
Groot-Letaba ≃ 158 23.58 S 31.50 E
Groot-Marico 158 25.37 S 26.26 E
Grootpan 158 25.58 S 26.33 E
Groot-Swartberge ∧ 158 33.22 S 22.20 E
Groot-Vis ≃ 158 33.30 S 27.08 E
Grootvlei 158 26.44 S 28.32 E
Grootvloer ≃ 158 30.00 S 20.40 E
Gröpelingen ✦⁸ 52 53.07 N 8.46 E
Gropello Cairoli 62 45.11 N 9.00 E
Gropeni 38 45.04 N 27.53 E
Grosbliederstroff 56 49.09 N 7.01 E
Gros Bois, Parc de ♦ 261 48.44 N 2.32 E
Groscavallo 62 45.22 N 7.15 E
Grose ≃ 170 33.36 S 150.41 E
Grosio 64 46.18 N 10.16 E
Gros Islet 241f 14.05 N 60.58 W
Gros Islet Bay ⊂ 241f 14.05 N 60.58 W
Groslay 261 48.59 N 2.21 E
Gros Mécatina, Cap du › 186 50.45 N 59.00 W
Gros-Morne 240e 14.43 N 61.01 W
Gros Morne ∧ 186 49.36 N 57.48 W
Gros Morne National Park ♦ 186 49.40 N 57.45 W
Grosne ≃ 58 46.42 N 4.56 E
Grosnez Point › 43b 49.16 N 2.15 W
Grosotto 64 46.17 N 10.15 E
Gros Piton ∧ 241f 13.49 N 61.04 W
Grosrouvre 261 48.47 N 1.46 E
Grossa, Ponta ›, Bra. 256 23.35 S 45.13 W
Grossa, Ponta ›, Bra. 287a 22.47 S 43.11 W
Grossache (Tiroler Ache) ≃ 60 47.51 N 12.30 E
Grossaitingen 58 48.14 N 10.47 E
Grossalmerode 56 51.15 N 9.46 E
Grossalsleben 54 51.59 N 11.13 E
Gross Ammensleben 54 52.14 N 11.31 E
Grossarl 64 47.14 N 13.12 E
Gross-Beeren 54 52.21 N 13.18 E
Gross Berkel 52 52.04 N 9.19 E
Grossbodungen 54 51.28 N 10.28 E
Gross Börnecke 54 51.50 N 11.29 E
Grossbothen 54 51.11 N 12.44 E
Grossbottwar 56 49.00 N 9.17 E
Grossbreitenbach 54 50.35 N 11.02 E
Grossdeuben 54 51.14 N 12.23 E
Grossdubrau 54 51.15 N 14.28 E
Gross Düngen 52 52.06 N 10.01 E
Grosse Antillen → Greater Antilles ıı 238 20.00 N 74.00 W
Grosse Aue ≃ 52 52.37 N 9.10 E
Grosse Australische Bucht → Great Australian Bight ⊂³ 162 35.00 S 135.00 E
Grossebersdorf 54 50.47 N 11.57 E
Grosse Ebene → Great Plains ≃ 16 42.00 N 100.00 W
Grossefehn 52 53.24 N 7.36 E
Grosse Herrenwiese ≡ 264a 52.17 N 13.20 E
Grosse Ile 216 42.08 N 83.09 W
Grosse Ile ı 216 42.08 N 83.09 W
Grosse Île, La ı 186 47.37 N 61.31 W
Grosse Laber ≃ 60 48.56 N 12.30 E
Grosse Mühl ≃ 61 48.25 N 13.59 E
Grossenbaum ✦⁸ 263 51.22 N 6.47 E
Grossenbrode 54 54.22 N 11.05 E
Grossengottern 54 51.09 N 10.34 E
Grossengstingen 58 48.23 N 9.17 E
Grossenhain 54 51.17 N 13.31 E
Grossenheidorn 52 52.27 N 9.23 E
Grossenkneten 52 52.56 N 8.16 E
Grossen-Linden 56 50.31 N 8.39 E
Grossenlüder 56 50.35 N 9.32 E
Grossenritte 56 51.15 N 9.23 E
Grossenwiehe 41 54.43 N 9.15 E
Gross-Enzersdorf 61 48.12 N 16.33 E
Grosse Pointe 214 42.23 N 82.54 W
Grosse Pointe › 241o 16.01 N 61.16 W
Grosse Pointe Farms 214 42.25 N 82.53 W
Grosse Pointe Park 214 42.22 N 82.56 W
Grosse Pointe Shores 214 42.26 N 82.53 W
Grosse Pointe Woods 214 42.26 N 82.54 W
Grosser Arber ∧ 60 49.07 N 13.07 E
Grosser Bären-See → Great Bear Lake ◎ 176 66.00 N 120.00 W
Grosser Beerberg ∧ 54 50.37 N 10.44 E
Grosser Bösenstein ∧ 61 47.26 N 14.24 E
Grosser Buchstein ∧ 61 47.36 N 14.35 E
Grosser Chingan → Da Hinggan Ling ∧ 90 49.00 N 122.00 E
Grosser Feldberg ∧ 56 50.14 N 8.26 E
Grosser Galtenberg ∧ 64 47.20 N 11.58 E
Grosser Gleichberg ∧ 54 50.23 N 10.35 E
Grosser Graben ≡ 264a 52.28 N 13.03 E
Grosser Heuberg ∧¹ 58 48.06 N 8.55 E
Grosser Inselsberg ∧ 54 50.52 N 10.28 E
Grosser Jasmunder Bodden ⊂ 54 54.31 N 13.29 E
Grosser Knallstein ∧ 61 47.19 N 13.58 E
Grosser Königstuhl ∧ 64 46.57 N 13.47 E
Grosser Müggelsee ◎ 54 52.26 N 13.39 E
Grosser Röder ≃ 54 51.30 N 13.25 E
Grosser oder Kaiser-Kanal → Da Yunhe ≍ 90 32.12 N 119.31 E
Grosser Rodl ≃ 61 48.20 N 14.09 E
Grosser Peilstein ∧ 61 48.18 N 15.16 E
Grosser Plessower See ◎ 264a 52.23 N 12.54 E
Grosser Plöner See ◎ 54 54.06 N 10.25 E
Grosser Priel ∧ 61 47.43 N 14.04 E
Grosser Rachel ∧ 60 48.59 N 13.24 E
Grosser Ravensberg ∧² 264a 52.21 N 13.04 E
Grosser Riedelstein ∧ 60 49.10 N 12.59 E
Grosser Salz-See → Great Salt Lake ◎ 200 41.10 N 112.30 W
Grosser Seddiner See ◎ 264a 52.17 N 13.02 E
Grosser Selchower See ◎ 54 52.14 N 13.53 E
Grosser Sklaven-See → Great Slave Lake ◎ 176 61.30 N 114.00 W
Grosser Speikkogel ∧ 61 46.47 N 14.58 E
Grosser Walfisch-Fluss → Baleine, Grande rivière de la ≃ 176 55.16 N 77.47 W
Grosser Wannsee ◎ 264a 52.26 N 13.11 E
Grosser Winterberg ∧² 54 50.54 N 14.16 E
Grosser Zern-See ◎ 264a 52.24 N 12.56 E
Grosse Sandspitze ∧ 64 46.46 N 12.49 E
Grosse Sandwüste → Great Sandy Desert ✦² 162 21.30 S 125.00 E
Grosses Barrier-Riff → Great Barrier Reef ✦² 160 18.00 S 145.50 E
Grosses Meer ◎ 52 53.25 N 7.17 E
Grosses Moor ✦³, B.R.D. 52 52.40 N 8.20 E
Grosses Moor ✦³, B.R.D. 52 52.35 N 8.45 E
Grosses Schulerloch ✦ 60 48.55 N 11.48 E
Grosse Sundainseln → Greater Sunda Islands ıı 108 2.00 S 110.00 E
Grosses Walsertal ∨ 58 47.14 N 9.56 E
Grosse Syrte → Surt, Khalīj ⊂ 146 31.30 N 18.00 E
Grosseto 66 42.46 N 11.08 E
Grosseto □⁴ 66 42.50 N 11.15 E
Grosse Tulln ≃ 61 48.20 N 16.02 E
Grossevichi 89 47.59 N 139.30 E
Gross-Gerau 56 49.55 N 8.29 E
Gross-Gerungs 61 48.34 N 14.57 E
Gross Gleidingen 52 52.14 N 10.25 E
Gross Glienicke 264a 52.28 N 13.07 E
Gross-Glienicker See ◎ 264a 52.28 N 13.06 E
Grossglockner ∧ 64 47.04 N 12.42 E
Grossgmain 64 47.43 N 12.55 E
Grossgörschen 54 51.13 N 12.11 E
Gross Grönau 54 53.48 N 10.45 E
Grosshansdorf 52 53.40 N 10.17 E
Grossharthmannsdorf 54 50.48 N 13.19 E
Gross-Hehlen 52 52.39 N 10.03 E
Grossheide 52 53.35 N 7.20 E
Grossheinnersdorf 54 50.59 N 14.47 E
Grosshöchstetten 58 46.55 N 7.38 E
Grossholzleute 58 47.41 N 10.05 E
Grossjedlersdorf ✦⁸ 264b 48.17 N 16.25 E
Grosskayna 54 51.17 N 11.56 E
Gross Kienitz 264a 52.19 N 13.28 E
Gross-Kollmar 52 53.44 N 9.30 E
Grosskorbetha 54 51.16 N 12.01 E
Gross Kreutz 54 52.24 N 12.46 E
Grosskrut 61 48.38 N 16.43 E
Grosslehna 54 51.18 N 12.10 E
Gross Leine 54 52.00 N 14.03 E
Grosslittgen 56 50.02 N 6.47 E
Grossmachnow 54 52.16 N 13.28 E
Grossmehring 60 48.46 N 11.32 E
Gross Möllen → Mielno 30 54.16 N 16.01 E
Grossmont 228 32.47 N 116.59 W
Gross Muckrow 54 52.04 N 14.26 E
Grössnöbach 60 48.21 N 11.35 E
Gross Oesingen 52 52.38 N 10.29 E
Grossörner 54 51.37 N 11.29 E
Grossos 250 4.59 S 37.09 W
Grossostheim 56 49.55 N 9.04 E
Grosspetersdorf 61 47.14 N 16.19 E
Grosspostwitz 54 51.07 N 14.26 E
Grossquenstedt 54 51.56 N 11.07 E
Grossraming 61 47.53 N 14.33 E
Grossräschen 54 51.35 N 14.00 E
Gross Rhüden 52 51.56 N 10.07 E
Grossrinderfeld 56 49.39 N 9.44 E
Gross Rodensleben 54 52.08 N 11.25 E
Grossröhrsdorf 54 51.08 N 14.01 E
Gross Rosenburg 54 51.55 N 11.53 E
Grossrückerswalde 54 50.38 N 13.07 E
Grossrudestedt 54 51.05 N 11.06 E
Gross Sankt Florian 61 46.49 N 15.19 E
Gross-Sarau 54 53.45 N 10.44 E
Grossschirma 54 50.58 N 13.17 E
Grossschönau 54 50.54 N 14.40 E
Gross Schönebeck 54 52.54 N 13.32 E
Gross-Schulzendorf 264a 52.16 N 13.21 E
Gross-Siegharts 61 48.48 N 15.24 E
Grosssölk 64 47.25 N 13.58 E
Gross Strehlitz → Strzelce Opolskie 30 50.31 N 18.19 E
Grosssimmern 56 49.52 N 8.50 E
Gross-Umstadt 56 49.52 N 8.55 E
Grossvenediger ∧ 64 47.06 N 12.21 E
Grosswardein → Oradea 38 47.03 N 21.57 E
Gross Wartenberg → Syców 30 51.19 N 17.43 E
Grossweil 64 47.41 N 11.18 E
Grossweissenbach 61 48.33 N 15.10 E
Gross Windgällen ∧ 58 46.49 N 8.44 E
Gross Wittensee 41 54.24 N 9.46 E
Gross Ziethen, D.D.R. 264a 52.24 N 13.28 E
Gross Ziethen, D.D.R. 264a 52.44 N 13.01 E
Gross-Zimmern 56 49.52 N 8.50 E
Grostenquin 56 48.59 N 6.44 E
Grosvenor, Lake ◎ 180 58.40 N 155.15 W
Grosvenor Dale 207 41.58 N 71.53 W
Gros Ventre ≃ 202 43.33 N 110.46 W
Groswater Bay ⊂ 176 54.20 N 57.30 W
Grote Nete ≃ 56 51.07 N 4.34 E
Groton, Ct., U.S. 207 41.21 N 72.04 W
Groton, Ma., U.S. 207 42.36 N 71.34 W
Groton, N.Y., U.S. 210 42.35 N 76.22 W
Groton, S.D., U.S. 198 45.26 N 98.05 W
Grottaferrata 66 41.47 N 12.40 E
Grottaglie 68 40.32 N 17.26 E
Grottaminarda 68 41.04 N 15.02 E
Grottammare 66 42.59 N 13.52 E
Grotte 70 37.24 N 13.42 E
Grotte di Castro 66 42.40 N 11.52 E
Grotteria 68 38.22 N 16.17 E
Grottkau → Grodków 30 50.43 N 17.22 E
Grottoes 188 38.16 N 78.49 W
Grottole 68 40.36 N 16.23 E
Grou, Oued ∨ 148 33.56 N 6.45 W
Grouard Mission 182 55.31 N 116.09 W
Groundbirch 182 55.47 N 120.55 W
Groundhog ≃ 176 49.43 N 81.58 W
Grouse Creek ≃, Ks., U.S. 198 37.00 N 96.55 W
Grouse Creek ≃, Ut., U.S. 200 41.22 N 113.55 W
Grouse Creek Mountain ∧ 202 44.22 N 113.54 W
Grouw 52 53.05 N 5.45 E
Grove, Eng., U.K. 42 51.36 N 1.25 W
Grove, Ok., U.S. 196 36.35 N 94.46 W
Grove, Pa., U.S. 285 40.01 N 75.38 W
Grove City, Fl., U.S. 220 26.54 N 82.19 W
Grove City, Mn., U.S. 198 45.09 N 94.40 W
Grove City, Oh., U.S. 218 39.52 N 83.05 W
Grove City, Pa., U.S. 214 41.09 N 80.05 W
Grove Hill 194 31.42 N 87.46 W
Groveland, Ca., U.S. 226 37.50 N 120.13 W
Groveland, Fl., U.S. 220 28.33 N 81.51 W
Groveland, Ma., U.S. 207 42.45 N 71.01 W
Groveland, N.Y., U.S. 210 42.39 N 77.46 W
Grovely Ridge ∧ 42 51.08 N 2.04 W
Grove Mountains ∧ 9 72.53 S 74.53 E
Grove Park ✦⁸ 260 51.26 N 0.01 E
Groveport 218 39.52 N 82.53 W
Grover 210 41.37 N 76.52 W
Grover City 204 35.07 N 120.37 W
Grover Cleveland Birthplace ⊥ 276 40.50 N 74.16 W
Grover Cleveland Park ♦ 284a 42.57 N 78.49 W
Grover Hill 216 41.01 N 84.28 W
Grovers Mills 276 40.19 N 74.37 W
Groves 194 29.56 N 93.55 W
Groveton, N.H., U.S. 188 44.35 N 71.30 W
Groveton, Pa., U.S. 279b 40.30 N 80.06 W
Groveton, Tx., U.S. 222 31.03 N 95.07 W
Groveton, Va., U.S. 284c 38.46 N 77.05 W
Grovetown 192 33.27 N 82.11 W
Groveville 208 40.10 N 74.40 W
Growa Point › 150 4.21 N 7.37 W
Growler Peak ∧ 200 32.24 N 113.07 W
Growler Wash ∨ 200 32.35 N 113.30 W
Groznoje 85 42.36 N 71.12 E
Groznyj 84 43.20 N 45.42 E
Groznyy → Groznyj 84 43.20 N 45.42 E
Grube, B.R.D. 54 54.14 N 11.01 E
Grube, D.D.R. 264a 52.26 N 12.57 E
Grubišno Polje 36 45.42 N 17.10 E
Grubweg 60 48.35 N 13.29 E
Grudovo 38 42.21 N 27.10 E
Grudziądz 30 53.29 N 18.45 E
Gruesa, Punta › 248 20.22 S 70.11 W
Gruetli-Laager 194 35.22 N 85.40 W
Grugapark ♦ 263 51.26 N 7.00 E
Grugliasco 62 45.04 N 7.35 E
Gruia 38 44.16 N 22.42 E
Gruinard Bay ⊂ 46 57.53 N 5.31 W
Gruinart, Loch ⊂ 46 55.52 N 6.20 W
Gruiten 56 51.14 N 7.01 E
Gruitrode 56 51.05 N 5.35 E
Grulla 196 26.16 N 98.39 W
Grumello del Monte 62 45.38 N 9.52 E
Grumento Nova 68 40.17 N 15.53 E
Grumentum ⊥ 68 40.17 N 15.55 E
Grumman-Bethpage Airport ⊗ 276 40.45 N 73.29 W
Grumman Corporation ▽³ 276 40.45 N 73.30 W
Grumme ✦⁸ 263 51.30 N 7.14 E
Grumo Appula 68 41.01 N 16.42 E
Grums 26 59.21 N 13.06 E
Grun' 78 50.16 N 34.36 E
Grüna 54 50.49 N 12.47 E
Grünau 156 27.44 S 18.23 E
Grünau ✦⁸ 264a 52.25 N 13.34 E
Grünau im Almtal 64 47.51 N 13.57 E
Grunavat, Loch ◎ 46 58.10 N 6.55 W
Grünbach 54 50.26 N 12.22 E
Grünberg, B.R.D. 56 50.35 N 8.58 E
Grünberg → Zielona Góra, Pol. 30 51.56 N 15.31 E
Grünburg 61 47.57 N 14.15 E
Grundlsee ◎ 61 47.38 N 13.52 E
Grundy 192 37.16 N 82.05 W
Grundy □⁶ 216 41.22 N 88.26 W
Grundy Center 190 42.21 N 92.46 W
Grundy Lake Provincial Park ♦ 190 45.48 N 80.34 W
Grünefeld 264a 52.41 N 12.58 E
Grünenplan 52 51.57 N 9.44 E
Grünewald, B.R.D. 263 51.13 N 7.37 E
Grünewald, D.D.R. 54 51.24 N 14.00 E
Grunewald ✦⁸ 264a 52.30 N 13.17 E
Grunewald, Jagdschloss ⊥ 264a 52.28 N 13.16 E
Grünhain 54 50.35 N 12.48 E
Grünhainichen 54 50.46 N 13.08 E
Grünheide 54 52.25 N 13.49 E
Grünsfeld 56 49.36 N 9.44 E
Grünstadt 56 49.34 N 8.10 E
Grüntal 264a 52.45 N 13.44 E
Grunthal 184 49.25 N 96.52 W
Grünwald 60 48.02 N 11.32 E
Gruševka 78 47.55 N 40.40 E
Gruševka ≃ 83 47.26 N 40.00 E
Gruševskaja 83 47.26 N 39.57 E
Grušino 76 59.27 N 44.09 E
Gruting 46 60.14 N 1.30 W
Gruver 196 36.16 N 101.24 W
Gruyère, Lac de la ◎ 58 46.38 N 7.06 E
Gruyères 58 46.35 N 7.05 E
Gruzdžiai 76 56.06 N 23.16 E
Gruzinskaja Sovetskaja Socialističeskaja Respublika □³ 84 42.00 N 44.00 E
Gruznovka 88 55.09 N 105.12 E
Gruzskaja Balka 78 46.25 N 40.19 E
Gruzskij Jelančik ≃ 83 47.07 N 38.04 E
Gruzskoje 83 48.33 N 37.18 E
Gruzsko-Zor'anskoje 83 47.56 N 38.06 E
Grybów 30 49.38 N 20.56 E
Grycken ◎ 40 60.27 N 16.13 E
Gryfice 30 53.56 N 15.12 E
Gryfino 30 53.12 N 14.30 E
Grytdalen Nasjonalpark ♦ 26 63.25 N 9.45 E
Grytgöl 40 58.48 N 15.33 E
Grythyttan 40 59.42 N 14.32 E
Grytviken ▽³ 9 54.17 S 36.30 W
Gschnitz 64 47.03 N 11.22 E
Gschütt, Pass)(64 47.35 N 13.30 E
Gschwend 56 48.56 N 9.44 E
Gstaad 58 46.28 N 7.17 E
Gsteig 58 46.23 N 7.16 E
Gu ≃ 100 27.02 N 115.03 E
Gua 124 22.12 N 85.23 E
Guabaria ≃¹ 126 22.10 N 90.30 E
Guabito 238 9.30 N 82.37 W
Guabu 106 32.16 N 118.53 E
Guacanayabo, Golfo de ⊂ 240p 20.28 N 77.30 W
Guacara 246 10.14 N 67.53 W
Guacari 246 3.46 N 76.20 W
Gu Achi 200 32.19 N 112.02 W
Guachinango 234 20.32 N 104.24 W
Guachiría ≃ 246 5.27 N 70.36 W
Guachochic 232 26.51 N 107.05 W
Guaçuí 255 20.46 S 41.41 W
Guadajira ≃ 34 38.52 N 6.41 W
Guadajoz ≃ 34 37.50 N 4.51 W
Guadalajara, Esp. 34 40.38 N 3.10 W
Guadalajara, Méx. 234 20.40 N 103.20 W
Guadalamar ≃ 34 38.05 N 3.06 W
Guadalaviar ≃ 34 40.21 N 1.08 W
Guadalcanal 34 38.06 N 5.49 W
Guadalcanal □⁴ 175e 9.50 S 160.00 E
Guadalcanal ı 175e 9.32 S 160.12 E
Guadalcázar 234 22.37 N 100.24 W
Guadalén, Embalse de ◎¹ 34 38.05 N 3.32 W
Guadalentín ≃ 34 38.25 N 3.15 W
Guadalentín ≃ 34 37.59 N 1.04 W
Guadalete ≃ 34 36.35 N 6.13 W
Guadalhorce ≃ 34 36.41 N 4.27 W
Guadalimar ≃ 34 38.19 N 2.56 W
Guadalmez ≃ 34 38.46 N 5.04 W
Guadalope ≃ 34 41.15 N 0.03 W
Guadalquivir ≃ 34 36.47 N 6.22 W
Guadalupe, Bol. 248 18.33 S 64.05 W
Guadalupe, Col. 246 2.01 N 75.45 W
Guadalupe, C.R. 236 9.57 N 84.03 W
Guadalupe, Méx. 196 28.09 N 100.36 W
Guadalupe, Méx. 232 16.16 N 91.27 W
Guadalupe, Méx. 234 25.41 N 100.15 W
Guadalupe, Méx. 234 22.45 N 102.31 W
Guadalupe, Perú 248 7.15 S 79.29 W
Guadalupe, Ca., U.S. 204 34.58 N 120.34 W
Guadalupe □⁶ 222 29.37 N 97.45 W
Guadalupe ✦⁸ 287a 22.50 S 43.23 W
Guadalupe → Guadeloupe □² 241o 16.15 N 61.35 W
Guadalupe ≃, Méx. 204 32.05 N 116.53 W
Guadalupe ≃, Ca., U.S. 282 37.25 N 121.58 W
Guadalupe ≃, Tx., U.S. 196 28.30 N 96.53 W
Guadalupe, Basílica de ▽¹ 286a 19.29 N 99.07 W
Guadalupe, Isla ı 178 29.00 N 118.16 W
Guadalupe, Presa de ◎¹ 286a 19.37 N 99.16 W
Guadalupe, Sierra de ∧, Esp. 34 39.26 N 5.25 W
Guadalupe, Sierra de ∧, Méx. 286a 19.35 N 99.08 W
Guadalupe [Bravos] 232 31.23 N 106.07 W
Guadalupe del Norte ≍ 286a 19.34 N 99.01 W
Guadalupe de Ramírez 234 17.45 N 98.10 W
Guadalupe Garzarón 232 24.35 N 101.15 W
Guadalupe Mountains ∧ 196 32.20 N 105.00 W
Guadalupe Mountains National Park ♦ 196 31.55 N 104.55 W
Guadalupe Peak ∧ 196 31.50 N 104.52 W
Guadalupe Seamount ✦³ 14 27.50 N 168.45 E
Guadalupe Slough ≃ 282 37.27 N 122.02 W
Guadalupe Victoria, Méx. 196 27.47 N 101.04 W
Guadalupe Victoria, Méx. 232 24.27 N 104.07 W
Guadalupe Victoria, Méx. 234 19.17 N 97.21 W
Guadalupe Victoria, Presa ◎¹ 234 23.50 N 104.46 W
Guadalupita 200 36.08 N 105.14 W
Guadarrama, Puerto de)(34 40.43 N 4.10 W
Guadarrama, Sierra de ∧ 34 40.55 N 4.00 W
Guadazaón ≃ 34 39.42 N 1.36 W
Guadeloupe □², N.A. 230 16.15 N 61.35 W
Guadeloupe □², N.A. 241o 16.15 N 61.35 W
Guadeloupe Passage ᴜ 238 16.45 N 61.30 W
Guadiana ≃ 34 37.14 N 7.22 W
Guadiana, Ensenada de ⊂ 240p 22.05 N 84.24 W
Guadiana Menor ≃ 34 37.56 N 3.15 W
Guadiaro ≃ 34 36.17 N 5.17 W
Guadiela ≃ 34 40.22 N 2.49 W
Guadix 34 37.18 N 3.08 W
Guafo, Isla ı 254 43.36 S 74.43 W
Guagnano 68 40.24 N 17.57 E
Guagua 116 14.58 N 120.38 E
Guahe 105 39.12 N 115.00 E
Guaianases ✦⁸ 287b 23.33 S 46.25 W
Guaíba 252 30.06 S 51.19 W
Guaíba ⊂¹ 252 30.15 S 51.12 W
Guaicaipuro □⁵ 286c 10.25 N 66.57 W
Guaihe 100 33.28 N 112.59 E
Guaimaca 236 14.32 N 86.51 W
Guáimaro 240p 21.03 N 77.21 W
Guaimoreto, Laguna de ⊂ 236 15.58 N 85.55 W
Guaimozi 98 41.31 N 125.26 E
Guainía □⁵ 246 2.30 N 69.00 W
Guainía ≃ 246 2.01 N 67.07 W
Guaió ≃ 287b 23.31 S 46.19 W
Guaipava 256 21.40 S 45.43 W
Guaiquica 256 22.25 S 47.14 W
Guaiquinima, Cerro ∧ 246 5.49 N 63.40 W
Guaíra, Bra. 252 24.04 S 54.15 W
Guaíra, Bra. 255 20.19 S 48.18 W
Guairá □⁵ 252 25.45 S 56.30 W
Guaire ≃ 286c 10.25 N 66.46 W
Guáitara ≃ 246 1.34 N 77.27 W
Guaitecas, Islas ıı 254 43.57 S 73.50 W
Guaiúba 250 4.02 S 38.38 W
Guajaba, Cayo ı 240p 21.50 N 77.30 W
Guajará ≃ 250 1.48 S 53.02 W
Guajará-Açu 250 1.38 S 48.07 W
Guajará-Mirim 248 10.48 S 65.22 W
Guajataca ≃ 240m 18.29 N 66.57 W
Guajataca, Lago de ◎¹ 240m 18.23 N 66.55 W
Guajiasi 104 41.15 N 120.54 E
Gualaca 236 8.32 N 82.18 W
Gualaceo 246 2.54 S 78.47 W
Gualala 204 38.45 N 123.31 W
Gualán 236 15.08 N 89.22 W
Gualaquiza 246 3.24 S 78.33 W
Gualdo Tadino 66 43.14 N 12.47 E
Gualeguay 252 33.09 S 59.20 W
Gualeguay ≃ 252 33.19 S 59.39 W
Gualeguaychú 252 33.01 S 58.31 W
Gualicho, Salina del ≡ 254 40.24 S 65.15 W
Gualjaina 254 42.42 S 70.30 W
Gualtieri 64 44.54 N 10.38 E
Guam □², Oc. 14 13.28 N 144.47 E
Guam □², Oc. 174p 13.28 N 144.47 E
Guamá ≃, Bra. 250 1.29 S 48.30 W
Guamá ≃, Cuba 240p 22.11 N 83.41 W
Guamal, Col. 246 9.09 N 74.14 W
Guamal, Col. 246 3.52 N 73.44 W
Guamal, Quebrada ≃ 286c 10.31 N 66.59 W
Guamblin, Isla ı 254 44.51 S 75.05 W
Guaminí 252 37.02 S 62.25 W
Guam International Airport ⊗ 174p 13.29 N 144.48 E
Guamo 246 4.02 N 74.58 W
Guamo Embarcadero 240p 20.37 N 76.58 W
Guamote 246 1.56 S 78.43 W
Guamúchil, Méx. 232 25.28 N 108.06 W
Guamúchil, Méx. 234 23.55 N 106.05 W
Guamués ≃ 246 0.32 N 76.33 W
Gua Musang 114 4.53 N 101.58 E
Gu'an 105 39.26 N 116.18 E
Guan ≃, Zhg. 100 34.29 N 119.49 E
Guan ≃, Zhg. 100 32.16 N 115.43 E
Guanábana 240m 18.01 N 67.07 W
Guanabara, Baía de ⊂ 287a 22.50 S 43.10 W
Guanabara, Palácio de ▽ 287a 22.56 S 43.11 W
Guanacaste □⁴ 236 10.30 N 85.15 W
Guanacaste, Cordillera de ∧ 236 10.45 N 85.05 W
Guanacaure, Cerro ∧ 236 13.14 N 87.07 W
Guanaceví 232 25.56 N 105.57 W
Guanache ≃ 248 5.53 S 74.21 W
Guanahacabibes, Golfo de ⊂ 240p 22.08 N 84.35 W
Guanahacabibes, Península de ›¹ 240p 21.57 N 84.35 W
Guana Island ı 240m 18.29 N 64.34 W
Guanaja 236 16.27 N 85.54 W
Guanaja, Isla de ı 236 16.30 N 85.55 W
Guanajay 240p 22.55 N 82.42 W
Guanajibo ≃ 240m 18.10 N 67.11 W
Guanajibo, Punta › 240m 18.10 N 67.11 W
Guanajuato 234 21.01 N 101.15 W
Guanajuato □³ 234 21.00 N 101.00 W
Guanambi 255 14.13 S 42.47 W
Guañape, Isla ı 248 8.33 S 78.57 W
Guanare 246 9.03 N 69.45 W
Guanare ≃ 246 8.13 N 67.46 W
Guanare Viejo ≃ 246 8.19 N 68.10 W
Guanarito 246 8.42 N 69.12 W
Guanay 248 15.28 S 67.52 W
Guanay, Cerro ∧ 246 5.51 N 66.18 W
Guanay, Cerro ∧² 286d 12.07 S 77.13 W
Guanbuqiao 100 29.56 N 114.21 E
Guanchao 100 26.41 N 114.58 E
Guancheng, Zhg. 100 30.11 N 121.25 E
Guancheng, Zhg. 100 32.47 N 115.27 E
Guancun 106 31.30 N 119.43 E
Guandacol 252 29.31 S 68.32 W
Guandanghu 100 30.06 N 113.37 E
Guandi, Zhg. 98 41.48 N 116.52 E
Guandi, Zhg. 98 42.37 N 118.27 E
Guandian 100 32.40 N 118.24 E
Guandu 100 33.21 N 113.53 E
Guandu, Zhg. 107 30.04 N 106.25 E
Guane 240p 22.12 N 84.05 W
Guang'an 107 30.28 N 106.39 E
Guang'anmen Station ✦⁵ 271a 39.53 N 116.20 E
Guangchang 100 26.50 N 116.14 E

	English	Deutsch	Español	Français	Português
≃	River	Fluss	Río	Rivière	Rio
≍	Canal	Kanal	Canal	Canal	Canal
⌇	Waterfall, Rapids	Wasserfall, Stromschnellen	Cascada, Rápidos	Chute d'eau, Rapides	Cascata, Rápidos
ᴜ	Strait	Meeresstrasse	Estrecho	Détroit	Estreito
⊂	Bay, Gulf	Bucht, Golf	Bahía, Golfo	Baie, Golfe	Baía, Golfo
◎	Lake, Lakes	See, Seen	Lago, Lagos	Lac, Lacs	Lago, Lagos
≡	Swamp	Sumpf	Pantano	Marais	Pântano
⁂	Ice Features, Glacier	Eis- und Gletscherformen	Accidentes Glaciales	Formes glaciaires	Acidentes glaciares
✦	Other Hydrographic Features	Andere Hydrographische Objekte	Otros Elementos Hidrográficos	Autres données hydrographiques	Outros acidentes hidrográficos

	English	Deutsch	Español	Français	Português
✦	Submarine Features	Untermeerische Objekte	Accidentes Submarinos	Formes de relief sous-marin	Acidentes submarinos
□	Political Unit	Politische Einheit	Unidad Política	Entité politique	Unidade política
▽	Cultural Institution	Kulturelle Institution	Institución Cultural	Institution culturelle	Instituição cultural
⊥	Historical Site	Historische Stätte	Sitio Histórico	Site historique	Sítio histórico
♦	Recreational Site	Erholungs- und Ferienort	Sitio de Recreo	Centre de loisirs	Área de Lazer
⊗	Airport	Flughafen	Aeropuerto	Aéroport	Aeroporto
■	Military Installation	Militäranlage	Instalación Militar	Installation militaire	Instalação militar
◆	Miscellaneous	Verschiedenes	Misceláneo	Divers	Diversos

ENGLISH Name	Page	Lat.°′	Long.°′	DEUTSCH Name	Seite	Breite°′	Länge°′ E = Ost

Symbols in the index entries represent the broad categories identified in the key at the right. Symbols with superior numbers (⩘[1]) identify subcategories (see complete key on page *I · 1).*

Kartensymbole in dem Registerverzeichnis stellen die rechts in Schlüssel erklärten Kategorien dar. Symbole mit hochgestellten Ziffern (⩘[1]) bezeichnen Unterabteilungen einer Kategorie (vgl. vollständiger Schlüssel auf Seite *I · 1).*

Los símbolos incluídos en el texto del índice representan las grandes categorias identificadas con la clave a la derecha. Los símbolos con numeros en su parte superior (⩘[1]) identifican las subcategorías (véase la clave completa en la página *I · 1).*

Les symboles de l'index représentent les catégories indiquées dans la légende à droite. Les symboles suivis d'un indice (⩘[1]) représentent des sous-catégories (voir légende complète à la page *I · 1).*

Os símbolos incluídos no texto do índice representam as grandes categorias identificadas com a chave à direita. Os símbolos com números em sua parte superior (⩘[1]) identificam as subcategorias (veja-se a chave completa à página *I · 1).*

∧ Mountain	Berg	Montaña	Montagne	Montanha
⩘ Mountains	Berge	Montañas	Montagnes	Montanhas
)(Pass	Pass	Paso	Col	Passo
V Valley, Canyon	Tal, Cañon	Valle, Cañón	Vallée, Canyon	Vale, Canhão
≚ Plain	Ebene	Llano	Plaine	Planície
› Cape	Kap	Cabo	Cap	Cabo
I Island	Insel	Isla	Île	Ilha
II Islands	Inseln	Islas	Îles	Ilhas
⊥ Other Topographic Features	Andere Topographische Objekte	Otros Elementos Topográficos	Autres données topographiques	Outros acidentes topográficos

ESPAÑOL · FRANÇAIS · PORTUGUÊS

Nombre / Nom / Nome	Página / Page	Lat.°′	Long.°′ W = Oeste / Ouest
Guxian, Zhg.	100	27.09 N	115.31 E
Guxiandu	100	29.06 N	116.50 E
Guxiansi	100	32.01 N	116.20 E
Guxiong	106	31.55 N	118.38 E
Guy	222	29.21 N	95.47 W
Guyana □[1], S.A.	242	5.00 N	59.00 W
Guyana □[1], S.A.	246	5.00 N	59.00 W
Guyancourt	261	48.46 N	2.04 E
Guyancourt, Aéroport de ⊠	261	48.45 N	2.05 E
Guyandotte ≃	188	38.26 N	82.23 W
Guyane → Guyana □[1]	246	5.00 N	59.00 W
Guyane française → French Guiana □[2]	250	4.00 N	53.00 W
Guyang, Zhg.	98	34.58 N	114.58 E
Guyang, Zhg.	102	41.03 N	110.03 E
Guye	105	39.44 N	118.25 E
Guyi, Zhg.	100	25.38 N	118.47 E
Guyi, Zhg.	107	30.22 N	103.33 E
Guyin	102	23.58 N	105.47 E
Guymon	196	36.40 N	101.28 W
Guyonne, Ruisseau la ≃	261	48.49 N	1.52 E
Guyot, Mount ʌ	192	35.42 N	83.15 W
Guyra	166	30.14 S	151.40 E
Guysborough	186	45.23 N	61.30 W
Guys Mills	214	41.38 N	79.59 W
Guyton	192	32.20 N	81.23 W
Guyuan (Pingdingbu), Zhg.	98	41.40 N	115.41 E
Guyuan, Zhg.	102	36.01 N	106.17 E
Guzar	72	38.36 N	66.15 E
Güzel ≃	84	39.44 N	43.01 E
Güzelbahçe	130	38.21 N	26.54 E
Güzelsu	130	36.54 N	31.53 E
Guzhang	102	28.31 N	109.57 E
Guzhen, Zhg.	100	22.37 N	113.11 E
Guzhen, Zhg.	100	33.19 N	117.21 E
Guzhu	100	26.58 N	116.16 E
Guzmán, Méx.	232	31.13 N	107.27 W
Guzmán → Ciudad Guzmán, Méx.	234	19.41 N	103.29 W
Guzmán, Laguna de ⊜	232	31.20 N	107.30 W
Gvardejsk	76	54.39 N	21.05 E
Gvardejskoje, S.S.S.R.	78	45.07 N	34.01 E
Gvardejskoje, S.S.S.R.	78	48.44 N	35.19 E
Gvardejskoje, S.S.S.R.	78	49.20 N	26.42 E
Gvazda	78	50.44 N	40.30 E
Gvozdec	78	48.34 N	25.17 E
Gwa	110	17.36 N	94.35 E
Gwabegar	166	30.36 S	148.58 E
Gwadabawa	150	13.20 N	5.15 E
Gwādar	128	25.07 N	62.19 E
Gwagwada	150	10.14 N	7.14 E
Gwai	154	19.15 S	27.42 E
Gwai ≃	154	17.59 S	26.52 E
Gwalangu	152	2.19 N	18.11 E
Gwalchmai	44	53.15 N	4.25 W
Gwāl Haidarzai	120	30.44 N	68.48 E
Gwalia	162	28.55 S	121.20 E
Gwalior	124	26.13 N	78.10 E
Gwambygine	168a	31.59 S	116.48 E
Gwanda	154	20.57 S	29.01 E
Gwandu	150	12.30 N	4.41 E
Gwane	154	4.43 N	25.50 E
Gwangjang Bridge ◆[5]	271b	37.33 N	127.05 E
Gwangju → Kwangju	98	35.09 N	126.54 E
Gwarzo	150	11.56 N	7.56 E
Gwasero	150	9.29 N	3.30 E
Gwash ≃	42	52.39 N	0.27 W
Gwātar Bay ⊂	128	25.04 N	61.36 E
Gwatt	58	46.43 N	7.38 E
Gwaun ≃	42	52.00 N	4.58 W
Gwda ≃	30	53.04 N	16.44 E
Gweebarra ≃	48	54.50 N	8.20 W
Gweebarra Bay ⊂	48	54.52 N	8.20 W
Gweedore	48	55.03 N	8.14 W
Gweesalia	48	54.07 N	9.54 W
Gwelo ≃	154	18.45 S	28.36 E
Gwembe	154	16.30 S	27.35 E
Gwendraeth Fâch ≃	42	51.44 N	4.18 W
Gwendraeth Fawr ≃	42	51.43 N	4.18 W
Gwent □[6]	42	51.43 N	2.57 W
Gweru	154	19.27 S	29.49 E
Gweta	156	20.10 S	25.18 E
Gwinhurst	285	39.47 N	75.29 W
Gwinn	190	46.16 N	87.26 W
Gwinner	198	46.13 N	97.39 W
Gwobu	154	2.37 N	26.13 E
Gwydir ≃	166	29.27 S	149.48 E
Gwynedd	285	40.12 N	75.15 W
Gwynedd □[6]	28	53.00 N	4.00 W
Gwynedd Square	285	40.13 N	75.18 W
Gwynedd Valley	285	40.11 N	75.15 W
Gwynn	208	37.30 N	76.17 W
Gwynneville	218	39.39 N	85.38 W
Gwynn Island I	208	37.30 N	76.17 W
Gwynn Oak Amusement Park ♠	284b	39.20 N	76.43 W
Gwynns Falls ≃	284b	39.16 N	76.37 W
Gwynns Falls Park ♠	284b	39.18 N	76.41 W
Gy	58	47.24 N	5.49 E
Gyál	264c	47.23 N	19.14 E
Gya La)(	124	28.44 N	84.40 E
Gyáli-patak ≃	264c	47.24 N	19.07 E
Gyangtse → Jiangzi	120	28.57 N	89.35 E
Gyaring Hu ⊜	102	34.53 N	97.58 E
Gybdan	80	56.33 N	51.39 E
Gyda	74	70.52 N	78.30 E
Gydanskaja guba ⊂	74	71.20 N	76.30 E
Gydanskij poluostrov ≻[1]	74	70.50 N	79.00 E
Gyebu	164	3.03 S	133.51 E
Gyemo Chen ʌ	124	27.20 N	88.52 E
Gyeongbog Palace ʋ	271b	37.36 N	126.57 E
Gyeongju → Kyŏngju	98	35.51 N	129.14 E
Gyldenløves Fjord ⊂[2]	176	64.30 N	41.30 W
Gyldenløveshøj ʌ[2]	41	55.33 N	11.52 E
Gylling	41	55.53 N	10.11 E
Gymea Bay	274a	34.02 S	151.05 E
Gym Peak ʌ	200	32.04 N	107.35 W
Gympie	166	26.11 S	152.40 E
Gyobingauk	110	18.13 N	95.39 E
Gyōda	94	36.08 N	139.28 E
Gyoma	30	46.56 N	20.50 E
Gyöngyös	30	47.47 N	19.56 E
Gyöngyös ≃	61	47.14 N	16.55 E
Győr	30	47.42 N	17.38 E
Győr-Sopron □[6]	30	47.35 N	17.15 E
Gypsey Race ≃	44	54.05 N	0.12 W
Gypsum, Co., U.S.	200	39.38 N	106.57 W
Gypsum, Ks., U.S.	198	38.42 N	97.25 W
Gypsum, Oh., U.S.	214	41.29 N	82.52 W
Gypsum Creek ≃, U.S.	200	37.09 N	109.52 W
Gypsum Creek ≃, Ks., U.S.	198	38.51 N	97.25 W
Gypsum Hills ⋏[2]	196	36.25 N	99.20 W
Gypsum Point ≻	176	61.53 N	114.35 W
Gypsumville	184	51.45 N	98.35 W
Gyrbovec	78	46.50 N	29.21 E
Gysinge	40	60.17 N	16.53 E
Gyttorp	40	59.31 N	14.58 E
Gyula	30	46.39 N	21.17 E
Gyulafehérvár → Alba-Iulia	38	46.04 N	23.35 E
Gžat' ≃	76	55.56 N	34.33 E
Gžatsk	86	55.42 N	78.11 E
Gžel'	82	55.36 N	38.24 E
Gzhatsk → Gagarin	76	55.33 N	35.00 E
H			
Haag → 's-Gravenhage, Ned.	52	52.06 N	4.18 E
Haag, Öst.	61	48.07 N	14.34 E
Haag am Hausruck	60	48.11 N	13.38 E
Haagen	58	47.38 N	7.40 E
Haag in Oberbayern	60	48.10 N	12.11 E
Haaksbergen	52	52.09 N	6.44 E
Haalenberg	156	26.52 S	15.30 E
Haaltert	50	50.54 N	4.00 E
Haamstede	52	51.43 N	3.45 E
Haan	56	51.11 N	7.00 E
Haapajärvi	26	63.45 N	25.20 E
Haapajärvi ⊜	26	63.33 N	27.00 E
Haapamäki	26	62.15 N	24.28 E
Haapavesi	26	64.08 N	25.22 E
Haapiti	174s	17.34 S	149.52 W
Haapsalu	76	58.56 N	23.33 E
Haar	60	48.06 N	11.44 E
Haar ◆[8]	263	51.26 N	7.13 E
Ha'Arava (Wādī al-Jayb) ∨	132	30.58 N	35.24 E
Haardt ⋏	56	49.15 N	8.00 E
Haaren, B.R.D.	52	51.34 N	8.44 E
Haaren, Ned.	52	51.36 N	5.12 E
Haarlem, Ned.	52	52.23 N	4.38 E
Haarlem, S. Afr.	158	33.44 S	23.20 E
Haarlemmermeer ◆[1]	52	52.15 N	4.38 E
Haarstrang ʌ	52	51.35 N	8.10 E
Haarzopf ◆[8]	263	51.25 N	6.58 E
Haast	172	43.53 S	169.03 E
Haast ≃	172	43.50 S	169.02 E
Haast Bluff	162	23.30 S	131.50 E
Haast Pass)(	172	44.06 S	169.21 E
Haasts Bluff Aboriginal Reserve ◆[4]	162	23.30 S	130.30 E
Haatinao, Pointe ≻	174y	9.47 S	138.51 W
Haava, Canal ≋	174y	9.53 S	139.04 W
Hab ≃	120	24.53 N	66.41 E
Habahe	86	47.53 N	86.12 E
Habaqi, Zhg.	104	42.36 N	122.52 E
Habaqi, Zhg.	104	42.38 N	122.02 E
Habaqila	102	42.01 N	106.02 E
Habartov	54	50.08 N	12.33 E
Ḥabashīyah, Jabal ⋏	144	16.40 N	49.40 E
Habaswein	154	1.01 N	39.29 E
Ḥabawnah, Wādī ∨	144	17.51 N	44.59 E
Habay-la-Neuve	56	49.44 N	5.39 E
Ḥabbān	144	14.21 N	47.05 E
Ḥabbānīyah, Hawr al- ⊜	128	33.17 N	43.29 E
Ḥabbūsh	132	33.24 N	35.29 E
Habelschwerdt → Bystrzyca Kłodzka	30	50.18 N	16.38 E
Habère-Poche	58	46.15 N	6.29 E
Haberfield	274a	33.53 S	151.08 E
Habermehl Peak ʌ	9	71.49 S	6.38 E
Ḥabīb, Wādī ∨	142	27.20 N	31.30 E
Habiganj	120	24.23 N	91.25 E
Habikino	96	34.33 N	135.37 E
Habīlah	140	12.41 N	22.33 E
Habinghorst ◆[8]	263	51.35 N	7.18 E
Hab Nadi Chowki	120	25.01 N	66.53 E
Habo	26	57.55 N	14.04 E
Habob, Wādī ∨	140	18.07 N	35.01 E
Habomai-shotō → Malaja Kuril'skaja Gr'ada II	92a	43.30 N	146.10 E
Haboro	92a	44.22 N	141.42 E
Hābra	126	22.50 N	88.38 E
Habsburg ⊥	58	47.28 N	8.13 E
Habsheim	58	47.44 N	7.25 E
Habu	270	34.27 N	135.24 E
Habutaki	270	34.25 N	135.26 E
Hache, Lac la ⊜	182	51.50 N	121.30 W
Hachen	56	51.22 N	7.59 E
Hachenburg	56	50.39 N	7.50 E
Hachi	120	27.46 N	94.01 E
Hachijō	270	34.37 N	135.48 E
Hachijō-jima I	90	33.05 N	139.48 E
Hachiman → Ōmi-hachiman	94	35.08 N	136.06 E
Hachiman	94	35.45 N	136.57 E
Hachiman-misaki ≻	94	35.08 N	140.19 E
Hachinohe	92	40.30 N	141.29 E
Hachiōji	94	35.39 N	139.20 E
Hachmühlen	52	52.10 N	9.28 E
Hacıbektaş	130	38.57 N	34.35 E
Hacienda Heights	228	34.00 N	117.57 W
Hacienda Miravalles	236	10.41 N	85.14 W
Hacihamza	130	41.05 N	34.28 E
Hacıishaklı	130	36.11 N	33.40 E
Hacıköy	130	40.04 N	35.31 E
Hacılar	130	38.39 N	35.27 E
Hack, Mount ʌ	166	30.46 S	138.48 E
Hackås	26	62.55 N	14.31 E
Hackberry, Az., U.S.	200	35.22 N	113.43 W
Hackberry, La., U.S.	194	29.59 N	93.20 W
Hackberry Creek ≃, Ks., U.S.	198	38.48 N	100.03 W
Hackberry Creek ≃, Tx., U.S.	222	31.53 N	97.12 W
Hackensack	210	40.53 N	74.02 W
Hackensack ≃	276	40.43 N	74.06 W
Hacketstown	48	52.52 N	6.33 W
Hackett, Ar., U.S.	194	35.11 N	94.24 W
Hackett, Pa., U.S.	279b	40.15 N	80.01 W
Hacketts	260	51.45 N	0.05 W
Hackettstown	210	40.52 N	74.48 W
Hacking ≃	274a	34.04 S	151.06 E
Hacking, Port ⊂	274a	34.05 S	151.09 E
Hackleburg	194	34.16 N	87.49 W
Hackney ◆[8]	260	51.33 N	0.03 W
Hack Point	208	39.27 N	75.52 W
Håckren ⊜	26	63.11 N	13.35 E
Haçlı Gölü ⊜	130	39.00 N	42.18 E
Haco	152	10.12 S	15.44 E
Hacreş Dağları ⋏	130	38.38 N	41.37 E
Hadāli	123	32.18 N	72.12 E
Hadalīya	140	16.10 N	36.06 E
Hadamar	56	50.27 N	8.02 E
Ḥaḍan, Ḥarrat ⊥[9]	144	21.30 N	41.23 E
Hadano	94	35.22 N	139.14 E
Ḥadāribah, Ra's al- ≻	140	22.04 N	36.54 E
HaDarom □[5]	132	30.40 N	34.50 E
Hadat	89	49.40 N	119.40 E
Hadayingzi	104	42.22 N	121.40 E
Ḥadd, Ra's al- ≻	118	22.32 N	59.48 E
Haddad, Ouadi ∨	146	14.40 N	18.46 E
Ḥaddādīn, Qārat al- ʌ[2]	142	30.04 N	30.58 E
Haddam, Ct., U.S.	207	41.28 N	72.30 W
Haddam, Ks., U.S.	198	39.51 N	97.18 W
Haddenham, Eng., U.K.	42	51.46 N	0.56 W
Haddenham, Eng., U.K.	42	52.22 N	0.09 E
Haddington	46	55.58 N	2.47 W
Haddock	192	33.01 N	83.25 W
Haddon Downs	166	26.21 S	140.50 E
Haddonfield	208	39.53 N	75.02 W
Haddon Heights	208	39.52 N	75.03 W
Haddon Hills	285	39.54 N	75.03 W
Hadejia	150	12.30 N	9.59 E
Hadejia ≃	134	12.50 N	10.51 E
Hadeln, Land ◆[1]	52	53.45 N	8.45 E
Haden	171a	27.14 S	151.53 E
Ḥadera	132	32.26 N	34.55 E
Ḥadera ≃	132	32.27 N	34.53 E
Hadersdorf ◆[8]	264b	48.13 N	16.14 E
Hadersfeld	264b	48.20 N	16.15 E
Haderslev	41	55.15 N	9.30 E
Haderslev Fjord ⊂	41	55.17 N	9.40 E
Hadfield, Austl.	274b	37.42 S	144.56 E
Hadfield, Eng., U.K.	262	53.28 N	1.58 W
Hadībū	118	12.38 N	54.02 E
Ḥadīd, Jabal ʌ[2]	142	30.20 N	30.06 E
Ḥadīd, Jabal al- ʌ[2]	142	28.47 N	31.04 E
Hadım	130	36.59 N	32.28 E
Hadīyah	128	25.34 N	38.41 E
Hadjout	34	36.31 N	2.25 E
Hadleigh, Eng., U.K.	42	52.03 N	0.58 E
Hadleigh, Eng., U.K.	260	51.33 N	0.37 E
Hadleigh Castle ⊥	260	51.33 N	0.36 E
Hadley, Eng., U.K.	42	52.42 N	2.29 W
Hadley, Ma., U.S.	207	42.20 N	72.35 W
Hadley, Mi., U.S.	216	42.57 N	83.24 W
Hadley, N.Y., U.S.	210	43.19 N	73.50 W
Hadley, Pa., U.S.	214	41.25 N	80.14 W
Hadley Bay ⊂	176	72.30 N	107.45 W
Hadley Creek ≃	219	39.37 N	91.12 W
Hadlock	224	48.01 N	122.45 W
Hadlow	260	51.14 N	0.20 E
Hadlyme	207	41.25 N	72.24 W
Hadmersleben	54	51.59 N	11.18 E
Hadong, Taehan	98	35.05 N	127.44 E
Ha-dong, Viet.	110	20.58 N	105.46 E
Ḥaḍramawt ◆[1]	144	15.00 N	50.00 E
Hadrian's Wall ⊥	44	54.59 N	2.26 W
Hadsten	41	56.20 N	10.03 E
Hadsund	26	56.43 N	10.07 E
Hadyai → Hat Yai	110	7.01 N	100.28 E
Haeju	98	38.02 N	125.42 E
Haemgon-ni ◆[8]	271b	37.35 N	126.49 E
Haena	229b	22.14 N	159.34 W
Haenam	98	34.34 N	126.35 E
Haena Point ≻	229b	22.14 N	159.34 W
Haenertsburg	156	24.00 S	29.50 E
Haengyŏng-ni	98	42.33 N	129.56 E
Haernao	104	41.46 N	120.28 E
Hafeïra, Oued el ∨	148	25.18 N	10.48 W
Hafelekarspitze ʌ	64	47.19 N	11.23 E
Haffen-Mehr	52	51.44 N	6.28 E
Hafford	184	52.43 N	107.21 W
Haffouz	36	35.38 N	9.41 E
Hafik	130	39.52 N	37.24 E
Ḥafīra, Qā'al- ≃	132	31.06 N	36.14 E
Ḥafīrat al-'Aydā	128	26.26 N	39.10 E
Ḥafīt, Jabal ʌ	128	24.03 N	55.46 E
Ḥāfiẓ, Bi'r ⫪[4]	142	30.51 N	29.40 E
Hāfizābād	123	32.04 N	73.41 E
Hafızbey	130	37.12 N	30.31 E
Hāflong	120	25.11 N	93.02 E
Hafnarfjördur	24a	64.03 N	21.56 W
Haft Gel	128	31.27 N	49.27 E
Hafun, Ras ≻	144	10.27 N	51.24 E
Haga, Nihon	94	36.32 N	140.04 E
Haga, Nihon	96	35.09 N	134.33 E
Hagachi-zaki ≻	94	34.41 N	138.45 E
HaGadol, HaMakhtesh ⊥[7]	132	30.56 N	34.59 E
Haga-Haga	158	32.46 S	28.14 E
Hagal	98	40.23 N	127.15 E
HaGalil (Galilee) □[9]	132	32.54 N	35.20 E
Hagaman	210	42.59 N	74.09 W
Hagan	192	32.09 N	81.56 W
Hagari ≃	122	15.45 N	76.56 E
Hagar Shores	216	42.13 N	86.22 W
Hagarstown	219	38.57 N	89.10 W
Hage	52	53.36 N	7.17 E
Hagelberg ʌ[2]	54	52.08 N	12.32 E
Hagemeister Island I	180	58.40 N	161.00 W
Hagen, B.R.D.	52	52.34 N	9.26 E
Hagen, B.R.D.	52	52.12 N	7.59 E
Hagen, B.R.D.	56	51.22 N	7.28 E
Hagenbrunn	264b	48.20 N	16.25 E
Hagen-Gebirge ⋏	64	47.32 N	13.07 E
Hagenow	54	53.26 N	11.11 E
Hagensborg	182	52.23 N	126.33 W
Hagenwerder	54	51.04 N	14.58 E
Hagere Hiywet	144	8.59 N	37.51 E
Hagere Selam	144	6.29 N	38.31 E
Hagerman, Id., U.S.	202	42.48 N	114.53 W
Hagerman, N.M., U.S.	196	33.06 N	104.19 W
Hagerman Corners	275b	43.50 N	79.18 W
Hagerstown, In., U.S.	218	39.54 N	85.09 W
Hagerstown, Md., U.S.	188	39.38 N	77.43 W
Hagersville	212	42.58 N	80.03 W
Hagetmau	32	43.40 N	0.35 W
Hagfors	40	60.02 N	13.42 E
Haggen ⊜	40	60.06 N	15.13 E
Haggetts Pond ⊜	283	42.39 N	71.12 W
Haggin, Mount ʌ	202	46.05 N	113.05 W
Hagi	96	34.24 N	131.25 E
Ha-giang	110	22.50 N	104.59 E
Hagitani	270	34.54 N	135.35 E
Hagiwara	94	35.52 N	137.12 E
Hagley	42	52.26 N	2.08 W
Hagley Museum ʋ	285	39.46 N	75.35 W
Hagondange	56	49.15 N	6.10 E
HaGosherim	132	33.13 N	35.37 E
Hags Head ≻	48	52.57 N	9.30 W
Hague, Sk., Can.	184	52.30 N	106.25 W
Hague, N.D., U.S.	198	46.01 N	99.59 W
Hague, Cap de la ≻	32	49.43 N	1.57 W
Haguenau	56	48.49 N	7.47 E
Hagues Peak ʌ	200	40.29 N	105.38 W
Hahaïa	157a	11.33 S	43.17 E
Hahajima-rettō II	14	26.37 N	142.10 E
Haharro, Uebi ≃	144	1.37 N	44.13 E
Hāhipur	272b	22.47 N	88.10 E
Hahira	192	30.59 N	83.22 W
Hahlen	52	52.18 N	8.50 E
Hahn am See	56	50.31 N	7.53 E
Hahnbach	60	49.32 N	11.48 E
Hahnenberg	263	51.12 N	7.24 E
Hahnenkamm ʌ	64	47.25 N	12.22 E
Hahnenklee-Bockswiese	52	51.51 N	10.20 E
Hahnerberg ◆[8]	263	51.13 N	7.09 E
Hahnstätten	56	50.18 N	8.04 E
Hahntown	279b	40.19 N	79.44 W
Haho ≃	150	6.17 N	1.23 E
Hahyŏn-ni	98	38.33 N	127.57 E
Hai ≃	105	39.00 N	117.43 E
Hai'an	100	32.34 N	120.28 E
Haian Shanmo ⋏	100	23.25 N	121.25 E
Haibara, Nihon	94	34.32 N	135.57 E
Haibara, Nihon	94	34.44 N	138.13 E
Haibatpur	272a	28.37 N	77.26 E
Haibei	89	47.39 N	126.51 E
Haicheng, Zhg.	100	24.25 N	117.51 E
Haicheng, Zhg.	104	40.52 N	122.45 E
Haicheng ≃	104	40.56 N	122.21 E
Haidargarh	124	26.37 N	81.22 E
Haidārpur ◆[8]	272a	28.43 N	77.09 E
Haidenaab ≃	60	49.36 N	12.08 E
Haiderabad → Hyderābād, India	122	17.23 N	78.29 E
Haiderabad → Hyderābād, Pāk.	120	25.22 N	68.22 E
Haidershofen	61	48.05 N	14.28 E
Haidian	105	39.59 N	116.18 E
Haiding	60	48.13 N	13.58 E
Haidmühle	60	48.50 N	13.46 E
Haïdra	36	35.34 N	8.27 E
Haidstein ʌ	60	49.13 N	12.48 E
Haidun	100	29.36 N	121.49 E
Hai-duong	110	20.56 N	106.19 E
Haifa → Ḥefa	132	32.50 N	35.00 E
Haifa, Bay of → Ḥefa, Mifraẕ ⊂	132	32.52 N	35.03 E
Haifeng	100	22.59 N	115.21 E
Haifengzheng	106	31.53 N	121.46 E
Haifuzhen	106	31.59 N	121.42 E
Haig	162	31.01 S	126.05 E
Haig, Mount ʌ	182	49.17 N	114.29 W
Haiger	56	50.44 N	8.13 E
Haigerloch	58	48.22 N	8.48 E
Haigh	262	53.35 N	2.36 W
Haigler	198	40.00 N	101.56 W
Haihezhen	100	33.44 N	120.02 E
Haijima	268	35.42 N	139.21 E
Haikang	102	20.56 N	110.04 E
Haikou, Zhg.	100	28.20 N	120.06 E
Haikou, Zhg.	100	25.43 N	119.28 E
Haikou, Zhg.	100	29.04 N	117.46 E
Haikou, Zhg.	102	20.03 N	110.19 E
Haiku	229a	20.55 N	156.19 W
Ḥā'il	128	27.33 N	41.42 E
Hailākāndi	120	24.41 N	92.34 E
Hailar	89	49.12 N	119.42 E
Hailar ≃	90	49.35 N	117.55 E
Hailasen	89	46.13 N	121.00 E
Hailesboro	212	44.18 N	75.27 W
Hailey, Eng., U.K.	260	51.46 N	0.01 W
Hailey, Id., U.S.	202	43.31 N	114.18 W
Haileybury	190	47.27 N	79.38 W
Haileyville	196	34.51 N	95.34 W
Hailin	89	44.35 N	129.22 E
Hailing Dao I	102	21.37 N	111.55 E
Haillicourt	50	50.28 N	2.35 E
Hailong (Meihekou)	98	42.32 N	125.38 E
Hailsham	42	50.52 N	0.16 E
Hailun	89	47.28 N	126.58 E
Hailuoto	26	65.00 N	24.43 E
Hailuoto I	26	65.02 N	24.42 E
Haiman Tepesi ʌ[2]	267b	41.12 N	29.15 E
Haimen, Zhg.	100	28.41 N	121.27 E
Haimen, Zhg.	100	23.14 N	116.38 E
Haimen, Zhg.	106	31.55 N	121.10 E
Haimen Wan ⊂	100	23.09 N	116.34 E
Haimhausen	60	48.19 N	11.34 E
Haimiao	98	37.13 N	119.51 E
Haiming	58	47.15 N	10.53 E
Haina	56	51.02 N	8.58 E
Hainan → Hainandao I	110	19.00 N	109.30 E
Hainan Dao I	110	19.00 N	109.30 E
Hainault ◆[8]	260	51.36 N	0.06 E
Hainaut □[4]	50	50.30 N	3.50 E
Hainaut □[9]	50	50.30 N	3.50 E
Hainburg an der Donau	61	48.09 N	16.57 E
Hainchen	56	50.51 N	8.12 E
Haines, Ak., U.S.	180	59.14 N	135.27 W
Haines, Or., U.S.	202	44.54 N	117.56 W
Haines City	220	28.06 N	81.37 W
Haines Falls	210	42.11 N	74.05 W
Haines Junction	180	60.45 N	137.30 W
Hainesport	208	39.59 N	74.49 W
Hainesville	278	42.21 N	88.04 W
Hainewalde	54	50.54 N	14.41 E
Hainfeld	61	48.02 N	15.46 E
Hainich ⋏	54	51.05 N	10.27 E
Hainichen	54	50.58 N	13.07 E
Haining (Xiashi)	106	30.32 N	120.41 E
Hainleite ⋏	54	51.20 N	10.48 E
Hainsberg	54	50.59 N	13.38 E
Hainzenberg	64	47.13 N	11.54 E
Hai-phong	110	20.52 N	106.41 E
Haiqiao	106	31.47 N	121.19 E
Haiqing	89	47.53 N	134.40 E
Haitangxi	107	29.33 N	106.35 E
Haitan Xia ≋	100	25.27 N	119.38 E
Haiti (Haïti) □[1], N.A.	230	19.00 N	72.25 W
Haiti (Haïti) □[1], N.A.	238	19.00 N	72.25 W
Haitou, Zhg.	98	34.56 N	119.10 E
Haitou, Zhg.	110	19.34 N	108.58 E
Haitouji	98	35.23 N	115.19 E
Haitun	102	38.50 N	96.41 E
Haiwee Reservoirs ⊜[1]	204	36.10 N	117.57 W
Haiyan, Zhg.	102	36.54 N	101.12 E
Haiyan, Zhg.	106	30.31 N	120.57 E
Haiyang (Dongcun)	98	36.46 N	121.10 E
Haiyang Dao I	98	39.02 N	123.14 E
Haiyuan	102	36.35 N	105.40 E
Haizhou, Zhg.	98	34.34 N	119.11 E
Haizhou, Zhg.	100	22.40 N	113.10 E
Haizhoumiao	104	42.00 N	121.39 E
Haizhou Wan ⊂	98	35.00 N	119.30 E
Haizhouyingzi	104	42.07 N	121.46 E
Ḥajar, Tall al- ʌ[2]	132	33.21 N	37.03 E
Hajar Banga	140	11.30 N	23.00 E
Hajdú-Bihar □[6]	30	47.25 N	21.30 E
Hajdúböszörmény	30	47.41 N	21.30 E
Hajdúnánás	30	47.51 N	21.26 E
Hajdúszoboszló	30	47.27 N	21.24 E
Hajeb el Ayoun	36	35.24 N	9.33 E
Hajiadian	98	41.32 N	117.10 E
Hājīganj	126	23.15 N	90.50 E
Hajiki-saki ≻	92	38.19 N	138.31 E
Haji Langar	120	35.52 N	79.21 E
Hājīpur, India	124	25.41 N	85.13 E
Hājīpur, India	126	22.49 N	87.38 E
Hajipur, India	272b	22.57 N	88.19 E
Ḥājj, Wādī al- ∨	142	30.03 N	32.45 E
Hajnówka	30	52.45 N	23.36 E
Hajo-do I	98	34.17 N	126.03 E
Ḥajr, Wādī ∨	144	14.04 N	48.40 E
Ḥajūl, Wādī ∨	142	29.42 N	32.22 E
Haka	110	22.39 N	93.37 E
HaKarmel, Har (Mount Carmel) ʌ	132	32.44 N	35.02 E
Hakata	96	34.12 N	133.07 E
Hakata-jima I	96	34.13 N	133.05 E
Hakataramea ≃	172	44.44 S	170.29 E
Hakendover	56	50.48 N	4.59 E
Haki	96	33.20 N	130.50 E
Ḥakīm, Abyār al- ⫪[4]	146	31.36 N	23.29 E
Hakkâri	128	37.34 N	43.45 E
Hakkâri □[4]	128	37.20 N	43.45 E
Hakken-san ʌ	92	34.10 N	135.54 E
Hakkōda-san ʌ	92	40.40 N	140.53 E
Hako-dake ʌ	92a	44.40 N	142.25 E
Hakodate	92a	41.45 N	140.43 E
Hakone	94	35.12 N	139.06 E
Hakone-no-seki-ato ⊥	94	35.10 N	139.02 E
Hakone-tōge)(	94	35.11 N	139.01 E
Hakone-yama ʌ	94	35.14 N	139.02 E
Håksberg	40	60.11 N	15.12 E
Hakskeenpan ≚	158	26.48 S	20.12 E
Hakuba	94	36.42 N	137.52 E
Hakui	94	36.53 N	136.47 E
Hakupu	174v	19.06 S	169.50 W
Hakusan	94	34.38 N	136.21 E
Haku-san ʌ	94	36.09 N	136.46 E
Haku-san-kokuritsu-kōen ♠	94	36.12 N	136.47 E
Hakushū	94	35.48 N	138.20 E
Hakuta	96	35.21 N	133.17 E
Hakuta ≃	96	35.26 N	133.15 E
Hāla	120	25.49 N	68.25 E
Halaaobao	102	42.11 N	107.20 E
Ḥalab (Aleppo)	130	36.12 N	37.10 E
Ḥalab □[8]	130	36.00 N	37.00 E
Ḥalabjah	128	35.10 N	45.59 E
Halachó	232	20.29 N	90.05 W
Halaerjige	104	42.24 N	122.11 E
Halagetu	104	42.34 N	122.40 E
Halahai	89	44.39 N	125.07 E
Halahushao	104	42.11 N	121.44 E
Ḥalā'ib	140	22.13 N	36.38 E
Halalii Lake ⊜	229b	21.52 N	160.11 W
Halamutai	86	46.10 N	84.52 E
Halangingie Point ≻	174v	19.03 S	169.57 W
Halasa	140	14.26 N	30.39 E
Halas-patak ≃	264c	47.24 N	19.20 E
Halataojie	104	42.30 N	122.06 E
Halatieke Shan ⋏	85	40.30 N	77.05 E
Halaula	229d	20.14 N	155.48 W
Hålaveden ⋏[2]	26	58.05 N	14.45 E
Halawa, Cape ≻	229a	21.10 N	156.43 W
Halawa Bay ⊂	229a	21.10 N	156.44 W
Halawa Heights	229c	21.22 N	157.55 W
Halawotelake	120	37.17 N	90.20 E
Ḥalbā	130	34.33 N	36.05 E
Halbach ◆[8]	263	51.12 N	7.12 E
Halba Deset I	144	12.56 N	42.55 E
Halbau → Iłowa	30	51.30 N	15.12 E
Halbe	54	52.06 N	13.42 E
Halberstadt	54	51.54 N	11.02 E
Halbert, Lake ⊜[1]	222	32.04 N	96.25 W
Halberton	42	50.55 N	3.25 W
Halbrite	184	49.30 N	103.33 W
Ḥalbūn	132	33.40 N	36.15 E
Halbury	168b	34.05 S	138.31 E
Halcombe	172	40.09 S	175.30 E
Halcon, Mount ʌ	116	13.16 N	121.00 E
Halcottsville	210	42.12 N	74.36 W
Haldeman	218	38.15 N	83.19 W
Halden	26	59.09 N	11.23 E
Halden ◆[8]	263	51.23 N	7.31 E
Haldensleben	54	52.18 N	11.26 E
Haldern	52	51.46 N	6.27 E
Haldi ≃	126	22.01 N	88.03 E
Haldībāri	124	26.20 N	88.46 E
Haldībunia	126	22.26 N	89.38 E
Haldimand-Norfolk □[6]	212	42.48 N	80.10 W
Haldwāni	124	29.13 N	79.31 E
Hale, Eng., U.K.	44	53.22 N	2.18 W
Hale, Eng., U.K.	262	53.23 N	2.21 W
Hale, Eng., U.K.	262	53.20 N	2.48 W
Hale, Mo., U.S.	194	39.36 N	93.20 W
Hale ≃	162	24.56 S	135.53 E
Haleakala Crater ⊥[6]	229a	20.43 N	156.13 W
Haleakala National Park ♠	229a	20.44 N	156.13 W
Haleb → Ḥalab	130	36.12 N	37.10 E
Halebarns	262	53.22 N	2.19 W
Hale Center	196	34.03 N	101.50 W
Hale Creek ≃	282	37.23 N	122.06 W
Haledon	276	40.56 N	74.11 W
Haledon Reservoir ⊜[1]	276	40.59 N	74.12 W
Hale Eddy	210	42.00 N	75.23 W
Hale Head ʌ	262	53.19 N	2.48 W
Haleiwa	229c	21.35 N	158.06 W
Halekii-Pihana Heiaus State Monument ⊥	229a	20.54 N	156.29 W
Halenkov	30	49.19 N	18.08 E
Hales Corners	216	42.56 N	88.02 W
Halesite	207	40.52 N	73.25 W
Halesowen ◆[8]	42	52.26 N	2.05 W
Hale Street	260	51.13 N	0.24 E
Halesworth	42	52.21 N	1.30 E
Halethorpe	284b	39.14 N	76.40 W
Halewood	262	53.22 N	2.49 W
Haleyville	194	34.13 N	87.37 W
Half Assini	150	5.03 N	2.53 W
Ḥalfāyah, Naqb al- (Halfaya Pass))(	140	31.30 N	25.11 E
Halfaya Pass → Ḥalfāyah, Naqb al-)(	140	31.30 N	25.11 E
Half Day	278	42.12 N	87.56 W
Halfeti	130	37.15 N	37.52 E
Half Hollow Hills	276	40.48 N	73.21 W
Halfing	64	47.57 N	12.16 E
Halfmoon Bay, B.C., Can.	182	49.31 N	123.54 W
Half-Moon Bay, N.Z.	172	46.54 S	168.08 E
Half Moon Bay, Ca., U.S.	226	37.27 N	122.25 W
Halfmoon Bay ⊂, Austl.	274b	37.58 S	145.00 E
Half Moon Bay ⊂, Ca., U.S.	282	37.29 N	122.28 W
Half Moon Bay Airport ⊠	282	37.31 N	122.30 W
Half Moon Bay State Beach ♠	282	37.29 N	122.27 W
Halfway, Md., U.S.	188	39.37 N	77.45 W
Halfway, Or., U.S.	202	44.52 N	117.06 W
Halfway ≃	176	56.10 N	121.35 W
Halfway Lake ⊜	184	55.03 N	98.24 W
Halgån ≃	40	60.16 N	13.27 E
Ḥalḥūl	132	31.35 N	35.07 E
Ḥalī ⫪[4]	144	18.42 N	41.20 E
Haliburton	212	45.03 N	78.31 W
Haliburton □[6]	212	44.10 N	78.30 W
Haliburton Lake ⊜	212	45.12 N	78.24 W
Halibut Point ≻	283	42.42 N	70.38 W
Haliç ⊂	267b	41.02 N	28.58 E
Halicarnassus ⊥	130	37.03 N	27.23 E
Halidmand	212	42.56 N	79.51 W
Halifax, Austl.	166	18.35 S	146.18 E
Halifax, N.S., Can.	186	44.39 N	63.36 W
Halifax, Eng., U.K.	44	53.44 N	1.52 W
Halifax, Ma., U.S.	207	41.59 N	70.51 W
Halifax, N.C., U.S.	192	36.19 N	77.35 W
Halifax, Pa., U.S.	208	40.28 N	76.55 W
Halifax, Va., U.S.	192	36.45 N	78.55 W
Halifax, Canadian Forces Base ■	186	44.43 N	63.38 W
Halifax Bay ⊂	166	18.50 S	146.30 E
Halifax Citadel National Historic Park ♠	186	44.36 N	63.39 W
Halifax Harbour ⊂	186	44.35 N	63.31 W
Haliimaile	229a	20.52 N	156.20 W
Ḥalīl ≃	128	27.28 N	58.44 E
Halimatazi	104	42.37 N	122.35 E
Halimiye	130	36.40 N	32.45 E
Halim Perdanakusuma Airfield ■	269e	6.16 S	106.54 E
Halimun, Gunung ʌ	115a	6.42 S	106.26 E
Halingen	263	51.27 N	7.44 E
Hālisahar	126	22.56 N	88.25 E
Haliyāl	122	15.20 N	74.46 E
Haljala	76	59.26 N	26.16 E
Halkalı	267b	41.02 N	28.47 E
Halkett, Cape ≻	180	70.49 N	152.12 W
Halkirk	46	58.30 N	3.30 W
Halkyn	262	53.14 N	3.11 W
Halkyn Mountain ʌ	262	53.14 N	3.13 W
Hall, Austl.	171b	35.10 S	149.04 E
Hall, In., U.S.	218	39.33 N	86.32 W
Hall, N.Y., U.S.	210	42.48 N	77.04 W
Hällabrottet	40	59.07 N	15.12 E
Halladale ≃	46	58.33 N	3.55 W
Hallam	274b	38.01 S	145.06 E
Hallam Peak ʌ	182	52.11 N	118.46 W
Halland □[9]	26	57.00 N	12.40 E
Hallandale	220	25.58 N	80.08 W
Hallandsås ⋏[2]	26	56.23 N	13.00 E
Hallands Län □[6]	26	56.45 N	13.00 E
Hallands Väderö I	26	56.26 N	12.33 E
Halla-san ʌ	90	33.22 N	126.32 E
Hallau	58	47.42 N	8.27 E
Hällberga	40	59.19 N	16.36 E
Hällbybrunn	40	59.24 N	16.25 E
Halle, Bel.	50	50.44 N	4.13 E
Halle, B.R.D.	52	52.04 N	8.22 E
Halle, B.R.D.	52	51.59 N	9.33 E
Halle, D.D.R.	54	51.29 N	11.58 E
Halle □[5]	54	51.30 N	11.45 E
Halleberg ʌ[2]	26	58.23 N	12.27 E
Hällefors	40	59.47 N	14.30 E
Hälleforsnäs	40	59.10 N	16.30 E
Hallein	64	47.41 N	13.06 E
Hällekis	26	58.38 N	13.25 E
Hallen	26	63.11 N	14.05 E
Hallenberg	56	51.06 N	8.37 E
Hallencourt	50	49.59 N	1.53 E
Halle-Neustadt	54	51.29 N	11.56 E
Hallertau ◆[1]	60	48.35 N	11.45 E
Hällestad	40	58.44 N	15.34 E
Hallett, Cape ≻	9	72.19 S	170.18 E
Hallettsville	222	29.26 N	96.56 W
Halley Bay ʋ[3]	9	75.31 S	26.56 W
Halliday	198	47.21 N	102.20 W
Halligen II	30	54.35 N	8.35 E
Halling	260	51.21 N	0.27 E
Hallingdalselvi ≃	26	60.24 N	9.35 E
Hällingsåfallet ∟	26	64.20 N	14.20 E
Hall in Tirol	64	47.17 N	11.31 E
Hall Island I	180	60.40 N	173.05 W
Hall Islands II	14	8.37 N	152.00 E
Halliste ≃	76	58.31 N	25.03 E
Hall-i'-th'-Wood ♠	262	53.36 N	2.26 W
Hall Lake ⊜	176	68.41 N	82.17 W
Hall Meadow Brook Reservoir ⊜[1]	207	41.52 N	73.10 W
Hall Mountain ʌ	202	48.49 N	117.15 W
Hällnäs	26	64.19 N	19.38 E
Hallock	198	48.46 N	96.56 W
Hallowell	188	44.17 N	69.47 W
Hall Peninsula ≻[1]	176	63.30 N	66.00 W
Halls	194	35.52 N	89.23 W
Halls Bayou ≃	222	29.12 N	95.07 W
Hallsberg	40	59.04 N	15.07 E
Halls Brook ≃	283	42.00 N	70.43 W
Halls Creek	162	18.16 S	127.46 E
Halls Creek ≃	200	37.18 N	110.45 W
Hållsfjärden ⊂[2]	40	59.08 N	17.40 E
Halls Lake ⊜	212	45.07 N	78.45 W
Halls Stream ≃	206	45.01 N	71.30 W
Hållsta	40	59.18 N	16.27 E
Hallstadt	56	49.55 N	10.52 E
Hallstahammar	40	59.37 N	16.13 E
Hallstatt	64	47.33 N	13.39 E
Hallstätter See ⊜	64	47.35 N	13.39 E
Hallstavik	40	60.03 N	18.36 E
Hallstead	210	41.57 N	75.44 W
Hallsville, Mo., U.S.	219	39.07 N	92.13 W
Hallsville, Tx., U.S.	222	32.30 N	94.34 W
Halluin	50	50.47 N	3.08 E
Hallwiler See ⊜	58	47.18 N	8.13 E
Hallwood	208	37.52 N	75.35 W
Halma	56	50.05 N	5.08 E
Halmahera I	108	1.00 N	128.00 E
Halmahera, Laut (Halmahera Sea) ⫪[2]	108	1.00 S	129.00 E
Halmstad	26	56.39 N	12.50 E
Halpine Village	284c	39.04 N	77.07 W
Hals	26	57.00 N	10.19 E
Halsafjorden ⊂[2]	26	63.03 N	8.11 E
Halsall	262	53.35 N	2.57 W
Halsbrücke	54	50.57 N	13.21 E
Halsey, Ne., U.S.	198	41.54 N	100.16 W
Halsey, Or., U.S.	202	44.23 N	123.06 W
Halsey Harbor ⊂	116	11.45 N	119.56 E
Halsey Valley	210	42.08 N	76.27 W
Hälsingborg → Helsingborg	41	56.03 N	12.42 E
Hälsingland □[9]	26	61.30 N	17.00 E
Halstad	198	47.21 N	96.49 W
Halstead, Eng., U.K.	42	51.57 N	0.38 E
Halstead, Eng., U.K.	260	51.20 N	0.08 E
Halstead, Ks., U.S.	198	38.00 N	97.30 W
Halstenbek	52	53.38 N	9.50 E
Halsteren	52	51.32 N	4.16 E
Halstow Marshes ☷	260	51.29 N	0.33 E
Haltang ≃	102	39.00 N	94.40 E
Haltern	52	51.46 N	7.10 E
Haltiatunturi ʌ	24	69.18 N	21.16 E
Haltom City	222	32.47 N	97.16 W
Halton, Eng., U.K.	44	54.05 N	2.46 W
Halton, Eng., U.K.	262	53.20 N	2.42 W
Halton □[6]	212	43.30 N	79.53 W
Halton □[8]	262	53.20 N	2.44 W
Halton Hills	212	43.39 N	79.55 W
Haltwhistle	44	54.58 N	2.27 W
Halura, Pulau I	115b	10.19 S	120.07 E
Halūzonī, Wādī al- ∨	273c	30.05 N	31.24 E
Halvarsgårdarna	40	60.24 N	15.23 E
Halvarsnoren ⊜	40	59.35 N	14.36 E
Halver	56	51.11 N	7.30 E
Halvorson, Mount ʌ	182	53.15 N	120.33 W
Halwell	42	50.22 N	3.43 W
Ham, Fr.	50	49.45 N	3.04 E
Ham, Tchad	146	10.00 N	15.41 E
Ham ◆[8]	260	51.26 N	0.19 W
Ham ≃	158	28.32 S	19.34 E
Ham, Oued el ≃	34	35.42 N	4.52 E
Ḥamad	140	15.19 N	33.43 E
Hamada	96	34.53 N	132.05 E
Hamadān	128	34.48 N	48.30 E
Hamadān □[4]	128	35.00 N	48.40 E
Ḥamāh	130	35.08 N	36.45 E
Ḥamāh □[8]	130	35.10 N	37.00 E
Hamahika-jima I	174m	26.19 N	127.57 E
Hamakeza	89	47.05 N	120.52 E
Hamakita	94	34.48 N	137.47 E
Hamale	150	10.59 N	2.44 W
Hamam	130	39.30 N	35.24 E
Hamamatsu	94	34.42 N	137.44 E
Hamamatsukita-kichi, Kōkū-jieitai- ■	94	34.45 N	137.42 E
Hamamözü	130	40.48 N	35.02 E
Haman	98	35.15 N	128.24 E
Hamanaka	92a	43.05 N	145.10 E
Hamana-ko ⊜	94	34.45 N	137.34 E
Hamano	268	35.33 N	140.08 E
Hamaoka	94	34.39 N	138.08 E
Hamar	26	60.48 N	11.06 E
Hamasaka	96	35.37 N	134.27 E
Ḥamāṭah, Jabal ʌ	140	24.12 N	35.00 E
Hamatang	98	40.12 N	124.20 E
Hama-tombetsu	92a	45.07 N	142.23 E
Hambach	56	49.04 N	7.02 E
Hambaek-san ʌ	98	37.09 N	128.55 E
Hambantota	122	6.07 N	81.07 E
Hambergen	52	53.18 N	8.49 E
Hamber Provincial Park ♠	182	52.25 N	117.40 W
Hamble	42	50.52 N	1.19 W
Hambledon	42	50.56 N	1.04 W
Hambleton	44	53.52 N	2.57 E
Hambleton Hills ⋏[2]	44	54.16 N	1.12 W
Hamborn ◆[8]	263	51.29 N	6.46 E
Hambourg → Hamburg	52	53.33 N	9.59 E
Hamburg, B.R.D.	52	53.33 N	9.59 E
Hamburg, Ciskei	158	33.17 S	27.28 E
Hamburg, Ar., U.S.	194	33.13 N	91.47 W
Hamburg, Ct., U.S.	207	41.23 N	72.21 W
Hamburg, Il., U.S.	219	39.14 N	90.43 W
Hamburg, Ia., U.S.	198	40.36 N	95.39 W
Hamburg, Mi., U.S.	216	42.27 N	83.48 W
Hamburg, N.J., U.S.	210	41.09 N	74.34 W
Hamburg, N.Y., U.S.	210	42.42 N	78.49 W
Hamburg, Pa., U.S.	208	40.33 N	75.58 W
Hamburg □[3]	52	53.35 N	10.00 E
Hamburg, Flughafen ⊠	52	53.38 N	10.00 E
Hamburg Airport ⊠	284a	42.42 N	78.55 W
Hamburg Ditch ≋	208	36.31 N	76.33 W
Hamburger Hallig ≻[1]	41	54.36 N	8.49 E
Hamburg Mountains ⋏	276	41.08 N	74.32 W
Hamburgo → Hamburg	52	53.33 N	9.59 E
Hamburgsund	26	58.33 N	11.16 E
Ḥamḍ, Wādī al- ∨	128	25.54 N	36.38 E
Ḥamḍah	144	19.02 N	43.36 E
Hamdallay Timbou	150	12.03 N	10.37 W
Hamdam Āb, Dasht-e ≚	128	34.45 N	61.30 E
Ḥamdānah	144	19.58 N	40.35 E
Hamden, Ct., U.S.	207	41.23 N	72.53 W
Hamden, N.Y., U.S.	210	42.12 N	75.00 W
Hamden, Oh., U.S.	188	39.09 N	82.31 W
Häme ◆[1]	26	61.30 N	24.30 E
Hämeenkangas ◆[3]	26	61.45 N	22.40 E
Hämeenkylä	26	60.16 N	24.47 E
Hämeen lääni □[4]	26	61.30 N	24.30 E
Hämeenlinna	26	61.00 N	24.27 E
Hamel	168a	32.52 S	115.55 E
HaMelah, Yam → Dead Sea ⊜	132	31.30 N	35.30 E
Hämelerwald	52	52.22 N	10.05 E
Hamelin Pool	162	26.26 S	114.11 E
Hamelin Pool ⊂	162	26.15 S	114.05 E
Hameln	52	52.06 N	9.21 E
HaMerkaz □[5]	132	32.05 N	34.55 E
Hamer Koke	144	5.12 N	36.45 E
Hamero Hadad	144	7.34 N	42.18 E
Hamersleben	54	52.04 N	11.05 E
Hamersley Range ⋏	162	21.53 S	116.46 E
Hamersley Range National Park ♠	162	22.40 S	118.15 E
Hamersville	218	38.55 N	83.59 W
Hames Creek ≃	226	35.53 N	120.50 W

Symbol	English	Deutsch	Español	Français	Português
≃	River	Fluss	Río	Rivière	Rio
≋	Canal	Kanal	Canal	Canal	Canal
∟	Waterfall, Rapids	Wasserfall, Stromschnellen	Cascada, Rápidos	Chute d'eau, Rapides	Cascata, Rápidos
≍	Strait	Meeresstrasse	Estrecho	Détroit	Estreito
⊂	Bay, Gulf	Bucht, Golf	Bahía, Golfo	Baie, Golfe	Baía, Golfo
⊜	Lake, Lakes	See, Seen	Lago, Lagos	Lac, Lacs	Lago, Lagos
☷	Swamp	Sumpf	Pantano	Marais	Pântano
⊞	Ice Features, Glacier	Eis- und Gletscherformen	Accidentes Glaciales	Formes glaciaires	Acidentes glaciares
⫪	Other Hydrographic Features	Andere Hydrographische Objekte	Otros Elementos Hidrográficos	Autres données hydrographiques	Outros acidentes hidrográficos

Symbol	English	Deutsch	Español	Français	Português
✦	Submarine Features	Untermeerische Objekte	Accidentes Submarinos	Formes de relief sous-marin	Acidentes submarinos
□	Political Unit	Politische Einheit	Unidad Politica	Entité politique	Unidade política
ʋ	Cultural Institution	Kulturelle Institution	Institución Cultural	Institution culturelle	Instituição cultural
⊥	Historical Site	Historische Stätte	Sitio Histórico	Site historique	Sítio histórico
♠	Recreational Site	Erholungs- und Ferienort	Sitio de Recreo	Centre de loisirs	Area de Lazer
⊠	Airport	Flughafen	Aeropuerto	Aéroport	Aeroporto
■	Military Installation	Militäranlage	Instalación Militar	Installation militaire	Instalação militar
◆	Miscellaneous	Verschiedenes	Misceláneo	Divers	Diversos

Name	Page	Lat.°′	Long.°′
Hamgyŏng Namdo □[4]	98	40.00 N	127.30 E
Hamgyŏng Pukdo □[4]	98	41.45 N	129.50 E
Hamgyŏng-sanmaek ⋀	98	41.00 N	128.30 E
Ham House ⊥	260	51.27 N	0.19 W
Hamhŭng	98	39.54 N	127.32 E
Hami (Kumul)	102	42.48 N	93.27 E
Hamidiye	130	41.09 N	26.40 E
Hamiguitan, Mount ∧	116	6.44 N	126.11 E
Hamilton, Austl.	166	37.45 S	142.02 E
Hamilton, Ber.	240a	32.17 N	64.46 W
Hamilton, On., Can.	212	43.15 N	79.51 W
Hamilton, N.Z.	172	37.47 S	175.17 E
Hamilton, Scot., U.K.	46	55.47 N	4.03 W
Hamilton, Al., U.S.	194	34.08 N	87.59 W
Hamilton, Ak., U.S.	180	62.54 N	163.53 W
Hamilton, Ga., U.S.	192	32.45 N	84.52 W
Hamilton, Il., U.S.	190	40.23 N	91.20 W
Hamilton, In., U.S.	216	41.32 N	84.54 W
Hamilton, Ks., U.S.	198	37.58 N	96.09 W
Hamilton, Ma., U.S.	207	42.37 N	70.52 W
Hamilton, Mi., U.S.	216	42.40 N	86.00 W
Hamilton, Mo., U.S.	194	39.44 N	93.59 W
Hamilton, Mt., U.S.	202	46.14 N	114.09 W
Hamilton, N.Y., U.S.	210	42.49 N	75.32 W
Hamilton, N.C., U.S.	192	35.56 N	77.12 W
Hamilton, Oh., U.S.	218	39.23 N	84.33 W
Hamilton, R.I., U.S.	207	41.32 N	71.26 W
Hamilton, Tx., U.S.	196	31.42 N	98.07 W
Hamilton, Wa., U.S.	224	48.31 N	121.59 W
Hamilton □[6], In., U.S.	218	40.03 N	86.01 W
Hamilton □[6], N.Y., U.S.	210	43.24 N	74.25 W
Hamilton □[6], Oh., U.S.	218	39.06 N	84.31 W
Hamilton ◆[8]	284b	39.21 N	76.33 W
Hamilton ≐	166	23.30 S	139.47 E
Hamilton, Lake ⊜	220	28.03 N	81.39 W
Hamilton, Lake ⊜[1]	194	34.30 N	93.05 W
Hamilton, Mount ∧, Ak., U.S.	180	61.10 N	159.46 W
Hamilton, Mount ∧, Ca., U.S.	226	37.21 N	121.38 W
Hamilton, Mount ∧, Nv., U.S.	204	39.14 N	115.32 W
Hamilton Acres	180	64.51 N	147.40 W
Hamilton Air Force Base ■	282	38.03 N	122.31 W
Hamilton City	204	39.44 N	122.00 W
Hamilton Creek ≐	162	26.40 S	135.19 E
Hamilton Creek Indian Reserve ◆[4]	182	50.11 N	120.30 W
Hamilton Dome	200	43.46 N	108.34 W
Hamilton Harbour ⊂	212	43.17 N	79.50 W
Hamilton Hill	168a	32.05 S	115.46 E
Hamilton Hotel	166	22.50 S	140.35 E
Hamilton Inlet ⊂	176	54.00 N	57.30 W
Hamilton Lake ⊜	216	41.33 N	84.55 W
Hamilton Mountain ∧	188	43.25 N	74.22 W
Hamilton Park, In., U.S.	216	40.17 N	85.19 W
Hamilton Park, Pa., U.S.	208	40.02 N	76.20 W
Hamilton Sound Ц	186	49.30 N	54.30 W
Hamilton Square	285	40.13 N	74.39 W
Hamilton-Wentworth □[6]	212	43.15 N	80.00 W
Ḥamīm, Wādī al- V	146	30.10 N	21.32 E
Hamina	26	60.34 N	27.12 E
Hamiota	184	50.11 N	100.36 W
Ḥāmir, Wādī V	128	31.37 N	42.12 E
Hamīrpur, India	123	31.41 N	76.31 E
Hamīrpur, India	124	25.57 N	80.09 E
Hamīrpur □[5]	124	25.30 N	26.40 E
Hamjong-ni	98	38.59 N	125.17 E
Hamler	216	41.13 N	84.02 W
Hamlet, In., U.S.	216	41.32 N	86.34 W
Hamlet, N.C., U.S.	192	34.53 N	79.41 W
Hamlet, Oh., U.S.	218	39.01 N	84.12 W
Hamlet, Mount ∧	180	68.47 N	165.57 W
Hamley Bridge	168b	34.21 S	138.41 E
Hamlin, N.Y., U.S.	210	43.18 N	77.55 W
Hamlin, Pa., U.S.	210	41.24 N	75.24 W
Hamlin, Tx., U.S.	196	32.53 N	100.08 W
Hamlin, W.V., U.S.	188	38.16 N	82.06 W
Hamlin Beach State Park ♦	210	43.22 N	77.58 W
Hamlin Lake ⊜	190	44.03 N	86.27 W
Hamlin Valley Wash V	200	38.53 N	114.01 W
Hamm	52	51.41 N	7.49 E
Hamm ◆[8], B.R.D.	263	51.15 N	6.25 E
Hamm ◆[8], B.R.D.	263	51.12 N	6.44 E
Hamm ◆[8], B.R.D.	263	51.23 N	7.03 E
Ḥammād, Wādī V	142	29.45 N	32.24 E
Hamma Hamma ≐	224	47.33 N	123.03 W
Ḥammām at-Turkumān	130	36.32 N	39.03 E
Hammamet, Alg.	36	35.27 N	7.58 E
Hammamet, Tun.	148	36.24 N	10.37 E
Hammamet, Golfe de ⊂	36	36.05 N	10.40 E
Hammam Lif	148	36.44 N	10.20 E
Ḥammānā	132	33.49 N	35.44 E
Hammar	40	58.49 N	14.57 E
Ḥammār, Hawr al- ⊜	128	30.50 N	47.10 E
Hammarby	40	60.33 N	16.34 E
Hammarn	40	59.45 N	14.30 E
Hammarö	40	59.20 N	13.31 E
Hammarön I	40	59.19 N	13.31 E
Hammarstrand	26	63.06 N	16.21 E
Hamme	50	51.06 N	4.08 E
Hamme ≐	52	53.10 N	8.44 E
Hammel	41	56.15 N	9.52 E
Hammelburg	56	50.07 N	9.53 E
Hamme-Mille	56	50.47 N	4.43 E
Hammerdal	26	63.36 N	15.21 E
Hammerfest	24	70.40 N	23.42 E
Hammermühle → Kępice	30	54.15 N	16.52 E
Hämmern	263	51.08 N	7.21 E
Hammershus ⊥	26	55.16 N	14.45 E
Hammersley Inlet ⊂	224	47.12 N	123.00 W
Hammersmith ◆[8]	260	51.30 N	0.14 W
Hammerstein → Czarne	30	53.42 N	16.57 E
Hammerum	41	56.08 N	9.04 E
Hamminkeln	52	51.44 N	6.35 E
Hammon	196	35.37 N	99.22 W
Hammonasset ≐	207	41.16 N	72.33 W
Hammond, In., U.S.	216	41.35 N	87.30 W
Hammond, La., U.S.	194	30.30 N	90.27 W
Hammond, N.Y., U.S.	212	44.26 N	75.41 W
Hammond, Or., U.S.	224	46.12 N	123.57 W
Hammond, Wi., U.S.	190	44.58 N	92.26 W
Hammond Island I, Austl.	164	10.35 S	142.13 E
Hammond Island I, Ca., U.S.	282	38.06 N	121.57 W
Hammond Pond Park ♦	283	42.19 N	71.11 W
Hammondsport	210	42.24 N	77.13 W
Hammondsville	214	40.33 N	80.43 W
Hammondville	274a	33.57 S	150.57 E
Hammonia	158	28.43 S	27.49 E
Hammonton	208	39.38 N	74.48 W
Hamningberg	24	70.31 N	30.37 E
Ham-Nord	206	45.54 N	71.39 W
Hamo	130	39.36 N	38.11 E
Hamoir	56	50.26 N	5.32 E
Hamont	56	51.15 N	5.33 E
HaMore, Giv'at ∧	132	32.37 N	35.21 E
Hamorton	285	39.52 N	75.39 W
Hamoyet, Jabal ∧	144	17.33 N	38.02 E
Hampden, Austl.	168b	34.09 S	139.03 E
Hampden, Nf., Can.	186	49.33 N	56.51 W
Hampden, N.Z.	172	45.19 S	170.49 E
Hampden, Me., U.S.	188	44.44 N	68.50 W
Hampden, Ma., U.S.	207	42.03 N	72.24 W
Hampden, N.D., U.S.	198	48.32 N	98.39 W
Hampden □[6]	207	42.07 N	72.36 W
Hampden Sydney	192	37.15 N	78.29 W
Hampetorp	40	59.09 N	15.40 E
Hampshire	216	42.05 N	88.31 W
Hampshire □[6], Eng., U.K.	42	51.05 N	1.15 W
Hampshire □[6], Ma., U.S.	207	42.19 N	72.38 W
Hampshire Downs ⋀[1]	42	51.15 N	1.17 W
Hampshire Heights	279b	40.20 N	79.33 W
Hampstead, P.Q., Can.	275a	45.29 N	73.38 W
Hampstead, Md., U.S.	208	39.36 N	76.51 W
Hampstead, N.C., U.S.	192	34.22 N	77.42 W
Hampstead ◆[8]	260	51.33 N	0.11 W
Hampstead Heath ♦	260	51.34 N	0.10 W
Hampton, Austl.	274b	37.56 S	145.00 E
Hampton, N.B., Can.	186	45.32 N	65.51 W
Hampton, On., Can.	212	43.58 N	78.45 W
Hampton, Ar., U.S.	194	33.32 N	92.28 W
Hampton, Ct., U.S.	207	41.47 N	72.03 W
Hampton, Fl., U.S.	192	29.51 N	82.07 W
Hampton, Ga., U.S.	192	33.23 N	84.16 W
Hampton, Ia., U.S.	190	42.44 N	93.12 W
Hampton, Ne., U.S.	198	40.52 N	97.53 W
Hampton, N.H., U.S.	188	42.56 N	70.50 W
Hampton, N.J., U.S.	210	40.42 N	74.57 W
Hampton, Pa., U.S.	208	39.56 N	77.04 W
Hampton, S.C., U.S.	192	32.52 N	81.06 W
Hampton, Tn., U.S.	192	36.17 N	82.10 W
Hampton, Va., U.S.	208	37.01 N	76.20 W
Hampton ◆[8]	260	51.25 N	0.22 W
Hampton Bays	207	40.52 N	72.31 W
Hampton Butte ∧	202	43.46 N	120.17 W
Hampton Court Palace ⊛	260	51.24 N	0.20 W
Hampton Harbour ⊂	162	20.40 S	116.30 E
Hampton National Historic Site ⊥	284b	39.25 N	76.35 W
Hampton Park	274b	38.02 S	145.15 E
Hampton Roads ⊤[3]	208	36.58 N	76.20 W
Hampton Roads Bridge-Tunnel ◆[5]	208	37.00 N	76.18 W
Hampton Tableland ⋀[1]	162	32.10 S	126.10 E
Hamp'yŏng	98	35.05 N	126.30 E
Hamr	54	50.35 N	13.35 E
Hamra	26	61.39 N	15.00 E
Ḥamrā', Al-Ḥamādah al- ◆[2]	146	30.00 N	12.00 E
Hamra, As Saquia al V	148	27.15 N	13.21 W
Hamra, Ouadi V	146	12.52 N	21.15 E
Ḥamrah, Jabal al- ∧	132	29.39 N	34.47 E
Ḥamran, Har ∧	132	30.41 N	34.34 E
Hamra Nationalpark ♦	26	61.45 N	14.55 E
Ḥamrat ash-Shaykh	140	14.35 N	27.58 E
Hams Bluff ±[4]	241n	17.46 N	64.52 W
Hams Fork ≐	200	41.35 N	109.59 W
Hamstreet	42	51.04 N	0.51 E
Ham-Sud	206	45.46 N	71.36 W
Ham-tan	110	10.40 N	107.46 E
Hamtramck	216	42.23 N	83.02 W
Hamur	84	39.36 N	42.59 E
Hamura	94	35.45 N	139.19 E
Hamyang	98	35.32 N	127.42 E
Han	150	10.41 N	2.27 W
Han ≐, Zhg.	100	23.41 N	116.38 E
Han ≐, Zhg.	102	30.35 N	114.17 E
Han, Grottes de ±[5]	56	50.08 N	5.15 E
Han, Nong ⊜	110	17.12 N	104.11 E
Hana	229a	20.45 N	155.59 W
Hanábana ≐	240p	22.23 N	80.58 W
Hanahan	192	32.55 N	80.01 W
Hanailike	85	39.16 N	76.26 E
Ḥanak	128	25.33 N	36.56 E
Hanakaoo Point ≻	229a	20.55 N	156.42 W
Hanalei	229b	22.12 N	159.30 W
Hanalei Bay ⊂	229b	22.13 N	159.31 W
Hanamaki	92	39.23 N	141.07 E
Hanamaulu	229b	21.59 N	159.21 W
Hanamenu, Baie ⊂	174y	9.46 S	139.08 W
Hanam-ni	98	38.23 N	126.43 E
Hanang ∧	154	4.26 S	35.24 E
Hanapepe	229b	21.54 N	159.35 W
Hānār Char	126	23.08 N	90.38 E
Hanataka-sen ∧	96	35.24 N	132.45 E
Hanateio	174y	9.59 S	139.06 W
Hanatetena	174y	9.58 S	139.04 W
Hanau	56	50.08 N	8.55 E
Hanaui	174y	9.45 S	139.05 W
Hanawa, Nihon	94	36.57 N	140.25 E
Hanawa, Nihon	268	35.13 N	139.53 E
Hanbury ≐	176	63.37 N	104.33 W
Hanceville, B.C., Can.	182	51.55 N	123.03 W
Hanceville, Al., U.S.	194	34.03 N	86.46 W
Hanchang	107	30.26 N	103.43 E
Hancheng, Zhg.	102	35.29 N	110.25 E
Hancheng, Zhg.	105	39.39 N	118.02 E
Hanches	261	48.36 N	1.39 E
Hanchō	270	34.49 N	135.27 E
Han-ch'ŏn ≐	271b	37.33 N	127.02 E
Hanchuan	100	30.39 N	113.48 E
Hanchung → Hanzhong	102	33.08 N	107.02 E
Hancock, Md., U.S.	188	39.41 N	78.10 W
Hancock, Mi., U.S.	190	47.07 N	88.34 W
Hancock, Mn., U.S.	198	45.29 N	95.47 W
Hancock, N.Y., U.S.	210	41.57 N	75.17 W
Hancock, Wi., U.S.	190	44.08 N	89.31 W
Hancock □[6], Il., U.S.	219	40.13 N	91.15 W
Hancock □[6], In., U.S.	218	39.47 N	85.46 W
Hancock □[6], Oh., U.S.	216	41.02 N	83.39 W
Hancock □[6], W.V., U.S.	214	40.30 N	80.33 W
Hancock, Lake ⊜	220	27.58 N	81.50 W
Hancocks Bridge	208	39.30 N	75.27 W
Hancun	105	39.24 N	116.36 E
Handa, Nihon	94	34.53 N	136.56 E
Handa, Nihon	96	34.02 N	134.02 E
Handa, Som.	144	10.40 N	51.07 E
Handa I	46	58.22 N	5.12 W
Handan	98	36.37 N	114.29 E
Handaokou	98	34.16 N	116.24 E
Handawor	123	34.24 N	74.17 E
Handen	40	59.10 N	18.08 E
Handeni	154	5.26 S	38.01 E
Handforth	262	53.21 N	2.13 W
Handlová	30	48.44 N	18.46 E
Handöl	26	63.16 N	12.26 E
Handorf	52	51.59 N	7.41 E
Handsworth	184	49.48 N	103.00 W
Handub	140	19.14 N	37.16 E
Handzame	50	51.02 N	3.00 E
Haneda Airport ⊠	268	35.33 N	139.46 E
HaNegev ◆[2]	132	30.30 N	34.55 E
Haney	224	49.13 N	122.36 W
Hane-yama ∧	96	33.14 N	131.08 E
Hane-zaki ≻	96	33.22 N	134.02 E
Hanford	226	36.19 N	119.38 W
Hanford Site ⊛[3]	202	46.35 N	119.30 W
Han'gang	98	34.39 N	114.38 E
Han-gang ≐	98	37.45 N	126.11 E
Hanga Roa	174z	27.09 S	109.26 W
Hangatiki	172	38.15 S	175.10 E
Hangbu	100	28.53 N	118.49 E
Hangchow → Hangzhou	106	30.15 N	120.10 E
Hangchow Bay → Hangzhou Wan ⊂	100	30.25 N	121.00 E
Hanger ≐	144	9.35 N	36.02 E
Hanggai	106	40.55 N	107.15 E
Hanggin Houqi	102	40.55 N	107.15 E
Hanggin Qi	102	39.56 N	108.54 E
Hang Hau Town	271d	22.19 N	114.16 E
Hanging Gardens ♦	272c	18.58 N	72.48 E
Hanging Rock State Park ♦	192	36.25 N	80.15 W
Hangingstone Hill ∧[2]	42	50.39 N	3.57 W
Hanging Woman Creek ≐	202	45.19 N	106.31 W
Hangklip, Kaap ≻	158	34.26 S	18.48 E
Hangkou	100	29.03 N	114.27 E
Hangman Creek ≐	202	47.38 N	117.27 W
Hangö (Hanko)	26	59.50 N	22.57 E
Hangou	105	39.18 N	117.07 E
Hang-Tcheou → Hangzhou	106	30.15 N	120.10 E
Hangtou	106	31.01 N	121.35 E
Hangtschou → Hangzhou	106	30.15 N	120.10 E
Hangu, Pāk.	123	33.32 N	71.04 E
Hangu, Zhg.	105	39.15 N	117.47 E
Hangu, Zhg.	107	28.58 N	104.30 E
Hanguang	100	24.16 N	113.08 E
Hanguchang	107	29.32 N	106.21 E
Hangugang	105	39.15 N	116.56 E
Hangzhou (Hangchow)	106	30.15 N	120.10 E
Hangzhou Wan (Hangchow Bay) ⊂	100	30.25 N	121.00 E
Hani	130	38.24 N	40.24 E
Hänigsen	52	52.29 N	10.05 E
Hanimadu I	122	6.45 N	73.09 E
Ḥanīsh II	144	13.45 N	42.45 E
Ḥanīsh al-Kabīr, Jazīrat al- I	144	13.43 N	42.45 E
Ḥanita	132	33.05 N	35.10 E
Hanjalipan	112	2.15 S	112.47 E
Hanjiagou	104	40.42 N	120.47 E
Hanjiang	100	25.30 N	119.06 E
Hanjiapuzi	104	40.48 N	123.14 E
Hanjiashu	105	39.11 N	117.04 E
Hanjiawa	106	31.16 N	119.18 E
Hankamer	222	29.51 N	94.38 W
Hankasalmi	26	62.23 N	26.26 E
Hanke	26	59.12 N	10.47 E
Hankensbüttel	54	52.44 N	10.36 E
Hankey	158	33.50 S	24.53 E
Hankins	210	41.49 N	75.05 W
Hankinson	198	46.04 N	96.54 W
Hanko → Hangö	26	59.50 N	22.57 E
Hankow → Wuhan	100	30.36 N	114.17 E
Hanköyü	130	38.35 N	39.04 E
Hanks Pond ⊜	276	41.05 N	74.26 W
Hanku → Hangu	105	39.15 N	117.47 E
Hānle	120	32.48 N	79.00 E
Hanley	184	51.37 N	106.27 W
Hanmer	190	46.39 N	80.56 W
Hanmer Springs	172	42.31 S	172.49 E
Hanmiao	89	44.33 N	119.59 E
Hann ≐	164	17.10 S	126.10 E
Hann, Mount ∧	164	15.51 S	125.48 E
Hanna, Ab., Can.	182	51.38 N	111.54 W
Hanna, In., U.S.	216	41.24 N	86.46 W
Hanna, Ok., U.S.	196	35.12 N	95.53 W
Hanna, Wy., U.S.	200	41.52 N	106.33 W
Hanna City	190	40.41 N	89.47 W
Hannaford	198	47.18 N	98.11 W
Hannah	198	48.58 N	98.41 W
Hannah Bay ⊂	176	51.05 N	79.45 W
Hannastown	214	40.21 N	79.30 W
Hannibal, Mo., U.S.	219	39.42 N	91.21 W
Hannibal, N.Y., U.S.	210	43.19 N	76.34 W
Hanningfield Reservoir ⊜[1]	260	51.39 N	0.31 E
Hannō	94	35.51 N	139.19 E
Hannover	52	52.24 N	9.44 E
Hannover □[6]	52	52.30 N	9.00 E
Hannover, Flughafen ⊠	52	52.27 N	9.42 E
Hannut	56	50.40 N	5.05 E
Hanö I	26	56.00 N	14.50 E
Hanobası	130	38.35 N	33.50 E
Hanöbukten ⊂	26	55.45 N	14.30 E
Ha-noi	110	21.02 N	105.51 E
Hanönü	130	41.38 N	34.28 E
Hanoura	96	33.57 N	134.38 E
Hanover → Hannover, B.R.D.	52	52.24 N	9.44 E
Hanover, On., Can.	212	44.09 N	81.02 W
Hanover, S. Afr.	158	31.04 S	24.29 E
Hanover, Ct., U.S.	207	41.38 N	72.03 W
Hanover, Il., U.S.	190	42.15 N	90.16 W
Hanover, In., U.S.	218	38.42 N	85.28 W
Hanover, Ks., U.S.	198	39.53 N	96.52 W
Hanover, Ma., U.S.	207	42.06 N	70.48 W
Hanover, Mi., U.S.	216	42.06 N	84.33 W
Hanover, N.H., U.S.	188	43.42 N	72.17 W
Hanover, N.M., U.S.	200	32.48 N	108.05 W
Hanover, Oh., U.S.	214	40.04 N	82.15 W
Hanover, Pa., U.S.	208	39.48 N	76.59 W
Hanover, Va., U.S.	208	37.45 N	77.22 W
Hanover, Wi., U.S.	216	42.38 N	89.10 W
Hanover □[6]	208	37.42 N	77.20 W
Hanover, Isla I	254	51.00 S	74.40 W
Hanover Airport ⊠	276	40.50 N	74.21 W
Hanover Center	283	42.07 N	70.50 W
Hanover Park	216	42.00 N	88.09 W
Hanover Road	158	30.58 S	24.33 E
Hanoverton	214	40.45 N	80.56 W
Hanovre → Hannover	52	52.24 N	9.44 E
Hanpan, Cape ≻	175e	5.01 S	154.37 E
Hanryeosudo Kukrip Kongwŏn ♦	98	34.46 N	128.30 E
Hansanjiazi	104	41.44 N	122.57 E
Hansard	182	54.05 N	121.52 W
Hansa-Viertel ⊛	264a	52.31 N	13.21 E
Hanscom Air Force Base ■	207	42.28 N	71.17 W
Hans Creek ≐	210	43.06 N	74.08 W
Hānsdiha	124	24.36 N	87.05 E
Hansen Dam ◆[6]	280	34.16 N	118.23 W
Hansen Flood Control Basin ≚[1]	228	34.16 N	118.23 W
Hanshan	100	31.44 N	118.08 E
Hansharo ⊥	94	35.02 N	138.56 E
Hansi, India	120	32.27 N	77.50 E
Hānsi, India	123	29.06 N	75.58 E
Hansia	272b	22.48 N	88.24 E
Hanska	198	44.08 N	94.29 W
Hānskhāli	126	23.21 N	88.37 E
Hans Lollik Island I	240m	18.24 N	64.55 W
Hanslope	42	52.06 N	0.49 W
Hans Meyer Range ⋀	164	4.20 S	152.55 E
Hanson	207	42.04 N	70.52 W
Hanson ≐	162	20.15 S	133.25 E
Hanson Lake ⊜	184	54.42 N	102.49 W
Hanstholm	26	57.07 N	8.38 E
Han-sur-Lesse	56	50.08 N	5.11 E
Han-sur-Nied	56	48.59 N	6.26 E
Hansville	224	47.55 N	122.33 W
Hansweert	52	51.26 N	4.00 E
Hantaj	88	49.31 N	103.13 E
Hāntālbunia	126	22.44 N	89.31 E
Hantamsberg ⋀	158	31.22 S	19.45 E
Hantan → Handan	98	36.37 N	114.29 E
Hantes ≐	50	50.19 N	4.11 E
Hant's Harbour	186	48.01 N	53.16 W
Hantsport	186	45.04 N	64.11 W
Hantu, Pulau I	271c	1.14 N	103.45 E
Hantu, Tanjong ≻	114	4.18 N	100.34 E
Hantzsch ≐	176	67.33 N	72.25 W
Hanumännagar	124	26.30 N	86.51 E
Hanušovce nad Topľou	30	49.02 N	21.30 E
Hanušovice	30	50.05 N	16.55 E
Hanveden ◆[2]	40	59.07 N	18.00 E
Hanwood	166	34.20 S	146.03 E
Hanworth ◆[8]	260	51.26 N	0.23 W
Hanxinzhuang	105	40.16 N	116.44 E
Hanyang	107	29.44 N	103.44 E
Hanyangping	102	32.41 N	108.34 E
Hanyin	102	32.42 N	108.50 E
Hanyū	94	36.10 N	139.32 E
Hanyuan	102	29.22 N	102.38 E
Hanyuangai	102	29.30 N	102.31 E
Hanzhong	102	33.08 N	107.02 E
Hanzhuang	98	34.38 N	117.24 E
Hao I[1]	14	18.15 S	140.54 W
Hao ≐	100	28.27 N	119.56 E
Haohekou	100	28.38 N	112.49 E
Haojiadian	100	31.47 N	113.44 E
Haoli → Hegang	89	47.24 N	130.17 E
Haoluqi	106	30.38 N	119.34 E
HaOn	132	32.43 N	35.38 E
Haouach, Ouadi V	146	16.45 N	19.35 E
Haoxue	102	30.00 N	112.20 E
Haozhikou	107	29.36 N	105.02 E
Haparanda	26	65.50 N	24.10 E
Hapatoni, Baie ⊂	174y	9.58 S	139.07 W
Hapert	52	51.23 N	5.15 E
Hapeville	192	33.39 N	84.24 W
Happ'o-ri	98	40.40 N	127.49 E
Happy	196	34.45 N	101.52 W
Happy Camp	204	41.47 N	123.22 W
Happy Jack	200	34.45 N	111.11 W
Happy Valley-Goose Bay	176	53.20 N	60.25 W
Happy Valley Race Course ♦	271d	22.16 N	114.10 E
Hapsford	262	53.16 N	2.48 W
Hapsu	98	41.13 N	128.51 E
Hapton	262	53.47 N	2.19 W
Hāpur	124	28.43 N	77.47 E
HaQatan, HaMakhtesh ±[7]	132	30.58 N	35.12 E
Ḥaql	128	29.18 N	34.57 E
Haquira	248	14.13 S	72.11 W
Har	164	5.20 S	133.10 E
Har, Laga ≐	154	1.40 N	39.36 E
Hara, Nihon	94	35.58 N	138.14 E
Hara, Nihon	268	35.50 N	139.46 E
Ḥaraḍ, Ar. Su.	128	24.08 N	49.05 E
Härad, Sve.	40	59.23 N	16.55 E
Ḥaraḍ, Yaman	144	16.28 N	43.04 E
Haraiki I[1]	14	17.28 S	143.27 W
Harajuku	268	35.54 N	139.21 E
Haraldsted	41	55.30 N	11.47 E
Haramachi	92	37.38 N	140.58 E
Haramachida	268	35.33 N	139.27 E
Haramosh ∧	123	35.50 N	74.54 E
Harappa	123	30.38 N	72.52 E
Harappa Road	123	30.36 N	72.55 E
Harar → Harer	144	9.18 N	42.08 E
Harare (Salisbury)	154	17.50 S	31.03 E
Ḥarash, Bi'r al- ⊤[4]	146	25.30 N	22.12 E
Ḥarastā al-Başal	132	33.34 N	36.22 E
Hārāt	272b	22.53 N	88.11 E
Ḥārat Ḥurayk	132	33.51 N	35.30 E
Haraz-Djombo	146	13.57 N	19.26 E
Haraze-Mangueigne	146	9.55 N	20.48 E
Harbāti	272b	22.55 N	88.33 E
Harbert	216	41.52 N	86.38 W
Harbeson	208	38.43 N	75.17 W
Harbin	89	45.45 N	126.41 E
Harbiye	130	36.11 N	36.05 E
Harbke	54	52.12 N	11.03 E
Harbo	40	60.06 N	17.12 E
Harbonnières	50	49.51 N	2.40 E
Harboør	26	56.37 N	8.12 E
Harbor	202	42.03 N	124.15 W
Harbor Beach	190	43.50 N	82.39 W
Harbor City ◆[8]	280	33.48 N	118.17 W
Harborcreek	214	42.10 N	79.57 W
Harbord	170	33.45 S	151.26 E
Harbor Isle	276	40.36 N	73.40 W
Harbor Side	228	32.37 N	117.05 W
Harbor Springs	190	45.25 N	84.59 W
Harborton	208	37.39 N	75.49 W
Harbor Tunnel ◆[5]	284b	39.15 N	76.34 W
Harbor View	214	41.42 N	83.27 W
Harbour Breton	186	47.29 N	55.48 W
Harbour Buffett	186	47.31 N	54.05 W
Harbour Deep	186	50.22 N	56.31 W
Harbour Grace	186	47.42 N	53.13 W
Harbours, Bay of ⊂	254	52.15 S	59.15 W
Harbourville	186	45.09 N	64.49 W
Harburg	56	48.47 N	10.41 E
Harburg ◆[8]	52	53.28 N	9.59 E
Hårby	41	55.13 N	10.07 E
Harchies	50	50.29 N	3.41 E
Harcourt, Austl.	169	37.00 S	144.15 E
Harcourt, Fr.	50	49.10 N	0.48 E
Harcuvar Mountains ⋀	200	34.00 N	113.30 W
Hard	58	47.29 N	9.41 E
Harda	124	22.20 N	77.06 E
Hardangerfjorden ⊂[2]	26	60.10 N	6.00 E
Hardangerjøkulen ⊓	26	60.33 N	7.26 E
Hardangervidda ⋀[1]	26	60.20 N	7.30 E
Hardangervidda Nasjonalpark ♦	26	60.15 N	7.05 E
Hardapdam ⊜[1]	156	24.28 S	17.48 E
Hardee □[6]	220	27.29 N	81.48 W
Hardeeville	192	32.17 N	81.04 W
Hardegarijp	52	53.13 N	5.56 E
Hardegsen	52	51.39 N	9.49 E
Hardelot-Plage	50	50.38 N	1.35 E
Hardenberg	52	52.34 N	6.37 E
Harderwijk	52	52.21 N	5.36 E
Hardesty	196	36.36 N	101.11 W
Hardey ≐	162	22.45 S	116.07 E
Hardgrave, Mount ∧[2]	171a	27.30 S	153.29 E
Hardheim	56	49.36 N	9.28 E
Hardin, Il., U.S.	219	39.09 N	90.37 W
Hardin, Mt., U.S.	202	45.43 N	107.36 W
Hardin, Tx., U.S.	222	30.09 N	94.44 W
Hardin □[6], Oh., U.S.	216	40.39 N	83.36 W
Hardin □[6], Tx., U.S.	222	30.20 N	94.35 W
Harding, S. Afr.	158	30.34 S	29.58 E
Harding, Il., U.S.	216	41.31 N	88.51 W
Harding, Ma., U.S.	283	42.12 N	71.27 W
Harding, Lake ⊜[1]	192	32.40 N	85.06 W
Harding Lake ⊜	184	56.13 N	98.23 W
Harding Lakes	208	39.27 N	74.45 W
Hardinsburg, In., U.S.	218	38.27 N	86.16 W
Hardinsburg, Ky., U.S.	194	37.46 N	86.27 W
Hardisty	182	52.40 N	111.18 W
Hardisty Lake ⊜	176	64.30 N	117.45 W
Hardoi	124	27.25 N	80.07 E
Hardoi □[5]	124	27.25 N	80.10 E
Hardricourt	261	49.01 N	1.54 E
Hardscrabble Wash V	200	34.39 N	109.28 W
Hardt	263	51.07 N	6.58 E
Hardtner	198	37.00 N	98.38 W
Hardwār	124	29.58 N	78.10 E
Hardwick, Ga., U.S.	192	33.04 N	83.13 W
Hardwick, Ma., U.S.	207	42.21 N	72.12 W
Hardwick, Vt., U.S.	188	44.30 N	72.22 W
Hardwood	194	30.49 N	91.23 W
Hardwood Ridge ∧	210	41.15 N	75.23 W
Hardy, Ar., U.S.	194	36.18 N	91.28 W
Hardy, Ne., U.S.	198	40.00 N	97.55 W
Hardy, Península ≻[1]	254	55.25 S	68.30 W
Hardy Bay ⊂	176	75.02 N	115.16 W
Hardy Creek ≐	214	42.52 N	81.52 W
Hardy Lake ⊜[1]	218	38.47 N	85.42 W
Hardy Lake State Recreation Area ♦	218	38.44 N	86.26 W
Hardys Pond ⊜	283	42.25 N	71.15 W
Hare, Mount ∧	180	66.38 N	136.12 E
Hare Bay	186	48.51 N	54.01 W
Hare Bay ⊂	186	51.18 N	55.50 W
Harefield ◆[8]	260	51.36 N	0.29 W
Hareid	26	62.22 N	6.02 E
Hare Indian ≐	180	66.18 N	128.38 W
Harelbeke	50	50.51 N	3.18 E
Haren, B.R.D.	52	52.47 N	7.14 E
Haren, Ned.	52	53.10 N	6.35 E
Hareøen I	176	70.25 N	54.50 W
Harer	144	9.18 N	42.08 E
Harerge □[4]	144	8.00 N	43.00 E
Hareskov	41	55.46 N	12.25 E
Hareto	144	9.20 N	37.06 E
Harewa	144	9.55 N	41.59 E
Harewood	172	43.29 S	172.35 E
Harewood Park	284b	39.23 N	76.22 W
Harfaz	130	38.01 N	41.19 E
Harfleur	50	49.30 N	0.12 E
Harford, N.Y., U.S.	210	42.26 N	76.14 W
Harford, Pa., U.S.	210	41.47 N	75.42 W
Harford □[6]	208	39.32 N	76.21 W
Harford Heights	279b	40.22 N	79.46 W
Harford Mills	210	42.25 N	76.12 W
Harg, Sve.	40	60.11 N	18.24 E
Harg, Sve.	40	59.49 N	18.57 E
Hargele	144	5.20 N	42.05 E
Hargeville	261	48.53 N	1.45 E
Hargeysa	144	9.35 N	44.04 E
Harghita □[6]	38	46.35 N	25.30 E
Hargrave ≐	184	54.24 N	98.48 W
Hargrave Lake ⊜	184	54.29 N	99.40 W
Hargshamn	40	60.10 N	18.28 E
Har Hu (Heihai) ⊜	102	38.15 N	97.40 E
Harhur	130	37.49 N	42.20 E
Hāriabhānga ≐[1]	126	21.43 N	89.05 E
Hariāna	123	31.38 N	75.51 E
Hariarapitu	114	2.33 N	98.35 E
Ḥarīb	144	14.57 N	45.30 E
Haribes	156	24.20 S	17.40 E
Ḥaricha, Ḥamâda el ◆[2]	148	22.36 N	3.31 W
Harigabessho	270	34.37 N	135.58 E
Harihar	122	14.31 N	75.48 E
Harihari	172	43.09 S	170.33 E
Hariharpāra	126	24.02 N	88.27 E
Hariharpur Garhi	124	27.19 N	85.29 E
Harike	123	31.10 N	74.57 E
Ḥārim	130	36.12 N	36.31 E
Ḥarim, Jabal al- ∧	128	23.58 N	56.14 E
Harima	96	34.42 N	134.53 E
Harima-nada ⊤[2]	96	34.29 N	134.35 E
Harinagab	124	27.09 N	84.19 E
Harinākunda	126	23.39 N	89.03 E
Haringey ◆[8]	260	51.35 N	0.07 W
Hāringhāta ≐[1]	124	21.54 N	89.57 E
Haringvliet Ц	52	51.47 N	4.10 E
Haringvlietbrug ◆[5]	52	51.43 N	4.20 E
Haringvlietdam ◆[5]	52	51.50 N	4.03 E
Haripād	122	9.18 N	76.28 E
Haripāl	272b	22.49 N	88.07 E
Haripur, India	126	24.18 N	87.05 E
Haripur, India	272b	22.56 N	88.14 E
Harīpur, Pāk.	123	33.59 N	72.56 E
Ḥarīr, Wādī al- V	132	32.44 N	35.54 E
Harirāmpur	126	23.42 N	89.57 E
Harīrūd (Tedžen) ≐	128	37.24 N	60.38 E
Harischandra Range ⋀	122	19.15 N	74.05 E
Ḥārithān	130	36.16 N	37.05 E
Hariyo	144	5.00 N	47.23 E
Harjavalta	26	61.19 N	22.08 E
Härjedalen □[9]	26	62.20 N	13.00 E
Harkaway	274b	38.00 S	145.21 E
Härkeberga	40	59.42 N	17.11 E
Harkema-Opeinde	52	53.11 N	6.08 E
Harker Heights	222	31.05 N	97.40 W
Harkers Island	192	34.41 N	76.33 W
Harker Village	285	39.51 N	75.09 W
Harkness Memorial State Park ♦	207	41.18 N	72.07 W
Harkortsee ⊜	263	51.24 N	7.25 E
Harlaching ◆[8]	60	48.06 N	11.33 E
Harlan, In., U.S.	216	41.11 N	84.55 W
Harlan, Ia., U.S.	198	41.39 N	95.19 W
Harlan, Ky., U.S.	192	36.50 N	83.19 W
Harlan County Lake ⊜[1]	198	40.04 N	99.16 W
Harlech	42	52.52 N	4.07 W
Harlem, Fl., U.S.	220	26.44 N	80.57 W
Harlem, Ga., U.S.	192	33.24 N	82.18 W
Harlem, Mt., U.S.	202	48.32 N	108.47 W
Harlem ◆[8]	276	40.49 N	73.56 W
Harlem River Ц	276	40.48 N	73.54 W
Harlem Springs	214	40.31 N	81.02 W
Harlesden ◆[8]	260	51.32 N	0.15 W
Harlesiel	52	53.43 N	7.49 E
Harleston	42	52.24 N	1.18 E
Harleton	222	32.41 N	94.35 W
Hårlev	41	55.21 N	12.15 E
Harleysville	208	40.17 N	75.23 W
Harlin	171a	26.59 S	152.22 E
Harlingen, Ned.	52	53.10 N	5.24 E
Harlingen, Tx., U.S.	196	26.11 N	97.41 W
Harlinger Land ◆[1]	52	53.40 N	7.30 E
Harlingerode	54	51.54 N	10.31 E
Harlington ◆[8]	260	51.29 N	0.26 W
Harlösa	41	55.43 N	13.32 E
Harlow	260	51.47 N	0.08 E
Harlow □[8]	260	51.44 N	0.07 E
Harlowton	202	46.26 N	109.50 W
Harlpur	272b	22.42 N	88.10 E
Harman	188	38.55 N	79.31 W
Harmånger	26	61.56 N	17.13 E
Harmanli, Blg.	38	41.56 N	25.54 E
Harmanlı, Tür.	130	37.51 N	37.45 E
Harmanschlag	61	48.39 N	14.47 E
Harmar Heights	279b	40.33 N	79.49 W
Harmarville	279b	40.32 N	79.51 W
Hármashatár-hegy ∧	264c	47.33 N	19.00 E
Harmelen	52	52.05 N	4.58 E
Harmil I	144	16.31 N	40.09 E
Harmonsburg	214	41.40 N	80.19 W
Harmonville	285	40.06 N	75.17 W
Harmony, Ca., U.S.	226	35.35 N	121.01 W
Harmony, In., U.S.	194	39.32 N	87.06 W
Harmony, Mn., U.S.	190	43.33 N	92.00 W
Harmony, N.J., U.S.	210	40.44 N	75.08 W
Harmony, Pa., U.S.	214	40.48 N	80.07 W
Harmony, R.I., U.S.	207	41.53 N	71.35 W
Harmony Brook ≐	276	40.48 N	74.34 W
Harmony Heights	220	27.29 N	80.21 W
Harmony Hills	285	39.42 N	75.41 W
Harmonyville	285	40.11 N	75.43 W
Harnai, India	122	17.48 N	73.06 E
Harnai, Pāk.	120	30.06 N	67.56 E
Harnäs	40	60.39 N	17.22 E
Harnātānr	124	27.19 N	84.01 E
Harndrup	41	55.28 N	10.02 E
Harnes	50	50.27 N	2.54 E
Härnevi	40	59.44 N	17.05 E
Harney ≐	220	25.25 N	81.10 W
Harney, Lake ⊜	220	28.45 N	81.03 W
Harney Basin ≚[1]	202	43.15 N	119.00 W
Harney Lake ⊜	202	43.14 N	119.07 W
Harney Peak ∧	198	43.51 N	103.31 W
Harney Pond Canal ≊	220	27.00 N	81.04 W
Härnösand	26	62.38 N	17.56 E
Haro, Esp.	34	42.35 N	2.51 W
Haro, Ityo.	144	8.28 N	38.37 E
Ḥarod ≐	132	32.31 N	35.33 E
Harola	272a	28.36 N	77.19 E
Harold Hill ◆[8]	260	51.36 N	0.13 E
Harold Parker State Forest ♦	283	42.37 N	71.05 W
Haroldswick	46a	60.41 N	0.50 W
Harold Wood ◆[8]	260	51.36 N	0.14 E
Haro Strait Ц	224	48.30 N	123.15 W
Haroué	58	48.28 N	6.11 E
Harpālpur	124	25.17 N	79.20 E
Harpanahalli	122	14.48 N	75.59 E
Harpen ◆[8]	263	51.29 N	7.16 E
Harpenden	42	51.49 N	0.22 W
Harper, Liber.	150	4.25 N	7.43 W
Harper, Ks., U.S.	198	37.17 N	98.01 W
Harper, Tx., U.S.	196	30.18 N	99.15 W
Harper, Wa., U.S.	224	47.31 N	122.31 W
Harper, Mount ∧	180	64.14 N	143.50 W
Harper Lake ⊜	228	35.02 N	117.17 W
Harpers Ferry National Historical Park ♦	188	39.13 N	77.45 W
Harpersfield	210	42.26 N	74.41 W
Harper Town	44	54.55 N	2.31 W
Harper Woods	214	42.25 N	82.55 W
Harpille ∧	62	43.50 N	6.48 E
Harpstedt	52	52.54 N	8.35 E
Harpster	214	40.44 N	83.15 W
Harpsund ⊛	40	59.06 N	16.29 E
Harpurhey ◆[8]	262	53.31 N	2.13 W
Harpur Hill	262	53.14 N	1.54 W
Harpursville	210	42.11 N	75.38 W
Harqin	98	41.08 N	119.38 E
Harqin Qi (Jinshan)	98	41.56 N	118.36 E
Harquahala Mountain ∧	200	33.49 N	113.21 W
Harrah	144	14.57 N	50.19 E
Ḥārrah, Jabal al- ∧	132	33.04 N	35.59 E
Harrai	124	22.37 N	79.13 E
Harran	130	36.51 N	39.00 E
Ḥarrān al-ʿAwāmīd	132	33.27 N	36.34 E
Harray, Loch of ⊜	46	59.01 N	3.13 W
Harrell	194	33.30 N	92.23 W
Harricana ≐	176	51.15 N	79.45 W
Harrietfield	46	56.25 N	3.39 W
Harrietsham	260	51.15 N	0.41 E
Harriman, N.Y., U.S.	210	41.18 N	74.09 W
Harriman, Tn., U.S.	192	35.56 N	84.33 W
Harriman Reservoir ⊜[1]	207	42.50 N	72.53 W
Harriman State Park ♦	210	41.14 N	74.09 W
Harrington, Eng., U.K.	44	54.37 N	3.34 W
Harrington, De., U.S.	208	38.55 N	75.34 W
Harrington, Me., U.S.	188	44.37 N	67.48 W
Harrington, Wa., U.S.	202	47.28 N	118.15 W
Harrington Creek ≐	282	37.19 N	122.18 W
Harrington Drain ≊	281	42.36 N	82.54 W
Harrington Park	276	40.59 N	73.58 W
Harris, Sk., Can.	184	51.44 N	107.35 W
Harris, Scot., U.K.	46	56.59 N	6.20 W
Harris, Mn., U.S.	190	45.35 N	92.58 W
Harris, N.Y., U.S.	210	41.43 N	74.44 W
Harris, R.I., U.S.	207	41.43 N	71.31 W
Harris □[6]	222	29.50 N	95.22 W
Harris ≐	168a	33.18 S	116.09 E
Harris ◆[1]	46	57.55 N	6.50 W
Harris, Lake ⊜, Austl.	162	31.08 S	135.14 E
Harris, Lake ⊜, Fl., U.S.	220	28.46 N	81.49 W
Harris, Sound of Ц	46	57.45 N	7.10 W
Harris Bay ⊂	212	45.23 N	77.50 W
Harris Brook ≐	283	42.44 N	71.13 W
Harrisburg, Ar., U.S.	194	35.33 N	90.43 W
Harrisburg, Il., U.S.	194	37.44 N	88.32 W
Harrisburg, In., U.S.	218	39.41 N	85.11 W
Harrisburg, Ne., U.S.	198	41.33 N	103.44 W
Harrisburg, Oh., U.S.	214	40.53 N	81.13 W
Harrisburg, Or., U.S.	202	44.16 N	123.10 W
Harrisburg, Pa., U.S.	208	40.16 N	76.53 W
Harrisburg International Airport ⊠	208	40.12 N	76.45 W
Harris Creek ⊂	208	38.45 N	76.18 W
Harris Creek ≐, Austl.	274a	33.57 S	150.57 E
Harris Creek ≐, Tx., U.S.	222	32.33 N	95.08 W
Harrisfield	274b	37.57 S	145.11 E
Harris Hill	210	42.58 N	78.40 W
Harrislee	41	54.48 N	9.22 E
Harrismith, Austl.	162	32.56 S	117.52 E
Harrismith, S. Afr.	158	28.18 S	29.03 E
Harrison, Ar., U.S.	194	36.13 N	93.06 W
Harrison, Id., U.S.	202	47.27 N	116.47 W
Harrison, Il., U.S.	216	42.25 N	89.11 W
Harrison, Mi., U.S.	190	44.01 N	84.47 W
Harrison, Ne., U.S.	198	42.41 N	103.53 W
Harrison, N.J., U.S.	276	40.44 N	74.09 W
Harrison, N.Y., U.S.	210	40.58 N	73.43 W
Harrison, Oh., U.S.	218	39.15 N	84.49 W
Harrison □[6], In., U.S.	218	38.17 N	86.07 W
Harrison □[6], Ky., U.S.	218	38.25 N	84.19 W
Harrison □[6], Oh., U.S.	214	40.16 N	81.05 W
Harrison □[6], Tx., U.S.	222	32.35 N	94.35 W
Harrison ≐	224	49.14 N	121.57 W
Harrison, Cape ≻	176	54.55 N	57.55 W
Harrison Bay ⊂	180	70.30 N	151.30 W
Harrisonburg, La., U.S.	194	31.46 N	91.49 W
Harrisonburg, Va., U.S.	188	38.26 N	78.52 W
Harrison City	279b	40.21 N	79.39 W
Harrison Hot Springs	224	49.18 N	121.47 W
Harrison Islands II	176	69.13 N	90.30 W
Harrison Lake ⊜	182	49.30 N	121.50 W
Harrison Mills	224	49.14 N	121.57 W
Harrisons Brook ≐	276	40.38 N	74.34 W
Harrison Tomb State Memorial ⊥	218	39.09 N	84.46 W
Harrison Valley	214	41.57 N	77.39 W
Harrisonville, Md., U.S.	284b	39.23 N	77.50 W
Harrisonville, Mo., U.S.	194	38.39 N	94.20 W
Harrisonville, N.J., U.S.	285	39.41 N	75.15 W
Harris Park	274a	33.49 S	151.01 E
Harris Pond ⊜	283	42.45 N	71.16 W
Harris Reservoir ⊜[1]	222	29.14 N	95.33 W
Harriston, On., Can.	212	43.54 N	80.53 W
Harriston, Ms., U.S.	194	31.43 N	91.01 W
Harristown	219	39.51 N	89.05 W
Harrisville, Austl.	171a	27.49 S	152.40 E
Harrisville, Mi., U.S.	190	44.39 N	83.17 W
Harrisville, N.Y., U.S.	212	44.09 N	75.19 W
Harrisville, Oh., U.S.	214	40.11 N	80.53 W
Harrisville, Pa., U.S.	214	41.08 N	80.00 W
Harrisville, R.I., U.S.	207	41.57 N	71.40 W
Harrisville, W.V., U.S.	188	39.12 N	81.03 W
Harrod	216	40.42 N	83.55 W
Harrodsburg	194	37.45 N	84.50 W
Harrods Creek ≐	218	38.20 N	85.38 W
Harrogate	44	54.00 N	1.33 W
Harrold	196	34.05 N	99.02 W
Harrop Lake ⊜	184	52.38 N	95.58 W
Harrow	214	42.02 N	82.55 W
Harrow ◆[8]	260	51.35 N	0.21 W
Harrow on the Hill ◆[8]	260	51.34 N	0.20 W
Harrow School ⊛[2]	260	51.34 N	0.20 W
Harrowsmith	212	44.24 N	76.40 W
Harry S. Truman Reservoir ⊜[1]	194	38.10 N	93.45 W
Harry Truman Field ⊠	240m	18.21 N	64.59 W
Har Sai Shan ∧	102	35.28 N	97.55 E
Harsefeld	52	53.27 N	9.30 E
Harsens Island	214	42.34 N	82.34 W
Harsens Island I	281	42.35 N	82.38 W
Harsewinkel	52	51.58 N	8.13 E
Harsīn	128	34.16 N	47.35 E
Harşit ≐	130	41.01 N	38.52 E
Harskamp	52	52.07 N	5.45 E
Harsleben	54	51.52 N	11.05 E
Harstad	24	68.46 N	16.30 E
Harstena	26	58.16 N	17.01 E
Harsūd	124	22.06 N	76.44 E
Har Sur ∧	89	48.09 N	122.25 E
Harsum	52	52.12 N	9.57 E
Hart, Tür.	130	40.24 N	40.09 E
Hart, Mi., U.S.	190	43.41 N	86.21 W
Hart, Tx., U.S.	196	34.23 N	102.07 W

Symbols in the index entries represent the broad categories identified in the key at the right. Symbols with superior numbers (⋀[1]) identify subcategories (see complete key on page I · 1).

Kartensymbole in dem Registerverzeichnis stellen die rechts in Schlüssel erklärten Kategorien dar. Symbole mit hochgestellten Ziffern (⋀[1]) bezeichnen Unterabteilungen einer Kategorie (vgl. vollständiger Schlüssel auf Seite I · 1).

Los símbolos incluidos en el texto del índice representan las grandes categorías identificadas con la clave a la derecha. Los símbolos con numeros en su parte superior (⋀[1]) identifican las subcategorías (véase la clave completa en la página I · 1).

Les symboles de l'index représentent les catégories indiquées dans la légende à droite. Les symboles suivis d'un indice (⋀[1]) représentent des sous-catégories (voir légende complète à la page I · 1).

Os símbolos incluídos no texto do índice representam as grandes categorias identificadas com a chave à direita. Os símbolos com números em sua parte superior (⋀[1]) identificam as subcategorias (veja-se a chave completa à página I · 1).

∧ Mountain	Berg	Montaña	Montagne	Montanha
⋀ Mountains	Berge	Montañas	Montagnes	Montanhas
)(Pass	Pass	Paso	Col	Passo
V Valley, Canyon	Tal, Cañon	Valle, Cañón	Vallée, Canyon	Vale, Canhão
⊻ Plain	Ebene	Llano	Plaine	Planície
≻ Cape	Kap	Cabo	Cap	Cabo
I Island	Insel	Isla	Île	Ilha
II Islands	Inseln	Islas	Îles	Ilhas
± Other Topographic Features	Andere Topographische Objekte	Otros Elementos Topográficos	Autres données topographiques	Outros acidentes topográficos

ESPAÑOL

Nombre	Página	Lat.°′	Long.°′ W = Oeste
Hart ≃	180	65.51 N	136.22 W
Hart, Lake ⊜, Austl.	166	31.08 S	136.24 E
Hart, Lake ⊜, Fl., U.S.	220	28.22 N	81.13 W
Ḥartā	132	32.42 N	35.51 E
Hartbees ≃	158	28.45 S	20.32 E
Hartbeesfontein	158	26.42 S	26.26 E
Hartbeespoort	158	25.44 S	27.52 E
Hartberg	61	47.17 N	15.59 E
Hartenholm	52	53.54 N	10.03 E
Hartenstein	54	50.39 N	12.40 E
Hart Fell ∧	44	55.25 N	3.25 W
Hartfield	208	37.34 N	76.30 W
Hartford, Eng., U.K.	262	53.15 N	2.33 W
Hartford, Al., U.S.	194	31.06 N	85.41 W
Hartford, Ar., U.S.	194	35.01 N	94.22 W
Hartford, Ct., U.S.	207	41.46 N	72.41 W
Hartford, Il., U.S.	219	38.50 N	90.05 W
Hartford, In., U.S.	218	38.59 N	84.57 W
Hartford, Ks., U.S.	198	38.18 N	95.57 W
Hartford, Ky., U.S.	194	37.27 N	86.54 W
Hartford, Mi., U.S.	216	42.12 N	86.10 W
Hartford, N.J., U.S.	285	39.58 N	74.53 W
Hartford, N.Y., U.S.	210	43.21 N	73.22 W
Hartford, Oh., U.S.	214	41.19 N	80.34 W
Hartford, S.D., U.S.	198	43.37 N	96.56 W
Hartford, Wi., U.S.	190	43.19 N	88.22 W
Hartford □ 6	207	41.46 N	72.41 W
Hartford City	216	40.27 N	85.22 W
Hartha	54	51.05 N	12.58 E
Hartington	198	42.37 N	97.15 W
Hart Island I	276	40.51 N	73.46 W
Hart Lake ⊜	202	42.24 N	119.51 W
Hartland, N.B., Can.	186	46.18 N	67.32 W
Hartland, Eng., U.K.	42	50.59 N	4.29 W
Hartland, Il., U.S.	216	42.22 N	88.31 W
Hartland, Me., U.S.	188	44.53 N	69.26 W
Hartland, Mi., U.S.	216	42.39 N	83.45 W
Hartland, N.Y., U.S.	210	43.14 N	78.35 W
Hartland, Wi., U.S.	216	43.06 N	88.20 W
Hartland Point >	42	51.02 N	4.31 W
Hartlepool	44	54.42 N	1.11 W
Hartleton	210	40.54 N	77.10 W
Hartley, Austl.	170	33.33 S	150.11 E
Hartley, Eng., U.K.	260	51.23 N	0.19 E
Hartley, Ia., U.S.	198	43.10 N	95.28 W
Hartley, Tx., U.S.	196	35.53 N	102.24 W
Hartley Bay	182	53.25 N	129.15 W
Hartlip	260	51.21 N	0.39 E
Hart Lot	210	43.01 N	76.28 W
Hartly	208	39.10 N	75.42 W
Hartmannsdorf	54	50.53 N	12.48 E
Hartmannshain	56	50.28 N	9.16 E
Hart-Miller Island I	208	39.15 N	76.23 W
Hart Mountain ∧	184	52.29 N	101.25 W
Hartney	184	49.28 N	100.30 W
Hartola	26	61.35 N	26.01 E
Harts ≃	158	28.24 S	24.17 E
Hartsburg	219	38.41 N	92.18 W
Hartsdale	210	41.01 N	73.47 W
Hartselle	194	34.26 N	86.56 W
Härtsfeld ◆ 1	56	48.50 N	10.15 E
Hartshill	42	52.37 N	1.32 W
Hartshorne	196	34.50 N	95.33 W
Harts Range	162	23.00 S	134.55 E
Hartstene Island I	224	47.14 N	122.53 W
Hartstown	214	41.33 N	80.23 W
Hartsville, In., U.S.	218	39.16 N	85.41 W
Hartsville, Pa., U.S.	285	40.14 N	75.05 W
Hartsville, S.C., U.S.	192	34.22 N	80.04 W
Hartsville, Tn., U.S.	194	36.23 N	86.10 W
Hartswater	158	27.34 S	24.43 E
Hartville, Mo., U.S.	194	37.15 N	92.30 W
Hartville, Oh., U.S.	214	40.57 N	81.19 W
Hartwell	192	34.21 N	82.55 W
Hartwell Lake ⊜ 1	192	34.30 N	82.55 W
Hartwick	210	42.39 N	75.02 W
Hartwick Pines State Park ♠	190	44.47 N	84.41 W
Hartz Mountains National Park ♠	166	43.15 S	146.50 E
Harue	94	36.08 N	136.14 E
Haruki	270	34.29 N	135.23 E
Haruku, Pulau I	164	3.34 S	128.29 E
Hārūn	140	11.20 N	25.43 E
Haruna	94	36.23 N	138.53 E
Hārūnābād	123	29.37 N	73.08 E
Haruna-san ∧	94	36.28 N	138.52 E
Haruniye	130	37.17 N	36.27 E
Haruno, Nihon	94	34.57 N	137.53 E
Haruno, Nihon	96	33.30 N	133.30 E
Harūr	122	12.04 N	78.30 E
Hārūt ≃	128	31.35 N	61.18 E
Harvard, Il., U.S.	216	42.25 N	88.36 W
Harvard, Ma., U.S.	207	42.30 N	71.35 W
Harvard, Ne., U.S.	198	40.37 N	98.05 W
Harvard University ⊛ 2	283	42.22 N	71.07 W
Harvel, Eng., U.K.	260	51.21 N	0.22 E
Harvel, Il., U.S.	219	39.21 N	89.32 W
Harvest, Mount ∧ 2	162	25.54 S	126.28 E
Harvey, Austl.	168a	33.05 S	115.54 E
Harvey, N.B., Can.	186	45.43 N	64.43 W
Harvey, Il., U.S.	216	41.36 N	87.38 W
Harvey, N.D., U.S.	198	47.46 N	99.56 W
Harvey ≃	168a	32.46 S	115.43 E
Harvey Estuary ⊂ 1	168a	32.43 S	115.42 E
Harvey Mountain ∧	207	42.18 N	73.25 W
Harvey Reservoir ⊜ 1	168a	33.05 S	115.58 E
Harveysburg	218	39.30 N	84.00 W
Harveys Lake	210	41.23 N	76.02 W
Harwell	42	51.37 N	1.18 W
Harwich, Eng., U.K.	42	51.57 N	1.17 E
Harwich, Ma., U.S.	207	41.41 N	70.04 W
Harwich Port	207	41.40 N	70.04 W
Harwick	279b	40.34 N	79.48 W
Harwinton	207	41.46 N	73.03 W
Harwood, Eng., U.K.	262	53.35 N	2.23 W
Harwood, Tx., U.S.	222	29.40 N	97.30 W
Harwood Heights	278	41.58 N	87.48 W
Harwood Mines	210	40.57 N	76.01 W
Harwood Park	284b	39.12 N	76.44 W
Haryana □ 3	120	29.20 N	76.20 E
Harz ⋏	54	51.45 N	10.30 E
Harzgerode	54	51.38 N	11.08 E
Ḥasā, Bi'r al- ⍑ 4	140	22.58 N	35.40 E
Ḥasā, Wādī al- V	132	31.05 N	35.27 E
Hasafen	86	45.14 N	90.20 E
Ḥaṣāh, Wādī al- V	132	30.38 N	37.09 E
Hasaki	94	35.44 N	140.50 E
Ḥasanābād	267d	35.44 N	51.19 E
Ḥasanābād-e Khāleṣeh	267d	35.37 N	51.12 E
Hasan Abdāl	123	33.49 N	72.41 E
Hasançelebi	130	38.58 N	37.54 E
Hasan Dağı ∧	130	38.08 N	34.12 E
Hasankale → Pasinler	130	39.59 N	41.41 E
Hasankeyf	130	37.43 N	41.25 E
Ḥasan Kīādeh	128	37.24 N	49.58 E
Hasanparti	122	18.04 N	79.32 E
Hasanpur	124	28.43 N	78.17 E
Hasayaz	130	40.15 N	33.20 E
Ḥāṣbānī, Nahr al- ≃	132	33.11 N	35.37 E
Ḥāṣbayyā	132	33.24 N	35.41 E
Hasbek	130	39.33 N	35.33 E
Hasbergen, B.R.D.	52	52.14 N	7.57 E
Hasbergen, B.R.D.	52	53.05 N	8.40 E
Hasbrouck Heights	276	40.51 N	74.04 W
Hascosay I	46	60.37 N	0.59 W
Hasdo ≃	120	21.44 N	82.44 E
Hasdo-Rāmpur Basin ≚ 1	124	22.50 N	82.35 E
Hase, Nihon	94	35.47 N	138.06 E
Hase, Nihon	270	34.32 N	135.54 E
Hase ≃, B.R.D.	52	52.41 N	7.18 E
Hase ≃, Nihon	270	34.34 N	135.38 E
Hasel ≃	54	50.32 N	10.27 E
Häselgehr	58	47.19 N	10.30 E
Haselhorst ◆ 8	264a	52.33 N	13.15 E
Haselünne	52	52.40 N	7.29 E
Hasenheide, Volkspark ♠	264a	52.29 N	13.25 E
Hasenkamp	252	31.31 S	59.51 W

FRANÇAIS

Nom	Page	Lat.°′	Long.°′ W = Ouest
Ḥashā', Jabal al- ∧	144	13.43 N	44.31 E
Ḩasharād	128	37.30 N	47.16 E
HaShefela ◆ 1	132	31.40 N	34.55 E
Hashima	94	35.19 N	136.42 E
Hashimoto, Nihon	96	34.19 N	135.37 E
Hashimoto, Nihon	270	34.26 N	135.23 E
Hashır	128	37.54 N	42.36 E
Hashira-jima I	96	34.01 N	132.25 E
Hashiri-jima I	96	34.21 N	133.27 E
Hashitai	89	49.24 N	125.18 E
Hashtpar	128	37.48 N	48.55 E
Hasht Sāl ◆ 8	272a	28.38 N	77.03 E
Hasil, Pulau I	164	1.06 S	128.24 E
Hāsilpur	123	29.43 N	72.33 E
Ḥāsīn-e Bozorg	84	39.23 N	44.42 E
Haskayne	262	53.34 N	2.58 W
Haskeir Islands II	46	57.42 N	7.41 W
Haskell, Ok., U.S.	196	35.49 N	95.40 W
Haskell, Tx., U.S.	196	33.09 N	99.44 W
Haskell Pond ⊜	283	42.37 N	70.44 W
Hasketh Bank	262	53.43 N	2.51 W
Haskins	216	41.27 N	83.42 W
Haskovo	38	41.56 N	25.33 E
Hasköy, Tür.	130	40.59 N	42.52 E
Hasköy, Tür.	130	41.38 N	26.41 E
Hasköy ◆ 8	267b	41.02 N	28.58 E
Haslach im Kinzigtal	58	48.16 N	8.06 E
Hasle, Dan.	41	55.11 N	14.43 E
Hasle, Schw.	58	47.01 N	7.39 E
Haslemere	42	51.06 N	0.43 W
Haslett	216	42.44 N	84.24 W
Haslev	41	55.20 N	11.58 E
Haslingden	262	53.43 N	2.18 W
Haslingden Grane	262	53.42 N	2.21 W
Haslington	44	53.06 N	2.24 W
Haslital V	58	46.42 N	8.10 E
Hasmark	41	55.33 N	10.28 E
Ḥasmat 'Umar, Bi'r ⍑ 4	140	21.46 N	34.00 E
Hāsnābād	126	22.35 N	88.55 E
Hasnācha	272b	22.26 N	88.09 E
Haspe ◆ 8	263	51.21 N	7.26 E
Hasperos Canyon V	200	33.50 N	105.02 W
Hasper-Stausee ⊜ 1	263	51.18 N	7.25 E
Haspres	50	50.15 N	3.25 E
Hasras	130	37.57 N	42.16 E
Ḥaṣṣ, Jabal al- ∧ 2	130	35.52 N	37.22 E
Hassa	130	36.50 N	36.29 E
Hassan	122	13.00 N	76.05 E
Hassard	219	39.39 N	91.40 W
Hassayampa ≃	200	33.20 N	112.43 W
Hassberge ⋏ 2	56	50.12 N	10.29 E
Hassbergen	52	52.44 N	9.13 E
Hassel, B.R.D.	52	52.48 N	9.11 E
Hassel, B.R.D.	263	51.39 N	7.30 E
Hassel ◆ 8	263	51.36 N	7.03 E
Hasselbeck-Schwarzbach	263	51.16 N	6.53 E
Hasselfelde	54	51.41 N	10.51 E
Hasselfors	40	59.05 N	14.39 E
Hassels ◆ 8	263	51.10 N	6.53 E
Hasselt, Bel.	56	50.56 N	5.20 E
Hasselt, Ned.	52	52.35 N	6.05 E
Hassfurt	56	50.02 N	10.31 E
Hassi Bel Guebbour	148	28.46 N	6.27 E
Hassi el Ghella	34	35.28 N	1.03 W
Hassi Mameche	34	35.52 N	0.04 E
Hassi Messaoud	148	31.43 N	5.59 E
Hassi Zehana	34	35.01 N	0.53 W
Hassleben	54	53.13 N	13.41 E
Hässleholm	41	56.09 N	13.46 E
Hasslinghausen	56	51.20 N	7.17 E
Hassloch	56	49.22 N	8.16 E
Hasson Heights	214	41.26 N	79.41 W
Hästbo	40	60.27 N	16.27 E
Hästen ◆ 8, B.R.D.	263	51.09 N	7.06 E
Hasten ◆ 8, B.R.D.	263	51.12 N	7.09 E
Hastière-Lavaux	56	50.13 N	4.50 E
Hastings, Austl.	169	38.18 S	145.11 E
Hastings, Barb.	241g	13.04 N	59.35 W
Hastings, On., Can.	212	44.18 N	77.57 W
Hastings, N.Z.	172	39.38 S	176.51 E
Hastings, Eng., U.K.	42	50.51 N	0.36 E
Hastings, Fl., U.S.	192	29.43 N	81.30 W
Hastings, Il., U.S.	278	41.41 N	87.58 W
Hastings, Mi., U.S.	216	42.39 N	85.17 W
Hastings, Mn., U.S.	190	44.44 N	92.51 W
Hastings, Ne., U.S.	198	40.35 N	98.23 W
Hastings, N.Y., U.S.	210	43.22 N	76.09 W
Hastings, Pa., U.S.	214	40.39 N	78.42 W
Hastings □ 6	212	44.45 N	77.40 W
Hastings Battlesite ⊥	42	50.53 N	0.31 E
Hastings-on-Hudson	276	40.59 N	73.52 W
Hastingwood	260	51.45 N	0.09 E
Hastrup	41	55.26 N	12.11 E
Hasty	198	38.06 N	102.57 W
Hasuda	94	35.59 N	139.40 E
Hasumi	96	34.52 N	132.37 E
Haswell	198	38.27 N	103.09 W
Hata	94	36.11 N	137.51 E
Hat'ae-do I	98	34.32 N	126.03 E
Ha-tan	110	18.30 N	105.20 E
Hatanagi-dam ◆ 6	94	35.18 N	138.12 E
Hatashō	94	35.10 N	136.15 E
Hatay □ 4	130	36.30 N	36.15 E
Hatboro	208	40.10 N	75.06 W
Hatch, N.M., U.S.	200	32.39 N	107.09 W
Hatch, Ut,. U.S.	200	37.38 N	112.26 W
Hatches Creek	162	20.56 S	135.12 E
Hatchet Creek ≃	194	32.52 N	86.20 W
Hatchet Lake	186	44.35 N	63.40 W
Hatchie ≃	194	35.35 N	89.53 W
Hatchineha, Lake ⊜	220	28.02 N	81.25 W
Hatchlands ⊥	260	51.15 N	0.28 W
Hatchmere	262	53.15 N	2.40 W
Hatchville	207	41.37 N	70.33 W
Hatch Wash V	200	38.32 N	109.36 W
Hat Creek ≃, U.S.	198	43.16 N	103.36 W
Hat Creek ≃, Ca., U.S.	204	40.59 N	121.33 W
Haţeg	38	45.37 N	22.57 E
Hateruma-shima I	175d	24.03 N	123.47 E
Hatfield, Austl.	166	33.52 S	143.45 E
Hatfield, Eng., U.K.	44	53.34 N	1.00 W
Hatfield, Eng., U.K.	260	51.46 N	0.13 W
Hatfield, Ar., U.S.	194	34.29 N	94.22 W
Hatfield, Ma., U.S.	207	42.22 N	72.35 W
Hatfield Aerodrome ⊠	260	51.46 N	0.16 W
Hatfield House ⊥	260	51.46 N	0.13 W
Hatfield Peverel	260	51.47 N	0.35 E
Hatfield Swamp ≡	276	40.50 N	74.20 W
Hathāla	123	32.03 N	70.34 E
Hathaway Pines	226	38.07 N	120.28 W
Hatherleigh	42	50.49 N	4.04 W
Hathersage	44	53.19 N	1.38 W
Hāthras	124	27.36 N	78.03 E
Hātia ʊ	124	22.30 N	91.15 E
Hātiāra	272b	22.37 N	88.27 E
Ḥāṭibah, Ra's >	144	21.55 N	38.58 E
Ha-tien	110	10.23 N	104.29 E
Hatillo	240m	18.29 N	66.49 W
Ha-tinh	110	18.20 N	105.54 E
Hatinoe → Hachinohe	92	40.30 N	141.29 E
Hatiozi → Hachiōji	94	35.39 N	139.20 E
Hatip	130	37.46 N	32.25 E
Hātisāla	272b	22.33 N	88.32 E
Hato	241s	12.12 N	68.57 W
Hato, Bocht van ⊂	241s	12.13 N	68.58 W
Hato del Volcán	236	8.46 N	82.38 W
Hatogaya	94	35.50 N	139.44 E
Hato Mayor [del Rey]	238	18.46 N	69.15 W
Hato Rey	240m	18.25 N	66.03 W
Hatoyama	94	35.59 N	139.20 E
Hāt Pīplia	124	22.46 N	76.18 E
Hatsukaichi	96	34.21 N	132.20 E
Hatsu-shima I	94	35.02 N	139.10 E
Hatsutomi	268	35.46 N	140.01 E
Hatta	124	24.07 N	79.36 E
Hattab, Oued el V	36	35.23 N	9.32 E

PORTUGUÊS

Nome	Página	Lat.°′	Long.°′ W = Oeste
Hattah-Kulkyne National Park ♠	166	34.40 S	142.30 E
Hattem	52	52.28 N	6.04 E
Hatten, B.R.D.	52	53.02 N	8.22 E
Hatten, Fr.	56	48.54 N	7.59 E
Hattenhofen	60	48.13 N	11.07 E
Hatteras	192	35.13 N	75.41 W
Hatteras, Cape >	192	35.13 N	75.32 W
Hatteras Island I	192	35.25 N	75.30 W
Hattiesburg	194	31.19 N	89.17 W
Hatting	41	55.51 N	9.46 E
Hattingen	56	51.23 N	7.10 E
Hattingspruit	158	28.09 S	30.11 E
Hatton, Eng., U.K.	262	53.20 N	2.36 W
Hatton, Scot., U.K.	46	57.25 N	1.54 W
Hatton, Al., U.S.	194	34.33 N	87.24 W
Hatton, N.D., U.S.	198	47.38 N	97.27 W
Hatton ◆ 8	260	51.28 N	0.25 W
Hatton Fields	226	36.33 N	121.54 W
Hattorf [am Harz]	52	51.39 N	10.14 E
Hattori, Nihon	270	34.46 N	135.27 E
Hattori, Nihon	270	34.52 N	135.36 E
Hattstatt	58	48.01 N	7.17 E
Hattstedt	41	54.31 N	9.01 E
Hatunsaray	130	37.35 N	32.21 E
Hatvan	30	47.40 N	19.41 E
Hat Yai	110	7.01 N	100.28 E
Hatzfeld ◆ 8	263	51.17 N	7.11 E
Hatzic	224	49.09 N	122.15 W
Hatzic Lake ⊜	224	49.10 N	122.14 W
Hau-bon (Cheo-reo)	110	13.24 N	108.27 E
Haubourdin	50	50.36 N	2.59 E
Haubstadt	194	38.12 N	87.34 W
Hau-duc	110	15.20 N	108.13 E
Hāudullāpur	272b	22.25 N	88.33 E
Hauge	26	58.18 N	6.15 E
Haugesund	26	59.25 N	5.18 E
Haugh of Urr	44	54.58 N	3.52 W
Haughton Green	262	53.27 N	2.06 W
Haugsdorf	61	48.42 N	16.05 E
Hau Hoi Wan ⊂	100	22.28 N	113.56 E
Hauhungaroa Range ⋏	172	38.50 S	175.34 E
Haukeligrend	26	59.45 N	7.31 E
Haukipudas	26	65.11 N	25.21 E
Haukivesi ⊜	26	62.06 N	28.28 E
Haukivuori	26	62.01 N	27.13 E
Hauldres, Rû des ≃	261	48.37 N	2.28 E
Haulerwijk	52	53.04 N	6.20 E
Haultain ≃	184	55.51 N	106.46 W
Haune ≃	56	50.52 N	9.43 E
Haunersdorf	60	48.36 N	12.43 E
Haunstetten	58	48.18 N	10.54 E
Haunts Creek ʊ	276	40.37 N	73.31 W
Hauppauge	210	40.49 N	73.12 W
Hauptsrus	158	26.33 S	26.18 E
Hauraki Gulf ⊂	172	36.20 S	175.05 E
Hauroko, Lake ⊜	172	46.00 S	167.20 E
Hauru, Pointe >	174s	17.29 S	149.55 W
Haus	64	47.25 N	13.49 E
Hausa	273a	6.37 N	3.21 E
Hausach	58	48.17 N	8.10 E
Hausham	64	47.45 N	11.50 E
Hausruck ⋏	60	48.07 N	13.35 E
Haussee ⊜	264a	52.38 N	13.41 E
Haussömmern	54	51.11 N	10.49 E
Haut, Isle au I	188	44.03 N	68.38 W
Haut Atlas ⋏	148	31.30 N	6.00 W
Haut-Bout	261	48.32 N	1.55 E
Haute Colme, Canal de la ≍	50	50.50 N	2.12 E
Hautecombe, Abbaye de ⊛ 1	62	45.45 N	5.50 E
Haute-Corse □ 5	36	42.30 N	9.00 E
Haute-Garonne □ 5	32	43.25 N	1.30 E
Haute-Kotto □ 5	152	7.00 N	23.00 E
Haute-Loire □ 5	32	45.05 N	3.50 E
Hauteluce	62	45.45 N	6.35 E
Haute-Marne □ 5	58	48.05 N	5.10 E
Hauterive	186	49.12 N	68.16 W
Hauterives	62	45.15 N	5.02 E
Hautes-Alpes □ 5	62	44.40 N	6.30 E
Haute-Sangha □ 5	152	4.30 N	16.00 E
Haute-Saône □ 5	58	47.40 N	6.10 E
Haute-Savoie □ 5	32	46.00 N	6.20 E
Haute Seine, Canal de la ≍	50	48.34 N	3.43 E
Hautes Fagnes ⋏	56	50.30 N	6.05 E
Hautes-Pyrénées □ 5	32	43.00 N	0.10 E
Haute Sûre, Lac de la ⊜ 1	56	49.52 N	5.52 E
Haute-Vienne □ 5	32	45.50 N	1.15 E
Hauteville-Lompnes	58	45.58 N	5.36 E
Haute Volta → Burkina Faso □ 1	150	13.00 N	1.30 W
Haut-Folin ∧	32	47.00 N	4.02 E
Haut-Kœnigsbourg, Château du ⊥	58	48.14 N	7.22 E
Haut-Mbomou □ 5	140	6.00 N	26.00 E
Hautmont	50	50.15 N	3.56 E
Haut-Ogooué □ 4	152	1.00 S	13.50 E
Haut-Rhin □ 5	58	47.53 N	7.13 E
Hauts-Bassins □ 5	150	11.00 N	4.30 W
Hauts-de-Seine □ 5	261	48.50 N	2.11 E
Hautvillers	50	49.05 N	3.57 E
Haut-Zaïre □ 4	154	2.20 N	27.00 E
Hauula	229c	21.36 N	157.54 W
Hauzenberg	60	48.39 N	13.38 E
Hauz Khas ⊥	272a	28.36 N	77.09 E
Hauz Rāni ◆ 8	272a	28.32 N	77.13 E
Havana → La Habana, Cuba	240p	23.08 N	82.22 W
Havana, Ar., U.S.	194	35.06 N	93.31 W
Havana, Fl., U.S.	192	30.37 N	84.24 W
Havana, Il., U.S.	194	40.18 N	90.03 W
Havana, N.D., U.S.	198	45.57 N	97.37 W
Havane, La → La Habana	240p	23.08 N	82.22 W
Havannah, Canal de la ʊ	175f	22.22 S	167.01 E
Havant	42	50.51 N	0.59 W
Havasu, Lake ⊜ 1	200	34.30 N	114.20 W
Havasu Creek ≃	200	36.19 N	112.46 W
Havasupai Indian Reservation ◆ 4	200	36.13 N	112.40 W
Havdrup	41	55.32 N	12.08 E
Havel ≃	54	52.53 N	11.58 E
Havelange	56	50.23 N	5.14 E
Havelberg	54	52.50 N	12.04 E
Havelberg ∧ 2	264a	52.28 N	13.12 E
Haveli	123	30.27 N	73.42 E
Haveliān	123	34.03 N	73.10 E
Havel-Kanal ≍	264a	52.36 N	13.12 E
Havelland ◆ 1	54	52.25 N	12.45 E
Havelländisches Luch ≡	54	52.40 N	12.40 E
Havelock, On., Can.	212	44.26 N	77.53 W
Havelock, N.Z.	172	41.17 S	173.46 E
Havelock, N.C., U.S.	192	34.52 N	76.54 W
Havelock Island I	110	11.58 N	93.00 E
Havelock North	172	39.40 S	176.53 E
Haven	198	37.53 N	97.46 W
Haverford	285	40.00 N	75.17 W
Haverford College ⊛ 2	285	40.00 N	75.18 W
Haverfordwest	42	51.49 N	4.58 W
Haverhill, Eng., U.K.	42	52.05 N	0.26 E
Haverhill, Ma., U.S.	207	42.46 N	71.04 W
Haverhill Airport ⊠	283	42.48 N	71.04 W
Haverhill-Riverside Airport ⊠	283	42.46 N	71.02 W
Hāveri	122	14.48 N	75.24 E
Haverigg	44	54.11 N	3.17 W
Havering ◆ 8	260	51.34 N	0.14 E
Havering-atte-Bower ◆ 8	260	51.37 N	0.11 E
Havering's Grove	260	51.38 N	0.23 E
Havern ⊜	26	62.17 N	15.07 E
Haverö	26	62.24 N	15.05 E
Haverstraw	210	41.11 N	73.57 W
Havertown	208	39.58 N	75.18 W
Haviland, Ks., U.S.	198	37.37 N	99.06 W

Haviland, Oh., U.S.	216	41.01 N	84.35 W
Haviland Brook ≃	276	41.07 N	73.33 W
Havilhanları	130	38.09 N	41.47 E
Ḥavīq	128	38.10 N	48.54 E
Havířov	30	49.47 N	18.27 E
Havixbeck	52	51.58 N	7.25 E
Hävla	40	58.55 N	15.52 E
Havlíčkův Brod	30	49.36 N	15.35 E
Havnbjerg	41	55.02 N	9.48 E
Havnsø	41	55.45 N	11.20 E
Havran	130	39.33 N	27.06 E
Havré, Bel.	50	50.28 N	4.02 E
Havre → Le Havre, Fr.	50	49.30 N	0.08 E
Havre, Mt., U.S.	202	48.32 N	109.40 W
Havre-Aubert	186	47.14 N	61.51 W
Havre Aubert, Île du I	186	47.14 N	61.57 W
Havre aux Maisons, Île du I	186	47.25 N	61.47 W
Havre de Grace	208	39.32 N	76.05 W
Havre de Grace Heights	208	39.35 N	76.07 W
Havre North	202	48.36 N	109.41 W
Havre-Saint-Pierre	186	50.14 N	63.36 W
Havsa	130	41.33 N	26.49 E
Havza	130	40.58 N	35.41 E
Haw ≃	192	35.36 N	79.03 W
Hawaii □ 3	229d	20.00 N	157.45 W
Hawaii I	229d	19.30 N	155.30 W
Hawaiian Gardens	280	33.49 N	118.04 W
Hawaiian Islands II	229d	20.30 N	157.30 W
Hawaiian Ridge ✦ 3	14	24.00 N	165.00 W
Hawaii Volcanoes National Park ♠	229d	19.23 N	155.17 W
Hawal ≃	146	10.00 N	12.05 E
Hawarden, Sk., Can.	184	51.23 N	106.36 W
Hawarden, N.Z.	172	42.56 S	172.38 E
Hawarden, Wales, U.K.	44	53.11 N	3.02 W
Hawarden, Ia., U.S.	198	42.59 N	96.29 W
Ḥawashīyah, Wādī V	140	28.31 N	32.58 E
Haw Creek ≃	218	39.11 N	85.55 W
Hawea, Lake ⊜	172	44.30 S	169.17 E
Hawera	172	39.35 S	174.17 E
Hawes	44	54.18 N	2.12 W
Hawesville	194	37.54 N	86.45 W
Haweswater Reservoir ⊜	44	54.32 N	2.48 W
Ḥawf, Jabal ⋏ 2	273c	29.55 N	31.21 E
Ḥawf, Wādī V	142	29.53 N	31.18 E
Hawi	229d	20.14 N	155.50 W
Hawick	44	55.25 N	2.47 W
Hawk Creek ≃	198	44.44 N	95.25 W
Hawkdun Range ⋏	172	44.46 S	170.00 E
Hawke, Cape >	166	32.13 S	152.34 E
Hawke Bay ⊂	172	39.20 S	177.30 E
Hawker	166	31.53 S	138.25 E
Hawkes, Mount ∧	9	83.56 S	55.45 W
Hawkes Brook ≃	283	42.45 N	71.08 W
Hawkesbury	206	45.36 N	74.37 W
Hawkesbury ≃	170	33.30 S	151.10 E
Hawkesbury Island I	182	53.38 N	129.00 W
Hawkes Pond ⊜	283	42.30 N	71.02 W
Hawkeye	190	42.56 N	91.57 W
Hawkhurst	42	51.02 N	0.30 E
Hawking	42	51.06 N	1.10 E
Hawkins, Tx., U.S.	222	32.35 N	95.12 W
Hawkins, Wi., U.S.	190	45.30 N	90.43 W
Hawkins, Lake ⊜ 1	222	32.38 N	95.15 W
Hawkins Island I	180	60.30 N	146.00 W
Hawkinsville	192	32.17 N	83.28 W
Hawk Junction	190	48.05 N	84.34 W
Hawk Lake	184	49.48 N	93.59 W
Haw Knob ∧	192	35.19 N	84.02 W
Hawk Point	219	38.58 N	91.07 W
Hawk Run	214	40.55 N	78.12 W
Hawksbill ∧	188	38.33 N	78.23 W
Hawksbill Creek ⊂	192	26.32 N	78.43 W
Hawks Nest Point >	238	24.09 N	75.32 W
Hawkwell	260	51.36 N	0.40 E
Hawkwood	166	25.47 S	150.50 E
Hawley, Eng., U.K.	260	51.25 N	0.14 E
Hawley, Mn., U.S.	198	46.52 N	96.18 W
Hawley, Pa., U.S.	210	41.28 N	75.10 W
Hawleyton	210	42.01 N	75.55 W
Hawleyville	207	41.25 N	73.21 W
Haworth	276	40.57 N	73.59 W
Haw Par Villa ⊛	271c	1.16 N	103.47 E
Hawr	142	27.52 N	30.44 E
Ḥawrān, Wādī V	128	33.58 N	42.34 E
Ḥawsh 'Īsā	142	30.55 N	30.17 E
Ḥawsh Mūsá	132	33.43 N	35.56 E
Hawthorn, Austl.	274b	37.49 S	145.02 E
Hawthorn, Pa., U.S.	214	41.01 N	79.17 W
Hawthorne, Ca., U.S.	228	33.54 N	118.21 W
Hawthorne, Fl., U.S.	192	29.35 N	82.05 W
Hawthorne, Nv., U.S.	204	38.31 N	118.37 W
Hawthorne, N.J., U.S.	210	40.56 N	74.09 W
Hawthorne, N.Y., U.S.	210	41.06 N	73.47 W
Hawthorne Lake ⊜	276	41.03 N	74.35 W
Hawthorne Municipal Airport ⊠	280	33.55 N	118.20 W
Hawthorne Race Course ♠	278	41.50 N	87.45 W
Hawthorn Woods	278	42.13 N	88.03 W
Ḥawwārah	132	32.32 N	35.54 E
Ḥawwārat 'Adlān	142	29.12 N	30.58 E
Ḥawwārat al-Maqṭa'	142	29.15 N	30.54 E
Hawza	148	27.06 N	10.55 W
Hawzen	144	13.56 N	39.28 E
Haxby	44	54.01 N	1.04 W
Haxey	44	53.29 N	0.50 W
Haxtun	198	40.38 N	102.37 W
Hay	166	34.30 S	144.51 E
Hay ≃, Austl.	166	25.14 S	138.00 E
Hay ≃, Can.	176	60.52 N	115.44 W
Hay ≃, Wi., U.S.	190	44.59 N	91.51 W
Hay, Cape >	176	74.25 N	113.00 W
Hay, Mount ∧, Austl.	162	23.28 S	133.05 E
Hay, Mount ∧, Austl.	170	33.37 S	150.26 E
Hay, Mount ∧, N.A.	180	59.15 N	137.37 W
Hay, South Fork ≃	190	45.03 N	91.57 W
Haya	164	3.27 S	129.33 E
Haya ≃, Nihon	94	35.25 N	138.27 E
Haya ≃, Nihon	94	35.14 N	139.09 E
Hayachine-san ∧	92	39.34 N	141.29 E
Haya'er	120	37.00 N	93.18 E
Hayakawa	94	35.25 N	138.22 E
Hayama, Nihon	94	35.16 N	139.35 E
Hayama, Nihon	96	33.26 N	133.13 E
Hayang	98	35.55 N	128.47 E
Hayange	56	49.20 N	6.03 E
HaYarden → Jordan ≃	132	31.46 N	35.33 E
Hayashima	96	34.36 N	133.50 E
Hayasui-seto ʊ	96	33.18 N	131.59 E
Haybān	140	11.13 N	30.31 E
Haybān, Jabal ∧	140	11.15 N	30.31 E
Hay Bay ⊂	212	44.10 N	76.55 W
Haybes	56	50.00 N	4.43 E
Haydān, Wādī al- V	132	31.27 N	35.36 E
Haydaran	130	39.14 N	39.43 E
Haydarlı	130	38.16 N	30.23 E
Haydarpaşa ◆ 8	267b	40.58 N	29.02 E
Haydarpaşa Garı ◆ 5	267b	41.00 N	29.01 E
Hayden, Az., U.S.	200	33.00 N	110.47 W
Hayden, Co., U.S.	200	40.29 N	107.15 W
Hayden, In., U.S.	218	38.58 N	85.44 W
Hayden Peak ∧	202	42.59 N	116.39 W
Haydenville, Ma., U.S.	207	42.22 N	72.42 W
Haydenville, Oh., U.S.	188	39.28 N	82.19 W
Haydock	262	53.28 N	2.39 W
Haydock Park Race Course ♠	262	53.29 N	2.37 W
Haydon Bridge	44	54.58 N	2.14 W

Haye, La → 's-Gravenhage	52	52.06 N	4.18 E
Hayes	194	30.06 N	92.55 W
Hayes ◆ 8, Eng., U.K.	260	51.31 N	0.25 W
Hayes ◆ 8, Eng., U.K.	260	51.23 N	0.01 E
Hayes ≃, Mb., Can.	184	57.03 N	92.09 W
Hayes ≃, N.T., Can.	176	67.18 N	95.02 W
Hayes, Mount ∧	180	63.37 N	146.43 W
Hayes Center	198	40.30 N	101.01 W
Hayes State Memorial ⊥	214	41.21 N	83.08 W
Hayesville, N.C., U.S.	192	35.02 N	83.49 W
Hayesville, Oh., U.S.	214	40.46 N	82.15 W
Hayesville, Or., U.S.	224	44.59 N	122.58 W
Hayfield, Eng., U.K.	262	53.23 N	1.57 W
Hayfield, Mn., U.S.	190	43.53 N	92.50 W
Hayford Peak ∧	204	36.40 N	115.11 W
Hayfork	204	40.33 N	123.10 W
Hayfork Bally ∧	204	40.39 N	123.13 W
Hayfork Creek ≃	204	40.37 N	123.26 W
Hay Island I	212	44.53 N	80.58 W
Hayk, Lake ⊜	144	11.21 N	39.43 E
Haykota	144	15.10 N	37.03 E
Hay Lake ⊜	212	45.23 N	78.11 W
Hay Lakes	182	53.13 N	113.03 W
Hayle	42	50.11 N	5.23 W
Haymakers Run ≃	279b	40.25 N	79.43 W
Haymana	130	39.27 N	32.30 E
Haynau → Chojnów	30	51.17 N	15.56 E
Haynes	194	34.53 N	90.47 W
Haynes Creek ≃	285	39.53 N	74.50 W
Haynesville, La., U.S.	194	32.57 N	93.08 W
Haynesville, Va., U.S.	208	37.57 N	76.40 W
Hayneville	194	32.11 N	86.34 W
Haynin	144	15.50 N	48.19 E
Hay-on-Wye	42	52.04 N	3.07 W
Hay Point >	166	21.17 S	149.18 E
Hayrabolu	130	41.12 N	27.06 E
Hay River	176	60.51 N	115.40 W
Hays, Ab., Can.	182	50.06 N	111.48 W
Hays, Ks., U.S.	198	38.52 N	99.19 W
Hays, Mt., U.S.	202	47.59 N	108.41 W
Hays □ 6	222	30.02 N	97.45 W
Hays ◆ 8	279b	40.23 N	79.56 W
Hayshah, Sabkhat al- ≡	146	31.45 N	15.20 E
Hays Mill Creek ≃	285	39.44 N	74.50 W
Hay Springs	198	42.41 N	102.41 W
Haystack Mountain ∧	204	41.39 N	115.38 W
Haysville, Ks., U.S.	198	37.33 N	97.21 W
Haysville, Pa., U.S.	279b	40.32 N	80.09 W
Hayti, Mo., U.S.	194	36.14 N	89.44 W
Hayti, Pa., U.S.	208	39.59 N	75.51 W
Hayti, S.D., U.S.	198	44.39 N	97.12 W
Hayward, Ca., U.S.	226	37.40 N	122.04 W
Hayward, Wi., U.S.	190	46.00 N	91.29 W
Hayward Brook ≃	283	42.22 N	71.20 W
Hayward Municipal Airport ⊠	282	37.40 N	122.08 W
Haywards Heath	42	51.00 N	0.06 W
Haywood	184	49.40 N	98.12 W
Ḥayy, Jabal al- ∧	142	29.43 N	31.35 E
HaZafon □ 5	132	32.50 N	35.20 E
Hazak	130	37.21 N	41.54 E
Hazara □ 8	123	34.30 N	73.15 E
Hazard	192	37.14 N	83.11 W
Hazardville	207	41.59 N	72.32 W
Hazāreh Toghāy	120	37.11 N	67.13 E
Hazar Gölü ⊜	130	38.30 N	39.25 E
Hazāribāgh	124	23.59 N	85.21 E
Hazāribāgh □ 5	126	24.00 N	85.30 E
Hazāribāgh Plateau ⋏ 1	124	24.00 N	85.10 E
Haze, Cape >	220	26.46 N	82.10 W
Hazebrouck	50	50.43 N	2.32 E
Hazel ≃	188	38.33 N	77.51 W
Hazelbrook	170	33.44 S	150.27 E
Hazel Crest	278	41.34 N	87.41 W
Hazel Dell	224	45.40 N	122.39 W
Hazel Green, Il., U.S.	278	41.41 N	87.45 W
Hazel Green, Wi., U.S.	190	42.31 N	90.26 W
Hazelgrove, Austl.	170	33.40 S	149.52 E
Hazel Grove, Eng., U.K.	262	53.23 N	2.08 W
Hazel Hurst	214	41.42 N	78.35 W
Hazel Kirk	279b	40.11 N	79.57 W
Hazel Park	216	42.27 N	83.06 W
Hazel Park Race Track ♠	281	42.29 N	83.05 W
Hazelton, B.C., Can.	182	55.15 N	127.40 W
Hazelton, Id., U.S.	202	42.35 N	114.08 W
Hazelton, N.D., U.S.	198	46.29 N	100.16 W
Hazelton Mountains ⋏	182	54.30 N	128.20 W
Hazelton Peak ∧	202	44.06 N	107.03 W
Hazelwood, Mo., U.S.	219	38.46 N	90.22 W
Hazelwood, N.C., U.S.	192	35.28 N	83.00 W
Hazelwood ◆ 8	279b	40.25 N	79.56 W
Hazen, Ar., U.S.	194	34.46 N	91.34 W
Hazen, Nv., U.S.	226	39.33 N	119.02 W
Hazen, N.D., U.S.	198	47.17 N	101.37 W
Hazen, Pa., U.S.	214	41.12 N	78.58 W
Hazen Bay ⊂	180	61.00 N	165.10 W
Ḥazerim	132	31.14 N	34.43 E
Hazlehurst, Ga., U.S.	192	31.52 N	82.35 W
Hazlehurst, Ms., U.S.	194	31.51 N	90.23 W
Hazlet, Sk., Can.	184	50.25 N	108.36 W
Hazlet, N.J., U.S.	208	40.26 N	74.13 W
Hazleton, Ia., U.S.	190	42.37 N	91.54 W
Hazleton, Pa., U.S.	210	40.57 N	75.58 W
Hazlett, Lake ⊜	162	21.30 S	128.48 E
Ḥazor	132	32.59 N	35.33 E
Hazro, Pāk.	123	33.54 N	72.29 E
Hazro, Tür.	130	38.15 N	40.47 E
Hazu	94	34.47 N	137.08 E
Hazzo	130	38.11 N	41.29 E
He ≃, Zhg.	100	27.05 N	114.59 E
He ≃, Zhg.	102	23.26 N	111.30 E
Heacham	42	52.55 N	0.30 E
Head ≃	212	44.44 N	79.15 W
Head Bay d'Espoir	186	47.56 N	55.45 W
Headcorn	42	51.11 N	0.37 E
Headford	48	53.28 N	9.05 W
Head Lake ⊜	212	44.45 N	78.55 W
Headland	194	31.21 N	85.20 W
Headlands	154	18.14 S	32.03 E
Headley, Eng., U.K.	42	51.07 N	0.50 W
Headley, Eng., U.K.	260	51.17 N	0.16 W
Headley, Mount ∧	202	47.44 N	115.15 W
Head of the Harbor	276	40.54 N	73.10 W
Heald Green	262	53.22 N	2.14 W
Heald Moor ◆ 3	262	53.44 N	2.10 W
Healdsburg	204	38.36 N	122.52 W
Healdton	196	34.13 N	97.29 W
Healesville	169	37.40 S	145.31 E
Healing	44	53.34 N	0.10 W
Healy, Ak., U.S.	180	63.52 N	148.58 W
Healy, Ks., U.S.	198	38.36 N	100.37 W
Healy, Mount ∧	180	63.46 N	149.01 W
Healy Lake ⊜	212	45.10 N	79.55 W
Heani, Mont ∧	174y	9.47 S	139.04 W
Heanna	174m	26.19 N	127.54 E
Heanor	44	53.01 N	1.22 W
Heany Junction	154	20.06 S	28.54 E
Heard Island I	6	53.06 S	73.30 E
Heard Pond ⊜	283	42.21 N	71.22 W
Hearne	222	30.52 N	96.35 W
Hearst	176	49.41 N	83.40 W
Hearst Island I	9	69.25 S	62.10 W
Hearst San Simeon State Historical Park ♠	226	35.42 N	121.10 W

Heart ≃, Ab., Can.	182	56.14 N	117.17 W
Heart ≃, N.D., U.S.	198	46.47 N	100.51 W
Heart Lake ⊜, Ab., Can.	182	55.02 N	111.30 W
Heart Lake ⊜, On., Can.	275b	43.44 N	79.48 W
Heart Lake Indian Reserve ◆ 4	182	55.02 N	111.30 W
Heart Pond ⊜	283	42.34 N	71.23 W
Heart's Content	186	47.53 N	53.22 W
Heath, Ma., U.S.	207	42.40 N	72.49 W
Heath, Oh., U.S.	214	40.02 N	82.28 W
Heath, Tx., U.S.	222	32.50 N	96.29 W
Heath ≃	248	12.31 S	68.38 W
Heath, Pointe >	186	49.05 N	61.42 W
Heathcote, Austl.	169	36.55 S	144.42 E
Heathcote, Austl.	274a	34.05 S	151.01 E
Heathcote Brook ≃	276	40.23 N	74.37 W
Heath End	42	51.22 N	1.09 W
Heatherton	274b	37.58 S	145.06 E
Heathfield	42	50.59 N	0.17 E
Heathmont	274b	37.49 S	145.15 E
Heath Springs	192	34.35 N	80.40 W
Heathsville	208	37.55 N	76.28 W
Heatley	262	53.24 N	2.27 W
Heaton Hall ⊥	262	53.32 N	2.15 W
Heaton Moor	262	53.25 N	2.11 W
Heaven, Temple of ⊛ 1	271a	39.53 N	116.25 E
Heavener	194	34.53 N	94.36 W
Heaverham	260	51.18 N	0.15 E
Heaviley	262	53.24 N	2.09 W
Hebaochang	107	29.33 N	105.32 E
Hebao Dao I	100	21.52 N	113.09 E
Hebbronville	196	27.18 N	98.40 W
Hebburn	44	54.59 N	1.30 W
Hebbville	284b	39.20 N	77.46 W
Hebden Bridge	262	53.45 N	2.00 W
Hebden Water ≃	262	53.44 N	2.00 W
Hebei, Zhg.	104	40.43 N	122.12 E
Hebei, Zhg.	104	41.01 N	123.51 E
Hebei (Hopeh) □ 4	98	38.00 N	116.00 E
Hebeitun	105	39.35 N	117.07 E
Hebel	166	28.59 S	147.48 E
Heber, Az., U.S.	200	34.25 N	110.35 W
Heber, Ca., U.S.	204	32.44 N	115.32 W
Heber City	200	40.30 N	111.24 W
Heber Springs	194	35.29 N	92.01 W
Hebgen Lake ⊜ 1	202	44.47 N	111.14 W
Hebi	98	35.59 N	114.11 E
Hebian	107	30.29 N	105.08 E
Hebo, Or., U.S.	224	45.13 N	123.51 W
Hebo, Zhg.	102	31.29 N	98.58 E
Hebo, Mount ∧	224	45.12 N	123.45 W
Hébridas, Islas → Hebrides II	46	57.00 N	6.30 W
Hebrides II	46	57.00 N	6.30 W
Hebrides, Sea of the ⍑ 2	46	57.07 N	6.55 W
Hebron, Nf., Can.	176	58.12 N	62.38 W
Hebron → Al-Khalīl, Ghaz.	132	31.32 N	35.06 E
Hebron, Ct., U.S.	207	41.39 N	72.21 W
Hebron, Il., U.S.	216	42.28 N	88.25 W
Hebron, In., U.S.	216	41.19 N	87.12 W
Hebron, Ky., U.S.	218	39.03 N	84.42 W
Hebron, Md., U.S.	208	38.25 N	75.41 W
Hebron, Ne., U.S.	198	40.09 N	97.35 W
Hebron, N.D., U.S.	198	46.54 N	102.02 W
Hebron, Pa., U.S.	208	40.21 N	76.24 W
Hebron, Tx., U.S.	222	33.01 N	96.52 W
Hebron, Wi., U.S.	216	42.56 N	88.42 W
Hebu	100	27.50 N	115.22 E
Hebutu	104	42.19 N	122.20 E
Heby	40	59.56 N	16.53 E
Hecao	105	40.21 N	116.47 E
Hecate Strait ʊ	182	53.00 N	131.00 W
Hecelchakán	232	20.10 N	90.08 W
Heceta Island I	180	55.45 N	133.35 W
Hechi	102	24.42 N	108.02 E
Hechiceros	196	28.33 N	103.38 W
Hechingen	58	48.21 N	8.58 E
Hechtel	56	51.08 N	5.21 E
Hechthausen	52	53.38 N	9.14 E
Hechuan	107	30.00 N	106.16 E
Heckelberg	54	52.44 N	13.50 E
Hecker	219	38.18 N	90.00 W
Heckington	42	52.59 N	0.18 W
Hecklingen	54	51.51 N	11.32 E
Heckscher State Park ♠	210	40.43 N	73.10 W
Hecla, Mb., Can.	184	51.08 N	96.40 W
Hecla, S.D., U.S.	198	45.52 N	98.09 W
Hecla Island I	184	51.08 N	96.45 W
Hectanooga	186	44.06 N	66.02 W
Hector, N.Z.	172	41.36 S	171.53 E
Hector, Mn., U.S.	198	44.44 N	94.42 W
Hector, Mount ∧	172	40.57 S	175.17 E
Heda	94	34.58 N	138.46 E
Hedal	26	60.37 N	9.42 E
Hedaru	154	4.30 S	37.54 E
Heddal ⊛ 1	26	59.35 N	9.11 E
Hedding	285	40.06 N	74.44 W
Hédé, Fr.	32	48.18 N	1.48 W
Hede, Sve.	26	62.25 N	13.30 E
Hedehusene	41	55.39 N	12.12 E
Hedel	52	51.45 N	5.15 E
Hedemora	40	60.17 N	15.59 E
Hedemünden	56	51.23 N	9.46 E
Hedensted	41	55.46 N	9.42 E
Hedersleben	54	51.51 N	11.15 E
Hedesunda	40	60.24 N	16.59 E
Hedesundafjärdarna ⊜	40	60.20 N	17.00 E
He Devil ∧	202	45.21 N	116.33 W
Hedge End	42	50.54 N	1.18 W
Hedgerley	260	51.35 N	0.36 W
Hedian	100	32.45 N	114.18 E
Hedley, B.C., Can.	182	49.21 N	120.04 W
Hedley, Tx., U.S.	196	34.52 N	100.39 W
Hedmark □ 6	26	61.30 N	11.45 E
Hednesford	42	52.43 N	2.00 W
Hedo	174m	26.51 N	128.16 E
Hedo-misaki >	174m	26.52 N	128.16 E
Hedon	44	53.44 N	0.12 W
Hedrick	190	41.10 N	92.18 W
Hedströmmen ≃	40	59.28 N	16.04 E
Hedutne	272c	19.10 N	73.06 E
Hedwig Village	222	29.47 N	95.27 W
Heek	52	52.07 N	7.06 E
Heel	52	51.11 N	5.53 E
Heel Point >	174a	19.19 N	166.37 E
Heemskerk	52	52.31 N	4.40 E
Heemstede	52	52.21 N	4.37 E
Heepen	52	52.01 N	8.35 E
Heer, Bel.	56	50.10 N	4.50 E
Heer, Ned.	56	50.50 N	5.44 E
Heerde	52	52.23 N	6.03 E
Heerdt ◆ 8	263	51.13 N	6.43 E
Heerenveen	52	52.57 N	5.55 E
Heeren-Werve	52	51.35 N	7.43 E
Heeres-Museum ⊛	264b	48.11 N	16.23 E
Heerhugowaard	52	52.40 N	4.50 E
Heerkan	107	29.32 N	103.56 E
Heerlen	56	50.54 N	5.59 E
Heesch	52	51.44 N	5.32 E
Heeslingen	52	53.19 N	9.20 E
Heessen	52	51.42 N	7.50 E
Heeze	52	51.24 N	5.35 E
Ḥefa (Haifa)	132	32.50 N	35.00 E
Ḥefa □ 5	132	32.35 N	35.00 E
Ḥefa, Mifraẓ ⊂	132	32.53 N	35.03 E
Ḥefa, Sede-Te'ufa ⊠	132	32.49 N	35.02 E
Hefei	100	31.51 N	117.17 E
Hefengchang	107	30.26 N	104.43 E
Heffron Park ♠	274a	33.57 S	151.15 E
Heflin	194	33.38 N	85.35 W
Hegang	89	47.24 N	130.22 E
Hegau ◆ 1	58	47.50 N	8.45 E
Hégenheim	58	47.34 N	7.32 E
Hegewisch ◆ 8	278	41.40 N	87.33 W
Hegins	208	40.39 N	76.29 W
Hegra	26	63.28 N	11.07 E
Hegura-jima I	92	37.51 N	136.55 E

≃	River	Fluss	Río	Rivière	Rio
≍	Canal	Kanal	Canal	Canal	Canal
ʟ	Waterfall, Rapids	Wasserfall, Stromschnellen	Cascada, Rápidos	Chute d'eau, Rapides	Cascata, Rápidos
ʊ	Strait	Meeresstrasse	Estrecho	Détroit	Estreito
⊂	Bay, Gulf	Bucht, Golf	Bahía, Golfo	Baie, Golfe	Baía, Golfo
⊜	Lake, Lakes	See, Seen	Lago, Lagos	Lac, Lacs	Lago, Lagos
≡	Swamp	Sumpf	Pantano	Marais	Pântano
⊓	Ice Features, Glacier	Eis- und Gletscherformen	Accidentes Glaciales	Formes glaciaires	Acidentes glaciares
⍑	Other Hydrographic Features	Andere Hydrographische Objekte	Otros Elementos Hidrográficos	Autres données hydrographiques	Outros acidentes hidrográficos

✦	Submarine Features	Untermeerische Objekte	Accidentes Submarinos	Formes de relief sous-marin	Acidentes submarinos
□	Political Unit	Politische Einheit	Unidad Politica	Entité politique	Unidade política
⊛	Cultural Institution	Kulturelle Institution	Institución Cultural	Institution culturelle	Institução cultural
⊥	Historical Site	Historische Stätte	Sitio Histórico	Site historique	Sitio histórico
♠	Recreational Site	Erholungs- und Ferienort	Sitio de Recreo	Centre de loisirs	Area de Lazer
⊠	Airport	Flughafen	Aeropuerto	Aéroport	Aeroporto
■	Military Installation	Militäranlage	Instalación Militar	Installation militaire	Instalação militar
◆	Miscellaneous	Verschiedenes	Misceláneo	Divers	Diversos

Heguri 270 34.38 N 135.42 E
Hegyeshalom 61 47.55 N 17.10 E
Hehlen 52 51.59 N 9.28 E
Heho 110 20.43 N 96.49 E
Hehou 100 28.40 N 114.28 E
Hei ≃, Zhg. 102 40.18 N 99.26 E
Hei ≃, Zhg. 105 40.44 N 116.27 E
Heicheng (Karakhoto) ⊥ 102 41.47 N 101.03 E
Heichengzhen 102 36.16 N 106.06 E
Heichengzi 104 42.10 N 121.01 E
Heidayingzi 98 40.52 N 116.12 E.
Heidberg ∧2 263 51.15 N 7.21 E
Heide 30 54.12 N 9.06 E
Heide ◆8, B.R.D. 263 51.26 N 7.01 E
Heide ◆8, B.R.D. 263 51.31 N 6.52 E
Heideck 60 49.08 N 11.07 E
Heidelberg, Austl. 169 37.45 S 145.04 E
Heidelberg, B.R.D. 56 49.25 N 8.43 E
Heidelberg, On., Can. 212 43.31 N 80.37 W
Heidelberg, S. Afr. 158 34.06 S 20.59 E
Heidelberg, S. Afr. 158 26.32 S 28.18 E
Heidelberg, Ms., U.S. 194 31.53 N 88.59 W
Heidelberg, Pa., U.S. 279b 40.23 N 80.05 W
Heidelberg □5 273d 26.19 S 28.16 E
Heidelberg, Schloss ⊥ 56 49.24 N 8.42 E
Heidelsheim 56 49.06 N 8.38 E
Heiden, B.R.D. 52 51.59 N 8.50 E
Heiden, Schw. 58 47.27 N 9.33 E
Heiden, Port c 180 56.55 N 158.45 W
Heidenau, B.R.D. 52 53.19 N 9.39 E
Heidenau, D.D.R. 54 50.59 N 13.52 E
Heidenheim 56 49.01 N 10.44 E
Heidenheim an der Brenz 56 48.40 N 10.08 E
Heidenheimer 222 31.01 N 97.18 W
Heidenoldendorf 52 51.57 N 8.50 E
Heidenreichstein 61 48.52 N 15.07 E
Heider Ditch ≍ 279a 41.31 N 82.01 W
Heiderscheid 56 49.53 N 5.54 E
Heidhausen ◆8 263 51.23 N 7.01 E
Heidhof ◆8 263 51.11 N 7.11 E
Heidlersburg 208 39.57 N 77.09 W
Heidouwo 105 39.42 N 117.15 E
Heigenbrücken 56 50.02 N 9.23 E
Heigoutaicun 104 41.30 N 123.01 E
Heigun-tō I 96 33.47 N 132.14 E
Heihai → Har Hu ⊜ 102 38.15 N 97.40 E
Heihe → Aihui 89 50.16 N 127.28 E
Heihe (Naquka) 120 31.34 N 92.00 E
Heijō → P'yŏngyang 98 39.01 N 125.45 E
Heikega-dake ∧ 96 34.19 N 131.54 E
Heikendorf 54 54.22 N 10.12 E
Heil 263 51.38 N 7.35 E
Heilangkou 105 39.37 N 117.24 E
Heilbron 158 27.21 S 27.58 E
Heilbronn 56 49.08 N 9.13 E
Heilenbecker-Stausee ⊜1 263 51.15 N 7.22 E
Heiligenberg 58 47.49 N 9.19 E
Heiligenblut 64 47.02 N 12.50 E
Heiligendamm 54 54.08 N 11.50 E
Heiligenhafen 54 54.22 N 10.58 E
Heiligenhaus 56 51.19 N 6.59 E
Heiligensee ◆8 264a 52.36 N 13.13 E
Heiligenstadt, B.R.D. 60 49.51 N 11.10 E
Heiligenstadt, D.D.R. 56 51.23 N 10.09 E
Heilin 98 35.01 N 118.58 E
Hei Ling Chau I 271d 22.15 N 114.02 E
Heilong (Amur) ≃ 89 52.56 N 141.10 E
Heilongguan 102 36.19 N 111.11 E
Heilongjiang □4 89 48.00 N 128.00 E
Heilongtan, Zhg. 105 40.44 N 116.31 E
Heilongtan, Zhg. 105 40.02 N 116.11 E
Heilongtan Shuiku ⊜1 107 30.03 N 104.02 E
Heiloo 52 52.36 N 4.43 E
Heilsberg → Lidzbark Warmiński 30 54.09 N 20.35 E
Heilsbronn 56 49.20 N 10.47 E
Heiltz-le-Maurupt 56 48.48 N 4.49 E
Heilungkiang → Heilongjiang □4 89 48.00 N 128.00 E
Heilwood 214 40.37 N 78.54 W
Heimaey I 24a 63.26 N 20.17 W
Heimbach 56 50.38 N 6.28 E
Heimbuchenthal 56 49.53 N 9.17 E
Heimburg 54 51.49 N 10.54 E
Heimdal 26 63.21 N 10.22 E
Heimenkirch 58 47.37 N 9.53 E
Heimsheim 56 48.48 N 8.51 E
Heinävesi 26 62.26 N 28.36 E
Heinersdorf, D.D.R. 54 52.27 N 14.13 E
Heinersdorf, D.D.R. 264a 52.23 N 13.20 E
Heinersdorf ◆8 264a 52.34 N 13.27 E
Heiniuyingzi 98 41.07 N 120.19 E
Heino 52 52.26 N 6.14 E
Heinola 26 61.13 N 26.02 E
Heinrichshorst 54 52.20 N 11.42 E
Heinsberg 56 51.03 N 6.05 E
Heiquan 102 39.32 N 99.42 E
Heirnkut 110 25.14 N 94.45 E
Heisfelde 52 53.15 N 7.26 E
Heishan 104 41.41 N 122.07 E
Heishanguan 98 38.33 N 113.41 E
Heishantou, Zhg. 89 50.13 N 119.28 E
Heishantou, Zhg. 98 42.28 N 125.33 E
Heishui 98 42.09 N 119.28 E
Heishuisi 102 36.08 N 108.42 E
Heisingen ◆8 263 51.25 N 7.04 E
Heisker Islands II 46 57.31 N 7.40 W
Heisler 182 52.41 N 112.13 W
Heislerville 208 39.13 N 74.59 W
Heissen ◆8 263 51.26 N 6.56 E
Heist-aan-Zee 50 51.21 N 3.15 E
Heist-op-den-Berg 56 51.05 N 4.43 E
Heitang 102 26.29 N 105.09 E
Heitersheim 58 47.53 N 7.40 E
Heiwa 94 35.12 N 136.44 E
Heiyanghebao 105 39.07 N 118.15 E
Heiyantang 102 27.28 N 101.11 E
Heiyanzi 105 39.13 N 118.08 E
Hejaz → Al-Ḥijāz ◆1 118 24.30 N 38.30 E
Hejiachang 107 29.24 N 104.56 E
Hejian, Zhg. 98 38.26 N 116.05 E
Hejian, Zhg. 105 39.25 N 116.25 E
Hejiang 107 28.49 N 105.50 E
Hejiangzhen 107 29.16 N 104.16 E
Hejiaqiao 100 27.24 N 113.21 E
Hejiawopeng 104 41.32 N 122.07 E
Hejiaying 105 39.55 N 118.19 E
Hejiazhen 107 29.52 N 104.26 E
Hejin 102 35.39 N 110.40 E
Hejlsminde 41 55.22 N 9.37 E
Hejnsvig 41 55.41 N 8.59 E
Hekelgem 50 50.54 N 4.06 E
Hekili Point › 229a 20.48 N 156.37 W
Hekimhan 130 38.49 N 37.56 E
Hekinan 94 34.51 N 136.58 E
Hekla ∧1 24a 64.00 N 19.39 W
Hekou, Zhg. 100 31.22 N 114.26 E
Hekou, Zhg. 102 36.09 N 103.22 E
Hekou, Zhg. 102 28.22 N 108.14 E
Hekou, Zhg. 102 29.57 N 111.04 E
Hekou, Zhg. 102 22.38 N 103.56 E
Hekouchang 107 29.21 N 104.21 E
Hekouji 100 32.09 N 116.04 E
Hekoujie 102 26.31 N 100.39 E
Hekpoort 158 25.55 S 27.38 E
Hel 30 54.37 N 18.48 E
Helagsfjället ∧ 26 62.55 N 12.27 E
Helaluo 102 33.56 N 102.10 E
Helangou 104 41.00 N 123.25 E
Helan Shan ⋏ 102 38.40 N 105.57 E
Helbe ≃ 54 51.13 N 11.06 E
Helbra 54 51.33 N 11.29 E
Helchteren 56 51.03 N 5.22 E
Heldburg 54 50.17 N 10.44 E
Helden 56 51.07 N 7.56 E
Heldra 56 51.07 N 10.11 E
Heldrungen 54 51.18 N 11.13 E
Helechos, Cañada de los ≃ 286a 19.22 N 99.12 W
Helemano Stream ≃ 229c 21.35 N 158.06 W
Helen, Mount ∧ 166 21.34 S 141.13 E
Helena, Ar., U.S. 194 34.31 N 90.35 W
Helena, Mt., U.S. 202 46.35 N 112.02 W
Helena, N.Y., U.S. 206 44.55 N 74.44 W
Helena, Oh., U.S. 214 41.21 N 83.18 W
Helena, Ok., U.S. 196 36.32 N 98.16 W
Helena ≃ 168a 31.54 S 116.00 E
Helena Reservoir ⊜1 168a 31.59 S 116.13 E
Helendale 228 34.45 N 117.18 W
Helenenberg 56 49.51 N 6.32 E
Helenental ◆1 264b 48.01 N 16.11 E
Helen Island I 108 2.58 N 131.49 E
Helensburgh, Austl. 170 34.11 S 150.59 E
Helensburgh, Scot., U.K. 46 56.01 N 4.44 W
Helen Springs 162 18.26 S 133.52 E
Helensville 172 36.40 S 174.28 E
Helenville 216 43.01 N 88.41 W
Helenwood 192 36.25 N 84.32 W
Ḥeleẓ 132 31.35 N 34.40 E
Helfenberg 61 48.32 N 14.08 E
Helfenstein 208 40.45 N 76.27 W
Helfta 54 51.30 N 11.34 E
Helgaå ≃ 26 55.53 N 14.08 E
Helgenæs I 41 56.08 N 10.32 E
Helgoland I 30 54.12 N 7.53 E
Helgoländer Bucht c 30 54.10 N 8.04 E
Heli 89 47.05 N 130.16 E
Helicoide ◆9 286c 10.29 N 66.55 W
Helidon 171a 27.33 S 152.08 E
Heliodora 256 22.04 S 45.32 W
Heliópolis 287a 22.45 S 43.25 W
Heliopolis → Miṣr al-Jadīdah ◆8 273c 30.06 N 31.20 E
Heliopolis ⊥ 142 30.08 N 31.17 E
Heliopolis Aerodrome ⊠ 273c 30.04 N 31.19 E
Heliopolis Racing Club ♠ 273c 30.06 N 31.19 E
Heliuji 100 33.02 N 116.57 E
Helixi 106 30.40 N 118.59 E
Hell 26 63.26 N 10.54 E
Hellam 208 40.00 N 76.36 W
Hellberge ⋏2 54 52.34 N 11.17 E
Hellbrunn, Schloss ⊥ 64 47.46 N 13.04 E
Hellebæk 41 56.04 N 12.34 E
Helleh ≃ 128 29.10 N 50.40 E
Hellen Blazes, Lake ⊜ 220 28.01 N 80.47 W
Hellendoorn 52 52.24 N 6.26 E
Hellenthal 56 50.29 N 6.26 E
Hellerau ◆8 54 51.07 N 13.44 E
Hellern 52 52.15 N 7.58 E
Hellersen 263 51.12 N 7.39 E
Hellertown 208 40.34 N 75.20 W
Hellesylt 26 62.05 N 6.54 E
Hellevad 41 55.05 N 9.13 E
Hellevoetsluis 52 51.49 N 4.08 E
Hell Gate 276 40.47 N 73.56 W
Hell Hole Reservoir ⊜1 226 39.04 N 120.22 W
Hellifield 44 54.01 N 2.12 W
Hellín 34 38.31 N 1.41 W
Helli Ness › 46 60.02 N 1.10 W
Hellmonsödt 61 48.26 N 14.18 E
Hell Point › 186 44.16 N 64.15 W
Hells Canyon V 202 45.20 N 116.45 W
Hellsee ⊜ 264a 52.45 N 13.35 E
Hells Gate V 182 49.47 N 121.27 W
Hell-Ville 157b 13.25 S 48.16 E
Hellweg ◆1 52 51.32 N 7.47 E
Helm 226 36.31 N 120.05 W
Helmand □4 128 31.00 N 64.00 E
Helmand ≃ 128 31.12 N 61.34 E
Helmbrechts 54 50.14 N 11.43 E
Helmcken Falls ∟ 182 51.57 N 120.11 W
Helme ≃ 54 51.20 N 11.20 E
Helmeringhausen 156 25.54 S 16.57 E
Helmetta 276 40.22 N 74.25 W
Helmetta Pond ⊜ 276 40.23 N 74.26 W
Helmond 52 51.29 N 5.40 E
Helmsburg 218 39.16 N 86.18 W
Helmsdale 46 58.07 N 3.40 W
Helmsdale ≃ 46 58.07 N 3.40 W
Helmshore 262 53.41 N 2.20 W
Helmsley 44 54.14 N 1.04 W
Helmstedt 54 52.13 N 11.00 E
Helnæs I 41 55.08 N 10.02 E
Helong 98 42.32 N 128.59 E
Helper 200 39.41 N 110.51 W
Helpmekaar 158 28.29 S 30.29 E
Helpter Berg ∧2 54 53.30 N 13.36 E
Helsby 262 53.16 N 2.46 W
Helsby Hill ∧2 262 53.16 N 2.46 W
Helsingborg 41 56.03 N 12.42 E
Helsinge 41 56.01 N 12.12 E
Helsingfors → Helsinki 26 60.10 N 24.58 E
Helsingør (Elsinore) 41 56.02 N 12.37 E
Helsinki (Helsingfors) 26 60.10 N 24.58 E
Helska, Mierzeja ›2 30 54.45 N 18.39 E
Helston 42 50.05 N 5.16 W
Heltonville 218 38.55 N 86.22 W
Helvecia 252 31.06 S 60.05 W
Helvellyn ∧ 44 54.31 N 3.01 W
Helvick Head › 48 52.03 N 7.33 W
Helvoirt 52 51.38 N 5.13 E
Hem ≃ 50 50.51 N 2.06 E
Ḥemar, Naḥal V 132 31.08 N 35.22 E
Hemau 60 49.03 N 11.47 E
Hemāvati ≃ 122 12.31 N 76.27 E
Hembe 152 1.54 N 22.42 E
Hemel Hempstead 260 51.46 N 0.28 W
Hemelingen ◆8 52 53.03 N 8.53 E
Hemeln 52 51.30 N 9.36 E
Hemer 56 51.23 N 7.46 E
Hemet 228 33.44 N 116.58 W
Hemfjärden c 40 59.17 N 15.20 E
Hemford 186 44.30 N 64.47 W
Hemfurth-Edersee 56 51.10 N 9.02 E
Hemiksem 50 51.09 N 4.21 E
Héming 58 48.42 N 6.57 E
Hemingford 198 42.19 N 103.04 W
Hemingway 192 33.45 N 79.26 W
Hemlock, In., U.S. 216 40.25 N 86.03 W
Hemlock, N.Y., U.S. 210 42.47 N 77.36 W
Hemlock Lake ⊜ 210 42.43 N 77.37 W
Hemmerde 52 51.33 N 7.48 E
Hemmerden 263 51.07 N 6.36 E
Hemmingen-Westerfeld 52 52.19 N 9.45 E
Hemmoor 52 53.41 N 9.08 E
Hemphill 194 31.20 N 93.50 W
Hempnall 42 52.30 N 1.19 E
Hempstead, N.Y., U.S. 210 40.42 N 73.37 W
Hempstead, Tx., U.S. 222 30.05 N 96.04 W
Hempstead Harbor c 276 40.50 N 73.39 W
Hempstead Lake ⊜ 276 40.41 N 73.38 W
Hempstead Lake State Park ♠ 276 40.41 N 73.38 W
Hemsby 42 52.41 N 1.42 E
Hemse 26 57.14 N 18.22 E
Hemsedal 26 60.52 N 8.34 E
Hemsön I 26 62.43 N 18.05 E
Hemstreet Park 210 42.54 N 73.41 W
Hemsworth 44 53.38 N 1.21 W
Hemujing 98 37.54 N 115.22 E
Henan 102 34.35 N 101.34 E
Henan (Honan) □4 90 34.00 N 114.00 E
Hen and Chickens II 172 35.55 S 174.45 E
Henares ≃ 34 40.24 N 3.30 W
Henbury, Austl. 162 24.35 S 133.15 E
Henbury, Eng., U.K. 262 53.15 N 2.11 W
Hendek 130 40.48 N 30.45 E
Henderson, Arg. 252 36.18 S 61.43 W
Henderson, In., U.S. 218 39.40 N 85.31 W
Henderson, Ky., U.S. 194 37.50 N 87.35 W
Henderson, Mn., U.S. 190 44.31 N 93.54 W
Henderson, Ne., U.S. 198 40.46 N 97.48 W
Henderson, Nv., U.S. 204 36.02 N 114.58 W
Henderson, N.Y., U.S. 212 43.51 N 76.11 W
Henderson, N.C., U.S. 192 36.19 N 78.23 W
Henderson, Tn., U.S. 194 35.26 N 88.38 W
Henderson, Tx., U.S. 222 32.09 N 94.47 W
Henderson □6 222 32.13 N 95.50 W
Henderson Bay c, N.Y., U.S. 212 43.54 N 76.10 W
Henderson Bay c, Wa., U.S. 224 47.18 N 122.42 W
Henderson Creek ≃ 190 40.52 N 91.02 W
Henderson Island I 6 24.22 S 128.19 W
Hendersonville, N.C., U.S. 192 35.19 N 82.27 W
Hendersonville, Pa., U.S. 214 40.18 N 80.09 W
Hendersonville, Tn., U.S. 194 36.18 N 86.37 W
Hendījān 128 30.14 N 49.43 E
Hendon ◆8 260 51.35 N 0.14 W
Hendorābī, Jazīreh-ye I 128 26.40 N 53.37 E
Hendricks, Mn., U.S. 198 44.30 N 96.25 W
Hendricks, W.V., U.S. 188 39.04 N 79.37 W
Hendricks □6 218 39.46 N 86.26 W
Hendrik Verwoerddam ⊜1 158 30.40 S 25.40 E
Hendrina 158 26.11 S 29.45 E
Hendry □6 220 26.36 N 81.13 W
Hendrysburg 214 40.04 N 81.10 W
Hendy 42 51.43 N 4.04 W
Henefer 200 41.01 N 111.29 W
Henfield 42 50.56 N 0.17 W
Heng ≃, Zhg. 102 28.40 N 104.25 E
Heng ≃, Zhg. 107 28.57 N 105.22 E
Hengām, Jazīreh-ye I 128 26.39 N 55.53 E
Henganofi 164 6.15 S 145.35 E
Hengchow → Hengyang 102 26.54 N 112.36 E
Hengdaochuan 98 41.15 N 125.31 E
Hengdaohe 104 42.02 N 123.51 E
Hengdaohezi 89 43.13 N 126.44 E
Hengdaozi 89 43.18 N 127.18 E
Hengdong 100 27.03 N 112.57 E
Hengelo 52 52.15 N 6.45 E
Hengersberg 60 48.47 N 13.03 E
Hengfan 106 30.20 N 119.45 E
Hengfeng 100 28.24 N 117.34 E
Henggang 100 29.32 N 115.27 E
Henggouzi 89 43.12 N 124.47 E
Henghutou 104 42.05 N 124.00 E
Hengjie 106 31.13 N 119.30 E
Hengjing 106 31.11 N 120.32 E
Hengjinghong 106 30.34 N 120.59 E
Hengli 100 23.12 N 114.37 E
Henglin 106 31.42 N 120.06 E
Henglu 98 41.26 N 126.04 E
Henglutou 106 30.19 N 119.19 E
Hengmian 106 31.09 N 121.38 E
Hengoed 42 51.39 N 3.10 W
Hengsen 263 51.29 N 7.38 E
Heng Sha I 106 31.20 N 121.50 E
Hengshan, Zhg. 100 27.15 N 112.51 E
Hengshan, Zhg. 102 37.56 N 108.53 E
Hengshan, Zhg. 106 31.01 N 120.32 E
Heng Shan ∧ 100 27.16 N 112.35 E
Heng Shan ⋏ 102 39.30 N 113.45 E
Hengshanchang 107 30.33 N 105.24 E
Hengshanqiao 106 31.46 N 120.07 E
Hengshanxia 106 30.18 N 118.44 E
Hengshi, Zhg. 100 26.05 N 114.38 E
Hengshi, Zhg. 100 23.52 N 113.15 E
Hengshi, Zhg. 100 29.32 N 114.41 E
Hengshui 98 37.43 N 115.40 E
Hengsteysee ⊜1 263 51.25 N 7.28 E
Hengtangshi 106 31.41 N 121.02 E
Hengtianchi 107 29.07 N 105.01 E
Hengtianxi 107 29.05 N 105.03 E
Hengxi, Zhg. 100 29.42 N 121.35 E
Hengxi, Zhg. 100 28.46 N 120.29 E
Hengxi, Zhg. 106 31.43 N 118.46 E
Hengxian 102 22.42 N 109.13 E
Hengxiang 106 32.12 N 120.15 E
Hengxikou 100 29.26 N 121.26 E
Hengyang 102 26.54 N 112.36 E
Hénin-Beaumont 50 50.25 N 2.56 E
Henley Beach 168b 34.55 S 138.30 E
Henley-in-Arden 42 52.17 N 1.46 W
Henley-on-Thames 42 51.32 N 0.56 W
Henlopen, Cape › 208 38.48 N 75.05 W
Henlow 42 52.02 N 0.18 W
Hennan ⊜ 26 62.06 N 15.46 E
Hennaya 34 34.58 N 1.22 W
Henneberg 54 50.29 N 10.21 E
Hennebont 32 47.48 N 3.17 W
Hennef 56 50.46 N 7.16 E
Hennen 56 51.27 N 7.39 E
Hennenman 158 27.59 S 27.01 E
Hennepin 190 41.15 N 89.21 W
Hennepin, Point › 281 42.12 N 83.09 W
Hennersdorf 264b 48.07 N 16.22 E
Hennessey 196 36.06 N 97.53 W
Hennessey, Lake ⊜1 226 38.29 N 122.22 W
Hennickendorf 54 52.30 N 13.51 E
Henniez 58 46.44 N 6.54 E
Hennigsdorf 54 52.38 N 13.12 E
Henniker 188 43.10 N 71.49 W
Henning, Il., U.S. 216 40.18 N 87.42 W
Henning, Mn., U.S. 198 46.19 N 95.26 W
Henning, Tn., U.S. 194 35.40 N 89.34 W
Henri ≃ 206 46.30 N 71.47 W
Henri, Cap › 186 49.48 N 64.23 W
Henri-Chapelle 56 50.40 N 5.56 E
Henrichemont 50 47.18 N 2.32 E
Henrichenburg 263 51.35 N 7.19 E
Henrico □6 208 37.30 N 77.20 W
Henrietta, N.Y., U.S. 210 43.03 N 77.36 W
Henrietta, N.C., U.S. 192 35.15 N 81.47 W
Henrietta, Tx., U.S. 196 33.49 N 98.11 W
Henrietta Maria, Cape › 176 55.09 N 82.20 W
Henry, Il., U.S. 190 41.06 N 89.21 W
Henry, S.D., U.S. 198 44.52 N 97.27 W
Henry □6, In., U.S. 218 39.55 N 85.22 W
Henry □6, Ky., U.S. 218 38.26 N 85.09 W
Henry □6, Oh., U.S. 216 41.20 N 84.04 W
Henry ≃ 162 22.40 S 115.40 E
Henry, Cape › 208 36.55 N 76.01 W
Henry, Mount ∧ 202 48.53 N 115.31 W
Henry, Mount ∧2 274a 33.50 S 150.38 E
Henry, Point › 162 34.29 S 119.23 E
Henry Cowell Redwoods State Park ♠ 226 37.02 N 122.03 W
Henryetta 196 35.26 N 95.58 W
Henry Island I 224 48.35 N 123.11 W
Henry Kater, Cape › 176 69.05 N 66.44 W
Henry Mountains ⋏ 200 38.00 N 110.50 W
Henry Pittier, Parque Nacional ♠ 246 10.25 N 67.43 W
Henrys Bend 214 41.28 N 79.37 W
Henrys Fork ≃, U.S. 200 41.00 N 109.39 W
Henrys Fork ≃, Id., U.S. 202 43.45 N 111.56 W
Henryville, P.Q., Can. 206 45.08 N 73.11 W
Henryville, In., U.S. 218 38.32 N 85.46 W
Henry W. Coe State Park ♠ 226 37.12 N 121.30 W
Hensall 190 43.26 N 81.30 W
Henshaw, Lake ⊜1 204 33.15 N 116.45 W
Hensley 194 34.30 N 92.12 W
Hensley Lake ⊜1 226 37.07 N 119.53 W
Henslow, Cape › 175e 9.56 S 160.38 E
Henson Creek ≃ 284b 38.46 N 77.00 W
Hensonville 210 42.17 N 74.13 W
Henstedt-Ulzburg 52 53.47 N 9.58 E
Henstridge 42 50.59 N 2.24 W
Hentiesbaai 156 22.08 S 14.18 E
Henty 166 35.31 S 147.02 E
Henzada 110 17.38 N 95.28 E
Hepburn 184 52.31 N 106.43 W
Hepburn Springs 169 37.19 S 144.09 E
Hephzibah 192 33.18 N 82.05 W
Heping, Zhg. 100 23.17 N 116.29 E
Heping, Zhg. 100 24.28 N 114.58 E
Heping, Zhg. 100 27.10 N 117.18 E
Heping, Zhg. 100 22.01 N 112.59 E
Heping, Zhg. 106 30.50 N 119.54 E
Heppenheim 56 49.39 N 8.38 E
Heppner 202 45.21 N 119.33 W
Heptonstall 262 53.45 N 2.01 W
Heptonstall Moor ≃ 262 53.46 N 2.05 W
Hepu (Lianzhou) 102 21.39 N 109.11 E
Hepworth 212 44.37 N 81.09 W
Heqiao, Zhg. 100 32.55 N 118.22 E
Heqiao, Zhg. 106 31.30 N 119.53 E
Heqing 102 26.34 N 100.12 E
Hequ 102 39.26 N 111.08 E
Héraðsflói c 24a 65.45 N 14.10 W
Hera Lacinia, Tempio di ⊥ 68 39.01 N 17.13 E
Herāt 128 34.20 N 62.12 E
Herāt □4 128 34.30 N 62.00 E
Hérault □5 32 43.40 N 3.30 E
Hérault ≃ 32 43.17 N 3.26 E
Herbasse ≃ 62 45.02 N 4.57 E
Herbault 50 47.36 N 1.08 E
Herbede 56 51.25 N 7.16 E
Herbern 52 51.44 N 7.39 E
Herbert, Sk., Can. 184 50.26 N 107.12 W
Herbert, N.Z. 172 45.14 S 170.47 E
Herbert ≃ 166 18.32 S 146.17 E
Herbertabad 110 11.43 N 92.37 E
Herbert Hoover National Historic Site ⊥ 190 41.38 N 91.23 W
Herbertingen 58 48.04 N 9.26 E
Herbert Island I 180 52.45 N 170.10 W
Herberton 166 17.23 S 145.23 E
Herbert Peak ∧ 172 43.41 S 172.44 E
Herbertsdale 158 34.01 S 21.46 E
Herbeumont 56 49.47 N 5.14 E
Herbignac 32 47.27 N 2.19 W
Herb Lake 184 54.47 N 99.47 W
Herblay 50 49.00 N 2.10 E
Herblet Lake ⊜ 184 54.56 N 99.54 W
Herbolzheim 58 48.13 N 7.47 E
Herborn 56 50.40 N 8.17 E
Herbrechtingen 56 48.37 N 10.10 E
Herbsleben 54 51.07 N 10.50 E
Herbstein 56 50.34 N 9.20 E
Herceg-Novi 38 42.27 N 18.32 E
Herculaneum 219 38.16 N 90.22 W
Hercules 282 38.01 N 122.17 W
Herdecke 56 51.24 N 7.26 E
Herdorf 56 50.46 N 7.56 E
Herðubreið ∧ 24a 65.13 N 16.18 W
Heredia 236 10.00 N 84.07 W
Heredia □4 236 10.30 N 84.00 W
Hereford, Eng., U.K. 42 52.04 N 2.43 W
Hereford, Az., U.S. 200 31.26 N 110.05 W
Hereford, Md., U.S. 208 39.35 N 76.39 W
Hereford, Tx., U.S. 196 34.48 N 102.23 W
Hereford and Worcester □6 42 52.10 N 2.30 W
Hereford Cathedral ♁1 42 52.04 N 2.43 W
Hereford Mountain ∧ 206 45.05 N 71.36 W
Hereke 130 40.48 N 29.39 E
Herekino 172 35.15 S 173.13 E
Herencia 34 39.21 N 3.22 W
Herent 56 50.54 N 4.40 E
Herentals 56 51.11 N 4.50 E
Hereroland Oos □5 156 21.00 S 20.00 E
Hereroland Wes □5 156 20.30 S 18.15 E
Herfølge 41 55.25 N 12.10 E
Herford 52 52.06 N 8.40 E
Hergatz 58 47.39 N 9.50 E
Hergisdorf 54 51.32 N 11.28 E
Hergla 36 36.02 N 10.31 E
Herhahn 56 50.33 N 6.26 E
Herheri 130 37.41 N 39.00 E
Héricourt 58 47.35 N 6.45 E
Hérimoncourt 58 47.26 N 6.53 E
Heringen 54 51.27 N 10.52 E
Heringsdorf 54 54.18 N 11.00 E
Herington 198 38.40 N 96.56 W
Heriot 172 45.50 S 169.16 E
Herisau 58 47.23 N 9.17 E
Heritage Range ⋏ 9 79.30 S 84.00 W
Herk ≃ 56 50.58 N 5.07 E
Herk-de-Stad 56 50.56 N 5.10 E
Herkimer 210 43.01 N 74.59 W
Herkimer □6 210 43.02 N 74.59 W
Herlen → Kerulen ≃ 90 48.48 N 117.00 E
Herleshausen 56 51.00 N 10.09 E
Herlev 41 55.43 N 12.27 E
Herlong 204 40.09 N 120.08 W
Herlufmagle 41 55.19 N 11.46 E
Herlufsholm 41 55.15 N 11.46 E
Hermagor 64 46.37 N 13.22 E
Herman, Mn., U.S. 198 45.48 N 96.08 W
Herman, Ne., U.S. 198 41.40 N 96.12 W
Herman, Pa., U.S. 214 40.50 N 79.49 W
Herman, Lake ⊜ 282 38.05 N 122.09 W
Hermana Mayor Island I 116 15.48 N 119.48 E
Hermanas 196 27.13 N 101.14 W
Herman Eksteen Park ♠ 273d 26.10 S 28.02 E
Herma Ness › 46a 60.50 N 0.55 W
Hermann 219 38.42 N 91.26 W
Hermannsburg, Austl. 162 23.57 S 132.45 E
Hermannsburg, B.R.D. 52 52.50 N 10.05 E
Hermanns-Denkmal ⊥ 52 51.55 N 8.50 E
Hermannskogel ∧ 264b 48.16 N 16.18 E
Hermannstadt → Sibiu 38 45.48 N 24.09 E
Hermano Peak ∧ 200 37.13 N 108.48 W
Hermansverk 26 61.11 N 6.51 E
Hermansville 190 45.42 N 87.36 W
Hermanus 158 34.25 S 19.16 E
Hermanville 194 31.57 N 90.50 W
Hermeray 261 48.38 N 1.41 E
Hermes 50 49.22 N 2.15 E
Hermeskeil 56 49.39 N 6.56 E
Hermidale 166 31.33 S 146.43 E
Hermies 50 50.07 N 3.02 E
Herminie 214 40.15 N 79.43 W
Hermiston 202 45.50 N 119.17 W
Hermitage, Nf., Can. 186 47.33 N 55.56 W
Hermitage, N.Z. 172 43.44 S 170.06 E
Hermitage, Eng., U.K. 42 51.27 N 1.16 W
Hermitage, Ar., U.S. 194 33.26 N 92.10 W
Hermitage, Mo., U.S. 194 37.56 N 93.18 W
Hermitage Bay c 186 47.35 N 56.05 W
Hermitage Park 284c 39.05 N 77.04 W
Hermit Islands II 164 1.30 S 145.05 E
Hermleigh 196 32.38 N 100.46 W
Hermon, S. Afr. 158 33.27 S 18.59 E
Hermon, N.Y., U.S. 212 44.28 N 75.13 W
Hermon, Mount → Shaykh, Jabal ash- ∧ 132 33.26 N 35.51 E

ENGLISH				DEUTSCH			
Name	Page	Lat.°′	Long.°′	Name	Seite	Breite°′	Länge°′ E = Ost

Hermosa Beach 280 33.51 N 118.23 W
Hermosillo, Méx. 200 32.30 N 114.59 W
Hermosillo, Méx. 232 29.04 N 110.58 W
Hermoso, Cerro ∧ 246 1.10 S 78.12 W
Hermsdorf 54 50.54 N 11.52 E
Hermsdorf ◆8 264a 52.37 N 13.18 E
Hermyingyi 110 14.15 N 98.21 E
Hernád ≃ 30 47.56 N 21.08 E
Hernals ◆8 264b 48.13 N 16.20 E
Hernandarias 252 25.22 S 54.45 W
Hernández 234 23.01 N 102.01 W
Hernandez Reservoir ⊜1 226 36.22 N 120.49 W
Hernando, Arg. 252 32.25 S 63.44 W
Hernando, Fl., U.S. 220 28.54 N 82.22 W
Hernando, Ms., U.S. 194 34.49 N 89.59 W
Hernando □6 220 28.34 N 82.22 W
Hernani 116 11.20 N 125.37 E
Herndon, Ca., U.S. 226 36.49 N 119.54 W
Herndon, Ks., U.S. 198 39.54 N 100.47 W
Herndon, Pa., U.S. 210 40.42 N 76.50 W
Herndon, Va., U.S. 208 38.58 N 77.23 W
Herndon Canal ≍ 226 36.46 N 119.46 W
Herne 52 51.32 N 7.13 E
Herne Bay 42 51.23 N 1.08 E
Herne Hill 168a 31.50 S 116.01 E
Herning 41 56.08 N 8.59 E
Hernwood Heights 284b 39.22 N 77.50 W
Heroica Caborca 232 30.37 N 112.06 W
Heroica Nogales 232 31.20 N 110.56 W
Herongate 260 51.36 N 0.21 E
Herongen 56 51.24 N 6.15 E
Heron Lake 198 43.47 N 95.19 W
Hérons, Île aux I 275a 45.25 N 73.35 W
Heronsgate 260 51.38 N 0.31 W
Hérouville 261 49.06 N 2.08 E
Hérouville-Saint-Clair 32 49.12 N 0.21 W
Herpf 54 50.34 N 10.20 E
Herradura 252 26.29 S 58.18 W
Herräng 40 60.08 N 18.39 E
Herreid 198 45.50 N 100.04 W
Herrenalb 56 48.48 N 8.26 E
Herrenberg 56 48.35 N 8.52 E
Herrenchiemsee, Schloss ⊥ 64 47.52 N 12.23 E
Herrera 252 28.29 S 63.04 W
Herrera □4 236 7.54 N 80.38 W
Herrera del Duque 34 39.10 N 5.03 W
Herrera de Pisuerga 34 42.36 N 4.20 W
Herrick, Austl. 166 41.06 S 147.52 E
Herrick, Il., U.S. 219 39.13 N 88.59 W
Herrick Creek ≃ 182 54.20 N 121.30 W
Herrick Grove 212 44.04 N 76.12 W
Herricks 276 40.45 N 73.40 W
Herrieden 56 49.14 N 10.30 E
Herrin 194 37.48 N 89.01 W
Herring Bay c 208 38.44 N 76.33 W
Herring Brook ≃ 283 42.10 N 70.44 W
Herring Cove, N.S., Can. 186 44.34 N 63.34 W
Herring Cove, Ak., U.S. 182 55.21 N 131.41 W
Herring Creek ≃ 208 37.49 N 77.07 W
Herringen 52 51.40 N 7.44 E
Herring Run ≃ 284b 39.18 N 76.31 W
Herring Run Park ♠ 284b 39.19 N 76.33 W
Herritslev 41 54.42 N 11.41 E
Herrljunga 26 58.05 N 13.02 E
Herrnburg 54 53.47 N 10.45 E
Herrnhut 54 51.01 N 14.44 E
Herrnstadt → Wąsosz 30 51.34 N 16.42 E
Herrsching am Ammersee 60 48.00 N 11.10 E
Herrs Island I 279b 40.28 N 79.58 W
Herrskogen 40 59.32 N 16.15 E
Herry 50 47.13 N 2.57 E
Hersbruck 60 49.30 N 11.26 E
Herschbach 56 50.34 N 7.44 E
Herscheid 56 51.10 N 7.44 E
Herschel, Sk., Can. 184 51.38 N 108.21 W
Herschel, Transkei 158 30.37 S 27.12 E
Herschel Island I 180 69.35 N 139.05 W
Herscher 216 41.03 N 88.06 W
Herselt 56 51.03 N 4.53 E
Herserange 56 49.31 N 5.47 E
Hersham 260 51.22 N 0.23 W
Hershey, Ne., U.S. 198 41.09 N 101.00 W
Hershey, Pa., U.S. 208 40.17 N 76.39 W
Hersman 219 39.57 N 90.44 W
Herstadberg 40 58.38 N 16.10 E
Herstal 56 50.40 N 5.38 E
Herstmonceux 42 50.53 N 0.20 E
Herten 52 51.35 N 7.07 E
Hertford, Eng., U.K. 260 51.48 N 0.05 W
Hertford, N.C., U.S. 192 36.11 N 76.27 W
Hertford □6 208 36.28 N 77.01 W
Hertfordshire □6 42 51.50 N 0.10 W
Hertingfordbury 260 51.48 N 0.06 W
Hertsmere □8 260 51.41 N 0.17 W
Hertzogville 158 28.08 S 25.33 E
Heruncun 104 40.58 N 123.27 E
Hervás 34 40.16 N 5.51 W
Herve 56 50.38 N 5.48 E
Hervel d'Oeste 252 27.13 S 51.34 W
Hervest 263 51.40 N 7.01 E
Hervey Bay c 166 25.00 S 153.00 E
Herxheim 56 49.09 N 8.13 E
Héry, Fr. 50 47.54 N 3.38 E
Héry, Fr. 62 45.46 N 6.28 E
Herzberg, D.D.R. 54 52.54 N 12.58 E
Herzberg, D.D.R. 54 51.41 N 13.14 E
Herzberg am Harz 52 51.39 N 10.20 E
Herzebrock 52 51.53 N 8.14 E
Herzfelde 54 52.29 N 13.50 E
Herzhausen 56 51.11 N 8.53 E
Herzliyya 132 32.10 N 34.51 E
Herznach 58 47.28 N 8.03 E
Herzogenaurach 56 49.34 N 10.53 E
Herzogenbuchsee 58 47.12 N 7.41 E
Herzogenburg 61 48.17 N 15.42 E
Herzogenrath 56 50.52 N 6.06 E
Herzsprung 54 53.04 N 12.28 E
Ḥeṣār, Kūh-e ⋏ 120 34.50 N 66.35 E
Hesarak 267d 35.47 N 51.19 E
Hesdin 50 50.22 N 2.02 E
Hesel 52 53.18 N 7.35 E
Hesepe 52 52.26 N 7.58 E
Heshachang 107 30.37 N 105.40 E
Heshangqiao 100 34.15 N 113.47 E
Heshe 110 19.41 N 109.42 E
Heshengqiao 100 30.00 N 114.22 E
Heshi, Zhg. 100 25.04 N 118.37 E
Heshi, Zhg. 107 29.10 N 104.22 E
Heshui, Zhg. 100 24.24 N 114.56 E
Heshui, Zhg. 102 22.48 N 112.29 E
Heshuijian 100 30.33 N 116.05 E
Heshun, Zhg. 100 27.30 N 117.24 E
Heshun, Zhg. 102 37.21 N 113.35 E
Heshuo 86 42.15 N 86.53 E
Hesketh Bank 262 53.42 N 2.51 W
Hesketh Out Marsh ≡ 262 53.43 N 2.55 W
Heskin Green 262 53.38 N 2.42 W
Hesler 218 38.28 N 84.47 W
Hesperange 56 49.34 N 6.09 E
Hesperia, Ca., U.S. 228 34.25 N 117.18 W
Hesperia, Mi., U.S. 190 43.34 N 86.02 W
Hesperus Mountain ∧ 200 37.27 N 108.05 W
Hess ≃ 180 63.34 N 133.57 W
Hesselager 41 55.10 N 10.45 E
Hesselberg ∧ 56 49.04 N 10.32 E
Hesselø I 41 56.12 N 11.43 E
Hesselte 52 52.25 N 7.22 E
Hessen 54 52.02 N 10.15 E
Hessen □3 30 50.30 N 9.15 E
Hessen Cassal 216 41.00 N 85.05 W
Hessenthal 56 49.55 N 9.17 E
Hessisch Lichtenau 56 51.12 N 9.43 E
Hessisch Oldendorf 52 52.10 N 9.15 E
Hessle 44 53.44 N 0.26 W
Hesso 166 32.08 S 137.27 E
Hess Tablemount ✦3 14 17.50 N 174.15 W
Hesston, Ks., U.S. 198 38.08 N 97.25 W
Hesston, Pa., U.S. 214 40.26 N 78.07 W
Heston ◆8 260 51.29 N 0.22 W
Heswall 262 53.20 N 3.06 W
Het ≃ 110 20.49 N 104.01 E
Hetai 102 23.22 N 112.19 E
Hetanbu 100 28.21 N 117.11 E
Hetang, Zhg. 100 26.40 N 119.09 E
Hetang, Zhg. 106 31.43 N 120.27 E
Hetang, Zhg. 107 28.58 N 106.03 E
Hetch Hetchy Aqueduct ≍1 226 37.29 N 122.19 W
Hetch Hetchy Reservoir ⊜1 226 37.57 N 119.43 W
Hethersett 42 52.36 N 1.11 E
Hetian, Zhg. 100 25.41 N 116.26 E
Hetian, Zhg. 100 23.19 N 115.38 E
Hetian, Zhg. 120 37.08 N 79.54 E
Het Loo, Paleis ♁ 52 52.14 N 5.56 E
Hetou 100 24.18 N 113.29 E
Hetoudian 98 37.02 N 120.35 E
Hettange-Grande 56 49.24 N 6.09 E
Hettenleidelheim 56 49.32 N 8.04 E
Hettick 219 39.21 N 90.02 W
Hettingen 58 48.13 N 9.14 E
Hettinger 198 46.00 N 102.38 W
Hetton-le-Hole 44 54.50 N 1.27 W
Hettstedt 54 51.38 N 11.30 E
Hetupu 100 30.50 N 116.03 E
Hetzendorf ◆8 264b 48.10 N 16.18 E
Hetzerath 56 49.52 N 6.49 E
Het Zoute 50 51.21 N 3.18 E
Heuchin 50 50.28 N 2.16 E
Heudeber 54 51.54 N 10.50 E
Heule 50 50.50 N 3.14 E
Heuningspruit 158 27.26 S 27.28 E
Heusden 50 51.02 N 5.16 E
Heustreu 56 50.21 N 10.15 E
Heusweiler 56 49.20 N 6.55 E
Heuvelton 212 44.37 N 75.24 W
Hève, Cap de la › 50 49.31 N 0.04 E
Heven ◆8 263 51.26 N 7.17 E
Heverlee 56 50.52 N 4.42 E
Heves 30 47.36 N 20.17 E
Heves □6 30 47.50 N 20.15 E
Hevlín 61 48.45 N 16.23 E
Hewitt, N.J., U.S. 210 41.08 N 74.18 W
Hewitt, Tx., U.S. 222 31.27 N 97.11 W
Hewittsville 219 39.32 N 89.19 W
Hewlett, N.Y., U.S. 276 40.38 N 73.41 W
Hewlett, Va., U.S. 208 37.55 N 77.35 W
Hewlett Bay Park 276 40.38 N 73.42 W
Hewlett Harbor 276 40.38 N 73.41 W
Hewlett Neck 276 40.37 N 73.42 W
Hewlett Point › 276 40.50 N 73.45 W
Hewopu 104 41.14 N 122.24 E
Hewu 100 26.41 N 113.40 E
Hexen Kopf ∧ 58 47.01 N 10.28 E
Hexham 44 54.58 N 2.06 W
Hexi, Zhg. 100 24.52 N 117.15 E
Hexi, Zhg. 102 24.09 N 102.39 E
Hexi, Zhg. 106 31.03 N 119.49 E
Hexian, Zhg. 100 31.43 N 118.22 E
Hexian, Zhg. 102 24.15 N 111.43 E
Hexibao 102 38.34 N 102.11 E
Hexingchang 107 30.05 N 104.35 E
Hexingjie 106 31.55 N 120.36 E
Hexiwu 105 39.38 N 116.58 E
Hex Rivierberge ⋏ 158 33.25 S 19.37 E
Hextable 260 51.25 N 0.11 E
Hexton 172 38.37 S 177.58 E
Heyan 104 42.30 N 120.29 E
Heyang, Zhg. 98 35.27 N 118.33 E
Heyang, Zhg. 102 35.15 N 110.06 E
Heybeli ◆8 267b 40.53 N 29.05 E
Heybeliada I 267b 40.53 N 29.05 E
Heybridge 260 51.44 N 0.41 E
Heyburn 202 42.33 N 113.45 W
Heyderbreck → Kędzierzyn 30 50.20 N 18.12 E
Heyerode 54 51.10 N 10.25 E
Heyrieux 62 45.38 N 5.03 E
Heysham 44 54.02 N 2.54 W
Heyuan 100 23.44 N 114.41 E
Heywood, Austl. 166 38.08 S 141.38 E
Heywood, Eng., U.K. 262 53.36 N 2.13 W
Heyworth 216 40.18 N 88.58 W
Hezan 130 38.21 N 40.38 E
Heze (Caozhou) 98 35.17 N 115.27 E
Hezhang 102 27.00 N 104.37 E
Hezhao 98 37.08 N 115.17 E
Hezhen 100 29.56 N 120.10 E
Hezheng 102 35.25 N 103.10 E
Hezijian 105 40.13 N 116.03 E
Hezixu 100 24.54 N 115.14 E
Hezuo 102 34.58 N 102.57 E
Hiale 110 15.55 N 107.34 E
Hialeah 220 25.51 N 80.16 W
Hialeah Park Race Track ♠ 220 25.51 N 80.17 W
Hiaohexi 100 31.21 N 114.02 E
Hiawassee 192 34.56 N 83.45 W
Hiawatha, Ks., U.S. 198 39.51 N 95.32 W
Hiawatha, Ut,. U.S. 200 39.29 N 111.00 W
Hiba-Dōgo-Taishaku-kokutei-kōen ♠ 96 35.07 N 133.08 E
Hibaiyo 116 10.16 N 123.20 E
Hibaldstow 44 53.31 N 0.32 W
Hibbing 190 47.25 N 92.56 W
Hibbs, Point › 166 42.38 S 145.15 E
Hibernia 276 40.57 N 74.30 W
Hibernia Reef ✦2 160 12.00 S 123.23 E
Hibiki-nada ⫪2 96 34.00 N 130.30 E
Hiburi-shima I 96 33.10 N 132.17 E
Hibuson Island I 116 10.27 N 125.29 E
Hickam Air Force Base ■ 229c 21.20 N 157.57 W
Hickman, Ca., U.S. 226 37.37 N 120.45 W
Hickman, Ky., U.S. 194 36.34 N 89.11 W
Hickman, Ne., U.S. 198 40.37 N 96.37 W
Hickman, Pa., U.S. 279b 40.23 N 80.09 W
Hickman's Harbour 186 48.06 N 53.44 W
Hickory, Ms., U.S. 194 32.19 N 89.01 W
Hickory, N.C., U.S. 192 35.43 N 81.20 W
Hickory, Pa., U.S. 214 40.18 N 80.18 W
Hickory Corners 216 42.26 N 85.22 W
Hickory Creek ≃, Il., U.S. 278 41.30 N 88.06 W
Hickory Creek ≃, Mi., U.S. 216 42.05 N 86.29 W
Hickory Creek ≃, Tx., U.S. 222 31.29 N 95.07 W
Hickory Flat 194 34.36 N 89.11 W
Hickory Hills 216 41.43 N 87.49 W
Hickory Run State Park ♠ 210 41.02 N 75.41 W
Hickory Township 214 41.15 N 80.27 W
Hicks, Point › 166 37.48 S 149.17 E
Hicks Bay 172 37.36 S 178.18 E
Hickson Lake ⊜ 184 56.17 N 104.25 W
Hicksville, N.Y., U.S. 210 40.46 N 73.31 W
Hicksville, Oh., U.S. 216 41.17 N 84.45 W
Hico 196 31.58 N 98.02 W
Hicpochee, Lake ⊜ 220 26.50 N 81.10 W
Hida → Hita 96 33.19 N 130.56 E
Hida ≃ 94 35.26 N 137.03 E
Hidaka, Nihon 94 35.54 N 139.21 E
Hidaka, Nihon 96 35.28 N 134.47 E
Hidaka, Nihon 96 33.55 N 135.09 E
Hidaka ≃ 96 33.52 N 135.09 E
Hidaka-sammyaku ⋏ 92a 42.35 N 142.45 E
Hida-Kiso-gawa-kokutei-kōen ♠ 94 35.37 N 137.15 E
Hida-kōchi ⋏1 94 36.16 N 137.05 E
Hidalgo, Méx. 232 27.47 N 99.52 W
Hidalgo, Méx. 232 25.59 N 100.27 W
Hidalgo, Méx. 232 24.15 N 99.26 W
Hidalgo, Méx. 234 23.10 N 103.13 W
Hidalgo □3 234 20.30 N 99.00 W
Hidalgo del Parral 232 26.56 N 105.40 W

Symbols in the index entries represent the broad categories identified in the key at the right. Symbols with superior numbers (⋏1) identify subcategories (see complete key on page *I · 1).*

Kartensymbole in dem Registerverzeichnis stellen die rechts in Schlüssel erklärten Kategorien dar. Symbole mit hochgestellten Ziffern (⋏1) bezeichnen Unterabteilungen einer Kategorie (vgl. vollständiger Schlüssel auf Seite *I · 1).*

Los símbolos incluídos en el texto del índice representan las grandes categorias identificadas con la clave a la derecha. Los símbolos con numeros en su parte superior (⋏1) identifican las subcategorías (véase la clave completa en la página *I · 1).*

Les symboles de l'index représentent les catégories indiquées dans la légende à droite. Les symboles suivis d'un indice (⋏1) représentent des sous-catégories (voir légende complète à la page *I · 1).*

Os símbolos incluídos no texto do índice representam as grandes categorias identificadas com a chave à direita. Os símbolos com números em sua parte superior (⋏1) identificam as subcategorias (veja-se a chave completa à página *I · 1).*

∧ Mountain	Berg	Montaña	Montagne	Montanha
⋏ Mountains	Berge	Montañas	Montagnes	Montanhas
)(Pass	Pass	Paso	Col	Passo
V Valley, Canyon	Tal, Cañon	Valle, Cañón	Vallée, Canyon	Vale, Canhão
≚ Plain	Ebene	Llano	Plaine	Planície
› Cape	Kap	Cabo	Cap	Cabo
I Island	Insel	Isla	Île	Ilha
II Islands	Inseln	Islas	Îles	Ilhas
⊥ Other Topographic Features	Andere Topographische Objekte	Otros Elementos Topográficos	Autres données topographiques	Outros acidentes topográficos

ESPAÑOL · FRANÇAIS · PORTUGUÊS

Nombre / Nom / Nome	Página / Page	Lat.°′	Long.°′ W = Oeste / W = Ouest
Hidalgo Yalalag	234	17.11 N	96.11 W
Hida-sammyaku ⩕	94	36.25 N	137.40 E
Hiddenhausen	52	52.08 N	8.38 E
Hidden Hills	228	34.09 N	118.43 W
Hiddensee I	54	54.33 N	13.07 E
Hidden Valley, Ca., U.S.	226	38.46 N	121.09 W
Hidden Valley, Tx., U.S.	222	29.54 N	95.25 W
Hiddesen	52	51.55 N	8.50 E
Hiddinghausen	263	51.22 N	7.17 E
Hidrolândia	255	16.58 S	49.14 W
Hidrolina	255	14.37 S	49.25 W
Hieflau	61	47.36 N	14.44 E
Hienghène	175f	20.41 S	164.56 E
Hierapolis ⊥	130	37.58 N	29.19 E
Hierges	56	50.06 N	4.44 E
Hierro (Ferro) I	148	27.45 N	18.00 W
Hiesfeld	263	51.33 N	6.46 E
Hietzing ◆[8]	264b	48.11 N	16.18 E
Higashi	174m	26.38 N	128.09 E
Higashi ◆[8]	270	34.41 N	135.31 E
Higashibetsuin	270	34.56 N	135.34 E
Higashifuji-enshūjō ■	94	35.17 N	138.51 E
Higashihiroshima	96	34.26 N	132.42 E
Higashiichiki	92	31.40 N	130.20 E
Higashiiyayama	96	33.52 N	133.54 E
Higashiizu	94	34.48 N	139.04 E
Higashi-jima I	174f	24.47 N	141.23 E
Higashikurume	268	35.45 N	139.32 E
Higashimatsuyama	94	36.02 N	139.24 E
Higashimonzen	268	35.56 N	139.40 E
Higashimurayama	94	35.46 N	139.29 E
Higashinada ◆[8]	270	34.43 N	135.16 E
Higashinakano	268	35.38 N	139.25 E
Higashinari ◆[8]	270	34.40 N	135.33 E
Higashine	92	38.26 N	140.24 E
Higashinose	270	34.55 N	135.30 E
Higashiōizumi ◆[8]	268	35.45 N	139.36 E
Higashiōsaka	96	34.39 N	135.35 E
Higashishirakawa	94	35.39 N	137.19 E
Higashisumiyoshi ◆[8]	270	34.37 N	135.32 E
Higashitokonoo-san ∧	96	35.25 N	134.55 E
Higashitsuno	96	33.23 N	133.02 E
Higashiura, Nihon	94	34.59 N	136.58 E
Higashiura, Nihon	270	34.33 N	135.00 E
Higashiyama ◆[8]	270	35.00 N	135.48 E
Higashiyamato	268	35.44 N	139.26 E
Higashiyodogawa ◆[8]	270	34.44 N	135.31 E
Higashiyoshino	94	34.24 N	135.58 E
Higbee	194	39.18 N	92.30 W
Higganum	207	41.29 N	72.33 W
Higgins	196	36.07 N	100.02 W
Higgins, Mount ∧	224	48.19 N	121.45 W
Higgins Lake ⊜	190	44.30 N	84.45 W
Higginsport	218	38.47 N	83.58 W
Higginsville, Austl.	162	31.45 S	121.43 E
Higginsville, Mo., U.S.	194	39.04 N	93.43 W
Higgs' Hope	158	29.19 S	23.16 E
Higham Ferrers	42	52.18 N	0.36 W
Higham Upshire	260	51.26 N	0.28 E
Highbank	222	31.10 N	96.50 W
High Bank Creek ≃	216	42.37 N	85.11 W
High Bar Indian Reserve ◆[4]	182	51.06 N	122.00 W
High Beach	260	51.39 N	0.02 E
High Bentham	44	54.08 N	2.30 W
High Bluff Island I	212	43.58 N	77.45 W
Highbridge, Eng., U.K.	42	51.13 N	2.49 W
High Bridge, N.J., U.S.	210	40.40 N	74.53 W
Highbury	164	16.25 S	143.09 E
Highcliff	279b	40.32 N	80.03 W
Higher Ballam	262	53.46 N	2.59 W
Higher Broughton ◆[8]	262	53.30 N	2.15 W
Higher Hogshead ∧[2]	262	53.42 N	2.09 W
Higher Penwortham	262	53.45 N	2.44 W
Higher Walton, Eng., U.K.	44	53.44 N	2.39 W
Higher Walton, Eng., U.K.	262	53.22 N	2.37 W
Higher Walton, Eng., U.K.	262	53.45 N	2.38 W
Higher Whitley	262	53.19 N	2.35 W
Highett	274b	37.57 S	145.03 E
High Falls	210	41.50 N	74.08 W
High Falls ∟	212	43.56 N	75.23 W
High Force ∟	44	54.38 N	2.13 W
Highgate	214	42.30 N	81.49 W
Highgate Center	206	44.56 N	73.02 W
Highgate Springs	206	44.58 N	73.06 W
Highgrove	228	34.01 N	117.20 W
High Halstow	260	51.27 N	0.34 E
High Hesket	44	54.48 N	2.48 W
High Hill	219	38.52 N	91.23 W
High Hill ∧[2]	276	40.49 N	73.25 W
High Hill ≃, Can.	184	56.45 N	110.30 W
High Hill ≃, Mb., Can.	184	55.52 N	94.42 W
High Hill Lake ⊜	184	55.34 N	95.40 W
High Island I, H.K.	271d	22.22 N	114.21 E
High Island I, Mi., U.S.	190	45.42 N	85.40 W
High Island Creek ≃	190	44.35 N	93.54 W
High Island Reservoir ⊜[1]	271d	22.23 N	114.21 E
Highland, Ca., U.S.	228	34.07 N	117.12 W
Highland, Il., U.S.	219	38.44 N	89.40 W
Highland, In., U.S.	216	41.33 N	87.27 W
Highland, Ks., U.S.	198	39.51 N	95.16 W
Highland, Md., U.S.	208	39.11 N	76.57 W
Highland, Mi., U.S.	281	42.38 N	83.37 W
Highland, N.Y., U.S.	210	41.43 N	73.57 W
Highland, Oh., U.S.	218	39.21 N	83.36 W
Highland, Pa., U.S.	279b	40.33 N	80.04 W
Highland □[4]	46	57.40 N	5.00 W
Highland □[6]	218	39.12 N	83.37 W
Highland Beach	220	26.25 N	80.04 W
Highland City	220	27.58 N	81.53 W
Highland Creek ≃, On., Can.	275b	43.46 N	79.08 W
Highland Creek ≃, Ca., U.S.	226	38.24 N	121.14 W
Highland Falls	210	41.22 N	73.58 W
Highland Heights, Ky., U.S.	218	39.04 N	84.27 W
Highland Heights, Oh., U.S.	214	41.33 N	81.28 W
Highland Hills	278	41.52 N	88.01 W
Highland Home	194	31.57 N	86.18 W
Highland Lake, Il., U.S.	278	42.21 N	88.04 W
Highland Lake, Ma., U.S.	283	42.41 N	72.37 W
Highland Lake, N.Y., U.S.	210	41.32 N	74.51 W
Highland Lake ⊜, Ct., U.S.	207	41.54 N	73.06 W
Highland Lake ⊜, Il., U.S.	278	42.22 N	88.04 W
Highland Lake ⊜, N.J., U.S.	276	41.10 N	74.28 W
Highland Lakes	210	41.10 N	74.28 W
Highland-on-the-Lake	284a	42.42 N	79.59 W
Highland Park, Il., U.S.	216	42.10 N	87.48 W
Highland Park, Md., U.S.	284c	38.54 N	76.54 W
Highland Park, Mi., U.S.	216	42.24 N	83.05 W
Highland Park, N.J., U.S.	210	40.29 N	74.25 W
Highland Park, Pa., U.S.	210	40.38 N	77.35 W
Highland Park, Tx., U.S.	222	32.50 N	96.48 W
Highland Park ◆[8]	280	34.07 N	118.13 W
Highland Park ♠, Ma., U.S.	283	42.30 N	70.55 W
Highland Park ♠, Pa., U.S.	279b	40.29 N	79.55 W
Highland Peak ∧	226	38.33 N	119.45 W
Highland Point ›	220	25.30 N	81.12 W
Highlands, N.J., U.S.	208	40.24 N	73.59 W
Highlands, N.C., U.S.	192	35.03 N	83.11 W
Highlands, Tx., U.S.	222	29.49 N	95.03 W
Highlands □[6]	220	27.20 N	81.16 W
Highlands Hammock State Park ♠	220	27.28 N	81.33 W
Highland Silver Lake ⊜[1]	219	38.47 N	89.39 W
Highlands North ◆[8]	273d	26.09 S	28.05 E
Highland Springs	208	37.32 N	77.19 W
Highlands Reservoir ⊜[1]	222	29.50 N	95.02 W
Highland State Recreation Area ♠	216	42.39 N	83.33 W
Highlandtown ◆[8]	284b	39.17 N	76.33 W
High Laver	260	51.45 N	0.13 E
High Legh	262	53.21 N	2.27 W
Highley	42	52.27 N	2.23 W
Highmore	198	44.31 N	99.26 W
High Ongar	260	51.43 N	0.16 E
High Park ♠	275b	43.39 N	79.28 W
High Peak □[8]	262	53.23 N	1.55 W
High Peak ∧, Pil.	116	15.29 N	120.07 E
High Peak ∧, N.Y., U.S.	210	42.09 N	74.05 W
High Peak ◆[1]	44	53.22 N	1.50 W
High Point, Fl., U.S.	220	27.55 N	82.42 W
High Point, N.C., U.S.	192	35.57 N	80.00 W
Highpoint, Oh., U.S.	218	39.14 N	84.24 W
High Point ∧, N.J., U.S.	210	41.19 N	74.40 W
High Point ∧, Wy., U.S.	202	41.37 N	107.47 W
High Point State Park ♠	210	41.18 N	74.41 W
High Prairie	182	55.26 N	116.29 W
High Ridge	219	38.27 N	90.32 W
High River	182	50.35 N	113.52 W
High Rock	192	26.36 N	76.18 W
High Rock ∧	188	39.33 N	79.06 W
Highrock Indian Reserve ◆[4]	184	55.54 N	100.30 W
Highrock Lake ⊜, Mb., Can.	184	55.45 N	100.30 W
Highrock Lake ⊜, Sk., Can.	184	57.04 N	105.30 W
High Rock Lake ⊜[1]	192	35.40 N	80.17 W
High Seat ∧	44	54.24 N	2.18 W
High Spire	208	40.12 N	76.47 W
High Springs	192	29.49 N	82.35 W
High Street ∧	44	54.29 N	2.52 W
Hightown, Eng., U.K.	44	53.31 N	3.03 W
Hightown, Eng., U.K.	262	53.32 N	3.04 W
Hightstown	208	40.16 N	74.31 W
High View	210	41.33 N	74.27 W
Highwater	206	45.01 N	72.26 W
Highway City	226	36.49 N	119.54 W
High Willhays ∧	42	50.41 N	3.59 W
Highwood, Il., U.S.	216	42.11 N	87.48 W
Highwood, Mt., U.S.	202	47.35 N	110.47 W
Highwood ≃	182	50.49 N	113.47 W
Highwood Baldy ∧	202	47.27 N	110.37 W
Highwood Creek ≃	202	47.40 N	111.00 W
Highwood Mountains ⩕	202	47.25 N	110.30 W
Highworth	42	51.38 N	1.43 W
High Wycombe	42	51.38 N	0.46 W
Higlet	154	1.04 S	40.19 E
Higuera Blanca	234	19.42 N	105.10 W
Higuera de Zaragoza	232	25.59 N	109.16 W
Higuera Gorda	234	22.04 N	104.29 W
Higueras	196	25.58 N	100.01 W
Higüero, Punta ›	240m	18.22 N	67.16 W
Higuerote	246	10.29 N	66.06 W
Higuito ≃	236	14.43 N	88.40 W
Hihétro	150	7.32 N	1.06 E
Hihyā	142	30.40 N	31.36 E
Hii ≃	96	35.26 N	132.54 E
Hiiraan □[4]	144	4.00 N	45.30 E
Hiiumaa I	76	58.52 N	22.40 E
Hījānah, Buḥayrat al- ⊜	132	33.18 N	36.36 E
Híjar	34	41.10 N	0.27 W
Hiji	96	33.22 N	131.32 E
Hiji ≃	96	33.36 N	132.29 E
Hijikawa	96	33.27 N	132.41 E
Hijiri-dake ∧	94	35.26 N	138.10 E
Hikami	96	35.10 N	135.02 E
Hikari, Nihon	94	35.39 N	140.30 E
Hikari, Nihon	96	33.58 N	131.56 E
Hikarigaoka	268	35.50 N	139.58 E
Hikawa	96	35.25 N	132.50 E
Hikawa Shrine ⊍[1]	268	35.54 N	139.38 E
Hiketa	96	34.13 N	134.24 E
Hiki ≃	96	33.33 N	135.27 E
Hikigawa	96	33.34 N	135.27 E
Hikimi	96	34.34 N	132.01 E
Hikimi ≃	96	34.37 N	131.48 E
Hikiura	270	34.33 N	134.58 E
Hikone	94	35.15 N	136.15 E
Hikone-jō ⊥	94	35.15 N	136.14 E
Hiko-san ∧	96	33.27 N	130.54 E
Hikueru I[1]	14	17.36 S	142.37 W
Hikurangi	172	35.36 S	174.18 E
Hikurangi ∧	172	37.55 S	178.04 E
Hikutaia	172	37.17 S	175.39 E
Hikutivake	174v	18.56 S	169.53 W
Hila	112	7.35 S	127.24 E
Hilaban Island I	116	12.03 N	125.34 E
Hilāl, Jabal ⩕	132	30.40 N	34.00 E
Hilāl, Ra's al- ›	146	32.57 N	22.10 E
Hilbersdorf	54	50.55 N	13.23 E
Hilbert	190	44.08 N	88.09 W
Hilbre Islands II	262	53.23 N	3.13 W
Hilbre Point ›	262	53.23 N	3.12 W
Hilchenbach	56	51.00 N	8.06 E
Hilda	184	50.28 N	110.03 W
Hildburghausen	54	50.25 N	10.44 E
Hilden	56	51.10 N	6.56 E
Hildenborough	260	51.13 N	0.15 E
Hilders	56	50.34 N	10.00 E
Hildesheim	52	52.09 N	9.57 E
Hildreth	198	40.20 N	99.02 W
Hilgen	263	51.06 N	7.09 E
Hiliaława	114	0.41 N	97.53 E
Hiligeo	114	1.22 N	97.10 E
Hiliotaluwa	114	0.44 N	97.53 E
Hill □[6]	222	32.02 N	97.10 W
Hillaby, Mount ∧	241g	13.12 N	59.35 W
Hill Air Force Base ■	202	41.05 N	111.58 W
Hillandale, S. Afr.	158	33.06 S	20.36 E
Hillandale, Md., U.S.	284c	39.01 N	76.58 W
Hillandale Heights	284c	39.01 N	76.59 W
Hill Bank	232	17.35 N	88.42 W
Hillburn	210	41.08 N	74.10 W
Hill City, Ks., U.S.	198	39.21 N	99.50 W
Hill City, Mn., U.S.	190	46.59 N	93.35 W
Hill City, S.D., U.S.	198	43.55 N	103.34 W
Hill Creek ≃	200	39.55 N	109.40 W
Hillcrest, Il., U.S.	216	41.57 N	89.04 W
Hillcrest, N.Y., U.S.	210	41.07 N	74.02 W
Hillcrest, N.Y., U.S.	210	42.09 N	75.53 W
Hillcrest Center	228	35.23 N	118.57 W
Hillcrest Heights	284c	38.49 N	76.57 W
Hillcrest Mines	182	49.34 N	114.23 W
Hillcrest Orchard	216	41.51 N	83.29 W
Hillcrest Park	226	38.07 N	122.16 W
Hill Cumorah ⊥	210	43.01 N	77.15 W
Hille, B.R.D.	52	52.20 N	8.44 E
Hille, Sve.	40	60.44 N	17.11 E
Hillegom	52	52.18 N	4.35 E
Hillegossen	52	51.59 N	8.37 E
Hillen ◆[8]	263	51.37 N	7.13 E
Hillerød	41	55.56 N	12.19 E
Hillers Creek ≃	219	38.38 N	91.54 W
Hillesheim	56	50.18 N	6.38 E
Hilli	124	25.17 N	89.01 E
Hilliard, Fl., U.S.	192	30.41 N	81.55 W
Hilliard, Oh., U.S.	218	40.02 N	83.09 W
Hilliards	214	41.05 N	79.50 W
Hillingdon ◆[8]	260	51.32 N	0.27 W
Hillisburg	216	40.17 N	86.20 W
Hill Island Lake ⊜	176	60.29 N	109.50 W
Hillister	194	30.40 N	94.23 W
Hillman	190	45.03 N	83.54 W
Hillman ≃	168a	33.26 S	116.48 E
Hillmersdorf	54	51.42 N	13.29 E
Hill of Fearn	46	57.45 N	3.56 W
Hills	198	43.31 N	96.21 W
Hills and Dales	214	39.42 N	84.13 W
Hillsboro, Il., U.S.	219	39.09 N	89.29 W
Hillsboro, Ks., U.S.	198	38.21 N	97.12 W
Hillsboro, Ky., U.S.	218	38.18 N	83.40 W
Hillsboro, Md., U.S.	208	38.55 N	75.56 W
Hillsboro, Mo., U.S.	219	38.13 N	90.33 W
Hillsboro, N.H., U.S.	188	43.06 N	71.53 W
Hillsboro, N.M., U.S.	200	32.55 N	107.33 W
Hillsboro, N.D., U.S.	198	47.24 N	97.03 W
Hillsboro, Oh., U.S.	218	39.12 N	83.36 W
Hillsboro, Or., U.S.	224	45.31 N	122.59 W
Hillsboro, Tx., U.S.	222	32.00 N	97.07 W
Hillsboro, Wi., U.S.	190	43.39 N	90.20 W
Hillsboro Beach	220	26.18 N	80.05 W
Hillsboro Canal ≍	220	26.19 N	80.05 W
Hillsborough, N.B., Can.	186	45.56 N	64.39 W
Hillsborough, N. Ire., U.K.	48	54.28 N	6.05 W
Hillsborough, Ca., U.S.	226	37.34 N	122.22 W
Hillsborough, N.C., U.S.	192	36.04 N	79.06 W
Hillsborough □[6], Fl., U.S.	220	27.55 N	82.15 W
Hillsborough □[6], N.H., U.S.	207	42.49 N	71.41 W
Hillsborough ≃	220	27.56 N	82.27 W
Hillsborough, Cape ›	166	20.54 S	149.03 E
Hillsborough Bay c, P.E., Can.	186	46.10 N	63.05 W
Hillsborough Bay c, Fl., U.S.	220	27.52 N	82.27 W
Hillsborough River State Park ♠	220	28.09 N	82.14 W
Hillsburgh	212	43.47 N	80.09 W
Hills Creek Lake ⊜[1]	202	43.40 N	122.26 W
Hillsdale, Mi., U.S.	216	41.55 N	84.37 W
Hillsdale, N.J., U.S.	276	41.00 N	74.02 W
Hillsdale, N.Y., U.S.	210	42.10 N	73.31 W
Hillsdale, Pa., U.S.	214	40.45 N	78.53 W
Hillsdale □[6]	216	41.53 N	84.36 W
Hillsdale ◆[9]	282	37.32 N	122.18 W
Hillsdale Lake ⊜[1]	198	38.40 N	94.55 W
Hills Flat	226	39.14 N	121.03 W
Hillsgrove	210	41.27 N	76.42 W
Hillside, Austl.	162	21.44 S	119.23 E
Hillside, Scot., U.K.	46	56.44 N	2.29 W
Hillside, Il., U.S.	278	41.52 N	87.54 W
Hillside, Md., U.S.	284c	38.52 N	76.55 W
Hillside, N.J., U.S.	276	40.42 N	74.13 W
Hillside ◆[8]	276	40.42 N	73.47 W
Hillside Gardens	216	42.16 N	84.27 W
Hillside Heights	285	39.41 N	75.41 W
Hillside Lake	210	41.36 N	73.50 W
Hillston	166	33.29 S	145.32 E
Hillsville, Pa., U.S.	214	41.00 N	80.29 W
Hillsville, Va., U.S.	192	36.45 N	80.44 W
Hillswick	46a	60.28 N	1.30 W
Hilltop	208	39.49 N	75.04 W
Hilltop Center ◆[9]	282	37.59 N	122.19 W
Hilltown, N. Ire., U.K.	48	54.12 N	6.09 W
Hilltown, Pa., U.S.	208	40.20 N	75.14 W
Hillview	219	39.27 N	90.33 W
Hillview Reservoir ⊜[1]	276	40.55 N	73.52 W
Hillwood	284c	38.52 N	77.10 W
Hilmar	226	37.25 N	120.51 W
Hilo	229d	19.43 N	155.05 W
Hilo Bay c	229d	19.44 N	155.05 W
Hilonghilong, Mount ∧	116	9.06 N	125.44 E
Hilongos	116	10.23 N	124.45 E
Hilpotstein	60	49.12 N	11.12 E
Hilpsford Point ›	44	54.03 N	3.12 W
Hils ∧	52	51.55 N	9.40 E
Hilshire Village	222	29.49 N	95.26 W
Hiltaba, Mount ∧	162	32.09 S	135.03 E
Hilter	52	52.08 N	8.08 E
Hilton, N.Y., U.S.	210	43.17 N	77.47 W
Hilton, Pa., U.S.	208	40.00 N	76.49 W
Hilton Head Island I	192	32.12 N	80.45 W
Hiltpoltstein	60	49.40 N	11.19 E
Hiltrop ◆[8]	263	51.30 N	7.15 E
Hiltrup	52	51.54 N	7.38 E
Hilvarenbeek	52	51.29 N	5.09 E
Hilversum	52	52.14 N	5.10 E
Hima	192	37.07 N	83.46 W
Himachal Pradesh □[8]	120	32.00 N	77.00 E
Himalayas ⩕	120	28.00 N	84.00 E
Himalchuli ∧	124	28.25 N	84.39 E
Himamaylan	116	10.06 N	122.52 E
Himanka	26	64.04 N	23.39 E
Himarë	38	40.07 N	19.44 E
Himatnagar	120	23.36 N	72.57 E
Himberg	61	48.05 N	16.26 E
Hime ≃	94	37.02 N	137.49 E
Himeji	96	34.49 N	134.42 E
Hime-shima I	96	33.43 N	131.40 E
Himeville	158	29.44 S	29.31 E
Himi	94	36.51 N	136.59 E
Himmelbjerget ⩕[2]	41	56.06 N	9.42 E
Himmelgeist ◆[8]	263	51.10 N	6.49 E
Himmelpforten	52	53.36 N	9.18 E
Himmelsthür	52	52.09 N	9.55 E
Himmerfjärden c[2]	40	59.00 N	17.43 E
Himmerland ◆[1]	26	56.50 N	9.45 E
Himmetdede	130	38.55 N	35.07 E
Himrod	210	42.35 N	76.57 W
Ḥimṣ (Homs)	130	34.44 N	36.43 E
Ḥimṣ □[8]	130	34.15 N	38.00 E
Ḥimṣ, Baḥrat ⊜[1]	130	34.39 N	36.34 E
Hinabangan	116	11.42 N	125.04 E
Ḥīnah	132	33.21 N	35.56 E
Hinako, Kepulauan II	114	0.52 N	97.21 E
Hinase	96	34.44 N	134.16 E
Hinatuan	116	8.23 N	126.20 E
Hinatuan Island I	116	9.47 N	125.43 E
Hinatuan Passage ʮ	116	9.45 N	125.47 E
Hinche	238	19.09 N	72.01 W
Hinchinbrook Entrance ʮ	180	60.25 N	146.50 W
Hinchinbrook Island I, Austl.	166	18.23 S	146.17 E
Hinchinbrook Island I, Ak., U.S.	180	60.22 N	146.30 W
Hinchinbrook Island National Park ♠	166	18.20 S	146.20 E
Hinckley, Eng., U.K.	42	52.33 N	1.21 W
Hinckley, Il., U.S.	216	41.46 N	88.38 W
Hinckley, Mn., U.S.	190	46.00 N	92.56 W
Hinckley, Oh., U.S.	214	41.14 N	81.45 W
Hinckley, Ut,. U.S.	200	39.19 N	112.40 W
Hinckley Reservoir ⊜[1]	210	43.20 N	75.05 W
Hindan ≃	272a	28.30 N	77.27 E
Hindang	116	10.26 N	124.44 E
Hindaun	124	26.43 N	77.01 E
Hindelang	58	47.30 N	10.22 E
Hindelbank	58	47.03 N	7.32 E
Hindeloopen	52	52.56 N	5.24 E
Hindenburg → Zabrze	30	50.18 N	18.46 E
Hindhead	42	51.07 N	0.44 W
Hindley	262	53.32 N	2.35 W
Hindley Green	262	53.31 N	2.32 W
Hindman	192	37.20 N	82.58 W
Hindmarsh, Lake ⊜	166	36.03 S	141.55 E
Hindmarsh Island I	168b	35.32 S	138.52 E
Hindmarsh Valley	168b	35.30 S	138.38 E
Hindon	42	51.06 N	2.08 W
Hinds	172	44.00 S	171.34 E
Hindsholm I	41	55.33 N	10.40 E
Hinds Lake ⊜	186	48.57 N	57.00 W
Hindubāgh	120	30.49 N	67.45 E
Hindu Kush ⩕	120	36.00 N	71.30 E
Hindu Malkot	123	30.09 N	73.55 E
Hindupur	122	13.49 N	77.29 E
Hi-Nella	285	39.50 N	75.01 W
Hines	202	43.33 N	119.04 W
Hines Creek	182	56.15 N	118.36 W
Hines Creek ≃	182	55.54 N	118.37 W
Hines Peak ∧	228	34.31 N	119.05 W
Hinesville	192	31.50 N	81.35 W
Hinganghāt	122	20.34 N	78.50 E
Hingatungan	116	10.35 N	125.11 E
Hingham, Eng., U.K.	42	52.35 N	0.59 E
Hingham, Ma., U.S.	207	42.14 N	70.53 W
Hingham Bay c	207	42.17 N	70.55 W
Hingham Harbor c	283	42.15 N	70.53 W
Hingol ≃	128	25.23 N	65.28 E
Hingoli	122	19.43 N	77.09 E
Hinigaran	116	10.17 N	122.51 E
Hınıs	130	39.22 N	41.44 E
Hınıs ≃	130	39.18 N	42.12 E
Hinish Bay c	46	56.28 N	6.50 W
Hinkley	228	34.56 N	117.11 W
Hinkson Creek ≃	219	38.56 N	92.23 W
Hinkston Creek ≃	188	38.18 N	84.14 W
Hinnerjoki	26	61.00 N	22.00 E
Hinnerup	41	56.16 N	10.04 E
Hinnøya I	24	68.30 N	16.00 E
Hino, Nihon	94	35.00 N	136.15 E
Hino, Nihon	94	35.41 N	139.24 E
Hino, Nihon	96	35.14 N	133.27 E
Hino ≃, Nihon	94	35.09 N	136.02 E
Hino ≃, Nihon	94	36.04 N	136.11 E
Hino ≃, Nihon	96	35.27 N	133.23 E
Hinoba-an	116	9.35 N	122.28 E
Hinode	94	35.45 N	139.14 E
Hinoemata	94	37.01 N	139.23 E
Hinohara	94	35.43 N	139.09 E
Hinojosa del Duque	34	38.30 N	5.09 W
Hinokage	92	32.39 N	131.24 E
Hinomi-saki ›, Nihon	96	33.53 N	135.04 E
Hinomi-saki ›, Nihon	96	35.26 N	132.38 E
Hinsbeck	56	51.21 N	6.17 E
Hinsdale, Il., U.S.	216	41.48 N	87.56 W
Hinsdale, Ma., U.S.	207	42.26 N	73.07 W
Hinsdale, Mt., U.S.	202	48.23 N	107.05 W
Hinsdale, N.H., U.S.	207	42.47 N	72.29 W
Hinsdale, N.Y., U.S.	210	42.10 N	78.23 W
Hinsel ◆[8]	263	51.26 N	7.05 E
Hinsen ⊜	40	60.39 N	16.05 E
Hinte	52	53.25 N	7.11 E
Hinterbichl	64	47.01 N	12.20 E
Hinterbrühl	61	48.05 N	16.15 E
Hinterhermsdorf	54	50.55 N	14.22 E
Hinterrhein	58	46.32 N	9.12 E
Hinterrhein ≃	58	46.49 N	9.25 E
Hintersdorf	264b	48.18 N	16.13 E
Hintersee	54	53.37 N	14.16 E
Hinterstoder	61	47.41 N	14.09 E
Hintertux	64	47.07 N	11.41 E
Hinterweidenthal	56	49.12 N	7.45 E
Hinterzarten	58	47.54 N	8.06 E
Hinton, Ab., Can.	182	53.25 N	117.34 W
Hinton, Mo., U.S.	219	39.03 N	92.21 W
Hinton, Ok., U.S.	196	35.28 N	98.21 W
Hinton, W.V., U.S.	192	37.40 N	80.53 W
Hi-numa ⊜	94	36.16 N	140.30 E
Hinuma ≃	94	36.16 N	140.28 E
Hinundayan	116	10.21 N	125.15 E
Hinwil	58	47.18 N	8.51 E
Hinzik	84	40.08 N	40.58 E
Hípico, Club ♠	286e	33.28 S	70.41 W
Hipólito	232	25.41 N	101.26 W
Hipólito Yrigoyen	252	32.55 S	66.20 W
Hippolytushoef	52	52.54 N	4.57 E
Hirado	92	33.22 N	129.33 E
Hirado-shima I	92	33.20 N	129.30 E
Hiraiwa-hana ›	174f	24.48 N	141.18 E
Hiraizumi	92	38.59 N	141.07 E
Hirakata, Nihon	96	34.48 N	135.38 E
Hirakata, Nihon	268	35.56 N	139.33 E
Hirakawa	270	34.52 N	135.47 E
Hīrākud	122	21.31 N	83.57 E
Hīrākud ⊜[1]	120	21.31 N	83.52 E
Hiram, Me., U.S.	188	43.52 N	70.48 W
Hiram, Oh., U.S.	214	41.18 N	81.08 W
Hiraman ≃	154	1.07 S	39.55 E
Hirano	175d	24.35 N	124.19 E
Hirano ◆[8]	270	34.36 N	135.34 E
Hirao	96	33.56 N	132.04 E
Hirao-dai ♠	96	33.45 N	130.52 E
Hiraoka → Higashiōsaka	96	34.39 N	135.35 E
Hīrāpur	124	24.22 N	79.13 E
Hirara	175d	24.48 N	125.17 E
Hirata, Nihon	94	35.15 N	136.38 E
Hirata, Nihon	96	35.26 N	132.49 E
Hiratsuka	94	35.19 N	139.21 E
Hiraya	94	35.19 N	137.37 E
Hirfanlı Barajı ◆[6]	130	39.18 N	33.29 E
Hirhafok	148	23.49 N	5.45 E
Hiriyūr	122	13.58 N	76.36 E
Hirjillah	132	33.22 N	36.18 E
Hîrlău	38	47.25 N	26.54 E
Hīrmand, Hāmūn-e ⊜	128	30.45 N	61.10 E
Hirokawa, Nihon	96	33.15 N	130.32 E
Hirokawa, Nihon	96	34.01 N	135.11 E
Hirok Sāmi	128	26.02 N	63.25 E
Hiromi	96	33.15 N	132.41 E
Hiroo	92a	42.17 N	143.19 E
Hirooka	268	35.15 N	140.04 E
Hirosaki	92	40.35 N	140.28 E
Hiroschima → Hiroshima	96	34.24 N	132.27 E
Hirose	96	35.22 N	133.10 E
Hiroshima	96	34.24 N	132.27 E
Hiroshima □[5]	96	34.30 N	133.00 E
Hiro-shima I	96	34.22 N	133.43 E
Hiroshima-wan c	96	34.06 N	132.20 E
Hirosima → Hiroshima	96	34.24 N	132.27 E
Hirota	270	34.45 N	135.21 E
Hirsau	56	48.44 N	8.44 E
Hirschaid	56	49.49 N	10.59 E
Hirschau	60	49.33 N	11.57 E
Hirschbach	54	50.33 N	10.44 E
Hirschberg, D.D.R.	54	50.24 N	11.49 E
Hirschberg → Jelenia Góra, Pol.	30	50.55 N	15.46 E
Hirschfeld	54	51.23 N	13.37 E
Hirschfelde, D.D.R.	54	50.57 N	14.53 E
Hirschfelde, D.D.R.	264a	52.38 N	13.48 E
Hirschhorn	56	49.27 N	8.53 E
Hirschstetten ◆[8]	264b	48.14 N	16.29 E
Hirshfeld Brook ≃	276	40.57 N	74.02 W
Hirsingue	58	47.35 N	7.15 E
Hirson	50	49.55 N	4.05 E
Hîrşova	38	44.41 N	27.57 E
Hirtshals	26	57.35 N	9.58 E
Hirtzfelden	58	47.55 N	7.27 E
Hirukawa	94	35.31 N	137.23 E
Hiru-zen ∧	96	35.19 N	133.40 E
Hirwaun	42	51.45 N	3.30 W
Hisābpur	272b	22.51 N	88.32 E
Hisai, Nihon	94	34.40 N	136.28 E
Hisai, Nihon	270	34.25 N	135.28 E
Hisār	123	29.10 N	75.43 E
Hisarköy	130	39.48 N	29.37 E
Hisarönu	130	41.33 N	32.02 E
Ḥisbān	132	31.48 N	35.48 E
Hisiu	164	9.05 S	146.45 E
Ḥismā ≚	128	29.00 N	35.40 E
Hisn al-ʿAbr	144	16.05 N	47.22 E
Ḥiṣn al-Qarn	144	15.11 N	49.05 E
Hispaniola I	238	19.00 N	71.00 W
Histon	42	52.15 N	0.06 E
Hisua	124	24.50 N	85.25 E
Ḥisyah	130	34.24 N	36.45 E
Hīt	128	33.38 N	42.49 E
Hita	96	33.19 N	130.56 E
Hitachi	94	36.36 N	140.39 E
Hitachi-ōta	94	36.32 N	140.31 E
Hitati → Hitachi	94	36.36 N	140.39 E
Hitchcock	222	29.20 N	95.00 W
Hitchin	42	51.57 N	0.17 W
Hitchins	218	38.16 N	82.55 W
Hither Green ◆[8]	260	51.27 N	0.01 W
Hither Hills State Park ♠	207	41.01 N	72.01 W
Hitiaa	174s	17.36 S	149.18 W
Hitokura	270	34.55 N	135.25 E
Hitotsubashi University ⊍[2]	268	35.42 N	139.27 E
Hitoyoshi	92	32.13 N	130.45 E
Hitra I	26	63.33 N	8.45 E
Hittarp	41	56.06 N	12.38 E
Hittisau	58	47.27 N	9.57 E
Hitzacker	54	53.09 N	11.02 E
Hitze-Berge ⩕[2]	264a	52.35 N	13.07 E
Hiu I	175f	13.10 S	166.35 E
Hiuchiga-take ∧	94	36.57 N	139.17 E
Hiuchi-nada ⫧[2]	96	34.05 N	133.20 E
Hiūnchuli Pātan ∧	124	28.50 N	82.37 E
Hiva Oa I	174y	9.45 S	139.00 W
Hi Vista	228	34.44 N	117.47 W
Hivris	130	38.18 N	42.10 E
Hiwa	96	34.59 N	132.59 E
Hiwannee	194	31.48 N	88.41 W
Hiwasa	96	33.44 N	134.32 E
Hiwassee ≃	192	35.19 N	84.47 W
Hiwassee Lake ⊜[1]	192	35.10 N	84.05 W
Hixon	182	53.27 N	122.36 W
Hixson	192	35.09 N	85.14 W
Hiyoshi, Nihon	94	35.53 N	137.45 E
Hiyoshi, Nihon	96	33.20 N	132.48 E
Hiyoshi, Nihon	96	35.09 N	135.31 E
Hiyoshi ◆[8]	268	35.33 N	139.39 E
Ḥiyyon, Naḥal ∨	132	30.12 N	35.07 E
Hizaonna	174m	26.24 N	127.50 E
Hjälmare kanal ≍	40	59.24 N	15.56 E
Hjälmaren ⊜	40	59.15 N	15.45 E
Hjälmaresund ʮ	40	59.15 N	16.06 E
Hjarnø I	41	55.50 N	10.05 E
Hjelm I	41	56.08 N	10.48 E
Hjelmelandsvågen	26	59.14 N	6.11 E
Hjeltefjorden c[2]	26	60.40 N	4.55 E
Hjembæk	41	55.42 N	11.25 E
Hjo	26	58.18 N	14.17 E
Hjøllund	41	56.05 N	9.25 E
Hjordkær	41	55.01 N	9.19 E
Hjørring	26	57.28 N	9.59 E
Hjort Basin ✦[1]	9	58.00 S	157.30 E
Hjortkvarn	40	58.53 N	15.25 E
Hjørundfjorden c[2]	26	62.21 N	6.23 E
Hkakabo Razi ∧	102	28.20 N	97.32 E
Hkok (Kok) ≃	110	20.14 N	100.09 E
Hlabisa	158	28.08 S	31.52 E
Hlaingbwe	110	17.08 N	97.50 E
Hlatikulu	158	27.00 S	31.25 E
Hlegu	110	17.06 N	96.14 E
Hlinsko	30	49.45 N	15.55 E
Hlobane	158	27.42 S	31.00 E
Hlohovec	30	48.25 N	17.47 E
Hluboká ⊥	61	49.05 N	14.25 E
Hluboká nad Vltavou	61	49.03 N	14.27 E
Hluboš	60	49.45 N	14.02 E
Hlučín	30	49.54 N	18.12 E
Hluhluwe	158	28.01 S	32.15 E
Hluhluwe Game Reserve ◆[4]	158	28.05 S	32.04 E
Hluti	158	27.13 S	31.35 E
Hmawbi	110	17.06 N	96.02 E
H. Neely Henry Lake ⊜[1]	194	33.55 N	86.05 W
Ho	150	6.35 N	0.30 E
Hoa-binh	110	20.50 N	105.20 E
Hoa-da	110	11.11 N	108.33 E
Hoagland	216	40.56 N	84.59 W
Hoagland Ditch ≍	216	40.48 N	86.48 W
Hoai-nhon	110	14.26 N	109.01 E
Hoanib ≃	156	19.27 S	12.46 E
Hoare Bay c	176	65.20 N	62.30 W
Hoarusib ≃	156	19.03 S	12.36 E
Hoa-thoi	269c	10.44 N	106.35 E
Hoback ≃	202	43.19 N	110.44 W
Hobart, Austl.	166	42.53 S	147.19 E
Hobart, In., U.S.	216	41.31 N	87.15 W
Hobart, N.Y., U.S.	210	42.22 N	74.40 W
Hobart, Ok., U.S.	196	35.01 N	99.05 W
Hobart, Wa., U.S.	224	47.25 N	121.58 W
Hobbs, In., U.S.	216	40.17 N	85.57 W
Hobbs, N.M., U.S.	196	32.42 N	103.08 W
Hobbs Coast ⫠[2]	9	74.45 S	131.00 W
Hobe Sound	220	27.03 N	80.08 W
Hobgood	192	36.01 N	77.23 W
Hobhole Drain ≍	44	52.59 N	0.02 E
Hobhouse	158	29.31 S	27.08 E
Hobo	246	2.35 N	75.27 W
Hoboken, Bel.	50	51.10 N	4.21 E
Hoboken, N.J., U.S.	210	40.44 N	74.01 W
Hoboksar	86	46.47 N	85.43 E
Hobq Shamo ◆[2]	102	40.30 N	107.55 E
Hobro	26	56.38 N	9.48 E
Hobson	202	47.00 N	109.52 W
Hobson Lake ⊜	182	52.30 N	120.20 W
Hobsons Bay c	274b	37.51 S	144.56 E
Hoburgen ›	26	56.55 N	18.07 E
Hobyo	144	5.21 N	48.32 E
Hocaköy, Tür.	130	41.03 N	30.17 E
Hocaköy, Tür.	130	37.08 N	32.16 E
Hocalar	130	38.34 N	30.00 E
Hocalı	130	38.41 N	27.41 E
Hochalmspitze ∧	64	47.01 N	13.19 E
Hochandochtla Mountain ∧	180	65.32 N	154.50 W
Höchberg	56	49.49 N	9.51 E
Hochburg	60	48.07 N	12.52 E
Hochdahl	56	51.13 N	6.56 E
Hochdorf	58	47.10 N	8.17 E
Höchenschwand	58	47.44 N	8.10 E
Hochfeiler (Gran Pilastro) ∧	64	46.58 N	11.44 E
Hochfeld	156	21.28 S	17.58 E
Hochfeld ◆[8]	263	51.25 N	6.46 E
Hochfelden	56	48.45 N	7.34 E
Hochfilzen	64	47.28 N	12.37 E
Hochfinstermünz	58	46.56 N	10.29 E
Hochgern ∧	64	47.45 N	12.30 E
Hochgolling ∧	64	47.16 N	13.45 E
Hochheide	263	51.27 N	6.41 E
Hochheim, B.R.D.	56	50.01 N	8.20 E
Hochheim, Tx., U.S.	222	29.19 N	97.17 W
Hochiss ∧	64	47.27 N	11.46 E
Hochkirch	54	51.09 N	14.34 E
Hochkönig ∧	64	47.25 N	13.04 E
Hochkreuz ∧	64	46.49 N	13.04 E
Hochlantsch ∧	61	47.21 N	15.25 E
Hochlar ◆[8]	263	51.36 N	7.10 E
Hochlarmark ◆[8]	263	51.34 N	7.11 E
Hochneukirch	56	51.06 N	6.26 E
Hochobir ∧	61	46.30 N	14.29 E
Hochreichhart ∧	61	47.22 N	14.41 E
Hochries ∧	64	47.45 N	12.14 E
Hochschwab ∧	61	47.37 N	15.09 E
Hochschwab ⩕	61	47.36 N	15.05 E
Hochsimmer ∧	56	50.21 N	7.12 E
Hochspeyer	56	49.26 N	7.54 E
Höchst, B.R.D.	56	49.48 N	8.59 E
Höchst, Öst.	58	47.28 N	9.38 E
Höchst ◆[8]	56	50.07 N	8.33 E
Höchstadt an der Aisch	56	49.42 N	10.44 E
Höchstädt an der Donau	56	48.36 N	10.34 E
Höchsten	263	51.27 N	7.29 E
Höchstenbach	56	50.38 N	7.44 E
Hochstuhl (Veliki Stol) ∧	61	46.26 N	14.10 E
Hochtor)(	64	47.05 N	12.51 E
Hoch'uan → Hechuan	107	30.00 N	106.16 E
Ho Chung	271d	22.22 N	114.14 E
Hochvogel ∧	58	47.23 N	10.26 E
Hochwildstelle ∧	64	47.20 N	13.50 E
Hockenheim	56	49.19 N	8.33 E
Hockeroda	54	50.35 N	11.26 E
Hockessin	285	39.47 N	75.41 W
Hocking ≃	188	39.12 N	81.45 W
Hocking Hills State Park ♠	188	39.30 N	82.32 W
Hockley, Eng., U.K.	260	51.37 N	0.40 E
Hockley, Tx., U.S.	222	30.02 N	95.51 W
Hockomock Swamp ≣	283	41.59 N	71.05 W
Hôḍ ◆[1]	150	16.10 N	8.40 W
Hodal	124	27.54 N	77.22 E
Hōdatsu-zan ∧	94	36.47 N	136.49 E
Hodder ≃	44	53.50 N	2.25 W
Hoddesdon	260	51.46 N	0.01 W
Hoddlesden	262	53.42 N	2.26 W
Hodeida → Al-Ḥudaydah	144	14.48 N	42.57 E
Hodenhagen	52	52.46 N	9.35 E
Hodge	194	32.16 N	92.43 W
Hodgenville	194	37.34 N	85.44 W
Hodges, Lake ⊜[1]	228	33.03 N	117.05 W
Hodges Brook ≃	283	41.58 N	71.14 W
Hodges Hill ∧[2]	186	49.04 N	55.53 W
Hodgeville	184	50.08 N	106.58 W
Hodgkins	278	41.46 N	87.51 W
Hodgson	184	51.13 N	97.34 W
Hodgson ≃	164	14.48 S	134.35 E
Hodgson, Mount ∧[2]	162	22.26 S	121.10 E
Hod HaSharon	132	32.09 N	34.53 E
Hodh ech Chargui □[4]	150	18.10 N	7.15 W
Hodh el Gharbi □[4]	150	16.30 N	10.00 W
Hódmezővásárhely	30	46.25 N	20.20 E
Hodmo ∨	144	10.41 N	46.13 E
Hodna, Chott el ⊜	148	35.25 N	4.45 E
Hodna, Monts du ⩕	34	35.50 N	4.50 E
Hodna, Plaine du ≚	34	35.38 N	4.30 E
Hodnet	42	52.51 N	2.35 W
Hodogaya ◆[8]	268	35.27 N	139.36 E
Hodogaya Baseball Ground ♠	268	35.27 N	139.35 E
Hodonín	30	48.51 N	17.08 E
Hodoš	61	46.50 N	16.20 E
Hodzana ≃	180	66.15 N	147.48 W
Hoed	41	56.19 N	10.49 E
Hoedekenskerke	52	51.25 N	3.55 E
Hoehne	198	37.16 N	104.22 W
Hoeksche Waard I	52	51.45 N	4.30 E
Hoek van Holland	52	51.59 N	4.09 E
Hoeningen	263	51.05 N	6.41 E
Hoensbroek	56	50.55 N	5.55 E
Hœrdt	58	48.42 N	7.47 E
Hoerstgen	263	51.30 N	6.27 E
Hoeryŏng	98	42.27 N	129.44 E
Hoeyang	98	38.43 N	127.36 E
Hof, B.R.D.	54	50.18 N	11.55 E
Hof, Ísland	24a	64.34 N	14.39 W
Hofburg ⊍	264b	48.12 N	16.22 E
Höfðakaupstaður	24a	65.50 N	20.19 W
Hofei → Hefei	100	31.51 N	117.17 E
Höfen	56	50.32 N	6.15 E
Hoffman, Il., U.S.	219	38.32 N	89.16 W
Hoffman, Mn., U.S.	198	45.49 N	95.47 W
Hoffman Estates	216	42.02 N	88.04 W
Hoffman Island I	276	40.35 N	74.03 W
Hoffmans	210	42.54 N	74.05 W
Hoffman Station	284a	43.04 N	78.50 W
Hoffnung	263	51.07 N	7.13 E
Hofgeismar	52	51.30 N	9.22 E
Hofheim	56	50.07 N	8.26 E
Hofheim in Unterfranken	56	50.08 N	10.31 E
Hofkirchen an der Trattnac	60	48.13 N	13.44 E
Höflein an der Donau	264b	48.21 N	16.17 E
Hofmeyr	158	31.39 S	25.50 E
Höfn	24a	64.17 N	15.10 W
Hofors	40	60.33 N	16.17 E
Hofsjökull ⊓	24a	64.48 N	18.50 W
Hofstade	50	50.58 N	4.02 E
Hofstede ◆[8]	263	51.30 N	7.12 E
Hofstra University ⊍[2]	276	40.43 N	73.36 W
Hōfu	96	34.03 N	131.34 E
Hofuf → Al-Hufūf	128	25.22 N	49.34 E
Hofweier	58	48.25 N	7.55 E
Hog, Tanjong ›	116	5.18 N	119.16 E
Hogalbāria	126	23.53 N	88.51 E
Höganäs	41	56.12 N	12.33 E
Hogan Lake ⊜	190	45.52 N	78.30 W
Hogansburg	206	44.58 N	74.39 W
Hogansville	192	33.10 N	84.54 W
Hogarth, Mount ∧[2]	166	21.48 S	136.58 E
Hogatza ≃	180	66.00 N	155.29 W
Hogback Mountain ∧, U.S.	207	42.43 N	72.25 W
Hogback Mountain ∧, Mt., U.S.	202	44.54 N	112.07 W
Hogback Mountain ∧, Ne., U.S.	198	41.40 N	103.44 W
Hogback Mountain ∧, S.C., U.S.	192	35.10 N	82.17 W
Högbo	40	60.40 N	16.48 E
Hog Canyon ∨	226	35.42 N	120.35 W
Hog Creek ≃	222	31.32 N	97.18 W
Hoge Veluwe, Nationale Park de ♠	52	52.02 N	5.55 E
Högfors	40	59.59 N	15.01 E
Hoggar → Ahaggar ⩕	148	23.00 N	6.30 E
Hoghton	262	53.44 N	2.35 W
Hoghton Tower ⊥	262	53.44 N	2.34 W
Hog Island I, Ma., U.S.	283	42.40 N	70.46 W
Hog Island I, Mi., U.S.	190	45.48 N	85.22 W
Hog Island I, Vt., U.S.	206	44.57 N	73.13 W
Hog Island I, Va., U.S.	208	37.25 N	75.41 W
Hog Island Bay c	208	37.27 N	75.46 W
Hogoro	154	5.57 S	36.27 E
Hog Point ›	208	37.12 N	76.41 W
Hogs Back ⫠[4]	42	51.13 N	0.40 W
Högsby	26	57.10 N	16.02 E
Högsjö	40	59.02 N	15.41 E
Hoh ≃	224	47.45 N	124.29 W
Hoh, South Fork ≃	224	47.46 N	124.01 W
Hohe Acht ∧	56	50.23 N	7.00 E
Hohebach	56	49.22 N	9.44 E
Hohegeiss	54	51.40 N	10.40 E
Hohelimburg, Schloss ⊥	263	51.21 N	7.34 E
Hohenau	252	27.05 S	55.45 W
Hohenau an der March	61	48.36 N	16.55 E
Höhenberg	61	48.46 N	14.53 E
Hohenbrunn	60	48.03 N	11.42 E
Hohenbucko	54	51.46 N	13.28 E
Hohenbudberg ◆[8]	263	51.23 N	6.40 E
Hohenburg	60	49.16 N	11.30 E
Hohendorf	54	54.01 N	13.44 E
Hohenebra	54	51.18 N	10.49 E
Hohenems	58	47.22 N	9.41 E
Hohenfels	60	49.12 N	11.51 E
Hohenfurch	58	47.51 N	10.54 E
Hohengüstow	54	53.14 N	13.59 E
Hohenhameln	52	52.15 N	10.03 E
Hohenheide	263	51.29 N	7.47 E
Hohenkammer	60	48.25 N	11.32 E
Hohenkirchen, B.R.D.	52	53.39 N	7.55 E
Hohenkirchen, B.R.D.	56	51.23 N	9.29 E
Hohenkirchen, D.D.R.	54	50.51 N	10.41 E
Hohenkirchen, D.D.R.	54	53.51 N	11.17 E

Símbolo	English	Deutsch	Español	Français	Português
≃	River	Fluss	Río	Rivière	Rio
≍	Canal	Kanal	Canal	Canal	Canal
∟	Waterfall, Rapids	Wasserfall, Stromschnellen	Cascada, Rápidos	Chute d'eau, Rapides	Cascata, Rápidos
ʮ	Strait	Meeresstrasse	Estrecho	Détroit	Estreito
c	Bay, Gulf	Bucht, Golf	Bahía, Golfo	Baie, Golfe	Baía, Golfo
⊜	Lake, Lakes	See, Seen	Lago, Lagos	Lac, Lacs	Lago, Lagos
≣	Swamp	Sumpf	Pantano	Marais	Pântano
⊓	Ice Features, Glacier	Eis- und Gletscherformen	Accidentes Glaciales	Formes glaciaires	Acidentes glaciares
⫧	Other Hydrographic Features	Andere Hydrographische Objekte	Otros Elementos Hidrográficos	Autres données hydrographiques	Outros acidentes hidrográficos

Símbolo	English	Deutsch	Español	Français	Português
✦	Submarine Features	Untermeerische Objekte	Accidentes Submarinos	Formes de relief sous-marin	Acidentes submarinos
□	Political Unit	Politische Einheit	Unidad Politica	Entité politique	Unidade política
⊍	Cultural Institution	Kulturelle Institution	Institución Cultural	Institution culturelle	Institução cultural
⊥	Historical Site	Historische Stätte	Sitio Histórico	Site historique	Sitio histórico
♠	Recreational Site	Erholungs- und Ferienort	Sitio de Recreo	Centre de loisirs	Area de Lazer
⊠	Airport	Flughafen	Aeropuerto	Aéroport	Aeroporto
■	Military Installation	Militäranlage	Instalación Militar	Installation militaire	Instalação militar
◆	Miscellaneous	Verschiedenes	Misceláneo	Divers	Diversos

ENGLISH — Name | Page | Lat.°′ | Long.°′

DEUTSCH — Name | Seite | Breite°′ | Länge°′ E = Ost

Hohenleipisch 54 51.30 N 13.34 E
Hohenleuben 54 50.43 N 12.03 E
Hohenlimburg 56 51.21 N 7.35 E
Hohenlimburg, Schloss ⊥ 263 51.21 N 7.34 E
Hohenlinden 60 48.09 N 12.00 E
Hohenmölsen 54 51.09 N 12.06 E
Hohen Neuendorf 54 52.40 N 13.16 E
Hohenpolding 60 48.23 N 12.08 E
Hohensalza → Inowrocław 30 52.48 N 18.15 E
Hohenschönhausen ◆[8] 264a 52.33 N 13.30 E
Hohenseeden 54 52.19 N 12.01 E
Hohenseefeld 54 51.53 N 13.18 E
Hohenstaufen 56 48.44 N 9.43 E
Hohenstein → Olsztynek 30 53.36 N 20.17 E
Hohenstein-Ernstthal 54 50.48 N 12.42 E
Hohensyburg ⊥ 56 51.25 N 7.29 E
Hohentauern 61 47.26 N 14.29 E
Hohenthurm 54 51.31 N 12.05 E
Hohenthurn 64 46.33 N 13.40 E
Hohentwiel ʌ 58 47.46 N 8.49 E
Hohenwald 194 35.32 N 87.33 W
Hohenwart 60 48.36 N 11.23 E
Hohenwarte-Stausee ⊜[1] 54 50.32 N 11.30 E
Hohenwarthe 54 52.13 N 11.42 E
Hohenwutzen 54 52.51 N 14.07 E
Hohenzethen 54 53.03 N 10.49 E
Hohenzollern, Burg ⊥ 58 48.19 N 8.58 E
Hohenzollernkanal ≆ 264a 52.32 N 13.20 E
Hoher Bogen ʌ 60 49.15 N 12.55 E
Hoher Dachstein ʌ 64 47.28 N 13.35 E
Hoher Freschen ʌ 58 47.18 N 9.46 E
Hohe Rhön ʌʌ 56 50.30 N 10.00 E
Hoher Ifen ʌ 58 47.21 N 10.05 E
Hoherlehme 264a 52.19 N 13.37 E
Hoher Mechtin ʌ[2] 54 53.03 N 10.55 E
Hoher Riffler ʌ 58 47.07 N 10.22 E
Hoher Sonnblick ʌ 64 47.03 N 12.57 E
Hoher Zinken ʌ 64 47.40 N 13.20 E
Hohe Tauern ʌʌ 64 47.10 N 12.45 E
Hohe Warte (Monte Coglians) ʌ 64 46.37 N 12.53 E
Hoh Head ≻ 224 47.46 N 124.29 W
Hohhot 102 40.51 N 111.40 E
Höhn 56 50.37 N 8.00 E
Hohndorf 54 50.45 N 12.40 E
Hohne 52 52.35 N 10.22 E
Hohneck, Le ʌ 58 48.02 N 7.01 E
Hohnstein 54 50.59 N 14.10 E
Hohoe 150 7.09 N 0.28 E
Hōhoku 96 34.17 N 130.57 E
Ho-Ho-Kus 276 40.59 N 74.06 W
Hohokus Brook ≃ 276 40.57 N 74.06 W
Hoholitna ≃ 180 61.31 N 157.00 W
Höhscheid ◆[8] 263 51.09 N 7.04 E
Hohultslätt 26 56.58 N 15.39 E
Hohwacht 54 54.19 N 10.41 E
Hohwachter Bucht ⊂ 41 54.20 N 10.45 E
Hoh Xil Shan ʌʌ 120 35.20 N 90.00 E
Hoi-an 110 15.52 N 108.19 E
Hoihow → Haikou 102 20.03 N 110.19 E
Hoima 154 1.26 N 31.21 E
Hoisdorf 52 53.39 N 10.20 E
Hoisington 198 38.31 N 98.46 W
Hoisten 263 51.08 N 6.42 E
Hoi-xuan 110 20.22 N 105.07 E
Hojāi 120 26.00 N 92.51 E
Højby, Dan. 41 55.55 N 11.37 E
Højby, Dan. 41 55.20 N 10.27 E
Höje 40 59.54 N 13.33 E
Højer 26 54.58 N 8.43 E
Højerup 41 55.17 N 12.27 E
Hōjō → Kasai, Nihon 96 34.56 N 134.50 E
Hōjō, Nihon 96 34.54 N 134.56 E
Hōjō, Nihon 96 33.58 N 132.46 E
Hoka 130 40.21 N 40.55 E
Hokah 190 43.45 N 91.20 W
Hokang → Hegang 89 47.24 N 130.17 E
Hökåsen 40 59.40 N 16.35 E
Hokendauqua 208 40.39 N 75.29 W
Hökensås ʌʌ[2] 26 58.11 N 14.08 E
Hokes Bluff 194 33.59 N 85.51 W
Hoketçe 130 38.16 N 36.13 E
Hōki ≃ 94 36.47 N 140.08 E
Hokianga Harbour ⊂ 172 35.32 S 173.22 E
Hokitika 172 42.43 S 170.58 E
Hokkaidō □[5] 92a 44.00 N 143.00 E
Hokkaidō I 92a 44.00 N 143.00 E
Hokksund 26 59.47 N 9.59 E
Hoko ≃ 224 48.17 N 124.22 W
Hōkōji 270 34.52 N 135.07 E
Hököpinge 41 55.30 N 13.00 E
Hokota 94 36.09 N 140.31 E
Hok So Wan 271d 22.13 N 114.14 E
Hokubo 96 34.57 N 133.38 E
Hokudan 96 34.32 N 134.56 E
Hokura ≃ 94 37.10 N 138.16 E
Hokuriku-tunnel ◆[5] 94 35.42 N 136.10 E
Hokusei 94 35.09 N 136.31 E
Hola 154 1.29 S 40.02 E
Holalkere 122 14.02 N 76.11 E
Holanda → Netherlands □[1] 30 52.15 N 5.30 E
Holbæk 41 55.43 N 11.43 E
Holbeach 42 52.49 N 0.01 E
Holbeach Marsh ≡ 42 52.52 N 0.05 E
Holberg 182 50.39 N 128.00 W
Holborn ◆[8] 260 51.31 N 0.07 W
Holbrook, Austl. 171b 35.44 S 147.19 E
Holbrook, Az., U.S. 200 34.54 N 110.09 W
Holbrook, Il., U.S. 278 41.32 N 87.38 W
Holbrook, Md., U.S. 284b 39.24 N 76.51 W
Holbrook, Ma., U.S. 207 42.09 N 71.00 W
Holbrook, Ne., U.S. 198 40.18 N 100.00 W
Holbrook, N.Y., U.S. 210 40.48 N 73.04 W
Holbrook, Lake ⊜[1] 222 32.42 N 95.33 W
Holbrook Mountain ʌ[2] 212 44.25 N 77.51 W
Holckenhavn 41 55.17 N 10.47 E
Holcomb, Il., U.S. 216 42.04 N 89.06 W
Holcomb, N.Y., U.S. 210 42.54 N 77.25 W
Holcomb Creek ≃ 228 34.17 N 117.08 W
Holden, Ab., Can. 182 53.14 N 112.14 W
Holden, Ma., U.S. 207 42.21 N 71.51 W
Holden, Mo., U.S. 194 38.42 N 93.59 W
Holden, Ut,. U.S. 200 39.05 N 112.16 W
Holden, W.V., U.S. 188 37.49 N 82.03 W
Holden, Mount ʌ[2] 216 41.40 N 87.03 W
Holdenstedt 52 52.55 N 10.31 E
Holden Village 224 48.12 N 120.47 W
Holdenville 196 35.04 N 96.23 W
Holder 220 28.58 N 82.25 W
Holderness ≻[1] 44 53.47 N 0.10 W
Holdfast 184 50.58 N 105.25 W
Holdich 254 45.57 S 68.13 W
Holdingford 190 45.43 N 94.28 W
Holdorf 52 52.35 N 8.07 E
Holdrege 198 40.26 N 99.22 W
Holeby 41 54.43 N 11.28 E
Hole in the Mountain Peak ʌ 204 40.55 N 115.05 W
Hole Narsipur 122 12.47 N 76.15 E
Holešov 30 49.20 N 17.35 E
Holetown 241g 13.11 N 59.39 W
Holgate, S. Afr. 158 33.59 S 22.21 E
Holgate, Oh., U.S. 216 41.14 N 84.07 W
Holguín 240p 20.53 N 76.15 W
Holguín □[4] 240p 20.55 N 75.50 W
Hol-Hol, Dji. 144 11.19 N 42.57 E
Holhol, Tür. 130 39.14 N 40.03 E
Holíč 30 48.49 N 17.10 E
Holice 30 50.04 N 15.59 E
Holiday Beach Provincial Park ♠ 214 42.02 N 83.05 W
Holiday Hills 216 42.18 N 88.13 W
Holiday Lake Amusement Park ♠ 285 40.02 N 74.56 W
Holiday Shores 219 38.55 N 89.56 W
Holitna ≃ 180 61.40 N 157.12 W
Höljes 26 60.54 N 12.36 E
Hollabrunn 61 48.34 N 16.05 E
Holladay 200 40.40 N 111.49 W
Holland, Mb., Can. 184 49.36 N 98.53 W
Holland, Mi., U.S. 216 42.47 N 86.06 W
Holland, N.Y., U.S. 210 42.38 N 78.32 W
Holland, Oh., U.S. 216 41.37 N 83.42 W
Holland, Pa., U.S. 285 40.10 N 74.59 W
Holland, Tx., U.S. 222 30.53 N 97.24 W
Holland, Va., U.S. 208 36.41 N 76.47 W
Holland □[9] 52 52.20 N 4.45 E
Holland → Netherlands □[1] 30 52.15 N 5.30 E
Holland ≃ 212 44.12 N 79.31 W
Holland, Mount ʌ 162 32.12 S 119.44 E
Hollandale 194 33.10 N 90.51 W
Holland Creek ≃ 169 36.43 S 146.06 E
Hollande, Étang de ⊜ 261 48.44 N 1.48 E
Holland Fen ≡ 42 53.00 N 0.10 W
Hollandia → Jayapura 164 2.32 S 140.42 E
Holland Landing 212 44.06 N 79.29 W
Holland Park 171a 27.31 S 153.03 E
Holland Patent 210 43.14 N 75.15 W
Holland Point ≻ 208 38.43 N 76.32 W
Holland Pond State Park ♠ 207 42.04 N 72.09 W
Hollandsbird Island I 156 24.45 S 14.34 E
Hollandsch Diep ⊔ 52 51.42 N 4.30 E
Hollandstoun 46 59.21 N 2.16 W
Holland Straits ⊔ 208 38.08 N 76.02 W
Holland Tunnel ◆[5] 276 40.44 N 74.02 W
Hollansburg 218 39.59 N 84.47 W
Holleben 54 51.26 N 11.53 E
Hollenfels, Château ⊥ 56 49.43 N 6.03 E
Höllengebirge ʌʌ 64 47.48 N 13.39 E
Hollenstedt 52 53.22 N 9.43 E
Hollenstein an der Ybbs 61 47.48 N 14.46 E
Höllenstein Berg ʌ 264b 48.06 N 16.11 E
Höllental V 61 47.45 N 15.47 E
Hollern 52 53.36 N 9.32 E
Holleton 162 31.57 S 119.02 E
Holley 210 43.13 N 78.01 W
Hollfeld 60 49.56 N 11.18 E
Hollick-Kenyon Plateau ʌʌ[1] 9 79.00 S 97.00 W
Holliday, Mo., U.S. 219 39.29 N 92.07 W
Holliday, Tx., U.S. 196 33.49 N 98.42 W
Holliday Creek ≃ 196 33.55 N 98.28 W
Holliday Park ♠ 281 42.21 N 83.24 W
Hollidaysburg 214 40.25 N 78.23 W
Hollingbourne 260 51.16 N 0.38 E
Hollingstedt 41 54.27 N 9.19 E
Hollingworth 262 53.28 N 1.59 W
Hollingworth Lake ⊜ 262 53.38 N 2.06 W
Hollins, Eng., U.K. 262 53.34 N 2.17 W
Hollins, Va., U.S. 192 37.20 N 79.56 W
Hollins Green 262 53.25 N 2.27 W
Hollinswood 284c 38.55 N 77.13 W
Hollis, N.H., U.S. 207 42.44 N 71.35 W
Hollis, Ok., U.S. 196 34.41 N 99.54 W
Hollis ◆[8] 276 40.43 N 73.46 W
Hollister 226 36.51 N 121.24 W
Hollister, Mount ʌ[2] 162 22.08 S 114.01 E
Holliston 207 42.12 N 71.25 W
Hollman, Cape ≻ 164 4.59 S 150.06 E
Holloman Air Force Base ■ 200 32.51 N 106.05 W
Holloway 214 40.10 N 81.08 W
Holloway Terrace 285 39.42 N 75.32 W
Hollow Rock 194 36.02 N 88.16 W
Hollowville 210 42.12 N 73.42 W
Hollsopple 214 40.13 N 78.56 W
Hollum 52 53.26 N 5.37 E
Höllviken ⊂ 41 55.26 N 12.54 E
Höllviksnäs 41 55.25 N 12.57 E
Holly, Co., U.S. 198 38.03 N 102.07 W
Holly, Mi., U.S. 216 42.47 N 83.37 W
Holly, Wa., U.S. 224 47.34 N 122.58 W
Holly, Mount ʌ[2] 285 40.00 N 74.47 W
Holly Brook 285 39.59 N 74.48 W
Holly Grove 194 34.35 N 91.11 W
Holly Hill, Fl., U.S. 192 29.14 N 81.02 W
Holly Hill, S.C., U.S. 192 33.19 N 80.24 W
Holly Park, N.J., U.S. 208 39.53 N 74.10 W
Holly Park, Va., U.S. 284c 38.50 N 77.17 W
Holly Pond ⊜ 276 41.03 N 73.30 W
Holly River State Park ♠ 188 38.40 N 80.21 W
Holly Run ≃ 285 39.47 N 75.03 W
Holly Springs 194 34.46 N 89.26 W
Holly State Recreation Area ♠ 216 42.49 N 83.32 W
Hollywood, Ire. 48 53.06 N 6.35 W
Hollywood, Fl., U.S. 220 26.00 N 80.08 W
Hollywood, Md., U.S. 208 38.20 N 76.34 W
Hollywood, Pa., U.S. 285 40.05 N 75.06 W
Hollywood ◆[8] 228 34.06 N 118.21 W
Hollywood, Mount ʌ 280 34.08 N 118.18 W
Hollywood Bowl ♠ 280 34.07 N 118.20 W
Hollywood-Burbank Airport ⊠ 228 34.12 N 118.21 W
Hollywood Heights 219 38.39 N 89.59 W
Hollywood Indian Reservation ◆[4] 220 26.02 N 80.13 W
Hollywood Park Race Track ♠ 280 33.57 N 118.20 W
Hollywood Reservoir ⊜[1] 280 34.07 N 118.20 W
Holman 176 70.43 N 117.43 W
Hólmavík 24a 65.43 N 21.43 W
Holmdel 208 40.20 N 74.11 W
Holme, Dan. 41 56.07 N 10.11 E
Holme, Eng., U.K. 262 53.33 N 1.50 W
Holme ≃ 44 53.41 N 1.43 W
Holme Chapel 262 53.45 N 2.11 W
Holmen, Nor. 26 60.40 N 10.22 E
Holmen, Wi., U.S. 190 43.57 N 91.15 W
Holmenkollen 26 59.58 N 10.40 E
Holme-on-Spaulding-Moor 44 53.50 N 0.46 W
Holmes, N.Y., U.S. 210 41.31 N 73.39 W
Holmes, Pa., U.S. 285 39.54 N 75.19 W
Holmes □[6] 214 40.33 N 81.55 W
Holmes, Mount ʌ 202 44.49 N 110.51 W
Holmes Beach 220 27.31 N 82.43 W
Holmesburg ◆[8] 285 40.02 N 75.03 W
Holmes Chapel 44 53.12 N 2.22 W
Holmes Creek ≃ 194 30.30 N 85.47 W
Holmesglen 274b 37.53 S 145.06 E
Holmes Harbor ⊂ 224 48.04 N 122.32 W
Holmes Lake ⊜ 184 57.05 N 96.45 W
Holmes Reefs ✧[2] 164 16.27 S 148.00 E
Holmes Run ≃ 284c 38.48 N 77.07 W
Holmes Run Acres 284c 38.51 N 77.13 W
Holmestrand 26 59.29 N 10.18 E
Holmesville, N.Y., U.S. 210 42.31 N 75.24 W
Holmesville, Oh., U.S. 214 40.37 N 81.55 W
Holmeswood 262 53.39 N 2.52 W
Holmfirth 44 53.35 N 1.46 W
Holmia 246 4.58 N 59.35 W
Holmön I 26 63.47 N 20.53 E
Holmsbu 26 59.33 N 10.27 E
Holmsjön ⊜, Sve. 26 62.41 N 16.33 E
Holmsjön ⊜, Sve. 26 62.25 N 15.20 E
Holmsund 26 63.42 N 20.21 E
Hölö 40 59.01 N 17.35 E
Holod 38 46.47 N 22.08 E
Holoit, Punta ≻ 232 21.37 N 88.08 W
Holon 132 32.01 N 34.46 E
Holoog 156 27.22 S 17.55 E
Holopaw 220 28.08 N 81.04 W
Holroyd 274a 33.50 S 150.58 E
Holroyd ≃ 164 14.10 S 141.36 E
Holsloot 52 52.44 N 6.48 E
Holstebro 26 56.21 N 8.38 E
Holsted 41 55.30 N 8.55 E
Holstein 198 42.29 N 95.32 W
Holsteinborg ⊥ 41 55.13 N 11.28 E
Holsteinische Schweiz ◆[1] 54 54.11 N 10.36 E
Holsteinsborg 176 66.55 N 53.40 W
Holsterhausen 263 51.41 N 6.57 E
Holston ≃ 192 35.57 N 83.51 W
Holston, North Fork ≃ 192 36.33 N 82.36 W
Holston High Knob ʌ 192 36.27 N 82.05 W
Holsworthy 42 50.49 N 4.21 W
Holt, Eng., U.K. 42 52.55 N 1.05 E
Holt, Wales, U.K. 42 53.05 N 2.53 W
Holt, Al., U.S. 194 33.14 N 87.29 W
Holt, Ca., U.S. 226 37.56 N 121.26 W
Holt, Fl., U.S. 194 30.42 N 86.44 W
Holt, Mi., U.S. 216 42.38 N 84.30 W
Holt Creek ≃ 198 42.28 N 98.50 W
Holte 41 55.49 N 12.28 E
Holtemme ≃ 54 51.57 N 11.10 E
Holten 52 52.17 N 6.25 E
Holten ◆[8] 263 51.31 N 6.48 E
Holtenau ◆[8] 54 54.22 N 10.08 E
Holter Lake ⊜[1] 202 46.55 N 111.57 W
Holthausen, B.R.D. 52 52.33 N 7.17 E
Holthausen, B.R.D. 263 51.23 N 7.13 E
Holthausen ◆[8] 263 51.34 N 7.26 E
Holthusen 52 53.08 N 7.18 E
Holton, In., U.S. 218 39.04 N 85.23 W
Holton, Ks., U.S. 198 39.27 N 95.44 W
Holtorf 52 52.40 N 9.13 E
Holts Summit 219 38.39 N 92.07 W
Holtsville 210 40.49 N 73.02 W
Holtug 41 55.21 N 12.25 E
Holtville 204 32.48 N 115.22 W
Holtwick 52 52.00 N 7.05 E
Holtwood 208 39.50 N 76.19 W
Holwerd 52 53.22 N 5.54 E
Holycross, Ire. 48 52.38 N 7.52 W
Holy Cross, Ak., U.S. 180 62.12 N 159.47 W
Holy Cross Mountain ʌ 182 53.47 N 120.47 W
Holyhead 44 53.19 N 4.38 W
Holyhead Bay ⊂ 44 53.23 N 4.37 W
Holy Island I, Eng., U.K. 44 55.41 N 1.48 W
Holy Island I, Scot., U.K. 46 55.32 N 5.04 W
Holy Island I, Wales, U.K. 44 53.18 N 4.37 W
Holy Island I, Ma., U.S. 283 42.43 N 70.50 W
Holyoke, Co., U.S. 198 40.35 N 102.18 W
Holyoke, Ma., U.S. 207 42.12 N 72.37 W
Holyrood 198 38.35 N 98.24 W
Holyrood Palace ⊍ 46 55.56 N 3.12 W
Holy Sepulchre, The Church of the ⊍[1] 132 31.46 N 35.14 E
Holýšov 60 49.36 N 13.05 E
Holywell 44 53.17 N 3.13 W
Holywell Green 262 53.41 N 1.52 W
Holywood 48 54.38 N 5.50 W
Holzbüttgen 263 51.12 N 6.37 E
Holzen 56 51.26 N 7.31 E
Holzgau 58 47.16 N 10.21 E
Holzgerlingen 56 48.38 N 9.00 E
Holzhausen, B.R.D. 52 52.17 N 8.32 E
Holzhausen, B.R.D. 52 52.13 N 8.01 E
Holzhausen, B.R.D. 52 52.01 N 8.44 E
Holzhausen, D.D.R. 54 51.18 N 12.28 E
Holzhausen an der Haide 56 50.13 N 7.55 E
Holzheim 56 51.09 N 6.39 E
Holzkirchen 64 47.52 N 11.42 E
Holzminden 52 51.50 N 9.27 E
Holzweissig 54 51.36 N 12.18 E
Holzwickede 52 51.30 N 7.36 E
Hom ≃ 158 28.51 S 18.37 E
Homa 130 38.14 N 30.01 E
Homa Bay 154 0.31 S 34.27 E
Homalin 110 24.52 N 94.55 E
Homathko ≃ 182 50.55 N 124.50 W
Homathko Icefield ⊓ 182 51.05 N 124.30 W
Homberg, B.R.D. 56 50.43 N 8.59 E
Homberg, B.R.D. 56 51.02 N 9.24 E
Homberg, B.R.D. 56 51.28 N 6.43 E
Homberg, B.R.D. 263 51.18 N 6.56 E
Hombori 150 15.17 N 1.42 W
Hombori Tondo ʌ 150 15.16 N 1.40 W
Hombourg-Haut 56 49.08 N 6.46 E
Hombre Muerto, Salar del ≚ 252 25.23 S 67.06 W
Hombruch ◆[8] 263 51.29 N 7.26 E
Homburg, B.R.D. 56 49.19 N 7.20 E
Homburg → Bad Homburg vor der Höhe, B.R.D. 56 50.13 N 8.37 E
Home, Pa., U.S. 214 40.44 N 79.06 W
Home, Wa., U.S. 224 47.17 N 122.46 W
Homeacre 214 40.51 N 79.55 W
Home Bay ⊂, N.T., Can. 176 68.45 N 67.10 W
Home Bay ⊂, Kiribati 174d 0.53 S 169.35 E
Homebush Bay ⊂ 274a 33.50 S 151.05 E
Home Corner 216 40.31 N 85.38 W
Homécourt 56 49.14 N 5.59 E
Home Creek ≃ 196 31.29 N 99.14 W
Homedale, Id., U.S. 202 43.37 N 116.55 W
Homedale, Oh., U.S. 214 40.04 N 83.02 W
Home Gardens 228 33.52 N 117.31 W
Home Hill 166 19.40 S 147.25 E
Homeland, Ca., U.S. 228 33.44 N 117.07 W
Homeland, Fl., U.S. 220 27.49 N 81.49 W
Homeland Canal ≆ 226 35.57 N 119.27 W
Homeland Park 192 34.27 N 82.41 W
Home Place 218 39.56 N 86.08 W
Homer, Ak., U.S. 180 59.39 N 151.33 W
Homer, Ga., U.S. 192 34.20 N 83.29 W
Homer, La., U.S. 194 32.47 N 93.03 W
Homer, Mi., U.S. 216 42.08 N 84.48 W
Homer, Ne., U.S. 198 42.19 N 96.29 W
Homer, N.Y., U.S. 210 42.38 N 76.10 W
Homer, Oh., U.S. 214 40.15 N 82.31 W
Homer, Tx., U.S. 222 31.18 N 94.36 W
Homer City 214 40.32 N 79.09 W
Homert ʌ[2] 263 51.11 N 7.39 E
Homer Tunnel ◆[5] 172 44.45 S 168.00 E
Homerville, Ga., U.S. 192 31.02 N 82.44 W
Homerville, Oh., U.S. 214 41.02 N 82.08 W
Homer Wash V 204 34.20 N 115.02 W
Homer Youngs Peak ʌ 202 45.19 N 113.41 W
Home Seamount ✧[3] 14 12.55 S 175.37 W
Homestead, Austl. 166 20.22 S 145.39 E
Homestead, Fl., U.S. 220 25.28 N 80.28 W
Homestead, Pa., U.S. 279b 40.24 N 79.54 W
Homestead Air Force Base ■ 220 25.29 N 80.23 W
Homestead National Monument of America ♠ 198 40.14 N 96.54 W
Homestead Valley 282 37.54 N 122.32 W
Hometown, Il., U.S. 278 41.44 N 87.43 W
Hometown, Pa., U.S. 210 40.49 N 75.59 W
Homewood, Al., U.S. 194 33.28 N 86.48 W
Homewood, Ca., U.S. 226 39.05 N 120.09 W
Homewood, Il., U.S. 216 41.33 N 87.39 W
Homewood, Oh., U.S. 218 39.23 N 84.33 W
Homewood ◆[8] 279b 40.27 N 79.54 W
Homewood Acres 278 41.34 N 87.43 W
Homeworth 214 40.50 N 81.03 W
Hominy 196 36.24 N 96.23 W
Hominy Creek ≃ 196 36.20 N 96.00 W
Hommersåk 26 58.58 N 5.42 E
Hommura 92 34.22 N 139.15 E
Homnābād 122 17.46 N 77.08 E
Homochitto ≃ 194 31.09 N 91.31 W
Homoíne 156 23.52 S 35.09 E
Homonhon Island I 116 10.44 N 125.43 E
Homosassa 220 28.46 N 82.36 W
Homosassa Bay ⊂ 220 28.45 N 82.43 W
Homosassa Springs 220 28.48 N 82.35 W
Homs → Al-Khums 146 32.39 N 14.16 E
Homs → Ḥimṣ 130 34.44 N 36.43 E
Honai 96 33.30 N 132.25 E
Honaker 192 37.00 N 81.58 W
Honami 96 33.36 N 130.42 E
Honan → Luoyang 102 34.41 N 112.28 E
Honan → Henan □[4] 90 34.00 N 114.00 E
Honāvar 122 14.17 N 74.27 E
Honaz 130 37.45 N 29.17 E
Honbetsu 92a 43.07 N 143.37 E
Hon-chong 110 10.10 N 104.37 E
Honda 246 5.12 N 74.45 W
Honda, Bahía ⊂, Col. 246 12.21 N 71.47 W
Honda, Bahía ⊂, Cuba 240p 22.57 N 83.10 W
Honda, Cañada ≃ 258 33.57 S 59.21 W
Honda Bay ⊂ 116 9.53 N 118.49 E
Honddu ≃, Wales, U.K. 42 51.54 N 2.58 W
Honddu ≃, Wales, U.K. 42 51.57 N 3.23 W
Hondeklipbaai 156 30.20 S 17.18 E
Honderfontein 158 32.12 S 21.22 E
Hondo, Ab., Can. 182 55.04 N 114.02 W
Hondo, Nihon 92 32.27 N 130.12 E
Hondo, N.M., U.S. 200 33.23 N 105.16 W
Hondo, Tx., U.S. 196 29.20 N 99.08 W
Hondo ≃, Cuba 286b 22.55 N 82.16 W
Hondo ≃, Méx. 286a 19.26 N 99.15 W
Hondo ≃, N.A. 232 18.29 N 88.19 W
Hondo, Arroyo ≃ 226 37.28 N 121.47 W
Hondo, Rio ≃, Ca., U.S. 280 33.55 N 118.10 W
Hondo, Rio ≃, N.M., U.S. 196 33.22 N 104.24 W
Hondo Creek ≃ 196 28.45 N 99.11 W
Hondoji Temple ⊍[1] 268 35.51 N 139.56 E
Hondschoote 50 50.59 N 2.35 E
Hondsrug ʌʌ[2] 52 52.55 N 6.50 E
Honduras □[1], N.A. 230 15.00 N 86.30 W
Honduras □[1], N.A. 236 15.00 N 86.30 W
Honduras, Cabo de ≻ 236 16.01 N 86.02 W
Honduras, Gulf of ⊂ 230 16.10 N 87.50 W
Honduras, Port ⊂ 236 16.13 N 88.41 W
Honea Path 192 34.26 N 82.23 W
Hönebach 56 50.56 N 9.56 E
Hønefoss 26 60.10 N 10.18 E
Honeoye 210 42.47 N 77.31 W
Honeoye Creek ≃ 210 42.58 N 77.43 W
Honeoye Falls 210 42.57 N 77.35 W
Honeoye Lake ⊜ 210 42.45 N 77.31 W
Honesdale 210 41.34 N 75.15 W
Honey Brook 208 40.05 N 75.54 W
Honey Creek 216 42.44 N 88.18 W
Honey Creek ≃, Ia., U.S. 190 42.09 N 93.03 W
Honey Creek ≃, Mo., U.S. 194 39.53 N 93.34 W
Honey Creek ≃, Oh., U.S. 214 41.05 N 83.12 W
Honey Creek ≃, Pa., U.S. 208 40.36 N 77.35 W
Honey Creek ≃, Wi., U.S. 216 42.41 N 88.17 W
Honeydew 273d 26.05 S 27.55 E
Honeygo Run ≃ 284b 39.22 N 76.25 W
Honey Grove 196 33.35 N 95.54 W
Honey Lake ⊜ 204 40.16 N 120.19 W
Honeymoon Bay 224 48.49 N 124.10 W
Honeyville 200 41.38 N 112.04 W
Honfleur 50 49.25 N 0.14 E
Høng 41 55.31 N 11.18 E
Hong ≃ 100 32.25 N 115.35 E
Honga 152 15.09 S 15.12 E
Hong'an 100 31.18 N 114.37 E
Honga River ⊂ 208 38.19 N 76.10 W
Hongawa 96 33.43 N 133.19 E
Hon-gay 110 20.57 N 107.05 E
Hongchang 100 34.05 N 113.20 E
Hongch'ŏn 98 37.42 N 127.52 E
Hongchoudai 100 29.03 N 121.11 E
Hongcun, Zhg. 100 27.10 N 116.48 E
Hongcun, Zhg. 106 31.01 N 119.15 E
Höngen 56 51.02 N 5.56 E
Honggun 98 40.46 N 128.27 E
Hong-ha → Red ≃ 110 20.17 N 106.34 E
Honghai Wan ⊂ 100 22.40 N 115.10 E
Honghe 102 23.23 N 102.35 E
Honghu 100 29.48 N 113.27 E
Hong Hu ⊜ 100 29.52 N 113.23 E
Honghuaerji 89 48.15 N 120.01 E
Honghuaji 100 33.52 N 114.26 E
Honghualiangzi 89 48.06 N 123.12 E
Honghuamu 89 48.33 N 125.39 E
Hongjiang, Zhg. 100 26.49 N 120.03 E
Hongjiang, Zhg. 102 27.07 N 109.56 E
Hong Kong → Victoria 271d 22.17 N 114.09 E
Hong Kong □[2], Asia 90 22.15 N 114.10 E
Hong Kong □[2], Asia 100 22.15 N 114.10 E
Hong Kong I 271d 22.15 N 114.11 E
Hong Kong, University of ⊍[2] 271d 22.17 N 114.08 E
Hongkou Park ♠ 269b 31.16 N 121.28 E
Honglai 100 25.08 N 118.32 E
Honglanbu 106 31.37 N 118.57 E
Honglinqiao 106 30.59 N 118.59 E
Hongliutai 85 39.48 N 77.26 E
Hongliuyuan 102 41.04 N 95.26 E
Honglongdian 106 30.30 N 119.00 E
Honglongtang 105 40.41 N 117.37 E
Honglu 100 25.44 N 119.20 E
Hongluan 100 28.31 N 117.01 E
Hongluo Shan ʌ 104 40.56 N 120.42 E
Hongluoxian 104 41.01 N 120.53 E
Hongmeichang 105 39.50 N 115.51 E
Hongmendu 102 26.10 N 102.37 E
Hongmenkou 102 27.22 N 100.30 E
Hongmenpu 107 30.37 N 104.08 E
Hongmiaozi 107 28.47 N 104.02 E
Hong-ngu 110 10.48 N 105.21 E
Hongō, Nihon 96 34.24 N 132.59 E
Hongō, Nihon 96 34.17 N 132.02 E
Hongō ◆[8] 268 35.42 N 139.47 E
Hongpailou 107 30.38 N 104.01 E
Hongqi 89 44.23 N 126.32 E
Hongqiao, Zhg. 100 28.14 N 121.01 E
Hongqiao, Zhg. 105 39.50 N 117.44 E
Hongqiao, Zhg. 106 31.29 N 121.49 E
Hongqiao, Zhg. 269b 31.12 N 121.22 E
Hongqiao Ji Chang ⊠ 106 31.12 N 121.20 E
Hongrie → Hungary □[1] 30 47.00 N 20.00 E
Hongshan, Zhg. 89 48.02 N 129.00 E
Hongshan, Zhg. 98 36.37 N 118.00 E
Hongshanzi 98 42.34 N 117.14 E
Hongshi, Zhg. 89 43.00 N 127.04 E
Hongshi, Zhg. 98 41.21 N 119.32 E
Hongshidou 104 41.52 N 122.11 E
Hongshili 98 40.41 N 125.03 E
Hongshui 102 37.24 N 104.00 E
Hongshui ≃ 102 23.45 N 109.30 E
Hongshuichuan 105 40.06 N 117.55 E
Hongshuyangzi 105 40.36 N 116.36 E
Hongsŏng 98 36.36 N 126.39 E
Hongtang 100 26.06 N 119.14 E
Hongtian 100 25.52 N 117.15 E
Hongtong 102 36.19 N 111.39 E
Hongtugou 120 38.08 N 91.10 E
Hongtuwan 98 41.03 N 113.39 E
Hongtu Zhang ʌ 100 23.46 N 115.56 E
Honguedo, Détroit d' ⊔ 186 49.15 N 64.00 W
Hongwŏn 98 40.02 N 127.57 E
Hongxin 100 32.43 N 117.47 E
Hongxing 105 39.48 N 116.27 E
Hongxingqiao 106 30.55 N 119.52 E
Hongyang, Zhg. 100 26.32 N 119.27 E
Hongyang, Zhg. 100 23.28 N 116.13 E
Hongyanzi 104 40.38 N 120.31 E
Hongyōtoku 268 35.41 N 139.55 E
Hongze 100 33.19 N 118.53 E
Hongze Hu ⊜ 100 33.16 N 118.34 E
Honiara 175e 9.26 S 159.57 E
Honiton 42 50.48 N 3.13 W
Hon-jima I 96 34.23 N 133.47 E
Honjō, Nihon 92 39.23 N 140.03 E
Honjō, Nihon 94 36.24 N 138.01 E
Honjō, Nihon 94 36.14 N 139.11 E
Honkamäki ʌ[2] 26 62.58 N 27.05 E
Hon-kawane 94 35.07 N 138.09 E
Honker Bay ⊂ 282 38.04 N 121.56 W
Hönne ≃ 263 51.28 N 7.46 E
Honnecourt-sur-Escaut 50 50.02 N 3.12 E
Honningsvåg 24 70.59 N 25.59 E
Hönö 26 57.42 N 11.39 E
Honokaa 229d 20.04 N 155.28 W
Honokahua 229a 21.00 N 156.39 W
Honokawai 229a 20.57 N 156.41 W
Honolulu 229c 21.18 N 157.51 W
Honolulu □[6] 229c 21.19 N 157.52 W
Honolulu International Airport ⊠ 229c 21.20 N 157.55 W
Honomu 229d 19.52 N 155.07 W
Honouliuli 229c 21.22 N 158.02 W
Hönow 54 52.32 N 13.38 E
Honshū I 92 36.00 N 138.00 E
Hontoon Island State Park ♠ 220 28.59 N 81.22 W
Höntrop ◆[8] 263 51.27 N 7.08 E
Honuapo Bay ⊂ 229d 19.05 N 155.33 W
Hoo 260 51.25 N 0.34 E
Hood 226 38.22 N 121.31 W
Hood □[6] 222 32.25 N 97.45 W
Hood ≃, N.T., Can. 176 67.26 N 108.53 W
Hood ≃, Or., U.S. 224 45.42 N 121.30 W
Hood, East Fork ≃ 224 45.36 N 121.38 W
Hood, Mount ʌ 224 45.23 N 121.41 W
Hood, West Fork ≃ 224 45.36 N 121.38 W
Hood Canal ⊂ 224 47.35 N 123.00 W
Hood Canal Floating Bridge ◆[5] 224 47.52 N 122.38 W
Hoodoo Peak ʌ 202 48.15 N 120.19 W
Hood Point ≻, Austl. 162 34.23 S 119.34 E
Hood Point ≻, Pap. N. Gui. 164 10.05 S 147.45 E
Hood Pond ⊜ 283 42.40 N 70.57 W
Hood River 224 45.42 N 121.31 W
Hoodsport 224 47.24 N 123.08 W
Hoods Range ʌʌ 166 28.35 S 144.30 E
Hoof 56 51.17 N 9.20 E
Hoogerheide 52 51.25 N 4.20 E
Hoogeveen 52 52.43 N 6.29 E
Hoogeveense Vaart ≃ 52 52.42 N 6.11 E
Hoogezand-Sappemeer 52 53.09 N 6.47 E
Hooghly □[5] 126 22.50 N 88.15 E
Hooghly ≃ 126 21.55 N 88.05 E
Hooghly-Chinsura 126 22.54 N 88.24 E
Hoogkerk 52 53.13 N 6.30 E
Hooglede 50 50.59 N 3.05 E
Hoogstede 52 52.34 N 6.56 E
Hoogstraten 56 51.24 N 4.46 E
Hoogte 158 27.28 S 28.03 E
Hoogvliet 52 51.52 N 4.21 E
Hook 42 51.17 N 0.58 W
Hook ◆[8] 260 51.22 N 0.18 W
Hooker 196 36.51 N 101.12 W
Hooker, Bi'r ⊤[4] 142 30.23 N 30.20 E
Hooker Creek 162 18.20 S 130.40 E
Hooker Creek Aboriginal Reserve ◆[4] 162 18.10 S 130.25 E
Hook Head ≻ 48 52.07 N 6.55 W
Hookina 166 31.45 S 138.20 E
Hook Island I 166 20.08 S 148.55 E
Hook Mountain State Park ♠ 276 41.09 N 73.55 W
Hook Norton 42 51.59 N 1.29 W
Hook Point ≻ 166 25.48 S 153.05 E
Hooks 194 33.28 N 94.15 W
Hooksiel 52 53.38 N 8.01 E
Hoolehua 229a 21.10 N 157.04 W
Hoonah 180 58.07 N 135.26 W
Hoopa 204 41.03 N 123.40 W
Hoopa Valley Indian Reservation ◆[4] 204 41.08 N 123.40 W
Hooper 198 41.36 N 96.32 W
Hooper Bay 180 61.31 N 166.06 W
Hooper Islands II 208 38.20 N 76.13 W
Hooper Strait ⊔ 208 38.12 N 76.03 W
Hoopersville 208 38.15 N 76.10 W
Hoopes Reservoir ⊜[1] 285 39.47 N 75.37 W
Hoopeston 216 40.28 N 87.40 W
Hooping Harbour 186 50.37 N 56.17 W
Hoople 198 48.32 N 97.38 W
Hoopstad 158 27.54 S 25.58 E
Hoopstick Brook ≃ 276 40.39 N 74.41 W
Höör 41 55.56 N 13.32 E
Hoorn 52 52.38 N 5.04 E
Hoorn, Kap → Hornos. Cabo de ≻ 254 55.59 S 67.16 W
Hoosac Range ʌʌ 207 42.45 N 73.02 W
Hoosac Tunnel ◆[5] 207 42.41 N 73.03 W
Hoosic ≃ 210 42.54 N 73.39 W
Hoosick 210 42.52 N 73.20 W
Hoosick Falls 210 42.54 N 73.21 W
Hooton 262 53.18 N 2.57 W
Hoot Owl Estates 285 39.53 N 74.50 W
Hoover Dam ◆[6] 200 36.00 N 114.27 W
Hoover Reservoir ⊜[1] 214 40.08 N 82.53 W
Hooversville 214 40.08 N 78.54 W
Hopa 130 41.25 N 41.24 E
Hopatcong 210 40.55 N 74.39 W
Hopatcong, Lake ⊜ 210 40.57 N 74.38 W
Hopatcong State Park ♠ 276 40.55 N 74.40 W
Hop Bottom 210 41.42 N 75.46 W
Hop Brook ≃ 276 40.19 N 74.08 W
Hope, B.C., Can. 182 49.23 N 121.26 W
Hope, Ak., U.S. 180 60.55 N 149.38 W
Hope, Ar., U.S. 194 33.40 N 93.35 W
Hope, In., U.S. 218 39.18 N 85.46 W
Hope, N.J., U.S. 210 40.54 N 74.58 W
Hope, N.D., U.S. 198 47.19 N 97.43 W
Hope, R.I., U.S. 207 41.44 N 71.33 W
Hope, Ben ʌ 46 58.24 N 4.37 W
Hope, Loch ⊜ 46 58.27 N 4.39 W
Hope, Point ≻ 180 68.21 N 166.50 W
Hope Bay ⊂ 212 44.55 N 81.08 W
Hopedale, Nf., Can. 176 55.28 N 60.13 W
Hopedale, Il., U.S. 194 40.25 N 89.24 W
Hopedale, La., U.S. 194 29.49 N 89.39 W
Hopedale, Ma., U.S. 207 42.07 N 71.32 W
Hopedale, Oh., U.S. 214 40.19 N 80.54 W
Hope Farm 210 41.44 N 73.40 W
Hopefield 158 33.04 S 18.22 E
Hopeh → Hebei □[4] 98 38.00 N 116.00 E
Hope Island I, B.C., Can. 182 50.55 N 127.53 W
Hope Island I, On., Can. 212 44.55 N 80.12 W
Hopeland 208 40.14 N 76.16 W
Hopelawn 276 40.31 N 74.17 W
Hopelchén 232 19.46 N 89.51 W
Hopeman 46 57.42 N 3.25 W
Hope Mills 192 34.58 N 78.56 W
Hopes Advance, Cap ≻ 176 61.04 N 69.34 W
Hopetoun, Austl. 162 33.57 S 120.07 E
Hopetoun, Austl. 166 35.44 S 142.22 E
Hopetown 158 29.34 S 24.03 E
Hope Valley, Austl. 168b 34.50 S 138.44 E
Hope Valley, R.I., U.S. 207 41.30 N 71.43 W
Hopewell, N.J., U.S. 208 40.23 N 74.45 W
Hopewell, Pa., U.S. 214 40.08 N 78.16 W
Hopewell, Va., U.S. 208 37.18 N 77.17 W
Hopewell Islands II 176 58.25 N 78.00 W
Hopewell Junction 210 41.35 N 73.48 W
Hopewell Village National Historic Site ⊥ 208 40.12 N 75.46 W
Hopfgarten 64 47.27 N 12.10 E
Hopfgarten in Defereggen 64 46.55 N 12.31 E
Hopi → Hebi 98 35.59 N 114.11 E
Hopi Buttes ʌ 200 35.20 N 110.15 W
Hopi Indian Reservation ◆[4] 200 35.45 N 110.35 W
Hopkins, Mi., U.S. 216 42.37 N 85.45 W
Hopkins, Mo., U.S. 194 40.33 N 94.49 W
Hopkins □[6] 222 33.07 N 95.35 W
Hopkins ≃ 166 38.24 S 142.31 E
Hopkins, Lake ⊜ 162 24.15 S 128.50 E
Hopkins Creek ≃ 284a 43.17 N 78.46 W
Hopkinsville 194 36.51 N 87.29 W
Hopkinton, Ia., U.S. 190 42.20 N 91.14 W
Hopkinton, Ma., U.S. 207 42.13 N 71.31 W
Hopkinton, R.I., U.S. 207 41.27 N 71.46 W
Hopland 204 38.58 N 123.06 W
Hoppegarten 264a 52.31 N 13.40 E
Hoppenrade 264a 52.32 N 12.56 E
Hoppo → Hepu 102 21.39 N 109.11 E
Hopsten 52 52.23 N 7.36 E
Hoptrup 41 55.11 N 9.28 E
Ho Pui 271d 22.25 N 114.03 E
Hopwood, Mount ʌ 166 21.49 S 144.26 E
Hoque 152 14.39 S 13.54 E
Hoquiam 224 46.58 N 123.53 W
Hoquiam, East Fork ≃ 224 46.58 N 123.54 W
Hora Califo 144 8.49 N 43.07 E
Horace Mountain ʌ 180 67.40 N 149.06 W
Horado 94 35.36 N 136.50 E
Hōrai 94 34.56 N 137.34 E
Horancia 144 6.31 N 38.44 E
Horasan 130 40.03 N 42.11 E
Horatio 194 33.56 N 94.21 W
Horatio Gardens 278 42.10 N 87.57 W
Horažd'ovice 60 49.20 N 13.43 E
Horb am Neckar 58 48.26 N 8.41 E
Horbelev 41 54.49 N 12.04 E
Horbourg 58 48.05 N 7.23 E
Hörby 41 55.51 N 13.39 E
Horconcitos 236 8.19 N 82.10 W
Hordaland □[6] 26 60.15 N 6.30 E
Hörde ◆[8] 263 51.29 N 7.30 E
Horden 44 54.46 N 1.18 W
Horden ≃ 164 3.50 S 141.25 E
Horezu 38 45.08 N 23.59 E
Horgen 58 47.15 N 8.36 E
Hořice 30 50.22 N 15.38 E
Horicon 190 43.27 N 88.37 W
Horigane 268 35.50 N 139.27 E
Horine 219 38.16 N 90.25 W
Horinger 102 40.26 N 111.55 E
Horinouchi 94 37.14 N 138.56 E
Horinouchi ◆[8] 268 35.41 N 139.40 E
Horizon Tablemount ✧[3] 14 19.40 N 168.30 W
Horizontina 252 27.37 S 54.19 W
Horka 54 51.16 N 14.56 E
Hörken 40 60.02 N 14.56 E
Horley 42 51.11 N 0.11 W
Horlick Mountains ʌʌ 9 85.23 S 121.00 W
Horloff ≃ 56 50.20 N 8.52 E
Hormigueros 240m 18.09 N 67.08 W
Hormoz, Jazīreh-ye I 128 27.04 N 56.28 E
Hormozgān □[4] 128 27.50 N 56.00 E
Hormuz, Strait of ⊔ 128 26.34 N 56.15 E
Horn, B.R.D. 52 51.52 N 8.56 E
Horn, Öst. 61 48.40 N 15.40 E
Horn ◆[8] 52 53.38 N 10.05 E
Horn ≻ 24a 66.28 N 22.28 W
Horn ≃, N.T., Can. 176 61.30 N 118.01 W
Horn ≃, Europe 56 49.15 N 7.20 E
Horn, Ben ʌ[2] 46 58.01 N 4.02 W
Horn, Cape → Hornos, Cabo de ≻ 254 55.59 S 67.16 W
Hornaday ≃ 180 69.22 N 123.50 W
Hornafjörður ⊂ 24a 64.17 N 15.16 W
Hornavan ⊜ 24 66.10 N 17.30 E
Hornbach 56 49.11 N 7.22 E
Hornbæk 41 56.05 N 12.28 E
Hornbeak 194 36.19 N 89.17 W
Hornbeck 194 31.19 N 93.23 W
Hornberg 58 48.13 N 8.13 E
Hornbrook 204 41.55 N 122.33 W
Hornburg 54 52.01 N 10.36 E
Hornby, On., Can. 275b 43.34 N 79.50 W
Hornby, N.Z. 172 43.33 S 172.32 E
Hornby Bay ⊂ 176 66.35 N 117.50 W
Horncastle 44 53.13 N 0.07 W
Hornchurch ◆[8] 260 51.34 N 0.12 E
Horndal 40 60.18 N 16.25 E
Horndean 42 50.55 N 1.00 W
Horndon on the Hill 260 51.31 N 0.25 E
Horne 41 55.06 N 10.11 E
Horne, Îles de II 14 14.16 S 178.05 W
Hornebach ≃ 263 51.39 N 7.38 E
Horneburg, B.R.D. 52 53.30 N 9.34 E
Horneburg, B.R.D. 263 51.38 N 7.18 E
Hörnefors 26 63.38 N 19.54 E
Hornell 210 42.19 N 77.39 W
Hornepayne 176 49.13 N 84.47 W
Hornerstown 208 40.06 N 74.30 W
Hornhausen 54 52.02 N 11.10 E
Horn Head ≻ 48 55.14 N 7.59 W
Horn Hill 260 51.37 N 0.32 W
Horní Jiřetín 54 50.35 N 13.32 E
Hornindal 26 61.58 N 6.31 E
Hornindalsvatnet ⊜ 26 61.56 N 6.22 E
Hørning 41 56.05 N 10.03 E
Hörningsholm 40 59.03 N 17.40 E
Horní Počernice 54 50.06 N 14.38 E
Hornisgrinde ʌ 56 48.36 N 8.12 E
Horn Island I, Austl. 164 10.37 S 142.17 E
Horn Island I, Ms., U.S. 194 30.13 N 88.38 W
Horní Slavkov 54 50.07 N 12.46 E
Horní Stropnice 61 48.46 N 14.44 E
Hornito, Cerro ʌ 236 8.42 N 82.06 W
Hornitos 226 37.30 N 120.14 W
Horní Vltavice 60 48.57 N 13.46 E
Horn Lake 194 34.58 N 90.02 W
Horn Lake ⊜ 212 45.24 N 79.36 W
Hornos, Cabo de (Cape Horn) ≻ 254 55.59 S 67.16 W
Hornos, Isla I 254 55.57 S 67.17 W
Hornos, Islas de II 288 34.25 S 57.55 W
Hornow 54 51.38 N 14.31 E
Hornoy 50 49.51 N 1.54 E
Horn Plateau ʌʌ[1] 176 62.15 N 119.15 W
Horn Pond ⊜ 283 42.28 N 71.09 W
Hornsby, Austl. 170 33.42 S 150.06 E
Hornsby, Il., U.S. 219 39.10 N 89.45 W
Hornsbyville 208 37.11 N 76.28 W
Hornsea 44 53.55 N 0.10 W
Hornsey ◆[8] 260 51.35 N 0.07 W
Hornslet 41 56.19 N 10.20 E
Hornstorf 54 53.54 N 11.32 E
Hornsyld 41 55.45 N 9.51 E

Symbols in the index entries represent the broad categories identified in the key at the right. Symbols with superior numbers (ʌʌ[1]) identify subcategories (see complete key on page *I · 1)*.

Kartensymbole in dem Registerverzeichnis stellen die rechts in Schlüssel erklärten Kategorien dar. Symbole mit hochgestellten Ziffern (ʌʌ[1]) bezeichnen Unterabteilungen einer Kategorie (vgl. vollständiger Schlüssel auf Seite *I · 1)*.

Los símbolos incluídos en el texto del índice representan las grandes categorias identificadas con la clave a la derecha. Los símbolos con numeros en su parte superior (ʌʌ[1]) identifican las subcategorías (véase la clave completa en la página *I · 1)*.

Les symboles de l'index représentent les catégories indiquées dans la légende à droite. Les symboles suivis d'un indice (ʌʌ[1]) représentent des sous-catégories (voir légende complète à la page *I · 1)*.

Os símbolos incluídos no texto do índice representam as grandes categorias identificadas com a chave à direita. Os símbolos com números em sua parte superior (ʌʌ[1]) identificam as subcategorias (veja-se a chave completa à página *I · 1)*.

ʌ	Mountain	Berg	Montaña	Montagne	Montanha
ʌʌ	Mountains	Berge	Montañas	Montagnes	Montanhas
)(	Pass	Pass	Paso	Col	Passo
V	Valley, Canyon	Tal, Cañon	Valle, Cañón	Vallée, Canyon	Vale, Canhão
≡	Plain	Ebene	Llano	Plaine	Planície
≻	Cape	Kap	Cabo	Cap	Cabo
I	Island	Insel	Isla	Île	Ilha
II	Islands	Inseln	Islas	Îles	Ilhas
⊥	Other Topographic Features	Andere Topographische Objekte	Otros Elementos Topográficos	Autres données topographiques	Outros acidentes topográficos

ESPAÑOL · FRANÇAIS · PORTUGUÊS

Nombre / Nom / Nome	Página / Page / Página	Lat.°′	Long.°′ W = Oeste / W = Ouest / W = Oeste
Horntown	208	37.58 N	75.28 W
Hornu	50	50.26 N	3.49 E
Horoshiri-dake ∧	92a	42.43 N	142.41 E
Horotiu	172	37.43 S	175.12 E
Hořovice	60	49.50 N	13.54 E
Horqin Youyi Qianqi (Ulan Hot)	89	46.05 N	122.05 E
Horqin Youyi Zhongqi	89	45.09 N	121.24 E
Horqin Zuoyi Houqi	89	42.58 N	122.20 E
Horqin Zuoyi Zhongqi	89	44.07 N	123.18 E
Horqueta	252	23.24 S	56.53 W
Horrabridge	42	50.31 N	4.05 W
Horrelville	172	43.20 S	172.20 E
Horrem	263	51.06 N	6.48 E
Hörsching	61	48.14 N	14.11 E
Horse ≃	184	56.43 N	111.23 W
Horseback Knob ∧[2]	218	39.14 N	83.06 W
Horse Cave	194	37.10 N	85.54 W
Horse Creek	200	41.25 N	105.11 W
Horse Creek ≃, U.S.	198	41.57 N	103.58 W
Horse Creek ≃, Co., U.S.	198	38.05 N	103.19 W
Horse Creek ≃, Fl., U.S.	220	27.06 N	81.58 W
Horse Creek ≃, Il., U.S.	219	39.45 N	89.34 W
Horse Creek ≃, Mo., U.S.	194	37.46 N	93.53 W
Horsefly	182	52.20 N	121.24 W
Horsefly Lake ⊜	182	52.25 N	121.00 W
Horsehead Creek ≃	198	43.17 N	103.22 W
Horsehead Lake ⊜	198	47.02 N	99.47 W
Horseheads	210	42.10 N	76.49 W
Horse Islands II	186	50.13 N	55.45 W
Horsell	260	51.19 N	0.34 W
Horseneck Brook ≃	276	41.01 N	73.38 W
Horsens	41	55.52 N	9.52 E
Horsens Fjord c	41	55.50 N	10.05 E
Horseshoe Bend, Ar., U.S.	194	36.15 N	91.43 W
Horseshoe Bend, Id., U.S.	202	43.55 N	116.12 W
Horseshoe Bend National Military Park ♠	194	33.00 N	85.46 W
Horseshoe Cove c	276	40.27 N	74.00 W
Horseshoe Creek ≃	198	42.27 N	104.58 W
Horseshoe Falls ∟	284a	43.05 N	79.04 W
Horseshoe Lake ⊜, Mb., Can.	184	52.12 N	95.50 W
Horseshoe Lake ⊜, Mi., U.S.	281	42.24 N	83.45 W
Horseshoe Lake ⊜, N.J., U.S.	276	40.52 N	74.38 W
Horse Shoe Reef ✢[2]	240m	18.40 N	64.12 W
Horsfjärden c	40	59.04 N	18.09 E
Horsford	42	52.41 N	1.15 E
Horsforth	44	53.51 N	1.39 W
Horsham, Austl.	166	36.43 S	142.13 E
Horsham, Eng., U.K.	42	51.04 N	0.21 W
Horsham, Pa., U.S.	208	40.10 N	75.07 W
Hørsholm	41	55.53 N	12.30 E
Hörsingen	54	52.16 N	11.09 E
Horsley, Austl.	274a	33.51 S	150.51 E
Horsley, Eng., U.K.	260	51.16 N	0.26 W
Horslunde	41	54.54 N	11.14 E
Horšovský Týn	60	49.32 N	12.56 E
Horst, B.R.D.	52	53.48 N	9.37 E
Horst, D.D.R.	54	53.22 N	10.37 E
Horst, Ned.	52	51.27 N	6.04 E
Horst ◆[8]	263	51.32 N	7.02 E
Horsted Keynes	42	51.02 N	0.01 W
Hörstel	52	52.18 N	7.35 E
Horsthausen ◆[8]	263	51.33 N	7.13 E
Horstmar	52	52.05 N	7.17 E
Horstmar ◆[8]	263	51.36 N	7.33 E
Horsunlu	130	37.55 N	28.36 E
Horta	148a	38.32 N	28.38 W
Horta □[5]	148a	38.30 N	29.00 W
Horta ◆[8]	266d	41.26 N	2.00 E
Hortaleza ◆[8]	266a	40.28 N	3.39 W
Horten	26	59.25 N	10.30 E
Hortobágy □[9]	30	47.35 N	21.00 E
Horton, Eng., U.K.	260	51.28 N	0.32 W
Horton, In., U.S.	218	40.05 N	86.09 W
Horton, Ks., U.S.	198	39.39 N	95.31 W
Horton, Mi., U.S.	216	42.09 N	84.31 W
Horton ≃	180	70.00 N	126.53 W
Horton in Ribblesdale	44	54.09 N	2.17 W
Horton Kirby	260	51.23 N	0.15 E
Horton Lake ⊜	180	67.29 N	122.31 W
Hortonville, N.Y., U.S.	210	41.46 N	75.02 W
Hortonville, Wi., U.S.	190	44.20 N	88.38 W
Horumersiel	52	53.41 N	8.00 E
Hørup	41	54.56 N	9.55 E
Hørve	41	55.45 N	11.28 E
Horw	58	47.01 N	8.18 E
Horwich	262	53.37 N	2.33 W
Horwood Lake ⊜	190	48.03 N	82.20 W
Hory Matky Boží	60	49.16 N	13.27 E
Hōryūji Temple ʊ[1]	270	34.36 N	135.44 E
Horzum	130	37.10 N	29.30 E
Hosaina	144	7.38 N	37.52 E
Hoşalay	130	42.00 N	33.27 E
Hösbach	56	50.00 N	9.12 E
Hosei University ʊ[2]	268	35.42 N	139.44 E
Hösel	56	51.19 N	6.54 E
Hosena	54	51.27 N	14.01 E
Hoséré Vokré ∧	146	8.20 N	13.15 E
Ḥoseynābād	128	35.33 N	47.08 E
Ḥoseynīyeh-ye Khodā-Dād	128	32.42 N	48.14 E
Hosford	192	30.23 N	84.47 W
Hoshāb	128	26.01 N	63.56 E
Hoshangābād	124	22.45 N	77.43 E
Hoshangābād □[5]	124	22.30 N	77.30 E
Hoshangābād Plain ≚	124	22.35 N	77.25 E
Hoshiārpur, India	123	31.32 N	75.54 E
Hoshiarpur, India	272a	28.35 N	77.22 E
Hoshigajō ∧	96	34.31 N	134.19 E
Hosingen	56	50.01 N	6.05 E
Hosjö	40	60.35 N	15.46 E
Hoskins	164	5.27 S	150.30 E
Hosmer, B.C., Can.	182	49.35 N	114.57 W
Hosmer, S.D., U.S.	198	45.34 N	99.28 W
Hosoe	94	34.49 N	137.39 E
Hospental	58	46.37 N	8.34 E
Hospers	198	43.04 N	95.54 W
Hospet	122	15.16 N	76.24 E
Hospital	48	52.29 N	8.25 W
Hospital de Orbigo	34	42.28 N	5.53 W
Hospitalet	34	41.22 N	2.08 E
Hossegor	32	43.40 N	1.27 W
Hosston	194	32.53 N	93.52 W
Hosta Butte ∧	200	35.35 N	108.12 W
Hoste, Isla I	254	55.15 S	69.00 W
Hostěradice	61	48.57 N	16.15 E
Hostetter	214	40.16 N	79.24 W
Hostigrām	272b	22.26 N	88.31 E
Hostivař ◆[8]	54	50.01 N	14.32 E
Hostivice	54	50.04 N	14.15 E
Hošťka	54	50.30 N	14.20 E
Hostomice	54	50.35 N	13.46 E
Hostotipaquillo	234	21.04 N	104.04 W
Hostouň	60	49.34 N	12.46 E
Hosūr	122	12.43 N	77.49 E
Hot	110	18.06 N	98.36 E
Hota	268	35.08 N	139.51 E
Hotagen	26	63.59 N	14.15 E
Hotagen ⊜	26	63.53 N	14.29 E
Hotagsfjällen ⋏	26	64.20 N	14.30 E
Hotaka	94	36.20 N	137.53 E
Hotaka-dake ∧	94	36.17 N	137.39 E
Hotamış	130	37.36 N	33.13 E
Hotan ≃	90	40.30 N	80.45 E
Hotarele	38	44.10 N	26.22 E
Hotazel	158	27.15 S	23.00 E
Hotchkiss	200	38.47 N	107.43 W
Hotchkissville	207	41.34 N	73.13 W
Hot Creek Range ⋏	204	38.30 N	116.25 W
Hötensleben	54	52.08 N	11.01 E
Hotevilla	200	35.55 N	110.40 W
Hotham ≃	168a	32.58 S	116.22 E
Hotham Inlet c	180	66.45 N	162.00 W
Hotham Peak ∧	180	66.48 N	160.42 W
Hoting	26	64.07 N	16.10 E
Hot Springs, Mt., U.S.	202	47.36 N	114.40 W
Hot Springs → Truth or Consequences, N.M., U.S.	200	33.08 N	107.15 W
Hot Springs, N.C., U.S.	192	35.53 N	82.49 W
Hot Springs, S.D., U.S.	198	43.25 N	103.28 W
Hot Springs, Va., U.S.	192	37.59 N	79.49 W
Hot Springs National Park	194	34.30 N	93.04 W
Hot Springs Peak ∧, Ca., U.S.	204	40.22 N	120.07 W
Hot Springs Peak ∧, Nv., U.S.	204	41.22 N	117.26 W
Hot Springs State Park ♠	202	43.40 N	108.10 W
Hot Sulphur Springs	200	40.04 N	106.06 W
Hottah Lake ⊜	176	65.04 N	118.29 W
Hotte, Massif de la ⋏	238	18.25 N	73.55 W
Hottentotbaai c	156	26.05 S	14.58 E
Hottentotskloof	158	33.15 S	19.40 E
Hotton	56	50.16 N	5.27 E
Hötzum	54	52.13 N	10.37 E
Houaïlou	175f	21.17 S	165.38 E
Houamuang	110	20.09 N	103.38 E
Houbaishu	106	31.49 N	119.10 E
Houbao	98	41.54 N	125.14 E
Houcheng	106	31.55 N	120.26 E
Houdahepao	104	41.49 N	123.01 E
Houdain	50	50.27 N	2.32 E
Houdan	50	48.47 N	1.36 E
Houdelaincourt	58	48.33 N	5.28 E
Houdeng-Aimeries	50	50.29 N	4.08 E
Houeillès	32	44.12 N	0.02 E
Houffalize	56	50.08 N	5.47 E
Hough Green	262	53.23 N	2.47 W
Houghton, Mi., U.S.	190	47.07 N	88.34 W
Houghton, N.Y., U.S.	210	42.25 N	78.09 W
Houghton, Wa., U.S.	224	47.40 N	122.12 W
Houghton Estates ◆[8]	273d	26.10 S	28.04 E
Houghton Green	262	53.25 N	2.34 W
Houghton Lake	190	44.18 N	84.45 W
Houghton Lake ⊜, Sk., Can.	184	52.23 N	105.08 W
Houghton Lake ⊜, Mi., U.S.	190	44.20 N	84.45 W
Houghton-le-Spring	44	54.51 N	1.28 W
Houghton Regis	42	51.55 N	0.31 W
Houguangzhengtai	104	41.13 N	122.07 E
Hougujiazi	104	42.21 N	123.22 E
Houhuangtukan	104	41.02 N	122.29 E
Houille ≃	56	50.08 N	4.49 E
Houillères de la Sarre, Canal des ⩧	56	48.42 N	6.55 E
Houilles	261	48.56 N	2.11 E
Houjiangfushan	105	40.03 N	117.09 E
Houjiaping	107	30.02 N	104.38 E
Houjiaying	105	39.51 N	117.15 E
Houjie	100	22.58 N	113.39 E
Houjiumen	104	42.38 N	123.18 E
Houkou	98	37.34 N	115.09 E
Houliujia	104	40.47 N	122.19 E
Houlka	194	34.02 N	89.01 W
Houlton	188	46.07 N	67.50 W
Houluan	105	39.13 N	116.32 E
Houma, Tonga	174w	21.09 S	175.19 W
Houma, La., U.S.	194	29.35 N	90.43 W
Houma, Zhg.	102	35.36 N	111.21 E
Houmanzhoutun	104	42.29 N	123.14 E
Houmen	100	22.51 N	115.09 E
Houmet Essouq	148	33.59 N	10.51 E
Houmont Park	222	29.50 N	95.13 W
Hound Creek ≃	202	47.13 N	111.23 W
Houndé	150	11.30 N	3.31 W
Hounslow ◆[8]	260	51.29 N	0.22 W
Houplines	50	50.42 N	2.55 E
Houqianjiayu	104	40.50 N	120.41 E
Houqiao	105	40.04 N	116.39 E
Hourn, Loch c	46	57.08 N	5.36 W
Housatonic	207	42.15 N	73.22 W
Housatonic ≃	207	41.10 N	73.07 W
House	196	34.38 N	103.54 W
House ≃	184	56.13 N	112.31 W
House of Seven Gables ⊥	283	42.32 N	70.53 W
Houserville	214	40.50 N	77.50 W
House Springs	219	38.24 N	90.34 W
Houshan	106	31.03 N	120.21 E
Houston, B.C., Can.	182	54.24 N	126.38 W
Houston, De., U.S.	208	38.55 N	75.30 W
Houston, Mn., U.S.	190	43.45 N	91.34 W
Houston, Ms., U.S.	194	33.53 N	88.59 W
Houston, Mo., U.S.	194	37.19 N	91.57 W
Houston, Oh., U.S.	216	40.15 N	84.20 W
Houston, Pa., U.S.	214	40.14 N	80.12 W
Houston, Tx., U.S.	222	29.45 N	95.21 W
Houston □[6]	222	31.20 N	95.20 W
Houston ≃	194	30.16 N	93.13 W
Houston, Lake ⊜[1]	222	29.58 N	95.07 W
Houston County Lake ⊜[1]	222	31.25 N	95.35 W
Houston Creek ≃	218	38.13 N	84.15 W
Houston Intercontinental Airport ⊠	222	29.59 N	95.27 W
Houston Ship Channel ⩧	222	29.21 N	94.47 W
Hout ≃	156	23.04 S	29.36 E
Houtbaai	158	34.03 S	18.21 E
Houthalen	56	51.02 N	5.22 E
Houthulst	50	50.59 N	2.57 E
Houtkop	158	26.36 S	27.52 E
Houtkraal	158	30.23 S	24.05 E
Houtman Abrolhos II	162	28.43 S	113.48 E
Houtskär I	26	60.12 N	21.22 E
Houtzdale	214	40.49 N	78.21 W
Houwuliangdian	104	41.31 N	121.55 E
Houwutaigou	104	41.46 N	121.42 E
Houx	261	48.34 N	1.37 E
Houxijie	100	28.46 N	118.49 E
Houxinlitun	104	41.05 N	122.33 E
Houxinqiu	104	42.34 N	122.43 E
Houyatai	104	41.26 N	121.49 E
Houying	105	39.42 N	118.18 E
Houyingzi	98	40.24 N	123.50 E
Houzhangcun	105	40.08 N	116.11 E
Houzhou	106	31.35 N	119.22 E
Houzitun	104	41.04 N	121.18 E
Hov	41	55.55 N	10.16 E
Hova	40	58.52 N	14.13 E
Hovborg	41	55.36 N	8.57 E
Høve, Dan.	41	55.50 N	11.30 E
Hove, Eng., U.K.	42	50.49 N	0.10 W
Hovedgård	41	55.57 N	9.58 E
Hövelhof	52	51.49 N	8.40 E
Hoven, Dan.	41	55.51 N	8.46 E
Hoven, S.D., U.S.	198	45.14 N	99.46 W
Hovenweep National Monument ♠	200	37.25 N	109.04 W
Hovmantorp	26	56.47 N	15.08 E
Hovran ⊜	40	60.16 N	16.03 E
Hovsta	40	59.21 N	15.13 E
Howa, Ouadi (Wādī Howar) V	140	17.30 N	27.08 E
Howakil I	144	15.10 N	40.16 E
Howar, Wādī (Ouadi Howa) V	140	17.30 N	27.08 E
Howard, Austl.	166	25.19 S	152.34 E
Howard, Ks., U.S.	198	37.28 N	96.15 W
Howard, Oh., U.S.	214	40.24 N	82.19 W
Howard, Pa., U.S.	214	41.00 N	77.39 W
Howard, S.D., U.S.	198	44.00 N	97.31 W
Howard, Wi., U.S.	190	44.32 N	88.05 W
Howard □[6], In., U.S.	216	40.29 N	86.08 W
Howard □[6], Md., U.S.	208	39.16 N	76.48 W
Howard Beach ◆[8]	276	40.40 N	73.51 W
Howard City	190	43.23 N	85.28 W
Howard Draw V	196	30.08 N	101.35 W
Howard Hanson Reservoir ⊜[1]	224	47.15 N	121.45 W
Howard Heights	284b	39.17 N	76.50 W
Howardian Hills ⋏[2]	44	54.07 N	1.00 W
Howard Island I	164	12.10 S	135.24 E
Howard Lake	190	45.03 N	94.04 W
Howard Prairie Lake ⊜[1]	202	42.15 N	122.20 W
Howard University ʊ[2]	284c	38.55 N	77.01 W
Howden	44	53.45 N	0.52 W
Howe, In., U.S.	216	41.43 N	85.25 W
Howe, Tx., U.S.	196	33.30 N	96.37 W
Howe, Cape ›	166	37.31 S	149.59 E
Howe Caverns ⌓[5]	210	42.42 N	74.25 W
Howe Green	260	51.42 N	0.32 E
Howe Island I	212	44.17 N	76.15 W
Howeke	150	4.50 N	7.45 W
Howell	216	42.36 N	83.55 W
Howell Airport ⊠	278	41.39 N	87.45 W
Howell Island I	219	38.40 N	90.42 W
Howells	198	41.43 N	97.00 W
Howells Pond ⊜	276	41.03 N	74.42 W
Howes Cave	210	42.41 N	74.23 W
Howe Sound ⊻	182	49.22 N	123.18 W
Howe's Range ⋏	170	33.08 S	150.47 E
Howes Valley	170	32.50 S	150.51 E
Howey In The Hills	220	28.43 N	81.47 W
Howick, P.Q., Can.	206	45.11 N	73.51 W
Howick, S. Afr.	158	29.28 S	30.14 E
Howitt, Mount ∧	166	37.10 S	146.40 E
Howland	188	45.14 N	68.39 W
Howland Island I	14	0.48 N	176.38 W
Howley	186	49.10 N	57.07 W
Howley, Mount ∧	186	48.17 N	58.26 W
Howmore	46	57.18 N	7.23 W
Howqua ≃	169	37.14 S	146.08 E
Howrah	126	22.35 N	88.20 E
Howrah □[5]	126	22.36 N	88.10 E
Howrah Bridge ◆[5]	272b	22.35 N	88.21 E
Howrah Railroad Station ◆[5]	272b	22.35 N	88.21 E
Howse Peak ∧	182	51.49 N	116.41 W
Howser	182	50.18 N	116.57 W
Howson Peak ∧	182	54.25 N	127.44 W
Howth	48	53.23 N	6.04 W
Howth Head ›	48	53.22 N	6.03 W
Hoxie, Ar., U.S.	194	36.03 N	90.58 W
Hoxie, Ks., U.S.	198	39.21 N	100.26 W
Höxter	52	51.46 N	9.23 E
Hoxtolgay	86	46.35 N	86.01 E
Hoxton Park	274a	33.55 S	150.51 E
Hoxton Park Aerodrome ⊠	274a	33.54 S	150.50 E
Hoy I	46	58.51 N	3.18 W
Hoya, B.R.D.	52	52.48 N	9.08 E
Hōya, Nihon	94	35.43 N	139.34 E
Høyanger	26	61.13 N	6.05 E
Hoyerswerda	54	51.26 N	14.14 E
Hoylake	262	53.23 N	3.11 W
Hoyleton, Austl.	168b	34.01 S	138.33 E
Hoyleton, Il., U.S.	219	38.27 N	89.16 W
Hoym	54	51.47 N	11.19 E
Hoyos	34	40.10 N	6.43 W
Hōyo-shotō II	96	33.52 N	132.18 E
Hoyran	130	38.19 N	30.59 E
Hoyran Gölü ⊜	130	38.12 N	30.50 E
Höytiäinen ⊜	26	62.48 N	29.39 E
Hoyt Lakes	190	47.31 N	92.08 W
Hoytville, Mi., U.S.	216	42.45 N	84.53 W
Hoytville, Oh., U.S.	216	41.11 N	83.47 W
Hozain ≃	50	48.16 N	4.06 E
Hozat	130	39.07 N	39.14 E
Hozumi	94	35.24 N	136.41 E
Hpru-so	110	19.25 N	97.08 E
Hracholusky, údolní nádrž ⊜[1]	60	49.47 N	13.07 E
Hradec Králové	30	50.12 N	15.50 E
Hrádek	61	48.46 N	16.16 E
Hrádek nad Nisou	54	50.48 N	14.51 E
Hradiště ⩓	54	50.13 N	13.08 E
Hranice, Česko.	30	49.33 N	17.44 E
Hranice, Česko.	54	50.15 N	12.10 E
Hrdlovka	54	50.36 N	13.40 E
Hřensko	54	50.50 N	14.14 E
Hriňová	30	48.36 N	19.31 E
Hrob	54	50.39 N	13.44 E
Hron ≃	30	47.49 N	18.45 E
Hronov	30	50.29 N	16.12 E
Hrotovice	61	49.06 N	16.07 E
Hrubieszów	30	50.49 N	23.55 E
Hrubý Jeseník ⋏	30	50.00 N	17.20 E
Hrušovany	61	48.50 N	16.23 E
Hrvatska (Croatia) □[3]	36	45.10 N	15.30 E
Hsenwi	110	23.18 N	97.58 E
Hsiakuan → Xiaguan	102	25.34 N	100.14 E
Hsiamen → Xiamen	100	24.28 N	118.07 E
Hsian → Xi'an	102	34.15 N	108.52 E
Hsiangt'an → Xiangtan	100	27.51 N	112.54 E
Hsiangyang → Xiangfan	102	32.03 N	112.01 E
Hsiaohungt'ou Yü I	100	21.57 N	121.36 E
Hsichih	269d	25.04 N	121.39 E
Hsichi Yü I	100	23.15 N	119.37 E
Hsich'üan Tao I	100	25.59 N	119.56 E
Hsientung	269d	25.09 N	121.44 E
Hsienyang → Xianyang	102	34.22 N	108.42 E
Hsi-hseng	110	20.09 N	97.15 E
Hsihu	100	23.58 N	120.28 E
Hsilo	100	23.48 N	120.27 E
Hsilo ≃	100	23.50 N	120.15 E
Hsim ≃	110	20.48 N	98.31 E
Hsinch'eng	100	24.08 N	121.39 E
Hsinchu	100	24.48 N	120.58 E
Hsinchuang	100	25.02 N	121.27 E
Hsinghua → Xinghua	100	32.57 N	119.50 E
Hsingt'ai → Xingtai	98	37.04 N	114.29 E
Hsinhailien → Lianyungang	98	34.39 N	119.16 E
Hsinhsiang → Xinxiang	98	35.20 N	113.51 E
Hsinhua	100	23.02 N	120.18 E
Hsining → Xining	102	36.38 N	101.55 E
Hsinking → Changchun	89	43.53 N	125.19 E
Hsinpeit'ou ◆[8]	269d	25.09 N	121.30 E
Hsinp'u → Lianyungang	98	34.39 N	119.16 E
Hsinshih	100	23.05 N	120.17 E
Hsintien	100	24.57 N	121.32 E
Hsintien ≃	269d	25.02 N	121.29 E
Hsinyang → Xinyang	100	32.08 N	114.04 E
Hsipaw	110	22.37 N	97.18 E
Hsiukuluan ≃	100	23.28 N	121.30 E
Hsiyü	100	23.36 N	119.30 E
Hsüanhua → Xuanhua	105	40.37 N	115.03 E
Hsüch'ang → Xuchang	100	34.03 N	113.49 E
Hsüchou → Xuzhou	98	34.16 N	117.11 E
Hsüehchia	100	23.14 N	120.10 E
Hsüeh Shan ∧	100	24.23 N	121.13 E
Hsuphāng	110	20.18 N	98.42 E
Hua'an	100	25.02 N	117.34 E
Huab ≃	156	20.52 S	13.25 E
Huabu	100	29.00 N	118.20 E
Huaca Juliana ⊥	286d	12.07 S	77.02 W
Huacaña	248	14.02 S	74.02 W
Huacao	269b	31.14 N	121.19 E
Huacaraje	248	13.33 S	63.45 W
Huachacalla	248	18.45 S	68.17 W
Huacheng	100	24.04 N	115.38 E
Huachi	102	36.43 N	107.52 E
Huachi, Laguna ⊜	248	14.11 S	63.30 W
Huachipa	286d	12.00 S	76.56 W
Huacho	248	11.07 S	77.37 W
Huachón	248	10.40 S	75.57 W
Huachos	248	13.12 S	75.31 W
Huachuca City	200	31.37 N	110.20 W
Huaco	252	30.09 S	68.31 W
Huacrachuco	248	8.39 S	77.05 W
Huade	98	41.46 N	114.16 E
Huadian	89	42.58 N	126.43 E
Huading Shan ∧	100	29.15 N	121.05 E
Huafeng	106	32.14 N	121.16 E
Huagutang	106	30.55 N	119.18 E
Hua Hin	110	12.34 N	99.58 E
Huai ≃, Zhg.	98	37.28 N	114.55 E
Huai ≃, Zhg.	100	32.58 N	118.17 E
Huaiá-Miçu ≃	250	10.52 S	53.15 W
Huai'an (Chaigoubu), Zhg.	98	40.39 N	114.27 E
Huai'an, Zhg.	100	33.32 N	119.10 E
Huaibin	100	32.28 N	115.24 E
Huaide	89	43.32 N	124.50 E
Huaidezhen, Zhg.	89	43.54 N	124.47 E
Huaidezhen, Zhg.	107	28.59 N	105.15 E
Huaihuazhenshi	106	31.05 N	119.41 E
Huaiji	102	24.01 N	112.18 E
Huailai (Shacheng)	105	40.23 N	115.33 E
Huailin	100	31.26 N	117.36 E
Huaillati	248	14.05 S	72.31 W
Huainan	100	32.40 N	117.00 E
Huaining	100	30.25 N	116.38 E
Huairou	105	40.19 N	116.37 E
Huaite → Huaide	89	43.32 N	124.50 E
Huaiyang	100	33.44 N	114.53 E
Huai Yot	110	7.45 N	99.37 E
Huaiyuan	100	32.57 N	117.12 E
Huaiyu Shan ⋏	100	28.50 N	117.50 E
Huaji	100	32.46 N	115.20 E
Huajiang	102	25.50 N	110.21 E
Huajianzi	104	40.48 N	122.12 E
Huajiapuzi	104	40.52 N	123.14 E
Huajiayingzi	104	42.20 N	121.00 E
Huajimic	234	21.42 N	104.20 W
Huajintepec	234	16.36 N	98.14 W
Huajuapan de León	234	17.48 N	97.46 W
Huakou	100	25.13 N	117.35 E
Hualahuises	232	24.53 N	99.41 W
Hualalai ∧[1]	229d	19.42 N	155.52 W
Hualañé	252	34.59 S	71.49 W
Hualapai Indian Reservation ◆[4]	200	35.38 N	113.30 W
Hualapai Mountains ⋏	200	34.50 N	113.55 W
Hualapai Peak ∧	200	35.04 N	113.54 W
Hualfín	252	27.14 S	66.50 W
Hualgayoc	248	6.46 S	78.37 W
Hualien	100	23.59 N	121.36 E
Hualien ≃	100	23.57 N	121.36 E
Hualingpuzi	104	41.31 N	123.54 E
Hualla	248	13.44 S	73.55 W
Huallaga ≃	248	5.10 S	75.32 W
Huallanca, Perú	248	8.49 S	77.52 W
Huallanca, Perú	248	9.51 S	76.56 W
Hualong	102	36.05 N	102.36 E
Huamachuco	248	7.48 S	78.04 W
Huamanquiquia	248	13.44 S	74.15 W
Huamantla	234	19.19 N	97.56 W
Huambo (Nova Lisboa), Ang.	152	12.44 S	15.47 E
Huambo, Perú	248	15.44 S	72.07 W
Huambo □[5]	152	12.30 S	15.40 E
Huambo ≃	248	7.04 S	77.10 W
Huambos	248	6.28 S	78.58 W
Huameiao	100	26.32 N	115.47 E
Huamei Shan ∧	100	25.28 N	113.58 E
Huamuxtitlán	234	17.49 N	98.34 W
Huan ≃	100	30.40 N	114.05 E
Huanan	89	46.13 N	130.32 E
Huancabamba, Perú	248	10.21 S	75.32 W
Huancabamba, Perú	248	5.14 S	79.28 W
Huancané	248	15.12 S	69.46 W
Huancapi	248	13.41 S	74.04 W
Huancarama	248	13.39 S	73.05 W
Huancarqui	248	16.06 S	72.29 W
Huancavelica	248	12.46 S	75.02 W
Huancavelica □[5]	248	13.00 S	75.00 W
Huancaybamba	248	9.05 S	76.50 W
Huancayo	248	12.04 S	75.14 W
Huanchaca	248	20.20 S	66.39 W
Huanchaca, Serranía de ⋏	248	14.30 S	60.39 W
Huandacareo	234	19.59 N	101.17 W
Huando	248	12.29 S	74.58 W
Huang ≃, Asia	110	17.49 N	101.33 E
Huang ≃, T'aiwan	269d	25.14 N	121.37 E
Huang (Yellow) ≃, Zhg.	90	37.32 N	118.19 E
Huang'aicun	106	31.43 N	118.40 E
Huang'an	98	35.28 N	115.42 E
Huang'anshi	100	29.06 N	113.34 E
Huangbai	98	41.17 N	126.21 E
Huangbaozi	102	39.54 N	99.26 E
Huangbeipu	104	42.21 N	123.25 E
Huangcaoping	100	25.42 N	113.27 E
Huangchong	100	22.18 N	113.03 E
Huangchuan	100	32.09 N	115.03 E
Huangcun	105	39.56 N	116.11 E
Huangdaizhen	106	31.26 N	120.33 E
Huangdan	107	29.10 N	103.44 E
Huangda Yang ⊻	100	30.03 N	122.26 E
Huangdi, Zhg.	98	40.14 N	120.15 E
Huangdi, Zhg.	105	40.57 N	118.24 E
Huangdu, Zhg.	106	30.47 N	118.51 E
Huangdu, Zhg.	106	31.16 N	121.13 E
Huangduqiao	100	29.18 N	120.55 E
Huanggai Hu ⊜	100	29.44 N	113.23 E
Huanggang	100	30.27 N	114.52 E
Huanggangji	98	34.39 N	116.03 E
Huanggangkou	100	28.32 N	114.33 E
Huanggang Shan ∧	100	27.50 N	117.45 E
Huanggangshi	100	33.09 N	115.55 E
Huangguayingzi	104	41.46 N	120.46 E
Huangguoshu	102	26.02 N	105.32 E
Huang Hai → Yellow Sea ⊤[2]	90	36.00 N	123.00 E
Huanghe Kou ≃[1]	98	37.54 N	118.48 E
Huangho → Huang ≃	90	37.32 N	118.19 E
Huanghu	106	30.27 N	119.48 E
Huanghua	98	38.22 N	117.21 E
Huanghuadianzi	104	41.44 N	122.48 E
Huanghuashi	100	28.14 N	113.14 E
Huangjialing	104	42.12 N	122.55 E
Huangjialu	106	31.00 N	121.45 E
Huangjiatun	104	41.11 N	122.54 E
Huangjiazhai	106	32.01 N	121.36 E
Huangjinbu	100	28.27 N	116.47 E
Huangjing	106	31.39 N	121.06 E
Huangjinggou	107	29.37 N	104.35 E
Huangjinjing	107	29.44 N	104.38 E
Huangjinzi	89	50.02 N	127.20 E
Huangjuezhen	107	29.50 N	106.27 E
Huangkan	105	40.22 N	116.28 E
Huangkeng	100	27.35 N	117.39 E
Huangkou	102	42.46 N	93.58 E
Huanglaomen	100	29.30 N	115.49 E
Huangli	106	31.39 N	119.42 E
Huanglian	107	29.17 N	106.18 E
Huangling	102	35.41 N	109.09 E
Huanglingji	100	30.25 N	114.03 E
Huanglong, Zhg.	100	31.58 N	112.28 E
Huanglong, Zhg.	102	35.45 N	109.42 E
Huanglongxi	107	30.19 N	103.58 E
Huangmao	100	28.07 N	114.04 E
Huangmapi	100	23.30 N	114.33 E
Huangmei	100	30.04 N	115.56 E
Huangnihe, Zhg.	89	43.32 N	127.59 E
Huangnihe, Zhg.	100	31.06 N	117.22 E
Huangpi, Zhg.	100	30.53 N	114.22 E
Huangpi, Zhg.	100	26.39 N	115.51 E
Huangpu ≃	106	31.24 N	121.31 E
Huangqi	100	26.21 N	119.54 E
Huangqiao	106	32.15 N	120.13 E
Huangqiao ≃	106	32.00 N	120.20 E
Huangshahe	102	26.03 N	110.58 E
Huangshajie	100	29.03 N	113.08 E
Huangshan	98	36.57 N	122.18 E
Huangshanguan	98	37.32 N	120.16 E
Huangshapu, Zhg.	100	26.50 N	113.26 E
Huangshapu, Zhg.	100	25.08 N	112.44 E
Huangshaqiao	100	28.56 N	114.40 E
Huangshatuo	104	41.12 N	122.31 E
Huangshi, Zhg.	100	25.23 N	119.04 E
Huangshi, Zhg.	100	30.13 N	115.05 E
Huangshi, Zhg.	102	29.00 N	111.02 E
Huangshidu	100	27.44 N	116.44 E
Huangshiguan	100	26.15 N	115.54 E
Huangshui	107	30.32 N	103.55 E
Huangtan, Zhg.	100	27.44 N	119.58 E
Huangtan, Zhg.	100	26.41 N	117.17 E
Huangtan ≃	100	24.48 N	116.31 E
Huangtang, Zhg.	100	23.44 N	114.58 E
Huangtang, Zhg.	106	31.46 N	120.21 E
Huangtang, Zhg.	106	31.47 N	119.40 E
Huangtang Hu ⊜	100	30.00 N	114.12 E
Huangtankou	100	28.50 N	118.53 E
Huangtantuan	100	30.53 N	113.33 E
Huangtian	100	23.52 N	114.58 E
Huangtianfan	100	29.10 N	120.08 E
Huangtu, Zhg.	100	27.36 N	118.00 E
Huangtu, Zhg.	106	31.52 N	120.03 E
Huangtuchang	107	30.41 N	104.18 E
Huangtugang	100	31.25 N	115.05 E
Huangtukan	104	41.21 N	122.45 E
Huangtuliangzi	98	41.14 N	118.39 E
Huangtuling	100	27.18 N	113.30 E
Huangtupo	105	39.47 N	116.16 E
Huanguelén	252	37.02 S	61.57 W
Huangwan	106	30.22 N	120.48 E
Huangxian	98	37.38 N	120.29 E
Huangxu	106	32.06 N	119.37 E
Huangyaguan	105	40.14 N	117.26 E
Huangyan	100	28.39 N	121.15 E
Huangyang Shan ⋏	105	40.20 N	115.00 E
Huangyanzhuang	105	40.01 N	118.21 E
Huangyuan	102	36.40 N	101.12 E
Huangyuzeng	104	42.05 N	124.11 E
Huangze	100	29.35 N	120.55 E
Huangze Yang ⊻	100	30.36 N	122.28 E
Huangzhai	100	29.27 N	120.00 E
Huangzhong	102	36.31 N	101.40 E
Huangzhu	110	19.29 N	110.24 E
Huangzhuang, Zhg.	100	34.05 N	112.15 E
Huangzhuang, Zhg.	105	39.29 N	117.31 E
Huangzhuang, Zhg.	105	39.53 N	117.05 E
Huangzhuang Wa ⊜	105	39.33 N	117.33 E
Huaning	102	24.14 N	102.56 E
Huaniqueo [de Morales]	234	19.54 N	101.26 W
Huaniugouzi	104	41.34 N	122.35 E
Huaniupuzi	104	41.23 N	123.31 E
Huanjiang	102	24.54 N	108.21 E
Huanren	98	41.14 N	125.21 E
Huanta	248	12.56 S	74.15 W
Huantai (Suozhen)	98	36.59 N	118.06 E
Huantan	100	31.49 N	113.04 E
Huántar	248	9.26 S	77.15 W
Huánuco	248	9.55 S	76.14 W
Huánuco □[5]	248	9.30 S	75.50 W
Huanuni	248	18.16 S	66.51 W
Huanxi	100	26.34 N	113.36 E
Huanxian	102	36.39 N	107.18 E
Huanxiang ≃	105	39.34 N	117.45 E
Huanxiling	104	41.17 N	123.54 E
Huanzo, Cordillera de ⋏	248	14.30 S	73.20 W
Huapí, Serranía ⋏	236	12.30 N	85.00 W
Huap'ing Yü I	100	25.26 N	121.56 E
Huaqiao, Zhg.	100	28.56 N	121.27 E
Huaqiao, Zhg.	100	29.32 N	117.11 E
Huaqiao, Zhg.	102	27.28 N	110.02 E
Huaqiao, Zhg.	107	30.28 N	103.52 E
Huaqiaozhen	107	30.47 N	106.41 E
Huaqiying	106	32.10 N	118.38 E
Huara	248	19.59 S	69.47 W
Huaral	248	11.30 S	77.12 W
Huaraz	248	9.32 S	77.32 W
Huari, Bol.	248	19.00 S	66.48 W
Huari, Perú	248	9.20 S	77.14 W
Huariaca	248	10.27 S	76.07 W
Huaribamba	248	12.16 S	74.57 W
Huarina	248	16.12 S	68.38 W
Huarmey	248	10.04 S	78.10 W
Huarochirí	248	12.09 S	76.14 W
Huarocondo	248	13.25 S	72.13 W
Huarong	100	29.30 N	112.34 E
Huásabas	232	29.47 N	109.18 W
Huasaga ≃	246	3.42 S	76.26 W
Hua Sai	110	8.02 N	100.18 E
Huasamota	234	22.30 N	104.30 W
Huascarán, Nevado ∧	248	9.07 S	77.37 W
Huasco	252	28.28 S	71.14 W
Huasco ≃	252	28.27 S	71.13 W
Huashan	98	34.39 N	116.44 E
Huashaoying	98	40.12 N	114.36 E
Huashi	106	31.50 N	120.28 E
Huatabampo	232	26.50 N	109.38 W
Huatangpu	100	25.48 N	112.52 E
Huating	102	35.09 N	106.38 E
Huatong, Zhg.	98	40.03 N	121.56 E
Huatong, Zhg.	102	23.01 N	106.36 E
Huatunas, Lagunas ⊜	248	13.06 S	66.15 W
Huatusco de Chicuellar	234	19.09 N	96.57 W
Huauchinango	234	20.11 N	98.03 W
Huaura	248	11.04 S	77.36 W
Huaura ≃	248	11.06 S	77.39 W
Huautla	234	21.02 N	98.17 W
Huautla de Jiménez	234	18.08 N	96.51 W
Huaxian (Daokou), Zhg.	98	35.37 N	114.32 E
Huaxian, Zhg.	100	23.22 N	113.12 E
Huaxian, Zhg.	102	34.30 N	109.40 E
Huayan	107	30.01 N	105.02 E
Huayang	107	30.32 N	104.04 E
Huayangzhen	102	33.25 N	107.44 E
Huaying Shan ∧	107	30.10 N	106.42 E
Huayingtai	104	40.43 N	122.19 E
Huayllay	248	11.01 S	76.21 W
Huayna Potosí, Nevado ∧	248	16.16 S	68.11 W
Huaytará	248	13.36 S	75.22 W
Hua Yü I	100	23.24 N	119.19 E
Huayuan, Zhg.	98	42.17 N	127.07 E
Huayuan, Zhg.	100	31.16 N	113.58 E
Huayuan, Zhg.	102	28.34 N	109.13 E
Huayuanzui	100	33.00 N	118.16 E
Huayunca, Nevado ∧	248	14.39 S	72.28 W
Huayuri, Pampa de ≚	248	14.30 S	75.30 W
Huazhou	102	21.40 N	110.33 E
Huazi	104	41.25 N	123.29 E
Huazigou	104	41.50 N	121.01 E
Huazikou	106	32.13 N	118.57 E
Huazolotitlán	234	16.17 N	97.56 W
Ḥubārah, Wādī V	142	27.21 N	31.39 E
Ḥubayṭah, Bi'r ⊤[4]	142	30.27 N	32.27 E
Hubbard, Ia., U.S.	190	42.18 N	93.18 W
Hubbard, Oh., U.S.	214	41.09 N	80.34 W
Hubbard, Or., U.S.	224	45.10 N	122.48 W
Hubbard, Tx., U.S.	222	31.50 N	96.47 W
Hubbard Creek ≃	196	32.54 N	98.53 W
Hubbard Creek Reservoir ⊜[1]	196	32.45 N	99.00 W
Hubbard Lake ⊜	190	44.49 N	83.34 W
Hubbards	186	44.38 N	64.04 W
Hubbardston	207	42.28 N	72.00 W
Hubbard Woods	278	42.06 N	87.44 W
Hubbell	190	47.10 N	88.25 W
Hubbell Trading Post National Historical Site ⊥	200	35.43 N	109.33 W
Hubbelrath	263	51.16 N	6.55 E
Hubei (Hupeh) □[4]	90	31.00 N	112.00 E
Huben, Öst.	64	47.03 N	10.58 E
Huben, Öst.	64	46.56 N	12.34 E
Huberdeau	206	45.58 N	74.38 W
Huber Heights	218	39.50 N	84.07 W
Hublersburg	210	40.58 N	77.37 W
Hubli	122	15.21 N	75.10 E
Hubuleng	102	41.19 N	111.08 E
Hucaogang	106	32.00 N	120.29 E
Hucclecote	42	51.51 N	2.11 W
Huch'ang	98	41.25 N	127.03 E
Hucheng	100	25.26 N	118.27 E
Huchi	100	31.08 N	117.40 E
Huchow → Huzhou	106	30.52 N	120.06 E
Huckarde ◆[8]	263	51.32 N	7.24 E
Hückelhoven	56	51.04 N	6.10 E
Hückeswagen	56	51.08 N	7.20 E
Hucking	260	51.18 N	0.39 E
Huckingen ◆[8]	263	51.22 N	6.43 E
Huckitta Creek ≃	162	22.38 S	135.30 E
Huckleberry Island I	276	40.53 N	73.45 W
Huckleberry Mountain ∧	202	43.51 N	122.19 W
Huckleberry Mountain ∧[2]	212	44.28 N	75.28 W
Hucknall	42	53.02 N	1.11 W
Hucqueliers	50	50.34 N	1.54 E
Hucun	105	39.02 N	115.56 E
Hudangtou	106	30.48 N	121.22 E
Huddart Park ♠	282	37.26 N	122.19 W
Hudderfield Narrow Canal ⩧	262	53.29 N	2.06 W
Huddersfield	262	53.39 N	1.47 W
Huddinge	40	59.14 N	17.59 E
Huddle Park Municipal Golf Course ♠	273d	26.09 S	28.07 E
Huddunge	40	60.03 N	16.59 E
Hude	52	53.07 N	8.27 E
Huder	89	50.00 N	121.37 E
Hudgin Creek ≃	194	33.40 N	91.59 W
Hūdī	140	17.42 N	34.17 E
Hudiksvall	26	61.44 N	17.07 E
Hudong	100	22.51 N	115.56 E
Hudson, P.Q., Can.	206	45.27 N	74.09 W
Hudson, Il., U.S.	216	40.36 N	88.59 W
Hudson, In., U.S.	216	41.31 N	85.04 W
Hudson, Ia., U.S.	190	42.24 N	92.27 W
Hudson, Md., U.S.	208	38.35 N	76.15 W
Hudson, Ma., U.S.	207	42.23 N	71.34 W
Hudson, Mi., U.S.	216	41.51 N	84.21 W
Hudson, N.H., U.S.	207	42.45 N	71.26 W
Hudson, N.Y., U.S.	210	42.15 N	73.47 W
Hudson, N.C., U.S.	192	35.50 N	81.29 W
Hudson, Oh., U.S.	214	41.14 N	81.26 W
Hudson, S.D., U.S.	198	43.07 N	96.27 W
Hudson, Tx., U.S.	222	31.19 N	94.50 W
Hudson, Wi., U.S.	190	44.58 N	92.45 W
Hudson, Wy., U.S.	200	42.54 N	108.34 W
Hudson □[6]	276	40.44 N	74.02 W
Hudson ≃, U.S.	188	40.42 N	74.02 W
Hudson ≃, Ga., U.S.	192	34.14 N	83.10 W
Hudson, Lake ⊜[1]	194	36.20 N	95.05 W
Hudson Bay	184	52.52 N	102.25 W
Hudson Bay c	176	60.00 N	86.00 W
Hudson-Bayonet Point	220	28.21 N	82.41 W
Hudson Falls	210	43.18 N	73.35 W
Hudson Highlands State Park ♠	210	41.26 N	73.58 W
Hudson Hope	182	56.02 N	121.55 W
Hudson Lake	216	41.42 N	86.32 W
Hudson Mountains ⋏	9	74.32 S	99.20 W
Hudsons Peak ∧	171b	36.26 S	149.10 E
Hudson Strait ⊻	176	62.30 N	72.00 W
Hudsonville	216	42.52 N	85.51 W
Hudwin Lake ⊜	184	53.12 N	95.42 W
Hue	110	16.28 N	107.36 E
Huebra ≃	34	41.02 N	6.48 W
Huechucuicui, Punta ›	254	41.47 S	74.02 W
Huechulafquén, Lago ⊜	254	39.46 S	71.28 W
Huedin	38	46.52 N	23.02 E
Huehuetán	236	15.01 N	92.22 W
Huehuetenango	236	15.20 N	91.28 W
Huehuetenango □[5]	236	15.40 N	91.35 W
Huehuetlán el Chico	234	18.21 N	98.42 W
Huejúcar	234	22.21 N	103.13 W
Huejuquilla el Alto	234	22.36 N	103.52 W
Huejutla de Reyes	234	21.08 N	98.25 W
Huelgoat	32	48.22 N	3.45 W
Huelma	34	37.39 N	3.27 W
Huelva	34	37.16 N	6.57 W
Huelva, Río de ≃	34	37.27 N	6.00 W
Huenque ≃	248	16.12 S	69.44 W
Huentelauquén	252	31.35 S	71.32 W
Huércal-Overa	34	37.23 N	1.57 W
Huerfano ≃	198	38.14 N	104.15 W
Huerfano Mountain ∧	200	36.26 N	107.51 W
Huerhuero Creek ≃	226	35.40 N	120.42 W
Huerlumada	120	32.45 N	90.00 E
Huerva ≃	34	41.39 N	0.52 W
Huesca	34	42.08 N	0.25 W
Huéscar	34	37.49 N	2.32 W
Hueston Woods State Park ♠	218	39.34 N	84.44 W
Huetamo de Núñez	234	18.35 N	100.53 W
Huete	34	40.08 N	2.41 W
Huey	219	38.36 N	89.17 W
Hueyapan	234	18.52 N	98.40 W
Hueyapan de Ocampo	234	18.07 N	95.09 W
Hueytown	194	33.27 N	86.59 W
Hufengzhen	107	29.43 N	106.07 E
Hüffenhardt	56	49.18 N	9.04 E
Huffman	222	30.01 N	95.05 W
Huffman Dam ◆[6]	218	39.48 N	84.05 W
Hüfingen	58	47.55 N	8.29 E
Ḥufrat an-Naḥās	140	9.45 N	24.19 E
Hufu	106	31.16 N	119.47 E
Hügel, Villa ʊ	263	51.25 N	7.01 E
Huggins, Mount ∧	9	78.17 S	162.28 E
Hugh ≃	162	25.01 S	134.01 E
Hugh Butler Lake ⊜[1]	198	40.22 N	100.42 W
Hughenden	166	20.51 S	144.12 E
Hughes, Austl.	162	30.42 S	129.31 E
Hughes, Ak., U.S.	180	66.03 N	154.16 W
Hughes, Ar., U.S.	194	34.56 N	90.28 W
Hughes ≃	184	56.46 N	100.01 W
Hughes, South Fork ≃	188	39.08 N	81.20 W
Hughes Airport ⊠	280	33.58 N	118.25 W
Hughes Creek ≃	169	36.53 S	145.08 E
Hughes Springs	222	33.05 N	94.38 W
Hughesville, Md., U.S.	208	38.31 N	76.47 W
Hughesville, Pa., U.S.	210	41.14 N	76.43 W
Hugh Keenleyside Dam ◆[6]	182	49.20 N	117.49 W
Hughson	226	37.36 N	120.52 W
Hughsonville	210	41.35 N	73.56 W
Hugh Town	42a	49.55 N	6.17 W
Hugo, Co., U.S.	198	39.08 N	103.28 W
Hugo, Ok., U.S.	196	34.00 N	95.30 W
Hugo Lake ⊜[1]	196	34.05 N	95.25 W
Hugoton	198	37.10 N	101.20 W
Hugou	100	33.23 N	117.08 E
Huguenot	210	41.25 N	74.38 W
Huguenot Lake ⊜	276	40.56 N	73.47 W

Symbol	English	Deutsch	Español	Français	Português
≃	River	Fluss	Río	Rivière	Rio
⩧	Canal	Kanal	Canal	Canal	Canal
∟	Waterfall, Rapids	Wasserfall, Stromschnellen	Cascada, Rápidos	Chute d'eau, Rapides	Cascata, Rápidos
⊻	Strait	Meeresstrasse	Estrecho	Détroit	Estreito
c	Bay, Gulf	Bucht, Golf	Bahía, Golfo	Baie, Golfe	Baía, Golfo
⊜	Lake, Lakes	See, Seen	Lago, Lagos	Lac, Lacs	Lago, Lagos
≡	Swamp	Sumpf	Pantano	Marais	Pântano
⌂	Ice Features, Glacier	Eis- und Gletscherformen	Accidentes Glaciales	Formes glaciaires	Acidentes glaciares
⊤	Other Hydrographic Features	Andere Hydrographische Objekte	Otros Elementos Hidrográficos	Autres données hydrographiques	Outros acidentes hidrográficos
✢	Submarine Features	Untermeerische Objekte	Accidentes Submarinos	Formes de relief sous-marin	Acidentes submarinos
□	Political Unit	Politische Einheit	Unidad Politica	Entité politique	Unidade política
ʊ	Cultural Institution	Kulturelle Institution	Institución Cultural	Institution culturelle	Institução cultural
⊥	Historical Site	Historische Stätte	Sitio Histórico	Site historique	Sitio histórico
♠	Recreational Site	Erholungs- und Ferienort	Sitio de Recreo	Centre de loisirs	Area de Lazer
⊠	Airport	Flughafen	Aeropuerto	Aéroport	Aeroporto
■	Military Installation	Militäranlage	Instalación Militar	Installation militaire	Instalação militar
◆	Miscellaneous	Verschiedenes	Misceláneo	Divers	Diversos

Name	Page	Lat.°′	Long.°′
Huhehot → Hohhot	102	40.51 N	111.40 E
Huhsi	100	23.35 N	119.39 E
Hui'an, Zhg.	100	25.04 N	118.47 E
Huian, Zhg.	106	31.47 N	121.45 E
Huiarau Range ✗	172	38.45 S	177.00 E
Huib-Hoch Plateau ✗[1]	156	27.00 S	16.45 E
Huibie Yang ɰ	100	30.08 N	121.44 E
Huibu	100	28.18 N	115.15 E
Huichang, Zhg.	100	25.34 N	115.49 E
Huichang, Zhg.	105	39.04 N	115.04 E
Huichapan	234	20.23 N	99.39 W
Hŭich'ŏn	98	40.10 N	126.17 E
Huichou → Huizhou	100	23.05 N	114.24 E
Huichuan	102	35.11 N	104.02 E
Huicungo	248	7.17 S	76.48 W
Huidong	102	26.41 N	102.36 E
Huidui	105	39.04 N	117.16 E
Huihe, Zhg.	89	48.12 N	119.17 E
Huihe, Zhg.	106	31.45 N	121.43 E
Huiji ≃	100	33.53 N	115.36 E
Huíla	152	15.04 S	13.32 E
Huíla □[5], Ang.	152	15.00 S	15.00 E
Huila □[5], Col.	246	2.30 N	75.45 W
Huila, Nevado del ∧	246	3.00 N	76.00 W
Huilai	100	23.04 N	116.18 E
Huili	102	26.43 N	102.10 E
Huiliuji	100	32.50 N	115.58 E
Huillapima	252	28.44 S	65.59 W
Huilong, Zhg.	100	27.30 N	118.24 E
Huilong, Zhg.	100	25.22 N	116.24 E
Huilong, Zhg.	100	24.09 N	113.58 E
Huilong, Zhg.	107	30.28 N	105.26 E
Huilong, Zhg.	107	30.35 N	105.49 E
Huilongchang, Zhg.	107	29.41 N	104.17 E
Huilongchang, Zhg.	107	30.18 N	103.39 E
Huilongchang, Zhg.	107	30.41 N	106.34 E
Huilongchang, Zhg.	107	29.17 N	105.01 E
Huimanguillo	234	17.51 N	93.23 W
Huimin	98	37.29 N	117.29 E
Huinan (Chaoyang)	98	42.40 N	126.00 E
Huinca Renancó	252	34.50 S	64.23 W
Hüinghausen	263	51.11 N	7.48 E
Huining	102	35.41 N	105.08 E
Huisachal	196	26.47 N	101.07 W
Huisduinen	52	52.56 N	4.44 E
Huishan	106	31.35 N	120.16 E
Huishui	102	26.07 N	106.24 E
Huismes	50	47.14 N	0.15 E
Huisne ≃	50	47.59 N	0.11 E
Huissen	52	51.57 N	5.56 E
Huistepec	234	16.39 N	98.20 W
Huiting	98	34.05 N	116.04 E
Huitiupan	234	17.13 N	92.39 W
Huitong	102	26.54 N	109.31 E
Huitongqiao	102	24.43 N	98.56 E
Huittinen (Lauttakylä)	26	61.11 N	22.42 E
Huitzilán	234	19.58 N	97.41 W
Huitzuco de los Figueroa	234	18.18 N	99.21 W
Huixian	102	33.47 N	106.16 E
Huixquilucan □[7]	286a	19.24 N	99.18 W
Huixtla	232	15.09 N	92.28 W
Huiyang → Huizhou	100	23.05 N	114.24 E
Huiyao	100	27.16 N	118.05 E
Huizache	234	22.55 N	100.25 W
Huize	102	26.27 N	103.09 E
Huizen	52	52.17 N	5.14 E
Huizhou	100	23.05 N	114.24 E
Hujia, Zhg.	104	41.20 N	121.52 E
Hujia, Zhg.	106	31.25 N	121.37 E
Hujiadian	107	29.41 N	104.07 E
Hujiajie	104	41.06 N	122.10 E
Hujiasi	107	29.16 N	105.13 E
Hujiawopu	104	42.34 N	122.11 E
Hujiayu	105	39.28 N	115.27 E
Hujiazhuang, Zhg.	105	39.51 N	117.07 E
Hujiazhuang, Zhg.	269b	31.21 N	121.25 E
Hujie	102	24.56 N	100.32 E
Hukeng	100	27.29 N	114.18 E
Hukou	100	29.45 N	116.13 E
Hŭksan-chedo II	98	34.30 N	125.20 E
Hukui → Fukui	94	36.04 N	136.13 E
Ḥukūmah	140	13.52 N	36.07 E
Hukuntsi	156	24.02 S	21.48 E
Hukuoka → Fukuoka	96	33.35 N	130.24 E
Hukusima → Fukushima	92	37.45 N	140.28 E
Hukuyama → Fukuyama	96	34.29 N	133.22 E
Ḥula, 'Emeq ≚[1]	132	33.08 N	35.37 E
Hulahula ≃	180	70.00 N	144.01 W
Hulan	89	46.00 N	126.38 E
Hulan ≃	89	45.55 N	126.41 E
Hulan Ergi	89	47.13 N	123.39 E
Hulbert, Mi., U.S.	190	46.21 N	85.09 W
Hulbert, Ok., U.S.	194	35.55 N	95.08 W
Hulberton	210	43.15 N	78.04 W
Ḥulda	132	31.50 N	34.53 E
Huldrefossen ∟	26	61.28 N	5.58 E
Hulei	100	24.50 N	116.48 E
Huleia Stream ≃	229b	21.57 N	159.22 W
Hulett	198	44.40 N	104.36 W
Hulim	114	1.12 N	99.31 E
Hulín, Česko.	30	49.19 N	17.28 E
Hulin, Zhg.	89	45.46 N	132.59 E
Hulin ≃, Zhg.	89	44.55 N	122.35 E
Hulin ≃, Zhg.	89	45.19 N	124.06 E
Huliu ≃	98	40.10 N	114.33 E
Hull, P.Q., Can.	212	45.26 N	75.43 W
Hull → Kingston upon Hull, Eng., U.K.	44	53.45 N	0.20 W
Hull, Il., U.S.	219	39.43 N	91.13 W
Hull, Ia., U.S.	198	43.11 N	96.08 W
Hull, Ma., U.S.	207	42.18 N	70.54 W
Hull, Tx., U.S.	222	30.09 N	94.39 W
Hull □[6]	212	45.40 N	75.35 W
Hull ≃	44	53.44 N	0.19 W
Hullavington	42	51.33 N	2.09 W
Hull Bay ⊂	283	42.18 N	70.53 W
Hullbridge	260	51.37 N	0.38 E
Hull Glacier ⊏	9	75.05 S	137.15 W
Hullo	76	59.00 N	23.14 E
Hulmeville	285	40.08 N	74.55 W
Hüls, B.R.D.	56	51.22 N	6.30 E
Hüls, B.R.D.	263	51.40 N	7.08 E
Hülscheid	56	51.16 N	7.34 E
Hülser Berg ●[8]	263	51.24 N	6.31 E
Hülser Berg ∧[2]	263	51.23 N	6.33 E
Hulst	52	51.17 N	4.03 E
Hult	40	58.40 N	16.07 E
Hultsfred	26	57.29 N	15.50 E
Huludao	104	40.43 N	121.00 E
Hulufa	105	39.42 N	116.12 E
Hulun → Hailar	89	49.12 N	119.42 E
Hulun Nur ⊜	88	49.01 N	117.32 E
Huluyu	105	40.14 N	116.53 E
Ḥulwān	142	29.51 N	31.20 E
Ḥulwān Observatory ʊ[3]	142	29.52 N	31.21 E
Huma, Tonga	174w	21.19 S	175.57 W
Huma, Zhg.	89	51.43 N	126.38 E
Huma ≃	89	51.40 N	126.44 E
Humacao	240m	18.09 N	65.50 W
Humahuaca	252	23.12 S	65.21 W
Humaitá, Bra.	248	7.31 S	63.02 W
Humaitá, Para.	252	27.03 S	58.33 W
Humaitá ≃	248	8.16 S	72.44 W
Humansdorp	158	34.02 S	24.46 E
Humansville	194	37.47 N	93.34 W
Humara, Jabal al- ∧	140	16.16 N	30.59 E
Humarock	283	42.08 N	70.41 W
Ḥumaydah	140	14.22 N	22.31 E
Humayingzi	98	41.06 N	116.48 E
Humayun's Tomb ⊥	272a	28.36 N	77.15 E
Humbe	152	16.40 S	14.55 E
Humbe, Serra do ✗	152	12.13 S	15.25 E
Humbeek	50	50.58 N	4.23 E
Humber ≃, On., Can.	212	43.38 N	79.28 W
Humber ≃, Eng., U.K.	44	53.40 N	0.10 W
Humber, Mouth of the ≃[1]	44	53.32 N	0.08 E
Humber Bay ⊂	275b	43.38 N	79.29 W
Humber Bridge ●[5]	44	53.42 N	0.27 W
Humberside □[6]	44	53.55 N	0.40 W
Humberston	44	53.32 N	0.02 W
Humberto de Campos	250	2.37 S	43.27 W
Humberto Primo	252	30.52 S	61.22 W
Humber Valley Park ♦	275b	43.39 N	79.30 W
Humbird	190	44.31 N	90.53 W
Humble, Dan.	41	54.50 N	10.42 E
Humble, Tx., U.S.	222	29.59 N	95.15 W
Humboldt, Sk., Can.	184	52.12 N	105.07 W
Humboldt, Az., U.S.	200	34.30 N	112.14 W
Humboldt, Il., U.S.	194	39.36 N	88.19 W
Humboldt, Ia., U.S.	198	42.43 N	94.12 W
Humboldt, Ks., U.S.	198	37.48 N	95.26 W
Humboldt, Ne., U.S.	198	40.09 N	95.56 W
Humboldt, S.D., U.S.	198	43.38 N	97.04 W
Humboldt, Tn., U.S.	194	35.49 N	88.54 W
Humboldt ∧	175f	21.53 S	166.25 E
Humboldt ≃	204	40.02 N	118.31 W
Humboldt, North Fork ≃	204	40.56 N	115.32 W
Humboldt, Parque ♦	286c	10.28 N	66.54 W
Humboldt, Planetario ʊ	286c	10.30 N	66.50 W
Humboldt, South Fork ≃	204	40.47 N	115.53 W
Humboldt Bay ⊂	204	40.47 N	124.11 W
Humboldt Lake ⊜	204	39.58 N	118.38 W
Humboldt Mountains ✗	9	71.45 S	11.30 E
Humboldt Park ♦	278	41.54 N	87.42 W
Humboldt Redwoods State Park ♦	204	40.19 N	124.00 W
Humboldt Salt Marsh ≡	204	39.50 N	117.55 W
Humboldt-Universität ʊ[2]	264a	52.31 N	13.24 E
Hume, Ca., U.S.	204	36.47 N	118.55 W
Hume, N.Y., U.S.	210	42.29 N	78.08 W
Hume, Lake ⊜[1]	166	36.06 S	147.05 E
Hume and Hovell Lookout ♦	169	37.15 S	144.59 E
Hume and Hovell Memorial ⊥	170	34.10 S	150.47 E
Humeburn	166	27.24 S	145.14 E
Hūmedān	128	25.24 N	59.39 E
Hu Men ⊂[1]	100	22.44 N	113.40 E
Humenné	30	48.56 N	21.55 E
Húmera	266a	40.26 N	3.47 W
Humeston	190	40.51 N	93.29 W
Humla Karnāli ≃	124	29.38 N	81.52 E
Humlebæk	41	55.58 N	12.33 E
Hummelfjell ∧	26	62.27 N	11.17 E
Hummelo	52	52.00 N	6.14 E
Hummelstown	208	40.16 N	76.43 W
Hummels Wharf	210	40.49 N	76.50 W
Hümmling ✗	52	52.52 N	7.31 E
Humos, Isla I	254	45.38 S	73.59 W
Humpata	152	15.02 S	13.24 E
Hümpfershausen	56	50.40 N	10.13 E
Humphrey, Ar., U.S.	194	34.25 N	91.42 W
Humphrey, Ne., U.S.	198	41.41 N	97.29 W
Humphreys, Mount ∧	204	37.17 N	118.40 W
Humphreys Peak ∧	200	35.20 N	111.40 W
Humpolec	30	49.32 N	15.22 E
Humppila	26	60.56 N	23.22 E
Humptulips	224	47.13 N	123.57 W
Humptulips ≃	224	47.03 N	124.03 W
Humptulips, East Fork ≃	224	47.15 N	123.54 W
Humptulips, West Fork ≃	224	47.15 N	123.54 W
Humptulips Ridge ∧	224	47.20 N	123.45 W
Humula	171b	35.29 S	147.45 E
Humuya ≃	236	15.13 N	87.57 W
Hūn	146	29.07 N	15.56 E
Hun ≃, Zhg.	98	41.01 N	122.27 E
Hun ≃, Zhg.	98	40.52 N	125.42 E
Hunabasi → Funabashi	94	35.42 N	139.59 E
Húnaflói ⊂	24a	65.50 N	20.50 W
Hunan □[4]	102	28.00 N	111.00 E
Ḥunayshāt, Ghurd al- ⊥[8]	142	30.07 N	29.47 E
Hunchun	98	42.54 N	130.22 E
Huncoat	262	53.46 N	2.20 W
Hundeluft	54	51.58 N	12.20 E
Hundested	41	55.58 N	11.52 E
Hundewāli	123	31.55 N	72.38 E
Hundezler, Tür.	84	40.40 N	40.24 E
Hundezler, Tür.	130	40.45 N	40.15 E
Hundorp	26	61.33 N	9.54 E
Hundred	188	39.41 N	80.27 W
Hundred End	262	53.42 N	2.53 W
Hundred Islands National Park ♦	116	16.13 N	120.01 E
Hundslund	41	55.55 N	10.04 E
Hundstein ∧	64	47.20 N	12.54 E
Hundwil	58	47.22 N	9.19 E
Hunedoara	38	45.45 N	22.54 E
Hunedoara □[6]	38	45.45 N	23.00 E
Hünfeld	56	50.40 N	9.46 E
Hungary (Magyarország) □[1], Europe	22	47.00 N	20.00 E
Hungary (Magyarország) □[1], Europe	30	47.00 N	20.00 E
Hungchiang → Hongjiang	102	27.07 N	109.56 E
Hungen	56	50.28 N	8.54 E
Hungerford, Austl.	166	29.00 S	144.25 E
Hungerford, Eng., U.K.	42	51.26 N	1.30 W
Hungerford, Tx., U.S.	222	29.24 N	96.05 W
Hŭngho-ri	98	37.14 N	127.44 E
Hŭngin-ni	98	39.03 N	126.26 E
Hung-long	269c	10.40 N	106.39 E
Hungmao	100	24.55 N	120.58 E
Hŭngnam	98	39.50 N	127.38 E
Hungría → Hungary □[1]	30	47.00 N	20.00 E
Hungry Horse	202	48.23 N	114.03 W
Hungry Horse Dam ●[6]	202	48.14 N	114.04 W
Hungry Horse Reservoir ⊜[1]	202	48.15 N	113.50 W
Hungry Lake ⊜	212	44.48 N	76.53 W
Hungry Law ∧[2]	44	55.21 N	2.24 W
Hung-yen	110	20.39 N	106.04 E
Hunhe	104	41.43 N	123.22 E
Huningue	58	47.36 N	7.35 E
Hunish, Rubha >	46	57.41 N	6.21 W
Huni Valley	150	5.28 N	1.55 W
Hunjiang (Badaojiang)	98	41.56 N	126.29 E
Hunker	279b	40.12 N	79.38 W
Ḥunkurāb, Ra's >	140	24.34 N	35.10 E
Hunlen Falls ∟	182	52.17 N	125.47 W
Hunmanby	44	54.10 N	0.19 W
Hunn ⊜	40	58.51 N	15.57 E
Hunneberg ∧[2]	26	58.20 N	12.27 E
Hunnebostrand	26	58.27 N	11.18 E
Hunnewell	219	39.40 N	91.51 W
Hunnewell Lake ⊜	219	39.42 N	91.52 W
Hunsberge ✗	156	27.45 S	17.12 E
Hunseby	41	54.48 N	11.32 E
Hunspach	56	48.57 N	7.57 E
Hunsrück ✗	56	49.50 N	6.40 E
Hunstanton	42	52.57 N	0.30 E
Hunstein Range ✗	164	4.30 S	142.40 E
Hunsūr	122	12.18 N	76.17 E
Hunswinkel	263	51.05 N	7.48 E
Hunt □[6]	222	33.03 N	96.05 W
Hunte ≃	52	52.30 N	8.19 E
Hunter, N.Y., U.S.	210	42.13 N	74.13 W
Hunter, N.D., U.S.	198	47.11 N	97.13 W
Hunter ≃, Austl.	170	32.50 S	151.42 E
Hunter ≃, N.Z.	172	44.22 S	169.25 E
Hunter, Île I	14	22.24 S	172.03 E
Hunter, Mount ∧	180	62.57 N	151.05 W
Hunter, Port ⊂	170	32.55 S	151.48 E
Hunterdon □[6]	208	40.31 N	74.52 W
Hunter Island I, Austl.	166	40.32 S	144.45 E
Hunter Island I, B.C., Can.	182	51.55 N	128.05 W
Hunter Island I, N.Y., U.S.	276	40.53 N	73.47 W
Hunter Mountain ∧	210	42.10 N	74.14 W
Hunter Mountains ✗	172	45.42 S	167.25 E
Hunter Range ✗	170	32.50 S	150.50 E
Hunter Ridge ✢[3]	14	21.30 S	174.30 E
Hunter River	186	46.21 N	63.21 W
Hunters	182	48.07 N	118.12 W
Hunters Bay ⊂	110	19.57 N	93.19 E
Hunters Creek Village	222	29.46 N	95.24 W
Huntersfield Mountain ∧	210	42.21 N	74.21 W
Hunters Hill	274a	33.50 S	151.09 E
Hunters Point >	282	37.43 N	122.22 W
Hunter's Quay	46	55.58 N	4.55 W
Hunters Road	154	19.09 S	29.48 E
Hunters Run	208	40.05 N	77.11 W
Huntersville	192	35.25 N	80.50 W
Huntertown	216	41.13 N	85.10 W
Hunterville	172	39.56 S	175.34 E
Hunter Wash V	200	36.17 N	108.34 W
Huntingburg	194	38.17 N	86.57 W
Huntingdon, B.C., Can.	224	49.00 N	122.16 W
Huntingdon, P.Q., Can.	206	45.05 N	74.10 W
Huntingdon, Eng., U.K.	42	52.20 N	0.12 W
Huntingdon, Pa., U.S.	214	40.29 N	78.00 W
Huntingdon, Tn., U.S.	194	36.00 N	88.25 W
Huntingdon □[6], P.Q., Can.	206	45.05 N	74.00 W
Huntingdon □[6], Pa., U.S.	214	40.29 N	78.01 W
Huntingdon Valley	285	40.07 N	75.03 W
Huntingdon Valley Creek ≃	285	40.07 N	75.04 W
Hunting Island State Park ♦	192	32.20 N	80.30 W
Hunting Ridge	284c	38.55 N	77.12 W
Huntington, Eng., U.K.	44	54.01 N	1.04 W
Huntington, In., U.S.	216	40.52 N	85.29 W
Huntington, Ma., U.S.	207	42.14 N	72.52 W
Huntington, N.Y., U.S.	210	40.51 N	73.25 W
Huntington, Or., U.S.	202	44.21 N	117.15 W
Huntington, Tx., U.S.	222	31.16 N	94.34 W
Huntington, Ut,. U.S.	200	39.19 N	110.57 W
Huntington, Va., U.S.	284c	38.48 N	77.15 W
Huntington, W.V., U.S.	188	38.25 N	82.26 W
Huntington □[6]	216	40.53 N	85.30 W
Huntington Bay	276	40.53 N	73.24 W
Huntington Bay ⊂	276	40.55 N	73.25 W
Huntington Beach, Ca., U.S.	228	33.39 N	117.59 W
Huntington Beach, N.Y., U.S.	276	40.54 N	73.23 W
Huntington Creek ≃, Nv., U.S.	204	40.37 N	115.43 W
Huntington Creek ≃, Pa., U.S.	210	41.06 N	76.22 W
Huntington Creek ≃, Ut,. U.S.	200	39.09 N	110.55 W
Huntington Harbor ⊂	276	40.54 N	73.26 W
Huntington Lake	226	37.15 N	119.14 W
Huntington Lake ⊜[1], Ca., U.S.	226	37.14 N	119.12 W
Huntington Lake ⊜[1], In., U.S.	216	40.50 N	85.25 W
Huntington Library ʊ[3]	280	34.08 N	118.07 W
Huntington Mills	210	41.11 N	76.14 W
Huntington Park	228	33.58 N	118.13 W
Huntington Park ♦	279a	41.29 N	81.56 W
Huntington Station	210	40.51 N	73.24 W
Huntington Woods	281	42.28 N	83.10 W
Huntingtown	208	38.36 N	76.36 W
Hunting Valley	279a	41.31 N	81.23 W
Huntingville	206	45.20 N	71.51 W
Huntland	194	35.03 N	86.16 W
Huntley, Il., U.S.	216	42.10 N	88.25 W
Huntley, Mt., U.S.	202	45.53 N	108.18 W
Huntly, N.Z.	172	37.33 S	175.10 E
Huntly, Scot., U.K.	46	57.27 N	2.47 W
Hunt Mountain ∧	202	44.44 N	107.45 W
Hunton	260	51.13 N	0.28 E
Huntsburg	214	41.32 N	81.03 W
Hunt's Cross ●[8]	262	53.21 N	2.51 W
Hunts Point	224	47.39 N	122.14 W
Huntsville, On., Can.	212	45.20 N	79.13 W
Huntsville, Al., U.S.	194	34.43 N	86.35 W
Huntsville, Ar., U.S.	194	36.05 N	93.44 W
Huntsville, Il., U.S.	219	40.11 N	90.52 W
Huntsville, In., U.S.	218	40.00 N	85.43 W
Huntsville, Mo., U.S.	194	39.26 N	92.33 W
Huntsville, Oh., U.S.	216	40.26 N	83.49 W
Huntsville, Tn., U.S.	192	36.24 N	84.29 W
Huntsville, Tx., U.S.	222	30.43 N	95.33 W
Huntsville, Ut,. U.S.	200	41.15 N	111.46 W
Huntsville State Park ♦	222	30.37 N	95.32 W
Hunū, Kathīb al- ⊥[8]	142	30.37 N	32.49 E
Hunucmá	232	21.01 N	89.52 W
Hunut	130	40.39 N	41.09 E
Hünxe	52	51.38 N	6.46 E
Hünxer Wald ♦	263	51.40 N	6.50 E
Hunyani ≃	154	15.37 S	30.39 E
Hunyuan	98	39.48 N	113.41 E
Hun-yung	98	42.53 N	130.12 E
Hunza ≃	123	35.55 N	74.22 E
Huocheng	86	44.12 N	80.26 E
Huoergeluo	89	45.35 N	120.56 E
Huoerpahu ⊜	120	34.32 N	81.03 E
Huokou	100	26.28 N	119.16 E
Huolong	106	32.04 N	121.17 E
Huolongmen	89	49.48 N	125.47 E
Huolu	98	38.05 N	114.18 E
Huong-hoa	110	16.37 N	106.45 E
Huong-khe	110	18.13 N	105.41 E
Huong-thuy	110	16.25 N	107.40 E
Huon Gulf ⊂	164	7.10 S	147.25 E
Huon Peninsula >[1]	164	6.25 S	147.25 E
Huonville	166	43.01 S	147.02 E
Huoqiu	100	32.20 N	116.16 E
Huorili	89	49.00 N	124.41 E
Huoshan	100	31.25 N	116.20 E
Huo Shan ∧	100	31.06 N	116.12 E
Huoshaoliao	100	25.00 N	121.45 E
Huotong	100	26.53 N	119.25 E
Huotong ≃	100	26.50 N	119.32 E
Huotuolaihuduke	102	40.19 N	104.18 E
Huoxian, Zhg.	102	36.37 N	111.40 E
Huoxian, Zhg.	105	39.46 N	116.46 E
Huoyan	100	33.42 N	113.40 E
Hupeh → Hubei □[4]	90	31.00 N	112.00 E
Huqiao	106	31.25 N	119.24 E
Hura	126	23.18 N	86.39 E
Hūrand	84	38.51 N	47.22 E
Hurāsāgar ≃	126	24.04 N	89.40 E
Ḥuraydīn, Wādī V	132	30.59 N	33.53 E
Ḥuraymilā	128	25.08 N	46.08 E
Hūrayn	142	30.39 N	31.08 E
Hurd, Cape >	190	45.13 N	81.44 W
Hurdalssjøen ⊜	26	60.20 N	11.05 E
Hurdiyo	144	10.33 N	51.08 E
Hurdland	219	40.09 N	92.18 W
Hurdsfield	262	53.16 N	2.06 W
Hurepoix ●[1]	261	48.40 N	2.10 E
Hure Qi	98	42.44 N	121.40 E
Hurffville	285	39.46 N	75.07 W
Huri ∧[2]	154	3.41 N	37.51 E
Huriel	32	46.23 N	2.29 E
Hurleg Hu ⊜	102	37.20 N	96.54 E
Hurley, Ms., U.S.	194	30.39 N	88.29 W
Hurley, N.M., U.S.	200	32.41 N	108.07 W
Hurley, N.Y., U.S.	210	41.55 N	74.03 W
Hurley, S.D., U.S.	198	43.16 N	97.05 W
Hurley, Wi., U.S.	190	46.26 N	90.11 W
Hurleyville	210	41.44 N	74.40 W
Hurlford	46	55.36 N	4.28 W
Hurliness	46	58.47 N	3.15 W
Hurlingham	258	34.36 S	58.38 W
Hurlock	208	38.37 N	75.51 W
Hurmāgai	128	28.18 N	64.26 E
Huron, Ca., U.S.	226	36.12 N	120.06 W
Huron, Oh., U.S.	214	41.22 N	82.33 W
Huron, S.D., U.S.	198	44.21 N	98.12 W
Huron □[6], On., Can.	212	43.45 N	81.10 W
Huron □[6], Oh., U.S.	214	41.15 N	82.37 W
Huron ≃, Mi., U.S.	216	42.03 N	83.14 W
Huron ≃, Oh., U.S.	214	41.23 N	82.33 W
Huron, East Branch ≃	214	41.17 N	82.38 W
Huron, Lake ⊜	190	44.30 N	82.15 W
Huron, Point >	214	42.34 N	82.47 W
Huron, West Branch ≃	214	41.17 N	82.38 W
Huron Gardens	216	42.38 N	83.20 W
Huron Mountains ✗[2]	190	46.50 N	87.55 W
Hurons, Rivière des ≃	206	45.28 N	73.16 W
Hurricane, Ak., U.S.	180	62.59 N	149.38 W
Hurricane, Ut,. U.S.	200	37.10 N	113.17 W
Hurricane, W.V., U.S.	188	38.25 N	82.01 W
Hurricane Bayou ≃	222	31.21 N	95.35 W
Hurricane Cliffs ⊥[4]	200	37.20 N	113.10 W
Hurricane Creek ≃, Ar., U.S.	194	34.05 N	92.23 W
Hurricane Creek ≃, Ga., U.S.	192	31.23 N	82.19 W
Hurricane Creek ≃, Il., U.S.	219	38.53 N	89.13 W
Hurricane Lake ⊜	198	48.25 N	99.30 W
Hurricane Wash V	200	37.00 N	113.23 W
Hurshi	126	24.17 N	88.28 E
Hursley	42	51.02 N	1.24 W
Hurso	144	9.38 N	41.38 E
Hurst	222	32.49 N	97.10 W
Hurstbourne Tarrant	42	51.17 N	1.23 W
Hurstbridge	169	37.38 S	145.12 E
Hurstpierpoint	42	50.56 N	0.11 W
Hurstville	170	33.58 S	151.06 E
Hurstwood Reservoir ⊜[1]	262	53.47 N	2.10 W
Hurt	192	37.05 N	79.17 W
Hurtado ≃	252	30.35 S	71.11 W
Hurtaut ≃	50	49.42 N	4.01 E
Hürth	56	50.52 N	6.51 E
Hurtsboro	194	32.14 N	85.24 W
Hurunui ≃	172	42.55 S	173.17 E
Hurup	26	56.45 N	8.25 E
Hurworth-on-Tees	44	54.29 N	1.31 W
Husainābād	124	24.32 N	84.01 E
Husainīwāla	123	30.59 N	74.34 E
Husainpur	124	24.25 N	90.40 E
Húsavík	24a	66.04 N	17.18 W
Husby-Långhundra	40	59.45 N	18.01 E
Huse → Higashiōsaka	96	34.39 N	135.35 E
Husen ●[8]	263	51.33 N	7.36 E
Hüseyinli	130	40.21 N	33.59 E
Hushan, Zhg.	89	45.35 N	130.35 E
Hushan, Zhg.	100	28.36 N	118.59 E
Hushan, Zhg.	100	22.09 N	113.10 E
Husheib	140	14.54 N	35.07 E
Hushi	107	28.57 N	105.22 E
Hushiha	98	40.52 N	116.59 E
Hushitai	104	41.57 N	123.30 E
Hushu, Zhg.	106	31.52 N	118.59 E
Hushu, Zhg.	106	30.18 N	120.08 E
Huși	38	46.40 N	28.04 E
Husinec	60	49.03 N	13.58 E
Huskisson	170	35.02 S	150.40 E
Huskvarna	26	57.48 N	14.16 E
Huslia	180	65.42 N	156.25 W
Hussar	182	51.03 N	112.41 W
Hussigny-Godbrange	56	49.29 N	5.52 E
Hustisford	190	43.21 N	88.36 W
Huston ≃	220	25.42 N	81.17 W
Hustontown	214	40.03 N	78.02 W
Hustopeče	61	48.57 N	16.44 E
Husum, B.R.D.	41	54.28 N	9.03 E
Husum, Sve.	26	63.20 N	19.10 E
Husum, Wa., U.S.	224	45.47 N	121.29 W
Hutaimbaru	114	1.34 N	99.44 E
Hutangqiao	106	31.46 N	119.57 E
Hutan Melintang	114	3.53 N	100.56 E
Hutanopan	114	0.41 N	99.42 E
Hutaym, Ḥarrat ⊥[9]	128	26.15 N	40.20 E
Hutberg ∧[2]	54	52.09 N	14.33 E
Hutchins	222	32.39 N	96.43 W
Hutchinson, S. Afr.	158	31.30 S	23.09 E
Hutchinson, Ks., U.S.	198	38.03 N	97.55 W
Hutchinson, Mn., U.S.	190	44.53 N	94.22 W
Hutchinson, Pa., U.S.	214	40.13 N	79.44 W
Hutchinson ≃	276	40.52 N	73.50 W
Hutchinson Island I	220	27.25 N	80.17 W
Hutch Mountain ∧	200	34.47 N	111.22 W
Huthwaite	44	53.09 N	1.17 W
Hutou, Zhg.	100	25.15 N	118.03 E
Hutou, Zhg.	100	26.04 N	118.46 E
Hutou, Zhg.	106	31.37 N	119.37 E
Hutou, Zhg.	106	32.14 N	120.17 E
Hutouya	98	37.13 N	119.46 E
Hutsonville	194	39.06 N	87.39 W
Hüttau	64	47.25 N	13.18 E
Hütteldorf ●[8]	264b	48.12 N	16.16 E
Hüttener Berge ✗[2]	41	54.26 N	9.40 E
Hüttenheim ●[8]	263	51.22 N	6.43 E
Hüttental	56	50.54 N	8.02 E
Hutte Sauvage, Lac de la ⊜	176	56.15 N	64.45 W
Huttig	194	33.02 N	92.10 W
Hütting	60	48.48 N	11.07 E
Hutto	222	30.33 N	97.33 W
Hutton, Eng., U.K.	260	51.38 N	0.22 E
Hutton, Eng., U.K.	262	53.44 N	2.46 W
Hutton, Mount ∧	166	25.51 S	148.20 E
Hutton Rudby	44	54.27 N	1.17 W
Huttonsville	212	43.38 N	79.48 W
Huttrop ●[8]	263	51.27 N	7.03 E
Hüttschlag	64	47.10 N	13.14 E
Huttwil	58	47.07 N	7.51 E
Hutubi	86	44.07 N	86.57 E
Hutuo ≃	98	38.14 N	116.05 E
Hutwisch ∧	61	47.28 N	16.13 E
Huu	115b	8.48 S	118.25 E
Huvalu Forest ●[3]	174v	19.03 S	169.51 W
Huveaune ≃	62	43.15 N	5.23 E
Hüvek	130	37.22 N	38.31 E
Huvudskär I	40	58.57 N	18.34 E
Huwan	100	31.41 N	114.53 E
Huwei	100	23.43 N	120.26 E
Huwun	144	4.23 N	40.08 E
Ḥuwwārah	132	32.09 N	35.15 E
Huxford	194	31.13 N	87.28 W
Huxi	100	26.12 N	114.44 E
Huxian	102	34.09 N	108.32 E
Huxley	182	51.56 N	113.14 W
Huy	56	50.31 N	5.14 E
Huy ∧	54	51.57 N	10.57 E
Huyangzhen	100	32.25 N	112.45 E
Huyton-with-Roby	262	53.25 N	2.52 W
Huyuesi	106	30.23 N	118.45 E
Hüyük	130	37.57 N	31.37 E
Huyutou	100	26.44 N	119.49 E
Huzgan	128	31.27 N	48.04 E
Huzhen	100	28.50 N	120.15 E
Huzhou	106	30.52 N	120.06 E
Huzhu	102	37.00 N	102.00 E
Huzhuangtun	104	40.43 N	122.33 E
Huzi	100	30.56 N	113.42 E
Huzisawa → Fujisawa	94	35.21 N	139.29 E
Hvalsø	41	55.36 N	11.50 E
Hvannadalshnúkur ∧	24a	64.01 N	16.41 W
Hvar	36	43.10 N	16.27 E
Hvar, Otok I	36	43.09 N	16.45 E
Hvarski Kanal ɰ	36	43.15 N	16.37 E
Hveragerði	24a	64.03 N	21.10 W
Hvide Sande	26	55.59 N	8.08 E
Hvidovre	41	55.39 N	12.29 E
Hvittingfoss	26	59.29 N	10.01 E
Hvolsvöllur	24a	63.45 N	20.10 W
Hwach'ŏn	98	38.06 N	127.41 E
Hwach'ŏn-chŏsuji ⊜[1]	98	38.07 N	127.52 E
Hwach'ŏn-ni	98	39.01 N	126.02 E
Hwainan → Huainan	100	32.40 N	117.00 E
Hwaining → Anqing	100	30.31 N	117.02 E
Hwange	154	18.22 S	26.29 E
Hwange National Park ♦	154	19.00 S	26.35 E
Hwanggong-ni	98	40.03 N	129.27 E
Hwanghae Namdo □[4]	98	38.15 N	125.30 E
Hwanghae Pukdo □[4]	98	38.30 N	126.25 E
Hwang Ho → Huang ≃	90	37.32 N	118.19 E
Hwangju	98	38.42 N	125.46 E
Hwangshih → Huangshi	100	30.13 N	115.05 E
Hyak	224	47.23 N	121.23 W
Hyakuna	174m	26.08 N	127.48 E
Hyakuri-ga-dake ∧	94	35.23 N	135.49 E
Hyakuri-kichi, Kōkū-jieitai- ■	94	36.11 N	140.25 E
Hyannis, Ma., U.S.	207	41.39 N	70.17 W
Hyannis, Ne., U.S.	198	42.00 N	101.45 W
Hyannis Port	207	41.38 N	70.18 W
Hyattsville	208	38.57 N	76.56 W
Hyattville	202	44.14 N	107.36 W
Hybla Valley	208	38.44 N	77.05 W
Hyco ≃	192	36.40 N	78.45 W
Hyco Lake ⊜[1]	192	36.30 N	79.05 W
Hydaburg	182	55.12 N	132.49 W
Hyde, N.Z.	172	45.18 S	170.15 E
Hyde, Eng., U.K.	262	53.27 N	2.04 W
Hyde, Pa., U.S.	214	41.00 N	78.28 W
Hyden, Austl.	162	32.27 S	118.53 E
Hyden, Ky., U.S.	192	37.10 N	83.22 W
Hyde Park, Guy.	246	6.30 N	58.16 W
Hyde Park, N.Y., U.S.	210	41.47 N	73.56 W
Hyde Park, Vt., U.S.	188	44.35 N	72.37 W
Hyde Park ●[8], Il., U.S.	278	41.48 N	87.36 W
Hyde Park ●[8], Ma., U.S.	283	42.15 N	71.08 W
Hyde Park ♦, Austl.	274a	33.53 S	151.13 E
Hyde Park ♦, Eng., U.K.	260	51.20 N	0.10 W
Hyde Park ♦, N.Y., U.S.	284a	43.06 N	79.01 W
Hyder	182	55.55 N	130.01 W
Hyderābād, India	122	17.23 N	78.29 E
Hyderābād, Pāk.	120	25.22 N	68.22 E
Hydetown	214	41.40 N	79.44 W
Hydra → Ídhra I	38	37.20 N	23.32 E
Hydraulic	182	52.36 N	121.42 W
Hydro	196	35.21 N	98.22 W
Hydrographers Passage ɰ	166	20.00 S	150.00 E
Hyen ⊜	40	60.36 N	16.12 E
Hyères	62	43.07 N	6.07 E
Hyères, Îles d' II	62	43.00 N	6.20 E
Hyères-Plage	62	43.06 N	6.10 E
Hyesan	98	41.23 N	128.12 E
Hyland ≃	180	59.50 N	128.10 W
Hylestad	26	59.05 N	7.32 E
Hyllekrog I	41	54.36 N	11.30 E
Hyllinge, Dan.	41	55.16 N	11.37 E
Hyllinge, Sve.	41	56.06 N	12.51 E
Hyllstofta	41	56.08 N	13.16 E
Hyltebruk	26	57.00 N	13.14 E
Hymera	194	39.11 N	87.18 W
Hyndburn □[8]	262	53.45 N	2.23 W
Hyndman	188	39.49 N	78.43 W
Hyndman Peak ∧	202	43.45 N	114.08 W
Hyne Field ⊠	281	42.34 N	83.47 W
Hyōgo □[5]	96	35.00 N	135.00 E
Hyōgo ●[8]	270	34.39 N	135.10 E
Hyŏn-ni	98	37.57 N	128.20 E
Hyōno-sen ∧	96	35.21 N	134.31 E
Hyōnosen-Ushiroyama-Nagisan-kokutei-kōen ♦	96	35.15 N	134.30 E
Hyŏpch'ŏn	98	35.35 N	128.08 E
Hyrum	200	41.38 N	111.51 W
Hyrynsalmi	26	64.40 N	28.32 E
Hysham	202	46.17 N	107.14 W
Hythe, Austl.	166	43.25 S	146.59 E
Hythe, Ab., Can.	182	55.20 N	119.33 W
Hythe, Eng., U.K.	42	51.05 N	1.05 E
Hythe, Eng., U.K.	42	50.51 N	1.24 W
Hythe End	260	51.27 N	0.32 W
Hyūga	92	32.25 N	131.38 E
Hyūga-nada Ŧ[2]	92	32.00 N	131.35 E
Hyvinge → Hyvinkää	26	60.38 N	24.52 E
Hyvinkää	26	60.38 N	24.52 E
I			
Iacanga	255	21.54 S	49.01 W
Iaciara	255	14.09 S	46.40 W
Iaco (Yaco) ≃	248	9.03 S	68.34 W
Iaçu	255	12.45 S	40.13 W
Iaeger	192	37.27 N	81.48 W
Iago	222	29.17 N	95.58 W
Iakora	157b	23.06 S	46.40 E
Ialomița □[6]	38	44.30 N	27.20 E
Ialomița ≃	38	44.42 N	27.51 E
Ialomiței, Balta ≡	38	44.30 N	28.00 E
Iamonia, Lake ⊜	192	30.38 N	84.14 W
Ianaivo ≃	157b	22.56 S	46.54 E
Ianakafy	157b	23.21 S	45.28 E
Ĭanga	146	9.07 N	18.11 E
Iango	152	9.11 S	17.39 E
Iano, Monte ∧	267a	41.46 N	12.44 E
Iapó ≃	252	24.30 S	50.24 W
Iapu	255	19.26 S	42.13 W
Iași	38	47.10 N	27.35 E
Iași □[6]	38	47.15 N	27.15 E
Iato	70	37.58 N	13.07 E
Iatt, Lake ⊜[1]	194	31.35 N	92.40 W
Iauaretê	246	0.36 N	69.12 W
Iaú-labu ≃	250	3.06 S	51.46 W
Iazu	38	44.44 N	27.25 E
Ib ≃	120	21.34 N	83.48 E
Iba, Pil.	116	15.20 N	119.58 E
Iba, Zaïre	152	3.05 S	17.38 E
'Ibādah, Wādī V	142	27.49 N	30.54 E
Ibadan	150	7.17 N	3.30 E
Ibagué	246	4.27 N	75.14 W
Ibaiti	255	23.50 S	50.10 W
Ibajay	116	11.49 N	122.10 E
Ibajay ≃	116	11.49 N	122.10 E
Ibaka	152	4.16 S	23.12 E
Ibambi	154	2.22 N	27.37 E
Ibanda	154	0.08 S	30.29 E
Ibănești	38	48.04 N	26.22 E
Ibans, Laguna de ⊂	236	15.53 N	84.52 W
Ibanshe	152	4.58 S	21.30 E
Ibapah Peak ∧	200	39.50 N	113.55 W
Ibar ≃	38	43.44 N	20.45 E
Ibara	96	34.36 N	133.28 E
Ibaraki, Nihon	94	36.17 N	140.26 E
Ibaraki, Nihon	96	34.49 N	135.34 E
Ibaraki □[5]	94	36.30 N	140.30 E
Ibarra	246	0.21 N	78.07 W
Ibarreta	252	25.13 S	59.51 W
Ibb	144	14.01 N	44.10 E
Ibba	154	4.48 N	29.06 E
Ibba ≃	140	7.09 N	28.41 E
Ibbenbüren	52	52.16 N	7.43 E
Ibeke Gembo	152	1.24 S	18.51 E
Ibembo	152	2.38 N	23.37 E
Ibenga ≃	152	2.20 N	18.08 E
Iberia, Mo., U.S.	194	38.05 N	92.17 W
Iberia, Oh., U.S.	214	40.40 N	82.51 W
Ibérica, Península >[1]	4	40.00 N	5.00 W
Ibérico, Sistema ✗	34	41.00 N	2.30 W
Iberoamericana, Universidad ʊ[2]	286a	19.21 N	99.08 W
Ibertioga	256	21.25 S	43.58 W
Iberville	206	45.18 N	73.14 W
Iberville □[6]	206	45.15 N	73.10 W
Iberville, Mont d' (Mount Caubvick) ∧	176	58.53 N	63.43 W
Ibese	273a	6.33 N	3.29 E
Ibeto	150	10.29 N	5.09 E
Ibi	150	8.12 N	9.45 E
Ibi ≃	94	35.03 N	136.42 E
Ibiá	255	19.29 S	46.32 W
Ibiapaba, Serra da ✗	250	4.00 S	41.00 W
Ibiapina	250	3.55 S	40.54 W
Ibìara	250	7.30 S	38.25 W
Ibicaraí	255	14.51 S	39.36 W
Ibicuí	255	14.51 S	39.59 W
Ibicuí ≃	252	29.25 S	56.47 W
Ibicuicito, Arroyo ≃	258	33.49 S	58.49 W
Ibicuy	258	33.44 S	59.10 W
Ibigawa	94	35.29 N	136.34 E
Ibipetuba	250	11.00 S	44.32 W
Ibipira	250	6.31 S	44.38 W
Ibiquera	255	12.38 S	40.57 W
Ibiraci	255	20.28 S	47.08 W
Ibiraçu	255	19.50 S	40.22 W
Ibirama	252	27.04 S	49.31 W
Ibirapuã	255	17.39 S	40.07 W
Ibirapuera ●[8]	287b	23.37 S	46.40 W
Ibirapuera, Parque ♦	287b	23.35 S	46.39 W
Ibirapuitã ≃	252	29.22 S	55.57 W
Ibirataia	255	14.04 S	39.38 W
Ibiri	154	4.56 S	32.33 E
Ibirubá	252	28.38 S	53.06 W
Ibitiara	255	12.39 S	42.13 W
Ibitiguaia	256	21.57 S	43.25 W
Ibitinga	255	21.45 S	48.49 W
Ibitiúra De Minas	256	22.04 S	46.26 W
Ibituporanga	256	22.45 S	43.47 W
Ibiúna	256	23.39 S	47.13 W
Ibiza	34	38.54 N	1.26 E
Ibiza I	34	39.00 N	1.25 E
Iblei, Monti ✗	70	37.10 N	14.50 E
Ibnahs	142	30.34 N	31.07 E
Ibn Hāni', Ra's >	130	35.35 N	35.43 E
Ibn Sarrār, Bi'r Ŧ[4]	144	19.30 N	42.41 E
Ibo	154	12.20 S	40.35 E
Ibo ≃	96	34.46 N	134.35 E
Ibondo	154	2.38 S	32.40 E
Ibonma	164	3.28 S	133.28 E
Ibor ≃	34	39.49 N	5.33 W
Ibotirama	255	12.11 S	43.13 W
Iboundji, Mont ∧	152	1.08 S	11.48 E
İbradı	130	37.06 N	31.36 E
Ibrah, Wādī V	140	10.36 N	24.58 E
Ibrāhīmīyah, Qārah al- ≚	142	29.10 N	31.10 E
İbrala	130	37.09 N	33.31 E
Ibresi	80	55.18 N	47.03 E
'Ibrī	128	23.14 N	56.30 E
İbriktepe	130	41.00 N	26.30 E
Ibshān	142	31.10 N	31.10 E
Ibshawāy	142	29.22 N	30.41 E
Ibstock	42	52.42 N	1.23 W
Ibta'	132	32.47 N	36.09 E
Ibu	174m	26.45 N	128.19 E
Ibuki	94	35.24 N	136.23 E
Ibuki-jima I	96	34.08 N	133.32 E
Ibuki-sanchi ✗	94	35.35 N	136.18 E
Ibuki-yama ∧	94	35.25 N	136.24 E
Iburg	52	52.09 N	8.02 E
Ibusuki	92	31.16 N	130.39 E
Ibwe Munyama	154	16.09 S	28.34 E
Ibychen, gora ∧	88	51.36 N	109.45 E
Ica	248	14.04 S	75.42 W
Ica □[5]	248	14.20 S	75.30 W
Ica ≃, Perú	248	14.54 S	75.34 W
Ića ≃, S.S.S.R.	76	56.52 N	26.59 E
Ića ≃, S.S.S.R.	86	55.30 N	77.13 E
Içá (Putumayo) ≃, S.A.	246	3.07 S	67.58 W
Icabarú ≃	246	4.45 N	62.15 W
Icadambanauan Island I	116	10.49 N	119.38 E
Icamaquã ≃	252	28.34 S	56.00 W
Icamole	196	25.55 N	100.43 W
Içana	246	0.21 N	67.19 W
Içana (Isana) ≃	246	0.26 N	67.19 W
Icaño, Arg.	252	28.41 S	62.54 W
Icaño, Arg.	252	28.54 S	65.19 W
Icatu	250	2.46 S	44.04 W
Icatuaçu	256	23.44 S	46.24 W
Iceberg Pass)(	200	40.25 N	105.45 W
Ice House Reservoir ⊜[1]	226	38.49 N	120.23 W
İçel □[4]	130	36.45 N	34.00 E
Iceland (Ísland) □[1], Europe	22	65.00 N	18.00 W
Iceland (Ísland) □[1], Europe	24a	65.00 N	18.00 W
Iceland Basin ✢[1]	10	69.00 N	10.00 W
Icém	255	20.21 S	49.12 W
Ice Mountain ∧	182	54.25 N	121.08 W
Ičera	88	58.32 N	109.47 E
İçerenköy ●[8]	267b	40.58 N	29.06 E
Ichalkaranji	122	16.42 N	74.28 E
Ichāmati ≃, Bngl.	126	24.00 N	89.15 E
Ichāmāti ≃, India	126	22.35 N	88.57 E
Ichang → Yichang	102	30.42 N	111.17 E
Ichāpur	126	22.50 N	88.24 E
Ichawaynochaway Creek ≃	192	31.10 N	84.28 W
Ich Bajan Ajrag uul ∧	88	47.55 N	95.02 E
Ichbulag	102	45.21 N	113.10 E
Ich Buural uul ∧	88	48.00 N	94.30 E
Ichchāpuram	122	19.07 N	84.42 E
Ichdžargalan	102	45.31 N	108.48 E
Ichenhausen	58	48.22 N	10.18 E
Ichenheim	58	48.26 N	7.49 E
Ichhāwar	124	23.01 N	77.01 E
Ichi ≃	96	34.46 N	134.41 E
Ichiba	96	34.05 N	134.17 E
Ichihara	94	35.31 N	140.05 E
Ichikai	94	36.32 N	140.06 E
Ichikawa, Nihon	94	35.44 N	139.55 E
Ichikawa, Nihon	96	34.59 N	134.46 E
Ichikawa-daimon	94	35.34 N	138.30 E
Ichilo ≃	248	15.57 S	64.42 W
Ichinohe	92	40.13 N	141.17 E
Ichinomiya, Nihon	94	35.18 N	136.48 E
Ichinomiya, Nihon	94	35.22 N	140.22 E
Ichinomiya, Nihon	94	35.39 N	138.41 E

Symbols in the index entries represent the broad categories identified in the key at the right. Symbols with superior numbers (✗[1]) identify subcategories (see complete key on page *I · 1).*

Kartensymbole in dem Registerverzeichnis stellen die rechts in Schlüssel erklärten Kategorien dar. Symbole mit hochgestellten Ziffern (✗[1]) bezeichnen Unterabteilungen einer Kategorie (vgl. vollständiger Schlüssel auf Seite *I · 1).*

Los símbolos incluídos en el texto del índice representan las grandes categorias identificadas con la clave a la derecha. Los símbolos con numeros en su parte superior (✗[1]) identifican las subcategorías (véase la clave completa en la página *I · 1).*

Les symboles de l'index représentent les catégories indiquées dans la légende à droite. Les symboles suivis d'un indice (✗[1]) représentent des sous-catégories (voir légende complète à la page *I · 1).*

Os símbolos incluídos no texto do índice representam as grandes categorias identificadas com a chave à direita. Os símbolos com números em sua parte superior (✗[1]) identificam as subcategorias (veja-se a chave completa à página *I · 1).*

∧ Mountain	Berg	Montaña	Montagne	Montanha
✗ Mountains	Berge	Montañas	Montagnes	Montanhas
)(Pass	Pass	Paso	Col	Passo
V Valley, Canyon	Tal, Cañon	Valle, Cañón	Vallée, Canyon	Vale, Canhão
≚ Plain	Ebene	Llano	Plaine	Planície
> Cape	Kap	Cabo	Cap	Cabo
I Island	Insel	Isla	Île	Ilha
II Islands	Inseln	Islas	Îles	Ilhas
⊥ Other Topographic Features	Andere Topographische Objekte	Otros Elementos Topográficos	Autres données topographiques	Outros acidentes topográficos

≃	River	Fluss	Río	Rivière	Rio
≊	Canal	Kanal	Canal	Canal	Canal
∟	Waterfall, Rapids	Wasserfall, Stromschnellen	Cascada, Rápidos	Chute d'eau, Rapides	Cascata, Rápidos
ɥ	Strait	Meeresstrasse	Estrecho	Détroit	Estreito
c	Bay, Gulf	Bucht, Golf	Bahía, Golfo	Baie, Golfe	Baía, Golfo
⊜	Lake, Lakes	See, Seen	Lago, Lagos	Lac, Lacs	Lago, Lagos
☷	Swamp	Sumpf	Pantano	Marais	Pântano
⛉	Ice Features, Glacier	Eis- und Gletscherformen	Accidentes Glaciales	Formes glaciaires	Acidentes glaciares
╤	Other Hydrographic Features	Andere Hydrographische Objekte	Otros Elementos Hidrográficos	Autres données hydrographiques	Outros acidentes hidrográficos

✧	Submarine Features	Untermeerische Objekte	Accidentes Submarinos	Formes de relief sous-marin	Acidentes submarinos
□	Political Unit	Politische Einheit	Unidad Politica	Entité politique	Unidade política
ʋ	Cultural Institution	Kulturelle Institution	Institución Cultural	Institution culturelle	Instituição cultural
⊥	Historical Site	Historische Stätte	Sitio Histórico	Site historique	Sitio histórico
♠	Recreational Site	Erholungs- und Ferienort	Sitio de Recreo	Centre de loisirs	Area de Lazer
⊠	Airport	Flughafen	Aeropuerto	Aéroport	Aeroporto
■	Military Installation	Militäranlage	Instalación Militar	Installation militaire	Instalação militar
◆	Miscellaneous	Verschiedenes	Misceláneo	Divers	Diversos

ENGLISH — DEUTSCH

Name	Page	Lat.°′	Long.°′
Indi	122	17.10 N	75.58 E
India (Bhārat) □[1]	118	20.00 N	77.00 E
India Brook ≃	276	40.47 N	74.37 W
India Gate ⊥	272a	28.37 N	77.18 E
Indialantic	220	28.05 N	80.34 W
Indian ≃, On., Can.	212	45.16 N	76.14 W
Indian ≃, On., Can.	212	44.13 N	78.08 W
Indian ≃, De., U.S.	208	38.36 N	75.10 W
Indian ≃, Ma., U.S.	283	42.47 N	70.58 W
Indian ≃, Mi., U.S.	190	45.59 N	86.15 W
Indian ≃, N.Y., U.S.	212	44.24 N	75.39 W
Indiana	214	40.37 N	79.09 W
Indiana □[6]	214	40.37 N	79.09 W
Indiana □[3], U.S.	178	40.00 N	86.15 W
Indiana □[3], U.S.	194	40.00 N	86.15 W
Indiana Dunes National Lakeshore ♠	216	41.40 N	87.00 W
Indiana Dunes State Park ♠	216	41.40 N	87.02 W
Indian Agricultural Research Institute ʊ[3]	272a	28.38 N	77.10 E
Indiana Harbor c	278	41.40 N	87.27 W
Indiana Harbor Canal ≍	278	41.40 N	87.27 W
Indianapolis	218	39.46 N	86.09 W
Indianapolis International Airport ⊠	218	39.43 N	86.16 W
Indianapolis Motor Speedway ♠	218	39.48 N	86.14 W
Indian Bayou ≃	194	34.14 N	91.52 W
Indian Brook	186	46.23 N	60.32 W
Indian Caverns ±[5]	214	40.38 N	78.05 W
Indian Church	232	17.45 N	88.40 W
Indian Creek	278	42.14 N	87.59 W
Indian Creek ≃, U.S.	218	39.19 N	84.38 W
Indian Creek ≃, Ca., U.S.	228	35.18 N	118.26 W
Indian Creek ≃, Il., U.S.	216	41.26 N	88.46 W
Indian Creek ≃, Il., U.S.	219	39.56 N	90.32 W
Indian Creek ≃, Il., U.S.	278	42.11 N	87.55 W
Indian Creek ≃, In., U.S.	216	40.55 N	86.42 W
Indian Creek ≃, In., U.S.	218	38.43 N	85.06 W
Indian Creek ≃, In., U.S.	218	39.23 N	86.29 W
Indian Creek ≃, In., U.S.	218	38.10 N	86.14 W
Indian Creek ≃, Md., U.S.	284c	38.59 N	76.55 W
Indian Creek ≃, Mo., U.S.	194	36.33 N	94.29 W
Indian Creek ≃, Mo., U.S.	219	39.10 N	91.11 W
Indian Creek ≃, N.M., U.S.	200	36.11 N	108.23 W
Indian Creek ≃, N.Y., U.S.	276	40.43 N	73.06 W
Indian Creek ≃, Oh., U.S.	218	39.19 N	84.38 W
Indian Creek ≃, Oh., U.S.	279a	41.17 N	81.31 W
Indian Creek ≃, S.D., U.S.	198	44.39 N	103.19 W
Indian Creek ≃, Tn., U.S.	194	35.13 N	88.08 W
Indian Creek Lake ⊜[1]	222	31.44 N	95.58 W
Indianford	216	42.49 N	88.35 W
Indian Grave Mountain ∧[2]	192	32.59 N	84.21 W
Indian Harbour Beach	220	28.08 N	80.35 W
Indian Head, Sk., Can.	184	50.32 N	103.40 W
Indian Head, Md., U.S.	208	38.36 N	77.09 W
Indian Head ≃	283	42.04 N	70.52 W
Indian Head Park	278	41.47 N	87.54 W
Indian Head Pond ⊜	283	42.03 N	70.51 W
Indian Heights	216	40.25 N	86.07 W
Indian Island I	224	48.04 N	122.43 W
Indian Kentuck Creek ≃	218	38.43 N	85.16 W
Indian Lake, Mi., U.S.	216	41.59 N	86.12 W
Indian Lake, N.Y., U.S.	188	43.46 N	74.16 W
Indian Lake ⊜, On., Can.	190	47.08 N	82.08 W
Indian Lake ⊜, Mi., U.S.	190	45.59 N	86.20 W
Indian Lake ⊜, Mi., U.S.	216	42.09 N	85.29 W
Indian Lake ⊜, Mi., U.S.	216	42.00 N	86.13 W
Indian Lake ⊜, N.J., U.S.	276	40.53 N	74.29 W
Indian Lake ⊜, Oh., U.S.	216	40.29 N	83.53 W
Indian Lake Estates	220	27.48 N	81.19 W
Indian Lakes ⊜	216	41.33 N	85.25 W
Indian Lake State Park ♠	216	40.29 N	83.52 W
Indian Mills Brook ≃	285	39.47 N	74.44 W
Indian Mills Lake ⊜	285	39.48 N	74.44 W
Indian Neck	207	41.15 N	72.48 W
Indian Ocean ⊤[1]	4	10.00 S	70.00 E
Indian Ocean ⊤[1]	6	10.00 S	70.00 E
Indianola, Ia., U.S.	190	41.21 N	93.33 W
Indianola, Ms., U.S.	194	33.27 N	90.39 W
Indianola, Ne., U.S.	198	40.14 N	100.25 W
Indianola, Pa., U.S.	279b	40.34 N	79.51 W
Indianola, Wa., U.S.	224	47.45 N	122.31 W
Indianópolis	255	19.02 S	47.55 W
Indianópolis ◆[8]	287b	23.36 S	46.38 W
Indian Peak ∧, Ut,. U.S.	200	38.16 N	113.53 W
Indian Peak ∧, Wy., U.S.	202	44.47 N	109.51 W
Indian Point ≻	212	44.37 N	78.49 W
Indian Prairie Canal ≍	220	27.02 N	80.57 W
Indian Queen Estates	284c	38.46 N	77.02 W
Indian River	190	45.24 N	84.36 W
Indian River □[6]	220	27.43 N	80.36 W
Indian River c	220	28.00 N	80.30 W
Indian River Bay c	208	38.36 N	75.05 W
Indian River Inlet c	208	38.37 N	75.03 W
Indian Rock ∧	224	45.59 N	120.49 W
Indian Rock Dam ◆[6]	208	39.57 N	76.45 W
Indian Rock Paintings ⊥	224	46.38 N	120.31 W
Indian Rocks Beach	220	27.52 N	82.51 W
Indian Springs, Nv., U.S.	204	36.34 N	115.40 W
Indian Springs, Va., U.S.	284c	38.49 N	77.10 W
Indian Stream ≃	206	45.03 N	71.26 W
Indiantown	220	27.01 N	80.29 W
Indian Town Point ≻	240c	17.06 N	61.40 W
Indian Valley Reservoir ⊜[1]	226	39.07 N	122.32 W
Indian Village, In., U.S.	218	40.10 N	85.22 W
Indian Village, N.Y., U.S.	210	42.57 N	76.10 W
Indiaporã	255	19.57 S	50.17 W
Indiaroba	250	11.32 S	37.31 W
Indibir	144	8.05 N	37.58 E
Indico, Océano → Indian Ocean ⊤[1]	6	10.00 S	70.00 E
Indien → India □[1]	118	20.00 N	77.00 E
Indien, Océan → Indian Ocean ⊤[1]	6	10.00 S	70.00 E
Indien, territoires britanniques de l'Ocean → British Indian Ocean Territory □[2]	12	7.00 S	72.00 E
Indiera Alta	240m	18.09 N	66.53 W
Indiga	24	67.41 N	49.00 E
Indigirka ≃	74	70.48 N	148.54 E
Inđija	38	45.03 N	20.05 E
Indin	120	20.16 N	92.57 E
Indio	204	33.43 N	116.12 W
Indio ≃, Nic.	236	10.57 N	83.44 W
Indio ≃, Pan.	236	9.12 N	80.11 W
Indio, Punta ≻	258	35.16 S	57.13 W
Indischer Ozean → Indian Ocean ⊤[1]	6	10.00 S	70.00 E
Indispensable Reefs ✣[2]	160	12.40 S	160.25 E
Indispensable Strait ⋓	175e	9.00 S	160.30 E
Indo → Indus ≃	120	24.20 N	67.47 E
Indochina ◆[1]	12	16.00 N	107.00 E
Indom	24	64.36 N	55.22 E
Indonesia □[1]	108	5.00 S	120.00 E
Indonesia, University of ʊ[2]	269e	6.12 S	106.51 E
Indonesian Culture, Museum of ʊ[3]	269e	6.09 N	106.49 E
Indonésie → Indonesia □[1]	108	5.00 S	120.00 E
Indonesien → Indonesia □[1]	108	5.00 S	120.00 E
Indooroopilly	171a	27.30 S	152.58 E
Indore	120	22.43 N	75.50 E
Indpur	126	23.10 N	86.56 E
Indragiri ≃	112	0.22 S	103.26 E
Indramayu	115a	6.20 S	108.19 E
Indramayu, Tanjung ≻	115a	6.14 S	108.17 E
Indrapuri	114	5.26 N	95.27 E
Indrāvati ≃	122	18.44 N	80.16 E
Indre □[5]	32	46.45 N	1.30 E
Indre ≃	32	47.16 N	0.19 E
Indre-et-Loire □[5]	32	47.15 N	0.45 E
Indrois ≃	50	47.13 N	0.56 E
Indungo	152	14.48 S	16.17 E
Induno Olona	62	45.52 N	8.51 E
Indur → Indore	120	22.43 N	75.50 E
Indura	76	53.27 N	23.53 E
Indus ≃	120	24.20 N	67.47 E
Industry, Il., U.S.	194	40.20 N	90.36 W
Industry, Pa., U.S.	214	40.39 N	80.25 W
Industry, Tx., U.S.	222	29.58 N	96.30 W
Indwe	158	31.27 S	27.23 E
Indwe ≃	158	32.01 S	27.21 E
Ine	96	35.39 N	135.17 E
İnebolu	130	41.58 N	33.46 E
İnece	130	41.41 N	27.04 E
İnecik	130	40.56 N	27.16 E
In Ecker	148	24.09 N	5.03 E
İnegöl	130	40.05 N	29.31 E
İnekollar	130	39.33 N	28.56 E
Inerie, Gunung ∧	115b	8.52 S	120.56 E
Inés, Monte ∧	254	48.29 S	69.40 W
Ineu	38	46.26 N	21.49 E
İnevi	130	38.40 N	32.56 E
Inez, Ky., U.S.	192	37.51 N	82.32 W
Inez, Tx., U.S.	222	28.54 N	96.47 W
Inez, Lake ⊜	276	41.01 N	74.17 W
Infanta, Pil.	116	15.50 N	119.55 E
Infanta, Pil.	116	14.45 N	121.39 E
Infantas	286d	11.57 S	77.04 W
Infante, Kaap ≻	158	34.29 S	20.51 E
Inferior, Laguna c	234	16.20 N	94.40 W
Inferno, Cachoeira do ⌞	250	1.00 S	56.04 W
Infiernillo, Canal del ⋓	232	29.09 N	112.15 W
Infiernillo, Presa del ⊜[1]	234	18.35 N	101.45 W
Infiesto	34	43.21 N	5.22 W
Infreschi, Ponta degli ≻	68	39.59 N	15.25 E
Ing ≃	110	20.13 N	100.27 E
Ingá	250	7.17 S	35.36 W
Ingabu	110	17.49 N	95.16 E
Ingaí	256	21.24 S	44.55 W
Ingaí ≃	256	21.23 S	44.52 W
Ingal	150	16.47 N	6.56 E
Ingalls	218	39.57 N	85.48 W
Ingalls Creek ≃	224	47.28 N	120.39 W
Ingalls Park	216	41.32 N	88.03 W
Inganda	152	0.05 S	20.57 E
Inganno ≃	70	38.04 N	14.37 E
Ingarö I	40	59.16 N	18.28 E
Ingatestone	42	51.41 N	0.22 E
Ingatestone Hall ⊥	260	51.39 N	0.23 E
Ingelfingen	56	49.18 N	9.39 E
Ingelheim	56	49.59 N	8.05 E
Ingelmunster	50	50.55 N	3.15 E
Ingelstad	26	56.45 N	14.55 E
Ingende	152	0.15 S	18.57 E
Ingeniero Budge ◆[8]	288	34.43 S	58.28 W
Ingeniero Jacobacci	254	41.18 S	69.35 W
Ingeniero Juan Allan	258	34.53 S	58.11 W
Ingeniero Luiggi	252	35.25 S	64.29 W
Ingeniero Luis A. Huergo	252	39.05 S	67.14 W
Ingeniero Maschwitz	258	34.23 S	58.44 W
Ingeniero Romulo Otamendi	258	34.13 S	58.54 W
Ingeniero White	252	38.47 S	62.16 W
Ingeniero Williams	258	34.54 S	59.22 W
Ingenio La Esperanza	252	24.13 S	64.51 W
Ingenio Santa Ana	252	27.28 S	65.41 W
Ingeringbach ≃	61	47.12 N	14.49 E
Ingersheim	58	48.06 N	7.18 E
Ingersoll	212	43.02 N	80.53 W
Ingham	166	18.39 S	146.10 E
Ingham □[6]	216	42.37 N	84.22 W
Ingička	85	39.52 N	67.20 E
Ingleborough ∧	44	54.11 N	2.23 W
Ingleburn	170	34.00 S	150.52 E
Inglesa, Costa → English Coast ±[2]	9	73.45 S	73.00 W
Ingleside, Austl.	274a	33.41 S	151.13 E
Ingleside, On., Can.	206	45.00 N	75.00 W
Ingleside, Il., U.S.	216	42.23 N	88.09 W
Ingleside, Tx., U.S.	196	27.52 N	97.12 W
Ingleside ◆[8]	282	37.43 N	122.28 W
Ingleton	44	54.10 N	2.27 W
Inglewood, Austl.	166	28.25 S	151.05 E
Inglewood, Austl.	166	36.34 S	143.52 E
Inglewood, On., Can.	212	43.47 N	79.56 W
Inglewood, N.Z.	172	39.09 S	174.12 E
Inglewood, Ca., U.S.	228	33.57 N	118.21 W
Inglewood, Wa., U.S.	224	47.44 N	122.15 W
Inglewood Forest ◆[3]	44	54.45 N	2.50 W
Inglis, Mb., Can.	184	50.57 N	101.15 W
Inglis, Fl., U.S.	220	29.02 N	82.40 W
Inglis Lock ◆[5]	220	29.02 N	82.37 W
Ingoda ≃	88	51.42 N	115.48 E
Ingogo	158	27.32 S	29.56 E
Ingoldmells	44	53.11 N	0.20 E
Ingolstadt	60	48.46 N	11.27 E
Ingomar	279b	40.35 N	80.05 W
Ingonish	186	46.42 N	60.22 W
Ingornachoix Bay c	186	50.38 N	57.20 W
Ingraham, Lake ⊜	220	25.09 N	81.08 W
Ingram, Pa., U.S.	279b	40.26 N	80.04 W
Ingram, Tx., U.S.	196	30.04 N	99.14 W
Ingram Bay c	208	37.48 N	76.17 W
Ingrave	260	51.36 N	0.21 E
Ingrid Christensen Coast ±[2]	9	69.30 S	76.00 E
In Guezzam	150	19.32 N	5.42 E
Ingul ≃	78	47.00 N	31.59 E
Ingulec	78	47.43 N	33.14 E
Ingulec ≃	78	46.41 N	32.48 E
Ingulo-Kamenka	78	48.17 N	32.30 E
Inguri ≃	84	42.24 N	41.33 E
Inguzet	86	58.50 N	83.52 E
Ingvallsbenning	40	60.15 N	15.53 E
Ingwavuma	158	27.09 S	32.00 E
Ingwe	154	13.02 S	26.25 E
Ingwiller	56	48.52 N	7.29 E
Inhaca, Ilha da I	158	26.03 S	32.57 E
Inhafenga	156	20.35 S	33.53 E
Inhambane	156	23.51 S	35.29 E
Inhambane □[5]	156	23.00 S	34.30 E
Inhambane, Baía de c	156	23.58 S	35.51 E
Inhambupe	255	11.47 S	38.21 W
Inhaminga	156	18.24 S	35.00 E
Inhapim	255	19.33 S	42.07 W
Inharrime	156	24.29 S	35.01 E
Inharrime ≃	156	24.29 S	35.01 E
Inhassoro	156	21.33 S	35.11 E
Inhaúma	255	19.29 S	44.22 W
Inhaúma ◆[8]	287a	22.52 S	43.17 W
İnhisar	130	40.03 N	30.23 E
Inhoaíba ◆[8]	256	22.54 S	43.36 W
Inhobi ≃	255	23.45 S	54.40 W
Inhomirim	256	22.35 S	43.10 W
Inhuma	250	6.40 S	41.42 W
Inhumas	255	16.22 S	49.30 W
Ini ≃	146	9.30 N	12.20 E
Iniesta	34	39.26 N	1.45 W
Inimutaba	255	18.45 S	44.22 W
Ining → Yining	86	43.54 N	81.21 E
Inini ≃	250	3.39 N	54.00 W
Inírida ≃	246	3.55 N	67.52 W
Inisa	150	7.52 N	4.20 E
Inishbofin I, Ire.	48	55.09 N	8.11 W
Inishbofin I, Ire.	48	53.37 N	10.15 W
Inishcrone	48	54.12 N	9.06 W
Inisheer I	48	53.02 N	9.26 W
Inishmaan I	48	53.05 N	9.32 W
Inishmore I	48	53.07 N	9.45 W
Inishowen ≻[1]	48	55.12 N	7.20 W
Inishowen Head ≻	44	55.14 N	6.56 W
Inishowen Point ≻	48	55.14 N	6.56 W
Inishshark I	48	53.37 N	10.18 W
Inishtrahull I	48	55.26 N	7.14 W
Inishturk I	48	53.43 N	10.08 W
Inistioge	48	52.29 N	7.04 W
Initao	116	8.30 N	124.18 E
Inje	98	38.05 N	128.09 E
Injibara	144	11.00 N	36.59 E
Injune	166	25.51 S	148.34 E
Inkeroinen	26	60.42 N	26.51 E
Inketete	152	2.37 S	21.53 E
Inkisi (Zadi) ≃	152	4.46 S	14.52 E
Inkom	202	42.47 N	112.15 W
Inkster, Mi., U.S.	216	42.17 N	83.18 W
Inkster, N.D., U.S.	198	48.09 N	97.38 W
Inland Kaikoura Range ⋏	172	42.00 S	173.40 E
Inland Lake ⊜, Mb., Can.	184	52.17 N	99.42 W
Inland Lake ⊜, Ak., U.S.	180	66.27 N	159.47 W
Inland Sea → Seto-naikai ⊤[2]	96	34.20 N	133.30 E
Inle Lake ⊜	110	20.32 N	96.55 E
Inmaculadita	232	29.55 N	111.48 W
Inman, Ks., U.S.	198	38.13 N	97.46 W
Inman, S.C., U.S.	192	35.02 N	82.05 W
Inman Mills	192	35.02 N	82.06 W
Inman Valley	168b	35.30 S	138.28 E
Inn (En) ≃	32	48.35 N	13.28 E
Innamincka	166	27.45 S	140.44 E
Innbach ≃	61	48.18 N	14.07 E
Innellan	46	55.54 N	4.57 W
Inner Bay c	214	42.37 N	80.24 W
Innerbraz	58	47.09 N	9.55 E
Innerferrera	58	46.31 N	9.28 E
Innerfragant	64	46.58 N	13.04 E
Inner Harbor c	276	40.52 N	73.28 W
Inner Hebrides II	46	56.30 N	6.00 W
Innerkip	212	43.13 N	80.42 W
Innerleithen	46	55.38 N	3.05 W
Inner Mongolia → Nei Monggol Zizhiqu □[4]	90	43.00 N	115.00 E
Inner Sound ⋓	46	57.25 N	5.56 W
Innerste ≃	52	52.15 N	9.50 E
Innerstetalsperre ◆[6]	52	51.55 N	10.17 E
Innerthal	58	47.06 N	8.56 E
Innertkirchen	58	46.42 N	8.14 E
Innervillgraten	64	46.48 N	12.23 E
Innichen → San Candido	64	46.44 N	12.17 E
Inning	60	48.05 N	11.09 E
Innisfail, Austl.	166	17.32 S	146.02 E
Innisfail, Ab., Can.	182	52.02 N	113.57 W
Innisfil Creek ≃	212	44.08 N	79.49 W
Innisfree	182	53.22 N	111.32 W
Innisplain	171a	28.10 S	152.55 E
Innokentjevka	89	49.42 N	136.57 E
Innokentjevskij	89	48.37 N	140.10 E
Innoko ≃	180	62.14 N	159.45 W
Innolovo	265a	59.47 N	29.59 E
Innoshima	96	34.17 N	133.11 E
Inno-shima I	96	34.19 N	133.10 E
Innsbruck	64	47.16 N	11.24 E
Innviertel ◆[1]	60	48.10 N	13.15 E
Inny ≃, Ire.	48	53.33 N	7.48 W
Inny ≃, Eng., U.K.	42	50.35 N	4.17 W
Ino, Nihon	96	33.33 N	133.26 E
Ino, Va., U.S.	208	37.46 N	76.48 W
Inoã	256	22.55 S	42.57 W
Inobonto	112	0.52 N	123.57 E
Inocência	255	19.47 S	51.48 W
Inokashira Park ♠	268	35.42 N	139.34 E
Inokovka	80	52.33 N	42.34 E
Inola	196	36.09 N	95.30 W
Ino-misaki ≻	96	33.01 N	133.06 E
Inongo	152	1.57 S	18.16 E
Inoni	152	3.04 S	15.39 E
İnönü	130	39.48 N	30.09 E
Inoue	270	34.48 N	135.03 E
Inowrocław	30	52.48 N	18.15 E
Inozemcevo	84	44.06 N	43.06 E
Inp'ung-dong	98	41.25 N	126.34 E
Inrath ◆[8]	263	51.21 N	6.32 E
In Rhar	148	27.10 N	1.59 E
Ins	58	47.00 N	7.06 E
In Salah	148	27.12 N	2.28 E
Insan-ni	98	41.01 N	127.21 E
Insar	80	53.52 N	44.21 E
Insar ≃	80	54.43 N	45.18 E
Insch	46	57.21 N	2.37 W
Inscription, Cape ≻	162	25.29 S	112.59 E
Inscription Point ≻	274a	34.00 S	151.13 E
Insein	110	16.53 N	96.07 E
Insel Man → Isle of Man □[2]	44	54.15 N	4.30 W
Inshar	150	8.49 N	9.40 E
Inshāṣ ar-Raml	142	30.23 N	31.27 E
Insjön	26	60.41 N	15.05 E
Ińsko	30	53.27 N	15.33 E
In Sokki, Oued V	148	29.37 N	4.13 E
Inspiration	200	33.24 N	110.52 W
Insterburg → Černʼachovsk	76	54.38 N	21.49 E
Instow	184	49.44 N	108.16 W
Insurgente José María Morelos, Parque Nacional ♠	234	19.51 N	101.18 W
Inta	24	66.02 N	60.08 E
Intendente Alvear	252	35.14 S	63.35 W
İntepe	130	40.00 N	26.20 E
Intercession City	220	28.15 N	81.30 W
Intercourse	208	40.02 N	76.06 W
Interlagos ◆[8]	287b	23.42 S	46.42 W
Interlaken, Schw.	58	46.41 N	7.51 E
Interlaken, Ma., U.S.	210	42.18 N	73.19 W
Interlaken, N.J., U.S.	208	40.14 N	74.01 W
Interlaken, N.Y., U.S.	210	42.37 N	76.43 W
Interlândia	255	16.12 S	49.02 W
International Amphitheatre ʊ	278	41.49 N	87.39 W
International Falls	190	48.36 N	93.24 W
International Peace Garden ♠	198	49.00 N	100.04 W
Interstate State Park ♠	190	45.23 N	92.40 W
Inthanon, Doi ∧	110	18.35 N	98.29 E
Intibucá	236	14.16 N	88.10 W
Intibucá □[5]	236	14.20 N	88.15 W
Intipucá	236	13.12 N	88.04 W
Intiyaco	252	28.39 S	60.05 W
Intracoastal Waterway ≍, U.S.	192	24.33 N	81.46 W
Intracoastal Waterway ≍, U.S.	196	26.04 N	97.12 W
Intragna	58	46.10 N	8.42 E
Intrånget	40	60.20 N	16.09 E
Introbio	58	45.57 N	9.27 E
Introdacqua	66	42.00 N	13.54 E
Intschön → Inch'ŏn	98	37.28 N	126.38 E
Intu	112	0.15 S	115.21 E
Intuto	246	3.39 S	74.44 W
Inubō-saki ≻	94	35.42 N	140.53 E
Inukai	96	33.04 N	131.38 E
Inukjuak	176	58.27 N	78.06 W
Inútil, Bahía c	254	53.30 S	69.50 W
Inuvik	180	68.25 N	133.30 W
Inuya ≃	248	10.41 S	73.30 W
Inuyama	94	35.23 N	136.56 E
In'va ≃	86	58.59 N	55.40 E
Inver	46	57.49 N	3.55 W
Inverallochy	46	57.40 N	1.55 W
Inveralochy	170	34.57 S	149.39 E
Inveraray	46	56.13 N	5.05 W
Inverarity	46	56.35 N	2.53 W
Inverbervie	46	56.51 N	2.17 W
Invercargill	172	46.24 S	168.21 E
Inverdruie	46	57.10 N	3.48 W
Inverell	166	29.47 S	151.07 E
Invergarry	46	57.02 N	4.47 W
Invergordon	46	57.42 N	4.10 W
Inverkeilor	46	56.38 N	2.32 W
Inverkeithing	46	56.02 N	3.25 W
Inverkeithny	46	57.30 N	2.37 W
Inverleigh	169	38.06 S	144.03 E
Inverloch	169	38.38 S	145.43 E
Invermay	184	51.48 N	103.09 W
Invermere	182	50.30 N	116.02 W
Invermoriston	46	57.13 N	4.38 W
Inverness, N.S., Can.	186	46.14 N	61.18 W
Inverness, P.Q., Can.	206	46.15 N	71.31 W
Inverness, Scot., U.K.	46	57.27 N	4.15 W
Inverness, Ca., U.S.	204	38.06 N	122.51 W
Inverness, Fl., U.S.	220	28.50 N	82.19 W
Inverness, Il., U.S.	216	42.07 N	88.05 W
Inverness, Ms., U.S.	194	33.21 N	90.35 W
Inveruglas	46	56.15 N	4.43 W
Inveruno	62	45.31 N	8.51 E
Inverurie	46	57.17 N	2.23 W
Inverway	162	17.50 S	129.38 E
Investigator Group II	162	33.45 S	134.30 E
Investigator Shoal ✣[2]	108	8.09 N	114.44 E
Investigator Strait ⋓	166	35.25 S	137.10 E
Inwood, Mb., Can.	184	50.30 N	97.30 W
Inwood, On., Can.	214	42.49 N	81.59 W
Inwood, Fl., U.S.	220	28.02 N	81.45 W
Inwood, In., U.S.	216	41.19 N	86.12 W
Inwood, Ia., U.S.	198	43.18 N	96.25 W
Inwood, N.Y., U.S.	276	40.37 N	73.44 W
Inwood Hill Park ♠	276	40.52 N	73.56 W
Inyanga	154	18.13 S	32.46 E
Inyanga Mountains ⋏	154	18.00 S	33.00 E
Inyangani ∧	154	18.20 S	32.50 E
Inyan Kara Mountain ∧	198	44.13 N	104.21 W
Inyantue	154	18.32 S	26.41 E
Inyati	154	19.39 S	28.54 E
Inyo, Mount ∧	204	36.44 N	117.59 W
Inyokern	204	35.38 N	117.48 W
Inyo Mountains ⋏	204	36.40 N	118.10 W
Inyonga	154	6.43 S	32.04 E
Inywa	110	23.56 N	96.17 E
Inza	80	53.51 N	46.21 E
Inza ≃	80	53.54 N	45.44 E
Inzago	62	45.32 N	9.29 E
Inzai	94	35.50 N	140.09 E
Inzana Lake ⊜	182	54.58 N	124.40 W
Inžavino	80	52.19 N	42.30 E
Inzell	64	47.46 N	12.44 E
Inzer	86	54.14 N	57.34 E
Inzer ≃	86	54.30 N	56.28 E
Inzersdorf ◆[8]	264b	48.09 N	16.21 E
Inzia ≃	152	3.45 S	17.57 E
Ioanna, gora ∧	180	64.50 N	178.08 E
Ioánnina	38	39.40 N	20.50 E
Ioco	224	49.18 N	122.52 W
Iō-jima (Iwo Jima) I, Nihon	14	24.47 N	141.20 E
Iō-jima (Iwo Jima) I, Nihon	174f	24.47 N	141.20 E
Iokanga ≃	24	68.00 N	39.43 E
Iola, Ks., U.S.	198	37.55 N	95.23 W
Iola, Pa., U.S.	210	45.08 N	76.32 W
Iola, Tx., U.S.	222	30.46 N	96.05 W
Iola, Wi., U.S.	190	44.30 N	89.07 W
Iolgo, chrebet ⋏	86	51.30 N	86.25 E
Iolotan'	72	37.18 N	62.21 E
Ioma	164	8.20 S	147.50 E
Iôna, Ang.	152	16.50 S	12.20 E
Iona, N.S., Can.	186	45.58 N	60.48 W
Iona, Id., U.S.	202	43.31 N	111.55 W
Iona I	46	56.19 N	6.25 W
Iôna, Parque Nacional do ♠	152	16.30 S	12.00 E
Iona, Sound of ⋓	46	56.19 N	6.24 W
Iona College ʊ[2]	276	40.56 N	73.47 W
Ione, Ca., U.S.	226	38.21 N	120.55 W
Ione, Or., U.S.	202	45.30 N	119.50 W
Ione, Wa., U.S.	202	48.44 N	117.24 W
Ionia, Mi., U.S.	216	42.59 N	85.04 W
Ionia, N.Y., U.S.	210	42.56 N	77.30 W
Ionia □[6]	216	42.56 N	85.04 W
Ionian Islands → Iónioi Nísoi II	38	38.30 N	20.30 E
Ionian Sea ⊤[2]	22	39.00 N	19.00 E
Ionia State Recreation Area ♠	216	42.58 N	85.36 W
Ionico, Mare → Ionian Sea ⊤[2]	22	39.00 N	19.00 E
Ionienne, Mer → Ionian Sea ⊤[2]	22	39.00 N	19.00 E
Iónioi Nísoi II	38	38.30 N	20.30 E
Ionisches Meer → Ionian Sea ⊤[2]	22	39.00 N	19.00 E
Ionivejem ≃	180	66.12 N	174.00 W
Iony, ostrov I	74	56.26 N	143.25 E
Ioppolo	68	38.35 N	15.53 E
Ioppolo Giancaxio	70	37.23 N	13.33 E
Iordan	85	39.58 N	71.46 E
Iori ≃	84	41.03 N	46.17 E
Iorskoje ploskogorje ⋏[1]	84	41.20 N	46.00 E
Iory	85	39.30 N	67.53 E
Íos	38	36.44 N	25.17 E
Íos I	38	36.42 N	25.24 E
Ioscoe, Lake ⊜	276	41.02 N	74.19 W
Iosegun ≃	182	54.44 N	117.11 W
Iosegun Lake	182	54.29 N	116.50 W
Iō-shima I	93b	30.48 N	130.18 E
Iota	194	30.19 N	92.29 W
Iovlevo	82	56.10 N	38.20 E
Iowa	194	30.14 N	93.00 W
Iowa □[3]	178	42.15 N	93.15 W
Iowa ≃	190	41.10 N	91.02 W
Iowa, South Fork ≃	190	42.18 N	93.04 W
Iowa City	190	41.39 N	91.31 W
Iowa Falls	190	42.31 N	93.15 W
Iowa Park	196	33.57 N	98.40 W
Iō-zen ∧	94	36.31 N	136.48 E
Ipa ≃	76	52.13 N	29.08 E
Ipala	154	4.30 S	32.53 E
Ipameri	255	17.43 S	48.09 W
Ipanema ◆[8]	256	22.59 S	43.12 W
Ipanema ≃	250	9.53 S	37.15 W
Ipanguaçu	250	5.30 S	36.52 W
Ipat	24	66.13 N	56.33 E
Ipatinga	255	19.30 S	42.32 W
Ipatovo	80	45.43 N	42.53 E
Ipaumirim	250	6.47 S	38.43 W
Ipava	194	40.21 N	90.19 W
Ípeiros □[9]	38	39.40 N	20.50 E
Ipel'(Ipoly) ≃	30	47.49 N	18.52 E
Iperu	150	6.52 N	3.38 E
Iphigenia Bay c	180	55.40 N	133.55 W
Iphofen	56	49.42 N	10.15 E
Ipiabas	256	22.23 S	43.53 W
Ipiales	246	0.50 N	77.37 W
Ipiaú	255	14.08 S	39.44 W
Ipiíba	256	22.52 S	42.57 W
Ipil	116	7.47 N	122.35 E
Ipin → Yibin	107	28.47 N	104.38 E
Ipirá	255	12.10 S	39.44 W
Ipiranga, Bra.	246	3.12 S	66.01 W
Ipiranga, Bra.	252	25.01 S	50.35 W
Ipiranga, Bra.	287a	22.43 S	43.12 W
Ipiranga ◆[8]	287b	23.36 S	46.35 W
Ipiranga ≃, Bra.	256	23.21 S	45.10 W
Ipiranga ≃, Bra.	287a	22.48 S	43.37 W
Ipiranga, Canal ≍	287a	22.46 S	43.37 W
Ipiranga, Museu do ʊ	287b	23.35 S	46.36 W
Ipitá	248	19.20 S	63.32 W
Ipitinga ≃	250	0.02 N	53.01 W
Ipixuna	250	4.22 S	44.34 W
Ipixuna ≃, Bra.	248	7.11 S	71.51 W
Ipixuna ≃, Bra.	248	5.45 S	63.02 W
Ipixuna ≃, Bra.	248	6.16 S	61.52 W
Ipixuna, Igarapé ≃	250	4.32 S	52.40 W
İpkaiye	130	40.12 N	27.06 E
Ipoh	114	4.35 N	101.05 E
Ipojuca	250	8.24 S	35.04 W
Ipojuca ≃	250	8.25 S	34.58 W
Ipokera	154	8.03 S	35.41 E
Ipole	154	5.47 S	32.44 E
Ipoly (Ipel') ≃	30	47.49 N	18.52 E
Iporã, Bra.	255	23.59 S	53.37 W
Iporá, Bra.	255	16.28 S	51.07 W
Ipota	175f	18.48 S	169.16 E
Ippari ≃	70	36.52 N	14.26 E
Ippinghausen	56	51.17 N	9.08 E
Ipplepen	42	50.29 N	3.38 W
Ippy	152	6.15 N	21.12 E
İpsala	130	40.55 N	26.23 E
İpsile	130	40.14 N	37.33 E
Ipswich, Austl.	171a	27.36 S	152.46 E
Ipswich, Eng., U.K.	42	52.04 N	1.10 E
Ipswich, Ma., U.S.	207	42.40 N	70.50 W
Ipswich, S.D., U.S.	198	45.26 N	99.01 W
Ipswich ≃	207	42.42 N	70.48 W
Ipswich Bay c	207	42.41 N	70.42 W
Ipu	250	4.20 S	40.42 W
Ipubi	250	7.39 S	40.07 W
Ipueiras	250	4.33 S	40.43 W
Ipuh	112	3.00 S	101.30 E
Ipuiúna	256	22.06 S	46.11 W
Ipun, Isla I	254	44.37 S	74.46 W
Ipupiara	255	11.49 S	42.37 W
Iput' ≃	76	52.26 N	31.02 E
Iqe ≃	102	38.14 N	94.18 E
Iqfahṣ	142	28.47 N	30.49 E
Iquique	248	20.13 S	70.10 W
Iquitos	246	3.46 S	73.15 W
Ira	196	32.35 N	101.00 W
Iraan, Pil.	116	9.04 N	117.42 E
Iraan, Tx., U.S.	196	30.54 N	101.53 W
Ira Banda	152	5.57 N	22.04 E
Irabu	175d	24.50 N	125.09 E
Irabu-jima I	175d	24.50 N	125.10 E
Iracema	250	5.48 S	38.18 W
Iracoubo	250	5.29 N	53.13 W
Irago-misaki ≻	94	34.35 N	137.01 E
Irago-suidō ⋓	94	34.35 N	137.00 E
Iraí	252	27.11 S	53.15 W
Irajá ◆[8]	287a	22.51 S	43.19 W
Irajá ≃	287a	22.49 S	43.17 W
Irajol'	24	64.27 N	55.08 E
Irak → Iraq □[1]	128	33.00 N	44.00 E
Iráklion, Ellás	38	35.20 N	25.09 E
Iráklion, Ellás	267c	38.04 N	23.46 E
Irámuco	234	19.57 N	100.55 W
Iran (Īrān) □[1], Asia	118	32.00 N	53.00 E
Iran (Īrān) □[1], Asia	128	32.00 N	53.00 E
Iran, Pegunungan ⋏	112	2.05 N	114.55 E
Īrānshahr	128	27.13 N	60.41 E
Irapa	246	10.34 N	62.35 W
Irapuato	234	20.41 N	101.21 W
Iraq (Al-ʿIrāq) □[1], Asia	118	33.00 N	44.00 E
Iraq (Al-ʿIrāq) □[1], Asia	128	33.00 N	44.00 E
Irará	255	12.02 S	38.46 W
Iratapuru ≃	250	0.36 S	52.35 W
Irati	252	25.27 S	50.39 W
Irati ≃	34	42.35 N	1.16 W
Irauçuba	250	3.45 S	39.47 W
Irazú, Volcán ∧[1]	236	9.58 N	83.53 W
Irba	88	58.07 N	99.00 E
Irbejskoje	88	55.39 N	95.28 E
Irbeni väin (Irves šaurums) ⋓	76	57.48 N	22.05 E
Irbid	132	32.33 N	35.51 E
Irbid □[8]	132	32.33 N	35.51 E
Irbīl	128	36.11 N	44.01 E
Irbīl □[4]	128	36.10 N	44.00 E
Irbit	86	57.41 N	63.03 E
Irby	262	53.21 N	3.07 W
Irchester	42	52.16 N	0.38 W
Irdning	61	47.33 N	14.01 E
Irdyn'	78	49.23 N	31.44 E
Ire, Mount ∧	175e	9.10 S	161.05 E
Irebu	152	0.37 S	17.45 E
Irecê	250	11.18 S	41.52 W
Iregua ≃	34	42.27 N	2.24 W
Ireland (Eire) □[1], Europe	22	53.00 N	8.00 W
Ireland (Eire) □[1], Europe	48	53.00 N	8.00 W
Ireland Brook ≃	276	40.25 N	74.29 W
Ireland Island I	240a	32.19 N	64.50 W
Iren' ≃	86	57.27 N	56.56 E
Irene, S. Afr.	158	25.53 S	28.13 E
Irene, S.D., U.S.	198	43.05 N	97.10 W
Irene, Tx., U.S.	222	31.59 N	96.52 W
Irene, Mount ∧	172	45.10 S	167.22 E
Ireng (Maú) ≃	246	3.33 N	59.51 W
İresi	130	39.09 N	39.53 E
Iresick Brook ≃	276	40.24 N	74.22 W
Ireton	198	42.58 N	96.19 W
Irfon ≃	42	52.09 N	3.24 W
Irgakly	84	44.22 N	44.45 E
Irgiz	86	48.37 N	61.16 E
Irgiz ≃	86	48.13 N	62.08 E
Iri	98	35.56 N	126.57 E
Irian Jaya □[4]	164	5.00 S	138.00 E
Iriba	146	15.07 N	22.15 E
Irié	150	8.17 N	9.11 W
Iriga	116	13.25 N	123.25 E
Irigny	62	45.40 N	4.49 E
Irîgui ◆[1]	150	16.43 N	5.30 W
Iriklinskij	86	51.39 N	58.38 E
Iringa	154	7.46 S	35.42 E
Iringa □[4]	154	9.00 S	35.00 E
Irinjālakuda	122	10.20 N	76.14 E
Iriomote-jima I	175d	24.20 N	123.50 E
Iriona	236	15.57 N	85.11 W
Iriri ≃, Bra.	250	3.52 S	52.37 W
Iriri ≃, Bra.	287a	22.41 S	43.05 W
Iriri Novo ≃	250	8.46 S	53.22 W
Irische See → Irish Sea ⊤[2]	28	53.30 N	5.20 W
Irish, Mount ∧	204	37.38 N	115.24 W
Irish Sea ⊤[2]	28	53.30 N	5.20 W
Irishtown	166	40.55 S	145.08 E
Irituia	250	1.46 S	47.26 W
Iriyamazu	268	35.16 N	139.39 E
Irkās, Wādī V	142	28.57 N	32.00 E
Irkeštam	85	39.41 N	73.55 E
Irkinejeva ≃	88	58.30 N	96.48 E
Irkinejevo	88	58.30 N	96.49 E
Irklijev	78	49.32 N	32.18 E
Irklijevskaja	78	45.51 N	39.39 E
Irkoutsk → Irkutsk	88	52.16 N	104.20 E
Irkut ≃	88	52.18 N	104.15 E
Irkutsk	88	52.16 N	104.20 E
Irkutsk □[4]	88	56.00 N	106.00 E
Irlam	44	53.28 N	2.25 W
Irland → Ireland □[1]	48	53.00 N	8.00 W
Irlanda, Mar de → Irish Sea ⊤[2]	28	53.30 N	5.20 W
Irlande → Ireland □[1]	48	53.00 N	8.00 W
Irlande, Mer d' → Irish Sea ⊤[2]	28	53.30 N	5.20 W
Irma	182	52.55 N	111.14 W
Irmauw	164	7.25 S	131.42 E
Irminger Basin ✣[1]	10	61.00 N	35.00 W
Irminio ≃	70	36.46 N	14.36 E
Irmino ◆[8]	83	48.36 N	38.36 E
Irnijärvi ⊜	26	65.36 N	29.05 E
Irnsum	52	53.05 N	5.47 E
Iro, Lac ⊜	146	10.06 N	19.25 E
Iroise c	32	48.15 N	4.55 W
Iron Baron	166	32.59 S	137.09 E
Iron Belt	190	46.24 N	90.19 W
Iron Bottom Sound ⋓	175e	9.15 S	160.00 E
Iron Bridge, On., Can.	190	46.17 N	83.14 W
Iron Bridge, Eng., U.K.	42	52.38 N	2.29 W
Iron Bridge Dam ◆[6]	222	32.50 N	95.54 W
Iron City	194	35.01 N	87.34 W
Iron Cove c	274a	33.52 S	151.10 E
Iron Creek ≃	182	52.43 N	111.14 W
Irondale, Al., U.S.	194	33.32 N	86.42 W
Irondale, Mo., U.S.	194	37.49 N	90.40 W
Irondale, Oh., U.S.	214	40.34 N	80.43 W
Irondale ≃	212	44.49 N	78.37 W
Irondequoit	210	43.12 N	77.36 W
Irondequoit Bay c	210	43.12 N	77.32 W
Iron Gate V	38	44.41 N	22.31 E
Iron Gate Reservoir ⊜[1]	38	44.30 N	22.00 E
Ironia	276	40.49 N	74.37 W
Iron Knob	166	32.44 S	137.08 E
Iron Mountain	190	45.49 N	88.03 W
Iron Mountain ∧, Az., U.S.	200	33.27 N	111.10 W
Iron Mountain ∧, Ca., U.S.	280	34.17 N	117.43 W
Iron Mountains ⋏	192	36.30 N	81.50 W
Iron Range	164	12.42 S	143.18 E
Iron River, Mi., U.S.	190	46.05 N	88.38 W
Iron River, Wi., U.S.	190	46.33 N	91.24 W
Iron Springs	208	39.46 N	77.25 W
Ironton, Mn., U.S.	190	46.28 N	93.58 W
Ironton, Mo., U.S.	194	37.35 N	90.37 W
Ironton, Oh., U.S.	188	38.32 N	82.40 W
Ironwood	190	46.27 N	90.10 W
Ironworks Creek ≃	285	40.10 N	74.59 W
Iroquois, On., Can.	212	44.51 N	75.19 W
Iroquois, Il., U.S.	216	40.50 N	87.35 W
Iroquois, S.D., U.S.	198	44.22 N	97.51 W
Iroquois □[6]	216	40.47 N	87.44 W
Iroquois ≃	216	41.05 N	87.49 W
Iroquois Falls	190	48.46 N	80.41 W
Iroquois Lock and Dam ◆[5]	212	44.45 N	75.23 W
Irosin	116	12.42 N	124.02 E
Írottkö (Geschriebenstein) ∧	61	47.21 N	16.26 E
Irō-zaki ≻	94	34.36 N	138.51 E
Irpen'	78	50.31 N	30.15 E
Irpen' ≃	78	50.34 N	30.16 E
Irrawaddy □[8]	110	17.00 N	95.00 E
Irrawaddy ≃	110	15.50 N	95.06 E
Irrawaddy, Mouths of the ≃[1]	110	15.45 N	94.50 E
Irregully Creek ≃	162	23.06 S	116.21 E
Irrel	56	49.51 N	6.28 E
Irricana	182	51.19 N	113.37 W
Irrigon	202	45.53 N	119.29 W
Irša ≃	78	50.45 N	29.30 E
Iršava	78	48.20 N	23.03 E
Irschenberg	64	47.50 N	11.55 E
Irsee	58	47.54 N	10.34 E
Irsina	68	40.45 N	16.15 E
Irt ≃	44	54.22 N	3.26 W
Irtek ≃	80	51.28 N	52.39 E
Irthing ≃	44	54.55 N	2.50 W
Irthlingborough	42	52.20 N	0.37 W
Irtyš	86	54.29 N	74.22 E
Irtyš (Ertix) ≃	74	61.04 N	68.52 E
Irtysch → Irtyš ≃	72	61.04 N	68.52 E
Irtysh → Irtyš ≃	72	61.04 N	68.52 E
Irtyšsk	86	53.21 N	75.27 E
Irubaj	80	50.11 N	51.21 E
Iruma	94	35.50 N	139.24 E
Iruma ≃	94	35.57 N	139.30 E
Iruma Air Base ■	268	35.50 N	139.24 E
Iruma-kichi, Kaijō-jieitai- ■	94	35.50 N	139.24 E
Irumu	154	1.27 N	29.52 E
Irún	34	43.21 N	1.47 W
Irupana	248	16.28 S	67.28 W
Irurzun	34	42.55 N	1.50 W
Irú Tepuy ∧	246	5.25 N	61.02 W
Irves šaurums (Irbeni väin) ⋓	76	57.48 N	22.05 E
Irvine, Ab., Can.	184	49.57 N	110.16 W
Irvine, Scot., U.K.	46	55.37 N	4.40 W
Irvine, Ca., U.S.	228	33.40 N	117.49 W
Irvine, Ky., U.S.	192	37.42 N	83.58 W
Irvine, Pa., U.S.	214	41.50 N	79.17 W
Irvine ≃	46	55.37 N	4.41 W
Irvine, Mount ∧	210	42.03 N	78.40 W
Irvine Creek ≃	212	43.41 N	80.25 W
Irvine Park ♠	280	33.48 N	117.45 W
Irvines Landing	182	49.38 N	124.03 W
Irvinestown	48	54.28 N	7.38 W
Irving, Il., U.S.	219	39.12 N	89.24 W
Irving, N.Y., U.S.	214	42.34 N	79.07 W
Irving, Tx., U.S.	222	32.48 N	96.56 W
Irving Park ◆[8]	278	41.57 N	87.43 W
Irvington, Il., U.S.	219	38.26 N	89.10 W
Irvington, Ky., U.S.	194	37.52 N	86.17 W
Irvington, N.J., U.S.	210	40.43 N	74.13 W
Irvington, N.Y., U.S.	210	41.02 N	73.51 W
Irvington, Oh., U.S.	218	39.51 N	84.15 W
Irvington, Va., U.S.	208	37.39 N	76.25 W
Irvington ◆[8]	284b	39.17 N	76.41 W
Irvona	214	40.46 N	78.33 W
Irwell ≃	44	53.27 N	2.17 W
Irwin, Austl.	162	29.12 S	115.04 E
Irwin, Oh., U.S.	218	40.07 N	83.29 W
Irwin, Pa., U.S.	279b	40.19 N	79.42 W
Irwin ≃	162	29.15 S	114.56 E
Irwin, Point ≻	162	35.04 S	116.56 E
Irwindale	280	34.06 N	117.56 W

Symbols in the index entries represent the broad categories identified in the key at the right. Symbols with superior numbers (⋏[1]) identify subcategories (see complete key on page I · 1).

Kartensymbole in dem Registerverzeichnis stellen die rechts in Schlüssel erklärten Kategorien dar. Symbole mit hochgestellten Ziffern (⋏[1]) bezeichnen Unterabteilungen einer Kategorie (vgl. vollständiger Schlüssel auf Seite I · 1).

Los símbolos incluídos en el texto del índice representan las grandes categorias identificadas con la clave a la derecha. Los símbolos con numeros en su parte superior (⋏[1]) identifican las subcategorias (véase la clave completa en la página I · 1).

Les symboles de l'index représentent les catégories indiquées dans la légende à droite. Les symboles suivis d'un indice (⋏[1]) représentent des sous-catégories (voir légende complète à la page I · 1).

Os símbolos incluídos no texto do índice representam as grandes categorias identificadas com a chave à direita. Os símbolos com números em sua parte superior (⋏[1]) identificam as subcategorias (veja-se a chave completa à página I · 1).

∧	Mountain	Berg	Montaña	Montagne	Montanha
⋏	Mountains	Berge	Montañas	Montagnes	Montanhas
)(	Pass	Pass	Paso	Col	Passo
V	Valley, Canyon	Tal, Cañon	Valle, Cañón	Vallée, Canyon	Vale, Canhão
≚	Plain	Ebene	Llano	Plaine	Planície
≻	Cape	Kap	Cabo	Cap	Cabo
I	Island	Insel	Isla	Île	Ilha
II	Islands	Inseln	Islas	Îles	Ilhas
±	Other Topographic Features	Andere Topographische Objekte	Otros Elementos Topográficos	Autres données topographiques	Outros acidentes topográficos

ESPAÑOL — Nombre | Página | Lat.°′ | Long.°′ W = Oeste
FRANÇAIS — Nom | Page | Lat.°′ | Long.°′ W = Ouest
PORTUGUÊS — Nome | Página | Lat.°′ | Long.°′ W = Oeste

Irwinton 192 32.48 N 83.10 W
Is 86 58.48 N 59.43 E
Is, Jabal ʌ 140 21.49 N 35.39 E
Isa 150 13.14 N 6.24 E
ʿĪsā, Ra's › 144 15.11 N 42.39 E
Isaac ≃ 166 22.52 S 149.20 E
Isaac Lake ⊜, B.C., Can. 182 53.10 N 120.50 W
Isaac Lake ⊜, On., Can. 212 44.47 N 81.14 W
Isaba 34 42.52 N 0.55 W
Isabel, Pil. 116 10.56 N 124.26 E
Isabel, S.D., U.S. 198 45.23 N 101.25 W
Isabel □[4] 175e 7.55 S 159.10 E
Isabel, Bahía c 246a 0.38 S 91.27 W
Isabela, Pil. 116 10.12 N 122.59 E
Isabela (Basilan), Pil. 116 6.42 N 121.58 E
Isabela, P.R. 240m 18.30 N 67.01 W
Isabela □[4] 116 17.00 N 122.00 E
Isabela, Cabo › 238 19.56 N 71.01 W
Isabela, Canal ʯ 246a 0.20 S 90.55 W
Isabela, Isla I, Ec. 246a 0.30 S 91.06 W
Isabela, Isla I, Méx. 234 21.51 N 105.55 W
Isabelia, Cordillera ⋏ 236 13.45 N 85.15 W
Isabella Indian Reservation ◆[4] 190 43.41 N 84.48 W
Isabella Lake ⊜ 212 45.24 N 79.49 W
Isabella Lake ⊜[1] 204 35.40 N 118.26 W
Isabelle ≃ 190 47.50 N 91.41 W
Isábena ≃ 34 42.11 N 0.21 E
Isaccea 38 45.16 N 28.28 E
Ísafjarðardjúp c[2] 24a 66.10 N 23.00 W
Ísafjörður 24a 66.08 N 23.13 W
Isāgarh 124 24.50 N 77.53 E
Isagatedo 273a 6.32 N 3.20 E
Isahaya 92 32.50 N 130.03 E
Isak 114 4.28 N 96.55 E
Isaka, Tan. 154 3.54 S 32.56 E
Isaka, Zaïre 152 2.35 S 18.48 E
Isaka-Buku 152 3.55 S 22.03 E
Īsa Khel 123 32.41 N 71.17 E
Isakly 80 54.08 N 51.32 E
Isakovka 86 55.45 N 74.24 E
Isakovo, S.S.S.R. 76 55.11 N 34.40 E
Isakovo, S.S.S.R. 76 60.30 N 41.13 E
Isakovo, S.S.S.R. 82 54.36 N 37.02 E
Isakovo, S.S.S.R. 265b 55.59 N 37.23 E
Isalnița 38 44.24 N 23.44 E
Isalo, Massif de l' ⋏ 157b 22.45 S 45.15 E
Isalo, Parc National de l' ♦ 157b 22.45 S 45.15 E
Isana (Içana) ≃ 246 0.26 N 67.19 W
Īsānagar 124 27.54 N 81.13 E
Isandhlwana ⊥ 158 28.21 S 30.39 E
Isandja Etat 152 2.59 S 22.00 E
Isando 273d 26.09 S 28.12 E
Isanga 152 1.26 S 22.18 E
Isangano National Park ♦ 154 11.10 S 30.40 E
Isangel 175f 19.32 S 169.16 E
Isangi 152 0.46 N 24.15 E
Is'angulovo 86 52.12 N 56.36 E
Isanlu Makutu 150 8.17 N 5.46 E
Isan-ni 98 40.46 N 128.55 E
Isanti 190 45.29 N 93.14 W
Isar ≃ 30 48.49 N 12.58 E
Isara 150 6.59 N 3.41 E
Isarco (Eisack) ≃ 64 46.27 N 11.18 E
Isarco, Valle V 64 46.45 N 11.37 E
Isarog, Mount ʌ 116 13.39 N 123.23 E
Isasi 273a 6.40 N 3.23 E
Isawa 94 35.39 N 138.38 E
Isbergues 50 50.37 N 2.27 E
Isbister 46 60.36 N 1.19 W
İşcehisar 130 38.51 N 30.45 E
Iščeino 76 52.57 N 38.50 E
Iščerskaja 84 43.43 N 45.08 E
Ischgl 58 47.01 N 10.17 E
Ischia 68 40.44 N 13.57 E
Ischia, Isola d' I 68 40.43 N 13.54 E
Ischia di Castro 66 42.33 N 11.45 E
Ischim → Išim ≃ 86 57.45 N 71.12 E
Ischitella 68 41.54 N 15.54 E
Ischma → Ižma ≃ 24 65.19 N 52.54 E
Ischodnaja, gora ʌ 180 64.50 N 173.26 W
Ischua 210 42.15 N 78.24 W
Ischua Creek ≃ 210 42.10 N 78.23 W
Iscuandé ≃ 246 2.38 N 78.04 W
Isdell ≃ 162 16.27 S 124.51 E
Isdes 50 47.40 N 2.15 E
Ise (Uji-yamada) 94 34.29 N 136.42 E
Ise ≃ 54 52.30 N 10.33 E
Isefjord c 41 55.52 N 11.49 E
Isehara 94 35.24 N 139.18 E
Išejevka 80 54.25 N 48.16 E
Iseke 154 6.25 S 35.01 E
Isel ≃ 64 46.50 N 12.47 E
Iselin, N.J., U.S. 210 40.34 N 74.19 W
Iselin, Pa., U.S. 214 40.33 N 79.23 W
Iselle 58 46.12 N 8.12 E
Iseltwald 58 46.43 N 7.58 E
Isen 60 48.13 N 12.04 E
Isen ≃ 60 48.15 N 12.40 E
Isenbajevo 80 56.03 N 53.25 E
Isenbüttel 52 52.26 N 10.34 E
Isenyela 154 8.36 S 33.30 E
Iseo 64 45.39 N 10.03 E
Iseo, Lago d' ⊜ 64 45.43 N 10.04 E
Iseramagazi 154 4.40 S 32.09 E
Iseran, Col de l')(62 45.25 N 7.02 E
Isère □[5] 62 45.10 N 5.50 E
Isère ≃ 62 44.59 N 4.51 E
Iseri 273a 6.39 N 3.23 E
Iseri-Oke 273a 6.38 N 3.23 E
Iseri-Osun 273a 6.31 N 3.17 E
Iserlohn 56 51.22 N 7.41 E
Iserlohn □[8] 263 51.24 N 7.36 E
Iserlohnerheide ◆[8] 263 51.24 N 7.42 E
Isernhagen 52 52.26 N 9.51 E
Isernia 66 41.36 N 14.14 E
Isernia □[4] 66 41.40 N 14.15 E
Isesaki 94 36.19 N 139.12 E
Ise-Shima-kokuritsu-kōen ♦ 92 34.23 N 136.48 E
Iset' ≃ 86 56.36 N 66.24 E
Isetskoje 86 56.29 N 65.21 E
Ise-wan c 94 34.43 N 136.43 E
Iseyin 150 7.58 N 3.36 E
Isezaki → Isesaki 92 36.19 N 139.12 E
Isfahan → Eșfahān 128 32.40 N 51.38 E
Isfana 85 39.50 N 69.31 E
Isfana ≃ 85 40.13 N 69.26 E
Isfara 85 40.07 N 70.38 E
ʿIsfiyā 132 32.43 N 35.04 E
Ishenga Oswe 152 3.46 S 22.34 E
Isheri-Olofin 273a 6.35 N 3.17 E
Isherton 246 2.19 N 59.22 W
Ishi ≃ 270 34.35 N 135.38 E
Ishibashi 94 36.26 N 139.52 E
Ishibe 94 35.00 N 136.04 E
Ishigaki 175d 24.20 N 124.09 E
Ishigaki-shima I 175d 24.24 N 124.12 E
Ishige 94 36.07 N 139.58 E
Ishii 96 34.04 N 134.26 E
Ishikari ≃ 92a 43.15 N 141.23 E
Ishikari-dake ʌ 92a 43.33 N 143.02 E
Ishikari-heiya ≌ 92a 43.15 N 141.23 E
Ishikari-sanchi ⋏ 92a 43.35 N 143.00 E
Ishikari-wan c 92a 43.25 N 141.01 E
Ishikawa, Nihon 94 37.09 N 140.27 E
Ishikawa, Nihon 174m 26.25 N 127.50 E
Ishikawa □[5] 94 36.45 N 136.45 E
Ishiki 94 34.48 N 137.01 E
Ishikiri 270 34.41 N 135.39 E
I-shima I 96 33.51 N 134.49 E
Ishinomaki 92 38.25 N 141.18 E
Ishinomaki-wan c 92 38.18 N 141.18 E
Ishioka 94 36.11 N 140.16 E
Ishiyama 270 34.58 N 135.55 E
Ishizuchi-san ʌ 96 33.46 N 133.07 E
Ishkumān 123 36.32 N 73.49 E
Ishmant 142 29.12 N 31.11 E
Ishpeming 190 46.29 N 87.40 W
Ishuizu ≃ 270 34.33 N 135.27 E
Ishurdi 124 24.08 N 89.05 E
Isidro Casanova 288 34.42 S 58.35 W
Isigny 32 49.19 N 1.06 W
Işıklı 130 38.19 N 29.51 E
Isili 71 39.44 N 9.06 E
Isil'kul' 86 54.55 N 71.16 E
Išim 86 56.09 N 69.27 E
Išim ≃ 86 57.45 N 71.12 E
Išimbaj 86 53.28 N 56.02 E
Išimka 86 51.24 N 67.08 E
Išimskaja step' ≌ 86 55.00 N 70.00 E
Isimu 112 0.40 N 122.51 E
Isinga 88 52.55 N 112.00 E
Isiolo 154 0.21 N 37.35 E
Isiolo Game Reserve ◆[4] 154 0.32 N 37.34 E
Isipingo 158 29.59 S 30.56 E
Isipingo Beach 158 29.59 S 30.57 E
Isiro (Paulis) 154 2.47 N 27.37 E
Isis 166 25.12 S 152.13 E
Isisford 166 24.16 S 144.26 E
Iskandar 85 41.36 N 69.43 E
Iskâr ≃ 38 43.44 N 24.27 E
Iškašim 123 36.44 N 71.37 E
Iskaten', chrebet ⋏ 180 66.30 N 179.00 W
Iškejevo 80 55.51 N 50.56 E
İskenderun 130 36.37 N 36.07 E
İskenderun Körfezi c 130 36.30 N 35.40 E
Iske-R'az'ap 80 54.36 N 49.42 E
İskilip 130 40.45 N 34.29 E
Iski-Naukat 85 40.16 N 72.36 E
Iskininskij 80 47.13 N 52.41 E
Iskitim 86 54.38 N 83.18 E
Iskona ≃ 82 55.34 N 36.05 E
Iskushuban 144 10.17 N 50.14 E
Iskut ≃ 180 56.42 N 131.45 W
Isla 234 18.01 N 95.30 W
Isla ≃ 46 57.30 N 2.47 W
Isla, Salar de la ≌ 252 25.49 S 68.53 W
Isla Cristina 34 37.12 N 7.19 W
Isla de Maipo 252 33.45 S 70.54 W
İslâhiye 130 37.03 N 36.36 E
Islāmābād → Anantnāg, India 123 33.44 N 75.09 E
Islāmābād, Pāk. 123 33.42 N 73.10 E
Isla Mala 258 34.12 S 56.21 W
Islāmkot 120 24.42 N 70.11 E
Islamorada 220 24.55 N 80.37 W
Islāmpur, India 124 25.09 N 85.12 E
Islāmpur, India 124 26.16 N 88.12 E
Islāmpur, India 126 21.43 N 87.39 E
Islāmpur, India 126 24.09 N 88.28 E
Isla Mujeres 232 21.12 N 86.43 W
Island 194 37.26 N 87.08 W
Island □[6] 224 48.07 N 122.36 W
Island → Iceland □[1] 24a 65.00 N 18.00 W
Island ≃ 262 53.44 N 2.51 W
Island Bay c 116 9.06 N 118.10 E
Island Beach State Park ♦ 208 39.50 N 74.06 W
Island Bend 171b 36.19 S 148.29 E
Island Creek 283 42.00 N 70.43 W
Island Falls, Sk., Can. 184 55.32 N 102.21 W
Island Falls, Me., U.S. 188 46.00 N 68.16 W
Island Heights 208 39.56 N 74.09 W
Islandia → Iceland □[1] 24a 65.00 N 18.00 W
Island Lagoon ⊜ 166 31.30 S 136.40 E
Island Lake, Mb., Can. 184 53.58 N 94.47 W
Island Lake, Il., U.S. 216 42.17 N 88.12 W
Island Lake, Mi., U.S. 281 42.31 N 83.44 W
Island Lake ⊜ 184 53.47 N 94.25 W
Island Lake State Recreation Area ♦ 216 42.30 N 83.43 W
Island Park, Id., U.S. 202 44.24 N 111.19 W
Island Park, N.Y., U.S. 276 40.36 N 73.39 W
Island Park, R.I., U.S. 207 41.37 N 71.13 W
Island Park Reservoir ⊜[1] 202 44.25 N 111.29 W
Island Point › 162 30.20 S 115.02 E
Island Pond 188 44.48 N 71.52 W
Island Pond ⊜ 186 48.25 N 56.23 W
Islands, Bay of c, Nf., Can. 186 49.10 N 58.15 W
Islands, Bay of c, N.Z. 172 35.12 S 174.10 E
Island View 216 40.31 N 83.53 W
Isla Patrulla 252 32.59 S 54.35 W
Islas de la Bahía □[5] 236 16.20 N 86.30 W
Islas Malvinas → Falkland Islands □[2] 254 51.45 S 59.00 W
Isla Verde 252 33.14 S 62.24 W
Isla Vista 204 34.25 N 119.50 W
Islay I 46 55.46 N 6.10 W
Islay, Punta › 248 17.01 S 72.07 W
Islay, Sound of ʯ 46 55.50 N 6.01 W
Isle 190 46.08 N 93.28 W
Isle ≃, Fr. 32 44.55 N 0.15 W
Isle ≃, Eng., U.K. 42 50.59 N 2.53 W
Isle-Adam, Forêt de l' ♦ 261 49.05 N 2.15 E
Isle-aux-Morts 186 47.35 N 58.59 W
Isle of Hope 192 31.58 N 81.05 W
Isle of Man □[2], Europe 22 54.15 N 4.30 W
Isle of Man □[2], Europe 44 54.15 N 4.30 W
Isle of Man (Ronaldsway) Airport ⊠ 44 54.06 N 4.36 W
Isle of Palms 192 32.47 N 79.48 W
Isle of Wight 208 36.54 N 76.42 W
Isle of Wight □[6], Eng., U.K. 42 50.40 N 1.20 W
Isle of Wight □[6], Va., U.S. 208 36.50 N 76.42 W
Isle of Wight Bay c 208 38.22 N 75.06 W
Isle Royale National Park ♦ 190 48.00 N 89.00 W
Isles, Lake of the ⊜ 212 44.19 N 75.59 W
Isle Saint George 214 41.43 N 82.49 W
Islesboro Island I 188 44.20 N 68.53 W
Isleta 200 34.54 N 106.41 W
Isleta Indian Reservation ◆[4] 200 34.55 N 106.45 W
Isleton 226 38.09 N 121.36 W
Islets-Caribou 186 49.30 N 67.14 W
Isleworth ◆[8] 260 51.28 N 0.20 W
Islington 207 42.13 N 71.11 W
Islington ◆[8], On., Can. 275b 43.39 N 79.32 W
Islington ◆[8], Eng., U.K. 42 51.34 N 0.06 W
Islip, Eng., U.K. 42 51.50 N 1.14 W
Islip, N.Y., U.S. 276 40.43 N 73.12 W
Islip Terrace 276 40.44 N 73.11 W
Islivig 46 58.05 N 7.11 W
Isloč' ≃ 76 53.55 N 26.13 E
Islón 252 29.54 S 71.12 W
Ismael Cortinas (Arroyo Grande) 258 33.58 S 57.06 W
Ismailia → Al-Ismāʿīlīyah 142 30.35 N 32.16 E
Ismāʿīlīyah ◆[8] 273c 30.03 N 31.14 E
Ismāʿīlīyah, Tur'at al- ≊ 142 30.04 N 31.16 E
İsmailli 130 38.56 N 27.13 E
Ismailly 84 40.47 N 48.09 E
Ismailovo 80 55.34 N 54.39 E
Ismaning 60 48.14 N 11.41 E
Isnā 140 25.18 N 32.33 E
Isny 58 47.41 N 10.02 E
Isoanala 157b 23.50 S 45.44 E
Isobe 94 34.22 N 136.49 E
Isogo ◆[8] 268 35.23 N 139.37 E
Isojoki 26 62.07 N 21.58 E
Isoka 154 10.10 S 32.35 E
Isokyrö 26 63.00 N 22.19 E
Isola, Fr. 62 44.11 N 7.03 E
Isola, Ms., U.S. 194 33.15 N 90.35 W
Isola, Monte ʌ 64 45.42 N 10.05 E
Isola d'Asti 62 44.50 N 8.11 E
Isola del Cantone 62 44.39 N 8.57 E
Isola del Gran Sasso d'Italia 66 42.30 N 13.40 E
Isola della Scala 64 45.16 N 11.00 E
Isola del Liri 66 41.41 N 13.34 E
Isola di Capo Rizzuto 68 38.58 N 17.06 E
Isola Dovarese 64 45.10 N 10.18 E
Isola Farnese ◆[8] 66 42.01 N 12.23 E
Isola Vicentina 64 45.38 N 11.25 E
Isoletta 66 41.30 N 13.34 E
Isolillock Peak ʌ 224 49.18 N 121.27 W
Isolo 273a 6.32 N 3.19 E
Isone 58 46.08 N 8.59 E
Isonzo (Soča) ≃ 64 45.47 N 13.32 E
Isorella 64 45.18 N 10.19 E
Isosyöte ʌ[2] 26 65.37 N 27.35 E
Iso-zaki › 94 36.23 N 140.38 E
İspanak 130 36.52 N 37.07 E
Ispani 68 40.08 N 15.34 E
Isparta 130 37.46 N 30.33 E
Isparta □[4] 130 38.00 N 31.00 E
Isperih 38 43.43 N 26.50 E
Ispica 70 36.47 N 14.55 E
Ispica, Cava d' ⊥[5] 70 36.51 N 14.51 E
Ispikān 128 26.14 N 62.12 E
İspir 130 40.29 N 41.00 E
Ispra 62 45.49 N 8.37 E
Ispringen 56 48.55 N 8.40 E
Israel (Yisra'el) □[1], Asia 118 31.30 N 35.00 E
Israel (Yisra'el) □[1], Asia 132 31.30 N 35.00 E
Israel ≃ 188 44.29 N 71.35 W
Issa 80 53.52 N 44.51 E
Issa ≃ 76 56.58 N 28.47 E
Issano 246 5.49 N 59.25 W
Issaquah 224 47.31 N 122.01 W
Issaran, Ra's › 142 28.48 N 32.47 E
Issel (Oude IJssel) ≃ 52 52.00 N 6.10 E
Isselburg 52 51.51 N 6.28 E
Isselhorst 52 51.57 N 8.24 E
Isser, Oued ≃, Alg. 34 36.52 N 3.48 E
Isser, Oued ≃, Alg. 34 35.08 N 1.28 W
Issia 150 6.29 N 6.35 W
Issia □[5] 150 6.25 N 6.35 W
Issigeac 32 44.44 N 0.36 E
Issime 62 45.41 N 7.51 E
Issogne 62 45.39 N 7.41 E
Issoire 32 45.33 N 3.15 E
Issole ≃ 62 43.27 N 6.12 E
Issou 261 48.59 N 1.48 E
Issoudun 32 46.57 N 2.00 E
Issum 52 51.32 N 6.25 E
Issuna 154 5.23 S 34.46 E
Is-sur-Tille 58 47.31 N 5.06 E
Issy 50 48.49 N 2.17 E
Issyk 85 43.22 N 77.28 E
Issyk-Kul', ozero ⊜ 85 42.25 N 77.15 E
Issy-les-Moulineaux 261 48.49 N 2.17 E
Īstādeh-ye Moqor, Āb-e ⊜ 120 32.32 N 67.57 E
İstanbul, Tür. 130 41.01 N 28.58 E
İstanbul, Tür. 267b 41.01 N 28.58 E
İstanbul □[4] 130 41.10 N 28.45 E
İstanbul (Yeşilköy) hava alanı ⊠ 267b 40.58 N 28.49 E
İstanbul Boğazı (Bosporus) ʯ 130 41.06 N 29.04 E
İstanbul Üniversitesi ʊ[2] 267b 41.00 N 28.58 E
Isṭanhā 142 30.28 N 31.07 E
Istead Rise 260 51.24 N 0.22 E
Isteren ⊜ 26 61.58 N 11.48 E
Isthmus Bay c 212 45.00 N 81.15 W
Istiaía 38 38.57 N 23.09 E
İstilil 130 37.14 N 41.04 E
İstinye ◆[8] 267b 41.06 N 29.03 E
Istisu 84 39.57 N 45.59 E
Istmina 246 5.10 N 76.39 W
Isto, Mount ʌ 180 69.12 N 143.48 W
Istobensk 80 58.25 N 48.48 E
Istobnoje, S.S.S.R. 78 51.08 N 37.21 E
Istobnoje, S.S.S.R. 78 51.16 N 38.39 E
Istok 38 42.47 N 20.29 E
Istokpoga, Lake ⊜ 220 27.22 N 81.17 W
Istra 82 55.55 N 36.52 E
Istra ›[1] 36 45.15 N 14.00 E
Istra ≃ 82 55.44 N 37.08 E
Istrana 64 45.41 N 12.07 E
Istranca Dağları ⋏ 130 41.50 N 27.30 E
Istres 62 43.31 N 4.59 E
Istria → Istra ›[1] 36 45.15 N 14.00 E
Istrinskoje vodochranilišče ⊜[1] 82 56.04 N 36.49 E
Isulan 116 6.34 N 124.37 E
Isumi 94 35.17 N 140.19 E
Isumi ≃ 94 35.18 N 140.25 E
Isumrud Strait ʯ 164 4.45 S 145.50 E
Isunba 273a 6.27 N 3.17 E
Iswarīpur 126 22.19 N 89.07 E
Iswepe 158 26.50 S 30.31 E
Itá 252 25.29 S 57.21 W
Itabaiana, Bra. 250 7.20 S 35.20 W
Itabaiana, Bra. 250 10.41 S 37.26 W
Itabaiana, Bra. 250 11.16 S 37.47 W
Itabapoana 255 21.18 S 40.58 W
Itabashi ◆[8] 268 35.45 N 139.43 E
Itaberá 255 23.51 S 49.09 W
Itaberaba 255 12.32 S 40.18 W
Itaberaí 255 16.02 S 49.48 W
Itabi 250 10.08 S 37.06 W
Itabira 255 19.37 S 43.13 W
Itaboca 256 22.03 S 44.05 W
Itaboraí 256 22.45 S 42.52 W
Itaboraí □[7] 287a 22.43 S 43.00 W
Itabuna 255 14.48 S 39.16 W
Itacaiunas ≃ 250 5.21 S 49.08 W
Itacajá 250 8.19 S 47.46 W
Itacambiruçu ≃ 255 16.44 S 42.45 W
Itacaré 255 14.18 S 39.00 W
Itacoatiara 250 3.08 S 58.25 W
Itacoatiara, Ponta de › 287a 22.59 S 43.02 W
Itacuaí ≃ 246 4.20 S 70.12 W
Itacurubí del Rosario 252 24.29 S 56.41 W
Itacuruça, Ilha de I 256 22.56 S 43.53 W
Itacurussá 256 22.55 S 43.55 W
Itaetê 255 12.59 S 40.58 W
Itagacaba ≃ 256 22.34 S 44.56 W
Itagi 255 14.10 S 40.01 W
Itaguaçu 255 19.48 S 40.51 W
Itaguaí 256 22.52 S 43.47 W
Itaguajé 255 22.37 S 51.59 W
Itaguara 255 20.23 S 44.29 W
Itaguaré, Pico do ʌ 256 22.30 S 45.10 W
Ítaguari ≃ 255 14.11 S 44.40 W
Itaguaru 255 15.44 S 49.37 W
Itaguatins 250 5.47 S 47.29 W
Itagüí 246 6.10 N 75.36 W
Itaí 255 23.24 S 49.06 W
Itá-Ibaté 252 27.26 S 57.20 W
Itaiçaba 250 4.40 S 37.51 W
Itaim 256 22.24 S 45.53 W
Itaim ≃, Bra. 250 7.02 S 42.02 W
Itaim ≃, Bra. 256 23.07 S 45.08 W
Itaim ≃, Bra. 256 22.19 S 45.51 W
Itainópolis 250 7.24 S 41.31 W
Itaiópolis 252 26.20 S 49.56 W
Itaipava 256 22.23 S 43.08 W
Itaipu, Bra. 256 22.58 S 43.02 W
Itaipu, Bra. 287a 22.44 S 43.26 W
Itaipu, Lagoa de c 287a 22.58 S 43.02 W
Itaipu, Ponta de › 287a 22.59 S 43.03 W
Itaituba 250 4.17 S 55.59 W
Itajá 255 19.07 S 51.37 W
Itajaí 252 26.53 S 48.39 W
Itajaí do Sul ≃ 252 27.12 S 49.39 W
Itajubá 256 22.26 S 45.27 W
Itaju do Colônia 255 15.09 S 39.44 W
Itajuípe 255 14.41 S 39.22 W
Itaka, S.S.S.R. 88 53.53 N 118.42 E
Itaka, Tan. 154 8.52 S 32.47 E
Itaki 273a 6.43 N 3.17 E
Itako 94 35.56 N 140.33 E
Itakura, Nihon 94 36.13 N 139.36 E
Itakura, Nihon 94 37.03 N 138.18 E
Itala Game Reserve ◆[4] 158 27.31 S 31.19 E
Italia → Italy □[1] 36 42.50 N 12.50 E
Itálica ⊥ 34 37.30 N 6.05 W
Italie → Italy □[1] 36 42.50 N 12.50 E
Italien → Italy □[1] 36 42.50 N 12.50 E
Italy 222 32.11 N 96.53 W
Italy (Italia) □[1], Europe 22 42.50 N 12.50 E
Italy (Italia) □[1], Europe 36 42.50 N 12.50 E
Itamaraju 255 17.05 S 39.31 W
Itamarandiba 255 17.51 S 42.51 W
Itamarandiba ≃ 255 17.18 S 42.48 W
Itamarati 256 21.25 S 42.49 W
Itamari 255 13.47 S 39.37 W
Itamataré 250 2.16 S 46.24 W
Itambacuri 255 18.01 S 41.42 W
Itambé 255 15.15 S 40.37 W
Itambi 256 22.44 S 42.58 W
Itami 96 34.46 N 135.25 E
Itami, Camp ■ 270 34.47 N 135.24 E
Itamonte 256 22.17 S 44.53 W
Itampolo 157b 24.41 S 43.57 E
Itānagar 120 27.09 N 93.33 E
Itandéua, Lago ⊜ 250 2.01 S 55.10 W
Itandrano 157b 21.47 S 45.17 E
Itanhaém 255 24.11 S 46.47 W
Itanhandu 256 22.18 S 44.57 W
Itanhauã ≃ 248 4.45 S 63.48 W
Itanhém 255 17.09 S 40.20 W
Itanhém ≃ 255 17.32 S 39.12 W
Itanhomi 255 19.10 S 41.52 W
Itano 96 34.07 N 134.28 E
Itany (Litani) ≃ 250 3.40 N 54.00 W
Itaobim 255 16.34 S 41.30 W
Itaocaia 287a 22.58 S 43.01 W
Itapaci 255 14.57 S 49.34 W
Itapagé 250 3.41 S 39.34 W
Itapagipe 255 19.54 S 49.22 W
Itapanhaú ≃ 256 23.51 S 46.10 W
Itaparaná ≃ 248 5.47 S 63.03 W
Itaparica, Ilha de I 255 13.00 S 38.42 W
Itapaya 248 17.34 S 66.21 W
Itapé 255 14.54 S 39.26 W
Itapebi 255 15.56 S 39.32 W
Itapecerica 255 20.28 S 45.07 W
Itapecerica da Serra 256 23.43 S 46.50 W
Itapecerica da Serra □[7] 287b 23.44 S 46.52 W
Itapechinga 256 22.58 S 46.35 W
Itapecuru ≃ 250 2.52 S 44.12 W
Itapecuru-Mirim 250 3.24 S 44.20 W
Itapemirim 255 21.01 S 40.50 W
Itapera 250 2.32 S 43.47 W
Itaperina, Pointe › 157b 24.59 S 47.06 E
Itaperuna 255 21.12 S 41.54 W
Itapeteiú 256 22.54 S 42.47 W
Itapetim 250 7.22 S 37.11 W
Itapetinga 255 15.15 S 40.15 W
Itapetininga 255 23.36 S 48.03 W
Itapetininga ≃ 255 23.35 S 48.27 W
Itapeva, Bra. 255 23.58 S 48.52 W
Itapeva, Bra. 256 22.46 S 46.13 W
Itapevi 256 23.33 S 46.56 W
Itapevi □[7] 287b 23.31 S 46.55 W
Itapicuru 250 11.19 S 38.15 W
Itapicuru ≃ 250 11.47 S 37.32 W
Itapipoca 250 3.30 S 39.35 W
Itapira 256 22.26 S 46.50 W
Itapiranga, Bra. 250 2.45 S 58.01 W
Itapiranga, Bra. 252 27.08 S 53.43 W
Itapirapuã 255 15.52 S 50.36 W
Itapitanga 255 14.26 S 39.34 W
Itapiúna 250 4.33 S 38.57 W
Itápolis 255 21.35 S 48.46 W
Itaporã 255 22.01 S 54.54 W
Itaporã de Goiás 250 8.02 S 48.39 W
Itaporanga, Bra. 250 7.18 S 38.10 W
Itaporanga, Bra. 255 23.42 S 49.29 W
Itaporanga d'Ajuda 250 10.59 S 37.18 W
Itapúa □[5] 252 26.50 S 55.50 W
Itapuranga 255 15.35 S 49.59 W
Itaquaciara 287b 23.47 S 46.51 W
Itaquaquecetuba 256 23.29 S 46.21 W
Itaquaquecetuba □[7] 287b 23.28 S 46.20 W
Itaquara 255 13.27 S 39.57 W
Itaquari 255 20.20 S 40.22 W
Itaquera ◆[8] 256 23.32 S 46.27 W
Itaquera, Ribeirão ≃ 287b 23.28 S 46.26 W
Itaqui 252 29.08 S 56.33 W
Itaqui, Serra do ʌ 287b 23.28 S 46.55 W
Itaquyry 252 24.56 S 55.13 W
Itarantim 255 15.39 S 40.03 W
Itararé 255 24.07 S 49.20 W
Itararé ≃ 252 23.10 S 49.42 W
Itārsi 124 22.37 N 77.45 E
Itarumã 255 18.42 S 51.25 W
Itasca, Il., U.S. 278 41.58 N 88.00 W
Itasca, Tx., U.S. 222 32.09 N 97.08 W
Itasca, Lake ⊜ 198 47.11 N 95.12 W
Itasca State Park ♦ 198 47.18 N 95.18 W
Itatá ≃, Bra. 250 3.28 S 51.57 W
Itata ≃, Chile 252 36.23 S 72.52 W
Itatí 252 27.16 S 58.15 W
Itatiaia 256 22.30 S 44.34 W
Itatiaia, Parque Nacional do ♦ 256 22.28 S 44.37 W
Itatiba 256 23.00 S 46.51 W
Itatinga 255 23.07 S 48.36 W
Itatira 250 4.30 S 39.37 W
Itatka 86 56.49 N 85.37 E
Itatolo 273b 4.09 S 15.15 E
Itatskij 86 56.04 N 89.05 E
Itatupã 250 0.37 S 51.12 W
Itaú 250 5.50 S 37.59 W
Itauaiuri, Serra ʌ[2] 250 1.47 S 54.06 W
Itauçu 255 16.13 S 49.37 W
Itaueira 250 7.36 S 43.02 W
Itaueiras ≃ 250 6.41 S 42.55 W
Itaúna 255 20.04 S 44.34 W
Itaúna, Morro do ʌ[2] 287a 22.46 S 43.02 W
Itazuke-kūkō ⊠ 96 33.35 N 130.28 E
Itbayat Island I 108 20.46 N 121.50 E
Ité ≃ 246 7.00 N 74.15 W
Itéa 38 38.26 N 22.24 E
Iténez (Guaporé) ≃ 248 11.54 S 65.01 W
Ith ʌ 52 52.05 N 9.35 E
Ithaca, Mi., U.S. 190 43.17 N 84.36 W
Ithaca, N.Y., U.S. 210 42.26 N 76.29 W
Itháki 38 38.23 N 20.42 E
Itháki I 38 38.24 N 20.42 E
Ithan Creek ≃ 285 40.00 N 75.21 W
Ithnayn 142 30.41 N 32.21 E
Itigi 154 5.42 S 34.29 E
Itikawa → Ichikawa 94 35.44 N 139.55 E
Itimādpur 124 27.15 N 78.12 E
Itimbiri ≃ 152 2.02 N 22.44 E
Itinga 255 16.36 S 41.47 W
Itinga ≃ 255 16.35 S 41.45 W
Itinomiya → Ichinomiya 94 35.18 N 136.48 E
Itipo 152 0.50 S 18.35 E
Itiquira 255 17.12 S 54.07 W
Itiquira ≃ 248 17.18 S 56.44 W
Itirapina 255 22.15 S 47.49 W
Itire 273a 6.31 N 3.21 E
Itiruçu 255 13.31 S 40.09 W
Itiúba 250 10.43 S 39.51 W
Itkillik ≃ 180 70.08 N 150.57 W
Itlar' 82 56.51 N 39.17 E
Itlīdim 142 27.52 N 30.48 E
Itmīdah 142 30.46 N 31.20 E
Itmuryn, ozero ⊜ 80 49.30 N 52.22 E
Itō 94 34.58 N 139.05 E
Itobi 256 21.44 S 46.58 W
Itobo 154 4.10 S 33.01 E
Itóca, Ilha de I 287a 22.46 S 43.04 W
Itoculo 154 14.42 S 40.18 E
Itoigawa 94 37.02 N 137.51 E
Itoko 152 1.00 S 21.45 E
Itomamo, Lac ⊜ 186 49.11 N 70.28 W
Itoman 174m 26.08 N 127.40 E
Iton ≃ 50 49.09 N 1.12 E
Itonamas ≃ 248 12.28 S 64.24 W
Itororó 255 15.07 S 40.06 W
Itri 66 41.17 N 13.32 E
Itsā 142 29.15 N 30.48 E
Itsukaichi, Nihon 94 35.44 N 139.13 E
Itsukaichi, Nihon 96 34.24 N 132.22 E
Itsuki 92 32.24 N 130.50 E
Itsuku-shima I 96 34.16 N 132.19 E
Itsuwa 92 32.30 N 130.10 E
Itta Bena 194 33.29 N 90.19 W
Ittel, Oued V 148 34.19 N 6.01 E
Itter ≃ 263 51.09 N 6.52 E
Ittersum 52 52.28 N 6.07 E
Itteville 261 48.31 N 2.21 E
Ittiḥād al-Imārāt al-ʿArabīyah → United Arab Emirates □[1] 128 24.00 N 54.00 E
Ittiri 71 40.36 N 8.34 E
Itu 255 23.16 S 47.19 W
Itu ≃ 252 29.25 S 55.51 W
Ituaçu 255 13.49 S 41.18 W
Ituango 246 7.04 N 75.45 W
Ituberá 255 13.44 S 39.09 W
Itucumã ≃ 248 6.59 S 69.48 W
Itueta 255 19.23 S 41.11 W
Ituí 256 21.32 S 42.55 W
Ituí ≃ 246 4.38 S 70.19 W
Ituim ≃ 252 28.35 S 51.20 W
Ituiutaba 255 18.58 S 49.28 W
Itula 154 3.29 S 27.52 E
Itumbiara 255 18.25 S 49.13 W
Itumirim 256 21.19 S 44.53 W
Itum-Kale 84 42.43 N 45.35 E
Ituna 184 51.10 N 103.30 W
Itungi Port 154 9.35 S 33.56 E
Ituni 246 5.30 N 58.14 W
Itupeva 256 23.09 S 47.04 W
Itupeva ≃ 256 22.03 S 47.15 W
Itupiranga 250 5.09 S 49.20 W
Ituporanga 252 27.25 S 49.36 W
Iturama 255 19.44 S 50.11 W
Iturbe 252 26.01 S 56.30 W
Iturbide 232 19.40 N 89.37 W
Ituri ≃ 154 1.40 N 27.01 E
Iturup, ostrov (Etorofu-Tō) I 92a 44.54 N 147.30 E
Itutinga 256 21.18 S 44.40 W
Ituverava 255 20.20 S 47.47 W
Ituxi ≃ 248 7.18 S 64.51 W
Ituzaingó, Arg. 252 27.36 S 56.41 W
Ituzaingó, Arg. 258 34.40 S 58.40 W
Ituzaingó, Ur. 258 34.25 S 56.26 W
Itwa 124 27.20 N 82.42 E
Ityāy al-Bārūd 142 30.53 N 30.40 E
Ityopiya → Ethiopia □[1] 144 9.00 N 39.00 E
Itz ≃ 56 49.58 N 10.52 E
Itzehoe 52 53.55 N 9.31 E
Iuka, Il., U.S. 219 38.37 N 88.47 W
Iuka, Ms., U.S. 194 34.48 N 88.11 W
Iul'tin 180 67.50 N 178.48 W
Iul'tin, gora ʌ 180 67.50 N 178.25 W
Iúna 255 20.21 S 41.32 W
Iupeba 256 23.41 S 46.22 W
Iva 192 34.18 N 82.39 W
Ivacevići 76 52.43 N 25.21 E
Ivačovo 76 60.32 N 36.22 E
Ivahona 157b 23.27 S 46.10 E
Ivaí ≃ 255 23.18 S 53.42 W
Ivaiporã 252 24.15 S 51.45 W
Ivajlovgrad 38 41.32 N 26.08 E
Ivakoany, Massif de l' ⋏ 157b 23.50 S 46.25 E
Ivalo 24 68.42 N 27.30 E
Ivalojoki ≃ 24 68.43 N 27.36 E
Ivancevo 82 55.58 N 36.07 E
Ivančice 61 49.06 N 16.23 E
Ivancovo 82 56.39 N 35.50 E
Ivanec 36 46.13 N 16.08 E
Ivane-Puste 78 48.39 N 26.11 E
Ivangorod 76 59.24 N 28.10 E
Ivangrad 38 42.50 N 19.52 E
Ivanhoe, Austl. 166 32.54 S 144.18 E
Ivanhoe, Austl. 274b 37.46 S 145.03 E
Ivanhoe, Ca., U.S. 226 36.23 N 119.13 W
Ivanhoe, Il., U.S. 278 42.17 N 88.02 W
Ivanhoe, Mn., U.S. 198 44.27 N 96.14 W
Ivanhoe, Va., U.S. 192 36.50 N 80.58 W
Ivanhoe ≃ 190 48.40 N 82.11 W
Ivanhoe Lake ⊜ 190 48.05 N 82.38 W
Ivanica 78 50.47 N 32.36 E
Ivanić Grad 36 45.42 N 16.24 E
Ivaniči 78 50.39 N 24.20 E
Ivanišči, S.S.S.R. 76 56.36 N 35.13 E
Ivanišči, S.S.S.R. 80 55.46 N 40.26 E
Ivanjci 61 46.38 N 15.54 E
Ivanjica 38 43.35 N 20.14 E
Ivankov 78 50.56 N 29.54 E
Ivankovcy 89 49.06 N 134.28 E
Ivan'kovo 82 54.44 N 37.57 E
Ivan'kovskij 80 56.39 N 40.05 E
Ivan'kovskoje vodochranilišče ⊜[1] 82 56.37 N 36.32 E
Ivanof Bay 180 55.54 N 159.29 W
Ivano-Frankovo 78 49.55 N 23.43 E
Ivano-Frankovsk 78 48.55 N 24.43 E
Ivanopol' 78 49.52 N 28.12 E
Ivanopolje 83 48.28 N 37.46 E
Ivano-Šamševo 83 46.52 N 39.54 E
Ivanov 78 49.28 N 28.21 E
Ivanovka, S.S.S.R. 78 46.43 N 34.33 E
Ivanovka, S.S.S.R. 78 46.58 N 30.28 E
Ivanovka, S.S.S.R. 80 52.51 N 53.48 E
Ivanovka, S.S.S.R. 80 51.54 N 43.46 E
Ivanovka, S.S.S.R. 80 52.15 N 41.35 E
Ivanovka, S.S.S.R. 83 48.14 N 38.58 E
Ivanovka, S.S.S.R. 83 47.35 N 37.19 E
Ivanovka, S.S.S.R. 85 42.54 N 75.05 E
Ivanovka, S.S.S.R. 89 50.22 N 128.02 E
Ivanovka, S.S.S.R. 89 43.58 N 132.30 E
Ivanovo, S.S.S.R. 78 52.09 N 25.32 E
Ivanovo, S.S.S.R. 80 57.00 N 40.59 E
Ivanovo-Voznesensk → Ivanovo 80 57.00 N 40.59 E
Ivanovskaja, S.S.S.R. 24 60.48 N 55.52 E
Ivanovskaja, S.S.S.R. 78 45.17 N 38.29 E
Ivanovskoje, S.S.S.R. 76 59.17 N 28.49 E
Ivanovskoje, S.S.S.R. 78 51.37 N 34.57 E
Ivanovskoje, S.S.S.R. 82 55.05 N 37.50 E
Ivanovskoje, S.S.S.R. 82 54.55 N 36.50 E
Ivanovskoje, S.S.S.R. 82 55.52 N 36.55 E
Ivanovskoje, S.S.S.R. 82 56.23 N 37.07 E
Ivanovskoje, S.S.S.R. 265a 59.46 N 30.47 E
Ivan-Ozero 82 54.04 N 38.20 E
Ivan-Ozero, ozero ⊜ 82 54.07 N 38.17 E
Ivanpah Lake ⊜ 204 35.35 N 115.25 W
Ivantejevka, S.S.S.R. 80 52.16 N 49.07 E
Ivantejevka, S.S.S.R. 82 55.58 N 37.55 E
Ivantejevo 76 57.48 N 33.09 E
Ivato 157b 20.37 S 47.12 E
Ivatuva 255 23.37 S 52.13 W
Ivdel' 72 60.42 N 60.24 E
Ivenec 76 53.53 N 26.45 E
Iver 260 51.31 N 0.30 W
Iver Heath 260 51.32 N 0.31 W
Iverny 261 49.00 N 2.47 E
Ivigtut 176 61.12 N 48.10 W
Ivindo ≃ 152 0.09 S 12.09 E
Ivinghoe 42 51.50 N 0.37 W
Ivinheima ≃ 255 23.14 S 53.42 W
Ivje 76 53.56 N 25.46 E
Ivn'a 78 51.04 N 36.08 E
Ivnica 78 50.09 N 29.03 E
Ivo 248 20.27 S 63.26 W
Ivohibe 157b 22.29 S 46.52 E
Ivolginsk 88 51.45 N 107.14 E
Ivon ≃ 248 11.06 S 66.08 W
Ivondro 157b 24.47 S 46.52 E
Ivor 208 36.54 N 76.54 W
Ivorogbo 150 5.30 N 6.21 E
Ivory Coast (Côte d'Ivoire) □[1], Afr. 134 8.00 N 5.00 W
Ivory Coast (Côte d'Ivoire) □[1], Afr. 150 8.00 N 5.00 W
Ivory Coast ⊥[2] 150 5.10 N 5.00 W
Ivoryton 207 41.20 N 72.26 W
Ivösjön ⊜ 26 56.06 N 14.27 E
Ivot, S.S.S.R. 76 53.42 N 34.12 E
Ivot, S.S.S.R. 78 51.58 N 33.28 E
Ivotka ≃ 78 51.57 N 33.22 E
Ivrea 62 45.28 N 7.52 E
İvrindi 130 39.34 N 27.29 E
Ivry-la-Bataille 50 48.53 N 1.28 E
Ivry [-sur-Seine] 50 48.49 N 2.23 E
Ivujivik 176 62.24 N 77.55 W
Ivybridge 42 50.23 N 3.56 W
Ivy Hatch 260 51.16 N 0.16 E
Ivyland 285 40.12 N 75.04 W
Iwade 96 34.15 N 135.19 E
Iwafune, Nihon 94 36.19 N 139.40 E
Iwafune, Nihon 270 34.44 N 135.54 E
Iwagi 96 34.15 N 133.09 E
Iwai 94 36.03 N 139.54 E
Iwai-shima I 96 33.47 N 131.58 E
Iwaizumi 92 39.50 N 141.48 E
Iwaki (Taira) 94 37.03 N 140.55 E
Iwaki ≃ 92 41.01 N 140.22 E
Iwaki-san ʌ 92 40.39 N 140.18 E
Iwakuni 96 34.09 N 132.11 E
Iwakuni Marine Corps Air Station ■ 96 34.08 N 132.14 E
Iwakura 94 35.17 N 136.52 E
Iwama 94 36.18 N 140.16 E
Iwami, Nihon 96 34.53 N 132.26 E
Iwami, Nihon 96 35.35 N 134.20 E
Iwami-kōgen ⋏[1] 96 35.00 N 132.30 E
Iwami-kokubun-ji ʊ[1] 96 34.56 N 132.08 E
Iwamizawa 92a 43.12 N 141.46 E
Iwamura 94 35.22 N 137.26 E
Iwanai 92a 42.58 N 140.30 E
Iwanowo → Ivanovo 80 57.00 N 40.59 E
Iwanuma 92 38.06 N 140.52 E
Iwaoka ◆[8] 270 34.44 N 134.58 E
Iwase, Nihon 94 36.21 N 140.06 E
Iwase, Nihon 268 35.17 N 139.52 E
Iwata 94 34.42 N 137.48 E
Iwataki 96 35.34 N 135.09 E
Iwate □[5] 92 39.37 N 141.22 E
Iwate-san ʌ 92 39.51 N 141.00 E
Iwatsuki 94 35.57 N 139.42 E
Iwaya → Awaji, Nihon 96 34.35 N 135.01 E
Iwaya, Nihon 270 34.35 N 135.02 E
Iwayama 270 34.52 N 135.52 E
Iwazono 270 34.45 N 135.19 E
Iwo 150 7.38 N 4.11 E
Iwo Jima → Iō-jima I 174f 24.47 N 141.20 E
Iwŏn 98 40.19 N 128.39 E
Iwuy 50 50.14 N 3.19 E
Ixcán ≃ 236 16.07 N 91.05 W
Ixchiguán 236 15.12 N 91.53 W
Ixcuintepec ≃ 234 17.21 N 95.24 W
Ixelles 50 50.50 N 4.22 E
Ixhuatlán del Café 234 19.04 N 96.59 W
Ixiamas 248 13.45 S 68.09 W
Iximché ⊥ 236 14.44 N 90.59 W
Ixmiquilpan 234 20.29 N 99.14 W
Ixonia 216 43.09 N 88.36 W
Ixopo 158 30.08 S 30.00 E
Ixtacalco □[7] 286a 19.24 N 99.06 W
Ixtacalco ◆[8] 286a 19.23 N 99.07 W
Ixtacihuatl y Popocatépetl, Parques Nacionales ♦ 234 19.10 N 98.38 W
Ixtaltepec 234 16.30 N 95.03 W
Ixtapa, Punta › 234 17.39 N 101.40 W
Ixtapalapa □[7] 286a 19.21 N 99.04 W
Ixtapalapa ◆[8] 286a 19.21 N 99.06 W
Ixtapan de la Sal 234 18.50 N 99.41 W
Ixtlahuacán del Río 234 20.52 N 103.15 W
Ixtlán 234 20.11 N 102.24 W
Ixtlán de Juárez 234 17.20 N 96.29 W
Ixtlán del Río 234 21.02 N 104.22 W
Ixworth 42 52.18 N 0.50 E
Iya ≃ 96 33.58 N 133.47 E
ʿIyādh 144 14.59 N 46.51 E
ʿIyāl Bakhīt 140 13.25 N 28.41 E
Iyang, Taehan 98 34.53 N 127.01 E
Iyang → Yiyang, Zhg. 102 28.36 N 112.20 E
Iyang, Gili I 115a 6.59 S 114.10 E
Iyo 96 33.46 N 132.42 E
Iyo-mishima 96 33.58 N 133.33 E
Iyo-nada ⫪[2] 96 33.40 N 132.20 E
Iž ≃ 80 55.58 N 52.38 E
Izabal 236 15.24 N 89.08 W
Izabal □[5] 236 15.30 N 89.00 W
Izabal, Lago de ⊜ 236 15.30 N 89.10 W
ʿIzab al-Başāriṭah 142 31.23 N 31.47 E
Īzad Khvāst 128 31.31 N 52.07 E
Izalco 236 13.45 N 89.40 W
ʿIzam, Jabal al- ʌ 132 30.51 N 35.46 E
Izapa ⊥ 232 14.55 N 92.10 W
Iz'aslav 78 50.07 N 26.51 E
ʿIzbat Abū Şuql 132 31.09 N 33.49 E
Izberbaš 84 42.33 N 47.52 E
Izbica, Pol. 30 54.42 N 17.26 E
Izbica, Pol. 30 50.54 N 23.09 E
Izd'oškovo 76 55.08 N 33.37 E
Izegem 50 50.55 N 3.12 E
Īzeh 128 31.50 N 49.50 E
Izena-shima I 174m 26.56 N 127.56 E
Izendy 86 45.48 N 59.28 E
Izernore 58 46.13 N 5.33 E
Iževskoje 80 54.34 N 40.53 E
Izhevsk → Ustinov 80 56.51 N 53.14 E
Izkī 128 22.56 N 57.46 E
Ižma 24 65.02 N 53.55 E
Ižma ≃ 24 65.19 N 52.54 E
Izmail 78 45.21 N 28.50 E
Izmajlovo 80 53.43 N 47.14 E
Izmajlovo ◆[8] 265b 55.48 N 37.46 E
Izmajlovskij park ♦ 265b 55.46 N 37.47 E
Izmalkovo 76 52.41 N 37.58 E
İzmir 130 38.25 N 27.09 E
İzmir □[4] 130 38.30 N 27.15 E
İzmir Körfezi c 130 38.30 N 26.50 E
İzmit (Kocaeli) 130 40.46 N 29.55 E
İzmit Körfezi c 130 40.45 N 29.35 E
Ižmorskij 86 56.11 N 86.38 E
Iznajar, Embalse de ⊜[1] 34 37.15 N 4.30 W
Iznalloz 34 37.23 N 3.31 W
İznik 130 40.26 N 29.43 E
İznik Gölü ⊜ 130 40.26 N 29.30 E

Symbol	English	Deutsch	Español	Français	Português
≃	River	Fluss	Río	Rivière	Rio
≊	Canal	Kanal	Canal	Canal	Canal
ᒪ	Waterfall, Rapids	Wasserfall, Stromschnellen	Cascada, Rápidos	Chute d'eau, Rapides	Cascata, Rápidos
ʯ	Strait	Meeresstrasse	Estrecho	Détroit	Estreito
c	Bay, Gulf	Bucht, Golf	Bahía, Golfo	Baie, Golfe	Baía, Golfo
⊜	Lake, Lakes	See, Seen	Lago, Lagos	Lac, Lacs	Lago, Lagos
≌	Swamp	Sumpf	Pantano	Marais	Pântano
⍓	Ice Features, Glacier	Eis- und Gletscherformen	Accidentes Glaciales	Formes glaciaires	Acidentes glaciares
⫪	Other Hydrographic Features	Andere Hydrographische Objekte	Otros Elementos Hidrográficos	Autres données hydrographiques	Outros acidentes hidrográficos
✢	Submarine Features	Untermeerische Objekte	Accidentes Submarinos	Formes de relief sous-marin	Acidentes submarinos
□	Political Unit	Politische Einheit	Unidad Politica	Entité politique	Unidade política
ʊ	Cultural Institution	Kulturelle Institution	Institución Cultural	Institution culturelle	Institução cultural
⊥	Historical Site	Historische Stätte	Sitio Histórico	Site historique	Sitio histórico
♦	Recreational Site	Erholungs- und Ferienort	Sitio de Recreo	Centre de loisirs	Area de Lazer
⊠	Airport	Flughafen	Aeropuerto	Aéroport	Aeroporto
■	Military Installation	Militäranlage	Instalación Militar	Installation militaire	Instalação militar
◆	Miscellaneous	Verschiedenes	Misceláneo	Divers	Diversos

Iznoski 76 54.59 N 35.19 E
Izola 64 45.32 N 13.40 E
Izoplit 82 56.38 N 36.12 E
Izopo, Punta ≻ 236 15.48 N 87.23 W
Izora ≐ 265a 59.48 N 30.36 E
Izozog, Bañados de ⊞ 248 18.48 S 62.10 W
Izra' 132 32.51 N 36.15 E
Izsák 30 46.48 N 19.22 E
Iztaccíhuatl ʌ¹ 234 19.11 N 98.39 W
Iztapa 236 13.56 N 90.43 W
Izúcar de Matamoros 234 18.36 N 98.28 W
Izu-hantō ≻¹ 94 34.45 N 139.00 E
Izuhara 92 34.12 N 129.17 E
Iz'um 83 49.12 N 37.19 E
Izumi, Nihon 92 32.05 N 130.22 E
Izumi, Nihon 92 38.20 N 140.53 E
Izumi, Nihon 94 35.54 N 136.40 E
Izumi, Nihon 96 34.55 N 134.55 E
Izumi, Nihon 96 34.29 N 135.26 E
Izumi ◆⁸ 268 35.25 N 139.30 E
Izumi-ōtsu 96 34.30 N 135.24 E
Izumi-sano 96 34.25 N 135.19 E
Izumizaki 94 37.09 N 140.17 E
Izumo 96 35.22 N 132.46 E
Izumo ≐ 94 34.38 N 136.33 E
Izumo-kokubun-ji ⅴ¹ 96 35.26 N 133.06 E
Izumrud 86 57.05 N 61.23 E
Izu-nagaoka 94 35.02 N 138.56 E
Izushi 96 35.28 N 134.52 E
Izu-shotō II 6 32.00 N 140.00 E
Izu Trench ◆¹ 6 31.00 N 142.00 E
Izuwara 270 34.53 N 135.32 E
Izvarino 83 48.17 N 39.52 E
Izvestij CIK, ostrova II 74 75.55 N 82.30 E
Izvestkovyj 89 48.59 N 131.33 E
Izynžul' 86 52.24 N 90.13 E

J

Ja'ār, Birkat al- ⊜ 142 30.28 N 30.10 E
Jääsjärvi ⊜ 26 61.36 N 26.07 E
Jaba, Ityo. 144 6.17 N 35.12 E
Jaba, Pap. N. Gui. 175e 6.32 S 155.12 E
Jabā, Sūrīy. 132 33.10 N 35.56 E
Jabal, Bahr al- → Mountain Nile ≐ 136 9.30 N 30.30 E
Jabal Abyad Plateau ʌ¹ 140 19.00 N 29.00 E
Jabal al-Awliyā' 140 15.14 N 32.30 E
Jabal al-Awliyā', Khazzān (White Nile Dam) ◆⁶ 140 15.14 N 32.29 E
Jabal an-Nūr 142 28.57 N 31.02 E
Jabal Aṭ-Ṭayr 142 28.14 N 30.45 E
Jabal Dūd 140 13.25 N 33.09 E
Jabal Lubnān □⁴ 132 33.50 N 35.40 E
Jabalón ≐ 34 38.53 N 4.05 W
Jabal Os Sarāj 120 35.07 N 69.14 E
Jabalpur 124 23.10 N 79.57 E
Jabal Qerri 140 16.15 N 32.48 E
Jabal 'Uwaybid 142 30.09 N 32.12 E
Jabālyah 132 31.32 N 34.29 E
Jabal Zuqar, Jazīrat I 144 14.00 N 42.45 E
Jabbān, Arḍ al- ◆¹ 132 32.08 N 36.35 E
Jabbeke 50 51.11 N 3.05 E
Jabbi 123 33.08 N 72.38 E
Jabbūl, Sabkhat al- ⊜ 130 36.03 N 37.39 E
Jabel 54 53.32 N 12.32 E
Jabi 114 2.32 N 102.48 E
Jabjabah, Wādī ⋁ 140 22.37 N 33.17 E
Jablah 130 35.21 N 35.55 E
Jablanac 36 44.42 N 14.54 E
Jablanica 36 43.39 N 17.45 E
Jablanica ≐ 38 43.07 N 21.57 E
Jablaničko Jezero ⊜¹ 36 43.40 N 17.50 E
Jablines 261 48.55 N 2.46 E
Jabločnoje 78 50.18 N 35.14 E
Jabločnyj 89 47.10 N 142.04 E
Jablonec nad Nisou 30 50.44 N 15.10 E
Jablonica 30 48.37 N 17.25 E
Jabłonka 30 49.29 N 19.41 E
Jablonné v Podještědí 54 50.48 N 14.47 E
Jablonoj → Jablonovyj chrebet ʌ 88 53.30 N 115.00 E
Jablonov 78 48.24 N 24.57 E
Jablonovo 88 51.51 N 112.49 E
Jablonovyj chrebet ʌ 88 53.30 N 115.00 E
Jabłonowo 30 53.24 N 19.09 E
Jablonowo-Gebirge → Jablonovyj chrebet ʌ 88 53.30 N 115.00 E
Jablunkov 30 49.35 N 18.47 E
Jaboatão 250 8.07 S 35.01 W
Jaboncillos 232 28.57 N 102.39 W
Jaboncillos Creek ≐ 196 27.23 N 97.45 W
Jabonga 116 9.20 N 125.32 E
Jaborandi 255 20.40 S 48.25 W
Jabori 123 34.36 N 73.16 E
Jaboticabal 255 21.16 S 48.19 W
Jabrat Sa'īd ⊽⁴ 140 16.06 N 31.50 E
Jabrīn ⊽⁴ 118 23.17 N 48.58 E
Jabron ≐ 62 44.33 N 4.45 E
Jabron, Torrent le ≐ 62 44.09 N 5.57 E
Jabung 115a 5.29 S 105.40 E
Jabung, Tanjung ≻ 112 1.01 S 104.22 E
Jaca 34 42.34 N 0.33 W
Jacala de Ledesma 234 21.01 N 99.11 W
Jacaleapa 236 14.00 N 86.40 W
Jacaltenango 236 15.40 N 91.44 W
Jacana 274b 37.42 S 144.55 E
Jacaraci 255 14.51 S 42.26 W
Jacaré 256 21.20 S 42.51 W
Jacaré ≐, Bra. 248 5.49 S 63.35 W
Jacaré ≐, Bra. 250 10.03 S 42.13 W
Jacaré ≐, Bra. 255 13.50 S 40.42 W
Jacaré ≐, Bra. 287a 22.56 S 43.04 W
Jacareí 256 23.19 S 45.58 W
Jacareí ≐ 256 22.54 S 46.28 W
Jacarepaguá ◆⁸ 256 22.56 S 43.20 W
Jacarepaguá, Lagoa de ⊂ 256 22.59 S 43.24 W
Jacarèzinho 255 23.09 S 49.59 W
Jaceel ⋁ 144 10.25 N 51.01 E
Jaceruba 256 22.35 S 43.34 W
Jáchal ≐ 252 30.44 S 68.08 W
Jachenau 64 47.36 N 11.25 E
Jachniki 78 50.26 N 33.10 E
Jachroma 82 56.17 N 37.30 E
Jachroma ≐ 82 56.31 N 37.07 E
Jáchymov 54 50.20 N 12.55 E
Jaciara 255 15.59 S 54.57 W
Jacinto 255 16.10 S 40.17 W
Jacinto Aráuz 252 38.04 S 63.26 W
Jacinto City 222 29.46 N 95.14 W
Jacinto Machado 252 29.00 S 49.46 W
Jaci Paraná 248 9.15 S 64.23 W
Jaciparaná ≐ 248 9.22 S 64.22 W
Jackass Creek ≐ 226 37.22 N 119.23 W
Jack Creek ≐ 202 42.59 N 121.32 W
Jackfish Lake ⊜ 184 53.05 N 108.25 W
Jackhead Harbour 184 51.52 N 97.16 W
Jack Lake ⊜ 212 44.42 N 78.03 W
Jack London State Historical Park ◆ 226 38.21 N 122.32 W
Jackman 188 45.38 N 70.15 W
Jackman Creek ≐ 224 48.30 N 121.43 W
Jack Mountain ʌ, Mt., U.S. 202 46.21 N 112.18 W
Jack Mountain ʌ, Wa., U.S. 224 48.47 N 120.57 W
Jackpot 204 41.59 N 114.40 W
Jacksboro, Tn., U.S. 192 36.19 N 84.11 W
Jacksboro, Tx., U.S. 196 33.13 N 98.09 W
Jacks Creek ≐ 208 40.35 N 77.33 W
Jacks Fork ≐ 194 37.12 N 91.17 W
Jacks Island I 279b 40.37 N 79.43 W
Jacks Mountain ʌ 210 40.45 N 77.30 W
Jackson, Al., U.S. 194 31.30 N 87.53 W
Jackson, Ca., U.S. 226 38.20 N 120.46 W
Jackson, Ga., U.S. 192 33.17 N 83.57 W
Jackson, Ky., U.S. 192 37.33 N 83.23 W
Jackson, La., U.S. 194 30.50 N 91.13 W
Jackson, Mi., U.S. 216 42.14 N 84.24 W
Jackson, Mn., U.S. 198 43.37 N 94.59 W
Jackson, Ms., U.S. 194 32.17 N 90.11 W
Jackson, Mo., U.S. 194 37.22 N 89.39 W
Jackson, N.J., U.S. 208 40.08 N 74.19 W
Jackson, N.C., U.S. 192 36.23 N 77.25 W
Jackson, Oh., U.S. 188 39.03 N 82.38 W
Jackson, Pa., U.S. 210 41.50 N 75.36 W
Jackson, S.C., U.S. 192 33.19 N 81.47 W
Jackson, Tn., U.S. 194 35.36 N 88.48 W
Jackson, Wy., U.S. 200 43.28 N 110.45 W
Jackson □⁶, In., U.S. 218 38.53 N 86.03 W
Jackson □⁶, Mi., U.S. 216 42.15 N 84.24 W
Jackson □⁶, Tx., U.S. 222 29.00 N 96.35 W
Jackson ≐ 188 37.47 N 79.46 W
Jackson, Cape ≻ 172 41.00 S 174.18 E
Jackson, Lake ⊜, Fl., U.S. 192 30.30 N 84.17 W
Jackson, Lake ⊜, Fl., U.S. 220 27.29 N 81.28 W
Jackson, Lake ⊜, Fl., U.S. 220 27.55 N 81.10 W
Jackson, Mount ʌ, Ant. 9 71.23 S 63.22 W
Jackson, Mount ʌ, Austl. 162 30.15 S 119.16 E
Jackson, Port ⊂ 170 33.50 S 151.16 E
Jackson Bay ⊂ 172 43.58 S 168.42 E
Jackson Brook ≐ 276 40.53 N 74.34 W
Jackson Butte ʌ 226 38.20 N 120.43 W
Jackson Center, Oh., U.S. 216 40.27 N 84.02 W
Jackson Center, Pa., U.S. 214 41.16 N 80.09 W
Jackson Creek ≐, Can. 184 49.18 N 100.50 W
Jackson Creek ≐, Ca., U.S. 226 38.18 N 121.01 W
Jackson Creek ≐, Il., U.S. 216 41.26 N 88.10 W
Jackson Heights ◆⁸ 276 40.45 N 73.53 W
Jackson Lake ⊜ 202 43.55 N 110.40 W
Jackson Lake ⊜¹ 192 33.22 N 83.52 W
Jackson Meadows Reservoir ⊜¹ 226 39.29 N 120.32 W
Jackson Mountain ʌ 188 44.46 N 70.32 W
Jackson Park ◆, On., Can. 281 42.17 N 83.01 W
Jackson Park ◆, Il., U.S. 278 41.47 N 87.35 W
Jackson's Arm 186 49.52 N 56.47 W
Jacksons Creek ≐ 169 37.40 S 144.48 E
Jacksons Head ≻ 172 43.58 S 168.37 E
Jacksonville, Al., U.S. 194 33.48 N 85.45 W
Jacksonville, Ar., U.S. 194 34.51 N 92.06 W
Jacksonville, Fl., U.S. 192 30.19 N 81.39 W
Jacksonville, Il., U.S. 219 39.44 N 90.13 W
Jacksonville, N.J., U.S. 285 40.03 N 74.46 W
Jacksonville, N.Y., U.S. 210 42.31 N 76.37 W
Jacksonville, N.C., U.S. 192 34.45 N 77.25 W
Jacksonville, Or., U.S. 202 42.18 N 122.57 W
Jacksonville, Tx., U.S. 222 31.57 N 95.16 W
Jacksonville, Vt., U.S. 207 42.47 N 72.49 W
Jacksonville, Lake ⊜¹ 222 31.55 N 95.17 W
Jacksonville Beach 192 30.17 N 81.23 W
Jacksonville Naval Air Station ■ 192 30.14 N 81.41 W
Jacks Reef 210 43.06 N 76.25 W
Jacks Run ≐ 279b 40.13 N 79.35 W
Jacktown Acres 279b 40.19 N 79.45 W
Jacmel 238 18.14 N 72.32 W
Jacob, Morne ʌ 240e 14.46 N 61.06 W
Jacobābād 120 28.17 N 68.26 E
Jacobina 250 11.11 S 40.31 W
Jacob Island I 212 44.28 N 78.28 W
Jacob Riis Park ◆ 276 40.34 N 73.52 W
Jacobs Creek ≐ 214 40.07 N 79.44 W
Jacobsdal 158 29.13 S 24.41 E
Jacobus 208 39.53 N 76.43 W
Jacona de Plancarte 234 19.57 N 102.16 W
Jacques, Lac à ⊜ 180 66.10 N 127.25 W
Jacques-Cartier ≐ 275a 45.31 N 73.29 W
Jacques-Cartier ≐ 206 46.40 N 71.45 W
Jacques-Cartier, Détroit de ⊔ 186 50.00 N 63.30 W
Jacques-Cartier, Mont ʌ 186 48.59 N 65.57 W
Jacques-Cartier, Pont ◆⁵ 275a 45.31 N 73.32 W
Jacquet River 186 47.55 N 66.00 W
Jacqueville 150 5.12 N 4.25 W
Jacquinot Bay ⊂ 164 5.35 S 151.30 E
Jacu ≐, Bra. 250 6.13 S 35.09 W
Jacú ≐, Bra. 256 23.05 S 45.08 W
Jacu, Rio do ≐ 287b 23.29 S 46.27 W
Jacuba 255 18.25 S 52.48 W
Jacuecanga 256 23.01 S 44.13 W
Jacuí ≐ 252 30.02 S 51.15 W
Jacuípe 255 12.29 S 38.38 W
Jacuípe ≐ 255 12.30 S 39.05 W
Jacumba 204 32.37 N 116.11 W
Jacundá 250 4.33 S 49.28 W
Jacundá ≐ 250 1.57 S 50.26 W
Jacupiranga 252 24.42 S 48.00 W
Jacuriaí ≐ 250 10.57 S 39.35 W
Jacutinga 256 22.17 S 46.37 W
Jada 146 8.46 N 12.09 E
Jada'ah, Jabal ʌ² 142 29.58 N 32.46 E
Jaddi, Rās ≻ 128 25.14 N 63.31 E
Jade 52 53.20 N 8.14 E
Jade Buddha, Temple of the ⅴ¹ 269b 31.14 N 121.26 E
Jadebusen ⊂ 52 53.30 N 8.10 E
Jäder 40 59.25 N 16.41 E
Jäderfors 40 60.41 N 16.49 E
Jade Run ≐ 285 39.56 N 74.43 W
Jadīdah 128 34.01 N 42.28 E
Jadito Wash ⋁ 200 35.22 N 110.50 W
J.A.D. Jensens Nunatakker ʌ 176 62.45 N 48.00 W
Jadotville → Likasi 154 10.59 S 26.44 E
Jadraque 34 40.55 N 2.55 W
Jadrin 80 55.56 N 46.12 E
Jadromino 82 55.57 N 36.36 E
Jādū 146 31.57 N 12.01 E
Jaduty 78 51.22 N 32.19 E
Jægerspris 41 55.51 N 11.59 E
Jaeger Summit ʌ 154 2.52 S 35.47 E
Jaén, Esp. 34 37.46 N 3.47 W
Jaén, Perú 248 5.42 S 78.47 W
Jæren ◆¹ 26 58.45 N 5.45 E
Jāfarābād, India 120 20.52 N 71.22 E
Ja'farābād, Īrān 128 37.26 N 56.16 E
Jāfarpur 126 22.29 N 89.06 E
Jāfarpur ◆⁸ 272a 28.40 N 77.01 E
Jaffa, Cape ≻ 166 36.58 S 139.40 E
Jaffa, Tel Aviv- → Tel Aviv-Yafo 132 32.04 N 34.46 E
Jaffna 122 9.40 N 80.00 E
Jaffna Lagoon ⊂ 122 9.35 N 80.15 E
Jaffrey 207 42.48 N 72.01 W
Jafr, Qā' al- ⊥⁷ 132 30.17 N 36.20 E
Jagādhri 124 30.10 N 77.18 E
Jägala ≐ 76 59.29 N 25.09 E
Jagalūr 122 14.32 N 76.21 E
Jāgan 120 28.05 N 68.30 E
Jagannāthganj Ghāt 124 24.45 N 89.49 E
Jagannāthpūr 272b 22.43 N 88.19 E
Jagati 126 23.54 N 89.06 E
Jagatnagar 272b 22.47 N 88.13 E
Jagatpur ◆⁸ 272a 28.44 N 77.14 E
Jagatsingpur 120 20.16 N 86.10 E
Jagdalpur 122 19.04 N 82.02 E
Jagdīspur 124 25.29 N 84.25 E
Jagel 41 54.27 N 9.32 E
Jagel'urta, gora ʌ² 24 67.33 N 38.02 E
Jagenbach 61 48.38 N 15.02 E
Jägerndorf → Krnov 30 50.05 N 17.41 E
Jagersfontein 158 29.44 S 25.29 E
Jaggayyapeta 122 16.54 N 80.06 E
Jagged Mountain ʌ 180 58.38 N 162.02 W
Jagnob ≐ 85 39.15 N 68.35 E
Jagny-sous-Bois 261 49.05 N 2.27 E
Jagodnoje, S.S.S.R. 74 62.33 N 149.40 E
Jagodnoje, S.S.S.R. 80 53.36 N 49.04 E
Jagodnyj 86 59.44 N 65.04 E
Jagorlyckij zaliv ⊂ 78 46.24 N 31.50 E
Jagotin 78 50.17 N 31.46 E
Jagraon 123 30.47 N 75.29 E
Jagst ≐ 56 49.14 N 9.11 E
Jagsthausen 56 49.19 N 9.28 E
Jagstzell 56 49.02 N 10.05 E
Jagtiāl 122 18.48 N 78.56 E
Jaguaquara 255 13.32 S 39.58 W
Jaguarão 252 32.34 S 53.23 W
Jaguarão (Yaguarón) ≐ 252 32.39 S 53.12 W
Jaguarari 250 10.16 S 40.12 W
Jaguaretama 250 5.37 S 38.46 W
Jaguari 252 29.30 S 54.41 W
Jaguari ≐, Bra. 256 22.41 S 47.17 W
Jaguari ≐, Bra. 256 23.10 S 45.55 W
Jaguariaíva 252 24.15 S 49.42 W
Jaguaribara 250 5.40 S 38.37 W
Jaguaribe 250 5.53 S 38.37 W
Jaguaribe ≐ 250 4.25 S 37.45 W
Jaguari-Mirim ≐ 256 21.59 S 47.17 W
Jaguaripe 255 13.06 S 38.53 W
Jaguariúna 256 22.41 S 46.59 W
Jaguaruana 250 4.50 S 37.47 W
Jaguaruna 252 28.36 S 49.02 W
Jagüé 252 28.38 S 68.24 W
Jagüey Grande 240p 22.32 N 81.08 W
Jāguli 126 22.56 N 88.32 E
Jāguli 272b 22.44 N 88.32 E
Jagungal, Mount ʌ 171b 36.09 S 148.23 E
Jagunovskij 86 55.17 N 85.59 E
Jahānābād, India 124 25.13 N 84.59 E
Jahānābād, Pāk. 123 32.11 N 72.29 E
Jahāngīra 123 33.58 N 72.13 E
Jahāngīrābād 124 28.25 N 78.06 E
Jahangirpur ◆⁸ 272a 28.44 N 77.13 E
Jahannam, Qārat ʌ² 142 29.19 N 30.09 E
Jahnsdorf 54 50.44 N 12.51 E
Jahrom 128 28.31 N 53.33 E
Jahú → Jaú 255 22.18 S 48.33 W
Jai 250 3.58 N 54.49 W
Jaicós 250 7.21 S 41.08 W
Jaidak 120 31.58 N 66.43 E
Jaihti ≐ 126 24.08 N 86.48 E
Jaijōn 123 31.21 N 76.09 E
Jailolo 108 1.05 N 127.30 E
Jaimanitas ≐ 286b 23.05 N 82.29 W
Jainca 102 35.59 N 102.02 E
Jainti 124 26.42 N 89.36 E
Jaintiāpur 120 25.08 N 92.07 E
Jaipur 120 26.55 N 75.49 E
Jaipur □⁵ 124 27.00 N 76.10 E
Jāis 124 26.15 N 81.32 E
Jaisalmer 120 26.55 N 70.54 E
Jaito 123 30.28 N 74.53 E
Jaja 86 56.12 N 86.26 E
Jaja ≐ 86 56.58 N 86.23 E
Jājarkot 124 28.42 N 82.12 E
Jājarm 128 36.58 N 56.27 E
Jajce 36 44.21 N 17.16 E
Jajichi 174m 26.47 N 128.13 E
Jajjha 123 28.45 N 70.34 E
Jajl'u 86 51.48 N 87.36 E
Jajpan 85 40.23 N 70.48 E
Jājpur 120 20.51 N 86.20 E
Jajsan 86 50.51 N 56.14 E
Jajva 86 59.20 N 57.15 E
Jajva ≐ 86 59.13 N 56.40 E
Ják 61 47.08 N 16.35 E
Jakarta, Indon. 115a 6.10 S 106.48 E
Jakarta, Indon. 269e 6.10 S 106.48 E
Jakarta, Teluk ⊂ 115a 6.05 S 106.48 E
Jakarta Kota Station ◆⁵ 269e 6.08 S 106.49 E
Jakarta Raya □⁴ 115a 6.10 S 106.45 E
Jakdūl ⊜ 140 17.39 N 32.59 E
Jake Creek Mountain ʌ 204 41.13 N 116.54 W
Jakenan 115a 6.45 S 111.11 E
Jākhal 123 29.48 N 75.50 E
Jakhāu 120 23.13 N 68.43 E
Jakkonen 24 66.33 N 29.52 E
Jakobsberg 40 59.26 N 17.50 E
Jakobsdalsberget ʌ² 40 58.41 N 16.07 E
Jakobshagen → Dobrzany 30 53.22 N 15.25 E
Jakobshavn 176 69.13 N 51.06 W
Jakobstad (Pietarsaari) 26 63.40 N 22.42 E
Jakovleviči 76 54.20 N 30.31 E
Jakovlevka 89 44.26 N 133.28 E
Jakovlevo, S.S.S.R. 78 50.51 N 36.27 E
Jakovlevo, S.S.S.R. 82 54.48 N 37.26 E
Jakša 24 61.48 N 56.49 E
Jakšanga 80 58.23 N 45.56 E
Jakšur-Bodja 80 57.11 N 53.09 E
Jakupica ʌ 38 41.43 N 21.26 E
Jakutsk 74 62.00 N 129.40 E
Jakutskaja Avtonomnaja Sovetskaja Socialističeskaja Respublika □³ 88 58.00 N 121.00 E
Jal 196 32.06 N 103.11 W
Jala 234 21.05 N 104.26 W
Jalacingo 234 19.48 N 97.18 W
Jalaid Qi 89 46.40 N 122.55 E
Jalājil 128 25.41 N 45.28 E
Jalālābād, Afg. 120 34.26 N 70.28 E
Jalālābād, India 123 30.37 N 74.15 E
Jalālābād, India 124 27.43 N 79.40 E
Jalāl al-Bahrīyah, Jabal ʌ¹ 142 29.20 N 32.00 E
Jalālat al-Qiblīyah, Jabal ʌ¹ 142 28.42 N 32.22 E
Jalaliyeh Race Track ◆ 267d 35.43 N 51.24 E
Jalālpur, India 124 26.19 N 82.44 E
Jalālpur, Pāk. 123 32.38 N 74.12 E
Jalālpur Pīrwāla 123 29.30 N 71.13 E
Jalandhar 123 31.19 N 75.34 E
Jalan' 86 58.21 N 60.51 E
Jalán ≐ 236 14.39 N 86.12 W
Jalan Besar Stadium ◆ 271c 1.18 N 103.52 E
Jalangi 126 24.08 N 88.42 E
Jalangi ≐ 126 23.23 N 88.22 E
Jalan Kayu 271c 1.24 N 103.52 E
Jalapa, Guat. 236 14.38 N 89.59 W
Jalapa, Méx. 234 17.43 N 92.49 W
Jalapa, Nic. 236 13.55 N 86.08 W
Jalapa □⁵ 236 14.35 N 89.55 W
Jalapa de Díaz 234 18.04 N 96.32 W
Jalapa Enríquez 234 19.32 N 96.55 W
Jalasjärvi 26 62.30 N 22.45 E
Jalaud ≐ 116 10.45 N 122.40 E
Jālaun 124 26.09 N 79.21 E
Jālaun □⁵ 124 26.00 N 79.30 E
Jal'čiki 80 55.09 N 48.01 E
Jalcocotán 234 21.28 N 105.07 W
Jalcomulco ≐ 234 19.20 N 96.33 W
Jalda 126 21.56 N 87.30 E
Jalea de Catalán 234 17.26 N 99.51 W
Jālesar 124 27.29 N 78.19 E
Jaleshwar 124 26.38 N 85.48 E
Jāleswar 126 21.49 N 87.13 E
Jālgaon, India 122 21.01 N 75.34 E
Jālgaon, India 122 21.03 N 76.32 E
Jal'gelevo 265a 59.44 N 29.57 E
Jalhay 56 50.34 N 5.58 E
Jalingo 146 8.53 N 11.22 E
Jālīrpār 126 23.13 N 89.58 E
Jalisco 234 21.27 N 104.54 W
Jalisco □³ 234 20.20 N 103.40 W
Jallas ≐ 34 42.54 N 9.08 W
Jallieu 62 45.35 N 5.16 E
Jālna 122 19.50 N 75.53 E
Jalón ≐ 34 41.47 N 1.04 W
Jālor 120 25.21 N 72.37 E
Jalostotitlán 234 21.12 N 102.28 W
Jalpa 234 21.38 N 102.58 W
Jalpa de Méndez 234 18.08 N 93.05 W
Jalpaiguri 124 26.31 N 88.44 E
Jalpaiguri □⁵ 124 26.40 N 89.00 E
Jalpan 234 21.14 N 99.29 W
Jalpug ≐ 78 45.41 N 28.35 E
Jalpug, ozero ⊜ 78 45.25 N 28.37 E
Jalta (Yalta), S.S.S.R. 78 44.30 N 34.10 E
Jalta, S.S.S.R. 83 46.58 N 37.16 E
Jaltenango de la Paz 234 15.55 N 92.43 W
Jaltepec ≐ 234 17.26 N 94.59 W
Jáltipan 234 17.58 N 94.42 W
Jaltocán 234 21.09 N 98.32 W
Jaltuškov 78 48.58 N 27.30 E
Jaluit I¹ 14 6.00 N 169.35 E
Jalutorovsk 86 56.40 N 66.18 E
Jam, S.S.S.R. 82 55.29 N 37.45 E
Jam, S.S.S.R. 85 40.07 N 68.11 E
Jama 83 48.52 N 38.06 E
Jamaame (Margherita) 144 0.04 N 42.45 E
Jamaare ≐ 146 12.06 N 10.14 E
Jamāibāti 272b 22.51 N 88.08 E
Jamaica 240p 20.12 N 75.09 W
Jamaica ◆⁸ 276 40.42 N 73.47 W
Jamaica □¹, N.A. 230 18.15 N 77.30 W
Jamaica □¹, N.A. 241q 18.15 N 77.30 W
Jamaica Bay ⊂ 210 40.36 N 73.51 W
Jamaica Channel ⊔ 238 18.00 N 75.30 W
Jamaica Plain ◆⁸ 283 42.19 N 71.06 W
Jamaika → Jamaica □¹ 241q 18.15 N 77.30 W
Jamaïque → Jamaica □¹ 241q 18.15 N 77.30 W
Jamal, poluostrov ≻¹ 74 70.00 N 70.00 E
Jam-Alin', chrebet ʌ 89 53.00 N 134.36 E
Jamāliyah ◆⁸ 273c 30.03 N 31.16 E
Jamalo-neneckij Nacional'nyj Okrug □⁸ 24 66.30 N 64.00 E
Jamālpur, Bngl. 124 24.55 N 89.56 E
Jamālpur, India 124 25.18 N 86.30 E
Jamālpurganj 126 23.04 N 87.59 E
Jamanari ≐ 246 2.58 S 68.53 W
Jamanchalinka 80 47.40 N 51.35 E
Jamantau, gora ʌ 86 54.15 N 58.06 E
Jamanxim ≐ 250 4.43 S 56.18 W
Jamapará 256 21.55 S 42.43 W
Jamari 248 8.27 S 63.30 W
Jamari, Lago ⊜ 250 1.26 S 56.35 W
Jamarovka 88 50.38 N 110.16 E
Jamašurma 80 55.58 N 49.36 E
Jamay 234 20.18 N 102.43 W
Jamba 152 13.50 S 15.30 E
Jāmbād 126 22.42 N 86.35 E
Jambeiro 256 23.16 S 45.41 W
Jambeiro, Serra do ʌ² 256 23.23 S 45.38 W
Jambelí, Canal de ⊔ 246 3.00 S 80.00 W
Jamberoo 170 34.39 S 150.47 E
Jambes 56 50.28 N 4.52 E
Jambi 112 1.36 S 103.37 E
Jambi □⁴ 112 1.30 S 103.00 E
Jambin 166 24.12 S 150.22 E
Jamboaye ≐ 114 5.16 N 97.26 E
Jambol 38 42.29 N 26.30 E
Jambol □⁴ 130 42.10 N 26.30 E
Jambongan, Pulau I 112 6.40 N 117.27 E
Jambuair, Tanjung ≻ 114 5.16 N 97.30 E
Jambusar 120 22.03 N 72.48 E
James ≐, Austl. 166 20.36 S 137.41 E
James ≐, Ab., Can. 182 51.55 N 114.34 W
James ≐, U.S. 198 42.52 N 97.18 W
James ≐, Mo., U.S. 194 36.45 N 93.30 W
James ≐, Va., U.S. 192 36.57 N 76.26 W
James, Isla I 254 44.57 S 74.07 W
James, Lake ⊜ 216 41.42 N 85.02 W
James, Lake ⊜¹ 192 35.45 N 81.55 W
Jamesābād 120 25.17 N 69.15 E
James Bay ⊂ 176 53.30 N 80.30 W
Jamesburg 208 40.21 N 74.26 W
James Bypass ≅ 226 36.41 N 120.16 W
James City, N.C., U.S. 192 35.05 N 77.02 W
James City, Pa., U.S. 214 41.37 N 78.50 W
James City □⁶ 208 37.17 N 76.48 W
James Craik 252 32.09 S 63.28 W
James Creek 214 40.23 N 78.10 W
James Gardens ◆ 275b 43.40 N 79.31 W
James Island, B.C., Can. 224 48.37 N 123.22 W
James Island, S.C., U.S. 192 32.44 N 79.57 W
James Island I 208 38.31 N 76.20 W
Jameson Raid Memorial ⊥ 273d 26.11 S 27.49 E
James Point ≻ 192 25.21 N 76.24 W
Jamesport 194 39.58 N 93.48 W
James Price Point ≻ 162 17.30 S 122.08 E
James Ranges ʌʌ 162 24.06 S 132.30 E
James River Bridge ◆⁵ 208 37.00 N 76.30 W
James Ross, Cape ≻ 176 74.40 N 114.25 W
James Ross Island I 9 64.15 S 57.45 W
James Ross Strait ⊔ 176 69.40 N 95.30 W
James Smith Indian Reserve ◆⁴ 184 53.08 N 104.52 W
Jamestown, Austl. 166 33.12 S 138.36 E
Jamestown, Ire. 48 53.55 N 8.02 W
Jamestown, S. Afr. 158 31.06 S 26.45 E
Jamestown, Ca., U.S. 226 37.57 N 120.25 W
Jamestown, Ks., U.S. 198 39.35 N 97.51 W
Jamestown, Ky., U.S. 194 36.59 N 85.03 W
Jamestown, Mi., U.S. 216 42.50 N 85.51 W
Jamestown, N.Y., U.S. 188 42.05 N 79.14 W
Jamestown, N.C., U.S. 192 35.59 N 79.56 W
Jamestown, N.D., U.S. 198 46.54 N 98.42 W
Jamestown, Oh., U.S. 218 39.39 N 83.44 W
Jamestown, Pa., U.S. 214 41.29 N 80.26 W
Jamestown, R.I., U.S. 207 41.29 N 71.22 W
Jamestown, Tn., U.S. 194 36.25 N 84.55 W
Jamestown ∴ 208 37.12 N 76.46 W
Jamestown Festival Park ◆ 208 37.14 N 76.48 W
Jamestown Island I 208 37.12 N 76.46 W

ENGLISH Name	Page	Lat.°′	Long.°′

Jamestown Reservoir ⊜¹ 198 47.15 N 98.40 W
Jamesville, N.Y., U.S. 210 42.59 N 76.04 W
Jamesville, Va., U.S. 208 37.30 N 75.55 W
Jamet, Lac ⊜ 206 46.34 N 74.30 W
Jametz 56 49.26 N 5.23 E
Jamieson ≐ 169 37.18 S 146.08 E
Jamiltepec 234 16.17 N 97.49 W
Jaminauá ≐ 248 9.20 S 70.59 W
Jaminsk 76 52.46 N 28.16 E
Jaminskij 80 50.21 N 42.14 E
Jāmira ≐ 126 21.45 N 87.02 E
Jamira ≐¹ 126 21.35 N 88.28 E
Jamison 208 40.16 N 75.05 W
Jamison City 210 41.18 N 76.22 W
Jamison Town 274a 33.46 S 150.41 E
Jam-Ižora 265a 59.42 N 30.36 E
Jamjodhpur 120 21.54 N 70.01 E
Jamkhandi 122 16.31 N 75.18 E
Jamki 86 59.33 N 66.47 E
Jamkino 82 55.55 N 38.24 E
Jamm 76 58.26 N 28.03 E
Jammalamadugu 122 14.50 N 78.24 E
Jammerbugten ⊂ 26 57.20 N 9.30 E
Jammerland Bugt ⊂ 41 55.35 N 11.05 E
Jammu 123 32.42 N 74.52 E
Jammu Airport ≋ 123 32.42 N 74.51 E
Jammu and Kashmir □² 120 34.00 N 76.00 E
Jāmnagar 120 22.28 N 70.04 E
Jamnotri 120 31.01 N 78.27 E
Jamoigne 56 49.42 N 5.25 E
Jamor ≐ 266c 38.42 N 9.15 W
Jampang-kulon 115a 7.16 S 106.37 E
Jampol', S.S.S.R. 78 48.16 N 28.17 E
Jampol', S.S.S.R. 78 49.58 N 26.14 E
Jampol', S.S.S.R. 78 51.57 N 33.46 E
Jampol', S.S.S.R. 83 48.56 N 37.58 E
Jāmpur, India 272b 22.56 N 88.12 E
Jāmpur, Pāk. 123 29.39 N 70.36 E
Jämsä 26 61.52 N 25.12 E
Jamsah 140 27.38 N 33.35 E
Jämsänkoski 26 61.55 N 25.11 E
Jamshedpur 126 22.48 N 86.11 E
Jamsk 74 59.35 N 154.10 E
Jamskaja Sloboda 82 55.29 N 36.01 E
Jāmtāra 126 23.57 N 86.48 E
Jämtland □⁹ 26 63.30 N 14.00 E
Jämtlands Län □⁶ 24 63.00 N 14.40 E
Jamuāni 126 21.57 N 86.14 E
Jamuga 82 56.24 N 36.40 E
Jamūī 124 24.55 N 86.13 E
Jamuna ≐ 124 23.51 N 89.45 E
Jamundí 246 3.15 N 76.32 W
Jamuria 126 23.44 N 87.02 E
Jāmurki 126 24.09 N 90.02 E
Jana ≐ 74 71.31 N 136.32 E
Janāi 272b 22.43 N 88.16 E
Janāj 142 31.00 N 30.46 E
Janajkino 80 50.43 N 51.06 E
Janas 266c 38.49 N 9.26 W
Janauacá, Lago ⊜ 246 3.28 S 60.17 W
Janaúba 255 15.48 S 43.19 W
Janaucu, Ilha I 250 0.30 N 50.10 W
Janaul 86 56.16 N 54.56 E
Jand 123 33.26 N 72.01 E
Janda, Laguna de la ⊜ 34 36.15 N 5.51 W
Jandaia 255 17.06 S 50.07 W
Jandaia do Sul 255 23.36 S 51.39 W
Jandaíra 250 11.34 S 37.47 W
Jandalī, Wādī al- ⋁ 142 30.05 N 31.52 E
Jandaq 128 34.02 N 54.26 E
Jandelsbrunn 60 48.44 N 13.42 E
Jandiāla 123 31.36 N 75.03 E
Jandiatuba ≐ 246 3.28 S 68.42 W
Jandira 256 23.31 S 46.54 W
Jandira □⁷ 287b 23.32 S 46.54 W
Jandowae 166 26.47 S 151.06 E
Jandrakinot 180 64.54 N 172.32 W
Jándula ≐ 34 38.03 N 4.06 W
Jándula, Embalse de ⊜¹ 34 38.30 N 4.00 W
Janeiro, Rio de ≐ 250 11.51 S 45.09 W
Jane Peak ʌ 172 45.20 S 168.19 E
Janes Island I 208 38.00 N 75.52 W
Janes Island State Park ◆ 208 38.00 N 75.52 W
Janesville, Ca., U.S. 204 40.17 N 120.31 W
Janesville, Mn., U.S. 190 44.06 N 93.42 W
Janesville, Wi., U.S. 216 42.40 N 89.01 W
Jangal Bādhāl 126 23.08 N 88.06 E
Jangamo 156 24.06 S 35.21 E
Jangany 157b 23.14 S 45.27 E
Jangaon 122 17.43 N 79.11 E
Jangarej 24 68.46 N 61.25 E
Jangel'skij 86 53.08 N 59.06 E
Jangeru 112 2.20 S 116.29 E
Jangi 85 41.08 N 70.05 E
Jangiabad 85 41.08 N 70.05 E
Jangi-Bazar 85 41.40 N 70.53 E
Jangijer 85 40.17 N 68.50 E
Jangijul' 85 41.07 N 69.03 E
Jangikišlak 85 40.25 N 67.10 E
Jangikurgan, S.S.S.R. 85 40.34 N 71.09 E
Jangikurgan, S.S.S.R. 85 41.12 N 71.44 E
Jangipāra 126 22.45 N 88.04 E
Jangipur 124 24.28 N 88.04 E
Jangong 114 4.23 N 96.48 E
Jangulovo 80 56.26 N 50.25 E
Janikowo 30 52.45 N 18.07 E
Janīn 132 32.28 N 35.18 E
Janina → Ioánnina 38 39.40 N 20.50 E
Janino 265a 59.56 N 30.36 E
Janisjarvi, ozero ⊜ 24 61.59 N 30.57 E
Janiuay 116 10.58 N 122.30 E
Janja 38 44.40 N 19.15 E
Janjina, Jugo. 36 42.56 N 17.26 E
Janjina, Madag. 157b 20.30 S 45.50 E
Janka 126 21.52 N 87.56 E
Jankan, chrebet ʌʌ 88 55.45 N 118.00 E
Jankāpur 126 21.54 N 87.23 E
Jan Kempdorp (Andalusia) 158 27.55 S 24.51 E
Jan Lake ⊜ 184 54.55 N 102.55 W
Janlohong 112 2.15 N 117.03 E
Jan Mayen I 12 71.00 N 8.20 W
Jan Mayen Ridge ◆³ 10 69.00 N 8.00 W
Jannaale 144 1.48 N 44.42 E
Jannali 274a 34.01 S 151.04 E
Jannali Park ◆ 274a 34.01 S 151.03 E
Janos 232 30.54 N 108.08 W
Janos, Rio de ≐ 232 30.56 N 108.09 W
Jánoshalma 30 46.18 N 19.20 E
Jánosháza 30 47.08 N 17.10 E
János-hegy ʌ 264c 47.31 N 18.58 E
Jánossomorja 61 47.47 N 17.08 E
Janoviči 76 55.17 N 30.42 E
Janowiec Wielkopolski 30 52.46 N 17.31 E
Janów Lubelski 30 50.43 N 22.24 E
Jansath 124 29.20 N 77.51 E
Jansen 184 51.47 N 104.43 W
Jansenville 158 32.56 S 24.40 E
Jänsmässholmen 26 63.40 N 14.30 E
Janskij zaliv ⊂ 74 71.50 N 136.00 E
Jantarnyj 76 54.52 N 19.57 E
Jantetelco 234 18.42 N 98.46 W
Jantikovo 80 55.32 N 47.48 E
Jantra ≐ 38 43.38 N 25.34 E
Januária 255 15.29 S 44.22 W
Januário Cicco 250 6.09 S 35.35 W
Jan Van Riebeeck Park ◆ 273d 26.10 S 27.59 E
Janvarcevo 80 51.26 N 52.15 E
Janville 50 48.12 N 1.53 E
Janville-sur-Juine 261 48.31 N 2.16 E
Janvry 261 48.39 N 2.09 E
Jany-Kurgan 85 43.55 N 67.15 E

DEUTSCH Name	Seite	Breite°′	Länge°′ E = Ost

Janzé 32 47.58 N 1.30 W
Janzūr 142 30.41 N 31.02 E
Jaora 120 23.38 N 75.08 E
Japan (Nihon) □¹, Asia 90 36.00 N 138.00 E
Japan (Nihon) □¹, Asia 92 36.00 N 138.00 E
Japan, Sea of ⊽² 90 40.00 N 135.00 E
Japan Basin ◆¹ 12 40.00 N 135.00 E
Japanisches Meer → Japan, Sea of ⊽² 90 40.00 N 135.00 E
Japan Trench ◆¹ 6 37.00 N 143.00 E
Japaratinga 250 9.05 S 35.15 W
Japaratuba 250 10.35 S 36.57 W
Japeri 256 22.39 S 43.40 W
Japi 250 6.27 S 35.56 W
Japichaua, Ilha I 250 0.55 S 50.35 W
Japiim 248 7.37 S 72.54 W
Japla 124 24.33 N 84.01 E
Japoatã 250 10.20 S 36.48 W
Japon → Japan □¹ 92 36.00 N 138.00 E
Japón, Mar del → Japan, Sea of ⊽² 90 40.00 N 135.00 E
Japtiksal'a 74 69.21 N 72.32 E
Japuíba 256 22.35 S 42.42 W
Japurá 246 1.48 S 66.30 W
Japurá (Caquetá) ≐ 246 3.08 S 64.46 W
Jaqué 246 7.31 N 78.10 W
Jaqui 248 15.30 S 74.26 W
Jar 80 58.15 N 52.06 E
Jarābulus 130 36.49 N 38.01 E
Jarad 144 18.59 N 41.24 E
Jarad 142 29.18 N 30.42 E
Jaraguá 255 15.45 S 49.20 W
Jaraguá ◆⁸ 287b 23.27 S 46.44 W
Jaraguá, Pico do ʌ 287b 23.26 S 46.46 W
Jaraguá do Sul 252 26.29 S 49.04 W
Jaraicejo 34 39.40 N 5.49 W
Jaraiz de la Vera 34 40.04 N 5.45 W
Jaral del Progreso 234 20.22 N 101.04 W
Jarales 200 34.36 N 106.45 W
Jarama ≐ 34 40.02 N 3.39 W
Jarama, Canal del ≅ 266a 40.18 N 3.32 W
Jaramānah 132 33.29 N 36.21 E
Jaramillo 254 47.11 S 67.09 W
Jaramor 80 56.07 N 48.44 E
Jaran' ≐ 80 57.35 N 48.14 E
Jarandilla 34 40.08 N 5.39 W
Jaransk 80 57.19 N 47.54 E
Jarānwāla 123 31.20 N 73.26 E
Jarash 132 32.17 N 35.54 E
Jaraucu ≐ 250 1.48 S 52.22 W
Jarawī, Wādī ⋁ 142 29.47 N 31.19 E
Jarbah, Jabal al- ʌ 142 30.16 N 32.03 E
Jarbah, Wāhat ⊽⁴ 140 29.21 N 25.20 E
Jarbidge ≐ 202 42.19 N 115.39 W
Järbo 40 60.43 N 16.36 E
Jarcevo 76 55.04 N 32.41 E
Jardas al-'Abīd 146 32.19 N 20.56 E
Jardim, Bra. 248 21.28 S 56.09 W
Jardim, Bra. 250 7.35 S 39.16 W
Jardim América ◆⁸ 287b 23.34 S 46.41 W
Jardim de Angicos 250 5.39 S 35.59 W
Jardim de Piranhas 250 6.22 S 37.20 W
Jardim do Seridó 250 6.35 S 36.46 W
Jardim Paulista ◆⁸ 287b 23.35 S 46.40 W
Jardín América 252 27.03 S 55.14 W
Jardine ≐ 164 10.55 S 142.13 E
Jardine River National Park ◆ 164 11.20 S 142.40 E
Jardines de la Reina, Archipiélago de los II 240p 20.50 N 78.55 W
Jardinópolis 255 21.02 S 47.46 W
Jardymly 84 38.55 N 48.15 E
Jaredi 150 12.46 N 5.05 E
Jaremča 78 48.27 N 24.33 E
Jaren'ga, S.S.S.R. 24 63.27 N 53.26 E
Jarenga, S.S.S.R. 24 62.43 N 49.30 E
Jarensk 24 62.11 N 49.02 E
Järfälla 40 59.24 N 17.50 E
Jargalang 89 43.06 N 122.54 E
Jargara 78 46.27 N 28.27 E
Jargeau 50 47.52 N 2.07 E
Jari ≐, Bra. 248 5.07 S 62.21 W
Jari ≐, Bra. 250 1.09 S 51.54 W
Jari, Lago ⊜ 246 5.00 S 62.19 W
Jāria Jhānjail 124 25.02 N 90.39 E
Jaridih 124 23.38 N 86.04 E
Jarinu 256 23.06 S 46.44 W
Jarkino 88 59.08 N 99.23 E
Jarkovo 86 57.24 N 67.05 E
Jarkul'-Mat'uškino 86 55.51 N 76.06 E
Järlåsa 40 59.53 N 17.12 E
Jarmen 54 53.55 N 13.20 E
Jarmolincy 78 49.12 N 26.50 E
Järna 40 59.06 N 17.34 E
Jarnac 32 45.41 N 0.10 W
Jarny 56 49.09 N 5.53 E
Jaro 116 11.11 N 124.47 E
Jarochta 88 58.58 N 98.58 E
Jarocin 30 51.59 N 17.31 E
Jaroměř 30 50.21 N 15.55 E
Jaroměřice 61 49.05 N 15.53 E
Jaropolec 82 56.08 N 35.49 E
Jaroslavec 78 51.33 N 33.40 E
Jaroslavl' 80 57.37 N 39.52 E
Jaroslavl' □⁴ 82 56.45 N 38.45 E
Jaroslavl' Station ◆⁵ 265b 55.47 N 37.39 E
Jaroslavskaja 84 44.36 N 40.27 E
Jaroslavskij 89 44.10 N 132.13 E
Jarosław 30 50.02 N 22.42 E
Jarovaja 83 49.03 N 37.37 E
Järpen 26 63.21 N 13.29 E
Jarrahdale 168a 32.21 S 116.04 E
Jarratt 208 36.48 N 77.28 W
Jarreau 194 30.39 N 91.29 W
Jarrell 222 30.49 N 97.36 W
Jarrettsville 208 39.36 N 76.28 W
Jarrīs 142 27.55 N 31.46 E
Jarrow 44 54.59 N 1.29 W
Jarry, Parc ◆ 275a 45.32 N 73.38 W
Jar-Sale 74 66.50 N 70.50 E
Jarsomovy 86 60.15 N 73.38 E
Jartai Yanchi ⊜ 102 39.43 N 105.41 E
Jaru 248 10.26 S 62.27 W
Jaru ≐ 248 10.05 S 61.59 W
Jarud Qi 89 44.37 N 120.58 E
Jaruga 88 48.08 N 96.45 E
Järva-Jaani 76 59.02 N 25.53 E
Järvakandi 76 58.47 N 24.49 E
Järvelä 26 60.53 N 25.17 E
Järvenpää 26 60.28 N 25.06 E
Jarvie 182 54.27 N 113.59 W
Jarville-la-Malgrange 58 48.40 N 6.13 E
Jarvis 212 42.53 N 80.06 W
Jarvisburg 192 36.12 N 75.52 W
Jarvis Island I 14 0.23 S 160.02 W
Järvsö 26 61.43 N 16.10 E
Jarwa 124 27.39 N 82.31 E
Jasaan 116 8.39 N 124.45 E
Jasai 272c 18.56 N 73.01 E
Jašalta 80 46.20 N 42.17 E
Jasašnaja Tašla 80 53.55 N 48.16 E
Jaša Tomić 38 45.27 N 20.51 E
Jasdan 120 22.02 N 71.12 E
Jasel'da ≐ 76 52.07 N 26.28 E
Jasenevo ◆⁸ 265b 55.36 N 37.33 E
Jasenki 78 51.32 N 38.12 E
Jasenovoje 82 54.10 N 36.47 E
Jasenovskij 83 48.10 N 39.10 E
Jasenskaja 78 46.22 N 38.16 E
Jashpurnagar 124 22.54 N 84.09 E
Jāshpur Pāts ◆¹ 124 22.55 N 84.00 E
Jasidih 124 24.31 N 86.39 E
Jasień 30 51.46 N 15.01 E
Jasienica 54 53.37 N 14.32 E
Jasikan 150 7.24 N 0.28 E
Jašil'kul', Ozero ⊜ 120 37.45 N 72.55 E

Symbols in the index entries represent the broad categories identified in the key at the right. Symbols with superior numbers (ʌ¹) identify subcategories (see complete key on page *I · 1*).

Kartensymbole in dem Registerverzeichnis stellen die rechts in Schlüssel erklärten Kategorien dar. Symbole mit hochgestellten Ziffern (ʌ¹) bezeichnen Unterabteilungen einer Kategorie (vgl. vollständiger Schlüssel auf Seite *I · 1*).

Los símbolos incluídos en el texto del índice representan las grandes categorías identificadas con la clave a la derecha. Los símbolos con numeros en su parte superior (ʌ¹) identifican las subcategorías (véase la clave completa en la página *I · 1*).

Les symboles de l'index représentent les catégories indiquées dans la légende à droite. Les symboles suivis d'un indice (ʌ¹) représentent des sous-catégories (voir légende complète à la page *I · 1*).

Os símbolos incluídos no texto do índice representam as grandes categorias identificadas com a chave à direita. Os símbolos com números em sua parte superior (ʌ¹) identificam as subcategorias (veja-se a chave completa à página *I · 1*).

English	Deutsch	Español	Français	Português
ʌ Mountain	Berg	Montaña	Montagne	Montanha
ʌʌ Mountains	Berge	Montañas	Montagnes	Montanhas
⋈ Pass	Pass	Paso	Col	Passo
⋁ Valley, Canyon	Tal, Cañon	Valle, Cañón	Vallée, Canyon	Vale, Canhão
⊞ Plain	Ebene	Llano	Plaine	Planície
≻ Cape	Kap	Cabo	Cap	Cabo
I Island	Insel	Isla	Île	Ilha
II Islands	Inseln	Islas	Îles	Ilhas
◆ Other Topographic Features	Andere Topographische Objekte	Otros Elementos Topográficos	Autres données topographiques	Outros acidentes topográficos

ESPAÑOL

Nombre	Página	Lat.°′	Long.°′ W = Oeste
Jasin	114	2.19 N	102.26 E
Jasin'a	78	48.16 N	24.20 E
Jasinga	115a	6.29 S	106.27 E
Jasinovataja	83	48.08 N	37.51 E
Jasinovka	83	48.08 N	37.57 E
Jāsk	128	25.38 N	57.46 E
Jaskhar	272c	18.54 N	72.59 E
Jaškino, S.S.S.R.	80	52.41 N	53.26 E
Jaškino, S.S.S.R.	86	55.54 N	85.26 E
Jaskino, S.S.S.R.	265b	55.40 N	37.16 E
Jaškul'	80	46.11 N	45.21 E
Jaškul' ≃	80	46.15 N	45.05 E
Jasło	30	49.45 N	21.29 E
Jasmine Estates	220	28.17 N	82.42 W
Jasmund >[1]	54	54.32 N	13.35 E
Jasnaja Pol'ana ⊥	82	54.05 N	37.32 E
Jasnogorka	83	48.47 N	37.33 E
Jasnogorsk	82	54.29 N	37.42 E
Jasnomorskij	89	46.45 N	141.54 E
Jasnyj, S.S.S.R.	86	51.04 N	59.58 E
Jasnyj, S.S.S.R.	89	53.17 N	127.59 E
Jason Islands II	254	51.05 S	61.00 W
Jason Peninsula >[1]	9	66.10 S	61.00 W
Jasonville	194	39.09 N	87.11 W
Jasper, Ab., Can.	182	52.53 N	118.05 W
Jasper, Al., U.S.	194	33.49 N	87.16 W
Jasper, Ar., U.S.	194	36.00 N	93.11 W
Jasper, Fl., U.S.	192	30.31 N	82.56 W
Jasper, Ga., U.S.	192	34.28 N	84.25 W
Jasper, In., U.S.	194	38.23 N	86.55 W
Jasper, Mi., U.S.	216	41.48 N	84.02 W
Jasper, Mn., U.S.	198	43.51 N	96.23 W
Jasper, Mo., U.S.	194	37.20 N	94.18 W
Jasper, N.Y., U.S.	210	42.07 N	77.30 W
Jasper, Tn., U.S.	194	35.04 N	85.37 W
Jasper, Tx., U.S.	194	30.55 N	93.59 W
Jasper □[6]	216	40.57 N	87.09 W
Jasper Lake ⊜	182	53.07 N	118.00 W
Jasper National Park ♦	182	52.53 N	118.03 W
Jaspur	124	29.17 N	78.49 E
Jasra	124	25.17 N	81.48 E
Jassans-Riottier	58	45.59 N	4.45 E
Jassar	123	32.06 N	74.57 E
Jassy → Iași	38	47.10 N	27.35 E
Jassy ≃	85	40.46 N	73.05 E
Jastarnia	30	54.43 N	18.40 E
Jastrebarsko	36	45.40 N	15.39 E
Jastrebovka, S.S.S.R.	78	51.27 N	37.32 E
Jastrebovka, S.S.S.R.	82	54.36 N	36.24 E
Jastrow → Jastrowie	30	53.26 N	16.49 E
Jastrowie	30	53.26 N	16.49 E
Jaswantnagar	124	26.53 N	78.55 E
Jászapáti	30	47.31 N	20.09 E
Jászberény	30	47.30 N	19.55 E
Jataí	255	17.53 S	51.43 W
Jatapu ≃	246	2.13 S	58.17 W
Jataté ≃	236	16.15 N	91.17 W
Jati, Bra.	250	7.41 S	39.01 W
Jāti, Pāk.	120	24.21 N	68.16 E
Jatibarang	115a	6.28 S	108.17 E
Jatibonico	240p	21.56 N	79.10 W
Jatibonico del Sur ≃	240p	21.33 N	79.09 W
Jatilawang	115a	7.32 S	109.06 E
Jatiluhur, Bendung ⊜[1]	115a	6.35 S	107.20 E
Jatinegara ✦[8]	269e	6.13 S	106.52 E
Jatiroto	115a	8.07 S	113.21 E
Jatisrono	115a	7.49 S	111.07 E
Játiva	34	38.59 N	0.31 W
Jatiwangi	115a	6.44 S	108.15 E
Jatni	120	20.10 N	85.42 E
Jatniel	273d	26.07 S	28.19 E
Jatobá ≃	255	12.23 S	54.07 W
Jatoi Janūbi	123	29.31 N	70.51 E
Jātrāpur	126	22.44 N	89.45 E
Jatt (Tel Gat)	132	32.24 N	35.02 E
Jatznick	54	53.35 N	13.56 E
Jáu, Ang.	152	15.12 S	13.31 E
Jaú, Bra.	255	22.18 S	48.33 W
Jaú ≃	246	1.54 S	61.26 W
Jauaperi ≃	246	1.26 S	61.35 W
Jauer → Jawor	30	51.03 N	16.11 E
Jauerling ∧	61	48.20 N	15.20 E
Jaugrām	126	23.06 N	88.05 E
Jauja	248	11.48 S	75.30 W
Jauli	272a	28.44 N	77.21 E
Jaumave	234	23.25 N	99.23 W
Jaúna ≃	248	6.24 S	59.57 W
Jaunde → Yaoundé	152	3.52 N	11.31 E
Jaune, Mer → Yellow Sea ⊤[2]	90	36.00 N	123.00 E
Jaungulbene	76	57.04 N	26.36 E
Jaunjelgava	76	56.37 N	25.05 E
Jaunpass)(	58	46.36 N	7.20 E
Jaunpiebalga	76	57.11 N	26.03 E
Jaunpils	76	56.44 N	23.01 E
Jaunpur	124	25.44 N	82.41 E
Jaunpur □[5]	124	25.40 N	82.40 E
Jaupaci	255	16.18 S	50.54 W
Jauquara ≃	248	15.06 S	57.06 W
Jáuregui	258	34.36 S	59.10 W
Jauru ≃, Bra.	248	16.22 S	57.46 W
Jauru ≃, Bra.	255	18.40 S	54.36 W
Jausiers	62	44.25 N	6.44 E
Jauza ≃, S.S.S.R.	82	56.25 N	36.05 E
Jauza ≃, S.S.S.R.	265b	55.45 N	37.38 E
Java	198	45.30 N	99.53 W
Java → Jawa I	115a	7.30 S	110.00 E
Java Center	210	42.39 N	78.23 W
Javādi Hills ⩘[2]	122	12.35 N	78.50 E
Javalambre ∧	34	40.06 N	1.03 W
Javan	85	38.19 N	69.02 E
Javari (Yavarí) ≃	242	4.21 S	70.02 W
Javas	80	54.26 N	42.51 E
Java Sea → Jawa, Laut ⊤[2]	112	5.00 S	110.00 E
Java Trench ✢[1]	12	10.30 S	110.00 E
Java Village	210	42.40 N	78.26 W
Jávea	34	38.47 N	0.10 E
Jävenitz	54	52.31 N	11.30 E
Javier, Isla I	254	47.06 S	74.24 W
Javkino	78	47.16 N	32.37 E
Javlenka	86	54.21 N	68.27 E
Javor ⩘	38	44.05 N	18.55 E
Javořice ∧	61	49.14 N	15.20 E
Javorie ∧	30	48.27 N	19.18 E
Javorná	60	49.13 N	13.18 E
Javorník	30	50.23 N	17.00 E
Javorov	78	49.56 N	23.23 E
Javorová skála ∧	30	49.31 N	14.30 E
Javr ≃	24	68.09 N	30.06 E
Jävre	26	65.09 N	21.59 E
Jawa (Java) I	115a	7.30 S	110.00 E
Jawa, Laut (Java Sea) ⊤[2]	112	5.00 S	110.00 E
Jawa Barat □[4]	115a	7.00 S	107.00 E
Jaw'āliyāt, Jabal al- ∧	132	31.26 N	36.26 E
Jawāla Mukhi	123	31.53 N	76.19 E
Jawa Tengah □[4]	115a	7.30 S	110.00 E
Jawa Timur □[4]	115a	8.00 S	113.00 E
Jawbar	132	33.31 N	36.19 E
Jawf, Wādī V	144	15.50 N	45.35 E
Jawi	112	0.48 S	109.16 E
Jawor	30	51.03 N	16.11 E
Jaworzno	30	50.13 N	19.15 E
Jay, Fl., U.S.	194	30.57 N	87.09 W
Jay, Ok., U.S.	196	36.25 N	94.47 W
Jay □[6]	216	40.26 N	84.59 W
Jaya, Puncak ∧	164	4.05 S	137.11 E
Jayamkondachola-Puram	122	11.13 N	79.22 E
Jayanca	248	6.24 S	79.50 W
Jayapura (Sukarnapura)	164	2.32 S	140.42 E

FRANÇAIS

Nom	Page	Lat.°′	Long.°′ W = Ouest
Jayb, Wādī al- (Ha'Arava) V	132	30.58 N	35.24 E
Jay Cooke State Park ♦	190	46.41 N	92.23 W
Jay Creek Aboriginal Reserve ✦[4]	162	23.45 S	133.35 E
Jaydebpur	124	24.00 N	90.26 E
Jaynagar	126	22.36 N	90.42 E
Jaynagar Majilpur	126	22.11 N	88.25 E
Jaynes	200	32.16 N	111.01 W
Jay Peak ∧	188	44.55 N	72.32 W
Jaypur	126	23.03 N	87.27 E
Jayrūd	130	33.49 N	36.44 E
Jayton	196	33.15 N	100.34 W
Jayuya	240m	18.13 N	66.36 W
Jaywick	42	51.47 N	1.08 E
Jaz	80	54.54 N	45.13 E
Jaželbicy	76	58.02 N	32.58 E
Jazevec	24	65.43 N	46.30 E
Jazgulem ≃	85	38.12 N	71.21 E
Jazīrat Muḥammad	273c	30.07 N	31.12 E
Jazjavan	85	40.39 N	71.44 E
Jažma	24	66.56 N	44.29 E
Jaz Mūrīān, Hāmūn-e ⊜	128	27.20 N	58.55 E
Jazovaja	86	49.27 N	85.20 E
Jazykovo	80	54.18 N	47.24 E
Jazzīn	132	33.32 N	35.34 E
Jbā'	132	33.29 N	35.31 E
J.B. Thomas, Lake ⊜[1]	196	32.35 N	101.10 W
J. C. Murphey Lake ⊜	216	40.58 N	87.30 W
Jdiouia	34	35.57 N	0.50 E
Jeanerette	194	29.54 N	91.39 W
Jeanesville	210	40.56 N	75.58 W
Jeannette	214	40.19 N	79.36 W
Jebāl Bārez, Kūh-e ⩘	128	28.30 N	58.20 E
Jebba	150	9.08 N	4.50 E
Jebel	38	45.33 N	21.14 E
Jebeniana	148	35.02 N	10.55 E
Jeber-Bergfrieden	54	51.59 N	12.20 E
Jeberos	248	5.17 S	76.13 W
Jebri	120	27.18 N	65.44 E
Jebus	112	1.44 S	105.29 E
Jechegnadzor	84	39.46 N	45.21 E
Jéci, Serra ∧	154	12.48 S	35.12 E
Jedane, Oued ti-n- V	148	24.55 N	6.30 E
Jedarma	88	58.44 N	102.36 E
Jedburgh	44	55.29 N	2.34 W
Jedburgh Abbey ʋ[1]	44	55.27 N	2.34 W
Jeddore Lake ⊜[1]	186	48.03 N	55.55 W
Jedelevo	80	53.24 N	47.45 E
Jedepo	150	5.16 N	8.20 W
Jedincy	78	48.10 N	27.19 E
Jedisa	84	42.31 N	44.16 E
Jedlesee ✦[8]	264b	48.16 N	16.23 E
Jednevo	82	56.06 N	36.14 E
Jedogon	88	54.15 N	100.15 E
Jedrovo	76	57.55 N	33.38 E
Jędrzejów	30	50.39 N	20.18 E
Jedwabne	30	53.17 N	22.19 E
Jed Water ≃	46	55.32 N	2.33 W
Jeetzel (Jeetze) ≃	54	53.09 N	11.04 E
Jefawa	140	10.57 N	23.48 E
Jeffara (Al-Jifārah) ≡	146	32.30 N	11.45 E
Jeffers	198	44.03 N	95.11 W
Jefferson, Ga., U.S.	192	34.07 N	83.34 W
Jefferson, In., U.S.	216	40.17 N	86.36 W
Jefferson, Ia., U.S.	198	42.00 N	94.22 W
Jefferson, Md., U.S.	208	39.21 N	77.31 W
Jefferson, Ma., U.S.	207	42.21 N	71.52 W
Jefferson, N.J., U.S.	285	39.45 N	75.13 W
Jefferson, N.Y., U.S.	210	42.14 N	73.54 W
Jefferson, N.Y., U.S.	210	42.29 N	74.37 W
Jefferson, N.C., U.S.	192	36.25 N	81.28 W
Jefferson, Oh., U.S.	214	41.44 N	80.46 W
Jefferson, Or., U.S.	202	44.43 N	123.00 W
Jefferson, Pa., U.S.	279b	40.18 N	80.03 W
Jefferson, S.C., U.S.	192	34.39 N	80.23 W
Jefferson, S.D., U.S.	198	42.36 N	96.33 W
Jefferson, Tx., U.S.	194	32.45 N	94.20 W
Jefferson, Wi., U.S.	216	43.00 N	88.48 W
Jefferson □[6], Il., U.S.	219	38.19 N	88.55 W
Jefferson □[6], In., U.S.	218	38.44 N	85.23 W
Jefferson □[6], Ky., U.S.	218	38.14 N	85.10 W
Jefferson □[6], Mo., U.S.	219	38.20 N	90.34 W
Jefferson □[6], N.Y., U.S.	212	43.59 N	75.55 W
Jefferson □[6], Oh., U.S.	214	40.22 N	80.37 W
Jefferson □[6], Pa., U.S.	214	41.09 N	79.05 W
Jefferson □[6], Wa., U.S.	224	47.50 N	122.36 W
Jefferson □[6], Wi., U.S.	216	43.02 N	88.46 W
Jefferson ≃	202	45.56 N	111.30 W
Jefferson, Mount ∧, U.S.	202	44.34 N	111.30 W
Jefferson, Mount ∧, Nv., U.S.	204	38.46 N	116.55 W
Jefferson, Mount ∧, Or., U.S.	202	44.40 N	121.47 W
Jefferson City, Mo., U.S.	219	38.34 N	92.10 W
Jefferson City, Tn., U.S.	192	36.07 N	83.29 W
Jefferson Farms	285	39.40 N	75.34 W
Jefferson Manor	284c	38.47 N	77.04 W
Jefferson Park ✦[8]	278	41.59 N	87.46 W
Jefferson Proving Ground ■	218	38.50 N	85.25 W
Jeffersonton	188	38.38 N	77.55 W
Jeffersontown	218	38.11 N	85.33 W
Jefferson Village	284c	38.52 N	77.10 W
Jeffersonville, Ga., U.S.	192	32.41 N	83.20 W
Jeffersonville, In., U.S.	218	38.16 N	85.44 W
Jeffersonville, N.Y., U.S.	210	41.46 N	74.56 W
Jeffersonville, Oh., U.S.	218	39.39 N	83.33 W
Jeffrey City	200	42.29 N	107.49 W
Jeffreys Bay	158	34.02 S	24.54 E
Jeffries Creek ≃	192	34.05 N	79.32 W
Jefimovka	80	52.13 N	52.03 E
Jefimovskij	76	59.30 N	35.02 E
Jefremov	76	53.09 N	38.07 E
Jefremova	82	56.13 N	38.59 E
Jefremovka	83	47.19 N	38.29 E
Jefremovo-Stepanovka	78	48.43 N	40.50 E
Jefremovskaja	82	55.25 N	38.59 E
Jega	150	12.15 N	4.23 E
Jegenstorf	58	47.03 N	7.30 E
Jegindybulak, S.S.S.R.	86	49.45 N	76.23 E
Jegindybulak, S.S.S.R.	86	48.42 N	81.48 E
Jegizkara, gora ∧	86	46.24 N	64.09 E
Jegorjevka	89	50.42 N	127.42 E
Jegorjevsk	82	55.23 N	39.02 E
Jegorlyk ≃	80	46.33 N	41.52 E
Jehol → Chengde	105	40.58 N	117.53 E
Jeja ≃	78	46.41 N	38.36 E
Jejsk	78	46.42 N	38.16 E
Jejskij liman ⊂	78	46.42 N	38.25 E
Jeju → Cheju	90	33.31 N	126.32 E
Jejur	272b	22.53 N	88.08 E
Jēkabpils	76	56.29 N	25.51 E
Jekaterinburg → Sverdlovsk	86	56.51 N	60.36 E
Jekaterinino	76	55.49 N	33.58 E
Jekaterininskoje	86	56.53 N	74.34 E

PORTUGUÊS

Nome	Página	Lat.°′	Long.°′ W = Oeste
Jekaterinoslav → Dnepropetrovsk	78	48.27 N	34.59 E
Jekaterinoslavka	89	50.23 N	129.08 E
Jekaterinovka, S.S.S.R.	78	46.42 N	38.46 E
Jekaterinovka, S.S.S.R.	80	53.04 N	49.28 E
Jekaterinovka, S.S.S.R.	80	46.32 N	41.42 E
Jekaterinovka, S.S.S.R.	80	52.03 N	44.21 E
Jekaterinovka, S.S.S.R.	83	47.33 N	38.23 E
Jekaterinovka, S.S.S.R.	86	54.36 N	70.58 E
Jekaterinovka ✦[8]	265b	55.46 N	37.23 E
Jekaterinovskaja	78	46.20 N	39.58 E
Jekateriny, proliv ⊔, S.S.S.R.	74	44.30 N	146.45 E
Jekateriny, proliv ⊔, S.S.S.R.	92a	44.25 N	146.40 E
Jekimoviči	76	54.07 N	33.18 E
Jekpindykurylys	80	47.49 N	47.17 E
Jekyll Island I	192	31.04 N	81.25 W
Jekyll Island State Park ♦	192	31.02 N	81.25 W
Jelabuga	80	55.47 N	52.04 E
Jelai ≃, Indon.	112	2.59 S	110.45 E
Jelai ≃, Malay.	114	4.04 N	102.20 E
Jelan', S.S.S.R.	80	52.13 N	44.11 E
Jelan', S.S.S.R.	80	50.57 N	43.44 E
Jelan', S.S.S.R.	83	48.41 N	39.47 E
Jelan', S.S.S.R.	86	57.39 N	63.42 E
Jelan' ≃, S.S.S.R.	78	51.07 N	41.25 E
Jelan' ≃, S.S.S.R.	80	50.57 N	43.44 E
Jelan' ≃, S.S.S.R.	80	51.07 N	41.26 E
Jelancy	88	52.49 N	106.25 E
Jelanec	78	47.42 N	31.51 E
Jelanka	86	55.37 N	75.18 E
Jelan'-Koleno	78	51.09 N	41.14 E
Jelan'-Kolenovskij	78	51.10 N	41.10 E
Jelat'ma	80	54.58 N	41.45 E
Jelaur, S.S.S.R.	80	54.34 N	50.21 E
Jelaur, S.S.S.R.	80	53.50 N	48.48 E
Jelchovka	80	53.51 N	50.18 E
Jel'covka	86	53.15 N	86.15 E
Jel'cy, S.S.S.R.	76	56.40 N	33.51 E
Jel'cy, S.S.S.R.	82	56.11 N	38.46 E
Jelec	76	52.37 N	38.30 E
Jeleckij	24	67.03 N	64.10 E
Jelenia Góra (Hirschberg)	30	50.55 N	15.46 E
Jelenia Góra □[4]	30	51.10 N	15.30 E
Jelenskij	76	53.29 N	35.23 E
Jelgava	76	56.39 N	23.42 E
Jelgavkrasti	76	57.28 N	24.26 E
Jelisejevka	78	47.02 N	36.24 E
Jelizarovo, S.S.S.R.	78	48.12 N	34.33 E
Jelizarovo, S.S.S.R.	80	58.33 N	44.50 E
Jelizavetgradka	78	48.48 N	32.24 E
Jelizavetinka	86	51.28 N	71.12 E
Jelizavetopol'skoje	86	52.51 N	60.36 E
Jelizavetovka	78	46.39 N	38.53 E
Jelizavety, mys >	89	54.26 N	142.42 E
Jelizovo	76	53.24 N	29.01 E
Jelli	154	5.22 N	31.48 E
Jellico	192	36.35 N	84.07 W
Jelling	41	55.45 N	9.26 E
Jelloway	214	40.33 N	82.18 W
Jelm Mountain ∧	200	41.06 N	105.58 W
Jel'n'a	76	54.35 N	33.11 E
Jelnat'	80	57.20 N	42.49 E
Jel'niki	80	54.37 N	43.53 E
Jeloguj ≃	74	63.13 N	87.45 E
Jel'onovka, S.S.S.R.	83	47.50 N	37.40 E
Jel'onovka, S.S.S.R.	83	48.39 N	38.01 E
Jelošnoje	86	55.27 N	66.44 E
Jelovo	80	57.03 N	54.54 E
Jels	41	55.21 N	9.12 E
Jelšanka, S.S.S.R.	80	51.49 N	46.23 E
Jelšanka, S.S.S.R.	80	52.35 N	47.59 E
Jelšanka Pervaja	80	52.53 N	52.02 E
Jelšava	30	48.39 N	20.14 E
Jel'sk	78	51.48 N	29.09 E
Jema ≃	144	10.09 N	38.20 E
Jemaa	150	9.27 N	8.23 E
Jemaja, Pulau I	112	2.55 N	105.45 E
Jemaluang	114	2.17 N	103.52 E
Jemantajevo	80	53.34 N	53.50 E
Jemanželinsk	86	54.45 N	61.20 E
Jemappes	50	50.27 N	3.53 E
Jember	115a	8.10 S	113.42 E
Jemca	24	63.04 N	40.20 E
Jemca ≃	24	63.15 N	41.20 E
Jemeljanovka	78	45.32 N	34.53 E
Jemeljanovo	86	56.11 N	92.40 E
Jemel'stan	24	61.13 N	52.29 E
Jemen → Yemen □[1]	144	15.00 N	44.00 E
Jemen, Volksrepublik → Yemen, People's Democratic Republic of □[1]	144	15.00 N	48.00 E
Jemez ≃	200	35.22 N	106.31 W
Jemez Canyon Reservoir ⊜[1]	200	35.28 N	106.39 W
Jemez Indian Reservation ✦[4]	200	35.35 N	106.45 W
Jemez Springs	200	35.46 N	106.41 W
Jemgum	52	53.16 N	7.23 E
Jemil'čino	78	50.52 N	27.48 E
Jeminary	86	47.32 N	85.38 E
Jemmal	148	35.38 N	10.46 E
Jemnice	61	49.01 N	15.35 E
Jempang, Danau ⊜	112	0.26 S	116.12 E
Jena, D.D.R.	54	50.56 N	11.35 E
Jena, La., U.S.	194	31.40 N	92.08 W
Jenakijevo	83	48.14 N	38.13 E
Jenašimskij Polkan, gora ∧	74	59.50 N	92.52 E
Jenaz	58	46.55 N	9.45 E
Jenbach	64	47.24 N	11.47 E
Jenbek	86	48.53 N	77.12 E
Jendarata	114	3.55 N	100.57 E
Jendongin	88	53.27 N	113.01 E
Jendouba (Souk el Arba)	148	36.30 N	8.47 E
Jendouba □[8]	148	36.30 N	8.45 E
Jeneponto	112	5.41 S	119.42 E
Jenera	216	40.54 N	83.44 W
Jeniang	114	5.49 N	100.38 E
Jenisej ≃	72	71.50 N	82.40 E
Jenisejsk	86	58.27 N	92.10 E
Jenisejskij kr'až ⩘	74	59.00 N	93.00 E
Jenisejskij zaliv ⊂	74	72.30 N	80.00 E
Jenison	216	42.54 N	85.47 W
Jenkins, Ky., U.S.	192	37.10 N	82.37 W
Jenkins, Tx., U.S.	222	32.59 N	94.44 W
Jenkins, Mount ∧	162	25.36 S	129.41 E
Jenkinson Lake ⊜[1]	226	38.44 N	120.33 W
Jenkinsville	192	34.16 N	81.17 W
Jenkintown	208	40.05 N	75.07 W
Jenks	196	36.01 N	95.58 W
Jenli	100	23.15 N	120.08 E
Jenners	214	40.08 N	79.02 W
Jennersdorf	61	46.57 N	16.08 E
Jennerstown	214	40.10 N	79.04 W
Jennifer Branch ≃	284b	39.25 N	76.30 W
Jennings, Fl., U.S.	192	30.36 N	83.05 W
Jennings, La., U.S.	194	30.13 N	92.39 W
Jennings, Mo., U.S.	219	38.43 N	90.15 W
Jennings □[6]	218	38.59 N	85.36 W
Jennings Creek ≃	216	40.53 N	84.17 W
Jennings Lodge	224	45.23 N	122.36 W
Jenotajevka	80	47.15 N	47.03 E
Jenpeg Dam ✦[6]	184	54.33 N	98.02 W
Jensen	200	40.22 N	109.20 W
Jensen Beach	220	27.15 N	80.13 W
Jens Munk Island I	176	69.42 N	79.30 W
Jens Munks Ø I	176	64.40 N	40.30 W
Jenu	112	0.36 S	109.52 E
Jen'uka	88	57.58 N	121.42 E
Jeonju → Chŏnju	98	35.49 N	127.08 E
Jepač	24	66.58 N	61.22 E
Jepara	115a	6.35 S	110.39 E
Jeparit	166	36.09 S	141.59 E
Jepelacio	248	6.07 S	76.57 W
Jepichin	80	48.16 N	45.14 E
Jepifan'	76	53.49 N	38.33 E
Jeppener	258	35.17 S	58.12 W
Jeptha Knob ∧[2]	218	38.11 N	85.07 W
Jepua (Jeppo)	26	63.24 N	22.37 E
Jequeri	255	20.27 S	42.40 W
Jequetepeque ≃	248	7.21 S	79.36 W
Jequié	255	13.51 S	40.05 W
Jequitaí	255	17.15 S	44.28 W
Jequitinhonha	255	16.26 S	41.00 W
Jequitinhonha ≃	255	15.51 S	38.53 W
Jerachtur	80	54.43 N	41.09 E
Jerada	148	34.17 N	2.13 W
Jeradou	36	36.15 N	10.23 E
Jerangle	171b	35.52 S	149.22 E
Jeransang	114	3.52 N	102.22 E
Jerantut	114	3.56 N	102.22 E
Jerba, Île de I	148	33.48 N	10.54 E
Jerbar	140	5.39 N	31.05 E
Jerbent	128	39.19 N	58.36 E
Jerbogačon	74	61.16 N	108.00 E
Jercevo	24	60.48 N	40.05 E
Jerdenevo	82	54.55 N	36.27 E
Jerécuaro	234	20.09 N	100.31 W
Jeremejevka	83	46.58 N	39.33 E
Jeremejevo	82	55.57 N	37.01 E
Jérémie	238	18.39 N	74.07 W
Jeremino	82	56.27 N	37.58 E
Jeremoabo	250	10.04 S	38.21 W
Jeremy Hill ∧[2]	207	42.45 N	71.21 W
Jeremy Point >	207	41.53 N	70.04 W
Jerevan	84	40.11 N	44.30 E
Jerez ≃	234	22.15 N	103.11 W
Jerez, Punta >	234	22.54 N	97.46 W
Jerez de García Salinas	234	22.39 N	103.00 W
Jerez de la Frontera	34	36.41 N	6.08 W
Jerez de los Caballeros	34	38.19 N	6.46 W
Jergač	86	57.28 N	56.39 E
Jergeni ⩘[2]	80	47.00 N	44.00 E
Jergeninskij	80	47.07 N	44.28 E
Jericho, Austl.	166	23.36 S	146.08 E
Jericho → Arīḥā, Ghaz.	132	31.52 N	35.27 E
Jericho, N.J., U.S.	285	39.48 N	75.09 W
Jericho, N.Y., U.S.	210	40.47 N	73.32 W
Jericho Dam ⊜[1]	158	26.39 S	30.28 E
Jerichow	54	52.30 N	12.01 E
Jericó, Bra.	250	6.33 S	37.48 W
Jericó, Col.	246	5.47 N	75.47 W
Jerid, Chott ≡	148	33.42 N	8.26 E
Jerik ≃	83	48.59 N	38.30 E
Jerilderie	166	35.22 S	145.44 E
Jerimoth Hill ∧[2]	207	41.52 N	71.47 W
Jerki	78	48.59 N	31.00 E
Jermak	86	52.02 N	76.55 E
Jermakovo	80	53.11 N	49.38 E
Jermakovskaja	80	48.03 N	41.17 E
Jermakovskoje	86	53.16 N	92.24 E
Jermekejevo	80	54.05 N	53.40 E
Jermentau	86	51.38 N	73.10 E
Jermentau ⩘	86	51.10 N	73.10 E
Jermica	24	66.56 N	52.15 E
Jermilovka	86	57.40 N	72.55 E
Jermiš'	80	54.46 N	42.16 E
Jermolajevo, S.S.S.R.	86	55.13 N	92.10 E
Jermolajevo, S.S.S.R.	86	52.43 N	55.48 E
Jermolino, S.S.S.R.	82	55.12 N	36.36 E
Jermolino, S.S.S.R.	82	55.57 N	36.54 E
Jermolino, S.S.S.R.	82	56.48 N	37.49 E
Jermolino, S.S.S.R.	86	57.20 N	64.43 E
Jermyn	210	41.31 N	75.32 W
Jernhatten ∧[2]	41	56.15 N	10.48 E
Jernih	114	4.25 N	97.43 E
Jeroaquara	255	15.23 S	50.25 W
Jerofej Pavlovič	89	53.58 N	122.01 E
Jerome, Az., U.S.	200	34.44 N	112.06 W
Jerome, Id., U.S.	202	42.43 N	114.31 W
Jerome, Il., U.S.	219	39.46 N	89.41 W
Jerome, Mi., U.S.	216	42.01 N	84.28 W
Jerome, Pa., U.S.	214	40.12 N	78.59 W
Jeromesville	214	40.48 N	82.11 W
Jer'omino	86	58.35 N	79.25 E
Jerônimo Monteiro	255	20.47 S	41.24 W
Jerónimos de Belém, Mosteiro dos ʋ[1]	266c	38.42 N	9.12 W
Jeröö	88	49.45 N	106.40 E
Jeröö ≃	88	49.54 N	106.08 E
Jeropol	74	65.15 N	168.40 E
Jerpoint Abbey ⊥	48	53.29 N	7.08 W
Jerry City	216	41.15 N	83.36 W
Jerry Slough ≃	226	35.33 N	119.31 W
Jersey	214	40.03 N	82.46 W
Jersey □[6]	219	39.07 N	90.20 W
Jersey □[2], Europe	22	49.15 N	2.10 W
Jersey □[2], Europe	43b	49.15 N	2.10 W
Jersey City	210	40.43 N	74.04 W
Jersey City State College ʋ[2]	276	40.43 N	74.05 W
Jersey Mountain ∧	202	45.29 N	115.34 W
Jersey Shore	210	41.12 N	77.16 W
Jersey Village	222	29.52 N	95.35 W
Jerseyville	219	39.07 N	90.19 W
Jerši	76	54.24 N	34.12 E
Jeršiči	76	53.40 N	32.44 E
Jeršov	80	51.20 N	48.17 E
Jeršovka	86	54.07 N	64.59 E
Jeršovo	82	55.46 N	36.52 E
Jeršovskij	86	52.29 N	59.08 E
Jertarskij	86	56.47 N	64.18 E
Jerte ≃	34	39.58 N	6.17 W
Jerteh	114	5.45 N	102.30 E
Jertoma	24	63.32 N	47.48 E
Jerumenha	250	7.05 S	43.30 W
Jerusalem → Yerushalayim	132	31.46 N	35.14 E
Jerusalem Airport ⊠	132	31.52 N	35.12 E
Jerusalim (Talusan)	116	7.26 N	122.49 E
Jeruslan ≃	80	50.15 N	45.42 E
Jervaulx Abbey ʋ[1]	44	54.16 N	1.43 W
Jervis, Cape >	168b	35.38 S	138.06 E
Jervis Bay	170	35.08 S	150.42 E
Jervis Bay ⊂	170	35.05 S	150.44 E
Jervis Inlet ⊂	182	49.46 N	124.10 W
Jervois Range ⩘	162	22.38 S	136.05 E
Jerxheim	54	52.05 N	10.54 E
Jerykly	80	55.11 N	51.26 E
Jerzens	58	47.10 N	10.45 E
Jesaulovka	83	48.03 N	39.02 E
Jesenankaty ≃	80	50.32 N	51.47 E
Jesenice, Česko.	54	50.04 N	13.29 E
Jesenice, Jugo.	61	46.27 N	14.04 E
Jesenice, údolní nádrž ⊜[1]	60	50.04 N	12.27 E
Jeseník	30	50.14 N	17.13 E
Jesenoviči	76	57.17 N	34.14 E
Jesensaj	80	49.54 N	51.28 E
Ješera	84	43.04 N	40.55 E
Jeserig bei Wiesenburg	54	52.05 N	12.27 E
Jesi	66	43.31 N	13.14 E
Jesil'	86	51.58 N	66.24 E
Jes'ki	76	57.56 N	36.23 E
Jesönbulag → Altaj	90	46.20 N	96.18 E
Jessej	74	68.29 N	102.10 E
Jesselton → Kota Kinabalu	112	5.59 N	116.04 E
Jessen	54	51.47 N	12.58 E
Jessentuki	84	44.03 N	42.51 E
Jesser Point >	158	27.32 S	32.40 E
Jessheim	26	60.09 N	11.11 E
Jessnitz	54	51.41 N	12.17 E
Jessore	124	23.10 N	89.13 E
Jessup, Md., U.S.	208	39.08 N	76.46 W
Jessup, Pa., U.S.	210	41.28 N	75.33 W
Jessup Park ♦	280	34.15 N	118.24 W
Jestetten	58	47.39 N	8.34 E
Jestřebí	54	50.38 N	14.36 E
Jesuânia	256	22.00 S	45.18 W
Jésuite, Lac du ⊜	206	46.53 N	72.36 W
Jesup, Ga., U.S.	192	31.36 N	81.53 W
Jesup, Ia., U.S.	190	42.28 N	92.03 W
Jesup, Lake ⊜	220	28.43 N	81.14 W
Jesús	252	27.03 S	55.47 W
Jésus, Île I	206	45.35 N	73.45 W
Jesús Carranza	234	17.26 N	95.02 W
Jesús del Monte ✦[8]	286b	23.06 N	82.22 W
Jesús de Otoro	236	14.26 N	87.59 W
Jesús María, Arg.	252	30.59 S	64.06 W
Jesús María, Méx.	232	25.06 N	107.28 W
Jesús María, Méx.	234	21.58 N	102.21 W
Jesús María, Perú	286d	12.04 S	77.04 W
Jesús María ≃	234	21.51 N	104.42 W
Jesús María, Punta >	258	34.39 S	56.55 W
Jet	196	36.39 N	98.10 W
Jeta, Ilha de I	150	11.53 N	16.15 W
Jetafe	116	10.09 N	124.09 E
Jetmore	198	38.05 N	99.53 W
Jet Propulsion Laboratory ʋ[3]	280	34.12 N	118.11 W
Jetpur	120	21.44 N	70.37 E
Jetřichovice	54	50.49 N	14.25 E
Jett	218	38.11 N	84.49 W
Jette	50	50.52 N	4.20 E
Jettingen	58	48.23 N	10.26 E
Jeumont	50	50.18 N	4.06 E
Jeune Landing	182	50.27 N	127.30 W
Jeunieb	114	5.10 N	96.29 E
Jeuram	114	4.14 N	96.18 E
Jever	52	53.34 N	7.54 E
Jeverland ✦[1]	52	53.35 N	8.00 E
Jevgaščino	86	56.26 N	74.41 E
Jevgenjevka	85	43.31 N	77.40 E
Jevičko	30	49.38 N	16.43 E
Jevišovice	61	48.59 N	16.00 E
Jevišovka ≃	61	48.49 N	16.28 E
Jevlach	84	40.36 N	47.09 E
Jevlaš'ovo	80	53.07 N	46.51 E
Jevnaker	26	60.15 N	10.28 E
Jevpatorija	78	45.12 N	33.22 E
Jevra	86	59.56 N	64.27 E
Jevrejskaja Avtonomnaja Oblast' □[8]	89	48.30 N	132.00 E
Jevsug	83	49.13 N	39.18 E
Jevsug ≃	83	48.47 N	39.19 E
Jewel Cave National Monument ♦	198	43.42 N	103.50 W
Jewell, Ia., U.S.	190	42.18 N	93.38 W
Jewell, Ks., U.S.	198	39.40 N	98.09 W
Jewell, N.Y., U.S.	210	43.13 N	75.48 W
Jewell, Oh., U.S.	216	41.20 N	84.17 W
Jewell, Or., U.S.	224	45.56 N	123.30 W
Jewell Ridge	192	37.11 N	81.47 W
Jewell Village	218	39.10 N	85.51 W
Jewett, Il., U.S.	194	39.13 N	88.15 W
Jewett, Oh., U.S.	214	40.22 N	81.00 W
Jewett, Tx., U.S.	222	31.22 N	96.09 W
Jewett City	207	41.36 N	71.58 W
Jewett Creek ≃	212	44.22 N	75.45 W
Jewett Lake ⊜	184	56.09 N	104.40 W
Jewettville	284a	42.43 N	78.52 W
Jeypore	122	18.51 N	82.35 E
Jezerce ∧	38	42.26 N	19.49 E
Jezerišče	76	55.50 N	29.59 E
Jezerní hora ∧	60	49.10 N	13.11 E
Ježicha	80	58.06 N	47.40 E
Jeziorany	30	53.58 N	20.46 E
Ježovo	80	58.02 N	52.14 E
Jezreel, Valley of → Yizre'el, 'Emeq ≡	132	32.36 N	35.14 E
J. G. Strijdomdam ⊜[1]	158	27.25 S	32.05 E
Jhābua	120	22.46 N	74.36 E
Jhāhtipahāri	126	23.22 N	86.54 E
Jhajha	124	24.46 N	86.22 E
Jhajjar	124	28.37 N	76.39 E
Jhal	120	28.17 N	67.27 E
Jhālakāti	124	22.39 N	90.12 E
Jhālawār	124	24.36 N	76.09 E
Jhālawār □[5]	124	24.30 N	76.20 E
Jhalida	124	23.22 N	85.58 E
Jhal Jhao	120	26.18 N	65.35 E
Jhālod	120	23.06 N	74.09 E
Jhālrapātan	124	24.33 N	76.10 E
Jhang Maghiāna	123	31.16 N	72.19 E
Jhānsi	124	25.26 N	78.35 E
Jhānsi □[5]	124	25.40 N	79.00 E
Jhānsi Post	123	33.52 N	71.24 E
Jhāpa	124	26.29 N	87.51 E
Jhārgrām	126	22.27 N	86.59 E
Jharia	126	23.45 N	86.24 E
Jhārpokhariā	126	22.10 N	86.38 E
Jhārsuguda	120	21.51 N	84.02 E
Jhawāni	124	27.35 N	84.31 E
Jhawāriān	123	32.22 N	72.38 E
Jhelum	123	32.56 N	73.44 E
Jhelum ≃	123	31.12 N	72.08 E
Jhenida	124	23.33 N	89.10 E
Jhenkāri	272b	22.46 N	88.18 E
Jhikra	126	22.37 N	87.55 E
Jhilimili	126	22.49 N	86.37 E
Jhil Kuranga ✦[8]	272a	28.40 N	77.17 E
Jhilla ≃[1]	126	21.58 N	88.56 E
Jhingergācha	126	23.07 N	89.07 E
Jhinkpāni	124	22.25 N	85.47 E
Jhok Rind	120	31.27 N	70.26 E
Jhūnjhunu	120	28.08 N	75.24 E
Jiaban, Zhg.	102	25.10 N	107.03 E
Jiaban, Zhg.	102	25.38 N	107.07 E
Jiabong	116	11.46 N	124.57 E
Jiacha	120	29.11 N	92.44 E
Jiading	106	31.23 N	121.15 E
Jiaganj	126	24.14 N	88.16 E
Jiagedan	89	51.35 N	120.55 E
Jiahashitai	89	46.25 N	122.17 E
Jiahe	102	25.43 N	112.05 E
Jiajiachang, Zhg.	107	29.44 N	105.06 E
Jiajiachang, Zhg.	107	30.26 N	104.21 E
Jiajiagou, Zhg.	104	41.44 N	120.58 E
Jiajiagou, Zhg.	104	42.20 N	121.46 E
Jiajiang	107	29.45 N	103.34 E
Jiajiayuan	106	32.18 N	120.55 E
Jiakou	100	30.10 N	119.03 E
Jiakou Wa ≡	105	38.58 N	116.50 E
Jiali	120	30.47 N	93.24 E
Jialing ≃	102	29.34 N	106.35 E
Jialou	100	32.54 N	113.26 E
Jialu	106	30.26 N	118.50 E
Jialu ≃	100	33.38 N	114.36 E
Jiamingzhen	107	29.16 N	105.20 E
Jiamusi (Kiamusze)	89	46.50 N	130.21 E
Jiamuyingzi	104	41.56 N	121.43 E
Ji'an, Zhg.	98	41.06 N	126.08 E
Ji'an, Zhg.	100	27.07 N	114.58 E
Jian ≃, Zhg.	100	26.38 N	118.12 E
Jian ≃, Zhg.	104	40.59 N	121.51 E
Jian'an	89	43.04 N	125.03 E
Jianba	106	31.59 N	120.35 E
Jianbi	106	32.11 N	119.35 E
Jianchang, Zhg.	98	39.58 N	122.35 E
Jianchang, Zhg.	98	41.16 N	124.29 E
Jianchang, Zhg.	98	40.51 N	119.46 E
Ji'anchang, Zhg.	107	30.31 N	106.02 E
Jianchangying	98	40.06 N	118.49 E
Jianchapu	105	39.06 N	116.31 E
Jianchaxi, Zhg.	102	28.08 N	108.04 E
Jianchaxi, Zhg.	107	30.22 N	104.03 E
Jianchuan	102	26.34 N	99.53 E
Jiande	100	29.29 N	119.16 E
Jiang'an	107	28.44 N	105.05 E
Jiangba	100	33.08 N	118.45 E
Jiangbei (Lianglukou)	107	29.44 N	106.38 E
Jiangbeixu	100	26.20 N	115.26 E
Jiangbian	102	24.03 N	103.37 E
Jiangbianzhai	102	23.49 N	100.11 E
Jiangcheng, Zhg.	102	22.40 N	101.48 E
Jiangcheng, Zhg.	105	38.52 N	115.22 E
Jiangcun	100	28.17 N	117.49 E
Jiangdi	102	25.08 N	104.45 E
Jiangdihe	102	25.55 N	101.31 E
Jiangdu	100	32.26 N	119.34 E
Jiangduo	100	32.22 N	120.15 E
Jiange	102	32.06 N	105.29 E
Jianggeer	120	36.41 N	76.07 E
Jianggezhuang	98	39.27 N	119.09 E
Jianghua (Shuikou)	102	24.58 N	111.38 E
Jianghuaqiao	106	32.05 N	120.00 E
Jiangji	100	32.19 N	115.44 E
Jiangjia, Zhg.	106	31.40 N	121.09 E
Jiangjia, Zhg.	106	31.58 N	121.28 E
Jiangjiadian	104	41.41 N	121.03 E
Jiangjiagou	104	41.44 N	121.44 E
Jiangjiaji	100	31.59 N	115.16 E
Jiangjiatun, Zhg.	104	41.42 N	122.02 E
Jiangjiatun, Zhg.	104	41.42 N	122.25 E
Jiangjin	107	29.17 N	106.15 E
Jiangjing	100	25.34 N	119.25 E
Jiangjunmiao	86	44.43 N	90.05 E
Jiangjunqiao	102	31.18 N	100.55 E
Jiangkou, Zhg.	100	29.43 N	121.25 E
Jiangkou, Zhg.	100	27.27 N	118.03 E
Jiangkou, Zhg.	100	25.29 N	119.12 E
Jiangkou, Zhg.	100	27.21 N	115.31 E
Jiangkou, Zhg.	100	27.44 N	114.49 E
Jiangkou, Zhg.	102	23.31 N	110.17 E
Jiangkou, Zhg.	102	27.37 N	108.48 E
Jiangkou, Zhg.	102	30.26 N	111.42 E
Jiangkou, Zhg.	102	33.39 N	107.12 E
Jiangkou, Zhg.	102	29.38 N	110.20 E
Jiangkou, Zhg.	107	30.14 N	103.55 E
Jiangkouji	100	32.50 N	116.16 E
Jiangkoutang	100	27.30 N	112.44 E
Jiangle	100	26.42 N	117.25 E
Jiangliadian	98	42.33 N	117.27 E
Jiangling	102	30.20 N	112.06 E
Jianglingxi	102	31.28 N	107.13 E
Jiangmen	100	22.35 N	113.05 E
Jiangmifeng	89	43.58 N	126.45 E
Jiangning	106	31.58 N	118.50 E
Jiangpu	100	32.04 N	118.37 E
Jiangqiao	89	46.48 N	123.45 E
Jiangqiaotou	106	30.37 N	120.38 E
Jiangshan	100	28.45 N	118.37 E
Jiangshan ≃	100	28.57 N	118.50 E
Jiangshe	106	31.34 N	120.08 E
Jiangshui	98	37.13 N	113.59 E
Jiangsu (Kiangsu) □[4]	90	33.00 N	120.00 E
Jiangtian	100	25.52 N	119.34 E
Jiangtun, Zhg.	102	23.41 N	112.37 E
Jiangtun, Zhg.	104	41.37 N	122.22 E
Jiangwakou	105	39.31 N	117.42 E
Jiangwan, Zhg.	100	29.25 N	118.02 E
Jiangwan, Zhg.	106	31.18 N	121.29 E
Jiangwan Airport ⊠	269b	31.20 N	121.30 E
Jiangxi	102	22.51 N	101.50 E
Jiangxi (Kiangsi) □[4]	100	28.00 N	116.00 E
Jiangxiacun	106	31.44 N	121.50 E
Jiangxiang	100	32.16 N	117.37 E
Jiangxikou	100	27.36 N	118.23 E
Jiangya	102	29.17 N	110.39 E
Jiangyi	100	29.12 N	115.46 E
Jiangyin	106	31.55 N	120.16 E
Jiangyou	102	31.47 N	104.45 E
Jiangyu, Zhg.	98	36.16 N	118.40 E
Jiangyu, Zhg.	100	27.50 N	112.46 E
Jiangyuanzhen	107	30.35 N	103.48 E
Jiangzaogang	106	32.01 N	121.03 E
Jiangzhasiji	120	30.28 N	88.55 E
Jiangzhong	120	29.10 N	93.32 E
Jiangzi	120	28.57 N	89.35 E
Jianhe, Zhg.	102	26.27 N	108.33 E
Jianhe, Zhg.	105	39.14 N	118.03 E
Jianhu	100	33.28 N	119.50 E
Jianli	100	29.49 N	112.53 E
Jianling	100	32.45 N	113.12 E
Jianning	100	26.50 N	116.49 E
Jian'ou	100	27.03 N	118.19 E
Jianping (Yebaishou)	98	41.24 N	119.37 E
Jianqiao	106	30.20 N	120.12 E
Jianqigou	104	40.54 N	123.17 E
Jianshan, Zhg.	100	29.14 N	120.44 E
Jianshan, Zhg.	100	29.58 N	120.16 E
Jian Shan ∧	104	41.49 N	121.44 E
Jianshi	102	30.36 N	109.38 E
Jianshui	102	23.38 N	102.49 E
Jiantiao	100	29.04 N	121.36 E
Jiantou	105	39.26 N	115.41 E
Jiantouji	98	34.35 N	117.34 E
Jianyang, Zhg.	100	27.22 N	118.04 E
Jianyang, Zhg.	100	33.27 N	119.40 E
Jianyang, Zhg.	107	30.24 N	104.32 E
Jiao ≃	100	26.48 N	119.42 E
Jiaocheng	102	37.33 N	112.02 E
Jiaodao	105	39.39 N	116.06 E
Jiaodianzi	104	41.32 N	121.49 E
Jiaodonggou	104	40.50 N	123.58 E
Jiaohe, Zhg.	89	43.42 N	127.19 E
Jiaohe, Zhg.	98	38.01 N	116.17 E
Jiaojiapuzi	104	40.47 N	123.48 E
Jiaolai ≃, Zhg.	89	43.43 N	123.05 E
Jiaolai ≃, Zhg.	98	37.07 N	119.35 E
Jiaolai ≃, Zhg.	98	42.47 N	120.44 E
Jiaoling	100	24.41 N	116.10 E
Jiaomei	100	24.32 N	117.54 E
Jiaonan (Wanggezhuang)	98	35.51 N	119.59 E
Jiao Shan I	106	31.21 N	120.06 E
Jiaoshanhe	100	29.38 N	112.33 E
Jiaoxi	106	31.49 N	120.10 E
Jiaoxian	98	36.18 N	119.58 E
Jiaoyang	100	27.56 N	119.16 E
Jiaozhou Wan ⊂	98	36.10 N	120.15 E
Jiaozhuang	100	33.14 N	114.02 E
Jiaozuo	102	35.15 N	113.13 E
Jiapu	106	31.06 N	119.56 E
Jiashan, Zhg.	100	32.47 N	118.00 E
Jiashan, Zhg.	106	30.51 N	120.54 E
Jiashi	85	39.28 N	76.45 E
Jiashunhu ⊜	120	34.35 N	86.05 E
Jiasi	107	29.06 N	106.24 E
Jiatan	107	30.12 N	106.29 E
Jiatanchang	107	29.09 N	106.16 E
Jiawang	98	34.27 N	117.27 E
Jiaxian, Zhg.	100	33.58 N	113.13 E
Jiaxian, Zhg.	102	38.01 N	110.31 E
Jiaxiang	98	35.25 N	116.21 E
Jiaxing	106	30.46 N	120.45 E
Jiayin	89	48.53 N	130.24 E
Jiayu	100	29.58 N	113.55 E
Jiayunhu ⊜	120	35.02 N	85.40 E
Jiaze	106	31.42 N	119.47 E
Jiazhai	98	34.33 N	115.48 E
Jiazhuang	105	39.19 N	117.22 E
Jiazi	100	22.55 N	116.04 E
Jiazier	85	38.40 N	76.33 E
Jibacoa ≃	240p	20.15 N	77.12 W
Jibagalle	144	8.04 N	48.39 E
Jibalei	144	10.09 N	50.53 E
Jibannagar	126	23.25 N	88.50 E
Jíbaro, Arroyo ≃	286b	23.03 N	82.23 W
Jibat ∧	144	8.45 N	37.29 E
Jibiya	150	13.05 N	7.12 E
Jiboa ≃	236	13.22 N	89.04 W
Jibóia, Ilha da I	256	23.03 S	44.22 W
Jibuti → Djibouti	144	11.36 N	43.09 E
Jicamarca, Quebrada V	286d	12.02 S	76.57 W
Jicarilla Apache Indian Reservation ✦[4]	200	36.40 N	107.00 W
Jicarón, Isla I	246	7.16 N	81.47 W
Jicatuyo ≃	236	14.43 N	88.39 W
Jicheng	105	39.23 N	116.17 E
Jičín	30	50.26 N	15.21 E
Jicotea ≃	286b	23.01 N	82.14 W
Jidād	140	11.05 N	24.44 E
Jiddah	144	21.30 N	39.12 E
Jidingxilin	120	32.52 N	92.21 E

	English	Deutsch	Español	Français	Português
≃	River	Fluss	Río	Rivière	Rio
≊	Canal	Kanal	Canal	Canal	Canal
ʟ	Waterfall, Rapids	Wasserfall, Stromschnellen	Cascada, Rápidos	Chute d'eau, Rapides	Cascata, Rápidos
⊔	Strait	Meeresstrasse	Estrecho	Détroit	Estreito
⊂	Bay, Gulf	Bucht, Golf	Bahía, Golfo	Baie, Golfe	Baía, Golfo
⊜	Lake, Lakes	See, Seen	Lago, Lagos	Lac, Lacs	Lago, Lagos
≡	Swamp	Sumpf	Pantano	Marais	Pântano
⊓	Ice Features, Glacier	Eis- und Gletscherformen	Accidentes Glaciales	Formes glaciaires	Acidentes glaciares
⊤	Other Hydrographic Features	Andere Hydrographische Objekte	Otros Elementos Hidrográficos	Autres données hydrographiques	Outros acidentes hidrográficos
✢	Submarine Features	Untermeerische Objekte	Accidentes Submarinos	Formes de relief sous-marin	Acidentes submarinos
□	Political Unit	Politische Einheit	Unidad Politica	Entité politique	Unidade política
ʋ	Cultural Institution	Kulturelle Institution	Institución Cultural	Institution culturelle	Institução cultural
⊥	Historical Site	Historische Stätte	Sitio Histórico	Site historique	Sitio histórico
♦	Recreational Site	Erholungs- und Ferienort	Sitio de Recreo	Centre de loisirs	Area de Lazer
⊠	Airport	Flughafen	Aeropuerto	Aéroport	Aeroporto
■	Military Installation	Militäranlage	Instalación Militar	Installation militaire	Instalação militar
✦	Miscellaneous	Verschiedenes	Misceláneo	Divers	Diversos

Symbols in the index entries represent the broad categories identified in the key at the right. Symbols with superior numbers (⋏[1]) identify subcategories (see complete key on page *I · 1).*

Kartensymbole in dem Registerverzeichnis stellen die rechts in Schlüssel erklärten Kategorien dar. Symbole mit hochgestellten Ziffern (⋏[1]) bezeichnen Unterabteilungen einer Kategorie (vgl. vollständiger Schlüssel auf Seite *I · 1).*

Los símbolos incluídos en el texto del índice representan las grandes categorias identificadas con la clave a la derecha. Los símbolos con numeros en su parte superior (⋏[1]) identifican las subcategorías (véase la clave completa en la página *I · 1).*

Les symboles de l'index représentent les catégories indiquées dans la légende à droite. Les symboles suivis d'un indice (⋏[1]) représentent des sous-catégories (voir légende complète à la page *I · 1).*

Os símbolos incluídos no texto do índice representam as grandes categorias identificadas com a chave à direita. Os símbolos com números em sua parte superior (⋏[1]) identificam as subcategorias (veja-se a chave completa à página *I · 1).*

∧	Mountain	Berg	Montaña	Montagne	Montanha
⋏	Mountains	Berge	Montañas	Montagnes	Montanhas
✕	Pass	Pass	Paso	Col	Passo
∨	Valley, Canyon	Tal, Cañon	Valle, Cañón	Vallée, Canyon	Vale, Canhão
≚	Plain	Ebene	Llano	Plaine	Planície
≻	Cape	Kap	Cabo	Cap	Cabo
I	Island	Insel	Isla	Île	Ilha
II	Islands	Inseln	Islas	Îles	Ilhas
⊥	Other Topographic Features	Andere Topographische Objekte	Otros Elementos Topográficos	Autres données topographiques	Outros acidentes topográficos

Symbol	English	Deutsch	Español	Français	Português
≏	River	Fluss	Río	Rivière	Rio
≊	Canal	Kanal	Canal	Canal	Canal
⌊	Waterfall, Rapids	Wasserfall, Stromschnellen	Cascada, Rápidos	Chute d'eau, Rapides	Cascata, Rápidos
ʯ	Strait	Meeresstrasse	Estrecho	Détroit	Estreito
⊂	Bay, Gulf	Bucht, Golf	Bahía, Golfo	Baie, Golfe	Baía, Golfo
⊜	Lake, Lakes	See, Seen	Lago, Lagos	Lac, Lacs	Lago, Lagos
≡	Swamp	Sumpf	Pantano	Marais	Pântano
≚	Ice Features, Glacier	Eis- und Gletscherformen	Accidentes Glaciales	Formes glaciaires	Acidentes glaciares
⍑	Other Hydrographic Features	Andere Hydrographische Objekte	Otros Elementos Hidrográficos	Autres données hydrographiques	Outros acidentes hidrográficos
✢	Submarine Features	Untermeerische Objekte	Accidentes Submarinos	Formes de relief sous-marin	Acidentes submarinos
□	Political Unit	Politische Einheit	Unidad Politica	Entité politique	Unidade política
⊎	Cultural Institution	Kulturelle Institution	Institución Cultural	Institution culturelle	Institução cultural
⊥	Historical Site	Historische Stätte	Sitio Histórico	Site historique	Sitio histórico
♠	Recreational Site	Erholungs- und Ferienort	Sitio de Recreo	Centre de loisirs	Area de Lazer
⊠	Airport	Flughafen	Aeropuerto	Aéroport	Aeroporto
■	Military Installation	Militäranlage	Instalación Militar	Installation militaire	Instalação militar
⬥	Miscellaneous	Verschiedenes	Misceláneo	Divers	Diversos

ENGLISH — Name | Page | Lat.°′ | Long.°′
DEUTSCH — Name | Seite | Breite°′ | Länge°′ E = Ost

Name	Page	Lat.	Long.
Kakagi Lake ⊜	184	49.13 N	93.52 W
Kakamas	158	28.45 S	20.33 E
Kakamega	154	0.17 N	34.45 E
Kakamigahara	94	35.24 N	136.54 E
Kakana	110	9.07 N	92.49 E
Kakanui Mountains ⋏	172	45.09 S	170.26 E
Kaka Point	172	46.23 S	169.47 E
Kakaramea	172	39.43 S	174.27 E
Kakasa	164	9.20 S	148.45 E
Kakata	150	6.35 N	10.19 W
Kakatahi	172	39.41 S	175.20 E
Kākdwīp	126	21.53 N	88.11 E
Kake, Nihon	96	34.36 N	132.19 E
Kake, Ak., U.S.	180	56.58 N	133.56 W
Kakegawa	94	34.46 N	138.01 E
Kakehashi ≃	94	36.25 N	136.25 E
Kakelwe	154	4.49 S	29.00 E
Kakenge	152	4.51 S	21.55 E
Kakeya	96	35.11 N	132.49 E
Kakhonak	180	59.26 N	154.51 W
Kakhra	126	21.38 N	87.27 E
Kākī	128	28.19 N	51.34 E
Kākināda	122	16.56 N	82.13 E
Kakino	80	55.12 N	44.53 E
Kakinoki	96	34.26 N	131.52 E
Kakisa Lake ⊜	176	60.55 N	117.40 W
Kakizaki	92	37.15 N	138.25 E
Kako ≃, Guy.	246	5.46 N	60.35 W
Kako ≃, Nihon	96	34.44 N	134.49 E
Kakoaka	156	18.40 S	24.22 E
Kakogawa	96	34.46 N	134.51 E
Kakrāla	272a	28.33 N	77.25 E
Kāksa	126	23.28 N	87.28 E
Kaktovik	180	70.08 N	143.37 W
Kakuda	92	37.58 N	140.47 E
Kakui-shima I	96	34.43 N	134.19 E
Kakuma	154	3.43 N	34.52 E
Kakunodate	92	39.35 N	140.34 E
Kakus ≃	112	2.46 N	113.01 E
Kakwa ≃	182	54.36 N	118.28 W
Kala, Nig.	146	12.05 N	14.27 E
Kala, Zhg.	120	36.47 N	83.48 E
Kala, Zhg.	124	28.16 N	89.23 E
Kala ≃	122	8.18 N	79.50 E
Kalaa Kebira	148	35.52 N	10.32 E
Kalaallit Nunaat → Greenland □[2]	16	70.00 N	40.00 W
Kalaa Sghira	36	35.49 N	10.33 E
Kālābagh	123	32.58 N	71.34 E
Kalabahi	112	8.13 S	124.31 E
Kalabáka	38	39.42 N	21.43 E
Kalabakan	112	4.25 N	117.29 E
Kalabo	152	14.57 S	22.40 E
Kalabula	86	43.24 N	83.06 E
Kalač	78	50.25 N	41.01 E
Kalacık	130	37.17 N	39.02 E
Kalačinsk	86	55.03 N	74.34 E
Kalač-Kurtlak	80	49.00 N	42.26 E
Kalač-Na-Donu	80	48.43 N	43.31 E
Kalačskaja vozvyšennost' ⋏[1]	80	50.30 N	41.30 E
Kaladan ≃	110	20.09 N	92.57 E
Kaladar	212	44.39 N	77.07 W
Kalae	229a	21.10 N	157.00 W
Ka Lae ≻	229d	18.55 N	155.41 W
Kalaena ≃	112	2.40 S	120.53 E
Kalagan	89	50.30 N	119.55 E
Kalagwe	110	22.31 N	96.31 E
Kalahari Desert ◆[2]	156	24.00 S	21.30 E
Kalahari Gemsbok National Park ♦	156	25.30 S	20.30 E
Kālahasti	122	13.45 N	79.43 E
Kalaheo	229b	21.55 N	159.31 W
Kālaia	126	22.23 N	90.36 E
Kalai-Chumb	85	38.28 N	70.46 E
Kalai-Mor	128	35.39 N	62.33 E
Kalais	80	52.38 N	42.38 E
Kalaiya	124	27.02 N	85.00 E
Kalajka	88	58.28 N	111.46 E
Kalajoki	26	64.15 N	23.57 E
Kalajoki ≃	26	64.17 N	23.55 E
Kalakamate	156	20.39 S	27.21 E
Kalakan	88	55.08 N	116.45 E
Kalakan ≃	88	55.07 N	116.46 E
Kalakashihe ≃	120	37.00 N	79.45 E
Kalakepen	114	2.45 N	97.50 E
Kalām	123	35.32 N	72.35 E
Kalama, Wa., U.S.	224	46.00 N	122.50 W
Kalama, Zaïre	154	2.55 S	28.33 E
Kalama ≃	224	46.02 N	122.52 W
Kalama, Pulau I	112	3.15 N	125.28 E
Kalámai	38	37.04 N	22.07 E
Kalamaki	130	36.15 N	29.24 E
Kalamákion	267c	37.55 N	23.43 E
Kalamalka Lake ⊜	182	50.09 N	119.22 W
Kalamariá	38	40.35 N	22.58 E
Kalamazoo	216	42.17 N	85.35 W
Kalamazoo □[6]	216	42.14 N	85.32 W
Kalamazoo ≃	216	42.40 N	86.10 W
Kalamazoo, North Branch ≃	216	42.14 N	84.44 W
Kalamazoo, South Branch ≃	216	42.14 N	84.44 W
Kalamazoo Lake ⊂	216	42.39 N	86.13 W
Kalamb	122	19.03 N	73.57 E
Kalamba	152	0.26 S	18.17 E
Kalambau, Pulau I	112	4.55 S	115.39 E
Kalambo Falls ∟	154	8.36 S	31.14 E
Kalamboli	272c	19.01 N	73.06 E
Kalamitskij zaliv ⊂	78	45.05 N	33.23 E
Kalamo	216	42.32 N	85.01 W
Kalampáka	38	39.42 N	21.39 E
Kalampising	112	3.44 N	116.42 E
Kalamunda	168a	31.57 S	116.03 E
Kalana	150	10.47 N	8.12 W
Kalančak	78	46.16 N	33.17 E
Kalandula	152	9.06 S	15.57 E
Kalang ≃	271c	1.19 N	103.52 E
Kalange-Bushimaie ≃	152	7.55 S	23.11 E
Kalanguj	88	51.01 N	116.31 E
Kalankalan	150	10.07 N	8.54 W
Kalannie	162	30.21 S	117.04 E
Kalanshiyū ar-Ramlī al-Kabīr, Sarīr ≛[8]	146	28.00 N	23.00 E
Kālānwāli	123	29.51 N	74.57 E
Kalao, Pulau I	112	7.18 S	120.58 E
Kalaong	116	6.04 N	124.28 E
Kalaotoa, Pulau I	112	7.22 S	121.47 E
Kalapana	229d	19.21 N	154.58 W
Kalapāra	126	21.59 N	90.14 E
Kalar ≃	88	55.23 N	116.18 E
Kalaraš	78	47.16 N	28.19 E
Kälarne	26	62.59 N	16.05 E
Kalāroa	126	22.52 N	89.02 E
Kalasarv	84	39.11 N	48.03 E
Kalashankou	120	35.06 N	91.51 E
Kalasi	86	48.43 N	86.59 E
Kalasin, Indon.	112	0.12 N	114.16 E
Kalasin, Thai	110	16.29 N	103.30 E
Kalašnikovo	76	57.17 N	35.13 E
Kalāt	120	29.02 N	66.35 E
Kalatungan Mountain ∧	116	7.58 N	124.47 E
Kalaupapa	229a	21.11 N	156.59 W
Kalaupapa National Historical Park ♦	229a	21.12 N	156.58 W
Kalaupapa Peninsula ≻[1]	229a	21.13 N	156.58 W
Kalauri	84	41.49 N	45.42 E
Kalaus ≃	80	45.43 N	44.07 E
Kalaus-Kr'akovka	83	48.46 N	38.52 E
Kalavárdha	38	36.20 N	27.57 E
Kalávrita	38	38.01 N	22.06 E
Kalaw	110	20.38 N	96.34 E
Kalawao □[6]	229a	21.12 N	156.58 W
Kal'azin	76	57.15 N	37.52 E
Kalb, Nahr al- ≃	132	33.57 N	35.35 E
Kalb, Ra's al- ≻	144	14.02 N	48.40 E
Kalbā'	128	25.03 N	56.21 E
Kalbar	171a	27.56 S	152.37 E
Kalbarri National Park ♦	162	27.45 S	114.25 E
Kalbe	54	52.40 N	11.25 E
Kalbinskij chrebet ⋏	86	49.10 N	83.00 E
Kalchās	120	29.21 N	69.42 E
Kal'čik ≃	83	47.07 N	37.36 E
Kaldırım ≃	267b	41.10 N	29.12 E
Kaldygajty ≃	80	49.20 N	52.38 E
Kale, Tür.	130	37.26 N	28.51 E
Kale, Tür.	130	40.23 N	39.39 E
Kalecik	130	40.06 N	33.25 E
Kaleden	182	49.23 N	119.35 W
Kaledupa, Pulau I	112	5.32 S	123.47 E
Kalegauk Island I	110	15.32 N	97.40 E
Kalehe	154	2.06 S	28.55 E
Kaleindaung ≃	110	18.50 N	94.00 E
Kalema, Tan.	154	1.12 S	31.50 E
Kalema, Zaïre	152	4.08 S	24.15 E
Kalemie (Albertville)	154	5.56 S	29.12 E
Kalemyo	120	23.12 N	94.10 E
Kalene Hill	152	11.11 S	24.10 E
Kaleščatovka	83	49.35 N	39.55 E
Kaletwa	110	21.45 N	92.48 E
Kalety	30	50.34 N	18.54 E
Kalevala	24	65.13 N	31.08 E
Kalewa	110	23.12 N	94.17 E
Kale Water ≃	46	55.32 N	2.28 W
Kaleybar	84	38.47 N	47.02 E
Kálfafell	24a	63.58 N	17.40 W
Kalga	88	50.57 N	118.48 E
Kalgačicha	24	63.20 N	36.44 E
Kalgan, Austl.	162	34.53 S	118.01 E
Kalgan → Zhangjiakou, Zhg.	105	40.50 N	114.53 E
Kalgin Island I	180	60.28 N	151.55 W
Kalgoorlie	162	30.45 S	121.28 E
Kalhe	272c	18.52 N	73.06 E
Kali	150	12.10 N	11.29 W
Kāli (Sārda) ≃	124	27.21 N	81.23 E
Kālia	126	23.03 N	89.38 E
Kāliāghaj ≃	126	22.10 N	87.50 E
Kāliākair	126	24.05 N	90.14 E
Kaliakra, nos ≻	38	43.21 N	28.27 E
Kalianda	115a	5.45 S	105.38 E
Kalianget	115a	7.03 S	113.56 E
Kalibek, ozero ⊜	86	53.52 N	70.40 E
Kālībhīt Hills ⋏[2]	124	22.10 N	77.30 E
Kalibo	116	11.43 N	122.22 E
Kalida	216	40.59 N	84.12 W
Kalifornien, Golf von → California, Golfo de ⊂	232	28.00 N	112.00 W
Kāli Gandaki ≃	124	27.42 N	84.25 E
Kāliganga ≃	126	23.43 N	90.15 E
Kāli Ganga ≃[1]	126	23.40 N	89.12 E
Kālīganj, Bngl.	126	23.25 N	89.08 E
Kālīganj, Bngl.	126	22.28 N	89.02 E
Kāliganj, India	126	23.44 N	88.14 E
Kalihiwai ≃	229b	22.13 N	159.26 W
Kalijati	115a	6.32 S	107.40 E
Kālikāpur, Bngl.	126	22.43 N	89.26 E
Kālikāpur, Bngl.	126	23.46 N	89.55 E
Kālikāpur, India	126	22.37 N	86.17 E
Kālikāpur, India	272b	22.29 N	88.32 E
Kalikino, S.S.S.R.	76	52.57 N	39.50 E
Kalikino, S.S.S.R.	80	52.55 N	54.05 E
Kalima, Zaïre	154	2.34 S	26.37 E
Kalima, Zhg.	104	41.32 N	122.40 E
Kalimantan → Borneo I	112	0.30 N	114.00 E
Kalimantan Barat □[4]	112	0.30 N	110.00 E
Kalimantan Selatan □[4]	112	2.30 S	115.30 E
Kalimantan Tengah □[4]	112	2.00 S	113.30 E
Kalimantan Timur □[4]	112	1.30 N	116.30 E
Kálimnos	38	36.57 N	26.59 E
Kálimnos I	38	37.00 N	27.00 E
Kālimpong	124	27.04 N	88.29 E
Kalina, Pointe de ≻	273b	4.18 S	15.16 E
Kālīnadi ≃	122	14.50 N	74.08 E
Kālinagar	126	22.26 N	88.51 E
Kalinga-Apayao □[4]	116	17.50 N	121.10 E
Kalinga Bil ⊜	272b	22.33 N	88.33 E
Kalinin, S.S.S.R.	80	47.11 N	42.10 E
Kalinin, S.S.S.R.	82	56.52 N	35.55 E
Kalinin □[4]	82	56.45 N	36.30 E
Kalininabad	85	39.45 N	69.08 E
Kaliningrad (Königsberg), S.S.S.R.	76	54.43 N	20.30 E
Kaliningrad, S.S.S.R.	82	55.55 N	37.49 E
Kalinino, S.S.S.R.	78	45.07 N	39.00 E
Kalinino, S.S.S.R.	80	46.21 N	48.53 E
Kalinino, S.S.S.R.	83	47.27 N	37.28 E
Kalinino, S.S.S.R.	84	41.07 N	44.17 E
Kalinino, S.S.S.R.	86	57.20 N	56.20 E
Kalinino, S.S.S.R.	89	49.24 N	129.20 E
Kalininsk, S.S.S.R.	80	51.30 N	44.28 E
Kalininsk, S.S.S.R.	85	42.29 N	72.06 E
Kalininskaja, S.S.S.R.	78	45.29 N	38.40 E
Kalininskaja, S.S.S.R.	80	47.52 N	42.15 E
Kalininskij	83	48.01 N	39.36 E
Kalininskoje, S.S.S.R.	78	47.07 N	32.59 E
Kalininskoje, S.S.S.R.	85	42.50 N	73.49 E
Kalinkoviči	78	52.08 N	29.21 E
Kalinku	154	11.12 S	33.12 E
Kalinovik	38	43.31 N	18.26 E
Kalinovka, S.S.S.R.	78	51.54 N	34.28 E
Kalinovka, S.S.S.R.	78	50.14 N	30.14 E
Kalinovka, S.S.S.R.	78	49.27 N	28.32 E
Kalinovka, S.S.S.R.	86	49.58 N	55.22 E
Kalinovo, S.S.S.R.	82	54.54 N	37.17 E
Kalinovo, S.S.S.R.	83	48.34 N	38.31 E
Kalipara	126	22.09 N	89.16 E
Kālipur	272b	22.41 N	88.17 E
Kaliro	154	0.54 N	33.30 E
Kalis	144	8.23 N	49.05 E
Kalisat	115a	8.08 S	113.48 E
Kalisch → Kalisz	30	51.46 N	18.06 E
Kāli Sindh ≃	124	25.32 N	76.17 E
Kalispell	202	48.11 N	114.18 W
Kalistraticha	86	52.59 N	83.35 E
Kalisz	30	51.46 N	18.06 E
Kalisz □[4]	30	51.40 N	17.45 E
Kalisz Pomorski	30	53.19 N	15.54 E
Kalitva ≃	78	48.10 N	40.46 E
Kaliua	154	5.04 S	31.48 E
Kaliveli Tank ⊜[1]	122	12.05 N	79.50 E
Kaliwiro	115a	7.27 S	109.51 E
Kaliwungu	115a	6.57 S	110.14 E
Kalix	26	65.51 N	23.08 E
Kalixälven ≃	24	65.50 N	23.11 E
Kāliyāganj	124	25.38 N	88.19 E
Kālka	123	30.50 N	76.56 E
Kālkāji ◆[8]	272a	28.33 N	77.16 E
Kalkaman	86	51.58 N	76.02 E
Kalkar	52	50.36 N	6.46 E
Kalkaska	190	44.44 N	85.10 W
Kalkfeld	156	20.53 S	16.11 E
Kalkfontein	156	22.08 S	20.53 E
Kalkfonteindam ⊜[1]	158	29.30 S	25.15 E
Kalkhorst	54	53.58 N	11.02 E
Kālkini	126	23.06 N	90.16 E
Kalkmond	158	28.40 S	20.26 E
Kalkrand	156	24.03 S	17.33 E
Kalksburg ◆[8]	264b	48.08 N	16.15 E
Kalk-See ⊜	264a	52.26 N	13.46 E
Kalkstasie	158	30.00 S	18.55 E
Kalkum	263	51.18 N	6.46 E
Kalkutta → Calcutta	126	22.32 N	88.22 E
Kalkwerf	158	28.39 S	21.43 E
Kall	56	50.32 N	6.32 E
Kallakkurichchi	122	11.44 N	78.58 E
Kallakoopah Creek ≃	166	27.29 S	138.15 E
Kållandsö I	26	58.40 N	13.09 E
Kallar Kahār	123	32.47 N	72.42 E
Kallaste	76	58.39 N	27.09 E
Kallavesi ⊜	26	62.50 N	27.45 E
Kalletal	52	52.06 N	8.56 E
Källfallet	40	59.50 N	15.31 E
Kallhäll	40	59.27 N	17.48 E
Kalliecahoolie Lake ⊜	184	54.14 N	95.29 W
Kallies → Kalisz Pomorski	30	53.19 N	15.54 E
Kallinge	26	56.14 N	15.17 E
Kallista	274b	37.53 S	145.22 E
Kallithéa	267c	37.57 N	23.42 E
Kallmünz	60	49.09 N	11.58 E
Kallnach	58	47.01 N	7.14 E
Kallsjön ⊜	26	63.37 N	13.00 E
Kalmakkora	86	44.03 N	78.44 E
Kalmakkyrgan ≃	86	46.58 N	64.30 E
Kalmar	26	56.40 N	16.22 E
Kalmar Län □[6]	26	57.20 N	16.00 E
Kalmarsund ų	26	56.40 N	16.25 E
Kalmit ∧	56	49.19 N	8.05 E
Kal'mius ≃	83	47.05 N	37.34 E
Kalmthout	50	51.23 N	4.28 E
Kalmyckaja Avtonomnaja Sovetskaja Socialističeskaja Respublika □[3]	80	46.30 N	45.30 E
Kalmyckije Mysy	86	51.53 N	82.16 E
Kalmykov	80	49.01 N	42.49 E
Kalmykovka, S.S.S.R.	83	49.17 N	38.39 E
Kalmykovka, S.S.S.R.	83	49.17 N	39.52 E
Kalmykovo	80	49.03 N	51.47 E
Kālna	126	23.13 N	88.22 E
Kalnciems	76	56.50 N	23.37 E
Kal'niboloto	78	48.44 N	31.00 E
Kalnibolotskaja	78	46.01 N	40.28 E
Kalničko Gorje ⋏	36	46.10 N	16.30 E
Kalo	164	10.00 S	147.45 E
Kálócfa	61	46.45 N	16.34 E
Kalocsa	30	46.32 N	18.59 E
Kalofer	38	42.37 N	24.59 E
Kalohi Channel ų	229a	21.00 N	156.56 W
Kaloko	154	6.47 S	25.48 E
Kālol, India	120	22.36 N	73.27 E
Kālol, India	120	23.15 N	72.29 E
Kalole	154	3.42 S	27.22 E
Kalolio	112	0.11 S	121.38 E
Kaloli Point ≻	229d	19.38 N	154.57 W
Kalomo	154	17.02 S	26.30 E
Kalomo ≃	154	17.57 S	26.24 E
Kalona	190	41.28 N	91.42 W
Kalonda	152	4.48 S	17.33 E
Kalone Peak ∧	182	52.38 N	126.37 W
Kalonga	154	9.10 S	27.25 E
Kalorama	274b	37.49 S	145.22 E
Kaloran	115a	7.15 S	110.15 E
Kalø Vig ⊂	41	56.15 N	10.25 E
Kalpáki	38	39.55 N	20.20 E
Kalpeni Island I	122	10.05 N	73.38 E
Kālpi	124	26.07 N	79.44 E
Kāl Qal'eh	128	32.38 N	62.32 E
Kalri	123	31.39 N	72.33 E
Kalsdorf bei Graz	61	46.57 N	15.28 E
Kalskag	180	61.30 N	160.23 W
Kalsūbai ∧	122	19.36 N	73.43 E
Kaltag	180	64.20 N	158.44 W
Kaltan	86	53.30 N	87.17 E
Kaltbrunn	58	47.12 N	9.02 E
Kalte Herberge ∧	56	50.03 N	7.59 E
Kalteneber	56	51.19 N	10.08 E
Kaltenhouse	56	48.48 N	7.50 E
Kaltenkirchen	52	53.50 N	9.58 E
Kaltenleutgeben	264b	48.07 N	16.12 E
Kaltennordheim	56	50.38 N	10.10 E
Kaltensundheim	56	50.36 N	10.10 E
Kalter Gang ≃	264b	48.02 N	16.25 E
Kalthof	263	51.26 N	7.40 E
Kal'tino	265a	59.58 N	30.40 E
Kaltungo	146	9.50 N	11.19 E
Kaluga	82	54.31 N	36.16 E
Kaluga □[4]	82	54.45 N	36.30 E
Kalugino, S.S.S.R.	80	48.22 N	51.33 E
Kalugino, S.S.S.R.	82	54.59 N	37.11 E
Kalukalukuang, Pulau I	112	5.14 S	117.38 E
Kalulushi	154	12.50 S	28.03 E
Kalumba, Mount ∧	166	31.49 S	146.22 E
Kalumburu	164	14.18 S	126.39 E
Kalumburu Aboriginal Reserve ◆[4]	164	14.15 S	126.50 E
Kalundborg	41	55.41 N	11.06 E
Kalundborg Fjord ⊂	41	55.41 N	11.00 E
Kālundri	272c	18.59 N	73.08 E
Kalundu, Zaïre	154	3.26 S	29.08 E
Kalundu, Zam.	154	10.16 S	29.24 E
Kalungwishi ≃	154	9.01 S	28.57 E
Kālupāra	126	22.58 N	90.10 E
Kalūr Kot	123	32.09 N	71.16 E
Kaluš	78	49.03 N	24.23 E
Kałuszyn	30	52.13 N	21.49 E
Kalutara	122	6.35 N	79.58 E
Kalvåg	26	61.46 N	4.53 E
Kalvarija	76	54.21 N	23.14 E
K'alvaz	84	38.39 N	48.18 E
Kalvehave	41	55.00 N	12.10 E
Kälviä	26	63.52 N	23.26 E
Kalwa	272c	19.12 N	72.59 E
Kalwang	61	47.26 N	14.46 E
Kalwaria Zebrzydowska	30	49.52 N	19.41 E
Kalyān	122	19.15 N	73.09 E
Kalyāndrug	122	14.33 N	77.06 E
Kam ≃	146	8.15 N	11.00 E
Kama, Mya.	110	19.02 N	95.06 E
Kama, S.S.S.R.	80	56.19 N	54.06 E
Kama, S.S.S.R.	86	60.08 N	62.10 E
Kama, Zaïre	154	3.32 S	27.07 E
Kama ≃, S.S.S.R.	72	55.45 N	52.00 E
Kama ≃, S.S.S.R.	86	55.35 N	76.54 E
Kamachumu	154	1.35 S	31.37 E
Kamado-zaki ≻	96	33.04 N	132.02 E
Kamae	92	32.48 N	131.56 E
Kamagaya	94	35.45 N	140.01 E
Kamaiki Point ≻	229a	20.46 N	156.50 W
Kamaishi	92	39.16 N	141.53 E
Kama-iwa I	174f	24.47 N	141.17 E
Kamajai	76	55.49 N	25.30 E
Kamakou ∧	229a	21.07 N	156.52 W
Kamakura	94	35.19 N	139.33 E
Kamakwie	150	9.30 N	12.14 W
Kamal	115a	7.10 S	112.42 E
Kamālia	123	30.44 N	72.39 E
Kamamaung	110	17.21 N	97.40 E
Kāman, India	124	27.39 N	77.16 E
Kaman, Tür.	130	39.22 N	33.44 E
Kaman ≃	110	14.48 N	106.51 E
Kamana	154	5.59 S	24.56 E
Kamanashi ≃	94	35.33 N	138.28 E
Kamango	154	0.39 N	29.53 E
Kamaniskeg Lake ⊜	212	45.25 N	77.42 W
Kamanjab	156	19.35 S	14.51 E
Kamapanda	152	12.00 S	24.10 E
Kamaraerdő ◆[3]	264c	47.26 N	19.00 E
Kamarān I	144	15.21 N	42.34 E
Kamaran, Hadjer ∧	146	12.41 N	21.46 E
Kamarang ≃	246	5.53 N	60.35 W
Kāmāreddi	122	18.19 N	78.21 E
Kāmārhāti	272b	22.40 N	88.22 E
Kamarik	130	39.37 N	39.18 E
Kāmārkhāli Ghāt	126	23.32 N	89.33 E
Kāmārkunda	272b	22.49 N	88.13 E
Kamas	200	40.38 N	111.16 W
Kamata ◆[8]	268	35.33 N	139.43 E
Kamatsi Lake ⊜	184	56.10 N	102.15 W
Kamay	196	33.51 N	98.48 W
Kamba, Nig.	150	11.53 N	3.36 E
Kamba, Zhg.	120	28.17 N	88.32 E
Kamba Kota	152	7.10 N	17.54 E
Kamballie	162	30.48 S	121.30 E
Kambam	122	9.44 N	77.18 E
Kambang	112	1.42 S	100.42 E
Kambanga	152	13.23 S	23.03 E
Kambar	120	27.36 N	68.00 E
Kambara	94	35.07 N	138.36 E
Kambara Island I	175g	18.57 S	178.57 W
Kambara-tunnel ◆[5]	94	35.02 N	138.31 E
Kambarka	80	56.17 N	54.12 E
Kambia	150	9.07 N	12.55 W
Kambing, Pulau I	112	8.13 S	125.35 E
Kambja	76	58.14 N	26.42 E
Kambolé	150	8.45 N	1.36 E
Kambole Mission	154	8.46 S	30.46 E
Kambove	154	10.52 S	26.38 E
Kambu	115b	8.23 S	118.20 E
Kambuye	152	7.18 S	22.50 E
Kamčatka ≃	74	56.15 N	162.30 E
Kamčatka, poluostrov ≻[1]	74	56.00 N	160.00 E
Kamčatskij poluostrov ≻[1]	74	56.15 N	163.00 E
Kamčatskij zaliv ⊂	74	55.35 N	162.21 E
Kâmchay Méa	110	11.35 N	105.40 E
Kamčija ≃	38	43.02 N	27.53 E
Kāmdebpur, India	272b	22.47 N	88.30 E
Kāmdebpur, India	272b	22.54 N	88.20 E
Kamdēsh	123	35.24 N	71.20 E
Kameari ◆[8]	268	35.46 N	139.51 E
Kameda	92	37.52 N	139.07 E
Kameel	158	26.38 S	24.58 E
Kamegamori ∧	96	33.47 N	133.12 E
Kameido ◆[8]	268	35.42 N	139.50 E
Kamelik ≃	80	52.06 N	49.30 E
Kamen, B.R.D.	52	51.35 N	7.40 E
Kamen', S.S.S.R.	76	55.01 N	28.53 E
Kamen', gora ∧	74	69.06 N	94.48 E
Kamenda	154	6.28 S	24.33 E
Kamenec	76	52.24 N	23.49 E
Kamenec-Podol'skij	78	48.41 N	26.36 E
Kamenický Šenov	54	50.45 N	14.29 E
Kamenjak, Rt ≻	36	44.46 N	13.55 E
Kamenka, S.S.S.R.	24	65.54 N	44.05 E
Kamenka, S.S.S.R.	78	50.43 N	39.25 E
Kamenka, S.S.S.R.	78	49.02 N	32.06 E
Kamenka, S.S.S.R.	78	48.03 N	28.42 E
Kamenka, S.S.S.R.	80	51.07 N	50.19 E
Kamenka, S.S.S.R.	80	56.11 N	45.35 E
Kamenka, S.S.S.R.	80	57.23 N	41.49 E
Kamenka, S.S.S.R.	80	53.13 N	44.03 E
Kamenka, S.S.S.R.	80	52.04 N	41.49 E
Kamenka, S.S.S.R.	82	56.11 N	37.18 E
Kamenka, S.S.S.R.	82	55.13 N	36.59 E
Kamenka, S.S.S.R.	82	54.43 N	38.19 E
Kamenka, S.S.S.R.	83	49.38 N	39.22 E
Kamenka, S.S.S.R.	83	49.07 N	37.18 E
Kamenka, S.S.S.R.	83	47.25 N	37.42 E
Kamenka, S.S.S.R.	85	42.55 N	72.50 E
Kamenka, S.S.S.R.	86	58.33 N	95.51 E
Kamenka, S.S.S.R.	86	52.22 N	69.04 E
Kamenka, S.S.S.R.	89	44.28 N	136.01 E
Kamenka, S.S.S.R.	265a	59.59 N	30.53 E
Kamenka ◆[8]	265a	60.03 N	30.11 E
Kamenka ≃, S.S.S.R.	78	49.47 N	30.01 E
Kamenka ≃, S.S.S.R.	78	47.39 N	34.02 E
Kamenka ≃, S.S.S.R.	83	49.35 N	39.05 E
Kamenka ≃, S.S.S.R.	83	47.30 N	38.54 E
Kamenka ≃, S.S.S.R.	88	58.33 N	95.51 E
Kamenka ≃, S.S.S.R.	265a	60.01 N	30.12 E
Kamenka-Bugskaja	78	50.07 N	24.20 E
Kamenka-Dneprovskaja	78	47.29 N	34.25 E
Kamen'-Kaširskij	78	51.38 N	24.58 E
Kamen'-Na-Obi	86	53.47 N	81.20 E
Kamennogorsk	24	60.58 N	29.07 E
Kamennoje, S.S.S.R.	78	51.31 N	27.38 E
Kamennoje, S.S.S.R.	78	47.53 N	35.25 E
Kamennomostskij	84	44.18 N	40.12 E
Kamennye Mogily, zapovednik ♦	78	47.18 N	37.04 E
Kamennyj Brod, S.S.S.R.	78	50.25 N	27.49 E
Kamennyj Brod, S.S.S.R.	83	47.26 N	39.51 E
Kamennyj Jar	80	48.27 N	45.34 E
Kamenolomni	83	47.40 N	40.13 E
Kamen'-Rybolov	89	44.46 N	132.02 E
Kamensk	88	51.58 N	106.36 E
Kamenskij	80	50.53 N	45.29 E
Kamenskoje, S.S.S.R.	74	62.30 N	166.12 E
Kamenskoje, S.S.S.R.	78	45.49 N	29.16 E
Kamenskoje, S.S.S.R.	82	55.16 N	36.50 E
Kamensk-Šachtinskij	83	48.21 N	40.19 E
Kamensk-Ural'skij	86	56.28 N	61.54 E
Kamenz	54	51.16 N	14.06 E
Kameoka	96	35.00 N	135.35 E
Kamerik	52	52.06 N	4.54 E
Kamerun → Cameroon □[1]	134	6.00 N	12.00 E
Kamerunberg → Cameroon Mountain ∧	152	4.12 N	9.11 E
Kames	46	55.54 N	5.15 W
Kameškovo	80	56.21 N	41.00 E
Kāmet ∧	120	30.54 N	79.37 E
Kameur, Bahr ≃	146	9.26 N	20.50 E
Kameyama	94	34.51 N	136.27 E
Kami, Nihon	94	34.41 N	137.42 E
Kami, Nihon	96	35.05 N	134.53 E
Kamiah	202	46.13 N	116.01 W
Kamiak Butte ∧	202	46.52 N	117.10 W
Kamiakotani	270	34.56 N	135.23 E
Kamiasō	268	35.35 N	139.30 E
Kamień Krajeńskie	30	53.33 N	17.32 E
Kamienna ≃	30	51.06 N	21.47 E
Kamienna Góra	30	50.47 N	16.01 E
Kamień Pomorski	30	53.58 N	14.46 E
Kamieńsk	30	51.12 N	19.30 E
Kamieskroon	156	30.09 S	17.56 E
Kamifukuoka	94	35.52 N	139.32 E
Kamigōri	96	34.52 N	134.22 E
Kamigyō ◆[8]	270	35.02 N	135.45 E
Kamiichi	94	36.42 N	137.22 E
Kamiishihara	268	35.39 N	139.32 E
Kamiiso	92a	41.49 N	140.39 E
Kamiita	96	34.07 N	134.24 E
Kami-jima I	94	34.33 N	136.59 E
Kamikamagari-jima I	96	34.11 N	132.44 E
Kamikatsu	96	33.53 N	134.24 E
Kamikawa, Nihon	92a	43.51 N	142.46 E
Kamikawa, Nihon	94	36.13 N	139.07 E
Kamikitazawa ◆[8]	268	35.40 N	139.38 E
Kamikume	270	34.55 N	135.03 E
Kâmil	130	41.07 N	34.47 E
Kamilukuak Lake ⊜	176	62.22 N	101.40 W
Kamimaki	270	34.34 N	135.43 E
Kamimizo	268	35.33 N	139.22 E
Kamina	154	8.44 S	25.00 E
Kaminaka, Nihon	94	35.28 N	135.51 E
Kaminaka, Nihon	96	33.48 N	134.22 E
Kaminak Lake ⊜	176	62.10 N	95.00 W
Kaminaljuyú ⊥	236	14.38 N	90.33 W
Kaminoho	94	35.37 N	137.03 E
Kaminokawa	94	36.26 N	139.55 E
Kaminokuni	92a	41.48 N	140.06 E
Kaminoseki	96	33.49 N	132.07 E
Kaminoyama	92	38.09 N	140.17 E
Kaminskij	80	57.10 N	41.28 E
Kaminuriak Lake ⊜	176	63.00 N	95.40 W
Kamioka	94	36.16 N	137.18 E
Kamiotawa	270	34.54 N	135.31 E
Kamioyamada	268	35.35 N	139.24 E
Kámiros ⊥	38	36.19 N	27.57 E
Kamisato	94	36.15 N	139.09 E
Kamishak Bay ⊂	180	59.15 N	153.45 W
Kamishii	94	36.04 N	136.24 E
Kamishinden	270	34.49 N	135.30 E
Kamisunagawa	92a	43.30 N	142.00 E
Kamitaira	94	36.24 N	136.54 E
Kamitakara	94	36.17 N	137.22 E
Kamitakino	270	34.57 N	134.59 E
Kamitomi	268	35.49 N	139.31 E
Kamitonda	96	33.43 N	135.27 E
Kamitsuruma	268	35.31 N	139.25 E
Kamitsushima	92	34.50 N	129.28 E
Kamituga	154	3.04 S	28.11 E
Kamiura	96	33.03 N	131.55 E
Kamiyahagi	94	35.18 N	137.29 E
Kamiyama	96	33.58 N	134.23 E
Kamiyamada	94	36.28 N	138.09 E
Kamiyama-jima I	174m	26.15 N	127.35 E
Kamiyugi	268	35.37 N	139.23 E
Kamīzgān	84	38.58 N	47.44 E
Kamkhat Muḥaywir ∧[2]	132	31.08 N	36.30 E
Kamku	120	27.30 N	96.30 E
Kamla ≃	124	25.37 N	86.40 E
Kamlach ≃	58	48.30 N	10.22 E
Kamloops	182	50.40 N	120.20 W
Kamloops Indian Reserve ◆[4]	182	50.42 N	120.20 W
Kamloops Lake ⊜	182	50.43 N	120.33 W
Kammon-kaikyō ų	96	33.56 N	130.56 E
Kammon-kyō ◆[5]	96	33.56 N	130.55 E
Kammuri-yama ∧	96	34.28 N	132.05 E
Kamnik	36	46.13 N	14.37 E
Kamniokan	88	56.17 N	111.57 E
Kamo, N.Z.	172	35.41 S	174.19 E
Kamo, Nihon	92	37.39 N	139.03 E
Kamo, Nihon	94	34.50 N	138.46 E
Kamo, Nihon	96	34.45 N	135.52 E
Kamo, Nihon	96	35.10 N	134.04 E
Kamo, Nihon	96	35.20 N	132.55 E
Kamo, Nihon	270	34.55 N	135.13 E
Kamo, S.S.S.R.	84	40.22 N	45.08 E
Kamo ≃, Nihon	94	35.06 N	140.06 E
Kamo ≃, Nihon	96	33.56 N	133.09 E
Kamo ≃, Nihon	270	34.56 N	135.44 E
Kamoa Mountains ⋏	246	1.37 N	59.00 W
Kamoda-misaki ≻	96	33.50 N	134.45 E
Kamogata	96	34.32 N	133.35 E
Kamogawa, Nihon	94	35.06 N	140.06 E
Kamogawa, Nihon	96	34.51 N	133.49 E
Kamohio Bay ⊂	229a	20.31 N	156.36 W
Kamojima	96	34.04 N	134.21 E
Kāmoke	123	31.58 N	74.13 E
Kamoshida ◆[8]	268	35.34 N	139.30 E
Kamoto	96	33.00 N	130.45 E
Kamp	56	50.14 N	7.37 E
Kamp ≃	61	48.23 N	15.48 E
Kāmpa	272b	22.56 N	88.28 E
Kampala	154	0.19 N	32.25 E
Kampar	114	4.18 N	101.09 E
Kampar ≃	112	0.32 N	103.08 E
Kamparkalns ∧[2]	76	57.18 N	22.47 E
Kampar-kanan ≃	112	0.16 N	101.41 E
Kampen	52	52.33 N	5.54 E
Kampene	154	3.36 S	26.40 E
Kampfe, Lake ⊜	276	41.02 N	74.21 W
Kamphaeng, Khao ∧	110	14.37 N	99.18 E
Kamphaeng Phet	110	16.28 N	99.30 E
Kampil	124	27.37 N	79.17 E
Kampinoski Park Narodowy ♦	30	52.20 N	20.35 E
Kampli	122	15.24 N	76.37 E
Kamp-Lintfort	52	51.30 N	6.31 E
Kamp'o	98	35.48 N	129.29 E
Kampolombo, Lake ⊜	154	11.37 S	29.42 E
Kampong Ayer Puteh	114	4.16 N	103.12 E
Kampong Baharu	114	3.43 N	103.17 E
Kampong Benta	114	3.32 N	103.22 E
Kampong Buloh	114	5.32 N	102.45 E
Kâmpóng Cham	110	12.00 N	105.27 E
Kampong Chenor	114	3.29 N	102.36 E
Kâmpóng Chhnăng	110	12.15 N	104.40 E
Kampong Dong	114	3.54 N	101.54 E
Kampong Guchil	114	5.33 N	102.14 E
Kampong Jabor	114	3.57 N	103.20 E
Kampong Jerangau	114	4.51 N	103.12 E
Kampong Kandang	114	2.11 N	102.18 E
Kâmpóng Kântuŏt	110	11.26 N	104.49 E
Kampong Kenyam	114	4.31 N	102.28 E
Kampong Kranji	271c	1.26 N	103.46 E
Kampong Kuala Kemaman	114	4.14 N	103.27 E
Kampong Lamir	114	3.36 N	103.21 E
Kampong Lawa	114	5.40 N	101.42 E
Kampong Loyang	271c	1.22 N	103.58 E
Kampong Mengkarak	114	3.19 N	102.27 E
Kampong Merang	114	5.32 N	102.57 E
Kampong Nuri	114	5.02 N	102.23 E
Kampong Penarek	114	5.37 N	102.48 E
Kampong Raja	114	5.48 N	102.35 E
Kampong Renggong	114	4.33 N	102.35 E
Kâmpóng Saôm	110	10.38 N	103.30 E
Kâmpóng Saôm, Chhâk ⊂	110	10.50 N	103.32 E
Kampong Sebuyau	112	1.31 N	110.56 E
Kampong Sekendi	114	3.43 N	100.56 E
Kampong Surau	114	5.49 N	100.54 E
Kampong Tanjong Batu	114	3.12 N	103.27 E
Kampong Tanjong Keling	271c	1.18 N	103.42 E
Kampong Tebing Runtoh	271c	1.26 N	103.40 E
Kâmpóng Thum	110	12.42 N	104.54 E
Kâmpóng Trâlach	110	11.54 N	104.47 E
Kampong Ulu	110	10.03 N	98.33 E
Kampong Ulu Chalok	114	5.26 N	102.50 E
Kâmpôt	110	10.37 N	104.11 E
Kampsville	194	39.18 N	90.37 W
Kampti	150	10.08 N	3.27 W
Kampuchea □[1], Asia	108	13.00 N	105.00 E
Kampuchea □[1], Asia	110	13.00 N	105.00 E
Kampung ≃	164	5.44 S	138.24 E
Kampungbaru	¥12	1.12 S	102.57 E
Kampung Sailolof	164	1.15 S	130.46 E
Kampville	219	38.51 N	90.33 W
Kāmrānga	126	23.14 N	90.47 E
Kamrau, Teluk ⊂	164	3.32 S	133.37 E
Kamrup □[5]	124	26.30 N	90.00 E
Kamsack	184	51.34 N	101.54 W
Kamsdorf	54	50.38 N	11.28 E
Kamskij	24	60.04 N	53.13 E
Kamskoje Ustje	80	55.13 N	49.16 E
Kamskoje vodochranilišče ⊜[1]	86	58.52 N	56.15 E
Kamslybas, ozero ⊜	86	46.12 N	61.48 E
Kamsu-ri	98	38.03 N	125.54 E
Kamsuuma	144	0.15 N	42.47 E
Kāmthi	120	21.14 N	79.12 E
Kam Tin	271d	22.27 N	114.03 E
Kamuchawie Lake ⊜	184	56.18 N	101.59 W
Kamudilo	154	7.42 S	27.18 E
Kamuela (Waimea)	229d	20.01 N	155.48 W
Kamui-misaki ≻	92a	43.20 N	140.21 E
Kámuk, Cerro ∧	236	9.17 N	83.04 W
Kamuli	154	0.57 N	33.07 E
Kamundan ≃	164	2.17 S	132.39 E
Kamutambaie ≃	152	7.17 S	23.41 E
Kamwandu	152	6.04 S	22.42 E
Kamyšet	88	55.12 N	98.42 E
Kamyšev, S.S.S.R.	80	46.39 N	42.38 E
Kamyšev, S.S.S.R.	80	46.53 N	42.31 E
Kamyševacha, S.S.S.R.	78	47.43 N	35.32 E
Kamyševacha, S.S.S.R.	83	48.42 N	38.23 E
Kamyševatskaja	78	46.25 N	37.57 E
Kamyševskaja	80	47.37 N	41.49 E
Kamyšin	80	50.06 N	45.24 E
Kamyškurgon	85	40.34 N	70.24 E
Kamyšla	80	54.07 N	52.10 E
Kamyšlov	86	56.52 N	62.43 E
Kamyslybas	86	46.11 N	61.57 E
Kamyšnaja ≃	83	48.55 N	39.55 E
Kamyšnoje	86	51.58 N	61.47 E
Kamyšovyj	80	46.26 N	45.12 E
Kamyš-Samarskich Ozer, razlivy ≡	80	48.50 N	50.50 E
Kamyz'ak	80	46.07 N	48.05 E
Kamyz'ak ≃	80	46.00 N	48.06 E
Kan, Īrān	128	35.45 N	51.16 E
Kan, Sūd.	140	9.01 N	31.47 E
Kan ≃	86	56.31 N	93.47 E
Kana ≃	154	18.30 S	27.22 E
Kanaaupscow ≃	176	53.39 N	77.09 W
Kanab	200	37.02 N	112.31 W
Kanab Creek ≃	200	36.24 N	112.38 W
Kanab Plateau ⋏[1]	200	36.40 N	112.45 W
Kanada	96	33.41 N	130.47 E
Kanada → Canada □[1]	176	60.00 N	95.00 W
Kanadej	80	53.10 N	47.30 E
Kanae	94	35.30 N	137.49 E
Kanafis	140	9.48 N	25.40 E
Kanaga Island I	180	51.45 N	177.10 W
Kanaga Volcano ∧[1]	180	51.50 N	177.09 W
Kanagawa □[5]	94	35.30 N	139.30 E
Kanagawa ◆[8]	268	35.28 N	139.38 E
Kanagi	96	34.53 N	132.11 E
Kanai	268	35.35 N	139.28 E
Kānāipur	126	23.33 N	89.47 E
Kanairiktok ≃	176	55.05 N	60.20 W
Kanā'is, Ra's al- ≻	140	31.15 N	27.51 E
Kanajevka, S.S.S.R.	80	53.07 N	45.35 E
Kanajevka, S.S.S.R.	80	52.12 N	49.40 E
Kanaka Creek ≃	226	39.25 N	120.57 W
Kanakapura	122	12.33 N	77.25 E
Kanakeswar	126	23.09 N	90.25 E
Kanákia I	267c	37.55 N	23.24 E
Kanākir	132	33.15 N	36.05 E
Kanal	64	46.05 N	13.38 E
Kanal-Inseln → Channel Islands II	28	49.20 N	2.20 W
Kanam	164	3.25 S	152.10 E
Kanamachi ◆[8]	268	35.46 N	139.53 E
Kanamori	268	35.32 N	139.28 E
Kanan	270	34.29 N	135.38 E
Kananaskis ≃	182	51.05 N	115.03 W
Kananga (Luluabourg)	152	5.54 S	22.25 E
Kananggar	115b	10.03 S	120.22 E
Kanangra-Boyd National Park ♦	170	34.00 S	150.06 E
Kanangra Walls ≛[4]	170	34.00 S	150.07 E
Kananikol'skoje	86	52.47 N	57.29 E
Kanaoka	270	34.33 N	135.32 E
Kanapou Bay ⊂	229a	20.33 N	156.33 W
Kanarase-yama ∧	96	33.26 N	131.15 E
Kanarraville	200	37.32 N	113.10 W
Kanaš	80	55.31 N	47.30 E
Kanasagō	94	36.33 N	140.28 E
Kanata	212	45.19 N	75.54 W
Kanaudi	124	23.36 N	81.23 E
Kanava, S.S.S.R.	24	61.07 N	54.58 E
Kanava, S.S.S.R.	80	47.13 N	45.24 E
Kanavka	80	50.19 N	48.33 E
Kanawha	190	42.56 N	93.47 W
Kanawha ≃	188	38.50 N	82.08 W
Kanaya, Nihon	94	34.49 N	138.08 E
Kanaya, Nihon	96	34.04 N	135.15 E
Kanaya, Nihon	268	35.10 N	139.50 E
Kanayama	94	35.39 N	137.09 E
Kanazawa	94	36.34 N	136.39 E
Kanazawa ◆[8]	268	35.20 N	139.38 E
Kanazu	94	36.13 N	136.14 E
Kanbalu	110	23.12 N	95.31 E
Kanbauk	110	14.36 N	98.02 E
Kanbe	110	16.42 N	96.01 E
Kančalan ≃	180	65.08 N	176.25 E
Kanchanaburi	110	14.01 N	99.32 E
Kanchanadit	110	9.10 N	99.28 E
Kānchenjunga ∧	124	27.42 N	88.08 E
Kānchipuram	122	12.50 N	79.43 E
Kanchow → Ganzhou	100	25.54 N	114.55 E
Kānchrāpāra	126	22.57 N	88.28 E
Kańczuga	30	49.59 N	22.24 E
Kanda	96	33.47 N	130.59 E
Kanda ◆[8]	268	35.42 N	139.46 E
Kandabulak	80	53.58 N	50.44 E
Kandāghat	123	30.59 N	77.07 E
Kandahar	184	51.46 N	104.21 W
Kandāhu	120	27.33 N	69.24 E
Kanda-Kanda	152	6.56 S	23.36 E
Kandala	152	6.02 S	19.24 E
Kandalakša	24	67.09 N	32.21 E
Kandalakšskaja guba ⊂	24	66.55 N	32.45 E
Kandalakšskij zapovednik ♦	24	68.50 N	37.30 E
Kandang	114	3.03 N	97.20 E
Kandangan	112	2.47 S	115.16 E
Kandanghaur	115a	6.21 S	108.06 E
Kandat	86	57.08 N	89.02 E
Kandava	76	57.05 N	22.49 E
Kandavu Island I	175g	19.03 S	178.13 E
Kandavu Passage ų	175g	18.45 S	178.00 E
Kandé	150	9.57 N	1.03 E
Kandel	56	49.05 N	8.11 E
Kandel ∧	58	48.04 N	8.01 E
Kander ≃	58	46.43 N	7.38 E
Kandern	58	47.43 N	7.40 E
Kandersteg	58	46.30 N	7.40 E
Kandhkot	120	28.14 N	69.11 E
Kāndhla	124	29.19 N	77.16 E
Kandi, Bénin	150	11.08 N	2.56 E
Kāndi, India	126	23.57 N	88.02 E
Kandi, Tanjung ≻	112	1.19 N	121.28 E
Kandia ≃	123	35.28 N	73.18 E
Kandiāro	120	27.04 N	68.13 E
Kandik ≃	180	65.24 N	142.34 W
Kandilli ◆[8]	267b	41.04 N	29.03 E
Kandıra	130	41.04 N	30.09 E
Kandivli ◆[8]	272c	19.12 N	72.51 E
Kando ≃	96	35.22 N	132.40 E
Kandor, Ouadi V	146	17.13 N	20.52 E
Kandos	170	32.52 S	149.58 E
Kāndra	126	23.44 N	87.58 E
Kandrāch	120	25.29 N	65.29 E
Kāndrāng Garhi	124	27.43 N	84.47 E
Kandreho	157b	17.29 S	46.06 E
Kandrian	164	6.15 S	149.35 E
Kandry	80	54.34 N	54.07 E
Kandufuri I	122	7.05 N	72.48 E
Kandukūr	122	15.13 N	79.55 E
Kandute I	122	6.20 N	72.57 E
Kandy	122	7.18 N	80.38 E
Kane, Il., U.S.	219	39.11 N	90.21 W
Kane, Pa., U.S.	214	41.39 N	78.48 W
Kane □[6]	216	41.53 N	88.18 W
Kaneda	268	35.28 N	139.22 E
Kaneilio Point ≻	229c	21.27 N	158.12 W
Kanektok ≃	180	59.45 N	161.55 W
Kanem □[5]	146	15.00 N	16.00 E
Kanemi	116	6.55 N	123.58 E
Kaneohe	229c	21.25 N	157.48 W
Kaneohe Bay ⊂	229c	21.28 N	157.49 W
Kaneohe Bay Marine Corps Air Station ■	229c	21.27 N	157.46 W
Kaneville	216	41.50 N	88.31 W
Kanevskaja	78	46.05 N	38.57 E
Kaneyama	94	35.28 N	137.06 E
Kanfanar	64	45.07 N	13.51 E
Kang	156	23.41 S	22.50 E
Kangaba	150	11.56 N	8.25 W
Kangal	130	39.15 N	37.24 E
Kangalassy	74	62.23 N	129.59 E
Kangān	128	27.50 N	52.03 E
Kānganheri ◆[8]	272a	28.33 N	76.59 E
Kanganpur	123	30.46 N	74.08 E
Kangar	114	6.26 N	100.12 E
Kangaré	150	11.35 N	8.10 W
Kangarilla	168b	35.09 S	138.40 E
Kangaroo ≃	170	34.46 S	150.18 E
Kangaroo Creek Reservoir ⊜[1]	168b	34.52 S	138.46 E
Kangaroo Flat	168b	34.33 S	138.40 E

Symbols in the index entries represent the broad categories identified in the key at the right. Symbols with superior numbers (⋏[1]) identify subcategories (see complete key on page *I · 1).*

Kartensymbole in dem Registerverzeichnis stellen die rechts in Schlüssel erklärten Kategorien dar. Symbole mit hochgestellten Ziffern (⋏[1]) bezeichnen Unterabteilungen einer Kategorie (vgl. vollständiger Schlüssel auf Seite *I · 1).*

Los símbolos incluídos en el texto del índice representan las grandes categorias identificadas con la clave a la derecha. Los símbolos con numeros en su parte superior (⋏[1]) identifican las subcategorías (véase la clave completa en la página *I · 1).*

Les symboles de l'index représentent les catégories indiquées dans la légende à droite. Les symboles suivis d'un indice (⋏[1]) représentent des sous-catégories (voir légende complète à la page *I · 1).*

Os símbolos incluídos no texto do índice representam as grandes categorias identificadas com a chave à direita. Os símbolos com números em sua parte superior (⋏[1]) identificam as subcategorias (veja-se a chave completa à página *I · 1).*

	English	Deutsch	Español	Français	Português
∧	Mountain	Berg	Montaña	Montagne	Montanha
⋏	Mountains	Berge	Montañas	Montagnes	Montanhas
)(	Pass	Pass	Paso	Col	Passo
V	Valley, Canyon	Tal, Cañon	Valle, Cañón	Vallée, Canyon	Vale, Canhão
≚	Plain	Ebene	Llano	Plaine	Planície
≻	Cape	Kap	Cabo	Cap	Cabo
I	Island	Insel	Isla	Île	Ilha
II	Islands	Inseln	Islas	Îles	Ilhas
≛	Other Topographic Features	Andere Topographische Objekte	Otros Elementos Topográficos	Autres données topographiques	Outros acidentes topográficos

ESPAÑOL: Nombre · Página · Lat.°′ · Long.°′ W = Oeste
FRANÇAIS: Nom · Page · Lat.°′ · Long.°′ W = Ouest
PORTUGUÊS: Nome · Página · Lat.°′ · Long.°′ W = Oeste

Nombre / Nom / Nome	Página / Page	Lat.°′	Long.°′
Kangaroo Ground	274b	37.41 S	145.13 E
Kangaroo Island I	166	35.50 S	137.06 E
Kangaroo Valley	170	34.44 S	150.32 E
Kangasala	26	61.28 N	24.05 E
Kangasniemi	26	61.59 N	26.38 E
Kangāvar	128	34.30 N	47.58 E
Kangaz	78	46.07 N	28.33 E
Kangbao	98	41.53 N	114.40 E
Kangding	102	30.03 N	102.02 E
Kangdong	98	39.09 N	126.05 E
Kangdu	100	27.00 N	116.36 E
Kangean, Kepulauan II	112	6.55 S	115.30 E
Kangean, Pulau I	112	6.54 S	115.20 E
Kangen ≃	140	6.47 N	33.09 E
Kanggezhuang	105	40.26 N	116.44 E
Kanggup'o	98	41.07 N	127.31 E
Kanggye	98	40.58 N	126.34 E
Kanggyŏng	98	36.10 N	127.00 E
Kanghwa	98	37.45 N	126.30 E
Kanghwa-do I	98	37.40 N	126.27 E
Kanghwa-man ⊂	98	37.20 N	126.35 E
Kangil	88	52.15 N	116.20 E
Kangiqsualujjuaq	176	58.41 N	65.57 W
Kangiqsujuaq	176	61.36 N	71.58 W
Kangirsuk	176	60.01 N	70.01 W
Kangjin	98	34.39 N	126.45 E
Kangjinjing	89	46.12 N	126.48 E
Kangkar Lenggor	114	2.16 N	103.44 E
Kangkar Teberau	114	1.32 N	103.45 E
Kangley	216	41.09 N	88.53 W
Kangly	85	40.07 N	67.54 E
Kangma	120	28.34 N	89.51 E
Kangmaer	124	30.45 N	85.34 E
Kangnam ◆[8]	271b	37.30 N	127.01 E
Kangnam-sanmaek ⋏	98	40.30 N	125.30 E
Kangnichumike	120	33.10 N	80.59 E
Kangnŭng	98	37.45 N	128.54 E
Kango	152	0.09 N	10.08 E
Kangoku-iwa I	174f	24.48 N	141.17 E
Kangombe	152	14.03 S	23.40 E
Kangongo	152	17.57 S	21.02 E
Kangowa	152	9.55 S	22.48 E
Kangping	98	42.44 N	123.21 E
Kāngpokpi	120	25.08 N	93.58 E
Kangpu	102	27.43 N	99.00 E
Kāngra	123	32.06 N	76.16 E
Kāngra □[5]	123	32.00 N	76.15 E
Kangrinboqê Feng ∧	90	31.04 N	81.18 E
Kangshan	100	22.48 N	120.17 E
Kangsŏ	98	38.58 N	125.26 E
Kangsŏ-ri	98	38.06 N	126.58 E
Kangto ∧	120	27.52 N	92.30 E
Kangtuyingzi	104	41.47 N	121.31 E
Känguruh-Insel → Kangaroo Island I	166	35.50 S	137.06 E
Kangwŏn Do □[4], C.M.I.K.	98	38.45 N	127.35 E
Kangwŏn Do □[4], Taehan	98	37.45 N	128.15 E
Kangxianzhuang	105	39.06 N	116.27 E
Kangyidaung	110	16.56 N	94.54 E
Kangzhuang	105	40.23 N	115.53 E
Kanhangad	122	12.19 N	75.04 E
Kanhar ≃	124	24.28 N	83.08 E
Kanheri Caves ⊥[5]	272c	19.13 N	72.52 E
Kanholmsfjärden ⊔	40	59.20 N	18.47 E
Kanhsien → Ganzhou	100	25.54 N	114.55 E
Kani, C. Iv.	150	8.29 N	6.36 W
Kani, Mya.	110	22.26 N	94.50 E
Kani, Nihon	94	35.22 N	137.04 E
Kaniama	152	7.31 S	24.11 E
Kaniamba	154	7.27 S	26.57 E
Kanibadam	85	40.17 N	70.25 E
Kanie	94	35.08 N	136.48 E
Kaniepa	154	9.00 S	27.21 E
Kaniere	172	42.45 S	171.00 E
Kaniere, Lake ⊜	172	42.50 S	171.09 E
Kaniet Islands II	164	0.53 S	145.30 E
Kanifay	174q	46.30 N	1.18 W
Kanigiri	122	15.24 N	79.31 E
Kanihāula ◆[8]	272a	28.44 N	77.01 E
Kanin	54	52.17 N	12.50 E
Kanin, poluostrov ≻[1]	24	68.00 N	45.00 E
Kanina	124	28.20 N	76.19 E
Kaningo	154	0.49 S	38.32 E
Kanin-Kamen' ∧	24	68.18 N	45.00 E
Kanin Nos	24	68.39 N	43.14 E
Kanin Nos, mys ≻	24	68.39 N	43.16 E
Kânireş	130	39.18 N	41.01 E
Kaniva	166	36.23 S	141.15 E
Kanjiža	38	46.04 N	20.04 E
Kānjur ◆[8]	272c	19.08 N	72.56 E
Kanjut Sār ∧	123	36.14 N	75.22 E
Kankaanpää	26	61.48 N	22.25 E
Kankakee	216	41.07 N	87.51 W
Kankakee □[6]	216	41.07 N	87.52 W
Kankakee ≃	216	41.23 N	88.16 W
Kankakee River State Park ♠	216	41.12 N	87.59 W
Kankan	150	10.23 N	9.18 W
Kankar ◆[8]	272a	28.46 N	77.06 E
Kankéla	150	10.50 N	6.40 W
Kānker	122	20.17 N	81.29 E
Kankō → Hamhŭng	98	39.54 N	127.32 E
Kankossa	150	15.56 N	11.31 W
Kankunskij	74	57.37 N	126.08 E
Kanlıavşar	130	37.13 N	38.16 E
Kanlıca ◆[8]	267b	41.06 N	29.04 E
Kanmaw Kyun I	110	11.40 N	98.28 E
Kanmen	100	28.06 N	121.16 E
Kanmuri-jima I	96	35.41 N	135.25 E
Kanmuri-yama ∧	92	34.28 N	132.05 E
Kanna ≃	94	36.17 N	139.09 E
Kannabe	96	34.32 N	133.23 E
Kannabi-san ∧[2]	270	34.48 N	135.44 E
Kannack	110	14.07 N	108.37 E
Kannad	122	20.16 N	75.08 E
Kanna-kō ⊂	174m	26.28 N	127.58 E
Kannami	94	35.05 N	138.57 E
Kannapolis	192	35.29 N	80.37 W
Kannauj	124	27.04 N	79.55 E
Kanniyākumāri	122	8.05 N	77.34 E
Kannod	124	22.40 N	76.44 E
Kannonkoski	26	62.58 N	25.15 E
Kannon-zaki ≻	268	35.15 N	139.45 E
Kannose ≃	96	34.54 N	132.49 E
Kannus	26	63.54 N	23.54 E
Kano, Nig.	150	12.00 N	8.30 E
Kano, Nihon	96	34.14 N	131.49 E
Kano □[3]	150	11.45 N	9.00 E
Kano ≃, Nig.	150	11.50 N	8.31 E
Kano ≃, Nihon	94	35.05 N	138.52 E
Kanona	210	42.22 N	77.22 W
Kanoneiland	158	28.39 S	21.05 E
Kanonerskij, ostrov I	265a	59.54 N	30.13 E
Kanonji	96	34.07 N	133.39 E
Kanopolis	198	38.42 N	98.09 W
Kanopolis Lake ⊜[1]	198	38.38 N	98.00 W
Kanorado	198	39.19 N	102.02 W
Kanosh	200	38.48 N	112.26 W
Kanouse Brook ≃	276	41.02 N	74.26 W
Kanouse Mountain ∧	276	41.04 N	74.25 W
Kan'ov	78	49.44 N	31.28 E
Kan'ovka	24	67.08 N	39.40 E
Kanovlei	156	19.10 S	19.23 E
Kan'ovskoje vodochranilišče ⊜[1]	78	50.00 N	31.20 E
Kanowit	112	2.06 N	112.09 E
Kanowna	162	30.36 S	121.36 E
Kanoya	92	31.23 N	130.51 E
Kanō-zan ∧[2]	268	35.15 N	139.57 E
Kanpetlet	110	21.12 N	94.02 E
Kanpoli	272c	19.04 N	73.09 E
Kānpur	124	26.28 N	80.21 E
Kānpur □[5]	124	26.30 N	80.00 E
Kanra	94	36.13 N	138.55 E
Kan Rūd ≃	267d	33.35 N	51.17 E
Kansa ≃	94	34.55 N	137.34 E
Kansaj	85	40.30 N	69.41 E
Kansanshi	154	12.05 S	26.26 E
Kānsāripāra	272b	22.56 N	88.14 E
Kansas, Il., U.S.	194	39.33 N	87.56 W
Kansas, Oh., U.S.	214	41.14 N	83.17 W
Kansas □[3], U.S.	178	38.45 N	98.15 W
Kansas □[3], U.S.	198	38.45 N	98.15 W
Kansas ≃	198	39.07 N	94.36 W
Kansas City, Ks., U.S.	198	39.06 N	94.37 W
Kansas City, Mo., U.S.	194	39.05 N	94.34 W
Kansau	110	23.50 N	93.35 E
Kansei Gakuin University ⊍[2]	270	34.46 N	135.21 E
Kansei University ⊍[2]	270	34.46 N	135.31 E
Kansenia	154	10.19 S	26.02 E
Kanshan	106	30.12 N	120.25 E
Kanshi	100	24.56 N	116.54 E
Kansk	86	56.13 N	95.41 E
Kansŏng	98	38.22 N	128.29 E
Kansu	85	39.45 N	75.02 E
Kansu → Gansu □[4]	102	37.00 N	103.00 E
Kansyat	164	2.15 S	138.51 E
Kant	85	42.55 N	74.55 E
Kantābānji	122	20.29 N	82.55 E
Kantabrisches Gebirge → Cantábrica, Cordillera ⋏	34	43.00 N	5.00 W
Kantalvi	272c	18.54 N	73.03 E
Kantang	110	7.25 N	99.31 E
Kāntāphor	124	22.35 N	76.34 E
Kantchari	150	12.29 N	1.31 E
Kantché	150	13.33 N	8.28 E
Kantemirovka, S.S.S.R.	83	49.41 N	39.51 E
Kantemirovka, S.S.S.R.	85	42.51 N	70.20 E
Kānth, India	124	29.04 N	78.38 E
Kanth → Kąty Wrocławskie, Pol.	30	51.02 N	16.46 E
Kantharalak	110	14.39 N	104.39 E
Kānthi Coastal Plain ≚	126	21.45 N	87.45 E
Kantishna ≃	180	64.45 N	149.58 W
Kantner	214	40.06 N	78.56 W
Kantō-heiya ≚	94	36.00 N	139.30 E
Kanton → Guangzhou	100	23.06 N	113.16 E
Kanton I, Kiribati	14	2.50 S	171.41 W
Kanton (Canton) I, Kiribati	174h	2.50 S	171.40 W
Kantorp	40	59.01 N	16.28 E
Kantō-sanchi ⋏, Nihon	92	35.50 N	138.50 E
Kantō-sanchi ⋏, Nihon	94	35.59 N	138.43 E
Kantuanji	100	32.59 N	116.19 E
Kantubek	86	45.07 N	59.16 E
Kantu-long	110	19.57 N	97.36 E
Kantunilkín	232	21.06 N	87.29 W
Kanturk	48	52.10 N	8.55 W
Kanuku Mountains ⋏	246	3.12 N	59.30 W
Kanuma	94	36.33 N	139.44 E
Kanus	156	27.54 S	18.40 E
Kanuti ≃	180	66.26 N	153.02 W
Kan'utino	76	55.33 N	33.14 E
Kanye	156	24.59 S	25.19 E
Kanygtokynmangkyn, laguna ⊂	180	69.20 N	178.45 E
Kanyu	156	20.05 S	24.39 E
Kanyutkwin	110	18.21 N	96.30 E
Kanzaki ≃	270	34.42 N	135.25 E
Kanzanavolok	24	62.23 N	36.58 E
Kanzenze	154	10.31 S	25.12 E
Kanzi	98	39.34 N	122.39 E
Kaohiung → Kaohsiung	100	22.38 N	120.17 E
Kaohsiung	100	22.38 N	120.17 E
Kaohsiunghsien	100	22.38 N	120.21 E
Kaoje	150	11.14 N	4.07 E
Kaoka Bay ⊂	175e	9.42 S	160.40 E
Kaokoland □[5]	156	18.15 S	13.00 E
Kaoko Otavi	156	18.14 S	13.40 E
Kaoko Veld ⋏[1]	156	20.00 S	14.00 E
Kaolack	150	14.09 N	16.04 W
Kaolin	285	39.48 N	75.43 W
Kaolun → Kowloon	271d	22.18 N	114.10 E
Kaoma	154	14.47 S	24.48 E
Kaongweshi ≃	152	7.53 S	22.20 E
Kaoping → Changzhi	102	36.11 N	113.08 E
Kaoshanji	105	40.11 N	117.17 E
Kaoshanpu	100	30.54 N	114.32 E
Kaouadja ≃	140	6.45 N	24.15 E
Kaouar ◆[1]	146	19.00 N	12.40 E
Kao Valley V	158	28.54 S	18.06 E
Kapaa	229b	22.04 N	159.19 W
Kapadvanj	120	23.01 N	73.04 E
Kapal	86	45.08 N	79.03 E
Kapalong	116	7.35 N	125.42 E
Kapan	112	9.44 S	124.17 E
Kapanga, Zaïre	152	8.21 S	22.35 E
Kapanga, Zaïre	152	5.04 S	16.58 E
Kapangan	116	16.35 N	120.35 E
Kapaonik ⋏	38	43.20 N	20.50 E
Kāpāsia	126	24.07 N	90.32 E
Kapatagan	116	7.52 N	123.44 E
Kapatu	154	9.43 S	30.42 E
Kapčagaj	85	43.53 N	77.12 E
Kapčagajskoje vodochranilišče ⊜[1]	86	43.50 N	78.00 E
Kapchorwa	154	1.24 N	34.27 E
Kapedo	154	1.10 N	36.06 E
Kapelle	52	51.28 N	3.58 E
Kapellen, Bel.	50	51.19 N	4.26 E
Kapellen, B.R.D.	56	51.25 N	6.35 E
Kapellen, B.R.D.	263	51.08 N	6.38 E
Kapellen, Öst.	61	47.38 N	15.37 E
Kapelle-op-den-Bos	50	51.01 N	4.22 E
Kapellerfeld	264b	48.19 N	16.30 E
Kapelln	61	48.15 N	15.45 E
Kapellskär	40	59.43 N	19.04 E
Kapema	154	10.42 S	28.24 E
Kapenguria	154	1.04 N	35.07 E
Kapfenberg	61	47.26 N	15.18 E
Kapia	152	4.17 S	19.46 E
Kapıdağı Yarımadası ≻[1]	130	40.28 N	27.50 E
Kapikik Lake ⊜	184	51.32 N	91.57 W
Kapikog Lake ⊜	212	45.09 N	79.53 W
Kapilavastu	124	27.28 N	83.16 E
Kapilmuni	126	22.42 N	89.20 E
Kapingamarangi I[1]	14	1.04 N	154.46 E
Kapiri Mposhi	154	13.58 S	28.41 E
Kāpīsā □[4]	120	34.45 N	69.30 E
Kapiskau ≃	176	52.47 N	81.55 W
Kapit	112	2.01 N	112.56 E
Kapitanovka	78	48.54 N	31.42 E
Kapiti Island I	172	40.52 S	174.54 E
Kapiura ≃	164	5.45 S	150.35 E
Kapka, Massif du ⋏	146	15.07 N	21.45 E
Kapkataš	85	40.23 N	74.20 E
Kapkatas, chrebet ⋏	85	41.50 N	76.10 E
Kapkinka	80	48.08 N	43.51 E
Kaplan	194	29.59 N	92.17 W
Kaplice	61	48.45 N	14.30 E
Kapoe	110	9.35 N	98.40 E
Kapoeta	154	4.47 N	33.35 E
Kapogere	164	9.50 S	147.45 E
Kapona	154	7.11 S	29.09 E
Kaponga	172	39.26 S	174.09 E
Kaporskoje	265a	59.45 N	29.58 E
Kapos ≃	30	46.44 N	18.30 E
Kaposvár	30	46.22 N	17.47 E
Kaposvar Creek ≃	184	50.31 N	101.55 W
Kapotn'a ◆[8]	265b	55.38 N	37.48 E
Kapowsin	224	46.59 N	122.13 W
Kapowsin, Lake ⊜	224	46.58 N	122.13 W
Kapp	26	60.42 N	10.52 E
Kappar	128	25.19 N	62.42 E
Kappel	56	50.00 N	7.21 E
Kappeln	41	54.40 N	9.56 E
Kappelshamn	26	57.51 N	18.47 E
Kapps	156	22.22 S	17.52 E
Kapralicha	86	56.11 N	67.15 E
Kaprijke	50	51.13 N	3.36 E
Kaprun	64	47.16 N	12.46 E
Kapsabet	154	0.12 N	35.06 E
Kapsan	98	41.04 N	128.19 E
Kapstadt → Cape Town	158	33.55 S	18.22 E
Kapsukas	76	54.33 N	23.21 E
Kaptai	120	22.21 N	92.17 E
Kaptipada	126	21.31 N	86.32 E
Kaptol	38	45.26 N	17.44 E
Kapuas ≃, Indon.	112	0.25 S	109.40 E
Kapuas ≃, Indon.	112	3.01 S	114.20 E
Kapuas Hulu, Pegunungan ⋏	112	1.25 N	113.30 E
Kapulo	154	8.18 S	29.15 E
Kapunda	168b	34.21 S	138.54 E
Kapūrthala	123	31.23 N	75.23 E
Kapur Utara, Pegunungan ⋏	115a	6.52 S	111.30 E
Kapuskasing	176	49.25 N	82.26 W
Kapuskasing ≃	176	49.49 N	82.00 W
Kapuskasing Lake ⊜	190	48.30 N	82.55 W
Kapustin Jar	80	48.36 N	45.45 E
Kapustino	78	48.57 N	31.14 E
Kapuvár	30	47.36 N	17.02 E
Kap Verde → Cape Verde □[1]	150a	16.00 N	24.00 W
Kapyrevščina	76	55.15 N	32.53 E
Kapytdžuch, gora ∧	84	39.13 N	46.00 E
Kara	74	69.14 N	65.00 E
Kara ≃	150	10.01 N	0.25 E
Karaali	130	39.40 N	32.57 E
Karaaul	86	48.57 N	79.15 E
Karabachskij chrebet ⋏	84	39.42 N	46.36 E
Karabagl'ar	84	39.26 N	45.12 E
Kara-Balta	85	42.50 N	73.52 E
Karabanovo	82	56.19 N	38.42 E
Karabaš, S.S.S.R.	80	54.42 N	52.36 E
Karabaš, S.S.S.R.	86	55.29 N	60.14 E
Karabau	80	48.26 N	52.54 E
Karabekaul	128	38.30 N	64.08 E
Karabiğa	130	40.24 N	27.18 E
Karabil', vozvyšennost' ⋏[1]	128	36.25 N	64.00 E
Kara-Bogaz-Gol, zaliv ⊂	72	41.00 N	53.15 E
Karabudachkent	84	42.41 N	47.34 E
Karabük	130	41.12 N	32.37 E
Karabula	88	58.08 N	97.23 E
Karabula ≃	88	58.22 N	97.02 E
Karabulak, S.S.S.R.	85	42.32 N	69.46 E
Karabulak, S.S.S.R.	85	39.51 N	69.38 E
Karabulak, S.S.S.R.	86	44.54 N	78.30 E
Karabulak, S.S.S.R.	86	47.34 N	84.41 E
Karabulduk	130	40.50 N	38.34 E
Karabutak	86	49.59 N	60.10 E
Karaca	130	40.12 N	39.08 E
Karacabey	130	40.13 N	28.21 E
Karacadağ	130	41.57 N	27.40 E
Karaca Dağ ∧	130	37.40 N	39.50 E
Karačaj ≃	84	41.28 N	49.00 E
Karačajevo-Čerkesskaja Avtonomnaja Oblast' □[4]	84	44.00 N	42.00 E
Karačajevsk	84	43.45 N	41.54 E
Karacaköy	130	41.24 N	28.22 E
Karačala	84	39.48 N	48.57 E
Karacali	130	40.53 N	37.17 E
Karacasu	130	37.43 N	28.37 E
Karacaviran, Tür.	130	39.44 N	38.08 E
Karacaviran, Tür.	130	37.33 N	39.22 E
Karaçayır	130	39.55 N	37.01 E
Karačev	76	53.07 N	35.00 E
Karāchi	120	24.52 N	67.03 E
Karachtaj	85	40.55 N	69.46 E
Karači	80	57.59 N	50.28 E
Karaçürun	130	37.35 N	38.57 E
Karād	122	17.17 N	74.12 E
Karadarja ≃	85	40.54 N	71.45 E
Karadeniz → Black Sea ⊤[2]	22	43.00 N	35.00 E
Karadere	130	40.59 N	30.50 E
Karadoğan	130	40.25 N	31.51 E
Karadoruk	130	38.53 N	37.22 E
Karaftit	88	54.12 N	111.54 E
Karagaj, S.S.S.R.	80	58.16 N	54.56 E
Karagaj, S.S.S.R.	80	48.39 N	47.38 E
Karagajly	86	49.20 N	75.48 E
Karaganda	86	49.50 N	73.10 E
Karagel	128	39.23 N	53.11 E
Karagičevskij	80	50.11 N	42.55 E
Karaginskij, ostrov I	74	58.50 N	164.00 E
Karaginskij zaliv ⊂	74	58.50 N	164.00 E
Karagola Road	124	25.29 N	87.23 E
Karagölü ⊜	130	36.42 N	29.50 E
Karagoš, gora ∧	86	51.44 N	89.24 E
Karagužicha	86	50.47 N	83.00 E
Karahallı	130	38.20 N	29.32 E
Karaia	124	25.54 N	78.01 E
Karaičev	80	48.37 N	42.13 E
Karaidel'	86	55.50 N	56.53 E
Karaidel'skij	86	55.49 N	57.05 E
Kāraikkudi	122	10.04 N	78.47 E
Karaisalı	130	37.16 N	35.03 E
Karaitivu I	122	8.23 N	79.47 E
Karaj	128	35.48 N	50.59 E
Karaj, Rūdkhāneh-ye ≃	267d	35.35 N	51.11 E
Karajantak	85	40.03 N	67.54 E
Karak	114	3.24 N	102.02 E
Karakabak	86	50.33 N	75.09 E
Karakain	85	41.26 N	74.19 E
Kara-Kala	128	38.26 N	56.18 E
Karakalpakskaja Avtonomnaja Sovetskaja Socialističeskaja Respublika □[3]	86	43.00 N	59.00 E
Karakastek	85	43.08 N	76.06 E
Karakavak	85	39.41 N	72.43 E
Karakecili	130	39.36 N	33.23 E
Karakelong, Pulau I	108	4.15 N	126.48 E
Karakemer	85	42.55 N	75.20 E
Karakendža	85	39.14 N	71.31 E
Karakitang, Pulau I	112	3.11 N	125.32 E
Karakoin, ozero ⊜	86	46.10 N	68.45 E
Karakojsu ≃	84	42.33 N	46.58 E
Karakojun ≃	85	41.10 N	75.45 E
Karakolka	85	41.32 N	77.23 E
Karakoram Range ⋏	120	35.30 N	77.00 E
Karakoro ≃	150	14.43 N	12.03 W
Karaksar	88	51.16 N	115.58 E
Karakudžur ≃	85	41.59 N	75.42 E
Karakul', S.S.S.R.	85	39.02 N	73.33 E
Karakul', S.S.S.R.	86	57.26 N	70.51 E
Karakul', S.S.S.R.	128	39.32 N	63.50 E
Karakul', ozero ⊜	85	39.05 N	73.25 E
Karakulak	130	39.59 N	40.01 E
Kara-Kul'dža	85	40.37 N	73.35 E
Karakul'dža ≃	85	40.39 N	73.26 E
Karakulino	80	56.01 N	53.43 E
Karakul'skoje	86	54.04 N	62.26 E
Karakum	86	46.49 N	79.33 E
Karakumskij Kanal ≊	128	37.35 N	61.50 E
Karakumy ◆[2]	72	39.00 N	60.00 E
Karakuni	270	34.28 N	135.28 E
Karakurt	130	40.10 N	42.36 E
Karala ◆[8]	272a	28.44 N	77.02 E
Karalat	80	45.55 N	48.18 E
Karalon	88	57.02 N	115.52 E
Karam	88	55.09 N	107.37 E
Karama ≃	112	2.18 S	119.06 E
Karamağara	130	39.42 N	35.31 E
Karamai → Karamay	86	45.30 N	84.55 E
Karaman, Tür.	130	37.05 N	29.20 E
Karaman, Tür.	130	37.11 N	33.14 E
Karamanlı	130	37.22 N	29.49 E
Karamay	86	45.30 N	84.55 E
Karambu	112	3.51 S	116.04 E
Karamea	172	41.15 S	172.07 E
Karamea ≃	172	41.16 S	172.06 E
Karamea Bight ⊂[3]	172	41.30 S	171.40 E
Karamıkbataklığı ≡	130	38.25 N	30.50 E
Karamoja □[5]	154	2.50 N	34.15 E
Karamola, gora ∧	86	47.58 N	66.35 E
Karamürsel	130	40.42 N	29.36 E
Karamurt	85	42.19 N	69.58 E
Karamyš ≃	80	51.20 N	45.00 E
Karamyševo, S.S.S.R.	76	57.45 N	28.45 E
Karamyševo, S.S.S.R.	82	54.46 N	36.07 E
Karamyševo, S.S.S.R.	88	57.34 N	100.55 E
Karamzino	76	56.00 N	34.33 E
Karang, Gunung ∧	115a	6.16 S	106.03 E
Karang, Tanjung ≻	112	0.38 S	119.44 E
Karangagung	112	2.22 S	104.27 E
Karangampel	115a	6.28 S	108.27 E
Karangana	150	12.13 N	5.02 W
Karangasem	115b	8.27 S	115.37 E
Karangbinangun	115a	7.01 S	112.30 E
Karangbolong	115a	7.45 S	109.28 E
Karangbolong, Tanjung ≻	115a	7.46 S	109.03 E
Karanggede	115a	7.22 S	110.37 E
Karang Kates, Bendung ⊜[1]	115a	8.10 S	112.30 E
Karangkobar	115a	7.16 S	109.44 E
Karangnunggal	115a	7.38 S	108.06 E
Karangpandan	115a	7.37 S	111.04 E
Karangsembung	115a	6.51 S	108.39 E
Kāranja	122	20.29 N	77.29 E
Karanjia	120	21.47 N	85.58 E
Karanti	130	40.15 N	27.07 E
Karaoba, S.S.S.R.	86	53.17 N	65.06 E
Karaoba, S.S.S.R.	86	47.03 N	56.20 E
Karaoglan	130	39.14 N	39.13 E
Karaoj	86	45.54 N	74.45 E
Karaozek, S.S.S.R.	85	43.43 N	77.23 E
Karaozek, S.S.S.R.	86	45.03 N	65.18 E
Karaozek, S.S.S.R.	86	43.16 N	58.40 E
Karapınar, Tür.	130	37.43 N	33.33 E
Karapınar, Tür.	130	41.30 N	32.12 E
Karapyši	78	49.38 N	30.47 E
Karaš	80	56.54 N	39.24 E
Karas, Pulau I	164	3.27 S	132.40 E
Karasaj	85	41.34 N	77.49 E
Kara-Sal ≃	80	47.22 N	43.38 E
Karaşar	130	40.20 N	32.00 E
Karasburg	156	28.00 S	18.43 E
Karasburg □[5]	156	28.00 S	18.45 E
Kara Sea → Karskoje more ⊤[2]	72	76.00 N	80.00 E
Karašengel'	86	47.29 N	75.35 E
Karašjåkka ≃	24	69.26 N	25.49 E
Karasjok	24	69.27 N	25.30 E
Karaskan	85	41.03 N	71.49 E
Karasor, ozero ⊜, S.S.S.R.	86	51.57 N	75.45 E
Karasor, ozero ⊜, S.S.S.R.	86	49.54 N	75.32 E
Karasu, Nihon	94	34.39 N	136.32 E
Karasu, S.S.S.R.	84	40.11 N	48.41 E
Karasu, S.S.S.R.	85	43.03 N	73.57 E
Kara-Su, S.S.S.R.	85	40.44 N	72.53 E
Karasu, S.S.S.R.	86	52.40 N	65.28 E
Karasu, S.S.S.R.	86	51.20 N	62.21 E
Karasu, Tür.	130	41.06 N	30.41 E
Karasu ≃, Nihon	94	36.15 N	139.17 E
Karasu ≃, Tür.	130	39.42 N	39.32 E
Karasuk	86	53.44 N	78.02 E
Karasuk ≃	86	53.35 N	77.30 E
Karasuyama	94	36.39 N	140.09 E
Karata	84	42.35 N	46.21 E
Karatá, Laguna ⊂	236	13.56 N	83.30 W
Karatal, S.S.S.R.	86	45.07 N	77.54 E
Karatal, S.S.S.R.	86	47.36 N	85.12 E
Karatal ≃	86	46.26 N	77.10 E
Karataş	130	36.36 N	35.21 E
Karatau	85	43.10 N	70.28 E
Karatau, chrebet ⋏, S.S.S.R.	72	43.50 N	68.30 E
Karatau, chrebet ⋏, S.S.S.R.	85	38.10 N	69.00 E
Karateginskij chrebet ⋏	85	38.50 N	69.40 E
Karatepe ⊥	130	37.17 N	36.13 E
Karatia	126	24.14 N	89.58 E
Karatobe	80	49.41 N	53.31 E
Karatogaj	86	48.42 N	59.40 E
Karaton	86	46.25 N	53.30 E
Karatoya ≃	124	24.13 N	89.36 E
Karatschi → Karāchi	120	24.52 N	67.03 E
Karatsu	92	33.26 N	129.58 E
Karaturuk	85	43.33 N	77.59 E
Karatuzskoje	86	53.36 N	92.53 E
Karau	164	3.45 S	144.20 E
Karaul	74	70.06 N	83.08 E
Karauli	124	26.30 N	77.01 E
Karault'ob'o	85	40.33 N	75.57 E
Karaunk'ur ≃	85	40.54 N	72.20 E
Karaurğan	130	40.15 N	42.17 E
Karauzak	86	42.59 N	60.02 E
Karauzek	80	47.15 N	48.25 E
Karavan	85	41.30 N	71.45 E
Karavannoje, S.S.S.R.	80	45.59 N	47.08 E
Karavannoje, S.S.S.R.	80	57.47 N	47.41 E
Karavás	38	36.21 N	22.57 E
Karave	272c	19.01 N	73.01 E
Karawa	152	3.20 N	20.18 E
Karawanken ⋏	36	46.30 N	14.25 E
Karayaka	130	40.45 N	36.37 E
Karaye	150	11.48 N	8.02 E
Karayün	130	39.41 N	37.19 E
Karažal	86	48.02 N	70.49 E
Karbalā'	128	32.36 N	44.02 E
Karbalā' □[4]	128	32.00 N	42.15 E
Karbenning	40	60.02 N	16.04 E
Kårberg	40	58.58 N	14.57 E
Karbeyaz	130	36.02 N	36.12 E
Kårböle	26	61.59 N	15.19 E
Karby	40	59.34 N	18.13 E
Karcag	30	47.19 N	20.56 E
Karczew	30	52.06 N	21.15 E
Kardail ≃	80	50.43 N	42.54 E
Kardašova Řečice	61	49.11 N	14.53 E
Karden	56	50.11 N	7.17 E
Kardhámaina	38	36.47 N	27.09 E
Kardhámila	38	38.32 N	26.05 E
Kardhítsa	38	39.21 N	21.55 E
Kärdla	76	59.00 N	22.45 E
Kardymovo	76	54.54 N	32.26 E
Kârdžali	38	41.39 N	25.22 E
Kardžin	84	43.16 N	44.16 E
Karea	272b	22.42 N	88.33 E
Kareeberge ⋏	158	30.53 S	21.57 E
Kareedouw	158	33.57 S	24.18 E
Kareli, India	124	22.55 N	79.04 E
Kareli, S.S.S.R.	84	42.01 N	43.54 E
Karelia □[9]	24	63.00 N	32.00 E
Karel'skij Gorodok	76	58.04 N	36.30 E
Karema, Pap. N. Gui.	164	9.12 S	147.14 E
Karema, Tan.	154	6.49 S	30.26 E
Karen	110	12.51 N	92.53 E
Karen □[3]	110	17.30 N	97.45 E
Karenga ≃	88	54.28 N	116.32 E
Karepino	24	61.02 N	57.02 E
Karera	272a	28.41 N	77.23 E
Karesuando	24	68.25 N	22.30 E
Kärevere	76	58.26 N	26.29 E
Kargali	80	55.12 N	50.54 E
Kargalinskaja	84	43.44 N	46.30 E
Karganaj	180	65.21 N	175.25 E
Kargapazarı Dağları ⋏	84	40.07 N	41.35 E
Kargapolje	86	55.57 N	64.27 E
Kargasok	86	59.07 N	80.53 E
Kargat	86	55.10 N	80.17 E
Kargat ≃	86	54.37 N	78.12 E
Kargı	130	41.08 N	34.30 E
Kargil	123	34.34 N	76.06 E
Karginskaja	80	49.21 N	41.38 E
Karginskij ≃	265a	59.50 N	30.01 E
Kargopol'	24	61.30 N	38.58 E
Karguéri	146	13.27 N	10.25 E
Karhal	124	27.01 N	78.57 E
Karhijärvi ⊜	26	61.35 N	22.30 E
Karhula	26	60.31 N	26.57 E
Kari	146	11.14 N	10.34 E
Karia-Ba-Mohammed	148	34.19 N	5.10 W
Kariaí	38	40.16 N	24.15 E
Karianga	157b	22.22 S	47.26 E
Kariba	154	16.30 S	28.45 E
Kariba, Lake ⊜[1]	154	17.00 S	28.00 E
Karibib	156	21.58 S	15.51 E
Karibib □[5]	156	22.20 S	16.00 E
Karibisches Meer → Caribbean Sea ⊤[2]	230	15.00 N	73.00 W
Karibumba	154	0.22 N	29.22 E
Kariega ≃	158	33.03 S	23.28 E
Karigasniemi	24	69.24 N	25.50 E
Kārikāl	122	10.55 N	79.50 E
Karikari, Cape ≻	172	34.47 S	173.24 E
Karimata	175d	24.54 N	125.17 E
Karimata, Kepulauan II	112	1.25 S	109.05 E
Karimata, Pulau I	112	1.36 S	108.55 E
Karimata, Selat (Karimata Strait) ⊔	112	2.05 S	108.40 E
Karīmnagar	122	18.26 N	79.09 E
Karīmpur	126	23.58 N	88.37 E
Karimun, Pulau I	114	1.03 N	103.22 E
Karimunjawa, Kepulauan II	115a	5.50 S	110.25 E
Karimunjawa, Pulau I	115a	5.51 S	110.27 E
Karin, Som.	144	10.59 N	49.13 E
Karin, Som.	144	10.51 N	45.47 E
Karino	82	54.42 N	38.56 E
Karin Seamount ✢[3]	14	17.55 N	168.58 W
Karinskoje	82	55.42 N	36.41 E
Karintorf	80	58.33 N	50.11 E
Karis (Karjaa)	26	60.05 N	23.40 E
Karise	41	55.18 N	12.13 E
Karisimbi, Volcan ∧[1]	154	1.30 S	29.27 E
Káristos	38	38.00 N	24.24 E
Kariya	94	34.59 N	136.59 E
Kārīz	128	34.49 N	60.47 E
Kārīz-e Elyās	128	35.25 N	61.20 E
Karjaa → Karis	26	60.05 N	23.40 E
Karjala ◆[1]	26	64.00 N	32.00 E
Karjepolje	24	65.34 N	43.40 E
Kārkal	122	13.12 N	74.59 E
Karkalaj	80	57.00 N	52.24 E
Karkaralinsk	86	49.23 N	75.21 E
Karkar Dūmān ◆[8]	272a	28.39 N	77.18 E
Karkar Island I	164	4.40 S	146.00 E
Karkas, Kūh-e ∧	128	33.27 N	51.48 E
Karkheh ≃	128	31.46 N	47.55 E
Kārkīn Dar	128	25.47 N	59.15 E
Karkinitskij zaliv ⊂	78	45.55 N	33.00 E
Karkkila	26	60.32 N	24.11 E
Karkku	26	61.25 N	23.01 E
Karkom, Har ∧	132	30.17 N	34.44 E
Karkonoski Park Narodowy ♠	30	50.45 N	15.35 E
Karkur	132	32.28 N	35.00 E
Kärla	76	58.20 N	22.15 E
Karlholmsbruk	40	60.31 N	17.35 E
Karlik Shan ∧	102	43.08 N	94.20 E
Karlino	30	54.03 N	15.51 E
Karl-Marx-Stadt (Chemnitz)	54	50.50 N	12.55 E
Karl-Marx-Stadt □[5]	54	50.45 N	12.45 E
Karlobag	36	44.32 N	15.05 E
Karlo-Libknechtovsk	83	48.42 N	38.04 E
Karlo-Marksovo	83	48.16 N	38.09 E
Karloske ≃	184	55.41 N	93.56 W
Karlovac	36	45.29 N	15.34 E
Karlovka	78	49.27 N	35.08 E
Karlovo	38	42.38 N	24.48 E
Karlovy Vary (Carlsbad)	54	50.11 N	12.52 E
Karlsbad → Karlovy Vary	54	50.11 N	12.52 E
Karlsborg, Sve.	26	58.32 N	14.31 E
Karlsborg, Sve.	26	65.48 N	23.17 E
Karlsburg → Alba-Iulia	38	46.04 N	23.35 E
Karlsby	40	58.38 N	15.08 E
Karlsdalssjön ⊜	40	59.27 N	14.42 E
Karlsfeld	60	48.13 N	11.28 E
Karlshafen	52	51.38 N	9.27 E
Karlshamn	26	56.10 N	14.51 E
Karlshorst ◆[8]	264a	52.29 N	13.32 E
Karlshorst, Trabrennbahn ♠	264a	52.29 N	13.31 E
Karlshuld	60	48.41 N	11.18 E
Karlskoga	40	59.20 N	14.31 E
Karlskrona	26	56.10 N	15.35 E
Karlslunde	41	55.34 N	12.14 E
Karlsöarna II	26	57.17 N	17.58 E
Karlsruhe	56	49.03 N	8.24 E
Karlsruhe □[5], B.R.D.	56	49.20 N	8.45 E
Karlsruhe □[5], B.R.D.	58	48.30 N	8.30 E
Karlstad, Sve.	40	59.22 N	13.30 E
Karlstad, Mn., U.S.	198	48.34 N	96.31 W
Karlstadt	56	49.57 N	9.45 E
Karlstift	61	48.35 N	14.45 E
Karl'uk, S.S.S.R.	85	38.12 N	67.42 E
Karluk, S.S.S.R.	88	53.27 N	105.58 E
Karluk, Ak., U.S.	180	57.34 N	154.28 W
Karma	150	13.40 N	1.49 E
Karma, Ouadi V	146	15.38 N	20.01 E
Karmah	140	19.38 N	30.25 E
Karmāla	122	18.25 N	75.12 E
Karmanovka	80	49.24 N	50.22 E
Karmanovo	76	55.52 N	34.52 E
Karmansbo	40	59.42 N	15.44 E
Karmatānr	126	24.05 N	86.42 E
Karmi'el	132	32.55 N	35.18 E
Karmiyya	132	31.36 N	34.33 E
Karmøy I	26	59.15 N	5.15 E
Karnack	194	32.40 N	94.10 W
Karnak → Al-Karnak, Mişr	140	25.43 N	32.39 E
Karnak, Il., U.S.	194	37.17 N	88.58 W
Karnāl	124	29.41 N	76.59 E
Karnāl □[5]	124	29.40 N	76.50 E
Karnāla Fort ⊥	272c	18.53 N	73.07 E
Karnāli ≃	124	28.45 N	81.16 E
Karnap ◆[8]	263	51.31 N	7.01 E
Karnaphuli Reservoir ⊜[1]	120	22.42 N	92.12 E
Karnataka □[3]	122	14.00 N	76.00 E
Karnauchovka	78	48.28 N	34.44 E
Karnes □[6]	222	29.00 N	97.47 W
Karnes City	196	28.53 N	97.54 W
Karni	150	10.40 N	2.37 W
Karniki	82	54.12 N	38.05 E
Karnische Alpen (Alpi Carniche) ⋏	64	46.40 N	13.00 E
Karnobat	38	42.39 N	26.59 E
Karns City	214	41.00 N	79.44 W
Kärnten □[3]	30	46.50 N	13.50 E
Karnzow	54	52.59 N	12.26 E
Karoi	154	16.50 S	29.40 E
Karokh	128	34.28 N	62.35 E
Karolinenhof ◆[8]	264a	52.23 N	13.38 E
Karomatan	116	7.46 N	123.44 E
Karompa-lompo, Pulau I	112	7.15 S	121.45 E
Karon	126	24.07 N	86.44 E
Karonga	154	9.56 S	33.56 E
Karonie	162	30.58 S	122.32 E
Karoonda	166	35.06 S	139.54 E
Karor	123	31.13 N	70.57 E
Karora	140	17.42 N	38.22 E
Karos	158	28.24 S	21.35 E
Karosa	112	1.48 S	119.20 E
Karossa, Tanjung ≻	115b	9.33 S	118.50 E
Karotho Post	154	5.11 N	35.50 E
Karou	150	15.07 N	0.39 E
Karow, D.D.R.	54	52.20 N	12.15 E
Karow, D.D.R.	54	53.32 N	12.15 E
Karow ◆[8]	264a	52.37 N	13.29 E
Karpathen → Carpathian Mountains ⋏	22	48.00 N	24.00 E
Kárpathos	38	35.30 N	27.14 E
Kárpathos I	38	35.40 N	27.10 E
Karpenísion	38	38.55 N	21.40 E
Karpinsk	86	59.45 N	60.01 E
Karpogory	24	64.00 N	44.24 E
Karpovka, S.S.S.R.	83	49.10 N	37.43 E
Karpovka, S.S.S.R.	83	47.57 N	39.36 E
Karpovo, S.S.S.R.	76	60.02 N	36.43 E
Karpovo, S.S.S.R.	82	55.35 N	38.34 E
Karpunicha	80	57.42 N	45.20 E
Karpuninskij	86	58.43 N	61.50 E
Karrats Fjord ⊂[2]	176	71.20 N	54.00 W
Karrebæksminde	41	55.11 N	11.40 E
Karres	58	47.13 N	10.47 E
Kärrgruvan	40	60.05 N	15.56 E
Karridale	162	34.13 S	115.05 E
Kars	84	40.36 N	43.05 E
Kars □[4]	84	40.35 N	43.00 E
Kars ≃	84	40.37 N	43.41 E
Karša	80	49.48 N	51.27 E
Karsakpaj	86	47.49 N	66.41 E
Karsakuwigamak Lake ⊜	184	56.22 N	99.30 W
Kärsämäki	26	63.58 N	25.46 E
Karsantı	130	37.33 N	35.24 E
Kārsava	76	56.47 N	27.40 E
Karsdorf	54	51.17 N	11.39 E
Karši	128	38.53 N	65.48 E
Karsin	30	53.54 N	17.56 E
Karšinskaja step' ≚	128	39.10 N	65.00 E
Karşıyaka	130	38.27 N	27.07 E
Karskije Vorota, proliv ⊔	72	70.30 N	58.00 E
Karskoje more (Kara Sea) ⊤[2]	72	76.00 N	80.00 E
Karsovaj	80	58.14 N	53.11 E
Karst → Kras ⋏[1]	64	45.48 N	14.00 E
Kårsta, Sve.	40	59.39 N	18.14 E
Kärsta, Sve.	40	59.40 N	16.49 E
Karstädt	54	53.09 N	11.44 E
Karstula	26	62.52 N	24.47 E
Karsun	80	54.11 N	46.59 E
Kartajol'	24	64.32 N	53.14 E
Kartal	130	40.53 N	29.10 E
Kartala ∧	157a	11.45 S	43.22 E
Kartaly	86	53.03 N	60.40 E
Kartārpur	123	31.27 N	75.30 E
Karthaus	214	41.07 N	78.07 W
Kartlijskij chrebet ⋏	84	42.10 N	44.55 E
Kartosuro	115a	7.33 S	110.44 E
Karttula	26	62.53 N	26.58 E
Kartuzy	30	54.20 N	18.12 E
Kartzow	54	52.29 N	12.58 E
Käru	76	58.50 N	25.11 E
Karuah ≃	170	32.39 S	151.58 E
Karufa	164	3.50 S	133.27 E
Karuizawa	94	36.21 N	138.38 E
Karukuwisa	156	18.56 S	19.40 E
Karumai	92	40.19 N	141.28 E
Karumba	166	17.29 S	140.50 E
Kārūn ≃	128	30.26 N	48.10 E
Karungi	26	66.03 N	23.57 E
Karungu	154	0.51 S	34.09 E
Karuni	115b	9.26 S	119.19 E
Karunjie	164	16.18 S	127.12 E
Karunki	26	66.02 N	24.01 E
Karup	41	56.18 N	9.10 E
Karup Å ≃	41	56.18 N	9.10 E
Karup Lufthavn ⊠	41	56.20 N	9.08 E
Karūr	122	10.57 N	78.05 E
Karuscia, Punta ≻	70	36.49 N	11.59 E
Karvala	265a	59.41 N	30.09 E
Karviná	30	49.50 N	18.30 E
Kārwār	122	14.48 N	74.08 E
Karwendel ⋏	64	47.27 N	11.20 E
Karwi	124	25.12 N	80.54 E
Karym	86	60.07 N	66.41 E
Karymskoje, S.S.S.R.	88	51.37 N	114.21 E
Karymskoje, S.S.S.R.	88	54.07 N	101.49 E
Karza	86	58.35 N	80.50 E
Karzachi	84	41.15 N	43.16 E
Kas, Sūd.	140	12.30 N	24.17 E
Kaş, Tür.	130	36.12 N	29.38 E
Kas ≃	86	59.40 N	90.00 E
Kasaan	182	55.32 N	132.24 W
Kasabi	152	14.48 S	23.42 E
Kasach ≃	84	40.03 N	43.52 E
Kasadi ≃	272c	18.59 N	72.59 E
Kasa-do I	98	34.28 N	126.03 E
Kasado-shima I	96	33.57 N	131.51 E
Kasagi	94	34.45 N	135.56 E
Kasagi-sanchi ⋏	270	34.37 N	135.56 E
Kasagi-yama ∧	94	35.31 N	137.21 E
Kasahara	94	35.17 N	137.09 E
Kasahata	268	35.54 N	139.25 E
Kasai	96	34.56 N	134.50 E
Kasai ◆[8]	268	35.39 N	139.53 E
Kasai (Cassai) ≃, Afr.	152	3.02 S	16.57 E
Kāsai ≃, India	124	22.09 N	87.50 E
Kasai-Occidental □[4]	152	5.30 S	21.40 E
Kasai-Oriental □[4]	152	4.00 S	23.30 E
Kasaji	152	10.22 S	23.27 E
Kasakake	94	36.23 N	139.17 E
Kasama, Nihon	94	36.23 N	140.16 E
Kasama, Zam.	154	10.13 S	31.12 E
Kasamatsu	94	35.22 N	136.46 E
Kasan → Kazan', S.S.S.R.	80	55.49 N	49.08 E
Kasan, S.S.S.R.	128	39.02 N	65.35 E
Kasan-dong	98	41.18 N	126.55 E
Kasane	156	17.50 S	25.05 E
Kasanga	154	8.28 S	31.09 E
Kasangale	152	6.20 S	22.42 E
Kasangeshi ≃	152	8.24 S	21.56 E
Kasangulu	152	4.36 S	15.10 E
Kasanka National Park ♠	154	12.35 S	30.12 E
Kasano-misaki ≻	94	36.21 N	136.18 E
Kasansaj	85	41.15 N	71.32 E
Kasansaj ≃	85	40.57 N	71.30 E
Kasaoka	96	34.30 N	133.30 E
Kāsaragod	122	12.30 N	75.00 E
Kasari ≃	76	58.45 N	23.49 E
Kašary	78	49.03 N	41.00 E
Kasatori-yama ∧, Nihon	94	34.44 N	136.18 E
Kasatori-yama ∧, Nihon	96	33.33 N	132.55 E
Kasauli	123	30.55 N	76.57 E
Kasba	124	25.51 N	87.33 E
Kasbagoas	126	24.11 N	88.30 E
Kasba Kamarda	126	21.46 N	87.21 E
Kasba Lake ⊜	176	60.18 N	102.07 W
Kasba Mirgoda	126	21.42 N	87.28 E
Kasba Nārāyangarh	126	22.10 N	87.23 E
Kasba Patāspur	126	22.02 N	87.32 E
Kasba-Tadla	148	32.34 N	6.18 W
Kaschau → Košice	30	48.43 N	21.15 E
Kaşçiftliği	130	36.36 N	29.45 E
Kåseberga	26	55.23 N	14.04 E
Kaseda	92	31.25 N	130.19 E
Kasempa	154	13.27 S	25.50 E
Kasenga	154	10.22 S	28.38 E
Kasenyi	154	1.24 N	30.26 E
Kasese, Ug.	154	0.10 N	30.05 E
Kasese, Zaïre	154	1.38 S	27.07 E
Kaset Sombun	110	16.17 N	101.57 E

≃	River	Fluss	Río	Rivière	Rio
≊	Canal	Kanal	Canal	Canal	Canal
∟	Waterfall, Rapids	Wasserfall, Stromschnellen	Cascada, Rápidos	Chute d'eau, Rapides	Cascata, Rápidos
⊔	Strait	Meeresstrasse	Estrecho	Détroit	Estreito
⊂	Bay, Gulf	Bucht, Golf	Bahía, Golfo	Baie, Golfe	Baía, Golfo
⊜	Lake, Lakes	See, Seen	Lago, Lagos	Lac, Lacs	Lago, Lagos
≡	Swamp	Sumpf	Pantano	Marais	Pântano
⍓	Ice Features, Glacier	Eis- und Gletscherformen	Accidentes Glaciales	Formes glaciaires	Acidentes glaciares
⊤	Other Hydrographic Features	Andere Hydrographische Objekte	Otros Elementos Hidrográficos	Autres données hydrographiques	Outros acidentes hidrográficos

✢	Submarine Features	Untermeerische Objekte	Accidentes Submarinos	Formes de relief sous-marin	Acidentes submarinos
□	Political Unit	Politische Einheit	Unidad Politica	Entité politique	Unidade política
⊍	Cultural Institution	Kulturelle Institution	Institución Cultural	Institution culturelle	Instituição cultural
⊥	Historical Site	Historische Stätte	Sitio Histórico	Site historique	Sitio histórico
♠	Recreational Site	Erholungs- und Ferienort	Sitio de Recreo	Centre de loisirs	Area de Lazer
⊠	Airport	Flughafen	Aeropuerto	Aéroport	Aeroporto
■	Military Installation	Militäranlage	Instalación Militar	Installation militaire	Instalação militar
◆	Miscellaneous	Verschiedenes	Misceláneo	Divers	Diversos

ENGLISH: Name, Page, Lat.°′, Long.°′ — DEUTSCH: Name, Seite, Breite°′, Länge°′ E = Ost

Name	Page	Lat.	Long.
Kasfareet Military Base ■	142	30.15 N	32.24 E
Kāsganj	124	27.49 N	78.39 E
Kashabowie Lake ⊜	190	48.42 N	90.25 W
Kashaf ≐	128	35.58 N	61.07 E
Kashagawigamog Lake ⊜	212	44.59 N	78.37 W
Kāshān	128	33.59 N	51.29 E
Kashasha	154	1.44 S	31.37 E
Kashegelok	180	60.50 N	157.50 W
Kashgar → Kashi	85	39.29 N	75.59 E
Kashi	85	39.29 N	75.59 E
Kashiba	96	34.33 N	135.42 E
Kashihara	96	34.30 N	135.46 E
Kashiji Plain ≚	152	13.20 S	22.30 E
Kashileshi ≐	152	9.46 S	23.05 E
Kashima, Nihon	92	33.07 N	130.06 E
Kashima, Nihon	94	35.58 N	140.38 E
Kashima, Nihon	94	36.58 N	136.55 E
Kashima, Nihon	96	35.30 N	133.01 E
Kashima-jingū ⛩[1]	94	35.59 N	140.40 E
Kashima-nada ⩒[2]	94	36.15 N	140.45 E
Kashima-Yariga-take ʌ	94	36.37 N	137.45 E
Kashimo	94	35.43 N	137.23 E
Kashing → Jiaxing	106	30.46 N	120.45 E
Kashio ◆[8]	268	35.25 N	139.33 E
Kashīpur, India	124	29.13 N	78.57 E
Kāshipur, India	126	23.26 N	86.40 E
Kashitu	154	13.42 S	28.40 E
Kashiwa	94	35.52 N	139.59 E
Kashiwara, Nihon	94	34.35 N	135.37 E
Kashiwara, Nihon	96	34.35 N	135.37 E
Kashiwazaki, Nihon	92	37.22 N	138.33 E
Kashiwazaki, Nihon	268	35.56 N	139.42 E
Kāshmar	128	35.12 N	58.27 E
Kashmir → Jammu and Kashmir □[2]	120	34.00 N	76.00 E
Kashmir, Vale of V	123	34.00 N	75.00 E
Kashmor	120	28.26 N	69.35 E
Kashunuk ≐	180	61.18 N	165.36 W
Kashwakamak Lake ⊜	212	44.50 N	77.04 W
Kasia	124	26.45 N	83.55 E
Kāsiāni	126	23.14 N	89.45 E
Kasiāri	126	22.08 N	87.14 E
Kasidiji ≐	152	7.57 S	23.12 E
Kasigau ʌ	154	3.50 S	38.40 E
Kasigluk	180	60.52 N	162.32 W
Kasilof	180	60.24 N	151.18 W
Kasilovo	78	50.38 N	35.37 E
Kasimbar	112	0.09 S	120.00 E
Kasimov	80	54.56 N	41.24 E
Kāsimpur, Bngl.	126	23.59 N	90.19 E
Kāsimpur, India	272b	22.46 N	88.31 E
Kašin	76	57.21 N	37.37 E
Kāsināthpur, Bngl.	126	23.58 N	89.37 E
Kāsināthpur, India	272b	22.35 N	88.31 E
Kasinge	154	6.20 S	26.59 E
Kasinka	156	18.13 S	24.22 E
Kāsipur	272b	22.25 N	88.10 E
Kasır	130	37.10 N	40.52 E
Kašira	82	54.51 N	38.10 E
Kaširka ≐	82	54.52 N	38.13 E
Kasiruta, Pulau I	108	0.25 S	127.12 E
Kasiui, Pulau I	164	4.30 S	131.40 E
Kasiwa → Kashiwa	94	35.52 N	139.59 E
Kaskabulak	86	49.34 N	79.52 E
Kaškadarjinskaja Oblast' □[4]	85	39.00 N	67.00 E
Kaskaden-Kette → Cascade Range ⋏	202	45.00 N	121.30 W
Kaskana	85	40.45 N	69.36 E
Kaskaskia ≐	194	37.59 N	89.56 W
Kaskaskia, East Fork ≐	219	38.43 N	89.09 W
Kaskaskia, North Fork ≐	219	38.46 N	89.09 W
Kaskattama ≐	176	57.03 N	90.07 W
Kaskelen	85	43.12 N	76.37 E
Kaskelen ≐	85	43.53 N	77.08 E
Kaskinen → Kaskö	26	62.23 N	21.13 E
Kaskö (Kaskinen)	26	62.23 N	21.13 E
Kašlagač ≐	83	47.45 N	37.16 E
Kaslātu ʌ	124	23.58 N	84.54 E
Kasli	86	55.53 N	60.46 E
Kaslo	182	49.55 N	116.55 W
Käsmark → Kežmarok	30	49.08 N	20.25 E
Kasn'a	76	55.24 N	34.20 E
Kasn'a ≐	76	55.51 N	34.25 E
Kaso ≐	115a	7.25 S	106.40 E
Kasongo	154	4.27 S	26.40 E
Kasongo-Lunda	152	6.28 S	16.49 E
Kásos I	38	35.22 N	26.56 E
Kasota	190	44.18 N	93.57 W
Kašperovka	78	49.26 N	29.41 E
Kaspi	84	41.57 N	44.25 E
Kaspijsk	84	42.52 N	47.38 E
Kaspijskij	22	45.22 N	47.24 E
Kaspijskoje more → Caspian Sea ⩒[2]	72	42.00 N	50.30 E
Kaspische Senke → Prikaspijskaja nizmennost' ≚	80	48.00 N	52.00 E
Kaspisches Meer → Caspian Sea ⩒[2]	72	42.00 N	50.30 E
Kaspl'a	76	55.00 N	31.38 E
Kaspl'a ≐	76	55.24 N	30.43 E
Kasr, Ra's ≻	140	18.02 N	38.35 E
Kasrat Muraybiṭ	130	36.02 N	38.08 E
Kasrik	130	38.13 N	41.54 E
Kassa → Košice	30	48.43 N	21.15 E
Kassab	130	35.56 N	35.59 E
Kassai → Cassai (Kasai) ≐	152	3.02 S	16.57 E
Kassalā	140	15.28 N	36.24 E
Kassalā □[4]	140	15.00 N	35.00 E
Kassándra ≻[1]	38	40.06 N	23.22 E
Kassándras, Kólpos c	38	40.06 N	23.30 E
Kassel	56	51.19 N	9.29 E
Kassel □[5]	56	51.10 N	9.20 E
Kasserine	148	35.11 N	8.48 E
Kasserine □[8]	148	35.00 N	8.45 E
Kasshabog Lake ⊜	212	44.38 N	77.58 W
Kassikaityu ≐	246	1.49 N	58.32 W
Kassinger	140	18.45 N	31.54 E
Kassîr, Sabkhat al- ⊜	130	35.03 N	41.07 E
Kasslerfeld ◆[8]	263	51.26 N	6.45 E
Kasson	190	44.01 N	92.45 W
Kassou	150	11.35 N	2.03 W
Kassoum	150	13.05 N	3.18 W
Kastamonu	130	41.22 N	33.47 E
Kastamonu □[4]	130	41.40 N	33.45 E
Kastanéai	38	41.38 N	26.28 E
Kastelholm	26	60.14 N	20.04 E
Kastellaun	56	50.04 N	7.26 E
Kastellórizon I	130	36.08 N	29.34 E
Kasterlee	56	51.15 N	4.57 E
Kastiyu, Puntan ≻	174n	14.57 N	145.40 E
Kastl, B.R.D.	60	49.50 N	11.54 E
Kastl, B.R.D.	60	49.22 N	11.42 E
Kastorf	52	53.44 N	10.34 E
Kastoría	38	40.31 N	21.15 E
Kastorías, Límni ⊜	38	40.30 N	21.17 E
Kastornoje	78	51.50 N	38.06 E
Kastrávion, Tekhnití Límni ⊜[1]	38	38.50 N	21.20 E
Kastrup Lufthavn ⊠	41	55.38 N	12.39 E
Kasuga, Nihon	94	35.28 N	136.29 E
Kasuga, Nihon	96	33.32 N	130.27 E
Kasuga, Nihon	96	35.10 N	135.06 E
Kasugai, Nihon	94	35.14 N	136.58 E
Kasugai, Nihon	94	35.39 N	138.39 E
Kasuga-kōkūkichi, Kaijō-jieitai- ■	96	33.31 N	130.28 E
Kasuga Shrine ⛩[1]	270	34.41 N	135.51 E
Kasuka	158	33.40 S	26.41 E
Kasukabe	94	35.58 N	139.45 E
Kasukawa	94	36.24 N	139.13 E
Kasulu	154	4.34 S	30.06 E
Kasumi	96	35.38 N	134.38 E
Kasumiga-ura ⊜	94	36.00 N	140.25 E
Kasum-Ismailov	84	40.36 N	46.47 E
Kasumkent	84	41.41 N	48.07 E
Kasungan	112	1.58 S	113.24 E
Kasungu	154	13.01 S	33.30 E
Kasungu National Park ♠	154	12.55 S	33.15 E
Kasupe	154	15.10 S	35.15 E
Kasūr	123	31.07 N	74.27 E
Kaszuby ◆[1]	30	54.10 N	18.15 E
Kata	88	58.46 N	102.40 E
Kataba	154	16.05 S	25.10 E
Kataeregi	150	9.22 N	6.17 E
Katagum	146	12.17 N	10.21 E
Katahdin, Mount ʌ	188	45.55 N	68.55 W
Katai	272c	19.10 N	73.05 E
Katajevo	88	50.57 N	108.41 E
Katajsk	86	56.18 N	62.35 E
Katako-Kombe	152	3.24 S	24.25 E
Katakura	270	34.29 N	135.31 E
Katakwi	154	1.55 N	33.57 E
Katale	154	4.59 S	31.03 E
Katalla	180	60.12 N	144.31 W
Katanda	154	0.50 S	29.22 E
Katanga □[9]	138	10.00 S	26.00 E
Katanga ≐	74	60.08 N	102.13 E
Katangi	124	23.27 N	79.47 E
Katanglad Mountains ⋏	116	8.06 N	124.54 E
Katangli	89	51.42 N	143.14 E
Katanimara	126	22.17 N	87.11 E
Katanning	162	33.42 S	117.33 E
Katano	270	34.47 N	135.40 E
Katano-hana ≻	174f	24.49 N	141.20 E
Katanti	154	2.18 S	27.08 E
Kataoka	270	35.03 N	135.58 E
Katapakishi	152	8.15 S	22.49 E
Katar → Qatar □[1]	128	25.00 N	51.10 E
Katara, Depresión de → Qaṭṭārah, Munkhafaḍ al- ⊥[7]	140	30.00 N	27.30 E
Katarniān Ghāt	124	28.20 N	81.09 E
Katase	268	35.19 N	139.29 E
Katashina	94	36.46 N	139.14 E
Katašin	76	52.36 N	32.10 E
Katav-Ivanovsk	86	54.45 N	58.12 E
Katayama	268	35.46 N	139.34 E
Katchall Island I	110	7.57 N	93.22 E
Katchewanooka Lake ⊜	212	44.27 N	78.16 W
Katchin-wan c	174m	26.18 N	127.53 E
Katchirga	150	14.03 N	0.06 E
Katchiungo	152	12.35 S	16.13 E
Katech	84	41.39 N	46.34 E
Kateel ≐	180	65.28 N	157.35 W
Katélé	150	10.38 N	5.37 W
Katena-wan c	174m	26.22 N	128.05 E
Katepwa Beach	184	50.42 N	103.38 W
Katerbow	54	52.59 N	12.39 E
Kateríni	38	40.16 N	22.30 E
Katerinopol'	78	48.56 N	30.59 E
Katerloch ⊥[5]	61	47.16 N	15.32 E
Katernberg ◆[8], B.R.D.	263	51.16 N	7.06 E
Katernberg ◆[8], B.R.D.	263	51.29 N	7.04 E
Katesbridge	48	54.18 N	6.08 W
Kates Needle ʌ	180	57.03 N	132.03 W
Katešovo	82	54.08 N	37.00 E
Katete, Malawi	154	12.17 S	33.39 E
Katete, Zam.	154	14.05 S	32.07 E
Katghora	124	22.30 N	82.33 E
Katha	110	24.11 N	96.21 E
Kathangor, Jabal ʌ	140	5.45 N	33.59 E
Katherine	164	14.28 S	132.16 E
Katherine ≐	164	14.39 S	131.42 E
Katherine Creek ≐	166	23.48 S	143.42 E
Katherine Gorge National Park ♠	164	14.10 S	132.30 E
Kāthgodām	124	29.16 N	79.32 E
Kathiār	120	25.32 N	87.35 E
Kāthiāwār ≻[1]	120	22.00 N	71.00 E
Kathīb, Ra's ≻	144	14.55 N	42.53 E
Kathla	123	31.59 N	76.47 E
Kathleen	220	28.07 N	82.01 W
Kathleen Valley	162	27.23 S	120.38 E
Kathlow	54	51.43 N	14.29 E
Kathmandu	124	27.43 N	85.19 E
Kathor	120	21.18 N	72.56 E
Kathrabbā	132	31.08 N	35.37 E
Kathua	123	32.22 N	75.31 E
Kāthuli	126	23.52 N	88.40 E
Kati	150	12.44 N	8.04 W
Kātiādi	126	24.15 N	90.48 E
Katibas ≐	112	2.01 N	112.33 E
Katihār	124	25.32 N	87.35 E
Katikati	172	37.33 S	175.55 E
Katima Mulilo	152	17.27 S	24.14 E
Katimik Lake ⊜	184	52.54 N	99.22 W
Katiola	150	8.08 N	5.06 W
Katiola □[5]	150	8.30 N	5.25 W
Katipunan	116	8.31 N	123.17 E
Kātlang	123	34.22 N	72.05 E
Katlehong	273d	26.19 S	28.09 E
Katlenburg-Duhm	52	51.41 N	10.06 E
Katmai, Mount ʌ	180	58.17 N	154.56 W
Katmai National Park ♠	180	58.30 N	155.00 W
Kātmāndu → Kathmandu	124	27.43 N	85.19 E
Katni → Murwāra, India	124	23.51 N	80.24 E
Katni, S.S.S.R.	80	57.59 N	47.46 E
Káto Akhaïa	38	38.09 N	21.32 E
Kātol	120	21.16 N	78.35 E
Katompi	154	6.11 S	26.20 E
Katonah	210	41.16 N	73.41 W
Katonga ≐	154	0.34 N	31.50 E
Katon-Karagaj	86	49.11 N	85.37 E
Katoomba	170	33.42 S	150.18 E
Katopa	154	2.45 S	25.06 E
Katori-jingū ⛩[1]	94	35.52 N	140.30 E
Katoúna	38	38.47 N	21.07 E
Katovice	60	49.16 N	13.49 E
Katowice	30	50.16 N	19.00 E
Katowice □[4]	30	50.15 N	19.00 E
Katra	123	32.59 N	74.57 E
Kātrās	126	23.48 N	86.17 E
Katričev	80	49.23 N	45.33 E
Kātrīnā, Jabal ʌ	140	28.31 N	33.57 E
Katrine, Loch ⊜	46	56.15 N	4.31 W
Katrineholm	40	59.00 N	16.12 E
Katsch, Golf von → Kutch, Gulf of c	120	22.36 N	69.30 E
Katschbach ≐	61	47.08 N	14.17 E
Katschberg)(	64	47.03 N	13.37 E
Katscher → Kietrz	30	50.05 N	18.01 E
Katsepe	157b	15.45 S	46.15 E
Katshungu	154	2.27 S	27.23 E
Katsina	150	13.00 N	7.32 E
Katsina Ala	150	7.10 N	9.17 E
Katsina Ala ≐	152	7.48 N	8.52 E
Katsunuma	94	35.39 N	138.44 E
Katsura ◆[8]	270	34.59 N	135.42 E
Katsura ≐, Nihon	94	35.36 N	139.15 E
Katsura ≐, Nihon	94	34.53 N	135.42 E
Katsura ≐, Nihon	96	34.02 N	134.35 E
Katsura ≐, Nihon	270	34.53 N	135.42 E
Katsuragi	96	34.30 N	135.30 E
Katsuragi-san ʌ	96	34.20 N	135.27 E
Katsushika ◆[8]	268	35.43 N	139.51 E
Katsuta, Nihon	94	36.24 N	140.30 E
Katsuta, Nihon	96	35.04 N	134.11 E
Katsuura, Nihon	94	35.08 N	140.18 E
Katsuura, Nihon	96	33.56 N	134.30 E
Katsuyama, Nihon	94	36.03 N	136.30 E
Katsuyama, Nihon	96	35.05 N	133.41 E
Kattakurgan	72	39.55 N	66.15 E
Kattara-Senke → Qaṭṭārah, Munkhafaḍ al- ⊥[7]	140	30.00 N	27.30 E
Kattarp	41	56.09 N	12.46 E
Katta-Taldyk	85	40.19 N	73.12 E
Kattaviá	38	35.57 N	27.46 E
Kattegat ⋓	26	57.00 N	11.00 E
Katternberg ◆[8]	263	51.09 N	7.02 E
Katthammarsvik	26	57.26 N	18.50 E
Kattonghu ⊜	120	35.30 N	92.00 E
Kattowitz → Katowice	30	50.16 N	19.00 E
Kattrup	41	55.57 N	9.56 E
Kāttuputtūr	122	10.59 N	78.14 E
Katul, Jabal ʌ	140	14.16 N	29.23 E
Katuma	154	6.10 S	30.34 E
Katumba	154	7.45 S	25.18 E
Katun' ≐	86	52.25 N	85.05 E
Katunino	80	58.01 N	45.39 E
Katunki	80	56.50 N	43.14 E
Kātūria	124	24.44 N	86.43 E
Katu Shan ʌ	86	45.40 N	82.55 E
Katusice	54	50.26 N	14.50 E
Kātwa	126	23.39 N	88.08 E
Katwijk aan de Rijn	52	52.11 N	4.26 E
Katwijk aan Zee	52	52.13 N	4.24 E
Katy	222	29.47 N	95.49 W
Kąty Wrocławskie	30	51.02 N	16.46 E
Katzenbuckel ʌ	56	49.28 N	9.02 E
Katzenelnbogen	56	50.17 N	7.59 E
Katzenfurt	56	50.37 N	8.21 E
Katzhütte	54	50.33 N	11.03 E
Kaua ≐	156	19.24 S	22.03 E
Kauai □[6]	229b	21.59 N	159.22 W
Kauai I	229b	22.00 N	159.30 W
Kauai Channel ⋓	229b	21.45 N	158.50 W
Kaub	56	50.05 N	7.46 E
Kau Desert ◆[2]	229d	19.21 N	155.19 W
Kaufbeuren	58	47.53 N	10.37 E
Kaufering	58	48.05 N	10.52 E
Kauffung → Wojcieszów	30	50.58 N	15.56 E
Kaufman	222	32.35 N	96.18 W
Kaufman □[6]	222	32.38 N	96.18 W
Kaufungen, B.R.D.	52	51.17 N	9.38 E
Kaufungen, B.R.D.	56	51.17 N	9.38 E
Kaugama	150	12.28 N	9.44 E
Kauhajoki	26	62.26 N	22.11 E
Kauhava	26	63.06 N	23.05 E
Kauiki Head ≻	229a	20.45 N	155.59 W
Kaukapakapa	172	36.37 S	174.30 E
Kaukasus → Bol'šoj Kavkaz ⋏	84	42.30 N	45.00 E
Kaukauna	190	44.16 N	88.16 W
Kaukau Veld ⋏[1]	156	19.30 S	20.30 E
Kaukhāli	126	22.38 N	90.04 E
Kaukura I[1]	14	15.45 S	146.42 W
Kaula I	229d	21.45 N	160.30 W
Kaulakahi Channel ⋓	229b	22.00 N	159.53 W
Kaulille	56	51.11 N	5.31 E
Kauliranta	24	66.27 N	23.41 E
Kaŭl-li	98	37.58 N	124.37 E
Kaulsdorf	54	50.37 N	11.26 E
Kaulsdorf ◆[8]	264a	52.31 N	13.33 E
Kaulsdorf-Süd ◆[8]	264a	52.29 N	13.34 E
Kaumakani	229b	21.55 N	159.37 W
Kaumalapau	229a	20.47 N	156.59 W
Kaunakakai	229a	21.05 N	157.01 W
Kaunas	76	54.54 N	23.54 E
Kauneonga Lake	210	41.41 N	74.50 W
Kauner Tal V	58	47.01 N	10.44 E
Kaunghein	110	25.40 N	95.26 E
Kauniainen → Grankulla	26	60.13 N	24.45 E
Kaununui ≻	229b	21.56 N	160.10 W
Kaup	164	3.50 S	144.00 E
Kaupanger	26	61.11 N	7.14 E
Kaura Namoda	150	12.35 N	6.35 E
Kauriāla Ghāt	124	28.23 N	81.02 E
Kauru	150	10.33 N	8.12 E
Kausa	272c	19.10 N	73.02 E
Kau Sai Chau I	271d	22.22 N	114.18 E
Kausala	26	60.54 N	26.22 E
Kaušany	78	46.38 N	29.25 E
Kaustinen	26	63.32 N	23.42 E
Kauswagan	116	8.11 N	124.05 E
Kautokeino	24	69.00 N	23.02 E
Kauttua	26	61.06 N	22.10 E
Kau-ye Kyun I	110	11.01 N	98.32 E
Kavača	74	60.16 N	169.51 E
Kavacık	130	39.40 N	28.30 E
Kavadarci	38	41.26 N	22.00 E
Kavajë	38	41.11 N	19.33 E
Kavak, Tür.	130	38.24 N	39.26 E
Kavak, Tür.	130	41.05 N	36.03 E
Kavak, Tür.	130	39.18 N	37.30 E
Kavakköy	130	40.13 N	27.46 E
Kavaklıdere	130	37.26 N	28.22 E
Kavála	38	40.56 N	24.25 E
Kavalerovo	89	44.15 N	135.04 E
Kāvali	122	14.55 N	79.59 E
Kavango □[5]	156	18.30 S	20.15 E
Kavaratti	122	10.34 N	72.39 E
Kavaratti Island I	122	10.33 N	72.38 E
Kavarna	38	43.25 N	28.20 E
Kavendou, Mont ʌ	150	10.41 N	12.12 W
Kaverino, S.S.S.R.	80	54.10 N	41.47 E
Kaverino, S.S.S.R.	82	56.11 N	36.15 E
Kavieng	164	2.35 S	150.50 E
Kavimba	156	18.02 S	24.38 E
Kavīr, Dasht-e ◆[2]	128	34.40 N	54.30 E
Kavkazskij zapovednik ♠	84	43.55 N	40.30 E
Kävlinge	41	55.48 N	13.06 E
Kävlingeån ≐	41	55.47 N	13.06 E
Kavungo	152	11.31 S	23.03 E
Kavuu ≐	154	7.40 S	31.46 E
Kavykuči-Gazimurskije	88	51.22 N	118.10 E
Kaw, Guy. fr.	250	4.29 N	52.02 W
Kaw, Ok., U.S.	196	36.46 N	96.50 W
Kawa	110	17.05 N	96.28 E
Kawaba	94	36.41 N	139.07 E
Kawabe, Nihon	94	35.29 N	137.04 E
Kawabe, Nihon	96	33.55 N	135.11 E
Kawachi, Nihon	94	35.53 N	140.15 E
Kawachi, Nihon	94	36.37 N	139.56 E
Kawachi, Nihon	94	36.24 N	136.38 E
Kawachi-nagano	96	34.27 N	135.34 E
Kawagama Lake ⊜	212	45.18 N	78.45 W
Kawage	94	34.47 N	136.33 E
Kawagoe	94	35.55 N	139.29 E
Kawaguchi	94	35.48 N	139.43 E
Kawaguchiko	94	35.30 N	138.46 E
Kawaguchi-ko ⊜	94	35.31 N	138.45 E
Kawahara	96	35.24 N	134.12 E
Kawai, Nihon	94	36.18 N	137.07 E
Kawai, Nihon	270	34.35 N	135.45 E
Kawaihae Bay c	229d	20.02 N	155.50 W
Kawaihoa ≻	229b	21.47 N	160.12 W
Kawaikini ʌ	229b	22.05 N	159.29 W
Kawailoa	229c	21.36 N	158.05 W
Kawailoa Beach	229c	21.37 N	158.04 W
Kawajiri	96	34.14 N	132.42 E
Kawakami, Nihon	94	35.58 N	138.35 E
Kawakami, Nihon	96	34.44 N	133.29 E
Kawakami, Nihon	96	35.17 N	133.39 E
Kawakawa	172	35.23 S	174.04 E
Kawakubo	270	34.54 N	135.38 E
Kawali	115a	7.11 S	108.22 E
Kawama Mission	154	10.04 S	28.37 E
Kawamata	92	37.39 N	140.36 E
Kawambwa	154	9.47 S	29.05 E
Kawamoto, Nihon	94	36.09 N	139.17 E
Kawamoto, Nihon	96	34.59 N	132.30 E
Kawane	94	34.57 N	138.05 E
Kawanishi, Nihon	94	37.09 N	138.45 E
Kawanishi, Nihon	96	34.49 N	135.24 E
Kawanishi, Nihon	270	34.35 N	135.47 E
Kawanoe	96	34.01 N	133.34 E
Kawara, Nihon	96	33.40 N	130.51 E
Kawara, Nihon	270	34.59 N	135.18 E
Kawara Débé	150	12.20 N	3.26 E
Kawarai	268	35.25 N	140.05 E
Kawardha	124	22.01 N	81.15 E
Kawartha Park	212	44.32 N	78.12 W
Kawasaki, Nihon	94	35.32 N	139.43 E
Kawasaki, Nihon	96	33.35 N	130.49 E
Kawasaki-kō c	268	35.30 N	139.47 E
Kawasaki Stadium ♠	268	35.32 N	139.43 E
Kawashima, Nihon	94	35.21 N	136.50 E
Kawashima, Nihon	94	35.59 N	139.30 E
Kawashima, Nihon	96	34.04 N	134.19 E
Kawashima ◆[8]	268	35.28 N	139.35 E
Kawashiri-misaki ≻	96	34.26 N	130.58 E
Kawatana	92	33.04 N	129.52 E
Kawauchi	96	33.48 N	132.55 E
Kawau Island I	172	36.25 S	174.51 E
Kawawa ◆[8]	268	35.31 N	139.33 E
Kawayan	116	11.41 N	124.21 E
Kawazu	94	34.44 N	138.59 E
Kawbein	110	16.33 N	97.52 E
Kawdut	110	15.31 N	97.47 E
Kawe	164	7.50 S	138.14 E
Kawe, Pulau I	164	0.03 S	130.07 E
Kaweenakumik Lake ⊜	184	52.52 N	99.30 W
Kaweka ʌ	172	39.17 S	176.23 E
Kaweka Range ⋏	172	39.15 S	176.20 E
Kawerau	172	38.03 S	176.43 E
Kawhia	172	38.04 S	174.49 E
Kawhia Harbour c	172	38.05 S	174.50 E
Kawich Peak ʌ	204	37.58 N	116.27 W
Kawich Range ⋏	204	37.40 N	116.30 W
Kawin	164	2.45 S	150.45 E
Kawinda	115b	8.07 S	118.04 E
Kawio, Kepulauan II	112	4.30 N	125.30 E
Kawit	269f	14.27 N	120.54 E
Kawkabān	144	15.40 N	43.52 E
Kawkareik	110	16.33 N	98.14 E
Kaw Lake ⊜[1]	196	36.55 N	96.57 W
Kawludo	110	18.29 N	97.19 E
Kawm	140	13.31 N	22.50 E
Kawm al-Farāʿin (Buto) ⊥	142	31.11 N	30.45 E
Kawm ar-Rāhib	142	28.20 N	30.37 E
Kawm Bīrah	273c	30.05 N	31.08 E
Kawm Dafanah (Daphnæ) ⊥	142	30.52 N	32.11 E
Kawm Ḥamādah	142	30.46 N	30.42 E
Kawm Ishfīn	273c	30.11 N	31.15 E
Kawm Ishū	142	31.07 N	30.00 E
Kawm Juʿayf (Naucratis) ⊥	142	30.54 N	30.36 E
Kawm Umbū	140	24.28 N	32.57 E
Kawnglanghpu	102	27.04 N	98.21 E
Kawnipi Lake ⊜	190	48.24 N	91.14 W
Kawthaung	110	9.59 N	98.33 E
Kax ≐	86	43.40 N	81.45 E
Kaxgar ≐	85	39.40 N	78.00 E
Kaya, Burkina	150	13.05 N	1.05 W
Kaya, Nihon	96	35.30 N	135.06 E
Kayaapu	112	5.26 S	102.24 E
Kayadibi, Tür.	130	39.55 N	34.15 E
Kayadibi, Tür.	130	39.29 N	36.43 E
Kayah □[3]	110	19.15 N	97.30 E
Kayak Island I	180	59.52 N	144.30 W
Kāyalpattinam	122	8.34 N	78.07 E
Kāyamba	272b	22.41 N	88.32 E
Kayambi	154	9.27 S	31.58 E
Kayan	110	16.54 N	96.34 E
Kayan ≐	112	2.55 N	117.35 E
Kayangel Islands II	108	8.04 N	134.43 E
Kayang-san ʌ[2]	271b	37.33 N	126.43 E
Kayankulam	122	9.11 N	76.30 E
Kayapa	116	16.22 N	120.53 E
Kayaş	130	39.56 N	32.58 E
Kaya-san ʌ	98	35.49 N	128.07 E
Kaya-san Kukrip Kongwŏn ♠	98	35.47 N	128.06 E
Kaycee	200	43.42 N	106.38 W
Kayeli	164	3.23 S	127.06 E
Kayembe-Mukulu	152	9.03 S	23.57 E
Kayen	115a	6.54 S	110.59 E
Kayenta	200	36.43 N	110.15 W
Kayes, Congo	152	4.25 S	11.41 E
Kayes, Mali	150	14.27 N	11.26 W
Kayes □[4]	150	14.00 N	11.00 W
Kay Gardens	285	39.45 N	75.25 W
Kayima	150	8.53 N	11.10 W
Kayış Dağı ʌ	267b	40.59 N	29.09 E
Kaymakçı	130	38.10 N	28.08 E
Kaymaz	130	39.31 N	31.11 E
Kayna	54	50.59 N	12.14 E
Kaynak	130	37.43 N	39.37 E
Kaynar	130	38.55 N	36.28 E
Kayō, Nihon	96	34.51 N	133.42 E
Kayō, Nihon	174m	26.33 N	128.07 E
Kayoa, Pulau I	164	0.05 S	127.25 E
Kayombo	154	9.36 S	25.37 E
Kay Point ≻	180	69.18 N	138.22 W
Kayser Gebergte ⋏	250	3.03 N	56.35 W
Kayseri	130	38.43 N	35.30 E
Kayseri □[4]	130	38.30 N	35.55 E
Kaysersberg	58	48.08 N	7.15 E
Kaysville	200	41.02 N	111.56 W
Kayuadi, Pulau I	112	6.49 S	120.47 E
Kayuagung	112	3.24 S	104.50 E
Kayumas	115a	7.50 S	114.08 E
Kayuta Lake ⊜	210	43.25 N	75.12 W
Kayuyu	154	3.39 S	26.21 E
Kazach	84	41.06 N	45.22 E
Kazachskaja Sovetskaja Socialističeskaja Respublika □[3]	72	48.00 N	68.00 E
Kazachskij melkosopočnik ⋏[2]	86	49.00 N	72.00 E
Kazačij	83	46.58 N	40.03 E
Kazačinskoje, S.S.S.R.	86	57.49 N	93.17 E
Kazačinskoje, S.S.S.R.	88	56.16 N	107.36 E
Kazačja Lopan'	78	50.21 N	36.11 E
Kazačje	74	70.44 N	136.13 E
Kazačji Lageri	78	46.42 N	32.59 E
Kazačka	80	51.28 N	43.56 E
Kazackij	86	49.20 N	58.31 E
Kazackoje	78	51.18 N	33.29 E
Kazakdarja	86	43.27 N	59.46 E
Kazakevičevo	89	48.17 N	134.46 E
Kazakh Soviet Socialist Republic → Kazachskaja Sovetskaja Socialističeskaja Respublika □[3]	72	48.00 N	68.00 E
Kazaki	76	52.38 N	38.16 E
Kazaklija	78	46.00 N	28.37 E
Kazal'cevo	86	59.18 N	80.30 E
Kazalinsk	86	45.46 N	62.07 E
Kazan'	80	55.49 N	49.08 E
Kazan ≐	176	64.02 N	95.30 W
Kazanbulak	84	40.38 N	46.41 E
Kazancı	130	36.30 N	32.53 E
Kazandžik	128	39.16 N	55.32 E
Kazanka, S.S.S.R.	78	47.50 N	32.49 E
Kazanka, S.S.S.R.	86	53.20 N	67.27 E
Kazanka ≐	80	55.48 N	49.01 E
Kazanlâk	38	42.38 N	25.21 E
Kazan Lake ⊜	184	55.33 N	108.21 W
Kazanlı	130	36.50 N	34.45 E
Kazanovka	76	53.46 N	38.34 E
Kazan-rettō II	14	25.00 N	141.00 E
Kazanskaja	78	49.48 N	41.09 E
Kazanskoje, S.S.S.R.	82	54.59 N	37.39 E
Kazanskoje, S.S.S.R.	86	55.38 N	69.14 E
Kazan' Station ◆[5]	265b	55.46 N	37.40 E
Kazantip, mys ≻	78	45.28 N	35.51 E
Kazarman	85	41.24 N	74.03 E
Kazatin	78	49.43 N	28.50 E
Kazatkul'	86	55.02 N	76.03 E
Kazbegi	84	42.39 N	44.39 E
Kazbek, gora ʌ	84	42.42 N	44.31 E
Kaz Dağı ʌ	130	39.42 N	26.50 E
Kazembe	154	12.11 S	32.37 E
Kāzerūn	128	29.37 N	51.38 E
Kazgorodok, S.S.S.R.	86	52.53 N	70.42 E
Kazgorodok, S.S.S.R.	86	49.56 N	71.36 E
Kažim	24	60.20 N	51.30 E
Kazi-Magomed	84	40.03 N	48.56 E
Kazimierza Wielka	30	50.16 N	20.30 E
Kazimierz Dolny	30	51.20 N	21.58 E
Kazincbarcika	30	48.16 N	20.37 E
Kazinka, S.S.S.R.	76	52.32 N	39.42 E
Kazinka, S.S.S.R.	78	50.14 N	37.50 E
Kāzipāra	272b	22.43 N	88.31 E
Kāzīr Char	126	22.46 N	90.33 E
Kaziza	152	10.42 S	23.52 E
Kazlų Rūda	76	54.46 N	23.30 E
Kaz'minskoje	84	44.35 N	41.41 E
Kaznačejevo	82	54.31 N	37.16 E
Kazo	94	36.07 N	139.36 E
Kaz'onnyj Torec ≐	83	48.54 N	37.46 E
Kaztalovka	80	49.46 N	48.42 E
Kazuma Pan National Park ♠	154	18.15 S	25.33 E
Kazumba	152	6.25 S	22.02 E
Kazungula	154	17.45 S	25.20 E
Kazuno	92	40.11 N	140.47 E
Kazvin → Qazvīn	128	36.16 N	50.00 E
Kazy	128	39.13 N	57.30 E
Kazym	74	63.40 N	67.14 E
Kazym ≐	74	63.54 N	65.50 E
Kazyr ≐	86	53.47 N	92.53 E
Kbal Dâmrei	110	14.07 N	105.21 E
Kbelnice	60	49.18 N	13.59 E
Kbely ◆[8]	54	50.07 N	14.32 E
Kcynia	30	53.00 N	17.30 E
Kdyně	60	49.23 N	13.02 E
Kéa	38	37.38 N	24.21 E
Kéa I	38	37.34 N	24.22 E
Keaau	229d	19.37 N	155.02 W
Keady	48	54.15 N	6.42 W
Keahole Point ≻	229d	19.44 N	156.03 W
Keal, Loch na c	46	56.28 N	6.04 W
Kealaikahiki, Lae o ≻	229a	20.32 N	156.42 W
Kealaikahiki Channel ⋓	229a	20.37 N	156.50 W
Kealakekua Bay c	229d	19.28 N	155.56 W
Kealia	229b	22.06 N	159.18 W
Keams Canyon	200	35.48 N	110.11 W
Keanae	229a	20.51 N	156.09 W
Keanapapa Point ≻	229a	20.54 N	157.04 W
Kean College of New Jersey ⛩[2]	276	40.41 N	74.14 W
Keansburg	208	40.25 N	74.12 W
Kearney, Mo., U.S.	194	39.22 N	94.21 W
Kearney, Ne., U.S.	198	40.41 N	99.04 W
Kearney, Pa., U.S.	214	40.08 N	78.12 W
Kearns	200	40.39 N	111.59 W
Kearny, Az., U.S.	200	33.03 N	110.54 W
Kearny, N.J., U.S.	210	40.46 N	74.08 W
Kearsley	262	53.32 N	2.23 W
Kearsley Creek ≐	216	43.04 N	83.40 W
Keasbey	276	40.31 N	74.19 W
Keb' ≐	76	57.44 N	28.28 E
Kebajoran ◆[8]	269e	6.13 S	106.46 E
Keban	130	38.48 N	38.45 E
Keban Gölü ⊜[1]	130	38.50 N	39.15 E
Kebanyartimur	115a	7.09 S	112.52 E
Kébara	152	2.27 S	14.25 E
Kebbi	150	12.08 N	4.44 E
Kebeiti	120	36.47 N	79.29 E
Kébémer	150	15.22 N	16.27 W
Kébi, Mayo ≐	146	9.18 N	13.33 E
Kebili	148	33.42 N	8.58 E
Kebîr, Oued el ≐	34	36.50 N	6.07 E
Kebnekaise ʌ	24	67.53 N	18.33 E
Kebock Head ≻	46	58.01 N	6.20 W
Kebri Dehar	144	6.47 N	44.17 E
Kebumen	115a	7.40 S	109.39 E
Keb'uty	80	45.50 N	44.14 E
Keče	85	43.14 N	71.22 E
Kecel	30	46.32 N	19.16 E
Kech ≐	128	26.00 N	62.44 E
Kechika ≐	176	59.36 N	127.05 W
Keçiborlu	130	37.57 N	30.18 E
Kecksburg	214	40.11 N	79.28 W
Kecskemét	30	46.54 N	19.42 E
Kedabek	84	40.34 N	45.49 E
Kedah □[3]	114	6.00 N	100.40 E
Kėdainiai	76	55.17 N	24.00 E
Kédange-sur-Canner	56	49.19 N	6.20 E
Kedarnath	124	30.44 N	79.04 E
Kedārpur	126	23.18 N	90.27 E
Kedawung	115a	6.42 S	108.31 E
Kedges Straits ⋓	208	38.03 N	76.02 W
Kedgwick	186	47.39 N	67.21 W
Kedgwick ≐	186	47.40 N	67.29 W
Kédhron	38	39.13 N	22.03 E
Kedian	100	31.23 N	112.51 E
Kediri	115a	7.49 S	112.01 E
Kedjebi	150	8.12 N	0.25 E
Kedon	74	64.08 N	159.14 E
Kedong	89	48.02 N	126.15 E
Kédougou	150	12.33 N	12.11 W
Kedrasju	24	64.36 N	60.24 E
Kedrovka	86	55.32 N	86.03 E
Kedu	102	26.33 N	104.21 E
Kedungdung	115a	7.06 S	113.15 E
Kedungjati	115a	7.10 S	110.37 E
Kedungwuni	115a	6.58 S	109.39 E
Kedvavom	24	64.15 N	53.27 E
Kędzierzyn Kozle	30	50.20 N	18.12 E
Keecheus Lake ⊜	224	47.22 N	121.22 W
Keefer	218	38.32 N	84.38 W
Keefers	182	50.02 N	121.33 W
Keego Harbor	216	42.36 N	83.20 W
Keelby	44	53.34 N	0.15 W
Keele	42	53.00 N	2.17 W
Keele ≐	180	64.24 N	124.50 W
Keele Peak ʌ	180	63.26 N	130.19 W
Keeley Lake ⊜	184	54.54 N	108.08 W
Keeling Islands → Cocos Islands □[2]	12	12.10 S	96.55 E
Keels	186	48.36 N	53.24 W
Keelung → Chilung	100	25.08 N	121.44 E
Keen, Mount ʌ	46	56.58 N	2.54 W
Keene, On., Can.	212	44.15 N	78.10 W
Keene, Ca., U.S.	228	35.13 N	118.33 W
Keene, Ky., U.S.	192	37.56 N	84.38 W
Keene, N.H., U.S.	188	42.56 N	72.16 W
Keene, Oh., U.S.	214	40.21 N	81.52 W
Keene, Tx., U.S.	222	32.23 N	97.19 W
Keenesburg	200	40.06 N	104.31 W
Keeney Knob ʌ	192	37.47 N	80.42 W
Keeneyville	278	41.59 N	88.07 W
Keerbergen	56	51.00 N	4.37 E
Keer-Weer, Cape ≻	164	13.58 S	141.30 E
Keerzong	120	32.11 N	79.59 E
Keeseg ʌ	64	46.58 N	12.14 E
Keeseville	188	44.30 N	73.28 W
Keesler Air Force Base ■	194	30.26 N	88.55 W
Keetmanshoop	156	26.36 S	18.08 E
Keetmanshoop □[5]	156	26.30 S	19.00 E
Keewatin, On., Can.	184	49.46 N	94.34 W
Keewatin, Mn., U.S.	190	47.23 N	93.04 W
Keewatin □[5]	176	65.00 N	95.00 W
Kefa □[4]	144	6.50 N	36.00 E
Kefallinía I	38	38.15 N	20.35 E
Kéfalos	38	36.45 N	27.00 E
Kefamenanu	112	9.27 S	124.29 E
Kefar Ata	132	32.48 N	35.06 E
Kefar ʿAzza	132	31.29 N	34.32 E
Kefar Blum	132	33.10 N	35.36 E
Kefar ʿEqron	132	31.51 N	34.49 E
Kefar Sava	132	32.10 N	34.54 E
Kefar Shammay	132	32.57 N	35.27 E
Kefar Syrkin	132	32.04 N	34.56 E
Kefar Szold	132	33.11 N	35.39 E
Kefar Vitkin	132	32.23 N	34.53 E
Kefar Warburg	132	31.43 N	34.44 E
Keferdiz	130	38.19 N	39.03 E
Kefermarkt	61	48.26 N	14.32 E
Keffi	150	8.51 N	7.52 E
Keffin Hausa	150	12.15 N	9.58 E
Keflavík	24a	64.02 N	22.36 W
Keftya	144	13.54 N	37.07 E
Kega	24	65.10 N	36.54 E
Kegalla	122	7.15 N	80.21 E
Kégashka	186	50.12 N	61.17 W
Kégashka, Lac ⊜	186	50.20 N	61.25 W
Kegejli	86	42.45 N	59.35 E
Kegičovka	78	49.17 N	35.46 E
Kegnæs ≻[1]	41	54.52 N	9.59 E
Kegon-no-taki ᒪ	94	36.44 N	139.31 E
Kegonsa, Lake ⊜	216	42.58 N	89.15 W
Kegonzhake	120	33.00 N	87.53 E
Keg River	176	57.48 N	117.52 W
Kegums	76	56.46 N	24.45 E
Kegworth	42	52.50 N	1.16 W
Kehdingen, Land ◆[1]	52	53.45 N	9.15 E
Kehiwin Indian Reserve ◆[4]	182	54.07 N	110.48 W
Kehl	56	48.35 N	7.50 E
Kehlen	58	47.41 N	9.33 E
Kehoe	218	38.28 N	83.03 W
Kehra	76	59.20 N	25.20 E
Kehrigk	54	52.09 N	13.55 E
Ke-hsi Mānsām	110	21.56 N	97.50 E
Keig	46	57.15 N	2.39 W
Keighley	44	53.52 N	1.54 W
Keihoku	96	35.09 N	135.38 E
Keijō → Sŏul	98	37.33 N	126.58 E
Keila	76	59.18 N	24.25 E
Keilor	169	37.43 S	144.50 E
Keimoes	158	28.41 S	21.00 E
Kei Mouth	158	32.41 S	28.22 E
Keio University ⛩[2]	268	35.38 N	139.45 E
Kei Road	158	32.42 S	27.32 E
Keiser	194	35.40 N	90.05 W
Keiskammahoek	158	32.41 S	27.09 E
Keiskammapunt ≻	158	32.40 S	27.10 E
Keïta	150	14.46 N	5.46 E
Kéita, Bahr ≐	146	9.14 N	18.21 E
Keitele	26	63.11 N	26.22 E
Keitele ⊜	26	62.55 N	26.00 E
Keith, Austl.	166	36.06 S	140.21 E
Keith, Scot., U.K.	46	57.32 N	2.57 W
Keith Arm c	176	65.20 N	122.15 W
Keithley Creek	182	52.45 N	121.24 W
Keithsburg	190	41.05 N	90.56 W
Keiyasi	175g	17.54 S	177.45 E
Keizer	224	44.59 N	123.01 W
Kejaman	112	2.39 N	113.45 E
Kejimkujik National Park ♠	186	44.21 N	65.18 W
Kejngypil'gyn, laguna c	180	63.30 N	178.50 E
Kejni, gora ʌ	180	64.30 N	174.54 W
Kejvy ⋏	24	67.35 N	38.00 E
Kekaha	229b	21.58 N	159.42 W
Kekek ≐	190	48.24 N	75.48 W
Kekerengu	172	42.00 S	174.01 E
Kékes ʌ	30	47.55 N	20.02 E
Kekexili	120	35.11 N	93.35 E
Kekeyaer	85	38.02 N	75.05 E
Kek Lok Si ⛩[1]	114	5.23 N	100.14 E
Kekpāra	126	22.27 N	86.35 E
Kekri	120	25.58 N	75.09 E
Kekurnoi, Cape ≻	180	57.44 N	155.15 W
Kelafo	144	5.40 N	44.20 E
Kelai ≐	112	2.10 N	117.29 E
Kelalihu ⊜	120	34.36 N	87.16 E
Kelan	102	38.43 N	111.32 E
Kelanang	114	2.48 N	101.26 E
Kelang	114	3.02 N	101.27 E
Kelang, Pulau I, Indon.	164	3.12 S	127.44 E
Kelang, Pulau I, Malay.	114	3.00 N	101.18 E
Kelani ≐	122	6.58 N	79.52 E
Kelantan	114	0.51 N	101.40 E
Kelantan □[3]	114	5.20 N	102.00 E
Kelantan ≐	114	6.11 N	102.15 E
Kelapa	112	1.52 S	105.42 E
Kelasuri	84	43.08 N	41.13 E
Kelat	218	38.32 N	84.19 W
Kelayres	210	40.54 N	76.00 W
Kelb, Ouadi V	146	15.19 N	18.51 E
Kel'badžar	84	40.07 N	46.02 E
Kelberg	56	50.17 N	6.55 E
Kelbia, Sebkhet ⊜	36	35.51 N	10.16 E
Kelbra	54	51.26 N	11.02 E
Keld Ula ʌ	86	43.20 N	85.25 E
Kel'd'ušovo	80	55.01 N	44.59 E
Kelegou	98	41.57 N	118.11 E
Kélékélé	273b	4.20 S	15.08 E
Kelem	144	4.48 N	35.58 E
Kelenföld ◆[8]	264c	47.28 N	19.03 E
Kelenken, gora ʌ	180	66.07 N	170.52 W
Keles, S.S.S.R.	85	41.24 N	69.12 E
Keles, Tür.	130	39.55 N	29.14 E
Keles ≐	85	41.02 N	68.37 E
Keleti-főcsatorna ≖	30	48.01 N	21.20 E
Keleti Pályaudvar ◆[5]	264c	47.30 N	19.06 E
Kelheim	60	48.55 N	11.52 E
Kelibia	148	36.51 N	11.06 E
Kelif	128	37.21 N	66.15 E
Keliyahe ≐	120	38.30 N	82.10 E
Kelkheim	56	50.08 N	8.26 E
Kelkit ≐	130	40.46 N	36.32 E
Kell	219	38.30 N	88.54 W
Kellé	152	0.06 S	14.33 E
Kellen	52	51.48 N	6.10 E
Kellenhusen	54	54.11 N	11.03 E
Keller, Tx., U.S.	222	32.56 N	97.15 W
Keller, Va., U.S.	208	37.37 N	75.45 W
Keller, Wa., U.S.	182	48.04 N	118.41 W
Kellerberg	64	46.40 N	13.42 E
Kellerberrin	162	31.38 S	117.43 E
Kellerjoch ʌ	64	47.19 N	11.46 E
Keller Lake ⊜, N.T., Can.	176	64.00 N	121.30 W
Keller Lake ⊜, Sk., Can.	184	56.04 N	106.46 W
Kellerovka	86	53.50 N	69.17 E
Keller Peak ʌ	228	34.12 N	117.03 W
Kellett, Cape ≻	176	71.59 N	125.34 W
Kellettville	214	41.33 N	79.16 W
Kelleys Island	214	41.36 N	82.42 W
Kelleys Island I	214	41.36 N	82.42 W
Kelliher	184	51.15 N	103.44 W
Kellinghusen	52	53.57 N	9.43 E
Kellmünz	58	48.07 N	10.08 E
Kelloe	44	54.43 N	1.28 W
Kellogg, Id., U.S.	202	47.32 N	116.07 W
Kellogg, Ia., U.S.	190	41.43 N	92.54 W
Kellogg, Mn., U.S.	190	44.18 N	91.59 W
Kellogg Marsh	224	48.05 N	122.07 W
Kelloggsville	214	41.52 N	80.36 W
Kellojärvi ⊜	26	64.16 N	29.03 E
Kelloselkä	24	66.56 N	28.50 E
Kells → Ceanannus Mór	48	53.44 N	6.53 W
Kelly Air Force Base ■	196	29.24 N	98.35 W
Kelly Lake ⊜	180	65.30 N	126.10 W

Symbols in the index entries represent the broad categories identified in the key at the right. Symbols with superior numbers (⋏[1]) identify subcategories (see complete key on page I · 1).

Kartensymbole in dem Registerverzeichnis stellen die rechts in Schlüssel erklärten Kategorien dar. Symbole mit hochgestellten Ziffern (⋏[1]) bezeichnen Unterabteilungen einer Kategorie (vgl. vollständiger Schlüssel auf Seite I · 1).

Los símbolos incluidos en el texto del índice representan las grandes categorías identificadas con la clave a la derecha. Los símbolos con numeros en su parte superior (⋏[1]) identifican las subcategorías (véase la clave completa en la página I · 1).

Les symboles de l'index représentent les catégories indiquées dans la légende à droite. Les symboles suivis d'un indice (⋏[1]) représentent des sous-catégories (voir légende complète à la page I · 1).

Os símbolos incluídos no texto do índice representam as grandes categorias identificadas com a chave à direita. Os símbolos com números em sua parte superior (⋏[1]) identificam as subcategorias (veja-se a chave completa à página I · 1).

ʌ Mountain	Berg	Montaña	Montagne	Montanha
⋏ Mountains	Berge	Montañas	Montagnes	Montanhas
)(Pass	Pass	Paso	Col	Passo
V Valley, Canyon	Tal, Cañon	Valle, Cañón	Vallée, Canyon	Vale, Canhão
≚ Plain	Ebene	Llano	Plaine	Planície
≻ Cape	Kap	Cabo	Cap	Cabo
I Island	Insel	Isla	Île	Ilha
II Islands	Inseln	Islas	Îles	Ilhas
⊥ Other Topographic Features	Andere Topographische Objekte	Otros Elementos Topográficos	Autres données topographiques	Outros acidentes topográficos

ESPAÑOL — Nombre | Página | Lat.°′ | Long.°′ W = Oeste

Kelly Run ≃, Pa., U.S. 279b 40.15 N 79.55 W
Kelly Run ≃, Pa., U.S. 279b 40.13 N 79.45 W
Kellyville, Austl. 274a 33.43 S 150.57 E
Kellyville, Ok., U.S. 196 35.56 N 96.12 W
Kelmė 76 55.38 N 22.56 E
Kel'mency 78 48.27 N 26.50 E
Kelmet 144 16.04 N 38.55 E
Kelmscott 168a 32.07 S 116.01 E
Kelo 146 9.19 N 15.48 E
Kelolokan 112 1.08 N 117.54 E
Kelottijärvi 24 68.31 N 22.04 E
Kelowna 182 49.53 N 119.29 W
Kelsall 44 53.13 N 2.43 W
Kelsey Bay 182 50.24 N 125.57 W
Kelsey Head ≻ 42 50.24 N 5.08 W
Kelsey Lake ⊜ 184 53.37 N 101.02 W
Kelseyville 204 38.58 N 122.50 W
Kelso, Scot., U.K. 46 55.36 N 2.25 W
Kelso, Wa., U.S. 224 46.08 N 122.54 W
Kelsterbach 56 50.04 N 8.32 E
Kel'temašat 85 42.30 N 70.17 E
Kelty 46 56.08 N 3.23 W
Keluang 114 2.02 N 103.19 E
Keluang, Tanjung ≻ 112 3.02 S 110.39 E
Kelud, Gunung ∧ 115a 7.56 S 112.18 E
Keluo ≃ 89 49.22 N 125.15 E
Keluotun 89 49.16 N 125.44 E
Kelvedon 42 51.51 N 0.42 E
Kelvedon Hatch 260 51.40 N 0.16 E
Kelvington 184 52.10 N 103.30 W
Kelvin Seamount ✢[3] 16 38.50 N 64.00 W
Kelyexeed 144 8.46 N 49.12 E
Kelzenberg 263 51.07 N 6.30 E
Kem' 24 64.57 N 34.36 E
Kem' ≃, S.S.S.R. 24 64.57 N 34.41 E
Kem' ≃, S.S.S.R. 86 58.31 N 92.04 E
Kema 112 1.23 N 125.04 E
Kema ≃, S.S.S.R. 76 60.16 N 37.20 E
Kema ≃, S.S.S.R. 76 59.21 N 44.29 E
Ké Macina 150 13.58 N 5.22 W
Kémah, Congo 273b 4.11 S 15.13 E
Kemah, Tür. 130 39.36 N 39.02 E
Kemah, Tx., U.S. 222 29.32 N 95.01 W
Kemaliye 130 39.16 N 38.29 E
Kemalpaşa, Tür. 130 41.30 N 41.30 E
Kemalpaşa, Tür. 130 38.25 N 27.26 E
Kemano 182 53.34 N 127.56 W
Kemasik 114 4.25 N 103.27 E
Kemayan 114 3.08 N 102.22 E
Kemayoran Airport ⊠ 269e 6.09 S 106.51 E
Kembani 112 1.34 S 122.54 E
Kembé 152 4.36 N 21.54 E
Kemberg 54 51.46 N 12.38 E
Kemblesville 208 39.45 N 75.50 W
Kembolcha 144 11.02 N 39.43 E
Kembs 58 47.41 N 7.30 E
Kembul 164 5.55 S 150.40 E
Kemčug ≃ 86 57.14 N 90.31 E
Kemena ≃ 112 3.10 N 113.03 E
Kemeneshát ⋀[2] 61 46.58 N 16.40 E
Kemer 130 36.38 N 29.21 E
Kemer ≃ 267b 41.04 N 29.07 E
Kemer Barajı ⬥[6] 130 37.34 N 28.31 E
Kemerburgaz 267b 41.09 N 28.54 E
Kemerhisar 130 37.49 N 34.36 E
Kemerovo 86 55.20 N 86.05 E
Kemi 24 65.49 N 24.32 E
Kemie 26 62.14 N 30.20 E
Kemijärvi 24 66.40 N 27.25 E
Kemijärvi ⊜ 24 66.36 N 27.24 E
Kemijoki ≃ 26 65.47 N 24.30 E
Kemiö → Kimito 26 60.10 N 22.45 E
Keml'a 80 54.42 N 45.15 E
Kemmel 50 50.47 N 2.49 E
Kemmelberg ∧[2] 50 50.47 N 2.50 E
Kemmerer 200 41.47 N 110.32 W
Kemminghausen ⬥[8] 263 51.34 N 7.29 E
Kemmuna I 36 36.00 N 14.20 E
Kemnath 60 49.52 N 11.54 E
Kemnay 46 57.14 N 2.27 W
Kemnitz 54 54.04 N 13.31 E
Kémo-Gribingui □[5] 152 6.00 N 19.00 E
Kemp 222 32.26 N 96.13 W
Kemp, Lake ⊜[1] 196 33.45 N 99.13 W
Kemparana 150 12.50 N 4.56 W
Kemp Coast ⫠[2] 9 67.10 S 58.00 E
Kempele 26 64.55 N 25.30 E
Kempen 56 51.22 N 6.25 E
Kempen □[9] 56 51.10 N 5.20 E
Kempener Land ⬥[1] 263 51.19 N 6.29 E
Kempenfelt Bay ⊂ 212 44.23 N 79.36 W
Kempenich 56 50.25 N 7.07 E
Kempen-Krefeld □[8] 263 51.17 N 6.31 E
Kemper → Quimper 32 48.00 N 4.06 W
Kempisch Kanaal ≅ 56 51.10 N 4.49 E
Kemp Mill 284c 39.02 N 77.01 W
Kempner 196 31.05 N 98.00 W
Kemp Peninsula ≻[1] 9 73.08 S 60.15 W
Kemps Bay 238 24.02 N 77.33 W
Kemps Creek ≃ 274a 33.51 S 150.46 E
Kempsey, Austl. 166 31.05 S 152.50 E
Kempsey, Eng., U.K. 42 52.08 N 2.12 W
Kempston 42 52.07 N 0.30 W
Kempt, Lac ⊜ 176 47.25 N 74.22 W
Kempten (Allgäu) 58 47.43 N 10.19 E
Kempton, Il., U.S. 216 40.56 N 88.14 W
Kempton, In., U.S. 216 40.17 N 86.13 W
Kempton Park 158 26.06 S 28.14 E
Kempton Park □[5] 273d 26.06 S 28.14 E
Kempton Park Race Course ♠ 260 51.25 N 0.23 W
Kemptville 212 45.01 N 75.38 W
Kemptville Creek ≃ 212 45.03 N 75.39 W
Kemsing 260 51.18 N 0.14 E
Kemubu 114 5.18 N 102.01 E
Kemujan, Pulau I 115a 5.48 S 110.28 E
Kemul, Kong ∧ 112 1.52 N 116.11 E
Ken ≃ 124 25.46 N 80.31 E
Ken, Loch ⊜ 44 55.02 N 4.02 W
Ken, Water of ≃ 44 55.04 N 4.08 W
Kena ≃ 24 62.05 N 39.06 E
Kenai 180 60.33 N 151.15 W
Kenai Fjords National Park ♠ 180 59.45 N 150.00 W
Kenai Mountains ⋀ 180 60.00 N 150.00 W
Kenai Peninsula ≻[1] 180 60.10 N 150.00 W
Kenamuke Swamp ≣ 140 6.15 N 33.48 E
Kenansville, Fl., U.S. 220 27.52 N 80.59 W
Kenansville, N.C., U.S. 192 34.57 N 77.57 W
Kenaral 85 42.32 N 72.08 E
Kenašči 80 50.32 N 53.20 E
Kenashiga-sen ∧ 96 35.14 N 133.31 E
Kenaston 184 51.30 N 106.18 W
Kenberma 283 42.17 N 70.52 W
Kenbridge 192 36.57 N 78.07 W
Kenda 126 23.12 N 86.32 E
Kendai 124 22.45 N 82.37 E
Kendal, Sk., Can. 184 50.15 N 103.37 W
Kendal, Indon. 115a 6.55 S 110.12 E
Kendal, S. Afr. 158 26.04 S 28.58 E
Kendal, Eng., U.K. 44 54.20 N 2.45 W
Kendall, Austl. 166 31.38 S 152.43 E
Kendall, Fl., U.S. 220 25.40 N 80.19 W
Kendall, Mi., U.S. 216 42.22 N 85.49 W
Kendall, N.Y., U.S. 210 43.20 N 78.02 W
Kendall, Wi., U.S. 190 43.47 N 90.22 W
Kendall □[6] 216 41.38 N 88.27 W
Kendall, Cape ≻ 176 63.36 N 87.09 W
Kendall, Mount ∧ 172 41.22 S 172.24 E
Kendall Park 208 40.31 N 74.24 W
Kendallville 216 41.26 N 85.15 W
Kendari 112 3.57 S 122.35 E
Kendari, Teluk ⊂ 112 3.57 S 122.38 E
Kendawangan 112 2.32 S 110.12 E
Kende 150 11.30 N 4.12 E
Kendenup 162 34.29 S 117.39 E
Kendghāta 126 24.05 N 87.10 E
Kendikolu I 122 5.57 N 73.24 E
Kendiktas ⋀ 85 43.35 N 74.45 E

FRANÇAIS — Nom | Page | Lat.°′ | Long.°′ W = Ouest

Kendleton 222 29.27 N 96.00 W
Kendrāpāra 120 20.30 N 86.25 E
Kendrew 158 32.31 S 24.30 E
Kendrick, Fl., U.S. 192 29.22 N 82.12 W
Kendrick, Id., U.S. 202 46.36 N 116.38 W
Kendrick Creek ≃ 226 38.00 N 119.50 W
Kendua 272b 22.34 N 88.10 E
Kendu Bay 154 0.22 S 34.39 E
Kendyrlik 86 47.30 N 85.12 E
Kenedy 196 28.49 N 97.50 W
Kenefick 222 30.07 N 94.51 W
Kenema 150 7.52 N 11.12 W
Kenes, S.S.S.R. 85 43.41 N 67.49 E
Kenes, S.S.S.R. 85 43.59 N 73.35 E
Kenesaw 198 40.37 N 98.39 W
Kenga 86 57.27 N 80.57 E
Kenga ≃ 86 58.05 N 80.37 E
Kenge 152 4.52 S 16.59 E
Kengeja 154 5.25 S 39.44 E
Kēng Hkam, Mya. 110 21.01 N 98.29 E
Keng Hkam, Mya. 110 21.27 N 97.03 E
Kengkou, Zhg. 100 29.48 N 117.22 E
Kengkou, Zhg. 100 28.27 N 120.26 E
Kengtian 100 25.54 N 119.26 E
Kēng Tung 110 21.17 N 99.36 E
Kengun-chūtonchi, Rikujō-jieitai- ■ 92 32.46 N 130.45 E
Kenhardt 158 29.19 S 21.12 E
Kenhorst 208 40.18 N 75.57 W
Kenia 152 2.43 S 17.04 E
Kenia → Kenya □[1] 154 1.00 N 38.00 E
Kenia → Kirinyaga ∧ 154 0.10 S 37.20 E
Kéniéba 150 12.50 N 11.14 W
Kenilworth, Eng., U.K. 42 52.21 N 1.34 W
Kenilworth, Il., U.S. 278 42.05 N 87.43 W
Kenilworth, N.J., U.S. 276 40.40 N 74.17 W
Kenilworth, Pa., U.S. 208 40.14 N 75.38 W
Kenilworth, Ut,. U.S. 200 39.41 N 110.48 W
Kenilworth Castle ⊥ 42 52.21 N 1.34 W
Keningau 112 5.20 N 116.10 E
Kenitra 148 34.16 N 6.40 W
Kenitra □[4] 148 34.30 N 6.00 W
Kenley ⬥[8] 260 51.19 N 0.06 W
Kenli (Xishuanghe) 98 37.40 N 118.35 E
Kenly 192 35.35 N 78.07 W
Kenmare, Ire. 48 51.53 N 9.35 W
Kenmare, N.D., U.S. 198 48.40 N 102.04 W
Kenmare River ≃ 48 51.45 N 10.00 W
Kenmawr 279b 40.28 N 80.06 W
Kenmore, Scot., U.K. 46 56.34 N 3.59 W
Kenmore, N.Y., U.S. 210 42.57 N 78.52 W
Kenmore, Wa., U.S. 224 47.45 N 122.14 W
Kennard, In., U.S. 218 39.54 N 85.31 W
Kennard, Pa., U.S. 214 41.28 N 80.20 W
Kennard, Tx., U.S. 222 31.22 N 95.11 W
Kennebec 198 43.54 N 99.51 W
Kennebec ≃ 188 44.00 N 69.50 W
Kennebecasis Bay ⊂ 186 45.25 N 66.00 W
Kennebec Lake ⊜ 212 44.43 N 77.00 W
Kennebunk 188 43.23 N 70.32 W
Kennedale 222 32.38 N 97.13 W
Kennedy, Al., U.S. 194 33.35 N 87.59 W
Kennedy, N.Y., U.S. 214 42.09 N 79.06 W
Kennedy, Zimb. 154 18.52 S 27.10 E
Kennedy, Cape → Canaveral, Cape ≻ 220 28.27 N 80.32 W
Kennedy, Mount ∧, B.C., Can. 182 50.49 N 125.33 W
Kennedy, Mount ∧, Yk., Can. 180 60.30 N 139.00 W
Kennedy Entrance ⋓ 180 59.00 N 152.00 W
Kennedy Lake ⊜ 182 49.05 N 125.40 W
Kennedy Peak ∧ 110 23.19 N 93.45 E
Kennedy Range ⋀ 162 24.30 S 115.00 E
Kennedyville 208 39.18 N 75.59 W
Kennemerduinen, Nationale Park de ♠ 52 52.25 N 4.35 E
Kenner 194 29.59 N 90.14 W
Kennerdell 214 41.16 N 79.51 W
Kennet ≃, Eng., U.K. 42 52.26 N 0.28 E
Kennet ≃, Eng., U.K. 42 51.28 N 0.57 W
Kennetcook 186 45.11 N 63.44 W
Kenneth City 220 27.49 N 82.44 W
Kennett 194 36.14 N 90.03 W
Kennett Square 208 39.50 N 75.42 W
Kennewick 202 46.12 N 119.08 W
Kenney 219 40.06 N 89.05 W
Kenney Dam ⬥[6] 182 53.37 N 124.58 W
Kennington, Eng., U.K. 42 51.10 N 0.54 E
Kennington, Eng., U.K. 42 51.43 N 1.15 W
Kennisis Lake ⊜ 212 45.13 N 78.39 W
Kenn Reef ✢[2] 160 21.12 S 155.46 E
Kenny 222 30.03 N 96.20 W
Kennydale 224 47.31 N 122.12 W
Kennywood Park ♠ 279b 40.23 N 79.52 W
Kénogami 186 48.26 N 71.14 W
Kenogami ≃ 176 51.06 N 84.28 W
Kénogami, Lac ⊜ 186 48.20 N 71.23 W
Kenogamissi Lake ⊜ 190 48.15 N 81.31 W
Keno Hill 180 63.55 N 135.18 W
Kenora 184 49.47 N 94.29 W
Kenosha 216 42.35 N 87.49 W
Kenosha □[6] 216 42.35 N 88.03 W
Kenova 188 38.23 N 82.34 W
Kenoza Lake 210 41.44 N 74.57 W
Kenoza Lake ⊜ 283 42.47 N 71.03 W
Kenozero, ozero ⊜ 24 62.03 N 38.14 E
Ken Rock 216 42.15 N 89.03 W
Kensal 198 47.18 N 98.43 W
Kense 86 46.49 N 68.20 E
Kensett 194 35.13 N 91.40 W
Kensico Lake ⊜ 276 41.07 N 73.45 W
Kensico Reservoir ⊜[1] 210 41.05 N 73.46 W
Kensington, Austl. 274a 33.55 S 151.14 E
Kensington, P.E., Can. 186 46.26 N 63.38 W
Kensington, Ca., U.S. 226 37.54 N 122.16 W
Kensington, Ct., U.S. 207 41.38 N 72.46 W
Kensington, Ks., U.S. 198 39.46 N 99.01 W
Kensington, Md., U.S. 284c 39.01 N 77.04 W
Kensington, Oh., U.S. 214 40.44 N 80.57 W
Kensington ⬥[8], S. Afr. 273d 26.12 S 28.06 E
Kensington ⬥[8], N.Y., U.S. 276 40.39 N 73.58 W
Kensington ⬥[8], Pa., U.S. 285 39.58 N 75.08 W
Kensington and Chelsea ⬥[8] 260 51.29 N 0.11 W
Kensington Estates 284c 39.02 N 77.05 W
Kensington Metropolitan Park ♠ 281 42.32 N 83.39 W
Kensington Park 220 27.22 N 82.31 W
Kent, S.L. 150 8.10 N 13.10 W
Kent, Ct., U.S. 207 41.43 N 73.28 W
Kent, N.Y., U.S. 210 43.20 N 78.08 W
Kent, Oh., U.S. 214 41.09 N 81.21 W
Kent, Or., U.S. 224 45.11 N 120.41 W
Kent, Wa., U.S. 224 47.22 N 122.14 W
Kent □[6], On., Can. 214 42.25 N 82.10 W
Kent □[6], Eng., U.K. 42 51.15 N 0.40 E
Kent □[6], De., U.S. 208 39.10 N 75.32 W
Kent □[6], Md., U.S. 208 39.13 N 76.04 W
Kent □[6], Mi., U.S. 216 42.56 N 85.33 W
Kent □[6], R.I., U.S. 207 41.40 N 71.38 W
Kent ≃ 44 54.15 N 2.48 W
Kent, Vale of V 42 51.10 N 0.30 E
Kent Acres 208 39.07 N 75.31 W

PORTUGUÊS — Nome | Página | Lat.°′ | Long.°′ W = Oeste

Kentallen 46 56.39 N 5.15 W
Kentani 158 32.31 S 28.19 E
Kentau 85 43.36 N 68.36 E
Kent Bridge 214 42.31 N 82.04 W
Kent County Airport ⊠ 216 42.54 N 85.39 W
Kentfield 282 37.57 N 122.33 W
Kent Group II 166 39.27 S 147.20 E
Kenthurst 274a 33.40 S 151.00 E
Kent Island I 208 38.55 N 76.20 W
Kent Lake ⊜ 216 42.32 N 83.40 W
Kentland, In., U.S. 216 40.46 N 87.26 W
Kentland, Md., U.S. 284c 38.55 N 76.53 W
Kenton, Eng., U.K. 42 50.38 N 3.28 W
Kenton, De., U.S. 208 39.13 N 75.39 W
Kenton, Mi., U.S. 190 46.29 N 88.53 W
Kenton, Oh., U.S. 216 40.38 N 83.36 W
Kenton, Tn., U.S. 194 36.12 N 89.00 W
Kenton □[6] 218 38.56 N 84.33 W
Kent Park 283 42.06 N 70.41 W
Kent Park ♠ 273d 26.08 S 28.04 E
Kent Peninsula ≻[1] 176 68.30 N 107.00 W
Kent Point ≻ 208 38.50 N 76.22 W
Kentucky □[3] 178 37.30 N 85.15 W
Kentucky ≃ 218 38.41 N 85.11 W
Kentucky, Middle Fork ≃ 192 37.35 N 83.40 W
Kentucky, North Fork ≃ 192 37.34 N 83.42 W
Kentucky, South Fork ≃ 192 37.34 N 83.42 W
Kentucky Horse Park ♠ 218 38.08 N 84.31 W
Kentucky Lake ⊜[1] 194 36.25 N 88.05 W
Kent Village 284c 38.55 N 76.53 W
Kentville 186 45.05 N 64.30 W
Kentwood, La., U.S. 194 30.56 N 90.30 W
Kentwood, Mi., U.S. 216 42.52 N 85.38 W
Kent Woodlands 282 37.57 N 122.34 W
Kenvil 276 40.52 N 74.37 W
Kenwick 168a 32.02 S 115.58 E
Kenwood, Ca., U.S. 226 38.25 N 122.33 W
Kenwood, Md., U.S. 284b 39.21 N 76.31 W
Kenwood, Oh., U.S. 218 39.12 N 84.22 W
Kenwood ⬥[8] 278 41.49 N 87.36 W
Kenwood ⊥ 260 51.34 N 0.10 W
Kenya □[1] 154 1.00 N 38.00 E
Kenya, Mount → Kirinyaga ∧ 154 0.10 S 37.20 E
Kenyon, Eng., U.K. 262 53.27 N 2.34 W
Kenyon, Mn., U.S. 190 44.16 N 92.59 W
Kenyon, R.I., U.S. 207 41.26 N 71.37 W
Ken-zaki ≻ 268 35.08 N 139.41 E
Kenzingen 58 48.11 N 7.46 E
Kenzou 152 4.10 N 15.02 E
Keokea 229a 20.42 N 156.21 W
Keokuk 190 40.23 N 91.23 W
Keonchi 124 22.38 N 81.47 E
Keo Neua, Col de)(110 18.23 N 105.09 E
Keonjhar □[5] 124 22.00 N 85.30 E
Keonjhargarh 120 21.38 N 85.35 E
Keon Park 274b 37.42 S 145.01 E
Keosauqua 190 40.43 N 91.57 W
Keota, Ia., U.S. 190 41.21 N 91.57 W
Keota, Ok., U.S. 196 35.15 N 94.55 W
Keowee, Lake ⊜[1] 192 34.45 N 82.55 W
Kepa (Mittagskogel) ∧ 61 46.31 N 13.57 E
Kepahiang 112 3.39 S 102.34 E
Kepala Batas 114 5.31 N 100.26 E
Kepanjen 115a 8.07 S 112.34 E
Kepi 164 6.32 S 139.19 E
Kępice 30 54.15 N 16.52 E
Kepina 24 65.24 N 41.50 E
Keping Shan ⋀ 85 40.00 N 77.10 E
Kępno 30 51.17 N 17.59 E
Kepo 112 2.56 S 106.33 E
Keppel Bay ⊂ 166 23.21 S 150.55 E
Keppel Harbour ⊂ 271c 1.16 N 103.50 E
Kepsut 130 39.41 N 28.09 E
Keptown 219 39.05 N 88.40 W
Kequan 98 36.04 N 114.00 E
Kerala □[3] 122 10.00 N 76.30 E
Keram ≃ 164 4.07 S 144.07 E
Keramian, Pulau I 112 5.04 S 114.36 E
Kerandin 112 0.12 S 104.46 E
Kerang 166 35.44 S 143.55 E
Keranyo 144 5.04 N 38.18 E
Keratéa 38 37.48 N 23.59 E
Keratsínion 267c 37.58 N 23.37 E
Keraudren, Cape ≻ 162 19.57 S 119.45 E
Kerava 26 60.24 N 25.07 E
Keravat 164 4.19 S 152.01 E
Kerbat ≃ 114 5.01 N 102.51 E
Kerbela → Karbalā' 128 32.36 N 44.02 E
Kerbi ≃ 89 52.28 N 136.25 E
Kerburan 130 37.33 N 41.44 E
Kerby 202 42.11 N 123.39 W
Kerč' 78 45.22 N 36.27 E
Kerčel' 86 59.18 N 64.46 E
Kerčemja 24 61.28 N 53.50 E
Kerčenskij poluostrov ≻[1] 78 45.15 N 36.00 E
Kerčenskij proliv ⋓ 78 45.22 N 36.38 E
Kerčevskij 24 59.55 N 56.17 E
Kerch → Kerč' 78 45.22 N 36.27 E
Kerckhoff Lake ⊜[1] 226 37.09 N 119.31 W
Kéré 154 5.16 N 26.11 E
Kéré ≃ 140 5.19 N 25.40 E
Kerec, mys ≻ 24 65.20 N 39.40 E
Kerej, ozero ⊜ 86 50.08 N 68.45 E
Kerema 164 8.00 S 145.45 E
Keremeos 182 49.12 N 119.50 W
Kerem Maharal 132 32.39 N 34.59 E
Kerempe Burnu ≻ 130 42.01 N 33.21 E
Keren 144 15.46 N 38.28 E
Kerend 128 34.16 N 46.15 E
Kerens 222 32.07 N 96.13 W
Kerepes 264c 47.34 N 19.18 E
Keret' 24 66.16 N 33.34 E
Keret', ozero ⊜ 24 65.55 N 32.56 E
Kerewan 150 13.29 N 16.10 W
Kerga 24 62.39 N 46.00 E
Kergez 84 40.18 N 49.38 E
Kerguélen, Îles II 6 49.15 S 69.10 E
Kerguelen Plateau ✢[3] 6 55.00 S 75.00 E
Kerhonkson 210 41.46 N 74.17 W
Kerian ≃ 114 5.10 N 100.26 E
Kericho 154 0.22 S 35.17 E
Keri Kera 140 12.21 N 32.46 E
Kerikeri 172 35.13 S 173.58 E
Kerimäki 26 61.55 N 29.17 E
Kerinci, Gunung ∧ 112 1.42 S 101.16 E
Kerio ≃ 154 2.59 N 36.07 E
Keríon 38 37.40 N 20.48 E
Keritang 112 0.51 S 102.39 E
Kerka ≃ 61 46.28 N 16.36 E
Kerkafalva 61 46.46 N 16.30 E
Kerkdriel 52 51.46 N 5.20 E
Kerkebet 144 16.18 N 37.24 E
Kerken 56 51.27 N 6.22 E
Kerkenna, Îles II 148 34.44 N 11.12 E
Kerkhove 50 50.48 N 3.30 E
Kerkhoven 198 45.11 N 95.19 W
Kerki, S.S.S.R. 24 63.43 N 54.05 E
Kerki, S.S.S.R. 128 37.50 N 65.12 E
Kérkira (Corfu) 38 39.36 N 19.56 E
Kérkira I 38 39.40 N 19.42 E
Kerkrade [-Holz] 56 50.52 N 6.04 E
Kerling 114 3.35 N 101.36 E
Kermadec Islands II 14 29.16 S 177.55 W
Kermadec Ridge ✢[3] 14 30.30 S 178.30 W
Kermadec Trench ✢[1] 14 30.00 S 177.00 W
Kermajärvi ⊜ 26 62.28 N 28.40 E
Kermān, Īrān 128 30.17 N 57.05 E
Kerman, Ca., U.S. 226 36.43 N 120.04 W
Kermān □[4] 128 29.00 N 57.30 E
Kerme Körfezi ⊂ 130 36.50 N 28.00 E
Kermit 196 31.51 N 103.05 W

Kermit Roosevelt Seamount ✢[3] 16 39.35 N 146.00 W
Kermode, Mount ∧ 182 52.57 N 131.51 W
Kern □[6] 228 35.20 N 118.55 W
Kern ≃ 204 35.13 N 119.17 W
Kern, South Fork ≃ 204 35.40 N 118.27 W
Kern City 228 35.18 N 119.05 W
Kernersville 192 36.07 N 80.04 W
Kernforschungszentrum ◍[3] 56 49.07 N 8.26 E
Kernhof 61 47.49 N 15.32 E
Kern Island Canal ≅ 228 35.22 N 119.01 W
Kern Lake Bed ⊜ 228 35.10 N 119.05 W
Kern River Channel ≃[1] 226 35.49 N 119.40 W
Kernville 204 35.45 N 118.25 W
Keroh 114 5.43 N 101.00 E
Keros 24 60.44 N 52.50 E
Kérou 150 10.50 N 2.06 E
Kérouané 150 9.16 N 9.01 W
Kerowagi 164 5.50 S 144.50 E
Kerpe Burnu ≻ 130 41.10 N 30.11 E
Kerpen 56 50.52 N 6.41 E
Kerpinen' 78 46.47 N 28.22 E
Kerr 214 41.03 N 78.25 W
Kerrera I 46 56.23 N 5.34 W
Kerridge 262 53.17 N 2.06 W
Kerridge Hill ∧[2] 262 53.17 N 2.06 W
Kerrobert 184 51.55 N 109.08 W
Kerrtown 214 41.38 N 80.10 W
Kerruish Park ♠ 279a 41.26 N 81.34 W
Kerrville 196 30.02 N 99.08 W
Kerry 42 52.30 N 3.16 W
Kerry □[6] 48 52.10 N 9.30 W
Kerry Head ≻ 48 52.25 N 9.57 W
Kersa 144 9.28 N 41.53 E
Kersbrook 168b 34.47 S 138.51 E
Kersey 214 41.21 N 78.35 W
Kershaw 192 34.33 N 80.35 W
Kersinyane 150 15.24 N 10.10 W
Kersley 182 52.49 N 122.25 W
Kerspestausee ⊜[1] 263 51.08 N 7.30 E
Kerstenhausen 56 51.04 N 9.13 E
Kert, Oued ≃ 34 35.15 N 3.15 W
Kertamulia 112 0.23 S 109.09 E
Kerteh 114 4.31 N 103.27 E
Kerteminde 41 55.27 N 10.40 E
Kertosono 115a 7.35 S 112.06 E
Kerulen (Cherlen) (Herlen) ≃ 90 48.48 N 117.00 E
Kerva 80 55.37 N 39.35 E
Kerzaz 148 29.30 N 1.37 W
Kerzendorf 264a 52.16 N 13.17 E
Keržence 80 56.28 N 44.26 E
Keržence ≃ 80 56.05 N 45.03 E
Kerzers 58 46.58 N 7.12 E
Kesabpur 126 22.55 N 89.13 E
Ke-sach 110 9.46 N 105.59 E
Kesagami Lake ⊜ 176 50.23 N 80.15 W
Kesälahti 26 61.54 N 29.50 E
Keşan 130 40.51 N 26.37 E
Keşap 130 40.55 N 38.31 E
Kesbern 263 51.20 N 7.42 E
Kesch, Piz ∧ 58 46.38 N 9.52 E
Kesem ≃ 144 9.14 N 40.06 E
Kesennuma 92 38.54 N 141.35 E
Kesh 48 54.32 N 7.43 W
Keshan 89 48.02 N 125.51 E
Keshena 190 44.53 N 88.38 W
Keshequa Creek ≃ 210 42.43 N 77.50 W
Keshitage 120 37.23 N 78.05 E
Keshod 120 21.18 N 70.15 E
Keşirlik 130 41.58 N 27.12 E
Keşiş Dağları ⋀ 130 39.50 N 39.45 E
Keskastel 56 48.58 N 7.02 E
Keskin 130 39.41 N 33.37 E
Keski-Suomen lääni □[4] 26 62.30 N 25.30 E
Keskozero 24 61.24 N 33.12 E
Keskuvejem, gora ∧ 180 66.12 N 177.40 W
Kes'ma 76 58.27 N 37.04 E
Kesova Gora 76 57.35 N 37.17 E
Kespur 126 22.35 N 87.29 E
Kesra 36 35.49 N 9.22 E
Kessebüren 263 51.31 N 7.43 E
Kessel 56 51.08 N 4.37 E
Kesselsdorf 54 51.02 N 13.35 E
Kessingland 42 52.25 N 1.42 E
Kesswil 58 47.36 N 9.20 E
Kestel Gölü ⊜ 130 37.26 N 30.28 E
Kestell 158 28.19 S 28.38 E
Kesten'ga 24 65.55 N 31.47 E
Kestep 130 36.27 N 29.16 E
Kestilä 26 64.21 N 26.17 E
Keston ⬥[8] 260 51.22 N 0.02 E
Keswick, On., Can. 212 44.15 N 79.28 W
Keswick, Eng., U.K. 44 54.37 N 3.08 W
Keszthely 30 46.46 N 17.15 E
Ket' ≃ 86 58.55 N 81.32 E
Keta 150 5.55 N 1.00 E
Keta ≃ 94 34.56 N 137.50 E
Keta, ozero ⊜ 74 68.44 N 90.00 E
Ketaka 96 35.30 N 134.03 E
Keta Lagoon ⊂ 150 5.54 N 0.56 E
Ketam, Pulau I 271c 1.24 N 103.57 E
Ketama 34 34.50 N 4.37 W
Ketang 100 22.58 N 115.28 E
Ketapang, Indon. 112 1.52 S 109.59 E
Ketapang, Indon. 115a 6.54 S 113.17 E
Ketapang, Indon. 115a 5.44 S 105.48 E
Ketaun 112 3.23 S 101.49 E
Ketchikan 182 55.21 N 131.35 W
Ketchum 202 43.40 N 114.21 W
Kete Krachi 150 7.46 N 0.03 W
Ketelmeer ⊜ 52 52.35 N 5.45 E
Keti Bandar 120 24.08 N 67.27 E
Ketingwan ∧ 154 0.40 N 35.50 E
Ketoj, ostrov I 74 47.20 N 152.28 E
Kétou 150 7.22 N 2.36 E
Ketovo 86 55.21 N 65.18 E
Kętrzyn (Rastenburg) 30 54.06 N 21.23 E
Ketsch 56 49.22 N 8.31 E
Ketta 152 1.28 N 15.56 E
Kettering, Eng., U.K. 42 52.24 N 0.44 W
Kettering, Md., U.S. 284c 38.53 N 76.49 W
Kettering, Oh., U.S. 218 39.41 N 84.10 W
Kettinge 41 54.42 N 11.45 E
Kettle ≃, Mb., Can. 184 56.23 N 94.34 W
Kettle ≃, N.A. 182 48.42 N 118.07 W
Kettle ≃, Mn., U.S. 190 45.52 N 92.45 W
Kettle Creek ≃, On., Can. 212 42.40 N 81.13 W
Kettle Creek ≃, Pa., U.S. 210 41.18 N 77.51 W
Kettle Creek State Park ♠ 214 41.23 N 77.56 W
Kettle Falls 202 48.36 N 118.03 W
Kettleman City 226 36.00 N 119.57 W
Kettleman Hills ⋀[2] 226 36.00 N 120.00 W
Kettle Rapids Dam ⬥[6] 184 56.23 N 94.38 W
Kettlersville 216 40.22 N 84.16 W
Kettleshulme 262 53.19 N 2.01 W
Kettlewell 44 54.09 N 2.02 W
Kettwig 56 51.22 N 6.56 E
Kęty 30 49.53 N 19.13 E
Ketzin 54 52.28 N 12.50 E
Keudemane 114 5.15 N 96.55 E
Keudepasi 114 4.18 N 95.56 E
Keudeteunom 114 4.27 N 95.48 E
Keudeunga 114 5.01 N 95.22 E
Keuka Lake ⊜ 210 42.27 N 77.10 W
Keuka Lake, West Branch ⊂ 210 42.33 N 77.09 W
Keuka Park 210 42.37 N 77.06 W
Keukenhof ♠ 52 52.16 N 4.33 E
Keul' 88 58.25 N 102.49 E
Keula 54 51.20 N 10.31 E
Keum ≃ 86 59.32 N 70.35 E
Keurboomsrivier 158 34.00 S 23.24 E
Keurusselkä ⊜ 26 62.10 N 24.40 E
Keuruu 26 62.16 N 24.42 E
Kevdo-Mel'sitovo 80 53.09 N 43.54 E

Kevelaer 52 51.35 N 6.15 E
Kevin 202 48.44 N 111.57 W
Kevsala 80 45.48 N 42.41 E
Kew, Austl. 169 37.49 S 145.02 E
Kew, T./C. Is. 238 21.54 N 72.02 W
Kewanee 190 41.14 N 89.55 W
Kewanna 216 41.01 N 86.25 W
Kewāre 124 27.57 N 83.47 E
Kewaunee 190 44.27 N 87.30 W
Keweenaw Bay ⊂ 190 46.56 N 88.23 W
Keweenaw Peninsula ≻[1] 190 47.12 N 88.25 W
Keweenaw Point ≻ 190 47.30 N 87.50 W
Kew Gardens ♠, On., Can. 275b 43.40 N 79.18 W
Kew Gardens ♠, Eng., U.K. 260 51.28 N 0.18 W
Keyala 154 4.27 N 32.52 E
Keyangkeershan ∧ 120 31.20 N 87.13 E
Keya Paha ≃ 198 42.54 N 99.00 W
Key Biscayne 220 25.42 N 80.10 W
Keyes, Ca., U.S. 226 37.33 N 120.54 W
Keyes, Ok., U.S. 196 36.48 N 102.15 W
Keyesport 219 38.44 N 89.17 W
Keyhole Reservoir ⊜[1] 198 44.21 N 104.51 W
Keyhole State Park ♠ 198 44.19 N 104.48 W
Keyihe 89 50.40 N 122.27 E
Keyingham 44 53.42 N 0.07 W
Key Largo 220 25.04 N 80.28 W
Key Largo I 220 25.16 N 80.19 W
Keymer 42 50.55 N 0.08 W
Keynes Hill ∧[2] 168b 34.37 S 139.06 E
Keyneton 168b 34.34 S 139.08 E
Keynsham 42 51.26 N 2.30 W
Keynshamburg 154 19.15 S 29.39 E
Keyport, N.J., U.S. 276 40.25 N 74.12 W
Keyport, Wa., U.S. 224 47.42 N 122.38 W
Keyport Harbor ⊂ 276 40.26 N 74.12 W
Keysborough 274b 38.00 S 145.10 E
Keysbrook 168a 32.26 S 115.59 E
Keyser 188 39.26 N 78.58 W
Keystone, In., U.S. 216 40.36 N 85.16 W
Keystone, Ia., U.S. 190 41.59 N 92.11 W
Keystone, S.D., U.S. 198 43.53 N 103.25 W
Keystone, W.V., U.S. 192 37.24 N 81.27 W
Keystone Lake ⊜[1], Ok., U.S. 196 36.15 N 96.25 W
Keystone Lake ⊜[1], Pa., U.S. 214 40.45 N 79.15 W
Keystone Peak ∧ 200 31.53 N 111.13 W
Keystone Race Track ♠ 285 40.07 N 74.57 W
Keystone State Park ♠ 214 40.23 N 79.24 W
Keysun 130 37.34 N 37.50 E
Keysville, Fl., U.S. 220 27.52 N 82.06 W
Keysville, Va., U.S. 192 37.02 N 78.29 W
Keytesville 194 39.26 N 92.56 W
Key West 220 24.33 N 81.46 W
Key West Island I 220 24.33 N 81.47 W
Key West Naval Air Station ■ 220 24.34 N 81.41 W
Keyworth 42 52.52 N 1.05 W
Kez 80 57.53 N 53.43 E
Kezar Stadium ♠ 282 37.46 N 122.27 W
Kezi 154 20.58 S 28.32 E
Kezilesu Zizhizhou □[8] 85 40.00 N 75.30 E
Kežma 88 58.59 N 101.09 E
Kežmarok 30 49.08 N 20.25 E
Kgalagadi □[5] 156 25.00 S 22.00 E
Kgatleng □[5] 156 24.28 S 26.05 E
Kgokgole ≃ 158 26.44 S 22.28 E
Kgun Lake ⊜ 180 61.32 N 163.45 W
Khaanziir, Ras ≻ 144 10.55 N 45.47 E
Khabab 132 33.00 N 36.16 E
Khābūr, Nahr al- ≃ 130 35.08 N 40.26 E
Khādar 272a 28.33 N 77.22 E
Khadari, Wādī al- V 140 10.29 N 26.15 E
Khadaungnge Taung ∧ 110 18.57 N 94.37 E
Khadki (Kirkee) 122 18.34 N 73.52 E
Khadra 34 36.15 N 0.35 E
Khafūrī, Wādī V 142 29.37 N 32.04 E
Khagaria 124 25.30 N 86.29 E
Khagdon ≃[1] 126 22.09 N 90.05 E
Khāgrāmuri 272b 22.26 N 88.14 E
Khaïdhárion 267c 37.33 N 22.53 E
Khair 124 27.57 N 77.50 E
Khairābād 124 27.32 N 80.45 E
Khairāgarh 120 21.25 N 80.58 E
Khairbani 126 24.14 N 87.05 E
Khairna 272c 19.06 N 73.01 E
Khairpur, Pāk. 120 27.32 N 68.46 E
Khairpur, Pāk. 123 29.35 N 72.14 E
Khajrāho 120 24.50 N 79.58 E
Khājuri 126 21.52 N 87.58 E
Khajuri ⬥[8] 272a 28.43 N 77.16 E
Kha Khaeng ≃ 110 14.55 N 99.07 E
Khakhea 156 24.51 S 23.20 E
Khalándrion 267c 38.01 N 23.48 E
Khalatse 123 34.20 N 76.49 E
Khālidī, Khirbat al- ⊥ 132 29.39 N 35.14 E
Khālid Ibn al-Walīd ⬥[6] 132 32.43 N 35.41 E
Khalkhāl 128 37.37 N 48.32 E
Khalkhalah 132 33.04 N 36.32 E
Khálki I 130 36.17 N 27.35 E
Khalkidhikí □[9] 38 40.25 N 23.27 E
Khalkís 38 38.28 N 23.36 E
Khālsar 120 34.31 N 77.41 E
Khambhāliya 120 22.12 N 69.39 E
Khambhāt, Gulf of ⊂ 122 21.00 N 72.30 E
Khāmgaon 122 20.41 N 76.34 E
Khamir 144 16.05 N 43.55 E
Khāmis, Ash-Shallāl al- (Fifth Cataract) ∟ 140 18.23 N 33.47 E
Khamīs Mushayṭ 144 18.18 N 42.44 E
Khamkeut 110 18.15 N 104.43 E
Khamma 70 36.47 N 12.02 E
Khammam 122 17.15 N 80.09 E
Khamsah 142 30.25 N 32.23 E
Khan ≃, Lao 110 19.54 N 102.09 E
Khan ≃, Namibia 156 22.37 S 14.56 E
Khāna 126 23.20 N 87.44 E
Khānābād 120 36.41 N 69.07 E
Khān Abū Shāmāt 132 33.40 N 36.54 E
Khānākul 126 22.43 N 87.51 E
Khān al-Baghdādī 128 33.51 N 42.33 E
Khānaqīn 128 34.21 N 45.22 E
Khān Arnabah 132 33.11 N 35.53 E
Khancoban 171b 36.12 S 148.05 E
Khandaghosh 126 23.13 N 87.41 E
Khandela 120 27.36 N 75.30 E
Khandwa 124 21.50 N 76.20 E
Khāneh Khvodī 128 36.05 N 56.04 E
Khānewāl 123 30.18 N 71.56 E
Khāngāh Dogrān 123 31.50 N 73.37 E
Khāngarh, Pāk. 120 28.22 N 71.43 E
Khāngarh, Pāk. 123 29.55 N 71.10 E
Khangkhai 110 19.28 N 103.15 E
Khanh-hoa 110 12.15 N 109.06 E
Khanh-hung 110 9.36 N 105.58 E
Khaniá 38 35.31 N 24.02 E
Khaníon, Kólpos ⊂ 38 35.34 N 23.48 E
Khānkurda 126 22.00 N 87.25 E
Khanna 123 30.42 N 76.13 E
Khannā, Qā' ≣ 132 32.04 N 36.26 E
Khānozai 120 30.37 N 67.19 E
Khānpur, India 272b 22.40 N 88.16 E
Khānpur, Pāk. 123 28.39 N 70.39 E
Khānpur ⬥[8], India 272a 28.34 N 77.01 E
Khānpur ⬥[8], India 272a 28.31 N 77.14 E
Khān Shaykhūn 130 35.26 N 36.38 E
Khanty-Mansiysk → Chanty-Mansijsk 74 61.00 N 69.06 E
Khān Yūnus 132 31.21 N 34.19 E
Khao Saming 110 12.21 N 102.27 E
Khao Yoi 110 13.14 N 99.50 E

Khapalu 123 35.10 N 76.20 E
Kharab, Ghoubet al ⊂ 144 11.30 N 42.35 E
Kharabā 132 32.34 N 36.27 E
Kharagdiha 124 24.25 N 86.10 E
Kharagpur, India 124 25.07 N 86.33 E
Kharagpur, India 126 22.20 N 87.20 E
Kharak 123 33.07 N 71.06 E
Khārān 120 28.35 N 65.25 E
Kharānaq 128 32.20 N 54.39 E
Kharar, India 123 30.45 N 76.39 E
Kharar, India 126 22.42 N 87.41 E
Khāravli ∧[2] 272c 18.54 N 72.55 E
Kharāyij, Sabkhat al- ⊜ 130 35.40 N 37.20 E
Kharaz, Jabal ∧ 144 12.44 N 44.09 E
Kharbatā 132 31.57 N 35.04 E
Kharbine → Harbin 89 45.45 N 126.41 E
Khardah 126 22.44 N 88.22 E
Kharg → Khārk, Jazīreh-ye I 128 29.15 N 50.20 E
Khārghar 272c 19.03 N 73.04 E
Khargon 120 21.49 N 75.36 E
Khāriān 123 32.49 N 73.52 E
Khariār Road 122 20.54 N 82.31 E
Khārijah, Al-Wāḥāt al- ⏉[4] 140 25.20 N 30.35 E
Kharīm, Jabal ∧ 132 30.17 N 33.58 E
Kharīṭ, Wādī al- V 140 24.26 N 33.03 E
Khārk, Jazīreh-ye I 128 29.15 N 50.20 E
Kharkov → Char'kov 78 50.00 N 36.15 E
Kharmān, Kūh-e ∧ 128 29.13 N 53.35 E
Kharri 272b 22.55 N 88.14 E
Kharsāwān 124 22.48 N 85.50 E
Kharsia 124 21.58 N 83.07 E
Khartoum → Al-Kharṭūm 140 15.36 N 32.32 E
Khartoum North → Al-Kharṭūm Baḥrī 140 15.38 N 32.33 E
Khartum → Al-Kharṭūm 140 15.36 N 32.32 E
Kharumwa 154 3.12 S 32.39 E
Khāsbāti 272b 22.55 N 88.25 E
Khasebake 156 20.41 S 24.29 E
Khāsh, Afg. 128 31.31 N 62.52 E
Khāsh, Īrān 128 28.14 N 61.14 E
Khāsh ≃ 128 31.11 N 62.05 E
Khāsh, Dasht-e ⬥[2] 128 31.50 N 62.30 E
Khashab, Jabal al- ∧[2] 142 29.56 N 31.01 E
Khashm al-Qirbah 140 14.58 N 35.55 E
Khashm al-Qirbah, Khazzān ⊜[1] 140 14.40 N 35.55 E
Khashshab, Tur'at al- ≅ 273c 29.53 N 31.17 E
Khashum 140 12.27 N 28.02 E
Khaskovo → Haskovo 38 41.56 N 25.33 E
Khatauli 124 29.17 N 77.43 E
Khātegaon 124 22.36 N 76.55 E
Khātra 126 22.59 N 86.51 E
Khatt, Oued al V 148 26.45 N 13.03 W
Khaur 123 33.16 N 72.28 E
Khāvda 120 23.51 N 69.43 E
Khawrah 144 14.26 N 46.09 E
Khawsa 110 15.03 N 97.50 E
Khayāla ⬥[8] 272a 28.40 N 77.06 E
Khaybar 128 25.42 N 39.31 E
Khaybar, Ḥarrat ⫠[9] 128 25.30 N 39.45 E
Khayerpur 272b 22.35 N 88.33 E
Khayl, Kathīb al- ⫠[8] 142 30.33 N 32.28 E
Khayra Bil ⊜ 272b 22.52 N 88.29 E
Khayrasole 126 23.48 N 87.16 E
Khayung ≃ 110 15.07 N 104.42 E
Khazar, Baḥr-e → Caspian Sea ⏉[2] 72 42.00 N 50.30 E
Kheardaha 272b 22.29 N 88.28 E
Khe-bo 110 19.08 N 104.41 E
Khed 122 17.43 N 73.23 E
Khefapur 272a 28.30 N 77.05 E
Khejurdaha 272b 22.59 N 88.10 E
Khemis 148 36.16 N 2.13 E
Khemis el Khechna 34 36.39 N 3.20 E
Khemisset 148 33.50 N 6.03 W
Khemisset □[4] 148 33.50 N 6.05 W
Khem Karan 123 31.09 N 74.34 E
Khemmarat 110 16.03 N 105.13 E
Khenchla 148 35.28 N 7.11 E
Khenifra 148 33.00 N 5.40 W
Khenifra □[4] 148 32.35 N 5.10 W
Khenjān 120 35.36 N 70.59 E
Khenyen 272b 22.59 N 88.19 E
Khera ⬥[8] 272a 28.46 N 77.08 E
Kheri 124 27.54 N 80.48 E
Kheri □[5] 124 28.10 N 80.40 E
Kherli 124 27.12 N 77.02 E
Kherrata 148 36.31 N 5.26 E
Khersan ≃ 128 31.33 N 50.22 E
Kherson → Cherson 78 46.38 N 32.35 E
Kherwāra 120 23.59 N 73.35 E
Khetia 120 21.40 N 74.35 E
Khevāj 120 38.13 N 71.02 E
Khewāri 120 26.36 N 68.52 E
Khewra 123 32.39 N 73.01 E
Kheyr Khāneh 128 34.57 N 63.37 E
Khichīwāra Plateau ⋀[1] 124 24.25 N 77.30 E
Khichripur ⬥[8] 272a 28.37 N 77.19 E
Khilchipur 124 24.02 N 76.34 E
Khilkāpur 272b 22.46 N 88.29 E
Khimki → Chimki 82 55.54 N 37.26 E
Khíos 38 38.22 N 26.08 E
Khíos I 38 38.22 N 26.00 E
Khipro 120 25.50 N 69.22 E
Khirbat Abū Qashṭah 132 31.16 N 34.16 E
Khirbat al-Ghazālah 132 32.44 N 36.12 E
Khirbat 'Awwād 132 32.19 N 36.43 E
Khirbat Qanāfār 132 33.38 N 35.43 E
Khirbat Umm as-Surab 132 32.26 N 36.19 E
Khirbitā 142 30.45 N 30.40 E
Khiri Mat 110 16.50 N 99.48 E
Khirpai 126 22.42 N 87.37 E
Khisfīn 132 32.51 N 35.49 E
Khiuri Khala ∧ 124 29.58 N 81.18 E
Khiva → Chiva 72 41.24 N 60.22 E
Khīyāv 128 38.24 N 47.40 E
Khlong Khlung 110 16.12 N 99.43 E
Khlong Thom 110 7.56 N 99.09 E
Khlong Yai 110 11.46 N 102.54 E
Khlung 110 12.27 N 102.14 E
Khmel'nitskiy → Chmel'nickij 78 49.25 N 27.00 E
Khoai, Hon I 110 8.26 N 104.50 E
Khogali 140 6.08 N 27.47 E
Khojāng ∧ 124 28.41 N 85.09 E
Khok Kloi 110 8.17 N 98.19 E
Khok Pho 110 6.43 N 101.06 E
Khoksa 126 23.48 N 89.17 E
Khok Samrong 110 15.04 N 100.44 E
Kholargós 267c 38.00 N 23.48 E
Kholm 120 36.42 N 67.41 E
Kholombidzo Falls ∟ 154 15.54 S 34.44 E
Khomām 128 37.22 N 49.40 E
Khomas Hochland ⋀[1] 156 22.30 S 16.30 E
Khomeyn 128 33.38 N 50.04 E
Khomeynīshahr 128 32.41 N 51.31 E
Khomodimo 156 22.46 S 23.52 E
Khondmāl Hills ⋀[2] 122 20.20 N 84.00 E
Khoni 272c 19.10 N 73.07 E
Khon Kaen 110 16.26 N 102.50 E
Khóra 38 37.04 N 21.43 E
Khorāsān □[4] 128 35.00 N 58.00 E
Khóra Sfakíon 38 35.12 N 24.09 E
Khorel 272b 22.42 N 88.19 E

≃	River	Fluss	Río	Rivière	Rio
≅	Canal	Kanal	Canal	Canal	Canal
∟	Waterfall, Rapids	Wasserfall, Stromschnellen	Cascada, Rápidos	Chute d'eau, Rapides	Cascata, Rápidos
⋓	Strait	Meeresstrasse	Estrecho	Détroit	Estreito
⊂	Bay, Gulf	Bucht, Golf	Bahía, Golfo	Baie, Golfe	Baía, Golfo
⊜	Lake, Lakes	See, Seen	Lago, Lagos	Lac, Lacs	Lago, Lagos
≣	Swamp	Sumpf	Pantano	Marais	Pântano
⫠	Ice Features, Glacier	Eis- und Gletscherformen	Accidentes Glaciales	Formes glaciaires	Acidentes glaciares
⏉	Other Hydrographic Features	Andere Hydrographische Objekte	Otros Elementos Hidrográficos	Autres données hydrographiques	Outros acidentes hidrográficos

✢	Submarine Features	Untermeerische Objekte	Accidentes Submarinos	Formes de relief sous-marin	Acidentes submarinos
□	Political Unit	Politische Einheit	Unidad Politica	Entité politique	Unidade política
◍	Cultural Institution	Kulturelle Institution	Institución Cultural	Institution culturelle	Instituição cultural
⊥	Historical Site	Historische Stätte	Sitio Histórico	Site historique	Sitio histórico
♠	Recreational Site	Erholungs- und Ferienort	Sitio de Recreo	Centre de loisirs	Area de Lazer
⊠	Airport	Flughafen	Aeropuerto	Aéroport	Aeroporto
■	Military Installation	Militäranlage	Instalación Militar	Installation militaire	Instalação militar
⬥	Miscellaneous	Verschiedenes	Misceláneo	Divers	Diversos

Symbols in the index entries represent the broad categories identified in the key at the right. Symbols with superior numbers (⩘[1]) identify subcategories (see complete key on page *I* · 1).

Kartensymbole in dem Registerverzeichnis stellen die rechts in Schlüssel erklärten Kategorien dar. Symbole mit hochgestellten Ziffern (⩘[1]) bezeichnen Unterabteilungen einer Kategorie (vgl. vollständiger Schlüssel auf Seite *I* · 1).

Los símbolos incluídos en el texto del índice representan las grandes categorías identificadas con la clave a la derecha. Los símbolos con números en su parte superior (⩘[1]) identifican las subcategorías (véase la clave completa en la página *I* · 1).

Les symboles de l'index représentent les catégories indiquées dans la légende à droite. Les symboles suivis d'un indice (⩘[1]) représentent des sous-catégories (voir légende complète à la page *I* · 1).

Os símbolos incluídos no texto do índice representam as grandes categorias identificadas com a chave à direita. Os símbolos com números em sua parte superior (⩘[1]) identificam as subcategorias (veja-se a chave completa à página *I* · 1).

∧ Mountain	Berg	Montaña	Montagne	Montanha
⩘ Mountains	Berge	Montañas	Montagnes	Montanhas
✕ Pass	Pass	Paso	Col	Passo
V Valley, Canyon	Tal, Cañon	Valle, Cañón	Vallée, Canyon	Vale, Canhão
≚ Plain	Ebene	Llano	Plaine	Planície
› Cape	Kap	Cabo	Cap	Cabo
I Island	Insel	Isla	Île	Ilha
II Islands	Inseln	Islas	Îles	Ilhas
≐ Other Topographic Features	Andere Topographische Objekte	Otros Elementos Topográficos	Autres données topographiques	Outros acidentes topográficos

ESPAÑOL · FRANÇAIS · PORTUGUÊS

Nombre / Nom / Nome	Página / Page / Página	Lat.°′	Long.°′ W = Oeste / W = Ouest
Kioto → Kyōto	94	35.00 N	135.45 E
Kiowa, Co., U.S.	198	39.20 N	104.27 W
Kiowa, Ks., U.S.	198	37.01 N	98.29 W
Kiowa, Ok., U.S.	196	34.43 N	95.53 W
Kiowa Creek ≃, U.S.	196	36.46 N	99.55 W
Kiowa Creek ≃, Co., U.S.	198	40.20 N	104.05 W
Kipahigan Lake ⊜	184	55.20 N	101.55 W
Kipandi	152	5.19 S	16.46 E
Kipanga	154	6.14 S	35.21 E
Kiparissía	38	37.14 N	21.40 E
Kiparissiakós Kólpos c	38	37.37 N	21.24 E
Kipatimu	154	8.29 S	38.56 E
Kipawa ≃	190	47.03 N	79.23 W
Kipawa, Lac ⊜	190	46.55 N	79.00 W
Kipawa, Réserve ♠	190	47.15 N	78.15 W
Kipembawe	154	7.39 S	33.24 E
Kipengere Range ⋏	154	9.10 S	34.15 E
Kiperčeny	78	47.32 N	28.50 E
Kipijevo	24	65.40 N	54.30 E
Kipili	154	7.26 S	30.36 E
Kipini	154	2.32 S	40.31 E
Kipling	184	50.10 N	102.38 W
Kipnuk	180	59.56 N	164.03 W
Kippax	44	53.46 N	1.22 W
Kippen	46	56.08 N	4.11 W
Kippenheim	58	48.17 N	7.49 E
Kippure ∧	48	53.10 N	6.18 W
Kípros → Cyprus □[1]	130	35.00 N	33.00 E
Kipsdorf	54	50.47 N	13.32 E
Kipton	214	41.16 N	82.18 W
Kipushi	154	11.46 S	27.14 E
Kipushia, Zaïre	154	6.10 S	25.12 E
Kipushia, Zaïre	154	12.58 S	29.30 E
Kira, Nihon	94	34.49 N	137.05 E
Kir'a, S.S.S.R.	80	55.04 N	46.53 E
Kirakira	175e	10.27 S	161.55 E
Kirane	150	15.25 N	10.14 W
Kiranlık	130	39.07 N	41.41 E
Kiranomena	157b	18.17 S	46.03 E
Kīratpur	124	29.31 N	78.12 E
Kiraz	130	38.13 N	28.13 E
Kirazlı	130	40.02 N	26.41 E
Kırbaçbayırı ∧	267b	40.56 N	29.10 E
Kirbla	76	58.44 N	23.57 E
Kirbymoorside	44	54.16 N	0.55 W
Kirby Muxloe	42	52.38 N	1.13 W
Kirbys Creek ≃	208	36.28 N	77.06 W
Kirbyville	194	30.39 N	93.53 W
Kırçal	130	41.39 N	35.16 E
Kırcasalih	130	41.23 N	26.48 E
Kirchardt	56	49.12 N	8.59 E
Kirchbach in Steiermark	61	46.54 N	15.44 E
Kirchberg, B.R.D.	56	49.12 N	9.58 E
Kirchberg, B.R.D.	56	49.56 N	7.24 E
Kirchberg, B.R.D.	60	48.54 N	13.11 E
Kirchberg, D.D.R.	54	50.37 N	12.32 E
Kirchberg, Schw.	58	47.05 N	7.35 E
Kirchberg, Schw.	58	47.25 N	9.03 E
Kirch-Berg ∧[2]	264a	52.27 N	13.02 E
Kirchberg am Wagram	61	48.26 N	15.53 E
Kirchberg an der Pielach	61	48.02 N	15.26 E
Kirchberg in Tirol	64	47.27 N	12.19 E
Kirchbichl	64	47.31 N	12.05 E
Kirchderne ◆[8]	263	51.33 N	7.30 E
Kirchdorf, B.R.D.	52	52.36 N	8.49 E
Kirchdorf, D.D.R.	54	54.00 N	11.26 E
Kirchdorf an der Krems	61	47.56 N	14.07 E
Kirchdorf im Wald	60	48.55 N	13.16 E
Kirchen	56	50.48 N	7.53 E
Kirchende	263	51.25 N	7.26 E
Kirchenlaibach	60	49.53 N	11.46 E
Kirchenlamitz	54	50.09 N	11.56 E
Kirchenthumbach	60	49.45 N	11.43 E
Kirchhain	56	50.49 N	8.55 E
Kirchham	60	48.21 N	13.16 E
Kirchheiligen	54	51.11 N	10.42 E
Kirchheimbolanden	56	49.40 N	8.00 E
Kirchheim in Schwaben	58	48.10 N	10.30 E
Kirchheim unter Teck	56	48.39 N	9.27 E
Kirchhellen	52	51.36 N	6.55 E
Kirchhellen Heide ◆[3]	263	51.36 N	6.53 E
Kirchhofen	264a	52.22 N	13.53 E
Kirchhörde ◆[8]	263	51.27 N	7.27 E
Kirchhundem	56	51.05 N	8.05 E
Kirchlengern	52	52.12 N	8.35 E
Kirchlinde ◆[8]	263	51.32 N	7.22 E
Kirchlinteln	52	52.56 N	9.19 E
Kirchmöser	54	52.22 N	12.25 E
Kirchroth	60	48.57 N	12.33 E
Kirchschlag in der Buckligen Welt	61	47.31 N	16.18 E
Kirchveischede	56	51.05 N	7.59 E
Kirchwalsede	52	53.01 N	9.23 E
Kirchwerder ◆[8]	52	53.25 N	10.11 E
Kirchzarten	58	47.58 N	7.56 E
Kircubbin	48	54.29 N	5.32 W
Kirda	85	41.06 N	69.00 E
Kirdāsah	142	30.02 N	31.07 E
Kireç, Tür.	130	39.33 N	28.22 E
Kireç, Tür.	130	40.59 N	39.10 E
Kirej ≃	88	54.12 N	100.40 E
Kirejevo	80	50.01 N	44.29 E
Kirejevsk	76	53.56 N	37.56 E
Kirejkovo	76	53.38 N	35.49 E
Kirenga ≃	88	57.47 N	108.07 E
Kirensk	88	57.46 N	108.08 E
Kirgali	130	37.55 N	40.00 E
Kirghiz Soviet Socialist Republic → Kirgizskaja Sovetskaja Socialističeskaja Respublika □[3]	85	41.30 N	75.00 E
Kirgili	85	40.24 N	71.43 E
Kirgiz-Mijaki	86	53.38 N	54.47 E
Kirgizskaja Sovetskaja Socialističeskaja Respublika □[3]	85	41.30 N	75.00 E
Kirgizskij chrebet ⋏	85	42.30 N	74.00 E
Kiri	152	1.27 S	19.00 E
Kiribati □[1]	14	5.00 S	170.00 W
Kiries West	158	26.34 S	19.00 E
Kirigalpotta Mountain ∧	122	6.48 N	80.46 E
Kiriga-mine ∧	94	36.06 N	138.12 E
Kırıkhan, Tür.	130	39.32 N	41.20 E
Kırıkhan, Tür.	130	36.32 N	36.19 E
Kirikiri Prisons ⊍	273a	6.27 N	3.19 E
Kırıkkale	130	39.50 N	33.31 E
Kirikovka	78	50.22 N	35.07 E
Kirillov	76	59.52 N	38.23 E
Kirillovka	265b	55.57 N	37.20 E
Kirillovo, S.S.S.R.	80	57.07 N	45.27 E
Kirillovo, S.S.S.R.	80	53.47 N	42.40 E
Kirillovskoje	76	60.28 N	29.17 E
Kirin → Jilin	89	43.51 N	126.33 E
Kirin → Jilin □[4]	90	44.00 N	126.00 E
Kirínia (Kyrenia)	130	35.20 N	33.19 E
Kirinyaga (Mount Kenya) ∧	154	0.10 S	37.20 E
Kirishima-Yaku-kokuritsu-kōen ♠	92	31.55 N	130.51 E
Kirishima-yama ∧	92	31.56 N	130.52 E
Kiriši	76	59.27 N	32.02 E
Kiritimati (Christmas Island) I[1]	174o	1.52 N	157.20 W
Kirizume-tōge ∧[2]	270	34.56 N	135.16 E
Kirjanovskaja Kontora	88	58.18 N	104.13 E
Kirka	130	39.17 N	30.33 E
Kirkabister	46	60.07 N	1.08 W
Kırkağaç	130	39.06 N	27.40 E
Kirkbride	44	54.54 N	3.12 W
Kirkburton	44	53.37 N	1.42 W
Kirkby ◆[8]	44	53.29 N	2.54 W
Kirkby in Ashfield	44	53.06 N	1.15 W
Kirkby Lonsdale	44	54.13 N	2.36 W
Kirkby Malzeard	44	54.11 N	1.38 W
Kirkby Stephen	44	54.28 N	2.20 W
Kirkcaldy	46	56.07 N	3.10 W
Kirkcolm	44	54.58 N	5.05 W
Kirkconnel	44	55.23 N	4.00 W
Kirkcudbright	44	54.50 N	4.03 W
Kirkcudbright Bay c	44	54.48 N	4.04 W
Kirkdale ◆[8]	262	53.26 N	2.59 W
Kirkeby	41	56.09 N	9.27 E
Kirkee → Khadki	122	18.34 N	73.52 E
Kirkenær	26	60.28 N	12.03 E
Kirkenes	24	69.40 N	30.03 E
Kirke Stillinge	41	55.26 N	11.15 E
Kirkham	44	53.47 N	2.53 W
Kirkhill	46	57.28 N	4.26 W
Kirkintilloch	46	55.57 N	4.10 W
Kirkjubæjarklaustur	24a	63.47 N	18.04 W
Kirkkonummi → Kyrkslätt	26	60.07 N	24.26 E
Kirkland, P.Q., Can.	275a	45.27 N	73.52 W
Kirkland, Il., U.S.	216	42.05 N	88.51 W
Kirkland, Tx., U.S.	196	34.23 N	100.04 W
Kirkland, Wa., U.S.	224	47.40 N	122.12 W
Kirkland Creek ≃	200	34.32 N	113.00 W
Kirkland Lake	190	48.09 N	80.02 W
Kırklar Dağı ∧	84	40.34 N	40.35 E
Kırklareli	130	41.44 N	27.12 E
Kırklareli □[4]	130	41.40 N	27.30 E
Kirklees □[8]	262	53.36 N	1.52 W
Kirkleyditch	262	53.18 N	2.12 W
Kirklin	194	40.11 N	86.21 W
Kirkliston	46	55.58 N	3.25 W
Kirk Michael, I. of Man	44	54.17 N	4.35 W
Kirkmichael, Scot., U.K.	46	56.43 N	3.29 W
Kirkmuirhill	46	55.40 N	3.55 W
Kirkness Lake ⊜	184	51.32 N	93.56 W
Kirkpatrick, Mount ∧	9	84.20 S	166.19 E
Kirkpatrick Lake ⊜	182	51.52 N	111.18 W
Kirk Sandall	44	53.33 N	1.04 W
Kirksville, Il., U.S.	219	39.34 N	88.40 W
Kirksville, Mo., U.S.	194	40.11 N	92.34 W
Kirkton of Culsalmond	46	57.23 N	2.34 W
Kirkton of Glenisla	46	56.44 N	3.17 W
Kirktown of Auchterless	46	57.27 N	2.28 W
Kirkūk	128	35.28 N	44.28 E
Kirkville	210	43.05 N	75.57 W
Kirkwall	46	58.59 N	2.58 W
Kirkwood, S. Afr.	158	33.24 S	25.26 E
Kirkwood, De., U.S.	208	39.34 N	75.41 W
Kirkwood, Il., U.S.	190	40.51 N	90.44 W
Kirkwood, Mo., U.S.	219	38.35 N	90.24 W
Kirkwood, N.J., U.S.	285	39.50 N	75.01 W
Kirkwood, N.Y., U.S.	210	42.02 N	75.48 W
Kırmıt	130	37.11 N	35.41 E
Kirn	56	49.47 N	7.28 E
Kirnāhar	126	23.45 N	87.52 E
Kirotshe	154	1.37 S	29.02 E
Kirov, S.S.S.R.	76	54.05 N	34.20 E
Kirov, S.S.S.R.	80	58.38 N	49.42 E
Kirova, zaliv c	84	39.09 N	49.03 E
Kirovabad	84	40.40 N	46.22 E
Kirovakan	84	40.48 N	44.30 E
Kirovgrad	86	57.26 N	60.04 E
Kirovka	86	47.07 N	82.00 E
Kirovo, S.S.S.R.	78	51.29 N	29.24 E
Kirovo, S.S.S.R.	78	47.41 N	35.46 E
Kirovo, S.S.S.R.	83	48.23 N	37.55 E
Kirovo, S.S.S.R.	83	48.50 N	38.03 E
Kirovo, S.S.S.R.	85	40.26 N	70.34 E
Kirovo, S.S.S.R.	86	55.33 N	63.46 E
Kirovo-Čepeck	80	58.33 N	50.01 E
Kirovograd	78	48.30 N	32.18 E
Kirovograd □[4]	38	48.10 N	30.20 E
Kirovsk, S.S.S.R.	24	67.37 N	33.35 E
Kirovsk, S.S.S.R.	76	53.16 N	29.29 E
Kirovsk, S.S.S.R.	83	49.01 N	37.56 E
Kirovsk, S.S.S.R.	83	48.38 N	38.39 E
Kirovsk, S.S.S.R.	84	38.48 N	48.43 E
Kirovsk, S.S.S.R.	128	37.42 N	60.23 E
Kirovsk, S.S.S.R.	265a	59.52 N	31.00 E
Kirovskij, S.S.S.R.	74	54.18 N	155.47 E
Kirovskij, S.S.S.R.	80	45.51 N	48.07 E
Kirovskij, S.S.S.R.	84	40.26 N	49.51 E
Kirovskij, S.S.S.R.	86	44.52 N	78.12 E
Kirovskij, S.S.S.R.	89	54.26 N	126.55 E
Kirovskij, S.S.S.R.	89	45.07 N	133.30 E
Kirovskije ostrova II	265a	59.58 N	30.15 E
Kirovskoje, S.S.S.R.	78	48.33 N	34.53 E
Kirovskoje, S.S.S.R.	78	45.14 N	35.13 E
Kirovskoje, S.S.S.R.	83	48.09 N	38.21 E
Kirovskoje, S.S.S.R.	85	42.39 N	71.35 E
Kirov Stadium ♠	265a	59.58 N	30.14 E
Kirov Theatre ⊍	265a	59.55 N	30.18 E
Kirpičnyj Zavod	265a	60.01 N	30.48 E
Kirpil'skaja	78	45.23 N	39.43 E
Kirriemuir	46	56.41 N	3.01 W
Kirs	86	59.21 N	52.14 E
Kirsanov	80	52.38 N	42.43 E
Kirsanovka	80	52.30 N	52.53 E
Kirschau	54	51.04 N	14.27 E
Kırşehir	130	39.09 N	34.10 E
Kırşehir □[4]	130	39.20 N	34.10 E
Kīrthar Range ⋏	120	27.00 N	67.10 E
Kirtland, N.M., U.S.	200	36.44 N	108.21 W
Kirtland, Oh., U.S.	214	41.37 N	81.21 W
Kirtland Air Force Base ■	200	35.02 N	106.37 W
Kirtland Hills	214	41.37 N	81.24 W
Kirtle Water ≃	44	54.58 N	3.05 W
Kirton	42	52.56 N	0.04 W
Kirton in Lindsey	44	53.28 N	0.36 W
Kirton of Largo	46	56.13 N	2.55 W
Kirtorf	56	50.46 N	9.06 E
Kiruna	24	67.51 N	20.16 E
Kirundu	154	0.44 S	25.32 E
Kirurumo	154	5.53 S	34.11 E
Kirvin	222	31.46 N	96.20 W
Kirwan Heights	279b	40.22 N	80.06 W
Kirwee	172	43.30 S	172.13 E
Kirwin	198	39.40 N	99.07 W
Kirwin Reservoir ⊜[1]	198	39.39 N	99.10 W
Kiryandongo	154	1.53 N	32.03 E
Kiryū	94	36.24 N	139.20 E
Kirza	86	54.14 N	81.40 E
Kiržač	82	56.09 N	38.52 E
Kiržač ≃	82	55.52 N	39.04 E
Kisa, Nihon	96	34.43 N	132.59 E
Kisa, Sve.	26	57.59 N	15.37 E
Kisai	94	36.06 N	139.35 E
Kisaichi	270	34.46 N	135.42 E
Kisakata	92	39.13 N	139.54 E
Kisaki	154	7.28 S	37.36 E
Kišaly	76	54.23 N	43.12 E
Kisambo	152	6.25 S	18.14 E
Kisanga	154	2.29 N	26.35 E
Kisangani (Stanleyville)	154	0.30 S	25.12 E
Kisantu	152	5.07 S	15.05 E
Kisar, Pulau I	112	8.05 S	127.10 E
Kisaralik ≃	180	60.51 N	161.16 W
Kisaran	114	2.59 N	99.37 E
Kisarawe	154	6.54 S	39.04 E
Kisarazu	94	35.23 N	139.55 E
Kisarazu-Kichi, Kōkū-jieitai ■	94	35.24 N	139.55 E
Kisawa	96	33.49 N	134.18 E
K.I. Sawyer Air Force Base ■	190	46.21 N	87.25 W
Kisbér	30	47.30 N	18.02 E
Kisbey	184	49.38 N	102.41 W
Kise ≃	94	35.06 N	138.53 E
Kiselevsk → Kisel'ovsk	86	54.00 N	86.39 E
Kisel'ovka	80	47.18 N	44.07 E
Kisel'ovsk	86	54.00 N	86.39 E
Kisengwa	154	6.00 S	25.50 E
Kisen-yama ∧[2]	270	34.54 N	135.51 E
Kiser Lake ⊜	218	40.11 N	83.58 W
Kisha	130	40.28 N	41.28 E
Kishanda	154	1.42 S	31.34 E
Kishanganga ≃	123	34.22 N	73.30 E
Kishanganj	124	26.07 N	87.56 E
Kishangarh, India	120	26.34 N	74.52 E
Kishangarh, India	120	27.52 N	70.34 E
Kishangarh ◆[8]	272a	28.31 N	77.08 E
Kishar Bāla	267d	35.49 N	51.13 E
Kishb, Harrat al- ⏏[9]	144	23.00 N	41.25 E
Kishi, Nig.	150	9.05 N	3.52 E
Kishi, Zaïre	154	10.04 S	26.26 E
Kishida ≃	96	35.38 N	134.27 E
Kishigawa	96	34.13 N	135.20 E
Kishikas ≃	184	52.45 N	91.43 W
Kishimoto	96	35.23 N	133.25 E
Kishinev → Kišin'ov	78	47.00 N	28.50 E
Kishiwada	96	34.28 N	135.22 E
Kishorganj	124	24.26 N	90.46 E
Kishorn, Loch c	46	57.21 N	5.41 W
Kishtwār	123	33.19 N	75.46 E
Kishwaukee ≃	216	42.11 N	89.08 W
Kishwaukee, South Branch ≃	216	42.12 N	88.59 W
Kisia	152	4.35 S	18.22 E
Kisigo ≃	154	7.03 S	35.50 E
Kisii	154	0.41 S	34.46 E
Kisiju	154	7.24 S	39.20 E
Kiši-Karoj, ozero ⊜	86	54.03 N	71.20 E
Kisika-zaki ≻	93b	30.50 N	131.04 E
Kısıklı ◆[8]	267b	41.01 N	29.03 E
Kišin	78	51.08 N	27.41 E
Kišin'ov (Kishinev)	78	47.00 N	28.50 E
Kısır Dağı ∧	84	40.58 N	43.06 E
Kısırkaya	267b	41.14 N	28.58 E
Kısırmandıra	267b	41.14 N	28.49 E
Kisiwada → Kishiwada	96	34.28 N	135.22 E
Kisiwani	154	4.08 S	37.57 E
Kisizi	154	1.00 S	29.56 E
Kiska Island I	181a	52.00 N	177.30 E
Kiskatinaw ≃	182	56.06 N	120.08 W
Kiska Volcano ∧[1]	181a	52.07 N	177.36 E
Kis-Kevély ∧[2]	264c	47.38 N	18.59 E
Kiski Lake ⊜	184	54.46 N	98.55 W
Kiskimere	279b	40.37 N	79.35 W
Kiskiminetas ≃	214	40.41 N	79.40 W
Kiskittogisu Lake ⊜	184	54.13 N	98.20 W
Kiskitto Lake ⊜	184	54.16 N	98.34 W
Kiskörei-víztároló ⊜[1]	30	47.35 N	20.40 E
Kiskőrös	30	46.38 N	19.17 E
Kiskunfélegyháza	30	46.43 N	19.52 E
Kiskunhalas	30	46.26 N	19.30 E
Kiskunmajsa	30	46.30 N	19.45 E
Kışla	130	40.51 N	30.57 E
Kisl'akovka	78	46.44 N	31.59 E
Kisl'akovskaja	78	46.27 N	39.40 E
Kislovka	83	49.38 N	37.53 E
Kislovo	80	49.54 N	45.25 E
Kislovodsk	84	43.55 N	42.44 E
Kismaayo	144	0.22 S	42.32 E
Kismet	276	40.38 N	73.12 W
Kisnema	76	60.20 N	37.39 E
Kiso, Nihon	94	35.56 N	137.47 E
Kiso, Nihon	268	35.34 N	139.26 E
Kiso ≃	94	35.02 N	136.45 E
Kisofukushima	94	35.51 N	137.42 E
Kisogawa	94	35.20 N	136.47 E
Kisoripur	126	22.05 N	88.34 E
Kisoro	154	1.17 S	29.41 E
Kiso-sammyaku ⋏	94	35.43 N	137.50 E
Kisozaki	94	35.04 N	136.44 E
Kispest ◆[8]	264c	47.27 N	19.08 E
Kispiox	182	55.21 N	127.41 W
Kispiox ≃	182	55.16 N	127.41 W
Kispiox Mountain ∧	182	55.25 N	127.57 W
Kissamos	38	35.30 N	23.38 E
Kissena Park ♠	276	40.45 N	73.49 W
Kisseynew Lake ⊜	184	54.58 N	101.35 W
Kissidougou	150	9.11 N	10.06 W
Kissimmee	220	28.17 N	81.24 W
Kissimmee ≃	220	27.10 N	80.53 W
Kissimmee, Lake ⊜	220	27.55 N	81.16 W
Kissing	60	48.18 N	10.59 E
Kississing	184	55.07 N	101.07 W
Kississing Lake ⊜	184	55.10 N	101.20 W
Kisslegg	58	47.47 N	9.53 E
Kissū, Jabal ∧	140	21.35 N	25.09 E
Kista	80	46.05 N	43.06 E
Kistanje	36	43.59 N	15.58 E
Kistarcsa	264c	47.33 N	19.16 E
Kistendej	80	52.08 N	43.39 E
Kistigan Lake ⊜	184	54.38 N	92.37 W
Kistler	214	40.22 N	77.51 W
Kisújszállás	30	47.13 N	20.46 E
Kisuki	96	35.17 N	132.54 E
Kisumu	154	0.06 S	34.45 E
Kisvárda	30	48.13 N	22.05 E
Kiswere	154	9.26 S	39.33 E
Kita	150	13.03 N	9.29 W
Kita ◆[8], Nihon	268	35.45 N	139.44 E
Kita ◆[8], Nihon	270	34.42 N	135.30 E
Kita ◆[8], Nihon	270	35.03 N	135.45 E
Kita ◆[8], Nihon	270	34.45 N	135.08 E
Kitaaiki	94	36.04 N	138.34 E
Kita-Daitō-jima I	90	25.57 N	131.18 E
Kitafuji-enshūjō ■	94	35.25 N	138.48 E
Kitagata	94	35.26 N	136.41 E
Kitagawa	96	33.27 N	134.03 E
Kitagi-shima I	96	34.23 N	133.32 E
Kitaibaraki	94	36.48 N	140.45 E
Kitain Temple ⊍[1]	268	35.54 N	139.30 E
Kita-Iō-jima I	14	25.26 N	141.17 E
Kitairiso	268	35.50 N	139.26 E
Kitajima	96	34.05 N	134.35 E
Kitakami	92	39.18 N	141.07 E
Kitakami ≃	92	38.25 N	141.19 E
Kitakami-kōchi ⋏	92	39.30 N	141.30 E
Kitakata	92	37.39 N	139.52 E
Kitakyuschu → Kitakyūshū	96	33.53 N	130.50 E
Kitakyūshū	96	33.53 N	130.50 E
Kitakyushu-kokutei-kōen ♠	96	33.45 N	130.50 E
Kitale	154	1.01 N	35.00 E
Kitamachi ◆[8]	268	35.46 N	139.39 E
Kitamba ◆[8]	273b	4.19 S	15.14 E
Kitami	92a	43.48 N	143.54 E
Kitami-sanchi ⋏	92a	44.22 N	142.43 E
Kitamoto	94	36.02 N	139.32 E
Kita-Nagato-kaigan-kokutei-kōen ♠	96	34.24 N	131.16 E
Kitanakagusuku	174m	26.21 N	127.51 E
Kitanda, Zaïre	154	6.36 S	26.27 E
Kitanda, Zaïre	154	9.59 S	27.28 E
Kitangari	154	10.39 S	39.20 E
Kitangiri, Lake ⊜	154	4.05 S	34.19 E
Kitangua	152	6.17 S	20.22 E
Kitano, Nihon	96	33.20 N	130.35 E
Kitano, Nihon	268	35.47 N	139.26 E
Kitanoshinden	268	35.48 N	139.26 E
Kitatachibana	94	36.29 N	139.03 E
Kitatajima	268	35.56 N	139.30 E
Kitatawara	270	34.44 N	135.42 E
Kitaura	94	36.04 N	140.32 E
Kita-ura ⊜	94	36.00 N	140.34 E
Kitava Island I	164	8.40 S	151.20 E
Kitaya	154	10.39 S	40.10 E
Kit Carson, Ca., U.S.	226	38.41 N	120.07 W
Kit Carson, Co., U.S.	198	38.45 N	102.47 W
Kitchener, Austl.	162	31.02 S	124.11 E
Kitchener, On., Can.	212	43.27 N	80.29 W
Kitee	26	62.06 N	30.09 E
Kitega → Gitega	154	3.26 S	29.56 E
Kiteiyab	140	17.12 N	33.43 E
Kitenda	152	6.53 S	17.21 E
Kitenevo	82	56.21 N	36.13 E
Kitengo	152	7.26 S	24.08 E
Kitéssa	154	5.20 N	25.20 E
Kitgum	154	3.18 N	32.53 E
Kíthira	38	36.09 N	23.00 E
Kíthira I	38	36.20 N	22.58 E
Kíthnos	38	37.26 N	24.26 E
Kíthnos I	38	37.25 N	24.28 E
Kithraía	130	35.15 N	33.29 E
Kitimat	182	54.03 N	128.33 W
Kitimat ≃	182	54.06 N	128.38 W
Kitimat Ranges ⋏	182	53.30 N	128.50 W
Kitinen ≃	24	67.08 N	27.29 E
Kitíou, Akrotírion ≻	130	34.48 N	33.36 E
Kitlope ≃	182	53.10 N	127.45 W
Kitlope Lake ⊜	182	53.07 N	127.47 W
Kitō, Nihon	94	34.42 N	138.03 E
Kitō, Nihon	96	33.46 N	134.12 E
Kitoj ≃	88	52.39 N	103.56 E
Kitridge Point ≻	241g	13.09 N	59.25 W
Kitsap □[6]	224	47.41 N	122.44 W
Kitscoty	184	53.20 N	110.20 W
Kit's Coty House ⊍	260	51.19 N	0.30 E
Kitshua-Nseke	152	4.26 S	19.36 E
Kitsuki	92	33.25 N	131.37 E
Kitsuregawa	94	36.43 N	140.01 E
Kittanning	214	40.48 N	79.31 W
Kittatinny Mountain ∧	210	41.10 N	74.55 W
Kittatinny Tunnel ◆[5]	214	40.09 N	77.41 W
Kittendorf	54	53.37 N	12.54 E
Kittery	188	43.05 N	70.44 W
Kitt Green	262	53.33 N	2.41 W
Kittilä	24	67.40 N	24.54 E
Kittitas	202	46.59 N	120.24 W
Kittitas □[6]	224	47.13 N	121.01 W
Kitt Peak National Observatory ⊍[3]	200	31.58 N	111.36 W
Kittsee	61	48.05 N	17.04 E
Kitu	154	7.38 S	27.42 E
Kitui	154	1.22 S	38.01 E
Kitumbeine ∧[1]	154	2.44 S	36.16 E
Kitunda	154	6.48 S	33.13 E
Kitutu	154	3.17 S	28.05 E
Kitwanga	182	55.06 N	128.03 W
Kitwangar Indian Reserve ◆[4]	182	55.06 N	128.04 W
Kitwe	154	12.49 S	28.13 E
Kitwitwi	156	17.25 S	18.25 E
Kityang → Jieyang	100	23.35 N	116.21 E
Kitzbühel	64	47.27 N	12.23 E
Kitzbüheler Alpen ⋏	64	47.20 N	12.20 E
Kitzingen	56	49.44 N	10.09 E
Kitzscher	54	51.09 N	12.33 E
Kiukiang → Jiujiang	100	29.44 N	115.59 E
Kiukiu, Pointe ≻	174y	9.47 S	139.09 W
Kiul	124	25.09 N	86.06 E
Kiunga, Kenya	154	1.45 S	41.29 E
Kiunga, Pap. N. Gui.	164	6.10 S	141.15 E
Kiuruvesi	26	63.39 N	26.37 E
Kiuschu → Kyūshū I	92	33.00 N	131.00 E
Kivak	180	64.16 N	172.57 W
Kivalina	180	67.44 N	164.33 W
Kivercy	78	50.50 N	25.27 E
Kiveriči	76	57.22 N	36.36 E
Kivijärvi	26	63.04 N	25.03 E
Kivijärvi ⊜	26	63.10 N	25.09 E
Kivik	26	55.41 N	14.15 E
Kiviõli	76	59.21 N	26.57 E
Kivu □[4]	154	2.30 S	27.00 E
Kivu, Lac ⊜	154	2.00 S	29.10 E
Kiwaba N'zogi	152	8.57 S	16.32 E
Kiwai Island I	164	8.30 S	143.25 E
Kiwalik	180	66.02 N	161.50 W
Kiwanis Lake	214	41.28 N	81.09 W
Kiyama	96	33.25 N	130.32 E
Kīyāmakī Dāgh ∧	84	38.47 N	45.53 E
Kiyan	174m	26.05 N	127.40 E
Kiyan-zaki ≻	174m	26.05 N	127.39 E
Kıyıköy	130	41.38 N	28.05 E
Kiyiu Lake ⊜	184	51.38 N	108.55 W
Kiyl ≃	86	49.25 N	54.50 E
Kiyokawa	94	35.29 N	139.17 E
Kiyomi	94	36.07 N	137.11 E
Kiyosawa	94	35.03 N	138.15 E
Kiyose	94	35.47 N	139.32 E
Kiyosu	94	35.13 N	136.50 E
Kiyosumi-yama ∧	94	35.09 N	140.09 E
Kiyotani	270	34.52 N	134.59 E
Kiyotsu ≃	94	37.03 N	138.41 E
Kizel	86	59.03 N	57.40 E
Kizevatovo	80	53.13 N	45.18 E
Kizhake Chālakudi	122	10.18 N	76.20 E
Kızıl ≃	130	41.44 N	35.58 E
Kızıl Adalar II	130	40.52 N	29.05 E
Kızılcabölük	130	37.37 N	29.01 E
Kızılcahamam	130	40.28 N	32.39 E
Kızılçakçak	84	40.46 N	43.37 E
Kızıldağ ∧	130	36.25 N	32.42 E
Kızıldikme	130	39.05 N	37.01 E
Kızılhisar	130	37.33 N	29.18 E
Kızıloğlan	130	41.20 N	34.52 E
Kizil'skoje	86	52.44 N	58.54 E
Kiziltašskij liman c	78	45.07 N	37.05 E
Kızıltepe	130	37.12 N	40.36 E
Kızıltoprak ◆[8]	267b	40.58 N	29.03 E
Kizil'unt	84	43.12 N	46.53 E
Kızılveran	130	40.27 N	34.28 E
Kızılviran	130	37.52 N	32.07 E
Kızılyaka	130	37.09 N	32.54 E
Kižimiz, gora ∧	24	63.12 N	58.48 E
Kizimkazi	154	6.27 S	39.28 E
Kižinga	88	51.51 N	109.55 E
Kizir ≃	86	53.51 N	93.06 E
Kızkalesi ⊥	130	36.28 N	34.04 E
Kızkulesi ◆[5]	267b	41.01 N	29.00 E
Kizl'ar	84	43.50 N	46.40 E
Kizl'arskij zaliv c	84	44.33 N	46.55 E
Kizner	80	56.17 N	51.31 E
Kiz'oma	24	61.08 N	44.50 E
Kizu	96	34.44 N	135.49 E
Kizu ≃	94	34.53 N	135.42 E
Kizuki	268	35.34 N	139.40 E
Kizuri	270	34.39 N	135.34 E
Kizyl-Ajak	128	37.40 N	65.23 E
Kizyl-Arvat	128	38.58 N	56.15 E
Kizyl-Atrek	128	37.36 N	54.46 E
Kizyl-Su	128	39.48 N	53.01 E
Kjellerup	41	56.17 N	9.26 E
Kjøbenhavn → København	41	55.40 N	12.35 E
Kjustendil	38	42.17 N	22.41 E
Klaarstroom	158	33.20 S	22.32 E
Klaaswaal	52	51.46 N	4.26 E
Klabat, Gunung ∧	112	1.28 N	125.02 E
Kladanj	38	44.13 N	18.41 E
Kladbišči	80	55.32 N	45.33 E
Kläden	54	52.38 N	11.39 E
Kladkovo	82	55.24 N	38.51 E
Kladno	54	50.08 N	14.05 E
Kladovo	38	44.37 N	22.37 E
Kladow ◆[8]	264a	52.27 N	13.09 E
Kladruby	60	49.43 N	12.59 E
Klaeng	110	12.47 N	101.39 E
Klagan	112	5.58 N	117.27 E
Klagenfurt	61	46.37 N	14.18 E
Klågerup	41	55.36 N	13.15 E
Klagshamn	41	55.32 N	12.55 E
Klagstorp	41	55.24 N	13.22 E
Klahoose Indian Reserve ◆[4]	182	50.31 N	124.19 W
Klaipėda (Memel)	76	55.43 N	21.07 E
Klakah	115a	7.59 S	113.15 E
Klamath	204	41.31 N	124.02 W
Klamath ≃	204	41.33 N	124.04 W
Klamath Falls	202	42.13 N	121.46 W
Klamath Marsh ≡	202	42.54 N	121.44 W
Klamath Mountains ⋏	204	41.40 N	123.20 W
K. Lamido	146	9.21 N	11.12 E
Klämmingen ⊜	40	59.07 N	17.15 E
Klammpass)(	64	47.17 N	13.05 E
Klamono	164	1.08 S	131.30 E
Klang → Kelang	114	3.02 N	101.27 E
Klangpi	110	22.59 N	93.20 E
Klarälven (Trysilelva) ≃	26	59.23 N	13.32 E
Kl'as'ma	265b	55.59 N	37.50 E
Klášterec	54	50.24 N	13.10 E
Kl'asticy	76	55.53 N	28.36 E
Klaten	115a	7.42 S	110.35 E
Klatovy	60	49.24 N	13.18 E
Klausdorf, B.R.D.	54	54.18 N	10.15 E
Klausdorf, D.D.R.	54	54.20 N	13.01 E
Klausenburg → Cluj-Napoca	38	46.47 N	23.36 E
Klausenpass)(	58	46.52 N	8.51 E
Kl'avlino	80	54.17 N	52.01 E
Klawer	158	31.44 S	18.36 E
Klawock	182	55.33 N	133.06 W
Klazienaveen	52	52.44 N	7.00 E
Kl'az'ma	82	55.58 N	37.27 E
Kl'az'ma ≃	80	56.10 N	42.58 E
Kl'az'minskoje vodochranilišče ⊜[1]	265b	55.59 N	37.35 E
Kleberg	222	32.40 N	96.37 W
Kleck	76	53.04 N	26.38 E
Kłecko	30	52.38 N	17.26 E
Kleczew	30	52.23 N	18.10 E
Kledering ◆[8]	264b	48.08 N	16.26 E
Kleef	263	51.11 N	6.56 E
Kleena Kleene	182	51.57 N	124.50 W
Kleinasien → Asia Minor □[9]	22	39.00 N	32.00 E
Kleinbeeren	264a	52.22 N	13.20 E
Kleinbegin	158	28.50 S	21.36 E
Klein-Blesbokspruit ≃	273d	26.16 S	28.29 E
Kleinbodungen	54	51.28 N	10.32 E
Klein Bonaire I	241s	12.10 N	68.18 W
Klein Bünzow	54	53.53 N	13.48 E
Kleinburg	275b	43.50 N	79.38 W
Klein Curaçao I	241s	12.00 N	68.40 W
Kleine Elster ≃	54	51.32 N	13.23 E
Kleine Emme ≃	58	47.04 N	8.17 E
Kleine Emscher ≃	263	51.31 N	6.43 E
Kleine Erlauf ≃	61	48.07 N	15.08 E
Kleineichen	263	51.08 N	7.21 E
Kleine Laber ≃	60	48.55 N	12.31 E
Kleinenberg	52	51.35 N	8.58 E
Kleinenbroich	263	51.12 N	6.35 E
Kleinengstingen	58	48.23 N	9.18 E
Kleiner Jasmunder Bodden c	54	54.28 N	13.32 E
Kleiner Ravens-Berg ∧[2]	264a	52.22 N	13.04 E
Kleiner Wannsee ⊜	264a	52.25 N	13.10 E
Kleiner Zern-See ⊜	264a	52.26 N	12.55 E
Kleine Spree ≃	54	51.31 N	14.24 E
Kleines Walsertal V	64	47.23 N	10.12 E
Kleinfeltersville	208	40.18 N	76.15 W
Kleinglödnitz	61	46.51 N	14.08 E
Kleinhammer	263	51.14 N	7.46 E
Klein-Jukskei ≃	273d	26.08 S	27.56 E
Klein-Karas	156	27.32 S	18.06 E
Klein Karroo → Little Karroo ⋏[1]	158	33.45 S	21.30 E
Klein Kienitz	264a	52.18 N	13.29 E
Kleinlützel	58	47.26 N	7.25 E
Kleinmachnow	54	52.24 N	13.15 E
Klein Marzehns	54	52.01 N	12.37 E
Kleinmond	158	34.21 S	19.03 E
Klein-Olifants ≃	158	25.41 S	29.19 E
Kleinschönebeck	264a	52.29 N	13.43 E
Klein-Soutpan	158	30.26 S	22.26 E
Klein Stöckheim	54	52.12 N	10.31 E
Klein-Vis ≃	158	33.05 S	26.00 E
Klein Wanzleben	54	52.04 N	11.21 E
Klein Ziethen	264a	52.23 N	13.27 E
Klein Ziethener-Berge ∧[2]	264a	52.22 N	13.26 E
Klekovača ∧	36	44.26 N	16.31 E
Klementjevka	86	50.16 N	80.56 E
Klementjevo	82	55.38 N	36.01 E
Klemme	190	43.00 N	93.36 W
Klemtu	182	52.36 N	128.31 W
Klenovka	80	57.45 N	54.19 E
Klenovo	82	55.19 N	37.21 E
Klerksdorp	158	26.58 S	26.39 E
Klerkskraal	158	26.15 S	27.10 E
Klesov	78	51.19 N	26.54 E
Klésso	150	10.57 N	3.59 W
Klet' ∧	61	48.52 N	14.17 E
Kletn'a	76	53.23 N	33.12 E
Kletskij	80	49.19 N	43.04 E
Kletsko-Počtovskij	80	49.36 N	43.03 E
Klettgau ◆[1]	58	47.40 N	8.25 E
Klettwitz	54	51.32 N	13.53 E
Klevan'	78	50.44 N	26.02 E
Kleve	52	51.48 N	6.09 E
Klevenka	80	52.07 N	49.33 E
Kley ◆[8]	263	51.30 N	7.22 E
Klibreck, Ben ∧	46	58.14 N	4.22 W
Kličev	76	53.29 N	29.21 E
Klička	88	50.26 N	118.00 E
Klickitat	224	45.49 N	121.09 W
Klickitat □[6]	224	45.50 N	121.07 W
Klickitat ≃	224	45.42 N	121.17 W
Kliedbruch ◆[1]	263	51.22 N	6.33 E
Klietz	54	52.40 N	12.04 E
Klimino	88	58.39 N	98.42 E
Klimoviči	76	53.37 N	31.58 E
Klimovo, S.S.S.R.	76	52.23 N	32.11 E
Klimovo, S.S.S.R.	82	55.22 N	38.52 E
Klimovsk	82	55.22 N	37.32 E
Klimovskoje	82	54.42 N	37.48 E
Klimov Zavod	76	54.50 N	34.55 E
Klimpfjäll	24	65.04 N	14.52 E
Klin, S.S.S.R.	82	56.20 N	36.44 E
Klin, S.S.S.R.	82	55.19 N	36.20 E
Klinaklini ≃	182	51.05 N	125.36 W
Klin-Bel'din	82	54.45 N	39.13 E
Klincovka	80	51.41 N	49.11 E
Klincy	76	52.47 N	32.14 E
Kline Ditch ≅	279a	41.28 N	82.04 W
Kling	116	5.58 N	124.42 E
Klingbach ≃	56	50.17 N	9.22 E
Klingenberg	54	50.55 N	13.31 E
Klingenberg am Main	56	49.47 N	9.11 E
Klingenmünster	56	49.08 N	8.01 E
Klingenthal	54	50.21 N	12.28 E
Klinger Lake ⊜	216	41.47 N	85.33 W
Klingerstown	208	40.40 N	76.41 W
Klinghardtberge ∧	156	27.18 S	15.48 E
Klingnau	58	47.35 N	8.15 E
Klink	54	53.29 N	12.37 E
Klinkino	83	47.17 N	38.15 E
Klínovec ∧	54	50.24 N	12.58 E
Klinsko-Dmitrovskaja gr'ada ∧	82	56.15 N	37.30 E
Klintehamn	26	57.24 N	18.12 E
Klintsy → Klincy	76	52.47 N	32.14 E
Klip ≃, S. Afr.	158	27.03 S	29.03 E
Klip ≃, S. Afr.	273d	26.19 S	27.53 E
Klipbakken	158	28.50 S	21.21 E
Klipdale	158	34.19 S	19.57 E
Klipdam	158	27.35 S	19.56 E
Kliplev	41	54.56 N	9.25 E
Klippan	41	56.08 N	13.06 E
Klipplaat	158	33.02 S	24.21 E
Klippoortjie	273d	26.13 S	28.10 E
Klipriviersberg ⋏	273d	26.17 S	28.02 E
Kliptown	273d	26.17 S	27.53 E
Klipwerf	158	31.09 S	19.52 E
Kliškovcy	78	48.26 N	26.15 E
Klisura	38	42.42 N	24.27 E
Klitmøller	26	57.02 N	8.31 E
Klitten	54	51.20 N	14.36 E
Klixbüll	41	54.48 N	8.53 E
Ključ	36	44.32 N	16.47 E
Klobbicke	264a	52.46 N	13.48 E
Klobouky	61	49.00 N	16.52 E
Kłobuck	30	50.55 N	18.57 E
Klobuticy	76	58.35 N	29.35 E
Kłodawa	30	52.16 N	18.55 E
Kłodzko	30	50.27 N	16.39 E
Kløfta	26	60.04 N	11.09 E
Kłomnice	30	50.56 N	19.21 E
Klondike	216	40.28 N	86.57 W
Klondike □[9]	180	63.30 N	139.00 W
Klondike ≃	180	64.05 N	139.26 W
Klöntaler See ⊜	58	47.02 N	8.58 E
Klooga	76	59.19 N	24.16 E
Kloosterveen	52	52.59 N	6.33 E
Kloosterzande	52	51.22 N	4.02 E
Kloster	54	54.35 N	13.06 E
Klosterfelde	54	52.48 N	13.28 E
Klosterhardt ◆[8]	263	51.31 N	6.53 E
Klösterle	58	47.08 N	10.05 E
Klostermansfeld	54	51.35 N	11.29 E
Klosterneuburg	264b	48.18 N	16.20 E
Kloster Oesede	52	52.12 N	8.07 E
Klosters	58	46.54 N	9.53 E
Klostertal V	58	47.08 N	9.59 E
Kloster Zinna	54	52.01 N	13.07 E
Kloten, Schw.	58	47.27 N	8.35 E
Kloten, Sve.	40	59.54 N	15.17 E
Klotz, Lac ⊜	176	60.32 N	73.40 W
Klötze	54	52.38 N	11.10 E
Kloulklubed	175b	7.02 N	134.15 E
Klouto	150	6.57 N	0.34 E
Kluane ≃	180	61.53 N	139.43 W
Kluane Lake ⊜	180	61.15 N	138.40 W
Kluane National Park ♠	180	60.45 N	139.30 W
Kluang	112	2.41 S	103.54 E
Kl'učevaja	24	65.16 N	41.32 E
Kl'učevskaja Sopka, vulkan ∧[1]	74	56.04 N	160.38 E
Kl'učevskij	88	53.33 N	119.26 E
Kluchorskij, pereval)(	84	43.15 N	41.54 E
Kl'uči, S.S.S.R.	74	56.18 N	160.51 E
Kl'uči, S.S.S.R.	80	51.59 N	46.31 E
Kl'uči, S.S.S.R.	80	51.26 N	45.11 E
Kl'uči, S.S.S.R.	86	52.16 N	79.10 E
Kl'učovka, S.S.S.R.	85	42.34 N	71.48 E
Kl'učovka, S.S.S.R.	86	51.22 N	55.48 E
Kluczbork	30	50.59 N	18.13 E
Kluess	54	53.46 N	12.14 E
Kluet ≃	114	3.04 N	97.20 E
Kl'ukvenka	86	58.34 N	85.55 E
Klukwan	180	59.24 N	135.54 W
Klundert	52	51.40 N	4.32 E
Klungkung	115b	8.32 S	115.24 E
Klüppelberg	56	51.06 N	7.28 E
Klüterthöhle ⏏[5]	52	51.18 N	7.21 E
Klutina Lake ⊜	180	61.37 N	146.55 W
Klütz	54	53.58 N	11.10 E
Knaben gruver	26	58.39 N	7.04 E
Knaddah	130	35.45 N	36.12 E
Kn'aginino	80	55.49 N	45.03 E
Knaik ≃	46	56.14 N	3.52 W
Knapdaar	158	30.43 S	26.09 E
Knapdale ◆[1]	46	55.55 N	5.30 W
Knaphill	260	51.19 N	0.37 W
Knapp	190	44.57 N	92.04 W
Knapp Creek	210	42.00 N	78.30 W
Knappenberg	61	46.56 N	14.35 E
Knäred	26	56.32 N	13.19 E
Knaresborough	44	54.00 N	1.27 W
Knargram	126	24.01 N	87.59 E
Knauertown	285	40.10 N	75.44 W
Knauthain ◆[8]	54	51.16 N	12.18 E
Kn'ažaja Bajgora	76	52.23 N	40.02 E
Kn'azevka	86	57.35 N	74.10 E
Kn'ažji Gory	76	56.05 N	35.14 E
Kn'ažovo	76	59.40 N	43.54 E
Knebel	41	56.13 N	10.30 E
Knebworth	42	51.52 N	0.12 W
Kneehills Creek ≃	182	51.30 N	112.50 W
Knee Lake ⊜, Mb., Can.	184	55.03 N	94.40 W
Knee Lake ⊜, Sk., Can.	184	55.51 N	107.00 W
Knesebeck	54	52.41 N	10.42 E
Knesselare	50	51.08 N	3.25 E
Knetzgau	56	50.00 N	10.33 E
Knevicy	76	57.56 N	32.14 E
Kneža	38	43.30 N	24.05 E
Knić	38	43.55 N	20.43 E
Knickerbocker	196	31.16 N	100.38 W
Kniebis	58	48.28 N	8.17 E
Knife ≃	198	47.20 N	101.23 W
Knife Lake ⊜	184	53.47 N	91.20 W
Knife River Indian Villages National Historical Site ⊥	198	47.21 N	101.23 W
Knight Inlet c	182	50.41 N	125.40 W
Knight Island I	180	60.20 N	147.45 W
Knighton	42	52.21 N	3.03 W
Knightsen	226	37.58 N	121.40 W
Knights Landing	226	38.47 N	121.43 W
Knightstown	218	39.47 N	85.31 W
Knightville Dam ◆[6]	207	42.17 N	72.52 W
Knik Arm c	180	61.25 N	149.45 W
Knin	36	44.02 N	16.12 E
Knippa	196	29.18 N	99.38 W
Knislinge	26	56.11 N	14.05 E
Knittelfeld	61	47.14 N	14.50 E
Knittlingen	56	49.01 N	8.45 E
Knivsbjerg ∧[2]	41	55.08 N	9.27 E
Knivsta	40	59.43 N	17.48 E
Knjaževac	38	43.34 N	22.16 E
Knob, Cape ≻	162	34.32 S	119.16 E
Knobby Head ≻	162	29.40 S	114.58 E
Knob Noster	194	38.45 N	93.33 W
Knob Peak ∧	116	12.28 N	121.21 E
Knoc	48	52.38 N	9.20 W
Knock	46	57.33 N	2.45 W
Knockholt	260	51.18 N	0.06 E
Knockholt Pound	260	51.19 N	0.08 E
Knocklayd ∧	44	55.09 N	6.15 W
Knocklong	48	52.26 N	8.24 W
Knockmealdown Mountains ⋏	48	52.10 N	8.00 W
Knokke	50	51.21 N	3.17 E
Knole ⊥	260	51.16 N	0.12 E
Knolls Green	262	53.19 N	2.18 W
Knollwood, Ct., U.S.	207	41.16 N	72.23 W
Knollwood, Il., U.S.	278	42.17 N	87.53 W
Knollwood, Md., U.S.	284c	39.02 N	76.58 W
Knollwood Park	216	42.14 N	84.22 W
Knon ⊜	40	60.12 N	13.40 E
Knossos ⊥	38	35.20 N	25.10 E
Knottingley	44	53.43 N	1.14 W
Knott's Berry Farm ♠	280	33.50 N	118.00 W
Knotts Island	208	36.31 N	75.56 W
Knotty Ash ◆[8]	262	53.25 N	2.54 W
Knotty Green	260	51.37 N	0.39 W
Knowland State Arboretum and Park ♠	282	37.45 N	122.09 W
Knowle	42	52.23 N	1.43 W
Knowlesville	210	43.14 N	78.19 W
Knowlton Lake ⊜	212	44.28 N	76.41 W
Knowltonwood	285	39.53 N	75.24 W
Knowsley ◆[8], Eng., U.K.	262	53.27 N	2.50 W
Knowsley ◆[8], Eng., U.K.	262	53.27 N	2.51 W
Knowsley Hall ⊍	262	53.26 N	2.50 W
Knowsley Park ♠	262	53.27 N	2.49 W
Knox, In., U.S.	216	41.17 N	86.37 W
Knox, N.Y., U.S.	210	42.40 N	74.07 W
Knox, Pa., U.S.	214	41.14 N	79.32 W
Knox □[6], Mo., U.S.	219	40.08 N	92.09 W
Knox □[6], Oh., U.S.	214	40.23 N	82.29 W
Knox, Cape ≻	182	54.11 N	133.04 W
Knoxboro	210	42.58 N	75.36 W
Knox City, Mo., U.S.	219	40.08 N	92.00 W
Knox City, Tx., U.S.	196	33.25 N	99.49 W
Knox Coast ⏏[2]	9	66.30 S	105.00 E
Knox Dale	214	41.05 N	79.02 W
Knox Lake ⊜[1]	214	40.31 N	82.30 W
Knoxville, Ga., U.S.	192	32.43 N	83.59 W

	English	Deutsch	Español	Français	Português
≃	River	Fluss	Río	Rivière	Rio
≅	Canal	Kanal	Canal	Canal	Canal
˪	Waterfall, Rapids	Wasserfall, Stromschnellen	Cascada, Rápidos	Chute d'eau, Rapides	Cascata, Rápidos
)(	Strait	Meeresstrasse	Estrecho	Détroit	Estreito
c	Bay, Gulf	Bucht, Golf	Bahía, Golfo	Baie, Golfe	Baía, Golfo
⊜	Lake, Lakes	See, Seen	Lago, Lagos	Lac, Lacs	Lago, Lagos
≡	Swamp	Sumpf	Pantano	Marais	Pântano
⌂	Ice Features, Glacier	Eis- und Gletscherformen	Accidentes Glaciales	Formes glaciaires	Acidentes glaciares
⊤	Other Hydrographic Features	Andere Hydrographische Objekte	Otros Elementos Hidrográficos	Autres données hydrographiques	Outros acidentes hidrográficos
✤	Submarine Features	Untermeerische Objekte	Accidentes Submarinos	Formes de relief sous-marin	Acidentes submarinos
□	Political Unit	Politische Einheit	Unidad Politica	Entité politique	Unidade política
⊍	Cultural Institution	Kulturelle Institution	Institución Cultural	Institution culturelle	Instituição cultural
⊥	Historical Site	Historische Stätte	Sitio Histórico	Site historique	Sitio histórico
♠	Recreational Site	Erholungs- und Ferienort	Sitio de Recreo	Centre de loisirs	Area de Lazer
⊠	Airport	Flughafen	Aeropuerto	Aéroport	Aeroporto
■	Military Installation	Militäranlage	Instalación Militar	Installation militaire	Instalação militar
◆	Miscellaneous	Verschiedenes	Misceláneo	Divers	Diversos

Knoxville, Il., U.S. 190 40.54 N 90.17 W
Knoxville, Ia., U.S. 190 41.19 N 93.06 W
Knoxville, Pa., U.S. 210 41.57 N 77.26 W
Knoxville, Tn., U.S. 192 35.57 N 83.55 W
Knuckles ∧ 122 7.24 N 80.48 E
Knudshoved Odde ≻[1] 41 55.03 N 11.45 E
Knüll ∧ 56 50.53 N 9.24 E
Knutby 40 59.55 N 18.15 E
Knuthenborg 41 54.50 N 11.30 E
Knutsford 44 53.19 N 2.22 W
Knysna 158 34.02 S 23.02 E
Knyszyn 30 53.19 N 22.55 E
Koala Sanctuary ◆[4] 274a 33.40 S 151.10 E
Koani 154 6.08 S 39.17 E
Kob' 88 55.25 N 101.24 E
Koba 112 2.29 S 106.24 E
Kob'aj 74 63.34 N 126.30 E
Kőbánya ◆[8] 264c 47.29 N 19.10 E
Kobarid 36 46.15 N 13.35 E
Kobar Sink ±[7] 144 13.35 N 40.50 E
Kobayashi 92 31.59 N 130.59 E
Kōbe, Nihon 96 34.41 N 135.10 E
Kōbe, Nihon 270 34.41 N 135.10 E
Kōbe-kō c 270 34.40 N 135.12 E
Kobel'aki 78 49.09 N 34.12 E
København (Copenhagen) 41 55.40 N 12.35 E
København □[6] 41 55.45 N 12.25 E
Kōbe University ʊ[2] 270 34.43 N 135.14 E
Kobi 84 42.33 N 44.32 E
Koblenz, B.R.D. 56 50.21 N 7.35 E
Koblenz, Schw. 58 47.37 N 8.14 E
Koblenz □[5] 56 50.10 N 7.30 E
Kobo, Ityo. 144 12.11 N 39.33 E
Kobo, Zaïre 152 4.54 S 17.09 E
Ko-boke ♦ 96 33.50 N 133.46 E
Koboko 154 3.25 N 30.58 E
Koboldo 89 52.58 N 132.42 E
Kobona 76 60.01 N 31.36 E
Kobou ≃ 152 6.13 N 23.19 E
Kobowen Swamp ≡ 144 5.38 N 33.54 E
Koboža 76 58.49 N 35.01 E
Koboža ≃ 76 58.52 N 36.17 E
Kobra 24 60.03 N 50.44 E
Kobrin 76 52.13 N 24.21 E
Kobrinskoje 76 59.25 N 30.07 E
Kobroor, Pulau I 164 6.12 S 134.32 E
Kobuchizawa 94 35.52 N 138.19 E
Kobuga-hara ♦ 94 36.40 N 139.35 E
Kobuk 180 66.54 N 156.52 W
Kobuk ≃ 180 66.45 N 161.00 W
Kobuk Valley National Park ♦ 180 67.20 N 159.00 W
Kobuleti 84 41.50 N 41.47 E
Kobushiga-take ∧ 94 35.54 N 138.44 E
Kobylanka 54 53.19 N 14.50 E
Kobylin 30 51.43 N 17.13 E
Kobyl'nik 76 54.56 N 26.41 E
Kobyžča 78 50.49 N 31.30 E
Köca ≃ 130 36.16 N 29.15 E
Kocaali 130 41.03 N 30.52 E
Kocaaliler 130 37.19 N 30.44 E
Kocaeli → İzmit 130 40.46 N 29.55 E
Kocaeli □[4] 130 40.55 N 29.55 E
Koçali 130 37.55 N 38.15 E
Kočani 38 41.55 N 22.25 E
Koçarlı 130 37.45 N 27.42 E
Kocasinan 267b 41.01 N 28.50 E
Kocasu ≃ 84 39.18 N 42.12 E
Koçbaşı Tepe ∧ 84 39.24 N 43.21 E
Kočečum ≃ 74 64.17 N 101.10 E
Kočelajevo 80 54.01 N 44.02 E
Kočemary 80 54.50 N 40.58 E
Kočen'ajevka 80 53.52 N 46.59 E
Kočen'ga, S.S.S.R. 76 60.09 N 43.33 E
Kočenga, S.S.S.R. 88 55.55 N 104.06 E
Kočenga ≃ 88 55.55 N 104.06 E
Kočerdyk 86 54.35 N 62.58 E
Kočerga 88 55.15 N 103.46 E
Kočerov 78 50.21 N 29.21 E
Kočetovka, S.S.S.R. 80 55.16 N 46.07 E
Kočetovka, S.S.S.R. 80 52.58 N 40.29 E
Kočevar 76 60.26 N 42.11 E
Kočevje 36 45.38 N 14.52 E
Kočevo 86 59.36 N 54.18 E
Koch'am-ni 98 41.06 N 129.23 E
Kŏch'ang, Taehan 98 35.26 N 126.42 E
Kŏch'ang, Taehan 98 35.41 N 127.55 E
Kochanoviči 76 55.52 N 28.08 E
Kochanovo 76 54.28 N 30.01 E
Kochel 64 47.39 N 11.22 E
Kochelsee ⊜ 64 47.38 N 11.20 E
Kochena 158 27.00 S 18.50 E
Kocher ≃ 56 49.14 N 9.12 E
Kōchi, Nihon 96 33.33 N 133.33 E
Kōchi, Nihon 96 34.28 N 132.53 E
Kōchi □[5] 96 33.40 N 133.30 E
Kōchi-dani ♦ 94 34.34 N 136.10 E
Kochinda 174m 26.08 N 127.43 E
Koch Island I 176 69.38 N 78.15 W
Kochiu → Gejiu 90 23.22 N 103.06 E
Kochma 80 56.56 N 41.06 E
Koch Peak ∧ 202 45.02 N 111.28 W
Kochugaon 124 26.34 N 90.04 E
Kock 30 51.39 N 22.27 E
Kočki, S.S.S.R. 86 52.24 N 80.40 E
Kočki, S.S.S.R. 86 54.20 N 80.29 E
Kočkor-Ata 85 41.04 N 72.29 E
Kočkorka 85 42.14 N 75.45 E
Kocksoord 273d 26.13 S 27.39 E
Kočkurovo 80 54.06 N 45.26 E
Kočmes 24 66.12 N 60.44 E
Kočon'ovo 86 55.02 N 82.12 E
Kočov 60 49.49 N 12.44 E
Kočubej 84 44.24 N 46.33 E
Kočubejevskoje 84 44.41 N 41.41 E
Kōda, Nihon 94 34.52 N 137.10 E
Kōda, Nihon 96 34.42 N 132.45 E
Kodačdikost 24 63.11 N 55.49 E
Kodaikānal 122 10.14 N 77.29 E
Kodaira 94 35.44 N 139.29 E
Kodama 94 36.11 N 139.08 E
Kodar, chrebet ⩓ 88 57.15 N 118.10 E
Kodari 124 27.56 N 85.56 E
Kodarma 124 24.28 N 85.36 E
Kodera ◆[8] 270 34.41 N 135.04 E
Kodersdorf 54 51.15 N 14.53 E
Kodi 152 3.34 S 22.12 E
Kodiak 180 57.48 N 152.23 W
Kodiak Island I 180 57.30 N 153.30 W
Kodiang 114 6.24 N 100.18 E
Kodinār 120 20.47 N 70.42 E
Kodino 24 63.43 N 39.41 E
Kodo ≃ 152 7.05 N 19.10 E
Kodo, Jabal ∧ 140 12.26 N 23.38 E
Kodok 140 9.53 N 32.07 E
Kodori ≃ 84 42.47 N 41.10 E
Kodorskij chrebet ⩓ 84 43.00 N 42.00 E
Kodra 78 50.36 N 29.34 E
Kodry ⩓[2] 78 47.10 N 28.25 E
Kodyma 78 48.07 N 29.07 E
Kodyma ≃ 78 48.01 N 30.48 E
Kodžori 84 41.40 N 44.41 E
Koegas 158 29.16 S 22.20 E
Koehn Lake ⊜ 228 35.20 N 117.53 W
Koekelare 50 51.05 N 2.58 E
Koekenaap 158 31.30 S 18.18 E
Koeltztown 219 38.19 N 92.03 W
Koenigsmacker 56 49.24 N 6.17 E
Koersel 56 51.04 N 5.16 E
Koes 156 25.59 S 19.08 E
Kofa Mountains ⩓ 200 33.20 N 114.00 W
Kofeld 58 47.44 N 9.41 E
Köfering 60 48.56 N 12.12 E
Koffiefontein 158 29.30 S 25.00 E
Kofiau, Pulau I 164 1.11 S 129.50 E
Köflach 61 47.04 N 15.05 E
Koforidua 150 6.03 N 0.17 W
Kōfu, Nihon 94 35.39 N 138.35 E
Kōfu, Nihon 96 35.17 N 133.30 E
Koga, Nihon 94 36.11 N 139.43 E
Koga, Nihon 96 33.40 N 130.30 E
Koga, Tan. 154 6.14 S 32.25 E
Kogaluc ≃ 176 59.40 N 77.35 W
Kogaluc, Baie c 176 59.20 N 77.50 W
Kogaluk ≃ 176 56.12 N 61.44 W
Kogan 166 27.03 S 150.46 E
Kogane 268 35.50 N 139.56 E
Koganei 94 35.42 N 139.32 E
Kogarah 274a 33.58 S 151.08 E
Kogarah Bay c 274a 33.59 S 151.07 E
Køge, Dan. 41 55.27 N 12.11 E
Kōge, Nihon 96 35.24 N 134.15 E
Køge Bugt c, Dan. 41 55.30 N 12.20 E
Køge Bugt c, Kal. Nun. 176 65.00 N 40.30 W
Kogil'nik ≃ 78 45.51 N 29.38 E
Kogin Baba 146 7.55 N 11.30 E
Koglhof 61 47.19 N 15.40 E
Kogon ≃ 150 11.09 N 14.42 W
Kogoni 150 14.44 N 6.02 W
Kōgŭm-do I 98 34.27 N 127.11 E
Kohak 128 25.44 N 62.33 E
Kohala Mountains ⩓ 229d 20.05 N 155.45 W
Kohama-shima I 175d 24.19 N 123.59 E
Kohāt 123 33.35 N 71.26 E
Kohāt ≃ 123 33.24 N 71.48 E
Kohatk Wash V 200 32.38 N 111.55 W
Kohila 76 59.10 N 24.45 E
Kohīma 120 25.40 N 94.07 E
Kohistān □[9] 123 35.03 N 72.52 W
Kohlberg ∧[2] 263 51.18 N 7.46 E
Kohler 190 43.44 N 87.46 W
Kohlfurt → Węgliniec 30 51.17 N 15.13 E
Kohlstädt 52 51.50 N 8.52 E
Kohoku 94 35.26 N 136.15 E
Kōhoku ◆[8] 268 35.31 N 139.38 E
Kohren-Sahlis 54 51.01 N 12.36 E
Kohsān 128 34.39 N 61.12 E
Kohtla-Järve 76 59.24 N 27.15 E
Kohu → Kōfu 94 35.39 N 138.35 E
Kohukohu 172 35.21 S 173.32 E
Kohŭng 98 34.37 N 127.16 E
Kohuratahi 172 39.06 S 174.46 E
Koide 94 37.13 N 138.57 E
Koidern 180 61.58 N 140.25 W
Koidu 150 8.38 N 10.59 W
Koigi 76 58.50 N 25.45 E
Koihoa 110 8.12 N 93.29 E
Koil-Aligarh → Alīgarh 124 27.53 N 78.05 E
Koilkuntla 122 15.14 N 78.19 E
Koimbani 157a 11.37 S 43.23 E
Koindu 150 8.26 N 10.19 W
Koin-ni 98 40.28 N 126.22 E
Koitere ⊜ 26 62.58 N 30.45 E
Koito ≃ 94 35.21 N 139.52 E
Kojā ≃ 128 25.34 N 61.13 E
Kojandy 86 49.51 N 75.40 E
Kojda 24 66.23 N 42.31 E
Kŏje-do I 98 34.52 N 128.37 E
Kojetin 30 49.21 N 17.18 E
Kojgorodok 24 60.26 N 50.58 E
Ko-jima I 92a 41.22 N 139.48 E
Kojima-ko ⊜[1] 96 34.37 N 134.00 E
Kojŏ 98 38.57 N 127.51 E
Kojonup 162 33.50 S 117.09 E
Kojsary 85 42.33 N 78.10 E
Kojsug 83 47.07 N 39.41 E
Kojtaš, S.S.S.R. 85 40.11 N 67.19 E
Kojtas, S.S.S.R. 86 51.32 N 76.15 E
Kok (Hkok) ≃ 110 20.14 N 100.09 E
Kōka 94 34.54 N 136.13 E
Koka, Lake ⊜[1] 144 8.23 N 39.05 E
Kokai ≃ 94 35.52 N 140.08 E
K'okajgyr 85 40.43 N 75.37 E
Kokalaat 86 49.47 N 64.15 E
Kokand 85 40.33 N 70.57 E
Kokanee Glacier Provincial Park ♦ 182 49.47 N 117.10 W
Kokankišlak 85 40.56 N 72.30 E
Kökar I 26 59.56 N 20.55 E
Kokaral, ostrov I 86 46.12 N 60.30 E
Kokas 164 2.42 S 132.26 E
Kokašice 60 49.53 N 12.57 E
Kokava nad Rimavicou 30 48.34 N 19.50 E
Kokawa 96 34.16 N 135.24 E
K'okbel' 85 40.17 N 72.55 E
Kokčetav 86 53.17 N 69.25 E
Kokčetavskaja vozvyšennost' ⩓[1] 86 52.50 N 69.00 E
Kokee State Park ♦ 229b 22.08 N 159.40 W
Kokemäenjoki ≃ 26 61.33 N 21.42 E
Kokemäki 26 61.15 N 22.21 E
Ko Kha 110 18.11 N 99.24 E
Kokhav 132 31.38 N 34.40 E
Koki 150 15.30 N 15.59 W
Kokinu 268 35.59 N 139.59 E
Kokiu → Gejiu 102 23.22 N 103.06 E
Kok-Jangak 85 41.02 N 73.12 E
Kokka 140 20.00 N 30.35 E
Kokkilai Lagoon c 122 9.00 N 80.56 E
Kokkola (Gamlakarleby) 26 63.50 N 23.07 E
Kokku 98 40.22 N 128.44 E
Koknese 76 56.39 N 25.29 E
Koko 150 11.26 N 4.32 E
Kokoda 164 8.52 S 147.45 E
Koko Head ≻ 229c 21.16 N 157.42 W
Kokola 154 0.47 N 29.36 E
Kokole Point ≻ 229b 21.59 N 159.46 W
Kokolik ≃ 180 69.46 N 163.00 W
Kokolopozo 150 5.08 N 6.05 W
K'ok'omeren ≃ 85 41.43 N 73.54 E
Kokomo, Hi., U.S. 229a 20.52 N 156.18 W
Kokomo, In., U.S. 216 40.29 N 86.08 W
Kokomo, Ms., U.S. 194 31.11 N 90.00 W
Kokonau 164 4.43 S 136.26 E
Kokong 156 24.27 S 23.03 E
Kokonoe 96 33.10 N 131.10 E
Koko Nor → Qinghai Hu ⊜ 102 36.50 N 100.20 E
Kokopo 164 4.20 S 152.15 E
Kokorevka 76 52.35 N 34.16 E
Kokosing ≃ 214 40.22 N 82.12 W
Kokos-Inseln → Cocos (Keeling) Islands □[2] 14 12.10 S 96.55 E
Kokoškino 265b 55.38 N 37.11 E
Kokpāra Narsinghgarh 126 22.31 N 86.33 E
Kokpaš 86 51.12 N 87.45 E
Kokpekty 86 48.45 N 82.24 E
Kokrajhar 124 26.24 N 90.16 E
Kokrines 180 64.56 N 154.42 W
Kokrines Hills ⩓[2] 180 65.15 N 154.00 W
Koksa ≃ 86 50.16 N 85.36 E
Kokšaalatau, chrebet ⩓ 72 41.00 N 78.00 E
Koksan 98 38.46 N 126.40 E
Koksaraj 85 42.40 N 68.08 E
Kokšekol', ozero ⊜ 86 46.05 N 62.00 E
Koksijde 50 51.07 N 2.38 E
Koksilah 224 48.40 N 123.38 W
Koksilah ≃ 224 48.45 N 123.39 W
Koksoak ≃ 176 58.32 N 68.10 W
Koksŏng 98 35.17 N 127.17 E
Koksovyj 78 48.12 N 40.39 E
Kokstad 158 30.32 S 29.29 E
Koksu, S.S.S.R. 85 41.27 N 68.01 E
Koksu, S.S.S.R. 86 44.59 N 77.56 E
Koktal 86 44.09 N 79.48 E
Kok-Taš, S.S.S.R. 85 41.12 N 72.25 E
Koktas, S.S.S.R. 86 47.33 N 70.55 E
Koktas, S.S.S.R. 86 45.59 N 73.32 E
Kokterek 80 49.25 N 49.15 E
Koktubek 86 48.07 N 56.51 E
Kokubu, Nihon 92 31.44 N 130.46 E
Kokubu, Nihon 96 34.56 N 132.07 E
Kokubunji, Nihon 94 36.22 N 139.51 E
Kokubunji, Nihon 96 34.18 N 133.58 E
Kokubunji, Nihon 268 35.42 N 139.29 E
Kokubunji Temple ʊ[1] 268 35.44 N 139.55 E
Kokufu 96 35.28 N 134.16 E
Kokuj 88 52.13 N 117.33 E
Kokujbel' ≃ 85 38.21 N 72.46 E
Kokžar 86 49.01 N 60.10 E
Kol ≃ 128 26.59 N 55.47 E
Kola, Indon. 164 5.26 S 134.29 E
Kola, S.S.S.R. 24 68.53 N 33.01 E
Kola ≃ 24 68.53 N 33.02 E
Kolāba □[5] 272c 18.56 N 73.07 E
Kolachel 122 8.10 N 77.15 E
Kolāchi ≃ 120 27.08 N 67.02 E
Kol'adovka 83 49.05 N 39.12 E
Kolageran 84 40.58 N 44.37 E
Kolahun 150 8.24 N 10.02 W
Kolaka 112 4.03 S 121.36 E
Kolambo 152 7.34 S 21.58 E
Kolambugan 116 8.07 N 123.55 E
Kola Peninsula → Kol'skij poluostrov ≻[1] 24 67.30 N 37.00 E
Kolār 122 13.08 N 78.08 E
Kolāras 124 25.14 N 77.36 E
Kolār Gold Fields 122 12.55 N 78.17 E
Kolari 24 67.20 N 23.48 E
Kolarovgrad → Šumen 38 43.16 N 26.55 E
Kolárovo 30 47.52 N 18.02 E
Kolašin 38 42.49 N 19.31 E
Kolāyat 120 27.50 N 72.57 E
Kolbači 89 54.22 N 123.02 E
Kolbäck 40 59.34 N 16.15 E
Kolbäcksån ≃ 40 59.32 N 16.16 E
Kol'baj, gora ∧[2] 86 43.43 N 53.57 E
Kolbano 112 10.02 S 124.31 E
Kolbasna 78 47.47 N 29.13 E
Kolbča 76 53.39 N 29.14 E
Kolberg → Kołobrzeg 30 54.12 N 15.33 E
Kolbermoor 64 47.51 N 12.04 E
Kolbio 144 1.10 S 41.15 E
Kolbnitz 64 46.52 N 13.19 E
Kolbotn 26 59.49 N 10.48 E
Kolbuszowa 30 50.15 N 21.47 E
Kolby Kås 41 55.48 N 10.33 E
Kolchida ≚ 84 42.15 N 42.00 E
Kolchozabad 120 37.27 N 68.31 E
Kol'covo 82 54.27 N 36.40 E
Kol'čuga 82 55.43 N 37.12 E
Kol'čugino 80 56.18 N 39.23 E
Kołczewo 54 53.58 N 14.38 E
Kolda 150 12.53 N 14.57 W
Kolding 41 55.31 N 9.29 E
Kolding Fjord c 41 55.30 N 9.35 E
Kole, Zaïre 152 3.27 S 22.29 E
Kole, Zaïre 154 2.07 N 25.26 E
Kolea 34 36.38 N 2.46 E
Kolebira 124 22.43 N 84.42 E
Kole Kalyan ◆[8] 272c 19.06 N 72.51 E
Kolenfeld 52 52.24 N 9.27 E
Koleno 80 51.52 N 44.07 E
Kolenté 150 10.06 N 12.37 W
Kolenté (Great Scarcies) ≃ 150 8.55 N 13.08 W
Kolga 76 59.32 N 25.42 E
Kolgujev, ostrov I 24 69.05 N 49.15 E
Kolhāpur, India 122 16.06 N 78.16 E
Kolhāpur, India 122 16.42 N 74.13 E
Kolho 26 62.08 N 24.31 E
Koli 76 59.30 N 34.30 E
Koli ∧[2] 26 63.06 N 29.48 E
Koli, Jabal ∧ 140 14.05 N 25.31 E
Kolia 150 9.46 N 6.28 W
Koliba (Corubal) ≃ 150 11.57 N 15.06 W
Koliganek 180 59.48 N 157.25 W
Kolima ⊜ 26 63.16 N 25.50 E
Kolimbine ≃ 150 14.26 N 11.23 W
Kolín 30 50.01 N 15.13 E
Kolka 76 57.45 N 22.35 E
Kølkær 41 56.04 N 9.06 E
Kolkasrags ≻ 76 57.47 N 22.36 E
Kolki, S.S.S.R. 78 51.37 N 26.37 E
Kolki, S.S.S.R. 78 51.07 N 25.41 E
Kolkwitz 54 51.45 N 14.15 E
Kollbach ≃ 60 48.36 N 12.58 E
Kölleda 54 51.11 N 11.15 E
Kollegāl 122 12.09 N 77.07 E
Kolleru Lake ⊜ 122 16.39 N 81.13 E
Kollum 52 53.16 N 6.09 E
Kollund 41 54.51 N 9.27 E
Kolmanskop 156 26.40 S 15.12 E
Kolmården 40 58.40 N 16.23 E
Kolmården ⩓[2] 40 58.41 N 16.35 E
Kolmårdens Djurpark ♦ 40 58.40 N 16.29 E
Kolmogorovo 86 59.15 N 91.20 E
Köln (Cologne) 56 50.56 N 6.59 E
Köln □[5] 56 50.55 N 6.40 E
Köln-Bonn, Flughafen ⊠ 56 50.50 N 7.10 E
Kolno 30 53.25 N 21.56 E
Kolo, Niger 150 13.14 N 2.20 E
Koło, Pol. 30 52.12 N 18.38 E
Kolo, Tan. 154 4.44 S 35.50 E
Koloa 229b 21.54 N 159.28 W
Kolobovo 80 56.42 N 41.21 E
Kołobrzeg 30 54.12 N 15.33 E
Koloč' ≃ 82 55.34 N 35.52 E
Kolochau 54 51.44 N 13.16 E
Kolodn'a 76 54.48 N 32.09 E
Kologriv 76 58.51 N 44.17 E
Kologrivovka 80 51.44 N 45.20 E
Kolojar 80 52.34 N 46.58 E
Kolok (Golok) ≃ 114 6.15 N 102.05 E
Kolokani 150 13.35 N 8.02 W
Koloko 150 11.05 N 5.19 W
Kolokol'covka, S.S.S.R. 80 52.36 N 49.48 E
Kolokol'covka, S.S.S.R. 80 51.12 N 44.36 E
Kololo 144 7.29 N 41.58 E
Kolom'agi ◆[8] 265a 60.00 N 30.17 E
Kolom'agi Airport ⊠ 265a 60.01 N 30.17 E
Kolomak 78 49.50 N 35.18 E
Kolombangara Island I 175e 8.00 S 157.05 E
Kolomea → Kolomyja 78 48.32 N 25.04 E
Kolomenka ≃ 82 55.06 N 38.46 E
Kolomenskaja Sloboda 82 54.22 N 38.15 E
Kolomenskoje ◆[8] 265b 55.40 N 37.41 E
Kolomna 82 55.05 N 38.49 E
Kolomyja 78 48.32 N 25.04 E
Kolondiéba 150 11.05 N 6.54 W
Kolonga 174w 21.08 S 175.04 W
Kolonia 174r 6.58 N 158.13 E
Kolonie Stolp 264a 52.28 N 13.46 E
Kolono 112 4.18 S 122.41 E
Kolonodale 112 2.00 S 121.19 E
Kolora 272b 22.55 N 88.22 E
Kolosib 120 24.14 N 92.42 E
Kol'osnoje 78 46.02 N 29.56 E
Kolosovka 86 56.28 N 73.36 E
Kolovai 174w 21.06 S 175.20 W
Kolovertnoje 80 50.36 N 51.06 E
Kolowana Watobo, Teluk c 112 5.00 S 123.06 E
Kolozsvár → Cluj-Napoca 38 46.47 N 23.36 E
Kolp' ≃ 76 59.20 N 36.49 E
Kolpaševo 86 58.20 N 82.50 E
Kolpino 76 59.45 N 30.36 E
Kölpinsee ⊜ 54 53.30 N 12.34 E
Kolpny 76 52.15 N 37.02 E
Kölsa 54 51.28 N 12.13 E
Kol'skij poluostrov (Kola Peninsula) ≻[1] 24 67.30 N 37.00 E
Kolsnaren ⊜ 40 59.02 N 16.01 E
Kolsva 40 59.36 N 15.50 E
Kol'togan 85 43.51 N 67.25 E
Koltovskaja 80 52.47 N 44.16 E
Koltubanovskij 80 52.57 N 52.02 E
Koltuši 265a 59.56 N 30.40 E
Kol'ubakino 82 55.40 N 36.32 E
Kolubara ≃ 38 44.40 N 20.15 E
Kol'učinskaja guba c 180 66.40 N 174.30 W
Koluel Kayke 254 46.43 S 68.14 W
Kölük 130 37.46 N 38.36 E
Kolumbien → Colombia □[1] 246 4.00 N 72.00 W
Kol'upanovo 82 54.26 N 36.14 E
Koluškino 78 48.39 N 40.56 E
Koluszki 30 51.44 N 19.49 E
Koluton 86 51.43 N 69.25 E
Koluton ≃ 86 51.42 N 69.10 E
Kolva ≃ 24 65.55 N 57.15 E
Kolvereid 24 64.51 N 11.32 E
Kølvrå 41 56.18 N 9.08 E
Kolwezi 154 10.43 S 25.28 E
Kolyberovo 82 55.16 N 38.44 E
Kolyčevo 82 55.30 N 37.52 E
Kolyma ≃ 74 69.30 N 161.00 W
Kolymskaja 74 68.44 N 158.44 E
Kolymskaja nizmennost' ≚ 74 68.30 N 154.00 E
Kolyšlej 80 52.42 N 44.32 E
Kolyšovo 82 54.54 N 36.57 E
Kolyvan', S.S.S.R. 86 51.18 N 82.34 E
Kolyvan', S.S.S.R. 86 55.18 N 82.45 E
Kom → Qom 128 34.39 N 50.54 E
Kom ∧ 38 43.10 N 23.03 E
Kom ≃ 152 2.18 N 11.40 E
Koma, Ityo. 144 8.27 N 36.52 E
Koma, Mya. 110 15.39 N 98.12 E
Koma, S.S.S.R. 86 55.02 N 91.19 E
Koma ≃ 94 35.59 N 139.26 E
Komadougou Yobé (Komadugu Yobe) ≃ 146 13.43 N 13.20 E
Komadugu Gana ≃ 146 13.05 N 12.24 E
Komadugu Yobe (Komadougou Yobé) ≃ 146 13.43 N 13.20 E
Komae 94 35.38 N 139.35 E
Komagane 94 35.43 N 137.55 E
Komaga-take ∧, Nihon 92a 42.04 N 140.41 E
Komaga-take ∧, Nihon 94 35.45 N 138.14 E
Komaga-take ∧, Nihon 94 35.47 N 137.48 E
Komagome ◆[8] 268 35.44 N 139.45 E
Komaki 94 35.17 N 136.55 E
Komandorskije ostrova II 74 55.00 N 167.00 E
Komandorski Village 226 37.43 N 121.54 W
Komariči 76 52.27 N 34.47 E
Komarin 78 51.26 N 30.31 E
Komarniki 78 49.00 N 23.04 E
Komárno, Česko. 30 47.45 N 18.09 E
Komarno, S.S.S.R. 78 49.38 N 23.42 E
Komárom 30 47.44 N 18.08 E
Komárom □[6] 30 47.40 N 18.15 E
Komarovka 78 51.14 N 32.07 E
Komarovo 76 58.39 N 33.26 E
Komarovy 86 60.26 N 75.50 E
Komati (Incomáti) ≃ 156 25.46 S 32.43 E
Komatipoort 156 25.25 S 31.55 E
Komatsu, Nihon 94 36.24 N 136.27 E
Komatsu, Nihon 96 33.53 N 133.07 E
Komatsu-kūkō ⊠ 94 36.24 N 136.26 E
Komatsushima 96 34.00 N 134.35 E
Kombissiri 150 12.04 N 1.20 W
Kombone 152 4.37 N 9.19 E
Komdhārā 272b 22.53 N 88.14 E
Kome Island I 154 0.06 S 32.45 E
Komen 64 45.49 N 13.44 E
Komenda 150 5.03 N 1.29 W
Komenoi 268 35.55 N 140.01 E
Komering ≃ 112 2.59 S 104.50 E
Komeshia 154 8.01 S 27.07 E
Komfane 164 5.39 S 134.44 E
Komga 158 32.35 S 27.55 E
Kominato → Amatsu-kominato 94 35.07 N 140.10 E
Kominternovskoje 78 46.49 N 30.56 E
Komin Yanga 150 11.42 N 0.08 E
Komi-Perm'ackij Nacional'nyj Okrug □[8] 24 60.00 N 54.30 E
Komissarovka, S.S.S.R. 83 48.23 N 38.32 E
Komissarovka, S.S.S.R. 83 48.07 N 40.09 E
Komissarovo 89 44.59 N 131.46 E
Komissarovskij 80 47.29 N 42.59 E
Komkans 158 31.16 S 18.09 E
Komló 30 46.12 N 18.16 E
Kommadagga 158 33.09 S 25.55 E
Kommandodrif 158 27.30 S 26.14 E
Kommandokraal 158 33.06 S 22.51 E
Kommetjie 158 34.08 S 18.21 E
Kommunal'naja 88 52.03 N 115.06 E
Kommunar, S.S.S.R. 80 58.10 N 43.33 E
Kommunar, S.S.S.R. 86 54.20 N 89.18 E
Kommunarka 265b 55.34 N 37.29 E
Kommunarsk 83 48.30 N 38.47 E
Kommunary 26 60.54 N 29.47 E
Kommunizma, pik ∧ 85 38.57 N 72.01 E
Komo ≃ 152 0.09 N 9.50 E
Komodo 115b 8.35 S 119.30 E
Komodo, Pulau I 115b 8.36 S 119.30 E
Komoé ≃ 150 5.12 N 3.44 W
Komoé, Parc National de la ♦ 150 9.00 N 3.30 W
Komoka 214 42.57 N 81.26 W
Komono, Congo 152 3.15 S 13.14 E
Komono, Nihon 94 35.00 N 136.31 E
Komoran, Pulau I 164 8.18 S 138.45 E
Komoren → Comoros □[1] 157a 12.10 S 44.10 E
Komorin, Kap → Comorin, Cape ≻ 122 8.04 N 77.34 E
Komorn → Komárno 30 47.45 N 18.09 E
Komoro 94 36.19 N 138.26 E
Komotau → Chomutov 54 50.28 N 13.26 E
Komotiní 38 41.08 N 25.25 E
Kompanejevka 78 48.15 N 32.12 E
Kompasberg ∧ 158 31.45 S 24.32 E
Kompiam 164 5.20 S 143.55 E
Kompot 112 0.24 N 124.10 E
Komrat 78 46.18 N 28.38 E
Komsomolabad 85 38.52 N 69.57 E
Komsomolec 86 53.45 N 62.02 E
Komsomolec, ostrov I 74 80.30 N 95.00 E
Komsomolec, zaliv c 72 45.30 N 52.45 E
Komsomol'sk, S.S.S.R. 80 57.02 N 40.21 E
Komsomol'sk, S.S.S.R. 86 55.38 N 88.11 E
Komsomol'sk, S.S.S.R. 86 57.27 N 86.02 E
Komsomol'sk, S.S.S.R. 128 39.02 N 63.36 E
Komsomol'skij, S.S.S.R. 80 54.27 N 45.49 E
Komsomol'skij, S.S.S.R. 83 47.40 N 37.26 E
Komsomol'skij, S.S.S.R. 86 51.40 N 66.39 E
Komsomol'skij, S.S.S.R. 86 47.20 N 53.42 E
Komsomol'skij, S.S.S.R. 89 50.22 N 142.10 E
Komsomol'sk-Na-Amure 89 50.35 N 137.02 E
Komsomol'sk-Na-Ust'urte 86 44.03 N 58.20 E
Komsomol'skoje, S.S.S.R. 78 49.35 N 36.30 E
Komsomol'skoje, S.S.S.R. 78 49.43 N 28.40 E
Komsomol'skoje, S.S.S.R. 80 55.16 N 47.33 E
Komsomol'skoje, S.S.S.R. 80 50.46 N 47.03 E
Komsomol'skoje, S.S.S.R. 83 47.40 N 38.05 E
Komsomol'skoje, S.S.S.R. 88 52.29 N 111.06 E
Komsomol'skoj Pravdy, ostrova II 74 77.20 N 107.40 E
Kŏmun-do I 98 34.02 N 127.19 E
Kömürcüpınar 267b 41.15 N 28.51 E
Komusan 98 42.08 N 129.41 E
Komyšn'a 78 50.12 N 33.41 E
Kona, India 272b 22.37 N 88.18 E
Kona, Mali 150 14.57 N 3.53 W
Kona Coast ±[2] 229d 19.25 N 155.55 W
Konagkend 84 41.04 N 48.37 E
Konakovo 82 56.42 N 36.46 E
Konakpınar 130 39.26 N 27.53 E
Konan → Hŭngnam, C.M.I.K. 98 39.50 N 127.38 E
Konan, C. Iv. 150 8.21 N 8.00 W
Kōnan, Nihon 94 35.20 N 136.53 E
Kōnan, Nihon 94 34.56 N 136.11 E
Kōnan ◆[8] 268 35.22 N 139.35 E
Konar (Kunar) ≃ 123 34.25 N 70.32 E
Konārak 120 19.54 N 86.07 E
Konār Dam ◆[6] 124 23.58 N 85.45 E
Konar-e Khāṣ 120 34.39 N 70.54 E
Konarha □[4] 120 35.15 N 71.00 E
Konawa 196 34.57 N 96.45 W
Končanskoje-Suvorovskoje 76 58.39 N 34.04 E
Konceba 78 48.07 N 29.56 E
Konch 124 25.59 N 79.09 E
Konda 74 61.20 N 63.58 E
Konda ≃, S.S.S.R. 86 60.40 N 69.46 E
Konda ≃, S.S.S.R. 88 53.30 N 113.32 E
Kondagaon 122 19.36 N 81.40 E
Konde 154 4.57 S 39.45 E
Kondega 76 60.14 N 33.30 E
Kondiaronk, Lac ⊜ 190 46.56 N 76.45 W
Kondinin 162 32.30 S 118.16 E
Kondinskoje 86 59.40 N 67.22 E
Kondli ◆[8] 272a 28.37 N 77.19 E
Kondoa 154 4.54 S 35.47 E
Kondol' 80 52.49 N 45.03 E
Kondolole 154 1.20 N 25.58 E
Kondopoga 24 62.12 N 34.17 E
Kondorfa 61 46.54 N 16.24 E
Kondratjevo, S.S.S.R. 76 60.38 N 28.08 E
Kondratjevo, S.S.S.R. 88 57.21 N 98.11 E
Kondrovka 80 54.36 N 43.17 E
Kondrovo 82 54.48 N 35.56 E
Konduga 146 11.39 N 13.24 E
Kondurča ≃ 80 53.31 N 50.24 E
Koné 175f 21.04 S 164.52 E
Koné, Passe de)(175f 21.08 S 164.41 E
Konecbor 24 64.52 N 57.44 E
Konergino 180 65.54 N 178.50 W
Konfara 150 11.55 N 8.50 W
Kong, C. Iv. 150 9.09 N 4.37 W
Køng, Dan. 41 55.07 N 11.50 E
Kông ≃ 110 13.32 N 105.58 E
Kông, Kaôh I 110 11.20 N 103.00 E
Kongakut ≃ 180 69.48 N 141.50 W
Kongbo 152 4.44 N 21.23 E
Kongcheng 100 31.02 N 117.05 E
Kongeå ≃ 41 55.23 N 8.40 E
Kongens Lyngby 41 55.46 N 12.31 E
Kongfang 100 27.58 N 116.53 E
Kongiganak 180 59.58 N 162.45 W
Konginkangas 26 62.46 N 25.48 E
Kongjiamatou 105 39.07 N 116.10 E
Kongjiatun 104 40.42 N 124.04 E
Kongjiawopeng 89 43.58 N 122.41 E
Kongjiazhuang 105 40.47 N 114.48 E
Kongju 98 36.27 N 127.07 E
Konglong 100 29.56 N 115.54 E
Konglongshan 105 40.33 N 117.17 E
Konglu 102 27.16 N 97.56 E
Kongmoon → Jiangmen 100 22.35 N 113.05 E
Kongo → Congo ≃ 138 6.04 S 12.24 E
Kongo, Republik → Zaire □[1] 138 4.00 S 25.00 E
Kongō-Ikoma-kokutei-kōen ♦ 96 34.28 N 135.40 E
Kongolo, Zaïre 154 5.26 S 24.49 E
Kongolo, Zaïre 154 5.23 S 27.00 E
Kongor 140 7.10 N 31.21 E
Kongō-sanchi ⩓ 270 34.27 N 135.41 E
Kongoussi 150 13.19 N 1.32 W
Kongō-zan ∧ 96 34.25 N 135.41 E
Kongsberg 26 59.39 N 9.39 E
Kongsvinger 26 60.12 N 12.00 E
Kongsvoll 26 62.18 N 9.37 E
Kongsvoll-Hjerkinn Nasjonalpark ♦ 26 62.15 N 9.35 E
Kongtan 107 29.10 N 104.42 E
Kongur Shan ∧ 85 38.37 N 75.20 E
Kongwa 154 6.12 S 36.25 E
Kongyangcun 106 31.23 N 118.54 E
Kongzhen 106 31.29 N 119.00 E
Koni 154 10.42 S 27.15 E
Koni ≃ 150 13.05 N 5.37 W
Koniakari 150 14.34 N 10.54 W
Konice 30 49.35 N 16.53 E
Koniecpol 30 50.48 N 19.41 E
Königgrätz → Hradec Králové 30 50.12 N 15.50 E
Königheim 56 49.37 N 9.35 E
Königin Alexandra-Kette → Queen Alexandra Range ⩓ 9 84.00 S 168.00 E
Königin Fabiola-Gebirge → Queen Fabiola Mountains ⩓ 9 71.30 S 35.40 E
Königin Mary-Küste → Queen Mary Coast ±[2] 9 67.00 S 96.00 E
Königin Maud-Land → Queen Maud Land ◆[1] 9 72.30 S 12.00 E
König-Otto-Höhle ±[5] 60 49.15 N 11.42 E
Königsbach 56 48.58 N 8.36 E
Königsberg, B.R.D. 56 50.05 N 10.34 E
Königsberg → Chojna, Pol. 30 52.58 N 14.28 E
Königsberg → Kaliningrad, S.S.S.R. 76 54.43 N 20.30 E
Königsborn 263 51.33 N 7.41 E
Königsbrück 54 51.16 N 13.54 E
Königsbrunn, B.R.D. 58 48.16 N 10.53 E
Königsbrunn, Öst. 264b 48.21 N 16.25 E
Königsdorf 64 47.49 N 11.28 E
Königsee 54 50.39 N 11.05 E
Königsfelden ʊ[1] 58 47.29 N 8.14 E
Königsfeld im Schwarzwald 58 48.08 N 8.25 E
Königshain 54 51.11 N 14.52 E
Königshardt ◆[8] 263 51.33 N 6.51 E
Königsheim 58 48.06 N 8.51 E
Königslutter 54 52.15 N 10.49 E
Königsmoor ◆[3] 52 53.15 N 9.40 E
Königssee 64 47.33 N 12.58 E
Königssee ⊜ 64 47.36 N 12.59 E
Königsstuhl ±[4] 54 54.34 N 13.40 E
Königstein, B.R.D. 56 50.11 N 8.29 E
Königstein, B.R.D. 60 49.37 N 11.38 E
Königstein, D.D.R. 54 50.55 N 14.04 E
Königstetten 264b 48.18 N 16.09 E
Königswalde 54 50.33 N 13.02 E
Königswartha 54 51.18 N 14.20 E
Königswiesen 61 48.24 N 14.50 E
Königswinter 56 50.40 N 7.11 E
Königs Wusterhausen 54 52.18 N 13.37 E
Konin 30 52.13 N 18.16 E
Konin □[4] 30 52.20 N 18.20 E
Konispol 38 39.39 N 20.10 E
Kónitsa 38 40.02 N 20.45 E
Köniz 58 46.56 N 7.25 E
Konjic 38 43.39 N 17.57 E
Konka ≃ 78 47.40 N 35.22 E
Könkämäälven ≃ 24 68.29 N 22.17 E
Konkapot ≃ 210 42.03 N 73.20 W
Konkiep ≃ 156 28.03 S 17.21 E
Konkō 96 34.32 N 133.37 E
Kon'-Kolodez' 76 52.08 N 39.11 E
Konkouré ≃ 150 9.58 N 13.42 W
Kon'kovo 83 47.20 N 38.10 E
Konkudera 88 57.33 N 112.30 E
Konkug University ʊ[2] 271b 37.32 N 127.05 E
Konnagar 126 22.42 N 88.22 E
Könnern 54 51.40 N 11.46 E
Konnevesi ⊜ 26 62.40 N 26.35 E
Konnur 122 16.12 N 74.45 E
Kōno 94 35.49 N 136.04 E
Konobejevo 82 55.24 N 38.40 E
Konohana ◆[8] 270 34.41 N 135.26 E
Kōnoike 270 34.42 N 135.37 E
Konolfingen 58 46.53 N 7.38 E
Konongo 150 6.37 N 1.11 W
Konoša 24 60.58 N 40.15 E
Kōno-shima I 96 34.28 N 133.31 E
Kōnosu 94 36.03 N 139.31 E
Konotop 78 51.14 N 33.12 E
Konovalovka 80 53.06 N 51.34 E
Kon'ovo, S.S.S.R. 24 62.08 N 39.16 E
Kon'ovo, S.S.S.R. 86 56.18 N 70.43 E
Konqi ≃ 90 40.40 N 90.10 E
Konradshöhe ◆[8] 264a 52.35 N 13.14 E
Konradsreuth 54 50.16 N 11.50 E
Konsankoro 150 9.02 N 9.00 W
Konsen-daichi ⩓[1] 92a 43.25 N 144.52 E
Końskie 30 51.12 N 20.26 E
Konstabel 158 33.16 S 20.17 E
Konstadt → Wołczyn 30 51.01 N 18.03 E
Konstantinopel → İstanbul 130 41.01 N 28.58 E
Konstantinovka, S.S.S.R. 78 49.57 N 35.07 E
Konstantinovka, S.S.S.R. 78 47.51 N 31.09 E
Konstantinovka, S.S.S.R. 80 56.41 N 50.53 E
Konstantinovka, S.S.S.R. 83 48.32 N 37.43 E
Konstantinovka, S.S.S.R. 83 47.52 N 37.24 E
Konstantinovka, S.S.S.R. 265a 59.47 N 30.08 E
Konstantinovo 82 56.33 N 38.02 E
Konstantinovsk 80 47.35 N 41.06 E
Konstantinovskij 76 57.50 N 39.36 E
Konstantinovskije Porogi 76 60.34 N 37.04 E
Konstantynów Łódzki 30 51.45 N 19.20 E
Konstanz 58 47.40 N 9.10 E
Kontagora 150 10.24 N 5.28 E
Kontcha 152 7.58 N 12.14 E
Kontejevo 80 58.26 N 41.21 E
Kontha 110 19.30 N 96.03 E
Kontich 50 51.08 N 4.27 E
Kontiolahti 26 62.46 N 29.51 E
Kontiomäki 26 64.21 N 28.09 E
Konto 115a 7.46 S 112.19 E
Kontum 110 14.21 N 108.00 E
Kontum, Plateau du ⩓[1] 110 13.55 N 108.05 E
Kōnu 96 34.42 N 133.05 E
Kon'uchovo 86 55.08 N 70.38 E
Konus, gora ∧ 180 67.34 N 178.10 E
Konya 130 37.52 N 32.31 E
Konya □[4] 130 38.00 N 33.00 E
Konyr 80 50.25 N 53.25 E
Konyrat 80 49.36 N 47.01 E
Konyrolen 86 44.16 N 79.19 E
Konyševka 78 51.51 N 35.18 E
Konystanu 80 48.51 N 53.20 E
Konz 56 49.42 N 6.34 E
Konza 154 1.45 S 37.07 E
Konžakovskij Kamen', gora ∧ 86 59.38 N 59.08 E
Konzell 60 49.04 N 12.43 E
Koocanusa, Lake ⊜[1] 202 49.00 N 115.10 W
Koog [aan de Zaan] 52 52.27 N 4.49 E
Kookynie 162 29.20 S 121.29 E
Koolamarra 166 20.12 S 140.14 E
Koolatah 164 15.53 S 142.27 E
Koolau Range ⩓ 229c 21.35 N 158.00 W
Kooloonong 166 34.53 S 143.09 E
Koolskamp 50 51.00 N 3.12 E
Koolyanobbing 162 30.50 S 119.35 E
Koolywurtie 168b 34.38 S 137.37 E
Koombana Bay c 168a 33.18 S 115.36 E
Koonap ≃ 158 33.03 S 26.39 E
Koondrook 166 35.39 S 144.08 E
Koonga 76 58.35 N 24.12 E
Koonibba 162 31.58 S 133.27 E
Koontz Lake 216 41.25 N 86.29 W
Koontz Lake ⊜ 216 41.25 N 86.28 W
Koopan-Noord 158 26.53 S 20.41 E
Koopan-Suid 158 27.15 S 20.22 E
Koopmansfontein 158 28.14 S 24.01 E
Koorawatha 166 34.02 S 148.33 E
Koorda 162 30.50 S 117.29 E
Koosa 76 58.33 N 27.07 E
Koosfontein 158 27.22 S 25.27 E
Koosharem 200 38.30 N 111.52 W
Kooskia 202 46.08 N 115.58 W
Koossa 150 9.32 N 8.32 W
Kootenai (Kootenay) ≃ 182 49.15 N 117.39 W
Kootenay (Kootenai) ≃ 182 49.15 N 117.39 W
Kootenay Indian Reserve ◆[4] 182 49.37 N 115.45 W
Kootenay Lake ⊜ 182 49.35 N 116.50 W
Kootenay National Park ♦ 182 51.00 N 116.00 W
Kootjieskolk 158 31.15 S 20.21 E
Kootwijk 52 52.12 N 5.45 E
Koo-Wee-Rup 169 38.12 S 145.30 E
Kooyong 274b 37.50 S 145.02 E
Kopa 85 43.32 N 75.50 E
Kopa ≃ 85 43.40 N 76.15 E
Kopāganj 124 26.01 N 83.34 E
Kopāi ≃ 126 23.48 N 87.47 E
Kopajgorod 78 48.51 N 27.48 E
Kopanbulak 86 48.56 N 80.52 E
Kopang 115b 8.39 S 116.21 E
Kopanovka 80 47.27 N 46.48 E
Kopanskaja 78 46.17 N 38.29 E
Kopapan 80 50.20 N 50.26 E
Kopargaon 122 19.53 N 74.29 E
Koparkhairna 272c 19.06 N 72.59 E
Koparpāda 272c 19.02 N 73.04 E
Kópasker 24a 66.20 N 16.24 W
Kopatkeviči 76 52.19 N 28.49 E
Kópavogur 24a 64.06 N 21.50 W
Kopceviči 78 52.14 N 28.19 E
Kopdağı Geçidi)(130 40.03 N 40.33 E
Kopé, Mont ∧[2] 150 4.59 N 7.27 W
Kopejsk 86 55.07 N 61.37 E

Symbols in the index entries represent the broad categories identified in the key at the right. Symbols with superior numbers (⩓[1]) identify subcategories (see complete key on page I · 1).

Kartensymbole in dem Registerverzeichnis stellen die rechts in Schlüssel erklärten Kategorien dar. Symbole mit hochgestellten Ziffern (⩓[1]) bezeichnen Unterabteilungen einer Kategorie (vgl. vollständiger Schlüssel auf Seite I · 1).

Los símbolos incluídos en el texto del índice representan las grandes categorias identificadas con la clave a la derecha. Los símbolos con numeros en su parte superior (⩓[1]) identifican las subcategorias (véase la clave completa en la página I · 1).

Les symboles de l'index représentent les catégories indiquées dans la légende à droite. Les symboles suivis d'un indice (⩓[1]) représentent des sous-catégories (voir légende complète à la page I · 1).

Os símbolos incluídos no texto do índice representam as grandes categorias identificadas com a chave à direita. Os símbolos com números em sua parte superior (⩓[1]) identificam as subcategorias (veja-se a chave completa à página I · 1).

∧ Mountain	Berg	Montaña	Montagne	Montanha
⩓ Mountains	Berge	Montañas	Montagnes	Montanhas
)(Pass	Pass	Paso	Col	Passo
V Valley, Canyon	Tal, Cañon	Valle, Cañón	Vallée, Canyon	Vale, Canhão
≚ Plain	Ebene	Llano	Plaine	Planície
≻ Cape	Kap	Cabo	Cap	Cabo
I Island	Insel	Isla	Île	Ilha
II Islands	Inseln	Islas	Îles	Ilhas
± Other Topographic Features	Andere Topographische Objekte	Otros Elementos Topográficos	Autres données topographiques	Outros acidentes topográficos

ESPAÑOL — Nombre / Página / Lat.°′ / Long.°′ W = Oeste
FRANÇAIS — Nom / Page / Lat.°′ / Long.°′ W = Ouest
PORTUGUÊS — Nome / Página / Lat.°′ / Long.°′ W = Oeste

Symbol	English	Deutsch	Español	Français	Português
≃	River	Fluss	Río	Rivière	Rio
≅	Canal	Kanal	Canal	Canal	Canal
∟	Waterfall, Rapids	Wasserfall, Stromschnellen	Cascada, Rápidos	Chute d'eau, Rapides	Cascata, Rápidos
⋓	Strait	Meeresstrasse	Estrecho	Détroit	Estreito
c	Bay, Gulf	Bucht, Golf	Bahía, Golfo	Baie, Golfe	Baía, Golfo
⊜	Lake, Lakes	See, Seen	Lago, Lagos	Lac, Lacs	Lago, Lagos
⌗	Swamp	Sumpf	Pantano	Marais	Pântano
⍓	Ice Features, Glacier	Eis- und Gletscherformen	Accidentes Glaciales	Formes glaciaires	Acidentes glaciares
⊤	Other Hydrographic Features	Andere Hydrographische Objekte	Otros Elementos Hidrográficos	Autres données hydrographiques	Outros acidentes hidrográficos
✢	Submarine Features	Untermeerische Objekte	Accidentes Submarinos	Formes de relief sous-marin	Acidentes submarinos
□	Political Unit	Politische Einheit	Unidad Política	Entité politique	Unidade política
⚜	Cultural Institution	Kulturelle Institution	Institución Cultural	Institution culturelle	Instituição cultural
⊥	Historical Site	Historische Stätte	Sitio Histórico	Site historique	Sitio histórico
♠	Recreational Site	Erholungs- und Ferienort	Sitio de Recreo	Centre de loisirs	Area de Lazer
⊠	Airport	Flughafen	Aeropuerto	Aéroport	Aeroporto
■	Military Installation	Militäranlage	Instalación Militar	Installation militaire	Instalação militar
◆	Miscellaneous	Verschiedenes	Misceláneo	Divers	Diversos

Name	Page	Lat.°′	Long.°′
Krasnopolje, S.S.S.R.	78	50.46 N	35.16 E
Krasnorečenskij	89	44.41 N	135.14 E
Krasnoščelje	24	67.21 N	37.02 E
Krasnoščokovo	86	51.40 N	82.45 E
Krasnosel'kup	74	65.41 N	82.28 E
Krasnosel'sk	84	40.36 N	45.21 E
Krasnosel'skoje	78	45.25 N	32.42 E
Krasnosielc	30	53.03 N	21.10 E
Krasnoslobodsk, S.S.S.R.	80	54.26 N	43.48 E
Krasnoslobodsk, S.S.S.R.	80	48.42 N	44.34 E
Krasnotorka	83	48.41 N	37.31 E
Krasnoturansk	86	54.16 N	91.29 E
Krasnoturjinsk	86	59.46 N	60.12 E
Krasnoufimsk	86	56.37 N	57.46 E
Krasnoural'sk	86	58.21 N	60.03 E
Krasnousol'skij	86	53.54 N	56.27 E
Krasnovidovo	80	55.21 N	49.04 E
Krasnovišersk	24	60.23 N	56.59 E
Krasnovka, S.S.S.R.	83	48.47 N	40.07 E
Krasnovka, S.S.S.R.	83	47.24 N	37.26 E
Krasnovodsk	128	40.00 N	53.00 E
Krasnovodsk □[4]	128	39.30 N	55.00 E
Krasnovodskij poluostrov >[1]	128	40.30 N	53.15 E
Krasnovodskij zaliv c	128	39.55 N	53.15 E
Krasnoyarsk → Krasnojarsk	86	56.01 N	92.50 E
Krasnozatonskij	24	61.41 N	50.58 E
Krasnozavodsk	82	56.27 N	38.13 E
Krasnoznamensk	76	54.57 N	22.30 E
Krasnoznamenskij	86	51.03 N	69.30 E
Krasnoz'orskoje	86	53.59 N	79.14 E
Krásný Dvůr	54	50.10 N	13.24 E
Krasnyj, S.S.S.R.	76	54.34 N	31.26 E
Krasnyj, S.S.S.R.	92a	46.15 N	141.15 E
Krasnyj Aul	86	51.03 N	81.02 E
Krasnyj Bazar	84	39.41 N	46.58 E
Krasnyj Bogatyr'	80	56.02 N	41.08 E
Krasnyj Bor, S.S.S.R.	80	55.17 N	43.59 E
Krasnyj Bor, S.S.S.R.	80	55.53 N	53.06 E
Krasnyj Bor, S.S.S.R.	265a	59.41 N	30.41 E
Krasnyj Cholm, S.S.S.R.	76	58.03 N	37.07 E
Krasnyj Cholm, S.S.S.R.	80	54.11 N	40.42 E
Krasnyj Cholm, S.S.S.R.	86	51.35 N	54.09 E
Krasnyj Chuduk	80	46.18 N	46.56 E
Krasnyj Čikoj	88	50.22 N	108.15 E
Krasnyje Baki	80	57.08 N	45.10 E
Krasnyje Barrikady	80	46.14 N	47.53 E
Krasnyje Četai	80	55.42 N	46.09 E
Krasnyje Gory	76	58.57 N	29.29 E
Krasnyje Okny	78	47.32 N	29.27 E
Krasnyje Partizany	78	50.57 N	31.47 E
Krasnyje Tkači	80	57.30 N	39.45 E
Krasnyj Gorodok	76	57.11 N	33.44 E
Krasnyj Gul'aj	80	54.01 N	48.22 E
Krasnyj Jar, S.S.S.R.	80	46.33 N	48.21 E
Krasnyj Jar, S.S.S.R.	80	53.30 N	50.22 E
Krasnyj Jar, S.S.S.R.	80	51.38 N	46.25 E
Krasnyj Jar, S.S.S.R.	80	50.37 N	45.47 E
Krasnyj Jar, S.S.S.R.	80	50.42 N	44.46 E
Krasnyj Jar, S.S.S.R.	86	55.54 N	86.57 E
Krasnyj Jar, S.S.S.R.	86	55.14 N	72.56 E
Krasnyj Jar, S.S.S.R.	86	57.07 N	84.33 E
Krasnyj Jar, S.S.S.R.	86	53.20 N	69.14 E
Krasnyj Kl'ič	86	55.26 N	56.12 E
Krasnyj Kut, S.S.S.R.	80	50.57 N	46.58 E
Krasnyj Kut, S.S.S.R.	83	48.12 N	38.48 E
Krasnyj Liman, S.S.S.R.	78	51.32 N	39.50 E
Krasnyj Liman, S.S.S.R.	83	48.59 N	37.49 E
Krasnyj Log	78	51.23 N	39.46 E
Krasnyj Luč, S.S.S.R.	76	57.04 N	30.05 E
Krasnyj Luč, S.S.S.R.	83	48.08 N	38.56 E
Krasnyj Majak	80	56.03 N	41.23 E
Krasnyj Manyč, S.S.S.R.	80	46.33 N	42.10 E
Krasnyj Manyč, S.S.S.R.	80	45.31 N	44.42 E
Krasnyj Manyč, S.S.S.R.	80	46.59 N	41.07 E
Krasnyj Meliorator	80	50.02 N	46.06 E
Krasnyj Okt'abr', S.S.S.R.	80	51.33 N	45.42 E
Krasnyj Okt'abr', S.S.S.R.	80	56.06 N	41.23 E
Krasnyj Okt'abr', S.S.S.R.	82	56.07 N	38.53 E
Krasnyj Okt'abr', S.S.S.R.	82	55.37 N	36.30 E
Krasnyj Okt'abr', S.S.S.R.	83	48.15 N	38.12 E
Krasnyj Okt'abr', S.S.S.R.	83	48.56 N	39.23 E
Krasnyj Okt'abr', S.S.S.R.	86	55.37 N	64.48 E
Krasnyj Okt'abr', S.S.S.R.	86	46.50 N	75.59 E
Krasnyj Oskol	83	49.11 N	37.26 E
Krasnyj Partizan	80	46.20 N	43.10 E
Krasnyj Perekop	78	46.41 N	33.46 E
Krasnyj Profintern	80	57.45 N	40.27 E
Krasnyj Rog	76	52.57 N	33.45 E
Krasnyj Steklovar	80	56.13 N	48.47 E
Krasnyj Stroitel' ◆[8]	265b	55.35 N	37.37 E
Krasnyj Sulin	83	47.54 N	40.03 E
Krasnyj Tekstil'ščik	80	51.23 N	45.50 E
Krasnyj Tkač	82	55.28 N	39.05 E
Krasnystaw	30	50.59 N	23.10 E
Krasnyy Luch → Krasnyj Luč	83	48.08 N	38.56 E
Krasucha	76	57.23 N	33.12 E
Kras'ukovskaja	83	47.31 N	40.06 E
Kraszna (Crasna) ≃	38	48.09 N	22.20 E
Kratke Range ⩘	164	6.25 S	145.35 E
Kratovo	38	42.05 N	22.11 E
Krauchenwies	58	48.01 N	9.14 E
Kraul Mountains ⩘	9	73.10 S	14.10 W
Krauschwitz	54	51.31 N	14.41 E
Kräuterin ⩘	61	47.41 N	15.05 E
Krautheim	56	49.23 N	9.38 E
Kravaře, Česko.	30	49.56 N	18.01 E
Kravaře, Česko.	54	50.38 N	14.23 E
Krawang	115a	6.19 S	107.17 E
Krawang, Tanjung >	115a	5.56 S	107.00 E
Kray ◆[8]	263	51.28 N	7.05 E
Kražiai	76	55.36 N	22.40 E
Krbava ◆[1]	36	44.40 N	15.35 E
Kreamer Island I	220	26.46 N	80.44 W
Kreba	54	51.20 N	14.40 E
Krebs	196	34.55 N	95.42 W
Krečetovo	24	60.56 N	38.30 E
Krečevicy	76	58.37 N	31.21 E
Krefeld	56	51.20 N	6.34 E
Kregme	41	55.57 N	12.04 E
Kreiensen	52	51.51 N	9.58 E
Kreischa	54	50.56 N	13.45 E
Kreitzer Glacier ⊓	9	70.25 S	72.30 E
Kremastón, Tekhnití Límni ⊜[1]	38	38.55 N	21.30 E
Kremenčug	78	49.04 N	33.25 E
Kremenčugskoje vodochranilišče ⊜[1]	78	49.20 N	32.30 E
Kremenec	78	50.07 N	25.45 E
Kremennaja	83	49.03 N	38.14 E
Kremen'ovka	83	47.20 N	37.29 E
Kremenskoj	80	47.49 N	41.08 E
Kremenskoje	82	55.06 N	35.57 E
Kremlin ʊ	265b	55.45 N	37.37 E
Kremmen	54	52.45 N	13.01 E
Kremmling	200	40.03 N	106.23 W
Kremnica	30	48.43 N	18.54 E
Krempe	52	53.50 N	9.29 E
Krems ≃, Öst.	61	48.25 N	15.36 E
Krems ≃, Öst.	61	48.14 N	14.19 E
Krems an der Donau	61	48.25 N	15.36 E
Kremsbrücke	64	46.57 N	13.37 E
Kremsmünster	61	48.03 N	14.08 E
Krenitzin Islands II	180	54.08 N	166.00 W
Krensitz	54	51.29 N	12.27 E
Krepenskij	83	48.06 N	39.03 E
Krepkaja ≃	83	47.35 N	39.23 E
Krepoljin	38	44.16 N	21.37 E
Kreščhonka	86	55.52 N	80.06 E
Kresgeville	210	40.54 N	75.30 W
Kress	196	34.22 N	101.45 W
Kressbronn	58	47.35 N	9.36 E
Kressey Lake ⊜	285	39.44 N	75.07 W
Kresta, zaliv c	180	66.00 N	179.15 W
Krestcy, S.S.S.R.	76	58.15 N	32.31 E
Krestcy, S.S.S.R.	76	58.23 N	39.00 E
Krestjanskij	85	40.32 N	69.02 E
Krestjanskoje	80	45.34 N	42.56 E
Krest-Major	74	67.37 N	144.45 E
Krestovaja Guba	72	74.07 N	55.33 E
Krestovo-Gorodišče	80	54.10 N	48.36 E
Krestovyj, pereval)(	84	42.32 N	44.28 E
Kresty	82	55.16 N	37.06 E
Kreta → Kríti I	38	35.29 N	24.42 E
Kretek	115a	7.59 S	110.19 E
Kretinga	76	55.53 N	21.13 E
Kreuth	64	47.38 N	11.44 E
Kreuz an der Ostbahn → Krzyż	30	52.54 N	16.01 E
Kreuzau	56	50.45 N	6.29 E
Kreuzberg	263	51.09 N	7.27 E
Kreuzberg ◆[8]	264a	52.30 N	13.23 E
Kreuzberg ∧	56	50.22 N	9.58 E
Kreuzburg → Kluczbork	30	50.59 N	18.13 E
Kreuzeck-Gruppe ⩘	64	46.51 N	13.06 E
Kreuzen	64	46.40 N	13.35 E
Kreuzlingen	58	47.39 N	9.11 E
Kreuznach → Bad Kreuznach	56	49.52 N	7.51 E
Kreuztal	56	50.58 N	7.59 E
Krevo	76	54.19 N	26.17 E
Kreyenhagen	54	52.55 N	10.52 E
Krian	115a	7.24 S	112.35 E
Kría Vrísi	38	40.41 N	22.18 E
Kribi	152	2.57 N	9.55 E
Kričov	76	53.42 N	31.43 E
Kriebstein, Burg ⊥	54	51.02 N	13.00 E
Krieglach	61	47.33 N	15.34 E
Kriel	158	26.16 S	29.14 E
Kriens	58	47.02 N	8.17 E
Krigujgun, mys >	180	65.30 N	171.05 W
Kriljon, mys >	89	45.53 N	142.05 E
Krim → Krymskij poluostrov >[1]	78	45.00 N	34.00 E
Křimice	60	49.46 N	13.15 E
Krim-Krim	146	8.58 N	15.48 E
Krimmler Wasserfälle ˪	64	47.12 N	12.10 E
Krimnicksee ⊜	264a	52.18 N	13.39 E
Krimpen aan de IJssel	52	51.54 N	4.35 E
Krimskij	80	47.39 N	40.44 E
Krinič
no-Lugskoje	83	47.45 N	39.12 E
Kriničk i	78	48.22 N	34.27 E
Kriničnaja	83	48.08 N	38.02 E
Kriničnoje	78	45.32 N	28.40 E
Krishna ≃	122	15.57 N	80.59 E
Krishna, Mouths of the ≃[1]	122	15.43 N	80.55 E
Krishnachaadrapur	126	21.50 N	86.49 E
Krishnagiri	122	12.32 N	78.14 E
Krishnamāti	272b	22.40 N	88.32 E
Krishnanagar, India	126	23.24 N	88.30 E
Krishnanagar, India	126	23.13 N	87.33 E
Krishnapur, Bngl.	126	23.30 N	89.56 E
Krishnapur, India	272b	22.36 N	88.26 E
Krishnarāja Sāgara ⊜[1]	122	12.30 N	76.26 E
Krishnarājpet	122	12.40 N	76.30 E
Krishnarāmpur	126	22.43 N	88.14 E
Kristdala	26	57.24 N	16.11 E
Kristiania → Oslo	26	59.55 N	10.45 E
Kristianopel	26	56.15 N	16.02 E
Kristiansand	26	58.10 N	8.00 E
Kristianstad	26	56.02 N	14.08 E
Kristianstads Län □[6]	26	56.15 N	14.00 E
Kristiansund	26	63.07 N	7.45 E
Kristiinankaupunki → Kristinestad	26	62.17 N	21.23 E
Kristineberg	26	65.04 N	18.35 E
Kristinehamn	40	59.20 N	14.07 E
Kristinestad (Kristiinankau-Punki)	26	62.17 N	21.23 E
Kríti (Crete) I	38	35.29 N	24.42 E
Kritikón Pélagos (Sea of Crete) ⩡[2]	38	35.46 N	23.54 E
Kritzendorf	264b	48.20 N	16.18 E
Kriul'any	78	47.13 N	29.09 E
Kriuša	82	54.28 N	36.24 E
Kriv'ačka	80	58.40 N	45.27 E
Krivaja ≃	38	44.27 N	18.09 E
Krivaja, kosa >[2]	83	47.02 N	38.06 E
Krivaja Ruda	78	49.31 N	32.59 E
Kriv'anskaja	83	47.24 N	40.10 E
Kriva Palanka	38	42.12 N	22.20 E
Krivcy	82	55.28 N	38.12 E
Kriviči	76	54.43 N	27.17 E
Krivinka	86	51.08 N	78.10 E
Krivodol	38	43.23 N	23.29 E
Krivoj Buzan	80	46.31 N	48.33 E
Krivoje Ozero	78	47.56 N	30.21 E
Krivoj Rog	78	47.55 N	33.21 E
Krivoj Torec ≃	83	48.39 N	37.32 E
Křivoklát	60	50.02 N	13.54 E
Krivonosovo	78	49.55 N	39.16 E
Krivorožje, S.S.S.R.	78	48.51 N	40.45 E
Krivorožje, S.S.S.R.	78	48.31 N	38.40 E
Krivorožje, S.S.S.R.	83	48.31 N	38.40 E
Krivošeino	86	57.20 N	83.57 E
Krivošin	76	52.52 N	26.08 E
Krivoy Rog → Krivoj Rog	78	47.55 N	33.21 E
Kriwoi-Rog → Krivoj Rog	78	47.55 N	33.21 E
Križevci	36	46.02 N	16.33 E
Krizskoje	83	49.28 N	39.38 E
Krk, Otok I	36	45.05 N	14.35 E
Krkonošský národní park ♠	30	50.45 N	15.35 E
Krn ∧	64	46.16 N	13.40 E
Krnov	30	50.05 N	17.41 E
Krobia	30	51.47 N	16.58 E
Krøderen ⊜	26	60.15 N	9.38 E
Krogager	41	55.42 N	8.51 E
Krögis	54	51.07 N	13.22 E
Krojanke → Krajenka	30	53.19 N	17.00 E
Krokek	40	58.40 N	16.24 E
Kroken	24	65.22 N	14.20 E
Krokodil ≃, S. Afr.	156	24.12 S	26.52 E
Krokodil ≃, S. Afr.	156	25.26 S	31.58 E
Krokom	26	63.19 N	14.30 E
Krokowa	30	54.48 N	18.11 E
Krolevec	78	51.33 N	33.23 E
Kröller-Müller, Rijksmuseum ʊ	52	52.05 N	5.50 E
Krölpa	54	50.41 N	11.32 E
Krom ≃	158	30.53 S	19.01 E
Krombi Pits	156	19.30 S	25.02 E
Kroměříž	30	49.18 N	17.24 E
Krommenie	52	52.29 N	4.45 E
Krompachy	30	48.56 N	20.52 E
Kromy	76	52.43 N	35.46 E
Kronach	54	50.14 N	11.20 E
Kronberg	56	50.10 N	8.30 E
Kronborg Slot ⊥	41	56.02 N	12.38 E
Krone ◆[8]	263	51.27 N	7.20 E
Krong Ana ⊜[1]	110	12.30 N	108.00 E
Kröng Kaôh Kŏng	110	11.37 N	102.59 E
Kröng Kêb	110	10.29 N	104.19 E
Kronobergs Län □[6]	26	56.40 N	14.40 E
Kronoby (Kruunupyy)	26	63.43 N	23.02 E
Kronockij zaliv c	74	54.12 N	160.36 E
Kronoki	74	54.36 N	161.10 E
Kronshagen	41	54.20 N	10.05 E
Kronstadt → Brașov, Rom.	38	45.39 N	25.37 E
Kronštadt, S.S.S.R.	76	59.59 N	29.45 E
Kronwa	110	15.25 N	98.26 E
Kroondal	158	25.45 S	27.19 E
Kroonstad	158	27.46 S	27.12 E
Kröpelin	54	54.04 N	11.48 E
Kropotkin, S.S.S.R.	72	45.26 N	40.34 E
Kropotkin, S.S.S.R.	88	58.30 N	115.17 E
Kropotkina, gora ∧	88	53.43 N	117.32 E
Kropp	41	54.24 N	9.31 E
Kroppefjäll ∧[2]	26	58.40 N	12.13 E
Kroppenstedt	54	51.56 N	11.18 E
Kropstädt	54	51.58 N	12.44 E
Kropufino	76	60.23 N	39.10 E
Krościenko	30	49.27 N	20.26 E
Kröslin	54	54.07 N	13.45 E
Krošn'a	78	50.18 N	28.39 E
Krośniewice	30	52.16 N	19.10 E
Krosno	30	49.42 N	21.46 E
Krosno □[4]	30	49.30 N	22.00 E
Krosno Odrzańskie	30	52.04 N	15.05 E
Krossen	54	50.58 N	11.59 E
Krostitz	54	51.28 N	12.27 E
Krotoszyn	30	51.42 N	17.26 E
Krotovka	80	53.18 N	51.12 E
Krotovo	86	56.57 N	69.20 E
Krotz Springs	194	30.32 N	91.45 W
Kröv	56	49.59 N	7.05 E
Kroya	115a	7.38 S	109.14 E
Krško	36	45.58 N	15.29 E
Krsy	60	49.54 N	13.03 E
Kr'učkov	80	48.01 N	45.40 E
Kr'učkovo	76	57.03 N	35.34 E
Kruckow	54	53.54 N	13.14 E
Krudenburg	263	51.39 N	6.45 E
Kruenggeukueh	114	5.15 N	97.02 E
Kruengluak	114	2.50 N	97.45 E
Kruft	56	50.23 N	7.20 E
Kruger National Park ♠	156	24.00 S	31.40 E
Krugersdorp	158	26.05 S	27.35 E
Krugersdorp □[5]	273d	26.05 S	27.35 E
Krugersdorp Race Course ♠	273d	26.08 S	27.45 E
Krugersdorp West	273d	26.06 S	27.45 E
Krugloje, S.S.S.R.	76	54.15 N	29.48 E
Krugloje, S.S.S.R.	83	47.01 N	39.15 E
Kruglooz'ornoje	86	55.13 N	79.01 E
Kruglooz'ornyj	80	51.06 N	51.17 E
Kruglyži	80	58.31 N	47.42 E
Krugzell	58	47.47 N	10.16 E
Krui	112	5.11 S	103.56 E
Kruidfontein	158	32.51 S	21.57 E
Kruiningen	52	51.27 N	4.02 E
Kruis, Kaap >	156	21.49 S	13.57 E
Kruisfontein	158	34.00 S	24.43 E
Kruishoutem	50	50.54 N	3.31 E
Kruisland	52	51.34 N	4.24 E
Kruisrivier	158	33.26 S	21.55 E
Kruisvallei	158	33.53 S	23.10 E
Krujë	38	41.30 N	19.48 E
Kr'ukov	80	47.24 N	42.28 E
Kr'ukovo, S.S.S.R.	74	66.30 N	159.31 E
Kr'ukovo, S.S.S.R.	82	55.59 N	37.10 E
Kr'ukovo, S.S.S.R.	82	55.28 N	36.32 E
Kr'ukovo, S.S.S.R.	83	47.40 N	39.13 E
Krukut, Kali ≃	269e	6.12 S	106.48 E
Krulevščina	76	55.02 N	27.45 E
Krumasye	164	1.40 S	133.09 E
Krumbach, B.R.D.	58	47.58 N	9.02 E
Krumbach, B.R.D.	58	48.14 N	10.22 E
Krumme Lanke ⊜	264a	52.27 N	13.14 E
Krummendammer Heide ◆[3]	264a	52.28 N	13.39 E
Krummenerl	263	51.05 N	7.45 E
Krummensee	264a	52.36 N	13.42 E
Krumme Steyrling ≃	61	47.54 N	14.14 E
Krummhörn	52	53.26 N	7.06 E
Krummhörn ◆[1]	52	53.25 N	7.10 E
Krumovgrad	38	41.28 N	25.39 E
Krumroy	214	39.58 N	81.24 W
Krün	64	47.30 N	11.16 E
Krung Thep (Bangkok), Thai	110	13.45 N	100.31 E
Krung Thep (Bangkok), Thai	269a	13.45 N	100.31 E
Krung Thep Mahanakhon □[4]	269a	13.47 N	100.43 E
Krung Thon Bridge ◆[5]	269a	13.47 N	100.30 E
Krupá	54	50.08 N	13.41 E
Krupec	78	51.38 N	34.21 E
Krüpel-See ⊜	264a	52.18 N	13.42 E
Krupka	54	50.43 N	13.46 E
Krupki	76	54.19 N	29.08 E
Kruså	41	54.50 N	9.25 E
Kruščica jezero ⊜[1]	36	44.39 N	15.19 E
Krusenstern, Cape >	180	67.07 N	163.43 W
Kruševac	38	43.35 N	21.20 E
Kruševo	38	41.22 N	21.14 E
Krušinovka	76	53.14 N	29.50 E
Krušné hory (Erzgebirge) ⩘	54	50.30 N	13.15 E
Kruszwica	30	52.41 N	18.19 E
Krutaja, S.S.S.R.	24	63.02 N	54.38 E
Krutaja, S.S.S.R.	86	57.24 N	76.27 E
Krutaja Gorka	86	55.25 N	73.15 E
Krutcy	76	57.10 N	29.23 E
Krutec, S.S.S.R.	76	60.17 N	39.25 E
Krutec, S.S.S.R.	82	56.10 N	38.33 E
Kruticha, S.S.S.R.	86	53.58 N	81.14 E
Kruticha, S.S.S.R.	86	56.49 N	77.10 E
Krutinka	86	56.01 N	71.31 E
Krutoje	76	52.26 N	37.28 E
Krutoj Log	86	57.53 N	58.14 E
Krutoj Majdan	80	55.35 N	44.04 E
Krutyje Verchi	82	54.19 N	36.26 E
Kruunupyy → Kronoby	26	63.43 N	23.02 E
Kruzenšterna, proliv ɰ	74	48.30 N	153.50 E
Kruzof Island I	180	57.10 N	135.40 W
Krydor	184	52.47 N	107.03 W
Krylatskoje ◆[8]	265b	55.45 N	37.26 E
Krylbo	40	60.08 N	16.13 E
Krylovskaja	78	46.07 N	39.19 E
Krym	83	47.19 N	39.31 E
Krymsk	78	44.56 N	37.59 E
Krymskaja Oblast' □[4]	78	45.00 N	34.00 E
Krymskij	78	47.40 N	40.46 E
Krymskije gory ⩘	78	44.45 N	34.25 E
Krymskij poluostrov (Crimea) >[1]	78	45.00 N	34.00 E
Krymskij Zapovednik ◆[4]	78	44.42 N	34.12 E
Krymskoje	83	48.45 N	38.48 E
Krynica	30	49.25 N	20.56 E
Krynka ≃	83	47.36 N	38.47 E
Kryžina, chrebet ⩘	88	54.00 N	95.00 E
Kryžopol'	78	48.23 N	28.52 E
Krzepice	30	50.58 N	18.44 E
Krzeszowice	30	50.09 N	19.39 E
Krzeszyce	54	52.36 N	15.01 E
Krzna ≃	30	52.08 N	23.31 E
Krzywiń	30	51.58 N	16.49 E
Krzyż	30	52.54 N	16.01 E
Ksar Chellala	148	35.13 N	2.18 E
Ksar el Barka	150	18.24 N	12.13 W
Ksar-El-Kebir	148	35.01 N	5.54 W
Ksar-Es-Seghir	34	35.50 N	5.32 W
Ksar Hellal	36	35.39 N	10.54 E
Ksaverovka	78	50.03 N	30.12 E
Ksel, Djebel ∧	148	33.44 N	1.10 E
Kšen' ≃	76	52.23 N	37.44 E
Ksenjevka	88	53.34 N	118.44 E
Ksenofontova	24	60.58 N	56.12 E
Kšenskij	78	51.52 N	37.43 E
Książ Wielkopolski	30	52.05 N	17.14 E
Ksob, Oued ≃, Alg.	34	35.46 N	4.34 E
Ksob, Oued ≃, Alg.	36	35.49 N	7.53 E
Ksour, Monts des ⩘	148	32.45 N	0.30 W
Ksour Essaf	148	35.25 N	11.00 E
Kstovo	80	56.11 N	44.11 E
Kū', Wādī al- V	140	13.37 N	25.15 E
Kuah	114	6.19 N	99.51 E
Kuai ≃	100	33.09 N	117.32 E
Kuala, Indon.	112	2.55 N	105.48 E
Kuala, Indon.	114	3.32 N	98.24 E
Kuala ≃	114	2.45 N	100.00 E
Kualabee	114	4.24 N	96.03 E
Kuala Berang	114	5.04 N	103.01 E
Kualacenako	112	0.28 S	102.40 E
Kuala Dungun	114	4.47 N	103.26 E
Kuala Kangsar	114	4.46 N	100.56 E
Kualakapuas	112	3.01 S	114.21 E
Kuala Kedah	114	6.06 N	100.18 E
Kuala Kelawang	114	2.56 N	102.05 E
Kuala Kerai	114	5.32 N	102.12 E
Kuala Kerau	114	3.43 N	102.22 E
Kualakeriau	112	0.50 N	113.20 E
Kuala Ketil	114	5.36 N	100.39 E
Kuala Kubu Baharu	114	3.34 N	101.39 E
Kuala Kurau	114	5.01 N	100.26 E
Kualakurun	112	1.07 S	113.53 E
Kualalangsa	114	4.32 N	98.01 E
Kuala Lipis	114	4.11 N	102.03 E
Kuala Lumpur	114	3.10 N	101.42 E
Kuala Lumpur □[3]	114	3.10 N	101.42 E
Kualamanjual	112	1.25 S	112.00 E
Kuala Nerang	114	6.15 N	100.36 E
Kualapesaguan	112	2.01 S	110.08 E
Kuala Pilah	114	2.44 N	102.15 E
Kualapuu	229a	21.09 N	157.02 W
Kuala Selangor	114	3.21 N	101.15 E
Kualasimpang	114	4.17 N	98.03 E
Kuala Terengganu	114	5.20 N	103.08 E
Kualu ≃	114	2.45 N	100.00 E
Kuamut	112	5.13 N	117.30 E
Kuamut ≃	112	5.13 N	117.32 E
Kuanbang	98	40.29 N	120.04 E
Kuancheng, Zhg.	98	40.37 N	118.31 E
Kuancheng, Zhg.	105	40.38 N	118.27 E
Kuandang	112	0.52 N	122.55 E
Kuandian	98	40.43 N	124.44 E
Kuando → Cuando ≃	152	18.27 S	23.32 E
Kuanhsi	100	24.48 N	121.10 E
Kuanmiao	100	22.58 N	120.19 E
Kuanshan	100	23.03 N	121.09 E
Kuan Shan ∧	100	23.14 N	120.54 E
Kuantan	114	3.48 N	103.20 E
Kuantan ≃	114	3.50 N	103.17 E
Kuanyin	100	25.02 N	121.04 E
Kuanyün → Guanyun	98	34.20 N	119.17 E
Kuanza → Cuanza ≃	152	9.19 S	13.08 E
Kuba	84	41.22 N	48.31 E
Kuba → Cuba □[1]	240p	21.30 N	80.00 W
Kuban' ≃	72	45.20 N	37.30 E
Kubatly	84	39.22 N	46.34 E
Kubbī	140	11.08 N	25.14 E
Kubbum	140	11.47 N	23.47 E
Kubena ≃	76	59.36 N	39.39 E
Kubenskoje	76	59.26 N	39.40 E
Kubenskoje, ozero ⊜	76	59.40 N	39.25 E
Kubiki	94	37.11 N	138.20 E
Kubinka	82	55.35 N	36.43 E
Kubitzer Bodden c	54	54.24 N	13.12 E
Küblis	58	46.55 N	9.47 E
Kubn'a ≃	80	55.31 N	48.27 E
Kubokawa	96	33.12 N	133.08 E
Kubor, Mount ∧	164	6.05 S	144.45 E
Kubr' ≃	82	56.52 N	38.17 E
Kubrat	38	43.48 N	26.30 E
Kubu	115b	8.16 S	115.35 E
Kubuchaj	88	50.30 N	114.48 E
Kubu Gajah	114	5.10 N	100.41 E
Kubumesaai	112	1.31 N	115.06 E
Kubutambahan	115b	8.05 S	115.10 E
Kučema	24	65.37 N	42.28 E
Kučen'ajevo	80	54.44 N	46.24 E
Kučevo	38	44.27 N	21.44 E
Kuchaiburi	126	22.16 N	86.10 E
Kuchāman	120	27.09 N	74.52 E
Kuch'ang-ni	98	40.09 N	124.46 E
Kuchelebai	154	1.29 N	35.01 E
Kuchen Spitze ∧	58	47.03 N	10.14 E
Kuchinarai	110	16.32 N	104.04 E
Kuching	112	1.33 N	110.20 E
Kuchinoerabu-jima I	93b	30.28 N	130.12 E
Kuchino-shima I	93b	29.57 N	129.57 E
Kuchiwa	96	34.53 N	132.55 E
Kuchl	64	47.37 N	13.09 E
Kūchnay Darvīshān	128	30.59 N	64.11 E
Kuchterin Lug	89	52.25 N	128.05 E
Kuchtinka	82	54.29 N	38.10 E
Kučino	265b	55.45 N	37.58 E
Kučkak	85	40.15 N	70.20 E
Kučki	80	53.01 N	44.29 E
Kuçovë → Stalin	38	40.48 N	19.54 E
Küçük Ağrı Dağı ∧	84	39.38 N	44.25 E
Küçükbahce	130	38.33 N	26.24 E
Küçükbakkal	267b	40.58 N	29.06 E
Küçükçekmece	267b	40.59 N	28.46 E
Küçükköy	267b	41.04 N	28.54 E
Küçükkuyu	130	39.32 N	26.36 E
Kučukskoje, ozero ⊜	86	52.42 N	79.46 E
Kucur, Tanjung >	115a	8.39 S	114.34 E
Kučurgan ≃	78	46.43 N	29.53 E
Kūd	123	33.05 N	75.17 E
Kuda ≃	88	52.25 N	104.08 E
Kudaka-jima I	174m	26.09 N	127.54 E
Kudamatsu	96	34.00 N	131.52 E
Kudanggou	104	41.06 N	124.00 E
Kudap	114	1.17 N	102.26 E
Kudara, S.S.S.R.	85	38.25 N	72.41 E
Kudara, S.S.S.R.	88	52.13 N	106.39 E
Kudara ≃	85	38.19 N	72.28 E
Kudara-Somon	88	50.10 N	107.25 E
Kudat	112	6.53 N	116.50 E
Kudbrooke ◆[8]	260	51.28 N	0.03 E
Kudejevskij	86	54.52 N	56.46 E
Kudene	164	6.14 S	134.39 E
Kudever'	76	56.47 N	29.23 E
Kudinovo	82	55.45 N	38.12 E
Kudirkos Naumiestis	76	54.46 N	22.53 E
Kudongho	98	35.31 N	126.29 E
Kudoyama	96	34.17 N	135.34 E
Kudremukh ∧	122	13.08 N	75.16 E
Kudrovo	265a	59.54 N	30.31 E
Kudus	115a	6.48 S	110.50 E
Kudyat al-Islām	142	27.32 N	30.45 E
Kudymkar	86	59.01 N	54.37 E
Kuee Ruins ⊥	229d	19.21 N	155.23 W
Kueishan Tao I	100	24.51 N	121.57 E
Kueisui → Hohhot	102	40.51 N	111.40 E
Kueiyang → Guiyang	102	26.35 N	106.43 E
Kuekvun' ≃	180	69.14 N	179.25 E
Kuënlun → Kunlun Shan ⩘	120	36.30 N	88.00 E
Kuerbin	89	49.25 N	128.59 E
K'uerhlo → Korla	90	41.44 N	86.09 E
Kufayr Yabūs	132	33.42 N	36.01 E
Küfre	130	38.02 N	42.00 E
Kufrinjah	132	32.18 N	35.42 E
Kufstein	64	47.35 N	12.10 E
Kufūr Bilshāy	142	30.51 N	30.48 E
Kufūr Najm	142	30.44 N	31.35 E
Kuga, Nihon	96	34.05 N	132.05 E
Kuga, Nihon	96	33.56 N	132.16 E
Kuga, Zhg.	90	41.43 N	82.54 E
Kugaluk ≃	180	69.10 N	131.00 W
Kugaly	86	44.29 N	78.40 E
Kugarčino	80	55.33 N	50.29 E
Kugart ≃	85	40.52 N	72.53 E
Kugas	85	38.21 N	70.48 E
Kugej	83	46.53 N	39.19 E
Kugesi	80	56.02 N	47.18 E
Kugmallit Bay c	180	69.33 N	133.25 W
Kugojeja ≃	78	46.34 N	39.38 E
Kuguno	94	36.03 N	137.16 E
Kuḥaylī	140	19.25 N	32.50 E
Kühbach	60	48.29 N	11.11 E
Kūhdasht	128	33.32 N	47.36 E
Kuḥlīyah, Wādī V	142	30.05 N	31.58 E
Kühlungsborn	54	54.09 N	11.43 E
Kuhmo	26	64.08 N	29.31 E
Kuhmoinen	26	61.34 N	25.11 E
Kühnhausen	54	51.02 N	10.58 E
Kühnsdorf	61	46.37 N	14.37 E
Kūhpāyeh	128	32.43 N	52.26 E
Kūhrān, Kūh-e ∧	128	26.46 N	58.12 E
Kühren	54	51.20 N	12.50 E
Kuhstedt	52	53.23 N	8.58 E
Kui	164	7.30 S	147.15 E
Kuibyschew → Kujbyšev	80	53.12 N	50.09 E
Kuidesu	98	41.46 N	119.29 E
Kuidou	100	25.10 N	118.11 E
Kuikkol', ozero ⊜	86	50.57 N	64.30 E
Kuikui, Lae o >	229a	20.36 N	156.35 W
Kuilāpāl	126	22.50 N	86.38 E
Kuinre	52	52.47 N	5.50 E
Kuiseb ≃	156	22.59 S	14.31 E
Kuishi-yama ∧, Nihon	96	33.51 N	133.35 E
Kuishi-yama ∧, Nihon	96	33.40 N	133.31 E
Kuitan	100	23.05 N	115.58 E
Kuito	152	12.22 S	16.56 E
Kuiu Island I	180	56.45 N	134.10 W
Kuivaniemi	26	65.35 N	25.11 E
Kuivastu	76	58.35 N	23.22 E
Kuja, S.S.S.R.	24	67.46 N	53.10 E
Kuja, S.S.S.R.	24	65.05 N	40.06 E
Kujal'nickij liman ⊜	78	46.40 N	30.42 E
Kujang	98	39.52 N	126.01 E
Kujani Game Reserve ◆[4]	150	7.10 N	0.50 W
Kujawy ◆[1]	30	52.45 N	18.30 E
Kujbyšev, S.S.S.R.	80	53.12 N	50.09 E
Kujbyšev, S.S.S.R.	80	54.57 N	49.05 E
Kujbyšev, S.S.S.R.	86	55.27 N	78.19 E
Kujbyševka	78	47.37 N	31.42 E
Kujbyševo, S.S.S.R.	78	44.38 N	33.52 E
Kujbyševo, S.S.S.R.	78	47.22 N	36.39 E
Kujbyševo, S.S.S.R.	83	47.49 N	38.55 E
Kujbyševo, S.S.S.R.	85	40.22 N	71.17 E
Kujbyševskij, S.S.S.R.	72	37.52 N	68.44 E
Kujbyševskij, S.S.S.R.	86	53.15 N	66.51 E
Kujbyševskij Zaton	80	55.09 N	49.12 E
Kujbyševskoje vodochranilišče ⊜[1]	80	54.30 N	48.30 E
Kujeda	86	56.26 N	55.35 E
Kujgan	86	45.25 N	74.10 E
Kujgenkol'	80	49.17 N	47.59 E
Kuji	92	40.11 N	141.46 E
Kuji ≃	94	36.29 N	140.37 E
Kujirai	268	35.56 N	139.27 E
Kujl'uk	85	41.15 N	69.20 E
Kujman'	76	52.52 N	39.16 E
Kujŏng-ni	98	37.53 N	125.54 E
Kujtun	88	54.21 N	101.29 E
Kujū	96	33.01 N	131.18 E
Kujūkuri	94	35.32 N	140.25 E
Kujūkuri-hama ⊥[2]	94	35.35 N	140.30 E
Kujū-san ∧	96	33.05 N	131.15 E
Kuk ∧	64	46.16 N	13.45 E
Kuk ≃	180	70.36 N	160.00 W
Kukaklek Lake ⊜	180	59.09 N	155.20 W
Kukalaya ≃	236	13.39 N	83.37 W
Kukan	89	49.12 N	133.28 E
Kukarino	82	55.31 N	35.59 E
Kukawa	146	12.56 N	13.35 E
Kukerin	162	33.11 S	118.05 E
Kukës	38	42.05 N	20.24 E
Kuke Shan ⩘	85	40.00 N	75.00 E
Kuki	94	36.04 N	139.40 E
Kukipi	164	8.10 S	146.05 E
Kukkola	26	65.59 N	24.04 E
Kukmirn	61	47.04 N	16.13 E
Kukmor	80	56.13 N	50.54 E
Kukoboj	76	58.42 N	39.54 E
Kukol'	76	59.52 N	32.35 E
Kükong → Shaoguan	100	24.50 N	113.37 E
Kukpowruk ≃	180	69.35 N	163.00 W
Kukpuk ≃	180	68.23 N	166.20 W
Kukshi	120	22.12 N	74.45 E
Kukuj	76	59.21 N	32.33 E
Kuku-Nor → Qinghai Hu ⊜	102	36.50 N	100.20 E
Kukup	114	1.19 N	103.27 E
Kuku Point >	174a	19.18 N	166.34 E
Kukuri Mukuri Char I	126	21.56 N	90.39 E
Kukuštan	86	57.38 N	56.30 E
Kula, Blg.	38	43.53 N	22.31 E
Kula, Jugo.	38	45.36 N	19.32 E
Kula, Tür.	130	38.32 N	28.40 E
Kula, Hi., U.S.	229a	20.52 N	156.40 W
Kul'ab	120	37.55 N	69.46 E
Kulāchi	123	31.56 N	70.27 E
Kulagi	76	52.56 N	32.24 E
Kula Gulf ɰ	175e	8.05 S	157.18 E
Kulai	114	1.40 N	103.36 E
Kulaj	86	57.42 N	75.15 E
Kula Kangri ∧	124	28.03 N	90.27 E
Kulākh	144	21.18 N	40.41 E
Kulakovo, S.S.S.R.	82	55.06 N	37.28 E
Kulakovo, S.S.S.R.	86	58.06 N	93.57 E
Kulakši	86	47.12 N	55.24 E
Kulal, Mount ∧	154	2.43 N	36.56 E
Kulanak	85	41.22 N	75.31 E
Kulandy	86	46.08 N	59.31 E
Kular	74	70.41 N	134.22 E
Kulasekharapatnam	122	8.24 N	78.03 E
Kulassein Island I	116	6.25 N	120.41 E
Kulautuva	76	54.58 N	23.38 E
Kulaykilī	140	11.21 N	25.36 E
Kul'či	89	53.33 N	139.36 E
Kuldīga	76	56.58 N	21.59 E
Kuldja → Yining	86	43.54 N	81.21 E
Kul'dur	89	49.13 N	131.38 E
Kule	156	23.05 S	20.05 E
Kulebaki	80	55.24 N	42.32 E
Kulejevo	86	59.40 N	80.59 E
Kulen Vakuf	36	44.34 N	16.06 E
Kulešovka	83	47.05 N	39.33 E
Kulevčinskij	86	53.12 N	61.26 E
Kulgam	123	33.39 N	75.01 E
Kulgera	162	25.50 S	133.18 E
Kulgunino	86	53.35 N	56.56 E
Kuligi	80	58.11 N	53.46 E
Kulikov	78	49.58 N	24.04 E
Kulikovka, S.S.S.R.	78	51.23 N	31.37 E
Kulikovka, S.S.S.R.	80	52.14 N	47.36 E
Kulikovo	76	52.14 N	39.35 E
Kulikovskij	80	50.51 N	42.34 E
Kulim	114	5.22 N	100.34 E
Kulin	162	32.40 S	118.10 E
Kuliushucun	105	40.07 N	116.34 E
Kulju	26	61.23 N	23.46 E
Kulkyne Creek ≃	166	30.16 S	144.12 E
Kullaberg ⩘[2]	41	56.18 N	12.30 E
Kullamaa	76	58.53 N	24.05 E
Küllenhahn ◆[8]	263	51.14 N	7.08 E
Küllstedt	56	51.16 N	10.17 E
Kulm	198	46.18 N	98.57 W
Kulmbach	54	50.06 N	11.27 E
Kulnura	170	33.14 S	151.13 E
Kuloj, S.S.S.R.	24	64.58 N	43.28 E
Kuloj, S.S.S.R.	24	61.02 N	42.29 E
Kuloj ≃, S.S.S.R.	24	66.03 N	43.22 E
Kuloj ≃, S.S.S.R.	76	60.25 N	42.30 E
Kuloli	85	39.22 N	68.03 E
Kulon, Ujung >[1]	115a	6.45 S	105.20 E
Kulongshan	98	41.43 N	116.54 E
Kulongshanpuzi	104	41.16 N	123.59 E
Kulotino	76	58.27 N	33.21 E
Kulpahār	124	25.19 N	79.39 E
Kulpara	168b	34.04 S	138.02 E
Kulpawn ≃	150	10.21 N	1.05 W
Kulpi	126	22.06 N	88.15 E
Kul'pino	82	56.18 N	37.09 E
Kulpmont	208	40.47 N	76.28 W
Kulpsville	285	40.15 N	75.20 W
Kul'sary	86	46.59 N	54.01 E
Kulsbjerge ⩘[2]	41	55.01 N	12.01 E
Külsheim	56	49.40 N	9.31 E
Kültepe ⊥	130	38.44 N	35.34 E
Kulti	126	23.44 N	86.51 E
Kultikri	126	22.10 N	87.09 E
Kultuk	88	51.44 N	103.42 E
Kulu, India	123	31.58 N	77.06 E
Kulu, Tür.	130	39.06 N	33.05 E
Kulu □[5]	123	32.00 N	77.05 E
Kuluha, Jabal ∧	140	15.31 N	23.25 E
Kulumadau	164	9.03 S	152.43 E
Kulunda	86	52.35 N	78.57 E
Kulunda ≃	86	52.59 N	79.48 E
Kulundinskaja step' ≚	86	53.00 N	79.00 E
Kulundinskoje, ozero ⊜	86	53.00 N	79.36 E
Kuluqi	89	50.23 N	124.13 E
Kulwin	166	35.02 S	142.33 E
Kuma	96	33.39 N	132.54 E
Kuma ≃, Nihon	92	32.30 N	130.34 E
Kuma ≃, S.S.S.R.	72	44.56 N	47.00 E
Kuma ≃, S.S.S.R.	86	59.32 N	66.45 E
Kumagaya	94	36.08 N	139.23 E
Kumai, Indon.	112	3.23 S	112.33 E
Kumai, Indon.	112	2.44 S	111.43 E
Kumai, Teluk c	112	3.00 S	111.43 E
Kumaishi	92a	42.08 N	139.59 E
Kumakanda	88	52.44 N	116.55 E
Kumalarang	116	7.44 N	123.08 E
Kumamba, Kepulauan II	164	1.36 S	138.45 E
Kumamoto	92	32.48 N	130.43 E
Kumamoto □[5]	96	32.58 N	130.55 E
Kumano, Nihon	92	33.54 N	136.05 E
Kumano, Nihon	96	34.20 N	132.34 E
Kumano ≃	92	33.44 N	136.01 E
Kumano-nada ⩡[2]	92	33.47 N	136.20 E
Kumanovo	38	42.08 N	21.43 E
Kumār ≃[1], Bngl.	126	23.11 N	90.10 E
Kumār ≃[1], Bngl.	126	23.31 N	89.28 E
Kumara, N.Z.	172	42.38 S	171.11 E
Kumara, S.S.S.R.	89	51.37 N	126.47 E
Kumārapālaiyam	122	11.28 N	77.43 E
Kumarganj	126	22.59 N	87.44 E
Kumārgrām	124	26.37 N	89.50 E
Kumāri ≃	126	22.57 N	86.48 E
Kumārkhāli	124	23.51 N	89.15 E
Kumarl	162	32.47 S	121.33 E
Kumasi	150	6.41 N	1.35 W
Kumatori	270	34.24 N	135.22 E
Kumawa, Pegunungan ⩘	164	3.50 S	132.50 E
Kumba	152	4.38 N	9.25 E
Kumbakonam	122	10.58 N	79.23 E
Kumba Pits	156	18.45 S	24.45 E
Kumbar	140	12.03 N	30.16 E
Kumbarilla	166	27.19 S	150.53 E
Kumbe	164	8.21 S	140.13 E
Kumbel'	85	42.30 N	73.11 E
Kumbher	124	28.16 N	81.24 E
Kŭmch'ŏn	98	38.10 N	126.29 E
Kum-Dag	128	39.16 N	54.35 E
Kumdah ⩡[4]	144	20.23 N	45.05 E
Kumdan ∧	123	35.09 N	77.35 E
Kume	96	35.03 N	133.54 E
Kume-jima I	93b	26.20 N	126.47 E
Kumenan	96	34.56 N	133.58 E
Kumeny	80	58.07 N	49.56 E
Kumertau	86	52.46 N	55.47 E
Kŭm-gang ≃	98	36.00 N	126.40 E
Kŭmgang-san ∧	98	38.35 N	128.10 E
Kŭmhwa	98	38.17 N	127.28 E
Kumi	154	1.29 N	33.56 E
Kumihama	96	35.36 N	134.55 E
Kuminovskoje	86	57.48 N	64.07 E
Kuminskij	86	58.40 N	66.04 E
Kumiyama	270	34.53 N	135.45 E
Kumizawa ◆[8]	268	35.23 N	139.31 E
Kumköy	267b	41.15 N	29.02 E
Kumla	40	59.08 N	15.08 E
Kumli	84	43.58 N	46.04 E
Kumlinge I	26	60.16 N	20.47 E
Kumluca, Tür.	130	36.22 N	30.18 E
Kumluca, Tür.	130	41.27 N	32.28 E
Kummelnäs	40	59.21 N	18.17 E
Kummerow	54	54.17 N	12.53 E
Kummerower See ⊜	54	53.49 N	12.52 E
Kümmersbruck	60	49.25 N	11.53 E
Kumo	146	10.03 N	11.13 E
Kŭmŏ-do I	98	34.31 N	127.45 E
Kumon Range ⩘	102	26.30 N	97.15 E
Kumora	88	55.53 N	111.13 E
Kumosō-yama ∧	96	33.54 N	134.18 E
Kumotori-yama ∧	94	35.51 N	138.57 E
Kumphawapi	110	17.07 N	103.01 E
Kumrābād	126	24.10 N	87.16 E
Kŭmsan	98	36.07 N	127.30 E
Kŭmsan-ni	98	37.55 N	125.41 E
Kumsenga	154	3.47 S	30.25 E
Kumta	122	14.25 N	74.24 E
Kumu	154	3.04 N	25.09 E
Kumu ≃	114	1.24 N	100.43 E
Kumuch	84	42.11 N	47.07 E
Kumukahi, Cape >	229d	19.31 N	154.49 W
Kumukuli	120	37.33 N	88.50 E
Kumusi ≃	164	8.35 S	148.00 E
Kümüx	86	42.14 N	88.11 E
Kumzār	128	26.20 N	56.25 E
Kuna	202	43.29 N	116.25 W
Kunar (Konar) ≃	123	34.25 N	70.32 E
Kunašak	86	55.43 N	61.36 E
Kunashiri-tō → Kunašir, ostrov I	92a	44.10 N	146.00 E
Kunašir, ostrov (Kunashiri-Tō) I	92a	44.10 N	146.00 E
Kun'batar	84	44.17 N	45.34 E
Kuncheng Hu ⊜	106	31.35 N	120.45 E
Kunchha	124	28.08 N	84.20 E
Kunc'ovo ◆[8]	265b	55.44 N	37.26 E
Kunda, S.S.S.R.	76	59.29 N	26.32 E
Kunda, Zaïre	154	3.57 S	26.35 E
Kunda Hills ⩘[2]	122	11.10 N	76.30 E
Kundahit	126	23.58 N	87.10 E
Kundam	124	23.13 N	80.21 E
Kundar ≃, Asia	120	31.56 N	69.19 E
Kundar ≃, Pāk.	123	34.17 N	73.29 E
Kundara	122	8.57 N	76.41 E
Kundat	86	55.14 N	87.51 E

Symbols in the index entries represent the broad categories identified in the key at the right. Symbols with superior numbers (⩘[1]) identify subcategories (see complete key on page *I · 1).*

Kartensymbole in dem Registerverzeichnis stellen die rechts in Schlüssel erklärten Kategorien dar. Symbole mit hochgestellten Ziffern (⩘[1]) bezeichnen Unterabteilungen einer Kategorie (vgl. vollständiger Schlüssel auf Seite *I · 1).*

Los símbolos incluídos en el texto del índice representan las grandes categorias identificadas con la clave a la derecha. Los símbolos con numeros en su parte superior (⩘[1]) identifican las subcategorías (véase la clave completa en la página *I · 1).*

Les symboles de l'index représentent les catégories indiquées dans la légende à droite. Les symboles suivis d'un indice (⩘[1]) représentent des sous-catégories (voir légende complète à la page *I · 1).*

Os símbolos incluídos no texto do índice representam as grandes categorias identificadas com a chave à direita. Os símbolos com números em sua parte superior (⩘[1]) identificam as subcategorias (veja-se a chave completa à página *I · 1).*

	English	Deutsch	Español	Français	Português
∧	Mountain	Berg	Montaña	Montagne	Montanha
⩘	Mountains	Berge	Montañas	Montagnes	Montanhas
)(	Pass	Pass	Paso	Col	Passo
V	Valley, Canyon	Tal, Cañon	Valle, Cañón	Vallée, Canyon	Vale, Canhão
≚	Plain	Ebene	Llano	Plaine	Planície
>	Cape	Kap	Cabo	Cap	Cabo
I	Island	Insel	Isla	Île	Ilha
II	Islands	Inseln	Islas	Îles	Ilhas
⊥	Other Topographic Features	Andere Topographische Objekte	Otros Elementos Topográficos	Autres données topographiques	Outros acidentes topográficos

ESPAÑOL

Nombre	Página	Lat.°′	Long.°′ W = Oeste
Kundelungu, Parc National de ♠	154	10.30 S	27.45 E
Kunderu ≃	122	14.38 N	78.42 E
Kundi	154	1.08 S	40.41 E
Kundiān	123	32.27 N	71.28 E
Kundiawa	164	6.00 S	145.00 E
Kundima	164	4.14 S	143.52 E
Kundip	162	33.42 S	120.10 E
Kundl	64	47.28 N	11.59 E
Kundla	120	21.20 N	71.18 E
Kundr'učje ≃	83	47.52 N	40.15 E
Kundur, Pulau ɪ	112	0.45 N	103.26 E
Kunene (Cunene) ≃	152	17.20 S	11.50 E
Kunersdorf, Forst ⬥ [3]	264a	52.17 N	12.59 E
Kunes	24	70.21 N	26.31 E
Künes ≃	86	43.55 N	80.55 E
Kunga ≃ [1]	124	21.45 N	89.30 E
Kungälv	26	57.52 N	11.58 E
Kungana	146	7.50 N	10.42 E
Kungchuling → Huaide	89	43.32 N	124.50 E
Kungej-Alatau, chrebet ⋏	85	42.50 N	77.00 E
Kunghit Island ɪ	.182	52.06 N	131.04 W
Kunghsi	100	24.37 N	121.16 E
Kung-pei-tien	269d	25.06 N	121.38 E
Kungrad	86	43.06 N	58.54 E
Kungsängen	40	59.29 N	17.45 E
Kungsbacka	26	57.29 N	12.04 E
Kungsgården	40	60.36 N	16.37 E
Kungshamn	26	58.22 N	11.15 E
Kungsör	40	59.25 N	16.05 E
Kungu	152	2.47 N	19.12 E
Kungur	86	57.25 N	56.57 E
Kungurri	166	21.05 S	148.44 E
Kunhegyes	30	47.22 N	20.38 E
Kunhing	110	21.18 N	98.26 E
Kuni	94	36.35 N	138.38 E
Kunia	229c	21.29 N	158.07 W
Kunigami	174m	26.45 N	128.10 E
Kunimi	96	33.41 N	131.36 E
Kuningan	115a	6.59 S	108.29 E
Kunisaki	96	33.33 N	131.45 E
Kunisaki-hantō ≻ [1]	96	33.30 N	131.40 E
Kunitachi	268	35.41 N	139.26 E
Kuni Vyselki	82	54.18 N	38.41 E
Kunja	76	56.18 N	30.59 E
Kunja ≃, S.S.S.R.	76	57.09 N	31.10 E
Kunja ≃, S.S.S.R.	82	56.31 N	38.12 E
Kunjāh	123	32.32 N	73.59 E
Kunje	83	49.23 N	37.15 E
Kunkle	216	41.38 N	84.30 W
Kunkletown	210	40.51 N	75.27 W
Kunkuri	124	22.45 N	83.57 E
Kunlong	110	23.25 N	98.39 E
Kunlun Shan ⋏	120	36.30 N	88.00 E
Kunming	102	25.05 N	102.40 E
Kunming Hu ⊜	271a	39.59 N	116.15 E
Kunnamkulam	122	10.39 N	76.05 E
Kunost'	76	60.01 N	37.38 E
Kunovice	30	49.03 N	17.29 E
Kunow	54	53.00 N	12.07 E
Kunowice	54	52.20 N	14.50 E
Kunrau	54	52.35 N	11.01 E
Kunsan	98	35.58 N	126.41 E
Kunsangen Flygplats ⊠	40	58.36 N	16.15 E
Kunshan	106	31.23 N	120.57 E
Kunstmuseum ☗	263	51.14 N	6.46 E
Kunszentmárton	30	46.51 N	20.18 E
Kuntair	150	13.32 N	16.13 W
Kuntaur	150	13.40 N	14.48 W
Kuntiki	86	58.29 N	76.24 E
Kunting	100	29.48 N	121.56 E
Kuntshankoie	152	3.20 S	23.34 E
Kuntuolun	102	45.13 N	115.21 E
Kununurra	164	15.47 S	128.44 E
Kunwi	98	36.15 N	128.34 E
Kunya	150	12.14 N	8.34 E
Kunyo	144	6.17 N	42.33 E
Kunžak	61	49.07 N	15.11 E
Künzell	56	50.33 N	9.42 E
Künzelsau	56	49.16 N	9.41 E
Künzing	60	48.40 N	13.05 E
Kunzulu	152	3.29 S	16.09 E
Kuocang Shan ⋏	100	28.36 N	120.30 E
Kuohsing	100	24.02 N	120.51 E
Kuokegan	120	37.30 N	89.55 E
Kuolajarvi	24	66.58 N	29.12 E
Kuop ɪ [1]	175c	7.03 N	151.56 E
Kuopio	26	62.54 N	27.41 E
Kuopion lääni □ [4]	26	63.00 N	27.30 E
Kuortane	26	62.48 N	23.30 E
Kupa ≃	36	45.28 N	16.24 E
Kup'abal	271b	37.37 N	126.54 E
Kupang	112	10.10 S	123.35 E
Kupang, Teluk c	112	10.04 S	123.40 E
Kup'ansk	83	49.42 N	37.38 E
Kupanskoje	82	56.51 N	38.43 E
Kup'ansk-Uzlovoj	83	49.39 N	37.39 E
Kuparuk ≃	180	70.25 N	148.55 W
Kupava	80	51.07 N	42.57 E
Kupavna	265b	55.45 N	38.08 E
Kuper Island ɪ	224	48.58 N	123.39 W
Kupferberg	263	51.09 N	7.27 E
Kupferdreh ⬥ [8]	263	51.23 N	7.05 E
Kupfermühle	41	54.50 N	9.24 E
Kupferzell	56	49.14 N	9.41 E
Kupičev	78	51.00 N	24.44 E
Kupino	86	54.22 N	77.18 E
Kupiškis	76	55.50 N	24.58 E
Küplü, Tür.	130	41.07 N	26.21 E
Küplu, Tür.	130	40.06 N	30.00 E
Kupol, gora ∧	180	68.38 N	174.45 E
Kuppenheim	56	48.49 N	8.15 E
Kupper Airport ⊠	276	40.31 N	74.36 W
Kupreanof	180	56.49 N	132.57 W
Kupreanof Island ɪ	180	56.50 N	133.30 W
Kupreanof Point ≻	180	55.34 N	159.35 W
Kupres	36	44.00 N	17.17 E
Küps	54	50.11 N	11.16 E
Kupuri	89	54.44 N	130.30 E
Kur ≃	89	48.44 N	134.14 E
Kur, Pulau ɪ	164	5.20 S	132.00 E
Kura (Kuruçay) ≃, Asia	84	39.24 N	49.24 E
Kura ≃, S.S.S.R.	84	44.06 N	44.57 E
Kurabuchi	94	36.25 N	138.48 E
Kur'ačeje	83	48.10 N	39.37 E
Kur'ačevka, S.S.S.R.	83	49.39 N	38.42 E
Kur'ačevka, S.S.S.R.	83	49.22 N	39.36 E
Kurach	84	41.36 N	47.46 E
Kurach ≃	84	41.40 N	48.11 E
Kurachovka	83	48.02 N	37.23 E
Kurachovo	83	47.59 N	37.16 E
Kuragaty	85	43.06 N	72.59 E
Kuragaty ≃	85	43.57 N	73.34 E
Kuragino	86	53.53 N	92.40 E
Kurahashi	96	34.06 N	132.30 E
Kurahashi-jima ɪ	96	34.08 N	132.31 E
Kuraj	86	56.42 N	95.29 E
Kurajlysaj	80	50.07 N	51.51 E
Kurakaki	270	34.59 N	135.28 E
Kurakino, S.S.S.R.	80	52.33 N	44.03 E
Kurakino, S.S.S.R.	82	54.30 N	35.48 E
Kurakovo	82	54.05 N	37.14 E
Kūrāli	123	30.50 N	76.35 E
Kuram	85	43.33 N	78.08 E
Kuramā', Ḥarrat ⩦ [9]	128	24.30 N	40.15 E
Kurama-yama ∧	96	35.07 N	135.46 E
Kuraminskij chrebet ⋏	85	40.45 N	70.10 E
Kuramo Waters c	273a	6.26 N	3.26 E
Kuranami	268	35.27 N	140.00 E
Kurāon	124	24.59 N	82.05 E
Kurar ⬥ [8]	272c	19.11 N	72.52 E
Kurašasaj	86	50.18 N	56.55 E
Kurashiki	96	34.35 N	133.46 E
Kurasiki → Kurashiki	96	34.35 N	133.46 E
Kurate	96	33.47 N	130.41 E
Kurauli	124	27.24 N	78.59 E
Kuraymah	140	18.33 N	31.51 E

FRANÇAIS

Nom	Page	Lat.°′	Long.°′ W = Ouest
Kurayoshi	96	35.26 N	133.49 E
Kurayyimah	132	32.16 N	35.36 E
Kurba	80	57.34 N	39.32 E
Kurba ≃	88	52.02 N	108.30 E
Kurbağa Gölü ⊜	130	38.21 N	35.17 E
Kurbalı Dere ≃	267b	40.59 N	29.02 E
Kurbatovo	86	55.34 N	91.10 E
Kurbulik	88	53.45 N	108.57 E
Kurčaloj	84	43.12 N	46.05 E
Kurchatov	78	51.39 N	35.36 E
Kur-Čilik ≃	85	43.50 N	78.06 E
Kurčum	86	48.37 N	83.40 E
Kurdaj	85	43.21 N	74.59 E
K'urdamir	84	40.21 N	48.08 E
Kurdgelauri	84	41.58 N	45.32 E
Kurdistan □ [9]	118	37.00 N	45.00 E
Kurdufān al-Janūbīyah □ [4]	140	11.00 N	30.00 E
Kurdufān ash-Shamālīyah □ [4]	140	14.00 N	29.45 E
Kurd'umovka	83	48.28 N	37.59 E
Kurduvādi	122	18.05 N	75.26 E
Kure, Austl.	164	15.27 S	124.33 E
Kure, Nihon	96	34.14 N	132.34 E
Küre, Tür.	130	41.48 N	33.43 E
Kure Island ɪ [1]	14	28.25 N	178.25 W
Kurejka ≃	74	66.30 N	87.12 E
Kurejskaja	88	58.56 N	111.20 E
Kuren'	78	51.09 N	32.44 E
Kurenalus	26	65.21 N	26.59 E
Kurenec	76	54.33 N	26.57 E
Kuressaare	76	58.15 N	22.28 E
Kurgal'džinskij	86	50.36 N	70.01 E
Kurgan	86	55.26 N	65.18 E
Kurgan Mečetnyj, gora ∧ [2]	83	48.06 N	39.21 E
Kurgan-T'ube	120	37.50 N	68.48 E
Kurgasyn	86	49.15 N	66.43 E
Kurgatej	88	54.23 N	99.27 E
Kurgolovo	76	59.46 N	28.06 E
Kuria ɪ	14	0.14 N	173.25 E
Kuria Muria Islands → Khūryān Mūryān ɪɪ	118	17.30 N	56.00 E
Kuriasol	126	22.06 N	86.39 E
Kuridala	166	21.17 S	140.30 E
Kurīgrām	124	25.49 N	89.39 E
Kurihama	268	35.13 N	139.43 E
Kurihashi	94	36.08 N	139.42 E
Kurikka	26	62.37 N	22.25 E
Kurilen → Kuril'skije ostrova ɪɪ	74	46.10 N	152.00 E
Kurilen-Strasse → Pervyj Kuril'skij proliv ⌇	74	50.50 N	156.36 E
Kuriles, Islas → Kuril'skije ostrova ɪɪ	74	46.10 N	152.00 E
Kuril Islands → Kuril'skije ostrova ɪɪ	74	46.10 N	152.00 E
Kurilovka	80	50.44 N	48.02 E
Kuril'sk	74	45.14 N	147.53 E
Kuril'skije ostrova (Kuril Islands) ɪɪ	74	46.10 N	152.00 E
Kuril Strait → Pervyj Kuril'skij proliv ⌇	74	50.50 N	156.36 E
Kuril Trench ⊹ [1]	6	47.00 N	155.00 E
Kuřim	30	49.18 N	16.32 E
Kurimoto	94	35.49 N	140.30 E
Ku-Ring-Gai Chase National Park ♠	170	33.38 S	151.15 E
Kurinjippadi	122	11.34 N	79.36 E
Kurinskaja kosa ≻ [2]	84	39.03 N	49.13 E
Kurinwás ≃	236	12.49 N	83.41 W
Kuripapango	172	39.23 S	176.21 E
Kuriyama, Nihon	92a	43.03 N	141.47 E
Kuriyama, Nihon	94	36.52 N	139.37 E
Kurja, S.S.S.R.	24	61.42 N	57.09 E
Kurja, S.S.S.R.	86	51.36 N	82.19 E
Kurjanovskaja	76	60.19 N	41.33 E
Kurkijoki	26	61.18 N	29.54 E
Kurkino, S.S.S.R.	76	53.26 N	38.40 E
Kurkino, S.S.S.R.	265b	55.53 N	37.23 E
Kurkliai	76	55.25 N	25.03 E
Kurl ⬥ [8]	263	51.35 N	7.35 E
Kurla ⬥ [8]	272c	19.05 N	72.53 E
Kurlackoje	83	47.21 N	39.03 E
Kurleja	88	52.11 N	119.11 E
Kurlin	80	51.48 N	51.00 E
Kurlovskij	80	55.27 N	40.36 E
Kurmanajevka, S.S.S.R.	80	52.31 N	52.06 E
Kurmanajevka, S.S.S.R.	80	49.53 N	42.36 E
Kurmani	126	22.47 N	89.53 E
Kurmankol'	80	49.09 N	48.27 E
Kurmenty	85	42.48 N	78.15 E
Kurmitala Airport ⊠	126	23.46 N	90.23 E
Kurmuk	140	10.33 N	34.17 E
Kurnell	274a	34.01 S	151.13 E
Kurnool	122	15.50 N	78.03 E
Kurobane	94	36.51 N	140.07 E
Kurobe	94	36.51 N	137.26 E
Kurobe ≃	94	36.55 N	137.25 E
Kurobe-dam ⬥ [6]	94	36.36 N	137.38 E
Kurodashō	96	35.01 N	135.00 E
Kurogi	96	33.12 N	130.40 E
Kurohone	94	36.30 N	139.17 E
Kuroishi	92	40.38 N	140.36 E
Kuroiso	94	36.58 N	140.03 E
Kuroo-tōge)(	96	35.11 N	134.12 E
Kuropatkino, S.S.S.R.	80	46.32 N	45.20 E
Kuropatkino, S.S.S.R.	85	39.57 N	67.27 E
Kurort-Darasun	88	51.12 N	113.44 E
Kurose	96	34.19 N	132.40 E
Kurose ≃	96	34.13 N	132.36 E
Kuro-shima ɪ, Nihon	93b	30.50 N	129.57 E
Kuro-shima ɪ, Nihon	175d	24.19 N	124.05 E
Kurosu	268	35.51 N	139.23 E
Kurovo	82	55.49 N	36.00 E
Kurovskoje	82	55.34 N	38.55 E
Kurow	172	44.44 S	170.28 E
Kuroya	268	35.55 N	139.44 E
Kurrajong	170	33.33 S	150.40 E
Kurram	120	30.06 N	66.31 E
Kurram □ [5]	123	33.45 N	70.20 E
Kurram ≃	123	32.36 N	71.20 E
Kurri Kurri	170	32.49 S	151.29 E
Kuršab ≃	85	40.46 N	73.06 E
Kursavka	84	44.28 N	42.31 E
Kursela	124	25.27 N	87.15 E
Kuršėnai	76	56.00 N	22.56 E
Kurseong	120	26.53 N	88.17 E
Kursk	78	51.42 N	36.12 E
Kursk □ [4]	76	52.14 N	35.30 E
Kurskaja	84	44.03 N	44.27 E
Kurskaja kosa ≻ [2]	76	55.18 N	21.00 E
Kurskij zaliv c	76	55.00 N	21.00 E
Kursk Station ⬥ [5]	265b	55.46 N	37.40 E
Kuršumlija	38	43.08 N	21.17 E
Kurşunlu, Tür.	130	40.51 N	33.16 E
Kurşunlu, Tür.	130	38.40 N	37.51 E
Kurtalan	130	37.57 N	41.42 E
Kurtamyš	86	54.55 N	64.27 E
Kurtatsch → Cortaccia	64	46.19 N	11.13 E
Kürten, B.R.D.	56	51.03 N	7.16 E
Kurten, Tx., U.S.	222	30.47 N	96.16 W
Kürteşe	130	41.14 N	33.44 E
Kurthasanlı	130	38.20 N	32.11 E
Kurth Lake ⊜	222	31.26 N	94.42 W
Kūrtī	140	18.07 N	31.33 E
Kurtino	82	54.59 N	38.17 E
Kurtinskoje vodochranilišče ⊜ [1]	85	43.50 N	76.20 E
Kurtistown	229d	19.36 N	155.03 W
Kurtušibinskij chrebet ⋏	88	52.10 N	93.30 E
Kurty ≃	85	44.05 N	76.20 E

PORTUGUÊS

Nome	Página	Lat.°′	Long.°′ W = Oeste
Kurtz	218	38.58 N	86.12 W
Kuru, Sūd.	140	7.43 N	26.31 E
Kuru, Suomi	26	61.52 N	23.44 E
Kuru ≃	140	9.08 N	26.57 E
Kuruca Geçidi)(	130	38.58 N	40.16 E
Kurucaşile	130	41.50 N	32.43 E
Kuruçay	130	39.39 N	38.29 E
Kuruçay (Kura) ≃	84	39.24 N	49.24 E
Kuruçeşme ⬥ [8]	267b	41.03 N	29.02 E
Kurudu, Pulau ɪ	164	1.51 S	137.01 E
Kurukshetra	124	29.59 N	76.51 E
Kuruktag ⋏	90	41.30 N	90.00 E
Kurum	164	4.45 S	145.55 E
Kuruman	158	27.28 S	23.28 E
Kuruman ≃	158	26.56 S	20.39 E
Kurumanheuwels ⋏ [2]	158	27.40 S	23.25 E
Kurumdy, gora ∧	85	39.28 N	73.32 E
Kurume	96	33.19 N	130.31 E
Kurumkan	88	54.18 N	110.18 E
Kurun ≃	144	5.30 N	34.17 E
Kurunegala	122	7.29 N	80.22 E
Kurungbaja, Tanjung ≻	115b	8.15 S	120.35 E
Kurung Tank ⊜ [1]	124	22.19 N	82.14 E
Kurunzulaj	88	51.00 N	117.10 E
Kuruqi	89	48.58 N	123.50 E
Kurur, Jabal ∧	140	20.31 N	31.32 E
Kurusaj	85	40.35 N	69.24 E
Kurushima-kaikyo ⌇	96	34.07 N	133.00 E
Kuruson-zan ∧	96	34.12 N	130.58 E
Kurylys	86	48.38 N	60.47 E
Kuryongp'o	98	35.59 N	129.32 E
Kurzeme □ [9]	76	56.50 N	22.30 E
Kusa	86	55.20 N	59.29 E
Kusabe	270	34.31 N	135.29 E
Kuşadası	130	37.51 N	27.15 E
Kuşadası Körfezi c	130	37.50 N	27.08 E
Kusak ≃	86	47.50 N	75.45 E
Kušalino	76	57.07 N	36.05 E
Kusan-ni, Taehan	98	37.43 N	128.49 E
Kusan-ni, Taehan	271b	37.29 N	126.45 E
Kusathu ⊜	120	35.43 N	92.45 E
Kusatsu, Nihon	94	36.37 N	138.36 E
Kusatsu, Nihon	94	35.00 N	135.57 E
Kusawa Lake ⊜	180	60.20 N	136.15 W
Kusaybah, Bi'r ⍑ [4]	140	22.41 N	29.55 E
Kuščovskaja	78	46.33 N	39.37 E
Kuse	96	35.04 N	133.45 E
Kusel	56	49.32 N	7.24 E
Kušen'ki	78	48.53 N	34.07 E
Kusey	54	52.36 N	11.05 E
Kuş Gölü ⊜	130	40.10 N	27.57 E
Kushaka	150	10.32 N	6.48 E
Kushālgarh	120	23.10 N	74.27 E
Kusheriki	150	10.33 N	6.28 E
Kushi	174m	26.33 N	128.06 E
Kushida ≃	94	34.36 N	136.34 E
Kushigata	94	35.36 N	138.28 E
Kushihiki	268	35.55 N	139.36 E
Kushikino	92	31.44 N	130.16 E
Kushima	92	31.29 N	131.14 E
Kushimoto	92	33.28 N	135.47 E
Kushira	270	34.28 N	135.43 E
Kushiro	92a	42.58 N	144.23 E
Kushog Lake ⊜	212	45.05 N	78.48 W
Kushtia	124	23.55 N	89.07 E
Kushui	102	42.11 N	94.25 E
Kusiro → Kushiro	92a	42.58 N	144.23 E
Kusiyāra ≃	120	24.36 N	91.44 E
Kuška	128	35.16 N	62.20 E
Kuška ≃	128	36.00 N	62.40 E
Kuskokwim ≃	180	60.17 N	162.27 W
Kuskokwim, North Fork ≃	180	63.06 N	154.37 W
Kuskokwim, South Fork ≃	180	63.06 N	154.37 W
Kuskokwim Bay c	180	59.45 N	162.25 W
Kuskokwim Mountains ⋏	180	62.30 N	156.00 W
Kuskovo ⬥ [8]	265b	55.44 N	37.49 E
Kuškušara	24	64.58 N	40.21 E
Kusma	124	28.14 N	83.41 E
Kušmurun	86	52.27 N	64.36 E
Kušmurun, ozero ⊜	86	52.40 N	64.48 E
Küsnacht	58	47.19 N	8.35 E
Kušnarenkovo	86	55.06 N	55.22 E
Kušnica	78	48.27 N	23.14 E
Kusŏng	98	39.59 N	125.15 E
Kusria	272b	22.58 N	88.14 E
Kussharo-ko ⊜	92a	43.38 N	144.21 E
Küssnacht am Rigi	58	47.05 N	8.27 E
Kustanaj	86	53.10 N	63.35 E
Kustanajskaja □ [4]	86	52.20 N	63.40 E
Kustar'ovka	80	54.16 N	42.16 E
Küsten-Gebirge → Coast Mountains ⋏	176	55.00 N	129.00 W
Küstenkanal ≅	52	52.57 N	7.18 E
Küsten-Ketten → Coast Ranges ⋏	178	41.00 N	123.30 W
Kusthalia	126	23.29 N	87.03 E
Kūstī	140	13.10 N	32.40 E
Küstrin → Kostrzyn	30	52.37 N	14.39 E
Kusu, Nihon	94	34.55 N	136.38 E
Kusu, Nihon	96	33.16 N	131.09 E
Kušugum	78	47.42 N	35.14 E
Kušum ≃	80	48.54 N	50.32 E
Kusumba	272b	22.27 N	88.24 E
Kusumbāni ∧	126	21.57 N	86.26 E
Kušumskij	80	51.38 N	48.21 E
Kusung	98	36.18 N	128.55 E
Kusunoki	96	34.03 N	131.15 E
K'us'ur	74	70.39 N	127.15 E
Kušva	86	58.18 N	59.45 E
Kut, Ko ɪ	110	11.40 N	102.35 E
Kuta	150	9.52 N	6.43 E
Kuta ≃	88	56.46 N	105.40 E
Kutabaru	112	0.44 S	102.56 E
Kutabuloh	114	3.28 N	97.04 E
Kutacane	114	3.30 N	97.48 E
Kütahya	130	39.25 N	29.59 E
Kütahya □ [4]	130	39.20 N	29.30 E
Kutais	78	44.32 N	39.18 E
Kutaisi	84	42.15 N	42.40 E
Kutāmat al-Ghābah	142	30.55 N	30.54 E
Kutanibong	114	3.53 N	96.22 E
Kutaradja → Banda Aceh	114	5.34 N	95.20 E
Kutarere	172	38.03 S	177.09 E
Kutasawang	114	5.08 N	96.54 E
Kutch, Gulf of c	120	22.36 N	69.30 E
Kutch, Rann of ⩦	120	24.05 N	70.10 E
Kutchan	92a	42.54 N	140.45 E
Kutcharo-ko ⊜	92a	45.09 N	142.19 E
Kutejnikovo, S.S.S.R.	83	47.49 N	38.18 E
Kutejnikovo, S.S.S.R.	83	47.34 N	39.46 E
Kutenholz	52	53.29 N	9.19 E
Kutima	88	57.10 N	108.16 E
Kutima ≃	88	57.08 N	108.14 E
Kutina	36	45.29 N	16.46 E
Kutiyāna	120	21.38 N	69.59 E
Kutkai	110	23.27 N	97.56 E
Kutkašen	84	40.59 N	47.50 E
Kutluškino	80	55.14 N	50.24 E
Kutná Hora	30	49.57 N	15.16 E
Kutno	30	52.15 N	19.23 E
Kutoarjo	115a	7.43 S	109.54 E
Kutomara	88	51.06 N	118.49 E
Kutse Game Reserve ⬥ [4]	156	23.30 S	24.05 E
Kutsuki	94	35.21 N	135.55 E
Küttigen	58	47.25 N	8.03 E
Kuttura	24	68.24 N	26.28 E
Kuttusoja	24	67.46 N	28.50 E
Kuttuzi	265a	59.45 N	30.04 E
Kutu	152	2.44 S	18.09 E
Kutubdia Island ɪ	120	21.50 N	91.52 E
Kutubu, Lake ⊜	164	6.23 S	143.18 E
Kutukovo	80	54.26 N	40.31 E

Kutulik	88	53.21 N	102.48 E
Kutulo, Lagh ≃	154	2.08 N	40.56 E
Kutuluk ≃	80	53.19 N	51.09 E
Kutum	140	14.12 N	24.40 E
Kutu-Moke	152	3.12 S	17.21 E
Kúty, Česko.	30	48.40 N	17.03 E
Kuty, S.S.S.R.	78	48.16 N	25.10 E
Kutztown	210	40.31 N	75.46 W
Kuujjuaq	176	58.06 N	68.25 W
Kuuli-Majak	128	40.14 N	52.42 E
Kuurne	50	50.51 N	3.17 E
Kuusamo	26	65.58 N	29.11 E
Kuusankoski	26	60.54 N	26.38 E
Kuva	85	40.32 N	72.05 E
Kuvak-Nikol'skoje	80	53.37 N	43.30 E
Kuvandyk	86	51.28 N	57.21 E
Kuvango	152	14.28 S	16.20 E
Kuvasaj	85	40.18 N	71.58 E
Kuvet ≃	180	69.14 N	175.00 E
Kuvšinovo	76	57.02 N	34.10 E
Kuwabara	270	34.53 N	135.15 E
Kuwait (Al-Kuwayt) □ [1], Asia	118	29.30 N	47.45 E
Kuwait (Al-Kuwayt) □ [1], Asia	128	29.30 N	47.45 E
Kuwait Bay → Kuwayt, Khalīj al- c	128	29.30 N	48.00 E
Kuwana	94	35.04 N	136.42 E
Kuwayt, Khalīj al- c	128	29.30 N	48.00 E
Kuyāli	126	22.31 N	86.11 E
Kuybyshev → Kujbyšev	80	53.12 N	50.09 E
Kuye ≃	102	38.30 N	110.44 E
Kūysanjaq	128	36.05 N	44.38 E
Kuyucak, Tür.	130	37.51 N	38.21 E
Kuyucak, Tür.	130	37.55 N	28.28 E
Kuyuwini ≃	246	2.16 N	58.16 W
Kuyuyukak, Cape ≻	180	56.54 N	156.50 W
Kuzaranda	24	62.22 N	35.37 E
Kuze	94	35.33 N	136.30 E
Kuze ⬥ [8]	270	34.57 N	135.43 E
Kuzedejevo	86	53.20 N	87.10 E
Kuzemin	78	50.09 N	34.39 E
Kuzemovka	83	49.31 N	37.59 E
Kužener	80	56.48 N	48.56 E
Kuženkino	76	57.44 N	33.59 E
Kuzitrin ≃	180	65.10 N	165.28 W
Kuzkejevo	80	55.46 N	52.48 E
Kuz'miniči	76	54.16 N	33.42 E
Kuz'minka ≃	265a	59.48 N	30.31 E
Kuz'minki ⬥ [8]	265b	55.42 N	37.48 E
Kuz'mino, S.S.S.R.	82	55.09 N	37.53 E
Kuz'mino, S.S.S.R.	82	56.36 N	37.55 E
Kuzmiščevo	82	54.46 N	37.12 E
Kuz'movka	74	62.19 N	92.02 E
Kuznečicha	80	54.43 N	49.38 E
Kuznečikovo	82	56.13 N	36.35 E
Kuzneck, S.S.S.R.	80	53.07 N	46.36 E
Kuzneck → Novokuzneck, S.S.S.R.	86	53.45 N	87.06 E
Kuzneckij Alatau ⋏	86	54.45 N	88.00 E
Kuznečnoje	26	61.09 N	29.52 E
Kuznecova	89	46.16 N	138.03 E
Kuznecovka	76	56.18 N	28.33 E
Kuznecovo, S.S.S.R.	82	55.30 N	38.21 E
Kuznecovo, S.S.S.R.	82	55.27 N	36.57 E
Kuznecovo, S.S.S.R.	86	59.15 N	63.28 E
Kuznecovo-Michajlovka	83	47.27 N	38.13 E
Kuznecovskij	80	47.25 N	40.57 E
Kuznecy	82	55.51 N	38.40 E
Kuznetsk → Kuzneck	80	53.07 N	46.36 E
Kuznetsovsk	78	51.22 N	25.53 E
Kuzomen', S.S.S.R.	24	64.17 N	42.53 E
Kuzomen', S.S.S.R.	24	66.17 N	36.54 E
Kuzovatovo	80	53.33 N	47.41 E
Kuztekke	130	41.48 N	33.16 E
Kuzucubelen	130	36.51 N	34.27 E
Kuzuha	270	34.52 N	135.41 E
Kuzuryū ≃	94	36.13 N	136.08 E
Kuzuu	94	36.24 N	139.37 E
Kvænangen c [2]	24	70.05 N	21.13 E
Kværndrup	41	55.10 N	10.32 E
Kvaisi	84	42.31 N	43.40 E
Kvaløya ɪ, Nor.	24	69.40 N	18.30 E
Kvaløya ɪ, Nor.	24	70.37 N	23.52 E
Kvam	26	61.40 N	9.42 E
Kvanløse	41	55.39 N	11.41 E
Kvanndal	26	60.29 N	6.36 E
Kvareli	84	41.56 N	45.54 E
Kvarner c	36	44.45 N	14.15 E
Kvarnerić ⌇	36	44.45 N	14.35 E
Kvarnsveden	40	60.31 N	15.24 E
Kvarntorp	40	59.08 N	15.15 E
Kvarsa	80	56.58 N	53.57 E
Kvarsebo	40	58.39 N	16.39 E
Kvašenki	82	56.48 N	37.33 E
Kvenna ≃	26	60.01 N	7.56 E
Kverkfjöll ∧	24a	64.43 N	16.38 W
Kvichak Bay c	180	58.48 N	157.30 W
Kvicksund	40	59.27 N	16.19 E
Kvidinge	41	56.08 N	13.04 E
Kvien ⊜	40	60.24 N	13.48 E
Kvikkjokk	24	66.55 N	17.50 E
Kvilda	60	49.01 N	13.35 E
Kvina ≃	26	58.17 N	6.56 E
Kvismare kanal ≅	40	59.12 N	15.11 E
Kvissleby	26	62.17 N	17.21 E
Kvistbro	40	59.09 N	14.49 E
Kvistgård	41	55.59 N	12.30 E
Kvitok	88	56.03 N	98.30 E
Kwa ≃	152	3.10 S	16.11 E
Kwachaga	154	5.38 S	38.08 E
Kwada	164	6.09 S	141.53 E
Kwahae-ri ⬥ [8]	271b	37.33 N	126.50 E
Kwahu Plateau ⋏ [1]	150	6.30 N	0.30 W
Kwai → Khwae Noi ≃	110	14.00 N	99.33 E
Kwajalein ɪ [1]	14	9.05 N	167.20 E
Kwajok	140	8.19 N	28.00 E
Kwakoegron	250	5.15 N	55.20 W
Kwale, Kenya	154	4.11 S	39.27 E
Kwale, Nig.	150	5.46 N	6.26 E
Kwambilo ≃	273b	4.26 S	15.20 E
Kwa-Mbonambi	158	28.36 S	32.05 E
Kwamisa ∧	150	7.08 N	1.53 W
Kwamouth	152	3.10 S	16.12 E
Kwa Mtoro	154	5.14 S	35.26 E
Kwanak-san ∧	271b	37.27 N	126.58 E
Kwando (Cuando) ≃	152	18.27 S	23.32 E
Kwangchow → Guangzhou	100	23.06 N	113.16 E
Kwangju	98	35.09 N	126.54 E
Kwangju □ [4]	98	35.09 N	126.55 E
Kwango (Cuango) ≃	152	3.14 S	17.23 E
Kwangsi Chuang Autonomous Region → Guangxi Zhuangzu Zizhiqu □ [4]	102	24.00 N	109.00 E
Kwangtung → Guangdong □ [4]	90	23.00 N	113.00 E
Kwangwazi	154	7.47 S	38.15 E
Kwangyang	98	34.59 N	127.34 E
Kwania, Lake ⊜	154	1.45 N	32.45 E
Kwanmo-bong ∧	98	41.42 N	129.13 E
Kwansan-ni	271b	37.43 N	126.51 E
Kwanto Plain → Kantō-heiya ⩦	94	36.00 N	139.30 E
Kwara □ [3]	150	8.45 N	5.00 E
Kware	150	13.12 N	5.14 E
Kwa-Thema	273d	26.18 S	28.23 E
Kwatisore	164	3.15 S	134.57 E
Kweichow → Guizhou □ [4]	102	27.00 N	107.00 E
Kweihwa → Hohhot	102	40.51 N	111.40 E
Kweijang → Guiyang	102	26.35 N	106.43 E

Kweilin → Guilin	102	25.17 N	110.17 E
Kweisui → Hohhot	102	40.51 N	111.40 E
Kweiyang → Guiyang	102	26.35 N	106.43 E
Kwekwe	154	18.55 S	29.49 E
Kweneng □ [5]	156	24.00 S	24.00 E
Kwenge (Caengo) ≃	152	4.50 S	18.42 E
Kwesimintim	150	4.54 N	1.47 W
Kwethluk	180	60.49 N	161.27 W
Kwethluk ≃	180	60.46 N	161.26 W
Kwidzyn	30	53.45 N	18.56 E
Kwigillingok	180	59.51 N	163.08 W
Kwiguk	180	62.45 N	164.28 W
Kwiha	144	13.31 N	39.32 E
Kwilu (Cuilo) ≃	152	3.22 S	17.22 E
Kwinana	168a	32.15 S	115.48 E
Kwitaro ≃	246	3.19 N	58.47 W
Kwobrup	162	33.37 S	117.46 E
Kwoka, Gunung ∧	164	0.31 S	132.27 E
Kwolla	150	9.00 N	9.15 E
Kwun Tong	271d	22.19 N	114.12 E
Kyabé	146	9.27 N	18.57 E
Kyabra	166	26.18 S	143.10 E
Kyabra Creek ≃	166	25.36 S	142.55 E
Kyabram	166	36.19 S	145.03 E
Kyaikkami	110	16.04 N	97.34 E
Kyaiklat	110	16.26 N	95.44 E
Kyaikto	110	17.18 N	97.01 E
Kya-in	110	16.02 N	98.08 E
Kyaka	154	1.16 S	31.25 E
Kyancutta	166	33.08 S	135.34 E
Ky-anh	110	18.05 N	106.18 E
Kyat-aw	110	12.29 N	98.19 E
Kyaukhnyat	110	18.15 N	97.31 E
Kyaukkyi	110	18.19 N	96.46 E
Kyaukme	110	22.32 N	97.02 E
Kyaukpa	110	13.05 N	98.59 E
Kyaukpyu, Mya.	110	19.05 N	93.52 E
Kyaukpyu, Mya.	110	19.26 N	93.33 E
Kyaukse	110	21.36 N	96.08 E
Kyauktaw	110	20.51 N	92.59 E
Kyaunggon	110	17.06 N	95.11 E
Kybartai	76	54.39 N	22.45 E
Kybean	171b	36.22 S	149.25 E
Kybeyan Range ⋏	171b	36.20 S	149.32 E
Kyburz	226	38.47 N	120.18 W
Kydra	171b	36.27 S	149.23 E
Kyeamba	171b	35.26 S	147.37 E
Kyeamba Creek ≃	171b	35.06 S	147.29 E
Kyebang-san ∧	98	37.43 N	128.29 E
Kyegegwa	154	0.29 N	31.03 E
Kyeikdon	110	16.00 N	98.24 E
Kyeintali	110	18.00 N	94.29 E
Kyenjojo	154	0.37 N	30.38 E
Kyeryong-san Kukrip Kongwŏn ♠	98	36.21 N	127.13 E
Kyes Peak ∧	224	47.57 N	121.19 W
Kyffhäuser-Denkmal ⊥	54	51.23 N	11.06 E
Kyffhäuser Gebirge ⋏	54	51.23 N	11.05 E
Kyidaunggan	110	19.53 N	96.12 E
Kyindwe	110	20.58 N	93.51 E
Kyje ⬥ [8]	54	50.04 N	14.32 E
Kyjov	30	49.01 N	17.08 E
Kykladen → Kikládhes ɪɪ	38	37.30 N	25.00 E
Kykotsmovi Village	200	35.52 N	110.37 W
Kykva	80	57.22 N	53.50 E
Kylās ∧	124	25.18 N	90.45 E
Kyle, Sk., Can.	184	50.50 N	108.02 W
Kyle, S.D., U.S.	198	43.25 N	102.10 W
Kyle, Tx., U.S.	196	29.59 N	97.52 W
Kyle □ [9]	44	55.29 N	4.24 W
Kyle, Lake ⊜ [1]	154	20.14 S	31.00 E
Kyleakin	46	57.16 N	5.44 W
Kyle of Lochalsh	46	57.17 N	5.43 W
Kylerhea	46	57.14 N	5.41 W
Kylertown	214	41.00 N	78.10 W
Kylestrome	46	58.16 N	5.02 W
Kyll ≃	56	49.48 N	6.42 E
Kyllburg	56	50.02 N	6.35 E
Kym ≃	42	52.14 N	0.17 W
Kymen lääni □ [4]	26	61.00 N	28.00 E
Kymijoki ≃	26	60.30 N	26.52 E
Kyn	86	57.52 N	58.38 E
Kyndby	41	55.48 N	11.56 E
Kyneton	169	37.15 S	144.27 E
Kynnefjäll ∧ [2]	26	58.42 N	11.41 E
Kynšperk nad Ohří	54	50.04 N	12.32 E
Kynuna	166	21.35 S	141.55 E
Kyodong-do ɪ	98	37.45 N	126.16 E
Kyoga, Lake ⊜	154	1.30 N	33.00 E
Kyōga-misaki ≻	96	35.46 N	135.13 E
Kyogle	166	28.37 S	153.00 E
Kyoha-ri	271b	37.46 N	126.46 E
Kyohyŏn-ni	271b	37.43 N	126.58 E
Kyom ≃	140	8.58 N	28.13 E
Kyŏmip'o → Songnim	98	38.44 N	125.38 E
Kyonan	94	35.07 N	139.50 E
Kyondo	110	16.35 N	98.03 E
Kyŏnggi Do □ [4]	98	37.30 N	127.15 E
Kyŏnggi-man c	98	37.25 N	126.00 E
Kyŏngju	98	35.51 N	129.14 E
Kyŏngju Kukrip Kongwŏn ♠	98	35.47 N	129.15 E
Kyŏngsan	98	35.48 N	128.43 E
Kyŏngsang Namdo □ [4]	98	35.15 N	128.30 E
Kyŏngsang Pukdo □ [4]	98	36.15 N	128.45 E
Kyŏngsŏng, C.M.I.K.	98	41.35 N	129.36 E
Kyŏngsŏng → Sŏul, Taehan	98	37.33 N	126.58 E
Kyŏngwŏn	98	42.48 N	130.09 E
Kyônkadun	110	16.04 N	95.38 E
Kyonmange	110	16.30 N	95.50 E
Kyonpyaw	110	17.18 N	95.12 E
Kyotera	154	0.33 S	31.19 E
Kyōto, Nihon	94	35.00 N	135.45 E
Kyōto, Nihon	270	35.00 N	135.45 E
Kyōto □ [5]	94	35.05 N	135.45 E
Kyōto-bonchi ⋏	270	35.03 N	135.45 E
Kyōto Race Track ♠	270	34.54 N	135.44 E
Kyōto University ☗ [2]	270	35.02 N	135.46 E
Kyōwa	94	36.19 N	140.03 E
Kyōyomi-dake ∧	96	33.31 N	131.02 E
Kypšak, ozero ⊜	86	50.09 N	68.28 E
Kyra	88	49.36 N	111.58 E
Kyra ≃	88	49.24 N	112.19 E
Kyrčany	80	57.37 N	50.10 E
Kyren	88	51.41 N	102.08 E
Kyrenia → Kirínia	130	35.20 N	33.19 E
Kyritz	54	52.56 N	12.23 E
Kyrkheden	40	60.10 N	13.29 E
Kyrkkazyk	85	42.30 N	72.20 E
Kyrksæterøra	26	63.17 N	9.06 E
Kyrkslätt (Kirkkonummi)	26	60.07 N	24.26 E
Kyrö	26	60.42 N	22.45 E
Kyrönjoki ≃	26	63.14 N	21.45 E
Kyrösjärvi ⊜	26	61.45 N	23.10 E
Kyröskoski	26	61.40 N	23.11 E
Kyrta	24	64.04 N	57.42 E
Kyrykkuduk	80	49.51 N	51.54 E
Kyštovka	86	56.33 N	76.38 E
Kyštym	86	55.42 N	60.34 E
Kysykkamys	80	49.14 N	50.19 E
Kyte ≃	190	42.00 N	89.19 W
Kytlym	86	59.30 N	59.12 E
Kytmanovo	86	53.28 N	85.28 E
Kyūhōji	270	34.38 N	135.35 E
Kyunchaung	110	15.33 N	98.15 E
Kyundon	110	20.31 N	95.44 E
Kyungyi ɪ	110	15.04 N	97.44 E
Kyunhla	110	23.21 N	95.18 E
Kyuquot	182	50.02 N	127.23 W
Kyuquot Sound ⌇	182	50.05 N	127.15 W
Kyūroku-jima ɪ	92	40.32 N	139.29 E

Kyū-shizudani-gakkō ⊥	96	34.45 N	134.13 E
Kyūshū ɪ	92	33.00 N	131.00 E
Kyushu-Palau Ridge ⊹ [3]	14	20.00 N	136.00 E
Kyūshū-sanchi ⋏	92	32.35 N	131.17 E
Kywebwe	110	18.42 N	96.25 E
Kywong	166	34.59 S	146.44 E
Kyyjärvi	26	63.02 N	24.34 E
Kyzas	86	52.20 N	89.20 E
Kyzyl	88	51.42 N	94.27 E
Kyzylagadžskij zapovednik ⬥ [4]	84	39.10 N	49.00 E
Kyzylagaš	86	45.54 N	81.37 E
Kyzylaryk	85	43.57 N	70.42 E
Kyzylbejit	85	41.30 N	72.24 E
Kyzyl-Chaja	86	50.03 N	89.54 E
Kyzyl-Chem (Šišchid) ≃	88	51.21 N	96.58 E
Kyzyl-Džar	85	41.17 N	72.02 E
Kyzylemgek	85	41.57 N	74.56 E
Kyzylespe	86	47.27 N	73.53 E
Kyzylkak, ozero ⊜	86	53.25 N	73.48 E
Kyzyl-Kija	85	40.16 N	72.08 E
Kyzyl-Kommuna	86	48.44 N	67.32 E
Kyzylkum ⬥ [2]	72	42.00 N	64.00 E
Kyzylkup	128	40.38 N	53.58 E
Kyzyl-Mažalyk	86	51.10 N	90.32 E
Kyzylmazar	85	39.39 N	68.25 E
Kyzyloba	80	49.37 N	50.38 E
Kyzylsu ≃	85	39.17 N	71.23 E
Kyzyltas, gory ⋏	86	48.30 N	74.50 E
Kyzyltau	86	47.53 N	72.05 E
Kyzylt'ob'o	85	42.13 N	75.16 E
Kyzyltu, S.S.S.R.	85	42.11 N	76.40 E
Kyzyltu, S.S.S.R.	86	47.46 N	59.08 E
Kyzyltu, S.S.S.R.	86	47.43 N	75.42 E
Kyzyluj	86	48.07 N	65.28 E
Kyzylžar	86	48.17 N	69.39 E
Kzyl-Kuga	80	48.28 N	53.01 E
Kzyl-Orda	86	44.48 N	65.28 E
Kzyl-Orda □ [4]	85	43.30 N	67.00 E
Kzyltu	86	53.38 N	72.20 E

L

La'a	102	29.44 N	101.26 E
Laa an der Thaya	61	48.43 N	16.23 E
Laaben	61	48.06 N	15.52 E
Laaber	60	49.04 N	11.53 E
Laaberberg	60	48.46 N	12.01 E
Laab im Walde	264b	48.09 N	16.11 E
Laacher See ⊜	56	50.25 N	7.16 E
Laaerberg ∧ [2]	264b	48.09 N	16.24 E
Laage	54	53.56 N	12.20 E
La Aguada, Zanjón de ≃	286e	33.30 S	70.47 W
La Aguja, Cabo de ≻	246	11.18 N	74.12 W
Laakajärvi ⊜	26	63.50 N	27.55 E
Laaken ⬥ [8]	263	51.15 N	7.15 E
Laakirchen	64	47.58 N	13.49 E
La Albuera	34	38.43 N	6.49 W
La Albufera ⊜	34	39.20 N	0.22 W
La Alcarria ⬥ [1]	34	40.30 N	2.45 W
La Aldea	234	20.54 N	101.29 W
La Aldehuela	266a	40.18 N	3.36 W
La Algaba	34	37.28 N	6.01 W
La Almarcha	34	39.41 N	2.22 W
La Almunia de Doña Godina	34	41.29 N	1.22 W
Laanecoorie Reservoir ⊜ [1]	169	36.52 S	143.53 E
La Antigua, Salina ⩦	252	30.00 S	66.06 W
La Antorcha, Cerro ∧	234	21.43 N	102.45 W
Laar ⬥ [8]	263	51.28 N	6.43 E
La Araucanía □ [4]	252	38.45 S	72.30 W
La Arena	236	7.58 N	80.28 W
Laas → Lasa	64	46.37 N	10.42 E
Laas Caanood	144	8.28 N	47.21 E
Laas Dawaco	144	10.28 N	49.05 E
Laas Dhaareed	144	10.10 N	45.59 E
Laase	54	53.04 N	11.18 E
Laas Qoray	144	11.10 N	48.13 E
La Asunción	246	11.02 N	63.53 W
Laatzen	52	52.19 N	9.47 E
Laau Point ≻	229a	21.06 N	157.19 W
La Aurora	286e	33.36 S	70.38 W
La Azufrosa	196	28.14 N	100.50 W
Laba ≃	78	45.11 N	39.42 E
La Babia	232	28.34 N	102.04 W
L'Abacou, Pointe ≻	238	18.03 N	73.47 W
Labadie	219	38.31 N	90.51 W
Labadieville	194	29.50 N	90.57 W
La Baie	186	48.19 N	70.53 W
La Balme-de-Sillingy	58	45.58 N	6.02 E
La Balme-les-Grottes	62	45.51 N	5.20 E
Laban	208	37.24 N	76.17 W
La Banda	252	27.44 S	64.15 W
La Bandera	286e	33.34 S	70.39 W
La Bañeza	34	42.18 N	5.54 W
La Barca	234	20.17 N	102.34 W
La Barge	200	42.15 N	110.11 W
La Barge Creek ≃	200	42.14 N	110.10 W
La Barre-en-Ouche	50	48.57 N	0.40 E
La Barr Meadows	226	39.11 N	121.02 W
Labason	116	8.04 N	122.31 E
La Bassée	50	50.32 N	2.48 E
Labastide-Murat	32	44.39 N	1.34 E
La Bastide-Puylaurent	62	44.36 N	3.54 E
La Bâte	261	48.35 N	2.01 E
La Baule-Escoublac	32	47.17 N	2.24 W
La Bazoche-Gouet	50	48.08 N	0.59 E
L'Abbé	261	48.34 N	1.50 E
Labdah (Leptis Magna) ⊥	146	32.38 N	14.18 E
Labé	150	11.19 N	12.17 W
Labe (Elbe) ≃	30	53.50 N	9.00 E
Labégude	62	44.39 N	4.22 E
La Bégude-Blanche	62	43.55 N	6.08 E
La Bégude-de-Mazenc	62	44.32 N	4.56 E
Labelle, P.Q., Can.	206	46.16 N	74.44 W
La Belle, Fl., U.S.	220	26.45 N	81.26 W
La Belle, Mo., U.S.	219	40.07 N	91.54 W
Labelle □ [6]	206	46.20 N	75.00 W
Labelle, Lac ⊜, P.Q., Can.	206	46.13 N	74.52 W
La Belle, Lac ⊜, Wi., U.S.	216	43.08 N	88.31 W
Labengke, Pulau ɪ	112	3.27 S	122.25 E
La Bérarde	62	44.56 N	6.18 E
Laberge, Lake ⊜	180	61.11 N	135.12 W
Laberinto de las Doce Leguas ɪɪ	240p	20.35 N	78.30 W
La Berra ∧	58	46.41 N	7.11 E
Laberweinting	60	48.48 N	12.19 E
Labes → Łobez	30	53.39 N	15.36 E
La Besace	56	49.34 N	4.58 E
Labette Creek ≃	198	37.03 N	95.05 W
Labi	112	4.25 N	114.22 E
La Biche ≃	182	55.01 N	112.44 W
Labico	66	41.47 N	12.53 E
Labin	36	45.05 N	14.07 E
Labinsk	84	44.38 N	40.44 E
Labis	114	2.23 N	103.02 E
La Bisbal	34	41.57 N	3.03 E
Łabiszyn	30	52.57 N	17.55 E
Lablābah, Wādī al- ∨	273c	30.02 N	31.19 E
La Blanca	286e	33.31 S	70.41 W
Labná ⊥	232	20.11 N	89.34 W
Labo	116	14.09 N	122.51 E
Labo ≃	116	14.11 N	122.56 E
Labo, Mount ∧	116	14.01 N	122.48 E
La Boca	234	23.56 N	99.17 W
Laboe	54	54.24 N	10.15 E
La Boissière	261	48.46 N	1.59 E

≃	River	Fluss	Río	Rivière	Rio
≅	Canal	Kanal	Canal	Canal	Canal
ʟ	Waterfall, Rapids	Wasserfall, Stromschnellen	Cascada, Rápidos	Chute d'eau, Rapides	Cascata, Rápidos
⌇	Strait	Meeresstrasse	Estrecho	Détroit	Estreito
c	Bay, Gulf	Bucht, Golf	Bahía, Golfo	Baie, Golfe	Baía, Golfo
⊜	Lake, Lakes	See, Seen	Lago, Lagos	Lac, Lacs	Lago, Lagos
⩦	Swamp	Sumpf	Pantano	Marais	Pântano
⛉	Ice Features, Glacier	Eis- und Gletscherformen	Accidentes Glaciales	Formes glaciaires	Acidentes glaciares
⍑	Other Hydrographic Features	Andere Hydrographische Objekte	Otros Elementos Hidrográficos	Autres données hydrographiques	Outros acidentes hidrográficos

⊹	Submarine Features	Untermeerische Objekte	Accidentes Submarinos	Formes de relief sous-marin	Acidentes submarinos
□	Political Unit	Politische Einheit	Unidad Politica	Entité politique	Unidade política
☗	Cultural Institution	Kulturelle Institution	Institución Cultural	Institution culturelle	Instituição cultural
⊥	Historical Site	Historische Stätte	Sitio Histórico	Site historique	Sitio histórico
♠	Recreational Site	Erholungs- und Ferienort	Sitio de Recreo	Centre de loisirs	Area de Lazer
⊠	Airport	Flughafen	Aeropuerto	Aéroport	Aeroporto
■	Military Installation	Militäranlage	Instalación Militar	Installation militaire	Instalação militar
⬥	Miscellaneous	Verschiedenes	Misceláneo	Divers	Diversos

ENGLISH — Name, Page, Lat.°′, Long.°′
DEUTSCH — Name, Seite, Breite°′, Länge°′ E = Ost

Name	Page	Lat.°′	Long.°′
La Boissière-Ecole	261	48.41 N	1.39 E
La Bollène-Vésubie	62	43.59 N	7.20 E
La Bonneville-sur-Iton	50	49.00 N	1.02 E
Laboratory	214	40.09 N	80.13 W
Laborde, Arg.	252	33.09 S	62.51 W
La Borde, Fr.	261	48.32 N	2.50 E
Laborec ≃	30	48.36 N	22.00 E
Laborie	241f	13.45 N	61.00 W
Laborie Bay c	241f	13.45 N	61.01 W
Labouchere, Mount ∧	162	25.12 S	118.18 E
Labouheyre	32	44.13 N	0.55 W
Laboulaye	252	34.07 S	63.24 W
La Bouverie	50	50.24 N	3.52 E
La Boyera, Ven.	286c	10.23 N	66.57 W
La Boyera, Ven.	286c	10.25 N	66.50 W
Lābpur	126	23.50 N	87.49 E
Labrador ◆[1]	176	54.00 N	62.00 W
Labrador Basin ✢[1]	16	53.00 N	48.00 W
Labrador City	176	52.57 N	66.55 W
Labrador Sea ⊤[2]	176	57.00 N	53.00 W
Lábrea, Bra.	248	7.16 S	64.47 W
La Brea, Trin.	241r	10.15 N	61.37 W
Labrède	32	44.41 N	0.31 W
La Bresse	58	48.00 N	6.53 E
La Brévine	58	46.59 N	6.36 E
Labrieville, Réserve ♠	186	49.20 N	69.40 W
La Brigue	62	44.04 N	7.37 E
La Brillanne	62	43.55 N	5.53 E
Labrit	32	44.07 N	0.33 W
La Broquerie	184	49.28 N	96.27 W
Labroye	50	50.17 N	1.59 E
Labry	56	49.10 N	5.52 E
Labuan, Pulau I	112	5.21 N	115.13 E
Labuchongshan ⋏	120	30.30 N	85.00 E
Labuha	164	0.37 S	127.29 E
Labuhan	115a	6.22 S	105.50 E
Labuhanbajo	115b	8.29 S	119.54 E
Labuhanbatu	114	2.12 N	100.12 E
Labuhanbilik	114	2.31 N	100.10 E
Labuhandeli	114	3.45 N	98.41 E
Labuhanhaji, Indon.	114	3.33 N	97.00 E
Labuhanhaji, Indon.	115b	8.42 S	116.34 E
Labuhanmarege	112	7.06 S	120.40 E
Labuhanmaringgai	115a	5.21 S	105.48 E
Labuhanpandan	115b	8.23 S	116.43 E
Labuhanruku	114	3.13 N	99.35 E
Labuhanwaiharu	112	5.44 S	104.26 E
Labuk ≃	112	5.54 N	117.30 E
Labuk, Teluk c	112	6.07 N	117.46 E
Labu Kananga	115b	8.08 S	117.47 E
Labutta	110	16.09 N	94.46 E
Labytnangi	72	66.39 N	66.21 E
Laç, Shq.	38	41.38 N	19.43 E
Lač, S.S.S.R.	24	63.18 N	54.28 E
Lac □[5]	146	13.30 N	14.15 E
Lača, ozero ⊜	24	61.20 N	38.48 E
La Cadena	196	25.53 N	104.12 W
L'Acadie	275a	45.19 N	73.21 W
L'Acadie ≃	206	45.29 N	73.16 W
La Cadière-d'Azur	62	43.12 N	5.46 E
Lacadivas, Islas → Lakshadweep II	122	10.00 N	73.00 E
Laca Jahuira ≃	248	19.21 S	67.54 W
La Cal ≃	248	17.27 S	58.15 W
Lac-à-la-Tortue	206	46.37 N	72.38 W
La Calera, Chile	252	32.47 S	71.12 W
La Calera, Perú	286d	12.12 S	76.54 W
Lac-Allard	186	50.33 N	63.25 W
Lacamas Creek ≃	224	46.20 N	122.55 W
Lacamas Lake ⊜	224	45.37 N	122.26 W
La Campana, Esp.	34	37.34 N	5.26 W
La Campana, Méx.	234	22.45 N	105.35 W
La Cañada	234	20.37 N	100.19 W
La Canada Flintridge	228	34.12 N	118.12 W
La Canada Verde Creek ≃	280	33.52 N	118.02 W
Lacanau	32	44.59 N	1.05 W
Lacanau, Lac de c	32	44.58 N	1.07 W
La Candelaria, Arg.	252	26.06 S	65.06 W
La Candelaria, Méx.	200	31.07 N	106.29 W
La Cañiza	34	42.13 N	8.16 W
La Canourgue	32	44.26 N	3.13 E
Lacantum ≃	232	16.36 N	90.39 W
La Capelle-en-Thiérache	50	49.58 N	3.55 E
La Capelle-lès-Boulogne	50	50.44 N	1.42 E
Lacapelle-Marival	32	44.44 N	1.54 E
La Capilla, Méx.	234	18.30 N	96.40 W
La Capilla, Méx.	234	23.59 N	98.25 W
La Carlota, Arg.	252	33.26 S	63.18 W
La Carlota, Pil.	116	10.25 N	122.55 E
La Carlota, Aeropuerto ⊠	286c	10.29 N	66.50 W
Lacarne	214	41.31 N	83.03 W
La Carolina	34	38.15 N	3.37 W
La Casita	234	23.43 N	104.46 W
La Castellana	116	10.20 N	123.03 E
La Castrina, Aeropuerto ⊠	286e	33.31 S	70.38 W
Lacaune	32	43.43 N	2.42 E
Lac-Bellemare	206	46.34 N	72.55 W
Lac-Brome	206	45.13 N	72.31 W
Laccadive, Minicoy, and Amīndīvi → Lakshadweep □[3]	122	10.00 N	73.00 E
Laccadive Islands → Lakshadweep II	122	10.00 N	73.00 E
Laccadive Sea ⊤[2]	12	7.00 N	76.00 E
Lacchiarella	62	45.19 N	9.08 E
Lacco Ameno	68	40.45 N	13.54 E
Lac Courte Oreilles Indian Reservation ◆[4]	190	45.55 N	91.19 W
Lac du Flambeau	190	45.59 N	89.51 W
Lac du Flambeau Indian Reservation ◆[4]	190	45.59 N	89.53 W
Laceby	44	53.32 N	0.10 W
Lacedonia	68	41.03 N	15.25 E
La Ceiba, Hond.	236	15.47 N	86.50 W
La Ceiba, Ven.	246	9.28 N	71.04 W
La Celle-les-Bordes	261	48.38 N	1.57 E
La Celle-Saint-Cyr	50	47.58 N	3.18 E
La Center, Ky., U.S.	194	37.04 N	88.58 W
La Center, Wa., U.S.	224	45.52 N	122.40 W
Lacepede Bay c	166	36.47 S	139.45 E
Lacerdónia	156	18.01 S	35.30 E
Laces (Latsch)	64	46.37 N	10.52 E
Lac-Etchemin	186	46.24 N	70.30 W
Lacey	224	47.02 N	122.49 W
Lacey Creek ≃	278	41.50 N	88.03 W
Laceyville	210	41.39 N	76.10 W
Lac-Frontière	186	46.42 N	70.00 W
Lac-giao	110	12.40 N	108.03 E
La Chaise-Dieu	62	45.19 N	3.42 E
La Chambre	62	45.22 N	6.18 E
La Chapelle-d'Angillon	50	47.22 N	2.26 E
La Chapelle-en-Vercors	62	44.58 N	5.25 E
La Chapelle-Gauthier	261	48.33 N	2.54 E
La Chapelle-la-Reine	50	48.19 N	2.35 E
La Chapelle-Saint-Luc	50	48.20 N	4.03 E
La Chapelle-Vendômoise	50	47.40 N	1.15 E
La Charité-sur-Loire	50	47.11 N	3.01 E
La Chartre-sur-le-Loir	50	47.44 N	0.35 E
La Châtaigneraie	32	46.39 N	0.44 W
La Châtre	32	46.35 N	1.59 E
Lachaussée, Étang de ⊜	56	49.02 N	5.48 E
La Chaux-de-Fonds	58	47.06 N	6.50 E
Lachay, Punta ›	248	11.18 S	77.39 W
Lach Dennis	262	53.15 N	2.26 W
Lachdenpochja	24	61.31 N	30.08 E
Lachen	58	47.12 N	8.51 E
Lachenaie	275a	45.42 N	73.34 W
Lachendorf	52	52.37 N	10.14 E
Lachhmangarh	120	27.49 N	75.02 E
L'achi	80	55.20 N	41.56 E
Lachine	206	45.26 N	73.40 W
Lachine, Canal de ≍	275a	45.26 N	73.40 W
Lachine, Rapides de ∟	275a	45.25 N	73.36 W
La Chira, Punta ›	286d	12.13 S	77.03 W
La Chivera	286c	10.37 N	66.54 W
Lachkaltsap Indian Reserve ◆[4]	182	55.03 N	129.34 W
Lachlan ≃	166	34.21 S	143.57 E
La Chorrera, Col.	246	0.44 S	73.01 W
La Chorrera, Pan.	236	8.53 N	79.47 W
L'achoviči, S.S.S.R.	76	53.02 N	26.16 E
L'achoviči, S.S.S.R.	76	52.23 N	27.55 E
L'achovskije ostrova II	74	73.30 N	141.00 E
La Choza	258	34.47 S	59.07 W
La Choza, Arroyo ≃	258	34.40 S	58.58 W
Lachta ◆[8]	265a	60.00 N	30.09 E
Lachtinskij Razliv, ozero ⊜	265a	60.00 N	30.11 E
Lachute	206	45.38 N	74.20 W
Lachva	78	52.13 N	27.04 E
La Ciénaga	252	27.30 S	66.57 W
La Ciénega	234	16.54 N	96.46 W
La Cinta Creek ≃	196	35.24 N	104.06 W
La Ciotat	62	43.10 N	5.36 E
La Cisterna	286e	33.33 S	70.41 W
La Citadelle ⊥	238	19.35 N	72.14 W
La Ciudad, Parque Nacional ♠	234	23.55 N	105.35 W
Lack	48	54.33 N	7.35 W
Lackawanna	210	42.49 N	78.49 W
Lackawanna □[6]	210	41.24 N	75.40 W
Lackawanna ≃	210	41.21 N	75.47 W
Lackawanna, Lake ⊜	276	40.57 N	74.42 W
Lackawanna State Park ♠	210	41.33 N	75.44 W
Lackawaxen	210	41.29 N	74.59 W
Lackawaxen ≃	210	41.29 N	74.59 W
Lackey	208	37.14 N	76.33 W
Lackland Air Force Base ■	196	29.27 N	98.37 W
Läckö	26	58.41 N	13.13 E
Lackoje	76	58.05 N	38.08 E
Lac La Belle	216	43.09 N	88.32 W
Lac la Biche	182	54.46 N	111.58 W
Lac la Hache	182	51.49 N	121.28 W
Lac la Ronge Provincial Park ♠	184	55.15 N	104.55 W
La Clayette	32	46.18 N	4.19 E
Laclede, Id., U.S.	182	48.10 N	116.45 W
La Clede, Il., U.S.	219	38.53 N	88.43 W
Laclede, Mo., U.S.	194	39.47 N	93.09 W
La Clotilde	252	27.08 S	60.40 W
La Clusaz	58	45.54 N	6.25 E
La Cluse	58	46.10 N	5.34 E
La Cluse-et-Mijoux	58	46.53 N	6.23 E
Lacmalac	171b	35.19 S	148.19 E
Lac-Masson	206	46.02 N	74.04 W
Lac-Mégantic	188	45.36 N	70.53 W
Lacob ti-Duyong, Mount ∧	116	17.35 N	121.09 E
La Cocha	252	27.47 S	65.34 W
Lacolle	206	45.05 N	73.22 W
Lacolle ≃	206	45.04 N	73.20 W
La Colle-sur-Loup	62	43.41 N	7.06 E
La Colmena	286a	19.36 N	99.18 W
La Colorada	232	28.41 N	110.25 W
La Columna → Bolívar, Pico ∧	246	8.30 N	71.02 W
Lacombe, Ab., Can.	182	52.28 N	113.44 W
Lacombe, La., U.S.	194	30.18 N	89.56 W
Lacon	190	41.01 N	89.24 W
Lacona, Ia., U.S.	190	41.11 N	93.22 W
Lacona, N.Y., U.S.	212	43.38 N	76.04 W
La Concepción, Méx.	234	18.15 N	102.27 W
La Concepción, Pan.	236	8.31 N	82.37 W
La Concepción, Ven.	246	10.38 N	71.50 W
La Condamine-Châtelard	62	44.27 N	6.45 E
Laconi	71	39.51 N	9.03 E
Laconia	188	43.31 N	71.28 W
La Conner	224	48.23 N	122.29 W
La Consulta	252	33.44 S	69.07 W
Lacoochee	220	28.27 N	82.10 W
La Coruña	34	43.22 N	8.23 W
Lacoste, Fr.	62	43.50 N	5.18 E
La Coste, Tx., U.S.	196	29.19 N	98.49 W
La Côte-Saint-André	62	45.23 N	5.15 E
La Courneuve	261	48.56 N	2.23 E
La Couronne	62	43.20 N	5.03 E
La Courtine	32	45.42 N	2.16 E
Lac qui Parle ≃	198	45.01 N	95.53 W
Lac qui Parle, West Branch ≃	198	44.55 N	96.02 W
La Crau	62	43.09 N	6.04 E
Lacre Punt ›	241s	12.02 N	68.15 W
La Crescent	190	43.49 N	91.18 W
La Crescenta	228	34.13 N	118.14 W
La Creu	266d	41.32 N	2.07 E
La Croft	214	40.39 N	80.35 W
Lacroix-Saint-Ouen	50	49.21 N	2.47 E
La Crosse, In., U.S.	216	41.19 N	86.53 W
La Crosse, Ks., U.S.	198	38.31 N	99.18 W
La Crosse, Va., U.S.	192	36.41 N	78.05 W
Lacrosse, Wa., U.S.	202	46.49 N	117.53 W
La Crosse, Wi., U.S.	190	43.48 N	91.14 W
La Crosse ≃	190	43.49 N	91.16 W
La Cruz, Arg.	252	29.10 S	56.38 W
La Cruz, Col.	246	1.35 N	76.58 W
La Cruz, C.R.	236	11.04 N	85.39 W
La Cruz, Méx.	196	28.33 N	100.48 W
La Cruz, Ur.	258	33.56 S	56.15 W
La Cruz de Río Grande	236	13.06 N	84.10 W
Lac-Saguay	206	46.30 N	75.09 W
Lac Seul	184	50.20 N	92.16 W
Lac Seul Indian Reserve ◆[4]	184	50.15 N	92.10 W
La Cuchilla	234	18.54 N	103.19 W
La Cuesta, C.R.	236	8.30 N	82.50 W
La Cuesta, Méx.	234	20.10 N	104.51 W
La Cuesta, P.R.	240m	18.25 N	66.49 W
La Cumbre, Arg.	252	30.58 S	64.30 W
La Cumbre, Ven.	286c	10.32 N	66.57 W
La Cumbre, Volcán ∧[1]	246a	0.20 S	91.30 W
La Cure	58	46.28 N	6.05 E
Lacy Fork ≃	222	32.24 N	96.08 W
La Cygne	198	38.21 N	94.45 W
Lacy-Lakeview	222	31.37 N	97.06 W
Lada, Teluk c	115a	6.29 S	105.44 E
Ladainha	255	17.39 S	41.44 W
Ladākh □[5]	123	34.45 N	76.30 E
Ladākh Range ⋏	120	34.00 N	78.00 E
Ladan	78	50.31 N	32.35 E
La Dang, Ko I	114	6.33 N	99.18 E
Ladang Jagor	114	4.42 N	101.35 E
Ladara	114	1.28 N	97.28 E
Ladário	248	19.01 S	57.35 W
Ladbergen	52	52.08 N	7.44 E
Ladby	41	55.26 N	10.38 E
Ladd	190	41.22 N	89.13 W
Ladder Creek ≃	198	38.48 N	100.52 W
Laddingford	260	51.12 N	0.25 E
Laddonia	219	39.14 N	91.38 W
Ladeburg	264a	52.42 N	13.35 E
La Défense ʊ	261	48.53 N	2.15 E
La Dehesa	286e	33.22 S	70.33 W
La Dent d'Oche ∧	58	46.21 N	6.44 E
Ladera Heights	280	33.59 N	118.22 W
La Désirade I	241o	16.19 N	61.03 W
Ládhi	38	41.27 N	26.17 E
Ladhurka	126	23.22 N	86.32 E
La Digue I	138	4.21 S	55.50 E
Lâdik	130	40.55 N	35.55 E
Ladinger Spitze ∧	61	46.51 N	14.39 E
L'adiny	24	61.33 N	38.20 E
Ladismith	158	33.30 S	21.16 E
Ladispoli	66	41.56 N	12.05 E
Lādīz	128	28.56 N	61.19 E
Ladner	224	49.05 N	123.05 W
Lādnun	120	27.39 N	74.23 E
Ladoga	194	39.54 N	86.48 W
Ladoga, Lake → Ladožskoje ozero ⊜	24	61.00 N	31.30 E
La Dolorita	286c	10.29 N	66.47 W
Ladon	50	48.00 N	2.32 E
Ladonia	196	33.25 N	95.56 W
La Dorada	246	5.27 N	74.40 W
La Dormida	252	33.21 S	67.55 W
Lado Sarāi ◆[8]	272a	28.32 N	77.12 E
L'adova ≃	78	48.28 N	27.37 E
Ladovskaja Balka	80	45.38 N	41.25 E
Ladožskaja	78	45.19 N	39.54 E
Ladožskoje Ozero	76	60.08 N	31.04 E
Ladožskoje ozero (Lake Ladoga) ⊜	24	61.00 N	31.30 E
Lādpur ◆[8]	272a	28.44 N	76.59 E
Ladrillero, Golfo c	254	49.20 S	75.37 W
Ladson	192	32.59 N	80.06 W
Ladue	219	38.38 N	90.23 W
Ladue ≃	180	63.09 N	140.25 W
Laduozong	102	31.27 N	97.19 E
Laduškin	76	54.36 N	20.11 E
Ladva	24	61.21 N	34.34 E
Ladva-Vetka	24	61.21 N	34.27 E
Lādwa	124	29.59 N	77.03 E
Lady, Fr.	261	48.35 N	2.54 E
L'ady, S.S.S.R.	76	58.38 N	28.47 E
L'ady, S.S.S.R.	76	54.36 N	31.10 E
Lady Ann Strait ɥ	176	75.40 N	79.50 W
Ladybank	46	56.16 N	3.08 W
Lady Barron	166	40.12 S	148.14 E
Ladybower Reservoir ⊜[1]	44	53.20 N	1.45 W
Ladybrand	158	29.19 S	27.25 E
Lady Elliot Island I	166	24.07 S	152.42 E
Lady Evelyn Lake ⊜	190	47.20 N	80.10 W
Lady Frere	158	31.44 S	27.16 E
Lady Grey	158	30.45 S	27.13 E
Lady Lake	220	28.55 N	81.55 W
Ladysmith, Austl.	171b	35.12 S	147.31 E
Ladysmith, B.C., Can.	182	48.58 N	123.49 W
Ladysmith, S. Afr.	158	28.34 S	29.45 E
Ladysmith, Wi., U.S.	190	45.27 N	91.06 W
Ladyženka	86	51.00 N	68.42 E
Ladyžin	78	48.41 N	29.15 E
Ladžanurges	84	42.37 N	42.50 E
Lae	164	6.45 S	147.00 E
Lae I[1]	14	8.56 N	166.14 E
Laem, Khao ∧	110	14.27 N	101.30 E
Laem Ngop	110	12.10 N	102.26 E
La Encantada, Cerro de ∧	232	31.00 N	115.24 W
La Encarnacion	234	23.23 N	98.01 W
Laer	52	52.03 N	7.21 E
Laer ◆[8]	263	51.28 N	7.16 E
Lærdalsøyri	26	61.06 N	7.29 E
La Escondida, Méx.	196	26.17 N	99.46 W
La Escondida, Méx.	232	25.40 N	98.18 W
La Esmeralda, Méx.	232	27.17 N	103.39 W
La Esmeralda, Para.	252	22.13 S	62.38 W
La Esmeralda, Ven.	246	3.10 N	65.33 W
Læsø I	26	57.16 N	11.01 E
La Esperanza, Cuba	240p	22.27 N	80.06 W
La Esperanza, Cuba	240p	22.46 N	83.44 W
La Esperanza, Hond.	236	14.20 N	88.10 W
La Esperanza, Méx.	196	26.46 N	104.00 W
La Esperanza, Méx.	200	32.06 N	114.47 W
La Esperanza, P.R.	240m	18.22 N	66.07 W
La Esperanza ◆[8]	286b	23.03 N	82.22 W
La Estación	266d	41.34 N	2.14 E
La Estación ◆[8]	266a	40.27 N	3.48 W
La Estancia	234	18.05 N	101.25 W
La Estrada	34	42.41 N	8.29 W
La Estrella, Bol.	248	16.30 S	63.45 W
La Estrella, Ven.	286c	10.25 N	66.48 W
Lafa	89	43.50 N	127.19 E
La Falda	252	31.05 S	64.30 W
La Farge	190	43.34 N	90.38 W
LaFargeville	212	44.11 N	75.57 W
Lafayette, Fr.	62	45.35 N	5.04 E
Lafayette, Al., U.S.	194	32.53 N	85.24 W
Lafayette, Ca., U.S.	226	37.53 N	122.07 W
Lafayette, Co., U.S.	198	39.59 N	105.05 W
Lafayette, Ga., U.S.	192	34.42 N	85.16 W
Lafayette, In., U.S.	216	40.25 N	86.52 W
Lafayette, La., U.S.	194	30.13 N	92.01 W
Lafayette, Mn., U.S.	190	44.26 N	94.23 W
Lafayette, N.J., U.S.	210	41.05 N	74.41 W
La Fayette, N.Y., U.S.	210	42.54 N	76.06 W
Lafayette, Oh., U.S.	216	40.46 N	83.57 W
Lafayette, Or., U.S.	224	45.14 N	123.06 W
La Fayette, R.I., U.S.	207	41.34 N	71.28 W
Lafayette, Tn., U.S.	194	36.31 N	86.01 W
La Fayette, Tx., U.S.	222	32.54 N	94.51 W
Lafayette, Mount ∧	188	44.10 N	71.38 W
Lafayette Hill	285	40.05 N	75.15 W
Lafayette Reservoir ⊜[1]	282	37.53 N	122.08 W
Lafayette Water Tunnel ◆[5]	282	37.54 N	122.12 W
La Fère	50	49.40 N	3.22 E
La Feria	196	26.09 N	97.49 W
Laferrere	288	34.45 S	58.35 W
La Ferrière-sur-Risle	50	48.59 N	0.48 E
La Ferté-Alais	50	48.29 N	2.21 E
La Ferté-Bernard	50	48.11 N	0.40 E
La Ferté-Frênel	50	48.50 N	0.30 E
La Ferté-Gaucher	50	48.47 N	3.18 E
La Ferté-Imbault	50	47.23 N	1.58 E
La Ferté-Macé	32	48.36 N	0.22 W
La Ferté-Milon	50	49.10 N	3.07 E
La Ferté-Saint-Aubin	50	47.43 N	1.56 E
La Ferté-sous-Jouarre	50	48.57 N	3.08 E
Laferté-sur-Amance	58	47.50 N	5.42 E
La Ferté-Vidame	50	48.37 N	0.55 E
La Ferté-Villeneuil	50	47.59 N	1.21 E
Lafferty	214	40.06 N	81.01 W
Laffrey	62	45.02 N	5.46 E
Lafia	150	8.30 N	8.30 E
Lafiagi	150	8.52 N	5.25 E
Laflamme ≃	190	48.56 N	77.18 W
Laflèche, P.Q., Can.	275a	45.30 N	73.28 W
Lafleche, Sk., Can.	184	49.43 N	106.35 W
La Flèche, Fr.	32	47.42 N	0.05 W
La Floresta	266d	41.27 N	2.04 E
La Florida, Chile	286e	33.33 S	70.34 W
La Florida, Esp.	266d	41.31 N	2.12 E
La Florida, Guat.	232	16.33 N	90.27 W
Lafnitz ≃	61	46.57 N	16.16 E
La Foa	175f	21.43 S	165.50 E
La Foce	62	44.08 N	9.47 E
La Follette	192	36.22 N	84.07 W
Lafon	154	5.02 N	32.27 E
Lafontaine, P.Q., Can.	206	45.48 N	74.01 W
La Fontaine, In., U.S.	216	40.40 N	85.43 W
Lafontaine, Parc ♠	275a	45.32 N	73.34 W
La Fortuna	236	10.30 N	84.35 W
Lafourche, Bayou ≃	194	29.05 N	90.14 W
La Foux, Fr.	62	43.16 N	6.35 E
La Foux, Fr.	62	44.17 N	6.34 E
La Fragua	252	26.05 S	64.20 W
La Francia	252	31.24 S	62.38 W
La Fregeneda	34	40.59 N	6.52 W
La Frette-sur-Seine	261	48.58 N	2.11 E
La Fría	246	8.13 N	72.15 W
Lafrimbolle	58	48.36 N	7.01 E
La Fuente de San Esteban	34	40.48 N	6.15 W
Laga, Monti della ⋏	66	42.37 N	13.24 E
La Gacilly	28	47.46 N	2.09 W
Lagaip ≃	164	5.05 S	142.40 E
La Galite I	36	37.32 N	8.56 E
La Gallareta	252	29.34 S	60.23 W
La Gallega	34	41.54 N	3.16 W
Lagan	26	56.55 N	13.59 E
Lagan ≃, Sve.	26	56.33 N	12.56 E
Lagan ≃, N. Ire., U.K.	44	54.37 N	5.53 W
Lagangzong	120	28.05 N	91.04 E
Lagantu	102	42.20 N	108.22 E
La Garde	62	43.07 N	6.01 E
La Garde-Freinet	62	43.19 N	6.28 E
La Garenne-Colombes	261	48.55 N	2.15 E
Lagarina, Val V	64	45.50 N	11.10 E
La Garita	234	19.43 N	103.10 W
Lagarto, Bra.	250	10.54 S	37.41 W
Lagarto, C.R.	236	10.07 N	84.56 W
Lagarto Creek ≃	196	28.08 N	97.56 W
Lagawe	116	16.49 N	121.06 E
Lagay	116	14.06 N	122.12 E
Lagayan	116	17.43 N	120.42 E
Lage, B.R.D.	52	51.59 N	8.48 E
Lage, Esp.	34	43.13 N	9.00 W
Lage, Zhg.	120	29.26 N	85.51 E
Lagechi ⊜	124	30.42 N	81.16 E
Lagedu	102	26.24 N	101.11 E
Lågen ≃, Nor.	26	59.03 N	10.05 E
Lågen ≃, Nor.	26	61.08 N	10.25 E
Lägerdorf	52	53.53 N	9.34 E
Lageuen	114	4.44 N	95.31 E
Lage Zwaluwe	52	51.43 N	4.41 E
Laggan	46	57.02 N	4.16 W
Laggan, Loch ⊜[1]	46	56.57 N	4.28 W
Laggan Bay c	46	55.41 N	6.19 W
Lagginhorn ∧	58	46.11 N	8.01 E
Laghmān □[4]	120	35.00 N	70.15 E
Laghouat	148	33.50 N	2.59 E
Laghouat □[5]	148	32.00 N	3.30 E
Laghy	48	54.37 N	8.05 W
Lagič	84	40.51 N	48.24 E
La Giettaz	62	45.52 N	6.30 E
La Giustiniana ◆[8]	267a	41.59 N	12.24 E
La Gleize	56	50.25 N	5.51 E
La Gloria	246	8.37 N	73.48 W
Lagnieu	58	45.54 N	5.21 E
Lagny	50	48.52 N	2.43 E
Lagny-le-Sac	261	49.05 N	2.45 E
Lago	68	39.10 N	16.09 E
Lago, Mount ∧	224	48.51 N	120.32 W
Lagoa	256	23.18 S	45.36 W
Lagoa Branca	256	21.54 S	47.02 W
Lagoa da Prata	255	20.01 S	45.33 W
Lagoa Dourada	255	20.55 S	44.05 W
Lagoa Formosa	255	18.47 S	46.24 W
Lago Argentino → Calafate	254	50.20 S	72.18 W
Lagoa Santa	255	19.38 S	43.53 W
Lagoa Vermelha	252	28.13 S	51.32 W
Lago Blanco	254	45.55 S	71.15 W
Lago da Pedra	250	4.20 S	45.10 W
Lago de Camécuaro, Parque Nacional ♠	234	19.51 N	102.18 W
Lagodechi	84	41.49 N	46.18 E
Lagodechskij zapovednik ♠	84	41.53 N	46.22 E
Lago Futalaufquen	254	42.53 S	71.37 W
Lagoinha	256	23.06 S	45.11 W
Lagolândia	255	15.37 S	49.02 W
Lagolovo	265a	59.42 N	30.00 E
La Gomera	236	14.05 N	91.03 W
Lagonegro	68	40.07 N	15.46 E
Lagonglong	116	8.48 N	124.47 E
Lagonoy	116	13.44 N	123.31 E
Lagonoy Gulf c	116	13.35 N	123.45 E
Lagopesole, Castel di ⊥	68	40.48 N	15.45 E
Lago Posadas	254	47.32 S	71.45 W
Lagorai, Catena del ⋏	64	46.18 N	11.35 E
Lago Ranco	254	40.20 S	72.38 W
La Gorgue	50	50.38 N	2.42 E
Lagos, Ang.	152	16.04 S	17.03 E
Lagos, Nig.	150	6.27 N	3.24 E
Lagos, Nig.	273a	6.27 N	3.24 E
Lagos, Port.	34	37.06 N	8.40 W
Lagos □[3]	150	6.30 N	3.30 E
Lagos (Ikeja) Airport ⊠	273a	6.35 N	3.20 E
Lagos, University of ʊ[2]	273a	6.32 N	3.24 E
Lagosanto	66	44.46 N	12.08 E
Lagos de Moreno	234	21.21 N	101.55 W
Lagos Harbour c	273a	6.26 N	3.24 E
Lagos Island I	273a	6.27 N	3.26 E
Lagos Lagoon c	273a	6.30 N	3.26 E
Lagos Terminus ◆[5]	273a	6.28 N	3.23 E
La Gouèra	148	20.48 N	17.08 W
La Goulette	148	36.49 N	10.18 E
Lago Viedma	254	49.48 S	72.07 W
La Grand'Combe	62	44.13 N	4.02 E
La Grande	202	45.19 N	118.05 W
La Grande Anse c	241o	16.19 N	61.48 W
La Grande Deux, Réservoir ⊜[1]	176	53.40 N	76.55 W
La Grande Moucherolle ∧	62	45.00 N	5.34 E
La Grande Quatre, Réservoir ⊜[1]	176	54.00 N	73.15 W
La Grange, Austl.	162	18.41 S	121.45 E
LaGrange, Ca., U.S.	226	37.40 N	120.28 W
La Grange, Ga., U.S.	192	33.02 N	85.01 W
La Grange, Il., U.S.	216	41.48 N	87.52 W
Lagrange, In., U.S.	216	41.39 N	85.25 W
La Grange, Ky., U.S.	218	38.24 N	85.22 W
La Grange, Mo., U.S.	219	40.02 N	91.29 W
La Grange, N.C., U.S.	192	35.18 N	77.47 W
Lagrange, Oh., U.S.	214	41.14 N	82.07 W
La Grange, Tx., U.S.	222	29.54 N	96.52 W
Lagrange, Wy., U.S.	198	41.38 N	104.10 W
Lagrange □[6]	216	41.39 N	85.25 W
Lagrange Bay c	162	18.38 S	121.42 E
La Grange Highlands	278	41.50 N	87.51 W
La Grange Lock and Dam ◆[5]	219	39.57 N	90.32 W
La Grange Park	278	41.50 N	87.51 W
Lagrangeville	210	41.39 N	73.46 W
La Granja	286e	33.32 S	70.39 W
La Gran Sabana ≚	246	5.30 N	61.30 W
La Grave	62	45.03 N	6.18 E
La Grita	246	8.08 N	71.59 W
Lagro	216	40.50 N	85.43 W
La Groise	50	50.05 N	3.41 E
La Grue Bayou ≃	194	34.05 N	91.10 W
Lagu	102	26.26 N	101.30 E
La Guadeloupe (Saint-Évariste)	188	45.57 N	70.56 W
La Guaira	246	10.36 N	66.56 W
La Guajira □[5]	246	11.30 N	72.30 W
La Guajira, Península de ›[1]	246	12.00 N	71.40 W
La Guardia, Arg.	252	29.33 S	65.27 W
La Guardia, Bol.	248	17.54 S	63.20 W
Laguardia, Esp.	34	42.33 N	2.35 W
La Guardia, Esp.	34	41.54 N	8.53 W
La Guardia Airport ⊠	210	40.46 N	73.53 W
Lagubu	124	29.08 N	87.14 E
La Gudiña	34	42.04 N	7.08 W
La Guêpière	261	48.35 N	1.50 E
La Guerche-de-Bretagne	32	47.56 N	1.14 W
La Guerche-sur-l'Aubois	32	46.57 N	2.57 E
Laguiole	32	44.41 N	2.51 E
Laguna, Bra.	252	28.29 S	48.47 W
Laguna, N.M., U.S.	200	35.02 N	107.22 W
Laguna □[4]	116	14.10 N	121.20 E
Laguna ≃, Bra.	250	1.17 S	50.50 W
Laguna ≃, Ca., U.S.	226	38.16 N	121.23 W
Laguna, Ilha da I	250	1.40 S	51.00 W
Laguna Beach	228	33.32 N	117.46 W
Laguna Blanca	240p	20.27 N	76.07 W
Laguna Blanca, Parque Nacional ♠	254	39.00 S	70.18 W
Laguna Carapã	255	22.27 S	55.01 W
Laguna Creek ≃	200	36.54 N	109.45 W
Laguna Dam ◆[6]	200	32.50 N	114.31 W
Laguna de Jaco	232	27.50 N	104.00 W
Laguna Hills	228	33.36 N	117.42 W
Laguna Indian Reservation ◆[4]	200	35.00 N	107.20 W
Laguna Lake ⊜	226	35.16 S	120.42 W
Laguna Larga	252	31.46 S	63.48 W
Laguna Limpia	252	26.29 S	59.41 W
Laguna Niguel	228	33.31 N	117.43 W
Laguna Paiva	252	31.19 S	60.39 W
Laguna Park	222	31.52 N	97.23 W
Lagunas	248	5.14 S	75.38 W
Lagundo	64	46.41 N	11.08 E
Lagunillas, Bol.	248	19.38 S	63.43 W
Lagunillas, Méx.	234	21.34 N	99.35 W
Lagunillas, Ven.	246	8.31 N	71.24 W
Lagunillas → Ciudad Ojeda, Ven.	246	10.12 N	71.19 W
Lagunillás, Laguna ⊜	248	15.44 S	70.43 W
Laguntara c	236	15.12 N	83.30 W
L'agušje	86	54.24 N	77.59 E
Laguyu	104	41.43 N	123.49 E
Laha	89	48.10 N	124.39 E
La Habana (Havana), Cuba	240p	23.08 N	82.22 W
La Habana (Havana), Cuba	286b	23.08 N	82.22 W
La Habana □[4]	240p	22.45 N	82.10 W
La Habana, Bahía de c	286b	23.08 N	82.20 W
La Habana, Universidad de ʊ[2]	286b	23.08 N	82.22 W
La Habra	228	33.55 N	117.56 W
La Habra Heights	280	33.57 N	117.57 W
Lahad Datu	112	5.02 N	118.19 E
Lahaina	229a	20.52 N	156.40 W
Laham	112	0.22 N	115.24 E
Lahār	124	26.12 N	78.57 E
La Harpe, Il., U.S.	190	40.35 N	90.58 W
La Harpe, Ks., U.S.	198	37.55 N	95.17 W
Lāharpur	124	27.43 N	80.54 E
Lahaska	208	40.21 N	75.02 W
Lahat, Indon.	112	3.48 S	103.32 E
Lahat, Malay.	114	4.33 N	101.02 E
Lahaul and Spiti □[5]	123	32.40 N	77.15 E
La Hauteville	261	48.42 N	1.37 E
La Havane → La Habana	240p	23.08 N	82.22 W
LaHave ≃	186	44.14 N	64.20 W
La Haye → 's-Gravenhage	52	52.06 N	4.18 E
La Haye-du-Puits	32	49.18 N	1.33 W
La Häy-les-Rosas	261	48.47 N	2.21 E
Lähden	52	52.45 N	7.34 E
Lāhe	110	26.20 N	95.26 E
Laheria Sarai	124	26.07 N	85.54 E
Lahewa	114	1.24 N	97.11 E
Lahfān, Bi'r ⊤[4]	132	31.01 N	33.52 E
Lahi, Ava ɥ	174w	21.02 S	175.11 W
La Higuera	252	29.30 S	71.17 W
Lahij	144	13.02 N	44.54 E
Lāhījān	128	37.12 N	50.01 E
Lāhitah	132	32.59 N	36.35 E
Lähn → Wleń	30	51.01 N	15.40 E
Lahn ≃	56	50.18 N	7.37 E
Lahnstein	56	50.19 N	7.36 E
Laholm	26	56.31 N	13.02 E
Laholmsbukten c	26	56.35 N	12.50 E
La Honda	226	37.19 N	122.16 W
La Honda Creek ≃	282	37.18 N	122.16 W
Lahontan Reservoir ⊜[1]	226	39.23 N	119.09 W
Lahontan State Recreation Area ♠	226	39.28 N	119.03 W
Lahor → Lahore, Pāk.	123	31.35 N	74.18 E
Lāhor, Pāk.	123	34.03 N	72.22 E
Lahore	123	31.35 N	74.18 E
La Horqueta	246	3.06 N	72.50 W
La Horqueta, Arroyo ≃	288	34.41 S	58.51 W
La Houssaye-en-Brie	261	48.45 N	2.53 E
Lahr	58	48.20 N	7.52 E
Lahri	120	29.11 N	68.13 E
Laḥtah, Wādī V	142	29.44 N	32.45 E
Lahti	26	60.58 N	25.40 E
La Huaca	248	4.54 S	80.57 W
La Huacana	234	18.58 N	101.49 W
La Huerta, Méx.	234	19.28 N	104.39 W
La Huerta, N.M., U.S.	196	32.27 N	104.13 W
La Hunière	261	48.36 N	1.52 E
Lahuy Island I	116	13.56 N	123.50 E
Laï	146	9.24 N	16.18 E
Laiagam	164	5.30 S	143.20 E
Lai'an	100	32.27 N	118.25 E
Laibach → Ljubljana	36	46.03 N	14.31 E
Laibin	102	23.42 N	109.22 E
Lai-chau	110	22.02 N	103.10 E
Laichingen	58	48.29 N	9.41 E
Laichow Bay → Laizhou Wan c	98	37.36 N	119.30 E
Laide	46	57.52 N	5.32 W
Laidley	171a	27.38 S	152.24 E
Laidley Creek ≃	171a	27.31 S	152.24 E
Laidon, Loch ⊜	46	56.39 N	4.40 W
Laie	229c	21.39 N	157.55 W
Laifang	100	25.56 N	116.54 E
Laifeng, Zhg.	102	29.31 N	109.15 E
Laifeng, Zhg.	107	30.14 N	105.17 E
Laifengzhen	107	29.26 N	106.13 E
L'Aigle	50	48.45 N	0.38 E
L'Aigle Creek ≃	194	33.12 N	92.08 W
Laignes	50	47.50 N	4.22 E
Laigou	100	33.56 N	117.06 E
Laigueglia	62	43.58 N	8.09 E
Laihia	26	62.58 N	22.01 E
Lai-hka	110	21.16 N	97.40 E
Lailly-en-Val	50	47.46 N	1.41 E
Laïmbélé, Mont ∧	175f	16.20 S	167.31 E
Lainate	266b	45.34 N	9.02 E
Lainbach	61	47.38 N	14.46 E
La Independencia, Bahía de c	248	14.15 S	76.10 W
Laingsburg, S. Afr.	158	33.11 S	20.51 E
Laingsburg, Mi., U.S.	216	42.53 N	84.21 W
Lainioälven ≃	24	67.22 N	23.39 E
Laino Borgo	68	39.57 N	15.59 E
Lainsitz (Lužnice) ≃	61	49.13 N	14.42 E
Lainville	261	49.04 N	1.49 E
Lainz ◆[8]	264b	48.11 N	16.17 E
Lainzer Tiergarten ♠	264b	48.10 N	16.14 E
Lair, Scot., U.K.	46	57.29 N	5.20 W
Lair, Ky., U.S.	218	38.20 N	84.18 W
Laird Hill	222	32.21 N	94.54 W
Lairdsville	210	41.14 N	76.37 W
Lairg	46	58.01 N	4.25 W
Laïri	146	10.49 N	17.06 E
Laïri, Batha de ≃	146	12.28 N	16.45 E
Laïriri, Pic ∧	175f	15.27 S	166.48 E
Lais, Indon.	112	0.47 N	120.27 E
Lais, Indon.	112	3.32 S	102.03 E
Lais, Pil.	116	6.20 N	125.39 E
La Isabela	240p	22.57 N	80.01 W
Laisamis	154	1.36 N	37.48 E
Laiševo	80	55.24 N	49.32 E
Laishan	98	37.24 N	121.23 E
Laishui	105	39.23 N	115.42 E
Laissac	32	44.23 N	2.49 E
Laissey	58	47.18 N	6.14 E
Laisu	107	29.16 N	105.47 E
Laisvall	24	66.05 N	17.10 E
Laitan	107	29.06 N	106.10 E
Laitila	26	60.53 N	21.41 E
Laives (Leifers)	64	46.26 N	11.20 E
Laiwu	98	36.12 N	117.42 E
Laiwui	164	1.22 S	127.40 E
Laixi (Shuiji)	98	36.51 N	120.29 E
Laiya	116	13.40 N	121.24 E
Laiyang	98	36.58 N	120.44 E
Laiyuan, Zhg.	98	39.18 N	114.44 E
Laiyuan, Zhg.	100	25.36 N	117.01 E
Laizhou Wan (Laichow Bay) c	98	37.36 N	119.30 E
Laja ≃, Chile	252	37.16 S	72.43 W
Laja ≃, S.S.S.R.	24	66.20 N	56.16 E
Laja, Laguna de la ⊜	252	37.21 S	71.19 W
Laja, Río de la ≃	234	20.30 N	100.46 W
Laja, Salto del ∟	252	37.22 S	71.25 W
La Jalca	248	6.29 S	77.43 W
La Jara	200	37.16 N	105.57 W
La Jara ◆[1]	34	39.42 N	4.54 W
La Jara Canyon V	200	36.50 N	107.30 W
La Jara Creek ≃	200	37.22 N	105.46 W
La Jarita	232	28.03 N	103.20 W
La Jarrie	32	46.08 N	1.00 W
Lajas, Méx.	234	23.07 N	105.07 W
Lajas, P.R.	240m	18.03 N	67.04 W
La Javie	62	44.10 N	6.21 E
Laje, Bra.	255	13.10 S	39.25 W
Laje, Bra.	256	21.22 S	44.31 W
Laje, Ilha da I	287a	22.57 S	43.09 W
Laje, Ponta da ›	266c	38.40 N	9.19 W
Laje, Ribeira de ≃	266c	38.41 N	9.19 W
Lajeado	252	29.27 S	51.58 W
Lajeado Velho ◆[8]	287b	23.32 S	46.23 W
Lajedo	250	8.40 S	36.19 W
Lajes, Bra.	250	5.41 S	36.14 W
Lajes, Bra.	252	27.48 S	50.19 W
Lajes, Ribeirão das ≃	256	22.38 S	43.42 W
Lajinha	255	20.09 S	41.37 W
Laji Shan ⋏	102	36.13 N	102.15 E
Lajkovo	265b	55.42 N	37.13 E
La Jolla	228	32.51 N	117.16 W
La Jolla, Point ›	228	32.51 N	117.17 W
Lajord	184	50.14 N	104.09 W
La Jose	214	40.50 N	78.41 W
Lajosmizse	30	47.02 N	19.34 E
La Joya, Méx.	196	26.26 N	101.08 W
La Joya, Méx.	232	32.08 N	114.01 W
La Joya, Perú	248	16.44 S	71.51 W
Lajta (Leitha) ≃	61	47.54 N	17.17 E
Lajtamak	86	58.25 N	67.25 E
Lajturi	84	41.55 N	41.55 E
La Junta, Méx.	232	28.28 N	107.20 W
La Junta, Co., U.S.	198	37.59 N	103.32 W
Lakaband	120	31.00 N	69.30 E
Lakahia, Teluk c	164	4.00 S	134.38 E
Lakamané	150	14.31 N	9.55 W
Lakatoro	175f	16.07 S	167.25 E
Lakazangbuhe ≃	124	29.24 N	87.58 E
Lake	194	32.20 N	89.19 W
Lake □[6], Ca., U.S.	226	39.01 N	122.33 W
Lake □[6], Fl., U.S.	220	28.42 N	81.39 W
Lake □[6], Il., U.S.	216	42.22 N	87.50 W
Lake □[6], In., U.S.	216	41.25 N	87.22 W
Lake □[6], Oh., U.S.	214	41.43 N	81.15 W
Lake Accotink Park ♠	284c	38.48 N	77.14 W
Lake Albert	171b	35.10 S	147.23 E
Lake Alfred	220	28.05 N	81.43 W
Lake Alpine	226	38.28 N	120.00 W
Lake Andes	198	43.09 N	98.32 W
Lake Angelus	281	42.42 N	83.19 W
Lake Ariel	210	41.27 N	75.23 W
Lake Arrowhead	228	34.14 N	117.11 W
Lake Arthur, La., U.S.	194	30.04 N	92.40 W
Lake Arthur, N.M., U.S.	196	32.59 N	104.21 W
Lake Barcroft	284c	38.51 N	77.09 W
Lake Bathurst	170	35.01 S	149.36 E
Lake Benton	198	44.15 N	96.17 W
Lake Beseck	207	41.31 N	72.44 W
Lake Biddy	162	33.00 S	118.57 E
Lake Bluff	216	42.16 N	87.50 W
Lake Brownwood	196	31.49 N	99.02 W
Lake Buena Vista	220	28.23 N	81.31 W
Lake Butler	192	30.01 N	82.20 W
Lake Cable	214	40.52 N	81.27 W
Lake Camm	162	32.59 S	119.35 E
Lake Cargelligo	166	33.18 S	146.23 E
Lake Carmel	210	41.27 N	73.40 W
Lake Charles	194	30.13 N	93.13 W
Lake Chelan National Recreation Area ♠	224	48.20 N	120.40 W
Lake City, Ar., U.S.	194	35.48 N	90.26 W
Lake City, Co., U.S.	200	38.01 N	107.18 W
Lake City, Fl., U.S.	192	30.11 N	82.38 W
Lake City, Il., U.S.	219	39.45 N	88.43 W
Lake City, Ia., U.S.	198	42.16 N	94.44 W
Lake City, Mi., U.S.	190	44.20 N	85.12 W
Lake City, Mn., U.S.	190	44.26 N	92.16 W
Lake City, Pa., U.S.	214	42.00 N	80.20 W
Lake City, S.C., U.S.	192	33.52 N	79.45 W
Lake City, Tn., U.S.	192	36.13 N	84.09 W
Lake Clarke Shores	220	26.39 N	80.04 W
Lake Clark National Park ♠	180	60.30 N	153.15 W
Lake Coleridge	172	43.22 S	171.32 E
Lake Como, N.Y., U.S.	210	42.41 N	76.18 W
Lake Como, Pa., U.S.	210	41.51 N	75.20 W
Lake Corpus Christi State Park ♠	196	28.05 N	97.52 W
Lake Cowichan	224	48.50 N	124.03 W
Lake Creek ≃	222	30.16 N	95.29 W
Lake Crescent	224	48.06 N	123.50 W
Lake Crystal	190	44.06 N	94.13 W
Lake Dalecarlia	216	41.20 N	87.24 W
Lake Dallas	222	33.07 N	97.02 W
Lake Delta	210	43.17 N	75.28 W
Lake Delton	190	43.36 N	89.47 W
Lakedemonovka	83	47.12 N	38.33 E
Lake Dennison State Park ♠	207	42.38 N	72.05 W
Lake District ◆[1]	44	54.30 N	3.10 W
Lake District National Park ♠	44	54.30 N	3.05 W
Lake Eliza	216	41.26 N	87.10 W
Lake Elsinore	228	33.38 N	117.20 W
Lake Elsinore State Recreation Area ♠	228	33.41 N	117.22 W
Lake Entrance ɥ	170	33.05 S	151.39 E
Lake Errock	224	49.13 N	122.02 W
Lake Fairfax County Park ♠	284c	38.58 N	77.19 W
Lake Fenton	216	42.52 N	83.43 W
Lakefield, On., Can.	212	44.26 N	78.16 W
Lakefield, S. Afr.	273d	26.11 S	28.18 E
Lakefield, Mn., U.S.	198	43.40 N	95.10 W
Lakefield National Park ♠	164	15.00 S	144.05 E
Lake Forest, Fl., U.S.	192	25.58 N	80.11 W
Lake Forest, Il., U.S.	216	42.12 N	87.53 W
Lake Forest, N.J., U.S.	276	40.58 N	74.36 W
Lake Forest Park	224	47.45 N	122.17 W
Lake Fork	219	39.58 N	89.21 W
Lake Fork ≃, Il., U.S.	219	40.05 N	89.25 W
Lake Fork ≃, Ut,. U.S.	200	40.13 N	110.07 W
Lake Fork, North Fork ≃	219	39.56 N	89.14 W
Lake Fork Creek ≃	222	32.36 N	95.21 W
Lake Fork Reservoir ⊜[1]	222	32.50 N	95.35 W
Lake Geneva	216	42.36 N	88.26 W
Lake George	188	43.25 N	73.42 W
Lake Grace	162	33.06 S	118.28 E
Lake Grinnell	276	41.06 N	74.38 W
Lake Grove	276	40.51 N	73.06 W
Lake Hamilton	220	28.07 N	81.42 W
Lake Harbor	220	26.42 N	80.48 W
Lake Harbour	176	62.51 N	69.53 W

Symbols in the index entries represent the broad categories identified in the key at the right. Symbols with superior numbers (⋏[1]) identify subcategories (see complete key on page *I · 1).*

Kartensymbole in dem Registerverzeichnis stellen die rechts in Schlüssel erklärten Kategorien dar. Symbole mit hochgestellten Ziffern (⋏[1]) bezeichnen Unterabteilungen einer Kategorie (vgl. vollständiger Schlüssel auf Seite *I · 1).*

Los símbolos incluídos en el texto del índice representan las grandes categorias identificadas con la clave a la derecha. Los símbolos con numeros en su parte superior (⋏[1]) identifican las subcategorías (véase la clave completa en la página *I · 1).*

Les symboles de l'index représentent les catégories indiquées dans la légende à droite. Les symboles suivis d'un indice (⋏[1]) représentent des sous-catégories (voir légende complète à la page *I · 1).*

Os símbolos incluídos no texto do índice representam as grandes categorias identificadas com a chave à direita. Os símbolos com números em sua parte superior (⋏[1]) identificam as subcategorias (veja-se a chave completa à página *I · 1).*

∧ Mountain	Berg	Montaña	Montagne	Montanha
⋏ Mountains	Berge	Montañas	Montagnes	Montanhas
)(Pass	Pass	Paso	Col	Passo
V Valley, Canyon	Tal, Cañon	Valle, Cañón	Vallée, Canyon	Vale, Canhão
≚ Plain	Ebene	Llano	Plaine	Planície
› Cape	Kap	Cabo	Cap	Cabo
I Island	Insel	Isla	Île	Ilha
II Islands	Inseln	Islas	Îles	Ilhas
⊥ Other Topographic Features	Andere Topographische Objekte	Otros Elementos Topográficos	Autres données topographiques	Outros acidentes topográficos

ESPAÑOL / FRANÇAIS / PORTUGUÊS

Nombre / Nom / Nome	Página / Page	Lat.°′	Long.°′ W = Oeste / Ouest
Lake Harmony	210	41.04 N	75.36 W
Lake Havasu City	200	34.29 N	114.19 W
Lake Havasu State Park ♠	200	34.29 N	114.21 W
Lake Helen	220	28.58 N	81.14 W
Lake Hiawatha	210	40.52 N	74.22 W
Lake Hill	210	42.04 N	74.11 W
Lake Hills, In., U.S.	216	41.28 N	87.27 W
Lake Hills, Wa., U.S.	224	47.36 N	122.08 W
Lake Hopatcong	210	40.55 N	74.39 W
Lake Hughes	228	34.40 N	118.26 W
Lake Huntington	210	41.41 N	75.00 W
Lakehurst	208	40.00 N	74.18 W
Lakehurst Naval Air Station ■	208	40.01 N	74.18 W
Lake Illawarra	170	34.33 S	150.52 E
Lake Intervale	276	40.53 N	74.25 W
Lake in the Hills	216	42.10 N	88.19 W
Lake Isabella	204	35.39 N	118.28 W
Lake Jackson	222	29.02 N	95.26 W
Lake Jem	220	28.45 N	81.40 W
Lakekamu ≃	164	8.10 S	146.15 E
Lake Katrine	210	41.59 N	73.59 W
Lake King	162	33.05 S	119.40 E
Lake Lackawanna	210	40.57 N	74.42 W
Lakeland, Fl., U.S.	220	28.03 N	81.57 W
Lakeland, Ga., U.S.	192	31.02 N	83.04 W
Lakeland, Mi., U.S.	216	42.28 N	83.51 W
Lakeland, N.Y., U.S.	210	43.06 N	76.15 W
Lakeland Park	216	42.21 N	88.17 W
Lakeland Village	228	33.39 N	117.22 W
Lake Lenape	210	41.01 N	74.44 W
Lake Linden	190	47.11 N	88.26 W
Lake Lookover	276	41.09 N	74.24 W
Lake Loramie State Park ♠	216	40.23 N	84.20 W
Lake Louise, Ab., Can.	182	51.26 N	116.11 W
Lake Louise, Wa., U.S.	224	47.05 N	122.36 W
Lake Lucerne	214	41.24 N	81.21 W
Lake Luzerne	210	43.18 N	73.50 W
Lake Mackay Aboriginal Reserve ◆[4]	162	22.00 S	129.45 E
Lake Magdalene	220	28.05 N	82.28 W
Lake Malawi National Park ♠	154	14.00 S	34.55 E
Lake Manyara National Park ♠	154	3.30 S	36.25 E
Lake Mary	220	28.45 N	81.19 W
Lakemba	274a	33.55 S	151.05 E
Lakemba Island I	175g	18.13 S	178.47 W
Lakemba Passage ʉ	175g	17.53 S	178.32 W
Lake Mead National Recreation Area ♠	200	36.00 N	114.30 W
Lake Meredith National Recreation Area ♠	196	35.40 N	101.40 W
Lake Mills, Ia., U.S.	190	43.25 N	93.31 W
Lake Mills, Wi., U.S.	216	43.04 N	88.54 W
Lake Milton	214	41.06 N	80.58 W
Lake Minchumina	180	63.53 N	152.19 W
Lake Monroe	220	28.50 N	81.19 W
Lakemont, N.Y., U.S.	210	42.31 N	76.56 W
Lakemont, Pa., U.S.	214	40.28 N	78.23 W
Lakemoor	216	42.20 N	88.12 W
Lakemore	214	41.01 N	81.25 W
Lake Mountain ∧	169	37.31 S	145.54 E
Lake Murray State Park ♠	196	34.01 N	97.00 W
Lake Nakuru National Park ♠	154	0.20 S	36.05 E
Lake Nash	166	21.00 S	137.55 E
Lake Nepessing	216	43.02 N	83.22 W
Lakenheath	42	52.25 N	0.31 E
Lake Norden	198	44.34 N	97.12 W
Lake Normandy Estates	284c	39.03 N	77.11 W
Lake Odessa	216	42.47 N	85.08 W
Lake of the Ozarks State Park ♠	194	38.08 N	92.40 W
Lake of the Woods	216	41.26 N	86.14 W
Lake on the Mountain Provincial Park ♠	212	44.02 N	77.05 W
Lake Orion	216	42.47 N	83.14 W
Lake Orion Heights	216	42.46 N	83.18 W
Lake Oroville State Recreational Area ♠	226	39.32 N	121.27 W
Lake Oswego	224	45.25 N	122.39 W
Lake Ozark	194	38.11 N	92.38 W
Lakepa	174v	18.59 S	169.48 W
Lake Panasoffkee	220	28.46 N	82.07 W
Lake Paringa	172	43.43 S	169.29 E
Lake Park, Fl., U.S.	220	26.48 N	80.04 W
Lake Park, Ia., U.S.	198	43.27 N	95.19 W
Lake Park, Mn., U.S.	198	46.53 N	96.05 W
Lake Pine	208	39.52 N	74.51 W
Lake Placid, Fl., U.S.	220	27.17 N	81.21 W
Lake Placid, N.Y., U.S.	188	44.16 N	73.58 W
Lake Pleasant	188	43.28 N	74.25 W
Lakeport, Ca., U.S.	204	39.02 N	122.54 W
Lakeport, Mi., U.S.	190	43.07 N	82.30 W
Lakeport, N.Y., U.S.	210	43.09 N	75.52 W
Lake Preston	198	44.21 N	97.22 W
Lake Providence	194	32.48 N	91.10 W
Lake Pukaki	172	44.11 S	170.09 E
Lakeridge, Nv., U.S.	226	39.02 N	119.56 W
Lake Ridge, N.J., U.S.	276	40.24 N	74.15 W
Lake Riviera	208	40.03 N	74.10 W
Lake Ronkonkoma	276	40.50 N	73.07 W
Lake Saint Louis	219	38.48 N	90.45 W
Lake Sammamish State Park ♠	224	47.33 N	122.03 W
Lake San Marcos	228	33.09 N	117.12 W
Lake Sawyer	224	47.20 N	122.03 W
Lakes Bay c	208	39.22 N	74.30 W
Lakes District	224	47.10 N	122.31 W
Lakes Entrance	166	37.53 S	147.59 E
Lake Shawnee	276	40.59 N	74.36 W
Lakeshore, Ca., U.S.	226	37.15 N	119.12 W
Lake Shore, Md., U.S.	208	39.06 N	76.29 W
Lake Shore, Mi., U.S.	216	42.38 N	86.14 W
Lakeshore, Ms., U.S.	194	30.14 N	89.26 W
Lake Shore, Wa., U.S.	224	45.42 N	122.42 W
Lakeside, N.S., Can.	186	44.38 N	63.41 W
Lakeside, S. Afr.	273d	26.06 S	28.09 E
Lakeside, Az., U.S.	200	34.09 N	109.58 W
Lakeside, Ca., U.S.	228	32.51 N	116.55 W
Lakeside, Ct., U.S.	207	41.25 N	73.13 W
Lakeside, Ct., U.S.	207	41.40 N	73.14 W
Lakeside, Mi., U.S.	216	41.51 N	86.40 W
Lakeside, Mt., U.S.	202	48.01 N	114.13 W
Lakeside, Oh., U.S.	214	41.32 N	82.44 W
Lakeside, Or., U.S.	202	43.34 N	124.10 W
Lakeside, Va., U.S.	208	37.36 N	77.28 W
Lakeside ◆[9]	281	42.37 N	83.00 W
Lakeside Village	222	32.02 N	97.30 W
Lake Station	216	41.34 N	87.14 W
Lake Stevens	224	48.01 N	122.04 W
Lake Stockholm	276	41.04 N	74.31 W
Lake Success	276	40.46 N	73.43 W
Lake Superior Provincial Park ♠	190	47.32 N	84.50 W
Lake Swannanoa	276	41.01 N	74.31 W
Lake Taghkanic State Park ♠	210	42.06 N	73.43 W
Lake Tahoe Airport ⊠	226	38.54 N	120.00 W
Lake Tahoe-Nevada State Park ♠	226	39.13 N	119.55 W
Lake Tamarack	210	41.06 N	74.32 W
Lake Tekapo	172	44.01 S	170.30 E
Lake Telemark	276	40.57 N	74.30 W
Lake Temescal Regional Park ♠	282	37.51 N	122.14 W
Laketon	216	40.58 N	85.50 W
Laketown	200	41.49 N	111.19 W
Lake Varley	162	32.46 S	119.27 E
Lake View, Ar., U.S.	194	34.24 N	90.50 W
Lakeview, Ca., U.S.	228	33.50 N	117.07 W
Lakeview, Ga., U.S.	192	34.58 N	85.15 W
Lake View, Ia., U.S.	198	42.18 N	95.03 W
Lakeview, Mi., U.S.	190	43.26 N	85.16 W
Lake View, N.Y., U.S.	210	42.42 N	78.56 W
Lakeview, Oh., U.S.	216	40.29 N	83.56 W
Lakeview, Or., U.S.	202	42.11 N	120.20 W
Lake View, S.C., U.S.	192	34.20 N	79.09 W
Lakeview, Tx., U.S.	194	29.55 N	93.54 W
Lakeview, Tx., U.S.	196	34.40 N	100.42 W
Lakeview, Wa., U.S.	224	47.10 N	122.30 W
Lakeview ◆[8]	278	41.57 N	87.39 W
Lakeview Mountain ∧, B.C., Can.	182	49.03 N	120.09 W
Lakeview Mountain ∧, Wa., U.S.	224	46.22 N	121.24 W
Lakeview Park ♠	285	40.12 N	75.32 W
Lake Village, Ar., U.S.	194	33.19 N	91.16 W
Lake Village, In., U.S.	216	41.08 N	87.27 W
Lakeville, Ct., U.S.	207	41.57 N	73.26 W
Lakeville, In., U.S.	216	41.31 N	86.16 W
Lakeville, Mi., U.S.	214	42.49 N	83.09 W
Lakeville, Mn., U.S.	190	44.38 N	93.14 W
Lakeville, N.Y., U.S.	210	42.50 N	77.42 W
Lakeville, Oh., U.S.	214	40.40 N	82.07 W
Lakeville Lake ⊜	214	42.50 N	83.09 W
Lake Wales	220	27.54 N	81.35 W
Lake Whitney State Park ♠	222	31.55 N	97.22 W
Lake Wilson	198	43.59 N	95.57 W
Lake Winola	210	41.30 N	75.50 W
Lakewood, Ca., U.S.	228	33.51 N	118.07 W
Lakewood, Co., U.S.	200	39.42 N	105.04 W
Lakewood, Il., U.S.	216	39.19 N	88.54 W
Lakewood, Mi., U.S.	216	42.18 N	85.31 W
Lakewood, N.J., U.S.	208	40.05 N	74.13 W
Lakewood, N.Y., U.S.	214	42.06 N	79.20 W
Lakewood, Oh., U.S.	214	41.28 N	81.47 W
Lakewood, Pa., U.S.	210	41.51 N	75.22 W
Lakewood, Wa., U.S.	224	48.09 N	122.12 W
Lakewood, Wi., U.S.	190	45.18 N	88.31 W
Lakewood Center ◆[9]	280	33.51 N	118.09 W
Lakewood Park	198	48.04 N	98.56 W
Lakewood Park ♠	279a	41.29 N	81.47 W
Lakewood Shores	216	41.17 N	88.10 W
Lake Worth, Fl., U.S.	220	26.36 N	80.03 W
Lake Worth, Tx., U.S.	222	32.49 N	97.27 W
Lake Zurich	216	42.11 N	88.05 W
Lakhdaria	34	36.34 N	3.35 E
Lākheri	124	25.40 N	76.10 E
Lakhīmpur	124	27.57 N	80.46 E
Lakhipur, India	120	24.48 N	93.01 E
Lakhipur, India	124	26.02 N	90.18 E
Lakhish	132	31.34 N	34.51 E
Lakhnādon	124	22.36 N	79.36 E
Lakhpat	120	23.49 N	68.47 E
Lakhya ≃	126	23.35 N	90.31 E
L'aki	84	40.34 N	47.26 E
Laki ≃	115a	7.30 S	107.25 E
Lakin	198	37.56 N	101.15 W
Lakinsk	80	56.01 N	39.57 E
Lakkadiven → Lakshadweep II	122	10.00 N	73.00 E
Lakki	123	32.36 N	70.55 E
Laknau → Lucknow	124	26.51 N	80.55 E
Lakonikós Kólpos c	38	36.25 N	22.37 E
Lakor, Pulau I	164	8.14 S	128.10 E
Lakota, C. Iv.	150	5.51 N	5.41 W
Lakota, Ia., U.S.	190	43.22 N	94.05 W
Lakota, N.D., U.S.	198	48.02 N	98.20 W
Lakota □[5]	150	5.50 N	5.40 W
Laksefjorden c[2]	24	70.58 N	27.00 E
Lakselv	24	70.04 N	24.56 E
Lakshadweep □[3]	122	10.00 N	73.00 E
Lakshadweep II	122	10.00 N	73.00 E
Lākshām	124	23.14 N	91.08 E
Lakshamannāth	126	21.51 N	87.13 E
Lakshmanpur	272b	22.38 N	88.16 E
Lakshmeshwar	122	15.08 N	75.28 E
Lakshmi, Char I	126	21.57 N	90.33 E
Lakshmikantapur	126	22.07 N	88.20 E
Lakshmīpur	126	22.57 N	90.50 E
Lakshmisāgar	126	22.55 N	87.01 E
Lala	116	7.59 N	123.46 E
Lalafuta ≃	154	13.57 S	24.41 E
La Laguna → San Cristóbal de la Laguna	148	28.29 N	16.19 W
La Lajilla	232	26.47 N	99.37 W
Lāla Mūsa	123	32.42 N	73.58 E
Lalapansi	154	19.16 S	30.15 E
Lâlapaşa	130	41.50 N	26.44 E
Lalatuncun	104	41.44 N	122.00 E
Lalbenque	32	44.20 N	1.33 E
Laleham, Austl.	166	23.58 S	148.46 E
Laleham, Eng., U.K.	260	51.25 N	0.30 W
Lāleh Zār, Kūh-e ∧	128	29.24 N	56.46 E
Lâleli	130	41.03 N	37.37 E
La Leona	196	25.52 N	101.05 W
La Leonesa	252	27.03 S	58.43 W
Lalera	152	0.22 N	11.28 E
Lalevade-d'Ardèche	62	44.39 N	4.19 E
Lālganj	124	25.52 N	85.11 E
Lālgarh	126	22.35 N	87.03 E
Lāliān	123	31.49 N	72.48 E
Lalibela	144	12.02 N	39.02 E
La Libertad, El Sal.	236	13.29 N	89.19 W
La Libertad, Guat.	232	16.47 N	90.07 W
La Libertad, Hond.	236	14.43 N	87.36 W
La Libertad, Nic.	236	12.13 N	85.10 W
La Libertad □[5]	248	8.00 S	78.30 W
La Ligua	252	32.27 S	71.14 W
La Lima, Hond.	236	15.24 N	87.56 W
La Lima, It.	66	44.04 N	10.46 E
La Limpia, Laguna ⊜	258	35.37 S	57.49 W
Lalín	34	42.39 N	8.07 W
Lalin ≃	89	45.29 N	125.26 E
Lalinde	32	44.51 N	0.44 E
Lalindi	115b	10.12 S	120.10 E
Lalindu ≃	112	3.28 S	122.05 E
La Línea	34	36.10 N	5.19 W
L'alino	82	54.29 N	39.06 E
La Lisa ◆[8]	286b	23.04 N	82.26 W
Lalitpur, India	124	24.41 N	78.25 E
Lalitpur, Nepāl	124	27.41 N	85.20 E
La Llagosta	266d	41.31 N	2.12 E
Lalla Khedidja, Tamgout de ∧	34	36.27 N	4.15 E
Lālmai	124	23.19 N	91.07 E
Lālmanir Hāt	124	25.54 N	89.27 E
Laloa	112	4.50 S	121.54 E
La Loche	184	56.29 N	109.27 W
La Loche ≃	184	56.09 N	109.08 W
La Loche, Lac ⊜	184	56.25 N	109.30 W
Laloki	164	9.25 S	147.15 E
La Loma	234	22.53 N	105.51 W
La Londe	62	43.08 N	6.14 E
La Lora ⋏[1]	34	42.45 N	4.00 W
Lalor Park	274a	33.45 S	150.56 E
La Loupe	50	48.28 N	1.01 E
Lalouvesc	62	45.07 N	4.32 E
La Louvière	50	50.28 N	4.11 E
L'Alpe-d'Huez	62	45.06 N	6.04 E
Lālpur, Bngl.	126	24.11 N	88.58 E
Lālpur, India	120	22.12 N	69.58 E
Lal'sk	24	60.44 N	47.34 E
Lālsot	124	26.34 N	76.20 E
Lālua	126	21.57 N	90.18 E
La Luz, Méx.	196	25.52 N	97.37 W
La Luz, N.M., U.S.	200	32.58 N	105.56 W
Lam	60	49.12 N	13.03 E
Lama ≃, S.S.S.R.	82	56.29 N	36.10 E
Lama ≃, Zhg.	104	42.11 N	123.29 E
Lama, ozero ⊜	74	69.30 N	90.30 E
L'Amable Lake ⊜	212	45.01 N	77.49 W
La Macarena, Serranía de ⋏	246	2.45 N	73.55 W
La Maddalena	71	41.13 N	9.24 E
Lama dei Peligni	66	42.02 N	14.11 E
La Madeleine	50	50.39 N	3.04 E
Lamadong	98	40.39 N	119.39 E
La Madrague	62	43.14 N	5.22 E
La Madrid, Arg.	252	27.38 S	65.15 W
Lamadrid, Méx.	196	27.05 N	101.50 W
Lamag	112	5.29 N	117.49 E
La Magdalena, Río de ≃	286a	19.21 N	99.11 W
Lamagoumen	105	40.52 N	116.39 E
Lamahuang	104	42.27 N	121.33 E
La Mailleraye-sur-Seine	50	49.29 N	0.46 E
Lamainong	114	3.49 N	96.46 E
La Majada	286c	10.27 N	67.01 W
Lama-Kara	150	9.33 N	1.12 E
La Malbaie	186	47.39 N	70.10 W
La Malinche, Parque Nacional ♠	234	19.15 N	98.05 W
Lamaline	186	46.52 N	55.49 W
La Malmaison ⊥	261	48.52 N	2.10 E
Lamaload Reservoir ⊜[1]	262	53.16 N	2.02 W
Lama Mocogno	64	44.18 N	10.45 E
La Mancha	232	24.52 N	102.47 W
La Mancha ◆[1]	34	38.50 N	3.00 W
La Mancha, Canal de → English Channel ʉ	28	50.20 N	1.00 W
La Manche (English Channel) ʉ	28	50.20 N	1.00 W
Lamandau ≃	112	2.42 S	111.34 E
La Mansión	236	10.06 N	85.22 W
Lamap	175f	16.26 S	167.43 E
Lamar, Co., U.S.	198	38.05 N	102.37 W
Lamar, Mo., U.S.	194	37.29 N	94.16 W
Lamar, Pa., U.S.	210	41.01 N	77.32 W
Lamar, S.C., U.S.	192	34.10 N	80.03 W
Lamar ≃	202	44.56 N	110.24 W
La Mar, Parque ♠	286d	12.04 S	77.02 W
La Marañosa	266a	40.17 N	3.35 W
Lamarche	58	48.04 N	5.47 E
Lamarche-sur-Saône	58	47.16 N	5.23 E
La Mare, Pointe ≻	240e	14.47 N	61.13 W
La Mariposa, Embalse ⊜[1]	286c	10.24 N	66.56 W
La Mariscala	252	34.03 S	54.47 W
La Marmora, Punta ∧	71	39.59 N	9.20 E
La Marolle-en-Sologne	50	47.35 N	1.47 E
La Maroma	196	28.34 N	100.45 W
Lamarque, Arg.	252	39.24 S	65.42 W
La Marque, Tx., U.S.	222	29.22 N	94.58 W
La Marsa	36	36.53 N	10.20 E
La Martre	62	43.46 N	6.36 E
Lamas	248	6.25 S	76.35 W
La Masica	236	15.37 N	87.07 W
Lamastre	62	44.59 N	4.35 E
La Matanza → San Justo	258	34.40 S	58.33 W
Lama Temple ♥[1]	271a	39.56 N	116.25 E
La Mauricie, Parc National de(La Mauricie National Park) ♠	206	46.50 N	73.00 W
La Maya, Cuba	240p	20.10 N	75.39 W
Lamaya, Zhg.	102	29.50 N	99.53 E
Lamayingzi	104	42.09 N	121.50 E
Lambach	60	48.05 N	13.53 E
Lamballe	32	48.28 N	2.31 W
Lambaréné	152	0.42 S	10.13 E
Lambari	256	21.58 S	45.21 W
Lambari ≃, Bra.	255	19.30 S	45.00 W
Lambari ≃, Bra.	256	21.47 S	45.13 W
Lambasa	175g	16.26 S	179.24 E
Lambayeque	248	6.42 S	79.55 W
Lambayeque □[5]	248	6.20 S	80.00 W
Lambayeque ≃	248	6.43 S	79.54 W
Lambay Island I	48	53.29 N	6.01 W
Lambe	273a	6.42 N	3.21 E
Lambersart	50	50.39 N	3.02 E
Lambert, Ms., U.S.	194	34.12 N	90.17 W
Lambert, Mt., U.S.	198	47.41 N	104.37 W
Lambert, Cape ≻, Austl.	162	20.35 S	117.10 E
Lambert, Cape ≻, Pap. N. Gui.	164	4.12 S	151.32 E
Lambert Glacier ⊓	9	71.00 S	70.00 E
Lamberton	198	44.13 N	95.15 W
Lambert-Saint Louis International Airport ⊠	219	38.45 N	90.22 W
Lambertsbaai → Lambert's Bay	158	32.05 S	18.17 E
Lambert's Bay	158	32.05 S	18.17 E
Lambertville, Mi., U.S.	216	41.45 N	83.37 W
Lambertville, N.J., U.S.	208	40.21 N	74.56 W
Lambesc	62	43.39 N	5.16 E
Lambeth	214	42.54 N	81.18 W
Lambeth ◆[8]	42	51.30 N	0.07 W
L'ambir'	80	54.17 N	45.07 E
Lambo Katenga	154	5.02 S	28.48 E
Lambomakondro	157b	22.41 S	44.44 E
Lambourn	42	51.31 N	1.31 W
Lambourne ≃	42	51.24 N	1.18 W
Lambourne End	260	51.38 N	0.08 E
Lambrama	248	13.52 S	72.46 W
Lambrate ◆[8]	266b	45.29 N	9.15 E
Lambrecht	56	50.08 N	8.56 E
Lambrechten	60	48.19 N	13.31 E
Lambrechts Drift	158	28.31 S	21.43 E
Lambro ≃	62	45.08 N	9.32 E
Lambro, Parco ♠	266b	45.30 N	9.15 E
Lambs Creek	210	41.51 N	77.06 W
Lambs Terrace	285	39.46 N	75.02 W
Lambton	273d	26.15 S	28.10 E
Lambton □[6]	214	42.45 N	82.15 W
Lambton, Cape ≻	176	71.05 N	123.10 W
Lambu	164	3.09 S	151.41 E
Lambunao	116	11.03 N	122.29 E
L'amca	24	64.27 N	37.04 E
Lamdessar-timur	164	7.12 S	131.58 E
Lame, Nig.	150	10.23 N	9.13 E
Lamé, Tchad	146	9.15 N	14.32 E
La Meca → Makkah	144	21.27 N	39.49 E
La Mecque → Makkah	144	21.27 N	39.49 E
Lame Deer	202	45.37 N	106.39 W
La Media Luna, Arrecifes de ✦[2]	236	15.13 N	82.36 W
La Méditerranée → Mediterranean Sea ∓[2]	10	35.00 N	20.00 E
Lamego	34	41.06 N	7.49 W
La Meije ∧	62	45.00 N	6.18 E
La Membrolle-sur-Choisille	50	47.26 N	0.38 E
La Mendieta	252	24.19 S	64.58 W
L'amen'ga	76	59.51 N	44.31 E
Lamentin	241o	16.16 N	61.38 W
Lamèque	186	47.47 N	64.38 W
Lamèque, Île I	186	47.48 N	64.36 W
La Merced, Arg.	252	28.10 S	65.41 W
La Merced, Arg.	252	24.58 S	65.29 W
La Merced, Perú	248	11.03 S	75.19 W
Lameroo	166	35.20 S	140.31 E
La Mesa, Pan.	236	8.09 N	81.11 W
La Mesa, Ca., U.S.	228	32.46 N	117.01 W
La Mesa, N.M., U.S.	200	32.07 N	106.42 W
Lamesa, Tx., U.S.	196	32.44 N	101.57 W
La Mesa, Cerro ∧	232	26.59 N	113.44 W
La Mesa Dam ◆[6]	269f	14.43 N	121.04 E
La Meta ∧	66	41.41 N	13.56 E
Lamía	38	38.54 N	22.26 E
L'amin ≃	74	61.18 N	71.48 E
Lamine ≃	194	38.59 N	92.51 W
La Minerve	206	46.15 N	74.56 W
Laming ≃	61	47.25 N	15.16 E
Lamington ≃	210	40.38 N	74.41 W
Lamington National Park ♠	166	28.15 S	153.12 E
La Mira	234	18.02 N	102.19 W
La Mirada	228	33.55 N	118.00 W
La Mirada Creek ≃	280	33.53 N	118.01 W
La Misión	204	32.05 N	116.50 W
Lamitan	116	6.39 N	122.08 E
Lamlam, Mount ∧[2]	174p	13.20 N	144.40 E
Lamlash	46	55.32 N	5.08 W
Lamma Island I	271d	22.12 N	114.07 E
Lammefjord c	41	55.48 N	11.43 E
Lammerlaw Top ∧	172	45.40 S	169.38 E
Lammermuir ◆[1]	46	55.50 N	2.25 W
Lammermuir Hills ⋏[2]	46	55.50 N	2.44 W
Lammeulo	114	5.15 N	95.56 E
Lammhult	26	57.10 N	14.35 E
Lammi	26	61.05 N	25.01 E
Lamming Mills	182	53.22 N	120.18 W
Lamogai	164	5.50 S	149.20 E
La Moille, Il., U.S.	190	41.31 N	89.16 W
Lamoille, Nv., U.S.	204	40.43 N	115.28 W
Lamoille ≃	188	44.35 N	73.10 W
La Moine ≃	194	39.59 N	90.31 W
La Moine, East Fork ≃	194	40.24 N	90.56 W
Lamoka Lake ⊜	210	42.24 N	77.05 W
La Molina	286d	12.05 S	76.57 W
Lamon Bay c	116	14.25 N	122.00 E
La Moncada	234	20.16 N	100.48 W
Lamone ≃	66	44.31 N	12.15 E
Lamongan	115a	7.07 S	112.25 E
Lamongan, Gunung ∧	115a	7.58 S	113.20 E
Lamoni	190	40.37 N	93.56 W
Lamont, Ab., Can.	182	53.46 N	112.48 W
Lamont, Ca., U.S.	228	35.15 N	118.54 W
Lamont, Ia., U.S.	190	42.35 N	91.38 W
Lamont, Mi., U.S.	216	43.01 N	86.09 W
Lamont, Ok., U.S.	196	36.41 N	97.33 W
La Monte	194	38.46 N	93.25 W
La Mora, Monte ∧	236	15.06 N	86.16 W
La Mosquitia □[9]	236	15.00 N	83.45 W
La Mothe, Lac ⊜[1]	186	48.46 N	71.09 W
La Mothe-Achard	32	46.37 N	1.40 W
Lamotrek I[1]	14	7.30 N	146.20 E
La Mott	285	40.04 N	75.08 W
La Motte, Lac ⊜	190	48.24 N	78.03 W
Lamotte-Beuvron	50	47.36 N	2.01 E
La Motte-Chalançon	62	44.29 N	5.23 E
La Motte-du-Caire	62	44.21 N	6.02 E
Lamoura	58	46.24 N	5.58 E
La Moure	198	46.21 N	98.17 W
La Moustique ≃	241o	16.11 N	61.35 W
Lampa	248	15.21 S	70.22 W
Lampang	110	18.18 N	99.31 E
Lampasas	196	31.03 N	98.10 W
Lampasas ≃	196	30.59 N	97.24 W
Lampazos de Naranjo	232	27.01 N	100.31 W
Lampedusa	70a	35.30 N	12.56 E
Lampedusa, Isola di I	70a	35.31 N	12.35 E
Lampertheim	56	49.35 N	8.28 E
Lampeter, Wales, U.K.	42	52.07 N	4.05 W
Lampeter, Pa., U.S.	208	39.58 N	76.14 W
Lamphun	110	18.35 N	99.01 E
Lampinsaari	26	64.25 N	25.09 E
Lampione, Isolotto di I	70a	35.34 N	12.19 E
Lampman	184	49.23 N	102.45 W
Lamprechtshausen	64	47.59 N	12.57 E
Lampung □[4]	112	5.00 S	105.00 E
Lampung, Teluk c	115a	5.40 S	105.20 E
Lamskoje	76	52.57 N	38.02 E
Lamspringe	52	51.58 N	10.00 E
Lamstedt	52	53.38 N	9.05 E
Lāmta	124	22.08 N	80.07 E
Lam Tong Hoi Hap ʉ	271d	22.15 N	114.15 E
Lamu, Kenya	154	2.16 S	40.54 E
Lāmu, Mya.	110	19.14 N	94.10 E
Lamud	248	6.09 S	77.55 W
La Muerte, Cerro ∧	236	9.33 N	83.44 W
Lam Uk Wei	271d	22.26 N	114.22 E
La Mure	62	44.54 N	5.47 E
Lamure-sur-Azergues	58	46.04 N	4.30 E
La Mutua	234	22.23 N	99.18 W
Lan' ≃, S.S.S.R.	76	52.09 N	27.18 E
Lan ≃, Zhg.	104	41.14 N	123.32 E
Lan, Loi ∧	110	19.40 N	97.55 E
Lana	64	46.37 N	11.09 E
Lana, Río de la ≃	234	17.49 N	95.09 W
Lanai I	229a	20.50 N	156.55 W
Lanai City	229a	20.49 N	156.55 W
Lanaihale ∧	229a	20.49 N	156.52 W
Lanaken	56	50.53 N	5.39 E
Lanalhue, Lago ⊜	252	37.55 S	73.18 W
La Nana, Bayou ≃	222	31.27 N	94.43 W
Lanao del Norte □[4]	116	8.10 N	124.00 E
Lanao del Sur □[4]	116	7.50 N	124.25 E
La Napoule	62	43.31 N	6.56 E
Lanarce	62	44.44 N	4.00 E
Lanark, On., Can.	212	45.01 N	76.22 W
Lanark, Scot., U.K.	46	55.41 N	3.46 W
Lanark, Il., U.S.	190	42.06 N	89.50 W
Lanark, Pa., U.S.	208	40.33 N	75.26 W
Lanark □[6]	212	45.05 N	76.20 W
La Nartelle	62	43.19 N	6.39 E
Lanas	112	5.20 N	116.30 E
La Nava de Ricomalillo	34	39.39 N	4.59 W
Lanbi Kyun I	110	10.50 N	98.15 E
Lanboyan Point ≻	116	8.18 N	122.56 E
Lancang	102	23.00 N	100.02 E
Lancang → Mekong ≃	12	10.33 N	105.24 E
Lancashire	285	39.49 N	75.29 W
Lancashire □[6]	44	53.45 N	2.40 W
Lancashire Plain ≡	44	53.40 N	2.45 W
Lancaster, On., Can.	206	45.08 N	74.30 W
Lancaster, Eng., U.K.	44	54.03 N	2.48 W
Lancaster, Ca., U.S.	228	34.41 N	118.08 W
Lancaster, Ky., U.S.	192	37.37 N	84.34 W
Lancaster, Ma., U.S.	207	42.27 N	71.40 W
Lancaster, Mn., U.S.	198	48.51 N	96.48 W
Lancaster, Mo., U.S.	194	40.31 N	92.31 W
Lancaster, N.H., U.S.	188	44.29 N	71.34 W
Lancaster, N.Y., U.S.	210	42.54 N	78.40 W
Lancaster, Oh., U.S.	188	39.43 N	82.36 W
Lancaster, Pa., U.S.	208	40.02 N	76.18 W
Lancaster, S.C., U.S.	192	34.43 N	80.46 W
Lancaster, Tx., U.S.	222	32.38 N	96.47 W
Lancaster, Va., U.S.	208	37.46 N	76.28 W
Lancaster, Wi., U.S.	190	42.50 N	90.42 W
Lancaster □[6], Pa., U.S.	208	40.02 N	76.19 W
Lancaster □[6], Va., U.S.	208	37.45 N	76.30 W
Lancaster Canal ≍	262	53.46 N	2.43 W
Lancaster Sound ʉ	176	74.13 N	84.00 W
Lancaster Village	285	39.45 N	75.35 W
Lančchuti	84	42.06 N	42.01 E
Lance Creek	200	43.01 N	104.38 W
Lance Creek ≃	198	43.22 N	104.16 W
Lancefield	169	37.17 S	144.44 E
Lancelot, Mount ∧	162	26.13 S	123.12 E
Lancey	62	45.14 N	5.53 E
Lanchang	114	3.30 N	102.11 E
Lanchester	44	54.49 N	1.44 W
Lanchow → Lanzhou	102	36.03 N	103.41 E
Lanciano	66	42.14 N	14.23 E
Lancin, Fr.	62	45.43 N	5.24 E
Lančin, S.S.S.R.	78	48.34 N	24.45 E
Lancing	42	50.50 N	0.19 W
Lanco	254	39.24 S	72.46 W
Lancones	246	4.35 S	80.30 W
Lancun	98	36.24 N	120.10 E
Łańcut	30	50.05 N	22.13 E
Lancy	58	46.11 N	6.07 E
Lândana	152	5.13 S	12.08 E
Landang Gua	116	6.58 N	122.15 E
Landau	56	49.12 N	8.07 E
Landau an der Isar	60	48.40 N	12.43 E
Landay	128	30.31 N	63.47 E
Land Between the Lakes ♠	194	36.55 N	88.05 W
Landeck	58	47.08 N	10.34 E
Landeck in Westpreussen → Lędyczek	30	53.33 N	16.58 E
Landen	56	50.45 N	5.05 E
Landenberg	208	39.47 N	75.46 W
Landenhausen	56	50.36 N	9.28 E
Lander	200	42.49 N	108.43 W
Lander ≃	162	20.25 S	132.00 E
Landerneau	32	48.27 N	4.15 W
Landes □[5]	32	44.20 N	1.00 W
Landes ◆[1]	32	44.15 N	1.00 W
Landesbergen	52	52.33 N	9.07 E
Landeskrone ∧[2]	54	51.08 N	14.56 E
Landess	216	40.37 N	85.34 W
Landete	34	39.54 N	1.22 W
Landham Brook ≃	283	42.22 N	71.25 W
Landhausen	263	51.24 N	7.45 E
Landi	98	36.35 N	119.59 E
Landi Kotal	123	34.06 N	71.09 E
Landina	86	59.12 N	67.02 E
Landing	210	40.54 N	74.40 W
Landing Lake ⊜	184	55.17 N	97.26 W
Landis, Sk., Can.	184	52.12 N	108.28 W
Landis, N.C., U.S.	192	35.32 N	80.36 W
Landisburg	208	40.20 N	77.18 W
Landisville	208	40.06 N	76.25 W
Landivisiau	32	48.31 N	4.04 W
Landkey	42	51.04 N	4.00 W
Landkirchen	54	54.27 N	11.08 E
Lando	192	34.46 N	81.00 W
Land O'Lakes, Fl., U.S.	220	28.11 N	82.34 W
Land O'Lakes, Wi., U.S.	190	46.10 N	89.13 W
Landor	162	25.09 S	116.54 E
Landos	62	44.51 N	3.50 E
Landösjön ⊜	26	63.35 N	14.04 E
Landover Estates	284c	38.56 N	76.54 W
Landover Hills	284c	38.57 N	76.53 W
Landover Mall ◆[9]	284c	38.55 N	76.51 W
Landquart	58	46.58 N	9.33 E
Landquart ≃	58	46.58 N	9.32 E
Landrecies	50	50.08 N	3.42 E
Landres	56	49.19 N	5.48 E
Landreth Draw V	196	31.14 N	102.29 W
Landriano	62	45.19 N	9.15 E
Landri Sales	250	7.16 S	43.55 W
Landro (Höhlenstein)	64	46.39 N	12.14 E
Landrum	192	35.10 N	82.11 W
Landry	62	45.34 N	6.45 E
Landsberg	54	51.31 N	12.10 E
Landsberg am Lech	58	48.05 N	10.55 E
Landsberg an der Warthe → Gorzów Wielkopolski	30	52.44 N	15.15 E
Landsberg in Oberschlesien → Gorzów Śląski	30	51.02 N	18.24 E
Landsberg in Ostpreussen → Górowo Iławeckie	30	54.17 N	20.30 E
Landsborough	166	26.49 S	152.58 E
Landsborough Creek ≃	166	22.30 S	144.33 E
Landsbro	26	57.22 N	14.54 E
Land's End ≻, Eng., U.K.	42	50.03 N	5.44 W
Lands End ≻, Ca., U.S.	228	33.28 N	118.36 W
Lands End ≻, R.I., U.S.	207	41.27 N	71.19 W
Landshut	60	48.33 N	12.09 E
Landskrona	41	55.52 N	12.50 E
Landsman Creek ≃	198	39.35 N	102.19 W
Landsmeer	52	52.26 N	4.52 E
Landštejn	61	49.00 N	15.13 E
Landstuhl	56	49.25 N	7.34 E
Landweg	263	51.29 N	7.37 E
Landwehrbach ≃	263	51.26 N	6.26 E
Land Wursten ◆[1]	52	53.40 N	8.35 E
Lane	219	40.07 N	88.51 W
Lane ≃	50	47.17 N	0.05 E
Lane City	222	29.13 N	96.02 W
Lane Cove	274a	33.49 S	151.10 E
Lane Cove c	274a	33.48 S	151.09 E
Lane Cove National Park ♠	274a	33.47 S	151.09 E
La Negra	252	23.45 S	70.19 W
Lane Mountain ∧	228	35.05 N	116.56 W
Lanersbach	64	47.09 N	11.44 E
Lanesboro, Ma., U.S.	207	42.31 N	73.14 W
Lanesboro, Mn., U.S.	190	43.43 N	91.58 W
Lanesboro, Pa., U.S.	210	41.57 N	75.35 W
Lanester	32	47.46 N	3.21 W
Lanesville, In., U.S.	218	38.14 N	85.59 W
Lanesville, N.Y., U.S.	210	42.08 N	74.16 W
Lanesville, Va., U.S.	208	37.37 N	76.59 W
Lanett	194	32.52 N	85.11 W
La Neuveville	58	47.04 N	7.06 E
Laneville	222	31.58 N	94.49 W
Lanexa	208	37.24 N	76.55 W
Lanezi Lake ⊜	182	53.03 N	120.56 W
Lang	184	49.56 N	104.23 W
La-nga ≃	110	11.12 N	107.16 E
Langadhás	38	40.45 N	23.04 E
Langádhia	38	37.41 N	22.02 E
Langa-Langa	152	3.54 S	15.56 E
Langan Creek ≃	216	40.57 N	87.49 W
Langano, Lake ⊜	144	7.35 N	38.48 E
Langao	102	32.13 N	109.02 E
Langar, Afg.	120	37.02 N	73.47 E
L'angar, S.S.S.R.	85	40.25 N	73.07 E
L'angar, S.S.S.R.	123	37.02 N	72.42 E
Langara	112	4.02 S	123.00 E
Langara Island I	182	54.14 N	133.00 W
Langarūd	128	37.11 N	50.10 E
L'angasovo	80	58.32 N	49.30 E
Langat ≃	114	2.54 N	101.22 E
Langau	61	48.49 N	15.42 E
Langavat, Loch ⊜	46	58.04 N	6.48 W
Långban	40	59.51 N	14.15 E
Langbank	184	50.05 N	102.20 W
Lang Bay	182	49.47 N	124.21 W
Langberg ⋏	158	28.20 S	22.35 E
Langburkersdorf	54	51.02 N	14.14 E
Langda	102	31.12 N	96.59 E
Langdai	102	26.06 N	105.20 E
Langdon	198	48.45 N	98.22 W
Langdondale	214	40.08 N	78.15 W
Langdon Hills	260	51.34 N	0.25 E
Langeac	32	45.06 N	3.30 E
Langeais	50	47.20 N	0.24 E
Langebaan	158	33.06 S	18.02 E
Langeberg ⋏	158	33.55 S	20.30 E
Lange Berge ⋏[2]	56	50.20 N	10.55 E
Langebrück	54	51.07 N	13.50 E
Langeland I	41	55.00 N	10.50 E
Langelands Bælt ʉ	41	54.50 N	10.55 E
Längelmävesi ⊜	26	61.32 N	24.22 E
Langeloth	214	40.21 N	80.24 W
Langelsheim	52	51.56 N	10.19 E
Langemark	50	50.55 N	2.55 E
Langen, B.R.D.	52	53.36 N	8.35 E
Langen, B.R.D.	56	49.59 N	8.41 E
Langenargen	58	47.35 N	9.32 E
Langenau, B.R.D.	58	48.30 N	10.07 E
Langenau, D.D.R.	54	50.50 N	13.18 E
Langenberg, B.R.D.	52	51.46 N	8.19 E
Langenberg, B.R.D.	56	51.21 N	7.09 E
Langenbernsdorf	54	50.45 N	12.19 E
Langenbielau → Bielawa	30	50.41 N	16.38 E
Langenbochum	263	51.37 N	7.07 E
Langenbruck	58	47.21 N	7.46 E
Langenburg, B.R.D.	56	49.15 N	9.50 E
Langenburg, Sk., Can.	184	50.50 N	101.43 W
Langendorf	54	51.11 N	11.58 E
Langendreer ◆[8]	263	51.28 N	7.19 E
Langeneichstädt	54	51.20 N	11.41 E
Langenfeld, B.R.D.	56	51.07 N	6.56 E
Längenfeld, Öst.	64	47.04 N	10.58 E
Langenhagen	52	52.27 N	9.44 E
Langenhessen	54	50.45 N	12.22 E
Langenhorn	41	54.41 N	8.53 E
Langenhorst	263	51.22 N	7.02 E
Langenlois	61	48.28 N	15.40 E
Langennaundorf	54	51.36 N	13.20 E
Langenneufnach	58	48.16 N	10.36 E
Langenselbold	56	50.10 N	9.02 E
Langensteinach	56	49.30 N	10.10 E
Langenthal	58	47.13 N	7.47 E
Langenwang	61	47.34 N	15.37 E
Langenweddingen	54	52.02 N	11.31 E
Langenwetzendorf	54	50.41 N	12.05 E
Langenzenn	56	49.30 N	10.48 E
Langenzersdorf	61	48.18 N	16.22 E
Langeoog	52	53.45 N	7.29 E
Langeoog I	52	53.46 N	7.32 E
Langerfeld ◆[8]	263	51.16 N	7.15 E
Langer See ⊜	264a	52.25 N	13.38 E
Langerwehe	56	50.49 N	6.22 E
Langeskov	41	55.22 N	10.36 E
Langesund	26	59.00 N	9.45 E
Langevåg	26	62.27 N	6.12 E
Langewiesen	54	50.40 N	10.58 E
Langfang → Anci	105	39.31 N	116.41 E
Langfjorden c[2]	26	62.43 N	7.30 E
Langford, B.C., Can.	224	48.27 N	123.30 W
Langford, Eng., U.K.	260	51.45 N	0.40 E
Langford, N.Y., U.S.	210	42.35 N	78.51 W
Langford, S.D., U.S.	198	45.36 N	97.49 W
Langförden	52	52.47 N	8.14 E
Langgam	112	0.15 N	101.43 E
Langgapayung	114	1.43 N	99.59 E
Langgöns	56	50.30 N	8.40 E
Långhalsen ⊜	40	58.56 N	16.41 E
Langham	184	52.22 N	106.57 W
Langhe □[9]	62	44.30 N	8.00 E
Langhirano	64	44.37 N	10.16 E
Langho	262	53.48 N	2.27 W
Langholm	44	55.09 N	3.00 W
Langhorne	208	40.10 N	74.55 W
Langhorne Acres	284c	38.51 N	77.16 W
Langhorne Creek	168b	35.18 S	139.02 E
Langhorne Gardens	285	40.11 N	74.53 W
Langhorne Manor	285	40.10 N	74.55 W
Langhorne Terrace	285	40.10 N	74.57 W
Langji Shan I	100	28.32 N	121.36 E
Langjökull ⊓	24a	64.42 N	20.12 W
Langju	100	27.52 N	116.36 E
Lang Ka, Doi ∧	110	19.00 N	99.24 E
Langkawi, Pulau I	114	6.22 N	99.50 E
Langkazi	124	28.59 N	90.25 E
Langkesi, Kepulauan II	112	5.18 S	124.20 E
Langklip	158	28.12 S	20.20 E
Langkrans	158	27.47 S	31.03 E
Langlade I	186	46.50 N	56.20 W
Lang Lang ≃	169	38.17 S	145.31 E
Langley, B.C., Can.	224	49.06 N	122.39 W
Langley, Eng., U.K.	260	51.30 N	0.33 W
Langley, Eng., U.K.	260	51.14 N	0.35 E
Langley, Eng., U.K.	262	53.15 N	2.05 W
Langley, Ok., U.S.	196	36.27 N	95.02 W
Langley, S.C., U.S.	192	33.31 N	81.50 W
Langley, Va., U.S.	284c	38.57 N	77.10 W
Langley, Wa., U.S.	224	48.02 N	122.24 W
Langley Air Force Base ■	208	37.05 N	76.21 W
Langley Hill ∧[2]	282	37.20 N	122.14 W
Langley Park	284c	38.59 N	76.58 W
Langleyville	219	39.34 N	89.21 W
Langlo ≃	166	26.26 S	146.05 E
Langlois	202	42.55 N	124.26 W
Langmazong	120	30.52 N	89.58 E
Lang-mo	110	17.14 N	106.27 E
Långnäs	26	60.06 N	20.17 E
Langnau	58	46.57 N	7.47 E
Langogne	62	44.43 N	3.51 E
Langon	32	44.33 N	0.15 W
Langøya I	24	68.44 N	14.50 E
Lang-phuoc-hai	110	10.26 N	107.18 E
Langping	102	30.38 N	110.21 E
Langport	42	51.02 N	2.50 W
Langqiao	100	30.30 N	118.24 E
Langquaid	60	48.49 N	12.03 E
Langreo → Sama [de Langreo]	34	43.18 N	5.41 W
Langres	58	47.52 N	5.20 E
Langres, Plateau de ⋏[1]	58	47.41 N	5.03 E
Langruth	184	50.24 N	98.38 W
Langruzong	120	31.50 N	91.25 E
Langsa	114	4.28 N	97.58 E
Langsa, Teluk c	114	4.35 N	98.00 E
Langschede	263	51.29 N	7.43 E
Långsele	26	63.11 N	17.04 E
Langshan, Zhg.	102	41.12 N	107.22 E
Langshan, Zhg.	105	40.22 N	115.41 E
Långshyttan	40	60.27 N	16.01 E
Långsjön ⊜	40	59.00 N	17.27 E
Langsnek ⊥	158	27.28 S	29.55 E
Lang-son	110	21.50 N	106.44 E
Langstaff	275b	43.50 N	79.25 W
Langst-Kierst	263	51.18 N	6.43 E
Lang Suan	110	9.57 N	99.04 E
Långsvan ⊜	40	59.43 N	15.49 E
Langtian	100	25.11 N	113.28 E
Langting	120	25.30 N	93.07 E
Langton	212	42.45 N	80.35 W
Langtoutun	89	46.51 N	121.54 E
Langtuozi	104	41.01 N	121.43 E
Langu	100	27.56 N	118.11 E
Langue	236	13.37 N	87.39 W
Languedoc □[9]	32	44.00 N	4.00 E
L'Anguille ≃	194	34.44 N	90.40 W
Langui y Layo, Laguna de ⊜	248	14.29 S	71.13 W
Langula	54	51.09 N	10.25 E
Langundu, Tanjung ≻	115b	8.49 S	118.58 E
Langwarden	52	53.36 N	8.19 E
Langwedel	52	52.59 N	9.12 E
Langweer	52	52.57 N	5.43 E
Langweid	58	48.29 N	10.51 E
Langweiler	56	49.40 N	7.31 E
Langwies	58	46.49 N	9.43 E
Langwo	104	41.13 N	121.44 E
Langwozhuang	105	39.05 N	115.37 E
Langxi	106	31.08 N	119.10 E
Langxi ≃	106	31.10 N	118.59 E
Langzhong	102	31.35 N	105.59 E
Langzishan	104	41.02 N	123.23 E
Lanham	284c	38.58 N	76.51 W
Lanhil Island I	116	6.46 N	122.22 E
Lanibga, Mount ∧	116	10.27 N	123.56 E
Lanigan	184	51.52 N	105.02 W
Lanigan Creek ≃	184	51.23 N	105.13 W
Lanín, Parque Nacional ♠	254	39.36 S	71.24 W
Lanín, Volcán ∧[1]	254	39.38 S	71.30 W

Symbol	English	Deutsch	Español	Français	Português
≃	River	Fluss	Río	Rivière	Rio
≍	Canal	Kanal	Canal	Canal	Canal
∟	Waterfall, Rapids	Wasserfall, Stromschnellen	Cascada, Rápidos	Chute d'eau, Rapides	Cascata, Rápidos
ʉ	Strait	Meeresstrasse	Estrecho	Détroit	Estreito
c	Bay, Gulf	Bucht, Golf	Bahía, Golfo	Baie, Golfe	Baía, Golfo
⊜	Lake, Lakes	See, Seen	Lago, Lagos	Lac, Lacs	Lago, Lagos
≡	Swamp	Sumpf	Pantano	Marais	Pântano
⊓	Ice Features, Glacier	Eis- und Gletscherformen	Accidentes Glaciales	Formes glaciaires	Acidentes glaciares
∓	Other Hydrographic Features	Andere Hydrographische Objekte	Otros Elementos Hidrográficos	Autres données hydrographiques	Outros acidentes hidrográficos
✦	Submarine Features	Untermeerische Objekte	Accidentes Submarinos	Formes de relief sous-marin	Acidentes submarinos
□	Political Unit	Politische Einheit	Unidad Política	Entité politique	Unidade política
♥	Cultural Institution	Kulturelle Institution	Institución Cultural	Institution culturelle	Institução cultural
⊥	Historical Site	Historische Stätte	Sitio Histórico	Site historique	Sitio histórico
♠	Recreational Site	Erholungs- und Ferienort	Sitio de Recreo	Centre de loisirs	Area de Lazer
⊠	Airport	Flughafen	Aeropuerto	Aéroport	Aeroporto
■	Military Installation	Militäranlage	Instalación Militar	Installation militaire	Instalação militar
◆	Miscellaneous	Verschiedenes	Misceláneo	Divers	Diversos

ENGLISH

Name	Page	Lat.°′	Long.°′

DEUTSCH

Name	Seite	Breite°′	Länge°′ E = Ost

Symbols in the index entries represent the broad categories identified in the key at the right. Symbols with superior numbers (⋏ [1]) identify subcategories (see complete key on page *I · 1).*

Kartensymbole in dem Registerverzeichnis stellen die rechts in Schlüssel erklärten Kategorien dar. Symbole mit hochgestellten Ziffern (⋏ [1]) bezeichnen Unterabteilungen einer Kategorie (vgl. vollständiger Schlüssel auf Seite *I · 1).*

Los símbolos incluídos en el texto del índice representan las grandes categorias identificadas con la clave a la derecha. Los símbolos con numeros en su parte superior (⋏ [1]) identifican las subcategorías (véase la clave completa en la página *I · 1).*

Les symboles de l'index représentent les catégories indiquées dans la légende à droite. Les symboles suivis d'un indice (⋏ [1]) représentent des sous-catégories (voir légende complète à la page *I · 1).*

Os símbolos incluídos no texto do índice representam as grandes categorias identificadas com a chave à direita. Os símbolos com números em sua parte superior (⋏ [1]) identificam as subcategorias (veja-se a chave completa à página *I · 1).*

∧ Mountain	Berg	Montaña	Montagne	Montanha
⋏ Mountains	Berge	Montañas	Montagnes	Montanhas
)(Pass	Pass	Paso	Col	Passo
V Valley, Canyon	Tal, Cañon	Valle, Cañón	Vallée, Canyon	Vale, Canhão
≚ Plain	Ebene	Llano	Plaine	Planície
> Cape	Kap	Cabo	Cap	Cabo
I Island	Insel	Isla	Île	Ilha
II Islands	Inseln	Islas	Îles	Ilhas
⊥ Other Topographic Features	Andere Topographische Objekte	Otros Elementos Topográficos	Autres données topographiques	Outros acidentes topográficos

ESPAÑOL: Nombre · Página · Lat.°′ · Long.°′ W = Oeste
FRANÇAIS: Nom · Page · Lat.°′ · Long.°′ W = Ouest
PORTUGUÊS: Nome · Página · Lat.°′ · Long.°′ W = Oeste

Nombre / Nom / Nome	Página / Page	Lat.°′	Long.°′ W = Oeste / Ouest
Laurelville, Pa., U.S.	214	40.09 N	79.29 W
Laurenburg	56	50.20 N	7.54 E
Laurence Harbor	276	40.27 N	74.14 W
Laurencekirk	46	56.50 N	2.29 W
Laurens, Ia., U.S.	198	42.50 N	94.51 W
Laurens, N.Y., U.S.	210	42.32 N	75.06 W
Laurens, S.C., U.S.	192	34.29 N	82.00 W
Laurentides	206	45.51 N	73.46 W
Laurentides, Les ⋀[1]	176	48.00 N	71.00 W
Laurentides, Parc Provincial des ♠	186	47.40 N	71.30 W
Laurenzana	68	40.28 N	15.58 E
Lauria	68	40.02 N	15.50 E
Lau Ridge ✤[3]	14	21.00 S	178.30 W
Laurie Island I	9	60.45 S	44.35 W
Laurie Lake ⊜	184	56.34 N	101.54 W
Laurier, Mb., Can.	184	50.54 N	99.33 W
Laurier, P.Q., Can.	206	46.32 N	71.38 W
Laurière	32	46.05 N	1.28 E
Laurierville	206	46.18 N	71.39 W
Laurinburg	192	34.46 N	79.27 W
Laurino	68	40.20 N	15.20 E
Laurito	68	40.10 N	15.24 E
Lauritsala	26	61.04 N	28.16 E
Lauritzen Bay c	9	69.05 S	156.50 E
Laurium	190	47.14 N	88.26 W
Lauriya Nandangarh	124	26.59 N	84.24 E
Lauro, Monte ∧	70	37.07 N	14.49 E
Lauro Müller	252	28.24 S	49.23 W
Laurys Station	208	40.43 N	75.32 W
Lausanne	58	46.31 N	6.38 E
Lauscha	54	50.28 N	11.10 E
Laut	86	59.18 N	66.02 E
Laut, Pulau I, Indon.	112	3.40 S	116.10 E
Laut, Pulau I, Indon.	112	4.43 N	107.59 E
Laut, Selat ʮ	112	3.25 S	116.03 E
Lauta	54	51.27 N	14.04 E
Lautaro	252	38.31 S	72.27 W
Lautém	112	8.22 S	126.54 E
Lautenbach	58	47.57 N	7.09 E
Lautenthal	52	51.52 N	10.17 E
Lauter ≃, B.R.D.	56	49.39 N	7.35 E
Lauter ≃, Europe	56	48.58 N	8.11 E
Lauterach	58	47.29 N	9.44 E
Lauterbach, B.R.D.	56	50.38 N	9.24 E
Lauterbach, B.R.D.	58	48.14 N	8.20 E
Lauterbourg	56	48.59 N	8.11 E
Lauterbrunnen	58	46.36 N	7.55 E
Lauterecken	56	49.39 N	7.35 E
Lauterhofen	60	49.22 N	11.37 E
Lauter [Sachsen]	54	50.33 N	12.44 E
Laut Kecil, Kepulauan II	112	4.50 S	115.45 E
Lautoka	175g	17.37 S	177.27 E
Lauttakylä → Huittinen	26	61.11 N	22.42 E
Lauwe	50	50.48 N	3.11 E
Lauwerszee c	52	53.20 N	6.12 E
Lauzerte	32	44.15 N	1.08 E
Lauzon	206	46.50 N	71.10 W
Lauzun	32	44.38 N	0.28 E
Lava (Łyna) ≃	76	54.37 N	21.14 E
Lava, Nosy I	157b	14.33 S	47.36 E
Lava Beds National Monument ♠	204	41.42 N	121.30 W
Lavaca □[6]	222	29.22 N	96.55 W
Lavaca ≃	196	28.50 N	96.36 W
Lavaca Bay c	196	28.35 N	96.35 W
La Vacherie	62	44.53 N	5.11 E
Lavagh More ∧	48	54.45 N	8.05 W
Lavagna	62	44.18 N	9.20 E
Lavagna ≃	62	44.21 N	9.20 E
Lava Hot Springs	202	42.37 N	112.00 W
Lavaisse	252	33.49 S	65.25 W
Laval, P.Q., Can.	206	45.35 N	73.45 W
Laval, Fr.	32	48.04 N	0.46 W
Laval-des-Rapides ◆[8]	275a	45.33 N	73.42 W
La Valette → Valletta	36	35.54 N	14.31 E
La Valette-du-Var	62	43.08 N	5.59 E
Lavalle, Arg.	252	29.01 S	59.11 W
Lavalle, Arg.	252	28.12 S	65.08 W
Lavalleja → Minas	252	34.23 S	55.14 W
Lavallette	208	39.58 N	74.04 W
La Valley	200	37.06 N	105.20 W
Laval-Ouest ◆[8]	275a	45.33 N	73.52 W
Lavaltrie	206	45.53 N	73.17 W
Lavamünd	61	46.39 N	14.56 E
Lāvān, Jazīreh-ye I	128	26.48 N	53.15 E
Lavanono	157b	25.24 S	44.55 E
Lavant ≃	61	46.38 N	14.57 E
Lavapié, Punta ›	252	37.09 S	73.35 W
Lávara	38	41.16 N	26.22 E
Lavaraty	157b	23.16 S	46.59 E
Lavardac	32	44.11 N	0.18 E
Lāvar Meydān ≚	128	30.20 N	54.30 E
Lavarone	64	45.56 N	11.15 E
Lavassaare	76	58.31 N	24.22 E
Lava Tudo ≃	252	28.26 S	50.25 W
Laveaga Peak ∧	226	36.53 N	121.11 W
La Vecilla de Curueño	34	42.51 N	5.24 W
La Vega ◆[8]	286c	10.28 N	66.57 W
Lavela	24	63.38 N	45.31 E
La Vela, Cabo de ›	246	12.15 N	72.11 W
La Vela de Coro	246	11.27 N	69.34 W
Lavelanet	32	42.56 N	1.51 E
Lavelle	208	40.46 N	76.22 W
Lavello	68	41.03 N	15.48 E
Laven	41	56.07 N	9.43 E
La Venada	196	25.50 N	97.30 W
Lavendon	42	52.11 N	0.40 W
Lavenham	42	52.06 N	0.47 E
Laveno	58	45.55 N	8.37 E
Lavenone	64	45.44 N	10.26 E
La Venta ⊥	234	18.08 N	94.03 W
Laventie	50	50.38 N	2.46 E
La Ventura	232	24.38 N	100.54 W
Laver ≃	44	54.08 N	1.30 W
Lavéra	62	43.23 N	5.02 E
La Vera ◆[1]	34	40.20 N	5.30 W
La Verde, Arg.	252	27.08 S	59.23 W
La Verde, Arg.	258	34.44 S	59.16 W
Laverdière, Lac ⊜	206	46.50 N	74.28 W
L'Averdy, Cape ›	175e	5.33 S	155.04 E
La Vérendrye, Réserve ♠	190	47.30 N	77.30 W
La Vergne	194	36.00 N	86.34 W
La Verna ʋ[1]	66	43.42 N	11.54 E
La Verne, Ca., U.S.	280	34.06 N	117.46 W
Laverne, Ok., U.S.	196	36.42 N	99.53 W
La Vernia	196	29.21 N	98.07 W
Laverock	285	40.05 N	75.11 W
La Verpillière	62	45.38 N	5.09 E
La Verrière	261	48.45 N	1.57 E
Lavers Hill	169	38.40 S	143.24 E
Laverton, Austl.	162	28.38 S	122.25 E
Laverton, Austl.	169	37.52 S	144.45 E
Laverton Royal Australian Air Force Base ■	169	37.52 S	144.43 E
La Veta	200	37.30 N	105.00 W
Lavezares	116	12.32 N	124.20 E
Lavezzi, Îles II	71	41.20 N	9.15 E
Lavezzola	66	44.34 N	11.52 E
Lavia	26	61.36 N	22.36 E
Laviano	68	40.47 N	15.18 E
Lavic Lake ⊜	204	34.40 N	116.21 W
La Victoria, Perú	286d	12.04 S	77.02 W
La Victoria, Ven.	246	10.14 N	67.20 W
Lavieille, Lake ⊜	190	45.51 N	78.14 W
Lavik	26	61.06 N	5.30 E
La Villa	64	46.36 N	11.54 E
La Villa ≃	236	7.59 N	80.23 W
La Ville-du-Bois	261	48.40 N	2.16 E
La Villeneuve-Saint-Martin	261	49.04 N	1.58 E
Lavillette	186	47.16 N	65.18 W
Lavin	58	46.46 N	10.06 E
La Viña, Arg.	252	25.27 S	65.35 W
Lavina, Mt., U.S.	202	46.17 N	108.56 W
Lavinio Lido di Enea	66	41.30 N	12.05 E
Laviolette, Lac ⊜	206	46.51 N	73.58 W
La Virginia	246	4.54 N	75.53 W
Lavis	64	46.08 N	11.07 E
La Vista	198	41.11 N	96.01 W
La Volla	204	32.51 N	117.16 W
Lavon	222	33.02 N	96.26 W
Lavonia	192	34.26 N	83.06 W
Lavon Lake ⊜[1]	222	33.05 N	96.28 W
Lavougba	152	5.46 N	23.21 E
La Voulte-sur-Rhône	62	44.48 N	4.47 E
Lavoûte-sur-Loire	62	45.07 N	3.54 E
Lavoutte, Anse c	241f	14.06 N	60.56 W
Lavras	256	21.14 S	45.00 W
Lavras ≃	287a	23.00 S	43.33 W
Lavras da Mangabeira	250	6.45 S	38.57 W
Lavras do Sul	252	30.49 S	53.55 W
Lavrentija	180	65.35 N	171.00 W
Lavrentija, zaliv c	180	65.40 N	171.15 W
Lavrinhas	256	22.35 S	44.54 W
Lávrion	38	37.44 N	24.04 E
Lavumisa	158	27.19 S	31.54 E
Lavushi Manda National Park ♠	154	12.20 S	30.50 E
Lawa	116	6.12 N	125.41 E
Lawai	229b	21.55 N	159.30 W
Lawang	115a	7.49 S	112.42 E
La Wantzenau	58	48.40 N	7.50 E
La Ward	222	28.51 N	96.28 W
Lawas	112	4.51 N	115.24 E
Lawatu	112	2.53 S	120.18 E
Lawdar	144	13.53 N	45.52 E
Lawele	112	5.13 S	122.57 E
Lawers, Ben ∧	46	56.34 N	4.13 W
Laweueng	114	5.31 N	95.52 E
Lawford Lake ⊜	184	54.30 N	96.43 W
Lawgi	166	24.34 S	150.39 E
Lawin	114	5.18 N	101.04 E
Lawin, Pulau I	164	1.31 S	128.44 E
Lawit, Gunong ∧	114	5.25 N	102.35 E
Lawksawk	110	21.15 N	96.52 E
Lawler	190	43.04 N	92.09 W
Lawlor, Mount ∧	280	34.16 N	118.06 W
Lawn, Nf., Can.	186	46.57 N	55.32 W
Lawn, Pa., U.S.	208	40.13 N	76.32 W
Lawn, Tx., U.S.	196	32.08 N	99.49 W
Lawn Bay c	186	46.53 N	55.35 W
Lawndale, Ca., U.S.	228	33.53 N	118.21 W
Lawndale, Il., U.S.	219	40.13 N	89.17 W
Lawndale, N.C., U.S.	192	35.24 N	81.33 W
Lawndale ◆[8], Il., U.S.	278	41.51 N	87.43 W
Lawndale ◆[8], Pa., U.S.	285	40.03 N	75.05 W
Lawnes Creek ≃	208	37.08 N	76.40 W
Lawn Hill	166	18.35 S	138.35 E
Lawn Hill Creek ≃	166	18.03 S	139.09 E
Lawnside	285	39.51 N	75.01 W
Lawowa	112	4.26 S	122.56 E
Lawqah	128	29.49 N	42.45 E
Lawra	150	10.39 N	2.52 W
Lawrence, N.Z.	172	45.55 S	169.41 E
Lawrence, In., U.S.	218	39.50 N	86.01 W
Lawrence, Ks., U.S.	198	38.58 N	95.14 W
Lawrence, Ma., U.S.	207	42.42 N	71.09 W
Lawrence, Mi., U.S.	216	42.13 N	86.03 W
Lawrence, Ne., U.S.	198	40.17 N	98.15 W
Lawrence, N.Y., U.S.	276	40.36 N	73.43 W
Lawrence, Pa., U.S.	279b	40.18 N	80.09 W
Lawrence, Tx., U.S.	222	32.45 N	96.21 W
Lawrence □[6], In., U.S.	218	38.52 N	86.29 W
Lawrence □[6], Pa., U.S.	214	41.00 N	80.20 W
Lawrence, Lake ⊜	224	46.51 N	122.34 W
Lawrence Brook ≃	276	40.29 N	74.24 W
Lawrenceburg, In., U.S.	218	39.05 N	84.51 W
Lawrenceburg, Ky., U.S.	218	38.02 N	84.54 W
Lawrenceburg, Tn., U.S.	194	35.14 N	87.20 W
Lawrence Fork ≃	198	41.36 N	103.14 W
Lawrence Institute of Technology ʋ[2]	281	42.28 N	83.15 W
Lawrence Marsh ⊞	276	40.36 N	73.42 W
Lawrence Municipal Airport ⊠	283	42.43 N	71.07 W
Lawrence Park	214	42.09 N	80.01 W
Lawrencepur	123	33.50 N	72.30 E
Lawrenceville, Il., U.S.	194	38.43 N	87.40 W
Lawrenceville, N.J., U.S.	208	40.17 N	74.43 W
Lawrenceville, Pa., U.S.	210	42.00 N	77.08 W
Lawrenceville, Va., U.S.	192	36.45 N	77.50 W
Lawrenceville ◆[8]	279b	40.28 N	79.57 W
Lawson, Austl.	170	33.43 S	150.26 E
Lawson, Mo., U.S.	194	39.26 N	94.12 W
Lawson Heights	214	40.18 N	79.23 W
Lawsonia	208	37.58 N	75.50 W
Lawsons Creek ≃	170	32.35 S	149.43 E
Lawtey	192	30.02 N	82.04 W
Lawton, Ky., U.S.	218	38.16 N	83.13 W
Lawton, Mi., U.S.	216	42.10 N	85.50 W
Lawton, N.D., U.S.	198	48.18 N	98.22 W
Lawton, Ok., U.S.	196	34.36 N	98.23 W
Lawton ◆[8]	286b	23.06 N	82.21 W
Lawu, Gunung ∧	115a	7.38 S	111.11 E
Lawyer Creek ≃	202	46.14 N	116.01 W
Lawyersville	210	42.42 N	74.30 W
Lawz, Jabal al- ∧	128	28.40 N	35.18 E
Laxå	40	58.59 N	14.37 E
Laxay	46	58.09 N	6.35 W
Laxenburg	264b	48.04 N	16.21 E
Laxenburger Park ♠	264b	48.04 N	16.22 E
Laxey	44	54.14 N	4.23 W
Laxford, Loch c	46	58.23 N	5.06 W
Laxou	58	48.41 N	6.09 E
Layang Layang	114	1.49 N	103.29 E
Laye ≃	62	43.54 N	5.48 E
La Yesca	234	21.19 N	104.02 W
Layhill	208	39.05 N	77.03 W
Laylā	144	22.17 N	46.45 E
Lay Lake ⊜[1]	194	33.10 N	86.35 W
Layou	241h	13.12 N	61.17 W
Layou ≃	240d	15.23 N	61.26 W
La'youn □[4]	148	27.55 N	12.15 W
Lay-Saint-Christophe	56	48.45 N	6.12 E
Laysan Island I	14	25.50 N	171.50 W
Layton, N.J., U.S.	210	41.13 N	74.50 W
Layton, Ut,. U.S.	200	41.03 N	111.58 W
Laytons Lake ⊜	285	39.42 N	75.26 W
Laytonville	204	39.41 N	123.28 W
Laytown	48	53.40 N	6.14 W
Laž	80	57.11 N	49.14 E
La Zarca	232	25.50 N	104.44 W
Lazarev	89	52.13 N	141.32 E
Lazarevo	80	56.49 N	50.15 E
Lazarevskoje	84	43.55 N	39.20 E
Lazarivo	157b	23.54 S	44.59 E
Lazaro Cárdenas	196	25.23 N	103.10 W
Lázaro Cárdenas, Presa ⊜[1]	232	25.35 N	105.02 W
Lazdijai	76	54.14 N	23.31 E
Lazha	102	26.26 N	101.50 E
Lazhulong	120	35.08 N	81.33 E
Lazi, Pil.	116	9.08 N	123.38 E
Lazi, Zhg.	120	29.10 N	87.42 E
Lazio □[4]	66	42.00 N	12.30 E
Lazise	64	45.30 N	10.44 E
Lazo	89	43.25 N	133.55 E
Lazorki	78	50.06 N	32.39 E
La Zorra, Quebrada ≃	286c	10.36 N	67.03 W
Lazovskij zapovednik ♠	89	44.00 N	133.55 E
Lazzaro	68	37.58 N	15.40 E
Lazzate	266b	45.40 N	9.05 E
Lea ≃	42	51.30 N	0.01 E
Léach	110	12.21 N	103.46 E
Leach ≃	42	51.41 N	1.39 W
Leach Pond ⊜	283	42.04 N	71.09 W
Leachville	194	35.56 N	90.15 W
Leacock	208	40.05 N	76.12 W
Lead	198	44.21 N	103.45 W
Leadbetter Point ›	224	46.38 N	124.03 W
Leadburn	46	55.47 N	3.14 W
Leadenham	42	53.05 N	0.34 W
Leaden Roding	260	51.48 N	0.19 E
Leader	184	50.53 N	109.31 W
Leader Water ≃	46	55.36 N	2.41 W
Leadgate	44	54.52 N	1.48 W
Lead Hill ∧[2]	194	37.06 N	92.38 W
Leadhills	44	55.25 N	3.47 W
Leadon ≃	42	51.53 N	2.16 W
Leadore	202	44.40 N	113.21 W
Leadville	200	39.15 N	106.17 W
Leaf ≃, Mn., U.S.	198	46.29 N	94.53 W
Leaf ≃, Ms., U.S.	194	31.00 N	88.45 W
Leaf Lake ⊜	184	53.02 N	102.07 W
Leaghur, Lake ⊜	166	33.35 S	143.04 E
League ∧	48	54.39 N	8.44 W
League City	222	29.30 N	95.05 W
Leakesville	194	31.09 N	88.33 W
Leakey	196	29.43 N	99.45 W
Leakin Park ♠	284b	39.18 N	76.42 W
Leak Run ≃	279b	40.27 N	79.47 W
Leaksville	192	36.29 N	79.53 W
Lealman	220	27.49 N	82.40 W
Lealui	152	15.10 S	23.02 E
Leam ≃	42	52.17 N	1.14 W
Leamington	214	42.03 N	82.36 W
Leamington Spa → Royal Leamington Spa	42	52.18 N	1.31 W
Le'an	100	27.24 N	115.48 E
Leán ≃	236	15.47 N	87.20 W
Leander Point ›	162	29.16 S	114.56 E
Leandro	250	5.59 S	44.55 W
Leandro, Serra do ⋀	256	22.55 S	43.55 W
Leandro N. Alem	252	27.36 S	55.19 W
Leane, Lough ⊜	48	52.05 N	9.35 W
Leannan ≃	48	55.02 N	7.38 W
Leano, Monte ∧	66	41.20 N	13.13 E
Leary	192	31.29 N	84.30 W
Leaside □[8]	275b	43.42 N	79.22 W
Leask	184	53.00 N	106.45 W
Leatherhead	42	51.18 N	0.20 W
Leatherman Peak ∧	202	44.05 N	113.44 W
Leatherwood Creek ≃	218	38.49 N	86.30 W
Lea Town	262	53.46 N	2.48 W
Leavenworth, Ks., U.S.	198	39.18 N	94.55 W
Leavenworth, Wa., U.S.	224	47.35 N	120.39 W
Leavesden Aerodrome ⊠	260	51.42 N	0.27 W
Leavittsburg	214	41.14 N	80.52 W
Leawood	194	37.03 N	94.31 W
Łeba	30	54.47 N	17.33 E
Łeba ≃	30	54.47 N	17.33 E
Lebach	56	49.24 N	6.54 E
Lebak	116	6.32 N	124.03 E
Lebam	224	46.33 N	123.32 W
Lébamba	152	2.12 S	11.30 E
Lebango	152	0.22 N	14.49 E
Lebanon, Ct., U.S.	207	41.38 N	72.13 W
Lebanon, Il., U.S.	219	38.36 N	89.48 W
Lebanon, In., U.S.	218	40.02 N	86.28 W
Lebanon, Ks., U.S.	198	39.48 N	98.33 W
Lebanon, Ky., U.S.	194	37.34 N	85.15 W
Lebanon, Mo., U.S.	194	37.40 N	92.39 W
Lebanon, N.H., U.S.	188	43.38 N	72.15 W
Lebanon, N.J., U.S.	210	40.38 N	74.50 W
Lebanon, N.Y., U.S.	210	42.47 N	75.39 W
Lebanon, Oh., U.S.	218	39.26 N	84.12 W
Lebanon, Or., U.S.	202	44.32 N	122.54 W
Lebanon, Pa., U.S.	208	40.20 N	76.24 W
Lebanon, S.D., U.S.	198	45.04 N	99.46 W
Lebanon, Tn., U.S.	194	36.12 N	86.17 W
Lebanon, Va., U.S.	192	36.54 N	82.04 W
Lebanon □[6]	208	40.20 N	76.25 W
Lebanon (Al-Lubnān) □[1], Asia	118	33.50 N	35.50 E
Lebanon (Al-Lubnān) □[1], Asia	128	33.50 N	35.50 E
Lebanon Junction	194	37.50 N	85.43 W
Lebanon Mountains → Lubnān, Jabal ⋀	132	34.00 N	36.00 E
Lebanon Springs	210	42.29 N	73.23 W
Le Ban-Saint-Martin	56	49.07 N	6.09 E
Le Bar-sur-le-Loup	62	43.42 N	6.59 E
Leb'ažje, S.S.S.R.	80	57.25 N	49.32 E
Leb'ažje, S.S.S.R.	86	55.16 N	66.29 E
Leb'ažje, S.S.S.R.	86	51.28 N	77.46 E
Lebbeke	50	51.00 N	4.08 E
Le Béage	62	44.51 N	4.07 E
Le Beausset	62	43.12 N	5.48 E
Lebec	228	34.50 N	118.51 W
Lebed'an'	76	53.01 N	39.09 E
Lebedevka, S.S.S.R.	80	51.06 N	47.09 E
Lebedevka, S.S.S.R.	86	56.48 N	66.57 E
Lebedevka, S.S.S.R.	86	50.09 N	54.07 E
Lebedi	78	51.17 N	37.38 E
Lebedin, S.S.S.R.	78	48.59 N	31.31 E
Lebedin, S.S.S.R.	78	50.36 N	34.30 E
Lebedino	80	55.14 N	49.50 E
Leben, Oued el V	148	34.37 N	10.01 E
Lebesby	24	70.34 N	26.59 E
Le Bessat	62	45.22 N	4.31 E
Le Bihan Falls ∟	158	29.51 S	28.03 E
Le Biot	58	46.16 N	6.38 E
Lebir ≃	114	5.33 N	102.12 E
Le Blanc	32	46.38 N	1.04 E
Le Blanc-Mesnil	261	48.56 N	2.28 E
Le Bleymard	62	44.29 N	3.44 E
Leblon ◆[8]	287a	22.59 S	43.13 W
Lebo, Ks., U.S.	198	38.25 N	95.51 W
Lebo, Zaïre	152	4.29 N	23.57 E
Le Bois-de-Cise	50	50.05 N	1.26 E
Le Bois-Dieu	261	48.39 N	1.43 E
Le Bois-D'Oingt	58	45.55 N	4.35 E
Lebombo Mountains ⋀[2]	156	25.15 S	32.00 E
Lebongtandai	112	3.01 S	101.54 E
Lebon Régis	252	26.56 S	50.42 W
Le Boréon	62	44.07 N	7.17 E
Lębork	30	54.33 N	17.44 E
Le Boulay	261	48.47 N	1.40 E
Le Bourg-d'Oisans	62	45.03 N	6.02 E
Le Bourget	261	48.56 N	2.26 E
Le Bourget-du-Lac	62	45.39 N	5.52 E
Le Brassus	58	46.35 N	6.13 E
Lebrija	34	36.55 N	6.04 W
Lebrija ≃	246	8.08 N	73.47 W
Le Broc	62	43.49 N	7.10 E
Le Brugeron	62	45.43 N	3.43 E
Łebsko, Jezioro c	30	54.44 N	17.24 E
Lebu	252	37.37 S	73.39 W
Le Bugue	32	44.55 N	0.56 E
Le Buisson de Massoury ♠	261	48.30 N	2.43 E
Lebus	54	52.25 N	14.32 E
Le Caire → Al-Qāhirah	142	30.03 N	31.15 E
Le Camp-du-Castellet	62	43.15 N	5.45 E
Le Cannet	62	43.34 N	7.01 E
Lecanto	220	28.51 N	82.29 W
Le Cap → Cap-Haïtien, Haï.	238	19.45 N	72.12 W
Le Cap → Cape Town, S. Afr.	158	33.55 S	18.22 E
Le Carbet	240e	14.43 N	61.11 W
Le Cateau	50	50.06 N	3.33 E
Le Catelet	50	50.00 N	3.15 E
Lecce	68	40.23 N	18.11 E
Lecce □[4]	68	40.13 N	18.10 E
Lecce, Tavoliere di ≚	68	40.30 N	17.35 E
Lecce nei Marsi	66	41.56 N	13.41 E
Lečchumskij chrebet ⋀	84	42.45 N	43.05 E
Lecco	62	45.51 N	9.23 E
Lecco, Lago di ⊜	58	45.55 N	9.19 E
Le Center	190	44.23 N	93.43 W
Lech	58	47.12 N	10.09 E
Lech ≃	30	48.44 N	10.56 E
Le Châble, Fr.	58	46.06 N	6.06 E
Le Châble, Schw.	58	46.05 N	7.12 E
L'Échalp	62	44.45 N	7.00 E
Le Chambon-Feugerolles	62	45.24 N	4.19 E
Le Chambon-sur-Lignon	62	45.03 N	4.18 E
Le Champ-Renault	261	49.06 N	2.31 E
Lechang	100	25.09 N	113.21 E
Le Chasseral ∧	58	47.08 N	7.03 E
Le-Château-d'Oléron	32	45.53 N	1.11 W
Le Châtelard, Fr.	62	45.41 N	6.08 E
Le Châtelard, Schw.	58	46.04 N	6.58 E
Le Châtelet	32	46.39 N	2.17 E
Le Châtelet-en-Brie	50	48.30 N	2.48 E
Lechbruck	58	47.42 N	10.47 E
Leche, Laguna de la c	240p	22.13 N	78.38 W
Le Chêne-Rogneux	261	48.46 N	1.46 E
Lecheng	110	19.14 N	110.34 E
Le Chesnay	261	48.50 N	2.07 E
Le Chesne	56	49.31 N	4.46 E
Le Cheylard	62	44.54 N	4.25 E
Lechfeld ≚	58	48.10 N	10.50 E
Lechiguanas, Islas de las II	252	33.26 S	59.42 W
Lechiguiri, Cerro ∧	234	16.43 N	95.30 W
Lechlade	42	51.43 N	1.41 W
Lechleiten	58	47.16 N	10.12 E
Lechta	24	60.49 N	48.28 E
Lechtaler Alpen ⋀	64	47.15 N	10.30 E
Lechuga, Arroyo ≃	286b	23.01 N	82.16 W
Lechuguilla, Cerro ∧	234	22.19 N	104.15 W
Lecinone, Monte ∧	267a	41.59 N	12.48 E
Leck	41	54.46 N	8.58 E
Le Claire	190	41.36 N	90.21 W
Lecompte	194	31.16 N	92.24 W
Leconfield	44	53.52 N	0.27 W
Léconi	152	1.35 S	14.14 E
Lecontes Mills	214	41.05 N	78.17 W
Le Cornate ∧	66	43.10 N	10.57 E
Le Coudray-Montceaux	261	48.34 N	2.31 E
Le Coudray-Saint-Germer	50	49.25 N	1.50 E
Le Creusot	58	46.48 N	4.26 E
Le Croci di Acerno)(	68	40.47 N	15.02 E
Le Croisic	32	47.18 N	2.31 W
Le Crotoy	50	50.13 N	1.37 E
Łęczna	30	51.19 N	22.52 E
Łęczyca	30	52.04 N	19.13 E
Leda ≃	52	53.12 N	7.26 E
Ledaig	46	56.30 N	5.23 W
Led'anaja, gora ∧	74	61.53 N	171.09 E
Ledang, Gunong ∧	114	2.22 N	102.37 E
Ledava ≃	61	46.29 N	16.35 E
Ledbetter	222	30.09 N	96.48 W
Ledbury	42	52.02 N	2.25 W
Lede	50	50.58 N	3.58 E
Ledenice	61	48.57 N	14.37 E
Lederach	285	40.16 N	75.24 W
Le Deschaux	58	46.57 N	5.30 E
Ledesma	34	41.05 N	6.00 W
Ledgewood	276	40.52 N	74.39 W
Ledi, Ben ∧	46	56.15 N	4.19 W
Le Diamant	240e	14.29 N	61.02 W
Lediba	152	3.03 S	16.32 E
Lédignan	62	43.59 N	4.06 E
Ledkovo	24	67.14 N	50.30 E
Lednice	61	48.48 N	16.48 E
Ledo, India	120	27.18 N	95.44 E
Ledo, Indon.	112	1.02 N	109.36 E
Lêdo, Cabo ›	152	9.41 S	13.12 E
Ledong	110	18.45 N	109.12 E
Le Donjon	32	46.21 N	3.48 E
Le Dorat	32	46.13 N	1.05 E
Le Doré, Lac ⊜	186	51.17 N	61.23 W
Ledra ≃	64	46.13 N	13.02 E
Ledsham	262	53.16 N	2.58 W
Ledu	102	36.32 N	102.25 E
Leduc	182	53.16 N	113.33 W
Ledung	114	2.45 N	99.59 E
Ledyard Bay c	180	69.30 N	164.30 W
Lędyczek	30	53.33 N	16.58 E
Lee, Il., U.S.	216	41.48 N	88.56 W
Lee, Ma., U.S.	207	42.18 N	73.14 W
Lee □[6], Fl., U.S.	220	26.34 N	81.55 W
Lee □[6], Il., U.S.	216	41.50 N	89.29 W
Lee □[6], Tx., U.S.	222	30.20 N	96.55 W
Lee ≃	48	51.54 N	8.22 W
Lee Boulevard Heights	284c	38.52 N	77.09 W
Lee Center	210	43.18 N	75.31 W
Leechburg	214	40.37 N	79.36 W
Leechburg Airport ⊠	279b	40.37 N	79.34 W
Leech Lake ⊜, Sk., Can.	184	51.04 N	102.30 W
Leech Lake ⊜, Mn., U.S.	190	47.09 N	94.23 W
Leech Lake Indian Reservation ◆[4]	190	47.30 N	94.27 W
Leechtown	224	48.30 N	123.42 W
Leedey	196	35.52 N	99.20 W
Leedom Estates	285	39.41 N	75.35 W
Leeds, Eng., U.K.	44	53.50 N	1.35 W
Leeds, Al., U.S.	194	33.32 N	86.32 W
Leeds, N.Y., U.S.	210	42.15 N	73.54 W
Leeds, N.D., U.S.	198	48.17 N	99.26 W
Leeds and Bradford (Yeadon) Airport ⊠	44	53.52 N	1.38 W
Leeds and Grenville □[6]	212	44.45 N	75.50 W
Leeds and Liverpool Canal ≊	262	53.25 N	2.59 W
Leeds Point	208	39.29 N	74.25 W
Leedstown	42	50.10 N	5.22 W
Leegebruch	54	52.43 N	13.11 E
Leek, Ned.	52	53.09 N	6.24 E
Leek, Eng., U.K.	44	53.06 N	2.01 W
Leelanau, Lake ⊜	190	44.55 N	85.43 W
Leelanau Peninsula ›[1]	190	45.10 N	85.35 W
Leeming	44	54.17 N	1.32 W
Leen ≃	42	52.57 N	1.11 W
Leenaun	48	53.36 N	9.45 W
Leende	52	51.21 N	5.33 E
Lee-on-the-Solent	42	50.47 N	1.12 W
Lee Park	210	41.14 N	75.55 W
Leeper	214	41.22 N	79.18 W
Leer	52	53.14 N	7.26 E
Leerdam	52	51.54 N	5.05 E
Leerhafe	52	53.32 N	7.47 E
Leersum	52	52.01 N	5.26 E
Lees	262	53.32 N	2.04 W
Leesburg, Fl., U.S.	220	28.48 N	81.52 W
Leesburg, Ga., U.S.	192	31.43 N	84.10 W
Leesburg, In., U.S.	216	41.19 N	85.51 W
Leesburg, N.J., U.S.	208	39.15 N	74.59 W
Leesburg, Oh., U.S.	218	39.20 N	83.33 W
Leesburg, Tx., U.S.	222	32.59 N	95.05 W
Leesburg, Va., U.S.	208	39.06 N	77.33 W
Lees Creek ≃	218	39.21 N	83.29 W
Leese	52	52.30 N	9.06 E
Leesport	208	40.27 N	75.58 W
Lees Summit	194	38.55 N	94.23 W
Leeste	52	52.59 N	8.49 E
Leeston	172	43.46 S	172.18 E
Leesville, Il., U.S.	216	41.01 N	87.33 W
Leesville, In., U.S.	218	38.51 N	86.18 W
Leesville, La., U.S.	194	31.08 N	93.15 W
Leesville, Oh., U.S.	214	40.27 N	81.13 W
Leesville, S.C., U.S.	192	33.54 N	81.30 W
Leesville, Tx., U.S.	222	29.24 N	97.45 W
Leesville Lake ⊜[1], Oh., U.S.	214	40.30 N	81.10 W
Leesville Lake ⊜[1], Va., U.S.	192	37.05 N	79.25 W
Leeton	166	34.33 S	146.24 E
Leetonia	214	40.52 N	80.45 W
Leetsdale	214	40.33 N	80.12 W
Leeudoringstad	158	27.15 S	26.10 E
Leeu-Gamka	158	32.47 S	21.59 E
Leeupan ≚	273d	26.14 S	28.19 E
Leeuwarden	52	53.12 N	5.46 E
Leeuwin, Cape ›	162	34.22 S	115.08 E
Lee Vining	226	37.57 N	119.07 W
Leeward Islands II	238	17.00 N	63.00 W
Le Faouët	28	48.02 N	3.29 W
Le Fayet	58	45.55 N	6.42 E
Lefèvre, Pointe ›	175f	20.54 S	167.01 E
Leffe	62	45.48 N	9.53 E
Lefferts, Lake ⊜	276	40.25 N	74.14 W
Léfini ≃	152	2.57 S	16.10 E
Léfini, Réserve de Chasse de la ◆[4]	152	2.58 S	15.25 E
Le Focette	64	43.55 N	10.13 E
Leforest	50	50.26 N	3.04 E
Lefors	196	35.26 N	100.48 W
Le François	240e	14.37 N	60.54 W
Le Freney-d'Oisans	62	45.02 N	6.07 E
Lefroy	212	44.16 N	79.34 W
Lefroy, Lake ⊜	162	31.15 S	121.40 E
Leftrook Lake ⊜	184	56.05 N	98.36 W
Lega Hida	144	7.56 N	41.04 E
Legal	182	53.57 N	113.35 W
Leganés	266a	40.19 N	3.45 W
Le Gardeur	206	45.45 N	73.28 W
Legaspi → Legazpi	116	13.08 N	123.44 E
Legau	58	47.51 N	10.07 E
Legazpi	116	13.08 N	123.44 E
Legden	52	52.02 N	7.07 E
Legendre ≃	206	45.44 N	71.08 W
Legendre Island I	162	20.23 S	116.54 E
Legges Tor ∧	166	41.32 S	147.40 E
Leggett, Ca., U.S.	204	39.51 N	123.42 W
Leggett, Tx., U.S.	222	30.49 N	94.52 W
Leghorn → Livorno	66	43.33 N	10.19 E
Legion Mine	154	21.23 S	28.33 E
Legion of Honor, Palace of the ʋ	282	37.47 N	122.30 W
Legionowo	30	52.25 N	20.56 E
Legnago	64	45.11 N	11.18 E
Legnano	62	45.36 N	8.54 E
Legnica (Liegnitz)	30	51.13 N	16.09 E
Legnica □[4]	30	51.25 N	16.10 E
Le Gosier	241o	16.12 N	61.30 W
Le Grand	226	37.13 N	120.14 W
LeGrand, Cape ›	162	34.01 S	122.06 E
Le Grand-Lucé	50	47.52 N	0.28 E
Le Grand-Quevilly	50	49.25 N	1.02 E
Le Grand-Serre	62	45.16 N	5.06 E
Le Grand Wintersberg ∧[2]	56	48.59 N	7.37 E
Le Grau-du-Roi	62	43.32 N	4.08 E
Le Gua	62	45.01 N	5.37 E
Le Guelta	34	36.22 N	0.50 E
Leguga	154	3.23 N	25.02 E
Legume	166	28.25 S	152.19 E
Legundi, Pulau I	115a	5.50 S	105.16 E
Leh	123	34.10 N	77.35 E
Le Havre	50	49.30 N	0.08 E
Lehčevo	38	43.32 N	23.32 E
Le Hérie-la-Viéville	50	49.49 N	3.38 E
Lehesten	54	50.29 N	11.28 E
Lehi	200	40.23 N	111.50 W
Lehigh, Ia., U.S.	190	42.21 N	94.03 W
Lehigh, Ok., U.S.	196	34.28 N	96.12 W
Lehigh □[6]	208	40.36 N	75.29 W
Lehigh ≃	210	40.41 N	75.12 W
Lehigh Acres	220	26.37 N	81.37 W
Lehighton	210	40.50 N	75.42 W
Lehinch	48	52.56 N	9.21 W
Lehman Caves National Monument ♠	204	39.01 N	114.14 W
Lehnin	54	52.19 N	12.44 E
Lehnitz	54	52.44 N	13.15 E
Lehnitz See ⊜	264a	52.45 N	13.16 E
Leho	140	7.07 N	33.52 E
Le Hohwald	58	48.24 N	7.20 E
Le Houlme	50	49.31 N	1.02 E
Lehr	198	45.59 N	99.32 W
Lehra Gāga	123	29.55 N	75.49 E
Lehrbach	56	50.47 N	9.04 E
Lehrberg	56	49.21 N	10.30 E
Lehre	54	52.19 N	10.40 E
Lehrte	52	52.22 N	9.59 E
Lehstedt	52	52.14 N	10.12 E
Lehtar	123	33.42 N	73.26 E
Lehtimäki	26	62.47 N	23.55 E
Lehtse	76	59.15 N	25.50 E
Lehua I	229b	22.01 N	160.06 W
Lehututu	156	23.58 S	21.51 E
Lei ≃	100	26.54 N	112.39 E
Leiah	123	30.58 N	70.56 E
Leião	266c	38.44 N	9.18 W
Leibnitz	61	46.47 N	15.32 E
Leibo	102	28.19 N	103.21 E
Leicester, Eng., U.K.	42	52.38 N	1.05 W
Leicester, Ma., U.S.	207	42.14 N	71.54 W
Leicester, N.Y., U.S.	210	42.46 N	77.53 W
Leicestershire □[6]	42	52.40 N	1.10 W
Leichhardt	274a	33.53 S	151.07 E
Leichhardt ≃	166	17.35 S	139.48 E
Leichhardt Falls ∟	166	18.14 S	139.53 E
Leichhardt Range ⋀	166	20.40 S	147.25 E
Leichlingen	56	51.06 N	7.01 E
Leiden	52	52.09 N	4.30 E
Leiderdorp	52	52.09 N	4.32 E
Leidschendam	52	52.05 N	4.24 E
Leie (Lys) ≃	50	51.03 N	3.43 E
Leiferde	52	52.26 N	10.26 E
Leigh, N.Z.	172	36.17 S	174.49 E
Leigh, Eng., U.K.	44	53.30 N	2.33 W
Leigh, Eng., U.K.	260	51.12 N	0.13 E
Leigh Canal ≊	262	53.28 N	2.21 W
Leigh Creek	166	30.28 S	138.25 E
Leighlinbridge	48	52.44 N	6.59 W
Leigh-on-Sea	42	51.33 N	0.38 E
Leighton	194	34.42 N	87.31 W
Leighton Buzzard	42	51.55 N	0.40 W
Leikanger	26	61.10 N	6.52 E
Leiktho	110	19.13 N	96.35 E
Leimbach	54	51.36 N	11.28 E
Leimstruth	56	50.59 N	8.19 E
Lein ≃	56	48.54 N	10.01 E
Leinan	184	50.30 N	107.46 W
Leinburg	60	49.27 N	11.19 E
Leine ≃	52	52.43 N	9.36 E
Leinefelde	54	51.23 N	10.20 E
Leinfelden-Echterdingen	56	48.41 N	9.08 E
Leinster □[9]	48	53.05 N	7.00 W
Leinster, Mount ∧	48	52.37 N	6.44 W
Leintwardine	42	52.23 N	2.51 W
Leipalingis	76	54.05 N	23.51 E
Leipheim	58	48.27 N	10.13 E
Leipoldtville	158	32.14 S	18.30 E
Leipsic, De., U.S.	208	39.14 N	75.31 W
Leipsic, In., U.S.	218	38.40 N	86.22 W
Leipsic, Oh., U.S.	216	41.05 N	83.59 W
Leipsic ≃	208	39.15 N	75.24 W
Leipzig	54	51.19 N	12.20 E
Leipzig □[5]	54	51.15 N	12.45 E
Leiria	34	39.45 N	8.48 W
Leirvik	26	59.45 N	5.30 E
Leisach	64	46.48 N	12.45 E
Leishendian	107	28.58 N	106.40 E
Leisi	76	58.34 N	22.39 E
Leisler, Mount ∧	162	23.28 S	129.17 E
Leisnig	54	51.09 N	12.56 E
Leiston	42	52.12 N	1.34 E
Leisure City	220	25.29 N	80.25 W
Leitariegos, Puerto de)(	34	43.00 N	6.25 W
Leitchfield	194	37.28 N	86.17 W
Leiters Ford	216	41.07 N	86.23 W
Leith	46	55.59 N	3.10 W
Leith, Water of ≃	46	55.59 N	3.11 W
Leitha (Lajta) ≃, Europe	61	47.54 N	17.17 E
Leitha ≃, Öst.	264b	48.00 N	16.35 E
Leithagebirge ⋀	61	47.52 N	16.35 E
Leithe ◆[8]	263	51.29 N	7.06 E
Leith Hill ∧[2]	42	51.11 N	0.23 W
Leitre	164	2.50 S	141.40 E
Leitrim	48	54.00 N	8.04 W
Leitrim □[6]	48	54.20 N	8.20 W
Leitzkau	54	52.03 N	11.57 E
Leiva	246	5.38 N	73.34 W
Leixi	100	27.10 N	112.52 E
Leixlip	48	53.22 N	6.29 W
Leiyang	100	26.24 N	112.51 E
Lei Yue Mun ʮ	271d	22.16 N	114.14 E
Leizhou Bandao ›[1]	102	21.15 N	110.09 E
Leizhuang	98	39.47 N	118.34 E
Lejasciems	76	57.17 N	26.35 E
Lek ≃	52	51.55 N	4.34 E
Lékana	152	2.19 S	14.36 E
Le Kef → El Kef	148	36.11 N	8.43 E
Lékéti ≃	152	1.36 S	14.57 E
Lekhainá	38	37.56 N	21.17 E
Lekir	114	4.07 N	100.44 E
Lekitobi	112	1.58 S	124.33 E
Lekkeroog	158	30.43 S	20.00 E
Lekkerwater	156	23.38 S	17.14 E
Lekkous, Oued ≃	34	35.12 N	6.09 W
Lekma ≃	80	58.18 N	52.04 E
Łęknice	54	51.35 N	14.45 E
Lékoni ≃	152	1.11 S	13.16 E
Lekotero	152	0.46 S	23.51 E
Lékoumou □[5]	152	3.00 S	13.30 E
Le Kreïder	148	34.06 N	0.02 E
Le Kremlin-Bicêtre	261	48.49 N	2.21 E
Leksand	26	60.44 N	14.59 E
Leksberg	40	59.41 N	13.49 E
Leksozero, ozero ⊜	24	63.46 N	30.58 E
Leksvik	26	63.40 N	10.37 E
Lela	152	5.03 S	12.29 E
Le Lac-d'Issarlès	62	44.49 N	4.04 E
Le Lamentin	240e	14.37 N	61.01 W
Leland, Il., U.S.	216	41.37 N	88.48 W
Leland, Mi., U.S.	190	45.01 N	85.45 W
Leland, Ms., U.S.	194	33.24 N	90.53 W
Leland Grove	219	39.47 N	89.41 W
Leland Lake ⊜	224	47.53 N	122.53 W
Lelång ⊜	26	59.08 N	12.10 E
Lelant	42	50.11 N	5.26 W
Le Laus	62	44.31 N	6.09 E
Le Lauzet-Ubaye	62	44.26 N	6.26 E
Le Lavandou	62	43.08 N	6.22 E
Lel'čicy	78	51.47 N	28.19 E
Leleiwi Point ›	229d	19.44 N	155.00 W
Leleque	254	42.23 S	71.03 W
Leles	115a	7.07 S	107.53 E
Lelewau	112	3.02 S	121.05 E
Lélex	58	46.18 N	5.57 E
Le Liège	50	47.13 N	1.06 E
Leling	98	37.45 N	117.12 E
Lelingluang	164	7.09 S	131.43 E
Lelintah	164	2.03 S	130.16 E
Le Lion-d'Angers	32	47.38 N	0.43 W
Lelishan ∧	120	33.26 N	81.42 E
Le Locle	58	47.03 N	6.45 E
Lelogama	112	9.44 S	123.57 E
Le Lorrain	240e	14.50 N	61.04 W
Le Luc	62	43.23 N	6.19 E
Le Lude	50	47.39 N	0.09 E
Lelystad	52	52.31 N	5.27 E
Lema	150	12.57 N	4.14 E
Le Madonie ⋀	70	37.52 N	13.58 E
Lemahabang	115a	6.17 S	107.27 E
Le Maire, Estrecho de ʮ	254	54.50 S	65.00 W
Léman, Lac → Geneva, Lake ⊜	58	46.25 N	6.30 E
Lemankoa	175e	5.02 S	154.35 E
Le Mans	50	48.00 N	0.12 E
Le Marin	240e	14.28 N	60.53 W
Le Markstein	58	47.56 N	7.02 E
Le Mars	198	42.47 N	96.09 W
Lema Shilindi	144	4.55 N	42.02 E
Lemay	219	38.32 N	90.17 W
Lemay, Lac ⊜	186	50.35 N	68.25 W
Lembach	56	49.00 N	7.48 E
Lembach im Mühlkreis	60	48.29 N	13.53 E
Lemba-Gaba	273b	4.27 S	15.18 E
Lembak	112	0.52 N	117.32 E
Lembang	115a	6.49 S	107.36 E
Lembeck	52	51.45 N	7.00 E
Lembeek	50	50.43 N	4.13 E
Lembeh, Pulau I	112	1.26 N	125.13 E
Lembeni	154	3.47 S	37.37 E
Lemberg, Sk., Can.	184	50.44 N	103.13 W
Lemberg, Fr.	56	49.00 N	7.23 E
Lemberg → L'vov, S.S.S.R.	78	49.50 N	24.00 E
Lemberg ∧	58	48.09 N	8.45 E
Lembruch	52	52.31 N	8.22 E
Lembu, Gunung ∧	114	4.12 N	97.24 E
Lemdiyya	148	36.12 N	2.50 E
Lemdiyya □[5]	148	35.50 N	3.00 E
Leme	255	22.12 S	47.24 W
Leme, Morro do ∧[2]	287a	22.58 S	43.10 W
Le Mée-sur-Seine	261	48.32 N	2.38 E
Lemei Rock ∧	224	46.01 N	121.46 W
Lemele	52	52.27 N	6.25 E
Le Mêle-sur-Sarthe	50	48.31 N	0.21 E
Lemene ≃	64	45.37 N	12.53 E
Lemeris, Cape ›	164	3.15 S	152.03 E
Le Merlerault	50	48.42 N	0.18 E
Lemery	116	13.53 N	120.55 E
Lemeškino	80	51.01 N	44.27 E
Le Mesle	261	48.43 N	1.41 E
Le Mesnil-Amelot	261	49.01 N	2.36 E
Le Mesnil-Aubry	261	49.03 N	2.24 E
Le Mesnil-le-Roi	261	48.56 N	2.08 E
Le Mesnil-Saint-Denis	261	48.45 N	1.58 E
Le Mesnil-sur-Oger	50	48.57 N	4.01 E
Lemesós (Limassol)	130	34.40 N	33.02 E
Lemešovka	78	52.04 N	31.38 E
Lemeta	180	64.52 N	147.44 W
Lemförde	52	52.28 N	8.22 E
Lemfu	152	5.18 S	15.13 E
Lemgo	52	52.02 N	8.54 E
Lemhi ≃	202	45.12 N	113.53 W
Lemhi Pass)(	202	44.58 N	113.27 W
Lemhi Range ⋀	202	44.30 N	113.25 W
Lemie	62	45.14 N	7.17 E
Lemierzyce	54	52.35 N	14.56 E
Lemieux Islands II	176	64.30 N	64.40 W
Lemin	102	21.11 N	109.42 E
Leming	196	29.04 N	98.29 W
Lemitar	200	34.09 N	106.54 W
Lemke	52	52.39 N	9.09 E
Lemland I	26	60.03 N	20.09 E
Lemmatsi	76	58.20 N	26.37 E
Lemmenjoen Kansallispuisto ♠	24	68.40 N	26.00 E
Lemmer	52	52.50 N	5.42 E
Lemmon	198	45.56 N	102.09 W
Lemmon, Mount ∧	200	32.26 N	110.47 W
Lemnos → Límnos I	38	39.54 N	25.21 E
Lemoenshoek	158	33.51 S	20.51 E
Lemoine, Lac ⊜	190	48.00 N	78.00 W
Lemon, Lake ⊜	218	39.16 N	86.25 W
Le Monastier	62	44.56 N	4.00 E
Lemoncove	204	36.23 N	119.01 W
Lemon Creek ≃	276	40.31 N	74.12 W
Le Monêtier-les-Bains	62	44.59 N	6.31 E
Lemon Grove	228	32.44 N	117.01 W
Lemon Heights	280	33.46 N	117.48 W
Lemont, Il., U.S.	216	41.40 N	88.00 W
Lemont, Pa., U.S.	214	40.49 N	77.49 W
Le Montet	32	46.25 N	3.03 E
Le Mont-Saint-Michel ʋ[1]	32	48.38 N	1.32 W

≃	River	Fluss	Río	Rivière	Rio
≊	Canal	Kanal	Canal	Canal	Canal
∟	Waterfall, Rapids	Wasserfall, Stromschnellen	Cascada, Rápidos	Chute d'eau, Rapides	Cascata, Rápidos
ʮ	Strait	Meeresstrasse	Estrecho	Détroit	Estreito
c	Bay, Gulf	Bucht, Golf	Bahía, Golfo	Baie, Golfe	Baía, Golfo
⊜	Lake, Lakes	See, Seen	Lago, Lagos	Lac, Lacs	Lago, Lagos
⊞	Swamp	Sumpf	Pantano	Marais	Pântano
≚	Ice Features, Glacier	Eis- und Gletscherformen	Accidentes Glaciales	Formes glaciaires	Acidentes glaciares
⊤	Other Hydrographic Features	Andere Hydrographische Objekte	Otros Elementos Hidrográficos	Autres données hydrographiques	Outros acidentes hidrográficos

✤	Submarine Features	Untermeerische Objekte	Accidentes Submarinos	Formes de relief sous-marin	Acidentes submarinos
□	Political Unit	Politische Einheit	Unidad Politica	Entité politique	Unidade política
ʋ	Cultural Institution	Kulturelle Institution	Institución Cultural	Institution culturelle	Institução cultural
⊥	Historical Site	Historische Stätte	Sitio Histórico	Site historique	Sitio histórico
♠	Recreational Site	Erholungs- und Ferienort	Sitio de Recreo	Centre de loisirs	Area de Lazer
⊠	Airport	Flughafen	Aeropuerto	Aéroport	Aeroporto
■	Military Installation	Militäranlage	Instalación Militar	Installation militaire	Instalação militar
◆	Miscellaneous	Verschiedenes	Misceláneo	Divers	Diversos

Lemoore 226 36.18 N 119.46 W
Lemoore Naval Air Station ■ 226 36.15 N 119.57 W
Lemoro 112 1.25 S 121.05 E
Le Moule 241o 16.20 N 61.21 W
Le Moutier 261 48.50 N 1.42 E
LeMoyne, P.Q., Can. 275a 45.31 N 73.29 W
Lemoyne, Oh., U.S. 214 41.30 N 83.28 W
Lemoyne, Pa., U.S. 208 40.15 N 76.54 W
Lempa ≃ 236 13.14 N 88.49 W
Lempäälä 26 61.19 N 23.45 E
Lempe 112 1.40 S 120.14 E
Lempira □5 236 14.20 N 88.40 W
Lemro ≃ 110 20.25 N 93.20 E
Lemsid 148 26.32 N 13.49 W
Lemukutan, Pulau I 112 0.45 N 108.43 E
Le Murge ⁎1 68 40.52 N 16.42 E
Lemutan 112 3.03 N 115.49 E
Le Muy 62 43.28 N 6.33 E
Lemva ≃ 24 66.30 N 61.48 E
Lemvig 26 56.32 N 8.18 E
Lemyethna 110 17.36 N 95.09 E
Len ≃ 260 51.16 N 0.31 E
Lena, Il., U.S. 190 42.22 N 89.49 W
Lena, Wi., U.S. 190 44.57 N 88.02 W
Lena ≃ 74 72.25 N 126.40 E
Lenangguar 115b 8.44 S 117.24 E
Lenape 285 39.55 N 75.38 W
Lenart 61 46.35 N 15.50 E
Lenasia 273d 26.17 S 27.50 E
Lenawee □6 216 41.53 N 84.04 W
Lencloître 32 46.49 N 0.20 E
Lençóis 255 12.34 S 41.23 W
Lend 64 47.18 N 13.04 E
Lenda ≃ 154 1.20 N 28.01 E
Lendava 61 46.34 N 16.27 E
Lendelede 50 50.53 N 3.14 E
Lendery 24 63.26 N 31.03 E
Lendinara 64 45.05 N 11.36 E
Lendorf 64 46.50 N 13.26 E
Lendringsen 56 51.24 N 7.49 E
Le Neubourg 50 49.09 N 0.55 E
Lenga 114 2.17 N 102.49 E
Lengduqiao 106 30.27 N 119.15 E
Lengede 52 52.12 N 10.18 E
Lengefeld 54 50.43 N 13.11 E
Lengelscheid 263 51.08 N 7.40 E
Lengenfeld, D.D.R. 54 50.34 N 12.22 E
Lengenfeld, D.D.R. 56 51.13 N 10.13 E
Lenger 85 42.12 N 69.54 E
Lengerich, B.R.D. 52 52.33 N 7.32 E
Lengerich, B.R.D. 52 52.11 N 7.50 E
Lenggor ≃ 114 2.25 N 103.37 E
Lenggries 64 47.41 N 11.34 E
Lenghu 90 38.30 N 93.15 E
Lengjiagou 104 41.40 N 121.37 E
Lengkong 115a 7.32 S 112.04 E
Lenglingen ⊜ 26 64.14 N 13.45 E
Lengnau 58 47.11 N 7.22 E
Lengoué 152 1.13 N 15.43 E
Lengoué ≃ 152 0.49 N 15.47 E
Lengshuijiang 107 27.29 N 106.26 E
Lengshuikeng 100 27.55 N 117.08 E
Lengshuitan 102 26.27 N 111.35 E
Lengua de Vaca, Punta ⟩ 252 30.14 S 71.38 W
Lengulu 154 3.15 N 26.30 E
Lengwe National Park ♦ 154 16.15 S 34.45 E
Lengzipu 104 41.42 N 122.47 E
Lenham, Eng., U.K. 42 51.14 N 0.43 E
Lenham, Eng., U.K. 260 51.14 N 0.43 E
Lenhartsville 208 40.34 N 75.53 W
Lenhovda 26 57.00 N 15.17 E
Lenina, gora ⋏2 265b 55.42 N 37.31 E
Lenina, ozero ⊜ 78 48.33 N 35.12 E
Lenina, pik ⋏ 85 39.20 N 72.55 E
Leninabad 85 40.17 N 69.37 E
Leninabad □4 85 39.45 N 69.00 E
Leninakan 84 40.48 N 43.50 E
Lenin Central Stadium ♦ 265b 55.43 N 37.33 E
Lenin-Džol 85 41.03 N 72.38 E
Leningori 84 42.07 N 44.29 E
Leningrad, S.S.S.R. 76 59.55 N 30.15 E
Leningrad, S.S.S.R. 265a 59.55 N 30.15 E
Leningrad □4 265a 59.55 N 30.15 E
Leningrad, Gorod □7 265a 59.55 N 30.15 E
Leningrad Airport ⊠ 265a 59.48 N 30.16 E
Leningrado → Leningrad 76 59.55 N 30.15 E
Leningradskaja 78 46.19 N 39.24 E
Leningradskaja ⋓3 9 69.30 S 159.23 E
Leningradskij 85 38.06 N 70.01 E
Leningradskoje 86 53.33 N 71.35 E
Leningrad State University ⋓2 265a 59.56 N 30.18 E
Leningrad Station ⇥5 265b 55.47 N 37.39 E
Lenino 78 45.18 N 35.47 E
Lenino ⇥8 265b 55.37 N 37.41 E
Leninogorsk, S.S.S.R. 80 54.36 N 52.30 E
Leninogorsk, S.S.S.R. 86 50.27 N 83.32 E
Leninpol' 85 42.29 N 71.55 E
Leninsk, S.S.S.R. 80 46.08 N 43.46 E
Leninsk, S.S.S.R. 80 48.42 N 45.11 E
Leninsk, S.S.S.R. 85 40.38 N 72.15 E
Leninsk, S.S.S.R. 86 45.40 N 63.20 E
Leninsk, S.S.S.R. 86 54.55 N 59.54 E
Leninskaja Sloboda 80 56.05 N 44.28 E
Leninskij, S.S.S.R. 78 47.53 N 28.23 E
Leninskij, S.S.S.R. 80 46.31 N 44.28 E
Leninskij, S.S.S.R. 80 56.34 N 45.56 E
Leninskij, S.S.S.R. 82 54.18 N 37.28 E
Leninskij, S.S.S.R. 83 48.05 N 39.31 E
Leninskij, S.S.S.R. 86 52.13 N 76.47 E
Leninsk-Kuzneckij 86 54.38 N 86.10 E
Leninskoje, S.S.S.R. 78 51.27 N 33.18 E
Leninskoje, S.S.S.R. 78 45.16 N 35.54 E
Leninskoje, S.S.S.R. 80 49.03 N 49.56 E
Leninskoje, S.S.S.R. 80 58.19 N 47.06 E
Leninskoje, S.S.S.R. 85 40.42 N 73.11 E
Leninskoje, S.S.S.R. 85 41.45 N 69.23 E
Leninskoje, S.S.S.R. 86 50.44 N 57.53 E
Leninskoje, S.S.S.R. 86 54.04 N 65.22 E
Leninskoje, S.S.S.R. 89 47.56 N 132.38 E
Lenin-Stausee → Kujbyševskoje vodochranilišče ⊜1 80 54.30 N 48.30 E
Leninžol 80 49.20 N 47.05 E
Lenk 58 46.28 N 7.27 E
Lenkerville 208 40.32 N 76.58 W
Len'ki 86 52.57 N 80.26 E
Lenkoran' 84 38.45 N 48.50 E
Lenmalu 164 1.44 S 130.13 E
Lennard, Mount ⋏2 168a 33.21 S 115.53 E
Lenne ≃ 56 51.25 N 7.30 E
Lennegebirge ⁎ 52 51.15 N 8.00 E
Lennep 56 51.11 N 7.15 E
Lennep ⇥8 56 51.12 N 7.15 E
Lennestadt 56 51.08 N 8.01 E
Lenni 285 39.54 N 75.27 W
Lennon 216 42.59 N 83.56 W
Lennonville 162 27.58 S 117.50 E
Lennox, Ca., U.S. 228 33.56 N 118.21 W
Lennox, S.D., U.S. 198 43.21 N 96.53 W
Lennox, Isla I 254 55.18 S 66.50 W
Lennox □9 46 56.02 N 4.15 W
Lennox and Addington □6 212 44.30 N 77.00 W
Lennoxtown 46 55.59 N 4.12 W
Lennoxville 206 45.22 N 71.51 W
Leno 64 45.22 N 10.13 E
Lenoir 192 35.54 N 81.32 W
Lenoir City 192 35.47 N 84.15 W
Le Noirmont 58 47.13 N 6.58 E
Lenola 66 41.24 N 13.28 E
Lenora 60 48.56 N 13.48 E
Lenore Lake ⊜ 184 52.30 N 105.00 W
Le Nouvion-en-Thiérache 50 50.01 N 3.47 E
Lenox, Ga., U.S. 192 31.16 N 83.27 W
Lenox, Ia., U.S. 198 40.52 N 94.33 W
Lenox, Ma., U.S. 207 42.22 N 73.17 W
Lenox, Tn., U.S. 194 36.05 N 89.29 W
Lenox Dale 207 42.20 N 73.14 W
Lens 50 50.26 N 2.50 E
Lensahn 54 54.13 N 10.52 E
Lensk 74 61.00 N 114.50 E
Lenskoje 86 58.09 N 63.11 E
Lenswood 168b 34.55 S 138.49 E
Lentate sul Seveso 266b 45.41 N 9.07 E
Lentechi 84 42.48 N 42.44 E
Lenti 61 46.37 N 16.33 E
Lenting 60 48.48 N 11.28 E
Lentini 70 37.17 N 15.00 E
Lentner 219 39.43 N 92.09 W
Lentua ⊜ 26 64.14 N 29.36 E
Lentvaris 76 54.39 N 25.03 E
Lenwood 228 34.53 N 117.07 W
Lenya 110 11.28 N 99.00 E
Lenya ≃ 110 11.40 N 98.43 E
Lenz 273d 26.19 S 27.49 E
Lenzburg 58 47.23 N 8.11 E
Lenzen 54 53.05 N 11.28 E
Lenzerheide (Lai) 58 46.44 N 9.33 E
Lenzinghausen 52 52.07 N 8.28 E
Lenzkirch 58 47.52 N 8.12 E
Léo, Burkina 150 11.06 N 2.06 W
Leo, In., U.S. 216 41.13 N 85.00 W
Leoben 61 47.23 N 15.06 E
Leobschütz → Głubczyce 30 50.13 N 17.49 E
Leo Carrillo State Beach ♦ 228 34.03 N 118.56 W
Léogâne 238 18.31 N 72.38 W
Leogang 64 47.26 N 12.45 E
Leola, Ar., U.S. 194 34.10 N 92.35 W
Leola, Pa., U.S. 208 40.05 N 76.11 W
Leola, S.D., U.S. 198 45.43 N 98.56 W
Leominster, Eng., U.K. 42 52.14 N 2.45 W
Leominster, Ma., U.S. 207 42.31 N 71.45 W
León, Esp. 34 42.36 N 5.34 W
Léon, Fr. 32 43.53 N 1.18 W
León, Nic. 236 12.26 N 86.53 W
Leon, Pil. 116 10.47 N 122.23 E
Leon, Ia., U.S. 190 40.44 N 93.44 W
Leon, Ks., U.S. 198 37.41 N 96.46 W
Leon, N.Y., U.S. 210 42.18 N 79.01 W
León □5 236 12.35 N 86.35 W
León □6 222 31.18 N 95.55 W
León □9 34 42.00 N 6.00 W
Leon ≃ 196 30.59 N 97.24 W
León, Arroyo ≃ 282 37.28 N 122.25 W
León, Montes de ⁎ 34 42.30 N 6.18 W
Leona 222 31.09 N 95.58 W
Leona ≃ 196 28.45 N 99.11 W
Leona, Punta ⟩ 236 9.41 N 84.41 W
Leonard, Mi., U.S. 214 42.51 N 83.08 W
Leonard, Mo., U.S. 219 39.53 N 92.10 W
Leonard, N.D., U.S. 198 46.39 N 97.14 W
Leonard, Tx., U.S. 196 33.22 N 96.14 W
Leonardo 276 40.25 N 74.03 W
Leonardo da Vinci, Aeroporto Intercontinentale ⊠ 66 41.48 N 12.13 E
Leonardsburg 214 40.21 N 82.59 W
Leonardsville 210 42.48 N 75.15 W
Leonardtown 208 38.17 N 76.38 W
Leonardville, Namibia 156 23.29 S 18.49 E
Leonardville, Ks., U.S. 198 39.21 N 96.51 W
Leonarisson 130 35.28 N 34.08 E
Leona Vicario 200 32.10 N 115.10 W
Leonberg 56 48.48 N 9.01 E
Leonbronn 56 49.03 N 8.53 E
Leondale 273d 26.18 S 28.12 E
Leondárion 267c 37.59 N 23.51 E
León [de los Aldamas] 234 21.07 N 101.40 W
Leonding 61 48.16 N 14.15 E
Leone 174u 14.20 S 170.47 W
Leone, Golfo del → Lion, Golfe du ⊂ 32 43.00 N 4.00 E
Leone, Monte ⋏ 58 46.15 N 8.06 E
Leones 252 32.39 S 62.18 W
Leonessa 66 42.34 N 12.58 E
Leonforte 70 37.38 N 14.23 E
Leongatha 169 38.29 S 145.57 E
Leon Guzmán 196 25.31 N 103.34 W
Leonía 276 40.51 N 73.59 W
Leonicha 76 59.37 N 38.51 E
Leonidas 216 42.01 N 85.21 W
Leonídhion 38 37.10 N 22.52 E
Leonidovo 89 49.17 N 142.50 E
Leon Junction 222 31.20 N 97.36 W
Leonora 162 28.53 S 121.20 E
Leonovo 82 55.26 N 38.42 E
León Rougés 252 27.13 S 65.32 W
Leontjevka 85 43.03 N 69.50 E
Leontjevo 76 58.58 N 36.37 E
Leonville 194 30.28 N 91.58 W
Leopard 285 40.01 N 75.27 W
Leopold 169 38.11 S 144.28 E
Leopold and Astrid Coast ⊥2 9 67.10 S 84.10 E
Leopoldau ⇥8 264b 48.16 N 16.27 E
Leopold Downs 162 17.52 S 125.25 E
Léopold II, Lac → Mai-Ndombe, Lac ⊜ 152 2.00 S 18.20 E
Leopoldina 256 21.32 S 42.38 W
Leopoldkanaal ≅ 50 51.14 N 3.46 E
Leopoldo de Bulhões 255 16.37 S 48.46 W
Leopoldo y Astrid, Costa → Leopold and Astrid Coast ⊥2 9 67.10 S 84.10 E
Leopoldsburg 56 51.07 N 5.15 E
Leopoldsdorf 264b 48.06 N 16.24 E
Leopoldshagen 54 53.46 N 13.53 E
Leopoldstadt ⇥8 264b 48.13 N 16.23 E
Léopoldville → Kinshasa 152 4.18 S 15.18 E
Leoti 198 38.28 N 101.21 W
Leova 184 53.37 N 107.35 W
Leovo 78 46.29 N 28.15 E
Le Pailly 58 47.48 N 5.25 E
Le Palais 32 47.21 N 3.09 W
Lepanto, C.R. 236 9.57 N 85.02 W
Lepanto → Návpaktos, Ellás 38 38.23 N 21.50 E
Lepanto, Ar., U.S. 194 35.36 N 90.19 W
Lepar, Pulau I 112 2.57 S 106.50 E
Le Parcq 50 50.23 N 2.06 E
Le Pâté 261 48.32 N 2.18 E
Lepaterique 34 37.15 N 7.12 W
Le Péage-de-Roussillon 62 45.22 N 4.48 E
Le Pecq 261 48.54 N 2.07 E
Lepel' 76 54.53 N 28.42 E
Le Pellerin 32 47.12 N 1.45 W
Lepembusu, Keli ⋏ 115b 8.40 S 121.49 E
Le Perray-en-Yvelines 261 48.42 N 1.51 E
Le Perreux-sur-Marne 261 48.51 N 2.30 E
Lepeški 82 56.05 N 38.07 E
Le Petit-Clamart ⇥ 261 48.47 N 2.14 E
Le Petit-Couronne 50 49.23 N 1.01 E
Le Petit-Quevilly 50 49.26 N 1.02 E
Lephepe 156 23.20 S 25.50 E
Lépi 152 12.52 S 15.26 E
Le Piastre 66 44.00 N 10.50 E
Lepihué 254 41.37 S 73.36 W
Le Pin 261 48.55 N 2.38 E
Le Pin-au-Haras 50 48.44 N 0.09 E
L'Épine, Fr. 56 48.58 N 4.28 E
L'Épine, Fr. 261 48.32 N 2.21 E
Leping 100 28.57 N 117.05 E
Lepini, Monti ⁎ 66 41.35 N 13.00 E
Lépin-le-Lac 62 45.32 N 5.47 E
L'Épiphanie 206 45.51 N 73.30 W
Lepl'avo 78 49.48 N 31.32 E
Le Plessis-aux-Bois 261 49.00 N 2.46 E
Le Plessis-Belleville 50 49.06 N 2.46 E
Le Plessis-Bouchard 261 49.00 N 2.14 E
Le Plessis-Pâté 261 48.37 N 2.20 E
Le Plessis-Trévise 261 48.49 N 2.34 E
Lépo, Lagoa de ⊜ 152 17.08 S 19.00 E
Le Poët 62 44.17 N 5.53 E
Le Pont 58 46.40 N 6.20 E
Le Pont-de-Beauvoisin 62 45.32 N 5.40 E
Le Pont-de-Montvert 62 44.22 N 3.45 E
Le Pontet 261 48.49 N 1.53 E
Lepontine, Alpi ⁎ 58 46.25 N 8.40 E
Leporano 68 40.23 N 17.20 E
Le Port 157c 20.55 S 55.18 E
Le Portel 50 50.42 N 1.34 E
Le Port-Marly 261 48.53 N 2.06 E
Le Pouzin 62 44.45 N 4.45 E
Leppävirta 26 62.29 N 27.47 E
Lepperton 172 39.04 S 174.13 E
Leppin 54 52.53 N 11.34 E
Leppington 274a 33.58 S 150.49 E
Le Pradet 62 43.06 N 6.01 E
Lepreau, Point ⟩ 186 45.04 N 66.27 W
Le Prêcheur 240e 14.48 N 61.14 W
Le Pré-Saint-Gervais 261 48.53 N 2.25 E
Le Prese 58 46.18 N 10.04 E
Lepsinsk 86 45.32 N 80.37 E
Lepsy, S.S.S.R. 86 46.18 N 78.20 E
Lepsy, S.S.S.R. 86 46.15 N 78.55 E
Le Puy 62 45.02 N 3.53 E
Lequeitio 34 43.22 N 2.30 W
Le Quesnoy 50 50.15 N 3.38 E
Léraba ≃ 150 9.42 N 4.35 W
Le Raincy 261 48.54 N 2.31 E
Le Rayol-Canadel-sur-Mer 62 43.10 N 6.28 E
Le Raysville 210 41.51 N 76.11 W
Lerberget 41 56.11 N 12.33 E
Lercara Friddi 70 37.45 N 13.36 E
Lerche 263 51.37 N 7.43 E
Lerderderg ≃ 169 37.42 S 144.30 E
Lerdo → Ciudad Lerdo 196 25.32 N 103.32 W
Lerdo de Tejada 234 18.37 N 95.31 W
Léré, Fr. 50 47.28 N 2.52 E
Léré, Mali 150 15.43 N 4.55 W
Lere, Nig. 150 9.43 N 9.21 E
Léré, Tchad 146 9.39 N 14.13 E
Lereh 164 3.08 S 139.54 E
Lerek ⋏ 114 3.47 N 102.47 E
Le Reposoir 58 46.00 N 6.33 E
Leri ≃ 42 52.32 N 4.02 W
Leribe 158 28.58 S 28.00 E
Lerici 64 44.04 N 9.55 E
Lérida, Col. 246 0.10 N 70.42 W
Lérida, Esp. 34 41.37 N 0.37 E
Lerik 84 38.46 N 48.25 E
Lérins, Îles de II 62 43.31 N 7.03 E
Lerma 34 42.02 N 3.45 W
Lerma ≃ 234 20.13 N 102.46 W
Lermontovka 89 47.10 N 134.20 E
Lermoos 58 47.24 N 10.53 E
Lerno, Monte ⋏ 71 40.37 N 9.10 E
Le Robert 240e 14.41 N 60.57 W
Léros 38 37.08 N 26.52 E
Léros I, Ellás 38 37.10 N 26.50 E
Léros I, Ellás 267c 37.59 N 23.34 E
Lérouville 56 48.47 N 5.33 E
Leroux Wash ⋁ 200 34.54 N 110.12 W
Le Roy, Il., U.S. 216 40.21 N 88.45 W
Leroy, In., U.S. 216 41.22 N 87.16 W
Le Roy, Ks., U.S. 198 38.05 N 95.38 W
Le Roy, Mn., U.S. 190 43.30 N 92.30 W
Le Roy, N.Y., U.S. 210 42.58 N 77.59 W
Le Roy, Pa., U.S. 210 41.41 N 76.43 W
Leroy, Tx., U.S. 222 31.44 N 97.01 W
Lerum 26 57.46 N 12.16 E
Le Russey 58 47.10 N 6.44 E
Lerwick 46a 60.09 N 1.09 W
Léry 206 45.21 N 73.48 W
Les 62 45.50 N 8.34 E
Les Abrets 62 45.32 N 5.35 E
Les Abymes 241o 16.16 N 61.31 W
Lesage, Lac ⊜ 206 46.19 N 75.03 W
Le Saint-Esprit 240e 14.34 N 60.57 W
Les Aix-d'Angillon 50 47.12 N 2.34 E
Les Allues 62 45.26 N 6.33 E
Les Alluets-le-Roi 261 48.55 N 1.55 E
Les Andelys 50 49.15 N 1.25 E
Les Anses-d'Arlets 240e 14.29 N 61.05 W
Le Sappey-en-Chartreuse 62 45.16 N 5.47 E
Les Arcs 62 43.27 N 6.29 E
Lesatima, Oldoinyo ⋏ 154 0.19 S 36.37 E
Le Sauze 62 44.22 N 6.41 E
Les Baux-en-Provence 62 43.45 N 4.48 E
Les Bézards 50 47.48 N 2.44 E
Les Bordes 261 48.39 N 1.58 E
Lesbos → Lésvos I 38 39.10 N 26.20 E
Les Bouchoux 58 46.18 N 5.49 E
Les Bréviaires 261 48.42 N 1.49 E
Lesbury 44 55.24 N 1.36 W
L'Escarène 62 43.50 N 7.21 E
Les Cayes 238 18.12 N 73.45 W
Les Chaises 261 48.39 N 1.42 E
Les Chapieux 62 45.42 N 6.44 E
Leschenault, Cape ⟩ 162 31.18 S 115.27 E
Leschenault Inlet ⊂ 168a 33.15 S 115.42 E
Leschnitz → Leśnica 30 50.26 N 18.11 E
Les Clayes-sous-Bois 261 48.49 N 1.59 E
Les Contamines-Montjoie 62 45.50 N 6.44 E
Les Diablerets 58 46.21 N 7.10 E
Les Diablerets ⋏ 58 46.19 N 7.12 E
Lesdiboderi 146 8.28 N 12.35 E
Les Écharmeaux 62 46.10 N 4.27 E
Les Échelles 62 45.26 N 5.45 E
Les Écureuils 206 46.39 N 71.38 W
Le Sentier 58 46.37 N 6.14 E
Le Sernoz ⋏ 62 45.48 N 6.01 E
Leseru 154 0.35 N 35.10 E
Les Essarts 50 49.21 N 1.14 W
Les Essarts-le-Roi 261 48.43 N 1.54 E
Les Estables 62 44.54 N 4.10 E
Les Étangs 56 49.09 N 6.23 E
Leseur, Mount ⋏ 162 30.15 S 115.11 E
Les Fonts 266d 41.32 N 2.02 E
Les Fourgs 58 46.50 N 6.25 E
Les Galleries d'Anjou ⇥9 275a 45.35 N 73.34 W
Les Gâtines 261 48.48 N 1.58 E
Les Gets 58 46.09 N 6.40 E
Les Granges-le-Roi 261 48.30 N 2.01 E
Les Grésillons 261 48.56 N 2.01 E
Les Halles 62 45.43 N 4.26 E
Leshan 107 29.34 N 103.45 E
Les Haudères 58 46.05 N 7.31 E
Les Hautes-Rivières 56 49.53 N 4.50 E
Les Herbiers 32 46.52 N 1.01 W
Les Houches 62 45.53 N 6.48 E
Lesignano de'Bagni 64 44.39 N 10.18 E
Lésigny 261 48.45 N 2.37 E
Lesima, Monte ⋏ 62 44.41 N 9.15 E
Lesina 64 41.52 N 15.21 E
Lesina, Lago di ⊂ 68 41.53 N 15.26 E
Lesja 26 62.07 N 8.52 E
Lesjaskog 26 62.15 N 8.22 E
Lesjöfors 40 59.59 N 14.11 E
Lesken 84 43.16 N 43.48 E
Les'ki 78 49.23 N 32.09 E
Lesko 30 49.29 N 22.21 E
Leskovac 38 42.59 N 21.57 E
Leskov Island I 18 56.40 S 28.10 W
Les Laumes 58 47.32 N 4.27 E
Les Lecques 62 43.11 N 5.40 E
Leslie, S. Afr. 158 26.27 S 28.55 E
Leslie, Scot., U.K. 46 56.12 N 3.13 W
Leslie, Ar., U.S. 194 35.49 N 92.33 W
Leslie, Ga., U.S. 192 31.57 N 84.05 W
Leslie, Mi., U.S. 216 42.27 N 84.25 W
Leslie, W.V., U.S. 188 38.02 N 80.43 W
Les Lilas 261 48.53 N 2.25 E
Les Loges 261 48.34 N 2.03 E
Les Loges-en-Josas 261 48.46 N 2.09 E
Lesmahagow 46 55.39 N 3.55 W
Les Marécottes 58 46.07 N 7.00 E
Les Mées 62 44.02 N 5.59 E
Les Mesnuls 50 48.45 N 1.50 E
Lesmo 266b 45.39 N 9.18 E
Les Molières 261 48.40 N 2.04 E
Les Monges ⋏ 62 44.16 N 6.12 E
Lesmont 50 48.26 N 4.25 E
Les Mosses 58 46.24 N 7.07 E
Lesmurdie Falls National Park ♦ 168a 32.01 S 116.04 E
Les Mureaux 261 49.00 N 1.55 E
Lešna 30 51.02 N 15.16 E
Lesna ≃ 76 52.10 N 23.33 E
Lesnaja 76 52.59 N 25.46 E
Lesneven 32 48.34 N 4.19 W
Les Neyrolles 58 46.08 N 5.38 E
Lešnica 38 44.39 N 19.19 E
Lesnoj, S.S.S.R. 24 59.48 N 52.08 E
Lesnoj, S.S.S.R. 80 54.11 N 40.27 E
Lesnoj, S.S.S.R. 86 56.57 N 67.15 E
Lesnoj ⇥8 265a 60.00 N 30.19 E
Lesnoje 76 58.17 N 35.32 E
Lesnoje Konobejevo 80 54.02 N 41.55 E
Lesnoje Mat'unino 80 53.27 N 47.26 E
Lesnoj Gorodok 265b 55.39 N 37.13 E
Lesnoj park ♦ 265a 59.59 N 30.21 E
Lesný ⋏ 60 50.02 N 12.37 E
Lesnyje Pol'any, S.S.S.R. 24 58.58 N 52.26 E
Lesnyje Pol'any, S.S.S.R. 265b 55.57 N 37.53 E
Lesogorsk, S.S.S.R. 80 55.06 N 43.56 E
Lesogorsk, S.S.S.R. 86 56.03 N 99.33 E
Lesogorsk, S.S.S.R. 89 49.27 N 142.08 E
Lesogorskij 24 61.02 N 28.53 E
Lesong, Gunong ⋏ 114 2.44 N 103.17 E
Lesopil'noje 89 46.44 N 134.20 E
Lesosibirsk 86 58.16 N 92.29 E
Lesotho □1, Afr. 138 29.30 S 28.30 E
Lesotho □1, Afr. 158 29.30 S 28.30 E
Lesovščina 78 50.47 N 28.35 E
Lesozavodsk 89 45.28 N 133.27 E
Lesozavodskij 24 66.44 N 32.49 E
Lesparre-Médoc 32 45.18 N 0.56 W
Les Pavillons-sous-Bois 261 48.55 N 2.30 E
Les Pieux 32 49.31 N 1.48 W
Les Planches-en-Montagne 58 46.40 N 6.01 E
Les Ponts-de-Martel 58 46.54 N 6.41 E
Les Praz-de-Chamonix 58 45.56 N 6.52 E
Lesquin 50 50.35 N 3.07 E
Les Riceys 50 47.59 N 4.22 E
Les Roches-l'Evêque 50 47.47 N 0.53 E
Les Rousses 58 46.29 N 6.04 E
Les Ruelles 261 48.40 N 1.37 E
Les Sables-d'Olonne 32 46.30 N 1.47 W
Lessach 64 47.11 N 13.49 E
Les Salles-sur-Verdon 62 43.46 N 6.12 E
Lessay 32 49.13 N 1.32 W
Les Scaffarels 62 43.57 N 6.41 E
Lesse ≃ 56 50.14 N 4.54 E
Lessebo 26 56.45 N 15.16 E
Lessen → Lessines 50 50.43 N 3.50 E
Lesser Antilles II 238 15.00 N 61.00 W
Lesser Khingan Range → Xiao Hinggan Ling ⁎ 89 48.45 N 127.00 E
Lesser Slave ≃ 182 55.10 N 114.03 W
Lesser Slave Lake ⊜ 182 55.25 N 115.30 W
Lesser Sunda Islands → Nusa Tenggara II 108 9.00 S 120.00 E
Lessines (Lessen) 50 50.43 N 3.50 E
Lessini, Monti ⁎ 64 45.41 N 11.13 E
L'Estaque 62 43.22 N 5.20 E
Le Stanghe 64 46.57 N 11.24 E
Lester, Pa., U.S. 285 39.52 N 75.17 W
Lester, Wa., U.S. 224 47.12 N 121.29 W
Lester B. Pearson International Airport ⊠ 212 43.41 N 79.38 W
Les Tessiers 62 44.24 N 4.16 E
Les Thilliers-en-Vexin 50 49.14 N 1.36 E
Lestijärvi 26 63.32 N 24.39 E
Lestijoki ≃ 26 64.04 N 23.38 E
Lestkov 60 49.54 N 12.52 E
Lestock 184 51.18 N 104.00 W
L'Estréchure 62 44.06 N 3.47 E
Les Trois Lacs ⊜ 206 45.48 N 71.54 W
Le Sueur 190 44.30 N 93.52 W
Le Sueur ≃ 190 44.07 N 94.03 W
Leśukonskoje 24 64.54 N 45.40 E
Lesung, Tanjung ⟩ 115a 6.29 S 105.40 E
Lesunovo 80 55.40 N 43.07 E
Les Vans 62 44.24 N 4.08 E
Les Verrières 58 46.54 N 6.30 E
Lésvos I 38 39.10 N 26.20 E
Leszno 30 51.51 N 16.35 E
Leszno □4 30 51.50 N 16.35 E
Letälven ≃ 40 59.05 N 14.20 E
L'Étang-La-Ville 261 48.52 N 2.05 E
Letcher 198 43.53 N 98.08 W
Letchmore Heath 260 51.40 N 0.20 W
Letchworth 42 51.58 N 0.14 W
Letchworth State Park ♦ 210 42.42 N 77.56 W
Letea, Ostrovul I 38 45.20 N 29.20 E
Le Teil 62 44.33 N 4.41 E
Le Temple 261 49.00 N 1.58 E
Letenye 30 46.26 N 16.43 E
Le Tertre-Saint-Denis 261 48.56 N 1.36 E
Lethbridge, Austl. 274a 33.44 S 150.48 E
Lethbridge, Ab., Can. 182 49.42 N 112.50 W
Lethbridge, Nf., Can. 186 48.21 N 53.52 W
Le Theil-sur-Huisne 50 48.16 N 0.41 E
Lethem 246 3.23 N 59.48 W
Le Thillay 261 49.00 N 2.28 E
Le Thillot 58 47.53 N 6.46 E
Le Tholy 58 48.05 N 6.45 E
Le Thor 62 43.56 N 5.00 E
Le Thoronet 62 43.27 N 6.18 E
Leti, Kepulauan II 164 8.13 S 127.50 E
Leti, Pulau I 112 8.12 S 127.41 E
Letičev 78 49.23 N 27.37 E
Leticia 246 4.09 S 69.57 W
Leting 98 39.27 N 118.53 E
Letino 68 41.26 N 14.17 E
Letjiesbos 158 32.34 S 22.16 E
Letka 24 59.36 N 49.22 E
Lethakane 156 21.27 S 25.30 E
Lethakeng 156 24.08 S 25.02 E
Letmathe 56 51.22 N 7.37 E
Letnaja zolotica 24 64.57 N 36.50 E
Letnerečenskij 24 64.18 N 34.25 E
Letong 112 2.58 N 105.42 E
Le Touquet-Paris-Plage 50 50.31 N 1.35 E
Le Touvet 62 45.21 N 5.57 E
Letovo 265b 55.34 N 37.24 E
Letpadan 110 17.47 N 95.45 E
Le Trait 50 49.28 N 0.49 E
Le Trayas 62 43.28 N 6.55 E
Le Tremblay-sur-Mauldre 261 48.47 N 1.53 E
Le Tréport 50 50.04 N 1.22 E
Letschin 54 52.39 N 14.21 E
Letsôk-aw Kyun I 110 11.37 N 98.15 E
Letter 52 52.24 N 9.38 E
Letterfrack 48 53.33 N 10.00 W
Letterkenny 48 54.57 N 7.44 W
Lettermullan 48 53.13 N 9.42 W
Letterston 42 51.56 N 5.00 W
Lettonie → Latvijskaja Sovetskaja Socialističeskaja Respublika □3 76 57.00 N 25.00 E
Letts 218 39.14 N 85.35 W
Letzlingen 54 52.26 N 11.29 E
Leu 38 44.11 N 24.00 E
Léua 152 11.34 S 20.32 E
Leubnitz 54 50.43 N 12.21 E
Leubsdorf 54 50.48 N 13.08 E
Leuca 68 39.48 N 18.21 E
Leucadia 228 33.04 N 117.18 W
Leucate, Étang de ⊂ 32 42.51 N 3.00 E
Leuchars 46 56.23 N 2.53 W
Leuchtenberg 60 49.36 N 12.15 E
Leudeville 261 48.34 N 2.20 E
Leuenberger Forst ⇥3 264a 52.40 N 13.53 E
Leuglay 58 47.49 N 4.48 E
Leuk 58 46.19 N 7.38 E
Leukerbad 58 46.23 N 7.38 E
Leulumoega 175a 13.49 S 171.55 W
Leumeah 274a 34.03 S 150.50 E
Leuna 54 51.19 N 12.01 E
Leupoldsgrün 54 50.17 N 11.47 E
Leura 170 33.43 S 150.20 E
Leura, Mount ⋏2 169 38.15 S 143.09 E
Leuser, Gunung ⋏ 114 3.45 N 97.11 E
Leušinskij Tuman, ozero ⊜ 86 59.42 N 65.35 E
Leutenberg 54 50.34 N 11.28 E
Leutersdorf 54 50.57 N 14.40 E
Leutershausen 56 49.18 N 10.24 E
Leutesdorf 56 50.27 N 7.23 E
Leutkirch 58 47.49 N 10.01 E
Leuven (Louvain) 56 50.53 N 4.42 E
Leuville-sur-Orge 261 48.37 N 2.16 E
Leuwiliang 115a 6.34 S 106.37 E
Leuze, Bel. 50 50.36 N 3.36 E
Leuze, Bel. 56 50.34 N 4.54 E
Levack 190 46.38 N 81.23 W
Levádhia 38 38.25 N 22.54 E
Levaja Mama ≃ 88 57.10 N 111.54 E
Le Val-d'Ajol 58 47.55 N 6.29 E
Le Val-d'Albian 261 48.45 N 2.11 E
Levallois-Perret 261 48.54 N 2.18 E
Le Val-Saint-Germain 261 48.34 N 2.04 E
Levan 200 39.33 N 111.51 W
Levanger 26 63.45 N 11.18 E
Levanna, Monte ⋏ 62 45.24 N 7.12 E
Levant, Île du I 62 43.03 N 6.28 E
Levante, Riviera di ⊥2 62 44.15 N 9.30 E
Levanto 62 44.10 N 9.38 E
Levanzo 70 37.59 N 12.20 E
Levanzo, Isola di I 70 38.00 N 12.20 E
Levaši 84 42.27 N 47.20 E
Le Vauclin 240e 14.33 N 60.51 W
Levdym 86 60.29 N 66.19 E
Leveaux Mountain ⋏2 190 47.37 N 90.47 W
Levél 61 47.54 N 17.12 E
Level, Isla I 254 44.29 S 74.23 W
Level Green 279b 40.24 N 79.43 W
Levelland 196 33.35 N 102.22 W
Levelock 180 59.07 N 156.52 W
Level Park 216 42.22 N 85.18 W
Leven, Eng., U.K. 44 53.53 N 0.19 W
Leven, Scot., U.K. 46 56.12 N 3.00 W
Leven ≃, Eng., U.K. 44 54.14 N 3.01 W
Leven ≃, Eng., U.K. 44 54.31 N 1.21 W
Leven, Loch ⊜, Scot., U.K. 46 56.41 N 5.07 W
Leven, Loch ⊜, Scot., U.K. 46 56.12 N 3.22 W
Leven Point ⟩ 158 27.55 S 32.35 E
Levens 62 43.52 N 7.13 E
Levenshulme ⇥8 262 53.27 N 2.10 W
Levent 38 38.27 N 37.52 E
Leventina, Valle ⋁ 58 46.25 N 9.52 E
Leveque, Cape ⟩ 162 16.24 S 122.56 E
Leverano 68 40.17 N 18.00 E
Leverburgh 46 57.45 N 7.00 W
Leverett Glacier ⊓ 9 85.30 S 150.00 W
Leveretts Chapel 222 32.19 N 94.55 W
Levering 190 45.38 N 84.47 W
Leverkusen 56 51.03 N 6.59 E
Levern 52 52.22 N 8.26 E
Lever Park ♦ 262 53.37 N 2.34 W
Le Vésinet 261 48.54 N 2.08 E
Le Vésuve → Vesuvio ⋏1 68 40.49 N 14.26 E
Leviathan Peak ⋏ 226 38.41 N 119.37 W
Levice 30 48.13 N 18.37 E
Levicha 86 57.36 N 59.55 E
Levick, Mount ⋏ 9 74.08 S 163.12 E
Levico 64 46.01 N 11.18 E
Levie 36 41.42 N 9.07 E
Levier 58 46.57 N 6.08 E
Le Vigan 32 43.59 N 3.35 E
Levin 172 40.37 S 175.17 E
Levino 76 60.29 N 37.30 E
Lévis 206 46.48 N 71.11 W
Lévis □6 206 46.40 N 71.15 W
Levisa Fork ≃ 192 38.06 N 82.36 W
Levis-Saint Nom 261 48.43 N 1.58 E
Levítha I 38 37.00 N 26.28 E
Levittown → Willingboro, N.J., U.S. 208 40.03 N 74.53 W
Levittown, N.Y., U.S. 210 40.43 N 73.30 W
Levittown, Pa., U.S. 208 40.09 N 74.49 W
Levittown Discount World ⇥9 285 40.09 N 74.49 W
Lévka 130 35.07 N 32.51 E
Lévka Óri ⋏ 38 35.18 N 24.01 E
Levkás 38 38.50 N 20.41 E
Levkás I 38 39.00 N 20.27 E
Levkímmi 38 39.25 N 20.04 E
Levkónoikon 130 35.15 N 33.50 E
Levkosía (Nicosia) 130 35.10 N 33.22 E
Levoča 30 49.02 N 20.36 E
Levokumskoje 84 44.48 N 44.39 E
Levroux 50 46.59 N 1.37 E
Levski 38 43.22 N 25.08 E
Lev Tolstoj 76 53.13 N 39.27 E
Levuka 175g 17.41 S 178.50 E
Lévuo ≃ 76 56.04 N 24.23 E
Levyj Tuzlov ≃ 83 47.35 N 39.23 E
Lewapaku 115b 9.43 S 119.55 E
Lewbeach 210 42.00 N 74.47 W
Lewe 110 19.38 N 96.07 E
Lewes 52 51.30 N 3.45 E
Lewedorp 198 41.19 N 102.08 W
Lewellen 156 25.30 S 17.45 E
Lewer ≃ 42 50.52 N 0.01 E
Lewes, Eng., U.K. 208 38.46 N 75.08 W
Lewes, De., U.S. 30 50.46 N 17.37 E
Lewin Brzeski 218 41.18 N 95.04 W
Lewis, Ia., U.S. 198 37.56 N 99.15 W
Lewis, Ks., U.S. 218 38.32 N 83.21 W
Lewis □6, Ky., U.S. 219 40.08 N 91.45 W
Lewis □6, Mo., U.S. 210 43.48 N 75.30 W
Lewis □6, N.Y., U.S. 224 46.35 N 122.22 W
Lewis □6, Wa., U.S. 224 45.51 N 122.48 W
Lewis ≃ 46 58.10 N 6.40 W
Lewis, Butt of ⟩ 46 58.31 N 6.16 W
Lewis, East Fork ≃ 224 45.52 N 122.43 W
Lewis, Isle of I 46 58.10 N 6.40 W
Lewis, Mount ⋏ 204 40.24 N 116.51 W
Lewis and Clark ≃ 224 46.10 N 123.52 W
Lewis and Clark Cavern State Park ♦ 202 45.49 N 111.13 W
Lewis and Clark Lake ⊜1 198 42.50 N 97.45 W
Lewis and Clark Range ⁎ 202 47.30 N 113.00 W
Lewisberry 208 40.08 N 76.52 W
Lewisburg, Ky., U.S. 194 36.59 N 86.56 W
Lewisburg, Oh., U.S. 218 39.50 N 84.32 W
Lewisburg, Pa., U.S. 210 40.57 N 76.53 W
Lewisburg, Tn., U.S. 194 35.26 N 86.47 W
Lewisburg, W.V., U.S. 188 37.48 N 80.26 W
Lewis Center 214 40.12 N 83.01 W
Lewis Creek ≃, Ca., U.S. 226 35.17 N 120.58 W
Lewis Creek ≃, In., U.S. 218 39.22 N 85.51 W
Lewis Creek Reservoir ⊜1 222 30.26 N 95.32 W
Lewisdale 284c 38.58 N 76.58 W
Lewisetta 208 38.01 N 76.28 W
Lewis Gut ⊂ 276 41.09 N 73.09 W
Lewisham 273d 26.07 S 27.49 E
Lewisham ⇥8 42 51.27 N 0.01 E
Lewisham Location 273d 26.10 S 27.47 E
Lewis-Lockport Airport ⊠ 278 41.36 N 88.05 W
Lewis Pass ⋊ 172 42.23 S 172.24 E
Lewisport 194 37.56 N 86.54 W
Lewisporte 186 49.15 N 55.03 W
Lewis Range ⁎, Austl. 162 20.20 S 128.40 E
Lewis Range ⁎, Mt., U.S. 202 48.35 N 113.40 W
Lewis Run 214 41.52 N 78.39 W
Lewis Run ≃ 279b 40.17 N 79.55 W
Lewis Smith Lake ⊜1 194 34.05 N 87.07 W
Lewiston, Ca., U.S. 204 40.43 N 122.48 W
Lewiston, Id., U.S. 202 46.25 N 117.01 W
Lewiston, Me., U.S. 188 44.06 N 70.12 W
Lewiston, Mi., U.S. 190 44.53 N 84.18 W
Lewiston, Mn., U.S. 190 43.59 N 91.52 W
Lewiston, N.Y., U.S. 210 43.10 N 79.02 W
Lewiston, Ut., U.S. 200 41.58 N 111.51 W
Lewiston Orchards 202 46.23 N 116.59 W
Lewistown, Il., U.S. 194 40.23 N 90.09 W
Lewistown, Md., U.S. 208 39.32 N 77.24 W
Lewistown, Mo., U.S. 219 40.05 N 91.48 W
Lewistown, Mt., U.S. 202 47.03 N 109.25 W
Lewistown, Oh., U.S. 216 40.25 N 83.53 W
Lewistown, Pa., U.S. 208 40.35 N 77.34 W
Lewisville, N.B., Can. 186 46.06 N 64.46 W
Lewisville, Ar., U.S. 194 33.21 N 93.34 W
Lewisville, In., U.S. 218 39.48 N 85.21 W
Lewisville, Pa., U.S. 208 39.43 N 75.53 W
Lewisville, Tx., U.S. 222 33.02 N 96.59 W
Lewisville Dam ⇥6 222 33.05 N 96.55 W
Lewisville Lake ⊜1 196 33.08 N 97.00 W
Lewoleba 112 8.23 S 123.24 E
Lewotobi Lakilaki, Ili ⋏ 115b 8.32 S 122.46 E
Lewvan 184 50.00 N 104.06 W
Lexa 194 34.35 N 90.44 W
Lexington, Ga., U.S. 192 33.52 N 83.06 W
Lexington, Il., U.S. 216 40.38 N 88.47 W
Lexington, In., U.S. 218 38.39 N 85.37 W
Lexington, Ky., U.S. 218 38.02 N 84.30 W
Lexington, Ma., U.S. 207 42.26 N 71.13 W
Lexington, Mi., U.S. 190 43.16 N 82.31 W
Lexington, Ms., U.S. 194 33.06 N 90.03 W
Lexington, Mo., U.S. 194 39.11 N 93.52 W
Lexington, Ne., U.S. 198 40.46 N 99.44 W
Lexington, N.Y., U.S. 210 42.15 N 74.22 W
Lexington, N.C., U.S. 192 35.49 N 80.15 W
Lexington, Oh., U.S. 214 40.40 N 82.34 W
Lexington, Ok., U.S. 196 35.00 N 97.20 W
Lexington, Or., U.S. 202 45.26 N 119.41 W
Lexington, S.C., U.S. 192 33.58 N 81.14 W
Lexington, Tn., U.S. 194 35.39 N 88.23 W
Lexington, Tx., U.S. 222 30.25 N 97.01 W
Lexington, Va., U.S. 192 37.47 N 79.26 W
Lexington Park 208 38.16 N 76.27 W
Lexington Reservoir ⊜1 226 37.12 N 121.59 W
Lexton 169 37.17 S 143.31 E
Leybourne 260 51.18 N 0.25 E
Leyburn 44 54.19 N 1.49 W
Leyden → Leiden 52 52.09 N 4.30 E
Leye 102 24.48 N 106.34 E
Leyland 44 53.42 N 2.42 W
Leyne 130 37.22 N 28.02 E
Le Yonne 184 51.40 N 96.32 W
Leyond ≃ 152 1.07 S 13.08 E
Léyou ≃ 32 44.39 N 1.01 W
Leyre ≃ 42 51.24 N 0.55 E
Leysdown-on-Sea 58 46.21 N 7.01 E
Leysin 116 11.23 N 124.29 E
Leyte 116 10.50 N 124.55 E
Leyte □4 116 10.50 N 124.50 E
Leyte I 116 10.50 N 125.25 E
Leyte Gulf ⊂ 100 31.55 N 120.43 E
Leyu 62 44.13 N 4.43 E
Lez ≃ 62 43.31 N 3.55 E
Lèz ≅ 76 58.56 N 40.45 E
Leža 76 59.15 N 40.10 E
Leža ≃ 30 50.16 N 22.24 E
Lezajsk 84 43.12 N 46.24 W
Lezama 241o 16.08 N 61.47 W
Lézard, Pointe à ⟩ 240e 14.36 N 61.01 W
Lézarde ≃ 58 46.30 N 5.56 E
Lézat 62 43.40 N 5.28 E
Lezay 38 41.47 N 19.39 E
Lezhë 107 30.17 N 104.55 E
Lezhi 80 56.46 N 40.53 E
Ležn'ovo 58 45.56 N 9.11 E
Lezzeno 78 51.43 N 35.17 E
L'gov 46 57.37 N 3.13 W
Lhanbryde 120 29.40 N 91.09 E
Lhasa 120 29.50 N 91.00 E
Lhasa ≃ 261 49.00 N 2.01 E
L'Hautil 254 55.52 S 67.20 W
L'Hermite, Isla I 34 41.21 N 2.06 E
L'Hillil 114 4.52 N 95.24 E
Lhokkruet 114 5.29 N 95.15 E
Lhoknga 114 5.10 N 97.08 E
Lhokseumawe 114 5.03 N 97.19 E
Lhoksukon
L'Hôpital-sous-Rochefort 62 45.46 N 3.56 E
Lhorong 102 30.45 N 96.09 E
Lhotse ⋏ 124 27.57 N 86.56 E
Lhuis 62 45.45 N 5.32 E
Lhuntsi Dzong 120 27.39 N 91.09 E
Li 110 18.26 N 98.42 E
Li ≃, Thai 100 33.11 N 115.07 E
Li ≃, Zhg. 102 29.24 N 112.01 E
Lian ≃, Zhg. 100 24.02 N 113.18 E
Lian ≃, Zhg. 100 25.46 N 115.48 E
Lian ≃, Zhg. 100 26.23 N 111.23 E
Lian ≃, Zhg. 102 25.44 N 116.46 E
Lian ≃, Zhg. 50 49.20 N 2.28 E
Liancourt 60 50.43 N 1.36 E
Liane ≃ 164 3.30 S 128.19 E
Liang 116 8.38 N 126.06 E
Lianga 116 8.37 N 126.12 E
Lianga Bay ⊂ 107 30.30 N 104.56 E
Liang'anchang 102 34.37 N 110.45 E
Liangbao 89 45.48 N 128.19 E
Liangbingbao 83 45.12 N 128.47 E
Liangbinghe 112 0.05 N 116.46 E
Liangbuaya 107 29.03 N 106.18 E
Liangchahe 98 35.35 N 119.35 E
Liangcheng

Symbols in the index entries represent the broad categories identified in the key at the right. Symbols with superior numbers (⁎1) identify subcategories (see complete key on page I · 1).

Kartensymbole in dem Registerverzeichnis stellen die rechts in Schlüssel erklärten Kategorien dar. Symbole mit hochgestellten Ziffern (⁎1) bezeichnen Unterabteilungen einer Kategorie (vgl. vollständiger Schlüssel auf Seite I · 1).

Los símbolos incluídos en el texto del índice representan las grandes categorías identificadas con la clave a la derecha. Los símbolos con números en su parte superior (⁎1) identifican las subcategorías (véase la clave completa en la página I · 1).

Les symboles de l'index représentent les catégories indiquées dans la légende à droite. Les symboles suivis d'un indice (⁎1) représentent des sous-catégories (voir légende complète à la page I · 1).

Os símbolos incluídos no texto do índice representam as grandes categorias identificadas com a chave à direita. Os símbolos com números em sua parte superior (⁎1) identificam as subcategorias (veja-se a chave completa à página I · 1).

⋏ Mountain	Berg	Montaña	Montagne	Montanha
⋏ Mountains	Berge	Montañas	Montagnes	Montanhas
⋊ Pass	Pass	Paso	Col	Passo
⋁ Valley, Canyon	Tal, Cañon	Valle, Cañón	Vallée, Canyon	Vale, Canhão
≚ Plain	Ebene	Llano	Plaine	Planície
⟩ Cape	Kap	Cabo	Cap	Cabo
I Island	Insel	Isla	Île	Ilha
II Islands	Inseln	Islas	Îles	Ilhas
⊥ Other Topographic Features	Andere Topographische Objekte	Otros Elementos Topográficos	Autres données topographiques	Outros acidentes topográficos

ESPAÑOL Nombre	Página	Lat.°′	Long.°′ W = Oeste
Liangcun	100	26.36 N	115.34 E
Liangdang	102	33.56 N	106.12 E
Liangdawa	105	40.39 N	117.37 E
Liangfengwu	107	30.11 N	105.22 E
Lianggezhuang	105	39.21 N	115.22 E
Lianghe, Zhg.	89	45.09 N	128.45 E
Lianghe, Zhg.	102	24.51 N	98.25 E
Liangheguan	102	32.52 N	109.19 E
Lianghekou, Zhg.	102	33.42 N	104.25 E
Lianghekou, Zhg.	102	29.14 N	108.40 E
Lianghekou, Zhg.	102	31.27 N	102.13 E
Lianghekou, Zhg.	107	28.55 N	106.03 E
Liangiu	98	35.12 N	117.47 E
Liangjia	107	29.29 N	105.33 E
Liangjiadian	98	39.10 N	121.54 E
Liangjiafang	98	41.04 N	117.18 E
Liangjianfang	105	40.45 N	117.20 E
Liangjiang	102	23.23 N	108.22 E
Liangjiangkou	98	42.38 N	128.05 E
Liangjiawazi	104	40.40 N	120.42 E
Liangjiazi	104	42.13 N	122.31 E
Liangkou	100	23.43 N	113.43 E
Lianglukou	107	29.18 N	106.15 E
Liangmen	98	35.34 N	114.54 E
Liangmentou	100	28.58 N	121.12 E
Liangmushi	106	30.46 N	119.35 E
Liangpa	102	24.10 N	106.13 E
Liangpeng	106	30.47 N	119.38 E
Liangping	102	30.41 N	107.49 E
Liang Shan ∧, Zhg.	102	23.45 N	99.45 E
Liang Shan ∧, Zhg.	102	23.45 N	99.45 E
Liangshui ≃	271a	39.49 N	116.40 E
Liangtian	100	25.37 N	113.00 E
Liangtinghe	100	30.20 N	116.12 E
Liangtoumen	100	29.31 N	120.45 E
Liangtun	98	40.14 N	122.34 E
Liangwangzhuang	105	39.01 N	116.58 E
Liangxiangzhen	105	39.44 N	116.08 E
Liangying	100	23.14 N	116.21 E
Liangyuan	100	32.00 N	117.34 E
Liangzhu	106	30.23 N	120.03 E
Liangzi Hu ◎	100	30.16 N	114.34 E
Lianhe	98	42.36 N	125.37 E
Lian Hu ◎	106	32.02 N	119.32 E
Lianhua	100	27.07 N	113.57 E
Lianhuachi	105	40.28 N	116.33 E
Lianhuapao	89	45.32 N	129.50 E
Lianhua Shan ⋏	100	23.40 N	116.00 E
Lianjiang, Zhg.	100	26.12 N	119.31 E
Lianjiang, Zhg.	102	21.38 N	110.15 E
Lianjiechang	107	29.41 N	104.30 E
Liannan (Sanjiang)	102	24.38 N	112.10 E
Lianozovo ◆[8]	265b	55.54 N	37.35 E
Lianping	100	24.22 N	114.31 E
Lianpu	100	26.02 N	118.38 E
Lianshanguan	104	40.58 N	123.46 E
Lianshi	106	30.42 N	120.26 E
Lianshui	100	33.47 N	119.16 E
Liansiji	98	33.58 N	114.24 E
Liantang	106	31.37 N	120.38 E
Lianxian	102	24.48 N	112.25 E
Lianyin	89	53.28 N	123.51 E
Lianyuan (Lantian)	102	27.42 N	111.19 E
Lianyungang, Zhg.	98	34.44 N	119.30 E
Lianyungang (Xinpu), Zhg.	98	34.39 N	119.16 E
Lianyun Shan ∧	100	28.32 N	113.50 E
Lianzhou → Hepu	102	21.39 N	109.11 E
Liao ≃	90	40.50 N	121.48 E
Liaobinta	104	42.08 N	123.04 E
Liaocheng	98	36.30 N	115.59 E
Liaodong Bandao (Liaotung Peninsula) ≻[1]	98	40.00 N	122.20 E
Liaodong Wan (Gulf of Liaotung) ⊂	98	40.30 N	121.30 E
Liaohe Kou ⊂[1]	104	40.42 N	122.05 E
Liaojiangshi	100	26.05 N	113.17 E
Liaoning □[4]	90	41.00 N	123.00 E
Liaotung, Gulf of → Liaodong Wan ⊂	98	40.30 N	121.30 E
Liaotung Peninsula → Liaodong Bandao ≻[1]	98	40.00 N	122.20 E
Liaoyang	104	41.17 N	123.11 E
Liaoyangwopu	89	43.00 N	123.28 E
Liaoyuan	89	42.54 N	125.07 E
Liaozhong	104	41.31 N	122.44 E
Liapádhes	38	39.40 N	19.44 E
Liāquatpur	123	28.56 N	70.57 E
Liard ≃	176	61.52 N	121.18 W
Liāri	120	25.41 N	66.29 E
Liart	50	49.46 N	4.20 E
Liat, Pulau I	112	2.53 S	107.05 E
Liathach ∧	46	57.35 N	5.29 W
Lib I	14	8.19 N	167.25 E
Libagon	116	10.18 N	125.03 E
Liban → Lebanon □[1]	128	33.50 N	35.50 E
Libanga	152	0.19 N	18.41 E
Líbano	246	4.55 N	75.04 W
Libano → Lebanon □[1]	128	33.50 N	35.50 E
Libanon → Lebanon □[1]	128	33.50 N	35.50 E
Libau → Liepāja	76	56.31 N	21.01 E
Libby	202	48.23 N	115.33 W
Libby Dam ◆[6]	202	48.24 N	115.20 W
Libčeves	54	50.26 N	13.50 E
Libčice nad Vltavou	54	50.10 N	14.20 E
Liběchov	54	50.20 N	14.28 E
Libenge	152	3.39 N	18.38 E
Liberal, Ks., U.S.	198	37.02 N	100.55 W
Liberal, Mo., U.S.	194	37.33 N	94.31 W
Liberdade	256	22.01 S	44.19 W
Liberdade ◆[8]	287b	23.35 S	46.37 W
Liberdade ≃	250	9.40 S	52.17 W
Liberdade, Riozinho da ≃	248	7.10 S	71.51 W
Liberec	30	50.46 N	15.03 E
Liberia	236	10.38 N	85.27 W
Liberia □[1], Afr.	134	6.30 N	9.30 W
Liberia □[1], Afr.	150	6.30 N	9.30 W
Liberta	240c	17.02 N	61.47 W
Libertad, Arg.	258	34.42 S	58.41 W
Libertad, Ur.	258	34.38 S	56.39 W
Libertad, Ven.	246	8.20 N	69.37 W
Libertad, Ven.	246	9.23 N	68.44 W
Libertador □[5]	286c	10.27 N	66.57 W
Libertador General Bernardo O'Higgins □[4]	252	34.30 S	71.00 W
Libertador General San Martín	252	23.48 S	64.48 W
Liberty, Il., U.S.	219	39.53 N	91.06 W
Liberty, In., U.S.	218	39.38 N	84.55 W
Liberty, Ky., U.S.	194	37.19 N	84.56 W
Liberty, Ms., U.S.	194	31.09 N	90.48 W
Liberty, Mo., U.S.	194	39.14 N	94.25 W
Liberty, Ne., U.S.	198	40.05 N	96.28 W
Liberty, N.Y., U.S.	210	41.48 N	74.44 W
Liberty, N.C., U.S.	192	35.51 N	79.34 W
Liberty, Pa., U.S.	210	41.34 N	77.06 W
Liberty, Pa., U.S.	279b	40.20 N	79.51 W
Liberty, S.C., U.S.	192	34.47 N	82.41 W
Liberty, Tx., U.S.	222	30.03 N	94.47 W
Liberty □[6]	222	30.12 N	94.50 W
Liberty Acres	280	34.04 N	118.12 W
Liberty Bell Race Track ♠	285	40.05 N	74.58 W
Liberty Center, In., U.S.	216	40.41 N	85.16 W
Liberty Center, Oh., U.S.	216	41.26 N	84.00 W
Liberty City	222	32.27 N	94.57 W
Liberty Corner	276	40.39 N	74.34 W
Liberty Ditch ≊	226	36.31 N	120.02 W
Liberty Farms	226	38.19 N	121.42 W
Liberty Hill	196	30.40 N	97.55 W
Liberty Island I	276	40.41 N	74.03 W
Liberty Lake ◎[1]	208	39.25 N	76.53 W

FRANÇAIS Nom	Page	Lat.°′	Long.°′ W = Ouest
Liberty Manor	284b	39.21 N	76.47 W
Liberty Mills	216	41.02 N	85.44 W
Liberty Park	216	41.26 N	87.22 W
Libertytown	208	39.29 N	77.14 W
Liberty Tree Mall ◆[9]	283	42.33 N	70.57 W
Liberty Tunnel ◆[5]	279b	40.26 N	80.01 W
Libertyville	216	42.16 N	87.57 W
Líbeznice	54	50.10 N	14.30 E
Libia → Libya □[1]	146	27.00 N	17.00 E
Libibi	152	14.42 S	17.44 E
Libishan	106	30.45 N	119.20 E
Lībiyā → Libya □[1]	146	27.00 N	17.00 E
Lībīyah, Aṣ-Ṣaḥrā' al- (Libyan Desert) ◆[2]	136	24.00 N	25.00 E
Liblín	60	49.55 N	13.32 E
Libni, Jabal ∧[2]	132	30.44 N	33.50 E
Libo	102	25.28 N	107.53 E
Libobo, Tanjung ≻	164	0.54 S	128.28 E
Liboc ≃	54	50.10 N	13.31 E
Libochovice	54	50.22 N	14.03 E
Libode	158	31.33 S	29.02 E
Liboi	154	0.24 N	40.57 E
Liboko	152	2.43 N	21.28 E
Libomyšl	60	49.52 N	14.00 E
Libona	116	8.20 N	124.44 E
Liboumba ≃	152	0.38 N	12.54 E
Libourne	32	44.55 N	0.14 W
Libramont	56	49.55 N	5.23 E
Library	214	40.18 N	80.02 W
Librazhd	38	41.11 N	20.19 E
Libres	234	19.28 N	97.41 W
Libreville	152	0.23 N	9.27 E
Librizzi	70	38.06 N	14.57 E
Libro Point ≻	116	11.26 N	119.29 E
Libu	102	23.41 N	111.30 E
Libucan Island I	116	11.54 N	124.39 E
Libuganon ≃	116	7.27 N	125.47 E
Libunga	154	1.49 N	26.35 E
Liburung	112	3.55 S	120.09 E
Libušín	54	50.09 N	14.04 E
Libya (Lībiyā) □[1], Afr.	136	27.00 N	17.00 E
Libya (Lībiyā) □[1], Afr.	146	27.00 N	17.00 E
Libyan Desert → Lībīyah, Aṣ-Ṣaḥrā' al- ◆[2]	136	24.00 N	25.00 E
Libyan Plateau → Aḍ-Diffah ⋏[1]	140	30.30 N	25.30 E
Libye → Libya □[1]	146	27.00 N	17.00 E
Libyen → Libya □[1]	146	27.00 N	17.00 E
Libysche Wüste → Lībīyah, Aṣ-Ṣaḥrā' al- ◆[2]	136	24.00 N	25.00 E
Licantén	252	34.59 S	72.00 W
Licata	70	37.06 N	13.56 E
Licciana Nardi	64	44.16 N	10.02 E
Lice	130	38.28 N	40.39 E
Lich	56	50.33 N	8.50 E
Lichačova, mys ≻	89	42.44 N	132.51 E
Lichaja ≃	83	48.08 N	40.15 E
Lichang	107	28.53 N	104.26 E
Licheng	102	36.30 N	113.21 E
Lichères-Près-Aigremont	50	47.43 N	3.51 E
Lichfield	42	52.42 N	1.48 W
Lich-hoi-thuong	110	9.26 N	106.08 E
Lichinga	154	13.18 S	35.14 E
Lichitiseni	38	46.23 N	27.17 E
Lichoborka ≃	265b	55.50 N	37.38 E
Lichoslavl'	76	57.07 N	35.28 E
Lichovka	78	48.41 N	33.55 E
Lichovskoj	83	48.07 N	40.12 E
Lichtaart	56	51.14 N	4.54 E
Lichte	54	50.31 N	11.10 E
Lichtenau	56	48.43 N	8.01 E
Lichtenberg, B.R.D.	54	50.23 N	11.40 E
Lichtenberg, Fr.	56	48.55 N	7.29 E
Lichtenberg ◆[8]	264a	52.31 N	13.29 E
Lichtenburg	158	26.08 S	26.08 E
Lichtendorf	263	51.28 N	7.37 E
Lichtenfels	56	50.09 N	11.04 E
Lichtenplatz ◆[8]	263	51.15 N	7.12 E
Lichtenrade ◆[8]	264a	52.23 N	13.25 E
Lichtensee	54	51.23 N	13.22 E
Lichtensteig	58	47.19 N	9.05 E
Lichtenstein	54	50.45 N	12.37 E
Lichtenstein, Schloss ♁	58	48.24 N	9.15 E
Lichtentanne	54	50.42 N	12.25 E
Lichtenvoorde	52	51.59 N	6.34 E
Lichterfelde ◆[8]	264a	52.26 N	13.19 E
Lichtervelde	50	51.02 N	3.09 E
Lichuan, Zhg.	100	27.18 N	116.53 E
Lichuan, Zhg.	102	30.18 N	108.51 E
Lick Creek ≃, Il., U.S.	219	39.42 N	89.41 W
Lick Creek ≃, In., U.S.	218	38.33 N	86.31 W
Lick Creek ≃, Mo., U.S.	219	39.31 N	91.39 W
Lick Creek ≃, Oh., U.S.	216	41.21 N	84.25 W
Lick Creek ≃, Tn., U.S.	192	36.11 N	83.10 W
Lickershamn	26	57.50 N	18.31 E
Licking	194	37.29 N	91.51 W
Licking □[6]	214	40.10 N	82.30 W
Licking ≃, Ky., U.S.	188	39.06 N	84.30 W
Licking ≃, Oh., U.S.	214	40.03 N	82.20 W
Licking, North Fork ≃, Ky., U.S.	218	38.35 N	84.13 W
Licking, North Fork ≃, Oh., U.S.	214	40.03 N	82.23 W
Licking, South Fork ≃	218	38.41 N	84.20 W
Lickingville	214	41.23 N	79.22 W
Lick Observatory ♁[3]	226	37.22 N	121.37 W
Ličko Polje ≡	36	44.35 N	15.25 E
Lick Run ≃, Pa., U.S.	210	41.12 N	77.32 W
Lick Run ≃, Pa., U.S.	279b	40.17 N	79.57 W
Licodia Eubea	70	37.09 N	14.42 E
Licosa, Punta ≻	68	40.15 N	14.54 E
Licun	98	38.32 N	117.08 E
Licungo ≃	154	17.40 S	37.15 E
Lid'	76	59.39 N	35.05 E
Lida	76	53.53 N	25.18 E
Lidan ≃	26	58.31 N	13.09 E
Lidao	98	37.15 N	122.32 E
Lidarentuncun	104	41.32 N	123.12 E
Lidcombe	274a	33.52 S	151.03 E
Liddel Water ≃	44	55.04 N	2.57 W
Liddesdale V	44	55.12 N	2.46 W
Liddon Gulf ⊂	176	75.03 N	113.00 W
Liden	26	62.42 N	16.48 E
Lidesi	100	33.33 N	115.53 E
Lidgerwood	198	46.04 N	97.09 W
Lidgetton	158	29.25 S	30.05 E
Lidian	107	28.57 N	103.44 E
Lídice, Bra.	256	22.51 S	44.12 W
Lídice, Pan.	236	8.45 N	79.54 W
Lidice ⊥	54	50.03 N	14.08 E
Lidingö	40	59.22 N	18.08 E
Lidköping	26	58.30 N	13.10 E
Lido	64	45.25 N	12.22 E
Lido, Litorale di ⍊[2]	64	45.23 N	12.21 E
Lido, Porto di ⊂	64	45.26 N	12.25 E
Lido Beach	276	40.35 N	73.38 W
Lido di Camaiore	64	43.54 N	10.13 E
Lido di Castel Fusano ◆[8]	66	41.43 N	12.20 E
Lido di Iesolo	64	45.30 N	12.39 E
Lido di Metaponto	68	40.22 N	16.50 E
Lido di Ostia ◆[8]	66	41.44 N	12.14 E
Lido di Pomposa	66	44.45 N	12.14 E
Lido di Siponto	68	41.37 N	15.55 E
Lido Key I	220	27.19 N	82.35 W
Lidsjön ◎	40	58.55 N	16.51 E
Lidu	107	30.35 N	106.04 E
Lidzbark	30	53.17 N	19.49 E
Lidzbark Warmiński	30	54.09 N	20.35 E

PORTUGUÊS Nome	Página	Lat.°′	Long.°′ W = Oeste
Liebenau, B.R.D.	52	52.36 N	9.05 E
Liebenau, Öst.	61	48.32 N	14.49 E
Liebenbergsvlei ≃	158	27.20 S	28.31 E
Liebenburg	52	52.01 N	10.26 E
Liebenthal → Lubomierz	30	51.01 N	15.30 E
Liebenwalde	54	52.52 N	13.23 E
Lieberhausen	56	51.03 N	7.40 E
Lieberose	54	51.59 N	14.17 E
Liebertwolkwitz	54	51.17 N	12.28 E
Liebstadt	54	50.52 N	13.51 E
Liechtenstein □[1], Europe	22	47.09 N	9.35 E
Liechtenstein □[1], Europe	58	47.09 N	9.35 E
Liechtensteinklamm V	64	47.18 N	13.12 E
Liedberg	263	51.10 N	6.32 E
Liedekerke	50	50.52 N	4.05 E
Liège (Luik)	56	50.38 N	5.34 E
Liège □[4]	56	50.30 N	5.30 E
Liège, Aéroport ⊠	56	50.39 N	5.30 E
Liegnitz → Legnica	30	51.13 N	16.09 E
Lieja → Liège	56	50.38 N	5.34 E
Lieksa	26	63.19 N	30.01 E
Lielais Liepu kalns ∧[2]	76	56.25 N	27.50 E
Lielupe ≃	76	57.01 N	23.56 E
Lielvārde	76	56.43 N	24.51 E
Liemienzhen	107	30.29 N	106.05 E
Lienart	154	3.04 N	25.31 E
Lienchou → Hepu	102	21.39 N	109.11 E
Lienen	52	52.09 N	7.58 E
Lien-huong	110	11.13 N	108.44 E
Lienz	64	46.50 N	12.47 E
Liepāja	76	56.31 N	21.01 E
Liepājas ezers ◎	76	56.27 N	21.03 E
Liepe	54	53.58 N	13.56 E
Liepna	76	57.25 N	27.25 E
Liepnitzsee ◎	264a	52.45 N	13.30 E
Lièpvre	58	48.16 N	7.17 E
Lier (Lierre)	50	51.08 N	4.34 E
Lierenfeld ◆[8]	263	51.13 N	6.51 E
Lierna	58	45.57 N	9.18 E
Liernais	50	47.12 N	4.17 E
Lierneux	56	50.18 N	5.48 E
Liershizhai	104	41.49 N	123.43 E
Liesborn	52	51.43 N	8.15 E
Lieser ≃, B.R.D.	56	49.55 N	7.01 E
Lieser ≃, Öst.	64	46.47 N	13.39 E
Lieshout	52	51.32 N	5.35 E
Liesing ◆[8]	264b	48.08 N	16.17 E
Liesing ≃	264b	48.08 N	16.28 E
Liesingbach ≃	61	47.20 N	15.02 E
Liesjärven Kansallispuisto ♠	26	60.40 N	23.54 E
Lieskau	54	51.37 N	13.48 E
Liesse	50	49.37 N	3.48 E
Liessies	50	50.07 N	4.05 E
Liestal	58	47.29 N	7.44 E
Liești	38	45.38 N	27.32 E
Lietzow	54	54.29 N	13.30 E
Lieurey	50	49.14 N	0.29 E
Lieusaint	261	48.38 N	2.33 E
Lieutel, Ruisseau le ≃	261	48.49 N	1.52 E
Lieutenant Robert J. Palenscar Memorial Airport ⊠	285	39.51 N	75.03 W
Liévin	50	50.25 N	2.46 E
Lièvre, Rivière du ≃	176	45.31 N	75.26 W
Lièvres, Île aux I	186	47.51 N	69.44 W
Liezen	61	47.35 N	14.15 E
Lifanga	152	0.19 N	21.57 E
Liffey ≃	44	53.21 N	6.16 W
Liffol-le-Grand	58	48.19 N	5.35 E
Lifford	48	54.50 N	7.29 W
Liffré	32	48.13 N	1.30 W
Lifjell ∧	26	59.30 N	8.52 E
Lifoku	152	0.04 S	21.18 E
Lifou I	175f	20.53 S	167.13 E
Lifoula	273b	4.06 S	15.25 E
Lifton	42	50.39 N	4.17 W
Liftwood	285	39.47 N	75.31 W
Lifune ≃	152	8.21 S	13.22 E
Ligačovo	265b	55.56 N	37.15 E
Ligang	100	30.04 N	121.52 E
Ligao, Pil.	116	13.14 N	123.32 E
Ligao, Pil.	116	6.17 N	124.09 E
Ligasa	152	0.42 N	23.45 E
Līgatne	76	57.14 N	25.02 E
Ligezhuang, Zhg.	105	39.42 N	118.12 E
Ligezhuang, Zhg.	105	39.49 N	115.56 E
Light ≃	168b	34.35 S	138.22 E
Lightfoot	208	37.20 N	76.45 W
Lighthouse Beach ⍊[2]	273a	6.24 N	3.22 E
Lighthouse Point	220	26.16 N	80.05 W
Lighthouse Point ≻, On., Can.	214	41.50 N	82.38 W
Lighthouse Point ≻, Fl., U.S.	192	29.54 N	84.21 W
Lighthouse Point ≻, Mi., U.S.	190	45.13 N	85.32 W
Lighthouse Reef ✧[2]	232	17.20 N	87.32 W
Lightning Creek ≃, Sk., Can.	184	49.12 N	101.43 W
Lightning Creek ≃, N.A.	224	48.50 N	121.03 W
Lightning Creek ≃, Wy., U.S.	198	43.11 N	104.44 W
Lightstreet	210	41.02 N	76.25 W
Lightsville	216	40.18 N	84.42 W
Ligist	61	46.59 N	15.12 E
Lignano Pineta	64	45.40 N	13.07 E
Lignano Sabbiadoro	64	45.42 N	13.09 E
Lignières	32	46.45 N	2.11 E
Lignite	198	48.52 N	102.33 W
Lignon ≃	62	45.44 N	4.08 E
Lignumvitae Key I	220	24.55 N	80.42 W
Ligny-en-Barrois	58	48.41 N	5.20 E
Ligny-en-Cambrésis	50	50.06 N	3.22 E
Ligny-le-Châtel	50	47.54 N	3.45 E
Ligny-le-Ribault	50	47.41 N	1.47 E
Ligonha ≃	154	16.54 S	39.09 E
Ligonier, In., U.S.	216	41.27 N	85.35 W
Ligonier, Pa., U.S.	214	40.14 N	79.14 W
Ligovka	78	49.08 N	36.03 E
Ligovo	76	60.13 N	31.48 E
Ligovo ◆[8]	265a	59.50 N	30.12 E
Ligovskij kanal ≊	265a	59.47 N	30.10 E
Liguantu	105	40.24 N	115.45 E
Ligueil	32	47.03 N	0.49 E
Ligui	232	25.43 N	111.16 W
Ligure, Mar → Ligurian Sea ⍑[2]	36	43.30 N	9.00 E
Liguria □[4]	62	44.30 N	8.50 E
Liguria, Mar de → Ligurian Sea ⍑[2]	36	43.30 N	9.00 E
Ligurian Sea ⍑[2]	36	43.30 N	9.00 E
Ligurisches Meer → Ligurian Sea ⍑[2]	36	43.30 N	9.00 E
Lihir Group II	164	3.05 S	152.40 E
Lihir Island I	164	3.05 S	152.35 E
Lihou Reef and Cays ✧[2]	166	17.25 S	151.40 E
Lihu	100	23.23 N	116.03 E
Lihue	229b	21.58 N	159.22 W
Lihue Airport ⊠	229b	21.59 N	159.21 W
Lihula	76	58.41 N	23.50 E
Liji, Zhg.	100	31.59 N	115.51 E
Liji, Zhg.	100	33.48 N	117.48 E
Lijia, Zhg.	98	37.49 N	118.01 E
Lijia, Zhg.	104	41.43 N	122.20 E
Lijiaba	107	29.37 N	105.33 E
Lijiadian	104	42.07 N	121.14 E
Lijiajie	107	29.49 N	105.30 E
Lijiakou	105	39.12 N	116.29 E
Lijiang	102	26.57 N	100.15 E
Lijiapuzi	104	40.59 N	123.38 E
Lijiaqiao, Zhg.	105	40.03 N	116.40 E
Lijiaqiao, Zhg.	105	39.47 N	117.47 E
Lijiaqiao, Zhg.	106	31.38 N	120.00 E
Lijiatun	104	41.19 N	121.23 E
Lijiatuo	107	29.28 N	106.33 E
Lijiawobao	104	41.00 N	122.26 E
Lijiaxiang	106	30.57 N	119.59 E
Lijiazao	105	39.17 N	118.19 E
Lijin, Zhg.	98	37.29 N	118.16 E
Lijin, Zhg.	104	41.40 N	121.20 E
Lik ≃	110	18.31 N	102.31 E
Likako	152	0.15 N	21.00 E
Likang	100	22.47 N	120.29 E
Likasi (Jadotville)	154	10.59 S	26.44 E
Likati	152	3.21 N	23.53 E
Likati ≃	152	2.53 N	24.03 E
Likely	182	52.37 N	121.34 W
Likėnai	76	56.12 N	24.37 E
Likete	152	0.43 S	21.25 E
Likhu ≃	124	27.15 N	86.12 E
Liki	112	1.36 S	101.11 E
Likimi	152	2.50 N	20.45 E
Likino	82	55.38 N	37.08 E
Likino-Dulevo	82	55.43 N	38.58 E
Liknes	26	58.19 N	6.59 E
Likoma Island I	154	12.05 S	34.45 E
Likou, Zhg.	100	29.53 N	117.28 E
Likou, Zhg.	100	33.51 N	113.20 E
Likou, Zhg.	106	31.24 N	120.37 E
Likouala □[5]	152	2.00 N	17.30 E
Likouala ≃	152	1.13 S	16.48 E
Likouala aux Herbes ≃	152	0.50 S	17.11 E
Likova ≃	265b	55.34 N	37.21 E
Likstammen ◎	40	58.58 N	17.12 E
Liku	174v	19.02 S	169.47 W
Likupang	112	1.41 N	125.04 E
Likus ≃	236	14.14 N	83.35 W
Likuyu	154	10.20 S	36.14 E
Lilanchengzhen	105	39.12 N	116.43 E
Lilanga	152	0.34 S	23.55 E
Lilasi	124	29.22 N	84.30 E
Lilbert	222	31.44 N	94.54 W
Lilbourn	194	36.35 N	89.36 W
L'Île-Bouchard	32	47.07 N	0.25 E
Lilenga	152	0.54 N	22.06 E
L'Île-Rousse	32	42.38 N	8.56 E
Lili	106	31.00 N	120.42 E
Lilian Point ≻	174d	0.53 S	169.35 E
Lilienfeld	61	48.03 N	15.36 E
Lilienthal	52	53.08 N	8.55 E
Liling	100	27.40 N	113.30 E
Lilio	116	14.08 N	121.26 E
Liljendal	40	60.08 N	14.04 E
Lilla Edet	26	58.08 N	12.08 E
Lillafüred ♠	38	48.07 N	20.38 E
Lillah Bharwanah	123	32.34 N	72.45 E
Lillån	40	59.19 N	15.13 E
Lillby	26	63.28 N	23.00 E
Lille	50	50.38 N	3.04 E
Lille Bælt ʊ	41	55.20 N	9.45 E
Lillebonne	50	49.31 N	0.33 E
Lillehammer	26	61.08 N	10.30 E
Lille-Lesquin, Aéroport ⊠	50	50.35 N	3.07 E
Lillerød	41	55.52 N	12.22 E
Lillers	50	50.34 N	2.29 E
Lillesand	26	58.15 N	8.24 E
Lilleshall	42	52.44 N	2.21 W
Lillestrøm	26	59.57 N	11.05 E
Lille Værløse	41	55.47 N	12.23 E
Lillhärdal	26	61.51 N	14.04 E
Lillian	222	32.30 N	97.11 W
Lillington	192	35.23 N	78.48 W
Lillinonah Lake ◎[1]	207	41.28 N	73.21 W
Lilli Pilli	274a	34.04 S	151.07 E
Lillo	34	39.43 N	3.18 W
Lillooet	182	50.42 N	121.56 W
Lillooet ≃	182	49.45 N	122.08 W
Lillooet Lake ◎	182	50.13 N	122.29 W
Lilly	214	40.25 N	78.37 W
Lilly Creek ≃	222	32.47 N	94.56 W
Liloan	116	10.09 N	125.07 E
Lilongwe	154	13.59 S	33.44 E
Lilo Viejo	252	26.56 S	62.58 W
Liloy	116	8.08 N	122.40 E
Liluāh	272b	22.35 N	88.23 E
Lily	192	37.01 N	84.04 W
Lily Cache Creek ≃	278	41.41 N	88.07 W
Lilydale, Austl.	166	41.15 S	147.13 E
Lilydale, Austl.	169	37.45 S	145.21 E
Lily Dale, N.Y., U.S.	214	42.21 N	79.19 W
Lilyfield	274a	33.52 S	151.10 E
Lilyvale	273d	26.06 S	28.25 E
Lim ≃, Afr.	152	7.54 N	15.46 E
Lim ≃, Jugo.	38	43.45 N	19.13 E
Lima, Arg.	258	34.03 S	59.12 W
Lima, Para.	252	23.54 S	56.20 W
Lima, Perú	248	12.03 S	77.03 W
Lima, Perú	286d	12.03 S	77.03 W
Lima, Sve.	26	60.56 N	13.26 E
Lima, Il., U.S.	219	40.11 N	91.23 W
Lima, Mt., U.S.	202	44.38 N	112.35 W
Lima, N.Y., U.S.	210	42.54 N	77.36 W
Lima, Oh., U.S.	216	40.44 N	84.06 W
Lima, Pa., U.S.	285	39.55 N	75.26 W
Lima □[5]	248	12.00 S	76.35 W
Lima (Limia) ≃, Europe	34	41.41 N	8.50 W
Lima ≃, It.	64	44.00 N	10.35 E
Lima, Punta ≻	240m	18.11 N	65.41 W
Lima-Callao, Aeropuerto Internacional ⊠	286d	12.02 S	77.07 W
Lima Center	216	42.47 N	88.49 W
Limache	252	33.01 S	71.16 W
Lima Duarte	256	21.51 S	43.48 W
Lima Duarte, Serra de ⋏[2]	256	21.54 S	43.52 W
Liman, S.S.S.R.	78	49.36 N	36.27 E
Liman, S.S.S.R.	78	45.41 N	29.45 E
Liman, S.S.S.R.	80	45.47 N	47.14 E
Liman, S.S.S.R.	83	49.21 N	38.57 E
Liman, Yis.	132	33.03 N	35.06 E
Liman ≃	115a	6.29 S	105.48 E
Limanowa	30	49.43 N	20.26 E
Limanskoje	78	46.38 N	30.00 E
Lima Nueva	236	15.23 N	87.56 W
Limão ◆[8]	287b	23.30 S	46.40 W
Limapuluh	114	3.10 N	99.26 E
Lima Reservoir ◎[1]	202	44.38 N	112.17 W
Limarí ≃	252	30.44 S	71.43 W
Limas	112	0.14 N	104.31 E
Limasawa Island I	116	9.56 N	125.05 E
Limassa	152	4.14 N	22.02 E
Limassol → Lemesós	130	34.40 N	33.02 E
Limavady	48	55.03 N	6.57 W
Limaville	214	40.59 N	81.09 W
Limay, Fr.	50	49.00 N	1.44 E
Limay, Pil.	116	14.34 N	120.36 E
Limay ≃	254	38.59 S	68.00 W
Limay Mahuida	252	37.12 S	66.42 W
Limbach-Oberfrohna	54	50.51 N	12.45 E
Limbadi	68	38.33 N	15.58 E
Limbang	108	4.45 N	115.00 E
Limbani	248	14.08 S	69.42 W
Limbara, Monte ∧	71	40.51 N	9.10 E
Limbaži	76	57.31 N	24.42 E
Limbdi	120	22.34 N	71.48 E
Limbe	154	15.49 S	35.03 E
Limbiate	62	45.36 N	9.07 E
Limboto	112	0.37 N	122.57 E
Limbourg	56	50.37 N	5.56 E
Limbrick	262	53.38 N	2.36 W
Limbueta	152	12.30 S	18.42 E
Limbunya	164	17.14 S	129.50 E
Limburg □[4], Bel.	56	51.00 N	5.30 E
Limburg □[4], Ned.	52	51.14 N	5.50 E
Limburg an der Lahn	56	50.23 N	8.04 E
Limburgerhof	56	49.25 N	8.24 E
Limecrest	218	39.54 N	83.48 W
Limefield	262	53.37 N	2.18 W
Limeira	255	22.34 S	47.24 W
Limekiln Canyon V	280	34.18 N	118.33 W
Lime Lake	210	42.26 N	78.29 W
Limen	100	27.07 N	119.19 E
Limena	64	45.29 N	11.50 E
Limentra ≃	64	44.14 N	11.03 E
Limerick, Sk., Can.	184	49.40 N	106.15 W
Limerick, Ire.	48	52.40 N	8.38 W
Limerick, Pa., U.S.	285	40.14 N	75.32 W
Limerick (Luimneach) □[6]	48	52.30 N	9.00 W
Limerick Lake ◎	212	44.54 N	77.37 W
Limerock	207	41.55 N	71.28 W
Lime Springs	190	43.27 N	92.17 W
Limestone, Austl.	162	21.11 S	119.50 E
Limestone, Fl., U.S.	220	27.21 N	81.53 W
Limestone, Me., U.S.	186	46.54 N	67.49 W
Limestone, N.Y., U.S.	210	42.01 N	78.37 W
Limestone, Pa., U.S.	214	41.08 N	79.20 W
Limestone □[6]	222	31.35 N	96.35 W
Limestone ≃	184	56.31 N	94.07 W
Limestone, Lake ◎[1]	222	31.25 N	96.20 W
Limestone Bay ⊂	184	53.50 N	98.50 W
Limestone Canyon V	280	33.45 N	117.41 W
Limestone Creek ≃	210	43.06 N	75.58 W
Limestone Lake ◎, Mb., Can.	184	56.35 N	96.00 W
Limestone Lake ◎, Sk., Can.	184	54.36 N	103.18 W
Limestone Point ≻[1]	184	53.50 N	98.50 W
Limestone Point Lake ◎	184	55.07 N	100.32 W
Lime Street Station ◆[5]	262	53.25 N	2.59 W
Lime Village	180	61.21 N	155.28 W
Limfjorden ʊ	26	56.55 N	9.10 E
Limhamn ◆[8]	41	55.35 N	12.54 E
Limia (Lima) ≃	34	41.41 N	8.50 W
Limina	70	37.56 N	15.17 E
Liminka	26	64.49 N	25.24 E
Liminzhen	98	34.31 N	115.56 E
Limit Brook ≃	283	42.42 N	71.25 W
Limmared	26	57.32 N	13.21 E
Limmaren ◎	40	59.44 N	18.43 E
Limmen	52	52.34 N	4.41 E
Limmen Bight ⊂[3]	164	14.45 S	135.40 E
Limmen Bight ≃	164	15.07 S	135.44 E
Límnos I	38	39.54 N	25.21 E
Limoeiro	250	7.52 S	35.27 W
Limoeiro do Norte	250	5.08 S	38.05 W
Limoges, On., Can.	212	45.20 N	75.15 W
Limoges, Fr.	32	45.50 N	1.16 E
Limoges-Fourches	261	48.38 N	2.40 E
Limogne	32	44.24 N	1.46 E
Limón, C.R.	236	10.00 N	83.02 W
Limón, Hond.	236	15.52 N	85.33 W
Limon, Co., U.S.	198	39.15 N	103.41 W
Limón □[4]	236	10.00 N	83.15 W
Limonar	240p	22.57 N	81.24 W
Limón de Ramos	232	24.43 N	107.08 W
Limone Piemonte	62	44.12 N	7.34 E
Limone sul Garda	64	45.49 N	10.47 E
Limours	50	48.39 N	2.05 E
Limousin, Plateaux du ⋏[1]	32	45.30 N	1.15 E
Limoux	32	43.04 N	2.14 E
Limpopo ≃	156	25.15 S	33.30 E
Limpsfield	42	51.16 N	0.01 E
Limski kanal ⊂	64	45.07 N	13.38 E
Limu	102	25.02 N	110.51 E
Limuling ⋏	110	19.10 N	109.30 E
Limuru	154	1.06 S	36.39 E
Linachamari	24	69.40 N	31.20 E
Līnah	128	28.42 N	43.48 E
Lin'an	106	30.14 N	119.43 E
Linanäs	40	59.28 N	18.31 E
Linao Bay ⊂	116	6.45 N	124.00 E
Linapacan Island I	116	11.27 N	119.49 E
Linapacan Strait ʊ	116	11.37 N	119.56 E
Linares, Chile	252	35.51 S	71.36 W
Linares, Col.	246	1.23 N	77.31 W
Linares, Esp.	34	38.05 N	3.38 W
Linares, Méx.	232	24.52 N	99.34 W
Linariá	38	37.24 N	24.57 E
Linaro, Capo ≻	66	42.02 N	11.50 E
Linas	261	48.38 N	2.16 E
Linas, Monte ∧	71	39.27 N	8.37 E
Linas-Montlhery, Domaine Militaire de ■	261	48.37 N	2.13 E
Linate, Aeroporto di ⊠	62	45.27 N	9.16 E
Lincai	100	33.50 N	114.56 E
Lincang	102	23.45 N	102.20 E
Lince	286d	12.06 S	77.03 W
Linch	200	43.36 N	106.11 W
Lincheng, Zhg.	98	37.27 N	114.29 E
Lincheng, Zhg.	106	30.55 N	119.47 E
Linch'ing → Linqing	98	36.53 N	115.41 E
Lincoln, Arg.	252	34.52 S	61.32 W
Lincoln, On., Can.	212	43.10 N	79.29 W
Lincoln, N.Z.	172	43.39 S	172.29 E
Lincoln, Eng., U.K.	44	53.14 N	0.33 W
Lincoln, Ar., U.S.	194	35.56 N	94.25 W
Lincoln, Ca., U.S.	226	38.53 N	121.17 W
Lincoln, De., U.S.	208	38.52 N	75.25 W
Lincoln, Il., U.S.	219	40.08 N	89.21 W
Lincoln, In., U.S.	216	40.37 N	86.12 W
Lincoln, Ks., U.S.	198	39.02 N	98.08 W
Lincoln, Me., U.S.	188	45.21 N	68.30 W
Lincoln, Ma., U.S.	207	42.25 N	71.18 W
Lincoln, Mi., U.S.	190	44.41 N	83.24 W
Lincoln, Mo., U.S.	194	38.23 N	93.20 W
Lincoln, Mt., U.S.	202	46.57 N	112.40 W
Lincoln, Ne., U.S.	198	40.48 N	96.40 W
Lincoln, N.H., U.S.	188	44.02 N	71.40 W
Lincoln, Pa., U.S.	208	40.12 N	76.12 W
Lincoln, Pa., U.S.	279b	40.18 N	79.51 W
Lincoln, R.I., U.S.	207	41.54 N	71.25 W
Lincoln, Tx., U.S.	222	30.17 N	96.52 W
Lincoln □[6], Mo., U.S.	219	39.05 N	90.57 W
Lincoln □[6], Or., U.S.	224	44.59 N	123.52 W
Lincoln, Mount ∧	200	39.21 N	106.07 W
Lincoln Acres	228	32.40 N	117.04 W
Lincoln Boyhood National Memorial ⊥	194	38.10 N	86.58 W
Lincoln Cathedral ♁[1]	44	53.14 N	0.33 W
Lincoln Center ♁	276	40.46 N	73.59 W
Lincoln City	224	44.57 N	124.00 W
Lincoln Creek ≃, Ne., U.S.	198	40.54 N	97.06 W
Lincoln Creek ≃, Wa., U.S.	224	46.45 N	123.02 W
Lincolndale	210	41.19 N	73.43 W
Lincoln Estates	278	41.31 N	87.49 W
Lincoln Gap	166	32.37 S	137.35 E
Lincoln Heights, Oh., U.S.	214	40.47 N	82.30 W
Lincoln Heights, Oh., U.S.	218	39.15 N	84.28 W
Lincoln Heights, Pa., U.S.	279b	40.19 N	79.37 W
Lincoln Home National Historical Site ⊥	219	39.47 N	89.38 W
Lincolnia Heights	284c	38.50 N	77.09 W
Lincoln Memorial ⊥	284c	38.53 N	77.03 W
Lincoln Park, Co., U.S.	200	38.25 N	105.13 W
Lincoln Park, Ga., U.S.	192	32.52 N	84.19 W
Lincoln Park, Mi., U.S.	216	42.15 N	83.10 W
Lincoln Park, N.J., U.S.	276	40.55 N	74.18 W
Lincoln Park, N.Y., U.S.	210	41.57 N	74.00 W
Lincoln Park ♠, Ca., U.S.	282	37.46 N	122.30 W
Lincoln Park ♠, Il., U.S.	278	41.56 N	87.38 W
Lincoln Park Airport ⊠	276	40.57 N	74.19 W
Lincoln Place ◆[8]	279b	40.22 N	79.55 W
Lincoln Sea ⍑[2]	16	83.00 N	56.00 W
Lincolnshire	216	42.11 N	87.54 W
Lincolnshire □[6]	42	52.55 N	0.22 W
Lincoln's New Salem State Park ♠	219	39.58 N	89.52 W
Lincoln Tomb State Memorial ⊥	219	39.50 N	89.39 W
Lincolnton, Ga., U.S.	192	33.47 N	82.28 W
Lincolnton, N.C., U.S.	192	35.28 N	81.15 W
Lincoln Tunnel ◆[5]	276	40.46 N	74.01 W
Lincoln University	208	39.48 N	75.55 W
Lincoln Village, Ca., U.S.	226	38.00 N	121.19 W
Lincoln Village, Oh., U.S.	218	39.57 N	83.08 W
Lincolnville	214	41.47 N	79.51 W
Lincolnwood	278	42.00 N	87.43 W
Lincolnwood Hills	278	41.31 N	87.54 W
Linconia	285	40.08 N	74.59 W
Lincroft	208	40.19 N	74.07 W
Lind	202	46.58 N	118.36 W
Linda, S.S.S.R.	80	56.37 N	44.07 E
Linda, Ca., U.S.	226	39.07 N	121.32 W
Linda-a-Velha	266c	38.43 N	9.14 W
Lindale, Ga., U.S.	192	34.11 N	85.10 W
Lindale, Tx., U.S.	222	32.30 N	95.24 W
Lindau, B.R.D.	41	54.36 N	9.47 E
Lindau, B.R.D.	52	51.39 N	10.07 E
Lindau, B.R.D.	58	47.33 N	9.41 E
Lindau, D.D.R.	54	52.02 N	12.06 E
Lindbergh	219	39.02 N	92.08 W
Lindbergh Field ⊠	228	32.44 N	117.11 W
Lind Coulee V	202	47.00 N	119.10 W
Linde ≃	74	64.57 N	124.36 E
Lindelse	41	54.52 N	10.44 E
Linden, Al., U.S.	194	32.18 N	87.47 W
Linden, Ca., U.S.	226	38.01 N	121.05 W
Linden, In., U.S.	194	40.11 N	86.54 W
Linden, Mi., U.S.	216	42.48 N	83.46 W
Linden, N.J., U.S.	210	40.37 N	74.14 W
Linden, Pa., U.S.	210	41.14 N	77.08 W
Linden, Pa., U.S.	279b	40.14 N	80.08 W
Linden, Tn., U.S.	194	35.37 N	87.50 W
Linden, Tx., U.S.	194	33.00 N	94.21 W
Linden ◆[8]	273d	26.08 S	28.00 E
Linden Airport ⊠	276	40.37 N	74.15 W
Lindenberg, D.D.R.	54	53.02 N	12.07 E
Lindenberg, D.D.R.	54	52.36 N	13.31 E
Lindenberg, D.D.R.	54	52.12 N	14.07 E
Lindenberg im Allgäu	58	47.36 N	9.53 E
Linden-Dahlhausen ◆[8]	263	51.26 N	7.09 E
Lindenfels	56	49.41 N	8.47 E
Lindenhorst ◆[8]	263	51.33 N	7.27 E
Lindenhurst, Il., U.S.	216	42.24 N	88.01 W
Lindenhurst, N.Y., U.S.	210	40.41 N	73.22 W
Lindenhurst, Pa., U.S.	285	40.14 N	74.54 W
Linden Park	216	40.13 N	85.23 W
Lindenthal	54	51.24 N	12.20 E
Lindenwold	208	39.49 N	74.59 W
Lindenwood, Il., U.S.	216	42.03 N	89.02 W
Lindenwood, In., U.S.	218	39.41 N	86.09 W
Linderhausen	263	51.18 N	7.17 E
Linderhof, Schloss ⊥	64	47.34 N	10.57 E
Lindern	52	52.50 N	7.46 E
Linderöd	41	55.56 N	13.49 E
Linderödsåsen ⋏[2]	26	55.53 N	13.56 E
Lindesay, Mount ∧	162	34.49 S	117.18 E
Lindesberg	40	59.35 N	15.15 E
Lindesnäs	40	60.20 N	14.32 E
Lindesnes ≻	26	58.00 N	7.02 E
Lindfield, Austl.	274a	33.47 S	151.10 E
Lindfield, Eng., U.K.	42	51.01 N	0.05 W
Lindfors	40	59.36 N	13.49 E
Lindholmen	40	59.35 N	18.06 E
Lindhorst	52	52.21 N	9.17 E
Líndhos	38	36.06 N	28.04 E
Líndhos ⊥	38	36.06 N	28.05 E
Lindi	154	10.00 S	39.43 E
Lindi □[4]	154	9.15 S	38.45 E
Lindi ≃	154	0.33 N	25.05 E
Lindian	89	47.11 N	124.52 E
Lindis Pass)(	172	44.36 S	169.40 E
Lindkirchen	60	48.40 N	11.47 E
Lindlar	56	51.01 N	7.23 E
Lindley, S. Afr.	158	28.00 S	27.57 E
Lindley, N.Y., U.S.	210	42.02 N	77.08 W
Lind National Park ♠	166	37.35 S	149.05 E
Lindö	40	58.37 N	16.15 E
Lindóia	256	22.31 S	46.39 W
Lindome	26	57.34 N	12.05 E
Lindon	198	39.44 N	103.24 W
Lindong, Zhg.	100	26.03 N	118.49 E
Lindong, Zhg.	105	39.51 N	117.41 E
Lindow	54	52.58 N	13.00 E
Lind Point ≻	240m	18.20 N	64.48 W
Lindre, Étang de ◎[1]	56	48.47 N	6.45 E
Lindsay, On., Can.	212	44.21 N	78.44 W
Lindsay, Ca., U.S.	204	36.12 N	119.05 W
Lindsay, Ne., U.S.	198	41.42 N	97.41 W
Lindsay, Ok., U.S.	196	34.50 N	97.36 W
Lindsborg	198	38.34 N	97.40 W
Lindsey	214	41.25 N	83.13 W
Lindved	41	55.47 N	9.35 E
Lindy Lake	276	41.05 N	74.22 W
Lineboro	208	39.43 N	76.50 W
Line Creek ≃	194	33.34 N	88.42 W
Line Islands II	14	0.05 N	157.00 W
Line Lexington	208	40.17 N	75.16 W
Line Mountain ∧	210	40.45 N	76.37 W
Linesville	214	41.39 N	80.25 W
Lineville, Al., U.S.	194	33.18 N	85.45 W
Lineville, Ia., U.S.	190	40.34 N	93.31 W
Línevo	86	54.05 N	83.24 E
Linfa	287b	23.44 S	46.56 W
Linfen	102	36.05 N	111.32 E
Linfield	208	40.13 N	75.34 W
Linford	260	51.29 N	0.25 E
Ling ≃	46	57.19 N	5.27 W
Ling'an	106	30.36 N	120.30 E
Linganamakki Reservoir ◎[1]	122	14.04 N	74.54 E
Lingao	102	19.54 N	109.40 E
Lingayen	116	16.01 N	120.14 E
Lingayen Gulf ⊂	116	16.15 N	120.14 E
Lingbi	100	33.33 N	117.33 E
Lingbo	26	61.03 N	16.41 E
Lingchuan, Zhg.	102	25.26 N	110.15 E
Lingchuan, Zhg.	102	35.46 N	113.26 E
Lingda	106	31.12 N	119.18 E
Lingdale	44	54.32 N	0.57 W
Lingdianzhen	106	31.51 N	121.25 E
Lingdou	100	26.22 N	118.56 E
Lingekeke	120	29.59 N	87.33 E
Lingen	52	52.31 N	7.19 E
Lingesestausee ◎[1]	263	51.06 N	7.32 E
Lingfengwei	100	24.44 N	115.35 E
Lingfield	42	51.11 N	0.01 W
Lingga, Kepulauan II	112	0.05 S	104.35 E
Lingga, Pulau I	112	0.12 S	104.35 E
Lingham Lake ◎	212	44.46 N	77.25 W
Linghe	98	36.23 N	119.03 E
Linghu	106	30.44 N	120.10 E
Lingig	116	8.02 N	126.24 E
Lingjiachang	107	29.28 N	104.54 E
Lingjiaqiao	106	30.09 N	120.04 E
Lingkar Dzong	124	28.45 N	90.36 E
Lingkou, Zhg.	100	29.16 N	120.38 E
Lingkou, Zhg.	106	31.57 N	119.38 E
Lingle	200	42.08 N	104.20 W
Linglestown	208	40.21 N	76.48 W
Lingling	102	26.13 N	111.37 E
Linglongta	98	40.54 N	119.59 E
Lingma	102	23.22 N	107.53 E
Lingolsheim	58	48.34 N	7.41 E

	English	Deutsch	Español	Français	Português
≃	River	Fluss	Río	Rivière	Rio
≊	Canal	Kanal	Canal	Canal	Canal
∟	Waterfall, Rapids	Wasserfall, Stromschnellen	Cascada, Rápidos	Chute d'eau, Rapides	Cascata, Rápidos
ʊ	Strait	Meeresstrasse	Estrecho	Détroit	Estreito
⊂	Bay, Gulf	Bucht, Golf	Bahía, Golfo	Baie, Golfe	Baía, Golfo
◎	Lake, Lakes	See, Seen	Lago, Lagos	Lac, Lacs	Lago, Lagos
≡	Swamp	Sumpf	Pantano	Marais	Pântano
⌂	Ice Features, Glacier	Eis- und Gletscherformen	Accidentes Glaciales	Formes glaciaires	Acidentes glaciares
⍑	Other Hydrographic Features	Andere Hydrographische Objekte	Otros Elementos Hidrográficos	Autres données hydrographiques	Outros acidentes hidrográficos
✧	Submarine Features	Untermeerische Objekte	Accidentes Submarinos	Formes de relief sous-marin	Acidentes submarinos
□	Political Unit	Politische Einheit	Unidad Politica	Entité politique	Unidade política
♁	Cultural Institution	Kulturelle Institution	Institución Cultural	Institution culturelle	Institução cultural
⊥	Historical Site	Historische Stätte	Sitio Histórico	Site historique	Sitio histórico
♠	Recreational Site	Erholungs- und Ferienort	Sitio de Recreo	Centre de loisirs	Area de Lazer
⊠	Airport	Flughafen	Aeropuerto	Aéroport	Aeroporto
■	Military Installation	Militäranlage	Instalación Militar	Installation militaire	Instalação militar
◆	Miscellaneous	Verschiedenes	Misceláneo	Divers	Diversos

ENGLISH | DEUTSCH

Name / Name	Page / Seite	Lat.°′ / Breite°′	Long.°′ / Länge°′ E = Ost
Lingomo	152	0.38 N	21.59 E
Lingqiu	98	39.24 N	114.13 E
Lingshan, Zhg.	98	36.33 N	120.27 E
Lingshan, Zhg.	102	22.28 N	109.17 E
Lingshanwei	98	35.58 N	120.13 E
Lingshi	102	36.54 N	111.43 E
Lingshou	98	38.18 N	114.24 E
Lingshui	110	18.31 N	110.01 E
Lingtangqiao	100	32.43 N	119.14 E
Lingu	120	29.26 N	87.36 E
Linguaglossa	70	37.50 N	15.08 E
Linguère	150	15.24 N	15.07 W
Lingwala	273b	4.22 S	15.17 E
Lingwood	42	52.37 N	1.29 E
Lingwu	102	38.06 N	106.21 E
Lingxian, Zhg.	98	37.21 N	116.34 E
Lingxian, Zhg.	100	26.30 N	113.46 E
Lingxiazhu	100	29.03 N	119.46 E
Lingyuan	98	41.15 N	119.16 E
Lingzhuangzi	105	39.04 N	117.09 E
Lingzinan	105	39.29 N	115.15 E
Linh, Ngoc ∧	110	15.04 N	107.59 E
Linhai	100	28.51 N	121.07 E
Linhares	255	19.25 S	40.04 W
Linh-cam	110	18.31 N	105.34 E
Linhe	102	40.51 N	107.30 E
Linhezhuang	105	40.04 N	117.39 E
Linhigh	284b	39.21 N	76.31 W
Linhó	266c	38.46 N	9.23 W
Linhsia → Linxia	102	35.35 N	103.13 E
Linhuaiguan	100	32.55 N	117.40 E
Linhuanji	100	33.42 N	116.33 E
Lini → Linyi	98	35.04 N	118.22 E
Linjiang, Zhg.	98	41.44 N	126.55 E
Linjiang, Zhg.	100	27.50 N	118.26 E
Linjiang, Zhg.	100	28.04 N	115.21 E
Linjiang, Zhg.	102	33.01 N	105.01 E
Linjiangchang	107	29.14 N	105.58 E
Linjianghu	100	28.41 N	117.54 E
Linjiangsi	107	30.15 N	104.37 E
Linjiatai	104	40.43 N	123.57 E
Linkenheim	56	49.07 N	8.24 E
Linköping	26	58.25 N	15.37 E
Linkou	89	45.15 N	130.16 E
Linksfield ◆[8]	273d	26.10 S	28.06 E
Linksmakalnis	76	54.45 N	23.55 E
Linkuva	76	56.05 N	23.59 E
Linkwood	208	38.32 N	75.57 W
Linli	102	29.18 N	111.30 E
Linlithgow	46	55.59 N	3.37 W
Linmeyer	273d	26.16 S	28.04 E
Linn, Ks., U.S.	198	39.40 N	97.05 W
Linn, Mo., U.S.	219	38.29 N	91.51 W
Linn ◆[8]	263	51.20 N	6.38 E
Linnancang	105	39.50 N	117.37 E
Linnansaaren Kansallispuisto ♠	26	62.07 N	28.31 E
Linndale	279a	41.27 N	81.46 W
Linne	52	51.10 N	5.57 E
Linnell	226	36.21 N	119.11 W
Linnés Hammarby ⊥	40	59.49 N	17.46 E
Linney Head >	42	51.38 N	5.04 W
Linn Grove	216	40.38 N	85.01 W
Linnhe, Loch c	46	56.39 N	5.21 W
Linnich	56	50.59 N	6.16 E
Linntown	210	40.58 N	76.54 W
Linnville Bayou ≃	222	28.57 N	95.42 W
Linosa	70a	35.51 N	12.52 E
Linosa, Isola di I	70a	35.51 N	12.52 E
Linovica	78	50.28 N	32.22 E
Lin'ovo	80	50.53 N	44.51 E
Linow	54	53.06 N	12.49 E
Linping → Yuhang	106	30.25 N	120.18 E
Linpu	100	30.03 N	120.15 E
Linqi, Zhg.	98	35.48 N	113.53 E
Linqi, Zhg.	100	29.51 N	119.06 E
Linqing	98	36.53 N	115.41 E
Linqu	98	36.32 N	118.31 E
Linquan	100	33.06 N	115.13 E
Linru	100	34.11 N	112.49 E
Linruzhen	100	34.17 N	112.35 E
Lins	255	21.40 S	49.45 W
Linshan	100	30.09 N	120.59 E
Linshanhe	100	30.44 N	114.52 E
Linshengpu	104	41.34 N	123.20 E
Linshui	102	30.21 N	106.59 E
Linslade	42	51.55 N	0.41 W
Linstead	241q	18.08 N	77.02 W
Linta ≃	157b	25.02 S	44.05 E
Lintan	102	34.37 N	103.40 E
Lintao	102	35.27 N	103.46 E
Linté	152	5.24 N	11.42 E
Linth ≃	58	47.07 N	9.07 E
Linthal, Fr.	58	47.56 N	7.08 E
Linthal, Schw.	58	46.55 N	9.00 E
Linthicum Heights	284b	39.12 N	76.39 W
Linthkanal ≅	58	47.13 N	8.57 E
Linthwaite	262	53.37 N	1.51 W
Lintingkou	105	39.39 N	117.30 E
Linton, Austl.	169	37.41 S	143.34 E
Linton, N.Z.	172	40.26 S	175.33 E
Linton, Eng., U.K.	42	52.06 N	0.17 E
Linton, Eng., U.K.	260	51.13 N	0.31 E
Linton, In., U.S.	194	39.02 N	87.09 W
Linton, N.D., U.S.	198	46.16 N	100.13 W
Lintong	102	34.21 N	109.11 E
Linton Park ♠	260	51.13 N	0.31 E
Linum	264a	52.46 N	12.53 E
Linville, Austl.	171a	26.51 S	152.16 E
Linville, N.C., U.S.	192	36.03 N	81.52 W
Linwood, Austl.	168b	34.21 S	138.46 E
Linwood, In., U.S.	218	40.12 N	85.41 W
Linwood, Ma., U.S.	207	42.05 N	71.38 W
Linwood, N.J., U.S.	208	39.20 N	74.34 W
Linwood, Pa., U.S.	285	39.49 N	75.24 W
Linworth	214	40.06 N	83.04 W
Linwu, Zhg.	98	36.14 N	119.17 E
Linwu, Zhg.	102	25.16 N	112.20 E
Linxi, Zhg.	90	43.30 N	118.00 E
Linxi, Zhg.	98	36.52 N	115.32 E
Linxia	102	35.35 N	103.13 E
Linxian, Zhg.	98	36.04 N	113.50 E
Linxian, Zhg.	102	37.58 N	110.59 E
Linxiang	100	29.28 N	113.30 E
Linyanti	156	18.04 S	24.01 E
Linyanti ≃	156	17.58 S	24.16 E
Linyi, Zhg.	98	35.04 N	118.22 E
Linyi, Zhg.	98	37.13 N	116.51 E
Linyi, Zhg.	102	35.15 N	110.59 E
Linying	100	33.50 N	113.57 E
Linyü → Shanhaiguan	98	40.01 N	119.44 E
Linyüan	100	22.30 N	120.23 E
Linz, B.R.D.	56	50.34 N	7.17 E
Linz, Öst.	61	48.18 N	14.18 E
Linze, Zhg.	100	33.03 N	119.38 E
Linze, Zhg.	102	39.19 N	100.17 E
Linzgau ◆[1]	58	47.45 N	9.16 E
Linzhai	100	24.18 N	115.03 E
Linzhang	98	36.21 N	114.36 E
Linzhi	120	29.25 N	94.22 E
Linzikou	100	28.42 N	112.46 E
Linzolo	152	4.25 S	15.07 E
Lioko, Zaïre	152	0.02 N	22.04 E
Lioko, Zaïre	152	1.25 N	23.07 E
Lio Matoh	112	3.10 N	115.14 E
Liomer	50	49.51 N	1.49 E
Lion, Golfe du c	32	43.00 N	4.00 E
Lionel Town	241q	17.48 N	77.14 W
Lioni	68	40.52 N	15.11 E
Lion Rock ∧[2]	271d	22.22 N	114.11 E
Lion Rock Tunnel ◆[5]	271d	22.21 N	114.09 E
Lions Den	154	17.16 S	30.02 E
Lion's Head	212	44.59 N	81.15 W
Lionville	208	40.03 N	75.39 W
Lioppa	112	7.40 S	126.00 E
Liouesso	152	1.02 N	15.43 E
Liozno	76	55.02 N	30.48 E
Lipa	116	13.57 N	121.10 E
Lipan	196	32.31 N	98.03 W
Lipany	30	49.10 N	20.58 E
Lipari	70	38.28 N	14.57 E
Lipari, Isola I	70	38.29 N	14.56 E
Lipatkain	112	0.01 S	101.13 E
Lipayan	104	42.13 N	123.23 E
Lipcy	78	50.13 N	36.25 E
Lipeck	76	52.37 N	39.35 E
Lipeck □[4]	80	52.15 N	40.30 E
Lipeckoje Vtoroje	78	47.46 N	29.41 E
Liperi	26	62.32 N	29.22 E
Lipetsk → Lipeck	76	52.37 N	39.35 E
Lipez, Cerro ∧	248	21.53 S	66.52 W
Liphook	42	51.05 N	0.49 W
Lipiany	30	53.00 N	14.59 E
Lipicy	76	53.22 N	37.17 E
Lipin Bor	76	60.16 N	37.57 E
Liping	102	26.17 N	109.00 E
Lipis ≃	114	4.10 N	102.04 E
Lipiyu	104	41.09 N	123.36 E
Lipka ≃	265b	55.45 N	37.11 E
Lipkany	78	48.16 N	26.48 E
Lipki	76	53.58 N	37.42 E
Lipník nad Bečvou	30	49.31 N	17.35 E
Lipniški	76	54.00 N	25.37 E
Lipno	30	52.51 N	19.10 E
Lipno, údolní nádrž ⊜[1]	60	48.43 N	14.04 E
Lipno nad Vltavou	61	48.38 N	14.14 E
Lipoa Point >	229a	21.02 N	156.38 W
Lipova	38	46.05 N	21.40 E
Lipovaja Dolina	78	50.35 N	33.48 E
Lipovcy	89	44.11 N	131.44 E
Lipovec	78	49.14 N	29.03 E
Lipovka, S.S.S.R.	78	50.52 N	40.02 E
Lipovka, S.S.S.R.	80	49.46 N	44.56 E
Lipovka, S.S.S.R.	80	52.26 N	46.11 E
Lippborg	52	51.40 N	8.02 E
Lippe ≃	52	51.39 N	6.38 E
Lipperode	52	51.41 N	8.22 E
Lippetal	52	51.40 N	8.06 E
Lippoldsberg	52	51.37 N	9.33 E
Lippolthausen ◆[8]	263	51.37 N	7.29 E
Lippstadt	52	51.40 N	8.19 E
Lipscomb	196	36.14 N	100.16 W
Lipsko	30	51.09 N	21.39 E
Lipsoí I	38	37.20 N	26.45 E
Lipsós I	130	37.20 N	26.45 E
Lipton	184	50.54 N	103.50 W
Liptovská Teplička	30	48.59 N	20.06 E
Liptovský Mikuláš	30	49.06 N	19.37 E
Liptrap, Cape >	166	38.54 S	145.55 E
Lipu	102	24.25 N	110.29 E
Lipu La)(	124	30.21 N	81.05 E
Liqiao	107	29.03 N	104.48 E
Lira, Ug.	154	2.15 N	32.54 E
Lira, Ven.	286c	10.26 N	66.46 W
Liranga	152	0.40 S	17.36 E
Lirangdian	105	39.14 N	116.14 E
Lircay	248	12.56 S	74.43 W
Liren	100	33.55 N	118.47 E
Lirentuncun	104	41.24 N	122.59 E
Liri ≃	66	41.25 N	13.52 E
Liria	34	39.38 N	0.36 W
Liro	175f	16.27 S	168.13 E
Liro ≃	58	46.18 N	9.23 E
Lisa, Punta >	236	8.00 N	80.22 W
Lisakovsk	86	52.36 N	62.37 E
Lisala	152	2.09 N	21.31 E
Lisavy	82	56.33 N	38.32 E
Lisboa (Lisbon), Port.	34	38.43 N	9.08 W
Lisboa (Lisbon), Port.	266c	38.43 N	9.08 W
Lisboa □[5]	266c	38.48 N	9.16 W
Lisboa, Universidade de ❦[2]	266c	38.45 N	9.09 W
Lisbon → Lisboa, Port.	34	38.43 N	9.08 W
Lisbon, Il., U.S.	216	41.29 N	88.29 W
Lisbon, Md., U.S.	208	39.20 N	77.04 W
Lisbon, N.H., U.S.	188	44.12 N	71.54 W
Lisbon, N.D., U.S.	198	46.26 N	97.40 W
Lisbon, Oh., U.S.	214	40.46 N	80.46 W
Lisbon Falls	188	43.59 N	70.03 W
Lisbonne → Lisboa	34	38.43 N	9.08 W
Lisburn	48	54.31 N	6.03 W
Lisburne, Cape >	180	68.52 N	166.14 W
Lisburne Peninsula >[1]	180	68.30 N	165.15 W
Liscannor Bay c	48	52.55 N	9.25 W
Liscarney	48	53.43 N	9.35 W
Liscia ≃, It.	36	41.11 N	9.19 E
Liscia ≃, It.	71	41.11 N	9.19 E
Liscia, Lago di ⊜	71	41.00 N	9.16 E
Lisdoonvarna	48	53.01 N	9.15 W
Lisec	78	48.52 N	24.36 E
Liseleje	41	56.01 N	11.59 E
Lishan, Zhg.	100	31.50 N	113.16 E
Lishan, Zhg.	104	41.10 N	123.00 E
Lishangzhuang	105	39.35 N	118.11 E
Lishanke	98	40.41 N	119.53 E
Lishe	100	29.48 N	121.28 E
Lishe ≃	102	24.18 N	101.32 E
Lishi, Zhg.	102	37.32 N	111.09 E
Lishi, Zhg.	106	31.14 N	120.37 E
Lishi, Zhg.	107	29.10 N	105.42 E
Lishizhen, Zhg.	107	29.04 N	106.15 E
Lishizhen, Zhg.	107	29.20 N	105.24 E
Lishu	89	43.21 N	124.37 E
Lishui, Zhg.	100	28.27 N	119.54 E
Lishui, Zhg.	106	31.39 N	119.01 E
Lishuzhen	89	45.05 N	130.41 E
Lísi	130	35.06 N	33.41 E
Lisianski Island I	14	26.02 N	174.00 W
Lisica ≃	86	58.34 N	85.11 E
Lisičansk	83	48.55 N	38.26 E
Lisichansk → Lisičansk	83	48.55 N	38.26 E
Lisicy	82	56.47 N	36.21 E
Lisieux, Sk., Can.	184	49.17 N	105.59 W
Lisieux, Fr.	50	49.09 N	0.14 E
Lisij Nos	265a	60.01 N	30.00 E
Líšina	60	49.37 N	13.10 E
Lisitu	154	9.39 S	34.39 E
Lisizhuang	105	38.55 N	115.07 E
Lisja	80	57.15 N	54.22 E
Liska ≃	80	48.32 N	43.08 E
Liskeard	42	50.28 N	4.28 W
Liski, S.S.S.R.	78	50.56 N	39.29 E
Liski → Georgiu-Dež, S.S.S.R.	78	50.59 N	39.30 E
Lískova	60	49.25 N	12.43 E
L'Isle, Schw.	58	46.37 N	6.25 E
Lisle, Il., U.S.	216	41.48 N	88.04 W
Lisle, N.Y., U.S.	210	42.21 N	76.00 W
L'Isle-Adam	50	49.07 N	2.14 E
L'Isle Jourdain	32	46.14 N	0.41 E
L'Isle-sur-la-Sorgue	62	43.55 N	5.03 E
L'Isle-sur-le-Doubs	58	47.27 N	6.35 E
L'Isle-sur-Serein	50	47.35 N	4.00 E
Lisman	194	32.10 N	88.16 W
Lismore, Austl.	166	28.48 S	153.17 E
Lismore, Austl.	169	37.58 S	143.20 E
Lismore, N.S., Can.	186	45.42 N	62.16 W
Lismore, Ire.	48	52.08 N	7.55 W
Lismore Castle ⊥	48	52.08 N	7.52 W
Lismore Island I	46	56.29 N	5.33 W
Lisnaskea	48	54.15 N	7.27 W
Lišn'ovka	78	51.28 N	25.25 E
Lisö >[1]	40	58.55 N	17.45 E
Lišov	61	49.01 N	14.37 E
Liss	42	51.03 N	0.55 W
Lissabon → Lisboa	34	38.43 N	9.08 W
Lissberg	56	50.22 N	9.05 E
Lisse	52	52.15 N	4.33 E
Lisses	261	48.36 N	2.26 E
Lissewege	50	51.18 N	3.11 E
Lissie	222	29.33 N	96.13 W
Lissingen	56	50.14 N	6.38 E
Lissone	62	45.37 N	9.14 E
Lissy	261	48.38 N	2.42 E
Lista	80	47.44 N	45.54 E
Lista >[1]	26	58.07 N	6.40 E
Lister ≃	263	51.05 N	7.45 E
Lištica	36	43.23 N	17.36 E
Listowel, On., Can.	212	43.44 N	80.57 W
Listowel, Ire.	48	52.27 N	9.29 W
Listv'anka	88	51.52 N	104.51 E
Listv'anskij	86	54.27 N	83.29 E
Lisui	105	40.05 N	116.44 E
Lit	26	63.19 N	14.49 E
Lita	100	27.22 N	116.34 E
Litang, Malay.	112	5.20 N	118.31 E
Litang, Zhg.	102	23.11 N	109.05 E
Litang, Zhg.	102	30.00 N	100.16 E
Litang ≃	102	28.04 N	101.30 E
Litani (Itany) ≃	250	3.40 N	54.00 W
Līṭānī, Nahr al- ≃	132	33.20 N	35.14 E
Litava ≃	61	49.02 N	16.36 E
Litcham	42	52.44 N	0.47 E
Litchfield, Ct., U.S.	207	41.44 N	73.11 W
Litchfield, Il., U.S.	219	39.10 N	89.39 W
Litchfield, Mi., U.S.	216	42.02 N	84.45 W
Litchfield, Mn., U.S.	190	45.07 N	94.31 W
Litchfield, Ne., U.S.	198	41.09 N	99.09 W
Litchfield, Oh., U.S.	214	41.10 N	82.02 W
Litchfield □[6]	207	41.45 N	73.11 W
Litchfield Park	200	33.29 N	112.21 W
Litchville	198	46.39 N	98.11 W
Literberry	219	39.51 N	90.12 W
Līth, Wādī al- V	144	20.40 N	40.35 E
Litherland	44	53.28 N	2.59 W
Lithgow	170	33.29 S	150.09 E
Lithia	220	27.51 N	82.10 W
Líthinon, Ákra >	38	34.55 N	24.44 E
Lithonia	192	33.42 N	84.06 W
Lithuania → Litovskaja Sovetskaja Socialističeskaja Respublika □[3]	76	56.00 N	24.00 E
Litian	100	26.58 N	114.10 E
Litija	36	46.03 N	14.50 E
Litin	78	49.20 N	28.05 E
Litipāra	124	24.42 N	87.37 E
Lititz	208	40.09 N	76.18 W
Litke	89	53.57 N	140.15 E
Litókhoron	38	40.06 N	22.30 E
Litoko	154	1.13 S	24.47 E
Litoměřice	54	50.35 N	14.09 E
Litomyšl	30	49.52 N	16.19 E
Litoo	154	9.54 S	38.24 E
Litoral, Cordillera del ⋏	286c	10.33 N	66.52 W
Litouqiao	106	31.15 N	118.54 E
Litovel	30	49.42 N	17.05 E
Litovko	89	49.15 N	135.11 E
Litovskaja Sovetskaja Socialističeskaja Respublika □[3]	76	56.00 N	24.00 E
Litschau	61	48.57 N	15.03 E
Littau	58	47.03 N	8.16 E
Little ≃, Austl.	169	38.01 S	144.35 E
Little ≃, On., Can.	281	42.20 N	82.56 W
Little ≃, U.S.	194	35.32 N	90.25 W
Little ≃, U.S.	194	33.37 N	93.52 W
Little ≃, Al., U.S.	194	31.18 N	87.46 W
Little ≃, Al., U.S.	194	34.16 N	85.40 W
Little ≃, Ct., U.S.	207	41.36 N	72.03 W
Little ≃, Ga., U.S.	192	33.14 N	83.24 W
Little ≃, Ga., U.S.	192	30.51 N	83.21 W
Little ≃, Ga., U.S.	192	33.39 N	82.32 W
Little ≃, In., U.S.	216	40.53 N	85.32 W
Little ≃, Ky., U.S.	194	36.51 N	87.58 W
Little ≃, La., U.S.	194	31.38 N	91.49 W
Little ≃, Ma., U.S.	283	42.37 N	70.42 W
Little ≃, Ma., U.S.	283	42.46 N	70.51 W
Little ≃, N.Y., U.S.	210	43.18 N	75.43 W
Little ≃, N.C., U.S.	192	35.15 N	78.42 W
Little ≃, N.C., U.S.	192	35.21 N	78.02 W
Little ≃, Ok., U.S.	196	35.00 N	96.25 W
Little ≃, S.C., U.S.	192	34.10 N	81.11 W
Little ≃, S.C., U.S.	192	33.56 N	82.25 W
Little ≃, S.C., U.S.	192	34.11 N	81.45 W
Little ≃, Tn., U.S.	192	35.51 N	83.57 W
Little ≃, Tx., U.S.	222	30.51 N	96.41 W
Little ≃, Va., U.S.	192	37.05 N	80.32 W
Little ≃, Va., U.S.	208	37.49 N	77.26 W
Little, Mountain Fork ≃	194	33.57 N	94.34 W
Little Abaco Island I	238	26.53 N	77.43 W
Little Amwell	260	51.47 N	0.02 W
Little Andaman I	110	10.45 N	92.30 E
Little Arkansas ≃	198	37.43 N	97.22 W
Little Auglaize ≃	216	41.07 N	84.25 W
Little Averill Lake ⊜	206	44.57 N	71.44 W
Little Avon ≃	42	51.42 N	2.28 W
Little Baddow	260	51.44 N	0.35 E
Little Barrier Island I	172	36.12 S	175.05 E
Little Bay	186	47.41 N	58.24 W
Little Bay c	276	40.48 N	73.47 W
Little Bay Islands	186	49.39 N	55.47 W
Little Bear ≃	200	41.42 N	111.57 W
Little Bear Creek ≃	196	37.43 N	101.43 W
Little Bear Creek Reservoir ⊜[1]	194	34.25 N	87.57 W
Little Beaver Creek ≃, U.S.	198	46.17 N	103.56 W
Little Beaver Creek ≃, U.S.	198	39.49 N	101.03 W
Little Beaver Creek ≃, U.S.	214	40.38 N	80.31 W
Little Beaver Creek ≃, Wa., U.S.	224	48.54 N	121.06 W
Little Beaver Creek, Middle Fork ≃	214	40.43 N	80.37 W
Little Beaver Creek, North Fork ≃	214	40.43 N	80.33 W
Little Beaver Creek, West Fork ≃	214	40.43 N	80.37 W
Little Belt Mountains ⋏	202	46.45 N	110.35 W
Little Berkhamsted	260	51.45 N	0.08 W
Little Bighorn ≃	202	45.44 N	107.34 W
Little Billabong	171b	35.35 S	147.32 E
Little Bitter Lake → Murrah aṣ-Ṣughrā, Al-Buḥayrah al- ⊜	142	30.13 N	32.33 E
Little Bitterroot ≃	202	47.30 N	114.19 W
Little Black ≃, U.S.	194	36.25 N	90.45 W
Little Black ≃, Ak., U.S.	180	66.26 N	143.49 W
Little Black Bear Indian Reserve ◆[4]	184	51.00 N	103.23 W
Little Blackfoot ≃	202	46.31 N	112.48 W
Little Blue ≃, U.S.	198	39.41 N	96.40 W
Little Blue ≃, In., U.S.	218	39.32 N	85.46 W
Littleborough	44	53.39 N	2.05 W
Little Bow ≃	182	49.53 N	112.29 W
Little Brazos ≃	222	30.38 N	96.31 W
Little Brokenstraw Creek ≃	214	41.50 N	79.23 W
Little Brosna ≃	48	53.10 N	8.05 W
Little Buffalo ≃	176	61.00 N	113.46 W
Little Bullhead	184	51.40 N	96.51 W
Little Burstead	260	51.36 N	0.24 E
Little Calumet ≃	278	41.39 N	87.34 W
Little Catalina	186	48.33 N	53.02 W
Little Cayman I	238	19.41 N	80.03 W
Little Cedar ≃	190	42.57 N	92.31 W
Little Chalfont	260	51.40 N	0.34 W
Little Chartiers Creek ≃	279b	40.17 N	80.08 W
Little Choptank River c	208	38.32 N	76.13 W
Little Churchill ≃	184	57.15 N	95.21 W
Little Chute	190	44.16 N	88.19 W
Little Coco Island I	110	14.00 N	93.13 E
Little Colorado ≃	200	36.11 N	111.48 W
Little Compton	207	41.30 N	71.10 W
Little Cooley	214	41.44 N	79.53 W
Little Cottonwood ≃	198	44.15 N	94.20 W
Little Creek	208	39.10 N	75.26 W
Little Creek ≃	285	39.56 N	74.48 W
Little Creek Naval Amphibious Base ■	208	36.55 N	76.10 W
Little Creek Reservoir ⊜[1]	208	37.20 N	76.50 W
Little Cumbrae Island I	46	55.43 N	4.57 W
Little Current	190	45.58 N	81.56 W
Little Current ≃	176	50.57 N	84.36 W
Little Cypress Bayou ≃	194	32.41 N	94.15 W
Little Cypress Creek ≃	222	32.39 N	94.42 W
Little Darby Creek ≃	218	39.53 N	83.13 W
Little Dart ≃	42	50.54 N	3.51 W
Little Deep Creek ≃	198	48.35 N	100.52 W
Little Deer Creek ≃, In., U.S.	216	40.36 N	86.28 W
Little Deer Creek ≃, Pa., U.S.	279b	40.33 N	79.50 W
Little Deschutes ≃	202	43.51 N	121.27 W
Little Desert ◆[2]	166	36.35 S	141.20 E
Little Diomede Island I	180	65.45 N	168.57 W
Little Don ≃	275b	43.42 N	79.20 W
Little Dry Creek ≃, Ca., U.S.	226	39.22 N	121.52 W
Little Dry Creek ≃, Mt., U.S.	202	47.21 N	106.22 W
Little Ease Run ≃	285	39.39 N	75.04 W
Little Eau Pleine ≃	190	44.40 N	89.41 W
Little Egg Harbor c	208	39.35 N	74.18 W
Little Elkhart ≃	216	41.43 N	85.49 W
Little End	260	51.41 N	0.14 E
Little Etobicoke Creek ≃	275b	43.37 N	79.34 W
Little Fabius ≃	219	39.59 N	91.59 W
Little Falls, Mn., U.S.	190	45.58 N	94.21 W
Little Falls, N.J., U.S.	276	40.52 N	74.12 W
Little Falls, N.Y., U.S.	210	43.02 N	74.51 W
Little Falls ≃	208	39.36 N	76.38 W
Little Falls Dam ◆[6]	284c	38.57 N	77.08 W
Little Farms	218	39.57 N	83.10 W
Little Ferry	276	40.51 N	74.02 W
Littlefield	196	33.55 N	102.19 W
Little Flatrock ≃	218	39.26 N	85.33 W
Littlefork	190	48.23 N	93.33 W
Little Fork ≃	190	48.31 N	93.35 W
Little Fort	182	51.25 N	120.12 W
Little Genesee	210	42.02 N	78.13 W
Little Gold ≃	162	18.01 S	126.29 E
Little Gunpowder Falls ≃	208	39.23 N	76.22 W
Littlehampton	42	50.48 N	0.33 W
Little Harbour Deep	186	50.15 N	56.33 W
Little Haw Creek ≃	192	29.23 N	81.24 W
Little Hawk Lake ⊜	212	45.10 N	78.42 W
Little Hoosic ≃	210	42.49 N	73.20 W
Little Hope	214	42.06 N	79.49 W
Little Hulton	262	53.32 N	2.25 W
Little Humboldt ≃	204	41.00 N	117.43 W
Little Humboldt, North Fork ≃	204	41.24 N	117.10 W
Little Humboldt, South Fork ≃	204	41.24 N	117.10 W
Little Hurricane Creek ≃	192	31.23 N	82.19 W
Little Inagua I	238	21.30 N	73.00 W
Little Indian Creek ≃, Il., U.S.	216	41.31 N	88.46 W
Little Indian Creek ≃, In., U.S.	218	38.12 N	86.08 W
Little Island Pond ⊜	283	42.43 N	71.17 W
Littlejohns Creek ≃	226	37.52 N	121.14 W
Little Juniata ≃	214	40.34 N	78.03 W
Little Juniata Creek ≃	208	40.23 N	77.02 W
Little Kanawha ≃	188	39.16 N	81.34 W
Little Kanawha, West Fork ≃	188	38.57 N	81.16 W
Little Karroo (Klein Karroo) ⋏[1]	158	33.45 S	21.30 E
Little Kentucky ≃	218	38.41 N	85.12 W
Little Klickitat ≃	224	45.51 N	121.04 W
Little Koniuji Island I	180	55.01 N	159.26 W
Little Lake ⊜, On., Can.	212	44.26 N	79.40 W
Little Lake ⊜, La., U.S.	194	29.30 N	90.10 W
Little Laramie ≃	200	41.28 N	105.44 W
Little Laver	260	51.46 N	0.14 E
Little Leigh	262	53.17 N	2.35 W
Little Lever	262	53.34 N	2.22 W
Little Limestone Lake ⊜	184	53.46 N	99.18 W
Little London	241q	18.15 N	78.13 W
Little Lost ≃	202	43.46 N	112.58 W
Little Lun ≃	116	6.02 N	125.17 E
Little Mahoning Creek ≃	214	40.49 N	79.00 W
Little Maitland ≃	212	43.52 N	81.18 W
Little Manatee ≃	220	27.42 N	82.28 W
Little Manatee, South Fork ≃	220	27.39 N	82.18 W
Little Manistee ≃	190	44.15 N	86.19 W
Little Manitou Lake ⊜	184	51.45 N	105.30 W
Little Marco Pass c	220	26.01 N	81.46 W
Little Marsh	210	41.53 N	77.24 W
Little Meadows	210	41.59 N	76.08 W
Little Mecatina ≃	176	50.28 N	59.35 W
Little Medicine Bow ≃	200	41.58 N	106.18 W
Little Mexico	196	30.57 N	102.52 W
Little Miami ≃	218	39.05 N	84.26 W
Little Miami, East Fork ≃	218	39.09 N	84.18 W
Little Miami, North Fork ≃	218	39.48 N	83.47 W
Little Miami, Todd Fork ≃	218	39.21 N	84.08 W
Little Miami, Todd Fork, East Fork ≃	218	39.24 N	84.00 W
Littlemill	46	57.32 N	3.49 W
Little Minch ʊ	46	57.35 N	6.55 W
Little Mississippi ≃	212	45.17 N	77.35 W
Little Missouri ≃, U.S.	198	47.30 N	102.25 W
Little Missouri ≃, Ar., U.S.	194	33.49 N	92.54 W
Little Mountain ∧	208	40.47 N	76.40 W
Little Muddy ≃, Il., U.S.	194	37.50 N	89.11 W
Little Muddy ≃, N.D., U.S.	198	48.12 N	103.36 W
Little Mulberry Creek ≃	194	32.26 N	86.51 W
Little Naches ≃	224	46.58 N	121.08 W
Little Nahant	283	42.25 N	70.56 W
Little Namaqualand □[9]	156	29.00 S	17.00 E
Little Neck	283	42.42 N	70.48 W
Little Neck ◆[8]	276	40.46 N	73.44 W
Little Neck Bay c	276	40.47 N	73.46 W
Little Nemaha ≃	198	40.19 N	95.40 W
Little Neshaminy Creek ≃	285	40.15 N	75.02 W
Little Niangua ≃	194	38.04 N	92.54 W
Little Nicobar I	110	7.20 N	93.40 E
Little Ohoopee ≃	192	32.27 N	82.24 W
Little Osage ≃	194	38.02 N	94.14 W
Little Otter Creek ≃	212	42.44 N	80.51 W
Little Ouse ≃	42	52.30 N	0.22 E
Little Panoche Creek ≃	226	36.50 N	120.42 W
Little Patuxent ≃	284b	39.11 N	76.52 W
Little Paxton	42	52.15 N	0.15 W
Little Peconic Bay c	207	40.59 N	72.24 W
Little Pee Dee ≃	192	33.42 N	79.11 W
Little Pic ≃	190	48.48 N	86.37 W
Little Pine and Lucky Man Indian Reserve ◆[4]	184	52.56 N	109.05 W
Little Pine Creek ≃, Pa., U.S.	210	41.18 N	77.22 W
Little Pine Creek ≃, Pa., U.S.	279b	40.31 N	79.57 W
Little Pine Island I	220	26.36 N	82.05 W
Little Pine Key I	220	24.44 N	81.19 W
Little Pine State Park ♠	210	41.22 N	77.20 W
Little Pipe Creek ≃	208	39.36 N	77.16 W
Little Platte ≃	194	39.24 N	94.41 W
Little Plum Creek ≃	279b	40.30 N	79.51 W
Little Popo Aggie ≃	202	42.54 N	108.35 W
Little Porcupine Creek ≃, Mt., U.S.	202	46.18 N	106.34 W
Little Porcupine Creek ≃, Mt., U.S.	202	48.02 N	106.04 W
Littleport	42	52.28 N	0.19 E
Little Portage Creek ≃	216	42.00 N	85.27 W
Little Powder ≃	198	45.28 N	105.20 W
Little Pucketa Creek ≃	279b	40.33 N	79.45 W
Little Quill Lake ⊜	184	51.55 N	104.05 W
Little Rann of Kutch ≚	120	23.25 N	71.15 E
Little Red ≃	194	35.11 N	91.27 W
Little Red, Middle Fork ≃	194	35.37 N	92.11 W
Little Red Deer ≃	182	52.04 N	114.09 W
Little Red River Indian Reserve ◆[4]	184	53.30 N	105.58 W
Little Redstone Lake ⊜	212	45.13 N	78.34 W
Little River, Austl.	169	37.58 S	144.30 E
Little River, N.Z.	172	43.46 S	172.47 E
Little River, Ks., U.S.	198	38.23 N	98.00 W
Little River, Tx., U.S.	222	30.59 N	97.22 W
Little Rock, Ar., U.S.	194	34.44 N	92.17 W
Littlerock, Ca., U.S.	228	34.31 N	117.59 W
Little Rock, Il., U.S.	216	41.43 N	88.34 W
Little Rock, Ia., U.S.	198	43.26 N	95.52 W
Littlerock, Wa., U.S.	224	46.54 N	123.01 W
Little Rock ≃	198	43.16 N	96.15 W
Little Rock Air Force Base ■	194	34.55 N	92.10 W
Little Rock Creek ≃	228	34.28 N	118.01 W
Little Rock Wash V	228	34.42 N	118.02 W
Little Rocky Mountains ⋏	202	47.50 N	108.10 W
Little Rouge Creek ≃	212	43.48 N	79.08 W
Little Ruaha ≃	154	7.17 S	35.28 E
Little Sable Point >	190	43.38 N	86.32 W
Little Sac ≃	194	37.39 N	93.46 W
Little Sachigo Lake ⊜	184	54.09 N	92.11 W
Little Saint Bernard Pass → Petit-Saint-Bernard, Col du)(	62	45.41 N	6.53 E
Little Salkehatchie ≃	192	32.37 N	80.53 W
Little Salmon ≃, Id., U.S.	202	45.25 N	116.19 W
Little Salmon ≃, N.Y., U.S.	212	43.32 N	76.16 W
Little Salmon, North Branch ≃	212	43.24 N	76.09 W
Little Salmon, South Branch ≃	212	43.24 N	76.09 W
Little Salmon Lake ⊜	180	62.12 N	134.45 W
Little Salt Lake ⊜	200	37.55 N	112.53 W
Little Sandy ≃	188	38.35 N	82.51 W
Little Sandy, East Fork ≃	188	38.30 N	82.50 W
Little Sandy Creek ≃	200	42.06 N	109.27 W
Little Saskatchewan ≃	184	49.52 N	100.07 W
Little Scarcies ≃	150	8.51 N	13.09 W
Little Scioto ≃, Oh., U.S.	214	40.31 N	83.12 W
Little Scioto ≃, Oh., U.S.	218	38.46 N	82.53 W
Little Sewickley Creek ≃, Pa., U.S.	279b	40.15 N	79.45 W
Little Sewickley Creek ≃, Pa., U.S.	279b	40.33 N	80.12 W
Little Silver	276	40.20 N	74.02 W
Little Sioux ≃	198	41.49 N	96.04 W
Little Sioux, West Fork ≃	198	42.04 N	96.00 W
Little Sitkin Island I	181a	51.55 N	178.30 E
Little Smoky ≃	182	55.42 N	117.38 W
Little Snake ≃	200	40.27 N	108.26 W
Little Sodus Bay c	210	43.20 N	76.43 W
Little Southwest Miramichi ≃	186	46.57 N	65.50 W
Little Stanney	262	53.15 N	2.53 W
Little Stony Creek ≃	226	39.20 N	122.31 W
Little Stour ≃	42	51.19 N	1.15 E
Littlestown	208	39.44 N	77.05 W
Little Stukeley	42	52.21 N	0.13 W
Little Sugarloaf ∧[2]	274b	37.41 S	145.19 E
Little Sur ≃	226	36.20 N	121.54 W
Little Sutton	262	53.17 N	2.57 W
Little Swatara Creek ≃	208	40.24 N	76.29 W
Little Tallapoosa ≃	192	33.18 N	85.34 W
Little Tanaga Island I	180	51.48 N	176.10 W
Little Tennessee ≃	192	35.47 N	84.15 W
Little Thurrock	260	51.28 N	0.21 E
Little Timber Creek ≃	285	39.53 N	75.08 W
Little Tinicum Island I	285	39.51 N	75.17 W
Little Tobago I, Br. Vir. Is.	240m	18.26 N	64.51 W
Little Tobago I, Trin.	241r	11.18 N	60.30 W
Little Toby Creek ≃	214	41.22 N	78.49 W
Littleton, Eng., U.K.	260	51.24 N	0.28 W
Littleton, Co., U.S.	200	39.36 N	105.00 W
Littleton, Ma., U.S.	207	42.32 N	71.30 W
Littleton, N.H., U.S.	188	44.18 N	71.46 W
Littleton, N.C., U.S.	192	36.26 N	77.54 W
Littleton, W.V., U.S.	188	39.41 N	80.31 W
Little Traverse Bay c	190	45.24 N	85.03 W
Little Truckee ≃	226	39.25 N	120.05 W
Little Turtle ≃	184	48.46 N	92.36 W
Little Turtle State Recreation Area ♠	216	40.50 N	85.26 W
Little Valley	210	42.15 N	78.48 W
Little Vermilion ≃	216	41.20 N	89.05 W
Little Vermilion Lake ⊜	184	51.16 N	93.50 W
Little Vienna Estates	284c	38.54 N	77.18 W
Little Wabash ≃	194	37.54 N	88.05 W
Little Walsingham	42	52.54 N	0.51 E
Little Waltham	260	51.47 N	0.29 E
Little Warley	260	51.35 N	0.19 E
Little Washita ≃	196	34.58 N	97.51 W
Little White ≃	198	43.44 N	100.40 W
Little White Mountain ∧	182	49.42 N	119.20 W
Little White Salmon ≃	224	45.43 N	121.38 W
Little Wichita ≃	196	33.54 N	97.59 W
Little Wichita, East Fork ≃	196	33.52 N	98.07 W
Little Wind ≃	202	42.57 N	108.29 W
Little Wind, North Fork ≃	202	43.01 N	108.53 W
Little Wind, South Fork ≃	202	43.01 N	108.53 W
Little Wolf ≃	190	44.23 N	88.48 W
Little Wood ≃	202	42.57 N	114.21 W
Little York, In., U.S.	218	38.42 N	85.54 W
Little York, N.Y., U.S.	210	42.42 N	76.10 W
Little Zab (Zāb-e Kūchek) (Az-Zāb aṣ-Ṣaghīr) ≃	128	35.12 N	43.25 E
Littoral □[4]	152	4.13 N	10.25 E
Litunga	152	13.17 S	16.43 E
Litvínov	54	50.37 N	13.36 E
Litvinovka	83	49.18 N	39.27 E
Litvinovo	76	59.34 N	38.01 E
Litvinskoje	86	50.42 N	72.42 E
Litzmannstadt → Łódź	30	51.46 N	19.30 E
Liu ≃, Zhg.	98	41.48 N	122.43 E
Liu ≃, Zhg.	98	42.45 N	126.04 E
Liu ≃, Zhg.	98	40.38 N	118.09 E
Liu ≃, Zhg.	102	23.52 N	109.45 E
Liu ≃, Zhg.	105	40.38 N	118.09 E
Liu ≃, Zhg.	106	31.31 N	121.18 E
Liuanzhuang	105	39.14 N	117.11 E
Liuba	102	33.32 N	107.07 E
Liubotong	100	31.26 N	116.00 E
Liucao	106	31.07 N	121.41 E
Liuchen	102	23.09 N	110.29 E
Liucheng, Zhg.	100	24.03 N	115.08 E
Liucheng, Zhg.	100	28.36 N	119.34 E
Liucheng, Zhg.	102	24.32 N	109.21 E
Liuchengba	102	27.27 N	102.53 E
Liuch'iu Hsü I	100	22.21 N	120.22 E
Liuchow → Liuzhou	102	24.19 N	109.24 E
Liucun	106	30.44 N	119.23 E
Liucura	252	38.39 S	71.05 W
Liudaogou	98	41.34 N	127.12 E
Liudaohe	105	40.39 N	116.12 E
Liudongqiao	106	31.03 N	119.32 E
Liudu	100	26.44 N	119.33 E
Liuduo	100	34.01 N	120.17 E
Liuduzhuang	105	39.27 N	117.50 E
Liuerbao	104	41.13 N	122.55 E
Liufang	100	27.56 N	116.22 E
Liufangling	100	30.27 N	114.27 E
Liufentzu	269d	24.57 N	121.35 E
Liugezhuang, Zhg.	98	38.33 N	116.30 E
Liugezhuang, Zhg.	105	40.03 N	118.16 E
Liugou	105	40.57 N	118.18 E
Liugu ≃	98	40.22 N	120.26 E
Liuguan	100	29.56 N	113.08 E
Liuguantun	104	41.20 N	121.21 E
Liuhang	106	31.21 N	121.22 E
Liuhe, Zhg.	98	42.15 N	125.43 E
Liuhe, Zhg.	100	33.20 N	112.48 E
Liuhe, Zhg.	100	30.20 N	115.36 E
Liuhe, Zhg.	100	30.46 N	113.12 E
Liuhe, Zhg.	100	32.22 N	118.49 E
Liuhe, Zhg.	105	39.31 N	118.17 E
Liuhe, Zhg.	106	31.30 N	121.15 E
Liuhegou	104	41.56 N	122.44 E
Liuheita	104	42.09 N	123.56 E
Liuhejie	102	24.26 N	101.35 E
Liuhekou	105	40.39 N	118.09 E
Liuheng Dao I	100	29.43 N	122.08 E
Liuhuang	100	23.58 N	116.28 E
Liuhudang	104	42.31 N	122.22 E
Liujia	102	24.54 N	107.49 E
Liujiachang	107	29.46 N	103.49 E
Liujiachuan	105	40.07 N	114.47 E
Liujiadai	106	31.57 N	120.23 E
Liujiadian	89	50.07 N	124.17 E
Liujiadu	106	32.15 N	120.33 E
Liujiafen	105	39.58 N	115.47 E
Liujiagangzi	104	41.28 N	122.33 E
Liujiagou	98	37.47 N	120.53 E
Liujiahe, Zhg.	100	32.06 N	113.21 E
Liujiahe, Zhg.	104	40.40 N	123.58 E
Liujiang	98	40.04 N	119.34 E
Liujiashan	105	40.14 N	114.49 E
Liujiatun, Zhg.	104	41.52 N	122.44 E
Liujiatun, Zhg.	104	41.51 N	122.05 E
Liujiatun, Zhg.	104	42.08 N	122.44 E
Liujiawopeng	104	42.16 N	123.01 E
Liujiazhai	269b	31.21 N	121.27 E
Liujiazhen	106	32.04 N	121.30 E
Liujiazi, Zhg.	98	41.00 N	120.13 E
Liujiazi, Zhg.	104	42.36 N	122.15 E
Liujiazi, Zhg.	104	41.48 N	123.47 E
Liujingcun	105	39.27 N	115.26 E
Liujisu	105	40.01 N	117.13 E
Liukang Tenggaya, Kepulauan II	112	6.45 S	118.50 E
Liukeshu	86	44.59 N	90.12 E
Liuku	102	25.48 N	98.52 E
Liuli	154	11.05 S	34.38 E
Liulicun	271a	39.56 N	116.28 E
Liulidian	106	31.31 N	119.17 E
Liuligou	104	41.24 N	121.29 E
Liulihezhen	105	39.36 N	116.01 E
Liulin	100	31.34 N	113.14 E
Liuliwei	100	24.20 N	114.03 E
Liulongtai	104	41.32 N	120.56 E
Liumachang	107	29.51 N	104.54 E
Liumaogou	89	48.12 N	127.13 E
Liupangtun	104	41.36 N	123.28 E
Liupan Shan ⋏	102	35.40 N	106.40 E
Liuqianhutun	104	42.01 N	123.41 E
Liuqiao	106	32.11 N	120.51 E
Liuquan, Zhg.	98	34.27 N	117.20 E
Liuquan, Zhg.	105	39.22 N	116.18 E
Liurenba	100	29.57 N	114.49 E
Liushi, Zhg.	98	38.33 N	115.44 E
Liushi, Zhg.	100	28.03 N	120.51 E
Liushilipu	100	32.45 N	115.58 E
Liushishan ∧	120	36.15 N	82.05 E
Liushouying	98	39.48 N	119.19 E
Liushudian	98	35.54 N	119.30 E
Liushudixia	104	42.26 N	121.14 E
Liushui	89	44.17 N	124.15 E
Liushuigou	100	31.34 N	112.27 E
Liushuquan	105	39.21 N	118.06 E
Liusiqiao	100	29.47 N	116.21 E
Liusong	105	39.40 N	117.08 E
Liuta	98	35.52 N	115.18 E
Liutai	98	41.20 N	113.43 E
Liutaizi	104	41.46 N	122.39 E
Liutang	102	24.58 N	110.21 E
Liutiaozhaicun	104	41.29 N	123.12 E
Liutuan	98	36.56 N	119.22 E
Liutuhutun	104	40.44 N	120.32 E
Liuwanglou	98	34.48 N	116.28 E
Liuwa Plain ≚	152	14.30 S	22.40 E
Liuwa Plain National Park ♠	152	14.30 S	22.40 E
Liuwei	106	32.16 N	119.28 E
Liuwudian	100	24.36 N	118.13 E
Liuxi ≃	100	23.22 N	112.54 E
Liuxia	106	30.15 N	120.03 E
Liuyang	100	28.09 N	113.38 E
Liuyang ≃	100	28.13 N	112.58 E
Liuyuan	98	36.10 N	114.34 E
Liuyuankou	98	34.54 N	114.20 E
Liuzhai	102	25.15 N	107.20 E
Liuzhou	102	24.19 N	109.24 E
Liuzhuang	100	33.10 N	120.19 E
Livada	38	47.52 N	23.07 E
Livadija	89	42.50 N	132.39 E
Livanátai	38	38.42 N	23.03 E
Līvāni	76	56.22 N	26.11 E
Livanjsko Polje ≚	36	43.55 N	16.45 E
Livanovka	86	52.06 N	61.59 E
Livarot	50	49.01 N	0.09 E
Lively, On., Can.	190	46.26 N	81.09 W
Lively, Va., U.S.	208	37.47 N	76.31 W
Lively Island I	254	52.02 S	58.30 W
Livengood	180	65.32 N	148.33 W
Livenka, S.S.S.R.	78	50.44 N	40.14 E
Livenka, S.S.S.R.	78	50.26 N	38.18 E
Livenza ≃	64	45.35 N	12.51 E
Live Oak, Ca., U.S.	226	39.16 N	121.39 W
Live Oak, Fl., U.S.	192	30.17 N	82.59 W
Live Oak Creek ≃	196	30.39 N	101.42 W
Liverdun	56	48.45 N	6.03 E
Liverdy-en-Brie	261	48.42 N	2.47 E
Livergnano	66	44.19 N	11.21 E
Liveringa	162	18.03 S	124.10 E
Livermore, Ca., U.S.	226	37.40 N	121.46 W

Symbols in the index entries represent the broad categories identified in the key at the right. Symbols with superior numbers (⋏[1]) identify subcategories (see complete key on page *I* · *1*).

Kartensymbole in dem Registerverzeichnis stellen die rechts in Schlüssel erklärten Kategorien dar. Symbole mit hochgestellten Ziffern (⋏[1]) bezeichnen Unterabteilungen einer Kategorie (vgl. vollständiger Schlüssel auf Seite *I* · *1*).

Los símbolos incluídos en el texto del índice representan las grandes categorias identificadas con la clave a la derecha. Los símbolos con numeros en su parte superior (⋏[1]) identifican las subcategorías (véase la clave completa en la página *I* · *1*).

Les symboles de l'index représentent les catégories indiquées dans la légende à droite. Les symboles suivis d'un indice (⋏[1]) représentent des sous-catégories (voir légende complète à la page *I* · *1*).

Os símbolos incluídos no texto do índice representam as grandes categorias identificadas com a chave à direita. Os símbolos com números em sua parte superior (⋏[1]) identificam as subcategorias (veja-se a chave completa à página *I* · *1*).

∧	Mountain	Berg	Montaña	Montagne	Montanha
⋏	Mountains	Berge	Montañas	Montagnes	Montanhas
)(	Pass	Pass	Paso	Col	Passo
V	Valley, Canyon	Tal, Cañon	Valle, Cañón	Vallée, Canyon	Vale, Canhão
≚	Plain	Ebene	Llano	Plaine	Planície
>	Cape	Kap	Cabo	Cap	Cabo
I	Island	Insel	Isla	Île	Ilha
II	Islands	Inseln	Islas	Îles	Ilhas
⊥	Other Topographic Features	Andere Topographische Objekte	Otros Elementos Topográficos	Autres données topographiques	Outros acidentes topográficos

≃	River	Fluss	Río	Rivière	Rio
≊	Canal	Kanal	Canal	Canal	Canal
ᒪ	Waterfall, Rapids	Wasserfall, Stromschnellen	Cascada, Rápidos	Chute d'eau, Rapides	Cascata, Rápidos
ɥ	Strait	Meeresstrasse	Estrecho	Détroit	Estreito
c	Bay, Gulf	Bucht, Golf	Bahía, Golfo	Baie, Golfe	Baía, Golfo
⊜	Lake, Lakes	See, Seen	Lago, Lagos	Lac, Lacs	Lago, Lagos
≚	Swamp	Sumpf	Pantano	Marais	Pântano
⟎	Ice Features, Glacier	Eis- und Gletscherformen	Accidentes Glaciales	Formes glaciaires	Acidentes glaciares
⫟	Other Hydrographic Features	Andere Hydrographische Objekte	Otros Elementos Hidrográficos	Autres données hydrographiques	Outros acidentes hidrográficos

✦	Submarine Features	Untermeerische Objekte	Accidentes Submarinos	Formes de relief sous-marin	Acidentes submarinos
□	Political Unit	Politische Einheit	Unidad Politica	Entité politique	Unidade política
ʋ	Cultural Institution	Kulturelle Institution	Institución Cultural	Institution culturelle	Institução cultural
⊥	Historical Site	Historische Stätte	Sitio Histórico	Site historique	Sitio histórico
♠	Recreational Site	Erholungs- und Ferienort	Sitio de Recreo	Centre de loisirs	Area de Lazer
⊠	Airport	Flughafen	Aeropuerto	Aéroport	Aeroporto
■	Military Installation	Militäranlage	Instalación Militar	Installation militaire	Instalação militar
◆	Miscellaneous	Verschiedenes	Misceláneo	Divers	Diversos

Name (Name)	Page (Seite)	Lat.°′ (Breite°′)	Long.°′ (Länge°′ E = Ost)
Long Branch Lake ⊜[1]	**194**	39.49 N	92.31 W
Longbu	**100**	25.32 N	115.24 E
Long Buckby	**42**	52.19 N	1.04 W
Long Cane Creek ≃	**192**	33.57 N	82.24 W
Long Canyon V	**226**	38.59 N	120.41 W
Longchamp, Hippodrome de ♦	**261**	48.51 N	2.14 E
Longchamps, Arg.	**258**	34.52 S	58.23 W
Longchamps, Bel.	**56**	50.03 N	5.42 E
Longchang, Zhg.	**104**	40.53 N	123.08 E
Longchang, Zhg.	**107**	29.21 N	105.17 E
Longchaumois	**58**	46.27 N	5.56 E
Longchêne	**261**	48.38 N	2.00 E
Longchuan, Zhg.	**100**	24.07 N	115.17 E
Longchuan, Zhg.	**102**	24.14 N	97.45 E
Longchuan (Shweli) ≃	**102**	23.56 N	96.17 E
Long Creek, Il., U.S.	**219**	39.48 N	88.50 W
Long Creek, Or., U.S.	**202**	44.42 N	119.06 W
Long Creek ≃	**184**	49.07 N	103.00 W
Long Crendon	**42**	51.47 N	1.01 W
Longcun	**100**	23.34 N	115.33 E
Longde	**102**	35.28 N	106.22 E
Longdendale V	**262**	53.29 N	1.56 W
Long Ditton	**260**	51.23 N	0.20 W
Longdongtuo	**107**	29.59 N	106.21 E
Longdor, gora ∧	**88**	58.24 N	116.47 E
Longdou	**100**	27.25 N	117.24 E
Longdu	**106**	31.51 N	118.56 E
Long Eaton	**42**	52.54 N	1.15 W
Longeau	**58**	47.46 N	5.18 E
Long Eddy	**210**	41.51 N	75.08 W
Longfellow National Historical Site ⊥	**283**	42.23 N	71.08 W
Longfengchang	**107**	30.26 N	105.38 E
Longfengkan	**104**	41.51 N	124.01 E
Longfengyutun	**104**	40.39 N	122.57 E
Longfield	**260**	51.24 N	0.18 E
Longford, Austl.	**166**	38.10 S	147.05 E
Longford, Ire.	**48**	53.44 N	7.47 W
Longford, Md., U.S.	**284b**	39.25 N	76.39 W
Longford □[6]	**48**	53.40 N	7.40 W
Longford Park ♦	**262**	53.27 N	2.17 W
Longframlington	**44**	55.18 N	1.47 W
Longgang, Zhg.	**100**	29.38 N	114.57 E
Longgang, Zhg.	**100**	33.22 N	120.04 E
Longgang, Zhg.	**102**	24.41 N	101.09 E
Longgangzi	**104**	42.09 N	123.26 E
Long Green	**208**	39.28 N	76.31 W
Long Grove	**216**	42.11 N	88.00 W
Longguan	**105**	40.47 N	115.34 E
Longgudu	**100**	27.45 N	116.14 E
Longguntur	**112**	0.13 N	112.12 E
Long Harbour	**186**	47.26 N	53.48 W
Long Harbour c, Nf., Can.	**186**	47.44 N	55.01 W
Long Harbour c, H.K.	**271d**	22.27 N	114.20 E
Longhorn Cavern State Park ♦	**196**	30.20 N	98.30 W
Longhorsley	**44**	55.15 N	1.46 W
Longhoughton	**44**	55.26 N	1.36 W
Long Hu ⊜	**100**	29.58 N	116.10 E
Longhua, Zhg.	**98**	41.17 N	117.37 E
Longhua, Zhg.	**100**	22.42 N	113.59 E
Longhua, Zhg.	**100**	23.37 N	114.14 E
Longhua, Zhg.	**106**	31.09 N	121.26 E
Longhua Airport ⊠	**269b**	31.10 N	121.26 E
Longhua Pagoda ʋ[1]	**269b**	31.11 N	121.26 E
Longhui, Zhg.	**100**	25.32 N	114.47 E
Longhui (Taohuaping), Zhg.	**102**	27.00 N	110.59 E
Longhui, Zhg.	**107**	29.32 N	104.48 E
Longhutang	**106**	31.52 N	119.59 E
Longi	**70**	38.01 N	14.45 E
Longido	**154**	2.44 S	36.41 E
Longiram	**112**	0.02 S	115.38 E
Long Island I, Antig.	**240c**	17.08 N	61.45 W
Long Island I, Austl.	**166**	22.09 S	149.54 E
Long Island I, Ba.	**238**	23.15 N	75.07 W
Long Island I, Nf., Can.	**186**	47.35 N	54.05 W
Long Island I, N.T., Can.	**176**	54.50 N	79.20 W
Long Island I, N.S., Can.	**186**	44.20 N	66.15 W
Long Island I, Pap. N. Gui.	**164**	5.20 S	147.05 E
Long Island I, Ak., U.S.	**182**	54.54 N	132.45 W
Long Island I, Ma., U.S.	**283**	42.19 N	70.58 W
Long Island I, N.Y., U.S.	**188**	40.50 N	73.00 W
Long Island I, Wa., U.S.	**224**	46.27 N	123.58 W
Long Island City ◂[8]	**276**	40.45 N	73.56 W
Long Island MacArthur Airport ⊠	**210**	40.48 N	73.06 W
Long Island Sound ʮ	**188**	41.05 N	72.58 W
Long Island University (C.W. Post Center) ʋ[2], N.Y., U.S.	**276**	40.49 N	73.36 W
Long Island University ʋ[2], N.Y., U.S.	**276**	40.41 N	73.59 W
Longitudinal, Valle V	**252**	36.00 S	72.00 W
Long Jetty	**170**	33.22 S	151.29 E
Longji	**107**	29.23 N	106.04 E
Longjiadian	**104**	42.10 N	120.47 E
Longjiang, Zhg.	**89**	47.19 N	123.12 E
Longjiang, Zhg.	**100**	22.53 N	113.04 E
Longjiang, Zhg.	**100**	22.59 N	116.13 E
Longjiang, Zhg.	**107**	29.48 N	105.03 E
Longjie	**107**	29.53 N	104.32 E
Longjin	**100**	28.37 N	116.37 E
Longjing	**100**	23.53 N	112.52 E
Longjohn Slough ≃	**278**	41.43 N	87.53 W
Longjumeau	**50**	48.42 N	2.18 E
Longka, Zhg.	**120**	31.10 N	84.00 E
Longka, Zhg.	**120**	33.12 N	79.47 E
Longkamp	**56**	49.53 N	7.07 E
Longkangji	**100**	33.09 N	116.54 E
Long Ke	**271d**	22.23 N	114.22 E
Long Key I, Fl., U.S.	**220**	24.49 N	80.49 W
Long Key I, Fl., U.S.	**220**	27.44 N	82.45 W
Long King Creek ≃	**222**	30.34 N	94.58 W
Longkou, Zhg.	**98**	37.38 N	120.18 E
Longkou, Zhg.	**100**	32.56 N	114.57 E
Longkou, Zhg.	**100**	29.57 N	113.47 E
Longkou, Zhg.	**100**	26.11 N	115.15 E
Longkouqiao	**85**	39.40 N	77.09 E
Long Lake, Il., U.S.	**216**	42.22 N	88.08 W
Long Lake, N.Y., U.S.	**188**	43.58 N	74.25 W
Long Lake, Tx., U.S.	**222**	31.39 N	95.47 W
Long Lake ⊜, On., Can.	**212**	44.41 N	76.45 W
Long Lake ⊜, Mi., U.S.	**190**	45.12 N	83.30 W
Long Lake ⊜, Mi., U.S.	**281**	42.37 N	83.44 W
Long Lake ⊜, Mi., U.S.	**281**	42.36 N	83.28 W
Long Lake ⊜, N.Y., U.S.	**188**	44.04 N	74.20 W
Long Lake ⊜, N.D., U.S.	**198**	46.43 N	100.07 W
Long Lake ⊜, Wa., U.S.	**224**	47.03 N	122.47 W
Long Lake ⊜[1]	**202**	47.50 N	117.40 W
Long Lake Creek ≃	**198**	46.40 N	100.13 W
Long Lake Shores	**281**	42.35 N	83.19 W
Long Lama	**112**	3.46 N	114.24 E
Longlaville	**56**	49.32 N	5.47 E
Longleaf	**194**	31.00 N	92.34 W
Long Leaf Park	**192**	34.12 N	77.56 W
Longleat ʋ	**42**	51.12 N	2.17 W
Longlegged Lake ⊜	**184**	50.46 N	94.08 W
Longli	**102**	26.26 N	106.58 E
Longlin	**102**	24.49 N	105.31 E
Longling	**102**	24.39 N	98.40 E
Longmeadow	**207**	42.03 N	72.35 W
Long Melford	**42**	52.05 N	0.43 E
Longmen, Zhg.	**89**	48.55 N	126.54 E
Longmen, Zhg.	**100**	23.44 N	114.15 E
Longmen, Zhg.	**100**	29.53 N	119.57 E
Longmen, Zhg.	**100**	24.56 N	118.04 E
Longmen, Zhg.	**100**	25.06 N	116.58 E
Longmen, Zhg.	**107**	29.27 N	104.59 E
Longmen, Zhg.	**107**	29.12 N	106.13 E
Longmenchang	**107**	30.53 N	106.10 E
Longmensuo	**98**	40.56 N	115.54 E
Longmenzhang	**107**	28.59 N	106.13 E
Longming	**102**	22.59 N	107.11 E
Longmire	**224**	46.45 N	121.49 W
Longmont	**200**	40.10 N	105.06 W
Longmorn	**46**	57.36 N	3.17 W
Long Mountain ∧	**194**	36.41 N	92.26 W
Long Mountain ∧[2]	**42**	52.39 N	3.09 W
Longmu	**100**	24.16 N	115.28 E
Longnan	**100**	24.54 N	114.48 E
Longnawan	**112**	1.54 N	114.53 E
Long Neck >[1]	**276**	41.03 N	73.29 W
Long Neck Point >	**276**	41.02 N	73.29 W
Longniddry	**46**	55.58 N	2.53 W
Longnüsi	**107**	30.23 N	106.11 E
Longny-au-Perche	**50**	48.32 N	0.45 E
Longobucco	**68**	39.27 N	16.37 E
Longperrier	**261**	49.03 N	2.40 E
Long Pine	**198**	42.32 N	99.42 W
Longping	**100**	29.53 N	115.41 E
Long Plains	**168b**	34.21 S	138.22 E
Long Point, Austl.	**274a**	34.01 S	150.54 E
Long Point, Il., U.S.	**216**	41.00 N	88.54 W
Long Point >, Ba.	**240b**	25.01 N	77.20 W
Long Point >, Nf., Can.	**186**	48.48 N	58.46 W
Long Point >, N.S., Can.	**186**	46.51 N	60.18 W
Long Point >, On., Can.	**212**	44.06 N	76.29 W
Long Point >, On., Can.	**212**	44.32 N	80.18 W
Long Point >, Pil.	**116**	9.39 N	118.20 E
Long Point >, Ca., U.S.	**280**	33.44 N	118.23 W
Long Point >, Vir. Is., U.S.	**240m**	18.18 N	64.53 W
Long Point >, Vir. Is., U.S.	**241n**	17.41 N	64.50 W
Long Point >[1], Mb., Can.	**184**	53.02 N	98.40 W
Long Point >[1], On., Can.	**214**	42.34 N	80.15 W
Long Point Bay c	**212**	42.40 N	80.14 W
Long Point Creek ≃	**216**	41.02 N	88.48 W
Long Point Provincial Park ♦	**214**	42.35 N	80.35 W
Long Pond ⊜, U.S.	**283**	42.41 N	71.21 W
Long Pond ⊜, Ma., U.S.	**207**	41.43 N	70.04 W
Long Pond ⊜, Ma., U.S.	**207**	41.48 N	70.57 W
Longpont, Fr.	**50**	49.16 N	3.13 E
Longpont, Fr.	**261**	48.38 N	2.17 E
Longport	**208**	39.18 N	74.31 W
Long Prairie	**198**	45.58 N	94.51 W
Long Prairie ≃	**198**	46.20 N	94.36 W
Longpré-les-Corps-Saints	**50**	50.01 N	1.59 E
Long Preston	**44**	54.02 N	2.15 W
Longqiantai	**104**	41.23 N	120.52 E
Longqu, Zhg.	**98**	34.16 N	114.49 E
Longqu, Zhg.	**98**	34.54 N	116.47 E
Longquan	**100**	28.04 N	119.07 E
Longquan ≃	**100**	28.17 N	119.44 E
Longquanguan	**98**	38.55 N	113.51 E
Longquan Shan ⋀	**107**	30.25 N	104.15 E
Longquanyi	**107**	30.34 N	104.16 E
Longquanzhen	**107**	30.21 N	104.39 E
Long Range Mountains ⋀	**186**	49.20 N	57.30 W
Longreach	**166**	23.26 S	144.15 E
Long Reach c	**186**	45.26 N	66.09 W
Long Reach ʮ	**212**	44.07 N	77.04 W
Long Reef ✥[2]	**164**	11.11 S	151.40 E
Long Reef Point >	**274a**	33.45 S	151.19 E
Longridge	**44**	53.51 N	2.36 W
Long Run ≃, Il., U.S.	**278**	41.37 N	88.03 W
Long Run ≃, Pa., U.S.	**279b**	40.20 N	79.48 W
Long-Sault	**206**	45.02 N	74.53 W
Long Sault Dam ◂[6]	**206**	45.00 N	74.45 W
Long Sault Islands II	**206**	45.00 N	74.55 W
Longsegah	**112**	2.15 N	116.42 E
Longshan, Zhg.	**100**	33.36 N	116.18 E
Longshan, Zhg.	**102**	29.28 N	109.20 E
Longshansuo	**100**	30.05 N	121.33 E
Longsheng, Zhg.	**102**	25.48 N	110.00 E
Longsheng, Zhg.	**107**	30.36 N	105.21 E
Longshizhen, Zhg.	**107**	30.12 N	106.26 E
Longshizhen, Zhg.	**107**	29.23 N	105.10 E
Longshu	**107**	29.33 N	105.45 E
Longs Peak ∧	**200**	40.15 N	105.37 W
Long Stratton	**42**	52.29 N	1.14 E
Long Sutton	**42**	52.47 N	0.08 E
Longtaichang	**107**	30.04 N	105.34 E
Longtan, Zhg.	**100**	23.40 N	113.24 E
Longtan, Zhg.	**102**	28.20 N	108.52 E
Longtan, Zhg.	**106**	31.20 N	118.45 E
Longtan, Zhg.	**106**	32.11 N	119.04 E
Longtansi	**107**	30.42 N	104.10 E
Longtanzhen	**107**	29.19 N	104.35 E
Long Teru	**112**	3.52 N	114.15 E
Long-thanh	**110**	10.47 N	106.57 E
Longtian	**100**	25.38 N	119.28 E
Longtian'an	**106**	31.10 N	120.49 E
Long Tom ≃	**202**	44.23 N	123.15 W
Longton, Eng., U.K.	**44**	53.43 N	2.47 W
Longton, Eng., U.K.	**262**	53.44 N	2.48 W
Longton, Ks., U.S.	**198**	37.22 N	96.04 W
Longtou	**98**	38.51 N	121.18 E
Longtoupu	**100**	27.54 N	113.12 E
Longtouwei	**100**	25.14 N	115.24 E
Longtown	**44**	55.01 N	2.58 W
Long-truong	**269c**	10.49 N	106.49 E
Longué	**32**	47.23 N	0.06 W
Longueau	**50**	49.52 N	2.21 E
Longuenesse	**50**	50.44 N	2.14 E
Longuesse	**261**	49.04 N	1.56 E
Longueuil	**206**	45.32 N	73.30 W
Longueville, Austl.	**274a**	33.50 S	151.10 E
Longueville, Fr.	**50**	48.31 N	3.15 E
Longueville-sur-Scie	**50**	49.48 N	1.06 E
Longuyon	**56**	49.26 N	5.36 E
Long Valley	**210**	40.47 N	74.46 W
Long Valley Creek ≃, Ca., U.S.	**226**	39.03 N	122.34 W
Long Valley Creek ≃, Nv., U.S.	**226**	39.31 N	119.39 W
Longvic	**58**	47.17 N	5.04 E
Longview, Ab., Can.	**182**	50.32 N	114.14 W
Longview, N.C., U.S.	**192**	35.43 N	81.23 W
Longview, Tx., U.S.	**222**	32.30 N	94.44 W
Longview, Wa., U.S.	**224**	46.08 N	122.56 W
Longview Heights	**222**	32.30 N	94.41 W
Longvilliers	**261**	48.35 N	2.00 E
Longvilly	**56**	50.01 N	5.50 E
Longwai	**112**	0.42 N	116.39 E
Longwan	**105**	38.57 N	116.10 E
Longwangmiao, Zhg.	**98**	36.12 N	115.13 E
Longwangmiao, Zhg.	**102**	40.36 N	95.52 E
Longwangmiao, Zhg.	**104**	41.38 N	121.04 E
Longwangmiao, Zhg.	**104**	42.35 N	123.42 E
Longwarry	**169**	38.07 S	145.46 E
Longwen	**100**	24.36 N	116.21 E
Longwo	**100**	23.28 N	115.17 E
Longwokou	**106**	32.18 N	119.52 E
Longwood	**220**	28.42 N	81.20 W
Longwood Gardens ♦	**285**	39.52 N	75.40 W
Longwood Lake	**276**	40.59 N	74.52 W
Longwood Park	**192**	34.55 N	79.42 W
Longworth	**182**	53.55 N	121.28 W
Longwy	**56**	49.31 N	5.46 E
Longxi → Zhangzhou, Zhg.	**100**	24.33 N	117.39 E
Longxi, Zhg.	**102**	34.56 N	104.47 E
Longxi, Zhg.	**107**	29.59 N	106.09 E
Longxian, Zhg.	**102**	34.51 N	106.59 E
Longxian, Zhg.	**107**	29.09 N	105.50 E
Long-xuyen	**110**	10.23 N	105.25 E
Longyan	**100**	25.08 N	117.02 E
Longyao	**98**	37.23 N	114.41 E
Longyou	**100**	29.02 N	119.10 E
Longyou ≃	**106**	32.08 N	120.38 E
Longyuanba	**100**	24.56 N	114.27 E
Longzhaogou	**98**	40.49 N	124.36 E
Longzhen	**89**	48.41 N	126.42 E
Longzhou	**102**	22.22 N	106.52 E
Longzi	**120**	28.25 N	92.31 E
Loni	**272a**	28.45 N	77.17 E
Lonigo	**64**	45.23 N	11.23 E
Löningen	**52**	52.44 N	7.46 E
Lonkala	**152**	4.37 S	23.14 E
Lönnewitz	**54**	51.34 N	13.11 E
Lonny	**56**	49.49 N	4.35 E
Lonoke	**194**	34.47 N	91.53 W
Lönsboda	**26**	56.24 N	14.19 E
Lønsdal	**24**	66.44 N	15.28 E
Lonsdale	**190**	44.28 N	93.25 W
Lonsdale, Point >	**169**	38.17 S	144.37 E
Lons-le-Saunier	**58**	46.40 N	5.33 E
Lonton	**110**	25.06 N	96.17 E
Lontra ≃	**250**	6.37 S	48.39 W
Lontra, Ribeirão ≃	**255**	21.28 S	53.37 W
Lonua ≃	**152**	1.16 N	22.38 E
Lonzhen	**107**	30.00 N	103.59 E
Loo	**84**	43.43 N	39.36 E
Looc	**116**	12.16 N	121.59 E
Loogootee	**194**	38.40 N	86.54 W
Looking Glass ≃	**216**	42.52 N	84.54 W
Lookout	**210**	41.47 N	75.11 W
Lookout, Cape >, N.C., U.S.	**192**	34.35 N	76.32 W
Lookout, Cape >, Or., U.S.	**224**	45.20 N	124.00 W
Lookout, Point >, Austl.	**171a**	27.26 S	153.33 E
Lookout, Point >, Md., U.S.	**208**	38.02 N	76.19 W
Lookout Mountain ∧, U.S.	**194**	34.25 N	85.40 W
Lookout Mountain ∧, Or., U.S.	**202**	44.20 N	120.22 W
Lookout Mountain ∧, Or., U.S.	**224**	45.21 N	121.31 W
Lookout Mountain ∧, Wa., U.S.	**224**	48.40 N	122.22 W
Lookout Pass)(	**202**	47.27 N	115.42 W
Lookout Point Lake ⊜[1]	**202**	43.52 N	122.40 W
Lookout Ridge ⋀	**180**	69.07 N	158.36 W
Loolmalassin ∧[1]	**154**	3.03 S	35.49 E
Loomis, Ca., U.S.	**226**	38.49 N	121.12 W
Loomis, Ne., U.S.	**198**	40.28 N	99.30 W
Loomis, Wa., U.S.	**182**	48.49 N	119.37 W
Loon	**116**	9.48 N	123.47 E
Loon ≃	**184**	55.50 N	101.59 W
Loon Creek ≃	**202**	44.49 N	114.49 W
Loongana	**162**	30.57 S	127.02 E
Loon Lake ⊜, Can.	**184**	55.51 N	102.00 W
Loon Lake ⊜, Mi., U.S.	**281**	42.41 N	83.22 W
Loon Lake ⊜[1]	**226**	39.00 N	120.18 W
Loon op Zand	**52**	51.38 N	5.04 E
Loop	**196**	32.55 N	102.25 W
Loop ◂[8]	**278**	41.53 N	87.38 W
Loop Head >	**48**	52.34 N	9.56 W
Lo Ortuzar	**286e**	33.28 S	70.45 W
Loos	**50**	50.37 N	3.01 E
Loosdorf	**61**	48.12 N	15.24 E
Loosduinen ◂[8]	**52**	52.04 N	4.13 E
Loose, B.R.D.	**41**	54.31 N	9.53 E
Loose, Eng., U.K.	**260**	51.14 N	0.31 E
Loose Creek	**219**	38.30 N	91.57 W
Lop ≃	**110**	13.18 N	107.37 E
Lopandino	**76**	52.28 N	34.49 E
Lopanka	**80**	46.24 N	40.59 E
Lopar'ovo	**80**	58.20 N	42.41 E
Lopasn'a ≃	**82**	54.51 N	37.52 E
Lopatiči	**76**	53.34 N	30.53 E
Lopatin, S.S.S.R.	**78**	50.13 N	24.50 E
Lopatin, S.S.S.R.	**84**	43.53 N	47.41 E
Lopatina, gora ∧	**89**	50.52 N	143.10 E
Lopatino, S.S.S.R.	**80**	52.37 N	45.47 E
Lopatino, S.S.S.R.	**82**	54.45 N	37.00 E
Lopatino, S.S.S.R.	**89**	48.24 N	142.15 E
Lopatinskij	**82**	55.21 N	38.34 E
Lopatka, mys >	**74**	50.52 N	156.40 E
Lopatovo	**76**	56.08 N	29.12 E
Lop Buri	**110**	14.48 N	100.37 E
Lopé-Okanda, Réserve de Chasse de ◂[4]	**152**	0.30 S	11.40 E
Lopévi I	**175f**	16.30 S	168.21 E
Lopez, Pa., U.S.	**210**	41.27 N	76.20 W
Lopez, Wa., U.S.	**224**	48.31 N	122.54 W
López, Arroyo de ≃	**258**	35.26 S	57.35 W
Lopez, Cap >	**152**	0.37 S	8.43 E
Lopez Bay c	**116**	13.56 N	122.12 E
López Collada	**232**	31.45 N	113.55 W
Lopez Island I	**224**	48.30 N	122.54 W
Lopez Lake ⊜[1]	**226**	35.12 N	120.28 W
Lopik	**52**	51.58 N	4.56 E
Lop Nor → Lop Nur ⊜	**90**	40.20 N	90.15 E
Lop Nur (Lop Nor) ⊜	**90**	40.20 N	90.15 E
Lopori ≃	**152**	1.14 N	19.49 E
Lopotovo	**82**	56.04 N	36.49 E
Loppersum	**52**	53.19 N	6.45 E
Loppi	**26**	60.43 N	24.27 E
Lo Prado, Embalse ⊜[1]	**286e**	33.26 S	70.48 W
Lo Prado Arriba	**286e**	33.26 S	70.45 W
Lopšen'ga	**24**	64.58 N	37.41 E
L'Opton Ruisseau ≃	**261**	48.52 N	1.29 E
Lopt'uga	**24**	63.16 N	47.56 E
Lopuchovka, S.S.S.R.	**80**	51.59 N	44.42 E
Lopuchovka, S.S.S.R.	**80**	50.37 N	44.29 E
Łopuszno	**30**	50.57 N	20.15 E
Lora	**123**	33.53 N	73.17 E
Lora ≃	**246**	9.25 N	72.25 W
Lora, Hāmūn-i- ⊜	**128**	29.20 N	64.50 E
Lora Creek ≃	**162**	28.10 S	135.22 E
Lora del Río	**34**	37.39 N	5.32 W
Lorain	**214**	41.27 N	82.10 W
Lorain □[6]	**214**	41.22 N	82.06 W
Lorain County Regional Airport ⊠	**279a**	41.20 N	82.11 W
Loraine, Ca., U.S.	**228**	35.19 N	118.25 W
Loraine, Il., U.S.	**219**	40.09 N	91.13 W
Loraine, Tx., U.S.	**196**	32.24 N	100.42 W
Loralai	**120**	30.22 N	68.36 E
Loramie, Lake ⊜[1]	**216**	40.23 N	84.18 W
Loramie Creek ≃	**216**	40.11 N	84.14 W
Lorca	**34**	37.40 N	1.42 W
Lorch, B.R.D.	**56**	48.49 N	9.40 E
Lorch, B.R.D.	**56**	50.02 N	7.48 E
Lorchhausen	**56**	50.03 N	7.47 E
Lord Howe Island I	**160**	31.33 S	159.05 E
Lord Howe Rise ✥[3]	**14**	32.00 S	162.00 E
Lord Howe Seamounts ✥[3]	**14**	28.00 S	159.00 E
Lord Mayor Bay c	**176**	69.44 N	92.00 W
Lordsburg	**200**	32.21 N	108.42 W
Lord's Cricket Ground ♦	**260**	51.32 N	0.10 W
Lordstown	**214**	41.09 N	80.53 W
Lords Valley	**210**	41.23 N	75.04 W
Loreauville	**194**	30.03 N	91.44 W
Loreley ♦	**56**	50.08 N	7.44 E
Lorena, Bra.	**256**	22.44 S	45.08 W
Lorena, Tx., U.S.	**222**	31.23 N	97.13 W
Lorengau	**164**	2.00 S	147.15 E
Lorentz ≃	**164**	5.23 S	138.04 E
Lorentzen	**56**	48.57 N	7.10 E
Lorenzago di Cadore	**64**	46.29 N	12.28 E
Lorenzo	**196**	33.40 N	101.32 W
Lorenzo Geyres (Queguay)	**252**	32.05 S	57.55 W
Loreo	**64**	45.04 N	12.11 E
Lorestān □[8]	**128**	33.30 N	48.30 E
Loreto, Arg.	**252**	27.46 S	57.17 W
Loreto, Bol.	**248**	15.13 S	64.40 W
Loreto, Bra.	**250**	7.05 S	45.09 W
Loreto, Col.	**246**	3.48 S	70.15 W
Loreto, It.	**66**	43.26 N	13.36 E
Loreto, Méx.	**232**	26.01 N	111.21 W
Loreto, Méx.	**234**	22.16 N	101.58 W
Loreto, Para.	**252**	23.16 S	57.11 W
Loreto, Pil.	**116**	10.21 N	125.34 E
Loreto, Pil.	**116**	8.12 N	125.45 E
Loreto □[5]	**246**	3.00 S	75.00 W
Loreto Aprutino	**66**	42.26 N	13.59 E
Lorette, Mb., Can.	**184**	49.44 N	96.52 W
Lorette, Fr.	**62**	45.31 N	4.35 E
Loretteville	**206**	46.51 N	71.21 W
Loretto → Loreto, It.	**66**	43.26 N	13.36 E
Loretto, Ky., U.S.	**194**	37.38 N	85.24 W
Loretto, Pa., U.S.	**214**	40.30 N	78.37 W
Loretto, Tn., U.S.	**194**	35.04 N	87.26 W
Lorgues	**62**	43.29 N	6.22 E
Lorian Swamp ≡	**154**	0.40 N	39.35 E
Lorica	**246**	9.14 N	75.49 W
Lorida	**220**	27.26 N	81.15 W
Lorient	**32**	47.45 N	3.22 W
L'Orignal	**206**	45.37 N	74.42 W
Lorimer Park ♦	**285**	40.06 N	75.05 W
Lorimor	**194**	41.07 N	94.03 W
Loring, Aeródromo de ⊠	**266a**	40.22 N	3.47 W
Loring Air Force Base ■	**186**	46.57 N	67.54 W
Lorino	**180**	65.30 N	171.43 W
Loriol-sur-Drôme	**62**	44.45 N	4.49 E
Loris	**192**	34.03 N	78.53 W
Lorman	**194**	31.49 N	91.03 W
L'Orme	**261**	48.39 N	1.41 E
Lormes	**50**	47.17 N	3.49 E
Lorn, Firth of c[1]	**46**	56.20 N	5.45 W
Lorna Glen	**162**	26.14 S	121.33 E
Lorne, Austl.	**169**	38.33 S	143.59 E
Lorne, N.B., Can.	**186**	47.53 N	66.08 W
Loro Ciuffenna	**66**	43.35 N	11.38 E
Loronyo	**154**	4.39 N	32.38 E
Lorquin	**58**	48.40 N	7.00 E
Lörrach	**58**	47.37 N	7.40 E
Lorrain, Rivière du ≃	**240e**	14.50 N	61.03 W
Lorraine □[9]	**32**	49.00 N	6.00 E
Lorrez-le-Bocage	**50**	48.14 N	2.54 E
Lorris	**50**	47.53 N	2.31 E
Lorsch	**56**	49.39 N	8.34 E
Lorsica	**62**	44.26 N	9.16 E
Lorup	**52**	52.55 N	7.38 E
Lorze ≃	**58**	47.15 N	8.25 E
Los	**26**	61.44 N	15.10 E
Los, Îles de II	**150**	9.30 N	13.48 W
Losa, Nuraghe ⊥	**71**	40.07 N	8.46 E
Losada ≃	**246**	2.12 N	73.55 W
Los Aguacates	**286c**	10.35 N	66.48 W
Los Alamitos	**280**	33.48 N	118.04 W
Los Alamitos Armed Forces Reserve Center ■	**280**	33.47 N	118.03 W
Los Alamitos Race Course ♦	**280**	33.48 N	118.03 W
Los Alamos, Méx.	**232**	28.40 N	103.30 W
Los Alamos, Ca., U.S.	**204**	34.44 N	120.16 W
Los Alamos, N.M., U.S.	**200**	35.53 N	106.19 W
Los Aldamas	**232**	26.03 N	99.11 W
Los Altos, Méx.	**196**	26.14 N	98.28 W
Los Altos, Ca., U.S.	**226**	37.23 N	122.06 W
Los Altos Hills	**226**	37.22 N	122.08 W
Los Amates, Guat.	**236**	15.16 N	89.06 W
Los Amates, Méx.	**234**	18.08 N	102.15 W
Los Andes	**252**	32.50 S	70.37 W
Los Ángeles, Chile	**252**	37.28 S	72.21 W
Los Angeles, Ca., U.S.	**228**	34.03 N	118.14 W
Los Angeles, Ca., U.S.	**280**	34.03 N	118.14 W
Los Angeles □[6]	**228**	34.20 N	118.10 W
Los Angeles ≃	**228**	33.46 N	118.12 W
Los Angeles Aqueduct ≍[1]	**204**	35.22 N	118.05 W
Los Angeles Coliseum and Sports Arena ♦	**280**	34.01 N	118.17 W
Los Angeles Convention Center ʋ	**280**	34.03 N	118.17 W
Los Angeles County Fairgrounds ♦	**280**	34.05 N	117.46 W
Los Angeles County Museum of Art ʋ	**280**	34.05 N	118.22 W
Los Angeles Harbor c	**280**	33.42 N	118.16 W
Los Angeles International Airport ⊠	**228**	33.56 N	118.24 W
Los Antiguos	**254**	46.33 S	71.37 W
Losantville	**218**	40.01 N	85.10 W
Losap I[1]	**14**	6.54 N	152.44 E
Los Arabos	**240p**	22.44 N	80.43 W
Losarang	**115a**	6.24 S	108.10 E
Los Arroyos, Laguna de ⊜	**248**	12.38 S	65.00 W
Los Banos	**226**	37.03 N	120.50 W
Los Banos Creek ≃	**226**	37.20 N	120.57 W
Los Banos Creek, North Fork ≃	**226**	36.57 N	121.07 W
Los Banos Creek, South Fork ≃	**226**	36.57 N	121.07 W
Los Banos Reservoir ⊜[1]	**226**	36.59 N	120.57 W
Los Berros	**252**	31.57 S	68.39 W
Los Blancos	**252**	23.36 S	62.36 W
Los Burros	**232**	25.03 N	110.50 W
Los Cardales	**258**	34.20 S	58.59 W
Los Cerrillos, Arg.	**252**	31.57 S	65.28 W
Los Cerrillos, Ur.	**258**	34.37 S	56.22 W
Los Cerrillos, Aeropuerto ⊠	**286e**	33.30 S	70.43 W
Los Cerritos Center ◂[9]	**280**	33.52 N	118.05 W
Los Chacos	**248**	14.33 S	62.11 W
Löschenrod	**56**	50.30 N	9.41 E
Los Chiles	**236**	11.02 N	84.43 W
Los Conquistadores	**252**	30.36 S	58.28 W
Los Coronados, Islas II	**204**	32.25 N	117.15 W
Los Coyotes Indian Reservation ◂[4]	**204**	33.20 N	116.35 W
Los Cuatro Álamos	**286e**	33.32 S	70.44 W
Los Dos Caminos	**286c**	10.31 N	66.50 W
Los Ebanos, Méx.	**232**	24.40 N	97.45 W
Los Ebanos, Tx., U.S.	**196**	26.14 N	98.34 W
Loseley House ⊥	**260**	51.13 N	0.36 W
Los Esclavos ≃	**236**	13.50 N	90.20 W
Losevo	**78**	50.40 N	40.02 E
Los Flamencos, Laguna ⊜	**258**	35.36 S	58.42 W
Los Frentones	**252**	26.25 S	61.25 W
Los Fresnos	**196**	26.04 N	97.29 W
Los Garzas	**196**	26.23 N	99.46 W
Los Gatos	**226**	37.13 N	121.58 W
Los Gatos Creek ≃, Ca., U.S.	**226**	36.13 N	120.08 W
Los Gatos Creek ≃, Ca., U.S.	**226**	37.20 N	121.54 W
Los Glaciares, Parque Nacional ♦	**254**	49.52 S	73.05 W
Los Guerras	**196**	26.25 N	99.05 W
Loshan → Leshan	**107**	29.34 N	103.45 E
Los Haros	**234**	22.46 N	102.57 W
Losheim	**56**	49.30 N	6.44 E
Los Hermanos, Islas II	**246**	11.45 N	64.25 W
Los Herreras, Méx.	**196**	25.55 N	99.24 W
Los Herreras, Méx.	**232**	25.10 N	105.31 W
Losi	**273a**	6.40 N	3.31 E
Łosice	**30**	52.14 N	22.43 E
Los Indios, Canal de ʮ	**240p**	21.56 N	83.16 W
Lošinj, Otok I	**36**	44.36 N	14.24 E
Losinoborskaja	**86**	58.27 N	89.28 E
Losino-Petrovskij	**82**	55.52 N	38.12 E
Losinovka	**78**	50.51 N	31.54 E
Los Jazmines, Presa ⊜[1]	**286a**	19.25 N	99.16 W
Los Juríes	**252**	28.28 S	62.06 W
Loškar'ovka	**78**	47.57 N	34.12 E
Loskopdam ⊜[1]	**156**	25.23 S	29.20 E
Loskop Dam Game Reserve ◂[4]	**156**	25.23 S	29.20 E
Los Lagos	**254**	39.51 S	72.50 W
Los Lagos □[4]	**254**	41.45 S	73.00 W
Los Llanos	**240m**	18.03 N	66.24 W
Los Llanos [de Aridane]	**148**	28.39 N	17.54 W
Los López	**196**	26.15 N	99.05 W
Los Lunas	**200**	34.48 N	106.43 W
Los Mármoles, Parque Nacional ♦	**234**	20.55 N	99.12 W
Los Médanos, Istmo de ⊥[3]	**241s**	11.35 N	69.45 W
Los Menucos	**254**	40.50 S	68.08 W
Los Metates	**234**	23.46 N	106.02 W
Los Micos, Laguna de c	**236**	15.45 N	87.36 W
Los'mino	**76**	55.04 N	34.24 E
Los Mochis	**232**	25.45 N	108.57 W
Los Molinos	**204**	40.01 N	122.05 W
Los Muermos	**254**	41.24 S	73.29 W
Los Naranjos	**286c**	10.27 N	66.48 W
Los Navalmorales	**34**	39.43 N	4.38 W
Lošnica	**76**	54.17 N	28.46 E
Los Nietos	**280**	33.58 N	118.04 W
Løsning	**41**	55.48 N	9.42 E
Los Nogales	**196**	26.16 N	99.43 W
Losolava	**175f**	14.11 S	167.34 E
Los Olmos Creek ≃, Tx., U.S.	**196**	27.20 N	97.40 W
Los Olmos Creek ≃, Tx., U.S.	**196**	26.21 N	98.48 W
Los Osos	**226**	35.19 N	120.50 W
Los Padillas	**200**	34.58 N	106.41 W
Los Palacios, Arg.	**252**	29.22 S	68.11 W
Los Palacios, Cuba	**240p**	22.35 N	83.15 W
Los Palacios y Villafranca	**34**	37.10 N	5.56 W
Los Perros, Arroyo ≃	**288**	34.37 S	58.46 W
Los Pinos ◂[8]	**286b**	23.04 N	82.23 W
Los Pinos ≃	**200**	36.56 N	107.36 W
Los Placeres	**234**	18.13 N	100.54 W
Los Polvorines	**288**	34.30 S	58.41 W
Los Quillayes	**286e**	33.34 S	70.37 W
Los Quirquinchos	**252**	33.22 S	61.43 W
Los Rábanos	**240m**	18.11 N	66.50 W
Los Ramones	**196**	25.42 N	99.37 W
Los Remedios ≃	**286a**	19.31 N	99.05 W
Los Reyes de Salgado	**234**	19.35 N	102.29 W
Los Reyes la Paz	**286a**	19.21 N	98.58 W
Los Ríos □[4]	**246**	1.30 S	79.25 W
Los Rodríguez	**232**	27.11 N	101.21 W
Los Roques, Islas II	**246**	11.50 N	66.45 W
Lossa	**54**	51.13 N	11.25 E
Lossa ≃	**54**	51.18 N	11.10 E
Los Santos	**246**	7.56 N	80.25 W
Los Santos □[4]	**236**	7.55 N	80.25 W
Los Santos de Maimona	**34**	38.27 N	6.23 W
Los Sauces	**252**	37.58 S	72.50 W
Lossburg	**58**	48.25 N	8.27 E
Lössel	**263**	51.21 N	7.39 E
Losser	**52**	52.15 N	7.00 E
Los Serranos	**228**	33.59 N	117.42 W
Lossie ≃	**46**	57.43 N	3.16 W
Lossiemouth	**46**	57.43 N	3.18 W
Lössnitz	**54**	50.37 N	12.43 E
Lost ≃, U.S.	**202**	41.56 N	121.30 W
Lost ≃, In., U.S.	**194**	38.33 N	86.49 W
Lost ≃, Mn., U.S.	**198**	47.51 N	96.02 W
Lost ≃, W.V., U.S.	**188**	39.05 N	78.36 W
Lostant	**216**	41.09 N	89.04 W
Los Taques	**246**	11.50 N	70.16 W
Lost Bridge State Recreation Area ♦	**216**	40.45 N	85.37 W
Lost Creek ≃, Al., U.S.	**194**	33.38 N	87.14 W
Lost Creek ≃, Ar., U.S.	**194**	34.10 N	92.31 W
Lost Creek ≃, Oh., U.S.	**218**	39.58 N	84.09 W
Lost Creek ≃, Ut,. U.S.	**200**	41.04 N	111.32 W
Lost Creek ≃, Wy., U.S.	**200**	42.01 N	108.11 W
Lost Draw V	**196**	32.58 N	102.02 W
Los Telares	**252**	28.59 S	63.26 W
Los Teques	**246**	10.21 N	67.02 W
Los Testigos, Islas II	**246**	11.22 N	63.06 W
Lost Hills	**226**	35.36 N	119.41 W
Lostine ≃	**202**	45.33 N	117.29 W
Lost Lake ⊜, Or., U.S.	**224**	45.29 N	121.49 W
Lost Lake ⊜, Wa., U.S.	**224**	47.20 N	121.24 W
Lost Nation	**190**	41.57 N	90.49 W
Lostock ≃	**262**	53.40 N	2.48 W
Lostock Gralam	**262**	53.16 N	2.28 W
Los Trancos Creek ≃	**282**	37.25 N	122.12 W
Los Trancos Woods	**282**	37.21 N	122.12 W
Los Tres Palos	**232**	24.33 N	98.18 W
Lost River Range ⋀	**202**	44.10 N	113.35 W
Lost Trail Pass)(	**202**	45.41 N	113.57 W
Lostwithiel	**42**	50.25 N	4.40 W
Losuia	**164**	8.32 S	151.04 E
Los Vidrios	**232**	31.59 N	113.28 W
Los Vilos	**252**	31.55 S	71.31 W
Los Yébenes	**34**	39.34 N	3.53 W
Lot □[5]	**32**	44.35 N	1.40 E
Lot ≃	**32**	44.18 N	0.20 E
Lota	**252**	37.05 S	73.10 W
Lotagipi Swamp (Lotikipi Plain) ≚	**144**	4.36 N	34.55 E
Lotak	**112**	0.11 S	115.54 E
Lotbinière □[6]	**206**	46.30 N	71.40 W
Lotela, Lake ⊜	**220**	27.34 N	81.29 W
Løten	**26**	60.49 N	11.19 E
Lot-et-Garonne □[5]	**32**	44.20 N	0.20 E
Lotfābād	**128**	37.32 N	59.20 E
Lothair, S. Afr.	**158**	26.26 S	30.27 E
Lothair, Ky., U.S.	**192**	37.14 N	83.10 W
Lothian □[4]	**46**	55.55 N	3.05 W
Lothian Region □[4]	**46**	55.50 N	3.15 W
Lothringen → Lorraine □[9]	**32**	49.00 N	6.00 E
Lotikipi Plain (Lotagipi Swamp) ≚	**144**	4.36 N	34.55 E
Loto	**152**	2.49 S	22.29 E
Loto ≃	**152**	1.55 S	22.09 E
Lotofaga	**175a**	13.59 S	171.50 W
Lotoi ≃	**152**	1.35 S	18.30 E
Lotorp	**40**	58.44 N	15.50 E
Lotošino	**76**	56.14 N	35.38 E
Lotrului, Munții ⋀	**38**	45.30 N	23.52 E
Lotsane ≃	**156**	22.41 S	28.11 E
Lötschberg Tunnel ◂[5]	**58**	46.25 N	7.45 E
Lötschental V	**58**	46.25 N	7.50 E
Lotseninsel I	**41**	54.40 N	10.01 E
Lott	**222**	31.12 N	97.02 W
Lotta ≃	**24**	68.36 N	31.06 E
Lottaville	**278**	41.31 N	87.22 W
Lotte	**52**	52.17 N	7.55 E
Lottivue	**214**	42.40 N	82.46 W
Löttringhausen ◂[8]	**263**	51.27 N	7.27 E
Lottsburg	**208**	37.57 N	76.31 W
Lotts Creek ≃	**192**	32.09 N	81.47 W
Lottsford Branch ≃	**284c**	38.55 N	76.49 W
Lottstetten	**58**	47.38 N	8.34 E
Lotuke, Jabal ∧	**154**	4.07 N	33.48 E
Lotung	**100**	24.41 N	121.46 E
Lötzen → Giżycko	**30**	54.03 N	21.47 E
Lotzorai	**71**	39.58 N	9.39 E
Louang Namtha	**110**	20.57 N	101.25 E
Louangphrabang	**110**	19.52 N	102.08 E
L'Ouarsenis, Massif de ⋀	**34**	35.40 N	1.50 E
Loubaresse	**62**	44.36 N	4.03 E
Loube, Montagne de la ∧	**62**	43.22 N	5.59 E
Loubetsi	**152**	3.12 S	12.10 E
Louchi	**24**	66.04 N	33.00 E
Loučim	**60**	49.22 N	13.07 E
Loučná ∧	**54**	50.39 N	13.37 E
Loude	**98**	35.54 N	117.18 E
Loudéac	**32**	48.10 N	2.45 W
Louden Cove c	**276**	41.05 N	73.43 W
Loudes	**62**	45.05 N	3.45 E
Loudima Poste	**152**	4.07 S	13.04 E
Loudon	**192**	35.43 N	84.20 W
Loudonville, N.Y., U.S.	**210**	42.42 N	73.45 W
Loudonville, Oh., U.S.	**214**	40.38 N	82.14 W
Loudoun □[6]	**208**	39.05 N	77.30 W
Loudun	**32**	47.01 N	0.05 E
Loué	**32**	48.00 N	0.09 W
Loue ≃	**58**	47.01 N	5.27 E
Louga	**150**	15.37 N	16.13 W
Louga □[4]	**150**	15.25 N	15.30 W
Louge	**252**	36.57 S	61.40 W
Louge ≃	**32**	43.27 N	1.20 E
Lougguéré ≃	**150**	15.35 N	14.47 W
Loughborough	**42**	52.47 N	1.11 W
Loughborough Lake ⊜	**212**	44.23 N	76.30 W
Loughermore ∧[2]	**44**	54.59 N	7.05 W
Loughman	**220**	28.14 N	81.34 W
Loughor	**42**	51.40 N	4.04 W
Loughor ≃	**42**	51.40 N	4.04 W
Loughrea	**48**	53.12 N	8.34 W
Loughros More Bay c	**48**	54.47 N	8.35 W
Loughton	**260**	51.39 N	0.03 E
Louhans	**58**	46.38 N	5.13 E
Louin	**194**	32.04 N	89.15 W
Louisa, Ky., U.S.	**192**	38.06 N	82.36 W
Louisa, Va., U.S.	**192**	38.01 N	78.00 W
Louisa, Lake ⊜, On., Can.	**212**	45.28 N	78.30 W
Louisa, Lake ⊜, Fl., U.S.	**220**	28.29 N	81.44 W
Louisbourg	**186**	45.55 N	59.58 W
Louis Bull Indian Reserve ◂[4]	**182**	52.53 N	113.31 W
Louisburg, Ks., U.S.	**198**	38.37 N	94.40 W
Louisburg, N.C., U.S.	**192**	36.05 N	78.18 W
Louisburgh	**48**	53.46 N	9.51 W
Louisdale	**186**	45.36 N	61.04 W
Louise, Ms., U.S.	**194**	32.58 N	90.35 W
Louise, Tx., U.S.	**222**	29.06 N	96.25 W
Louise, Lac ⊜, P.Q., Can.	**206**	45.46 N	74.25 W
Louise, Lac ⊜, P.Q., Can.	**206**	45.43 N	71.25 W
Louise, Lake ⊜	**180**	62.20 N	146.30 W
Louise Island I	**182**	52.58 N	131.50 W
Louiseville	**206**	46.15 N	72.57 W
Louis Gentil → Youssoufia	**148**	32.16 N	8.33 W
Louisiade Archipelago II	**160**	11.00 S	153.00 E
Louisiana	**219**	39.26 N	91.03 W
Louisiana □[3], U.S.	**178**	31.15 N	92.15 W
Louisiana □[3], U.S.	**194**	31.15 N	92.15 W
Louisiana ʋ	**41**	55.58 N	12.33 E
Lou Island I	**164**	2.25 S	147.20 E
Louis Trichardt	**156**	23.01 S	29.43 E
Louisvale	**158**	28.33 S	21.12 E
Louisville, On., Can.	**214**	42.28 N	82.07 W
Louisville, Al., U.S.	**194**	31.47 N	85.33 W
Louisville, Ga., U.S.	**192**	33.00 N	82.24 W
Louisville, Il., U.S.	**194**	38.46 N	88.30 W
Louisville, Ky., U.S.	**218**	38.15 N	85.45 W
Louisville, Ms., U.S.	**194**	33.07 N	89.03 W
Louisville, Ne., U.S.	**198**	40.59 N	96.09 W
Louisville, Oh., U.S.	**214**	40.50 N	81.15 W
Louisville Ridge ✥[3]	**14**	31.00 S	172.30 W
Louisville Seamount ✥[3]	**14**	31.15 S	172.15 W
Louis-XIV, Pointe >	**176**	54.37 N	79.45 W
Loujiaying	**98**	42.04 N	116.04 E
Loukanga	**273b**	4.20 S	15.09 E
Loukoua ≃	**273b**	4.09 S	15.08 E
Loulé	**34**	37.08 N	8.02 W
Loum	**152**	4.43 N	9.44 E
Loumou	**273b**	4.08 S	15.09 E
Lount Lake ⊜	**184**	50.10 N	94.20 W
Louny	**54**	50.19 N	13.46 E
Loup ≃, Fr.	**62**	43.38 N	7.09 E
Loup ≃, Ne., U.S.	**198**	41.24 N	97.19 W
Loup, Gorge du V	**56**	49.47 N	6.23 E
Loup, Rivière du ≃	**206**	46.13 N	72.55 W
Loup City	**198**	41.16 N	98.57 W
Loups Marins, Lacs des ⊜	**176**	56.30 N	73.45 W
Lourches	**50**	50.19 N	3.21 E
Lourdes, Nf., Can.	**186**	48.39 N	59.00 W
Lourdes, Fr.	**32**	43.06 N	0.03 W
Lourel de Baixo	**266c**	38.49 N	9.22 W
Lourenço	**250**	2.30 N	51.40 W
Lourenço Marques → Maputo	**156**	25.58 S	32.35 E
Lourenço Marques → Maputo □[5]	**156**	26.00 S	32.25 E
Lourenço Velho	**256**	22.22 S	45.19 W
Lourenço Velho ≃, Bra.	**256**	23.26 S	45.35 W
Lourenço Velho ≃, Bra.	**256**	22.22 S	45.31 W
Loures	**34**	38.50 N	9.10 W
Loures ≃	**266c**	38.50 N	9.08 W
Lourinhã	**34**	39.14 N	9.19 W
Lourmarin	**62**	43.46 N	5.22 E
Lourosa	**34**	40.19 N	7.56 W
Loury	**50**	48.00 N	2.05 E
Lousã, Port.	**34**	40.07 N	8.15 W
Lousa, Port.	**266c**	38.53 N	9.12 W
Louse Creek ≃	**198**	46.22 N	100.57 W
Lou Shan ∧	**89**	45.15 N	128.58 E
Louta	**150**	13.30 N	3.10 W
Loutang	**106**	31.26 N	121.12 E
Loutézou, Île de I	**273b**	4.22 S	15.10 E
Louth, Austl.	**166**	30.32 S	145.07 E
Louth, Ire.	**44**	53.57 N	6.33 W
Louth, Ire.	**48**	53.37 N	6.53 W
Louth, Eng., U.K.	**44**	53.22 N	0.01 W
Louth □[6]	**48**	53.55 N	6.30 W
Louth Bay c	**166**	34.34 S	136.02 E
Louti, Mayo ≃	**146**	9.38 N	13.56 E
Loutit Bay c	**169**	38.33 S	144.00 E
Loutrá Aidhipsoú	**38**	38.51 N	23.02 E
Loutre ≃	**219**	38.42 N	91.25 W
Loutre, Bayou de ≃	**194**	32.41 N	92.08 W
Loutrópirgos	**267c**	38.02 N	23.28 E

Symbols in the index entries represent the broad categories identified in the key at the right. Symbols with superior numbers (⋀[1]) identify subcategories (see complete key on page *I · 1).*

Kartensymbole in dem Registerverzeichnis stellen die rechts in Schlüssel erklärten Kategorien dar. Symbole mit hochgestellten Ziffern (⋀[1]) bezeichnen Unterabteilungen einer Kategorie (vgl. vollständiger Schlüssel auf Seite *I · 1).*

Los símbolos incluídos en el texto del índice representan las grandes categorias identificadas con la clave a la derecha. Los símbolos con numeros en su parte superior (⋀[1]) identifican las subcategorías (véase la clave completa en la página *I · 1).*

Les symboles de l'index représentent les catégories indiquées dans la légende à droite. Les symboles suivis d'un indice (⋀[1]) représentent des sous-catégories (voir légende complète à la page *I · 1).*

Os símbolos incluídos no texto do índice representam as grandes categorias identificadas com a chave à direita. Os símbolos com números em sua parte superior (⋀[1]) identificam as subcategorias (veja-se a chave completa à página *I · 1).*

∧ Mountain	Berg	Montaña	Montagne	Montanha
⋀ Mountains	Berge	Montañas	Montagnes	Montanhas
)(Pass	Pass	Paso	Col	Passo
V Valley, Canyon	Tal, Cañon	Valle, Cañón	Vallée, Canyon	Vale, Canhão
≚ Plain	Ebene	Llano	Plaine	Planície
> Cape	Kap	Cabo	Cap	Cabo
I Island	Insel	Isla	Île	Ilha
II Islands	Inseln	Islas	Îles	Ilhas
⊥ Other Topographic Features	Andere Topographische Objekte	Otros Elementos Topográficos	Autres données topographiques	Outros acidentes topográficos

	English	Deutsch	Español	Français	Português
≃	River	Fluss	Río	Rivière	Rio
≌	Canal	Kanal	Canal	Canal	Canal
∟	Waterfall, Rapids	Wasserfall, Stromschnellen	Cascada, Rápidos	Chute d'eau, Rapides	Cascata, Rápidos
)(	Strait	Meeresstrasse	Estrecho	Détroit	Estreito
c	Bay, Gulf	Bucht, Golf	Bahía, Golfo	Baie, Golfe	Baía, Golfo
⊜	Lake, Lakes	See, Seen	Lago, Lagos	Lac, Lacs	Lago, Lagos
≡	Swamp	Sumpf	Pantano	Marais	Pântano
⊼	Ice Features, Glacier	Eis- und Gletscherformen	Accidentes Glaciales	Formes glaciaires	Acidentes glaciares
⊤	Other Hydrographic Features	Andere Hydrographische Objekte	Otros Elementos Hidrográficos	Autres données hydrographiques	Outros acidentes hidrográficos
✦	Submarine Features	Untermeerische Objekte	Accidentes Submarinos	Formes de relief sous-marin	Acidentes submarinos
□	Political Unit	Politische Einheit	Unidad Política	Entité politique	Unidade política
ʋ	Cultural Institution	Kulturelle Institution	Institución Cultural	Institution culturelle	Institução cultural
⊥	Historical Site	Historische Stätte	Sitio Histórico	Site historique	Sitio histórico
♠	Recreational Site	Erholungs- und Ferienort	Sitio de Recreo	Centre de loisirs	Area de Lazer
⊠	Airport	Flughafen	Aeropuerto	Aéroport	Aeroporto
■	Military Installation	Militäranlage	Instalación Militar	Installation militaire	Instalação militar
◆	Miscellaneous	Verschiedenes	Misceláneo	Divers	Diversos

Name	Page	Lat.°′	Long.°′
Luni ⊥	64	44.04 N	10.01 E
Lunia-Bubi	154	7.30 S	24.49 E
Lunigiana ◆[1]	64	44.15 N	9.50 E
Lunin	76	52.18 N	26.38 E
Luninec	76	52.15 N	26.48 E
Lunino, S.S.S.R.	80	53.35 N	45.14 E
Lunino, S.S.S.R.	82	54.09 N	38.29 E
Lunjiao	100	22.53 N	113.13 E
Lūnkaransar	120	28.29 N	73.44 E
Lunnaja, gora ∧	180	68.14 N	174.20 E
Lunndörrsfjällen ∧	26	63.00 N	13.00 E
Lunno	76	53.27 N	24.16 E
Lunongzha	106	31.59 N	120.55 E
Lunsar	150	8.41 N	12.32 W
Lunsemfwa ≃	154	14.54 S	30.12 E
Lunt	262	53.31 N	2.59 W
Lunteren	52	52.05 N	5.37 E
Lunyuk	115b	8.57 S	117.14 E
Lunz am See	61	47.51 N	15.03 E
Lunzenau	54	50.58 N	12.45 E
Lunzhen	98	36.47 N	116.34 E
Luo ≃, Zhg.	102	34.48 N	113.04 E
Luo ≃, Zhg.	102	34.42 N	110.15 E
Luoba, Zhg.	100	24.51 N	114.13 E
Luoba, Zhg.	107	29.08 N	106.11 E
Luobei (Fengxiang)	89	47.34 N	130.50 E
Luobo	102	28.22 N	101.38 E
Luobu	102	24.30 N	109.40 E
Luobumiao	102	40.19 N	107.30 E
Luobuqiongzi	124	29.02 N	89.15 E
Luochanghe	100	31.01 N	117.18 E
Luocheng, Zhg.	102	24.51 N	108.59 E
Luocheng, Zhg.	107	29.23 N	104.01 E
Luochuan	102	35.55 N	109.26 E
Luoci	102	25.19 N	102.18 E
Luodian	106	31.25 N	121.20 E
Luoding	102	22.47 N	111.31 E
Luoduoke	120	33.28 N	79.40 E
Luoduzhen	107	30.22 N	106.35 E
Luofa	105	39.25 N	116.50 E
Luofang, Zhg.	100	28.40 N	115.04 E
Luofang, Zhg.	100	27.52 N	115.06 E
Luofu, Zaïre	154	0.10 S	29.14 E
Luofu, Zhg.	100	24.32 N	115.35 E
Luogang, Zhg.	100	23.11 N	113.30 E
Luogang, Zhg.	100	24.25 N	115.38 E
Luogosanto	71	41.03 N	9.13 E
Luoguhe	89	53.18 N	121.30 E
Luohan Shan ∧	100	25.51 N	119.13 E
Luohe	100	33.35 N	114.01 E
Luoheya	98	35.46 N	118.54 E
Luohua	100	26.35 N	118.43 E
Luoji	100	32.06 N	117.16 E
Luojiachang	107	30.49 N	106.32 E
Luojiang	102	31.21 N	104.28 E
Luojiatang	106	30.18 N	120.13 E
Luojiatun, Zhg.	98	40.11 N	118.34 E
Luojiatun, Zhg.	104	42.06 N	122.44 E
Luojiatun, Zhg.	104	40.55 N	122.04 E
Luojiawei	100	26.55 N	115.02 E
Luoke	100	24.07 N	114.28 E
Luokeng	100	24.32 N	113.23 E
Luokou, Zhg.	100	28.54 N	117.24 E
Luokou, Zhg.	100	25.46 N	115.39 E
Luolong	107	28.49 N	104.46 E
L'Uomo di Cagna ∧	71	41.33 N	9.04 E
Luonan	102	34.05 N	110.04 E
Luoning	102	34.25 N	111.42 E
Luoping	102	24.59 N	104.21 E
Luopu	120	37.02 N	80.15 E
Luoqi	102	29.48 N	106.56 E
Luoqiao	100	26.28 N	119.01 E
Luoquanzhen	107	29.50 N	104.31 E
Luoshan, Zhg.	100	32.13 N	114.32 E
Luoshan, Zhg.	100	29.41 N	113.18 E
Luoshan, Zhg.	105	39.55 N	117.33 E
Luoshe, Zhg.	106	31.39 N	120.11 E
Luoshe, Zhg.	106	30.41 N	120.04 E
Luoshuihe	98	39.27 N	114.19 E
Luossa ≃	152	8.24 S	17.03 E
Luotian	100	30.48 N	115.22 E
Luotuodian	100	32.13 N	113.49 E
Luotuoqiao	100	29.56 N	121.32 E
Luotuo Shan ∧	104	42.14 N	121.42 E
Luowenba	102	31.48 N	107.48 E
Luowenyu	105	40.16 N	117.57 E
Luoxi	100	29.05 N	114.58 E
Luoxiao Shan ⩘	100	26.00 N	114.00 E
Luoyang (Loyang), Zhg.	102	34.41 N	112.28 E
Luoyang, Zhg.	106	31.39 N	120.05 E
Luoyuan	100	26.31 N	119.32 E
Luoyuan Wan ⊂	100	26.25 N	119.43 E
Luoyukou	102	38.23 N	110.43 E
Luozha	120	28.24 N	90.49 E
Luozhexi	107	29.02 N	103.54 E
Luozi	152	4.57 S	14.08 E
Lupala	156	17.50 S	19.06 E
Lupani	154	18.54 S	27.44 E
Lupao	116	15.53 N	120.54 E
Lupar ≃	112	1.30 N	111.00 E
Łupawa	30	54.26 N	17.24 E
Lupberg	60	49.09 N	11.45 E
Lupembe	154	9.15 S	35.15 E
Lupeni	38	45.22 N	23.13 E
Lupire	152	14.36 S	19.29 E
Lupiro	154	8.23 S	36.40 E
Lupon	116	6.54 N	126.00 E
Lupow → Łupawa	30	54.26 N	17.24 E
Luppa	54	51.20 N	12.57 E
Luputa	152	7.10 S	23.42 E
Luqiao, Zhg.	100	32.34 N	117.14 E
Luqiao, Zhg.	100	28.35 N	121.22 E
Luqu	102	34.41 N	102.22 E
Luque	34	37.33 N	4.16 W
Luquillo	240m	18.22 N	65.43 W
Luquillo, Sierra de ⩘	240m	18.17 N	65.47 W
Lūrah ≃	120	31.33 N	66.33 E
Luray	188	38.39 N	78.27 W
Lure	58	47.41 N	6.30 E
Lure, Montagne de ⩘	62	44.07 N	5.47 E
Lureco ≃	154	12.28 S	37.40 E
Luremo	152	8.31 S	17.50 E
Lurgan	48	54.28 N	6.20 W
Luribay	248	17.06 S	67.39 W
Lurigancho	286d	12.02 S	77.01 W
Lurín	248	12.17 S	76.52 W
Lúrio	154	13.35 S	40.30 E
Lúrio ≃, Moç.	154	13.35 S	40.32 E
Lurio ≃, Suomi	24	67.08 N	27.29 E
Lurisia	62	44.18 N	7.42 E
Lurnea	274a	33.56 S	150.54 E
Lurö I	26	58.48 N	13.14 E
Lürrip ◆[8]	263	51.12 N	6.28 E
Lusahunga	154	2.52 S	31.15 E
Lusaka, Zaïre	154	7.10 S	29.27 E
Lusaka, Zam.	154	15.25 S	28.17 E
Lusaka □[4]	154	15.25 S	29.00 E
Lusakert	84	40.23 N	44.36 E
Lusambo	152	4.58 S	23.27 E
Lusancay Islands and Reefs II	164	8.25 S	150.20 E
Lusanga	152	4.50 S	18.44 E
Lusangaye	154	4.54 S	26.00 E
Lusangi	154	4.37 S	27.08 E
Luscar	182	53.04 N	117.24 W
Luseke	152	2.51 S	23.08 E
Luseland	184	52.05 N	109.24 W
Lusen ∧	60	48.56 N	13.31 E
Lusenga Plain National Park ♦	154	9.30 S	29.10 E
Lusengo	152	1.46 N	19.29 E
Luserna San Giovanni	62	44.48 N	7.15 E
Lush, Mount ∧	164	17.02 S	127.30 E
Lushan, Zhg.	100	33.45 N	112.53 E
Lushan, Zhg.	102	30.15 N	102.58 E
Lu Shan ∧	100	29.31 N	115.58 E
Lu Shan ⩘	98	36.05 N	118.05 E
Lushanguanliju	100	29.33 N	115.58 E
Lushi	102	34.05 N	111.01 E
Lushiko (Luchico) ≃	152	6.13 S	19.40 E
Lüshikou	100	29.16 N	120.17 E
Lushnje	38	40.56 N	19.42 E
Lushoto	154	4.47 S	38.17 E
Lushui	102	26.00 N	98.51 E
Lüshun (Port Arthur)	98	38.48 N	121.16 E
Lüsi	106	32.03 N	121.36 E
Lusi ≃	115a	7.05 S	110.55 E
Lusiana	64	45.47 N	11.34 E
Lusignan	32	46.26 N	0.07 E
Lusignan, Lac ⊜	206	46.40 N	74.09 W
Lusigny-sur-Barse	50	48.15 N	4.16 E
Lusikisiki	158	31.25 S	29.30 E
L'usino	76	52.38 N	26.31 E
Lusk, Ire.	48	53.32 N	6.10 W
Lusk, Wy., U.S.	200	42.45 N	104.27 W
Lus-la-Croix-Haute	62	44.40 N	5.42 E
Lusongwa	152	12.58 S	24.16 E
Luspebryggan	24	67.01 N	19.51 E
Lussac-les-Châteaux	32	46.24 N	0.44 E
Lussan	62	44.09 N	4.22 E
Lustenau	58	47.26 N	9.39 E
Luster	26	61.26 N	7.24 E
Lustin	56	50.23 N	4.53 E
Lustrafjorden ⊂[2]	26	61.20 N	7.22 E
Lüstringen	52	52.16 N	8.08 E
Lusutfu (Maputo) (Great Usutu) ≃	158	26.11 S	32.42 E
Luswishi ≃	154	13.55 S	27.24 E
Lūt, Dasht-e ◆[2]	128	33.00 N	57.00 E
Lü-ta → Lüda	98	38.53 N	121.35 E
L'uta ≃	76	58.37 N	28.40 E
Lutago (Luttach)	64	46.57 N	11.55 E
Lutai	100	33.32 N	115.03 E
Lütan, Zhg.	98	34.07 N	114.27 E
Lütan, Zhg.	100	28.57 N	119.46 E
Lutang	100	25.39 N	112.46 E
Lutao	116	10.00 N	124.04 E
Lü Tao I	100	22.40 N	121.29 E
Lutcher	194	30.02 N	90.41 W
Lute	284c	39.04 N	77.03 W
Lutembo	152	13.26 S	21.16 E
Lutembo ≃	152	12.03 S	22.15 E
L'uten'ka	78	50.13 N	34.02 E
Lutesville	194	37.18 N	89.58 W
Lutéte ≃	152	9.21 S	15.14 E
Lutexu ≃	273b	4.24 S	15.12 E
Lütgendortmund ◆[8]	263	51.30 N	7.21 E
Luthe	52	52.26 N	9.28 E
Luther, Mi., U.S.	190	44.02 N	85.40 W
Luther, Ok., U.S.	196	35.39 N	97.11 W
Luther Lake ⊜	212	43.55 N	80.26 W
Luthersburg	214	41.03 N	78.43 W
Lutherville-Timonium	284b	39.25 N	76.37 W
Luthrie	46	56.21 N	3.05 W
Luti	175e	7.14 S	156.59 E
Lutian, Zhg.	100	26.33 N	114.38 E
Lütian, Zhg.	100	23.48 N	113.56 E
Lütjenburg	54	54.17 N	10.35 E
Lütjensee	52	53.39 N	10.22 E
Luton, Eng., U.K.	42	51.53 N	0.25 W
Luton, Eng., U.K.	260	51.22 N	0.32 E
Lutong	112	4.28 N	114.00 E
Lutosn'a ≃	82	56.26 N	36.52 E
Lutou	100	32.16 N	112.53 E
Lutry	58	46.30 N	6.41 E
Lutshi	154	4.09 S	26.30 E
Lutshima ≃	152	5.22 S	18.59 E
Lutsk → Luck	78	50.44 N	25.20 E
Luttach → Lutago	64	46.57 N	11.55 E
Lutter am Barenberge	52	51.59 N	10.16 E
Lutterbach	58	47.46 N	7.17 E
Lutterworth	42	52.28 N	1.10 W
Lüttich → Liège	56	50.38 N	5.34 E
Luttrell	192	36.11 N	83.44 W
Lüttringhausen ◆[8]	263	51.13 N	7.14 E
Lutuai ≃	152	12.33 S	20.16 E
Lutugino	83	48.24 N	39.13 E
Lutz	220	28.09 N	82.27 W
Lützel	56	50.58 N	8.10 E
Lutzelbourg	56	48.44 N	7.15 E
Lützelflüh	58	47.00 N	7.41 E
Lützen	54	51.15 N	12.08 E
Lutzerath	56	50.07 N	7.00 E
Lutz Hill	284b	39.20 N	76.32 W
Lützow	54	53.40 N	11.11 E
Lützow-Holm Bay ⊂	9	69.10 S	37.30 E
Lutzputs	158	28.03 S	20.40 E
Lützschena	54	51.23 N	12.16 E
Lutzville	158	31.33 S	18.22 E
Luud, Waadi V	144	10.17 N	50.14 E
Luuq	144	3.48 N	42.33 E
Luus	102	45.30 N	105.45 E
Luverne, Al., U.S.	194	31.42 N	86.15 W
Lu Verne, Ia., U.S.	190	42.54 N	94.04 W
Luverne, Mn., U.S.	198	43.39 N	96.12 W
Luvo	152	5.51 S	14.05 E
Luvo ≃	152	10.18 S	17.08 E
Luvua	154	8.48 S	25.19 E
Lúvua ≃, Ang.	152	11.57 S	22.30 E
Luvua ≃, Zaïre	154	6.46 S	26.58 E
Luvuvhu ≃	156	22.40 S	30.55 E
Luwegu ≃	154	8.31 S	37.23 E
Luwingu	154	10.15 S	29.55 E
Luwuk → Banggai, Indon.	112	1.34 S	123.30 E
Luwuk, Indon.	112	0.56 S	122.47 E
Luxana Bay ⊂	182	52.03 N	131.00 W
Luxapallila Creek ≃	194	33.28 N	88.26 W
Luxembourg	56	49.36 N	6.09 E
Luxembourg □[4]	56	50.00 N	5.30 E
Luxembourg □[1], Europe	22	49.45 N	6.05 E
Luxembourg □[1], Europe	56	49.45 N	6.05 E
Luxembourg, Aéroport de ⊠	56	49.37 N	6.10 E
Luxembourg, Jardin du ♦	261	48.51 N	2.19 E
Luxemburg	190	44.32 N	87.42 W
Luxemburg → Luxembourg □[1]	56	49.45 N	6.05 E
Luxemburgo → Luxembourg □[1]	56	49.45 N	6.05 E
Luxeuil-les-Bains	58	47.49 N	6.23 E
Luxi, Zhg.	102	24.32 N	103.41 E
Luxi (Mangshi), Zhg.	102	24.20 N	98.25 E
Lüxia	100	26.41 N	120.06 E
Luxian	107	28.55 N	105.29 E
Luxiang, Zhg.	106	31.32 N	120.45 E
Lüxiang, Zhg.	106	30.50 N	121.10 E
Luxi Dao I	100	27.59 N	121.11 E
Luxikou	100	29.54 N	113.42 E
Luxmanor	284c	39.02 N	77.07 W
Luxor → Al-Uqṣur, Miṣr	140	25.41 N	32.39 E
Luxor, Pa., U.S.	214	40.20 N	79.28 W
Luxora	194	35.45 N	89.55 W
Luxu	106	31.01 N	120.50 E
Lu Xun Museum ⊕	269b	31.16 N	121.28 E
Lüxuqiao	106	31.50 N	119.31 E
Luy ≃	32	43.39 N	1.08 W
Luyan	106	30.25 N	120.53 E
Lüyang	104	41.23 N	121.40 E
Luyanó ≃	286b	23.07 N	82.21 W
Luyeh	100	22.55 N	121.08 E
Luyi	100	33.53 N	115.28 E
Luynes	50	47.23 N	0.33 E
Luyu	106	31.34 N	121.41 E
Luyuan, Zhg.	106	31.51 N	120.38 E
Luyuan, Zhg.	271a	39.54 N	116.27 E
Luz, Bra.	255	19.48 S	45.40 W
Luz, Bra.	287a	22.48 S	43.05 W
Luz ◆[8]	266c	38.46 N	9.10 W
Luz, Estação da ◆[5]	287b	23.32 S	46.38 W
Luz, Isla I	254	45.30 S	73.59 W
Luz, Ponta da ›	287a	22.47 S	43.05 W
Luza, S.S.S.R.	24	62.42 N	37.06 E
Luza, S.S.S.R.	24	60.39 N	47.10 E
Luža, S.S.S.R.	76	59.58 N	31.56 E
Luža ≃	82	55.03 N	36.35 E
Luzarches	50	49.07 N	2.25 E
Luzern	58	47.03 N	8.18 E
Luzern □[3]	58	47.05 N	8.05 E
Luzerne	210	41.17 N	75.54 W
Luzerne □[6]	210	41.14 N	75.53 W
Luzhai, Zhg.	102	24.31 N	109.50 E
Luzhai, Zhg.	269b	31.20 N	121.22 E
Luzhi	106	31.16 N	120.52 E
Luzhou	107	28.54 N	105.27 E
Luziânia	255	16.15 S	47.56 W
Lužické hory ⩘	54	50.48 N	14.40 E
Luzilândia	250	3.28 S	42.22 W
Lužki, S.S.S.R.	76	55.21 N	27.52 E
Lužki, S.S.S.R.	82	54.51 N	37.36 E
Lužná	54	50.06 N	13.45 E
Lužnice ≃, Europe	30	49.14 N	14.23 E
Lužnice (Lainsitz) ≃, Europe	61	49.13 N	14.42 E
Lužniki ◆[8]	265b	55.43 N	37.33 E
Luzon	236	9.25 N	82.32 W
Luzon I	116	16.00 N	121.00 E
Luzon Strait ⊔	108	20.30 N	121.00 E
Lužskaja guba ⊂	76	59.45 N	28.20 E
Luzy	32	46.48 N	3.58 E
Luzzara	64	44.58 N	10.41 E
Luzzi	68	39.27 N	16.17 E
L'va ≃	78	52.00 N	27.36 E
L'va Tolstogo	82	54.37 N	36.03 E
L'vov	78	49.50 N	24.00 E
L'vovskij	82	55.19 N	37.31 E
Lwów → L'vov	78	49.50 N	24.00 E
Lwówek	30	52.28 N	16.10 E
Lwówek Śląski	30	51.07 N	15.35 E
Lyall, Mount ∧	172	45.17 S	167.34 E
Lyallpur → Faisalabad	123	31.25 N	73.05 E
Lyantonde	154	0.24 S	31.09 E
Lybster	46	58.18 N	3.18 W
Lycaonia □[9]	130	37.50 N	33.15 E
Lychen	54	53.12 N	13.19 E
Lycia □[9]	130	36.20 N	30.00 E
Lyck → Ełk	30	53.50 N	22.22 E
Lyckeby	26	56.12 N	15.39 E
Lyčkovo, S.S.S.R.	76	57.55 N	32.24 E
Lyčkovo, S.S.S.R.	78	49.06 N	35.12 E
Lycksele	26	64.36 N	18.40 E
Lycoming □[6]	210	41.14 N	77.00 W
Lycoming Creek ≃	210	41.13 N	77.02 W
Lydd	42	50.57 N	0.55 E
Lydda → Lod	132	31.58 N	34.54 E
Lydden V	42	50.56 N	2.22 W
Lydenburg	156	25.10 S	30.29 E
Lydenburgh County Park ♦	276	40.50 N	73.14 W
Lydford	42	50.39 N	4.06 W
Lydgate	262	53.44 N	2.07 W
Lydham	42	52.31 N	2.58 W
Lydia □[9]	130	38.40 N	27.30 E
Lydia Mills	192	34.28 N	81.55 W
Lydiate	262	53.32 N	2.57 W
Lydick	216	41.42 N	86.22 W
Lydney	42	51.44 N	2.32 W
Lye Green	260	51.43 N	0.35 W
Lyell, Mount ∧, Can.	182	51.57 N	117.06 W
Lyell, Mount ∧, Ca., U.S.	226	37.44 N	119.16 W
Lyell Brown, Mount ∧	162	23.21 S	130.24 E
Lyell Island I	182	52.40 N	131.30 W
Lyerly	192	34.24 N	85.24 W
Lyford	196	26.24 N	97.47 W
Lygnern ⊜	26	57.29 N	12.20 E
Lykens	208	40.34 N	76.42 W
Lykošino	76	58.07 N	33.43 E
Lyle, Mn., U.S.	190	43.30 N	92.56 W
Lyle, Wa., U.S.	224	45.41 N	121.17 W
Lyles	194	35.55 N	87.20 W
Lyman, Ne., U.S.	198	41.55 N	104.02 W
Lyman, S.C., U.S.	192	34.56 N	82.07 W
Lyman, Wa., U.S.	224	48.31 N	122.03 W
Lyman, Wy., U.S.	200	41.19 N	110.17 W
Lymbel'karamo	86	60.15 N	83.32 E
Lyme	207	41.18 N	72.19 W
Lyme Bay ⊂	42	50.38 N	3.00 W
Lyme Hall ⊥	262	53.20 N	2.03 W
Lyme Park ♦	262	53.21 N	2.04 W
Lyme Regis	42	50.44 N	2.57 W
Lyminge	42	51.08 N	1.05 E
Lymington	42	50.46 N	1.33 W
Lymkoj	86	59.31 N	70.22 E
Lymm	262	53.23 N	2.29 W
Lympne	42	51.05 N	1.02 E
Lympstone	42	50.39 N	3.25 W
Lyn	212	44.35 N	75.47 W
Łyna (Lava) ≃	76	54.37 N	21.14 E
Lynæs	41	55.57 N	11.52 E
Lynbrook	276	40.39 N	73.41 W
Lynch, Ky., U.S.	192	36.57 N	82.55 W
Lynch, Ne., U.S.	198	42.49 N	98.27 W
Lynch, Lac ⊜	190	46.25 N	77.05 W
Lynchburg, Oh., U.S.	218	39.14 N	83.47 W
Lynchburg, S.C., U.S.	192	34.03 N	80.04 W
Lynchburg, Tn., U.S.	194	35.16 N	86.22 W
Lynchburg, Va., U.S.	192	37.24 N	79.08 W
Lynches ≃	192	33.50 N	79.22 W
Lynchville	214	41.26 N	78.34 W
Lynd ≃	164	16.28 S	143.18 E
Lynde Creek ≃	212	43.51 N	78.57 W
Lynden, On., Can.	212	43.14 N	80.09 W
Lynden, Wa., U.S.	224	48.56 N	122.27 W
Lyndhurst, Austl.	166	19.12 S	144.23 E
Lyndhurst, Austl.	166	30.17 S	138.21 E
Lyndhurst, Austl.	274b	38.03 S	145.15 E
Lyndhurst, Eng., U.K.	42	50.52 N	1.34 W
Lyndhurst, N.J., U.S.	276	40.48 N	74.07 W
Lyndhurst, Oh., U.S.	214	41.31 N	81.29 W
Lyndoch	168b	34.37 S	138.53 E
Lyndon, Austl.	162	23.37 S	115.15 E
Lyndon, Ks., U.S.	198	38.38 N	95.41 W
Lyndon, Ky., U.S.	218	38.15 N	85.36 W
Lyndon ≃	162	23.29 S	114.06 E
Lyndon B. Johnson, Lake ⊜[1]	196	30.35 N	98.25 W
Lyndon B. Johnson Historical Park ⊥	196	30.15 N	98.38 W
Lyndon B. Johnson Space Center ⊕[3]	222	29.34 N	95.05 W
Lyndonville, N.Y., U.S.	210	43.19 N	78.23 W
Lyndonville, Vt., U.S.	188	44.32 N	72.00 W
Lyndora	214	40.51 N	79.55 W
Lyne	260	51.23 N	0.33 W
Lyne ≃	44	54.58 N	3.01 W
Lyneham	42	51.31 N	1.58 W
Lynemouth	44	55.12 N	1.31 W
Lyne Water ≃	46	54.39 N	3.16 W
Lynga	80	57.17 N	53.04 E
Lyngdal	26	58.08 N	7.05 E
Lynge	41	55.51 N	12.17 E
Lyngen	24	69.34 N	20.10 E
Lyngen ⊂[2]	24	69.58 N	20.30 E
Lyngør	26	58.38 N	9.10 E
Lynher ≃	42	50.28 N	4.12 W
Lynmouth	42	51.15 N	3.50 W
Lynn, Al., U.S.	194	34.02 N	87.32 W
Lynn, In., U.S.	218	40.02 N	84.56 W
Lynn, Ma., U.S.	207	42.28 N	70.57 W
Lynn ≃	212	42.47 N	80.12 W
Lynn Canal ⊂	180	58.50 N	135.15 W
Lynndyl	200	39.31 N	112.22 W
Lynne Acres	284b	39.21 N	76.45 W
Lynnfield	207	42.32 N	71.02 W
Lynn Garden	192	36.34 N	82.34 W
Lynn Harbor ⊂	283	42.27 N	70.57 W
Lynn Haven	194	30.14 N	85.38 W
Lynn Lake	184	56.51 N	101.03 W
Lynnville	190	41.34 N	92.47 W
Lynnwood, Pa., U.S.	210	41.14 N	75.56 W
Lynnwood, Pa., U.S.	214	40.07 N	79.51 W
Lynnwood, Wa., U.S.	224	47.49 N	122.18 W
Lynn Woods ♦	283	42.29 N	70.59 W
Lynton	42	51.15 N	3.50 W
Lyntupy	76	55.03 N	26.19 E
Lynwood, Ca., U.S.	228	33.55 N	118.12 W
Lynwood, Il., U.S.	278	41.32 N	87.32 W
Lynx Lake ⊜	176	62.25 N	106.15 W
Lyø I	41	55.02 N	10.10 E
Lyon	62	45.45 N	4.51 E
Lyon □[6]	226	39.00 N	119.15 W
Lyon ≃	46	56.37 N	4.01 W
Lyon ◆[5]	261	48.51 N	2.23 E
Lyon, Glen V	46	56.35 N	4.20 W
Lyon, Loch ⊜	46	56.32 N	4.36 W
Lyon Inlet ⊂	176	66.32 N	83.53 W
Lyon Mountain	188	44.43 N	73.54 W
Lyon Mountain ∧	188	44.41 N	73.53 W
Lyonnais □[9]	62	45.45 N	4.30 E
Lyonnais, Monts du ⩘	62	45.40 N	4.30 E
Lyons, Co., U.S.	200	40.13 N	105.16 W
Lyons, Ga., U.S.	192	32.12 N	82.19 W
Lyons, Il., U.S.	216	41.48 N	87.49 W
Lyons, In., U.S.	194	38.59 N	87.04 W
Lyons, Ks., U.S.	198	38.20 N	98.12 W
Lyons, Mi., U.S.	216	42.58 N	84.56 W
Lyons, Ne., U.S.	198	41.56 N	96.28 W
Lyons, N.Y., U.S.	210	43.03 N	76.59 W
Lyons, Oh., U.S.	216	41.41 N	84.04 W
Lyons, Tx., U.S.	222	30.23 N	96.34 W
Lyons, Wi., U.S.	216	42.39 N	88.21 W
Lyons ≃	162	25.02 S	115.09 E
Lyon-Satolas, Aéroport de ⊠	62	45.43 N	5.04 E
Lyons Creek ≃	284a	43.03 N	79.04 W
Lyons Falls	212	43.37 N	75.22 W
Lyons-la-Forêt	50	49.24 N	1.28 E
Lyons Plains	207	41.13 N	73.21 W
Lyons Run ≃	279b	40.25 N	79.43 W
Lyon Station	208	40.28 N	75.45 W
Lyonsville	276	40.57 N	74.25 W
Lyracrumpane	48	52.20 N	9.30 W
Lyrestad	40	58.48 N	14.04 E
Lys (Leie) ≃, Europe	50	51.03 N	3.43 E
Lys ≃, It.	62	45.36 N	7.47 E
Lysá ∧	60	49.29 N	12.42 E
Lysaja Gora	78	48.11 N	31.06 E
Lysaker	26	59.54 N	10.36 E
Lys'anka	78	49.16 N	30.50 E
Lysá pod Makytou	30	49.12 N	18.13 E
Lysefjorden ⊂[2]	26	59.00 N	6.14 E
Lysekil	26	58.16 N	11.26 E
Łysica ∧	30	50.54 N	20.55 E
Lysjön ⊜	40	60.07 N	14.18 E
Lyskovo	80	56.04 N	45.02 E
Lysogorka	83	47.42 N	39.12 E
Lyss	58	47.04 N	7.18 E
Lysterfield	274b	37.56 S	145.18 E
Lysterfield Hills ⩘[2]	274b	37.56 S	145.16 E
Lysterfield Reservoir ⊜[1]	274b	37.58 S	145.18 E
Lyster Station	206	46.22 N	71.37 W
Lys'va	86	58.07 N	57.47 E
Lys'va ≃	80	58.15 N	54.47 E
Lysyje Gory	80	51.32 N	44.46 E
Lytham Saint Anne's	44	53.45 N	2.57 W
Lytkarino	82	55.35 N	37.54 E
Lytle	196	29.13 N	98.47 W
Lytle Creek ≃	228	34.09 N	117.23 W
Lyttelton, N.Z.	172	43.35 S	172.42 E
Lyttelton, S. Afr.	158	25.50 S	28.11 E
Lytton	182	50.14 N	121.34 W
Lytton Springs	222	30.00 N	97.37 W
Lyubertsy → L'ubercy	82	55.41 N	37.53 E

M

Name	Page	Lat.°′	Long.°′
Ma ≃	110	19.47 N	105.56 E
Ma, Oued el V, Alg.	148	27.45 N	7.45 W
Ma, Oued el V, Maur.	148	24.03 N	9.10 W
Maad, Djebel bou ∧	34	36.26 N	2.08 E
Maadid, Djebel ∧	34	35.52 N	4.46 E
Maalaea Bay ⊂	229a	20.47 N	156.29 W
Ma'alot-Tarshiḥa	132	33.01 N	35.17 E
Maam Cross	48	53.27 N	9.31 W
Maan, Tür.	130	36.51 N	38.50 E
Ma'ān, Urd.	132	30.12 N	35.44 E
Ma'ān □[8]	132	30.20 N	36.30 E
Maaninka	26	63.09 N	27.18 E
Ma'anshan, Zhg.	100	31.42 N	118.30 E
Maanshan, Zhg.	107	29.52 N	104.59 E
Ma-ao	116	10.29 N	122.59 E
Maap I	174q	9.35 N	138.11 E
Maar	140	6.54 N	31.33 E
Maardu	76	59.28 N	25.02 E
Maarianhamina → Mariehamn	26	60.06 N	19.57 E
Ma'ārik, Qārat al- ∧[2]	142	29.59 N	30.52 E
Ma'arrat an-Nu'mān	130	35.38 N	36.40 E
Ma'arrat Miṣrīn	130	36.01 N	36.40 E
Ma'arrat Ṣaydnāyā	132	33.41 N	36.23 E
Maarssen	52	52.08 N	5.08 E
Maas	48	54.50 N	8.22 W
Maas (Meuse) ≃	30	51.49 N	5.01 E
Maasbracht	52	51.08 N	5.53 E
Maasdam	52	51.47 N	4.32 E
Maaseik	56	51.06 N	5.48 E
Maasholm	41	54.41 N	9.59 E
Maasin	116	10.08 N	124.50 E
Ma'āṣir ash-Shūf	132	33.40 N	35.40 E
Maasmechelen	56	50.58 N	5.44 E
Maasniel	52	51.13 N	6.01 E
Maassluis	52	51.55 N	4.15 E
Maastricht	56	50.52 N	5.43 E
Maave	156	21.03 S	34.47 E
Ma-ayon ≃	116	11.25 N	122.46 E
Maba	100	32.59 N	118.48 E
Maba, Ouadi V	146	15.10 N	21.00 E
Mababe Depression ⊥[7]	156	18.50 S	24.15 E
Mabaduan	164	9.16 S	142.44 E
Mabaho, Mount ∧	116	9.15 N	125.42 E
Mabaia	152	7.13 S	14.03 E
Mabalane	156	23.37 S	32.31 E
Mabana	224	48.05 N	122.24 W
Mabanga	152	1.30 N	19.06 E
Mabank	222	32.21 N	96.06 W
Mabaoquan	105	40.09 N	115.53 E
Ma'barot	132	32.22 N	34.54 E
Mabaruma	246	8.12 N	59.47 W
Mabashi	268	35.49 N	139.55 E
Mabau	112	2.14 S	111.54 E
Mabay	240p	20.16 N	76.40 W
Mabber, Ras ›	144	9.28 N	50.50 E
Mabel Creek	162	29.01 S	134.17 E
Mabeleapodi	156	20.58 S	22.36 E
Mabel Lake ⊜	182	50.35 N	118.44 W
Maben	194	33.33 N	89.05 W
Mabenga-Cité	152	3.39 S	18.40 E
Mabenge	152	4.14 N	24.09 E
Maberry, Loch ⊜	44	55.02 N	4.41 W
Mabeti ≃	92	40.31 N	141.31 E
Mabeul	36	36.27 N	10.46 E
Mabi, Nihon	96	34.38 N	133.41 E
Mabi, Zhg.	100	26.21 N	119.36 E
Mabi, Zhg.	102	35.59 N	112.15 E
Mabian	107	28.48 N	103.41 E
Mabian ≃	107	29.08 N	103.58 E
Mablethorpe	44	53.21 N	0.15 E
Mableton	192	33.49 N	84.34 W
Mabole ≃	150	9.01 N	12.44 W

ENGLISH Name	Page	Lat.°′	Long.°′
Maboma	154	2.32 N	28.13 E
Mabonto	150	8.52 N	11.49 W
Mabote	156	22.03 S	34.09 E
Mabou	186	46.05 N	61.22 W
Mabrak, Jabal ∧	132	30.13 N	35.29 E
Mabrous ⊤[4]	146	21.13 N	13.38 E
Mabrūk, Lībiyā	146	29.50 N	17.10 E
Mabrūk, Sūd.	140	8.07 N	29.25 E
Mabton	202	46.12 N	119.59 W
Mabuasehube Game Reserve ◆[4]	156	25.10 S	22.10 E
Mabuguai	100	29.49 N	112.42 E
Mabuki	154	2.59 S	33.11 E
Mabuni	174m	26.05 N	127.43 E
Mabwe	154	8.39 S	26.31 E
Mača, S.S.S.R.	74	59.54 N	117.35 E
Maca, Ven.	286c	10.28 N	66.48 W
Macá, Cerro ∧	254	45.06 S	73.12 W
Macachín	252	37.09 S	63.39 W
Macaco, Morro do ∧[2]	287a	22.56 S	43.07 W
Macacos, Ilha dos I	250	1.20 S	50.35 W
Macacu ≃	256	22.42 S	43.02 W
McAdam	186	45.36 N	67.20 W
McAdams Peak ∧[2]	219	38.58 N	90.32 W
McAdoo	210	40.54 N	75.59 W
McAdoo Heights	210	40.54 N	76.01 W
Macaé	255	22.23 S	41.47 W
McAfee	210	41.10 N	74.32 W
Macaíba	250	5.51 S	35.21 W
Macajalar Bay ⊂	116	8.37 N	124.38 E
Macajuba	255	12.09 S	40.22 W
Macalaya	116	12.53 N	123.46 E
Macalelon	116	13.45 N	122.08 E
McAlester	196	34.56 N	95.46 W
Macalister	182	52.27 N	122.24 W
Macalister ≃	166	38.02 S	146.59 E
Macalister, Mount ∧	170	34.27 S	149.45 E
McAlisterville	208	40.38 N	77.16 W
McAllen	196	26.12 N	98.13 W
Macallum Lake ⊜	184	55.02 N	108.25 W
Macaloge	154	12.25 S	35.25 E
McAlpine	208	39.16 N	76.50 W
McAlpine Dam ◆[6]	218	38.16 N	85.47 W
MacAlpine Lake ⊜	176	66.40 N	103.15 W
McAlveys Fort	214	40.39 N	77.50 W
Macambira	250	10.40 S	37.32 W
Macamic, Lac ⊜	190	48.48 N	78.59 W
Macão	34	39.33 N	8.00 W
Macao → Macau □[2]	100	22.10 N	113.33 E
Macapá	250	0.02 N	51.03 W
Macar	130	37.06 N	30.56 E
Macará	246	4.23 S	79.57 W
Macarani	255	15.33 S	40.24 W
Macarao	286c	10.26 N	67.02 W
Macarao ≃	286c	10.26 N	67.01 W
Macareo, Caño ≃[1]	246	9.47 N	61.37 W
Macari ≃	250	1.52 N	50.31 W
MacArthur, Pil.	116	10.50 N	125.00 E
MacArthur, Il., U.S.	278	41.39 N	87.44 W
McArthur	188	39.14 N	82.28 W
McArthur ≃	164	15.54 S	136.40 E
McArthur River	164	16.27 S	136.07 E
Macas	246	2.19 S	78.07 W
Macatawa ≃	216	42.48 N	86.05 W
Macatawa, Lake ⊂	216	42.47 N	86.10 W
Macaterick, Loch ⊜	44	55.12 N	4.26 W
Macau, Bra.	250	5.07 S	36.38 W
Macau (Aomen), Macau	100	22.14 N	113.35 E
Macau □[2], Asia	90	22.10 N	113.33 E
Macau □[2], Asia	100	22.10 N	113.33 E
Macau, Ilha I	156	20.55 S	35.05 E
Macauã ≃	248	9.13 S	68.44 W
Macaúbas	255	13.02 S	42.42 W
McAuley	184	50.16 N	101.23 W
Macaya, Pic de ∧	238	18.25 N	74.00 W
Macaza ≃	206	46.21 N	74.47 W
McBain	190	44.11 N	85.12 W
McBee	192	34.28 N	80.15 W
McBeth	222	29.11 N	95.30 W
McBeth Fjord ⊂[2]	176	69.38 N	68.30 W
McBride	182	53.18 N	120.10 W
McCall	202	44.54 N	116.05 W
McCall Creek	194	31.30 N	90.41 W
McCallum	186	47.38 N	56.15 W
McCallum Creek ≃	169	37.03 S	143.49 E
McCamey	196	31.08 N	102.13 W
McCammon	202	42.39 N	112.11 W
McCandless, Pa., U.S.	214	40.35 N	80.01 W
McCandless, Pa., U.S.	279b	40.34 N	80.02 W
Maccarese ◆[8]	267a	41.53 N	12.13 E
Maccarese, Bonifica di ◆[1]	267a	41.51 N	12.13 E
McCarteney Creek ≃	202	47.13 N	120.05 W
McCarthy	180	61.26 N	142.55 W
McCauley Island I	182	53.40 N	130.15 W
McCaysville	192	34.59 N	84.22 W
Macchiagodena	66	41.33 N	14.24 E
McChord Air Force Base ■	224	47.08 N	122.29 W
McClarens Run ≃	279b	40.27 N	80.12 W
McClarty Lake ⊜	184	54.28 N	100.20 W
McCleary	224	47.03 N	123.15 W
McClees Creek ≃	276	40.22 N	74.03 W
McClellan Air Force Base ■	226	38.39 N	121.23 W
McClellan Creek ≃	196	35.22 N	100.34 W
McClellanville	192	33.05 N	79.27 W
MacClenny	192	30.16 N	82.07 W
Macclesfield, Austl.	168b	35.10 S	138.50 E
Macclesfield, Eng., U.K.	44	53.16 N	2.07 W
Macclesfield □[8]	262	53.17 N	2.15 W
Macclesfield Canal ≋	262	53.24 N	2.03 W
Macclesfield Forest ◆[3]	262	53.15 N	2.03 W
McClintock, Mount ∧	9	80.13 S	157.26 E
McCloud	204	41.15 N	122.08 W
McCloud ≃	204	40.46 N	122.18 W
McClure, Il., U.S.	194	37.19 N	89.26 W
McClure, Oh., U.S.	216	41.22 N	83.56 W
McClure, Pa., U.S.	210	40.42 N	77.18 W
McClure, Lake ⊜[1]	226	37.37 N	120.16 W
McClusky	198	47.29 N	100.26 W
McColl	192	34.40 N	79.32 W
McComas	192	37.23 N	81.17 W
McComb, Ms., U.S.	194	31.14 N	90.27 W
McComb, Oh., U.S.	216	41.06 N	83.47 W
McConaughy, Lake ⊜[1]	198	41.15 N	101.50 W
McConnell Air Force Base ■	198	37.38 N	97.15 W
McConnell Range ⩘	180	64.00 N	123.50 W
McConnellsburg	188	39.55 N	77.59 W
McConnells Mill	279b	40.15 N	80.15 W
McConnells Mill State Park ♦	214	40.57 N	80.11 W
McConnellstown	214	40.27 N	78.05 W
McConnellsville	210	43.16 N	75.42 W
McConnelsville	188	39.38 N	81.51 W
McCook, Il., U.S.	278	41.48 N	87.50 W
McCook, Ne., U.S.	198	40.12 N	100.37 W
McCordsville	218	39.53 N	85.55 W
McCormick	192	33.54 N	82.17 W
McCormick Place ⊕	278	41.51 N	87.37 W
McCoy	224	45.03 N	123.13 W
McCoy Creek ≃	202	43.02 N	118.50 W
McCoy Lake ⊜	184	52.35 N	92.19 W
McCraney Creek ≃	219	39.39 N	91.12 W
McCreary	184	50.46 N	99.30 W
McCrory	194	35.15 N	91.12 W
McCulloch, Mount ∧	162	25.10 S	129.52 E
McCullom Lake	216	42.22 N	88.18 W
McCullough	279b	40.22 N	79.38 W
McCullough Mountain ∧	204	35.36 N	115.11 W
McCune	198	37.21 N	95.00 W
McCurtain	196	35.08 N	94.58 W
McCusker ≃	184	55.32 N	108.40 W

DEUTSCH Name	Seite	Breite°′	Länge°′ E = Ost
McCutchenville	214	40.59 N	83.15 W
McDade	222	30.17 N	97.15 W
McDavid	194	30.51 N	87.19 W
McDermitt	204	41.59 N	117.43 W
McDermott	218	38.50 N	83.03 W
Macdhui, Ben ∧	158	30.39 S	27.58 E
MacDill Air Force Base ■	220	27.51 N	82.29 W
McDonald, Ks., U.S.	198	39.47 N	101.22 W
McDonald, Pa., U.S.	214	40.22 N	80.14 W
Macdonald ≃	170	33.23 S	150.59 E
McDonald, Lac ⊜	206	45.52 N	74.35 W
Macdonald, Lake ⊜	162	23.30 S	129.00 E
McDonald, Lake ⊜	202	48.35 N	113.55 W
MacDonald Downs	162	22.27 S	135.13 E
Macdonald Lake ⊜	212	45.14 N	78.34 W
McDonald Park ♦	282	37.18 N	122.17 W
MacDonald Pass)(	202	46.34 N	112.18 W
Macdonald Range ⩘	182	49.12 N	114.46 W
Macdonnell Ranges ⩘	162	23.45 S	133.20 E
McDonogh	284c	39.24 N	76.46 W
McDonough, Ga., U.S.	192	33.26 N	84.08 W
McDonough, N.Y., U.S.	210	42.30 N	75.46 W
McDouall Peak	162	29.51 S	134.55 E
McDougal, Mount ∧	200	42.54 N	110.36 W
MacDowell Lake ⊜	184	52.15 N	92.45 W
McDowell Peak ∧	200	33.40 N	111.50 W
Macdowell Peninsula ›[1]	168b	35.47 S	138.00 E
Macduff	46	57.40 N	2.29 W
Macdui, Ben ∧	46	57.05 N	3.38 W
Mačecha	80	50.48 N	43.17 E
Mačechi	78	49.31 N	34.26 E
Maceday Lake ⊜	281	42.42 N	83.26 W
Macedo de Cavaleiros	34	41.32 N	6.58 W
Macedon, Austl.	169	37.25 S	144.34 E
Macedon, N.Y., U.S.	210	43.04 N	77.17 W
Macedon, Mount ∧	169	37.23 S	144.35 E
Macedonia, Ct., U.S.	207	41.47 N	73.30 W
Macedonia, Oh., U.S.	214	41.18 N	81.30 W
Macedonia → Makedonija □[3]	38	41.50 N	22.00 E
Macedonia □[9]	38	41.00 N	23.00 E
Macedonia Brook State Park ♦	207	41.47 N	73.29 W
Macedonio Alcalá	234	17.52 N	96.02 W
Maceió	250	9.40 S	35.43 W
Maceira	266c	38.52 N	9.19 W
McElhattan	210	41.09 N	77.22 W
McElmo Creek ≃	200	37.13 N	109.12 W
Mc Ennen Airport ⊠	281	42.12 N	83.37 W
Macenta	150	8.33 N	9.28 W
Maceo	246	6.33 N	74.47 W
Macerata	66	43.18 N	13.27 E
Macerata □[4]	66	43.12 N	13.10 E
Macerata Feltria	66	43.48 N	12.26 E
McEwen	194	36.06 N	87.37 W
McEwensville	210	41.05 N	76.49 W
McFadden	200	41.39 N	106.07 W
McFarland, Ca., U.S.	226	35.40 N	119.13 W
McFarland, Wi., U.S.	216	43.00 N	89.17 W
MacFarlane ≃	176	59.12 N	107.58 W
Macfarlane, Lake ⊜	166	31.55 S	136.42 E
Macfarlane, Mount ∧	172	43.56 S	169.23 E
McGavock Lake ⊜	184	56.32 N	101.25 W
McGehee	194	33.37 N	91.23 W
McGill	204	39.24 N	114.46 W
McGill, Université ⊕[2]	275a	45.30 N	73.35 W
McGillivray, Lac ⊜	190	46.04 N	77.06 W
Macgillycuddy's Reeks ⩘	48	51.55 N	9.45 W
McGinnis Slough Wildlife Refuge ◆[4]	278	41.39 N	87.52 W
McGovern	214	40.14 N	80.13 W
McGrann	214	40.47 N	79.31 W
McGrath	180	62.58 N	155.38 W
McGraw	210	42.35 N	76.05 W
MacGregor	184	49.57 N	98.49 W
McGregor, On., Can.	214	42.09 N	82.58 W
McGregor, S. Afr.	158	33.57 S	19.50 E
McGregor, Ia., U.S.	190	43.01 N	91.10 W
McGregor, Tx., U.S.	222	31.26 N	97.24 W
McGregor ≃	182	54.11 N	122.00 W
McGregor Creek ≃	214	42.24 N	82.11 W
McGregor Lake ⊜	182	50.31 N	112.53 W
McGregor Range ⩘	166	26.40 S	142.45 E
McGuffey	216	40.41 N	83.47 W
McGuire, Mount ∧	202	45.10 N	114.36 W
McGuire Air Force Base ■	208	40.02 N	74.35 W
McGuire Reservoir ⊜	224	45.19 N	123.26 W
Macha	248	18.49 S	66.05 W
Machacamarca	248	18.10 S	67.02 W
Machache ∧	158	29.21 S	27.55 E
Machachi	246	0.30 S	78.34 W
Machačkala	84	42.58 N	47.30 E
Machada, Mata Nacional da ♦	266c	38.36 N	9.02 W
Machadinho ≃	248	9.00 S	61.52 W
Machado	256	21.41 S	45.56 W
Machado ≃	256	21.38 S	45.52 W
Machadodorp	156	25.40 S	30.14 E
Machados	256	22.30 S	46.25 W
Machærus ⊥	132	31.34 N	35.38 E
Machagai	252	26.56 S	60.03 W
Machaila	156	22.15 S	32.55 E
Machakos	154	1.31 S	37.16 E
Machala	246	3.16 S	79.58 W
Machalí	252	34.11 S	70.40 W
Machalino	80	53.05 N	46.14 E
Māchalpur	124	24.08 N	76.18 E
Machaneng	156	23.10 S	27.26 E
Machang, Malay.	114	5.46 N	102.13 E
Machang, Zhg.	98	34.06 N	119.02 E
Machang, Zhg.	98	42.05 N	119.42 E
Machanga	156	20.58 S	34.59 E
Machangcun	105	38.54 N	115.26 E
Machangfu	102	25.14 N	103.45 E
Machang Jianhe ≃	105	39.00 N	117.40 E
Machaquilá ≃	236	16.13 N	90.01 W
Macharadze	84	41.56 N	42.00 E
Machattie, Lake ⊜	166	24.50 S	139.48 E
Machault	50	49.21 N	4.30 E
Machava	156	25.54 S	32.29 E
Machaze	156	20.51 S	33.26 E
Machecoul	32	47.00 N	1.50 W
Macheke	154	18.05 S	31.51 E
Machelen	50	50.55 N	4.26 E
Macheng	100	31.13 N	115.00 E
McHenry, Il., U.S.	216	42.20 N	88.16 W
McHenry, Ms., U.S.	194	30.42 N	89.08 W
McHenry □[6]	216	42.19 N	88.27 W
Macherio	266b	45.38 N	9.16 E
Mācherla	122	16.29 N	79.26 E
Machern	54	51.21 N	12.37 E
Machery	261	48.36 N	2.05 E
Machesna Mountain ∧	226	35.17 N	120.14 W
Machesney Park	216	42.20 N	89.03 W
Machhīwara	123	30.55 N	76.12 E
Machhlīshahr	124	25.41 N	82.25 E
Machhuakhali	126	22.05 N	90.21 E
Machias, Me., U.S.	188	44.42 N	67.27 W
Machias, N.Y., U.S.	210	42.25 N	78.30 W
Machias ≃	188	44.43 N	67.22 W
Machias Bay ⊂	188	44.40 N	67.20 W
Machichaco, Cabo ›	34	43.27 N	2.45 W
Machichi ≃	184	57.03 N	92.06 W
Machico	148	32.42 N	16.46 W
Machida	94	35.32 N	139.27 E
Machile ≃	154	17.26 S	25.02 E
Machilīpatnam (Bandar)	122	16.10 N	81.08 E
Machindžauri	84	41.40 N	41.43 E
Machiques	246	10.04 N	72.34 W
Machiya ≃	94	35.01 N	136.42 E
Machkund ⊜[1]	122	18.26 N	82.35 E

Symbols in the index entries represent the broad categories identified in the key at the right. Symbols with superior numbers (⩘[1]) identify subcategories (see complete key on page *I · 1).*

Kartensymbole in dem Registerverzeichnis stellen die rechts in Schlüssel erklärten Kategorien dar. Symbole mit hochgestellten Ziffern (⩘[1]) bezeichnen Unterabteilungen einer Kategorie (vgl. vollständiger Schlüssel auf Seite *I · 1).*

Los símbolos incluídos en el texto del índice representan las grandes categorias identificadas con la clave a la derecha. Los símbolos con numeros en su parte superior (⩘[1]) identifican las subcategorías (véase la clave completa en la página *I · 1).*

Les symboles de l'index représentent les catégories indiquées dans la légende à droite. Les symboles suivis d'un indice (⩘[1]) représentent des sous-catégories (voir légende complète à la page *I · 1).*

Os símbolos incluídos no texto do índice representam as grandes categorias identificadas com a chave à direita. Os símbolos com números em sua parte superior (⩘[1]) identificam as subcategorias (veja-se a chave completa à página *I · 1).*

Symbol	English	Deutsch	Español	Français	Português
∧	Mountain	Berg	Montaña	Montagne	Montanha
⩘	Mountains	Berge	Montañas	Montagnes	Montanhas
)(	Pass	Pass	Paso	Col	Passo
V	Valley, Canyon	Tal, Cañon	Valle, Cañón	Vallée, Canyon	Vale, Canhão
≌	Plain	Ebene	Llano	Plaine	Planície
›	Cape	Kap	Cabo	Cap	Cabo
I	Island	Insel	Isla	Île	Ilha
II	Islands	Inseln	Islas	Îles	Ilhas
⊥	Other Topographic Features	Andere Topographische Objekte	Otros Elementos Topográficos	Autres données topographiques	Outros acidentes topográficos

ESPAÑOL

Nombre	Página	Lat. °′	Long. °′ W = Oeste
Machmud-Mekteb	84	44.26 N	45.13 E
Machn'ovo	86	58.27 N	61.42 E
Macho, Arroyo del V	196	33.36 N	104.28 W
Machočen, porog ∟	88	57.23 N	121.29 E
Machona, Laguna ⊂	234	18.20 N	93.40 W
Machtaly	85	41.22 N	68.02 E
Machupicchu	248	13.07 S	72.34 W
Machupicchu ⊥	248	13.07 S	72.34 W
Machupo ≃	248	12.34 S	64.25 W
Machynlleth	42	52.35 N	3.51 W
Maciá, Arg.	252	32.10 S	59.23 W
Macia, Moç.	156	25.03 S	33.10 E
Maciel, Arroyo ≃	258	33.42 S	57.59 W
Măcin	38	45.15 N	28.08 E
Macina → Massina ◆[1]	150	14.30 N	5.00 W
McInnes Lake ⊜	184	52.12 N	93.45 W
McIntosh, Al., U.S.	194	31.15 N	88.01 W
McIntosh, Il., U.S.	216	42.03 N	88.23 W
McIntosh, Mn., U.S.	198	47.38 N	95.53 W
McIntosh, S.D., U.S.	198	45.55 N	101.20 W
McIntosh Lake ⊜	184	55.45 N	105.08 W
McIntyre	214	40.34 N	79.17 W
Macintyre ≃, Austl.	166	29.25 S	148.45 E
Macintyre ≃, Austl.	166	28.38 S	150.47 E
McIntyre Bay ⊂	182	54.05 N	131.55 W
Mačkassy	80	52.46 N	45.34 E
Mackay, Austl.	166	21.09 S	149.11 E
Mackay, Id., U.S.	202	43.54 N	113.36 W
MacKay ≃	184	57.03 N	111.55 W
Mackay, Lake ⊜	162	22.30 S	129.00 E
McKay, Mount ∧	162	22.26 S	120.01 E
McKay Creek ≃	202	45.40 N	118.50 W
MacKay Lake ⊜	176	63.55 N	110.25 W
McKean	214	41.59 N	80.09 W
McKean □[6]	214	41.49 N	78.27 W
McKeand ≃	176	65.26 N	68.10 W
McKee	192	37.25 N	83.59 W
McKee City	208	39.27 N	74.38 W
McKee Creek ≃	219	39.46 N	90.36 W
McKeesport	214	40.20 N	79.51 W
McKees Rocks	214	40.27 N	80.03 W
McKenna	224	46.56 N	122.33 W
Mackenrode	54	51.33 N	10.33 E
Mackenzie	246	6.00 N	58.17 W
McKenzie, Al., U.S.	194	31.32 N	86.42 W
McKenzie, Tn., U.S.	194	36.07 N	88.31 W
Mackenzie □[5]	176	65.00 N	115.00 W
Mackenzie ≃, Austl.	166	23.38 S	149.46 E
Mackenzie ≃, N.T., Can.	176	69.15 N	134.08 W
McKenzie ≃	202	44.07 N	123.06 W
MacKenzie Bay ⊂, Ant.	9	68.20 S	71.15 E
Mackenzie Bay ⊂, Can.	180	69.00 N	136.30 W
McKenzie Bridge	202	44.10 N	122.09 W
McKenzie Creek ≃	212	43.02 N	79.53 W
Mackenzie Delta ⩧[2]	180	68.50 N	135.25 W
McKenzie Island	184	51.05 N	93.48 W
McKenzie Lake ⊜, On., Can.	212	45.22 N	78.02 W
McKenzie Lake ⊜, Sk., Can.	184	54.12 N	102.30 W
Mackenzie Mountains ⋏	180	64.00 N	130.00 W
McKerrow, Lake ⊜	172	44.26 S	168.03 E
Mackeyville	210	41.03 N	77.28 W
McKillip Ditch ≅	216	40.50 N	86.51 W
Mackinac, Straits of ⊍	190	45.49 N	84.42 W
Mackinac Bridge ◆[5]	190	45.50 N	84.45 W
Mackinac Island	190	45.50 N	84.37 W
Mackinac Island I	190	45.51 N	84.38 W
Mackinac Island State Park ♠	190	45.52 N	84.40 W
Mackinaw	190	40.32 N	89.21 W
Mackinaw ≃	194	40.33 N	89.44 W
Mackinaw City	190	45.47 N	84.43 W
McKinlay	166	21.16 S	141.17 E
McKinlay ≃	166	20.50 S	141.28 E
McKinley, Mount ∧	180	63.04 N	151.00 W
McKinley Airport ⊠	281	42.33 N	82.58 W
McKinley Park ♠	279b	40.25 N	80.00 W
McKinleyville, Ca., U.S.	204	40.56 N	124.05 W
McKinleyville, W.V., U.S.	214	40.15 N	80.36 W
McKinney	222	33.11 N	96.36 W
Mackinnon Road	154	3.44 S	39.03 E
McKittrick, Ca., U.S.	226	35.18 N	119.37 W
McKittrick, Mo., U.S.	219	38.44 N	91.27 W
McKittrick Summit ∧	226	35.18 N	119.46 W
Macklin	184	52.20 N	109.56 W
McKnight Lake ⊜	184	56.03 N	101.08 W
McKnightstown	208	39.52 N	77.20 W
McKnight Village	279b	40.31 N	80.00 W
Mačkovci	61	46.47 N	16.09 E
M'ačkovo, S.S.S.R.	82	55.13 N	38.40 E
M'ačkovo, S.S.S.R.	82	56.21 N	39.03 E
McKownville	210	42.41 N	73.50 W
Macksville, Austl.	166	30.43 S	152.55 E
Macksville, Ks., U.S.	198	38.57 N	98.58 W
McLain	194	31.06 N	88.49 W
McLarty Hills ⋏[2]	162	19.29 S	123.33 E
McLaughlin	198	45.48 N	100.48 W
McLaughlin ≃	184	53.46 N	97.38 W
McLaughlin Run ≃	279b	40.22 N	80.07 W
McLaurin	194	31.10 N	89.13 W
Maclean	166	29.28 S	153.13 E
McLean, Sk., Can.	184	50.30 N	104.04 W
McLean, Il., U.S.	194	40.18 N	89.10 W
McLean, N.Y., U.S.	210	42.33 N	76.17 W
McLean, Tx., U.S.	196	35.13 N	100.35 W
McLean, Va., U.S.	208	38.56 N	77.10 W
McLean □[6]	216	40.29 N	88.45 W
McLean Hamlet	284c	38.56 N	77.13 W
McLean Lake ⊜	184	56.27 N	109.15 W
McLean Mountain ∧	186	47.07 N	68.50 W
McLeansboro	194	38.05 N	88.32 W
Macleantown	158	32.47 S	27.45 E
Maclear	158	31.02 S	28.23 E
Macleay ≃	166	30.52 S	153.01 E
McLennan	182	55.42 N	116.54 W
McLennan □[6]	222	31.35 N	97.13 W
Macleod	274b	37.43 S	145.04 E
McLeod ≃	182	54.08 N	115.42 W
Macleod, Lake ⊜	162	24.00 S	113.35 E
McLeod Bay ⊂	176	62.53 N	110.00 W
McLeodganj	123	30.15 N	73.42 E
McLeodganj Road	123	30.09 N	73.44 E
McLeod Lake	182	54.59 N	123.02 W
McLoughlin, Mount ∧	202	42.27 N	122.19 W
McLoughlin Bay ⊂	176	67.50 N	99.00 W
McLoughlin House National Historic Site ⊥	224	45.20 N	122.33 W
McLouth	198	39.11 N	95.12 W
Maclovio Herrera	232	29.05 N	105.08 W
McLure	182	51.03 N	120.14 W
McMahan	222	29.51 N	97.31 W
McMahon	184	50.05 N	107.32 W
McMasterville	206	45.33 N	73.15 W
McMichael Art Collection ❦	275b	43.50 N	79.37 W
Macmillan ≃	180	62.52 N	135.55 W
McMillan, Lake ⊜[1]	196	32.40 N	104.20 W
McMinnville, Or., U.S.	224	45.12 N	123.11 W
McMinnville, Tn., U.S.	194	35.41 N	85.46 W
McMurdo ❦[3]	9	77.50 S	166.25 E
McMurdo Sound ⊍	9	77.30 S	165.00 E
McMurray	214	40.17 N	80.05 W
McNair	222	29.48 N	95.02 W
McNary	200	34.04 N	109.51 W
McNeil, Ar., U.S.	194	33.20 N	93.12 W
McNeil, Tx., U.S.	222	30.27 N	97.43 W
McNeil, Mount ∧	182	54.35 N	130.14 W
McNeil Island I	224	47.13 N	122.41 W
McNeill	194	30.40 N	89.38 W
McNulty	224	45.50 N	122.50 W

FRANÇAIS

Nom	Page	Lat. °′	Long. °′ W = Ouest
Macocolo	152	6.47 S	16.08 E
Macolin	58	47.09 N	7.14 E
Macolla, Punta ≻	241s	12.06 N	70.13 W
Macolo	152	7.05 S	16.48 E
Macomb	190	40.27 N	90.40 W
Macomb □[6]	214	42.40 N	82.54 W
Macomb Mall ◆[9]	281	42.32 N	82.55 W
Macomer	71	40.16 N	8.47 E
Macomia	154	12.15 S	40.08 E
Macon, Bel.	50	50.03 N	4.13 E
Mâcon, Fr.	58	46.18 N	4.50 E
Macon, Ga., U.S.	192	32.50 N	83.37 W
Macon, Il., U.S.	219	39.42 N	88.59 W
Macon, Ms., U.S.	194	33.06 N	88.33 W
Macon, Mo., U.S.	194	39.44 N	92.28 W
Macon □[6], Il., U.S.	219	39.51 N	89.32 W
Macon □[6], Mo., U.S.	219	39.50 N	92.20 W
Macon, Bayou ≃	194	31.55 N	91.33 W
Macon Creek ≃	216	41.58 N	83.38 W
Macondo	152	12.35 S	23.44 E
Macondo ≃	152	13.23 S	23.03 E
Mâconnais, Monts du ⋏	58	46.18 N	4.45 E
Macorís, Cabo ≻	238	19.47 N	70.28 W
Macosquin	44	55.06 N	6.43 W
Macossa	156	17.52 S	33.56 E
Macouba, Pointe de ≻	240e	14.53 N	61.09 W
Macoun Lake ⊜	184	56.32 N	103.50 W
Macoupin □[6]	219	39.17 N	89.53 W
Macoupin Creek ≃	219	39.11 N	90.36 W
Macouria	250	4.55 N	52.22 W
Macovane	156	21.28 S	35.04 E
McPhail ≃	184	52.44 N	96.31 W
McPhee Bay ⊂	212	44.35 N	79.19 W
McPhee Reservoir ⊜[1]	200	37.32 N	108.35 W
McPherson	198	38.22 N	97.39 W
Macpherson, Mount ∧[2]	162	21.49 S	121.35 E
McPherson Range ⋏	166	28.20 S	153.00 E
Macquarie ≃, Austl.	166	41.44 S	147.08 E
Macquarie ≃, Austl.	166	30.07 S	147.24 E
Macquarie, Lake ⊜	170	33.05 S	151.35 E
Macquarie Fields	274a	33.59 S	150.53 E
Macquarie Harbour ⊂	166	42.19 S	145.23 E
Macquarie Island I	9	54.30 S	158.56 E
Macquarie Marshes ≡	166	30.50 S	147.32 E
Macquarie Ridge ⊹[3]	9	57.00 S	159.00 E
Macquarie University ❦[2]	274a	33.46 S	151.06 E
McQueeney	196	29.35 N	98.02 W
McRae, Ar., U.S.	194	35.06 N	91.49 W
McRae, Ga., U.S.	192	32.04 N	82.54 W
McRae, Mount ∧	162	22.17 S	117.35 E
McRae Point Provincial Park ♠	212	44.34 N	79.19 W
Macritchie Reservoir ⊜[1]	271c	1.21 N	103.50 E
McRoberts	192	37.12 N	82.40 W
Mac Robertson Coast ⌓[2]	9	68.10 S	65.00 E
Macrohon	116	10.05 N	124.56 E
Macroom	48	51.54 N	8.57 W
McSherrystown	208	39.48 N	77.00 W
Mactan Airfield ■	116	10.18 N	123.58 E
Mactan Island I	116	10.18 N	123.58 E
MacTier	212	45.08 N	79.47 W
Macuelizo	236	15.18 N	88.31 W
Macugnaga	58	45.58 N	7.58 E
Macujer	246	0.23 N	72.55 W
Macul	286e	33.30 S	70.34 W
Macúl, Parque de ♠	286e	33.30 S	70.35 W
Maculabo Island I	116	14.24 N	122.49 E
Macumba ≃	162	27.52 S	137.12 E
Macun	130	36.58 N	30.50 E
Macungie	208	40.30 N	75.33 W
Macunqiao	100	33.50 N	116.13 E
Macuro	246	10.39 N	61.56 W
Maçururé ≃	250	8.47 S	38.59 W
Macusani	248	14.05 S	70.26 W
Macuspana	234	17.46 N	92.36 W
Macusse	152	17.51 S	20.21 E
Macuto	286c	10.37 N	66.53 W
Macuze	156	17.42 S	37.11 E
McVeigh	192	37.32 N	82.15 W
McVeytown	214	40.30 N	77.44 W
McVickers Brook ≃	276	40.45 N	74.38 W
McVille	198	47.45 N	98.10 W
McWilliams	194	31.49 N	87.05 W
Macy	216	40.57 N	86.07 W
Mad ≃, On., Can.	212	44.25 N	79.54 W
Mad ≃, Ca., U.S.	204	40.57 N	124.07 W
Mad ≃, N.Y., U.S.	212	43.20 N	75.44 W
Mad ≃, Oh., U.S.	188	39.46 N	84.11 W
Mad ≃, Vt., U.S.	188	44.18 N	72.41 W
Mada ≃	150	7.59 N	7.55 E
Ma'dabā	132	31.43 N	35.48 E
Madagascar (Madagasikara) □[1], Afr.	138	19.00 S	46.00 E
Madagascar (Madagasikara) □[1], Afr.	157b	19.00 S	46.00 E
Madagascar Basin ⊹[1]	12	27.00 S	53.00 E
Madagascar Plateau ⊹[3]	10	30.00 S	45.00 E
Madagasikara → Madagascar □[1]	157b	19.00 S	46.00 E
Madagaskar → Madagascar □[1]	157b	19.00 S	46.00 E
Madagiz	84	40.19 N	46.44 E
Madagoi, Bohol V	144	0.44 N	42.56 E
Madā'in Şāliḩ	128	26.48 N	37.53 E
Madajevo	80	54.48 N	44.31 E
Madama	146	21.58 N	13.39 E
Madame, Isle I	186	45.33 N	61.02 W
Madan	38	41.30 N	24.57 E
Madanapalle	122	13.33 N	78.30 E
Madang, Pap. N. Gui.	164	5.15 S	145.50 E
Madang, Zhg.	100	29.58 N	116.40 E
Madang □[5]	164	5.00 S	145.30 E
Madanpur	272b	22.40 N	88.32 E
Madanpur Dabās ◆[8]	272a	28.43 N	77.02 E
Madaoua	150	14.05 N	5.58 E
Mādār Gāng ≃[1]	126	22.12 N	89.04 E
Mādāri Hāt	124	26.42 N	89.17 E
Mādārīpur	124	23.10 N	90.12 E
Madarounfa	150	13.18 N	7.09 E
Mādārpur	272b	22.54 N	88.27 E
Madawaska, On., Can.	212	45.30 N	77.59 W
Madawaska, Me., U.S.	186	47.21 N	68.19 W
Madawaska ≃	212	45.27 N	76.21 W
Madawaska Highlands ⋏[1]	212	45.15 N	77.35 W
Madawaska Lake ⊜	212	45.20 N	78.23 W
Madaxmaroodi	144	2.39 N	44.36 E
Madaya, Mya.	110	22.13 N	96.07 E
Maḑāyā, Sūrīy.	132	33.41 N	36.06 E
Madbar	140	6.19 N	30.40 E
Mad Creek ≃	210	42.55 N	77.59 W
Maddalena, Colle della (Col de Larche))(	62	44.25 N	6.53 E
Maddalena, Isola I	71	41.14 N	9.25 E
Maddaloni	68	41.02 N	14.23 E
Maddela	116	16.21 N	121.41 E
Madden, Mount ∧	162	33.12 S	119.51 E
Maddington	168a	32.03 S	115.59 E
Maddock	198	47.57 N	99.31 W
Maddy, Loch ⊂	46	57.36 N	7.08 W
Made	52	51.41 N	4.46 E
Madeir	140	7.50 N	29.12 E
Madeira	218	39.11 N	84.21 W
Madeira I	148	32.44 N	17.00 W
Madeira ≃	242	3.22 S	58.45 W

PORTUGUÊS

Nome	Página	Lat. °′	Long. °′ W = Oeste
Madeira, Arquipélago da II	148	32.40 N	16.45 W
Madeira Beach	220	27.48 N	82.48 W
Madeirinha ≃	248	8.31 S	60.46 W
Madeirinha, Paraná ≃[1]	246	3.25 S	58.51 W
M'adel'	76	54.53 N	26.57 E
Mädelegabel ∧	58	47.18 N	10.18 E
Madeleine, Îles de la II	186	47.30 N	61.45 W
Madeleine, Pointe ≻	275a	45.27 N	73.57 W
Madeleine-Centre	186	49.15 N	65.21 W
Madeley, Eng., U.K.	42	52.59 N	2.20 W
Madeley, Eng., U.K.	42	52.39 N	2.28 W
Madelia	190	44.03 N	94.25 W
Madeline Island I	190	46.50 N	90.40 W
Maden	130	38.23 N	39.40 E
Maden ◆[8]	267b	40.52 N	29.08 E
Madenhanları	130	40.11 N	40.25 E
Madenijet	86	47.53 N	78.37 E
Madera, Méx.	232	29.12 N	108.07 W
Madera, Ca., U.S.	226	36.57 N	120.03 W
Madera, Pa., U.S.	214	40.49 N	78.26 W
Madera □[6]	226	37.15 N	119.45 W
Madera Canal ≅	226	37.05 N	119.59 W
Madera Lake ⊜[1]	226	37.02 N	119.59 W
Madera Peak ∧	226	37.32 N	119.23 W
Maderas, Islas → Madeira, Arquipélago da II	148	32.40 N	16.45 W
Maderas, Volcán ∧[1]	236	11.27 N	85.31 W
Maderno	64	45.38 N	10.35 E
Madgaon (Margao)	122	15.18 N	73.57 E
Madh ◆[8]	272c	19.08 N	72.47 E
Madhipura	124	25.55 N	86.47 E
Madhkūr, Bi'r ⍑[4]	142	30.42 N	32.32 E
Mādhopur	123	32.22 N	75.36 E
Madhubani	124	26.22 N	86.05 E
Madhudaha	272b	22.31 N	88.25 E
Madhugiri	122	13.40 N	77.12 E
Madhukhāli	126	23.33 N	89.38 E
Madhumati ≃[1]	126	22.53 N	89.52 E
Madhupar	126	22.54 N	86.28 E
Madhupur	126	24.16 N	86.39 E
Madhya Bhārat Pathār ◆[1]	124	25.00 N	77.00 E
Madhyamgrām	272b	22.42 N	88.27 E
Madhya Pradesh □[3]	120	23.00 N	79.00 E
Mādi ≃	124	27.49 N	84.27 E
Madia	154	7.08 S	26.00 E
Madian	106	32.15 N	119.58 E
Madibi	152	4.18 S	18.24 E
Madibira	154	8.12 S	34.49 E
Madibogo	158	26.25 S	25.10 E
Madida	98	42.57 N	130.48 E
Madidi ≃	248	12.32 S	66.52 W
Madill	196	34.05 N	96.46 W
Madimba, Ang.	152	6.31 S	14.21 E
Madimba, Zaïre	152	4.58 S	15.08 E
Madina	150	13.24 N	8.51 W
Madina do Boé	150	11.45 N	14.13 W
Madinani	150	9.37 N	6.57 W
Madinat al-Abyār	146	32.11 N	20.36 E
Madīnat ash-Sha'b (Al-Ittihad)	144	12.50 N	44.56 E
Madine, Lac de ⊜	56	48.54 N	5.42 E
Madingo	152	4.07 S	11.22 E
Madingou	152	4.09 S	13.34 E
Madingzi	104	42.08 N	120.52 E
Madi Opei	154	3.37 N	33.05 E
Madirobe	157b	16.04 S	46.15 E
Madirovalo	157b	16.26 S	46.30 E
Madison, Al., U.S.	194	34.41 N	86.44 W
Madison, Ca., U.S.	226	38.41 N	121.58 W
Madison, Ct., U.S.	207	41.16 N	72.35 W
Madison, Fl., U.S.	192	30.28 N	83.24 W
Madison, Ga., U.S.	192	33.35 N	83.28 W
Madison, Il., U.S.	219	38.40 N	90.09 W
Madison, In., U.S.	218	38.44 N	85.22 W
Madison, Ks., U.S.	198	38.08 N	96.08 W
Madison, Me., U.S.	188	44.47 N	69.52 W
Madison, Md., U.S.	208	38.30 N	76.13 W
Madison, Mn., U.S.	198	45.00 N	96.11 W
Madison, Mo., U.S.	219	39.28 N	92.12 W
Madison, Ne., U.S.	198	41.49 N	97.27 W
Madison, N.J., U.S.	210	40.45 N	74.25 W
Madison, N.Y., U.S.	210	42.53 N	75.30 W
Madison, N.C., U.S.	192	36.23 N	79.57 W
Madison, Oh., U.S.	214	41.46 N	81.03 W
Madison, Pa., U.S.	279b	40.15 N	79.41 W
Madison, S.D., U.S.	198	44.00 N	97.06 W
Madison, Va., U.S.	188	38.22 N	78.15 W
Madison, W.V., U.S.	188	38.04 N	81.49 W
Madison, Wi., U.S.	216	43.04 N	89.24 W
Madison □[6], Il., U.S.	219	38.49 N	89.58 W
Madison □[6], In., U.S.	218	40.10 N	85.41 W
Madison □[6], N.Y., U.S.	210	43.05 N	75.42 W
Madison □[6], Oh., U.S.	218	39.53 N	83.27 W
Madison □[6], Tx., U.S.	222	30.58 N	95.55 W
Madison ≃	202	45.56 N	111.30 W
Madison, West Fork ≃	202	44.55 N	111.35 W
Madisonburg, Oh., U.S.	214	40.51 N	81.55 W
Madisonburg, Pa., U.S.	210	40.55 N	77.31 W
Madison Heights, Mi., U.S.	216	42.29 N	83.06 W
Madison Heights, Va., U.S.	192	37.25 N	79.07 W
Madison Mills	218	39.40 N	83.20 W
Madison-on-the-Lake	214	41.42 N	81.24 W
Madison Park	276	40.26 N	74.19 W
Madison Range ⋏	202	45.15 N	111.20 W
Madison Square Garden ♠	276	40.45 N	74.00 W
Madisonville, Ky., U.S.	194	37.19 N	87.29 W
Madisonville, La., U.S.	194	30.24 N	90.09 W
Madisonville, Tn., U.S.	192	35.31 N	84.21 W
Madisonville, Tx., U.S.	222	30.56 N	95.54 W
Madiun	115a	7.37 S	111.31 E
Madiun ≃	115a	7.23 S	111.27 E
Madiyi	102	28.14 N	110.30 E
Madjingo	152	1.23 N	14.06 E
Madjoari	150	11.26 N	1.15 E
Madley, Mount ∧	162	24.31 S	123.58 E
Madoc	212	44.30 N	77.28 W
Mado Gashi	154	0.44 N	39.10 E
Madoi	102	34.53 N	98.24 E
Madol	140	9.02 N	27.46 E
Madon ≃	58	48.36 N	6.06 E
Madona	76	56.51 N	26.13 E
Madonna (Unserfrau)	64	46.43 N	10.52 E
Madonna della Guardia ❦[1]	62	44.29 N	8.51 E
Madonna della Quercia ❦[1]	66	42.25 N	12.06 E
Madonna dell'Olmo	62	44.25 N	7.32 E
Madonna del Sasso ❦[1]	58	46.11 N	8.33 E
Madonna di Campiglio	64	46.14 N	10.49 E
Madonna di Tirano	64	46.13 N	10.09 E
Madora	76	53.09 N	30.11 E
Madougou	150	14.24 N	3.05 W
Madrakah	144	21.59 N	39.59 E
Madrakah, Ra's al- ≻	118	19.00 N	57.50 E
Madras, India	122	13.05 N	80.17 E
Madras, Or., U.S.	202	44.38 N	121.07 W
Madras → Tamil Nadu □[3]	122	11.00 N	78.15 E
Madre, Laguna ⊂, Méx.	232	25.00 N	97.40 W
Madre, Laguna ⊂, Tx., U.S.	196	27.00 N	97.35 W
Madre, Sierra ⋏, N.A.	236	15.20 N	92.20 W
Madre, Sierra ⋏, Pil.	116	16.20 N	122.00 E
Madre de Deus de Minas	256	21.29 S	44.20 W
Madre de Dios □[5]	248	12.00 S	70.15 W
Madre de Dios ≃	248	10.59 S	66.08 W
Madre de Dios, Isla I	254	50.15 S	75.05 W
Madre del Sur, Sierra ⋏	234	17.00 N	100.00 W
Madre Occidental, Sierra ⋏	232	25.00 N	105.00 W
Madre Oriental, Sierra ⋏	232	22.00 N	99.30 W
Madre Vieja ≃	236	14.01 N	91.26 W
Madrid, Col.	246	4.44 N	74.16 W
Madrid, Esp.	34	40.24 N	3.41 W
Madrid, Esp.	266a	40.24 N	3.41 W
Madrid, Pil.	116	9.15 N	126.00 E
Madrid, Al., U.S.	194	31.02 N	85.23 W
Madrid, Ia., U.S.	190	41.52 N	93.49 W
Madrid, Ne., U.S.	198	40.51 N	101.32 W
Madrid □[4]	34	40.30 N	3.40 W
Madridejos, Esp.	34	39.28 N	3.32 W
Madridejos, Pil.	116	11.18 N	123.44 E
Madrigalejo	34	39.09 N	5.37 W
Madrillon	284c	38.55 N	77.14 W
Madriz □[5]	236	13.30 N	86.30 W
Madroñera	34	39.26 N	5.46 W
Madruga	240p	22.55 N	81.51 W
Madrūsah	146	24.48 N	14.32 E
Madsen	184	50.58 N	93.55 W
Madsūs, Bi'r ⍑[4]	142	29.15 N	32.19 E
Maducang Island I	116	10.42 N	120.15 E
Maduda	152	4.55 S	13.06 E
Maduo	152	1.24 S	20.44 E
Madura, Austl.	162	31.55 S	127.00 E
Madura → Madurai, India	122	9.56 N	78.07 E
Madura I	115a	7.00 S	113.20 E
Madura, Selat ⊍	115a	7.25 S	113.25 E
Madurai	122	9.56 N	78.07 E
Madurāntakam	122	12.31 N	79.54 E
Madureira, Serra de ⋏	287a	22.49 S	43.31 W
Madurerira ◆[8]	287a	22.53 S	43.21 W
Maduru ≃	122	7.52 N	81.31 E
Madwar al-Bighāl ∧[2]	142	29.09 N	29.54 E
Madyan ◆[1]	128	27.40 N	35.35 E
Madžalis	84	42.08 N	47.50 E
Mãe, Ilha da I	287a	22.59 S	43.04 W
Maeander Reef ⊹[2]	116	8.05 N	119.18 E
Maebaru	92	33.33 N	130.12 E
Maebashi	94	36.23 N	139.04 E
Maeda	270	34.55 N	135.08 E
Mãe dos Homens	256	22.52 S	46.37 W
Maegye-ri	98	34.45 N	126.18 E
Mae Hong Son	110	19.16 N	97.56 E
Mae Klong ≃	110	13.21 N	100.00 E
Mae Nam Khong → Mekong ≃	12	10.33 N	105.24 E
Maenclochog	42	51.54 N	4.48 W
Maengsan	98	39.40 N	126.30 E
Maeno ◆[8]	268	35.46 N	139.42 E
Maenza	66	41.31 N	13.11 E
Mae Ramat	110	16.58 N	98.31 E
Mae Rim	110	18.54 N	98.57 E
Maerkansu	85	39.19 N	73.53 E
Ma'erna	102	31.13 N	102.02 E
Maershan ∧	102	26.18 N	100.20 E
Mae Sariang	110	18.10 N	97.56 E
Maeser	200	40.28 N	109.35 W
Mae Sot	110	16.43 N	98.34 E
Maesteg	42	51.37 N	3.40 W
Maestra, Sierra ⋏	240p	20.00 N	76.45 W
Maestre de Campo Island I	116	12.56 N	121.42 E
Maestu	34	42.44 N	2.27 W
Mae Tha	110	18.28 N	99.08 E
Maevarano ≃	157b	14.35 S	47.58 E
Maevatanana	157b	16.56 S	46.49 E
Maéwo I	175f	15.10 S	168.10 E
Ma'fan	146	25.55 N	14.29 E
Mafang	105	40.02 N	117.01 E
Mafangchang	107	29.24 N	106.06 E
Mafangcun	105	40.09 N	116.24 E
Ma Faro ⊹[2]	122	5.50 N	73.26 E
Mafeking	184	52.41 N	101.06 W
Mafembage	152	14.32 S	21.42 E
Mafengtun	104	40.49 N	122.54 E
Mafeteng	158	29.51 S	27.15 E
Maffliers	261	49.05 N	2.19 E
Maffra	166	37.58 S	146.59 E
Mafia Channel ⊍	154	8.10 S	39.40 E
Mafia Island I	154	7.50 S	39.50 E
Mafikeng	156	25.53 S	25.39 E
Mafou ≃	150	10.32 N	10.08 W
Mafra, Bra.	252	26.07 S	49.49 W
Mafra, Port.	34	38.56 N	9.20 W
Magadan	74	59.34 N	150.48 E
Magadan □[4]	180	66.00 N	178.00 E
Magadi	154	1.54 S	36.17 E
Magadi, Lake ⊜	154	1.52 S	36.17 E
Magaguadavic Lake ⊜	186	45.43 N	67.12 W
Magai-butsu ❦[1]	96	33.05 N	131.45 E
Magalhães Bastos ◆[8]	287a	22.53 S	43.23 W
Magalhães de Almeida	250	3.24 S	42.12 W
Magaliesberg ⋏	158	25.50 S	27.30 E
Magallanes → Punta Arenas, Chile	254	53.09 S	70.55 W
Magallanes, Pil.	116	12.50 N	123.50 E
Magallanes, Estrecho de (Strait of Magellan) ⊍	254	54.00 S	71.00 W
Magallanes y Antártica Chilena □[4]	254	53.00 S	72.00 W
Maganga	154	0.51 N	26.22 E
Magangué	246	9.14 N	74.45 W
Magansk	88	55.52 N	93.15 E
Maganuy ≃	116	6.55 N	124.30 E
Magara, India	126	22.34 N	87.34 E
Mağara, Tür.	130	36.43 N	33.52 E
Magaramkent	84	41.37 N	48.21 E
Magaria	150	13.00 N	8.54 E
Magat ≃	116	17.02 N	121.49 E
Magazine Mountain ∧	194	35.10 N	93.38 W
Magazzolo ≃	70	37.25 N	13.15 E
Magboro	273a	6.43 N	3.24 E
Magburaka	150	8.43 N	11.57 W
Magdagači	89	53.27 N	125.48 E
Magdalena, Arg.	258	35.04 S	57.32 W
Magdalena, Bol.	248	13.20 S	64.08 W
Magdalena, Méx.	234	20.55 N	103.57 W
Magdalena, Perú	248	6.21 S	77.49 W
Magdalena, N.M., U.S.	200	34.07 N	107.14 W
Magdalena □[5]	246	10.00 N	74.00 W
Magdalena ≃, Col.	246	11.06 N	74.51 W
Magdalena ≃, Méx.	232	30.48 N	112.32 W
Magdalena, Bahía ⊂	232	24.35 N	112.00 W
Magdalena, Isla I	254	44.40 S	73.10 W
Magdalena, Punta ≻	246	3.56 N	77.21 W
Magdalena Contreras ◆[8]	286a	19.18 N	99.17 W
Magdalena de Kino	232	30.38 N	110.57 W
Magdalena Nueva	286d	12.06 S	77.05 W
Magdalena Peñasco	234	17.14 N	97.34 W
Magdalena Tequisistlán	234	16.22 N	95.15 W
Magdalen Laver	260	51.45 N	0.11 E
Magdalinovka	78	48.55 N	34.54 E
Magdeborn	54	51.14 N	12.26 E
Magdeburg	54	52.07 N	11.38 E
Magdeburg □[5]	54	52.15 N	11.30 E
Magdeburger Börde ⩧	54	52.00 N	11.30 E
Magdeburgo → Magdeburg	54	52.07 N	11.38 E
Magdiwang	116	12.30 N	122.31 E
Magdonskij, porog ∟	88	57.45 N	100.55 E
Magé, Bra.	256	22.39 S	43.02 W
Māge, Mya.	110	26.33 N	98.33 E
Magé □[7]	287a	22.41 S	43.07 W
Magé ≃	256	22.41 S	43.03 W
Magee	194	31.52 N	89.44 W
Magee, Island ≻[1]	48	54.49 N	5.42 W
Magelang	115a	7.28 S	110.13 E
Magellan, Strait of → Magallanes, Estrecho de ⊍	254	54.00 S	71.00 W
Magellan-Strasse → Magallanes, Estrecho de ⊍	254	54.00 S	71.00 W
Magé-Mirim	287a	22.40 S	43.01 W
Magen	132	31.18 N	34.26 E
Magenta	62	45.28 N	8.53 E
Magenta, Lake ⊜	162	33.26 S	119.10 E
Magerov	78	50.08 N	23.43 E
Magerøya I	24	71.03 N	25.45 E
Magetan	115a	7.39 S	111.20 E
Magezhuang	105	40.08 N	117.59 E
Maggia	58	46.15 N	8.42 E
Maggia ≃	58	46.09 N	8.48 E
Maggia, Valle V	58	46.17 N	8.40 E
Maggie Creek ≃	204	40.43 N	116.05 W
Maggieville	166	17.27 S	141.10 E
Maggiorasca, Monte ∧	62	44.33 N	9.29 E
Maggiore ≃	267a	43.43 N	13.06 E
Maggiore, Fosso ≃	267a	41.54 N	12.16 E
Maggiore, Lago ⊜	36	46.00 N	8.40 E
Maggiore, Monte ∧	68	41.14 N	14.12 E
Maghāghah	142	28.39 N	30.50 E
Maghama	150	15.31 N	12.51 W
Maghār	132	32.53 N	35.24 E
Maghdūshah	132	33.31 N	35.23 E
Maghera	48	54.51 N	6.40 W
Magherafelt	48	54.45 N	6.36 W
Maghniyya	148	34.50 N	1.50 W
Magholpur ◆[8]	272a	28.42 N	77.06 E
Maghull	44	53.32 N	2.57 W
Magician Lake ⊜	216	42.04 N	86.10 W
Magic Mountain ♠	228	34.26 N	118.36 W
Magic Reservoir ⊜[1]	202	43.17 N	114.23 W
Magill, Lac ⊜	206	45.35 N	71.17 W
Magill Heights	279b	40.37 N	79.52 W
Magill Lake ⊜	184	54.45 N	94.58 W
Magina ∧	34	37.43 N	3.28 W
Maginu	268	35.35 N	139.36 E
Magione	66	43.08 N	12.12 E
Magisano	68	39.01 N	16.27 E
Magiscatzin	234	22.48 N	98.42 W
Magiss Lake ⊜	184	52.59 N	91.40 W
Maglaj	38	44.33 N	18.06 E
Magliana ◆[8]	267a	41.50 N	12.25 E
Magliana, Fosso ≃	267a	41.49 N	12.25 E
Magliano dei Marsi	66	42.05 N	13.22 E
Magliano in Toscana	66	42.36 N	11.17 E
Magliano Sabina	66	42.22 N	12.29 E
Maglie	68	40.07 N	18.19 E
Maglód	264c	47.27 N	19.21 E
M'aglovo	265a	59.53 N	30.41 E
Magnago	266b	45.35 N	8.48 E
Magnanville	261	48.58 N	1.41 E
Magnet	184	51.19 N	99.30 W
Magnetawan ≃	190	45.46 N	80.37 W
Magnetic Island I	166	19.08 S	146.50 E
Magnetic Springs	214	40.21 N	83.16 W
Magnetischer Nordpol → North Magnetic Pole ◆	16	77.19 N	101.49 W
Magnetischer Südpol → South Magnetic Pole ◆	9	65.53 S	139.28 E
Magnières	58	48.27 N	6.34 E
Magnitka	86	55.21 N	59.43 E
Magnitogorsk	86	53.27 N	59.04 E
Magnitostroj	80	51.43 N	53.05 E
Magnolia, Ar., U.S.	194	33.16 N	93.14 W
Magnolia, De., U.S.	208	39.04 N	75.28 W
Magnolia, Ma., U.S.	283	42.35 N	70.43 W
Magnolia, Mn., U.S.	198	43.38 N	96.04 W
Magnolia, Ms., U.S.	194	31.08 N	90.27 W
Magnolia, N.J., U.S.	285	39.51 N	75.02 W
Magnolia, Oh., U.S.	214	40.39 N	81.17 W
Magnolia, Tx., U.S.	222	30.13 N	95.45 W
Magnor	26	59.57 N	12.12 E
Magny-en-Vexin	50	49.09 N	1.47 E
Magny-le-Hongre	261	48.52 N	2.49 E
Magny-les-Hameaux	261	48.44 N	2.04 E
Mago	89	53.15 N	140.13 E
Magog	206	45.16 N	72.09 W
Magog ≃	206	45.24 N	71.54 W
Magog, Lake ⊜	206	45.18 N	72.03 W
Magoito	266c	38.52 N	9.26 W
Magome ◆[8]	268	35.35 N	139.43 E
Mago National Park ♠	144	5.30 N	36.15 E
Magonoy	116	6.54 N	124.33 E
Magoro	154	1.44 N	34.06 E
Magothy Bay ⊂	208	37.10 N	75.55 W
Magothy River ⊂	208	39.04 N	76.28 W
Magoúla	267c	38.04 N	23.32 E
Magoye	154	16.00 S	27.37 E
M'agozero	76	60.21 N	34.50 E
Magpie	186	50.19 N	64.30 W
Magpie ≃, On., Can.	190	47.56 N	84.50 W
Magpie ≃, P.Q., Can.	186	50.19 N	64.27 W
Magpie, Lac ⊜	186	51.00 N	64.41 W
Magpie Ouest ≃	186	51.02 N	64.42 W
Magra	126	22.59 N	88.22 E
Magra ≃	64	44.03 N	9.58 E
Magra Hāt	126	22.14 N	88.23 E
Magrath	182	49.25 N	112.52 W
Magrè (Margreid)	64	46.17 N	11.12 E
Magro ≃	34	39.11 N	0.25 W
Magruder Mountain ∧	204	37.25 N	117.33 W
Magsaysay (Linugos)	116	9.01 N	125.11 E
Magsingal	116	17.41 N	120.25 E
Magu ≃	250	2.56 S	41.55 W
Maguan	102	22.59 N	104.19 E
Maguanying	271a	39.52 N	116.17 E
Maguari, Cabo ≻	250	0.18 S	48.22 W
Magude	156	25.02 S	32.40 E
Magudu	158	27.31 S	31.40 E
Magueyes	196	25.44 N	97.47 W
Maguindanao □[4]	116	6.55 N	124.20 E
Magumeri	146	12.08 N	12.50 E
Māgura	124	23.29 N	89.25 E
Maguru	150	12.28 N	6.35 E
Maguse Lake ⊜	176	61.40 N	95.10 W
Maguzhan	120	31.15 N	88.00 E
Magwe, Mya.	110	20.09 N	94.55 E
Magwe, Sūd.	154	4.08 N	32.17 E
Magwe □[8]	110	23.00 N	95.00 E
Magwood Park ♠	275b	43.39 N	79.30 W
Magyarország → Hungary □[1]	30	47.00 N	20.00 E
Mahābād	128	36.45 N	45.43 E
Mahābaleshwar	122	17.55 N	73.40 E
Mahābalipuram	122	12.37 N	80.12 E
Mahabe	157b	17.05 S	45.20 E
Mahābhārat Range ⋏	124	27.40 N	84.30 E
Mahabo, Madag.	157b	23.40 S	46.08 E
Mahabo, Madag.	157b	20.23 S	44.40 E
Mahād	122	18.05 N	73.25 E
Mahadday Weyn	144	2.58 N	45.32 E
Mahādebpur	126	23.51 N	89.53 E
Mahādeo Hills ⋏[2]	122	22.22 N	78.34 E
Mahādeo Range ⋏	122	17.50 N	74.15 E
Mahaffey	214	40.52 N	78.43 W
Mahagi	154	2.18 N	30.59 E
Mahagi Port	154	2.09 N	31.14 E
Mahai	102	38.17 N	94.13 E
Mahaicony Village	246	6.36 N	57.48 W
Mahajamba ≃	157b	15.33 S	47.08 E
Mahajamba, Helodranon' i ⊂	157b	15.24 S	47.05 E
Mahājan	123	28.47 N	73.50 E
Mahajanga	157b	15.43 S	46.19 E
Mahajanga □[4]	157b	17.00 S	46.00 E
Mahajilo ≃	157b	19.42 S	45.22 E
Maḩajjah	132	32.57 N	36.14 E
Mahakam ≃	112	0.35 S	117.17 E
Mahālandi	126	24.04 N	88.07 E
Mahalatswe	156	23.05 S	26.51 E
Mahalla el-Kubra → Al-Maḩallah al-Kubrā	142	30.58 N	31.10 E
Maḩallāt	128	33.55 N	50.27 E
Maḩallat Kayl	142	31.01 N	30.17 E
Maḩallat Marḩūm	142	30.48 N	30.57 E
Maḩallat Minūf	142	30.53 N	30.58 E
Maḩallat Zayyād	142	31.02 N	31.14 E
Maham	124	28.59 N	76.18 E
Mahamba	158	27.07 S	31.10 E
Mahānadi ≃	118	20.19 N	86.45 E
Mahānadpati	126	23.00 N	88.16 E
Mahānanda ≃	124	24.29 N	88.18 E
Mahanay Island I	116	10.12 N	124.14 E
Mahanoro	157b	19.54 S	48.48 E
Mahanoy City	208	40.48 N	76.08 W
Mahanoy Creek ≃	208	40.42 N	76.51 W
Mahantango Creek ≃	208	40.47 N	76.56 W
Mahantango Mountain ∧	208	40.40 N	76.45 W
Mahao	89	43.10 N	127.59 E
Mahape	272c	19.07 N	73.01 E
Mahārājganj, India	124	26.07 N	84.29 E
Mahārājganj, India	124	27.09 N	83.34 E
Mahārājpur, India	124	25.01 N	79.44 E
Mahārājpur, India	272a	28.39 N	77.20 E
Mahārāshtra □[3]	122	19.00 N	76.00 E
Maḩārīq, Wādī V	142	27.48 N	31.47 E
Mahārlū, Daryācheh-ye ⊜	128	29.25 N	52.50 E
Mahāsamund	120	21.06 N	82.06 E
Maha Sarakham	110	16.11 N	103.18 E
Maha Sawat, Khlong ≅	269a	13.47 N	100.28 E
Mahasoa	157b	22.12 S	46.06 E
Mahasolo	157b	19.07 S	46.22 E
Mahāsu □[5]	123	31.10 N	77.10 E
Mahates	246	10.14 N	75.12 W
Mahatsinjo	157b	21.26 S	45.51 E
Maḩaţţat Abū al-Lasan	132	30.05 N	35.31 E
Maḩaţţat Abū Jirdhān	132	30.20 N	35.46 E
Maḩaţţat Abū Ţarafah	132	30.00 N	35.56 E
Maḩaţţat al-Furayfirah	132	30.54 N	35.59 E
Maḩaţţat al-Ḩasā	132	30.49 N	35.59 E
Maḩaţţat al-Jīzah	132	31.43 N	35.58 E
Maḩaţţat al-Manzil	132	31.03 N	36.01 E
Maḩaţţat al-Qaşr	132	31.54 N	35.56 E
Maḩaţţat al-Qaţrānah	132	31.15 N	36.03 E
Maḩaţţat 'Aqabat al-Ḩijāzīyah	132	29.44 N	35.52 E
Maḩaţţat ar-Ramlah	132	29.32 N	35.57 E
Maḩaţţat ash-Shīdīyah	132	29.56 N	35.56 E
Maḩaţţat as-Suwāqah	132	31.22 N	36.07 E
Maḩaţţat Baţn al-Ghūl	132	29.41 N	35.55 E
Maḩaţţat Bḩamdūn	132	33.48 N	35.39 E
Maḩaţţat Ḑab'ah	132	31.36 N	36.04 E
Maḩaţţat Faşşū'ah	132	29.46 N	35.54 E
Maḩaţţat Izaa'	132	32.50 N	36.14 E
Maḩaţţat Jurf ad-Darāwīsh	132	30.42 N	35.52 E
Maḩaţţat Muşawwal	132	30.05 N	35.52 E
Maḩaţţat Samnah	132	30.09 N	35.39 E
Maḩaţţat 'Unayzah	132	30.29 N	35.48 E
Mahaut	240d	15.21 N	61.25 W
Mahavavy ≃, Madag.	157b	15.57 S	45.54 E
Mahavavy ≃, Madag.	157b	13.00 S	48.55 E
Mahaweli ≃	122	8.27 N	81.13 E
Mahaxai	110	17.25 N	105.12 E
Maḩbas, Wādī al- V	140	15.50 N	29.45 E
Mahbūbābād	122	17.37 N	80.01 E
Mahbūbnagar	122	16.44 N	77.59 E
Mahd adh-Dhahab	128	23.30 N	40.52 E
Mahdāt, Bi'r al- ⍑[4]	142	30.44 N	32.32 E
Mahdia	148	35.30 N	11.04 E
Mahdia □[8]	148	35.18 N	10.45 E
Mahe	122	11.42 N	75.32 E
Mahébourg	157c	20.24 S	57.42 E
Mahé Island I	138	4.40 S	55.28 E
Mahendraganj	120	25.20 N	89.45 E
Mahendragarh	124	28.17 N	76.09 E
Mahendragarh □[5]	124	28.20 N	76.10 E
Mahendra Giri ∧	122	18.58 N	84.21 E
Mahenge, Tan.	154	7.38 S	36.16 E
Mahenge, Tan.	154	8.41 S	36.43 E
Maheno	172	45.10 S	170.50 E
Mahesgādi	272b	22.39 N	88.33 E
Maheshmunda	126	24.13 N	86.24 E
Maheshtala	272b	22.30 N	88.15 E
Maheshwar	120	22.11 N	75.35 E
Mahespur	124	23.21 N	88.55 E
Mahgawān	124	26.29 N	78.37 E
Mahi ≃	120	22.16 N	72.58 E
Mahia Peninsula ≻[1]	172	39.10 S	177.53 E
Mahiāri	272b	22.35 N	88.14 E
Māhikpur	272b	22.32 N	88.14 E
Mahilāra	126	22.56 N	90.16 E
Māhīm ◆[8]	272c	19.03 N	72.49 E
Māhīm ≃	272c	19.03 N	72.51 E
Māhīm Bay ⊂	272c	19.02 N	72.50 E
Mahina, Mali	150	13.46 N	10.51 W
Mahina, Poly. fr.	174s	17.31 S	149.30 W
Mahinerangi, Lake ⊜	172	45.51 S	169.57 E
Mahinog	116	9.09 N	124.47 E
Mahīshādal	126	22.11 N	87.59 E
Mahishdānga	272b	22.54 N	88.11 E
Mahlabatini	158	28.14 S	31.30 E
Mahlangasi	158	27.37 S	31.42 E
Mahlberg	58	48.17 N	7.48 E
Mahlow	54	52.22 N	13.24 E
Mahlsdorf	54	52.47 N	11.13 E
Mahlsdorf-Süd ◆[8]	264a	52.29 N	13.36 E
Mahmūdābād, India	124	27.18 N	81.07 E
Maḩmūdābād, Īrān	128	36.38 N	52.15 E
Maḩmūd-e 'Erāqī	120	35.01 N	69.20 E
Maḩmūdīyah, Tur'at al- ≅	142	31.11 N	29.53 E
Mahmudiye	130	39.30 N	31.00 E
Mahmūdpur, India	272a	28.46 N	77.22 E
Mahmudpur, India	272b	22.41 N	88.09 E
Mahmut Bendi ◆[6]	267b	41.10 N	28.57 E
Mahmutbey	267b	41.03 N	28.49 E
Mahmutşevketpaşa	267b	41.09 N	29.11 E
Mahnomen	198	47.18 N	95.58 W
Mahoba	124	25.17 N	79.52 E
Mahogany Mountain ∧	202	43.14 N	117.16 W
Mahomet	216	40.11 N	88.24 W
Mahón	34	39.53 N	4.15 E
Mahone Bay	186	44.27 N	64.23 W
Mahone Bay ⊂	186	44.30 N	64.15 W
Mahoning □[6]	214	41.06 N	80.39 W
Mahoning ≃	214	40.58 N	80.23 W
Mahoning, West Branch ≃	214	41.12 N	80.57 W
Mahoning Creek ≃	214	40.55 N	79.27 W
Mahoning Creek Lake ⊜[1]	214	40.50 N	79.10 W
Mahony Lake ⊜	180	65.30 N	125.20 W
Mahood Falls	182	51.50 N	120.39 W
Mahood Lake ⊜	182	51.55 N	120.24 W
Mahopac	210	41.22 N	73.44 W
Mahopac Falls	210	41.22 N	73.46 W
Mahora	34	39.13 N	1.44 W
Mahoras Brook ≃	276	40.25 N	74.08 W
Mahrāt, Jabal ⋏	144	17.05 N	51.30 E
Mahrauli ◆[8]	272a	28.31 N	77.11 E
Mähren → Morava □[9]	30	49.20 N	17.00 E
Mahres	148	34.32 N	10.30 E
Mähring	60	49.55 N	12.32 E
Mahroni	124	24.35 N	78.43 E

≃ River	Fluss	Río	Rivière	Rio		
≅ Canal	Kanal	Canal	Canal	Canal		
∟ Waterfall, Rapids	Wasserfall, Stromschnellen	Cascada, Rápidos	Chute d'eau, Rapides	Cascata, Rápidos		
⊍ Strait	Meeresstrasse	Estrecho	Détroit	Estreito		
⊂ Bay, Gulf	Bucht, Golf	Bahía, Golfo	Baie, Golfe	Baía, Golfo		
⊜ Lake, Lakes	See, Seen	Lago, Lagos	Lac, Lacs	Lago, Lagos		
≡ Swamp	Sumpf	Pantano	Marais	Pântano		
⊓ Ice Features, Glacier	Eis- und Gletscherformen	Accidentes Glaciales	Formes glaciaires	Acidentes glaciares		
⍑ Other Hydrographic Features	Andere Hydrographische Objekte	Otros Elementos Hidrográficos	Autres données hydrographiques	Outros acidentes hidrográficos		
⊹ Submarine Features	Untermeerische Objekte	Accidentes Submarinos	Formes de relief sous-marin	Acidentes submarinos		
□ Political Unit	Politische Einheit	Unidad Politica	Entité politique	Unidade política		
❦ Cultural Institution	Kulturelle Institution	Institución Cultural	Institution culturelle	Institução cultural		
⊥ Historical Site	Historische Stätte	Sitio Histórico	Site historique	Sitio histórico		
♠ Recreational Site	Erholungs- und Ferienort	Sitio de Recreo	Centre de loisirs	Area de Lazer		
⊠ Airport	Flughafen	Aeropuerto	Aéroport	Aeroporto		
■ Military Installation	Militäranlage	Instalación Militar	Installation militaire	Instalação militar		
◆ Miscellaneous	Verschiedenes	Misceláneo	Divers	Diversos		

Symbols in the index entries represent the broad categories identified in the key at the right. Symbols with superior numbers (⋏[1]) identify subcategories (see complete key on page I · 1).

Kartensymbole in dem Registerverzeichnis stellen die rechts in Schlüssel erklärten Kategorien dar. Symbole mit hochgestellten Ziffern (⋏[1]) bezeichnen Unterabteilungen einer Kategorie (vgl. vollständiger Schlüssel auf Seite I · 1).

Los símbolos incluídos en el texto del índice representan las grandes categorías identificadas con la clave a la derecha. Los símbolos con numeros en su parte superior (⋏[1]) identifican las subcategorías (véase la clave completa en la página I · 1).

Les symboles de l'index représentent les catégories indiquées dans la légende à droite. Les symboles suivis d'un indice (⋏[1]) représentent des sous-catégories (voir légende complète à la page I · 1).

Os símbolos incluídos no texto do índice representam as grandes categorias identificadas com a chave à direita. Os símbolos com números em sua parte superior (⋏[1]) identificam as subcategorias (veja-se a chave completa à página I · 1).

⋀ Mountain	Berg	Montaña	Montagne	Montanha
⋏ Mountains	Berge	Montañas	Montagnes	Montanhas
⋊ Pass	Pass	Paso	Col	Passo
V Valley, Canyon	Tal, Cañon	Valle, Cañón	Vallée, Canyon	Vale, Canhão
⌓ Plain	Ebene	Llano	Plaine	Planície
≻ Cape	Kap	Cabo	Cap	Cabo
I Island	Insel	Isla	Île	Ilha
II Islands	Inseln	Islas	Îles	Ilhas
✦ Other Topographic Features	Andere Topographische Objekte	Otros Elementos Topográficos	Autres données topographiques	Outros acidentes topográficos

	English	Deutsch	Español	Français	Português
≃	River	Fluss	Río	Rivière	Rio
≊	Canal	Kanal	Canal	Canal	Canal
∟	Waterfall, Rapids	Wasserfall, Stromschnellen	Cascada, Rápidos	Chute d'eau, Rapides	Cascata, Rápidos
⊍	Strait	Meeresstrasse	Estrecho	Détroit	Estreito
⊂	Bay, Gulf	Bucht, Golf	Bahía, Golfo	Baie, Golfe	Baía, Golfo
⊜	Lake, Lakes	See, Seen	Lago, Lagos	Lac, Lacs	Lago, Lagos
≡	Swamp	Sumpf	Pantano	Marais	Pântano
⊓	Ice Features, Glacier	Eis- und Gletscherformen	Accidentes Glaciales	Formes glaciaires	Acidentes glaciares
⍑	Other Hydrographic Features	Andere Hydrographische Objekte	Otros Elementos Hidrográficos	Autres données hydrographiques	Outros acidentes hidrográficos

	English	Deutsch	Español	Français	Português
✥	Submarine Features	Untermeerische Objekte	Accidentes Submarinos	Formes de relief sous-marin	Acidentes submarinos
□	Political Unit	Politische Einheit	Unidad Politica	Entité politique	Unidade política
ʊ	Cultural Institution	Kulturelle Institution	Institución Cultural	Institution culturelle	Institução cultural
⊥	Historical Site	Historische Stätte	Sitio Histórico	Site historique	Sitio histórico
♠	Recreational Site	Erholungs- und Ferienort	Sitio de Recreo	Centre de loisirs	Area de Lazer
⊠	Airport	Flughafen	Aeropuerto	Aéroport	Aeroporto
■	Military Installation	Militäranlage	Instalación Militar	Installation militaire	Instalação militar
◆	Miscellaneous	Verschiedenes	Misceláneo	Divers	Diversos

ENGLISH — DEUTSCH

Name	Page	Lat.°′	Long.°′
Manukau Harbour ⊂	172	37.01 S	174.44 E
Manulla ≃	48	53.57 N	9.12 W
Manulu Lagoon ⊂	174o	1.56 N	157.20 W
Manumuskin ≃	208	39.18 N	75.00 W
Manundi, Tanjung >	164	0.38 S	135.22 E
Manunui	172	38.53 S	175.20 E
Manuoha ∧	172	38.39 S	177.07 E
Manupari ≃	248	11.50 S	67.16 W
Manurimi ≃	248	11.42 S	67.16 W
Manuripe (Manuripi) ≃	248	11.06 S	67.36 W
Manursing Island I	276	40.58 N	73.40 W
Manursing Island Park ♠	276	40.58 N	73.40 W
Manus □[5]	164	2.00 S	147.00 E
Mānushmuria	126	22.22 N	86.47 E
Manus Island I	164	2.05 S	147.00 E
Manutahi	172	39.40 S	174.24 E
Manutuke	172	38.41 S	177.55 E
Manvel, N.D., U.S.	198	48.04 N	97.10 W
Manvel, Tx., U.S.	222	29.28 N	95.22 W
Manville, N.J., U.S.	210	40.32 N	74.35 W
Manville, R.I., U.S.	207	41.58 N	71.28 W
Mānwat	122	19.18 N	76.30 E
Many	194	31.34 N	93.29 W
Manyal Shīḥah	273c	29.57 N	31.14 E
Manyana	156	23.23 S	21.44 E
Manyani	154	3.05 S	38.30 E
Manyara, Lake ⊜	154	3.35 S	35.50 E
Manyberries	184	49.24 N	110.42 W
Manyč ≃	72	47.15 N	40.00 E
Manyč-Gudilo, ozero ⊜	80	46.24 N	42.38 E
Manyeleti Game Reserve ⇝[4]	156	25.42 S	31.30 E
Many Island Lake ⊜	184	50.08 N	110.03 W
Manyoni	154	5.45 S	34.50 E
Many Peaks	166	24.33 S	151.23 E
Manytsch → Manyč ≃	72	47.15 N	40.00 E
Manz'a	86	58.29 N	96.15 E
Mānzai	120	30.07 N	68.52 E
Manzanares	34	39.00 N	3.22 W
Manzanares ≃	34	40.19 N	3.32 W
Manzanares, Canal del ≡	266a	40.23 N	3.41 W
Manzanillo, Cuba	240p	20.21 N	77.07 W
Manzanillo, Méx.	234	19.03 N	104.20 W
Manzanillo, Bahía ⊂	234	19.04 N	104.22 W
Manzanillo, Punta >, Pan.	236	9.38 N	79.32 W
Manzanillo, Punta >, Ven.	241s	11.32 N	69.17 W
Manzanillo Bay ⊂	238	19.45 N	71.46 W
Manzanita, Or., U.S.	224	45.43 N	123.56 W
Manzanita, Wa., U.S.	224	47.42 N	122.33 W
Manzano, It.	64	45.59 N	13.23 E
Manzano, N.M., U.S.	200	34.38 N	106.20 W
Manzanola	198	38.06 N	103.51 W
Manzano Peak ∧	200	34.35 N	106.26 W
Manželija	78	49.19 N	33.38 E
Manzhouli	88	49.35 N	117.22 E
Manziana	66	42.08 N	12.08 E
Manzil	128	29.15 N	63.05 E
Manzilah, Birkat al- ⊜	142	31.08 N	31.56 E
Manzilah, Buḥayrat al- ⊜	142	31.15 N	32.00 E
Manzini	158	26.30 S	31.25 E
Manzone	258	34.29 S	58.52 W
Manzurka	88	53.30 N	106.04 E
Mao, Rep. Dom.	238	19.34 N	71.05 W
Mao, Tchad	146	14.07 N	15.19 E
Maoba	102	30.02 N	108.59 E
Maocifan	100	31.40 N	112.53 E
Maocun	98	34.25 N	117.16 E
Maodianzi, Zhg.	107	30.42 N	104.25 E
Maodianzi, Zhg.	107	29.45 N	104.55 E
Mao'ertuo	107	29.19 N	106.24 E
Maojiagou	104	40.58 N	120.51 E
Maojiaji	100	31.32 N	114.16 E
Maojiakou	100	29.53 N	112.58 E
Maojiaping	105	40.34 N	114.43 E
Maojiapuzi	104	41.10 N	123.32 E
Maojiatun	104	41.05 N	121.58 E
Maojiazao	98	39.53 N	113.26 E
Maoke, Pegunungan ⩘	164	4.00 S	138.00 E
Maolin, Zhg.	89	43.58 N	123.24 E
Maolin, Zhg.	100	30.32 N	118.14 E
Maomao Shan ∧	102	37.12 N	103.10 E
Maoming	102	21.39 N	110.54 E
Maomu	102	40.18 N	99.28 E
Ma On Shan ∧	271d	22.25 N	114.15 E
Ma On Shan Tsuen	271d	22.24 N	114.14 E
Maoping	102	30.23 N	110.33 E
Maopora, Pulau I	112	7.35 S	127.35 E
Maoshan	105	40.17 N	117.26 E
Mao Shan ⩘	106	31.43 N	119.17 E
Maoshi	100	26.57 N	113.05 E
Maospati	115a	7.36 S	111.26 E
Maouri, Dallol V	150	12.05 N	3.32 E
Maowen	102	31.30 N	103.39 E
Maoxing	89	45.32 N	124.33 E
Mao Yü I	100	23.19 N	119.19 E
Maozhou	105	38.51 N	116.06 E
Mapaga	112	0.06 S	119.48 E
Mapan	112	2.21 S	111.10 E
Mapanda	152	9.32 S	24.16 E
Mapane	112	1.24 S	120.40 E
Mapanza	154	16.15 S	26.55 E
Mapaoni ≃	250	1.55 N	54.13 W
Mapari ≃	250	0.45 N	53.07 W
Mapastepec	234	15.26 N	92.54 W
Mapaville	219	38.14 N	90.29 W
Mapi	164	7.07 S	139.23 E
Mapi ≃	164	7.00 S	139.16 E
Mapia, Kepulauan II	108	0.50 N	134.20 E
Mapida	112	0.33 S	119.46 E
Mapimí	232	25.49 N	103.51 W
Mapimí, Bolsón de ⇝[2]	232	27.30 N	103.30 W
Mapimí, Bufa de ∧	196	25.47 N	103.48 W
Maping, Zhg.	100	24.16 N	117.54 E
Maping, Zhg.	100	31.36 N	113.32 E
Mapinga	154	6.36 S	39.04 E
Mapinhane	156	22.19 S	35.03 E
Mapire	246	7.45 N	64.42 W
Mapiri	248	15.15 S	68.10 W
Mapiri ≃	248	9.52 S	66.21 W
Mapixari, Ilha I	246	2.10 S	65.08 W
Maple ⇝[8]	275b	43.51 N	79.31 W
Maple ≃, U.S.	198	45.47 N	98.33 W
Maple ≃, Ia., U.S.	198	42.00 N	95.59 W
Maple ≃, Mi., U.S.	190	42.59 N	84.57 W
Maple ≃, Mn., U.S.	190	44.05 N	94.00 W
Maple ≃, N.D., U.S.	198	46.56 N	96.55 W
Maple Airfield ⊠	275b	43.51 N	79.32 W
Maple Bay	224	48.49 N	123.36 W
Maple Bluff	216	43.07 N	89.22 W
Maple Creek	184	49.55 N	109.27 W
Maple Creek ≃	198	41.33 N	96.27 W
Maplecrest	210	42.17 N	74.11 W
Maple Cross	260	51.37 N	0.30 W
Mapledale	214	41.23 N	79.51 W
Maple Falls	224	48.55 N	122.04 W
Maple Glen	285	40.11 N	75.11 W
Maple Grove, On., Can.	212	43.55 N	78.44 W
Maple Grove, P.Q., Can.	206	45.19 N	73.50 W
Maple Heights	214	41.24 N	81.33 W
Maple Lake	198	45.14 N	94.00 W
Maple Lake ⊜	212	45.06 N	78.40 W
Maple Lane	216	41.46 N	86.14 W
Maple Leaf Gardens ♠	275b	43.40 N	79.23 W
Maple Meadow Brook ≃	283	42.33 N	71.09 W
Maple Mount	194	37.42 N	87.26 W
Maple Park	216	41.55 N	88.36 W
Maples	216	41.01 N	84.58 W
Maple Shade	285	39.57 N	74.59 W
Maple Springs	214	42.12 N	79.25 W
Maplesville	194	32.47 N	86.52 W
Mapleton, S. Afr.	158	26.20 S	28.14 E
Mapleton, Ia., U.S.	198	42.09 N	95.47 W
Mapleton, Mn., U.S.	190	43.55 N	93.57 W
Mapleton, Or., U.S.	202	44.01 N	123.51 W
Mapleton, Ut,. U.S.	200	40.07 N	111.34 W
Mapleton Depot	214	40.24 N	77.57 W
Maple Valley	224	47.25 N	122.03 W
Mapleville	207	41.56 N	71.38 W
Maplewood, Mo., U.S.	219	38.36 N	90.19 W
Maplewood, N.J., U.S.	276	40.43 N	74.14 W
Maplewood, Oh., U.S.	216	40.23 N	84.02 W
Maplewood, Wa., U.S.	224	47.30 N	122.07 W
Maplewood Terrace	279b	40.17 N	79.32 W
Mapocho ≃	286e	33.25 S	70.47 W
Mapocho, Estación ⇝[5]	286e	33.26 S	70.40 W
Mapoi	154	5.28 N	27.40 E
Mappsville	208	37.51 N	75.34 W
Maprik	164	3.40 S	143.05 E
Mapuera ≃	250	1.05 S	57.02 W
Mapujiang	105	40.24 N	114.56 E
Mapulanguene	156	24.29 S	32.06 E
Mapulau ≃	246	1.23 N	63.24 W
Mapumulo	158	29.11 S	31.02 E
Maputa	158	26.59 S	32.46 E
Maputo (Lourenço Marques)	156	25.58 S	32.35 E
Maputo □[5]	156	26.00 S	32.25 E
Maputo (Great Usutu) (Lusutfu) ≃	158	26.11 S	32.42 E
Maputo, Baia de ⊂	158	25.48 S	32.51 E
Maʿqalā'	128	26.31 N	47.19 E
Maqên Gangri ∧	102	34.55 N	99.18 E
Maqiangou	105	39.30 N	115.02 E
Maqiao, Zhg.	100	29.48 N	114.22 E
Maqiao, Zhg.	106	30.28 N	120.42 E
Maqṭeïr ⍑[4]	148	22.10 N	10.50 W
Maquanhe ≃	124	29.35 N	84.10 E
Maqueda	34	40.04 N	4.22 W
Maqueda Bay ⊂	116	11.44 N	124.58 E
Maqueda Channel ⋓	116	13.42 N	124.01 E
Maquela do Zombo	152	6.03 S	15.07 E
Maquereau, Pointe au >	186	48.12 N	64.47 W
Maquiling, Mount ∧	116	14.08 N	121.12 E
Maquinchao	254	41.15 S	68.44 W
Maquinchao ≃	254	41.13 S	69.25 W
Maquoketa	190	42.04 N	90.39 W
Maquoketa ≃	190	42.11 N	90.19 W
Maquoketa, North Fork ≃	190	42.05 N	90.40 W
Mar, Serra do ⊥[4]	252	26.00 S	48.00 W
Mara, India	120	28.11 N	94.06 E
Mara, Perú	248	14.06 S	72.07 W
Mara, Zhg.	120	28.11 N	94.08 E
Mara □[4]	154	1.45 S	34.30 E
Mara ≃, Afr.	154	1.31 S	33.56 E
Mara ≃, S.S.S.R.	88	58.06 N	104.06 E
Maraã, Bra.	246	1.50 S	65.22 W
Maraa, Poly. fr.	174s	17.46 S	149.34 W
Marabá	250	5.21 S	49.07 W
Marabahan	112	3.00 S	114.45 E
Marabut	116	11.07 N	125.13 E
Maracá ≃	250	0.26 S	51.26 W
Maracá, Ilha de I, Bra.	246	3.25 N	61.40 W
Maracá, Ilha de I, Bra.	250	2.05 N	50.25 W
Maracaçumé ≃	250	1.23 S	45.42 W
Maracaí	255	22.36 S	50.39 W
Maracaibo	246	10.40 N	71.37 W
Maracaibo, Lago de ⊜	246	9.50 N	71.30 W
Maracaju	255	21.38 S	55.09 W
Maracaju, Serra de ⩘[2]	255	20.45 S	55.00 W
Maracalagonis	71	39.17 N	9.13 E
Maracanã	250	0.46 S	47.27 W
Maracanã ⇝[8]	287a	22.54 S	43.14 W
Maracanã ≃	248	8.22 S	59.41 W
Maracanã, Estádio Municipal ♠	287a	22.55 S	43.14 W
Maracanaú	250	3.52 S	38.38 W
Maracás	255	13.26 S	40.27 W
Maracay	246	10.15 N	67.36 W
Maracossic Creek ≃	208	37.53 N	77.11 W
Marādah	146	29.14 N	19.13 E
Maradi	150	13.29 N	7.06 E
Maradi □[5]	150	14.00 N	7.00 E
Maradi, Goulbin ≃	150	13.38 N	6.20 E
Marāghah, Sabkhat al- ⊜	130	35.39 N	37.39 E
Marāgheh	128	37.23 N	46.13 E
Maragini	164	3.33 S	141.34 E
Maragiu, Capo >	71	40.20 N	8.23 E
Maragogi	250	9.01 S	35.13 W
Maragogipe	255	12.46 S	38.55 W
Marahoué, Parc National de la ♠	150	7.00 N	6.00 W
Mārahra	124	27.44 N	78.35 E
Marahuaca, Cerro ∧	246	3.34 N	65.27 W
Maraial	250	8.47 S	35.50 W
Maraiche Lake ⊜	184	54.28 N	102.01 W
Marainviller	58	48.35 N	6.36 E
Maraisburg → Roodepoort-Maraisburg	273d	26.11 S	27.56 E
Marais des Cygnes ≃	194	38.02 N	94.14 W
Marais Temps Clair ⊜	219	38.54 N	90.24 W
Marajó, Baía de ⊂	250	1.00 S	48.30 W
Marajó, Ilha de I	250	1.00 S	49.30 W
Marakabei	158	29.32 S	28.09 E
Maʿrakah	132	33.16 N	35.18 E
Mārākand	84	38.52 N	45.14 E
Maralal	154	1.06 N	36.42 E
Maralaleng	156	25.47 S	22.45 E
Maralal Game Sanctuary ⇝[4]	154	1.09 N	36.38 E
Maraldy	86	52.26 N	77.45 E
Marali	152	6.01 N	18.24 E
Maralik	84	40.35 N	43.52 E
Maram	120	25.25 N	94.06 E
Maramag	116	7.46 N	125.00 E
Maramasike I	175e	9.32 S	161.27 E
Marambaia ≃	256	21.44 S	46.25 W
Marambaia, Ilha da I	256	23.04 S	43.58 W
Marambaia, Pico da ∧	256	23.04 S	43.59 W
Marambio ⊌[3]	9	64.14 S	56.43 W
Marampa	150	8.41 N	12.28 W
Maramsilli Reservoir ⊜[1]	122	20.32 N	81.41 E
Maramureș □[6]	38	47.40 N	24.00 E
Maramureșului, Munții ⩘	38	47.50 N	24.45 E
Maran	114	3.35 N	102.46 E
Mārān, Koh-i- ∧	120	29.26 N	66.48 E
Marana, Mali	150	14.38 N	11.55 W
Marana, Az., U.S.	200	32.26 N	111.13 W
Maranalgo	162	29.23 S	117.48 E
Maranboy	164	14.30 S	132.45 E
Maranchón	34	41.03 N	2.12 W
Marand	128	38.26 N	45.46 E
Maranello	64	44.32 N	10.52 E
Marang, Malay.	114	5.12 N	103.13 E
Marang, Mya.	110	10.27 N	98.47 E
Marangá ⇝[8]	287a	22.51 S	43.23 W
Marangani	248	14.22 S	71.10 W
Marangas	116	8.40 N	117.38 E
Marange-Zondrange	56	49.07 N	6.32 E
Maranguape	250	3.53 S	38.40 W
Maranhão □[3]	250	5.00 S	45.00 W
Maranhão ≃	255	14.34 S	49.02 W
Maranhão, Cachoeira ⌞	250	4.49 S	56.18 W
Marano	266b	45.38 N	8.38 E
Marano, Laguna di ⊂	64	45.44 N	13.10 E
Maranoa ≃	166	27.50 S	148.37 E
Marano di Napoli	68	40.54 N	14.11 E
Marano Lagunare	64	45.46 N	13.10 E
Marañón ≃	242	4.30 S	73.27 W
Marano sul Panaro	64	44.27 N	10.58 E
Marano Vicentino	64	45.41 N	11.25 E
Marans	32	46.19 N	1.00 W
Maraoli ⇝[8]	272c	19.03 N	72.54 E
Marapanim	250	0.42 S	47.42 W
Marapendi, Lagoa de ⊂	287a	23.01 S	43.24 W
Marapi ≃	250	0.37 N	55.58 W
Marapicu	256	22.48 S	43.35 W
Marapicu, Morro do ∧	287a	22.50 S	43.36 W
Mararoa ≃	172	45.34 S	167.36 E
Mararui	154	1.56 S	41.18 E
Maras, Perú	248	13.20 S	72.09 W
Maraş, Tür.	130	37.36 N	36.55 E
Maraş □[4]	130	38.00 N	37.05 E
Marasany	80	57.27 N	54.25 E
Maraş Dağları ⩘	130	37.40 N	37.00 E
Marasende, Pulau I	112	5.08 S	118.09 E
Mărășești	38	45.52 N	27.14 E
Maratasã ≃	250	4.14 S	42.15 W
Maratea	68	39.59 N	15.45 E
Marathon, Austl.	166	20.49 S	143.34 E
Marathon, On., Can.	190	48.43 N	86.23 W
Marathón, Ellás	38	38.10 N	23.58 E
Marathon, Fl., U.S.	220	24.42 N	81.05 W
Marathon, N.Y., U.S.	210	42.26 N	76.01 W
Marathon, Tx., U.S.	196	30.12 N	103.15 W
Marathon, Wi., U.S.	190	44.55 N	89.50 W
Marathóvounon	130	35.13 N	33.37 E
Maratua, Pulau I	112	2.15 N	118.36 E
Marau, Bra.	252	28.27 S	52.12 W
Maraú, Bra.	255	14.06 S	39.00 W
Marauiá ≃	246	0.23 S	65.13 W
Marausa	70	37.56 N	12.30 E
Maravari	175e	7.51 S	156.42 E
Maravatío de Ocampo	234	19.54 N	100.27 W
Marāveh Tappeh	128	37.55 N	55.57 E
Maravilha, Bra.	250	9.14 S	37.21 W
Maravilha, Bra.	252	26.47 S	53.09 W
Maravillas	232	27.22 N	104.29 W
Maravillas Creek ≃	196	29.34 N	102.47 W
Mara Vista	207	41.33 N	70.34 W
Marav Lake ⊜	120	29.04 N	69.18 E
Maravovo	175e	9.17 S	159.38 E
Marāwah	146	32.29 N	21.25 E
Marawi, Pil.	116	8.01 N	124.18 E
Marawī, Sūd.	140	18.29 N	31.49 E
Maraye-en-Othe	50	48.10 N	3.51 E
Marayes	252	31.29 S	67.20 W
Marayong	274a	33.45 S	150.54 E
Maraza	84	40.33 N	48.56 E
Marazion	42	50.08 N	5.28 W
Marbach, B.R.D.	56	50.37 N	9.43 E
Marbach, D.D.R.	54	51.02 N	13.13 E
Marbach, Schw.	58	46.52 N	7.55 E
Marbach am Neckar	56	48.56 N	9.14 E
Marbache	56	48.48 N	6.05 E
Marbais	50	50.33 N	4.31 E
Marbeck	52	51.49 N	6.52 E
Marbella	34	36.31 N	4.53 W
Marble, Mn., U.S.	190	47.19 N	93.17 W
Marble, N.C., U.S.	192	35.10 N	83.55 W
Marble, Pa., U.S.	214	41.20 N	79.26 W
Marble Arch ⊥	146	30.29 N	18.35 E
Marble Bar	162	21.11 S	119.44 E
Marble Canyon V	200	36.30 N	111.50 W
Marble Falls	196	30.34 N	98.16 W
Marble Hall	156	24.57 S	29.13 E
Marblehead, Il., U.S.	219	39.50 N	91.22 W
Marblehead, Ma., U.S.	207	42.30 N	70.51 W
Marblehead, Oh., U.S.	214	41.32 N	82.44 W
Marblehead Neck >[1]	283	42.29 N	70.51 W
Marble Hill	194	37.18 N	89.58 W
Marble Lake ⊜	216	41.54 N	84.54 W
Marblemount	224	48.31 N	121.26 W
Marble Rock	190	42.57 N	92.52 W
Marbleton	206	45.37 N	71.35 W
Marburg, Austl.	171a	27.34 S	152.35 E
Marburg, B.R.D.	56	50.49 N	8.46 E
Marburg, S. Afr.	158	30.44 S	30.26 E
Marburg, Lake ⊜[1]	208	39.48 N	76.53 W
Marburg an der Drau → Maribor	36	46.33 N	15.39 E
Marbury	208	38.34 N	77.09 W
Marc ≃	50	50.43 N	3.50 E
Marca, Ponta da >	152	16.31 S	11.42 E
Marcaconga	248	13.59 S	71.34 W
Marcal ≃	30	47.41 N	17.32 E
Marcala	236	14.07 N	88.00 W
Marcali	30	46.35 N	17.25 E
Marcallo con Casone	266b	45.29 N	8.52 E
Marcaria	64	45.07 N	10.32 E
Marceau, Lac ⊜	186	51.25 N	66.41 W
Marcedusa	68	39.02 N	16.50 E
Marcelin	184	52.55 N	106.47 W
Marceline	194	39.42 N	92.56 W
Marcelino Ramos	252	27.28 S	51.54 W
Marcella	276	40.59 N	74.28 W
Marcellina	66	42.01 N	12.48 E
Marcellus, Mi., U.S.	216	42.01 N	85.48 W
Marcellus, N.Y., U.S.	210	42.59 N	76.20 W
Marcellus Falls	210	43.00 N	76.20 W
Marcevo	83	47.15 N	38.53 E
March	42	52.33 N	0.06 E
March (Morava) ≃	30	48.10 N	16.59 E
Marcha	74	60.37 N	123.18 E
Marcha ≃	74	63.28 N	118.50 E
March Air Force Base ■	228	33.54 N	117.15 W
Marchais	261	48.31 N	2.03 E
Marchal	152	5.16 S	14.58 E
Marchamat	85	40.30 N	72.19 E
Marchand	214	40.51 N	79.02 W
Marchaux	58	47.19 N	6.08 E
Marche □[4]	66	43.30 N	13.15 E
Marche □[9]	32	46.05 N	2.10 E
Marche-en-Famenne	56	50.12 N	5.20 E
Marchegg	61	48.17 N	16.55 E
Marche-les-Dames	56	50.29 N	4.58 E
Marchémoret	261	49.03 N	2.46 E
Marchena	34	37.20 N	5.24 W
Marchena, Isla I	246a	0.21 N	90.29 W
Marchenoir	50	47.49 N	1.24 E
Marchesa Bay ⊂	116	6.35 N	117.40 E
Marchesato	68	39.07 N	16.58 E
Marchfeld ⇝[1]	264b	48.17 N	16.31 E
Marchienne-au-Pont	50	50.24 N	4.23 E
Marchinbar Island I	164	11.15 S	136.45 E
Marching	60	48.49 N	11.43 E
Mar Chiquita, Laguna ⊂	252	37.37 S	57.24 W
Mar Chiquita, Laguna ⊜	252	30.42 S	62.36 W
Marchtrenk	61	48.11 N	14.07 E
Marciana	66	42.47 N	10.10 E
Marciana Marina	66	42.48 N	10.12 E
Marcianise	68	41.02 N	14.17 E
Marciano della Chiana	66	43.18 N	11.47 E
Marčichina Buda	78	51.58 N	34.03 E
Marcigny	32	46.17 N	4.02 E
Marcillac-Vallon	32	44.29 N	2.28 E
Marcilloles	62	45.20 N	5.11 E
Marcilly	261	49.02 N	2.53 E
Marcilly-la-Campagne	50	48.50 N	1.13 E
Marcilly-le-Hayer	50	48.21 N	3.38 E
Marcilly-sur-Eure	50	48.49 N	1.21 E
Marck	50	50.57 N	1.57 E
Marckolsheim	58	48.10 N	7.33 E
Marco, Bra.	250	3.08 S	40.09 W
Marco, It.	64	45.51 N	11.01 E
Marco, Fl., U.S.	220	25.58 N	81.43 W
Marcoing	50	50.07 N	3.11 E
Marco Island I	220	25.55 N	81.45 W
Marcola	202	44.10 N	122.51 W
Marcolino, Igarapé ≃	250	11.03 S	58.35 W
Marcona	248	15.03 S	75.01 W
Marco Polo, Aeroporto ⊠	64	45.30 N	12.21 E
Marco Polo Bridge ⇝[5]	271a	39.52 N	116.12 E
Marcos Juárez	252	32.42 S	62.06 W
Marcos Paz	258	34.46 S	58.50 W
Marcos Paz □[5]	288	34.49 S	58.49 W
Marcotte, Lac ⊜	206	46.47 N	73.12 W
Marcoussis	261	48.39 N	2.14 E
Marcq	261	48.52 N	1.49 E
Marcq-en-BarŒul	50	50.40 N	3.05 E
Marčugi	82	55.21 N	38.33 E
Marcus	198	42.49 N	95.48 W
Marcus Baker, Mount ∧	180	61.26 N	147.45 W
Marcus Hook	208	39.49 N	75.25 W
Marcus Hook Creek ≃	285	39.49 N	75.25 W
Marcus Island → Minami-Tori-shima I	14	24.18 N	153.58 E
Marcy, Mount ∧	188	44.07 N	73.56 W
Marda	162	30.13 S	119.17 E
Mardakert	84	40.12 N	46.48 E
Mardalsfossen ⌞	26	62.30 N	8.07 E
Mardān	123	34.12 N	72.02 E
Mardarovka	78	47.32 N	29.44 E
Mar de Cães, Vala de ≡	266c	38.51 N	8.59 W
Mar de Espanha	256	21.52 S	43.00 W
Mardela Springs	208	38.27 N	75.45 W
Mar del Plata	252	38.00 S	57.33 W
Marden	42	51.10 N	0.29 E
Mardie	162	21.11 S	115.57 E
Mardin	130	37.18 N	40.44 E
Mardin □[4]	130	37.25 N	41.00 E
Mar Dyke ≃	260	51.29 N	0.14 E
Mare	164	9.10 S	141.40 E
Maré I	175f	21.30 S	168.00 E
Mare, Muntele ∧	38	46.29 N	23.14 E
Marecchia ≃	66	44.04 N	12.34 E
Marechal Cândido Rondon	252	24.34 S	54.04 W
Marechal Deodoro	250	9.43 S	35.54 W
Maree, Loch ⊜	46	57.42 N	5.30 W
Mareeba	166	17.00 S	145.26 E
Mareetsane	158	26.09 S	25.25 E
Mareil-en-France	261	49.04 N	2.26 E
Mareil-le-Guyon	261	48.47 N	1.51 E
Mareil-Marly	261	48.53 N	2.05 E
Mare Island I	226	38.06 N	122.16 W
Mare Island Naval Shipyard ■	226	38.06 N	122.17 W
Mare Island Strait ⋓	282	38.06 N	122.17 W
Mareje, Gunung ∧	115b	8.46 S	116.08 E
Marek	112	4.48 S	120.21 E
Maremma ⇝[1]	66	42.30 N	11.30 E
Marene	62	44.39 N	7.44 E
Marengo, Il., U.S.	216	42.14 N	88.36 W
Marengo, In., U.S.	218	38.22 N	86.20 W
Marengo, Ia., U.S.	190	41.47 N	92.04 W
Marengo, Mi., U.S.	216	42.17 N	84.51 W
Marengo, Oh., U.S.	214	40.24 N	82.49 W
Marengo ⇝[1]	62	44.55 N	8.40 E
Marengo ⊥	62	44.49 N	8.40 E
Marengo Cave ⊥[5]	218	38.23 N	86.21 W
Marenisco	190	46.22 N	89.41 W
Marennes	32	45.50 N	1.06 W
Marerano	157b	21.23 S	44.52 E
Mareşalçakmak	130	39.22 N	39.13 E
Maresias	256	23.48 S	45.33 W
Marettimo	70	37.58 N	12.04 E
Marettimo, Isola I	70	37.58 N	12.03 E
Mareuil-en-Brie	50	48.57 N	3.45 E
Mareuil-lès-Meaux	261	48.56 N	2.52 E
Mareuil-sur-Aÿ	50	49.03 N	4.02 E
Mareuil-sur-Belle	32	45.28 N	0.28 E
Marevo	76	57.19 N	32.05 E
Marey-sur-Tille	58	47.35 N	5.03 E
Marfa	196	30.18 N	104.01 W
Marfinka	83	47.36 N	38.32 E
Marfino	80	46.25 N	48.44 E
Mar Forest ⇝[3]	46	57.00 N	3.35 W
Margam, Īrān	84	39.09 N	44.57 E
Margam, Wales, U.K.	42	51.34 N	3.44 W
Marganec	78	47.38 N	34.40 E
Margao → Madgaon	122	15.18 N	73.57 E
Margaree	186	46.24 N	61.05 W
Margaree Harbour	186	46.26 N	61.07 W
Margaret ≃	162	18.10 S	125.37 E
Margaret, Mount ∧	224	46.18 N	122.08 W
Margaret Bay	182	51.20 N	127.29 W
Margaret Creek ≃	166	29.26 S	137.07 E
Margarethenhöhe ⇝[8]	263	51.26 N	6.58 E
Margaret River, Austl.	162	33.57 S	115.04 E
Margaret River, Austl.	162	18.38 S	126.52 E
Margaret Roding	260	51.47 N	0.19 E
Margaretting	260	51.41 N	0.25 E
Margarettsville	208	36.32 N	77.21 W
Margaretville	210	42.08 N	74.38 W
Margarita, Bahía → Marguerite Bay ⊂	9	68.30 S	68.30 W
Margarita, Isla I	246	9.05 N	74.30 W
Margarita, Isla de I	246	11.00 N	64.00 W
Margarita Belén	252	27.16 S	58.58 W
Margarita Peak ∧	228	33.26 N	117.23 W
Margaritovka	83	46.55 N	38.52 E
Margate, S. Afr.	158	30.55 S	30.15 E
Margate, Eng., U.K.	42	51.24 N	1.24 E
Margate, Fl., U.S.	220	26.14 N	80.12 W
Margate City	208	39.19 N	74.30 W
Margecany	30	48.54 N	21.01 E
Margelan → Margilan	85	40.28 N	71.44 E
Margeride, Monts de la ⩘	32	44.50 N	3.30 E
Margès	62	45.09 N	5.03 E
Mārgherita	120	27.17 N	95.41 E
Margherita → Jamaame	144	0.04 N	42.45 E
Margherita di Savoia	68	41.23 N	16.09 E
Margherita Peak ∧	154	0.22 N	29.51 E
Marghī	120	34.58 N	66.31 E
Marghita	38	47.21 N	22.21 E
Marghūb, Kūh-e ∧	128	33.06 N	57.30 E
Margi ≃	70	37.16 N	14.58 E
Margilan	85	40.28 N	71.44 E
Margit Híd ⇝[5]	264c	47.31 N	19.02 E
Margit-sziget I	264c	47.32 N	19.03 E
Margny-lès-Compiègne	50	49.26 N	2.49 E
Margone	62	45.13 N	7.11 E
Margonin	30	52.59 N	17.05 E
Margos	248	10.04 S	76.26 W
Margosatubig	116	7.34 N	123.10 E
Margot Lake ⊜	184	52.28 N	93.10 W
Mārgow, Dasht-e ⇝[2]	128	30.45 N	63.10 E
Margreid → Magrè	64	46.17 N	11.12 E
Marguerite, Pic → Margherita Peak ∧	154	0.22 N	29.51 E
Marguerite Bay ⊂	9	68.30 S	68.30 W
Marguerittes	62	43.51 N	4.27 E
Margut	56	49.35 N	5.16 E
Mari	130	36.28 N	37.11 E
Mari ≃	248	7.05 S	64.34 W
Maria, Îles II	14	21.48 S	154.41 W
Mariabrunn ⇝[8]	264b	48.12 N	16.14 E
María Cleofas, Isla I	234	21.16 N	106.14 W
Maria da Fé	256	22.18 S	45.23 W
María Elena	252	22.21 S	69.40 W
Maria Enzersdorf	61	48.06 N	16.17 E
Maria Gail	64	46.36 N	13.52 E
Mariager	26	56.39 N	10.00 E
Mariāhu	124	25.37 N	82.37 E
María Ignacia (Vela)	252	37.24 S	59.30 W
Maria Island I, Austl.	164	14.52 S	135.40 E
Maria Island I, Austl.	166	42.39 S	148.04 E
Mariakani	154	3.52 S	39.28 E
Maria Laach ⊌[1]	56	50.24 N	7.14 E
María la Baja	246	9.59 N	75.17 W
Maria Lanzendorf	264b	48.06 N	16.25 E
Maria Luggau	64	46.42 N	12.45 E
María Madre, Isla I	234	21.35 N	106.33 W
María Magdalena, Isla I	234	21.25 N	106.24 W
Marian, Lake ⊜	220	27.52 N	81.06 W
Mariana	255	20.23 S	43.25 W
Mariana Basin ✣[1]	14	17.30 N	145.00 E
Mariana Islands II	108	16.00 N	145.30 E
Mariana Ridge ✣[3]	14	17.00 N	146.00 E
Mariana Trench ✣[1]	14	15.00 N	147.30 E
Mariāni	120	26.40 N	94.20 E
Marian Lake ⊜	176	63.00 N	116.10 W
Marianna, Ar., U.S.	194	34.46 N	90.45 W
Marianna, Fl., U.S.	192	30.46 N	85.13 W
Mariannelund	26	57.37 N	15.34 E
Mariannhill	158	29.52 S	30.50 E
Mariano Acosta	258	34.43 S	58.48 W
Mariano Comense	62	45.42 N	9.11 E
Mariano del Friuli	64	45.55 N	13.27 E
Mariano I. Loza	252	29.22 S	58.12 W
Mariano J. Haedo	288	34.38 S	58.36 W
Mariano Moreno, Arg.	252	38.44 S	70.01 W
Mariano Moreno → Moreno, Arg.	258	34.39 S	58.48 W
Marianopoli	70	37.36 N	13.55 E
Marianópolis	250	4.47 S	44.38 W
Mariánské Lázně	60	49.59 N	12.43 E
Maria Paula	287a	22.54 S	43.02 W
Mariar	164	2.48 S	132.50 E
Mariarano	157b	15.29 S	46.42 E
Marias ≃	202	47.56 N	110.30 W
Marias, Dry Fork ≃	202	48.22 N	111.45 W
Marías, Islas II	234	21.25 N	106.28 W
Maria Saal	61	46.41 N	14.21 E
Marias Pass)(	202	48.19 N	113.21 W
Maria Stein	216	40.24 N	84.28 W
María Teresa	252	34.01 S	61.54 W
Maria-Theresiopel → Subotica	38	46.06 N	19.39 E
Mariato, Punta >	246	7.13 N	80.53 W
Maria van Diemen, Cape >	172	34.28 S	172.39 E
Mariaville	210	42.49 N	74.08 W
Mariazell	61	47.47 N	15.19 E
Ma'rib	144	15.30 N	45.20 E
Maribios, Cordillera de los ⩘	236	12.35 N	86.50 W
Maribo	41	54.46 N	11.31 E
Maribojoc Bay ⊂	116	9.42 N	123.50 E
Maribor	61	46.33 N	15.39 E
Maribyrnong	274b	37.46 S	144.54 E
Maribyrnong ≃	169	37.49 S	144.55 E
Marica, Blg.	38	42.02 N	25.50 E
Maricá, Bra.	256	22.55 S	42.49 W
Marica, S.S.S.R.	78	51.45 N	35.16 E
Maricá □[7]	287a	22.57 S	42.59 W
Marica (Évros) (Meriç) ≃	38	40.52 N	26.12 E
Maricá, Lagoa de ⊂	256	22.56 S	42.50 W
Maricaban Island I	116	13.39 N	120.53 E
Maricao	240m	18.11 N	66.59 W
Maricás, Ilhas II	256	23.01 S	42.55 W
Maricha Bil ⊜	272b	22.55 N	88.31 E
Marico ≃	156	24.12 S	26.52 E
Maricopa, Az., U.S.	200	33.03 N	112.02 W
Maricopa, Ca., U.S.	204	35.03 N	119.24 W
Maricopa Indian Reservation ⇝[4]	200	33.02 N	112.05 W
Maricunga, Salar de ≚	252	26.55 S	69.05 W
Maridagao ≃	116	7.13 N	124.41 E
Marīdī	154	4.55 N	29.28 E
Maridi ≃	140	6.05 N	29.24 E
Marié ≃	246	0.27 S	66.26 W
Marie Byrd Land ⇝[1]	9	80.00 S	120.00 W
Marie Curtis Park ♠	275b	43.35 N	79.33 W
Mariedamm	40	58.51 N	15.09 E
Mariefred	40	59.16 N	17.13 E
Marie-Galante I	241o	15.56 N	61.16 W
Mariehamn	26	60.06 N	19.57 E
Marieholm	41	55.52 N	13.09 E
Mariel	240p	22.59 N	82.45 W
Marie Lake ⊜	184	54.37 N	110.18 W
Marie-Lefranc, Lac ⊜	206	46.08 N	75.00 W
Mariembourg	50	50.06 N	4.31 E
Marienbad → Mariánské Lázně	60	49.59 N	12.43 E
Marienbaum	52	51.41 N	6.22 E
Marienberg, B.R.D.	56	50.39 N	7.57 E
Marienberg, D.D.R.	54	50.39 N	13.10 E
Marienberg, Pap. N. Gui.	164	3.55 S	144.15 E
Marien-Berg ∧[2]	264a	52.22 N	13.32 E
Marienborn	54	52.12 N	11.08 E
Marienburg → Malbork	30	54.02 N	19.01 E
Mariendorf ⇝[8]	264a	52.26 N	13.23 E
Marienfelde ⇝[8]	264a	52.25 N	13.22 E
Marienhafe	52	53.31 N	7.16 E
Marienheide	56	51.05 N	7.32 E
Mariental, B.R.D.	54	52.16 N	10.59 E
Mariental, Namibia	156	24.36 S	17.59 E
Mariental □[5]	156	25.00 S	19.00 E
Marienville	214	41.28 N	79.07 W
Maries □[6]	219	38.15 N	91.56 W
Maries ≃	194	38.30 N	92.01 W
Mariestad	40	58.43 N	13.51 E
Marieta ≃	246	5.02 N	66.38 W
Marietta, Ga., U.S.	192	33.57 N	84.33 W
Marietta, In., U.S.	218	39.26 N	85.53 W
Marietta, Mn., U.S.	198	45.00 N	96.25 W
Marietta, Oh., U.S.	188	39.24 N	81.27 W
Marietta, Ok., U.S.	196	33.56 N	97.06 W
Marietta, Pa., U.S.	208	40.03 N	76.33 W
Marietta, Tx., U.S.	222	33.10 N	94.33 W
Marietta, Wa., U.S.	224	48.47 N	122.34 W
Marieville	206	45.26 N	73.10 W
Mariga ≃	150	9.40 N	5.55 E
Marigliano	66	40.56 N	14.27 E
Marignane	62	43.25 N	5.13 E
Marignier	58	46.06 N	6.31 E
Marigny-le-Châtel	50	48.24 N	3.44 E
Marigny-L'église	50	47.22 N	3.56 E
Marigot, Dom.	240d	15.32 N	61.18 W
Marigot, Guad.	238	18.04 N	63.06 W
Marihatag	116	8.48 N	126.18 E
Mariinsk	86	56.13 N	87.45 E
Mariinskoje	89	51.43 N	140.13 E
Marijec	80	56.32 N	49.50 E
Marijskaja Avtonomnaja Sovetskaja Socialističeskaja Respublika □[3]	80	56.30 N	48.00 E
Marikana	158	25.42 S	27.48 E
Marikina	269f	14.38 N	121.06 E
Marikina ≃	269f	14.33 N	121.04 E
Marília	255	22.13 S	49.56 W
Marilla	210	42.50 N	78.33 W
Mari-Malmyž	80	56.30 N	50.40 E
Marimari ≃	246	3.58 S	58.49 W
Marimba	152	8.28 S	17.08 E
Marín, Esp.	34	42.23 N	8.42 W
Marín, Méx.	232	25.52 N	100.03 W
Marin □[6]	226	38.03 N	122.33 W
Marina	226	36.41 N	121.48 W
Marina ⇝[8]	282	37.47 N	122.27 W
Marina del Rey	280	33.50 N	118.25 W
Marina del Rey ⊂	280	33.58 N	118.27 W
Marina di Andora	62	43.57 N	8.08 E
Marina di Campo	66	42.44 N	10.14 E
Marina di Caronia	70	38.02 N	14.28 E
Marina di Carrara	64	44.02 N	10.02 E
Marina di Cecina	66	43.18 N	10.29 E
Marina di Gioiosa Ionica	68	38.18 N	16.20 E
Marina di Grosseto	66	42.43 N	10.59 E
Marina di Massa	64	44.00 N	10.06 E
Marina di Minturno	66	41.16 N	13.45 E
Marina di Orosei	71	40.22 N	9.43 E
Marina di Palma ⇝[8]	70	37.10 N	13.43 E
Marina di Pietrasanta	64	43.56 N	10.12 E
Marina di Pisa	66	43.40 N	10.16 E
Marina di Ragusa	70	36.47 N	14.33 E
Marina di Ravenna	66	44.29 N	12.17 E
Marina Fall ⌞	246	5.22 N	59.29 W
Marin City	282	37.52 N	122.21 W
Marinduque □[4]	116	13.25 N	121.55 E
Marinduque Island I	116	13.24 N	121.58 E
Marine	219	38.47 N	89.46 W
Marine City	214	42.43 N	82.29 W
Marine-Ehrenmal ⊥	54	54.23 N	10.15 E
Marineland of the Pacific ⊌[3]	228	33.44 N	118.24 W
Marinella	70	37.35 N	12.50 E
Marine Museum ⊌	280	33.43 N	118.17 W
Marineo	70	37.57 N	13.25 E
Marine Park ♠	283	42.20 N	71.01 W
Marine Parkway Bridge ⇝[5]	276	40.34 N	73.53 W
Mariners Museum ⊌	208	37.03 N	76.30 W
Marines	50	49.09 N	1.59 E
Marinette	190	45.06 N	87.37 W
Marine World/Africa USA ♠	282	37.32 N	122.16 W
Maringá	255	23.25 S	51.55 W
Maringa ≃	152	1.14 N	19.48 E
Maringouin	194	30.29 N	91.31 W
Maríngue	154	17.55 S	34.24 E
Marinha Grande	34	39.45 N	8.56 W
Marin Mall ⇝[9]	282	37.56 N	122.31 W
Marino, It.	66	41.46 N	12.39 E
Marino, Vanuatu	175f	15.00 S	168.09 E
Marinovka, S.S.S.R.	78	47.46 N	30.53 E
Marinovka, S.S.S.R.	80	48.41 N	43.49 E
Marinovka, S.S.S.R.	83	47.54 N	38.51 E
Marin Peninsula >[1]	282	37.51 N	122.31 W
Marins	256	22.27 S	45.08 W
Marinskij Posad	80	56.07 N	47.43 E
Marintu	112	0.34 N	110.00 E
Marinwood	226	38.02 N	122.32 W
Mario, Monte ∧[2]	267a	41.55 N	12.27 E
Marion, Austl.	168b	35.01 S	138.34 E
Marion, Al., U.S.	194	32.37 N	87.19 W
Marion, Ar., U.S.	194	35.12 N	90.11 W
Marion, Ct., U.S.	207	41.33 N	72.55 W
Marion, Il., U.S.	194	37.43 N	88.55 W
Marion, In., U.S.	216	40.33 N	85.39 W
Marion, Ia., U.S.	190	42.02 N	91.35 W
Marion, Ks., U.S.	198	38.20 N	97.01 W
Marion, Ky., U.S.	194	37.19 N	88.04 W
Marion, La., U.S.	194	32.54 N	92.14 W
Marion, Ma., U.S.	207	41.42 N	70.45 W
Marion, Mi., U.S.	190	44.06 N	85.08 W
Marion, Ms., U.S.	194	32.25 N	88.38 W
Marion, N.Y., U.S.	210	43.08 N	77.11 W
Marion, N.C., U.S.	192	35.41 N	82.00 W
Marion, N.D., U.S.	198	46.36 N	98.19 W
Marion, Oh., U.S.	214	40.35 N	83.07 W
Marion, S.C., U.S.	192	34.10 N	79.24 W
Marion, S.D., U.S.	198	43.25 N	97.15 W
Marion, Va., U.S.	192	36.50 N	81.30 W
Marion, Wi., U.S.	190	44.40 N	88.53 W
Marion □[6], Fl., U.S.	220	29.00 N	82.03 W
Marion □[6], Il., U.S.	219	38.38 N	88.57 W
Marion □[6], In., U.S.	218	39.46 N	86.09 W
Marion □[6], Mo., U.S.	219	39.50 N	91.37 W
Marion □[6], Oh., U.S.	214	40.35 N	83.08 W
Marion □[6], Or., U.S.	224	45.06 N	122.47 W
Marion □[6], Tx., U.S.	222	32.48 N	94.33 W
Marion, Lake ⊜	220	28.05 N	81.32 W
Marion, Lake ⊜[1]	192	33.30 N	80.25 W
Marion Bay ⊂	166	42.48 S	147.55 E
Marion Center	214	40.46 N	79.03 W
Marion Downs	166	23.22 S	139.39 E
Marion Heights	210	40.48 N	76.28 W
Marion Hill	214	40.44 N	80.18 W
Marion Hills	278	41.45 N	87.57 W
Marion Junction	194	32.26 N	87.14 W
Marion Lake ⊜[1]	198	38.24 N	97.08 W
Marion Reef ✣[2]	166	19.10 S	152.17 E
Marion Station	208	38.02 N	75.46 W
Marionville	194	37.00 N	93.38 W
Mariópolis	252	26.20 S	52.33 W
Maripa	246	7.26 N	65.09 W
Maripá de Minas	256	21.48 S	42.58 W
Maripipi Island I	116	11.47 N	124.19 E
Mariposa	226	37.29 N	119.57 W
Mariposa □[6]	226	37.29 N	119.58 W
Mariposa Creek ≃	226	37.14 N	120.26 W
Mariposa Slough ≃	226	37.12 N	120.46 W
Mariquita	246	5.12 N	74.54 W
Mariquita, Cerro ∧	234	23.13 N	98.22 W
Marisa	112	0.28 N	121.56 E
Marisa ≃	112	0.28 N	121.56 E
Mariscal Estigarribia	252	22.02 S	60.38 W
Marisco, Ponta do >	287a	23.01 S	43.17 W
Mariškino	82	55.21 N	38.37 E
Marissa	219	38.15 N	89.45 W
Maritime Alps (Alpes Maritimes) (Alpi Marittime) ⩘	62	44.15 N	7.10 E
Maritimes, Alpes → Maritime Alps ⩘	62	44.15 N	7.10 E
Marittime, Alpi → Maritime Alps ⩘	62	44.15 N	7.10 E
Mari-Turek	80	56.47 N	49.36 E
Maritzburg → Pietermaritzburg	158	29.37 S	30.16 E
Mariupol' → Ždanov	83	47.06 N	37.33 E
Mariusa, Caño ≃[1]	246	9.43 N	61.26 W
Mariusa, Isla I	241r	9.39 N	61.19 W
Marīvān	128	35.31 N	46.10 E
Mariveles	116	14.26 N	120.29 E
Märjamaa	76	58.54 N	24.26 E
Marjanovka, S.S.S.R.	78	50.28 N	24.48 E
Marjanovka, S.S.S.R.	86	54.58 N	72.38 E
Marjanskaja	78	45.06 N	38.38 E
Marjevka	86	53.46 N	67.24 E
Marjina Gorka	76	53.31 N	28.09 E
Marjinka	83	47.56 N	37.31 E
Marjino, S.S.S.R.	82	54.28 N	37.12 E
Marjino, S.S.S.R.	89	48.31 N	130.38 E
Marjino, S.S.S.R.	265a	59.50 N	29.56 E
Marjino, S.S.S.R.	265a	59.54 N	31.00 E
Marjino, S.S.S.R.	265b	55.52 N	37.18 E
Marjinskaja	84	43.53 N	43.29 E
Marjinsko	76	58.49 N	28.32 E
Mār Jirjis, Jūn ⊂	132	33.54 N	35.33 E
Marj ʿUyūn	132	33.22 N	35.35 E
Marka, Šom.	144	1.43 N	44.53 E
Markā, Urd.	132	31.59 N	35.59 E
Markā I	138	18.13 N	41.20 E
Mark Acres	279b	40.21 N	79.42 W
Markakol', ozero ⊜	86	48.45 N	85.56 E
Markala	150	13.41 N	6.05 W
Markam	102	29.40 N	98.30 E
Markansu	85	39.18 N	73.20 E
Mārkāpur	122	15.44 N	79.17 E
Markaryd	26	56.26 N	13.36 E
Markazī □[4]	128	35.30 N	51.00 E
Markdale	212	44.19 N	80.39 W
Markdorf	58	47.43 N	9.23 E
Marked Tree	194	35.31 N	90.25 W
Markelo	52	52.14 N	6.30 E

Symbols in the index entries represent the broad categories identified in the key at the right. Symbols with superior numbers (⩘[1]) identify subcategories (see complete key on page *I · 1*).

Kartensymbole in dem Registerverzeichnis stellen die rechts in Schlüssel erklärten Kategorien dar. Symbole mit hochgestellten Ziffern (⩘[1]) bezeichnen Unterabteilungen einer Kategorie (vgl. vollständiger Schlüssel auf Seite *I · 1*).

Los símbolos incluidos en el texto del índice representan las grandes categorías identificadas con la clave a la derecha. Los símbolos con números en su parte superior (⩘[1]) identifican las subcategorías (véase la clave completa en la página *I · 1*).

Les symboles de l'index représentent les catégories indiquées dans la légende à droite. Les symboles suivis d'un indice (⩘[1]) représentent des sous-catégories (voir légende complète à la page *I · 1*).

Os símbolos incluídos no texto do índice representam as grandes categorias identificadas com a chave à direita. Os símbolos com números em sua parte superior (⩘[1]) identificam as subcategorias (veja-se a chave completa à página *I · 1*).

∧ Mountain	Berg	Montaña	Montagne	Montanha
⩘ Mountains	Berge	Montañas	Montagnes	Montanhas
)(Pass	Pass	Paso	Col	Passo
V Valley, Canyon	Tal, Cañon	Valle, Cañón	Vallée, Canyon	Vale, Canhão
≚ Plain	Ebene	Llano	Plaine	Planície
> Cape	Kap	Cabo	Cap	Cabo
I Island	Insel	Isla	Île	Ilha
II Islands	Inseln	Islas	Îles	Ilhas
⊥ Other Topographic Features	Andere Topographische Objekte	Otros Elementos Topográficos	Autres données topographiques	Outros acidentes topográficos

ESPAÑOL — Nombre | Página | Lat.°′ | Long.°′ W = Oeste
FRANÇAIS — Nom | Page | Lat.°′ | Long.°′ W = Ouest
PORTUGUÊS — Nome | Página | Lat.°′ | Long.°′ W = Oeste

Markelovo 86 56.42 N 83.33 E
Marken I 52 52.28 N 5.03 E
Markendorf 54 51.59 N 13.10 E
Markermeer ⊜ 52 52.33 N 5.15 E
Markesan 190 43.42 N 88.59 W
Märket I 40 60.18 N 19.08 E
Market Bosworth 42 52.37 N 1.24 W
Market Deeping 42 52.41 N 0.19 W
Market Drayton 42 52.54 N 2.29 W
Market Harborough 42 52.29 N 0.55 W
Markethill 44 54.18 N 6.31 W
Market Lavington 42 51.18 N 1.59 W
Market Rasen 44 53.24 N 0.21 W
Market Weighton 44 53.52 N 0.40 W
Markfield 42 52.40 N 1.17 W
Markgröningen 56 48.54 N 9.05 E
Markham, On., Can. 212 43.52 N 79.16 W
Markham, Il., U.S. 278 41.35 N 87.41 W
Markham, Tx., U.S. 222 28.57 N 96.04 W
Markham ≃ 164 6.35 S 146.25 E
Markham, Mount ∧ 9 82.51 S 161.21 E
Markham Bay c 176 63.30 N 71.48 W
Markinch 46 56.12 N 3.08 W
Märkisch Buchholz 54 52.07 N 13.46 E
Märkisch Friedland
→ Mirosławiec 30 53.21 N 16.05 E
Markit 85 38.55 N 77.38 E
Markkleeberg 54 51.17 N 12.23 E
Markland Dam ◆[6] 218 38.47 N 84.58 W
Markle, In., U.S. 216 40.50 N 85.20 W
Markle, Pa., U.S. 279b 40.34 N 79.39 W
Markleeville 226 38.41 N 119.46 W
Markleville 218 39.58 N 85.36 W
Markley Canyon V 282 38.00 N 121.50 W
Marklissa
→ Leśna 30 51.02 N 15.16 E
Marknesse 52 52.43 N 5.52 E
Markneukirchen 54 50.18 N 12.19 E
Markoldendorf 52 51.48 N 9.46 E
Markópoulon 267c 37.54 N 23.54 E
Markounda 152 7.37 N 16.59 E
Markovka 83 49.31 N 39.34 E
Markovo, S.S.S.R. 74 64.40 N 170.25 E
Markovo, S.S.S.R. 80 57.01 N 40.30 E
Markovo, S.S.S.R. 82 55.52 N 39.17 E
Markovo, S.S.S.R. 88 57.20 N 107.04 E
Markoy 150 14.39 N 0.02 E
Markranstädt 54 51.18 N 12.13 E
Marks, S.S.S.R. 80 51.42 N 46.46 E
Marks, Ms., U.S. 194 34.15 N 90.16 W
Marks Tey 42 51.52 N 0.47 E
Marksuhl 56 50.55 N 10.11 E
Marksville 194 31.07 N 92.03 W
Markt Bibart 56 49.39 N 10.26 E
Marktbreit 56 49.40 N 10.08 E
Markt Erlbach 56 49.29 N 10.38 E
Marktheidenfeld 56 49.50 N 9.36 E
Markt Indersdorf 60 48.22 N 11.23 E
Marktl 60 48.15 N 12.51 E
Marktleugast 54 50.10 N 11.38 E
Marktleuthen 54 50.08 N 12.00 E
Marktoberdorf 58 47.47 N 10.37 E
Marktredwitz 30 50.00 N 12.06 E
Markt Rettenbach 58 47.57 N 10.23 E
Marktschellenberg 64 47.42 N 13.02 E
Markt Schwaben 60 48.11 N 11.51 E
Mark Twain Cave ⩣[5] 219 39.42 N 91.21 W
Mark Twain Lake ⊜[1] 219 39.30 N 91.45 W
Mark Twain State Park ♠ 219 39.29 N 91.48 W
Markulešty 78 47.52 N 28.14 E
Markundi 140 11.33 N 23.49 E
Markvue Manor 279b 40.20 N 79.46 W
Mark West Creek ≃ 226 38.30 N 122.42 W
Marl 52 51.38 N 7.05 E
Marlasi 164 5.30 S 134.38 E
Marlboro, Ab., Can. 182 53.33 N 116.45 W
Marlboro, N.J., U.S. 208 40.18 N 74.14 W
Marlboro, N.Y., U.S. 210 41.36 N 73.58 W
Marlboro, Oh., U.S. 214 40.53 N 81.12 W
Marlboro, Pa., U.S. 285 39.54 N 75.42 W
Marlborough, Austl. 166 22.49 S 149.53 E
Marlborough, Guy. 246 7.29 N 58.38 W
Marlborough, Eng., U.K. 42 51.26 N 1.43 W
Marlborough, Ct., U.S. 207 41.37 N 72.27 W
Marlborough, Ma., U.S. 207 42.20 N 71.33 W
Marlborough Downs ⋏[1] 42 51.30 N 1.45 W
Marldon 42 50.28 N 3.36 W
Marle 50 49.44 N 3.46 E
Marlenheim 58 48.37 N 7.30 E
Marles-en-Brie 261 48.44 N 2.53 E
Marles-les-Mines 50 50.30 N 2.31 E
Marlette 190 43.19 N 83.04 W
Marlette Lake ⊜ 226 39.10 N 119.54 W
Marley, Il., U.S. 278 41.33 N 87.55 W
Marley, Md., U.S. 208 39.09 N 76.35 W
Marley Creek ≃ 278 41.31 N 87.57 W
Marley Neck ›[1] 284b 39.12 N 76.33 W
Marlieux 58 46.04 N 5.04 E
Marlin 222 31.18 N 96.53 W
Marlinton 188 38.13 N 80.05 W
Marl-Loemühle, Flughafen ⊠ 263 51.39 N 7.10 E
Marlow, D.D.R. 54 54.09 N 12.34 E
Marlow, Eng., U.K. 42 51.35 N 0.48 W
Marlow, Ok., U.S. 196 34.38 N 97.57 W
Marlpit Hill 260 51.13 N 0.04 E
Marlton 208 39.53 N 74.55 W
Marlton Heights 285 39.40 N 75.21 W
Marly 50 50.20 N 3.32 E
Marly, Forêt de ♠ 261 48.50 N 2.00 E
Marly-la-Ville 261 49.05 N 2.30 E
Marly-le-Roi 50 48.52 N 2.05 E
Marma, Sve. 26 61.16 N 16.52 E
Marma, Sve. 40 60.30 N 17.25 E
Marmaduke 194 36.11 N 90.22 W
Marmagne 58 46.50 N 4.21 E
Marmande 32 44.30 N 0.10 E
Marmara, Sea of
→ Marmara Denizi ⊤[2] 130 40.40 N 28.15 E
Marmara Adası I 130 40.38 N 27.37 E
Marmara Denizi (Sea of Marmara) ⊤[2] 130 40.40 N 28.15 E
Marmara Ereğlisi 130 40.58 N 27.57 E
Marmara Gölü ⊜ 130 38.37 N 28.02 E
Marmaris 130 36.51 N 28.16 E
Marmarītā 130 34.47 N 36.15 E
Marmarth 198 46.17 N 103.55 W
Marmaton ≃ 194 38.00 N 94.19 W
Marmelos 248 6.08 S 61.50 W
Marmelos, Rio dos ≃ 248 6.06 S 61.46 W
Marmet 188 38.14 N 81.34 W
Marmion Lake ⊜[1] 190 48.54 N 91.30 W
Marmirolo 64 45.13 N 10.45 E
Marmolada ∧ 64 46.26 N 11.51 E
Marmora, On., Can. 212 44.29 N 77.41 W
Marmora, N.J., U.S. 208 39.16 N 74.38 W
Marmore 66 42.33 N 12.43 E
Marmore ≃ 62 45.44 N 7.37 E
Marmore, Cascàta delle ʟ 66 42.33 N 12.43 E
Marmot Bay c 180 58.00 N 152.20 W
Marmot Island I 180 58.13 N 151.51 W
Marmoutier 58 48.41 N 7.23 E
Marnate 266b 45.38 N 8.54 E
Marnay 58 47.17 N 5.46 E
Marnaz 58 46.04 N 6.32 E
Marne, B.R.D. 52 53.57 N 9.00 E
Marne, Mi., U.S. 216 43.02 N 85.49 W
Marne □[5] 32 48.55 N 4.10 E
Marne ≃, Austl. 168b 34.40 S 139.18 E
Marne ≃, Fr. 32 48.49 N 2.24 E
Marne à la Saône, Canal de la ≊ 58 48.44 N 4.36 E
Marne au Rhin, Canal de la ≊ 56 48.35 N 7.47 E
Marneuli 84 41.28 N 44.50 E
Marnhull 42 50.58 N 2.18 W

Marnitz 54 53.19 N 11.56 E
Maroa, Il., U.S. 219 40.02 N 88.57 W
Maroa, Ven. 246 2.43 N 67.33 W
Maroala 157b 15.23 S 47.59 E
Maroantsetra 157b 15.26 S 49.44 E
Maroc
→ Morocco □[1] 148 32.00 N 5.00 W
Maroelaboom 156 19.15 S 18.53 E
Marofandilia 157b 20.07 S 44.34 E
Maroglio ≃ 70 37.03 N 14.15 E
Marokko
→ Morocco □[1] 148 32.00 N 5.00 W
Marol ◆[8] 272c 19.07 N 72.53 E
Marolambo 157b 20.02 S 48.07 E
Maroldsweisach 56 50.12 N 10.39 E
Marolles-en-Brie 261 48.44 N 2.33 E
Marolles-en-Hurepoix 261 48.34 N 2.18 E
Marolles-les-Braults 50 48.15 N 0.19 E
Maromandia 157b 14.13 S 48.08 E
Maromme 50 49.28 N 1.02 E
Maromokotro ∧ 157b 14.01 S 48.59 E
Marondera 154 18.10 S 31.36 E
Marone 64 45.44 N 10.05 E
Marong 102 31.07 N 99.20 E
Maronghi Creek ≃ 171a 26.58 S 152.22 E
Maroni (Marowijne) ≃ 250 5.45 N 53.58 W
Maroon 171a 28.10 S 152.44 E
Maroon, Mount ∧ 171a 28.13 S 152.44 E
Maroondah Aqueduct ≊[1] 274b 37.42 S 145.01 E
Maros 112 5.00 S 119.34 E
Maros (Mureș) ≃ 38 46.15 N 20.13 E
Maroseranana 157b 18.32 S 48.51 E
Marostica 64 45.45 N 11.39 E
Marosvásárhely
→ Tîrgu Mureș 38 46.33 N 24.33 E
Marotandrano 157b 16.10 S 48.50 E
Marotiri, Îles II 14 27.55 S 143.26 W
Marotta 66 43.46 N 13.08 E
Maroua 146 10.36 N 14.20 E
Maroubra 274a 33.57 S 151.16 E
Maroubra Bay c 274a 33.57 S 151.16 E
Marouini ≃ 250 3.18 N 54.04 W
Marovato, Madag. 157b 13.59 S 48.36 E
Marovato, Madag. 157b 15.48 S 48.05 E
Marovato, Madag. 157b 16.28 S 48.25 E
Marovoay 157b 16.06 S 46.39 E
Marovoay Nord 157b 16.57 S 44.34 E
Marowijne □[5] 250 4.15 N 54.35 W
Marowijne (Maroni) ≃ 250 5.45 N 53.58 W
Marpent 50 50.18 N 4.05 E
Marple 44 53.24 N 2.03 W
Marquam 224 45.04 N 122.41 W
Marquand 194 37.25 N 90.10 W
Marquard 158 28.54 S 27.28 E
Marquardt 54 52.27 N 12.57 E
Marquartstein 64 47.45 N 12.28 E
Marquesas Islands
→ Marquises, Îles II 6 9.00 S 139.30 W
Marquesas Keys II 220 24.34 N 82.08 W
Marquette, Ks., U.S. 198 38.33 N 97.50 W
Marquette, Mi., U.S. 190 46.32 N 87.23 W
Marquette Park ♠ 278 41.46 N 87.42 W
Márquez, Perú 286d 11.57 S 77.08 W
Marquez, Tx., U.S. 222 31.14 N 96.15 W
Marquina-Jemein 34 43.16 N 2.30 W
Marquion 50 50.13 N 3.05 E
Marquis 241k 12.06 N 61.37 W
Marquis, Cape › 241f 14.03 N 60.54 W
Marquise 50 50.49 N 1.42 E
Marquises, Îles (Marquesas Islands) II 6 9.00 S 139.30 W
Marrabel 168b 34.08 S 138.53 E
Marra Creek ≃ 166 30.05 S 147.05 E
Marradi 66 44.04 N 11.37 E
Marradong 168a 32.52 S 116.27 E
Marrah, Jabal ∧ 140 13.04 N 24.21 E
Marra Hills ⋏[2] 140 6.05 N 27.33 E
Marrakech 148 31.38 N 8.00 W
Marrakech □[4] 148 31.30 N 8.05 W
Marrawah 166 40.56 S 144.41 E
Marree 166 29.39 S 138.04 E
Marrero 194 29.53 N 90.06 W
Marrickville 274a 33.55 S 151.09 E
Marromeu 156 18.20 S 35.56 E
Marrowstone Island I 224 48.04 N 122.41 W
Marrubiu 71 39.45 N 8.38 E
Marruecos
→ Morocco □[1] 148 32.00 N 5.00 W
Marrupa 154 13.08 S 37.30 E
Mars 214 40.41 N 80.00 W
Marsā al-Burayqah 146 30.25 N 19.34 E
Marsabit 154 2.20 N 37.59 E
Marsabit National Park ♠ 154 2.20 N 38.00 E
Marsac-en-Livradois 62 45.29 N 3.44 E
Marṣafā wa Kafr Aḥmad Ḥashīsh 142 30.25 N 31.15 E
Marsal 56 48.48 N 6.36 E
Marsala 70 37.48 N 12.26 E
Marsā Maṭrūḥ 140 31.21 N 27.14 E
Marsā Maṭrūḥ □[4] 142 29.00 N 30.00 E
Marsangue, Ruisseau la ≃ 261 48.43 N 2.45 E
Marsannay-la-Côte 58 47.16 N 4.59 E
Marsanne 62 44.39 N 4.52 E
Marsassoum 150 12.50 N 16.00 W
Mars'aty 86 60.05 N 60.29 E
Marscheid ◆[8] 263 51.14 N 7.14 E
Marsciano 66 42.54 N 12.20 E
Marsden, Austl. 166 33.45 S 147.32 E
Marsden, Eng., U.K. 262 53.36 N 1.56 W
Marsden, Point › 168b 35.35 S 137.38 E
Marsden Park 274a 33.42 S 150.50 E
Marsdiep ʉ 52 52.59 N 4.45 E
Marseille 62 43.18 N 5.24 E
Marseille-en-Beauvaisis 50 49.35 N 1.57 E
Marseille-Marignane, Aéroport de ⊠ 62 43.27 N 5.13 E
Marseilles, Il., U.S. 216 41.19 N 88.42 W
Marseilles, Oh., U.S. 214 40.42 N 83.23 W
Marsella
→ Marseille 62 43.18 N 5.24 E
Marsfield 274a 33.47 S 151.07 E
Marsfjället ∧ 24 65.05 N 15.28 E
Marshall, Liber. 150 6.10 N 10.23 W
Marshall, Ar., U.S. 194 35.54 N 92.37 W
Marshall, Il., U.S. 194 39.23 N 87.41 W
Marshall, Mi., U.S. 216 42.16 N 84.57 W
Marshall, Mn., U.S. 198 44.26 N 95.47 W
Marshall, Mo., U.S. 194 39.07 N 93.11 W
Marshall, N.C., U.S. 192 35.47 N 82.41 W
Marshall, Tx., U.S. 194 32.32 N 94.22 W
Marshall, Va., U.S. 188 38.51 N 77.51 W
Marshall, Wi., U.S. 216 43.10 N 89.04 W
Marshall □[6], Il., U.S. 216 41.02 N 89.24 W
Marshall □[6], In., U.S. 216 41.21 N 86.19 W
Marshall ≃ 162 22.59 S 136.59 E
Marshall Bennett Islands II 164 8.50 S 151.50 E
Marshallberg 192 34.43 N 76.30 W
Marshall Canyon Regional Park ♠ 280 34.09 N 117.43 W
Marshall Gold Discovery State Historical Park ♠ 226 38.48 N 120.53 W
Marshall Hall 208 38.41 N 77.06 W
Marshall Islands □[2] 14 11.00 N 168.00 E
Marshall Islands II 14 9.00 N 168.00 E
Marshalls Creek 210 41.03 N 75.08 W
Marshallton, De., U.S. 208 39.43 N 75.39 W
Marshallton, Pa., U.S. 210 40.47 N 76.33 W
Marshallton, Pa., U.S. 285 39.57 N 75.41 W
Marshalltown 190 42.02 N 92.54 W
Marshallville, Ga., U.S. 192 32.27 N 83.56 W

Marshallville, Oh., U.S. 214 40.54 N 81.44 W
Marshbank Metropolitan Park ♠ 281 42.36 N 83.23 W
Marsh Creek ≃, Ca., U.S. 282 37.53 N 121.49 W
Marsh Creek ≃, Mi., U.S. 281 42.06 N 83.13 W
Marsh Creek ≃, Pa., U.S. 214 41.03 N 77.36 W
Marsh Creek ≃, Pa., U.S. 285 40.03 N 75.43 W
Marsh Creek ≃, Wi., U.S. 216 42.13 N 89.04 W
Marsh Creek Lake ⊜[1] 208 40.04 N 75.44 W
Marshes Creek ≃ 276 40.36 N 74.13 W
Marshfield, Eng., U.K. 42 51.28 N 2.19 W
Marshfield, Ma., U.S. 207 42.05 N 70.42 W
Marshfield, Mo., U.S. 194 37.20 N 92.54 W
Marshfield, Wi., U.S. 190 44.40 N 90.10 W
Marshfield Airport ⊠ 283 42.06 N 70.40 W
Marshfield Center 283 42.07 N 70.43 W
Marshfield Hills 207 42.08 N 70.44 W
Marsh Harbour 238 26.33 N 77.03 W
Marsh Hill 210 41.29 N 76.58 W
Mars Hill, In., U.S. 218 39.43 N 86.09 W
Mars Hill, Me., U.S. 186 46.30 N 67.52 W
Mars Hill, N.C., U.S. 192 35.49 N 82.32 W
Marsh Island I 194 29.35 N 91.53 W
Marsh Lake ⊜ 180 60.25 N 134.18 W
Marsh Peak ∧ 200 40.43 N 109.50 W
Marshside 262 53.40 N 2.58 W
Marshville 192 34.59 N 80.22 W
Marshyhope Creek ≃ 208 38.32 N 75.45 W
Marsica ◆[1] 66 41.50 N 13.45 E
Marsico Nuovo 68 40.25 N 15.44 E
Marsico Vetere 68 40.23 N 15.49 E
Marsillargues 62 43.40 N 4.11 E
Marsing 202 43.32 N 116.48 W
Marske-by-the-Sea 44 54.36 N 1.01 W
Mars-la-Tour 56 49.06 N 5.54 E
Marson 56 48.55 N 4.32 E
Marssum 52 53.12 N 5.42 E
Märsta 40 59.37 N 17.51 E
Marstal 41 54.51 N 10.31 E
Marsteller 214 40.39 N 78.48 W
Märstetten 58 47.36 N 9.04 E
Marston 262 53.16 N 2.30 W
Marston Moor ≡ 44 53.57 N 1.17 W
Marston Moor Battlesite ⊥ 44 53.57 N 1.17 W
Marstons Mills 207 41.39 N 70.25 W
Marstrand 26 57.53 N 11.35 E
Marsyandi ≃ 124 28.05 N 84.28 E
Mart 222 31.32 N 96.50 W
Marta 66 42.32 N 11.55 E
Marta ≃ 66 42.14 N 11.42 E
Martaban 110 16.32 N 97.37 E
Martaban, Gulf of c 110 16.30 N 97.00 E
Martano 68 40.12 N 18.18 E
Martap 152 6.54 N 13.03 E
Martapura, Indon. 112 3.25 S 114.51 E
Martapura, Indon. 112 4.19 S 104.22 E
Marte 146 12.22 N 13.51 E
Marteg ≃ 42 52.20 N 3.33 W
Martel, Fr. 32 44.56 N 1.37 E
Martel, Oh., U.S. 214 40.40 N 82.55 W
Martelange 56 49.50 N 5.44 E
Martell 226 38.22 N 120.48 W
Martello 64 46.34 N 10.47 E
Martello, Val V 64 46.31 N 10.45 E
Martemjanovskij 86 55.54 N 80.22 E
Marten ◆[8] 263 51.31 N 7.23 E
Marten Lake ⊜ 190 46.42 N 79.41 W
Marten Mountain ∧ 182 55.28 N 114.43 W
Marte R. Gomez, Presa ⊜[1] 196 26.10 N 99.00 W
Martfeld 52 52.52 N 9.04 E
Marthaguy Creek ≃ 166 30.16 S 147.35 E
Martha Lake 224 47.51 N 122.20 W
Marthall 262 53.17 N 2.18 W
Martham 42 52.42 N 1.38 E
Marthasville 219 38.37 N 91.03 W
Martha's Vineyard I 207 41.25 N 70.40 W
Martí, Cuba 240p 21.09 N 77.27 W
Martí, Cuba 240p 22.57 N 80.55 W
Martí, Pico ∧ 240p 20.01 N 76.35 W
Martignacco 64 46.05 N 13.08 E
Martignat 58 46.13 N 5.36 E
Martigny 58 46.06 N 7.04 E
Martigny-les-Bains 58 48.06 N 5.49 E
Martigues 62 43.24 N 5.03 E
Martil 34 35.37 N 5.17 W
Martim Francisco 256 22.31 S 46.57 W
Martin, Česko. 30 49.05 N 18.55 E
Martin, Ky., U.S. 192 37.34 N 82.45 W
Martin, Mi., U.S. 216 42.32 N 85.38 W
Martin, N.D., U.S. 198 47.49 N 100.06 W
Martin, Oh., U.S. 214 41.33 N 83.20 W
Martin, S.D., U.S. 198 43.10 N 101.43 W
Martin, Tn., U.S. 194 36.20 N 88.51 W
Martin □[6] 220 27.07 N 80.31 W
Martín ≃ 34 41.18 N 0.19 W
Martín, Arroyo ≃ 288 34.51 S 58.04 W
Martin, Isle I 46 57.55 N 5.14 W
Martina 58 46.53 N 10.30 E
Martina Franca 68 40.42 N 17.21 E
Martinborough 172 41.13 S 175.28 E
Martín Chico, Punta › 258 34.10 S 58.13 W
Martindale 196 29.50 N 97.51 W
Martindale Creek ≃, Austl. 170 32.32 S 150.42 E
Martindale Creek ≃, In., U.S. 218 39.48 N 85.09 W
Martindale Pond ⊜ 284a 43.11 N 79.16 W
Martin-Église 50 49.54 N 1.09 E
Martinengo 62 45.34 N 9.46 E
Mărtinești 38 45.30 N 27.18 E
Martinez, Ca., U.S. 226 38.01 N 122.07 W
Martinez, Ga., U.S. 192 33.31 N 82.04 W
Martínez ◆[8] 258 34.29 S 58.30 W
Martínez de la Torre 234 20.04 N 97.03 W
Martín García, Isla I 258 34.13 S 58.15 W
Martinho Campos 255 19.20 S 45.13 W
Martinica
→ Martinique □[2] 240e 14.40 N 61.00 W
Martini Creek ≃ 282 37.33 N 122.31 W
Martinique □[2], N.A. 230 14.40 N 61.00 W
Martinique □[2], N.A. 240e 14.40 N 61.00 W
Martin Lake ⊜[1], Al., U.S. 194 32.50 N 85.55 W
Martin Lake ⊜[1], Tx., U.S. 222 32.15 N 94.35 W
Martin Marietta Corporation ⊍[3] 284b 39.20 N 76.26 W
Martinniemi 26 65.13 N 25.18 E
Martinópole 250 3.15 S 40.41 W
Martin Peninsula ›[1] 9 74.25 S 114.10 W
Martín Pérez ≃ 286b 23.07 N 82.20 W
Martin Point › 180 70.08 N 143.16 W
Martin Run ≃ 279a 41.27 N 82.12 W
Martins 250 6.05 S 37.55 W
Martinsberg 61 48.22 N 15.09 E
Martins Brook ≃ 283 42.34 N 71.06 W
Martinsburg, Mo., U.S. 219 39.06 N 91.38 W
Martinsburg, N.Y., U.S. 212 43.44 N 75.28 W
Martinsburg, Oh., U.S. 214 40.16 N 82.21 W
Martinsburg, Pa., U.S. 214 40.18 N 78.19 W
Martinsburg, W.V., U.S. 188 39.27 N 77.57 W
Martins Creek 208 40.47 N 75.11 W
Martins Creek ≃ 210 41.37 N 75.46 W
Martinscroft 262 53.24 N 2.31 W
Martins Ferry 214 40.05 N 80.43 W
Martins Mills 222 32.25 N 95.47 W

Martins Pond ⊜ 283 42.36 N 71.08 W
Martinstein 56 49.48 N 7.32 E
Martinsthal 56 50.03 N 8.07 E
Martinsville, Austl. 170 33.03 S 151.25 E
Martinsville, Il., U.S. 194 39.20 N 87.52 W
Martinsville, In., U.S. 218 39.25 N 86.25 W
Martinsville, N.J., U.S. 276 40.36 N 74.34 W
Martinsville, Oh., U.S. 218 39.19 N 83.48 W
Martinsville, Va., U.S. 192 36.41 N 79.52 W
Martinton 216 40.55 N 87.44 W
Martintown 206 45.09 N 74.42 W
Martin Van Buren National Historic Site ⊥ 210 42.22 N 73.43 W
Martin Vaz, Ilhas II 244 20.30 S 28.51 W
Martis 71 40.47 N 8.49 E
Martisovo 76 56.34 N 31.55 E
Martock 42 50.59 N 2.46 W
Martofte 41 55.33 N 10.40 E
Marton, N.Z. 172 40.05 S 175.23 E
Marton, Eng., U.K. 262 53.12 N 2.13 W
Martorell 266d 41.28 N 1.56 E
Martorellas 266d 41.32 N 2.14 E
Martos 34 37.43 N 3.58 W
Martovaja 78 49.57 N 36.57 E
Martre, Lac la ⊜ 176 63.15 N 117.55 W
Martti 24 67.28 N 28.28 E
Martūbah 146 32.35 N 22.46 E
Martuk 86 50.46 N 56.31 E
Martuni, S.S.S.R. 84 39.48 N 47.06 E
Martuni, S.S.S.R. 84 40.08 N 45.19 E
Martville 210 43.17 N 76.38 W
Martynoviči 78 51.17 N 29.37 E
Martynovka 78 49.38 N 31.18 E
Martynovo 80 50.43 N 50.23 E
Martynovskij 80 50.29 N 42.18 E
Maru 150 12.22 N 6.22 E
Marua 164 9.30 S 149.20 E
Marudi 112 4.11 N 114.19 E
Marudu, Teluk c 112 6.45 N 116.55 E
Marugame 96 34.17 N 133.47 E
Maruggio 68 40.19 N 17.34 E
Marui 164 4.05 S 143.00 E
Maruia 172 42.11 S 172.13 E
Maruia ≃ 172 41.47 S 172.12 E
Maruim 250 10.45 S 37.05 W
Maruko 94 36.19 N 138.16 E
Marula 154 20.26 S 28.06 E
Marulan 170 34.43 S 150.00 E
Marulan South 170 34.46 S 150.02 E
Marum 52 53.08 N 6.16 E
Marum, Mont ∧ 175f 16.15 S 168.07 E
Marunga 152 17.27 S 20.02 E
Marungu 154 3.44 S 30.48 E
Marungu ⋏ 154 7.42 S 30.00 E
Maruoka 94 36.09 N 136.16 E
Mårup 41 55.57 N 10.35 E
Marusino 265b 55.42 N 37.59 E
Maruškino 82 55.36 N 37.12 E
Ma'rūt 120 31.34 N 67.03 E
Marutea I[1] 14 17.00 S 143.10 W
Maruyama 94 35.01 N 139.58 E
Maruyama ≃ 96 35.39 N 134.50 E
Marv Dasht 128 29.50 N 52.40 E
Marve ◆[8] 272c 19.12 N 72.49 E
Marvejols 32 44.33 N 3.18 E
Marvell 194 34.33 N 90.54 W
Marvel Loch 162 31.28 S 119.28 E
Marviken 40 58.34 N 16.51 E
Marvila ◆[8] 266c 38.44 N 9.06 W
Marville 56 49.27 N 5.27 E
Marvin Creek ≃ 214 41.48 N 78.26 W
Marvine, Mount ∧ 200 38.40 N 111.39 W
Mar Vista ◆[8] 280 34.00 N 118.27 W
Mārwār 120 25.44 N 73.36 E
Marwayne 184 53.32 N 110.20 W
Marwitz 264a 52.41 N 13.09 E
Marwitzer Heide ◆[3] 264a 52.40 N 13.06 E
Marwood 214 40.48 N 79.47 W
Marxhagen 54 53.37 N 12.36 E
Marxloh ◆[8] 263 51.31 N 6.46 E
Mary 128 37.36 N 61.50 E
Mary □[4] 128 37.30 N 62.30 E
Mary ≃, Austl. 164 12.53 S 131.38 E
Mary ≃, Austl. 166 25.26 S 152.55 E
Mary Anne Group II 162 21.13 S 115.32 E
Maryborough, Austl. 166 25.32 S 152.42 E
Maryborough, Austl. 169 37.03 S 143.45 E
Maryborough
→ Port Laoise 48 53.02 N 7.17 W
Mary D 208 40.45 N 76.04 W
Marydale 158 29.23 S 22.05 E
Marydel 208 39.06 N 75.44 W
Maryfield 184 49.48 N 101.32 W
Maryhill 224 45.41 N 120.49 W
Mary Jane, Lake ⊜ 220 28.22 N 81.11 W
Mary Kathleen 166 20.49 S 139.58 E
Maryknoll 210 41.11 N 73.50 W
Mary Lake ⊜ 212 45.15 N 79.15 W
Maryland 210 42.32 N 74.53 W
Maryland □[6] 150 4.40 N 8.00 W
Maryland □[3], U.S. 178 39.00 N 76.45 W
Maryland □[3], U.S. 188 39.00 N 76.45 W
Maryland, University of (Baltimore County Campus) ⊍[2], Md., U.S. 284b 39.15 N 76.43 W
Maryland, University of ⊍[2], Md., U.S. 284c 38.59 N 76.57 W
Maryland City 208 39.05 N 76.49 W
Maryland Gardens Park ♠ 275b 43.47 N 79.32 W
Maryland Heights 219 38.42 N 90.25 W
Maryland Historical Society ⊍ 284b 39.18 N 76.37 W
Maryland Line 208 39.42 N 76.39 W
Maryland Park 284c 38.53 N 76.54 W
Marylebone 262 53.34 N 2.38 W
Maryneal 196 32.14 N 100.27 W
Marypark 46 57.26 N 3.21 W
Maryport 44 54.43 N 3.30 W
Marys ≃, Il., U.S. 194 37.53 N 89.47 W
Marys ≃, Nv., U.S. 204 41.04 N 115.16 W
Marys Creek ≃ 202 42.18 N 115.48 W
Mary's Igloo 180 65.09 N 165.04 W
Marys Peak ∧ 202 44.30 N 123.33 W
Marystown 186 47.10 N 55.09 W
Marysvale 200 38.26 N 112.13 W
Marysville, Austl. 169 37.31 S 145.45 E
Marysville, B.C., Can. 182 49.38 N 115.57 W
Marysville, N.B., Can. 186 45.59 N 66.35 W
Marysville, Ca., U.S. 226 39.08 N 121.35 W
Marysville, Ks., U.S. 198 39.50 N 96.38 W
Marysville, Mi., U.S. 214 42.54 N 82.29 W
Marysville, Oh., U.S. 214 40.14 N 83.22 W
Marysville, Pa., U.S. 208 40.20 N 76.55 W
Marysville, Wa., U.S. 224 48.03 N 122.10 W
Mār Yūsuf 132 33.53 N 35.33 E
Maryūṭ, Buḥayrat ⊜ 142 31.08 N 29.56 E
Maryvale 171a 28.05 S 152.15 E
Maryvale ◆[8] 275b 43.46 N 79.18 W
Maryville, Mo., U.S. 194 40.20 N 94.52 W
Maryville, Tn., U.S. 192 35.45 N 83.58 W
Marywell 46 57.02 N 2.42 W
Marywood 216 41.48 N 88.18 W
Marzabotto 64 44.20 N 11.12 E
Marzagão 255 17.59 S 48.39 W
Marzahn ◆[8] 264a 52.33 N 13.33 E
Marzahna 54 52.00 N 12.46 E
Marzahne 54 52.31 N 12.31 E
Marzal, Aven de ⩣[5] 62 44.22 N 4.31 E
Marzo, Punta › 246 6.50 N 77.42 W
Marzolara 64 44.38 N 10.10 E
Marzūq 146 25.55 N 13.55 E
Marzūq, Ḥamādat ◆[2] 146 26.10 N 12.45 E
Marzūq, Ṣaḥrā' ◆[2] 146 24.30 N 13.00 E
Masa 152 3.45 S 15.29 E
Masachapa 236 11.47 N 86.31 W

Masada
→ Meẓada, Ḥorvot ⊥ 132 31.19 N 35.21 E
Mas'adah (Cæsarea Philippi) 132 33.14 N 35.45 E
Masada Landing Ground ⊠ 132 31.19 N 35.21 E
Más Afuera, Isla
→ Alejandro Selkirk, Isla I 244 33.45 S 80.46 W
Masagua 236 14.12 N 90.51 W
Masaguisi 116 12.41 N 121.32 E
Masai 114 1.29 N 103.53 E
Masai Mara Game Reserve ◆[4] 154 1.15 S 35.15 E
Masai Steppe ⋏[1] 154 4.45 S 37.00 E
Masak 85 43.37 N 78.18 E
Masaka 154 0.20 S 31.44 E
Masaki, Nihon 96 33.47 N 132.42 E
Masaki, Nihon 268 35.13 N 140.02 E
Masalembo-besar I 112 5.34 S 114.26 E
Masally 84 39.03 N 48.40 E
Masalok, Puntan › 174n 15.01 N 145.41 E
Masamba 112 2.32 S 120.20 E
Masan 98 35.11 N 128.32 E
Masangwe ∧ 154 5.28 S 30.05 E
Masānjor 126 24.07 N 87.19 E
Masapelid Island I 116 9.42 N 125.39 E
Masapun 112 7.47 S 126.38 E
Masaṙah 142 27.29 N 30.50 E
Masaran 115a 7.28 S 110.55 E
Ma'ṣarat Samālūṭ 142 28.19 N 30.43 E
Masaryktown 220 28.26 N 82.27 W
Masasi 154 10.43 S 38.48 E
Masatepe 236 11.55 N 86.09 W
Más a Tierra, Isla
→ Róbinson Crusoe, Isla I 244 33.38 S 78.52 W
Masaya 236 11.58 N 86.06 W
Masaya □[5] 236 12.00 N 86.10 W
Masba 146 11.30 N 13.00 E
Masbate 116 12.22 N 123.36 E
Masbate □[4] 116 12.20 N 123.30 E
Masbate Island I 116 12.15 N 123.30 E
Masbate Pass ʉ 116 12.30 N 123.35 E
Mascali 70 37.45 N 15.12 E
Mascarene Basin ✦[1] 12 15.00 S 56.00 E
Mascarene Islands II 157c 21.00 S 57.00 E
Mascarene Plateau ✦[3] 12 10.00 S 60.00 E
Mascasín 252 31.22 S 66.59 W
Maschen 52 53.24 N 10.02 E
Maschito 68 40.54 N 15.50 E
Mascot, Austl. 274a 33.56 S 151.12 E
Mascot, Tn., U.S. 192 36.03 N 83.44 W
Mascota 234 20.32 N 104.49 W
Mascota ≃ 234 20.38 N 104.59 W
Mascotte 220 28.35 N 81.53 W
Mascouche 206 45.45 N 73.36 W
Mascouche ≃ 206 45.41 N 73.40 W
Mascoutah 219 38.29 N 89.47 W
Mascuppic Lake ⊜ 283 42.41 N 71.23 W
Mase 102 27.16 N 104.08 E
Masefield 184 49.09 N 107.48 W
Masela, Pulau I 164 8.09 S 129.50 E
Masenberg ∧ 61 47.21 N 15.53 E
Maser 64 45.48 N 11.59 E
Maserada sul Piave 64 45.45 N 12.17 E
Maserti 130 37.24 N 40.58 E
Maseru 158 29.28 S 27.30 E
Masevaux 58 47.47 N 7.00 E
Maševka 78 49.26 N 34.52 E
Maševo 78 52.06 N 32.48 E
Masha 100 27.26 N 117.50 E
Mashaba 154 20.02 S 30.29 E
Mashaba Mountains ⋏ 154 18.45 S 30.32 E
Mash'abbe Sade 132 31.00 N 34.47 E
Mashābih I 128 25.37 N 36.29 E
Mashalah 142 30.44 N 31.08 E
Masham 44 54.13 N 1.40 W
Mashan, Zhg. 89 45.13 N 130.35 E
Mashan, Zhg. 100 27.33 N 113.46 E
Mashan, Zhg. 102 23.50 N 108.16 E
Mashar 140 9.14 N 26.52 E
Mashbury 260 51.47 N 0.24 E
Mashel ≃ 224 46.51 N 122.20 W
Mashenqiao 105 40.04 N 117.36 E
Masherbrum ∧ 123 35.43 N 76.18 E
Mashgharah 132 33.32 N 35.39 E
Mashhad, Īrān 128 36.18 N 59.36 E
Mashhad, Yis. 132 32.44 N 35.19 E
Mashi, Nig. 150 13.00 N 7.54 E
Mashi, Zhg. 100 29.05 N 114.22 E
Mashi, Zhg. 100 25.01 N 114.09 E
Mashike 92a 43.51 N 141.31 E
Mashiko 94 36.28 N 140.06 E
Mashita ≃ 94 35.40 N 137.10 E
Mashīz 128 29.56 N 56.37 E
Mashkai ≃ 128 26.02 N 65.19 E
Māshkel (Māshkīd) ≃ 128 28.02 N 63.25 E
Māshkel, Hāmūn-i- ⊜ 128 28.15 N 63.00 E
Mashki Chāh 128 29.01 N 62.27 E
Māshkīd (Māshkel) ≃ 128 28.02 N 63.25 E
Mashonaland North □[4] 154 16.30 S 30.00 E
Mashonaland South □[4] 154 18.15 S 30.45 E
Mashpee 207 41.38 N 70.28 W
Mashra'ur-Raqq 140 8.25 N 29.16 E
Mashtūl as-Sūq 142 30.22 N 31.22 E
Mashū-ko ⊜ 92a 43.35 N 144.32 E
Mashūray 120 32.12 N 68.21 E
Masibi 152 11.08 S 22.42 E
Masihi 114 2.47 N 99.40 E
Masīlah, Wādī al- V 144 15.10 N 51.05 E
Masi-Manimba 152 4.46 S 17.55 E
Masin 164 6.15 S 139.19 E
Masina 272b 22.55 N 88.32 E
Masindi 154 1.41 N 31.43 E
Masini Port 154 1.42 N 32.05 E
Masinloc 116 15.32 N 119.57 E
Masīr 142 31.03 N 31.00 E
Maṣīrah, Khalīj al- c 118 20.10 N 58.15 E
Masis 84 40.00 N 44.29 E
Masisea 248 8.36 S 74.19 W
Masisi 154 1.24 S 28.49 E
Masiwang, Tanjung › 164 3.27 S 130.49 E
Masjed Soleymān 128 31.58 N 49.18 E
Masjid Tanah 114 2.21 N 102.07 E
Mask, Lough ⊜ 48 53.35 N 9.20 W
Maska 150 11.20 N 7.20 E
Maskan, Ras › 144 11.10 N 43.33 E
Maskanah 130 36.01 N 38.05 E
Maskin 128 23.35 N 56.39 E
Maškino 82 54.53 N 36.08 E
Maskinongé □[6] 206 46.35 N 73.30 W
Maskinongé ≃, P.Q., Can. 206 46.10 N 73.01 W
Maskinongé ≃, P.Q., Can. 206 45.49 N 74.40 W
Maskinongé, Lac ⊜ 206 46.19 N 73.23 W
Maškoviči 82 54.11 N 36.17 E
Masku 26 60.34 N 22.06 E
Maskūtān 128 26.51 N 59.49 E
Maskwa ≃ 184 50.33 N 96.08 W
Masl'anino 86 54.20 N 84.13 E
Masl'anskaja 86 55.56 N 70.08 E
Maslova 265a 59.47 N 30.48 E
Maslovka 78 51.33 N 39.14 E
Maslovo 86 60.07 N 60.30 E
Masnières 50 50.07 N 3.13 E
Masnou 266d 41.29 N 2.19 E
Maso 150 7.14 N 2.53 W
Masoala 157b 15.59 S 50.10 E
Masoala, Cap › 157b 15.59 S 50.13 E
Masoala, Presqu'île de ›[1] 157b 15.40 S 50.12 E
Masoarivo 157b 19.03 S 44.19 E
Masomeloka 157b 20.17 S 48.37 E
Mason, Mi., U.S. 216 42.34 N 84.26 W
Mason, Oh., U.S. 218 39.21 N 84.18 W

Mason, Tn., U.S. 194 35.24 N 89.31 W
Mason, Tx., U.S. 196 30.44 N 99.13 W
Mason, W.V., U.S. 188 39.01 N 82.01 W
Mason □[6], Il., U.S. 219 40.18 N 90.04 W
Mason □[6], Ky., U.S. 218 38.35 N 83.48 W
Mason □[6], Wa., U.S. 224 47.20 N 123.09 W
Mason, Lake ⊜ 162 27.39 S 119.34 E
Mason Bay c 172 46.56 S 167.44 E
Mason City, Il., U.S. 219 40.12 N 89.41 W
Mason City, Ia., U.S. 190 43.09 N 93.12 W
Mason City, Ne., U.S. 198 41.13 N 99.18 W
Masone 62 44.30 N 8.42 E
Masonicus Brook ≃ 276 41.06 N 74.09 W
Mason Lake ⊜ 224 47.20 N 122.57 W
Masons Creek ≃ 285 39.59 N 74.51 W
Mason Valley V 226 39.07 N 119.10 W
Masonville, N.J., U.S. 285 39.59 N 74.52 W
Masonville, N.Y., U.S. 210 42.15 N 75.23 W
Maspeth ◆[8] 276 40.43 N 73.55 W
Masqaṭ (Muscat) 128 23.37 N 58.35 E
Maṣra' 142 27.14 N 31.02 E
Massa 64 44.01 N 10.09 E
Massa-Carrara □[4] 64 44.15 N 10.03 E
Massachusetts □[3], U.S. 178 42.15 N 71.50 W
Massachusetts □[3], U.S. 207 42.15 N 71.50 W
Massachusetts (Boston), University of ⊍[2] 283 42.19 N 71.03 W
Massachusetts Bay c 207 42.20 N 70.50 W
Massachusetts Correctional Institution ⊍ 283 42.07 N 71.18 W
Massachusetts Institute of Technology ⊍[2] 283 42.21 N 71.06 W
Massaciuccoli, Lago di ⊜ 66 43.50 N 10.20 E
Massacre Lake ⊜ 204 41.39 N 119.35 W
Massa Fermana 66 43.09 N 13.28 E
Massa Fiscaglia 66 44.48 N 12.01 E
Massafra 68 40.35 N 17.07 E
Massaguet 146 12.28 N 15.26 E
Massakory 146 13.00 N 15.44 E
Massalassef 146 11.43 N 17.08 E
Massa Lombarda 66 44.27 N 11.49 E
Massa Lubrense 68 40.36 N 14.20 E
Massa Marittima 66 43.03 N 10.53 E
Massa Martana 66 42.46 N 12.31 E
Massandra 78 44.32 N 34.12 E
Massangano 152 9.37 S 14.15 E
Massangena 156 21.32 S 32.57 E
Massapê 250 3.31 S 40.19 W
Massapequa 210 40.40 N 73.28 W
Massapequa Park 276 40.40 N 73.27 W
Massapequa Reserve County Park ♠ 276 40.42 N 73.27 W
Massapoag Brook ≃ 283 42.09 N 71.09 W
Massapoag Lake ⊜ 283 42.06 N 71.11 W
Massara 156 18.20 S 34.09 E
Massarosa 66 43.52 N 10.20 E
Massasoit State Park ♠ 207 41.53 N 71.01 W
Massaua
→ Mitsiwa 144 15.38 N 39.28 E
Massawa
→ Mitsiwa 144 15.38 N 39.28 E
Massawippi ≃ 206 45.22 N 71.51 W
Massawippi, Lake ⊜ 206 45.14 N 72.00 W
Massay 50 47.09 N 2.00 E
Massé, Ruisseau ≃ 275a 45.28 N 73.17 W
Massello 62 44.57 N 7.04 E
Massen 52 51.32 N 7.38 E
Massena, Ia., U.S. 198 41.15 N 94.46 W
Massena, N.Y., U.S. 206 44.55 N 74.53 W
Massenya 146 11.24 N 16.10 E
Masset 182 54.02 N 132.09 W
Masset Inlet c 182 53.42 N 132.20 W
Masseube 32 43.26 N 0.35 E
Massey 190 46.12 N 82.05 W
Massiac 32 45.15 N 3.12 E
Massiaru 76 58.00 N 24.35 E
Massico, Monte ∧ 68 41.10 N 13.55 E
Massieville 218 39.16 N 82.58 W
Massif Central
→ Central, Massif ⋏ 32 45.00 N 3.10 E
Massillon 214 40.48 N 81.32 W
Massima Camp 152 1.27 S 11.42 E
Massina 273b 4.22 S 15.22 E
Massina ◆[1] 150 14.30 N 5.00 W
Massinga 156 23.20 S 35.25 E
Massingir 156 23.51 S 32.04 E
Massive, Mount ∧ 200 39.12 N 106.28 W
Masson, Lac ⊜ 206 46.03 N 74.02 W
Masson Island I 9 66.08 S 96.34 E
Massy 261 48.44 N 2.17 E
Mastābah 144 20.49 N 39.20 E
Maštaga 84 40.32 N 50.00 E
Masterson 196 35.38 N 101.58 W
Masterton 172 40.57 S 175.40 E
Mas-Thibert 62 43.34 N 4.44 E
Mastic Point 192 25.03 N 77.57 W
Mastigouche ≃ 206 46.20 N 73.24 W
Mastigouche Nord ≃ 206 46.24 N 73.25 W
Mastūj 123 36.17 N 72.31 E
Mastūj ≃ 123 35.54 N 71.49 E
Mastung 120 29.48 N 66.51 E
Mastūrah 128 23.06 N 38.50 E
Masu 146 12.10 N 13.19 E
Masua 126 24.16 N 90.46 E
Masuda 96 34.40 N 131.51 E
Masuho 94 35.34 N 138.28 E
Masuika 152 7.37 S 22.32 E
Masuku 154 17.12 S 27.07 E
Māsūleh 128 37.10 N 48.59 E
Masulipatam
→ Machilīpatnam 122 16.10 N 81.08 E
Masura 126 23.16 N 90.24 E
Masurai, Gunung ∧ 112 2.30 S 101.51 E
Masury 214 41.12 N 80.32 W
Masvingo 154 20.05 S 30.50 E
Maṣyāf 130 35.03 N 36.21 E
Maszewo, Pol. 30 53.29 N 15.02 E
Maszewo, Pol. 54 52.06 N 14.55 E
Mat ≃ 38 41.39 N 19.34 E
Mata, Indon. 115b 8.12 S 122.56 E
Mata, Zaïre 152 7.53 S 21.58 E
Mata Amarilla 254 49.36 S 71.13 W
Mataba, Mount ∧ 269f 14.42 N 121.10 E
Matabeleland North □[4] 154 19.00 S 27.15 E
Matabeleland South □[4] 154 21.00 S 29.15 E
Mātābhānga 124 26.20 N 89.13 E
Matabuena 34 41.10 N 3.40 W
Matachel ≃ 34 38.50 N 6.17 W
Matachewan 190 47.56 N 80.39 W
Matacuni ≃ 246 3.02 N 65.16 W
Matad 88 46.58 N 115.18 E
Mata de Plátano, Quebrada ≃ 286c 10.35 N 66.46 W
Matadero Creek ≃ 282 37.26 N 122.08 W
Mata de São João 255 12.31 S 38.17 W
Matadi 152 5.49 S 13.27 E
Matador 196 34.00 N 100.49 W
Matagalpa 236 12.55 N 85.55 W
Matagalpa □[5] 236 13.00 N 85.30 W
Matagami 176 49.45 N 77.38 W
Matag-ob 116 11.07 N 124.29 E
Matagorda 196 28.41 N 95.58 W
Matagorda □[6] 222 28.57 N 96.00 W
Matagorda Bay c 196 28.35 N 96.20 W
Matagorda Island I 196 28.15 N 96.30 W
Matagorda Peninsula ›[1] 196 28.32 N 96.07 W
Mata Grande 250 9.07 S 37.44 W
Matahiae, Pointe › 174s 17.49 S 149.17 W

≃ River	Fluss	Río	Rivière	Rio	
≊ Canal	Kanal	Canal	Canal	Canal	
ʟ Waterfall, Rapids	Wasserfall, Stromschnellen	Cascada, Rápidos	Chute d'eau, Rapides	Cascata, Rápidos	
ʉ Strait	Meeresstrasse	Estrecho	Détroit	Estreito	
c Bay, Gulf	Bucht, Golf	Bahía, Golfo	Baie, Golfe	Baía, Golfo	
⊜ Lake, Lakes	See, Seen	Lago, Lagos	Lac, Lacs	Lago, Lagos	
≡ Swamp	Sumpf	Pantano	Marais	Pântano	
⍓ Ice Features, Glacier	Eis- und Gletscherformen	Accidentes Glaciales	Formes glaciaires	Acidentes glaciares	
⊤ Other Hydrographic Features	Andere Hydrographische Objekte	Otros Elementos Hidrográficos	Autres données hydrographiques	Outros acidentes hidrográficos	

✦ Submarine Features	Untermeerische Objekte	Accidentes Submarinos	Formes de relief sous-marin	Acidentes submarinos
□ Political Unit	Politische Einheit	Unidad Politica	Entité politique	Unidade política
⊍ Cultural Institution	Kulturelle Institution	Institución Cultural	Institution culturelle	Institução cultural
⊥ Historical Site	Historische Stätte	Sitio Histórico	Site historique	Sitio histórico
♠ Recreational Site	Erholungs- und Ferienort	Sitio de Recreo	Centre de loisirs	Area de Lazer
⊠ Airport	Flughafen	Aeropuerto	Aéroport	Aeroporto
■ Military Installation	Militäranlage	Instalación Militar	Installation militaire	Instalação militar
◆ Miscellaneous	Verschiedenes	Misceláneo	Divers	Diversos

Symbols in the index entries represent the broad categories identified in the key at the right. Symbols with superior numbers (⋏[1]) identify subcategories (see complete key on page *I · 1).*

Kartensymbole in dem Registerverzeichnis stellen die rechts in Schlüssel erklärten Kategorien dar. Symbole mit hochgestellten Ziffern (⋏[1]) bezeichnen Unterabteilungen einer Kategorie (vgl. vollständiger Schlüssel auf Seite *I · 1).*

Los símbolos incluídos en el texto del índice representan las grandes categorias identificadas con la clave a la derecha. Los símbolos con numeros en su parte superior (⋏[1]) identifican las subcategorías (véase la clave completa en la página *I · 1).*

Les symboles de l'index représentent les catégories indiquées dans la légende à droite. Les symboles suivis d'un indice (⋏[1]) représentent des sous-catégories (voir légende complète à la page *I · 1).*

Os símbolos incluídos no texto do índice representam as grandes categorias identificadas com a chave à direita. Os símbolos com números em sua parte superior (⋏[1]) identificam as subcategorias (veja-se a chave completa à página *I · 1).*

∧	Mountain	Berg	Montaña	Montagne	Montanha
⋏	Mountains	Berge	Montañas	Montagnes	Montanhas
)(	Pass	Pass	Paso	Col	Passo
V	Valley, Canyon	Tal, Cañon	Valle, Cañón	Vallée, Canyon	Vale, Canhão
≃	Plain	Ebene	Llano	Plaine	Planície
›	Cape	Kap	Cabo	Cap	Cabo
I	Island	Insel	Isla	Île	Ilha
II	Islands	Inseln	Islas	Îles	Ilhas
⊥	Other Topographic Features	Andere Topographische Objekte	Otros Elementos Topográficos	Autres données topographiques	Outros acidentes topográficos

ESPAÑOL

Nombre	Página	Lat.°′	Long.°′ W = Oeste
Measham	**42**	52.43 N	1.29 W
Meath □[6]	**48**	53.35 N	6.40 W
Meath □[9]	**48**	53.40 N	7.00 W
Meaux	**50**	48.57 N	2.52 E
Meaux-Esbly, Aérodrome de ⊠	**261**	48.55 N	2.50 E
Mebane	**192**	36.05 N	79.16 W
Mebisere	**273a**	6.42 N	3.31 E
Mebtoûh, Oued el ≃	**34**	35.16 N	0.32 W
Meča ≃	**82**	54.50 N	39.10 E
Meca, La → Makkah	**144**	21.27 N	39.49 E
Mecanhelas	**154**	15.12 S	35.54 E
Mecatán	**234**	21.32 N	105.08 W
Mecatlán	**234**	20.13 N	97.41 W
Mecaya ≃	**246**	0.29 N	75.11 W
Mecca → Makkah	**144**	21.27 N	39.49 E
Mečebilovo	**78**	49.04 N	36.41 E
Mečetinskaja	**78**	46.46 N	40.27 E
Mečetka	**78**	50.54 N	40.05 E
Mechanic Falls	**188**	44.06 N	70.23 W
Mechanicsburg, Il., U.S.	**219**	39.48 N	89.24 W
Mechanicsburg, In., U.S.	**218**	40.09 N	86.28 W
Mechanicsburg, Oh., U.S.	**218**	40.04 N	83.33 W
Mechanicsburg, Pa., U.S.	**208**	40.12 N	77.00 W
Mechanicstown, N.Y., U.S.	**210**	41.27 N	74.24 W
Mechanicstown, Oh., U.S.	**214**	40.37 N	80.57 W
Mechanicsville, Ia., U.S.	**190**	41.54 N	91.15 W
Mechanicsville, Md., U.S.	**208**	38.26 N	76.44 W
Mechanicsville, Va., U.S.	**192**	37.36 N	77.22 W
Mechanicville	**210**	42.54 N	73.41 W
Mechara	**144**	8.32 N	40.22 E
Mechelen (Malines)	**50**	51.02 N	4.28 E
Mechel'ta	**84**	42.48 N	46.30 E
Mechernich	**56**	50.35 N	6.38 E
Mechita	**252**	35.04 S	60.24 W
Mechlin → Mechelen	**50**	51.02 N	4.28 E
Mechonskoje	**86**	56.09 N	64.34 E
Mechra Safsaf	**34**	34.52 N	2.36 W
Mechren'ga	**24**	61.46 N	40.57 E
Mechrenga ≃	**24**	63.15 N	41.20 E
Mechriyya	**148**	33.35 N	0.18 W
Mechroha	**36**	36.21 N	7.51 E
Mecidiye, Tür.	**130**	38.53 N	27.42 E
Mecidiye, Tür.	**130**	40.38 N	26.32 E
Mečigmen	**180**	65.28 N	172.05 W
Mečigmeskij zaliv c	**180**	65.25 N	172.00 W
Meçitözü	**130**	40.31 N	35.19 E
Meckelfeld	**52**	53.25 N	10.01 E
Meckenbeuren	**58**	47.42 N	9.34 E
Meckenheim	**56**	50.37 N	7.07 E
Meckering	**162**	31.38 S	117.01 E
Meckesheim	**56**	49.19 N	8.49 E
Meckinghoven	**263**	51.37 N	7.19 E
Mecklenburg, D.D.R.	**54**	53.47 N	11.28 E
Mecklenburg, N.Y., U.S.	**210**	42.27 N	76.43 W
Mecklenburg □[9]	**54**	53.30 N	13.00 E
Mecklenburger Bucht c	**54**	54.20 N	11.40 E
Mecklenburgische Seenplatte ◆[1]	**54**	53.30 N	12.00 E
Meclov	**60**	49.31 N	12.52 E
Meco	**210**	43.03 N	74.23 W
Mecoacán	**234**	18.23 N	93.07 W
Mecoacán, Laguna c	**234**	18.22 N	93.09 W
Meconta	**154**	14.49 S	39.50 E
Mecox Bay c	**207**	40.54 N	72.20 W
Mecque, La → Makkah	**144**	21.27 N	39.49 E
Mecrihan	**130**	37.08 N	39.03 E
Mecsek ⋏	**30**	46.15 N	18.05 E
Mecubúri	**154**	14.39 S	38.54 E
Mecubúri ≃	**154**	14.10 S	40.31 E
Mecúfi	**154**	13.17 S	40.30 E
Mecula	**154**	12.04 S	37.40 E
Meda, It.	**62**	45.40 N	9.09 E
Meda, Port.	**34**	40.58 N	7.16 W
Medak	**122**	18.02 N	78.16 E
Medākul	**126**	23.03 N	90.11 E
Médan, Fr.	**261**	48.57 N	2.00 E
Medan, Indon.	**114**	3.35 N	98.40 E
Medang	**114**	2.06 N	101.38 E
Medang, Pulau I	**115b**	8.09 S	117.23 E
Medang, Tanjung ›	**114**	2.08 N	101.39 E
Médanos	**252**	38.50 S	62.41 W
Medanosa, Punta ›	**254**	48.06 S	65.55 W
Medaryville	**216**	41.04 N	86.53 W
Mede	**62**	45.06 N	8.44 E
Medebach	**56**	51.12 N	8.42 E
Medeiros Neto	**255**	17.20 S	40.14 W
Medel, Val V	**58**	46.37 N	8.50 E
Medellín, Col.	**246**	6.15 N	75.35 W
Medellín, Pil.	**116**	11.08 N	123.58 E
Medelpad □[9]	**26**	62.40 N	16.15 E
Medemblik	**52**	52.46 N	5.06 E
Měděnec	**54**	50.25 N	13.05 E
Medenica	**78**	49.26 N	23.45 E
Médenine	**148**	33.21 N	10.30 E
Médenine □[8]	**148**	32.00 N	10.00 E
Mederdra	**150**	16.55 N	15.39 W
Medesano	**64**	44.45 N	10.08 E
Medevi	**40**	58.40 N	14.57 E
Medfield	**207**	42.11 N	71.18 W
Medford, Ma., U.S.	**207**	42.25 N	71.06 W
Medford, N.J., U.S.	**208**	39.54 N	74.49 W
Medford, N.Y., U.S.	**210**	40.49 N	73.00 W
Medford, Ok., U.S.	**196**	36.48 N	97.44 W
Medford, Or., U.S.	**202**	42.19 N	122.52 W
Medford, Wi., U.S.	**190**	45.08 N	90.20 W
Medford Farms	**285**	39.52 N	74.45 W
Medford Lakes	**285**	39.51 N	74.48 W
Medfra	**180**	63.06 N	154.44 W
Medgidia	**38**	44.15 N	28.16 E
Medgyes → Mediaș	**38**	46.10 N	24.21 E
Medi	**154**	5.04 N	30.44 E
Media	**208**	39.55 N	75.23 W
Mediapolis	**190**	41.00 N	91.09 W
Mediaș	**38**	46.10 N	24.21 E
Medical Lake	**202**	47.34 N	117.40 W
Medicina	**66**	44.28 N	11.38 E
Medicine Bow	**200**	41.53 N	106.12 W
Medicine Bow ≃	**200**	42.00 N	106.40 W
Medicine Bow Mountains ⋏	**200**	41.10 N	106.10 W
Medicine Bow Peak ∧	**200**	41.21 N	106.19 W
Medicine Creek ≃, Mo., U.S.	**194**	39.43 N	93.24 W
Medicine Creek ≃, Ne., U.S.	**198**	40.17 N	100.10 W
Medicine Creek ≃, S.D., U.S.	**198**	44.06 N	99.42 W
Medicine Hat	**184**	50.03 N	110.40 W
Medicine Knoll Creek ≃	**198**	44.19 N	100.05 W
Medicine Lake	**198**	48.30 N	104.30 W
Medicine Lake ⊜	**198**	48.28 N	104.24 W
Medicine Lodge	**198**	37.16 N	98.34 W
Medicine Lodge ≃	**196**	36.49 N	98.20 W
Medicine Rocks State Park ♠	**198**	46.01 N	104.35 W
Medina → Al-Madīnah, Ar. Su.	**128**	24.28 N	39.36 E
Medina, Bra.	**255**	16.15 S	41.29 W
Medina, Pil.	**116**	8.55 N	125.01 E
Medina, N.Y., U.S.	**210**	43.13 N	78.23 W
Medina, N.D., U.S.	**198**	46.53 N	99.17 W
Medina, Oh., U.S.	**214**	41.08 N	81.51 W
Medina, Tx., U.S.	**196**	29.48 N	99.15 W

FRANÇAIS

Nom	Page	Lat.°′	Long.°′ W = Ouest
Medina, Wa., U.S.	**224**	47.37 N	122.13 W
Medina □[6]	**214**	41.08 N	81.52 W
Medina ≃	**196**	29.12 N	98.20 W
Medinaceli	**34**	41.10 N	2.26 W
Medina del Campo	**34**	41.18 N	4.55 W
Medina de Ríoseco	**34**	41.53 N	5.02 W
Médina Gonasse	**150**	13.08 N	13.45 W
Medinah	**278**	41.59 N	88.01 W
Medina Lake ⊜[1]	**196**	29.35 N	98.58 W
Médina Sabak	**150**	13.36 N	15.35 W
Medina-Sidonia	**34**	36.27 N	5.55 W
Medinat al-Faiyum → Al-Fayyūm	**142**	29.19 N	30.50 E
Medininkai	**76**	54.32 N	25.40 E
Medino	**164**	9.40 S	149.40 E
Medio, Arroyo del ≃	**258**	33.49 S	57.43 W
Medio Creek ≃	**196**	28.19 N	97.19 W
Mediterranean Sea ⩱[2]	**10**	35.00 N	20.00 E
Mediterraneo, Mare → Mediterranean Sea ⩱[2]	**10**	35.00 N	20.00 E
Mediterráneo, Mare → Mediterranean Sea ⩱[2]	**10**	35.00 N	20.00 E
Medjana	**34**	36.08 N	4.41 E
Medje	**154**	2.25 N	27.18 E
Medjerda, Monts de la ⋏	**36**	36.35 N	8.15 E
Medkovec	**38**	43.37 N	23.10 E
Mednogorsk	**86**	51.24 N	57.37 E
Mednoje	**76**	56.56 N	35.29 E
Mednyj, ostrov I	**74**	54.45 N	167.35 E
Médoc ◆[1]	**32**	45.20 N	1.00 W
Medolla	**64**	44.51 N	11.04 E
Medora, Il., U.S.	**219**	39.11 N	90.09 W
Medora, In., U.S.	**218**	38.49 N	86.10 W
Medora, N.D., U.S.	**198**	46.54 N	103.31 W
Médouneu	**152**	0.57 N	10.47 E
Medow	**54**	53.50 N	13.32 E
Medstead, Sk., Can.	**184**	53.19 N	108.02 W
Medstead, Eng., U.K.	**42**	51.08 N	1.04 W
Medua	**126**	22.38 N	90.44 E
Meductic	**186**	46.00 N	67.29 W
Medulla	**220**	27.58 N	81.58 W
Međumurje ◆[1]	**61**	46.25 N	16.30 E
Meduna ≃	**64**	45.49 N	12.34 E
Medveđa	**38**	42.50 N	21.35 E
Medvedevo, S.S.S.R.	**76**	60.02 N	43.01 E
Medvedevo, S.S.S.R.	**80**	56.37 N	47.47 E
Medvedevo, S.S.S.R.	**86**	60.37 N	77.21 E
Medvedevskoje	**76**	58.58 N	35.58 E
Medvedica ≃, S.S.S.R.	**76**	57.05 N	37.32 E
Medvedica ≃, S.S.S.R.	**80**	49.35 N	42.41 E
Medvedickij	**80**	50.47 N	44.43 E
Medvědí hora ∧	**60**	48.59 N	13.25 E
Medvedkovo ◆[8]	**265b**	55.53 N	37.38 E
Medvedok	**80**	57.23 N	50.05 E
Medvedovskaja	**78**	45.27 N	39.01 E
Medvenka, S.S.S.R.	**78**	51.26 N	36.07 E
Medvenka, S.S.S.R.	**82**	54.15 N	37.42 E
Medvežij, ostrov I	**89**	54.41 N	136.18 E
Medvežinka	**83**	48.10 N	39.31 E
Medvežje, ozero ⊜	**86**	55.07 N	68.00 E
Medvežjegorsk	**24**	62.55 N	34.23 E
Medvežji ostrova II	**74**	70.52 N	161.26 E
Medvežji ozera ⊜	**265b**	55.52 N	38.00 E
Medvežji Oz'ora	**265b**	55.52 N	37.59 E
Medvežskaja	**24**	64.57 N	57.34 E
Medviagalis ∧[2]	**76**	55.38 N	22.45 E
Medvin	**78**	49.23 N	30.47 E
Medv'onka ≃	**265b**	55.44 N	37.12 E
Medway, Ma., U.S.	**207**	42.08 N	71.23 W
Medway, Oh., U.S.	**218**	39.53 N	83.59 W
Medway □[8]	**260**	51.24 N	0.31 E
Medway ≃, N.S., Can.	**186**	44.08 N	64.36 W
Medway ≃, Eng., U.K.	**42**	51.27 N	0.44 E
Medyn'	**82**	54.58 N	35.52 E
Medynka ≃	**82**	54.44 N	36.02 E
Medynskij Zavorot, mys ›	**24**	68.58 N	59.17 E
Medžibož	**78**	49.26 N	27.25 E
Medzilaborce	**30**	49.16 N	21.55 E
Meeberrie	**162**	26.58 S	115.58 E
Meekatharra	**162**	26.36 S	118.29 E
Meeker, Co., U.S.	**200**	40.02 N	107.54 W
Meeker, Oh., U.S.	**214**	40.39 N	83.18 W
Meeks Bay	**226**	39.02 N	120.08 W
Meelpaeg Lake ⊜[1]	**186**	48.16 N	56.35 W
Meenaar	**168a**	31.38 S	116.53 E
Meentheena	**162**	21.17 S	120.28 E
Meer	**52**	51.27 N	4.44 E
Meeralpen → Maritime Alps ⋏	**62**	44.15 N	7.10 E
Meerane	**54**	50.51 N	12.28 E
Meerbeck	**263**	51.28 N	6.39 E
Meerbeke	**50**	50.50 N	4.02 E
Meerbusch	**56**	51.15 N	6.41 E
Meerhout	**56**	51.08 N	5.05 E
Meerhusener Moor ◆[3]	**52**	53.35 N	7.30 E
Meerkerk	**52**	51.45 N	5.00 E
Meerle	**52**	51.28 N	4.48 E
Meersburg	**58**	47.41 N	9.16 E
Meerssen	**56**	50.53 N	5.45 E
Meerut	**124**	28.59 N	77.42 E
Meerut □[5]	**124**	29.00 N	77.35 E
Meese ≃	**42**	52.40 N	2.39 W
Meeteetse	**202**	44.09 N	108.52 W
Mega, Indon.	**164**	0.41 S	131.53 E
Mega, Ityo.	**144**	4.07 N	38.16 E
Mega, Pulau I	**112**	4.00 S	101.02 E
Megalo	**144**	6.55 N	41.48 E
Megálon Khoríon	**38**	36.27 N	27.21 E
Megalópolis	**38**	37.24 N	22.08 E
Meganom, mys ›	**78**	44.48 N	35.05 E
Mégantic □[6]	**206**	46.10 N	71.30 W
Mégantic, Lac ⊜	**188**	45.32 N	70.53 W
Mégantic, Mont ∧	**206**	45.28 N	71.09 W
Mégara	**38**	38.01 N	23.21 E
Megargel	**196**	33.27 N	98.56 W
Mégaron, Kólpos c	**267c**	37.56 N	23.20 E
Megaruma ≃	**154**	13.28 S	40.32 E
Megasini ∧	**120**	21.38 N	86.21 E
Meget	**88**	52.24 N	104.03 E
Megève	**62**	45.52 N	6.37 E
Mégevette	**58**	46.12 N	6.30 E
Megezez ∧	**144**	9.17 N	39.32 E
Megget Reservoir ⊜[1]	**46**	55.29 N	3.17 W
Meghalaya □[3]	**120**	25.30 N	91.15 E
Meghna ≃	**120**	22.50 N	90.50 E
Megi-jima I	**96**	34.24 N	134.03 E
Mégiscane ≃	**190**	48.29 N	77.08 W
Mégiscane, Lac ⊜	**190**	48.35 N	75.55 W
Meglino, ozero ⊜	**76**	58.25 N	35.07 E
Megra, S.S.S.R.	**24**	66.09 N	41.37 E
Megra, S.S.S.R.	**76**	60.10 N	37.13 E
Megri	**84**	38.56 N	46.16 E
Meguro ◆[8]	**268**	35.38 N	139.42 E
Meguro ≃	**268**	35.37 N	139.45 E
Mehadia	**38**	44.55 N	22.22 E
Méhaigne ≃	**56**	50.32 N	5.13 E
Mehaïguene, Oued V	**148**	32.15 N	2.59 E
Mehakit	**112**	2.51 S	115.57 E
Mehar	**120**	27.11 N	67.49 E
Meharry, Mount ∧	**162**	22.59 S	118.35 E
Mehdia	**148**	35.26 N	1.40 E
Mehede	**40**	60.27 N	17.24 E
Mehedinți □[6]	**38**	44.30 N	22.50 E
Meheisa	**140**	19.37 N	32.57 E
Mehekar	**122**	20.09 N	76.34 E
Mehendiganj	**126**	22.49 N	90.32 E
Meherpur	**124**	23.46 N	88.38 E
Meherrin ≃	**192**	36.26 N	76.57 W

PORTUGUÊS

Nome	Página	Lat.°′	Long.°′ W = Oeste
Mehetia I	**14**	17.52 S	148.03 W
Mehidpur	**120**	23.49 N	75.40 E
Mehikoorma	**76**	58.14 N	27.28 E
Mehlsack → Pieniężno	**30**	54.15 N	20.08 E
Mehlteuer	**54**	50.32 N	12.02 E
Mehlville	**219**	38.30 N	90.19 W
Mehmetkân	**130**	38.26 N	41.17 E
Mehnagar	**124**	25.53 N	83.07 E
Mehndāwal	**124**	26.59 N	83.07 E
Mehoopany	**210**	41.34 N	76.04 W
Mehoopany Creek ≃	**210**	41.34 N	76.03 W
Mehpālpur ◆[8]	**272a**	28.33 N	77.08 E
Mehr	**52**	51.43 N	6.29 E
Mehrābād, Īrān	**128**	36.53 N	47.55 E
Mehrābād, Īrān	**267d**	35.40 N	51.20 E
Mehrābād Airport ⊠	**267d**	35.41 N	51.19 E
Mehram Nagar ◆[8]	**272a**	28.34 N	77.07 E
Mehrān	**128**	33.07 N	46.10 E
Mehring	**56**	49.48 N	6.49 E
Mehrīz	**128**	31.35 N	54.28 E
Mehrow	**264a**	52.34 N	13.37 E
Mehrum	**263**	51.35 N	6.37 E
Mehsāna	**120**	23.36 N	72.24 E
Mè-hsa-tè	**110**	19.33 N	97.38 E
Mehtar Lām	**120**	34.39 N	70.10 E
Mehun-sur-Yèvre	**50**	47.09 N	2.13 E
Mei ≃, Zhg.	**100**	24.24 N	116.34 E
Mei ≃, Zhg.	**100**	26.00 N	115.23 E
Mei ≃, Zhg.	**105**	39.21 N	117.50 E
Meia Meia	**154**	5.49 S	35.48 E
Meia Ponte ≃	**255**	18.32 S	49.36 W
Meichang	**105**	39.22 N	117.10 E
Meichuan	**100**	30.10 N	115.36 E
Meicun, Zhg.	**100**	25.30 N	116.56 E
Meicun, Zhg.	**106**	30.22 N	119.01 E
Meicun, Zhg.	**106**	30.40 N	119.04 E
Meicun, Zhg.	**106**	31.33 N	120.24 E
Meide	**263**	51.11 N	6.55 E
Meiderich ◆[8]	**263**	51.28 N	6.46 E
Meidling ◆[8]	**264b**	48.11 N	16.20 E
Méier ◆[8]	**287a**	22.54 S	43.16 W
Meierij ◆[1]	**52**	51.35 N	5.40 E
Meierkaisong	**120**	30.54 N	84.31 E
Meiersberg	**263**	51.17 N	6.57 E
Meig ≃	**46**	57.34 N	4.41 W
Meiganga	**152**	6.31 N	14.11 E
Meigle	**46**	56.35 N	3.09 W
Meigs	**192**	31.04 N	84.05 W
Meigs Field ⊠	**278**	41.51 N	87.36 W
Meihsien → Meixian	**100**	24.21 N	116.08 E
Meihua	**100**	26.02 N	119.40 E
Meihuajie	**100**	25.14 N	113.05 E
Meijel	**52**	51.21 N	5.53 E
Meijino-Mori-Minō-kokutei-kōen ♠	**94**	34.51 N	135.29 E
Meiji Shrine ⊍[1]	**268**	35.41 N	139.42 E
Meikeng	**100**	23.59 N	114.05 E
Meikle Millyea ∧	**44**	55.07 N	4.19 W
Meikle Says Law ∧	**46**	55.55 N	2.40 W
Meiktila	**110**	20.52 N	95.52 E
Meila	**54**	51.09 N	13.13 E
Meilen	**58**	47.16 N	8.38 E
Meili	**106**	31.42 N	120.53 E
Meilie	**100**	26.18 N	117.38 E
Meilin, Zhg.	**100**	23.18 N	115.58 E
Meilin, Zhg.	**106**	30.35 N	119.04 E
Meillerie	**58**	46.24 N	6.43 E
Meilong	**100**	22.56 N	115.17 E
Meilunyingzi	**104**	42.18 N	122.10 E
Meina	**62**	45.47 N	8.32 E
Meine	**52**	52.23 N	10.32 E
Meiners Oaks	**228**	34.26 N	119.17 W
Meinerzhagen	**56**	51.06 N	7.38 E
Meiningen	**54**	50.34 N	10.25 E
Meinung	**100**	22.54 N	120.32 E
Meio, Ilha do I	**287a**	23.02 S	43.17 W
Meio, Rio do ≃	**255**	17.47 S	39.47 W
Meiringen	**58**	46.43 N	8.12 E
Meisburg	**56**	50.06 N	6.41 E
Meisenheim	**56**	49.42 N	7.40 E
Meishan, Zhg.	**106**	31.06 N	119.43 E
Meishan, Zhg.	**107**	30.02 N	103.49 E
Meissen	**54**	51.10 N	13.28 E
Meissendorf	**52**	52.43 N	9.50 E
Meiss Lake ⊜	**204**	41.52 N	122.04 W
Meissner ∧	**56**	51.12 N	9.50 E
Meitan	**102**	27.46 N	107.35 E
Meitian	**100**	25.21 N	112.47 E
Meitingen	**56**	48.32 N	10.50 E
Meiwa	**94**	34.33 N	136.39 E
Meixi	**106**	30.48 N	119.45 E
Meixian, Zhg.	**100**	24.21 N	116.08 E
Meixian, Zhg.	**100**	28.52 N	113.38 E
Meiyao	**89**	49.37 N	124.30 E
Meiyino	**140**	6.12 N	34.40 E
Meizhai	**102**	25.30 N	108.50 E
Meizhou	**100**	23.50 N	117.20 E
Meizhou Dao I	**100**	25.06 N	119.07 E
Meizhou Wan c	**100**	25.06 N	119.00 E
Meizhu	**106**	31.16 N	119.13 E
Meječkyn, ostrov I	**180**	65.26 N	178.00 W
Mejerda, Oued (Oued Medjerda) ≃	**36**	37.07 N	10.13 E
Mejez el Bab	**148**	36.39 N	9.37 E
Mejia	**126**	23.34 N	87.06 E
Mejicanos	**236**	13.43 N	89.12 W
Mejillones	**252**	23.06 S	70.27 W
Mejillones, Península ›[1]	**252**	23.17 S	70.34 W
Mejillones del Sur, Bahía de c	**252**	23.03 S	70.27 W
Mejnypil'gyno	**74**	62.32 N	177.02 E
Mejorada del Campo	**266a**	40.24 N	3.29 W
Meka	**162**	27.26 S	116.48 E
Mekada, Garaet el ≡	**36**	36.48 N	8.00 E
Mékambo	**152**	1.01 N	13.56 E
Mekele	**144**	13.33 N	39.30 E
Mekerra, Oued ≃	**34**	35.00 N	0.45 W
Mekhé	**150**	15.07 N	16.38 W
Mekhliganj	**124**	26.21 N	88.55 E
Mekhtar	**120**	30.28 N	69.22 E
Mékinac ≃	**206**	46.51 N	72.46 W
Mekka → Makkah	**144**	21.27 N	39.49 E
Meknès	**148**	33.53 N	5.37 W
Meknès □[4]	**148**	33.50 N	5.30 W
Mekong ≃	**12**	10.33 N	105.24 E
Mekongga, Gunung ∧	**112**	3.38 S	121.15 E
Mekongga, Pegunungan ⋏	**112**	3.35 S	121.15 E
Mékôngk → Mekong ≃	**12**	10.33 N	105.24 E
Mekoryuk	**180**	60.23 N	166.12 W
Mékrou ≃	**150**	12.24 N	2.49 E
Mel	**64**	46.04 N	12.05 E
Melado ≃	**252**	35.43 S	71.05 W
Melah, Oued el V, Alg.	**148**	28.21 N	6.00 E
Melah, Oued el V, Tun.	**148**	34.03 N	8.06 E
Melah, Sebkhet el ⊜	**148**	29.05 N	1.10 W
Melaka	**114**	2.12 N	102.15 E
Melaka □[3]	**114**	2.15 N	102.15 E
Melalap	**112**	5.14 N	116.00 E
Melandro ≃	**68**	40.37 N	15.27 E
Melanesia II	**14**	13.00 S	164.00 E
Melanesian Basin ✦[1]	**14**	0.05 N	160.35 E
Melappālaiyam	**122**	8.42 N	77.43 E
Melara	**64**	45.03 N	11.11 E
Melaune	**54**	51.11 N	14.44 E
Melawi ≃	**112**	0.05 N	111.29 E
Melayu ≃	**271c**	1.27 N	103.42 E
Melbern	**216**	41.28 N	84.39 W
Melbost	**46**	58.15 N	6.22 W
Melbourn	**42**	52.05 N	0.01 E
Melbourne, Austl.	**169**	37.49 S	144.58 E
Melbourne, Austl.	**274b**	37.49 S	144.58 E
Melbourne, On., Can.	**214**	42.49 N	81.33 W

Melbourne, Eng., U.K.	**42**	52.49 N	1.25 W
Melbourne, Ar., U.S.	**194**	36.03 N	91.54 W
Melbourne, Fl., U.S.	**220**	28.04 N	80.36 W
Melbourne, Ia., U.S.	**190**	41.56 N	93.06 W
Melbourne, University of ⊍[2]	**274b**	37.48 S	144.58 E
Melbourne Beach	**220**	28.04 N	80.33 W
Melbourne Island I	**176**	68.30 N	104.45 W
Melbourne Regional Airport ⊠	**220**	28.06 N	80.38 W
Melby House	**46**	60.18 N	1.39 W
Mel'cany	**80**	54.28 N	44.43 E
Melcher	**190**	41.13 N	93.14 W
Melchor, Isla I	**254**	45.08 S	73.57 W
Melchor Ocampo	**196**	26.03 N	99.33 W
Melchor Romero ◆[8]	**258**	34.56 S	58.03 W
Melchtal	**58**	46.50 N	8.17 E
Melcroft	**214**	40.03 N	79.24 W
Melderskin ∧	**26**	60.01 N	6.05 E
Meldola	**66**	44.07 N	12.05 E
Meldorf	**30**	54.05 N	9.05 E
Meldrum Bay	**190**	45.56 N	83.07 W
Meldrum Creek	**182**	52.07 N	122.20 W
Mélé, Centraf.	**146**	9.46 N	21.33 E
Mele, India	**272b**	22.49 N	88.09 E
Mele, It.	**62**	44.27 N	8.45 E
Mélé, Baie c	**175f**	17.43 S	168.15 E
Mele, Capo ›	**62**	43.57 N	8.10 E
Melechovo	**80**	56.17 N	41.17 E
Meleck	**86**	57.25 N	90.12 E
Meleden	**144**	10.25 N	49.51 E
Melefan	**130**	38.11 N	41.34 E
Melegnano	**62**	45.21 N	9.19 E
Meleješt'	**78**	46.59 N	29.33 E
Melekeok	**175b**	7.29 N	134.38 E
Melekess → Dimitrovgrad	**80**	54.14 N	49.39 E
Melela ≃	**154**	17.04 S	38.36 E
Melena del Sur	**240p**	22.47 N	82.09 W
Melendiz Dağı ∧	**130**	38.07 N	34.25 E
Melendugno	**68**	40.16 N	18.20 E
Melenki	**80**	55.20 N	41.38 E
Meleškoviči	**78**	51.56 N	28.59 E
Meleuz	**86**	52.58 N	55.55 E
Mélèzes, Rivière aux ≃	**176**	57.40 N	69.29 W
Melfa	**208**	37.39 N	75.45 W
Melfa ≃	**66**	41.30 N	13.35 E
Melfi, It.	**68**	41.00 N	15.39 E
Melfi, Tchad	**146**	11.04 N	17.56 E
Melfort, Sk., Can.	**184**	52.52 N	104.36 W
Melfort, Zimb.	**154**	17.59 S	31.19 E
Melfort, Loch c	**46**	56.15 N	5.31 W
Melgaço, Bra.	**250**	1.47 S	50.44 W
Melgaço, Port.	**34**	42.07 N	8.16 W
Melgar	**246**	4.12 N	74.39 W
Melghir, Chott ⊜	**148**	34.20 N	6.20 E
Mel'guny	**80**	52.09 N	40.52 E
Melhus	**26**	63.17 N	10.16 E
Meli ≃	**150**	8.16 N	10.42 W
Meliane, Oued ≃	**36**	36.46 N	10.18 E
Meliau	**112**	0.08 S	110.18 E
Meliau, Gunong ∧	**116**	5.50 N	117.14 E
Melibocus ∧	**56**	49.42 N	8.40 E
Melichovo, S.S.S.R.	**78**	50.42 N	36.48 E
Melichovo, S.S.S.R.	**82**	55.07 N	37.39 E
Melicuccà	**68**	38.18 N	15.53 E
Melide	**58**	45.57 N	8.57 E
Meligalás	**38**	37.13 N	21.59 E
Melilla	**34**	35.19 N	2.58 W
Melilli	**70**	37.11 N	15.07 E
Melimoyu, Cerro ∧	**254**	44.05 S	72.52 W
Melincué	**252**	33.39 S	61.27 W
Melipilla	**252**	33.42 S	71.13 W
Mélisey	**58**	47.45 N	6.35 E
Melissa	**68**	39.18 N	17.01 E
Melissano	**68**	39.58 N	18.07 E
Melíssia	**267c**	38.03 N	23.50 E
Melita	**184**	49.16 N	101.00 W
Melito di Porto Salvo	**68**	37.55 N	15.47 E
Melitopol'	**78**	46.50 N	35.22 E
Melívoia	**38**	39.45 N	22.48 E
Melk	**61**	48.14 N	15.20 E
Melk ≃	**61**	48.14 N	15.19 E
Melk ⊍[1]	**61**	48.14 N	15.20 E
Melka Teka	**144**	6.05 N	43.08 E
Melkbosstrand	**158**	33.43 S	18.27 E
Melksham	**42**	51.23 N	2.09 W
Mella ≃	**64**	45.13 N	10.13 E
Mellansel	**26**	63.26 N	18.19 E
Mellau	**58**	47.21 N	9.53 E
Melle, B.R.D.	**52**	52.12 N	8.20 E
Melle, Fr.	**32**	46.13 N	0.09 W
Melleck	**64**	47.40 N	12.45 E
Mellègue, Oued ≃	**36**	36.32 N	8.51 E
Mellen	**190**	46.19 N	90.39 W
Mellendorf	**52**	52.33 N	9.43 E
Mellenville	**210**	42.15 N	73.40 W
Mellerud	**26**	58.42 N	12.28 E
Mellette	**198**	45.09 N	98.29 W
Mellid	**34**	42.55 N	8.00 W
Mellier ≃	**56**	49.43 N	5.32 E
Melling	**262**	53.30 N	2.56 W
Mellingen	**54**	50.56 N	11.23 E
Mellish Reef I[1]	**160**	17.25 S	155.50 E
Mellish Rise ✦[3]	**14**	17.00 S	156.00 E
Mellit	**140**	14.08 N	25.33 E
Mellone, Monte ∧	**267a**	41.50 N	12.43 E
Mellong Range ⋏	**170**	33.06 S	150.43 E
Mellon Udrigle	**46**	57.55 N	5.39 W
Mellor	**262**	53.46 N	2.32 W
Mellor Brook	**262**	53.47 N	2.33 W
Mellor Glacier ⊓	**9**	73.30 S	66.30 E
Mellösa	**40**	59.06 N	16.33 E
Mellrichstadt	**56**	50.26 N	10.18 E
Mellum I	**52**	53.40 N	8.10 E
Melmerby	**44**	54.44 N	2.35 W
Melmore	**214**	41.02 N	83.07 W
Melmoth	**158**	28.38 S	31.24 E
Mel'nica-Podol'skaja	**78**	48.37 N	26.10 E
Mělník	**54**	50.20 N	14.29 E
Mel'nikovo, S.S.S.R.	**26**	61.05 N	29.22 E
Mel'nikovo, S.S.S.R.	**85**	40.19 N	70.19 E
Mel'nikovo, S.S.S.R.	**86**	56.34 N	84.05 E
Melo	**252**	32.22 S	54.11 W
Melo ≃	**248**	21.27 S	57.52 W
Melo, Ilha de I	**150**	11.02 N	15.13 W
Melocheville	**206**	45.19 N	73.56 W
Meloco	**154**	13.25 S	39.08 E
Melolo	**115b**	9.53 S	120.40 E
Melolo ≃	**115b**	9.52 S	120.41 E
Melong	**152**	5.07 N	9.57 E
Melos → Mílos I	**38**	36.41 N	24.15 E
Melovaja ≃	**83**	49.23 N	40.16 E
Melovatka	**83**	49.21 N	38.11 E
Melovoje	**83**	49.22 N	40.06 E
Melovoj Syrt ∧	**80**	52.15 N	52.35 E
Melozitna ≃	**180**	64.46 N	155.29 W
Melrose, Austl.	**162**	27.56 S	121.19 E
Melrose, Austl.	**166**	32.42 S	146.58 E
Melrose, Scot., U.K.	**46**	55.36 N	2.44 W
Melrose, Ma., U.S.	**207**	42.27 N	71.04 W
Melrose, Mn., U.S.	**198**	45.40 N	94.48 W
Melrose, N.M., U.S.	**196**	34.25 N	103.37 W
Melrose, N.Y., U.S.	**210**	42.50 N	73.37 W
Melrose, Oh., U.S.	**216**	41.05 N	84.25 W
Melrose, Wi., U.S.	**190**	44.07 N	90.59 W
Melrose ◆[8]	**276**	40.49 N	73.55 W
Melrose Abbey ⊍[1]	**46**	55.37 N	2.45 W
Melrose Park, Fl., U.S.	**220**	26.06 N	80.12 W
Melrose Park, Il., U.S.	**216**	41.54 N	87.51 W
Melrose Park, N.Y., U.S.	**212**	42.54 N	76.32 W
Melrose Park, Pa., U.S.	**285**	40.04 N	75.08 W
Mels	**58**	47.03 N	9.25 E
Melstone	**202**	46.35 N	107.52 W
Melsungen	**56**	51.08 N	9.32 E
Meltaus	**24**	66.54 N	25.22 E
Meltham, Eng., U.K.	**44**	53.35 N	1.51 W

Meltham, Eng., U.K.	**262**	53.36 N	1.51 W
Melton, Austl.	**168b**	34.05 S	137.59 E
Melton, Austl.	**169**	37.41 S	144.35 E
Melton Constable	**42**	52.53 N	1.01 E
Melton Hill Lake ⊜[1]	**192**	36.00 N	84.15 W
Melton Mowbray	**42**	52.46 N	0.53 W
Melton Reservoir ⊜[1]	**169**	37.43 S	144.32 E
Melúa	**246**	3.55 N	72.50 W
Meluan	**112**	1.52 N	111.56 E
Meluco	**154**	12.36 S	39.38 E
Melúli ≃	**154**	16.28 S	39.44 E
Melun, Fr.	**50**	48.32 N	2.40 E
Melun, Mya.	**110**	20.14 N	93.24 E
Melunga	**152**	17.16 S	16.24 E
Melun-Villaroche, Aérodrome de ⊠	**261**	48.37 N	2.40 E
Melūr	**122**	10.03 N	78.20 E
Melvaig	**46**	57.48 N	5.49 W
Melvern	**198**	38.30 N	95.38 W
Melvern Lake ⊜[1]	**198**	38.30 N	95.50 W
Melvich	**46**	58.33 N	3.55 W
Melville, Austl.	**168a**	32.03 S	115.49 E
Melville, Sk., Can.	**184**	50.55 N	102.48 W
Melville, La., U.S.	**194**	30.41 N	91.44 W
Melville, N.Y., U.S.	**276**	40.47 N	73.24 W
Melville ◆[8]	**273d**	26.11 S	28.00 E
Melville, Cape ›, Austl.	**164**	14.11 S	144.30 E
Melville, Cape ›, Pil.	**116**	7.49 N	117.01 E
Melville, Détroit de → Viscount Melville Sound Ц	**176**	74.10 N	108.00 W
Melville, Lake ⊜	**176**	53.45 N	59.30 W
Melville Bugt c	**16**	75.30 N	63.00 W
Melville Hall Airport ⊠	**240d**	15.33 N	61.18 W
Melville Hills ⋏[2]	**180**	69.15 N	124.00 W
Melville Island I, Austl.	**164**	11.40 S	131.00 E
Melville Island I, N.T., Can.	**16**	75.15 N	110.00 W
Melville Peninsula ›[1]	**176**	68.00 N	84.00 W
Melville Sound Ц, N.T., Can.	**176**	68.05 N	107.30 W
Melville Sound Ц, On., Can.	**212**	44.57 N	81.05 W
Melvin, Il., U.S.	**216**	40.34 N	88.15 W
Melvin, Ky., U.S.	**192**	37.21 N	82.41 W
Melvin, Tx., U.S.	**196**	31.13 N	99.35 W
Melvin, Lough ⊜	**48**	54.26 N	8.10 W
Melvindale	**214**	42.16 N	83.10 W
Melvin Lake ⊜	**184**	57.08 N	100.15 W
Melyana	**148**	36.15 N	2.15 E
Mélykút	**30**	46.13 N	19.24 E
Melzo	**62**	45.30 N	9.25 E
Memala	**112**	1.44 S	112.36 E
Memāri	**126**	23.12 N	88.07 E
Memba	**154**	14.11 S	40.30 E
Membalong	**112**	3.09 S	107.38 E
Memboro	**115b**	9.22 S	119.32 E
Membre	**56**	49.52 N	4.54 E
Même ≃	**50**	48.11 N	0.39 E
Memel → Klaipėda, S.S.S.R.	**76**	55.43 N	21.07 E
Memel, S. Afr.	**158**	27.43 S	29.30 E
Memel → Nemunas ≃	**76**	55.18 N	21.23 E
Mēmele ≃	**76**	56.24 N	24.10 E
Memewin, Lac ⊜	**190**	46.29 N	78.42 W
Memmert I	**52**	53.39 N	6.53 E
Memmingen	**58**	47.59 N	10.11 E
Memo ≃	**246**	9.16 N	66.40 W
Memori, Tanjung ›	**164**	0.52 S	134.08 E
Memorial Bridge ◆[5]	**269a**	13.44 N	100.30 E
Memorial Stadium ♠	**284b**	39.20 N	76.36 W
Mémót	**110**	11.49 N	106.11 E
Mempawah	**112**	0.22 N	108.58 E
Memphis, Fl., U.S.	**220**	27.32 N	82.33 W
Memphis, In., U.S.	**218**	38.29 N	85.45 W
Memphis, Mi., U.S.	**214**	42.54 N	82.46 W
Memphis, Mo., U.S.	**194**	40.27 N	92.10 W
Memphis, Tn., U.S.	**194**	35.08 N	90.02 W
Memphis, Tx., U.S.	**196**	34.43 N	100.32 W
Memphis → Mīt Ruhaynah ⊥	**142**	29.51 N	31.15 E
Memphis Naval Air Station ■	**194**	35.21 N	89.52 W
Memphremagog, Lake ⊜	**206**	45.05 N	72.15 W
Memsie	**46**	57.39 N	2.02 W
Mena, Ityo.	**144**	6.25 N	39.51 E
Mena, S.S.S.R.	**78**	51.31 N	32.13 E
Mena, Ar., U.S.	**194**	34.35 N	94.14 W
Menado → Manado	**112**	1.29 N	124.51 E
Menaggio	**58**	46.01 N	9.14 E
Menahga	**198**	46.45 N	95.06 W
Menai	**274a**	34.01 S	151.01 E
Menai Bridge	**44**	53.14 N	4.10 W
Menai Strait Ц	**44**	53.12 N	4.12 W
Ménaka	**150**	15.55 N	2.24 E
Menaldum	**52**	53.12 N	5.39 E
Mènam Khong → Mekong ≃	**12**	10.33 N	105.24 E
Menan	**202**	43.43 N	111.59 W
Menands	**210**	42.41 N	73.43 W
Menangina	**162**	29.50 S	121.54 E
Menantico Creek ≃	**208**	39.20 N	75.00 W
Menarandra ≃	**157b**	25.17 S	44.30 E
Menard	**196**	30.55 N	99.47 W
Menard □[6]	**219**	40.01 N	89.51 W
Menard Creek ≃	**222**	30.29 N	94.50 W
Menars	**50**	47.38 N	1.24 E
Menasha	**190**	44.12 N	88.26 W
Menate	**112**	0.14 S	113.02 E
Menawashei	**140**	12.40 N	24.59 E
Menchang	**105**	38.54 N	117.01 E
Menčikury	**78**	47.04 N	34.48 E
Mencué	**254**	40.25 S	69.38 W
Mend	**89**	43.40 N	123.08 E
Mendanau, Pulau I	**112**	2.51 S	107.26 E
Mendarik, Pulau I	**112**	1.18 N	107.02 E
Mendatai	**102**	38.51 N	94.39 E
Mendatica	**62**	44.05 N	7.49 E
Mendawai	**112**	2.59 S	113.16 E
Mendawai ≃	**112**	3.17 S	113.21 E
Mendaya	**115a**	8.23 S	114.42 E
Mende	**32**	44.30 N	3.30 E
Mendebo ⋏	**144**	6.50 N	39.40 E
Mendel' ≃	**86**	58.13 N	90.08 E
Mendelejevsk	**80**	55.54 N	52.20 E
Menden	**56**	51.26 N	7.47 E
Menden ◆[8]	**263**	51.24 N	6.54 E
Mendenhall, Ms., U.S.	**194**	31.57 N	89.52 W
Mendenhall, Pa., U.S.	**285**	39.51 N	75.38 W
Mendenhall, Cape ›	**180**	59.51 N	166.15 W
Mendes	**256**	22.32 S	43.44 W
Méndez	**246**	2.43 S	78.19 W
Mendez-Nuñez	**116**	14.08 N	120.54 E
Mendham	**210**	40.46 N	74.36 W
Mendi, Ityo.	**144**	9.50 N	35.06 E
Mendi, Pap. N. Gui.	**164**	6.10 S	143.40 E
Mendig	**56**	50.21 N	7.15 E
Mendip Hills ⋏[2]	**42**	51.15 N	2.40 W
Mendlesham	**42**	52.16 N	1.05 E
Mendocino	**204**	39.18 N	123.47 W
Mendocino, Cape ›	**204**	40.25 N	124.25 W
Mendocino Fracture Zone ✦	**16**	40.00 N	145.00 W
Mendola ≃	**70**	37.44 N	13.32 E
Mendon, Il., U.S.	**219**	40.05 N	91.17 W
Mendon, Ma., U.S.	**207**	42.06 N	71.33 W
Mendon, Mi., U.S.	**216**	42.00 N	85.27 W
Mendon, N.Y., U.S.	**210**	43.00 N	77.34 W
Mendon, Oh., U.S.	**216**	40.40 N	84.31 W
Mendon, Pa., U.S.	**279b**	40.11 N	79.41 W
Mendota, Ca., U.S.	**226**	36.45 N	120.22 W
Mendota, Il., U.S.	**216**	41.32 N	89.07 W
Mendota, Lake ⊜	**216**	43.05 N	89.25 W
Mendoza, Arg.	**252**	32.53 S	68.49 W
Mendoza, Perú	**248**	6.20 S	77.24 W

Mendoza, Perú	**286d**	12.06 S	76.59 W
Mendoza, Ur.	**258**	34.17 S	56.13 W
Mendoza □[4]	**252**	34.30 S	68.30 W
Mendoza ≃	**252**	32.21 S	68.18 W
Mendoza, Arroyo de ≃	**258**	34.21 S	56.18 W
Mendrisio	**58**	45.52 N	8.59 E
Mend'ukino	**82**	54.47 N	38.51 E
Mendung	**112**	0.31 N	103.13 E
Ménéac	**32**	48.09 N	2.28 W
Mene de Mauroa	**246**	10.43 N	71.01 W
Mene Grande	**246**	9.49 N	70.56 W
Menemen	**130**	38.36 N	27.04 E
Menen	**50**	50.48 N	3.07 E
Meneng Point ›	**174b**	0.32 S	166.57 E
Menes	**115a**	6.23 S	105.55 E
Menfi	**70**	37.36 N	12.58 E
Mengalum, Pulau I	**112**	6.16 N	115.12 E
Mengban	**102**	23.08 N	100.19 E
Mengbang	**102**	21.28 N	101.19 E
Mengcheng	**100**	33.17 N	116.33 E
Mengchi ≃	**107**	29.47 N	104.56 E
Mengcun	**98**	38.06 N	117.05 E
Mengdapu	**104**	41.35 N	123.12 E
Mengede ◆[8]	**263**	51.34 N	7.23 E
Mengeh Jek	**120**	37.02 N	66.07 E
Mengen, B.R.D.	**58**	48.03 N	9.20 E
Mengen, Tür.	**130**	40.59 N	31.37 E
Mengeringhausen	**56**	51.22 N	8.59 E
Mengersgereuth-Hämmern	**54**	50.24 N	11.07 E
Menges Mills	**208**	39.52 N	76.54 W
Menggala	**112**	4.28 S	105.17 E
Menggu	**102**	26.34 N	102.57 E
Menggubao	**104**	42.27 N	122.23 E
Menggudai	**102**	38.10 N	108.15 E
Menghai	**102**	22.00 N	100.26 E
Menghe	**106**	32.03 N	119.47 E
Menghun	**102**	21.44 N	100.23 E
Mengjiacun	**106**	31.33 N	118.46 E
Mengjiagang	**89**	46.22 N	130.40 E
Mengjiatai	**104**	42.06 N	123.21 E
Mengjiawan	**102**	38.35 N	109.25 E
Mengjiawopeng	**104**	41.22 N	121.51 E
Mengjiayuanjia	**105**	40.52 N	118.08 E
Mengjiazhai	**269b**	31.18 N	121.19 E
Mengka	**102**	25.10 N	98.01 E
Mengkibol	**114**	1.58 N	103.20 E
Mengkuang	**114**	3.11 N	102.24 E
Menglian	**102**	22.20 N	99.38 E
Menglinghausen ◆[8]	**263**	51.28 N	7.25 E
Mengluchang	**107**	29.19 N	103.35 E
Mengmucun	**106**	31.59 N	119.01 E
Mengong	**152**	2.56 N	11.25 E
Mengqigou	**104**	42.00 N	121.08 E
Mengshan	**102**	24.07 N	110.33 E
Meng Shan ⋏, Zhg.	**98**	35.44 N	117.45 E
Meng Shan ⋏, Zhg.	**104**	41.50 N	121.10 E
Mengtong	**107**	30.44 N	105.53 E
Mengulek, gora ∧	**86**	50.58 N	89.30 E
Mengwang	**102**	22.26 N	100.34 E
Mengyin	**98**	35.45 N	117.57 E
Mengzhe	**102**	22.02 N	100.16 E
Mengzhi	**102**	24.10 N	99.46 E
Mengzi	**102**	23.22 N	103.20 E
Menihek Lakes ⊜	**176**	54.00 N	66.35 W
Ménil-la-Tour	**56**	48.46 N	5.52 E
Menindee	**166**	32.24 S	142.26 E
Menindee Lake ⊜	**166**	32.21 S	142.20 E
Meningie	**166**	35.42 S	139.20 E
Menjiaqiangzi	**104**	42.29 N	121.19 E
Menkoutang	**106**	31.01 N	119.27 E
Menlo	**224**	46.37 N	123.38 W
Menlo Park	**226**	37.27 N	122.10 W
Menlo Park Mall ◆[9]	**276**	40.32 N	74.20 W
Menlo Park Terrace	**276**	40.32 N	74.20 W
Mennecy	**261**	48.34 N	2.26 E
Mennetou-sur-Cher	**50**	47.16 N	1.53 E
Mennighüffen	**52**	52.13 N	8.43 E
Menno	**198**	43.14 N	97.34 W
Meno, Indon.	**164**	3.52 S	135.31 E
Meno, Ok., U.S.	**196**	36.23 N	98.10 W
Menominee	**190**	45.06 N	87.36 W
Menominee ≃	**190**	45.05 N	87.36 W
Menominee Indian Reservation ◆[4]	**190**	45.00 N	88.45 W
Menomonee ≃	**216**	43.02 N	87.54 W
Menomonee Falls	**216**	43.10 N	88.07 W
Menomonie	**190**	44.52 N	91.55 W
Menongue	**152**	14.36 S	17.48 E
Menor, Mar c	**34**	37.43 N	0.48 W
Menorca I	**34**	40.00 N	4.00 E
Mens	**62**	44.49 N	5.45 E
Menslage	**52**	52.41 N	7.49 E
Menston	**44**	53.53 N	1.44 W
Menstrup	**41**	55.13 N	11.36 E
Mentana	**66**	42.02 N	12.38 E
Mentasta Lake	**180**	62.55 N	143.45 W
Mentasta Mountains ⋏	**180**	62.40 N	143.07 W
Mentawai, Kepulauan II	**108**	2.00 S	99.30 E
Mentawai, Selat Ц	**112**	1.56 S	100.12 E
Mentekab	**114**	3.29 N	102.21 E
Menteke, peski ◆[2]	**80**	47.20 N	50.40 E
Menteng ◆[8]	**269e**	6.12 S	106.50 E
Menteroda	**54**	51.18 N	10.33 E
Menteşpiri	**130**	41.41 N	32.39 E
Menthon-Saint-Bernard	**62**	45.51 N	6.12 E
Menton	**62**	43.47 N	7.30 E
Mentone, Austl.	**274b**	37.59 S	145.05 E
Mentone → Menton, Fr.	**62**	43.47 N	7.30 E
Mentone, Ca., U.S.	**228**	34.05 N	117.08 W
Mentone, In., U.S.	**216**	41.10 N	86.02 W
Mentone, Tx., U.S.	**196**	31.42 N	103.36 W
Mentor, Ky., U.S.	**218**	38.53 N	84.14 W
Mentor, Oh., U.S.	**214**	41.39 N	81.20 W
Mentor-on-the-Lake	**214**	41.42 N	81.21 W
Mentougou	**105**	39.56 N	116.03 E
Mentzdam ⊜[1]	**158**	33.10 S	25.09 E
Menucourt	**261**	49.02 N	1.59 E
Menuma	**94**	36.13 N	139.23 E
Men'uša	**76**	58.23 N	30.42 E
Menyamya	**164**	7.10 S	146.00 E
Menyapa, Gunung ∧	**112**	1.05 N	116.05 E
Menyuan	**102**	37.27 N	101.48 E
Menza ≃	**88**	50.14 N	108.38 E
Menzel Bourguiba	**148**	37.10 N	9.48 E
Menzel Bou Zelfa	**36**	36.41 N	10.36 E
Menzel Djemil	**36**	37.14 N	9.55 E
Menzelen	**52**	51.37 N	6.32 E
Menzelerheide	**263**	51.37 N	6.31 E
Menzelinsk	**80**	55.43 N	53.08 E
Menzel Temime	**148**	36.47 N	10.59 E
Menzenschwand	**58**	47.49 N	8.04 E
Menzies	**162**	29.41 S	121.02 E
Menzies, Mount ∧	**9**	73.30 S	61.50 E
Menziken	**58**	47.14 N	8.12 E
Meobbaai c	**156**	24.25 S	14.34 E
Meola Āgri	**272a**	28.42 N	77.23 E
Meolo	**64**	45.37 N	12.27 E
Meon ≃	**42**	50.48 N	1.15 W
Meopham	**260**	51.22 N	0.22 E
Meopham Station	**260**	51.23 N	0.21 E
Meoqui	**232**	28.17 N	105.29 W
Meota	**184**	53.02 N	108.27 W
Méouge ≃	**62**	44.16 N	5.50 E
Méounes-lès-Montrieux	**62**	43.17 N	5.58 E
Mepal	**42**	52.24 N	0.07 E
Mepisckaro, gora ∧	**84**	41.50 N	42.40 E
Meppel	**52**	52.42 N	6.11 E
Meppen	**52**	52.41 N	7.17 E
Meqerghane, Sebkha ≚	**148**	26.19 N	1.20 E
Meqruur	**174q**	9.31 N	138.09 E
Mequon	**216**	43.13 N	87.59 W
Mer	**50**	47.42 N	1.30 E
Mera ≃	**58**	46.11 N	9.25 E
Merah	**112**	0.50 N	116.48 E
Merai	**164**	4.50 S	152.20 E
Merak	**115a**	5.56 S	106.00 E

≃ River	Fluss	Río	Rivière	Rio
≊ Canal	Kanal	Canal	Canal	Canal
⌊ Waterfall, Rapids	Wasserfall, Stromschnellen	Cascada, Rápidos	Chute d'eau, Rapides	Cascata, Rápidos
Ц Strait	Meeresstrasse	Estrecho	Détroit	Estreito
c Bay, Gulf	Bucht, Golf	Bahía, Golfo	Baie, Golfe	Baía, Golfo
⊜ Lake, Lakes	See, Seen	Lago, Lagos	Lac, Lacs	Lago, Lagos
≡ Swamp	Sumpf	Pantano	Marais	Pântano
⊓ Ice Features, Glacier	Eis- und Gletscherformen	Accidentes Glaciales	Formes glaciaires	Acidentes glaciares
⩱ Other Hydrographic Features	Andere Hydrographische Objekte	Otros Elementos Hidrográficos	Autres données hydrographiques	Outros acidentes hidrográficos

✦ Submarine Features	Untermeerische Objekte	Accidentes Submarinos	Formes de relief sous-marin	Acidentes submarinos
□ Political Unit	Politische Einheit	Unidad Politica	Entité politique	Unidade política
⊍ Cultural Institution	Kulturelle Institution	Institución Cultural	Institution culturelle	Institução cultural
⊥ Historical Site	Historische Stätte	Sitio Histórico	Site historique	Sitio histórico
♠ Recreational Site	Erholungs- und Ferienort	Sitio de Recreo	Centre de loisirs	Area de Lazer
⊠ Airport	Flughafen	Aeropuerto	Aéroport	Aeroporto
■ Military Installation	Militäranlage	Instalación Militar	Installation militaire	Instalação militar
◆ Miscellaneous	Verschiedenes	Misceláneo	Divers	Diversos

Symbols in the index entries represent the broad categories identified in the key at the right. Symbols with superior numbers (⋏[1]) identify subcategories (see complete key on page *I · 1).*

Kartensymbole in dem Registerverzeichnis stellen die rechts in Schlüssel erklärten Kategorien dar. Symbole mit hochgestellten Ziffern (⋏[1]) bezeichnen Unterabteilungen einer Kategorie (vgl. vollständiger Schlüssel auf Seite *I · 1).*

Los símbolos incluídos en el texto del índice representan las grandes categorías identificadas con la clave a la derecha. Los símbolos con numeros en su parte superior (⋏[1]) identifican las subcategorías (véase la clave completa en la página *I · 1).*

Les symboles de l'index représentent les catégories indiquées dans la légende à droite. Les symboles suivis d'un indice (⋏[1]) représentent des sous-catégories (voir légende complète à la page *I · 1).*

Os símbolos incluídos no texto do índice representam as grandes categorias identificadas com a chave à direita. Os símbolos com números em sua parte superior (⋏[1]) identificam as subcategorias (veja-se a chave completa à página *I · 1).*

∧ Mountain	Berg	Montaña	Montagne	Montanha
⋏ Mountains	Berge	Montañas	Montagnes	Montanhas
)(Pass	Pass	Paso	Col	Passo
V Valley, Canyon	Tal, Cañon	Valle, Cañón	Vallée, Canyon	Vale, Canhão
≚ Plain	Ebene	Llano	Plaine	Planície
≻ Cape	Kap	Cabo	Cap	Cabo
I Island	Insel	Isla	Île	Ilha
II Islands	Inseln	Islas	Îles	Ilhas
≗ Other Topographic Features	Andere Topographische Objekte	Otros Elementos Topográficos	Autres données topographiques	Outros acidentes topográficos

ESPAÑOL

Nombre	Página	Lat.°′	Long.°′ W = Oeste
Middle Brook ≃, N.J., U.S.	276	40.33 N	74.33 W
Middle Brook, East Branch ≃	276	40.35 N	74.33 W
Middle Brook, West Branch ≃	276	40.35 N	74.33 W
Middleburg, Md., U.S.	208	39.35 N	77.12 W
Middleburg, N.Y., U.S.	210	42.36 N	74.20 W
Middleburg, Oh., U.S.	216	40.17 N	83.34 W
Middleburg, Pa., U.S.	208	40.47 N	77.02 W
Middleburg Heights	214	41.22 N	81.48 W
Middlebury, Ct., U.S.	207	41.31 N	73.07 W
Middlebury, In., U.S.	216	41.40 N	85.42 W
Middlebury, Vt., U.S.	188	44.00 N	73.10 W
Middlebush	276	40.29 N	74.32 W
Middle Caicos I	238	21.47 N	71.43 W
Middle Cape ≻	220	25.09 N	81.09 W
Middle Castor ≃	212	45.16 N	75.24 W
Middle Channel ≃[1], N.T., Can.	180	69.21 N	135.33 W
Middle Channel ≃[1], Mi., U.S.	281	42.33 N	82.42 W
Middle Concho ≃	196	31.27 N	100.25 W
Middle Creek ≃, U.S.	208	39.41 N	76.18 W
Middle Creek ≃, Pa., U.S.	210	40.46 N	76.52 W
Middle Creek ≃, Pa., U.S.	210	41.28 N	75.11 W
Middle Fabius ≃	194	39.58 N	91.35 W
Middle Falls	210	43.07 N	73.32 W
Middlefield, Ct., U.S.	207	41.31 N	72.42 W
Middlefield, N.Y., U.S.	210	42.41 N	74.50 W
Middlefield, Oh., U.S.	214	41.27 N	81.04 W
Middle Fork Reservoir ⊜[1]	218	39.51 N	84.51 W
Middle Ground I	272c	18.55 N	72.51 E
Middle Ground ✦[2]	174g	28.15 N	177.25 W
Middle Grove, Mo., U.S.	219	39.24 N	92.16 W
Middle Grove, N.Y., U.S.	210	43.05 N	73.55 W
Middle Haddam	207	41.33 N	72.33 W
Middleham	44	54.17 N	1.49 W
Middle Harbour c	274a	33.48 S	151.14 E
Middle Head ≻	274a	33.50 S	151.16 E
Middle Hope	210	41.34 N	74.01 W
Middle Island	210	40.53 N	72.56 W
Middle Island I	162	34.07 S	123.12 E
Middle Level Main Drain ≅	42	52.43 N	0.22 E
Middle Loup ≃	198	41.17 N	98.23 W
Middle Maitland ≃	212	43.53 N	81.19 W
Middlemarch	172	45.31 S	170.07 E
Middle Musquodoboit	186	45.03 N	63.09 W
Middle Nodaway ≃	194	40.54 N	95.00 W
Middle Pease ≃	196	34.15 N	100.07 W
Middle Point	216	40.51 N	84.27 W
Middleport, N.Y., U.S.	210	43.12 N	78.28 W
Middleport, Oh., U.S.	188	39.00 N	82.02 W
Middleport, Pa., U.S.	208	40.44 N	76.05 W
Middle Raccoon ≃	198	41.34 N	94.12 W
Middle Reservoir ⊜[1]	283	42.27 N	71.07 W
Middle River	208	39.20 N	76.26 W
Middle River c	208	39.19 N	76.25 W
Middle River Neck ≻[1]	284b	39.22 N	76.23 W
Middle River Rouge ≃	281	42.20 N	83.15 W
Middle Rouge Parkway ♠	281	42.21 N	83.21 W
Middle Run ≃	285	39.41 N	75.43 W
Middlesboro	192	36.36 N	83.43 W
Middlesbrough	44	54.35 N	1.14 W
Middlesex, Belize	232	17.02 N	88.31 W
Middlesex, N.J., U.S.	276	40.34 N	74.29 W
Middlesex, N.Y., U.S.	210	42.42 N	77.16 W
Middlesex, N.C., U.S.	192	35.47 N	78.12 W
Middlesex □[6], On., Can.	212	43.00 N	81.08 W
Middlesex □[6], Ct., U.S.	207	41.33 N	72.39 W
Middlesex □[6], Ma., U.S.	207	42.30 N	71.25 W
Middlesex □[6], N.J., U.S.	208	40.29 N	74.27 W
Middlesex □[6], Va., U.S.	208	37.40 N	76.35 W
Middlesex Fells Reservation ♠	283	42.27 N	71.07 W
Middlesex Reservoir ⊜[1]	276	40.37 N	74.19 W
Middle Stewiacke	186	45.13 N	63.08 W
Middle Swan	168a	31.52 S	116.00 E
Middle Thames ≃	212	42.59 N	80.58 W
Middleton, Austl.	166	22.22 S	141.32 E
Middleton, N.S., Can.	186	44.57 N	65.04 W
Middleton, Eng., U.K.	42	52.43 N	0.28 E
Middleton, Eng., U.K.	44	53.33 N	2.13 W
Middleton, Ma., U.S.	207	42.35 N	71.01 W
Middleton, Mi., U.S.	190	43.11 N	84.42 W
Middleton, Tn., U.S.	194	35.03 N	88.53 W
Middleton, Wi., U.S.	216	43.05 N	89.30 W
Middleton ≃	166	22.35 S	141.51 E
Middleton in Teesdale	44	54.38 N	2.04 W
Middleton Island I	180	59.25 N	146.25 W
Middleton-on-the-Wolds	44	53.56 N	0.33 W
Middleton Pond ⊜	283	42.36 N	71.02 W
Middleton Reef I[1]	160	29.28 S	159.06 E
Middleton Saint George	44	54.30 N	1.28 W
Middletown, N. Ire., U.K.	48	54.18 N	6.50 W
Middletown, Ca., U.S.	226	38.45 N	122.36 W
Middletown, Ct., U.S.	207	41.33 N	72.39 W
Middletown, De., U.S.	208	39.26 N	75.43 W
Middletown, Il., U.S.	219	40.11 N	89.35 W
Middletown, In., U.S.	218	40.03 N	85.32 W
Middletown, Ky., U.S.	218	38.14 N	85.32 W
Middletown, Md., U.S.	208	39.26 N	77.32 W
Middletown, Mo., U.S.	219	39.07 N	91.24 W
Middletown, N.J., U.S.	208	40.23 N	74.07 W
Middletown, N.Y., U.S.	210	41.26 N	74.25 W
Middletown, Oh., U.S.	218	39.30 N	84.23 W
Middletown, Pa., U.S.	208	40.11 N	76.43 W
Middletown, R.I., U.S.	207	41.32 N	71.17 W
Middletown, Va., U.S.	188	39.01 N	78.16 W
Middletown Park	218	40.09 N	85.26 W
Middle Tuolumne ≃	226	37.50 N	120.01 W
Middleville, Mi., U.S.	216	42.42 N	85.27 W
Middleville, N.Y., U.S.	210	43.08 N	74.58 W
Middleville, N.Y., U.S.	276	43.08 N	74.58 W
Middlewich	44	53.11 N	2.27 W
Middle Yegua Creek ≃	222	30.19 N	96.47 W

FRANÇAIS

Nom	Page	Lat.°′	Long.°′ W = Ouest
Middle Yuba ≃	226	39.22 N	121.12 W
Midelt	148	32.41 N	4.43 W
Midfield	222	28.56 N	96.13 W
Midge Hall	262	53.42 N	2.45 W
Midgic	186	45.59 N	64.18 W
Mid Glamorgan □[6]	42	51.40 N	3.30 W
Midgley	262	53.44 N	1.58 W
Midhurst, On., Can.	212	44.27 N	79.44 W
Midhurst, Eng., U.K.	42	50.59 N	0.45 W
Midi, Aiguille du ∧	62	45.52 N	6.53 E
Midi, Canal du ≅	32	43.26 N	1.58 E
Midi de Bigorre, Pic du ∧	32	42.56 N	0.08 E
Mid Illovo	158	29.59 S	30.25 E
Mid-Indian Basin ✦[1]	12	10.00 S	80.00 E
Mid-Indian Ridge ✦[3]	6	30.00 S	75.00 E
Midland, Austl.	168a	31.53 S	116.00 E
Midland, On., Can.	212	44.45 N	79.53 W
Midland, Ca., U.S.	204	33.52 N	114.48 W
Midland, Mi., U.S.	190	43.36 N	84.14 W
Midland, N.C., U.S.	192	35.13 N	80.30 W
Midland, Oh., U.S.	218	39.18 N	83.54 W
Midland, Pa., U.S.	214	40.37 N	80.26 W
Midland, Pa., U.S.	214	40.37 N	80.26 W
Midland, S.D., U.S.	198	44.04 N	101.09 W
Midland, Tx., U.S.	196	31.59 N	102.04 W
Midland, Wa., U.S.	224	47.10 N	122.24 W
Midland Bay c	212	44.47 N	79.52 W
Midland Beach ◆[8]	276	40.34 N	74.05 W
Midland City	219	40.09 N	89.08 W
Midland Park, Mi., U.S.	216	42.23 N	85.22 W
Midland Park, N.J., U.S.	276	40.59 N	74.08 W
Midland Park Lake ⊜	212	44.44 N	79.53 W
Midlands □[4]	154	19.00 S	29.45 E
Midleton	48	51.55 N	8.10 W
Midlothian, Il., U.S.	216	41.37 N	87.43 W
Midlothian, Tx., U.S.	222	32.28 N	96.59 W
Midlothian Creek ≃	278	41.39 N	87.40 W
Midlum	52	53.43 N	8.37 E
Midnapore, Ab., Can.	182	50.55 N	114.05 W
Midnapore, India	126	22.26 N	87.20 E
Midnapore □[5]	126	22.25 N	87.20 E
Midnapore Canal ≅	126	22.25 N	87.53 E
Midnapore Plain ≚	126	22.00 N	87.45 E
Mid-Ohio Sports Car Course ♠	214	40.40 N	82.38 W
Midongy Nord	157b	20.45 S	46.13 E
Midongy Sud	157b	23.35 S	47.01 E
Midori	96	34.43 N	132.37 E
Midori ◆[8]	268	35.32 N	139.34 E
Midori ≃	92	32.42 N	130.37 E
Midou ≃	32	43.54 N	0.30 W
Mid-Pacific Mountains ✦[3]	14	20.00 N	170.00 E
Midpines	226	37.32 N	119.55 W
Midsayap	116	7.12 N	124.32 E
Midshipman Point ≻	282	38.07 N	122.27 W
Midsland	52	53.22 N	5.16 E
Midsomer Norton	42	51.18 N	2.28 W
Midu	102	25.22 N	100.31 E
Midvale, De., U.S.	285	39.39 N	75.37 W
Midvale, Id., U.S.	202	44.28 N	116.44 W
Midvale, Oh., U.S.	214	40.26 N	81.22 W
Midville	192	32.49 N	82.14 W
Midway, B.C., Can.	182	49.01 N	118.47 W
Midway, B.C., Can.	202	49.01 N	118.46 W
Midway, Al., U.S.	194	32.04 N	85.31 W
Midway, In., U.S.	216	41.37 N	85.55 W
Midway, Ky., U.S.	218	38.09 N	84.41 W
Midway, Pa., U.S.	279b	40.22 N	80.17 W
Midway, Tx., U.S.	222	31.02 N	95.45 W
Midway, Ut,. U.S.	200	40.30 N	111.28 W
Midway City	280	33.45 N	118.00 W
Midway Islands □[2], Oc.	6	28.13 N	177.22 W
Midway Islands □[2], Oc.	174g	28.13 N	177.22 W
Midway Mall ◆[9]	279a	41.24 N	82.07 W
Midway Naval Station ■	174g	28.13 N	177.26 W
Midway Park	192	34.43 N	77.21 W
Midwest	200	43.24 N	106.16 W
Midwest City	196	35.26 N	97.23 W
Midwolda	52	53.12 N	7.00 E
Midyat	130	37.25 N	41.23 E
Midyobe	152	1.21 N	10.18 E
Midžor (Midžur) ∧	38	43.23 N	22.42 E
Mie	96	32.58 N	131.35 E
Mie □[5]	92	34.30 N	136.30 E
Miechów	30	50.23 N	20.01 E
Miedwie, Jezioro ⊜	54	53.17 N	14.52 E
Międzybórz	30	51.24 N	17.40 E
Międzychód	30	52.36 N	15.55 E
Międzylesie	30	50.10 N	16.40 E
Międzyrzec Podlaski	30	52.00 N	22.47 E
Międzyrzecz	30	52.28 N	15.35 E
Międzyzdroje	30	53.55 N	14.28 E
Miehuapu	105	39.11 N	117.44 E
Miejska Górka	30	51.40 N	16.58 E
Miélan	32	43.26 N	0.19 E
Mielec	30	50.18 N	21.25 E
Mielno	30	54.16 N	16.01 E
Mien ⊜	26	56.25 N	14.51 E
Mienga	152	17.17 S	19.48 E
Mienhua Yü I	100	25.29 N	122.06 E
Mient'ienhuo Shan ∧	269d	25.11 N	121.30 E
Miercurea-Ciuc	38	46.22 N	25.48 E
Mieres	34	43.15 N	5.46 W
Mierlo	52	51.27 N	5.37 E
Mieroszów	30	50.41 N	16.10 E
Miersdorf	264a	52.20 N	13.37 E
Miersig	38	46.53 N	21.51 E
Mier y Noriega	234	23.25 N	100.07 W
Miesaituo	120	35.52 N	93.40 E
Miesbach	64	47.47 N	11.50 E
Miesenbach	61	47.22 N	15.46 E
Mieso	144	9.15 N	40.48 E
Mieste	54	52.28 N	11.11 E
Miesterhorst	54	52.27 N	11.09 E
Mieszkowice	30	52.46 N	14.30 E
Mifflin, Oh., U.S.	214	40.47 N	82.22 W
Mifflin, Pa., U.S.	208	40.34 N	77.24 W
Mifflin □[6]	210	40.40 N	77.33 W
Mifflinburg	210	40.55 N	77.02 W
Mifflintown	208	40.34 N	77.23 W
Mifflinville	210	41.01 N	76.18 W
Miftāḥ, Wādī V	142	30.15 N	31.46 E
Migdal	132	32.50 N	35.30 E
Migdal Ha'Emeq	132	32.41 N	35.15 E
Migdol	158	26.54 S	25.27 E
Migennes	50	47.58 N	3.31 E
Mīghān	128	31.49 N	59.28 E
Mıgırtepe ∧	130	36.50 N	36.22 E
Migliarino	66	44.46 N	11.56 E
Migliaro	64	44.48 N	11.58 E
Miglionico	68	40.34 N	16.30 E
Mignano Monte Lungo	68	41.23 N	13.58 E
Mignone ≃	66	42.11 N	11.44 E
Mignoviči	76	54.16 N	31.34 E
Mignovillard	58	46.48 N	6.08 E
Migori ≃	154	0.59 S	34.15 E
Miguel Alemán, Presa ⊜[1]	234	18.13 N	96.32 W
Miguel Alves	250	4.10 S	42.54 W
Miguel Auza	232	24.18 N	103.25 W
Miguel Calmon	250	11.26 S	40.36 W
Miguel Couto	287a	22.43 S	43.27 W
Miguel de la Borda	236	9.09 N	80.19 W
Migueles, Arroyo de los ≃	266a	40.20 N	3.32 W
Miguelete	258	34.01 S	57.39 W
Miguelete, Arroyo ≃	258	34.14 S	57.54 W
Miguel Hidalgo □[7]	286a	19.26 N	99.11 W
Miguel Hidalgo, Presa ⊜[1]	232	26.30 N	108.35 W
Miguelópolis	255	20.12 S	48.03 W
Miguel Pereira	256	22.27 S	43.22 W
Miguel Riglos	252	36.51 S	63.42 W
Migulinskaja	80	49.42 N	41.16 E
Migvie	46	57.08 N	2.56 W

PORTUGUÊS

Nome	Página	Lat.°′	Long.°′ W = Oeste
Migyaunglaung	110	14.40 N	98.09 E
Mihăești	38	45.07 N	25.00 E
Mihai Viteazu	38	44.39 N	28.41 E
Mihajlovgrad	38	43.25 N	23.13 E
Mihalıççık	130	39.52 N	31.30 E
Mihama, Nihon	94	34.46 N	136.54 E
Mihama, Nihon	94	35.36 N	135.56 E
Mihama, Nihon	96	33.54 N	135.08 E
Mihara, Nihon	96	34.24 N	133.05 E
Mihara, Nihon	96	34.17 N	134.46 E
Mihara, Nihon	96	34.32 N	135.34 E
Mihara-yama ∧	94	34.43 N	139.23 E
Mihla	54	51.04 N	10.20 E
Mihmandar	130	36.52 N	35.18 E
Miho	94	36.00 N	140.18 E
Mihonoseki	96	35.34 N	133.19 E
Miho-wan c	96	35.30 N	133.23 E
Mihuangzhuang	105	39.07 N	116.12 E
Mijaly	86	48.57 N	53.42 E
Mijares ≃	34	39.55 N	0.01 W
Mijdaḥah	144	14.00 N	48.26 E
Mijdrecht	52	52.13 N	4.52 E
Mijiang	98	43.01 N	130.08 E
Mijoux	58	46.22 N	6.00 E
Mikabo-yama ∧	94	36.09 N	138.55 E
Mikame	96	33.25 N	132.27 E
Mikamo	96	35.09 N	133.37 E
Mikasa	92a	43.14 N	141.53 E
Mikaševiči	78	52.13 N	27.28 E
Mikata	94	35.33 N	135.55 E
Mikata-ko ⊜	94	35.34 N	135.53 E
Mikatou	273b	4.16 S	15.08 E
Mikawa, Nihon	94	36.29 N	136.29 E
Mikawa, Nihon	96	33.37 N	132.58 E
Mikawa-wan c	94	34.43 N	137.10 E
Mikawa-wan-kokutei-kōen ♠	94	34.42 N	137.10 E
Mikazuki	96	34.58 N	134.27 E
Mikese	154	6.46 S	37.54 E
Mikhaylov, Cape ≻	9	66.51 S	118.33 E
Miki, Nihon	96	34.48 N	134.59 E
Miki, Nihon	96	34.17 N	134.05 E
Mikínai ⊥	38	37.44 N	22.45 E
Mikindani	154	10.17 S	40.07 E
Mikinduri	154	0.07 N	37.50 E
Mikkabi	94	34.48 N	137.33 E
Mikkaichi	270	34.26 N	135.35 E
Mikkeli	26	61.41 N	27.15 E
Mikkelin lääni □[4]	26	62.00 N	27.30 E
Mikkwa ≃	176	58.25 N	114.45 W
Mikołajki	30	53.49 N	21.36 E
Mikołów	30	50.11 N	18.55 E
Mikomeseng	152	2.08 N	10.37 E
Mikomoto-jima I	94	34.34 N	138.56 E
Míkonos	38	37.26 N	25.20 E
Míkonos I	38	37.29 N	25.25 E
Mikope	152	5.03 S	20.48 E
Mikre	38	43.02 N	24.31 E
Mikrí Préspa, Límni ⊜	38	40.46 N	21.04 E
Miksimil	126	22.52 N	89.23 E
Mikšino	76	57.15 N	35.43 E
Mikstat	30	51.32 N	17.59 E
Mikulášovice	54	50.58 N	14.20 E
Mikulincy	78	49.24 N	25.38 E
Mikulino	76	55.02 N	31.07 E
Mikulkin, mys ≻	24	67.48 N	46.40 E
Mikulov	61	48.49 N	16.39 E
Mikumi	154	7.24 S	36.59 E
Mikumi National Park ♠	154	7.12 S	37.05 E
Mikun'	24	62.21 N	50.06 E
Mikuni	94	36.13 N	136.09 E
Mikuni-sammyaku ⋏	94	36.50 N	138.40 E
Mikuni-tōge)(	94	36.46 N	138.50 E
Mikuni-yama ∧	94	35.59 N	138.43 E
Mikura-jima I	92	33.52 N	139.36 E
Mila	34	36.27 N	6.16 E
Milaca	190	45.45 N	93.39 W
Miladummadulu Atoll I[1]	122	6.15 N	73.15 E
Milagre	256	21.18 S	47.00 W
Milagres	250	7.17 S	38.57 W
Milagro	246	2.07 S	79.36 W
Milagros	116	12.13 N	123.30 E
Milam □[6]	222	30.47 N	96.57 W
Milan → Milano, It.	62	45.28 N	9.12 E
Milan, Ga., U.S.	192	32.01 N	83.03 W
Milan, In., U.S.	218	39.07 N	85.07 W
Milan, Mi., U.S.	216	42.05 N	83.40 W
Milan, Mn., U.S.	198	45.06 N	95.54 W
Milan, Mo., U.S.	194	40.12 N	93.07 W
Milan, N.M., U.S.	200	35.10 N	107.53 W
Milan, Oh., U.S.	214	41.17 N	82.36 W
Milan, Pa., U.S.	210	41.54 N	76.32 W
Milan, Tn., U.S.	194	35.55 N	88.45 W
Milando	152	8.45 S	17.36 E
Milan Federal Correctional Institution ʋ	281	42.06 N	83.40 W
Milang	168b	35.25 S	138.58 E
Milano (Milan), It.	62	45.28 N	9.12 E
Milano (Milan), It.	266b	45.28 N	9.12 E
Milano, Tx., U.S.	222	30.43 N	96.52 W
Milano □[4]	62	45.30 N	9.30 E
Milanoa	157b	13.35 S	49.47 E
Milano Marittima	66	44.16 N	12.21 E
Milanville	210	41.40 N	75.04 W
Milâs	130	37.19 N	27.47 E
Milaševiči	78	51.39 N	27.56 E
Mil'atino, S.S.S.R.	76	54.29 N	34.18 E
Mil'atino, S.S.S.R.	82	55.41 N	35.48 E
Milazzo	70	38.13 N	15.14 E
Milazzo, Capo di ≻	70	38.16 N	15.14 E
Milazzo, Golfo di c	70	38.15 N	15.20 E
Milbank	198	45.13 N	96.38 W
Milbanke Sound ʊ	182	52.18 N	128.33 W
Milborne Port	42	50.58 N	2.27 W
Milbuk	116	6.10 N	124.16 E
Milburn	196	34.14 N	96.32 W
Milburn Creek ≃	276	40.38 N	73.36 W
Milden	184	51.30 N	107.31 W
Mildenau	54	50.35 N	13.04 E
Mildenhall	42	52.21 N	0.30 E
Milders	64	47.06 N	11.16 E
Mildmay	212	44.03 N	81.07 W
Mildred, Il., U.S.	219	39.46 N	89.38 W
Mildred, Pa., U.S.	210	41.28 N	76.22 W
Mildura	166	34.12 S	142.09 E
Mile	102	24.26 N	103.26 E
Miléai	38	39.20 N	23.09 E
Milena	70	37.28 N	13.44 E
Milepa	154	11.43 S	36.20 E
Miles, Austl.	166	26.40 S	150.11 E
Miles, Tx., U.S.	196	31.35 N	100.10 W
Miles ≃	283	42.40 N	70.51 W
Milesburg	214	40.56 N	77.47 W
Miles City	202	46.24 N	105.50 W
Miles Creek c	208	38.46 N	76.12 W
Miles Creek ≃	226	37.12 N	120.21 W
Mile Seven Hundred Thirty Three	180	60.03 N	131.07 W
Milešovka ∧	54	50.33 N	13.56 E
Milestone	184	50.00 N	104.30 W
Milesville	279b	40.12 N	79.52 W
Mileto	68	38.36 N	16.04 E
Miletto, Monte ∧	68	41.27 N	14.22 E
Miletus ⊥	130	37.28 N	27.15 E
Mileura	162	26.23 S	117.20 E
Milevsko	30	49.27 N	14.22 E
Milford, Eng., U.K.	42	51.11 N	1.38 W
Milford, Ct., U.S.	207	41.13 N	73.04 W
Milford, De., U.S.	208	38.54 N	75.25 W
Milford, Il., U.S.	216	40.37 N	87.41 W
Milford, In., U.S.	216	41.24 N	85.50 W
Milford, Ia., U.S.	198	43.19 N	95.08 W
Milford, Ky., U.S.	218	38.34 N	84.09 W
Milford, Me., U.S.	188	44.56 N	68.38 W
Milford, Md., U.S.	284b	39.21 N	76.44 W
Milford, Ma., U.S.	207	42.08 N	71.31 W
Milford, Mi., U.S.	216	42.35 N	83.35 W
Milford, N.H., U.S.	207	42.50 N	71.38 W
Milford, N.J., U.S.	210	40.34 N	75.05 W
Milford, N.Y., U.S.	210	42.35 N	74.56 W
Milford, Oh., U.S.	218	39.10 N	84.17 W
Milford, Pa., U.S.	210	41.19 N	74.48 W
Milford, Tx., U.S.	222	32.07 N	96.57 W
Milford, Ut,. U.S.	200	38.23 N	113.00 W
Milford, Va., U.S.	208	38.01 N	77.22 W
Milford Brook ≃	276	40.19 N	74.17 W
Milford Center	218	40.10 N	83.26 W
Milford Cross Roads	285	39.43 N	75.44 W
Milford Haven	42	51.40 N	5.02 W
Milford Haven c	42	51.42 N	5.03 W
Milford Lake ⊜[1]	198	39.15 N	97.00 W
Milford on Sea	42	50.44 N	1.36 W
Milford Ridge	284b	39.21 N	76.45 W
Milford Sound	172	44.40 S	167.54 E
Milford Sound ʊ	172	44.35 S	167.47 E
Milford Station	186	45.03 N	63.26 W
Milgis ≃	154	1.48 N	38.06 E
Milgoo ∧	162	28.51 S	118.07 E
Mil'guvejem ≃	180	68.22 N	171.30 E
Milḥ, Baḥr al- ⊜	128	32.40 N	43.35 E
Milḥat Ashqar ⊜	128	35.18 N	41.55 E
Milhaud	62	43.47 N	4.18 E
Mili I[1]	14	6.08 N	171.55 E
Milian ≃	112	5.13 N	117.25 E
Milibangalala, Ponta ≻	158	26.26 S	32.56 E
Milicia ≃	70	38.04 N	13.33 E
Milicz	30	51.32 N	17.17 E
Milieu, Rivière du ≃	206	46.47 N	73.56 W
Milij	142	30.36 N	31.03 E
Milín	60	49.39 N	14.02 E
Miling	162	30.30 S	116.21 E
Milis	71	40.03 N	8.38 E
Militello in Val di Catania	70	37.16 N	14.48 E
Militello Rosmarino	70	38.03 N	14.41 E
Militsch → Milicz	30	51.32 N	17.17 E
Milk ≃	202	48.05 N	106.15 W
Milk Creek ≃, Co., U.S.	200	40.24 N	107.45 W
Milk Creek ≃, Or., U.S.	224	45.15 N	122.41 W
Milk Hill ∧[2]	42	51.23 N	1.51 W
Mil'kovo	74	54.43 N	158.37 E
Milk River	182	49.09 N	112.05 W
Milk River Ridge Reservoir ⊜[1]	182	49.22 N	112.35 W
Mill	52	51.41 N	5.47 E
Mill ≃, Ct., U.S.	276	41.08 N	73.16 W
Mill ≃, Ma., U.S.	207	42.18 N	72.37 W
Mill ≃, Ma., U.S.	283	42.38 N	70.41 W
Mill ≃, Ma., U.S.	283	42.12 N	70.57 W
Mill ≃, Ma., U.S.	283	42.08 N	71.21 W
Mill ≃, Ma., U.S.	283	42.44 N	70.52 W
Mill ≃, N.Y., U.S.	276	40.38 N	73.39 W
Millard	198	41.13 N	96.07 W
Millau	32	44.06 N	3.05 E
Mill Bay	224	48.39 N	123.34 W
Millboro	192	37.59 N	79.36 W
Millbourne	285	39.58 N	75.15 W
Millbrae	226	37.35 N	122.23 W
Millbrook, On., Can.	212	44.09 N	78.27 W
Millbrook, Eng., U.K.	42	50.20 N	4.13 W
Millbrook, Ma., U.S.	283	42.03 N	70.41 W
Millbrook, N.J., U.S.	276	40.52 N	74.33 W
Millbrook, N.Y., U.S.	210	41.47 N	73.41 W
Mill Brook ≃, Ma., U.S.	283	42.31 N	71.18 W
Mill Brook ≃, N.J., U.S.	276	40.53 N	74.32 W
Mill Brook ≃, N.J., U.S.	276	40.25 N	74.06 W
Mill Brook ≃, N.J., U.S.	276	40.29 N	74.23 W
Millburn	276	40.44 N	74.18 W
Millbury, Ma., U.S.	207	42.11 N	71.45 W
Millbury, Oh., U.S.	214	41.33 N	83.25 W
Mill City	202	44.45 N	122.29 W
Mill Creek, Pa., U.S.	214	40.26 N	77.56 W
Millcreek, Ut,. U.S.	200	40.27 N	111.54 W
Mill Creek, W.V., U.S.	188	38.43 N	79.58 W
Mill Creek ≃, Austl.	274a	33.59 S	151.01 E
Mill Creek ≃, Ca., U.S.	226	36.49 N	119.21 W
Mill Creek ≃, Ca., U.S.	228	34.05 N	117.06 W
Mill Creek ≃, De., U.S.	285	39.42 N	75.39 W
Mill Creek ≃, Il., U.S.	219	39.50 N	91.24 W
Mill Creek ≃, In., U.S.	194	39.30 N	86.57 W
Mill Creek ≃, In., U.S.	216	41.01 N	86.36 W
Mill Creek ≃, Ia., U.S.	198	42.47 N	95.31 W
Mill Creek ≃, Ks., U.S.	198	39.55 N	96.56 W
Mill Creek ≃, Ky., U.S.	218	38.28 N	84.20 W
Mill Creek ≃, N.J., U.S.	276	40.48 N	74.03 W
Mill Creek ≃, N.J., U.S.	285	40.02 N	74.55 W
Mill Creek ≃, N.Y., U.S.	212	43.57 N	76.08 W
Mill Creek ≃, Oh., U.S.	214	41.06 N	80.40 W
Mill Creek ≃, Oh., U.S.	214	40.14 N	83.09 W
Mill Creek ≃, Oh., U.S.	218	39.06 N	84.32 W
Mill Creek ≃, Oh., U.S.	279a	41.25 N	81.38 W
Mill Creek ≃, Or., U.S.	224	45.36 N	121.11 W
Mill Creek ≃, Pa., U.S.	208	40.00 N	76.18 W
Mill Creek ≃, Pa., U.S.	210	41.53 N	77.08 W
Mill Creek ≃, Pa., U.S.	214	41.09 N	79.03 W
Mill Creek ≃, Pa., U.S.	285	40.03 N	75.16 W
Mill Creek ≃, Pa., U.S.	285	40.08 N	74.52 W
Mill Creek ≃, Tx., U.S.	222	32.46 N	95.46 W
Mill Creek ≃, Tx., U.S.	222	29.50 N	96.07 W
Mill Creek ≃, Tx., U.S.	222	30.08 N	95.37 W
Mill Creek ≃, Va., U.S.	208	38.09 N	77.10 W
Mill Creek, North Fork ≃	224	45.33 N	121.18 W
Mill Creek, South Fork ≃	224	45.36 N	121.12 W
Millcreek Township	214	42.05 N	80.10 W
Milldale	207	41.33 N	72.53 W
Milledgeville, Ga., U.S.	192	33.04 N	83.13 W
Milledgeville, Il., U.S.	190	41.57 N	89.46 W
Milledgeville, Oh., U.S.	218	39.36 N	83.35 W
Mille Îles, Rivière des ≃	206	45.42 N	73.32 W
Mille Lacs, Lac des ⊜	190	48.50 N	90.30 W
Mille Lacs Kathio State Park ♠	190	46.08 N	93.43 W
Mille Lacs Lake ⊜	190	46.15 N	93.40 W
Millemont	261	48.49 N	1.45 E
Millen	192	32.48 N	81.56 W
Millendon	168a	31.48 S	116.02 E
Miller, Mo., U.S.	194	37.13 N	93.50 W
Miller, S.D., U.S.	198	44.31 N	98.59 W
Miller □[6]	219	38.15 N	92.15 W
Miller, Mount ∧	180	60.25 N	142.23 W
Miller City	216	41.06 N	84.08 W
Miller Creek ≃	282	38.02 N	122.30 W
Miller House	180	65.32 N	145.11 W
Miller Mountain ∧	204	38.03 N	118.12 W
Millerovo, S.S.S.R.	78	48.55 N	40.25 E
Millerovo, S.S.S.R.	83	47.49 N	39.15 E
Miller Peak ∧	200	31.23 N	110.17 W
Miller Place	210	40.58 N	73.00 W
Millers ≃	207	42.35 N	72.30 W
Millersburg, In., U.S.	216	41.31 N	85.41 W
Millersburg, In., U.S.	218	41.31 N	85.41 W
Millersburg, Ky., U.S.	218	38.18 N	84.08 W
Millersburg, Mi., U.S.	190	45.20 N	84.03 W
Millersburg, Oh., U.S.	214	40.33 N	81.55 W
Millersburg, Pa., U.S.	208	40.32 N	76.57 W
Millers Creek ≃	196	33.27 N	99.14 W
Miller Seamount ✦[3]	16	53.30 N	144.20 W
Millers Falls	207	42.34 N	72.29 W
Millers Ferry	194	32.05 N	87.22 W
Millers Flat	172	45.40 S	169.25 E
Millers Island	284b	39.14 N	76.24 W
Millers Pond ⊜	276	40.51 N	73.12 W
Millersport	188	39.54 N	82.32 W
Millers Run ≃	279b	40.22 N	80.07 W
Millerstown	210	40.32 N	77.09 W
Millersville, Il., U.S.	219	39.25 N	89.07 W
Millersville, Oh., U.S.	214	41.18 N	83.16 W
Millersville, Pa., U.S.	208	39.59 N	76.21 W
Millerton, N.Y., U.S.	210	41.57 N	73.30 W
Millerton, Pa., U.S.	210	41.59 N	76.56 W
Millerton Lake ⊜[1]	226	37.01 N	119.41 W
Millerton Lake State Recreation Area ♠	226	37.02 N	119.37 W
Millertown	186	48.49 N	56.33 W
Millertown Junction	186	49.01 N	56.21 W
Millesimo	62	44.22 N	8.12 E
Millet	182	53.06 N	113.28 W
Millett, Mi., U.S.	216	42.42 N	84.38 W
Millett, Tx., U.S.	196	28.35 N	99.12 W
Milleur Point ≻	44	55.01 N	5.06 W
Millevaches, Plateau de ⋏[1]	32	45.30 N	2.10 E
Millford	48	55.07 N	7.43 W
Mill Green	260	51.41 N	0.22 E
Mill Grove	216	40.25 N	85.17 W
Mill Hall	210	41.06 N	77.29 W
Millheim	210	40.53 N	77.28 W
Mill Hill ◆[8]	260	51.37 N	0.13 W
Mill Hill ∧[2]	262	53.25 N	1.54 W
Millhousen	218	39.13 N	85.26 W
Millican	222	30.28 N	96.12 W
Millicent	166	37.36 S	140.22 E
Milligan, Fl., U.S.	194	30.45 N	86.38 W
Milligan, Ne., U.S.	198	40.30 N	97.23 W
Milligan Gulch V	200	33.37 N	107.02 W
Milligantown	279b	40.33 N	79.41 W
Milliken	275b	43.49 N	79.18 W
Millingen aan de Rijn	52	51.52 N	6.02 E
Millington, Il., U.S.	216	41.34 N	88.36 W
Millington, Md., U.S.	208	39.15 N	75.50 W
Millington, Mi., U.S.	190	43.16 N	83.31 W
Millington, N.J., U.S.	210	40.40 N	74.31 W
Millington, Tn., U.S.	194	35.20 N	89.53 W
Millinocket	188	45.39 N	68.42 W
Millionnyj	89	54.30 N	126.19 E
Millis	207	42.10 N	71.21 W
Mill Island I, Ant.	9	65.30 S	100.40 E
Mill Island I, N.T., Can.	176	64.00 N	78.00 W
Millisle	48	54.36 N	5.32 W
Mill Lake ⊜	212	45.22 N	80.00 W
Millmerran	166	27.52 S	151.16 E
Millmont	210	40.53 N	77.08 W
Mill Neck	276	40.52 N	73.34 W
Mill Neck ≻[1]	276	40.53 N	73.33 W
Mill Neck Creek c	276	40.54 N	73.33 W
Millom	44	54.13 N	3.18 W
Mill Pond ⊜	276	40.53 N	73.22 W
Millport, Scot., U.K.	46	55.46 N	4.55 W
Millport, Al., U.S.	194	33.33 N	88.04 W
Millport, N.Y., U.S.	210	42.16 N	76.50 W
Millport, Pa., U.S.	214	41.55 N	78.07 W
Millrift	210	41.25 N	74.45 W
Mill River	207	42.06 N	73.16 W
Mill Run Acres	284c	38.58 N	77.17 W
Millry	194	31.38 N	88.18 W
Mills, Pa., U.S.	214	41.57 N	77.41 W
Mills, Wy., U.S.	202	42.50 N	106.21 W
Mills, Lake ⊜[1]	224	47.59 N	123.36 W
Millsboro	208	38.35 N	75.17 W
Mills Creek ≃, Austl.	166	22.23 S	143.05 E
Mills Creek ≃, Ca., U.S.	282	37.27 N	122.25 W
Mills Lake ⊜	176	61.30 N	118.10 W
Mills Mansion State Historic Site ⊥	210	41.52 N	73.57 W
Millstadt	219	38.27 N	90.05 W
Millstatt	64	46.48 N	13.35 E
Millstätter See ⊜	64	46.47 N	13.35 E
Millstone	276	40.29 N	74.35 W
Millstone ≃	276	40.33 N	74.34 W
Millstream, Austl.	162	21.35 S	117.04 E
Millstream, B.C., Can.	224	48.30 N	123.31 W
Millstreet	48	52.03 N	9.04 W
Milltown, In., U.S.	218	38.20 N	86.16 W
Milltown, Mt., U.S.	202	46.52 N	113.52 W
Milltown, N.J., U.S.	208	40.27 N	74.26 W
Milltown, Wi., U.S.	190	45.31 N	92.30 W
Milltown Malbay	48	52.50 N	9.23 W
Millvale	279b	40.28 N	79.58 W
Mill Valley	226	37.54 N	122.32 W
Mill Village	214	41.53 N	79.58 W
Millville, Ma., U.S.	207	42.01 N	71.34 W
Millville, N.J., U.S.	208	39.24 N	75.02 W
Millville, Oh., U.S.	218	39.24 N	84.40 W
Millville, Pa., U.S.	210	41.07 N	76.31 W
Millville Lake	283	42.48 N	71.13 W
Millville Lake ⊜	283	42.48 N	71.13 W
Millwood, Md., U.S.	284c	38.53 N	76.53 W
Millwood, N.Y., U.S.	210	41.11 N	73.48 W
Millwood, Va., U.S.	188	39.04 N	78.02 W
Millwood Lake ⊜[1]	194	33.45 N	94.00 W
Milly-la-Forêt	50	48.24 N	2.28 E
Milly-Lamartine	58	46.21 N	4.42 E
Milmay	208	39.26 N	74.51 W
Milmersdorf	54	53.06 N	13.38 E
Milmine	219	39.54 N	88.39 W
Milmont Park	285	39.53 N	75.20 W
Milne Bay □[5]	164	10.00 S	152.30 E
Milne Bay c	164	10.22 S	150.30 E
Milner	224	49.20 N	122.42 W
Milnesville	210	40.59 N	75.59 W
Milngavie	46	55.57 N	4.20 W
Milnor	198	46.15 N	97.27 W
Milnrow	44	53.37 N	2.06 W
Milnthorpe	44	54.14 N	2.46 W
Milo, Ab., Can.	182	50.34 N	112.53 W
Milo, Ia., U.S.	190	41.17 N	93.26 W
Milo, Me., U.S.	188	45.15 N	68.59 W
Milo ≃	150	11.04 N	9.14 W
Milon-la-Chapelle	261	48.44 N	2.03 E
Mílos	38	36.45 N	24.27 E
Mílos I	38	36.41 N	24.15 E
Miloslaviči	76	53.41 N	32.15 E
Miloslavskoje	76	53.34 N	39.24 E
Miłosław	30	52.13 N	17.29 E
Milow, D.D.R.	54	53.11 N	11.32 E
Milow, D.D.R.	54	52.31 N	12.18 E
Milpa Alta □[7]	286a	19.11 N	99.02 W
Milpa Alta ◆[8]	286a	19.11 N	99.01 W
Milparinka	166	29.44 S	141.53 E
Milpitas	226	37.25 N	121.54 W
Milpitas Wash V	204	33.18 N	114.44 W
Milroy, In., U.S.	218	39.29 N	85.28 W
Milroy, Pa., U.S.	208	40.42 N	77.35 W
Milseburg ∧	56	50.32 N	9.53 E
Mil'skaja ravnina ≚	84	40.00 N	48.00 E
Milspe	263	51.18 N	7.21 E
Miltach	60	49.09 N	12.46 E
Miltenberg	56	49.42 N	9.15 E
Miltitz	54	51.19 N	12.16 E
Milton, Austl.	170	35.19 S	150.26 E
Milton, On., Can.	212	43.31 N	79.53 W
Milton, N.Z.	172	46.07 S	169.58 E
Milton, Eng., U.K.	42	52.14 N	0.09 W
Milton, De., U.S.	208	38.46 N	75.18 W
Milton, Fl., U.S.	194	30.37 N	87.02 W
Milton, Il., U.S.	219	39.34 N	90.39 W
Milton, In., U.S.	218	39.47 N	85.09 W
Milton, In., U.S.	218	38.58 N	85.01 W
Milton, Ia., U.S.	190	40.40 N	92.09 W
Milton, Ky., U.S.	218	38.43 N	85.22 W
Milton, Ma., U.S.	207	42.15 N	71.05 W
Milton, N.J., U.S.	276	41.02 N	74.32 W
Milton, N.Y., U.S.	210	41.39 N	73.57 W
Milton, N.D., U.S.	198	48.37 N	98.02 W
Milton, Pa., U.S.	210	41.00 N	76.50 W
Milton, Vt., U.S.	188	44.38 N	73.06 W
Milton, Wa., U.S.	224	47.14 N	122.18 W
Milton, W.V., U.S.	188	38.26 N	82.07 W
Milton, Wi., U.S.	216	42.46 N	88.56 W
Milton, Lake ⊜	214	41.06 N	80.58 W
Milton Abbot	42	50.35 N	4.15 W
Milton-Freewater	202	45.55 N	118.23 W
Milton Harbor c	276	40.57 N	73.42 W
Milton Keynes	42	52.02 N	0.42 W
Milton Point ≻	276	40.57 N	73.42 W
Miltonvale	198	39.20 N	97.26 W
Miltou	146	10.14 N	17.26 E
Miltzow	54	54.12 N	13.13 E
Milumba	154	7.06 S	31.04 E
Miluo	100	28.50 N	113.04 E
Miluo ≃	100	28.50 N	113.06 E
Mil'utinskaja	80	48.38 N	41.40 E
Mil'utkej, gora ∧	180	65.42 N	178.03 W
Milverton, On., Can.	212	43.34 N	80.55 W
Milverton, Eng., U.K.	42	51.02 N	3.16 W
Milwaukee	216	43.02 N	87.54 W
Milwaukee □[6]	216	43.02 N	87.58 W
Milwaukee ≃	190	43.02 N	87.54 W
Milwaukee Bay c	216	43.02 N	87.53 W
Milwaukie	224	45.26 N	122.38 W
Mim	150	6.54 N	2.34 W
Mima	96	33.17 N	132.36 E
Mimasaka	96	35.00 N	134.10 E
Mimbres ≃	200	32.13 N	107.28 W
Mimbres Mountains ⋏	200	32.45 N	107.45 W
Mimi ≃	92	32.20 N	131.37 E
Mimico ◆[8]	275b	43.37 N	79.30 W
Mimico Creek ≃	275b	43.37 N	79.29 W
Mimizan	32	44.12 N	1.14 W
Mimmaya	92	41.12 N	140.26 E
Mimoň	54	50.40 N	14.44 E
Mimongo	152	1.11 S	11.36 E
Mimoso, Bra.	248	16.17 S	55.48 W
Mimoso, Bra.	255	15.10 S	48.05 W
Mimoso do Sul	255	21.04 S	41.22 W
Mims	220	28.39 N	80.50 W
Mimuro-yama ∧	96	35.14 N	134.28 E
Min ≃, Zhg.	100	26.05 N	119.32 E
Min ≃, Zhg.	102	28.46 N	104.38 E
Mina, Méx.	196	26.01 N	100.32 W
Mina, Nv., U.S.	204	38.23 N	118.06 W
Mina ≃	112	10.09 S	124.12 E
Mîna, Oued ≃	34	35.47 N	0.30 E
Mīnā' al-Aḥmadī	128	29.04 N	48.08 E
Mīnāb	128	27.09 N	57.05 E
Mīnāb ≃	128	27.01 N	56.53 E
Minabe	96	33.46 N	135.19 E
Minabegawa	96	33.47 N	135.20 E
Mina el Limón	236	12.45 N	86.44 W
Minago ≃	184	54.34 N	98.08 W
Minahasa ≻[1]	112	1.00 N	124.35 E
Minâj ≃[1]	126	22.31 N	89.22 E
Minakami	94	36.46 N	138.58 E
Minakuchi	94	34.58 N	136.10 E
Minam ≃	202	45.37 N	117.43 W
Minamata	92	32.13 N	130.24 E
Minami	94	35.39 N	136.57 E
Minami ◆[8], Nihon	268	35.24 N	139.36 E
Minami ◆[8], Nihon	270	34.40 N	135.31 E
Minami ◆[8], Nihon	270	34.58 N	135.45 E
Minami ≃	94	35.30 N	135.49 E
Minamiaiki	94	36.02 N	138.33 E
Minami-Alps-kokuritsu-kōen ♠	94	35.40 N	138.13 E
Minamiashigara	94	35.19 N	139.07 E
Minami-Bōsō-kokutei-kōen ♠	94	35.10 N	140.05 E
Minamichita	94	34.44 N	136.52 E
Minami-Daitō-jima I	90	25.50 N	131.15 E
Minami-Iō-jima I	14	24.14 N	141.28 E
Minamiizu	94	34.39 N	138.50 E
Minamimaki	94	36.00 N	138.30 E
Minaminasu	94	36.39 N	140.06 E
Minamisenju ◆[8]	268	35.44 N	139.48 E
Minamishinano	94	35.19 N	137.56 E
Minami-Tori-shima (Marcus Island) I	14	24.18 N	153.58 E
Minano	94	36.04 N	139.06 E
Mina Pirquitas	252	22.41 S	66.31 W
Minard, S. Afr.	158	31.17 S	27.35 E
Minard, Scot., U.K.	46	56.07 N	5.15 W
Minas, Cuba	240p	21.29 N	77.37 W
Minas, Indon.	114	0.50 N	101.29 E
Minas, Ur.	252	34.23 S	55.14 W
Minas, Sierra de las ⋏	236	15.10 N	89.40 W
Minas Basin c	186	45.20 N	64.00 W
Minas Channel ʊ	186	45.15 N	64.45 W
Minas de Barroterán	232	27.40 N	101.20 W
Minas de Corrales	252	31.35 S	55.28 W
Minas de Matahambre	240p	22.35 N	83.57 W
Minas de Oro	236	14.46 N	87.20 W
Minas de Ríotinto	34	37.42 N	6.35 W
Minas Gerais □[3]	255	18.00 S	44.00 W
Minas Novas	255	17.15 S	42.36 W
Mînăstirea	38	44.13 N	26.54 E
Minatare	198	41.48 N	103.30 W
Minatitlán	234	17.59 N	94.31 W
Minato	268	35.13 N	139.52 E
Minato ◆[8], Nihon	268	35.39 N	139.45 E
Minato ◆[8], Nihon	270	34.39 N	135.26 E
Minato ≃	268	35.13 N	139.52 E
Minbāl	142	28.24 N	30.41 E
Minbu	110	20.11 N	94.52 E
Minbulak	85	41.30 N	75.53 E
Minbya	110	20.22 N	93.15 E
Minbyin	110	19.17 N	93.32 E
Minchinābād	123	30.10 N	73.34 E
Minchinhampton	42	51.42 N	2.10 W
Minchinmávida, Volcán ∧[1]	254	42.49 S	72.28 W
Minchumina, Lake ⊜	180	63.52 N	152.15 W
Mincio ≃	64	45.04 N	10.59 E
Minco	196	35.18 N	97.56 W
Minčol ∧	30	49.15 N	20.59 E
Mind'ak	86	54.02 N	58.48 E
Mindanao I	116	8.00 N	125.00 E
Mindanao ≃	116	7.07 N	124.24 E
Mindanao Sea ⫧[2]	116	9.10 N	124.25 E
Mindego Creek ≃	282	37.18 N	122.15 W
Mindego Hill ∧[2]	282	37.18 N	122.13 W
Mindel ≃	58	48.31 N	10.23 E
Mindelheim	58	48.03 N	10.29 E
Mindelo	150a	16.53 N	25.00 W
Mindemoya	190	45.44 N	82.10 W
Minden, B.R.D.	52	52.17 N	8.55 E
Minden, On., Can.	212	44.55 N	78.43 W
Minden, La., U.S.	194	32.36 N	93.17 W
Minden, Ne., U.S.	198	40.29 N	98.56 W
Minden, Nv., U.S.	226	38.57 N	119.45 W
Minden, W.V., U.S.	188	37.58 N	81.07 W
Minden City	190	43.40 N	82.46 W
Mindenmines	194	37.28 N	94.35 W
Minderoo	162	22.00 S	115.02 E
Mindif	146	10.24 N	14.26 E
Mindiptana	164	5.45 S	140.42 E
Mindon	110	19.21 N	94.44 E
Mindoro I	116	12.50 N	121.05 E
Mindoro Occidental □[4]	116	13.00 N	121.00 E
Mindoro Oriental □[4]	116	13.00 N	121.20 E
Mindoro Strait ʊ	116	12.20 N	120.40 E
Mindouli	152	4.17 S	14.21 E
Mindourou, Cam.	152	4.06 N	14.34 E
Mindourou, Cam.	152	3.25 N	13.32 E
Minduri	256	21.41 S	44.37 W

≃ River	Fluss	Río	Rivière	Rio
≅ Canal	Kanal	Canal	Canal	Canal
ʟ Waterfall, Rapids	Wasserfall, Stromschnellen	Cascada, Rápidos	Chute d'eau, Rapides	Cascata, Rápidos
ʊ Strait	Meeresstrasse	Estrecho	Détroit	Estreito
c Bay, Gulf	Bucht, Golf	Bahía, Golfo	Baie, Golfe	Baía, Golfo
⊜ Lake, Lakes	See, Seen	Lago, Lagos	Lac, Lacs	Lago, Lagos
≡ Swamp	Sumpf	Pantano	Marais	Pântano
✱ Ice Features, Glacier	Eis- und Gletscherformen	Accidentes Glaciales	Formes glaciaires	Acidentes glaciares
⫧ Other Hydrographic Features	Andere Hydrographische Objekte	Otros Elementos Hidrográficos	Autres données hydrographiques	Outros acidentes hidrográficos
✦ Submarine Features	Untermeerische Objekte	Accidentes Submarinos	Formes de relief sous-marin	Acidentes submarinos
□ Political Unit	Politische Einheit	Unidad Política	Entité politique	Unidade política
ʋ Cultural Institution	Kulturelle Institution	Institución Cultural	Institution culturelle	Instituição cultural
⊥ Historical Site	Historische Stätte	Sitio Histórico	Site historique	Sítio histórico
♠ Recreational Site	Erholungs- und Ferienort	Sitio de Recreo	Centre de loisirs	Área de Lazer
✈ Airport	Flughafen	Aeropuerto	Aéroport	Aeroporto
■ Military Installation	Militäranlage	Instalación Militar	Installation militaire	Instalação militar
◆ Miscellaneous	Verschiedenes	Misceláneo	Divers	Diversos

ENGLISH · **DEUTSCH**

Symbols in the index entries represent the broad categories identified in the key at the right. Symbols with superior numbers (⋏[1]) identify subcategories (see complete key on page *I · 1).*

Kartensymbole in dem Registerverzeichnis stellen die rechts in Schlüssel erklärten Kategorien dar. Symbole mit hochgestellten Ziffern (⋏[1]) bezeichnen Unterabteilungen einer Kategorie (vgl. vollständiger Schlüssel auf Seite *I · 1).*

Los símbolos incluídos en el texto del índice representan las grandes categorias identificadas con la clave a la derecha. Los símbolos con numeros en su parte superior (⋏[1]) identifican las subcategorías (véase la clave completa en la página *I · 1).*

Les symboles de l'index représentent les catégories indiquées dans la légende à droite. Les symboles suivis d'un indice (⋏[1]) représentent des sous-catégories (voir légende complète à la page *I · 1).*

Os símbolos incluídos no texto do índice representam as grandes categorias identificadas com a chave à direita. Os símbolos com números em sua parte superior (⋏[1]) identificam as subcategorias (veja-se a chave completa à página *I · 1).*

Symbol	English	Deutsch	Español	Français	Português
∧	Mountain	Berg	Montaña	Montagne	Montanha
⋏	Mountains	Berge	Montañas	Montagnes	Montanhas
)(	Pass	Pass	Paso	Col	Passo
V	Valley, Canyon	Tal, Cañon	Valle, Cañón	Vallée, Canyon	Vale, Canhão
≚	Plain	Ebene	Llano	Plaine	Planície
≻	Cape	Kap	Cabo	Cap	Cabo
I	Island	Insel	Isla	Île	Ilha
II	Islands	Inseln	Islas	Îles	Ilhas
⊥	Other Topographic Features	Andere Topographische Objekte	Otros Elementos Topográficos	Autres données topographiques	Outros acidentes topográficos

ESPAÑOL — Nombre | Página | Lat.°′ | Long.°′ W = Oeste
FRANÇAIS — Nom | Page | Lat.°′ | Long.°′ W = Ouest
PORTUGUÊS — Nome | Página | Lat.°′ | Long.°′ W = Oeste

Nombre / Nom / Nome	Página / Page	Lat.°′	Long.°′ W = Oeste / Ouest
Mochtín	60	49.22 N	13.21 E
Mochudi	156	24.28 S	26.05 E
Močily	82	54.20 N	38.41 E
Mocímboa da Praia	154	11.20 S	40.21 E
Mocímboa do Rovuma	154	11.20 S	39.18 E
Möckeln ⊜, Sve.	26	56.40 N	14.10 E
Möckeln ⊜, Sve.	40	59.18 N	14.30 E
Möckern	54	52.08 N	11.57 E
Mockfjärd	40	60.30 N	14.58 E
Mockhorn Island I	208	37.13 N	75.53 W
Möckmühl	56	49.19 N	9.22 E
Mockrehna	54	51.30 N	12.49 E
Mocksville	192	35.53 N	80.33 W
Moclips	224	47.14 N	124.12 W
Mocó ≃	246	1.49 S	66.48 W
Môco, Serra do ∧	152	12.28 S	15.10 E
Mocoa	246	1.09 N	76.37 W
Mococa	256	21.28 S	47.01 W
Mocoduene	156	23.40 S	35.10 E
Mocomoco	248	15.22 S	68.59 W
Mocoretá	252	30.38 S	57.58 W
Mocorito	232	25.29 N	107.55 W
Moctezuma, Méx.	232	29.48 N	109.42 W
Moctezuma, Méx.	234	22.45 N	101.05 W
Moctezuma ≃, Méx.	232	29.09 N	109.40 W
Moctezuma ≃, Méx.	234	21.59 N	98.34 W
Mocuba	154	16.50 S	36.59 E
Močurica ≃	38	42.31 N	26.32 E
Modane	62	45.12 N	6.40 E
Modāsa	120	23.28 N	73.18 E
Modau ≃	56	49.49 N	8.28 E
Modbury	42	50.21 N	3.53 W
Modder ≃	158	29.02 S	24.37 E
Modderbee	273d	26.10 S	28.24 E
Modder East	273d	26.11 S	28.26 E
Modderfontein	273d	26.06 S	28.09 E
Modderfontein ≃	273d	26.13 S	28.10 E
Modderrivier	158	29.02 S	24.38 E
Model City	284a	43.11 N	78.59 W
Modena, It.	64	44.40 N	10.55 E
Modena, N.Y., U.S.	210	41.40 N	74.07 W
Modena □[4]	64	44.30 N	10.54 E
Moder ≃	56	48.49 N	8.06 E
Möderbrugg	61	47.17 N	14.29 E
Modern Art, Museum of ʊ	276	40.46 N	73.58 W
Modeste, Mount ∧	224	48.37 N	124.06 W
Modesto, Ca., U.S.	226	37.38 N	120.59 W
Modesto, Il., U.S.	219	39.29 N	89.59 W
Modesto City-County Airport ⊠	226	37.39 N	120.57 W
Modesto Main Canal ≊	226	37.39 N	120.27 W
Modesto Reservoir ⊜[1]	226	37.26 N	121.58 W
Modica	70	36.52 N	14.46 E
Modigliana	66	44.09 N	11.47 E
Modione ≃	70	37.34 N	12.49 E
Modjamboli	152	2.28 N	22.06 E
Modjeska	280	33.43 N	117.37 W
Mödling	264b	48.05 N	16.17 E
Mödling ≃	264b	48.04 N	16.22 E
Modoc	218	40.02 N	85.07 W
Modon ≃	50	47.16 N	1.27 E
Modowi	164	4.05 S	134.39 E
Modra, Česko.	30	48.21 N	17.17 E
Modra, Tchad	146	20.43 N	17.42 E
Modra špilja ⌂[5]	36	43.00 N	16.02 E
Mödrath	56	50.53 N	6.43 E
Modriča	38	44.57 N	18.18 E
Modřice	61	49.07 N	16.37 E
Mo-duc	110	14.57 N	108.53 E
Modugno	68	41.05 N	16.47 E
Moe	169	38.10 S	146.15 E
Moe ≃, Austl.	169	38.08 S	146.17 E
Moe ≃, P.Q., Can.	206	45.19 N	71.49 W
Moecherville	216	41.44 N	88.17 W
Moeda	255	20.20 S	44.03 W
Moehau ∧	172	36.35 S	175.24 E
Moel Fferna ∧	42	52.57 N	3.18 W
Moelv	26	60.56 N	10.42 E
Moema	255	19.50 S	45.24 W
Moen	50	50.46 N	3.24 E
Moen I	175c	7.26 N	151.52 E
Moena	64	46.22 N	11.39 E
Moengo	250	5.37 N	54.24 W
Moenkopi	200	36.06 N	111.13 W
Moenkopi Wash V	200	36.54 N	111.26 W
Moeraki Point >	172	45.22 S	170.52 E
Moeranyah Lake ⊜	166	33.02 S	143.58 E
Moerbeke, Bel.	50	50.45 N	3.55 E
Moerbeke, Bel.	50	51.10 N	3.56 E
Moerdijk	52	51.43 N	4.38 E
Moerewa	172	35.23 S	174.02 E
Moergestel	52	51.33 N	5.11 E
Moero, Lago → Mweru, Lake ⊜	154	9.00 S	28.45 E
Moers	56	51.27 N	6.37 E
Moers □[8]	263	51.32 N	6.36 E
Moersbach ≃	263	51.33 N	6.36 E
Moesa ≃	58	46.13 N	9.03 E
Moffat	44	55.20 N	3.27 W
Moffat Peak ∧	172	45.02 S	168.07 E
Moffatt	222	31.12 N	97.28 W
Moffatt, Lac ⊜	206	45.34 N	71.19 W
Moffat Water ≃	44	55.18 N	3.25 W
Moffet Point >	180	55.26 N	162.32 W
Moffett Field Naval Air Station ■	226	37.24 N	122.03 W
Moffit	198	46.40 N	100.17 W
Mofoluku	273a	6.33 N	3.20 E
Moga	123	30.48 N	75.10 E
Mogadiscio → Muqdisho	144	2.04 N	45.22 E
Mogadishu → Muqdisho	144	2.04 N	45.22 E
Mogador → Essaouira	148	31.30 N	9.47 W
Mogadore	214	41.02 N	81.23 W
Mogadore Reservoir ⊜[1]	214	41.04 N	81.21 W
Mogadouro	34	41.20 N	6.39 W
Mogalakwena ≃	156	23.00 S	28.40 E
Mogalo	152	3.10 N	19.04 E
Mogami ≃	92	38.55 N	139.48 E
Mogan Shan ∧	106	30.36 N	119.52 E
Mogapinyana	156	22.19 S	27.27 E
Mogaung	110	25.18 N	96.56 E
Mogdy	89	50.35 N	133.51 E
Mogees	285	40.06 N	75.19 W
Møgeltønder	41	54.56 N	8.49 E
Mogenstrup	41	55.11 N	11.53 E
Mogent ≃	266d	41.33 N	2.15 E
Moggio Udinese	64	46.25 N	13.12 E
Mogi, Serra do ⩘	287b	23.47 S	46.20 W
Mogi das Cruzes	256	23.31 S	46.11 W
Mogielnica	30	51.42 N	20.43 E
Mogi-Guaçu	256	22.22 S	46.57 W
Mogila-Bel'mak, gora ∧[2]	78	47.20 N	36.35 E
Mogila-Mečetnaja, gora ∧[2]	83	48.16 N	38.53 E
Mogilev → Mogil'ov	76	53.54 N	30.21 E
Mogilno	30	52.40 N	17.58 E
Mogil'ov, S.S.S.R.	76	53.54 N	30.21 E
Mogil'ov, S.S.S.R.	78	48.52 N	34.29 E
Mogil'ov-Podol'skij	78	48.27 N	27.48 E
Mogi-Mirim	256	22.26 S	46.57 W
Mogincual	154	15.35 S	40.25 E
Moglal, Wādī V	140	19.18 N	34.29 E
Moglia	64	44.56 N	10.55 E
Mogliano Veneto	64	45.33 N	12.14 E
Mogoča	88	53.44 N	119.44 E
Mogoča ≃	76	58.00 N	36.26 E
Mogočin	86	57.43 N	83.34 E
Mogod	88	48.24 N	103.00 E
Mogogh	140	8.26 N	31.19 E
Mogojto	88	54.25 N	110.27 E
Mogojtuj	88	51.17 N	114.55 E
Mogok	110	22.55 N	96.30 E
Mogollon Mountains ⩘	200	33.25 N	108.40 W
Mogollon Rim ⌂[4]	200	34.25 N	110.50 W
Mogor	120	32.52 N	67.47 E
Mogorella	71	39.52 N	8.51 E
Mogoro	71	39.41 N	8.47 E
Mogotes	246	6.30 N	72.58 W
Mogotón, Pico ∧	236	13.45 N	86.23 W
Mograt Island I	140	19.30 N	33.15 E
Mogroum	146	11.06 N	15.25 E
Moguer	34	37.16 N	6.50 W
Mogyoród	264c	47.36 N	19.15 E
Mogyoródi-patak ≃	264c	47.36 N	19.05 E
Mogzon	88	51.45 N	111.58 E
Mohács	30	45.59 N	18.42 E
Mohaka	172	39.07 S	177.11 E
Mohaka ≃	172	39.07 S	177.12 E
Mohall	198	48.45 N	101.30 W
Moḥammadābād	128	30.53 N	61.28 E
Mohammedia (Fedala)	148	33.44 N	7.24 W
Mohana	124	25.54 N	77.45 E
Mohangi	154	0.03 N	29.05 E
Mohania	124	25.11 N	83.37 E
Mohanpur, Bngl.	126	23.24 N	90.36 E
Mohanpur, India	126	21.51 N	87.26 E
Mohanpur, India	272a	28.44 N	77.10 E
Mohave, Lake ⊜[1]	204	35.25 N	114.38 W
Mohawk, Mi., U.S.	190	47.18 N	88.21 W
Mohawk, N.Y., U.S.	210	43.00 N	75.00 W
Mohawk ≃	210	42.47 N	73.42 W
Mohawk, East Branch ≃	212	43.22 N	75.28 W
Mohawk, Lake ⊜	276	41.02 N	74.41 W
Mohawk Dam ◆[6]	214	40.20 N	82.05 W
Mohawk Mountain ∧	207	41.49 N	73.17 W
Mohawk Point >	212	42.51 N	79.29 W
Mohe	89	53.29 N	122.19 E
Moheda	26	57.00 N	14.34 E
Mohegan	207	41.28 N	72.06 W
Mohegan Lake	210	41.19 N	73.51 W
Mohelnice	30	49.46 N	16.55 E
Moher, Cliffs of ⌂[4]	48	52.57 N	9.26 W
Mohican ≃	214	40.22 N	82.09 W
Mohican, Black Fork ≃	214	40.35 N	82.17 W
Mohican, Cape >	180	60.12 N	167.28 W
Mohican, Clear Fork ≃	214	40.35 N	82.12 W
Mohican, Jerome Fork ≃	214	40.45 N	82.23 W
Mohican, Lake Fork ≃	214	40.27 N	82.12 W
Mohican, Muddy Fork ≃	214	40.45 N	82.08 W
Mohican State Park ♠	214	40.37 N	82.16 W
Mohicanville Dam ◆[6]	214	40.44 N	82.09 W
Mohili ◆[8]	272c	19.06 N	72.53 E
Mohill	48	53.54 N	7.52 W
Mohinora, Cerro ∧	232	26.06 N	107.04 W
Mohlakeng	273d	26.13 S	27.42 E
Möhlau	54	51.44 N	12.21 E
Möhlin	58	47.34 N	7.51 E
Mohmand □[8]	123	34.30 N	71.20 E
Möhne ≃	52	51.27 N	7.57 E
Möhnestausee ⊜[1]	52	51.29 N	8.08 E
Mohns Ridge ✢[3]	16	72.30 N	5.00 E
Mohnton	208	40.17 N	75.59 W
Mohnyin	110	24.47 N	96.22 E
Moho ≃	236	16.04 N	88.52 W
Mohokare (Caledon) ≃	158	30.31 S	26.05 E
Moholm	40	58.37 N	14.02 E
Mohon	56	49.45 N	4.44 E
Mohorn	54	51.00 N	13.28 E
Mohoro	154	8.08 S	39.10 E
Möhringen	58	47.57 N	8.46 E
Mohrsville	208	40.28 N	75.59 W
Mohrungen → Morąg	30	53.56 N	19.56 E
Moi	26	58.28 N	6.32 E
Moiano, It.	68	40.39 N	14.28 E
Moiano, It.	68	41.05 N	14.32 E
Moindou	175f	21.42 S	165.41 E
Moinești	38	46.28 N	26.29 E
Moingbi	140	5.46 N	28.49 E
Moinhos	256	22.43 S	46.20 W
Moinkum	85	43.48 N	73.41 E
Mointy	86	47.13 N	73.21 E
Moio Alcantara	70	37.54 N	15.03 E
Moiporá	255	16.34 S	50.42 W
Moira	48	54.30 N	6.17 W
Moira ≃	212	44.09 N	77.23 W
Moiraba	250	2.27 S	49.25 W
Moira Lake ⊜	212	44.29 N	77.27 W
Moirans	62	45.20 N	5.34 E
Moirans-en-Montagne	58	46.26 N	5.44 E
Mõisaküla	76	58.06 N	25.11 E
Moisdon	32	47.37 N	1.22 W
Moisejeviči	76	53.13 N	28.17 E
Moisejevka, S.S.S.R.	83	49.14 N	39.51 E
Moisejevka, S.S.S.R.	86	58.05 N	76.16 E
Moisejevo Alabuška	76	51.54 N	42.06 E
Moisenay	261	48.34 N	2.44 E
Moisés Ville	252	30.43 S	61.29 W
Moisie	186	50.11 N	66.05 W
Moisie ≃	176	50.11 N	66.05 W
Moisie, Baie de ⊂	186	50.16 N	65.56 W
Moisling ◆[8]	52	53.50 N	10.38 E
Moison Creek ≃	281	42.18 N	82.40 W
Moissac	32	44.06 N	1.05 E
Moïssala	146	8.21 N	17.46 E
Moisselles	261	49.03 N	2.20 E
Moisson	261	49.05 N	1.40 E
Moisson, Forêt de ♠	261	49.03 N	1.39 E
Moissy-Cramayel	261	48.38 N	2.36 E
Moita	34	38.39 N	8.59 W
Moitaco	246	8.01 N	64.21 W
Moivre ≃	56	48.52 N	4.28 E
Möja I	26	59.26 N	18.55 E
Mojácar	34	37.08 N	1.51 W
Mojana, Caño ≃[1]	246	9.02 N	74.46 W
Mojave	228	35.03 N	118.10 W
Mojave ≃	204	35.06 N	116.04 W
Mojave Desert ◆[2]	204	35.00 N	117.00 W
Mojave River Forks Reservoir ⊜[1]	228	34.20 N	117.15 W
Moji	85	38.59 N	74.24 E
Mojiang	102	23.28 N	101.39 E
Moji-Guaçu ≃	255	20.53 S	48.10 W
Mojjero ≃	74	68.44 N	103.42 E
Mojnalyk	88	51.18 N	95.33 E
Mojo	144	8.36 N	39.07 E
Mojoagung	115a	7.34 S	112.21 E
Mojokerto	115a	7.28 S	112.26 E
Mojosari	115a	7.31 S	112.33 E
Mojstrana	64	46.27 N	13.56 E
Moju	250	1.53 S	48.46 W
Moju ≃	250	1.40 S	48.25 W
Mōka	94	36.26 N	140.01 E
Mokai	172	38.32 S	175.54 E
Mokambo	154	12.25 S	28.21 E
Mokameh	124	25.24 N	85.55 E
Mokane	219	38.40 N	91.52 W
Mokapu Peninsula >[1]	229c	21.27 N	157.45 W
Mokaria	152	2.00 N	23.20 E
Mokarta, Castello di ⊥	70	37.48 N	12.45 E
Mokau	172	38.41 S	174.37 E
Mokau ≃	172	38.42 S	174.37 E
Moke	102	30.14 N	100.01 E
Mokelumne ≃	226	38.13 N	121.28 W
Mokelumne, Middle Fork ≃	226	38.22 N	120.37 W
Mokelumne, North Fork ≃	226	38.22 N	120.37 W
Mokelumne, South Fork ≃	226	38.23 N	120.35 W
Mokelumne Aqueduct ≊[1]	226	37.54 N	122.07 W
Mokelumne Hill	226	38.18 N	120.42 W
Mokena	216	41.31 N	87.53 W
Mokhotlong	158	29.22 S	29.02 E
Mokil I[1]	14	6.40 N	159.47 E
Mokimbo	154	6.20 S	28.42 E
Mokino	80	57.27 N	49.11 E
Moklakan	88	54.56 N	118.56 E
Möklinta	40	60.05 N	16.32 E
Moknine	148	35.38 N	10.54 E
Mokochu, Khao ∧	110	15.56 N	99.06 E
Mokohinau Islands II	172	35.55 S	175.07 E
Mokokchūng	120	26.20 N	94.32 E
Mokolo, Cam.	146	10.45 N	13.48 E
Mokolo, Zaïre	152	1.57 N	18.05 E
Mokolo ≃	156	23.14 S	27.43 E
Mokombe	152	0.14 S	23.48 E
Mokoreta ≃	172	46.21 S	168.51 E
Mokou	273b	4.13 S	15.13 E
Mokpalin	110	17.26 N	96.53 E
Mokp'o	98	34.48 N	126.22 E
Mokraja Jel'muta	80	46.51 N	41.41 E
Mokraja Ol'chovka	80	50.28 N	44.59 E
Mokraja Sura ≃	78	48.19 N	35.09 E
Mokraja Volnovacha ≃	83	47.30 N	37.15 E
Mokrany	78	51.50 N	24.14 E
Mokrisset	34	34.59 N	5.20 W
Mokro-Jelančik	83	47.42 N	38.31 E
Mokrous	80	51.14 N	47.37 E
Mokrousovo	86	55.48 N	66.45 E
Mokrušinskoje	86	57.31 N	93.11 E
Mokryje Jaly ≃	78	48.05 N	36.44 E
Mokryj Gašun	80	46.53 N	42.45 E
Mokryj Jelančik ≃	83	47.08 N	38.20 E
Mokryj Kor	82	54.34 N	37.58 E
Mokša ≃	80	54.44 N	41.53 E
Mokšan	80	53.26 N	44.37 E
Moku	154	2.57 N	29.22 E
Mokuleia	229c	21.35 N	158.09 W
Mokumbusu	152	1.44 N	21.04 E
Mokvin	78	50.57 N	26.48 E
Mokwa	150	9.20 N	5.02 E
Mol	56	51.11 N	5.06 E
Mola di Bari	68	41.04 N	17.05 E
Molale	144	10.08 N	39.42 E
Molalla	224	45.08 N	122.34 W
Molalla ≃	224	45.18 N	122.43 W
Molalla, North Fork ≃	224	45.05 N	122.29 W
Molanda	152	2.28 N	20.48 E
Molanosa	184	54.30 N	105.33 W
Moláoi	38	36.48 N	22.52 E
Molara, Isola I	71	40.52 N	9.43 E
Molaretto	62	45.10 N	7.00 E
Molat, Otok I	36	44.15 N	14.49 E
Molbergen	52	52.51 N	7.55 E
Molčanovka	83	46.52 N	38.37 E
Molčanovo	86	57.35 N	83.48 E
Mold	44	53.10 N	3.08 W
Moldary	86	50.47 N	78.29 E
Moldau → Vltava ≃	30	50.21 N	14.30 E
Moldavia → Moldavskaja Sovetskaja Socialističeskaja Respublika □[3]	78	47.00 N	29.00 E
Moldavia □[9]	38	47.00 N	27.15 E
Moldavskaja Sovetskaja Socialističeskaja Respublika □[3]	78	47.00 N	29.00 E
Molde	26	62.44 N	7.11 E
Moldotau, chrebet ⩘	85	41.35 N	74.40 E
Moldova ≃	38	46.54 N	26.58 E
Moldova-Nouă	38	44.44 N	21.40 E
Moldoveanu ∧	38	45.36 N	24.44 E
Môle ≃, Fr.	62	43.15 N	6.32 E
Mole ≃, Eng., U.K.	42	50.57 N	3.54 W
Mole ≃, Eng., U.K.	42	51.24 N	0.21 W
Môle, Cap du >	238	19.50 N	73.25 W
Mole Creek	166	41.33 S	146.24 E
Molega Lake ⊜	186	44.22 N	64.53 W
Mole Game Reserve ◆[4]	150	9.30 N	2.00 W
Molegbe	152	4.14 N	20.53 E
Molenbeek-St.-Jean	50	50.51 N	4.19 E
Molepolole	156	24.25 S	25.30 E
Moléson ∧	58	46.33 N	7.01 E
Molėtai	76	55.14 N	25.25 E
Mole Valley □[8]	260	51.16 N	0.18 W
Molfetta	68	41.12 N	16.36 E
Molibagu	112	0.23 N	123.59 E
Molières-sur-Cèze	62	44.15 N	4.09 E
Molimiao	89	43.34 N	121.54 E
Molina	252	35.07 S	71.17 W
Molina de Aragón	34	40.51 N	1.53 W
Molina de Segura	34	38.03 N	1.12 W
Molina di Ledro	64	45.56 N	10.46 E
Molinara	68	41.18 N	14.54 E
Moline, Il., U.S.	190	41.30 N	90.30 W
Moline, Ks., U.S.	198	37.21 N	96.18 W
Moline, Mi., U.S.	216	42.44 N	85.39 W
Molinella	64	44.37 N	11.40 E
Molinges	58	46.21 N	5.46 E
Molingguan	106	31.50 N	118.50 E
Molini di Tures (Mühlen)	64	46.54 N	11.56 E
Moliniere Point >	241k	12.05 N	61.45 W
Molino	194	30.43 N	87.18 W
Molino de Rosas ◆[8]	286a	19.22 N	99.13 W
Molinos	252	25.25 S	66.19 W
Molins de Rey	34	41.25 N	2.01 E
Moliro	154	8.13 S	30.34 E
Molise □[4]	66	41.35 N	14.30 E
Moliterno	68	40.14 N	50.52 E
Molkābād	128	34.32 N	52.35 E
Mölkau	54	51.20 N	12.26 E
Molkom	40	59.36 N	13.43 E
Möll ≃	64	46.50 N	13.26 E
Mollahasan	130	39.22 N	42.37 E
Mollāhāt	126	22.56 N	89.48 E
Mollakendi	130	38.36 N	39.20 E
Mollaro	64	46.16 N	11.05 E
Möllbrücke	64	46.50 N	13.22 E
Mölle	41	56.17 N	12.29 E
Möllen	263	51.35 N	6.42 E
Möllenbeck, D.D.R.	54	53.17 N	11.44 E
Möllenbeck, D.D.R.	54	53.23 N	13.20 E
Mollendo	248	17.02 S	72.01 W
Möllensee ⊜	264a	52.26 N	13.51 E
Mollepata	248	13.31 S	72.32 W
Moller, Port ⊂	180	55.51 N	160.25 W
Möllersdorf	264b	48.02 N	16.18 E
Mollet	266d	41.33 N	2.13 E
Mollia	62	45.49 N	8.02 E
Molliens-Vidame	50	49.53 N	2.01 E
Mollington	262	53.13 N	2.55 W
Mollis	58	47.05 N	9.04 E
Mölln, B.R.D.	54	53.37 N	10.41 E
Mölln, Öst.	61	47.53 N	14.15 E
Mollösund	26	58.04 N	11.28 E
Mollusk	208	37.43 N	76.32 W
Molly Ann Brook ≃	276	40.55 N	74.11 W
Mölnbo	40	59.03 N	17.25 E
Mölndal	26	57.39 N	12.01 E
Mölnlycke	26	57.39 N	12.09 E
Mölntorp	40	59.33 N	16.15 E
Molocaboc Island I	116	10.58 N	123.34 E
Moločansk	78	47.12 N	35.36 E
Molochio	68	38.18 N	16.02 E
Moločnaja ≃	78	46.42 N	35.20 E
Moločnoje	76	59.17 N	39.41 E
Moločnoje, ozero ⊜	78	46.30 N	35.20 E
Molócuè ≃	154	17.03 S	38.52 E
Molodečno	76	54.19 N	26.49 E
Molodežnaja ʊ[3]	9	67.35 S	46.35 E
Molodi	82	55.17 N	37.31 E
Molodo	150	14.14 N	6.02 W
Molodogvardejsk	83	48.20 N	39.40 E
Molodoj Tud	76	56.26 N	33.36 E
Molod'ožnyj	89	50.23 N	136.48 E
Mologa ≃	76	58.50 N	37.11 E
Molokai I	229a	21.07 N	157.00 W
Molokai Fracture Zone ✢	14	23.00 N	148.00 W
Molokai Fracture Zone ✢	16	23.00 N	130.00 W
Molokča ≃	82	56.15 N	38.45 E
Molokini I	229a	20.38 N	156.30 W
Molokovo, S.S.S.R.	76	58.10 N	36.45 E
Molokovo, S.S.S.R.	82	55.34 N	37.52 E
Moloma ≃	24	58.20 N	48.28 E
Molong	166	33.06 S	148.52 E
Molonglo ≃	171b	35.15 S	148.58 E
Molopo ≃	156	28.30 S	20.13 E
Molotkoviči	78	52.07 N	25.56 E
Molotov → Perm'	86	58.00 N	56.15 E
Molotovsk → Severodvinsk	24	64.34 N	39.50 E
Molou	146	13.42 N	21.44 E
Moloundou	152	2.03 N	15.10 E
Molowaie	152	5.47 S	23.20 E
Moloy	58	47.32 N	4.55 E
Molsheim	58	48.32 N	7.29 E
Molson Lake ⊜	184	54.12 N	96.45 W
Molteno	158	31.22 S	26.22 E
Moltrasio	58	45.52 N	9.05 E
Molu, Pulau I	164	6.45 S	131.33 E
Moluca, Mar de la → Maluku, Laut ⍑[2]	108	0.00	125.00 E
Molucas, Islas → Maluku II	108	2.00 S	128.00 E
Moluccas → Maluku II	108	2.00 S	128.00 E
Molucca Sea → Maluku, Laut ⍑[2]	108	0.00	125.00 E
Molukken → Maluku II	108	2.00 S	128.00 E
Molumbo	154	15.27 S	30.15 E
Molundo	116	7.56 N	124.23 E
Moluques → Maluku II	108	2.00 S	128.00 E
Molveno, Lago di ⊜	64	46.08 N	10.57 E
Molvoticy	76	57.25 N	32.20 E
Molžaninovo	82	55.56 N	37.22 E
Moma, Moç.	154	16.44 S	39.14 E
Moma, Zaïre	152	1.36 S	23.57 E
Moma ≃	74	66.26 N	143.06 E
Momanga	156	18.12 S	21.42 E
Momats ≃	164	5.20 S	137.47 E
Momax	234	21.56 N	103.19 W
Momba ≃	154	8.28 S	32.40 E
Mombaça	250	5.45 S	39.38 W
Mombachito, Cerro ∧	236	12.24 N	85.34 W
Mombacho, Volcán ∧[1]	236	11.50 N	85.58 W
Mombango	152	1.45 N	24.26 E
Mombaruzzo	62	44.46 N	8.27 E
Mombasa	154	4.03 S	39.40 E
Mombetsu	92a	44.21 N	143.22 E
Mombo	154	4.53 S	38.17 E
Mombongo	152	1.39 N	23.09 E
Momboyo ≃	152	0.16 S	19.00 E
Mombuey	34	42.02 N	6.20 W
Mombum	164	8.23 S	138.51 E
Momčilgrad	38	41.32 N	25.25 E
Momence	216	41.10 N	87.39 W
Momfafa, Tanjung >	164	0.18 S	131.20 E
Momi	175g	17.55 S	177.17 E
Momignies	50	50.02 N	4.10 E
Mommark	41	54.55 N	10.03 E
Mommenheim	56	48.45 N	7.39 E
Momo	152	1.52 N	11.48 E
Momotombo, Volcán ∧[1]	236	12.26 N	86.33 W
Momozaka	270	34.51 N	135.02 E
Mompog Island I	116	13.31 N	122.11 E
Mompog Pass ꓴ	116	13.34 N	122.13 E
Mompono	152	0.04 N	21.48 E
Mompós	246	9.14 N	74.26 W
Momskij chrebet ⩘	74	66.00 N	146.00 E
Mon	110	18.31 N	96.38 E
Mon □[8]	110	17.30 N	97.00 E
Møn I	41	55.00 N	12.20 E
Mon ≃	110	20.20 N	94.54 E
Mona	200	39.48 N	111.51 W
Mona, Canal de la ꓴ	238	18.30 N	67.45 W
Mona, Isla de I	238	18.05 N	67.54 W
Mona, Punta >	236	9.38 N	82.37 W
Monaca	214	40.41 N	80.16 W
Monach, Sound of ꓴ	46	57.34 N	7.35 W
Monachovo	83	48.09 N	38.07 E
Monaci, Fiume dei ≃	70	37.24 N	14.48 E
Monaco	62	43.42 N	7.23 E
Monaco □[1], Europe	22	43.45 N	7.25 E
Monaco □[1], Europe	62	43.45 N	7.25 E
Monadhliath Mountains ⩘	46	57.10 N	4.00 W
Monadnock Mountain ∧	207	42.52 N	72.07 W
Monagas □[3]	246	9.20 N	63.00 W
Monaghan	48	54.15 N	6.58 W
Monaghan □[6]	48	54.10 N	7.00 W
Monagrillo	236	7.59 N	80.26 W
Monahans	196	31.35 N	102.53 W
Monahans Draw V	196	31.55 N	101.46 W
Monahans Sandhills State Park ♠	196	31.38 N	102.50 W
Monakino	89	43.24 N	133.29 E
Mona Lake ⊜	216	43.11 N	86.17 W
Monamolin	48	52.33 N	6.20 W
Monango	198	46.10 N	98.35 W
Monapo	154	14.57 S	40.17 E
Monapo ≃	154	15.07 S	40.33 E
Mona Quimbundo	152	9.55 S	19.58 E
Monar, Loch ⊜	46	57.25 N	5.06 W
Monarch	192	34.43 N	81.35 W
Monarch Mountain ∧	182	51.54 N	125.53 W
Monarch Pass)(	200	38.30 N	106.19 W
Monaro Range ⩘	171b	36.22 S	149.03 E
Monarto South	168b	35.08 S	139.08 E
Monaš	80	46.58 N	50.36 E
Monashee Mountains ⩘	182	50.30 N	118.30 W
Monashee Provincial Park ♠	182	50.28 N	118.11 W
Monash University ʊ[2]	274b	37.55 S	145.08 E
Monasterace	68	38.27 N	16.33 E
Monasterevin	48	53.07 N	7.02 W
Monasterolo di Savigliano	62	44.40 N	7.37 E
Monastir, It.	71	39.23 N	9.02 E
Monastir → Bitola, Jugo.	38	41.01 N	21.20 E
Monastir, Tun.	148	35.47 N	10.50 E
Monastir □[8]	148	35.15 N	10.45 E
Monastyrišče	78	49.00 N	29.49 E
Monastyriska	78	49.06 N	25.11 E
Monastyrščina	76	54.21 N	31.50 E
Monatélé	152	4.16 N	11.12 E
Mona Vale	170	33.41 S	151.18 E
Monbulk	274b	37.52 S	145.25 E
Monbulk Creek ≃	274b	37.54 S	145.15 E
Moncada, Esp.	266d	41.29 N	2.11 E
Moncada, Pil.	116	15.44 N	120.34 E
Moncalieri	62	45.00 N	7.41 E
Moncalvo	62	45.03 N	8.16 E
Monção, Bra.	250	3.30 S	45.15 W
Moncão, Port.	34	42.05 N	8.29 W
Monceau-sur-Sambre	50	50.25 N	4.22 E
Mončegorsk	24	67.54 N	32.58 E
Mönchdorf	61	48.21 N	14.48 E
Mönchengladbach	56	51.12 N	6.28 E
Mönchengladbach, Flughafen ⊠	263	51.14 N	6.29 E
Mönchhof	61	47.52 N	16.56 E
Monchique	34	37.19 N	8.33 W
Mönchweiler	58	48.06 N	8.25 E
Moncks Corner	192	33.11 N	80.00 W
Monclova	232	26.54 N	101.25 W
Moncontour	32	48.21 N	2.39 W
Moncoutant	32	46.43 N	0.35 W
Moncton	186	46.06 N	64.47 W
Mondaí	252	27.05 S	53.25 W
Mondaino	66	43.51 N	12.41 E
Mondavio	66	43.40 N	12.58 E
Monday ≃	252	25.33 S	54.41 W
Mondego ≃	34	40.09 N	8.52 W
Mondego, Cabo >	34	40.11 N	8.55 W
Mondello	70	38.13 N	13.20 E
Mondeodo	112	3.33 S	122.12 E
Mondeor	273d	26.17 S	28.00 E
Mondimbi	152	1.43 N	22.58 E
Mondo, Tan.	154	4.59 S	35.54 E
Mondo, Tchad	146	13.47 N	15.32 E
Mondolè, Monte ∧	62	44.13 N	7.46 E
Mondolfo	66	43.45 N	13.06 E
Mondombe	152	0.53 S	22.45 E
Mondoñedo	34	43.26 N	7.22 W
Mondorf-les-Bains	56	49.31 N	6.16 E
Mondoro	150	14.40 N	1.57 W
Mondoubleau	50	47.59 N	0.54 E
Mondovi	190	44.34 N	91.40 W
Mondragon, Fr.	62	44.14 N	4.43 E
Mondragon, Pil.	116	12.31 N	124.45 E
Mondragone	68	41.07 N	13.53 E
Mondrain Island I	162	34.08 S	122.15 E
Mondsee	64	47.52 N	13.21 E
Mondsee ⊜	64	47.49 N	13.23 E
Monds Island I	285	39.50 N	75.19 W
Mondy	88	51.40 N	100.59 E
Monee	216	41.25 N	87.45 W
Moneglia	62	44.14 N	9.30 E
Monemvasía	38	36.41 N	23.03 E
Monero	200	36.54 N	106.52 W
Moneron, ostrov I	89	46.17 N	141.15 E
Monesiglio	62	44.28 N	8.07 E
Monessen	214	40.08 N	79.53 W
Monesterio	34	38.05 N	6.16 W
Monestier-de-Clermont	62	44.54 N	5.38 E
Monetnyj	86	57.03 N	60.53 E
Monett	194	36.55 N	93.55 W
Monette	194	35.53 N	90.20 W
Money Creek ≃	216	40.40 N	88.58 W
Moneygall	48	52.53 N	7.57 W
Moneymore	48	54.42 N	6.40 W
Monfalcone	64	45.49 N	13.32 E
Monferrato □[9]	62	44.55 N	8.05 E
Monflanquin	32	44.32 N	0.46 E
Monforte	34	39.03 N	7.26 W
Monforte de Lemos	34	42.31 N	7.30 W
Monforte San Giorgio	70	38.09 N	15.23 E
Monfort Heights	218	39.12 N	84.37 W
Monga	152	4.12 N	22.49 E
Mongaguá	256	24.06 S	46.37 W
Mongai-Musenge	152	4.04 S	19.34 E
Mongala ≃	152	1.53 N	19.46 E
Mongalla	154	5.12 N	31.46 E
Mongalla Game Reserve ◆[4]	154	5.12 N	31.33 E
Mongandjo	152	1.21 N	24.20 E
Mongarlowe ≃	170	35.15 S	149.52 E
Mongat	266d	41.28 N	2.17 E
Mongaup ≃	210	41.25 N	74.45 W
Mongaup Valley	210	41.40 N	74.47 W
Mongbwalu	154	1.57 N	30.02 E
Mongbyŏn-ni	271b	37.40 N	126.44 E
Mong-cai	110	21.32 N	107.58 E
Monge ∧	266c	38.46 N	9.26 W
Monger, Îles II	186	51.05 N	58.45 W
Mongeri	150	8.19 N	11.44 W
Mongers Lake ⊜	162	29.15 S	117.05 E
Monggon Qulu	89	48.35 N	119.49 E
Monggŭmp'o	98	38.09 N	124.47 E
Möng Hai	110	20.46 N	99.49 E
Möng Hawm	110	23.51 N	98.20 E
Monghidoro	66	44.13 N	11.19 E
Möng Hpāyak	110	20.53 N	99.54 E
Möng Hsat	110	20.32 N	99.15 E
Monghyr	124	25.23 N	86.28 E
Monghyr □[5]	124	25.10 N	86.10 E
Mongi ≃	164	6.35 S	147.35 E
Mongiana	68	38.31 N	16.19 E
Mongibello → Etna, Monte ∧[1]	70	37.46 N	15.00 E
Mongiuffi	70	37.55 N	15.17 E
Möng Küng	110	21.36 N	97.32 E
Möng Ma	110	21.37 N	99.54 E
Möng Mit	110	23.07 N	96.41 E
Möng Nai	110	20.31 N	97.52 E
Möng Nawng	110	21.39 N	98.08 E
Mongo, Tchad	146	12.11 N	18.42 E
Mongo, In., U.S.	216	41.41 N	85.17 W
Mongo ≃	150	9.34 N	12.11 W
Mongoj	88	53.57 N	113.50 E
Mongol Altajn nuruu ⩘	90	46.30 N	93.00 E
Mongol Ard Uls → Mongolia □[1]	90	46.00 N	105.00 E
Mongolei → Mongolia □[1]	90	46.00 N	105.00 E
Mongol els ◆[2]	88	47.45 N	94.30 E
Mongolia (Mongol Ard Uls) □[1]	90	46.00 N	105.00 E
Mongolie → Mongolia □[1]	90	46.00 N	105.00 E
Mongomo	152	1.38 N	11.19 E
Möngön Mor't	88	48.11 N	108.29 E
Mongororo	146	12.01 N	22.28 E
Mongoumba	152	3.38 N	18.36 E
Möng Pai	110	19.44 N	97.05 E
Möng Pan	110	20.19 N	98.22 E
Möng Pawn	110	20.49 N	97.28 E
Möng Ping	110	22.22 N	99.02 E
Mongpong ≃	116	12.44 N	120.48 E
Mongrando	62	45.31 N	8.00 E
Mongrove, Punta >	234	17.56 N	102.11 W
Möng Si	110	23.40 N	98.23 E
Mong Tung Hang	271d	22.20 N	114.02 E
Mongu	152	15.15 S	23.09 E
Môngua	152	16.43 S	15.23 E
Monguelfo (Welsberg)	64	46.45 N	12.06 E
Monguno	146	12.40 N	13.38 E
Möng Yai	110	22.25 N	98.02 E
Möng Yawng	110	21.11 N	100.22 E
Monheim, B.R.D.	56	48.50 N	10.51 E
Monheim, B.R.D.	56	51.05 N	6.52 E
Moniaive	44	55.12 N	3.55 W
Mönichkirchen	61	47.31 N	16.02 E
Monico	190	45.34 N	89.09 W
Monida Pass)(	202	44.33 N	112.18 W
Mon Idée	50	49.53 N	4.23 E
Monie	152	4.00 S	17.22 E
Monie Bay ⊂	208	38.13 N	75.51 W
Monie Creek ≃	208	38.14 N	75.50 W
Monifieth	46	56.29 N	2.49 W
Monimail	46	56.18 N	3.08 W
Moninger	214	40.14 N	80.13 W
Monino	82	55.50 N	38.11 E
Moniquirá	246	5.52 N	73.36 W
Mõniste	76	57.35 N	26.33 E
Monistrol-d'Allier	62	44.57 N	3.38 E
Monistrol-sur-Loire	62	45.17 N	4.10 E
Monitor Range ⩘	204	38.45 N	116.30 W
Monitor Valley V	204	39.00 N	116.40 W
Monívea	48	53.23 N	8.43 W
Monjolo	256	22.49 S	42.57 W
Monk, Pointe >	275a	45.29 N	73.57 W
Monkayo	116	7.50 N	126.03 E
Mönkebude	54	53.46 N	13.57 E
Monken Hadley ◆[8]	260	51.40 N	0.11 W
Monkey Bay	154	14.05 S	34.55 E
Monkey Point >	236	11.36 N	83.39 W
Monkey River	236	16.22 N	88.29 W
Mońki	30	53.24 N	22.49 E
Monkira	166	24.49 S	140.34 E
Monkoto	152	1.38 S	20.39 E
Monks Heath	262	53.16 N	2.14 W
Monkton	212	43.35 N	81.05 W
Monmouth, Wales, U.K.	42	51.50 N	2.43 W
Monmouth, Il., U.S.	190	40.54 N	90.38 W
Monmouth, In., U.S.	216	40.52 N	84.57 W
Monmouth, Or., U.S.	202	44.50 N	123.13 W
Monmouth □[6]	208	40.16 N	74.17 W
Monmouth Beach	276	40.19 N	73.58 W
Monmouth Hills	276	40.24 N	74.00 W
Monmouth Junction	208	40.22 N	74.32 W
Monmouth Mountain ∧	182	51.00 N	123.47 W
Monnickendam	52	52.27 N	5.02 E
Monnow ≃	42	51.48 N	2.42 W
Mono □[5]	150	6.45 N	1.50 E
Mono □[6]	226	38.18 N	119.22 W
Mono ≃	150	6.17 N	1.51 E
Mono, Caño ≃	246	4.25 N	67.47 W
Monobe	96	33.42 N	133.53 E
Monobe ≃	96	33.32 N	133.41 E
Monocacy ≃	208	39.13 N	77.27 W
Monocacy Station	208	40.16 N	75.46 W
Monogarovo	82	54.42 N	38.45 E
Mono Island I	175e	7.21 S	155.34 E
Mono Lake ⊜	204	38.00 N	119.00 W
Monolith	228	35.07 N	118.22 W
Monomoy Island I	207	41.35 N	69.59 W
Monomoy Point >	207	41.33 N	70.02 W
Monon	216	40.52 N	86.52 W
Monona, Ia., U.S.	190	43.03 N	91.23 W
Monona, Wi., U.S.	216	43.03 N	89.20 W
Monona, Lake ⊜	216	43.03 N	89.22 W
Monongahela	214	40.12 N	79.55 W
Monongahela ≃	188	40.27 N	80.00 W
Monongahela Brook ≃	285	39.47 N	75.09 W
Monopoli	68	40.57 N	17.19 E
Monor	30	47.21 N	19.27 E
Mono Road Station	275b	43.51 N	79.51 W
Monos ⊥	232	18.27 N	89.02 W
Monóvar	34	38.26 N	0.50 W
Monowai, Lake ⊜	172	45.52 S	167.27 E
Monponsett	207	42.01 N	70.50 W
Monponsett Pond ⊜	283	42.01 N	70.51 W
Monreal	34	42.42 N	1.30 W
Monreal del Campo	34	40.47 N	1.21 W
Monreale	70	38.05 N	13.17 E
Monreale, Castello di ⊥	71	39.38 N	8.49 E
Monroe, Ct., U.S.	207	41.19 N	73.12 W
Monroe, Fl., U.S.	220	25.52 N	81.06 W
Monroe, Ga., U.S.	192	33.47 N	83.42 W
Monroe, In., U.S.	216	40.44 N	84.56 W
Monroe, Ia., U.S.	190	41.31 N	93.06 W
Monroe, La., U.S.	194	32.30 N	92.07 W
Monroe, Mi., U.S.	214	41.54 N	83.23 W
Monroe, Ne., U.S.	198	41.28 N	97.35 W
Monroe, N.J., U.S.	276	41.06 N	74.38 W
Monroe, N.Y., U.S.	210	41.19 N	74.11 W
Monroe, N.C., U.S.	192	34.59 N	80.32 W
Monroe, Oh., U.S.	218	39.26 N	84.21 W
Monroe, Or., U.S.	202	44.18 N	123.17 W
Monroe, Ut,. U.S.	200	38.37 N	112.07 W
Monroe, Va., U.S.	192	37.30 N	79.07 W
Monroe, Wa., U.S.	224	47.51 N	121.58 W
Monroe, Wi., U.S.	190	42.36 N	89.38 W
Monroe □[6], Fl., U.S.	220	25.10 N	81.10 W
Monroe □[6], Il., U.S.	219	38.20 N	90.09 W
Monroe □[6], In., U.S.	218	39.10 N	86.26 W
Monroe □[6], Mi., U.S.	216	41.55 N	83.26 W
Monroe □[6], Mo., U.S.	219	39.30 N	92.00 W
Monroe □[6], N.Y., U.S.	210	43.10 N	77.36 W
Monroe □[6], Pa., U.S.	210	40.59 N	75.12 W
Monroe, Lake ⊜	220	28.52 N	81.16 W
Monroe Bridge	207	42.43 N	72.56 W
Monroe Center, Ct., U.S.	207	41.20 N	73.12 W
Monroe Center, Il., U.S.	216	42.06 N	89.00 W
Monroe City, In., U.S.	194	38.36 N	87.21 W
Monroe City, Mo., U.S.	219	39.39 N	91.44 W
Monroe City, Tx., U.S.	222	29.47 N	94.35 W
Monroe Lake ⊜[1]	218	39.05 N	86.25 W
Monroe Manor	216	41.36 N	86.40 W
Monroeton	210	41.43 N	76.30 W
Monroeville, Al., U.S.	194	31.31 N	87.19 W
Monroeville, In., U.S.	216	40.58 N	84.52 W
Monroeville, N.J., U.S.	208	39.37 N	75.09 W
Monroeville, Oh., U.S.	214	41.14 N	82.41 W
Monroeville, Pa., U.S.	214	40.26 N	79.47 W
Monroeville Mall ◆[9]	279b	40.26 N	79.48 W
Monrovia, Liber.	150	6.18 N	10.47 W
Monrovia, Ca., U.S.	228	34.08 N	117.59 W
Monrovia, In., U.S.	218	39.34 N	86.28 W
Monrovia Mountain Park ♠	280	34.10 N	118.10 W
Monrovia Peak ∧	280	34.13 N	117.58 W
Mons (Bergen), Bel.	50	50.27 N	3.56 E
Mons, Fr.	62	43.41 N	6.43 E
Monsanto, Parque Florestal de ♠	266c	38.43 N	9.11 W
Monsarás, Ponta do >	255	19.35 S	39.45 W
Monschau	56	50.33 N	6.14 E
Monse	112	4.07 S	123.15 E
Monsefú	248	6.52 S	79.52 W
Monselice	64	45.14 N	11.45 E
Monsenhor Hipólito	250	6.59 S	41.07 W
Monsenhor Paulo	256	21.46 S	45.33 W
Monsenhor Tabosa	250	4.47 S	40.04 W
Monserrato	71	39.15 N	9.08 E
Monsey	210	41.06 N	74.04 W
Monsheim, B.R.D.	56	49.38 N	8.12 E
Mönsheim, B.R.D.	56	48.52 N	8.52 E
Møns Klint ⌂[4]	41	54.58 N	12.33 E
Monsols	58	46.13 N	4.31 E
Monson, Me., U.S.	188	45.17 N	69.30 W
Monson, Ma., U.S.	207	42.06 N	72.19 W
Monster	52	52.02 N	4.10 E
Mönsterås	26	57.02 N	16.26 E
Monsummano Terme	66	43.52 N	10.49 E
Montà	62	44.48 N	7.57 E
Montabaur	56	50.26 N	7.50 E
Montabaur □[5]	56	50.30 N	7.40 E
Montafon V	58	47.02 N	9.57 E
Montagano	66	41.39 N	14.40 E
Montagnana	64	45.14 N	11.28 E
Montagnareale	70	38.07 N	14.57 E
Montagne d'Ambre, Parque National de la ♠	157b	12.40 S	49.05 E
Montagnola ⩘	66	43.17 N	11.11 E
Montagrier	32	45.16 N	0.29 E
Montagu	158	33.45 S	20.08 E
Montague, P.E., Can.	186	46.10 N	62.39 W
Montague, Ca., U.S.	204	41.43 N	122.31 W
Montague, Ma., U.S.	207	42.32 N	72.32 W
Montague, Mi., U.S.	190	43.25 N	86.21 W
Montague, Tx., U.S.	196	33.40 N	97.43 W
Montague, Isla I	232	31.45 N	114.48 W
Montague City	207	42.35 N	72.35 W
Montague Island I	180	60.00 N	147.30 W
Montague Peak ∧	180	60.15 N	147.01 W
Montagu Island I	18	58.25 S	26.20 W
Montaigle, Château de ⊥	56	50.18 N	4.49 E
Montaigu	32	46.59 N	1.19 W
Montaigut-en-Combraille	32	46.11 N	2.48 E
Montainville	261	48.53 N	1.52 E
Montaione	66	43.33 N	10.55 E
Montaj-Taš	85	42.06 N	68.58 E
Montalba	222	31.53 N	95.38 W
Montalbán	34	40.50 N	0.48 W
Montalbancito	286c	10.28 N	66.59 W
Montalbano Elicona	70	38.02 N	15.01 E
Montalbano Ionico	68	40.17 N	16.34 E
Montalcino	66	43.03 N	11.29 E
Montaldo di Cosola	62	44.40 N	9.11 E
Montale	66	43.56 N	11.01 E

Symbol	English	Deutsch	Español	Français	Português
≃	River	Fluss	Río	Rivière	Rio
≊	Canal	Kanal	Canal	Canal	Canal
⌊	Waterfall, Rapids	Wasserfall, Stromschnellen	Cascada, Rápidos	Chute d'eau, Rapides	Cascata, Rápidos
ꓴ	Strait	Meeresstrasse	Estrecho	Détroit	Estreito
⊂	Bay, Gulf	Bucht, Golf	Bahía, Golfo	Baie, Golfe	Baía, Golfo
⊜	Lake, Lakes	See, Seen	Lago, Lagos	Lac, Lacs	Lago, Lagos
≡	Swamp	Sumpf	Pantano	Marais	Pântano
⊓	Ice Features, Glacier	Eis- und Gletscherformen	Accidentes Glaciales	Formes glaciaires	Acidentes glaciares
⍑	Other Hydrographic Features	Andere Hydrographische Objekte	Otros Elementos Hidrográficos	Autres données hydrographiques	Outros acidentes hidrográficos
✢	Submarine Features	Untermeerische Objekte	Accidentes Submarinos	Formes de relief sous-marin	Acidentes submarinos
□	Political Unit	Politische Einheit	Unidad Politica	Entité politique	Unidade política
ʊ	Cultural Institution	Kulturelle Institution	Institución Cultural	Institution culturelle	Institução cultural
⊥	Historical Site	Historische Stätte	Sitio Histórico	Site historique	Sitio histórico
♠	Recreational Site	Erholungs- und Ferienort	Sitio de Recreo	Centre de loisirs	Area de Lazer
⊠	Airport	Flughafen	Aeropuerto	Aéroport	Aeroporto
■	Military Installation	Militäranlage	Instalación Militar	Installation militaire	Instalação militar
◆	Miscellaneous	Verschiedenes	Misceláneo	Divers	Diversos

ENGLISH — Name / Page / Lat.°′ / Long.°′
DEUTSCH — Name / Seite / Breite°′ / Länge°′ E = Ost

Montalegre 34 41.49 N 7.48 W
Montalet-le-Bois 261 49.03 N 1.50 E
Montalieu-Vercieu 62 45.49 N 5.24 E
Montallegro 70 37.23 N 13.21 E
Mont Alto 208 39.50 N 77.33 W
Montalto ∧ 68 38.10 N 15.55 E
Montalto delle Marche 66 42.59 N 13.36 E
Montalto di Castro 66 42.21 N 11.37 E
Montalto Ligure 62 43.56 N 7.51 E
Montalto Uffugo 68 39.25 N 16.10 E
Montalvin Manor 226 37.59 N 122.21 W
Montalvo 228 34.15 N 119.12 W
Montana, Schw. 58 46.18 N 7.29 E
Montana, Ak., U.S. 180 62.05 N 150.04 W
Montana □3, U.S. 178 47.00 N 110.00 W
Montana □3, U.S. 202 47.00 N 110.00 W
Montana de Oro State Park ♠ 226 35.15 N 120.50 W
Montana Indian Reserve ➔4 182 52.43 N 113.25 W
Montanaro 62 45.14 N 7.51 E
Montánchez 34 39.13 N 6.09 W
Montandon 210 40.58 N 76.51 W
Montano Antilia 68 40.10 N 15.22 E
Montara 226 37.33 N 122.31 W
Montara Beach ♠ 282 37.33 N 122.31 W
Montara Mountain ⋏ 282 37.32 N 122.27 W
Montargil 34 39.05 N 8.10 W
Montargis 50 48.00 N 2.45 E
Montataire 50 49.16 N 2.26 E
Montauban 32 44.01 N 1.21 E
Montauban, Lac ⊜ 206 46.52 N 72.10 W
Montauban-les-Mines 206 46.50 N 72.20 W
Montauk 207 41.02 N 71.57 W
Montauk, Lake ⊜ 207 41.04 N 71.55 W
Montauk Point › 207 41.04 N 71.52 W
Montauroux 62 43.37 N 6.46 E
Monta Vista 226 37.19 N 122.03 W
Montazzoli 66 41.57 N 14.26 E
Montbard 50 47.37 N 4.20 E
Montbarrey 58 47.01 N 5.39 E
Montbazon 50 47.17 N 0.43 E
Montbéliard 58 47.31 N 6.48 E
Mont Belvieu 222 29.50 N 94.53 W
Montbenoît 58 46.59 N 6.28 E
Mont Blanc, Tunnel du ➔5 58 45.50 N 6.53 E
Montblanch 34 41.22 N 1.10 E
Mont-Bonvillers 56 49.20 N 5.51 E
Montbovon 58 46.29 N 7.03 E
Montbozon 58 47.28 N 6.16 E
Montbrison 62 45.36 N 4.03 E
Montbron 32 45.40 N 0.30 E
Montbronn 56 48.59 N 7.19 E
Montcalm □6 206 46.20 N 74.20 W
Montceau-les-Mines 58 46.40 N 4.22 E
Montcenis 58 46.47 N 4.23 E
Mont Cenis, Col du)(62 45.15 N 6.54 E
Mont Cenis, Lac du ⊜ 62 45.14 N 6.55 E
Montcevelles, Lac ⊜ 186 51.07 N 60.38 W
Montchanin, Fr. 58 46.45 N 4.27 E
Montchanin, De., U.S. 285 39.47 N 75.35 W
Montchauvet 261 48.54 N 1.38 E
Montclair, Ca., U.S. 228 34.06 N 117.41 W
Montclair, N.J., U.S. 210 40.49 N 74.12 W
Montclair State College ⊕2 276 40.51 N 74.12 W
Mont Clare 285 40.08 N 75.30 W
Montcornet 50 49.41 N 4.01 E
Montdale 210 41.32 N 75.37 W
Mont-de-Marsan 32 43.53 N 0.30 W
Montdidier 50 49.39 N 2.34 E
Mont-Dore 175f 22.16 S 166.34 E
Monte, Castel del ⊥ 68 41.05 N 16.16 E
Monte, Laguna del ⊜, Arg. 252 37.00 S 62.28 W
Monte, Laguna del ⊜, Arg. 258 35.28 S 58.49 W
Montea ∧ 68 39.40 N 15.57 E
Monte Adone, Galleria di ➔5 64 44.21 N 11.25 E
Monteagle 194 35.15 N 85.50 W
Monteagudo 248 19.49 S 63.59 W
Monte Albán ⊥ 234 17.02 N 96.45 W
Monte Alegre, Bra. 250 2.01 S 54.04 W
Monte Alegre, Bra. 250 6.04 S 35.20 W
Monte Alegre de Goiás 255 13.14 S 47.10 W
Monte Alegre de Minas 255 18.52 S 48.52 W
Monte Alegre de Sergipe 250 10.02 S 37.33 W
Monte Alegre do Piauí 250 9.46 S 45.18 W
Monte Alegre do Sul 256 22.40 S 46.41 W
Monte Azul 255 15.09 S 42.53 W
Monte Azul Paulista 255 20.55 S 48.38 W
Montebello, P.Q., Can. 206 45.39 N 74.56 W
Montebello, It. 62 45.00 N 9.06 E
Montebello, P.R. 240m 18.22 N 66.31 W
Montebello, Ca., U.S. 228 34.00 N 118.06 W
Montebello Iónico 68 37.59 N 15.45 E
Montebello Islands II 162 20.25 S 115.32 E
Montebello Vicentino 64 45.27 N 11.23 E
Montebelluna 64 45.47 N 12.03 E
Monte Belo 256 21.20 S 46.23 W
Montebruno 62 44.31 N 9.15 E
Monte Buey 252 32.55 S 62.27 W
Montecalvo Irpino 68 41.11 N 15.02 E
Monte Campatri 267a 41.48 N 12.44 E
Montecarlo 252 26.34 S 54.47 W
Monte Carlo ➔8 62 43.44 N 7.25 E
Montecarotto 66 43.31 N 13.04 E
Monte Caseros 252 30.15 S 57.39 W
Montecassiano 66 43.21 N 13.26 E
Montecassino, Abbazia di ⊕1 66 41.29 N 13.48 E
Montecastrilli 66 42.39 N 12.29 E
Montecatini-Terme 66 43.53 N 10.46 E
Monte Cavallo 66 42.59 N 13.00 E
Montecchio 66 43.51 N 12.46 E
Montecchio Emilia 64 44.42 N 10.27 E
Montecchio Maggiore 64 45.30 N 11.24 E
Montecelio 66 42.01 N 12.44 E
Montechiaro d'Asti 62 45.01 N 8.07 E
Montechiarugolo 64 44.42 N 10.25 E
Monte Chingolo ➔8 288 34.45 S 58.20 W
Monteciccardo 66 43.49 N 12.48 E
Montecilfone 66 41.54 N 14.50 E
Montecillos, Cordillera de ⋏ 236 14.25 N 87.51 W
Montecito 204 34.26 N 119.37 W
Monte Comán 252 34.36 S 67.54 W
Montecorice 68 40.14 N 14.59 E
Montecorvino Pugliano 68 40.41 N 14.57 E
Montecorvino Rovella 68 40.42 N 14.59 E
Montecosaro 66 43.19 N 13.37 E
Monte Creek 182 50.39 N 119.57 W
Montecreto 64 44.14 N 10.41 E
Montecristi 246 1.03 S 80.40 W
Monte Cristo 248 14.43 S 61.14 W
Monte Cristo, Cerro ∧ 236 14.25 N 89.21 W
Montecristo, Isola di I 36 42.20 N 10.19 E
Montecuccolo ⊕1 64 44.19 N 10.50 E
Montedinove 66 42.58 N 13.35 E
Monte di Procida 68 40.48 N 14.03 E
Monte do Carmo 250 10.45 S 48.07 W
Montedoro 70 37.27 N 13.49 E
Monte Escobedo 234 22.18 N 103.35 W
Monte Estoril 266c 38.42 N 9.24 W
Montefalcione 68 40.58 N 14.53 E
Montefalco 66 42.54 N 12.39 E
Montefalcone di Val Fortore 68 41.20 N 15.00 E
Montefano 66 43.25 N 13.26 E
Montefeltro ➔1 66 43.50 N 12.15 E
Montefiascone 66 42.32 N 12.02 E
Montefiorino 64 44.22 N 10.37 E
Monteforte d'Alpone 64 45.25 N 11.17 E
Monteforte Irpino 68 40.54 N 14.42 E
Montefrío 34 37.19 N 4.01 W
Montegallo 66 42.50 N 13.19 E
Montegiordano 68 40.02 N 16.32 E
Montegiorgio 66 43.08 N 13.32 E
Monte Giovi, Passo di (Jaufen Pass))(64 46.50 N 11.19 E
Montego Bay 241q 18.28 N 77.55 W
Montegranaro 66 43.14 N 13.38 E
Monte Grande 252 30.06 S 70.31 W
Monte Grande, Aeródromo ⊠ 288 34.48 S 58.28 W
Monte Grimano 66 43.52 N 12.29 E
Montegrotto Terme 64 45.19 N 11.46 E
Montegut 194 29.28 N 90.33 W
Monteiasi 68 40.30 N 17.23 E
Monteiro 250 7.53 S 37.07 W
Monteiro Lobato 256 22.58 S 45.50 W
Monteith, Mount ∧ 182 55.45 N 122.30 W
Montejicar 34 37.34 N 3.30 W
Montejinni 164 16.40 S 131.45 E
Montelavar 266c 38.51 N 9.20 W
Monteleone di Puglia 68 41.10 N 15.15 E
Monteleone di Spoleto 66 42.39 N 12.58 E
Monteleone Rocco Doria 71 40.29 N 8.34 E
Monteleone Sabino 66 42.14 N 12.51 E
Montelepre 70 38.05 N 13.10 E
Montelíbano 246 8.05 N 75.29 W
Montélimar 62 44.34 N 4.45 E
Montelindo ≃ 252 23.56 S 57.12 W
Montella 68 40.51 N 15.01 E
Montellano 34 37.00 N 5.34 W
Montello, Nv., U.S. 204 41.15 N 114.11 W
Montello, Wi., U.S. 190 43.47 N 89.19 W
Monteluco ⊕1 66 42.43 N 12.45 E
Montelungo 64 44.24 N 9.54 E
Montelupo Fiorentino 66 43.44 N 11.01 E
Montemaggiore Belsito 70 37.51 N 13.46 E
Montemagno 62 44.59 N 8.20 E
Monte Maíz 252 33.12 S 62.36 W
Montemarano 68 40.55 N 15.00 E
Montemarciano 66 43.38 N 13.19 E
Montemayor, Meseta de ⋏1 254 44.20 S 66.10 W
Montemesola 68 40.34 N 17.20 E
Montemiletto 68 41.01 N 14.54 E
Montemilone 68 41.02 N 15.38 E
Montemor 266c 38.49 N 9.12 W
Montemor ∧ 266c 38.49 N 9.12 W
Montemorelos 232 25.12 N 99.49 W
Montemor-o-Novo 34 38.39 N 8.13 W
Montemor-o-Vehlo 34 40.10 N 8.41 W
Montemurro 68 40.18 N 15.59 E
Montendre 32 45.17 N 0.24 W
Montenegro 252 29.42 S 51.28 W
Montenegro → Crna Gora □3 38 42.30 N 19.18 E
Montenero 66 43.30 N 10.21 E
Montenero ∧ 68 39.13 N 16.35 E
Montenero di Bisaccia 66 41.57 N 14.47 E
Monteodorisio 66 42.05 N 14.39 E
Monte Oliveto Maggiore, Abbazia del ⊕1 66 43.12 N 11.32 E
Monte Pascoal, Parque Nacional de ♠ 255 16.54 S 39.24 W
Monte Patria 252 30.42 S 70.58 W
Montepescali 66 42.53 N 11.05 E
Monte Porzio Catone 267a 41.49 N 12.43 E
Monteprandone 66 42.55 N 13.50 E
Montepuez 154 13.07 S 39.00 E
Montepuez ≃ 154 12.32 S 40.27 E
Montepulciano 66 43.05 N 11.47 E
Monte Quemado 252 25.48 S 62.52 W
Monterado 112 0.45 N 109.08 E
Monterchi 66 43.29 N 12.07 E
Montereale 66 42.31 N 13.15 E
Montereale Valcellina 64 46.10 N 12.39 E
Montereau 50 47.51 N 2.34 E
Montereau-Faut-Yonne 50 48.23 N 2.57 E
Montereau-sur-le-Jard 261 48.35 N 2.40 E
Monterey, Ca., U.S. 226 36.36 N 121.53 W
Monterey, In., U.S. 216 41.09 N 86.28 W
Monterey, Ky., U.S. 218 38.25 N 84.52 W
Monterey, Ma., U.S. 207 42.10 N 73.12 W
Monterey, N.Y., U.S. 210 42.18 N 77.03 W
Monterey, Tn., U.S. 194 36.08 N 85.16 W
Monterey, Va., U.S. 188 38.24 N 79.34 W
Monterey □6 226 36.40 N 121.38 W
Monterey Bay ⊂ 226 36.45 N 121.55 W
Monterey Park 228 34.03 N 118.07 W
Monterey Peninsula Airport ⊠ 226 36.35 N 121.51 W
Montería 246 8.46 N 75.53 W
Monteriggioni 66 43.23 N 11.13 E
Montero 248 17.20 S 63.15 W
Monte Romano 66 42.16 N 11.54 E
Monteroni d'Arbia 66 43.14 N 11.25 E
Monteroni di Lecce 68 40.19 N 18.06 E
Monteros 252 27.10 S 65.30 W
Monterosso al Mare 62 44.09 N 9.39 E
Monterosso Almo 70 37.05 N 14.46 E
Monterosso Calabro 68 38.43 N 16.17 E
Monterotondo 66 42.03 N 12.37 E
Monterotondo Marittimo 66 43.09 N 10.51 E
Monterrey, Méx. 232 25.40 N 100.19 W
Monterrey, Méx. 234 16.05 N 93.23 W
Monterrico, Hipódromo de ♠ 286d 12.06 S 76.59 W
Monterubbiano 66 43.05 N 13.43 E
Montes Altos 250 5.50 S 47.04 W
Monte San Biagio 66 41.21 N 13.21 E
Monte San Giovanni Campano 66 41.38 N 13.31 E
Montesano, It. 36 40.16 N 15.43 E
Montesano, Wa., U.S. 224 46.58 N 123.36 W
Montesano sulla Marcellana 68 40.16 N 15.42 E
Monte San Savino 66 43.20 N 11.43 E
Monte Santa Maria Tiberina 66 43.26 N 12.09 E
Monte Sant'Angelo 68 41.42 N 15.57 E
Monte Santo, Bra. 250 10.26 S 39.20 W
Monte Santo, Bra. 250 9.54 S 49.03 W
Monte Santo de Minas 256 21.12 S 46.59 W
Monte Santu, Capo di › 71 40.05 N 9.44 E
Montesarchio 68 41.04 N 14.38 E
Montescaglioso 68 40.33 N 16.40 E
Montes Claros 255 16.43 S 43.52 W
Montescudaio 66 43.18 N 10.40 E
Montese 64 44.16 N 10.56 E
Monte Sereno 226 37.15 N 122.01 W
Monte Sião 256 22.26 S 46.34 W
Montesilvano Marina 66 42.31 N 14.09 E
Montespaccato ➔8 267a 41.54 N 12.23 E
Montespertoli 66 43.38 N 11.04 E
Montespluga 58 46.30 N 9.21 E
Montesson 261 48.55 N 2.09 E
Montets, Col des)(58 46.00 N 6.55 E
Monteux 62 44.02 N 5.00 E
Montevago 70 37.42 N 12.58 E
Montevallo 194 33.06 N 86.51 W
Montevarchi 66 43.31 N 11.34 E
Monteverde 68 41.00 N 15.32 E
Monte Verde ≃ 256 21.55 S 43.33 W
Monteverde Nuovo ➔8 267a 41.51 N 12.27 E
Montevergine, Santuario di ⊕1 68 40.55 N 14.45 E
Montevideo, Mn., U.S. 198 44.56 N 95.43 W
Montevideo, Ur. 258 34.53 S 56.11 W
Montevideo □5 258 34.50 S 56.12 W
Monte Vista 200 37.34 N 106.08 W
Montévrain 261 48.53 N 2.45 E
Montezemolo 62 44.22 N 8.08 E
Montezuma, Ca., U.S. 282 38.05 N 121.53 W
Montezuma, Ga., U.S. 192 32.18 N 84.01 W
Montezuma, In., U.S. 194 39.47 N 87.22 W
Montezuma, Ia., U.S. 190 41.35 N 92.31 W
Montezuma, Ks., U.S. 198 37.35 N 100.26 W
Montezuma, N.Y., U.S. 210 43.00 N 76.42 W
Montezuma, Oh., U.S. 216 40.29 N 84.33 W
Montezuma Castle National Monument ♠ 200 34.38 N 110.49 W
Montezuma Creek ≃ 200 37.17 N 109.20 W
Montezuma Hills ⋏2 282 38.07 N 121.51 W
Montezuma Slough ≃ 226 38.04 N 121.52 W
Montfaucon, Fr. 56 49.17 N 5.08 E
Montfaucon, Fr. 62 45.10 N 4.18 E
Montfaucon, Schw. 58 47.17 N 7.03 E
Montfermeil 261 48.54 N 2.34 E
Montfleur 58 46.19 N 5.26 E
Montflorit 266d 41.29 N 2.08 E
Montfort, Fr. 32 48.08 N 1.58 W
Montfort, Wi., U.S. 190 42.58 N 90.25 W
Montfort-l'Amaury 50 48.47 N 1.49 E
Montfort-le-Rotrou 50 48.03 N 0.25 E
Montfort-sur-Risle 50 49.18 N 0.40 E
Montfrin 62 43.53 N 4.36 E
Montgé 261 49.02 N 2.45 E
Montgenèvre 62 44.56 N 6.43 E
Montgenèvre, Col de)(62 44.56 N 6.44 E
Montgeron 261 48.42 N 2.27 E
Montgeroult 261 49.05 N 2.00 E
Montgesoye 58 47.05 N 6.12 E
Montgomery → Sāhiwāl, Pāk. 123 30.40 N 73.06 E
Montgomery, Wales, U.K. 42 52.33 N 3.03 W
Montgomery, Al., U.S. 194 32.23 N 86.18 W
Montgomery, Il., U.S. 216 41.43 N 88.20 W
Montgomery, La., U.S. 194 31.40 N 92.53 W
Montgomery, Mi., U.S. 216 41.46 N 84.48 W
Montgomery, Mn., U.S. 190 44.26 N 93.34 W
Montgomery, N.Y., U.S. 210 41.31 N 74.14 W
Montgomery, Oh., U.S. 218 39.13 N 84.21 W
Montgomery, Pa., U.S. 210 41.10 N 76.52 W
Montgomery, Tx., U.S. 222 30.23 N 95.42 W
Montgomery, W.V., U.S. 188 38.11 N 81.19 W
Montgomery □6, Il., U.S. 219 39.09 N 89.29 W
Montgomery □6, Md., U.S. 208 39.05 N 77.09 W
Montgomery □6, Mo., U.S. 219 38.57 N 91.27 W
Montgomery □6, N.Y., U.S. 210 42.57 N 74.22 W
Montgomery □6, Oh., U.S. 218 39.45 N 84.15 W
Montgomery □6, Pa., U.S. 208 40.07 N 75.21 W
Montgomery □6, Tx., U.S. 222 30.18 N 95.30 W
Montgomery City 219 38.58 N 91.30 W
Montgomery Dam ➔6 214 40.39 N 80.24 W
Montgomery Knolls 284b 39.14 N 76.48 W
Montgomery Mall ➔9 284c 39.01 N 77.09 W
Montgomery Square 284c 39.04 N 77.09 W
Montgomeryville 285 40.15 N 75.15 W
Montgomeryville Airport ⊠ 285 40.15 N 75.14 W
Montguyon 32 45.13 N 0.11 W
Monthermé 56 49.53 N 4.44 E
Monthey 58 46.15 N 6.57 E
Monthois 56 49.19 N 4.43 E
Monthureux-sur-Saône 58 48.02 N 5.58 E
Monthyon 261 49.00 N 2.50 E
Monti 71 40.49 N 9.19 E
Monticelli d'Ongina 64 45.05 N 9.56 E
Monticello, Ar., U.S. 194 33.37 N 91.47 W
Monticello, Fl., U.S. 192 30.32 N 83.52 W
Monticello, Ga., U.S. 192 33.18 N 83.41 W
Monticello, Il., U.S. 194 40.01 N 88.34 W
Monticello, In., U.S. 216 40.44 N 86.45 W
Monticello, Ia., U.S. 190 42.14 N 91.11 W
Monticello, Ky., U.S. 194 36.49 N 84.50 W
Monticello, Mn., U.S. 190 45.18 N 93.47 W
Monticello, Ms., U.S. 194 31.33 N 90.06 W
Monticello, Mo., U.S. 219 40.07 N 91.42 W
Monticello, N.Y., U.S. 210 41.39 N 74.41 W
Monticello, Ut,. U.S. 200 37.52 N 109.20 W
Monticello, Wi., U.S. 190 42.44 N 89.35 W
Monticello ⊥ 188 38.00 N 78.30 W
Monticello Conte Otto 64 45.35 N 11.35 E
Monticello Dam ➔6 226 38.30 N 122.07 W
Monticello Woods 284c 38.47 N 77.10 W
Montichiari 64 45.25 N 10.23 E
Monticiano 66 43.08 N 11.11 E
Montiel, Campo de ≚ 34 38.46 N 2.44 W
Montier-en-Der 58 48.29 N 4.46 E
Montieri 66 43.08 N 11.01 E
Montieri, Poggio di ∧ 66 43.08 N 11.00 E
Montiers-sur-Saulx 58 48.32 N 5.16 E
Montignac 32 45.04 N 1.10 E
Montigny 58 48.31 N 6.48 E
Montigny-Devant-Sassey 56 49.26 N 5.09 E
Montigny-le-Bretonneux 261 48.46 N 2.02 E
Montigny-le-Roi 58 48.00 N 5.30 E
Montigny-lès-Cormeilles 261 48.59 N 2.12 E
Montigny-lès-Metz 56 49.06 N 6.09 E
Montigny-sur-Aube 58 47.57 N 4.46 E
Montijo, Esp. 34 38.55 N 6.37 W
Montijo, Pan. 236 7.59 N 81.03 W
Montijo, Port. 34 38.42 N 8.58 W
Montijo, Aeroporto ⊠ 266c 38.42 N 9.02 W
Montijo, Golfo de ⊂ 246 7.40 N 81.07 W
Montilla 34 37.35 N 4.38 W
Montividiu 255 17.24 S 51.14 W
Montivilliers 50 49.33 N 0.12 E
Montjay-la-Tour 261 48.55 N 2.40 E
Montjoie, Lac ⊜, P.Q., Can. 206 46.17 N 75.08 W
Montjoie, Lac ⊜, P.Q., Can. 206 45.25 N 72.06 W
Mont-Joli 186 48.35 N 68.11 W
Montjovet 62 45.43 N 7.40 E
Montjuich, Castillo de ⊥ 266d 41.22 N 2.10 E
Montjuich, Estadio de ♠ 266d 41.22 N 2.09 E
Montjuich, Faro de ➔5 266d 41.21 N 2.11 E
Montjuich, Parque de ♠ 266d 41.21 N 2.09 E
Mont-Laurier 176 46.33 N 75.30 W
Montlebon 58 47.02 N 6.37 E
Montlhéry 50 48.38 N 2.16 E
Montlhéry, Tour de ⊕ 261 48.38 N 2.16 E
Montlhéry, Tour de ♠ 261 48.38 N 2.16 E
Montlignon 261 49.01 N 2.17 E
Montlouet 261 48.31 N 1.43 E
Mont-Louis 32 42.31 N 2.07 E
Montlouis-sur-Loire 50 47.23 N 0.50 E
Montluçon 32 46.21 N 2.36 E
Montluel 62 45.51 N 5.03 E
Montmagny, P.Q., Can. 186 46.59 N 70.33 W
Montmagny, Fr. 261 48.58 N 2.21 E
Montmajour, Abbaye de ⊕1 62 43.43 N 4.40 E
Montmartre ➔8 261 48.53 N 2.21 E
Montmédy 56 49.31 N 5.22 E
Montmélian 62 45.30 N 6.04 E
Montmeló 266d 41.33 N 2.15 E
Montmerle-sur-Saône 58 46.05 N 4.46 E
Montmin 62 45.48 N 6.16 E
Montmirail, Fr. 50 48.52 N 3.32 E
Montmirail, Fr. 50 48.06 N 0.48 E
Montmirey-le-Château 58 47.13 N 5.32 E
Montmoreau-Saint-Cybard 32 45.24 N 0.08 E
Montmorenci 216 40.28 N 87.02 W
Montmorency 274b 37.43 S 145.07 E
Montmorency → Beauport 186 46.52 N 71.11 W
Montmorency 261 49.00 N 2.20 E
Montmorency ≃ 186 46.53 N 71.07 W
Montmorency, Forêt de ♠ 261 49.02 N 2.16 E
Montmorillon 32 46.26 N 0.52 E
Montmort 50 48.55 N 3.49 E
Monto 166 24.52 S 151.07 E
Montodine 62 45.17 N 9.42 E
Montoggio 62 44.31 N 9.03 E
Montoire-sur-le-Loir 50 47.45 N 0.52 E
Montone 66 43.22 N 12.20 E
Montone ≃, It. 64 44.24 N 12.14 E
Montone ≃, It. 66 43.22 N 12.20 E
Montopoli in Val d'Arno 66 43.40 N 10.45 E
Mont Orford, Parc du ♠ 206 45.22 N 72.05 W
Montorio al Vomano 66 42.35 N 13.38 E
Montorio nei Frentani 66 41.46 N 14.55 E
Montornés del Vallés 266d 41.33 N 2.16 E
Montoro 34 38.01 N 4.23 W
Mont'Orso, Galleria di ➔5 66 41.20 N 13.15 E
Montour □6 210 40.58 N 76.37 W
Montour Falls 210 42.20 N 76.50 W
Montour Run ≃, Pa., U.S. 279b 40.36 N 79.57 W
Montour Run ≃, Pa., U.S. 279b 40.31 N 80.08 W
Montoursville 210 41.15 N 76.55 W
Mont Park 274b 37.43 S 145.04 E
Montparnasse ➔5 261 48.51 N 2.19 E
Mont Peko, Parc National du ♠ 150 7.00 N 7.15 W
Montpelier, Jam. 241q 18.22 N 77.56 W
Montpelier, Id., U.S. 202 42.19 N 111.17 W
Montpelier, In., U.S. 216 40.33 N 85.16 W
Montpelier, Md., U.S. 284c 39.04 N 76.51 W
Montpelier, Ms., U.S. 194 33.43 N 88.56 W
Montpelier, Oh., U.S. 216 41.35 N 84.36 W
Montpelier, Vt., U.S. 188 44.15 N 72.34 W
Montpellier 62 43.36 N 3.53 E
Montpellier-Fréjorgues, Aéroport de ⊠ 62 43.33 N 4.00 E
Montpezat-sous-Bauzon 62 44.43 N 4.12 E
Mont-Pichet 261 48.53 N 2.54 E
Montpon-Ménesterol 32 45.00 N 0.10 E
Montpont-en-Bresse 58 46.33 N 5.09 E
Montréal, P.Q., Can. 206 45.31 N 73.34 W
Montréal, P.Q., Can. 275a 45.31 N 73.34 W
Montréal, Fr. 50 47.32 N 4.02 E
Montreal, Wi., U.S. 190 46.25 N 90.14 W
Montreal ≃, On., Can. 190 47.14 N 84.39 W
Montreal ≃, On., Can. 190 47.08 N 79.27 W
Montreal ≃, Sk., Can. 184 55.06 N 105.19 W
Montreal ≃, U.S. 190 46.44 N 90.25 W
Montréal, Base des Forces Canadiennes ■ 275a 45.31 N 73.25 W
Montréal, Île de I 206 45.30 N 73.40 W
Montréal, Université de ⊕2 275a 45.30 N 73.37 W
Montréal-Est 206 45.38 N 73.31 W
Montreal International Airport ⊠ 206 45.28 N 73.45 W
Montreal Lake 184 54.03 N 105.46 W
Montreal Lake ⊜ 184 54.20 N 105.40 W
Montreal Lake Indian Reserve ➔4 184 54.00 N 105.45 W
Montréal-Nord 206 45.36 N 73.38 W
Montréal-Quest 275a 45.27 N 73.39 W
Montreal Water Works Aqueduct ≖1 275a 45.26 N 73.36 W
Montrésor 50 47.09 N 1.12 E
Montresta 71 40.22 N 8.30 E
Montret 58 46.41 N 5.07 E
Montreuil 261 48.52 N 2.26 E
Montreuil-Bellay 32 47.08 N 0.09 W
Montreuil-sous-Bois 50 48.52 N 2.26 E
Montreuil-sur-Mer 50 50.28 N 1.46 E
Montreux 58 46.26 N 6.55 E
Montrevel-en-Bresse 58 46.20 N 5.08 E
Montrichard 50 47.21 N 1.11 E
Montriond 58 46.12 N 6.41 E
Mont-Rolland 206 45.57 N 74.07 W
Montrond-les-Bains 62 45.38 N 4.14 E
Montrose, Austl. 274b 37.49 S 145.21 E
Montrose, Scot., U.K. 46 56.43 N 2.29 W
Montrose, Ca., U.S. 228 34.12 N 118.13 W
Montrose, Co., U.S. 200 38.28 N 107.52 W
Montrose, Ia., U.S. 190 40.31 N 91.24 W
Montrose, Mi., U.S. 190 43.10 N 83.53 W
Montrose, N.Y., U.S. 210 41.15 N 73.56 W
Montrose, Oh., U.S. 214 41.08 N 81.37 W
Montrose, Pa., U.S. 210 41.50 N 75.52 W
Montrose, S.D., U.S. 198 43.41 N 97.11 W
Montrose Harbor ⊂ 278 41.58 N 87.38 W
Montrose Hill 279b 40.30 N 79.51 W
Montross 208 38.05 N 76.49 W
Montrouge 261 48.49 N 2.19 E
Mont-Royal 206 45.31 N 73.39 W
Mont Royal, Parc ♠ 275a 45.31 N 73.35 W
Mont Royal Tunnel ➔5 275a 45.31 N 73.38 W
Montry 261 48.53 N 2.50 E
Monts 50 47.17 N 0.37 E
Monts, Pointe des › 186 49.20 N 67.23 W
Mont-Saint-Aignan 50 49.28 N 1.05 E
Mont-Sainte-Anne, Parc du ♠ 186 47.08 N 70.55 W
Mont-Saint-Hilaire 206 45.34 N 73.11 W
Mont-Saint-Martin 56 49.32 N 5.47 E
Mont-Saint-Michel → Le Mont-Saint-Michel ⊕1 32 48.38 N 1.32 W
Mont-Saint-Vincent 58 46.38 N 4.29 E
Montsauche 50 47.13 N 4.01 E
Montsec 56 48.53 N 5.43 E
Montserrado □6 150 6.40 N 10.40 W
Montserrat □2, N.A. 230 16.45 N 62.12 W
Montserrat □2, N.A. 238 16.45 N 62.12 W
Montserrat, Monasterio de ⊕1 34 41.36 N 1.49 E
Montsoult 261 49.04 N 2.19 E
Montsûrs 28 48.08 N 0.33 W
Mont-sur-Vaudrey 58 46.58 N 5.36 E
Mont-Tremblant, Parc provincial du ♠ 206 46.42 N 74.20 W
Montuenga 34 41.03 N 4.37 W
Montvale, N.J., U.S. 276 41.02 N 74.01 W
Montvale, Va., U.S. 192 37.23 N 79.43 W
Montverde 220 28.36 N 81.41 W
Montville, Ct., U.S. 207 41.27 N 72.08 W
Montville, N.J., U.S. 276 40.54 N 74.23 W
Montville, Oh., U.S. 214 41.36 N 81.03 W
Montville Airpark ⊠ 276 40.56 N 74.20 W
Monument, S. Afr. 273d 26.06 S 27.43 E
Monument, Or., U.S. 202 44.49 N 119.25 W
Monument, Pa., U.S. 214 41.07 N 77.42 W
Monument Beach 207 41.43 N 70.36 W
Monument Draw V, U.S. 196 32.27 N 102.20 W
Monument Draw V, Tx., U.S. 196 30.51 N 102.33 W
Monument Hill State Historic Site ⊥ 222 29.53 N 96.54 W
Monumento 256 22.44 S 43.51 W
Monument Peak ∧, Co., U.S. 200 39.43 N 107.55 W
Monument Peak ∧, Id., U.S. 202 42.07 N 114.14 W
Monument Valley V 200 37.05 N 110.20 W
Monundilla, Mount ∧ 170 32.45 S 150.29 E
Monveda 152 2.57 N 21.27 E
Monymusk 46 57.13 N 2.31 W
Monyo 110 17.59 N 95.30 E
Monywa 110 22.05 N 95.08 E
Monza 62 45.35 N 9.16 E
Monze 154 16.16 S 27.28 E
Monzen 92 37.17 N 136.46 E
Monzie 46 56.24 N 3.48 W
Monzón, Esp. 34 41.55 N 0.12 E
Monzón, Perú 248 9.10 S 76.23 W
Moóca ➔8 287b 23.33 S 46.35 W
Moóca, Ribeirão da ≃ 287b 23.36 S 46.35 W
Moodie Island I 176 64.37 N 65.30 W
Moodus 207 41.30 N 72.27 W
Moodus Reservoir ⊜1 207 41.30 N 72.24 W
Moody 222 31.18 N 97.21 W
Moody Air Force Base ■ 192 30.59 N 83.11 W
Moody Wood Dale Airport ⊠ 278 41.59 N 87.58 W
Mooers 206 44.58 N 73.35 W
Mooi ≃, S. Afr. 158 28.45 S 30.34 E
Mooi ≃, S. Afr. 158 26.53 S 26.56 E
Mooirivier 158 29.13 S 29.50 E
Mook 52 51.45 N 5.54 E
Mookane 156 24.59 S 24.33 E
Mooketsi 156 23.35 S 30.05 E
Moolalloo Point › 168a 31.48 S 115.44 E
Moolawatana 166 29.55 S 139.43 E
Moolman 158 27.10 S 30.53 E
Mooloogool 162 26.06 S 119.05 E
Moon 214 40.31 N 80.14 W
Moon ≃ 212 45.08 N 79.59 W
Moon, Mountains of the → Ruwenzori Range ⋏ 154 0.23 N 29.54 E
Moonachie 276 40.50 N 74.02 W
Moonachie Creek ≃ 276 40.48 N 74.03 W
Moonah Creek ≃ 166 22.03 S 138.33 E
Moon Crest 279b 40.32 N 80.11 W
Moondarra Reservoir ⊜1 169 38.04 S 146.22 E
Moonee Valley Racecourse ♠ 274b 37.46 S 144.56 E
Moonie ≃ 166 29.19 S 148.43 E
Moon Island I, On., Can. 212 45.09 N 80.01 W
Moon Island I, Ma., U.S. 283 42.18 N 71.00 W
Moon Run 214 40.27 N 80.06 W
Moonta 168b 34.04 S 137.35 E
Moonyoonooka 162 28.47 S 114.43 E
Moor, Kepulauan II 164 2.57 S 135.45 E
Moora 162 30.39 S 116.00 E
Moorabbin 169 37.56 S 145.02 E
Moorabbin Airport ⊠ 274b 37.59 S 145.09 E
Mooraberree 166 25.14 S 140.59 E
Moorabool ≃ 169 38.09 S 144.19 E
Moorarie 162 25.56 S 117.35 E
Moorburg 52 53.17 N 7.53 E
Moorcroft 198 44.15 N 104.56 W
Moordorf 52 53.28 N 7.23 E
Moordrecht 52 51.59 N 4.40 E
Moore, Austl. 171a 26.53 S 152.18 E
Moore, Eng., U.K. 262 53.21 N 2.38 W
Moore, Id., U.S. 202 43.44 N 113.21 W
Moore, Mt., U.S. 202 46.58 N 109.41 W
Moore, Ok., U.S. 196 35.20 N 97.29 W
Moore, Tx., U.S. 196 29.03 N 99.01 W
Moore ≃ 162 31.22 S 115.29 E
Moore, Lake ⊜ 162 29.50 S 117.35 E
Moorea I 174s 17.32 S 149.50 W
Moorebank 274a 33.56 S 150.56 E
Moore Creek ≃ 212 45.29 N 77.58 W
Moorefield, Ky., U.S. 218 38.16 N 83.55 W
Moorefield, Oh., U.S. 214 40.12 N 81.10 W
Moorefield, W.V., U.S. 188 39.03 N 78.58 W
Moore Haven 220 26.49 N 81.05 W
Moore Haven Lock ➔5 220 26.51 N 81.05 W
Moore Lake ⊜, On., Can. 212 45.26 N 78.01 W
Moore Lake ⊜, On., Can. 212 44.48 N 78.48 W
Moore Lake ⊜, Mi., U.S. 281 42.37 N 83.36 W
Mooreland, In., U.S. 218 39.59 N 85.15 W
Mooreland, Ok., U.S. 196 36.26 N 99.12 W
Moore Park ♠ 274a 33.54 S 151.13 E
Moore Point › 275b 43.48 N 79.03 W
Moore Reservoir ⊜1 188 44.25 N 71.50 W
Mooresburg 210 40.59 N 76.43 W
Moores Creek National Battlefield ♠ 192 34.24 N 78.08 W
Moores Hill 218 39.06 N 85.05 W
Moore Station 222 32.11 N 95.35 W
Moorestown 208 39.58 N 74.56 W
Moorestown Mall ➔9 285 39.56 N 74.58 W
Mooresville, In., U.S. 218 39.36 N 86.22 W
Mooresville, N.C., U.S. 192 35.35 N 80.48 W
Mooreville 281 42.06 N 83.44 W
Moorfoot Hills ⋏2 46 55.45 N 3.02 W
Moorhead, Mn., U.S. 198 46.52 N 96.46 W
Moorhead, Ms., U.S. 194 33.27 N 90.30 W
Mooring 222 30.41 N 96.33 W
Mooringsport 194 32.41 N 93.57 W
Moormerland 52 53.20 N 7.27 E
Moorooka 171a 27.32 S 153.02 E
Mooroolbark 274b 37.47 S 145.19 E
Moorpark 228 34.17 N 118.53 W
Moorreesburg 158 33.08 S 18.40 E
Moorrege 52 53.40 N 9.39 E
Moorriem 52 53.15 N 8.19 E
Moorsel 50 50.57 N 4.06 E
Moorside 262 53.34 N 2.04 W
Moorslede 50 50.53 N 3.04 E
Moos → Moso, It. 64 46.41 N 12.23 E
Moos → Moso in Passiria, It. 64 46.50 N 11.10 E
Moosach ➔8 60 48.11 N 11.31 E
Moosbrunn 264b 48.01 N 16.28 E
Moosburg, B.R.D. 30 48.29 N 11.57 E
Moosburg, Öst. 61 46.39 N 14.10 E
Moosburg an der Isar 60 48.29 N 11.57 E
Moose ≃, Me., U.S. 188 45.40 N 69.42 W
Moose ≃, N.Y., U.S. 212 43.37 N 75.22 W
Moose Creek 206 45.15 N 74.58 W
Moose Creek ≃ 206 45.23 N 75.04 W
Moosehead Lake ⊜ 188 45.40 N 69.40 W
Mooseheart 216 41.49 N 88.20 W
Moose Heights 182 53.05 N 122.30 W
Moose Hill ∧2 283 42.07 N 71.13 W
Moose Island I 184 51.42 N 97.10 W
Moose Jaw 184 50.23 N 105.32 W
Moose Jaw ≃ 184 50.34 N 105.17 W
Moose Lake, Mb., Can. 184 53.43 N 100.20 W
Moose Lake, Mn., U.S. 190 46.27 N 92.45 W
Moose Lake ⊜, Ab., Can. 182 54.15 N 110.55 W
Moose Lake ⊜, Mb., Can. 184 53.55 N 99.45 W
Moose Lake ⊜, On., Can. 212 45.09 N 78.28 W
Mooselookmeguntic Lake ⊜ 188 44.53 N 70.48 W
Moose Mountain ∧ 184 49.45 N 102.37 W
Moose Mountain Creek ≃ 184 49.12 N 102.10 W
Moose Mountain Provincial Park ♠ 184 49.48 N 102.25 W
Moose Pass 180 60.29 N 149.22 W
Moosomin 184 50.07 N 101.40 W
Moosomin Indian Reserve ➔4 184 53.06 N 108.14 W
Moosonee 176 51.17 N 80.39 W
Moosup 207 41.42 N 71.52 W
Mooti 144 0.35 N 41.56 E
Moots Creek ≃ 216 40.32 N 86.47 W
Mopane 156 22.37 S 29.52 E
Mopeia Velha 156 17.59 S 35.44 E
Mopipi 156 21.07 S 24.55 E
Mopo 100 33.07 N 113.02 E
Moppo → Mokp'o 98 34.48 N 126.22 E
Mopti 150 14.30 N 4.12 W
Mopti □4 150 14.40 N 4.15 W
Moqokorei 144 4.04 N 46.08 E
Moquegua 248 17.12 S 70.56 W
Moquegua □5 248 16.50 S 70.55 W
Mór 30 47.23 N 18.12 E
Mor ≃ 126 24.01 N 88.03 E
Mòr, Glen V 46 57.10 N 4.40 W
Mor, Sgurr ∧ 46 57.42 N 5.03 W
Mora, Cam. 146 11.03 N 14.09 E
Mora, Esp. 34 39.41 N 3.46 W
Mora, India 272c 18.54 N 72.56 E
Mora, Port. 34 38.56 N 8.10 W
Mora, Sve. 26 61.00 N 14.33 E
Mora, Mn., U.S. 190 45.52 N 93.17 W
Mora, N.M., U.S. 200 35.58 N 105.19 W
Mora ≃ 196 35.44 N 104.23 W
Mora, Arroyo de la ≃ 196 34.05 N 104.18 W
Moraby 40 60.23 N 15.35 E
Morača, Manastir ⊕1 38 42.44 N 19.20 E
Morada 226 38.01 N 121.15 W
Morādābād 124 28.50 N 78.47 E
Morādābād □5 124 28.50 N 78.30 E
Morada Nova 250 5.07 S 38.23 W
Morada Nova de Minas 255 18.37 S 45.22 W
Mora de Rubielos 34 40.15 N 0.45 W
Morado Primero, Cerro ∧ 252 22.49 S 65.26 W
Moraduccio 66 44.10 N 11.29 E
Morafenobe 157b 17.49 S 44.55 E
Morąg 30 53.56 N 19.56 E
Moraga 226 37.50 N 122.08 W
Mórahalom 30 46.13 N 19.54 E
Moraine 218 39.42 N 84.13 W
Moraine Hills State Park ♠ 216 42.18 N 88.15 W
Moraine State Park ♠ 214 40.56 N 80.07 W
Morainvilliers 261 48.56 N 1.56 E
Morākhi ≃ 126 24.01 N 88.10 E
Mor'akovskij Zaton 86 56.45 N 84.41 E
Moral de Calatrava 34 38.50 N 3.35 W
Moraleda, Canal de ʉ 254 44.30 S 73.30 W
Morales, Guat. 236 15.29 N 88.49 W
Morales, Perú 248 6.28 S 76.28 W
Morales, Arroyo ≃ 258 34.48 S 58.36 W
Morales, Laguna de ⊂ 234 23.35 N 97.47 W
Moramanga 157b 18.56 S 48.12 E
Moran, Ks., U.S. 198 37.54 N 95.10 W
Moran, Mi., U.S. 190 45.59 N 84.49 W
Moran, Tx., U.S. 196 32.33 N 99.10 W
Moran ≃ 164 15.16 S 125.33 E
Morangis 261 48.42 N 2.20 E
Morangup Hill ∧2 168a 31.41 S 116.19 E
Morann 214 40.48 N 78.21 W
Morano Calabro 68 39.50 N 16.08 E
Morano sul Po 62 45.10 N 8.22 E
Moran State Park ♠ 224 48.41 N 122.52 W
Morant Bay 241q 17.53 N 76.25 W
Morant Cays II 238 17.24 N 75.59 W
Morant Point › 241q 17.55 N 76.10 W
Morar, Loch ⊜ 46 56.57 N 5.43 W
Mörarp 41 56.04 N 12.52 E
Morasverdes 34 40.36 N 6.16 W
Morat, Lac de (Murtensee) ⊜ 58 46.55 N 7.05 E
Moratalla 34 38.12 N 1.53 W
Morattico 208 37.47 N 76.37 W
Moratuwa 122 6.46 N 79.53 E
Morava □9 30 49.30 N 17.00 E
Morava (March) ≃ 30 48.10 N 16.59 E
Moravia, C.R. 236 9.51 N 83.26 W
Moravia, Ia., U.S. 190 40.53 N 92.48 W
Moravia, N.Y., U.S. 210 42.42 N 76.25 W
Moravia → Morava □9 30 49.20 N 17.00 E
Moravian Indian Reserve ➔4 214 42.34 N 81.53 W
Moravská Dyje ≃ 61 48.51 N 15.30 E
Moravská Ostrava → Ostrava 30 49.50 N 18.17 E
Moravská Třebová 30 49.45 N 16.40 E
Moravské Budějovice 61 49.03 N 15.49 E
Moravský Krumlov 61 49.03 N 16.19 E
Morawa 162 29.13 S 116.00 E
Morawhanna 246 8.16 N 59.45 W
Moraya 248 21.45 S 65.32 W
Morayfield 171a 27.07 S 152.57 E
Moray Firth ⊂1 46 57.50 N 3.30 W
Morazán, Guat. 236 14.56 N 90.09 W
Morazán, Hond. 236 15.17 N 87.34 W
Morbach 56 49.48 N 7.07 E
Morbegno 36 46.08 N 9.34 E
Morbihan □5 32 47.55 N 2.50 W
Mörbisch am See 61 47.45 N 16.40 E
Morbras ≃ 261 48.47 N 2.29 E
Mörbylånga 26 56.31 N 16.23 E
Morcenx 32 44.02 N 0.55 W
Morciano di Romagna 66 43.55 N 12.38 E
Morcone 68 41.20 N 14.40 E
Morcote 58 45.56 N 8.55 E
Morcy 80 51.18 N 47.51 E
Morden 184 49.11 N 98.05 W

Symbols in the index entries represent the broad categories identified in the key at the right. Symbols with superior numbers (⋏1) identify subcategories (see complete key on page I · 1).

Kartensymbole in dem Registerverzeichnis stellen die rechts in Schlüssel erklärten Kategorien dar. Symbole mit hochgestellten Ziffern (⋏1) bezeichnen Unterabteilungen einer Kategorie (vgl. vollständiger Schlüssel auf Seite I · 1).

Los símbolos incluídos en el texto del índice representan las grandes categorias identificadas con la clave a la derecha. Los símbolos con numeros en su parte superior (⋏1) identifican las subcategorías (véase la clave completa en la página I · 1).

Les symboles de l'index représentent les catégories indiquées dans la légende à droite. Les symboles suivis d'un indice (⋏1) représentent des sous-catégories (voir légende complète à la page I · 1).

Os símbolos incluídos no texto do índice representam as grandes categorias identificadas com a chave à direita. Os símbolos com números em sua parte superior (⋏1) identificam as subcategorias (veja-se a chave completa à página I · 1).

	English	Deutsch	Español	Français	Português
∧	Mountain	Berg	Montaña	Montagne	Montanha
⋏	Mountains	Berge	Montañas	Montagnes	Montanhas
)(	Pass	Pass	Paso	Col	Passo
V	Valley, Canyon	Tal, Cañon	Valle, Cañón	Vallée, Canyon	Vale, Canhão
≚	Plain	Ebene	Llano	Plaine	Planície
›	Cape	Kap	Cabo	Cap	Cabo
I	Island	Insel	Isla	Île	Ilha
II	Islands	Inseln	Islas	Îles	Ilhas
⊥	Other Topographic Features	Andere Topographische Objekte	Otros Elementos Topográficos	Autres données topographiques	Outros acidentes topográficos

ESPAÑOL: Nombre · Página · Lat.°′ · Long.°′ W = Oeste
FRANÇAIS: Nom · Page · Lat.°′ · Long.°′ W = Ouest
PORTUGUÊS: Nome · Página · Lat.°′ · Long.°′ W = Oeste

Symbol	English	Deutsch	Español	Français	Português
≃	River	Fluss	Río	Rivière	Rio
⩩	Canal	Kanal	Canal	Canal	Canal
⌊	Waterfall, Rapids	Wasserfall, Stromschnellen	Cascada, Rápidos	Chute d'eau, Rapides	Cascata, Rápidos
⟗	Strait	Meeresstrasse	Estrecho	Détroit	Estreito
⊂	Bay, Gulf	Bucht, Golf	Bahía, Golfo	Baie, Golfe	Baía, Golfo
◎	Lake, Lakes	See, Seen	Lago, Lagos	Lac, Lacs	Lago, Lagos
≡	Swamp	Sumpf	Pantano	Marais	Pântano
⊓	Ice Features, Glacier	Eis- und Gletscherformen	Accidentes Glaciales	Formes glaciaires	Acidentes glaciares
⊤	Other Hydrographic Features	Andere Hydrographische Objekte	Otros Elementos Hidrográficos	Autres données hydrographiques	Outros acidentes hidrográficos
✤	Submarine Features	Untermeerische Objekte	Accidentes Submarinos	Formes de relief sous-marin	Acidentes submarinos
□	Political Unit	Politische Einheit	Unidad Politica	Entité politique	Unidade política
⊕	Cultural Institution	Kulturelle Institution	Institución Cultural	Institution culturelle	Instituição cultural
⊥	Historical Site	Historische Stätte	Sitio Histórico	Site historique	Sítio histórico
♠	Recreational Site	Erholungs- und Ferienort	Sitio de Recreo	Centre de loisirs	Área de Lazer
⊠	Airport	Flughafen	Aeropuerto	Aéroport	Aeroporto
■	Military Installation	Militäranlage	Instalación Militar	Installation militaire	Instalação militar
◆	Miscellaneous	Verschiedenes	Misceláneo	Divers	Diversos

Name	Page	Lat.°′	Long.°′
Mount Cavenagh	162	25.58 S	133.15 E
Mount Charles	275b	43.41 N	79.40 W
Mount Clare	188	39.13 N	80.21 W
Mount Clemens	214	42.35 N	82.52 W
Mount Colah	274a	33.41 S	151.07 E
Mount Compass	168b	35.22 S	138.37 E
Mount Cook National Park ♦	172	43.35 S	170.15 E
Mount Cory	216	40.56 N	83.50 W
Mount Crawford	168b	34.40 S	138.57 E
Mount Crosby	171a	27.32 S	152.48 E
Mount Currie Indian Reserve ⊸[4]	182	50.19 N	122.42 W
Mount Dandenong	274b	37.50 S	145.22 E
Mount Dennis ⊸[8]	275b	43.42 N	79.30 W
Mount Desert Island I	188	44.20 N	68.20 W
Mount Diablo Creek ≐	282	38.02 N	122.02 W
Mount Diablo State Park ♦	226	37.51 N	121.55 W
Mount Dora	220	28.48 N	81.38 W
Mount Doreen	162	22.03 S	131.18 E
Mount Druitt	274a	33.46 S	150.49 E
Mount Dutton	162	27.50 S	135.43 E
Mount Eaton	214	40.42 N	81.42 W
Mount Eba	166	30.12 S	135.40 E
Mount Eden	226	37.38 N	122.06 W
Mount Edgecumbe	180	57.03 N	135.21 W
Mount Edwards	171a	28.01 S	152.31 E
Mount Elgon National Park ♦	154	1.07 N	34.44 E
Mount Elizabeth	164	16.15 S	126.12 E
Mount Emu Creek ≐	169	38.18 S	142.55 E
Mount Enterprise	222	31.55 N	94.41 W
Mount Ephraim	285	39.52 N	75.05 W
Mount Evelyn	274b	37.47 S	145.23 E
Mount Fern	276	40.52 N	74.34 W
Mount Field National Park ♦	166	43.10 S	146.45 E
Mount Fletcher	158	30.40 S	28.30 E
Mount Forest	212	43.59 N	80.44 W
Mount Freedom	210	40.49 N	74.34 W
Mount Frere	158	31.00 S	28.58 E
Mount Gambier	166	37.50 S	140.46 E
Mount Garnet	166	17.41 S	145.07 E
Mount Gay	188	37.51 N	82.00 W
Mount Gilead, N.C., U.S.	192	35.12 N	80.00 W
Mount Gilead, Oh., U.S.	214	40.32 N	82.49 W
Mount Glorious National Park ♦	171a	27.19 S	152.47 E
Mount Gravatt	171a	27.33 S	153.06 E
Mount Greenwood ⊸[8]	278	41.42 N	87.43 W
Mount Hagen	164	5.50 S	144.15 E
Mount Hawke	42	50.17 N	5.12 W
Mount Hawthorn	168a	31.55 S	115.50 E
Mount Healthy	218	39.14 N	84.32 W
Mount Hebron	284b	39.18 N	76.50 W
Mount Helena	168a	31.53 S	116.13 E
Mount Hermon, Ca., U.S.	226	37.03 N	122.04 W
Mount Hermon, Ma., U.S.	207	42.40 N	72.29 W
Mount Holly, N.J., U.S.	208	39.59 N	74.47 W
Mount Holly, N.C., U.S.	192	35.17 N	81.00 W
Mount Holly Springs	208	40.07 N	77.11 W
Mount Hope, Austl.	166	34.07 S	135.23 E
Mount Hope, On., Can.	212	43.09 N	79.55 W
Mount Hope, Ks., U.S.	198	37.52 N	97.39 W
Mount Hope, N.J., U.S.	276	40.56 N	74.33 W
Mount Hope, Oh., U.S.	214	40.38 N	81.47 W
Mount Hope, W.V., U.S.	188	37.53 N	81.09 W
Mount Hope Lake ⊜	276	40.56 N	74.32 W
Mount Horeb	190	43.00 N	89.44 W
Mount Houston	222	29.54 N	95.18 W
Mount Howitt	166	26.31 S	142.16 E
Mount Hunter Rivulet ≐	274a	34.02 S	150.40 E
Mount Ida	194	34.33 N	93.38 W
Mount Isa	166	20.44 S	139.30 E
Mount Jackson, Pa., U.S.	214	40.58 N	80.26 W
Mount Jackson, Va., U.S.	188	38.44 N	78.38 W
Mount Jewett	214	41.43 N	78.38 W
Mount Juliet	194	36.12 N	86.31 W
Mount Kenya National Park ♦	154	0.09 S	37.19 E
Mount Kisco	210	41.12 N	73.43 W
Mount Kokeby	168a	32.13 S	116.58 E
Mountlake Terrace	224	47.47 N	122.18 W
Mount Laurel	285	39.56 N	74.54 W
Mount Lebanon	214	40.21 N	80.02 W
Mount Liberty	214	40.21 N	82.38 W
Mount Lofty Ranges ⋏	168b	34.45 S	139.00 E
Mount Magnet	162	28.04 S	117.49 E
Mount Manara	166	32.29 S	143.56 E
Mount Margaret	166	26.54 S	143.21 E
Mount Marion	210	42.02 N	73.59 W
Mount Maroon National Park ♦	166	28.14 S	152.42 E
Mount Martha	169	38.17 S	145.01 E
Mount Maunganui	172	37.37 S	176.11 E
Mount McKinley National Park → Denali National Park ♦	180	63.15 N	150.30 W
Mount Mee	171a	27.04 S	152.46 E
Mountmellick	48	53.07 N	7.20 W
Mount Misery Point ›	276	40.58 N	73.05 W
Mount Molloy	164	16.41 S	145.20 E
Mount Monger	162	30.59 S	121.53 E
Mount Moorosi	158	30.16 S	27.53 E
Mount Morgan	166	23.39 S	150.23 E
Mount Morris, Il., U.S.	190	42.03 N	89.25 W
Mount Morris, Mi., U.S.	190	43.07 N	83.41 W
Mount Morris, N.Y., U.S.	210	42.43 N	77.52 W
Mount Morris Dam ⊸[6]	210	42.44 N	77.53 W
Mount Mulligan	166	16.51 S	144.52 E
Mount Nebo	279b	40.33 N	80.06 W
Mountnessing	260	51.39 N	0.21 E
Mount Olive, Il., U.S.	219	39.04 N	89.43 W
Mount Olive, Ms., U.S.	194	31.45 N	89.39 W
Mount Olive, N.C., U.S.	192	35.11 N	78.04 W
Mount Oliver	279b	40.28 N	79.59 W
Mount Olivet	218	38.31 N	84.02 W
Mount Orab	218	39.01 N	83.55 W
Mount Penn	208	40.20 N	75.54 W
Mount Perry	166	25.11 S	151.39 E
Mount Pleasant, Austl.	168b	34.47 S	139.02 E
Mount Pleasant, On., Can.	212	43.05 N	80.19 W
Mount Pleasant, In., U.S.	218	38.07 N	86.31 W
Mount Pleasant, Ia., U.S.	190	40.57 N	91.33 W
Mount Pleasant, Mi., U.S.	190	43.35 N	84.46 W
Mount Pleasant, N.C., U.S.	192	35.23 N	80.26 W
Mount Pleasant, Oh., U.S.	214	40.11 N	80.48 W
Mount Pleasant, Pa., U.S.	214	40.08 N	79.32 W
Mount Pleasant, S.C., U.S.	192	32.47 N	79.51 W
Mount Pleasant, Tn., U.S.	194	35.32 N	87.12 W
Mount Pleasant, Tx., U.S.	222	33.09 N	94.58 W
Mount Pleasant, Ut., U.S.	200	39.32 N	111.27 W
Mount Pleasant Mills	208	40.43 N	77.01 W
Mount Pleasant Park ♦	284b	39.22 N	76.35 W
Mount Pocono	210	41.07 N	75.21 W
Mount Pritchard	274a	33.54 S	150.54 E
Mount Prospect, S. Afr.	158	27.29 S	29.53 E
Mount Prospect, Il., U.S.	216	42.03 N	87.56 W
Mount Pulaski	219	40.00 N	89.16 W
Mount Rainier	284c	38.56 N	76.57 W
Mount Rainier National Park ♦	224	46.52 N	121.43 W
Mountrath	48	53.00 N	7.27 W
Mount Rebecca	162	26.48 S	135.10 E
Mount Repose	218	39.10 N	84.14 W
Mount Revelstoke National Park ♦	182	51.06 N	118.00 W
Mount Riddock	162	23.03 S	134.40 E
Mount Robson Provincial Park ♦	182	52.58 N	118.50 W
Mount Rogers National Recreation Area ♦	192	36.42 N	81.30 W
Mount Roskill	172	36.55 S	174.45 E
Mount Royal	285	39.49 N	75.13 W
Mount Rushmore National Memorial ⊥	198	43.50 N	103.24 W
Mount Saint Helens National Volcanic Monument ♦	224	46.12 N	122.11 W
Mount Sandiman	162	24.24 S	115.23 E
Mount Sarah	162	26.57 S	135.22 E
Mount Savage	188	39.41 N	78.52 W
Mount's Bay c	42	50.03 N	5.25 W
Mount Selinda	154	20.25 S	32.43 E
Mount Selman	222	32.04 N	95.17 W
Mount Seymour Provincial Park ♦	182	49.23 N	122.57 W
Mount Shasta	204	41.18 N	122.18 W
Mount Sinai	276	40.57 N	73.02 W
Mount Sinai Harbor c	276	40.57 N	73.02 W
Mount Sinai Ridge ∧	218	39.04 N	84.58 W
Mount Somers	172	43.43 S	171.24 E
Mountsorrel	42	52.44 N	1.07 W
Mount Spokane State Park ♦	202	47.58 N	117.13 W
Mount Sterling, Il., U.S.	219	39.59 N	90.45 W
Mount Sterling, Ky., U.S.	192	38.03 N	83.56 W
Mount Sterling, Mo., U.S.	219	38.28 N	91.38 W
Mount Sterling, Oh., U.S.	218	39.43 N	83.15 W
Mount Stewart, P.E., Can.	186	46.22 N	62.52 W
Mount Stewart, S. Afr.	158	33.10 S	24.26 E
Mount Stromlo Observatory ʊ[3]	171b	35.20 S	149.00 E
Mount Summit	218	40.00 N	85.23 W
Mount Surprise	166	18.09 S	144.19 E
Mount Sylvia	171a	27.44 S	152.14 E
Mount Tamalpais State Park ♦	226	37.54 N	122.34 W
Mount Tempest National Park ♦	171a	27.10 S	153.24 E
Mount Torrens	168b	34.52 S	138.57 E
Mount Tremper	210	42.03 N	74.17 W
Mount Uniacke	186	44.54 N	63.50 W
Mount Union	214	40.23 N	77.52 W
Mount Upton	210	42.25 N	75.23 W
Mount Vernon, Austl.	162	24.13 S	118.14 E
Mount Vernon, Al., U.S.	194	31.05 N	88.00 W
Mount Vernon, Ga., U.S.	192	32.10 N	82.35 W
Mount Vernon, Il., U.S.	219	38.19 N	88.54 W
Mount Vernon, In., U.S.	194	37.55 N	87.53 W
Mount Vernon, Ia., U.S.	190	41.55 N	91.25 W
Mount Vernon, Ky., U.S.	192	37.21 N	84.20 W
Mount Vernon, Md., U.S.	208	38.14 N	75.49 W
Mount Vernon, Mo., U.S.	194	37.06 N	93.49 W
Mount Vernon, N.Y., U.S.	210	42.45 N	78.53 W
Mount Vernon, N.Y., U.S.	210	40.54 N	73.50 W
Mount Vernon, Oh., U.S.	214	40.23 N	82.29 W
Mount Vernon, Or., U.S.	202	44.25 N	119.06 W
Mount Vernon, Pa., U.S.	279b	40.17 N	79.48 W
Mount Vernon, S.D., U.S.	198	43.42 N	98.15 W
Mount Vernon, Tx., U.S.	222	33.11 N	95.13 W
Mount Vernon, Wa., U.S.	224	48.25 N	122.19 W
Mount Vernon ⊥	208	38.47 N	77.06 W
Mount Victoria	170	33.35 S	150.15 E
Mount Victory	216	40.32 N	83.31 W
Mount View	207	41.38 N	71.24 W
Mountville	208	40.02 N	76.26 W
Mount Vision	210	42.35 N	75.04 W
Mount Washington	284b	39.23 N	76.41 W
Mount Washington ⊸[8]	284b	39.22 N	76.40 W
Mount Waverley	274b	37.53 S	145.08 E
Mount Wedge, Austl.	162	22.45 S	132.09 E
Mount Wedge, Austl.	162	33.29 S	135.10 E
Mount Wellington	172	36.54 S	174.51 E
Mount Willoughby	162	27.58 S	134.08 E
Mount Wilson Observatory ʊ[3]	228	34.14 N	118.03 W
Mount Wolf	208	40.03 N	76.42 W
Mount Zion	219	39.46 N	88.53 W
Mounyaz	146	10.41 N	21.18 E
Moura, Austl.	166	24.35 S	149.58 E
Moura, Bra.	246	1.27 S	61.38 W
Moura, Port.	34	38.08 N	7.27 W
Moura, Tchad	146	13.47 N	21.13 E
Mouraya	146	11.27 N	20.59 E
Mourdi, Dépression du ±[7]	146	18.10 N	23.00 E
Mourdiah	150	14.28 N	7.28 W
Mouriès	62	43.41 N	4.52 E
Mourindi	152	2.32 S	10.48 E
Mourmelon-le-Grand	50	49.08 N	4.22 E
Mourne ≐	48	54.49 N	7.28 W
Mourne Beg ≐	48	54.41 N	7.39 W
Mourne Mountains ⋏	48	54.10 N	6.04 W
Mousa I	46	60.00 N	1.11 W
Mouscron	50	50.44 N	3.13 E
Mousgougou	146	10.47 N	16.09 E
Moussa Ali ∧	144	12.28 N	42.24 E
Mousseaux-sur-Seine	261	49.03 N	1.39 E
Moussey	58	48.40 N	6.47 E
Moussoro	146	13.39 N	16.29 E
Moussy-le-Neuf	261	49.04 N	2.36 E
Moussy-le-Vieux	261	49.03 N	2.38 E
Moustiers-Sainte-Marie	62	43.51 N	6.13 E
Mouthe	58	46.43 N	6.12 E
Mouthier-Haute-Pierre	58	47.02 N	6.16 E
Moutier	58	47.17 N	7.23 E
Moûtiers	62	45.29 N	6.32 E
Moutiers-au-Perche	50	48.29 N	0.51 E
Moutnice	61	49.02 N	16.46 E
Moutohora	172	38.17 S	177.32 E
Moutomoukadi	152	4.41 S	13.15 E
Moutong	112	0.28 N	121.13 E
Mouy	50	49.19 N	2.19 E
Mouydir ⋏	148	24.45 N	4.05 E
Mouyondzi	152	3.58 S	13.57 E
Mouzákion	38	39.26 N	21.40 E
Mouzarak	146	13.11 N	15.58 E
Mouzon	56	49.36 N	5.05 E
Mouzon ≐	58	48.21 N	5.41 E
Móvano	232	26.42 N	103.39 W
Moville, Ire.	48	55.11 N	7.03 W
Moville, Ia., U.S.	198	42.29 N	96.04 W
Mowang	100	30.31 N	113.34 E
Moweaqua	219	39.37 N	89.01 W
Mowein	140	7.36 N	28.11 E
Mowry Slough ≐	282	37.29 N	122.03 W
Mowrystown	218	39.02 N	83.44 W
Mowshera	123	34.01 N	71.59 E
Mowu	100	26.50 N	117.42 E
Moxhe	56	50.38 N	5.05 E
Moxi	107	30.18 N	105.41 E
Moxico □[5]	152	13.00 S	20.30 E
Moxotó ≐	250	9.19 S	38.14 W
Moy	48	54.27 N	6.42 W
Moy ≐	48	54.12 N	9.08 W
Moy, Cnoc ∧[2], Scot., U.K.	44	55.22 N	5.46 W
Moy, Cnoc ∧[2], Scot., U.K.	46	55.22 N	5.46 W
Moya, Comores	157a	12.18 S	44.27 E
Moya, Perú	248	12.24 S	75.10 W
Moyagee	162	27.45 S	117.54 E
Moyahua	234	21.16 N	103.10 W
Moyale, Ityo.	144	3.30 N	39.07 E
Moyale, Kenya	154	3.32 N	39.03 E
Moyamba	150	8.10 N	12.26 W
Moycullen	48	53.21 N	9.09 W
Moydans	62	44.24 N	5.30 E
Moÿ-de-l'Aisne	50	49.45 N	3.22 E
Moye Dao I	98	36.55 N	122.32 E
Moyen Atlas ⋏	148	33.30 N	5.00 W
Moyen-Chari □[5]	146	9.00 N	18.00 E
Moyenmoutier	58	48.23 N	6.55 E
Moyenne-Sido	146	8.13 N	18.43 E
Moyenneville	50	50.04 N	1.45 E
Moyen-Ogooué □[4]	152	0.30 S	10.30 E
Moyenvic	56	48.47 N	6.33 E
Moyeuvre-Grande	56	49.15 N	6.02 E
Moyie	182	49.17 N	115.50 W
Moyie ≐	202	48.42 N	116.11 W
Moyie Springs	202	48.43 N	116.11 W
Moylan	285	39.54 N	75.23 W
Moyle ≐	48	52.24 N	7.39 W
Moyo	154	3.39 N	31.43 E
Moyo ≐	115b	8.26 S	117.28 E
Moyo, Pulau I	115b	8.15 S	117.34 E
Moyobamba	248	6.03 S	76.58 W
Moyock	208	36.31 N	76.10 W
Moyogalpa	236	11.32 N	85.42 W
Moyowosi ≐	154	4.50 S	31.24 E
Moyu	120	37.17 N	79.44 E
Moyuta, Volcán ∧[1]	236	14.02 N	90.06 W
Moza	132	31.47 N	35.09 E
M'oža ≐, S.S.S.R.	76	55.27 N	30.43 E
M'oža ≐, S.S.S.R.	80	58.23 N	44.54 E
Možajevka	83	48.44 N	39.45 E
Možajsk	82	55.30 N	36.01 E
Možajskij	265a	59.43 N	30.07 E
Možajskoje vodochranilišče ⊜[1]	82	55.35 N	35.50 E
Mozambique → Moçambique	154	15.03 S	40.42 E
Mozambique (Moçambique) □[1]	138	18.15 S	35.00 E
Mozambique Channel ᛘ	138	19.00 S	41.00 E
Mozambique Plateau ✣[3]	10	32.00 S	35.00 E
Mozarlândia	255	14.47 S	50.35 W
Možarovka	86	51.09 N	59.05 E
Možarov Majdan	80	55.37 N	45.53 E
Možary	80	53.53 N	41.02 E
Mozdok	84	43.44 N	44.38 E
Možga	80	56.23 N	52.17 E
Mozhabong Lake ⊜	190	46.57 N	82.05 W
Mozhugongka	120	29.50 N	91.45 E
Mozia ⊥	70	37.52 N	12.28 E
Mozichang	107	29.20 N	103.53 E
Mozolevo	76	59.19 N	33.51 E
Mozu	270	34.34 N	135.29 E
Mozuli	76	56.36 N	28.11 E
Mozyr'	78	52.03 N	29.14 E
Mozzanica	62	45.29 N	9.41 E
Mozzano	66	42.50 N	13.31 E
Mozzate	266b	45.41 N	8.57 E
Mpaka	158	26.26 S	31.47 E
Mpala	154	6.45 S	29.31 E
Mpama ≐	152	0.57 S	15.39 E
Mpanda	154	6.22 S	31.02 E
Mpé	152	2.54 S	14.43 E
Mpese	152	5.14 S	15.33 E
Mpessoba	150	12.40 N	5.43 W
Mphoengs	154	21.10 S	27.51 E
Mpigi	154	0.13 N	32.42 E
Mpika	154	11.54 S	31.26 E
Mpila ⊸[8]	273b	4.14 S	15.18 E
Mpoka	152	1.26 S	17.02 E
Mpoko ≐	152	4.19 N	18.33 E
Mporokoso	154	9.23 S	30.05 E
Mpouya	152	2.37 S	16.13 E
Mpraeso	150	6.35 N	0.44 W
Mpui	154	8.21 S	31.50 E
Mpulungu	154	8.46 S	31.07 E
Mpwapwa	154	6.21 S	36.29 E
Mqanduli	158	31.48 S	28.46 E
Mrągowo	30	53.52 N	21.19 E
Mrakovo	86	52.43 N	56.38 E
M'Ramani	157a	12.21 S	44.32 E
Mranggen	115a	7.01 S	110.31 E
Mras-Su ≐	86	53.45 N	87.49 E
Mrhila, Jebel ∧	36	35.25 N	9.14 E
Mrijo	154	5.10 S	36.15 E
Mrkonjić Grad	36	44.25 N	17.05 E
Mrkopalj	36	45.19 N	14.51 E
Mrocza	30	53.14 N	17.36 E
Msagali	154	6.21 S	36.18 E
M'Saken	148	35.44 N	10.35 E
Msata	154	6.20 S	38.23 E
Mšec	54	50.10 N	13.54 E
Mšeno	54	50.27 N	14.38 E
M'Sila	148	35.46 N	4.31 E
M'sila □[5]	148	35.00 N	4.20 E
Mšinskaja	76	59.01 N	29.57 E
Msoro	154	13.36 S	31.55 E
Msta	76	57.55 N	34.29 E
Msta ≐	76	58.25 N	31.20 E
Mstera	80	56.23 N	41.56 E
Mstislavl'	76	54.02 N	31.42 E
Mstiž	76	54.34 N	28.10 E
Mszana Dolna	30	49.42 N	20.05 E
Mszczonów	30	51.58 N	20.31 E
Mtakataka	154	14.12 S	34.32 E
Mtakuja	154	7.22 S	30.37 E
Mtama	154	10.18 S	39.22 E
Mtamvuna ≐	158	31.06 S	30.12 E
Mtarazi National Park ♦	158	18.36 S	32.50 E
Mtata ≐	158	31.58 S	29.10 E
Mtelo ∧	154	1.39 N	35.23 E
Mtilikwe ≐	154	21.09 S	31.30 E
Mtito Andei	154	2.41 S	38.10 E
Mtowabaga	154	2.30 S	35.53 E
Mtsensk → Mcensk	76	53.17 N	36.35 E
Mtubatuba	158	28.30 S	32.08 E
Mtunzini	158	28.57 S	31.46 E
Mtwara	154	10.16 S	40.11 E
Mtwara □[4]	154	11.00 S	39.00 E
Mtyangimbori	154	10.16 S	35.31 E
Mu ≐, Mya.	110	21.56 N	95.38 E
Mu ≐, Nihon	92a	42.33 N	141.56 E
Mu, Cerro ∧	246	9.29 N	73.07 W
Mu'a	174w	21.11 S	175.07 W
Muacandala	152	10.02 S	19.40 E
Mualama	154	16.53 S	38.17 E
Mualang	112	0.42 N	111.18 E
Mu 'Allaqah	140	13.28 N	23.57 E
Muan	98	34.58 N	126.26 E
Muaná	250	1.32 S	49.13 W
Muanda	152	5.56 S	12.21 E
Muangai	152	12.32 S	19.51 E
Muang Bèng	110	20.22 N	101.44 E
Muang Hay	110	21.03 N	101.49 E
Muang Hinboun	110	17.35 N	104.36 E
Muang Hôngsa	110	19.43 N	101.20 E
Muang Houn	110	20.09 N	101.27 E
Muang Hounxianghoung	110	21.37 N	102.18 E
Muang Huang	110	18.45 N	103.42 E
Muang Khammouan	110	17.24 N	104.48 E
Muang Khao	110	19.47 N	103.29 E
Muang Khi	110	18.27 N	101.46 E
Muang Không	110	14.07 N	105.51 E
Muang Khôngxédôn	110	15.34 N	105.49 E
Muang La	110	20.52 N	102.07 E
Muang Liap	110	18.29 N	101.40 E
Muang Long	110	20.57 N	100.48 E
Muang Meung	110	20.43 N	100.28 E
Muang Ngoy, Lao	102	20.43 N	102.41 E
Muang Ngoy, Lao	110	20.43 N	102.41 E
Muang Nong	110	16.22 N	106.30 E
Muang Ou Nua	110	22.18 N	101.48 E
Muang Ou Tai	110	22.07 N	101.48 E
Muang Pakbèng	110	19.54 N	101.08 E
Muang Pak-Lay	110	18.12 N	101.25 E
Muang Paktha	110	20.06 N	100.36 E
Muang Pakxan	110	18.22 N	103.39 E
Muang Peun	110	20.13 N	103.52 E
Muang Phalan	110	16.39 N	105.34 E
Muang Phiang	110	19.06 N	101.32 E
Muang Phônthong	110	15.05 N	105.39 E
Muang Phoun	110	19.07 N	102.43 E
Muang Sam Sip	110	15.31 N	104.44 E
Muang Sing	110	21.11 N	101.09 E
Muang Soum	110	18.45 N	102.36 E
Muang Souvannakhili	110	15.23 N	105.49 E
Muang Souy	110	19.33 N	102.52 E
Muang Sung	110	20.19 N	102.27 E
Muang Thadua	110	19.26 N	101.50 E
Muang Thatèng	110	15.26 N	106.23 E
Muang Thathôm	110	19.00 N	103.36 E
Muang Va	110	21.53 N	102.19 E
Muang Vangviang	110	18.56 N	102.27 E
Muang Vapi	110	15.40 N	105.55 E
Muang Xaignabouri	110	19.15 N	101.45 E
Muang Xamtong	110	19.51 N	103.51 E
Muang Xay	110	20.42 N	101.59 E
Muang Xépôn	110	16.41 N	106.14 E
Muang Xon	110	20.27 N	103.19 E
Muang Yo	110	21.31 N	101.51 E
Muang You	110	19.49 N	102.50 E
Muanza	156	18.59 S	34.48 E
Muar (Bandar Maharani)	114	2.02 N	102.34 E
Muar ≐	114	2.03 N	102.35 E
Muara	112	5.02 N	115.02 E
Muaraaman	112	3.07 S	102.12 E
Muaraancalung	112	0.27 N	116.41 E
Muarabeliti	112	3.15 S	103.02 E
Muarabenangin	112	0.58 S	115.19 E
Muarabinuangeun	115a	6.50 S	105.53 E
Muarabulian	112	1.43 S	103.15 E
Muarabungo	112	1.28 S	102.07 E
Muaradua	112	4.32 S	104.05 E
Muaraenim	112	3.39 S	103.48 E
Muaragusung	112	1.35 N	117.17 E
Muarajuloi	112	0.12 S	114.03 E
Muarakaman	112	0.09 S	116.43 E
Muarakelingi	112	3.05 S	103.14 E
Muarakumpe	112	1.24 S	104.00 E
Muaralabuh	112	1.29 S	101.03 E
Muaralakitan	112	2.51 S	103.19 E
Muaralasan	112	1.48 N	117.12 E
Muaralembu	112	0.24 S	101.21 E
Muaramawai	112	0.37 N	116.49 E
Muarapangean	112	2.38 N	116.41 E
Muarapantai	112	0.45 S	101.43 E
Muarapayang	112	1.32 S	115.48 E
Muararupit	112	2.44 S	102.54 E
Muarasabak	112	1.08 S	103.51 E
Muarasiberut	108	1.36 S	99.11 E
Muarasipongi	112	0.37 N	99.51 E
Muaratais	114	1.17 N	99.21 E
Muaratebo	112	1.30 S	102.26 E
Muarateladang	112	2.50 S	103.58 E
Muaratembesi	112	1.42 S	103.07 E
Muaratewe	112	0.57 S	114.53 E
Muaratuhup	112	0.37 S	114.50 E
Muaratunan	112	1.24 S	116.39 E
Muarawahau	112	1.02 N	116.52 E
Muāri, Rās ›	120	24.49 N	66.40 E
Muasdale	46	55.36 N	5.41 W
Muá Ximica	152	9.50 S	18.41 E
Mubārakpur	124	26.05 N	83.18 E
Mubārakpur Dabās ⊸[8]	272a	28.43 N	77.03 E
Mubayyad ⊤[4]	142	30.55 N	32.48 E
Mubende	154	0.35 N	31.23 E
Mubi	146	10.18 N	13.20 E
Mubur, Pulau I	112	3.20 N	106.12 E
Mucaitá ≐	250	6.59 S	42.40 W
Mucajaí ≐	246	2.25 N	60.52 W
Mucambo	250	3.54 S	40.44 W
Mucári	152	9.30 S	16.54 E
Muccan	162	20.38 S	120.04 E
Muccia	66	43.05 N	13.02 E
Much	56	50.54 N	7.25 E
Mucha	269d	24.59 N	121.34 E
Muchangpu	100	31.55 N	116.35 E
Muchanovo	82	56.31 N	38.20 E
Muchavec ≐	76	52.05 N	23.39 E
Much Dewchurch	42	51.59 N	2.46 W
Muchea	168a	31.35 S	115.59 E
Mücheln	54	51.18 N	11.48 E
Muchen	89	48.10 N	136.13 E
Muchengzhen	107	29.47 N	103.29 E
Much Hoole	262	53.42 N	2.48 W
Muchinga Escarpment ±[4]	154	14.45 S	29.30 E
Muchinga Mountains ⋏	154	12.20 S	31.00 E
Muchino, S.S.S.R.	80	58.11 N	51.02 E
Muchino, S.S.S.R.	89	52.16 N	127.14 E
Muchor-Konduj	88	52.25 N	113.16 E
Muchoršibir'	88	51.03 N	107.50 E
Muchrani	84	41.56 N	44.35 E
Muchtadir	84	41.41 N	48.46 E
Muchtolovo	80	55.27 N	43.13 E
Muchuan	107	28.55 N	103.58 E
Much Wenlock	42	52.36 N	2.34 W
Mucifal	266c	38.48 N	9.26 W
Mučikan	88	53.02 N	120.27 E
Muck I	46	56.50 N	6.15 W
Mücka	54	51.18 N	14.40 E
Muckadilla	166	26.35 S	148.23 E
Muckalee Creek ≐	192	31.38 N	84.09 W
Muckamore	48	54.41 N	6.10 W
Mučkapskij	80	51.52 N	42.28 E
Mučkas	24	64.02 N	48.27 E
Mücke	56	50.38 N	9.03 E
Muckendorf an der Donau	264b	48.20 N	16.09 E
Mucking	260	51.30 N	0.26 E
Muckle Roe I	46a	60.22 N	1.27 W
Muckleshoot Indian Reservation ⊸[4]	224	47.16 N	122.09 W
Muckno Lake ⊜	48	54.07 N	6.42 W
Mucojo	154	12.04 S	40.28 E
Mucoma	152	15.18 S	13.39 E
Muconda	152	10.34 S	21.17 E
Mucope, Ang.	152	16.24 S	14.53 E
Mucope, Ang.	152	8.42 S	21.43 E
Mucrone, Monte ∧	62	45.36 N	7.56 E
Mucubela	154	16.55 S	37.52 E
Mucuchíes	246	8.45 N	70.55 W
M'uc'ucl'u	84	40.28 N	47.55 E
Mucucuaú ≐	246	0.37 S	61.24 W
Mucugê	255	13.00 S	41.23 W
Mucuim ≐	248	6.33 S	64.18 W
Muculo	152	16.47 S	14.51 E
Muçum	252	29.10 S	51.53 W
Mucumbura	154	16.09 S	31.31 E
Mucun	100	26.44 N	114.00 E
Mucupia	156	18.01 S	36.48 E
Mucupina, Monte ∧	236	15.08 N	86.38 W
Mucur	130	39.04 N	34.23 E
Mucuri	255	18.05 S	39.34 W
Mucuri ≐	255	18.05 S	39.34 W
Mucusso	152	18.01 S	21.25 E
Mud ≐, Ky., U.S.	194	37.13 N	86.54 W
Mud ≐, W.V., U.S.	188	38.25 N	82.17 W
Muda ≐	114	5.33 N	100.22 E
Mudan ≐	89	46.22 N	129.33 E
Mudanjiang	89	44.35 N	129.36 E
Mudanya	130	40.22 N	28.52 E
Mudau	56	49.32 N	9.11 E
Mudaysīsāt, Jabal ∧	132	31.39 N	36.14 E
Mud Creek ≐, N.A.	206	45.01 N	72.24 W
Mud Creek ≐, U.S.	198	43.17 N	96.15 W
Mud Creek ≐, Il., U.S.	219	38.21 N	89.48 W
Mud Creek ≐, In., U.S.	216	41.06 N	86.21 W
Mud Creek ≐, In., U.S.	216	40.26 N	85.55 W
Mud Creek ≐, Ne., U.S.	198	41.01 N	98.54 W
Mud Creek ≐, N.Y., U.S.	210	43.05 N	78.43 W
Mud Creek ≐, N.Y., U.S.	210	42.17 N	77.13 W
Mud Creek ≐, N.Y., U.S.	210	42.59 N	77.23 W
Mud Creek ≐, Ok., U.S.	196	33.55 N	97.28 W
Mud Creek ≐, S.D., U.S.	198	45.11 N	98.24 W
Mud Creek ≐, Tx., U.S.	222	31.48 N	94.58 W
Muddus Nationalpark ♦	24	67.00 N	20.16 E
Muddy ≐, Nv., U.S.	204	36.27 N	114.22 W
Muddy ≐, Wa., U.S.	224	46.04 N	122.01 W
Muddy Boggy Creek ≐	196	34.03 N	95.47 W
Muddy Branch ≐	284c	39.03 N	77.18 W
Muddy Brook ≐	276	41.07 N	73.20 W
Muddy Creek ≐, U.S.	276	41.03 N	74.02 W
Muddy Creek ≐, Mo., U.S.	194	38.51 N	93.03 W
Muddy Creek ≐, Mt., U.S.	202	47.56 N	111.46 W
Muddy Creek ≐, Oh., U.S.	214	41.27 N	83.03 W
Muddy Creek ≐, Pa., U.S.	208	39.47 N	76.18 W
Muddy Creek ≐, Ut., U.S.	200	38.24 N	110.42 W
Muddy Creek ≐, Wy., U.S.	198	42.35 N	104.57 W
Muddy Creek ≐, Wy., U.S.	200	41.59 N	106.08 W
Muddy Creek ≐, Wy., U.S.	200	41.32 N	110.13 W
Muddy Creek ≐, Wy., U.S.	200	41.01 N	107.42 W
Muddy Creek ≐, Wy., U.S.	202	43.17 N	108.14 W
Muddy Fork ≐	224	46.22 N	121.34 W
Muddy Gut c	284b	39.17 N	76.26 W
Muddy Peak ∧	204	36.18 N	114.42 W
Müden, B.R.D.	52	52.52 N	10.07 E
Müden, B.R.D.	54	52.31 N	10.22 E
Mudgee	166	32.36 S	149.35 E
Mudgeeraba	171a	28.04 S	153.22 E
Mudhol	122	16.21 N	75.17 E
Mud Island I	171a	27.20 S	153.15 E
Mud Islands II	169	38.17 S	144.45 E
Mudjatik ≐	184	56.02 N	107.36 W
Mudjuga	24	63.46 N	39.15 E
Mud Lake ⊜, Id., U.S.	202	43.53 N	112.24 W
Mud Lake ⊜, Nv., U.S.	204	37.52 N	117.04 W
Mud Lake ⊜, N.Y., U.S.	212	44.30 N	75.28 W
Mud Lake Reservoir ⊜[1]	198	45.50 N	98.10 W
Mudon	110	16.15 N	97.44 E
Mudongzhen	102	29.35 N	106.51 E
Mudu	106	31.15 N	120.30 E
Mudug □[4]	144	6.15 N	48.00 E
Mudurnu	130	40.28 N	31.13 E
Mudurnu ≐	130	40.49 N	30.33 E
M'ud'ur'um ≐	85	40.53 N	76.36 E
Mueda	154	11.39 S	39.33 E
Muelle de los Bueyes	236	12.04 N	84.32 W
Mueller, Mount ∧	162	19.54 S	127.51 E
Muenster	196	33.39 N	97.23 W
Mu'er	107	29.48 N	106.37 E
Muerte, Valle de la → Death Valley V	204	36.30 N	117.00 W
Muerto ≐	252	23.02 S	62.29 W
Muerto, Mar c	234	16.10 N	94.10 W
Muerto, Mar → Dead Sea ⊜	132	31.30 N	35.30 E
Mufulira	154	12.33 S	28.14 E
Mufuma	152	9.04 S	17.06 E
Mufu Shan ∧	100	29.02 N	113.54 E
Mufu Shan ⋏	100	29.00 N	114.00 E
Mugang	100	29.44 N	115.14 E
Muganskaja ravnina ≚	84	39.40 N	48.15 E
Mugazine	158	26.07 S	32.30 E
Mugegawa	94	35.31 N	136.51 E
Mugello V	66	43.55 N	11.30 E
Mügeln	54	51.14 N	13.02 E
Muger ≐	144	9.54 N	37.57 E
Müggelberge ⋏[2]	264a	52.25 N	13.39 E
Müggelheim ⊸[8]	264a	52.25 N	13.40 E
Muggia	64	45.36 N	13.46 E
Muggio	266b	45.36 N	9.14 E
Mughalsarai	124	25.18 N	83.07 E
Mughr	132	33.05 N	35.43 E
Mugi, Nihon	94	35.34 N	137.01 E
Mugi, Nihon	96	33.40 N	134.25 E
Mu Gia, Deo ≍	110	17.40 N	105.47 E
Muginga	152	8.20 S	17.37 E
Muğla	130	37.12 N	28.22 E
Muğla □[4]	130	37.10 N	28.30 E
Mugodžarskaja	86	48.36 N	58.27 E
Mugodžary, gory ⋏[2]	86	49.00 N	58.40 E
Mugombazi	154	5.50 S	30.14 E
Mugo-ri	98	38.58 N	126.31 E
Mugrejevskij	80	56.36 N	42.21 E
Mugron	32	43.45 N	0.45 W
Mugu Karnāli ≐	124	29.38 N	81.53 E
Mugur-Aksy	86	50.21 N	90.30 E
Mūh, Sabkhat ⊜	130	34.30 N	38.20 E
Muhala	154	5.40 S	28.43 E
Muhamdi	124	27.57 N	80.13 E
Muhammad, Ra's ›	140	27.44 N	34.15 E
Muhammadābād	124	26.02 N	83.23 E
Muhammadpur	124	23.24 N	89.36 E
Muhammad Qawl	140	20.54 N	37.05 E
Muhayshir, Birkat ⊜	142	30.43 N	31.56 E
Muheza	154	5.10 S	38.47 E
Muḥīṭ, Maṣrif al- ≚	273c	30.07 N	31.06 E
Mühlacker	56	48.57 N	8.50 E
Mühlau	54	50.54 N	12.45 E
Mühlbach am Hochkönig	64	47.22 N	13.08 E
Muhlbach-sur-Munster	58	48.02 N	7.05 E
Mühlberg	54	51.26 N	13.13 E
Mühldorf	61	48.22 N	15.21 E
Mühldorf am Inn	60	48.15 N	12.32 E
Mühlen → Molini di Tures	64	46.54 N	11.56 E
Mühlenbeck	54	52.40 N	13.22 E
Mühlenbecker See ⊜	264a	52.41 N	13.24 E
Muhlenberg	210	41.14 N	76.09 W
Mühlen-Berg ∧[2]	264a	52.23 N	13.15 E
Mühlen Eichsen	54	53.45 N	11.15 E
Mühlenfliess ≐	264a	52.26 N	13.41 E
Mühlenrahmede	263	51.16 N	7.40 E
Mühlhausen, B.R.D.	263	51.33 N	7.44 E
Mühlhausen, D.D.R.	54	51.12 N	10.27 E
Mühlhausen im Täle	56	48.34 N	9.39 E
Mühlheim	56	50.07 N	8.50 E
Mühlheim an der Donau	58	48.01 N	8.53 E
Mühlig-Hofmann Mountains ⋏	9	72.00 S	5.20 E
Mühlleiten	264b	48.10 N	16.34 E
Mühltroff	54	50.32 N	11.55 E
Mühlviertel ⊸[1]	30	48.25 N	14.10 E
Muhola	26	63.20 N	25.05 E
Muhoro	154	1.01 S	34.07 E
Muhos	26	64.48 N	25.59 E
Muḥradah	130	35.15 N	36.35 E
Mühringen	58	48.25 N	8.46 E
Muhu I	76	58.38 N	23.15 E
Muhula	154	13.53 S	39.30 E
Muhulu	154	1.03 S	27.17 E
Muhutwe	154	1.33 S	31.42 E
Muhu väin ᛘ	76	58.45 N	23.20 E
Muhuwesi ≐	154	11.16 S	37.58 E
Mui Ba-lang-an ›	110	15.14 N	108.56 E
Mui Ca-mau ›	110	8.38 N	104.44 E
Muick, Loch ⊜	46	56.55 N	3.10 W
Muiden	52	52.19 N	5.04 E
Muiderslot ⊥	52	52.20 N	5.10 E
Muides-sur-Loire	50	47.40 N	1.31 E
Muié	152	14.25 S	20.36 E
Mui Hopohoponga Point ›	174w	21.09 S	175.02 W
Muikaichi	96	34.21 N	131.56 E
Muikamachi	94	37.04 N	138.53 E
Mui Ke-ga ›, Viet.	110	12.53 N	109.28 E
Mui Ke-ga ›, Viet.	110	10.42 N	107.58 E
Muine Bheag	48	52.41 N	6.58 W
Muir, Mi., U.S.	216	42.59 N	84.56 W
Muir, Pa., U.S.	208	40.36 N	76.31 W
Muir, Mount ∧	180	61.06 N	148.24 W
Muir Beach	282	37.52 N	122.35 W
Muirdrum	46	56.31 N	2.42 W
Muirkirk, Scot., U.K.	46	55.31 N	4.04 W
Muirkirk, Md., U.S.	284c	39.03 N	76.53 W
Muir of Ord	46	57.31 N	4.27 W
Muiron Islands II	162	21.35 S	114.20 E
Mui Ron-ma ›	110	18.07 N	106.22 E
Muir Seamount ✣[3]	16	33.41 N	62.30 W
Muirtown	46	56.16 N	3.45 W
Muir Woods	282	37.53 N	122.34 W
Muir Woods National Monument ♦	226	37.54 N	122.33 W
Muiskraal	158	33.56 S	21.13 E
Muisne	246	0.36 N	80.02 W
Muite	154	14.02 S	39.00 E
Mui Wo	271d	22.16 N	113.59 E
Muizen	50	51.01 N	4.31 E
Muja, Ityo.	144	12.02 N	39.29 E
Muja, S.S.S.R.	88	56.24 N	115.39 E
Muja ≐	88	56.24 N	115.39 E
Mujāhidpur ⊸[8]	272a	28.34 N	77.13 E
Mujang-ni	98	35.26 N	126.32 E
Mujezerskij	24	63.57 N	31.55 E
Mujiapucun	104	41.06 N	122.48 E
Mujiayu	105	40.24 N	116.55 E
Mujimbeji Mission	154	12.11 S	24.57 E
Mujnak	86	43.48 N	59.02 E
Muju	98	36.02 N	127.40 E
Mujunkum, peski ⊸[2]	86	44.20 N	71.00 E
Mukačevo	78	48.27 N	22.45 E
Mukah	112	2.54 N	112.06 E
Mukaishima	96	34.20 N	133.10 E
Mukalla → Al-Mukallā	144	14.32 N	49.08 E
Mukandpur ⊸[8]	272a	28.44 N	77.11 E
Mukandwara	120	24.49 N	75.59 E
Mukawa	94	35.47 N	138.23 E
Mukāwir	132	31.34 N	35.38 E
Mukawwar I	140	20.48 N	37.13 E
Mukdahan	110	16.32 N	104.43 E
Mukden → Shenyang	104	41.48 N	123.27 E
Muke Arba	144	8.57 N	42.09 E
Mukebo	154	6.49 S	28.03 E
Mukeriān	123	31.57 N	75.37 E
Mukharram al-Fawqānī	130	34.49 N	37.04 E
Mukhmās	132	31.52 N	35.17 E
Mukho	98	37.33 N	129.06 E
Mukilteo	224	47.56 N	122.18 W
Mukinbudin	162	30.54 S	118.13 E
Mukinge Hill	154	13.29 S	25.52 E
Mukō	96	34.56 N	135.42 E
Muko ≐	96	34.41 N	135.23 E
Mukomuko	112	2.35 S	101.07 E
Mukomwenze	154	6.52 S	27.16 E
Mukoshima-rettō II	14	27.37 N	142.10 E
Mukry	128	37.36 N	65.44 E
Muksi-ri	98	39.52 N	125.54 E
Muksu ≐	85	39.15 N	71.23 E
Muksūdpur	126	23.18 N	89.51 E
Muktāgācha	124	24.46 N	90.14 E
Muktsar	123	30.29 N	74.31 E
Mukuku	154	12.09 S	29.49 E
Mukuleshi ≐	154	10.21 S	24.30 E
Mukur	86	48.03 N	54.30 E
Mukusaki	115b	8.33 S	121.37 E
Mukutan	154	0.38 N	36.16 E
Mukutawa ≐	184	53.10 N	97.28 W
Mukwela	154	17.02 S	26.39 E
Mukwonago	216	42.51 N	88.19 W
Mūl	122	20.04 N	79.40 E
Mula, Esp.	34	38.03 N	1.30 W
Mula, Zhg.	102	29.40 N	100.39 E
Mula ≐, India	122	18.34 N	74.20 E
Mūla ≐, Pāk.	120	27.57 N	67.36 E
Mulādi	126	22.54 N	90.25 E
Muladu I	122	7.01 N	72.59 E
Mulaly	86	45.27 N	78.19 E
Mulan	89	45.57 N	128.03 E
Muland ⊸[8]	272c	19.10 N	72.57 E
Mulanda	152	14.41 S	21.48 E
Mulanje, Malawi	154	16.03 S	35.31 E
Mulanje, Moç.	154	16.03 S	35.45 E
Mulargia, Lago ⊜	71	39.37 N	9.14 E
Mulas, Punta ›	240m	18.09 N	65.27 W
Mulas, Punta de ›	240p	21.01 N	75.35 W
Mulatos	232	28.39 N	108.51 W
Mulatupo	246	8.57 N	77.45 W
Mulayit Taung ∧	110	16.11 N	98.32 E
Mulazzo	64	44.19 N	9.53 E
Mulbāgal	122	13.10 N	78.24 E
Mulben	46	57.31 N	3.06 W
Mulberry, Ar., U.S.	194	35.30 N	94.03 W
Mulberry, Fl., U.S.	220	27.53 N	81.58 W
Mulberry, In., U.S.	216	40.20 N	86.39 W
Mulberry, Oh., U.S.	218	39.11 N	84.14 W
Mulberry ≐	194	35.28 N	94.03 W
Mulberry Creek ≐, Al., U.S.	194	32.27 N	86.52 W
Mulberry Creek ≐, Tx., U.S.	196	34.37 N	100.55 W
Mulberry Fork ≐	194	33.33 N	87.11 W

Symbols in the index entries represent the broad categories identified in the key at the right. Symbols with superior numbers (⋏[1]) identify subcategories (see complete key on page I · 1).

Kartensymbole in dem Registerverzeichnis stellen die rechts in Schlüssel erklärten Kategorien dar. Symbole mit hochgestellten Ziffern (⋏[1]) bezeichnen Unterabteilungen einer Kategorie (vgl. vollständiger Schlüssel auf Seite I · 1).

Los símbolos incluídos en el texto del índice representan las grandes categorías identificadas con la clave a la derecha. Los símbolos con numeros en su parte superior (⋏[1]) identifican las subcategorías (véase la clave completa en la página I · 1).

Les symboles de l'index représentent les catégories indiquées dans la légende à droite. Les symboles suivis d'un indice (⋏[1]) représentent des sous-catégories (voir légende complète à la page I · 1).

Os símbolos incluídos no texto do índice representam as grandes categorias identificadas com a chave à direita. Os símbolos com números em sua parte superior (⋏[1]) identificam as subcategorias (veja-se a chave completa à página I · 1).

English	Deutsch	Español	Français	Português
∧ Mountain	Berg	Montaña	Montagne	Montanha
⋏ Mountains	Berge	Montañas	Montagnes	Montanhas
≍ Pass	Pass	Paso	Col	Passo
V Valley, Canyon	Tal, Cañon	Valle, Cañón	Vallée, Canyon	Vale, Canhão
≚ Plain	Ebene	Llano	Plaine	Planície
› Cape	Kap	Cabo	Cap	Cabo
I Island	Insel	Isla	Île	Ilha
II Islands	Inseln	Islas	Îles	Ilhas
± Other Topographic Features	Andere Topographische Objekte	Otros Elementos Topográficos	Autres données topographiques	Outros acidentes topográficos

ESPAÑOL

Nombre	Página	Lat.°′	Long.°′ W = Oeste
Mulberry Grove	219	38.55 N	89.16 W
Mulberry Mountain ∧	194	35.42 N	92.56 W
Mulchatna ≃	180	59.39 N	157.08 W
Mulchén	252	37.43 S	72.14 W
Mulda, D.D.R.	54	50.48 N	13.25 E
Mul'da, S.S.S.R.	24	67.28 N	63.34 E
Mulde ≃	54	51.52 N	12.15 E
Muldenstein	54	51.40 N	12.19 E
Muldersdrif se Loop ≃	273d	26.06 S	27.51 E
Muldersvlei	158	30.41 S	22.13 E
Muldoon	222	29.49 N	97.04 W
Muldraugh	194	37.56 N	85.59 W
Muldrow	194	35.24 N	94.35 W
Mule, Lac la ⊜	186	51.33 N	65.35 W
Muleba	154	1.49 S	31.40 E
Mule Creek ≃	198	37.05 N	99.00 W
Mulegé	232	26.53 N	112.01 W
Mulegns	58	46.33 N	9.37 E
Mulei	86	43.49 N	90.11 E
Mules (Mauls)	64	46.51 N	11.31 E
Mules, Pulau I	115b	8.54 S	120.17 E
Muleshoe	196	34.13 N	102.43 W
Mulevala	154	16.30 S	37.30 E
Mulga Downs	162	22.08 S	118.26 E
Mulgathing	162	30.15 S	134.00 E
Mulgathing Rocks ∧	162	30.14 S	133.58 E
Mulghar	126	22.46 N	89.45 E
Mulgoa	170	33.50 S	150.40 E
Mulgoa Creek ≃	274a	33.46 S	150.39 E
Mulgowie	171a	27.43 S	152.22 E
Mulgrave, Austl.	274b	37.56 S	145.12 E
Mulgrave, N.S., Can.	186	45.37 N	61.23 W
Mulgrave Hills ⩘[2]	180	67.42 N	163.24 W
Mulgul	162	24.49 S	118.26 E
Mulhacén ∧	34	37.03 N	3.19 W
Mulhall	196	36.03 N	97.24 W
Mülhausen → Mulhouse	58	47.45 N	7.20 E
Mülheim	56	49.54 N	7.01 E
Mülheim an der Ruhr	56	51.24 N	6.54 E
Mülheimer Ruhrtalbrüke ◆[5]	263	51.23 N	6.54 E
Mülheim-Karlich	56	50.21 N	7.28 E
Mulhouse (Mülhausen)	58	47.45 N	7.20 E
Muli	102	27.50 N	101.15 E
Muling, Zhg.	89	44.56 N	130.31 E
Muling, Zhg.	89	44.31 N	130.13 E
Muling ≃	89	45.53 N	133.30 E
Mulini, Capo ›	70	37.34 N	15.10 E
Mulino	224	45.13 N	122.34 W
Mulinu'u, Cape ›	175a	13.26 S	172.43 W
Mulita ≃	116	7.18 N	124.52 E
Mulkear ≃	48	52.40 N	8.33 W
Mūlki	122	13.06 N	74.48 E
Mull, Island of I	46	56.27 N	6.00 W
Mull, Sound of Ʉ	46	56.32 N	5.50 W
Mullagh	48	53.49 N	6.57 W
Mullaghareirk Mountains ⩘	48	52.20 N	9.10 W
Mullaghcleevaun ∧	48	53.06 N	6.24 W
Mullaghmore ∧	48	54.52 N	6.51 W
Mullan	202	47.28 N	115.48 W
Mullen	198	42.02 N	101.02 W
Müllenbach	56	50.19 N	6.55 E
Mullengudgery	166	31.41 S	147.26 E
Mullens	192	37.34 N	81.22 W
Muller, Pegunungan ⩘	112	0.40 N	113.50 E
Muller Creek ≃	162	22.29 S	134.30 E
Muller Range ⩘	164	5.35 S	142.15 E
Mullerup	41	55.30 N	11.13 E
Mullet Key I	220	27.37 N	82.44 W
Mullet Peninsula ›[1]	48	54.12 N	10.00 W
Mullett Lake ⊜	190	45.30 N	84.30 W
Mullewa	162	28.33 S	115.31 E
Mull Head ›, Scot., U.K.	46	58.58 N	2.43 W
Mull Head ›, Scot., U.K.	46	59.23 N	2.54 W
Müllheim	58	47.48 N	7.38 E
Mullhyttan	40	59.09 N	14.41 E
Mullica ≃	208	39.33 N	74.25 W
Mullica, Alquatka Branch ≃	285	39.47 N	74.48 W
Mullica, Sleeper Branch ≃	285	39.39 N	74.40 W
Mullica Hill	208	39.44 N	75.13 W
Mulligan ≃	166	25.00 S	138.30 E
Mulliken	216	42.45 N	84.53 W
Mullin	196	31.33 N	98.40 W
Mullinahone	48	52.30 N	7.30 W
Mullinavat	48	52.21 N	7.10 W
Mullingar	48	53.32 N	7.20 W
Mullins	192	34.12 N	79.15 W
Mullinville	198	37.35 N	99.28 W
Mullion	42	50.01 N	5.15 W
Mulloon Creek ≃	171b	35.12 S	149.38 E
Mullovka	80	54.13 N	49.25 E
Müllrose	54	52.14 N	14.25 E
Mullsjö	26	57.55 N	13.53 E
Mullumbimby	166	28.33 S	153.30 E
Mulobezi	154	16.48 S	25.09 E
Mulonda Funda	154	11.06 S	25.28 E
Mulondo	152	15.39 S	15.14 E
Mulongo	154	7.50 S	27.00 E
Mulshi Lake ⊜	122	18.30 N	73.30 E
Multai	120	21.46 N	78.15 E
Multān	123	30.11 N	71.29 E
Multé	232	17.41 N	91.24 W
Multen ⊜	40	59.10 N	14.37 E
Multia	26	62.25 N	24.47 E
Multnomah □[6]	224	45.30 N	122.22 W
Multnomah Channel ≃[1]	224	45.51 N	122.52 W
Multnomah Falls ∟	224	45.35 N	122.07 W
Mulu, Gunong ∧	112	4.04 N	114.56 E
Mulumbe, Monts ⩘	154	8.16 S	28.16 E
Mulungu	250	7.02 S	35.28 W
Mulungushi	154	14.40 S	28.50 E
Mulungushi Dam ◆[6]	154	14.40 S	28.50 E
Muluwusuhe ≃	120	34.40 N	95.00 E
Mulvane	198	37.28 N	97.14 W
Mulwad	140	18.39 N	30.35 E
Mulyah Mountain ∧	166	30.37 S	144.31 E
Muma	152	3.24 N	23.15 E
Mumbles Head ›	42	51.35 N	3.59 W
Mumbondo	152	10.09 S	14.15 E
Mumbra	272c	19.11 N	73.01 E
Mumbwa	154	14.59 S	27.04 E
Mumcular	130	37.05 N	27.40 E
Mume	154	9.40 S	27.26 E
Mumen	102	32.09 N	106.28 E
Mumeng	164	7.00 S	146.35 E
Mumford, N.Y., U.S.	210	42.59 N	77.52 W
Mumford, Tx., U.S.	222	30.44 N	96.34 W
Mumias	154	0.20 N	34.29 E
Mümling ≃	56	49.50 N	9.09 E
Mumoni ∧	154	0.31 S	38.01 E
Mumra	80	45.47 N	47.41 E
Mumu	140	12.06 N	23.42 E
Mumungwe	156	21.59 S	26.24 E
Mun ≃	110	15.19 N	105.30 E
Mun, Jabal ∧	140	14.08 N	22.42 E
Munā, Ar. Su.	144	21.25 N	39.52 E
Muna, Méx.	232	20.29 N	89.43 W
Muna ≃	74	67.52 N	123.06 E
Muna, Pulau I	112	5.00 S	122.30 E
Muna, Selat Ʉ	112	5.15 S	122.10 E
Munā al-Amīr	142	29.54 N	31.15 E
Munābāo	120	25.45 N	70.17 E
Munajly	86	46.47 N	54.31 E
Munakata	96	33.50 N	130.35 E
Munamägi ∧[2]	76	57.43 N	27.04 E
Munam-ni	98	38.41 N	126.54 E
Munam-san ∧	98	40.26 N	127.22 E
Munbong-ni	271b	37.43 N	126.49 E
Muncar	115a	8.26 S	114.20 E
Münchberg	54	50.11 N	11.47 E
Müncheberg	54	52.30 N	14.08 E
Münchehofe	264a	52.30 N	13.40 E
München	60	48.08 N	11.34 E
Münchenbernsdorf	54	50.49 N	11.56 E

FRANÇAIS

Nom	Page	Lat.°′	Long.°′ W = Ouest
Münchenbuchsee	58	47.01 N	7.27 E
Münchendorf	264b	48.02 N	16.23 E
München-Gladbach → Mönchen-gladbach	56	51.12 N	6.28 E
München-Riem, Flughafen ⊠	60	48.08 N	11.41 E
Münchenstein	58	47.31 N	7.37 E
Münchhausen	56	50.57 N	8.43 E
Munchique, Cerro ∧	246	2.32 N	76.57 W
Munch'ŏn	98	39.16 N	127.15 E
Muncie	216	40.11 N	85.23 W
Muncusun	130	38.54 N	35.38 E
Muncy	210	41.12 N	76.47 W
Muncy Creek ≃	210	41.13 N	76.48 W
Muncy Valley	210	41.21 N	76.35 W
Mundare	182	53.36 N	112.20 W
Mundaring	168a	31.54 S	116.10 E
Munday	196	33.26 N	99.37 W
Mundelein	216	42.15 N	88.00 W
Mündelheim ◆[8]	263	51.21 N	6.41 E
Münden	56	51.25 N	9.39 E
Munderfing	60	48.05 N	13.11 E
Munderkingen	58	48.14 N	9.38 E
Munderoo ∧	171b	35.48 S	147.47 E
Mundesley	42	52.53 N	1.26 E
Mundijong	168a	32.18 S	115.59 E
Mundiwindi	162	23.52 S	120.09 E
Mūndka ◆[8]	272a	28.41 N	77.02 E
Mundo ≃	34	38.19 N	1.40 W
Mundolsheim	58	48.39 N	7.42 E
Mundon Hill	260	51.41 N	0.42 E
Mundo Novo	255	11.52 S	40.28 W
Mundra	120	22.51 N	69.44 E
Mundrabilla	162	31.52 S	127.51 E
Mundubbera	166	25.36 S	151.18 E
Mundybaš	86	53.14 N	87.19 E
Mundytau, gora ∧	85	38.00 N	68.27 E
Munene	154	20.38 S	30.03 E
Munenga	152	10.02 S	14.41 E
Munera	34	39.02 N	2.28 W
Munford	194	35.26 N	89.48 W
Munfordville	194	37.16 N	85.53 W
Mungallala	166	26.27 S	147.33 E
Mungallala Creek ≃	166	28.05 S	147.15 E
Mungana	166	17.07 S	144.24 E
Mungaoli	124	24.25 N	78.06 E
Mungári	154	17.12 S	33.31 E
Mungar Junction	166	25.36 S	152.36 E
Mungau	152	13.56 S	21.55 E
Mungbere	154	2.38 N	28.30 E
Mungeli	124	22.04 N	81.41 E
Mungeranie	162	28.00 S	138.36 E
Mungindi	166	28.58 S	148.59 E
Mungla	126	22.19 N	89.36 E
Mungo	152	11.49 S	16.16 E
Mungra Badshāhpur	124	25.40 N	82.11 E
Mungun-Tajga, gora ∧	86	50.16 N	90.05 E
Mun'gyŏng	98	36.44 N	128.07 E
Munhall	214	40.23 N	79.54 W
Munhamade	154	16.37 S	36.58 E
Munhango	152	12.12 S	18.42 E
Munhango ≃	152	11.20 S	19.50 E
Munhoz	256	22.37 S	46.22 W
Munhye-ri	98	38.10 N	127.19 E
Munich → München	60	48.08 N	11.34 E
Muniesa	34	41.02 N	0.48 W
Munim ≃	250	2.45 S	44.04 W
Munirka ◆[8]	272a	28.34 N	77.10 E
Munising	190	46.24 N	86.38 W
Munith	216	42.23 N	84.15 W
Muñiz	258	34.33 S	58.42 W
Muniz Freire	255	20.28 S	41.25 W
Munkács → Mukačevo	78	48.27 N	22.45 E
Munka-Ljungby	41	56.15 N	12.58 E
Munkebjerg ∧[2]	41	55.41 N	9.37 E
Munkebo	41	55.27 N	10.34 E
Munkedal	26	58.29 N	11.41 E
Munkerud	40	59.50 N	13.31 E
Munkfors	40	59.50 N	13.32 E
Munksund	26	65.17 N	21.29 E
Munktorp	40	59.32 N	16.08 E
Munku-Sardyk, gora ∧	88	51.45 N	100.32 E
Munlochy	46	57.32 N	4.15 W
Münnerstadt	56	50.15 N	10.11 E
Munnsville	210	42.58 N	75.35 W
Muñoz	116	15.43 N	120.54 E
Muñoz ≃	240p	21.22 N	78.32 W
Munozero	24	67.05 N	34.12 E
Muñoz Gamero, Península ›[1]	254	52.30 S	73.10 W
Munpal-li	271b	37.45 N	126.43 E
Munro ◆[8]	288	34.32 S	58.31 W
Munroe Falls	214	41.08 N	81.26 W
Munro Lake ⊜	184	54.38 N	95.16 W
Munsan	98	37.51 N	126.48 E
Munsarpur	126	24.18 N	88.26 E
Munsey Park	276	40.48 N	73.41 W
Munshiganj	124	23.33 N	90.32 E
Münsing	64	47.54 N	11.22 E
Münsingen, B.R.D.	58	48.25 N	9.29 E
Münsingen, Schw.	58	46.53 N	7.34 E
Munsö I	40	59.23 N	17.35 E
Munson, Ab., Can.	182	51.34 N	112.45 W
Munson, Pa., U.S.	214	40.57 N	78.10 W
Munson Knob ∧[2]	214	40.40 N	81.54 W
Munsons Corners	210	42.35 N	76.13 W
Münster, B.R.D.	52	51.57 N	7.37 E
Münster, B.R.D.	52	52.59 N	10.05 E
Münster, B.R.D.	56	49.55 N	8.52 E
Munster, Fr.	56	48.55 N	6.54 E
Munster, Fr.	58	48.03 N	7.08 E
Münster, Schw.	58	46.29 N	8.16 E
Munster, In., U.S.	216	41.33 N	87.30 W
Münster □[6]	52	51.50 N	7.25 E
Munster □[9]	48	52.25 N	8.20 W
Munster ≃	48	52.33 N	7.12 W
Münsterberg → Ziębice	30	50.37 N	17.00 E
Münsterkirche ʋ[1]	263	51.27 N	7.01 E
Münsterland ◆[1]	52	52.00 N	7.30 E
Münsterlingen	58	47.38 N	9.14 E
Münstermaifeld	56	50.15 N	7.22 E
Muntadgin	162	31.45 S	118.34 E
Muntahak ∧	114	1.52 N	103.47 E
Munte	112	0.30 N	119.55 E
Muntendam	52	53.07 N	6.53 E
Muntok	112	2.04 S	105.11 E
Mununzi	154	0.36 N	29.15 E
Munuscong Lake ⊜	190	46.10 N	84.08 W
Münzenberg	56	50.27 N	8.46 E
Münzkirchen	60	48.29 N	13.34 E
Munzur Silsilesi ⩘	130	39.30 N	39.10 E
Muojärvi ⊜	26	65.56 N	29.36 E
Muolea Point ›	229a	20.41 N	156.01 W
Muong Het	110	20.49 N	104.01 E
Muong-hinh	110	19.49 N	105.03 E
Muong Khoua	110	21.05 N	102.31 E
Muong Saiapoun	110	18.24 N	101.31 E
Muong-sen	110	19.24 N	104.08 E
Muong-te	110	22.28 N	102.37 E
Muonio	24	67.57 N	23.42 E
Muoro	36	40.20 N	9.20 E
Muotathal	58	46.59 N	8.46 E
Mupa	152	16.10 S	15.44 E
Mupa, Parque Nacional da ◆[4]	152	16.00 S	15.35 E
Muping	98	37.24 N	121.35 E
Mupini	156	17.50 S	19.40 E
Mup'ungjang	98	35.58 N	127.49 E
Muqaddam, Wādī V	140	18.04 N	31.30 E
Muqatta'	140	14.40 N	35.51 E
Muqaybirah, Bi'r al- ⍑[4]	142	30.53 N	32.50 E
Muqayshit I	128	24.12 N	53.42 E
Muqdisho (Mogadishu)	144	2.04 N	45.22 E
Muqi	98	41.46 N	124.39 E
Muqsam, Jabal ∧	140	13.38 N	27.42 E
Muquequete	152	14.50 S	14.16 E

PORTUGUÊS

Nome	Página	Lat.°′	Long.°′ W = Oeste
Muqui	255	20.57 S	41.20 W
Mur (Mura) ≃	30	46.18 N	16.53 E
Mura (Mur) ≃, Europe	30	46.18 N	16.53 E
Mura ≃, S.S.S.R.	88	58.27 N	98.34 E
Muradiye, Tür.	128	38.59 N	43.46 E
Muradiye, Tür.	130	38.39 N	27.21 E
Murādnagar	124	28.47 N	77.30 E
Murafa ≃	78	48.13 N	28.14 E
Murāgācha	126	23.32 N	88.24 E
Muraglione, Passo del)(	66	43.56 N	11.39 E
Murajá	250	0.47 S	47.57 W
Murakami	92	38.14 N	139.29 E
Murallón, Cerro ∧	254	49.48 S	73.25 W
Murambi	154	1.46 S	30.23 E
Muramvya	154	3.16 S	29.37 E
Muráň	30	48.46 N	20.02 E
Murana	164	3.33 S	133.49 E
Murang'a	154	0.43 S	37.09 E
Murano, Isola di I	64	45.28 N	12.21 E
Muranskij porog ∟	88	58.02 N	112.16 E
Muraoka	96	35.28 N	134.35 E
Murarai	124	24.27 N	87.52 E
Muraši	24	59.24 N	48.55 E
Muraški	265b	55.59 N	37.45 E
Murat	32	45.07 N	2.52 E
Murat ≃	130	38.39 N	39.50 E
Muratdağı ∧	130	38.55 N	29.43 E
Muratkovo	86	58.26 N	62.23 E
Muratlı	130	41.10 N	27.30 E
Muratovo	83	48.48 N	38.45 E
Muratpur	272b	22.59 N	88.27 E
Murau	61	47.07 N	14.10 E
Murauaú ≃	246	0.09 N	60.40 W
Muravera	71	39.25 N	9.34 E
Muravjovka	89	49.50 N	127.44 E
Muravjovo	76	56.14 N	34.14 E
Murayama	92	38.28 N	140.22 E
Murayama-chosuichi ⊜[1]	268	35.45 N	139.25 E
Muraysah, Ra's al- ›	146	31.55 N	25.02 E
Murča	34	41.24 N	7.27 W
Murcanyo	144	11.41 N	50.27 E
Mūrcheh Khvort	128	33.06 N	51.30 E
Murchin	54	53.54 N	13.44 E
Murchison, Austl.	166	36.37 S	145.14 E
Murchison, N.Z.	172	41.48 S	172.20 E
Murchison, Tx., U.S.	222	32.17 N	95.45 W
Murchison ≃	162	27.42 S	114.09 E
Murchison, Mount ∧, Austl.	162	26.46 S	116.25 E
Murchison, Mount ∧, N.Z.	172	43.01 S	171.22 E
Murchison Falls → Kabalega Falls ∟	154	2.17 N	31.41 E
Murchison Range ⩘	162	20.11 S	134.26 E
Murcia, Esp.	34	37.59 N	1.07 W
Murcia, Pil.	116	10.36 N	123.02 E
Murcia □[4], Esp.	34	38.00 N	1.30 W
Murcia □[4], Esp.	148	37.55 N	1.30 W
Murciélago	236	10.55 N	85.44 W
Murciélago, Islas II	236	10.51 N	85.57 W
Murcielagos Bay ᑕ	116	8.39 N	123.33 E
Mur-de-Barrez	32	44.51 N	2.39 E
Murdeduke, Lake ⊜	169	38.11 S	143.53 E
Murder Creek ≃, Al., U.S.	194	31.04 N	87.06 W
Murder Creek ≃, N.Y., U.S.	210	43.05 N	78.31 W
Murderkill ≃	208	39.03 N	75.24 W
Murdo	198	43.53 N	100.42 W
Murdock	220	27.00 N	82.08 W
Mure	94	36.45 N	138.14 E
Mureaux, Aérodrome des ⊠	261	49.00 N	1.57 E
Mureck	61	46.42 N	15.46 E
Mürefte	130	40.40 N	27.14 E
Mureș □[6]	38	46.35 N	24.40 E
Mureș (Maros) ≃	38	46.15 N	20.13 E
Muret	32	43.28 N	1.21 E
Murewa	154	17.39 S	31.47 E
Murfreesboro, Ar., U.S.	194	34.03 N	93.41 W
Murfreesboro, N.C., U.S.	192	36.26 N	77.05 W
Murfreesboro, Tn., U.S.	194	35.50 N	86.23 W
Murg	58	47.33 N	8.01 E
Murg ≃	56	48.55 N	8.10 E
Murgab	85	38.10 N	73.59 E
Murgab (Morghāb) ≃, Asia	128	38.18 N	61.12 E
Murgab ≃, S.S.S.R.	85	38.05 N	71.55 E
Murgeni	38	46.12 N	28.01 E
Murgenthal	58	47.16 N	7.50 E
Murgha Faqīrzai	120	30.11 N	67.48 E
Murgha Kibzai	120	30.44 N	69.25 E
Murgon	166	26.15 S	151.57 E
Murguía	34	42.57 N	2.49 W
Murgul	130	41.17 N	41.46 E
Muri, Cook Is.	174k	21.14 S	159.43 W
Muri, Nig.	146	9.11 N	10.53 E
Muri, Schw.	58	46.56 N	7.29 E
Muri, Schw.	58	47.16 N	8.21 E
Muria, Gunung ∧	112	6.36 S	110.53 E
Muriaé	255	21.08 S	42.22 W
Muriaé ≃	255	21.43 S	41.22 W
Murias de Paredes	34	42.51 N	6.11 W
Muribeca	250	10.26 S	36.59 W
Muribeca dos Guararapes	250	8.10 S	35.01 W
Murici	250	9.19 S	35.56 W
Muricizal ≃	250	6.40 S	48.40 W
Murīdke	123	31.48 N	74.16 E
Muriége	152	9.58 S	21.11 E
Muriel Lake ⊜	182	54.10 N	110.40 W
Murih, Pulau I	112	1.54 N	108.38 E
Murila	152	10.44 S	20.20 E
Murilo I[1]	14	8.40 N	152.11 E
Mūrinda	123	30.47 N	76.29 E
Murinéli	256	22.07 S	42.39 W
Murinja	88	54.47 N	107.21 E
Murino, S.S.S.R.	88	51.30 N	104.23 E
Murino, S.S.S.R.	265a	60.03 N	30.27 E
Murinskij ≃	265a	60.01 N	30.28 E
Muriqui ≃	287a	22.52 S	43.02 W
Murisengo	62	45.05 N	8.08 E
Mūrītāniyā → Mauritania □[1]	134	20.00 N	12.00 W
Muritiba	255	12.39 S	38.59 W
Müritz ⊜	54	53.25 N	12.43 E
Muriwai	172	38.46 S	177.55 E
Murkong Selek	120	27.49 N	95.16 E
Murliganj	124	25.54 N	86.59 E
Murlo	66	43.09 N	11.23 E
Murmansk	24	68.58 N	33.05 E
Murmansk Rise ✦[3]	12	75.00 N	37.00 E
Murmerwoude	52	53.16 N	6.00 E
Murmino	80	54.36 N	40.03 E
Murnau	64	47.40 N	11.12 E
Murnei	140	12.57 N	22.52 E
Murō	94	34.34 N	136.02 E
Murō-Akame-Aoyama-kokutei-kōen ♠	94	34.30 N	136.10 E
Muro Lucano	68	40.45 N	15.29 E
Murom	80	55.34 N	42.02 E
Muromcevo	86	56.23 N	75.14 E
Muroran	92a	42.18 N	140.59 E
Muros	34	42.47 N	9.02 W
Muros y Noya, Ría de ᑕ[1]	34	42.45 N	9.00 W
Muroto	96	33.18 N	134.09 E
Muroto-Anan-kaigan-kokutei-kōen ♠	96	33.41 N	134.32 E
Muroto-zaki ›	96	33.15 N	134.11 E
Murovanyje Kurilovcy	78	48.43 N	27.31 E
Murowana Goślina	30	52.35 N	17.01 E
Murphy, Id., U.S.	202	43.13 N	116.33 W
Murphy, Mo., U.S.	219	38.29 N	90.29 W
Murphy, N.C., U.S.	192	35.05 N	84.02 W
Murphy Lake ⊜	182	52.03 N	121.14 W

Murphys	226	38.08 N	120.27 W
Murphysboro	194	37.45 N	89.20 W
Murphy Slough ≃	226	36.28 N	120.00 W
Murr ≃	56	48.57 N	9.16 E
Murr, Wādī V	142	28.27 N	32.18 E
Murrah, Qārat al- ∧[2]	142	30.00 N	32.41 E
Murrah al-Kubrā, Al-Buḥayrah al- (Great Bitter Lake) ⊜	142	30.20 N	32.23 E
Murrah aṣ-Ṣughrā, Al-Buḥayrah al- (Little Bitter Lake) ⊜	142	30.13 N	32.33 E
Murra Murra	166	28.16 S	146.48 E
Murrāt, Ābār ⍑[4]	140	21.03 N	32.55 E
Murray, Ia., U.S.	190	41.02 N	93.56 W
Murray, Ky., U.S.	194	36.36 N	88.18 W
Murray, Ut., U.S.	200	40.40 N	111.53 W
Murray ≃, Austl.	166	35.22 S	139.22 E
Murray ≃, Austl.	168a	32.35 S	115.46 E
Murray ≃, B.C., Can.	182	55.40 N	121.10 W
Murray, Lake ⊜	164	7.00 S	141.30 E
Murray, Lake ⊜[1]	192	34.04 N	81.23 W
Murray, Mount ∧, Yk., Can.	180	60.54 N	128.49 W
Murray, Mount ∧, Pap. N. Gui.	164	6.46 S	144.01 E
Murray Bay → La Malbaie	186	47.39 N	70.10 W
Murray Bridge	168b	35.07 S	139.17 E
Murray Canal ≊	212	44.04 N	77.35 W
Murray City	188	39.30 N	82.09 W
Murray Downs	162	21.04 S	134.40 E
Murray Fracture Zone ✦	16	34.00 N	135.00 W
Murray Harbour	186	46.00 N	62.31 W
Murray Head ›	186	46.00 N	62.28 W
Murray Maxwell Bay ᑕ	176	70.00 N	80.00 W
Murray Mouth ≃[1]	168b	35.34 S	138.54 E
Murray River	186	46.01 N	62.37 W
Murraysburg	158	31.58 S	23.47 E
Murrayville, B.C., Can.	224	49.10 N	122.36 W
Murrayville, Il., U.S.	194	39.35 N	90.15 W
Murrébuè	154	13.02 S	40.30 E
Murree	123	33.54 N	73.24 E
Mürren	58	46.34 N	7.54 E
Murrhardt	56	48.59 N	9.34 E
Murrí ≃	246	6.33 N	76.52 W
Murrieta	228	33.33 N	117.12 W
Murrin Murrin	162	28.55 S	121.49 E
Murro di Porca, Capo ›	70	37.00 N	15.20 E
Murrumbidgee ≃	166	34.43 S	143.12 E
Murrumburrah	166	34.33 S	148.21 E
Murrupula	154	15.27 S	38.47 E
Murrurundi	166	31.46 S	150.50 E
Murry Hill	279b	40.17 N	80.09 W
Murrysville	279b	40.25 N	79.41 W
Mursala, Pulau I	114	1.38 N	98.32 E
Mürsel	130	39.11 N	37.59 E
Murshidābād	126	24.11 N	88.16 E
Murshidābād □[5]	126	24.05 N	88.10 E
Mürşitpınar	130	36.54 N	38.19 E
Murska Sobota	61	46.40 N	16.10 E
Murskij, porog ∟	88	58.27 N	98.30 E
Mursko središče	61	46.31 N	16.27 E
Murtajāpur	122	20.44 N	77.23 E
Murtal	266c	38.42 N	9.22 W
Murtee	166	31.35 S	143.30 E
Murten	58	46.56 N	7.07 E
Murtensee → Morat, Lac de ⊜	58	46.55 N	7.05 E
Murter, Otok I	36	43.48 N	15.37 E
Murtle Lake ⊜	182	52.08 N	119.38 W
Murtoa	166	36.37 S	142.28 E
Murton	44	54.49 N	1.24 W
Murtosa	34	40.44 N	8.38 W
Muru	140	6.36 N	29.15 E
Muru ≃	248	8.09 S	70.45 W
Muru, Capu di ›	36	41.44 N	8.40 E
Murud	122	18.19 N	72.58 E
Murud, Gunong ∧	112	3.52 N	115.30 E
Murukta	74	67.46 N	102.01 E
Murung ≃	112	0.12 S	114.03 E
Murupara	172	38.28 S	176.42 E
Murutinga	246	3.26 S	59.12 W
Murvaul, Lake ⊜[1]	222	32.03 N	94.28 W
Murvaul Creek ≃	194	32.05 N	94.12 W
Murwāra	124	23.51 N	80.24 E
Murwillumbah	166	28.19 S	153.24 E
Mürz ≃	61	47.24 N	15.17 E
Mürzsteg	61	47.40 N	15.29 E
Mürzzuschlag	61	47.36 N	15.41 E
Muş	130	38.44 N	41.30 E
Muş □[4]	128	39.00 N	42.00 E
Musa	152	2.40 N	19.18 E
Musa ≃, Pap. N. Gui.	164	9.25 S	148.50 E
Mūša ≃, S.S.S.R.	76	56.24 N	24.10 E
Mūsā, Jabal (Mount Sinai) ∧	140	28.32 N	33.59 E
Mūsā, 'Uyūn (Springs of Moses) ⍑[4]	142	29.52 N	32.39 E
Musabeyli	130	39.51 N	34.37 E
Musadi	152	2.34 S	22.47 E
Musaid	146	31.35 N	25.03 E
Mūsa Khel	123	32.38 N	71.44 E
Mūsa Khel Bāzār	120	30.52 N	69.49 E
Musala ∧	38	42.11 N	23.34 E
Musan	98	42.14 N	129.13 E
Musao	154	7.43 S	26.17 E
Mūsá Qal'eh	120	32.22 N	64.46 E
Mūsā Qal'eh ≃	128	32.05 N	64.51 E
Musar	272b	22.54 N	88.14 E
Musara	164	10.00 S	149.50 E
Musasa	154	3.21 S	31.33 E
Musashi → Iruma, Nihon	94	35.50 N	139.24 E
Musashi, Nihon	96	33.30 N	131.43 E
Musashimurayama	268	35.45 N	139.23 E
Musashino	94	35.42 N	139.34 E
Musashino-daichi ⩘[1]	268	35.45 N	139.35 E
Musau	58	47.32 N	10.40 E
Musay'īd	128	24.59 N	51.32 E
Musaymīr	144	13.27 N	44.37 E
Musazade	130	41.22 N	41.16 E
Mūsāzai	120	30.23 N	66.32 E
Muscat → Masqaṭ	128	23.37 N	58.35 E
Muscat and Oman → Oman □[1]	118	22.00 N	58.00 E
Muscatatuck ≃	218	38.46 N	86.10 W
Muscatatuck, Grassy Fork ≃	218	38.45 N	85.07 W
Muscatatuck, Vernon Fork ≃	218	38.46 N	85.54 W
Muscatine	190	41.25 N	91.03 W
Müsch	56	50.23 N	6.49 E
Mus-Chaja, gora ∧	74	62.35 N	140.50 E
Muschwitz	54	51.11 N	12.07 E
Muscle Shoals	194	34.44 N	87.40 W
Musclow, Mount ∧	182	53.17 N	127.09 W
Musclow Lake ⊜	184	51.25 N	94.56 W
Muscoda	190	43.11 N	90.26 W
Musconetcong ≃	210	40.36 N	75.11 W
Musconetcong, Lake ⊜	276	40.54 N	74.42 W
Muscongus Bay ᑕ	188	43.55 N	69.20 W
Muscote Bay ᑕ	212	44.06 N	77.18 W
Muscowpetung Indian Reserve ◆[4]	184	50.45 N	104.15 W
Muscoy	228	34.09 N	117.20 W
Muse	214	40.17 N	80.12 W
Musengezi ≃	154	15.43 S	31.14 E
Museo Nacional de Antropologia ʋ	286a	19.25 N	99.11 W
Müsgebi	130	37.02 N	27.21 E
Musgrave, Austl.	164	14.47 S	143.30 E

Musgrave, B.C., Can.	224	48.45 N	123.32 W
Musgrave, Mount ∧	172	43.48 S	170.43 E
Musgrave Ranges ⩘	162	26.10 S	131.50 E
Musgravetown	186	48.24 N	53.53 W
Mūshā	142	27.08 N	31.18 E
Mushābani	126	22.31 N	86.27 E
Mushāsh, Jabal al- ∧[2]	142	28.54 N	31.11 E
Mushenge	152	4.32 S	21.21 E
Mushie	152	3.01 S	16.54 E
Mushima	154	14.13 S	25.05 E
Mushin	150	6.32 N	3.22 E
Mushu Island I	164	3.25 S	143.35 E
Mūsi ≃, India	122	16.41 N	79.40 E
Musi ≃, Indon.	112	2.20 S	104.56 E
Musicians Seamounts ✦[3]	6	31.00 N	162.00 W
Musishan ∧	120	36.03 N	80.07 E
Muskauer Heide ◆[3]	54	51.25 N	14.40 E
Muskeg ≃	182	54.01 N	119.03 W
Muskeget Channel Ʉ	207	41.25 N	70.20 W
Muskeget Island I	207	41.20 N	70.18 W
Muskeg Lake Indian Reserve ◆[4]	184	52.58 N	106.57 W
Muskego	216	42.54 N	88.08 W
Muskego Lake ⊜	216	42.53 N	88.07 W
Muskegon	216	43.14 N	86.14 W
Muskegon □[6]	216	43.12 N	86.08 W
Muskegon ≃	190	43.14 N	86.20 W
Muskegon County Airport ⊠	216	43.10 N	86.14 W
Muskegon Heights	216	43.12 N	86.14 W
Muskegon Lake ⊜	216	43.14 N	86.17 W
Muskegon State Park ♠	216	43.14 N	86.20 W
Muškětova, gora ∧	88	53.35 N	113.32 E
Muskingum □[6]	214	40.06 N	81.51 W
Muskingum ≃	188	39.27 N	81.30 W
Muskingum Brook ≃	285	39.48 N	74.44 W
Muskira	124	25.40 N	79.48 E
Muskö I	40	59.00 N	18.06 E
Muskoday Indian Reserve ◆[4]	184	53.06 N	105.30 W
Muskogee	196	35.44 N	95.22 W
Muskoka □[6]	212	45.05 N	79.03 W
Muskoka, Lake ⊜	212	45.00 N	79.25 W
Muskoka, North Branch ≃	212	45.02 N	79.19 W
Muskoka, South Branch ≃	212	45.02 N	79.19 W
Muskosh Channel Ʉ	212	44.55 N	79.53 W
Muskowekwan Indian Reserve ◆[4]	184	51.19 N	104.06 W
Muskrat Creek ≃	202	43.09 N	108.11 W
Muskrat Dam Lake ⊜	184	53.25 N	91.40 W
Muskrat Lake ⊜	190	45.40 N	76.55 W
Muskwa ≃	176	58.45 N	122.35 W
Muskwa Lake ⊜	182	56.09 N	114.38 W
Musl'umovo	80	55.18 N	53.12 E
Muşmuş	132	32.32 N	35.09 E
Musocco ◆[8]	266b	45.30 N	9.08 E
Musofu Mission	154	13.31 S	29.02 E
Musoma	154	1.30 S	33.48 E
Musone ≃, It.	64	45.50 N	11.55 E
Musone ≃, It.	66	43.28 N	13.38 E
Musoshi	154	11.54 S	27.46 E
Musquanousse, Lac ⊜	186	50.22 N	61.05 W
Musquapsink Brook ≃	276	40.59 N	74.01 W
Musquaro, Lac ⊜	186	50.38 N	61.05 W
Musquash ≃	212	44.57 N	79.52 W
Musquash Brook ≃	283	42.42 N	71.26 W
Musquashcut Pond ⊜	283	42.13 N	70.46 W
Musquodoboit Harbour	186	44.47 N	63.09 W
Mussau Island I	164	1.30 S	149.40 E
Musselburgh	46	55.57 N	3.04 W
Musselkanaal	52	52.56 N	7.00 E
Musselshell ≃	202	47.21 N	107.58 W
Mussende	152	10.32 S	16.05 E
Mussidan	32	45.02 N	0.22 E
Mussolo	152	9.59 S	17.19 E
Mussomeli	70	37.35 N	13.45 E
Mussoorie	124	30.27 N	78.05 E
Mussuco	152	17.08 S	19.05 E
Mussum	52	51.48 N	6.34 E
Mussuma	152	14.14 S	21.59 E
Mussy-sur-Seine	58	47.58 N	4.30 E
Mustafakemalpaşa	130	40.02 N	28.24 E
Mustafino	80	55.01 N	53.38 E
Mustahil	144	5.12 N	44.17 E
Müstair	58	46.37 N	10.27 E
Mustajevo	80	51.48 N	53.25 E
Mustajõe	76	57.59 N	26.58 E
Mustāng	124	29.11 N	83.58 E
Mustang Draw V	196	32.12 N	101.36 W
Mustang Island I	196	28.00 N	96.55 W
Mustāy	142	30.37 N	31.09 E
Musters, Lago ⊜	254	45.27 S	69.13 W
Mustinka ≃	198	45.45 N	96.38 W
Mustjala	76	58.28 N	22.14 E
Mustla	76	58.14 N	25.52 E
Musṭurud	273c	30.08 N	31.17 E
Mustvee	76	58.51 N	26.56 E
Musu-dan ›	98	40.50 N	129.43 E
Musun	84	39.42 N	43.49 E
Muswellbrook	166	32.16 S	150.53 E
Muszyna	30	49.21 N	20.54 E
Mūt, Miṣr	140	25.29 N	28.59 E
Mut, Tür.	130	36.39 N	33.27 E
Muta	61	46.37 N	15.10 E
Mutá, Ponta do ›	255	13.52 S	38.56 W
Mu'tah	132	31.06 N	35.42 E
Mutalau	174v	18.56 S	169.50 W
Mutambara	154	19.36 S	32.33 E
Mutanchiang → Mudanjiang	89	44.35 N	129.36 E
Mutanda, Moç.	156	21.02 S	33.31 E
Mutanda, Zaïre	152	5.17 S	16.34 E
Mutanda Mission	154	12.24 S	26.16 E
Mutankiang → Mudanjiang	89	44.35 N	129.36 E
Mutarammil, Jabal al- ∧	132	31.04 N	36.06 E
Mutare	154	18.58 S	32.40 E
Mutbīn	132	33.09 N	36.15 E
Mutějovice	54	50.09 N	13.41 E
Mutha	154	1.48 S	38.26 E
Muthill	46	56.19 N	3.50 W
Mutiko	154	1.39 S	28.12 E
Muting	164	7.23 S	140.20 E
Mutis, Gunung ∧	112	9.34 S	124.14 E
Mutmur	130	38.51 N	38.31 E
Mutoko	154	17.24 S	32.13 E
Mutombo-Mukulu	152	7.58 S	24.00 E
Mutoraj	74	61.20 N	100.30 E
Mutoto	152	5.42 S	22.42 E
Mutouchengzi	98	41.20 N	119.59 E
Mutouhao	107	28.49 N	105.04 E
Mutsamudu	157a	12.09 S	44.25 E
Mutshatsha	152	10.39 S	24.27 E
Mutsu	92	41.17 N	141.10 E
Mutsuai	268	35.08 N	139.38 E
Mutsumi	96	34.26 N	131.34 E
Mutsuura ◆[8]	268	35.19 N	139.37 E
Mutsu-wan ᑕ	92	41.05 N	140.55 E
Muttaburra	166	22.36 S	144.33 E
Mutte Kopf ∧	58	47.16 N	10.39 E
Muttenz	58	47.32 N	7.39 E
Mutters	64	47.14 N	11.23 E
Mutterstadt	56	49.26 N	8.21 E
Mutton Bird Islands II	172	47.15 S	167.24 E
Muttontown	276	40.49 N	73.33 W
Muttra → Mathura	124	27.30 N	77.41 E
Muttyāluppettai	122	11.57 N	79.50 E
Mutual, Oh., U.S.	218	40.05 N	83.38 W
Mutual, Pa., U.S.	279b	40.14 N	79.30 W

Muṭūbis	142	31.18 N	30.31 E
Mutuca, Ribeirão da ≃	256	21.36 S	45.39 W
Mutucu, Lago ⊜	250	1.21 N	50.24 W
Mutuípe	255	13.15 S	39.31 W
Mutum	255	19.49 S	41.26 W
Mutum ≃	246	4.25 S	68.03 W
Mutum Biyu	146	8.38 N	10.46 E
Mutumbo	152	13.14 S	17.17 E
Mutunópolis	255	13.40 S	49.15 W
Muturi	164	2.06 S	133.43 E
Muturi ≃	164	2.13 S	133.40 E
Mututi, Ilha I	250	0.45 S	51.00 W
Mutzig	58	48.32 N	7.28 E
Mutzschen	54	51.16 N	12.53 E
Mu Us Shamo ◆[2]	102	38.45 N	109.10 E
Mūvattupula	122	9.58 N	76.35 E
Muvukoni	154	0.24 S	38.14 E
Muwopu	104	41.03 N	121.12 E
Muxaluando	152	8.07 S	14.17 E
Muxihe	100	31.03 N	115.21 E
Muxima	152	9.31 S	13.56 E
Muyaga	154	3.14 S	30.33 E
Muyang	100	27.06 N	119.34 E
Muyang ≃	100	27.00 N	119.41 E
Muyinga	154	2.51 S	30.20 E
Muymanu ≃	248	11.27 S	69.03 W
Muy Muy	236	12.46 N	85.38 W
Muyuka	152	4.17 N	9.25 E
Muyumba	154	7.15 S	26.59 E
Mužač'	82	54.22 N	36.21 E
Muzaffarābād	123	34.22 N	73.28 E
Muzaffargarh	123	30.04 N	71.12 E
Muzaffarnagar	124	29.28 N	77.41 E
Muzaffarnagar □[5]	124	29.30 N	77.30 E
Muzaffarpur	124	26.07 N	85.24 E
Muzaffarpur □[5]	124	26.00 N	85.20 E
Muzambinho	256	21.22 S	46.32 W
Muzambinho ≃	256	21.15 S	46.26 W
Muzambo ≃	256	21.17 S	46.16 W
Muzat ≃	90	41.15 N	83.27 E
Muzayrīb	132	32.42 N	36.01 E
Muzbek, gora ∧	85	40.23 N	69.39 E
Muzbel' ◆[1]	86	50.15 N	70.50 E
Muzeze	152	15.03 S	17.43 E
Muzhen	100	30.43 N	117.56 E
Muži	74	65.22 N	64.40 E
Mužiči	84	43.03 N	44.59 E
Mužiksu	86	47.42 N	84.58 E
Muzillac	32	47.33 N	2.29 W
Muzkol, chrebet ⩘	85	38.25 N	73.30 E
Muzoka	154	16.41 S	27.19 E
Muzon, Cape ›	182	54.41 N	132.44 W
Muztag ∧	90	36.25 N	87.25 E
Muztagata ∧	85	38.17 N	75.11 E
Muz Tau ∧	86	43.50 N	85.40 E
Muzūrah	142	28.53 N	30.48 E
Muzzana del Turgnano	64	45.49 N	13.08 E
Mvam	152	0.13 S	9.39 E
Mvangan	152	2.38 N	11.44 E
Mvela	154	14.46 S	35.16 E
Mvengué	152	3.17 N	11.01 E
Mvolo	140	6.03 N	29.56 E
Mvomero	154	6.20 S	37.25 E
Mvoti ≃	158	29.24 S	31.22 E
Mvoung ≃	152	0.04 N	12.18 E
Mvouti	152	4.15 S	12.29 E
Mvuha	154	7.12 S	37.51 E
Mvuma	154	19.19 S	30.35 E
Mwadi-Kalumba	152	7.53 S	18.46 E
Mwadui	154	3.33 S	33.36 E
Mwali (Mohéli) I	157a	12.15 S	43.45 E
Mwami	154	16.40 S	29.46 E
Mwanangumune	152	15.31 S	23.30 E
Mwango	152	6.51 S	24.13 E
Mwanza, Malawi	154	15.37 S	34.31 E
Mwanza, Tan.	154	2.31 S	32.54 E
Mwanza, Zaïre	154	7.54 S	26.45 E
Mwanza, Zam.	152	17.02 S	24.27 E
Mwanza □[4]	154	2.45 S	32.45 E
Mwanza Gulf ᑕ	154	2.35 S	32.51 E
Mwaya, Tan.	154	9.33 S	33.57 E
Mwaya, Tan.	154	8.55 S	36.50 E
Mweelrea ∧	48	53.38 N	9.50 W
Mwehu	154	5.44 S	26.40 E
Mweka	152	4.51 S	21.34 E
Mwemena	154	10.19 S	27.28 E
Mwenda	154	12.01 S	28.44 E
Mwendjila	152	7.12 S	18.51 E
Mwene-Ditu	152	7.03 S	23.27 E
Mwenezi	154	21.22 S	30.45 E
Mwenga	154	3.02 S	28.26 E
Mwepo	154	11.56 S	26.11 E
Mwerasandu	154	0.59 S	30.23 E
Mwereni	154	4.20 S	39.08 E
Mweru, Lake ⊜	154	9.00 S	28.45 E
Mweru Mantipa National Park ♠	154	8.45 S	29.30 E
Mweru Wantipa, Lake ⊜	154	8.45 S	29.40 E
Mwetshi	152	4.42 S	22.39 E
Mwilambwe	154	8.07 S	25.00 E
Mwimbi	154	8.39 S	31.40 E
Mwingi	154	0.56 S	38.04 E
Mwinilunga	152	11.44 S	24.26 E
Mwitikira	154	6.31 S	35.39 E
Mwombezhi ≃	154	12.52 S	25.00 E
Myaing	110	21.37 N	94.51 E
Myakka ≃	220	26.56 N	82.11 W
Myakka, Lake ⊜	220	27.16 N	82.17 W
Myakka City	220	27.20 N	82.09 W
Myakka River State Park ♠	220	27.15 N	82.17 W
Myall Range ⩘	170	32.58 S	151.22 E
Myanaung	110	18.17 N	95.19 E
Myanma → Burma □[1]	110	22.00 N	98.00 E
Myaungmya	110	16.36 N	94.56 E
Myawadi	110	16.41 N	98.31 E
Mybster	46	58.27 N	3.25 W
Myckelgensjö	26	63.34 N	17.37 E
Myebon	110	20.03 N	93.22 E
Myeik → Mergui	110	12.26 N	98.36 E
Myers, Ky., U.S.	218	38.21 N	83.57 W
Myers, N.Y., U.S.	210	42.32 N	76.32 W
Myerstown	208	40.22 N	76.19 W
Myingyan	110	21.28 N	95.23 E
Myinmoletkat Taung ∧	110	13.28 N	98.48 E
Myitkyinā	110	25.23 N	97.24 E
Myitnge ≃	110	21.52 N	95.59 E
Myitta	110	14.10 N	98.31 E
Myittha	110	21.25 N	96.08 E
Myittha ≃	110	23.12 N	94.17 E
Myjava	30	48.45 N	17.34 E
Myjeldino	24	61.46 N	54.48 E
Myjlybulak	86	48.57 N	75.13 E
Myla	24	65.25 N	50.48 E
Mylau	54	50.37 N	12.16 E
Myl'džino	86	59.03 N	78.29 E
Myllendonk, Schloss ⊥	263	51.13 N	6.29 E
Myllykoski	26	60.47 N	26.48 E
Myllymäki	26	62.32 N	24.17 E
Mylor	168b	35.03 S	138.45 E
Mymensingh	124	24.45 N	90.24 E
Mynämäki	26	60.40 N	22.00 E
Mynaral	86	45.25 N	73.41 E
Mynbulak, gora ∧	85	41.43 N	69.49 E
Mynfontein	158	30.55 S	23.57 E
Mynydd Bach ∧[2]	42	52.15 N	4.05 W
Mynydd Eppynt ∧	42	52.05 N	3.30 W
Mynydd Hiraethog ∧	42	53.05 N	3.33 W
Mynydd Pencarreg ∧[2]	42	52.04 N	4.04 W
Mynydd Preseli ∧	42	51.58 N	4.42 W
Myōgata	94	35.51 N	137.02 E
Myōgi	94	36.17 N	138.49 E
Myōgi-Arafune-Saku-kōgen-kokutei-kōen ♠	94	36.12 N	138.10 E
Myōgi-san ∧	94	36.17 N	138.44 E

≃	River	Fluss	Río	Rivière	Rio
≊	Canal	Kanal	Canal	Canal	Canal
∟	Waterfall, Rapids	Wasserfall, Stromschnellen	Cascada, Rápidos	Chute d'eau, Rapides	Cascata, Rápidos
Ʉ	Strait	Meeresstrasse	Estrecho	Détroit	Estreito
ᑕ	Bay, Gulf	Bucht, Golf	Bahía, Golfo	Baie, Golfe	Baía, Golfo
⊜	Lake, Lakes	See, Seen	Lago, Lagos	Lac, Lacs	Lago, Lagos
≡	Swamp	Sumpf	Pantano	Marais	Pântano
⊓	Ice Features, Glacier	Eis- und Gletscherformen	Accidentes Glaciales	Formes glaciaires	Acidentes glaciares
⍑	Other Hydrographic Features	Andere Hydrographische Objekte	Otros Elementos Hidrográficos	Autres données hydrographiques	Outros acidentes hidrográficos

✦	Submarine Features	Untermeerische Objekte	Accidentes Submarinos	Formes de relief sous-marin	Acidentes submarinos
□	Political Unit	Politische Einheit	Unidad Politica	Entité politique	Unidade política
ʋ	Cultural Institution	Kulturelle Institution	Institución Cultural	Institution culturelle	Institução cultural
⊥	Historical Site	Historische Stätte	Sitio Histórico	Site historique	Sitio histórico
♠	Recreational Site	Erholungs- und Ferienort	Sitio de Recreo	Centre de loisirs	Area de Lazer
⊠	Airport	Flughafen	Aeropuerto	Aéroport	Aeroporto
■	Military Installation	Militäranlage	Instalación Militar	Installation militaire	Instalação militar
◆	Miscellaneous	Verschiedenes	Misceláneo	Divers	Diversos

ENGLISH / DEUTSCH

Name / Name	Page / Seite	Lat.°′ / Breite°′	Long.°′ / Länge°′ E = Ost
Myo-gyi	110	21.27 N	96.22 E
Myohaung	110	20.36 N	93.10 E
Myohyang-san ∧	98	40.02 N	126.17 E
Myohyang-sanmaek ⋏	98	40.30 N	127.00 E
Myojin-dake ∧	270	34.57 N	135.36 E
Myōjin-san ∧	96	33.34 N	133.04 E
Myōken-san ∧	96	35.24 N	134.39 E
Myōken-zan ∧	270	34.56 N	135.28 E
Myōken-zan ∧[2]	270	34.30 N	134.57 E
Myōkō	94	36.56 N	138.13 E
Myōkō-kōgen	94	36.52 N	138.12 E
Myōkō-san ∧	94	36.52 N	138.07 E
Myŏnmong-ni ◆[8]	271b	37.35 N	127.05 E
Myponga	168b	35.24 S	138.28 E
Myponga Reservoir ⊜[1]	168b	35.24 S	138.26 E
Myra ⊥	130	36.15 N	29.54 E
Mýrdalsjökull ⊓	24a	63.40 N	19.05 W
Myrnam	182	53.40 N	111.14 W
Myroodah	162	18.08 S	124.16 E
Myrskylä (Mörskom)	26	60.40 N	25.51 E
Myrtle Beach	192	33.41 N	78.53 W
Myrtle Beach Air Force Base ■	192	33.41 N	78.56 W
Myrtle Beach State Park ♦	192	33.37 N	78.58 W
Myrtle Creek	202	43.01 N	123.17 W
Myrtle Grove	194	30.25 N	87.18 W
Myrtle Point	202	43.03 N	124.08 W
Myrtle Springs	222	32.37 N	95.56 W
Myrtletowne	204	40.47 N	124.04 W
Myrtleville	170	34.29 S	149.49 E
Myšega	82	54.31 N	37.02 E
Mysen	26	59.33 N	11.20 E
Mysia □[9]	130	39.15 N	28.00 E
Mysingen ʊ	40	59.00 N	18.15 E
Myski	86	53.42 N	87.48 E
Myškino	76	57.47 N	38.27 E
Myśla ≃	54	52.40 N	14.29 E
Myślenice	30	49.51 N	19.56 E
Myślibórz	30	52.55 N	14.52 E
Mysłowice	30	50.15 N	19.07 E
Mysore	122	12.18 N	76.39 E
Mys Šmidta	180	68.56 N	179.26 W
Mystic, Ct., U.S.	207	41.21 N	71.58 W
Mystic, Ia., U.S.	190	40.46 N	92.56 W
Mystic ≃	283	42.23 N	71.03 W
Mystic Seaport ʋ	207	41.22 N	71.58 W
Mys Vchodnoj	74	73.53 N	86.43 E
Mysy	24	60.34 N	53.57 E
Mys Želanija	72	76.56 N	68.35 E
Myszków	30	50.36 N	19.20 E
Myszyniec	30	53.24 N	21.21 E
Myt	80	56.48 N	42.21 E
My-tho	110	10.21 N	106.21 E
Mytholm	262	53.44 N	2.01 W
Mytholmroyd	262	53.44 N	1.59 W
Mytilene → Mitilíni	38	39.06 N	26.32 E
Mytišči	82	55.55 N	37.46 E
Mytishchi → Mytišči	82	55.55 N	37.46 E
Mytišino	76	54.48 N	34.01 E
Mýto	60	49.47 N	13.44 E
Myton	200	40.11 N	110.03 W
Mývatn ⊜	24a	65.37 N	16.58 W
Myzovo	78	51.22 N	24.31 E
M'zab, Oued V	148	32.19 N	5.24 E
Mže ≃	60	49.46 N	13.24 E
Mzenga	154	6.56 S	38.43 E
Mziha	154	5.54 S	37.47 E
Mzimba	154	11.52 S	33.34 E
Mzimkulu ≃	158	30.44 S	30.28 E
Mzimvubu ≃	158	31.38 S	29.32 E
Mzintlava ≃	158	31.12 S	29.18 E
Mzuzu	154	11.27 S	33.55 E
Mzymta ≃	84	43.27 N	39.56 E

N

Name / Name	Page / Seite	Lat.°′ / Breite°′	Long.°′ / Länge°′ E = Ost
Na I	174r	6.52 N	158.22 E
Na (Tengtiaohe) ≃	110	22.05 N	103.09 E
Naab ≃	60	49.01 N	12.02 E
Naach, Jbel ∧	34	34.53 N	3.22 W
Naachtpunkt Brook ≃	276	40.54 N	74.15 W
Naaldwijk	52	52.00 N	4.12 E
Naalehu	229d	19.03 N	155.35 W
Na'ām	140	9.42 N	28.27 E
Na'âma, Sebkhet en ⁙	148	33.20 N	0.16 W
Naaman Creek ≃	285	39.48 N	75.27 W
Naaman Creek, South Branch ≃	285	39.49 N	75.27 W
Naamans Garden	285	39.49 N	75.31 W
Naantali	26	60.27 N	22.02 E
Naarden	52	52.17 N	5.09 E
Naarn ≃	61	48.11 N	14.49 E
Naas	48	53.13 N	6.39 W
Naas ≃	171b	35.36 S	149.04 E
Naast	50	50.33 N	4.05 E
Na'azuz, Har ∧	132	30.01 N	35.00 E
Nabā, Jabal an- (Mount Nebo) ∧	132	31.46 N	35.45 E
Nababiep	156	29.36 S	17.46 E
Nabābpur	272b	22.42 N	88.12 E
Nabadwīp	126	23.25 N	88.22 E
Nabaganga ≃[1]	126	22.59 N	89.34 E
Nabagram	126	24.12 N	88.06 E
Nabalat Al-Ḥajanah	140	13.13 N	29.02 E
Nabari	94	34.37 N	136.05 E
Nabari ≃	94	34.45 N	136.01 E
Nabarūh	142	31.06 N	31.18 E
Nabas	116	11.50 N	122.05 E
Nabasta	126	23.15 N	88.01 E
Nabb	218	38.36 N	85.38 W
Nabberu, Lake ⊜	162	25.36 S	120.30 E
Nabburg	60	49.28 N	12.11 E
Nabeina	174t	1.26 N	173.05 E
Naberera	154	4.12 S	36.56 E
Naberežnoje	265b	55.57 N	37.58 E
Nabesna	180	62.22 N	143.00 W
Nabesna ≃	180	63.03 N	141.52 W
Nabeul	148	36.27 N	10.44 E
Nabeul □[8]	148	36.35 N	10.45 E
Nābha	123	30.22 N	76.09 E
Nab Hill ∧[2]	262	53.47 N	1.57 W
Nabigou	152	1.12 S	9.31 E
Nabī Hārūn, Jabal an- ∧	132	30.19 N	35.24 E
Nabileque ≃	248	20.55 S	57.49 W
Nabire	164	3.22 S	135.29 E
Nabī Shu'ayb, Jabal an- ∧	144	15.18 N	43.59 E
Nabisipi ≃	186	50.14 N	62.13 W
Nabiswera	154	1.28 N	32.16 E
Nabī Yūnus, Ra's an- ›	132	33.39 N	35.24 E
Nabnasset	207	42.36 N	71.25 W
Nabnasset Pond ⊜	283	42.37 N	71.26 W
Nabogame	232	26.14 N	106.57 W
Naboomspruit	156	24.32 S	28.36 E
Nabordo	150	10.10 N	9.20 E
Nabou	150	11.27 N	2.43 W
Nabq	140	28.04 N	34.25 E
Nabua	116	13.24 N	123.22 E
Nabula	120	31.55 N	80.10 E
Nābulus	132	32.13 N	35.16 E
Nabunturan	116	7.35 N	125.58 E
Nacajuca	234	18.08 N	93.01 W
Nacala	154	14.34 S	40.41 E
Nacala-Velha	154	14.32 S	40.37 E
Načalovo	80	46.20 N	48.11 E
Nacaome	236	13.31 N	87.30 W
Nacastillo	234	19.35 N	104.55 W
Nacchie	144	7.23 N	40.10 E
Nacereddine	34	36.08 N	3.26 E
Nachabinka ≃	265b	55.51 N	37.12 E
Nachabino	82	55.51 N	37.11 E
Naches	224	46.43 N	120.41 W
Naches ≃	202	46.38 N	120.31 W
Nachičevan'	84	39.13 N	45.24 E
Nachičevanskaja Avtonomnaja Sovetskaja Socialističeskaja Respublika □[3]	84	39.20 N	45.30 E
Nachi-katsuura	92	33.30 N	135.55 E
Nāchinda	126	21.53 N	87.46 E
Nachingwea	154	10.23 S	38.46 E
Nāchna	120	27.30 N	71.43 E
Náchod	30	50.25 N	16.10 E
Nachodka	89	42.48 N	132.52 E
Nächstebreck ◆[8]	263	51.18 N	7.14 E
Nachterstedt	54	51.49 N	11.20 E
Nachuge	110	10.45 N	92.22 E
Nachvak Fiord c[2]	176	59.03 N	63.45 W
Naci, Pil.	116	14.19 N	120.46 E
Naci, Pil.	116	6.19 N	124.46 E
Nacimiento	252	37.30 S	72.40 W
Nacimiento ≃	226	35.49 N	120.45 W
Nacimiento, Lake ⊜[1]	226	35.45 N	121.00 W
Načinskij Golec, gora ∧	89	52.24 N	118.53 E
Nacka	40	59.18 N	18.10 E
Naco, Méx.	232	31.20 N	109.56 W
Naco, Az., U.S.	200	31.20 N	109.56 W
Nacogdoches	222	31.36 N	94.39 W
Nacogdoches □[6]	222	31.40 N	94.45 W
Nacogdoches, Lake ⊜[1]	222	31.37 N	94.50 W
Nácori Chico	232	29.39 N	109.01 W
Nacozari [de García]	232	30.24 N	109.39 W
Ñacunday	252	26.01 S	54.46 W
Nada	222	29.24 N	96.23 W
Nada ◆[8]	270	34.44 N	135.14 E
Nadābhānga	272b	22.24 N	88.14 E
Nadachi	94	37.09 N	138.06 E
Nadaleen Mountain ∧	180	64.15 N	133.04 W
Nadasaki	96	34.32 N	133.52 E
Nádasd	61	46.58 N	16.37 E
Nadbai	124	27.14 N	77.12 E
Nadder ≃	42	51.03 N	1.48 W
Nadela	34	42.58 N	7.30 W
Nadelkap → Agulhas, Cape ›	158	34.52 S	20.00 E
Naden Harbour c	182	54.00 N	132.35 W
Nadeždinskoje	89	48.18 N	133.11 E
Nadi	140	18.40 N	33.42 E
Nadia □[5]	126	23.30 N	88.30 E
Nadiād	120	22.42 N	72.52 E
Nādir, Miṣr	142	30.33 N	30.51 E
Nadir, Vir. Is., U.S.	240m	18.19 N	64.53 W
Nădlac	38	46.10 N	20.45 E
Nador	148	35.12 N	2.55 W
Nador □[4]	148	35.09 N	3.04 W
Nadporožje	76	60.28 N	34.17 E
Nadrin	56	50.10 N	5.41 E
Nadterečnaja	84	43.37 N	45.22 E
Nadvoicy	24	63.52 N	34.15 E
Nadvornaja	78	48.38 N	24.34 E
Nadym	72	65.35 N	72.42 E
Nadym ≃	74	66.12 N	72.00 E
Nadyrovo	80	54.53 N	52.28 E
Naeba-san ∧	94	36.51 N	138.41 E
Nae-dong	98	37.16 N	126.27 E
Naejang-san Kukrip Kongwŏn ♦	98	35.28 N	126.52 E
Naenwa	120	25.46 N	75.51 E
Nærbø	26	58.40 N	5.39 E
Næsby	41	55.25 N	10.22 E
Næstved	41	55.14 N	11.46 E
Nafada	146	11.08 N	11.20 E
Nafadji	150	12.37 N	11.37 W
Nafarros	266c	38.49 N	9.25 W
Nafāzah, 'Alam ∧[2]	142	30.30 N	29.42 E
Näfels	58	47.06 N	9.04 E
Nafīshah	142	30.34 N	32.15 E
Naftalan	84	40.31 N	46.50 E
Nāfūrah	146	29.20 N	21.20 E
Nafūsah, Jabal ⋏[2]	146	31.50 N	12.00 E
Nāg	120	27.24 N	65.08 E
Naga, Nihon	96	34.16 N	135.26 E
Naga, Pil.	116	13.37 N	123.11 E
Naga, Pil.	116	10.13 N	123.45 E
Nâga, Kreb en ≗[4]	148	24.00 N	6.00 W
Naga, Oued en V	148	27.53 N	7.10 W
Nagaga	154	10.54 S	39.07 E
Nagahama, Nihon	94	35.23 N	136.16 E
Nagahama, Nihon	96	33.36 N	132.29 E
Nagahama, Nihon	174m	26.25 N	127.44 E
Naga Hills ⋏	110	26.00 N	95.00 E
Nagai, Nihon	92	38.06 N	140.02 E
Nagai, Nihon	268	35.12 N	139.37 E
Nagai Island I	180	55.11 N	159.55 W
Nagai Park ♦	270	34.36 N	135.31 E
Nagaizumi	94	35.08 N	138.54 E
Nāgāland □[3]	120	26.00 N	95.00 E
Nagambie	169	36.47 S	145.10 E
Nagannu-shima I	174m	26.16 N	127.33 E
Nagano	94	36.39 N	138.11 E
Nagano □[5]	94	36.00 N	138.00 E
Nagano-dam ◆[6]	94	35.50 N	136.33 E
Naganohara	94	36.33 N	138.38 E
Nagao, Nihon	96	34.16 N	134.10 E
Nagao, Nihon	270	34.50 N	135.43 E
Nagao-hana ›	96	35.32 N	134.01 E
Nagaoka	92	37.27 N	138.51 E
Nagaokakyō	94	34.55 N	135.42 E
Nāgappattinam	122	10.46 N	79.50 E
Nagar, India	123	32.07 N	77.10 E
Nagar, India	124	27.26 N	77.06 E
Nagara	270	34.26 N	135.44 E
Nagara ≃	94	35.01 N	136.43 E
Nagareyama	94	35.51 N	139.54 E
Nāgārjuna Sāgar ⊜[1]	122	16.35 N	79.21 E
Nagarote	236	12.16 N	86.34 W
Nagar Pārkar	120	24.22 N	70.45 E
Nāgarpur	124	24.03 N	89.53 E
Nagar Untāri	124	24.17 N	83.30 E
Nagas	116	13.06 N	123.18 E
Nagasaka	94	35.49 N	138.22 E
Nagasaki	92	32.48 N	129.55 E
Nagasawa	268	35.12 N	139.41 E
Nagashima	94	35.05 N	136.42 E
Naga-shima I, Nihon	96	33.49 N	132.05 E
Naga-shima I, Nihon	96	34.41 N	134.15 E
Nagashino ⊥	94	34.56 N	137.32 E
Nagasin Lake ⊜	190	47.44 N	83.37 W
Nagasu, Nihon	96	32.56 N	130.27 E
Nagasu → Usa, Nihon	96	33.31 N	131.22 E
Nagata ◆[8]	270	34.40 N	135.09 E
Nagataki	270	34.23 N	135.20 E
Nagatino ◆[8]	265b	55.41 N	37.41 E
Nagato, Nihon	94	36.15 N	138.16 E
Nagato, Nihon	96	34.21 N	131.10 E
Nagatsuda ◆[8]	268	35.32 N	139.30 E
Nāgaur	120	27.12 N	73.44 E
Nāgāvali ≃	122	18.13 N	83.56 E
Nagavskaja	80	47.47 N	42.50 E
Nagawa	94	36.05 N	137.41 E
Nagawicka Lake ⊜	216	43.05 N	88.23 W
Nagcarlan	116	14.08 N	121.25 E
Nāgda	120	23.27 N	75.25 E
Nagele	52	52.37 N	5.44 E
Nāgercoil	122	8.10 N	77.26 E
Nagi	96	35.07 N	134.11 E
Nagiba	116	13.41 N	120.53 E
Nagibino	86	55.46 N	72.43 E
Nagichot	154	4.16 N	33.34 E
Nagīna	124	29.27 N	78.27 E
Nāgirāt	126	23.38 N	89.18 E
Nagi-san ∧	96	35.10 N	134.11 E
Nagiso	94	35.36 N	137.37 E
Nagla	272a	28.31 N	77.22 E
Naglarby	40	60.25 N	15.34 E
Nagles Mountains ⋏	48	52.05 N	8.30 W
Nagłowice	30	50.41 N	20.06 E
Nago	174m	26.35 N	127.59 E
Nāgod	124	24.34 N	80.36 E
Nagog Pond ⊜	283	42.31 N	71.26 W
Nagoja → Nagoya	94	35.10 N	136.55 E
Nagold	56	48.33 N	8.43 E
Nagold ≃	56	48.52 N	8.42 E
Nagol'naja ≃	83	47.57 N	38.58 E
Nagol'no-Tarasovka	83	48.00 N	39.29 E
Nagorje	76	56.55 N	38.16 E
Nagornoje	78	45.26 N	28.27 E
Nagorno-Karabachskaja Avtonomnaja Oblast' □[4]	84	40.00 N	46.40 E
Nagornyj, S.S.S.R.	74	55.58 N	124.57 E
Nagornyj, S.S.S.R.	265a	59.43 N	30.16 E
Nagorsk	24	59.18 N	50.48 E
Nagorskoje	82	56.54 N	38.06 E
Nago-wan c	174m	26.34 N	127.57 E
Nagoya	94	35.10 N	136.55 E
Nagoya-kūkō ⊠	94	35.15 N	136.55 E
Nāgpur	120	21.09 N	79.06 E
Nagrai	123	34.23 N	72.41 E
Nāgrākata	124	26.54 N	88.55 E
Nagrota	123	32.03 N	76.05 E
Nagu I	26	60.10 N	21.48 E
Nagua	238	19.23 N	69.50 W
Naguabo	240m	18.13 N	65.44 W
Naguilian	116	17.01 N	121.50 E
Nagumbuaya Point ›	116	13.34 N	124.21 E
Naguri	94	35.53 N	139.11 E
Naguri I	122	6.39 N	72.55 E
Nagyatád	30	46.14 N	17.22 E
Nagybajom	30	46.23 N	17.31 E
Nagybánya → Baia-Mare	38	47.40 N	23.35 E
Nagycenk	61	47.36 N	16.42 E
Nagyecsed	30	47.52 N	22.24 E
Nagykálló	78	47.53 N	21.51 E
Nagykanizsa	30	46.27 N	17.00 E
Nagykáta	30	47.25 N	19.45 E
Nagy-Kevély ∧	264c	47.37 N	18.59 E
Nagykőrös	30	47.02 N	19.43 E
Nagy-Milic ∧	30	48.35 N	21.28 E
Nagytarcsa	264c	47.32 N	19.17 E
Nagytétény ◆[8]	264c	47.24 N	18.58 E
Nagyvarad → Oradea	38	47.03 N	21.57 E
Naha	174m	26.13 N	127.40 E
Naha Airfield ⊠	174m	26.13 N	127.40 E
Nahabuan	112	0.49 N	114.05 E
Nahakki	123	34.25 N	71.20 E
Nahalal	132	32.41 N	35.12 E
Naḥal 'Oz	132	31.28 N	34.30 E
Naḥam	132	31.46 N	35.00 E
Nāhan	124	30.33 N	77.18 E
Nahang (Nihing) ≃	128	26.00 N	62.44 E
Nahanni National Park ♦	180	61.40 N	126.00 W
Nahant	207	42.25 N	70.55 W
Nahant Bay c	207	42.27 N	70.55 W
Nahant Beach ≗[2]	283	42.27 N	70.56 W
Nahari	96	33.25 N	134.01 E
Nahari ≃	96	33.25 N	134.01 E
Nahariyya	132	33.00 N	35.05 E
Naharpur ◆[8]	272a	28.42 N	77.07 E
Nahāta	126	23.20 N	89.31 E
Nahāvand	128	34.12 N	48.22 E
Nahcotta	224	46.30 N	124.02 W
Nahe	89	48.28 N	124.52 E
Nahe ≃	56	49.58 N	7.57 E
Naḥf	132	32.56 N	35.19 E
Nahma	190	45.50 N	86.39 W
Nahmer	263	51.20 N	7.35 E
Nahmer ≃	263	51.21 N	7.35 E
Nahoe	174y	9.45 S	138.55 W
Nahoï, Cap ›	175f	14.39 S	166.37 E
Nahon ≃	50	47.14 N	1.39 E
Nahr Ouassel, Oued ≃	148	35.42 N	2.33 E
Nahuala, Laguna c	234	16.46 N	99.44 W
Nahualate ≃	236	14.03 N	91.32 W
Nahuatzén	234	19.42 N	101.50 W
Nahuel Huapi	254	41.03 S	71.09 W
Nahuel Huapi, Lago ⊜	254	40.58 S	71.30 W
Nahuel Huapi, Parque Nacional ♦	254	41.00 S	71.48 W
Nahuel Niyeu	254	40.30 S	66.33 W
Nahuizalco	236	13.46 N	89.45 W
Nahunta	192	31.12 N	81.58 W
Nāhyā	142	30.03 N	31.07 E
Naia ≃	66	42.46 N	12.22 E
Naicá	232	27.53 N	105.31 W
Naicam	184	52.25 N	104.30 W
Naidong	120	29.14 N	91.46 E
Nai Ga	102	27.48 N	97.30 E
Naiguatá, Pico ∧	286c	10.33 N	66.46 W
Naihāti, Bngl.	126	22.49 N	89.37 E
Naihāti, India	126	22.54 N	88.25 E
Naij Gol ≃	102	36.20 N	94.49 E
Naikliu	112	9.30 S	123.50 E
Naikoon Provincial Park ♦	182	53.50 N	131.50 W
Naila	54	50.19 N	11.42 E
Nailin	98	41.53 N	119.15 E
Nails Creek ≃	222	30.16 N	96.44 W
Nailsea	42	51.26 N	2.43 W
Nailsworth	42	51.42 N	2.14 W
Nā'im, Jabal an- ∧	132	31.04 N	35.55 E
Naiman Qi	89	42.55 N	120.43 E
Nain, Nf., Can.	176	56.32 N	61.41 W
Nā'īn, Īrān	128	32.52 N	53.05 E
Nain ⊜	40	60.14 N	13.50 E
Naini Tāl	124	29.23 N	79.27 E
Naini Tāl □[5]	124	29.20 N	79.30 E
Nainpur	124	22.26 N	80.07 E
Naipli, Tür.	130	39.48 N	27.13 E
Naipli, Tür.	130	40.19 N	38.07 E
Naiqiguolehe ≃	120	35.58 N	95.00 E
Nairai I	175g	17.49 S	179.24 E
Nairn, Scot., U.K.	46	57.35 N	3.53 W
Nairn, La., U.S.	194	29.27 N	89.38 W
Nairn ≃	46	57.35 N	3.52 W
Nairne	168b	35.02 S	138.54 E
Nairobi	154	1.17 S	36.49 E
Nairobi Airport ⊠	276	41.08 N	74.21 W
Nairobi National Park ♦	154	1.24 S	36.50 E
Naissaar I	76	59.33 N	24.32 E
Naita ∧	144	5.30 N	35.18 E
Naitamba Island I	175g	17.31 S	179.17 W
Naivasha	154	0.43 S	36.26 E
Naivasha, Lake ⊜	154	0.46 S	36.21 E
Naivos	114	2.30 N	96.10 E
Naizifang	105	39.36 N	116.47 E
N'aizishen	89	43.41 N	127.29 E
Najac	32	44.13 N	1.59 E
Najafābād	128	32.37 N	51.21 E
Najafgarh ◆[8]	272a	28.37 N	76.59 E
Najafgarh Drain ≊	272a	28.43 N	77.14 E
Najasa ≃	240p	20.42 N	77.55 W
Najd □[8]	144	21.00 N	46.00 E
Nájera	34	42.25 N	2.44 W
Najhā	132	33.23 N	36.22 E
Naj' Ḥammādī	140	26.03 N	32.15 E
Najībābād	124	29.38 N	78.20 E
Najin	98	42.15 N	130.18 E
Najinkouzi	89	50.23 N	126.57 E
Najio	270	34.50 N	135.18 E
Najstenjarvi	24	62.16 N	32.38 E
Naju	98	35.03 N	126.43 E
Najza, gora ∧	86	49.24 N	70.42 E
Naka, Nihon	94	36.27 N	140.30 E
Naka, Nihon	96	35.02 N	134.55 E
Naka, Nihon	268	35.49 N	140.03 E
Naka, Nihon	270	34.50 N	135.48 E
Naka, Nihon	270	34.42 N	135.45 E
Naka, Nihon	270	34.50 N	135.56 E
Naka ◆[8]	268	35.27 N	139.39 E
Naka ≃, Nihon	94	36.20 N	140.36 E
Naka ≃, Nihon	96	33.56 N	134.42 E
Naka ≃, Nihon	268	35.39 N	139.51 E
Nakadōri-shima I	92	32.57 N	129.04 E
Nakagami	268	35.49 N	139.21 E
Nakagawa	94	35.38 N	137.56 E
Nakagawa ◆[8], Nihon	268	35.33 N	139.35 E
Nakagawa ◆[8], Nihon	268	35.31 N	139.33 E
Nakagō	94	36.58 N	138.14 E
Nakagusuku	174m	26.15 N	127.49 E
Nakagusuku-wan c	174m	26.14 N	127.53 E
Nakagyō ◆[8]	270	35.01 N	135.45 E
Nakaheji	96	33.47 N	135.31 E
Nakai	94	35.20 N	139.14 E
Nakaizu	94	34.57 N	139.00 E
Nakajima, Nihon	94	37.07 N	136.51 E
Nakajima, Nihon	96	33.58 N	132.07 E
Nakajima, Nihon	268	35.26 N	139.56 E
Nakajima, Nihon	268	35.18 N	139.58 E
Naka-jima I	96	33.58 N	132.37 E
Nakajō, Nihon	92	38.03 N	139.24 E
Nakajō, Nihon	94	36.36 N	138.02 E
Nakakawane	94	35.03 N	138.05 E
Nāka Khārari	120	25.15 N	66.44 E
Nakalele Point ›	229a	21.02 N	156.35 W
Nākālia	126	24.02 N	89.40 E
Nakama, Nihon	96	33.50 N	130.43 E
Nakama, Nihon	174m	26.16 N	127.44 E
Nakaminato	94	36.21 N	140.36 E
Nakamura	96	32.59 N	132.56 E
Nakanai Mountains ⋏	164	5.35 S	151.10 E
Nakano, Nihon	94	36.45 N	138.22 E
Nakano, Nihon	268	35.20 N	139.54 E
Nakano, Nihon	270	34.58 N	135.58 E
Nakano ◆[8]	268	35.42 N	139.42 E
Nakanobu ◆[8]	268	35.36 N	139.43 E
Nakanojō	94	36.35 N	138.51 E
Nakano-shima I	93b	29.49 N	129.52 E
Nakanoshima-suidō ʊ	93b	29.44 N	129.49 E
Nakanougan-jima I	175d	24.11 N	123.33 E
Nakaosu	174m	26.37 N	128.02 E
Nakaōzō ◆[8]	270	34.51 N	135.11 E
Nakape	140	5.47 N	28.37 E
Nakashibetsu	92a	43.33 N	144.59 E
Nākāsipāra	126	23.35 N	88.21 E
Nakasongola	154	1.19 N	32.28 E
Nakatō	268	35.45 N	139.24 E
Nakatomi, Nihon	94	35.28 N	138.26 E
Nakatomi, Nihon	268	35.49 N	139.30 E
Nakatosa	96	33.20 N	133.14 E
Nakatsu, Nihon	96	33.34 N	131.13 E
Nakatsu, Nihon	96	33.57 N	135.18 E
Nakatsu, Nihon	268	35.30 N	139.20 E
Nakatsu ≃	94	37.00 N	138.39 E
Nakatsue	96	33.08 N	130.56 E
Nakatsugawa	94	35.29 N	137.30 E
Nakatsumine-yama ∧	96	33.58 N	134.31 E
Nakauchigami	270	34.56 N	135.10 E
Naka-umi c	96	35.28 N	133.12 E
Nakayama, Nihon	96	33.38 N	132.42 E
Nakayama, Nihon	96	35.31 N	133.35 E
Nakayama ≃	96	33.55 N	133.08 E
Nakazato, Nihon	94	36.05 N	138.50 E
Nakazato, Nihon	94	37.03 N	138.42 E
Nakazuma	268	35.58 N	139.35 E
Nakechake	120	30.11 N	83.09 E
Nakehe ≃	120	31.29 N	93.51 E
Nakéty	175f	21.33 S	166.03 E
Nakfa	144	16.43 N	38.32 E
Nakhola	120	26.07 N	92.11 E
Nakhon Nayok	110	14.12 N	101.13 E
Nakhon Pathom	110	13.49 N	100.03 E
Nakhon Phanom	110	17.24 N	104.47 E
Nakhon Ratchasima	110	14.58 N	102.07 E
Nakhon Sawan	110	15.41 N	100.07 E
Nakhon Si Thammarat	110	8.26 N	99.58 E
Nakhon Thai	110	17.07 N	100.50 E
Nakhtarana	120	23.20 N	69.15 E
Nakina	176	50.10 N	86.42 W
Nakkaş ≃	267b	41.00 N	28.45 E
Nakło nad Notecią	30	53.08 N	17.35 E
Naknek	180	58.44 N	157.02 W
Naknek Lake ⊜	180	58.40 N	156.15 W
Nako	150	10.38 N	3.04 W
Nakodar	123	31.07 N	75.29 E
Nakonde	154	9.20 S	32.42 E
Nakoso-no-seki-ato ⊥	94	36.53 N	140.46 E
Nakou	100	27.09 N	117.38 E
Nakskov	41	54.50 N	11.09 E
Nakskov Fjord c	41	54.50 N	11.02 E
Näkten ⊜	26	62.52 N	14.38 E
Naktong-gang ≃	98	35.07 N	128.57 E
Nakūr	124	29.55 N	77.18 E
Nakuru	154	0.17 S	36.04 E
Nakuru, Lake ⊜	154	0.22 S	36.05 E
Nakusp	182	50.15 N	117.48 W
Nāl ≃	120	26.02 N	65.19 E
Nālāgarh	123	31.03 N	76.43 E
Nalajch	88	47.45 N	107.16 E
Nālanda	124	25.07 N	85.25 E
Nalao	102	24.22 N	105.23 E
Nalázi	156	24.03 S	33.20 E
Nalbāri	120	26.25 N	91.26 E
Nalcayec, Isla I	254	46.06 S	73.49 W
Nalchik → Nal'čik	84	43.29 N	43.37 E
Nālchiti	124	22.38 N	90.17 E
Nal'čik	84	43.29 N	43.37 E
Naldānga	126	23.26 N	89.11 E
Nāldera	123	31.11 N	77.11 E
Näldsjön ⊜	26	63.23 N	14.17 E
Nałęczów	30	51.18 N	22.11 E
Nalgonda	122	17.03 N	79.16 E
Nalgora	126	22.52 N	90.39 E
Nalhāti	126	24.18 N	87.49 E
Naliagrām	126	23.36 N	89.37 E
Naliang	102	21.43 N	107.51 E
Nālikul	272b	22.49 N	88.11 E
Nalinnes	50	50.19 N	4.26 E
Nalisan	104	42.06 N	122.12 E
Nallamalla Range ⋏	122	15.30 N	78.45 E
Nalles (Nals)	64	46.32 N	11.12 E
Nallıhan	130	40.11 N	31.21 E
Na Logu	64	46.23 N	13.45 E
Nalolo	152	15.35 S	23.07 E
Nalón ≃	34	43.32 N	6.04 W
Nalong	102	23.35 N	106.05 E
Nalusa	152	14.55 S	22.13 E
Nālūt	146	31.52 N	10.59 E
Nalžovské Hory	60	49.20 N	13.33 E
Nam ≃	110	21.33 N	98.38 E
Namaacha	156	25.58 S	32.01 E
Namachire	152	11.26 S	22.43 E
Namacunde	152	17.18 S	15.50 E
Namacurra	154	17.29 S	37.01 E
Namak, Daryācheh-ye ⊜	128	34.45 N	51.36 E
Namak, Kavīr-e ◆[2]	128	34.45 N	57.45 E
Namakan Lake ⊜	190	48.27 N	92.35 W
Nāmakkal	122	11.14 N	78.10 E
Namakula	174v	18.57 S	169.54 W
Namakzār, Daryācheh-ye ⊜	128	34.00 N	60.30 E
Namaland □[5]	156	25.50 S	18.00 E
Namamugi ◆[8]	268	35.29 N	139.41 E
Namanga	154	2.33 S	36.46 E
Namangan	85	41.00 N	71.40 E
Namanyere	154	7.31 S	31.03 E
Namapa	154	13.43 S	39.50 E
Namarodu, Cape ›	164	3.38 S	152.30 E
Namarrói	154	15.58 S	36.55 E
Namasagali	154	1.01 N	32.57 E
Namatanai	164	3.40 S	152.25 E
Nambe Indian Reservation ◆[4]	200	35.52 N	105.57 W
Namber	164	1.04 S	134.49 E
Nambi	162	28.54 S	121.41 E
Nambling	164	5.10 S	152.00 E
Nambour	166	26.38 S	152.58 E
Nambouwalu	175g	16.59 S	178.42 E
Nambuangongo	152	8.01 S	14.12 E
Nambucca Heads	166	30.39 S	153.00 E
Nam-can	110	8.46 N	104.59 E
Namcha Barwa → Namjagbarwa Feng ∧	102	29.38 N	95.04 E
Namch'ang	98	35.26 N	129.16 E
Namdae-ch'ŏn ≃	98	40.26 N	128.57 E
Namdanak	85	41.11 N	69.42 E
Nam-dinh	110	20.25 N	106.10 E
Nämdö I	40	59.12 N	18.41 E
Nämdöfjärden ʊ	40	59.12 N	18.34 E
Nam-du, Quan-dao II	110	9.42 N	104.22 E
Namegawa	94	36.04 N	139.22 E
Nameh	112	2.34 N	116.21 E
Nameigos Lake ⊜	190	48.46 N	84.43 W
Namekagon ≃	190	46.05 N	92.06 W
Namen → Namur	56	50.28 N	4.52 E
Namerikawa	94	36.46 N	137.20 E
Náměšť	61	49.12 N	16.10 E
Námestovo	30	49.25 N	19.30 E
Nametil	154	15.43 S	39.21 E
Namew Lake ⊜	184	54.13 N	101.56 W
Nam-gang ≃	98	39.03 N	125.52 E
Namhae	98	34.50 N	127.54 E
Namhae-do I	98	34.48 N	127.57 E
Namhan-gang ≃	98	37.31 N	127.18 E
Namhkam	110	23.50 N	97.41 E
Namho-ri	98	38.07 N	125.10 E
Namhsan	110	22.58 N	97.10 E
Namiai	94	35.22 N	137.41 E
Namib Desert ◆[2]	156	23.00 S	15.00 E
Namibe	152	15.10 S	12.09 E
Namibe □[5]	152	15.20 S	12.30 E
Namibia (South West Africa) □[2], Afr.	138	22.00 S	17.00 E
Namibia (South West Africa) □[2], Afr.	156	22.00 S	17.00 E
Namibie → Namibia (South West Africa) □[2]	156	22.00 S	17.00 E
Namib-Naukluft Park ♦	156	23.30 S	15.30 E
Namie	92	37.29 N	141.00 E
Namies	158	29.18 S	19.13 E
Namīn	128	38.25 N	48.30 E
Naminga	88	56.33 N	118.41 E
Namjagbarwa Feng ∧	102	29.38 N	95.04 E
Nāmja La)(	124	29.27 N	82.34 E
Namji-ri	98	35.23 N	128.29 E
Nāmkhāna	126	21.46 N	88.14 E
Nam Kwo Chau I	271d	22.15 N	114.21 E
Namlan	110	22.15 N	97.24 E
Namlea	164	3.18 S	127.06 E
Namlos	58	47.21 N	10.40 E
Namnoi, Khao ∧	110	10.36 N	98.38 E
Namo	112	1.24 S	119.57 E
Namoi ≃	166	30.00 S	148.07 E
Namoluk I[1]	14	5.55 N	153.08 E
Namonuito I[1]	14	8.46 N	150.02 E
Namorik I[1]	14	5.36 N	168.07 E
Namoruputh	154	4.34 N	35.57 E
Namounou	150	11.52 N	1.42 E
Namous, Oued en V	148	31.00 N	0.15 W
Namoya	154	4.01 S	27.34 E
Nampa, Ab., Can.	182	56.02 N	117.08 W
Nampa, Id., U.S.	202	43.32 N	116.33 W
Nampala	150	15.17 N	5.33 W
Nam Pat	110	17.43 N	100.41 E
Nampawng	110	22.45 N	97.52 E
Nam Phong	110	16.42 N	102.52 E
Nampicuan	116	15.44 N	120.38 E
Namp'o	98	38.45 N	125.23 E
Nampont-Saint-Martin	50	50.21 N	1.45 E
Namp'ot'ae-san ∧	98	41.44 N	128.24 E
Nampuecha	154	13.59 S	40.18 E
Nampula	154	15.07 S	39.15 E
Nampula □[5]	154	15.00 S	39.00 E
Namrun	130	37.09 N	34.36 E
Namsang	110	20.53 N	97.43 E
Namsan Park ♦	271b	37.34 N	126.59 E
Namsanyŏng-ni	98	38.59 N	127.26 E
Namsen ≃	24	64.27 N	11.28 E
Namsi	98	39.54 N	124.36 E
Namslau → Namysłów	30	51.05 N	17.42 E
Namsos	24	64.29 N	11.30 E
Nam Tok	110	14.14 N	99.04 E
Namtu	110	23.05 N	97.24 E
Namu	182	51.49 N	127.52 W
Namu I[1]	14	8.00 N	168.10 E
Namuhu ⊜	120	30.42 N	90.30 E
Namuka-I-Lau I	175g	18.51 S	178.38 W
Namúli, Serra ⋏	154	15.15 S	37.08 E
Namur, Bel.	56	50.28 N	4.52 E
Namur, P.Q., Can.	206	45.54 N	74.56 W
Namur □[4]	56	50.20 N	4.50 E
Namuruputh	154	4.34 N	35.57 E
Namutoni	156	18.49 S	16.55 E
Namwala	154	15.45 S	26.26 E
Namwera	154	14.22 S	35.30 E
Namwŏn	98	35.25 N	127.21 E
Namyang, C.M.I.K.	98	42.57 N	129.53 E
Namyang, Taehan	98	37.14 N	126.44 E
Namysłów	30	51.05 N	17.42 E
Nan	110	18.47 N	100.47 E
Nan ≃, Thai	110	15.42 N	100.09 E
Nan ≃, Zhg.	100	28.15 N	120.43 E
Nana ≃	152	5.00 N	15.50 E
Nana Barya ≃	146	7.59 N	17.43 E
Nana Barya, Réserve de Faune de la ◆[4]	146	7.30 N	17.30 E
Nanacamilpa	234	19.29 N	98.33 W
Nanaimo	224	49.10 N	123.56 W
Nanaimo ≃	224	49.08 N	123.54 W
Nanaimo Lakes ⊜	224	49.07 N	124.11 W
Nānakheri ◆[8]	272a	28.31 N	76.59 E
Nana Kru	150	4.50 N	8.44 W
Nanakuli	229c	21.23 N	158.09 W
Nanam	98	41.43 N	129.41 E
Nana-Mambéré □[5]	152	5.30 N	15.30 E
Nan'an	100	24.58 N	118.23 E
Nan'anba	107	28.46 N	104.38 E
Nanango	166	26.40 S	152.00 E
Nanantun	110	24.45 N	95.41 E
Nanao, Nihon	94	37.03 N	136.58 E
Nanao, T'aiwan	100	24.28 N	121.48 E
Nan'ao, Zhg.	100	23.27 N	117.02 E
Nan'ao Dao I	100	23.26 N	117.03 E
Nanao-wan c	94	37.06 N	137.00 E
Nanas Channel ʊ	271c	1.25 N	103.58 E
Nanatsu-jima II	92	37.36 N	136.53 E
Nanatsuka	94	36.44 N	136.41 E
Nanay ≃	246	3.42 S	73.16 W
Nanba	102	32.20 N	104.58 E
Nanbaita	105	38.58 N	115.39 E
Nanbaixia	98	35.45 N	117.23 E
Nanbaozhen	106	31.32 N	121.37 E
Nanbu, Nihon	94	35.17 N	138.27 E
Nanbu, Zhg.	102	31.23 N	106.02 E
Nancaicun	105	39.28 N	117.01 E
Nancefield	273d	26.17 S	27.53 E
Nancha	89	47.08 N	129.19 E
Nanchang, Zhg.	100	28.41 N	115.53 E
Nanchang (Liantang), Zhg.	100	28.34 N	115.56 E
Nancheng, Zhg.	100	25.39 N	118.26 E
Nancheng, Zhg.	100	27.35 N	116.40 E
Nancheng → Hanzhong, Zhg.	102	33.08 N	107.02 E
Nanching → Nanjing	106	32.03 N	118.47 E
Nanchital	234	18.04 N	94.24 W
Nanchong	107	30.48 N	106.04 E
Nanchuan	102	29.08 N	107.07 E
Nanchuang	100	24.36 N	120.59 E
Nanch'ung → Nanchong	107	30.48 N	106.04 E
Nancowry Island I	110	7.59 N	93.32 E
Nancroix	62	45.32 N	6.46 E
Nancun, Zhg.	98	39.46 N	114.07 E
Nancun, Zhg.	98	36.32 N	120.06 E
Nancy	58	48.41 N	6.12 E
Nanda Devi ∧	124	30.23 N	79.59 E
Nāndāha	272b	22.50 N	88.17 E
Nandaime	236	11.46 N	86.03 W
Nandan	96	34.15 N	134.43 E
Nandarivatu	175g	17.34 S	177.58 E
Nandashan	100	29.01 N	112.43 E
Nānded	122	19.09 N	77.20 E
Nāndgaon, India	122	20.19 N	74.39 E
Nāndgaon, India	272c	18.58 N	73.08 E
Nandi	175g	17.48 S	177.25 E
Nandi Bay c	175g	17.44 S	177.25 E
Nandi Drug ∧	122	13.25 N	77.42 E
Nandigrām	126	22.01 N	87.58 E
Nandikotkūr	122	15.52 N	78.16 E
Nanding ≃	102	23.25 N	98.41 E
Nandinghe ≃	110	23.25 N	98.41 E
Nandlstadt	60	48.32 N	11.48 E
Nandom	150	10.51 N	2.45 W
N'andoma	24	61.40 N	40.12 E
Nandu	106	31.27 N	119.19 E
Nanduhe ≃	110	20.04 N	110.22 E
Nanduluohe	105	40.11 N	117.13 E
Nāndūra	122	20.50 N	76.27 E
Nandurbār	122	21.22 N	74.15 E
Nanduri	175g	16.27 S	179.09 E
Nandy	261	48.35 N	2.34 E
Nandyāl	122	15.29 N	78.29 E
Nanfangquan	106	31.26 N	120.16 E
Nanfen	104	41.06 N	123.44 E
Nanfeng, Zhg.	100	27.15 N	116.32 E
Nanfeng, Zhg.	100	29.16 N	116.32 E
Nangabadau	112	1.02 N	111.54 E
Nangade	154	11.05 S	39.36 E
Nanga Eboko	152	4.41 N	12.22 E
Nangahale	115b	8.34 S	122.32 E
Nangakelawit	112	0.23 N	112.26 E
Nangalangki	112	1.15 S	111.40 E
Nangalao Island I	116	11.27 N	120.11 E
Nangal Dewat ◆[8]	272a	28.33 N	77.06 E
Nangamau	112	0.06 S	111.55 E
Nangamesi, Teluk c	115b	9.37 S	120.20 E
Nangamuntatai	112	0.22 S	112.23 E
Nangang	100	31.22 N	116.59 E
Nan Gang c	100	23.30 N	117.00 E
Nan'gangwa	105	39.46 N	116.09 E
Nangaobat	112	0.57 N	113.13 E
Nangaocun	105	39.25 N	115.58 E
Nanga Parbat ∧	123	35.15 N	74.36 E
Nangapinoh	112	0.20 S	111.44 E
Nangaraun	112	0.38 N	113.11 E
Nangarhār □[4]	120	34.15 N	70.30 E
Nangatayap	112	1.32 S	110.34 E
Nangezhuang	105	39.31 N	116.23 E
Nanggala Hill ∧	175e	8.16 S	157.43 E
Nanggulan	115a	7.46 S	110.12 E
Nangi	272b	22.31 N	88.13 E
Nangin	110	10.31 N	98.31 E
Nangis	50	48.33 N	3.00 E
Nangka ≃	269f	14.41 N	121.06 E
Nanglai ≃	126	24.20 N	90.04 E
Nangloi ◆[8], India	272a	28.41 N	77.05 E
Nāngloi ◆[8], India	272a	28.40 N	77.02 E
Nangloi Jat ◆[8]	272a	28.41 N	77.04 E
Nangnim	98	40.58 N	127.08 E
Nangnim-sanmaek ⋏	98	40.00 N	127.00 E
Nangō, Nihon	92	31.32 N	131.23 E
Nangō, Nihon	94	37.13 N	139.33 E
Nangola	150	12.40 N	6.36 W
Nangoma	152	15.30 S	23.08 E
Nangong	98	37.24 N	115.22 E
Nangou	89	43.17 N	128.37 E
Nangō-yama-tunnel ◆[6]	94	35.12 N	139.10 E
Nangqên	102	32.22 N	96.21 E
Nang Rong	110	14.38 N	102.48 E
Nanguan	102	37.00 N	112.31 E
Nangweshi	152	16.26 S	23.17 E
Nanhai → Foshan	100	23.03 N	113.09 E
Nanhai → South China Sea ⊤[2]	108	10.00 N	113.00 E
Nanhe	98	37.01 N	114.41 E
Nanhedian	100	33.23 N	112.25 E
Nanhekan	107	30.24 N	103.27 E
Nanhezhao	105	39.05 N	115.56 E
Nanhsi	100	23.11 N	120.29 E
Nanhu	102	39.57 N	94.13 E
Nanhua	102	25.14 N	101.13 E
Nanhualou	104	42.30 N	123.53 E
Nanhuang	98	36.58 N	121.47 E
Nanhui	106	31.03 N	121.45 E
Nan Hulsan Hu ⊜	102	36.39 N	96.20 E
Nanhuta Shan ∧	100	24.22 N	121.26 E
Nanhutou	89	43.44 N	128.55 E
Nanika Lake ⊜	182	53.45 N	127.40 W
Naniwa ◆[8]	270	34.39 N	135.30 E
Nanjangūd	122	12.06 N	76.42 E
Nanjemoy	208	38.27 N	77.13 W
Nanjemoy Creek c	208	38.25 N	77.07 W
Nanji I	100	27.28 N	121.04 E
Nanjiang, Zhg.	100	32.44 N	120.52 E
Nanjiang, Zhg.	102	32.33 N	107.30 E
Nanjiangqiao	100	28.58 N	113.44 E
Nanjie	107	29.11 N	105.00 E
Nanjing, Zhg.	100	24.41 N	114.25 E
Nanjing, Zhg.	100	24.32 N	117.22 E
Nanjing (Nanking), Zhg.	106	32.03 N	118.47 E
Nanjing, Zhg.	107	28.49 N	105.12 E
Nanjinyi	107	30.02 N	104.42 E
Nanjirinji	154	9.39 S	39.04 E
Nanjō	94	35.50 N	136.13 E
Nanjuma ≃	105	39.24 N	115.43 E
Nankan	96	33.03 N	130.32 E
Nankāna Sāhib	123	31.27 N	73.42 E
Nankang	100	25.42 N	114.44 E
Nankang ◆[8]	269d	25.03 N	121.36 E
Nankin	214	40.55 N	82.17 W
Nanking → Nanjing	106	32.03 N	118.47 E
Nanko-kōen ♦	94	37.05 N	140.14 E
Nankoku	96	33.39 N	133.44 E
Nankou	100	26.38 N	117.24 E
Nankouzhen	105	40.14 N	116.07 E
Nanku	106	31.06 N	120.37 E
Nankye	110	14.20 N	98.11 E
Nanle	98	36.04 N	115.10 E
Nanling, Zhg.	100	30.56 N	118.20 E
Nanling, Zhg.	100	23.21 N	115.25 E
Nanling, Zhg.	104	41.37 N	120.56 E
Nan Ling ⋏	90	25.00 N	112.00 E
Nanlinqiao	100	29.35 N	114.19 E
Nanliu ≃	102	21.38 N	109.00 E
Nanliucun	105	40.10 N	116.04 E
Nanlongba	102	28.02 N	107.31 E
Nanlou Shan ∧	89	43.27 N	126.42 E
Nanma	102	24.17 N	101.03 E
Nanmatang	106	32.18 N	120.38 E
Nanmeng	105	39.11 N	116.22 E
Nanmoku	94	36.10 N	138.44 E
Nanmulin	120	29.41 N	89.04 E
Nannerch	262	53.13 N	3.15 W
Nannine	162	26.53 S	118.20 E
Nanning	102	22.48 N	108.20 E
Nanniwan	102	36.29 N	109.40 E
Nannō	94	35.13 N	136.36 E
Nannup	162	33.59 S	115.45 E
Nanny ≃	44	53.40 N	6.14 W
Na Noi	110	18.19 N	100.43 E
Nānole ◆[8]	272c	19.01 N	72.55 E
Nanoose Bay	224	49.16 N	124.12 W
Nanoose Harbour c	224	49.20 N	124.10 W
Nanoshi	272c	18.56 N	73.05 E
Nanowin ≃	184	53.13 N	97.13 W
Nanpan ≃, Zhg.	102	25.07 N	106.00 E

Symbols in the index entries represent the broad categories identified in the key at the right. Symbols with superior numbers (⋏[1]) identify subcategories (see complete key on page I · 1).

Kartensymbole in dem Registerverzeichnis stellen die rechts in Schlüssel erklärten Kategorien dar. Symbole mit hochgestellten Ziffern (⋏[1]) bezeichnen Unterabteilungen einer Kategorie (vgl. vollständiger Schlüssel auf Seite I · 1).

Los símbolos incluídos en el texto del índice representan las grandes categorias identificadas con la clave a la derecha. Los símbolos con numeros en su parte superior (⋏[1]) identifican las subcategorías (véase la clave completa en la página I · 1).

Les symboles de l'index représentent les catégories indiquées dans la légende à droite. Les symboles suivis d'un indice (⋏[1]) représentent des sous-catégories (voir légende complète à la page I · 1).

Os símbolos incluídos no texto do índice representam as grandes categorias identificadas com a chave à direita. Os símbolos com números em sua parte superior (⋏[1]) identificam as subcategorias (veja-se a chave completa à página I · 1).

∧	Mountain	Berg	Montaña	Montagne	Montanha
⋏	Mountains	Berge	Montañas	Montagnes	Montanhas
)(	Pass	Pass	Paso	Col	Passo
V	Valley, Canyon	Tal, Cañon	Valle, Cañón	Vallée, Canyon	Vale, Canhão
≚	Plain	Ebene	Llano	Plaine	Planície
›	Cape	Kap	Cabo	Cap	Cabo
I	Island	Insel	Isla	Île	Ilha
II	Islands	Inseln	Islas	Îles	Ilhas
≗	Other Topographic Features	Andere Topographische Objekte	Otros Elementos Topográficos	Autres données topographiques	Outros acidentes topográficos

ESPAÑOL / FRANÇAIS / PORTUGUÊS

Nombre / Nom / Nome	Página / Page	Lat.°′	Long.°′ W = Oeste / Ouest
Nanpan ≏, Zhg.	102	24.34 N	103.04 E
Nānpāra	124	27.52 N	81.30 E
Nanpengchang	107	29.21 N	106.38 E
Nanpi	98	38.02 N	116.42 E
Nanpiao	104	41.12 N	120.39 E
Nanping, Zhg.	89	43.24 N	129.05 E
Nanping, Zhg.	98	42.16 N	129.09 E
Nanping, Zhg.	100	26.38 N	118.10 E
Nanping, Zhg.	102	21.50 N	107.28 E
Nanping, Zhg.	102	33.07 N	104.20 E
Nanpingji	100	33.30 N	116.51 E
Nanpu	105	39.16 N	118.12 E
Nanpu ≏	100	27.02 N	118.18 E
Nanqingtuo	105	39.37 N	117.53 E
Nanqu	104	40.44 N	122.08 E
Nanquan	98	36.24 N	120.17 E
Nanri Dao I	100	25.13 N	119.30 E
Nansa ≏	34	43.22 N	4.29 W
Nansei	92	34.22 N	136.41 E
Nansei-shotō (Ryukyu Islands) II	90	26.30 N	128.00 E
Nansemond □[6]	208	36.43 N	76.40 W
Nansen, Lago ⊜	254	47.57 S	72.21 W
Nan Sha I	106	31.36 N	121.22 E
Nanshahe	98	35.03 N	117.12 E
Nanshan, Zhg.	100	26.38 N	118.20 E
Nanshan, Zhg.	105	39.21 N	115.34 E
Nanshan → Qilian Shan ⋏	102	39.06 N	98.40 E
Nanshanba	100	25.34 N	116.32 E
Nanshanchengzi	98	42.09 N	125.19 E
Nanshan Island I	108	10.45 N	115.49 E
Nanshankou	102	43.09 N	93.41 E
Nanshanlingcun	105	39.09 N	117.26 E
Nanshuang Dao I	100	26.35 N	120.08 E
Nanshui	100	22.02 N	113.16 E
Nansifa	105	39.27 N	116.27 E
Nansio	154	2.08 S	33.03 E
Nans-les-Pins	62	43.22 N	5.47 E
Nanson	162	28.34 S	114.46 E
Nansunzhai	269b	31.21 N	121.27 E
Nant	32	44.01 N	3.18 E
Nant ≏	50	47.30 N	1.14 E
Nantai	104	40.55 N	122.47 E
Nantais, Lac ⊜	176	60.59 N	74.00 W
Nantai-san ∧	94	36.43 N	140.26 E
Nantai-zan ∧	94	36.46 N	139.29 E
Nantang	100	26.08 N	115.12 E
Nantangdun	106	31.15 N	120.56 E
Nantangmei	105	38.51 N	114.56 E
Nantasket Beach	283	42.16 N	70.52 W
Nantawarra	168b	34.00 S	138.14 E
Nant Bran ≏	42	51.57 N	3.28 W
Nanterre	50	48.53 N	2.12 E
Nantes	32	47.13 N	1.33 W
Nanteuil-le-Haudouin	50	49.08 N	2.48 E
Nanteuil-lès-Meaux	261	48.56 N	2.54 E
Nantian, Zhg.	100	27.57 N	119.56 E
Nantian, Zhg.	100	29.08 N	121.56 E
Nantianmen	104	40.56 N	123.04 E
Nanticoke, On., Can.	212	42.47 N	80.12 W
Nanticoke, Md., U.S.	208	38.16 N	75.54 W
Nanticoke, Pa., U.S.	210	41.12 N	76.00 W
Nanticoke ≏	208	38.16 N	75.56 W
Nanticoke Creek ≏, On., Can.	212	42.48 N	80.04 W
Nanticoke Creek ≏, N.Y., U.S.	210	42.05 N	76.05 W
Nantmeal Village	285	40.08 N	75.42 W
Nanto	92	34.20 N	136.31 E
Nanton	182	50.21 N	113.46 W
Nantong	106	32.02 N	120.53 E
Nant'ou, T'aiwan	100	23.55 N	120.41 E
Nantou, Zhg.	100	22.33 N	113.55 E
Nantouillet	261	49.00 N	2.42 E
Nantschang → Nanchang	100	28.41 N	115.53 E
Nantua	58	46.09 N	5.37 E
Nantuantingzhuang	105	40.17 N	118.17 E
Nantucket	207	41.17 N	70.06 W
Nantucket □[6]	207	41.17 N	70.06 W
Nantucket Island I	207	41.16 N	70.03 W
Nantucket Sound ɥ	207	41.30 N	70.15 W
Nantuego	154	11.21 S	38.24 E
Nantulo	154	12.17 S	39.03 E
Nantung → Nantong	106	32.02 N	120.53 E
Nantwich	42	53.04 N	2.32 W
Nanty Glo	214	40.28 N	78.50 W
Nant-y-Moch Reservoir ⊜[1]	42	52.27 N	3.50 W
Nanu	164	8.50 S	142.40 E
Nanuet	210	41.05 N	74.00 W
Nanuet Mall ◆[9]	276	41.06 N	74.01 W
Nanuku Passage ɥ	175g	16.45 S	179.15 W
Nanumanga I	14	6.18 S	176.20 E
Nanumea I[1]	14	5.39 S	176.08 E
Nanuque	255	17.50 S	40.21 W
Nānūr	126	23.42 N	87.52 E
Nanusa, Pulau-pulau II	108	4.42 N	127.06 E
Nanushuk ≏	180	69.18 N	151.00 W
Nanwan	100	32.09 N	113.57 E
Nan Wan ⊂	100	21.55 N	120.47 E
Nanwengkouzi	89	51.10 N	125.25 E
Nanwenquan	107	29.26 N	106.35 E
Nanxi, Zhg.	100	31.31 N	115.38 E
Nanxi, Zhg.	100	26.24 N	118.24 E
Nanxi, Zhg.	107	28.51 N	104.58 E
Nanxian	102	29.20 N	112.19 E
Nanxiang	106	31.17 N	121.18 E
Nanxikou	107	30.43 N	106.07 E
Nanxin, Zhg.	98	35.33 N	117.12 E
Nanxin, Zhg.	105	39.11 N	115.38 E
Nanxing Hu ⊜	106	31.08 N	120.48 E
Nanxinzhuang	98	36.39 N	115.15 E
Nanxiong	100	25.10 N	114.20 E
Nanxun	106	30.53 N	120.26 E
Nanya	100	26.52 N	118.19 E
Nanyandang Shan ∧	100	27.36 N	120.04 E
Nanyang, Zhg.	100	27.24 N	119.39 E
Nanyang, Zhg.	100	33.00 N	112.32 E
Nanyang, Zhg.	100	33.25 N	120.13 E
Nanyangcun	106	31.53 N	121.43 E
Nanyanggangzi	89	48.43 N	125.27 E
Nanyang Hu ⊜	98	35.12 N	116.41 E
Nanyang Shan ∧	106	31.20 N	120.28 E
Nanyang University ✿[2]	271c	1.21 N	103.41 E
Nanyi Hu ⊜	106	31.07 N	118.57 E
Nan-yō	92	38.03 N	140.10 E
Nanyu	100	25.59 N	119.14 E
Nanyuan	105	39.48 N	116.23 E
Nanyuan Airport ⊠	271a	39.47 N	116.23 E
Nanyue	100	27.13 N	112.43 E
Nanyuki	154	0.01 N	37.04 E
Nanyulin	105	40.09 N	115.23 E
Nanzamu	98	41.56 N	124.23 E
Nanzha	106	31.51 N	120.15 E
Nanzhai	106	31.34 N	120.02 E
Nanzhang, Zhg.	102	31.50 N	111.41 E
Nanzhang, Zhg.	105	39.03 N	115.46 E
Nanzhao	100	33.30 N	112.27 E
Nanzhaoji	100	32.38 N	115.58 E
Nanzhen	100	26.59 N	119.57 E
Nanzhenjie	106	31.48 N	119.17 E
Nanzhila	154	16.05 S	26.07 E
Nanzhuang, Zhg.	105	40.22 N	116.21 E
Nanzhuang, Zhg.	105	40.43 N	114.58 E
Nao	152	4.35 N	15.09 E
Nao, Cabo de la ›	34	38.44 N	0.14 E
Naoābād	272b	22.28 N	88.27 E
Naoāpāra	126	22.45 N	89.39 E
Naococane, Lac ⊜	176	52.52 N	70.40 W
Naoetsu	94	37.11 N	138.15 E
Naogaon	124	24.47 N	88.56 E
Naoiri	96	33.04 N	131.23 E
Naokot	120	24.51 N	69.27 E
Naoli ≏	89	47.20 N	134.10 E
Naolinco de Victoria	234	19.39 N	96.51 W
Não-me-Toque	252	28.28 S	52.49 W
Naong, Bukit ∧	112	2.40 N	112.45 E
Nāopāra	126	24.09 N	88.54 E
Naopukuria	272b	22.55 N	88.16 E
Naosap Lake ⊜	184	54.51 N	101.24 W
Naoshima	96	34.27 N	133.59 E
Naours	50	50.02 N	2.17 E
Náousa	38	40.37 N	22.05 E
Naozhou Dao I	102	20.57 N	110.34 E
Napa	226	38.17 N	122.17 W
Napa □[6]	226	38.18 N	122.17 W
Napa ≏	226	38.07 N	122.18 W
Napacao Point ›	116	9.43 N	124.31 E
Napajedla	30	49.10 N	17.31 E
Napakiak	180	60.42 N	161.57 W
Napaku	112	2.32 N	115.58 E
Na Pali Coast State Park ♠	229b	22.09 N	159.41 W
Napalkovo	74	70.03 N	73.47 E
Napamute	180	61.33 N	158.42 W
Napanee	212	44.15 N	76.57 W
Napanee ≏	212	44.12 N	77.02 W
Napanoch	210	41.44 N	74.22 W
Napareuli	84	42.03 N	45.31 E
Napas	86	59.53 N	81.58 E
Napaskiak	180	60.42 N	161.45 W
Napa Valley V	226	38.18 N	122.18 W
Napavine	224	46.34 N	122.54 W
Napayauan Island I	116	12.22 N	123.14 E
Napè	110	18.18 N	105.06 E
Napenay	252	26.44 S	60.37 W
Naperville	216	41.47 N	88.08 W
Napetipi ≏	186	51.21 N	58.08 W
Napf ∧	58	47.00 N	7.56 E
Napido	164	0.41 S	135.23 E
Napiéolédougou	150	9.18 N	5.35 W
Napier, N.Z.	172	39.29 S	176.55 E
Napier, S. Afr.	158	34.29 S	19.53 E
Napier, Mount ∧	162	17.32 S	129.10 E
Napier Mountains ⋏	9	66.30 S	53.40 E
Napierville	206	45.11 N	73.25 W
Napierville □[6]	206	45.10 N	73.35 W
Napinka	184	49.17 N	100.50 W
Naplate	216	41.20 N	88.54 W
Naples → Napoli, It.	68	40.51 N	14.17 E
Naples, Fl., U.S.	220	26.08 N	81.47 W
Naples, Id., U.S.	202	48.34 N	116.23 W
Naples, Il., U.S.	219	39.45 N	90.36 W
Naples, N.Y., U.S.	210	42.36 N	77.24 W
Naples, Tx., U.S.	222	33.12 N	94.40 W
Naples Park	220	26.16 N	81.48 W
Napo	102	23.16 N	105.54 E
Napo □[4]	246	0.20 S	76.50 W
Napo ≏	246	3.20 S	72.40 W
Napola	70	37.59 N	12.38 E
Napoleon, In., U.S.	218	39.12 N	85.19 W
Napoleon, Ky., U.S.	218	38.46 N	84.47 W
Napoleon, Mi., U.S.	216	42.10 N	84.15 W
Napoleon, N.D., U.S.	198	46.30 N	99.46 W
Napoleon, Oh., U.S.	216	41.23 N	84.07 W
Napoleonville	194	29.56 N	91.01 W
Nápoles → Napoli	68	40.51 N	14.17 E
Napoli (Naples)	68	40.51 N	14.17 E
Napoli □[4]	68	40.53 N	14.25 E
Napoli, Golfo di ⊂	68	40.43 N	14.10 E
Napopo	154	4.12 N	28.02 E
Nappamerry	166	27.36 S	141.07 E
Nappanee	216	41.26 N	86.00 W
Nappan Island I	212	44.23 N	77.49 W
Napton on the Hill	42	52.15 N	1.24 W
Napu	115b	9.24 S	119.56 E
Napudalutai Shan ∧	89	51.06 N	122.13 E
Naqādah	140	25.54 N	32.43 E
Naqadeh	128	36.57 N	45.23 E
Naqb, Ra's an- ∧	132	29.50 N	35.40 E
Naquhe ≏	120	31.15 N	94.37 E
Nar ≏	42	52.45 N	0.24 E
Nara, Mali	150	15.10 N	7.17 W
Nara, Nihon	96	34.41 N	135.50 E
Nara □[5]	96	34.30 N	135.50 E
Nāra ≏, Pāk.	120	24.07 N	69.07 E
Nara ≏, S.S.S.R.	82	54.53 N	37.26 E
Nara-bonchi ≌[1]	270	34.38 N	135.50 E
Naracoorte	166	36.58 S	140.44 E
Naradhan	166	33.37 S	146.19 E
Narai ≏	94	36.20 N	137.55 E
Naraina ◆[8]	272a	28.37 N	77.08 E
Naraini	124	25.11 N	80.29 E
Narainpur	126	24.03 N	86.36 E
Narakawa	94	35.59 N	137.50 E
Narāl	126	23.10 N	89.30 E
Naramata	182	49.36 N	119.35 W
Naran	88	48.34 N	98.17 E
Naran Bulag	86	49.22 N	92.33 E
Nārang	123	31.54 N	74.31 E
Narangba	171a	27.12 S	152.58 E
Naranja	220	25.31 N	80.25 W
Naranjal, Ec.	246	2.42 S	79.37 W
Naranjal, Perú	286d	11.58 S	77.06 W
Naranjal, Ven.	286c	10.28 N	67.02 W
Naranjito, Hond.	236	14.57 N	88.41 W
Naranjito, P.R.	240m	18.18 N	66.15 W
Naranjo	236	10.06 N	84.22 W
Naranjo ≏	236	14.30 N	92.11 W
Naranjo, Río del ≏	234	18.54 N	103.37 W
Naranjo Islands II	116	12.23 N	124.03 E
Naranjos	234	21.21 N	97.41 W
Narao	92	32.50 N	129.04 E
Nara Park ♠	270	34.41 N	135.52 E
Narasannapeta	122	18.25 N	84.03 E
Narasapur	122	16.27 N	81.40 E
Narasaraopet	122	16.15 N	80.04 E
Narashino	94	35.41 N	140.02 E
Narasinhapur	126	23.10 N	90.36 E
Narasun	88	50.06 N	112.58 E
Narat	86	43.28 N	83.44 E
Narathiwat	110	6.26 N	101.50 E
Nara Visa	196	35.36 N	103.05 W
Nara Women's University ✿[2]	270	34.42 N	135.49 E
Nārāyanganj	124	23.37 N	90.30 E
Nārāyani (Gandak) ≏	124	25.39 N	85.13 E
Nārāyanpāra	272b	22.54 N	88.19 E
Nārāyanpet	122	16.44 N	77.30 E
Nārāyanpur	272b	22.29 N	88.34 E
Narazeni	84	42.27 N	41.57 E
Narberth, Wales, U.K.	42	51.48 N	4.45 W
Narberth, Pa., U.S.	285	40.00 N	75.15 W
Narbonne	32	43.11 N	3.00 E
Narcao	71	39.10 N	8.40 E
Narcea ≏	34	43.28 N	6.06 W
Narcosli Creek ≏	182	52.49 N	122.28 W
Nardò	68	40.11 N	18.02 E
Nare ≏	246	6.12 N	74.35 W
Narellan	170	34.02 S	150.44 E
Narembeen	162	32.04 S	118.24 E
Narenbulake	89	49.52 N	120.23 E
Narendranagar	124	30.10 N	78.18 E
Nares Strait ɥ	16	80.30 N	68.00 W
Naretha	162	31.00 S	124.50 E
Narew ≏	30	52.26 N	20.42 E
Nargund	122	15.43 N	75.23 E
Narhan	272c	19.08 N	73.07 E
Nāri ≏	120	28.35 N	67.50 E
Naria	124	23.18 N	90.25 E
Nariai	270	34.53 N	135.38 E
Nariel	171b	36.26 S	147.50 E
Narijn ≏	88	50.20 N	93.24 E
Narijnteel	102	45.57 N	101.29 E
Nārikelbāria	126	23.17 N	89.21 E
Nariman	85	40.34 N	72.48 E
Narimanabad	84	38.53 N	48.52 E
Narimba, Her Majesty's Air Station (Royal Australian Navy Airfield) ■	274a	33.43 S	150.53 E
Narinca	130	37.52 N	38.46 E
Narinda, Baie de ⊂	157b	14.55 S	47.30 E
Nārīn Ghar	120	36.01 N	69.06 E
Nariño □[5]	246	1.30 N	78.00 W
Narita	94	35.47 N	140.19 E
Nariwa	96	34.47 N	133.33 E
Nariwa ≏	96	34.46 N	133.36 E
Narizón, Punta ›	232	27.52 N	110.54 W
Nar'jan-Mar	24	67.39 N	53.00 E
Nārkanda	123	31.16 N	77.27 E
Narkatiāganj	124	27.06 N	84.28 E
Närke □[9]	40	59.06 N	15.03 E
Närkes Marieberg	40	59.12 N	15.10 E
Narlı	130	37.27 N	37.09 E
Narma	80	54.46 N	42.01 E
Narmada ≏	118	21.38 N	72.36 E
Narmada Valley V	124	22.30 N	77.00 E
Narmak ◆[8]	267d	35.43 N	51.29 E
Narman	130	40.21 N	41.52 E
Narmušad'	80	54.40 N	41.07 E
Nar-Nar-Goon	169	38.05 S	145.34 E
Nārnaul	124	28.03 N	76.07 E
Narni	66	42.31 N	12.31 E
Naro	70	37.18 N	13.47 E
Naro ≏	70	37.14 N	13.37 E
Naroč' ≏	76	54.26 N	26.39 E
Naroč', ozero ⊜	76	54.52 N	26.45 E
Narodiči	78	51.13 N	29.03 E
Narodnaja, gora ∧	24	65.04 N	60.09 E
Naro-Fominsk	82	55.23 N	36.43 E
Naro Island I	116	11.53 N	123.40 E
Narok	154	1.05 S	35.52 E
Narol	30	50.22 N	23.21 E
Narón	34	43.32 N	8.10 W
Narooma	166	36.14 S	150.03 E
Naro-Osakovo	82	55.33 N	36.33 E
Narovčat	80	53.52 N	43.41 E
Narovl'a	78	51.48 N	29.29 E
Nārowāl	123	32.07 N	73.25 E
Närpes (Närpiö)	26	62.28 N	21.20 E
Närpiö → Närpes	26	62.28 N	21.20 E
Narrabeen	170	33.43 S	151.18 E
Narrabeen Lagoon ⊂	274a	33.43 S	151.17 E
Narrabri	166	30.19 S	149.47 E
Narragansett	207	41.25 N	71.27 W
Narragansett Bay ⊂	207	41.40 N	71.20 W
Narran ≏	166	29.45 S	147.20 E
Narra Narra ∧	171b	35.50 S	147.27 E
Narrandera	166	34.45 S	146.33 E
Narraway ≏	182	54.48 N	119.56 W
Narraweena	274a	33.45 S	151.16 E
Narre Warren	274b	38.02 S	145.19 E
Narre Warren North	274b	37.59 S	145.19 E
Narrogin	162	32.56 S	117.10 E
Narromine	166	32.14 S	148.15 E
Narrows, Md., U.S.	208	38.58 N	76.15 W
Narrows, Va., U.S.	192	37.19 N	80.48 W
Narrowsburg	210	41.36 N	75.03 W
Närsen ⊜	40	60.17 N	14.23 E
Narsimhapur	124	22.57 N	79.12 E
Narsingdi	124	23.55 N	90.43 E
Narsinghgarh	124	23.42 N	77.06 E
Narsinghpur □[5]	124	23.00 N	79.00 E
Narsīpatnam	122	17.40 N	82.37 E
Narskije Prudy, ozero ⊜[1]	82	55.32 N	36.36 E
Narssaq	176	60.54 N	46.00 W
Nartkala	84	43.33 N	43.50 E
Nartuby ≏	62	43.28 N	6.34 E
Naru	92	32.49 N	128.56 E
Narubis, Namibia	158	27.10 S	19.05 E
Narubis, Namibia	158	26.55 S	18.35 E
Naruko	92	38.44 N	140.43 E
Naruksovo	80	54.37 N	44.33 E
Naruo	270	34.43 N	135.23 E
Narusawa	94	35.29 N	138.41 E
Narutō, Nihon	94	35.36 N	140.25 E
Naruto, Nihon	96	34.11 N	134.37 E
Naruto-kaikyō ɥ	96	34.14 N	134.39 E
Narva, S.S.S.R.	76	59.23 N	28.12 E
Narva, S.S.S.R.	86	55.25 N	93.39 E
Narva ≏	76	59.27 N	28.02 E
Narvacan	116	17.25 N	120.28 E
Narva-Jõesuu	76	59.27 N	28.03 E
Narvan	85	40.15 N	67.12 E
Narvik	24	68.26 N	17.25 E
Narvskij zaliv (Narva laht) ⊂	76	59.30 N	27.40 E
Narvskoje vodochranilišče ⊜[1]	76	59.18 N	28.14 E
Narwāna	124	29.37 N	76.07 E
Narwietooma	162	23.15 S	132.35 E
Narym	86	58.58 N	81.30 E
Naryn, S.S.S.R.	85	41.26 N	75.59 E
Naryn, S.S.S.R.	88	50.13 N	96.27 E
Naryn □[4]	85	41.30 N	75.30 E
Naryn ≏	85	40.54 N	71.45 E
Narynkol	72	42.43 N	80.12 E
Naryntau, gory ⋏	85	41.25 N	76.50 E
Naryškino	76	52.58 N	35.44 E
Naryū-zaki ›	96	35.36 N	135.28 E
Narzole	62	44.35 N	7.52 E
Nås, Sve.	40	60.27 N	14.29 E
Näs, Sve.	40	58.41 N	15.50 E
Nasadkino	82	56.29 N	37.21 E
Näsåker	26	63.26 N	16.54 E
Na-san	110	21.12 N	104.02 E
Nasarawa	150	8.30 N	7.40 E
Năsăud	38	47.17 N	24.24 E
Nasawa	175f	15.13 S	168.09 E
NASA Wallops Station ✿[3]	208	37.52 N	75.28 W
Nasbinals	32	44.40 N	3.03 E
Naschel	252	32.55 S	65.23 W
Nase → Naze	93b	28.23 N	129.30 E
Naseby, N.Z.	172	45.02 S	170.09 E
Naseby, Eng., U.K.	42	52.25 N	0.58 W
Naselle	224	46.21 N	123.48 W
Naselle ≏	224	46.25 N	123.55 W
Nash	194	33.27 N	94.08 W
Nashawena Island I	207	41.26 N	70.53 W
Nashoba Brook ≏	283	42.28 N	71.24 W
Nashport	214	40.04 N	82.09 W
Nashū', Wādī an- V	146	26.25 N	14.15 E
Nashua, Ia., U.S.	190	42.57 N	92.32 W
Nashua, Mt., U.S.	202	48.07 N	106.21 W
Nashua, N.H., U.S.	207	42.45 N	71.28 W
Nashua ≏	207	42.46 N	71.27 W
Nashuixi	102	30.09 N	108.40 E
Näshultasjön ⊜	40	59.14 N	16.21 E
Nashville, On., Can.	275b	43.50 N	79.40 W
Nashville, Ar., U.S.	194	33.56 N	93.50 W
Nashville, Ga., U.S.	192	31.12 N	83.15 W
Nashville, Il., U.S.	219	38.20 N	89.22 W
Nashville, In., U.S.	218	39.12 N	86.15 W
Nashville, Mi., U.S.	216	42.36 N	85.05 W
Nashville, N.C., U.S.	192	35.58 N	77.57 W
Nashville, Oh., U.S.	214	40.36 N	82.07 W
Nashville, Tn., U.S.	194	36.09 N	86.47 W
Nashwaak ≏	186	45.57 N	66.37 W
Nashwaaksis	186	45.59 N	66.39 W
Nashwah	142	30.30 N	31.29 E
Nashwauk	190	47.22 N	93.10 W
Nasia	150	10.09 N	0.48 W
Naṣīb	132	32.33 N	36.11 E
Našice	38	45.29 N	18.06 E
Nasielsk	30	52.36 N	20.48 E
Näsijärvi ⊜	26	61.37 N	23.42 E
Nāsik	122	19.59 N	73.48 E
Nāṣir	140	8.36 N	33.04 E
Nāṣir, Buḥayrat (Lake Nasser) ⊜[1]	140	22.40 N	32.00 E
Nasīrābād, India	120	26.18 N	74.44 E
Nasīrābād, Pāk.	120	28.23 N	68.24 E
Naskaftym	80	52.57 N	45.38 E
Naskaupi ≏	176	53.45 N	60.50 W
Näsnaren ⊜	40	58.51 N	16.18 E
Naso	70	38.07 N	14.47 E
Nasondoye	154	10.22 S	25.06 E
Naso Point ›	116	10.25 N	121.57 E
Nasorolevu ∧	175g	16.38 S	178.42 E
Nasosnyj	84	40.37 N	49.34 E
Naṣr	142	30.36 N	30.23 E
Naṣrābād	128	34.08 N	51.26 E
Naṣrānī, Jabal an- ∧	130	34.06 N	37.24 E
Nasriddinbek	85	40.41 N	71.55 E
Nāsriganj	124	25.03 N	84.20 E
Nass ≏	182	55.00 N	129.50 W
Nassau, Ba.	240b	25.05 N	77.21 W
Nassau, B.R.D.	56	50.19 N	7.47 E
Nassau, D.D.R.	54	50.46 N	13.32 E
Nassau, N.Y., U.S.	210	42.30 N	73.36 W
Nassau □[6]	210	40.45 N	73.38 W
Nassau, Bahía ⊂	254	55.25 S	67.40 W
Nassau Bay	222	29.32 N	95.05 W
Nassau Coliseum ♠	276	40.43 N	73.36 W
Nassau International Airport ⊠	240b	25.02 N	77.28 W
Nassau Island I	14	11.33 S	165.25 W
Nassau Shores	276	40.39 N	73.26 W
Nassawadox	208	37.28 N	75.51 W
Nassawango Creek ≏	208	38.10 N	75.25 W
Nassenfels	60	48.48 N	11.16 E
Nassenheide	54	52.49 N	13.12 E
Nasser, Lake → Nāṣir, Buḥayrat ⊜[1]	140	22.40 N	32.00 E
Nassereith	58	47.19 N	10.50 E
Nassian	150	8.27 N	3.29 W
Nässjö	26	57.39 N	14.41 E
Nastapoca ≏	176	56.55 N	76.33 W
Nastapoka Islands II	176	57.00 N	76.50 W
Nastasjino	82	54.28 N	38.16 E
Nastaška	78	49.39 N	30.19 E
Nastätten	56	50.12 N	7.51 E
Nastauli	272a	28.43 N	77.22 E
Nastf, Bi'r ⩒[4]	142	30.18 N	30.28 E
Nasu	94	37.01 N	140.07 E
Nasu-dake ∧, Nihon	92	37.07 N	139.58 E
Nasu-dake ∧, Nihon	94	37.09 N	139.58 E
Nasugbu	116	14.05 N	120.38 E
Nasukoin Mountain ∧	202	48.48 N	114.35 W
Nasva	76	56.35 N	30.10 E
Nat ≏	190	48.48 N	82.07 W
Nata, Bots.	156	20.12 S	26.12 E
Natá, Pan.	236	8.20 N	80.31 W
Nata ≏	156	20.14 S	26.10 E
Natagaima	246	3.37 N	75.06 W
Nātāgarh	272b	22.42 N	88.25 E
Natal, Bra.	250	5.47 S	35.13 W
Natal, B.C., Can.	182	49.44 N	114.50 W
Natal, Indon.	110	0.33 N	99.07 E
Natal □[4]	158	28.40 S	30.40 E
Natal Basin ✦[1]	10	30.00 S	40.00 E
Natalia	196	29.11 N	98.51 W
Nataljevka	83	47.10 N	38.29 E
Nataljin Jar	80	51.46 N	50.35 E
Nataljino	80	52.56 N	49.02 E
Natalkuz Lake ⊜	182	53.26 N	125.20 W
Natalspruit ≏	273d	26.19 S	28.10 E
Natanes Plateau ⋏[1]	200	33.35 N	110.15 W
Natash, Wādī V	140	24.25 N	33.26 E
Natashō	96	35.24 N	135.38 E
Natashquan	186	50.12 N	61.49 W
Natashquan ≏	176	50.06 N	61.49 W
Natashquan, Pointe de ›	186	50.06 N	61.44 W
Natashquan Est ≏	186	51.20 N	61.40 W
Natchez	194	31.33 N	91.24 W
Natchez Trace Parkway ♠	194	32.00 N	91.00 W
Natchitoches	194	31.45 N	93.05 W
Natco Lake ⊜	276	40.26 N	74.09 W
Natércia	256	22.07 S	45.30 W
Naters	58	46.20 N	7.59 E
Natewa Bay ⊂	175g	16.35 S	179.40 E
Na Thawi	110	6.45 N	100.42 E
Nāthdwāra	120	24.56 N	73.49 E
Nathia Gali	123	34.04 N	73.24 E
Nathkaw	102	26.53 N	96.13 E
Nathula I	175g	16.53 S	177.25 E
Natick	207	42.17 N	71.21 W
Natick Laboratories ■	283	42.17 N	71.22 W
Natimuk	166	36.45 S	141.57 E
Nation ≏	182	55.28 N	123.35 W
National Agricultural Research Center ✿[3]	284c	39.02 N	76.52 W
National Airport ⊠	281	42.19 N	83.25 W
National Arboretum ♠	284c	38.54 N	76.58 W
National Assembly ✿	269a	13.46 N	100.31 E
National Baseball Hall of Fame and Museum ✿	210	42.42 N	74.57 W
National City	228	32.40 N	117.05 W
National Gallery ✿	260	51.31 N	0.08 W
National Institute of Health ✿	284c	39.00 N	77.06 W
National Maritime Museum ✿	260	51.29 N	0.00
National Park	285	39.51 N	75.10 W
National Taiwan Normal University ✿[2]	269d	25.02 N	121.31 E
National Taiwan University ✿[2]	269d	25.01 N	121.32 E
National Zoological Park ♠	284c	38.56 N	77.03 W
Natipi, Lac ⊜	186	51.27 N	71.23 W
Natisone ≏	64	45.57 N	13.22 E
Natitingou	150	10.19 N	1.22 E
Native Bay ⊂	176	63.52 N	82.30 W
Natividade	250	11.43 S	47.47 W
Natividade da Serra	256	23.24 S	45.26 W
Natívitas ◆[8]	286a	19.14 N	99.05 W
Nativity, Church of the ✿[1]	132	31.43 N	35.12 E
Natkyizin	110	14.55 N	97.57 E
Natl	132	31.39 N	35.52 E
Natoma	198	39.11 N	99.01 W
Natong	102	23.01 N	107.50 E
Nator	124	24.25 N	88.59 E
Natori	92	38.08 N	140.55 E
Natorp	263	51.30 N	7.38 E
Natron, Lake ⊜	154	2.25 S	36.00 E
Natrona Heights	214	40.37 N	79.43 W
Naṭrūn, Wādī an- ⊥[7]	142	30.25 N	30.13 E
Natsui ≏	94	37.03 N	140.59 E
Nattai ≏	170	34.05 S	150.25 E
Nattai River	170	34.04 S	150.27 E
Nattam	122	10.14 N	78.14 E
Nåttarö I	40	58.52 N	18.07 E
Nattastunturit ∧	24	68.12 N	27.20 E
Nattaung ∧	110	18.48 N	97.02 E
Natters	64	47.14 N	11.22 E
Nattwerder	264a	52.26 N	12.56 E
Natuchajevskaja	78	44.54 N	37.34 E
Nātudaha	126	23.39 N	88.41 E
Natukanaoka Pan ≌	156	18.40 S	15.45 E
Natu La)(	124	27.23 N	88.51 E
Natuna Besar I	112	4.00 N	108.15 E
Natural Bridge	212	44.04 N	75.29 W
Natural Bridge ♠	192	37.38 N	79.33 W
Natural Bridges National Monument ♠	200	37.30 N	110.08 W
Natural Bridge State Resort Park ♠	192	37.47 N	83.42 W
Naturaliste, Cape ›	162	33.32 S	115.01 E
Naturaliste Channel ɥ	162	25.25 S	113.00 E
Naturita	200	38.13 N	108.34 W
Naturita Creek ≏	200	38.13 N	108.32 W
Naturno (Naturns)	64	46.39 N	11.00 E
Natzungen	52	51.36 N	9.14 E
Nau	85	40.09 N	69.22 E
Naucalpan → Ciudad de Naucalpan de Juárez	286a	19.28 N	99.14 W
Naucalpan □[7]	286a	19.26 N	99.17 W
Naucelle	32	44.12 N	2.20 E
Naučnyj	78	44.44 N	34.01 E
Naude	272c	19.03 N	73.06 E
Nauders	58	46.53 N	10.30 E
Nauen	54	52.36 N	12.52 E
Nauener Luch ⩨	264a	52.37 N	12.55 E
Nauener Stadtforst ♠	264a	52.38 N	12.58 E
Naugachhia	124	25.24 N	87.06 E
Naugatuck	207	41.30 N	73.05 W
Naugatuck ≏	207	41.19 N	73.05 W
Naughton	190	46.24 N	81.12 W
Naugol'noje	82	56.22 N	38.11 E
Naui	140	18.28 N	30.43 E
Naujamiestis	76	55.41 N	24.04 E
Naujan	116	13.20 N	121.18 E
Naujan, Lake ⊜	116	13.10 N	121.21 E
Naujoji Akmenė	76	56.19 N	22.55 E
Naukan	180	66.01 N	169.43 W
Naulavaara ∧[2]	26	63.53 N	28.13 E
Naulila	152	17.12 S	14.42 E
Naumburg, B.R.D.	56	51.15 N	9.10 E
Naumburg, D.D.R.	54	51.09 N	11.48 E
Naumburg am Queiss → Nowogrodziec	30	51.12 N	15.25 E
Naumovščina	76	58.23 N	28.20 E
Naunak	86	59.00 N	80.13 E
Naundorf	54	50.56 N	13.25 E
Naunglon	110	16.48 N	97.45 E
Naungpale	110	19.33 N	97.08 E
Naunhof	54	51.16 N	12.35 E
Naupada ◆[8]	272c	19.04 N	72.50 E
Ñaupe	248	5.36 S	79.54 W
Nā'ūr	132	31.53 N	35.50 E
Nauraushaun Brook ≏	276	41.03 N	73.59 W
Nauroth	56	50.42 N	7.52 E
Nauroz Kalāt	128	28.47 N	65.38 E
Naurskaja	84	43.38 N	45.19 E
Nauru □[1], Oc.	14	0.32 S	166.55 E
Nauru □[1], Oc.	174b	0.32 S	166.55 E
Naurzumskij zapovednik ♠	86	52.30 N	64.20 E
Naushahra	123	33.09 N	74.14 E
Naushahro Fīroz	120	26.50 N	68.07 E
Naushon Island I	207	41.29 N	70.45 W
Nauški	88	50.28 N	106.07 E
Nausori	175g	18.02 S	178.32 E
Naussac, Barrage de ◆[6]	62	44.46 N	3.49 E
Naust	46	57.47 N	5.39 W
Naustdal	26	61.31 N	5.43 E
Nauta	246	4.32 S	73.33 W
Nautanwa	124	27.26 N	83.25 E
Nautilus Park	207	41.22 N	72.05 W
Nautla	234	20.13 N	96.47 W
Nautla ≏	234	20.15 N	96.47 W
Nauvoo	190	40.33 N	91.23 W
Nava	232	28.25 N	100.46 W
Nava, Arroyo de la ≏	266a	40.31 N	3.46 W
Nava, Colle di)(	62	44.05 N	7.53 E
Nava del Rey	34	41.20 N	5.05 W
Navahermosa	34	39.38 N	4.28 W
Navajo	200	35.55 N	109.01 W
Navajo ≏	200	37.01 N	107.10 W
Navajo Creek ≏	200	36.59 N	111.24 W
Navajo Hopi Joint Use Area ◆[4]	200	36.15 N	110.30 W
Navajo Indian Reservation ◆[4]	200	36.25 N	110.00 W
Navajo Mountain ∧	200	37.02 N	110.52 W
Navajo National Monument ♠	200	36.40 N	110.33 W
Navajo Reservoir ⊜[1]	200	36.55 N	107.30 W
Naval	116	11.34 N	124.23 E
Navalcarnero	34	40.18 N	4.00 W
Navalmoral de la Mata	34	39.54 N	5.32 W
Naval Ordnance Test Station ■	228	35.32 N	117.05 W
Navalvillar de Pela	34	39.06 N	5.28 W
Navan → An Uaimh, Ire.	48	52.07 N	7.16 W
Navan → An Uaimh, Ire.	48	53.39 N	6.41 W
Navāpur	122	21.09 N	73.48 E
Navarin, mys ›	180	62.16 N	179.10 E
Navarino → Pílos	38	36.55 N	21.43 E
Navarino, Isla I	254	55.05 S	67.40 W
Navarra □[4]	34	42.40 N	1.30 W
Navarre, Austl.	169	36.54 S	143.07 E
Navarre, Oh., U.S.	214	40.43 N	81.31 W
Navarro	258	35.01 S	59.16 W
Navarro □[6]	222	32.05 N	96.30 W
Navarro ≏	204	39.11 N	123.45 W
Navarro, Cañada ≏	258	35.00 S	59.18 W
Navarro, Laguna ⊜	258	35.01 S	59.18 W
Navarro Mills Lake ⊜[1]	222	31.56 N	96.45 W
Navašino	80	55.32 N	42.12 E
Navasota	222	30.23 N	96.05 W
Navasota ≏	222	30.20 N	96.09 W
Navassa	192	34.15 N	78.00 W
Navassa Island I	238	18.24 N	75.01 W
Nave	64	45.35 N	10.17 E
Nävekvarn	40	58.38 N	16.49 E
Navenne	58	47.36 N	6.10 E
Naver ≏	46	58.32 N	4.15 W
Naver, Loch ⊜	46	58.17 N	4.23 W
Navesink	276	40.23 N	74.02 W
Navesink River ⊂	276	40.23 N	73.58 W
Navesnoje	76	52.17 N	37.57 E
Nâves-Parmelan	58	45.56 N	6.11 E
Navesti ≏	76	58.30 N	24.54 E
Navestock	260	51.39 N	0.13 E
Navestock Side	260	51.39 N	0.16 E
Navia, Arg.	252	34.47 S	66.35 W
Navia, Esp.	34	43.32 N	6.43 W
Navia ≏	34	43.33 N	6.44 W
Navibandar	120	21.26 N	69.48 E
Navidad, Chile	252	33.57 S	71.50 W
Navidad, Méx.	234	20.35 N	104.42 W
Navidad ≏	196	28.41 N	96.35 W
Navidad, Bahía ⊂	234	19.12 N	104.43 W
Navidad Bank ✦[3]	238	20.00 N	68.50 W
Navio, Riacho do ≏	250	8.39 S	38.36 W
Naviraí	255	23.08 S	54.13 W
Navis	64	47.07 N	11.32 E
Naviti I	175g	17.07 S	177.15 E
Navl'a	76	52.51 N	34.30 E
Navl'a ≏	76	52.42 N	34.01 E
Navoi	72	40.15 N	65.15 E
Navojoa	232	27.06 N	109.26 W
Navolato	232	24.47 N	107.42 W
Navoloki	80	57.28 N	41.59 E
Navotas	269f	14.39 N	120.57 E
Návpaktos	38	38.23 N	21.50 E
Návplion	38	37.34 N	22.48 E
Navrongo	150	10.54 N	1.06 W
Navşar	128	37.18 N	44.35 E
Navsāri	120	20.51 N	72.55 E
Navua	175g	18.14 S	178.10 E
Navy Island I	284a	43.04 N	79.01 W
Navy Pier ◆[5]	278	41.53 N	87.36 W
Navy Yard City	224	47.32 N	122.41 W
Nawa, Nihon	96	35.30 N	133.30 E
Nawa → Naha, Nihon	174m	26.13 N	127.40 E
Nawá, Sūrīy.	132	32.53 N	36.03 E
Nawābganj, Bngl.	124	24.36 N	88.17 E
Nawābganj, Bngl.	126	23.40 N	90.10 E
Nawābganj, India	124	28.33 N	79.38 E
Nawābganj, India	124	26.52 N	82.08 E
Nawābganj, India	124	26.56 N	81.13 E
Nawābshāh	120	26.15 N	68.25 E
Nawāda	124	24.53 N	85.32 E
Nāwah	120	32.19 N	67.53 E
Nawākot, Nepāl	124	27.55 N	85.10 E
Nawa Kot, Pāk.	120	28.20 N	71.22 E
Nawalapitiya	122	7.03 N	80.32 E
Nawalgarh	120	27.51 N	75.16 E
Nawān Kot	123	31.06 N	71.32 E
Nawāpāra, Bngl.	126	23.02 N	89.23 E
Nawāpāra, India	122	20.58 N	81.51 E
Nawapārā, India	126	23.29 N	88.15 E
Nawasā al-Ghayṭ	142	30.58 N	31.19 E
Nawāshahr, India	123	31.07 N	76.08 E
Nawāshahr, Pāk.	123	34.10 N	73.16 E
Nawāṣīf, Ḥarrat ⊥[9]	144	21.20 N	42.10 E
Nawāy	142	27.47 N	30.46 E
Nawiliwili Bay ⊂	229b	21.57 N	159.21 W
Nawinda Kuta	152	16.25 S	24.28 E
Nawŏn-ni	98	36.25 N	126.40 E
Naxera	208	37.20 N	76.27 W
Naxi	107	28.47 N	105.22 E
Náxos	38	37.06 N	25.23 E
Náxos I	38	37.02 N	25.35 E
Naxos ⊥	70	37.49 N	15.17 E
Naxuebiruzong	120	31.30 N	93.51 E
Nayābās	272a	28.35 N	77.19 E
Nayāgaon	126	23.32 N	90.46 E
Nayāgarh	120	20.08 N	85.06 E
Nayāgrām	126	22.02 N	87.11 E
Nayak	120	34.44 N	66.57 E
Nayāpāra	126	21.35 N	87.01 E
Nayarit	204	32.20 N	115.19 W
Nayarit □[3]	234	22.00 N	105.00 W
Nayau Island I	175g	17.58 S	179.03 W
Nāy Band, Īrān	128	32.20 N	57.34 E
Nāy Band, Īrān	128	27.23 N	52.38 E
Nāy Band, Kūh-e ∧	128	32.27 N	57.23 E
Nayland	42	51.59 N	0.52 E
Naylor	194	36.34 N	90.36 W
Nayong	102	26.50 N	105.13 E
Nayoro	92a	44.21 N	142.28 E
Nayyāl, Wādī V	128	28.40 N	39.26 E
Nazālī Ṭāhā'	142	28.11 N	30.42 E
Nazaré, Bra.	250	6.23 S	47.40 W
Nazaré, Bra.	255	13.02 S	39.00 W
Nazaré, Port.	34	39.36 N	9.04 W
Nazaré da Mata	250	7.44 S	35.14 W
Nazaré do Piauí	250	6.59 S	42.40 W
Nazareno	256	21.13 S	44.37 W
Nazaré Paulista	256	23.11 S	46.24 W
Nazareth, Bel.	50	50.58 N	3.36 E
Nazareth, Pa., U.S.	208	40.44 N	75.18 W
Nazareth, Vanuatu	175f	15.29 S	168.10 E
Nazareth, Vanuatu	175f	15.21 S	167.50 E
Nazareth → Naẓerat, Yis.	132	32.42 N	35.18 E
Nazareth Bank ✦[4]	12	14.30 S	60.45 E
Nazário	255	16.36 S	49.54 W
Nazarjevo, S.S.S.R.	82	55.22 N	36.24 E
Nazarjevo, S.S.S.R.	265b	55.59 N	37.16 E
Nazarovo	86	56.01 N	90.26 E
Nazarovskij	78	49.33 N	40.56 E
Nazas	232	25.14 N	104.08 W
Nazas ≏	232	25.35 N	105.00 W
Nazca	248	14.50 S	74.57 W
Nazca Ridge ✦[3]	18	22.00 S	82.00 W
Naze	93b	28.23 N	129.30 E
Nazeing	260	51.44 N	0.03 E
N'azepetrovsk	86	56.03 N	59.36 E
Naẓerat (Nazareth)	132	32.42 N	35.18 E
Naẓerat 'Illit	132	32.42 N	35.19 E
Nazija	76	59.50 N	31.35 E
Nazik Gölü ⊜	130	38.53 N	42.16 E
Nazilli	130	37.55 N	28.21 E
Nazimicha	265b	55.59 N	38.08 E
Nazımiye	130	39.11 N	39.50 E
Nazimovo	86	59.30 N	90.58 E
Nazina	86	60.07 N	78.52 E
Nāzira	120	26.55 N	94.44 E
Nāzir Hāt	120	22.38 N	91.47 E
Nāzirpur	126	22.43 N	89.58 E
Nazko ≏	182	53.07 N	123.34 W
Nazlat al-'Amūdayn	142	28.14 N	30.42 E
Nazlat al-Badramān	142	27.40 N	30.44 E
Nazlat as-Sammān	273c	29.59 N	31.08 E
Nazlat Khalīfah	273c	30.01 N	31.10 E
Nazlat Quftan Bāshā	142	28.57 N	30.49 E
Nazlat Thābit	142	28.25 N	30.47 E
Nazran'	84	43.13 N	44.46 E
Nazret	144	8.33 N	39.16 E
Nazwā	128	22.56 N	57.32 E
Nazyvajevsk	86	55.34 N	71.21 E
N. B. C. Studios ✿[3]	280	34.09 N	118.20 W
Nchanga	154	12.30 S	27.53 E
Nchelenge	154	9.20 S	28.50 E
Ncue	152	2.01 N	10.28 E
Ndabala	154	13.28 S	29.50 E
Ndala	154	4.46 S	33.16 E
N'dalatando	152	9.18 S	14.54 E
Ndali	150	9.51 N	2.43 E
Ndanda	152	5.12 N	22.21 E
Ndande	150	15.16 N	16.30 W
Ndarassa	152	6.49 N	22.15 E
Ndélé	146	8.24 N	20.39 E
Ndélélé	152	4.02 N	14.56 E
Ndemba	152	0.11 N	14.19 E
Ndendé	152	2.23 S	11.23 E
Ndikiniméki	152	4.46 N	10.50 E
Ndindi	152	3.46 S	11.09 E
N'Djamena	146	12.07 N	15.03 E
Ndji ≏	152	6.47 N	22.14 E
Ndjili ◆[8]	273b	4.20 S	15.22 E
Ndjili ≏	273b	4.19 S	15.24 E
Ndjili, Grande Île de la I	273b	4.19 S	15.24 E
Ndjim ≏	152	4.38 N	11.24 E
Ndjo	152	1.15 S	14.30 E
Ndjolé	152	0.11 S	10.45 E
Ndogo, Lagune ⊂	152	2.35 S	10.00 E
Ndola	154	12.58 S	28.38 E
Ndolo ◆[8]	273b	4.19 S	15.19 E
Ndona	115b	8.46 S	121.45 E
Ndongo	152	2.19 S	13.38 E
Ndouba	152	0.11 S	14.09 E
Ndougou	152	1.39 S	9.40 E
Ndu	152	4.41 N	22.49 E
Nduguti	154	4.18 S	34.42 E
Nduindui	175f	15.24 S	167.46 E
Ndumbwe	154	10.14 S	39.58 E
Ndumu Game Reserve ◆[4]	158	26.53 S	32.15 E
Nduye	154	1.50 N	29.01 E
Ne	268	35.47 N	140.03 E
Nea ≏	26	63.13 N	11.02 E
Neabul Creek ≏	166	27.45 S	147.32 E
Néa Erithraía	267c	38.05 N	23.49 E
Néa Filadhélfia	267c	38.02 N	23.44 E
Neagari	94	36.27 N	136.27 E
Neagh, Lough ⊜	48	54.38 N	6.24 W
Neah Bay	224	48.22 N	124.37 W
Néa Ionía	267c	38.02 N	23.45 E
Neajlov ≏	38	44.11 N	26.12 E
Néa Khalkidhón	267c	38.02 N	23.43 E
Neale, Lake ⊜	162	24.22 S	130.00 E
Neales ≏	162	28.08 S	136.47 E
Neales Flat	168b	34.15 S	139.10 E
Néa Liósia	267c	38.02 N	23.42 E
Neamț □[6]	38	47.00 N	26.30 E
Neandertal, Naturschutzgebiet ♠	263	51.15 N	7.00 E
Néa Páfos (Paphos)	130	34.45 N	32.25 E
Neapel → Napoli	68	40.51 N	14.17 E
Néa Pendéli	267c	38.04 N	23.52 E
Néa Péramos	267c	38.00 N	23.26 E
Neápolis, Ellás	38	36.30 N	23.04 E
Neápolis, Ellás	38	35.15 N	25.37 E
Neapolis, Oh., U.S.	216	41.29 N	83.52 W
Néa Psará	38	38.23 N	23.48 E
Near Islands II	181a	52.40 N	173.30 E
Near North Side ◆[8]	278	41.54 N	87.38 W
Néa Smírni	267c	37.57 N	23.43 E
Neasons Hill	214	41.37 N	80.08 W
Neatahwanta, Lake ⊜	210	43.18 N	76.27 W
Neath	42	51.40 N	3.48 W
Neath ≏	42	51.37 N	3.50 W
Neauphle-le-Château	50	48.49 N	1.54 E
Neauphle-le-Vieux	261	48.49 N	1.52 E
Neavitt	208	38.43 N	76.16 W
Neba	94	35.15 N	137.35 E
Nebaj	236	15.24 N	91.08 W
Nebbou	150	11.18 N	1.53 W
Nebelhorn ∧	58	47.25 N	10.20 E
Nebesnaja, gora ∧	86	43.19 N	80.44 E
Nebeur	36	36.17 N	8.47 E
Nebine Creek ≏	166	29.07 S	146.56 E
Nebit-Dag	128	39.30 N	54.22 E
Neblina, Pico da ∧	246	0.48 N	66.02 W
Nebo	194	39.27 N	90.47 W
Nebo, Mount ∧, Ut,. U.S.	200	39.49 N	111.46 W

Symbol	English	Deutsch	Español	Français	Português
≏	River	Fluss	Río	Rivière	Rio
≊	Canal	Kanal	Canal	Canal	Canal
⌊	Waterfall, Rapids	Wasserfall, Stromschnellen	Cascada, Rápidos	Chute d'eau, Rapides	Cascata, Rápidos
ɥ	Strait	Meeresstrasse	Estrecho	Détroit	Estreito
⊂	Bay, Gulf	Bucht, Golf	Bahía, Golfo	Baie, Golfe	Baía, Golfo
⊜	Lake, Lakes	See, Seen	Lago, Lagos	Lac, Lacs	Lago, Lagos
⩨	Swamp	Sumpf	Pantano	Marais	Pântano
⌂	Ice Features, Glacier	Eis- und Gletscherformen	Accidentes Glaciales	Formes glaciaires	Acidentes glaciares
⩒	Other Hydrographic Features	Andere Hydrographische Objekte	Otros Elementos Hidrográficos	Autres données hydrographiques	Outros acidentes hidrográficos
✦	Submarine Features	Untermeerische Objekte	Accidentes Submarinos	Formes de relief sous-marin	Acidentes submarinos
□	Political Unit	Politische Einheit	Unidad Politica	Entité politique	Unidade política
✿	Cultural Institution	Kulturelle Institution	Institución Cultural	Institution culturelle	Institução cultural
⊥	Historical Site	Historische Stätte	Sitio Histórico	Site historique	Sitio histórico
♠	Recreational Site	Erholungs- und Ferienort	Sitio de Recreo	Centre de loisirs	Area de Lazer
⊠	Airport	Flughafen	Aeropuerto	Aéroport	Aeroporto
■	Military Installation	Militäranlage	Instalación Militar	Installation militaire	Instalação militar
◆	Miscellaneous	Verschiedenes	Misceláneo	Divers	Diversos

ENGLISH

Name	Page	Lat.°′	Long.°′
Nebo, Mount → Nabā, Jabal an- ∧, Urd.	132	31.46 N	35.45 E
Nebolči	76	59.08 N	33.18 E
Nebra	54	51.17 N	11.34 E
Nebraska	218	39.04 N	85.28 W
Nebraska □[3], U.S.	178	41.30 N	100.00 W
Nebraska □[3], U.S.	198	41.30 N	100.00 W
Nebraska City	198	40.40 N	95.51 W
Nebrodi ⋏	70	37.54 N	14.35 E
Nebyloje	80	56.22 N	39.59 E
Nečajannoje	78	46.57 N	31.33 E
Nečajevka	80	53.17 N	44.27 E
Nečajevo	82	54.42 N	37.23 E
Necaxa ≃	234	20.16 N	97.27 W
Necedah	190	44.01 N	90.04 W
Nechajevskij	80	50.25 N	41.44 E
Nechako ≃	182	53.56 N	122.42 W
Nechako Plateau ⋏[1]	182	54.00 N	124.30 W
Nechako Range ⋏	182	53.20 N	124.30 W
Nechako Reservoir ⊜[1]	182	53.25 N	125.10 W
Neche	198	48.59 N	97.33 W
Neches	222	31.52 N	95.30 W
Neches ≃	194	29.55 N	93.52 W
Nechí	246	8.07 N	74.46 W
Nechí ≃	246	8.08 N	74.46 W
Nechisar National Park ♦	144	6.00 N	37.50 E
Nechmeya	36	36.36 N	7.31 E
Nechranická Přehradová Nádrž ⊜[1]	54	50.20 N	13.20 E
Nechvorošča	78	49.09 N	34.44 E
Neckar ≃	30	49.31 N	8.26 E
Neckarbischofsheim	56	49.17 N	8.57 E
Neckarelz	56	49.20 N	9.06 E
Neckargemünd	56	49.23 N	8.47 E
Neckarsteinach	56	49.25 N	8.53 E
Neckarsulm	56	49.12 N	9.13 E
Neckartailfingen	56	48.36 N	9.16 E
Neckartenzlingen	56	48.35 N	9.14 E
Neck Creek ≃	276	40.36 N	74.12 W
Necker	284b	39.23 N	76.29 W
Necker Island I, Br. Vir. Is.	240m	18.33 N	64.21 W
Necker Island I, Hi., U.S.	14	23.35 N	164.42 W
Necker Ridge ✦[3]	14	22.00 N	167.15 W
Necochea	252	38.33 S	58.45 W
Necrópolis ◆	266a	40.25 N	3.38 W
Nedančiči	78	51.30 N	30.37 E
Ned Brown Preserve ♦	278	42.02 N	88.01 W
Nedel'noje	82	54.50 N	36.39 E
Nederland	194	29.58 N	93.59 W
Nederland → Netherlands □[1]	30	52.15 N	5.30 E
Nederlandse Antillen → Netherlands Antilles □[2]	241s	12.15 N	69.00 W
Neder-Rijn ≃[1]	52	51.58 N	5.20 E
Nederweert	52	51.17 N	5.45 E
Nederzwalm-Hermelgem	50	50.53 N	3.41 E
Nedlands	168a	31.59 S	115.49 E
Nedlitz	54	52.04 N	12.14 E
Nedlitz ◆[8]	264a	52.26 N	13.03 E
Nedre Soppero	24	68.01 N	21.44 E
Nedre Vättern ⊜	40	59.49 N	15.40 E
Nedrigajlov	78	50.50 N	33.53 E
Nédroma	148	35.01 N	1.45 W
Nedrow	210	42.58 N	76.08 W
Nedstrand	26	59.21 N	5.51 E
Neebish Island I	190	46.16 N	84.09 W
Neede	52	52.08 N	6.36 E
Needham, In., U.S.	218	39.32 N	85.58 W
Needham, Ma., U.S.	207	42.17 N	71.14 W
Needham Market	42	52.09 N	1.03 E
Needhams Point ≻	241g	13.05 N	59.36 W
Needle Mountain ∧	202	44.05 N	109.37 W
Needles	204	34.50 N	114.36 W
Needville	222	29.23 N	95.50 W
Neelyton	214	40.10 N	77.50 W
Ñeembucú □[5]	252	27.00 S	58.00 W
Neenah	190	44.11 N	88.27 W
Neepawa	184	50.13 N	99.29 W
Neerabup National Park ♦	168a	31.41 S	115.43 E
Neerim South	169	38.01 S	145.58 E
Neermoor	52	53.18 N	7.26 E
Neeroeteren	56	51.05 N	5.42 E
Neerpelt	56	51.13 N	5.25 E
Neersen	263	51.15 N	6.29 E
Nee Soon	271c	1.24 N	103.49 E
Neetze	52	53.15 N	10.39 E
Neetze ≃	54	53.20 N	10.28 E
Nefedjevo, S.S.S.R.	82	54.39 N	37.56 E
Nefedjevo, S.S.S.R.	265b	55.54 N	37.10 E
Nefern ≃	42	52.02 N	4.50 W
Neffs	208	40.42 N	75.37 W
Neffsville	208	40.06 N	76.18 W
Nef'odovo	86	58.48 N	72.34 E
Nefta	148	33.52 N	7.33 E
Nefteabad	85	40.12 N	70.34 E
Neftečala	84	39.23 N	49.16 E
Neftegorsk	84	44.22 N	39.42 E
Neftekamsk	80	56.06 N	54.17 E
Neftekumsk	84	44.45 N	44.48 E
Nefyn	42	52.57 N	4.31 W
Nefza	36	36.58 N	9.05 E
Negage	152	7.45 S	15.16 E
Négala	150	12.52 N	8.27 W
Negapatam → Nāgappattinam	122	10.46 N	79.50 E
Negara, Indon.	112	2.37 S	115.06 E
Negara, Indon.	115a	8.22 S	114.37 E
Negara ≃	112	3.00 S	114.45 E
Negast	54	54.15 N	13.01 E
Negaunee	190	46.29 N	87.36 W
Negba	132	31.40 N	34.41 E
Negele	144	5.20 N	39.36 E
Negenborn	52	51.53 N	9.34 E
Negeribatin	112	4.35 S	104.32 E
Negeri Sembilan □[3]	114	2.45 N	102.10 E
Negev Desert → HaNegev ◆[2]	132	30.30 N	34.55 E
Negishi	268	35.51 N	139.23 E
Negley	214	40.47 N	80.32 W
Negola	152	14.10 S	14.30 E
Negomano	154	11.27 S	38.31 E
Negombo	122	7.13 N	79.50 E
Negonego I[1]	14	18.47 S	141.48 W
Negoreloje	76	53.36 N	27.04 E
Negotin	38	44.14 N	22.32 E
Negra, Laguna ⊜	252	34.03 S	53.40 W
Negra, Ponta ≻	256	22.58 S	42.42 W
Negra, Punta ≻, Belize	232	16.17 N	88.34 W
Negra, Punta ≻, Perú	248	6.06 S	81.09 W
Negra, Serra ∧, Bra.	250	6.30 S	46.15 W
Negra, Serra ∧, Bra.	256	21.58 S	43.54 W
Negrais	266c	38.53 N	9.17 W
Negras, Lomas ∧[2]	286d	11.55 S	77.06 W
Negreira	34	42.54 N	8.44 W
Nègres, Pointe des ≻	240e	14.36 N	61.06 W
Negrești	38	46.50 N	27.27 E
Negrești-Oaș	38	47.52 N	23.25 E
Negrine	148	34.30 N	7.30 E
Negritos	246	4.38 S	81.19 W
Negro ≃, Arg.	254	41.02 S	62.47 W
Negro ≃, Bol.	248	9.49 S	65.42 W
Negro ≃, Bol.	248	14.11 S	63.07 W
Negro ≃, Bra.	248	5.15 S	70.53 W
Negro ≃, Bra.	248	19.13 S	57.17 W
Negro ≃, Bra.	250	9.15 S	47.34 W
Negro ≃, Bra.	252	26.01 S	50.30 W
Negro ≃, Col.	246	5.44 N	74.39 W
Negro ≃, N.A.	236	13.02 N	87.17 W
Negro ≃, Para.	252	24.23 S	57.11 W
Negro ≃, S.A.	246	3.08 S	59.55 W
Negro ≃, S.A.	252	33.24 S	58.22 W
Negro ≃, Ven.	246	9.36 N	72.15 W
Negro, Baia del ⊂	144	7.55 N	49.55 E
Negro, Cerro ∧, Arg.	254	46.55 S	70.12 W
Negro, Cerro ∧, Arg.	254	44.09 S	69.30 W
Negro, Mar → Black Sea ⊤[2]	22	43.00 N	35.00 E
Negros I	116	10.00 N	123.00 E
Negros Occidental □[4]	116	10.20 N	123.00 E
Negros Oriental □[4]	116	9.40 N	123.00 E
Negru-Vodă	38	43.50 N	28.12 E
Neguac	186	47.15 N	65.05 W
Nehalem	224	45.43 N	123.53 W
Nehalem ≃	224	45.40 N	123.56 W
Nehawka	198	40.49 N	95.59 W
Nehbandān	128	31.32 N	60.02 E
Neheim-Hüsten	56	51.27 N	7.57 E
Nehonsey Brook ≃	285	39.49 N	75.18 W
Néhoué, Baie de ⊂	175f	20.21 S	164.09 E
Neiba	238	18.28 N	71.25 W
Neiba, Bahía de ⊂	238	18.15 N	71.02 W
Neichiang → Neijiang	107	29.35 N	105.03 E
Neidenburg → Nidzica	30	53.22 N	20.26 E
Neidpath	184	50.13 N	107.15 W
Neige, Crêt de la ∧	58	46.16 N	5.56 E
Neiges, Piton des ∧	157c	21.05 S	55.29 E
Neihart	202	46.56 N	110.44 W
Neihe ≃	100	22.54 N	115.38 E
Neihu	269d	25.05 N	121.34 E
Neihuang	98	35.59 N	114.55 E
Neijiang	107	29.35 N	105.03 E
Neikiang → Neijiang	107	29.35 N	105.03 E
Neilburg	184	52.50 N	109.38 W
Neillsville	190	44.33 N	90.35 W
Neilston	46	55.47 N	4.27 W
Neimen	263	51.29 N	7.48 E
Nei Monggol Zizhiqu (Inner Mongolia) □[4]	90	43.00 N	115.00 E
Nein	132	32.38 N	35.21 E
Neindorf	54	52.20 N	10.50 E
Neinstedt	54	51.45 N	11.05 E
Neiqiu	98	37.17 N	114.31 E
Neira	246	5.10 N	75.32 W
Neirone	62	44.27 N	9.11 E
Neishuishan	269d	25.09 N	121.43 E
Neisse (Nysa Łużycka) (Nisa) ≃	30	52.04 N	14.46 E
Neiva	246	2.56 N	75.18 W
Neiwufuquan	105	40.11 N	117.39 E
Neixiang	102	33.12 N	111.57 E
Neizeng Shan ∧	100	24.02 N	117.32 E
Neja, S.S.S.R.	80	58.24 N	46.31 E
Neja, S.S.S.R.	80	58.18 N	43.54 E
Neja ≃	80	57.48 N	43.42 E
Nejapa de Madero	234	16.37 N	95.59 W
Nejdek	54	50.17 N	12.42 E
Nejo	144	9.30 N	35.30 E
Nejva ≃	86	57.54 N	62.18 E
Nejvo-Šajtanskij	86	57.44 N	61.15 E
Nekalagba	154	2.50 N	28.01 E
Nekemte	144	9.02 N	36.31 E
Nekhab ⊥	140	25.10 N	32.48 E
Nekl'udovo	80	56.24 N	43.59 E
Nekoosa	190	44.18 N	89.54 W
Neko-zaki ≻	96	35.40 N	134.46 E
Nekrasino	82	56.18 N	36.33 E
Nekrasovka	265b	55.41 N	37.56 E
Nekrasovo, S.S.S.R.	80	51.10 N	45.18 E
Nekrasovo, S.S.S.R.	82	54.30 N	38.57 E
Nekrasovskoje	80	57.41 N	40.22 E
Nekselø I	41	55.47 N	11.18 E
Neksø	26	55.04 N	15.09 E
Nela Park ♦	279a	41.33 N	81.33 W
Nel'aty	88	56.29 N	115.41 E
Nelichu ∧	140	6.08 N	34.25 E
Nelidovo	76	56.13 N	32.46 E
Neligh	198	42.07 N	98.01 W
Nel'kan	74	57.40 N	136.13 E
Nellie	214	40.20 N	82.04 W
Nellikuppam	122	11.46 N	79.41 E
Nellingen	56	48.33 N	9.47 E
Nellis Air Force Base ■	204	36.14 N	115.02 W
Nelliston	210	42.56 N	74.37 W
Nellis Weapons Range ■	204	37.15 N	116.20 W
Nellore	122	14.26 N	79.58 E
Nel'ma	89	47.39 N	139.09 E
Nelson, B.C., Can.	182	49.29 N	117.17 W
Nelson, N.Z.	172	41.17 S	173.17 E
Nelson, Eng., U.K.	44	53.51 N	2.13 W
Nelson, Ne., U.S.	198	40.12 N	98.04 W
Nelson, Pa., U.S.	210	41.59 N	77.14 W
Nelson ≃	184	57.04 N	92.30 W
Nelson, Cape ≻, Austl.	166	38.26 S	141.33 E
Nelson, Cape ≻, Pap. N. Gui.	164	9.00 S	149.15 E
Nelson, Estrecho Ʉ	254	51.37 S	75.00 W
Nelson Creek ≃	222	30.56 N	95.31 W
Nelson House	184	55.47 N	98.51 W
Nelson Island I	180	60.35 N	164.45 W
Nelson-Kennedy Ledges State Park ♦	214	41.18 N	81.04 W
Nelson Lake ⊜	184	55.44 N	100.00 W
Nelson Lakes National Park ♦	172	41.50 S	172.40 E
Nelson Reservoir ⊜[1]	202	48.30 N	107.34 W
Nelsons Dockyard ⊥	240c	17.00 N	61.46 W
Nelsonville, N.Y., U.S.	210	41.25 N	73.57 W
Nelsonville, Oh., U.S.	188	39.27 N	82.14 W
Nelspoort	158	32.07 S	23.00 E
Nelspoortjie	158	29.58 S	22.25 E
Nelspruit	156	25.30 S	30.58 E
Néma, Maur.	150	16.37 N	7.15 W
Nema, S.S.S.R.	80	57.31 N	50.31 E
Néma, Ḍahr ⊥[4]	150	16.40 N	7.13 W
Nemadji ≃	190	46.41 N	92.02 W
Nemah	224	46.31 N	123.51 W
Nemaha	198	40.20 N	95.40 W
Nemam	122	8.27 N	77.01 E
Neman	76	55.02 N	22.02 E
Neman (Nemunas) ≃	76	55.18 N	21.23 E
Nematābād	267d	35.38 N	51.21 E
Nembe	150	4.35 N	6.26 E
Nembrala	112	10.53 S	122.50 E
Nembro	62	45.45 N	9.45 E
Nemčinovka	265b	55.43 N	37.23 E
Nemda ≃, S.S.S.R.	80	57.35 N	48.56 E
Nemda ≃, S.S.S.R.	80	57.21 N	43.08 E
Nemegosenda ≃	190	48.31 N	82.53 W
Nemegt uul ⋏	102	43.40 N	101.10 E
Nemeiben Lake ⊜	184	55.20 N	105.20 W
Nemenčinė	76	54.51 N	25.29 E
Nementcha, Monts de ⋏	148	34.52 N	7.05 E
Nemeriči	76	53.51 N	33.59 E
Nemi	66	41.43 N	12.43 E
Nemi, Lago di ⊜	267a	41.43 N	12.42 E
Nemira ∧	38	46.15 N	26.19 E
Nemirov, S.S.S.R.	78	50.07 N	23.25 E
Nemirov, S.S.S.R.	78	48.58 N	28.50 E
Nemirovo	82	55.54 N	36.12 E
Nemo	222	32.16 N	97.39 W
Nemoli	68	40.04 N	15.48 E
Nemor ≃	89	48.23 N	124.32 E
Nemours	50	48.16 N	2.42 E
Nemoviči	78	51.16 N	26.38 E
Nemrut Gölü ⊜	130	38.37 N	42.12 E
Nemuna, Bjeshkët e ⋏	38	42.27 N	19.47 E
Nemunas (Neman) ≃	76	55.18 N	21.23 E
Nemuro	92a	43.20 N	145.35 E
Nemuro-hantō ≻[1]	92a	43.21 N	145.42 E
Nemuro Strait Ʉ	92a	44.00 N	145.20 E
Nemzeti Múzeum ʋ	264c	47.29 N	19.05 E
Nen ≃	89	45.25 N	124.40 E
Nena Creek ≃	224	45.07 N	121.07 W
Nenagh	48	52.52 N	8.12 W
Nenagh ≃	48	52.56 N	8.17 W
Nenana	180	64.34 N	149.07 W
Nenana ≃	180	64.30 N	149.00 W
Nenaševo	82	54.34 N	37.28 E
Nenasi	114	3.08 N	103.27 E
Nendaz	58	46.11 N	7.18 E
Nendeln	58	47.12 N	9.32 E
Nendo I	14	10.45 S	165.54 E
Nene ≃	42	52.48 N	0.13 E
Neneckij Nacional'nyj Okrug □[8]	24	67.30 N	54.00 E
Nenggiri ≃	114	4.53 N	101.48 E
Nengjia	104	41.38 N	120.46 E
Nengo ≃	152	14.27 S	22.09 E
Nenneper ≃	263	51.32 N	6.26 E
Neno	154	15.24 S	34.39 E
Nentón ≃	236	15.48 N	91.52 W
Nenzing	58	47.11 N	9.42 E
Neo	94	35.38 N	136.37 E
Neo ≃	94	35.24 N	136.34 E
Neodesha	198	37.25 N	95.40 W
Neoga	194	39.19 N	88.27 W
Neola, Ia., U.S.	198	41.26 N	95.36 W
Neola, Ut,. U.S.	200	40.26 N	110.01 W
Neoneli	71	40.04 N	8.57 E
Néon Fáliron	267c	37.57 N	23.40 E
Néon Karlovásion	38	37.48 N	26.44 E
Néon Psikhikón	267c	38.00 N	23.47 E
Neopit	190	44.58 N	88.49 W
Neópolis	250	10.18 S	36.35 W
Neosho	194	36.52 N	94.22 W
Neosho ≃	194	35.48 N	95.18 W
Neotsu	224	45.00 N	123.58 W
Nepa ≃	88	59.16 N	108.16 E
Nepal (Nepāl) □[1], Asia	118	28.00 N	84.00 E
Nepal (Nepāl) □[1], Asia	124	28.00 N	84.00 E
Nepālganj	124	28.03 N	81.37 E
Nepa Nagar	120	21.28 N	76.23 E
Nepaug Reservoir ⊜[1]	207	41.48 N	72.57 W
Nepean	212	45.18 N	75.47 W
Nepean ≃	170	33.27 S	150.53 E
Nepean, Point ≻	169	38.18 S	144.39 E
Nepean Bay ⊂	168b	35.42 S	137.44 E
Nepean Island I	174c	29.04 S	167.58 E
Nepean Reservoir ⊜[1]	170	34.22 S	150.35 E
Nepecino	82	55.12 N	38.37 E
Nepeña	248	9.10 S	78.23 W
Nepewassi Lake ⊜	190	46.20 N	80.40 W
Nephi	200	39.42 N	111.50 W
Nephin ∧	48	54.01 N	9.22 W
Nephin Beg Range ⋏	48	54.00 N	9.35 W
Nepi	66	42.14 N	12.21 E
Nepisiguit ≃	186	47.37 N	65.38 W
Nepisiguit Bay ⊂	186	47.46 N	65.32 W
Népliget ♦	264c	47.29 N	19.07 E
Nepoko ≃	154	1.40 N	27.01 E
Nepomuceno	256	21.14 S	45.15 W
Nepomuk, Česko.	60	49.29 N	13.35 E
Neponset ≃	283	42.17 N	71.02 W
Neponset Reservoir ⊜[1]	283	42.05 N	71.15 W
Neponset River Reservation ♦	283	42.13 N	71.08 W
Neppermin	54	53.56 N	14.02 E
Nepr'adva ≃	76	53.40 N	38.39 E
Népstadion ♦	264c	47.30 N	19.06 E
Nép-sziget I	264c	47.34 N	19.05 E
Neptune, N.J., U.S.	208	40.12 N	74.02 W
Neptune, Oh., U.S.	216	40.36 N	84.30 W
Neptune Beach	192	30.18 N	81.23 W
Neptune City	208	40.12 N	74.02 W
Neqarot, Naḥal V	132	30.40 N	35.15 E
Nera ≃, Europe	38	44.49 N	21.22 E
Nera ≃, It.	66	42.26 N	12.24 E
Nérac	32	44.08 N	0.20 E
Nerákion	267c	38.01 N	23.27 E
Nerang	171a	28.00 S	153.20 E
Nerang ≃	171a	28.03 S	153.17 E
Neratovice	54	50.14 N	14.31 E
Nerča ≃	88	51.56 N	116.40 E
Nerchau	54	51.16 N	12.47 E
Nerčinsk	88	51.58 N	116.35 E
Nerčinskij Zavod	88	51.19 N	119.36 E
Nère ≃	50	47.34 N	2.18 E
Nerechta	80	57.28 N	40.34 E
Nerenstetten	56	48.31 N	10.06 E
Neresheim	56	48.45 N	10.15 E
Nereta	76	56.13 N	25.18 E
Nereto	66	42.49 N	13.49 E
Neretva ≃	36	43.01 N	17.27 E
Nerevoznoje	80	56.53 N	53.54 E
Nerima ◆[8]	268	35.44 N	139.39 E
Neringa	76	55.18 N	21.01 E
Neris ≃	76	54.54 N	23.53 E
Nerito	66	42.32 N	13.28 E
Nerja	34	36.44 N	3.52 W
Nerka, Lake ⊜	180	59.30 N	158.45 W
Nerl', S.S.S.R.	76	57.03 N	37.59 E
Nerl', S.S.S.R.	80	56.40 N	40.24 E
Nerl' ≃, S.S.S.R.	76	57.07 N	37.39 E
Nerl' ≃, S.S.S.R.	80	56.11 N	40.34 E
Nero, ozero ⊜	80	57.07 N	39.27 E
Neroj	88	54.28 N	97.49 E
Néronde	62	45.50 N	4.14 E
Nérondes	32	47.00 N	2.49 E
Nerópolis	255	16.25 S	49.14 W
Nerriga	170	35.07 S	150.05 E
Nerrima	162	18.24 S	124.29 E
Nerrimunga Creek ≃	170	34.57 S	150.04 E
Nersingen	58	48.25 N	10.07 E
Nerskaja ≃	82	55.23 N	38.35 E
Nerul	272c	19.02 N	73.01 E
Nerus ≃	114	5.20 N	103.05 E
Nerussa ≃	76	52.33 N	33.47 E
Nerva	34	37.42 N	6.32 W
Nervi	62	44.23 N	9.02 E
Nervia ≃	62	43.47 N	7.38 E
Nerviano	266b	45.33 N	8.58 E
Nerville-la-Forêt	261	49.05 N	2.17 E
Nes, Ned.	52	53.04 N	5.51 E
Nes, Ned.	52	53.26 N	5.45 E
Nes, Nor.	26	60.34 N	9.59 E
Nes', S.S.S.R.	24	66.37 N	44.36 E
Nes, Har ∧	132	30.22 N	34.37 E
Nesbyen	26	60.34 N	9.09 E
Neščerdo, ozero ⊜	76	55.54 N	29.04 E
Neščeretovo	83	49.24 N	38.48 E
Nesco	208	39.38 N	74.41 W
Nescochague Creek ≃	285	39.39 N	74.41 W
Nescochague Creek, Great Swamp Branch ≃	285	39.41 N	74.43 W
Nesconset	276	40.51 N	73.09 W
Nescopeck	210	41.03 N	76.13 W
Nescopeck Creek ≃	210	41.03 N	76.14 W
Nescopeck Mountain ∧	210	41.03 N	76.05 W
Nesebâr	38	42.39 N	27.44 E
Neshaminy Creek ≃	208	40.04 N	74.55 W
Neshaminy Hills	285	40.10 N	74.57 W
Neshaminy Mall ◆[9]	285	40.08 N	74.57 W
Neshaminy State Park ♦	285	40.05 N	74.55 W
Neshaminy Woods	285	40.10 N	74.57 W
Neshannock Creek ≃	214	40.59 N	80.21 W
Nesher	132	32.46 N	35.03 E
Neškan	180	67.03 N	173.01 W
Neskaupstaður	24a	65.10 N	13.43 W
Neskowin	224	45.06 N	123.58 W
Neskynpil'gyn, laguna ⊂	180	66.57 N	172.45 W
Nesle	50	49.46 N	2.55 E
Nesna	24	66.12 N	13.02 E
Nespelem	182	48.10 N	118.58 W
Nesque ≃	62	43.59 N	4.59 E
Nesquehoning	210	40.51 N	75.48 W
Ness	262	53.17 N	3.03 W
Ness, Loch ⊜	46	57.15 N	4.30 W
Ness City	198	38.27 N	99.54 W
Nesse ≃	54	50.59 N	10.32 E
Nesselrode, Mount ∧	180	58.58 N	134.18 W
Nesselwang	58	47.37 N	10.30 E
Nesselwängle	58	47.29 N	10.37 E
Nesslau	58	47.13 N	9.13 E
Nessmersiel	52	53.40 N	7.21 E
Nesso	58	45.55 N	9.08 E
Neštěmice	54	50.40 N	14.07 E
Nesterkovo	76	59.10 N	30.33 E
Nesterov, S.S.S.R.	76	54.38 N	22.34 E
Nesterov, S.S.S.R.	78	50.04 N	23.58 E
Nesterovka	80	52.26 N	53.42 E
Nesterovo, S.S.S.R.	80	54.31 N	41.49 E
Nesterovo, S.S.S.R.	82	56.45 N	36.30 E
Nesterovo, S.S.S.R.	88	52.22 N	107.53 E
Nestiary	80	56.34 N	45.21 E
Nestoita	78	47.47 N	29.21 E
Neston	44	53.18 N	3.04 W
Nestore ≃	66	43.21 N	12.15 E
Néstos (Mesta) ≃	38	40.41 N	24.44 E
Nesttun	26	60.19 N	5.20 E
Nestucca ≃	224	45.12 N	123.57 W
Nesvetaj	83	47.27 N	39.40 E
Nesviž	76	53.13 N	26.40 E
Nes Ẓiyyona	132	31.55 N	34.48 E
Netanya	132	32.20 N	34.51 E
Netarhāt	124	23.29 N	84.16 E
Netarts	224	45.26 N	123.56 W
Netarts Bay ⊂	224	45.24 N	123.56 W
Netcong	210	40.53 N	74.42 W
Nethan ≃	46	55.42 N	3.52 W
Nether Alderley	262	53.17 N	2.14 W
Netherdale	166	21.08 S	148.32 E
Netherlands (Nederland) □[1], Europe	22	52.15 N	5.30 E
Netherlands (Nederland) □[1], Europe	30	52.15 N	5.30 E
Netherlands Antilles (Nederlandse Antillen) □[2], N.A.	230	12.15 N	68.45 W
Netherlands Antilles (Nederlandse Antillen) □[2], N.A.	241s	12.15 N	68.45 W
Netherton	262	53.30 N	2.58 W
Nethy Bridge	46	57.16 N	3.38 W
Netia	154	14.48 S	39.59 E
Netley Marsh	42	50.53 N	1.21 W
Neto ≃	68	39.13 N	17.08 E
Netolice	61	49.03 N	14.12 E
Netphen	56	50.55 N	8.06 E
Netra	56	51.06 N	10.05 E
Netrakona	124	24.53 N	90.43 E
Netstal	58	47.03 N	9.03 E
Nettancourt	56	48.52 N	4.57 E
Nette	52	52.02 N	10.05 E
Nette ◆[8]	263	51.33 N	7.25 E
Nettelstedt	52	52.18 N	8.41 E
Nettetal	56	51.18 N	6.16 E
Nettilling Fiord ⊂[2]	176	66.02 N	68.12 W
Nettilling Lake ⊜	176	66.30 N	70.40 W
Nett Lake ⊜	190	48.10 N	93.10 W
Nett Lake Indian Reservation ◆[4]	190	48.06 N	93.10 W
Nettlebed	42	51.35 N	1.00 W
Nettle Creek ≃	218	40.03 N	83.48 W
Nettleden	260	51.47 N	0.32 W
Nettleham	44	53.16 N	0.29 W
Nettlestead	260	51.15 N	0.25 E
Nettlestead Green	260	51.14 N	0.25 E
Nettleton	194	34.05 N	88.37 W
Nettuno	66	41.27 N	12.39 E
Nettuno, Grotta di ⊥[5]	71	40.34 N	8.09 E
Netze → Noteć ≃	30	52.44 N	15.26 E
Netzschkau	54	50.36 N	12.14 E
Neualbenreuth	60	49.59 N	12.27 E
Neu-Anspach	56	50.17 N	8.29 E
Neuastenberg	56	51.10 N	8.29 E
Neubeckum	52	51.48 N	8.01 E
Neu Bentschen → Zbąszynek	30	52.15 N	15.50 E
Neubrandenburg	54	53.33 N	13.15 E
Neubrandenburg □[5]	54	53.30 N	13.15 E
Neubraunschweig → New Brunswick □[4]	186	46.30 N	66.15 W
Neubritannien → New Britain I	164	6.00 S	150.00 E
Neu Büddenstedt	54	52.10 N	10.31 E
Neubukow	54	54.02 N	11.40 E
Neuburg am Inn	60	48.30 N	13.27 E
Neuburg an der Donau	60	48.44 N	11.11 E
Neuchâtel	58	46.59 N	6.56 E
Neuchâtel □[3]	58	47.00 N	6.55 E
Neuchâtel, Lac de ⊜	58	46.52 N	6.50 E
Neudamm → Dębno	30	52.45 N	14.40 E
Neu-Delhi → New Delhi	124	28.36 N	77.12 E
Neudenau	56	49.17 N	9.16 E
Neudietendorf	54	50.55 N	10.55 E
Neudorf, Sk., Can.	184	50.44 N	102.59 W
Neudorf, D.D.R.	54	50.29 N	12.58 E
Neudorf ◆[8]	263	51.25 N	6.47 E
Neudörfl	61	47.48 N	16.17 E
Neue Hebriden → Vanuatu □[1]	175f	16.00 S	167.00 E
Neuemühle	264a	52.18 N	13.39 E
Neuenburg, B.R.D.	52	53.23 N	7.57 E
Neuenbürg, B.R.D.	56	48.50 N	8.35 E
Neuenburg, B.R.D.	58	47.49 N	7.35 E
Neuenburg → Neuchâtel, Schw.	58	46.59 N	6.56 E
Neuendettelsau	56	49.17 N	10.47 E
Neuendorf	54	54.31 N	13.05 E
Neuendorfer See ⊜	54	52.07 N	13.55 E
Neuenegg	58	46.54 N	7.18 E
Neuenhagen bei Berlin	54	52.32 N	13.41 E
Neuenhaus	52	52.30 N	6.59 E
Neuenhof ◆[8]	263	51.10 N	7.13 E
Neuenhoven	263	51.08 N	6.31 E
Neue Niers ≃	263	51.16 N	6.26 E
Neuenkamp ◆[8]	263	51.26 N	6.44 E
Neuenkirchen, B.R.D.	52	52.30 N	8.04 E
Neuenkirchen, B.R.D.	52	51.50 N	8.26 E
Neuenkirchen, B.R.D.	52	53.14 N	8.31 E
Neuenkirchen, B.R.D.	52	53.02 N	9.42 E
Neuenkirchen, B.R.D.	52	52.14 N	7.22 E
Neuenkirchen, B.R.D.	52	53.46 N	8.53 E
Neuenkirchen, D.D.R.	54	54.32 N	13.20 E
Neuenrade	56	51.17 N	7.47 E
Neuensalz	54	50.30 N	12.13 E
Neuenstadt am Kocher	56	49.14 N	9.20 E
Neuenwalde	52	53.40 N	8.40 E
Neuerburg	56	50.00 N	6.17 E
Neu-Erlaa ◆[8]	264b	48.08 N	16.19 E
Neues Palais ⊥	264a	52.24 N	13.01 E
Neu Fahrland	264a	52.26 N	13.03 E
Neufahrn bei Freising	60	48.19 N	11.40 E
Neufahrn in Niederbayern	60	48.44 N	12.11 E
Neuf-Brisach	58	48.01 N	7.32 E
Neufchâteau, Bel.	56	49.50 N	5.26 E
Neufchâteau, Fr.	58	48.21 N	5.42 E
Neufchâtel-en-Bray	50	49.44 N	1.27 E
Neufchâtel-sur-Aisne	50	49.26 N	4.02 E
Neufelden	61	48.29 N	14.00 E
Neuffen	56	48.33 N	9.22 E
Neuffossé, Canal de ≖	50	50.45 N	2.15 E
Neufmanil	56	49.49 N	4.48 E
Neuf-Marché	50	49.25 N	1.43 E
Neufmontiers-lès-Meaux	261	48.58 N	2.50 E
Neufundland → Newfoundland □[4]	176	52.00 N	56.00 W
Neufvilles	50	50.34 N	4.00 E
Neugersdorf	54	50.59 N	14.36 E
Neuglobsow	54	53.09 N	13.02 E
Neugraben-Fischbek ◆[8]	52	53.28 N	9.52 E
Neuguinea → New Guinea I	164	5.00 S	140.00 E
Neuharlingersiel	52	53.42 N	7.42 E
Neu-Hartmannsdorf	264a	52.22 N	13.51 E
Neuhaus, B.R.D.	58	47.48 N	8.34 E
Neuhaus, D.D.R.	54	50.30 N	11.08 E
Neuhaus, D.D.R.	54	53.17 N	10.55 E
Neuhaus, Öst.	61	47.47 N	15.11 E
Neuhaus an der Oste	52	53.48 N	9.02 E
Neuhausen, B.R.D.	58	47.58 N	8.55 E
Neuhausen, D.D.R.	54	50.41 N	13.28 E
Neuhausen, Schw.	58	47.41 N	8.37 E
Neuhaus im Solling	52	51.45 N	9.31 E
Neuhaus-Schierschnitz	54	50.19 N	11.14 E
Neuheum	114	5.34 N	95.32 E
Neuhof	56	50.27 N	9.40 E
Neuhof an der Zenn	56	49.27 N	10.38 E
Neuhofen	56	49.25 N	8.26 E
Neuhofen an der Krems	61	48.08 N	14.14 E
Neuillé-Pont-Pierre	50	47.33 N	0.33 E
Neuilly-en-Thelle	50	49.13 N	2.17 E
Neuilly-L'Évêque	58	47.55 N	5.26 E
Neuilly-Saint-Front	50	49.10 N	3.16 E
Neuilly-sur-Marne	261	48.51 N	2.32 E
Neuilly-sur-Seine	50	48.53 N	2.16 E
Neuirland → New Ireland I	164	3.20 S	152.00 E
Neu-Isenburg	56	50.03 N	8.41 E
Neukagran ◆[8]	264b	48.14 N	16.27 E
Neu-Kaledonien → New Caledonia □[2]	175f	21.30 S	165.30 E
Neukalen	54	53.49 N	12.47 E
Neu Kaliss	54	53.10 N	11.17 E
Neukieritzsch	54	51.10 N	12.25 E
Neukirch, B.R.D.	58	47.39 N	9.41 E
Neukirch, D.D.R.	54	51.17 N	13.58 E
Neukirch, D.D.R.	54	51.05 N	14.20 E
Neukirchen, B.R.D.	41	54.52 N	8.44 E
Neukirchen, B.R.D.	54	54.19 N	11.01 E
Neukirchen, B.R.D.	56	50.46 N	9.41 E
Neukirchen, B.R.D.	56	49.29 N	6.50 E
Neukirchen, B.R.D.	60	49.05 N	11.45 E
Neukirchen, B.R.D.	263	51.07 N	6.41 E
Neukirchen, D.D.R.	54	51.05 N	12.32 E
Neukirchen, D.D.R.	54	50.47 N	12.22 E
Neukirchen, D.D.R.	54	50.46 N	12.52 E
Neukirchen, Öst.	64	47.15 N	12.17 E
Neukirchen am Walde	60	48.24 N	13.46 E
Neukirchen bei Sulzbach-Rosenberg	60	49.32 N	11.38 E
Neukirchen-Vluyn	56	51.27 N	6.33 E
Neukloster	54	53.52 N	11.41 E
Neukölln ◆[8]	264a	52.29 N	13.27 E
Neulangerwisch	264a	52.19 N	13.04 E
Neulengbach	61	48.12 N	15.55 E
Neulienken	54	53.27 N	14.22 E
Neu Lübbenau	54	52.04 N	13.53 E
Neulussheim	56	49.17 N	8.31 E
Neumagen	56	49.51 N	6.53 E
Neuman Creek ≃	284a	42.42 N	78.48 W
Neumark	54	50.39 N	12.21 E
Neumark ◆[1]	54	52.40 N	14.50 E
Neumarkt → Środa Śląska	30	51.10 N	16.36 E
Neumarkt → Tîrgu-Secuiesc, Rom.	38	46.00 N	26.08 E
Neumarkt → Tîrgu Mureș, Rom.	38	46.33 N	24.33 E
Neumarkt am Wallersee	64	47.57 N	13.14 E
Neumarkt im Hausruckkreis	60	48.16 N	13.45 E
Neumarkt in der Oberpfalz	60	49.16 N	11.28 E
Neumarkt in Steiermark	61	47.04 N	14.25 E
Neumarkt-Sankt Veit	60	48.22 N	12.30 E
Neumittelwalde → Międzybórz	30	51.24 N	17.40 E
Neumünster	30	54.04 N	9.59 E
Neun ≃	110	19.42 N	104.03 E
Neunburg vorm Wald	60	49.21 N	12.24 E
Neundorf	54	51.49 N	11.34 E
Neung-sur-Beuvron	50	47.32 N	1.48 E
Neunkirchen, B.R.D.	56	50.32 N	8.06 E
Neunkirchen, B.R.D.	56	49.20 N	7.10 E
Neunkirchen, B.R.D.	56	50.48 N	8.00 E
Neunkirchen, Öst.	61	47.43 N	16.05 E
Neunkirchen am Brand	60	49.37 N	11.08 E
Neunkirchen am Potzberg	56	49.30 N	7.29 E
Neunkirchen-Seelscheid	56	50.51 N	7.20 E
Neuötting	60	48.14 N	12.42 E
Neupetershain	54	51.36 N	14.09 E
Neuquén	252	38.57 S	68.04 W
Neuquén □[4]	254	39.00 S	70.00 W
Neuquén ≃	252	38.59 S	68.00 W
Neurara	252	24.10 S	68.29 W
Neuravensburg	58	47.38 N	9.46 E
Neureisenberg	264b	48.01 N	16.30 E
Neurode → Nowa Ruda	30	50.35 N	16.31 E
Neuruppin	54	52.55 N	12.48 E
Neusalz → Nowa Sól	30	51.48 N	15.44 E
Neusalza-Spremberg	54	51.02 N	14.32 E
Neu Sankt Johann	58	47.14 N	9.12 E
Neusatz → Novi Sad	38	45.15 N	19.50 E
Neuschottland → Nova Scotia □[4]	186	45.00 N	63.00 W
Neuschwanstein, Schloss ʋ	58	47.35 N	10.44 E
Neuse ≃	192	35.06 N	76.30 W
Neuseddin	264a	52.18 N	12.59 E
Neuseeland → New Zealand □[1]	172	41.00 S	174.00 E
Neusibirische Inseln → Novosibirskije ostrova II	74	75.00 N	142.00 E
Neusiedl am See	61	47.57 N	16.51 E
Neusiedler See (Fertő) ⊜	61	47.50 N	16.45 E
Neusohl → Banská Bystrica	30	48.44 N	19.07 E
Neusorg	60	49.56 N	11.58 E
Neuss	56	51.12 N	6.41 E
Neusserweyhe ◆[8]	263	51.13 N	6.39 E
Neustadt, B.R.D.	56	50.51 N	9.07 E
Neustadt, B.R.D.	56	50.37 N	7.26 E
Neustadt, On., Can.	212	44.05 N	81.00 W
Neustadt, D.D.R.	54	52.52 N	12.25 E
Neustadt, D.D.R.	54	51.01 N	14.13 E

DEUTSCH

Name	Seite	Breite°′	Länge°′ E = Ost
Neustadt, D.D.R.	54	50.44 N	11.44 E
Neustadt ◆[8]	52	53.04 N	8.47 E
Neustadt am Rübenberge	52	52.30 N	9.28 E
Neustadt an der Aisch	56	49.34 N	10.37 E
Neustadt an der Donau	60	48.48 N	11.46 E
Neustadt an der Waldnaab	60	49.44 N	12.11 E
Neustadt an der Weinstrasse	56	49.21 N	8.08 E
Neustadt bei Coburg	56	50.19 N	11.07 E
Neustädtel → Nowe Miasteczko	30	51.42 N	15.45 E
Neustädter Bucht ⊂	54	54.02 N	10.50 E
Neustadt-Glewe	54	53.25 N	11.36 E
Neustadt in Holstein	54	54.06 N	10.48 E
Neustadt in Oberschlesien → Prudnik	30	50.19 N	17.34 E
Neustettin → Szczecinek	30	53.43 N	16.42 E
Neustift am Walde ◆[8]	264b	48.15 N	16.18 E
Neustift im Stubaital	64	47.07 N	11.19 E
Neustrelitz	54	53.21 N	13.04 E
Neuteich → Nowy Staw	30	54.09 N	19.00 E
Neu Töplitz	264a	52.27 N	12.54 E
Neutral Hills ⋏[2]	184	52.10 N	110.50 W
Neutral Zone □[2]	128	29.10 N	45.30 E
Neutraubling	60	48.59 N	12.12 E
Neutrebbin	54	52.40 N	14.13 E
Neu-Ulm	58	48.23 N	10.01 E
Neuve-Chapelle	50	50.35 N	2.47 E
Neuves-Maisons	58	48.37 N	6.06 E
Neuvic	32	45.23 N	2.16 E
Neuville-aux-Bois	50	48.04 N	2.03 E
Neuville-de-Poitou	32	46.41 N	0.15 E
Neuville-en-Condroz	56	50.32 N	5.27 E
Neuville-lès-Dieppe	50	49.55 N	1.06 E
Neuville-sur-Oise	261	49.01 N	2.04 E
Neuville-sur-Saône	62	45.52 N	4.51 E
Neuvy-le-Roi	50	47.36 N	0.36 E
Neuvy-sur-Barangeon	50	47.19 N	2.15 E
Neuvy-sur-Loire	50	47.31 N	2.53 E
Neuwaldegg ◆[8]	264b	48.14 N	16.17 E
Neuwarp → Nowe Warpno	30	53.44 N	14.16 E
Neuwedell → Drawno	30	53.13 N	15.45 E
Neuwerk ◆[8]	263	51.13 N	6.28 E
Neuwerk I	52	53.55 N	8.30 E
Neuwied	56	50.25 N	7.27 E
Neuwiller-lès-Saverne	56	48.49 N	7.24 E
Neu Wulmstorf	52	53.28 N	9.48 E
Neuzelle	54	52.05 N	14.38 E
Neu Zittau	54	52.23 N	13.44 E
Neva ≃	265a	59.57 N	30.20 E
Névache	62	45.01 N	6.37 E
Nevada, Ia., U.S.	190	42.01 N	93.27 W
Nevada, Mo., U.S.	194	37.50 N	94.21 W
Nevada, Oh., U.S.	214	40.49 N	83.07 W
Nevada, Tx., U.S.	222	33.02 N	96.22 W
Nevada □[6]	226	39.16 N	121.01 W
Nevada □[3], U.S.	178	39.00 N	117.00 W
Nevada □[3], U.S.	204	39.00 N	117.00 W
Nevada, Sierra ⋏, Esp.	34	37.05 N	3.10 W
Nevada, Sierra ⋏, Ca., U.S.	204	38.00 N	119.15 W
Nevada City	226	39.15 N	121.00 W
Nevada Creek ≃	202	46.54 N	113.02 W
Nevado, Cerro ∧	246	3.59 N	74.04 W
Nevado de Toluca, Parque Nacional ♦	234	19.10 N	99.50 W
Neval'cevo	86	58.38 N	81.53 E
Nevali	272c	19.01 N	73.07 E
Nevanka	88	56.30 N	98.54 E
Neve, Serra da ⋏	152	13.52 S	13.26 E
Nevel'	76	56.02 N	29.55 E
Nevel'sk	89	46.40 N	141.53 E
Nevel'skogo, proliv Ʉ	89	52.05 N	141.35 E
Nevendon	260	51.36 N	0.30 E
Never	89	53.58 N	124.05 E
Neverkino	80	52.47 N	46.44 E
Neverovo	80	55.07 N	44.24 E
Nevers	32	47.00 N	3.09 E
Neversink ≃	210	41.21 N	74.42 W
Neversink Reservoir ⊜[1]	210	41.48 N	74.42 W
Nevertire	166	31.52 S	147.39 E
Neves	256	22.51 S	43.06 W
Nevesinje	38	43.15 N	18.07 E
Nevėžis ≃	76	54.56 N	23.46 E
Nevežkino	80	53.07 N	43.19 E
Neviano	68	40.06 N	18.06 E
Neviano degli Arduini	64	44.35 N	10.19 E
Neviges	56	51.19 N	7.05 E
Neville Island	279b	40.31 N	80.08 W
Neville Island I	279b	40.31 N	80.08 W
Nevinnomyssk	84	44.38 N	41.56 E
Nevis I	238	17.10 N	62.34 W
Nevis ≃	46	56.50 N	5.00 W
Nevis, Ben ∧	46	56.48 N	5.01 W
Nevis, Loch ⊂	46	57.01 N	5.43 W
Nevjansk	86	57.32 N	60.13 E
Nevlunghamn	26	58.58 N	9.52 E
Nevon	88	58.07 N	102.49 E
Nevşehir	130	38.38 N	34.43 E
Nevşehir □[4]	130	38.50 N	34.40 E
Nevskoje	76	58.08 N	30.26 E
New ≃, Belize	232	18.22 N	88.24 W
New ≃, Guy.	246	3.23 N	57.36 W
New ≃, N.A.	204	33.08 N	115.44 W
New ≃, Eng., U.K.	260	51.40 N	0.01 W
New ≃, U.S.	192	38.10 N	81.12 W
New ≃, Az., U.S.	200	33.31 N	112.18 W
New ≃, Fl., U.S.	192	29.50 N	84.40 W
New ≃, Fl., U.S.	192	29.55 N	82.25 W
New ≃, N.C., U.S.	192	34.32 N	77.20 W
New ≃, S.C., U.S.	192	32.09 N	80.50 W
New ≃, Tn., U.S.	192	36.25 N	84.38 W
New, North Fork ≃	192	36.33 N	81.21 W
Newabāgam	272b	22.48 N	88.24 E
New Abbey	44	54.59 N	3.38 W
New Addington ◆[8]	260	51.21 N	0.01 W
Newala	154	10.56 S	39.18 E
New Albany, In., U.S.	218	38.17 N	85.49 W
New Albany, Ms., U.S.	194	34.29 N	89.00 W
New Albany, Oh., U.S.	214	40.05 N	82.49 W
New Albany, Pa., U.S.	210	41.36 N	76.27 W
New Albin	190	43.29 N	91.17 W
New Alexandria, Oh., U.S.	214	40.17 N	80.40 W
New Alexandria, Pa., U.S.	214	40.24 N	79.25 W
New Alexandria, Va., U.S.	284c	38.47 N	77.03 W
New Alfa	140	15.10 N	35.40 E
New Almaden	226	37.11 N	121.49 W
New Alresford	42	51.06 N	1.10 W
New Amsterdam	246	6.15 N	57.31 W
New Angledool	166	29.07 S	147.57 E
Newark, Ar., U.S.	194	35.42 N	91.26 W
Newark, Ca., U.S.	226	37.31 N	122.02 W
Newark, De., U.S.	208	39.41 N	75.45 W
Newark, Il., U.S.	216	41.32 N	88.35 W
Newark, Md., U.S.	208	38.15 N	75.17 W
Newark, Mo., U.S.	219	39.59 N	91.59 W
Newark, N.J., U.S.	210	40.44 N	74.10 W
Newark, N.Y., U.S.	210	43.02 N	77.05 W
Newark, Oh., U.S.	214	40.04 N	82.24 W
Newark, Tx., U.S.	222	33.00 N	97.29 W

Symbols in the index entries represent the broad categories identified in the key at the right. Symbols with superior numbers (⋏[1]) identify subcategories (see complete key on page I · 1).

Kartensymbole in dem Registerverzeichnis stellen die rechts in Schlüssel erklärten Kategorien dar. Symbole mit hochgestellten Ziffern (⋏[1]) bezeichnen Unterabteilungen einer Kategorie (vgl. vollständiger Schlüssel auf Seite I · 1).

Los símbolos incluídos en el texto del índice representan las grandes categorias identificadas con la clave a la derecha. Los símbolos con numeros en su parte superior (⋏[1]) identifican las subcategorías (véase la clave completa en la página I · 1).

Les symboles de l'index représentent les catégories indiquées dans la légende à droite. Les symboles suivis d'un indice (⋏[1]) représentent des sous-catégories (voir légende complète à la page I · 1).

Os símbolos incluídos no texto do índice representam as grandes categorias identificadas com a chave à direita. Os símbolos com números em sua parte superior (⋏[1]) identificam as subcategorias (veja-se a chave completa à página I · 1).

∧ Mountain	Berg	Montaña	Montagne	Montanha
⋏ Mountains	Berge	Montañas	Montagnes	Montanhas
)(Pass	Pass	Paso	Col	Passo
V Valley, Canyon	Tal, Cañon	Valle, Cañón	Vallée, Canyon	Vale, Canhão
≚ Plain	Ebene	Llano	Plaine	Planície
≻ Cape	Kap	Cabo	Cap	Cabo
I Island	Insel	Isla	Île	Ilha
II Islands	Inseln	Islas	Îles	Ilhas
⊥ Other Topographic Features	Andere Topographische Objekte	Otros Elementos Topográficos	Autres données topographiques	Outros acidentes topográficos

Newark Bay c, U.S. 276 40.39 N 74.09 W
Newark Bay c, N.J., U.S. 276 40.40 N 74.08 W
Newark Bay Bridge ✦5 276 40.42 N 74.07 W
Newark International Airport ✈ 210 40.42 N 74.10 W
Newark Lake ◎ 204 39.41 N 115.44 W
Newark-on-Trent 42 53.05 N 0.49 W
Newark Slough ≐ 282 37.31 N 122.05 W
Newark Valley 210 42.13 N 76.11 W
New Athens, Il., U.S. 219 38.19 N 89.52 W
New Athens, Oh., U.S. 214 40.11 N 80.59 W
New Augusta 194 31.12 N 89.02 W
Newaukum, North Fork ≐ 224 46.36 N 122.51 W
Newaukum, South Fork ≐ 224 46.36 N 122.51 W
Newaygo 190 43.25 N 85.48 W
New Baden, Il., U.S. 219 38.32 N 89.42 W
New Baden, Tx., U.S. 222 31.03 N 96.26 W
New Baltimore, Mi., U.S. 214 42.40 N 82.44 W
New Baltimore, N.Y., U.S. 210 42.26 N 73.47 W
New Bavaria 216 41.12 N 84.10 W
New Bedford, Ma., U.S. 207 41.38 N 70.56 W
New Bedford, Pa., U.S. 214 41.06 N 80.30 W
New Bedford ≐ 42 52.35 N 0.20 E
Newberg 224 45.18 N 122.58 W
New Berlin, Il., U.S. 219 39.43 N 89.54 W
New Berlin, N.Y., U.S. 210 42.37 N 75.19 W
New Berlin, Pa., U.S. 210 40.53 N 76.59 W
New Berlin, Wi., U.S. 216 42.58 N 88.06 W
New Berlinville 208 40.20 N 75.38 W
Newbern, Al., U.S. 194 32.35 N 87.31 W
Newbern, Il., U.S. 219 39.01 N 90.20 W
New Bern, N.C., U.S. 192 35.06 N 77.02 W
Newbern, Tn., U.S. 194 36.06 N 89.15 W
Newberry, Fl., U.S. 192 29.38 N 82.36 W
Newberry, Mi., U.S. 190 46.21 N 85.30 W
Newberry, S.C., U.S. 192 34.16 N 81.37 W
New Bethlehem 214 41.00 N 79.19 W
Newbiggin-by-the-Sea 44 55.11 N 1.30 W
New Bloomfield, Mo., U.S. 219 38.43 N 92.05 W
New Bloomfield, Pa., U.S. 208 40.25 N 77.11 W
New Bloomington 214 40.35 N 83.19 W
Newbold Island I 285 40.08 N 74.45 W
New Boreo 212 44.39 N 76.19 W
Newboro Lake ◎ 212 44.38 N 76.20 W
Newborough, Austl. 169 38.11 S 146.17 E
Newborough, Wales, U.K. 44 53.09 N 4.22 W
New Boston, Il., U.S. 190 41.10 N 90.59 W
New Boston, Mi., U.S. 216 42.09 N 83.24 W
New Boston, Oh., U.S. 218 38.45 N 82.56 W
New Boston, Tx., U.S. 194 33.27 N 94.24 W
New Braintree 207 42.19 N 72.07 W
New Braunfels 196 29.42 N 98.07 W
New Bremen 216 40.26 N 84.22 W
Newbridge → Droichead Nua 48 53.11 N 6.48 W
Newbridge on Wye 42 52.13 N 3.27 W
New Brighton, N.Z. 172 43.31 S 172.44 E
New Brighton, Eng., U.K. 262 53.26 N 3.03 W
New Brighton, Pa., U.S. 214 40.43 N 80.18 W
New Brighton ✦8 276 40.38 N 74.06 W
New Britain, Ct., U.S. 207 41.39 N 72.46 W
New Britain, Pa., U.S. 208 40.18 N 75.11 W
New Britain I 164 6.00 S 150.00 E
New Britain Trench ✦1 14 6.00 S 153.00 E
New Brockton 194 31.23 N 85.55 W
Newbrook 182 54.19 N 112.57 W
New Brooklyn County Park ✦ 285 39.43 N 74.57 W
New Brunswick, In., U.S. 218 39.57 N 86.31 W
New Brunswick, N.J., U.S. 208 40.29 N 74.27 W
New Brunswick □4, Can. 176 46.30 N 66.15 W
New Brunswick □4, Can. 186 46.30 N 66.15 W
New Buffalo, Mi., U.S. 216 41.47 N 86.44 W
New Buffalo, Pa., U.S. 208 40.27 N 76.58 W
Newbuildings 48 54.57 N 7.21 W
New Bullards Bar Lake ◎1 226 39.25 N 121.08 W
Newburg, Mo., U.S. 194 37.54 N 91.54 W
Newburg, Pa., U.S. 208 40.08 N 77.32 W
Newburg, Pa., U.S. 214 40.31 N 78.25 W
Newburgh, On., Can. 212 44.19 N 76.52 W
Newburgh, Eng., U.K. 262 53.35 N 2.47 W
Newburgh, Scot., U.K. 46 57.18 N 2.00 W
Newburgh, Scot., U.K. 46 56.20 N 3.15 W
Newburgh, In., U.S. 194 37.56 N 87.24 W
Newburgh, N.Y., U.S. 210 41.30 N 74.00 W
Newburgh Heights 279a 41.27 N 81.39 W
Newburn 44 54.59 N 1.43 W
Newbury, On., Can. 214 42.41 N 81.48 W
Newbury, Eng., U.K. 42 51.25 N 1.20 W
Newbury, Ma., U.S. 207 42.49 N 70.53 W
Newbury Old Town 207 42.46 N 70.51 W
Newbury Park 228 34.11 N 118.53 W
Newburyport 207 42.48 N 70.52 W
Newby 44 54.20 N 0.28 W
Newby Bridge 44 54.16 N 2.58 W
New Caledonia (Nouvelle-Calédonie) □2, Oc. 14 21.30 S 165.30 E
New Caledonia (Nouvelle-Calédonie) □2, Oc. 175f 21.30 S 165.30 E
New Caledonia Basin ✦1 14 30.00 S 165.00 E
New Canaan 207 41.08 N 73.29 W
New Canada ✦8 273d 26.13 S 27.57 E
New Caney 222 30.09 N 95.13 W
New Canton 219 39.38 N 91.06 W
New-Carlisle, P.Q., Can. 186 48.01 N 65.20 W
New Carlisle, In., U.S. 216 41.42 N 86.30 W
New Carlisle, Oh., U.S. 218 39.56 N 84.01 W
New Carrollton 284c 38.58 N 76.52 W
New Cassel 276 40.45 N 73.34 W
Newcastle, Austl. 170 32.56 S 151.46 E
Newcastle, N.B., Can. 186 47.00 N 65.34 W
Newcastle, On., Can. 212 43.55 N 78.35 W
Newcastle, Ire. 48 52.16 N 7.48 W
Newcastle, S. Afr. 158 27.49 S 29.55 E
Newcastle, Eng., U.K. 42 52.26 N 3.06 W
Newcastle, N. Ire., U.K. 48 54.12 N 5.54 W
Newcastle, Ca., U.S. 226 38.53 N 121.08 W
New Castle, Co., U.S. 200 39.34 N 107.32 W
New Castle, De., U.S. 208 39.39 N 75.34 W
New Castle, In., U.S. 218 39.55 N 85.22 W
New Castle, Ky., U.S. 218 38.26 N 85.10 W
Newcastle, Ne., U.S. 198 42.33 N 96.42 W
New Castle, Oh., U.S. 214 40.20 N 82.10 W
Newcastle, Ok., U.S. 196 35.15 N 97.36 W
New Castle, Pa., U.S. 214 41.00 N 80.20 W
Newcastle, Tx., U.S. 196 33.11 N 98.44 W
New Castle, Va., U.S. 192 37.30 N 80.06 W
Newcastle, Wy., U.S. 198 43.51 N 104.12 W
New Castle □6 208 39.44 N 75.33 W
Newcastle (Ouston) Airport ✈ 44 55.01 N 1.53 W
Newcastle Bay c 164 10.50 S 142.37 E
Newcastle Bight c3 170 32.51 S 151.54 E
Newcastle Creek ≐ 164 17.20 S 133.23 E
Newcastle Emlyn 42 52.02 N 4.28 W
Newcastle Mine 182 51.28 N 112.46 W
Newcastleton 44 55.11 N 2.49 W
Newcastle-under-Lyme 44 53.00 N 2.14 W
Newcastle upon Tyne 44 54.59 N 1.35 W
Newcastle Waters 162 17.24 S 133.24 E
Newcastle West 48 52.27 N 9.03 W
New Centerville 285 40.04 N 75.26 W
Newcestown 48 51.47 N 8.51 W
New Chicago 216 41.34 N 87.16 W
Newchurch, Wales, U.K. 42 52.09 N 3.08 W
New Church, Va., U.S. 208 37.59 N 75.32 W
New City 210 41.08 N 73.59 W
Newclare ✦8 273d 26.11 S 27.58 E
New Columbia 210 41.02 N 76.52 W
New Columbus 210 41.10 N 76.18 W
Newcomerstown 214 40.16 N 81.36 W
New Concord 188 39.59 N 81.44 W
New Corydon 216 40.34 N 84.51 W
New Croton Aqueduct ≊1 276 41.11 N 73.49 W
New Croton Reservoir ◎1 210 41.14 N 73.46 W
New Cumberland, Pa., U.S. 208 40.13 N 76.53 W
New Cumberland, W.V., U.S. 214 40.29 N 80.36 W
New Cumberland Dam ✦6 214 40.32 N 80.37 W
New Cumnock 44 55.24 N 4.12 W
New Dayton 182 49.25 N 112.23 W
New Deer 46 57.30 N 2.12 W
Newdegate 162 33.06 S 119.01 E
New Delhi, India 124 28.36 N 77.12 E
New Delhi, India 272a 28.36 N 77.12 E
New Delhi Railroad Station ✦5 272a 28.39 N 77.13 E
New Denver 182 49.59 N 117.22 W
New Derry 214 40.21 N 79.19 W
New Dundee 212 43.21 N 80.31 W
New Eagle 214 40.12 N 79.56 W
New Edinburg 194 33.45 N 92.14 W
New Effington 198 45.51 N 96.55 W
New Egypt 208 40.04 N 74.31 W
Newell, Ia., U.S. 198 42.36 N 95.00 W
Newell, S.D., U.S. 198 44.42 N 103.25 W
Newell, W.V., U.S. 214 40.37 N 80.36 W
Newell, Lake ◎, Austl. 162 24.50 S 126.10 E
Newell, Lake ◎, Ab., Can. 182 50.25 N 111.56 W
New Ellenton 192 33.25 N 81.41 W
Newellton 194 32.04 N 91.14 W
New Eltham ✦8 260 51.26 N 0.04 E
New Empire 226 40.16 N 119.21 W
New England 198 46.32 N 102.52 W
New England National Park ✦ 166 30.30 S 152.15 E
New England Range ✦ 166 30.00 S 151.50 E
Newenham, Cape ⟩ 180 58.37 N 162.12 W
Newent 42 51.56 N 2.24 W
New Enterprise 214 40.10 N 78.25 W
New Ermelo 158 26.32 S 30.02 E
New Falconwood 284a 42.59 N 78.58 W
Newfane, N.Y., U.S. 210 43.17 N 78.42 W
Newfane, Vt., U.S. 188 42.59 N 72.39 W
New Ferry 262 53.22 N 2.59 W
Newfield, N.J., U.S. 208 39.32 N 75.01 W
Newfield, N.Y., U.S. 210 42.22 N 76.35 W
Newfield Pond ◎ 283 42.38 N 71.22 W
New Florence, Mo., U.S. 219 38.54 N 91.26 W
New Florence, Pa., U.S. 214 40.22 N 79.04 W
New Forest ✦3 42 50.53 N 1.35 W
New Fork ≐ 200 42.33 N 109.58 W
Newfound Gap ✕ 192 35.37 N 83.25 W
Newfoundland, N.J., U.S. 276 40.44 N 74.29 W
Newfoundland, Pa., U.S. 210 41.19 N 75.19 W
Newfoundland □4 176 52.00 N 56.00 W
Newfoundland I 186 48.30 N 56.00 W
Newfoundland Basin ✦1 8 45.00 N 40.00 W
Newfoundland Ridge ✦3 8 40.30 N 48.00 W
New Franklin 194 39.01 N 92.44 W
New Freedom 208 39.44 N 76.42 W
New Galilee 214 40.50 N 80.24 W
New Galloway 44 55.05 N 4.10 W
New Garden 285 39.49 N 75.45 W
Newgate 182 49.00 N 115.10 W
Newgate Street 260 51.44 N 0.07 W
New Georgia I 175e 8.15 S 157.30 E
New Georgia Group II 175e 8.30 S 157.20 E
New Georgia Sound ꜧ 175e 8.00 S 158.10 E
New Germantown 208 40.18 N 77.34 W
New Germany 186 44.33 N 64.43 W
New Glarus 190 42.48 N 89.38 W
New Glasgow 186 45.35 N 62.39 W
New Gretna 208 39.35 N 74.27 W
New Guinea I 164 5.00 S 140.00 E
New Guinea, Territory of → Papua New Guinea □1 164 6.00 S 150.00 E
Newgulf 222 29.16 N 95.54 W
Newhalem 224 48.40 N 121.14 W
Newhalen 180 59.43 N 154.54 W
Newhall, Eng., U.K. 42 52.48 N 1.34 W
Newhall, Ca., U.S. 228 34.23 N 118.31 W
Newham ✦8 42 51.32 N 0.03 E
New Hamburg, On., Can. 212 43.23 N 80.42 W
New Hamburg, N.Y., U.S. 210 41.35 N 73.57 W
New Hampshire 216 40.33 N 83.57 W
New Hampshire □3, U.S. 178 43.35 N 71.40 W
New Hampshire □3, U.S. 188 43.35 N 71.40 W
New Hampton, Ia., U.S. 190 43.03 N 92.19 W
New Hampton, N.Y., U.S. 210 41.25 N 74.24 W
New Hanover, S. Afr. 158 29.28 S 30.28 E
New Hanover, Il., U.S. 219 38.23 N 90.13 W
New Hanover I 164 2.30 S 150.15 E
New Harmony 194 38.07 N 87.56 W
New Hartford, Ct., U.S. 207 41.52 N 72.58 W
New Hartford, Ia., U.S. 190 42.34 N 92.37 W
New Hartford, Mo., U.S. 219 39.12 N 91.16 W
New Hartford, N.Y., U.S. 210 43.04 N 75.18 W
Newhaven, Eng., U.K. 42 50.47 N 0.03 E
New Haven, Ct., U.S. 207 41.18 N 72.56 W
New Haven, Il., U.S. 194 37.54 N 88.07 W
New Haven, In., U.S. 216 41.04 N 85.00 W
New Haven, Ky., U.S. 194 37.39 N 85.35 W
New Haven, Mi., U.S. 214 42.43 N 82.48 W
New Haven, Mo., U.S. 219 38.36 N 91.13 W
New Haven, N.Y., U.S. 212 43.29 N 76.19 W
New Haven, Oh., U.S. 214 41.02 N 82.41 W
New Haven, W.V., U.S. 188 38.59 N 81.58 W
New Haven □6 207 41.18 N 72.56 W
New Hazelton 182 55.15 N 127.35 W
New Hebrides → Vanuatu □1 175f 16.00 S 167.00 E
New Hebrides II 175f 16.00 S 167.00 E
New Hebrides Trench ✦1 14 22.30 S 170.00 E
Newhebron 194 31.44 N 89.58 W
New Hempstead 276 41.08 N 74.03 W
New Hey 262 53.36 N 2.06 W
New Hogan Lake ◎1 226 38.09 N 120.48 W
New Holland, Eng., U.K. 44 53.42 N 0.22 W
New Holland, Il., U.S. 219 40.11 N 89.36 W
New Holland, Oh., U.S. 218 39.33 N 83.15 W
New Holland, Pa., U.S. 208 40.06 N 76.05 W
New Holstein 190 43.57 N 88.05 W
New Hope, Al., U.S. 194 34.32 N 86.23 W
New Hope, Pa., U.S. 208 40.21 N 74.57 W
New Hudson 281 42.30 N 83.36 W
New Hyde Park 276 40.44 N 73.41 W
New Hythe 260 51.19 N 0.27 E
New Iberia 194 30.00 N 91.49 W
Newick 42 50.58 N 0.01 E
Newington, On., Can. 206 45.07 N 75.01 W
Newington, Eng., U.K. 42 51.05 N 1.08 E
Newington, Eng., U.K. 260 51.21 N 0.40 E
Newington, Ct., U.S. 207 41.42 N 72.43 W
New Inn 48 52.26 N 7.53 W
New Ipswich 207 42.44 N 71.51 W
New Ireland □5 164 3.00 S 151.30 E
New Ireland I 164 3.20 S 152.00 E
New Island I 126 21.31 N 88.12 E
New Jersey □3, U.S. 178 40.15 N 74.30 W
New Jersey □3, U.S. 188 40.15 N 74.30 W
New Jersey Institute of Technology ✧2 276 40.45 N 74.11 W
New Johnsonville 194 36.01 N 87.58 W
New Kensington 214 40.34 N 79.45 W
New Kent 208 37.31 N 76.58 W
New Kent □6 208 37.30 N 77.00 W
New Kingstown 208 40.13 N 77.07 W
Newkirk 196 36.52 N 97.03 W
Newkirk Estates 285 39.42 N 75.36 W
New Knoxville 216 40.29 N 84.18 W
New Kowloon (Xinjiulong) 271d 22.20 N 114.10 E
New Lagos ✦8 273a 6.30 N 3.22 E
New Lake ◎ 192 35.38 N 76.20 W
Newland 192 36.05 N 81.55 W
Newland Head ⟩ 168b 35.39 S 138.31 E
Newland Range ✦ 162 27.53 S 123.58 E
Newlands ✦8 273d 26.11 S 27.58 E
New Lane 262 53.37 N 2.52 W
New Lebanon, N.Y., U.S. 210 42.27 N 73.23 W
New Lebanon, Oh., U.S. 218 39.45 N 84.23 W
New Lebanon, Pa., U.S. 214 41.25 N 80.04 W
New Lebanon Center 210 42.28 N 73.25 W
New Leipzig 198 46.22 N 101.56 W
New Lenox 216 41.30 N 87.57 W
New Lexington 188 39.42 N 82.12 W
New Liberty 218 38.36 N 84.54 W
New Lisbon 190 43.52 N 90.09 W
New Liskeard 190 47.30 N 79.40 W
Newllano 194 31.06 N 93.16 W
New London, Ct., U.S. 207 41.21 N 72.07 W
New London, Ia., U.S. 190 40.55 N 91.23 W
New London, Mn., U.S. 198 45.18 N 94.56 W
New London, Mo., U.S. 219 39.35 N 91.24 W
New London, N.H., U.S. 188 43.24 N 71.59 W
New London, Oh., U.S. 214 41.05 N 82.24 W
New London, Pa., U.S. 208 39.47 N 75.52 W
New London, Tx., U.S. 222 32.15 N 94.56 W
New London, Wi., U.S. 190 44.23 N 88.44 W
New London □6 207 41.21 N 72.07 W
New London Submarine Base ■ 207 41.24 N 72.05 W
New Longton 262 53.44 N 2.45 W
Newlonsburg 279b 40.25 N 79.40 W
New Lyme 214 41.36 N 80.47 W
Newlyn 169 37.25 S 143.59 E
Newlyn East 42 50.22 N 5.03 W
Newmachar 46 57.16 N 2.11 W
New Machavie 158 26.48 S 26.57 E
New Madison 218 39.58 N 84.42 W
New Madrid 194 36.35 N 89.31 W
Newmains 44 55.47 N 3.53 W
Newman, Austl. 162 23.20 S 119.46 E
Newman, Ca., U.S. 226 37.18 N 121.01 W
Newman, Il., U.S. 194 39.47 N 87.59 W
Newman, Mount ʌ 162 23.16 S 119.33 E
New Manchester 214 40.31 N 80.34 W
Newmanstown 208 40.20 N 76.12 W
Newmansville 219 40.00 N 90.01 W
New Marion 218 39.00 N 85.22 W
Newmarket, Austl. 171a 27.25 S 153.01 E
Newmarket, On., Can. 212 44.03 N 79.28 W
Newmarket, Ire. 48 52.13 N 9.00 W
Newmarket, S. Afr. 273d 26.17 S 28.08 E
Newmarket, Eng., U.K. 42 52.15 N 0.25 E
New Market, Al., U.S. 194 34.54 N 86.25 W
New Market, Ia., U.S. 198 40.43 N 94.53 W
New Market, Md., U.S. 208 39.22 N 77.16 W
Newmarket, N.H., U.S. 188 43.04 N 70.56 W
New Market, N.J., U.S. 276 40.34 N 74.27 W
New Market, Va., U.S. 188 38.39 N 78.40 W
Newmarket on Fergus 48 52.45 N 8.53 W
Newmarket Race Course ✦ 273d 26.17 S 28.08 E
New Marske 44 54.34 N 1.02 W
New Martinsville 188 39.38 N 80.51 W
New Meadows 202 44.58 N 116.16 W
New Melle 219 38.42 N 90.52 W
New Melones Lake ◎1 226 38.00 N 120.32 W
New Memphis 219 38.29 N 89.41 W
New Mexico □3 178 34.30 N 106.00 W
New Miami 218 39.26 N 84.32 W
New Middletown 214 40.58 N 80.34 W
New Milford, Ct., U.S. 207 41.34 N 73.24 W
New Milford, Il., U.S. 216 42.11 N 89.04 W
New Milford, N.J., U.S. 276 40.56 N 74.01 W
New Milford, Pa., U.S. 210 41.52 N 75.43 W
New Millpond ◎ 276 40.50 N 73.13 W
New Millport 214 40.54 N 78.32 W
New Mills 44 53.23 N 2.00 W
Newmilns 46 55.37 N 4.20 W
New Milton 42 50.44 N 1.40 W
New Minden 219 38.26 N 89.22 W
New Munster 216 42.34 N 88.13 W
Newnan 192 33.22 N 84.47 W
Newnans Lake ◎ 192 29.39 N 82.13 W
Newnham 42 51.49 N 2.27 W
New Norcia 162 30.58 S 116.13 E
New Norfolk 166 42.47 S 147.03 E
New Norway 182 52.53 N 112.58 W
New Orleans 194 29.57 N 90.04 W
New Orleans Naval Air Station ■ 194 29.51 N 90.01 W
New Oxford 208 39.51 N 77.03 W
New Palestine 218 39.43 N 85.53 W
New Paltz 210 41.44 N 74.05 W
New Paris, In., U.S. 216 41.30 N 85.49 W
New Paris, Oh., U.S. 218 39.51 N 84.47 W
New Paris, Pa., U.S. 214 40.06 N 78.39 W
New Philadelphia, Oh., U.S. 214 40.30 N 81.27 W
New Philadelphia, Pa., U.S. 208 40.43 N 76.06 W
New Pine Creek 202 41.59 N 120.17 W
New Pitsligo 46 57.35 N 2.11 W
New Pittsburg 214 40.50 N 82.06 W
New Plymouth, N.Z. 172 39.04 S 174.05 E
New Plymouth, Id., U.S. 202 43.58 N 116.49 W
New Point 218 39.18 N 85.19 W
New Point Comfort ⟩ 208 37.18 N 76.17 W
Newport, Austl. 274a 33.40 S 151.19 E
Newport, Austl. 274b 37.51 S 144.53 E
Newport, P.Q., Can. 186 48.16 N 64.45 W
Newport, Ire. 48 52.42 N 8.24 W
Newport, Ire. 48 53.53 N 9.34 W
New Port, Ned. Ant. 241s 12.03 N 68.49 W
Newport, Eng., U.K. 42 50.42 N 1.18 W
Newport, Eng., U.K. 42 52.47 N 2.22 W
Newport, Eng., U.K. 42 51.59 N 0.15 E
Newport, Wales, U.K. 42 52.01 N 4.51 W
Newport, Wales, U.K. 42 51.35 N 3.00 W
Newport, Ar., U.S. 194 35.36 N 91.16 W
Newport, De., U.S. 208 39.42 N 75.36 W
Newport, In., U.S. 194 39.53 N 87.24 W
Newport, Ky., U.S. 218 39.05 N 84.29 W
Newport, Me., U.S. 188 44.50 N 69.16 W
Newport, Md., U.S. 208 38.25 N 76.54 W
Newport, Mi., U.S. 216 42.00 N 83.18 W
Newport, N.H., U.S. 188 43.21 N 72.10 W
Newport, N.J., U.S. 208 39.17 N 75.10 W
Newport, N.Y., U.S. 210 43.11 N 75.00 W
Newport, N.C., U.S. 192 34.47 N 76.51 W
Newport, Oh., U.S. 216 39.23 N 81.13 W
Newport, Or., U.S. 202 44.38 N 124.03 W
Newport, Pa., U.S. 208 40.28 N 77.07 W
Newport, R.I., U.S. 207 41.29 N 71.18 W
Newport, Tn., U.S. 192 35.58 N 83.11 W
Newport, Vt., U.S. 206 44.56 N 72.12 W
Newport, Wa., U.S. 202 48.11 N 117.02 W
Newport □6 207 41.35 N 71.15 W
Newport Bay c 228 33.37 N 117.53 W
Newport Beach 228 33.37 N 117.55 W
Newport Center 206 44.57 N 72.18 W
Newport Hills 224 47.32 N 122.10 W
Newport News 208 36.58 N 76.25 W
Newport-on-Tay 46 56.26 N 2.55 W
Newport Pagnell 42 52.05 N 0.44 W
New Port Richey 220 28.14 N 82.43 W
Newportville 285 40.09 N 74.53 W
Newportville Terrace 285 40.07 N 74.54 W
New Prague 190 44.32 N 93.34 W
New Preston 207 41.40 N 73.21 W
New Providence, N.J., U.S. 210 40.41 N 74.24 W
New Providence, Pa., U.S. 208 39.56 N 76.12 W
New Providence, Tn., U.S. 194 36.32 N 87.23 W
New Providence I 240b 25.02 N 77.24 W
Newquay, Eng., U.K. 42 50.25 N 5.05 W
New Quay, Wales, U.K. 42 52.13 N 4.22 W
New Redruth 273d 26.16 S 28.07 E
New Richland 190 43.53 N 93.29 W
New-Richmond, P.Q., Can. 186 48.10 N 65.52 W
New Richmond, Oh., U.S. 218 38.56 N 84.16 W
New Richmond, Wi., U.S. 190 45.07 N 92.32 W
New Riegel 214 41.03 N 83.19 W
New Rim Ditch ≊ 228 35.08 N 118.58 W
New Ringgold 208 40.41 N 76.00 W
New Road 186 44.45 N 63.28 W
New Roads 194 30.42 N 91.26 W
New Rochelle 210 40.54 N 73.46 W
New Rockford 198 47.40 N 99.08 W
New Romney 42 50.59 N 0.57 E
New Ross, N.S., Can. 186 44.44 N 64.27 W
New Ross, Ire. 48 52.24 N 6.56 W
New Rossington 44 53.29 N 1.04 W
Newry, N. Ire., U.K. 48 54.11 N 6.20 W
Newry, Pa., U.S. 214 40.24 N 78.26 W
Newry, S.C., U.S. 192 34.43 N 82.54 W
New Salem, In., U.S. 218 39.32 N 85.22 W
New Salem, N.D., U.S. 198 46.50 N 101.24 W
New Salisbury 218 38.19 N 86.06 W
New Sarum → Salisbury 42 51.05 N 1.48 W
New Schwabenland ✦1 9 72.30 S 1.00 E
New Scone 46 56.25 N 3.24 W
Newsham Park ✦ 262 53.25 N 2.57 W
New Sharon 190 41.28 N 92.39 W
New Sheffield 214 40.36 N 80.17 W
New Shrewsbury 276 40.19 N 74.04 W
New Smyrna Beach 220 29.01 N 80.55 W
Newsome 222 32.59 N 95.08 W
Newsoms 208 36.37 N 77.07 W
New South Wales □3 166 33.00 S 146.00 E
New South Wales, University of ✧2 274a 33.55 S 151.14 E
New South Wales Lawn Tennis Association Courts ✦ 274a 33.53 S 151.14 E
New Springfield 214 40.55 N 80.36 W
New Square 276 41.08 N 74.02 W
New Stanton 214 40.13 N 79.37 W
Newstead 169 37.07 S 144.04 E
New Stuyahok 180 59.29 N 157.20 W
New Suffolk 207 41.00 N 72.28 W
New Summerfield 222 31.59 N 95.06 W
New Tazewell 192 36.27 N 83.33 W
New Terrill City Lake ◎1 222 32.44 N 96.14 W
New Territories □8 271d 22.24 N 114.10 E
New Thunderchild Indian Reserve ✦4 184 53.30 N 108.50 W
Newtok 180 60.56 N 164.38 W
Newton, Eng., U.K. 44 53.57 N 2.27 W
Newton, Eng., U.K. 262 53.16 N 2.43 W
Newton, Ga., U.S. 192 31.18 N 84.20 W
Newton, Il., U.S. 194 38.59 N 88.09 W
Newton, Ia., U.S. 190 41.41 N 93.02 W
Newton, Ks., U.S. 198 38.02 N 97.20 W
Newton, Ma., U.S. 207 42.20 N 71.12 W
Newton, Ms., U.S. 194 32.19 N 89.09 W
Newton, N.J., U.S. 210 41.03 N 74.45 W
Newton, N.C., U.S. 192 35.40 N 81.13 W
Newton, Tx., U.S. 194 30.50 N 93.45 W
Newton □6 216 40.46 N 87.27 W
Newton Abbot 42 50.32 N 3.36 W
Newton Arlosh 44 54.53 N 3.15 W
Newton Aycliffe 44 54.36 N 1.32 W
Newton Brook ✦8 275b 43.48 N 79.24 W
Newton Center 283 42.20 N 71.12 W
Newton Falls, N.Y., U.S. 188 44.12 N 74.59 W
Newton Falls, Oh., U.S. 214 41.11 N 80.58 W
Newton Ferrers 42 50.18 N 4.02 W
Newton Flotman 42 52.32 N 1.16 E
Newton Hamilton 214 40.24 N 77.51 W
Newton Highlands 283 42.19 N 71.13 W
Newton-le-Willows 44 53.28 N 2.37 W
Newton Longville 42 51.58 N 0.46 W
Newton Lower Falls 283 42.19 N 71.23 W
Newtonmore 46 57.04 N 4.08 W
Newton Stewart 44 54.57 N 4.29 W
Newtonsville 218 39.11 N 84.05 W
Newton Upper Falls 283 42.19 N 71.13 W
Newtonville, On., Can. 212 43.56 N 78.30 W
Newtonville, Ma., U.S. 283 42.21 N 71.13 W
Newtonville, N.J., U.S. 208 39.33 N 74.51 W
New Toronto ✦8 275b 43.36 N 79.30 W
Newtown, Austl. 169 38.09 S 144.20 E
Newtown, Nf., Can. 186 49.12 N 53.31 W
Newtown, Eng., U.K. 262 53.21 N 2.00 W
Newtown, Wales, U.K. 42 52.32 N 3.19 W
Newtown, Ct., U.S. 207 41.24 N 73.18 W
Newtown, In., U.S. 216 40.12 N 87.08 W
Newtown, Ky., U.S. 218 38.13 N 84.57 W
New Town, N.D., U.S. 198 47.58 N 102.29 W
Newtown, Pa., U.S. 208 40.14 N 74.56 W
Newtown ✦8 274a 33.54 S 151.11 E
Newtownabbey 48 54.42 N 5.54 W
Newtownards 48 54.36 N 5.41 W
Newtownbutler 48 54.12 N 7.23 W
Newtown Creek ≐, N.Y., U.S. 276 40.44 N 73.58 W
Newtown Creek ≐, Pa., U.S. 285 40.13 N 74.56 W
Newtown Crommelin 48 54.59 N 6.13 W
Newtown Forbes 48 53.46 N 7.50 W
Newtownhamilton 48 54.12 N 6.35 W
Newtown Mount Kennedy 48 53.05 N 6.07 W
Newtown Saint Boswells 46 55.34 N 2.40 W
Newtown Square 208 39.59 N 75.24 W
Newtownstewart 48 54.43 N 7.24 W
New Tredegar 42 51.43 N 3.14 W
New Tripoli 208 40.41 N 75.45 W
New Troy 216 41.53 N 86.33 W
New Truxton 219 38.58 N 91.15 W
New Ulm, Mn., U.S. 190 44.18 N 94.27 W
New Ulm, Tx., U.S. 222 29.53 N 96.29 W
New Usenow 54 53.47 N 13.46 E
New Utrecht ✦8 276 40.36 N 73.59 W
New Vernon 276 40.45 N 74.30 W
New Vienna 218 39.19 N 83.41 W
Newville, In., U.S. 216 41.21 N 84.51 W
Newville, Pa., U.S. 208 40.10 N 77.23 W
New Vineyard 188 44.48 N 70.07 W
New Waltham 44 53.32 N 0.04 W
New Washington, Pil. 116 11.39 N 122.26 E
New Washington, In., U.S. 218 38.33 N 85.32 W
New Washington, Oh., U.S. 214 40.57 N 82.51 W
New Waterford, N.S., Can. 186 46.15 N 60.05 W
New Waterford, Oh., U.S. 214 40.50 N 80.36 W
New Waverly, In., U.S. 216 40.46 N 86.12 W
New Waverly, Tx., U.S. 222 30.32 N 95.29 W
New Westminster 224 49.12 N 122.55 W
New Whiteland 218 39.33 N 86.05 W
New Wilmington 214 41.07 N 80.19 W
New Windsor → Windsor, Eng., U.K. 42 51.29 N 0.38 W
New Windsor, Md., U.S. 208 39.32 N 77.06 W
New Windsor, N.Y., U.S. 210 41.30 N 74.01 W
New Woodbine Racetrack ✦ 275b 43.43 N 79.36 W
New Woodstock 210 42.50 N 75.51 W
New World Island I 186 49.35 N 54.40 W
New Year Creek ≐ 222 30.08 N 96.12 W
New York, N.Y., U.S. 210 40.43 N 74.01 W
New York, N.Y., U.S. 276 40.43 N 74.01 W
New York □6 276 40.47 N 73.58 W
New York □3, U.S. 178 43.00 N 75.00 W
New York □3, U.S. 188 43.00 N 75.00 W
New York, City College of ✧2 276 40.49 N 73.57 W
New York, Polytechnic Institute of ✧2 276 40.42 N 73.59 W
New York, State University of (Stony Brook) ✧2, N.Y., U.S. 276 40.55 N 73.08 W
New York, State University of (Buffalo) ✧2, N.Y., U.S. 284a 42.57 N 78.49 W
New York, State University of, College at Buffalo ✧2 284a 42.56 N 78.53 W
New York at Buffalo, State University of ✧2 284a 42.56 N 78.49 W
New York Mills, Mn., U.S. 198 46.31 N 95.22 W
New York Mills, N.Y., U.S. 210 43.06 N 75.18 W
New York State Barge Canal ≊ 210 43.05 N 78.43 W
New York Stock Exchange ✧ 276 40.42 N 74.01 W
New Zealand □1, Oc. 14 41.00 S 174.00 E
New Zealand □1, Oc. 172 41.00 S 174.00 E
New Zealand Plateau ✦3 9 51.00 S 170.00 E
Nexapa ≐ 234 18.07 N 98.46 W
Nexon 32 45.41 N 1.11 E
Nexpa ≐ 234 18.05 N 102.46 W
Ney 216 41.23 N 84.32 W
Neyagawa 96 34.46 N 135.38 E
Neye 263 51.07 N 7.22 E
Neyestausee ◎1 263 51.08 N 7.24 E
Ney Lake ◎ 184 54.38 N 92.25 W
Neyland 42 51.43 N 4.57 W
Neylandville 222 33.12 N 96.00 W
Neyrīz 128 29.12 N 54.19 E
Neyshābūr 128 36.12 N 58.50 E
Neyyāttinkara 122 8.24 N 77.05 E
Nezahualcóyotl, Presa ◎1 234 17.10 N 93.40 W
Nezamajevskaja 78 46.09 N 40.16 E
Nezameno-toko ✦ 94 35.46 N 137.42 E
Nežárka ≐ 61 49.11 N 14.41 E
Nezavertajlovka 78 46.37 N 29.56 E
Nežin 78 51.03 N 31.54 E
Nezlobnaja 84 44.08 N 43.23 E
Neznanka ≐ 265b 55.34 N 37.21 E
Neznanovo 80 54.02 N 40.06 E
Nezperce 202 46.14 N 116.14 W
Nez Perce Indian Reservation ✦4 202 46.20 N 116.30 W
Nez Perce National Historical Park ✦ 202 45.50 N 116.15 W
Nezpique, Bayou ≐ 194 30.12 N 92.35 W
Nezvěstice 60 49.39 N 13.32 E
Ngabang 112 0.23 N 109.57 E
Ngabé 152 3.12 S 16.11 E
Ngabordamlu, Tanjung ⟩ 164 6.56 S 134.11 E
Ngadda ≐ 146 12.40 N 13.50 E
Ngadirojo 115a 8.13 S 111.19 E
Ngadza 152 5.10 N 20.12 E
Ngahere 172 42.24 S 171.27 E
Ngala 146 12.20 N 14.10 E
Ngale 152 2.56 N 21.20 E
Ngali 152 2.27 S 19.20 E
Ngaliema, Baie de c 273b 4.19 S 15.16 E
Ngalipaeng 112 3.24 N 125.37 E
Ngaloa Harbour c 175g 19.06 S 178.11 E
Ngamaba 273b 4.14 S 15.16 E
Ngamba ✦8 273b 4.15 S 15.18 E
Ngambé 152 4.14 S 10.37 E
Ngamdu 146 11.48 N 12.18 E
Ngami, Lake ◎ 156 20.37 S 22.40 E
Ngamiland □5 156 19.09 S 22.47 E
Ngamo 154 19.08 S 27.32 E
Ngamouéri 273b 4.14 S 15.14 E
Nganda ʌ 154 10.25 S 33.50 E
Ngangala 154 4.42 N 31.55 E
Nganglong Kangri ʌ 120 32.00 N 83.00 E
Nganjuk 115a 7.36 S 111.55 E
Ngao 110 18.46 N 99.59 E
Ngaoui, Mont ʌ 152 6.40 N 14.57 E
Ngaoundéré 152 7.19 N 13.35 E
Ngapali 110 18.26 N 94.19 E
Ngapara 172 44.57 S 170.45 E
Ngape 110 20.04 N 94.38 E
Ngaputaw 110 16.32 N 94.42 E
Ngara 154 2.28 S 30.39 E
Ngaramasch 175b 6.54 N 134.08 E
Ngarimbi 154 8.28 S 38.36 E
Ngaruawahia 172 37.40 S 175.09 E
Ngaruroro ≐ 172 39.34 S 176.56 E
Ngasamo 154 2.33 S 33.53 E
Ngat ≐ 110 19.09 N 99.01 E
Ngatangiia 174k 21.14 S 159.43 W
Ngatangiia Harbour c 174k 21.14 S 159.45 W
Ngatea 172 37.17 S 175.30 E
Ngathainggyaung 110 17.24 N 95.05 E
Ngatik I[1] 14 5.51 N 157.16 E
Ngau I 175g 18.02 S 179.18 E
Ngauruhoe, Mount ʌ 172 39.09 S 175.38 E
Ngau Tau Kok → Kwun Tong 271d 22.19 N 114.12 E
Ngawen 115a 7.00 S 111.18 E
Ngawi 115a 7.24 S 111.26 E
Ngay Nua 110 21.50 N 101.54 E
Ngebel 115a 7.46 S 111.37 E
Ngela Sule I 175e 9.05 S 160.15 E
Ngele 152 0.29 S 20.25 E
Ngemelis Islands II 175b 7.07 N 134.15 E
Ngerengere 154 6.45 S 38.07 E
Ngerkeel 175b 7.25 N 134.30 E
Ngermechau 175b 7.35 N 134.39 E
Ngeruktabel I 175b 7.15 N 134.24 E
Ngetbong 175b 7.37 N 134.35 E
Ngetera 146 12.31 N 12.38 E
Nggamea Island I 175g 16.46 S 179.46 W
Nggatokae Island I 175e 8.46 S 158.11 E
Nggela Pile I 175e 9.05 S 160.15 E
Nggelelevu I 175g 16.05 S 179.09 W
Nggwavuma ≐ 158 26.58 S 32.17 E
Nghia-hanh 110 15.03 N 108.47 E
Nghia-hung 110 19.18 N 105.26 E
Nghia-lo 110 21.36 N 104.31 E
Ngiap ≐ 110 18.24 N 103.36 E
Ngidinga 152 5.37 S 15.17 E
Ngimbang 115a 7.17 S 112.12 E
Ng'iro ≐ 154 2.08 N 36.51 E
Ngiro, Ewaso ≐, Kenya 154 2.04 S 36.07 E
Ng'iro, Ewaso ≐, Kenya 154 0.28 N 39.55 E
Ngo 152 2.29 S 15.45 E
Ngoangoa ≐ 140 5.48 N 25.09 E
Ngoboli 154 4.57 N 32.37 E
Ngoko ≐, Afr. 152 1.40 N 16.03 E
Ngoko ≐, Congo 152 0.25 S 15.29 E
Ngol-Kedju Hill ʌ2 152 6.20 N 9.45 E
Ngolo 146 9.56 N 22.16 E
Ngom ≐ 102 31.11 N 97.15 E
Ngomahuru 154 20.26 S 30.43 E
Ngomba 154 8.23 S 32.53 E
Ngomba ʌ 154 5.43 S 35.52 E
Ngombe, Zaïre 152 6.35 S 20.42 E
Ngombe, Zaïre 273b 4.24 S 15.11 E
Ngome 158 27.46 S 31.28 E
Ngomedzap 152 3.15 N 11.12 E
Ngomeni, Ras ⟩ 154 2.59 S 40.14 E
Ngong 154 1.22 S 36.39 E
Ngongotaha 172 38.05 S 176.12 E
Ngono ≐ 154 1.08 S 31.35 E
Ngonye Falls ⌊ 152 16.35 S 23.35 E
Ngop 140 6.16 N 30.12 E
Ngora 154 1.27 N 33.46 E
Ngorengore 154 1.02 S 35.30 E
Ngoring Hu ◎ 102 34.50 N 97.35 E
Ngoro 115a 7.41 S 112.16 E
Ngorongoro Crater ⊥6 154 3.10 S 35.35 E
Ngote 154 2.14 N 30.48 E
Ngoto 152 4.00 N 17.21 E
Ngotwane ≐ 156 23.35 S 26.58 E
Ngoulémakong 152 3.07 N 11.25 E
Ngouma 150 15.38 N 3.22 W
Ngounié □4 152 1.15 S 11.00 E
Ngounié ≐ 152 0.37 S 10.18 E
Ngouri 146 13.38 N 15.22 E
Ngouroundou 152 6.27 N 22.37 E
Ngourti 146 15.19 N 13.12 E
Ngoywa 154 5.56 S 32.48 E
Ngozi 154 2.54 S 29.50 E
Ngqeleni 158 31.40 S 29.02 E
Ngudiabaka ≐ 273b 4.25 S 15.11 E
Nguélémendouka 152 4.23 N 12.55 E
Ngugha ≐ 156 19.21 S 23.15 E
Nguigmi 146 14.15 N 13.07 E
Nguila 152 4.43 N 11.41 E
Ngulu I[1] 108 8.27 N 137.29 E
Ngum ≐ 110 18.09 N 103.45 E
Nguna, Île I 175f 17.26 S 168.21 E
Ngunga 154 3.41 S 33.34 E
Ngunju, Tanjung ⟩ 115b 10.19 S 120.28 E
Ngunut 115a 8.06 S 112.01 E
Nguraw 110 9.18 N 12.14 E
Nguroro 146 12.52 N 10.27 E
Nguru 146 12.52 N 10.27 E
Ngwempisi ≐ 158 26.42 S 31.23 E
Ngweni 158 27.56 S 32.15 E
Ngwenya ʌ 158 26.11 S 31.02 E
Ngwerere 154 15.18 S 28.20 E
Ngweze ≐ 154 17.45 S 25.07 E
Nha-be 269c 10.42 N 106.44 E
Nhabe ≐, Bots. 156 20.22 S 22.58 E
Nha-be ≐, Viet. 269c 10.42 N 106.44 E
Nhacoongo 156 24.18 S 35.14 E
Nhamacolomo 156 18.05 S 34.26 E
Nhamundá 250 2.14 S 56.43 W

≐ River — Fluss — Río — Rivière — Rio
≊ Canal — Kanal — Canal — Canal — Canal
⌊ Waterfall, Rapids — Wasserfall, Stromschnellen — Cascada, Rápidos — Chute d'eau, Rapides — Cascata, Rápidos
ꜧ Strait — Meeresstrasse — Estrecho — Détroit — Estreito
c Bay, Gulf — Bucht, Golf — Bahía, Golfo — Baie, Golfe — Baía, Golfo
◎ Lake, Lakes — See, Seen — Lago, Lagos — Lac, Lacs — Lago, Lagos
⩸ Swamp — Sumpf — Pantano — Marais — Pântano
⊓ Ice Features, Glacier — Eis- und Gletscherformen — Accidentes Glaciales — Formes glaciaires — Acidentes glaciares
✦ Other Hydrographic Features — Andere Hydrographische Objekte — Otros Elementos Hidrográficos — Autres données hydrographiques — Outros acidentes hidrográficos

✦1 Submarine Features — Untermeerische Objekte — Accidentes Submarinos — Formes de relief sous-marin — Acidentes submarinos
□ Political Unit — Politische Einheit — Unidad Política — Entité politique — Unidade política
✧ Cultural Institution — Kulturelle Institution — Institución Cultural — Institution culturelle — Instituição cultural
⊥ Historical Site — Historische Stätte — Sitio Histórico — Site historique — Sítio histórico
✦ Recreational Site — Erholungs- und Ferienort — Sitio de Recreo — Centre de loisirs — Area de Lazer
✈ Airport — Flughafen — Aeropuerto — Aéroport — Aeroporto
■ Military Installation — Militäranlage — Instalación Militar — Installation militaire — Instalação militar
✦ Miscellaneous — Verschiedenes — Misceláneo — Divers — Diversos

Nhamundá ≃ 246 2.12 S 56.41 W
Nha-nam 110 21.27 N 106.06 E
Nhandeara 255 20.40 S 50.02 W
Nhareia 152 11.25 S 17.03 E
Nha-trang 110 12.15 N 109.11 E
Nhecolândia 248 19.16 S 57.04 W
Nhia ≃ 152 10.15 S 14.12 E
Nhill 166 36.20 S 141.39 E
Nhlangano 158 27.06 S 31.12 E
Nhlazatshe 158 28.10 S 31.14 E
Nhoma ≃ 156 18.52 S 20.53 E
Nhon-trach 269c 10.43 N 106.51 E
Nhulunbuy 164 12.11 S 136.47 E
Nhundo 152 14.25 S 21.23 E
Nhunguaçu 256 22.21 S 42.53 W
Niabembe 154 2.14 S 27.44 E
Niafounké 150 15.56 N 4.00 W
Niagara 190 45.46 N 87.59 W
Niagara □[6], On., Can. 212 43.05 N 79.20 W
Niagara □[6], N.Y., U.S. 210 43.10 N 78.42 W
Niagara ≃ 212 43.15 N 79.04 W
Niagara County Historical Center ʊ 284a 43.10 N 78.43 W
Niagara Falls, On., Can. 212 43.06 N 79.04 W
Niagara Falls, On., Can. 284a 43.06 N 79.04 W
Niagara Falls, N.Y., U.S. 210 43.05 N 79.03 W
Niagara Falls, N.Y., U.S. 284a 43.05 N 79.03 W
Niagara Falls ↳ 212 43.05 N 79.04 W
Niagara Falls Airport ⊠ 284a 43.02 N 79.08 W
Niagara Falls International Airport ⊠ 284a 43.06 N 78.56 W
Niagara-on-the-Lake 212 43.15 N 79.04 W
Niagara University ʊ[2] 284a 43.08 N 79.02 W
Niagassola 150 12.19 N 9.07 W
Niah 112 3.52 N 113.44 E
Niakaramandougou 150 8.40 N 5.17 W
Niamey 150 13.31 N 2.07 E
Niamey □[5] 150 14.00 N 2.00 E
Niamtougou 150 9.46 N 1.06 E
Nianbadu 100 28.17 N 118.28 E
Niandan ≃ 150 10.30 N 10.26 W
Niandan Koro 150 11.05 N 9.15 W
Nianforando 150 9.32 N 10.31 W
Niangara 154 3.42 N 27.52 E
Niangay, Lac ⊜ 150 15.50 N 3.00 W
Niangmake 102 30.14 N 99.40 E
Niangnianggong 104 41.00 N 121.13 E
Niangniangmiao 98 42.34 N 118.05 E
Niangniangwa 105 40.33 N 117.30 E
Niangoloko 150 10.17 N 4.55 W
Niangua ≃ 194 37.58 N 92.48 W
Niangzizhuang 105 40.02 N 118.05 E
Nia-Nia 154 1.24 N 27.36 E
Nianpan 104 41.48 N 124.02 E
Niantic, Ct., U.S. 207 41.19 N 72.11 W
Niantic, Il., U.S. 219 39.51 N 89.10 W
Nianyugou 104 42.00 N 123.59 E
Nianyushan 100 29.11 N 117.04 E
Nianzhuang 98 34.19 N 117.47 E
Nianzigang 100 31.03 N 114.18 E
Nianzishan 89 47.32 N 122.52 E
Niapu 154 2.25 N 26.28 E
Niari □[5] 152 3.15 S 12.30 E
Niari ≃ 152 3.56 S 12.12 E
Niaro 140 10.38 N 31.31 E
Nias, Pulau I 114 1.05 N 97.35 E
Niassa □[5] 154 13.30 S 36.00 E
Nibbiano 62 44.54 N 9.19 E
Nibe 26 56.59 N 9.38 E
Nibong Tebal 114 5.10 N 100.29 E
Nibria 272b 22.36 N 88.16 E
Nīca 76 56.19 N 21.04 E
Nica ≃ 86 57.29 N 64.33 E
Nicaragua □[1], N.A. 230 13.00 N 85.00 W
Nicaragua □[1], N.A. 236 13.00 N 85.00 W
Nicaragua, Lago de ⊜ 236 11.30 N 85.30 W
Nicaro 240p 20.42 N 75.33 W
Nicastro 68 38.59 N 16.20 E
Ničatka, ozero ⊜ 88 57.45 N 117.30 E
Nice 62 43.42 N 7.15 E
Nice-Côte d'Azur, Aéroport de ⊠ 62 43.40 N 7.14 E
Niceville 194 30.31 N 86.28 W
Nichelino 62 44.59 N 7.38 E
Nicheng 106 30.55 N 121.49 E
Nichihara 96 34.33 N 131.50 E
Nichinan, Nihon 92 31.36 N 131.23 E
Nichinan, Nihon 96 35.09 N 133.16 E
Nicholas □[6] 218 38.20 N 84.02 W
Nicholas Channel ɥ 238 23.25 N 80.05 W
Nicholas Research Institute ʊ[3] 274b 37.53 S 145.21 E
Nicholasville 192 37.52 N 84.34 W
Nicholls 192 31.31 N 82.38 W
Nichols, Ca., U.S. 282 38.02 N 121.59 W
Nichols, Fl., U.S. 220 27.54 N 82.02 W
Nichols, N.Y., U.S. 210 42.01 N 76.22 W
Nichols Brook ≃ 283 42.37 N 70.59 W
Nicholson, Austl. 162 18.02 S 128.54 E
Nicholson, Ky., U.S. 218 38.54 N 84.33 W
Nicholson, Ms., U.S. 194 30.28 N 89.41 W
Nicholson, Pa., U.S. 210 41.37 N 75.46 W
Nicholson ≃, Austl. 162 17.34 S 128.38 E
Nicholson ≃, Austl. 166 17.31 S 139.36 E
Nicholson Island I 212 43.56 N 77.31 W
Nicholson Range ⋀ 162 27.15 S 116.45 E
Nichols Run ≃ 284b 39.03 N 77.18 W
Nickerie □[5] 250 4.00 N 57.30 W
Nickerie ≃ 250 5.59 N 57.00 W
Nickerson 198 38.08 N 98.05 W
Nickol Bay c 162 20.39 S 116.52 E
Nicktown 214 40.37 N 78.48 W
Nicobar Islands II 110 8.00 N 93.30 E
Nicola 182 50.10 N 120.40 W
Nicola ≃ 182 50.25 N 121.18 W
Nicolae Bălcescu 38 47.34 N 26.52 E
Nicolai Mountain ∧ 224 46.05 N 123.28 W
Nicola Lake ⊜ 182 50.10 N 120.25 W
Nicola Mameet Indian Reserve ◆[4] 182 50.11 N 120.49 W
Nicolás Bravo 234 18.21 N 93.10 W
Nicolás Pérez, Sierra de ⋀ 234 22.27 N 99.08 W
Nicolás Romero □[7] 286a 19.37 N 99.17 W
Nicolaus 226 38.54 N 121.35 W
Nicolet 206 46.13 N 72.37 W
Nicolet □[6] 206 46.15 N 72.20 W
Nicolet ≃ 206 46.14 N 72.39 W
Nicolet, Lac ⊜ 206 45.50 N 71.33 W
Nicolet, Lake ⊜ 190 46.20 N 84.15 W
Nicolet Centre ≃ 206 45.46 N 71.50 W
Nicolet Sud-Ouest ≃ 206 46.13 N 72.36 W
Nicoll Bay c 276 40.43 N 73.07 W
Nicollet 190 44.16 N 94.11 W
Nicoll Point > 276 40.42 N 73.09 W
Nicolls Town 238 25.08 N 78.00 W
Nicolosi 70 37.37 N 15.01 E
Nicosia, It. 70 37.45 N 14.24 E
Nicosia → Levkosía, Kípros 130 35.10 N 33.22 E
Nicotera 68 38.34 N 15.57 E
Nicoya 236 10.09 N 85.27 W
Nicoya, Golfo de c 236 9.47 N 84.48 W
Nicoya, Península de >[1] 236 10.00 N 85.25 W
Nictheroy → Niterói 256 22.53 S 43.07 W
Nida ≃ 30 50.18 N 20.52 E
Nidadavole 122 16.55 N 81.40 E
Nidau 58 47.07 N 7.14 E
Nidd ≃ 44 54.01 N 1.12 W
Nidda 56 50.24 N 9.00 E
Nidda ≃ 56 50.06 N 8.34 E
Nidder ≃ 56 50.12 N 8.47 E
Nidderau 56 50.14 N 8.52 E
Nide 102 31.51 N 96.19 E
Nideggen 56 50.47 N 6.29 E
Nidelva ≃ 26 58.24 N 8.48 E
Nidwalden □[3] 58 46.55 N 8.28 E
Nidž 84 40.56 N 47.41 E
Nidzica 30 53.22 N 20.26 E
Niebüll 41 54.48 N 8.50 E
Nied ≃ 56 49.23 N 6.40 E
Nied Allemande ≃ 56 49.10 N 6.26 E
Nieddu, Monte ∧ 71 40.45 N 9.34 E
Niederaden ◆[8] 263 51.36 N 7.34 E
Niederanven 56 49.39 N 6.16 E
Niederau 54 51.10 N 13.32 E
Niederaula 56 50.48 N 9.36 E
Niederbayern □[5] 60 48.45 N 12.45 E
Niederbipp 58 47.16 N 7.39 E
Niederbobritzsch 54 50.54 N 13.26 E
Niederbonsfeld 263 51.23 N 7.08 E
Niederbronn-Les-Bains 56 48.57 N 7.38 E
Niederdonk 263 51.14 N 6.41 E
Niederelfringhausen 263 51.21 N 7.10 E
Niedere Tauern ⋀ 30 47.18 N 14.00 E
Niederfinow 54 52.50 N 13.55 E
Niederfrohna 54 50.53 N 12.43 E
Niederhaverbeck 52 53.09 N 9.54 E
Niederheimbach 56 50.02 N 7.48 E
Niederhone 56 51.13 N 10.06 E
Niederkassel 56 50.49 N 7.02 E
Nieder-Kassel ◆[8] 263 51.14 N 6.45 E
Niederkrüchten 56 51.12 N 6.13 E
Niederlande → Netherlands □[1] 30 52.15 N 5.30 E
Niederländische Antillen → Netherlands Antilles □[2] 241s 12.15 N 69.00 W
Niederlausitz □[9] 54 51.40 N 14.15 E
Niederlehme 54 52.19 N 13.39 E
Niedermarsberg 56 51.28 N 8.50 E
Niedermarschacht 52 53.25 N 10.21 E
Nieder-Mörlen 56 50.23 N 8.43 E
Niederndodeleben 54 52.08 N 11.30 E
Nieder-Neuendorf 264a 52.37 N 13.12 E
Niedernhall 56 49.17 N 9.36 E
Niedernwöhren 52 52.21 N 9.08 E
Niederoderwitz 54 50.57 N 14.44 E
Nieder-Ohmen 56 50.38 N 9.02 E
Nieder-Olm 56 49.55 N 8.11 E
Niederorschel 54 51.22 N 10.25 E
Niederösterreich □[3] 61 48.20 N 15.50 E
Niedersachsen □[3] 30 52.40 N 9.00 E
Niedersachswerfen 54 51.33 N 10.46 E
Niederschöneweide ◆[8] 264a 52.27 N 13.31 E
Niederschönhausen ◆[8] 54 52.35 N 13.23 E
Niedersee → Ruciane-Nida 30 53.39 N 21.35 E
Niedersonthofen 58 47.38 N 10.13 E
Niederstetten 56 49.24 N 9.55 E
Niederstotzingen 56 48.32 N 10.14 E
Niedersulz 61 48.29 N 16.40 E
Niederurnen 58 47.07 N 9.03 E
Niederwald 58 46.26 N 8.12 E
Niederwalgern 56 50.44 N 8.41 E
Niederweningen 58 47.30 N 8.23 E
Niederwiesa 54 50.51 N 13.01 E
Niederwürschnitz 54 50.43 N 12.45 E
Nied Française ≃ 56 49.10 N 6.26 E
Niedu 100 25.28 N 114.08 E
Niefang 152 1.50 N 10.14 E
Nieheim 52 51.48 N 9.06 E
Niekerkshoop 158 29.19 S 22.51 E
Niel 50 51.07 N 4.20 E
Niellé 150 10.12 N 5.38 W
Niellim 146 9.42 N 17.49 E
Niem 152 6.12 N 15.14 E
Niemba 154 5.57 S 28.26 E
Niemegk 54 52.04 N 12.41 E
Niemeyer ◆[8] 287a 23.00 S 43.15 W
Niemodlin 30 50.39 N 17.37 E
Niéna 150 11.26 N 6.21 W
Nienberge 52 52.00 N 7.34 E
Nienborg-Wigbold 52 52.08 N 7.06 E
Nienburg, B.R.D. 52 52.38 N 9.13 E
Nienburg, D.D.R. 54 51.50 N 11.46 E
Niendorf 54 53.59 N 10.50 E
Nienhagen, B.R.D. 52 52.33 N 10.05 E
Nienhagen, D.D.R. 54 51.57 N 11.09 E
Niénokoué, Mont ∧[2] 150 5.26 N 7.10 W
Niepkuhlen ≃ 263 51.29 N 6.31 E
Niepołomice 30 50.03 N 20.13 E
Nieppe 50 50.42 N 2.50 E
Nier ≃ 48 52.17 N 7.48 W
Niéré 146 14.30 N 21.09 E
Niéré, Hadjer ∧ 146 14.21 N 21.40 E
Niéri Ko ≃ 150 13.21 N 13.23 W
Nierong 120 32.09 N 92.11 E
Niers ≃ 52 51.43 N 5.57 E
Nierst 263 51.19 N 6.43 E
Nierstein 56 49.52 N 8.20 E
Niesen ∧ 58 46.39 N 7.39 E
Niesky 54 51.17 N 14.49 E
Nieszawa 30 52.50 N 18.55 E
Nieto, Cañada de ≃ 258 34.00 S 58.15 W
Nieu Bethesda 158 31.51 S 24.34 E
Nieuw-Amsterdam, Ned. 52 52.44 N 6.51 E
Nieuw Amsterdam, Sur. 250 5.53 N 55.05 W
Nieuw-Buinen 52 52.57 N 6.55 E
Nieuwefontein 158 28.01 S 19.06 E
Nieuwegein 52 52.03 N 5.05 E
Nieuwe-Niedorp 52 52.45 N 4.54 E
Nieuwe-Pekela 52 53.04 N 6.58 E
Nieuweschans 52 53.11 N 7.12 E
Nieuwkoop 52 52.08 N 4.47 E
Nieuw Nickerie 250 5.57 N 56.59 W
Nieuwolda 52 53.14 N 6.59 E
Nieuwoudtville 158 31.23 S 19.07 E
Nieuwpoort 50 51.08 N 2.45 E
Nieuwpoort-Bad 50 51.09 N 2.42 E
Nieuw-Schoonebeek 52 52.38 N 6.59 E
Nieuw-Vennep 52 52.16 N 4.38 E
Nieuw-Weerdinge 52 52.52 N 6.59 E
Nieva ≃ 246 4.35 S 77.53 W
Nievenheim 56 51.07 N 6.46 E
Nievería 286d 11.59 S 76.55 W
Nieves 234 24.00 N 103.01 W
Nièvre □[5] 32 47.05 N 3.30 E
Nièvre ≃ 50 47.10 N 3.13 E
Nīfī Ya'qūb 132 31.50 N 35.14 E
Niga 150 13.38 N 5.27 W
Nigan 126 23.30 N 87.59 E
Niğde 130 37.59 N 34.42 E
Niğde □[4] 130 38.15 N 34.15 E
Nigei Island I 182 50.55 N 127.50 W
Nigel 158 26.30 S 28.28 E
Niger □[3] 150 10.00 N 6.00 E
Niger □[1] 134 16.00 N 8.00 E
Niger ≃ 150 5.33 N 6.33 E
Niger Delta ≚[2] 150 4.50 N 6.00 E
Nigeria □[1] 134 10.00 N 8.00 E
Nigerian Museum ʊ 273a 6.20 N 3.24 E
Nigg 46 57.43 N 4.00 W
Nighāsan 124 28.14 N 80.52 E
Nightcaps 172 45.58 S 168.02 E
Nighthawk 182 48.58 N 119.38 W
Night Hawk Lake ⊜ 190 48.28 N 81.00 W
Nightingale Island I 10 37.24 S 12.28 W
Nightmute 180 60.29 N 164.43 W
Nigríta 38 40.55 N 23.30 E
Nihe 104 41.27 N 121.13 E
Nihing (Nahang) ≃ 128 26.00 N 62.44 E
Nihoa I 14 23.06 N 161.58 W
Nihommatsu 92 37.35 N 140.26 E
Nihon → Japan □[1] 92 36.00 N 138.00 E
Nihonbashi ◆[8] 268 35.41 N 139.47 E
Nihon-kai → Japan, Sea of ⊕[2] 90 40.00 N 135.00 E
Nihon University ʊ[2] 268 35.42 N 139.45 E
Nihtaur 124 29.20 N 78.23 E
Nihuil, Embalse del ⊜[1] 252 35.05 S 68.45 W
Niida ≃ 96 33.11 N 132.58 E
Niigata 92 37.55 N 139.03 E
Niigata □[5] 94 37.08 N 138.30 E
Niihama 96 33.58 N 133.16 E
Niihari 94 36.07 N 140.09 E
Niiharu 94 36.41 N 138.55 E
Niihau I 229b 21.55 N 160.10 W
Nii-jima I 92 34.22 N 139.16 E
Niimi 96 34.59 N 133.28 E
Niinisalo 26 61.50 N 22.29 E
Niitsu 92 37.48 N 139.07 E
Niiza 94 35.48 N 139.34 E
Níjar 34 36.58 N 2.12 W
Nijiaqiao 269b 31.14 N 121.21 E
Nijil 132 30.31 N 35.33 E
Nijkerk 52 52.13 N 5.30 E
Nijlen 56 51.10 N 4.39 E
Nijmegen 52 51.50 N 5.50 E
Nijo Castle ⊥ 270 35.01 N 135.45 E
Nijvel → Nivelles 50 50.36 N 4.20 E
Nijverdal 52 52.22 N 6.27 E
Níkaia 267c 37.58 N 23.39 E
Nikel' 24 69.24 N 30.12 E
Nikel'tau 86 50.23 N 58.13 E
Nikiforovo 265b 55.50 N 38.05 E
Nikiniki 112 9.49 S 124.28 E
Nikip Lake ⊜ 184 52.53 N 91.53 W
Nikitovka, S.S.S.R. 78 50.23 N 38.25 E
Nikitovka, S.S.S.R. 83 48.21 N 38.02 E
Nikitsch 61 47.32 N 16.40 E
Nikitskoje, S.S.S.R. 82 55.18 N 38.28 E
Nikitskoje, S.S.S.R. 82 55.13 N 35.46 E
Nikki 150 9.56 N 3.12 E
Nikkō 94 36.45 N 139.37 E
Nikkō-kokuritsu-kōen ♦ 94 36.49 N 139.33 E
Niklā al-'Inab 142 30.55 N 30.46 E
Niklasdorf 61 47.24 N 15.10 E
Nikobaren → Nicobar Islands II 110 8.00 N 93.30 E
Nikolai 180 62.58 N 154.09 W
Nikolaiken → Mikołajki 30 53.49 N 21.36 E
Nikolajev, S.S.S.R. 78 49.32 N 23.58 E
Nikolajev, S.S.S.R. 78 46.58 N 32.00 E
Nikolajevka, S.S.S.R. 78 47.38 N 33.12 E
Nikolajevka, S.S.S.R. 78 47.06 N 34.14 E
Nikolajevka, S.S.S.R. 78 44.58 N 33.37 E
Nikolajevka, S.S.S.R. 78 46.23 N 29.24 E
Nikolajevka, S.S.S.R. 78 47.33 N 30.25 E
Nikolajevka, S.S.S.R. 78 51.04 N 34.02 E
Nikolajevka, S.S.S.R. 80 52.28 N 49.14 E
Nikolajevka, S.S.S.R. 80 52.11 N 48.04 E
Nikolajevka, S.S.S.R. 80 53.08 N 47.12 E
Nikolajevka, S.S.S.R. 80 46.21 N 47.44 E
Nikolajevka, S.S.S.R. 83 47.39 N 37.41 E
Nikolajevka, S.S.S.R. 83 48.51 N 37.46 E
Nikolajevka, S.S.S.R. 83 47.18 N 38.50 E
Nikolajevka, S.S.S.R. 83 48.46 N 38.20 E
Nikolajevka, S.S.S.R. 86 56.29 N 95.06 E
Nikolajevka, S.S.S.R. 86 54.57 N 75.44 E
Nikolajevka, S.S.S.R. 86 49.10 N 81.59 E
Nikolajevka, S.S.S.R. 88 55.46 N 98.10 E
Nikolajevka, S.S.S.R. 89 48.34 N 134.47 E
Nikolajevo 76 58.16 N 29.29 E
Nikolajevo-Kozlovskij 83 47.13 N 38.21 E
Nikolajevsk 80 50.01 N 45.28 E
Nikolajevskaja 80 47.37 N 41.29 E
Nikolajevsk-Na-Amure 89 53.08 N 140.44 E
Nikolajevskoje, S.S.S.R. 78 45.08 N 39.36 E
Nikolajevskoje, S.S.S.R. 88 51.04 N 111.48 E
Nikolajevskoje, S.S.S.R. 88 52.21 N 117.00 E
Nikolassee ◆[8] 264a 52.26 N 13.12 E
Nikolayev → Nikolajev 78 46.58 N 32.00 E
Nikolo-Berezovec 76 58.38 N 42.17 E
Nikolo-Ber'ozovka 80 56.08 N 54.09 E
Nikolo-Chovanskoje 265b 55.36 N 37.27 E
Nikologory 80 56.09 N 41.59 E
Nikolo-Kropotki 82 56.44 N 37.55 E
Nikolo-L'vovsk 89 43.54 N 131.23 E
Nikolo-Makarovo 80 57.38 N 43.34 E
Nikolsdorf 64 46.47 N 12.55 E
Nikol'sk, S.S.S.R. 24 59.30 N 45.27 E
Nikol'sk, S.S.S.R. 80 53.45 N 46.05 E
Nikolski 180 52.56 N 168.52 W
Nikol'skij, S.S.S.R. 24 60.55 N 34.00 E
Nikol'skij, S.S.S.R. 86 56.18 N 68.58 E
Nikol'skij, S.S.S.R. 86 47.55 N 67.28 E
Nikol'skij Toržok 76 59.53 N 38.46 E
Nikol'skoje, S.S.S.R. 74 55.12 N 166.00 E
Nikol'skoje, S.S.S.R. 76 52.39 N 36.04 E
Nikol'skoje, S.S.S.R. 76 55.26 N 35.04 E
Nikol'skoje, S.S.S.R. 76 59.23 N 44.36 E
Nikol'skoje, S.S.S.R. 76 59.30 N 42.32 E
Nikol'skoje, S.S.S.R. 78 50.35 N 41.10 E
Nikol'skoje, S.S.S.R. 80 47.46 N 46.24 E
Nikol'skoje, S.S.S.R. 80 52.37 N 43.49 E
Nikol'skoje, S.S.S.R. 82 54.27 N 36.24 E
Nikol'skoje, S.S.S.R. 82 54.30 N 36.50 E
Nikol'skoje, S.S.S.R. 82 54.03 N 37.10 E
Nikol'skoje, S.S.S.R. 82 54.18 N 35.53 E
Nikol'skoje, S.S.S.R. 82 55.37 N 36.41 E
Nikol'skoje, S.S.S.R. 82 54.51 N 35.53 E
Nikol'skoje, S.S.S.R. 82 55.15 N 36.04 E
Nikol'skoje, S.S.S.R. 82 56.09 N 36.43 E
Nikol'skoje, S.S.S.R. 82 55.53 N 36.26 E
Nikol'skoje, S.S.S.R. 83 47.46 N 37.18 E
Nikol'skoje, S.S.S.R. 86 57.12 N 84.21 E
Nikol'skoje, S.S.S.R. 86 52.02 N 55.43 E
Nikol'skoje, S.S.S.R. 265a 59.41 N 30.47 E
Nikol'skoje, S.S.S.R. 265b 55.46 N 37.54 E
Nikol'skoje-na-Čeremšane 80 54.03 N 49.14 E
Nikol'skoje-na-Dnepre 78 48.12 N 35.12 E
Nikol'skoje-Ur'upino 265b 55.48 N 37.13 E
Nikonga ≃ 154 4.40 S 31.28 E
Nikonorovka 83 49.07 N 39.59 E
Nikonova Gora 76 60.22 N 36.07 E
Nikonovskoje 82 55.17 N 38.10 E
Nikopol, Blg. 38 43.42 N 24.54 E
Nikopol', S.S.S.R. 78 47.35 N 34.25 E
Niksar 130 40.36 N 36.58 E
Nīkshahr 128 26.13 N 60.12 E
Nikšić 38 42.46 N 18.56 E
Nikulino, S.S.S.R. 76 55.16 N 33.46 E
Nikulino, S.S.S.R. 80 58.05 N 44.14 E
Nikulino, S.S.S.R. 82 56.48 N 35.50 E
Nikulino ◆[8] 265b 55.40 N 37.28 E
Nikulkino 82 56.07 N 38.38 E
Nikul'skoje 82 55.10 N 38.41 E
Nikumaroro I[1] 14 4.40 S 174.32 W
Nikunau I 14 1.23 S 176.26 E
Nil → Nile ≃ 140 30.10 N 31.06 E
Nīl, Nahr an- → Nile ≃ 140 30.10 N 31.06 E
Nila, Pulau I 164 6.44 S 129.31 E
Nilakka ⊜ 26 63.07 N 26.33 E
Niland 204 33.14 N 115.31 W
Nil Blanc → White Nile ≃ 140 15.38 N 32.31 E
Nile □[5] 154 3.00 N 31.30 E
Nile (Nahr an-Nīl) ≃ 140 30.10 N 31.06 E
Nīleh, Kūh-e ∧ 128 32.59 N 50.32 E
Niles, Il., U.S. 216 42.01 N 87.48 W
Niles, Mi., U.S. 216 41.49 N 86.15 W
Niles, Oh., U.S. 214 41.10 N 80.45 W
Nileshwar 122 12.15 N 75.06 E
Niles Pond ⊜ 283 42.35 N 70.40 W
Nilgani 272b 22.46 N 88.26 E
Nilgaut, Lac ⊜ 190 46.36 N 77.15 W
Nīlgiri 126 21.28 N 86.46 E
Nilka 86 43.47 N 82.20 E
Nilkitkwa ≃ 182 55.27 N 126.43 W
Nillahcootie, Lake ⊜[1] 169 36.54 S 146.00 E
Nilo → Nile ≃ 140 30.10 N 31.06 E
Nilo Azul → Blue Nile ≃ 140 15.38 N 32.31 E
Nilo Blanco → White Nile ≃ 140 15.38 N 32.31 E
Nilo Peçanha 255 13.37 S 39.06 W
Nilópolis 256 22.49 S 43.25 W
Nilópolis □[7] 287a 22.49 S 43.26 W
Nilphāmāri 124 25.56 N 88.51 E
Nilsiä 26 63.12 N 28.05 E
Niltepec 234 16.34 N 94.37 W
Nīlwāl ◆[8] 272a 28.40 N 76.59 E
Nilwood 219 39.24 N 89.49 W
Nima 96 35.09 N 132.24 E
Nīmach 120 24.28 N 74.52 E
Niman ≃ 89 51.24 N 132.45 E
Nimančik 89 52.09 N 133.47 E
Nimba □[6] 150 7.40 N 8.50 W
Nimba, Mount ∧ 150 7.37 N 8.25 W
Nīmbahera 120 24.37 N 74.41 E
Nimba Range ⋀ 150 7.30 N 8.30 W
Nimboran, Pegunungan ⋀ 164 2.45 S 140.20 E
Nimelen ≃ 89 52.27 N 136.32 E
Nîmes 62 43.50 N 4.21 E
Nimis 64 46.12 N 13.16 E
Nimishillen Creek ≃ 214 40.38 N 81.22 W
Nimisila 214 40.56 N 81.34 W
Nimisila Reservoir ⊜[1] 214 40.57 N 81.31 W
Nīm Ka Thāna 120 27.44 N 75.48 E
Nimmitabel 166 36.31 S 149.16 E
Nimmonsburg 210 42.09 N 75.55 W
Nimpkish Lake ⊜ 182 50.25 N 126.59 W
Nimrod Glacier ⊓ 9 82.27 S 161.00 E
Nimrod Lake ⊜[1] 194 34.55 N 93.20 W
Nīmrūz □[4] 128 30.30 N 62.00 E
Nims ≃ 56 49.51 N 6.28 E
Nimta 272b 22.40 N 88.25 E
Nimule 154 3.36 N 32.03 E
Nimule National Park ♦ 154 3.50 N 31.35 E
Nimy 50 50.28 N 3.57 E
Nīnah, Wādī V 146 30.02 N 15.22 E
Nīnawā □[4] 128 36.10 N 42.35 E
Nin Bay c 116 12.13 N 123.15 E
Ninda 152 14.47 S 21.24 E
Nindigully 166 28.21 S 148.49 E
Nindirí 236 12.00 N 86.08 W
Nine Ashes 260 51.42 N 0.18 E
Nine Degree Channel ɥ 122 9.00 N 73.00 E
Ninemile Creek ≃, N.Y., U.S. 210 43.11 N 75.20 W
Ninemile Creek ≃, N.Y., U.S. 210 43.06 N 76.14 W
Ninemile Creek ≃, N.Y., U.S. 210 43.24 N 76.38 W
Nine Mile Creek ≃, Ut,. U.S. 200 39.50 N 109.53 W
Ninemile Island I 279b 40.29 N 79.52 W
Nine Mile Lake ⊜ 212 44.57 N 79.34 W
Nine Mile Point > 212 44.09 N 76.34 W
Ninepin Group II 271d 22.16 N 114.21 E
Nineteen Hundred Five Memorial Cemetery ◆ 265a 59.51 N 30.27 E
Ninette 184 49.24 N 99.38 W
Ninetyeast Ridge ⊕[3] 6 4.00 S 90.00 E
Ninety Mile Beach ⩦[2], Austl. 166 38.13 S 147.23 E
Ninety Mile Beach ⩦[2], N.Z. 172 34.48 S 173.00 E
Ninety Six 192 34.10 N 82.01 W
Nineveh, In., U.S. 218 39.22 N 86.05 W
Nineveh, N.Y., U.S. 210 42.12 N 75.36 W
Nineveh ⊥ 128 36.25 N 43.10 E
Ninfa ⊥ 66 41.36 N 12.58 E
Ninfas, Punta > 254 42.56 S 64.20 W
Ninfield 42 50.53 N 0.25 E
Ninga 184 49.13 N 99.51 W
Ning'an 89 44.22 N 129.25 E
Ningari 150 14.40 N 3.16 W
Ningbo 100 29.52 N 121.31 E
Ningcheng (Tianyi) 98 41.33 N 119.20 E
Ningde 100 26.43 N 119.33 E
Ningdu 100 26.31 N 115.58 E
Ninggang 100 26.50 N 114.02 E
Ningguo 106 30.38 N 118.58 E
Ninghai 100 29.17 N 121.25 E
Ninghe (Lutai) 105 39.20 N 117.48 E
Ninghepu 105 40.43 N 116.07 E
Ninghua 100 26.15 N 116.38 E
Ningi 150 11.04 N 9.32 E
Ningjin, Zhg. 98 37.37 N 114.55 E
Ningjin, Zhg. 98 37.39 N 116.48 E
Ningjing Shan ⋀ 102 29.45 N 98.45 E
Ningling 98 34.27 N 115.21 E
Ningming 102 22.07 N 107.05 E
Ningnan 102 27.11 N 102.36 E
Ningpo → Ningbo 100 29.52 N 121.31 E
Ningqiang 102 32.44 N 106.19 E
Ningshan 102 33.04 N 108.39 E
Ningsia → Yinchuan 102 38.30 N 106.18 E
Ningsia Hui Autonomous Region → Ningxia Huizu Zizhiqu □[4] 102 37.00 N 106.00 E
Ningwu 102 39.01 N 112.21 E
Ningxi 100 28.35 N 121.00 E
Ningxia Huizu Zizhiqu (Ningsia Hui) □[4] 102 37.00 N 106.00 E
Ningxian 102 35.31 N 108.01 E
Ningxiang 100 28.15 N 112.33 E
Ningyang 98 35.47 N 116.47 E
Ningyō-tōge)(96 35.19 N 133.56 E
Ningyuan 102 25.37 N 111.46 E
Ningyuanbao 102 38.38 N 102.30 E
Ningyuanpu 105 40.44 N 114.54 E
Ninh-binh 110 20.15 N 105.59 E
Ninh-hoa 110 12.29 N 109.08 E
Ninhue 252 36.24 S 72.24 W
Ninigo Group II 164 1.15 S 144.15 E
Ninilchik 180 60.03 N 151.41 W
Ninnescah ≃ 198 37.20 N 97.10 W
Ninnescah, North Fork ≃ 198 37.34 N 97.42 W
Ninnescah, South Fork ≃ 198 37.34 N 97.42 W
Ninnis Glacier Tongue ⊓ 9 68.12 S 147.12 E
Ninohe 92 40.16 N 141.18 E
Ninomiya, Nihon 94 36.22 N 139.58 E
Ninomiya, Nihon 94 35.18 N 139.16 E
Ninove 50 50.50 N 4.01 E
Niny 84 44.29 N 43.57 E
Nio 96 34.12 N 133.39 E
Nioaque 248 21.08 S 55.48 W
Nioaque ≃ 248 20.46 S 56.04 W
Niobe 214 42.01 N 79.27 W
Niobrara 198 42.45 N 98.01 W
Niobrara ≃ 198 42.45 N 98.00 W
Nioka 154 2.10 N 30.39 E
Nioki 152 2.43 S 17.41 E
Niokolo Koba 150 13.04 N 12.43 W
Niokolo Koba, Parc National du ♦ 150 13.00 N 13.00 W
Niono 150 14.15 N 6.00 W
Nionsamoridougou 150 8.43 N 8.50 W
Nioro du Rip 150 13.45 N 15.48 W
Nioro du Sahel 150 15.15 N 9.35 W
Niort 32 46.19 N 0.27 W
Niota 192 35.30 N 84.32 W
Nioût ⊕[4] 150 16.03 N 6.52 W
Nipan 166 24.47 S 150.01 E
Nipāni 122 16.24 N 74.23 E
Nipawin 184 53.22 N 104.00 W
Nipawin Provincial Park ♦ 184 54.00 N 104.40 W
Nipe, Bahía de c 240p 20.47 N 75.42 W
Nipe, Sierra de ⋀ 240p 20.28 N 75.49 W
Nipekamew ≃ 184 54.59 N 104.52 W
Nipekamew Lake ⊜ 184 54.24 N 104.58 W
Nipepe 154 14.01 S 37.55 E
Nipigon 190 49.01 N 88.16 W
Nipigon, Lake ⊜ 176 49.50 N 88.30 W
Nipigon Bay c 190 48.53 N 87.50 W
Nipin ≃ 184 55.45 N 109.02 W
Nipisi Lake ⊜ 182 55.47 N 114.57 W
Nipissing □[6] 212 45.30 N 78.50 W
Nipissing, Lake ⊜ 190 46.17 N 80.00 W
Nipissis, Lac ⊜ 186 51.02 N 66.10 W
Nipisso, Lac ⊜ 186 50.52 N 65.50 W
Nipomo 204 35.02 N 120.28 W
Nippenicket, Lake ⊜ 283 41.58 N 71.03 W
Nippers Harbour 186 49.48 N 55.52 W
Nippersink Creek ≃ 216 42.23 N 88.22 W
Niqiu 100 33.25 N 115.38 E
Niquelândia 255 14.27 S 48.27 W
Niquero 240p 20.03 N 77.35 W
Niquivil 252 30.25 S 68.42 W
Nīr 128 38.02 N 47.59 E
Nīr, Jabal an- ⋀[2] 128 24.10 N 43.20 E
Nīra ≃ 122 17.59 N 75.07 E
Nir'am 132 31.31 N 34.35 E
Nirasaki 94 35.42 N 138.27 E
Nirayama 94 35.03 N 138.57 E
Nirgua 246 10.09 N 68.34 W
Nirim 132 31.20 N 34.24 E
Nirmal 122 19.06 N 78.21 E
Nirmali 124 26.19 N 86.35 E
Nirsa 126 23.47 N 86.43 E
Nirwāno 128 26.22 N 62.43 E
Niš 38 43.19 N 21.54 E
Nisa 34 39.31 N 7.39 W
Nisa (Neisse) (Nysa Łużycka) ≃ 30 52.04 N 14.46 E
Niṣāb 144 14.31 N 46.30 E
Nišava ≃ 38 43.22 N 21.46 E
Nisbet 210 41.13 N 77.07 W
Niscemi 70 37.09 N 14.23 E
Nischintāpur 272b 22.26 N 88.22 E
Niṣf Thānī Bashbīsh 142 31.07 N 31.11 E
Nish → Niš 38 43.19 N 21.54 E
Nishan 120 33.35 N 85.30 E
Nishi ◆[8], Nihon 268 35.27 N 139.38 E
Nishi ◆[8], Nihon 270 34.41 N 135.30 E
Nishiarai ◆[8] 268 35.47 N 139.47 E
Nishiazai 94 35.31 N 136.10 E
Nishibetsuin 270 34.58 N 135.31 E
Nishi-Chūgoku-sanchi-kokutei-kōen ♦ 96 34.40 N 132.10 E
Nishigō 94 37.09 N 140.10 E
Nishiiyayama 96 33.53 N 133.49 E
Nishiizu 94 34.46 N 138.47 E
Nishi-jima I 96 34.39 N 134.29 E
Nishikata 94 36.28 N 139.45 E
Nishikatsura 94 35.31 N 138.51 E
Nishiki 96 34.16 N 131.57 E
Nishiki ≃ 96 34.09 N 132.15 E
Nishikiori 270 34.29 N 135.34 E
Nishikyō ◆[8] 270 34.59 N 135.40 E
Nishimori ◆[8] 270 34.45 N 135.01 E
Nishinari ◆[8] 270 34.38 N 135.28 E
Nishinasuno 94 36.53 N 139.59 E
Nishinomiya 96 34.43 N 135.20 E
Nishinoomote 93b 30.44 N 131.00 E
Nishio 94 34.52 N 137.03 E
Nishitoda ◆[8] 270 34.43 N 135.00 E
Nishitosa 96 33.09 N 132.47 E
Nishiwaki 96 34.59 N 134.58 E
Nishiyodogawa ◆[8] 270 34.42 N 135.27 E
Nisinomiya → Nishinomiya 96 34.43 N 135.20 E
Nísiros I 38 36.35 N 27.10 E
Niska Lake ⊜ 184 55.35 N 108.38 W
Niskayuna 210 42.46 N 73.50 W
Nisling ≃ 180 62.27 N 139.30 W
Nismes 56 50.05 N 4.33 E
Nispen 52 51.29 N 4.28 E
Nisporeny 78 47.06 N 28.11 E
Nisqually ≃ 224 47.06 N 122.42 W
Nisqually Indian Reservation ◆[4] 224 47.02 N 122.42 W
Nisqually Reach c 224 47.07 N 122.45 W
Nissan ≃ 26 56.40 N 12.51 E
Nissequogue 276 40.54 N 73.12 W
Nissequogue ≃ 276 40.54 N 73.13 W
Nissequogue, Northeast Branch ≃ 276 40.50 N 73.13 W
Nissequogue River State Park ♦ 276 40.51 N 73.13 W
Nisser ⊜ 26 59.10 N 8.30 E
Nisshin 94 35.08 N 137.02 E
Nissoria 70 37.39 N 14.27 E
Nissum Bredning c 26 56.38 N 8.22 E
Nissum Fjord c[2] 26 56.21 N 8.14 E
Nisswa 190 46.31 N 94.17 W
Nistelrode 52 51.43 N 5.33 E
Nister ≃ 56 50.47 N 7.43 E
Nisutlin ≃ 180 60.10 N 132.30 W
Nita, Indon. 115b 8.40 S 122.11 E
Nita, Nihon 96 35.12 N 133.01 E
Nitalas 272c 19.06 N 73.08 E
Nītaure 76 57.10 N 25.10 E
Niterói 256 22.53 S 43.07 W
Niterói □[7] 287a 22.56 S 43.04 W
Nith ≃, On., Can. 212 43.12 N 80.22 W
Nith ≃, Scot., U.K. 44 55.00 N 3.35 W
Nithāri 272a 28.35 N 77.21 E
Nithāri ◆[8] 272a 28.42 N 77.03 E
Nithi River 182 54.01 N 125.01 W
Nithsdale V 44 55.14 N 3.46 W
Nitibe 112 9.19 S 124.12 E
Nitinat 224 48.55 N 124.29 W
Nitinat ≃ 224 48.49 N 124.37 W
Nitinat Lake ⊜ 182 48.45 N 124.45 W
Niton 42 50.35 N 1.16 W
Nitra 30 48.20 N 18.05 E
Nitra ≃ 30 47.46 N 18.10 E
Nitro 188 38.24 N 81.50 W
Nitry 50 47.40 N 3.53 E
Nítse Óros (Nidže) ∧ 38 40.58 N 21.49 E
Nitta 94 36.17 N 139.18 E
Nittälven ≃ 40 59.51 N 14.50 E
Nittany Mountain ∧ 210 41.00 N 77.25 W
Nittedal 26 60.04 N 10.53 E
Nittenau 60 49.12 N 12.16 E
Nittendorf 60 49.02 N 11.58 E
Niu Aunfo Point > 174w 21.04 S 175.20 W
Niubaotun 105 39.46 N 116.41 E
Niubu 100 31.02 N 117.39 E
Niuchutuncun 104 41.28 N 122.58 E
Niudouguang 100 24.51 N 115.44 E
Niue □[2], Oc. 14 19.02 S 169.52 W
Niue □[2], Oc. 174v 19.02 S 169.52 W
Niu'erhe 89 51.30 N 121.49 E
Niufentai 89 47.05 N 120.02 E
Niufozhen 107 29.23 N 105.02 E
Niuhang 100 28.44 N 115.51 E
Niuhuaxi 107 29.29 N 103.48 E
Niujie 102 27.47 N 104.16 E
Niujingjie 110 25.46 N 100.33 E
Niuke 120 30.41 N 82.01 E
Niulakita I 14 10.45 S 179.30 E
Niulan ≃ 102 27.28 N 103.10 E
Niulanshan 105 40.13 N 116.39 E
Niumaowu 98 40.58 N 124.59 E
Niupeng 106 31.32 N 121.50 E
Niupichang 107 30.35 N 103.40 E
Niushitun 98 35.18 N 114.24 E
Niut, Gunung ∧ 112 1.00 N 109.55 E
Niutan 107 29.05 N 105.21 E
Niutao I 14 6.06 S 177.17 E
Niuti 100 32.58 N 113.35 E
Niutian 100 27.17 N 115.44 E
Niutoushan 89 45.09 N 126.45 E
Niutou Shan I 100 29.07 N 121.56 E
Niutuo 105 39.15 N 116.20 E
Niutuoshan 106 31.04 N 119.37 E
Niuxichang 107 28.47 N 104.31 E
Niuxintai 104 41.21 N 123.53 E
Niuxintun 104 41.56 N 121.21 E
Niuyuanzi 105 40.20 N 117.47 E
Niuzhuang, Zhg. 98 37.21 N 118.29 E
Niuzhuang, Zhg. 104 40.58 N 122.32 E
Nivå 41 55.56 N 12.31 E
Nivala 26 63.55 N 24.58 E
Nive ≃, Austl. 166 26.02 S 146.25 E
Nive ≃, Fr. 32 43.30 N 1.29 W
Nive Downs 166 25.30 S 146.32 E
Nivelles (Nijvel) 50 50.36 N 4.20 E
Nivernais □[9] 32 47.00 N 3.30 E
Nivernais, Canal du ≍ 50 47.40 N 3.40 E
Niverville, Mb., Can. 184 49.37 N 97.01 W
Niverville, N.Y., U.S. 210 42.26 N 73.40 W
Nivillers 50 49.28 N 2.10 E
Nivnoje 76 53.11 N 32.35 E
Nivskij 24 67.16 N 32.23 E
Nixa 194 37.02 N 93.17 W
Nixi 102 27.58 N 99.27 E
Nixis 107 30.08 N 106.19 E
Nixizhen 107 29.02 N 104.16 E
Nixon, Nv., U.S. 204 39.49 N 119.21 W
Nixon, Pa., U.S. 214 40.45 N 79.56 W
Nixon, Tx., U.S. 222 29.16 N 97.45 W
Niyodo 96 33.32 N 133.08 E
Niyodo ≃ 96 33.27 N 133.29 E
Niyor 114 2.05 N 103.17 E
Niyu Shan I 100 27.51 N 121.03 E
Niža 24 66.20 N 43.16 E
Nizam ◆[8] 267b 40.52 N 29.07 E
Nizāmābād 122 18.40 N 78.07 E
Nizamghāt 120 28.16 N 95.42 E
Nizām Sāgar ⊜[1] 122 18.10 N 77.55 E
Nižankoviči 78 49.40 N 22.47 E
Nīzgān ≃ 128 33.13 N 63.40 E
Nizhniy Tagil → Nižnij Tagil 86 57.55 N 59.57 E
Nizhny Novgorod → Gor'kij 80 56.20 N 44.00 E
Nižin 76 52.38 N 28.10 E
Nizino 265a 59.50 N 29.53 E
Nizip 130 37.01 N 37.46 E
Nízke Tatry ⋀ 30 48.54 N 19.40 E
Nízke Tatry, národní park ♦ 30 47.48 N 19.35 E
Nižn'aja 80 56.34 N 49.07 E
Nižn'aja Čvorovaja 86 59.11 N 77.31 E
Nižnaja Dobrinka 80 50.18 N 45.42 E
Nižn'aja Duvanka 83 49.35 N 38.10 E
Nižn'aja-Gerasimovka 83 48.46 N 39.44 E
Nižn'aja Grajvoronka 78 51.47 N 37.45 E
Nižn'aja Irga 86 56.51 N 57.26 E
Nižn'aja Ivanovka ◆[8] 83 48.09 N 38.46 E
Nižn'aja Karelina 88 57.55 N 107.44 E
Nižn'aja Keul'skaja, šivera ↳ 88 58.25 N 102.46 E
Nižn'aja Krynka 83 48.07 N 38.11 E
Nižnaja Matrenka 80 52.16 N 40.06 E
Nižn'aja-Ol'chovaja 83 48.44 N 39.35 E
Nižn'aja Omka 86 55.26 N 74.55 E
Nižn'aja Omra 24 62.46 N 55.46 E
Nižn'aja Ošma 80 55.44 N 51.18 E
Nižn'aja Peša 24 66.43 N 47.36 E
Nižn'aja Pojma 88 56.11 N 97.13 E
Nižn'aja Pokrovka 80 51.40 N 50.07 E
Nižn'aja Šachtama 88 51.24 N 117.40 E
Nižn'aja Salda 86 58.05 N 60.43 E
Nižn'aja Syzran' 80 53.04 N 48.34 E
Nižn'aja Tavda 86 57.40 N 66.12 E
Nižn'aja Tunguska ≃ 74 65.48 N 88.04 E
Nižn'aja Tura 86 58.37 N 59.49 E
Nižn'aja Vol'dža 86 58.19 N 79.20 E
Nižn'aja Zaimka 88 56.09 N 98.14 E
Nižneangarsk 88 55.47 N 109.33 E
Nižnebakanskij 78 44.52 N 37.52 E
Nižne-Baranikovka 83 49.05 N 39.51 E
Nižnečujskij 85 43.12 N 74.21 E
Nižnedevick 78 51.33 N 38.20 E
Nižne-Gnilovskoj ◆[8] 83 47.11 N 39.36 E
Nižnegnutov 80 48.02 N 42.22 E
Nižnegorskij 78 45.27 N 34.44 E
Nižneilimsk 88 57.11 N 103.16 E
Nižneje 83 48.46 N 38.37 E
Nižneje Al'kejevo 80 54.46 N 50.03 E
Nižn'eje Gir'unino 88 51.12 N 116.58 E
Nižneje Kučukovo 80 56.13 N 52.57 E
Nižneje Kujto, ozero ⊜ 24 64.58 N 31.38 E
Nižneje M'ačkovo 82 55.33 N 37.59 E
Nižneje Platino 83 48.48 N 39.30 E
Nižnejepravalje ≃ 83 48.17 N 39.57 E
Nižneje Romanovo 86 59.47 N 69.35 E
Nižneje Sančelejevo 80 53.40 N 49.27 E
Nižnekamsk 80 55.32 N 51.58 E
Nižnekundr'učen-Skaja 80 47.45 N 40.57 E
Nižnelemskij 24 64.01 N 56.16 E
Nižne-Mit'akin Pervyj 83 48.41 N 40.02 E
Nižne-Nagol'naja 83 49.00 N 39.59 E
Nižneoz'ornoje 80 51.37 N 53.56 E
Nižne-Podpol'nyj 83 47.12 N 40.01 E
Nižne-Pokrovka 83 49.13 N 38.38 E
Nižnetambovskoje 89 50.54 N 138.13 E
Nižne-T'oploje 83 48.48 N 39.23 E
Nižnetroickij 80 54.20 N 53.41 E
Nižneudinsk 88 54.54 N 99.03 E
Nižnevartovsk 74 60.56 N 76.31 E
Nižnij Baskunčak 80 48.13 N 46.50 E
Nižnij Časučej 88 50.31 N 115.08 E
Nižnij Čir 80 48.22 N 43.03 E
Nižnij Čulym 86 54.37 N 78.56 E
Nižnije Černi 80 47.41 N 43.26 E
Nižnije Čeršely 80 54.40 N 52.08 E
Nižnije Ostrovcy 82 55.35 N 38.01 E
Nižnije Sergi 86 56.40 N 59.18 E
Nižnije Serogozy 78 46.50 N 34.23 E
Nižnije Timers'any 80 54.34 N 47.45 E
Nižnije V'azovyje 80 55.49 N 48.32 E
Nižnij Ingaš 88 56.12 N 96.31 E
Nižnij Kisl'aj 78 50.50 N 40.11 E
Nižnij Kuranach 74 58.49 N 125.32 E
Nižnij Lomov 80 53.32 N 43.41 E
Nižnij Mamon 78 50.11 N 40.30 E
Nižnij Odes 24 63.40 N 54.52 E
Nižnij Ol'šan 78 50.45 N 38.55 E
Nižnij P'andž 120 37.08 N 68.32 E
Nižnij Paramonov 80 47.57 N 41.55 E

Symbols in the index entries represent the broad categories identified in the key at the right. Symbols with superior numbers (⋀[1]) identify subcategories (see complete key on page *I · 1).*

Kartensymbole in dem Registerverzeichnis stellen die rechts in Schlüssel erklärten Kategorien dar. Symbole mit hochgestellten Ziffern (⋀[1]) bezeichnen Unterabteilungen einer Kategorie (vgl. vollständiger Schlüssel auf Seite *I · 1).*

Los símbolos incluídos en el texto del índice representan las grandes categorias identificadas con la clave a la derecha. Los símbolos con numeros en su parte superior (⋀[1]) identifican las subcategorías (véase la clave completa en la página *I · 1).*

Les symboles de l'index représentent les catégories indiquées dans la légende à droite. Les symboles suivis d'un indice (⋀[1]) représentent des sous-catégories (voir légende complète à la page *I · 1).*

Os símbolos incluídos no texto do índice representam as grandes categorias identificadas com a chave à direita. Os símbolos com números em sua parte superior (⋀[1]) identificam as subcategorias (veja-se a chave completa à página *I · 1).*

∧ Mountain	Berg	Montaña	Montagne	Montanha
⋀ Mountains	Berge	Montañas	Montagnes	Montanhas
)(Pass	Pass	Paso	Col	Passo
V Valley, Canyon	Tal, Cañon	Valle, Cañón	Vallée, Canyon	Vale, Canhão
≚ Plain	Ebene	Llano	Plaine	Planície
> Cape	Kap	Cabo	Cap	Cabo
I Island	Insel	Isla	Île	Ilha
II Islands	Inseln	Islas	Îles	Ilhas
⩦ Other Topographic Features	Andere Topographische Objekte	Otros Elementos Topográficos	Autres données topographiques	Outros acidentes topográficos

ESPAÑOL · FRANÇAIS · PORTUGUÊS

Nombre / Nom / Nome	Página / Page	Lat.°′	Long.°′ W = Oeste / W = Ouest
Nižnij Rogačik	78	47.21 N	34.02 E
Nižnij Şerebr'akov	80	47.58 N	41.02 E
Nižnij Škaft	80	53.36 N	45.40 E
Nižnij Stan	88	52.18 N	115.44 E
Nižnij Tagil	86	57.55 N	59.57 E
Nižnij Takanyš	80	55.57 N	51.04 E
Nižnij Ufalej	86	55.55 N	59.59 E
Nižnij V'aloz'orskij	24	66.44 N	35.10 E
Nižnyj Nagol'čik	83	48.01 N	39.04 E
Nizy	78	50.47 N	34.46 E
Nizy-le-Comte	50	49.34 N	4.03 E
Nizza Monferrato	62	44.46 N	8.21 E
Niẕẕana, Naḥal V	132	30.57 N	34.23 E
Niẕẕanim	132	31.43 N	34.38 E
Njassa-See → Nyasa, Lake ⊜	154	12.00 S	34.30 E
Njazidja (Grande Comore) I	157a	11.35 S	43.20 E
Njinjo	154	8.48 S	38.54 E
Njoko ≃	152	17.10 S	24.05 E
Njombe	154	9.20 S	34.46 E
Njombe ≃	154	6.56 S	35.06 E
Njupeskär ∟	26	61.38 N	12.41 E
Njurunda	26	62.16 N	17.22 E
Nkambe	152	6.38 N	10.40 E
Nkandla	158	28.37 S	31.05 E
Nkawkaw	150	6.33 N	0.47 W
Nkayi	154	19.00 S	28.54 E
Nkhata Bay	154	11.33 S	34.18 E
Nkhotakota	154	12.57 S	34.17 E
Nkolabona	152	1.14 N	11.43 E
Nkomi, Lagune c	152	1.35 S	9.17 E
Nkongsamba	152	4.57 N	9.56 E
Nkonko	154	6.20 S	34.58 E
Nkoso	152	2.42 S	22.39 E
Nkoto	152	1.56 S	19.41 E
Nkunga	152	4.41 S	18.34 E
Nkurenkuru	152	17.38 S	18.35 E
Nkwalini	158	28.45 S	31.33 E
Nmai ≃	102	25.42 N	97.30 E
Nnewi	150	6.00 N	6.59 E
Nō	94	37.06 N	137.59 E
Noābād	272b	22.34 N	88.31 E
Noailles	50	49.20 N	2.12 E
Noākhāli	124	22.49 N	91.06 E
Noak Hill ◆^{8}	260	51.37 N	0.14 E
Noale	64	45.32 N	12.04 E
Noamundi	124	22.09 N	85.32 E
Noank	207	41.19 N	71.59 W
Noarlunga	168b	35.11 S	138.30 E
Noasca	62	45.27 N	7.19 E
Noatak	180	67.34 N	162.59 W
Noatak ≃	180	67.00 N	162.30 W
Nobby	171a	27.51 S	151.54 E
Nobel	212	45.25 N	80.06 W
Nobeoka	92	32.35 N	131.40 E
Nobidome	268	35.48 N	139.35 E
Nobidome-yōsui ≋^{1}	268	35.44 N	139.27 E
Nōbi-heiya ≚	94	35.15 N	136.45 E
Nobili	150	11.33 N	1.12 W
Nobitz	54	50.58 N	12.29 E
Noble, Il., U.S.	194	38.41 N	88.13 W
Noble, Ok., U.S.	196	35.08 N	97.23 W
Noble □^{6}	216	41.24 N	85.25 W
Noble Park	274b	37.58 S	145.10 E
Noblestown	279b	40.24 N	80.12 W
Noblesville	218	40.02 N	86.00 W
Nobleton, On., Can.	212	43.54 N	79.40 W
Nobleton, Fl., U.S.	220	28.38 N	82.15 W
Noboribetsu	92a	42.27 N	141.11 E
Noborito	268	35.37 N	139.34 E
Nobres	248	14.44 S	56.20 W
Nobsa	246	5.46 N	72.57 W
Nocatee	220	27.09 N	81.52 W
Noccundra	166	27.50 S	142.36 E
Nocé	50	48.22 N	0.42 E
Noce ≃	64	46.09 N	11.04 E
Nocera Inferiore	68	40.44 N	14.38 E
Nocera Superiore	68	40.44 N	14.40 E
Nocera Tirinese	68	39.02 N	16.09 E
Nocera Umbra	66	43.05 N	12.47 E
Noceto	64	44.48 N	10.11 E
Nochistlán	234	21.22 N	102.51 W
Nochten	54	51.26 N	14.36 E
Noci	68	40.48 N	17.08 E
Nociglia	68	40.02 N	18.20 E
Nockamixon Lake ⊜^{1}	208	40.28 N	75.14 W
Nockamixon State Park ♠	208	40.27 N	75.16 W
Nockatunga	166	27.43 S	142.43 E
Nocona	196	33.47 N	97.43 W
Nocupétaro	234	18.48 N	101.04 W
Noda	94	35.56 N	139.52 E
Nodagawa	96	35.31 N	135.06 E
Nodaway ≃	194	39.54 N	94.58 W
Nodera	270	34.45 N	134.56 E
Nods	58	47.06 N	6.20 E
Noé, Ouadi V	146	15.39 N	21.19 E
Noel	194	36.32 N	94.29 W
Noenieput	158	27.29 S	20.06 E
Noepoli	68	40.05 N	16.20 E
Noer	41	54.27 N	10.00 E
Noetinger	252	32.22 S	62.19 W
Nœux-les-Mines	50	50.29 N	2.40 E
Nofels	58	47.15 N	9.34 E
Nogajskaja step' ≚	84	44.17 N	46.05 E
Nogales, Chile	252	32.44 S	71.15 W
Nogales, Méx.	234	18.49 N	97.10 W
Nogales, Az., U.S.	200	31.20 N	110.56 W
Nogami	94	36.07 N	139.07 E
Nogangjin	98	39.30 N	125.23 E
Nogara, It.	64	45.11 N	11.04 E
Nogara, Ityo.	144	13.53 N	36.32 E
Nogaro	32	43.46 N	0.02 W
Nōgata	96	33.44 N	130.44 E
Nogent-en-Bassigny	58	48.02 N	5.21 E
Nogent-le-Roi	50	48.39 N	1.32 E
Nogent-le-Rotrou	50	48.19 N	0.50 E
Nogent-sur-Marne	261	48.50 N	2.29 E
Nogent-sur-Oise	50	49.16 N	2.28 E
Nogent-sur-Seine	50	48.29 N	3.30 E
Nogent-sur-Vernisson	50	47.51 N	2.45 E
Nogi	94	36.14 N	139.44 E
Nogies Creek ≃	212	44.35 N	78.31 W
Noginsk	82	55.51 N	38.27 E
Nogisaki	268	35.57 N	139.58 E
Nogliki	89	51.48 N	143.10 E
Nogmung	102	27.30 N	97.49 E
Nogoa ≃	166	23.33 S	148.32 E
Nōgohaku-san ∧	94	35.46 N	136.31 E
Nogoon Nuur	86	49.33 N	90.17 E
Nogoyá	252	32.24 S	59.48 W
Nógrád □^{6}	30	48.00 N	19.35 E
Noguera Pallarese ≃	34	42.15 N	0.54 E
Noguera Ribagorzana ≃	34	41.40 N	0.43 E
Nohain ≃	50	47.24 N	2.55 E
Nohar	123	29.11 N	74.46 E
Noheji	92	40.52 N	141.08 E
Nohili Point ≻	229b	22.04 N	159.47 W
Nohjhīl	124	27.51 N	77.39 E
Nohta	124	23.40 N	79.34 E
Nohwa-do I	98	34.12 N	126.35 E
Noicattaro	68	41.02 N	16.59 E
Noichi	96	33.33 N	133.42 E
Noir, Causse ⋏^{1}	32	44.10 N	3.15 E
Noir, Isla I	254	54.29 S	73.02 W
Noire ≃, P.Q., Can.	190	45.54 N	76.57 W
Noire ≃, P.Q., Can.	206	45.33 N	72.58 W
Noire ≃, P.Q., Can.	206	46.39 N	72.08 W
Noire, Mer du → Black Sea ⫧^{2}	22	43.00 N	35.00 E
Noire, Montagne ∧	206	46.14 N	74.18 W
Noire, Montagne ⋏	32	43.28 N	2.18 E
Noirétable	62	45.49 N	3.46 E
Noirmoutier	32	47.00 N	2.14 W
Noirmoutier, Île de I	32	47.00 N	2.15 W
Noiseau	261	48.47 N	2.33 E
Noisiel	261	48.51 N	2.37 E
Noisy ≃	212	44.19 N	80.08 W
Noisy-le-Grand	261	48.51 N	2.33 E
Noisy-le-Roi	261	48.51 N	2.04 E
Noisy-le-Sec	261	48.53 N	2.28 E
Nojember'an	84	41.12 N	45.01 E
Nojima-zaki ≻	94	34.56 N	139.53 E
Nojiri-ko ⊜	94	36.49 N	138.13 E
Nojon	102	43.10 N	102.07 E
Nojon uul ⋏	102	43.10 N	101.30 E
Nokami	96	34.15 N	135.20 E
Nokaneng	156	19.40 S	22.16 E
Nōke	270	34.26 N	135.29 E
Nokha	120	27.35 N	73.29 E
Nokia	26	61.28 N	23.30 E
Nokilalaki, Bulu ∧	112	1.13 S	120.08 E
Nok Kundi	128	28.46 N	62.46 E
Nokogiri-yama ∧^{2}	268	35.09 N	139.51 E
Nokomis, Sk., Can.	184	51.30 N	105.00 W
Nokomis, Fl., U.S.	220	27.07 N	82.26 W
Nokomis, Il., U.S.	219	39.18 N	89.17 W
Nokomis Lake ⊜	184	56.58 N	103.02 W
Nokou	146	14.35 N	14.47 E
Nokpan-ni ◆^{8}	271b	37.36 N	126.56 E
Nokrek ∧	124	25.27 N	90.20 E
Nokuku	175f	14.53 S	166.35 E
Nola, Centraf.	152	3.32 N	16.04 E
Nola, It.	68	40.55 N	14.33 E
Nolan ≃	222	32.07 N	97.26 W
Nolan Creek ≃	222	31.02 N	97.26 W
Nolanville	222	31.05 N	97.36 W
Nolay	58	46.57 N	4.38 E
Nole	62	45.15 N	7.35 E
Noli	62	44.12 N	8.26 E
Noli, Capo di ≻	62	44.12 N	8.25 E
Nolichucky ≃	192	36.07 N	83.14 W
Nolin ≃	194	37.13 N	86.15 W
Nolin Lake ⊜^{1}	194	37.20 N	86.10 W
Nolinsk	80	57.33 N	49.57 E
Nomahegan Brook ≃	276	40.41 N	74.18 W
Nomans Land I	207	41.15 N	70.49 W
Nombre de Dios, Méx.	232	28.41 N	106.05 W
Nombre de Dios, Méx.	234	23.51 N	104.14 W
Nombre de Dios, Pan.	236	9.35 N	79.28 W
Nombre de Dios, Cordillera ⋏	236	15.35 N	86.55 W
Nome	180	64.30 N	165.24 W
Nomény	56	48.54 N	6.14 E
Nomexy	58	48.18 N	6.23 E
Nomgon, Mong.	102	45.26 N	105.08 E
Nomgon, Mong.	102	42.50 N	105.07 E
Nomgon uul ⋏	102	42.50 N	104.20 E
Nomingue, Petit lac ⊜	206	46.21 N	75.00 W
Nomini Bay c	208	38.09 N	76.43 W
Nominingue	206	46.24 N	75.02 W
Nominingue, Lac ⊜	206	46.26 N	74.59 W
Nomoi Islands II	14	5.27 N	153.40 E
Nomoneas II	175c	7.24 N	151.53 E
Nomozaki	92	32.35 N	129.45 E
Nomtsas	156	24.22 S	16.47 E
Nomura	96	33.22 N	132.38 E
Nona, Lake ⊜	220	28.24 N	81.15 W
Nonacho Lake ⊜	176	61.42 N	109.40 W
Nonancourt	50	48.46 N	1.12 E
Nonant-le-Pin	50	48.42 N	0.13 E
Nonantola	64	44.41 N	11.02 E
Nonburg	24	65.34 N	50.32 E
Nonceveux	56	50.28 N	5.44 E
Nondalton	180	60.00 N	154.49 W
Nondwa	154	6.26 S	35.20 E
Nondweni	158	28.11 S	30.49 E
None	62	44.56 N	7.32 E
Nonette ≃	50	49.12 N	2.24 E
None-yama ∧	96	33.29 N	134.10 E
Nong'an	89	44.25 N	125.10 E
Nong Bua Lamphu	110	17.11 N	102.25 E
Nong Han	110	17.21 N	103.07 E
Nong Hèt	110	19.29 N	103.59 E
Nong Khai	110	17.52 N	102.44 E
Nongoma	158	27.58 S	31.35 E
Nongpoh	120	25.54 N	91.53 E
Nongstoin	120	25.31 N	91.16 E
Nonnenhorn	58	47.34 N	9.36 E
Nonnevitz	54	54.39 N	13.17 E
Nonning	166	32.30 S	136.30 E
Nonnweiler	56	49.36 N	6.58 E
Nono	144	8.32 N	37.26 E
Nonoai	252	27.21 S	52.47 W
Nonoava	232	27.28 N	106.44 W
Nonoc Island I	116	9.51 N	125.37 E
Nono de Julho, Túnel ◆^{5}	287b	23.34 S	46.39 W
Nonogasta	252	29.18 S	67.30 W
Nonoichi	94	36.32 N	136.37 E
Nonouti I^{1}	14	0.40 S	174.21 E
Nonsan	98	36.12 N	127.05 E
Nonsuch Bay c	240c	17.03 N	61.42 W
Nonthaburi	110	13.50 N	100.29 E
Nonthaburi □^{4}	269a	13.52 N	100.27 E
Non Thai	110	15.12 N	102.19 E
Nontron	32	45.32 N	0.40 E
Nonvianuk Lake ⊜	180	59.00 N	155.15 W
Noojee	169	37.55 S	146.00 E
Nookawarra	162	26.19 S	116.52 E
Nooksack	224	48.55 N	122.19 W
Nooksack ≃	224	48.46 N	122.35 W
Nooksack, Middle Fork ≃	224	48.50 N	122.08 W
Nooksack, North Fork ≃	224	48.50 N	122.11 W
Nooksack, South Fork ≃	224	48.50 N	122.11 W
Noonamah	164	12.38 S	131.04 E
Noonan	198	48.53 N	103.00 W
Noon Hill ∧^{2}	283	42.09 N	71.19 W
Noonkanbah	162	18.30 S	124.50 E
Noorat	169	38.12 S	142.56 E
Noord-Beveland I	52	51.35 N	3.45 E
Noord-Brabant □^{4}	52	51.30 N	5.00 E
Noord-Holland □^{4}	52	52.40 N	4.50 E
Noordhorn	52	53.16 N	6.24 E
Noordoewer	156	28.45 S	17.37 E
Noordoost Polder ◆^{1}	52	52.42 N	5.45 E
Noordpunt ≻	241s	12.23 N	69.10 W
Noord-Scharwoude	52	52.43 N	4.47 E
Noordwijk aan Zee	52	52.14 N	4.26 E
Noordwijk-Binnen	52	52.13 N	4.27 E
Noordwijkerhout	52	52.15 N	4.30 E
Noordwolde	52	52.54 N	6.09 E
Noormarkku	26	61.35 N	21.52 E
Noorvik	180	66.50 N	161.12 W
Noosaville	166	26.24 S	153.04 E
Nootka Island I	182	49.32 N	126.42 W
Nootka Sound Ʉ	182	49.33 N	126.38 W
Nopaltepec	234	18.17 N	95.59 W
No Point, Point ≻	276	41.09 N	73.08 W
Nóqui	152	5.51 S	13.25 E
Nora, Sve.	40	59.31 N	15.02 E
Nora, In., U.S.	218	39.55 N	86.08 W
Nora ≃	89	52.26 N	129.58 E
Nora ⊥	71	39.00 N	9.01 E
Nor Ačin	84	40.19 N	44.35 E
Norah Head ≻	170	33.17 S	151.35 E
Nora Islands II	144	16.02 N	40.03 E
Norala	116	6.28 N	124.38 E
Noralee	182	53.59 N	126.26 W
Noranda	190	48.15 N	79.02 W
Noraskög ⋏	40	59.39 N	14.50 E
Nora Springs	190	43.08 N	93.00 W
Norberg	40	60.04 N	15.56 E
Norberto de la Riestra	252	35.16 S	59.46 W
Norborne	194	39.18 N	93.40 W
Norcan Lake ⊜	212	45.10 N	76.53 W
Norcatur	198	39.50 N	100.11 W
Norchia ⊥	66	42.20 N	11.57 E
Norcia	66	42.48 N	13.05 E
Norco	228	33.56 N	117.33 W
Norcott, Mount ∧	162	32.07 S	121.59 E
Norcross	192	33.56 N	84.12 W
Nord □^{4}	146	9.00 N	13.30 E
Nord □^{5}, Burkina	150	13.30 N	2.15 W
Nord □^{5}, Fr.	50	50.20 N	3.40 E
Nord ◆^{5}	261	48.53 N	2.21 E
Nord, Canal du ≋	50	50.16 N	3.05 E
Nord, Cap → Nordkapp ≻	24	71.11 N	25.48 E
Nord, Grand lac du ⊜	186	50.54 N	67.06 W
Nord, Petit lac du ⊜	186	50.50 N	67.10 W
Nord, Rivière du ≃	206	45.31 N	74.20 W
Nordamerika → North America ⏏^{1}	16	45.00 N	100.00 W
Nordanholen	40	60.30 N	14.57 E
Nordausques	50	50.49 N	2.05 E
Nordaustlandet I	12	79.48 N	22.24 E
Nordbögge	263	51.37 N	7.44 E
Nordborg	41	55.03 N	9.45 E
Nordby	41	55.58 N	10.34 E
Nord Dakota → North Dakota □^{3}	198	47.30 N	100.15 W
Norddeich	52	53.37 N	7.09 E
Nordegg	182	52.28 N	116.04 W
Nordegg ≃	182	52.53 N	115.18 W
Norden, B.R.D.	52	53.36 N	7.12 E
Norden, Eng., U.K.	262	53.38 N	2.13 W
Norden, Ca., U.S.	226	39.20 N	120.22 W
Nordendorf	56	48.36 N	10.50 E
Nordenham	52	53.29 N	8.28 E
Nordenšel'da, archipelag II	74	76.45 N	96.00 E
Nordenskiold ≃	180	62.05 N	136.18 W
Norderney	52	53.42 N	7.08 E
Norderney I	52	53.42 N	7.10 E
Norderstapel	41	54.21 N	9.14 E
Norderstedt	52	53.43 N	10.00 E
Nordfjord c^{2}	26	61.54 N	5.12 E
Nordfjordeid	26	61.54 N	6.00 E
Nordfold	24	67.46 N	15.12 E
Nordfriesische Inseln → North Frisian Islands II	24	54.50 N	8.12 E
Nordfriesland ◆^{1}	41	54.40 N	9.10 E
Nordgermersleben	54	52.13 N	11.20 E
Nordhalben	54	50.22 N	11.30 E
Nordhausen	54	51.30 N	10.47 E
Nordheim	222	28.55 N	97.36 W
Nordheim von der Rhön	56	50.28 N	10.11 E
Nordhelle ∧^{2}	263	51.09 N	7.46 E
Nordhorn	52	52.27 N	7.05 E
Nordic Park	278	41.57 N	88.02 W
Nordingrå	26	62.56 N	18.16 E
Nordirland → Northern Ireland □^{8}	48	54.40 N	6.45 W
Nordiyya	132	32.19 N	34.54 E
Nordkanal ≋	263	51.10 N	6.42 E
Nordkapp ≻	24	71.11 N	25.48 E
Nordkinnhalvøya ≻^{1}	24	70.55 N	27.45 E
Nordkirchen	52	51.44 N	7.31 E
Nordkjosbotn	24	69.13 N	19.30 E
Nord-Korea → Korea, North □^{1}	98	40.00 N	127.00 E
Nordland	224	48.03 N	122.41 W
Nordland □^{6}	24	67.00 N	14.40 E
Nördliche Dwina → Severnaja Dvina ≃	24	64.32 N	40.30 E
Nördliches Eismeer → Arctic Ocean ⫧^{1}	16	85.00 N	170.00 E
Nördlingen	56	48.51 N	10.30 E
Nordmaling	26	63.34 N	19.30 E
Nordmark	40	59.50 N	14.06 E
Nordmarka ◆^{1}	26	60.00 N	10.25 E
Nordostrundingen ≻	16	81.36 N	12.09 W
Nord-Ostsee-Kanal ≋	30	53.53 N	9.08 E
Nord-Ouest □^{4}	152	6.30 N	10.30 E
Nordpfälzer Bergland ⋏	56	49.40 N	7.40 E
Nordradde ≃	52	52.43 N	7.17 E
Nordreisa	24	69.46 N	21.03 E
Nordre Strømfjord c^{2}	176	67.50 N	52.00 W
Nordrhein-Westfalen □^{3}	30	51.30 N	7.30 E
Nordsee → North Sea ⫧^{2}	22	55.20 N	3.00 E
Nordstemmen	52	52.09 N	9.46 E
Nordstrand I	41	54.30 N	8.53 E
Nordstrandischmoor I	41	54.33 N	8.48 E
Nord-Trøndelag □^{6}	24	64.25 N	12.00 E
Nordvik	74	74.02 N	111.32 E
Nordwalde	52	52.05 N	7.28 E
Nordwest-Kap → North West Cape ≻	162	21.45 S	114.10 E
Nore	26	60.10 N	9.01 E
Nore ≃	48	52.25 N	6.58 W
Noremberg → Nürnberg	60	49.27 N	11.04 E
Nörenberg → Ińsko	30	53.27 N	15.33 E
Norf	263	51.09 N	6.43 E
Norfbach ≃	263	51.11 N	6.44 E
Norfolk, Ct., U.S.	207	41.59 N	73.12 W
Norfolk, Ma., U.S.	283	42.07 N	71.19 W
Norfolk, Ne., U.S.	198	42.02 N	97.25 W
Norfolk, Va., U.S.	208	36.50 N	76.17 W
Norfolk □^{6}, On., Can.	214	42.48 N	80.25 W
Norfolk □^{6}, Eng., U.K.	42	52.35 N	1.00 E
Norfolk □^{6}, Ma., U.S.	207	42.10 N	71.15 W
Norfolk Broads ◆^{1}	42	52.40 N	1.30 E
Norfolk-Insel → Norfolk Island □^{2}	174c	29.02 S	167.57 E
Norfolk International Airport ⊠	208	36.54 N	76.12 W
Norfolk Island □^{2}, Oc.	14	29.02 S	167.57 E
Norfolk Island □^{2}, Oc.	174c	29.02 S	167.57 E
Norfolk Island Aerodome ⊠	174c	29.03 S	167.56 E
Norfolk Naval Shipyard ■	208	36.49 N	76.18 W
Norfolk Naval Station ■	208	36.57 N	76.18 W
Norfolk Ridge ✤^{3}	14	29.00 S	168.00 E
Norfork Lake ⊜^{1}	194	36.25 N	92.10 W
Norg	52	53.04 N	6.27 E
Norge	208	37.22 N	76.46 W
Norge → Norway □^{1}	24	62.00 N	10.00 E
Norham	44	55.43 N	2.10 W
Norheimsund	26	60.22 N	6.08 E
Norikura-dake ∧	94	36.06 N	137.33 E
Noril'sk	74	69.20 N	88.06 E
Noring, Gunong ∧	114	5.24 N	101.44 E
Norland, On., Can.	212	44.43 N	78.49 W
Norland, Fl., U.S.	220	25.57 N	80.12 W
Norlane	169	38.06 S	144.21 E
Norley	262	53.15 N	2.39 W
Norlina	192	36.26 N	78.11 W
Norma, It.	66	41.35 N	12.58 E
Norma, N.J., U.S.	208	39.29 N	75.05 W
Normal, Al., U.S.	194	34.47 N	86.34 W
Normal, Il., U.S.	216	40.30 N	88.59 W
Norman, Ar., U.S.	194	34.27 N	93.40 W
Norman, In., U.S.	218	38.57 N	86.16 W
Norman, Ok., U.S.	196	35.13 N	97.26 W
Norman ≃	166	17.28 S	140.49 E
Norman, Lake ⊜^{1}	192	35.35 N	80.55 W
Normanby, Austl.	171a	27.28 S	153.01 E
Normanby, N.Z.	172	39.32 S	174.17 E
Normanby ≃	164	14.25 S	144.08 E
Normanby Island I	164	10.05 S	151.05 E
Norman Creek c	284b	39.18 N	76.25 W
Normandie □^{9}	32	49.00 N	0.05 W
Normandie, Collines de ⋏^{2}	32	48.40 N	0.30 W
Normandien	158	27.57 S	29.47 E
Normandy → Normandie □^{9}	32	49.00 N	0.05 W
Normandy Heights	284b	39.17 N	76.48 W
Normandy Park	224	47.27 N	122.21 W
Normangee	222	31.02 N	96.07 W
Normanhurst	274a	33.43 S	151.06 E
Normanhurst, Mount ∧	162	25.04 S	122.32 E
Norman Island I	240m	18.20 N	64.37 W
Normannische Inseln → Channel Islands II	28	49.20 N	2.20 W
Norman Park	192	31.16 N	83.41 W
Normans Kill ≃	210	42.36 N	73.44 W
Normanton, Austl.	166	17.40 S	141.05 E
Normanton, Eng., U.K.	44	53.41 N	1.27 W
Normanville	168b	35.27 S	138.19 E
Norman Wells	180	65.17 N	126.51 W
Nor Marsh ≡	260	51.24 N	0.38 E
Nornalup	162	35.00 S	116.49 E
Norogachic	232	27.15 N	107.07 W
Noroton ≃	276	41.03 N	73.31 W
Noroton Point ≻	276	41.03 N	73.26 W
Norovlin	88	48.40 N	112.00 E
Noroy-le-Bourg	58	47.37 N	6.18 E
Norphlet	194	33.18 N	92.39 W
Norquay	184	51.53 N	102.05 W
Ñorquinco	254	41.51 S	70.54 W
Norra Björkfjärden c	40	59.27 N	17.28 E
Norrahammar	26	57.42 N	14.06 E
Norra Hörken ⊜	40	60.04 N	14.53 E
Norra Kvarken (Merenkurkku) Ʉ	26	63.36 N	20.43 E
Norra Kvills Nationalpark ♠	26	57.44 N	15.37 E
Norrälgen ⊜	40	59.50 N	14.34 E
Norra Rörum	41	56.01 N	13.30 E
Norra Storfjället ∧	24	65.52 N	15.18 E
Norrboda	40	60.28 N	18.25 E
Norrbotten □^{9}	26	66.45 N	23.00 E
Norrbottens Län □^{6}	24	66.00 N	20.00 E
Nørre Åby	41	55.27 N	9.54 E
Nørre Alslev	41	54.54 N	11.54 E
Nørre Broby	41	55.15 N	10.14 E
Nørre Næra	41	55.34 N	10.17 E
Norrent-Fontes	50	50.35 N	2.24 E
Nørre Snede	41	55.58 N	9.25 E
Nørresundby	26	57.04 N	9.55 E
Nørre Vejrup	41	55.31 N	8.47 E
Norrfjärden	26	65.25 N	21.27 E
Norridge	216	41.57 N	87.49 W
Norridgewock	188	44.42 N	69.47 W
Norris	192	36.11 N	84.04 W
Norris, Lake ⊜	220	28.57 N	81.32 W
Norris Arm	186	49.05 N	55.15 W
Norris Bridge ◆^{5}	208	37.37 N	76.26 W
Norris City	194	37.58 N	88.19 W
Norris Dam State Park ♠	192	36.14 N	84.07 W
Norrish Creek ≃	224	49.10 N	122.08 W
Norris Lake ⊜^{1}	192	36.20 N	83.55 W
Norris Point	186	49.31 N	57.53 W
Norristown	208	40.07 N	75.20 W
Norrköping	40	58.36 N	16.11 E
Norroway Brook ≃	283	42.11 N	71.03 W
Norrskedika	40	60.17 N	18.17 E
Norrsundet	26	60.56 N	17.08 E
Norrtälje	40	59.46 N	18.42 E
Norrtäljeviken c	40	59.47 N	18.53 E
Norseman	162	32.12 S	121.46 E
Norsewood	172	40.04 S	176.13 E
Norsjå ⊜	26	59.18 N	9.20 E
Norsjö	26	64.55 N	19.29 E
Norsk	89	52.20 N	129.55 E
Norsminde	41	56.01 N	10.16 E
Norsup	175f	16.05 S	167.23 E
Norte, Cabo ≻, Bra.	250	1.40 N	49.55 W
Norte, Cabo ≻, Chile	174z	27.03 S	109.24 W
Norte, Cabo → Nordkapp ≻	24	71.11 N	25.48 E
Norte, Canal do Ʉ	250	0.30 N	50.30 W
Norte, Cayo I	240m	18.20 N	65.15 W
Norte, Estación del ◆^{5}, Esp.	266a	40.25 N	3.43 W
Norte, Estación del ◆^{5}, Esp.	266d	41.24 N	2.02 E
Norte, Mar del → North Sea ⫧^{2}	22	55.20 N	3.00 E
Norte, Punta ≻, Arg.	252	36.17 S	56.47 W
Norte, Punta ≻, Arg.	254	42.04 S	63.45 W
Norte, Serra do ⋏^{1}	248	11.20 S	59.00 W
Norte de Santander □^{5}	246	8.00 N	73.00 W
Nortelândia	248	14.25 S	56.48 W
Nörten-Hardenberg	52	51.38 N	9.56 E
North, S.C., U.S.	192	33.36 N	81.06 W
North, Va., U.S.	208	37.26 N	76.24 W
North ≃, Nf., Can.	176	57.30 N	62.05 W
North ≃, On., Can.	212	44.44 N	79.39 W
North ≃, Al., U.S.	194	33.15 N	87.30 W
North ≃, Ia., U.S.	194	41.31 N	93.27 W
North ≃, Ma., U.S.	283	42.10 N	70.43 W
North ≃, Mo., U.S.	219	39.52 N	91.27 W
North ≃, Wa., U.S.	224	46.45 N	123.53 W
North, Cape ≻	186	47.02 N	60.25 W
North Abington	207	42.07 N	70.57 W
North Adams, Ma., U.S.	207	42.42 N	73.06 W
North Adams, Mi., U.S.	216	41.58 N	84.32 W
North Albany	202	44.39 N	123.06 W
Northallerton	44	54.20 N	1.26 W
Northam, Austl.	168a	31.39 S	116.40 E
Northam, S. Afr.	156	25.03 S	27.11 E
Northam, Eng., U.K.	42	51.02 N	4.12 W
North America ⏏^{1}	4	45.00 N	100.00 W
North America ⏏^{1}	16	45.00 N	100.00 W
North American Basin ✤^{1}	8	30.00 N	60.00 W
North Amherst	207	42.24 N	72.31 W
North Amityville	276	40.41 N	73.25 W
Northampton, Austl.	162	28.21 S	114.37 E
Northampton, Eng., U.K.	42	52.14 N	0.54 W
Northampton, Md., U.S.	284c	38.52 N	76.49 W
Northampton, Ma., U.S.	207	42.19 N	72.38 W
Northampton, N.Y., U.S.	207	40.54 N	72.40 W
Northampton, Pa., U.S.	208	40.41 N	75.29 W
Northampton □^{6}, N.C., U.S.	208	36.28 N	77.21 W
Northampton □^{6}, Pa., U.S.	210	40.45 N	75.18 W
Northampton □^{6}, Va., U.S.	208	37.20 N	75.50 W
Northamptonshire □^{6}	42	52.20 N	0.50 W
North Andaman I	110	13.15 N	92.55 E
North Andover	207	42.41 N	71.08 W
North Andrews Gardens	220	26.12 N	80.07 W
North Anna ≃	192	37.48 N	77.25 W
North Anson	188	44.51 N	69.54 W
North Apollo	214	40.35 N	79.33 W
North Arlington	276	40.47 N	74.08 W
North Arm ≃^{1}	224	49.12 N	123.10 W
North Asheboro	192	35.44 N	79.49 W
North Atlanta	192	33.51 N	84.20 W
North Attleboro	207	41.59 N	71.20 W
North Attleboro National Fish Hatchery ♠	283	42.00 N	71.17 W
North Auburn	274a	33.50 S	151.02 E
North Augusta	192	33.30 N	81.57 W
North Aulatsivik Island I	176	59.50 N	64.00 W
North Aurora	216	41.48 N	88.19 W
North Australian Basin ✤^{1}	14	14.30 S	116.30 E
Northaw	260	51.42 N	0.09 W
North Babylon	276	40.42 N	73.19 W
North Balabac Strait Ʉ	116	8.10 N	117.04 E
North Baltimore	216	41.10 N	83.40 W
North Balwyn	274b	37.48 S	145.05 E
North Bannister	168a	32.35 S	116.26 E
North Barrackpore	126	22.46 N	88.22 E
North Bass Island I	214	41.43 N	82.49 W
North Battleford	184	52.47 N	108.17 W
North Bay, On., Can.	190	46.19 N	79.28 W
North Bay, N.Y., U.S.	210	43.14 N	75.45 W
North Bay, Wi., U.S.	216	42.46 N	87.47 W
North Bay c, On., Can.	212	44.53 N	79.48 W
North Bay c, Wa., U.S.	224	46.59 N	124.04 W
North Bay Village	220	25.51 N	80.08 W
North Beach	168a	31.52 S	115.45 E
North Beach ◆^{8}	282	37.48 N	122.25 W
North Beach Peninsula ≻^{1}	224	46.30 N	124.02 W
North Belle Vernon	214	40.08 N	79.52 W
North Bellmore	276	40.41 N	73.32 W
North Bend, B.C., Can.	182	49.53 N	121.27 W
North Bend, Ne., U.S.	198	41.27 N	96.46 W
North Bend, Oh., U.S.	218	39.09 N	84.44 W
North Bend, Or., U.S.	202	43.24 N	124.13 W
North Bend, Pa., U.S.	214	41.21 N	77.42 W
North Bend, Wa., U.S.	224	47.29 N	121.47 W
North Benfleet	260	51.35 N	0.32 E
North Bengal Plains ≚	124	26.20 N	88.30 E
North Bennington	210	42.55 N	73.14 W
North Bergen	276	40.47 N	74.02 W
North Berwick, Scot., U.K.	46	56.04 N	2.44 W
North Berwick, Me., U.S.	188	43.18 N	70.44 W
North Bethlehem	210	42.40 N	73.50 W
North Bihar Plains ≚	124	26.20 N	86.00 E
North Billerica	207	42.35 N	71.17 W
North Bloomfield	214	41.27 N	80.52 W
North Boggy Creek ≃	196	34.23 N	96.04 W
North Bonneville	224	45.38 N	121.58 W
Northborough	207	42.19 N	71.38 W
North Bosque ≃	196	31.40 N	97.24 W
North Boston	210	42.41 N	78.47 W
North Bourke	166	30.03 S	145.57 E
North Box Hill	274b	37.48 S	145.07 E
North Braddock	279b	40.23 N	79.50 W
North Branch, Mi., U.S.	190	43.13 N	83.11 W
North Branch, Mn., U.S.	190	45.30 N	92.58 W
North Branch, N.J., U.S.	210	40.36 N	74.41 W
North Branch Canal ≋	224	47.12 N	120.40 W
North Branford	207	41.19 N	72.46 W
North Breakers ✤^{2}	174g	28.14 N	177.25 W
Northbridge, Austl.	274a	33.49 S	151.13 E
Northbridge, Ma., U.S.	207	42.09 N	71.39 W
North Bristol	214	41.24 N	80.52 W
Northbrook, On., Can.	212	44.44 N	77.10 W
Northbrook, Il., U.S.	216	42.07 N	87.49 W
Northbrook, Pa., U.S.	285	39.55 N	75.41 W
North Brookfield, Ma., U.S.	207	42.16 N	72.05 W
North Brookfield, N.Y., U.S.	210	42.51 N	75.24 W
North Brunswick	208	40.28 N	74.28 W
North Buganda □^{5}	154	1.00 N	32.15 E
North Caicos I	238	21.56 N	71.59 W
North Caldwell	276	40.51 N	74.16 W
North Canadian ≃	196	35.17 N	95.31 W
North Canton, Ct., U.S.	207	41.53 N	72.53 W
North Canton, Ga., U.S.	192	34.14 N	84.29 W
North Canton, Oh., U.S.	214	40.52 N	81.24 W
North Cape	216	42.47 N	88.05 W
North Cape ≻, P.E., Can.	186	47.05 N	64.00 W
North Cape ≻, N.Z.	172	34.25 S	173.02 E
North Cape → Nordkapp ≻, Nor.	24	71.11 N	25.48 E
North Cape ≻, Pap. N. Gui.	164	2.32 S	150.49 E
North Cape ≻, Mi., U.S.	216	41.44 N	83.25 W
North Cape May	208	38.58 N	74.57 W
North Captiva Island I	220	26.35 N	82.13 W
North Caribou Lake ⊜	176	52.50 N	90.40 W
North Carolina □^{3}, U.S.	178	35.30 N	80.00 W
North Carolina □^{3}, U.S.	192	35.30 N	80.00 W
North Carver	207	41.55 N	70.48 W
North Cascades National Park ♠	224	48.30 N	121.00 W
North Castor ≃	212	45.16 N	75.24 W
North Catasauqua	208	40.40 N	75.29 W
North Chagrin Reservation ♠	279a	41.34 N	81.26 W
North Channel Ʉ, On., Can.	190	46.02 N	82.50 W
North Channel Ʉ, On., Can.	212	44.10 N	76.45 W
North Channel Ʉ, U.K.	44	55.10 N	5.40 W
North Channel Ʉ, N.Y., U.S.	276	40.36 N	73.53 W
North Channel ≃^{1}	281	42.38 N	82.40 W
North Charleroi	214	40.09 N	79.54 W
North Charleston	192	32.51 N	79.58 W
North Chatham	210	42.29 N	73.38 W
North Chelmsford	207	42.38 N	71.23 W
North Chicago	216	42.19 N	87.50 W
North Chili	210	43.06 N	77.45 W
Northchurch	260	51.46 N	0.36 W
North City	224	47.45 N	122.18 W
North Cleveland	222	30.21 N	95.06 W
Northcliff ◆^{8}	273d	26.09 S	27.58 E
Northcliffe	162	34.36 S	116.07 E
North Clymer	214	42.04 N	79.34 W
North Cohasset	283	42.15 N	70.50 W
North Cohocton	210	42.34 N	77.28 W
North College Hill	218	39.13 N	84.33 W
North Collins	210	42.35 N	78.56 W
North Commerce Lake ⊜	281	42.35 N	83.30 W
North Concho ≃	196	31.27 N	100.25 W
North Conway	188	44.03 N	71.07 W
North Cotabato □^{4}	116	7.15 N	124.50 E
Northcote	274b	37.46 S	145.00 E
North Cray ◆^{8}	260	51.26 N	0.08 E
North Creek	188	43.41 N	73.59 W
North Creek ≃	278	41.33 N	87.37 W
Northcrest	222	31.38 N	97.06 W
North Crossett	194	33.09 N	91.56 W
North Crosswicks	285	40.10 N	74.39 W
North Croton Creek ≃	196	33.24 N	100.00 W
North Dakota □^{3}, U.S.	178	47.30 N	100.15 W
North Dakota □^{3}, U.S.	198	47.30 N	100.15 W
North Dandalup	168a	32.31 S	115.58 E
North Dandalup ≃	168a	32.36 S	115.53 E
North Dartmouth	207	41.38 N	70.58 W
North Dighton	207	41.51 N	71.07 W
North Dorset Downs ⋏^{1}	42	50.47 N	2.30 W
North Downs ⋏^{1}	42	51.20 N	0.10 E
North Dum-Dum	126	22.38 N	88.23 E
North Eagle Butte	198	45.02 N	101.15 W
North East, Md., U.S.	208	39.36 N	75.56 W
North East, Pa., U.S.	214	42.12 N	79.50 W
North-East □^{5}	156	21.00 S	27.30 E
Northeast Cape	180	63.18 N	168.42 W
Northeast Cape ≻	180	63.17 N	168.45 W
Northeast Cape Fear ≃	192	34.11 N	77.57 W
Northeast Creek ≃	284b	39.18 N	76.29 W
North Eastern □^{4}	154	1.00 N	40.15 E
Northeastern University ⊍^{2}	283	42.20 N	71.05 W
North Eastham	207	41.51 N	69.59 W
Northeast Henrietta	210	43.04 N	77.36 W
Northeast Islands II	175c	7.36 N	151.57 E
North Easton	207	42.04 N	71.06 W
Northeast Pass Ʉ	175c	7.30 N	151.59 E
Northeast Point ≻, Ba.	238	21.20 N	73.01 W
Northeast Point ≻, Ba.	238	22.43 N	73.50 W
North East Point ≻, Kiribati	174o	1.57 N	157.16 W
Northeast Point ≻, St. Vin.	241h	13.03 N	61.13 W
Northeast Providence Channel Ʉ	238	25.40 N	77.09 W
North Edwards	228	35.01 N	117.44 W
North Egremont	207	42.11 N	73.26 W
Northeim	52	51.42 N	10.00 E
North Elkhorn Creek ≃	218	38.13 N	84.48 W
North Elm Creek ≃	222	30.53 N	97.00 W
North English	190	41.30 N	92.04 W
Northern □^{4}, Ghana	150	9.30 N	1.00 W
Northern □^{4}, Malawi	154	11.00 S	34.00 E
Northern □^{4}, S.L.	150	9.15 N	11.45 W
Northern □^{4}, Zam.	154	11.00 S	31.00 E
Northern □^{5}, Pap. N. Gui.	164	9.00 S	148.30 E
Northern □^{5}, Ug.	154	2.50 N	32.45 E
Northern Aire Estates	278	42.08 N	88.02 W
Northern Arm	186	49.10 N	55.23 W
Northern Cheyenne Indian Reservation ◆^{4}	202	45.31 N	106.45 W
Northern Circārs ⋏^{2}	122	18.00 N	83.15 E
Northern Cook Islands II	14	10.00 S	161.00 W
Northern Division □^{5}	175g	16.30 S	179.30 E
Northern Dvina → Severnaja Dvina ≃	24	64.32 N	40.30 E
Northern Indian Lake ⊜	176	57.20 N	97.20 W
Northern Ireland □^{8}	48	54.40 N	6.45 W
Northern Light Lake ⊜	190	48.15 N	90.38 W
Northern Mariana Islands □^{2}	14	16.00 N	149.00 E
Northern Peninsula Aboriginal Reserve ◆^{4}	164	11.40 S	142.25 E
Northern Samar □^{4}	116	12.30 N	124.30 E
Northern Territory □^{8}	160	20.00 S	134.00 E
North Esk ≃, Scot., U.K.	46	56.44 N	2.28 W
North Esk ≃, Scot., U.K.	46	55.54 N	3.04 W
North Essendon	274b	37.45 S	144.54 E
North Evans	210	42.42 N	78.56 W
Northey Island I	260	51.44 N	0.43 E
North Fabius ≃	194	39.54 N	91.30 W
North Fairfield	214	41.06 N	82.36 W
North Fair Oaks	282	37.28 N	122.12 W
North Falmouth	207	41.38 N	70.37 W
North Ferriby	44	53.43 N	0.30 W
Northfield, B.C., Can.	224	49.11 N	123.59 W
Northfield, Ct., U.S.	207	41.41 N	73.06 W
Northfield, Il., U.S.	278	42.05 N	87.46 W
Northfield, Ma., U.S.	207	42.41 N	72.27 W
Northfield, Mn., U.S.	190	44.27 N	93.09 W
Northfield, N.J., U.S.	208	39.22 N	74.33 W
Northfield, Oh., U.S.	214	41.20 N	81.32 W
Northfield, Vt., U.S.	188	44.09 N	72.39 W
Northfield Airport ⊠	279a	41.17 N	81.31 W
Northfield Center	279a	41.19 N	81.32 W
Northfield Park Race Track ♠	279a	41.21 N	81.31 W
Northfield Village	279a	41.21 N	81.31 W
Northfield Woods	278	42.05 N	87.52 W
North Fiji Basin ✤^{1}	14	16.00 S	174.00 E
North Fillmore	228	34.24 N	118.56 W
North Fitzroy	274b	37.47 S	144.59 E
Northfleet	42	51.27 N	0.21 E
North Flinders Range ⋏	166	31.00 S	139.00 E
North Fond du Lac	190	43.48 N	88.29 W
Northford	207	41.23 N	72.47 W
North Foreland ≻	42	51.23 N	1.27 E
North Fork	226	37.13 N	119.30 W
North Fork ≃	194	36.13 N	92.17 W
North Fork Lake ⊜^{1}	226	38.56 N	121.00 W
North Fork Reservoir ⊜^{1}	224	45.13 N	122.15 W
North Fork Village	218	39.21 N	83.02 W
North Fort Myers	220	26.40 N	81.52 W
North Freedom	190	43.27 N	89.52 W
North Frisian Islands II	24	54.50 N	8.12 E
Northgate	216	43.01 N	85.36 W
Northgate ◆^{9}	282	38.00 N	122.33 W
North Georgetown	214	40.51 N	80.59 W
North Glanford	212	43.11 N	79.54 W
North Glen Ellyn	278	41.54 N	88.04 W
Northglenn	200	39.53 N	104.59 W
North Gower	212	45.08 N	75.43 W
North Grafton	207	42.14 N	71.42 W
North Granby	207	41.59 N	72.49 W
North Grand Island Bridge ◆^{5}	284a	43.04 N	78.59 W
North Great River	276	40.44 N	73.10 W
North Greece	212	43.15 N	77.44 W
North Grosvenordale	207	41.59 N	71.53 W
North Grove	216	40.37 N	85.58 W
North Gulfport	194	30.24 N	89.06 W
North Hadley	207	42.23 N	72.36 W
North Haledon	276	40.57 N	74.11 W
North Hampton	218	39.59 N	83.56 W
North Hanover	283	42.08 N	70.52 W
North Harbor c	269f	14.36 N	120.57 E
North Hātia Island I	124	22.40 N	91.00 E
North Haven	207	41.23 N	72.51 W
North Head ≻, Austl.	274a	33.49 S	151.18 E
North Head ≻, N.Z.	172	36.25 S	174.03 E
North Henderson	192	36.21 N	78.22 W
North Henik Lake ⊜	176	61.45 N	97.40 W
North Hero	188	44.49 N	73.17 W
North Highlands	226	38.41 N	121.22 W
North Hill	42	50.34 N	4.25 W
North Hills, De., U.S.	285	39.46 N	75.30 W
North Hills, Il., U.S.	278	42.18 N	88.01 W
North Hills, N.Y., U.S.	276	40.47 N	73.41 W
North Hinksey	42	51.45 N	1.16 W
North Hogan Creek ≃	218	39.03 N	84.54 W
North Hollywood ◆^{8}	280	34.10 N	118.23 W
North Holmwood	260	51.13 N	0.20 W
North Honcut Creek ≃	226	39.19 N	121.36 W

Symbol	English	Deutsch	Español	Français	Português
≃	River	Fluss	Río	Rivière	Rio
≋	Canal	Kanal	Canal	Canal	Canal
∟	Waterfall, Rapids	Wasserfall, Stromschnellen	Cascada, Rápidos	Chute d'eau, Rapides	Cascata, Rápidos
Ʉ	Strait	Meeresstrasse	Estrecho	Détroit	Estreito
c	Bay, Gulf	Bucht, Golf	Bahía, Golfo	Baie, Golfe	Baía, Golfo
⊜	Lake, Lakes	See, Seen	Lago, Lagos	Lac, Lacs	Lago, Lagos
≡	Swamp	Sumpf	Pantano	Marais	Pântano
⊼	Ice Features, Glacier	Eis- und Gletscherformen	Accidentes Glaciales	Formes glaciaires	Acidentes glaciares
⫧	Other Hydrographic Features	Andere Hydrographische Objekte	Otros Elementos Hidrográficos	Autres données hydrographiques	Outros acidentes hidrográficos
✤	Submarine Features	Untermeerische Objekte	Accidentes Submarinos	Formes de relief sous-marin	Acidentes submarinos
□	Political Unit	Politische Einheit	Unidad Politica	Entité politique	Unidade política
⊍	Cultural Institution	Kulturelle Institution	Institución Cultural	Institution culturelle	Instituição cultural
⊥	Historical Site	Historische Stätte	Sitio Histórico	Site historique	Sitio histórico
♠	Recreational Site	Erholungs- und Ferienort	Sitio de Recreo	Centre de loisirs	Area de Lazer
⊠	Airport	Flughafen	Aeropuerto	Aéroport	Aeroporto
■	Military Installation	Militäranlage	Instalación Militar	Installation militaire	Instalação militar
◆	Miscellaneous	Verschiedenes	Misceláneo	Divers	Diversos

Name	Page	Lat.°′	Long.°′
North Hoosick	210	42.56 N	73.21 W
North Hornell	210	42.21 N	77.40 W
North Horr	154	3.19 N	37.04 E
North Houston	222	29.54 N	95.31 W
Northiam	42	50.59 N	0.36 E
North Industry	214	40.44 N	81.22 W
North Irwin	279b	40.20 N	79.43 W
North Island I, India	122	10.08 N	72.20 E
North Island I, Kenya	154	4.04 N	36.03 E
North Island I, N.Z.	172	39.00 S	176.00 E
North Island Naval Air Station ■	228	32.42 N	117.12 W
North Islet I	116	8.56 N	120.02 E
North Jackson	214	41.06 N	80.52 W
North Java	210	42.41 N	78.20 W
North Judson	216	41.12 N	86.46 W
North Kenai	180	60.44 N	151.19 W
North Kingstown	207	41.38 N	71.25 W
North Kingsville	214	41.54 N	80.42 W
North Knife Lake ⊜	176	58.05 N	97.05 W
North Knob ∧	210	41.43 N	75.33 W
North Korea → Korea, North □1	98	40.00 N	127.00 E
North La Junta	198	37.59 N	103.31 W
Northlake, Il., U.S.	278	41.50 N	87.58 W
North Lake, Wi., U.S.	216	43.09 N	88.22 W
North Lake ⊜, N.Y., U.S.	276	41.09 N	73.41 W
North Lake ⊜, Tx., U.S.	222	32.57 N	96.58 W
North Lakhimpur	120	27.14 N	94.07 E
Northland ◆9	281	42.27 N	83.13 W
North Landing ≃	208	36.31 N	76.01 W
North Laramie ≃	198	42.08 N	104.56 W
North Las Vegas	204	36.11 N	115.07 W
North La Veta Pass)(	200	37.37 N	105.11 W
North Lawrence	214	40.51 N	81.38 W
Northleach	42	51.51 N	1.50 W
North Lewisburg	216	40.13 N	83.33 W
North Liberty	216	41.32 N	86.25 W
North Lima	214	40.56 N	80.39 W
North Lindenhurst	276	40.42 N	73.22 W
North Line Island I	276	40.38 N	73.29 W
Northline Terrace	222	29.55 N	95.25 W
North Little Rock	194	34.46 N	92.16 W
North Llano ≃	196	30.30 N	99.46 W
North Logan	202	41.46 N	111.48 W
North Loma Linda	228	34.02 N	117.05 W
North Loon Mountain ∧	202	45.07 N	115.52 W
North Loup	198	41.29 N	98.46 W
North Loup ≃	198	41.17 N	98.23 W
North Luangwa National Park ♦	154	11.50 S	32.15 E
North Luconia Shoals ◆2	108	5.40 N	112.35 E
North Macmillan ≃	180	63.03 N	133.18 W
North Madison	214	41.48 N	81.03 W
North Magnetic Pole ◆	16	77.19 N	101.49 W
North Malosmadulu Atoll I1	122	5.35 N	72.55 E
North Mamm Peak ∧	200	39.23 N	107.52 W
North Manchester	216	41.00 N	85.46 W
North Manitou Island I	190	45.06 N	86.01 W
North Mankato	190	44.10 N	94.02 W
North Manly	274a	33.46 S	151.16 E
North Maroota	170	33.29 S	150.56 E
North Marshfield	283	42.08 N	70.46 W
North Marysville	224	48.07 N	122.09 W
North Massapequa	276	40.42 N	73.27 W
Northmead, Austl.	274a	33.47 S	151.00 E
Northmead, S. Afr.	273d	26.10 S	28.20 E
North Merrick	276	40.41 N	73.33 W
North Miami	220	25.53 N	80.11 W
North Miami Beach	220	25.55 N	80.09 W
North Middleboro	207	41.56 N	70.58 W
North Milk ≃	202	49.08 N	112.23 W
North Mokelumne ≃	226	38.08 N	121.35 W
North Moose Lake ⊜	184	54.08 N	100.13 W
North Moreau Creek ≃	194	38.30 N	92.18 W
North Muskegon	216	43.15 N	86.16 W
North Myrtle Beach	192	33.49 N	78.40 W
North Nahanni ≃	180	62.05 N	124.30 W
North Naples	220	26.13 N	81.47 W
North Narrabeen	274a	33.42 S	151.18 E
North Nemah ≃	224	46.30 N	123.53 W
North New Hyde Park	276	40.44 N	73.41 W
North New River Canal ≡	220	26.05 N	80.12 W
North Newton	198	38.04 N	97.21 W
North Niles	216	41.52 N	86.15 W
North Norwich	210	42.37 N	75.31 W
North Oaks	222	30.22 N	97.41 W
North Ockendon ◆8	260	51.32 N	0.18 E
North Ogden	200	41.18 N	111.57 W
North Olmsted	214	41.24 N	81.55 W
Northolt Aerodrome ⊠	260	51.33 N	0.23 W
Northome	190	47.52 N	94.16 W
Northop	262	53.12 N	3.08 W
North Ore Creek ≃	281	42.43 N	83.47 W
North Orwell	210	41.55 N	76.19 W
Northowram	262	53.44 N	1.50 W
North Oxford	207	42.09 N	71.52 W
North Palisade ∧	204	37.06 N	118.31 W
North Palm Beach	220	26.49 N	80.04 W
North Para ≃	168b	34.36 S	138.45 E
North Park ◆8	278	41.59 N	87.43 W
North Park ♦	279b	40.36 N	80.00 W
North Park Lake ⊜	279b	40.36 N	80.00 W
North Parramatta	274a	33.48 S	151.00 E
North Pass ⊔	175c	7.41 N	151.48 E
North Patchogue	276	40.47 N	73.00 W
North Peak ∧, Ak., U.S.	180	62.34 N	162.23 W
North Peak ∧, Ca., U.S.	282	37.33 N	122.28 W
North Pease ≃	196	34.15 N	100.07 W
North Pelham, N.H., U.S.	283	42.46 N	71.21 W
North Pelham, N.Y., U.S.	276	40.55 N	73.48 W
North Pembroke	207	42.05 N	70.47 W
North Pender Island I	224	48.49 N	123.17 W
North Perry	214	41.47 N	81.07 W
North Petherton	42	51.06 N	3.01 W
North Philadelphia ◆8	285	39.58 N	75.09 W
North Philadelphia Airport ⊠	285	40.05 N	75.01 W
North Pine Grove	214	41.24 N	79.13 W
North Piney Creek ≃	200	42.31 N	110.05 W
North Pitcher	210	42.37 N	75.49 W
North Plainfield	210	40.37 N	74.25 W
North Plains	224	45.35 N	122.59 W
North Plains ≚	200	34.40 N	108.15 W
North Platte	198	41.07 N	100.45 W
North Platte ≃	178	41.07 N	100.42 W
North Pleasureville	218	38.22 N	85.07 W
North Plympton	283	41.59 N	70.48 W
North Point, H.K.	271d	22.17 N	114.12 E
Northpoint, Pa., U.S.	214	40.54 N	79.08 W
North Point ≻, Barb.	241g	13.20 N	59.36 W
North Point ≻, Md., U.S.	284b	39.12 N	76.27 W
North Point ≻, Mi., U.S.	190	45.02 N	83.16 W
North Pole	180	64.45 N	147.21 W
North Pole ◆	16	90.00 N	0.00
Northport, Al., U.S.	194	33.13 N	87.34 W
North Port, Fl., U.S.	220	27.03 N	82.15 W
Northport, Mi., U.S.	190	45.07 N	85.37 W
Northport, N.Y., U.S.	210	40.53 N	73.20 W
Northport, Wa., U.S.	202	48.54 N	117.46 W
North Portal	184	49.00 N	102.33 W
Northport Bay c	276	40.55 N	73.23 W
Northport Harbor c	276	40.53 N	73.22 W
North Powder	202	45.01 N	117.55 W
North Pownal	207	42.47 N	73.15 W
North Prairie	216	42.56 N	88.24 W
North Providence	207	41.50 N	71.25 W
North Puyallup	224	47.12 N	122.17 W
North Queensferry	46	56.01 N	3.25 W
North Quincy	219	39.58 N	91.24 W
North Raccoon ≃	198	41.50 N	94.08 W
North Raisin ≃	206	45.09 N	74.43 W
North Ram ≃	182	52.16 N	115.38 W
North Randall	279a	41.27 N	81.32 W
North Reading	207	42.34 N	71.04 W
North Reservoir ⊜1	283	42.28 N	71.07 W
North Richland Hills	222	32.50 N	97.13 W
North Richmond	282	37.57 N	122.22 W
Northridge, Oh., U.S.	218	39.59 N	83.46 W
Northridge, Oh., U.S.	218	39.48 N	84.11 W
Northridge ◆8	280	34.14 N	118.33 W
Northridge Fashion Center ◆9	280	34.13 N	118.33 W
North Ridge Village	218	39.57 N	86.09 W
North Ridgeville	214	41.23 N	82.01 W
North Rim	200	36.12 N	112.03 W
North River c	208	37.25 N	76.25 W
North Riverside	278	41.50 N	87.49 W
North Riverside Park Mall ◆9	278	41.51 N	87.49 W
North Robinson	214	40.48 N	82.51 W
North Rocks	274a	33.46 S	151.02 E
North Ronaldsay I	46	59.22 N	2.26 W
North Ronaldsay Firth ⊔	46	59.20 N	2.25 W
North Rose	210	43.11 N	76.53 W
North Royalton	214	41.18 N	81.43 W
North Rustico	186	46.27 N	63.19 W
North Ryde	274a	33.48 S	151.07 E
North Salem	214	40.09 N	81.33 W
North Salt Lake	200	40.50 N	111.54 W
North San Juan	226	39.22 N	121.06 W
North Santiam ≃	202	44.41 N	123.00 W
North Saskatchewan ≃	176	53.15 N	105.05 W
North Saugeen ≃	212	44.19 N	81.17 W
North Scituate, Ma., U.S.	207	42.13 N	70.47 W
North Scituate, R.I., U.S.	207	41.49 N	71.35 W
North Sea ⊤2	22	56.00 N	3.00 E
North Seaton Colliery	44	55.11 N	1.32 W
North Shafter	226	35.31 N	119.18 W
North Shields	44	55.01 N	1.27 W
Norths Highland ⋀1	9	66.40 S	126.00 E
North Shoal Lake ⊜	184	50.29 N	97.40 W
North Shore	216	42.16 N	88.23 W
Northshore ◆9	283	42.32 N	70.57 W
North Shore Channel ≡	278	42.05 N	87.41 W
North Shores	216	41.50 N	83.25 W
North Shoshone Peak ∧	204	39.09 N	117.29 W
North Siberian Lowland → Severo-Sibirskaja nizmennost' ≚	74	73.00 N	100.00 E
Northside	174h	2.47 S	171.43 W
North Sioux City	198	42.31 N	96.28 W
North Skunk ≃	190	41.15 N	92.02 W
North Somercotes	44	53.28 N	0.08 E
North Sound ⊔, Antig.	240c	17.07 N	61.45 W
North Sound ⊔, Ire.	48	53.11 N	9.43 W
North Sound ⊔, Scot., U.K.	46	59.18 N	2.46 W
North Spicer Island I	176	68.30 N	78.55 W
North Spirit Lake ⊜	184	52.30 N	92.53 W
North Spot I	236	16.15 N	88.11 W
North Springfield, Pa., U.S.	214	41.59 N	80.26 W
North Springfield, Va., U.S.	284c	38.48 N	77.12 W
North Stamford Reservoir ⊜1	276	41.08 N	73.32 W
North Star, De., U.S.	285	39.46 N	75.43 W
North Star, Oh., U.S.	216	40.19 N	84.34 W
North Sterling Reservoir ⊜1	198	40.47 N	103.17 W
North Stradbroke Island I	171a	27.35 S	153.28 E
North Sudbury	283	42.24 N	71.24 W
North Sulphur ≃	196	33.23 N	95.18 W
North Sunday Creek ≃	202	46.27 N	105.54 W
North Sunderland	44	55.34 N	1.39 W
North Swansea	207	41.46 N	71.15 W
North Sydenham ≃	214	42.35 N	82.23 W
North Sydney, Austl.	274a	33.50 S	151.13 E
North Sydney, N.S., Can.	186	46.13 N	60.15 W
North Syracuse	210	43.08 N	76.07 W
North Tamborine	171a	27.56 S	153.11 E
North Taranaki Bight c3	172	38.42 S	174.15 E
North Tarrytown	276	41.05 N	73.51 W
North Tawton	42	50.48 N	3.53 W
North Tea Lake ⊜	190	45.56 N	79.03 W
North Terre Haute	194	39.31 N	87.21 W
North Tewksbury	283	42.38 N	71.14 W
North Thames ≃	212	42.59 N	81.16 W
North Thompson ≃	182	50.41 N	120.21 W
North Tidworth	42	51.16 N	1.40 W
North Toe ≃	192	36.00 N	82.16 W
North Tolsta	46	58.20 N	6.13 W
North Tonawanda	210	43.02 N	78.51 W
North Towanda	210	41.47 N	76.28 W
North Troy	206	44.59 N	72.24 W
North Truro	207	42.02 N	70.05 W
North Tule Draw V	196	34.30 N	101.36 W
North Tunica	194	34.42 N	90.23 W
North Turlock	226	37.31 N	120.51 W
North Turramurra	274a	33.43 S	150.09 E
North Twin Lake ⊜	186	49.16 N	55.56 W
North Tyne ≃	44	54.59 N	2.08 W
North Ubian Island I	116	6.09 N	120.27 E
North Uist I	46	57.36 N	7.18 W
Northumberland	210	40.53 N	76.47 W
Northumberland □6, On., Can.	212	44.10 N	78.00 W
Northumberland □6, Eng., U.K.	44	55.15 N	2.05 W
Northumberland □6, Pa., U.S.	210	40.49 N	76.39 W
Northumberland □6, Va., U.S.	208	37.50 N	76.25 W
Northumberland Isles II	166	21.40 S	150.00 E
Northumberland National Park ♦	44	55.15 N	2.20 W
Northumberland Strait ⊔	186	46.00 N	63.30 W
North Umpqua ≃	202	43.16 N	123.27 W
North Uxbridge	207	42.05 N	71.38 W
Northvale	276	41.00 N	73.56 W
North Valley Hills ⋀2	285	40.02 N	75.40 W
North Valley Stream	276	40.41 N	73.42 W
North Vancouver	224	49.19 N	123.04 W
North Vandergrift	279b	40.36 N	79.34 W
North Vernon	218	39.00 N	85.37 W
North Versailles	279b	40.22 N	79.48 W
North Vietnam → Vietnam □1	108	16.00 N	108.00 E
North Vijayapuri	122	16.52 N	79.35 E
Northville, Mi., U.S.	216	42.25 N	83.29 W
Northville, N.Y., U.S.	210	43.13 N	74.10 W
Northville Downs ◆	281	42.26 N	83.29 W
Northvue	214	40.50 N	79.56 W
Northwaa	46	59.16 N	2.17 W
North Wabasca Lake ⊜	182	56.00 N	113.55 W
North Wales	208	40.12 N	75.16 W
North Walsham	42	52.50 N	1.24 E
North Wantagh	276	40.41 N	73.30 W
North Warren	214	41.52 N	79.09 W
North Washington, Pa., U.S.	214	41.03 N	79.49 W
North Washington, Pa., U.S.	279b	40.32 N	79.36 W
North Watuppa Pond ⊜	207	41.42 N	71.06 W
Northway	180	62.58 N	141.56 W
North Wazīristān □5	123	33.10 N	70.30 E
North Weald Bassett	42	51.43 N	0.10 E
North Webster	216	41.19 N	85.41 W
North Weissport	210	40.50 N	75.41 W
North West □5	246	7.45 N	59.30 W
Northwest ≃	208	36.31 N	76.05 W
North West Aboriginal Reserve ◆4	162	27.00 S	130.30 E
North West Cape ≻, Austl.	162	21.45 S	114.10 E
Northwest Cape ≻, Ak., U.S.	180	63.46 N	171.45 W
Northwest Cape ≻, Fl., U.S.	220	25.13 N	81.11 W
North Westchester	207	41.34 N	72.24 W
North Western	210	43.20 N	75.22 W
North-Western □4	154	13.00 S	25.00 E
Northwestern University ⊍2, Il., U.S.	278	42.04 N	87.40 W
Northwestern University (Chicago Campus) ⊍2, Il., U.S.	278	41.54 N	87.37 W
Northwest Frontier □4	120	34.30 N	72.00 E
Northwest Gander ≃	186	48.50 N	55.00 W
Northwest Harbor c	284b	39.16 N	76.35 W
Northwest Head ≻	116	10.08 N	118.45 E
Northwest Miramichi ≃	186	46.58 N	65.35 W
Northwest Pacific Basin ◆1	6	40.00 N	155.00 E
North West Point ≻	174o	2.02 N	157.29 W
Northwest Providence Channel ⊔	238	26.10 N	78.20 W
North West River	176	53.32 N	60.08 W
Northwest Territories □4	176	70.00 N	100.00 W
North Weymouth	283	42.15 N	70.57 W
Northwich	44	53.16 N	2.32 W
North Wichita ≃	196	33.43 N	99.29 W
North Wilbraham	207	42.09 N	72.25 W
North Wildwood	208	39.00 N	74.47 W
North Wilkesboro	192	36.09 N	81.08 W
North Willow Creek ≃	202	46.51 N	107.54 W
North Wilmington	283	42.34 N	71.09 W
North Windham, Ct., U.S.	207	41.44 N	72.09 W
North Windham, Me., U.S.	188	43.50 N	70.26 W
Northwold	42	52.33 N	0.35 E
Northwood, Eng., U.K.	42	50.44 N	1.19 W
Northwood, Ia., U.S.	190	43.26 N	93.13 W
Northwood, Mi., U.S.	216	42.19 N	85.38 W
Northwood, N.D., U.S.	198	47.44 N	97.33 W
Northwood, Oh., U.S.	214	41.36 N	83.28 W
Northwood ◆8	260	51.37 N	0.25 W
North Woodslee	281	42.13 N	82.43 W
Northwood Village	284c	39.02 N	77.01 W
North Yamhill ≃	224	45.13 N	123.08 W
North Yelta	168b	34.03 S	137.37 E
North York	212	43.46 N	79.25 W
North York Moors ⋀2	44	54.24 N	0.53 W
North York Moors National Park ♦	44	54.23 N	0.50 W
North Yorkshire □6	44	54.15 N	1.30 W
North Yuba ≃	226	39.22 N	121.08 W
North Zulch	222	30.55 N	96.07 W
Norton, N.B., Can.	186	45.38 N	65.42 W
Norton, Eng., U.K.	44	54.09 N	0.47 W
Norton, Eng., U.K.	262	53.20 N	2.40 W
Norton, Ks., U.S.	198	39.50 N	99.53 W
Norton, Ma., U.S.	207	41.58 N	71.11 W
Norton, Oh., U.S.	214	41.01 N	81.39 W
Norton, Vt., U.S.	206	45.00 N	71.47 W
Norton, Va., U.S.	192	36.56 N	82.37 W
Norton, Zimb.	154	17.53 S	30.42 E
Norton Air Force Base ■	228	34.06 N	117.14 W
Norton Basin c	276	40.36 N	73.47 W
Norton Bay c	180	64.45 N	161.15 W
Norton Creek ≃	281	42.34 N	83.34 W
Norton Fitzwarren	42	51.02 N	3.09 W
Norton Grove	207	42.00 N	71.12 W
Norton Heath	260	51.43 N	0.19 E
Norton Hill	210	42.25 N	74.04 W
Norton Pond ⊜	206	44.56 N	71.51 W
Norton Reservoir ⊜1	283	41.59 N	71.12 W
Norton Shores	216	43.10 N	86.15 W
Norton Sound ⊔	180	63.50 N	164.00 W
Nortonville, On., Can.	275b	43.43 N	79.44 W
Nortonville, Ks., U.S.	198	39.25 N	95.20 W
Nortorf, B.R.D.	30	54.10 N	9.50 E
Nortorf, B.R.D.	52	53.55 N	9.16 E
Nort-sur-Erdre	32	47.26 N	1.30 W
Noruega → Norway □1	24	62.00 N	10.00 E
Noruega, Mar de → Norwegian Sea ⊤2	10	70.00 N	2.00 E
Norumbega Reservoir ⊜1	283	42.20 N	71.18 W
Nørup	41	55.43 N	9.19 E
Norval	212	43.39 N	79.51 W
Norvalspont	158	30.38 S	25.27 E
Norvège → Norway □1	24	62.00 N	10.00 E
Norvegia, Cape ≻	9	71.25 S	12.18 W
Norvell	216	42.21 N	84.16 W
Norvelt	214	40.12 N	79.32 W
Norvin Green State Forest ♠	276	41.03 N	74.20 W
Norwalk, Ca., U.S.	228	33.54 N	118.04 W
Norwalk, Ct., U.S.	207	41.07 N	73.24 W
Norwalk, Ia., U.S.	190	41.28 N	93.40 W
Norwalk, Oh., U.S.	214	41.14 N	82.36 W
Norwalk ≃	207	41.06 N	73.25 W
Norwalk Harbor c	276	41.06 N	73.24 W
Norwalk Islands II	276	41.04 N	73.24 W
Norway, In., U.S.	216	40.47 N	86.46 W
Norway, Ia., U.S.	190	41.54 N	91.55 W
Norway, Me., U.S.	188	44.12 N	70.32 W
Norway, Mi., U.S.	190	45.47 N	87.54 W
Norway (Norge) □1, Europe	22	62.00 N	10.00 E
Norway (Norge) □1, Europe	24	62.00 N	10.00 E
Norway Bay c	176	71.08 N	104.35 W
Norway House	184	53.59 N	97.50 W
Norway Lake ⊜	212	45.20 N	76.43 W
Norwegen → Norway □1	24	62.00 N	10.00 E
Norwegian Basin ◆1	10	68.00 N	2.00 W
Norwegian Sea ⊤2	10	70.00 N	2.00 E
Norwegian Trench ◆1	10	59.00 N	4.30 E
Norwell	283	42.09 N	70.47 W
Norwich, On., Can.	212	42.59 N	80.36 W
Norwich, Eng., U.K.	42	52.38 N	1.18 E
Norwich, Ct., U.S.	207	41.32 N	72.05 W
Norwich, Ks., U.S.	198	37.27 N	97.50 W
Norwich, N.Y., U.S.	210	42.31 N	75.31 W
Norwich Airport ⊠	42	52.31 N	1.15 E
Norwin Heights	279b	40.20 N	79.44 W
Norwood, On., Can.	212	44.23 N	77.59 W
Norwood, Co., U.S.	200	38.07 N	108.17 W
Norwood, Ma., U.S.	207	42.11 N	71.12 W
Norwood, Mn., U.S.	190	44.46 N	93.55 W
Norwood, N.J., U.S.	276	40.59 N	73.57 W
Norwood, N.Y., U.S.	188	44.45 N	74.59 W
Norwood, N.C., U.S.	192	35.13 N	80.07 W
Norwood, Oh., U.S.	218	39.10 N	84.27 W
Norwood, Pa., U.S.	285	39.53 N	75.17 W
Norwood ◆8	273d	26.10 S	28.04 E
Norwood Memorial Airport ⊠	283	42.11 N	71.10 W
Norwood Park ◆8	278	41.59 N	87.48 W
Norwood Pond ⊜	283	42.35 N	70.52 W
Norwoodville	190	41.39 N	93.33 W
Noryang	98	34.56 N	127.52 E
Norzagaray	116	14.54 N	121.02 E
Nosaka	94	35.39 N	140.34 E
Nosappu-misaki ≻	92a	43.23 N	145.49 E
Nosate	266b	45.33 N	8.43 E
Nosbonsing, Lake ⊜	190	46.12 N	79.13 W
Nose	96	34.58 N	135.24 E
Nose ◆8	270	34.49 N	135.09 E
Nose Creek ≃	182	54.52 N	119.38 W
Noshiro	92	40.12 N	140.02 E
Noska ≃	86	58.53 N	68.40 E
Nosop (Nossob) ≃	156	26.55 S	20.37 E
Nosova	86	59.30 N	63.13 E
Nosovaja, S.S.S.R.	24	68.15 N	54.35 E
Nosovaja, S.S.S.R.	80	57.15 N	45.35 E
Nosovka	78	50.55 N	31.35 E
Nosovo, S.S.S.R.	76	57.07 N	27.50 E
Nosovo, S.S.S.R.	83	47.16 N	38.40 E
Nosovščina	24	62.56 N	37.03 E
Noṣratābād	128	29.54 N	59.59 E
Noss, Isle of I	46a	60.09 N	1.01 W
Nossa Senhora da Aparecida	256	22.02 S	42.48 W
Nossa Senhora das Dores	250	10.29 S	37.13 W
Nossa Senhora do Amparo	256	22.22 S	44.05 W
Nossa Senhora do Livramento	248	15.48 S	56.22 W
Nossa Senhora do Ó ◆8	287b	23.30 S	46.41 W
Nossebro	26	58.11 N	12.43 E
Nossen	54	51.03 N	13.17 E
Nossentiner Heide ◆3	54	53.35 N	12.25 E
Noss Head ≻	46	58.28 N	3.04 W
Nossob	156	22.18 S	17.10 E
Nossob (Nosop) ≃	156	26.55 S	20.37 E
Nossombougou	150	13.06 N	7.56 W
Nošul'	24	60.09 N	49.28 E
Nosy Varika	157b	20.35 S	48.32 E
Notasulga	194	32.33 N	85.40 W
Notch Cliff	284b	39.27 N	76.31 W
Notch Hill	182	50.52 N	119.26 W
Notch Peak ∧	200	39.08 N	113.24 W
Noteć ≃	30	52.44 N	15.26 E
Notengo, Laguna de c	234	16.12 N	98.07 W
Notigi Lake ⊜	184	55.57 N	99.18 W
Notikewin ≃	176	57.15 N	117.05 W
Noto, It.	70	36.53 N	15.04 E
Noto, Nihon	92	37.18 N	137.09 E
Noto, Golfo di c	70	36.50 N	15.12 E
Noto, Val di ◆1	70	37.05 N	14.35 E
Noto Antica ⊥	70	36.56 N	15.02 E
Notodden	26	59.34 N	9.17 E
Notogawa	94	35.10 N	136.10 E
Noto-hantō ≻1	92	37.20 N	137.00 E
Noto-hantō-kokutei-kōen ♠	94	37.10 N	136.50 E
Noto-jima	94	37.08 N	137.00 E
Noto-jima I	94	37.07 N	137.00 E
Nōtori-dake ∧	94	35.37 N	138.15 E
Notoro-ko ⊜	92a	44.05 N	144.10 E
Notozero, ozero ⊜	24	66.28 N	32.05 E
Notre-Dame	186	46.19 N	64.43 W
Notre-Dame ⊍1	261	48.51 N	2.21 E
Notre-Dame, Bois ♠	261	48.45 N	2.35 E
Notre-Dame, Monts ⋀	186	48.10 N	68.00 W
Notre-Dame, Ruisseau ≃	275a	45.41 N	73.26 W
Notre Dame Bay c	186	49.45 N	55.15 W
Notre-Dame-de-Bellecombe	62	45.48 N	6.31 E
Notre-Dame-de-Lorette ⊍1	50	50.25 N	2.42 E
Notre-Dame-de-Lourdes	184	49.32 N	98.33 W
Notre-Dame-de-Pierreville	206	46.06 N	72.53 W
Notre-Dame-des-Victoires ◆8	275a	45.35 N	73.34 W
Notre-Dame-du-Haut ⊍1, Fr.	32	47.43 N	6.37 E
Notre-Dame-du-Haut ⊍1, Fr.	58	47.43 N	6.37 E
Notre-Dame-du-Laus	188	46.05 N	75.37 W
Notre-Dame-du-Nord	190	47.36 N	79.30 W
Notrees	196	31.55 N	102.45 W
Notreure ≃	50	47.41 N	2.36 E
Notsu	96	33.02 N	131.42 E
Notsuharu	96	33.09 N	131.32 E
Nottawa	216	41.55 N	85.27 W
Nottawa Creek ≃	216	42.01 N	85.24 W
Nottawasaga ≃	212	44.32 N	80.01 W
Nottawasaga Bay c	212	44.35 N	80.15 W
Nottaway ≃	176	51.22 N	79.55 W
Nottingham, Eng., U.K.	42	52.58 N	1.10 W
Nottingham, Pa., U.S.	208	39.45 N	76.01 W
Nottingham, Pa., U.S.	285	40.07 N	74.58 W
Nottingham Island I	176	63.20 N	77.55 W
Nottingham Park	278	41.46 N	87.48 W
Nottingham Road	158	29.22 S	30.00 E
Nottinghamshire □6	44	53.00 N	1.00 W
Notting Hill	274b	37.54 S	145.08 E
Nottleben	54	50.58 N	10.50 E
Nottoway	192	37.08 N	78.05 W
Nottoway ≃	192	36.33 N	76.55 W
Nottuln	52	51.55 N	7.22 E
Notukeu Creek ≃	184	49.55 N	106.30 W
Nouâdhibou	148	20.54 N	17.04 W
Nouâdhibou, Râs ≻	148	20.46 N	17.03 W
Nouakchott	150	18.06 N	15.57 W
Nouâmghâr	150	19.22 N	16.31 W
Nouan-le-Fuzelier	50	47.32 N	2.02 E
Nouans-les-Fontaines	50	47.08 N	1.18 E
Nouméa	175f	22.16 S	166.27 E
Noun ≃	152	4.55 N	11.06 E
Nouna	150	12.44 N	3.52 W
Nounsley	260	51.46 N	0.36 E
Noupoort	158	31.10 S	24.57 E
Nous	158	28.44 S	19.52 E
Nouveau Brunswick → New Brunswick □4	186	46.30 N	66.15 W
Nouveau Mexique → New Mexico □3	178	34.30 N	106.00 W
Nouveau-Québec, Cratère du ±6	176	61.17 N	73.40 W
Nouvelle	186	48.08 N	66.19 W
Nouvelle ≃	186	48.07 N	66.18 W
Nouvelle-Calédonie → New Caledonia □2	175f	21.30 S	165.30 E
Nouvelle-Calédonie (New Caledonia) I	175f	21.30 S	165.30 E
Nouvelle Écosse → Nova Scotia □4	186	45.00 N	63.00 W
Nouvelle-France, Cap de ≻	176	62.27 N	73.42 W
Nouvelle Galles du Sud → New South Wales □3	166	33.00 S	146.00 E
Nouvelle-Orléans → New Orleans	194	29.58 N	90.07 W
Nouvelles-Hébrides → Vanuatu □1	175f	16.00 S	167.00 E
Nouvelle Zélande → New Zealand □1	172	41.00 S	174.00 E
Nouvelle Zemble → Novaja Zeml'a II	72	74.00 N	57.00 E
Nouvion-en-Ponthieu	50	50.12 N	1.47 E
Nouvion-sur-Meuse	56	49.42 N	4.48 E
Nouzonville	56	49.49 N	4.45 E
Nova, Magy.	61	46.41 N	16.41 E
Nova, Oh., U.S.	214	41.02 N	82.18 W
Nova, Ilha I	250	0.20 N	49.40 W
Nova América	255	15.01 S	49.56 W
Nova Andradina	255	22.10 S	53.15 W
Nova Aurora	255	18.04 S	48.16 W
Novabad, S.S.S.R.	85	39.01 N	70.09 E
Novabad, S.S.S.R.	85	38.37 N	68.45 E
Nová Baňa	30	48.26 N	18.39 E
Nová Bystřice	61	49.01 N	15.06 E
Nova Cachoeirinha ◆8	287b	23.28 S	46.40 W
Nova Caipemba	152	7.26 S	14.38 E
Novacella ⊍1	64	46.44 N	11.39 E
Nova Cintra	256	22.13 S	46.46 W
Nova Era	255	19.45 S	43.03 W
Nova Esperança	255	23.08 S	52.13 W
Nova Fátima	255	23.29 S	50.33 W
Novafeltria	66	43.53 N	12.17 E
Nova Friburgo	256	22.16 S	42.32 W
Nova Goa → Panaji	122	15.29 N	73.50 E
Nova Gorica	64	45.57 N	13.39 E
Nova Gradiška	36	45.16 N	17.23 E
Nova Granada	255	20.29 S	49.19 W
Nova Iguaçu	256	22.45 S	43.27 W
Nova Iguaçu □7	287a	22.45 S	43.29 W
Novaja, S.S.S.R.	82	55.13 N	38.54 E
Novaja, S.S.S.R.	265b	55.48 N	38.03 E
Novaja ◆8	265a	60.02 N	30.28 E
Novaja Astrachan'	83	49.07 N	38.36 E
Novaja Belaja	78	49.46 N	39.11 E
Novaja Belokoroviči	78	51.07 N	28.02 E
Novaja Binaradka	80	53.48 N	49.56 E
Novaja Borovaja	78	50.42 N	28.39 E
Novaja Čigla	78	51.13 N	40.28 E
Novaja Derevn'a, S.S.S.R.	82	54.01 N	38.53 E
Novaja Derevn'a, S.S.S.R.	88	57.15 N	103.08 E
Novaja Ivanovka	78	45.55 N	29.05 E
Novaja Janisol'	83	47.17 N	37.16 E
Novaja Kachovka	78	46.45 N	33.23 E
Novaja Kalitva	78	50.06 N	40.01 E
Novaja Kazanka	80	48.57 N	49.36 E
Novaja Kazmaska	80	56.49 N	53.31 E
Novaja Kriuša	78	50.16 N	41.16 E
Novaja Ladoga	76	60.05 N	32.16 E
Novaja L'al'a	86	59.03 N	60.36 E
Novaja Majačka	78	46.36 N	33.14 E
Novaja Maluksa	76	59.39 N	31.21 E
Novaja Malykla	80	54.13 N	49.57 E
Novaja Mojgora	82	54.27 N	38.32 E
Novaja Odessa	78	47.19 N	31.47 E
Novaja Porubežka	80	51.45 N	49.40 E
Novaja Praga	78	48.33 N	32.54 E
Novaja Ropša	265a	59.45 N	29.53 E
Novaja Sibir', ostrov I	74	75.00 N	149.00 E
Novaja Sloboda	78	51.23 N	34.08 E
Novaja Slobodka	82	54.56 N	36.47 E
Novaja Šul'ba	86	50.33 N	81.20 E
Novaja Uda	88	54.07 N	103.33 E
Novaja Ušica	78	48.49 N	27.16 E
Novaja Usman'	78	51.37 N	39.24 E
Novaja Vodolaga	78	49.43 N	35.52 E
Novaja Zburjevka	78	46.28 N	32.24 E
Novaja Zeml'a II	72	74.00 N	57.00 E
Nováky	30	48.43 N	18.34 E
Nova Lamego	150	12.19 N	14.11 W
Novale (Rauth)	64	46.24 N	11.30 E
Novalesa	62	45.11 N	7.01 E
Novaliches Reservoir ⊜1	269f	14.43 N	121.05 E
Nova Lima	255	19.59 S	43.51 W
Nova Lisboa → Huambo	152	12.44 S	15.47 E
Nova Lusitânia	156	19.54 S	34.35 E
Nova Mambone	156	20.59 S	35.01 E
Nova Milanese	266b	45.35 N	9.12 E
Nova Nabúri	154	16.46 S	38.57 E
Nova Olinda	250	7.06 S	39.40 W
Nova Olinda, Riacho ≃	250	8.05 S	42.34 W
Nova Olinda do Norte	246	3.45 S	59.03 W
Nová Paka	30	50.29 N	15.31 E
Nova Ponente (Deutschnofen)	64	46.25 N	11.25 E
Nova Ponte	255	19.08 S	47.41 W
Nova Prata	252	28.47 S	51.36 W
Novar	212	45.27 N	79.15 W
Novara	62	45.28 N	8.38 E
Novara □4	62	45.40 N	8.30 E
Novara di Sicilia	70	38.01 N	15.08 E
Nova Resende	255	21.08 S	46.25 W
Nová Role	54	50.15 N	12.47 E
Nova Roma	255	13.51 S	46.57 W
Nova Russas	250	4.42 S	40.34 W
Nova Scotia □4, Can.	176	45.00 N	63.00 W
Nova Scotia □4, Can.	186	45.00 N	63.00 W
Nova Siri	68	40.09 N	16.32 E
Nova Sofala	156	20.09 S	34.42 E
Nova Soure	250	11.14 S	38.29 W
Novate Mezzola	58	46.15 N	9.27 E
Novate Milanese	266b	45.32 N	9.08 E
Nova Timboteua	250	1.12 S	47.24 W
Novato	226	38.06 N	122.34 W
Novato Creek ≃	282	38.06 N	122.29 W
Nova Vandúzi	156	18.57 S	33.16 E
Nova Varoš	38	43.28 N	19.48 E
Nova Venécia	255	18.43 S	40.24 W
Nova Veneza	252	28.39 S	49.30 W
Nova Vida	248	10.11 S	62.47 W
Nova Vida, Cachoeira ∟	248	9.25 S	63.36 W
Nova Zagora	38	42.29 N	26.01 E
Nove	64	45.43 N	11.40 E
Nové Hrady	61	48.47 N	14.37 E
Novelda	34	38.23 N	0.46 W
Novellara	64	44.51 N	10.44 E
Novelty	219	40.00 N	92.12 W
Nové Město	30	50.21 N	16.09 E
Nové Město nad Váhom	30	48.46 N	17.49 E
Nové Město na Moravě	30	49.34 N	16.04 E
Nové Mlýny, údolní nádrž ⊜1	61	48.54 N	16.34 E
Noventa di Piave	64	45.39 N	12.31 E
Noventa Padovana	64	45.24 N	11.58 E
Noventa Vicentina	64	45.17 N	11.32 E
Noves	62	43.52 N	4.54 E
Nové Sedlo	54	50.10 N	12.42 E
Nové Strašecí	54	50.07 N	13.53 E
Nové Údolí	60	48.48 N	13.48 E
Nové Zámky	30	47.59 N	18.11 E
Novgorod	76	58.31 N	31.17 E
Novgorodka	78	48.21 N	32.39 E
Novgorod-Severskij	78	51.59 N	33.16 E
Novgorodskoje	83	48.20 N	37.50 E
Novi	216	42.28 N	83.28 W
Novi Bečej	38	45.36 N	20.08 E
Novice	196	31.59 N	99.37 W

Name	Seite	Breite°′	Länge°′ E = Ost
Novičicha	86	52.13 N	81.24 E
Novi di Modena	64	44.54 N	10.54 E
Novigrad, Jugo.	36	45.19 N	13.34 E
Novigrad, Jugo.	36	44.11 N	15.33 E
Novikovo, S.S.S.R.	86	58.15 N	80.39 E
Novikovo, S.S.S.R.	89	46.23 N	143.20 E
Novi Ligure	62	44.46 N	8.47 E
Noville	56	50.40 N	5.23 E
Novi Lyon Drain ≅	281	42.30 N	83.38 W
Novinger	194	40.13 N	92.42 W
Novinka	76	59.49 N	33.20 E
Novion-Porcien	50	49.36 N	4.25 E
Novi Pazar, Blg.	38	43.21 N	27.12 E
Novi Pazar, Jugo.	38	43.08 N	20.31 E
Novi Sad	38	45.15 N	19.50 E
Novi Vinodolski	36	45.08 N	14.48 E
Novka	76	55.27 N	30.24 E
Novki	80	56.22 N	41.06 E
Novl'anka	80	55.48 N	41.44 E
Novlenskoje	76	59.37 N	39.20 E
Nôvo ≃, Bra.	248	4.55 S	70.33 W
Nôvo ≃, Bra.	250	4.30 S	53.50 W
Nôvo ≃, Bra.	250	6.22 S	55.42 W
Novo ≃, Bra.	256	21.23 S	42.44 W
Novo, Lago ⊜	250	1.30 N	50.40 W
Novoachtyrka	83	48.55 N	38.49 E
Nôvo Acôrdo	255	13.10 S	46.48 W
Novoajdar	83	48.57 N	39.00 E
Novoaleksandrovka, S.S.S.R.	80	51.56 N	52.26 E
Novoaleksandrovka, S.S.S.R.	83	48.17 N	39.37 E
Novoaleksandrovka, S.S.S.R.	83	49.08 N	39.17 E
Novoaleksandrovka, S.S.S.R.	86	51.47 N	68.49 E
Novoaleksandrovo	265b	55.59 N	37.33 E
Novoaleksandrovsk	80	45.29 N	41.16 E
Novoaleksejevka, S.S.S.R.	78	46.06 N	32.30 E
Novoaleksejevka, S.S.S.R.	78	46.13 N	34.39 E
Novoaleksejevka, S.S.S.R.	86	52.56 N	64.41 E
Novoaleksejevka, S.S.S.R.	86	52.47 N	74.54 E
Novoaleksejevka, S.S.S.R.	86	50.08 N	55.39 E
Novoaltajsk	86	53.24 N	83.58 E
Novoamvrosijevskoje	83	47.49 N	38.29 E
Novoanninskij	80	50.32 N	42.41 E
Novoarchangel'sk	78	48.39 N	30.48 E
Novoarchangel'skoje	265b	55.55 N	37.33 E
Novo Aripuanã	246	5.08 S	60.22 W
Novoasbest	86	57.44 N	60.45 E
Novoazovsk	83	47.08 N	38.05 E
Novobachmutovka	83	48.15 N	37.48 E
Novobatajsk	83	46.54 N	39.47 E
Novobelaja	78	49.49 N	39.18 E
Novobessergenovka	83	47.11 N	38.51 E
Novobogatinskoje	80	47.22 N	51.11 E
Novobogdanovka	78	47.06 N	35.29 E
Novobogordskoje	80	53.11 N	53.56 E
Novoborovaja	83	49.15 N	38.33 E
Novo Brasil	255	16.11 S	50.38 W
Novobratcevskij	82	55.51 N	37.23 E
Novoburejskij	89	49.49 N	129.54 E
Novočeboksarsk	80	56.08 N	47.30 E
Novo Čeremšansk	80	54.21 N	50.10 E
Novočerkassk	83	47.25 N	40.06 E
Novočernorečenskij	86	56.16 N	91.06 E
Novocharitonovo	82	55.35 N	38.30 E
Novocherkassk → Novočerkassk	83	47.25 N	40.06 E
Novochop'orsk	80	51.07 N	41.37 E
Novochop'orskij	80	51.06 N	41.33 E
Novochovrino ◆8	265b	55.52 N	37.30 E
Novociml'anskaja	80	47.59 N	42.17 E
Nôvo Cruzeiro	255	17.29 S	41.53 W
Novodanilovka	78	46.38 N	35.00 E
Novoderev'ankov-Skaja	78	46.19 N	38.45 E
Novoderkul	83	49.08 N	39.38 E
Novodevičje	80	53.37 N	48.52 E
Novodolinka	86	51.12 N	72.33 E
Novodolinskij	86	49.44 N	72.45 E
Novodoroninskoje	88	51.08 N	112.08 E
Novodružesk	83	48.58 N	38.21 E
Novodubovoje	76	52.19 N	39.13 E
Novodugino	76	55.38 N	34.18 E
Novodvinsk	24	64.26 N	40.47 E
Novodžerelijevskaja	78	45.46 N	38.41 E
Novoekonomičeskoje	83	48.18 N	37.15 E
Novofetinino	82	56.14 N	39.17 E
Novogaritovo	80	52.47 N	40.07 E
Novogirejevo ◆8	265b	55.45 N	37.49 E
Novogorbovo	82	55.43 N	36.29 E
Novogornyj	86	55.37 N	60.47 E
Novograd-Volynskij	78	50.36 N	27.36 E
Novogrigorjevka	78	46.24 N	34.59 E
Novogrigorjevskaja	80	49.26 N	43.37 E
Novogrodovka	83	48.13 N	37.20 E
Novogroznenskij	84	43.15 N	46.15 E
Novogrudok	76	53.36 N	25.50 E
Novogupalovka	78	48.02 N	35.26 E
Novo Hamburgo	252	29.41 S	51.08 W
Novo Horizonte	255	21.28 S	49.13 W
Novoignatjevka	83	47.38 N	37.41 E
Novoiljinsk	88	51.42 N	108.41 E
Novoiljinskij	86	57.54 N	55.30 E
Novoivanovka, S.S.S.R.	78	49.44 N	33.28 E
Novoivanovka, S.S.S.R.	83	47.41 N	38.23 E
Novoivanovka, S.S.S.R.	85	43.08 N	71.26 E
Novoivanovskoje	265b	55.43 N	37.22 E
Novoizborsk	76	57.50 N	27.59 E
Novojampol'	89	52.55 N	127.38 E
Novojamskoje	76	52.14 N	34.28 E
Novoje, S.S.S.R.	82	55.38 N	38.55 E
Novoje, S.S.S.R.	86	58.53 N	68.40 E
Novoje Alechnovo	82	56.02 N	36.49 E
Novojegorjevskoje	86	51.46 N	80.53 E
Novojekaterinovka	83	47.43 N	38.07 E
Novoje Koval'ovo	265a	59.59 N	30.34 E
Novoje Leušino	80	56.48 N	40.32 E
Novojel'n'a	76	53.28 N	25.35 E
Novojenisejsk	86	58.16 N	92.24 E
Novoje Pavšino	82	54.15 N	37.07 E
Novoje Zarečje	76	57.43 N	34.22 E
Novokačalinsk	89	45.06 N	132.01 E
Novokadinsk	88	54.46 N	101.24 E
Novokamala	88	55.58 N	94.58 E
Novokarasuk	86	56.16 N	71.46 E
Novokaširovo	80	54.58 N	52.32 E
Novokaširsk	82	54.51 N	38.15 E
Novokazalinsk	86	45.50 N	62.10 E
Novokijevskij	80	50.27 N	43.08 E
Novokorsunskaja	78	45.38 N	39.09 E
Novokrasn'anka	83	49.08 N	38.18 E
Novokrasnoje	78	48.01 N	31.21 E
Novokručininskij	88	51.46 N	113.48 E
Novokubanka	86	51.40 N	70.44 E
Novokujbyševsk	80	53.07 N	49.58 E
Novokurovka	89	48.51 N	134.20 E
Novokuzneck	86	53.45 N	87.06 E
Novokuznetsk → Novokuzneck	86	53.45 N	87.06 E
Novolakskoje	84	43.07 N	46.29 E
Novolazarevskaja ⊍3	9	70.45 S	11.50 E
Novoleuškovskaja	78	45.59 N	39.58 E
Novoli	68	40.23 N	18.03 E
Novolimarevka	83	49.17 N	39.36 E
Novolukoml'	76	54.40 N	29.08 E
Novol'vovsk	76	53.55 N	38.47 E
Novomalorossijskaja	78	45.38 N	39.53 E
Novomansurkino	80	53.52 N	51.52 E
Novomargaritovka	83	46.54 N	38.50 E
Novomariinka	88	55.27 N	96.01 E
Novomarkovka	86	51.44 N	72.17 E
Novomel'nikov	84	43.56 N	45.09 E
Novomelovatka	78	50.27 N	40.46 E

Symbols in the index entries represent the broad categories identified in the key at the right. Symbols with superior numbers (⋀1) identify subcategories (see complete key on page *I* · *1*).

Kartensymbole in dem Registerverzeichnis stellen die rechts in Schlüssel erklärten Kategorien dar. Symbole mit hochgestellten Ziffern (⋀1) bezeichnen Unterabteilungen einer Kategorie (vgl. vollständiger Schlüssel auf Seite *I* · *1*).

Los símbolos incluídos en el texto del índice representan las grandes categorías identificadas con la clave a la derecha. Los símbolos con numeros en su parte superior (⋀1) identifican las subcategorías (véase la clave completa en la página *I* · *1*).

Les symboles de l'index représentent les catégories indiquées dans la légende à droite. Les symboles suivis d'un indice (⋀1) représentent des sous-catégories (voir légende complète à la page *I* · *1*).

Os símbolos incluídos no texto do índice representam as grandes categorias identificadas com a chave à direita. Os símbolos com números em sua parte superior (⋀1) identificam as subcategorias (veja-se a chave completa à página *I* · *1*).

English	Deutsch	Español	Français	Português
∧ Mountain	Berg	Montaña	Montagne	Montanha
⋀ Mountains	Berge	Montañas	Montagnes	Montanhas
)(Pass	Pass	Paso	Col	Passo
V Valley, Canyon	Tal, Cañon	Valle, Cañón	Vallée, Canyon	Vale, Canhão
≚ Plain	Ebene	Llano	Plaine	Planície
≻ Cape	Kap	Cabo	Cap	Cabo
I Island	Insel	Isla	Île	Ilha
II Islands	Inseln	Islas	Îles	Ilhas
± Other Topographic Features	Andere Topographische Objekte	Otros Elementos Topográficos	Autres données topographiques	Outros acidentes topográficos

O

Symbol	English	Deutsch	Español	Français	Português
≃	River	Fluss	Río	Rivière	Rio
≍	Canal	Kanal	Canal	Canal	Canal
∟	Waterfall, Rapids	Wasserfall, Stromschnellen	Cascada, Rápidos	Chute d'eau, Rapides	Cascata, Rápidos
⊔	Strait	Meeresstrasse	Estrecho	Détroit	Estreito
⊂	Bay, Gulf	Bucht, Golf	Bahía, Golfo	Baie, Golfe	Baía, Golfo
⊜	Lake, Lakes	See, Seen	Lago, Lagos	Lac, Lacs	Lago, Lagos
⁞	Swamp	Sumpf	Pantano	Marais	Pântano
◹	Ice Features, Glacier	Eis- und Gletscherformen	Accidentes Glaciales	Formes glaciaires	Acidentes glaciares
⫪	Other Hydrographic Features	Andere Hydrographische Objekte	Otros Elementos Hidrográficos	Autres données hydrographiques	Outros acidentes hidrográficos
✢	Submarine Features	Untermeerische Objekte	Accidentes Submarinos	Formes de relief sous-marin	Acidentes submarinos
□	Political Unit	Politische Einheit	Unidad Politica	Entité politique	Unidade política
♉	Cultural Institution	Kulturelle Institution	Institución Cultural	Institution culturelle	Institução cultural
⊥	Historical Site	Historische Stätte	Sitio Histórico	Site historique	Sitio histórico
♠	Recreational Site	Erholungs- und Ferienort	Sitio de Recreo	Centre de loisirs	Area de Lazer
⊠	Airport	Flughafen	Aeropuerto	Aéroport	Aeroporto
■	Military Installation	Militäranlage	Instalación Militar	Installation militaire	Instalação militar
◆	Miscellaneous	Verschiedenes	Misceláneo	Divers	Diversos

ENGLISH — Name · Page · Lat.°′ · Long.°′
DEUTSCH — Name · Seite · Breite°′ · Länge°′ E = Ost

Oakville, Wa., U.S. **224** 46.50 N 123.13 W
Oakwood, On., Can. **212** 44.20 N 78.53 W
Oakwood, N.J., U.S. **285** 39.52 N 74.50 W
Oakwood, Oh., U.S. **214** 41.23 N 81.29 W
Oakwood, Oh., U.S. **216** 41.05 N 84.22 W
Oakwood, Oh., U.S. **218** 39.44 N 84.10 W
Oakwood, Tx., U.S. **222** 31.35 N 95.50 W
Oakwood Beach **208** 39.33 N 75.31 W
Oakwood Park ♦ **279a** 41.26 N 82.06 W
Oamaru **172** 45.06 S 170.58 E
Ōamishirasato **94** 35.31 N 140.19 E
Ōana **268** 35.45 N 140.04 E
Oancea **38** 45.55 N 28.06 E
Ōarai **94** 36.18 N 140.34 E
Oaro **172** 42.31 S 173.30 E
Ōasa **96** 34.46 N 132.28 E
Oat Creek ≃ **226** 38.50 N 121.56 W
Oates Coast ⩡ [2] **9** 70.00 S 160.00 E
Oatka Creek ≃ **210** 43.01 N 77.44 W
Oatlands **166** 42.18 S 147.21 E
Oatley **274a** 33.59 S 151.05 E
Oatley Park ♦ **274a** 33.59 S 151.04 E
Oatman **200** 35.01 N 114.22 W
Oaxaca □ [3] **234** 17.00 N 96.30 W
Oaxaca [de Juárez] **234** 17.03 N 96.43 W
Ob' ≃ **72** 66.45 N 69.30 E
Oba ≃ **190** 48.55 N 84.17 W
Obaba **152** 2.00 S 16.10 E
Obabika Lake ◎ **190** 47.05 N 80.17 W
Obala **152** 4.10 N 11.32 E
Oba Lake ◎ **190** 48.38 N 84.18 W
Obama, Nihon **92** 32.43 N 130.13 E
Obama, Nihon **94** 35.30 N 135.45 E
Obama-wan ⊂ **94** 35.30 N 135.42 E
Oban, Austl. **166** 21.14 S 139.03 E
Oban, Nig. **150** 5.17 N 8.35 E
Oban, Scot., U.K. **46** 56.25 N 5.29 W
Obanazawa **92** 38.36 N 140.24 E
Obando **269f** 14.43 N 120.56 E
Oban Hills ⋏ [2] **150** 5.35 N 8.35 E
Obara **94** 35.15 N 137.18 E
Obata **94** 34.30 N 136.40 E
Ob' Bay ⊂ **9** 70.35 S 163.22 E
Obbo **144** 3.36 N 38.54 E
Obbola **26** 63.42 N 20.19 E
Občuga **76** 54.30 N 29.22 E
Obdach **61** 47.04 N 14.41 E
Obed **182** 53.33 N 117.12 W
Obed ≃ **192** 36.04 N 84.39 W
Obeliai **76** 55.56 N 25.48 E
Obelisk ∧ **172** 45.20 S 169.12 E
Oberá **252** 27.29 S 55.08 W
Oberägeri **58** 47.08 N 8.37 E
Oberalppass)(**58** 46.39 N 8.40 E
Oberalpstock ∧ **58** 46.44 N 8.46 E
Oberammergau **64** 47.35 N 11.04 E
Oberau **64** 47.33 N 11.08 E
Oberaudorf **64** 47.39 N 12.10 E
Oberbauer **263** 51.17 N 7.26 E
Oberbayern □ [5] **60** 48.15 N 11.45 E
Oberbieber **56** 50.28 N 7.29 E
Oberbonsfeld **263** 51.22 N 7.08 E
Oberbrügge **263** 51.11 N 7.34 E
Obercunnersdorf **54** 51.02 N 14.40 E
Oberdiessbach **58** 46.51 N 7.38 E
Oberdolling **60** 48.50 N 11.35 E
Oberdorla **54** 51.10 N 10.25 E
Oberdrauburg **64** 46.45 N 12.58 E
Oberelfringhausen **263** 51.20 N 7.11 E
Ober Engadin V **58** 46.37 N 9.58 E
Oberengstringen **58** 47.25 N 8.28 E
Oberer See
→ Superior, Lake ◎ **190** 48.00 N 88.00 W
Oberfranken □ [5] **60** 49.50 N 11.20 E
Obergeis **56** 50.54 N 9.35 E
Oberglogau
→ Głogówek **30** 50.22 N 17.51 E
Ober-Grafendorf **61** 48.09 N 15.33 E
Obergum **52** 53.20 N 6.31 E
Obergünzburg **58** 47.51 N 10.25 E
Obergurgl **64** 46.52 N 11.01 E
Obergurig **54** 51.07 N 14.24 E
Oberhaan **263** 51.13 N 7.02 E
Oberhaching **60** 48.02 N 11.37 E
Oberharmersbach **58** 48.22 N 8.07 E
Oberhaslach **58** 48.33 N 7.20 E
Oberhausen **56** 51.28 N 6.50 E
Oberhof **54** 50.41 N 10.44 E
Oberhofen **58** 46.44 N 7.40 E
Oberinntal V **64** 47.13 N 10.45 E
Oberjettingen **56** 48.34 N 8.46 E
Oberjoch **58** 47.31 N 10.23 E
Ober-Kassel -◆- [8] **263** 51.14 N 6.46 E
Oberkirch **58** 48.31 N 8.05 E
Ober-Kirchbach **264b** 48.17 N 16.12 E
Oberkirchen **56** 51.09 N 8.22 E
Oberkochen **56** 48.47 N 10.06 E
Oberkotzau **54** 50.16 N 11.56 E
Oberlaa -◆- [8] **264b** 48.08 N 16.24 E
Oberlausitz □ [9] **54** 51.15 N 14.30 E
Oberlin, Ks., U.S. **198** 39.49 N 100.31 W
Oberlin, La., U.S. **194** 30.37 N 92.45 W
Oberlin, Oh., U.S. **214** 41.17 N 82.13 W
Oberlin, Pa., U.S. **208** 40.14 N 76.49 W
Oberloisdorf **61** 47.27 N 16.30 E
Oberlungwitz **54** 50.47 N 12.44 E
Obermarchtal **58** 48.14 N 9.34 E
Obermeiser **56** 51.26 N 9.19 E
Obermieming **64** 47.18 N 10.59 E
Obermodern **56** 48.51 N 7.32 E
Obermoschel **56** 49.44 N 7.46 E
Obermünstertal **58** 47.52 N 7.49 E
Obernai **58** 48.28 N 7.29 E
Obernbeck **52** 52.12 N 8.41 E
Obernberg am Inn **60** 48.19 N 13.20 E
Obernburg am Main **56** 49.50 N 9.08 E
Oberndorf **52** 53.45 N 9.08 E
Oberndorf am
Neckar **58** 48.18 N 8.34 E
Oberndorf bei
Salzburg **64** 47.57 N 12.56 E
Oberndorf in Tirol **64** 47.30 N 12.23 E
Oberne **171b** 35.24 S 147.50 E
Oberne Hill ∧ [2] **171b** 35.26 S 147.53 E
Obernhausen **56** 50.29 N 9.56 E
Obernkirchen **52** 52.16 N 9.07 E
Obernzell **60** 48.34 N 13.39 E
Oberoderwitz **54** 50.58 N 14.42 E
Oberon **170** 33.43 S 149.52 E
Oberösterreich □ [3] **30** 48.15 N 14.00 E
Oberpfalz □ [5] **60** 49.30 N 12.10 E
Oberpleis **56** 50.43 N 7.16 E
Oberpullendorf **61** 47.31 N 16.31 E
Ober-Ramstadt **56** 49.49 N 8.44 E
Oberried **58** 46.44 N 7.58 E
Oberriet **58** 47.19 N 9.33 E
Oberrimsingen **58** 47.59 N 7.40 E
Oberröblingen **54** 51.26 N 11.18 E
Ober Sankt Veit -◆- [8] **264b** 48.11 N 16.16 E
Oberscheidental **56** 49.30 N 9.09 E
Oberscheinfeld **56** 49.42 N 10.26 E
Oberscheld **56** 50.44 N 8.20 E
Oberschleissheim **60** 48.15 N 11.34 E
Oberschöneweide
-◆- [8] **264a** 52.28 N 13.31 E
Oberseebach **56** 48.58 N 7.59 E
Obersickte **54** 52.13 N 10.38 E
Oberspier **54** 51.19 N 10.51 E
Oberstadtfeld **56** 50.10 N 6.46 E
Oberstaufen **58** 47.33 N 10.01 E
Oberstdorf **58** 47.24 N 10.16 E
Obersteinbach **56** 49.02 N 7.41 E
Oberstreu **56** 50.24 N 10.17 E
Obersuhl **56** 50.56 N 10.02 E
Obersulm **56** 49.08 N 9.27 E
Obertheres **56** 50.01 N 10.26 E
Obertilliach **64** 46.42 N 12.37 E
Obertin **78** 48.42 N 25.11 E
Obertraubling **60** 48.58 N 12.10 E
Obertraun **64** 47.33 N 13.41 E
Obertrum **64** 47.56 N 13.05 E
Obertrumer See ◎ **60** 47.58 N 13.06 E
Obertürken **60** 48.19 N 12.50 E
Oberueckersee ◎ **54** 53.12 N 13.52 E
Oberursel **56** 50.11 N 8.35 E
Oberuzwil **58** 47.26 N 9.08 E
Obervellach **64** 46.56 N 13.12 E
Oberviechtach **60** 49.28 N 12.25 E
Obervolta
→ Burkina Faso □ [1] **150** 13.00 N 1.30 W
Oberwald **58** 46.32 N 8.21 E
Oberwart **61** 47.17 N 16.13 E
Oberweissbach **54** 50.35 N 11.08 E
Oberwengern **263** 51.23 N 7.22 E
Oberwesel **56** 50.06 N 7.43 E
Oberwiesenthal **54** 50.25 N 12.59 E
Oberwolfach **58** 48.19 N 8.12 E
Oberwölz Stadt **61** 47.13 N 14.17 E
Oberzeiring **61** 47.15 N 14.29 E
Obetz **218** 39.52 N 82.57 W
Obey, East Fork ≃ **192** 36.27 N 85.07 W
Obey, West Fork ≃ **192** 36.27 N 85.09 W
Obgruiten **263** 51.13 N 7.01 E
Obhausen **54** 51.23 N 11.39 E
Obi **150** 8.22 N 8.46 E
Obi, Kepulauan II **164** 1.30 S 127.45 E
Obi, Pulau I **164** 1.30 S 127.45 E
Obi, Selat ⫫ **164** 0.52 S 127.33 E
Obiaruku **150** 5.51 N 6.09 E
Obichingou ≃ **85** 38.53 N 70.01 E
Obichody **78** 51.02 N 28.59 E
Óbidos **250** 1.55 S 55.31 W
Obi-Garm **85** 38.43 N 69.42 E
Obihiro **92a** 42.55 N 143.12 E
Obikanda **85** 39.10 N 67.10 E
Obilatu, Pulau I **108** 1.25 S 127.20 E
Obil'noje **80** 47.31 N 44.25 E
Obing **60** 48.00 N 12.24 E
Obion **194** 36.15 N 89.11 W
Obion ≃ **194** 35.55 N 89.39 W
Obion, Middle Fork ≃ **194** 36.13 N 88.56 W
Obion, Rutherford
Fork ≃ **194** 36.17 N 89.01 W
Obion, South Fork ≃ **194** 36.17 N 89.03 W
Obion Creek ≃ **194** 36.35 N 89.11 W
Obiou, Grande Tête
de l' ∧ **62** 44.46 N 5.50 E
Obira **92a** 44.00 N 141.35 E
Obitočnaja kosa ≻ [2] **78** 46.33 N 36.13 E
Obitočnyj zaliv ⊂ **78** 46.35 N 36.00 E
Obitsu ≃ **94** 35.24 N 139.54 E
Objačevo **24** 60.20 N 49.34 E
Oblačnaja, gora ∧ **89** 43.45 N 134.10 E
Öblarn **61** 47.27 N 13.59 E
Oblastnaja **80** 56.59 N 52.37 E
Oblivskaja **80** 48.32 N 42.30 E
Oblong **194** 39.00 N 87.54 W
Oblučje **89** 49.03 N 131.04 E
Obninsk **82** 55.05 N 36.37 E
Obnora ≃ **76** 58.14 N 40.58 E
Obnova **38** 43.26 N 24.59 E
Obo **154** 5.24 N 26.30 E
Obobogorap **158** 27.18 S 20.04 E
Obock **144** 11.59 N 43.16 E
Obojan' **78** 51.13 N 36.16 E
Ō-boke ♦ **96** 33.55 N 133.46 E
Obokote **154** 0.52 S 26.19 E
Obol' **76** 55.22 N 29.17 E
Obol' ≃ **76** 55.24 N 29.02 E
Oboldino **265b** 55.53 N 37.56 E
Obolon' **78** 49.36 N 32.52 E
Oborniki **30** 52.39 N 16.51 E
Obot **144** 4.30 N 37.20 E
Obouya **152** 0.56 S 15.43 E
Oboz'orskij **24** 63.28 N 40.18 E
Obra ≃ **30** 52.36 N 15.28 E
Obrazcovo-Travino **80** 45.58 N 48.02 E
Obree, Mount ∧ **164** 9.30 S 148.05 E
Obrenovac **38** 44.39 N 20.12 E
O'Brien **202** 42.04 N 123.42 W
O'Brien Coulee V **202** 48.38 N 110.22 W
Obrighoven-
Lackhausen **52** 51.40 N 6.38 E
Obrovac **36** 44.12 N 15.41 E
Obrovo **76** 52.30 N 25.34 E
Obručeva, gora ∧ **88** 53.36 N 113.52 E
Obručevka **85** 42.30 N 69.05 E
Obruk **130** 38.10 N 33.12 E
Obryta **54** 53.13 N 14.59 E
Obryvistoje **89** 48.46 N 144.40 E
Obša ≃ **76** 55.55 N 32.32 E
Obšarovka **80** 53.07 N 48.52 E
Obščij Syrt ∧ **80** 52.00 N 51.30 E
Observation Peak ∧ **204** 40.46 N 120.10 W
Observatoire, Caye
de l' I **160** 21.25 S 158.50 E
Observatory Inlet ⊂ **182** 55.10 N 129.54 W
Obskaja guba ⊂ **72** 69.00 N 73.00 E
Obsteig **64** 47.18 N 10.56 E
Obtovo **78** 51.37 N 33.13 E
Ob' Trench ⫧ [1] **14** 33.00 S 98.00 E
Ōbu **94** 35.00 N 136.58 E
Obu -◆- [8] **270** 34.44 N 135.09 E
Obuasi **150** 6.14 N 1.39 W
Obubra **150** 6.05 N 8.21 E
Obuchov **78** 50.08 N 30.37 E
Obuchova **76** 56.06 N 32.22 E
Obuchoviči **78** 51.00 N 29.46 E
Obuchovka **86** 46.13 N 81.05 E
Obuchovo, S.S.S.R. **82** 56.09 N 36.55 E
Obuchovo, S.S.S.R. **82** 55.50 N 38.16 E
Óbuda -◆- [8] **264c** 47.33 N 19.02 E
Óbudai-sziget I **264c** 47.33 N 19.04 E
Obudu **150** 6.40 N 9.09 E
Obuse **94** 36.42 N 138.19 E
Obushkong Lake ◎ **190** 47.42 N 80.48 W
Obuškovo **82** 55.47 N 37.02 E
Obu-tōge)(**270** 34.44 N 135.10 E
Obva ≃ **86** 58.32 N 55.18 E
Obvinsk **86** 58.29 N 54.51 E
Obwalden □ [3] **58** 46.50 N 8.14 E
Obžericha **80** 57.11 N 42.58 E
Očakov **78** 46.37 N 31.33 E
Očakovo -◆- [8] **265b** 55.41 N 37.27 E
Ocala **192** 29.11 N 82.08 W
Ocallí **248** 6.09 S 78.18 W
Očamčira **84** 42.44 N 41.28 E
Ocamo ≃ **246** 2.48 N 65.14 W
Ocampo, Méx. **232** 28.11 N 108.23 W
Ocampo, Méx. **232** 27.20 N 102.21 W
Ocampo, Méx. **234** 21.39 N 101.30 W
Ocaña, Col. **246** 8.15 N 73.20 W
Ocaña, Esp. **34** 39.56 N 3.31 W
Ocate Creek ≃ **196** 36.17 N 104.30 W
Occaquan ≃ **208** 38.40 N 77.14 W
Occaquan Reservoir
◎ [1] **208** 38.43 N 77.22 W
Očchamuri **84** 41.52 N 41.50 E
Occhieppo Inferiore **62** 45.33 N 8.01 E
Occhiobello **64** 44.55 N 11.35 E
Occidental,
Cordillera ⋏, Col. **246** 5.00 N 76.00 W
Occidental,
Cordillera ⋏, Perú **248** 10.00 S 77.00 W
Occidental College
❀ [2] **280** 34.08 N 118.13 W
Occidental de
Zapata, Ciénaga ⩸ **240p** 22.25 N 81.20 W
Occimiano **62** 45.03 N 8.30 E
Occoquan **208** 38.41 N 77.15 W
Occoquan Bay ⊂ **208** 38.37 N 77.13 W
Ocean □ [6] **208** 39.58 N 74.12 W
Oceana **192** 37.41 N 81.37 W
Oceana Naval Air
Station ■ **208** 36.50 N 76.02 W
Ocean Bay Park **276** 40.39 N 73.08 W
Ocean Beach **276** 40.38 N 73.18 W
Ocean Bluff **207** 42.05 N 70.39 W
Ocean Breeze Park **220** 27.15 N 80.14 W
Ocean Cape ≻ **180** 59.30 N 139.45 W
Ocean City, Md.,
U.S. **208** 38.20 N 75.05 W
Ocean City, N.J.,
U.S. **208** 39.16 N 74.34 W
Ocean City, Wa.,
U.S. **224** 47.04 N 124.09 W
Ocean Falls **182** 52.21 N 127.40 W
Ocean Gate **208** 39.55 N 74.08 W
Ocean Grove **207** 41.43 N 71.12 W
Ocean Heights **207** 41.24 N 70.33 W
Ocean Island
→ Banaba I **174d** 0.52 S 169.35 E
Ocean Lake ◎ [1] **202** 43.11 N 108.36 W
Oceano **204** 35.06 N 120.37 W
Ocean Park, B.C.,
Can. **224** 49.02 N 122.53 W
Ocean Park, Wa.,
U.S. **224** 46.29 N 124.02 W
Ocean Park ♦ **271d** 22.15 N 114.09 E
Ocean Port **276** 40.19 N 74.00 W
Ocean Shores **224** 47.01 N 124.09 W
Oceanside, Ca., U.S. **228** 33.11 N 117.22 W
Oceanside, N.Y.,
U.S. **210** 40.38 N 73.38 W
Ocean Springs **194** 30.24 N 88.49 W
Ocean View, De.,
U.S. **208** 38.32 N 75.05 W
Ocean View, N.J.,
U.S. **208** 39.10 N 74.44 W
Oceanville **208** 39.28 N 74.27 W
Oceola **214** 40.51 N 83.06 W
Očer **80** 57.53 N 54.42 E
Očeretino **83** 48.14 N 37.36 E
O. C. Fisher Lake
◎ [1] **196** 31.30 N 100.30 W
Ocha **89** 53.34 N 142.56 E
Ochagavía, Canal de
≊ **286e** 33.30 S 70.49 W
Ochanomizu
Women's
University ❀ [2] **268** 35.43 N 139.44 E
Ochansk **86** 57.43 N 55.23 E
Ochapowace Indian
Reserve -◆- [4] **184** 50.30 N 102.24 W
Ocheyedan **198** 43.24 N 95.32 W
Ocheyedan ≃ **198** 43.08 N 95.09 W
Ōchi, Nihon **96** 34.16 N 134.18 E
Ochi, Nihon **96** 33.32 N 133.15 E
Ōchi, Nihon **96** 35.04 N 132.36 E
Ochiai **96** 35.01 N 133.45 E
Ochiai -◆- [8] **268** 35.43 N 139.42 E
O'Chiese Indian
Reserve -◆- [4] **182** 52.50 N 115.28 W
Ochil Hills ⋏ [2] **46** 56.14 N 3.40 W
Ochiltree **44** 55.28 N 4.23 W
Ōchise ≃ **94** 35.03 N 137.46 E
Ochlocknee **192** 30.58 N 84.03 W
Ochlockonee ≃ **192** 29.58 N 84.21 W
Ochoco Creek ≃ **202** 44.19 N 120.53 W
Ochoco Mountains ⋏ **202** 44.30 N 120.35 W
Ochopee **220** 25.54 N 81.18 W
Ocho Rios **241q** 18.25 N 77.07 W
Ochota ≃ **74** 59.20 N 143.04 E
Ochotsk **74** 59.23 N 143.18 E
Ochotskisches Meer
→ Okhotsk, Sea
of ⫧ [2] **74** 53.00 N 150.00 E
Ochotskoje more
→ Okhotsk, Sea
of ⫧ [2] **74** 53.00 N 150.00 E
Ochre River **184** 51.03 N 99.47 W
Ochsenfurt **56** 49.40 N 10.03 E
Ochsenhausen **58** 48.04 N 9.56 E
Ochsenwerder -◆- [8] **52** 53.28 N 10.05 E
Ochta ≃ **265a** 59.57 N 30.24 E
Ochtrup **52** 52.13 N 7.11 E
Ochvat **76** 56.46 N 32.27 E
Oci ≃ **152** 15.14 S 15.16 E
Ocilla **192** 31.35 N 83.15 W
Ock ≃ **42** 51.39 N 1.17 W
Ockelbo **26** 60.53 N 16.43 E
Öckerö **26** 57.43 N 11.39 E
Ockham **260** 51.18 N 0.27 W
Ockholm **41** 54.40 N 8.49 E
Ockies **158** 31.31 S 21.41 E
Ocklawaha, Lake ◎ [1] **192** 29.30 N 81.50 W
Ocmulgee ≃ **192** 31.58 N 82.32 W
Ocmulgee National
Monument ♦ **192** 32.43 N 83.38 W
Ocna Mureș **38** 46.23 N 23.51 E
Ocoa, Bahía de ⊂ **238** 18.22 N 70.39 W
Ocoee **220** 28.34 N 81.32 W
Ocoee (Toccoa) ≃ **192** 35.12 N 84.40 W
Ocoña **248** 16.26 S 73.07 W
Ocoña ≃ **248** 16.28 S 73.07 W
Oconee **219** 39.17 N 89.07 W
Oconee ≃ **192** 31.58 N 82.32 W
Oconee, Lake ◎ [1] **192** 33.30 N 83.15 W
Ocongate **248** 13.38 S 71.24 W
O'Connell **170** 33.32 S 149.44 E
Oconomowoc **216** 43.06 N 88.29 W
Oconomowoc ≃ **216** 43.07 N 88.37 W
Oconomowoc Lake **216** 42.37 N 88.28 W
Oconomowoc Lake
◎ **216** 43.06 N 88.27 W
Oconto **190** 44.53 N 87.51 W
Oconto ≃ **190** 44.53 N 87.50 W
Oconto, North
Branch ≃ **190** 45.00 N 88.23 W
Oconto Falls **190** 44.52 N 88.08 W
Ocós **236** 14.31 N 92.11 W
Ocotal **236** 13.38 N 86.29 W
Ocotepec **234** 17.13 N 93.09 W
Ocotepeque □ [5] **236** 14.30 N 89.00 W
Ocotlán **234** 20.21 N 102.46 W
Ocotlán de Morelos **234** 16.48 N 96.40 W
Ocoyoacac **234** 19.16 N 99.26 W
Ocozingo **232** 16.54 N 92.07 W
Ocozocoautla [de
Espinosa] **234** 16.46 N 93.22 W
Ocracoke **192** 35.06 N 75.58 W
Ocracoke Island I **192** 35.09 N 75.53 W
Ocre, Monte ∧ **66** 42.15 N 13.26 E
Ocreza, Ribeira da ≃ **34** 39.32 N 7.50 W
Ocros **248** 10.24 S 77.24 W
Octoraro Creek ≃ **208** 39.39 N 76.09 W
Octoraro Creek,
East Branch ≃ **208** 39.49 N 76.02 W
Octoraro Creek,
West Branch ≃ **208** 39.49 N 76.05 W
Octoraro Lake ◎ [1] **208** 39.48 N 76.02 W
Ocú **236** 7.57 N 80.47 W
Ocuilán de Arteaga **234** 18.58 N 99.25 W
Ocumare del Tuy **246** 10.07 N 66.46 W
Ocurí **248** 18.50 S 65.50 W
Ocussi **112** 9.12 S 124.21 E
Oda, Ghana **150** 5.55 N 0.59 W
Ōda, Nihon **96** 33.34 N 132.48 E
Ōda, Nihon **96** 35.11 N 132.30 E
Oda ≃ **96** 34.37 N 133.44 E
Oda, Jabal ∧ **140** 20.21 N 36.39 E
Ŏdaejin **98** 41.34 N 129.40 E
Odae-san Kukrip
Kongwŏn ♦ **98** 37.46 N 128.37 E
Ōdai **94** 34.24 N 136.25 E
Ōdaigahara-zan ∧ **92** 34.11 N 136.05 E
Odaka **92** 37.34 N 141.00 E
Ödåkra **41** 56.06 N 12.44 E
Odanakumadona **156** 20.53 S 24.45 E
Ōdate **92** 40.16 N 140.34 E
Odawara **94** 35.15 N 139.10 E
Odayeri **267b** 41.14 N 28.51 E
Odda **26** 60.04 N 6.33 E
Odden **41** 55.58 N 11.22 E
Odder **41** 55.58 N 10.10 E
Oddville **218** 38.27 N 84.15 W
Odebolt **198** 42.18 N 95.15 W
Ödeby **40** 59.24 N 15.25 E
Odei ≃ **184** 56.06 N 96.55 W
Odeleite, Ribeira de
≃ **34** 37.21 N 7.27 W
Odell, Il., U.S. **216** 41.00 N 88.31 W
Odell, Ne., U.S. **198** 40.03 N 96.48 W
Odell, Or., U.S. **224** 45.37 N 121.32 W
Odell, Tx., U.S. **196** 34.21 N 99.25 W
Odell Lake ◎ **202** 43.34 N 122.00 W
Odelzhausen **60** 48.19 N 11.12 E
Odem **196** 27.57 N 97.34 W
Odemira **34** 37.36 N 8.38 W
Ödemiş **130** 38.13 N 27.59 E
Ödenburg
→ Sopron **61** 47.41 N 16.36 E
Odendaalsrus **158** 27.48 S 26.45 E
Odenkirchen -◆- [8] **263** 51.08 N 6.27 E
Odensbacken **40** 59.10 N 15.32 E
Odense **41** 55.24 N 10.23 E
Odense Å ≃ **41** 55.26 N 10.26 E
Odense Fjord ⊂ **41** 55.30 N 10.34 E
Odenthal **56** 51.02 N 7.07 E
Odenton **208** 39.05 N 76.42 W
Odenwald ⋏ **56** 49.40 N 9.00 E
Oder ≃, B.R.D. **52** 51.40 N 10.06 E
Oder (Odra) ≃,
Europe **30** 53.32 N 14.38 E
Oderberg **54** 52.52 N 14.02 E
Oderbruch -◆- [1] **54** 52.40 N 14.15 E
Oderen **58** 47.55 N 6.59 E
Oderhaff (Zalew
Szczeciński) ⊂ **54** 53.46 N 14.14 E
Oder-Havel-Kanal ≊ **54** 52.52 N 14.02 E
Oder-Spree-Kanal ≊ **54** 52.23 N 13.41 E
Odertalsperre -◆- [6] **54** 51.38 N 10.30 E
Oderzo **64** 45.47 N 12.29 E
Odesa
→ Odessa **78** 46.28 N 30.44 E
Ödeshög **26** 58.14 N 14.39 E
Odessa, On., Can. **212** 44.17 N 76.43 W
Odessa, S.S.S.R. **78** 46.28 N 30.44 E
Odessa, De., U.S. **208** 39.27 N 75.39 W
Odessa, Fl., U.S. **220** 28.11 N 82.35 W
Odessa, Mo., U.S. **194** 38.59 N 93.57 W
Odessa, N.Y., U.S. **210** 42.20 N 76.47 W
Odessa, Tx., U.S. **196** 31.50 N 102.22 W
Odessa, Wa., U.S. **202** 47.20 N 118.41 W
Odessa □ [4] **38** 47.30 N 30.00 E
Odessa Lake ◎ **212** 44.19 N 76.41 W
Odesskoje **86** 54.13 N 72.58 E
Odiakwe **156** 20.01 S 25.17 E
Odib, Wādī V **140** 22.38 N 36.06 E
Odiel ≃ **34** 37.10 N 6.54 W
Odienné **150** 9.30 N 7.34 W
Odienné □ [5] **150** 9.30 N 7.20 W
Odiham **42** 51.15 N 0.57 W
Odin **219** 38.37 N 89.03 W
Odin, Mount ∧ **182** 50.33 N 118.08 W
Odincovo, S.S.S.R. **82** 54.40 N 38.00 E
Odincovo, S.S.S.R. **82** 55.41 N 37.17 E
Odiongan **116** 12.24 N 121.59 E
Odiongan Bay ⊂ **116** 12.25 N 121.58 E
Odivelas **266c** 38.47 N 9.11 W
Odobești **38** 45.45 N 27.04 E
Odojev **76** 53.56 N 36.41 E
Odolanów **30** 51.35 N 17.39 E
Ōdomari-chosuichi ◎ **96** 34.43 N 132.18 E
Odon **194** 38.50 N 86.59 W
Ŏdŏngk **110** 11.48 N 104.45 E
O'Donnell **196** 32.57 N 101.49 W
O'Donnell ≃ **162** 18.22 S 126.36 E
Odoorn **52** 52.51 N 6.51 E
Odorheiu Secuiesc **38** 46.18 N 25.18 E
Odra
→ Oder ≃ **54** 53.32 N 14.38 E
Odra Port **54** 53.52 N 14.14 E
Odrinhas **266c** 38.53 N 9.22 W
Odrzywół **30** 51.32 N 20.33 E
Odsherred -◆- [1] **41** 55.52 N 11.37 E
Ødsted **41** 55.39 N 9.25 E
Odum **192** 31.39 N 82.01 W
Odžaci **38** 45.30 N 19.16 E
Odzala, Parc
National d' ♦ **152** 1.00 S 15.00 E
Odzi **154** 18.58 S 32.23 E
Odzi ≃ **154** 19.45 S 32.24 E
Odziba **152** 3.35 S 15.31 E
Ōe **96** 35.23 N 135.09 E
Oebisfelde **54** 52.25 N 10.59 E
Oedelem **50** 51.10 N 3.20 E
Oederan **54** 50.52 N 13.09 E
Oeding **52** 51.56 N 6.49 E
Oedt **56** 51.19 N 6.22 E
Oegstgeest **52** 52.10 N 4.29 E
Oeiras, Bra. **250** 7.01 S 42.08 W
Oeiras, Port. **266c** 38.41 N 9.21 W
Oeiras do Pará **250** 1.58 S 49.51 W
Oelde **52** 51.49 N 8.08 E
Oelemari ≃ **250** 3.13 N 54.09 W
Oella **284b** 39.16 N 76.47 W
Oels
→ Oleśnica **30** 51.13 N 17.23 E
Oelsig **54** 51.41 N 13.22 E
Oelsnitz, D.D.R. **54** 50.24 N 12.10 E
Oelsnitz, D.D.R. **54** 50.43 N 12.41 E
Oelwein **190** 42.40 N 91.54 W
Oenpelli Mission **164** 12.20 S 133.04 E
Oensingen **58** 47.17 N 7.44 E
Oepping **60** 48.36 N 13.56 E
Oeraro-do I **98** 34.27 N 127.30 E
Oer-Erkenschwick **52** 51.39 N 7.15 E
Oerlinghausen **52** 51.57 N 8.39 E
Oermten **263** 51.29 N 6.27 E
Oesede **52** 52.12 N 8.04 E
Oespel -◆- [8] **263** 51.30 N 7.23 E
Oeste, Canal del ≊ **266a** 40.32 N 3.42 W
Oeste, Parque del ♦ **266a** 40.26 N 3.44 W
Oesterdam -◆- [5] **52** 51.29 N 4.15 E
Oestrich **263** 51.22 N 7.38 E
Oestrich -◆- [8] **263** 51.34 N 7.22 E
Oestrum **263** 51.25 N 6.40 E
Ōetaka-yama ∧ **96** 35.04 N 132.26 E
Oettingen in Bayern **56** 48.57 N 10.36 E
Oetz **58** 47.12 N 10.54 E
Oeuf ≃ **50** 48.11 N 2.21 E
Oeventrop **56** 51.23 N 8.08 E
Oeversee **41** 54.42 N 9.26 E
Ōe-yama ∧ **96** 35.27 N 135.07 E
Oeyŏn-do I **98** 36.14 N 126.05 E
Of **130** 40.57 N 40.18 E
O'Fallon, Il., U.S. **219** 38.35 N 89.54 W
O'Fallon, Mo., U.S. **219** 38.48 N 90.41 W
O'Fallon Creek ≃ **198** 46.50 N 105.09 W
Ofanto ≃ **68** 41.22 N 16.13 E
Ofaqim **132** 31.17 N 34.37 E
Ofenpass
→ Fuorn, Pass dal
)(**58** 46.37 N 10.15 E
Offa **150** 8.09 N 4.44 E
Offaly □ [6] **48** 53.20 N 7.30 W
Offanengo **62** 45.22 N 9.44 E
Offemont **58** 47.40 N 6.53 E
Offenbach **56** 50.08 N 8.47 E
Offenburg **58** 48.28 N 7.57 E
Offendorf **58** 48.43 N 7.55 E
Offerdal **26** 63.28 N 14.00 E
Offham **260** 51.17 N 0.23 E
Officer **274b** 38.04 S 145.25 E
Officer Creek ≃ **162** 27.45 S 132.24 E
Offida **66** 42.56 N 13.41 E
Offingen **58** 48.29 N 10.21 E
Offranville **50** 49.52 N 1.03 E
Offutt Air Force
Base ■ **198** 41.08 N 95.56 W
Oficina Alianza **248** 20.46 S 69.42 W
Oficina Chile **252** 25.09 S 69.54 W
Oficina Pedro de
Valdivia **252** 22.36 S 69.40 W
Oficina Victoria **248** 20.44 S 69.42 W
Ofin **273a** 6.33 N 3.30 E
Öflingen **58** 47.35 N 7.55 E
Ofotfjorden ⊂ [2] **24** 68.23 N 16.10 E
Oftringen **58** 47.19 N 7.56 E
Ofu **174w** 14.10 S 169.42 W
Ofu I **174w** 14.11 S 169.42 W
Ōfukuroshinden **268** 35.53 N 139.27 E
Ōfuna **268** 35.21 N 139.32 E
Ōfunato **92** 39.04 N 141.43 E
Oga **92** 39.53 N 139.51 E
Ogaden -◆- [1] **144** 8.00 N 44.00 E
Oga-hantō ≻ [1] **92** 39.55 N 139.50 E
Ōgaki, Nihon **94** 35.21 N 136.37 E
Ōgaki, Nihon **96** 34.06 N 132.30 E
Ogallala **198** 41.07 N 101.43 W
Ogan ≃ **112** 3.01 S 104.44 E
Ogano **94** 36.01 N 139.00 E
Ogasa **94** 34.41 N 138.06 E
Ogasawara-guntō
(Bonin Islands) II **14** 27.00 N 142.10 E
Ōgata, Nihon **94** 37.13 N 138.20 E
Ōgata, Nihon **96** 33.01 N 133.01 E
Ogata, Nihon **96** 32.58 N 131.29 E
Ōga-tō ∧ **94** 36.13 N 138.06 E
Ogatsu **92** 38.31 N 141.28 E
Ogawa, Nihon **92** 32.35 N 130.43 E
Ogawa, Nihon **94** 36.37 N 137.58 E
Ogawa, Nihon **94** 36.03 N 139.16 E
Ogawa, Nihon **94** 36.45 N 140.08 E
Ogawa, Nihon **94** 36.10 N 140.21 E
Ogawa, Nihon **268** 35.44 N 139.28 E
Ogawara-ko ◎ **92** 40.47 N 141.20 E
Ogbomosho **150** 8.08 N 4.15 E
Ogden, Ia., U.S. **190** 42.02 N 94.01 W
Ogden, Ks., U.S. **198** 39.06 N 96.42 W
Ogden, Pa., U.S. **208** 39.49 N 75.27 W
Ogden, Ut,. U.S. **200** 41.13 N 111.58 W
Ogden, Mount ∧ **180** 58.26 N 133.23 W
Ogden Dunes **216** 41.38 N 87.12 W
Ogden Island I **212** 44.52 N 75.12 W
Ogden Reservoir ◎ [1] **262** 53.42 N 2.22 W
Ogdensburg, N.J.,
U.S. **210** 41.04 N 74.35 W
Ogdensburg, N.Y.,
U.S. **212** 44.41 N 75.29 W
Ogeechee ≃ **192** 31.51 N 81.06 W
Ōge-jima I **96** 34.12 N 134.38 E
Ogema **184** 49.35 N 104.55 W
Oggersheim **56** 49.29 N 8.22 E
Oghi **123** 34.31 N 73.01 E
Ogibalovo **76** 60.34 N 39.40 E
Ogidaki Mountain ∧ [2] **190** 46.58 N 83.58 W
Ogies **158** 26.02 S 29.04 E
Ogi-jima I **96** 34.26 N 134.04 E
Ogijo **273a** 6.42 N 3.31 E
Ogilvie, Austl. **162** 28.09 S 114.38 E
Ogilvie, Mn., U.S. **190** 45.49 N 93.25 W
Ogilvie ≃ **180** 65.52 N 137.16 W
Ogilvie Mountains ⋏ **180** 65.00 N 139.30 W
Ogilville **218** 39.08 N 86.01 W
Ōgimi **174m** 26.42 N 128.07 E
Ōgino-sen ∧ **96** 35.26 N 134.26 E
Ogle □ [6] **216** 42.01 N 89.20 W
Oglesby, Il., U.S. **216** 41.17 N 89.03 W
Oglesby, Tx., U.S. **222** 31.25 N 97.31 W
Oglethorpe **192** 32.17 N 84.03 W
Ogliastra -◆- [1] **71** 39.56 N 9.37 E
Ogliastro Cilento **68** 40.21 N 15.03 E
Oglio ≃ **64** 45.02 N 10.39 E
Ogmore **166** 22.37 S 149.40 E
Ogmore ≃ **42** 51.28 N 3.38 W
Ogmore Vale **42** 51.38 N 3.31 W
Ogni **86** 51.54 N 83.31 E
Ognica **54** 53.07 N 14.27 E
Ognon ≃ **58** 47.20 N 5.29 E
Ogn'ov Jar **86** 58.23 N 76.29 E
Ogn'ovka **86** 49.36 N 83.25 E
Oğnut **130** 39.08 N 40.53 E
Ōgo **94** 36.25 N 139.10 E
Ōgo -◆- [8] **270** 34.49 N 135.06 E
Ōgo ≃ **270** 34.47 N 135.04 E
Ogoamas, Gunung ∧ **112** 0.40 N 120.12 E
Ogōchi-dam -◆- [6] **94** 35.47 N 139.04 E
Ogodža **89** 52.44 N 132.31 E
Ogoja **150** 6.40 N 8.48 E
Ogoki ≃ **176** 51.38 N 85.57 W
'Ogol, Khaṭṭ el V **150** 20.01 N 15.29 W
Ogooué ≃ **152** 0.49 S 9.00 E
Ogooué-Ivindo □ [4] **152** 1.00 N 13.00 E
Ogooué-Lolo □ [4] **152** 1.00 S 12.30 E
Ogooué-Maritime □ [4] **152** 2.00 S 9.30 E
Ogōri, Nihon **96** 33.22 N 130.32 E
Ogōri, Nihon **96** 34.06 N 131.24 E
Ogo, odnoje **78** 45.53 N 28.50 E
Ogose **94** 35.58 N 139.18 E
Ogosta ≃ **38** 43.45 N 23.51 E
Ogou ≃ **150** 7.50 N 1.19 E
Ogoyo **273a** 6.26 N 3.29 E
Ogr **140** 12.02 N 27.06 E
Ogre **76** 56.51 N 24.36 E
Ogre ≃ **76** 56.48 N 24.36 E
Ogrodzieniec **30** 50.27 N 19.31 E
Ogrosen **54** 51.42 N 14.02 E
Ōguchi **94** 35.20 N 136.55 E
Ŏgu-dong **98** 38.57 N 126.56 E
Ogudu **273a** 6.34 N 3.24 E
Ogulin **36** 45.16 N 15.14 E
Ogun □ [3] **150** 6.45 N 3.25 E
Ogun ≃ **150** 6.36 N 3.27 E
Ogun Forest
Reserve ♦ **273a** 6.37 N 3.26 E
Oguni, Nihon **92** 38.04 N 139.45 E
Oguni, Nihon **96** 33.07 N 131.04 E
Ogunlogun **273a** 6.41 N 3.28 E
Ogunquit **188** 43.14 N 70.35 W
Ogura-san ∧ **94** 36.02 N 138.37 E
Ogurčinskij, ostrov I **128** 38.55 N 53.02 E
Oguta **150** 5.44 N 6.44 E
Oğuz **130** 39.32 N 38.51 E
Oğuzeli **130** 36.59 N 37.30 E
Ogwashi-Uku **150** 6.10 N 6.31 E
Ohai **172** 45.55 S 167.57 E
Ohakune **172** 39.25 S 175.24 E
Ohanapecosh ≃ **224** 46.38 N 121.37 W
Ohanet **148** 28.45 N 8.55 E
Ōhara, Nihon **94** 35.15 N 140.23 E
Ōhara, Nihon **96** 35.07 N 134.20 E
Ōharano -◆- [8] **270** 34.58 N 135.40 E
Ōhara-tunnel -◆- [5] **94** 35.12 N 137.50 E
Ōhata **92** 41.24 N 141.10 E
Ōhatake **268** 35.57 N 139.46 E
Ohau, Lake ◎ **172** 44.15 S 169.51 E
Ohaupo **172** 37.55 S 175.19 E
Ohey **56** 50.26 N 5.08 E
O'Higgins, Cabo ≻ **174z** 27.05 S 109.15 W
O'Higgins, Cerro ∧ **254** 48.48 S 73.11 W
O'Higgins, Lago
(Lago San Martín)
◎ **254** 49.00 S 72.40 W
Ohingaiti **172** 39.52 S 175.43 E
Ohio **190** 41.34 N 89.28 W
Ohio □ [6], In., U.S. **218** 38.57 N 84.51 W
Ohio □ [6], W.V., U.S. **214** 40.09 N 80.35 W
Ohio □ [3], U.S. **178** 40.15 N 82.45 W
Ohio □ [3], U.S. **188** 40.15 N 82.45 W
Ohio ≃ **178** 36.59 N 89.08 W
Ohio Brush Creek ≃ **218** 38.41 N 83.27 W
Ohio Brush Creek,
Baker Fork ≃ **218** 39.02 N 83.26 W
Ohio Brush Creek,
Little West Fork ≃ **218** 38.58 N 83.34 W
Ohio Brush Creek,
West Fork ≃ **218** 38.56 N 83.28 W
Ohio Canal ≊ **279a** 41.26 N 81.40 W
Ohio Caverns ⩡ [5] **216** 40.14 N 83.43 W
Ohio City **216** 40.46 N 84.36 W
Ohio Peak ∧ **200** 38.49 N 107.07 W
Ohiopyle State Park
♦ **188** 39.50 N 79.31 W
Ohioville, N.Y., U.S. **210** 41.45 N 74.03 W
Ohioville, Pa., U.S. **214** 40.40 N 80.29 W
Ōhira **94** 36.20 N 139.42 E
Ōhira-yama ∧ **96** 34.20 N 133.57 E
Ōhito **94** 35.01 N 138.56 E
Ohlau
→ Oława **30** 50.57 N 17.17 E
Ohligs -◆- [8] **263** 51.09 N 7.00 E
Ohlman **219** 39.21 N 89.13 W
Ohlsdorf **64** 47.57 N 13.47 E
Ohm ≃ **56** 50.51 N 8.48 E
Ōho **94** 36.08 N 140.06 E
Ohoitom **164** 5.56 S 132.41 E
'Ohonua **174w** 21.20 S 174.57 W
Ohoopee ≃ **192** 31.54 N 82.07 W
Ōhori **268** 35.20 N 139.52 E
Ohorn **54** 51.10 N 14.02 E
Ohra Stausee ◎ [1] **54** 50.46 N 10.42 E
Ohrdruf **54** 50.50 N 10.44 E
Ohře (Eger) ≃,
Europe **54** 50.32 N 14.08 E
Ohre ≃, Europe **54** 52.18 N 11.47 E
Ohrid **38** 41.07 N 20.47 E
Ohrid, Lake ◎ **38** 41.02 N 20.43 E
Ohrigstad **156** 24.49 S 30.33 E
Öhringen **56** 49.12 N 9.29 E
Ohrnberg **56** 49.15 N 9.27 E
Ohuira, Bahía de ⊂ **232** 25.38 N 108.58 W
Ohura **172** 38.50 S 174.59 E
Ōi, Nihon **96** 35.28 N 135.37 E
Ōi, Nihon **268** 35.51 N 139.30 E
Oi -◆- [8] **268** 35.35 N 139.45 E
Ōi ≃, Nihon **94** 34.46 N 138.18 E
Ōi ≃, Nihon **96** 35.01 N 135.39 E
Oiapoque **250** 3.50 N 51.50 W
Oiapoque (Oyapock)
≃ **250** 4.08 N 51.40 W
Oies, Île aux I **186** 47.07 N 70.30 W
Ōigawa **94** 34.48 N 138.17 E
Oignies **50** 50.28 N 2.59 E
Oil Center **196** 32.29 N 103.15 W
Oil City, La., U.S. **194** 32.44 N 93.58 W
Oil City, Pa., U.S. **214** 41.26 N 79.42 W
Oil Creek ≃ **214** 41.26 N 79.42 W
Oil Creek State Park
♦ **214** 41.33 N 79.40 W
Oildale **226** 35.25 N 119.01 W
Oilmont **182** 48.44 N 111.50 W
Oil Springs **214** 42.47 N 82.07 W
Oilton, Ok., U.S. **196** 36.05 N 96.35 W
Oilton, Tx., U.S. **196** 27.33 N 98.59 W
Oil Trough **194** 35.37 N 91.27 W
Oinville-sur-
Montcient **261** 49.02 N 1.51 E
Oir, Beinn an ∧ **46** 55.54 N 6.00 W
Oirschot **52** 51.30 N 5.18 E
Oise □ [5] **50** 49.30 N 2.30 E
Oise ≃ **50** 49.00 N 2.04 E
Oise à l'Aisne, Canal
de l' ≊ **50** 49.36 N 3.11 E
Oisemont **50** 49.57 N 1.46 E
Ōiso, Nihon **94** 35.18 N 139.19 E
Ōiso, Nihon **270** 34.33 N 135.01 E
Oissel **50** 49.20 N 1.06 E
Oissery **261** 49.04 N 2.49 E
Oisterwijk **52** 51.35 N 5.12 E
Oistins **241g** 13.04 N 59.32 W
Oistins Bay ⊂ **241g** 13.03 N 59.33 W
Ōita **96** 33.14 N 131.36 E
Ōita □ [5] **96** 33.15 N 131.30 E
Ōita ≃ **96** 33.15 N 131.37 E
Oiticica **250** 5.03 S 41.05 W
Oituz, Pasul)(**38** 46.03 N 26.23 E
Ōiwa **270** 34.53 N 135.33 E
Ōizumi, Nihon **94** 36.15 N 139.25 E
Ōizumi, Nihon **94** 35.52 N 138.23 E
Oizuruga-dake ∧ **94** 36.18 N 136.47 E
Öja I **40** 58.45 N 17.52 E
Oja ≃ **86** 53.26 N 91.55 E
Ojai **228** 34.26 N 119.14 W
Öjaren ◎ **40** 60.43 N 16.50 E
Ojat' ≃ **76** 60.31 N 33.00 E
Ojcowski Park
Narodowy ♦ **30** 50.15 N 19.50 E
Öje **26** 60.49 N 13.51 E
Ojgon nuur ◎ **88** 49.10 N 96.36 E
Ojgor **86** 49.10 N 89.17 E
Ōji **96** 34.35 N 135.42 E
Ōjima **94** 36.15 N 139.20 E
Ojinaga **232** 29.34 N 104.25 W
Ojitlán **234** 18.04 N 96.23 W
Ojiya **92** 37.18 N 138.48 E
Ojm'akon **74** 63.28 N 142.49 E
Ojocaliente **234** 22.34 N 102.15 W
Ojo de Agua de
Alférez **234** 22.51 N 99.42 W
Ojo de la Casa **200** 31.23 N 106.32 W
Ojo de Liebre,
Laguna ⊂ **232** 27.45 N 114.15 W
Ojok **88** 52.35 N 104.27 E
Ojos del Salado,
Nevado ∧ **252** 27.06 S 68.32 W
Ojota **273a** 6.35 N 3.23 E
Ojtal, S.S.S.R. **85** 42.55 N 73.17 E
Ojtal, S.S.S.R. **85** 40.24 N 74.06 E
Oju **150** 6.53 N 8.26 E
Ojuelos de Jalisco **234** 21.52 N 101.35 W
Ojus **220** 25.57 N 80.09 W
Oka **150** 7.29 N 5.49 E
Oka ≃, S.S.S.R. **80** 56.20 N 43.59 E
Oka ≃, S.S.S.R. **88** 55.15 N 102.10 E
Okaba **164** 8.06 S 139.42 E
Okabe, Nihon **94** 36.12 N 139.15 E
Okabe, Nihon **94** 34.55 N 138.17 E
Okagaki **96** 33.50 N 130.38 E
Okahandja **156** 21.59 S 16.58 E
Okahandja □ [5] **156** 21.30 S 17.00 E
Okahukura **172** 38.47 S 175.13 E
Okahumpka **220** 28.45 N 81.54 W
Okaihau **172** 35.19 S 173.47 E
Okalataka **152** 0.20 S 14.59 E
Okaloacoochee
Slough ≃ **220** 26.16 N 81.17 W
Okam **130** 40.53 N 42.36 E
Okamoto **270** 34.59 N 135.58 E
Okamoto -◆- [8] **270** 34.44 N 135.16 E
Okanagan
(Okanogan) ≃ **182** 48.06 N 119.43 W
Okanagan Centre **182** 50.03 N 119.27 W
Okanagan Falls **182** 49.21 N 119.34 W
Okanagan Indian
Reserve -◆- [4] **182** 50.21 N 119.17 W
Okanagan Lake ◎ **182** 50.00 N 119.28 W
Okanagan Landing **182** 50.14 N 119.22 W
Okanagan Mountain
Provincial Park ♦ **182** 49.45 N 119.40 W
Okanagan Range
(Okanogan Range)
⋏ **182** 49.00 N 120.00 W
Okanogan **202** 48.21 N 119.34 W
Okanogan □ [6] **224** 48.39 N 120.41 W
Okanogan
(Okanagan) ≃ **182** 48.06 N 119.43 W
Okanogan Range
(Okanagan Range)
⋏ **182** 49.00 N 120.00 W
Okapilco Creek ≃ **192** 30.45 N 83.30 W
Okaputa **156** 20.09 S 16.56 E
Okāra **123** 30.49 N 73.27 E
Okarche **196** 35.44 N 97.58 W
Okarito **172** 43.14 S 170.11 E
Okasaki **270** 34.46 N 135.52 E
Okatibbee Reservoir
◎ [1] **194** 32.30 N 88.47 W
Okato **172** 39.12 S 173.53 E
Okauchee **216** 43.06 N 88.26 W
Okauchee Lake ◎ **216** 43.07 N 88.26 W
Okaukuejo **156** 19.10 S 15.54 E
Okavango
(Cubango) ≃ **138** 18.50 S 22.25 E
Okavango Delta ≚ [2] **156** 18.45 S 22.45 E
Ōkawa, Nihon **92** 33.12 N 130.23 E
Ōkawa, Nihon **94** 35.05 N 138.15 E
Ōkawa, Nihon **96** 33.47 N 133.26 E
Ōkawachi **96** 35.04 N 134.45 E
Ōkawado **268** 35.56 N 139.50 E
Okawville **219** 38.26 N 89.33 W
Okaya **94** 36.03 N 138.03 E
Okayama **96** 34.39 N 133.55 E
Okayama □ [5] **96** 35.00 N 134.00 E
Okazaki **94** 34.57 N 137.10 E
Okch'ŏn **98** 36.20 N 127.34 E
Oke-Aro **273a** 6.41 N 3.19 E
Okeechobee **220** 27.14 N 80.49 W
Okeechobee □ [6] **220** 27.25 N 80.52 W
Okeechobee, Lake ◎ **220** 26.55 N 80.45 W
O'Keefe Centre ❀ **275b** 43.37 N 79.22 W
Okeene **196** 36.06 N 98.19 W
Okefenokee Swamp
⩸ **192** 30.42 N 82.20 W
Okegawa **94** 36.00 N 139.35 E

Symbols in the index entries represent the broad categories identified in the key at the right. Symbols with superior numbers (⋏ [1]) identify subcategories (see complete key on page *I · 1)*.

Kartensymbole in dem Registerverzeichnis stellen die rechts in Schlüssel erklärten Kategorien dar. Symbole mit hochgestellten Ziffern (⋏ [1]) bezeichnen Unterabteilungen einer Kategorie (vgl. vollständiger Schlüssel auf Seite *I · 1)*.

Los símbolos incluídos en el texto del índice representan las grandes categorias identificadas con la clave a la derecha. Los símbolos con numeros en su parte superior (⋏ [1]) identifican las subcategorías (véase la clave completa en la página *I · 1)*.

Les symboles de l'index représentent les catégories indiquées dans la légende à droite. Les symboles suivis d'un indice (⋏ [1]) représentent des sous-catégories (voir légende complète à la page *I · 1)*.

Os símbolos incluídos no texto do índice representam as grandes categorias identificadas com a chave à direita. Os símbolos com números em sua parte superior (⋏ [1]) identificam as subcategorias (veja-se a chave completa à página *I · 1)*.

	English	Deutsch	Español	Français	Português
∧	Mountain	Berg	Montaña	Montagne	Montanha
⋏	Mountains	Berge	Montañas	Montagnes	Montanhas
)(	Pass	Pass	Paso	Col	Passo
V	Valley, Canyon	Tal, Cañon	Valle, Cañón	Vallée, Canyon	Vale, Canhão
≚	Plain	Ebene	Llano	Plaine	Planície
≻	Cape	Kap	Cabo	Cap	Cabo
I	Island	Insel	Isla	Île	Ilha
II	Islands	Inseln	Islas	Îles	Ilhas
⩡	Other Topographic Features	Andere Topographische Objekte	Otros Elementos Topográficos	Autres données topographiques	Outros acidentes topográficos

Symbol	English	Deutsch	Español	Français	Português
≃	River	Fluss	Río	Rivière	Rio
≍	Canal	Kanal	Canal	Canal	Canal
ʟ	Waterfall, Rapids	Wasserfall, Stromschnellen	Cascada, Rápidos	Chute d'eau, Rapides	Cascata, Rápidos
ʉ	Strait	Meeresstrasse	Estrecho	Détroit	Estreito
c	Bay, Gulf	Bucht, Golf	Bahía, Golfo	Baie, Golfe	Baía, Golfo
◎	Lake, Lakes	See, Seen	Lago, Lagos	Lac, Lacs	Lago, Lagos
☷	Swamp	Sumpf	Pantano	Marais	Pântano
⊓	Ice Features, Glacier	Eis- und Gletscherformen	Accidentes Glaciales	Formes glaciaires	Acidentes glaciares
⍑	Other Hydrographic Features	Andere Hydrographische Objekte	Otros Elementos Hidrográficos	Autres données hydrographiques	Outros acidentes hidrográficos
✣	Submarine Features	Untermeerische Objekte	Accidentes Submarinos	Formes de relief sous-marin	Acidentes submarinos
□	Political Unit	Politische Einheit	Unidad Politica	Entité politique	Unidade política
ʊ	Cultural Institution	Kulturelle Institution	Institución Cultural	Institution culturelle	Institução cultural
⊥	Historical Site	Historische Stätte	Sitio Histórico	Site historique	Sitio histórico
♠	Recreational Site	Erholungs- und Ferienort	Sitio de Recreo	Centre de loisirs	Area de Lazer
⊠	Airport	Flughafen	Aeropuerto	Aéroport	Aeroporto
■	Military Installation	Militäranlage	Instalación Militar	Installation militaire	Instalação militar
◆	Miscellaneous	Verschiedenes	Misceláneo	Divers	Diversos

ENGLISH: Name | Page | Lat.°′ | Long.°′ — DEUTSCH: Name | Seite | Breite°′ | Länge°′ E = Ost

Symbols in the index entries represent the broad categories identified in the key at the right. Symbols with superior numbers (⩘[1]) identify subcategories (see complete key on page I · 1).

Kartensymbole in dem Registerverzeichnis stellen die rechts in Schlüssel erklärten Kategorien dar. Symbole mit hochgestellten Ziffern (⩘[1]) bezeichnen Unterabteilungen einer Kategorie (vgl. vollständiger Schlüssel auf Seite I · 1).

Los símbolos incluídos en el texto del índice representan las grandes categorias identificadas con la clave a la derecha. Los símbolos con numeros en su parte superior (⩘[1]) identifican las subcategorías (véase la clave completa en la página I · 1).

Les symboles de l'index représentent les catégories indiquées dans la légende à droite. Les symboles suivis d'un indice (⩘[1]) représentent des sous-catégories (voir légende complète à la page I · 1).

Os símbolos incluídos no texto do índice representam as grandes categorias identificadas com a chave à direita. Os símbolos com números em sua parte superior (⩘[1]) identificam as subcategorias (veja-se a chave completa à página I · 1).

	English	Deutsch	Español	Français	Português
ʌ	Mountain	Berg	Montaña	Montagne	Montanha
⩘	Mountains	Berge	Montañas	Montagnes	Montanhas
)(	Pass	Pass	Paso	Col	Passo
V	Valley, Canyon	Tal, Cañon	Valle, Cañón	Vallée, Canyon	Vale, Canhão
≚	Plain	Ebene	Llano	Plaine	Planície
›	Cape	Kap	Cabo	Cap	Cabo
I	Island	Insel	Isla	Île	Ilha
II	Islands	Inseln	Islas	Îles	Ilhas
⊥	Other Topographic Features	Andere Topographische Objekte	Otros Elementos Topográficos	Autres données topographiques	Outros acidentes topográficos

ESPAÑOL

Nombre	Página	Lat.°′	Long.°′ W = Oeste
Osilo	71	40.45 N	8.40 E
Osimo	66	43.29 N	13.29 E
Osini	71	39.50 N	9.29 E
Osinki	80	52.51 N	49.30 E
Osinniki, S.S.S.R.	80	58.03 N	47.02 E
Osinniki, S.S.S.R.	86	53.37 N	87.21 E
Osinovka, S.S.S.R.	83	49.34 N	39.05 E
Osinovka, S.S.S.R.	88	50.34 N	109.27 E
Osinovka, S.S.S.R.	88	56.19 N	101.56 E
Osinovskij chrebet ⋏	180	67.10 N	175.00 E
Osinów Dolny	54	52.48 N	14.10 E
Osintorf	76	54.42 N	30.39 E
Osio Sotto	62	45.36 N	9.35 E
Osipaonica	38	44.33 N	21.04 E
Osipenko, S.S.S.R.	78	46.54 N	36.49 E
Osipenko → Berd'ansk, S.S.S.R.	78	46.45 N	36.49 E
Osipoviči	76	53.18 N	28.38 E
Osipovo Selo	76	56.51 N	30.30 E
Osire	156	20.59 S	17.19 E
Oskaloosa, Ia., U.S.	190	41.17 N	92.38 W
Oskaloosa, Ks., U.S.	198	39.12 N	95.18 W
Oskar-Fredriksborg	40	59.24 N	18.26 E
Oskarshamn	26	57.16 N	16.26 E
Oskarström	26	56.48 N	12.58 E
Os'kino	78	51.14 N	39.02 E
Oskol ≃	78	49.06 N	37.25 E
Oskolkovo	24	67.58 N	53.42 E
Oskū	128	37.55 N	46.06 E
Oskuj	76	59.17 N	32.05 E
Oskuja ≃	76	59.14 N	31.54 E
Osl'anka, gora ∧	86	59.10 N	58.33 E
Oslava ≃	61	49.05 N	16.22 E
Ösling ◆[1]	56	49.55 N	6.00 E
Oslo	26	59.55 N	10.45 E
Oslob	116	9.31 N	123.26 E
Oslofjorden ⊂[2]	26	59.20 N	10.35 E
Os'ma ≃, S.S.S.R.	76	54.55 N	33.24 E
Ošma ≃, S.S.S.R.	80	57.52 N	47.45 E
Osmānābād	122	18.10 N	76.02 E
Osmancık	130	40.59 N	34.49 E
Osmaneli	130	40.22 N	30.01 E
Osmaniye	130	37.05 N	36.14 E
Osmanlı	130	41.52 N	34.37 E
Osmanpaşa	130	39.38 N	34.58 E
Ošm'anskaja vozvyšennosť ⋏[1]	76	54.20 N	26.00 E
Ošm'any	76	54.25 N	25.56 E
Osmeña	116	10.11 N	125.31 E
Osmington	42	50.38 N	2.22 W
Os'mino	76	59.01 N	29.06 E
Osminog, gora ∧	180	67.54 N	176.50 E
Ösmo	40	58.59 N	17.54 E
Osmond	198	42.21 N	97.35 W
Osmore, Río de ≃	248	17.33 S	71.12 W
Osmoy	261	48.52 N	1.43 E
Osmussaar I	76	59.18 N	23.22 E
Osnabrück	52	52.16 N	8.02 E
Ośno	30	52.28 N	14.50 E
Osny	261	49.04 N	2.04 E
Oso	224	48.16 N	121.56 W
Oso ≃	154	1.09 S	27.22 E
Oso, Gran Lago del → Great Bear Lake ⊜	176	66.00 N	120.00 W
Ošoba	85	40.44 N	70.26 E
Osogna	58	46.18 N	9.00 E
Osoppo	64	46.15 N	13.05 E
Osorakan-zan ∧	96	34.36 N	132.08 E
Osore-yama ∧	92	41.18 N	141.05 E
Osorio, Quebrada ≃	286c	10.36 N	66.56 W
Osório Fonseca	250	3.40 S	58.13 W
Osorno, Chile	254	40.34 S	73.09 W
Osorno, Esp.	34	42.24 N	4.22 W
Osorun	273a	6.33 N	3.29 E
Os'otr ≃	82	54.58 N	38.46 E
Osoyoos	182	49.02 N	119.28 W
Osoyoos Indian Reserve ◆[4]	182	49.08 N	119.30 W
Osoyoos Lake ⊜	182	49.00 N	119.26 W
Osøyra	26	60.11 N	5.28 E
Ospedaletti	62	43.48 N	7.43 E
Ospedaletto, It.	64	46.17 N	13.07 E
Ospedaletto, It.	64	46.03 N	11.33 E
Ospino	246	9.18 N	69.27 W
Ospitale di Cadore	64	46.20 N	12.19 E
Ospitaletto	64	45.33 N	10.04 E
Osprey	220	27.11 N	82.29 W
Osprey Reef ✢[2]	164	13.55 S	146.38 E
Ospwagan Lake ⊜	184	55.35 N	98.03 W
Os Ribeiros	256	22.06 S	46.49 W
Oss	52	51.46 N	5.31 E
Ossa, Mount ∧	166	41.54 S	146.01 E
Ossabaw Island I	192	31.47 N	81.06 W
Osse ≃, Fr.	32	44.07 N	0.17 E
Osse ≃, Nig.	150	6.10 N	5.20 E
Ossenberg	263	51.34 N	6.35 E
Ossendrecht	52	51.24 N	4.19 E
Osseo, Mi., U.S.	216	41.53 N	84.33 W
Osseo, Wi., U.S.	190	44.34 N	91.13 W
Ossett	44	53.41 N	1.35 W
Ossi	71	40.40 N	8.35 E
Ossiacher See ⊜	64	46.40 N	13.55 E
Ossian, In., U.S.	216	40.52 N	85.09 W
Ossian, Ia., U.S.	190	43.08 N	91.45 W
Ossian, Loch ⊜	46	56.46 N	4.38 W
Ossining	210	41.09 N	73.51 W
Ossipee	188	43.41 N	71.07 W
Ossjøen ⊜	26	61.13 N	11.53 E
Ossling	54	51.21 N	14.09 E
Ossona	266b	45.30 N	8.54 E
Ossora	74	59.20 N	163.13 E
Ossum-Bösinghoven	263	51.18 N	6.39 E
Ošta	24	60.49 N	35.32 E
Ostaboningue, Lac ⊜	190	47.09 N	78.53 W
Östanå, Sve.	40	59.33 N	18.35 E
Östanå, Sve.	40	60.38 N	16.48 E
Östanbyn	40	60.39 N	16.48 E
Ostankino ◆[8]	265b	55.49 N	37.37 E
Östansjö	40	59.03 N	14.59 E
Ostapje	78	49.33 N	33.46 E
Ostaškov	76	57.09 N	33.06 E
Ostašovo	82	55.52 N	35.52 E
Ost-Berlin → Berlin (Ost)	264a	52.30 N	13.25 E
Ostbevern	52	52.02 N	7.50 E
Østbirk	41	55.58 N	9.46 E
Ostbüren	263	51.31 N	7.46 E
Østby	26	61.15 N	12.32 E
Ostchinesisches Meer → East China Sea ╤[2]	90	30.00 N	126.00 E
Oste ≃	52	53.51 N	8.59 E
Osted	41	55.34 N	11.58 E
Osteen	220	28.50 N	81.09 W
Ostellato	66	44.45 N	11.56 E
Ostende → Oostende	50	51.13 N	2.55 E
Ostenfelde	52	51.52 N	8.04 E
Oster ≃	60	48.43 N	13.29 E
Osterath	56	51.16 N	6.37 E
Osterbönen	263	51.37 N	7.48 E
Osterburg, D.D.R.	54	52.47 N	11.44 E
Osterburg, Pa., U.S.	214	40.16 N	78.31 W
Osterburken	56	49.26 N	9.26 E
Österbybruk	40	60.12 N	17.54 E
Österbymo	26	57.50 N	15.16 E
Ostercappeln	52	52.20 N	8.13 E
Österdalälven ≃	26	60.33 N	15.08 E
Østerdalen V	26	61.15 N	11.10 E
Österfärnebo	40	60.18 N	16.48 E
Osterfeld	54	51.05 N	11.56 E
Osterfeld ◆[8]	263	51.30 N	6.53 E
Östergötland □[9]	26	58.24 N	15.34 E
Östergötlands Län □[6]	26	58.25 N	15.45 E
Österhaninge	40	59.08 N	18.12 E
Osterhofen	60	48.42 N	13.01 E
Øster Højst	41	55.00 N	9.03 E
Osterholz-Scharmbeck	52	53.14 N	8.47 E
Osterley Park ♠	260	51.30 N	0.21 W

FRANÇAIS

Nom	Page	Lat.°′	Long.°′ W = Ouest
Österlövsta	40	60.26 N	17.47 E
Ostermundigen	58	46.58 N	7.29 E
Osternienburg	54	51.48 N	12.01 E
Osterode, B.R.D.	52	51.44 N	10.11 E
Osterode → Ostróda, Pol.	30	53.43 N	19.59 E
Osterøya I	26	60.33 N	5.35 E
Österreich → Austria □[1]	30	47.20 N	13.20 E
Österreichisches Freilichtmuseum ⊍	61	47.10 N	15.19 E
Osterrönfeld	41	54.17 N	9.41 E
Östersjön → Baltic Sea ╤[2]	24	57.00 N	19.00 E
Österskär	40	59.28 N	18.18 E
Östersund	26	63.11 N	14.39 E
Östervåla	40	60.11 N	17.11 E
Osterville	207	41.37 N	70.23 W
Osterwick	52	52.01 N	7.13 E
Osterwieck	54	51.58 N	10.42 E
Ostfeld	263	51.40 N	7.45 E
Østfold □[6]	26	59.20 N	11.30 E
Ostfriesische Inseln II	52	53.44 N	7.25 E
Ostfriesland □[9]	52	53.20 N	7.40 E
Ost-Ghats → Eastern Ghāts ⋏	122	14.00 N	78.50 E
Östhammar	40	60.16 N	18.22 E
Ostheim vor der Rhön	56	50.27 N	10.14 E
Osthofen	56	49.42 N	8.19 E
Ostia, Bonifica di ◆[1]	267a	41.46 N	12.18 E
Ostia Antica ⊥	66	41.45 N	12.16 E
Ostiano	64	45.13 N	10.15 E
Ostiglia	64	45.04 N	11.08 E
Ostki	78	51.16 N	27.22 E
Östliche Sierra Madre → Madre Oriental, Sierra ⋏	232	22.00 N	99.30 W
Östmark	26	60.17 N	12.45 E
Ost'or, S.S.S.R.	76	54.01 N	32.48 E
Ost'or, S.S.S.R.	78	50.57 N	30.53 E
Ost'or ≃, S.S.S.R.	76	53.47 N	31.46 E
Ost'or ≃, S.S.S.R.	78	50.56 N	30.52 E
Ostpeene ≃	54	53.43 N	12.46 E
Ostra	66	43.37 N	13.09 E
Östraby	41	55.46 N	13.41 E
Ostrach	58	47.57 N	9.23 E
Ostrach ≃	58	48.04 N	9.24 E
Östra Grevie	41	55.28 N	13.08 E
Östra Husby	40	58.35 N	16.33 E
Östra Laxsjön ⊜	40	58.54 N	14.42 E
Östra Ljungby	41	56.11 N	13.04 E
Ostrander	214	40.15 N	83.12 W
Ostrau → Ostrava, Česko.	30	49.50 N	18.17 E
Ostrau, D.D.R.	54	51.12 N	13.09 E
Ostrava	30	49.50 N	18.17 E
Ostra Vetere	66	43.36 N	13.03 E
Ostrhauderfehn	52	53.08 N	7.37 E
Östrich	263	51.40 N	6.55 E
Ostricourt	50	50.27 N	3.02 E
Östringen	56	49.13 N	8.43 E
Ostritz	54	51.01 N	14.56 E
Ostróda	30	53.43 N	19.59 E
Ostrog	78	50.20 N	26.31 E
Ostrogožsk	78	50.52 N	39.05 E
Ostrokonje	76	59.52 N	42.02 E
Ostrołęka	30	53.06 N	21.34 E
Ostrołęka □[4]	30	53.00 N	21.30 E
Ostroróg	30	52.39 N	16.27 E
Ostrošickij Gorodok	76	54.04 N	27.42 E
Ostrov, Česko.	54	50.17 N	12.57 E
Ostrov, Rom.	38	44.06 N	27.22 E
Ostrov, S.S.S.R.	76	57.20 N	28.22 E
Ostrov, S.S.S.R.	76	60.34 N	37.55 E
Ostrov, S.S.S.R.	76	52.53 N	25.59 E
Ostrov, S.S.S.R.	265b	55.35 N	37.51 E
Ostrov I	30	47.55 N	17.35 E
Ostrov'anskij	80	46.45 N	42.13 E
Ostrovec	76	54.37 N	25.57 E
Ostrovki	265a	59.48 N	30.50 E
Ostrovno	76	55.08 N	29.53 E
Ostrovskaja	80	50.26 N	44.27 E
Ostrovskoje	80	57.48 N	42.15 E
Ostrov-Zalit	76	58.01 N	28.04 E
Ostrowiec Świętokrzyski	30	50.57 N	21.23 E
Ostrów Lubelski	30	51.30 N	22.52 E
Ostrów Mazowiecka	30	52.49 N	21.54 E
Ostrów Wielkopolski	30	51.39 N	17.49 E
Ostryna	76	53.44 N	24.32 E
Ostrzeszów	30	51.25 N	17.57 E
Ostsee → Baltic Sea ╤[2]	24	57.00 N	19.00 E
Ostseebad Ahrenshoop	54	54.23 N	12.25 E
Ostseebad Boltenhagen	54	54.00 N	11.12 E
Ostseebad Dierhagen	41	54.17 N	12.22 E
Ostseebad Graal-Müritz	54	54.15 N	12.12 E
Ostseebad Nienhagen	54	54.09 N	11.58 E
Ostseebad Rerik	54	54.06 N	11.37 E
Ostseebad Wustrow	54	54.21 N	12.23 E
Ost-Sümmern	263	51.26 N	7.44 E
Osttirol ◆[1]	64	46.55 N	12.30 E
Ostúa ≃	236	14.17 N	89.33 W
Ostuacán	234	17.25 N	93.18 W
Ostula	234	18.30 N	103.28 W
Ostuni	68	40.44 N	17.35 E
Ostwald	58	48.33 N	7.43 E
Osu	98	35.31 N	127.18 E
Osuga	76	56.02 N	34.18 E
Osuga ≃	76	57.16 N	34.49 E
Ōsuka	94	34.41 N	137.59 E
O'Sullivan, Lac ⊜	190	47.37 N	76.05 W
Osum ≃	38	40.48 N	19.52 E
Ōsumi	270	34.50 N	135.45 E
Ōsumi-hantō ≻[1]	92	31.20 N	130.55 E
Ōsumi-kaikyō ʯ	92	31.00 N	131.00 E
Ōsumi-shotō II	93b	30.30 N	130.00 E
Osuna	34	37.14 N	5.07 W
Osupugo ∧	154	1.40 N	35.49 E
Osvaldo Cruz	255	21.47 S	50.50 W
Osveja	76	56.01 N	28.06 E
Osvejskoje, ozero ⊜	76	56.03 N	28.08 E
Ošvor	24	66.58 N	62.53 E
Oswaldtwistle	44	53.43 N	2.26 W
Oswaldtwistle Moor ◆[3]	262	53.43 N	2.23 W
Oswald West State Park ♠	224	45.45 N	123.58 W
Oswayo	214	41.55 N	78.01 W
Oswayo Creek ≃	210	42.02 N	78.21 W
Oswegatchie ≃	188	44.42 N	75.30 W
Oswegatchie, Middle Branch ≃	212	44.07 N	75.19 W
Oswegatchie, West Branch ≃	188	44.18 N	75.20 W
Oswego, Il., U.S.	216	41.40 N	88.21 W
Oswego, In., U.S.	216	41.19 N	85.47 W
Oswego, Ks., U.S.	198	37.10 N	95.06 W
Oswego, N.Y., U.S.	212	43.27 N	76.30 W
Oswego □[6]	212	43.22 N	76.15 W
Oswego ≃, N.J., U.S.	208	39.40 N	74.32 W
Oswego ≃, N.Y., U.S.	212	43.28 N	76.31 W
Oswestry	42	52.52 N	3.04 W
Oświęcim	30	50.03 N	19.12 E
Osyka	194	31.00 N	90.28 W
Ota, Nihon	94	35.58 N	136.04 E
Ōta, Nihon	94	36.18 N	139.22 E
Ōta, Nihon	96	33.31 N	131.33 E
Ōta ◆[8]	268	35.34 N	139.43 E
Ōta ≃, Nihon	94	34.40 N	137.54 E
Ōta ≃, Nihon	96	34.22 N	132.25 E
Otago Peninsula ≻[1]	172	45.52 S	170.40 E

PORTUGUÊS

Nome	Página	Lat.°′	Long.°′ W = Oeste
Otahuhu	172	36.57 S	174.51 E
Ōtake	96	34.12 N	132.13 E
Otaki, N.Z.	172	40.45 S	175.09 E
Ōtaki, Nihon	94	35.17 N	140.15 E
Ōtaki, Nihon	94	35.48 N	137.33 E
Ōtaki, Nihon	94	35.57 N	138.56 E
Ōtaki ≃	94	35.49 N	137.40 E
Ōtaki-yama ∧	96	34.07 N	134.08 E
Ōta-Koizumi-hikojō ♠	94	36.16 N	139.24 E
Otane	172	39.53 S	176.38 E
Otanmäki	26	64.07 N	27.06 E
Otar	85	43.33 N	75.13 E
Otari	94	36.46 N	137.54 E
Otaru	92a	43.13 N	141.00 E
Otatara	172	46.26 S	168.18 E
Otatitlán	234	18.12 N	96.02 W
Otautau	172	46.09 S	168.00 E
Otava	26	61.39 N	27.04 E
Otava ≃	30	49.27 N	14.12 E
Otavalo	246	0.14 N	78.16 W
Otavi	156	19.39 S	17.20 E
Ōtawara	94	36.52 N	140.02 E
Otawa-yama ∧	270	34.28 N	135.53 E
Otay	228	32.35 N	117.03 W
Otchinjau	152	16.30 S	13.57 E
Oteapan	234	18.00 N	94.39 W
Otego	210	42.23 N	75.10 W
Otego Creek ≃	210	42.25 N	75.07 W
Otélé	152	3.35 N	11.15 E
Otematata	172	44.37 S	170.16 E
Oteotea	175e	9.05 S	161.11 E
Otepää	76	58.03 N	26.30 E
Oteros ≃	232	26.55 N	108.22 W
Otford, Austl.	170	34.12 S	151.01 E
Otford, Eng., U.K.	42	51.19 N	0.12 E
Otgon	88	47.11 N	97.33 E
Otgon Tenger uul ∧	88	47.36 N	97.36 E
Otham	260	51.15 N	0.35 E
Othello	202	46.49 N	119.10 W
Othery	42	51.05 N	2.53 W
Othfresen	52	52.00 N	10.23 E
Óthiris, Óros ⋏	38	39.02 N	22.37 E
Othis	261	49.04 N	2.41 E
Othonoí I	38	39.50 N	19.26 E
Oti ≃	150	8.40 N	0.13 E
Otibanda	164	7.15 S	146.30 E
Otinapa	232	24.11 N	105.02 W
Otira	172	42.50 S	171.33 E
Otis, Co., U.S.	198	40.08 N	102.57 W
Otis, In., U.S.	216	41.36 N	86.54 W
Otis, Ks., U.S.	198	38.32 N	99.03 W
Otis, Ma., U.S.	207	42.11 N	73.05 W
Otisco	218	38.32 N	85.40 W
Otisco Lake ⊜	210	42.52 N	76.18 W
Otish, Monts ⋏	176	52.22 N	70.30 W
Otis Reservoir ⊜[1]	207	42.09 N	73.02 W
Otisville	210	41.28 N	74.32 W
Otjassy	80	53.14 N	41.39 E
Otjikondo	156	19.50 S	15.23 E
Otjimbingue	156	22.19 S	16.10 E
Otjinene	156	21.13 S	18.42 E
Otjiwarongo	156	20.29 S	16.36 E
Otjiwarongo □[5]	156	20.45 S	16.30 E
Otjozondjou ≃	156	20.18 S	20.50 E
Otley	44	53.54 N	1.41 W
Otm'ok, pereval)(	85	42.20 N	73.10 E
Otmuchów	30	50.28 N	17.10 E
Otnes	26	61.45 N	11.14 E
Otnice	61	49.05 N	16.49 E
Ōtō	96	33.41 N	135.35 E
Otočac	36	44.52 N	15.14 E
Otog Qi	102	39.08 N	108.00 E
Ōtomi	175d	24.19 N	123.54 E
Oton	116	10.42 N	122.29 E
Otonabee ≃	212	44.08 N	78.14 W
Otoque, Isla I	236	8.36 N	79.36 W
Ōtori-kita	270	34.33 N	135.27 E
Otorma	80	53.32 N	42.32 E
Otoro ≃	236	15.00 N	88.16 W
Otorohanga	172	38.11 S	175.12 E
Otoskwin ≃	176	52.13 N	88.06 W
Otowa	94	34.51 N	137.18 E
Otowa-yama ∧	270	34.58 N	135.51 E
Otowa-yama-tunnel ◆[5]	94	34.58 N	135.51 E
Ōtoyo	96	33.46 N	133.40 E
Otra ≃	26	58.09 N	8.00 E
Otradnaja	84	44.23 N	41.31 E
Otradnoje	265a	59.47 N	30.49 E
Otradnyj	80	53.22 N	51.21 E
Otranto	68	40.09 N	18.30 E
Otranto, Capo d' ≻	68	40.06 N	18.31 E
Otranto, Strait of ʯ	38	40.00 N	19.00 E
Otricoli	66	42.25 N	12.29 E
Otrokovice	30	49.13 N	17.31 E
Ötscher ∧	61	47.52 N	15.12 E
Otsego	216	42.27 N	85.41 W
Otsego □[6]	210	42.42 N	74.56 W
Otsego Lake ⊜	210	42.45 N	74.52 W
Otselic ≃	210	42.20 N	75.58 W
Ōtsu, Nihon	96	35.00 N	135.52 E
Ōtsu, Nihon	268	35.16 N	139.42 E
Ōtsu ≃	270	34.30 N	135.24 E
Ōtsuchi	92	39.21 N	141.54 E
Ōtsuki	94	35.36 N	138.57 E
Ōtsu-shima I	96	34.00 N	131.42 E
Otta, Nig.	150	6.42 N	3.10 E
Otta, Nor.	26	61.46 N	9.32 E
Otta ≃	26	61.46 N	9.31 E
Ottakring ◆[8]	264b	48.12 N	16.19 E
Ottana	71	40.14 N	9.02 E
Otta Pass ʯ	175c	7.09 N	151.53 E
Ottarnic Pond ⊜	283	42.46 N	71.25 W
Ottati	68	40.28 N	15.19 E
Ottavia ◆[8]	267a	41.58 N	12.24 E
Ottaviano	68	40.51 N	14.28 E
Ottawa, On., Can.	212	45.25 N	75.42 W
Ottawa, Il., U.S.	216	41.20 N	88.50 W
Ottawa, Ks., U.S.	198	38.36 N	95.16 W
Ottawa, Oh., U.S.	216	41.01 N	84.02 W
Ottawa □[6], Mi., U.S.	216	42.57 N	86.02 W
Ottawa □[6], Oh., U.S.	214	41.31 N	82.56 W
Ottawa ≃, Can.	176	45.20 N	73.58 W
Ottawa ≃, Oh., U.S.	214	41.44 N	83.28 W
Ottawa ≃, Oh., U.S.	216	41.00 N	84.15 W
Ottawa-Carleton □[6]	212	45.15 N	75.45 W
Ottawa Hills	214	41.39 N	83.38 W
Ottawa International Airport ⊠	212	45.19 N	75.40 W
Ottawa Islands II	176	59.30 N	80.10 W
Ottbergen	52	51.42 N	9.18 E
Ottenby	26	56.14 N	16.25 E
Ottendorf-Okrilla	54	51.11 N	13.50 E
Ottenhöfen	58	48.34 N	8.09 E
Ottenschlag	61	48.25 N	15.13 E
Ottensheim	61	48.20 N	14.11 E
Ottenstein Stausee ⊜[1]	61	48.37 N	15.17 E
Otter ≃	42	50.46 N	3.17 W
Otterbach ≃	56	49.07 N	8.21 E
Otterbäcken	40	58.57 N	14.02 E
Otterbein	216	40.29 N	87.06 W
Otterburn	44	55.14 N	2.10 W
Otterburne	184	49.30 N	97.03 W
Otterburn Park	206	45.33 N	73.13 W
Otter Creek	192	29.19 N	82.46 W
Otter Creek ≃, On., Can.	212	44.06 N	81.07 W
Otter Creek ≃, Il., U.S.	219	39.18 N	90.07 W
Otter Creek ≃, In., U.S.	218	38.58 N	85.37 W
Otter Creek ≃, Ia., U.S.	190	41.20 N	93.30 W
Otter Creek ≃, Mo., U.S.	219	39.31 N	91.51 W
Otter Creek ≃, Mt., U.S.	202	45.36 N	106.17 W
Otter Creek ≃, N.Y., U.S.	212	43.43 N	75.23 W
Otter Creek ≃, Ut,. U.S.	200	38.10 N	112.02 W
Otter Creek ≃, Vt., U.S.	188	44.13 N	73.17 W

Otter Creek Reservoir ⊜[1]	200	38.12 N	111.59 W
Otterhöfen	56	48.33 N	8.12 E
Otter-Lake, P.Q., Can.	188	45.51 N	76.26 W
Otter Lake, Mi., U.S.	190	43.13 N	83.28 W
Otter Lake ⊜, On., Can.	212	44.47 N	76.07 W
Otter Lake ⊜, On., Can.	212	45.17 N	79.56 W
Otter Lake ⊜, Sk., Can.	184	55.35 N	104.39 W
Otter Lake ⊜[1]	219	39.26 N	89.54 W
Otterlo	52	52.06 N	5.45 E
Otterndorf	52	53.48 N	8.53 E
Otterøya I	26	62.42 N	6.48 E
Otter River	207	42.35 N	72.03 W
Ottersberg	52	53.06 N	9.08 E
Ottershaw	260	51.22 N	0.32 W
Ottersleben ◆[8]	54	52.05 N	11.34 E
Otter Tail ≃	198	46.16 N	96.36 W
Otter Tail Lake ⊜	198	46.23 N	95.40 W
Otterup	41	55.31 N	10.24 E
Otterville, On., Can.	212	42.55 N	80.36 W
Otterville, Il., U.S.	219	39.03 N	90.24 W
Otterville, Mo., U.S.	194	38.41 N	93.00 W
Ottery ≃	42	50.39 N	4.20 W
Ottery Saint Mary	42	50.45 N	3.17 W
Ottignies	56	50.40 N	4.34 E
Ottine	222	29.36 N	97.35 W
Ottleben	54	52.05 N	11.07 E
Ottmachau → Otmuchów	30	50.28 N	17.10 E
Ottmarsbocholt	52	51.49 N	7.32 E
Ottnang	60	48.06 N	13.40 E
Ottnaren ⊜	40	60.29 N	16.37 E
Otto, N.Y., U.S.	210	42.21 N	78.50 W
Otto, Tx., U.S.	222	31.27 N	96.49 W
Ottobeuren	58	47.56 N	10.18 E
Ottobeuren, Klosterkirche ⊍[1]	58	47.56 N	10.18 E
Ottobiano	62	45.09 N	8.50 E
Ottobrunn	60	48.04 N	11.40 E
Ottone	62	44.37 N	9.20 E
Ottoschwanden	58	48.12 N	7.52 E
Ottosdal	158	26.58 S	26.00 E
Ottoshoop	156	25.45 S	25.59 E
Ottoville	216	40.55 N	84.20 W
Ottuk, S.S.S.R.	85	41.38 N	75.51 E
Ottuk, S.S.S.R.	85	42.18 N	76.18 E
Ottumwa	190	41.00 N	92.22 W
Ottweiler	56	49.24 N	7.09 E
Otty Lake ⊜	212	44.50 N	76.13 W
Otu	150	8.14 N	3.24 E
Otu → Ōtsu	96	35.00 N	135.52 E
Otukpa	150	7.09 N	7.41 E
Otumpa	252	27.19 S	62.13 W
Otun	273a	6.42 N	3.22 E
Otuquis, Bañados de ⩩	248	19.20 S	58.30 W
Oturkpo	150	7.14 N	8.08 E
Otuzco	248	7.54 S	78.35 W
Otway, Bahía ʯ	254	53.20 S	74.00 W
Otway, Cape ≻	166	38.52 S	143.31 E
Otway, Seno ⊂	254	53.05 S	71.30 W
Otway Range ⋏	169	38.30 S	143.50 E
Otwock	30	52.07 N	21.16 E
Otyn'a	78	48.44 N	24.51 E
Ötztal V	64	47.05 N	10.55 E
Ötztaler Ache ≃	64	47.14 N	10.50 E
Ötztaler Alpen (Alpi Venoste) ⋏	64	46.45 N	10.55 E
Ou ≃, Lao	110	20.04 N	102.13 E
Ou ≃, Zhg.	100	28.01 N	120.44 E
Ou ≃, Zhg.	100	26.02 N	113.09 E
Oua ≃	152	0.43 N	12.55 E
Ouachita ≃	194	31.38 N	91.49 W
Ouachita, Lake ⊜[1]	194	34.40 N	93.25 W
Ouachita Mountains ⋏	194	34.40 N	94.25 W
Ouaco	175f	20.50 S	164.29 E
Ouadâne	148	20.56 N	11.37 W
Ouadda	152	8.04 N	22.24 E
Ouaddaï □[5]	146	13.00 N	21.00 E
Ouadey, Ouadi el V	146	13.34 N	18.03 E
Ouagadougou	150	12.22 N	1.31 W
Ouahigouya	150	13.35 N	2.25 W
Ouahran → Wahran	148	35.43 N	0.43 W
Ouaka □[5]	152	6.00 N	21.00 E
Ouaka ≃	152	4.59 N	19.56 E
Oualâta	150	17.18 N	7.02 W
Ouâlata, Dahr ⊥[4]	150	17.48 N	7.24 W
Oualé ≃	150	10.52 N	0.51 E
Oualidia	148	32.44 N	9.08 W
Ouallam	150	14.19 N	2.05 E
Ouallene	148	24.37 N	1.14 E
Oualto	150	9.01 N	10.06 W
Ouanary	250	4.13 N	51.40 W
Ouanda Djallé	146	8.54 N	22.48 E
Ouandago	146	7.10 N	18.42 E
Ouandja ≃	146	9.35 N	21.43 E
Ouandja-Vakaga, Réserve de la ◆[4]	146	9.00 N	21.30 E
Ouango	152	4.19 N	22.33 E
Ouangolodougou	150	9.58 N	5.09 W
Ouaninou	150	8.11 N	7.51 W
Ouanne ≃	50	47.57 N	2.47 E
Ouan Taredert	148	27.33 N	9.32 E
Ouaquaga	210	42.08 N	75.39 W
Ouara ≃	154	5.05 N	24.26 E
Ouarâne ◆[1]	134	21.00 N	10.30 W
Ouararda, Passe de)(	148	21.01 N	13.03 W
Ouareau ≃	206	45.56 N	73.25 W
Ouareau, Lac ⊜[1]	206	46.17 N	74.09 W
Ouargaye	150	11.32 N	0.01 E
Ouarkoye	150	12.05 N	3.40 W
Ouarkziz, Jbel ⋏	148	28.50 N	9.00 W
Ouarsenis, Djebel ∧	34	35.53 N	1.38 E
Ouarville	50	48.21 N	1.46 E
Ouarzazate	148	30.57 N	6.50 W
Ouarzazate □[4]	148	30.55 N	6.45 W
Ouassoulou ≃	150	11.35 N	8.11 W
Ouatcha	150	13.22 N	9.18 E
Oubangui (Ubangi) ≃	152	0.30 S	17.42 E
Ouche ≃	58	47.06 N	5.16 E
Oucques	50	47.49 N	1.18 E
Ōuda	94	34.28 N	135.56 E
Oudaze Lake ⊜	212	45.27 N	79.11 W
Oud-Beijerland	52	51.49 N	4.25 E
Ouddorp	52	51.18 N	3.56 E
Oude IJssel (Issel) ≃	52	52.00 N	6.10 E
Oudenaarde	50	50.51 N	3.36 E
Oudenbosch	52	51.35 N	4.31 E
Oudenburg	50	50.46 N	3.53 E
Oude-Pekela	52	53.04 N	6.58 E
Oude Rijn ≃	52	52.05 N	4.20 E
Oudeschild	52	53.02 N	4.50 E
Oude-Tonge	52	51.41 N	4.12 E
Oudewater	52	52.02 N	4.52 E
Oud-Gastel	52	51.35 N	4.27 E
Oudjda → Oujda	148	34.41 N	1.45 W
Oud-Loosdrecht	52	52.13 N	5.04 E
Oudtshoorn	158	33.35 S	22.14 E
Oudyoumoudi	150	14.04 N	0.28 W
Oued Athmenia	34	36.15 N	6.17 E
Oued Cheham	36	36.23 N	7.46 E
Oued edh Dheheb, Khlij ⊂	148	23.45 N	15.47 W
Oued Fodda	34	36.11 N	1.32 E
Oued Meliz	36	36.27 N	8.34 E
Oued Rhiou	34	35.58 N	0.55 E
Oued Tlelat	34	35.34 N	0.27 W
Oued Zarga	36	36.40 N	9.25 E
Oued-Zem	148	32.55 N	6.33 W
Ouellé	150	7.18 N	4.01 W
Ouémé □[5]	150	7.00 N	2.35 E
Ouémé ≃	150	6.29 N	2.32 E
Ouen, Île I	175f	22.26 S	166.49 E
Ouenkoro	150	13.23 N	3.50 W
Ouenza, Djebel ∧	36	35.57 N	8.05 E

Ouenzé ◆[8]	273b	4.14 S	15.17 E
Ouessa	150	11.03 N	2.47 W
Ouessant, Île d' I	32	48.28 N	5.05 W
Ouesso	152	1.37 N	16.04 E
Ouest □[4]	152	5.23 N	10.45 E
Ouest, Pointe de l' ≻	186	49.52 N	64.31 W
Ouest, Rivière de l' ≃	206	45.39 N	74.21 W
Ouezzane	148	34.52 N	5.35 W
Ouffet	56	50.26 N	5.28 E
Ouganda → Uganda □[1]	154	1.00 N	32.00 E
Ougarou	150	12.09 N	0.56 E
Oughter, Lough ⊜, Ire.	48	54.00 N	7.30 W
Oughter, Lough ⊜, Ire.	48	54.07 N	6.42 W
Oughterard	48	53.25 N	9.17 W
Oughtibridge	44	53.26 N	1.33 W
Ouham □[5]	152	7.00 N	18.00 E
Ouham ≃	136	9.18 N	18.14 E
Ouham-Pendé □[5]	152	7.00 N	16.00 E
Ouidah	150	6.22 N	2.05 E
Ouidi	146	14.07 N	12.58 E
Ouimet Canyon V	190	48.47 N	88.40 W
Oujda	148	34.41 N	1.45 W
Oujda □[4]	148	34.05 N	2.10 W
Oulad Naïl, Monts des ⋏	148	34.33 N	3.28 E
Oulainen	26	64.16 N	24.48 E
Oulangan Kansallispuisto ♠	24	66.12 N	29.30 E
Oulchy-le-Château	50	49.12 N	3.21 E
Oule ≃	62	44.25 N	5.21 E
Ouled Agla	34	35.58 N	4.45 E
Ouleout Creek ≃	210	42.20 N	75.18 W
Oulins	50	48.52 N	1.28 E
Oullins	62	45.43 N	4.48 E
Oulou, Bahr ≃	146	9.48 N	21.32 E
Oulton Broad	42	52.31 N	1.42 E
Oulu	26	65.01 N	25.28 E
Oulujärvi ⊜	26	64.20 N	27.15 E
Oulujoki ≃	26	65.01 N	25.25 E
Oulun lääni □[4]	24	65.00 N	27.00 E
Oulx	62	45.02 N	6.50 E
Oumba	152	4.55 N	19.04 E
Oum-Chalouba	146	15.48 N	20.46 E
Oumé	150	6.23 N	5.25 W
Oumé □[5]	150	6.20 N	5.30 W
Oum El Bouagui	148	35.53 N	7.07 E
Oum El Bouagui □[5]	148	35.50 N	7.15 E
Oum er Rbia, Oued ≃	148	33.19 N	8.21 W
Oum-Hadjer	146	13.18 N	19.41 E
Oum Hadjer, Ouadi V	146	16.38 N	20.14 E
Oumiao	102	31.55 N	112.09 E
Oumm eḍ Ḍroûs Guebli, Sebkhet ⊜	148	24.03 N	11.45 W
Oumm eḍ Ḍroûs Telli, Sebkhet ⊜	148	24.20 N	11.30 W
Ounâne, Bîr ╤[4]	148	21.28 N	3.56 W
Ounara	148	31.33 N	9.28 W
Ounasjoki ≃	24	66.30 N	25.45 E
Oundle	42	52.29 N	0.29 W
Ounianga Kébir	146	19.04 N	20.29 E
Ouolossébougou	150	12.00 N	7.55 W
Our ≃	56	49.53 N	6.18 E
Ouragahio	150	6.19 N	5.56 W
Ōura-wan ⊂	174m	26.32 N	128.04 E
Ouray	200	38.01 N	107.40 W
Ouray, Mount ∧	200	38.25 N	106.14 W
Ource ≃	58	48.06 N	4.23 E
Ourcq ≃	50	49.01 N	3.01 E
Ourcq, Canal de l' ≊	50	48.51 N	2.22 E
Ourém	250	1.33 S	47.06 W
Ouri	146	21.34 N	19.13 E
Ouri, Tarso ∧	146	21.25 N	18.56 E
Ouricuri	250	7.53 S	40.05 W
Ourimbah	170	33.22 S	151.23 E
Ourinhos	255	22.59 S	49.52 W
Ourique	34	37.39 N	8.13 W
Ournie	171b	35.56 S	147.51 E
Ouro, Paraná do ≃	248	8.29 S	70.30 W
Ouro, Ponta do ≻	158	26.51 S	32.54 E
Ouro, Rio d' ≃	287a	22.42 S	43.35 W
Ouro Branco	250	6.42 S	36.57 W
Ouro Fino	256	22.17 S	46.22 W
Ouro Prêto	255	20.23 S	43.30 W
Ouro Prêto ≃	248	11.02 S	65.13 W
Ouroufa, Vallée d' V	150	14.42 N	7.00 E
Ours, Grand Lac de l' → Great Bear Lake ⊜	176	66.00 N	120.00 W
Oursi	150	14.41 N	0.27 W
Ourthe ≃	56	50.38 N	5.35 E
Ourthe Occidentale ≃	56	50.08 N	5.41 E
Ourthe Orientale ≃	56	50.08 N	5.41 E
Ourville-en-Caux	50	49.44 N	0.36 E
Ōu-sammyaku ⋏	92	38.45 N	140.50 E
Ouse	166	42.29 S	146.42 E
Ouse ≃, On., Can.	212	44.17 N	78.03 W
Ouse ≃, Eng., U.K.	42	50.47 N	0.03 E
Ouse ≃, Eng., U.K.	44	53.42 N	0.41 W
Oust ≃	32	47.39 N	2.06 W
Outardes, Baie aux ⊂	186	49.02 N	68.30 W
Outardes, Rivière aux ≃	176	49.04 N	68.28 W
Outardes Est, Rivière aux ≃	206	45.06 N	74.04 W
Outardes Quatre, Réservoir ⊜[1]	186	49.50 N	68.58 W
Outardes Trois, Barrage ◆[6]	186	49.34 N	68.48 W
Outarville	50	48.13 N	2.01 E
Outcalt	276	40.23 N	74.24 W
Outeniekwaberge ⋏	158	33.53 S	22.35 E
Outerbridge Crossing ◆[5]	276	40.31 N	74.15 W
Outer Harbour	168b	34.47 S	138.30 E
Outer Hebrides II	46	57.45 N	7.00 W
Outer Island I	190	47.03 N	90.30 W
Outer Santa Barbara Passage ʯ	228	33.10 N	118.30 W
Outjo	156	20.08 S	16.08 E
Outjo □[5]	156	19.30 S	15.30 E
Outlane	262	53.39 N	1.53 W
Outlet Bay ⊂	208	37.22 N	75.49 W
Outlook, Sk., Can.	184	51.30 N	107.03 W
Outlook, Mt., U.S.	198	48.53 N	104.46 W
Outokumpu	26	62.44 N	29.01 E
Outpost Mountain ∧	180	69.08 N	151.12 W
Outreau	50	50.42 N	1.35 E
Outremont	206	45.31 N	73.38 W
Outside Canal ≊	226	37.13 N	121.02 W
Out Skerries II	46a	60.25 N	0.42 W
Outwell	42	52.37 N	0.14 E
Ouvéa I, N. Cal.	175f	20.30 S	166.35 E
Ouvéa I, N. Cal.	175f	20.30 S	166.35 E
Ouvéa I, N. Cal.	175f	20.30 S	166.35 E
Ouvéa, Lagon d' ⊂	175f	20.33 S	166.27 E
Ouvèze ≃	62	43.59 N	4.51 E
Ouvidor	255	18.14 S	47.50 W
Ouye, Forêt de l' ♠	261	48.32 N	2.00 E
Ouyen	166	35.04 S	142.20 E
Ouzinkie	180	57.55 N	152.30 W
Ouzouer-le-Marché	50	47.55 N	1.32 E
Ouzouer-sur-Loire	50	47.46 N	2.29 E
Ouzzal, Oued i-n- V	148	21.35 N	2.00 E
Ovacık	130	41.05 N	32.55 E
Ovada	62	44.38 N	8.38 E
Oval	210	41.09 N	77.11 W
Ovalau I	175g	17.40 S	178.48 E
Ovalle	252	30.36 S	71.12 W
Ovamboland □[9]	156	17.45 S	16.30 E
Ovana, Cerro ∧	246	4.38 N	66.57 W
Ovar	34	40.52 N	8.38 W
Ovaro	64	46.29 N	12.52 E
Ovčinino	82	56.02 N	39.03 E
Ovcyno	265a	59.48 N	30.37 E
Övedskloster	41	55.41 N	13.38 E
Ovejas	246	9.32 N	75.14 W
Ovelgönne	52	53.20 N	8.25 E
Ovenden	262	53.44 N	1.53 W

Oveng	152	2.25 N	12.16 E
Overath	56	50.55 N	7.14 E
Overberge	263	51.37 N	7.41 E
Overbrook	198	38.46 N	95.33 W
Overbrook ◆[8], Pa., U.S.	279b	40.24 N	79.59 W
Overbrook ◆[8], Pa., U.S.	285	39.58 N	75.16 W
Overdinkel	52	52.14 N	7.01 E
Overflakkee I	52	51.45 N	4.10 E
Overflowing ≃	184	53.10 N	101.05 W
Overhalla	24	64.30 N	11.57 E
Overijse	56	50.46 N	4.32 E
Overijssel □[4]	52	52.25 N	6.30 E
Over Jerstal	41	55.12 N	9.18 E
Överkalix	24	66.21 N	22.56 E
Overland	219	38.42 N	90.21 W
Overland Park	198	38.58 N	94.40 W
Overlea	208	39.22 N	76.31 W
Overloon	52	51.35 N	5.57 E
Övermark (Ylimarkku)	26	62.38 N	21.30 E
Overpeck Creek ≃	276	40.51 N	74.02 W
Overpelt	56	51.13 N	5.25 E
Overseal	42	52.44 N	1.34 W
Overstrand	42	52.56 N	1.20 E
Overton, Eng., U.K.	42	51.15 N	1.15 W
Overton, Ne., U.S.	198	40.44 N	99.32 W
Overton, Nv., U.S.	204	36.32 N	114.26 W
Overton, Tx., U.S.	222	32.16 N	94.58 W
Overton Arm ⊂	204	36.20 N	114.25 W
Övertorneå	24	66.23 N	23.40 E
Överum	26	57.59 N	16.19 E
Over Wallop	42	51.09 N	1.35 W
Ovett	194	31.29 N	89.01 W
Ovid, Mi., U.S.	216	43.00 N	84.22 W
Ovid, N.Y., U.S.	210	42.40 N	76.49 W
Ovidiopol'	78	46.17 N	30.27 E
Oviedo, Esp.	34	43.22 N	5.50 W
Oviedo, Fl., U.S.	220	28.40 N	81.13 W
Oviglio	62	44.52 N	8.29 E
Oviken	26	62.59 N	14.24 E
Oviksfjällen ⋏	26	63.02 N	13.51 E
Ovilla	222	32.32 N	96.53 W
Ovindoli	66	42.08 N	13.31 E
Ovinišče	76	58.22 N	37.02 E
Ovino	76	59.41 N	33.11 E
Oviši	76	57.34 N	21.45 E
Övörchangaj □[4]	102	46.00 N	102.30 E
Øvre Anarjokka Nasjonalpark ♠	24	69.00 N	25.00 E
Øvre Årdal	26	61.19 N	7.48 E
Øvre Dividalen Nasjonalpark ♠	24	68.39 N	19.45 E
Øvre Pasvik Nasjonalpark ♠	24	69.06 N	28.55 E
Øvre Rendal	26	61.53 N	11.05 E
Övre Vättern ⊜	40	59.52 N	15.40 E
Ovruč	78	51.21 N	28.49 E
Ovs'anikovo	76	60.09 N	45.16 E
Ovs'anka, S.S.S.R.	86	55.57 N	92.33 E
Ovs'anka, S.S.S.R.	89	53.35 N	126.57 E
Ovs'annikovo	82	56.54 N	37.33 E
Ovstug	76	53.24 N	33.52 E
Ōwada	268	35.49 N	139.33 E
Owaka	172	46.27 S	169.40 E
Owambo □[5]	156	18.00 S	16.00 E
Owambo ≃	156	18.45 S	17.03 E
Owando	152	0.29 S	15.55 E
Owaneco	219	39.29 N	89.12 W
Owariashi	94	35.12 N	137.02 E
Owasco	210	42.51 N	76.28 W
Owasco Inlet ≃	210	42.45 N	76.28 W
Owasco Lake ⊜	210	42.52 N	76.32 W
Owasco Outlet ≃	210	43.04 N	76.39 W
Owase	92	34.04 N	136.12 E
Owasso	196	36.16 N	95.51 W
Owatonna	190	44.05 N	93.13 W
Owbeh	128	34.22 N	63.10 E
Owe	272c	19.04 N	73.04 E
Owego	210	42.06 N	76.15 W
Owego Creek, East Branch ≃	210	42.10 N	76.15 W
Owego Creek, West Branch ≃	210	42.10 N	76.15 W
Owel, Lough ⊜	48	53.34 N	7.25 W
Owen, Austl.	168b	34.16 S	138.33 E
Owen, B.R.D.	56	48.35 N	9.27 E
Owen, In., U.S.	218	38.27 N	85.34 W
Owen, Wi., U.S.	190	44.57 N	90.33 W
Owen □[6]	218	38.33 N	84.49 W
Owen, Mount ∧	172	41.33 S	172.32 E
Owenboy ≃	48	51.48 N	8.18 W
Owendo	152	0.17 N	9.30 E
Owenea ≃	48	54.47 N	8.26 W
Owen Falls Dam ◆[6]	154	0.27 N	33.11 E
Owen Fracture Zone ✢	12	12.00 N	58.00 E
Owenkillew ≃	48	54.44 N	7.18 W
Owenmore ≃	48	54.07 N	9.50 W
Owen River	172	41.39 S	172.27 E
Owens ≃	204	36.31 N	117.57 W
Owensboro	194	37.46 N	87.06 W
Owens Creek ≃, Ca., U.S.	226	37.13 N	120.42 W
Owens Creek ≃, Md., U.S.	208	39.33 N	77.20 W
Owens Lake ⊜	204	36.25 N	117.56 W
Owen Sound	212	44.34 N	80.56 W
Owen Sound ⊂	212	44.40 N	80.55 W
Owen Stanley Range ⋏	164	9.20 S	147.55 E
Owensville, In., U.S.	194	38.16 N	87.41 W
Owensville, Mo., U.S.	219	38.20 N	91.30 W
Owensville, Oh., U.S.	218	39.07 N	84.08 W
Owenton, Ky., U.S.	218	38.32 N	84.50 W
Owenton, Va., U.S.	208	37.53 N	77.06 W
Owentown	222	32.26 N	95.12 W
Owerri	150	5.29 N	7.02 E
Owhango	172	39.00 S	175.23 E
Owikeno Lake ⊜	182	51.41 N	127.00 W
Owings	208	38.43 N	76.36 W
Owings Mills	284b	39.25 N	76.46 W
Owingsville	188	38.08 N	83.45 W
Owl ≃, Ab., Can.	182	54.54 N	111.57 W
Owl ≃, Mb., Can.	176	57.51 N	92.44 W
Owl Creek ≃, U.S.	198	44.41 N	103.29 W
Owl Creek ≃, Mt., U.S.	202	45.18 N	107.21 W
Owl Creek ≃, Wy., U.S.	202	43.41 N	108.11 W
Owl Creek, South Fork ≃	202	43.43 N	108.32 W
Owl Creek Mountains ⋏	202	43.30 N	108.35 W
Owo	150	7.15 N	5.37 E
Oworonsoki	273a	6.33 N	3.24 E
Owosso	216	42.59 N	84.10 W
Owuru ≃	273a	6.39 N	3.27 E
Owyhee	204	41.56 N	116.05 W
Owyhee ≃	202	43.46 N	117.02 W
Owyhee, Lake ⊜[1]	202	43.28 N	117.20 W
Owyhee, South Fork ≃	202	42.26 N	116.53 W
Oxapampa	248	10.34 S	75.24 W
Oxbow, Sk., Can.	184	49.14 N	102.11 W
Oxbow, Mi., U.S.	281	42.38 N	83.28 W
Oxbow, N.Y., U.S.	212	44.17 N	75.37 W
Oxbow Lake ⊜	281	42.38 N	83.28 W
Ox Creek ≃	198	48.37 N	100.17 W
Oxelösund	40	58.40 N	17.06 E
Oxford, N.S., Can.	186	45.44 N	63.52 W
Oxford, N.Z.	172	43.18 S	172.11 E
Oxford, Eng., U.K.	42	51.46 N	1.15 W
Oxford, Al., U.S.	194	33.36 N	85.50 W
Oxford, Ct., U.S.	207	41.26 N	73.07 W
Oxford, Fl., U.S.	220	28.55 N	82.02 W
Oxford, In., U.S.	216	40.31 N	87.14 W
Oxford, Ia., U.S.	190	41.43 N	91.47 W
Oxford, Ks., U.S.	198	37.16 N	97.10 W
Oxford, Ky., U.S.	218	38.16 N	84.30 W
Oxford, Me., U.S.	188	44.07 N	70.29 W

Symbol	English	Deutsch	Español	Français	Português
≃	River	Fluss	Río	Rivière	Rio
≊	Canal	Kanal	Canal	Canal	Canal
ʟ	Waterfall, Rapids	Wasserfall, Stromschnellen	Cascada, Rápidos	Chute d'eau, Rapides	Cascata, Rápidos
ʯ	Strait	Meeresstrasse	Estrecho	Détroit	Estreito
⊂	Bay, Gulf	Bucht, Golf	Bahía, Golfo	Baie, Golfe	Baía, Golfo
⊜	Lake, Lakes	See, Seen	Lago, Lagos	Lac, Lacs	Lago, Lagos
⩩	Swamp	Sumpf	Pantano	Marais	Pântano
⍓	Ice Features, Glacier	Eis- und Gletscherformen	Accidentes Glaciales	Formes glaciaires	Acidentes glaciares
╤	Other Hydrographic Features	Andere Hydrographische Objekte	Otros Elementos Hidrográficos	Autres données hydrographiques	Outros acidentes hidrográficos
✢	Submarine Features	Untermeerische Objekte	Accidentes Submarinos	Formes de relief sous-marin	Acidentes submarinos
□	Political Unit	Politische Einheit	Unidad Politica	Entité politique	Unidade política
⊍	Cultural Institution	Kulturelle Institution	Institución Cultural	Institution culturelle	Institução cultural
⊥	Historical Site	Historische Stätte	Sitio Histórico	Site historique	Sitio histórico
♠	Recreational Site	Erholungs- und Ferienort	Sitio de Recreo	Centre de loisirs	Area de Lazer
⊠	Airport	Flughafen	Aeropuerto	Aéroport	Aeroporto
■	Military Installation	Militäranlage	Instalación Militar	Installation militaire	Instalação militar
◆	Miscellaneous	Verschiedenes	Misceláneo	Divers	Diversos

Name	Page	Lat.°′	Long.°′
Oxford, Md., U.S.	**208**	38.41 N	76.10 W
Oxford, Ma., U.S.	**207**	42.07 N	71.51 W
Oxford, Mi., U.S.	**216**	42.49 N	83.15 W
Oxford, Ms., U.S.	**194**	34.21 N	89.31 W
Oxford, Ne., U.S.	**198**	40.15 N	99.38 W
Oxford, N.J., U.S.	**210**	40.48 N	74.59 W
Oxford, N.Y., U.S.	**210**	42.26 N	75.35 W
Oxford, N.C., U.S.	**192**	36.18 N	78.35 W
Oxford, Oh., U.S.	**218**	39.30 N	84.44 W
Oxford, Pa., U.S.	**208**	39.47 N	75.58 W
Oxford, Wi., U.S.	**190**	43.46 N	89.34 W
Oxford □[6]	**212**	43.08 N	80.50 W
Oxford Falls	**274a**	33.44 S	151.15 E
Oxford House	**184**	54.56 N	95.16 W
Oxford House Indian Reserve ◆[4]	**184**	54.54 N	95.15 W
Oxford Junction	**190**	41.59 N	90.57 W
Oxford Lake ⊜	**184**	54.51 N	95.37 W
Oxford Peak ∧	**202**	42.16 N	112.06 W
Oxfordshire □[6]	**42**	51.50 N	1.15 W
Oxford Valley Mall ◆[9]	**285**	40.11 N	74.53 W
Oxhey	**260**	51.39 N	0.23 W
Oxie	**41**	55.33 N	13.04 E
Oxley	**166**	34.12 S	144.06 E
Oxley Creek ≃	**171a**	27.32 S	153.00 E
Oxnard	**228**	34.11 N	119.10 W
Oxnard Beach	**228**	34.09 N	119.13 W
Oxon Hill	**284c**	38.48 N	76.59 W
Oxon Run ≃	**284b**	38.49 N	77.00 W
Ox Pasture Brook ≃	**283**	42.45 N	70.54 W
Oxshott	**260**	51.20 N	0.21 W
Oxted	**42**	51.16 N	0.01 W
Oxtongue ≃	**212**	45.19 N	79.01 W
Oxtongue Lake ⊜	**212**	45.22 N	78.55 W
Oxus → Amu Darya ≃	**72**	43.40 N	59.01 E
Oy	**58**	47.38 N	10.28 E
Oya, Malay.	**112**	2.52 N	111.53 E
Ōya, Nihon	**96**	35.20 N	134.40 E
Oya ≃	**112**	2.52 N	111.52 E
Oyabe	**94**	36.40 N	136.52 E
Oyabe ≃	**94**	36.48 N	137.04 E
Ōya-ji ʋ[1]	**94**	36.38 N	139.48 E
Ōyake-yama ∧[2]	**270**	34.48 N	135.51 E
Oyama, B.C., Can.	**182**	50.07 N	119.22 W
Oyama, Nihon	**94**	35.21 N	139.00 E
Oyama, Nihon	**94**	36.18 N	139.48 E
Ōyama, Nihon	**94**	36.36 N	137.18 E
Oyama, Nihon	**268**	35.36 N	139.22 E
Ōyamada	**94**	34.46 N	136.13 E
Ōyamazaki	**270**	34.54 N	135.42 E
Oyameles	**234**	19.43 N	97.32 W
Oyan	**152**	0.02 N	10.17 E
Ōyano	**92**	32.35 N	130.26 E
Oyapock (Oiapoque) ≃	**250**	4.08 N	51.40 W
Oyashirazu ♠	**94**	36.59 N	137.40 E
Oybin	**54**	50.50 N	14.44 E
Oye-et-Pallet	**58**	46.51 N	6.20 E
Oyem	**152**	1.37 N	11.35 E
Oyen	**184**	51.22 N	110.28 W
Øyeren ⊜	**26**	59.48 N	11.14 E
Oykel ≃	**46**	57.56 N	4.25 W
Oykel Bridge	**46**	57.58 N	4.43 W
Oymyakon → Ojm'akon	**74**	63.28 N	142.49 E
Oyo, Congo	**152**	0.01 N	15.54 E
Oyo, Nig.	**150**	7.51 N	3.56 E
Oyo □[3]	**150**	8.00 N	3.50 E
Oyo ≃	**115a**	7.57 S	110.22 E
Ōyodo	**96**	34.23 N	135.48 E
Ōyodo ◆[8]	**270**	34.43 N	135.30 E
Ōyodo ≃	**92**	31.53 N	131.28 E
Oyón	**248**	10.39 S	76.47 W
Oyonnax	**58**	46.15 N	5.40 E
Ōyorogi-san ∧	**96**	35.05 N	132.51 E
Oyotún	**248**	6.51 S	79.19 W
Oyster	**208**	37.17 N	75.55 W
Oyster Bay	**210**	40.51 N	73.31 W
Oyster Bay ⊂, Austl.	**168b**	34.54 S	137.48 E
Oyster Bay ⊂, Austl.	**274a**	34.00 S	151.06 E
Oyster Bay ⊂, N.Y., U.S.	**276**	40.55 N	73.30 W
Oyster Bay Cove	**276**	40.52 N	73.31 W
Oyster Bay Harbor ⊂	**276**	40.53 N	73.32 W
Oyster Creek	**222**	29.00 N	95.20 W
Oyster Creek ≃	**222**	28.59 N	95.18 W
Oyster Point ∧	**282**	37.50 N	121.52 W
Oyster Point ≻	**168b**	34.55 S	137.48 E
Oyster Rock I[2]	**272c**	18.54 N	72.50 E
Oysterville	**224**	46.33 N	124.02 W
Øystese	**26**	60.23 N	6.13 E
Oyten	**52**	53.04 N	9.01 E
Ozaki	**268**	35.59 N	139.51 E
Ozamiz	**116**	8.08 N	123.50 E
Ozanne ≃	**50**	48.11 N	1.22 E
Ozariči	**76**	52.28 N	29.16 E
Ozark, Al., U.S.	**194**	31.27 N	85.38 W
Ozark, Ar., U.S.	**194**	35.29 N	93.49 W
Ozark, Mo., U.S.	**194**	37.01 N	93.12 W
Ozark National Scenic Riverways ♠	**194**	37.10 N	91.10 W
Ozark Plateau ⋏[1]	**194**	37.00 N	93.00 W
Ozark Reservoir ⊜[1]	**194**	35.35 N	94.00 W
Ozarks, Lake of the ⊜[1]	**194**	38.10 N	92.50 W
Ozaukee □[6]	**216**	44.14 N	88.00 W
Ozbourn Seamount ✣[3]	**14**	26.00 S	174.50 W
Ózd	**30**	48.14 N	20.18 E
Ozd'atiči	**76**	54.06 N	28.50 E
Oze ≃	**96**	34.12 N	132.14 E
Ozeblin ∧	**36**	44.35 N	15.53 E
Ozek	**86**	46.35 N	60.41 E
Ozereckoje	**82**	56.04 N	37.23 E
Ožerelje	**82**	54.48 N	38.17 E
Ožerelki	**82**	55.51 N	38.52 E
Ozerišče	**76**	54.48 N	33.13 E
Ozerki, S.S.S.R.	**80**	51.13 N	53.56 E
Ozerki, S.S.S.R.	**80**	51.32 N	45.16 E
Ozerki, S.S.S.R.	**80**	52.01 N	45.29 E
Ozerki, S.S.S.R.	**86**	53.38 N	83.44 E
Ozerki, S.S.S.R.	**265a**	59.54 N	30.44 E
Ozerna ≃	**82**	55.44 N	36.08 E
Ozerninskoje vodochranilišče ⊜[1]	**82**	55.45 N	36.15 E
Ozernoje	**78**	50.11 N	28.42 E
Ozernovskij	**74**	51.30 N	156.31 E
Ozernyj	**180**	66.24 N	179.06 W
Ozero	**80**	56.58 N	44.43 E
Ozery	**82**	54.51 N	38.34 E
Ozette Lake ⊜	**224**	48.06 N	124.38 W
Ozgol	**267d**	35.47 N	51.30 E
Ozgoryš	**85**	41.15 N	74.45 E
Ozieri	**71**	40.35 N	9.00 E
Ozimek	**30**	50.41 N	18.13 E
Ozinki	**80**	51.12 N	49.45 E
Ožogino, ozero ⊜	**74**	69.16 N	146.36 E
Ozoir-la-Ferrière	**261**	48.46 N	2.40 E
Ozona, Fl., U.S.	**220**	28.04 N	82.46 W
Ozona, Tx., U.S.	**196**	30.42 N	101.12 W
Ozone Park ◆[8]	**276**	40.40 N	73.51 W
Ozorków	**30**	51.58 N	19.19 E
Oz'ornaja, S.S.S.R.	**86**	53.25 N	63.15 E
Oz'ornaja, S.S.S.R.	**86**	51.08 N	60.50 E
Oz'ornoje, S.S.S.R.	**80**	51.46 N	51.28 E
Oz'ornoje, S.S.S.R.	**80**	51.41 N	44.55 E
Oz'ornoje, S.S.S.R.	**86**	56.48 N	71.15 E
Oz'ornyj	**80**	57.10 N	40.59 E
Oz'orsk, S.S.S.R.	**76**	54.25 N	22.01 E
Oz'orsk, S.S.S.R.	**78**	51.43 N	26.24 E
Oz'orskij	**89**	46.36 N	143.08 E
Oz'ory	**76**	53.43 N	24.11 E
Ozouer-le-Voulgis	**261**	48.40 N	2.47 E
Ōzu, Nihon	**92**	32.52 N	130.52 E
Ōzu, Nihon	**96**	33.30 N	132.33 E
Ozubulu	**150**	5.57 N	6.51 E
Ozuluama	**234**	21.40 N	97.51 W
Ozumba de Alzate	**234**	19.03 N	98.48 W

P

Name	Page	Lat.°′	Long.°′
Pâ	**150**	11.33 N	3.15 W
Paagoumène	**175f**	20.29 S	164.11 E
Paal	**56**	51.02 N	5.11 E
Paama □[8]	**175f**	16.28 S	168.18 E
Paama I	**175f**	16.28 S	168.14 E
Pa-an	**110**	16.53 N	97.38 E
Paar ≃	**60**	48.45 N	11.33 E
Paardekraal Monument ⊥	**273d**	26.06 S	27.47 E
Paaren	**264a**	52.39 N	12.59 E
Paarl	**158**	33.45 S	18.56 E
Paasbach ≃	**263**	51.25 N	7.11 E
Paauilo	**229d**	20.02 N	155.22 W
Pabarabuk	**164**	6.05 S	144.05 E
Pabbay I, Scot., U.K.	**46**	57.46 N	7.15 W
Pabbay I, Scot., U.K.	**46**	56.51 N	7.35 W
Pabbi	**123**	34.01 N	71.47 E
Pabbiring, Kepulauan II	**112**	4.55 S	119.25 E
Pabean	**112**	6.50 S	115.19 E
Pabellón, Ensenada del ⊂	**232**	24.27 N	107.36 W
Pabellón, Punta ≻	**254**	43.14 S	74.23 W
Pabellon de Arteaga	**234**	22.10 N	102.21 W
Pabianice	**30**	51.40 N	19.22 E
Pabillonis	**71**	39.35 N	8.43 E
Pablo	**202**	47.36 N	114.07 W
Pābna	**124**	24.00 N	89.15 E
Pabo	**154**	3.00 N	32.09 E
Pabradė	**76**	54.59 N	25.44 E
Paca	**115b**	8.29 S	120.11 E
Pacaás Novos ≃	**248**	10.51 S	65.20 W
Pacaás Novos, Serra dos ⋏	**248**	10.45 S	64.15 W
Pacaembu	**255**	21.34 S	51.17 W
Pacaembú, Estádio do ♠	**287b**	23.33 S	46.39 W
Pacahuaras ≃	**248**	10.04 S	65.46 W
Pacajá ≃	**250**	1.56 S	50.50 W
Pacajus	**250**	4.10 S	38.28 W
Pacaltsdorp	**158**	34.00 S	22.28 E
Pacaraima, Sierra de → Pakaraima Mountains ⋏	**246**	5.30 N	60.40 W
Pacarán	**248**	12.52 S	76.03 W
Pacaraos	**248**	11.11 S	76.44 W
Pacasmayo	**248**	7.24 S	79.34 W
Pacatuba	**250**	3.58 S	38.37 W
Paccha ≃	**248**	9.05 S	76.54 W
Pace, Fl., U.S.	**194**	30.35 N	87.09 W
Pace, Ms., U.S.	**194**	33.47 N	90.51 W
Paceco	**70**	37.59 N	12.33 E
Pačelma, S.S.S.R.	**80**	53.15 N	43.21 E
Pačelma, S.S.S.R.	**80**	53.20 N	43.20 E
Pacet	**115a**	6.45 S	107.03 E
Pachača	**74**	60.34 N	169.03 E
Pachacamac	**248**	12.14 S	76.53 W
Pachacamac ⊥	**248**	12.14 S	76.52 W
Pachāgarh	**124**	26.20 N	88.34 E
Pachamba	**126**	24.12 N	86.16 E
Pachaug Pond ⊜	**207**	41.34 N	71.54 W
Pacheco	**226**	37.59 N	122.04 W
Pacheco Creek ≃	**226**	36.58 N	121.28 W
Pacheco Pass)(	**226**	37.03 N	121.13 W
Pachecos	**256**	22.48 S	42.50 W
Pāchh Elāsin	**126**	24.08 N	89.54 E
Páchi I	**267c**	37.58 N	23.22 E
Pachino	**70**	36.43 N	15.05 E
Pachitea ≃	**248**	8.46 S	74.32 W
Pachiza	**248**	7.16 S	76.46 W
Pachkoli ◆[8]	**272c**	19.08 N	72.54 E
Pachmarhi	**124**	22.28 N	78.26 E
Pacho	**246**	5.08 N	74.10 W
Pachomovo	**82**	54.38 N	37.33 E
Pachor	**124**	23.42 N	76.44 E
Pāchora	**122**	20.40 N	75.21 E
Pachotnyj Ugol	**80**	52.58 N	41.56 E
Pachra ≃	**82**	55.32 N	37.59 E
Pachtaabad	**85**	38.28 N	68.10 E
Pachuca [de Soto]	**234**	20.07 N	98.44 W
Paciência ◆[8]	**256**	22.55 S	43.38 W
Pacific, B.C., Can.	**182**	54.46 N	128.17 W
Pacific, Mo., U.S.	**219**	38.28 N	90.44 W
Pacific, Wa., U.S.	**224**	47.15 N	122.14 W
Pacific □[6]	**224**	46.30 N	123.39 W
Pacifica	**226**	37.37 N	122.29 W
Pacific-Antarctic Ridge ✣[3]	**6**	62.00 S	157.00 W
Pacific Beach	**224**	47.12 N	124.12 W
Pacific City	**224**	45.12 N	123.57 W
Pacific Creek ≃	**200**	42.08 N	109.24 W
Pacific Gardens	**226**	37.58 N	121.20 W
Pacific Grove	**226**	36.38 N	121.56 W
Pacific Islands, Trust Territory of the □[2]	**14**	10.00 N	155.00 E
Pacific Missile Test Center ▪	**228**	34.07 N	119.07 W
Pacífico, Océano → Pacific Ocean ⫪[1]	**6**	10.00 S	150.00 W
Pacific Ocean ⫪[1]	**4**	10.00 S	150.00 W
Pacific Ocean ⫪[1]	**6**	10.00 S	150.00 W
Pacifico Mountain ∧	**228**	34.23 N	118.02 W
Pacific Palisades ◆[8]	**280**	34.03 N	118.32 W
Pacific Ranges ⋏	**182**	50.45 N	125.30 W
Pacific Rim National Park ♠, B.C., Can.	**182**	48.45 N	125.40 W
Pacifique, Océan → Pacific Ocean ⫪[1]	**6**	10.00 S	150.00 W
Pacijan Island I	**116**	10.39 N	124.20 E
Pacinan, Tanjung ≻	**115a**	7.36 S	114.02 E
Paciran	**115a**	6.52 S	112.20 E
Pacitan	**115a**	8.12 S	111.07 E
Pack	**61**	46.58 N	14.59 E
Packanack Lake ⊜	**276**	40.56 N	74.15 W
Packard Mountain ∧[2]	**207**	42.28 N	72.21 W
Pack Monadnock Mountain ∧	**207**	42.52 N	71.52 W
Packsattel)(	**61**	46.58 N	14.58 E
Packwood	**224**	46.36 N	121.40 W
Packwood Lake ⊜	**224**	46.35 N	121.34 W
Pacllón	**248**	10.18 S	77.07 W
Pacock Brook ≃	**276**	41.05 N	74.31 W
Paço de Arcos	**266c**	38.42 N	9.17 W
Paço do Lumiar	**250**	2.31 S	44.07 W
Pacoima ◆[8]	**280**	34.16 N	118.26 W
Pacolet ≃	**192**	34.50 N	81.27 W
Pacolet Mills	**192**	34.55 N	81.44 W
Pácora, Col.	**246**	5.31 N	75.27 W
Pacora, Pan.	**246**	9.05 N	79.17 W
Pacoti	**250**	4.13 S	38.56 W
Pacov	**30**	49.28 N	15.00 E
Pacquet	**186**	49.59 N	55.53 W
Pacuare ≃	**236**	10.14 N	83.17 W
Pacuí ≃	**255**	16.46 S	45.01 W
Pacuneiro ≃	**255**	13.02 S	53.25 W
Pacy-sur-Eure	**50**	49.01 N	1.23 E
Paczkow	**30**	50.27 N	17.00 E
Padada	**116**	6.42 N	125.22 E
Padada ≃	**116**	6.42 N	125.23 E
Padaido, Kepulauan II	**164**	1.15 S	136.30 E
Padam	**123**	33.28 N	76.53 E
Padamarang, Pulau I	**112**	4.07 S	121.24 E
Padamo ≃	**246**	2.54 N	65.17 W
Padampur	**120**	20.59 N	83.04 E
Padang, Indon.	**112**	1.39 S	108.55 E
Padang, Indon.	**112**	2.59 N	105.40 E
Padang, Indon.	**112**	6.11 S	120.26 E
Padang, Indon.	**112**	0.57 S	100.21 E
Padang, Pulau I	**114**	1.10 N	102.20 E
Padang Besar	**114**	6.40 N	100.19 E
Padangbetuah	**112**	3.39 S	102.13 E
Padang Endau	**114**	2.40 N	103.37 E
Padangpanjang	**112**	0.27 S	100.25 E
Padangsidempuan	**114**	1.22 N	99.16 E
Padangtiji	**114**	5.22 N	95.50 E
Padangtikar, Pulau I	**112**	0.50 S	109.30 E
Padang Tungku	**114**	4.14 N	101.59 E
Padany	**24**	63.17 N	33.22 E
Padas	**115a**	7.25 S	111.32 E
Padas ≃	**112**	5.14 N	115.34 E
Padasjoki	**26**	61.21 N	25.17 E
Padauiri ≃	**246**	0.15 S	64.05 W
Padborg	**41**	54.49 N	9.22 E
Padcaya	**248**	21.52 S	64.48 W
Paddington ◆[8]	**260**	51.31 N	0.10 W
Paddington Station ◆[5]	**260**	51.31 N	0.11 W
Paddle ≃	**182**	54.05 N	114.15 W
Paddle Prairie	**176**	57.57 N	117.29 W
Paddock Lake	**216**	42.34 N	88.06 W
Paddock Wood	**42**	51.11 N	0.23 E
Padea	**38**	44.01 N	23.52 E
Padea-besar I	**112**	3.30 S	123.05 E
Padeghar	**272c**	18.58 N	73.03 E
Paden City	**188**	39.36 N	80.56 W
Paderborn	**52**	51.43 N	8.45 E
Paderno Dugnano	**266b**	45.34 N	9.10 E
Paderno Ponchielli	**64**	45.14 N	9.55 E
Padghe	**272c**	19.03 N	73.07 E
Padibe	**154**	3.28 N	32.50 E
Padiham	**44**	53.49 N	2.19 W
Padilla	**248**	19.19 S	64.20 W
Padilla Bay ⊂	**224**	48.35 N	122.32 W
Padingge	**120**	32.52 N	88.39 E
Padjelanta Nationalpark ♠	**24**	67.28 N	16.41 E
Padle	**272c**	19.09 N	73.03 E
Padloping Island I	**176**	67.07 N	62.35 W
Padma → Ganges ≃	**124**	23.22 N	90.32 E
Padmanābhapuram	**122**	8.14 N	77.20 E
Padola	**64**	46.36 N	12.28 E
Padoue → Padova	**64**	45.25 N	11.53 E
Padova	**64**	45.25 N	11.53 E
Padova □[4]	**64**	45.21 N	11.49 E
Padovka	**80**	52.28 N	49.31 E
Pādra	**120**	22.14 N	73.05 E
Padrão, Ponta do ≻	**152**	6.03 S	12.18 E
Padrauna	**124**	26.55 N	83.59 E
Padre Bernardo	**255**	15.21 S	48.30 W
Padre Brito	**256**	21.18 S	43.59 W
Padre Burgos	**116**	10.02 N	125.01 E
Padre Island I	**196**	27.00 N	97.15 W
Padre Island National Seashore ♠	**196**	27.00 N	97.25 W
Padre Miguel ◆[8]	**287a**	22.53 S	43.26 W
Padre Paraíso	**255**	17.06 S	41.31 W
Padria	**71**	40.24 N	8.38 E
Padrón	**34**	42.44 N	8.40 W
Padrone, Cape ≻	**158**	33.46 S	26.30 E
Padrt'	**60**	49.40 N	13.46 E
Padstow, Austl.	**274a**	33.57 S	151.02 E
Padstow, Eng., U.K.	**42**	50.33 N	4.56 W
Padua → Padova	**64**	45.25 N	11.53 E
Paduari ≃	**246**	2.08 S	61.15 W
Paducah, Ky., U.S.	**194**	37.05 N	88.36 W
Paducah, Tx., U.S.	**196**	34.00 N	100.18 W
Padula	**68**	40.20 N	15.39 E
Paduli	**68**	41.10 N	14.53 E
Padunskaja	**86**	55.02 N	85.02 E
Pădurea Craiului, Munții ⋏	**38**	46.55 N	22.20 E
Paea	**174s**	17.41 S	149.35 W
Paedun	**98**	35.03 N	128.21 E
Paekakariki	**172**	40.59 S	174.57 E
Paektu-san ∧	**98**	42.00 N	128.03 E
Paengaroa	**172**	37.49 S	176.25 E
Paengnyŏng-do I	**98**	37.57 N	124.40 E
Paerdegat Basin ⊂	**276**	40.37 N	73.54 W
Paeroa	**172**	37.23 S	175.40 E
Paesana	**62**	44.41 N	7.16 E
Paese	**64**	45.40 N	12.10 E
Paestum ⊥	**68**	40.25 N	15.00 E
Paete	**116**	14.23 N	121.29 E
Páez ≃	**246**	2.28 N	75.34 W
Pafúri	**156**	22.27 S	31.21 E
Pag	**36**	44.27 N	15.04 E
Pag, Otok I	**36**	44.30 N	15.00 E
Paga	**150**	10.58 N	1.06 W
Pagadenbaru	**115a**	6.28 S	107.48 E
Pagadian	**116**	7.49 N	123.25 E
Pagadian Bay ⊂	**116**	7.48 N	123.31 E
Pagai Selatan, Pulau I	**112**	3.00 S	100.20 E
Pagai Utara, Pulau I	**112**	2.42 S	100.07 E
Pagalungan	**116**	7.04 N	124.41 E
Pagan	**110**	21.10 N	94.51 E
Pagan I	**108**	18.07 N	145.46 E
Pagancillo	**252**	29.34 S	68.03 W
Paganella ∧	**64**	46.08 N	11.02 E
Pagani	**68**	40.45 N	14.37 E
Paganica	**66**	42.21 N	13.28 E
Paganico	**66**	42.56 N	11.16 E
Pagaralam	**112**	4.01 S	103.16 E
Pagaran Tonga	**114**	1.14 N	99.46 E
Pagasitikós Kólpos ⊂	**38**	39.15 N	22.51 E
Pagatan	**112**	3.36 S	115.56 E
Pagato ≃	**184**	55.49 N	102.05 W
Pagato Lake ⊜	**184**	56.08 N	102.30 W
Pagbilao	**116**	13.58 N	121.41 E
Pagbilao Grande Island I	**116**	13.55 N	121.46 E
Pagdanan Bay ⊂	**116**	10.31 N	119.15 E
Page, Az., U.S.	**200**	36.54 N	111.28 W
Page, N.D., U.S.	**198**	47.09 N	97.34 W
Page Field ⊠	**220**	26.35 N	81.52 W
Pagėgiai	**76**	55.09 N	21.54 E
Pageland	**192**	34.46 N	80.23 W
Page Manor	**218**	39.45 N	84.06 W
Pager ≃	**154**	3.09 N	32.30 E
Pagerdewa	**112**	3.46 S	105.18 E
Paget, Mount ∧	**244**	54.26 S	36.33 W
Paghmān	**120**	34.36 N	68.57 E
Paglia ≃	**66**	42.42 N	12.11 E
Pagliara	**70**	37.59 N	15.22 E
Paglieta	**66**	42.10 N	14.30 E
Pagliete, Bonifica delle ◆[1]	**267a**	41.53 N	12.12 E
Pagny-sur-Moselle	**56**	48.59 N	6.01 E
Pago Bay ⊂	**174p**	13.25 N	144.48 E
Pagoda Peak ∧	**200**	40.10 N	107.20 W
Pagoda Point ≻	**110**	15.57 N	94.15 E
Pagon, Bukit ∧	**112**	4.18 N	115.19 E
Pago Pago	**174u**	14.16 S	170.42 W
Pago Pago Harbor ⊂	**174u**	14.17 S	170.40 W
Pago Pago International Airport ⊠	**174u**	14.20 S	170.43 W
Pagosa Springs	**200**	37.16 N	107.00 W
Pagote	**272c**	18.54 N	72.59 E
Pagouda	**150**	9.45 N	1.19 E
Pagsangahan	**116**	13.13 N	122.33 E
Pagsanjan	**116**	14.15 N	121.25 E
Pagua Bay ⊂	**240d**	15.32 N	61.17 W
Paguate	**200**	35.08 N	107.22 W
Pagudpud	**116**	18.34 N	120.47 E
Pagueras, Torrente de ≃	**266d**	41.28 N	1.58 E
Paguyaman ≃	**112**	0.31 N	122.38 E
Pah, Tür.	**84**	39.08 N	39.40 E
Pah, Tür.	**130**	39.08 N	30.10 E
Pahādi ◆[8]	**272c**	19.10 N	72.51 E
Pahala	**229d**	19.12 N	155.28 W
Pahang □[3]	**114**	3.30 N	102.45 E
Pahang ≃	**114**	3.32 N	103.28 E
Páhara, Laguna ⊂	**236**	14.18 N	83.15 W
Pahāsu	**124**	28.11 N	78.03 E
Pahau Point ≻	**229b**	21.49 N	160.15 W
Pahi	**114**	5.28 N	102.13 E
Pahia Point ≻	**172**	46.19 S	167.41 E
Pahiatua	**172**	40.27 S	175.50 E
Pahlād Garhi	**272a**	28.40 N	77.21 E
Pahlevī → Bandar-e Anzalī	**128**	37.28 N	49.27 E
Pahlgām	**123**	34.02 N	75.20 E
Pahoa	**229d**	19.29 N	154.57 W
Pahokee	**220**	26.49 N	80.39 W
Pahrump	**204**	36.12 N	115.58 W
Pahsimeroi ≃	**202**	44.41 N	114.03 W
Pahuatlán de Valle	**234**	20.17 N	98.09 W
Pahvant Range ⋏	**200**	38.45 N	112.15 W
Pai	**110**	19.19 N	98.27 E
Pai ≃	**110**	19.09 N	97.33 E
Pai, Ilha do I	**287a**	22.59 S	43.05 W
Paia	**229a**	20.54 N	156.22 W
Paianía	**267c**	37.57 N	23.51 E
Paicines	**226**	36.44 N	121.17 W
Paico	**248**	14.02 S	73.39 W
Paide	**76**	58.54 N	25.33 E
Paidorzu, Monte ∧	**71**	40.30 N	9.05 E
Paifangchang	**107**	30.31 N	106.38 E
Paige	**222**	30.13 N	97.07 W
Paignton	**42**	50.26 N	3.34 W
Paiguano	**252**	30.01 S	70.32 W
Paiho	**100**	23.21 N	120.25 E
Paiján	**248**	7.44 S	79.19 W
Päijänne ⊜	**26**	61.35 N	25.30 E
Pāikgācha	**126**	22.35 N	89.20 E
Pail, India	**123**	30.43 N	76.03 E
Pail, Pāk.	**123**	32.38 N	72.27 E
Paila ≃	**248**	16.02 S	64.12 W
Paila, Sierra la ⋏	**196**	25.50 N	101.30 W
Pailīn	**110**	12.51 N	102.36 E
Pailitas	**246**	8.58 N	73.38 W
Paillaco	**254**	40.04 S	72.53 W
Pailolo Channel Ʉ	**229a**	21.05 N	156.42 W
Pailoutou	**106**	30.56 N	121.16 E
Pailoutun	**104**	40.44 N	122.49 E
Paimboeuf	**32**	47.17 N	2.02 W
Paimio	**26**	60.27 N	22.42 E
Paimpol	**32**	48.46 N	3.03 W
Painan	**112**	1.21 S	100.34 E
Paincourt	**214**	42.23 N	82.17 W
Painesdale	**190**	47.02 N	88.40 W
Painesville	**214**	41.43 N	81.14 W
Pains	**255**	20.22 S	45.40 W
Painscastle	**42**	52.07 N	3.12 W
Painshawfield	**44**	54.56 N	1.54 W
Painswick	**42**	51.48 N	2.11 W
Paint ≃	**190**	45.58 N	88.15 W
Paint Creek ≃, Mi., U.S.	**281**	42.06 N	83.36 W
Paint Creek ≃, Oh., U.S.	**218**	39.18 N	82.56 W
Paint Creek ≃, Pa., U.S.	**214**	41.10 N	79.28 W
Paint Creek ≃, Tx., U.S.	**196**	30.18 N	99.54 W
Paint Creek, East Fork ≃	**218**	39.32 N	83.25 W
Paint Creek, North Fork ≃	**218**	39.18 N	83.02 W
Paint Creek Lake ⊜[1]	**218**	39.15 N	83.22 W
Painted Desert ◆[2]	**200**	36.00 N	111.20 W
Painted Post	**210**	42.09 N	77.05 W
Painted Rock Reservoir ⊜[1]	**200**	33.00 N	112.50 W
Painten	**60**	49.00 N	11.49 E
Painter	**208**	37.35 N	75.47 W
Painter Creek ≃	**218**	40.05 N	84.21 W
Paintertown	**279b**	40.21 N	79.42 W
Paint Lake ⊜	**184**	55.28 N	97.57 W
Paint Rock	**196**	31.30 N	99.55 W
Paint Rock ≃	**194**	34.28 N	86.28 W
Paintsville	**192**	37.48 N	82.48 W
Paiol da Vargem	**256**	22.41 S	46.26 W
Paiolinho	**256**	21.52 S	45.54 W
Paisco	**64**	46.04 N	10.17 E
Paisha	**100**	23.40 N	119.35 E
Paisley, Austl.	**274b**	37.51 S	144.51 E
Paisley, On., Can.	**212**	44.18 N	81.16 W
Paisley, Scot., U.K.	**46**	55.50 N	4.26 W
Paisley, Fl., U.S.	**220**	28.59 N	81.32 W
Paisley, Or., U.S.	**202**	42.41 N	120.32 W
País Vasco □[4]	**34**	43.00 N	2.30 W
Païta, N. Cal.	**175f**	22.08 S	166.22 E
Paita, Perú	**248**	5.06 S	81.07 W
Paita, Bahía de ⊂	**248**	5.04 S	81.05 W
Paitan	**100**	23.31 N	113.46 E
Paitan ≃	**116**	6.30 N	117.30 E
Paitan, Teluk ⊂	**116**	6.45 N	117.20 E
Paiton	**115a**	7.43 S	113.30 E
Paiva	**256**	21.18 S	43.25 W
Paiva ≃	**34**	41.04 N	8.16 W
Paizhou	**100**	30.13 N	113.56 E
Paj	**24**	61.13 N	34.24 E
Pajacuarán	**234**	20.07 N	102.34 W
Pajala	**24**	67.11 N	23.22 E
Paján	**246**	1.34 S	80.25 W
Pajapan	**234**	18.15 N	94.42 W
Pajares, Puerto de)(	**34**	43.00 N	5.46 W
Pajaro	**226**	36.54 N	121.39 W
Pajaro ≃	**226**	36.51 N	121.48 W
Pajaros Point ≻	**240m**	18.31 N	64.18 W
Paj-Choj ⋏[2]	**72**	69.00 N	63.00 E
Pajdugina ≃	**86**	58.50 N	81.47 E
Pajęczno	**30**	51.09 N	19.00 E
Pajeú ≃	**250**	8.55 S	38.42 W
Pajiangkou	**100**	23.46 N	113.14 E
Pajjer, gora ∧	**24**	66.42 N	64.25 E
Pajtug	**85**	40.53 N	72.15 E
Pak ≃	**110**	21.05 N	102.31 E
Páka, Magy.	**61**	46.36 N	16.39 E
Paka, Malay.	**114**	4.39 N	103.26 E
Paka ≃	**114**	4.40 N	103.27 E
Pākāla	**122**	13.28 N	79.07 E
Pakanbaru	**112**	0.32 N	101.27 E
Pakaraima Mountains ⋏	**246**	5.30 N	60.40 W
Pakaur	**124**	24.38 N	87.51 E
Pak Ban	**110**	21.14 N	102.28 E
Pakch'ŏn	**98**	39.45 N	125.35 E
Pakeng	**140**	6.55 N	30.40 E
Pakenham, Austl.	**169**	38.04 S	145.29 E
Pakenham, On., Can.	**212**	45.20 N	76.17 W
Pākhāl ⊜[1]	**122**	17.57 N	79.59 E
Pákhi	**267c**	37.59 N	23.22 E
Pákhna	**130**	34.46 N	32.48 E
Pakhoi → Beihai	**102**	21.29 N	109.05 E
Pakin I[1]	**14**	7.04 N	157.48 E
Pakipaki	**172**	39.41 S	176.48 E
Pakistan (Pākistān) □[1], Asia	**118**	30.00 N	70.00 E
Pakistan (Pākistān) □[1], Asia	**120**	30.00 N	70.00 E
Pakistan, East → Bangladesh □[1]	**120**	24.00 N	90.00 E
Pak Kong	**271d**	22.23 N	114.15 E
Pak Kret	**269a**	13.55 N	100.30 E
Pak Kwo Chau I	**271d**	22.16 N	114.20 E
Paklenica Nacionalni Park ♠	**36**	44.21 N	15.23 E
Pakokku	**110**	21.20 N	95.05 E
Pakość	**30**	52.49 N	18.05 E
Pakouabo	**150**	7.10 N	5.48 W
Pakowki Lake ⊜	**184**	49.22 N	110.57 W
Pākpattan	**123**	30.21 N	73.24 E
Pak Phanang	**110**	8.21 N	100.12 E
Pak Phayun	**110**	7.21 N	100.19 E
Pakrac	**36**	45.26 N	17.12 E
Pākrāganj	**126**	24.00 N	90.41 E
Pakruojis	**76**	55.58 N	23.52 E
Paks	**30**	46.39 N	18.53 E
Pak Sane → Muang Pakxan	**110**	18.22 N	103.39 E
Pāksey	**126**	24.05 N	89.03 E
Pak Thong Chai	**110**	14.43 N	102.01 E
Paktīā □[4]	**120**	33.30 N	69.30 E
Pākundia	**126**	24.20 N	90.42 E
P'akupur ≃	**74**	65.00 N	77.48 E
Pakwach	**154**	2.28 N	31.30 E
Pakwash Lake ⊜	**184**	50.45 N	93.30 W
Pakxé	**110**	15.07 N	105.47 E
Pala, Mya.	**110**	12.51 N	98.40 E
Pala, Tchad	**146**	9.22 N	14.54 E
Pala, Ca., U.S.	**228**	33.22 N	117.05 W
Palaau State Park ♠	**229a**	21.11 N	157.00 W
Palabek	**154**	3.26 N	32.34 E
Palacios	**196**	28.42 N	96.13 W
Palacios ≃	**248**	16.36 S	64.18 W
Paladru	**62**	45.28 N	5.33 E
Palagano	**64**	44.20 N	10.39 E
Palagianello	**68**	40.37 N	16.58 E
Palagiano	**68**	40.35 N	17.02 E
Palagonia	**70**	37.19 N	14.45 E
Palagruža, Otoci II	**36**	42.24 N	16.15 E
Palai	**122**	9.44 N	76.41 E
Palai, Punta ∧	**71**	40.20 N	8.55 E
Palaia	**66**	43.36 N	10.46 E
Palaiá Epídhavros	**38**	37.38 N	23.09 E
Palaia Kórinthos ⊥	**38**	37.54 N	22.56 E
Palaiá Psará	**38**	38.46 N	25.36 E
Palaikhóri	**130**	34.55 N	33.05 E
Pala Indian Reservation ◆[4]	**228**	33.21 N	117.04 W
Palaiokhóra	**38**	35.14 N	23.41 E
Palaión Fáliron	**267c**	37.55 N	23.41 E
Palaiseau	**50**	48.43 N	2.15 E
Pālakollu	**122**	16.32 N	81.44 E
Pālam ◆[8]	**272a**	28.35 N	77.05 E
Palam Airport ⊠	**123**	28.35 N	77.07 E
Palamás	**38**	39.28 N	22.05 E
Palāmau □[5]	**124**	24.00 N	84.00 E
Pālam International Airport ⊠	**272a**	28.35 N	77.07 E
Palamós	**34**	41.51 N	3.08 E
Pālampur	**123**	32.07 N	76.32 E
Palamuse	**76**	58.41 N	26.35 E
Palamut	**130**	38.59 N	27.41 E
Palana	**74**	59.07 N	159.58 E
Palanan, Mount ∧	**116**	17.03 N	122.15 E
Palanan Bay ⊂	**116**	17.09 N	122.27 E
Palanan Point ≻	**116**	17.09 N	122.30 E
Palanas	**116**	12.09 N	123.55 E
Palandöken Dağları ⋏	**130**	39.47 N	41.15 E
Pālang	**126**	23.13 N	90.21 E
Pālang ≃[1]	**126**	23.15 N	90.21 E
Palanga	**76**	55.55 N	21.03 E
Palanganene	**152**	6.26 S	18.50 E
Palangkaraya	**112**	2.16 S	113.56 E
Pālanpur	**120**	24.10 N	72.26 E
Palanquinos	**34**	42.27 N	5.31 W
Palanzano	**64**	44.26 N	10.11 E
Palaoa Point ≻	**229a**	20.44 N	156.58 W
Palapag	**116**	12.33 N	125.07 E
Palapye	**156**	22.37 S	27.06 E
Palasan Island I	**116**	14.52 N	122.03 E
Palas del Rey	**34**	42.52 N	7.52 W
Palāshdānga	**126**	23.24 N	87.22 E
Palāspol	**126**	22.43 N	89.05 E
Palāstha	**126**	23.51 N	87.03 E
Palata	**66**	41.53 N	14.47 E
Palatcy	**86**	49.09 N	83.43 E
Palatine	**216**	42.06 N	88.02 W
Palatine Bridge	**210**	42.55 N	74.35 W
Palatka, S.S.S.R.	**74**	60.06 N	150.54 E
Palatka, Fl., U.S.	**192**	29.38 N	81.38 W
Palau, It.	**71**	41.11 N	9.23 E
Palau, Méx.	**196**	27.54 N	101.26 W
Palau → Belau □[2]	**14**	5.00 N	137.00 E
Palauig	**116**	15.26 N	119.54 E
Palaui Island I	**116**	18.33 N	122.08 E
Palau Islands II	**175b**	7.30 N	134.30 E
Palauk	**110**	13.16 N	98.38 E
Pal'avaam ≃	**180**	68.50 N	170.45 E
Pal'avaamskij chrebet ⋏	**180**	68.20 N	177.00 E
Palavas-les-Flots	**62**	43.32 N	3.56 E
Palaw	**110**	12.58 N	98.39 E
Palawai Basin ≚[1]	**229a**	20.47 N	156.55 W
Palawan □[4]	**116**	10.00 N	118.50 E
Palawan I	**116**	9.30 N	118.30 E
Palawan Passage Ʉ	**116**	10.00 N	118.00 E
Palayan	**116**	15.33 N	121.06 E
Pālayankottai	**122**	8.43 N	77.44 E
Palazzo Adriano	**70**	37.41 N	13.23 E
Palazzolo Acreide	**70**	37.04 N	14.54 E
Palazzolo dello Stella	**64**	45.48 N	13.05 E
Palazzolo sull'Oglio	**62**	45.36 N	9.53 E
Palazzolo Vercellese	**62**	45.11 N	8.14 E
Palazzo San Gervasio	**68**	40.56 N	16.00 E
Palazzuolo sul Senio	**66**	44.07 N	11.33 E
P'albong-san ∧	**98**	40.16 N	127.57 E
Palca, Bol.	**248**	16.34 S	67.59 W
Palca, Perú	**248**	11.21 S	75.31 W
Palcamayo	**248**	11.18 S	75.46 W
Pal'co	**76**	53.17 N	34.56 E
Paldi	**224**	48.48 N	123.51 W
Paldiski	**76**	59.20 N	24.06 E
Pāldor ∧	**124**	28.16 N	85.11 E
Palech	**80**	56.48 N	41.51 E
Palel	**120**	24.27 N	94.02 E
Paleleh	**112**	1.04 N	121.57 E
Palembang	**112**	2.55 S	104.45 E
Palena	**66**	41.59 N	14.08 E
Palena ≃	**254**	43.50 S	72.59 W
Palena, Lago (Lago General Vintter) ⊜	**254**	43.55 S	71.40 W
Palencia	**34**	42.01 N	4.32 W
Palen Lake ⊜	**204**	33.46 N	115.12 W
Palenque	**232**	17.31 N	91.58 W
Palenque ⊥	**232**	17.30 N	92.00 W
Palenque, Punta ≻	**238**	18.14 N	70.09 W
Palenville	**210**	42.10 N	74.01 W
Paleparto, Monte ∧	**68**	39.28 N	16.34 E
Palermo, Col.	**246**	2.54 N	75.26 W
Palermo, It.	**70**	38.07 N	13.21 E
Palermo, Ca., U.S.	**226**	39.26 N	121.33 W
Palermo, Ur.	**252**	33.48 S	55.59 W
Palermo □[4]	**70**	37.49 N	13.35 E
Palermo ◆[8]	**288**	34.35 S	58.25 W
Palermo, Golfo di ⊂	**70**	38.08 N	13.26 E
Palese, Aeroporto di ⊠	**68**	41.10 N	16.47 E
Palestina, Bra.	**255**	20.23 S	49.25 W
Palestina, Méx.	**196**	29.10 N	100.55 W
Palestine, Ar., U.S.	**194**	34.58 N	90.54 W
Palestine, Il., U.S.	**194**	39.00 N	87.36 W
Palestine, Oh., U.S.	**218**	40.03 N	84.45 W
Palestine, Tx., U.S.	**222**	31.45 N	95.37 W
Palestine □[9]	**132**	32.00 N	35.15 E
Palestine, Lake ⊜[1]	**222**	32.06 N	95.27 W
Palestrina	**66**	41.50 N	12.53 E
Paletwa	**110**	21.18 N	92.51 E
Palézieux	**58**	46.33 N	6.50 E
Palfau	**61**	47.42 N	14.48 E
Pālghāt	**122**	10.47 N	76.39 E
Palgrave, Mount ∧	**162**	23.22 S	115.58 E
Palgrave Point ≻	**156**	20.45 S	13.20 E
Palhais	**266c**	38.37 N	9.03 W
Palhano	**250**	4.44 S	37.57 W
Palhano ≃	**250**	4.33 S	37.42 W
Pāli, India	**120**	25.46 N	73.20 E
Pali, India	**124**	25.51 N	76.33 E
Paliano	**66**	41.48 N	13.03 E
Palikea ∧	**229c**	21.26 N	158.06 W
Palima	**112**	4.20 S	120.22 E
Palimanan	**115a**	6.42 S	108.26 E
Palimbang	**116**	6.12 N	124.12 E
Palimé	**150**	6.54 N	0.38 E
Palín	**236**	14.24 N	90.42 W
Palinges	**32**	46.33 N	4.13 E
Palinuro	**68**	40.02 N	15.17 E
Palinuro, Capo ≻	**68**	40.02 N	15.16 E
Palisade, Co., U.S.	**200**	39.06 N	108.21 W
Palisade, Ne., U.S.	**198**	40.20 N	101.06 W
Palisades, Id., U.S.	**202**	43.21 N	111.13 W
Palisades, N.Y., U.S.	**276**	41.01 N	73.55 W
Palisades Amusement Park ♠	**276**	40.50 N	73.59 W
Palisades Interstate Park ♠	**210**	40.56 N	73.55 W
Palisades Park, Mi., U.S.	**216**	42.18 N	86.19 W
Palisades Park, N.J., U.S.	**276**	40.50 N	73.59 W
Palisades Reservoir ⊜[1]	**202**	43.15 N	111.05 W
Paliseul	**56**	49.54 N	5.08 E
Palit, Kep i ≻	**38**	41.24 N	19.24 E
Pālitāna	**120**	21.31 N	71.50 E
Palivere	**76**	58.59 N	23.52 E
Palizada	**232**	18.15 N	92.05 W
Palizzi	**68**	37.58 N	15.59 E
Paljakka ∧[2]	**26**	64.41 N	28.08 E
Pälkäne	**26**	61.20 N	24.16 E
Palk Bay ⊂	**122**	9.30 N	79.15 E
Palkino, S.S.S.R.	**76**	57.32 N	28.01 E
Palkino, S.S.S.R.	**80**	58.15 N	42.56 E
Pālkonda	**122**	18.36 N	83.45 E
Pālkonda Hills ⋏[2]	**122**	14.05 N	79.05 E
Palk Strait Ʉ	**122**	10.00 N	79.45 E
Palla Bianca (Weisskugel) ∧	**64**	46.48 N	10.44 E
Pallagorio	**68**	39.18 N	16.54 E
Pallamana	**168b**	35.02 S	139.12 E
Pallasca	**248**	8.15 S	78.01 W
Pallas Grean	**48**	52.33 N	8.22 W
Pallaskenry	**48**	52.39 N	8.52 W
Pallas-Ounastunturin Kansallispuisto ♠	**24**	68.06 N	24.00 E
Pallasovka	**80**	50.03 N	46.53 E
Pallastunturi ∧	**24**	68.06 N	24.00 E
Pallejá	**266d**	41.25 N	2.00 E
Palling	**182**	54.21 N	125.55 W
Pallíni	**267c**	38.00 N	23.53 E
Pallinup ≃	**162**	34.29 S	118.54 E
Pallisa	**154**	1.10 N	33.42 E
Palliser, Cape ≻	**172**	41.37 S	175.17 E
Palliser Bay ⊂	**172**	41.25 S	175.05 E
Pallu	**123**	28.56 N	74.13 E
Palluau	**32**	46.48 N	1.37 W
Palma, Bra.	**255**	21.22 S	42.19 W
Palma, Moç.	**154**	10.46 S	40.29 E
P'al'ma, S.S.S.R.	**24**	62.26 N	35.53 E
Palma ≃	**255**	12.33 S	47.52 W
Palma, Bahía de ⊂	**34**	39.27 N	2.35 E
Palmácia	**250**	4.08 S	38.50 W
Palma del Río	**34**	37.42 N	5.17 W
Palma [de Mallorca]	**34**	39.34 N	2.39 E
Palma di Montechiaro	**70**	37.11 N	13.46 E
Palmaḥim	**132**	31.56 N	34.42 E
Palma Pegada	**234**	22.42 N	101.48 W
Palmar ≃	**246**	10.10 N	71.50 W
Palmar Camp	**232**	16.26 N	88.53 W
Palmar de Cariaco	**286c**	10.34 N	66.55 W
Palmar de Sepúlveda	**232**	25.43 N	107.55 W
Palmar de Varela	**246**	10.45 N	74.45 W
Palmarejo	**240m**	18.03 N	67.05 W
Palmares, Bra.	**250**	8.41 S	35.36 W
Palmares, C.R.	**236**	10.03 N	84.26 W
Palmares, C.R.	**236**	9.21 N	83.40 W
Palmares do Sul	**252**	30.16 S	50.31 W
Palmaria, Isola I	**62**	44.02 N	9.51 E
Palmarito	**246**	7.37 N	70.10 W
Palmarito [Tochapan]	**234**	18.54 N	97.37 W
Palmarola, Isola I	**66**	40.56 N	12.51 E
Palmar Sur	**236**	8.58 N	83.29 W
Palmas	**252**	26.30 S	52.00 W
Palmas, Canal de las Ʉ	**288**	34.36 S	58.18 W
Palmas, Golfo di ⊂	**71**	39.02 N	8.31 E
Palmas, Ilha das I, Bra.	**287a**	23.02 S	43.12 W
Palmas, Ilha das I, Bra.	**287a**	23.04 S	43.31 W
Palmas Bellas	**236**	9.14 N	80.05 W
Palmas de Monte Alto	**255**	14.16 S	43.10 W
Palma Sola	**220**	27.31 N	82.38 W
Palma Soriano	**240p**	20.13 N	76.00 W
Palm Bay	**220**	28.02 N	80.35 W
Palm Beach, Austl.	**170**	33.36 S	151.19 E
Palm Beach, Austl.	**171a**	28.08 S	153.28 E
Palm Beach, Fl., U.S.	**220**	26.42 N	80.02 W
Palm Beach □[6]	**220**	26.38 N	80.27 W
Palm Beach Gardens	**220**	26.49 N	80.06 W
Palm Beach International Airport ⊠	**220**	26.41 N	80.05 W
Palm City	**220**	27.09 N	80.16 W
Palmdale, Ca., U.S.	**228**	34.34 N	118.06 W
Palmdale, Fl., U.S.	**220**	26.56 N	81.18 W
Palmdale, Pa., U.S.	**208**	40.18 N	76.37 W
Palmdale, Lake ⊜[1]	**228**	34.33 N	118.07 W
Palm Desert	**204**	33.43 N	116.23 W
Palmeira, Bra.	**252**	25.25 S	50.00 W
Palmeira, C.V.	**150a**	16.46 N	22.59 W
Palmeira das Missões	**252**	27.55 S	53.17 W
Palmeira d'Oeste	**255**	20.23 S	50.47 W
Palmeira dos Indios	**250**	9.25 S	36.37 W
Palmeirais	**250**	5.58 S	43.04 W
Palmeiral	**256**	21.38 S	46.31 W
Palmeirante	**250**	7.49 S	48.09 W
Palmeiras	**255**	12.31 S	41.34 W
Palmeiras ≃, Bra.	**250**	12.22 S	47.08 W
Palmeiras ≃, Bra.	**255**	15.25 S	51.10 W
Palmeirina	**250**	8.56 S	36.17 W
Palmeirinhas, Ponta das ≻	**152**	9.05 S	13.00 E
Palmela ≃	**256**	21.38 S	45.23 W
Palmelo	**255**	17.20 S	48.27 W
Palmer, Austl.	**168b**	34.51 S	139.10 E
Palmer, P.R.	**240m**	18.22 N	65.46 W
Palmer, Ak., U.S.	**180**	61.36 N	149.07 W
Palmer, Il., U.S.	**219**	39.27 N	89.24 W
Palmer, Ma., U.S.	**207**	42.09 N	72.19 W
Palmer, Ms., U.S.	**194**	31.16 N	89.15 W
Palmer, Ne., U.S.	**198**	41.13 N	98.15 W
Palmer, Tn., U.S.	**194**	35.21 N	85.34 W
Palmer, Tx., U.S.	**222**	32.26 N	96.40 W
Palmer ≃, Austl.	**162**	24.46 S	133.25 E
Palmer ≃, Austl.	**164**	15.34 S	142.26 E
Palmer ≃, P.Q., Can.	**206**	46.19 N	71.27 W
Palmer ʋ[3]	**9**	64.46 S	64.03 W
Palmerah ◆[8]	**269e**	6.12 S	106.47 E
Palmer Heights	**208**	40.42 N	75.16 W
Palmer Lake	**200**	38.52 N	104.48 W
Palmer Land ◆[1]	**9**	71.30 S	65.00 W
Palmer Mill Brook ≃	**283**	41.58 N	70.52 W
Palmer Park	**284c**	38.55 N	76.52 W
Palmer Park ♠	**281**	42.26 N	83.07 W
Palmerston, On., Can.	**212**	43.50 N	80.51 W
Palmerston, N.Z.	**172**	45.29 S	170.43 E
Palmerston I[1]	**14**	18.04 S	163.10 W
Palmerston, Cape ≻	**166**	21.32 S	149.29 E
Palmerston Lake ⊜	**212**	45.01 N	76.50 W
Palmerston North	**172**	40.21 S	175.37 E
Palmerton	**210**	40.48 N	75.36 W
Palmerville	**164**	15.59 S	144.05 E
Palmetto, Fl., U.S.	**220**	27.31 N	82.34 W
Palmetto, Ga., U.S.	**192**	33.31 N	84.40 W
Palmetto, La., U.S.	**194**	30.43 N	91.54 W
Palmford	**158**	27.11 S	29.42 E
Palm Harbor	**220**	28.04 N	82.45 W
Palmi	**68**	38.21 N	15.51 E
Palminópolis	**255**	16.47 S	50.08 W
Palmira, Arg.	**252**	33.03 S	68.34 W
Palmira, Col.	**246**	3.32 N	76.16 W
Palmira, Cuba	**240p**	22.14 N	80.23 W
Palmira, Ec.	**246**	2.05 S	78.43 W
Palmira, Méx.	**196**	28.58 N	100.47 W
Palmitas	**252**	33.31 S	57.49 W
Palmitos	**252**	27.05 S	53.08 W
Palmnicken → Jantarnyj	**76**	54.52 N	19.57 E
Palmoli	**66**	41.56 N	14.32 E
Palm River	**220**	27.56 N	82.23 W
Palms ◆[8]	**280**	34.02 N	118.25 W
Palm Shores	**220**	28.11 N	80.35 W

Symbols in the index entries represent the broad categories identified in the key at the right. Symbols with superior numbers (⋏[1]) identify subcategories (see complete key on page *I · 1).*

Kartensymbole in dem Registerverzeichnis stellen die rechts in Schlüssel erklärten Kategorien dar. Symbole mit hochgestellten Ziffern (⋏[1]) bezeichnen Unterabteilungen einer Kategorie (vgl. vollständiger Schlüssel auf Seite *I · 1).*

Los símbolos incluídos en el texto del índice representan las grandes categorias identificadas con la clave a la derecha. Los símbolos con numeros en su parte superior (⋏[1]) identifican las subcategorías (véase la clave completa en la página *I · 1).*

Les symboles de l'index représentent les catégories indiquées dans la légende à droite. Les symboles suivis d'un indice (⋏[1]) représentent des sous-catégories (voir légende complète à la page *I · 1).*

Os símbolos incluídos no texto do índice representam as grandes categorias identificadas com a chave à direita. Os símbolos com números em sua parte superior (⋏[1]) identificam as subcategorias (veja-se a chave completa à página *I · 1).*

English	Deutsch	Español	Français	Português
∧ Mountain	Berg	Montaña	Montagne	Montanha
⋏ Mountains	Berge	Montañas	Montagnes	Montanhas
)(Pass	Pass	Paso	Col	Passo
∨ Valley, Canyon	Tal, Cañon	Valle, Cañón	Vallée, Canyon	Vale, Canhão
≚ Plain	Ebene	Llano	Plaine	Planície
≻ Cape	Kap	Cabo	Cap	Cabo
I Island	Insel	Isla	Île	Ilha
II Islands	Inseln	Islas	Îles	Ilhas
⊥ Other Topographic Features	Andere Topographische Objekte	Otros Elementos Topográficos	Autres données topographiques	Outros acidentes topográficos

≃	River	Fluss	Río	Rivière	Rio
≅	Canal	Kanal	Canal	Canal	Canal
∟	Waterfall, Rapids	Wasserfall, Stromschnellen	Cascada, Rápidos	Chute d'eau, Rapides	Cascata, Rápidos
ʊ	Strait	Meeresstrasse	Estrecho	Détroit	Estreito
c	Bay, Gulf	Bucht, Golf	Bahía, Golfo	Baie, Golfe	Baía, Golfo
⊜	Lake, Lakes	See, Seen	Lago, Lagos	Lac, Lacs	Lago, Lagos
≡	Swamp	Sumpf	Pantano	Marais	Pântano
⍓	Ice Features, Glacier	Eis- und Gletscherformen	Accidentes Glaciales	Formes glaciaires	Acidentes glaciares
⫪	Other Hydrographic Features	Andere Hydrographische Objekte	Otros Elementos Hidrográficos	Autres données hydrographiques	Outros acidentes hidrográficos
✢	Submarine Features	Untermeerische Objekte	Accidentes Submarinos	Formes de relief sous-marin	Acidentes submarinos
□	Political Unit	Politische Einheit	Unidad Politica	Entité politique	Unidade política
⊍	Cultural Institution	Kulturelle Institution	Institución Cultural	Institution culturelle	Institução cultural
⊥	Historical Site	Historische Stätte	Sitio Histórico	Site historique	Sitio histórico
♦	Recreational Site	Erholungs- und Ferienort	Sitio de Recreo	Centre de loisirs	Area de Lazer
⊠	Airport	Flughafen	Aeropuerto	Aéroport	Aeroporto
■	Military Installation	Militäranlage	Instalación Militar	Installation militaire	Instalação militar
◆	Miscellaneous	Verschiedenes	Misceláneo	Divers	Diversos

ENGLISH — Name / Page / Lat.°′ / Long.°′
DEUTSCH — Name / Seite / Breite°′ / Länge°′ E = Ost

Parksley 208 37.46 N 75.39 W
Park Station ◆5 273d 26.12 S 28.03 E
Parkstein 60 49.44 N 12.04 E
Parkstetten 60 48.55 N 12.36 E
Parkston 198 43.23 N 97.59 W
Parksville, B.C., Can. 182 49.19 N 124.19 W
Parksville, N.Y., U.S. 210 41.51 N 74.45 W
Parktown ◆8 273d 26.11 S 28.03 E
Parktown North ◆8 273d 26.09 S 28.02 E
Parkview 279b 40.30 N 79.56 W
Parkville, Md., U.S. 208 39.22 N 76.32 W
Parkville, Mo., U.S. 194 39.11 N 94.40 W
Parkwater 202 47.40 N 117.19 W
Parkway, Ca., U.S. 226 38.29 N 121.27 W
Parkway, Mo., U.S. 219 38.20 N 90.57 W
Parkwood 284c 39.01 N 77.05 W
Parlākimidi 122 18.47 N 84.06 E
Parlament ✧ 264b 48.12 N 16.22 E
Parle, Lac qui ⊜ 198 45.07 N 96.00 W
Parliament, Houses of ✧ 260 51.30 N 0.07 W
Parlier 226 36.36 N 119.31 W
Parma, It. 64 44.48 N 10.20 E
Parma, Id., U.S. 202 43.47 N 116.56 W
Parma, Mi., U.S. 216 42.15 N 84.35 W
Parma, Mo., U.S. 194 36.36 N 89.48 W
Parma, Oh., U.S. 214 41.24 N 81.43 W
Parma □4 64 44.40 N 10.10 E
Parma ≃ 64 44.56 N 10.26 E
Parma Heights 214 41.23 N 81.45 W
Parmain 261 49.07 N 2.12 E
Parmatown Mall ◆9 279a 41.23 N 81.44 W
Parnaguá 250 10.13 S 44.38 W
Parnahyba → Parnaíba 250 2.54 S 41.47 W
Parnaíba 250 2.54 S 41.47 W
Parnaíba ≃ 250 3.00 S 41.50 W
Parnaìbinha ≃ 250 9.17 S 45.55 W
Parnamirim, Bra. 250 8.05 S 39.34 W
Parnamirim, Bra. 250 5.55 S 35.15 W
Parnarama 250 5.41 S 43.06 W
Parnassós ∧ 38 38.32 N 22.35 E
Parnassus 172 42.43 S 173.18 E
Parndorf 61 47.59 N 16.51 E
Parnell 216 40.14 N 88.42 W
Párnis ∧ 38 38.11 N 23.42 E
Párnis Óros ⋏ 267c 38.07 N 23.41 E
Parnon ⋏ 38 37.18 N 22.35 E
Pärnu 76 58.24 N 24.32 E
Pärnu ≃ 76 58.23 N 24.29 E
Pärnu-Jaagupi 76 58.37 N 24.30 E
Pärnu laht c 76 58.15 N 24.25 E
Paro 124 27.26 N 89.25 E
Pārola 120 20.53 N 75.07 E
Paromaj 89 52.50 N 143.02 E
Parona 130 37.31 N 41.58 E
Paroo 162 26.16 S 119.46 E
Paroo ≃ 166 31.28 S 143.32 E
Parorā 272b 22.48 N 88.09 E
Páros 38 37.04 N 25.08 E
Páros I 38 37.08 N 25.12 E
Parow 158 33.53 S 18.37 E
Parowan 200 37.50 N 112.49 W
Parpaillon ⋏ 62 44.30 N 6.40 E
Parpan 58 46.46 N 9.33 E
Parr 216 41.02 N 87.13 W
Parral, Chile 252 36.09 S 71.50 W
Parral → Hidalgo del Parral, Méx. 232 26.56 N 105.40 W
Parral, Oh., U.S. 214 40.33 N 81.30 W
Parramatta 170 33.49 S 151.00 E
Parramatta ≃ 274a 33.51 S 151.14 E
Parramatta Park ♠ 274a 33.49 S 151.00 E
Parramore Island I 208 37.32 N 75.38 W
Parras de la Fuente 232 25.25 N 102.11 W
Parrett ≃ 42 51.13 N 3.01 W
Parrish, Al., U.S. 194 33.43 N 87.17 W
Parrish, Fl., U.S. 220 27.35 N 82.25 W
Parris Island Marine Corps Recruit Depot ■ 192 32.21 N 80.41 W
Parrita 236 9.30 N 84.19 W
Parrsboro 186 45.24 N 64.20 W
Parry, Cape > 176 70.08 N 124.24 W
Parry, Mount ∧ 182 52.53 N 128.45 W
Parry Bay c 176 68.07 N 82.00 W
Parry Channel ⊔ 16 74.20 N 98.00 W
Parry Island I 212 45.18 N 80.10 W
Parry Island Indian Reserve ◆4 212 45.18 N 80.10 W
Parry Peninsula >1 180 69.45 N 124.30 W
Parry Sound 212 45.21 N 80.02 W
Parry Sound □6 212 45.25 N 79.55 W
Parry Sound ⊔ 212 45.21 N 80.06 W
Parryville 208 40.49 N 75.40 W
Parsad 120 24.11 N 73.42 E
Parsberg 60 49.09 N 11.43 E
Parsdorf 60 48.09 N 11.47 E
Parseier Spitze ∧ 58 47.10 N 10.28 E
Parsęta ≃ 30 54.12 N 15.33 E
Parshall 198 47.57 N 102.08 W
Parshallville 281 42.41 N 83.46 W
Paršino 88 59.10 N 111.48 E
Parsippany 210 40.51 N 74.25 W
Parsippany, Lake ⊜ 276 40.51 N 74.26 W
Parsnāth ∧ 124 23.53 N 86.08 E
Parsnip ≃ 182 55.10 N 123.00 W
Parsoburan 114 2.19 N 99.20 E
Parsonage Island I 276 40.37 N 73.37 W
Parsons, Ks., U.S. 198 37.20 N 95.15 W
Parsons, Tn., U.S. 194 35.38 N 88.07 W
Parsons, W.V., U.S. 188 39.05 N 79.40 W
Parsons, Mount ∧2 164 13.33 S 135.09 E
Parson's Pond 186 50.02 N 57.43 W
Parsons Pond ⊜ 186 50.00 N 57.35 W
Parsons Range ⋏ 164 13.30 S 135.15 E
Parsteiner See ⊜ 54 52.55 N 13.59 E
Pärsti 76 58.25 N 25.32 E
Partābpur 124 23.29 N 83.13 E
Partanna 70 37.43 N 12.53 E
Partāppur 126 21.48 N 86.44 E
Partenen 58 46.58 N 10.03 E
Parthala 272a 28.36 N 77.24 E
Parthe ≃ 54 51.22 N 12.21 E
Parthenay 32 46.39 N 0.15 W
Partille 26 57.44 N 12.07 E
Partington 262 53.25 N 2.26 W
Partinico 70 38.03 N 13.07 E
Partizansk 89 43.08 N 133.09 E
Partizánske 30 48.39 N 18.23 E
Partizanskoje 86 55.30 N 94.24 E
Parton 44 54.34 N 3.35 W
Partridge, Point > 224 48.13 N 122.46 W
Partridge Creek ≃ 212 44.44 N 77.13 W
Partridge Crop Lake ⊜ 184 55.38 N 97.27 W
Partridge Point > 186 50.09 N 56.10 W
Partry 48 53.41 N 9.19 W
Partschins → Parcines 64 46.41 N 11.04 E
Paru ≃, Bra. 250 1.33 S 52.38 W
Parú ≃, Ven. 246 4.20 N 66.27 W
Parubcan 116 13.43 N 123.45 E
Parucito ≃ 246 5.18 N 65.59 W
Paru de Este ≃ 250 1.10 N 54.40 W
Paru de Oeste ≃ 250 1.30 S 56.00 W
Parung 115a 6.25 S 106.42 E
Pårup, Dan. 41 55.24 N 10.20 E
Pårup, Dan. 41 56.08 N 9.21 E
Parūr 122 10.09 N 76.14 E
Paruro 248 13.46 S 71.51 W
Parutino 78 46.43 N 31.53 E
Parvān □4 120 35.15 N 69.30 E
Pārvatīpuram 122 18.47 N 83.26 E
Parvin State Park ♠ 208 39.30 N 75.09 W
Pârvomaj 38 42.06 N 25.13 E
Påryd 26 56.34 N 15.55 E
Parys 158 27.04 S 27.16 E
Paša ≃ 76 60.29 N 32.55 E
Paşabahçe ◆8 267b 41.06 N 29.05 E
Pasacao 116 13.31 N 123.03 E
Pasaco 236 13.59 N 90.12 W
Pasadena, Nf., Can. 186 49.01 N 57.36 W
Pasadena, Ca., U.S. 228 34.08 N 118.08 W
Pasadena, Md., U.S. 208 39.06 N 76.34 W
Pasadena, Tx., U.S. 222 29.41 N 95.12 W
Pasado, Cabo > 246 0.22 S 80.30 W
Pasaje 246 3.20 S 79.49 W
Pasaje ≃ 252 25.35 S 63.57 W
Pasaje Talavera ≃1 258 33.53 S 58.55 W
Pa Sak ≃ 110 14.21 N 100.35 E
Pasaleng Bay c 116 18.36 N 120.56 E
Paşalimanı Adası I 130 40.28 N 27.37 E
Pasān 124 22.51 N 82.12 E
Pasanauri 84 42.21 N 44.41 E
Pasangkayu 112 1.10 S 119.20 E
Pasarbantal 112 2.45 S 101.20 E
Pasarseluma 112 4.09 S 102.32 E
Pasar Senen Station ◆5 269e 6.10 S 106.50 E
Pasarsorkam 114 1.53 N 98.34 E
Pasarwajo 112 5.29 S 122.50 E
Pasatiempo 226 37.02 N 122.02 W
Pasaunda 272a 28.42 N 77.21 E
Paşavenk 130 38.53 N 39.29 E
Pasawng 110 18.52 N 97.18 E
Pasay 269f 14.33 N 121.00 E
Pasayten ≃ 224 49.08 N 120.35 W
Pasayten, Middle Fork ≃ 224 48.53 N 120.37 W
Pasayten, West Fork ≃ 224 48.53 N 120.37 W
Pascack Brook ≃ 276 40.59 N 73.59 W
Pascagama, Lac ⊜ 190 48.34 N 75.36 W
Pascagoula 194 30.21 N 88.33 W
Pascagoula ≃ 194 30.21 N 88.34 W
Pascalis, Lac ⊜ 190 48.16 N 77.24 W
Paşcani 38 47.15 N 26.44 E
Pasching 61 48.15 N 14.12 E
Pasco 202 46.13 N 119.05 W
Pasco □5 248 10.30 S 75.15 W
Pasco □6 220 28.20 N 82.27 W
Pascoag 207 41.57 N 71.42 W
Pascoe Vale 274b 37.44 S 144.56 E
Pascua ≃ 254 48.13 S 73.22 W
Pascua, Isla de (Easter Island) (Rapa Nui) I 174z 27.07 S 109.22 W
Pascuales, Boca ≃1 234 18.52 N 103.58 W
Pas-de-Calais □5 50 50.30 N 2.20 E
Pas-en-Artois 50 50.09 N 2.30 E
Pasewalk 54 53.30 N 14.00 E
Pasian di Prato 64 46.03 N 13.11 E
Pasiano di Pordenone 64 45.51 N 12.37 E
Pasig 116 14.33 N 121.05 E
Pasig ≃ 269f 14.36 N 120.58 E
Pāsighāt 120 28.04 N 95.20 E
Pašija 86 58.26 N 58.16 E
P'asina ≃ 74 73.50 N 87.10 E
Pasinler (Hasankale) 130 39.59 N 41.41 E
Pašino 86 55.11 N 83.00 E
P'asino, ozero ⊜ 74 69.45 N 87.45 E
P'asinskij zaliv c 74 74.00 N 86.00 E
Pasión, Rió de la ≃ 232 16.28 N 90.33 W
Pasirganting 112 2.02 S 100.53 E
Pasir Gudang 271c 1.27 N 103.53 E
Pasirian 115a 8.13 S 113.06 E
Pasir Mas 114 6.02 N 102.08 E
Pasir Panjang 271c 1.17 N 103.47 E
Pasirpengarayan 114 0.51 N 100.16 E
Pasir Puteh, Malay. 114 5.50 N 102.24 E
Pasir Puteh, Malay. 271c 1.26 N 103.56 E
Påskallavik 26 57.10 N 16.27 E
Paskeville 168b 34.02 S 137.54 E
Paškovo, S.S.S.R. 80 53.39 N 42.25 E
Paškovo, S.S.S.R. 89 48.54 N 130.42 E
Paškovskij 78 45.02 N 39.06 E
Pasłęk 30 54.05 N 19.39 E
Pasłęka ≃ 30 54.26 N 19.45 E
Pasley, Cape > 162 33.57 S 123.31 E
Pasley Bay c 176 70.40 N 96.27 W
Pašman, Otok I 36 43.58 N 15.21 E
Pasmore ≃ 166 31.07 S 139.48 E
Pašn'a 24 63.21 N 56.28 E
Pasni 128 25.16 N 63.28 E
Paso de Indios 254 43.52 S 69.06 W
Paso del Cerro 252 31.29 S 55.50 W
Paso del Macho 234 18.58 N 96.43 W
Paso de los Libres 252 29.43 S 57.05 W
Paso de los Toros 252 32.49 S 56.31 W
Paso del Rey 288 34.39 S 58.46 W
Paso del Toro 234 19.02 N 96.07 W
Paso de Ovejas 234 19.17 N 96.26 W
Paso de Patria 252 27.13 S 58.35 W
Paso de San Antonio 196 29.05 N 103.55 W
Paso Hondo 232 15.49 N 92.02 W
Paso Limay 254 40.33 S 70.26 W
Pasorapa 248 18.16 S 64.37 W
Paso Real de Sarabia 234 17.03 N 95.01 W
Paso Robles 226 35.37 N 120.41 W
Paso Seco 240m 17.59 N 66.23 W
Pašozero 76 60.02 N 34.37 E
Pasqua Indian Reserve ◆4 184 50.45 N 104.02 W
Pasque Island I 207 41.27 N 70.50 W
Pasquia Hills ⋏2 184 53.13 N 102.37 W
Pasquotank □6 208 36.26 N 76.26 W
Pasquotank ≃ 192 36.10 N 76.03 W
Pasrūr 123 32.16 N 74.40 E
Passa-Cinco, Corredeira ⊥ 256 21.19 S 43.08 W
Passadumkeag 188 45.11 N 68.37 W
Passadumkeag Mountain ∧2 188 45.10 N 68.20 W
Passage East 48 52.13 N 6.59 W
Passagem Franca 250 6.10 S 43.47 W
Passage Point > 176 73.29 N 115.17 W
Passage West 48 51.52 N 8.20 W
Passaic 210 40.51 N 74.07 W
Passaic □6 210 40.55 N 74.10 W
Passaic ≃ 276 40.43 N 74.07 W
Passamaquoddy Bay c 186 45.06 N 66.59 W
Passa Quatro 256 22.23 S 44.58 W
Passa Três 256 22.42 S 44.00 W
Passau 60 48.35 N 13.28 E
Passa Vinte 256 22.13 S 44.15 W
Pass Creek ≃ 198 43.45 N 101.28 W
Passero, Capo > 70 36.40 N 15.09 E
Passignano sul Trasimeno 66 43.11 N 12.08 E
Passirio (Passer) ≃ 64 46.41 N 11.10 E
Pass Island 186 47.29 N 56.11 W
Pašskij Perevoz 76 60.24 N 32.59 E
Passo Corese 66 42.09 N 12.39 E
Passo de Camaragibe 250 9.14 S 35.29 W
Passo Fundo 252 28.15 S 52.24 W
Passo Fundo ≃ 252 27.16 S 52.42 W
Passopisciaro 70 37.52 N 15.02 E
Passos 255 20.43 S 46.37 W
Passow 54 53.08 N 14.06 E
Passy 58 45.55 N 6.41 E
Passy ◆8 261 48.52 N 2.17 E
Pastaza □4 246 1.45 S 76.50 W
Pastaza ≃ 246 4.50 S 76.25 W
Pastecho ≃ 182 56.07 N 114.15 W
Pasteur, Lac ⊜ 186 50.13 N 66.58 W
Pastillo 240m 17.59 N 66.29 W
Pasto 246 1.13 N 77.17 W
Pastol Bay c 180 63.07 N 163.15 W
Pastora Peak ∧ 200 36.47 N 109.10 W
Pastoría, Laguna de c 234 15.59 N 97.40 W
Pastoria Creek ≃ 228 35.01 N 118.51 W
Pastos Bons 250 6.36 S 44.05 W
Pastrana 34 40.25 N 2.55 W
Pastrengo 64 45.29 N 10.48 E
Pašukovo 82 55.55 N 38.16 E
Pasuquin 116 18.20 N 120.37 E
Pasur 130 38.30 N 41.02 E
Pasuruan 115a 7.38 S 112.54 E
Pasvalys 76 56.04 N 24.24 E
Pásztó 30 47.55 N 19.42 E
Pata 116 5.51 N 121.10 E
Patacamaya 248 17.14 S 67.55 W
Pātāchārkuchi 120 26.31 N 91.16 E
Patagonia 200 31.32 N 110.45 W
Patagonia ◆1 254 44.00 S 68.00 W
Pataha Creek ≃ 202 46.31 N 117.59 W
Pata Island I 116 5.49 N 121.10 E
Patamban 234 19.48 N 102.18 W
Pātan, India 120 23.50 N 72.07 E
Pātan, India 124 23.18 N 79.42 E
Patan → Lalitpur, Nepāl 124 27.41 N 85.20 E
Patapsco 208 39.32 N 76.53 W
Patapsco ≃ 208 39.09 N 76.27 W
Patapsco, Cooks Branch ≃ 284b 39.27 N 76.53 W
Patapsco, Davis Branch ≃ 284b 39.19 N 76.51 W
Patapsco, North Branch ≃ 208 39.21 N 76.53 W
Patapsco, Rockburn Branch ≃ 284b 39.14 N 76.43 W
Patapsco, Soapstone Branch ≃ 284b 39.13 N 76.43 W
Patapsco, South Branch ≃ 208 39.21 N 76.53 W
Patapsco River Neck >1 284b 39.14 N 76.27 W
Patapsco Valley State Park ♠ 208 39.20 N 76.55 W
Patargān, Daqq-e ⩩ 128 33.30 N 60.40 E
Pataudi 124 28.19 N 76.47 E
Pataula Creek ≃ 192 31.46 N 85.02 W
Patay 50 48.03 N 1.42 E
Pataz 248 7.44 S 77.37 W
Patcham 42 50.52 N 0.08 W
Patchewollock 166 35.23 S 142.11 E
Patchogue 210 40.45 N 73.00 W
Patchogue Bay c 276 40.44 N 73.01 W
Patchway 42 51.32 N 2.34 W
Pat Cleburne, Lake ⊜1 222 32.25 N 97.30 W
Pate 154 2.08 S 41.00 E
Patea 172 39.45 S 174.28 E
Patea ≃ 172 39.46 S 174.29 E
Patearoa 172 45.16 S 170.03 E
Pategi 150 8.44 N 5.44 E
Pate Island I 154 2.07 S 41.03 E
Pateley Bridge 44 54.05 N 1.45 W
Patel Nagar ◆8 272a 28.39 N 77.10 E
Patensie 158 33.46 S 24.49 E
Patéras Óros ∧ 267c 38.07 N 23.25 E
Patergassen 64 46.49 N 13.52 E
Paterna 34 39.30 N 0.26 W
Paternion 64 46.43 N 13.38 E
Paternò 70 37.34 N 14.54 E
Pateros, Pil. 269f 14.33 N 121.04 E
Pateros, Wa., U.S. 202 48.03 N 119.54 W
Patersdorf 60 49.01 N 12.59 E
Paterson, Austl. 170 32.36 S 151.37 E
Paterson, S. Afr. 158 33.26 S 25.58 E
Paterson, N.J., U.S. 210 40.55 N 74.10 W
Paterson ≃ 170 32.43 S 151.39 E
Paterson, Cape > 169 38.40 S 145.36 E
Paterson Inlet c 172 46.55 S 168.03 E
Paterswolde 52 53.08 N 6.35 E
Pātghāti 126 22.53 N 89.55 E
Pathalgaon 124 22.34 N 83.28 E
Pathānkot 123 32.17 N 75.39 E
Pathānkot Airport ⊠ 123 32.15 N 75.37 E
Pātharghāra 272b 22.34 N 88.35 E
Pātharghāta 126 22.02 N 89.58 E
Patharia 124 23.54 N 79.12 E
Pathfinder Reservoir ⊜1 200 42.30 N 106.50 W
Pathfinder Seamount ✢3 16 50.55 N 143.15 W
Pathiong 140 6.46 N 30.54 E
Pathiu 110 10.42 N 99.19 E
Path of Condie 46 56.15 N 3.30 W
Pāthrāil 126 24.12 N 89.56 E
Pathro ≃ 126 24.12 N 86.48 E
Pathum Thani 110 14.01 N 100.32 E
Pati, Indon. 112 0.33 S 111.19 E
Pati, Indon. 115a 6.45 S 111.01 E
Pati ≃ 246 3.41 S 67.37 W
Patía 246 2.04 N 77.04 W
Patía ≃ 246 2.13 N 78.40 W
Patiāla 123 30.19 N 76.24 E
Patiāla □5 124 30.20 N 76.20 E
Patiāla ∧ 123 32.32 N 72.11 E
P'atichatki 78 48.24 N 33.42 E
Pati do Alferes 256 22.25 S 43.25 W
P'atigorsk 84 44.03 N 43.04 E
Pātihāl 272b 22.39 N 88.08 E
Patikul 116 6.04 N 121.06 E
Patillas 240m 18.00 N 66.01 W
P'atimar 80 49.31 N 50.32 E
Patinti, Selat ⊔ 164 0.30 S 127.45 E
Patipāda 272c 19.04 N 73.05 E
Pati Point > 174p 13.36 N 144.57 E
Pātiram 124 25.19 N 88.45 E
Patire, Convento del ✧1 68 39.34 N 16.35 E
Pătîrlagele 38 45.19 N 26.22 E
Pativilca 248 10.42 S 77.47 W
Pativilca ≃ 248 10.44 S 77.48 W
Pātkai Range ⋏ 120 27.00 N 96.00 E
Pat Mayse Reservoir ⊜1 196 33.40 N 95.35 W
Pátmos I 130 37.20 N 26.33 E
Patna, India 124 25.36 N 85.07 E
Patna, India 126 21.56 N 87.52 E
Pātna, India 272b 22.59 N 88.18 E
Patna, Scot., U.K. 44 55.21 N 4.30 W
Patna □5 124 25.20 N 85.30 E
Patnāgarh 122 20.43 N 83.09 E
Patnanongan Island I 116 14.48 N 122.11 E
P'atnica, S.S.S.R. 82 54.46 N 38.09 E
P'atnica, S.S.S.R. 82 56.05 N 36.48 E
P'atnickoje, S.S.S.R. 78 50.25 N 37.51 E
P'atnickoje, S.S.S.R. 82 54.20 N 35.53 E
Pātnoli 272c 18.57 N 73.05 E
Patnoñgon 116 10.55 N 122.00 E
Patnos 84 39.14 N 42.52 E
Pato Branco 252 26.13 S 52.40 W
Patoka 219 38.45 N 89.05 W
Patoka ≃ 194 38.25 N 87.44 W
Patoka Lake ⊜1 194 38.20 N 86.40 W
Patokino 82 56.27 N 39.06 E
Patomskoje nagorje ⋏1 88 59.00 N 115.00 E
Paton, Île I 275a 45.31 N 73.45 W
Patonga 154 2.46 N 33.18 E
Patos 250 7.01 S 37.16 W
Patos, Cachoeira dos ⊥ 248 9.20 S 60.15 W
Patos, Lagoa dos c 252 31.06 S 51.15 W
Patos, Río de los ≃ 252 31.18 S 69.25 W
Patos, Rio dos ≃, Bra. 248 13.33 S 56.29 W
Patos, Rio dos ≃, Bra. 255 14.59 S 48.46 W
Patos de Minas 255 18.35 S 46.32 W
Patos Island I 224 48.47 N 122.56 W
P'atovskij 82 54.41 N 36.04 E
Patquía 252 30.03 S 66.53 W
Pátrai 38 38.15 N 21.44 E
Patraïkós Kólpos c 38 38.14 N 21.15 E
Patras → Pátrai 38 38.15 N 21.44 E
Pātrasāer 124 23.13 N 87.31 E
Patricio Lynch, Isla I 254 48.37 S 75.26 W
Patrick Air Force Base ■ 220 28.15 N 80.36 W
Patrick Henry International Airport ⊠ 208 37.08 N 76.30 W
Patrick Point > 214 42.35 N 81.28 W
Patrington 44 53.41 N 0.02 W
Patriot 218 38.50 N 84.49 W
Patrocínio 255 18.57 S 46.59 W
Patrocínio Paulista 255 20.38 S 47.17 W
Patsaliga Creek ≃ 194 31.22 N 86.31 W
Patscherkofel ∧ 64 47.13 N 11.28 E
Pattada 71 40.35 N 9.06 E
Pattani 110 6.52 N 101.16 E
Pattani ≃ 110 6.53 N 101.16 E
Patten 188 45.59 N 68.26 W
Pattenburg 210 40.38 N 75.01 W
Pattensen 52 52.15 N 9.46 E
Pattenville 283 42.35 N 71.14 W
Patterdale 44 54.32 N 2.56 W
Patterson, Ca., U.S. 226 37.28 N 121.07 W
Patterson, Ga., U.S. 192 31.23 N 82.08 W
Patterson, Il., U.S. 219 39.29 N 90.29 W
Patterson, La., U.S. 194 29.41 N 91.18 W
Patterson, N.Y., U.S. 210 41.30 N 73.36 W
Patterson, Oh., U.S. 216 40.47 N 83.32 W
Patterson ≃ 274b 38.05 S 145.07 E
Patterson, Mount ∧ 180 64.04 N 134.39 W
Patterson Creek ≃ 188 39.34 N 78.44 W
Patterson Gardens 216 41.56 N 83.25 W
Patterson Heights 214 40.45 N 80.19 W
Patterson Island I 190 48.39 N 87.00 W
Patterson Park ♠ 284b 39.17 N 76.35 W
Pattersonville 210 42.53 N 74.05 W
Patti, India 123 31.17 N 74.51 E
Patti, India 124 25.55 N 82.12 E
Patti, It. 70 38.08 N 14.58 E
Patti, Golfo di c 36 38.12 N 15.05 E
Pattison, Ms., U.S. 194 31.53 N 90.53 W
Pattison, Tx., U.S. 222 29.49 N 95.60 W
Pattoki 123 31.01 N 73.51 E
Patton 214 40.37 N 78.39 W
Patton, Cape > 169 38.42 S 143.50 E
Patton Park ♠ 281 42.19 N 83.10 W
Pattonsburg 194 40.02 N 94.08 W
Patton Seamounts ✢3 16 54.20 N 149.30 W
Pattscheid 263 51.05 N 7.03 E
Pattukkottai 122 10.26 N 79.19 E
Pattullo, Mount ∧ 180 56.14 N 129.39 W
Patu 250 6.06 S 37.38 W
Pātua 126 22.06 N 90.23 E
Patuākhāli 124 22.21 N 90.21 E
Patuca ≃ 236 15.50 N 84.17 W
Patuca, Punta > 236 15.51 N 84.18 W
Patuha, Gunung ∧ 115a 7.10 S 107.23 E
Pātul 272b 22.45 N 88.10 E
Patul ∧ 246 2.40 S 79.03 W
Pātuli, Bngl. 126 24.13 N 89.54 E
Pātuli, India 126 23.33 N 88.15 E
Patulul 236 14.25 N 91.10 W
Patumahoe 172 37.11 S 174.50 E
Pātūr 122 20.27 N 76.56 E
Patusi 164 2.10 S 147.10 E
Patutu ∧ 172 39.15 S 175.51 E
Patuxent ≃ 208 38.18 N 76.25 W
Patuxent, Western Branch ≃ 208 38.47 N 76.43 W
Patuxent River Naval Air Test Center ■ 208 38.17 N 76.25 W
Patuxent Wildlife Research Center ✧3 284c 39.03 N 76.48 W
Patwāri 272a 28.35 N 77.27 E
Pátzcuaro 234 19.31 N 101.36 W
Pátzcuaro, Lago de ⊜ 234 19.35 N 101.35 W
Patzicía 236 14.38 N 90.56 W
Patzig 54 54.28 N 13.24 E
Patzún 236 14.41 N 91.01 W
Pau 32 43.18 N 0.22 W
Pau, Gave de ≃ 32 43.33 N 1.12 W
Pau Brasil 255 15.27 S 39.39 W
Paucarbamba 248 12.25 S 74.36 W
Paucarpata 248 16.26 S 71.30 W
Paucartambo 248 13.18 S 71.40 W
Pau d'Arco 250 7.30 S 49.22 W
Paudash Lake ⊜ 212 44.58 N 78.04 W
Pau dos Ferros 250 6.07 S 38.10 W
Pauh 112 2.08 S 102.48 E
Pauhunri ∧ 124 27.58 N 88.50 E
Pauini 248 7.40 S 66.58 W
Pauini ≃, Bra. 246 1.42 S 62.50 W
Pauini ≃, Bra. 248 7.47 S 67.05 W
Pauk 110 21.27 N 94.27 E
Pauksa Taung ∧ 110 19.55 N 94.18 E
Paul 202 42.36 N 113.46 W
Paul, Lac à ⊜ 186 49.52 N 70.46 W
Paula Lima 256 21.35 S 43.29 W
Paularo 64 46.32 N 13.07 E
Paulaya ≃ 236 15.51 N 85.06 W
Paulding, Ms., U.S. 194 32.01 N 89.02 W
Paulding, Oh., U.S. 216 41.08 N 84.34 W
Paulding □6 216 41.08 N 84.35 W
Paulding Bay c 9 66.35 S 123.00 E
Paulhan 32 43.32 N 3.27 E
Paulicéia 255 21.17 S 51.51 W
Paulilatino 71 40.05 N 8.46 E
Paulina Peak ∧ 202 43.41 N 121.15 W
Pauline, Mount ∧ 182 53.33 N 119.54 W
Paulinenaue 54 52.40 N 12.43 E
Paulínia 256 22.45 S 47.10 W
Paulino Neves 250 2.43 S 42.33 W
Paulins Kill 210 41.03 N 74.49 W
Paulins Kill ≃ 210 40.55 N 75.05 W
Paulinzella ⊥ 54 50.42 N 11.06 E
Paulis → Isiro 154 2.47 N 27.37 E
Paulista 250 7.57 S 34.53 W
Paulistana 250 8.09 S 41.09 W
Paulistas 255 18.25 S 42.52 W
Paullina 198 42.58 N 95.41 W
Paull Lake ⊜ 184 56.08 N 104.50 W
Paullo 62 45.25 N 9.24 E
Paulo Afonso 250 9.21 S 38.14 W
Paulo Afonso, Parque Nacional de ♠ 250 9.20 S 38.12 W
Paulo de Faria 255 20.02 S 49.24 W
Paulo e Virginia, Gruta ⊥5 287a 22.57 S 43.18 W
Pauloff Harbor (Pavlof Harbor) 180 54.27 N 162.42 W
Paulpietersburg 158 27.30 S 30.51 E
Paul Roux 158 28.18 S 27.59 E
Paul-Sauvé, Parc ♠ 275a 45.28 N 74.02 W
Paulsboro 208 39.49 N 75.14 W
Pauls Cross Roads 208 37.52 N 76.53 W
Paul Seamount ✢3 14 23.26 N 172.36 W
Paulstown → Whitehall 48 52.41 N 7.01 W
Pauls Valley 196 34.44 N 97.13 W
Paulton, Eng., U.K. 42 51.18 N 2.30 W
Paulton, Pa., U.S. 279b 40.34 N 79.34 W
Pauma Indian Reservation ◆4 228 33.22 N 116.58 W
Pāunān 272b 22.57 N 88.17 E
Paung 110 16.37 N 97.28 E
Paungbyin 110 24.16 N 94.49 E
Paungde 110 18.29 N 95.30 E
Paunggyi 110 17.19 N 96.11 E
Pauni 122 20.47 N 79.38 E
Paup 164 3.15 S 142.35 E
Paupack 210 41.24 N 75.14 W
Pauri, India 124 25.32 N 77.21 E
Pauri, India 124 30.09 N 78.47 E
Pausa, D.D.R. 54 50.35 N 12.00 E
Pausa, Perú 248 15.16 S 73.20 W
Pausania 36 40.55 N 9.06 E
Pausin 264a 52.38 N 13.03 E
Paute 246 2.47 S 78.50 W
Paute ≃ 246 2.46 S 78.16 W
Pauto ≃ 246 5.09 N 70.55 W
Pautou → Baotou 102 40.40 N 109.59 E
Pauwalu Point > 229a 20.52 N 156.08 W
Pauwela 229a 20.56 N 156.19 W
Pauwela Point > 229a 20.57 N 156.19 W
Pavai ◆8 272c 19.07 N 72.55 E
Pavai Lake ⊜ 272c 19.07 N 72.55 E
Pavda 86 59.15 N 59.30 E
Pāveh 128 35.03 N 46.22 E
Pavel'cevo 82 56.15 N 36.26 E
Pavelec 76 53.50 N 39.16 E
Pavelec Station ◆5 265b 55.44 N 37.38 E
Pavia 62 45.10 N 9.10 E
Pavia □4 62 45.07 N 9.08 E
Pavia, Naviglio di ≚ 266b 45.27 N 9.11 E
Pavia di Udine 64 45.59 N 13.17 E
Pavilion, B.C., Can. 182 50.52 N 121.50 W
Pavilion, N.Y., U.S. 210 42.52 N 78.01 W
Pavilion Key I 220 25.42 N 81.22 W
Pavillion 200 43.14 N 108.41 W
Pavilly 50 49.34 N 0.58 E
Pāvilosta 76 56.53 N 21.14 E
Pavino 24 59.07 N 46.07 E
Pavione, Monte ∧ 64 46.07 N 11.50 E
Pavlice 61 48.59 N 15.53 E
Pavlikeni 38 43.14 N 25.18 E
Pavliščevo, S.S.S.R. 82 55.11 N 35.59 E
Pavliščevo, S.S.S.R. 82 55.34 N 35.59 E
Pavlodar 86 52.18 N 76.57 E
Pavlof Bay c 180 55.30 N 161.32 W
Pavlof Volcano ∧1 180 55.24 N 161.52 W
Pavlograd 78 48.32 N 35.53 E
Pavlogradka 86 54.12 N 73.33 E
Pavlopol' 83 47.16 N 37.47 E
Pavlovka, S.S.S.R. 78 47.45 N 37.14 E
Pavlovka, S.S.S.R. 80 52.41 N 47.09 E
Pavlovka, S.S.S.R. 83 48.08 N 39.33 E
Pavlovka, S.S.S.R. 83 49.36 N 38.42 E
Pavlovka, S.S.S.R. 86 55.25 N 56.33 E
Pavlovka, S.S.S.R. 86 51.55 N 54.47 E
Pavlovo, S.S.S.R. 76 60.05 N 45.17 E
Pavlovo, S.S.S.R. 80 55.58 N 43.04 E
Pavlovo, S.S.S.R. 265a 59.56 N 30.40 E
Pavlovo, S.S.S.R. 265a 59.49 N 30.54 E
Pavlovsk, S.S.S.R. 76 59.41 N 30.27 E
Pavlovsk, S.S.S.R. 78 50.27 N 40.08 E
Pavlovsk, S.S.S.R. 86 53.20 N 82.59 E
Pavlovskaja 78 46.08 N 39.48 E
Pavlovskaja Sloboda 82 55.49 N 37.05 E
Pavlovskij, S.S.S.R. 80 57.50 N 54.51 E
Pavlovskij, S.S.S.R. 86 52.32 N 63.06 E
Pavlovskij Posad 82 55.47 N 38.40 E
Pavlyš 78 48.55 N 33.21 E
Pavne 272c 19.05 N 73.01 E
Pavo 192 31.02 N 84.04 W
Pavón, Arg. 258 34.23 S 59.03 W
Pavón, Col. 246 3.37 N 72.15 W
Pavón, Arroyo ≃ 258 34.30 S 57.05 W
Pavona 267a 41.43 N 12.37 E
Pavonia 214 40.49 N 82.26 W
Pavšino 265b 55.49 N 37.21 E
Pavšozero 76 60.38 N 35.34 E
Pavullo nel Frignano 64 44.20 N 10.50 E
Pavuna, Arroio ≃ 287a 22.58 S 43.23 W
Pavuvu Island I 175e 9.03 S 159.06 E
Pavy 76 58.03 N 29.30 E
Pawai, Pulau I 271c 1.12 N 103.43 E
Pawan ≃ 112 1.51 S 109.57 E
Pawāyan 124 28.04 N 80.06 E
Pawcatuck 207 41.22 N 71.50 W
Paw Creek 192 35.16 N 80.56 W
Päwesin 54 52.31 N 12.42 E
Pawhuska 196 36.40 N 96.20 W
Pawling 210 41.33 N 73.36 W
Pawn ≃ 110 18.53 N 97.19 E
Pawnee, Il., U.S. 219 39.35 N 89.34 W
Pawnee, Ok., U.S. 196 36.20 N 96.48 W
Pawnee ≃ 198 38.10 N 99.06 W
Pawnee City 198 40.06 N 96.09 W
Pawnee Creek ≃ 198 40.34 N 103.14 W
Pawnee Rock 198 38.15 N 98.58 W
Pawota 110 17.46 N 97.17 E
Paw Paw, Il., U.S. 216 41.41 N 88.59 W
Paw Paw, Mi., U.S. 216 42.13 N 85.53 W
Paw Paw, W.V., U.S. 188 39.31 N 78.27 W
Paw Paw ≃ 216 42.07 N 86.29 W
Paw Paw Creek ≃ 216 40.52 N 85.58 W
Paw Paw Lake 216 42.12 N 86.15 W
Paw Paw Lake ⊜ 216 42.12 N 86.16 W
Pawtucket 207 41.52 N 71.22 W
Pawtucket Falls ⊥ 207 42.39 N 71.20 W
Paxoí I 38 39.12 N 20.12 E
Paxson 180 63.02 N 145.30 W
Paxton, Austl. 170 32.54 S 151.16 E
Paxton, Il., U.S. 216 40.27 N 88.05 W
Paxton, Ma., U.S. 207 42.18 N 71.55 W
Paxton, Ne., U.S. 198 41.07 N 101.21 W
Paxtonia 208 40.19 N 76.48 W
Paxtonville 208 40.46 N 77.05 W
Paya 236 15.37 N 85.17 W
Paya Besar 114 3.47 N 103.16 E
Payadapu 114 3.05 N 97.23 E
Payāgpur 124 27.25 N 81.48 E
Payagyi 110 17.29 N 96.32 E
Payakumbuh 112 0.14 S 100.38 E
Paya Lebar 271c 1.22 N 103.53 E
Paya Lebar Airport ⊠ 271c 1.21 N 103.54 E
Payamlı 130 37.01 N 38.35 E
Payangan 115b 8.26 S 115.15 E
Payas 130 36.47 N 36.10 E
Payas, Cerro ∧ 236 15.50 N 85.00 W
Payerne 58 46.49 N 6.56 E
Payeti 115b 9.41 S 120.20 E
Payette 202 44.04 N 116.55 W
Payette ≃ 202 44.05 N 116.57 W
Payette, Middle Fork ≃ 202 44.05 N 116.07 W
Payette, North Fork ≃ 202 44.05 N 116.07 W
Payette, South Fork ≃ 202 44.06 N 116.00 W
Payette Lake ⊜1 202 44.57 N 116.05 W
Paylampur 272b 22.47 N 88.16 E
Payne 216 41.04 N 84.43 W
Payne ≃ 206 45.14 N 75.08 W
Payne, Lac ⊜ 176 59.25 N 74.00 W
Payne Bay c 176 60.00 N 70.00 W
Payneham 168b 34.53 S 138.38 E
Paynes Creek ≃ 204 40.16 N 122.11 W
Paynes Find 162 29.15 S 117.41 E
Paynesville, S. Afr. 273d 26.14 S 28.28 E
Paynesville, Mn., U.S. 198 45.22 N 94.42 W
Paynesville, Mo., U.S. 219 39.16 N 90.54 W
Paynetown State Recreation Area ♠ 218 39.05 N 86.27 W
Paynton 184 53.01 N 108.56 W
Paysandú 252 32.19 S 58.05 W
Pays-Bas → Netherlands □1 30 52.15 N 5.30 E
Payson, Az., U.S. 200 34.13 N 111.19 W
Payson, Il., U.S. 219 39.49 N 91.14 W
Payson, Ut,. U.S. 200 40.02 N 111.43 W
Payún, Cerro ∧ 252 36.30 S 69.18 W
Paz ≃ 236 13.45 N 90.08 W
Paz, Cañada de la ≃ 288 34.53 S 58.38 W
Paz, Ribeirão da ≃ 250 9.14 S 52.01 W
Pazanji 122 10.41 N 76.04 E
Pazar, Tür. 130 41.11 N 40.53 E
Pazar, Tür. 130 40.17 N 36.18 E
Pazarcık, Tür. 130 40.00 N 29.54 E
Pazarcık, Tür. 130 37.31 N 37.19 E
Pazardžik 38 42.12 N 24.20 E
Pazarköy, Tür. 130 40.55 N 32.11 E
Pazarköy, Tür. 130 39.51 N 27.24 E
Pazarviran 130 38.41 N 36.11 E
Pazaryeri, Tür. 130 38.05 N 28.14 E
Pazaryeri, Tür. 130 41.57 N 34.01 E
Paz de Ariporo 246 5.53 N 71.54 W
Paz de Río 246 5.59 N 72.47 W
Pazifischer Ozean → Pacific Ocean ⊤1 6 10.00 S 150.00 W
P'ažijeva Sel'ga 24 61.29 N 34.29 E
Pazin 36 45.14 N 13.56 E
Pazña 248 18.36 S 66.55 W
Paznaun ∨ 58 47.03 N 10.20 E
Pčevža 76 59.23 N 32.20 E
Pčevža ≃ 76 59.21 N 31.54 E
Pchery 54 50.10 N 14.08 E
Pe 110 13.28 N 98.31 E
Pea 174w 21.10 S 175.14 W
Pea ≃ 194 31.01 N 85.51 W
Peabody, Ks., U.S. 198 38.10 N 97.06 W
Peabody, Ma., U.S. 207 42.31 N 70.55 W
Peace ≃, Can. 176 59.00 N 111.25 W
Peace ≃, Fl., U.S. 220 26.55 N 82.05 W
Peace Arch ⊥ 224 49.00 N 122.45 W
Peace Bridge ◆5 284a 42.54 N 78.55 W
Peace Canyon Dam ◆6 182 55.59 N 121.59 W
Peace Dale 207 41.27 N 71.29 W
Peacehaven 42 50.47 N 0.01 E
Peace River 182 56.14 N 117.17 W
Peach Creek 188 37.52 N 81.59 W
Peach Creek ≃, Tx., U.S. 222 30.07 N 95.10 W
Peach Creek ≃, Tx., U.S. 222 29.24 N 97.19 W
Peach Creek, Sandy Fork ≃ 222 29.34 N 97.19 W
Peachdale 158 26.30 S 24.42 E
Peachland 182 49.46 N 119.44 W
Peach Orchard 192 33.28 N 82.04 W
Peach Springs 200 35.31 N 113.25 W
Peacock Hills ⋏2 176 66.05 N 110.45 W
Peacock Point >, On., Can. 212 42.47 N 79.59 W
Peacock Point >, Wake I. 174a 19.16 N 166.37 E
Peacock Sound ⊔ 9 72.55 S 100.00 W
Pea Hill Branch ≃ 284c 38.45 N 76.57 W
Peak Crossing 171a 27.47 S 152.44 E
Peak Dale 262 53.17 N 1.52 W
Peak District National Park ♠ 44 53.17 N 1.45 W
Peak Downs 166 22.12 S 148.10 E
Peake Creek ≃ 162 28.05 S 136.07 E
Peaked Mountain ∧ 186 46.34 N 68.49 W
Peak Forest 262 53.19 N 1.50 W
Peak Forest Canal ≚ 262 53.29 N 2.06 W
Peak Hill, Austl. 162 25.38 S 118.43 E
Peak Hill, Austl. 166 32.44 S 148.12 E
Peakhurst 274a 33.58 S 151.04 E
Peakview 171b 36.04 S 149.24 E
Peäldoaivi ∧ 24 69.11 N 26.36 E
Peale, Mount ∧ 200 38.26 N 109.14 W
Peale Island I 174a 19.19 N 166.35 E
Peapack Brook ≃ 276 40.41 N 74.39 W
Pearblossom 228 34.30 N 117.55 W
Pearce 200 31.54 N 109.49 W
Pearce, Royal Australian Air Force Station ■ 168a 31.41 S 116.01 E
Pearce Point > 164 14.25 S 129.21 E
Peard Bay c 180 70.51 N 159.10 W
Pea Ridge ∧ 218 38.25 N 83.36 W
Pea Ridge National Military Park ♠ 194 36.29 N 94.06 W
Pearisburg 192 37.19 N 80.44 W
Pearl, Il., U.S. 194 39.28 N 90.38 W
Pearl, Ms., U.S. 194 32.16 N 90.07 W
Pearl ≃ 194 30.11 N 89.32 W
Pearl, Lake ⊜ 283 42.04 N 71.21 W
Pearland 222 29.33 N 95.17 W
Pearl and Hermes Reef ✢2 14 27.55 N 175.45 W
Pearl Bank ✢4 116 5.49 N 119.42 E
Pearl Beach 214 42.37 N 82.35 W
Pearl City 229c 21.23 N 157.58 W
Pearl Creek ≃ 198 44.15 N 98.08 W
Pearl Harbor c 229c 21.22 N 157.58 W
Pearl Harbor Naval Station ■ 229c 21.21 N 157.57 W
Pearl Peak ∧ 204 40.14 N 115.32 W
Pearl River, La., U.S. 194 30.22 N 89.44 W
Pearl River, N.Y., U.S. 210 41.03 N 74.01 W
Pearls Airport ⊠ 241k 12.09 N 61.37 W
Pearns Point > 240c 17.05 N 61.54 W
Pearsall 196 28.53 N 99.05 W
Pearse Island I 182 54.51 N 130.21 W
Pearsoll Peak ∧ 202 42.18 N 123.50 W
Pearson 192 31.17 N 82.51 W
Pearson Lake ⊜ 184 56.15 N 97.15 W
Pearston 158 32.35 S 25.08 E
Peary Land ◆1 16 83.00 N 35.00 W
Pease ≃ 196 34.12 N 99.07 W
Pease Air Force Base ■ 188 43.06 N 70.49 W
Peasedown Saint John 42 51.19 N 2.27 W
Peaster 222 32.52 N 97.52 W
Peat Inn 46 56.17 N 2.53 W
Pebane 154 17.10 S 38.08 E
Pebas 246 3.20 S 71.49 W
Pebble Beach 226 36.34 N 121.57 W
Pebble Island I 254 51.18 S 59.35 W
Peć 38 42.40 N 20.19 E
Pecan Bayou ≃ 196 31.28 N 98.43 W
Pecangakan 115a 6.41 S 110.42 E
Pecan Gap 196 33.26 N 95.51 W
Peçanha 255 18.33 S 42.34 W
Peças, Ilha das I 252 25.26 S 48.19 W
Pecatonica 190 42.18 N 89.21 W
Pecatonica ≃ 190 42.27 N 89.05 W
Pecatu 115b 8.50 S 115.07 E
Peccioli 66 43.33 N 10.43 E
Pécel 264c 47.29 N 19.21 E
Pečenegi 78 49.52 N 36.55 E
Peçenek 130 40.25 N 32.19 E
Pečenežin 78 48.32 N 24.54 E
Pečenga 24 69.33 N 31.07 E
Pečerniki 82 54.39 N 39.14 E
Pečernikovskije Vyselki 82 54.10 N 39.10 E
Pechanga Indian Reservation ◆4 228 33.27 N 117.04 W
Peche Island I 281 42.21 N 82.56 W
Pechincha ◆8 287a 22.56 S 43.21 W
Pechora → Pečora ≃ 24 68.13 N 54.15 E
Pechorka ≃ 265b 55.35 N 38.03 E
Pechra-Jakovlevskaja 265b 55.48 N 37.58 E
Pechra-Pokrovskoje 265b 55.50 N 37.57 E
Pechu 84 43.24 N 40.49 E
Peči 80 54.48 N 44.19 E
Pecica 38 46.10 N 21.05 E
Pečicy 82 55.36 N 38.27 E
Pecixe, Ilha de I 150 11.50 N 16.05 W
Peck 190 43.15 N 82.49 W
Peck Bay c 208 39.16 N 74.37 W
Peck-Berge ⋏2 264a 52.36 N 13.34 E
Peckeloh 52 52.01 N 8.07 E
Peckelsheim 52 51.36 N 9.07 E
Pecket Well 262 53.46 N 2.00 W
Peck Lake ⊜ 210 43.07 N 74.25 W
Peckman ≃ 276 40.53 N 74.13 W
Peconic ≃ 207 40.55 N 72.37 W
Pečora, S.S.S.R. 24 65.10 N 57.11 E
Pečora, S.S.S.R. 78 48.52 N 28.42 E
Pečora ≃ 24 68.13 N 54.15 E
Pecora, Capo > 71 39.27 N 8.23 E
Pecoraro, Monte ∧ 68 38.32 N 16.20 E
Pečoro-Ilyčskij Zapovednik ◆4 24 62.20 N 59.00 E
Pečorskaja guba c 24 68.40 N 54.45 E
Pečorskoje more ⊤2 24 70.00 N 54.00 E
Pečory 76 57.49 N 27.36 E
Pecos, N.M., U.S. 200 35.34 N 105.40 W
Pecos, Tx., U.S. 196 31.25 N 103.29 W
Pecos ≃ 178 29.42 N 101.22 W
Pecos National Monument ♠ 200 35.26 N 105.56 W
Pecos Plains ≚ 196 33.20 N 104.30 W
Pecq 50 50.41 N 3.20 E
Pecquencourt 50 50.23 N 3.13 E
Pecqueuse 261 48.39 N 2.03 E

Symbols in the index entries represent the broad categories identified in the key at the right. Symbols with superior numbers (⋏1) identify subcategories (see complete key on page *I · 1).*

Kartensymbole in dem Registerverzeichnis stellen die rechts in Schlüssel erklärten Kategorien dar. Symbole mit hochgestellten Ziffern (⋏1) bezeichnen Unterabteilungen einer Kategorie (vgl. vollständiger Schlüssel auf Seite *I · 1*).

Los símbolos incluídos en el texto del índice representan las grandes categorias identificadas con la clave a la derecha. Los símbolos con numeros en su parte superior (⋏1) identifican las subcategorías (véase la clave completa en la página *I · 1).*

Les symboles de l'index représentent les catégories indiquées dans la légende à droite. Les symboles suivis d'un indice (⋏1) représentent des sous-catégories (voir légende complète à la page *I · 1).*

Os símbolos incluídos no texto do índice representam as grandes categorias identificadas com a chave à direita. Os símbolos com números em sua parte superior (⋏1) identificam as subcategorias (veja-se a chave completa à página *I · 1).*

English	Deutsch	Español	Français	Português
∧ Mountain	Berg	Montaña	Montagne	Montanha
⋏ Mountains	Berge	Montañas	Montagnes	Montanhas
≍ Pass	Pass	Paso	Col	Passo
∨ Valley, Canyon	Tal, Cañon	Valle, Cañón	Vallée, Canyon	Vale, Canhão
≚ Plain	Ebene	Llano	Plaine	Planície
> Cape	Kap	Cabo	Cap	Cabo
I Island	Insel	Isla	Île	Ilha
II Islands	Inseln	Islas	Îles	Ilhas
◆ Other Topographic Features	Andere Topographische Objekte	Otros Elementos Topográficos	Autres données topographiques	Outros acidentes topográficos

ESPAÑOL — Nombre | Página | Lat.°′ | Long.°′ W = Oeste
FRANÇAIS — Nom | Page | Lat.°′ | Long.°′ W = Ouest
PORTUGUÊS — Nome | Página | Lat.°′ | Long.°′ W = Oeste

Pécs 30 46.05 N 18.13 E
Pedana 122 16.16 N 81.10 E
Pedas 114 2.37 N 102.04 E
Pedasí 246 7.32 N 80.02 W
Pedaso 66 43.06 N 13.50 E
Peddāpuram 122 17.05 N 82.08 E
Pedder, Lake ⊜[1] 166 42.54 S 146.12 E
Peddie 158 33.12 S 27.07 E
Peddocks Island I 283 42.17 N 70.56 W
Pededze ≃ 76 56.56 N 26.54 E
Pedernales, Arg. 252 35.15 S 59.39 W
Pedernales, Méx. 234 19.08 N 101.28 W
Pedernales, Rep. Dom. 238 18.02 N 71.45 W
Pedernales, Ven. 246 9.58 N 62.16 W
Pedernales ≃ 196 30.26 N 98.04 W
Pedernales, Salar de ☷ 252 26.15 S 69.10 W
Pedernales Falls State Park ♠ 196 30.20 N 98.14 W
Pederobba 64 45.53 N 11.58 E
Pedersborg 41 55.27 N 11.34 E
Pederstrup 41 54.54 N 11.16 E
Pedesina 58 46.05 N 9.33 E
Pedhoulás 130 34.58 N 32.50 E
Pedirka 162 26.40 S 135.14 E
Pedja ≃ 76 58.25 N 26.11 E
Pedley 228 33.59 N 117.28 W
Pé do Morro 256 22.20 S 44.57 W
Pedra 250 8.30 S 36.57 W
Pedra Azul 255 16.01 S 41.16 W
Pedra Bela 256 22.47 S 46.27 W
Pedra Branca 250 5.27 S 39.43 W
Pedra Branca ∧ 256 22.56 S 43.28 W
Pedra Branca, Serra da ∧ 287a 22.56 S 43.29 W
Pedra da Gávea ∧ 287a 23.00 S 43.17 W
Pedra de Guaratiba ◆[8] 256 23.00 S 43.39 W
Pedra do Sino ∧ 256 22.30 S 43.03 W
Pedra Grande, Recifes da ✢[2] 255 17.45 S 38.58 W
Pedra Lume 150a 16.46 N 22.54 W
Pedralva 256 22.14 S 45.28 W
Pedras 250 2.48 S 57.16 W
Pedras, Rio das ≃, Bra. 255 12.13 S 45.15 W
Pedras, Rio das ≃, Bra. 287a 22.51 S 43.01 W
Pedras de Fogo 250 7.23 S 35.07 W
Pedras Selada 256 22.21 S 44.26 W
Pedras Negras 248 12.51 S 62.54 W
Pedras Salgadas 34 41.32 N 7.36 W
Pedraza 246 10.11 N 74.55 W
Pedregal, Pan. 236 8.22 N 82.26 W
Pedregal, Ven. 246 11.01 N 70.08 W
Pedregulho 255 20.16 S 47.29 W
Pedreira 256 22.43 S 46.55 W
Pedreira ≃ 250 0.12 N 50.47 W
Pedreiras 250 4.34 S 44.39 W
Pedreros 286d 12.01 S 76.57 W
Pedriceña 232 25.06 N 103.47 W
Pedricktown 208 39.46 N 75.24 W
Pedrinhas 250 11.12 S 37.41 W
Pedro, Point ≻ 122 9.50 N 80.14 E
Pedro Afonso 250 8.59 S 48.11 W
Pedro Avelino 250 5.31 S 36.23 W
Pedro Bay 180 59.47 N 154.07 W
Pedro Betancourt 240p 22.44 N 81.17 W
Pedro Cays II 238 17.00 N 77.50 W
Pedro do Rio 256 22.20 S 43.09 W
Pedrógão Grande 34 39.55 N 8.09 W
Pedro Gomes 255 18.04 S 54.32 W
Pedro González, Isla I 246 8.24 N 79.06 W
Pedro II 250 4.25 S 41.28 W
Pedro II, Ilha I 246 1.10 N 66.40 W
Pedro Juan Caballero 252 22.34 S 55.37 W
Pedro Leopoldo 255 19.38 S 44.03 W
Pedro Luro 252 39.29 S 62.41 W
Pedro Muñoz 34 39.24 N 2.58 W
Pedro Osório 252 31.51 S 52.45 W
Pedro R. Fernández 252 28.45 S 58.39 W
Pedro Teixeira 256 21.43 S 43.44 W
Pedro Velho 250 6.26 S 35.14 W
Peebinga 166 34.56 S 140.55 E
Peebles, Scot., U.K. 46 55.39 N 3.12 W
Peebles, Oh., U.S. 218 38.56 N 83.24 W
Peedamullah 162 21.50 S 115.38 E
Pee Dee ≃ 192 34.43 N 79.52 W
Peekaboo Mountain ∧[2] 188 45.45 N 67.53 W
Peekskill 210 41.17 N 73.55 W
Peel, Austl. 170 33.19 S 149.38 E
Peel, I. of Man 44 54.13 N 4.40 W
Peel □[6] 212 43.45 N 79.47 W
Peel ≃ 180 67.37 N 134.40 W
Peel Channel ≃[1] 180 68.13 N 135.00 W
Peel Fell ∧ 44 55.17 N 2.35 W
Peel Inlet c 168a 32.35 S 115.44 E
Peel Island I 171a 27.30 S 153.22 E
Pe Ell 224 46.34 N 123.17 W
Peel Point ≻ 176 73.22 N 114.35 W
Peel Sound Ʉ 176 73.15 N 96.30 W
Peene ≃ 54 54.09 N 13.46 E
Peenemünde 54 54.08 N 13.46 E
Peepeekisis Indian Reserve ◆[4] 184 50.52 N 103.24 W
Peer 56 51.08 N 5.28 E
Peerless 202 48.46 N 105.49 W
Peers 182 53.40 N 116.00 W
Peesane 184 52.52 N 103.36 W
Peetz 198 40.57 N 103.06 W
Peetzsee ⊜ 264a 52.26 N 13.50 E
Pefferlaw 212 44.19 N 79.12 W
Pefferlaw Brook ≃ 212 44.15 N 79.13 W
Pegasus, Port c 172 47.12 S 167.41 E
Pegasus Bay c 172 43.20 S 173.00 E
Pegau 54 51.10 N 12.14 E
Pegli 62 44.26 N 8.48 E
Peglia, Monte ∧ 66 42.49 N 12.13 E
Pegnitz 60 49.45 N 11.33 E
Pegnitz ≃ 60 49.29 N 11.00 E
Pego 34 38.51 N 0.07 W
Pegolotte 64 45.12 N 12.02 E
Pegswood 44 55.11 N 1.38 W
Pegtymel' ≃ 180 69.25 N 174.35 E
Pegtymel'skij chrebet ✗ 180 68.30 N 177.00 E
Pegu 110 17.20 N 96.29 E
Pegu □[8] 110 18.00 N 96.00 E
Pegu ≃ 110 16.47 N 96.13 E
Pegueros 234 20.57 N 102.40 W
Peguis Indian Reserve ◆[4] 184 51.20 N 97.35 W
Pegu Yoma ✗ 110 19.00 N 95.50 E
Pegwell Bay c 42 51.18 N 1.26 E
Pegyš 24 63.26 N 50.30 E
Pehčevo 38 41.46 N 22.54 E
Pehladpur ◆[8] 272a 28.35 N 77.06 E
Pehlivanköy 130 41.21 N 26.55 E
Pehowa 124 29.59 N 76.35 E
Pehuajó 252 35.48 S 61.53 W
Pehula 26 61.17 N 22.42 E
Peian → Beian 89 48.16 N 126.36 E
Peiching → Beijing 105 39.55 N 116.25 E
Peigan Indian Reserve ◆[4] 182 49.35 N 113.40 W
Peihai → Beihai 102 21.29 N 109.05 E
Peij 52 51.06 N 5.53 E
Peijiatun 98 39.19 N 121.41 E
Peikang 100 23.34 N 120.18 E
Peikang ≃ 100 23.31 N 120.08 E
Peikant'ang Tao I 100 26.13 N 119.59 E
Peilstein im Mühlviertel 60 48.37 N 13.53 E
Peinan 100 22.47 N 121.07 E
Peinan ≃ 100 22.46 N 121.10 E
Peine 52 52.19 N 10.13 E
Peine, Pointe à ≻ 240d 15.23 N 61.15 W
Peinnechaung I 110 19.59 N 93.04 E
Peio 64 46.22 N 10.40 E
Peip'ing → Beijing 105 39.55 N 116.25 E
Peipsi järv → Čudskoje ozero ⊜ 76 58.45 N 27.25 E
Peipus, Lake → Čudskoje ozero ⊜ 76 58.45 N 27.25 E
Peïra-Cava 62 43.56 N 7.22 E
Peirce, Cape ≻ 180 58.35 N 161.47 W
Peirce Reservoir ⊜[1] 271c 1.22 N 103.49 E
Peisey-Nancroix 62 45.33 N 6.45 E
Peiskretscham → Pyskowice 30 50.24 N 18.38 E
Peissenberg 64 47.48 N 11.04 E
Peissenberg ∧, B.R.D. 60 47.48 N 11.01 E
Peissenberg ∧, B.R.D. 64 47.48 N 11.01 E
Peiting 58 47.47 N 10.55 E
Peit'ou ◆[8] 269d 25.08 N 121.30 E
Peitz 54 51.51 N 14.24 E
Peixe 255 12.03 S 48.32 W
Peixe, Rio do ≃, Bra. 255 14.06 S 50.51 W
Peixe, Rio do ≃, Bra. 255 21.31 S 51.58 W
Peixe, Rio do ≃, Bra. 256 23.24 S 45.28 W
Peixe, Rio do ≃, Bra. 256 21.55 S 43.21 W
Peixe, Rio do ≃, Bra. 256 22.23 S 46.51 W
Peixe, Rio do ≃, Bra. 256 23.12 S 46.06 W
Peixe, Rio do ≃, Bra. 256 21.38 S 45.11 W
Peixe-Boi 250 1.12 S 47.18 W
Peixes, Rio dos ≃ 250 10.42 S 57.56 W
Peixian (Yunhe), Zhg. 98 34.21 N 117.59 E
Peixian, Zhg. 98 34.44 N 116.59 E
Peixoto de Azevedo ≃ 250 10.06 S 55.31 W
Peiziyan 98 35.07 N 115.01 E
Pejantan, Pulau I 112 0.07 N 107.14 E
Pejelagartero 234 18.04 N 93.45 W
Pek ≃ 38 44.46 N 21.33 E
Pekalongan 115a 6.53 S 109.40 E
Pekan 114 3.30 N 103.25 E
Pekanheran 112 0.21 S 102.26 E
Pekin, Il., U.S. 190 40.34 N 89.38 W
Pekin, In., U.S. 218 38.29 N 86.01 W
Pekin, N.Y., U.S. 284a 43.10 N 78.53 W
Pekin, Oh., U.S. 214 40.43 N 81.07 W
Pékin → Beijing, Zhg. 105 39.55 N 116.25 E
Peking → Beijing 105 39.55 N 116.25 E
Peking National Library ʋ 271a 39.56 N 116.22 E
Peking Railway Station ◆[5] 271a 39.54 N 116.26 E
Peking University ʋ[2] 271a 39.59 N 116.18 E
Peking Zoo ♠ 271a 39.56 N 116.19 E
Peklino 76 53.33 N 33.32 E
Pekša ≃ 80 55.53 N 39.40 E
Pektubajevo 80 57.02 N 48.23 E
Pekul'nej, chrebet ✗ 180 66.00 N 175.00 E
Pekul'nejskoje, ozero ⊜ 180 62.40 N 177.00 E
Péla 150 7.37 N 9.07 W
Pelabuhandagaung 112 1.08 S 103.05 E
Pelabuhan Kelang 114 3.00 N 101.24 E
Pelabuhanratu 115a 6.59 S 106.33 E
Pelabuhan Ratu, Teluk c 115a 7.03 S 106.27 E
Pel'a-Chovanskaja 80 54.36 N 44.56 E
Pelado, Cerro ∧ 286a 19.09 N 99.13 W
Pelagejevka 83 48.06 N 38.36 E
Pelagie, Isole II 70a 35.40 N 12.40 E
Pelago 66 43.46 N 11.30 E
Pelahatchie 194 32.18 N 89.47 W
Pelaihari 112 3.48 S 114.45 E
Pelalawan 112 0.27 N 102.05 E
Pelat, Mont ∧ 62 44.16 N 6.42 E
Pelawan 114 2.47 N 102.55 E
Pełczyce 30 53.03 N 15.18 E
Pélé, Mont ∧ 152 3.15 S 11.14 E
Peleaga, Vîrful ∧ 38 45.22 N 22.54 E
Pelechuco 248 14.48 S 69.04 W
Peleduj 74 59.36 N 112.45 E
Pelée, Montagne ∧ 240e 14.48 N 61.10 W
Pelee, Point ≻ 214 41.54 N 82.30 W
Pelee Island I 214 41.46 N 82.39 W
Pelee Passage Ʉ 214 41.52 N 82.37 W
Pelekech ∧ 154 3.48 N 35.04 E
Peleliu I 175b 7.01 N 134.15 E
Peleng, Pulau I 112 1.20 S 123.10 E
Peleng, Selat Ʉ 112 1.10 S 122.45 E
Pelenija 78 47.53 N 27.50 E
Pelf, Monte ∧ 64 46.14 N 12.12 E
Pelham, On., Can. 212 43.02 N 79.17 W
Pelham, Al., U.S. 194 33.17 N 86.48 W
Pelham, Ga., U.S. 192 31.07 N 84.09 W
Pelham, Ma., U.S. 207 42.23 N 72.24 W
Pelham, N.H., U.S. 207 42.44 N 71.19 W
Pelham, N.Y., U.S. 276 40.54 N 73.48 W
Pelham Bay c 276 40.52 N 73.47 W
Pelham Bay Park ♠ 276 40.52 N 73.49 W
Pelham Manor 276 40.53 N 73.48 W
Pelhřimov 30 49.26 N 15.13 E
Pelican 180 57.57 N 136.14 W
Pelican ≃ 198 46.17 N 96.08 W
Pelican, Punta ≻ 200 31.19 N 113.43 W
Pelican Bay c 184 52.45 N 100.20 W
Pelican Island I, Mo., U.S. 219 38.52 N 90.18 W
Pelican Island I, Tx., U.S. 222 29.20 N 94.48 W
Pelican Lagoon c 168b 35.50 S 137.47 E
Pelican Lake 190 45.30 N 89.10 W
Pelican Lake ⊜, Ab., Can. 182 55.47 N 113.15 W
Pelican Lake ⊜, Mb., Can. 184 53.50 N 96.08 W
Pelican Lake ⊜, Mb., Can. 184 52.30 N 100.20 W
Pelican Lake ⊜, Mb., Can. 184 49.20 N 99.35 W
Pelican Lake ⊜, Sk., Can. 184 55.08 N 103.00 W
Pelican Lake ⊜, Sk., Can. 184 50.32 N 106.00 W
Pelican Lake ⊜, Mn., U.S. 190 48.05 N 92.54 W
Pelican Lake ⊜, S.D., U.S. 198 44.52 N 97.11 W
Pelican Mountain ∧ 182 55.35 N 113.40 W
Pelican Narrows 184 55.10 N 102.56 W
Pelican Point ≻ 168b 34.48 S 138.29 E
Pelican Rapids, Mb., Can. 184 52.45 N 100.42 W
Pelican Rapids, Mn., U.S. 198 46.34 N 96.04 W
Pelileo 246 1.19 S 78.32 W
Pelister ∧ 38 41.00 N 21.12 E
Peljekajse Nationalpark ♠ 24 66.18 N 16.58 E
Pelješac, Poluotok ≻[1] 36 42.58 N 17.20 E
Pelkosenniemi 24 67.07 N 27.30 E
Pelkum, B.R.D. 52 51.39 N 7.46 E
Pelkum, B.R.D. 263 51.40 N 7.24 E
Pella, S. Afr. 158 29.01 S 19.06 E
Pella, Ia., U.S. 190 41.24 N 92.54 W
Pélla ⊥ 38 40.45 N 22.33 E
Pellaro 68 38.01 N 15.39 E
Pell City 194 33.35 N 86.17 W
Pellechia, Monte ∧ 66 42.07 N 12.52 E
Pellegrini 252 36.16 S 63.09 W
Pellegrini, Lago ⊜ 252 38.40 S 68.00 W
Pellegrino, Cozzo ∧ 68 39.45 N 16.03 E
Pellegrino, Monte ∧ 70 38.10 N 13.21 E
Pellegrino Parmense 64 44.44 N 9.55 E
Pellendorf 264b 48.06 N 16.27 E
Peller, Monte ∧ 64 46.18 N 10.57 E
Pellestrina, Litorale di ⩡[2] 64 45.16 N 12.18 E
Pelletier Lake ⊜ 184 56.30 N 97.00 W
Pellice ≃ 62 44.50 N 7.38 E
Pellingen 56 49.40 N 6.40 E
Pell Lake 216 42.32 N 88.21 W
Pello 24 66.47 N 24.00 E
Pellston 190 45.33 N 84.47 W
Pellworm I 30 54.31 N 8.38 E
Pelly 184 51.52 N 101.55 W
Pelly ≃ 180 62.47 N 137.19 W
Pelly Bay c 176 68.53 N 89.51 W
Pelly Crossing 180 62.50 N 136.35 W
Pelly Lake ⊜ 176 65.59 N 101.12 W
Pelly Mountains ✗ 180 62.00 N 133.00 W
Peloncillo Mountains ✗ 200 32.15 N 109.00 W
Pelón de Ñado, Cerro ∧ 234 20.05 N 99.55 W
Pelopónnisos ≻[1] 38 37.30 N 22.00 E
Peloritani, Monti ✗ 70 38.03 N 15.20 E
Pelotas 252 31.46 S 52.20 W
Pelotas ≃ 252 27.28 S 51.55 W
Pelplin 30 53.56 N 18.42 E
Pelque ≃ 254 51.03 S 70.58 W
Pelsin 54 53.48 N 13.40 E
Pelusium Bay → Tīnah, Khalīj aț- c 140 31.08 N 32.40 E
Pel'ušn'a 76 58.56 N 32.52 E
Pélussin 62 45.25 N 4.41 E
Pelvo d'Elva ∧ 62 44.33 N 9.15 E
Pelym 86 59.38 N 63.05 E
Pemadumcook Lake ⊜ 188 45.40 N 68.55 W
Pemalang 115a 6.54 S 109.22 E
Pemalang, Ujung ≻ 115a 6.47 S 109.29 E
Pemali ≃ 115a 6.47 S 109.01 E
Pematang 112 0.12 S 102.04 E
Pematangsiantar 114 2.57 N 99.03 E
Pematangtanahjawa 114 2.53 N 99.12 E
Pemba, Moç. 154 12.58 S 40.30 E
Pemba, Zam. 154 16.31 S 27.22 E
Pemba I 154 5.10 S 39.48 E
Pemba Channel Ʉ 154 5.10 S 39.20 E
Pembarisan, Pegunungan ✗ 115a 7.13 S 108.45 E
Pemberton, Austl. 162 34.28 S 116.01 E
Pemberton, B.C., Can. 182 50.20 N 122.48 W
Pemberton, Eng., U.K. 262 53.32 N 2.41 W
Pemberton, N.J., U.S. 208 39.58 N 74.41 W
Pemberton, Oh., U.S. 216 40.18 N 84.02 W
Pemberton Airport ⊠ 285 39.59 N 74.41 W
Pemberton Heights 285 39.58 N 74.41 W
Pemberville 214 41.24 N 83.27 W
Pembina 198 48.57 N 97.14 W
Pembina ≃, Ab., Can. 182 54.45 N 114.15 W
Pembina ≃, N.A. 184 48.57 N 97.14 W
Pembina Hills ✗[2] 198 49.10 N 98.25 W
Pembine 190 45.38 N 87.59 W
Pembrey 42 51.42 N 4.16 W
Pembroke, On., Can. 190 45.49 N 77.07 W
Pembroke, Wales, U.K. 42 51.41 N 4.55 W
Pembroke, Ga., U.S. 192 32.08 N 81.37 W
Pembroke, Ky., U.S. 194 36.46 N 87.21 W
Pembroke, Me., U.S. 188 44.57 N 67.09 W
Pembroke, N.Y., U.S. 210 43.00 N 78.27 W
Pembroke, N.C., U.S. 192 34.40 N 79.11 W
Pembroke, Va., U.S. 192 37.19 N 80.38 W
Pembroke, Cape ≻ 176 62.56 N 81.55 W
Pembroke Castle ⊥ 42 51.41 N 4.56 W
Pembroke Dock 42 51.42 N 4.56 W
Pembroke Pines 220 26.00 N 80.13 W
Pembrokeshire Coast National Park ♠ 42 51.47 N 5.06 W
Pembuang 112 2.34 S 112.19 E
Pembuang ≃ 112 3.24 S 112.33 E
Pembury 42 51.09 N 0.20 E
Pemfling 60 49.16 N 12.37 E
Pemichigamau Lake ⊜ 184 56.16 N 99.33 W
Pemigewasset ≃ 188 43.26 N 71.40 W
Pemmican Portage 184 53.56 N 102.17 W
Pemuco 252 36.58 S 72.06 W
Pemynoos Indian Reserve ◆[4] 182 50.29 N 121.15 W
Pemzašen 84 40.35 N 43.57 E
Peña Blanca 236 8.27 N 81.40 W
Peña Blanca, Macizos de ∧ 236 13.15 N 85.41 W
Peñafiel, Esp. 34 41.36 N 4.07 W
Penafiel, Port. 34 41.12 N 8.17 W
Pen'agino 265b 55.50 N 37.21 E
Peñagolosa ∧ 34 40.13 N 0.21 W
Peña Gorda, Cerro ∧ 234 20.44 N 104.50 W
Peña Grande ◆[8] 266a 40.29 N 3.44 W
Pen'akša 80 56.22 N 44.56 E
Peñalara ∧ 34 40.51 N 3.57 W
Peñalolén 286e 33.29 S 70.32 W
Pena-Lunanga 154 4.16 S 28.10 E
Penalva 250 3.18 S 45.10 W
Penambulai, Pulau I 164 6.24 S 134.48 E
Peña Negra, Punta ≻ 246 4.17 S 81.15 W
Peña Nevada, Cerro ∧ 234 23.46 N 99.52 W
Penang → George Town 114 5.25 N 100.20 E
Penanjung, Teluk c 115a 7.45 S 108.37 E
Penápolis 255 21.24 S 50.04 W
Peñaranda de Bracamonte 34 40.54 N 5.12 W
Pen Argyl 210 40.52 N 75.15 W
Penaron 114 4.38 N 97.40 E
Peñarroya-Pueblonuevo 34 38.18 N 5.16 W
Penarth 42 51.27 N 3.11 W
Peñas, Cabo de ≻ 34 43.39 N 5.51 W
Penas, Golfo de c 254 47.22 S 74.50 W
Penasco 200 36.10 N 105.41 W
Peñasco, Rio ≃ 196 32.45 N 104.19 W
Penataquit Creek ≃ 276 40.43 N 73.14 W
Penbrook 208 40.16 N 76.50 W
Pencader 42 52.01 N 4.16 W
Pencahue 252 35.24 S 71.49 W
Pence 190 46.25 N 90.16 W
Pen Centre ◆[9] 284a 43.08 N 79.14 W
Penchard 261 48.59 N 2.52 E
Penck Trough V 9 73.00 S 2.45 W
Pencoed 42 51.32 N 3.30 W
Pendang, Indon. 112 1.28 S 114.51 E
Pendang, Malay. 114 6.00 N 100.28 E
Pendé ≃ 146 7.55 N 16.36 E
Pendéli 267c 38.03 N 23.52 E
Pendelikón Óros ∧ 267c 38.06 N 23.54 E
Pendembu, S.L. 150 8.06 N 10.42 W
Pendembu, S.L. 150 9.06 N 12.12 W
Pendências 250 5.15 S 36.43 W
Pendeng 114 4.06 N 97.36 E
Pender 198 42.06 N 96.42 W
Pender Bay c 162 16.45 S 122.42 E
Pendhar 272c 19.04 N 73.06 E
Pendik 267b 40.53 N 29.13 E
Pendjari ≃ 150 10.54 N 0.51 E
Pendjari, Parc National de la ♠ 150 11.20 N 1.15 E
Pendlebury 262 53.31 N 2.20 W
Pendle Hill 274a 33.48 S 150.57 E
Pendle Hill ∧[2] 44 53.52 N 2.17 W
Pendleton, In., U.S. 218 39.59 N 85.44 W
Pendleton, N.Y., U.S. 284a 43.05 N 78.44 W
Pendleton, Or., U.S. 202 45.40 N 118.47 W
Pendleton, S.C., U.S. 192 34.39 N 82.47 W
Pendleton □[6] 218 38.42 N 84.22 W
Pendolo 112 2.05 S 120.42 E
Pendopo 112 3.17 S 103.52 E
Pend Oreille ≃ 202 49.04 N 117.37 W
Pend Oreille, Lake ⊜ 202 48.10 N 116.11 W
Pend Oreille, Mount ∧ 202 48.25 N 116.10 W
Pendotiba ≃ 287a 22.53 S 43.02 W
Pendžikent 85 39.29 N 67.35 E
Penebel 115b 8.25 S 115.09 E
Penedo 250 10.17 S 36.36 W
Penedono 34 40.59 N 7.24 W
Penela 34 40.02 N 8.23 W
Penelope 222 31.52 N 96.56 W
Penetang Harbour c 212 44.47 N 79.57 W
Penetanguishene 212 44.47 N 79.55 W
Penfield, Il., U.S. 216 40.18 N 87.57 W
Penfield, N.Y., U.S. 210 43.07 N 77.28 W
Penfield, Oh., U.S. 214 41.10 N 82.08 W
Penfield, Pa., U.S. 214 41.13 N 78.34 W
Penganga ≃ 122 19.53 N 79.09 E
Pengastulan 115b 8.11 S 114.55 E
Peng Chau I 271d 22.17 N 114.02 E
P'engchia Yü I 100 25.38 N 122.04 E
Penge, S. Afr. 156 24.22 S 30.13 E
Penge, Zaïre 154 5.31 S 24.37 E
Penge ◆[8] 260 51.25 N 0.04 W
Penggong 106 30.27 N 119.57 E
Penggongmiao 100 26.07 N 113.34 E
Penghu 100 25.24 N 118.11 E
P'enghu Ch'üntao (Pescadores) II 100 23.30 N 119.30 E
P'enghu Shuitao Ʉ 100 23.30 N 119.50 E
Pengiki, Pulau I 112 0.15 N 108.03 E
Pengjiachang 107 30.36 N 103.53 E
Pengjialouzi 104 41.56 N 123.40 E
Pengjiawan 100 32.16 N 114.04 E
Pengjiawu 105 39.41 N 117.10 E
Pengkalan Baharu 114 4.28 N 100.38 E
Pengkou 100 25.32 N 116.42 E
Penglai (Dengzhou) 98 37.48 N 120.42 E
Penglaizhen 107 30.36 N 105.14 E
Penglang 106 31.23 N 121.05 E
Pengnan 107 30.25 N 105.53 E
Pengpu → Bengbu 100 32.58 N 117.24 E
Pengshan 107 30.13 N 103.52 E
Pengshi 100 30.28 N 113.10 E
Pengshui 102 29.18 N 108.09 E
Penguin 166 41.07 S 146.04 E
Pengwaluoteshan ∧ 120 33.30 N 86.35 E
Pengxi 102 30.49 N 105.40 E
Pengxian 102 31.00 N 103.50 E
Pengze 100 29.53 N 116.33 E
Pengzhai 100 24.23 N 115.06 E
Pengzhuangzi 105 40.06 N 114.51 E
Penha 252 26.46 S 48.39 W
Penha ◆[8] 287a 22.49 S 43.17 W
Penha, Ribeirão da ≃ 256 22.24 S 46.50 W
Penha de França ◆[8] 287b 23.32 S 46.32 W
Penha Longa, Bra. 256 22.04 S 43.05 W
Penhalonga, Zimb. 154 18.54 S 32.40 E
Penhold 182 52.08 N 113.52 W
Penhold, Canadian Forces Base ■ 182 52.12 N 113.53 W
Penhorn Creek ≃ 276 40.45 N 74.05 W
Penhsi → Benxi 104 41.18 N 123.45 E
Peniche 34 39.21 N 9.23 W
Penicuik 46 55.50 N 3.14 W
Penida, Nusa I 115b 8.44 S 115.32 E
Penig 54 50.56 N 12.41 E
Peningo Neck ≻[1] 276 40.57 N 73.41 W
Peninjai 112 1.26 S 101.50 E
Peninsula Lake ⊜ 212 45.20 N 79.05 W
Peninsula State Park ♠ 190 45.09 N 87.14 W
Peñíscola 34 40.21 N 0.25 E
Penistone 44 53.32 N 1.37 W
Penitas 196 26.17 N 98.27 W
Penitencia Creek ≃ 282 37.27 N 121.55 W
Penitente, Serra do ✗[2] 250 8.45 S 46.20 W
Penjamillo [de Degollado] 234 20.06 N 101.54 W
Pénjamo 234 20.26 N 101.44 W
Penketh 262 53.23 N 2.40 W
Penki → Benxi 104 41.18 N 123.45 E
Penkino 82 54.50 N 38.53 E
Penkridge 42 52.44 N 2.07 W
Penkun 54 53.17 N 14.14 E
Pen Lake ⊜ 212 45.28 N 78.23 W
Penllyn 285 40.10 N 75.15 W
Penmaenmawr 44 53.16 N 3.54 W
Penmarc'h, Pointe de ≻ 32 47.48 N 4.22 W
Penn 279b 40.20 N 79.38 W
Penna, Punta della ≻ 66 42.10 N 14.43 E
Pennabilli 66 43.49 N 12.16 E
Penn Acres 285 39.40 N 75.34 W
Pennant Hills 274a 33.44 S 151.04 E
Pennant Hills Park ♠ 274a 33.45 S 151.06 E
Pennant Point ≻ 186 44.26 N 63.39 W
Pennant Station 184 50.33 N 108.12 W
Pennask Lake ⊜ 182 50.00 N 120.05 W
Pennask Mountain ∧ 182 49.53 N 120.07 W
Penn Brook ≃ 283 42.44 N 70.59 W
Penn Cove c 224 48.14 N 122.41 W
Penn Cove Park 224 48.14 N 122.41 W
Penndel 285 40.09 N 74.55 W
Penne 66 42.27 N 13.55 E
Penne, Punta ≻ 68 40.41 N 17.56 E
Penne-d'Agenais 32 44.23 N 0.49 E
Pennedepie 50 49.25 N 0.11 E
Pennel Creek ≃ 198 46.34 N 104.52 W
Penner ≃ 122 14.35 N 80.10 E
Pennes (Pens) 64 46.47 N 11.25 E
Pennes, Val di V 64 46.47 N 11.25 E
Penneshaw 168b 35.44 S 137.56 E
Penngrove 226 38.18 N 122.40 W
Penn Hills 214 40.28 N 79.51 W
Penn Hills Center ◆[9] 279b 40.28 N 79.50 W
Pennines ✗ 44 54.10 N 2.05 W
Pennines, Alpes ✗ 58 46.05 N 7.50 E
Penningby 40 59.41 N 18.40 E
Penningby slott ⊥ 40 59.41 N 18.40 E
Pennington, N.J., U.S. 208 40.19 N 74.47 W
Pennington, Tx., U.S. 222 31.11 N 95.14 W
Pennington ≃[1] 150 4.45 N 5.35 E
Pennington Gap 192 36.45 N 83.01 W
Pennino, Monte ∧ 66 43.06 N 12.53 E
Penn Run 214 40.37 N 79.01 W
Pennsauken 208 39.58 N 75.04 W
Pennsauken Creek ≃ 285 39.59 N 75.03 W
Pennsauken Creek, North Branch ≃ 285 39.58 N 75.01 W
Pennsauken Creek, South Branch ≃ 285 39.58 N 75.01 W
Pennsboro 188 39.17 N 80.58 W
Penns Brook ≃ 276 40.43 N 74.32 W
Pennsburg 208 40.23 N 75.29 W
Pennsbury Heights 285 40.12 N 74.49 W
Pennsbury Manor ⊥ 285 40.08 N 74.46 W
Penn's Cave ⩡[5] 210 40.53 N 77.36 W
Penns Creek 210 40.52 N 77.04 W
Penns Creek ≃ 210 40.48 N 76.51 W
Pennsdale 210 41.15 N 76.48 W
Penns Grove 208 39.43 N 75.28 W
Pennside 208 40.20 N 75.53 W
Penns Neck 276 40.20 N 74.38 W
Pennsuco 220 25.53 N 80.22 W
Pennsville 208 39.39 N 75.31 W
Penns Woods 279b 40.21 N 79.46 W
Pennsylvania □[3], U.S. 178 40.45 N 77.30 W
Pennsylvania □[3], U.S. 188 40.45 N 77.30 W
Pennsylvania, University of ʋ[2] 285 39.57 N 75.12 W
Pennsylvania Canal ≊ 285 40.13 N 74.47 W
Pennsylvania Station ◆[5] 276 40.45 N 74.00 W
Penn Valley, Ca., U.S. 226 39.12 N 121.11 W
Penn Valley, Pa., U.S. 285 40.01 N 75.16 W
Penn Valley Terrace 285 40.11 N 74.47 W
Pennville 216 40.29 N 85.08 W
Penn Wynne 285 39.59 N 75.16 W
Penny 182 53.50 N 121.17 W
Penn Yan 210 42.39 N 77.03 W
Pennycutaway ≃ 184 56.43 N 92.44 W
Penny Hill 285 39.46 N 75.30 W
Penny Ice Cap ⊓ 176 67.10 N 66.00 W
Pennypack Creek ≃ 285 40.02 N 75.00 W
Pennypack Park ♠ 285 40.04 N 75.03 W
Penny Strait Ʉ 176 76.30 N 97.00 W
Peno 76 56.55 N 32.45 E
Penobscot 210 41.10 N 75.52 W
Penobscot ≃ 188 44.30 N 68.50 W
Penobscot, East Branch ≃ 186 45.35 N 68.32 W
Penobscot, West Branch ≃ 188 45.35 N 68.32 W
Penobscot Bay c 188 44.15 N 68.52 W
Peno Creek ≃ 219 39.32 N 91.16 W
Pen'ok 86 55.30 N 81.34 E
Penola 166 37.23 S 140.50 E
Peñoles 196 25.39 N 104.30 W
Peñon, Cerro ∧ 286a 19.19 N 99.00 W
Peñón Blanco 232 24.47 N 104.02 W
Peñón de Ifach ♠ 34 38.38 N 0.05 E
Peñón del Rosario, Cerro ∧ 234 19.40 N 98.11 W
Penong 162 31.55 S 133.01 E
Penonomé 236 8.31 N 80.22 W
Penrhyn I[1] 14 9.00 S 158.00 W
Penrhyn Bay 44 53.19 N 3.45 W
Penrhyndeudraeth 42 52.56 N 4.04 W
Penrith, Austl. 170 33.45 S 150.42 E
Penrith, Eng., U.K. 44 54.40 N 2.44 W
Penryn, Eng., U.K. 42 50.09 N 5.06 W
Penryn, Ca., U.S. 226 38.51 N 121.10 W
Penryn, Pa., U.S. 208 40.12 N 76.22 W
Pens → Pennes 64 46.47 N 11.25 E
Pensacola 194 30.25 N 87.13 W
Pensacola Bay c 194 30.25 N 87.06 W
Pensacola Mountains ✗ 9 83.45 S 55.00 W
Pensacola Naval Air Station ■ 194 30.21 N 87.19 W
Pensacola Seamount ✢[3] 14 18.17 N 157.20 W
Pensaukee ≃ 190 44.49 N 87.55 W
Pensby 262 53.21 N 3.06 W
Pense 184 50.25 N 105.00 W
Penshaw 44 54.53 N 1.29 W
Pensiangan 112 4.33 N 116.19 E
Pensilva 42 50.30 N 4.25 W
Pensilvania 246 5.31 N 75.05 W
Pentagna 256 22.09 S 43.45 W
Pentagon ʋ 284c 38.52 N 77.03 W
Pentagon Mountain ∧ 202 47.56 N 113.07 W
Pentecost □[8] 175f 15.45 S 168.12 E
Pentecoste 250 3.48 S 39.17 W
Pentecôte I 175f 15.42 S 168.10 E
Pentecôte ≃ 186 49.47 N 67.10 W
Pentecôte, Lac ⊜ 186 49.53 N 67.20 W
Penticton 182 49.30 N 119.35 W
Penticton Indian Reserve ◆[4] 182 49.30 N 119.40 W
Pentire Point ≻ 42 50.36 N 4.55 W
Pentland 166 20.32 S 145.24 E
Pentland Firth Ʉ 46 58.44 N 3.07 W
Pentland Hills ✗[2] 46 55.48 N 3.23 W
Pentraeth 44 53.17 N 4.12 W
Pentre Halkyn 262 53.15 N 3.12 W
Pentucket, Lake ⊜ 283 42.47 N 71.05 W
Pentucket Pond ⊜ 283 42.44 N 71.00 W
Pentwater 190 43.46 N 86.25 W
Penuba 112 0.20 S 104.28 E
Peñuelas 240m 18.03 N 66.43 W
Penugonda 122 16.40 N 81.44 E
Penuguan 112 2.27 S 104.31 E
Penukonda 122 14.05 N 77.35 E
Penunjok, Tanjong ≻ 114 4.22 N 103.29 E
Pènwègon 110 18.13 N 96.34 E
Penwell 196 31.44 N 102.35 W
Peny 78 51.04 N 35.54 E
Penyengat 114 0.54 N 102.20 E
Pen-y-Ghent ∧ 44 54.09 N 2.14 W
Penygroes, Wales, U.K. 42 51.49 N 4.02 W
Penygroes, Wales, U.K. 44 53.04 N 4.17 W
Penyu, Kepulauan II 164 5.22 S 127.46 E
Penyu, Teluk c 115a 7.45 S 109.15 E
Penza 80 53.13 N 45.00 E
Penza □[4] 76 53.30 N 43.00 E
Penzance 42 50.07 N 5.33 W
Penzberg 64 47.45 N 11.23 E
Penzig → Pieńsk 30 51.15 N 15.03 E
Penžina ≃ 74 62.28 N 165.18 E
Penzing ◆[8] 264b 48.12 N 16.18 E
Penzino 80 52.07 N 50.27 E
Penžinskaja guba c 74 61.00 N 162.00 E
Penžinskij chrebet ✗ 74 62.30 N 167.00 E
Penzlin 54 53.30 N 13.05 E
Péone 62 44.07 N 6.54 E
Peonias, Quebrada ≃ 286c 10.32 N 67.01 W
Peoples Creek ≃ 202 48.24 N 108.19 W
Peoples Ditch ≊ 226 36.15 N 119.41 W
Peoria, Az., U.S. 200 33.34 N 112.14 W
Peoria, Il., U.S. 190 40.41 N 89.35 W
Peoria, Oh., U.S. 216 40.19 N 83.27 W
Peoria Heights 190 40.44 N 89.34 W
Peotillos 234 22.30 N 100.37 W
Peotone 216 41.19 N 87.47 W
Peover Eye ≃ 262 53.15 N 2.31 W
Peover Heath 262 53.15 N 2.19 W
Pepa 154 7.42 S 29.47 E
Pepacton Reservoir ⊜[1] 210 42.06 N 74.54 W
Pepaw ≃ 184 52.40 N 102.23 W
Pepel 150 8.35 N 13.03 W
Peper 140 7.04 N 33.00 E
Pepin 190 44.26 N 92.08 W
Pepin, Lake ⊜ 190 44.30 N 92.15 W
Pepinster 56 50.34 N 5.49 E
Péplos 130 40.58 N 26.16 E
Pepperdine University ʋ[2] 280 33.58 N 118.18 W
Pepperell 207 42.40 N 71.35 W
Pepper Park State Recreation Area ♠ 220 27.30 N 80.18 W
Pepper Pike 279a 41.28 N 81.27 W
Peqi'in Hadasha 132 32.59 N 35.20 E
Peqin 38 41.03 N 19.45 E
Pequannock 210 40.57 N 74.17 W
Pequannock ≃ 276 40.58 N 74.17 W
Pequanticut Brook ≃ 283 42.01 N 71.08 W
Pequea Creek ≃ 208 39.53 N 76.22 W
Pequena ≃ 287a 22.55 S 43.25 W
Pequeno, Campo ♠ 266c 38.44 N 9.08 W
Pequeri 256 21.50 S 43.06 W
Pequeri ≃ 248 17.39 S 55.09 W
Pequest ≃ 210 40.50 N 75.05 W
Pequez 208 39.53 N 76.22 W
Pequizeiro 250 8.32 S 48.58 W
Pequop Mountains ✗ 204 40.45 N 114.40 W
Pequot Lakes 190 46.36 N 94.18 W
Perabumulih 112 3.27 S 104.15 E
Perak □[3] 114 5.00 N 101.00 E
Perak ≃ 114 3.58 N 100.53 E
Perak, Kuala c 114 4.00 N 100.47 E
Peralba, Monte ∧ 64 46.37 N 12.43 E
Perales de Alfambra 34 40.38 N 1.00 W
Perales del Rio 266a 40.19 N 3.38 W
Peralillo 252 34.29 S 71.29 W
Peralta 200 34.50 N 106.41 W
Pérama 267c 37.58 N 23.34 E
Perambalūr 122 11.14 N 78.53 E
Perämeri (Bottenviken) c 26 65.00 N 23.00 E
Peranāmbattu 122 12.56 N 78.43 E
Perarolo di Cadore 64 46.24 N 12.21 E
Peräseinäjoki 26 62.34 N 23.04 E
Percé 186 48.31 N 64.13 W
Percée, Pointe ∧ 58 45.57 N 6.33 E
Perch ≃ 212 44.00 N 76.05 W
Perchas 240m 18.19 N 66.59 W
Perchau 61 47.06 N 14.27 E
Perchauer Sattel)(61 47.07 N 14.27 E
Perche, Collines du ✗[2] 50 48.25 N 0.40 E
Perche Creek ≃ 194 38.49 N 92.24 W
Perch Lake ⊜ 212 44.07 N 75.54 W
Perchtoldsdorf 264b 48.07 N 16.17 E
Perchuškovo 265b 55.41 N 37.10 E
Percival Lakes ⊜ 162 21.25 S 125.00 E
Percy Creek ≃ 212 44.15 N 77.49 W
Percy Isles II 166 21.39 S 150.16 E
Percy Lake ⊜ 212 45.13 N 78.22 W
Percy Reach ⊜ 212 44.15 N 77.45 W
Perdagangan-tomuon 114 3.09 N 99.20 E
Perdasdefogu 71 39.41 N 9.26 E
Perdeberg 158 28.59 S 25.05 E
Perdekop 158 27.13 S 29.38 E
Perdices, Arroyo de las ≃ 288 34.41 S 58.22 W
Perdida ≃ 250 9.13 S 47.59 W
Perdido 194 31.00 N 87.37 W
Perdido ≃, Bra. 248 22.10 S 57.33 W
Perdido ≃, U.S. 194 30.29 N 87.26 W
Perdido, Arroyo ≃ 254 42.55 S 67.00 W
Perdido, Arroyo del ≃ 258 33.37 S 57.23 W
Perdido, Cuchilla del ✗[2] 258 33.43 S 57.17 W
Perdido, Monte ∧ 34 42.40 N 0.05 E
Perdido Bay c 194 30.21 N 87.27 W
Perdifumo 68 40.16 N 15.01 E
Perdix 208 40.22 N 76.57 W
Perdizes 255 19.21 S 47.17 W
Perdreauville 261 48.58 N 1.38 E
Perdu, Lac ⊜ 186 50.44 N 70.14 W
Perdue 184 52.04 N 107.32 W
Perebrody 78 51.43 N 27.00 E
Perečin 78 48.44 N 22.26 E
Peredel 76 55.12 N 35.41 E
Peredel'cy 82 55.36 N 37.21 E
Peredelkino 265b 55.39 N 37.21 E
Peregino 76 57.27 N 31.21 E
Pereginskoje 78 48.49 N 24.12 E
Peregonovka 78 48.32 N 30.31 E
Pereira 246 4.49 N 75.43 W
Pereira, Cachoeira ᒐ 250 4.25 S 56.17 W
Pereira Barreto 255 20.38 S 51.07 W
Pereiras 256 22.42 S 46.24 W
Pereiro 250 6.03 S 38.28 W
Perejaslav-Chmel'nickij 78 50.06 N 31.30 E
Perejaslavka 89 47.58 N 135.06 E
Perejaslavskaja 78 45.51 N 39.02 E
Perejezdnoje 83 48.47 N 38.04 E
Perejež'na 24 59.43 N 48.12 E
Perekopnoje 80 51.13 N 48.04 E
Perekopovka 78 50.37 N 33.25 E
Perekopskaja 80 49.21 N 43.20 E
Père-Lachaise, Cimetière du ◆ 261 48.51 N 2.25 E
Perelazovskij 80 49.09 N 42.33 E
Perelazy 76 53.02 N 31.28 E
Perelesinskij 78 51.44 N 40.07 E
Perel'ub 80 51.52 N 50.22 E
Pere Marquette ≃ 190 43.57 N 86.27 W
Pere Marquette, Big South Branch ≃ 190 43.56 N 86.10 W
Pere Marquette State Park ♠ 219 39.00 N 90.30 W
Perem'otnoje 80 51.11 N 50.49 E
Peremul Par I[1] 122 11.10 N 72.04 E
Peremyšl' 82 54.16 N 36.10 E
Peremyšl'any 78 49.41 N 24.33 E
Perené ≃ 248 11.09 S 74.18 W
Perenjori 162 29.26 S 116.17 E
Pereputje 92a 46.17 N 141.54 E
Pererov 78 52.04 N 28.00 E
Pereščepino 78 49.01 N 35.22 E
Pereščepnoje 80 50.32 N 45.06 E
Pereslavl'-Zalesskij 82 56.44 N 38.51 E
Peresypkino Pervoje 80 52.55 N 42.55 E
Peretrusovo 82 56.51 N 36.53 E
Pereval'sk 83 48.26 N 38.47 E
Perevoz, S.S.S.R. 80 55.36 N 44.32 E
Perevoz, S.S.S.R. 88 59.00 N 116.57 E
Perevoz, S.S.S.R. 265a 59.43 N 30.47 E
Pereyra, Arroyo ≃ 288 34.47 S 58.08 W
Pereyra, Punta ≻ 258 34.14 S 58.04 W
Pérez 252 33.00 S 60.46 W
Perfugas 71 40.50 N 8.53 E
Perg 61 48.15 N 14.37 E
Pergam, Pulau I 271c 1.24 N 103.40 E
Pergamino 252 33.53 S 60.35 W
Pergamum ⊥ 130 39.10 N 27.13 E
Pergau ≃ 114 5.23 N 102.02 E
Pergine Valdarno 66 43.28 N 11.41 E
Pergine Valsugana 64 46.04 N 11.14 E
Pergola 66 43.34 N 12.50 E
Pergusa, Lago di ⊜ 70 37.31 N 14.18 E
Perham 198 46.35 N 95.34 W
Perho 26 63.13 N 24.25 E
Peri 64 45.39 N 10.54 E
Peri ≃ 84 38.50 N 39.35 E
Peribán de Ramos 234 19.32 N 102.28 W
Péribonca ≃ 176 48.45 N 72.05 W
Péribonca, Lac ⊜ 186 50.04 N 71.15 W
Perico, Arg. 252 24.23 S 65.06 W
Perico, Cuba 240p 22.46 N 81.01 W
Pericos 232 25.03 N 107.42 W
Pericumã ≃ 250 2.17 S 44.42 W
Peridot 200 33.18 N 110.27 W
Périers 32 49.11 N 1.25 W
Perigiraja 112 0.16 S 103.30 E
Périgord □[9] 32 45.20 N 1.00 E
Perigoso, Canal Ʉ 250 0.05 N 49.40 W
Périgueux 32 45.11 N 0.43 E
Perijá, Sierra de ✗ 246 10.00 N 73.00 W
Perim → Barīm I 144 12.40 N 43.25 E
Peri-Mirim 250 2.38 S 44.54 W
Perinaldo 62 43.52 N 7.40 E
Peringat 114 6.02 N 102.17 E
Periprava 38 45.24 N 29.32 E
Peristérion 267c 38.01 N 23.42 E
Perito 68 40.18 N 15.09 E
Perito Moreno 254 46.36 S 70.56 W
Peritoró 250 4.20 S 44.18 W
Perivale ◆[8] 260 51.32 N 0.19 W
Periyakulam 122 10.07 N 77.33 E
Periyār ≃ 122 10.11 N 76.13 E
Perkam, Tanjung ≻ 164 1.28 S 137.54 E
Perkasie 208 40.22 N 75.17 W
Perkins 196 35.58 N 97.02 W
Perkinsfield 212 44.42 N 79.57 W
Perkins Observatory ʋ[3] 214 40.14 N 83.02 W
Perkinston 194 30.46 N 89.08 W
Perkinsville, In., U.S. 218 40.09 N 85.52 W
Perkinsville, N.Y., U.S. 210 42.32 N 77.38 W
Perkiomen Creek ≃ 208 40.07 N 75.28 W
Perkiomen Creek, East Branch ≃ 208 40.15 N 75.27 W
Perkiomen Junction Pawling 285 40.21 N 75.28 W
Perkiomen Valley Airport ⊠ 285 40.12 N 75.25 W
Perl 56 49.28 N 6.36 E
Perlas, Archipiélago de las II 246 8.25 N 79.00 W
Perlas, Laguna de c 236 12.30 N 83.40 W
Perlas, Punta ≻ 236 12.23 N 83.30 W
Perleberg 54 53.04 N 11.51 E
Perlez 38 45.12 N 20.24 E

Symbol	English	Deutsch	Español	Français	Português
≃	River	Fluss	Río	Rivière	Rio
≊	Canal	Kanal	Canal	Canal	Canal
ᒐ	Waterfall, Rapids	Wasserfall, Stromschnellen	Cascada, Rápidos	Chute d'eau, Rapides	Cascata, Rápidos
Ʉ	Strait	Meeresstrasse	Estrecho	Détroit	Estreito
c	Bay, Gulf	Bucht, Golf	Bahía, Golfo	Baie, Golfe	Baía, Golfo
⊜	Lake, Lakes	See, Seen	Lago, Lagos	Lac, Lacs	Lago, Lagos
☷	Swamp	Sumpf	Pantano	Marais	Pântano
⊓	Ice Features, Glacier	Eis- und Gletscherformen	Accidentes Glaciales	Formes glaciaires	Acidentes glaciares
⊤	Other Hydrographic Features	Andere Hydrographische Objekte	Otros Elementos Hidrográficos	Autres données hydrographiques	Outros acidentes hidrográficos

Symbol	English	Deutsch	Español	Français	Português
✢	Submarine Features	Untermeerische Objekte	Accidentes Submarinos	Formes de relief sous-marin	Acidentes submarinos
□	Political Unit	Politische Einheit	Unidad Politica	Entité politique	Unidade política
ʋ	Cultural Institution	Kulturelle Institution	Institución Cultural	Institution culturelle	Institução cultural
⊥	Historical Site	Historische Stätte	Sitio Histórico	Site historique	Sitio histórico
♠	Recreational Site	Erholungs- und Ferienort	Sitio de Recreo	Centre de loisirs	Area de Lazer
⊠	Airport	Flughafen	Aeropuerto	Aéroport	Aeroporto
■	Military Installation	Militäranlage	Instalación Militar	Installation militaire	Instalação militar
◆	Miscellaneous	Verschiedenes	Misceláneo	Divers	Diversos

Perlis □[3] 114 6.30 N 100.15 E
Perl'ovka 78 51.51 N 38.51 E
Perm' 86 58.00 N 56.15 E
Perm' □[4] 80 57.30 N 54.30 E
Permanente Creek ≃ 282 37.25 N 122.05 W
Permas 24 59.20 N 45.34 E
Përmet 38 40.14 N 20.21 E
Permisi 80 54.06 N 45.48 E
Permskaja Oblast' □[4] 24 59.00 N 56.00 E
Pernambuco → Recife 250 8.03 S 34.54 W
Pernambuco □[3] 250 8.00 S 37.00 W
Pernate 266b 45.27 N 8.41 E
Pernatty Lagoon ⊜ 166 31.31 S 137.14 E
Pernay 50 47.27 N 0.30 E
Pernegg an der Mur 61 47.22 N 15.21 E
Pernes-les-Fontaines 62 44.00 N 5.03 E
Pernik 38 42.36 N 23.02 E
Pernink 54 50.20 N 12.45 E
Perniö 26 60.12 N 23.08 E
Pernitz 61 47.54 N 15.58 E
Pernovo 82 55.58 N 39.10 E
Pero 266b 45.31 N 9.05 E
Peroba, Ribeirão do ≃ 287b 23.27 S 46.22 W
Pérols, Étang de c 62 43.33 N 3.56 E
Peron, Cape › 168a 32.17 S 115.41 E
Péronne 50 49.56 N 2.56 E
Péronnes 50 50.26 N 4.08 E
Peron Peninsula ›[1] 162 25.55 S 113.30 E
Pero Pinheiro 266c 38.51 N 9.20 W
Perosa Argentina 62 44.58 N 7.10 E
Perote 234 19.34 N 97.14 W
Perotó 248 14.50 S 64.31 W
Pérou → Peru □[1] 242 10.00 S 76.00 W
Pérouges 58 45.54 N 5.11 E
Peroulaz 62 45.42 N 7.19 E
Perovo ◆[8] 265b 55.44 N 37.46 E
Perow 182 54.31 N 126.26 W
Perpendicular, Point › 170 35.06 S 150.48 E
Perpignan 32 42.41 N 2.53 E
Perranporth 42 50.20 N 5.09 W
Perrault Falls 184 50.19 N 93.11 W
Perray ≃ 261 48.31 N 1.42 E
Perrero 62 44.56 N 7.05 E
Perriers-sur-Andelle 50 49.25 N 1.22 E
Perrignier 58 46.18 N 6.27 E
Perrigny 58 46.40 N 5.35 E
Perrin 196 33.02 N 98.04 W
Perrine 220 25.36 N 80.21 W
Perrineville 208 40.13 N 74.26 W
Perris 228 33.46 N 117.13 W
Perris, Lake ⊜[1] 228 33.50 N 117.10 W
Perro, Laguna del ⊜ 200 34.40 N 105.57 W
Perro, Punta del › 34 36.45 N 6.25 W
Perros ≃ 234 16.20 N 94.59 W
Perros, Bahía de los c 240p 22.25 N 78.30 W
Perros-Guirec 32 48.49 N 3.27 W
Perrot, Île I 206 45.22 N 73.57 W
Perry, Fl., U.S. 192 30.07 N 83.34 W
Perry, Ga., U.S. 192 32.27 N 83.43 W
Perry, Il., U.S. 219 39.47 N 90.45 W
Perry, Ia., U.S. 190 41.50 N 94.06 W
Perry, Ks., U.S. 198 39.04 N 95.23 W
Perry, Me., U.S. 186 44.58 N 67.04 W
Perry, Mi., U.S. 216 42.49 N 84.13 W
Perry, Mo., U.S. 219 39.25 N 91.40 W
Perry, N.Y., U.S. 210 42.42 N 78.00 W
Perry, Oh., U.S. 214 41.45 N 81.08 W
Perry, Ok., U.S. 196 36.17 N 97.17 W
Perry, Tx., U.S. 222 31.25 N 96.55 W
Perry, Ut,. U.S. 200 41.27 N 112.02 W
Perry □[6] 208 40.25 N 77.11 W
Perrydale 224 45.02 N 123.15 W
Perry Hall 208 39.24 N 76.27 W
Perry Heights 214 40.47 N 81.28 W
Perry-Jōriku-kinenhi ⊥ 94 35.14 N 139.43 E
Perry Lake ⊜[1] 198 39.20 N 95.30 W
Perryman 208 39.28 N 76.12 W
Perrymont 279b 40.33 N 80.02 W
Perryopolis 214 40.05 N 79.45 W
Perry Park 218 38.33 N 85.00 W
Perry Point 208 39.33 N 76.04 W
Perrysburg, N.Y., U.S. 210 42.27 N 79.00 W
Perrysburg, Oh., U.S. 214 41.33 N 83.37 W
Perry's Landing Monument ⊥ 268 35.13 N 139.43 E
Perry's Victory and International Peace Memorial ⊥ 214 41.33 N 82.50 W
Perrysville, Oh., U.S. 214 40.39 N 82.18 W
Perrysville, Pa., U.S. 279b 40.32 N 80.01 W
Perryton 196 36.24 N 100.48 W
Perryville, Ak., U.S. 180 55.54 N 159.10 W
Perryville, Ar., U.S. 194 35.00 N 92.48 W
Perryville, Ky., U.S. 192 37.39 N 84.57 W
Perryville, Md., U.S. 208 39.33 N 76.04 W
Perryville, Mo., U.S. 194 37.43 N 89.51 W
Perryville, N.Y., U.S. 210 43.01 N 75.48 W
Peršaj 76 54.02 N 26.41 E
Persan 50 49.09 N 2.16 E
Perșani, Munții ⋀ 38 45.40 N 25.15 E
Persberg 40 59.45 N 14.15 E
Perschling ≃ 61 48.20 N 15.58 E
Perşembe 130 41.04 N 37.46 E
Persepolis → Takht-e Jamshīd ⊥ 128 29.57 N 52.52 E
Perseverance, Mount ∧ 171a 27.25 S 152.10 E
Perseverancia 248 14.44 S 62.48 W
Pershagen 40 59.10 N 17.39 E
Pershing 218 39.49 N 84.53 W
Pershore 42 52.07 N 2.05 W
Pershyttan 40 59.30 N 15.00 E
Persia 198 41.34 N 95.34 W
Persia → Iran □[1] 128 32.00 N 53.00 E
Persian Gulf c 128 27.00 N 51.00 E
Pérsico, Golfo → Persian Gulf c 128 27.00 N 51.00 E
Persimmon Creek ≃ 194 31.31 N 86.50 W
Persique, Golfe → Persian Gulf c 128 27.00 N 51.00 E
Persischer Golf → Persian Gulf c 128 27.00 N 51.00 E
Peršotravensk, S.S.S.R. 78 50.12 N 27.39 E
Peršotravensk, S.S.S.R. 78 48.22 N 36.24 E
Peršotravnevoje, S.S.S.R. 78 51.24 N 28.53 E
Peršotravnevoje, S.S.S.R. 83 47.03 N 37.18 E
Perštejn 54 50.23 N 13.08 E
Perstorp 41 56.08 N 13.23 E
Pertandangan, Tanjung › 114 2.41 N 100.14 E
Pertang ≃ 114 3.14 N 102.19 E
Pertek 130 38.50 N 39.22 E
Perth, Austl. 168a 31.56 S 115.50 E
Perth, On., Can. 212 44.54 N 76.15 W
Perth, Scot., U.K. 46 56.24 N 3.28 W
Perth, N.Y., U.S. 210 43.03 N 74.12 W
Perth □[6] 212 43.30 N 81.05 W
Perth Amboy 210 40.30 N 74.15 W
Perth-Andover 186 46.45 N 67.42 W
Perth Basin ✧[1] 14 28.30 S 110.00 E
Perthes 58 48.39 N 4.49 E
Perth International Airport ⊠ 168a 31.57 S 115.58 E
Perthois ◆[1] 58 48.40 N 4.45 E
Pertokar 144 16.59 N 37.28 E
Pertominsk 24 64.47 N 38.25 E
Pertovo 80 54.22 N 41.31 E
Pertuis 62 43.41 N 5.30 E
Pertusato, Capo › 71 41.21 N 9.10 E
Peru, Il., U.S. 216 41.19 N 89.07 W
Peru, In., U.S. 216 40.45 N 86.04 W
Peru, Ne., U.S. 198 40.28 N 95.44 W
Peru, N.Y., U.S. 188 44.34 N 73.31 W
Peru □[1] 242 10.00 S 76.00 W
Peruaçu ≃ 255 15.11 S 44.07 W
Peru Basin ✧[1] 18 15.00 S 85.00 W
Peruc 54 50.19 N 13.59 E
Peru-Chile Trench ✧[1] 18 20.00 S 73.00 W
Perugia 66 43.08 N 12.22 E
Perugia □[4] 66 43.03 N 12.33 E
Perugorría 252 29.20 S 58.37 W
Peruíbe 252 24.19 S 47.00 W
Peruípe ≃ 255 17.43 S 39.16 W
Peruque Creek ≃ 219 38.53 N 90.39 W
Perus ◆[8] 256 23.25 S 46.45 W
Perus ≃ 287b 23.23 S 46.46 W
Perušić 36 44.39 N 15.23 E
Péruwelz 50 50.31 N 3.35 E
Pervaja Maja 86 48.55 N 67.25 E
Pervenchères 50 48.26 N 0.26 E
Pervesinka 80 52.13 N 43.15 E
Pervijze 50 51.05 N 2.47 E
Pervoavgustovskij 76 52.14 N 35.03 E
Pervoje Pole 180 63.05 N 179.19 E
Pervomajka, S.S.S.R. 83 49.09 N 37.58 E
Pervomajka, S.S.S.R. 86 51.17 N 70.08 E
Pervomajka ◆[8] 83 48.17 N 39.50 E
Pervomajsk, S.S.S.R. 78 48.04 N 30.52 E
Pervomajsk, S.S.S.R. 80 54.53 N 43.49 E
Pervomajsk, S.S.S.R. 83 48.37 N 38.35 E
Pervomajsk, S.S.S.R. 83 49.05 N 39.37 E
Pervomajsk, S.S.S.R. 88 58.02 N 94.05 E
Pervomajskij, S.S.S.R. 76 54.04 N 32.29 E
Pervomajskij, S.S.S.R. 76 53.54 N 25.23 E
Pervomajskij, S.S.S.R. 78 49.24 N 36.12 E
Pervomajskij, S.S.S.R. 80 53.22 N 51.38 E
Pervomajskij, S.S.S.R. 80 51.22 N 48.54 E
Pervomajskij, S.S.S.R. 80 53.15 N 40.18 E
Pervomajskij, S.S.S.R. 82 55.57 N 37.52 E
Pervomajskij, S.S.S.R. 82 54.03 N 37.32 E
Pervomajskij, S.S.S.R. 82 55.32 N 37.09 E
Pervomajskij, S.S.S.R. 83 47.58 N 38.47 E
Pervomajskij, S.S.S.R. 85 42.51 N 74.04 E
Pervomajskij, S.S.S.R. 86 54.52 N 61.08 E
Pervomajskij, S.S.S.R. 86 59.29 N 61.24 E
Pervomajskij, S.S.S.R. 86 53.41 N 55.57 E
Pervomajskij, S.S.S.R. 86 51.32 N 55.06 E
Pervomajskij, S.S.S.R. 88 51.44 N 115.39 E
Pervomajskoje, S.S.S.R. 76 52.56 N 33.36 E
Pervomajskoje, S.S.S.R. 78 45.43 N 33.51 E
Pervomajskoje, S.S.S.R. 80 55.05 N 47.22 E
Pervomajskoje, S.S.S.R. 80 46.03 N 42.13 E
Pervomajskoje, S.S.S.R. 80 46.21 N 43.37 E
Pervomajskoje, S.S.S.R. 80 48.50 N 41.14 E
Pervomajskoje, S.S.S.R. 80 51.28 N 47.37 E
Pervomajskoje, S.S.S.R. 80 50.56 N 46.46 E
Pervomajskoje, S.S.S.R. 85 42.05 N 69.53 E
Pervomajskoje, S.S.S.R. 86 53.45 N 84.08 E
Pervomajskoje, S.S.S.R. 86 57.06 N 86.12 E
Pervoural'sk 86 56.54 N 59.58 E
Pervušino 80 58.02 N 41.56 E
Pervyj Kuril'skij proliv ꓵ 74 50.50 N 156.36 E
Perwenitz 264a 52.40 N 13.01 E
Pes' 76 58.55 N 34.19 E
Pes' ≃ 76 59.08 N 35.18 E
Pesa ≃ 66 43.44 N 11.01 E
Pes'akov, ostrov I 24 68.47 N 57.35 E
Pesangrohan ≃ 269e 6.11 S 106.45 E
Pesaro 66 43.54 N 12.55 E
Pesaro e Urbino □[4] 66 43.40 N 12.38 E
Pesca 246 5.33 N 73.03 W
Pescadero 226 37.15 N 122.22 W
Pescadero, Laguna c 234 22.12 N 105.20 W
Pescadero Creek ≃, Ca., U.S. 226 36.42 N 121.17 W
Pescadero Creek ≃, Ca., U.S. 226 37.16 N 122.25 W
Pescadores → P'enghu Ch'üntao II 100 23.30 N 119.30 E
Pescadores, Punta ›, Méx. 232 23.46 N 109.43 W
Pescadores, Punta ›, Perú 248 16.21 S 73.15 W
Pescaglia 66 43.58 N 10.25 E
Pesčanaja 78 48.08 N 29.44 E
Pesčanka, S.S.S.R. 78 48.12 N 28.53 E
Pesčanka, S.S.S.R. 80 51.18 N 43.40 E
Pesčanoje, S.S.S.R. 24 62.09 N 35.48 E
Pesčanoje, S.S.S.R. 78 49.44 N 31.50 E
Pesčanoje, S.S.S.R. 83 49.34 N 37.51 E
Pesčanoje, S.S.S.R. 86 53.01 N 76.19 E
Pesčanokopskoje 80 46.12 N 41.04 E
Pescantina 64 45.29 N 10.51 E
Pesčanyj 83 47.02 N 37.28 E
Pesčanyje, ostrova II 83 46.52 N 38.17 E
Pescara 66 42.28 N 14.13 E
Pescara □[4] 66 42.20 N 13.57 E
Pescara ≃ 66 42.28 N 14.13 E
Pescasseroli 66 41.48 N 13.47 E
Pesch 263 51.11 N 6.32 E
Pesch, Schloss ⊥ 263 51.18 N 6.39 E
Peschici 68 41.57 N 16.01 E
Peschiera del Garda 64 45.26 N 10.42 E
Peschio, Monte ∧ 267a 41.43 N 12.46 E
Pescia 66 43.54 N 10.41 E
Pescina 66 42.02 N 13.39 E
Pescocostanzo 66 41.53 N 14.04 E
Pescolanciano 66 41.41 N 14.20 E
Pescopagano 68 40.50 N 15.24 E
Pescorocchiano 66 42.12 N 13.09 E
Pesco Sannita 68 41.14 N 14.49 E
Pesé 236 7.54 N 80.37 W
Pesek, Pulau I 271c 1.17 N 103.41 E
Peseux 58 46.59 N 6.53 E
Peshastin 224 47.34 N 120.36 W
Peshastin Creek ≃ 224 47.33 N 120.35 W
Peshāwar 123 34.01 N 71.33 E
Peshīn Jān 128 33.25 N 61.28 E
Peshkopi 38 41.41 N 20.26 E
Peshmāl 123 35.26 N 72.36 E
Peshtigo 190 45.03 N 87.44 W
Peshtigo ≃ 190 44.58 N 87.40 W
Pesio ≃ 62 44.28 N 7.53 E
Pesjane 82 56.01 N 38.48 E
Peski, S.S.S.R. 76 53.21 N 24.38 E
Peski, S.S.S.R. 78 50.23 N 33.27 E
Peski, S.S.S.R. 80 51.16 N 42.27 E
Peski, S.S.S.R. 82 55.13 N 38.46 E
Peški, S.S.S.R. 82 56.08 N 37.04 E
Peski, S.S.S.R. 83 49.26 N 38.59 E
Peski-Rad'kovskije 83 49.17 N 37.36 E
Peskovatskoje 82 54.03 N 36.16 E
Peskovka, S.S.S.R. 78 50.42 N 29.38 E
Peskovka, S.S.S.R. 86 59.04 N 52.22 E
Peškovo 83 47.02 N 39.24 E
Peškovo Grecovo 82 54.26 N 37.36 E
Peškovskoje 86 53.45 N 62.23 E
Pesmes 58 47.17 N 5.34 E
Pesnica 61 46.36 N 15.41 E
Pesnica ≃ 61 46.24 N 16.05 E
Pešnoj, poluostrov ›[2] 80 46.52 N 51.42 E
Pesočenskij 82 54.10 N 36.06 E
Pesočin 78 49.57 N 36.06 E
Pesočn'a 80 54.07 N 40.50 E
Pesočnoje, S.S.S.R. 76 53.20 N 27.06 E
Pesočnoje, S.S.S.R. 80 58.01 N 39.10 E
Pesočnyj 76 60.07 N 30.08 E
Peso da Régua 34 41.10 N 7.47 W
Pespire 236 13.35 N 87.22 W
Pesqueira 250 8.22 S 36.42 W
Pesquería 196 25.47 N 100.03 W
Pesquería ≃ 196 25.54 N 99.11 W
Pessac 32 44.48 N 0.38 W
Pessáni 130 41.05 N 26.06 E
Pessin 54 52.38 N 12.40 E
Pessinetto 62 45.17 N 7.24 E
Pest □[6] 30 47.25 N 19.20 E
Pest'aki 80 56.43 N 42.40 E
Peštera 38 42.02 N 24.18 E
Pesterzsébet ◆[8] 264c 47.26 N 19.07 E
Pesthidegkút ◆[8] 264c 47.34 N 18.58 E
Pestimre ◆[8] 264c 47.24 N 19.12 E
Pestlőrinc ◆[8] 264c 47.26 N 19.12 E
Pestovo, S.S.S.R. 76 58.36 N 35.48 E
Pestovo, S.S.S.R. 80 57.12 N 46.44 E
Pestovskoje vodochranilišče ⊜[1] 82 56.06 N 37.40 E
Pestravka 80 52.24 N 49.58 E
Pestrecy 80 55.46 N 49.39 E
Pestrikovo 82 55.05 N 38.53 E
Pestújhely ◆[8] 264c 47.32 N 19.07 E
Petacalco, Bahía de c 234 17.57 N 102.05 W
Petaḥ Tiqwa 132 32.05 N 34.53 E
Petäjävesi 26 62.15 N 25.12 E
Petal 194 31.20 N 89.15 W
Petalcingo 232 17.17 N 92.27 W
Petaling Jaya 114 3.05 N 101.39 E
Petalión, Kólpos c 38 37.59 N 24.02 E
Petaluma 226 38.13 N 122.38 W
Petaluma ≃ 226 38.06 N 122.30 W
Pétange 56 49.34 N 5.52 E
Petare 246 10.29 N 66.49 W
Petatlán 234 17.31 N 101.16 W
Petauke 154 14.15 S 31.20 E
Petawawa 190 45.54 N 77.17 W
Petawawa ≃ 190 45.55 N 77.15 W
Pété 146 10.58 N 14.30 E
Petegem 50 50.58 N 3.32 E
Petén □[5] 236 16.15 N 89.50 W
Peteń Itzá, Lago ⊜ 232 16.59 N 89.50 W
Petenwell Lake ⊜[1] 190 44.10 N 89.57 W
Peter and Paul Fortress ⊥ 265a 59.57 N 30.19 E
Peterboro 210 42.58 N 75.41 W
Peterborough, Austl. 166 32.58 S 138.50 E
Peterborough, On., Can. 212 44.18 N 78.19 W
Peterborough, Eng., U.K. 42 52.35 N 0.15 W
Peterborough, N.H., U.S. 188 42.52 N 71.57 W
Peterborough □[6] 212 44.33 N 78.15 W
Peterculter 46 57.05 N 2.16 W
Peterhead 46 57.30 N 1.49 W
Peter Hill ∧ 46 56.58 N 2.42 W
Peter I Island I 9 68.47 S 90.35 W
Peter Island I 240m 18.22 N 64.35 W
Peter Lake ⊜, N.T., Can. 176 63.08 N 92.48 W
Peter Lake ⊜, Sk., Can. 184 57.15 N 103.53 W
Peterlee 44 54.46 N 1.19 W
Peterman 194 31.35 N 87.15 W
Petermann Aboriginal Reserve ◆[4] 162 25.00 S 130.15 E
Petermann Ranges ⋀ 162 25.00 S 129.46 E
Peter Pond Lake ⊜ 184 55.55 N 108.44 W
Peter Pond Lake Indian Reserve ◆[4] 184 55.55 N 109.00 W
Petersberg 56 50.33 N 9.43 E
Peters Brook ≃ 276 40.33 N 74.37 W
Petersburg, Ak., U.S. 180 56.49 N 132.57 W
Petersburg, Il., U.S. 219 40.00 N 89.50 W
Petersburg, In., U.S. 194 38.29 N 87.16 W
Petersburg, Mi., U.S. 216 41.54 N 83.42 W
Petersburg, Ne., U.S. 198 41.51 N 98.04 W
Petersburg, N.J., U.S. 208 39.15 N 74.43 W
Petersburg, N.Y., U.S. 210 42.44 N 73.20 W
Petersburg, Oh., U.S. 214 40.54 N 80.31 W
Petersburg, Pa., U.S. 214 40.34 N 78.03 W
Petersburg, Tn., U.S. 194 35.19 N 86.38 W
Petersburg, Tx., U.S. 196 33.52 N 101.36 W
Petersburg, Va., U.S. 208 37.13 N 77.24 W
Petersburg, W.V., U.S. 188 38.59 N 79.07 W
Petersburg National Battlefield ♠ 208 37.14 N 77.22 W
Peters Canyon Reservoir ⊜[1] 280 33.47 N 117.45 W
Peters Creek ≃, Ca., U.S. 282 37.15 N 122.13 W
Peters Creek ≃, Pa., U.S. 279b 40.18 N 79.52 W
Peters Creek, Piney Fork ≃ 279b 40.16 N 79.58 W
Petersdorf 54 54.29 N 11.04 E
Petersfield, S. Afr. 273d 26.14 S 28.26 E
Petersfield, Eng., U.K. 42 51.00 N 0.56 W
Petershagen, B.R.D. 52 52.23 N 8.58 E
Petershagen, D.D.R. 54 52.24 N 14.20 E
Petershagen bei Berlin 54 52.31 N 13.46 E
Petersham, Austl. 274a 33.54 S 151.09 E
Petersham, Ma., U.S. 207 42.29 N 72.11 W
Peters Hill ∧[2] 168b 34.11 S 138.50 E
Peterson 198 42.55 N 95.20 W
Peterson Air Force Base ■ 198 38.49 N 104.42 W
Peters Pond ⊜ 283 42.43 N 71.16 W
Peterswald Hill ∧[2] 162 26.43 S 123.39 E
Peter the Great Bay → Petra Velikogo, zaliv c 89 42.40 N 132.00 E
Peter the Great Monument ⊥ 265a 59.56 N 30.18 E
Pétervására 30 48.01 N 20.06 E
Petilia Policastro 68 39.07 N 16.47 E
Pétionville 238 18.31 N 72.17 W
Petit 273d 26.06 S 28.22 E
Petit Bois Island I 194 30.12 N 88.26 W
Petit-Bourg 241o 16.12 N 61.36 W
Petit-Canal 241o 16.23 N 61.29 W
Petitcodiac 186 45.56 N 65.10 W
Petitcodiac ≃ 186 45.50 N 64.33 W
Petit Cul-de-Sac Marin c 241o 16.12 N 61.33 W
Petite Nation, Rivière de la ≃ 206 45.35 N 75.06 W
Petite Rivière du Chêne ≃ 206 46.34 N 72.02 W
Petite Rivière Noire, Piton de la ∧ 157c 20.24 S 57.24 E
Petite Rivière Rouge ≃ 206 45.45 N 75.00 W
Petite Sauldre ≃ 50 47.27 N 2.05 E
Petite Terre, Îles de la II 241o 16.10 N 61.07 W
Petit Forte 186 47.24 N 54.40 W
Petit-Fort-Philippe 50 51.00 N 2.07 E
Petit-Goâve 238 18.26 N 72.52 W
Petit Jean ≃ 194 35.10 N 92.56 W
Petit Jean State Park ♠ 194 35.06 N 92.57 W
Petit Loango 152 2.16 S 9.35 E
Petit Loango, Parc National du ♠ 152 2.15 S 9.36 E
Petit Mécatina, Île du I 186 50.33 N 59.20 W
Petit Morin ≃ 50 48.56 N 3.07 E
Petitot ≃ 176 60.14 N 123.29 W
Petit Rhône ≃ 62 43.27 N 4.24 E
Petit-Saint-Bernard, Col du)(62 45.41 N 6.53 E
Petitsikapau Lake ⊜ 176 54.45 N 66.25 W
Petkeljärven Kansallispuisto ♠ 24 62.35 N 31.12 E
Petkus 54 51.59 N 13.21 E
Petlād 120 22.28 N 72.48 E
Petlalcingo 234 18.05 N 97.54 W
Petnahor 267b 41.11 N 28.53 E
Petnjička Pećina ≗[5] 38 44.15 N 19.54 E
Peto 232 20.08 N 88.55 W
Petoh 114 2.53 N 103.15 E
Petone 172 41.13 S 174.52 E
Petorca 252 32.15 S 70.56 W
Petoskey 190 45.22 N 84.57 W
Petownikip Lake ⊜ 184 52.56 N 92.02 W
Petra ⊥ 132 30.20 N 35.26 E
Petralia Soprana 70 37.47 N 14.06 E
Petralia Sottana 70 37.48 N 14.05 E
Petras, Mount ∧ 9 75.52 S 128.38 W
Petra Velikogo, zaliv (Peter the Great Bay) c 89 42.40 N 132.00 E
Petre, Point › 212 43.50 N 77.09 W
Petrecovo 24 61.18 N 57.07 E
Petrella, Monte ∧ 66 41.18 N 13.40 E
Petrella Salto 66 42.18 N 13.04 E
Petrella Tifernina 66 41.41 N 14.42 E
Petrič 38 41.24 N 23.13 E
Petrie 171a 27.16 S 152.59 E
Petrified Forest National Park ♠ 200 34.55 N 109.49 W
Petrikov 78 52.08 N 28.30 E
Petrikovka 78 48.43 N 34.37 E
Petrila 38 45.27 N 23.25 E
Petrinja 36 45.26 N 16.17 E
Petriščevo, S.S.S.R. 82 54.37 N 36.57 E
Petriščevo, S.S.S.R. 82 55.30 N 36.18 E
Petrodvorec 76 59.53 N 29.54 E
Petroglyphs Provincial Park ♠ 212 44.33 N 77.53 W
Petrograd → Leningrad 76 59.55 N 30.15 E
Petrogrado-Doneckoje ◆[8] 83 48.42 N 38.41 E
Petrohanski prohod)(38 43.08 N 23.08 E
Petrohué 254 41.08 S 72.25 W
Petrokrepost' 76 59.57 N 31.02 E
Petrolândia 250 9.05 S 38.18 W
Petrólea 246 8.30 N 72.35 W
Petroleum 216 40.36 N 85.09 W
Petrolia, On., Can. 214 42.52 N 82.09 W
Petrolia, Pa., U.S. 214 41.01 N 79.43 W
Petrolia, Tx., U.S. 196 34.01 N 98.14 W
Petrolina 250 9.24 S 40.30 W
Petrolina de Goiás 255 16.06 S 49.20 W
Petronà 68 39.03 N 16.45 E
Petrona, Punta › 240m 17.56 N 66.23 W
Petronila Creek ≃ 196 27.32 N 97.32 W
Petropavlovka, S.S.S.R. 78 50.06 N 40.54 E
Petropavlovka, S.S.S.R. 78 48.27 N 36.26 E
Petropavlovka, S.S.S.R. 83 49.43 N 37.42 E
Petropavlovka, S.S.S.R. 88 50.38 N 105.19 E
Petropavlovsk, S.S.S.R. 86 54.54 N 69.06 E
Petropavlovsk, S.S.S.R. 86 56.20 N 57.09 E
Petropavlovsk-Kamčatskij 74 53.01 N 158.39 E
Petropavlovskoje, S.S.S.R. 86 52.04 N 84.08 E
Petropavlovskoje, S.S.S.R. 88 58.13 N 108.59 E
Petrópolis 256 22.31 S 43.10 W
Petros 192 36.05 N 84.26 W
Petroșani 38 45.25 N 23.22 E
Petrosino 70 37.43 N 12.29 E
Petro-Slav'anka 265a 59.48 N 30.31 E
Petroso, Monte ∧ 66 41.44 N 13.55 E
Petroúpolis 267c 38.03 N 23.41 E
Petrovac 38 44.22 N 21.27 E
Petrovgrad → Zrenjanin 38 45.23 N 20.24 E
Petrovka, S.S.S.R. 78 46.54 N 30.44 E
Petrovka, S.S.S.R. 80 53.13 N 51.58 E
Petrovka, S.S.S.R. 83 48.53 N 39.52 E
Petrovka, S.S.S.R. 83 48.48 N 39.16 E
Petrovo, S.S.S.R. 76 58.22 N 35.09 E
Petrovo, S.S.S.R. 78 48.20 N 33.16 E
Petrovo, S.S.S.R. 82 55.00 N 38.08 E
Petrovo, S.S.S.R. 88 54.30 N 105.15 E
Petrovo-Dal'neje 265b 55.45 N 37.11 E
Petrovo-Krasnoselje ◆[8] 83 48.18 N 38.52 E
Petrovsk 80 52.19 N 45.23 E
Petrovskaja 78 45.25 N 37.57 E
Petrovskij, S.S.S.R. 80 56.39 N 40.19 E
Petrovskij, S.S.S.R. 80 50.45 N 41.59 E
Petrovskij, S.S.S.R. 82 54.29 N 36.59 E
Petrovskoje, S.S.S.R. 78 49.10 N 36.54 E
Petrovskoje, S.S.S.R. 80 52.39 N 40.15 E
Petrovskoje, S.S.S.R. 80 57.01 N 39.16 E
Petrovskoje, S.S.S.R. 82 55.27 N 38.21 E
Petrovskoje, S.S.S.R. 82 55.32 N 36.59 E
Petrovskoje, S.S.S.R. 83 48.18 N 38.52 E
Petrovskoje, S.S.S.R. 265b 55.36 N 37.53 E
Petrovsko-Razumovskoje ◆[8] 265b 55.50 N 37.34 E
Petrovsk-Zabajkal'skij 88 51.17 N 108.50 E
Petrov Val 80 50.09 N 45.12 E
Petrozavodsk 24 61.47 N 34.20 E
Petrozsény → Petroșani 38 45.25 N 23.22 E
Petrun' 24 66.28 N 60.43 E
Petrusburg 158 29.08 S 25.27 E
Petrušino 265a 59.48 N 30.50 E
Petrus Steyn 158 27.38 S 28.08 E
Petrusville 158 30.05 S 24.41 E
Petschora → Pečora ≃ 24 68.13 N 54.15 E
Petten 52 52.45 N 4.39 E
Pettenbach 61 47.57 N 14.01 E
Petteril ≃ 44 54.54 N 2.55 W
Petticoat Creek ≃ 275b 43.48 N 79.06 W
Pettigo 48 54.33 N 7.50 W
Pettinascura, Monte ∧ 68 39.22 N 16.37 E
Pettineo 70 37.58 N 14.17 E
Pettisville 216 41.31 N 84.13 W
Pettnau 64 47.18 N 11.08 E
Pettneu am Arlberg 58 47.09 N 10.20 E
Pettus 196 28.37 N 97.48 W
Petty Harbour 186 47.28 N 52.43 W
Petty Island I 285 39.58 N 75.07 W
Petua 272b 22.25 N 88.27 E
Petuchovo 86 55.06 N 67.58 E
Petuški 80 55.55 N 39.28 E
Petworth 42 50.59 N 0.38 W
Petzow 264a 52.21 N 12.56 E
Peudada 114 5.12 N 96.35 E
Peuerbach 60 48.21 N 13.56 E
Peuetsagoe, Gunung ∧ 114 4.55 N 96.20 E
Peureulak 114 4.48 N 97.53 E
Peureulak ≃ 114 4.54 N 97.53 E
Peureulak, Ujung › 114 4.54 N 97.54 E
Peusangan ≃ 114 5.16 N 96.51 E
Peusangan, Ujung › 114 5.18 N 96.50 E
Pevek 74 69.42 N 170.17 E
Pevely 219 38.17 N 90.23 W
Pevensey 42 50.49 N 0.20 E
Pevensey Levels ≚ 42 50.50 N 0.20 E
Peveragno 62 44.20 N 7.37 E
Pewamo 216 43.00 N 84.50 W
Pewaukee 216 43.04 N 88.15 W
Pewaukee Lake ⊜ 216 43.04 N 88.19 W
Pewee Valley 218 38.18 N 85.29 W
Pews Creek ≃ 276 40.27 N 74.06 W
Pewsey 42 51.21 N 1.46 W
Pewsey, Vale of V 42 51.20 N 1.48 W
Péyia 130 34.53 N 32.23 E
Peykjahlið 24a 65.40 N 16.50 W
Peyrolles-en-Provence 62 43.39 N 5.35 E
Peyruis 62 44.02 N 5.56 E
Peza ≃ 24 65.36 N 44.35 E
Pezas 86 54.39 N 87.46 E
Pezawa Taung ∧ 110 19.33 N 94.31 E
Pézenas 32 43.27 N 3.25 E
Peženga 76 59.10 N 44.16 E
Pezinok 30 48.18 N 17.17 E
Pezu 123 32.19 N 70.44 E
Pezzana 62 45.16 N 8.29 E
Pfäfers 58 46.59 N 9.30 E
Pfaffenhausen 58 48.07 N 10.27 E
Pfaffenhofen an der Ilm 60 48.31 N 11.30 E
Pfaffenhoffen 56 48.51 N 7.37 E
Pfaffenöden ∧[2] 264b 48.04 N 16.33 E
Pfäffikersee ⊜ 58 47.21 N 8.48 E
Pfäffikon 58 47.22 N 8.47 E
Pfaffnau 58 47.14 N 7.54 E
Pfaffstätten 264b 48.01 N 16.16 E
Pfalz □[5] 56 49.20 N 8.00 E
Pfalzdorf 52 51.42 N 6.11 E
Pfalzel 56 49.47 N 6.41 E
Pfänder ∧ 58 47.30 N 9.47 E
Pfarrkirchen 60 48.27 N 12.56 E
Pfarrweisach 56 50.09 N 10.44 E
Pfastatt 58 47.47 N 7.18 E
Pfatter 60 48.58 N 12.23 E
Pfaueninsel, Schloss ⊥ 264a 52.26 N 13.07 E
Pfeddersheim 56 49.38 N 8.16 E
Pfeffenhausen 60 48.40 N 11.58 E
Pfeiffer-Big Sur State Park ♠ 226 36.15 N 121.47 W
Pferderennbahn ♠ 263 51.31 N 7.32 E
Pflugerville 222 30.26 N 97.37 W
Pförten → Brody 30 51.45 N 14.45 E
Pforzen 58 47.55 N 10.37 E
Pforzheim 56 48.54 N 8.42 E
Pfreimd ≃ 60 49.29 N 12.11 E
Pfrimm ≃ 56 49.39 N 8.22 E
Pfronten 58 47.34 N 10.33 E
Pfuhl 58 48.24 N 10.02 E
Pfullendorf 58 47.55 N 9.15 E
Pfullingen 58 48.28 N 9.13 E
Pfunds 58 46.58 N 10.33 E
Pfungstadt 56 49.48 N 8.36 E
Pfyn 58 47.36 N 8.57 E
Phachi ≃ 110 13.56 N 99.24 E
Phaéton, Port c 174s 17.44 S 149.21 W
Phagwāra 123 31.14 N 75.46 E
Phala 156 23.45 S 26.57 E
Phalaborwa 156 23.55 S 31.13 E
Phalanx 214 41.15 N 80.58 W
Phalempin 50 50.31 N 3.01 E
Phālia 123 32.26 N 73.35 E
Phalodi 120 27.08 N 72.22 E
Phalsbourg 56 48.46 N 7.16 E
Phaltan 122 17.59 N 74.26 E
Phalti 272b 22.46 N 88.34 E
Phan 110 19.28 N 99.43 E
Phanat Nikhom 110 13.27 N 101.11 E
Phangan, Ko I 110 9.45 N 100.04 E
Phang Hoei, Khao ∧ 110 15.15 N 101.23 E
Phangnga 110 8.28 N 98.32 E
Phaniang ≃ 110 16.49 N 102.24 E
Phanom Dongrak, Thiu Khao ⋀ 110 14.25 N 103.30 E
Phanom Thuan 110 14.07 N 99.42 E
Phan-rang 110 11.34 N 108.59 E
Phan-thiet 110 10.56 N 108.06 E
Phan Thong 110 13.28 N 101.06 E
Phantom Lake 216 42.52 N 88.21 W
Pharenda 124 27.06 N 83.17 E
Phariāro 120 27.12 N 68.59 E
Pharr 196 26.11 N 98.11 W
Phasi Charoen 269a 13.43 N 100.26 E
Phasi Charoen, Khlong ≋ 269a 13.44 N 100.30 E
Phat-diem 110 20.06 N 106.06 E
Phato 110 9.48 N 98.48 E
Phatthalung 110 7.37 N 100.05 E
Phayao 110 19.10 N 99.55 E
Pheasant Creek ≃ 184 50.35 N 103.28 W
Pheba 194 33.35 N 88.56 W
Phelan 228 34.25 N 117.34 W
Phelps, N.Y., U.S. 210 42.57 N 77.03 W
Phelps, Tx., U.S. 222 30.42 N 95.27 W
Phelps, Wi., U.S. 190 46.03 N 89.05 W
Phelps Lake ⊜ 192 35.46 N 76.27 W
Phenix City 192 32.28 N 85.00 W
Phepane ≃ 156 25.50 S 22.45 E
Phet Buri 110 13.06 N 99.57 E
Phet Buri ≃ 110 13.13 N 99.59 E
Phetchabun 110 16.25 N 101.08 E
Phetchabun, Thiu Khao ⋀ 110 16.20 N 100.55 E
Phibun Mangsahan 110 15.14 N 105.14 E
Phichai 110 17.17 N 100.05 E
Phichit 110 16.26 N 100.22 E
Philadelphia, S. Afr. 158 33.40 S 18.36 E
Philadelphia, Il., U.S. 219 39.58 N 90.07 W
Philadelphia, Ms., U.S. 194 32.46 N 89.07 W
Philadelphia, Mo., U.S. 219 39.50 N 91.44 W
Philadelphia, N.Y., U.S. 212 44.09 N 75.42 W
Philadelphia, Pa., U.S. 208 39.57 N 75.09 W
Philadelphia, Pa., U.S. 285 39.57 N 75.09 W
Philadelphia, Tn., U.S. 192 35.40 N 84.24 W
Philadelphia □[6] 285 39.57 N 75.07 W
Philadelphia International Airport ⊠ 208 39.53 N 75.14 W
Philadelphia Museum of Art ʊ 285 39.58 N 75.11 W
Philadelphia Naval Shipyard ■ 285 39.53 N 75.11 W
Philae ⊥ 140 24.01 N 32.53 E
Phil Campbell 194 34.21 N 87.42 W
Philip 198 44.02 N 101.39 W
Philipp 194 33.45 N 90.12 W
Philippeville → Skikda, Alg. 148 36.50 N 6.58 E
Philippeville, Bel. 50 50.12 N 4.32 E
Philippi 188 39.09 N 80.02 W
Philippi, Lake ⊜ 166 24.22 S 139.00 E
Philippi Glacier ⩍ 9 66.45 S 88.20 E
Philippine Basin ✧[1] 14 17.00 N 132.00 E
Philippine Miniature Village ʊ 269f 14.31 N 121.00 E
Philippinen → Philippines □[1] 116 13.00 N 122.00 E
Philippines (Pilipinas) □[1], Asia 108 13.00 N 122.00 E
Philippines (Pilipinas) □[1], Asia 116 13.00 N 122.00 E
Philippines, University of the ʊ[2] 269f 14.39 N 121.04 E
Philippine Sea ⊤[2] 14 20.00 N 135.00 E
Philippine Trench ✧[1] 14 9.00 N 127.00 E
Philippolis 158 30.19 S 25.13 E
Philippopolis → Plovdiv 38 42.09 N 24.45 E
Philippsreut 60 48.52 N 13.41 E
Philippsthal 264a 52.20 N 13.09 E
Philipsburg, P.Q., Can. 206 45.02 N 73.05 W
Philipsburg, Ned. Ant. 238 17.59 N 63.10 W
Philipsburg, Mt., U.S. 202 46.19 N 113.17 W
Philipsburg, Pa., U.S. 214 40.53 N 78.13 W
Philipsburg Manor ⊥ 276 41.05 N 73.52 W
Philipse Manor Hall State Historic Site ⊥ 276 40.56 N 73.54 W
Philip Smith Mountains ⋀ 180 68.30 N 148.00 W
Philipstown 158 30.26 S 24.29 E
Phillaur 123 31.01 N 75.47 E
Phillip Island I 169 38.29 S 145.14 E
Phillips, Me., U.S. 188 44.49 N 70.20 W
Phillips, Tx., U.S. 196 35.41 N 101.21 W
Phillips, Wi., U.S. 190 45.41 N 90.24 W
Phillipsburg, Ga., U.S. 192 31.34 N 83.31 W
Phillipsburg, Ks., U.S. 198 39.45 N 99.19 W
Phillipsburg, N.J., U.S. 210 40.41 N 75.11 W
Philmont 210 42.14 N 73.39 W
Philo, Il., U.S. 194 40.01 N 88.09 W
Philo, Oh., U.S. 188 39.51 N 81.54 W
Philomath 202 44.32 N 123.21 W
Philpots Island I 176 74.48 N 80.00 W
Phimai 110 15.13 N 102.30 E
Phinga 272b 22.41 N 88.25 E
Phitsanulok 110 16.50 N 100.15 E
Phnom Penh → Phnum Pénh 110 11.33 N 104.55 E
Phnum Pénh 110 11.33 N 104.55 E
Phnum Tbêng Méanchey 110 13.49 N 104.58 E
Pho ≃ 124 27.41 N 89.53 E
Phoenicia 210 42.05 N 74.18 W
Phoenix, Az., U.S. 200 33.26 N 112.04 W
Phoenix, Il., U.S. 278 41.36 N 87.38 W
Phoenix, Md., U.S. 208 39.30 N 76.36 W
Phoenix, N.Y., U.S. 210 43.13 N 76.18 W
Phoenix Islands II 14 4.00 S 172.00 W
Phoenix Lake ⊜[1] 282 37.57 N 122.35 W
Phoenix Park ♠ 281 42.24 N 83.27 W
Phoenixville 208 40.07 N 75.30 W
Phon 110 15.49 N 102.36 E
Phong ≃ 110 16.23 N 102.56 E
Phôngsali 110 21.41 N 102.06 E
Phong-tho 110 22.32 N 103.21 E
Phon Phisai 110 18.01 N 103.05 E
Phosphate Hill 166 21.52 S 139.51 E
Phrae 110 18.09 N 100.08 E
Phra Khanong ◆[8] 269a 13.42 N 100.35 E
Phra Nakhon → Krung Thep 110 13.45 N 100.31 E
Phra Nakhon Si Ayutthaya 110 14.21 N 100.33 E
Phran Kratai 110 16.40 N 99.36 E
Phrao 110 19.22 N 99.13 E
Phra Phutthabat 110 14.43 N 100.48 E
Phra Pradaeng 269a 13.40 N 100.32 E
Phra Rop, Khao ∧ 110 13.11 N 99.31 E
Phrom Phiram 110 17.02 N 100.12 E
Phrygia □[9] 130 39.00 N 30.00 E
Phsar Réam 110 10.30 N 103.37 E
Phu-cat 110 14.01 N 109.03 E
Phu-cuong 110 10.58 N 106.39 E
Phu-huu, Viet. 110 18.58 N 105.31 E
Phu-huu, Viet. 269c 10.43 N 106.47 E
Phuket 110 7.53 N 98.24 E
Phuket, Ko I 110 8.00 N 98.22 E
Phularwān 123 32.22 N 73.00 E
Phulbari 126 21.52 N 88.08 E
Phulbāria 126 23.22 N 89.50 E
Phuljhuri 126 22.12 N 90.04 E
Phulkusma 126 22.43 N 86.52 E
Phu-loc 110 16.16 N 107.53 E
Phūlpur 124 25.33 N 82.06 E
Phulra 123 34.20 N 73.03 E
Phultala 126 22.59 N 89.28 E
Phu-ly 110 20.32 N 105.56 E
Phum Duang ≃ 110 9.10 N 99.20 E
Phumĭ Bâ Khăm 110 13.51 N 107.22 E
Phumĭ Banam 110 11.19 N 105.18 E
Phumĭ Béng 110 13.05 N 104.18 E
Phumĭ Châmbák 110 11.14 N 104.49 E
Phumĭ Chângho Ândêng 110 12.39 N 104.35 E
Phumĭ Chhuk 110 10.50 N 104.28 E
Phumĭ Chruŏy Slêng 110 13.14 N 105.57 E
Phumĭ Dăk Dăm 110 12.20 N 107.21 E
Phumĭ Kâmpóng Srâlau 110 14.05 N 105.46 E
Phumĭ Kâmpóng Trâbâk 110 13.06 N 105.14 E
Phumĭ Kântuŏt Sâmraông 110 14.12 N 104.37 E
Phumĭ Kaôh Kért 110 13.47 N 104.32 E
Phumĭ Kaôh Kŏng 110 11.26 N 103.11 E
Phumĭ Khpôb 110 11.02 N 105.12 E
Phumĭ Krêk 110 11.46 N 105.56 E
Phumĭ Lvéa Kraôm 110 13.21 N 102.54 E
Phumĭ Moŭng 110 13.45 N 103.33 E
Phumĭ Narŭng 110 13.53 N 105.34 E
Phumĭ Phnum Srâlau 110 11.03 N 103.42 E
Phumĭ Prêk Kák 110 12.15 N 105.32 E
Phumĭ Prêk Sândêk 110 11.51 N 105.22 E
Phumĭ Prey Toch 110 12.54 N 103.23 E
Phumĭ Puŏk Chăs 110 13.26 N 103.44 E
Phumĭ Rôluŏs Chăs 110 13.19 N 104.00 E
Phumĭ Sâmraông 110 14.11 N 103.31 E
Phumĭ Spœ Tbong 110 12.20 N 105.19 E
Phumĭ Srê Kôkir 110 13.08 N 106.04 E
Phumĭ Srê Rônéam 110 12.16 N 106.25 E
Phumĭ Tbêng 110 13.35 N 104.55 E
Phumĭ Thalabârĭvăt 110 13.33 N 105.57 E
Phumĭ Thmâ Pôk 110 13.57 N 103.04 E
Phumĭ Tnaôt 110 12.56 N 104.34 E
Phumĭ Tœk Choŭ 110 13.36 N 103.24 E
Phu-my 110 14.10 N 109.03 E
Phung-hiep 110 9.49 N 105.50 E
Phuntsholing 124 26.53 N 89.23 E
Phuoc-binh 110 11.50 N 106.58 E

Symbols in the index entries represent the broad categories identified in the key at the right. Symbols with superior numbers (⋀[1]) identify subcategories (see complete key on page *I · 1).*

Kartensymbole in dem Registerverzeichnis stellen die rechts in Schlüssel erklärten Kategorien dar. Symbole mit hochgestellten Ziffern (⋀[1]) bezeichnen Unterabteilungen einer Kategorie (vgl. vollständiger Schlüssel auf Seite *I · 1).*

Los símbolos incluídos en el texto del índice representan las grandes categorias identificadas con la clave a la derecha. Los símbolos con numeros en su parte superior (⋀[1]) identifican las subcategorías (véase la clave completa en la página *I · 1).*

Les symboles de l'index représentent les catégories indiquées dans la légende à droite. Les symboles suivis d'un indice (⋀[1]) représentent des sous-catégories (voir légende complète à la page *I · 1).*

Os símbolos incluídos no texto do índice representam as grandes categorias identificadas com a chave à direita. Os símbolos com números em sua parte superior (⋀[1]) identificam as subcategorias (veja-se a chave completa à página *I · 1).*

∧ Mountain	Berg	Montaña	Montagne	Montanha
⋀ Mountains	Berge	Montañas	Montagnes	Montanhas
)(Pass	Pass	Paso	Col	Passo
V Valley, Canyon	Tal, Cañon	Valle, Cañón	Vallée, Canyon	Vale, Canhão
≚ Plain	Ebene	Llano	Plaine	Planície
› Cape	Kap	Cabo	Cap	Cabo
I Island	Insel	Isla	Île	Ilha
II Islands	Inseln	Islas	Îles	Ilhas
≗ Other Topographic Features	Andere Topographische Objekte	Otros Elementos Topográficos	Autres données topographiques	Outros acidentes topográficos

ESPAÑOL — Nombre | Página | Lat.°′ | Long.°′ W = Oeste
FRANÇAIS — Nom | Page | Lat.°′ | Long.°′ W = Ouest
PORTUGUÊS — Nome | Página | Lat.°′ | Long.°′ W = Oeste

Phuoc Khanh 269c 10.40 N 106.48 E
Phuoc-long 110 9.26 N 105.28 E
Phuoc-long-xa 269c 10.49 N 106.46 E
Phuoc-luong 269c 10.45 N 106.48 E
Phu-quoc, Dao I 110 10.12 N 104.00 E
Phurphura 272b 22.44 N 88.08 E
Phu-tho 110 21.24 N 105.13 E
Phu-tho-hoa 269c 10.46 N 106.38 E
Phu Tho Race Track ♦ 269c 10.46 N 106.40 E
Phutthaisong 110 15.32 N 103.01 E
Phu-vang 110 16.31 N 107.37 E
Phu-vinh 110 9.56 N 106.20 E
Phu-yen 110 21.16 N 104.39 E
Pi ≃ 100 32.26 N 116.34 E
Pia 154 4.00 N 26.17 E
Piaanu Pass ʮ 175c 7.20 N 151.26 E
Piabas 250 1.12 S 46.54 W
Piabetá 256 22.37 S 43.10 W
Piacá 250 7.42 S 47.18 W
Piaçabuçu 250 10.24 S 36.25 W
Piacatu 255 21.38 S 50.30 W
Piacatuba 256 21.29 S 42.47 W
Piacenza 62 45.01 N 9.40 E
Piacenza □[4] 62 44.53 N 9.35 E
Piacouadie, Lac ⊜ 186 51.16 N 70.54 W
Piadena 64 45.08 N 10.22 E
Piaggine 68 40.21 N 15.23 E
Piako ≃ 172 37.12 S 175.30 E
Pialba 166 25.17 S 152.51 E
Piāli ≃ 272b 22.23 N 88.35 E
Piana 36 42.14 N 8.38 E
Piana, Isola I 71 40.58 N 8.13 E
Piana Crixia 62 44.29 N 8.18 E
Piana degli Albanesi 70 38.00 N 13.17 E
Piana degli Albanesi, Lago di ⊜ 70 37.58 N 13.18 E
Piana Mwanga 154 7.40 S 28.10 E
Piancastagnaio 66 42.51 N 11.41 E
Piancó 250 7.12 S 37.57 W
Pian Creek ≃ 166 30.02 S 148.12 E
Pian di Sco 66 43.38 N 11.33 E
Pianella 66 42.24 N 14.02 E
Pianello Val Tidone 62 44.57 N 9.24 E
Pianezza 62 45.06 N 7.33 E
Pianguan 102 39.24 N 111.30 E
Pianjiaojie 102 26.01 N 100.32 E
Piankatank ≃ 208 37.32 N 76.18 W
Pianling 104 41.24 N 123.58 E
Piano 64 45.46 N 11.08 E
Piano d'Arta 64 46.29 N 13.01 E
Piano del Voglio 66 44.10 N 11.13 E
Pianoro 64 44.22 N 11.20 E
Pianosa, Isola I, It. 36 42.35 N 10.04 E
Pianosa, Isola I, It. 66 42.13 N 15.45 E
Pianosinatico 66 44.07 N 10.44 E
Pianottoli-Caldarello, Fr. 71 41.29 N 9.03 E
Pianottoli-Caldarello, Fr. 71 41.29 N 9.03 E
Pians 58 47.08 N 10.30 E
Piapot 184 49.59 N 109.07 W
Piapot Indian Reserve ✦[4] 184 50.45 N 104.26 W
Piares, Punta > 234 16.49 N 99.55 W
Piasa 219 39.07 N 90.07 W
Piasa Creek ≃ 219 38.56 N 90.17 W
Piaseczno 30 52.05 N 21.01 E
Piashti, Lac ⊜ 186 50.29 N 62.52 W
Piaski 30 51.08 N 22.51 E
Piat 116 17.48 N 121.29 E
Piatã 255 13.09 S 41.48 W
Piatra-Neamț 38 46.56 N 26.22 E
Piatra Olt 38 44.24 N 24.16 E
Piatt □[6] 219 40.00 N 88.35 W
Piau 256 21.31 S 43.19 W
Piauí □[3] 250 7.00 S 43.00 W
Piauí ≃, Bra. 250 6.38 S 42.42 W
Piauí ≃, Bra. 255 16.41 S 41.53 W
Piaus, Rio dos ≃ 255 12.27 S 49.32 W
Piave ≃ 64 45.32 N 12.44 E
Piawaning 162 30.51 S 116.22 E
Piaxtla ≃ 232 23.42 N 106.49 W
Piazza Armerina 70 37.23 N 14.22 E
Piazzola sul Brenta 64 45.32 N 11.47 E
Piberegg 61 47.05 N 15.05 E
Pibor ≃ 140 8.26 N 33.13 E
Pibor Post 140 6.48 N 33.08 E
Pibroch 182 54.16 N 113.52 W
Pic ≃ 190 48.36 N 86.18 W
Pica 248 20.30 S 69.21 W
Picacho 200 32.42 N 111.29 W
Picacho, Cerro del ∧ 286a 19.35 N 99.06 W
Pičajevo 80 53.15 N 42.12 E
Picanoc ≃ 190 46.05 N 76.03 W
Picardie □[9] 50 49.45 N 2.50 E
Picatinny Arsenal ■ 276 40.57 N 74.33 W
Picatinny Lake ⊜ 276 40.57 N 74.33 W
Picayune 194 30.31 N 89.40 W
Piccadilly 186 48.34 N 58.55 W
Piccadilly Station ✦[5] 262 53.28 N 2.14 W
Piccione 66 43.11 N 12.31 E
Piccolo, Mar (Taranto) ⊤[2] 68 40.29 N 17.16 E
Piccotts End 260 51.46 N 0.28 W
Pic de Tio ∧ 150 8.52 N 8.54 W
Piceance Creek ≃ 200 40.05 N 108.14 W
Picentini, Monti ∧ 68 40.45 N 15.00 E
Picerno 68 40.38 N 15.38 E
Pičeury 80 54.19 N 45.50 E
Pīch ≃ 123 34.52 N 71.09 E
Pichana ≃ 246 3.31 S 71.43 W
Pichanal 252 23.19 S 64.13 W
Pichátaro 234 19.30 N 101.46 W
Picheng 106 32.07 N 119.42 E
Picher 196 36.59 N 94.49 W
Pichhor 124 25.58 N 78.24 E
Pichilemu 252 34.23 S 72.00 W
Pichileufú, Arroyo ≃ 254 40.35 S 70.39 W
Pichimá 246 4.24 N 77.21 W
Pichi-Mahuida 252 38.50 S 64.57 W
Pichinango, Arroyo ≃ 258 34.10 S 57.15 W
Pichincha □[4] 246 0.10 S 78.40 W
Pichis ≃ 248 9.59 S 74.59 W
Pichl bei Wels 60 48.11 N 13.54 E
Pichor 124 25.11 N 78.11 E
Pichtovka 86 56.00 N 82.42 E
Pichucalco 234 17.31 N 93.09 W
Pichucalco ≃ 234 17.57 N 92.55 W
Picinguaba 256 23.22 S 44.50 W
Picinisco 66 41.39 N 13.52 E
Pic Island I 190 48.43 N 86.38 W
Pickardville 182 54.03 N 113.53 W
Pickaway □[6] 218 39.36 N 82.57 W
Pickens, Ms., U.S. 194 32.53 N 89.58 W
Pickens, S.C., U.S. 192 34.53 N 82.42 W
Pickens, W.V., U.S. 188 38.39 N 80.12 W
Pickensville 194 33.14 N 88.16 W
Pickerel ≃ 190 45.55 N 80.50 W
Pickerel Lake ⊜ 184 52.36 N 99.30 W
Pickering, On., Can. 212 43.52 N 79.02 W
Pickering, Eng., U.K. 44 54.14 N 0.46 W
Pickering, Vale of V 44 54.12 N 0.45 W
Pickering Beach 212 43.50 N 78.59 W
Pickering Brook 168a 32.03 S 116.08 E
Pickering Creek ≃ 285 40.08 N 75.30 W
Pickering Creek Reservoir ⊜[1] 285 40.07 N 75.30 W
Pickett, Lake ⊜ 220 28.36 N 81.07 W
Pickford 190 46.09 N 84.21 W
Pičkir'ajevo 80 54.12 N 42.27 E
Pickle Crow 176 51.30 N 90.04 W
Pickmere 262 53.17 N 2.28 W
Pick Mere ⊜ 262 53.17 N 2.29 W
Pickstown 198 43.04 N 98.31 W
Pickton 222 33.02 N 95.24 W
Pickwick Lake ⊜[1] 194 34.55 N 88.10 W
Pickwick Landing Dam ✦[6] 194 35.00 N 88.21 W
Picnic Point > 274b 37.57 S 145.00 E
Pico 66 41.27 N 13.34 E
Pico ∧ 150a 14.56 N 24.21 W
Pico I 148a 38.28 N 28.20 W
Pico, Ponta do ∧ 148a 38.28 N 28.25 W
Pico de Orizaba, Parque Nacional ♦ 234 19.05 N 97.16 W
Pico de Oro 234 18.01 N 93.37 W
Pico de Tancítaro, Parque Nacional ♦ 234 19.27 N 102.22 W
Pico Rivera 228 33.58 N 118.05 W
Picos 250 7.05 S 41.28 W
Picos, Riacho dos ≃ 255 12.46 S 41.47 W
Picota 248 6.55 S 76.20 W
Pico Truncado 254 46.48 S 67.58 W
Picquigny 50 49.57 N 2.09 E
Picton, Austl. 170 34.11 S 150.36 E
Picton, On., Can. 212 44.00 N 77.08 W
Picton, N.Z. 172 41.18 S 174.01 E
Picton, Eng., U.K. 262 53.14 N 2.51 W
Picton, Isla I 254 55.02 S 66.57 W
Picton Bay c 212 44.03 N 77.08 W
Picton Junction 168a 33.21 S 115.41 E
Pictou 186 45.41 N 62.43 W
Pictou Island I 186 45.50 N 62.34 W
Picture Butte 182 49.53 N 112.47 W
Pictured Rocks National Lakeshore ♦ 190 46.35 N 86.20 W
Picture Rocks 210 41.17 N 76.43 W
Picúa, Punta > 240m 18.25 N 65.46 W
Picuí 250 6.31 S 36.21 W
Picunda 84 43.12 N 40.21 E
Picún Leufú 254 39.31 S 69.15 W
Picún Leufú, Arroyo ≃ 254 39.31 S 69.08 W
Picuris Indian Reservation ✦[4] 200 36.12 N 105.42 W
Pidálion, Akrotírion > 130 34.56 N 34.05 E
Pidarak 128 25.51 N 63.14 E
Piddle ≃ 42 50.42 N 2.04 W
Piddletrenthide 42 50.48 N 2.25 W
Pide Adası I 267b 40.53 N 29.04 E
Pidie, Ujung > 114 5.30 N 95.53 E
Piding 64 47.46 N 12.55 E
Pidurutalagala ∧ 122 7.00 N 80.46 E
Piedade 287a 22.41 S 43.05 W
Piedade ✦[8] 287a 22.53 S 43.19 W
Piedade do Baruel 287b 23.37 S 46.18 W
Piedade do Rio Grande 256 21.28 S 44.12 W
Piedecuesta 246 6.59 N 73.03 W
Piedicavallo 62 45.42 N 7.57 E
Piedicroce 32 42.23 N 9.23 E
Piediluco 66 42.32 N 12.45 E
Piedimonte Etneo 70 37.48 N 15.12 E
Piedimonte Matese 68 41.21 N 14.22 E
Piedimonte San Germano 66 41.30 N 13.45 E
Piedimulera 58 46.01 N 8.16 E
Piè di Ripa 66 43.15 N 13.29 E
Piedmont, Al., U.S. 194 33.55 N 85.36 W
Piedmont, Ca., U.S. 226 37.49 N 122.13 W
Piedmont, Mo., U.S. 194 37.09 N 90.41 W
Piedmont, Oh., U.S. 214 40.11 N 81.12 W
Piedmont, S.C., U.S. 192 34.54 N 82.21 W
Piedmont Lake ⊜[1] 214 40.08 N 81.11 W
Piedra 226 36.48 N 119.22 W
Piedra ≃ 200 37.01 N 107.24 W
Piedra, Cerro ∧ 252 37.41 S 73.07 W
Piedra Azul, Quebrada ≃ 286c 10.36 N 66.57 W
Piedra Blanca 232 29.05 N 102.19 W
Piedrabuena 34 39.02 N 4.10 W
Piedra del Águila 254 40.03 S 70.05 W
Piedrafita, Puerto de)(34 42.40 N 7.01 W
Piedrahita 34 40.28 N 5.19 W
Piedra Roja 236 8.38 N 81.48 W
Piedras, Arroyo de las ≃ 288 34.43 S 58.19 W
Piedras, Punta >, Arg. 258 35.25 S 57.08 W
Piedras, Punta >, Ur. 258 33.59 S 58.17 W
Piedras, Punta >, Ven. 246 10.40 N 61.40 W
Piedras, Punta de > 234 20.50 N 97.14 W
Piedras Blancas 252 31.11 S 59.56 W
Piedras Blancas, Point > 226 35.40 N 121.17 W
Piedras Coloradas 252 32.23 S 57.36 W
Piedras de Tunja ♦ 246 4.49 N 74.20 W
Piedras Negras, Guat. 232 17.11 N 91.15 W
Piedras Negras, Méx. 232 28.42 N 100.31 W
Piedras Negras ⊥ 232 17.12 N 91.15 W
Piedra Sola 252 32.04 S 56.21 W
Piegaro 66 42.58 N 12.05 E
Pie Island I 190 48.15 N 89.05 W
Pieksämäki 26 62.18 N 27.08 E
Piéla 150 12.42 N 0.08 W
Pielach ≃ 61 48.15 N 15.22 E
Pielavesi 26 63.14 N 26.45 E
Pielavesi ⊜ 26 63.18 N 26.35 E
Pielinen ⊜ 26 63.15 N 29.40 E
Piemonte □[4] 62 45.00 N 8.00 E
Pienaarsrivier 156 25.15 S 28.18 E
Piendamó 246 2.38 N 76.30 W
Pieniężno 30 54.15 N 20.08 E
Pieniński Park Narodowy ♦ 30 49.25 N 20.25 E
Pieni-Salpausselkä ∧ 26 61.08 N 27.20 E
Piennes 56 49.19 N 5.47 E
Pieńsk 30 51.15 N 15.03 E
Pienza 66 43.04 N 11.41 E
Pierce, Co., U.S. 200 40.38 N 104.45 W
Pierce, Fl., U.S. 220 27.50 N 81.58 W
Pierce, Id., U.S. 202 46.29 N 115.47 W
Pierce, Ne., U.S. 198 42.11 N 97.31 W
Pierce, Tx., U.S. 222 29.14 N 96.12 W
Pierce □[6] 224 47.04 N 122.07 W
Pierce, Lake ⊜ 220 27.58 N 81.31 W
Pierce City 194 36.56 N 94.00 W
Pierce Lake ⊜, Can. 184 54.10 N 92.56 W
Pierce Lake ⊜, Sk., Can. 184 54.30 N 109.42 W
Pierceton 216 41.12 N 85.42 W
Piermont 210 41.03 N 73.55 W
Pierowall 46 59.20 N 2.59 W
Pierpont, Oh., U.S. 214 41.45 N 80.34 W
Pierpont, S.D., U.S. 198 45.29 N 97.49 W
Pierre 198 44.22 N 100.21 W
Pierre, Bayou ≃, La., U.S. 194 31.51 N 93.06 W
Pierre, Bayou ≃, Ms., U.S. 194 31.55 N 91.11 W
Pierre-Buffière 32 45.42 N 1.21 E
Pierreclos 58 46.20 N 4.41 E
Pierre-de-Bresse 58 46.53 N 5.15 E
Pierrefeu-du-Var 62 43.13 N 6.08 E
Pierrefitte-sur-Aire 56 48.54 N 5.20 E
Pierrefitte-sur-Sauldre 50 47.30 N 2.09 E
Pierrefitte-sur-Seine 261 48.58 N 2.22 E
Pierrefonds, P.Q., Can. 206 45.29 N 73.52 W
Pierrefonds, Fr. 50 49.21 N 2.59 E
Pierrefontaine-les-Varans 58 47.13 N 6.33 E
Pierrelatte 62 44.23 N 4.42 E
Pierrelaye 261 49.01 N 2.09 E
Pierre Part 194 29.57 N 91.12 W
Pierre Pertuis, Col de)(58 47.12 N 7.11 E
Pierrepont Manor 212 43.44 N 76.04 W
Pierre-sur-Haut ∧ 62 45.39 N 3.49 E
Pierreville, P.Q., Can. 206 46.04 N 72.49 W
Pierreville, Trin. 241r 10.18 N 61.01 W
Pierron 219 38.47 N 89.36 W
Pierron, Lac ⊜ 206 46.53 N 74.20 W
Pierry 50 49.01 N 3.56 E
Pierson 192 29.14 N 81.27 W
Piersonville 285 40.10 N 74.42 W
Pierz 190 45.58 N 94.06 W
Piesendorf 64 47.17 N 12.43 E
Piešt'any 30 48.36 N 17.50 E
Piesting ≃ 61 48.02 N 16.30 E
Pietarsaari → Jakobstad 26 63.40 N 22.42 E
Pieterburen 52 53.24 N 6.27 E
Pieterlen 58 47.11 N 7.20 E
Pietermaritzburg 158 29.37 S 30.16 E
Pietersburg 156 23.54 S 29.25 E
Pietrabbondante 66 41.45 N 14.23 E
Pietracamela 66 42.31 N 13.33 E
Pietracatella 66 41.35 N 14.52 E
Pietra del Pertusillo, Lago di ⊜ 68 40.17 N 15.58 E
Pietragalla 68 40.45 N 15.53 E
Pietra Ligure 62 44.09 N 8.17 E
Pietralunga 66 43.26 N 12.26 E
Pietramala 66 44.10 N 11.20 E
Pietramelara 68 41.16 N 14.11 E
Pietramontecorvino 68 41.32 N 15.07 E
Pietrapaola 68 39.29 N 16.49 E
Pietrapertosa 68 40.31 N 16.04 E
Pietraperzia 70 37.25 N 14.08 E
Pietrasanta 64 43.57 N 10.14 E
Pietrelcina 68 41.12 N 14.51 E
Piet Retief 158 27.01 S 30.50 E
Pietrosu, Vîrful ∧, Rom. 38 47.08 N 25.11 E
Pietrosu, Vîrful ∧, Rom. 38 47.36 N 24.38 E
Pieve 64 45.46 N 10.45 E
Pieve d'Alpago 64 46.10 N 12.21 E
Pieve del Cairo 62 45.03 N 8.48 E
Pieve di Cadore 64 46.26 N 12.22 E
Pieve di Cento 64 44.43 N 11.18 E
Pieve di Soligo 64 45.53 N 12.10 E
Pieve di Teco 62 44.03 N 7.56 E
Pieve Fosciana 64 44.08 N 10.25 E
Pievepelago 64 44.12 N 10.37 E
Pieve Porto Morone 62 45.07 N 9.26 E
Pieve Santo Stefano 66 43.40 N 12.02 E
Piffard 210 42.50 N 77.51 W
Piffgal 123 36.10 N 73.10 E
Pigádhia 130 35.31 N 27.12 E
Pigari 80 51.24 N 49.42 E
Pigeon, Mi., U.S. 190 43.49 N 83.16 W
Pigeon, Pa., U.S. 214 41.32 N 79.03 W
Pigeon ≃, Mb., Can. 184 52.15 N 97.00 W
Pigeon ≃, On., Can. 212 44.22 N 78.31 W
Pigeon ≃, N.A. 190 48.00 N 89.34 W
Pigeon ≃, U.S. 192 36.00 N 83.11 W
Pigeon ≃, U.S. 216 41.46 N 85.47 W
Pigeon ≃, Mi., U.S. 190 43.56 N 83.17 W
Pigeon ≃, Mi., U.S. 190 45.27 N 84.33 W
Pigeon ≃, Mi., U.S. 216 42.54 N 86.11 W
Pigeon Bay c 214 42.01 N 82.40 W
Pigeon Cove 207 42.40 N 70.38 W
Pigeon Creek ≃, Al., U.S. 194 31.20 N 86.42 W
Pigeon Creek ≃, In., U.S. 194 37.59 N 87.35 W
Pigeon Creek ≃, In., U.S. 216 41.41 N 85.17 W
Pigeon Creek ≃, Pa., U.S. 279b 40.12 N 79.55 W
Pigeon Creek ≃, Pa., U.S. 285 40.12 N 75.35 W
Pigeon Forge 192 35.47 N 83.33 W
Pigeon Lake ⊜, Ab., Can. 182 53.00 N 114.00 W
Pigeon Lake ⊜, On., Can. 212 44.30 N 78.30 W
Pigeon Run ≃ 285 40.06 N 75.35 W
Pigeon Swamp ≡ 276 40.23 N 74.29 W
Pigezhuang 105 39.39 N 116.15 E
Pigg ≃ 192 37.00 N 79.29 W
Piggott 194 36.22 N 90.11 W
Piggs Peak 158 25.38 S 31.15 E
Pigkawagan 116 7.12 N 124.32 E
Piglio 66 41.49 N 13.08 E
Pigna 62 43.56 N 7.40 E
Pignans 62 43.18 N 6.13 E
Pignataro Maggiore 68 41.11 N 14.10 E
Pignola 68 40.34 N 15.47 E
Pigs, Bay of → Cochinos, Bahía de c 240p 22.07 N 81.10 W
Pigüé 252 37.37 S 62.25 W
Pigŭm-do I 98 34.45 N 125.55 E
Pihama 172 39.30 S 173.56 E
Pihāni 124 27.38 N 80.12 E
Piha Passage ʮ 174w 21.07 S 175.05 W
Pihlajavesi ⊜ 26 61.45 N 28.50 E
Pihlava 26 61.33 N 21.36 E
Pihtipudas 26 63.23 N 25.34 E
Pihuamo 234 19.15 N 103.23 W
P'ihyŏn 98 40.01 N 124.37 E
Piikkiö 26 60.26 N 22.31 E
Piippola 26 64.10 N 25.58 E
Pijijiapan 234 15.42 N 93.14 W
Pijnacker 52 52.02 N 4.27 E
Pijol, Pico ∧ 236 15.06 N 87.35 W
Pikal'ovo 76 59.31 N 34.06 E
Pikangikum 184 51.49 N 94.00 W
Pikangikum Lake ⊜ 184 51.48 N 94.00 W
Pike 210 42.33 N 78.09 W
Pike □[6], Il., U.S. 219 39.36 N 90.48 W
Pike □[6], Mo., U.S. 219 39.21 N 91.10 W
Pike □[6], Oh., U.S. 218 39.05 N 83.06 W
Pike □[6], Pa., U.S. 210 41.19 N 74.48 W
Pike ≃, N.A. 206 45.04 N 73.06 W
Pike ≃, Wi., U.S. 190 45.26 N 87.52 W
Pike, North Branch ≃ 190 45.30 N 88.01 W
Pike, South Branch ≃ 190 45.30 N 88.01 W
Pike Creek ≃, On., Can. 281 42.19 N 82.51 W
Pike Creek ≃, De., U.S. 285 39.42 N 75.42 W
Pike Lake ⊜ 212 44.46 N 76.21 W
Pikelot I 14 8.05 N 147.38 E
Pike Lowe ∧[2] 262 53.42 N 2.34 W
Pike Run ≃ 276 40.25 N 74.38 W
Pikes Peak 218 39.08 N 86.09 W
Pikes Peak ∧ 200 38.51 N 105.03 W
Pikes Rocks ∧[2] 214 41.56 N 79.24 W
Pikesville 208 39.22 N 76.43 W
Piketberg 158 32.54 S 18.46 E
Piketon 218 39.04 N 83.00 W
Piketown 208 40.23 N 76.45 W
Pikeville, Ky., U.S. 192 37.28 N 82.31 W
Pikeville, Tn., U.S. 194 35.36 N 85.11 W
Pikkola 265a 59.42 N 30.08 E
Pikou 98 39.24 N 122.20 E
Pikounda 152 0.33 N 16.42 E
Pikwitonei 184 55.35 N 97.09 W
Pila, Arg. 252 36.01 S 58.08 W
Pila, It. 62 45.41 N 7.18 E
Piła (Schneidemühl), Pol. 30 53.10 N 16.44 E
Piła □[4] 30 53.15 N 16.30 E
Pilamedu 122 11.01 N 77.01 E
Pilanesberg ∧ 156 25.14 S 27.04 E
Pilão Arcado 250 10.09 S 42.26 W
Pilar, Arg. 252 31.41 S 63.54 W
Pilar, Arg. 252 31.27 S 61.15 W
Pilar, Arg. 258 34.27 S 58.54 W
Pilar, Bra. 250 9.36 S 35.56 W
Pilar, Bra. 287a 22.42 S 43.19 W
Pilar, Para. 252 26.52 S 58.23 W
Pilar, Pil. 116 11.29 N 123.00 E
Pilar, Pil. 116 9.52 N 126.06 E
Pilar □[5] 288 34.28 S 58.52 W
Pilar Bay c 116 11.34 N 123.00 E
Pilarcitos Creek ≃ 282 37.28 N 122.27 W
Pilarcitos Lake ⊜ 282 37.33 N 122.25 W
Pilar de Goiás 255 14.41 S 49.27 W
Pilar do Sul 255 23.49 S 47.42 W
Pilares 196 30.24 N 104.52 W
Pilas Group II 116 6.45 N 121.35 E
Pilas Island I 116 6.38 N 121.37 E
Pilatus ∧ 58 46.59 N 8.15 E
Pilawa 30 51.58 N 21.31 E
Pilaya ≃ 248 20.55 S 64.04 W
Pilcher Park ♦ 278 41.32 N 88.01 W
Pilchuck ≃ 224 47.55 N 122.02 W
Pilchuck Creek ≃ 224 48.12 N 122.13 W
Pilcomayo ≃ 18 25.21 S 57.42 W
Pilcomayo, Brazo Norte ≃ 252 24.56 S 58.16 W
Pilcomayo, Brazo Sur ≃ 252 24.56 S 58.16 W
Pil'dozero 24 65.43 N 33.28 E
Piles Creek ≃ 276 40.37 N 74.12 W
Pilga 162 21.29 S 119.25 E
Pilger 198 42.00 N 97.03 W
Pilgrim Gardens 285 39.57 N 75.19 W
Pilgrim Memorial Monument ⊥ 207 42.04 N 70.12 W
Pilgrims Hatch 260 51.38 N 0.17 E
Pilgrim's Rest 156 24.55 S 30.44 E
Pil'gyn 180 69.18 N 179.08 E
Pili 116 13.33 N 123.16 E
Pīlībhīt 124 28.38 N 79.48 E
Pīlībhīt □[5] 124 28.40 N 80.00 E
Pilica ≃ 30 51.52 N 21.17 E
Pilipinas → Philippines □[1] 116 13.00 N 122.00 E
Pilis ⋏ 264c 47.37 N 18.59 E
Pilisborosjenő 264c 47.36 N 19.00 E
Pilkhua 124 28.43 N 77.39 E
Píllaro 246 1.10 S 78.32 W
Pillar Point > 282 37.30 N 122.30 W
Pillar Point >[1] 212 43.59 N 76.09 W
Pillau → Baltijsk 76 54.39 N 19.55 E
Pilley's Island 186 49.31 N 55.44 W
Pilliga 166 30.21 S 148.54 E
Pillings Pond ⊜ 283 42.32 N 71.02 W
Pillnitz ✦[8] 54 51.00 N 13.52 E
Pillon, Col du)(58 46.22 N 7.13 E
Pillow 208 40.38 N 76.48 W
Pillsbury Sound ʮ 240m 18.20 N 64.49 W
Pil'na 80 55.33 N 45.55 E
Pilón ≃ 232 25.22 N 99.32 W
Pílos 38 36.55 N 21.43 E
Pilot Butte 184 50.28 N 104.25 W
Pilot Grove 194 38.52 N 92.54 W
Pilot Hill 226 38.50 N 121.02 W
Pilot Knob 194 37.37 N 90.38 W
Pilot Knob ∧, Ar., U.S. 194 35.42 N 93.57 W
Pilot Knob ∧, Id., U.S. 202 45.54 N 115.42 W
Pilot Mound 184 49.16 N 98.55 W
Pilot Mountain 192 36.23 N 80.28 W
Pilot Peak ∧, Nv., U.S. 204 38.21 N 117.58 W
Pilot Peak ∧, Nv., U.S. 204 41.02 N 114.06 W
Pilot Peak ∧, Wy., U.S. 202 44.58 N 109.53 W
Pilot Point, Ak., U.S. 180 57.34 N 157.35 W
Pilot Point, Tx., U.S. 196 33.23 N 96.57 W
Pilot Rock 202 45.29 N 118.49 W
Pilot Rock ∧ 200 35.09 N 109.53 W
Pilot Station 180 61.56 N 162.54 W
Pilottown 194 29.10 N 89.15 W
Pilpah Range ⋏ 166 20.23 S 138.34 E
Pilsen → Plzeň 60 49.45 N 13.23 E
Pilsensee ⊜ 60 48.01 N 11.11 E
Pilsum 52 53.29 N 7.04 E
Piltene 76 57.13 N 21.40 E
Pilu ≃ 110 19.33 N 97.24 E
Piluchang 107 29.13 N 105.37 E
Pil'ugino 80 53.25 N 52.26 E
Pilusi 106 32.05 N 120.05 E
Pilzno 30 49.59 N 21.17 E
Pim ≃ 74 61.18 N 71.57 E
Pima 200 32.53 N 109.49 W
Pimah 110 15.36 N 107.25 E
Pimba 166 31.15 S 136.47 E
Pimelles 50 47.50 N 4.10 E
Pimenteira, Vereda ≃ 250 10.04 S 42.25 W
Pimenteiras 250 6.14 S 41.25 W
Pimentel, Bra. 250 3.43 S 45.30 W
Pimentel, Perú 248 6.50 S 79.57 W
Pimlico Race Course ♦ 284b 39.21 N 76.40 W
Pimmit Hills 284c 38.54 N 77.12 W
Pimmit Run ≃ 284c 38.55 N 77.07 W
Pimu-Lendo 152 1.46 N 20.54 E
Pimville ✦[8] 273d 26.16 S 27.54 E
Pina, Cuba 240p 22.01 N 78.43 W
Pina, Esp. 34 41.29 N 0.32 W
Pina ≃ 78 52.10 N 26.14 E
Pinacanauan ≃ 116 17.37 N 121.44 E
Pinamalayan 116 13.02 N 121.29 E
Pinamungajan 116 10.16 N 123.35 E
Pinang → George Town 114 5.25 N 100.20 E
Pinang □[3] 114 5.20 N 100.20 E
Pinang, Pulau I 114 5.23 N 100.15 E
Pinangah 112 5.12 N 116.50 E
Pınar 130 37.02 N 27.57 E
Pınarbaşı, Tür. 130 41.36 N 33.07 E
Pınarbaşı, Tür. 130 38.44 N 36.24 E
Pinar del Río 240p 22.25 N 83.42 W
Pinar del Río □[4] 240p 22.30 N 83.45 W
Pilgrim's Rest 156 24.55 S 30.44 E
Pil'gyn 180 69.18 N 179.08 E
Pili 116 13.33 N 123.16 E
Pīlībhīt 124 28.38 N 79.48 E
Pīlībhīt □[5] 124 28.40 N 80.00 E
Pilica ≃ 30 51.52 N 21.17 E
Pilipinas → Philippines □[1] 116 13.00 N 122.00 E
Pilis ⋏ 264c 47.37 N 18.59 E
Pilisborosjenő 264c 47.36 N 19.00 E
Pilkhua 124 28.43 N 77.39 E
Píllaro 246 1.10 S 78.32 W
Pillar Point > 282 37.30 N 122.30 W
Pillar Point >[1] 212 43.59 N 76.09 W
Pillau → Baltijsk 76 54.39 N 19.55 E
Pilley's Island 186 49.31 N 55.44 W
Pilliga 166 30.21 S 148.54 E
Pillings Pond ⊜ 283 42.32 N 71.02 W
Pillnitz ✦[8] 54 51.00 N 13.52 E
Pillon, Col du)(58 46.22 N 7.13 E
Pillow 208 40.38 N 76.48 W
Pillsbury Sound ʮ 240m 18.20 N 64.49 W
Pil'na 80 55.33 N 45.55 E
Pilón ≃ 232 25.22 N 99.32 W
Pílos 38 36.55 N 21.43 E
Pilot Butte 184 50.28 N 104.25 W
Pilot Grove 194 38.52 N 92.54 W
Pilot Hill 226 38.50 N 121.02 W
Pilot Knob 194 37.37 N 90.38 W
Pilot Knob ∧, Ar., U.S. 194 35.42 N 93.57 W
Pilot Knob ∧, Id., U.S. 202 45.54 N 115.42 W
Pilot Mound 184 49.16 N 98.55 W
Pilot Mountain 192 36.23 N 80.28 W
Pilot Peak ∧, Nv., U.S. 204 38.21 N 117.58 W
Pilot Peak ∧, Nv., U.S. 204 41.02 N 114.06 W
Pilot Peak ∧, Wy., U.S. 202 44.58 N 109.53 W
Pilot Point, Ak., U.S. 180 57.34 N 157.35 W
Pilot Point, Tx., U.S. 196 33.23 N 96.57 W
Pilot Rock 202 45.29 N 118.49 W
Pilot Rock ∧ 200 35.09 N 109.53 W
Pilot Station 180 61.56 N 162.54 W
Pilottown 194 29.10 N 89.15 W
Pilpah Range ⋏ 166 20.23 S 138.34 E
Pilsen → Plzeň 60 49.45 N 13.23 E
Pilsensee ⊜ 60 48.01 N 11.11 E
Pilsum 52 53.29 N 7.04 E
Piltene 76 57.13 N 21.40 E
Pilu ≃ 110 19.33 N 97.24 E
Piluchang 107 29.13 N 105.37 E
Pil'ugino 80 53.25 N 52.26 E
Pilusi 106 32.05 N 120.05 E
Pilzno 30 49.59 N 21.17 E
Pim ≃ 74 61.18 N 71.57 E
Pima 200 32.53 N 109.49 W
Pimah 110 15.36 N 107.25 E
Pimba 166 31.15 S 136.47 E
Pimelles 50 47.50 N 4.10 E
Pimenteira, Vereda ≃ 250 10.04 S 42.25 W
Pimenteiras 250 6.14 S 41.25 W
Pimentel, Bra. 250 3.43 S 45.30 W
Pimentel, Perú 248 6.50 S 79.57 W
Pimlico Race Course ♦ 284b 39.21 N 76.40 W
Pimmit Hills 284c 38.54 N 77.12 W
Pimmit Run ≃ 284c 38.55 N 77.07 W
Pimu-Lendo 152 1.46 N 20.54 E
Pimville ✦[8] 273d 26.16 S 27.54 E
Pina, Cuba 240p 22.01 N 78.43 W
Pina, Esp. 34 41.29 N 0.32 W
Pina ≃ 78 52.10 N 26.14 E
Pinacanauan ≃ 116 17.37 N 121.44 E
Pinamalayan 116 13.02 N 121.29 E
Pinamungajan 116 10.16 N 123.35 E
Pinang → George Town 114 5.25 N 100.20 E
Pinang □[3] 114 5.20 N 100.20 E
Pinang, Pulau I 114 5.23 N 100.15 E
Pinangah 112 5.12 N 116.50 E
Pınar 130 37.02 N 27.57 E
Pınarbaşı, Tür. 130 41.36 N 33.07 E
Pınarbaşı, Tür. 130 38.44 N 36.24 E
Pinar del Río 240p 22.25 N 83.42 W
Pinar del Río □[4]
Pinardville 188 42.59 N 71.30 W
Pınarhisar 130 41.37 N 27.30 E
Pinas, Arg. 252 31.09 S 65.29 W
Piñas, Ec. 246 3.42 S 79.42 W
Piñas, Cerro ∧ 236 15.25 N 85.47 W
Pinatubo, Mount ∧ 116 15.08 N 120.21 E
Pinazo, Arroyo ≃ 288 34.24 S 58.48 W
Pinchbeck 42 52.48 N 0.09 W
Pincher Creek 182 49.29 N 113.57 W
Pinchi Lake ⊜ 182 54.35 N 124.20 W
Pinckney 216 42.27 N 83.56 W
Pinckney State Recreation Area ♦ 216 42.25 N 84.04 W
Pinckneyville 194 38.04 N 89.22 W
Pinconning 190 43.51 N 83.57 W
Pincourt 206 45.23 N 74.00 W
Pinčuga 86 58.23 N 96.59 E
Pińczów 30 50.32 N 20.35 E
Pindaíba, Ribeirão ≃ 255 14.18 S 51.45 W
Pindale 110 21.11 N 95.51 E
Pindamonhangaba 256 22.55 S 45.28 W
Pindar 162 28.29 S 115.48 E
Pindaré ≃ 250 3.17 S 44.47 W
Pindaré-Mirim 250 3.37 S 45.21 W
Pind Dādan Khān 123 32.35 N 73.03 E
Pinde → Píndhos Óros ⋏ 38 39.49 N 21.14 E
Pinder Point > 192 26.28 N 78.39 W
Píndhos Óros ⋏ 38 39.49 N 21.14 E
Pindi Bhattiān 123 31.54 N 73.16 E
Pindiga 146 9.59 N 10.54 E
Pindi Gheb 123 33.14 N 72.16 E
Pindo → Píndhos Óros ⋏ 38 39.49 N 21.14 E
Pindobaçu 250 10.44 S 40.21 W
Pindorama de Goiás 250 10.55 S 47.40 W
Pindoyacu ≃ 246 2.07 S 76.03 W
Pinduši 24 62.56 N 34.35 E
Pindus Mountains → Píndhos Óros ⋏ 38 39.49 N 21.14 E
Pindwāra 120 24.48 N 73.04 E
Pine ≃, Austl. 171a 27.17 S 153.04 E
Pine ≃, B.C., Can. 182 56.08 N 120.41 W
Pine ≃, Mb., Can. 184 52.00 N 100.09 W
Pine ≃, On., Can. 212 44.20 N 79.52 W
Pine ≃, Mi., U.S. 190 46.03 N 84.40 W
Pine ≃, Mi., U.S. 190 44.26 N 83.21 W
Pine ≃, Mi., U.S. 190 43.35 N 84.08 W
Pine ≃, Mi., U.S. 190 44.15 N 85.55 W
Pine ≃, Mi., U.S. 214 42.49 N 82.29 W
Pine ≃, Wi., U.S. 190 45.50 N 88.08 W
Pine ≃, Wi., U.S. 190 43.12 N 90.18 W
Pine ≃, Wi., U.S. 190 44.08 N 88.54 W
Pine Apple 194 31.52 N 86.59 W
Pine Banks Park ♦ 283 42.26 N 71.04 W
Pine Barrens ✦[1] 208 39.48 N 74.35 W
Pine Beach 206 45.32 N 73.57 W
Pine Bluff 194 34.13 N 92.00 W
Pine Bluffs 198 41.10 N 104.04 W
Pine Brook 276 40.52 N 74.20 W
Pine Brook ≃, U.S. 276 41.04 N 74.05 W
Pine Brook ≃, Ma., U.S. 283 42.00 N 70.47 W
Pine Brook ≃, N.J., U.S. 276 40.19 N 74.20 W
Pine Bush 210 41.36 N 74.17 W
Pine Castle 220 28.28 N 81.22 W
Pine City, Mn., U.S. 190 45.49 N 92.58 W
Pine City, N.Y., U.S. 210 42.02 N 76.52 W
Pinecliff Lake ⊜ 276 41.08 N 74.23 W
Pinecraft 220 27.19 N 82.30 W
Pine Creek 164 13.49 S 131.49 E
Pine Creek ≃, Ab., Can. 182 54.56 N 112.31 W
Pine Creek ≃, Ca., U.S. 204 40.40 N 120.46 W
Pine Creek ≃, Ca., U.S. 282 37.58 N 122.02 W
Pine Creek ≃, Nv., U.S. 204 40.36 N 116.10 W
Pine Creek ≃, Pa., U.S. 210 41.10 N 77.16 W
Pine Creek ≃, Pa., U.S. 279b 40.30 N 79.57 W
Pine Creek ≃, Pa., U.S. 285 40.05 N 75.37 W
Pine Creek, West Branch ≃ 210 41.43 N 77.38 W
Pine Creek Indian Reserve ✦[4] 184 52.03 N 100.14 W
Pine Creek Lake ⊜[1] 196 34.05 N 95.05 W
Pine Creek Point > 276 41.07 N 73.16 W
Pine Crest, Fl., U.S. 220 28.01 N 82.32 W
Pinecrest, Va., U.S. 208 38.50 N 77.09 W
Pinecrest Lake ⊜ 226 38.12 N 119.58 W
Pine Crest Point > 284a 42.52 N 79.11 W
Pinedale, Ca., U.S. 226 36.50 N 119.48 W
Pinedale, Wy., U.S. 200 42.52 N 109.51 W
Pine Falls 184 50.35 N 96.15 W
Pine Flat Lake ⊜[1] 226 36.52 N 119.18 W
Pinega 24 64.42 N 43.19 E
Pinega ≃ 24 64.08 N 41.54 E
Pine Glen 212 45.19 N 75.43 W
Pine Grove, On., Can. 275b 43.48 N 79.35 W
Pine Grove, Ca., U.S. 226 38.25 N 120.39 W
Pine Grove, Fl., U.S. 220 28.16 N 81.11 W
Pine Grove, N.J., U.S. 285 39.53 N 74.52 W
Pine Grove, Pa., U.S. 208 40.32 N 76.23 W
Pine Grove, W.V., U.S. 188 39.33 N 80.40 W
Pine Grove Mills 214 40.44 N 77.53 W
Pine Hill, Austl. 166 23.39 S 146.58 E
Pine Hill, Al., U.S. 194 31.58 N 87.35 W
Pine Hill, N.J., U.S. 208 39.47 N 74.59 W
Pine Hill, N.Y., U.S. 210 42.08 N 74.29 W
Pinehill, Tx., U.S. 222 32.06 N 94.36 W
Pine Hills 220 28.33 N 81.27 W
Pinehouse Lake 184 55.31 N 106.36 W
Pinehouse Lake ⊜ 184 55.32 N 106.35 W
Pinehurst, Ga., U.S. 192 32.11 N 83.45 W
Pinehurst, Id., U.S. 202 45.15 N 116.20 W
Pinehurst, Ma., U.S. 207 42.31 N 71.13 W
Pinehurst, N.Y., U.S. 284a 42.44 N 78.57 W
Pinehurst, N.C., U.S. 192 35.11 N 79.28 W
Pinehurst, Tx., U.S. 222 30.10 N 95.41 W
Pinehurst Lake ⊜ 182 54.39 N 111.25 W
Pine Island, Mn., U.S. 190 44.12 N 92.38 W
Pine Island, N.Y., U.S. 210 41.17 N 74.27 W
Pine Island I 220 26.35 N 82.06 W
Pine Island Bay c 9 74.50 S 102.05 W
Pine Island Bayou ≃ 194 30.10 N 94.07 W
Pine Island Creek ≃ 283 42.47 N 70.48 W
Pine Island Dam ✦[6] 214 40.08 N 80.43 W
Pine Island Sound ʮ 220 26.33 N 82.10 W
Pine Lake, In., U.S. 216 41.38 N 86.45 W
Pine Lake, Ma., U.S. 283 42.23 N 71.27 W
Pine Lake ⊜, On., Can. 212 44.57 N 79.27 W
Pine Lake ⊜, Mi., U.S. 281 42.35 N 83.20 W
Pine Lake ⊜, N.Y., U.S. 210 43.12 N 74.31 W
Pineland 194 31.14 N 93.58 W
Pine Lawn 219 38.41 N 90.16 W
Pinellas □[6] 220 27.53 N 82.43 W
Pinellas, Point > 220 27.42 N 82.38 W
Pinellas Park 220 27.50 N 82.41 W
Pine Marsh ≡ 276 40.37 N 73.34 W
Pine Meadow Lake ⊜ 276 41.11 N 74.07 W
Pine Mountain ∧, U.S. 192 36.55 N 83.20 W
Pine Mountain ∧, Ca., U.S. 226 35.41 N 121.05 W
Pine Mountain ∧, Ca., U.S. 280 34.13 N 117.54 W
Pine Mountain ∧, Ct., U.S. 207 41.58 N 72.56 W
Pine Mountain ∧, Ga., U.S. 192 32.51 N 84.47 W
Pine Mountain ∧, Or., U.S. 202 43.47 N 120.54 W
Pine Mountain ∧, Wy., U.S. 200 41.02 N 109.01 W
Pine Nut Mountains ⋏ 226 39.00 N 119.25 W
Pine Orchard Meadows 284b 39.17 N 76.52 W
Pine Pass)(182 55.22 N 122.40 W
Pine Plains 210 41.59 N 73.40 W
Pine Point, Austl. 168b 34.34 S 137.52 E
Pine Point, N.T., Can. 176 61.01 N 114.15 W
Pine Point Park ♦ 275b 43.43 N 79.33 W
Pine Portage Dam ✦[6] 176 49.18 N 88.19 W
Pine Prairie 194 30.47 N 92.25 W
Piner 218 38.50 N 84.32 W
Pine Rest 283 42.23 N 71.26 W
Pine Ridge, Pa., U.S. 285 39.55 N 75.22 W
Pine Ridge, S.D., U.S. 198 43.01 N 102.33 W
Pine Ridge, Va., U.S. 284c 38.52 N 77.14 W
Pine Ridge ∧ 198 42.40 N 103.00 W
Pine Ridge Estates 276 41.02 N 73.41 W
Pine Ridge Indian Reservation ✦[4] 198 43.25 N 102.21 W
Pine River, Mb., Can. 184 51.47 N 100.32 W
Pine River, Mn., U.S. 190 46.43 N 94.24 W
Piñero 258 34.32 S 58.45 W
Pinerolo 62 44.53 N 7.21 E
Piñeros, Isla I 240m 18.15 N 65.35 W
Pinerovka 80 51.34 N 43.04 E
Pine Run ≃ 279b 40.37 N 79.35 W
Pines ≃ 283 42.27 N 70.58 W
Pines, Isle of → Juventud, Isla de la I 240p 21.40 N 82.50 W
Pines, Lake o' the ⊜[1] 222 32.46 N 94.35 W
Pines, Point of > 283 42.26 N 70.58 W
Pine Shores 220 27.17 N 82.32 W
Pines Lake ⊜ 276 41.00 N 74.16 W
Pines Run ≃ 285 39.50 N 75.05 W
Pine Swamp Knob ∧ 188 39.33 N 79.31 W
Pineto 66 42.36 N 14.04 E
Pinetop 200 34.07 N 109.56 W
Pinetops 192 35.47 N 77.38 W
Pinetown 158 29.52 S 30.46 E
Pine Tree Hill ∧ 114 3.43 N 101.42 E
Pine Valley, Md., U.S. 284b 39.26 N 76.39 W
Pine Valley, N.Y., U.S. 210 42.14 N 76.51 W
Pine Valley V 204 38.25 N 113.40 W
Pine Village 216 40.27 N 87.15 W
Pineville, Ky., U.S. 192 36.45 N 83.41 W
Pineville, La., U.S. 194 31.19 N 92.26 W
Pineville, Mo., U.S. 194 36.35 N 94.23 W
Pineville, N.C., U.S. 192 35.04 N 80.53 W
Pineville, Pa., U.S. 208 40.18 N 75.00 W
Pineville, W.V., U.S. 192 37.34 N 81.32 W
Pinewood, Fl., U.S. 220 25.53 N 80.14 W
Pinewood, S.C., U.S. 192 33.44 N 80.27 W
Piney 50 48.22 N 4.20 E
Piney ≃ 194 35.49 N 87.33 W
Piney Branch ≃ 284c 38.56 N 77.18 W
Piney Creek ≃, Tx., U.S. 222 31.03 N 94.34 W
Piney Creek ≃, Wy., U.S. 202 44.34 N 106.32 W
Piney Fork 214 40.15 N 80.50 W
Piney Point 222 29.46 N 95.31 W
Piney Point > 208 38.08 N 76.32 W
Piney Run ≃ 284c 38.58 N 77.17 W
Piney Woods 194 32.03 N 89.59 W
Pinfold 262 53.36 N 2.55 W
Ping ≃, Thai 110 15.42 N 100.09 E
Ping ≃, Zhg. 100 25.59 N 115.07 E
Pinga 154 1.01 S 28.42 E
Ping'an, Zhg. 89 45.20 N 123.42 E
Ping'an, Zhg. 104 41.11 N 123.26 E
Ping'an, Zhg. 107 30.36 N 104.42 E
Ping'anbu 98 41.45 N 116.13 E
Ping'ancheng 105 40.03 N 117.48 E
Ping'andi 104 42.34 N 121.52 E
Pingaring 162 32.45 S 118.37 E
Pingba, Zhg. 100 31.19 N 113.18 E
Pingba, Zhg. 102 26.22 N 106.09 E
Pingchang 102 31.35 N 107.03 E
Pingchao 106 32.07 N 120.45 E
Pingding 98 37.48 N 113.37 E
Pingdingpu 104 42.22 N 123.55 E
Pingdingshan, Zhg. 98 41.26 N 124.45 E
Pingdingshan, Zhg. 100 33.45 N 113.17 E
Pingding Shan ∧ 89 46.38 N 128.27 E
Pingdu 98 36.47 N 119.54 E
Pingelap I[1] 14 6.13 N 160.42 E
Pingelly 162 32.32 S 117.05 E
Pingfang, Zhg. 100 30.07 N 113.48 E
Pingfang, Zhg. 104 41.17 N 120.40 E
Pingfang, Zhg. 104 41.28 N 120.48 E
Pingfang, Zhg. 104 42.14 N 120.38 E
Pingfang, Zhg. 104 42.27 N 120.38 E
Pingfang, Zhg. 271a 39.56 N 116.33 E
Pingfangdu 104 41.45 N 121.12 E
Pingfangzi 104 41.31 N 121.21 E
Pinggau 61 47.27 N 16.04 E
Pinggu 105 40.09 N 117.07 E
Pingguo 102 23.19 N 107.39 E
Pinghai, Zhg. 100 25.14 N 119.15 E
Pinghai, Zhg. 100 22.39 N 114.53 E
Pinghe, Zhg. 100 24.25 N 117.22 E
Pinghe, Zhg. 102 22.51 N 102.30 E
Pinghe ≃ 100 24.25 N 116.36 E
P'inghsiang → Pingxiang 102 22.09 N 106.43 E
Pinghu, Zhg. 100 26.46 N 118.48 E
Pinghu, Zhg. 100 30.56 N 115.22 E
Pinghu, Zhg. 100 22.42 N 114.08 E
Pinghu, Zhg. 106 30.42 N 121.01 E
Pingjiang 100 28.44 N 113.34 E
Pingjing 105 39.20 N 116.06 E
Pinglan 100 22.22 N 113.27 E
Pingle, Zhg. 102 24.37 N 110.40 E
Pingle, Zhg. 102 24.31 N 106.59 E
Pingli 102 32.19 N 109.21 E
Pingliang 102 35.32 N 106.41 E
Pinglidian 98 37.17 N 119.59 E
Pingling 100 23.39 N 114.23 E
Pinglucheng 102 39.50 N 112.19 E
Pingluo 102 38.57 N 106.35 E
Pingluopu 104 41.56 N 123.20 E
Pingnan, Zhg. 100 26.56 N 119.02 E

≃ River	Fluss	Río	Rivière	Rio
≚ Canal	Kanal	Canal	Canal	Canal
L Waterfall, Rapids	Wasserfall, Stromschnellen	Cascada, Rápidos	Chute d'eau, Rapides	Cascata, Rápidos
ʮ Strait	Meeresstrasse	Estrecho	Détroit	Estreito
c Bay, Gulf	Bucht, Golf	Bahía, Golfo	Baie, Golfe	Baía, Golfo
⊜ Lake, Lakes	See, Seen	Lago, Lagos	Lac, Lacs	Lago, Lagos
≡ Swamp	Sumpf	Pantano	Marais	Pântano
⊓ Ice Features, Glacier	Eis- und Gletscherformen	Accidentes Glaciales	Formes glaciaires	Acidentes glaciares
⊤ Other Hydrographic Features	Andere Hydrographische Objekte	Otros Elementos Hidrográficos	Autres données hydrographiques	Outros acidentes hidrográficos

✧ Submarine Features	Untermeerische Objekte	Accidentes Submarinos	Formes de relief sous-marin	Acidentes submarinos
□ Political Unit	Politische Einheit	Unidad Politica	Entité politique	Unidade política
ʊ Cultural Institution	Kulturelle Institution	Institución Cultural	Institution culturelle	Instituição cultural
⊥ Historical Site	Historische Stätte	Sitio Histórico	Site historique	Sitio histórico
♦ Recreational Site	Erholungs- und Ferienort	Sitio de Recreo	Centre de loisirs	Area de Lazer
⊠ Airport	Flughafen	Aeropuerto	Aéroport	Aeroporto
■ Military Installation	Militäranlage	Instalación Militar	Installation militaire	Instalação militar
✦ Miscellaneous	Verschiedenes	Misceláneo	Divers	Diversos

Name	Page	Lat.°′	Long.°′
Pingnan, Zhg.	102	23.30 N	110.30 E
Pingqiao	100	33.24 N	119.13 E
Pingquan	98	40.59 N	118.34 E
Pingrup	162	33.32 S	118.31 E
Ping Shan, H.K.	271d	22.27 N	114.00 E
Pingshan, Zhg.	100	25.36 N	117.52 E
Pingshan, Zhg.	100	23.26 N	113.15 E
Pingshan, Zhg.	100	22.43 N	114.22 E
Pingshan, Zhg.	102	38.15 N	114.10 E
Pingshang	98	35.11 N	119.07 E
Pingshi, Zhg.	100	32.32 N	113.03 E
Pingshi, Zhg.	100	25.20 N	113.02 E
Pingshui	100	29.53 N	120.38 E
Pingtaizi	105	40.44 N	116.25 E
Pingtan, Zhg.	100	25.31 N	119.47 E
Pingtan, Zhg.	100	23.04 N	114.38 E
Pingtan, Zhg.	107	29.38 N	105.16 E
Pingtan, Zhg.	107	29.50 N	105.56 E
Pingtan Dao I	100	25.33 N	119.48 E
Pingtang	102	25.50 N	107.19 E
Pingtian	100	25.19 N	113.31 E
P'ingtung	100	22.40 N	120.29 E
Pingües, Cayos II	240p	20.47 N	78.15 W
Pingüicas, Cerro ∧	234	21.10 N	99.42 W
Pingwang	106	30.59 N	120.38 E
Pingwu	102	32.29 N	104.37 E
Pingxiang, Zhg.	100	27.38 N	113.50 E
Pingxiang, Zhg.	102	22.09 N	106.43 E
Pingyang, Zhg.	89	48.13 N	124.23 E
Pingyang, Zhg.	100	27.41 N	120.33 E
Pingyao, Zhg.	102	37.16 N	112.09 E
Pingyao, Zhg.	106	30.24 N	119.58 E
Pingyi	98	35.34 N	117.37 E
Pingyin	98	36.19 N	116.22 E
Pingyu	100	32.57 N	114.41 E
Pingyuan, Zhg.	98	37.11 N	116.25 E
Pingyuan, Zhg.	100	24.36 N	115.54 E
Pingzhai	102	24.07 N	104.22 E
Pingzhuang	98	42.03 N	119.22 E
Pinhal	256	22.12 S	46.45 W
Pinhal, Ribeirão do ≃	256	22.42 S	46.42 W
Pinhal Novo	34	38.38 N	8.55 W
Pinhalzinho	256	22.46 S	46.36 W
Pinhão	250	10.34 S	37.44 W
Pinheiral	256	22.31 S	43.59 W
Pinheirinhos	256	22.26 S	44.59 W
Pinheiro	250	2.31 S	45.05 W
Pinheiro de Loures	266c	38.50 N	9.12 W
Pinheiro Machado	252	31.34 S	53.23 W
Pinheiros	256	22.32 S	44.54 W
Pinheiros ≃	287b	23.32 S	46.44 W
Pinhel	34	40.46 N	7.04 W
Pinhoe	42	50.44 N	3.27 W
Pinhuã ≃	248	6.21 S	65.00 W
Pini, Pulau I	110	0.08 N	98.40 E
Pinillos	246	8.55 N	74.28 W
Piniós ≃	38	39.54 N	22.45 E
Pinitos, Sierra de ⋏	200	31.08 N	110.50 W
Pinjar, Lake ⊜	168a	31.38 S	115.49 E
Pinjarra	168a	32.37 S	115.53 E
Pinjor Garden ♦	123	30.47 N	76.47 E
Pinka ≃	61	47.00 N	16.35 E
Pinkafeld	61	47.22 N	16.07 E
Pinkiang → Harbin	89	45.45 N	126.41 E
Pinlaung	110	20.08 N	96.47 E
Pinlebu	110	24.05 N	95.21 E
Pinn ≃	260	51.31 N	0.29 W
Pinnacle ∧, N.Z.	172	41.49 S	173.17 E
Pinnacle ∧, N.Y., U.S.	188	43.13 N	74.23 W
Pinnacle ∧, Va., U.S.	188	39.08 N	78.26 W
Pinnacle Buttes ∧	202	43.44 N	109.57 W
Pinnacle Island I	180	60.12 N	172.46 W
Pinnacle Peak ∧	224	46.45 N	121.43 W
Pinnacles National Monument ♦	226	36.28 N	121.19 W
Pinnaroo	166	35.16 S	140.55 E
Pinneberg	52	53.40 N	9.47 E
Pinner ◆[8]	260	51.36 N	0.23 W
Pino, Sierra del ⋏	196	28.15 N	103.03 W
Pin Oak Creek ≃	222	31.57 N	96.28 W
Pinocchio	66	43.35 N	13.30 E
Pinochle Peak ∧	224	45.43 N	123.36 W
Pinole	226	38.00 N	122.17 W
Pinole Creek ≃	282	38.01 N	122.18 W
Pinole Point ›	282	38.01 N	122.22 W
Pinole Ridge ∧	282	37.59 N	122.15 W
Pinos	234	22.18 N	101.34 W
Pinos, Mount ∧	228	34.50 N	119.09 W
Pinos, Point ›	226	36.38 N	121.56 W
Pinos-Puente	34	37.15 N	3.45 W
Pinotepa de Don Luis	234	16.25 N	97.55 W
Pinotepa Nacional	234	16.19 N	98.01 W
Pinrang	112	3.48 S	119.38 E
Pins, Île de → Juventud, Isla de la I	240p	21.40 N	82.50 W
Pins, Île des I	175f	22.37 S	167.30 E
Pins, Pointe aux ›	214	42.15 N	81.51 W
Pins, Rivière des ≃	206	46.01 N	72.03 W
Pinsk	78	52.07 N	26.04 E
Pinson	194	33.41 N	86.41 W
Pinsot	62	45.21 N	6.06 E
Pinta, Isla I	246a	0.35 N	90.44 W
Pintada Arroyo V	196	34.53 N	104.39 W
Pintado	258	33.50 S	56.18 W
Pintado ≃	255	13.33 S	50.16 W
Pintado, Arroyo de ≃	258	34.08 S	56.14 W
Pintado, Cuchilla del ⋏[2]	258	34.12 S	56.25 W
Pintados	248	20.37 S	69.38 W
Pintados, Salar de ≚	248	20.30 S	69.42 W
Pintasan	112	5.26 N	117.43 E
Pinteus	266c	38.52 N	9.09 W
Pintlala Creek ≃	194	32.21 N	86.30 W
Pinto	252	29.09 S	62.39 W
Pinto Butte ∧	184	49.22 N	107.25 W
Pinto Creek ≃, Ab., Can.	182	53.51 N	117.35 W
Pinto Creek ≃, Sk., Can.	184	49.40 N	106.42 W
Pintos, Arroyo de ≃	258	33.55 S	56.51 W
Pintos Negreiros	256	22.18 S	45.13 W
Pintoyacu ≃	246	3.35 S	73.55 W
Pinturas ≃	254	46.35 S	70.18 W
Pintuyan	116	9.57 N	125.15 E
Pin'ug	24	60.15 N	47.48 E
Pinukpuk	116	17.35 N	121.22 E
Pinwherry	44	55.09 N	4.50 W
Pinxton	42	53.06 N	1.19 W
Pinzano al Tagliamento	64	46.11 N	12.57 E
Pinzgau V	64	47.15 N	12.40 E
Pinzón, Isla I	246a	0.36 S	90.40 W
Piobbico	66	43.35 N	12.31 E
Pioche	204	37.55 N	114.27 W
Pio IX	250	6.50 S	40.37 W
Piolenc	62	44.11 N	4.46 E
Piombino	66	42.55 N	10.32 E
Piombino, Canale di ʊ	66	42.53 N	10.30 E
Pioneer, Austl.	162	31.48 S	121.43 E
Pioneer, Ca., U.S.	226	38.25 N	120.33 W
Pioneer, Oh., U.S.	216	41.40 N	84.33 W
Pioneer Mine	182	50.46 N	122.46 W
Pioneer Mountains ⋏	202	45.40 N	113.00 W
Pioneer Park ♦	273d	26.14 S	28.04 E
Pioner, ostrov I	74	79.50 N	92.30 E
Pionerskij	76	54.57 N	20.20 E
Pionierbivak	164	2.16 S	138.02 E
Pionki	30	51.30 N	21.27 E
Pio Pico State Historical Monument ♦	280	33.59 N	118.04 W
Piopio	172	38.28 S	175.01 E
Pioppo	70	38.03 N	13.14 E
Piora, Mount ∧	164	6.45 S	146.00 E
Pioraco	66	43.11 N	12.59 E
Piorini ≃	246	3.23 S	63.30 W
Piorini, Lago ⊜	246	3.34 S	63.15 W
Piotrków Trybunalski	30	51.25 N	19.42 E
Piotrków Trybunalski □[4]	30	51.30 N	19.45 E
Piotta	58	46.31 N	8.40 E
Pio V. Corpus (Limbujan)	116	11.53 N	124.03 E
Piove di Sacco	64	45.18 N	12.02 E
Piovene-Rocchette	64	45.45 N	11.25 E
Pio XII	250	3.53 S	45.17 W
Pipa	107	29.07 N	105.05 E
Pipalkoti	124	30.26 N	79.27 E
Pipanaco, Salar de ≚	252	28.07 S	66.25 W
Pīpār	120	26.23 N	73.32 E
Piparia	124	22.45 N	78.21 E
Pīpar Road	120	26.27 N	73.27 E
Pipas	152	14.56 S	12.12 E
Pipe Creek ≃, In., U.S.	194	40.08 N	85.52 W
Pipe Creek ≃, In., U.S.	216	40.45 N	86.13 W
Pipe Creek ≃, In., U.S.	218	39.26 N	85.06 W
Piper City	216	40.45 N	88.11 W
Pipe Spring National Monument ♦	200	36.43 N	112.33 W
Pipestem Creek ≃	198	46.54 N	98.43 W
Pipestem State Park ♦	192	37.32 N	81.00 W
Pipestone	198	44.00 N	96.19 W
Pipestone ≃	176	52.53 N	89.23 W
Pipestone Creek ≃, Can.	184	49.42 N	100.45 W
Pipestone Creek ≃, Mi., U.S.	216	42.04 N	86.24 W
Pipestone National Monument ♦	198	44.00 N	96.18 W
Pipi ≃	146	7.27 N	22.48 E
Pipinas	258	35.32 S	57.20 W
Piping Brook ≃	276	41.08 N	73.37 W
Pipiriki	172	39.29 S	175.03 E
Piplān	123	32.17 N	71.21 E
Piplūn	126	23.21 N	88.07 E
Pipmuacan, Réservoir ⊜[1]	186	49.35 N	70.30 W
Pipri	124	23.58 N	82.40 E
Pipriac	28	47.49 N	1.57 W
Piqiang	85	40.20 N	77.38 E
Piqiao	106	31.34 N	119.27 E
Piqua	218	40.08 N	84.14 W
Piquet Carneiro	250	5.48 S	39.25 W
Piquete	256	22.36 S	45.11 W
Piquete, Ribeirão ≃	256	22.36 S	45.01 W
Piquiri ≃	252	24.03 S	54.14 W
Pira	150	8.30 N	1.44 E
Piracaia	256	23.03 S	46.21 W
Piracanjuba	255	17.18 S	49.01 W
Piracanjuba ≃, Bra.	255	18.14 S	48.48 W
Piracanjuba ≃, Bra.	255	17.18 S	48.13 W
Piracão ≃	287a	23.02 S	43.36 W
Piracicaba	255	22.43 S	47.38 W
Piracicaba ≃	255	22.36 S	48.19 W
Piracuruca	250	3.56 S	41.42 W
Pirae	174s	17.32 S	149.33 W
Piraeus → Piraiévs	38	37.57 N	23.38 E
Pirahmet	130	38.11 N	39.51 E
Piraí	256	22.38 S	43.54 W
Piraí ≃	256	22.28 S	43.50 W
Piraí do Sul	252	24.31 S	49.56 W
Piraiévs (Piraeus)	38	37.57 N	23.38 E
Piraino	70	38.10 N	14.52 E
Piraju	255	23.12 S	49.23 W
Pirajuba	255	19.54 S	48.42 W
Pirajucara, Ribeirão ≃	287b	23.34 S	46.43 W
Pirajuí	255	21.59 S	49.29 W
Pirakata	126	22.34 N	87.11 E
Piramida, gora ∧	88	54.15 N	95.45 E
Piramidal'nyj, pik ∧	85	39.34 N	69.57 E
Pirámide de Cuicuilco ⊥	286a	19.18 N	99.11 W
Pirámide de Santa Cecilia ⊥	286a	19.35 N	99.11 W
Pirámide de Tenayuca ⊥	286a	19.32 N	99.11 W
Pirámide Xochicalco ⊥	234	18.48 N	99.19 W
Piram Island I	120	21.36 N	72.41 E
Piran, Jugo.	36	45.32 N	13.34 E
Piran, Tür.	130	38.22 N	40.04 E
Piraña, Arroyo ≃	288	34.24 S	58.30 W
Pirané	252	25.43 S	59.06 W
Piranga	255	20.41 S	43.18 W
Pirangaí	256	22.34 S	44.37 W
Piranguinho	256	22.24 S	45.32 W
Piranha ≃	250	5.56 S	48.15 W
Piranhas, Bra.	250	9.27 S	37.46 W
Piranhas, Bra.	255	16.31 S	51.51 W
Piranhas ≃, Bra.	250	5.15 S	36.45 W
Piranhas ≃, Bra.	250	8.40 S	49.28 W
Piranji ≃	250	4.23 S	37.48 W
Pīrān Shahr	128	36.41 N	45.08 E
Pirapemas	250	3.43 S	44.14 W
Pirapetinga	256	21.54 S	43.40 W
Pirapetinga ≃	256	21.37 S	42.32 W
Pirapetinga, Ribeirão ≃	256	21.49 S	43.36 W
Pirapó ≃	255	22.30 S	52.01 W
Pirapora	255	17.21 S	44.56 W
Pirapora do Bom Jesus	256	23.24 S	47.00 W
Pirapora do Bom Jesus □[7]	287b	23.24 S	46.56 W
Piraputanga	255	20.26 S	55.32 W
Piraquara	252	25.26 S	49.04 W
Piraquê ≃	287a	23.01 S	43.37 W
Pirarajá	252	33.44 S	54.45 W
Piraras, Cachoeira de ⌊	255	14.02 S	53.25 W
Pirassununga	255	21.59 S	47.25 W
Pirata, Monte ∧[2]	240m	18.06 N	65.33 W
Pirate Creek ≃	282	37.33 N	121.52 W
Pir'atin	78	50.15 N	32.30 E
Piratinga ≃	255	15.41 S	46.07 W
Piratini	252	31.27 S	53.06 W
Piratini ≃	252	28.06 S	55.27 W
Piratininga	287a	22.57 S	43.04 W
Piratininga, Lagoa de c	256	22.57 S	43.05 W
Piratuba	252	27.27 S	51.48 W
Piratuba, Lago c	250	1.37 N	50.10 W
Piratucu ≃	250	1.59 S	56.58 W
Piraúba	256	21.17 S	43.02 W
Piraube, Lac ⊜	186	50.33 N	71.42 W
Piray ≃	248	16.32 S	63.45 W
Pirbright	260	51.18 N	0.39 W
Pirdop	38	42.42 N	24.11 E
Pirenópolis	255	15.51 S	48.57 W
Pires, Ribeirão ≃	287b	23.43 S	46.25 W
Pires do Rio	255	17.18 S	48.17 W
Pírgos	38	37.41 N	21.28 E
Piriá	250	1.40 S	50.02 W
Piriápolis	252	34.54 S	55.17 W
Piribebuy	252	25.29 S	57.03 W
Pirin ⋏	38	41.40 N	23.30 E
Pirinççiköy	267b	41.10 N	28.50 E
Pirineos → Pyrenees ⋏	34	42.40 N	1.00 E
Piripiri	250	4.16 S	41.47 W
Piritiba	250	11.44 S	40.34 W
Píritu, Ven.	246	11.22 N	69.08 W
Píritu, Ven.	246	9.23 N	69.12 W
Pirituba ◆[8]	287b	23.29 S	46.43 W
Pīr Jo Goth	120	27.36 N	68.37 E
Pirk	54	50.25 N	12.04 E
Pirlerkondu	130	36.55 N	32.31 E
Pīr Mahal	123	30.46 N	72.26 E
Pirmasens	56	49.12 N	7.36 E
Pirna	54	50.58 N	13.56 E
Piroči	82	55.04 N	38.57 E
Pirogovka	78	51.54 N	33.18 E
Pirogovskij	265b	55.59 N	37.44 E
Pirogovskoje vodochranilišče ⊜[1]	82	55.58 N	37.40 E
Pirojpur	126	22.34 N	89.59 E
Pirón ≃	34	41.23 N	4.31 W
Pirongia	172	38.00 S	175.12 E
Pirot	38	43.09 N	22.35 E
Pirovano	252	36.30 S	61.34 W
Pirovskoje	86	57.37 N	92.16 E
Pīr Panjāl Range ⋏	123	33.37 N	74.32 E
Pirpirituba	250	6.46 S	35.30 W
Pirreşit Tepe ∧	84	38.56 N	43.51 E
Pirrís ≃	236	9.29 N	84.19 W
Pirsagat	84	39.54 N	49.24 E
Pirsagat ≃	84	39.53 N	49.19 E
Pirtleville	200	31.22 N	109.34 W
Piru, Indon.	164	3.04 S	128.12 E
Piru, Ca., U.S.	228	34.25 N	118.48 W
Piru, Lake ⊜[1]	228	34.30 N	118.45 W
Piru, Teluk c	164	3.10 S	128.08 E
Piru Creek ≃	228	34.23 N	118.47 W
Pisa	66	43.43 N	10.23 E
Pisa □[4]	66	43.25 N	10.43 E
Pisa ∧[2]	26	63.13 N	28.18 E
Pisa ≃	30	53.15 N	21.52 E
Pisa, Certosa di ⊍[1]	66	43.45 N	10.31 E
Pisa, Mount ∧	172	44.52 S	169.11 E
Pisac ⊥	248	13.25 S	71.53 W
Pisagua	248	19.36 S	70.13 W
Pisam-bong ∧	98	40.41 N	126.34 E
Pisang, Pulau I	164	1.23 S	128.55 E
Pisarevka	78	49.53 N	40.12 E
Pisarve	272c	19.06 N	73.05 E
Pisau, Tanjong ›	112	6.04 N	118.03 E
Piščalje	80	58.14 N	48.42 E
Piscasaw Creek ≃	216	42.16 N	88.49 W
Piscataway	210	40.29 N	74.23 W
Piscataway Creek ≃, Md., U.S.	208	38.42 N	77.02 W
Piscataway Creek ≃, Va., U.S.	208	37.54 N	76.50 W
Pişchia	38	45.55 N	21.20 E
Pisciotta	68	40.06 N	15.14 E
Pisco	248	13.42 S	76.13 W
Pisco ≃	248	13.42 S	76.15 W
Pişcolt	38	47.35 N	22.18 E
Piscovo	80	57.11 N	40.32 E
Piseco Lake ⊜	210	43.23 N	74.36 W
Písek	30	49.19 N	14.10 E
Pisgah, Md., U.S.	208	38.32 N	77.08 W
Pisgah, Oh., U.S.	218	39.19 N	84.22 W
Pisgah Forest	192	35.15 N	82.42 W
Pishan	120	37.37 N	78.18 E
Pishīn	120	30.35 N	67.00 E
Pishīn Lora (Lowrah) ≃	120	29.09 N	64.55 E
Pisidia □[9]	130	37.30 N	31.00 E
Pisinemo	200	32.02 N	112.18 W
Pising	112	5.05 S	121.54 E
Pis'mennoje	78	48.13 N	35.48 E
Pismo Beach	226	35.08 N	120.38 W
Pišnur	80	57.47 N	47.58 E
Piso, Lake ⊜	150	6.48 N	11.17 W
Pisogne	64	45.48 N	10.06 E
Pisqui ≃	248	7.45 S	75.01 W
Pissila	150	13.10 N	0.49 W
Pissos	32	44.19 N	0.47 W
Pistakee Highlands	216	42.25 N	88.11 W
Pistakee Lake ⊜	216	42.23 N	88.12 W
Pisticci	68	40.23 N	16.34 E
Pistoia	66	43.55 N	10.54 E
Pistoia □[4]	64	43.58 N	10.50 E
Pistolet Bay c	186	51.32 N	55.50 W
Pistuk Peak ∧	180	59.43 N	159.42 W
Pisuerga ≃	34	41.33 N	4.52 W
Pisz	30	53.38 N	21.49 E
Pit ≃	204	40.45 N	122.22 W
Pit, North Fork ≃	204	41.28 N	120.33 W
Pit, South Fork ≃	204	41.28 N	120.33 W
Pita	150	11.05 N	12.24 W
Pital	246	2.16 N	75.49 W
Pitalito	246	1.51 N	76.02 W
Pitampura Kālan ◆[8]	272a	28.42 N	77.08 E
Pitanga	252	24.46 S	51.44 W
Pitangueiras	255	21.02 S	48.13 W
Pitangueiras, Ribeirão das ≃	256	21.27 S	44.27 W
Pitangui	255	19.40 S	44.54 W
Pitcairn	279b	40.24 N	79.46 W
Pitcairn □[2], Oc.	6	25.04 S	130.05 W
Pitcairn □[2], Oc.	174e	25.04 S	130.05 W
Pitcairn Island I	6	25.04 S	130.06 W
Pitcher	210	42.35 N	75.52 W
Pitch Place	260	51.16 N	0.36 W
Piteå	26	65.20 N	21.30 E
Piteälven ≃	24	65.14 N	21.32 E
Piteglio	66	44.01 N	10.46 E
Pitelino	80	54.34 N	41.49 E
Piterka	80	50.42 N	47.27 E
Piteşti	38	44.52 N	24.52 E
Pithāpuram	122	17.07 N	82.16 E
Pithara	162	30.24 S	116.40 E
Pithiviers	50	48.10 N	2.15 E
Pithoragarh	124	29.35 N	80.13 E
Pithoragarh □[5]	124	30.10 N	80.30 E
Piti, Lagoa ⊜	158	26.34 S	32.53 E
Pitigliano	66	42.38 N	11.40 E
Pitillal del Norte	234	20.40 N	105.01 W
Pitim	80	53.12 N	42.21 E
Pitiquito	232	30.42 N	112.02 W
Pitk'aranta	24	61.34 N	31.27 E
Pitkas Point	180	62.02 N	163.17 W
Pitlochry	46	56.43 N	3.45 W
Pitman	208	39.43 N	75.07 W
Pitman Airport ⊠	285	39.45 N	75.08 W
Pitmedden	46	57.20 N	2.11 W
Pitner Ditch ≡	216	41.14 N	86.53 W
Pitogo	116	10.08 N	124.33 E
Pitomača	36	45.57 N	17.14 E
Pitou, Zhg.	100	25.01 N	114.35 E
Pitou, Zhg.	100	23.34 N	116.05 E
Pitou, Zhg.	100	24.26 N	114.22 E
Pitrufquén	254	38.59 S	72.39 W
Pitschen → Byczyna	30	51.07 N	18.11 E
Pitsea	260	51.34 N	0.31 E
Pitseng	158	28.58 S	28.16 E
Pitsford Reservoir ⊜[1]	42	52.20 N	0.52 W
Pitt ≃	224	49.12 N	122.47 W
Pitt, Mount ∧	174c	29.01 S	167.56 E
Pittem	50	51.00 N	3.16 E
Pitten ≃	61	47.44 N	16.14 E
Pittenweem	46	56.12 N	2.44 W
Pitti Island I	122	10.50 N	72.38 E
Pitt Island I	182	53.35 N	129.45 W
Pitt Lake ⊜	182	49.25 N	122.32 W
Pittsboro, In., U.S.	218	39.51 N	86.28 W
Pittsboro, Ms., U.S.	194	33.56 N	89.20 W
Pittsboro, N.C., U.S.	192	35.43 N	79.10 W
Pittsburg, Ca., U.S.	226	38.01 N	121.53 W
Pittsburg, In., U.S.	216	40.37 N	86.42 W
Pittsburg, Ks., U.S.	198	37.24 N	94.42 W
Pittsburg, N.H., U.S.	206	45.03 N	71.23 W
Pittsburg, Tx., U.S.	222	32.59 N	94.57 W
Pittsburgh, Pa., U.S.	214	40.26 N	79.59 W
Pittsburgh, Pa., U.S.	279b	40.26 N	79.59 W
Pittsburgh, University of ⊍[2]	279b	40.27 N	79.58 W
Pittsburgh-Monroeville Airport ⊠	279b	40.27 N	79.46 W
Pittsfield, Il., U.S.	219	39.36 N	90.48 W
Pittsfield, Me., U.S.	188	44.46 N	69.23 W
Pittsfield, Ma., U.S.	207	42.27 N	73.14 W
Pittsfield, N.H., U.S.	188	43.18 N	71.19 W
Pittsfield, Pa., U.S.	214	41.50 N	79.23 W
Pittsford, Mi., U.S.	216	41.52 N	84.28 W
Pittsford, N.Y., U.S.	210	43.05 N	77.31 W
Pitt Stadium ♦	279b	40.27 N	79.58 W
Pittston	210	41.19 N	75.47 W
Pittsview	194	32.11 N	85.09 W
Pittsville	208	38.23 N	75.24 W
Pittsworth	166	27.43 S	151.38 E
Pitt Water c	170	33.37 S	151.18 E
Pituil	252	28.34 S	67.27 W
Pitumarca	248	13.59 S	71.25 W
Pituri Creek ≃	166	22.58 S	138.50 E
Pitzbach ≃	64	47.13 N	10.46 E
Pitztal V	58	47.07 N	10.47 E
Pium	250	10.27 S	49.11 W
Pium ≃	250	10.12 S	49.57 W
Piura	248	5.12 S	80.38 W
Piura □[5]	248	5.10 S	80.00 W
Piura ≃	248	5.32 S	80.53 W
Piute Peak ∧	204	35.27 N	118.24 W
Piute Reservoir ⊜[1]	200	38.17 N	112.12 W
Piuthān	124	28.06 N	82.54 E
Piva ≃	38	43.21 N	18.51 E
Pivan'	89	50.29 N	137.06 E
Piverone	62	45.27 N	8.00 E
Pivijay	246	10.28 N	74.37 W
Piwniczna	30	49.27 N	20.42 E
Pixian	102	30.49 N	103.49 E
Pixley	226	35.58 N	119.17 W
Piyadin	130	37.01 N	29.58 E
Pižanka	80	57.28 N	48.33 E
Pižma	80	57.52 N	47.06 E
Pižma ≃	80	57.37 N	48.58 E
Pizzighettone	62	45.11 N	9.47 E
Pizzillo, Monte ∧	70	37.48 N	15.01 E
Pizzo	68	38.44 N	16.10 E
Pizzoferrato	66	41.55 N	14.14 E
Pizzoli	66	42.26 N	13.18 E
Pizzone	66	41.40 N	14.02 E
Pjalka	24	66.43 N	40.59 E
Pjana ≃	80	55.40 N	45.57 E
Pjöngjang → P'yŏngyang	98	39.01 N	125.45 E
P. K. le Rouxdam ⊜[1]	158	30.12 S	24.54 E
Placanica	68	38.25 N	16.27 E
Place Bonaventure ◆[9]	275a	45.30 N	73.34 W
Placentia, Nf., Can.	186	47.14 N	53.58 W
Placentia, Ca., U.S.	228	33.52 N	117.52 W
Placentia Bay c	186	47.15 N	54.30 W
Placer, Pil.	116	11.52 N	123.55 E
Placer, Pil.	116	9.39 N	125.36 E
Placer □[6]	226	38.54 N	121.04 W
Placeres de Picacho	234	23.11 N	105.42 W
Placerville	226	38.43 N	120.47 W
Placetas	240p	22.19 N	79.40 W
Place Versailles ◆[9]	275a	45.35 N	73.32 W
Plachino	76	54.28 N	39.20 E
Plachtejevka	78	46.07 N	29.43 E
Placid, Lake ⊜	220	27.14 N	81.22 W
Placida	220	26.49 N	82.15 W
Plácido de Castro	248	10.20 S	67.11 W
Plácido Rosas	252	32.45 S	53.44 W
Plačkovica ⋏	38	41.45 N	22.35 E
Plaffeien	58	46.44 N	7.17 E
Plages, Lac des ⊜	206	45.59 N	74.54 W
Plage-Sainte-Cécile	50	50.34 N	1.35 E
Plailly	261	49.06 N	2.35 E
Plai Mat ≃	110	15.22 N	102.45 E
Plain	224	47.46 N	120.39 W
Plain City, Oh., U.S.	214	40.06 N	83.16 W
Plain City, Ut,. U.S.	200	41.17 N	112.05 W
Plain Dealing	194	32.54 N	93.41 W
Plaines, Île aux I	275a	45.21 N	73.50 W
Plainfield, Ct., U.S.	207	41.40 N	71.54 W
Plainfield, Il., U.S.	216	41.37 N	88.12 W
Plainfield, In., U.S.	218	39.42 N	86.23 W
Plainfield, Ma., U.S.	207	42.30 N	72.55 W
Plainfield, N.J., U.S.	210	40.37 N	74.26 W
Plainfield, Oh., U.S.	214	40.13 N	81.43 W
Plainfield, Pa., U.S.	208	40.12 N	77.17 W
Plainfield, Wi., U.S.	190	44.12 N	89.29 W
Plainfield Heights	216	43.01 N	85.37 W
Plains, Ga., U.S.	192	32.02 N	84.23 W
Plains, Ks., U.S.	198	37.15 N	100.35 W
Plains, Mt., U.S.	202	47.27 N	114.52 W
Plains, Tx., U.S.	196	33.11 N	102.50 W
Plainsboro	208	40.20 N	74.36 W
Plainview, Ca., U.S.	226	36.08 N	119.08 W
Plainview, Il., U.S.	219	39.10 N	89.59 W
Plainview, Mn., U.S.	190	44.09 N	92.10 W
Plainview, Ne., U.S.	198	42.20 N	97.47 W
Plainview, N.Y., U.S.	210	40.46 N	73.28 W
Plainview, Tx., U.S.	196	34.11 N	101.42 W
Plainville, Ct., U.S.	207	41.40 N	72.51 W
Plainville, Il., U.S.	219	39.47 N	91.11 W
Plainville, In., U.S.	194	38.48 N	87.09 W
Plainville, Ks., U.S.	198	39.14 N	99.17 W
Plainville, Ma., U.S.	207	42.00 N	71.20 W
Plainville, N.Y., U.S.	210	43.10 N	76.27 W
Plainwell	216	42.26 N	85.38 W
Plaisance, Baie de c	186	47.18 N	61.53 W
Plaisir	261	48.49 N	1.57 E
Plaistow	207	42.50 N	71.05 W
Plaksino	76	56.11 N	30.42 E
Plamondon	182	54.51 N	112.19 W
Plampang	115b	8.48 S	117.48 E
Planá	60	49.52 N	12.44 E
Plana, Isla I	34	38.10 N	0.28 W
Planada	226	37.18 N	120.19 W
Planalto, Bra.	252	27.20 S	53.03 W
Planalto, Bra.	255	14.39 S	40.29 W
Planches	50	48.42 N	0.22 E
Plandome	276	40.48 N	73.42 W
Plandome Heights	276	40.48 N	73.42 W
Plandome Manor	276	40.49 N	73.42 W
Plan-d'Orgon	62	43.48 N	5.00 E
Plane ≃	54	52.23 N	12.30 E
Planegg	60	48.06 N	11.25 E
Planerskoje	78	44.57 N	35.14 E
Planeta Rica	246	8.25 N	75.36 W
Plangeross	58	46.59 N	10.52 E
Plankenfels	60	49.53 N	11.20 E
Plankinton	198	43.42 N	98.29 W
Plano, Il., U.S.	216	41.39 N	88.32 W
Plano, Tx., U.S.	222	33.01 N	96.41 W
Plansee ⊜	64	47.28 N	10.48 E
Planta de Evaporación ⊍[3]	286a	19.35 N	99.00 W
Plantagenet	206	45.32 N	75.00 W
Plantation, Fl., U.S.	220	26.07 N	80.14 W
Plantation, Fl., U.S.	220	24.59 N	80.33 W
Plantation, Ky., U.S.	218	38.17 N	85.36 W
Plantation Key I	220	24.58 N	80.33 W
Plant City	220	28.01 N	82.06 W
Plantersville, Al., U.S.	194	32.39 N	86.55 W
Plantersville, Ms., U.S.	194	34.12 N	88.39 W
Plantersville, Tx., U.S.	222	30.20 N	95.52 W
Planting Fields Arboretum State Park ♦	276	40.52 N	73.33 W
Plantsite	200	33.03 N	109.19 W
Plantsville	207	41.35 N	72.53 W
Plaquemine	194	30.17 N	91.14 W
Plaridel, Pil.	116	10.32 N	124.46 E
Plaridel, Pil.	116	8.37 N	123.43 E
Plasencia	34	40.02 N	6.05 W
Plaški	36	45.05 N	15.22 E
Plassenburg ⊥	60	50.06 N	11.28 E
Plassey	126	23.47 N	88.15 E
Plast	86	54.22 N	60.50 E
Plaster Rock	186	46.54 N	67.24 W
Plastovo	82	54.17 N	37.03 E
Plastun	89	44.45 N	136.19 E
Plastunovskaja	78	45.18 N	39.16 E
Plasy	60	49.56 N	13.24 E
Plata, Río de la c[1]	258	35.00 S	57.00 W
Plata, Río de la ≃	240m	18.29 N	66.15 W
Platani ≃	70	37.24 N	13.16 E
Platania ≃	68	39.00 N	16.19 E
Plátanos	288	34.47 S	58.11 W
Plátanos, Arroyo ≃	288	34.45 S	58.08 W
Plate, Île I	275a	45.22 N	73.48 W
Platea	214	41.57 N	80.20 W
Plateau □[3]	150	8.45 N	8.30 E
Plateau Creek ≃	200	39.11 N	108.18 W
Plateaux □[5]	152	2.15 S	15.30 E
Plathe → Płoty	30	53.49 N	15.16 E
Platì	68	38.13 N	16.03 E
Platinum	180	59.01 N	161.49 W
Platnirovskaja	78	45.23 N	39.23 E
Plato	246	9.47 N	74.47 W
Platono-Petrovka	83	46.59 N	39.28 E
Platonovka	80	52.43 N	41.57 E
Platón Sánchez	234	21.17 N	98.22 W
Platovo	83	48.05 N	39.53 E
Platrand	158	27.08 S	29.29 E
Platt	260	51.17 N	0.20 E
Platta	58	46.40 N	8.51 E
Platte	198	43.23 N	98.50 W
Platte ≃, U.S.	194	39.16 N	94.50 W
Platte ≃, Mn., U.S.	190	45.47 N	94.17 W
Platte ≃, Ne., U.S.	198	41.04 N	95.53 W
Platte ≃, Wi., U.S.	190	42.37 N	90.40 W
Platte Center	198	41.32 N	97.29 W
Platte City	194	39.22 N	94.46 W
Platte Creek ≃	198	43.19 N	99.00 W
Platte Island I	138	5.52 S	55.23 E
Plattekill	210	41.37 N	74.05 W
Platteville, Co., U.S.	200	40.12 N	104.49 W
Platteville, Wi., U.S.	190	42.44 N	90.28 W
Platt Hall ⊥	262	53.27 N	2.13 W
Plattling	60	48.47 N	12.53 E
Plattsburg	194	39.33 N	94.26 W
Plattsburgh	188	44.41 N	73.27 W
Plattsburgh Air Force Base ■	188	44.40 N	73.28 W
Plattsmouth	198	41.00 N	95.52 W
Plattsville	212	43.18 N	80.37 W
Platveld	156	19.58 S	17.07 E
Plau	54	53.27 N	12.16 E
Plaue, D.D.R.	54	52.24 N	12.25 E
Plaue, D.D.R.	54	50.47 N	10.54 E
Plauen	54	50.30 N	12.08 E
Plauer See ⊜	54	53.30 N	12.20 E
Plav	38	42.36 N	19.56 E
Plave	64	46.02 N	13.36 E
Plaviņas	76	56.37 N	25.43 E
Plavsk	76	53.43 N	37.18 E
Plaxtol	260	51.15 N	0.18 E
Playa Azul	234	17.59 N	102.24 W
Playa Baracoa	286b	23.03 N	82.34 W
Playa Bonita	236	9.39 N	84.27 W
Playa de Fajardo	240m	18.20 N	65.38 W
Playa de Guayanés	240m	18.04 N	65.49 W
Playa de Guayanilla	240m	18.01 N	66.46 W
Playa del Carmen	238	20.36 N	87.06 W
Playa del Rey ◆[8]	280	33.58 N	118.26 W
Playa de Naguabo	240m	18.12 N	65.43 W
Playa de Ponce	240m	17.59 N	66.37 W
Playa Noriega, Laguna ⊜	232	29.10 N	111.50 W
Playas Lake ⊜	200	31.50 N	108.34 W
Playa Vicente	234	17.50 N	95.49 W
Playa Vicente ≃	234	18.31 N	95.42 W
Playford ≃	162	19.03 S	135.35 E
Playgreen Lake ⊜	184	54.00 N	98.10 W
Playland ♦	276	40.58 N	73.41 W
Playon Grande	246	9.21 N	78.20 W
Plaza	198	48.01 N	101.57 W
Plaza at Mid Island ◆[9]	276	40.46 N	73.32 W
Plaza Caisan	236	8.46 N	82.45 W
Plaza de Mayo ♦	288	34.36 S	58.23 W
Plaza de Toros ♦	266a	40.26 N	3.39 W
Plaza de Toros Las Arenas ♦	266d	41.23 N	2.09 W
Plaza de Toros Monumental ♦	266d	41.24 N	2.11 E
Plaza Huincul	252	38.55 S	69.09 W
Plaza Park	285	40.04 N	74.53 W
Plazas de Soberanía en el Norte de África → Spanish North Africa □[2]	34	35.53 N	5.19 W
Pleasant	275b	43.41 N	79.49 W
Pleasant, Lake ⊜[1]	200	33.53 N	112.16 W
Pleasant, Mount ∧	192	37.44 N	79.10 W
Pleasant, Mount ∧[2]	186	45.26 N	66.49 W
Pleasant Bay	186	46.49 N	60.48 W
Pleasantdale, Sk., Can.	184	52.35 N	104.30 W
Pleasantdale, N.Y., U.S.	210	42.47 N	73.40 W
Pleasant Gap	214	40.52 N	77.44 W
Pleasant Garden	192	35.57 N	79.45 W
Pleasant Grove, Ca., U.S.	226	38.49 N	121.29 W
Pleasant Grove, Ut,. U.S.	200	40.21 N	111.44 W
Pleasant Grove Creek ≃	226	38.48 N	121.32 W
Pleasant Hill, Ca., U.S.	226	37.56 N	122.03 W
Pleasant Hill, Il., U.S.	219	39.26 N	90.52 W
Pleasant Hill, La., U.S.	194	31.49 N	93.31 W
Pleasant Hill, Mo., U.S.	194	38.47 N	94.16 W
Pleasant Hill, N.C., U.S.	208	36.32 N	77.32 W
Pleasant Hill, Oh., U.S.	218	40.03 N	84.20 W
Pleasant Hill Lake ⊜[1]	214	40.38 N	82.21 W
Pleasant Hills	214	40.20 N	79.57 W
Pleasant Lake, In., U.S.	216	41.34 N	85.00 W
Pleasant Lake, Mi., U.S.	216	42.23 N	84.22 W
Pleasant Lake ⊜	216	42.13 N	83.56 W
Pleasant Mills	216	40.47 N	84.51 W
Pleasant Mount	210	41.44 N	75.26 W
Pleasanton, Ca., U.S.	226	37.39 N	121.52 W
Pleasanton, Ks., U.S.	198	38.10 N	94.42 W
Pleasanton, Tx., U.S.	196	28.58 N	98.28 W
Pleasanton Ridge ∧	282	37.40 N	121.55 W
Pleasant Plains, Il., U.S.	219	39.52 N	89.55 W
Pleasant Plains, N.J., U.S.	208	40.00 N	74.13 W
Pleasant Point	172	44.16 S	171.08 E
Pleasant Prairie	216	42.33 N	87.57 W
Pleasant Ridge	281	42.31 N	83.10 W
Pleasant Unity	214	40.15 N	79.28 W
Pleasant Valley, N.Y., U.S.	210	41.44 N	73.49 W
Pleasant Valley, Oh., U.S.	218	39.22 N	83.03 W
Pleasant Valley, Pa., U.S.	279b	40.31 N	75.18 W
Pleasantville, Ia., U.S.	190	41.23 N	93.16 W
Pleasantville, Md., U.S.	284b	39.11 N	76.38 W
Pleasantville, N.J., U.S.	208	39.23 N	74.31 W
Pleasantville, N.Y., U.S.	210	41.07 N	73.47 W
Pleasantville, Pa., U.S.	214	41.35 N	79.34 W
Pleasington	262	53.44 N	2.34 W
Pleasure Beach	207	41.18 N	72.08 W
Pleasure Ridge Park	218	38.09 N	85.51 W
Pleasureville	218	38.33 N	85.04 W
Pléaux	32	45.08 N	2.14 E
Plechanovo	82	54.14 N	37.33 E
Plechanovskoje	76	52.39 N	39.50 E
Plechovo	78	51.07 N	35.18 E
Plechý (Plöckenstein) ∧	60	48.46 N	13.51 E
Pledger	222	29.11 N	95.55 W
Pleebo	150	4.35 N	7.40 W
Pleiku	110	13.59 N	108.00 E
Pleinfeld	56	49.06 N	10.59 E
Pleissa	54	50.50 N	12.46 E
Pleisse ≃	54	51.20 N	12.22 E
Pléneuf	32	48.36 N	2.33 W
Plenty	184	51.47 N	108.36 W
Plenty ≃, Austl.	162	23.25 S	136.31 E
Plenty ≃, Austl.	274b	37.45 S	145.07 E
Plenty, Bay of c	172	37.40 S	177.00 E
Plentywood	198	48.46 N	104.33 W
Plered	115a	6.38 S	107.23 E
Pleščejevo, ozero ⊜	82	56.46 N	38.47 E
Pleščenicy	76	54.25 N	27.50 E
Pleseck	24	62.43 N	40.20 E
Plešivka	82	54.23 N	37.09 E
Plesna ≃	54	50.07 N	12.28 E
Pless, B.R.D.	58	48.05 N	10.08 E
Pless → Pszczyna, Pol.	30	49.59 N	18.57 E
Plessa	54	51.28 N	13.37 E
Plessisville	206	46.14 N	71.47 W
Pleszew	30	51.54 N	17.48 E
Pletenevka	82	54.31 N	36.06 E
Pleternica	38	45.17 N	17.48 E
Plétipi, Lac ⊜	176	51.44 N	70.06 W
Plet'onyj Tašlyk	78	48.29 N	31.40 E
Plettenberg	56	51.13 N	7.52 E
Plettenbergbaai	158	34.04 S	23.22 E
Pleurs	50	48.41 N	3.52 E
Pleven	38	43.25 N	24.37 E
Plevna, Mo., U.S.	219	39.58 N	92.05 W
Plevna, Mt., U.S.	198	46.25 N	104.31 W
Pleyben	32	48.14 N	3.58 W
Pleystein	60	49.39 N	12.25 E
Pliening	60	48.12 N	11.48 E
Pliezhausen	56	48.33 N	9.12 E
Plimmerton	172	41.05 S	174.52 E
Plimoth Plantation ⊥	207	41.57 N	70.38 W
Plintovka	265a	60.01 N	30.46 E
Pliski	78	51.07 N	32.24 E
Pliskov	78	49.23 N	29.18 E
Pliszka ≃	54	52.14 N	14.42 E
Plitvička Jezera Nacionalni Park ♦	36	44.53 N	15.38 E
Plješevica ⋏	36	44.40 N	15.45 E
Pljevlja	38	43.21 N	19.21 E
Ploaghe	71	40.40 N	8.45 E
Ploče	36	43.04 N	17.26 E
Plochingen	56	48.42 N	9.25 E
Płock	30	52.33 N	19.43 E
Płock □[4]	30	52.25 N	19.45 E
Plöckenpass)(	64	46.36 N	12.58 E
Plöckenstein (Plechý) ∧	60	48.46 N	13.51 E
Pločno ∧	36	43.23 N	17.57 E
Plodorodnoje	80	46.44 N	41.06 E
Ploegsteert	50	50.43 N	2.53 E
Ploërmel	32	47.56 N	2.24 W
Ploeşti → Ploieşti	38	44.56 N	26.02 E
Plogastel-Saint-Germain	28	47.59 N	4.16 W
Ploieşti	38	44.56 N	26.02 E
Plomárion	38	38.59 N	26.22 E
Plomb du Cantal ∧	32	45.03 N	2.46 E
Plombières-les-Bains	58	47.58 N	6.29 E
Plombières-lès-Dijon	58	47.20 N	4.58 E
Plomer	258	34.48 S	59.02 W
Plomer, Point ›	166	31.19 S	152.58 E
Plön	54	54.09 N	10.25 E
Plonge, Lac la ⊜	184	55.08 N	107.25 W
Płońsk	30	52.38 N	20.23 E
Pl'os	80	57.27 N	41.31 E
Plose, Cima delle ∧	64	46.42 N	11.44 E
Ploskij	78	46.17 N	40.15 E
Ploskoje	76	52.45 N	38.21 E
Ploskoš'	76	56.46 N	31.16 E
Pl'oso	76	59.47 N	35.43 E
Plotbišče	80	56.50 N	50.35 E
Plotina	83	48.33 N	40.05 E
Plotnica	78	52.03 N	26.39 E
Plottier	252	38.58 S	68.14 W
Płoty	30	53.49 N	15.16 E
Plötz	54	51.38 N	11.56 E
Plouay	32	47.55 N	3.20 W
Ploučnice ≃	54	50.47 N	14.13 E
Ploudalmézeau	32	48.32 N	4.39 W
Plouguenast	32	48.17 N	2.43 W
Plouha	32	48.41 N	2.56 W
Plovdiv	38	42.09 N	24.45 E
Plover ≃	190	44.29 N	89.35 W
Plover Islands II	180	71.15 N	155.30 W
Pluckemin	276	40.39 N	74.39 W
Plum, Pa., U.S.	214	40.31 N	79.45 W
Plum, Pa., U.S.	214	41.35 N	79.51 W
Plum, Tx., U.S.	222	29.56 N	96.58 W
Pluma Hidalgo	234	15.55 N	96.25 W
Plumas	184	50.25 N	99.02 W
Plumbon	115a	6.42 S	108.28 E
Plumbridge	48	54.46 N	7.15 W
Plum Brook ≃	281	42.34 N	82.58 W
Plum Creek ≃, Il., U.S.	278	41.33 N	87.29 W
Plum Creek ≃, Ne., U.S.	198	41.52 N	96.44 W
Plum Creek ≃, Oh., U.S.	279a	41.18 N	82.09 W
Plum Creek ≃, Pa., U.S.	279b	40.31 N	79.51 W
Plum Creek ≃, S.D., U.S.	198	44.13 N	100.43 W
Plum Creek ≃, Tx., U.S.	196	29.38 N	97.36 W
Plum Creek, Clear Fork ≃	222	29.45 N	97.37 W
Plumerville	194	35.09 N	92.38 W
Plum Grove	222	30.15 N	95.05 W
Plum Grove Estates	278	42.04 N	88.02 W
Plum Island	283	42.49 N	70.59 W
Plum Island I, Ma., U.S.	207	42.45 N	70.48 W
Plum Island I, N.Y., U.S.	207	41.11 N	72.12 W
Plum Island Airport ⊠	283	42.48 N	70.50 W
Plum Island Sound ʊ	283	42.45 N	70.48 W
Plum Island State Park ♦	283	42.42 N	70.47 W
Plumley	262	53.17 N	2.25 W
Plummer	202	47.20 N	116.53 W
Plummers Landing	218	38.19 N	83.33 W
Plumper Sound ʊ	224	48.47 N	123.13 W
Plum Point ›	276	40.50 N	40.43 W
Plumpton	274a	33.45 S	150.50 E
Plumridge Lakes ⊜	162	29.30 S	125.25 E
Plum Run ≃	279b	40.15 N	80.13 W
Plumsteadville	208	40.23 N	75.09 W
Plumtree	154	20.30 S	27.50 E
Plumville	214	40.48 N	79.11 W
Plumwood	218	40.01 N	83.23 W
Plungė	76	55.55 N	21.51 E
Pl'usa	76	58.26 N	29.21 E
Pl'uskovo	76	52.46 N	33.49 E
Pl'ussa ≃	76	59.19 N	28.11 E
Pluvigner	32	47.46 N	3.01 E
Plym ≃	42	50.12 N	4.07 W
Plymouth, Monts.	238	16.42 N	62.13 W
Plymouth, Trin.	241r	11.13 N	60.47 W
Plymouth, Eng., U.K.	42	50.23 N	4.10 W
Plymouth, Ca., U.S.	226	38.29 N	120.51 W
Plymouth, Ct., U.S.	207	41.40 N	73.03 W
Plymouth, Il., U.S.	194	40.17 N	90.55 W
Plymouth, In., U.S.	216	41.20 N	86.18 W
Plymouth, Ma., U.S.	207	41.57 N	70.40 W
Plymouth, Mi., U.S.	216	42.22 N	83.28 W
Plymouth, Ne., U.S.	198	40.18 N	96.59 W
Plymouth, N.H., U.S.	188	43.45 N	71.41 W
Plymouth, N.Y., U.S.	210	42.37 N	75.36 W
Plymouth, N.C., U.S.	192	35.52 N	76.44 W
Plymouth, Oh., U.S.	214	41.00 N	82.40 W
Plymouth, Pa., U.S.	210	41.14 N	75.56 W
Plymouth, Wi., U.S.	190	43.44 N	87.58 W
Plymouth □[6]	207	41.58 N	70.41 W
Plymouth ≃	283	42.12 N	70.54 W
Plymouth Bay c	207	41.57 N	70.37 W
Plymouth Harbor c	283	41.58 N	70.39 W
Plymouth Meeting	285	40.06 N	75.16 W
Plymouth Meeting Mall ◆[9]	285	40.07 N	75.17 W
Plymouth Rock ⊥	207	41.57 N	70.39 W
Plymouth Valley	285	40.07 N	75.23 W
Plympton, Eng., U.K.	42	50.23 N	4.03 W
Plympton, Ma., U.S.	207	41.57 N	70.48 W
Plymptonville	214	41.03 N	78.28 W
Plymstock	42	50.22 N	4.04 W
Plynlimon ∧	42	52.28 N	3.47 W
Plzeň	60	49.45 N	13.23 E
Pniewy	30	52.31 N	16.15 E
Pô	150	11.10 N	1.09 W
Po ≃, It.	36	44.57 N	12.04 E
Po ≃, Zhg.	100	28.57 N	116.39 E
Po, Foci del ≃[1]	64	44.52 N	12.30 E
Pô, Parc National de ♦	150	11.30 N	1.15 W
Poá	256	23.32 S	46.20 W
Poá ≃	287b	23.37 S	46.45 W

Symbols in the index entries represent the broad categories identified in the key at the right. Symbols with superior numbers (⋏[1]) identify subcategories (see complete key on page *I · 1*).

Kartensymbole in dem Registerverzeichnis stellen die rechts in Schlüssel erklärten Kategorien dar. Symbole mit hochgestellten Ziffern (⋏[1]) bezeichnen Unterabteilungen einer Kategorie (vgl. vollständiger Schlüssel auf Seite *I · 1*).

Los símbolos incluídos en el texto del índice representan las grandes categorías identificadas con la clave a la derecha. Los símbolos con numeros en su parte superior (⋏[1]) identifican las subcategorías (véase la clave completa en la página *I · 1*).

Les symboles de l'index représentent les catégories indiquées dans la légende à droite. Les symboles suivis d'un indice (⋏[1]) représentent des sous-catégories (voir légende complète à la page *I · 1*).

Os símbolos incluídos no texto do índice representam as grandes categorias identificadas com a chave à direita. Os símbolos com números em sua parte superior (⋏[1]) identificam as subcategorias (veja-se a chave completa à página *I · 1*).

∧ Mountain	Berg	Montaña	Montagne	Montanha
⋏ Mountains	Berge	Montañas	Montagnes	Montanhas
)(Pass	Pass	Paso	Col	Passo
V Valley, Canyon	Tal, Cañon	Valle, Cañón	Vallée, Canyon	Vale, Canhão
⋍ Plain	Ebene	Llano	Plaine	Planície
› Cape	Kap	Cabo	Cap	Cabo
I Island	Insel	Isla	Île	Ilha
II Islands	Inseln	Islas	Îles	Ilhas
⊥ Other Topographic Features	Andere Topographische Objekte	Otros Elementos Topográficos	Autres données topographiques	Outros acidentes topográficos

ESPAÑOL

Nombre	Página	Lat.°′	Long.°′ W = Oeste
Poana ≃	250	0.56 N	57.03 W
Poás, Volcán ∧ [1]	236	10.11 N	84.13 W
Pobé, Bénin	150	6.58 N	2.41 E
Pobé, Burkina	150	13.53 N	1.45 W
Pobeda, gora ∧	74	65.12 N	146.12 E
Pobeda Ice Island I	9	64.30 S	97.00 E
Pobedino	74	49.51 N	142.49 E
Pobedy, pik ∧	72	42.02 N	80.05 E
Pobershau	54	50.38 N	13.13 E
Poběžovice	60	49.31 N	12.48 E
Poblado Cerro Gordo	240m	18.29 N	66.20 W
Poblado Jacaguas	240m	18.03 N	66.32 W
Poblado Medianía Alta	240m	18.26 N	65.50 W
Poblado Sábalos	240m	18.11 N	67.09 W
Poblado Santana	240m	18.27 N	66.40 W
Poblet	258	35.04 S	57.57 W
Pocahontas, Ar., U.S.	194	36.15 N	90.58 W
Pocahontas, Il., U.S.	219	38.49 N	89.32 W
Pocahontas, Ia., U.S.	198	42.44 N	94.40 W
Pocahontas State Park ♦	208	37.23 N	77.34 W
Počajev	78	50.01 N	25.31 E
Pocantico Hills	276	41.06 N	73.50 W
Pocantico Lake ⊜	276	41.07 N	73.50 W
Poção	250	8.11 S	36.42 W
Pocasset	207	41.41 N	70.37 W
Pocatalico ≃	188	38.29 N	81.49 W
Pocatello	202	42.52 N	112.26 W
Počep	76	52.56 N	33.27 E
Počepy	76	53.17 N	31.20 E
Pocé-sur-Cisse	50	47.26 N	0.59 E
Pöchlarn	61	48.12 N	15.13 E
Pochutla	234	15.44 N	96.28 W
Pochvistnevo	80	53.38 N	52.08 E
Pocinhos	250	7.04 S	36.03 W
Pocinhos do Rio Verde	256	21.56 S	46.25 W
Počinki	80	54.42 N	44.51 E
Počinnaja Sopka	76	58.25 N	34.22 E
Počinok	76	54.25 N	32.27 E
Pocitos, Salar ≃	252	24.30 S	67.03 W
Pockau	54	50.40 N	13.27 E
Pocking	60	48.24 N	13.19 E
Pocklington	44	53.56 N	0.46 W
Pocoata	248	18.41 S	66.11 W
Poçoda Cruz, Açude ⊜ [1]	250	8.30 S	37.35 W
Poço do Bispo ◆ [8]	266c	38.44 N	9.06 W
Poções	255	14.31 S	40.21 W
Poço Fundo	256	21.48 S	45.58 W
Poço Fundo, Cachoeira do ∟	256	22.10 S	44.13 W
Pocol	64	46.31 N	12.07 E
Pocola	194	35.13 N	94.28 W
Pocomoke ≃	208	37.58 N	75.39 W
Pocomoke City	208	38.04 N	75.34 W
Pocomoke Sound Ʉ	208	37.52 N	75.49 W
Pocona	248	17.39 S	65.24 W
Poconé	248	16.15 S	56.37 W
Pocono International Raceway ♦	210	41.03 N	75.31 W
Pocono Lake	210	41.06 N	75.31 W
Pocono Manor	210	41.06 N	75.22 W
Pocono Mountains ⩘ [2]	210	41.10 N	75.20 W
Pocono Pines	210	41.05 N	75.29 W
Pocono Summit	210	41.07 N	75.25 W
Pocopson	285	39.54 N	75.37 W
Pocopson Creek ≃	285	39.54 N	75.37 W
Poço Redondo	250	9.49 S	37.41 W
Poços de Caldas	256	21.48 S	46.34 W
Poço Verde	250	10.42 S	38.11 W
Pocrane	255	19.37 S	41.37 W
Pocrí	236	8.16 N	80.33 W
Podbel'skaja	80	53.37 N	51.50 E
Podberezje, S.S.S.R.	76	56.57 N	30.38 E
Podberezje, S.S.S.R.	82	56.46 N	37.10 E
Podbořany	54	50.11 N	13.25 E
Podborki	82	54.11 N	35.56 E
Podborovje	76	59.30 N	35.02 E
Podbuž	78	49.22 N	23.15 E
Podbužje	76	53.30 N	34.56 E
Podčerje	24	63.57 N	57.34 E
Podchožeje	82	54.19 N	38.34 E
Podčinnyj	80	50.52 N	45.13 E
Poddębice	30	51.53 N	18.58 E
Poddemjur	24	64.05 N	53.26 E
Poddolgoje	76	53.12 N	38.04 E
Poddorje	76	57.28 N	31.07 E
Poděbrady	30	50.08 N	15.07 E
Podejuch → Podjuchy ◆ [8]	54	53.20 N	14.36 E
Po della Donzella ≃	64	44.48 N	12.25 E
Po delle Tolle ≃	64	44.50 N	12.28 E
Podensac	32	44.39 N	0.22 W
Podenzano	62	44.57 N	9.41 E
Podersdorf am See	61	47.51 N	16.50 E
Podgajcy	78	49.16 N	25.08 E
Podgorenskij	78	50.24 N	39.39 E
Podgorica → Titograd	38	42.26 N	19.14 E
Podgornaja	78	50.28 N	41.10 E
Podgornoje, S.S.S.R.	78	51.43 N	39.07 E
Podgornoje, S.S.S.R.	78	50.27 N	39.37 E
Podgornoje, S.S.S.R.	80	46.33 N	43.07 E
Podgornoje, S.S.S.R.	85	42.55 N	72.25 E
Podgornoje, S.S.S.R.	86	57.47 N	82.36 E
Podgorodnaja	78	48.07 N	30.51 E
Podgorodnoje	78	48.34 N	35.08 E
Podhůří	60	49.28 N	13.40 E
Podi	112	1.08 S	121.16 E
Po di Goro ≃	64	44.48 N	12.27 E
Po di Volano ≃	64	44.49 N	12.15 E
Podjom-Michajlovka	80	52.49 N	50.32 E
Podjuchy ◆ [8]	54	53.20 N	14.36 E
Podkamen'	78	49.57 N	25.19 E
Podkamennaja Tunguska	74	61.36 N	90.09 E
Podkamennaja Tunguska ≃	74	61.36 N	90.18 E
Podkoren	64	46.30 N	13.45 E
Podkumok ≃	84	44.14 N	43.36 E
Podlasie ◆ [1]	30	52.30 N	23.00 E
Podlesnoje, S.S.S.R.	78	48.47 N	32.15 E
Podlesnoje, S.S.S.R.	80	51.50 N	47.03 E
Podlopatki	88	50.55 N	107.05 E
Podmošje	82	56.23 N	37.24 E
Podol'sk	82	55.26 N	37.33 E
Podol'skaja vozvyšennost' ⩘ [1]	78	49.00 N	27.00 E
Podor, Maur.	150	16.40 N	15.00 W
Podor, Sén.	150	16.40 N	14.57 W
Podora	24	62.22 N	54.19 E
Podosinovec	24	60.17 N	47.04 E
Podoz'orskij	80	57.14 N	40.20 E
Podporožje	24	60.53 N	34.07 E
Podravina ◆ [1]	38	45.40 N	17.40 E
Podravska Slatina	38	45.42 N	17.42 E
Podrezčicha	24	59.22 N	51.28 E
Podstepnyj	80	51.08 N	51.28 E
Podsvilje	76	55.09 N	27.58 E
Podt'osovo	88	58.36 N	92.06 E
Pod'uga	24	61.06 N	40.53 E
Podujevo	38	42.55 N	21.11 E
Poduškino	265b	55.43 N	37.17 E
Podu Turcului	38	46.12 N	27.23 E
Podvoločisk	78	49.33 N	26.09 E
Podymachino	88	56.59 N	106.11 E
Podyvotje	78	52.03 N	34.08 E
Poe	216	40.56 N	85.05 W
Poel I	54	54.00 N	11.26 E
Poeldijk	52	52.01 N	4.12 E
Poelela, Lagoa ⊜	156	24.38 S	35.00 E
Poelkapelle	50	50.55 N	2.57 E
Poestenkill	210	42.41 N	73.34 W
Poesten Kill ≃	210	42.43 N	73.42 W
Poetto	71	39.12 N	9.10 E

FRANÇAIS

Nom	Page	Lat.°′	Long.°′ W = Ouest
Pofadder	158	29.10 S	19.22 E
Pogamasing Lake ⊜	190	46.57 N	81.50 W
Pogan, Zhg.	100	28.18 N	116.46 E
Pogan, Zhg.	100	27.40 N	116.46 E
Pogăniș ≃	38	45.41 N	21.22 E
Pogar	76	52.33 N	33.16 E
Poge, Cape ≻	207	41.25 N	70.27 W
Poggendorf	54	54.03 N	13.07 E
Poggiardo	68	40.03 N	18.23 E
Poggibonsi	66	43.28 N	11.09 E
Poggio	64	44.30 N	10.00 E
Poggio Berni	66	44.02 N	12.24 E
Poggio Bustone	66	42.30 N	12.53 E
Poggio Imperiale	68	41.49 N	15.22 E
Poggiomarino	68	40.48 N	14.32 E
Poggio Mirteto	66	42.16 N	12.41 E
Poggio Moiano	66	42.12 N	12.53 E
Poggioreale	70	37.47 N	13.01 E
Poggio Renatico	64	44.46 N	11.29 E
Poggiorsini	68	40.55 N	16.15 E
Poggio Rusco	64	44.59 N	11.07 E
Poggio Sannita	66	41.47 N	14.25 E
Pöggstall	61	48.19 N	15.12 E
Pogibi	89	52.12 N	141.42 E
Pogil-to I	98	34.09 N	126.33 E
Pogliano	266b	45.32 N	8.59 E
Pogny	56	48.52 N	4.29 E
Pogoanele	38	44.54 N	27.00 E
Pogodajev	80	51.37 N	51.04 E
Pogonianí	38	40.00 N	20.25 E
Pogoreloje Gorodišče	76	56.08 N	34.56 E
Pogoso	152	6.46 S	17.12 E
Pogost, S.S.S.R.	76	52.51 N	27.39 E
Pogost, S.S.S.R.	76	53.51 N	29.09 E
Pogost, S.S.S.R.	80	57.39 N	42.33 E
Pogost, S.S.S.R.	82	56.52 N	39.04 E
Pogožeje	78	51.36 N	37.16 E
Pogradec	38	40.54 N	20.39 E
Po Grande ≃	64	44.57 N	12.26 E
Pograničnoje	80	50.32 N	48.38 E
Pograničnyj, S.S.S.R.	80	46.57 N	45.46 E
Pograničnyj, S.S.S.R.	89	44.25 N	131.24 E
Pogrebišče	78	49.29 N	29.16 E
Pogromni Volcano ∧ [1]	180	54.33 N	164.45 W
Pogromnoje	80	52.35 N	52.32 E
Pogruznaja	80	54.14 N	50.29 E
Poh	112	0.46 S	122.49 E
P'ohang	98	36.03 N	129.20 E
Pohatcong Creek ≃	210	40.37 N	75.11 W
Pohénégamook	186	47.31 N	69.16 W
Pohick Creek ≃	284c	38.46 N	77.14 W
Pohick Creek, Rabbit Branch ≃	284c	38.48 N	77.17 W
Pohick Creek, Sideburn Branch ≃	284c	38.48 N	77.17 W
Pohjanmaa ◆ [1]	26	64.00 N	25.00 E
Pohjois-Karjalan lääni □ [4]	24	63.00 N	30.00 E
Pöhl, Talsperre ◆ [6]	54	50.33 N	12.12 E
Pöhla	54	50.31 N	12.49 E
Pöhlde	52	51.37 N	10.18 E
Pohl-Göns	56	50.28 N	8.39 E
Pohlheim	56	50.34 N	8.45 E
Pohořelice	61	48.59 N	16.32 E
Pohorje ⩘	36	46.30 N	15.20 E
Pohsien → Boxian	100	33.53 N	115.45 E
Pohue Bay ⊂	229d	19.00 N	155.48 W
Poiana Mare	38	43.55 N	23.04 E
Poiana Rușcăi, Munții ⩘	38	45.41 N	22.30 E
Pöide	76	58.31 N	23.03 E
Poigny-la-Forêt	261	48.41 N	1.45 E
Poim	80	53.01 N	43.11 E
Poinsett, Cape ≻	9	65.42 S	113.18 E
Poinsett, Lake ⊜, Fl., U.S.	220	28.20 N	80.50 W
Poinsett, Lake ⊜, S.D., U.S.	198	44.34 N	97.05 W
Point	222	32.56 N	95.52 W
Point Arena	204	38.54 N	123.41 W
Point Au Fer Island I	194	29.15 N	91.15 W
Point Baker	180	56.21 N	133.37 W
Pointblank	222	30.45 N	95.13 W
Point Chautauqua	214	42.14 N	79.28 W
Point Cloates	162	22.35 S	113.41 E
Point Comfort	196	28.41 N	96.33 W
Point Cook	274b	37.56 S	144.45 E
Point Cook Royal Australian Air Force Station ■	169	37.56 S	144.45 E
Point du Jour, Ruisseau du ≃	206	45.50 N	73.25 W
Pointe-à-la-Frégate	186	49.12 N	64.55 W
Pointe-à-la-Garde	186	48.05 N	66.32 W
Pointe a la Hache	194	29.34 N	89.47 W
Pointe-à-Maurier	186	50.20 N	59.48 W
Pointe-à-Pitre	241o	16.14 N	61.32 W
Pointe-à-Pitre-le Raizet, Aérodrome de ⊠	241o	16.17 N	61.32 W
Pointe-au-Chêne	206	45.38 N	74.45 W
Pointe Aux Peaux Farms	216	41.57 N	83.16 W
Pointe-aux-Trembles	206	45.39 N	73.30 W
Pointe-Calumet	275a	45.30 N	73.58 W
Pointe-Claire	206	45.26 N	73.50 W
Pointe-des-Cascades	275a	45.20 N	73.58 W
Pointe-des-Galets → Le Port	157c	20.55 S	55.18 E
Pointe-du-Moulin	275a	45.22 N	73.52 W
Point Edward	214	43.00 N	82.24 W
Pointe-Noire, Congo	152	4.48 S	11.51 E
Pointe-Noire, Guad.	241o	16.14 N	61.47 W
Point Enterprise	222	31.40 N	96.26 W
Pointers	208	39.35 N	75.26 W
Point Fortin	241r	10.11 N	61.41 W
Point Hope	180	68.21 N	166.41 W
Point Imperial ∧	200	36.16 N	111.58 W
Point Independence	207	41.44 N	70.39 W
Point Lake ⊜	176	65.15 N	113.04 W
Point Leamington	186	49.20 N	55.24 W
Point Lookout, Md., U.S.	208	38.02 N	76.19 W
Point Lookout, N.Y., U.S.	276	40.35 N	73.35 W
Point Marion	188	39.44 N	79.53 W
Point McLeay	168b	35.32 S	139.06 E
Point of Rocks	208	39.16 N	77.32 W
Point O'Woods	276	40.39 N	73.08 W
Point Pass	168b	34.05 S	139.03 E
Point Pelee National Park ♦	214	41.57 N	82.30 W
Point Peninsula ≻ [1]	212	44.01 N	76.15 W
Point Pleasant, Md., U.S.	284b	39.11 N	76.35 W
Point Pleasant, N.J., U.S.	208	40.04 N	74.04 W
Point Pleasant, Oh., U.S.	218	38.54 N	84.14 W
Point Pleasant, Pa., U.S.	208	40.25 N	75.04 W
Point Pleasant, W.V., U.S.	188	38.50 N	82.08 W
Point Pleasant Beach	208	40.05 N	74.02 W
Point Reyes National Seashore ♦	204	38.00 N	122.58 W
Point Roberts	224	48.59 N	123.04 W
Point Samson	162	20.36 S	117.12 E
Point Sapin	186	46.58 N	64.50 W
Point View Reservoir ⊜ [1]	276	40.58 N	74.15 W
Point Whiteshed	180	60.28 N	145.57 W
Poirino	62	44.55 N	7.51 E
Poisevo	80	55.32 N	53.30 E
Poison Creek ≃	202	43.15 N	108.09 W
Poison Spider Creek ≃	200	42.46 N	106.31 W
Poisson Blanc, Réservoir du ⊜ [1]	188	46.00 N	75.45 W
Poissonnier Point ≻	162	19.57 S	119.11 E

PORTUGUÊS

Nome	Página	Lat.°′	Long.°′ W = Oeste
Poissons	58	48.25 N	5.13 E
Poissy	50	48.56 N	2.03 E
Poitiers	32	46.35 N	0.20 E
Poitou □ [9]	32	46.20 N	0.30 W
Poix	50	49.47 N	1.59 E
Poix-Terron	56	49.39 N	4.39 E
Pojarkovo	89	49.38 N	128.38 E
Pojma ≃	88	56.54 N	97.48 E
Pojo	248	17.45 S	64.49 W
Pojoaque Valley	200	35.59 N	106.00 W
Pojuca	255	12.21 S	38.20 W
Pojuca ≃	255	12.34 S	38.03 W
Pokagon State Park ♦	216	41.43 N	85.01 W
Pokaran	120	26.55 N	71.55 E
Pokataroo	166	29.35 S	148.42 E
Pokatejeva	88	56.59 N	97.25 E
Pokatilovka, S.S.S.R.	80	51.06 N	51.53 E
Pokatilovka, S.S.S.R.	86	45.23 N	80.10 E
Poke Run ≃	279b	40.30 N	79.33 W
Pokhara	124	28.14 N	83.59 E
Pokharia	126	23.55 N	86.37 E
Poko, Sūd.	140	5.38 N	31.50 E
Poko, Zaïre	154	3.09 N	26.53 E
Pokoinu	174k	21.12 S	159.49 W
Pokojnoje	84	44.48 N	44.16 E
Pokok Sena	114	6.10 N	100.32 E
Pokol'ubiči	76	52.30 N	31.02 E
Pokrov	82	55.55 N	39.10 E
Pokrovka, S.S.S.R.	80	48.22 N	46.04 E
Pokrovka, S.S.S.R.	80	53.47 N	53.19 E
Pokrovka, S.S.S.R.	85	42.20 N	78.01 E
Pokrovka, S.S.S.R.	85	42.45 N	71.36 E
Pokrovka, S.S.S.R.	86	54.17 N	68.15 E
Pokrovka, S.S.S.R.	86	49.28 N	81.28 E
Pokrovka, S.S.S.R.	89	43.57 N	131.39 E
Pokrovo-Kirejevo	83	47.38 N	38.16 E
Pokrovsk	74	61.29 N	129.06 E
Pokrovskaja Arčada	80	52.56 N	44.13 E
Pokrovskij	78	46.32 N	31.38 E
Pokrovskoje, S.S.S.R.	76	52.38 N	36.51 E
Pokrovskoje, S.S.S.R.	78	49.44 N	38.13 E
Pokrovskoje, S.S.S.R.	78	47.59 N	36.14 E
Pokrovskoje, S.S.S.R.	80	54.04 N	43.37 E
Pokrovskoje, S.S.S.R.	80	53.54 N	40.26 E
Pokrovskoje, S.S.S.R.	82	56.25 N	37.03 E
Pokrovskoje, S.S.S.R.	82	55.53 N	36.19 E
Pokrovskoje, S.S.S.R.	83	47.25 N	38.54 E
Pokrovskoje, S.S.S.R.	83	48.37 N	38.09 E
Pokrovskoje, S.S.S.R.	86	57.14 N	66.48 E
Pokrovskoje, S.S.S.R.	265a	59.44 N	30.46 E
Pokrovskoje ◆ [8]	265b	55.37 N	37.37 E
Pokrovsko-Strešnevo ◆ [8]	265b	55.49 N	37.29 E
Pokrovsk-Ural'skij	86	60.10 N	59.49 E
Pokur	74	61.02 N	75.26 E
Pola → Pula, Jugo.	64	44.52 N	13.50 E
Pola, Pil.	116	13.09 N	121.26 E
Pola, S.S.S.R.	76	57.56 N	31.50 E
Pola ≃	76	58.04 N	31.37 E
Pola Bay ⊂	116	13.10 N	121.28 E
Polacca	200	35.50 N	110.22 W
Polacca Wash V	200	35.22 N	110.50 W
Pola de Laviana	34	43.15 N	5.34 W
Pola de Lena	34	43.10 N	5.49 W
Pola de Siero	34	43.23 N	5.40 W
Polān	128	25.35 N	61.12 E
Polanco	252	33.54 S	55.09 W
Poland, Kiribati	174o	1.59 N	157.32 W
Poland, N.Y., U.S.	210	43.13 N	75.03 W
Poland, Oh., U.S.	214	41.01 N	80.37 W
Poland (Polska) □ [1], Europe	22	52.00 N	19.00 E
Poland (Polska) □ [1], Europe	30	52.00 N	19.00 E
Polangui	116	13.17 N	123.29 E
Polanów	30	54.08 N	16.39 E
Polapare ≃	115b	9.43 S	119.06 E
Pol'arnik	180	67.03 N	178.53 W
Pol'arnyj, S.S.S.R.	24	69.12 N	33.22 E
Pol'arnyj, S.S.S.R.	74	69.10 N	178.48 E
Pol'arnyj Ural ⩘	24	66.55 N	64.30 E
Polar Record Glacier ⌂	9	69.49 S	75.30 E
Polatlı	130	39.36 N	32.09 E
Polba	272b	22.57 N	88.18 E
Polbain	46	58.02 N	5.23 W
Polbeth	46	55.52 N	3.33 W
Polch	56	50.18 N	7.18 E
Polcirkeln	24	66.34 N	21.05 E
Polcura	252	37.17 S	71.43 W
Połczyn Zdrój	30	53.46 N	16.06 E
Polden Hills ⩘ [2]	42	51.08 N	2.50 W
Poldnevica	80	58.37 N	46.38 E
Pol'dorak	85	39.25 N	69.56 E
Poleang	112	4.42 S	121.46 E
Polebridge	182	48.45 N	114.17 W
Polecat Creek ≃	196	36.00 N	95.57 W
Poledník ∧	60	49.04 N	13.24 E
Polee, Pulau I	164	2.12 S	130.15 E
Polegate	42	50.49 N	0.15 E
Pol-e Khomrī	120	35.56 N	68.43 E
Pole Moor	262	53.39 N	1.54 W
Polen → Poland □ [1]	30	52.00 N	19.00 E
Polenezköy	267b	41.07 N	29.12 E
Pol-e Safīd	128	36.06 N	53.01 E
Polesden Lacey ⊥	260	51.15 N	0.22 W
Polesella	64	44.58 N	11.45 E
Polesine □ [9]	64	45.00 N	11.45 E
Polesine Parmense	64	45.01 N	10.04 E
Polesje	76	53.05 N	31.17 E
Polesje ◆ [1]	72	52.00 N	27.00 E
Polessk [Labiau]	76	54.52 N	21.05 E
Polesskoje	78	51.14 N	29.22 E
Polesworth	42	52.37 N	1.36 W
Polevaja	78	51.37 N	36.30 E
Polevskoj	86	56.26 N	60.11 E
Polewali	112	3.25 S	119.20 E
Polgár	30	47.52 N	21.08 E
Polgooth	42	50.19 N	4.48 W
Pŏlgyo	98	34.52 N	127.21 E
Poli, Cam.	146	8.29 N	13.15 E
Poli, Zhg.	98	35.43 N	119.47 E
Poli, Zhg.	98	35.57 N	118.17 E
Polia	68	38.45 N	16.19 E
Políaigos I	38	36.46 N	24.38 E
Policastro, Golfo di ⊂	68	40.00 N	15.30 E
Policastro Bussentino	68	40.09 N	15.32 E
Police	30	53.35 N	14.33 E
Polička	30	49.43 N	16.16 E
Policoro	68	40.13 N	16.41 E
Polignac	62	45.04 N	3.52 E
Polignano a Mare	68	41.00 N	17.13 E
Poligny	58	46.50 N	5.43 E
Polihale State Park ♦	229b	22.05 N	159.45 W
Políkastron	38	41.00 N	22.34 E
Polikhnítos	38	39.05 N	26.11 E
Polillo	116	14.43 N	121.56 E
Polillo Island I	116	14.50 N	121.57 E
Polillo Islands II	116	14.50 N	122.05 E
Polillo Strait Ʉ	116	14.44 N	121.51 E
Polinesia Francesa → French Polynesia □ [2]	14	15.00 S	140.00 W
Polinik ∧	64	46.54 N	13.09 E
Polinyá	266d	41.33 N	2.10 E
Pólis	130	35.02 N	32.25 E
Polist' ≃	76	58.06 N	31.31 E
Polistena	68	38.25 N	16.05 E
Politécnico Nacional, Instituto ʊ [2]	286a	19.30 N	99.08 W
Politotdel'skoje	83	47.33 N	39.05 E
Pölitz → Police	30	53.35 N	14.33 E
Polivanovo	80	53.36 N	47.23 E
Políyiros	38	40.23 N	23.27 E
Polizzi Generosa	70	37.49 N	14.00 E
Polizzo, Monte ∧	70	37.52 N	12.47 E
Polk, Ne., U.S.	198	41.04 N	97.47 W
Polk, Oh., U.S.	214	40.57 N	82.13 W
Polk, Pa., U.S.	214	41.22 N	79.55 W
Polk □ [6], Fl., U.S.	220	28.01 N	81.37 W
Polk □ [6], Or., U.S.	224	45.00 N	123.23 W
Polk □ [6], Tx., U.S.	222	30.45 N	94.48 W
Polk City	220	28.10 N	81.49 W
Pol'kino	74	71.10 N	99.13 E
Polkton	192	35.00 N	80.12 W
Polla	68	40.30 N	15.30 E
Pollāchi	122	10.40 N	77.01 E
Pollanten	60	49.09 N	11.28 E
Pöllau	61	47.18 N	15.51 E
Pöllauberg	61	47.19 N	15.52 E
Polleben	54	51.34 N	11.36 E
Pollenfeld	60	48.57 N	11.12 E
Pollenza	66	43.16 N	13.21 E
Pollica	68	40.11 N	15.03 E
Pollina	70	37.59 N	14.09 E
Polling	64	47.48 N	11.09 E
Pollino, Monte ∧	68	39.55 N	16.11 E
Pollnow → Polanów	30	54.08 N	16.39 E
Polloc Harbor ⊂	116	7.23 N	124.12 E
Pollock, La., U.S.	194	31.31 N	92.24 W
Pollock, S.D., U.S.	198	45.54 N	100.17 W
Pollock Pines	226	38.46 N	120.34 W
Pollock Run ≃	279b	40.14 N	79.47 W
Pollok	222	31.27 N	94.52 W
Pollutri	66	42.08 N	14.35 E
Pollux ∧	172	44.14 S	168.53 E
Polmak	24	70.04 N	28.00 E
Polmont	46	55.59 N	3.42 W
Polná	30	49.29 N	15.43 E
Polnaja ≃	83	48.54 N	39.50 E
Pol'noje-Jaltunovo	80	53.59 N	41.52 E
Polnovo-Seliger	76	57.32 N	32.55 E
Polo, Pil.	269f	14.42 N	120.57 E
Polo, Il., U.S.	190	41.59 N	89.34 W
Polo, Mo., U.S.	194	39.33 N	94.02 W
Polochic ≃	236	15.28 N	89.22 W
Polock, S.S.S.R.	76	55.31 N	28.46 E
Polock, S.S.S.R.	86	52.46 N	59.42 E
Pologi	78	47.29 N	36.15 E
Pologne → Poland □ [1]	30	52.00 N	19.00 E
Pologoje Zajmišče	80	48.29 N	45.57 E
Pologrudovo	86	57.07 N	74.13 E
Polom, S.S.S.R.	24	59.13 N	50.50 E
Polom, S.S.S.R.	80	57.47 N	53.29 E
Polo Magnético del Sur → South Magnetic Pole ◆	9	65.53 S	139.28 E
Pölömäki ∧ [2]	26	63.21 N	27.03 E
Polomet' ≃	76	57.41 N	32.12 E
Polonia → Poland □ [1]	30	52.00 N	19.00 E
Polonio, Cabo ≻	252	34.24 S	53.46 W
Polonnaruwa	122	7.56 N	81.00 E
Polonnaruwa ⊥	122	7.56 N	81.00 E
Polonnoje	78	50.07 N	27.30 E
Polos	130	41.50 N	27.04 E
Pološkovo	82	54.08 N	35.53 E
Polo Sur → South Pole ◆	9	90.00 S	0.00
Polotn'anyj	82	54.45 N	36.00 E
Polotsk → Polock	76	55.31 N	28.46 E
Polovinkino	83	49.14 N	38.55 E
Polovinnoje, S.S.S.R.	86	54.43 N	63.50 E
Polovinnoje, S.S.S.R.	86	53.46 N	79.15 E
Polovo	76	57.03 N	32.27 E
Polperro	42	50.19 N	4.31 W
Polruan	42	50.19 N	4.36 W
Pöls	61	47.11 N	14.45 E
Pölsbach ≃	61	47.11 N	14.45 E
Polska → Poland □ [1]	30	52.00 N	19.00 E
Polski Trâmbeš	38	43.22 N	25.38 E
Polson	202	47.41 N	114.09 W
Polster ∧	61	47.32 N	14.58 E
Polsum	52	51.37 N	7.03 E
Poltava	78	49.35 N	34.34 E
Poltavka	86	54.22 N	71.45 E
Poltevy Pen'ki	80	54.35 N	42.06 E
Poltimore	188	45.47 N	75.43 W
Põltsamaa	76	58.38 N	25.58 E
Põltsamaa ≃	76	58.27 N	26.09 E
Poludino	86	54.51 N	69.55 E
Poluj ≃	74	66.31 N	66.33 E
Polunočnoje	72	60.52 N	60.25 E
Polūr	122	12.30 N	79.08 E
Polur'adinki	82	54.51 N	38.41 E
Poluškino	265b	55.41 N	38.05 E
Pol'ustrovo ◆ [8]	265a	59.58 N	30.25 E
Põlva	76	58.03 N	27.03 E
Polvaredas	258	35.35 S	59.30 W
Polverigi	66	43.31 N	13.23 E
Polvijärvi	26	62.51 N	29.22 E
Polvoranca	266a	40.19 N	3.48 W
Polynesia II	14	4.00 S	156.00 W
Polynesian Cultural Center ʊ	229c	21.39 N	157.55 W
Polynésie française → French Polynesia □ [2]	14	15.00 S	140.00 W
Polynnoje	80	46.51 N	46.56 E
Polysajevo	86	54.35 N	86.14 E
Pölzig	54	50.57 N	12.11 E
Poma, Lago ⊜ [1]	70	37.55 N	13.06 E
Pomabamba	248	8.50 S	77.28 W
Pomacanchi	248	14.02 S	71.34 W
Pomahaka ≃	172	46.09 S	169.34 E
Pomarance	66	43.18 N	10.52 E
Pomarico	68	40.31 N	16.33 E
Pomarkku	26	61.42 N	22.00 E
Pomaro	234	18.20 N	103.18 W
Pomata	248	16.16 S	69.18 W
Pomáz	264c	47.39 N	19.02 E
Pomba ≃	256	21.24 S	42.32 W
Pombais, Ribeira de ≃	266c	38.48 N	9.07 W
Pombal, Bra.	250	6.46 S	37.47 W
Pombal, Port.	34	39.55 N	8.38 W
Pombas, Rio das ≃	248	6.27 S	60.18 W
Pombia	266b	45.39 N	8.38 E
Pomellen	54	53.20 N	14.23 E
Pomene	156	22.53 S	35.33 E
Pomerania □ [9]	30	54.00 N	16.00 E
Pomeranian Bay ⊂	54	54.00 N	14.15 E
Pomerene	200	31.59 N	110.17 W
Pomerode	252	26.45 S	49.11 W
Pomeroon ≃	246	7.37 N	58.45 W
Pomeroy, S. Afr.	158	28.33 S	30.26 E
Pomeroy, N. Ire., U.K.	48	54.36 N	6.55 W
Pomeroy, Ia., U.S.	198	42.33 N	94.41 W
Pomeroy, Oh., U.S.	188	39.01 N	82.02 W
Pomeroy, Pa., U.S.	208	39.58 N	75.53 W
Pomeroy, Wa., U.S.	202	46.28 N	117.36 W
Pomezia	66	41.40 N	12.30 E
Pomfret, S. Afr.	156	25.50 S	23.32 E
Pomfret, Ct., U.S.	207	41.53 N	71.57 W
Pomfret, Md., U.S.	208	38.34 N	77.01 W
Pomi	38	47.42 N	23.19 E
Pomigliano	66	40.54 N	14.23 E
Pominovo	82	55.26 N	39.11 E
Pomio	164	5.30 S	151.30 E
Pommard	58	47.01 N	4.47 E
Pomme de Terre ≃, Mn., U.S.	198	45.10 N	96.05 W
Pomme de Terre ≃, Mo., U.S.	194	38.11 N	93.24 W
Pomme de Terre Lake ⊜ [1]	194	37.51 N	93.19 W
Pommera	50	50.10 N	2.26 E
Pommern → Pomerania □ [9]	30	54.00 N	16.00 E
Pommersche Bucht → Pomeranian Bay ⊂	54	54.00 N	14.15 E
Pommersfelden	56	49.46 N	10.49 E
Pomona, Namibia	156	27.09 S	15.18 E
Pomona, Ca., U.S.	228	34.03 N	117.45 W
Pomona, Ks., U.S.	198	38.36 N	95.27 W
Pomona, N.J., U.S.	208	39.28 N	74.34 W
Pomona, N.Y., U.S.	276	41.10 N	74.02 W
Pomona College ʊ [2]	280	34.06 N	117.44 W
Pomona Estates	273d	26.06 S	28.15 E
Pomona Lake ⊜ [1]	198	38.40 N	95.35 W
Pomona Park	192	29.30 N	81.35 W
Pomongo	152	5.00 S	19.08 E
Pomor'any	78	49.38 N	24.56 E
Pomorie	38	42.33 N	27.39 E
Pomorskij proliv Ʉ	24	68.30 N	50.00 E
Pomorze → Pomerania □ [9]	30	54.00 N	16.00 E
Pomošnaja	78	48.14 N	31.26 E
Pomozdino	24	62.12 N	54.06 E
Pompano Beach	220	26.14 N	80.07 W
Pompano Beach Highlands	220	26.16 N	80.06 W
Pompei	68	40.45 N	14.30 E
Pompei ⊥	68	40.45 N	14.30 E
Pompéia	255	22.08 S	50.10 W
Pompejevka	89	48.23 N	130.46 E
Pompeston Creek ≃	285	40.01 N	75.01 W
Pompéu	255	19.12 S	44.59 W
Pompey, Fr.	56	48.46 N	6.07 E
Pompey, N.Y., U.S.	210	42.54 N	76.01 W
Pomponio Creek ≃	282	37.18 N	122.25 W
Pomponio State Beach ♦	282	37.17 N	122.24 W
Pomponne	261	48.53 N	2.41 E
Pompon-yama ∧	270	34.56 N	135.37 E
Pomposa	66	44.49 N	12.11 E
Pomposa, Abbazia di ʊ [1]	64	44.49 N	12.11 E
Pompton ≃	276	40.54 N	74.16 W
Pompton Lakes	210	41.00 N	74.17 W
Pompton Lakes ⊜	276	41.00 N	74.17 W
Pompton Plains	276	40.58 N	74.18 W
Pomquet	186	45.38 N	61.51 W
Pomssen	54	51.14 N	12.37 E
Ponape I	174r	6.55 N	158.15 E
Ponask Lake ⊜	184	54.00 N	92.41 W
Ponass Lakes ⊜	184	52.18 N	103.58 W
Ponazyrevo	80	58.21 N	46.19 E
Ponca	198	42.33 N	96.42 W
Ponca City	196	36.42 N	97.05 W
Ponca Creek ≃	198	42.48 N	98.05 W
Ponce	240m	18.01 N	66.37 W
Ponce de Leon	194	30.43 N	85.56 W
Ponce de Leon Bay ⊂	220	25.21 N	81.07 W
Ponce de Leon Inlet ⊂	192	29.04 N	80.55 W
Poncé-sur-le-Loir	50	47.46 N	0.40 E
Poncha Pass)(	200	38.25 N	106.05 W
Ponchatoula	194	30.26 N	90.26 W
Poncin	58	46.05 N	5.24 E
Poncitlán	234	20.22 N	102.55 W
Pond ≃	194	37.32 N	87.21 W
Pond Brook ≃, N.J., U.S.	276	41.02 N	74.15 W
Pond Brook ≃, Oh., U.S.	279a	41.17 N	81.24 W
Pondcreek	196	36.40 N	97.48 W
Pond Creek ≃, U.S.	196	36.40 N	97.33 W
Pond Creek ≃, Tx., U.S.	222	31.02 N	96.46 W
Pond Eddy	210	41.27 N	74.49 W
Ponder	222	33.11 N	97.17 W
Pondera Coulee V	202	48.16 N	111.03 W
Ponders End ◆ [8]	260	51.39 N	0.03 W
Pondicherry	122	11.56 N	79.53 E
Pondicherry □ [8]	122	11.56 N	79.50 E
Pond Inlet	176	72.41 N	78.00 W
Pond Inlet ⊂	176	72.46 N	77.00 W
Pondok Tanjong	114	5.00 N	100.44 E
Pondoland □ [9]	158	31.10 S	29.30 E
Pondosa	204	41.12 N	121.41 W
Pond Run ≃	285	40.13 N	74.44 W
Poneas Island I	116	9.55 N	125.57 E
Ponente, Capo ≻	70a	35.31 N	12.31 E
Ponente, Riviera di ⏏ [2]	62	44.10 N	8.20 E
Ponérihouen	175f	21.05 S	165.24 E
Poneto	216	40.39 N	85.13 W
Ponežukaj	78	44.53 N	39.22 E
Ponferrada	34	42.33 N	6.35 W
Pong	110	19.10 N	100.17 E
Pongani	164	9.05 S	148.35 E
Pongara, Pointe ≻	152	0.21 N	9.21 E
Pongaroa	172	40.33 S	176.11 E
Pongau V	64	47.21 N	13.14 E
Ponghyŏn	98	37.49 N	125.36 E
Pongo ≃	140	8.42 N	27.40 E
Pongolo ≃	158	26.57 S	32.17 E
Pon'goma	24	65.21 N	34.25 E
Pong Tamale	150	9.41 N	0.49 W
Ponhook Lake ⊜	186	44.19 N	64.53 W
Poni ≃	208	38.07 N	77.26 W
Poniatowa	30	51.11 N	22.05 E
Poniec	30	51.47 N	16.50 E
Ponil Creek ≃	196	36.29 N	104.48 W
Poninka	78	50.12 N	27.32 E
Ponino	80	58.16 N	52.49 E
Pönitz, B.R.D.	54	54.03 N	10.40 E
Ponitz, D.D.R.	54	50.51 N	12.25 E
Ponizovje	76	55.17 N	31.04 E
Ponkapog Pond ⊜	283	42.12 N	71.06 W
Pônley	110	12.26 N	104.27 E
Ponnaiyār ≃	122	11.46 N	79.47 E
Ponnāni	122	10.46 N	75.54 E
Ponnūru Nidubrolu	122	16.04 N	80.34 E
Pono	164	6.22 S	134.36 E
Ponoj	24	67.05 N	41.07 E
Ponoj ≃	24	66.59 N	41.17 E
Ponoka	182	52.42 N	113.35 W
Ponomar'ovka, S.S.S.R.	80	53.19 N	54.08 E
Ponomar'ovka, S.S.S.R.	86	56.08 N	82.23 E
Ponornica	78	51.43 N	32.49 E
Ponorogo	115a	7.52 S	111.27 E
Ponpāj	272b	22.56 N	88.15 E
Pons, Esp.	34	41.55 N	1.12 E
Pons, Fr.	32	45.35 N	0.33 W
Ponsacco	66	43.37 N	10.38 E
Ponson Island I	116	10.46 N	124.32 E
Ponsul ≃	34	39.40 N	7.31 W
Pont	62	45.34 N	7.07 E
Pont-à-Celles	50	50.30 N	4.21 E
Ponta Delgada	148a	37.44 N	25.40 W
Ponta Delgada □ [5]	148a	37.40 N	25.30 W
Ponta de Pedras	250	1.23 S	48.52 W
Ponta Grossa	252	25.05 S	50.09 W
Pontal ≃	250	9.08 S	40.12 W
Pontalete	256	21.27 S	45.40 W
Pontalina	255	17.31 S	49.27 W
Pontallier-sur-Saône	58	47.18 N	5.25 E
Pont-à-Marcq	50	50.31 N	3.07 E
Pont-à-Mousson	56	48.54 N	6.04 E
Pontão	34	39.55 N	8.22 W
Ponta Porã	255	22.32 S	55.43 W
Pontardawe	42	51.44 N	3.51 W
Pontardulais	42	51.43 N	4.03 W
Pontarlier	58	46.54 N	6.22 E
Pontas de Pedra	250	7.38 S	34.48 W
Pontassieve	66	43.46 N	11.26 E
Pontaubert	50	47.29 N	3.52 E
Pont-Audemer	50	49.21 N	0.31 E
Pontault-Combault	261	48.47 N	2.36 E
Pontaumur	32	45.52 N	2.40 E
Pont-Aven	32	47.51 N	3.45 W
Pontbriand	206	46.09 N	71.15 W
Pont Canavese	62	45.25 N	7.36 E
Pontcarré	261	48.48 N	2.42 E
Pontcharra	62	45.26 N	6.01 E
Pontchartrain	261	48.48 N	1.54 E
Pontchartrain, Lake ⊜	194	30.10 N	90.10 W
Pontchâteau	32	47.26 N	2.05 W
Pont-Croix	32	48.02 N	4.29 W
Pont-d'Ain	58	46.03 N	5.20 E
Pont d'Arc ♦	62	44.23 N	4.26 E
Pont-de-Bonne	56	50.27 N	5.17 E
Pont-de-Chéruy	62	45.45 N	5.11 E
Pont-de-l'Arche	50	49.18 N	1.10 E
Pont-de-Pany	58	47.18 N	4.49 E
Pont-de-Poitte	58	46.35 N	5.41 E
Pont-de-Roide	58	47.23 N	6.46 E
Pont-de-Ruan	50	47.15 N	0.35 E
Pont-de-Salars	32	44.17 N	2.44 E
Pont de Suert	34	42.24 N	0.45 E
Pont-de-Vaux	58	46.26 N	4.56 E
Pont-de-Veyle	58	46.16 N	4.53 E
Ponte a Elsa	66	43.41 N	10.54 E
Ponte Alta	256	22.26 S	47.06 W
Ponte Alta do Bom Jesus	255	12.06 S	46.29 W
Ponte Alta do Norte	250	10.45 S	47.34 W
Ponte a Moriano	66	43.54 N	10.31 E
Pontebba	64	46.30 N	13.18 E
Ponte Branca	255	16.27 S	52.40 W
Ponte Caffaro	64	45.50 N	10.32 E
Pontecagnano	68	40.39 N	14.52 E
Pontecchio Marconi	64	44.25 N	11.15 E
Pontecchio Polesine	64	45.01 N	11.49 E
Pontecorvo	66	41.27 N	13.40 E
Pontecurone	62	44.57 N	8.56 E
Ponte da Barca	34	41.48 N	8.25 W
Ponte d'Arbia	66	43.10 N	11.28 E
Ponte delle Arche	64	46.02 N	10.52 E
Ponte dell'Olio	62	44.52 N	9.39 E
Pontedera	66	43.40 N	10.38 E
Ponte de Sor	34	39.15 N	8.01 W
Ponte di Barbarano	64	45.23 N	11.34 E
Ponte di Legno	64	46.16 N	10.31 E
Ponte di Nava	62	44.08 N	7.53 E
Ponte di Piave	64	45.43 N	12.28 E
Ponte do Lima	34	41.46 N	8.35 W
Ponte do Púngoè	156	19.30 S	34.32 E
Pontefract	44	53.42 N	1.18 W
Ponte Galeria ◆ [8]	267a	41.49 N	12.21 E
Ponte Gardena (Waidbruck)	64	46.36 N	11.32 E
Ponte Ghiereto	66	43.59 N	11.15 E
Pontegrande	58	45.59 N	8.09 E
Ponte in Valtellina	64	46.12 N	9.59 E
Ponteix	184	49.45 N	107.29 W
Pontelagoscuro	64	44.53 N	11.36 E
Ponteland	44	55.03 N	1.44 W
Pontelandolfo	68	41.17 N	14.41 E
Pontelongo	64	45.15 N	12.02 E
Ponte nell'Alpi	64	46.11 N	12.16 E
Ponte Nova	255	20.24 S	42.54 W
Pont-en-Royans	62	45.04 N	5.21 E
Ponte Nuovo	66	43.01 N	12.28 E
Pontenure	62	44.59 N	9.47 E
Pontepetri	66	44.02 N	10.53 E
Pontericcioli	66	43.26 N	12.38 E
Ponte Rocchetta	64	46.14 N	11.04 E
Ponterwyd	42	52.25 N	3.50 W
Pontes	256	22.26 S	46.28 W
Ponte San Giovanni	66	43.05 N	12.26 E
Ponte San Pietro	62	45.42 N	9.35 E
Pontesbury	42	52.39 N	2.54 W
Ponte Selva	64	45.52 N	9.54 E
Ponte Serrada	252	26.52 S	51.58 W
Pontestura	62	45.08 N	8.20 E
Ponte Tresa	58	45.58 N	8.52 E
Pontevedra, Arg.	258	34.45 S	58.42 W
Pontevedra, Esp.	34	42.26 N	8.38 W
Pontevedra, Pil.	116	10.22 N	122.52 E
Pontevedra, Ría de ⊂ [1]	34	42.22 N	8.45 W
Ponte Vedra Beach	192	30.14 N	81.23 W
Pont-Évêque	62	45.32 N	4.55 E
Pontevico	64	45.16 N	10.05 E
Pontfaverger-Moronvilliers	50	49.18 N	4.19 E
Pontgibaud	32	45.50 N	2.52 E
Ponthévrard	261	48.33 N	1.55 E
Ponthierry	261	48.32 N	2.33 E
Ponthierville → Ubundu	154	0.21 S	25.29 E
Pontiac, Il., U.S.	216	40.52 N	88.37 W
Pontiac, Mi., U.S.	216	42.38 N	83.17 W
Pontiac □ [6]	212	46.30 N	77.00 W
Pontiac Lake	281	42.40 N	83.28 W
Pontiac Lake ⊜	281	42.40 N	83.28 W
Pontiac Lake State Recreation Area ♦	216	42.41 N	83.28 W
Pontiac Mall ◆ [9]	281	42.39 N	83.20 W
Pontiac State Recreation Area ♦	281	42.41 N	83.28 W
Pontianak	112	0.02 S	109.20 E
Pontian Kechil	114	1.29 N	103.23 E
Pontida	62	45.43 N	9.30 E
Pontigny	50	47.55 N	3.43 E
Pontinha ◆ [8]	266c	38.46 N	9.11 W
Pontinia	66	41.24 N	13.02 E
Pontivy	32	48.04 N	2.59 W
Pont-l'Abbé	32	47.52 N	4.13 W
Pont-lès-Moulins	58	47.19 N	6.22 E
Pont-L'Évêque	50	49.18 N	0.11 E
Pontlevoy	50	47.23 N	1.15 E
Pontoise	50	49.03 N	2.06 E
Pontoise-Corneilles-en-Vexin, Aérodrome ⊠	261	49.06 N	2.02 E
Ponton Creek ≃	162	31.10 S	124.25 E
Pontonnyj	265a	59.47 N	30.38 E
Pontoon Beach	219	38.43 N	90.04 W
Pontorson	32	48.33 N	1.31 W
Pontotoc, Ms., U.S.	194	34.14 N	88.59 W
Pontotoc, Tx., U.S.	196	30.54 N	98.59 W
Pontremoli	62	44.22 N	9.53 E
Pont-Remy	50	50.03 N	1.55 E
Pontresina	58	46.28 N	9.53 E
Pontrhydfendigaid	42	52.17 N	3.51 W
Pont-Rouge	206	46.45 N	71.42 W
Pont-Royal	62	43.43 N	5.11 E
Pont-Sainte-Marie	50	48.19 N	4.06 E
Pont-Sainte-Maxence	50	49.18 N	2.36 E
Pont-Saint-Esprit	62	44.15 N	4.39 E
Pont-Saint-Martin	62	45.36 N	7.48 E
Pont-Scorff	28	47.50 N	3.24 W
Ponts Quentin, Ruisseau des ≃	261	48.44 N	1.48 E
Pont-sur-Yonne	50	48.17 N	3.12 E
Pontuda, Ilha I	287a	23.02 S	43.18 W
Pontus □ [9]	130	40.15 N	38.00 E
Pontvallain	50	47.45 N	0.12 E
Pont-Viau ◆ [8]	275a	45.34 N	73.41 W
Pontyberem	42	51.17 N	4.09 W
Pontycymer	42	51.37 N	3.34 W
Pontypool	42	51.43 N	3.02 W
Pontypridd	42	51.37 N	3.22 W
Pony	202	45.39 N	111.53 W
Ponyri	76	52.19 N	36.20 E
Ponza	66	40.54 N	12.58 E
Ponza, Isola di I	66	40.55 N	12.57 E
Ponziane, Isole II	66	40.55 N	12.57 E
Ponzone	62	44.35 N	8.27 E
Poochera	162	32.43 S	134.51 E
Pool □ [5]	152	3.30 S	15.00 E
Poole	42	50.43 N	1.59 W
Poole, Mount ∧	166	29.37 S	141.46 E
Poole Bay ⊂	42	50.42 N	1.52 W
Pooler	192	32.06 N	81.14 W
Poole's Cavern ⏏ [5]	262	53.14 N	1.56 W
Pooles Island I	208	39.17 N	76.16 W
Poolesville	208	39.08 N	77.25 W
Poolewe	46	57.45 N	5.37 W
Pooley Island I	182	52.44 N	128.16 W
Pool's Cove	186	47.41 N	55.26 W
Poolville	222	32.58 N	97.52 W
Poona → Pune	122	18.32 N	73.52 E
Poona-Bayabo	116	7.51 N	124.22 E
Pooncarie	166	33.23 S	142.34 E

≃ River	Fluss	Río	Rivière	Rio
≅ Canal	Kanal	Canal	Canal	Canal
∟ Waterfall, Rapids	Wasserfall, Stromschnellen	Cascada, Rápidos	Chute d'eau, Rapides	Cascata, Rápidos
Ʉ Strait	Meeresstrasse	Estrecho	Détroit	Estreito
⊂ Bay, Gulf	Bucht, Golf	Bahía, Golfo	Baie, Golfe	Baía, Golfo
⊜ Lake, Lakes	See, Seen	Lago, Lagos	Lac, Lacs	Lago, Lagos
≡ Swamp	Sumpf	Pantano	Marais	Pântano
⌂ Ice Features, Glacier	Eis- und Gletscherformen	Accidentes Glaciales	Formes glaciaires	Acidentes glaciares
⊤ Other Hydrographic Features	Andere Hydrographische Objekte	Otros Elementos Hidrográficos	Autres données hydrographiques	Outros acidentes hidrográficos

✦ Submarine Features	Untermeerische Objekte	Accidentes Submarinos	Formes de relief sous-marin	Acidentes submarinos
□ Political Unit	Politische Einheit	Unidad Politica	Entité politique	Unidade política
ʊ Cultural Institution	Kulturelle Institution	Institución Cultural	Institution culturelle	Institução cultural
⊥ Historical Site	Historische Stätte	Sitio Histórico	Site historique	Sitio histórico
♦ Recreational Site	Erholungs- und Ferienort	Sitio de Recreo	Centre de loisirs	Area de Lazer
⊠ Airport	Flughafen	Aeropuerto	Aéroport	Aeroporto
■ Military Installation	Militäranlage	Instalación Militar	Installation militaire	Instalação militar
◆ Miscellaneous	Verschiedenes	Misceláneo	Divers	Diversos

ENGLISH
Name Page Lat.°' Long.°'

DEUTSCH
Name Seite Breite°' Länge°' E = Ost

Symbols in the index entries represent the broad categories identified in the key at the right. Symbols with superior numbers (ʌ[1]) identify subcategories (see complete key on page I · 1).

Kartensymbole in dem Registerverzeichnis stellen die rechts in Schlüssel erklärten Kategorien dar. Symbole mit hochgestellten Ziffern (ʌ[1]) bezeichnen Unterabteilungen einer Kategorie (vgl. vollständiger Schlüssel auf Seite I · 1).

Los símbolos incluídos en el texto del índice representan las grandes categorías identificadas con la clave a la derecha. Los símbolos con numeros en su parte superior (ʌ[1]) identifican las subcategorías (véase la clave completa en la página I · 1).

Les symboles de l'index représentent les catégories indiquées dans la légende à droite. Les symboles suivis d'un indice (ʌ[1]) représentent des sous-catégories (voir légende complète à la page I · 1).

Os símbolos incluídos no texto do índice representam as grandes categorias identificadas com a chave à direita. Os símbolos com números em sua parte superior (ʌ[1]) identificam as subcategorias (veja-se a chave completa à página I · 1).

ʌ Mountain	Berg	Montaña	Montagne	Montanha
ʌ Mountains	Berge	Montañas	Montagnes	Montanhas
)(Pass	Pass	Paso	Col	Passo
V Valley, Canyon	Tal, Cañon	Valle, Cañón	Vallée, Canyon	Vale, Canhão
≡ Plain	Ebene	Llano	Plaine	Planície
> Cape	Kap	Cabo	Cap	Cabo
I Island	Insel	Isla	Île	Ilha
II Islands	Inseln	Islas	Îles	Ilhas
♦ Other Topographic Features	Andere Topographische Objekte	Otros Elementos Topográficos	Autres données topographiques	Outros acidentes topográficos

ESPAÑOL — Nombre | Página | Lat.°′ | Long.°′ W = Oeste

FRANÇAIS — Nom | Page | Lat.°′ | Long.°′ W = Ouest

PORTUGUÊS — Nome | Página | Lat.°′ | Long.°′ W = Oeste

Nombre	Página	Lat.°′	Long.°′ W = Oeste
Poverennyj	**80**	46.45 N	43.12 E
Poverty Bay ⊂	**172**	38.42 S	177.58 E
Povetkino	**82**	54.20 N	38.23 E
Poviglio	**64**	44.51 N	10.32 E
Povljen ⋏	**38**	43.55 N	19.30 E
Póvoa, Mouchão da I	**266c**	38.51 N	9.03 W
Povoação	**148a**	37.45 N	25.15 W
Póvoa de Santa Iria	**266c**	38.52 N	9.04 W
Póvoa de Santo Adrião	**266c**	38.48 N	9.10 W
Póvoa de Varzim	**34**	41.23 N	8.46 W
Povorino	**80**	51.12 N	42.14 E
Povorotnyj, mys ›	**89**	42.42 N	133.04 E
Povorsk	**78**	51.16 N	25.07 E
Povrly	**54**	50.40 N	14.10 E
Povungnituk	**176**	60.02 N	77.10 W
Povungnituk, Rivière de ≃	**176**	60.03 N	77.15 W
Powassan	**190**	46.05 N	79.22 W
Poway	**228**	32.57 N	117.02 W
Powder ≃, U.S.	**178**	46.44 N	105.26 W
Powder ≃, Or., U.S.	**202**	44.45 N	117.03 W
Powder, Dry Fork ≃	**200**	43.47 N	106.15 W
Powder, Middle Fork ≃	**200**	43.42 N	106.33 W
Powder, North Fork ≃	**202**	43.42 N	106.33 W
Powder, Red Fork ≃	**202**	43.39 N	106.47 W
Powder, South Fork ≃	**202**	43.40 N	106.30 W
Powder Horn Lake ⊜	**278**	41.38 N	87.32 W
Powderly, Ky., U.S.	**194**	37.09 N	87.10 W
Powderly, Tx., U.S.	**196**	33.49 N	95.31 W
Powdermaker Ditch ≍	**279a**	41.30 N	82.02 W
Powder Mill Village	**284c**	39.03 N	76.57 W
Powder River Pass)(	**202**	44.09 N	107.04 W
Powell, Oh., U.S.	**214**	40.09 N	83.05 W
Powell, Pa., U.S.	**210**	41.42 N	76.31 W
Powell, Tx., U.S.	**222**	32.07 N	96.20 W
Powell, Wy., U.S.	**202**	44.45 N	108.45 W
Powell ≃	**192**	36.29 N	83.42 W
Powell, Lake ⊜ [1]	**200**	37.25 N	110.45 W
Powell, Mount ∧	**200**	39.46 N	106.20 W
Powell Creek ≃, Austl.	**166**	25.02 S	143.40 E
Powell Creek ≃, Oh., U.S.	**216**	41.17 N	84.21 W
Powellhurst	**224**	45.30 N	122.32 W
Powell Lake ⊜	**182**	50.11 N	124.24 W
Powell River	**182**	49.52 N	124.33 W
Powells Valley	**208**	40.26 N	76.56 W
Powellton	**188**	38.05 N	81.19 W
Powellville	**208**	38.19 N	75.22 W
Powers, Mi., U.S.	**190**	45.41 N	87.31 W
Powers, Or., U.S.	**202**	42.53 N	124.04 W
Powers Lake, N.D., U.S.	**198**	48.33 N	102.38 W
Powers Lake, Wi., U.S.	**216**	42.33 N	88.17 W
Powers Lookout ♠	**169**	36.50 S	146.22 E
Powhatan, La., U.S.	**194**	31.52 N	93.12 W
Powhatan, Va., U.S.	**192**	37.32 N	77.55 W
Powhatan Mill	**284b**	39.20 N	76.43 W
Powhatan Point	**188**	39.51 N	80.48 W
Powis, Vale of ∨	**42**	52.38 N	3.08 W
Powissett Brook ≃	**283**	42.16 N	71.14 W
Powlett ≃	**169**	38.35 S	145.32 E
Pownal	**210**	42.45 N	73.14 W
Powys □ [6]	**42**	52.17 N	3.20 W
Poxoréu	**255**	15.50 S	54.23 W
Poya	**175f**	21.19 S	165.07 E
Poyang Hu ⊜	**100**	29.00 N	116.25 E
Poyen	**194**	34.19 N	92.38 W
Poygan, Lake ⊜	**190**	44.09 N	88.50 W
Poyle	**260**	51.28 N	0.31 W
Poynette	**190**	43.23 N	89.24 W
Poynor	**222**	32.04 N	95.36 W
Poynton, Eng., U.K.	**44**	53.21 N	2.07 W
Poyntzpass	**48**	54.18 N	6.23 W
Poyraz	**267b**	41.12 N	29.07 E
Poyraz Burnu ›	**267b**	41.12 N	29.09 E
Poysdorf	**61**	48.40 N	16.38 E
Poza Grande	**232**	25.50 N	112.05 W
Pozantı	**130**	37.25 N	34.52 E
Požarevac	**38**	44.37 N	21.11 E
Poza Rica de Hidalgo	**234**	20.33 N	97.27 W
Požarskoje	**89**	46.16 N	134.04 E
Pozdejevka	**89**	50.36 N	128.56 E
Požega	**38**	43.50 N	20.02 E
Poznań	**30**	52.25 N	16.55 E
Poznań □ [4]	**30**	52.20 N	16.55 E
Pozo Alcón	**34**	37.42 N	2.56 W
Pozo Almonte	**248**	20.16 S	69.48 W
Pozoblanco	**34**	38.22 N	4.51 W
Pozo-Cañada	**34**	38.48 N	1.45 W
Pozo Colorado	**252**	23.28 S	58.51 W
Pozo del Molle	**252**	32.02 S	62.55 W
Pozo del Tigre	**252**	24.54 S	60.19 W
Pozo Hondo	**252**	27.10 S	64.30 W
Pozos	**234**	21.14 N	100.29 W
Pozos, Arroyo de los ≃	**288**	34.57 S	58.45 W
Pozos, Punta ›	**254**	47.57 S	65.47 W
Pozsony → Bratislava	**30**	48.09 N	17.07 E
Pozuelo de Alarcón	**34**	40.26 N	3.49 W
Pozuelo de Alarcón ◆ [8]	**266a**	40.26 N	3.49 W
Pozuelos	**246**	10.11 N	64.39 W
Pozuelos, Laguna de ⊜	**252**	22.22 S	66.01 W
Pozuzo	**248**	10.04 S	75.32 W
Pozuzo ≃	**248**	9.52 S	75.12 W
Požva	**86**	59.05 N	56.05 E
Pozzallo	**70**	36.43 N	14.51 E
Pozzillo, Lago di ⊜	**70**	37.40 N	14.35 E
Pozzolo Formigaro	**62**	44.48 N	8.47 E
Pozzomaggiore	**71**	40.24 N	8.39 E
Pozzuoli	**68**	40.49 N	14.07 E
Pozzuolo del Friuli	**64**	45.59 N	13.12 E
Pra ≃, Ghana	**150**	5.01 N	1.37 W
Pra ≃, S.S.S.R.	**80**	54.45 N	41.01 E
Prabuty	**30**	53.46 N	19.10 E
Pracai ≃	**250**	2.26 S	51.19 W
Praça Sêca ◆ [8]	**287a**	22.54 S	43.21 W
Prachantakham	**110**	14.04 N	101.31 E
Prachatice	**30**	49.01 N	14.00 E
Prachin Buri	**110**	14.03 N	101.22 E
Prachuap Khiri Khan	**110**	11.49 N	99.48 E
Prackenbach	**60**	49.06 N	12.50 E
Pracupi ≃	**250**	2.06 S	51.30 W
Pradelles	**62**	44.46 N	3.53 E
Pradera	**246**	3.25 N	76.15 W
Prades	**32**	42.37 N	2.26 E
Pradleves	**62**	44.25 N	7.17 E
Prado	**255**	17.21 S	39.13 W
Prado, Museo del ♥	**266a**	40.25 N	3.41 W
Prado Dam ◆ [6]	**280**	33.54 N	117.39 W
Prado Flood Control Basin ≚ [1]	**280**	33.54 N	117.38 W
Prados	**255**	21.03 S	44.05 W
Pr'adovka	**78**	48.55 N	34.41 E
Prads	**62**	44.13 N	6.27 E
Præstø	**41**	55.07 N	12.03 E
Prag → Praha	**54**	50.05 N	14.26 E
Praga → Praha	**54**	50.05 N	14.26 E
Pragelato	**62**	45.01 N	6.57 E
Pragersko	**61**	46.23 N	15.40 E
Praglia, Monastero di ♥ [1]	**64**	45.23 N	11.45 E
Prägraten	**64**	47.01 N	12.23 E
Prague → Praha, Česko.	**54**	50.05 N	14.26 E
Prague, Ne., U.S.	**198**	41.18 N	96.48 W
Prague, Ok., U.S.	**196**	35.29 N	96.41 W
Praha (Prague)	**54**	50.05 N	14.26 E
Praha ∧	**60**	49.40 N	13.49 E
Prahova □ [6]	**38**	45.00 N	26.00 E
Prahova ≃	**38**	44.43 N	26.27 E
Prahran	**274b**	37.51 S	144.59 E
Praia	**150a**	14.55 N	23.31 W
Praia a Mare	**68**	39.54 N	15.47 E
Praia da Cruz Quebrada	**266c**	38.42 N	9.14 W
Praia das Maçãs	**266c**	38.50 N	9.28 W
Praia da Vitória	**148a**	38.44 N	27.04 W
Praia de Araçatiba	**256**	23.06 S	44.15 W
Praia Funda, Ponta da ›	**287a**	23.05 S	43.33 W
Praia Grande, Bra.	**252**	29.12 S	49.57 W
Praia Grande, Bra.	**256**	24.01 S	46.25 W
Praiano	**68**	40.37 N	14.32 E
Praikalogu	**115b**	9.45 S	119.25 E
Prainha, Bra.	**248**	7.16 S	60.23 W
Prainha, Bra.	**250**	1.48 S	53.29 W
Prairie	**166**	20.52 S	144.36 E
Prairie ≃, Mi., U.S.	**216**	41.55 N	85.38 W
Prairie ≃, Mn., U.S.	**190**	47.18 N	93.29 W
Prairie ≃, Wi., U.S.	**190**	45.10 N	89.42 W
Prairie City, Il., U.S.	**190**	40.37 N	90.28 W
Prairie City, Ia., U.S.	**190**	41.35 N	93.14 W
Prairie City, Or., U.S.	**202**	44.27 N	118.42 W
Prairie Creek ≃, Fl., U.S.	**220**	26.59 N	81.56 W
Prairie Creek ≃, Il., U.S.	**216**	41.21 N	88.12 W
Prairie Creek ≃, Il., U.S.	**216**	40.55 N	87.49 W
Prairie Creek ≃, Il., U.S.	**278**	41.36 N	87.40 W
Prairie Creek ≃, Mi., U.S.	**216**	42.59 N	85.01 W
Prairie Creek ≃, Ne., U.S.	**198**	41.22 N	97.32 W
Prairie Creek Reservoir ⊜ [1]	**218**	40.08 N	85.17 W
Prairie Dog Creek ≃	**198**	40.00 N	99.23 W
Prairie du Chien	**190**	43.03 N	91.08 W
Prairie du Sac	**190**	43.17 N	89.43 W
Prairie Elk Creek ≃	**198**	48.00 N	105.51 W
Prairie Grove	**194**	35.58 N	94.19 W
Prairie Hill	**222**	31.39 N	96.47 W
Prairie Lea	**222**	29.44 N	97.45 W
Prairie River	**184**	52.52 N	103.00 W
Prairies, Coteau des ⋏ [2]	**198**	44.30 N	96.45 W
Prairies, Lake of the ⊜ [1]	**184**	51.05 N	101.25 W
Prairies, Rivière des ≃	**275a**	45.42 N	73.29 W
Prairie View, Il., U.S.	**278**	42.12 N	87.57 W
Prairie View, Tx., U.S.	**222**	30.05 N	95.59 W
Prairie Village	**198**	38.59 N	94.38 W
Prajekan	**115a**	7.47 S	113.59 E
Prakhon Chai	**110**	14.37 N	103.05 E
Pralboino	**64**	45.16 N	10.13 E
Prali	**62**	44.54 N	7.03 E
Pralls Island I	**276**	40.37 N	74.12 W
Pralognan-la-Vanoise	**62**	45.23 N	6.43 E
Pram	**60**	48.14 N	13.37 E
Pram ≃	**60**	48.28 N	13.26 E
Pramaggiore, Monte ∧	**64**	46.22 N	12.33 E
Prambachkirchen	**60**	48.19 N	13.55 E
Prambanan	**115a**	7.45 S	110.30 E
Pr'amicyno	**78**	51.39 N	35.56 E
Pramort	**54**	54.26 N	12.55 E
Prampram	**150**	5.42 N	0.07 E
Pran Buri	**110**	12.23 N	99.55 E
Pran Buri ≃	**110**	12.24 N	100.00 E
Prang	**150**	7.59 N	0.53 W
Prangli I	**76**	59.38 N	25.02 E
Pranzo	**64**	45.55 N	10.48 E
Prapa, Khlong ≍	**269a**	13.46 N	100.32 E
Prapat	**114**	2.40 N	98.56 E
Praraye	**58**	45.55 N	7.32 E
Prärien → Great Plains ≚	**16**	42.00 N	100.00 W
Praskoveja	**84**	44.43 N	44.12 E
Praskovejevka	**83**	48.40 N	38.00 E
Praslin, Lac ⊜	**186**	50.03 N	69.48 W
Praslin, Port ⊂	**241f**	13.53 N	60.54 W
Praslin Island I	**138**	4.19 S	55.44 E
Prasonísi, Ákra ›	**38**	35.42 N	27.46 E
Praszka	**30**	51.04 N	18.26 E
Prat, Isla I	**254**	48.15 S	75.00 W
Prata, Bra.	**250**	7.41 S	37.06 W
Prata, Bra.	**255**	19.18 S	48.55 W
Prata, Bra.	**287a**	22.45 S	43.25 W
Prata, Rio da ≃, Bra.	**255**	17.28 S	46.35 W
Prata, Rio da ≃, Bra.	**255**	18.49 S	49.54 W
Prata, Rio da ≃, Bra.	**255**	18.50 S	52.11 W
Prata, Rio da ≃, Bra.	**287a**	22.56 S	43.34 W
Pratāpgarh	**120**	24.02 N	74.47 E
Pratapgarh □ [5]	**124**	25.55 N	82.00 E
Pratāpnagar	**126**	22.23 N	89.13 E
Pratápolis	**255**	20.45 S	46.52 W
Pratas Island → Tungsha Tao I	**90**	20.42 N	116.43 E
Pratau	**54**	51.50 N	12.38 E
Prat de Llobregat	**34**	41.20 N	2.06 E
Pratella	**68**	41.24 N	14.11 E
Prater ♠	**264b**	48.12 N	16.25 E
Prathet Thai → Thailand □ [1]	**110**	15.00 N	100.00 E
Pratinha	**255**	19.46 S	46.24 W
Prato	**66**	43.53 N	11.06 E
Prato allo Stelvio	**64**	46.37 N	10.35 E
Pratola Peligna	**66**	42.06 N	13.52 E
Pratola Serra	**68**	40.59 N	14.51 E
Pratolino	**66**	43.52 N	11.18 E
Pratomagno ⋏	**66**	43.39 N	11.39 E
Pratt	**198**	37.38 N	98.44 W
Pratteln	**58**	47.31 N	7.42 E
Prättigau ∨	**58**	46.55 N	9.45 E
Pratt's Bottom ◆ [8]	**260**	51.20 N	0.07 E
Prattsburg	**210**	42.31 N	77.17 W
Prattsville	**210**	42.18 N	74.26 W
Prattville	**194**	32.27 N	86.27 W
Pratudão ≃	**255**	13.56 S	44.55 W
Prauthoy	**58**	47.40 N	5.17 E
Pravaja Mama ≃	**88**	57.10 N	111.54 E
Pravda	**89**	47.00 N	142.01 E
Pravdinsk, S.S.S.R.	**76**	54.27 N	21.01 E
Pravdinsk, S.S.S.R.	**80**	56.32 N	43.34 E
Pravdinskij	**82**	56.04 N	37.51 E
Pravia	**34**	43.29 N	6.07 W
Prawet Buri Rom, Khlong ≍	**269a**	13.42 N	100.35 E
Prawle Point ›	**42**	50.13 N	3.42 W
Praya	**115b**	8.42 S	116.17 E
Pr'aža	**24**	61.42 N	33.35 E
Praz-sur-Arly	**62**	45.50 N	6.34 E
Prazzo	**62**	44.29 N	7.03 E
Preakness Brook ≃	**276**	40.54 N	74.15 W
Preakness Mountain ∧	**276**	40.58 N	74.13 W
Preakness Valley Park ♠	**276**	40.55 N	74.14 W
Preble, In., U.S.	**216**	40.50 N	85.01 W
Preble, N.Y., U.S.	**210**	42.44 N	76.09 W
Preble □ [6]	**218**	39.45 N	84.38 W
Preci	**66**	42.53 N	13.02 E
Prečistoje, S.S.S.R.	**76**	55.41 N	34.56 E
Prečistoje, S.S.S.R.	**76**	55.31 N	32.22 E
Prečistoje, S.S.S.R.	**80**	58.27 N	40.19 E
Précy-sous-Thil	**50**	47.23 N	4.19 E
Précy-sur-Marne	**261**	48.56 N	2.47 E
Précy-sur-Oise	**50**	49.12 N	2.22 E
Preda	**58**	46.36 N	9.46 E
Predappio	**66**	44.06 N	11.58 E
Predazzo	**64**	46.19 N	11.36 E
Predeal	**38**	45.30 N	25.35 E
Prédecelle ≃	**261**	48.35 N	2.07 E
Predeşti	**38**	44.21 N	23.36 E
Predgornoje	**86**	47.10 N	81.02 E
Predigtstuhl ∧	**61**	48.48 N	15.22 E
Předin	**61**	49.12 N	15.40 E
Predivinsk	**86**	57.04 N	93.27 E
Predlitz	**64**	47.04 N	13.55 E
Predmostnoje	**78**	45.57 N	34.37 E
Predoi (Prettau)	**64**	47.02 N	12.06 E
Predore	**64**	45.40 N	10.01 E
Preeceville	**184**	51.58 N	102.40 W
Pré-en-Pail	**32**	48.27 N	0.12 W
Preesall	**44**	53.55 N	2.58 W
Preetz	**54**	54.14 N	10.16 E
Pregarten	**61**	48.21 N	14.32 E
Pregel → Pregol'a ≃	**76**	54.41 N	20.22 E
Pregnana	**266b**	45.31 N	9.00 E
Pregol'a ≃	**76**	54.41 N	20.22 E
Pregonero	**246**	8.01 N	71.46 W
Pregos	**256**	21.46 S	42.54 W
Pregradnaja	**84**	43.58 N	41.12 E
Pregradnoje	**80**	45.49 N	41.45 E
Preguiças ≃	**250**	2.34 S	42.44 W
Preila	**76**	55.22 N	21.04 E
Preiļi	**76**	56.18 N	26.43 E
Preissac, Lac ⊜	**190**	48.20 N	78.20 W
Prekestolen ♠	**26**	59.00 N	6.01 E
Preko	**36**	44.05 N	15.11 E
Prekomurje ◆ [1]	**61**	46.40 N	16.10 E
Prěk Poŭthĭ	**110**	11.51 N	105.07 E
Prelate	**184**	50.51 N	109.23 W
Přelouč	**30**	50.02 N	15.34 E
Premana	**58**	46.03 N	9.25 E
Prembun	**115a**	7.43 S	109.48 E
Prémery	**50**	47.10 N	3.20 E
Premiá de Mar	**266d**	41.29 N	2.21 E
Premnitz	**54**	52.32 N	12.19 E
Prémont, P.Q., Can.	**206**	46.22 N	73.03 W
Premont, Tx., U.S.	**196**	27.21 N	98.07 W
Prémontré	**50**	49.33 N	3.24 E
Premosello	**58**	46.00 N	8.20 E
Premuda, Otok I	**36**	44.20 N	14.37 E
Prenestini, Monti ⋏	**66**	41.50 N	12.55 E
Prenjas	**38**	41.04 N	20.32 E
Prentice	**190**	45.32 N	90.17 W
Prentiss	**194**	31.35 N	89.52 W
Prenton	**262**	53.22 N	3.03 W
Prenzlau	**54**	53.19 N	13.52 E
Prenzlauer Berg ◆ [8]	**264a**	52.32 N	13.26 E
Preobraženije	**89**	42.57 N	133.55 E
Preobražennoje	**83**	49.32 N	38.10 E
Preobraženovka	**89**	48.04 N	131.55 E
Preparis Island I	**110**	14.52 N	93.41 E
Preparis North Channel Ʊ	**110**	15.27 N	94.05 E
Preparis South Channel Ʊ	**110**	14.40 N	94.00 E
Přerov	**30**	49.27 N	17.27 E
Prerow	**54**	54.26 N	12.35 E
Pré-Saint-Didier	**62**	45.46 N	6.59 E
Presanella, Cima ∧	**64**	46.13 N	10.40 E
Prescot	**44**	53.26 N	2.48 W
Prescott, On., Can.	**212**	44.43 N	75.31 W
Prescott, Az., U.S.	**200**	34.32 N	112.28 W
Prescott, Ar., U.S.	**194**	33.48 N	93.22 W
Prescott, Or., U.S.	**224**	46.02 N	122.53 W
Prescott, Wi., U.S.	**190**	44.44 N	92.48 W
Prescott and Russell □ [6], On., Can.	**206**	45.25 N	75.00 W
Prescott and Russell □ [6], On., Can.	**212**	45.25 N	75.15 W
Prescott Island I	**176**	73.01 N	96.50 W
Preševo	**38**	42.18 N	21.39 E
Presho	**198**	43.54 N	100.03 W
Presicce	**68**	39.54 N	18.16 E
Presidencia de la Plaza	**252**	27.01 S	59.51 W
Presidencia Roca	**252**	26.08 S	59.36 W
Presidencia Roque Sáenz Peña	**252**	26.47 S	60.27 W
Presidente Costa e Silva, Ponte ◆ [5]	**287a**	22.53 S	43.10 W
Presidente Derqui	**258**	34.29 S	58.51 W
Presidente Dutra	**250**	5.15 S	44.30 W
Presidente Epitácio	**255**	21.46 S	52.06 W
Presidente Getúlio	**252**	27.03 S	49.37 W
Presidente Hayes □ [5]	**252**	24.00 S	59.00 W
Presidente Nicolás Avellaneda, Parque ♠	**288**	34.39 S	58.29 W
Presidente Olegário	**255**	18.25 S	46.25 W
Presidente Prudente	**255**	22.07 S	51.22 W
Presidente Ríos, Lago ⊜	**254**	46.28 S	74.25 W
Presidente Roosevelt, Estação ◆ [5]	**287b**	23.33 S	46.36 W
Presidente Venceslau	**255**	21.52 S	51.50 W
Presidential Heights	**279b**	40.34 N	80.03 W
President Roxas	**116**	11.26 N	122.56 E
Presidio	**196**	29.33 N	104.22 W
Presidio, Río del ≃	**234**	23.06 N	106.17 W
Presidio of San Francisco ■	**226**	37.48 N	122.28 W
Presles	**56**	50.23 N	4.35 E
Presles-en-Brie	**261**	48.43 N	2.45 E
Presnogor'kovka	**86**	54.30 N	65.45 E
Presnovka	**86**	54.40 N	67.09 E
Presolana, Passo della)(	**64**	45.55 N	10.06 E
Prešov	**30**	49.00 N	21.15 E
Prespa, Lake ⊜	**38**	40.55 N	21.00 E
Prespansko Jezero → Prespa, Lake ⊜	**38**	40.55 N	21.00 E
Presque Isle	**186**	46.40 N	68.00 W
Presque Isle › [1]	**214**	42.09 N	80.06 W
Presque Isle ≃	**190**	46.43 N	89.59 W
Presque Isle State Park ♠	**214**	42.09 N	80.06 W
Presqu'ile Bay ⊂	**212**	44.01 N	77.43 W
Presqu'ile Peninsula › [1]	**212**	44.00 N	77.41 W
Presqu'ile Provincial Park ♠	**212**	44.00 N	77.42 W
Pressana	**64**	45.17 N	11.24 E
Pressath	**60**	49.46 N	11.56 E
Pressbaum	**61**	48.11 N	16.05 E
Pressburg → Bratislava	**30**	48.09 N	17.07 E
Pressel	**54**	51.34 N	12.41 E
Prestatyn	**44**	53.20 N	3.24 W
Prestbury	**262**	53.17 N	2.09 W
Prestea	**150**	5.27 N	2.08 W
Presteigne	**42**	52.17 N	3.00 W
Přeštice	**60**	49.34 N	13.20 E
Presto, Bol.	**248**	18.55 S	64.56 W
Presto, Pa., U.S.	**279b**	40.23 N	80.07 W
Preston, Austl.	**169**	37.45 S	145.01 E
Preston, Cuba	**240p**	20.46 N	75.39 W
Preston, Eng., U.K.	**42**	50.39 N	2.25 W
Preston, Eng., U.K.	**44**	53.46 N	0.12 W
Preston, Eng., U.K.	**44**	53.46 N	2.42 W
Preston, Ga., U.S.	**192**	32.03 N	84.32 W
Preston, Id., U.S.	**202**	42.05 N	111.52 W
Preston, Ia., U.S.	**190**	42.03 N	90.24 W
Preston, Ks., U.S.	**198**	37.45 N	98.33 W
Preston, Md., U.S.	**208**	38.42 N	75.54 W
Preston, Mn., U.S.	**190**	43.40 N	92.04 W
Preston, Wa., U.S.	**224**	47.31 N	121.55 W
Preston □ [8]	**262**	53.48 N	2.42 W
Preston ≃, Austl.	**168a**	33.20 S	115.40 E
Preston ≃, P.Q., Can.	**206**	46.05 N	75.04 W
Preston, Cape ›	**162**	20.51 S	116.12 E
Preston, Lac ⊜	**206**	46.05 N	75.04 W
Preston, Lake ⊜, Austl.	**168a**	32.59 S	115.42 E
Preston, Lake ⊜, Fl., U.S.	**220**	28.18 N	81.08 W
Preston Airport ⊠	**276**	40.22 N	74.15 W
Preston Brook	**262**	53.19 N	2.39 W
Preston Brook Canal Tunnel ◆ [5]	**262**	53.19 N	2.38 W
Preston Heights	**216**	41.28 N	88.08 W
Preston Hollow	**210**	42.27 N	74.13 W
Preston North End Football Ground ♠	**262**	53.47 N	2.42 W
Prestonpans	**46**	55.57 N	3.00 W
Preston Peak ∧	**204**	41.50 N	123.37 W
Prestonsburg	**192**	37.39 N	82.46 W
Prestrud Inlet ⊂	**9**	78.18 S	156.00 W
Preststranda	**26**	59.06 N	9.04 E
Prestville	**182**	55.44 N	118.37 W
Prestwich	**44**	53.32 N	2.17 W
Prestwick	**46**	55.30 N	4.37 W
Prestwick Airport ⊠	**46**	55.30 N	4.36 W
Prêto ≃, Bra.	**246**	1.41 S	63.48 W
Prêto ≃, Bra.	**248**	8.03 S	62.54 W
Prêto ≃, Bra.	**250**	11.21 S	43.52 W
Prêto ≃, Bra.	**250**	3.32 S	43.46 W
Prêto ≃, Bra.	**255**	13.37 S	48.06 W
Prêto ≃, Bra.	**255**	17.00 S	46.12 W
Prêto ≃, Bra.	**255**	18.25 S	39.47 W
Prêto ≃, Bra.	**255**	18.44 S	50.23 W
Prêto ≃, Bra.	**255**	19.22 S	41.56 W
Prêto ≃, Bra.	**255**	20.08 S	49.38 W
Preto ≃, Bra.	**256**	22.14 S	43.07 W
Preto ≃, Bra.	**256**	22.01 S	43.20 W
Prêto, Igarapé ≃	**246**	4.10 S	68.57 W
Prêto do Igapó-Açu ≃	**246**	4.26 S	59.48 W
Pretoria	**158**	25.45 S	28.10 E
Pretoriusvlei	**158**	28.30 S	22.59 E
Prettau → Predoi	**64**	47.02 N	12.06 E
Prettin	**54**	51.39 N	12.55 E
Prettyboy Reservoir ⊜ [1]	**208**	39.38 N	76.45 W
Pretty Prairie	**198**	37.46 N	98.01 W
Pretzfeld	**60**	49.45 N	11.11 E
Pretzier	**54**	52.49 N	11.15 E
Pretzsch	**54**	51.42 N	12.48 E
Preussisch Eylau → Bagrationovsk	**76**	54.23 N	20.39 E
Preussisch Friedland → Debrzno	**30**	53.33 N	17.14 E
Preussisch Holland → Pasłęk	**30**	54.05 N	19.39 E
Preussisch Königsdorf → Olesno	**30**	50.53 N	18.25 E
Preussisch-Oldendorf	**52**	52.18 N	8.30 E
Preussisch-Ströhen	**52**	52.29 N	8.40 E
Prevalje	**61**	46.32 N	14.55 E
Préveza	**38**	38.57 N	20.44 E
Prévost	**206**	45.52 N	74.05 W
Prevost Island I	**224**	48.50 N	123.22 W
Prey Lvéa	**110**	11.10 N	104.57 E
Prey Nób	**110**	10.38 N	103.47 E
Prey Vêng	**110**	11.29 N	105.19 E
Prezza, Monte ∧	**66**	42.02 N	13.49 E
Priaral'skije Karakumy ◆ [2]	**86**	47.00 N	63.30 E
Priargunsk	**88**	50.27 N	119.00 E
Priay	**58**	46.00 N	5.17 E
Priazovskaja vozvyšennost' ⋏ [1]	**83**	47.30 N	37.30 E
Priazovskoje	**78**	46.43 N	35.38 E
Pribilof Islands II	**180**	57.00 N	170.00 W
Priboj	**38**	43.35 N	19.31 E
Příbram	**30**	49.42 N	14.01 E
Pribylovo	**76**	60.26 N	28.40 E
Priccio, Cozzo ∧	**70**	37.01 N	14.46 E
Price, Austl.	**168b**	34.17 S	138.00 E
Price, Tx., U.S.	**222**	32.08 N	94.57 W
Price, Ut,. U.S.	**200**	39.35 N	110.48 W
Price ≃	**200**	39.10 N	110.06 W
Price, Cape ›	**110**	13.34 N	93.03 E
Price Bend ⊂	**276**	40.55 N	73.24 W
Price Island I	**182**	52.23 N	128.36 W
Prichard	**194**	30.44 N	88.04 W
Prickly Point ›	**241k**	11.59 N	61.45 W
Pričornomorskaja nizmennost' ≚	**78**	47.00 N	33.00 E
Priddy	**196**	31.40 N	98.31 W
Pridneprovskaja nizmennost' ≚	**78**	50.00 N	32.00 E
Pridneprovskaja vozvyšennost' ⋏ [1]	**78**	49.00 N	32.00 E
Priego	**34**	40.27 N	2.18 W
Priego de Córdoba	**34**	37.26 N	4.11 W
Priekule, S.S.S.R.	**76**	56.26 N	21.35 E
Priekule, S.S.S.R.	**76**	55.33 N	21.19 E
Prienai	**76**	54.38 N	23.57 E
Prien am Chiemsee	**64**	47.51 N	12.20 E
Prieros	**54**	52.13 N	13.46 E
Prieska	**158**	29.40 S	22.42 E
Priest ≃	**202**	48.11 N	116.53 W
Priestewitz	**54**	51.15 N	13.30 E
Priest Island I	**46**	57.58 N	5.30 W
Priest Lake ⊜	**202**	48.34 N	116.52 W
Priestley, Mount ∧	**182**	55.13 N	128.53 W
Priest Rapids Lake ⊜ [1]	**202**	46.45 N	119.55 W
Priest River	**202**	48.10 N	116.54 W
Prieta, Loma ∧	**226**	37.07 N	121.51 W
Prieta, Peña ∧	**34**	43.01 N	4.44 W
Prieto ≃	**240m**	18.15 N	66.54 W
Prieto Diaz	**116**	13.02 N	124.12 E
Prievidza	**30**	48.47 N	18.37 E
Prignitz ◆ [1]	**54**	53.05 N	12.15 E
Priirtyšskaja ravnina ≚	**86**	52.30 N	76.15 E
Priiskovyj, S.S.S.R.	**86**	54.39 N	88.42 E
Priiskovyj, S.S.S.R.	**88**	51.57 N	116.39 E
Prijedor	**36**	44.59 N	16.43 E
Prijepolje	**38**	43.23 N	19.39 E
Prijutnoje	**80**	46.06 N	43.31 E
Prijutovo	**80**	53.54 N	53.56 E
Prikaspijskaja nizmennost' ≚	**80**	48.00 N	52.00 E
Prikolotnoje	**78**	50.09 N	37.21 E
Prikro	**150**	7.39 N	3.59 W
Prilep	**38**	41.20 N	21.33 E
Prilepy	**82**	54.03 N	37.42 E
Prilly	**58**	46.32 N	6.36 E
Priluki, S.S.S.R.	**76**	59.16 N	39.53 E
Priluki, S.S.S.R.	**78**	50.36 N	32.24 E
Priluki, S.S.S.R.	**82**	54.51 N	37.53 E
Prima Porta ◆ [8]	**267a**	42.00 N	12.29 E
Primavera	**250**	0.56 S	47.06 W
Primavera ♥ [3]	**9**	64.09 S	60.57 W
Přimda	**60**	49.41 N	12.41 E
Primeira Cruz	**250**	2.30 S	43.26 W
Primeiro de Maio	**255**	22.48 S	51.01 W
Primera	**196**	26.14 N	97.43 W
Primero ≃	**252**	31.00 S	63.12 W
Primero de Mayo	**196**	27.12 N	101.15 W
Primghar	**198**	43.05 N	95.37 W
Primkenau → Przemków	**30**	51.32 N	15.48 E
Primolano	**64**	45.58 N	11.42 E
Primorje [Warnicken]	**76**	54.57 N	20.02 E
Primorka	**83**	47.16 N	39.03 E
Primorsk, S.S.S.R.	**76**	54.44 N	20.01 E
Primorsk, S.S.S.R.	**76**	60.22 N	28.36 E
Primorsk, S.S.S.R.	**78**	46.44 N	36.20 E
Primorsk, S.S.S.R.	**80**	49.16 N	45.03 E
Primorsk, S.S.S.R.	**84**	40.13 N	49.33 E
Primorskij, S.S.S.R.	**78**	45.07 N	35.29 E
Primorskij, S.S.S.R.	**89**	43.07 N	131.38 E
Primorskij chrebet ⋏	**88**	52.30 N	106.00 E
Primorskij Kraj □ [4]	**89**	45.25 N	135.25 E
Primorsko	**38**	42.16 N	27.46 E
Primorsko-Achtarsk	**78**	46.03 N	38.11 E
Primorskoje	**83**	47.11 N	37.42 E
Primos	**285**	39.55 N	75.18 W
Primrose, S. Afr.	**273d**	26.12 S	28.10 E
Primrose, Pa., U.S.	**210**	40.42 N	76.17 W
Primrose, Pa., U.S.	**279b**	40.21 N	80.16 W
Primrose Brook ≃	**276**	40.43 N	74.31 W
Primrose Lake ⊜	**184**	54.55 N	109.45 W
Prims ≃	**56**	49.20 N	6.44 E
Primstal	**56**	49.32 N	6.58 E
Prince, Lake ⊜ [1]	**208**	36.48 N	76.38 W
Prince Albert, On., Can.	**212**	44.05 N	78.58 W
Prince Albert, Sk., Can.	**184**	53.12 N	105.46 W
Prince Albert, S. Afr.	**158**	33.13 S	22.02 E
Prince Albert Mountains ⋏	**9**	76.00 S	161.30 E
Prince Albert National Park ♠	**184**	54.00 N	106.25 W
Prince Albert Road	**158**	33.01 S	21.40 E
Prince Albert Sound Ʊ	**176**	70.25 N	115.00 W
Prince Alexander Mountains ⋏	**164**	3.30 S	142.50 E
Prince Alfred Hamlet	**158**	33.18 S	19.20 E
Prince Charles Island I	**176**	67.50 N	76.00 W
Prince Charles Mountains ⋏	**9**	72.00 S	67.00 E
Prince-de-Galles, Île du → Prince of Wales Island I, Austl.	**164**	10.40 S	142.10 E
Prince-de-Galles, Île du → Prince of Wales Island I, N.T., Can.	**176**	72.40 N	99.00 W
Prince Edward □ [6]	**212**	44.00 N	77.15 W
Prince Edward Bay ⊂	**212**	43.57 N	76.57 W
Prince Edward Island □ [4], Can.	**176**	46.20 N	63.20 W
Prince Edward Island □ [4], Can.	**186**	46.20 N	63.20 W
Prince Edward Island National Park ♠	**186**	46.31 N	63.26 W
Prince Edward Islands II	**6**	46.35 S	37.56 E
Prince Edward Park ♠	**274a**	34.02 S	151.03 E
Prince Edward Point ›	**212**	43.56 N	76.52 W
Prince Frederick	**208**	38.32 N	76.35 W
Prince Gallitzin State Park ♠	**214**	40.40 N	78.32 W
Prince George, B.C., Can.	**182**	53.55 N	122.45 W
Prince George, Va., U.S.	**208**	37.13 N	77.17 W
Prince George □ [6]	**208**	37.13 N	77.10 W
Prince Georges □ [6]	**208**	38.49 N	76.45 W
Prince Georges Plaza ◆ [9]	**284c**	38.58 N	76.57 W
Prince Leopold Island I	**176**	74.02 N	89.55 W
Prince of Wales, Cape ›	**180**	65.40 N	168.05 W
Prince of Wales Island I, Austl.	**164**	10.40 S	142.10 E
Prince of Wales Island I, N.T., Can.	**176**	72.40 N	99.00 W
Prince of Wales Island I, Ak., U.S.	**180**	55.47 N	132.50 W
Prince of Wales Strait Ʊ	**176**	73.00 N	117.00 W
Prince Olav Coast ⍓ [2]	**9**	68.30 S	42.30 E
Prince Patrick Island I	**16**	76.45 N	119.30 W
Prince Regent ≃	**164**	15.28 S	125.05 E
Prince Regent Inlet ⊂	**176**	73.00 N	90.30 W
Prince Rupert	**182**	54.19 N	130.19 W
Prince Rupert Bay ⊂	**240d**	15.34 N	61.29 W
Prince Rupert Bluff Point ›	**240d**	15.35 N	61.29 W
Princesa, Puerto ⊂	**116**	9.45 N	118.43 E
Princesa Astrid, Costa → Princess Astrid Coast ⍓ [2]	**9**	70.45 S	12.30 E
Princesa Carlota, Bahía → Princess Charlotte Bay ⊂	**164**	14.25 S	144.00 E
Princesa Isabel	**250**	7.44 S	38.00 W
Princesa Marta, Costa → Princess Martha Coast ⍓ [2]	**9**	72.00 S	7.30 W
Princesa Ragnhild, Costa → Princess Ragnhild Coast ⍓ [2]	**9**	70.15 S	27.30 E
Princes Bay ⊂	**276**	40.31 N	74.12 W
Princes Risborough	**42**	51.44 N	0.51 W
Princess Anne	**208**	38.12 N	75.41 W
Princess Astrid Coast ⍓ [2]	**9**	70.45 S	12.30 E
Princess Charlotte Bay ⊂	**164**	14.25 S	144.00 E
Princess Martha Coast ⍓ [2]	**9**	72.00 S	7.30 W
Princess Ragnhild Coast ⍓ [2]	**9**	70.15 S	27.30 E
Princess Ranges ⋏	**162**	26.08 S	121.55 E
Princess Royal Channel Ʊ	**182**	53.10 N	128.37 W
Princess Royal Island I	**182**	52.57 N	128.49 W
Princes Town	**241r**	10.16 N	61.23 W
Princeton, B.C., Can.	**182**	49.27 N	120.31 W
Princeton, Nf., Can.	**186**	48.25 N	53.36 W
Princeton, On., Can.	**212**	43.10 N	80.32 W
Princeton, Ca., U.S.	**226**	39.24 N	122.00 W
Princeton, Fl., U.S.	**220**	25.32 N	80.24 W
Princeton, Il., U.S.	**190**	41.22 N	89.27 W
Princeton, In., U.S.	**194**	38.21 N	87.34 W
Princeton, Ky., U.S.	**194**	37.06 N	87.52 W
Princeton, Me., U.S.	**188**	45.13 N	67.34 W
Princeton, Mi., U.S.	**190**	46.17 N	87.28 W
Princeton, Mn., U.S.	**190**	45.34 N	93.34 W
Princeton, Mo., U.S.	**194**	40.24 N	93.34 W
Princeton, N.J., U.S.	**208**	40.20 N	74.39 W
Princeton, N.C., U.S.	**192**	35.27 N	78.09 W
Princeton, Tx., U.S.	**222**	33.11 N	96.30 W
Princeton, W.V., U.S.	**192**	37.21 N	81.06 W
Princeton, Wi., U.S.	**190**	43.51 N	89.07 W
Princeton Airfield ⊠	**276**	40.24 N	74.39 W
Princeton Battlefield Park ⊥	**276**	40.20 N	74.41 W
Princeton Junction	**208**	40.19 N	74.37 W
Princeton Township	**276**	40.22 N	74.40 W
Princeton University ♥ [2]	**276**	40.21 N	74.39 W
Princetown	**42**	50.33 N	4.00 W
Princeville, P.Q., Can.	**206**	46.10 N	71.53 W
Princeville, Il., U.S.	**190**	40.56 N	89.45 W
Princeville, N.C., U.S.	**192**	35.53 N	77.31 W
Prince William □ [6]	**208**	38.42 N	77.27 W
Prince William Forest Park ♠	**208**	38.36 N	77.23 W
Prince William Sound Ʊ	**180**	60.40 N	147.00 W
Príncipe I	**152**	1.37 N	7.25 E
Príncipe Alberto, Montes → Prince Albert Mountains ⋏	**9**	76.00 S	161.30 E
Príncipe Carlos, Montes → Prince Charles Mountains ⋏	**9**	72.00 S	67.00 E
Principe Channel Ʊ	**182**	53.28 N	130.00 W
Príncipe da Beira	**248**	12.25 S	64.25 W
Príncipe de Gales, Isla → Prince of Wales Island I, Austl.	**164**	10.40 S	142.10 E
Príncipe de Gales, Isla → Prince of Wales Island I, N.T., Can.	**176**	72.40 N	99.00 W
Príncipe Eduardo, Isla → Prince Edward Island □ [4]	**186**	46.20 N	63.20 W
Príncipe Olav, Costa → Prince Olav Coast ⍓ [2]	**9**	68.30 S	42.30 E
Príncipe Patricio, Isla → Prince Patrick Island I	**16**	76.45 N	119.30 W
Prineville	**202**	44.18 N	120.51 W
Prineville Reservoir ⊜ [1]	**202**	44.08 N	120.42 W
Prineville Southeast	**202**	44.17 N	120.53 W
Pringgabaja	**115b**	8.34 S	116.37 E
Pringy	**261**	48.31 N	2.34 E
Prinsenbeek	**52**	51.36 N	4.42 E
Prinses Margrietkanaal ≍	**52**	53.10 N	5.55 E
Prinshof	**158**	32.06 S	20.53 E
Prinzapolka	**236**	13.24 N	83.34 W
Prinzapolka ≃	**236**	13.24 N	83.34 W
Prinzessin Astrid-Küste → Princess Astrid Coast ⍓ [2]	**9**	70.45 S	12.30 E
Prinzessin Charlotte Bucht → Princess Charlotte Bay ⊂	**164**	14.25 S	144.00 E
Prinzessin Martha-Küste → Princess Martha Coast ⍓ [2]	**9**	72.00 S	7.30 W
Prinzessin Ragnhild-Küste → Princess Ragnhild Coast ⍓ [2]	**9**	70.15 S	27.30 E
Priobskoje plato ⋏ [1]	**86**	52.40 N	83.00 E
Prioksko-Terrasnyj Zapovednik ◆ [4]	**82**	54.51 N	37.36 E
Priolo Gargallo	**70**	37.09 N	15.11 E
Prior, Cabo ›	**34**	43.34 N	8.19 W
Priort	**264a**	52.31 N	12.58 E
Priozernyj	**80**	47.23 N	45.14 E
Prioz'ornyj	**86**	47.50 N	84.13 E
Prioz'orsk	**24**	61.02 N	30.04 E
Prip'at' ≃	**78**	51.21 N	30.09 E
Pripet → Prip'at' ≃	**78**	51.21 N	30.09 E
Pripet Marshes → Polesje ◆ [1]	**72**	52.00 N	27.00 E
Pripol'arnyj Ural ⋏	**24**	65.00 N	60.00 E
Priputni	**78**	50.57 N	32.14 E
Prirečje	**88**	55.07 N	101.03 E
Prirečnyj	**80**	51.03 N	52.26 E
Přísečnice	**54**	50.27 N	13.06 E
Priselje	**76**	55.09 N	32.49 E
Prišib, S.S.S.R.	**78**	47.16 N	35.21 E
Prišib, S.S.S.R.	**84**	39.08 N	48.36 E
Prislon	**82**	56.48 N	37.16 E
Pristan'-Prževal'sk	**85**	42.34 N	78.18 E
Pristen', S.S.S.R.	**78**	51.15 N	36.41 E
Pristen', S.S.S.R.	**83**	49.36 N	37.38 E
Priština	**38**	42.39 N	21.10 E
Pritchett	**198**	37.22 N	102.51 W
Přítluky	**61**	48.51 N	16.46 E
Pritzerbe	**54**	52.30 N	12.27 E
Pritzier	**54**	53.22 N	11.04 E
Pritzwalk	**54**	53.09 N	12.10 E
Priural'nyj	**80**	51.29 N	53.06 E
Privas	**62**	44.44 N	4.36 E
Priverno	**66**	41.28 N	13.11 E
Privetnoje	**78**	44.50 N	34.41 E
Privodino	**24**	61.05 N	46.28 E
Privokzal'nyj, S.S.S.R.	**82**	55.59 N	35.56 E
Privokzal'nyj, S.S.S.R.	**86**	58.53 N	60.43 E
Privolje, S.S.S.R.	**83**	49.01 N	38.18 E
Privolje, S.S.S.R.	**83**	48.52 N	37.16 E
Privol'naja	**78**	46.09 N	38.42 E
Privol'n'anskij ◆ [8]	**83**	48.41 N	38.28 E
Privol'noje, S.S.S.R.	**78**	47.29 N	32.17 E
Privol'noje, S.S.S.R.	**80**	50.57 N	46.06 E
Privolžje	**80**	52.52 N	48.37 E
Privolžsk	**80**	57.23 N	41.17 E
Privolžskaja vozvyšennost' ⋏ [1]	**80**	52.00 N	46.00 E
Privolžskij, S.S.S.R.	**80**	46.24 N	48.00 E
Privolžskij, S.S.S.R.	**80**	51.24 N	46.02 E
Privolžskoje	**80**	51.06 N	45.57 E
Prizren	**38**	42.12 N	20.44 E
Prizzi	**70**	37.43 N	13.26 E
Prizzi, Lago di ⊜	**70**	37.44 N	13.25 E
Prnjavor	**36**	44.52 N	17.40 E
Pro	**286d**	11.57 S	77.05 W
Probolinggo	**115a**	7.45 S	113.13 E
Proboštov	**54**	50.39 N	13.50 E
Probstzella	**54**	50.32 N	11.22 E
Probus	**42**	50.17 N	4.57 W
Procchio	**66**	42.47 N	10.15 E
Prochladnoje	**86**	48.30 N	82.41 E
Prochladnyj	**84**	43.46 N	44.00 E
Prochorkino	**86**	59.34 N	79.26 E
Prochorovka	**82**	54.07 N	38.11 E
Prochowice	**30**	51.17 N	16.22 E
Procida	**68**	40.46 N	14.02 E
Procida, Isola di I	**68**	40.45 N	14.01 E
Procter	**182**	49.37 N	116.57 W
Proctor, Mn., U.S.	**190**	46.44 N	92.13 W
Proctor, Vt., U.S.	**188**	43.39 N	73.02 W
Proctor Brook ≃	**283**	42.32 N	70.54 W
Proctor Lake ⊜	**228**	35.07 N	118.21 W
Proctor Lake ⊜ [1]	**196**	32.02 N	98.32 W
Proddatūr	**122**	14.44 N	78.33 E
Proença-a-Nova	**34**	39.45 N	7.55 W
Profen	**54**	51.07 N	12.13 E
Pro Football Hall of Fame ♥	**214**	40.49 N	81.25 W
Prognoj	**83**	48.45 N	39.51 E
Progreso, Méx.	**196**	27.28 N	100.59 W
Progreso, Méx.	**232**	21.17 N	89.40 W
Progreso, Ur.	**258**	34.40 S	56.13 W
Progreso Industrial	**234**	19.38 N	99.21 W
Progress, S.S.S.R.	**89**	49.42 N	129.39 E
Progress, Or., U.S.	**224**	45.28 N	122.47 W
Progress, Pa., U.S.	**208**	40.08 N	76.34 W
Project City	**204**	40.41 N	122.21 W
Prokopjeva	**88**	58.03 N	100.39 E
Prokopjevsk	**86**	53.53 N	86.45 E
Prokopyevsk → Prokopjevsk	**86**	53.53 N	86.45 E
Prokuplje	**38**	43.14 N	21.36 E
Prokuševo	**76**	59.55 N	34.56 E
Prokutkino	**86**	56.19 N	69.46 E
Proletarij	**76**	58.26 N	31.44 E
Proletarsk, S.S.S.R.	**78**	48.56 N	38.23 E
Proletarsk, S.S.S.R.	**80**	46.42 N	41.44 E
Proletarsk, S.S.S.R.	**85**	40.10 N	69.30 E
Proletarsk ◆ [8]	**83**	48.56 N	38.23 E
Proletarskij, S.S.S.R.	**78**	50.47 N	35.47 E
Proletarskij, S.S.S.R.	**82**	55.01 N	37.23 E
Proletarskij ◆ [8]	**83**	48.08 N	39.18 E
Prolysovo	**76**	52.54 N	34.09 E
Prome (Pyè)	**110**	18.49 N	95.13 E
Promised Land State Park ♠	**210**	41.18 N	75.11 W
Promissão	**255**	21.32 S	49.52 W
Promitorio	**267a**	42.03 N	12.39 E
Promontogno	**58**	46.21 N	9.34 E
Prompton	**210**	41.35 N	75.19 W
Prompton Lake ⊜ [1]	**210**	41.36 N	75.20 W
Prompton Lake State Park ♠	**210**	41.37 N	75.22 W
Promyšlennaja	**86**	54.55 N	85.40 E
Promyšlennovskij	**86**	55.29 N	86.12 E
Promyšlennyj	**24**	67.35 N	63.55 E
Promyslovka	**80**	45.44 N	47.10 E
Pron'a ≃, S.S.S.R.	**76**	53.25 N	31.01 E
Pron'a ≃, S.S.S.R.	**80**	54.21 N	40.24 E
Pron'a Gorodišče	**82**	54.15 N	38.43 E
Pronin	**80**	49.12 N	42.11 E
Pronsfeld	**56**	50.10 N	6.20 E
Pronsk	**76**	54.07 N	39.37 E
Prony, Baie du ⊂	**175f**	22.22 S	166.53 E
Prophet ≃	**176**	58.45 N	122.45 W
Prophetstown	**190**	41.40 N	89.56 W
Propriá	**250**	10.13 S	36.51 W
Propriano	**36**	41.40 N	8.55 E
Prorer Wiek ⊂	**54**	54.27 N	13.38 E
Prorva	**86**	46.03 N	53.15 E
Proryvnoje	**86**	54.23 N	64.26 E
Pros'anaja	**78**	48.07 N	36.23 E
Pros'anov	**78**	49.42 N	35.47 E
Prösen	**54**	51.25 N	13.30 E
Proserpine	**166**	20.24 S	148.34 E
Prosigk	**54**	51.42 N	12.03 E

Symbol	English	Deutsch	Español	Français	Português
≃	River	Fluss	Río	Rivière	Rio
≍	Canal	Kanal	Canal	Canal	Canal
∟	Waterfall, Rapids	Wasserfall, Stromschnellen	Cascada, Rápidos	Chute d'eau, Rapides	Cascata, Rápidos
Ʊ	Strait	Meeresstrasse	Estrecho	Détroit	Estreito
⊂	Bay, Gulf	Bucht, Golf	Bahía, Golfo	Baie, Golfe	Baía, Golfo
⊜	Lake, Lakes	See, Seen	Lago, Lagos	Lac, Lacs	Lago, Lagos
☷	Swamp	Sumpf	Pantano	Marais	Pântano
⍓	Ice Features, Glacier	Eis- und Gletscherformen	Accidentes Glaciales	Formes glaciaires	Acidentes glaciares
⍑	Other Hydrographic Features	Andere Hydrographische Objekte	Otros Elementos Hidrográficos	Autres données hydrographiques	Outros acidentes hidrográficos
✥	Submarine Features	Untermeerische Objekte	Accidentes Submarinos	Formes de relief sous-marin	Acidentes submarinos
□	Political Unit	Politische Einheit	Unidad Politica	Entité politique	Unidade política
♥	Cultural Institution	Kulturelle Institution	Institución Cultural	Institution culturelle	Institução cultural
⊥	Historical Site	Historische Stätte	Sitio Histórico	Site historique	Sitio histórico
♠	Recreational Site	Erholungs- und Ferienort	Sitio de Recreo	Centre de loisirs	Area de Lazer
⊠	Airport	Flughafen	Aeropuerto	Aéroport	Aeroporto
■	Military Installation	Militäranlage	Instalación Militar	Installation militaire	Instalação militar
◆	Miscellaneous	Verschiedenes	Misceláneo	Divers	Diversos

ENGLISH: Name | Page | Lat.°′ | Long.°′
DEUTSCH: Name | Seite | Breite°′ | Länge°′ E = Ost

Name	Page	Lat.°′	Long.°′
Proskurov → Chmel'nickij	78	49.25 N	27.00 E
Prosna ≃	30	52.10 N	17.39 E
Prosnica	80	58.26 N	50.15 E
Prosotsáni	38	41.10 N	23.59 E
Prospect, Austl.	168b	34.54 S	138.35 E
Prospect, Austl.	274a	33.48 S	150.56 E
Prospect, Ct., U.S.	207	41.30 N	72.58 W
Prospect, N.Y., U.S.	210	43.18 N	75.09 W
Prospect, Oh., U.S.	214	40.27 N	83.11 W
Prospect, Pa., U.S.	214	40.54 N	80.03 W
Prospect Bay c	208	38.56 N	76.14 W
Prospect Creek ≃	274a	33.55 S	150.59 E
Prospect Heights	278	42.05 N	87.56 W
Prospect Hill	168b	35.13 S	138.44 E
Prospect Hill ∧[2], Ma., U.S.	207	41.21 N	70.45 W
Prospect Hill ∧[2], Ma., U.S.	283	42.23 N	71.15 W
Prospect Hill Park ♦	283	42.23 N	71.15 W
Prospect Meadows	278	42.05 N	87.57 W
Prospect Park, N.J., U.S.	276	40.56 N	74.10 W
Prospect Park, Pa., U.S.	214	41.31 N	78.13 W
Prospect Park, Pa., U.S.	285	39.53 N	75.18 W
Prospect Park ♦	276	40.40 N	73.58 W
Prospect Park Lake ⊜	276	40.39 N	73.57 W
Prospect Plains	276	40.19 N	74.28 W
Prospect Point	276	40.58 N	74.38 W
Prospect Point ≻	276	40.52 N	73.43 W
Prospect Reservoir ⊜[1]	274a	33.49 S	150.54 E
Prospectville	285	40.13 N	75.11 W
Prosper	222	33.14 N	96.48 W
Prosperi Airport ⊠	278	41.33 N	87.47 W
Prosperidad	116	8.34 N	125.52 E
Prosser	202	46.12 N	119.46 W
Prosser Creek Reservoir ⊜[1]	226	39.22 N	120.08 W
Prostějov	30	49.29 N	17.07 E
Prostken → Prostki	30	53.43 N	22.26 E
Prostki	30	53.43 N	22.26 E
Proston	166	26.10 S	151.36 E
Proszowice	30	50.12 N	20.18 E
Protasovo, S.S.S.R.	82	54.48 N	38.35 E
Protasovo, S.S.S.R.	82	54.11 N	37.00 E
Protasovo, S.S.S.R.	82	56.08 N	37.36 E
Protasy	76	52.47 N	29.05 E
Protea	273d	26.17 S	27.51 E
Protection	198	37.12 N	99.29 W
Protection Island I	224	48.07 N	122.55 W
Protem	158	34.16 S	20.05 E
Protestantes	256	22.44 S	46.18 W
Protivín	61	49.12 N	14.13 E
Protoka ≃	78	45.43 N	37.46 E
Protva	82	55.01 N	36.41 E
Protva ≃	82	54.51 N	37.16 E
Protville	36	36.54 N	10.01 E
Prötzel	54	52.38 N	13.59 E
Proud Lake State Recreation Area ♦	281	42.34 N	83.33 W
Proulxville	206	46.40 N	72.30 W
Provadija	38	43.11 N	27.26 E
Provencal	194	31.39 N	93.12 W
Provence □[9]	62	44.00 N	6.00 E
Provence, Alpes de ∧∧	62	43.40 N	6.00 E
Provenchères-sur-Fave	58	48.19 N	7.05 E
Providence, Ky., U.S.	194	37.23 N	87.45 W
Providence, R.I., U.S.	207	41.49 N	71.24 W
Providence, Ut,. U.S.	200	41.42 N	111.48 W
Providence □[6]	207	41.52 N	71.36 W
Providence ≃	207	41.43 N	71.21 W
Providence Forge	208	37.26 N	77.02 W
Providence Island I	138	9.14 S	51.02 E
Providência, Bra.	256	21.40 S	42.35 W
Providencia, Chile	286e	33.26 S	70.37 W
Providencia, Méx.	196	27.06 N	103.32 W
Providencia, Isla de I	236	13.21 N	81.22 W
Providenciales I	238	21.47 N	72.17 W
Providenija	180	64.23 N	173.18 W
Providenija, buchta c	180	64.30 N	173.20 W
Provincetown	207	42.03 N	70.10 W
Provincia, Cerro de la ∧	286e	33.25 S	70.26 W
Provins	50	48.33 N	3.18 E
Provo	200	40.14 N	111.39 W
Provo ≃	200	40.14 N	111.44 W
Provost	184	52.21 N	110.16 W
Provost, Lac ⊜	206	46.22 N	74.00 W
Prozor	36	43.49 N	17.37 E
Pru ≃	150	7.58 N	0.53 W
Prud'anka	78	50.14 N	36.09 E
Prudence Island I	207	41.37 N	71.19 W
Prudentópolis	252	25.12 S	50.57 W
Prudentov	80	49.39 N	46.19 E
Prudhoe	44	54.58 N	1.51 W
Prudhoe Bay c	180	70.20 N	148.20 W
Prudhoe Island I	166	21.19 S	149.40 E
Prudišči	82	54.24 N	38.26 E
Prudki	82	54.46 N	36.29 E
Prudnik	30	50.19 N	17.34 E
Prudy	76	53.47 N	26.32 E
Pruggern	64	47.25 N	13.52 E
Prüm	56	50.12 N	6.25 E
Prüm ≃	56	49.49 N	6.28 E
Pruna, Punta sa ∧	71	40.11 N	9.26 E
Prunay-le-Temple	261	48.52 N	1.40 E
Prunay-sous-Ablis	261	48.32 N	1.48 E
Prunedale	226	36.47 N	121.40 W
Prunéřov	54	50.25 N	13.16 E
Prunières	62	44.33 N	6.20 E
Prunn, Schloss ⊥	60	48.57 N	11.44 E
Pruszków	30	52.11 N	20.48 E
Prut ≃	78	45.30 N	28.12 E
Pruth → Prut ≃	78	45.30 N	28.12 E
Prutting	64	47.53 N	12.11 E
Prutz	58	47.05 N	10.40 E
Pružany	76	52.33 N	24.28 E
Prydz Bay c	9	69.00 S	76.00 E
Pryor	196	36.19 N	95.19 W
Pryor Creek ≃	202	45.54 N	108.19 W
Pryor Mountain ∧[2]	222	31.43 N	95.12 W
Prysor ≃	42	52.56 N	4.00 W
Przasnysz	30	53.01 N	20.55 E
Przedbórz	30	51.06 N	19.53 E
Przemków	30	51.32 N	15.48 E
Przemocze	54	53.27 N	14.55 E
Przemyśl	30	49.47 N	22.47 E
Przemyśl □[4]	30	50.00 N	22.40 E
Prževal'sk	85	42.29 N	78.24 E
Prževal'sk □[4]	85	42.00 N	77.45 E
Przeworsk	30	50.05 N	22.29 E
Przewóz	54	51.29 N	14.59 E
Przybiernów	54	53.46 N	14.46 E
Przysucha	30	51.22 N	20.38 E
Pšagar	85	39.58 N	68.08 E
Psakhná	38	38.35 N	23.38 E
Psará I	38	38.35 N	25.37 E
Psárion	38	37.20 N	21.51 E
Psebaj	84	44.07 N	40.47 E
Pšecha ≃	78	44.47 N	39.48 E
Psekups ≃	78	45.00 N	39.09 E
Pselec	78	51.17 N	36.32 E
Psikhikón	267c	38.01 N	23.46 E
Pšiš ≃	78	45.01 N	39.18 E
Pšiš, gora ∧	84	43.24 N	41.12 E
Psittália I	267c	37.56 N	23.35 E
Pskem	85	41.56 N	70.22 E
Pskem ≃	85	41.38 N	70.01 E
Pskent	85	40.54 N	69.20 E
Pskov	76	57.50 N	28.20 E
Pskovskoje ozero ⊜	76	58.00 N	28.00 E
Pskowsee → Pskovskoje ozero ⊜	76	58.00 N	28.00 E
Ps'ol ≃	78	49.02 N	33.33 E
Pšov	54	50.10 N	13.29 E
Pszczyna	30	49.59 N	18.57 E
Ptarmigan, Cape ≻	176	71.04 N	118.07 W
Ptič'	78	52.09 N	28.52 E
Ptič' ≃	76	52.09 N	28.52 E
Ptolemaís	38	40.31 N	21.41 E
Ptolemais ⊥	146	32.43 N	20.57 E
Ptuj	61	46.25 N	15.52 E
Pu ≃, Zhg.	104	41.21 N	122.47 E
Pu ≃, Zhg.	107	30.25 N	103.49 E
Puah, Pulau I	112	0.30 S	122.34 E
Puakonikai	174d	0.52 S	169.36 E
Puamau, Baie c	174y	9.46 S	138.52 W
Puán, Arg.	252	37.33 S	62.43 W
Puan, Taehan	98	35.45 N	126.44 E
Pubāil	126	23.56 N	90.29 E
Pubnico	186	43.42 N	65.47 W
Pucallpa	248	8.23 S	74.32 W
Pucará	248	18.43 S	64.11 W
Pucarani	248	16.23 S	68.30 W
Puccia, Serra di ∧	70	37.44 N	13.56 E
Puce	214	42.18 N	82.47 W
Puces ≃	281	42.18 N	82.47 W
Pučevejem ≃	180	68.48 N	170.30 E
Pučež	80	56.59 N	43.11 E
Puchberg am Schneeberg	61	47.47 N	15.54 E
Pucheng, Zhg.	100	27.55 N	118.31 E
Pucheng, Zhg.	102	34.59 N	109.29 E
Pucheta	252	29.54 S	57.34 W
Puchheim	60	48.09 N	11.20 E
Púchov	30	49.08 N	18.20 E
Puchoviči	76	53.32 N	28.15 E
Pucioasa	38	45.04 N	25.26 E
Pucio Point ≻	116	11.46 N	121.51 E
Pučišća	36	43.21 N	16.44 E
Puck	30	54.44 N	18.27 E
Pucketa Creek ≃	279b	40.33 N	79.45 W
Pudahuel, Aeropuerto de ⊠	286e	33.23 S	70.49 W
Pudding ≃	224	45.18 N	122.43 W
Puddingstone Reservoir ⊜[1]	280	34.05 N	117.48 W
Puddington	262	53.15 N	3.00 W
Puddletown	42	50.45 N	2.21 W
Pūdeh Tal ≃	128	31.03 N	62.15 E
Pudem	80	58.18 N	52.10 E
Pudi	102	27.58 N	99.05 E
Pudimoe	158	27.26 S	24.44 E
Puding	102	26.21 N	105.40 E
Pudino	86	57.34 N	79.24 E
Pudops Dam ⊷[6]	186	48.09 N	56.50 W
Pudož	24	61.48 N	36.32 E
Pudsey	44	53.48 N	1.40 W
Pudu ≃	102	26.19 N	102.45 E
Puduhe	102	25.39 N	102.39 E
Pudukkottai	122	10.23 N	78.49 E
Puebla □[3]	234	18.50 N	98.00 W
Puebla de Alcocer	34	38.59 N	5.15 W
Puebla de Don Fadrique	34	37.58 N	2.26 W
Puebla de Don Rodrigo	34	39.05 N	4.37 W
Puebla de Sanabria	34	42.03 N	6.38 W
Puebla de Trives	34	42.20 N	7.15 W
Puebla [de Zaragoza]	234	19.03 N	98.12 W
Pueblito de Ponce	240m	18.26 N	66.58 W
Pueblo	198	38.15 N	104.36 W
Pueblo Ledesma	252	23.50 S	64.46 W
Pueblo Libertador	252	30.13 S	59.23 W
Pueblo Libre	286d	12.05 S	77.04 W
Pueblo Mountain ∧	202	42.06 N	118.39 W
Pueblonuevo, Col.	246	8.31 N	75.15 W
Pueblo Nuevo, Méx.	234	20.31 N	101.22 W
Pueblo Nuevo, Nic.	236	13.23 N	86.29 W
Pueblo Nuevo, P.R.	240m	18.28 N	66.51 W
Pueblo Nuevo, Ur.	258	34.26 S	56.29 W
Pueblo Nuevo, Ven.	246	11.58 N	69.55 W
Pueblo Nuevo ⊷[8]	266a	40.26 N	3.39 W
Pueblo of Acoma	200	35.03 N	107.35 W
Pueblo Reservoir ⊜[1]	198	38.15 N	104.45 W
Puebloviejo, Ec.	246	1.34 S	79.30 W
Pueblo Viejo, Méx.	234	17.33 N	100.05 W
Pueblo Viejo, Méx.	234	17.24 N	93.47 W
Pueblo Viejo, Laguna de c	234	22.10 N	97.53 W
Puelches	252	38.09 S	65.55 W
Puente Alto	252	33.37 S	70.35 W
Puenteareas	34	42.11 N	8.30 W
Puente-Caldelas	34	42.23 N	8.30 W
Puente de Arganda	266a	40.19 N	3.31 W
Puente de Camotlán	234	21.32 N	104.12 W
Puente de Ixtla	234	18.37 N	99.20 W
Puentedeume	34	43.24 N	8.10 W
Puente-Genil	34	37.23 N	4.47 W
Puente Hills ∧∧[2]	280	34.00 N	117.55 W
Puente Hills Mall ⊷[9]	280	33.59 N	117.56 W
Puente la Reina	34	42.40 N	1.49 W
Puente Negro	196	27.55 N	101.01 W
Puente Nuevo, Embalse de ⊜[1]	34	38.00 N	5.00 W
Pueo Point ≻	229b	21.54 N	160.04 W
Pu'er	102	23.07 N	101.00 E
Puerca, Punta ≻	240m	18.14 N	65.36 W
Puerco ≃	200	34.53 N	110.07 W
Puerco, Rio ≃	200	34.22 N	106.50 W
Pu'erdu	102	28.08 N	104.24 E
Puerto Acosta	248	15.32 S	69.15 W
Puerto Adela	252	24.33 S	54.22 W
Puerto Aisén	254	45.24 S	72.42 W
Puerto Alegre	248	13.53 S	61.36 W
Puerto Alfonso	246	2.11 S	71.01 W
Puerto Ángel	234	15.40 N	96.29 W
Puerto Armuelles	236	8.17 N	82.52 W
Puerto Asís	246	0.30 N	76.31 W
Puerto Ayacucho	246	5.40 N	67.35 W
Puerto Bahía Negra	248	20.15 S	58.12 W
Puerto Baquerizo Moreno	246a	0.54 S	89.36 W
Puerto Barrios	236	15.43 N	88.36 W
Puerto Belgrano	252	38.54 S	62.06 W
Puerto Bermejo	252	26.56 S	58.30 W
Puerto Bermúdez	248	10.20 S	74.54 W
Puerto Berrío	246	6.29 N	74.24 W
Puerto Bolívar	246	3.16 S	79.59 W
Puerto Boyacá	246	5.45 N	74.39 W
Puerto Busch	248	20.02 S	57.55 W
Puerto Cabello	246	10.28 N	68.01 W
Puerto Cabezas	236	14.02 N	83.23 W
Puerto Carreño	246	6.12 N	67.22 W
Puerto Casado	252	22.20 S	57.55 W
Puerto Castilla	236	16.01 N	86.01 W
Puerto Chicama	248	7.42 S	79.27 W
Puerto Colombia	246	10.59 N	74.58 W
Puerto Constanza	258	33.50 S	59.03 W
Puerto Cortés, C.R.	236	8.58 N	83.32 W
Puerto Cortés, Hond.	236	15.48 N	87.56 W
Puerto Cumarebo	246	11.29 N	69.21 W
Puerto de Lajas, Cerro ∧	232	28.59 N	107.02 W
Puerto Delicia	252	26.12 S	54.35 W
Puerto Delón	236	14.22 N	85.53 W
Puerto de los Ángeles y Barranca de los Negros, Parques Nacionales de ♦	234	23.40 N	105.18 W
Puerto del Rosario	148	28.30 N	13.52 W
Puerto de Pollensa	34	39.55 N	3.05 E
Puerto de San José	236	13.55 N	90.49 W
Puerto de San Juan de Dios	234	22.19 N	99.33 W
Puerto Deseado	254	47.45 S	65.54 W
Puerto El Triunfo	236	13.17 N	88.33 W
Puerto Escondido	234	15.50 N	97.10 W
Puerto Espãna → Port of Spain	241r	10.39 N	61.31 W
Puerto Esperanza	252	26.01 S	54.39 W
Puerto Felipe, Bahía → Port Phillip Bay c	169	38.07 S	144.48 E
Puerto Fonciere	252	22.29 S	57.48 W
Puerto Francisco de Orellana	246	0.28 S	76.58 W
Puerto Guaraní	248	21.18 S	57.55 W
Puerto Heath	248	12.30 S	68.40 W
Puerto Iguazú	252	25.34 S	54.34 W
Puerto Ingeniero Ibáñez	254	46.18 S	71.56 W
Puerto Inírida	246	3.53 N	67.52 W
Puerto Jiménez	236	8.33 N	83.19 W
Puerto Juárez	232	21.11 N	86.49 W
Puerto la Cruz	246	10.13 N	64.38 W
Puerto la Plata, Zona Nacional □[5]	288	34.52 S	57.52 W
Puerto Leda	248	20.41 S	58.02 W
Puerto Leguízamo	246	0.12 S	74.46 W
Puerto Lempira	236	15.13 N	83.47 W
Puerto Libertad, Arg.	252	25.55 S	54.36 W
Puerto Libertad, Méx.	232	29.55 N	112.43 W
Puerto Limón, Col.	246	3.23 N	73.30 W
Puerto Limón → Limón, C.R.	236	10.00 N	83.02 W
Puertollano	34	38.41 N	4.07 W
Puerto Lobos	254	42.00 S	65.06 W
Puerto López	246	4.05 N	72.58 W
Puerto Madero	236	14.44 N	92.25 W
Puerto Madryn	254	42.46 S	65.03 W
Puerto Maldonado	248	12.36 S	69.11 W
Puerto Manatí	240p	21.22 N	76.50 W
Puerto Mihanovich	248	20.52 S	57.59 W
Puerto Montt	254	41.28 S	72.57 W
Puerto Morazán	236	12.51 N	87.11 W
Puerto Morelos	232	20.50 N	86.52 W
Puerto Morrito	236	11.37 N	85.05 W
Puerto Nariño	246	4.56 N	67.48 W
Puerto Natales	254	51.44 S	72.31 W
Puerto Nuevo, Punta ≻	240m	18.30 N	66.24 W
Puerto Octay	254	40.58 S	72.54 W
Puerto Ordaz → Ciudad Guayana	246	8.22 N	62.40 W
Puerto Padre	240p	21.12 N	76.36 W
Puerto Páez	246	6.13 N	67.28 W
Puerto Palmer, Pico ∧	196	27.08 N	101.47 W
Puerto Peñasco	232	31.20 N	113.33 W
Puerto Pilón	236	9.22 N	79.48 W
Puerto Pinasco	252	22.43 S	57.50 W
Puerto Pirámides	254	42.34 S	64.17 W
Puerto Piray	252	26.28 S	54.42 W
Puerto Píritu	246	10.04 N	65.03 W
Puerto Portillo	248	9.46 S	72.45 W
Puerto Potrero	236	10.28 N	85.47 W
Puerto Presidente Stroessner	252	25.30 S	54.36 W
Puerto Princesa, Pil.	116	9.44 N	118.44 E
Puerto Princesa, Pil.	116	10.06 N	125.29 E
Puerto Real, Esp.	34	36.32 N	6.11 W
Puerto Real, P.R.	240m	18.05 N	67.11 W
Puerto Reyes	246	0.59 S	73.17 W
Puerto Rico, Arg.	252	26.48 S	55.02 W
Puerto Rico, Bol.	248	11.05 S	67.38 W
Puerto Rico, Col.	246	1.54 N	75.10 W
Puerto Rico □[2], N.A.	230	18.15 N	66.30 W
Puerto Rico □[2], N.A.	240m	18.15 N	66.30 W
Puerto Rico, International Airport Of ⊠	240m	18.27 N	66.00 W
Puerto Rico Trench ⊹[1]	16	20.00 N	66.00 W
Puerto Rondón	246	6.17 N	71.06 W
Puerto Saavedra	252	38.47 S	73.24 W
Puerto Salgar	246	5.28 N	74.39 W
Puerto Sandino	236	12.12 N	86.46 W
Puerto Santa Cruz	254	50.01 S	68.31 W
Puerto Sastre	252	22.06 S	57.59 W
Puerto Siles	248	12.48 S	65.05 W
Puerto Suárez	248	18.57 S	57.51 W
Puerto Supe	248	10.49 S	77.45 W
Puerto Tejada	246	3.14 N	76.24 W
Puerto Toledo	246	0.59 S	74.09 W
Puerto Umbría	246	0.52 N	76.33 W
Puerto Vallarta	234	20.37 N	105.15 W
Puerto Varas	254	41.19 S	72.59 W
Puerto Victoria, Arg.	252	26.20 S	54.39 W
Puerto Victoria, Perú	248	9.54 S	74.58 W
Puerto Viejo, C.R.	236	10.26 N	83.59 W
Puerto Viejo, C.R.	236	9.39 N	82.45 W
Puerto Villamizar	246	8.19 N	72.26 W
Puerto Villaroel	248	16.50 S	64.47 W
Puerto Visser	254	45.24 S	67.08 W
Puerto Wilches	246	7.21 N	73.54 W
Puerto Ybapobó	252	23.42 S	57.12 W
Pueyrredón, Lago (Lago Cochrane) ⊜	254	47.20 S	72.00 W
Puffendorf	56	50.56 N	6.13 E
Puffing Billy ⊥	274b	37.55 S	145.21 E
Pugačov	80	52.01 N	48.50 E
Pugač'ovo	80	56.35 N	53.02 E
Puge, Tan.	154	4.45 S	33.07 E
Puge, Zhg.	102	27.28 N	102.31 E
Puget, Cape ≻	180	59.52 N	148.26 W
Puget Island I	224	46.10 N	123.23 W
Puget Sound ⋓	224	47.50 N	122.30 W
Puget Sound Naval Shipyard ■	224	47.33 N	122.38 W
Puget-sur-Argens	62	43.27 N	6.41 E
Puget-Théniers	62	43.57 N	6.54 E
Puget-Ville	62	43.17 N	6.08 E
Pugh Mountain ∧	224	48.08 N	121.22 W
Pughtown	285	40.10 N	75.40 W
Puglia □[4]	68	41.15 N	16.15 E
Pugong-ni	271b	37.43 N	126.58 E
Pugŏ-ri	98	42.01 N	129.59 E
Pugwash	186	45.51 N	63.40 W
Puhe	104	41.57 N	123.36 E
Puhi	229b	21.58 N	159.23 W
Puhja	76	58.20 N	26.19 E
Puhos	26	62.05 N	29.54 E
Puhosjärvi ⊜	26	65.19 N	27.55 E
Puica	248	15.04 S	72.42 W
Puiești	38	46.25 N	27.33 E
Puigcerdá	34	42.26 N	1.56 E
Puigmal ∧	34	42.23 N	2.07 E
Puimoisson	62	43.52 N	6.08 E
Puinahua, Canal de ≃[1]	248	5.20 S	74.13 W
Puinān	272b	22.56 N	88.13 E
Puir	89	53.10 N	141.25 E
Puisaye, Collines de la ∧∧[2]	50	47.40 N	3.15 E
Puiseaux	50	48.12 N	2.28 E
Puiseaux ≃	50	48.00 N	2.44 E
Puiseux-en-France	261	49.04 N	2.29 E
Puiseux-Pontoise	261	49.03 N	2.01 E
Puisieux	50	50.07 N	2.42 E
Puits ≃	50	48.31 N	4.15 E
Pujada Bay c	116	6.51 N	126.14 E
Pujehun	150	7.21 N	11.42 W
Puji, Zhg.	100	27.59 N	113.25 E
Puji, Zhg.	100	29.58 N	112.32 E
Pujiang, Zhg.	100	29.28 N	119.53 E
Pujiang, Zhg.	107	30.12 N	103.30 E
Pujilí	246	0.57 S	78.41 W
Pujon	115a	7.50 S	112.28 E
Pujun	112	1.20 S	114.20 E
Pujut	114	1.25 N	100.39 E
Pujut, Tanjung ≻	115a	5.52 S	106.02 E
Pukaki, Lake ⊜	172	44.07 S	170.10 E
Pukalani	229a	20.50 N	156.20 W
Pukaskwa ≃	190	48.00 N	85.53 W
Pukaskwa National Park ♦	190	48.20 N	85.50 W
Pukch'ang	98	39.36 N	126.17 E
Pukchin	98	40.10 N	125.43 E
Pukch'ŏn	98	36.13 N	126.45 E
Pukch'ŏng	98	40.15 N	128.20 E
Pukë	38	42.03 N	19.54 E
Pukeashun Mountain ∧	182	51.12 N	119.14 W
Pukekohe	172	37.12 S	174.55 E
Puketeraki Range ∧∧	172	42.58 S	172.12 E
Puketoi Range ∧∧	172	40.30 S	176.05 E
Pukeuri Junction	172	45.02 S	171.02 E
Pukhan-gang ≃	98	37.31 N	127.18 E
Pŭkhan-san ∧	271b	37.41 N	127.00 E
Pukhrāyān	124	26.14 N	79.51 E
Pukoo	229d	21.04 N	156.48 W
Pukou, Zhg.	100	26.16 N	119.35 E
Pukou, Zhg.	106	32.07 N	118.43 E
Puksoozero	24	62.38 N	40.36 E
Puksubaek-san ∧	98	40.42 N	127.44 E
Puktae-ch'ŏn ≃	98	40.28 N	129.00 E
Pula, It.	71	39.01 N	9.00 E
Pula, Jugo.	64	44.52 N	13.50 E
Pulacayo	248	20.25 S	66.41 W
Pulan	120	30.16 N	81.14 E
Pulandian Wan c	98	39.18 N	121.35 E
Pulanduta Point ≻	116	11.54 N	123.10 E
Pulangi ≃	116	7.18 N	124.50 E
Pulangpisau	112	2.46 S	114.14 E
Pulap I[1]	14	7.35 N	149.24 E
Púlar, Cerro ∧	252	24.11 S	68.04 W
Pulaski, In., U.S.	216	40.59 N	86.40 W
Pulaski, Mi., U.S.	216	42.07 N	84.40 W
Pulaski, N.Y., U.S.	212	43.34 N	76.07 W
Pulaski, Oh., U.S.	216	41.30 N	84.26 W
Pulaski, Pa., U.S.	214	41.07 N	80.26 W
Pulaski, Tn., U.S.	194	35.11 N	87.01 W
Pulaski, Va., U.S.	192	37.02 N	80.46 W
Pulaski, Wi., U.S.	190	44.40 N	88.14 W
Pulaski □[6]	216	41.03 N	86.36 W
Pulau ≃	164	5.50 S	138.15 E
Pulaukida	112	2.44 S	102.34 E
Pulaukijang	112	0.42 S	103.12 E
Pulaumerak	115a	5.56 S	106.00 E
Pulauraja	114	2.42 N	99.37 E
Pulautelo	110	0.03 N	98.16 E
Puławy	30	51.25 N	21.57 E
Pulborough	42	50.58 N	0.30 W
Pul'chakim	85	38.10 N	67.21 E
Pulehu Gulch V	229a	20.50 N	156.28 W
Pulfero	64	46.11 N	13.29 E
Pulga	123	31.59 N	77.26 E
Pulgaon	122	20.44 N	78.20 E
Pulham Market	42	52.26 N	1.14 E
Pulheim	56	51.00 N	6.47 E
Puli	100	23.58 N	120.57 E
Pulicat	122	13.25 N	80.19 E
Pulicat Lake c	122	13.40 N	80.10 E
Pulichatum	128	35.57 N	61.07 E
Puliciano	66	43.23 N	11.51 E
Puliyangudi	122	9.10 N	77.25 E
Pulj → Pula	64	44.52 N	13.50 E
Pulkau	61	48.42 N	15.51 E
Pulkau ≃	61	48.43 N	16.21 E
Pulkkila	26	64.16 N	25.52 E
Pulkovo ⊷[8]	265a	59.46 N	30.20 E
Pullman, Mi., U.S.	216	42.29 N	86.05 W
Pullman, Wa., U.S.	202	46.43 N	117.10 W
Pullman ⊷[8]	278	41.43 N	87.36 W
Pullo	248	15.14 S	73.50 W
Pully	58	46.31 N	6.39 E
Pul'mo	78	51.31 N	23.47 E
Pulo ⊥	68	41.12 N	16.34 E
Pulo Anna I	108	4.40 N	131.58 E
Pulog, Mount ∧	116	16.36 N	120.54 E
Pulogadung ⊷[8]	269e	6.11 S	106.54 E
Pulon'ga	24	66.17 N	40.02 E
Púlpito, Punta ≻	232	26.31 N	111.28 W
Púlpito do Sul	152	15.46 S	12.00 E
Pulsano	68	40.23 N	17.22 E
Pulsen	54	51.23 N	13.26 E
Pulsnitz	54	51.11 N	14.01 E
Pulsnitz ≃	54	51.27 N	13.30 E
Pulteney	210	42.31 N	77.10 W
Pultneyville	210	43.17 N	77.11 W
Pułtusk	30	52.43 N	21.05 E
Pulü	107	29.50 N	106.11 E
Pülümür Geçidi)(	130	39.31 N	39.54 E
Puluo	120	36.11 N	81.30 E
Pulupandan	116	10.31 N	122.48 E
Pulur	130	40.10 N	39.53 E
Pulusuk I	14	6.42 N	149.19 E
Pulversheim	58	47.51 N	7.18 E
Pumbi	152	3.26 N	22.11 E
Pumei	102	23.28 N	105.15 E
Pumphrey	284b	39.13 N	76.38 W
Pumpkin Buttes ∧	200	43.44 N	105.54 W
Pumpkin Center	228	35.18 N	119.05 W
Pumpkin Creek ≃, Mt., U.S.	198	46.15 N	105.45 W
Pumpkin Creek ≃, Ne., U.S.	198	41.38 N	103.01 W
Pumsaint	42	52.03 N	3.58 W
Pumsi	80	57.12 N	51.39 E
Puna	248	19.46 S	65.28 W
Puná, Isla I	246	2.50 S	80.08 W
Punaauia	174s	17.38 S	149.36 W
Punaauia, Pointe de ≻	174s	17.38 S	149.36 W
Punakha	124	27.37 N	89.52 E
Punaluu	229c	21.35 N	157.53 W
Punan, Indon.	112	1.20 N	115.34 E
Punan, Indon.	112	3.24 N	116.16 E
Punan, Zhg.	100	24.39 N	117.41 E
Punata	248	17.32 S	65.50 W
Pūnch	123	33.46 N	74.06 E
Punch □[8]	123	33.50 N	73.45 E
Pūnch ≃	123	33.12 N	73.40 E
Puncha	126	23.10 N	86.39 E
Punchaw	182	53.28 N	123.13 W
Punchbowl	274a	33.56 S	151.03 E
Pundaguitan	116	6.22 N	126.10 E
Punda Milia	156	22.40 S	31.05 E
Pünderich	56	50.02 N	7.08 E
Pūndri	124	29.45 N	76.33 E
Punduga	76	60.08 N	40.12 E
Pune (Poona)	122	18.32 N	73.52 E
P'ungam-ni	98	37.43 N	128.11 E
Pungan	85	40.45 N	70.49 E
Punganūru	122	13.22 N	78.35 E
Pungești	38	46.42 N	27.20 E
Punggol	271c	1.25 N	103.55 E
Punggol ≃	271c	1.25 N	103.54 E
Pungki	114	4.17 N	96.13 E
Pungo ≃	192	35.23 N	76.33 W
Pungo Andongo	152	9.40 S	15.35 E
Púngoè ≃	154	19.50 S	34.48 E
P'ungsan, C.M.I.K.	98	40.47 N	128.10 E
P'ungsan, C.M.I.K.	98	38.28 N	125.01 E
P'ungsong-ni	98	39.56 N	127.11 E
Punia	154	1.28 S	26.27 E
Punilla, Sierra de la ∧∧	252	28.55 S	69.00 W
Puning	100	23.18 N	116.12 E
Punitaqui	252	30.50 S	71.16 W
Punjab □[3]	123	31.00 N	75.30 E
Punjab □[4]	120	31.00 N	72.00 E
Punkaharju ♦	26	61.47 N	29.20 E
Punkalaidun	26	61.07 N	23.06 E
Punnichy	184	51.23 N	104.18 W
Puno	248	15.50 S	70.02 W
Puno □[5]	248	15.00 S	70.00 W
Punta, Castillo de la ⊥	286b	23.09 N	82.21 W
Punta, Cerro de ∧	240m	18.10 N	66.36 W
Punta Alegre	240p	22.23 N	78.49 W
Punta Alta	254	38.53 S	62.05 W
Punta Arenas	254	53.09 S	70.55 W
Punta Banda, Cabo ≻	232	31.45 N	116.45 W
Punta Brava ⊷[8]	286b	23.01 N	82.30 W
Punta Cardón	246	11.38 N	70.14 W
Punta de Agua Creek (Tramperos Creek) ≃	196	35.32 N	102.27 W
Punta de Bombón	248	17.11 S	71.48 W
Punta de Díaz	252	28.03 S	70.37 W
Punta del Cobre	252	27.30 S	70.16 W
Punta del Este	252	34.58 S	54.57 W
Punta Delgada	254	42.46 S	63.38 W
Punta de los Llanos	252	30.09 S	66.33 W
Punta de Mata	246	9.43 N	63.38 W
Punta Flecha	116	7.23 N	123.25 E
Punta Gorda, Belize	232	16.07 N	88.48 W
Punta Gorda, Fl., U.S.	220	26.55 N	82.02 W
Punta Gorda ≃	236	11.30 N	83.47 W
Punta Gorda, Bahía de c	236	11.15 N	83.45 W
Punta Indio, Canal ≚	258	34.36 S	58.16 W
Punta Moreno	248	7.36 S	78.54 W
Punta Negra, Salar de ≚	252	24.35 S	69.00 W
Punta Piedras	246	10.54 N	64.06 W
Punta Porá	252	25.13 S	58.31 W
Punta Prieta	232	28.58 N	114.17 W
Punta Raisi, Aeroporto di ⊠	70	38.11 N	13.06 E
Puntarenas	236	9.58 N	84.50 W
Puntarenas □[4]	236	9.00 N	83.15 W
Punta Santiago	240m	18.10 N	65.45 W
Puntas del Sauce	258	33.51 S	57.01 W
Punto Fijo	246	11.42 N	70.13 W
Puntzi Lake ⊜	182	52.12 N	124.02 W
Punung	115a	8.08 S	111.01 E
Punxsutawney	214	40.56 N	78.58 W
Puolanka	26	64.52 N	27.40 E
Puolo Point ≻	229b	21.54 N	159.36 W
Puper	164	0.10 S	131.18 E
Pup'yŏng	271b	37.30 N	126.43 E
Puqi, Zhg.	100	28.11 N	121.01 E
Puqi, Zhg.	100	29.43 N	113.53 E
Puqian, Zhg.	100	23.34 N	114.38 E
Puqian, Zhg.	102	20.03 N	110.36 E
Puquio	248	14.42 S	74.08 W
Pur ≃	74	67.31 N	77.55 E
Purabiya Plain ≚	124	25.50 N	82.30 E
Puracé, Volcán ∧[1]	246	2.21 N	76.23 W
Purandarpur	126	23.51 N	87.36 E
Pūranpur	124	28.31 N	80.09 E
Purari ≃	164	7.25 S	145.05 E
Purba	114	2.54 N	98.42 E
Purbashthāli	126	23.28 N	88.21 E
Purbeck, Isle of I	42	50.38 N	2.00 W
Purbolinggo	115a	7.24 S	109.22 E
Purcell	196	35.00 N	97.21 W
Purcell Mountains ∧∧	182	50.00 N	116.30 W
Purcellville	188	39.08 N	77.42 W
Purchase	276	41.02 N	73.43 W
Purchena	34	37.21 N	2.22 W
Purdon	222	31.57 N	96.37 W
Purdoški	80	54.40 N	43.32 E
Purdy	194	36.49 N	93.55 W
Purdy Islands II	164	2.50 S	146.20 E
Purech	80	56.39 N	43.05 E
Pureora, Mount ∧	172	38.33 S	175.38 E
Purépero	234	19.55 N	102.01 W
Purfleet	42	51.29 N	0.15 E
Purga	171a	27.43 S	152.44 E
Purga Creek ≃	171a	27.42 S	152.45 E
Purgatoire ≃	198	38.04 N	103.10 W
Purgatory Brook ≃	283	42.11 N	71.11 W
Purgg	61	47.32 N	14.04 E
Purgstall an der Erlauf	61	48.03 N	15.08 E
Puri	120	19.48 N	85.51 E
Purial, Sierra del ∧∧	240p	20.12 N	74.42 W
Purificación, Col.	246	3.51 N	74.55 W
Purificación, Méx.	234	19.43 N	104.38 W
Purificación ≃, Méx.	232	23.58 N	98.42 W
Purificación ≃, Méx.	234	19.18 N	104.54 W
Purikari neem ≻	76	59.40 N	25.43 E
Purísima, Méx.	196	29.09 N	100.46 W
Purísima, Méx.	232	25.25 N	105.26 W
Purísima, Sierra de la ∧∧	196	26.30 N	101.44 W
Purisima Creek ≃	282	37.24 N	122.26 W
Purísima de Bustos	234	21.02 N	101.52 W
Purkersdorf	264b	48.12 N	16.11 E
Purleigh	260	51.41 N	0.40 E
Purley	222	33.05 N	95.16 W
Purley ⊷[8]	260	51.20 N	0.07 W
Purli	122	18.51 N	76.32 E
Purling	210	42.17 N	74.00 W
Purmerend	52	52.31 N	4.57 E
Pūrna ≃, India	122	19.07 N	77.02 E
Pūrna ≃, India	122	21.05 N	76.00 E
Purnea	124	25.47 N	87.31 E
Purnea □[5]	124	26.00 N	87.30 E
Puronga	76	60.09 N	40.54 E
Purranque	254	40.55 S	73.10 W
Purrorumba Hill ∧	171b	35.10 S	149.23 E
Purros	156	18.38 S	12.59 E
Purrumbete, Lake ⊜	169	38.17 S	143.14 E
Pursat → Poŭthĭsăt	110	12.32 N	103.55 E
Purton	42	51.36 N	1.52 W
Puruándiro	234	20.05 N	101.30 W
Puruarán	234	19.06 N	101.32 W
Puruchuca	286d	12.04 S	76.57 W
Puruê ≃	246	1.40 S	68.08 W
Purukcahu	112	0.35 S	114.35 E
Purūlia	126	23.20 N	86.22 E
Purūlia □[5]	124	23.20 N	86.25 E
Puruni ≃	246	6.00 N	59.12 W
Purus (Purús) ≃	242	3.42 S	61.28 W
Puruvesi ⊜	26	61.50 N	29.27 E
Purvis	194	31.08 N	89.24 W
Purwakarta	115a	6.34 S	107.26 E
Purwantoro	115a	7.51 S	111.15 E
Purwareja	115a	7.28 S	109.25 E
Purwodadi, Indon.	115a	7.49 S	110.00 E
Purwodadi, Indon.	115a	7.05 S	110.54 E
Purwokerto	115a	7.25 S	109.14 E
Purworejo	115a	7.43 S	110.01 E
Pusa, India	124	25.59 N	85.41 E
Pusa, Malay.	112	1.36 N	111.17 E
Pusad	122	19.54 N	77.35 E
Pusan	98	35.06 N	129.03 E
Pusan □[4]	98	35.10 N	129.05 E
Pusat Gayo, Pegunungan ∧∧	114	4.15 N	97.05 E
Puščino	82	54.50 N	37.36 E
Pusgo Point ≻	116	13.31 N	122.38 E
Pushang	98	36.08 N	119.42 E
Pushkar	120	26.30 N	74.33 E
Pushkin → Puškin	76	59.43 N	30.25 E
Pushkin Airport ⊠	265a	59.41 N	30.21 E
Pushkin Drama Theatre ⊍	265a	59.56 N	30.21 E
Pushthrough	186	47.39 N	56.10 W
Puškar'ovka	78	48.40 N	34.16 E
Puskiakiwenin Indian Reserve ⊷[4]	184	53.57 N	110.26 W
Puškin	76	59.43 N	30.25 E
Puškino, S.S.S.R.	80	51.14 N	46.59 E
Puškino, S.S.S.R.	82	56.01 N	37.51 E
Puškino, S.S.S.R.	82	56.36 N	35.46 E
Puškino, S.S.S.R.	84	39.27 N	48.33 E
Puškinskij	265a	59.43 N	30.18 E
Puškinskije Gory	76	57.01 N	28.54 E
Puskwaskau ≃	182	55.29 N	118.10 W
Puslinch Lake ⊜	212	43.25 N	80.16 W
Pusŏng-ni	98	40.19 N	127.19 E
Püspökladány	30	47.19 N	21.07 E
Pussay	50	48.21 N	2.00 E
Püssi	76	59.24 N	27.01 E
Puster-Tal V	64	46.45 N	12.20 E
Pustin'	76	59.54 N	35.32 E
Pustomyty	78	49.42 N	23.56 E
Pustoš'	76	60.07 N	42.45 E
Pustoška	76	56.20 N	29.22 E
Pustozersk	24	67.33 N	52.27 E
Pusur ≃[1]	126	21.45 N	89.30 E
Puszczykowo	30	52.17 N	16.52 E
Putaendo	252	32.38 S	70.44 W
Putah Creek ≃	226	38.33 N	121.42 W
Putai	100	23.23 N	120.09 E
Putang ≃	269e	6.13 S	106.54 E
Putangqiao	106	31.34 N	118.59 E
Putao	102	27.21 N	97.24 E
Putaruru	172	38.03 S	175.47 E
Put'atin	89	42.52 N	132.25 E
Put'atino	80	54.10 N	41.07 E
Putbus	54	54.21 N	13.28 E
Puteaux	261	48.53 N	2.14 E
Puteran, Pulau I	115a	7.05 S	114.00 E
Putfontein Landbouhoewes	273d	26.08 S	28.24 E
Putgarten	54	54.40 N	13.25 E
Puth Kalān ⊷[8]	272a	28.43 N	77.05 E
Putian, Zhg.	100	29.16 N	114.58 E
Putian, Zhg.	100	25.28 N	119.02 E
Putifigari	71	40.34 N	8.27 E
Putignano	68	40.51 N	17.07 E
Putila	78	48.01 N	25.03 E
Putilkovo	265b	55.52 N	37.23 E
Putina	248	14.55 S	69.52 W
Put-in-Bay	214	41.39 N	82.49 W
Putincevo	86	49.50 N	84.22 E
Puting, Tanjung ≻	112	3.31 S	111.46 E
Putivl'	78	51.21 N	33.52 E
Putla de Guerrero	234	17.02 N	97.56 W
Putlitz	54	53.15 N	12.02 E
Putnam, Ct., U.S.	207	41.54 N	71.54 W
Putnam, Tx., U.S.	196	32.22 N	99.12 W
Putnam □[6], N.Y., U.S.	210	41.26 N	73.41 W
Putnam □[6], Oh., U.S.	216	41.01 N	84.03 W
Putnam Lake	210	41.28 N	73.35 W
Putnam Lake ⊜	276	41.05 N	73.38 W
Putnam Valley	210	41.20 N	73.52 W
Putnamville Reservoir ⊜[1]	283	42.36 N	70.57 W
Putney, Ga., U.S.	192	31.29 N	84.07 W
Putney, Vt., U.S.	188	42.58 N	72.31 W
Putney ⊷[8]	260	51.28 N	0.13 W
Puto	175e	5.41 S	154.43 E
Putorana, plato ∧∧[1]	74	69.00 N	95.00 E
Putorino	172	39.08 S	177.00 E
Putre	248	18.12 S	69.35 W
Putri Narrows ⋓	271c	1.27 N	103.42 E
Putsonderwater	158	29.09 S	21.51 E
Pütt	263	51.11 N	6.59 E
Puttalam	122	8.02 N	79.49 E
Puttalam Lagoon c	122	8.07 N	79.47 E
Putte, Bel.	56	51.04 N	4.38 E
Putte, Ned.	52	51.22 N	4.23 E
Puttelange-lès-Farschviller	56	49.03 N	6.56 E
Putten	52	52.15 N	5.36 E
Putten I	52	51.50 N	4.15 E
Puttgarden	41	54.30 N	11.13 E
Püttlingen	56	49.17 N	6.53 E
Puttūr	122	13.27 N	79.33 E
Putty	170	32.57 S	150.40 E
Putú	252	35.13 S	72.17 W
Putumayo □[8]	246	0.30 N	76.00 W
Putumayo (Içá) ≃	246	3.07 S	67.58 W
Putuo	100	29.58 N	122.17 E
Putu Range ∧∧	150	5.30 N	8.10 W
Putussibau	112	0.50 N	112.56 E
Putzkau	54	51.06 N	14.13 E
Putzu Idu	71	40.02 N	8.25 E
Pu'uhonua o Honaunau National Historical Park ♦	229d	19.25 N	155.54 W
Puu Kaaumakua ∧	229c	21.30 N	157.54 W
Puu Keahiakahoe ∧	229c	21.23 N	157.49 W
Puukohola National Historic Site ⊥	229d	20.00 N	155.46 W
Puukolii	229a	20.56 N	156.40 W
Puu Kukui ∧	229a	20.52 N	156.35 W
Puulavesi ⊜	26	61.50 N	26.42 E
Puumala	26	61.32 N	28.11 E
Puunene	229a	20.51 N	156.27 W
Pu'upu'a	175a	13.34 S	172.09 W
Puurmani	76	58.34 N	26.17 E
Puurs	50	51.05 N	4.17 E
Puuwai	229b	21.54 N	160.12 W
Puxcatán ≃	234	17.37 N	92.34 W
Puxi	100	25.10 N	119.08 E
Puxian	102	36.30 N	111.02 E
Puxico	194	36.56 N	90.09 W
Puxingchang	107	30.41 N	105.06 E
Puxmetacán ≃	234	17.22 N	95.36 W
Puyallup	224	47.11 N	122.17 W
Puyallup ≃	224	47.15 N	122.24 W
Puyang	98	35.42 N	114.59 E
Puyang ≃	100	30.05 N	120.11 E
Puyango (Tumbes) ≃	246	3.30 S	80.27 W
Puy-de-Dôme □[5]	32	45.45 N	3.05 E
Puyehue	254	40.40 S	72.37 W
Puyehue, Volcán ∧[1]	254	40.35 S	72.08 W
Puylaurens	32	43.34 N	2.01 E
Puy-l'Évêque	32	44.30 N	1.08 E
Puyloubier	62	43.31 N	5.41 E
Puymorens, Col de)(	32	42.30 N	1.50 E
Puyo, Ec.	246	1.28 S	77.59 W
Puyŏ, Taehan	98	36.18 N	126.54 E
Puysegur Point ≻	172	46.09 S	166.36 E
Puyuan	106	30.41 N	120.38 E
Puyuguapi, Canal ⋓	254	44.45 S	72.48 W
Puyun-dong	98	41.55 N	129.30 E
Pūzak, Jehīl-e ⊜	128	31.30 N	61.45 E
Puzhen	106	32.09 N	118.41 E
Puzzle Creek ≃	162	17.58 S	135.41 E
Puzzle Lake ⊜, On., Can.	212	44.36 N	76.58 W
Puzzle Lake ⊜, Fl., U.S.	220	28.41 N	81.02 W
Pwalagu	150	10.35 N	0.50 W
Pwani □[4]	154	7.00 S	39.00 E
Pweto	154	8.28 S	28.54 E
Pwinbyu	110	20.22 N	94.40 E
Pwllheli	42	52.53 N	4.25 W
Pyalo	110	19.09 N	95.11 E
Pyalong	169	37.07 S	144.54 E
Pyamalaw ≃[1]	110	15.49 N	94.42 E
Pyapon	110	16.17 N	95.41 E
Pyatigorsk → P'atigorsk	84	44.03 N	43.04 E
Pyawbwe	110	20.35 N	96.04 E
Pyaye	110	19.15 N	95.06 E
Pyčas	80	56.29 N	52.28 E
Pye Islands II	180	59.22 N	150.25 W
Pyhäjärvi ⊜, Suomi	26	61.53 N	30.00 E
Pyhäjärvi ⊜, Suomi	26	62.46 N	25.30 E
Pyhäjärvi ⊜, Suomi	26	63.35 N	25.57 E
Pyhäjärvi ⊜, Suomi	26	61.28 N	23.35 E
Pyhäjärvi ⊜, Suomi	26	61.00 N	22.18 E
Pyhäjoki	26	64.28 N	24.14 E
Pyhäjoki ≃	26	64.28 N	24.13 E
Pyhämaa I	26	60.57 N	21.20 E
Pyhän-Häkin kansallispuisto ♦	26	62.52 N	25.30 E
Pyhäsalmi	26	63.41 N	25.59 E
Pyhäselkä	26	62.26 N	29.58 E
Pyhäselkä ⊜	26	62.26 N	29.58 E
Pyhätunturi ∧	24	67.01 N	27.09 E
Pyhätunturin Kansallispuisto ♦	24	67.01 N	27.10 E
Pyhra	61	48.10 N	15.41 E
Pyhtää (Pyttis)	26	60.29 N	26.32 E
Pyinbongyi	110	17.34 N	96.34 E
Pyingaing	110	23.09 N	94.51 E
Pyinkayaing	110	15.58 N	94.24 E
Pyinmana	110	19.44 N	96.13 E
Pyle	42	51.32 N	3.42 W
Pylos → Pílos	38	36.55 N	21.43 E
Pymatuning Creek ≃	214	41.18 N	80.27 W
Pymatuning Reservoir ⊜[1]	214	41.37 N	80.30 W
Pymatuning State Park ♦, Oh., U.S.	214	41.38 N	80.33 W
Pymatuning State Park ♦, Pa., U.S.	214	41.30 N	80.27 W
Pymble	274a	33.45 S	151.09 E
Pyngopil'gyn, laguna c	180	67.24 N	175.10 W
Pyŏktong	98	40.35 N	125.20 E
Pyŏlch'ang-ni	98	39.17 N	126.26 E
P'yŏngan Namdo □[4]	98	39.20 N	126.00 E
P'yŏngan Pukdo □[4]	98	40.10 N	125.20 E
P'yŏngch'ang	98	37.23 N	128.22 E
P'yŏngdong-ni	98	37.10 N	128.02 E
P'yŏnggang	98	38.26 N	127.16 E
P'yonghae	98	36.46 N	129.28 E
P'yŏngsan	98	38.19 N	126.23 E
P'yŏngt'aek	98	37.00 N	127.05 E
P'yŏngyang	98	39.01 N	125.45 E
P'yŏngyang □[4]	98	39.05 N	125.50 E
Pyŏrha-ri	98	40.48 N	126.32 E
Pyote	196	31.32 N	103.08 W
Pyramid Head ≻	228	32.49 N	118.21 W
Pyramid Lake ⊜	204	40.00 N	119.35 W
Pyramid Lake ⊜[1]	228	34.39 N	118.47 W

Symbols in the index entries represent the broad categories identified in the key at the right. Symbols with superior numbers (∧∧[1]) identify subcategories (see complete key on page I · 1).

Kartensymbole in dem Registerverzeichnis stellen die rechts in Schlüssel erklärten Kategorien dar. Symbole mit hochgestellten Ziffern (∧∧[1]) bezeichnen Unterabteilungen einer Kategorie (vgl. vollständiger Schlüssel auf Seite I · 1).

Los símbolos incluídos en el texto del índice representan las grandes categorias identificadas con la clave a la derecha. Los símbolos con numeros en su parte superior (∧∧[1]) identifican las subcategorias (véase la clave completa en la página I · 1).

Les symboles de l'index représentent les catégories indiquées dans la légende à droite. Les symboles suivis d'un indice (∧∧[1]) représentent des sous-catégories (voir légende complète à la page I · 1).

Os símbolos incluídos no texto do índice representam as grandes categorias identificadas com a chave à direita. Os símbolos com números em sua parte superior (∧∧[1]) identificam as subcategorias (veja-se a chave completa à página I · 1).

∧ Mountain	Berg	Montaña	Montagne	Montanha
∧∧ Mountains	Berge	Montañas	Montagnes	Montanhas
)(Pass	Pass	Paso	Col	Passo
V Valley, Canyon	Tal, Cañon	Valle, Cañón	Vallée, Canyon	Vale, Canhão
≚ Plain	Ebene	Llano	Plaine	Planície
≻ Cape	Kap	Cabo	Cap	Cabo
I Island	Insel	Isla	Île	Ilha
II Islands	Inseln	Islas	Îles	Ilhas
⊥ Other Topographic Features	Andere Topographische Objekte	Otros Elementos Topográficos	Autres données topographiques	Outros acidentes topográficos

Symbol	English	Deutsch	Español	Français	Português
≃	River	Fluss	Río	Rivière	Rio
≡	Canal	Kanal	Canal	Canal	Canal
⌊	Waterfall, Rapids	Wasserfall, Stromschnellen	Cascada, Rápidos	Chute d'eau, Rapides	Cascata, Rápidos
ʯ	Strait	Meeresstrasse	Estrecho	Détroit	Estreito
c	Bay, Gulf	Bucht, Golf	Bahía, Golfo	Baie, Golfe	Baía, Golfo
⊜	Lake, Lakes	See, Seen	Lago, Lagos	Lac, Lacs	Lago, Lagos
⩶	Swamp	Sumpf	Pantano	Marais	Pântano
⊓	Ice Features, Glacier	Eis- und Gletscherformen	Accidentes Glaciales	Formes glaciaires	Acidentes glaciares
⊤	Other Hydrographic Features	Andere Hydrographische Objekte	Otros Elementos Hidrográficos	Autres données hydrographiques	Outros acidentes hidrográficos
✢	Submarine Features	Untermeerische Objekte	Accidentes Submarinos	Formes de relief sous-marin	Acidentes submarinos
□	Political Unit	Politische Einheit	Unidad Politica	Entité politique	Unidade política
ʊ	Cultural Institution	Kulturelle Institution	Institución Cultural	Institution culturelle	Instituição cultural
⊥	Historical Site	Historische Stätte	Sitio Histórico	Site historique	Sitio histórico
♠	Recreational Site	Erholungs- und Ferienort	Sitio de Recreo	Centre de loisirs	Area de Lazer
⊠	Airport	Flughafen	Aeropuerto	Aéroport	Aeroporto
■	Military Installation	Militäranlage	Instalación Militar	Installation militaire	Instalação militar
◆	Miscellaneous	Verschiedenes	Misceláneo	Divers	Diversos

Quiririm 256 23.02 S 45.38 W
Quirke Lake ⊚ 190 46.28 N 82.33 W
Quiroga, Esp. 34 42.29 N 7.16 W
Quiroga, Méx. 234 19.40 N 101.32 W
Quirós 252 28.47 S 65.07 W
Quiros, Cap › 175f 14.55 S 167.01 E
Quirpon Island I 186 51.35 N 55.25 W
Quirra, Salto di ◆[1] 71 39.35 N 9.33 E
Quiruvilca 248 8.00 S 78.19 W
Quissac 62 43.55 N 4.00 E
Quissanga 154 12.25 S 40.29 E
Quissico 156 24.42 S 34.44 E
Quissongo 152 10.01 S 15.07 E
Quistello 64 45.00 N 10.59 E
Quitapa 152 10.23 S 18.14 E
Quitaque 196 34.22 N 101.04 W
Quita Sueño Bank ◆[4] 236 14.20 N 81.15 W
Quitaúna 287b 23.31 S 46.47 W
Quiterajo 154 11.48 S 40.25 E
Quitéria ≃ 255 20.16 S 51.08 W
Quitilipi 252 26.52 S 60.13 W
Quitman, Ga., U.S. 192 30.47 N 83.33 W
Quitman, Ms., U.S. 194 32.02 N 88.43 W
Quitman, Tx., U.S. 222 32.47 N 95.27 W
Quitman, Lake ⊚[1] 222 32.52 N 95.27 W
Quito 246 0.13 S 78.30 W
Quitzdorf, Speicherbecken ⊚[1] 54 51.17 N 14.45 E
Quivilla 248 9.32 S 76.41 W
Quixadá 250 4.58 S 39.01 W
Quixeramobim 250 5.12 S 39.17 W
Quixeré 250 5.05 S 37.59 W
Quixico 152 7.59 S 14.25 E
Quixinge 152 9.52 S 14.23 E
Quixito ≃ 246 4.29 S 70.18 W
Quizenga 152 9.21 S 15.28 E
Qujiadian 89 43.13 N 123.53 E
Qujiang, Zhg. 100 28.15 N 115.45 E
Qujiang, Zhg. 100 24.48 N 113.17 E
Qujiang, Zhg. 100 24.41 N 113.35 E
Qujing 102 25.32 N 103.41 E
Qujiu 102 22.28 N 107.40 E
Quke 120 28.16 N 87.24 E
Qukou 105 39.46 N 117.07 E
Qulay'ah, Ra's al- › 128 28.53 N 48.18 E
Qulbān al-'Īsāwīyah 128 30.38 N 37.53 E
Qulin 194 36.35 N 90.14 W
Qulubbā 142 27.45 N 30.50 E
Qulūd, Jabal ∧[2] 140 11.41 N 29.31 E
Qulūṣanā 142 28.21 N 30.44 E
Qulzum, Baḥr al- ⊂ 142 29.55 N 32.31 E
Qumar ≃ 90 34.42 N 94.50 E
Qumarlêb 102 34.35 N 95.27 E
Qumbu 158 31.10 S 28.48 E
Qumrān, Khirbat ⊥ 132 31.44 N 35.27 E
Qunayfidhah, Nafūd ⊥[8] 128 24.45 N 45.30 E
Qunbush Al-Ḥamrā' 142 29.00 N 30.59 E
Qunshen'guan 105 39.49 N 117.59 E
Quobba, Point › 162 24.23 S 113.24 E
Quoich ≃ 176 64.00 N 93.30 W
Quoich, Loch ⊚ 46 57.04 N 5.17 W
Quoile ≃ 44 54.21 N 5.42 W
Quoin Point › 158 34.46 S 19.37 E
Quonochontaug 207 41.21 N 71.43 W
Quorn 166 32.21 S 138.03 E
Quorndon 42 52.45 N 1.09 W
Quoxo ≃ 156 22.16 S 24.02 E
Qurayyah, Wādī V 132 30.26 N 34.01 E
Qurayyāt, Al- □[4] 132 31.28 N 37.05 E
Qurdūd 140 10.17 N 29.56 E
Qurrāṣah 140 14.38 N 32.12 E
Qurūn Ḥarḥash ∧[2] 142 28.09 N 31.42 E
Qūṣ 140 25.55 N 32.45 E
Quṣayr ad-Daffah ⊥ 146 30.20 N 23.57 E
Qūshchī 128 37.59 N 45.03 E
Qushui, Zhg. 107 30.41 N 106.02 E
Qushui, Zhg. 120 29.22 N 90.43 E
Qutang 100 32.30 N 120.21 E
Qutbapur ◆[8] 272a 28.35 N 77.01 E
Qutb Minar Ʊ[1] 272a 28.32 N 77.11 E
Qutdligssat 176 70.04 N 53.01 W
Quthing 158 30.30 S 27.36 E
Quṭūr 142 30.59 N 30.57 E
Quwaysinā 142 30.34 N 31.09 E
Quxi, Zhg. 100 28.00 N 120.31 E
Quxi, Zhg. 100 23.36 N 116.26 E
Quxia 106 32.06 N 120.09 E
Quxian, Zhg. 100 28.58 N 118.52 E
Quxian, Zhg. 102 30.51 N 106.59 E
Quxingji 98 34.52 N 114.39 E
Quxiong 102 31.09 N 96.00 E
Quyang 98 38.34 N 114.42 E
Qūyjāq-e-Bālā 84 39.16 N 47.07 E
Quyon 188 45.31 N 76.14 W
Quyquyó 252 26.14 S 57.01 W
Quzaymah, Jabal ∧ 132 30.34 N 36.21 E
Quzhou 98 36.46 N 114.57 E
Quzong 102 30.08 N 96.00 E

R

Råå 41 56.00 N 12.44 E
Raab → Győr, Magy. 30 47.42 N 17.38 E
Raab, Öst. 60 48.21 N 13.39 E
Raab (Rába) ≃ 30 47.42 N 17.38 E
Raabs an der Thaya 61 48.51 N 15.30 E
Raadt ◆[8] 263 51.24 N 6.56 E
Raahe 26 64.41 N 24.29 E
Rääkkylä 26 62.19 N 29.37 E
Raalte 52 52.24 N 6.16 E
Raamsdonksveer 52 51.42 N 4.56 E
Ra'ananna 132 32.11 N 34.53 E
Raas, Pulau I 115a 7.09 S 114.32 E
Raasay I 46 57.23 N 6.04 W
Raasay, Sound of ⊔ 46 57.27 N 6.06 W
Raasdorf 264b 48.15 N 16.34 E
Raasiku 76 59.22 N 25.11 E
Rab 36 44.46 N 14.46 E
Rab, Otok I 36 44.47 N 14.45 E
Raba 115b 8.27 S 118.46 E
Rába (Raab) ≃, Europe 30 47.42 N 17.38 E
Raba ≃, Pol. 30 50.09 N 20.30 E
Rabaable 144 8.17 N 48.18 E
Rabaçal ≃ 34 41.30 N 7.12 W
Rábade 34 43.07 N 7.37 W
Rábahidvég 61 47.04 N 16.45 E
Rabai 154 3.58 S 39.37 E
Rabak 140 13.09 N 32.44 E
Rabal 164 6.22 S 134.52 E
Rabat, Magreb 148 34.02 N 6.51 W
Rabat, Malta 36 35.52 N 14.25 E
Rabat (Victoria), Malta 36 36.02 N 14.14 E
Rabat □[4] 148 33.57 N 6.50 W
Rabaul 164 4.12 S 152.12 E
Rabbit ≃ 216 42.38 N 86.06 W
Rabbit, Lac ⊚ 190 47.30 N 78.22 W
Rabbit Creek ≃, S.D., U.S. 198 45.13 N 102.10 W
Rabbit Creek ≃, Tx., U.S. 222 32.26 N 94.47 W
Rabbit Ears Pass)(200 40.23 N 106.37 W
Rabbit Lake ⊚, On., Can. 190 47.00 N 79.37 W
Rabbit Lake ⊚, Ca., U.S. 228 34.27 N 117.01 W
Rabbs Creek ≃ 222 29.59 N 96.55 W
Rábca ≃ 61 47.43 N 17.17 E
R'abcevo 76 54.39 N 32.19 E
Rabeira, Ponta da › 287a 22.49 S 43.10 W
Rabenau 54 50.57 N 13.38 E
Rabette, Ruisseau la ≃ 261 48.35 N 2.00 E
Rābi', Ash-Shallāl ar- (Fourth Cataract) ⌊ 140 18.47 N 32.03 E
Rābigh 128 22.48 N 39.01 E
Rabinal 236 15.06 N 90.27 W
Rabiusa ≃ 58 46.48 N 9.20 E
Rabka 30 49.36 N 19.56 E
Rabkavi Banhatti 122 16.28 N 75.06 E
Rabnābād Channel ⊔ 126 21.50 N 90.19 E
Rabočeostrovsk 24 64.59 N 34.48 E
Rabočij 86 59.07 N 79.00 E
Rabong, Gunong ∧ 114 4.48 N 102.07 E
Rabotki 80 56.03 N 44.38 E
R'abovskij 80 50.01 N 41.53 E
Rabun Bald ∧ 192 34.58 N 83.18 W
Rabwāh 120 31.44 N 72.50 E
Raby 262 53.19 N 3.02 W
Rabyānah ⊤[4] 146 24.15 N 22.00 E
Rabyānah, Ṣaḥrā' ◆[2] 146 24.30 N 21.00 E
Racale 68 39.57 N 18.06 E
Racalmuto 70 37.24 N 13.44 E
Răcari 38 44.38 N 25.45 E
Racconigi 62 44.46 N 7.46 E
Raccoon ≃ 194 41.35 N 93.37 W
Raccoon Creek ≃, N.J., U.S. 208 39.48 N 75.23 W
Raccoon Creek ≃, Oh., U.S. 188 38.43 N 82.11 W
Raccoon Creek ≃, Oh., U.S. 214 40.02 N 82.24 W
Raccoon Creek ≃, Pa., U.S. 214 40.38 N 80.22 W
Raccoon Creek ≃, Pa., U.S. 285 39.48 N 75.23 W
Raccoon Creek ≃, Va., U.S. 208 36.48 N 77.10 W
Raccoon Creek, South Branch ≃ 285 39.44 N 75.15 W
Raccoon Creek State Park ♠ 214 40.30 N 80.27 W
Raccoon Island I 285 39.49 N 75.22 W
Raccuia 70 38.03 N 14.54 E
Race, Cape › 186 46.40 N 53.10 W
Raceland 194 29.43 N 90.35 W
Race Point › 207 42.04 N 70.14 W
Racette, Lac ⊚ 206 46.34 N 74.03 W
Racette, Ruisseau ≃ 206 46.36 N 74.04 W
Raceview 273d 26.17 S 28.08 E
Rach'a 76 60.05 N 30.49 E
Rach Ben-cat ≃ 269c 10.50 N 106.42 E
Rach Dong-nhien ≃ 269c 10.49 N 106.46 E
Rach-gia 110 10.01 N 105.05 E
Rachmanovka, S.S.S.R. 78 47.48 N 33.13 E
Rachmanovka, S.S.S.R. 80 51.57 N 49.29 E
Rachmanovo 82 55.44 N 38.37 E
Rachny Lesovyje 78 48.47 N 28.29 E
Rachov 78 48.03 N 24.12 E
Raciąż 30 52.47 N 20.06 E
Racibórz (Ratibor) 30 50.06 N 18.13 E
Racine, Pa., U.S. 214 40.49 N 80.20 W
Racine, Wi., U.S. 216 42.43 N 87.46 W
Racine □[6] 216 42.45 N 88.05 W
Racines 64 46.52 N 11.18 E
Račinskij chrebet ⋀ 84 42.30 N 43.30 E
Rackerby 226 39.26 N 121.20 W
Ráckeve 30 47.10 N 18.56 E
Rackwick 46 58.52 N 3.23 W
R'ad 76 57.56 N 35.04 E
Råda 40 60.00 N 13.36 E
Radama, Nosy II 157b 14.00 S 47.47 E
Radama, Presqu'île ›[1] 157b 14.16 S 47.53 E
Rådasjön ⊚ 40 59.58 N 13.38 E
Radaur 124 30.02 N 77.09 E
Rădăuți 38 47.51 N 25.55 E
Radbuza ≃ 60 49.46 N 13.24 E
Radčenskoje 78 49.48 N 40.32 E
Radcliff 194 37.50 N 85.56 W
Radcliffe 44 53.34 N 2.20 W
Radcliffe on Trent 42 52.57 N 1.03 W
Radda in Chianti 66 43.29 N 11.22 E
Raddusa 70 37.28 N 14.32 E
Råde 26 59.21 N 10.51 E
Radebaugh 279b 40.19 N 79.35 W
Radeberg 54 51.07 N 13.55 E
Radebeul 54 51.06 N 13.40 E
Radeburg 54 51.13 N 13.43 E
Radeče 36 46.04 N 15.11 E
Radechov 78 50.18 N 24.37 E
Radegast 54 51.39 N 12.05 E
Radenci 61 46.38 N 16.03 E
Radenthein 64 46.48 N 13.43 E
Radevormwald 56 51.12 N 7.21 E
Radford 192 37.07 N 80.34 W
Rādhānagar, India 126 23.09 N 87.19 E
Rādhānagar, India 272b 22.27 N 88.28 E
Rādhanpur 120 23.50 N 71.36 E
Radici, Foce delle)(64 44.12 N 10.31 E
Radicofani 66 42.54 N 11.46 E
Radicondoli 66 43.16 N 11.02 E
Rădinești 38 44.48 N 23.46 E
Radiščevo 80 52.51 N 47.53 E
Radisson 184 52.27 N 107.23 W
Radiumbad Brambach 54 50.13 N 12.19 E
Radium Hot Springs 182 50.38 N 116.03 W
Radix, Point › 241r 10.20 N 60.59 W
Rad'kovka 78 51.06 N 36.58 E
Radlett 42 51.42 N 0.20 W
Radlett Aerodrome ⊠ 260 51.43 N 0.19 W
Radley Run ≃ 285 39.54 N 75.37 W
Radlje ob Dravi 61 46.37 N 15.13 E
Rådmansö ›[1] 40 59.45 N 18.55 E
Radnevo 38 42.18 N 25.56 E
Radnice 60 49.51 N 13.37 E
Radnor, Oh., U.S. 214 40.23 N 83.09 W
Radnor, Pa., U.S. 285 40.02 N 75.21 W
Radnor Forest ∧ 42 52.18 N 3.10 W
Radnor Mere ⊚ 262 53.17 N 2.14 W
Radofinnikovo 76 59.09 N 30.55 E
Radogošča 76 59.47 N 34.51 E
Radoj'a 78 47.44 N 28.09 E
Radolfzell 58 47.44 N 8.58 E
Radom, Pol. 30 51.25 N 21.10 E
Radom, Il., U.S. 219 38.17 N 89.12 W
Radom □[4] 30 51.25 N 21.15 E
Radomicko 54 52.10 N 14.58 E
Radomir 38 42.33 N 22.58 E
Radomka 78 51.56 N 32.32 E
Radomka ≃ 30 51.43 N 21.26 E
Radomsko 30 51.05 N 19.25 E
Radomyšl' 78 50.30 N 29.14 E
Radomyśl Wielki 30 50.12 N 21.16 E
Radošice 60 49.33 N 13.39 E
Radoškoviči 76 54.09 N 27.14 E
Radotin 30 50.00 N 14.22 E
Radovicy 80 55.06 N 39.32 E
Radoviš 38 41.38 N 22.28 E
Radovljica 36 46.21 N 14.11 E
Radstadt 64 47.23 N 13.27 E
Radstädter Tauern)(64 47.15 N 13.24 E
Radstock 42 51.18 N 2.28 W
Raduha ∧ 61 46.25 N 14.45 E
Radul' 78 51.49 N 30.42 E
Radun' 76 54.03 N 25.00 E
Radušnoje 78 47.49 N 33.29 E
Radutino 76 52.39 N 33.57 E
Radvaniči 78 52.02 N 24.02 E
Radviliškis 76 55.50 N 23.31 E
Radville 184 49.27 N 104.17 W
Raḍwā, Jabal ∧ 128 24.34 N 38.18 E
Radway 182 54.04 N 112.57 W
Radykovskoje 80 45.56 N 41.57 E
Radymno 30 49.57 N 22.48 E
Radyr 42 51.31 N 3.15 W
Radziejów 30 52.38 N 18.32 E
Radzyń Chełmiński 30 53.24 N 18.56 E
Radzyń Podlaski 30 51.48 N 22.38 E
Rae 176 62.50 N 116.03 W
Rae ≃ 176 67.55 N 115.30 W
Rāe Bareli 124 26.13 N 81.14 E
Rāe Bareli □[5] 124 26.20 N 81.20 E
Raeford 192 34.58 N 79.13 W
Rae Isthmus ⊥[3] 176 66.55 N 86.10 W
Rāenda 126 22.18 N 86.51 E
Raeren 56 50.41 N 6.07 E
Raesfeld 52 51.46 N 6.50 E
Raeside, Lake ⊚ 162 29.30 S 122.00 E
Rae Strait ⊔ 176 68.45 N 95.00 W
Raetihi 172 39.26 S 175.17 E
Rafael, Cachoeira do ⌊ 248 10.25 S 63.15 W
Rafaela 252 31.16 S 61.29 W
Rafael Calzada 258 34.48 S 58.22 W
Rafael Castillo 288 34.43 S 58.37 W
Rafael Perazza 258 34.32 S 56.47 W
Rafaḥ 132 31.18 N 34.15 E
Rafaï 152 4.58 N 23.56 E
Rafalovka 78 51.22 N 25.52 E
Raffadali 70 37.24 N 13.32 E
Raffelberg, Rennbahn ♠ 263 51.26 N 6.50 E
Raffili Mission 140 6.53 N 27.58 E
Rafḥā' 128 29.42 N 43.30 E
Rafinesque, Mount ∧[2] 210 42.47 N 73.37 W
Rafsanjān 128 30.24 N 56.01 E
Raft ≃ 202 42.37 N 113.15 W
Raft River Mountains ⋀ 200 41.55 N 113.25 W
Rafz 58 47.37 N 8.32 E
Raga 140 8.28 N 25.41 E
Ragada 64 46.10 N 10.38 E
Ragang, Mount ∧ 116 7.43 N 124.32 E
Ragay 116 13.49 N 122.47 E
Ragay Gulf ⊂ 116 13.30 N 122.45 E
Rågeleje 41 56.06 N 12.10 E
Rägelin 54 53.01 N 12.38 E
Ragewitz 54 51.14 N 12.51 E
Ragged, Mount ∧ 162 33.27 S 123.25 E
Ragged Island I 238 22.12 N 75.44 W
Ragged Island Range II 238 22.40 N 75.54 W
Ragged Lake ⊚ 212 45.28 N 78.38 W
Ragged Top Mountain ∧ 200 41.27 N 105.20 W
Raghabpur 272b 22.25 N 88.21 E
Rāghogarh 124 24.27 N 77.12 E
Raghumāthbāri 126 22.22 N 87.47 E
Raghunāthpur, Bngl. 126 23.12 N 89.31 E
Raghunāthpur, India 126 23.33 N 86.40 E
Raglan, Austl. 170 33.26 S 149.36 E
Raglan, N.Z. 172 37.48 S 174.53 E
Raglan, Wales, U.K. 42 51.47 N 2.51 W
Ragland 194 33.44 N 86.09 W
Ragnitz 61 46.50 N 15.35 E
Rago Nasjonalpark ♠ 24 67.26 N 16.00 E
Ragow 264a 52.17 N 13.33 E
Ragozino 86 59.15 N 77.52 E
Rågsveden 40 60.29 N 14.05 E
Raguda, Ghubbet ⊂ 144 10.45 N 46.34 E
Raguhn 54 51.42 N 12.17 E
Raguli 80 45.38 N 43.42 E
Ragusa, It. 70 36.55 N 14.44 E
Ragusa → Dubrovnik, Jugo. 38 42.38 N 18.07 E
Ragusa □[4] 70 36.55 N 14.36 E
Raguva 76 55.34 N 24.36 E
Raha 112 4.51 S 122.43 E
Rahad, Nahr ar- (Rahad) ≃ 140 14.28 N 33.31 E
Rahad al-Bardī 140 11.18 N 23.53 E
Rahad Game Reserve ◆[4] 140 13.06 N 35.05 E
Rahaṭ, Ḥarrat ⊥[9] 144 22.20 N 40.05 E
Rahatgaon 124 22.15 N 77.14 E
Rāhatgarh 124 23.47 N 78.22 E
Raḥbah 130 34.30 N 36.09 E
Rahden 52 52.26 N 8.36 E
Rahimatpur 122 17.36 N 74.12 E
Rahīm ki Bāzār 120 24.19 N 69.09 E
Rahīmyār Khān 120 28.25 N 70.18 E
Rahīmyār Khān □[5] 123 28.50 N 70.50 E
Rahlstedt ◆[8] 52 53.36 N 10.09 E
Rahm 263 51.26 N 6.26 E
Rahm ◆[8], B.R.D. 263 51.32 N 7.23 E
Rahm ◆[8], B.R.D. 263 51.21 N 6.47 E
Rahmer See ⊚ 264a 52.45 N 13.25 E
Rahns 285 40.12 N 75.27 W
Rahnsdorf ◆[8] 264a 52.26 N 13.42 E
Rāhon 123 31.03 N 76.07 E
Rahotu 172 39.20 S 173.48 E
Rahouia 34 35.32 N 1.01 E
Rāhwāli 123 32.15 N 74.10 E
Rahway 210 40.36 N 74.16 W
Rahway ≃ 276 40.35 N 74.12 W
Rahway, East Branch ≃ 276 40.42 N 74.18 W
Rahway, Robinsons Branch ≃ 276 40.37 N 74.17 W
Rahway, South Branch ≃ 276 40.36 N 74.17 W
Rahway, West Branch ≃ 276 40.42 N 74.18 W
Rahway River Parkway ♠ 276 40.41 N 74.19 W
Raiano 66 42.06 N 13.49 E
Raiatea I 14 16.50 S 151.25 W
Rāichūr 122 16.12 N 77.22 E
Raidak ≃ 124 26.22 N 89.45 E
Rāidighi 126 22.00 N 88.26 E
Raiding 61 47.34 N 16.32 E
Raiford 192 30.03 N 82.14 W
Raiganj 124 25.37 N 88.07 E
Raigarh 122 21.54 N 83.24 E
Raigarh □[5] 124 22.20 N 83.30 E
Raijua, Pulau I 112 10.37 S 121.36 E
Rāikot 123 30.39 N 75.36 E
Railroad 208 39.46 N 76.42 W
Railroad Canyon Reservoir ⊚[1] 228 33.42 N 117.16 W
Railroad Creek ≃ 224 48.12 N 120.36 W
Rail Road Flat 226 38.20 N 120.30 W
Railroad Valley V 204 38.25 N 115.40 W
Railton 166 41.21 S 146.25 E
Raimangal ≃ 126 21.47 N 89.08 E
Rain 56 48.41 N 10.55 E
Rainbach im Innkreis 60 48.27 N 13.32 E
Rainbow 228 33.24 N 117.10 W
Rainbow Bridge ◆[5] 284a 43.05 N 79.04 W
Rainbow Bridge National Monument ♠ 200 37.06 N 110.57 W
Rainbow City 236 9.21 N 79.53 W
Rainbow Falls ⌊ 182 52.23 N 119.59 W
Rainbow Lakes 276 40.52 N 74.28 W
Rainbow Park ♠ 278 41.46 N 87.33 W
Rainbow Shores 212 43.37 N 76.12 W
Rainelle 188 37.58 N 80.46 W
Rainford 44 53.30 N 2.48 W
Rainham 42 51.23 N 0.36 E
Rainham ◆[8] 260 51.31 N 0.12 E
Rainhill 262 53.26 N 2.46 W
Rainhill Stoops 262 53.24 N 2.45 W
Rainier, Or., U.S. 224 46.05 N 122.56 W
Rainier, Wa., U.S. 224 46.53 N 122.41 W
Rainier, Mount ∧ 224 46.52 N 121.46 W
Rainow 262 53.17 N 2.04 W
Rains → Riva di Tures 64 46.57 N 12.04 E
Rains □[6] 222 32.50 N 95.47 W
Rainsboro 218 39.13 N 83.25 W
Rainsford Island I 283 42.18 N 70.57 W
Rainworth 44 53.07 N 1.08 W
Rainy ≃, N.A. 184 48.50 N 94.41 W
Rainy ≃, Mi., U.S. 190 45.27 N 84.13 W
Rainy Lake ⊚, On., Can. 212 45.32 N 79.30 W
Rainy Lake ⊚, N.A. 184 48.42 N 93.10 W
Rainy Pass)(224 48.32 N 120.39 W
Rainy River 190 48.43 N 94.34 W
Rāipur, Bngl. 126 23.03 N 90.46 E
Raipur, India 122 21.14 N 81.38 E
Raipur, India 124 30.19 N 78.06 E
Raipur, India 126 22.48 N 86.57 E
Raipur, India 272a 28.32 N 77.20 E
Raipur, India 272b 22.24 N 88.09 E
Rāipura 126 23.59 N 90.53 E
Rāipur Uplands ⋀[1] 126 21.00 N 82.20 E
Rairākhol 122 21.04 N 84.21 E
Ra'īs 128 23.34 N 38.36 E
Raisdorf 54 54.17 N 10.16 E
Raisen 124 23.20 N 77.48 E
Raisen □[5] 124 23.10 N 78.10 E
Ráisi, Punta › 70 38.11 N 13.06 E
Raisin 226 36.36 N 119.54 W
Raisin ≃, On., Can. 206 45.08 N 74.29 W
Raisin ≃, Mi., U.S. 216 41.53 N 83.20 W
Raisinghnagar 123 29.32 N 73.27 E
Raismes 50 50.23 N 3.29 E
Raita 126 24.07 N 88.57 E
Raitenbuch 60 49.01 N 11.08 E
Raiti 236 14.35 N 85.02 W
Raivavae I 14 23.52 S 147.40 W
Rāiwind 123 31.15 N 74.13 E
Raizeux 261 48.37 N 1.41 E
Raja, Gili I 115a 7.14 S 113.47 E
Raja, Ujung › 114 3.45 N 96.33 E
Rājābari 126 23.23 N 90.28 E
Rajabasa 112 5.25 S 104.24 E
Rājābhāt Khāwa 124 26.37 N 89.32 E
Rājābhita 126 23.52 N 86.20 E
Rājahmundry 122 16.59 N 81.47 E
Rajāj 140 10.55 N 24.43 E
Rāja Jang 123 31.13 N 74.16 E
Raja-Jooseppi 24 68.28 N 28.21 E
Rājākhera 124 26.55 N 78.11 E
Rājaldesar 120 28.02 N 74.28 E
Raj-Aleksandrovka 83 48.48 N 37.51 E
Rājāluka 126 22.09 N 86.38 E
Rajamäki 26 60.32 N 24.45 E
Rājampet 122 14.11 N 79.10 E
Rajang ≃ 112 2.04 N 111.12 E
Rājanpur 120 29.06 N 70.19 E
Rājapālaiyam 122 9.27 N 77.34 E
Rājāpur, Bngl. 126 22.34 N 90.09 E
Rājāpur, India 122 16.40 N 73.31 E
Rājāpur, India 124 25.23 N 81.09 E
Rājāpur, India 272b 22.39 N 88.11 E
Rājapur Canal ≋ 272b 22.30 N 88.07 E
Rājasthān □[3] 120 27.00 N 74.00 E
Rājasthān Canal ≋ 120 31.10 N 75.00 E
Rājauri 123 33.23 N 74.18 E
Rājbāri, Bngl. 124 23.46 N 89.39 E
Rājbāri, India 126 22.25 N 88.48 E
Rājbāri ⊥ 120 25.52 N 93.44 E
Raj Bhawan Ʊ 272b 22.34 N 88.21 E
Rajčichinsk 89 49.46 N 129.25 E
Rājendrapur 126 24.06 N 90.27 E
Rajevskij 86 54.04 N 54.56 E
Rāj Gāngpur 124 22.11 N 84.36 E
Rājganj ≃[1] 126 22.21 N 90.16 E
Rājgarh, India 123 28.38 N 75.23 E
Rājgarh, India 124 23.56 N 76.58 E
Rājgarh, India 124 27.14 N 76.38 E
Rājgarh □[5] 124 23.45 N 76.50 E
Rajghat Ʊ[1] 272a 28.39 N 77.15 E
Rājgīr 124 25.02 N 85.25 E
Rajgorod 80 48.26 N 44.55 E
Rajgorodka, S.S.S.R. 83 49.22 N 37.57 E
Rajgorodka, S.S.S.R. 83 48.50 N 39.04 E
Rajgorodok, S.S.S.R. 80 48.48 N 52.53 E
Rajgorodok, S.S.S.R. 83 48.54 N 37.43 E
Rajgród 30 53.44 N 22.42 E
Rājhāt 272b 22.56 N 88.21 E
Rajhrad 61 49.05 N 16.37 E
Rājibpur 272b 22.49 N 88.34 E
Rajik 112 2.36 S 105.56 E
Rajka 61 48.02 N 17.11 E
Rājkot 120 22.18 N 70.47 E
Rajkuzi 265a 59.47 N 29.57 E
Rājmahāl 124 25.03 N 87.50 E
Rājmahāl Hills ⋀[2] 124 24.40 N 87.25 E
Rājnagar 126 23.57 N 87.19 E
Rāj-Nāndgaon 120 21.06 N 81.02 E
Rajokri ◆[8] 272a 28.31 N 77.07 E
Rājpīpla 120 21.47 N 73.34 E
Rājpur, India 120 21.56 N 75.08 E
Rājpur, India 126 22.25 N 88.25 E
Rājpur, India 272a 28.44 N 77.22 E
Rājpur ◆[8] 272a 28.41 N 77.12 E
Rājpura 124 30.29 N 76.36 E
Rājshāhi 124 24.22 N 88.36 E
Rajskoje 83 48.34 N 37.25 E
Rajula 122 21.03 N 71.26 E
Rakaia 172 43.45 S 172.01 E
Rakaia ≃ 172 43.56 S 172.13 E
Rakamaz 30 48.08 N 21.30 E
Rakaposhi ∧ 123 36.10 N 74.30 E
Rakata, Pulau I 115a 6.10 S 105.26 E
Rakha La)(124 27.53 N 87.34 E
Rakhawt, Wādī V 144 17.40 N 51.40 E
Rakhine □[8] 110 19.00 N 94.15 E
Rakhneh 128 31.39 N 59.13 E
Rakhni 120 30.03 N 69.55 E
Rakhshān ≃ 128 27.10 N 63.25 E
Rākīn 132 31.14 N 35.42 E
Rakitnoje, S.S.S.R. 78 50.51 N 35.50 E
Rakitnoje, S.S.S.R. 78 49.42 N 30.27 E
Rakitnoje, S.S.S.R. 78 51.17 N 27.14 E
Rakitnoje, S.S.S.R. 89 45.36 N 134.17 E
Rakke 76 58.59 N 26.15 E
Rakkestad 26 59.26 N 11.21 E
Rakoniewice 30 52.10 N 16.16 E
Rakops 156 21.00 S 24.32 E
Rákoscsaba ◆[8] 264c 47.29 N 19.17 E
Rákoshegy ◆[8] 264c 47.28 N 19.14 E
Rákoskeresztúr ◆[8] 264c 47.29 N 19.15 E
Rákoskert ◆[8] 264c 47.28 N 19.19 E
Rákosliget ◆[8] 264c 47.30 N 19.16 E
Rákospalota ◆[8] 264c 47.34 N 19.08 E
Rákos-patak ≃ 264c 47.33 N 19.04 E
Rákosszentmihály ◆[8] 264c 47.32 N 19.11 E
Rakovnická plošina ⋀[1] 54 50.08 N 13.47 E
Rakovník 54 50.05 N 13.43 E
Rakovski 38 42.18 N 24.58 E
Rakša 80 53.33 N 41.37 E
Raksakiny 86 60.37 N 73.52 E
Rakuša 80 47.03 N 52.47 E
Råkvåg 26 63.46 N 10.05 E
Rakvere 76 59.22 N 26.20 E
Rakwa 164 2.42 S 134.30 E
Raleigh, Nf., Can. 186 51.34 N 55.44 W
Raleigh, Ms., U.S. 194 32.02 N 89.31 W
Raleigh, N.C., U.S. 192 35.46 N 78.38 W
Raleigh Hills 224 45.29 N 122.45 W
Ralik Chain II 14 8.00 N 167.00 E
Ralls 196 33.40 N 101.23 W
Ralls □[6] 219 39.34 N 91.30 W
Ralsko ∧ 54 50.42 N 14.47 E
Ralston, Ne., U.S. 198 41.12 N 96.02 W
Ralston, Pa., U.S. 210 41.31 N 76.57 W
Ram ≃ 182 52.23 N 115.25 W
Rama, Nic. 236 12.09 N 84.15 W
Rama, Yis. 132 32.56 N 35.22 E
Rama ≃ 236 12.08 N 84.13 W
Ramacca 70 37.23 N 14.42 E
Ramachandrapuram 122 16.51 N 82.01 E
Ramādah 144 13.38 N 43.56 E
Ramah 200 35.07 N 108.29 W
Ramah Indian Reservation ◆[4] 200 34.50 N 108.25 W
Rama Indian Reserve ◆[4] 212 44.41 N 79.15 W
Ramales de la Victoria 34 43.15 N 3.27 W
Ramalho, Serra do ⋀ 255 13.45 S 44.00 W
Rām Allāh 132 31.54 N 35.12 E
Raman 123 29.58 N 74.58 E
Rāmanagaram 122 12.43 N 77.18 E
Rāmanāthapuram 122 9.23 N 78.50 E
Ramānāthpur 272b 22.41 N 88.14 E
Ramanbāti 272b 22.47 N 88.08 E
Rāmānuj Ganj 124 23.48 N 83.42 E
Ramapo 276 41.08 N 74.10 W
Ramapo ≃ 276 40.58 N 74.17 W
Ramapo Lake ⊚ 276 41.02 N 74.16 W
Ramapo Mountains ⋀ 276 41.08 N 74.12 W
Ramapo Valley Airport ⊠ 276 41.06 N 74.06 W
Ramas, Cape › 122 15.07 N 73.55 E
Ramasaig 46 57.24 N 6.44 W

ENGLISH

Name	Page	Lat.°′	Long.°′

Ramasucha 76 52.46 N 33.33 E
Ramat Gan 132 32.05 N 34.49 E
Ramat HaSharon 132 32.09 N 34.50 E
Ramat HaShofet 132 32.37 N 35.06 E
Ramathlabama 156 25.40 S 25.35 E
Ramatuelle 62 43.13 N 6.37 E
Ramat Yoḥanan 132 32.47 N 35.07 E
Rama VI Bridge ◆[5] 269a 13.48 N 100.31 E
Rāmban 123 33.15 N 75.15 E
Rambervillers 58 48.21 N 6.38 E
Rambi I 175g 16.30 S 179.59 E
Rambipuji 115a 8.13 S 113.36 E
Rambleton Acres 208 39.39 N 75.38 W
Ramblewood 285 39.55 N 74.56 W
Rambouillet 50 48.39 N 1.50 E
Rambouillet, Château de ⊥ 261 48.39 N 1.49 E
Rambouillet, Forêt de ♠ 261 48.40 N 1.50 E
Rambutyo Island I 164 2.20 S 147.50 E
Rām Dās 123 31.58 N 74.54 E
Rāmdia 126 23.42 N 89.32 E
Rāmdurg 122 15.57 N 75.18 E
Ramea 186 47.31 N 57.23 W
Ramea Islands II 186 47.31 N 57.21 W
Rāmechhāp 124 27.20 N 86.05 E
Rame Head ›, Transkei 158 31.48 S 29.22 E
Rame Head ›, Eng., U.K. 42 50.19 N 4.13 W
Rämen ⊚ 40 60.18 N 15.10 E
Ramenje, S.S.S.R. 76 60.17 N 43.46 E
Ramenje, S.S.S.R. 82 56.34 N 37.13 E
Ramenka ◆[8] 265b 55.41 N 37.30 E
Ramenskoje 82 55.34 N 38.14 E
Ramer 194 32.03 N 86.13 W
Ramerupt 50 48.31 N 4.18 E
Rameški 76 57.21 N 36.03 E
Rāmeswaram 122 9.17 N 79.18 E
Ramey 214 40.48 N 78.24 W
Ramey Air Force Base ■ 240m 18.30 N 67.08 W
Rāmganj 126 23.06 N 90.51 E
Rāmgarh, Bngl. 120 22.59 N 91.44 E
Rāmgarh, India 120 27.22 N 70.30 E
Rāmgarh, India 120 27.15 N 75.11 E
Rāmgarh, India 124 23.38 N 85.31 E
Rāmgarh, India 124 24.34 N 87.15 E
Rāmgarh, India 126 22.42 N 87.04 E
Rāmgarh Hills ⋀[2] 124 22.50 N 83.10 E
Ram Head › 240m 18.18 N 64.42 W
Rāmhormoz 128 31.16 N 49.36 E
Ramingstein 64 47.04 N 13.50 E
Ramírez, Méx. 196 25.57 N 97.46 W
Ramírez, Méx. 196 27.20 N 100.58 W
Ramiriquí 246 5.24 N 73.20 W
Ramis ≃ 144 7.59 N 41.34 E
Rāmjībanpur 126 22.50 N 87.37 E
Rāmkānāli 126 23.35 N 86.45 E
Raml, Qārat ar- ∧[2] 142 30.02 N 30.39 E
Ramla 132 31.55 N 34.52 E
Ramlu ∧ 144 13.24 N 41.51 E
Ramm, Jabal ∧ 132 29.35 N 35.24 E
Rämmen 40 60.07 N 14.08 E
Rāmnagar, India 123 32.49 N 75.19 E
Rāmnagar, India 124 25.17 N 83.02 E
Rāmnagar, India 124 29.24 N 79.07 E
Rāmnagar, India 126 21.41 N 87.33 E
Rāmnagar, India 272b 22.23 N 88.19 E
Ramnäs 40 59.46 N 16.12 E
Ramo 144 6.42 N 41.23 E
Ramon' 78 51.54 N 39.20 E
Ramon, Har ∧ 132 30.30 N 34.38 E
Ramon, Makhtesh ⊥[7] 132 30.36 N 34.49 E
Ramon, Naḥal V 132 30.36 N 34.55 E
Ramona, Ca., U.S. 228 33.02 N 116.52 W
Ramona, Ok., U.S. 196 36.31 N 95.55 W
Ramona, S.D., U.S. 198 44.07 N 97.12 W
Ramor, Lough ⊚ 48 53.49 N 7.05 W
Ramos 234 22.50 N 101.55 W
Ramos ◆[8] 287a 22.51 S 43.15 W
Ramos ≃[1] 150 5.08 N 5.22 E
Ramos Arizpe 232 25.33 N 100.58 W
Ramosch 58 46.50 N 10.22 E
Ramos Island I 116 8.06 N 117.02 E
Ramos Mejía 258 34.38 S 58.34 W
Ramotswa 156 24.56 S 25.50 E
Rāmpāl 126 22.34 N 89.39 E
Rampart 180 65.30 N 150.11 W
Ramparts ≃ 180 66.11 N 129.03 W
Rampillon 50 48.33 N 3.04 E
Rampside 44 54.05 N 3.10 W
Rāmpur, India 120 31.27 N 77.38 E
Rāmpur, India 123 29.49 N 77.27 E
Rāmpur, India 124 28.49 N 79.02 E
Rāmpur □[5] 124 28.50 N 79.05 E
Rāmpura 120 24.28 N 75.26 E
Rāmpura Phūl 123 30.17 N 75.14 E
Rampur Boalia → Rājshāhi 124 24.22 N 88.36 E
Rāmpur Hāt 126 24.10 N 87.47 E
Ramrath 263 51.06 N 6.41 E
Ramree Island I 110 19.06 N 93.48 E
Rāmsāgar 126 23.05 N 87.17 E
Ramsau 64 47.36 N 12.54 E
Ramsay Range ⋀ 162 18.31 S 127.03 E
Ramsbeck 56 51.18 N 8.24 E
Ramsberg 40 59.46 N 15.17 E
Ramsbottom 44 53.40 N 2.19 W
Ramsden Bellhouse 260 51.37 N 0.29 E
Ramsden Heath 260 51.38 N 0.28 E
Ramsdorf 52 51.54 N 6.55 E
Ramsele 26 63.33 N 16.29 E
Ramsenthal 60 50.01 N 11.35 E
Ramseur 192 35.44 N 79.39 W
Ramsey, I. of Man 44 54.20 N 4.21 W
Ramsey, Eng., U.K. 42 51.56 N 1.14 E
Ramsey, Eng., U.K. 42 52.27 N 0.07 W
Ramsey, Il., U.S. 219 39.08 N 89.06 W
Ramsey, N.J., U.S. 210 41.03 N 74.08 W
Ramsey Bay ⊂ 44 54.20 N 4.20 W
Ramsey Brook ≃ 276 41.02 N 74.08 W
Ramsey Creek ≃ 219 39.03 N 89.04 W
Ramsey Island I 42 51.52 N 5.10 W
Ramsey Lake ⊚ 190 47.15 N 82.16 W
Ramsey Lake State Park ♠ 219 39.10 N 89.08 W
Ramsgate, Austl. 274a 33.59 S 151.08 E
Ramsgate, S. Afr. 158 30.55 S 30.20 E
Ramsgate, Eng., U.K. 42 51.20 N 1.25 E
Rāmshai 124 26.44 N 88.51 E
Rāmshīr 128 30.54 N 49.24 E
Ramshorn Peak ∧ 202 45.09 N 111.06 W
Rämshyttan 40 60.18 N 15.13 E
Ramsjö 26 62.11 N 15.39 E
Ramsloh 52 53.06 N 7.40 E
Ramstein 56 49.27 N 7.33 E
Rāmtek 120 21.24 N 79.20 E
Rāmu, Bngl. 120 21.25 N 92.07 E
Ramu, Kenya 154 3.56 N 41.13 E
Ramu ≃ 164 5.00 S 144.40 E
Ramuševo 76 57.50 N 31.37 E
Ramvik 26 62.49 N 17.51 E
Ramville, Îlet I 240e 14.42 N 60.53 W
Ramygala 76 55.31 N 24.18 E
Ramzaj 80 53.18 N 44.44 E
Rānāghāt 126 23.11 N 88.35 E
Rana Kao, Volcán ∧[1] 174z 27.11 S 109.27 W
Ranalt 64 47.02 N 11.13 E
Rånäs 40 59.48 N 18.17 E
Ranau 112 5.58 N 116.41 E
Ranau, Danau ⊚ 112 4.50 S 103.55 E
Ranbīrsinghpura 123 32.38 N 74.44 E
Ranburne 194 33.31 N 85.20 W
Ranburn Woods 278 41.33 N 87.22 W
Rancabali 115a 7.08 S 107.21 E
Rancagua 252 34.10 S 70.45 W
Rancah 115a 7.12 S 108.30 E
Rance ≃ 32 48.31 N 1.59 W
Rancevo, S.S.S.R. 76 56.40 N 34.24 E
Rancevo, S.S.S.R. 76 56.50 N 33.02 E
Rancharia 255 22.15 S 50.55 W

DEUTSCH

Name	Seite	Breite°′	Länge°′ E = Ost

Rancheria 180 60.05 N 130.40 W
Ranchería ≃ 246 11.34 N 72.54 W
Rancheria Rock ∧ 202 44.53 N 120.08 W
Ranches of Taos 200 36.22 N 105.37 W
Ranchester 202 44.54 N 107.09 W
Rānchī 124 23.21 N 85.20 E
Rānchi □[5] 124 23.00 N 85.00 E
Ranchillos 252 26.57 S 65.03 W
Rānchi Plateau ⋀[1] 124 23.20 N 84.50 E
Ranch Lake ⊚ 184 52.30 N 104.46 W
Rancho Colorado, Presa de ⊚[1] 286a 19.29 N 99.17 W
Rancho Cordova 226 38.35 N 121.18 W
Rancho Del Mar 226 38.10 N 122.15 W
Rancho Nuevo, Méx. 196 26.22 N 99.54 W
Rancho Nuevo, Méx. 234 23.12 N 97.48 W
Rancho Palos Verdes 228 33.45 N 118.24 W
Rancho Rinconado 226 37.18 N 122.01 W
Rancho Santa Fe 228 33.01 N 117.12 W
Rancho Veloz 240p 22.53 N 80.23 W
Ranchuelo 240p 22.23 N 80.09 W
Ranco, Lago ⊚ 254 40.14 S 72.24 W
Rancocas 208 40.00 N 74.52 W
Rancocas Creek ≃ 285 40.02 N 74.59 W
Rancocas Creek, North Branch ≃ 208 40.00 N 74.52 W
Rancocas Creek, South Branch ≃ 208 40.00 N 74.52 W
Rancocas Creek, Southwest Branch ≃ 285 39.57 N 74.48 W
Rancocas Heights 285 39.59 N 74.51 W
Rancocas State Park ♠ 285 40.00 N 74.50 W
Rancocas Woods 285 39.59 N 74.51 W
Rancul 252 35.03 S 64.42 W
Rand 166 35.36 S 146.35 E
Rand (Germiston) Airport ⊠ 273d 26.15 S 28.09 E
Randa 58 46.07 N 7.47 E
Randall Lake ⊚ 216 41.57 N 85.02 W
Randall Park Mall ◆[9] 279a 41.26 N 81.32 W
Randalls Island I 276 40.48 N 73.55 W
Randallstown 284b 39.22 N 76.48 W
Randalstown 48 54.45 N 6.19 W
Randan 32 46.01 N 3.21 E
Randazzo 70 37.53 N 14.57 E
Randbøl 41 55.42 N 9.16 E
Randburg 273d 26.06 S 27.59 E
Rānder 120 21.14 N 72.47 E
Randers 26 56.28 N 10.03 E
Randfontein 158 26.11 S 27.42 E
Randfontein □[5] 273d 26.13 S 27.40 E
Randgate 273d 26.11 S 27.41 E
Randhurst ◆[9] 278 42.05 N 87.56 W
Randle 224 46.32 N 121.57 W
Randleman 192 35.49 N 79.48 W
Randlett 196 34.10 N 98.27 W
Randolph, Az., U.S. 200 32.55 N 111.30 W
Randolph, Me., U.S. 188 44.13 N 69.46 W
Randolph, Ma., U.S. 207 42.09 N 71.02 W
Randolph, Ne., U.S. 198 42.22 N 97.21 W
Randolph, N.Y., U.S. 210 42.09 N 78.58 W
Randolph, Oh., U.S. 214 41.01 N 81.14 W
Randolph, Ut,. U.S. 200 41.39 N 111.10 W
Randolph, Vt., U.S. 188 43.55 N 72.39 W
Randolph, Wi., U.S. 190 43.32 N 89.00 W
Randolph □[6], In., U.S. 218 40.10 N 85.00 W
Randolph □[6], Mo., U.S. 219 39.22 N 92.20 W
Randolph Air Force Base ■ 196 29.32 N 98.16 W
Randolph Hills 284c 39.03 N 77.05 W
Randolph Village 284c 38.53 N 76.52 W
Random Island I 186 48.08 N 53.45 W
Random Lake 190 43.33 N 87.57 W
Randow ≃ 54 53.41 N 14.04 E
Randowaya 164 1.52 S 136.31 E
Randowbruch ≋ 54 53.15 N 14.10 E
Randsburg 228 35.22 N 117.39 W
Randse Afrikaanse Universiteit Ʊ[2] 273d 26.11 S 27.50 E
Randsfjorden ⊚ 26 60.25 N 10.24 E
Rand Stadium ♠ 273d 26.14 S 28.03 E
Randublatung 115a 7.12 S 111.23 E
Randudongkal 115a 7.06 S 109.19 E
Randwick 170 33.55 S 151.15 E
Randwick Racecourse ♠ 274a 33.54 S 151.14 E
Råneå 26 65.52 N 22.18 E
Ranelagh 258 34.48 S 58.12 W
Rāner 123 28.53 N 73.17 E
Ranérou 150 15.18 N 13.58 W
Rāneswar 126 24.02 N 87.25 E
Raneue 114 5.03 N 95.20 E
Ranford 168a 32.48 S 116.31 E
Ranfurly, N.Z. 172 45.08 S 170.06 E
Ranfurly, Scot., U.K. 46 55.52 N 4.33 W
Rangae 114 6.17 N 101.44 E
Rāngāmāti 120 22.38 N 92.12 E
Rangantemiang 112 0.35 S 113.19 E
Rangasa, Tanjung › 112 2.38 S 118.49 E
Rangaunu Bay ⊂ 172 34.50 S 173.15 E
Range Creek ≃ 200 39.18 N 110.04 W
Range Indian Reserve ◆[4] 182 49.09 N 119.50 W
Rangeley 188 44.57 N 70.38 W
Rangely 200 40.05 N 108.48 W
Ranger 196 32.28 N 98.40 W
Ranger Lake ⊚ 190 46.54 N 83.35 W
Rangersdorf 64 46.51 N 12.58 E
Ranghe 100 33.43 N 112.51 E
Rangia 120 26.28 N 91.38 E
Rangiora 172 43.18 S 172.36 E
Rangitaiki ≃ 172 37.54 S 176.53 E
Rangitata ≃ 172 44.12 S 171.30 E
Rangitikei ≃ 172 40.18 S 175.14 E
Rangitukia 172 37.46 S 178.27 E
Rangkasbitung 115a 6.21 S 106.15 E
Rangkul' 85 38.29 N 74.22 E
Rangoon 110 16.47 N 96.10 E
Rangoon □[8] 110 16.50 N 96.10 E
Rangoon ≃ 110 16.29 N 96.21 E
Rangpo 124 27.11 N 88.32 E
Rangpur, Bngl. 124 25.45 N 89.15 E
Rangpur, Pāk. 123 30.31 N 71.34 E
Rangpuri ⊥ 272a 28.33 N 77.08 E
Rangsang, Pulau I 114 1.00 N 102.55 E
Rangsdorf 54 52.17 N 13.25 E
Rangsdorfer See ⊚ 264a 52.17 N 13.24 E
Ranguana Cay I 236 16.20 N 88.09 W
Ranguana Entrance ⊔ 236 16.19 N 88.09 W
Rangun → Rangoon 110 16.47 N 96.10 E
Ranholas 266c 38.47 N 9.22 W
Rānībāndh 126 22.52 N 86.47 E
Rānībennur 122 14.37 N 75.37 E
Rānīganj 126 23.37 N 87.08 E
Rānīkhet 124 29.39 N 79.25 E
Ranino 80 52.58 N 40.15 E
Rānipet 122 12.56 N 79.20 E
Ranis 54 50.39 N 11.34 E
Rāniwāra 120 24.45 N 72.13 E
Rāniyah 128 36.15 N 44.53 E
Ranken ≃ 166 20.31 S 137.36 E
Ranken Store 166 19.35 S 136.55 E
Rankin, Il., U.S. 216 40.27 N 87.53 W
Rankin, Mi., U.S. 216 42.55 N 83.46 W
Rankin, Pa., U.S. 279b 40.24 N 79.52 W
Rankin, Tx., U.S. 196 31.13 N 101.56 W
Rankin Inlet 176 62.45 N 92.10 W
Rankins Springs 166 33.50 S 146.16 E
Rānkūs 132 33.45 N 36.23 E
Rankweil 58 47.17 N 9.39 E
Ranlo 192 35.17 N 81.07 W
Ranneje 80 55.17 N 37.17 E
Rannersdorf 264b 48.08 N 16.28 E
Rannoch, Loch ⊚ 46 56.41 N 4.20 W
Rannoch Moor ◆[3] 46 56.38 N 4.40 W

Symbols in the index entries represent the broad categories identified in the key at the right. Symbols with superior numbers (⋀[1]) identify subcategories (see complete key on page I · 1).

Kartensymbole in dem Registerverzeichnis stellen die rechts in Schlüssel erklärten Kategorien dar. Symbole mit hochgestellten Ziffern (⋀[1]) bezeichnen Unterabteilungen einer Kategorie (vgl. vollständiger Schlüssel auf Seite I · 1).

Los símbolos incluidos en el texto del índice representan las grandes categorías identificadas con la clave a la derecha. Los símbolos con numeros en su parte superior (⋀[1]) identifican las subcategorías (véase la clave completa en la página I · 1).

Les symboles de l'index représentent les catégories indiquées dans la légende à droite. Les symboles suivis d'un indice (⋀[1]) représentent des sous-catégories (voir légende complète à la page I · 1).

Os símbolos incluídos no texto do índice representam as grandes categorias identificadas com a chave à direita. Os símbolos com números em sua parte superior (⋀[1]) identificam as subcategorias (veja-se a chave completa à página I · 1).

∧ Mountain	Berg	Montaña	Montagne	Montanha
⋀ Mountains	Berge	Montañas	Montagnes	Montanhas
)(Pass	Pass	Paso	Col	Passo
V Valley, Canyon	Tal, Cañon	Valle, Cañón	Vallée, Canyon	Vale, Canhão
≐ Plain	Ebene	Llano	Plaine	Planície
› Cape	Kap	Cabo	Cap	Cabo
I Island	Insel	Isla	Île	Ilha
II Islands	Inseln	Islas	Îles	Ilhas
⊥ Other Topographic Features	Andere Topographische Objekte	Otros Elementos Topográficos	Autres données topographiques	Outros acidentes topográficos

ESPAÑOL

Nombre	Página	Lat.°′	Long.°′ W = Oeste
Rann of Kutch → Kutch, Rann of ≃	120	24.05 N	70.10 E
Ranobe ≃	157b	17.10 S	44.08 E
Ranohira	157b	22.29 S	45.24 E
Ranomafana, Madag.	157b	18.57 S	48.50 E
Ranomafana, Madag.	157b	24.36 S	46.58 E
Ranomena	157b	23.25 S	47.17 E
Ranong	110	9.58 N	98.38 E
Ranongga Island I	175e	8.05 S	156.34 E
Ranopiso	157b	25.03 S	46.40 E
Ranot	110	7.46 N	100.19 E
Ranotsara Nord	157b	22.48 S	46.36 E
Rānsai	272c	18.53 N	73.05 E
Ransäter	40	59.46 N	13.26 E
Ransiki	164	1.30 S	134.10 E
Ransom, Il., U.S.	216	41.09 N	88.39 W
Ransom, Ks., U.S.	198	38.38 N	99.56 W
Ransom, Pa., U.S.	210	41.24 N	75.50 W
Ransom Creek ≃	284a	43.04 N	78.45 W
Ransomville	210	43.14 N	78.54 W
Ranson	188	39.17 N	77.51 W
Ransta	40	59.48 N	16.38 E
Ranstadt	56	50.21 N	8.59 E
Rantabe	157b	15.42 S	49.39 E
Rantasalmi	26	62.04 N	28.18 E
Rantau, Indon.	112	2.56 S	115.09 E
Rantau, Malay.	114	2.35 N	101.58 E
Rantaukampar	114	1.24 N	100.59 E
Rantaupanjang, Indon.	112	1.51 S	102.19 E
Rantaupanjang, Indon.	112	1.16 S	101.49 E
Rantaupanjang, Indon.	114	0.58 N	99.13 E
Rantauprapat	114	2.06 N	99.50 E
Rantekombola, Bulu ʌ	112	3.21 S	120.01 E
Ranten	61	47.09 N	14.05 E
Rantepao	112	2.59 S	119.54 E
Rantigny	50	49.20 N	2.26 E
Rantoul	216	40.09 N	88.20 W
Rantsila	26	64.31 N	25.39 E
Rantzau	54	54.15 N	10.30 E
Ranua	26	65.55 N	26.32 E
Rānvād	272c	18.53 N	72.55 E
Ranwanalenaus	156	19.35 S	22.47 E
Råö	26	57.24 N	11.56 E
Rao'er	100	28.48 N	117.40 E
Raohe	89	46.47 N	134.00 E
Raon-L'Étape	58	48.24 N	6.51 E
Raon-sur-Plaine	58	48.31 N	7.06 E
Raoping	100	23.43 N	117.01 E
Raoui, 'Erg er ◆[2]	148	29.17 N	2.20 W
Raoul	192	34.27 N	83.36 W
Raoul Island I	14	29.16 S	177.54 W
Raoyang	98	38.16 N	115.44 E
Raoyang ≃	104	41.50 N	122.35 E
Raoyanghe	104	41.46 N	122.26 E
Rapa I	14	27.36 S	144.20 W
Rapa, Ponta do >	252	27.22 S	48.26 W
Rapallo	62	44.21 N	9.14 E
Rapang	112	3.50 S	119.48 E
Rāpar	120	23.34 N	70.38 E
Raparo, Monte ʌ	68	40.12 N	15.59 E
Rapatovo	80	55.04 N	54.37 E
Rāpch ≃	128	25.28 N	59.21 E
Rapel ≃	252	33.55 S	71.51 W
Rapel, Embalse ◎[1]	252	34.12 S	71.30 W
Rapelli	252	26.24 S	64.29 W
Raphoe	48	54.52 N	7.36 W
Rapid ≃, Mi., U.S.	190	45.55 N	86.58 W
Rapid ≃, Mn., U.S.	198	48.42 N	94.26 W
Rapid ≃, Wa., U.S.	224	47.48 N	121.18 W
Rapidan ≃	188	38.22 N	77.37 W
Rapid Bay	168b	35.32 S	138.12 E
Rapid City, Mb., Can.	184	50.08 N	100.02 W
Rapid City, Mi., U.S.	190	44.50 N	85.16 W
Rapid City, S.D., U.S.	198	44.04 N	103.13 W
Rapid Creek ≃	198	43.54 N	102.37 W
Rapide Taureau, Barrage du ◆[6]	206	46.52 N	73.39 W
Rapid River	190	45.55 N	86.58 W
Räpina	76	58.06 N	27.27 E
Rapkan	85	40.22 N	70.40 E
Rapla	76	59.01 N	24.47 E
Rapness	46	59.14 N	2.51 W
Rapolano Terme	66	43.17 N	11.36 E
Rapolla	68	40.58 N	15.41 E
Rapone	68	40.51 N	15.30 E
Raposo ʌ[2]	266c	38.40 N	9.11 W
Rappahannock ≃	208	37.34 N	76.18 W
Rappbodestausee ◎[1]	54	51.09 N	10.58 E
Rappenlochschlucht ∟	58	47.23 N	9.47 E
Rappottenstein	61	48.31 N	15.05 E
Rāpti ≃, Asia	124	26.18 N	83.41 E
Rāpti ≃, Nepāl	124	27.33 N	84.07 E
Rápulo ≃	248	13.43 S	65.32 W
Rapu-Rapu	116	13.11 N	124.08 E
Rapu Rapu Island I	116	13.12 N	124.09 E
Raqabah, Khashm ar- ʌ[2]	142	28.18 N	31.43 E
Raquette ≃	206	45.00 N	74.42 W
Raraka I[1]	14	16.10 S	144.54 W
Rāribahāl	126	24.05 N	87.21 E
Raritan	210	40.34 N	74.38 W
Raritan ≃	208	40.29 N	74.17 W
Raritan, North Branch ≃	210	40.33 N	74.41 W
Raritan, South Branch ≃	210	40.33 N	74.41 W
Raritan Bay ⊂	208	40.28 N	74.12 W
Raroïa I	14	16.01 S	142.27 W
Raron	58	46.19 N	7.48 E
Rarotonga I	174k	21.14 S	159.46 W
Rarotonga International Airport ⊠	174k	21.12 S	159.49 W
Rarz	85	39.23 N	68.44 E
Rasa, Ilha I	287a	23.04 S	43.09 W
Rasa, Punta >	254	40.51 S	62.19 W
Rašaant	88	49.07 N	101.25 E
Rasa da Guaratiba, Ilha I	256	23.05 S	43.34 W
Rasa Island I	116	9.14 N	118.27 E
Ra's al-ʿAyn	130	36.51 N	40.04 E
Ra's al-Barr	142	31.31 N	31.50 E
Ra's al-Khalīj	142	31.15 N	31.39 E
Ra's al-Khaymah	128	25.47 N	55.57 E
Ra's al-Unūf	146	30.31 N	18.34 E
Ra's al-Ushsh ◆[8]	142	31.08 N	32.18 E
Ra's an-Naqb, Miṣr	132	29.36 N	34.51 E
Ra's an-Naqb, Urd.	132	30.00 N	35.29 E
Rasawi	164	2.04 S	134.01 E
Ra's Baʿlabakk	130	34.15 N	36.25 E
Rasbo	40	59.57 N	17.53 E
Raschau	54	50.32 N	12.50 E
Ras Dashen Terara ʌ	144	13.16 N	38.24 E
Rasdorf	56	50.43 N	9.53 E
Raseborg	26	59.59 N	23.39 E
Raseiniai	76	55.24 N	23.07 E
Râs el Aïoun	36	35.30 N	8.18 E
Ras el Ma, Alg.	148	34.31 N	0.46 W
Râs el Mâ, Mali	150	16.37 N	4.28 W
Ras el Oued	34	35.57 N	5.03 E
Rasen-Antholz → Anterselva di Sopra	64	46.52 N	12.08 E
Raševka	78	50.14 N	33.54 E
Rashād	140	11.51 N	31.04 E
Rāshayyā	132	33.30 N	35.51 E
Rashīd (Rosetta)	142	31.24 N	30.25 E
Rashīd, Farʿ (Rosetta Branch) ≃	142	31.30 N	30.21 E
Rashīd, Maṣabb (Rosetta Mouth) ≃[1]	142	31.30 N	30.20 E
Rashīd Qalʿeh	120	31.31 N	67.31 E

FRANÇAIS

Nom	Page	Lat.°′	Long.°′ W = Ouest
Rashin → Najin	98	42.15 N	130.18 E
Rasht	128	37.16 N	49.36 E
Rashtrapati Bhawan ✿	272a	28.37 N	77.12 E
Rasina ≃	38	43.37 N	21.22 E
Rāsipuram	122	11.28 N	78.10 E
Rasi Salai	110	15.20 N	104.09 E
Rāsk	128	26.13 N	61.25 E
Raška	38	43.17 N	20.37 E
Rask Mølle	41	55.52 N	9.37 E
Rās Koh ʌ	128	28.50 N	65.12 E
Raškov	78	47.57 N	28.50 E
Raskunda	126	22.48 N	87.26 E
Rasm al-Arwām, Sabkhat ◎	130	35.53 N	37.40 E
R'asna	76	54.01 N	31.12 E
R'asnopol'	78	47.04 N	31.12 E
Raso, Cabo >	266c	38.43 N	9.29 W
Raso, Ilhéu I	150a	16.37 N	24.36 W
Rasocolmo, Capo >	70	38.18 N	15.31 E
Rason Lake ◎	162	28.46 S	124.20 E
Raspberry Peak ʌ	194	34.23 N	94.01 W
Raspopinskaja	80	49.24 N	42.52 E
Rasra	124	25.51 N	83.51 E
Rass Jebel	36	37.13 N	10.09 E
Rasskazovka	265b	55.38 N	37.20 E
Rasskazovo	80	52.40 N	41.53 E
Rassšua, ostrov I	74	47.45 N	153.01 E
Rassudovo	82	55.29 N	36.54 E
Rassvet, S.S.S.R.	84	43.58 N	46.44 E
Rassvet, S.S.S.R.	84	43.58 N	46.44 E
Rassvet, S.S.S.R.	86	57.02 N	91.34 E
Rassvet, S.S.S.R.	88	57.02 N	91.34 E
Rassypnaja	80	51.35 N	53.37 E
Rassypnoje	83	48.08 N	38.34 E
Rast	38	43.53 N	23.17 E
Rastälven ≃	40	59.37 N	14.56 E
Rastatt	56	48.51 N	8.12 E
Rastavica ≃	78	49.44 N	30.01 E
Rastede	52	53.15 N	8.11 E
Rastegai'sa ʌ	24	70.00 N	26.18 E
Rastenberg	54	51.10 N	11.25 E
Rastenburg → Kętrzyn	30	54.06 N	21.23 E
Rastorf	54	54.16 N	10.19 E
Rastorgujevo	82	55.33 N	37.41 E
Rastovcy	82	56.39 N	37.35 E
Rastunovo	82	55.16 N	37.50 E
Rasu, Monte ʌ	71	40.25 N	9.00 E
Rasūl	123	32.42 N	73.34 E
Rasūlnagar	123	32.20 N	73.47 E
Rasulpur	272a	28.37 N	77.22 E
Rasulpur ◆[8]	272a	28.42 N	77.01 E
Rasun di sopra	64	46.48 N	12.03 E
Rasun di sotto	64	46.47 N	12.02 E
Rasura	58	46.06 N	9.33 E
Råsvalen ◎	40	59.40 N	15.10 E
Răsvani	38	44.25 N	26.53 E
Rat ≃, Mb., Can.	184	49.35 N	97.08 W
Rat ≃, Mb., Can.	184	55.41 N	99.04 W
Ratahan	112	1.04 N	124.48 E
Ratak Chain II	14	9.00 N	171.00 E
Ratangarh	120	28.05 N	74.36 E
Ratanpur, India	126	23.07 N	87.04 E
Ratanpur, India	272b	22.50 N	88.14 E
Rätansbyn	26	62.29 N	14.32 E
Rat Burana	269a	13.41 N	100.30 E
Ratčino, S.S.S.R.	80	53.02 N	39.55 E
Ratčino, S.S.S.R.	82	55.16 N	38.39 E
Ratcliff	222	31.24 N	95.08 W
Rateče	64	46.30 N	13.43 E
Ratekau	54	53.57 N	10.44 E
Rāth	124	25.35 N	79.34 E
Rath ◆[8]	263	51.17 N	6.49 E
Rathangan	48	53.12 N	6.59 W
Rathbone	210	42.08 N	77.19 W
Rathbun Lake ◎	212	44.47 N	78.12 W
Rathbun Lake ◎[1]	190	40.54 N	93.05 W
Rathcoole	48	53.16 N	6.28 W
Rathcormack	48	52.54 N	8.17 W
Rathdowney, Austl.	171a	28.12 S	152.52 E
Rathdowney, Ire.	48	52.50 N	7.34 W
Rathdrum, Ire.	48	52.56 N	6.13 W
Rathdrum, Id., U.S.	202	47.48 N	116.53 W
Rathebur	54	53.44 N	13.46 E
Ratheim	52	51.04 N	6.10 E
Rathen	46	57.38 N	2.02 W
Rathenow	54	52.36 N	12.20 E
Rathfriland	48	54.14 N	6.10 W
Rathkeale	48	52.32 N	8.56 W
Rathlin Island I	48	55.18 N	6.13 W
Rathlin Sound ⊔	48	55.15 N	6.15 W
Ráth Luirc (Charleville)	48	52.21 N	8.41 W
Rathmecke	263	51.15 N	7.38 E
Rathmelton	48	55.02 N	7.38 W
Rathmore	48	52.03 N	9.13 W
Rathmullen	48	55.06 N	7.33 W
Rathnew	48	53.00 N	6.05 W
Ratho	46	55.55 N	3.22 W
Rathowen	48	53.40 N	7.31 W
Rathstock	54	52.31 N	14.32 E
Rathwell	184	49.40 N	98.32 W
Ratibor → Racibórz	30	50.06 N	18.13 E
Raticosa, Passo della)(	66	44.10 N	11.20 E
Rätikon ⋀	58	47.03 N	9.40 E
Ratingen	56	51.18 N	6.51 E
Ratisbon → Regensburg	60	49.01 N	12.06 E
Rätische Alpen → Rhaetian Alps ⋀	58	46.30 N	10.00 E
Rat Island I	181a	51.55 N	178.20 E
Rat Islands II	181a	51.40 N	178.30 E
Rat'kovo	82	56.01 N	38.38 E
Rat Lake ◎	184	56.10 N	99.40 W
Ratlām	120	23.19 N	75.04 E
Ratmanova, ostrov I	180	65.46 N	169.02 W
Ratnāgiri	122	16.59 N	73.18 E
Ratnapura	122	6.41 N	80.24 E
Ratno	78	51.40 N	24.31 E
Ratodero	120	27.48 N	68.18 E
Ratomka	76	53.56 N	27.21 E
Raton	196	36.54 N	104.26 W
Raton Pass)(	196	36.59 N	104.29 W
Ratt ≃	224	47.27 N	124.21 W
Rattanaburi	110	15.19 N	103.51 E
Rattaphum	110	7.08 N	100.16 E
Ratten	61	47.29 N	15.43 E
Rattlesnake	202	46.56 N	113.59 W
Rattlesnake Creek ≃, Ks., U.S.	198	38.13 N	98.22 W
Rattlesnake Creek ≃, Oh., U.S.	218	39.16 N	83.23 W
Rattlesnake Creek ≃, Or., U.S.	202	42.44 N	117.47 W
Rattlesnake Creek ≃, Wa., U.S.	224	46.45 N	120.55 W
Rattlesnake Creek ≃, Wa., U.S.	224	45.48 N	121.29 W
Rattlesnake Mountain ʌ	207	41.42 N	72.50 W
Rattlesnake Peak ʌ	280	34.16 N	117.47 W
Rattling Brook	186	49.38 N	56.10 W
Rattling Run ≃	279b	40.33 N	79.32 W
Rattray Head >	46	57.37 N	1.49 W
Rattu	123	35.08 N	74.48 E
Rättvik	26	60.53 N	15.06 E
Ratz, Mount ʌ	180	57.23 N	132.19 W
Ratzebuhr → Okonek	30	53.33 N	16.50 E
Ratzeburg	54	53.42 N	10.46 E
Ratzeburger See ◎	54	53.45 N	10.47 E
Rätzlingen	54	52.23 N	11.08 E
Rau	112	0.34 N	100.01 E
Raub, Malay.	114	3.48 N	101.52 E
Raub, In., U.S.	216	40.44 N	87.29 W
Raubsville	208	40.38 N	75.12 W
Rauch	252	36.46 S	59.06 W
Raucheck ʌ	64	47.30 N	13.14 E
Rauchenwarth	264b	48.05 N	16.32 E
Rauchtown	210	41.07 N	77.14 W
Raucourt-et-Flaba	56	49.36 N	4.57 E

PORTUGUÊS

Nome	Página	Lat.°′	Long.°′ W = Oeste
Rauen	54	52.20 N	14.01 E
Rauenstein	54	50.24 N	11.03 E
Raufarhöfn	24a	66.30 N	15.57 W
Raufoss	26	60.43 N	10.37 E
Rauhe Ebrach ≃	56	49.50 N	10.56 E
Raukumara Range ⋀	172	37.47 S	178.02 E
Raul Soares	255	20.05 S	42.22 W
Rauma	26	61.08 N	21.30 E
Rauma ≃	26	62.33 N	7.43 E
Raumünzach	56	48.38 N	8.21 E
Rauna	76	57.20 N	25.43 E
Raunds	42	52.21 N	0.33 W
Raung, Gunung ʌ	115a	8.08 S	114.03 E
Raunheim	56	50.01 N	8.28 E
Raupal'an	180	65.28 N	171.59 W
Raurimu	172	39.07 S	175.24 E
Rauris	64	47.13 N	13.00 E
Raurkela	124	22.13 N	84.53 E
Rauschenberg	56	50.53 N	8.55 E
Rausu	92a	44.01 N	145.12 E
Rautalampi	26	62.38 N	26.50 E
Rāutara	272b	22.51 N	88.28 E
Rautavaara	26	63.29 N	28.18 E
Ravahere I[1]	14	18.14 S	142.09 W
Ravalgaon	122	20.38 N	74.25 E
Ravanica, Manastir ✿[1]	38	43.58 N	21.26 E
Ravānsar	128	34.43 N	46.40 E
Ravanusa	70	37.16 N	13.58 E
Rāvar	128	31.15 N	56.53 E
Ravarano	64	44.35 N	10.04 E
Ravarino	64	44.44 N	11.06 E
Rava-Russkaja	78	50.14 N	23.37 E
Ravascletto	64	46.32 N	12.57 E
Ravat	85	39.54 N	70.12 E
Ravello	68	40.39 N	14.37 E
Ravelo	248	18.48 S	65.32 W
Raven	192	37.05 N	81.51 W
Ravena	210	42.28 N	73.49 W
Ravenglass	44	54.21 N	3.24 W
Raven Lake ◎	212	45.13 N	78.51 W
Ravenna, It.	66	44.25 N	12.12 E
Ravenna, Ky., U.S.	192	37.41 N	83.57 W
Ravenna, Mi., U.S.	216	43.11 N	85.56 W
Ravenna, Ne., U.S.	198	41.01 N	98.54 W
Ravenna, Oh., U.S.	214	41.09 N	81.14 W
Ravenna □[4]	66	44.25 N	11.59 E
Ravensbourne	171a	27.22 S	152.10 E
Ravensbourne National Park ♠	171a	27.21 S	152.15 E
Ravensburg	58	47.47 N	9.37 E
Ravenscrag	184	49.30 N	109.05 W
Ravensdale	224	47.21 N	121.58 W
Ravenshoe	166	17.37 S	145.29 E
Ravensthorpe, Austl.	162	33.35 S	120.02 E
Ravensthorpe, Eng., U.K.	44	53.42 N	1.35 W
Ravenswood, S. Afr.	273d	26.11 S	28.15 E
Ravenswood, Mi., U.S.	216	42.45 N	84.36 W
Ravenswood, W.V., U.S.	188	38.56 N	81.45 W
Ravenswood Park ♠	283	42.36 N	70.42 W
Ravenswood Point >	282	37.30 N	122.08 W
Ravensworth	284c	38.48 N	77.13 W
Răver	120	21.15 N	76.02 E
Ravernet ≃	44	54.30 N	6.04 W
Rāvi ≃	123	30.35 N	71.49 E
Ravières	50	47.45 N	4.17 E
Ravine	208	40.34 N	76.24 W
Ravine Lake ◎[1]	276	40.43 N	74.38 W
Ravinia Park ♠	278	42.09 N	87.46 W
Ravlı	130	40.08 N	33.06 E
Ravna Gora	36	45.23 N	14.57 E
Ravne	61	46.33 N	14.58 E
Ravnina	128	37.57 N	62.40 E
Ravsted	41	55.01 N	9.08 E
Rāwah	128	34.28 N	41.55 E
Rawaki I[1]	14	3.43 S	170.43 W
Rāwala Kot	123	33.52 N	73.46 E
Rāwalpindi	123	33.36 N	73.04 E
Rawa Mazowiecka	30	51.46 N	20.16 E
Rāwāndūz	128	36.37 N	44.31 E
Rawang	114	3.19 N	101.35 E
Rawas ≃	112	2.42 S	103.24 E
Rawāwiṣ, Wādī V	146	30.26 N	15.24 E
Rawḍah ◎	130	35.15 N	41.05 E
Rawḍah, Wādī ar- V	130	34.22 N	37.21 E
Rawd al-Faraj ◆[8]	273c	30.05 N	31.14 E
Rawḍaw, Jazīrat ar- I	273c	30.01 N	31.13 E
Rawdon	206	46.03 N	73.43 W
Rawene	172	35.24 S	173.30 E
Rawḥah	144	19.28 N	41.48 E
Rawhide Creek ≃	198	42.06 N	104.20 W
Rawhide Lake ◎	190	46.39 N	82.37 W
Rawhide Mountain ʌ	204	38.17 N	116.25 W
Rawi	112	2.07 S	113.56 E
Rawi, Ko I	114	6.33 N	99.14 E
Rawicz	30	51.37 N	16.52 E
Rawlinna	162	31.01 S	125.20 E
Rawlins	200	41.47 N	107.14 W
Rawlinson, Mount ʌ	162	25.58 S	127.28 E
Rawlinson Range ⋀	162	24.51 S	128.00 E
Rawmarsh	44	53.27 N	1.21 W
Rawreth	260	51.37 N	0.35 E
Rawson, Arg.	252	34.36 S	60.04 W
Rawson, Arg.	254	43.18 S	65.06 W
Rawson, Oh., U.S.	216	40.57 N	83.47 W
Rawsonville	158	33.41 S	19.20 E
Rawtenstall	44	53.42 N	2.18 W
Rawu	102	29.30 N	96.45 E
Rax ⋀	61	47.42 N	15.43 E
Raxaul	124	26.59 N	84.51 E
Ray, Il., U.S.	219	40.12 N	90.29 W
Ray, In., U.S.	216	41.45 N	84.53 W
Ray, N.D., U.S.	198	48.20 N	103.09 W
Ray ≃	42	51.48 N	1.15 W
Ray, Cape >	186	47.40 N	59.18 W
Raya	112	1.05 N	118.32 E
Raya, Bukit ʌ	112	0.40 S	112.41 E
Raya, Gunong ʌ	114	6.22 N	99.49 E
Raya, Pulau I	114	4.52 N	95.22 E
Rāyachoti	122	14.03 N	78.45 E
Rāyadrug	122	14.42 N	76.52 E
Rāyagada	122	19.10 N	83.25 E
Rayburn	222	30.25 N	94.56 W
Rayen, B.R.D.	263	51.28 N	6.32 E
Rāyen, Īrān	128	29.34 N	57.26 E
Ray Hubbard, Lake ◎[1]	222	32.53 N	96.35 W
Rayland	214	40.11 N	80.41 W
Rayleigh	42	51.36 N	0.36 E
Raymond, Ab., Can.	182	49.27 N	112.39 W
Raymond, Ca., U.S.	226	37.13 N	119.54 W
Raymond, Il., U.S.	219	39.19 N	89.34 W
Raymond, Mn., U.S.	198	45.00 N	95.14 W
Raymond, Ms., U.S.	194	32.15 N	90.25 W
Raymond, Oh., U.S.	216	40.20 N	83.28 W
Raymond, Wa., U.S.	224	46.41 N	123.43 W
Raymond Terrace	170	32.46 S	151.44 E
Raymondville	196	26.29 N	97.47 W
Raymore	184	51.25 N	104.31 W
Ray Mountains ⋀	180	65.45 N	151.30 W
Rāyna	126	23.05 N	87.54 E
Rayne	194	30.14 N	92.16 W
Rayner Glacier ⌂	9	67.40 S	48.30 E
Raynham	207	41.56 N	71.04 W
Raynham Dog Track ♠	283	41.59 N	71.04 W
Rayón, Méx.	232	29.43 N	110.35 W
Rayón, Méx.	234	17.12 N	93.00 W
Rayón, Méx.	234	21.51 N	99.40 W
Rayón, Parque Nacional ♠	234	19.54 N	100.10 W
Rayones	232	25.01 N	100.05 W
Rayong	110	12.40 N	101.17 E
Rāypur	272b	22.25 N	88.31 E
Rayrah ⊤[4]	140	15.21 N	34.41 E
Rayse Creek ≃	219	38.13 N	89.00 W
Raystown Lake ◎[1]	214	40.20 N	78.05 W
Rayton	158	25.45 S	28.32 E
Raytown	194	39.00 N	94.27 W
Rayville	194	32.28 N	91.45 W
Raywood	222	30.02 N	94.40 W
Rayyikhah I	128	26.12 N	36.21 E
Raz, Pointe du >	32	48.02 N	4.44 W
Raza, Punta >	234	21.02 N	105.20 W
Razan, Īrān	128	35.23 N	49.02 E
R'azan', S.S.S.R.	80	54.38 N	39.44 E
R'azan □[4]	82	54.15 N	39.00 E
R'azancevo	82	56.42 N	39.12 E
Ražanj	38	43.40 N	21.33 E
R'azanovo	82	55.29 N	37.31 E
Razāq, Kūh-e ⋀	267d	35.42 N	51.35 E
Razbegaj	265a	59.47 N	29.56 E
Războeni	38	47.05 N	26.32 E
Razdan	84	40.30 N	44.46 E
Razdan ≃	84	39.58 N	44.27 E
Razdel'naja	78	46.51 N	30.05 E
Razdolinsk	86	58.25 N	94.38 E
Razdolje	88	52.27 N	103.13 E
Razdol'noje, S.S.S.R.	78	45.47 N	33.29 E
Razdol'noje, S.S.S.R.	83	47.37 N	38.01 E
Razdol'noje, S.S.S.R.	89	43.30 N	131.52 E
Razdol'nyj	80	46.38 N	42.57 E
Razdorskaja	78	47.33 N	40.38 E
Razdory, S.S.S.R.	78	48.21 N	35.42 E
Razdory, S.S.S.R.	265b	55.45 N	37.18 E
Razelm, Lacul ◎	38	44.54 N	28.57 E
R'aženoje	83	47.31 N	38.52 E
Raževo	86	56.09 N	68.25 E
Razgrad	38	43.32 N	26.31 E
Razlog	38	41.53 N	23.28 E
Razmachnino	88	51.47 N	115.28 E
Razmitelevo	265a	59.54 N	30.41 E
Raznočinovka	80	46.37 N	47.57 E
Raznomojka	86	52.29 N	55.52 E
Razorback Mountain ʌ	182	51.35 N	124.42 W
R'ažsk	80	53.43 N	40.04 E
Razvil'noje	80	46.14 N	41.18 E
Razzoli, Isola I	71	41.18 N	9.21 E
Ré, Île de I	32	46.12 N	1.25 W
Rea ≃, Eng., U.K.	42	52.30 N	1.51 W
Rea ≃, Eng., U.K.	42	52.18 N	2.32 W
Read	262	53.49 N	2.21 W
Reading, Eng., U.K.	42	51.28 N	0.59 W
Reading, Il., U.S.	216	41.05 N	88.51 W
Reading, Ks., U.S.	198	38.31 N	95.57 W
Reading, Ma., U.S.	207	42.31 N	71.05 W
Reading, Mi., U.S.	216	41.50 N	84.44 W
Reading, Oh., U.S.	218	39.13 N	84.26 W
Reading, Pa., U.S.	208	40.20 N	75.55 W
Reading Center	210	42.26 N	76.56 W
Reading Station ◆[5]	285	39.57 N	75.10 W
Readington	210	40.34 N	74.44 W
Readlyn	190	42.42 N	92.13 W
Readsboro	207	42.46 N	72.56 W
Readstown	190	43.26 N	90.45 W
Reagan	222	31.13 N	96.47 W
Real	116	14.40 N	121.36 E
Real ≃	250	11.27 S	37.22 W
Real, Cordillera ⋀	248	19.00 S	66.30 W
Real, Estero ≃	236	12.55 N	87.23 W
Real del Castillo	232	31.58 N	116.19 W
Real del Padre	252	34.50 S	67.46 W
Real de San Carlos	258	34.26 S	57.53 W
Realengo ◆[8]	256	22.53 S	43.25 W
Real Felipe, Castillo ⊥	286d	12.04 S	77.09 W
Realicó	252	35.02 S	64.15 W
Realitos	196	27.27 N	98.32 W
Realmonte	70	37.18 N	13.28 E
Reamstown	208	40.12 N	76.07 W
Reana del Roiale	64	46.12 N	13.13 E
Reardan	202	47.40 N	117.52 W
Reata	232	26.08 N	101.05 W
Reatini, Monti ⋀	66	42.28 N	13.00 E
Réau	261	48.37 N	2.38 E
Reay	46	58.33 N	3.47 W
Reay Forest ◆[3]	46	58.19 N	4.47 W
Rebecca, Lake ◎	162	29.53 S	122.10 E
Rebecq-Rognon	50	50.40 N	4.08 E
Rebeida, Wādī V	140	20.45 N	34.06 E
Rebel Hill	285	40.04 N	75.20 W
Rebersburg	210	40.57 N	77.27 W
Rebi	164	6.23 S	134.06 E
Rebiana Sand Sea → Rabyānah, Ṣaḥrā' ◆[2]	146	24.20 N	20.37 E
Rebild ✿	26	56.50 N	9.51 E
Reboly	24	63.50 N	30.47 E
Rebouças	252	25.36 S	50.42 W
Rebricha	86	53.05 N	82.20 E
Rebun-tō I	92a	45.23 N	141.02 E
Recalde	252	36.39 S	61.05 W
Recanati	66	43.24 N	13.32 E
Rečane	76	56.25 N	31.39 E
Recco	62	44.22 N	9.09 E
Recey-sur-Ource	58	47.47 N	4.52 E
Rechāh Lām	120	34.58 N	70.51 E
Rechberghausen	56	48.44 N	9.38 E
Recherche, Archipelago of the II	162	34.05 S	122.45 E
Recherche, Cape >	175e	10.11 S	161.19 E
Réchicourt-le-Château	58	48.40 N	6.51 E
Rechlin	54	53.21 N	12.43 E
Rechna Doāb ⋀[1]	123	31.35 N	73.30 E
Rechnitz	61	47.18 N	16.27 E
Rečica, S.S.S.R.	76	52.22 N	30.25 E
Rečica, S.S.S.R.	78	51.52 N	26.48 E
Recife	250	8.03 S	34.54 W
Recife, Kaap >	158	34.02 S	25.44 E
Recinto	252	36.48 S	71.44 W
Recke	52	52.22 N	7.43 E
Rečki	78	51.07 N	34.30 E
Recklinghausen	52	51.36 N	7.13 E
Recklinghausen □[8]	263	51.38 N	7.02 E
Recklinghausen-Süd ◆[8]	263	51.34 N	7.13 E
Recknitz ≃	54	54.14 N	12.28 E
Recoaro Terme	64	45.42 N	11.13 E
Recogne	56	49.55 N	5.22 E
Recologne	58	47.16 N	5.50 E
Reconquista	252	29.09 S	59.39 W
Reconquista ≃	288	34.25 S	58.35 W
Recovery Glacier ⌂	9	81.10 S	28.00 W
Recreio, Bra.	248	8.11 S	58.14 W
Recreio, Bra.	255	21.32 S	42.28 W
Recreo	252	29.16 S	65.04 W
Rector	194	36.15 N	90.17 W
Rectorville	218	38.34 N	83.39 W
Recuay	248	9.43 S	77.28 W
Recz	30	53.16 N	15.33 E
Red (Hong-ha) (Yuanjiang) ≃, Asia	110	20.17 N	106.34 E
Red ≃, N.A.	178	50.24 N	96.48 W
Red ≃, U.S.	178	31.00 N	91.40 W
Red ≃, U.S.	194	36.32 N	87.22 W
Red ≃, Ky., U.S.	192	37.51 N	84.05 W
Red ≃, N.M., U.S.	200	36.39 N	105.42 W
Red ≃, Wi., U.S.	190	44.49 N	88.38 W
Red, Elm Fork ≃	196	34.53 N	99.19 W
Red, North Fork ≃	196	34.24 N	99.14 W
Red, Prairie Dog Town Fork ≃	196	34.35 N	99.58 W
Red, Salt Fork ≃	196	34.27 N	99.22 W
Red, South Fork ≃	194	36.41 N	86.56 W
Red, West Fork ≃	194	36.32 N	87.21 W
Reda	30	54.37 N	18.21 E
Redang, Pulau I	114	5.47 N	103.00 E
Redange	56	49.46 N	5.54 E
Redang Panjang	114	5.07 N	100.47 E
Red Bank, N.J., U.S.	208	40.20 N	74.03 W
Red Bank, Tn., U.S.	194	35.07 N	85.17 W
Red Bank Battle Monument ⊥	285	39.52 N	75.11 W
Redbank Creek ≃	214	40.58 N	79.33 W
Red Banks	194	34.49 N	89.33 W
Red Bay, Nf., Can.	186	51.44 N	56.25 W
Red Bay, Al., U.S.	194	34.26 N	88.08 W
Redbay, Fl., U.S.	194	30.35 N	85.56 W
Red Bay ⊂	44	55.04 N	6.02 W
Redberry Lake ◎	184	52.40 N	107.10 W
Redbird	214	41.48 N	81.06 W
Red Bluff	204	40.10 N	122.14 W
Red Bluff Reservoir ◎[1]	196	31.57 N	103.56 W
Red Boiling Springs	194	36.31 N	85.50 W
Redbourn	42	51.48 N	0.24 W
Redbridge ◆[8]	42	51.34 N	0.05 E
Red Bud	219	38.12 N	89.59 W
Red Canyon V	198	43.18 N	103.49 W
Redcar	44	54.37 N	1.04 W
Red Cedar ≃, Mi., U.S.	216	42.43 N	84.33 W
Red Cedar ≃, Wi., U.S.	190	44.42 N	91.53 W
Red Cedar Lake ◎	190	46.45 N	79.54 W
Red Clay Creek ≃	285	39.43 N	75.39 W
Red Clay Creek, East Branch ≃	285	39.49 N	75.42 W
Red Clay Creek, West Branch ≃	285	39.49 N	75.42 W
Redcliff, Ab., Can.	184	50.05 N	110.47 W
Red Cliff, Co., U.S.	200	39.31 N	106.22 W
Redcliff, Zimb.	154	19.02 S	29.50 E
Redcliffe	171a	27.14 S	153.07 E
Redcliffe, Mount ʌ	162	28.25 S	121.32 E
Red Cliff Indian Reservation ◆[4]	190	46.50 N	90.47 W
Red Cliffs	166	34.19 S	142.11 E
Red Cloud	198	40.05 N	98.31 W
Red Creek	210	43.14 N	76.43 W
Red Creek ≃	194	30.41 N	88.40 W
Red Cross Lake ◎	184	55.05 N	92.55 W
Red Deer	182	52.16 N	113.48 W
Red Deer ≃, Can.	176	50.56 N	109.54 W
Red Deer ≃, Can.	184	52.53 N	101.01 W
Red Deer Creek ≃	196	35.56 N	100.24 W
Red Deer Lake ◎, Ab., Can.	182	52.43 N	113.02 W
Red Deer Lake ◎, Mb., Can.	184	52.56 N	101.20 W
Reddersburg	158	29.38 S	26.07 E
Red Devil	180	61.46 N	157.18 W
Red Dial	44	54.48 N	3.10 W
Reddick	216	41.06 N	88.15 W
Redding, Ca., U.S.	204	40.35 N	122.23 W
Redding, Ct., U.S.	207	41.18 N	73.23 W
Redding Ridge	207	41.18 N	73.21 W
Reddish	262	53.26 N	2.09 W
Redditch	42	52.19 N	1.56 W
Rede ≃	44	55.08 N	2.13 W
Redefin	54	53.21 N	11.11 E
Redelinghuys	158	32.30 S	18.33 E
Redenção	250	4.13 S	38.43 W
Redenção da Serra	256	23.16 S	45.33 W
Redesdale V	44	55.17 N	2.16 W
Redes Mere ◎	262	53.15 N	2.14 W
Redeye ≃	198	46.26 N	94.49 W
Redfield, Ia., U.S.	198	41.35 N	94.11 W
Redfield, N.Y., U.S.	212	43.32 N	75.49 W
Redfield, S.D., U.S.	198	44.52 N	98.31 W
Redfish Lake ◎	202	44.07 N	114.56 W
Redford	196	29.47 N	104.10 W
Redford ◆[8]	281	42.25 N	83.16 W
Redford Township	216	42.25 N	83.16 W
Red Fort ⊥	272a	28.40 N	77.14 E
Red Fox Forest	284c	38.49 N	77.15 W
Redhead	241r	10.47 N	60.57 W
Red Hill, Austl.	162	21.59 S	116.03 E
Redhill, Eng., U.K.	42	51.14 N	0.11 W
Red Hill, Ca., U.S.	280	33.45 N	117.48 W
Red Hill, Pa., U.S.	208	40.22 N	75.29 W
Red Hill ʌ	172	41.38 S	173.04 E
Redhill Aerodrome ⊠	260	51.12 N	0.07 W
Red Hill Branch ≃	284b	39.14 N	76.51 W
Red Hook	210	41.59 N	73.52 W
Redhouse Creek ≃	284b	39.18 N	76.31 W
Rédics	61	46.36 N	16.30 E
Red Indian Lake ◎	186	48.40 N	56.50 W
Redinger Lake ◎[1]	226	37.09 N	119.26 W
Redington Beach	220	27.49 N	82.49 W
Redington Shores	220	27.50 N	82.50 W
Red Island I	186	47.23 N	54.11 W
Redja ≃	76	58.05 N	31.33 E
Redkey	216	40.21 N	85.09 W
Redkino	82	56.38 N	36.17 E
Red Lake, On., Can.	184	51.03 N	93.49 W
Redlake, Mn., U.S.	198	47.53 N	95.01 W
Red Lake ◎, On., Can.	184	51.01 N	94.05 W
Red Lake ◎, Az., U.S.	200	35.40 N	114.04 W
Red Lake ◎, S.D., U.S.	198	43.44 N	99.13 W
Red Lake ◎[1]	222	31.40 N	95.58 W
Red Lake ≃	198	47.55 N	97.01 W
Red Lake Falls	198	47.52 N	96.16 W
Red Lake Indian Reservation ◆[4]	198	48.05 N	95.05 W
Red Lake Road	184	49.58 N	93.22 W
Redland, Scot., U.K.	46	59.05 N	3.05 W
Redland, Tx., U.S.	222	31.25 N	94.43 W
Redland Bay	171a	27.37 S	153.18 E
Redlands, S. Afr.	158	29.52 S	22.57 E
Redlands, Ca., U.S.	228	34.01 N	117.12 W
Redlands, Co., U.S.	200	39.04 N	108.38 W
Red Level	194	31.24 N	86.36 W
Red Lick	194	31.47 N	90.58 W
Redlin	54	53.22 N	12.01 E
Red Lion, Pa., U.S.	208	39.54 N	76.36 W
Red Lion, Pa., U.S.	285	39.53 N	75.41 W
Red Lion Airport ⊠	285	39.54 N	74.45 W
Red Lodge	202	45.11 N	109.14 W
Red Mill	206	46.25 N	72.28 W
Redmond, Or., U.S.	202	44.16 N	121.10 W
Redmond, Ut,. U.S.	200	39.00 N	111.51 W
Redmond, Wa., U.S.	224	47.40 N	122.07 W
Red Mountain	228	35.21 N	117.36 W
Red Mountain ʌ, Ca., U.S.	204	41.35 N	123.06 W
Red Mountain ʌ, Ca., U.S.	228	35.21 N	117.36 W
Red Mountain ʌ, Mt., U.S.	202	47.07 N	112.44 W
Red Mountain Pass)(	200	37.54 N	107.43 W
Rednitz ≃	56	49.28 N	10.59 E
Red Oak, Ia., U.S.	198	41.00 N	95.13 W
Red Oak, Ok., U.S.	196	34.57 N	95.04 W
Red Oak, Tx., U.S.	222	32.31 N	96.48 W
Red Oak Creek ≃	222	32.28 N	96.30 W
Red Oaks Mill	210	41.40 N	73.53 W
Redon	32	47.39 N	2.05 W
Redonda I	238	16.55 N	62.19 W
Redonda, Ilha I	256	23.04 S	43.12 W
Redonda, Isla I	241r	9.52 N	61.35 W
Redonda Islands II	182	50.13 N	124.48 W
Redondela	34	42.17 N	8.36 W
Redondo, Port.	34	38.39 N	7.33 W
Redondo, Wa., U.S.	224	47.20 N	122.19 W
Redondo, Mount ʌ	116	10.21 N	125.38 E
Redondo Beach	228	33.50 N	118.23 W
Redondo Beach State Park ♠	280	33.50 N	118.24 W
Redoubt, Mount ʌ	224	48.57 N	121.18 W
Redoubt Volcano ʌ[1]	180	60.29 N	152.45 W
Red Pass	182	52.59 N	118.59 W
Red Pheasant Indian Reserve ◆[4]	184	52.30 N	108.07 W
Red Pine Lake ◎	212	45.12 N	78.42 W
Red Point >	170	34.29 S	150.55 E
Red Rock, B.C., Can.	182	53.39 N	122.41 W
Red Rock, On., Can.	190	48.58 N	88.15 W
Red Rock, Tx., U.S.	222	29.58 N	97.27 W
Red Rock I	282	37.56 N	122.26 W
Red Rock ≃	202	44.59 N	112.52 W
Red Rock, Lake ◎[1]	190	41.30 N	93.02 W
Red Rock Canyon State Park ♠	228	35.23 N	118.00 W
Red Rock Creek ≃	196	36.36 N	97.03 W
Red Rocks Point >	162	32.13 S	127.32 E
Red Root Creek ≃	276	40.30 N	74.19 W
Red Run ≃, Md., U.S.	284b	39.24 N	76.47 W
Red Run ≃, Mi., U.S.	281	42.34 N	82.58 W
Redruth	42	50.13 N	5.14 W
Red Sea ⊤[2]	136	20.00 N	38.00 E
Red Springs	192	34.48 N	79.11 W
Redstone	182	52.08 N	123.42 W
Redstone ≃, N.T., Can.	180	64.17 N	124.33 W
Redstone ≃, On., Can.	190	48.27 N	81.03 W
Redstone Arsenal ■	194	34.38 N	86.38 W
Redstone Creek ≃	198	44.04 N	98.05 W
Redstone Lake ◎	212	45.11 N	78.32 W
Red Sucker ≃	184	55.19 N	92.31 W
Red Sucker Lake ◎	184	54.09 N	93.40 W
Reduction	279b	40.11 N	79.46 W
Redut	80	47.22 N	51.53 E
Redvers	184	49.33 N	101.39 W
Redwater	182	53.57 N	113.06 W
Redwater ≃	198	48.03 N	105.13 W
Red Wharf Bay ⊂	44	53.18 N	4.10 W
Redwillow ≃	182	55.04 N	119.21 W
Red Willow Creek ≃	198	40.13 N	100.29 W
Red Wing	190	44.33 N	92.32 W
Redwood	212	44.18 N	75.48 W
Redwood ≃	198	44.34 N	95.05 W
Redwood City	226	37.29 N	122.14 W
Redwood Creek ≃, Ca., U.S.	204	41.18 N	124.05 W
Redwood Creek ≃, Ca., U.S.	226	38.18 N	122.18 W
Redwood Creek ≃, Ca., U.S.	282	37.31 N	122.12 W
Redwood Creek ≃, Ca., U.S.	282	37.52 N	122.35 W
Redwood Estates	226	37.10 N	121.59 W
Redwood Falls	198	44.32 N	95.07 W
Redwood National Park ♠	204	41.30 N	124.05 W
Redwood Point >	282	37.32 N	122.12 W
Redwood Regional Park ♠	282	37.38 N	122.10 W
Redwood Terrace	282	37.19 N	122.18 W
Redwood Valley	204	39.15 N	123.12 W
Ree, Lough ◎	48	53.35 N	8.00 W
Reed City	190	43.52 N	85.30 W
Reeder	198	46.06 N	102.56 W
Reeders	210	41.01 N	75.20 W
Reeders Point >	171a	27.22 S	153.55 E
Reed Lake ◎, Mb., Can.	184	54.37 N	100.30 W
Reed Lake ◎, Sk., Can.	184	50.24 N	107.05 W
Reedley	226	36.35 N	119.26 W
Reedsburg, Oh., U.S.	214	40.49 N	82.07 W
Reedsburg, Wi., U.S.	190	43.31 N	90.00 W
Reeds Peak ʌ	200	33.09 N	107.51 W
Reedsport	202	43.42 N	124.05 W
Reedsville, Pa., U.S.	208	40.39 N	77.35 W
Reedsville, Wi., U.S.	190	44.09 N	87.57 W
Reedurban	214	40.47 N	81.26 W
Reedville	208	37.50 N	76.16 W
Reedy Creek ≃	220	28.04 N	81.21 W
Reedy Creek Swamp ☷	220	28.17 N	81.31 W
Reedy Lake ◎	220	27.44 N	81.22 W
Reefton	172	42.07 S	171.52 E
Reelfoot Lake ◎	194	36.25 N	89.22 W
Reepham	42	52.46 N	1.07 E
Reersø >[1]	41	55.31 N	11.06 E
Rees	52	51.45 N	6.23 E
Rees □[8]	263	51.41 N	6.45 E
Reese	190	43.27 N	83.41 W
Reese ≃	204	40.39 N	116.54 W
Reese Air Force Base ■	196	33.36 N	102.02 W
Reeseville	190	43.18 N	88.50 W
Reesville	218	39.29 N	83.41 W
Reetz	54	53.11 N	11.52 E
Reetz in der Neumark → Recz	30	53.16 N	15.33 E
Refaa, Djebel ʌ	34	35.34 N	5.52 E
Refahiye	130	39.54 N	38.46 E
Reform	194	33.22 N	88.00 W
Reforma de Pineda	234	16.24 N	94.28 W
Refton	208	39.57 N	76.14 W
Refuge Cove	182	50.07 N	124.50 W
Refugio	196	28.18 N	97.16 W
Refugio, Isla I	254	43.58 S	73.12 W
Refugio Creek ≃	282	38.01 N	122.17 W
Rega ≃	30	54.10 N	15.18 E
Regaïa	34	35.38 N	5.46 W
Regalbuto	70	37.39 N	14.38 E
Regau	64	47.59 N	13.41 E
Regen	60	48.59 N	13.07 E
Regen ≃	60	49.01 N	12.06 E
Regencia	255	19.36 S	39.49 W
Regency Estates	284c	39.03 N	77.10 W
Regeneração	250	6.15 S	42.41 W
Regensburg	60	49.01 N	12.06 E
Regensdorf	58	47.26 N	8.28 E
Regenstauf	60	49.08 N	12.08 E
Regent, Austl.	274b	37.44 S	145.00 E
Regent, N.D., U.S.	198	46.25 N	102.33 W
Regent Park	284c	39.03 N	77.10 W
Regents Park	274a	33.53 S	151.02 E
Regents Park ◆[8]	273d	26.15 S	28.04 E
Regent's Park ♠	260	51.32 N	0.09 W
Regentville	274a	33.47 S	150.40 E
Reggâne	148	26.42 N	0.10 E
Regge ≃	52	52.31 N	6.22 E
Reggello	66	43.41 N	11.32 E
Reggio di Calabria	68	38.07 N	15.39 E
Reggio di Calabria □[4]	68	38.10 N	16.00 E
Reggiolo	64	44.55 N	10.48 E
Reggio nell'Emilia	64	44.43 N	10.36 E
Reggio nell'Emilia □[4]	64	44.37 N	10.37 E
Regharen ◎	40	58.54 N	15.46 E
Reghin	38	46.47 N	24.42 E
Regina, Sk., Can.	184	50.25 N	104.39 W
Régina, Guy. fr.	250	4.19 N	52.08 W
Regina, S. Afr.	158	27.02 S	26.30 E
Regina Beach	184	50.47 N	105.00 W
Regina Elena, Canale ≊	266b	45.41 N	8.39 E
Regis-Breitingen	54	51.05 N	12.26 E
Registro	252	24.30 S	47.50 W
Registro do Araguaia	255	15.44 S	51.50 W
Regiwar	120	25.57 N	65.44 E
Regla ◆[8]	286b	23.08 N	82.20 W
Regnéville	32	49.01 N	1.33 W
Regnitz ≃	56	49.54 N	10.49 E
Rego Park ◆[8]	276	40.44 N	73.52 W
Regozero	24	65.28 N	31.10 E
Regresso, Cachoeira do ∟	250	0.58 S	54.51 W
Regstrup	41	55.40 N	11.37 E
Reguengos de Monsaraz	34	38.25 N	7.32 W
Reh	263	51.22 N	7.33 E
Rehau	54	50.15 N	12.02 E
Rehbach ≃	56	49.27 N	8.27 E
Rehberg	54	52.43 N	12.10 E
Reh-Berge ⋀[2]	264a	52.35 N	13.11 E
Rehberge, Volkspark ♠	264a	52.33 N	13.20 E
Rehburg	52	52.28 N	9.13 E
Rehden	52	52.37 N	8.29 E
Rehe	56	50.38 N	8.07 E
Rehefeld-Zaunhaus	54	50.43 N	13.42 E
Rehfelde	54	52.30 N	13.54 E
Rehli	124	23.38 N	79.05 E
Rehme	52	52.12 N	8.49 E
Rehna	54	53.47 N	11.03 E
Rehoboth, Namibia	156	23.18 S	17.03 E
Rehoboth, Namibia	156	17.53 S	15.04 E
Rehoboth □[5]	156	23.30 S	17.00 E
Rehoboth Bay ⊂	208	38.40 N	75.06 W
Rehoboth Beach	208	38.43 N	75.04 W
Rehoboth Seamount ✧[3]	16	37.30 N	59.50 W
Réhon	56	49.30 N	5.45 E
Reḥovot	132	31.54 N	34.49 E
Rehti	124	22.44 N	77.26 E
Reiche Ebrach ≃	56	49.49 N	10.58 E
Reiche Liesing ≃	264b	48.08 N	16.16 E

Symbol	English	Deutsch	Español	Français	Português
≃	River	Fluss	Río	Rivière	Rio
≊	Canal	Kanal	Canal	Canal	Canal
∟	Waterfall, Rapids	Wasserfall, Stromschnellen	Cascada, Rápidos	Chute d'eau, Rapides	Cascata, Rápidos
⊔	Strait	Meeresstrasse	Estrecho	Détroit	Estreito
⊂	Bay, Gulf	Bucht, Golf	Bahía, Golfo	Baie, Golfe	Baía, Golfo
◎	Lake, Lakes	See, Seen	Lago, Lagos	Lac, Lacs	Lago, Lagos
☷	Swamp	Sumpf	Pantano	Marais	Pântano
⌂	Ice Features, Glacier	Eis- und Gletscherformen	Accidentes Glaciales	Formes glaciaires	Acidentes glaciares
⊤	Other Hydrographic Features	Andere Hydrographische Objekte	Otros Elementos Hidrográficos	Autres données hydrographiques	Outros acidentes hidrográficos
✧	Submarine Features	Untermeerische Objekte	Accidentes Submarinos	Formes de relief sous-marin	Acidentes submarinos
□	Political Unit	Politische Einheit	Unidad Politica	Entité politique	Unidade política
✿	Cultural Institution	Kulturelle Institution	Institución Cultural	Institution culturelle	Institução cultural
⊥	Historical Site	Historische Stätte	Sitio Histórico	Site historique	Sitio histórico
♠	Recreational Site	Erholungs- und Ferienort	Sitio de Recreo	Centre de loisirs	Area de Lazer
⊠	Airport	Flughafen	Aeropuerto	Aéroport	Aeroporto
■	Military Installation	Militäranlage	Instalación Militar	Installation militaire	Instalação militar
◆	Miscellaneous	Verschiedenes	Misceláneo	Divers	Diversos

Name	Page	Lat.°′	Long.°′
Reichelsheim	56	49.43 N	8.50 E
Reichenau, B.R.D.	58	47.41 N	9.03 E
Reichenau → Bogatynia, Pol.	54	50.53 N	15.00 E
Reichenau, Schw.	58	46.49 N	9.24 E
Reichenau an der Rax	61	47.42 N	15.50 E
Reichenbach, D.D.R.	54	51.08 N	14.48 E
Reichenbach, D.D.R.	54	50.37 N	12.18 E
Reichenbach → Dzierżoniów, Pol.	30	50.44 N	16.39 E
Reichenbach, Schw.	58	46.38 N	7.42 E
Reichenberg → Liberec	30	50.46 N	15.03 E
Reichenhofen	58	47.50 N	9.58 E
Reichensachsen	56	51.09 N	9.59 E
Reichen Spitze ∧	64	47.09 N	12.07 E
Reichertshausen	60	48.28 N	11.31 E
Reichertsheim	60	48.12 N	12.17 E
Reichertshofen	60	48.40 N	11.28 E
Reichraming	61	47.53 N	14.27 E
Reichsbrücke ◆[5]	264b	48.14 N	16.25 E
Reichshoffen	56	48.56 N	7.40 E
Reid	162	30.49 S	128.26 E
Reid, Mount ∧, Austl.	162	17.58 S	130.38 E
Reid, Mount ∧, Ak., U.S.	182	55.42 N	131.15 W
Reid Lake ⊜[1]	184	50.02 N	108.05 W
Reidsville, Ga., U.S.	192	32.05 N	82.07 W
Reidsville, N.C., U.S.	192	36.21 N	79.39 W
Reiffton	208	40.19 N	75.53 W
Reigate	42	51.14 N	0.13 W
Reigate and Banstead □[8]	260	51.17 N	0.12 W
Reignac-sur-Indre	50	47.13 N	0.55 E
Reignier	58	46.08 N	6.16 E
Reigoldswil	58	47.24 N	7.41 E
Reihoku	92	32.31 N	130.02 E
Reillanne	62	43.53 N	5.40 E
Reims	50	49.15 N	4.02 E
Reims, Montagne de ⋏[2]	50	49.08 N	4.00 E
Reina Adelaida, Archipiélago II	254	52.10 S	74.25 W
Reina Alejandra → Queen Alexandra Range ⋏	9	84.00 S	168.00 E
Reina Carlota, Estrecho de la → Queen Charlotte Sound ʊ	182	51.30 N	129.30 W
Reinach, Schw.	58	47.15 N	8.11 E
Reinach, Schw.	58	47.30 N	7.35 E
Reina Fabiola → Queen Fabiola Mountains ⋏	9	71.30 S	35.40 E
Reina Maria, Costa de la → Queen Mary Coast ⊥[2]	9	67.00 S	96.00 E
Reina Maud, Tierras de la → Queen Maud Land ◆[1]	9	72.30 S	12.00 E
Reinbeck	190	42.19 N	92.35 W
Reinbek	52	53.31 N	10.14 E
Reinberg	54	54.12 N	13.15 E
Reindeer ≃	184	55.36 N	103.11 W
Reindeer Island I	184	52.25 N	98.00 W
Reindeer Lake ⊜	176	57.15 N	102.40 W
Reindeer Station	180	68.42 N	134.06 W
Reine Charlotte, Détroit de la → Queen Charlotte Sound ʊ	182	51.30 N	129.30 W
Reinerton	208	40.36 N	76.34 W
Reinfeld	52	53.49 N	10.28 E
Reinga, Cape ≻	172	34.25 S	172.41 E
Reinhardswald ◆[3]	52	51.30 N	9.30 E
Reinhardtsdorf	54	50.53 N	14.11 E
Reinheim	56	49.49 N	8.50 E
Reinickendorf ◆[8]	264a	52.35 N	13.21 E
Reinosa	34	43.00 N	4.08 W
Reino Unido → United Kingdom □[1]	28	54.00 N	2.00 W
Reinsdorf, D.D.R.	54	50.42 N	12.33 E
Reinsdorf, D.D.R.	54	51.54 N	12.37 E
Reinshagen ◆[8]	263	51.10 N	7.09 E
Reinstorf	54	53.50 N	11.38 E
Reis	130	38.16 N	31.35 E
Reisach	64	46.39 N	13.09 E
Reisaelva ≃	24	69.48 N	21.00 E
Reischach	60	48.17 N	12.44 E
Reisdorf	56	49.53 N	6.15 E
Reisdorf, Camp ■	273b	4.21 S	15.15 E
Reisholz ◆[8]	263	51.11 N	6.52 E
Reisjärvi	26	63.37 N	24.54 E
Reiss	46	58.28 N	3.10 W
Reisterstown	208	39.28 N	76.49 W
Reisterstown Road Plaza ◆[9]	284b	39.02 N	76.42 W
Reitano	70	37.58 N	14.20 E
Reitdiep ≊	52	53.20 N	6.18 E
Reith bei Seefeld	64	47.18 N	11.12 E
Reit im Winkl	64	47.40 N	12.28 E
Reitz	158	27.53 S	28.31 E
Reitzenhain	54	50.33 N	13.13 E
Reivilo	158	27.36 S	24.08 E
Reixach	266d	41.30 N	2.12 E
Rejinagar	126	23.53 N	88.15 E
Rejmyra	40	58.50 N	15.55 E
Rejowiec Fabryczny	30	51.08 N	23.13 E
Rejštejn	60	49.09 N	13.31 E
Rekarne	40	59.26 N	16.20 E
Rekarne □[9]	40	59.17 N	16.25 E
Reken	52	51.50 N	7.02 E
Rekjoāti	272b	22.37 N	88.28 E
Rela	120	29.27 N	89.45 E
Reliance, N.T., Can.	176	62.42 N	109.08 W
Reliance, Wy., U.S.	200	41.40 N	109.11 W
Relief Reservoir ⊜[1]	226	38.16 N	119.44 W
Religione, Punta ≻	70	36.42 N	14.46 E
Reliz Creek ≃	226	36.19 N	121.18 W
Rellingen	52	53.39 N	9.49 E
Rellinghausen ◆[8]	263	51.25 N	7.04 E
Reloncaví, Seno c	254	41.40 S	72.35 W
Remada	148	32.19 N	10.24 E
Remagen	56	50.34 N	7.13 E
Rémalard	50	48.26 N	0.47 E
Remansão	250	4.25 S	49.34 W
Remanso	250	9.41 S	42.04 W
Remarde ≃	261	48.35 N	2.15 E
Remarkable, Mount ∧	162	32.48 S	138.10 E
Rembang	115a	6.42 S	111.20 E
Rembau	114	2.35 N	102.06 E
Rembia	114	2.20 N	102.13 E
Remchi	34	35.04 N	1.26 W
Remecó	252	37.38 S	63.39 W
Remedios, Col.	246	7.02 N	74.41 W
Remedios, Cuba	240p	22.30 N	79.33 W
Remedios, Pan.	236	8.14 N	81.51 W
Remedios, Punta ≻	236	13.31 N	89.49 W
Remedios, Santuario de los ʋ[1]	286a	19.28 N	99.15 W
Remedios de Escalada ◆[8]	258	34.43 S	58.23 W
Remels	52	53.18 N	7.44 E
Remennicy	82	56.43 N	36.36 E
Remer	190	47.03 N	93.54 W
Remeshk	128	26.50 N	58.49 E
Remhoogte	158	29.33 S	23.01 E
Remich	56	49.33 N	6.22 E
Remich Airport ⊠	279b	40.36 N	79.49 W
Rémigny, Lac ⊜	190	47.51 N	79.12 W
Rémilly	56	49.01 N	6.24 E
Reminderville	214	41.20 N	81.23 W
Remington, In., U.S.	216	40.45 N	87.09 W
Remington, Va., U.S.	188	38.32 N	77.48 W
Rémire	250	4.53 N	52.17 W
Remiremont	58	48.01 N	6.35 E
Remo □[8]	273a	6.42 N	3.29 E
Remolá, Laguna del c	266d	41.17 N	2.04 E
Remollon	62	44.28 N	6.10 E
Remontnoje	80	46.33 N	43.39 E
Remoray	58	46.46 N	6.14 E
Remoulins	62	43.56 N	4.34 E
Removka ◆[8]	83	47.59 N	38.43 E
Rempang, Pulau I	114	0.51 N	104.10 E
Remptendorf	54	50.31 N	11.39 E
Rems ≃	56	48.52 N	9.16 E
Remscheid	56	51.11 N	7.11 E
Remscheider-Stausee ⊜[1]	263	51.10 N	7.14 E
Remsen, Ia., U.S.	198	42.48 N	95.58 W
Remsen, N.Y., U.S.	210	43.19 N	75.11 W
Remsfeld	56	51.00 N	9.29 E
Remuna	126	21.33 N	86.54 E
Remus	190	43.36 N	85.09 W
Rémuzat	62	44.24 N	5.21 E
Rena	26	61.08 N	11.22 E
Renaix → Ronse	50	50.45 N	3.36 E
Renāla Khurd	123	30.53 N	73.36 E
Rena Point ≻	116	16.10 N	119.45 E
Renard Islands II	164	10.50 S	153.05 E
Renascença	246	3.50 S	66.21 W
Renata	182	49.26 N	118.06 W
Renaud Island I	9	65.40 S	66.00 W
Renbu	124	29.10 N	89.59 E
Renca	286e	33.24 S	70.44 W
Renca, Cerro ∧	286e	33.23 S	70.43 W
Rencēni	76	57.44 N	25.26 E
Renchen	56	48.35 N	8.01 E
Rencontre East	186	47.38 N	55.12 W
Rencun	98	36.19 N	113.50 E
Renda, Ityo.	144	14.30 N	39.53 E
Renda, S.S.S.R.	76	57.09 N	22.22 E
Rende	68	39.19 N	16.11 E
Rendena, Valle V	58	46.08 N	10.42 E
Rend Lake ⊜[1]	194	38.05 N	88.58 W
Rendova Island I	175e	8.32 S	157.20 E
Rendsburg	41	54.18 N	9.40 E
Renens	58	46.32 N	6.35 E
Renesse	52	51.44 N	3.46 E
Renews	186	46.56 N	52.56 W
Renfrew, On., Can.	212	45.28 N	76.41 W
Renfrew, Scot., U.K.	46	55.53 N	4.24 W
Renfrew, Pa., U.S.	214	40.46 N	79.58 W
Renfrew □[6]	212	45.25 N	77.05 W
Rengam	114	1.53 N	103.24 E
Ren'gang	106	32.01 N	120.50 E
Rengasdengklok	115a	6.09 S	107.17 E
Rengat	112	0.24 S	102.33 E
Rengel	115a	7.04 S	112.00 E
Rengen ⊜	26	64.05 N	14.03 E
Rengezhuang	105	39.45 N	118.10 E
Rengit	114	1.41 N	103.09 E
Rengkang	112	1.07 N	112.10 E
Rengo	252	34.25 S	70.52 W
Rengsdorf	56	50.30 N	7.29 E
Reng Tlāng ∧	120	21.59 N	92.36 E
Renhe, Zhg.	100	33.32 N	114.02 E
Renhe, Zhg.	100	27.41 N	115.15 E
Renhechang	107	30.30 N	105.56 E
Renheji	100	31.56 N	115.07 E
Renhua	100	25.06 N	113.44 E
Renhuai	102	27.48 N	106.18 E
Reni, India	123	28.41 N	75.02 E
Reni, S.S.S.R.	78	45.27 N	28.17 E
Renick	188	37.59 N	80.21 W
Renish Point ≻	46	57.44 N	6.59 W
Renjiawopeng	104	41.27 N	122.18 E
Renjiaxu	106	30.49 N	121.00 E
Renju	100	24.51 N	115.54 E
Renko	26	60.54 N	24.17 E
Renkum	52	51.58 N	5.45 E
Renliuchang	107	29.13 N	106.39 E
Renlong	107	30.32 N	105.47 E
Renmark	166	34.11 S	140.45 E
Renmei	100	25.50 N	117.56 E
Renmin	89	46.37 N	125.32 E
Renna, Monte ∧	70	36.52 N	14.41 E
Rennau	54	52.17 N	10.55 E
Renne, Lac du → Reindeer Lake ⊜	176	57.15 N	102.40 W
Renne, Rivière le ≃	206	45.41 N	72.39 W
Rennell I	160	11.40 S	160.10 E
Rennell, Isla I	254	52.00 S	74.00 W
Rennell Sound ʊ	182	53.25 N	132.40 W
Renner	222	32.59 N	96.47 W
Rennerdale	279b	40.24 N	80.08 W
Rennerod	56	50.36 N	8.04 E
Renner Springs	162	18.20 S	133.48 E
Rennertshofen	60	48.45 N	11.02 E
Rennes	32	48.05 N	1.41 W
Rennick Bay c	9	70.18 S	161.45 E
Rennick Glacier ⊓	9	70.30 S	161.45 E
Rennie	184	49.51 N	95.33 W
Rennie's Mill	271d	22.18 N	114.15 E
Renningen	56	48.46 N	8.56 E
Renntier-See → Reindeer Lake ⊜	176	57.15 N	102.40 W
Rennweg	64	47.01 N	13.37 E
Reno, Nv., U.S.	226	39.31 N	119.48 W
Reno, Pa., U.S.	214	41.25 N	79.45 W
Reno, Tx., U.S.	222	32.56 N	97.05 W
Reno ≃	64	44.37 N	12.16 E
Reno Beach	214	41.40 N	83.15 W
Reno Hill ∧	200	42.35 N	106.03 W
Reno International Airport ⊠	226	39.30 N	119.46 W
Renoster ≃	158	31.37 S	20.37 E
Renous	186	46.49 N	65.48 W
Renous ≃	186	46.50 N	65.50 W
Renovo	214	41.19 N	77.45 W
Renqiao	100	33.27 N	117.16 E
Renqiu	98	38.43 N	116.05 E
Rens	41	54.54 N	9.06 E
Renshan	100	22.50 N	114.48 E
Renshou, Zhg.	100	27.08 N	117.51 E
Renshou, Zhg.	107	30.00 N	104.08 E
Rensjön	24	68.05 N	19.49 E
Rensselaer, In., U.S.	216	40.56 N	87.09 W
Rensselaer, Mo., U.S.	219	39.40 N	91.33 W
Rensselaer, N.Y., U.S.	210	42.38 N	73.44 W
Rensselaer □[6]	210	42.43 N	73.40 W
Rensselaer Falls	212	44.35 N	75.19 W
Rensselaerville	210	42.30 N	74.08 W
Rentería	34	43.19 N	1.54 W
Rentfort ◆[8]	263	51.35 N	6.57 E
Renton	224	47.28 N	122.12 W
Rentuo	107	29.14 N	106.23 E
Rentweinsdorf	56	50.04 N	10.47 E
Renun ≃	114	3.05 N	97.55 E
Renville	198	44.47 N	95.12 W
Renwez	56	49.50 N	4.36 E
Renwick, N.Z.	172	41.30 S	173.50 E
Renwick, Ia., U.S.	190	42.49 N	93.58 W
Renyichang	107	29.29 N	105.28 E
Renziehalusen Park ♦	279b	40.21 N	79.50 W
Réo, Burkina	150	12.19 N	2.28 W
Reo, Indon.	115b	8.19 S	120.30 E
Reola ◆[8]	272a	28.34 N	76.59 E
Repartición	286d	12.00 S	77.04 W
Repartimento ≃	250	6.06 S	50.40 W
Repaupo	285	39.48 N	75.18 W
Repbäcken	40	60.31 N	15.20 E
Répce ≃	30	47.41 N	17.03 E
Repentigny	206	45.44 N	73.28 W
Repetek	128	38.34 N	63.11 E
Repino	76	60.10 N	29.52 E
Repjovka, S.S.S.R.	78	51.05 N	38.39 E
Repjovka, S.S.S.R.	80	53.09 N	48.06 E
Repki	78	51.48 N	31.05 E
Repolka	76	59.16 N	29.34 E
Repolovo	86	60.40 N	69.50 E
Reporoa	172	38.26 S	176.21 E
Reposaari	26	61.37 N	21.27 E
Reppen → Rzepin	54	52.22 N	14.50 E
Repton	194	31.24 N	87.14 W
Republic, Ks., U.S.	198	39.55 N	97.49 W
Republic, Mi., U.S.	190	46.24 N	87.58 W
Republic, Mo., U.S.	194	37.07 N	93.28 W
Republic, Oh., U.S.	214	41.07 N	83.00 W
Republic, Wa., U.S.	202	48.38 N	118.44 W
República Centroafricana → Central African Republic □[1]	136	7.00 N	21.00 E
Republic Airport ⊠	276	40.44 N	73.25 W
Republican ≃	198	39.03 N	96.48 W
Republican, North Fork ≃	198	40.01 N	101.59 W
Republican, South Fork ≃	198	40.03 N	101.31 W
Republic Observatory ʋ[3]	273d	26.11 S	28.05 E
Republic Steel Corporation ʋ[3]	279a	41.28 N	81.40 W
République centrafricaine → Central African Republic □[1]	136	7.00 N	21.00 E
Repueblo de Oriente	196	25.51 N	99.39 W
Repulse Bay	176	66.32 N	86.15 W
Repulse Bay c	166	20.36 S	148.43 E
Repvåg	24	70.45 N	25.41 E
Requena, Esp.	34	39.29 N	1.06 W
Requena, Perú	248	4.58 S	73.50 W
Réquista	32	44.02 N	2.32 E
Rère ≃	50	47.22 N	1.50 E
Reriutaba	250	4.10 S	40.35 W
Reşadiye, Tür.	130	40.24 N	37.21 E
Reşadiye, Tür.	267b	41.05 N	29.15 E
Reşadiye Yarımadası ≻[1]	130	36.40 N	27.45 E
Resang, Tanjong ≻	114	2.35 N	103.51 E
Resarö	40	59.26 N	18.20 E
Rescalda	266b	45.38 N	8.56 E
Rescaldina	266b	45.37 N	8.57 E
Reschenpass (Passo di Resia))(	64	46.50 N	10.30 E
Reschenscheideck)(	64	46.51 N	10.31 E
Rescue	208	36.59 N	76.33 W
Research	274b	37.42 S	145.11 E
Reseda ◆[8]	280	34.12 N	118.31 W
Resen	38	41.05 N	21.00 E
Resende	256	22.28 S	44.27 W
Reserva	252	24.38 S	50.52 W
Reserve, La., U.S.	194	30.03 N	90.33 W
Reserve, N.M., U.S.	200	33.42 N	108.45 W
Reserve Township	279b	40.29 N	79.59 W
Reservoir	274b	37.43 S	145.00 E
Reservoir Pond ⊜	283	42.10 N	71.07 W
Rešetilovka	78	49.34 N	34.04 E
Rešetnikovo	82	56.27 N	36.34 E
Reshui	98	42.09 N	119.18 E
Reshuitang	102	24.10 N	103.09 E
Resia, Passo di (Reschenpass))(	64	46.50 N	10.30 E
Resipol, Beinn ∧	46	56.43 N	5.39 W
Resistencia	252	27.27 S	58.59 W
Reșița	38	45.17 N	21.53 E
Resiutta	64	46.23 N	13.13 E
Resko	30	53.47 N	15.25 E
Rešma	80	57.24 N	42.34 E
Rešn'ovka	78	49.47 N	27.25 E
Resolute	176	74.41 N	94.54 W
Resolution Island I, N.T., Can.	176	61.30 N	65.00 W
Resolution Island I, N.Z.	172	45.40 S	166.40 E
Resolven	42	51.42 N	3.42 W
Resort, Loch c	46	58.03 N	7.06 W
Rešoty	76	57.09 N	28.30 E
Resplandes	250	6.17 S	45.13 W
Resplendor	255	19.20 S	41.15 W
Ressa ≃	76	54.45 N	35.10 E
Ressaca, Ribeirão ≃	287b	23.38 S	46.51 W
Resse ◆[8]	263	51.34 N	7.07 E
Resseta ≃	76	53.49 N	35.15 E
Ressons-sur-Matz	50	49.33 N	2.45 E
Resta ≃	76	53.36 N	30.56 E
Resthaven	216	41.16 N	88.09 W
Restigouche (Ristigouche) ≃	186	48.04 N	66.20 W
Restinga	34	35.42 N	5.23 W
Restinga Sêca	252	29.49 S	53.23 W
Reston, Mb., Can.	184	49.35 N	101.02 W
Reston, Scot., U.K.	46	55.51 N	2.11 W
Reston, Va., U.S.	208	38.58 N	77.20 W
Restoule Lake ⊜	190	46.03 N	79.47 W
Restrepo, Col.	246	4.15 N	73.33 W
Restrepo, Col.	246	3.48 N	76.31 W
Resülhınzır ≻	130	36.22 N	35.45 E
Resurrección	234	19.06 N	98.07 W
Resuttano	70	37.41 N	14.02 E
Retalhuleu	236	14.32 N	91.41 W
Retalhuleu □[5]	236	14.20 N	91.50 W
Retamosa	252	33.35 S	54.44 W
Retem, Oued er V	148	33.30 N	5.45 E
Řetenice	54	50.38 N	13.46 E
Retezat, Munții ⋏	38	45.25 N	23.00 E
Retezat Parc Național ♦	78	45.20 N	22.50 E
Rethel	50	49.31 N	4.22 E
Rethem	52	52.45 N	9.23 E
Réthimnon	38	35.22 N	24.29 E
Retiche, Alpi → Rhaetian Alps ⋏	58	46.30 N	10.00 E
Retie	56	51.16 N	5.04 E
Retiers	28	47.55 N	1.23 W
Retiro, Estacion ◆[5]	288	34.36 S	58.22 W
Retiro, Parque del ♦	266a	40.25 N	3.41 W
Retournac	62	45.12 N	4.02 E
Retreat	222	32.03 N	96.29 W
Retreat ≃	170	34.07 S	149.38 E
Retsof	210	42.50 N	77.53 W
Rettenberg	58	47.35 N	10.17 E
Rettendon	260	51.39 N	0.33 E
Rettendon Place	260	51.38 N	0.34 E
Rettichovka	89	44.10 N	132.47 E
Rettin	54	54.06 N	10.53 E
Return Creek ≃	226	37.56 N	119.28 W
Retz	61	48.45 N	15.57 E
Retzow	54	52.37 N	12.41 E
Reuden	54	52.04 N	12.18 E
Reungeut	114	4.34 N	96.22 E
Reunion (Réunion) □[2], Afr.	138	21.06 S	55.36 E
Reunion (Réunion) □[2], Afr.	157c	21.06 S	55.36 E
Réunion I	157c	21.06 S	55.36 E
Reus	34	41.09 N	1.07 E
Reuschenberg ◆[8]	263	51.10 N	6.42 E
Reusel	52	51.21 N	5.22 E
Reusrath	263	51.06 N	6.57 E
Reuss ≃	58	47.28 N	8.14 E
Reut ≃	78	47.15 N	29.09 E
Reuterstadt Stavenhagen	54	53.42 N	12.53 E
Reutlingen	58	48.29 N	9.11 E
Reutov	82	55.46 N	37.52 E
Reutte	58	47.29 N	10.43 E
Reuver	52	51.17 N	6.05 E
Rev'akino	82	54.22 N	37.40 E
Reval → Tallinn	76	59.25 N	24.45 E
Revda, S.S.S.R.	24	67.58 N	34.32 E
Revda, S.S.S.R.	86	56.48 N	59.57 E
Réveillon, Ruisseau le ≃	261	48.42 N	2.30 E
Revel	62	45.11 N	5.52 E
Revelganj	124	25.47 N	84.40 E
Revelstoke	182	50.59 N	118.12 W
Reventazón	248	6.10 S	80.58 W
Reventazón ≃	236	10.17 N	83.24 W
Revere, It.	64	45.03 N	11.08 E
Revere, Ma., U.S.	207	42.24 N	71.00 W
Revere, Pa., U.S.	208	40.31 N	75.10 W
Revere Beach ⊥[2]	283	42.25 N	70.59 W
Revermont ⋏[2]	58	46.27 N	5.25 E
Revesby	274a	33.57 S	151.01 E
Revest-du-Bion	62	44.05 N	5.33 E
Révia	154	13.23 S	36.31 E
Reviga	38	44.42 N	27.06 E
Revigny-sur-Ornain	56	48.50 N	4.59 E
Revilla del Campo	34	42.13 N	3.32 W
Revillagigedo, Islas II	232	19.00 N	111.30 W
Revillagigedo Channel ʊ	182	55.10 N	131.13 W
Revillagigedo Island I	182	55.35 N	131.23 W
Revillo	198	45.01 N	96.34 W
Revin	56	49.56 N	4.38 E
Ŗevloc	214	40.29 N	78.45 W
Řevničov	54	50.08 N	13.45 E
Revò	64	46.23 N	11.03 E
Revol'ucii, pik ∧	85	38.31 N	72.21 E
Revolution, Museum of the ʋ	265b	55.46 N	37.36 E
Revsundssjön ⊜	26	62.49 N	15.17 E
Revúboè ≃	154	16.13 S	33.37 E
Revuè ≃	156	19.49 S	34.00 E
Rew	214	41.54 N	78.32 W
Rewa	124	24.32 N	81.18 E
Rewa □[5]	124	24.45 N	81.30 E
Rewa ≃	246	3.53 N	58.45 W
Rewāri	124	28.11 N	76.37 E
Rewataya, Taka ◆[2]	112	6.05 S	118.55 E
Rex, Mount ∧	9	74.57 S	76.00 W
Rexburg	202	43.49 N	111.47 W
Rexdale ◆[8]	275b	43.43 N	79.35 W
Rexford, Ks., U.S.	198	39.28 N	100.44 W
Rexford, Mt., U.S.	202	48.52 N	115.13 W
Rexhame	283	42.06 N	70.40 W
Rexton	186	46.39 N	64.52 W
Rexville, In., U.S.	278	41.31 N	87.21 W
Rexville, N.Y., U.S.	210	42.05 N	77.40 W
Rey	128	35.35 N	51.25 E
Rey, Arroyo del ≃	288	34.46 S	58.27 W
Rey, Estrecho del → King Sound ʊ	162	17.00 S	123.30 E
Rey, Isla del I	246	8.22 N	78.55 W
Rey, Laguna del ⊜	196	27.01 N	103.26 W
Rey Bouba	146	8.40 N	14.11 E
Reyes	248	14.19 S	67.23 W
Reyes, Point ≻	204	38.00 N	123.01 W
Reyes Peak ∧	228	34.38 N	119.17 W
Reyhanlı	130	36.18 N	36.32 E
Rey Jorge, Estrecho → King George Sound ʊ	162	35.03 S	117.57 E
Rey Jorge, Isla → King George Island I	9	62.00 S	58.15 W
Reykjanes ≻[1]	24a	63.49 N	22.43 W
Reykjanes Ridge ◆[3]	10	62.00 N	27.00 W
Reykjavík	24a	64.09 N	21.51 W
Reynella	168b	35.06 S	138.32 E
Reyno	194	36.21 N	90.45 W
Reynolds, Ga., U.S.	192	32.33 N	84.05 W
Reynolds, In., U.S.	216	40.44 N	86.52 W
Reynolds, N.D., U.S.	198	47.57 N	97.45 W
Reynolds Channel ʊ	276	40.36 N	73.40 W
Reynolds Creek ≃, Austl.	171a	27.56 S	152.36 E
Reynolds Creek ≃, On., Can.	212	43.00 N	80.58 W
Reynoldsville	214	41.05 N	78.53 W
Reynosa	232	26.07 N	98.18 W
Reyssouze ≃	58	46.27 N	4.54 E
Rež	86	57.23 N	61.24 E
Rež ≃	86	57.54 N	62.18 E
Reza, gora (Kūh-e Rīzeh) ∧	128	37.47 N	58.05 E
Rezé	32	47.12 N	1.34 W
Rēzekne	76	56.30 N	27.19 E
Rēzekne ≃	76	56.46 N	26.58 E
Rezeny	78	46.46 N	28.54 E
Rezina	78	47.44 N	28.58 E
Rezino	86	55.51 N	75.18 E
Rēznas ezers ⊜	76	56.20 N	27.27 E
Rezovo	38	41.59 N	28.02 E
Rezovska (Rezve) ≃	130	41.59 N	28.01 E
Rezvāndeh	128	37.33 N	49.09 E
Rezve (Rezovska) ≃	130	41.59 N	28.01 E
Rezzato	64	45.31 N	10.19 E
Rezzoaglio	62	44.32 N	9.23 E
Rezzonico	58	46.04 N	9.16 E
Rhade	52	53.19 N	9.07 E
Rhadeswood Reservoir ⊜[1]	262	53.29 N	1.56 W
Rhaetian Alps (Rätische Alpen) (Alpi Retiche) ⋏	58	46.30 N	10.00 E
Rhallamane, Sebkha de ≚	148	23.41 N	9.50 W
Rhame	198	46.13 N	103.39 W
Rharbi, Île I	148	34.39 N	11.03 E
Rharbi, Zahrez ⊜	148	34.50 N	2.50 E
Rhauderfehn	52	53.08 N	7.35 E
Rhaunen	56	49.52 N	7.20 E
Rhayader	42	52.18 N	3.30 W
Rhea Creek ≃	202	45.30 N	119.46 W
Rheda-Wiedenbrück	52	51.50 N	8.18 E
Rhede, B.R.D.	52	53.03 N	7.16 E
Rhede, B.R.D.	52	51.50 N	6.11 E
Rheden	52	52.01 N	6.02 E
Rheems	208	40.08 N	76.34 W
Rheem Valley	226	37.52 N	122.07 W
Rheidol ≃	42	52.25 N	4.05 W
Rheims → Reims	50	49.15 N	4.02 E
Rhein, Sk., Can.	184	51.22 N	102.10 W
Rhein → Ryn, Pol.	30	53.56 N	21.33 E
Rhein → Rhine ≃	30	51.52 N	6.02 E
Rheinau	56	48.41 N	7.56 E
Rheinbach	56	50.37 N	6.57 E
Rheinberg	52	51.33 N	6.35 E
Rheinböllen	56	50.00 N	7.40 E
Rheinbrohl	56	50.30 N	7.19 E
Rheinbrücke ◆[5]	263	51.12 N	6.44 E
Rheindürkheim	56	49.42 N	8.21 E
Rheine	52	52.17 N	7.26 E
Rheineck	58	47.28 N	9.35 E
Rheinen	263	51.27 N	7.38 E
Rheinfall ∟	58	47.41 N	8.38 E
Rheinfelden, B.R.D.	58	47.33 N	7.47 E
Rheinfelden, Schw.	58	47.33 N	7.48 E
Rheinhausen	56	51.24 N	6.44 E
Rhein-Herne-Kanal ≊	263	51.27 N	6.47 E
Rheinhessen □[5]	56	49.40 N	8.40 E
Rheinisch-Bergischer Kreis □[8]	263	51.06 N	7.25 E
Rheinkamp	52	51.30 N	6.37 E
Rheinland-Pfalz □[3]	56	50.00 N	7.00 E
Rheinpark ♦	263	51.15 N	6.46 E
Rheinsberg	54	53.06 N	12.53 E
Rheinstadion ♦	263	51.16 N	6.44 E
Rheinstein, Burg ⊥	56	50.00 N	7.50 E
Rheinwald V	58	46.32 N	9.17 E
Rheinwaldhorn ∧	58	46.30 N	9.02 E
Rhein-Wupper-Kreis □[8]	263	51.07 N	7.06 E
Rheirs, Oued V	148	30.39 N	4.26 W
Rhêmes-Notre-Dame	62	45.34 N	7.07 E
Rhenen	52	51.57 N	5.34 E
Rhens	56	50.17 N	7.37 E
Rheurdt	263	51.27 N	6.28 E
Rheydt	56	51.10 N	6.25 E
Rheydt, Schloss ⊥	263	51.11 N	6.29 E
Rhin ≃, D.D.R.	54	52.59 N	12.55 E
Rhin → Rhine ≃, Europe	30	51.52 N	6.02 E
Rhinau	58	48.19 N	7.42 E
Rhine	192	31.59 N	83.12 W
Rhine (Rhein) (Rhin) ≃	30	51.52 N	6.02 E
Rhinebeck	210	41.55 N	73.54 W
Rhinecliff	210	41.55 N	73.57 W
Rhineland	219	38.43 N	91.31 W
Rhinelander	190	45.38 N	89.24 W
Rhin Kanal ≊	54	52.47 N	12.24 E
Rhinluch ≡	54	52.50 N	12.50 E
Rhinns of Kells ⋏	44	55.07 N	4.22 W
Rhino Camp	154	2.58 N	31.24 E
Rhinow	54	52.45 N	12.20 E
Rhiou, Oued ≃	34	36.00 N	0.55 E
Rhir, Cap ≻	148	30.38 N	9.55 W
Rhis, Oued ≃	34	35.14 N	3.57 W
Rhiw ≃	42	52.36 N	3.11 W
Rho	62	45.32 N	9.02 E
Rhode Island □[3], U.S.	178	41.40 N	71.30 W
Rhode Island □[3], U.S.	207	41.40 N	71.30 W
Rhode Island I	207	41.33 N	71.15 W
Rhode Island Sound ʊ	207	41.25 N	71.15 W
Rhoden	52	51.28 N	9.00 E
Rhodes, Austl.	274a	33.50 S	151.05 E
Rhodes → Ródhos, Ellás	38	36.26 N	28.13 E
Rhodes, S. Afr.	158	30.47 S	27.59 E
Rhodes, Eng., U.K.	262	53.33 N	2.14 W
Rhodes → Ródhos I	38	36.10 N	28.00 E
Rhodesia → Zimbabwe □[1]	154	20.00 S	30.00 E
Rhodes Inyanga National Park ♦	154	18.12 S	32.45 E
Rhodes Matopos National Park ♦	154	20.33 S	28.20 E
Rhodes Park ♦	273d	26.12 S	28.06 E
Rhodes Peak ∧	202	46.41 N	114.47 W
Rhodes' Tomb ⊥	154	20.30 S	28.30 E
Rhododendron	224	45.20 N	121.55 W
Rhododendron State Park ♦	207	42.47 N	72.12 W
Rhodon	261	48.43 N	2.04 E
Rhodon, Ruisseau le ≃	261	48.42 N	2.04 E
Rhodope Mountains ⋏	38	41.30 N	24.30 E
Rhodt	56	49.16 N	8.07 E
Rhome	222	33.03 N	97.28 W
Rhondda	42	51.40 N	3.27 W
Rhône □[5]	32	45.55 N	4.40 E
Rhône ≃	32	43.20 N	4.50 E
Rhône à Sète, Canal du ≊	62	43.25 N	3.42 E
Rhône au Rhin, Canal du ≊	58	47.06 N	5.19 E
Rhoose	42	51.24 N	3.20 W
Rhosesmor	262	53.12 N	3.10 W
Rhosllanerchrugog	42	53.00 N	3.03 W
Rhosneigr	44	53.14 N	4.31 W
Rhos-on-Sea	44	53.19 N	3.45 W
Rhossili	42	51.34 N	4.17 W
Rhourde-El-Baguel	148	31.24 N	6.57 E
Rhuddlan	44	53.18 N	3.27 W
Rhue ≃	32	45.23 N	2.29 E
Rhum I	46	57.00 N	6.20 W
Rhum, Sound of ʊ	46	56.56 N	6.14 W
Rhyl	44	53.19 N	3.29 W
Rhymney	42	51.46 N	3.18 W
Rhymney ≃	42	51.28 N	3.10 W
Rhynie	46	57.19 N	2.50 W
Riaba	152	3.23 N	8.46 E
Riace	68	38.25 N	16.29 E
Riachão	250	7.22 S	46.37 W
Riachão do Dantas	250	11.04 S	37.44 W
Riachão do Jacuípe	250	11.48 S	39.21 W
Riacho de Santana	255	13.37 S	42.57 W
Riacho Grande	256	23.48 S	46.35 W
Riachos, Islas de los II	254	40.10 S	62.08 W
Riachuelo, Bra.	250	10.44 S	37.11 W
Riachuelo, Chile	254	40.49 S	73.21 W
Riachuelo, Ur.	258	34.28 S	57.43 W
Riachuelo, Arroyo ≃	258	34.27 S	57.44 W
Rialma	255	15.18 S	49.34 W
Rialto, Bra.	256	22.35 S	44.16 W
Rialto, Ca., U.S.	228	34.06 N	117.22 W
Rianápolis	255	15.29 S	49.28 W
Riāng	120	27.32 N	92.56 E
Riangnom	140	9.55 N	30.01 E
Riaño	34	42.58 N	5.01 W
Rians	62	43.37 N	5.45 E
Riánsares ≃	34	39.32 N	3.18 W
Riāsi	123	33.05 N	74.50 E
Riau □[4]	112	1.00 N	102.00 E
Riau, Kepulauan II	112	1.00 N	104.30 E
Riaz	58	46.38 N	7.04 E
Riaza	34	41.17 N	3.28 W
Riaza ≃	34	41.42 N	3.55 W
Rib ≃	42	51.48 N	0.04 W
Ribadavia	34	42.17 N	8.08 W
Ribadeo	34	43.32 N	7.02 W
Ribadesella	34	43.28 N	5.04 W
Ribamar	250	2.33 S	44.03 W
Ribarroja, Embalse de ⊜[1]	34	41.12 N	0.20 E
Ribas de Jarama	266a	40.23 N	3.31 W
Ribas do Rio Pardo	255	20.27 S	53.46 W
Ribauè	154	14.57 S	38.17 E
Ribble ≃	44	53.44 N	2.50 W
Ribbleton	262	53.46 N	2.40 W
Ribble Valley □[8]	262	53.48 N	2.31 W
Ribbon Fall ∟	226	37.44 N	119.39 W
Ribchester	262	53.49 N	2.32 W
Ribe	41	55.21 N	8.46 E
Ribe □[6]	41	55.35 N	8.50 E
Ribe Å ≃	41	55.21 N	8.40 E
Ribeauvillé	58	48.12 N	7.19 E
Ribécourt	50	49.31 N	2.55 E
Ribeira	252	24.40 S	49.01 W
Ribeira de Iguape ≃	252	24.40 S	47.24 W
Ribeira do Amparo	250	11.03 S	38.26 W
Ribeira do Pombal	250	10.50 S	38.32 W
Ribeira Grande, C.V.	150a	17.11 N	25.04 W
Ribeira Grande, Port.	148a	37.49 N	25.31 W
Ribeirão, Bra.	250	8.31 S	35.23 W
Ribeirão, Bra.	256	23.17 S	45.36 W
Ribeirão, Bra.	287b	23.35 S	46.55 W
Ribeirão das Lajes, Reprêsa do ⊜[1]	256	22.45 S	43.55 W
Ribeirão de São Joaquim	256	22.17 S	44.11 W
Ribeirão do Pinhal	255	23.24 S	50.18 W
Ribeirão do Pote	256	23.36 S	45.50 W
Ribeirão Fundo	256	22.40 S	46.15 W
Ribeirão Grande	256	22.48 S	45.27 W
Ribeirão Pires	256	23.43 S	46.25 W
Ribeirão Prêto	255	21.10 S	47.48 W
Ribeirão Vermelho	255	21.11 S	45.03 W
Ribeirãozinho	255	16.27 S	52.35 W
Ribeiro Gonçalves	250	7.32 S	45.14 W
Ribeiro Junqueira	256	21.28 S	42.31 W
Ribeiros	256	21.59 S	45.35 W
Ribemont	50	49.48 N	3.28 E
Ribera	70	37.30 N	13.16 E
Ribérac	32	45.15 N	0.20 E
Riberalta	248	10.59 S	66.06 W
Riberão Pires □[7]	287b	23.43 S	46.21 W
Ribiers	62	44.14 N	5.52 E
Rib Lake	190	45.19 N	90.12 W
Ribnica, Jugo.	36	45.44 N	14.44 E
Ribnica, Jugo.	61	46.32 N	15.16 E
Ribnitz-Damgarten	54	54.15 N	12.28 E
Ribstone Creek ≃	184	52.51 N	110.05 W
Ricadi	68	38.37 N	15.52 E
Ricarda, Laguna de la c	266d	41.18 N	2.07 E
Ricardo Flores Magón	232	29.58 N	106.58 W
Ricaurte	246	1.13 N	77.59 W
Riccall	44	53.50 N	1.04 W
Riccarton	172	43.32 S	172.36 E
Riccia	66	41.29 N	14.50 E
Riccione	66	43.59 N	12.39 E
Rice	222	32.15 N	96.30 W
Rice Creek ≃	216	42.16 N	84.57 W
Rice Lake	190	45.30 N	91.44 W
Rice Lake ⊜, On., Can.	190	47.42 N	82.08 W
Rice Lake ⊜, On., Can.	212	44.08 N	78.13 W
Rice Lake Indian Reserve ◆[4]	212	44.10 N	78.12 W
Riceville, Ia., U.S.	190	43.22 N	92.33 W
Riceville, Pa., U.S.	214	41.47 N	79.48 W
Riceville, Tn., U.S.	192	35.23 N	84.41 W
Rich, Cape ≻	212	44.43 N	80.38 W
Richan	184	49.59 N	92.49 W
Richard B. Russell Lake ⊜[1]	192	34.05 N	82.39 W
Richard Collinson Inlet c	176	72.45 N	113.45 W
Richards	222	30.32 N	95.51 W
Richard's Bay	158	28.47 S	32.06 E
Richard's Bay c	158	28.50 S	32.02 E
Richards-Gebaur Air Force Base ■	194	38.51 N	94.33 W
Richard's Harbour	186	47.37 N	56.24 W
Richards Island I	180	69.20 N	134.30 W
Richardson	222	32.56 N	96.43 W
Richardson ≃	176	58.30 N	111.30 W
Richardson, Mount ∧	162	28.49 S	119.59 E
Richardson Bay c	282	37.52 N	122.29 W
Richardson Mountains ⋏, Can.	180	67.15 N	136.30 W
Richardson Mountains ⋏, N.Z.	172	44.45 S	168.31 E
Richardson Park	285	39.44 N	75.35 W
Richardsville	214	41.14 N	79.01 W
Richard-Toll	150	16.28 N	15.41 W
Richardton	198	46.53 N	102.18 W
Rîchât, Guelb er ∧[2]	148	21.07 N	11.24 W
Richboro	208	40.13 N	75.01 W
Richburg	210	42.05 N	78.09 W
Riche, Pointe ≻	186	50.42 N	57.25 W
Richebourg	261	48.49 N	1.38 E
Richelieu, P.Q., Can.	206	45.27 N	73.15 W
Richelieu, Fr.	32	47.01 N	0.19 E
Richelieu □[6]	206	45.55 N	73.00 W
Richelieu ≃	206	46.03 N	73.07 W
Richer	184	49.39 N	96.28 W
Richey	198	47.38 N	105.04 W
Richfield, Id., U.S.	202	43.02 N	114.09 W
Richfield, Mn., U.S.	190	44.53 N	93.16 W
Richfield, Oh., U.S.	214	41.14 N	81.39 W
Richfield, Pa., U.S.	208	40.41 N	77.07 W
Richfield, Ut,. U.S.	200	38.46 N	112.05 W
Richfield Springs	210	42.51 N	74.59 W
Richford, N.Y., U.S.	210	42.21 N	76.12 W
Richford, Vt., U.S.	206	44.59 N	72.40 W
Rich Fountain	219	38.24 N	91.53 W
Richgrove	226	35.48 N	119.07 W
Rich Hill, N. Ire., U.K.	48	54.23 N	6.33 W
Rich Hill, Mo., U.S.	194	38.05 N	94.12 W
Richibucto	186	46.41 N	64.52 W
Richisau	58	47.02 N	8.54 E
Richland, Ga., U.S.	192	32.05 N	84.40 W
Richland, Mi., U.S.	216	42.22 N	85.27 W
Richland, Mo., U.S.	194	37.51 N	92.24 W
Richland, N.J., U.S.	208	39.29 N	74.52 W
Richland, N.Y., U.S.	212	43.34 N	76.03 W
Richland, Pa., U.S.	208	40.21 N	76.16 W
Richland, Tx., U.S.	222	32.57 N	95.49 W
Richland, Tx., U.S.	222	31.56 N	96.26 W
Richland, Wa., U.S.	202	46.17 N	119.17 W
Richland □[6]	214	40.46 N	82.31 W
Richland Center	190	43.20 N	90.23 W
Richland Creek ≃, Il., U.S.	219	38.14 N	89.54 W
Richland Creek ≃, Tn., U.S.	194	35.02 N	86.55 W
Richland Creek ≃, Tx., U.S.	222	31.58 N	96.03 W
Richlands, N.C., U.S.	192	34.53 N	77.32 W
Richlands, Va., U.S.	192	37.05 N	81.47 W
Richland Springs	196	31.16 N	98.57 W
Richmond, Austl.	166	20.44 S	143.08 E
Richmond, Austl.	170	33.36 S	150.46 E
Richmond, Austl.	274b	37.49 S	145.00 E
Richmond, B.C., Can.	224	49.09 N	123.06 W
Richmond, On., Can.	212	45.11 N	75.50 W
Richmond, P.Q., Can.	206	45.40 N	72.09 W
Richmond, N.Z.	172	41.20 S	173.11 E
Richmond, S. Afr.	158	31.23 S	23.56 E
Richmond, S. Afr.	158	29.54 S	30.08 E
Richmond, Eng., U.K.	44	54.24 N	1.44 W
Richmond, Ca., U.S.	226	37.56 N	122.20 W
Richmond, Il., U.S.	216	42.28 N	88.18 W
Richmond, In., U.S.	218	39.49 N	84.53 W
Richmond, Ks., U.S.	198	38.24 N	95.15 W
Richmond, Ky., U.S.	192	37.44 N	84.17 W
Richmond, Me., U.S.	188	44.05 N	69.47 W
Richmond, Ma., U.S.	207	42.22 N	73.22 W
Richmond, Mi., U.S.	214	42.48 N	82.45 W
Richmond, Mn., U.S.	190	45.27 N	94.31 W
Richmond, Mo., U.S.	194	39.16 N	93.58 W
Richmond, Oh., U.S.	214	40.26 N	80.46 W
Richmond, Tx., U.S.	222	29.34 N	95.45 W
Richmond, Ut,. U.S.	200	41.55 N	111.48 W
Richmond, Vt., U.S.	188	44.24 N	72.59 W
Richmond, Va., U.S.	208	37.33 N	77.27 W
Richmond □[6], P.Q., Can.	206	45.40 N	72.00 W
Richmond □[6], N.Y., U.S.	210	40.38 N	74.05 W
Richmond □[6], Va., U.S.	208	37.32 N	77.28 W
Richmond ◆[8], Eng., U.K.	42	51.28 N	0.18 W
Richmond ◆[8], Ca., U.S.	282	37.46 N	122.29 W
Richmond ◆[8], Pa., U.S.	285	39.59 N	75.06 W
Richmond, Mount ∧	172	41.29 S	173.24 E
Richmond, Point ≻	282	37.55 N	122.23 W
Richmond Beach	224	47.46 N	122.23 W
Richmond Creek ≃	276	40.34 N	74.11 W
Richmond Heights, Fl., U.S.	220	25.37 N	80.22 W
Richmond Heights, Mo., U.S.	219	38.37 N	90.19 W
Richmond Heights, Oh., U.S.	214	41.33 N	81.30 W
Richmond Highlands	224	47.45 N	122.20 W
Richmond Hill, On., Can.	212	43.52 N	79.27 W
Richmond Hill, Ga., U.S.	192	31.56 N	81.18 W
Richmond Hill ◆[8]	276	40.42 N	73.49 W
Richmond International Airport ⊠	208	37.30 N	77.19 W
Richmond Mall ◆[9]	279a	41.32 N	81.30 W
Richmond National Battlefield Park ♦	208	37.25 N	77.23 W
Richmond Park ♦	260	51.26 N	0.16 W
Richmond Peak ∧	241h	13.17 N	61.13 W
Richmond Range ⋏	172	41.27 S	173.30 E
Richmond Royal Australian Air Force Base ■	170	33.37 S	150.48 E
Richmond-San Rafael Bridge ◆[5]	282	37.56 N	122.27 W
Richmondtown Restoration ⊥	276	40.34 N	74.09 W
Richmond Valley ◆[8]	276	40.31 N	74.13 W
Richmondville	210	42.38 N	74.33 W
Richrath	263	51.08 N	6.56 E
Rich Square	192	36.16 N	77.17 W
Rich Stadium ♦	284a	42.57 N	78.47 W
Richtenberg	54	54.12 N	12.53 E
Richterswil	58	47.13 N	8.42 E
Richton	194	31.20 N	88.56 W
Richton Park	216	41.29 N	87.42 W
Richvale, On., Can.	212	43.51 N	79.26 W
Richvale, Ca., U.S.	226	39.30 N	121.45 W
Richview	219	38.23 N	89.11 W
Richville, N.Y., U.S.	212	44.25 N	75.23 E
Richville, Oh., U.S.	214	40.45 N	81.27 W
Richwood, N.J., U.S.	285	39.43 N	75.10 W
Richwood, Oh., U.S.	214	40.25 N	83.17 W
Richwood, W.V., U.S.	188	38.13 N	80.32 W
Richwood Village	222	29.04 N	95.25 W
Ricinskij zapovednik ♦	84	43.25 N	40.30 E

Symbols in the index entries represent the broad categories identified in the key at the right. Symbols with superior numbers (⋏[1]) identify subcategories (see complete key on page *I · 1).*

Kartensymbole in dem Registerverzeichnis stellen die rechts in Schlüssel erklärten Kategorien dar. Symbole mit hochgestellten Ziffern (⋏[1]) bezeichnen Unterabteilungen einer Kategorie (vgl. vollständiger Schlüssel auf Seite *I · 1).*

Los símbolos incluídos en el texto del índice representan las grandes categorias identificadas con la clave a la derecha. Los símbolos con numeros en su parte superior (⋏[1]) identifican las subcategorías (véase la clave completa en la página *I · 1).*

Les symboles de l'index représentent les catégories indiquées dans la légende à droite. Les symboles suivis d'un indice (⋏[1]) représentent des sous-catégories (voir légende complète à la page *I · 1).*

Os símbolos incluídos no texto do índice representam as grandes categorias identificadas com a chave à direita. Os símbolos com números em sua parte superior (⋏[1]) identificam as subcategorias (veja-se a chave completa à página *I · 1).*

∧ Mountain	Berg	Montaña	Montagne	Montanha
⋏ Mountains	Berge	Montañas	Montagnes	Montanhas
)(Pass	Pass	Paso	Col	Passo
V Valley, Canyon	Tal, Cañon	Valle, Cañón	Vallée, Canyon	Vale, Canhão
≚ Plain	Ebene	Llano	Plaine	Planície
≻ Cape	Kap	Cabo	Cap	Cabo
I Island	Insel	Isla	Île	Ilha
II Islands	Inseln	Islas	Îles	Ilhas
⊥ Other Topographic Features	Andere Topographische Objekte	Otros Elementos Topográficos	Autres données topographiques	Outros acidentes topográficos

ESPAÑOL — Nombre | Página | Lat.°′ | Long.°′ W = Oeste
FRANÇAIS — Nom | Page | Lat.°′ | Long.°′ W = Ouest
PORTUGUÊS — Nome | Página | Lat.°′ | Long.°′ W = Oeste

Nombre / Nom / Nome	Página / Page	Lat.°′	Long.°′ W = Oeste / Ouest
Rickenbacker Air Force Base ■	218	39.48 N	82.56 W
Rickenpass)(	58	47.14 N	9.02 E
Ricken Tunnel ◆[5]	58	47.12 N	9.05 E
Ricketts Glen State Park ♠	210	41.20 N	76.18 W
Ricketts Point ›	274b	38.00 S	145.02 E
Rickleån ≃	26	64.05 N	20.56 E
Rickling	54	54.01 N	10.13 E
Rickmansworth	42	51.39 N	0.29 W
Rico	200	37.41 N	108.01 W
Ricoa ≃	241s	11.30 N	69.12 W
Ricobayo, Embalse de ◎[1]	34	41.30 N	5.55 W
Ricupe	152	14.37 S	21.25 E
Ridā'	144	14.38 N	44.54 E
Ridanna (Ridnaun)	64	46.55 N	11.15 E
Riddarhyttan	40	59.48 N	15.33 E
Ridderkerk	52	51.52 N	4.36 E
Riddes	58	46.10 N	7.13 E
Riddle	202	42.57 N	123.21 W
Riddle Mountain ∧	202	43.07 N	118.30 W
Riddlesburg	214	40.10 N	78.15 W
Riddlewood	285	39.54 N	75.26 W
Riddon, Loch c	46	55.58 N	5.12 W
Rideau ≃	212	45.27 N	75.42 W
Ridge, Eng., U.K.	260	51.41 N	0.15 W
Ridge, N.Y., U.S.	207	40.54 N	72.53 W
Ridge, Tx., U.S.	222	31.09 N	96.19 W
Ridge Acres	276	40.41 N	74.32 W
Ridgecrest, Ca., U.S.	204	35.37 N	117.40 W
Ridgecrest, Wa., U.S.	224	47.45 N	122.21 W
Ridgedale	184	53.04 N	104.09 W
Ridge Farm	194	39.53 N	87.39 W
Ridgefield, Ct., U.S.	207	41.16 N	73.29 W
Ridgefield, Il., U.S.	216	42.16 N	88.22 W
Ridgefield, N.J., U.S.	210	40.50 N	74.00 W
Ridgefield, Wa., U.S.	224	45.48 N	122.44 W
Ridgefield Park	276	40.51 N	74.01 W
Ridgeland, Ms., U.S.	194	32.25 N	90.07 W
Ridgeland, S.C., U.S.	192	32.28 N	80.58 W
Ridgely, Md., U.S.	208	38.56 N	75.53 W
Ridgely, Tn., U.S.	194	36.15 N	89.29 W
Ridge Manor	220	28.31 N	82.10 W
Ridgemont	210	43.13 N	77.43 W
Ridgetown	214	42.26 N	81.54 W
Ridgeville, Mb., Can.	184	49.04 N	97.01 W
Ridgeville, In., U.S.	216	40.17 N	85.01 W
Ridgeville, S.C., U.S.	192	33.05 N	80.18 W
Ridgeville Corners	216	41.26 N	84.15 W
Ridgeway, On., Can.	284a	42.53 N	79.03 W
Ridgeway, Mi., U.S.	216	41.59 N	83.51 W
Ridgeway, Mo., U.S.	194	40.22 N	93.56 W
Ridgeway, N.J., U.S.	208	40.01 N	74.17 W
Ridgeway, Oh., U.S.	216	40.30 N	83.34 W
Ridgeway, Tx., U.S.	222	33.11 N	95.46 W
Ridgeway, Wi., U.S.	190	43.00 N	89.59 W
Ridgeway Ditch ≅	279a	41.25 N	82.05 W
Ridgewood	210	40.58 N	74.07 W
Ridgewood ◆[8]	276	40.42 N	73.53 W
Ridgewood Farm	285	39.57 N	75.34 W
Ridgewood Reservoir ◎[1]	276	40.41 N	73.53 W
Ridgway, Co., U.S.	200	38.09 N	107.46 W
Ridgway, Il., U.S.	194	37.47 N	88.15 W
Ridgway, Pa., U.S.	214	41.25 N	78.43 W
Riding Mountain ∧	184	50.37 N	99.37 W
Riding Mountain National Park ♠	184	50.55 N	100.25 W
Ridley Creek ≃	285	39.51 N	75.21 W
Ridley Creek State Park ♠	285	39.57 N	75.27 W
Ridley Park	285	39.52 N	75.19 W
Ridnaun → Ridanna	64	46.55 N	11.15 E
Riebeek-Kasteel	158	33.23 S	18.53 E
Riebeek-Oos	158	33.10 S	26.10 E
Riebeek-Wes	158	33.21 S	18.52 E
Riecawr, Loch ◎	44	55.13 N	4.27 W
Riedau	60	48.18 N	13.38 E
Riedelbach	56	50.18 N	8.23 E
Rieden	60	49.19 N	11.57 E
Riedenburg	60	48.58 N	11.41 E
Rieder	54	51.44 N	11.10 E
Riederalp	58	46.23 N	8.01 E
Riedern	56	49.40 N	9.23 E
Ried im Innkreis	60	48.13 N	13.30 E
Ried im Oberinntal	58	47.03 N	10.39 E
Riedisheim	58	47.45 N	7.22 E
Riedlingen	58	48.09 N	9.28 E
Riedstadt	56	49.50 N	8.30 E
Riegel	58	48.09 N	7.45 E
Riegelsville, N.J., U.S.	210	40.49 N	74.52 W
Riegelsville, Pa., U.S.	208	40.36 N	75.12 W
Riegelwood	192	34.20 N	78.15 W
Riegersburg	61	47.00 N	15.56 E
Riegersburg, Schloss ⊥	61	47.01 N	15.56 E
Riegersdorf	64	46.33 N	13.47 E
Riehen	58	47.35 N	7.39 E
Rieka → Rijeka	36	45.20 N	14.27 E
Rielasingen	58	47.44 N	8.50 E
Riemke ◆[8]	263	51.30 N	7.13 E
Riemst	56	50.48 N	5.36 E
Rieneck	56	50.05 N	9.38 E
Rienza (Rienz) ≃	64	46.43 N	11.39 E
Rienzi	194	34.45 N	88.31 W
Riesa	54	51.18 N	13.17 E
Riesco, Isla I	254	53.00 S	72.30 W
Rieseby	41	54.32 N	9.48 E
Riesel	222	31.28 N	96.56 W
Riesenbeck	52	52.16 N	7.37 E
Riesenburg → Prabuty	30	53.46 N	19.10 E
Riese Pio X	64	45.44 N	11.55 E
Riesi	70	37.17 N	14.05 E
Riestedt	54	51.29 N	11.21 E
Riet ≃, S. Afr.	158	29.00 S	23.54 E
Riet ≃, S. Afr.	158	31.20 S	20.17 E
Rietavas	76	55.44 N	21.56 E
Rietberg	52	51.47 N	8.25 E
Rietbron	158	32.54 S	23.10 E
Rietfontein	156	21.58 S	20.58 E
Riethuiskraal	158	34.20 S	21.22 E
Rieti	66	42.24 N	12.51 E
Rieti □[4]	66	42.18 N	12.52 E
Rietschen	54	51.23 N	14.47 E
Rietspruit ≃, S. Afr.	273d	26.19 S	28.18 E
Rietspruit ≃, S. Afr.	273d	26.06 S	27.39 E
Rietvlei	158	30.29 S	29.51 E
Rietzer See ◎	54	52.22 N	12.39 E
Riez	62	43.49 N	6.06 E
Riezlern	58	47.21 N	10.11 E
Rif ⩘	148	35.00 N	4.00 W
Riffe Lake ◎[1]	224	46.30 N	122.20 W
Rifflart	273b	4.25 S	15.21 E
Rifiano (Riffian)	64	46.42 N	11.11 E
Rifle	200	39.32 N	107.46 W
Rifle ≃	190	44.00 N	83.49 W
Rifstangi ›	24a	66.35 N	16.10 W
Rifton	210	41.50 N	74.03 W
Rift Valley □[4]	154	0.30 N	36.00 E
Rift Valley V	10	3.00 S	29.00 E
Rift Valley Lakes National Park ♠	144	7.30 N	38.30 E
Rīga, S.S.S.R.	76	56.57 N	24.06 E
Riga, S.S.S.R.	88	56.36 N	106.17 E
Riga, Mi., U.S.	216	41.49 N	83.50 W
Riga, Gulf of → Rižskij zaliv c	76	57.30 N	23.35 E
Riga, Mount ∧	162	21.59 S	116.25 E
Rigacikun	150	10.40 N	7.28 E
Rigaih	114	4.40 N	95.34 E
Rīgān	128	28.37 N	58.58 E
Rīgas Jūras līcis → Rižskij zaliv c	76	57.30 N	23.35 E
Rīga Station ◆[5]	265b	55.48 N	37.38 E
Rigaud	206	45.29 N	74.18 W
Rigaud ≃	206	45.29 N	74.18 W
Rigby	202	43.40 N	111.54 W
Rīgestān ◆[1]	128	31.00 N	65.00 E
Riggins	202	45.25 N	116.18 W
Riggisberg	58	46.48 N	7.29 E
Riggston	219	39.42 N	90.25 W
Righedo, Passo del)(	64	44.27 N	9.55 E
Rigi ∧	58	47.05 N	8.30 E
Rignano Flaminio	66	42.12 N	12.29 E
Rignano Garganico	68	41.40 N	15.35 E
Rignano sull'Arno	66	43.43 N	11.27 E
Rigney	58	47.23 N	6.11 E
Rigney Bluff	210	43.19 N	77.38 W
Rigny-Ussé	50	47.15 N	0.18 E
Rigo	164	9.47 S	147.34 E
Rigolet	176	54.20 N	58.35 W
Rig-Rig	146	14.16 N	14.21 E
Rigside	46	53.36 N	3.47 W
Riguldi	76	59.08 N	23.33 E
Rīḥ, Jazīrat ar- I	140	18.10 N	38.27 E
Riḥāb	132	32.19 N	36.06 E
Rihand ≃	124	24.33 N	82.59 E
Rihand Dam ◆[6]	124	24.05 N	82.45 E
Riihimäki	26	60.45 N	24.46 E
Riiser-Larsen Peninsula ›[1]	9	68.55 S	34.00 E
Rijau	150	11.07 N	5.14 E
Riječki Zaljev c	36	45.15 N	14.25 E
Rijeka	36	45.20 N	14.27 E
Rijen	52	51.35 N	4.55 E
Rijkevorsel	56	51.21 N	4.46 E
Rijksdorp	52	52.09 N	4.25 E
Rijn → Rhine ≃	30	51.52 N	6.02 E
Rijnsburg	52	52.12 N	4.27 E
Rijssel → Lille	50	50.38 N	3.04 E
Rijssen	52	52.18 N	6.30 E
Rijswijk	52	52.04 N	4.20 E
Rike	144	10.42 N	39.55 E
Rikers Island I	276	40.47 N	73.53 W
Rikers Island Channel ʯ	276	40.47 N	73.52 W
Rikkavesi ◎	26	62.50 N	28.44 E
Riksgränsen	24	68.24 N	18.12 E
Rikuchū-kaigan-kokuritsu-kōen ♠	92	39.25 N	141.57 E
Rikuzen-takata	92	39.01 N	141.38 E
Rila ⩘	38	42.08 N	23.33 E
Riley	198	39.17 N	96.49 W
Riley, Mount ∧	200	31.55 N	107.07 W
Riley, Point ›	168b	33.53 S	137.36 E
Riley Creek ≃	216	41.02 N	84.00 W
Riley Lake ◎	212	44.50 N	79.11 W
Rileys Range ⩘	170	34.21 S	150.10 E
Rilievo	70	37.55 N	12.33 E
Rillieux	62	45.49 N	4.54 E
Rillington	44	54.09 N	0.42 W
Rillito	200	32.24 N	111.09 W
Rillton	214	40.17 N	79.44 W
Rilly-la-Montagne	50	49.10 N	4.03 E
Rilski manastir ♁[1]	38	42.08 N	23.20 E
Rima ≃	150	13.04 N	5.10 E
Rímac	286d	12.03 S	77.03 W
Rímac ≃	248	12.02 S	77.09 W
Rímachi, Lago ◎	246	4.25 S	76.43 W
Rimāḥ, Jabal ar- ∧	132	32.19 N	36.52 E
Rima San Giuseppe	62	45.52 N	8.00 E
Rimatara I	14	22.38 S	152.51 W
Rimavská Sobota	30	48.23 N	20.02 E
Rimbey	182	52.38 N	114.14 W
Rimbo	40	59.45 N	18.22 E
Rimé, Ouadi V	146	14.02 N	18.03 E
Rimersburg	214	41.02 N	79.30 W
Rimforsa	26	58.08 N	15.40 E
Rimi	150	12.58 N	7.43 E
Rimini	66	44.04 N	12.34 E
Rîmna ≃	38	45.39 N	27.19 E
Rîmnicu-Sărat	38	45.23 N	27.03 E
Rîmnicu-Vîlcea	38	45.06 N	24.22 E
Rimo Glacier ⍓	123	35.25 N	77.30 E
Rimogne	56	49.50 N	4.33 E
Rimouski	186	48.26 N	68.33 W
Rimouski ≃	186	48.27 N	68.32 W
Rimouski, Réserve ♠	186	48.03 N	68.15 W
Rimpar	56	49.51 N	9.57 E
Rimrock Lake ◎[1]	224	46.38 N	121.12 W
Rimsko-Korsakovka	80	51.34 N	48.31 E
Rín → Rhine ≃	30	51.52 N	6.02 E
Rinca	115b	8.37 S	119.48 E
Rinca, Pulau I	115b	8.41 S	119.42 E
Rinchnach	60	48.57 N	13.12 E
Rinčin Lchumbe	88	51.07 N	99.40 E
Rincón, C.R.	236	8.42 N	83.29 W
Rincon, Ned. Ant.	241s	12.15 N	68.20 W
Rincón, P.R.	240m	18.20 N	67.15 W
Rincon, Ga., U.S.	192	32.17 N	81.14 W
Rincon, N.M., U.S.	200	32.40 N	107.03 W
Rincón, Bahía de c	240m	17.58 N	66.20 W
Rinconada	252	22.26 S	66.10 W
Rinconada, Hipódromo de la ♠	286c	10.26 N	66.56 W
Rincón del Bonete, Lago Artificial ◎[1]	252	32.45 S	56.00 W
Rincón del Ocote, Cerro ∧	236	13.36 N	87.10 W
Rincón de Romos	234	22.14 N	102.18 W
Rincón de Tamayo	234	20.25 N	100.45 W
Rincon Indian Reservation ◆[4]	228	33.15 N	116.57 W
Rincon Valley	226	38.28 N	122.39 W
Rindal	26	63.03 N	9.13 E
Rindown Castle ⊥	48	53.32 N	7.59 W
Ringdove	175f	16.38 S	168.09 E
Ringe	41	55.14 N	10.29 E
Ringebu	26	61.31 N	10.10 E
Ringenwalde	54	53.03 N	13.42 E
Ringertown	279b	40.25 N	79.36 W
Ringford	44	54.54 N	4.03 W
Ringgau ◆[1]	56	51.04 N	10.04 E
Ringgit, Gunung ∧	115a	7.43 S	113.50 E
Ringgold, Ga., U.S.	192	34.54 N	85.06 W
Ringgold, La., U.S.	194	32.19 N	93.16 W
Ringgold, Pa., U.S.	214	41.00 N	79.10 W
Ringgold Isles II	175g	16.15 S	179.25 W
Ringim	150	12.08 N	9.10 E
Ringkøbing	26	56.05 N	8.15 E
Ringkøbing □[6]	41	56.10 N	8.50 E
Ringkøbing Fjord c[2]	26	56.00 N	8.15 E
Ringlet	114	4.25 N	101.23 E
Ringling	196	34.10 N	97.35 W
Ringling Museums ♁	220	27.23 N	82.34 W
Ringmer	42	50.53 N	0.04 E
Ringoes	208	40.26 N	74.52 W
Rings Island	283	42.49 N	70.52 W
Ringsjön ◎	41	55.52 N	13.32 E
Ringsted, Dan.	41	55.27 N	11.49 E
Ringsted, Ia., U.S.	198	43.17 N	94.30 W
Ringtown	210	40.51 N	76.14 W
Rīngus	120	27.21 N	75.34 E
Ringvassøya I	24	69.55 N	19.15 E
Ringville	48	52.02 N	7.34 W
Ringwood, Austl.	169	37.49 S	145.14 E
Ringwood, Eng., U.K.	42	50.51 N	1.47 W
Ringwood, N.J., U.S.	210	41.06 N	74.14 W
Ringwood Manor ⊥	276	41.08 N	74.15 W
Ringwood North	274b	37.48 S	145.14 E
Ringwood State Park ♠	210	41.08 N	74.16 W
Riñihue	254	39.49 S	72.27 W
Riñihue, Lago ◎	254	39.50 S	72.18 W
Rinjani, Gunung ∧	115b	8.24 S	116.28 E
Rinkenæs	41	54.54 N	9.34 E
Rinkerode	52	51.50 N	7.41 E
Rinnes, Ben ∧	46	57.23 N	3.15 W
Rinns of Islay ⩘	46	55.45 N	6.25 W
Rinns Point ›	46	55.40 N	6.30 W
Rinnthal	56	49.13 N	7.55 E
Rinsumageest	52	53.18 N	5.57 E
Rinteln	52	52.11 N	9.04 E
Rinxent	50	50.48 N	1.44 E
Rio, Fl., U.S.	220	27.13 N	80.14 W
Rio, Wi., U.S.	190	43.26 N	89.14 W
Rio Azul	252	25.43 S	50.47 W
Río Balsas	234	17.59 N	99.47 W
Riobamba	246	1.40 S	78.38 W
Río Blanco, Chile	252	32.55 S	70.19 W
Río Blanco (Tenango de Rio Blanco), Méx.	234	18.50 N	97.09 W
Rio Bonito	256	22.43 S	42.37 W
Rio Bonito ◆[8]	287b	23.43 S	46.41 W
Rio Branco, Bra.	248	9.58 S	67.48 W
Río Branco, Ur.	252	32.34 S	53.25 W
Río Bravo, Méx.	196	28.17 N	100.55 W
Río Bravo, Méx.	232	25.59 N	98.06 W
Rio Brilhante	255	21.48 S	54.33 W
Río Bueno	254	40.19 S	72.58 W
Río Caribe	246	10.42 N	63.07 W
Rio Casca	255	20.13 S	42.39 W
Río Cauto	240p	20.33 N	76.55 W
Río Ceballos	252	31.10 S	64.20 W
Río Chico, Arg.	254	41.43 S	70.30 W
Río Chico, Ven.	246	10.18 N	65.59 W
Rio Claro, Bra.	255	22.24 S	47.33 W
Rio Claro, Bra.	256	22.43 S	44.09 W
Rio Claro, Trin.	241r	10.18 N	61.11 W
Rio Claro, Reprêsa do ◎[1]	256	23.39 S	45.54 W
Río Colorado	252	39.01 S	64.05 W
Rio Comprido ◆[8]	287a	22.55 S	43.12 W
Río Cuarto	252	33.08 S	64.21 W
Rio da Conceição	250	11.24 S	46.54 W
Rio das Antas	252	26.55 S	51.04 W
Rio das Flores	256	22.10 S	43.35 W
Rio das Pedras	156	23.12 S	35.23 E
Rio de Contas	255	13.36 S	41.48 W
Rio de Janeiro, Bra.	256	22.54 S	43.14 W
Rio de Janeiro, Bra.	287a	22.54 S	43.14 W
Rio de Janeiro □[3]	255	22.00 S	42.30 W
Rio de Janeiro □[7]	287a	22.55 S	43.30 W
Río de Jesús	236	7.59 N	81.10 W
Río de las Playas	234	17.51 N	94.02 W
Rio Dell	204	40.29 N	124.06 W
Rio de Mouro	266c	38.46 N	9.20 W
Río de Oro	246	8.17 N	73.23 W
Rio d'Oeste	252	27.12 S	49.48 W
Rio do Ouro	256	22.51 S	42.59 W
Rio do Prado	255	16.35 S	40.34 W
Rio do Sul	252	27.13 S	49.39 W
Rio d'Ouro	287a	22.39 S	43.32 W
Rio Espera	255	20.51 S	43.29 W
Rio Fortuna	252	28.06 S	49.07 W
Río Gallegos	254	51.38 S	69.13 W
Río Grande, Arg.	254	53.47 S	67.42 W
Rio Grande, Bra.	252	32.02 S	52.05 W
Río Grande, Méx.	234	15.59 N	97.27 W
Río Grande, Méx.	234	23.50 N	103.02 W
Río Grande, Pan.	236	8.37 N	81.17 W
Río Grande, P.R.	240m	18.23 N	65.50 W
Rio Grande, N.J., U.S.	208	39.00 N	74.52 W
Río Grande, Ven.	286c	10.35 N	66.57 W
Rio Grande → Grande, Rio ≃	178	25.57 N	97.09 W
Rio Grande, Barragem do ◆[6]	287b	23.42 S	46.40 W
Rio Grande, Ponte do ◆[5]	287b	23.46 S	46.31 W
Rio Grande, Reservatório do ◎[1]	256	23.47 S	46.37 W
Rio Grande City	196	26.22 N	98.49 W
Rio Grande da Serra	287b	23.44 S	46.24 W
Rio Grande da Serra □[7]	287b	23.45 S	46.23 W
Rio Grande do Norte □[3]	250	5.45 S	36.00 W
Rio Grande do Sul → Rio Grande	252	32.02 S	52.05 W
Rio Grande do Sul □[3]	252	30.00 S	54.00 W
Riograndina	256	22.11 S	42.30 W
Ríohacha	246	11.33 N	72.55 W
Río Hato	236	8.23 N	80.10 W
Río Hondo, Méx.	286a	19.25 N	99.16 W
Rio Hondo, Tx., U.S.	196	26.14 N	97.34 W
Rioja	248	6.05 S	77.09 W
Río Jueyes	240m	18.01 N	66.20 W
Riola	64	44.16 N	11.04 E
Río Lagartos	232	21.36 N	88.10 W
Riolândia	255	19.59 S	49.40 W
Rio Largo	250	9.29 S	35.51 W
Riola Sardo	71	39.59 N	8.32 E
Rio Linda	226	38.41 N	121.26 W
Riolo Terme	66	44.16 N	11.43 E
Río Luján	258	34.17 S	58.54 W
Riom	32	45.54 N	3.07 E
Riomaggiore	62	44.06 N	9.44 E
Rio Marina	66	42.49 N	10.25 E
Río Mayo	254	45.41 S	70.16 W
Río Mulatos	248	19.42 S	66.47 W
Río Muni □[4]	152	1.30 N	10.30 E
Riondel	182	49.46 N	116.52 W
Rio Negrinho	252	26.15 S	49.31 W
Rio Negro, Bra.	252	26.06 S	49.48 W
Rio Negro, Bra.	255	19.27 S	54.58 W
Río Negro, Chile	254	40.47 S	73.14 W
Ríonegro, Col.	246	6.09 N	75.22 W
Ríonegro, Col.	246	7.16 N	73.09 W
Río Negro □[4]	254	40.00 S	67.00 W
Rio Negro, Pantanal do ≡	248	19.00 S	56.00 W
Rionero in Vulture	68	40.56 N	15.41 E
Rionero Sannitico	66	41.42 N	14.08 E
Rioni ≃	84	42.08 N	41.39 E
Rio Novo	256	21.29 S	43.08 W
Rio Novo do Sul	255	20.52 S	40.56 W
Riópar	34	38.30 N	2.27 W
Rio Pardo	252	29.59 S	52.22 W
Rio Pardo de Minas	255	15.37 S	42.33 W
Rio Pequeno, Reservatório do ◎[1]	287b	23.46 S	46.30 W
Río Pico	254	44.13 S	71.21 W
Río Piedras, Arg.	252	25.18 S	64.54 W
Río Piedras, P.R.	240m	18.24 N	66.03 W
Río Pilcomayo, Parque Nacional ♠	252	25.10 S	58.00 W
Rio Piracicaba	255	19.55 S	43.11 W
Rio Pomba	256	21.17 S	43.11 W
Rio Prêto, Bra.	256	22.06 S	43.50 W
Rio Prêto, Bra.	256	22.48 S	45.46 W
Rio Prêto → São José do Rio Prêto, Bra.	256	22.10 S	42.57 W
Rio Rancho	200	35.14 N	106.38 W
Rio Real	250	11.28 S	37.56 W
Rio Saliceto	64	44.49 N	10.49 E
Río San Juan □[5]	236	11.10 N	84.30 W
Rio Sêco	256	22.46 S	42.40 W
Río Segundo	252	31.40 S	63.55 W
Rio Sorocaba, Reprêsa do ◎[1]	256	23.37 S	47.16 W
Río Sucio, Col.	246	5.25 N	75.42 W
Ríosucio, Col.	246	7.27 N	77.07 W
Río Tercero	252	32.11 S	64.06 W
Rio Tinto	250	6.48 S	35.05 W
Riotord	62	45.14 N	4.24 E
Rio Tuba	116	8.30 N	117.25 E
Riou, Île de I	62	43.11 N	5.24 E
Rioveggio	64	44.17 N	11.14 E
Rio Verde, Bra.	255	17.43 S	50.56 W
Ríoverde, Méx.	234	21.56 N	99.59 W
Rio Verde de Mato Grosso	255	18.56 S	54.52 W
Rio Vermelho	255	18.18 S	43.00 W
Rio Vista, Ca., U.S.	226	38.09 N	121.41 W
Rio Vista, Tx., U.S.	222	32.14 N	97.23 W
Rioz	58	47.25 N	6.04 E
Riozinho ≃, Bra.	246	2.55 S	67.07 W
Riozinho ≃, Bra.	250	10.22 S	49.50 W
Riozinho ≃, Bra.	250	8.25 S	45.43 W
Riozinho ≃, Bra.	250	7.06 S	51.40 W
Říp ∧	54	50.24 N	14.18 E
Ripacandida	68	40.55 N	15.43 E
Ripalti, Punta dei ›	66	42.42 N	10.25 E
Ripatransone	66	43.00 N	13.46 E
Ripley, Eng., U.K.	42	53.03 N	1.24 W
Ripley, Eng., U.K.	260	51.18 N	0.29 W
Ripley, Il., U.S.	219	40.01 N	90.38 W
Ripley, In., U.S.	216	41.06 N	86.39 W
Ripley, Ms., U.S.	194	34.43 N	88.57 W
Ripley, N.Y., U.S.	214	42.16 N	79.42 W
Ripley, Oh., U.S.	218	38.44 N	83.50 W
Ripley, Tn., U.S.	194	35.44 N	89.31 W
Ripley, W.V., U.S.	188	38.49 N	81.42 W
Ripley □[6]	218	39.04 N	85.15 W
Ripoll	34	42.12 N	2.12 E
Ripoll ≃	266d	41.29 N	2.12 E
Ripollet	266d	41.30 N	2.10 E
Ripon, P.Q., Can.	206	45.47 N	75.06 W
Ripon, Eng., U.K.	44	54.08 N	1.31 W
Ripon, Ca., U.S.	226	37.44 N	121.07 W
Ripon, Wi., U.S.	190	43.50 N	88.50 W
Riposto	70	37.44 N	15.12 E
Rippling Ridge	284b	39.11 N	76.37 W
Ripponden	44	53.41 N	1.57 W
Rippowam ≃, U.S.	276	41.03 N	73.33 W
Rippowam ≃, Ct., U.S.	276	41.03 N	73.33 W
Riquewihr	58	48.10 N	7.18 E
Ririba, Laga ≃	154	3.34 N	37.15 E
Riri Bāzār	124	27.57 N	83.26 E
Ririe	202	43.37 N	111.46 W
Risālpur Cantonment	123	34.04 N	72.00 E
Risaralda □[5]	246	5.00 N	76.00 W
Risasi	154	0.25 S	25.44 E
Risbäck	26	64.42 N	15.32 E
Risca	42	51.37 N	3.07 W
Rischenau	52	51.53 N	9.17 E
Risción, Punta de la ›	232	25.10 N	108.22 W
Riscle	32	43.40 N	0.05 W
Rī Shahr	128	28.55 N	50.50 E
Rishīkesh	124	30.07 N	78.19 E
Rishiri-Rebun-Sarobetsu-kokuritsu-kōen ♠	92a	45.10 N	141.35 E
Rishiri-suidō ʯ	92a	45.10 N	141.25 E
Rishiri-tō I	92a	45.11 N	141.15 E
Rishiri-zan ∧	92a	45.11 N	141.15 E
Rishmayyā	132	33.44 N	35.36 E
Rishon leẔiyyon	132	31.58 N	34.48 E
Rishpon	132	32.12 N	34.49 E
Rishra	272b	22.43 N	88.21 E
Rishrāsh, Wādī V	142	29.29 N	31.16 E
Rishton	262	53.46 N	2.25 W
Rishworth	262	53.40 N	1.57 W
Rishworth Moor ◆[3]	262	53.39 N	2.01 W
Risinge	40	58.42 N	15.51 E
Rising Star	196	32.05 N	98.57 W
Rising Sun, In., U.S.	218	38.56 N	84.51 W
Rising Sun, Md., U.S.	208	39.41 N	76.03 W
Risingsun, Oh., U.S.	214	41.16 N	83.25 W
Risle ≃	50	49.26 N	0.23 E
Risnjak ∧	36	45.26 N	14.37 E
Rîşnov	38	45.36 N	25.28 E
Risø	41	55.42 N	12.06 E
Rison, Ar., U.S.	194	33.57 N	92.11 W
Rison, Md., U.S.	208	38.32 N	77.10 W
Risør	26	58.43 N	9.14 E
Ris-Orangis	50	48.39 N	2.25 E
Riss ≃	58	48.17 N	9.49 E
Rissani	148	31.23 N	4.09 W
Risskov ◆[8]	41	56.11 N	10.14 E
Risstissen	58	48.16 N	9.49 E
Risti	76	58.59 N	24.03 E
Ristigouche (Restigouche) ≃	186	48.04 N	66.20 W
Ristiina	26	61.30 N	27.16 E
Ristijärvi	26	64.44 N	28.24 E
Ristinge	41	54.50 N	10.38 E
Ristna	76	58.56 N	22.05 E
Risum-Lindholm	41	54.45 N	8.53 E
Rita Blanca Creek ≃	196	35.40 N	102.29 W
Ritchie, S. Afr.	158	29.02 S	24.38 E
Ritchie, Md., U.S.	284c	38.52 N	76.52 W
Ritchie Branch ≃	284c	38.53 N	76.52 W
Rithāla ◆[8]	272a	28.43 N	77.06 E
Ritidian Point ›	174p	13.39 N	144.51 E
Ritscher Upland ⩘[1]	9	73.20 S	9.30 W
Ritsumeikan University ♁[2]	270	35.01 N	135.46 E
Ritsurin-kōen ♠	96	34.21 N	134.02 E
Ritta Island I	220	26.44 N	80.48 W
Ritter, Mount ∧	226	37.42 N	119.12 W
Ritterhude	52	53.11 N	8.45 E
Rittersgrün	54	50.29 N	12.47 E
Rittman	214	40.58 N	81.46 W
Rittō	94	35.01 N	136.00 E
Ritzleben	54	52.50 N	11.21 E
Ritzville	202	47.07 N	118.22 W
Riu	120	28.19 N	95.03 E
Riva	208	38.57 N	76.35 W
Rivadavia, Arg.	252	35.28 S	62.57 W
Rivadavia, Arg.	252	33.11 S	68.28 W
Rivadavia, Arg.	252	24.11 S	62.53 W
Rivadavia, Arg.	252	31.33 S	68.37 W
Rivadavia, Chile	252	29.58 S	70.34 W
Riva del Garda	64	45.53 N	10.50 E
Riva del Sole	66	42.46 N	10.52 E
Riva Deresi ≃	267b	41.14 N	29.12 E
Riva di Tures (Rain)	64	46.57 N	12.04 E
Rivaköy	267b	41.13 N	29.12 E
Rivanazzano	62	44.56 N	9.01 E
Rivanna ≃	192	37.45 N	78.10 W
Rivare	216	40.49 N	84.50 W
Rivarolo Canavese	62	45.19 N	7.43 E
Rivarolo Mantovano	64	45.04 N	10.26 E
Rivas	236	11.26 N	85.50 W
Rivas □[5]	236	11.25 N	85.50 W
Rivasdale	273d	26.17 S	27.56 E
Rīvash	128	35.26 N	58.26 E
Rivas-Vaciamadrid	266a	40.20 N	3.31 W
Riva Trigoso	62	44.16 N	9.26 E
Rive, Île de la I	273b	4.21 S	15.26 E
Rive d'Arcano	64	46.08 N	13.02 E
Rive-de-Gier	62	45.32 N	4.37 E
Rivello	68	40.04 N	15.45 E
Rivera, Arg.	252	37.12 S	63.14 W
Rivera, Col.	246	2.47 N	75.15 W
Rivera, Ur.	252	30.54 S	55.31 W
Riverbank	226	37.44 N	120.56 W
River Cess	150	5.28 N	9.32 W
Riverdale, Ca., U.S.	226	36.25 N	119.51 W
Riverdale, Il., U.S.	278	41.38 N	87.37 W
Riverdale, Md., U.S.	284c	38.57 N	76.55 W
Riverdale, N.J., U.S.	276	40.59 N	74.18 W
Riverdale, N.D., U.S.	198	47.29 N	101.22 W
Riverdale, Or., U.S.	224	45.27 N	122.41 W
Riverdale ◆[8]	276	40.54 N	73.54 W
Riverdale Heights	284c	38.58 N	76.55 W
Riverdale Park ♠	275b	43.40 N	79.21 W
River Drive Park	212	44.08 N	79.31 W
River Edge, N.J., U.S.	276	40.55 N	74.02 W
River Edge, Oh., U.S.	279a	41.25 N	81.51 W
River Falls, Al., U.S.	194	31.21 N	86.32 W
River Falls, Wi., U.S.	190	44.51 N	92.37 W
River Forest	278	41.53 N	87.48 W
Rivergaro	62	44.55 N	9.36 E
River Grove	278	41.55 N	87.50 W
Riverhaven	216	41.05 N	85.02 W
Riverhead, Eng., U.K.	260	51.17 N	0.10 E
Riverhead, N.Y., U.S.	207	40.55 N	72.39 W
River Hébert	186	45.42 N	64.23 W
River Hill	279b	40.12 N	79.54 W
River Hills	216	43.10 N	87.55 W
Riverhurst	184	50.53 N	106.52 W
Riverina ◆[1]	166	35.30 S	145.30 E
River John	186	45.45 N	63.03 W
River Jordan	224	48.25 N	124.03 W
Riverlea	214	40.05 N	83.02 W
River Lea Navigation ≅	260	51.32 N	0.02 W
River Meadow Brook ≃	283	42.38 N	71.17 W
Rivermont	192	35.13 N	77.38 W
Rivero, Isla I	254	45.37 S	74.20 W
River Oaks	284c	38.57 N	77.11 W
River of Ponds	186	50.32 N	57.24 W
River Pines, Ca., U.S.	226	38.33 N	120.45 W
River Pines, Ma., U.S.	207	42.33 N	71.17 W
River Plaza	208	40.21 N	74.05 W
River Ridge Estates	284c	38.47 N	77.00 W
River Road	202	44.03 N	123.05 W
River Rouge	216	42.16 N	83.08 W
River Rouge Park ♠	281	42.22 N	83.15 W
Rivers	184	50.02 N	100.12 W
Rivers □[3]	150	4.30 N	6.30 E
Rivers, Lake of the ◎	184	49.45 N	105.45 W
Riversdale, N.Z.	172	45.54 S	168.45 E
Riversdale, S. Afr.	158	34.07 S	21.15 E
Riverside, Ca., U.S.	228	33.57 N	117.23 W
Riverside, Ct., U.S.	276	41.02 N	73.35 W
Riverside, Il., U.S.	278	41.50 N	87.49 W
Riverside, Ia., U.S.	190	41.28 N	91.34 W
Riverside, Mi., U.S.	216	42.11 N	86.23 W
Riverside, Mi., U.S.	216	42.17 N	84.29 W
Riverside, N.J., U.S.	208	40.01 N	74.57 W
Riverside, N.Y., U.S.	210	42.55 N	73.40 W
Riverside, N.Y., U.S.	210	42.08 N	77.01 W
Riverside, Pa., U.S.	210	40.57 N	76.38 W
Riverside, Tx., U.S.	222	30.57 N	95.24 W
Riverside, Wa., U.S.	182	48.30 N	119.30 W
Riverside □[6]	228	33.45 N	117.10 W
Riverside ◆[8]	281	42.20 N	82.57 W
Riverside International Raceway ♠	228	33.57 N	117.17 W
Riverside Manors	284a	43.11 N	79.03 W
Riverside Park ♠, Mi., U.S.	281	42.22 N	83.26 W
Riverside Park ♠, N.Y., U.S.	284a	42.57 N	78.54 W
Rivers Inlet	182	51.41 N	127.15 W
Rivers Inlet c	182	51.39 N	127.30 W
Riversleigh	166	19.02 S	138.44 E
Riverstone	170	33.40 S	150.52 E
Riverton, Austl.	168b	34.09 S	138.45 E
Riverton, Mb., Can.	184	50.59 N	96.59 W
Riverton, N.Z.	172	46.21 S	168.01 E
Riverton, Il., U.S.	219	39.51 N	89.33 W
Riverton, Ne., U.S.	198	40.05 N	98.45 W
Riverton, N.J., U.S.	208	40.00 N	75.00 W
Riverton, Ut,. U.S.	200	40.31 N	111.56 W
Riverton, Va., U.S.	188	38.56 N	78.11 W
Riverton, Wy., U.S.	200	43.01 N	108.22 W
Riverton Heights	224	47.28 N	122.18 W
River Vale	276	40.59 N	74.00 W
Riverview, S. Afr.	158	28.27 S	32.10 E
River View, Al., U.S.	194	32.47 N	85.08 W
Riverview, Fl., U.S.	220	27.51 N	82.19 W
Riverview, Ks., U.S.	198	37.47 N	97.22 W
Riverview, Mi., U.S.	216	42.10 N	83.10 W
Riverview Park ♠	279b	40.29 N	80.01 W
Riverwood, Austl.	274a	33.57 S	151.03 E
Riverwood, In., U.S.	218	40.06 N	85.58 W
Riverwoods	278	42.10 N	87.54 W
Rives, Fr.	62	45.21 N	5.30 E
Rives, Tn., U.S.	194	36.21 N	89.02 W
Rivesaltes	32	42.46 N	2.52 E
Rives Junction	216	42.23 N	84.27 W
Rive Sud, Canal de la ≅	275a	45.25 N	73.41 W
Rivesville	188	39.31 N	80.07 W
Riviera, Az., U.S.	204	35.04 N	114.35 W
Riviera, Tx., U.S.	196	27.18 N	97.49 W
Riviera V	58	46.15 N	8.58 E
Riviera Beach, Fl., U.S.	220	26.46 N	80.03 W
Riviera Beach, Md., U.S.	208	39.10 N	76.30 W
Rivière-à-Claude	186	49.13 N	65.54 W
Rivière à Goyaves, Pointe de la ›	241o	16.11 N	61.35 W
Rivière-au-Tonnerre	186	50.16 N	64.47 W
Rivière-Bleue	186	47.26 N	69.03 W
Rivière-Bois-Clair	206	46.34 N	71.50 W
Rivière-de-la-Chaloupe	186	49.08 N	62.32 W
Rivière-des-Prairies ◆[8]	275a	45.39 N	73.33 W
Rivière-du-Loup	186	47.50 N	69.32 W
Rivière du Rempart	157c	20.06 S	57.41 E
Rivière-Matane	186	48.39 N	67.20 W
Rivière-Mékinac	206	46.47 N	72.48 W
Rivière-Pentecôte	186	49.47 N	67.10 W
Rivière-Pilote	240e	14.29 N	60.54 W
Rivière-Salée	240e	14.32 N	60.59 W
Rivière-Verte	186	47.19 N	68.09 W
Riviersonderend	158	34.09 S	19.55 E
Rivignano	64	45.52 N	13.03 E
Rivington	262	53.37 N	2.34 W
Rivington Reservoirs ◎[1]	262	53.37 N	2.34 W
Rivisondoli	66	41.52 N	14.04 E
Rivoli	62	45.04 N	7.31 E
Rivoli Bay c	166	37.32 S	140.04 E
Rivolta d'Adda	62	45.28 N	9.31 E
Rivoltella	64	45.27 N	10.33 E
Riwaka	172	41.05 S	173.00 E
Rixford	214	41.55 N	78.30 W
Rixheim	58	47.46 N	7.24 E
Riyadh → Ar-Riyāḍ	128	24.38 N	46.43 E
Rīyāq	132	33.51 N	36.00 E
Rīz	128	32.23 N	51.20 E
Rizal, Pil.	116	15.43 N	121.06 E
Rizal → Pasay, Pil.	269f	14.33 N	121.00 E
Rizal □[4]	116	14.35 N	121.10 E
Rizal Memorial Stadium ♠	269f	14.34 N	120.59 E
Rize	130	41.02 N	40.31 E
Rize □[4]	130	40.55 N	40.55 E
Rīzeh, Kūh-e (gora Reza) ∧	128	37.47 N	58.05 E
Rizhao	98	35.27 N	119.29 E
Rizokárpason	130	35.36 N	34.23 E
Rižskij zaliv (Rīgas Jūras līcis) (Gulf of Riga) c	76	57.30 N	23.35 E
Rizziconi	68	38.25 N	15.57 E
Rizzuto, Capo ›	68	38.54 N	17.06 E
Rjukan	26	59.52 N	8.34 E
Rkîz, Lac ◎	150	16.50 N	15.19 W
Rô	175f	21.22 S	167.50 E
Roa, Esp.	34	41.42 N	3.55 W
Roa, N.Z.	172	42.21 S	171.23 E
Roa, Nor.	26	60.17 N	10.37 E
Roa, Zaïre	154	3.49 N	24.56 E
Roachdale	194	39.50 N	86.48 W
Roade	42	52.09 N	0.53 W
Roadhead	44	55.04 N	2.46 W
Roadknight, Point ›	169	38.26 S	144.11 E
Roadside	158	27.31 S	28.52 E
Road Town	240m	18.27 N	64.37 W
Roaming Rock, Lake ◎[1]	214	41.38 N	80.49 W
Roaming Shores	214	41.39 N	80.49 W
Roana	64	45.52 N	11.28 E
Roan Cliffs ⌓[4]	200	39.20 N	109.40 W
Roan Creek ≃	200	39.20 N	108.13 W
Roan Fell ∧	44	55.13 N	2.52 W
Roan Mountain	192	36.11 N	82.04 W
Roann	216	40.54 N	85.55 W
Roanne	32	46.02 N	4.04 E
Roanoke, Al., U.S.	194	33.09 N	85.22 W
Roanoke, Il., U.S.	190	40.47 N	89.11 W
Roanoke, In., U.S.	216	40.57 N	85.22 W
Roanoke, Tx., U.S.	222	33.01 N	97.14 W
Roanoke, Va., U.S.	192	37.16 N	79.56 W
Roanoke (Staunton) ≃	192	35.56 N	76.43 W
Roanoke Island I	192	35.53 N	75.39 W
Roanoke Rapids	192	36.27 N	77.39 W
Roanoke Rapids Dam ◆[6]	192	36.24 N	77.40 W
Roanoke Rapids Lake ◎[1]	192	36.30 N	77.45 W
Roan Plateau ⩘[1]	200	39.30 N	109.40 W
Roans Prairie	222	30.35 N	95.57 W
Roaring ≃	224	45.13 N	122.12 W
Roaring Branch	210	41.34 N	76.57 W
Roaring Brook ≃	212	43.44 N	75.24 W
Roaring Fork ≃	200	39.33 N	107.20 W
Roaring River Slough ≃	282	38.05 N	121.55 W
Roaring Run ≃	279b	40.33 N	79.32 W
Roaring Spring	214	40.20 N	78.23 W
Roaring Springs	196	33.54 N	100.52 W
Roaringwater Bay c	48	51.25 N	9.35 W
Roatán	236	16.18 N	86.35 W
Roatán, Isla de I	236	16.23 N	86.30 W
Robâa Oued Yahia	36	36.05 N	9.35 E
Robāṭ	128	30.04 N	54.49 E
Robāṭ Karīm	128	35.28 N	51.05 E
Robbeneiland I	158	33.49 S	18.22 E
Robbers Cave State Park ♠	196	35.01 N	95.27 W
Robbins, Ca., U.S.	226	38.53 N	121.42 W
Robbins, Il., U.S.	216	41.38 N	87.42 W
Robbins, N.C., U.S.	192	35.26 N	79.35 W
Robbins, Tn., U.S.	192	36.21 N	84.35 W
Robbins Airport ⊠	283	42.34 N	70.58 W
Robbins Ditch ≅	216	41.21 N	86.43 W
Robbins Island I	166	40.41 S	144.57 E
Robbins Pond ◎	283	42.00 N	70.55 W
Robbins Rest	276	40.39 N	73.10 W
Robbinsville, N.J., U.S.	208	40.13 N	74.37 W
Robbinsville, N.C., U.S.	192	35.19 N	83.48 W
Robbio	62	45.17 N	8.35 E
Robe, Austl.	166	37.11 S	139.45 E
Robe, Ityo.	144	7.52 N	39.38 E
Robe ≃, Austl.	162	21.19 S	115.40 E
Robe ≃, Ire.	48	53.37 N	9.16 W
Robe, Mount ∧	166	31.40 S	141.20 E
Robecchetto con Induno	266b	45.32 N	8.46 E
Robecco d'Oglio	64	45.15 N	10.04 E
Robecco sul Naviglio	266b	45.26 N	8.53 E
Röbel	54	53.23 N	12.35 E
Robeline	194	31.41 N	93.18 W
Röberget ∧[2]	40	59.45 N	14.54 E
Robersonville	192	35.49 N	77.15 W
Robert, Havre du c	240e	14.40 N	60.55 W
Roberta	192	32.43 N	84.00 W
Roberta Mills	192	35.22 N	80.38 W
Robert College ♁[2]	267b	41.04 N	29.02 E
Robert E. Lee Memorial Park ♠	284b	39.23 N	76.39 W
Robert E. Lee's Birthplace ⊥	208	38.10 N	76.49 W
Robert-Espagne	56	48.45 N	5.02 E
Robert F. Kennedy Memorial Stadium ♠	284c	38.53 N	76.58 W
Robert H. Treman State Park ♠	210	42.24 N	76.35 W
Robert Lee	196	31.54 N	100.29 W
Robert Louis Stevenson Memorial State Park ♠	226	38.40 N	122.36 W
Robert Louis Stevenson's Tomb ⊥	175a	13.50 S	171.44 W
Robert Morse College ♁[2]	279b	40.31 N	80.12 W
Robert Moses State Park ♠	210	40.37 N	73.16 W
Robert Mueller Municipal Airport ⊠	222	30.18 N	97.42 W
Roberto Payró	258	35.10 S	57.39 W
Robert Point ›	168a	32.31 S	115.42 E
Roberts, Id., U.S.	202	43.43 N	112.07 W
Roberts, Il., U.S.	216	40.37 N	88.11 W
Roberts, Mt., U.S.	202	45.21 N	109.10 W
Roberts, Mount ∧	171a	28.13 S	152.28 E
Roberts, Point ›	224	49.00 N	123.06 W
Robert's Arm	186	49.29 N	55.49 W
Robertsbridge	42	50.59 N	0.29 E
Roberts Canyon V	280	34.11 N	117.54 W
Roberts Creek Mountain ∧	204	39.52 N	116.18 W
Robertsdale, Al., U.S.	194	30.33 N	87.42 W
Robertsdale, Pa., U.S.	214	40.11 N	78.06 W
Robertsfield	150	6.15 N	10.24 W
Robertsfors	26	64.11 N	20.51 E
Robertsganj	124	24.42 N	83.04 E
Robertsham ◆[8]	273d	26.15 S	28.00 E
Robertsholm	40	60.35 N	76.16 E
Robert S. Kerr Lake ◎[1]	194	35.25 N	95.00 W
Roberts Mountain ∧	180	60.03 N	166.16 W
Robertson, Austl.	170	34.35 S	150.35 E
Robertson, S. Afr.	158	33.46 S	19.50 E
Robertson □[6], Ky., U.S.	218	38.32 N	84.04 W
Robertson □[6], Tx., U.S.	222	31.00 N	96.30 W
Robertson, Lac ◎	186	51.00 N	59.10 W
Robertson Bay c	9	71.25 S	170.00 E
Robertson Range ⩘	162	23.10 S	121.00 E
Robertsonville	206	46.09 N	71.13 W
Roberts Park	278	41.44 N	87.49 W
Roberts Peak ∧	182	52.57 N	120.32 W
Robertsport	150	6.45 N	11.22 W
Robertstown, Austl.	168b	34.00 S	139.05 E
Robertstown, Ire.	48	53.15 N	6.59 W
Robertsville	214	40.46 N	81.11 W
Robertville	56	50.27 N	6.07 E
Roberval	176	48.31 N	72.13 W
Robin Hood's Bay	44	54.25 N	0.33 W
Robins Air Force Base ■	192	32.38 N	83.35 W
Robins Island I	207	40.58 N	72.28 W
Robinson, Il., U.S.	194	39.00 N	87.44 W
Robinson, Tx., U.S.	222	31.28 N	97.06 W
Robinson ≃	164	16.03 S	137.16 E
Robinson, Lake ◎[1]	192	34.26 N	80.10 W
Robinson Brook ≃	283	43.02 N	71.13 W
Robinson Creek ≃	226	38.16 N	119.15 W
Róbinson Crusoe, Isla (Isla Más A Tierra) I	244	33.38 S	78.52 W
Robinson Gorge National Park ♠	166	25.15 S	149.10 E
Robinson Lake ◎	222	29.35 N	94.36 W
Robinson Lake Aerodrome ⊠	273d	26.08 S	27.42 E
Robinson Pond ◎	283	42.48 N	71.23 W
Robinson Range ⩘	162	25.45 S	119.00 E
Robinson Run ≃	279b	40.23 N	80.06 W
Robinson Run, North Branch ≃	279b	40.23 N	80.11 W
Robinsons	186	48.15 N	58.48 W
Robinvale	166	34.36 S	142.46 E
Robleda	34	40.23 N	6.36 W
Robledo	34	38.46 N	2.26 W
Roblin	184	51.14 N	101.21 W
Röblingen	54	51.28 N	11.40 E
Roboré	248	18.20 S	59.45 W
Röbrinken	40	58.36 N	15.53 E
Rob Roy Island I	175e	7.25 S	157.35 E
Robson, Mount ∧	182	53.07 N	119.09 W
Robstown	196	27.47 N	97.40 W
Roby, Eng., U.K.	262	53.25 N	2.51 W
Roby, Il., U.S.	219	39.44 N	89.24 W
Roby, Tx., U.S.	196	32.44 N	100.22 W
Roby Mill	262	53.34 N	2.44 W
Roca, Cabo da ›	34	38.47 N	9.30 W
Roçado	250	6.40 S	44.19 W
Rocafuerte	246	0.55 S	80.28 W
Roça Grande	256	21.36 S	42.58 W
Rocanville	184	50.24 N	101.43 W
Roca Partida, Isla I	232	19.01 N	112.02 W
Roca Partida, Punta ›	234	18.42 N	95.10 W
Rocas, Atol das I[1]	250	3.52 S	33.59 W
Roccabernarda	68	39.08 N	16.52 E
Roccacasale	66	42.07 N	13.53 E
Roccadaspide	68	40.26 N	15.12 E
Rocca di Cambio	66	42.14 N	13.29 E
Rocca di Mezzo	66	42.12 N	13.31 E

Symbol	English	Deutsch	Español	Français	Português
≃	River	Fluss	Río	Rivière	Rio
≅	Canal	Kanal	Canal	Canal	Canal
ʟ	Waterfall, Rapids	Wasserfall, Stromschnellen	Cascada, Rápidos	Chute d'eau, Rapides	Cascata, Rápidos
ʯ	Strait	Meeresstrasse	Estrecho	Détroit	Estreito
c	Bay, Gulf	Bucht, Golf	Bahía, Golfo	Baie, Golfe	Baía, Golfo
◎	Lake, Lakes	See, Seen	Lago, Lagos	Lac, Lacs	Lago, Lagos
≡	Swamp	Sumpf	Pantano	Marais	Pântano
⍓	Ice Features, Glacier	Eis- und Gletscherformen	Accidentes Glaciales	Formes glaciaires	Acidentes glaciares
⊤	Other Hydrographic Features	Andere Hydrographische Objekte	Otros Elementos Hidrográficos	Autres données hydrographiques	Outros acidentes hidrográficos
✧	Submarine Features	Untermeerische Objekte	Accidentes Submarinos	Formes de relief sous-marin	Acidentes submarinos
□	Political Unit	Politische Einheit	Unidad Política	Entité politique	Unidade política
♁	Cultural Institution	Kulturelle Institution	Institución Cultural	Institution culturelle	Instituição cultural
⊥	Historical Site	Historische Stätte	Sitio Histórico	Site historique	Sitio histórico
♠	Recreational Site	Erholungs- und Ferienort	Sitio de Recreo	Centre de loisirs	Area de Lazer
⊠	Airport	Flughafen	Aeropuerto	Aéroport	Aeroporto
■	Military Installation	Militäranlage	Instalación Militar	Installation militaire	Instalação militar
◆	Miscellaneous	Verschiedenes	Misceláneo	Divers	Diversos

Name	Page	Lat.°′	Long.°′
Rocca di Neto	68	39.11 N	17.00 E
Rocca di Papa	66	41.46 N	12.42 E
Roccafluvione	66	42.51 N	13.29 E
Roccagloriosa	68	40.06 N	15.26 E
Roccalbegna	66	42.47 N	11.30 E
Roccalumera	70	37.58 N	15.24 E
Rocca Massima	66	41.41 N	12.55 E
Roccamena	70	37.50 N	13.09 E
Roccamonfina	68	41.17 N	13.59 E
Roccanova	68	40.13 N	16.12 E
Roccapalumba	70	37.48 N	13.39 E
Rocca Pia	66	41.56 N	13.59 E
Rocca Pietore	64	46.26 N	11.59 E
Roccaprebalza	64	44.31 N	9.57 E
Rocca Priora	267a	41.48 N	12.45 E
Roccaraso	66	41.51 N	14.05 E
Rocca San Casciano	66	44.03 N	11.50 E
Rocca Santa Maria	66	42.41 N	13.30 E
Roccasecca	66	41.33 N	13.40 E
Roccasecca dei Volsci	66	41.29 N	13.13 E
Roccastrada	66	43.00 N	11.10 E
Roccavione	62	44.19 N	7.29 E
Roccavivara	66	41.50 N	14.36 E
Roccelito, Monte ∧	70	37.50 N	13.47 E
Roccella Ionica	68	38.19 N	16.24 E
Roccella Valdemone	70	37.56 N	15.00 E
Rocchetta Sant'Antonio	68	41.06 N	15.27 E
Rocciamelone ∧	62	45.12 N	7.05 E
Ročegda	24	62.42 N	43.23 E
Roch ≃	44	53.34 N	2.18 W
Rocha, Bra.	256	21.28 S	45.49 W
Rocha, Ur.	252	34.29 S	54.20 W
Rocha da Gale, Barragem ◆[6]	34	37.42 N	7.35 W
Rocha Miranda ◆[8]	287a	22.52 S	43.22 W
Rocha Sobrinho	287a	22.47 S	43.25 W
Rochdale, Eng., U.K.	44	53.38 N	2.09 W
Rochdale, Ma., U.S.	207	42.11 N	71.54 W
Rochdale, N.Y., U.S.	210	41.43 N	73.50 W
Rochdale □[8]	262	53.37 N	2.08 W
Rochdale Canal ≋	262	53.43 N	1.54 W
Roche	42	50.24 N	4.48 W
Rochebrune, Pic de ∧	62	44.49 N	6.51 E
Rochechouart	32	45.50 N	0.50 E
Rochedinho	255	20.14 S	54.33 W
Rochedo	255	19.57 S	54.52 W
Rochedo de Minas	256	21.38 S	43.01 W
Rochefort, Bel.	56	50.10 N	5.13 E
Rochefort, Fr.	32	45.57 N	0.58 W
Rochefort-en-Yvelines	50	48.35 N	1.59 E
Rochefort-Montagne	32	45.41 N	2.48 E
Rochefort-sur-Nenon	58	47.07 N	5.34 E
Roche Harbor	224	48.36 N	123.08 W
Rochehaut	56	49.51 N	5.00 E
Roche-la-Molière	62	45.26 N	4.19 E
Roche-lez-Beaupré	58	47.17 N	6.07 E
Rochelle, Ga., U.S.	192	31.57 N	83.27 W
Rochelle, Il., U.S.	216	41.55 N	89.04 W
Rochelle, Tx., U.S.	196	31.13 N	99.13 W
Rochelle Park	276	40.54 N	74.04 W
Rochemaure	62	44.35 N	4.42 E
Roche-Percée	184	49.03 N	102.45 W
Rochepot, Château de la ⊥	58	46.57 N	4.40 E
Rocher Fendu, Rapides du ⌞	275a	45.19 N	73.57 W
Rochester, Austl.	166	36.22 S	144.42 E
Rochester, Eng., U.K.	42	51.24 N	0.30 E
Rochester, Eng., U.K.	44	55.16 N	2.16 W
Rochester, Il., U.S.	219	39.45 N	89.32 W
Rochester, In., U.S.	216	41.03 N	86.12 W
Rochester, Ma., U.S.	207	41.43 N	70.49 W
Rochester, Mi., U.S.	214	42.40 N	83.08 W
Rochester, Mn., U.S.	190	44.01 N	92.28 W
Rochester, N.H., U.S.	188	43.18 N	70.58 W
Rochester, N.Y., U.S.	210	43.09 N	77.36 W
Rochester, Oh., U.S.	214	41.07 N	82.18 W
Rochester, Pa., U.S.	214	40.42 N	80.17 W
Rochester, Tx., U.S.	196	33.19 N	99.51 W
Rochester, Wa., U.S.	224	46.49 N	123.05 W
Rochester, Wi., U.S.	216	42.44 N	88.13 W
Rochester City Airport ⊠	260	51.21 N	0.30 E
Rochester Hills	214	42.40 N	83.09 W
Rochester Mills	214	40.49 N	78.59 W
Rochester-Monroe County Airport ⊠	210	43.07 N	77.40 W
Rochester-Utica State Recreation Area ♦	214	42.39 N	83.04 W
Rochetaillée	62	45.25 N	4.27 E
Rocheuses → Rocky Mountains ⋏	16	48.00 N	116.00 W
Rochford	42	51.36 N	0.43 E
Rochford □[8]	260	51.36 N	0.39 E
Rochfortbridge	48	53.23 N	7.17 W
Rochlitz	54	51.03 N	12.47 E
Rochon, Lac ⊜	206	46.43 N	75.14 W
Rock	190	46.04 N	87.09 W
Rock □[6]	216	42.41 N	89.05 W
Rock ≃, U.S.	190	41.29 N	90.37 W
Rock ≃, U.S.	198	43.05 N	96.27 W
Rockall I	22	57.35 N	13.48 W
Rockall Rise ✦[3]	10	59.00 N	14.00 W
Rockanje	52	51.53 N	4.05 E
Rockaway, N.J., U.S.	210	40.54 N	74.30 W
Rockaway, Or., U.S.	224	45.36 N	123.56 W
Rockaway ≃	210	40.51 N	74.21 W
Rockaway Inlet ⊂	276	40.34 N	73.55 W
Rockaway Neck	276	40.51 N	74.21 W
Rockaway Park ◆[8]	276	40.35 N	73.50 W
Rockaway Point ◆[8]	276	40.33 N	73.55 W
Rockaway Point >	276	40.33 N	73.56 W
Rockaways' Playland ♦	276	40.35 N	73.49 W
Rockbank	274b	37.43 S	144.39 E
Rock Bay	182	50.20 N	125.29 W
Rockbridge	219	39.16 N	90.12 W
Rock Bridge State Park ♦	219	38.53 N	92.19 W
Rock Brook ≃	276	40.25 N	74.40 W
Rock Candy Mountain ∧	224	47.01 N	123.07 W
Rockcastle ≃	192	36.58 N	84.21 W
Rock City Falls	210	43.04 N	73.55 W
Rockcliffe Park	212	45.27 N	75.41 W
Rockcorry	48	54.07 N	7.01 W
Rock Creek, B.C., Can.	182	49.06 N	118.58 W
Rock Creek, Oh., U.S.	214	41.39 N	80.51 W
Rock Creek ≃, N.A.	202	48.25 N	107.05 W
Rock Creek ≃, U.S.	208	39.43 N	77.13 W
Rock Creek ≃, U.S.	284c	38.54 N	77.04 W
Rock Creek ≃, Ca., U.S.	226	37.55 N	120.58 W
Rock Creek ≃, Co., U.S.	198	40.20 N	102.31 W
Rock Creek ≃, Il., U.S.	216	41.12 N	87.59 W
Rock Creek ≃, In., U.S.	216	40.42 N	86.35 W
Rock Creek ≃, In., U.S.	216	40.49 N	85.23 W
Rock Creek ≃, Mt., U.S.	202	45.31 N	108.49 W
Rock Creek ≃, Mt., U.S.	202	46.43 N	113.40 W
Rock Creek ≃, Nv., U.S.	204	40.39 N	116.54 W
Rock Creek ≃, Or., U.S.	202	42.39 N	119.08 W
Rock Creek ≃, Or., U.S.	202	45.34 N	120.25 W
Rock Creek ≃, Or., U.S.	224	45.51 N	123.12 W
Rock Creek ≃, S.D., U.S.	198	43.44 N	97.58 W
Rock Creek ≃, Ut,. U.S.	200	40.17 N	110.30 W
Rock Creek ≃, Wa., U.S.	202	46.55 N	117.56 W
Rock Creek ≃, Wa., U.S.	202	45.42 N	120.29 W
Rock Creek ≃, Wy., U.S.	200	41.54 N	106.08 W
Rock Creek Butte ∧	202	44.49 N	118.07 W
Rock Creek Hills	284c	39.01 N	77.04 W
Rock Creek Park ♦	284c	38.58 N	77.03 W
Rock Cut State Park ♦	216	42.20 N	89.00 W
Rockdale, Austl.	170	33.57 S	151.08 E
Rockdale, Il., U.S.	216	41.30 N	88.06 W
Rockdale, Md., U.S.	284b	39.21 N	76.45 W
Rockdale, Pa., U.S.	285	39.53 N	75.26 W
Rockdale, Tx., U.S.	222	30.39 N	97.00 W
Rockdale, W.V., U.S.	214	40.18 N	80.35 W
Rockefeller Center ✿	276	40.45 N	74.00 W
Rockefeller Park ♦	279a	41.32 N	81.38 W
Rockefeller Plateau ⋏[1]	9	80.00 S	135.00 W
Rockenhausen	56	49.38 N	7.49 E
Rockensüss	56	51.03 N	9.50 E
Rockfall	207	41.31 N	72.41 W
Rock Falls	190	41.46 N	89.41 W
Rock Ferry	262	53.22 N	3.00 W
Rockfield	216	40.38 N	86.34 W
Rock Flat	171b	36.21 S	149.12 E
Rock Flat Creek ≃	171b	36.07 S	149.12 E
Rockford, Al., U.S.	194	32.53 N	86.13 W
Rockford, Il., U.S.	216	42.16 N	89.05 W
Rockford, In., U.S.	218	38.59 N	85.54 W
Rockford, Ia., U.S.	190	43.03 N	92.56 W
Rockford, Mi., U.S.	190	43.07 N	85.33 W
Rockford, Oh., U.S.	216	40.41 N	84.38 W
Rockford, Tn., U.S.	192	35.49 N	83.56 W
Rock Forest	206	45.20 N	71.59 W
Rockglen, Sk., Can.	184	49.10 N	105.57 W
Rock Glen, N.Y., U.S.	210	42.41 N	78.07 W
Rock Hall	208	39.08 N	76.14 W
Rockhammar	40	59.32 N	15.26 E
Rockhampton	166	23.23 S	150.31 E
Rockhampton Downs	162	18.57 S	135.01 E
Rock Hill, N.Y., U.S.	210	41.38 N	74.36 W
Rock Hill, S.C., U.S.	192	34.55 N	81.01 W
Rockhill Furnace	214	40.15 N	77.54 W
Rockingham, Austl.	168a	32.17 S	115.44 E
Rockingham, N.C., U.S.	192	34.56 N	79.46 W
Rockingham □[6]	207	42.50 N	71.15 W
Rockingham Bay ⊂	166	18.10 S	146.05 E
Rockingham Forest ◆[3]	42	52.30 N	0.37 W
Rockingham State Historic Site ⊥	276	40.24 N	74.37 W
Rock Island, P.Q., Can.	206	45.01 N	72.06 W
Rock Island, Il., U.S.	190	41.30 N	90.34 W
Rock Island, Tx., U.S.	222	29.32 N	96.35 W
Rocklake	198	48.47 N	99.15 W
Rock Lake ⊜, Mb., Can.	184	49.11 N	99.12 W
Rock Lake ⊜, On., Can.	212	45.30 N	78.23 W
Rock Lake ⊜, Il., U.S.	278	41.40 N	88.03 W
Rock Lake ⊜, N.D., U.S.	198	48.50 N	99.10 W
Rock Lake ⊜, Wi., U.S.	216	43.04 N	88.56 W
Rockland, On., Can.	188	45.33 N	75.17 W
Rockland, De., U.S.	285	39.47 N	75.34 W
Rockland, Id., U.S.	202	42.34 N	112.52 W
Rockland, Me., U.S.	188	44.06 N	69.06 W
Rockland, Ma., U.S.	207	42.07 N	70.55 W
Rockland, Mi., U.S.	190	46.44 N	89.10 W
Rockland, N.Y., U.S.	210	41.58 N	74.54 W
Rockland □[6]	210	41.09 N	73.59 W
Rockland Lake	276	41.09 N	73.55 W
Rockland Lake ⊜	276	41.08 N	73.55 W
Rockland Lake State Park ♦	276	41.08 N	73.55 W
Rocklands Reservoir ⊜[1]	166	37.15 S	142.00 E
Rockledge, Fl., U.S.	220	28.21 N	80.43 W
Rockledge, Pa., U.S.	285	40.03 N	75.05 W
Rockleigh	276	41.00 N	73.55 W
Rocklin	226	38.47 N	121.14 W
Rockmart	192	34.00 N	85.02 W
Rock Meadow Brook ≃	283	42.16 N	71.13 W
Rock of Cashel ⊥	48	52.31 N	7.53 W
Rock Point	208	38.16 N	76.50 W
Rock Point Provincial Park ♦	212	42.51 N	79.33 W
Rock Pond ⊜	283	42.44 N	71.00 W
Rockport, Il., U.S.	219	39.32 N	91.00 W
Rockport, Ky., U.S.	194	37.20 N	86.59 W
Rockport, Me., U.S.	188	44.11 N	69.04 W
Rockport, Ma., U.S.	207	42.39 N	70.37 W
Rock Port, Mo., U.S.	194	40.24 N	95.30 W
Rockport, Tx., U.S.	196	28.01 N	97.03 W
Rock Rapids	198	43.25 N	96.10 W
Rock River	200	41.44 N	105.58 W
Rock Run	208	39.59 N	75.50 W
Rock Run ≃	284c	38.58 N	77.11 W
Rock Sound	238	24.54 N	76.12 W
Rocksprings, Tx., U.S.	196	30.00 N	100.12 W
Rock Springs, Wy., U.S.	200	41.35 N	109.12 W
Rockstone	246	5.59 N	58.33 W
Rock Stream	210	42.28 N	76.56 W
Rockton, Il., U.S.	216	42.27 N	89.04 W
Rockton, Pa., U.S.	214	41.05 N	78.39 W
Rock Valley	198	43.12 N	96.17 W
Rockville, N.Z.	172	40.44 S	172.38 E
Rockville, Ct., U.S.	207	41.52 N	72.27 W
Rockville, In., U.S.	194	39.45 N	87.13 W
Rockville, Md., U.S.	208	39.05 N	77.09 W
Rockville, Ma., U.S.	283	42.08 N	71.21 W
Rockville, Pa., U.S.	208	40.20 N	76.54 W
Rockville, R.I., U.S.	207	41.27 N	71.30 W
Rockville Centre	210	40.39 N	73.38 W
Rockwall	222	32.55 N	96.27 W
Rockwall □[6]	222	32.55 N	96.23 W
Rockwell, Ia., U.S.	190	42.59 N	93.11 W
Rockwell, N.C., U.S.	192	35.33 N	80.24 W
Rockwell, Lake ⊜	214	41.12 N	81.19 W
Rockwell City	198	42.23 N	94.38 W
Rockwell International Corporation ✿[3]	280	33.52 N	117.51 W
Rockwood, On., Can.	212	43.37 N	80.08 W
Rockwood, Me., U.S.	188	45.41 N	69.44 W
Rockwood, Mi., U.S.	216	42.04 N	83.14 W
Rockwood, Or., U.S.	224	45.31 N	122.28 W
Rockwood, Pa., U.S.	188	39.54 N	79.09 W
Rockwood, Tn., U.S.	192	35.51 N	84.41 W
Rockwood Lake ⊜	276	41.06 N	73.38 W
Rockwood Lake Brook ≃	276	41.03 N	73.36 W
Rocky	196	35.09 N	99.03 W
Rocky ≃, Ab., Can.	182	53.08 N	117.59 W
Rocky ≃, Mi., U.S.	216	41.57 N	85.39 W
Rocky ≃, N.C., U.S.	192	35.37 N	79.09 W
Rocky ≃, Oh., U.S.	214	41.30 N	81.49 W
Rocky, East Branch ≃	279a	41.24 N	81.53 W
Rocky, West Branch ≃	214	41.24 N	81.53 W
Rocky Arroyo V	196	32.32 N	104.21 W
Rocky Boy's Indian Reservation ◆[4]	202	48.18 N	109.45 W
Rocky Branch ≃	284c	38.53 N	77.19 W
Rocky Comfort Creek ≃	192	32.59 N	82.25 W
Rocky Coulee V	202	47.10 N	119.16 W
Rocky Creek ≃	192	35.53 N	80.47 W
Rockyford, Ab., Can.	182	51.13 N	113.08 W
Rocky Ford, Co., U.S.	198	38.06 N	103.43 W
Rocky Ford Creek ≃	216	41.19 N	83.37 W
Rocky Fork Lake ⊜	218	39.11 N	83.28 W
Rocky Fork State Park ♦	218	39.11 N	83.30 W
Rocky Gorge Reservoir ⊜[1]	208	39.07 N	77.54 W
Rocky Grove	214	41.25 N	79.49 W
Rocky Gully	162	34.30 S	116.48 E
Rocky Harbour	186	49.36 N	57.55 W
Rocky Harbour ⊂	271d	22.20 N	114.19 E
Rocky Hill, Ct., U.S.	207	41.40 N	72.39 W
Rocky Hill, N.J., U.S.	276	40.24 N	74.38 W
Rocky Island Lake ⊜[1]	190	46.56 N	83.04 W
Rocky Lake ⊜	184	54.08 N	101.30 W
Rocky Mount, N.C., U.S.	192	35.57 N	77.48 W
Rocky Mount, Va., U.S.	192	36.59 N	79.53 W
Rocky Mountain ∧	202	47.49 N	112.49 W
Rocky Mountain House	182	52.22 N	114.55 W
Rocky Mountain National Park ♦	200	40.19 N	105.42 W
Rocky Mountains ⋏	16	48.00 N	116.00 W
Rocky Point, N.Y., U.S.	207	40.57 N	72.56 W
Rocky Point, Wa., U.S.	224	47.35 N	122.41 W
Rocky Point >, Ba.	192	26.00 N	77.25 W
Rocky Point >, Namibia	156	19.03 S	12.30 E
Rocky Point >, Norf. I.	174c	29.03 S	167.55 E
Rocky Point >, Ak., U.S.	180	64.25 N	163.10 W
Rocky Point >, Ma., U.S.	207	41.57 N	70.35 W
Rocky Point >, N.Y., U.S.	276	40.55 N	73.32 W
Rocky Ridge	214	41.32 N	83.13 W
Rocky Ridge ∧	282	37.48 N	122.03 W
Rocky River	214	41.28 N	81.50 W
Rocky River Reservation ♦	279a	41.27 N	81.50 W
Rocky Run ≃, N.D., U.S.	198	47.38 N	99.02 W
Rocky Run ≃, Pa., U.S.	285	39.54 N	75.28 W
Rocky Run ≃, Va., U.S.	284c	38.58 N	77.15 W
Rocky Saugeen ≃	212	44.13 N	80.53 W
Rocky Top ∧	202	44.47 N	122.17 W
Roclenge-sur-Geer	56	50.45 N	5.36 E
Rocosas, Montañas → Rocky Mountains ⋏	16	48.00 N	116.00 W
Rocquencourt	261	48.50 N	2.07 E
Rocroi	50	49.55 N	4.31 E
Roda	192	36.58 N	82.49 W
Roda ≃	54	50.52 N	11.44 E
Rodach	56	50.20 N	10.46 E
Rodach ≃	56	50.08 N	10.52 E
Rodakovo	83	48.33 N	39.02 E
Rodalben	56	49.14 N	7.38 E
Rodalquilar	34	37.40 N	2.08 W
Rodas	240p	22.20 N	80.33 W
Rodas, Isla de → Ródhos I	38	36.10 N	28.00 E
Rodaun ◆[8]	264b	48.08 N	16.16 E
Rødberg	26	60.16 N	8.58 E
Rødby	41	54.42 N	11.24 E
Rødbyhavn	41	54.39 N	11.21 E
Roddickton	186	50.52 N	56.08 W
Rødding	41	55.23 N	9.06 E
Rodeio	252	26.57 S	49.23 W
Rodeiro	256	21.12 S	42.52 W
Rødekro	41	55.04 N	9.21 E
Rodel	46	57.41 N	7.05 W
Roden	52	53.07 N	6.26 E
Roden ≃	42	52.43 N	2.36 W
Rodenberg	52	52.18 N	9.21 E
Rodenkirchen, B.R.D.	52	53.24 N	8.26 E
Rodenkirchen, B.R.D.	56	50.54 N	6.59 E
Rödentel	54	50.17 N	11.01 E
Rodeo, Arg.	252	30.12 S	69.06 W
Rodeo, Méx.	232	25.11 N	104.34 W
Rodeo, Ca., U.S.	226	38.01 N	122.15 W
Rodeo, N.M., U.S.	200	31.50 N	109.01 W
Rodeo Lagoon ⊂	282	37.50 N	122.31 W
Röderau	54	51.19 N	13.19 E
Roderick ≃	162	26.57 S	116.13 E
Roderick Island I	182	52.40 N	128.22 W
Rödermark	56	49.59 N	8.50 E
Rodewisch	54	50.32 N	12.24 E
Rodez	32	44.21 N	2.35 E
Rodgau	56	50.02 N	8.54 E
Rodheim-Bieber	56	50.37 N	8.35 E
Rodhópis, Orosirá → Rhodope Mountains ⋏	38	41.30 N	24.30 E
Ródhos (Rhodes)	38	36.26 N	28.13 E
Ródhos (Rhodes) I	38	36.10 N	28.00 E
Rodi Garganico	68	41.55 N	15.53 E
Roding	60	49.12 N	12.32 E
Roding ≃	42	51.31 N	0.06 E
Rodinga	162	24.34 S	134.05 E
Rodinka	80	57.24 N	43.34 E
Rodino, S.S.S.R.	76	58.57 N	44.59 E
Rodino, S.S.S.R.	86	52.30 N	80.15 E
Rodionovo-Nesvetajskaja	83	47.36 N	39.42 E
Rodman	180	57.28 N	135.21 W
Rodman Naval Station ■	236	8.56 N	79.36 W
Rodn'a	76	56.22 N	34.55 E
Rodnei, Munţii ⋏	38	47.35 N	24.40 E
Rodney, On., Can.	214	42.34 N	81.41 W
Rodney, Ms., U.S.	194	31.51 N	91.11 W
Rodney, Cape >, N.Z.	172	36.17 S	174.49 E
Rodney, Cape >, Ak., U.S.	180	64.39 N	166.24 W
Rodney Village	208	39.07 N	75.31 W
Rodničok	80	51.26 N	42.54 E
Rodniki, S.S.S.R.	80	57.06 N	41.44 E
Rodniki, S.S.S.R.	265b	55.39 N	38.04 E
Rodnikovskij	86	50.39 N	57.12 E
Rodolfo, Lago → Rudolf, Lake ⊜	144	3.30 N	36.05 E
Rodolfo Iselín	252	34.39 S	68.01 W
Rodonit, Kep i >	38	41.35 N	19.27 E
Rodostov	78	51.58 N	24.57 E
Rødovre	41	55.41 N	12.29 E
Rodrigo de Freitas, Lagoa ⊂	287a	22.58 S	43.13 W
Rodrigues I	12	19.42 S	63.25 E
Rodríguez, Méx.	196	27.10 N	100.01 W
Rodríguez, Ur.	258	34.23 S	56.33 W
Rodríguez, Arroyo ≃	288	34.52 S	58.02 W
Rodstock, Cape >	162	33.12 S	134.20 E
Roduco	208	36.27 N	76.48 W
Rødven	26	62.38 N	7.33 E
Rødvig	41	55.15 N	12.23 E
Roe ≃	44	55.07 N	6.59 W
Roebling	208	40.06 N	74.47 W
Roebourne	162	20.47 S	117.09 E
Roebuck Bay ⊂	162	18.04 S	122.17 E
Roehampton ◆[8]	260	51.27 N	0.14 W
Roe Island I	282	38.04 N	122.02 W
Roeland Park	198	39.02 N	94.37 W
Roelands	168a	33.18 S	115.50 E
Roeliff Jansen Kill ≃	210	42.11 N	73.52 W
Roelofarendsveen	52	52.12 N	4.38 E
Roelofskamp	158	26.10 S	24.24 E
Roen, Monte ∧	64	46.22 N	11.11 E
Roer (Rur) ≃	56	51.12 N	5.59 E
Roermond	52	51.12 N	6.00 E
Roesbrugge-Haringe	50	50.55 N	2.37 E
Roeselare (Roulers)	50	50.57 N	3.08 E
Roesinger, Lake ⊜	224	47.58 N	121.55 W
Roessleville	210	42.41 N	73.48 W
Roes Welcome Sound ⊔	176	64.00 N	88.00 W
Roetgen	56	50.39 N	6.12 E
Rœulx	50	50.30 N	4.06 E
Roff	196	34.37 N	96.50 W
Röfors	40	58.57 N	14.37 E
Rofrano	68	40.12 N	15.25 E
Rogačevo	82	56.26 N	37.10 E
Rogačov	76	53.05 N	30.03 E
Rogačovka	78	51.30 N	39.34 E
Rogagua, Laguna ⊜	248	13.43 S	66.54 W
Rogaguado, Laguna ⊜	248	12.52 S	65.43 W
Rogaland □[6]	26	59.00 N	6.15 E
Rogalik	83	48.56 N	40.03 E
Rogan'	78	49.54 N	36.29 E
Rogans Hill	274a	33.44 S	151.01 E
Rogan's Seat ∧	44	54.25 N	2.07 W
Rogart	46	58.00 N	4.08 W
Rogäsen	54	52.19 N	12.20 E
Rogaška Slatina	36	46.14 N	15.38 E
Rogatica	38	43.48 N	19.00 E
Rogatin	78	49.25 N	24.37 E
Rogätz	54	52.19 N	11.46 E
Rogen ⊜	26	62.19 N	12.23 E
Roger, Lac ⊜	190	47.50 N	78.51 W
Roger Island I	283	42.43 N	70.50 W
Rogers, Ar., U.S.	194	36.19 N	94.07 W
Rogers, Ct., U.S.	207	41.50 N	71.54 W
Rogers, Oh., U.S.	214	40.48 N	80.38 W
Rogers, Tx., U.S.	222	30.55 N	97.13 W
Rogers, Mount ∧	192	36.39 N	81.33 W
Rogers City	190	45.25 N	83.49 W
Rogers Lake ⊜	228	34.52 N	117.51 W
Rogers Park ◆[8]	278	42.01 N	87.40 W
Rogers Pass)(	182	51.17 N	117.31 W
Rogersville, N.B., Can.	186	46.44 N	65.26 W
Rogersville, Al., U.S.	194	34.49 N	87.17 W
Rogersville, Tn., U.S.	192	36.24 N	83.00 W
Roggeveldberge ⋏	158	32.17 S	20.08 E
Roggewein, Cabo >	174z	27.07 S	109.15 W
Roggiano Gravina	68	39.37 N	16.09 E
Roghudi	68	38.03 N	15.55 E
Rogliano, Fr.	62	42.57 N	9.25 E
Rogliano, It.	68	39.11 N	16.20 E
Rognac	62	43.29 N	5.14 E
Rognedino	76	53.48 N	33.33 E
Rögnitz ≃	54	53.19 N	10.57 E
Rognon ≃	58	48.23 N	5.10 E
Rogny	50	47.45 N	2.53 E
Rogojampi	115a	8.19 S	114.17 E
Rogovatoje	78	51.14 N	38.22 E
Rogovo	82	55.13 N	37.05 E
Rogovskaja	78	45.44 N	38.44 E
Rogovskoje	80	58.33 N	50.43 E
Rogožkino	83	47.10 N	39.21 E
Rogoźno	30	52.46 N	17.00 E
Rogozov	78	50.14 N	31.03 E
Rogue ≃, Mi., U.S.	190	43.04 N	85.35 W
Rogue ≃, Or., U.S.	202	42.26 N	124.25 W
Rogue River	202	42.26 N	123.10 W
Rohdenhaus	263	51.18 N	7.01 E
Rohilkhand Plains ≚	124	28.20 N	79.30 E
Rohinjan	272c	19.06 N	73.04 E
Rohitpur	126	23.42 N	90.19 E
Rohl ≃	140	6.22 N	29.46 E
Röhlinghausen ◆[8]	263	51.36 N	7.14 E
Rohnert Park	226	38.20 N	122.42 W
Rohr	60	48.46 N	11.58 E
Rohrbach in Oberösterreich	60	48.34 N	13.59 E
Rohrbach-lès-Bitche	56	49.03 N	7.16 E
Rohrbeck	264a	52.32 N	13.02 E
Rohrberg	54	52.42 N	11.02 E
Röhrenfurth	56	51.09 N	9.32 E
Rohri	120	27.41 N	68.54 E
Röhrsdorf	54	50.51 N	12.50 E
Rohtak	123	28.54 N	76.34 E
Rohtak □[5]	124	28.50 N	76.40 E
Roi, Île du → King Island I	166	39.50 S	144.00 E
Roia (Roya) ≃	62	43.48 N	7.35 E
Roi Et	110	16.03 N	103.40 E
Roi Georges, Îles du II	14	14.32 S	145.08 W
Roi Léopold, Monts du → King Leopold Ranges ⋏	160	17.30 S	125.45 E
Roine ⊜	26	61.24 N	24.06 E
Roinville	261	48.32 N	2.03 E
Roisel	50	49.57 N	3.06 E
Roissy	261	48.47 N	2.39 E
Roissy-en-France	261	49.00 N	2.31 E
Roitzsch	54	51.34 N	12.16 E
Roja, S.S.S.R.	76	57.30 N	22.49 E
Roja, S.S.S.R.	83	47.59 N	37.20 E
Rojas	252	34.12 S	60.44 W
Rojl'anka	78	46.17 N	29.46 E
Rojo → Red ≃	178	31.00 N	91.40 W
Rojo, Cabo >, Méx.	234	21.33 N	97.20 W
Rojo, Cabo >, P.R.	240m	17.56 N	67.11 W
Rojo, Mar → Red Sea ⊤[2]	136	20.00 N	38.00 E
Rokan	112	0.34 N	100.25 E
Rokan ≃	114	2.00 N	100.52 E
Rokan-kanan ≃	114	1.23 N	100.56 E
Rokan-kiri ≃	114	1.23 N	100.56 E
Röke	41	56.14 N	13.30 E
Rokel ≃	150	8.33 N	12.48 W
Rokewood	169	37.54 S	143.43 E
Rokewood Junction	169	37.51 S	143.41 E
Rokheh	120	35.16 N	69.28 E
Rokiškis	76	55.58 N	25.35 E
Rokkō-san ∧	96	34.46 N	135.16 E
Rokkō-sanchi ⋏	270	34.45 N	135.13 E
Roklum	54	52.04 N	10.44 E
Rokuan Kansallispuisto ♦	26	64.32 N	26.33 E
Rokugō	94	35.29 N	138.27 E
Rokugō ◆[8]	268	35.33 N	139.43 E
Rokusei	94	36.58 N	136.52 E
Rokycany	60	49.45 N	13.36 E
Rokytná ≃	61	49.05 N	16.22 E
Rolampont	58	47.57 N	5.16 E
Roland, Mb., Can.	184	49.25 N	97.55 W
Roland, Ar., U.S.	194	34.54 N	92.29 W
Roland, Ia., U.S.	190	42.09 N	93.30 W
Roland, Lake ⊜[1]	284b	39.23 N	76.38 W
Roland C. Nickerson State Park ♦	207	41.46 N	70.03 W
Rolândia	255	23.18 S	51.22 W
Roland Park ◆[8]	284b	39.22 N	76.39 W
Roland Run ≃	284b	39.23 N	76.39 W
Rolava ≃	54	50.15 N	12.51 E
Røldal	26	59.49 N	6.48 E
Roldán	252	32.54 S	60.54 W
Roldanillo	246	4.24 N	76.09 W
Rolde	52	52.58 N	6.38 E
Roldskov ◆[3]	26	56.48 N	9.50 E
Rolette	198	48.39 N	99.50 W
Roleystone	168a	32.08 S	116.04 E
Rolfe	198	42.48 N	94.31 W
Roll, Az., U.S.	200	32.45 N	113.59 W
Roll, In., U.S.	216	40.33 N	85.23 W
Rolla, B.C., Can.	182	55.54 N	120.09 W
Rolla, Ks., U.S.	198	37.07 N	101.07 W
Rolla, Mo., U.S.	194	37.57 N	91.46 W
Rolla, N.D., U.S.	198	48.51 N	99.37 W
Rolle	58	46.28 N	6.20 E
Rolle, Passo di)(	64	46.18 N	11.47 E
Rolleboise	261	49.01 N	1.36 E
Rolleston, Austl.	166	24.28 S	148.37 E
Rolleston, N.Z.	172	43.35 S	172.23 E
Rolling Acres	284b	39.17 N	76.52 W
Rollingbay	224	47.39 N	122.30 W
Rolling Fork	194	32.54 N	90.52 W
Rolling Fork ≃	194	37.55 N	85.50 W
Röllinghausen ◆[8]	263	51.31 N	7.08 E
Rolling Hills	280	33.46 N	118.21 W
Rolling Hills Estates	280	33.47 N	118.21 W
Rolling Meadows	216	42.05 N	88.00 W
Rolling Prairie	216	41.40 N	86.37 W
Rolling River Indian Reserve ◆[4]	184	50.27 N	100.00 W
Rollingstone	166	19.03 S	146.24 E
Rollingwood	226	37.57 N	122.20 W
Rollins	182	47.54 N	114.11 W
Rollins Reservoir ⊜[1]	226	39.08 N	120.57 W
Rolvsøya I	24	71.00 N	24.00 E
Rom → Roma	66	41.54 N	12.29 E
Roma, Austl.	166	26.35 S	148.47 E
Roma (Rome), It.	66	41.54 N	12.29 E
Roma (Rome), It.	267a	41.54 N	12.29 E
Roma, Leso.	158	29.27 S	27.45 E
Roma, Tx., U.S.	196	26.25 N	99.01 W
Roma □[4]	66	41.58 N	12.40 E
Romagna □[9]	64	44.30 N	12.15 E
Romagnano Sesia	62	45.38 N	8.23 E
Romagne-sous-Montfaucon	56	49.20 N	5.05 E
Romain, Cape >	192	33.00 N	79.22 W
Romaine ≃	176	50.18 N	63.47 W
Romainmôtier	58	46.42 N	6.29 E
Romainville	261	48.53 N	2.26 E
Romakloster	26	57.31 N	18.27 E
Roman, Blg.	38	43.09 N	23.55 E
Roman, Rom.	38	46.55 N	26.56 E
Roman ≃	42	51.51 N	0.57 E
Romanche ≃	62	45.05 N	5.43 E
Romanche Gap ✦[1]	10	0.10 S	18.15 W
Romang, Pulau I	164	7.35 S	127.26 E
Romang, Selat ⊔	164	7.30 S	127.00 E
Romania (România) □[1], Europe	22	46.00 N	25.30 E
Romania (România) □[1], Europe	38	46.00 N	25.30 E
Roman-Koš, gora ∧	78	44.37 N	34.15 E
Romankovcy	78	48.29 N	27.13 E
Roman Nose Mountain ∧	202	43.55 N	123.44 W
Romano, Cape >	220	25.50 N	81.41 W
Romano, Cayo I	240p	22.04 N	77.50 W
Romano di Lombardia	62	45.31 N	9.45 E
Romanova	88	57.04 N	103.24 E
Romanovka, S.S.S.R.	80	51.24 N	47.23 E
Romanovka, S.S.S.R.	80	51.45 N	42.45 E
Romanovka, S.S.S.R.	80	49.47 N	45.05 E
Romanovka, S.S.S.R.	86	54.38 N	76.03 E
Romanovka, S.S.S.R.	88	53.14 N	112.46 E
Romanovka, S.S.S.R.	265a	60.03 N	30.42 E
Romanovo, S.S.S.R.	82	56.39 N	39.14 E
Romanovo, S.S.S.R.	86	53.58 N	80.30 E
Romanovo, S.S.S.R.	86	52.37 N	81.14 E
Romanovo, S.S.S.R.	86	59.09 N	61.30 E
Romans d'Isonzo	64	45.53 N	13.26 E
Romanshorn	58	47.34 N	9.22 E
Romans-sur-Isère	62	45.03 N	5.03 E
Romansville	285	39.57 N	75.45 W
Romanzof Mountains ⋏	180	69.00 N	144.00 W
Romaški	80	50.13 N	46.41 E
Romaškino	80	52.29 N	51.48 E
Romaškovo	265b	55.44 N	37.20 E
Romayor	222	30.27 N	94.50 W
Rombari	154	4.33 N	31.02 E
Romblon	116	12.35 N	122.15 E
Romblon □[4]	116	12.30 N	122.10 E
Romblon Island I	116	12.33 N	122.17 E
Romblon Passage ⊔	116	12.27 N	122.12 E
Rombo, Ilhéus do II	150a	14.58 N	24.40 W
Rome → Roma, It.	66	41.54 N	12.29 E
Rome, Ga., U.S.	192	34.15 N	85.09 W
Rome, Il., U.S.	190	40.53 N	89.30 W
Rome, Ms., U.S.	194	33.57 N	90.28 W
Rome, N.Y., U.S.	210	43.12 N	75.27 W
Rome, Oh., U.S.	214	41.36 N	80.52 W
Rome, Pa., U.S.	210	41.51 N	76.21 W
Rome, Wi., U.S.	216	42.58 N	88.38 W
Rome City	216	41.29 N	85.22 W
Romeleåsen ⋏[2]	41	55.34 N	13.33 E
Romenay	58	46.30 N	5.04 E
Romeno	64	46.24 N	11.07 E
Romentino	62	45.28 N	8.42 E
Romeo	214	42.48 N	83.00 W
Romeoville	216	41.38 N	88.05 W
Römerberg	56	49.17 N	8.24 E
Romero, Isla I	258	33.48 S	59.20 W
Rometan	128	39.56 N	64.23 E
Rometta	70	38.10 N	15.25 E
Romfartuna	40	59.44 N	16.35 E
Romford ◆[8]	260	51.35 N	0.11 E
Römhild	54	50.24 N	10.32 E
Romiley	262	53.25 N	2.05 W
Romilly, Mount ∧	162	20.27 S	126.34 E
Romilly-sur-Seine	50	48.31 N	3.43 E
Romit	85	38.44 N	69.17 E
Romit, zapovednik ♦	85	38.52 N	69.20 E
Romita	234	20.52 N	101.31 W
Romitorio	267a	42.01 N	12.39 E
Rommani	148	34.34 N	6.37 W
Romme	40	60.26 N	15.30 E
Rommerskirchen	56	51.02 N	6.40 E
Romney, In., U.S.	216	40.14 N	86.54 W
Romney, W.V., U.S.	188	39.20 N	78.45 W
Romney Marsh ≡	42	51.03 N	0.55 E
Romny, S.S.S.R.	78	50.45 N	33.30 E
Romny, S.S.S.R.	89	50.44 N	129.15 E
Rømø I	26	55.08 N	8.31 E
Romodan	78	49.59 N	33.19 E
Romodanovo	80	54.26 N	45.20 E
Romoland	228	33.45 N	117.10 W
Romont	58	46.42 N	6.55 E
Romorantin-Lanthenay	50	47.22 N	1.45 E
Rompin, Malay.	114	2.42 N	102.31 E
Rompin, Malay.	114	2.48 N	103.29 E
Rompin ≃	114	2.49 N	103.29 E
Romrod	56	50.43 N	9.13 E
Romsdalen V	26	62.15 N	8.05 E
Romsdalsfjorden ⊂[2]	26	62.39 N	7.15 E
Romsey, Austl.	169	37.21 S	144.45 E
Romsey, Eng., U.K.	42	50.59 N	1.30 W
Romsø I	41	55.31 N	10.48 E
Romulus, Mi., U.S.	216	42.13 N	83.23 W
Romulus, N.Y., U.S.	210	42.45 N	76.50 W
Røn, Nor.	26	61.03 N	9.03 E
Ron, Viet.	110	17.53 N	106.27 E
Rona, Schw.	58	46.34 N	9.38 E
Rona, Zaïre	154	2.14 N	30.52 E
Rona I, Scot., U.K.	46	59.07 N	5.49 W
Rona I, Scot., U.K.	46	57.34 N	5.59 W
Ronald	224	47.14 N	121.01 W
Ronan	202	47.31 N	114.06 W
Ronas Hill ∧[2]	46a	60.31 N	1.28 W
Ronas Voe ⊂	46	60.32 N	1.29 W
Ronay I	46	57.29 N	7.11 W
Roncade	64	45.38 N	12.22 E
Roncador, Serra do ⋏[1]	242	12.00 S	52.00 W
Roncador Bank ✦[4]	236	13.32 N	80.03 W
Roncador Reef ✦[2]	175e	6.13 S	159.22 E
Roncegno	64	46.03 N	11.25 E
Roncesvalles	34	43.01 N	1.19 W
Ronceverte	192	37.44 N	80.27 W
Ronchamp	58	47.42 N	6.39 E
Ronchi dei Legionari	64	45.50 N	13.30 E
Ronchin	50	50.36 N	3.06 E
Ronchis	64	45.49 N	13.00 E
Ronciglione	66	42.17 N	12.13 E
Ronco	58	46.08 N	8.44 E
Ronco Canavese	62	45.30 N	7.32 E
Roncofreddo	66	44.02 N	12.20 E
Roncone	64	45.59 N	10.40 E
Ronco Scrivia	62	44.37 N	8.59 E
Roncq	50	50.45 N	3.07 E
Rond, Sommet ∧	206	45.05 N	72.33 W
Ronda	34	36.44 N	5.10 W
Ronda, Serranía de ⋏	34	36.44 N	5.03 W
Rondane ∧	26	61.55 N	9.45 E
Rondane Nasjonal Park ♦	26	61.50 N	9.50 E
Rønde	41	56.18 N	10.29 E
Rondeau Harbour ⊂	214	42.18 N	81.53 W
Rondeau Provincial Park ♦	214	42.16 N	81.51 W
Rondebult	273d	26.18 S	28.14 E
Ronde Island I	241k	12.18 N	61.35 W
Rondissone	62	45.15 N	7.58 E
Rondon	255	23.23 S	52.48 W
Rondônia	248	10.52 S	61.57 W
Rondônia □[3]	248	11.00 S	63.00 W
Rondonópolis	255	16.28 S	54.38 W
Rondout	278	42.17 N	87.53 W
Rondout Creek ≃	210	41.55 N	73.53 W
Rondout Reservoir ⊜[1]	210	41.50 N	74.29 W
Rone ≃	50	50.46 N	3.27 E
Ronehamn	26	57.10 N	18.29 E
Rong ≃	102	24.32 N	109.15 E
Ronga	80	56.43 N	48.32 E
Rongai	154	0.10 S	35.51 E
Rong'an	102	25.10 N	109.20 E
Rongbaca	102	31.48 N	99.40 E
Rongchang	107	29.24 N	105.36 E
Rongcheng, Zhg.	98	37.08 N	122.23 E
Rongcheng, Zhg.	105	39.03 N	115.52 E
Rongding	107	28.57 N	103.40 E
Ronge, Lac la ⊜	184	55.10 N	105.00 W
Rongelap I[1]	14	11.20 N	166.50 E
Rongjiang	102	25.52 N	108.37 E
Rongkop	115a	8.10 S	110.45 E
Rongola	158	27.22 S	31.37 E
Rongotea	172	40.18 S	175.25 E
Rõngu	76	58.09 N	26.15 E
Rongui, Ilha I	154	10.50 S	40.40 E
Rongwanshi	100	28.10 N	112.57 E
Rongxian, Zhg.	102	22.50 N	110.38 E
Rongxian, Zhg.	107	29.28 N	104.25 E
Ronkiti Harbor ⊂	174r	6.48 N	158.10 E
Ronkonkoma	276	40.48 N	73.06 W
Ronkonkoma, Lake ⊜	276	40.50 N	73.07 W
Rønne	26	55.06 N	14.42 E
Rönne ≃	41	56.16 N	12.50 E
Ronneburg	54	50.51 N	12.10 E
Ronneby	26	56.12 N	15.18 E
Ronne Entrance ⊂	9	72.30 S	74.00 W
Ronne Ice Shelf ⌂	9	78.30 S	61.00 W
Ronnenberg	52	52.20 N	9.40 E
Rönneshytta	40	58.56 N	15.02 E
Rönninge	40	59.12 N	17.44 E
Ronroni	175e	9.37 S	159.58 E
Rönsahl	263	51.07 N	7.30 E
Ronsdorf ◆[8]	263	51.14 N	7.12 E
Ronse (Renaix-Gleiche)	50	50.45 N	3.36 E
Röntgenmuseum ✿	263	51.12 N	7.16 E
Ronuro ≃	255	11.56 S	53.33 W
Roodepoort □[5]	273d	26.10 S	27.52 E
Roodepoort-Maraisburg	158	26.11 S	27.54 E
Roodeschool	52	53.25 N	6.45 E
Roodhouse	219	39.29 N	90.22 W
Roof Butte ∧	200	36.28 N	109.05 W
Rooiberge ∧	158	28.27 S	28.26 E
Rooiboklaagte ≃	156	20.50 S	21.00 E
Rooidam	158	28.07 S	21.15 E
Rooilyf	158	28.49 S	21.57 E
Rooiwal	158	27.18 S	27.32 E
Rooks Creek ≃	216	40.57 N	88.44 W
Rookwood Cemetery ◆	274a	33.53 S	151.04 E
Roon, Pulau I	164	2.23 S	134.33 E
Rooniu, Mont ∧	174s	17.49 S	149.12 W
Roordahuizum	52	53.06 N	5.46 E
Roorkee	124	29.52 N	77.53 E
Roosboom	158	28.36 S	29.44 E
Roosendaal	52	51.32 N	4.28 E
Roosevelt, Az., U.S.	200	33.40 N	111.08 W
Roosevelt, Mn., U.S.	198	48.48 N	95.05 W
Roosevelt, N.J., U.S.	208	40.13 N	74.28 W
Roosevelt, N.Y., U.S.	276	40.40 N	73.35 W
Roosevelt, Ok., U.S.	196	34.50 N	99.01 W
Roosevelt, Ut,. U.S.	200	40.17 N	109.59 W
Roosevelt ≃	248	7.35 S	60.20 W
Roosevelt Beach	210	43.19 N	78.52 W
Roosevelt Campobello International Park ♦	186	44.52 N	66.58 W
Roosevelt Field ◆[9]	276	40.45 N	73.37 W
Roosevelt Island I	9	79.30 S	162.00 W
Roosevelt Park	216	43.11 N	86.15 W
Roosevelt Park ♦	276	40.33 N	74.21 W
Roosevelt Raceway ♦	276	40.44 N	73.36 W
Roosevelt Roads Naval Station ■	240m	18.15 N	65.38 W
Roosevelt Terrace	226	38.08 N	122.16 W
Root	58	47.07 N	8.23 E
Root ≃, N.T., Can.	180	62.50 N	123.40 W
Root ≃, Mn., U.S.	190	43.46 N	91.15 W
Root ≃, Wi., U.S.	216	42.44 N	87.47 W
Root, North Branch ≃	190	43.49 N	92.10 W
Root, South Branch ≃	190	43.44 N	91.58 W
Root Lake ⊜	184	54.04 N	101.24 W
Rootstown	214	41.05 N	81.14 W
Rooty Hill	170	33.46 S	150.50 E
Ropang	115b	8.52 S	117.29 E
Ropaži	76	57.08 N	24.30 E
Ropča	24	63.02 N	52.16 E
Ropczyce	30	50.03 N	21.37 E
Roper	192	35.52 N	76.36 W
Roper ≃	164	14.43 S	135.27 E
Roper River Mission	164	14.44 S	134.44 E
Roper Valley	164	14.56 S	134.00 E
Rope's Creek ≃	274a	33.43 S	150.47 E
Ropesville	196	33.26 N	102.09 W
Roppe	58	47.40 N	6.55 E
Ropša	265a	59.44 N	29.52 E
Roque	250	3.01 S	45.23 W
Roquebillière	62	44.01 N	7.18 E
Roquebrune-Cap-Martin	62	43.46 N	7.28 E
Roquebrune-sur-Argens	62	43.26 N	6.38 E
Roquefavour, Aqueduc de ≋[1]	62	43.31 N	5.19 E
Roquefort	32	44.02 N	0.19 W
Roquemaure	62	44.03 N	4.47 E
Roque Pérez	258	35.25 S	59.20 W
Roquestéron	62	43.52 N	7.00 E
Roquevaire	62	43.21 N	5.36 E
Rora Head >	46	58.52 N	3.25 W
Roraima □[8]	246	1.00 N	61.00 W
Roraima, Mount ∧	246	5.12 N	60.44 W
Rörbäcksnäs	26	61.08 N	12.49 E
Roreto Chisone	62	44.59 N	7.06 E
Rorey Lake ⊜	180	66.55 N	128.25 W
Rørholtfjorden ⊜	26	59.01 N	9.15 E
Rorke Lake ⊜	184	54.33 N	92.30 W
Rorke's Drift ⊥	158	28.20 S	30.32 E
Rorketon	184	51.26 N	99.32 W
Røros	26	62.35 N	11.20 E
Rorschach	58	47.29 N	9.30 E
Rørvig	41	55.57 N	11.46 E
Rørvik	24	64.51 N	11.14 E
Ros' ≃	78	49.39 N	31.35 E
Rosà, It.	64	45.43 N	11.45 E
Rosa, Zam.	154	9.38 S	31.21 E
Rosa, Cap >	36	36.58 N	8.14 E
Rosa, Lake ⊜	238	21.00 N	73.30 W
Rosa, Monte ∧	58	45.55 N	7.53 E
Rosairinho	266c	38.40 N	9.01 W
Rošal'	80	55.40 N	39.51 E

Symbols in the index entries represent the broad categories identified in the key at the right. Symbols with superior numbers (⋏[1]) identify subcategories (see complete key on page *I* · *1*).

Kartensymbole in dem Registerverzeichnis stellen die rechts in Schlüssel erklärten Kategorien dar. Symbole mit hochgestellten Ziffern (⋏[1]) bezeichnen Unterabteilungen einer Kategorie (vgl. vollständiger Schlüssel auf Seite *I* · *1*).

Los símbolos incluídos en el texto del índice representan las grandes categorias identificadas con la clave a la derecha. Los símbolos con numeros en su parte superior (⋏[1]) identifican las subcategorías (véase la clave completa en la página *I* · *1*).

Les symboles de l'index représentent les catégories indiquées dans la légende à droite. Les symboles suivis d'un indice (⋏[1]) représentent des sous-catégories (voir légende complète à la page *I* · *1*).

Os símbolos incluídos no texto do índice representam as grandes categorias identificadas com a chave à direita. Os símbolos com números em sua parte superior (⋏[1]) identificam as subcategorias (veja-se a chave completa à página *I* · *1*).

English	Deutsch	Español	Français	Português
∧ Mountain	Berg	Montaña	Montagne	Montanha
⋏ Mountains	Berge	Montañas	Montagnes	Montanhas
)(Pass	Pass	Paso	Col	Passo
V Valley, Canyon	Tal, Cañon	Valle, Cañón	Vallée, Canyon	Vale, Canhão
≚ Plain	Ebene	Llano	Plaine	Planície
> Cape	Kap	Cabo	Cap	Cabo
I Island	Insel	Isla	Île	Ilha
II Islands	Inseln	Islas	Îles	Ilhas
⊥ Other Topographic Features	Andere Topographische Objekte	Otros Elementos Topográficos	Autres données topographiques	Outros acidentes topográficos

ESPAÑOL

Nombre	Página	Lat.°′	Long.°′ W = Oeste
Rosales, Méx.	232	28.12 N	105.33 W
Rosales, Pil.	116	15.54 N	120.38 E
Rosalia	202	47.14 N	117.22 W
Rosalie, Lake ⊜	220	27.58 N	81.28 W
Rosalind Bank ✣[4]	238	16.30 N	80.30 W
Rosamond, Ca., U.S.	228	34.51 N	118.09 W
Rosamond, Il., U.S.	219	39.23 N	89.10 W
Rosamond Lake ⊜	228	34.50 N	118.04 W
Rosamorada	234	22.08 N	105.12 W
Rosana	255	22.33 S	53.00 W
Rosander, Mount ∧	224	48.46 N	124.42 W
Rosanky	222	29.56 N	97.18 W
Rosanna	274b	37.45 S	145.04 E
Rosans	62	44.23 N	5.28 E
Rosario, Arg.	252	32.57 S	60.40 W
Rosário, Bra.	250	2.57 S	44.14 W
Rosario, Méx.	232	30.01 N	115.40 W
Rosario, Méx.	234	23.00 N	105.52 W
Rosario, Para.	252	24.27 S	57.03 W
Rosario, Pil.	116	13.51 N	121.12 E
Rosario, Pil.	116	16.14 N	120.29 E
Rosario, Ur.	258	34.19 S	57.21 W
Rosario, Ven.	246	10.19 N	72.19 W
Rosario ≃, Arg.	252	24.50 S	65.43 W
Rosario ≃, Ur.	258	34.26 S	57.21 W
Rosario, Bahía del ⊂	232	29.52 N	115.45 W
Rosario, Cayo del I	240p	21.38 N	81.53 W
Rosario, Islas del II	246	10.10 N	75.46 W
Rosario, Laguna ⊜	234	17.52 N	93.48 W
Rosario Bank ✣[2]	238	18.30 N	84.05 W
Rosario de la Frontera	252	25.48 S	64.58 W
Rosario de Lerma	252	24.59 S	65.35 W
Rosario del Tala	252	32.18 S	59.09 W
Rosário de Minas	256	21.43 S	43.38 W
Rosário do Sul	252	30.15 S	54.55 W
Rosário Oeste	248	14.50 S	56.25 W
Rosario Strait ⋓	224	48.30 N	122.45 W
Rosarito, Méx.	204	32.20 N	117.02 W
Rosarito, Méx.	232	28.38 N	114.04 W
Rosarito, Méx.	232	26.27 N	111.38 W
Rosarito, Embalse de ⊜[1]	34	40.05 N	5.15 W
Rosarno	68	38.29 N	15.59 E
Rosas	196	26.09 N	103.27 W
Rosas, Golfo de ⊂	34	42.10 N	3.15 E
Rosazza	62	45.41 N	7.58 E
Rošča	82	54.47 N	36.51 E
Roščino	76	60.15 N	29.37 E
Rosciolo	66	42.07 N	13.20 E
Roscoe, Il., U.S.	216	42.25 N	89.01 W
Roscoe, N.Y., U.S.	210	41.55 N	74.54 W
Roscoe, Pa., U.S.	214	40.04 N	79.51 W
Roscoe, S.D., U.S.	198	45.26 N	99.20 W
Roscoe, Tx., U.S.	196	32.26 N	100.32 W
Roscoe ≃	180	69.40 N	120.57 W
Roscoe Glacier ⌂	9	66.30 S	95.20 E
Roscoe Village ⊥	214	40.18 N	81.54 W
Roscoff	32	48.44 N	3.59 E
Roscommon, Ire.	48	53.38 N	8.11 W
Roscommon, Mi., U.S.	190	44.29 N	84.35 W
Roscommon □[6]	48	53.40 N	8.30 W
Roscrea	48	52.57 N	7.47 W
Rosdorf	52	51.30 N	9.53 E
Rose, It.	68	39.24 N	16.17 E
Rose, N.Y., U.S.	210	43.09 N	76.53 W
Rose, Monte ∧	70	37.39 N	13.25 E
Rose, Mount ∧	226	39.21 N	119.55 W
Rose, Pointe de la ›	240e	14.40 N	60.53 W
Roseau, Dom.	240d	15.18 N	61.24 W
Roseau, Mn., U.S.	198	48.50 N	95.45 W
Roseau ≃, Dom.	240d	15.18 N	61.24 W
Roseau ≃, N.A.	198	49.08 N	97.15 W
Roseau ≃, St. Luc.	241f	13.58 N	61.02 W
Rosebank ◆[8]	273d	26.09 S	28.02 E
Rosebank Station	275b	43.47 N	79.07 W
Roseberry Lakes ⊜	184	52.40 N	92.30 W
Roseberth	166	25.47 S	139.37 E
Rosebery	166	41.46 S	145.32 E
Rosebery ◆[8]	274a	33.55 S	151.12 E
Rose-Blanche	186	47.37 N	58.41 W
Roseboom	210	42.45 N	74.47 W
Roseboro	192	34.57 N	78.30 W
Rose Bowl ♠	280	34.10 N	118.09 W
Rosebud, Austl.	169	38.21 S	144.54 E
Rosebud, Mo., U.S.	219	38.23 N	91.24 W
Rosebud, Mt., U.S.	202	46.16 N	106.26 W
Rose Bud, Pa., U.S.	214	40.45 N	78.33 W
Rosebud, S.D., U.S.	198	43.13 N	100.51 W
Rosebud, Tx., U.S.	222	31.04 N	96.58 W
Rosebud ≃	182	51.25 N	112.37 W
Rosebud Creek ≃	202	46.16 N	106.28 W
Rosebud Indian Reservation ◆[4]	198	43.25 N	100.28 W
Roseburg	202	43.13 N	123.20 W
Rosebush	190	43.41 N	84.46 W
Rose City	190	44.25 N	84.07 W
Rose Creek ≃, U.S.	198	40.04 N	97.07 W
Rose Creek ≃, Ca., U.S.	226	38.07 N	120.24 W
Rosecroft Raceway ♠	284c	38.48 N	76.58 W
Rosedale, Austl.	166	24.38 S	151.55 E
Rosedale, Ab., Can.	182	51.25 N	112.38 W
Rosedale, B.C., Can.	224	49.11 N	121.48 W
Rosedale, In., U.S.	194	39.37 N	87.17 W
Rosedale, La., U.S.	194	30.27 N	91.27 W
Rosedale, Md., U.S.	284b	39.19 N	76.30 W
Rosedale, Ms., U.S.	194	33.51 N	91.01 W
Rosedale ◆[8], On., Can.	275b	43.41 N	79.22 W
Rosedale ◆[8], N.Y., U.S.	276	40.39 N	73.45 W
Rosedale Estates	284c	38.47 N	76.58 W
Rosedale Hills	218	39.42 N	86.07 W
Rosedene	158	32.01 S	22.07 E
Rose Hall	246	6.16 N	57.21 W
Rosehearty	46	57.42 N	2.07 W
Rose-Hill, Maus.	157c	20.14 S	57.27 E
Rose Hill, N.C., U.S.	192	34.49 N	78.01 W
Rose Hill, Va., U.S.	192	36.40 N	83.22 W
Rose Hill, Wa., U.S.	224	47.42 N	122.10 W
Rosehill Cemetery ◆	278	41.59 N	87.41 W
Rosehill Racecourse ♠	274a	33.49 S	151.02 E
Rose Hills Memorial Park ◆	280	34.01 N	118.02 W
Roseira	256	22.54 S	45.18 W
Roseiras	256	22.49 S	46.17 W
Rose Island I	192	25.06 N	77.14 W
Rose Lake	182	54.24 N	126.02 W
Roseland, Ca., U.S.	226	38.30 N	122.55 W
Roseland, In., U.S.	216	41.42 N	86.15 W
Roseland, La., U.S.	194	30.45 N	90.30 W
Roseland, N.J., U.S.	276	40.49 N	74.17 W
Roseland, Oh., U.S.	214	40.47 N	82.32 W
Roseland ◆[8]	278	41.42 N	87.38 W
Roselawn	216	41.09 N	87.19 W
Roselle, Il., U.S.	216	41.59 N	88.04 W
Roselle, N.J., U.S.	276	40.39 N	74.15 W
Roselle Field ⊠	278	41.59 N	88.06 W
Rosellen	263	51.08 N	6.43 E
Roselle Park	276	40.39 N	74.15 W
Rosellerheide	263	51.07 N	6.44 E
Rose Lodge	224	45.01 N	123.52 W
Rosemary	182	50.46 N	112.05 W
Rosemary Brook ≃	283	42.19 N	71.15 W
Rosemead	280	34.04 N	118.04 W
Rosemère	206	45.38 N	73.48 W
Rosemont, Ca., U.S.	226	38.34 N	121.20 W
Rosemont, Il., U.S.	278	41.59 N	87.52 W
Rosemont, Ky., U.S.	218	38.01 N	84.32 W
Rosemont, Oh., U.S.	214	41.03 N	80.53 W
Rosemont, Pa., U.S.	285	40.01 N	75.19 W
Rosemont Horizon ♠	278	42.00 N	87.53 W
Rosenberg → Susz, Pol.	30	53.44 N	19.20 E
Rosenberg, Tx., U.S.	222	29.33 N	95.48 W
Rosendaël	50	51.02 N	2.24 E
Rosendal, Nor.	26	59.59 N	6.01 E
Rosendal, S. Afr.	158	28.30 S	27.55 E
Rosendale	210	41.51 N	74.05 W
Roseneath	273d	26.17 S	28.11 E

FRANÇAIS

Nom	Page	Lat.°′	Long.°′ W = Ouest
Rosenfeld	58	48.17 N	8.43 E
Rosengarten	52	53.23 N	9.54 E
Rosenhayn	208	39.28 N	75.07 W
Rosenheim	64	47.51 N	12.07 E
Rosenhügel ◆[8]	263	51.10 N	7.12 E
Rosenthal, B.R.D.	56	50.58 N	8.52 E
Rosenthal, D.D.R.	54	50.51 N	14.04 E
Rosenthal ◆[8]	264a	52.36 N	13.23 E
Rose Peak ∧	200	33.26 N	109.22 W
Rosepine	194	30.55 N	93.17 W
Rose Point ›	182	54.13 N	131.35 W
Rosersberg	40	59.35 N	17.53 E
Rosersberg ⊥	40	59.34 N	17.50 E
Roseto	210	40.52 N	75.12 W
Roseto Capo Spulico	68	39.59 N	16.36 E
Roseto degli Abruzzi	66	42.41 N	14.01 E
Roseto Valfortore	68	41.22 N	15.06 E
Rosetown	184	51.33 N	108.00 W
Rose Tree	285	39.56 N	75.23 W
Rose Tree Park ♠	285	39.56 N	75.24 W
Rosetta → Rashīd	142	31.24 N	30.25 E
Rosetta Branch → Rashīd, Far‘OM	142	31.30 N	30.21 E
Rosetta Mouth → Rashīd, Maṣabb ≃[1]	142	31.30 N	30.20 E
Rosettenville ◆[8]	273d	26.15 S	28.03 E
Rosevale	171a	27.51 S	152.29 E
Rose Valley, Sk., Can.	184	52.18 N	103.50 W
Rose Valley, Pa., U.S.	285	39.53 N	75.23 W
Rose Valley, Pa., U.S.	285	40.10 N	75.13 W
Rose Valley, Wa., U.S.	224	46.06 N	122.50 W
Roseville, Austl.	274a	33.47 S	151.11 E
Roseville, Ca., U.S.	226	38.45 N	121.17 W
Roseville, Il., U.S.	190	40.43 N	90.39 W
Roseville, Mi., U.S.	214	42.29 N	82.56 W
Roseville, Mn., U.S.	190	45.00 N	93.09 W
Roseville, Oh., U.S.	188	39.48 N	82.04 W
Roseville, Pa., U.S.	210	41.51 N	76.57 W
Roseville Park	285	39.42 N	75.43 W
Rosewood, Austl.	171a	27.39 S	152.35 E
Rosewood, Austl.	171b	35.41 S	147.52 E
Rosewood, Oh., U.S.	216	40.13 N	83.58 W
Rosewood Heights	219	38.53 N	90.05 W
Roseworthy	168b	34.32 S	138.44 E
Roshanara Gardens ♠	272a	28.40 N	77.12 E
Rosharon	222	29.21 N	95.28 W
Rosheim	58	48.30 N	7.28 E
Rosherville Dam ⊜[1]	273d	26.14 S	28.07 E
Rosh Ha‘Ayin	132	32.06 N	34.57 E
Rosholt, S.D., U.S.	198	45.52 N	96.43 W
Rosholt, Wi., U.S.	190	44.37 N	89.18 W
Rosh Pinna	132	32.58 N	35.32 E
Rosh Pinna, Sede-Te‘ufa ⊠	132	32.59 N	35.34 E
Rosica ≃	38	43.15 N	25.42 E
Rosice	30	49.11 N	16.23 E
Rosiclare	194	37.25 N	88.20 W
Rosières-aux-Salines	58	48.36 N	6.20 E
Rosières-en-Santerre	50	49.49 N	2.43 E
Rosiers, Rivière des ≃	206	45.59 N	72.07 W
Rosignano Marittimo	66	43.24 N	10.28 E
Rosignano Solvay	66	43.23 N	10.26 E
Rosignol	246	6.17 N	57.32 W
Roșiori-de-Vede	38	44.07 N	25.00 E
Rosita	236	13.53 N	84.24 W
Rositz	54	51.01 N	12.22 E
Roskilde	41	55.39 N	12.05 E
Roskilde □[6]	41	55.30 N	12.05 E
Roskilde Fjord ⊂	41	55.56 N	12.00 E
Roskow	54	52.28 N	12.42 E
Roslagen □[9]	40	59.30 N	18.40 E
Roslags-Bro	40	59.50 N	18.44 E
Roslags-Näsby	40	59.26 N	18.04 E
Rosl'akovo	24	69.03 N	33.09 E
Rosl'atino	76	59.46 N	44.15 E
Roslavl'	76	53.57 N	32.52 E
Roslev	26	56.42 N	8.59 E
Roslindale ◆[8]	283	42.18 N	71.07 W
Roslyn, N.Y., U.S.	276	40.48 N	73.39 W
Roslyn, Pa., U.S.	208	40.07 N	75.08 W
Roslyn, Pa., U.S.	285	39.57 N	75.36 W
Roslyn, Wa., U.S.	224	47.13 N	120.59 W
Roslyn Estates	276	40.47 N	73.40 W
Roslyn Harbor	276	40.49 N	73.38 W
Roslyn Heights	276	40.47 N	73.38 W
Rosmalen	52	51.43 N	5.22 E
Rosman	192	35.08 N	82.49 W
Rosmead	158	31.29 S	25.08 E
Ros Mhic Thriúin → New Ross	48	52.24 N	6.56 W
Røsnæs ›[1]	41	55.44 N	10.59 E
Rosne, Ruisseau le ≃	261	48.58 N	2.25 E
Rosneath	46	56.01 N	4.49 W
Rosny-sous-Bois	261	48.53 N	2.29 E
Rosny-sur-Seine	50	49.00 N	1.38 E
Rosolina	64	45.05 N	12.15 E
Rosolini	70	36.49 N	14.57 E
Rošore	85	38.20 N	72.19 E
Rosporden	32	47.58 N	3.50 W
Rösrath	56	50.54 N	7.11 E
Ross, Austl.	166	42.02 S	147.29 E
Ross, N.Z.	172	42.54 S	170.49 E
Ross', S.S.S.R.	76	53.17 N	24.24 E
Ross, Ca., U.S.	226	37.55 N	122.32 W
Ross, In., U.S.	278	41.32 N	87.23 W
Ross, Oh., U.S.	218	39.19 N	84.39 W
Ross □[6]	218	39.20 N	83.06 W
Ross ≃	180	61.59 N	132.26 W
Ross, Cape ›	116	10.56 N	119.13 E
Ross, Mount ∧	172	41.28 S	175.21 E
Ross, Point ›	174c	29.04 S	167.56 E
Ross, Pointe ›	275a	45.21 N	73.48 W
Rossa	58	46.22 N	9.08 E
Rossach	56	50.09 N	10.56 E
Rossano	68	39.35 N	16.39 E
Rossan Point ›	48	54.42 N	8.48 W
Rossasna	76	54.39 N	30.53 E
Rossau	54	52.47 N	11.38 E
Rossbach	54	51.15 N	11.53 E
Ross-Béthio	150	16.16 N	16.08 W
Rossburg	216	40.17 N	84.38 W
Rossburn	184	50.40 N	100.52 W
Ross Carbery	48	51.35 N	9.01 W
Rosscott Manor	285	39.39 N	75.44 W
Ross Dam ◆[6]	224	48.44 N	121.04 W
Rossdorf	56	49.51 N	8.45 E
Rosseau	212	45.16 N	79.39 W
Rosseau, Lake ⊜	212	45.10 N	79.35 W
Rossel, Cap ›	175f	20.23 S	166.36 E
Rossel Island I	160	11.21 S	154.09 E
Rossell y Rius	252	33.11 S	55.42 W
Rossen ⊜	40	60.19 N	16.26 E
Rossendale □[8]	262	53.43 N	2.14 W
Rossendale V	44	53.45 N	2.47 W
Rosser	222	32.28 N	96.27 W
Rosses Bay ⊂	48	55.10 N	8.27 W
Rosses Point	48	54.18 N	8.33 W
Rossford	214	41.37 N	83.33 W
Ross Fork Creek ≃	202	47.05 N	109.43 W
Rosshaupten	58	47.39 N	10.43 E
Rosshyttan	40	60.04 N	16.21 E
Ross Ice Shelf ⌂	9	81.30 S	175.00 W
Rossiglione	62	44.34 N	8.40 E
Rossignol, Lake ⊜	186	44.10 N	65.10 W
Rossijskaja Sovetskaja Federativnaja Socialističeskaja Respublika (Russian Soviet Federative Socialist Republic) □[3]	72	60.00 N	80.00 E
Rössing	156	22.31 S	14.52 E

PORTUGUÊS

Nome	Página	Lat.°′	Long.°′ W = Oeste
Rossio, Estação do ◆[5]	266c	38.43 N	9.09 W
Ross Island I, Ant.	9	77.30 S	168.00 E
Ross Island I, Mb., Can.	184	54.14 N	97.45 W
Rossiter	214	40.53 N	78.55 W
Rossitten → Rybačij	76	55.09 N	20.51 E
Rossla	54	51.28 N	11.04 E
Ross Lake ⊜[1]	224	48.53 N	121.04 W
Ross Lake National Recreation Area ♠	224	48.45 N	121.00 W
Rossland	182	49.05 N	117.48 W
Rosslare	48	52.17 N	6.23 W
Rosslau	54	51.53 N	12.14 E
Rosslea	48	54.14 N	7.11 W
Rossleben	54	51.17 N	11.25 E
Rosslyn Farms	279b	40.26 N	80.05 W
Rossmoor	280	33.47 N	118.05 W
Rossmore	274a	33.57 S	150.46 E
Rossmoyne	208	40.13 N	76.57 W
Rosso	150	16.30 N	15.49 W
Rossön	26	63.55 N	16.21 E
Ross-on-Wye	42	51.55 N	2.35 W
Rossony	76	55.53 N	28.49 E
Rossoš', S.S.S.R.	78	51.08 N	38.29 E
Rossoš', S.S.S.R.	78	50.12 N	39.34 E
Rossouw	158	31.09 S	27.18 E
Ross R. Barnett Reservoir ⊜[1]	194	32.30 N	90.00 W
Ross River	180	61.59 N	132.27 W
Ross-Schelfeis → Ross Ice Shelf ⌂	9	81.30 S	175.00 W
Ross Sea ⊤[2]	9	76.00 S	175.00 W
Rosstal	56	49.25 N	10.52 E
Rosston	218	40.03 N	86.17 W
Rossu, Capu ›	36	42.14 N	8.33 E
Røssvatnet ⊜	24	65.45 N	14.00 E
Rossville, Ga., U.S.	192	34.58 N	85.17 W
Rossville, Il., U.S.	216	40.22 N	87.40 W
Rossville, In., U.S.	216	40.25 N	86.35 W
Rossville, Ks., U.S.	198	39.08 N	95.57 W
Rossville, Md., U.S.	284b	39.20 N	76.29 W
Rosswein	54	51.03 N	13.10 E
Røst II	24	67.28 N	11.59 E
Rostāg	120	37.07 N	69.49 E
Röstånga	41	56.00 N	13.17 E
Rosthern	184	52.40 N	106.17 W
Rostherne	262	53.21 N	2.23 W
Rostherne Mere ⊜	262	53.21 N	2.23 W
Roštkala	120	37.16 N	71.49 E
Rostock	54	54.05 N	12.07 E
Rostock □[5]	54	54.15 N	12.30 E
Rostov	80	57.11 N	39.25 E
Rostov □[4]	83	47.30 N	39.30 E
Rostov-na-Donu	83	47.14 N	39.42 E
Rostrataville	158	26.49 S	25.39 E
Rostraver Airport ⊠	279b	40.13 N	79.50 W
Rostrevor	48	54.06 N	6.12 W
Rosvinskoje	24	66.32 N	52.26 E
Roswell, Ga., U.S.	192	34.01 N	84.21 W
Roswell, N.M., U.S.	196	33.23 N	104.31 W
Roswell, Oh., U.S.	214	40.28 N	81.21 W
Rosyth	46	56.03 N	3.26 W
Rot ≃	58	48.19 N	9.54 E
Rota	34	36.37 N	6.21 W
Rota I	108	14.10 N	145.12 E
Rot am See	56	49.15 N	10.01 E
Rotan	196	32.51 N	100.27 W
Rotanda	156	19.33 S	32.50 E
Rotary Island I	285	40.14 N	74.49 W
Rotbach ≃	263	51.34 N	6.41 E
Rotberg	264a	52.21 N	13.31 E
Rote-Erde, Stadion ♠	263	51.30 N	7.27 E
Rotenburg	52	53.06 N	9.24 E
Rotenburg an der Fulda	56	51.00 N	9.45 E
Roter Main ≃	54	50.04 N	11.24 E
Rotes Meer → Red Sea ⊤[2]	136	20.00 N	38.00 E
Roth, B.R.D.	56	50.46 N	7.42 E
Roth, B.R.D.	60	49.15 N	11.06 E
Roth ≃	58	48.27 N	10.10 E
Rötha	54	51.12 N	12.25 E
Rothaargebirge ⋏	56	51.05 N	8.15 E
Rothbury	44	55.19 N	1.55 W
Rothbury Forest ◆[3]	44	55.18 N	1.54 W
Rothemühl	54	53.36 N	13.49 E
Röthenbach, B.R.D.	58	47.37 N	9.59 E
Röthenbach, Schw.	58	46.51 N	7.45 E
Röthenbach an der Pegnitz	60	49.29 N	11.15 E
Rothenburg	54	51.20 N	14.58 E
Rothenburg an der Oder → Czerwieńsk	30	52.01 N	15.25 E
Rothenburg ob der Tauber	56	49.23 N	10.10 E
Rothenkirchen	54	50.33 N	12.30 E
Rothenschirmbach	54	51.27 N	11.33 E
Rothenstein ∧[2]	263	51.07 N	7.41 E
Rother ≃	42	50.57 N	0.32 W
Rothera ⚘[3]	9	67.34 S	68.08 W
Rotherham, N.Z.	172	42.42 S	172.57 E
Rotherham, Eng., U.K.	44	53.26 N	1.20 W
Rothes	46	57.31 N	3.13 W
Rothesay, N.B., Can.	186	45.23 N	66.00 W
Rothesay, Scot., U.K.	46	55.51 N	5.03 W
Roth-Neusiedl ◆[8]	264b	48.08 N	16.23 E
Rothrist	58	47.19 N	7.53 E
Rothsay, Austl.	162	29.17 S	116.53 E
Rothsay, Mn., U.S.	198	46.28 N	96.16 W
Rothschild	190	44.53 N	89.37 W
Rothsville	208	40.09 N	76.15 W
Rothwell, N.B., Can.	186	46.04 N	66.04 W
Rothwell, Eng., U.K.	42	52.25 N	0.48 W
Rothwell, Eng., U.K.	44	53.46 N	1.29 W
Roti, Pulau I	112	10.45 S	123.10 E
Roti, Selat ⋓	112	10.25 S	123.25 E
Roto	166	33.03 S	145.28 E
Rotoiti, Lake ⊜	172	38.02 S	176.25 E
Rotomanu	172	42.39 S	171.32 E
Rotonda	68	39.57 N	16.02 E
Rotondella	68	40.10 N	16.32 E
Rotondo, Monte ∧	36	42.13 N	9.03 E
Rotoroa, Lake ⊜	172	41.52 S	172.38 E
Rotorua	172	38.09 S	176.15 E
Rotorua, Lake ⊜	172	38.05 S	176.16 E
Rotowaro	172	37.36 S	175.05 E
Rott	64	47.54 N	10.59 E
Rott ≃	60	48.27 N	13.26 E
Rottach-Egern	64	47.41 N	11.46 E
Rott am Inn	64	47.59 N	12.07 E
Rotten ≃	58	46.17 N	7.33 E
Röttenbach	60	49.09 N	11.02 E
Rottenbach-Tremersdorf	56	50.21 N	10.56 E
Rottenbuch	64	47.44 N	10.58 E
Rottenburg am Neckar	58	48.28 N	8.56 E
Rottenburg an der Laaber	60	48.42 N	12.02 E
Rottenmann	61	47.31 N	14.22 E
Rotterdam, Ned.	52	51.55 N	4.28 E
Rotterdam, N.Y., U.S.	210	42.48 N	73.59 W
Rotterdam, Luchthaven ⊠	52	51.58 N	4.30 E
Rotterdam Junction	210	42.52 N	74.03 W
Rotthalmünster	60	48.21 N	13.12 E
Rotthausen ◆[8]	263	51.30 N	7.05 E
Rottingdean	42	50.48 N	0.04 W
Röttingen	56	49.30 N	9.58 E
Rottleberode	54	51.31 N	10.57 E
Rottnest Island I	168a	32.00 S	115.30 E
Rottofreno	62	45.03 N	9.34 E
Rottum	263	51.36 N	7.42 E
Rottumeroog I	52	53.30 N	6.30 E
Rottumerplaat I	52	53.32 N	6.30 E
Rottweil	58	48.10 N	8.37 E
Rotuma I	14	12.30 S	177.05 E
Rotwand ∧	64	47.39 N	11.56 E

Rötz	60	49.21 N	12.32 E
Roubaix	50	50.42 N	3.10 E
Roubideau Creek ≃	200	38.44 N	108.10 W
Roubidoux Creek ≃	194	37.51 N	92.13 W
Roubion ≃	62	44.31 N	4.42 E
Rouceux	58	48.22 N	5.41 E
Roudnice [nad Labem]	54	50.22 N	14.16 E
Rouen	50	49.26 N	1.05 E
Rougé	32	47.47 N	1.27 W
Rouge ≃, On., Can.	212	43.48 N	79.07 W
Rouge ≃, P.Q., Can.	206	45.33 N	74.20 W
Rouge ≃, P.Q., Can.	206	45.39 N	74.42 W
Rouge → Red ≃, U.S.	178	31.00 N	91.40 W
Rouge, Bell Branch ≃	281	42.23 N	83.16 W
Rouge, Lac ⊜	206	46.56 N	74.38 W
Rouge, Mer → Red Sea ⊤[2]	136	20.00 N	38.00 E
Rouge, River ≃	281	42.17 N	83.06 W
Rougeau, Forêt de ♠	261	48.35 N	2.30 E
Rougemont, Fr.	58	47.29 N	6.21 E
Rougemont, Schw.	58	46.29 N	7.12 E
Rougemont-le-Château	58	47.44 N	6.58 E
Rough ≃	194	37.29 N	87.08 W
Rough And Ready	226	39.14 N	121.08 W
Rough River Lake ⊜[1]	194	37.40 N	86.25 W
Rouiba	34	36.44 N	3.17 E
Rouillac	32	45.47 N	0.04 W
Rouillon	261	48.33 N	2.00 E
Roujol, Pointe de ›	241o	16.12 N	61.35 W
Rouku	164	8.40 S	141.35 E
Roulans	58	47.19 N	6.14 E
Rouleau	184	50.11 N	104.55 W
Roulers → Roeselare	50	50.57 N	3.08 E
Roulette	214	41.46 N	78.09 W
Roumanie → Romania □[1]	38	46.00 N	25.30 E
Round, Point ›	240d	15.33 N	61.29 W
Round Harbour	186	49.51 N	55.40 W
Roundhead	216	40.34 N	83.50 W
Round Hill Head ›	166	24.10 S	151.53 E
Round Hill Regional Park ♠	279b	40.15 N	79.51 W
Round Knowe ∧[2]	44	55.08 N	7.05 W
Round Lake, Il., U.S.	278	42.21 N	88.05 W
Round Lake, Mn., U.S.	198	43.32 N	95.28 W
Round Lake, N.Y., U.S.	210	42.56 N	73.47 W
Round Lake ⊜, Nf., Can.	186	51.08 N	56.33 W
Round Lake ⊜, On., Can.	190	45.38 N	77.32 W
Round Lake ⊜, On., Can.	212	44.30 N	77.52 W
Round Lake ⊜, On., Can.	212	45.28 N	79.24 W
Round Lake ⊜, Sk., Can.	184	50.33 N	102.23 W
Round Lake ⊜, Il., U.S.	278	42.22 N	88.05 W
Round Lake ⊜, Mi., U.S.	216	41.58 N	84.17 W
Round Lake Beach	216	42.22 N	88.05 W
Round Lake Park	216	42.21 N	88.04 W
Round Mound ∧[2]	198	38.55 N	99.39 W
Round Mountain	204	38.42 N	117.04 W
Round Mountain ∧, Austl.	166	30.27 S	152.14 E
Round Mountain ∧, Austl.	171b	36.15 S	148.34 E
Round Pond ⊜, Nf., Can.	186	48.10 N	56.00 W
Round Pond ⊜, Ma., U.S.	283	42.36 N	70.49 W
Round Rock	222	30.30 N	97.40 W
Roundstone	48	53.23 N	9.53 W
Round Top	210	42.16 N	74.02 W
Round Top ∧[2]	208	40.30 N	76.42 W
Round Top Regional Park ♠	282	37.51 N	122.12 W
Roundup	202	46.26 N	108.32 W
Round Valley Indian Reservation ◆[4]	204	39.50 N	123.20 W
Round Valley Reservoir ⊜[1]	210	40.36 N	74.50 W
Roundwood	48	53.04 N	6.13 W
Roura	250	4.44 N	52.20 W
Rourkela → Raurkela	124	22.13 N	84.53 E
Rousay I	46	59.10 N	3.02 W
Rouse Hill	274a	33.41 S	150.56 E
Rouses Point	206	45.00 N	73.22 W
Rouseville	214	41.28 N	79.41 W
Rousies	50	50.16 N	4.00 E
Rousseau, Lake ⊜[1]	220	29.02 N	82.32 W
Rousset, Col de)(	62	44.50 N	5.24 E
Roussigny	261	48.39 N	2.06 E
Roussillon, Fr.	62	45.22 N	4.49 E
Roussillon, Fr.	62	43.54 N	5.17 E
Roussillon □[9]	32	42.30 N	2.30 E
Roussy-le-Village	56	49.27 N	6.10 E
Routhierville	186	48.11 N	67.09 W
Routot	50	49.23 N	0.44 E
Rouveen	52	52.36 N	6.11 E
Rouvignies	50	50.20 N	3.26 E
Rouville □[6]	206	45.23 N	73.04 W
Rouvray	50	47.25 N	4.06 E
Rouvray, Lac ⊜	186	49.18 N	70.49 W
Rouxville	158	30.29 S	26.46 E
Rouyn	190	48.15 N	79.01 W
Rouzerville	208	39.44 N	77.32 W
Rovaniemi	24	66.34 N	25.48 E
Rovasenda	62	45.32 N	8.19 E
Rovato	64	45.34 N	10.00 E
Rovbickskaja	76	52.40 N	24.05 E
Rove, Tunnel du ◆[5]	62	43.22 N	5.17 E
Rovegno	62	44.35 N	9.17 E
Rovellasca	62	45.40 N	9.03 E
Rovello Porro	62	45.39 N	9.02 E
Roven'ki, S.S.S.R.	78	49.56 N	38.54 E
Roven'ki, S.S.S.R.	83	48.05 N	39.21 E
Rovenskaja Sloboda	78	52.13 N	30.19 E
Roverbella	64	45.16 N	10.46 E
Rovere	66	42.10 N	13.31 E
Roverè della Luna	64	46.15 N	11.10 E
Roveredo	58	46.14 N	9.08 E
Rovereto	64	45.53 N	11.02 E
Roverè Veronese	64	45.36 N	11.03 E
Rövershagen	54	54.10 N	12.15 E
Roversi	252	27.35 S	61.57 W
Roverud	26	60.15 N	12.03 E
Roviano	66	42.01 N	13.00 E
Rovigo	64	45.04 N	11.47 E
Rovigo □[4]	64	45.02 N	11.50 E
Rovinj	36	45.05 N	13.38 E
Rovira	246	4.14 N	75.14 W
Rovno	78	50.37 N	26.15 E
Rovnoje, S.S.S.R.	78	48.15 N	31.45 E
Rovnoje, S.S.S.R.	80	50.47 N	46.05 E
Rovnoje, S.S.S.R.	85	42.53 N	73.32 E
Rovubu (Ruvubu) ≃	154	2.23 S	30.47 E
Rovuma (Ruvuma) ≃	154	10.29 S	40.28 E
Rów	54	52.58 N	14.45 E
Rowan □[6]	218	38.17 N	83.26 W
Rowan Lake ⊜	184	49.18 N	93.32 W
Rowanty Creek ≃	208	36.58 N	77.21 W
Rowena, Austl.	166	29.49 S	148.54 E
Rowena, Tx., U.S.	196	31.39 N	100.03 W
Rowe Park ♠	273a	6.30 N	3.23 E
Rowhill	273d	26.14 S	28.26 E
Rowland, N.C., U.S.	192	34.32 N	79.17 W
Rowland, Pa., U.S.	210	41.28 N	75.03 W
Rowland Flat	168b	34.35 S	138.56 E
Rowland Heights	280	33.58 N	117.54 W
Rowlands Gill	44	54.54 N	1.45 W
Rowlesburg	188	39.20 N	79.40 W
Rowlett	222	32.54 N	96.33 W
Rowlett, Isla I	254	44.48 S	74.25 W
Rowlett Creek ≃	222	32.49 N	96.31 W
Rowley	207	42.43 N	70.52 W
Rowley ≃, N.T., Can.	176	70.16 N	77.45 W

Rowley ≃, Ma., U.S.	283	42.43 N	70.49 W
Rowley Island I	176	69.08 N	78.50 W
Rowley Regis	42	52.29 N	2.03 W
Rowley Shoals ✣[2]	162	17.30 S	119.00 E
Rowntree Mill Park ♠	275b	43.45 N	79.35 W
Rowsburg	214	40.52 N	82.10 W
Rowville	274b	37.56 S	145.14 E
Roxa, Ilha I	150	11.15 N	15.40 W
Roxana	219	38.50 N	90.04 W
Roxas (Capiz), Pil.	108	11.35 N	122.45 E
Roxas, Pil.	116	17.08 N	121.36 E
Roxas, Pil.	116	12.35 N	121.31 E
Roxas, Pil.	116	10.20 N	119.21 E
Roxas (Capiz), Pil.	116	11.35 N	122.45 E
Roxboro, P.Q., Can.	275a	45.31 N	73.48 W
Roxboro, N.C., U.S.	192	36.23 N	78.58 W
Roxborough	241r	11.15 N	60.35 W
Roxborough ◆[8]	285	40.02 N	75.13 W
Roxborough Downs	166	22.30 S	138.50 E
Roxburgh, N.Z.	172	45.32 S	169.19 E
Roxburgh, Scot., U.K.	46	55.34 N	2.30 W
Roxbury, Ct., U.S.	207	41.33 N	73.18 W
Roxbury, N.Y., U.S.	210	42.17 N	74.33 W
Roxbury, Pa., U.S.	214	40.07 N	77.40 W
Roxbury, Va., U.S.	208	37.28 N	77.09 W
Roxbury ◆[8], Ma., U.S.	283	42.20 N	71.06 W
Roxbury ◆[8], N.Y., U.S.	276	40.34 N	73.54 W
Roxel	52	51.57 N	7.32 E
Roxen ⊜	26	58.30 N	15.41 E
Roxie	194	31.30 N	91.04 W
Roxo, Cap ›	150	12.20 N	16.43 W
Roxton	196	33.33 N	95.44 W
Roxton Pond (Sainte-Pudentienne)	206	45.29 N	72.40 W
Roxwell	260	51.45 N	0.23 E
Roy, N.M., U.S.	196	35.56 N	104.11 W
Roy, Ut,. U.S.	200	41.09 N	112.01 W
Roy, Wa., U.S.	224	47.00 N	122.32 W
Roya (Roia) ≃	62	43.48 N	7.35 E
Royal	198	43.03 N	95.17 W
Royal Albert Hall ⚘	260	51.30 N	0.11 W
Royal Bangkok Sports Club ♠	269a	13.44 N	100.33 E
Royal Botanic Gardens ♠, Austl.	274a	33.52 S	151.13 E
Royal Botanic Gardens ♠, Austl.	274b	37.50 S	144.59 E
Royal Canal ≌	48	53.21 N	6.15 W
Royal Center	216	40.51 N	86.29 W
Royal City	202	46.54 N	119.38 W
Royale, Isle I	190	48.00 N	89.00 W
Royal Festival Hall ⚘	260	51.30 N	0.07 W
Royal Gorge V	200	38.17 N	105.45 W
Royal Island I	192	25.31 N	76.51 W
Royalla	171b	35.31 S	149.09 E
Royal Leamington Spa	42	52.18 N	1.31 W
Royal Natal National Park ♠	158	28.45 S	28.57 E
Royal National Park ♠	170	34.10 S	151.05 E
Royal Naval College ⚘[2]	170	35.07 S	150.42 E
Royal Naval College ■	260	51.29 N	0.01 W
Royal Oak, B.C., Can.	224	48.30 N	123.23 W
Royal Oak, Md., U.S.	208	38.44 N	76.10 W
Royal Oak, Mi., U.S.	216	42.29 N	83.08 W
Royal Oak Township	281	42.27 N	83.10 W
Royal Ontario Museum ⚘	275b	43.40 N	79.24 W
Royal Opera House ⚘	260	51.30 N	0.08 W
Royal Palms State Beach ♠	280	33.44 N	118.19 W
Royal Park ♠	274b	37.47 S	144.57 E
Royal Roads ⊂	224	48.26 N	123.26 W
Royalton, In., U.S.	218	39.56 N	86.21 W
Royalton, Mn., U.S.	190	45.49 N	94.17 W
Royalton, Pa., U.S.	208	40.11 N	76.44 W
Royal Tunbridge Wells	42	51.08 N	0.16 E
Royal Turf Club ♠	269a	13.46 N	100.32 E
Royan	32	45.37 N	1.01 W
Royaume-Uni → United Kingdom □[1]	28	54.00 N	2.00 W
Roybon	62	45.15 N	5.15 E
Royce Brook ≃	276	40.32 N	70.35 W
Roydon, Eng., U.K.	42	52.50 N	0.32 E
Roydon, Eng., U.K.	42	51.46 N	0.03 E
Roye	50	49.42 N	2.48 E
Royersford	208	40.11 N	75.32 W
Royerton	216	40.15 N	85.21 W
Roy Hill	162	22.38 S	119.57 E
Royse City	222	32.58 N	96.19 W
Royston, Eng., U.K.	42	52.03 N	0.01 W
Royston, Eng., U.K.	44	53.37 N	1.27 W
Royston, Ga., U.S.	192	34.17 N	83.06 W
Royton	44	53.34 N	2.08 W
Rožaj	38	42.50 N	20.10 E
Różan	30	52.53 N	21.25 E
Rozay-en-Brie	50	48.41 N	2.58 E
Roždestvenka, S.S.S.R.	86	55.21 N	77.29 E
Roždestvenka, S.S.S.R.	86	55.42 N	70.00 E
Roždestvenka, S.S.S.R.	86	50.52 N	71.22 E
Roždestveno, S.S.S.R.	76	57.44 N	37.57 E
Roždestveno, S.S.S.R.	80	53.15 N	50.04 E
Roždestveno, S.S.S.R.	82	56.51 N	36.33 E
Roždestveno, S.S.S.R.	82	55.57 N	36.23 E
Roždestvenskaja Chava	78	51.38 N	39.40 E
Roždestvenskoje, S.S.S.R.	80	58.09 N	45.35 E
Roždestvenskoje, S.S.S.R.	80	52.47 N	42.10 E
Roždestvenskoje, S.S.S.R.	80	51.14 N	42.10 E
Roždestvo	76	57.36 N	33.48 E
Rozel	43b	49.14 N	2.03 W
Rozelle	274a	33.52 S	151.10 E
Roželov	60	49.33 N	13.48 E
Rozewie, Przylądek ›	30	54.51 N	18.21 E
Rozhnof, Cape ›	180	55.58 N	160.58 W
Rožišče	78	50.54 N	25.15 E
Rožki	80	56.41 N	50.31 E
Rožkov	80	51.39 N	52.19 E
Rožmberk ⊜	61	49.04 N	14.47 E
Rožmberk nad Vltava	61	48.39 N	14.22 E
Rožmitál pod Třemšínem	60	49.36 N	13.52 E
Rožn'atov	78	48.56 N	24.09 E
Rožňava	30	48.40 N	20.32 E
Roznov	38	46.50 N	26.31 E
Rožnov pod Radhoštěm	30	49.28 N	18.10 E
Rożnów	30	49.46 N	20.42 E
Rozovka	78	47.23 N	37.04 E
Rozoy-sur-Serre	50	49.43 N	4.08 E
Roztoczański Park Narodowy ♠	78	50.35 N	23.03 E
Roztocze ⋏[2]	30	50.30 N	23.20 E
Roztoky	54	50.09 N	14.22 E
Rozzano	62	45.20 N	9.06 E
Rrëshen	38	41.47 N	19.54 E
Rrogozhinë	38	41.05 N	19.40 E
Rtiščevo	80	52.16 N	43.47 E
Ru ≃	100	32.43 N	115.01 E
Ru, Tanjong ›	114	2.50 N	101.17 E
Ruabon	42	52.59 N	3.02 W
Ruacaná	152	17.25 S	14.12 E

Ruacana Falls ⌞	152	17.22 S	14.12 E
Ruaha National Park ♠	154	7.30 S	34.40 E
Ruahine Range ⋏	172	40.00 S	176.06 E
Ruahmi, Ra's ›	142	28.44 N	32.50 E
Ruanda	154	10.33 S	34.57 E
Ruanda → Rwanda □[1]	154	2.00 S	30.00 E
Ruango	164	5.35 S	150.10 E
Ruapehu, Mount ∧	172	39.17 S	175.34 E
Ruapuke Island I	172	46.47 S	168.30 E
Ruatahuna	172	38.33 S	176.57 E
Ruatapu	172	42.48 S	170.53 E
Ruathair, Lochan ⊜	46	58.18 N	3.56 W
Ruatoria	172	37.53 S	178.20 E
Ruawai	172	36.08 S	174.02 E
Rub‘al Khali → Ar-Rub‘al-Khālī ◆[2]	136	20.00 N	51.00 E
Rubanovka	78	47.00 N	34.10 E
Rubbestadneset	26	59.49 N	5.17 E
Rubcovsk	86	51.33 N	81.10 E
Rubcy	83	49.12 N	37.33 E
Rubeho Mountains ⋏	154	6.55 S	36.30 E
Rubel'	78	51.58 N	27.04 E
Rübeland	54	51.45 N	10.50 E
Rubelles	261	48.34 N	2.41 E
Rubery	42	52.24 N	2.00 W
Rubeshibe	92a	43.47 N	143.38 E
Rubežka	80	51.26 N	51.59 E
Rubežnoje	83	49.01 N	38.23 E
Rubí, Esp.	266d	41.29 N	2.02 E
Rubi, Zaïre	154	2.49 N	25.14 E
Rubi ≃	152	2.48 N	23.54 E
Rubiana	62	45.08 N	7.23 E
Rubiataba	255	15.08 S	49.48 W
Rubicon ≃	226	39.00 N	120.44 W
Rubicone ≃	66	44.08 N	12.28 E
Rubidoux	228	33.59 N	117.24 W
Rubiera	64	44.39 N	10.45 E
Rubim	255	16.23 S	40.32 W
Rubinéia	255	20.11 S	50.58 W
Rubino	150	6.04 N	4.18 W
Rubio	246	7.43 N	72.22 W
Rubio Woods ♠	278	41.38 N	87.46 W
Rubl'ovka	78	49.15 N	33.19 E
Rubl'ovo	82	55.47 N	37.21 E
Ruboani	140	8.06 N	30.45 E
Rubona	154	0.33 N	30.10 E
Rubondo Island I	154	2.20 S	31.52 E
Rubondo Island National Park ♠	154	2.20 S	31.52 E
Rubtsovsk → Rubcovsk	86	51.33 N	81.10 E
Ruby, Ak., U.S.	180	64.44 N	155.30 W
Ruby, N.Y., U.S.	210	42.01 N	74.01 W
Ruby ≃	202	45.34 N	112.21 W
Ruby Creek ≃	224	48.43 N	120.59 W
Ruby Dome ∧	204	40.37 N	115.28 W
Ruby Lake ≡	204	40.10 N	115.30 W
Ruby Mountains ⋏	204	40.25 N	115.35 W
Ruby Valley V	204	40.30 N	115.15 W
Rucava	76	56.09 N	21.10 E
Ruchan'	76	53.33 N	32.48 E
Ruche	261	49.02 N	2.27 E
Rucheng	100	25.34 N	113.41 E
Ruciane-Nida	30	53.39 N	21.35 E
Ručji ◆[8]	265a	60.01 N	30.24 E
Ručjuvom	24	66.42 N	61.08 E
Rucphen	52	51.32 N	4.34 E
Ruda	64	45.50 N	13.24 E
Rudall	166	33.41 S	136.16 E
Rudall ≃	162	22.16 S	122.47 E
Rudall River National Park ♠	162	22.25 S	122.40 E
Ruda Śląska	30	50.18 N	18.51 E
Rudauli	124	26.45 N	81.45 E
Ruḍaymah Lioûa	132	33.01 N	36.35 E
Rūdbār, Afg.	128	30.09 N	62.36 E
Rūdbār, Īrān	128	36.48 N	49.24 E
Rūdbar, Īrān	128	33.35 N	47.00 E
Rudbøl	41	54.54 N	8.45 E
Ruddervoorde	50	51.06 N	3.12 E
Ruddiman Terrace	216	43.12 N	86.17 W
Rudelsburg ⊥	54	51.07 N	11.43 E
Ruden I	54	54.12 N	13.46 E
Rudensk	76	53.36 N	27.52 E
Rüdersdorf, D.D.R.	54	52.29 N	13.47 E
Rudersdorf, Öst.	61	47.03 N	16.07 E
Rüdersdorf, Forst ◆[3]	264a	52.26 N	13.50 E
Rüdesheim am Rhein	56	49.59 N	7.56 E
Rudeville	276	41.09 N	74.33 W
Rudewa	154	10.06 S	34.39 E
Rudge Ramos	287b	23.41 S	46.34 W
Rüdinghausen ◆[8]	263	51.27 N	7.25 E
Rūdiškės	76	54.31 N	24.50 E
Rudki	78	49.39 N	23.29 E
Rudkino	78	51.27 N	39.01 E
Rudkøbing	41	54.56 N	10.43 E
Rudn'a, S.S.S.R.	76	54.57 N	31.06 E
Rudn'a, S.S.S.R.	80	50.48 N	44.33 E
Rudnaja Pristan'	89	44.22 N	135.48 E
Rudnevka ≃	265b	55.43 N	37.56 E
Rudnevo	82	54.44 N	38.09 E
Rudnica	78	48.15 N	28.55 E
Rudničnyj, S.S.S.R.	24	59.38 N	52.27 E
Rudničnyj, S.S.S.R.	86	56.08 N	86.12 E
Rudničnyj, S.S.S.R.	86	59.42 N	60.18 E
Rudničnyj, S.S.S.R.	86	44.40 N	78.55 E
Rudnik	30	50.28 N	22.15 E
Rüdnitz	54	52.43 N	13.37 E
Rudnyj, S.S.S.R.	86	52.57 N	63.07 E
Rudnyj, S.S.S.R.	89	44.21 N	134.58 E
Rudo	38	43.37 N	19.22 E
Rudolf, Lake (Lake Turkana) ⊜	144	3.30 N	36.00 E
Rudolfov	61	48.59 N	14.34 E
Rudolph	216	41.17 N	83.40 W
Rudolstadt	54	50.43 N	11.20 E
Rudong, Zhg.	102	21.39 N	111.23 E
Rudong, Zhg.	106	32.19 N	121.12 E
Rudovka, S.S.S.R.	80	53.07 N	42.23 E
Rudovka, S.S.S.R.	83	49.24 N	38.27 E
Rudow ◆[8]	264a	52.25 N	13.30 E
Rudrón ≃	34	42.47 N	3.45 W
Rūd Sar	128	37.08 N	50.18 E
Ruds Vedby	41	55.33 N	11.23 E
Rudyard, Mi., U.S.	190	46.13 N	84.36 W
Rudyard, Mt., U.S.	202	48.33 N	110.33 W
Rudyerd Bay ⊂	182	55.35 N	130.44 W
Rue, Fr.	50	50.16 N	1.40 E
Rue, Schw.	58	46.37 N	6.50 E
Ruecas ≃	34	39.00 N	5.55 W
Rueil-Malmaison	261	48.53 N	2.11 E
Ruen ∧	38	42.10 N	22.31 E
Ruenya (Luenha) ≃	154	16.24 S	33.48 E
Rufā‘ah	140	14.46 N	33.22 E
Ruffano	68	39.59 N	18.15 E
Ruffec	32	46.01 N	0.12 E
Ruffieu	58	46.00 N	5.40 E
Ruffieux	62	45.51 N	5.50 E
Ruffin	192	33.00 N	80.48 W
Ruffle Bar I	276	40.36 N	46.51 W
Rufford	262	53.38 N	2.49 W
Rufford Old Hall ⊥	262	53.38 N	2.49 W
Ruffs Dale	279b	40.10 N	79.37 W
Rufidschi → Rufiji ≃	154	8.00 S	39.20 E
Rufiji ≃	154	8.00 S	39.20 E
Rufina	66	43.49 N	11.29 E
Rufino	252	34.16 S	62.42 W
Rufisque	150	14.43 N	17.17 W
Rufunsa	154	15.05 S	29.40 E
Rufus	224	45.41 N	120.44 W
Rufus, Mount ∧	168b	34.20 S	139.07 E
Rugāji	76	57.00 N	27.08 E
Rugao	100	32.25 N	120.36 E
Rugby, Eng., U.K.	42	52.23 N	1.15 W
Rugby, N.D., U.S.	198	48.22 N	99.59 W
Rugeley	42	52.46 N	1.55 W
Rügen I, D.D.R.	30	54.25 N	13.24 E
Rügen I, D.D.R.	54	54.25 N	13.24 E
Rügenwalde → Darłowo	30	54.26 N	16.23 E

≃	River	Fluss	Río	Rivière	Rio
≌	Canal	Kanal	Canal	Canal	Canal
⌞	Waterfall, Rapids	Wasserfall, Stromschnellen	Cascada, Rápidos	Chute d'eau, Rapides	Cascata, Rápidos
⋓	Strait	Meeresstrasse	Estrecho	Détroit	Estreito
⊂	Bay, Gulf	Bucht, Golf	Bahía, Golfo	Baie, Golfe	Baía, Golfo
⊜	Lake, Lakes	See, Seen	Lago, Lagos	Lac, Lacs	Lago, Lagos
≡	Swamp	Sumpf	Pantano	Marais	Pântano
⌂	Ice Features, Glacier	Eis- und Gletscherformen	Accidentes Glaciales	Formes glaciaires	Acidentes glaciares
⊤	Other Hydrographic Features	Andere Hydrographische Objekte	Otros Elementos Hidrográficos	Autres données hydrographiques	Outros acidentes hidrográficos

✣	Submarine Features	Untermeerische Objekte	Accidentes Submarinos	Formes de relief sous-marin	Acidentes submarinos
□	Political Unit	Politische Einheit	Unidad Politica	Entité politique	Unidade política
⚘	Cultural Institution	Kulturelle Institution	Institución Cultural	Institution culturelle	Institução cultural
⊥	Historical Site	Historische Stätte	Sitio Histórico	Site historique	Sitio histórico
♠	Recreational Site	Erholungs- und Ferienort	Sitio de Recreo	Centre de loisirs	Area de Lazer
⊠	Airport	Flughafen	Aeropuerto	Aéroport	Aeroporto
■	Military Installation	Militäranlage	Instalación Militar	Installation militaire	Instalação militar
◆	Miscellaneous	Verschiedenes	Misceláneo	Divers	Diversos

ENGLISH / **DEUTSCH**

Name / Name	Page / Seite	Lat.°′ / Breite°′	Long.°′ / Länge°′ E = Ost
Rüggeberg	263	51.16 N	7.22 E
Rugged Mountain ʌ	182	50.02 N	126.41 W
Ruggles Beach	214	41.22 N	82.29 W
Rugles	50	48.49 N	0.42 E
Rugufu ≃	154	5.10 S	30.14 E
Ruguj	76	59.28 N	32.50 E
Ruḥama	132	31.30 N	34.42 E
Ruhea	124	26.10 N	88.25 E
Ruhengeri	154	1.30 S	29.38 E
Ruhla	54	50.53 N	10.22 E
Ruhland	54	51.27 N	13.52 E
Ruhlsdorf	264a	52.23 N	13.16 E
Ruhmannsfelden	60	48.59 N	12.59 E
Ruhner Berge ϰ[2]	54	53.17 N	11.55 E
Ruhnu saar I	76	57.48 N	23.15 E
Ruhpolding	64	47.45 N	12.38 E
Ruhr ≃	52	51.27 N	6.44 E
Ruhr, Universität ʋ[2]	263	51.27 N	7.16 E
Ruhrort ◆[8]	263	51.26 N	6.45 E
Ruhstorf an der Rott	60	48.26 N	13.20 E
Ruhudji ≃	154	8.52 S	36.01 E
Ruhuhu ≃	154	10.31 S	34.34 E
Rui'an	100	27.49 N	120.38 E
Ruichang	100	29.41 N	115.40 E
Ruicheng	102	34.45 N	110.45 E
Ruidoso	200	33.19 N	105.40 W
Ruidoso, Rio ≃	200	33.23 N	105.16 W
Ruidoso Downs	200	33.19 N	105.36 W
Ruifeng Sha I	106	31.25 N	121.36 E
Ruihong	100	28.45 N	116.23 E
Ruijin	100	25.50 N	116.00 E
Ruinen	52	52.46 N	6.22 E
Ruiselede	50	51.03 N	3.24 E
Ruislip ◆[8]	260	51.34 N	0.25 W
Ruivo, Pico ʌ	148	32.45 N	16.56 W
Ruiz	234	21.57 N	105.09 W
Ruiz de Montoya	252	26.59 S	55.03 W
Rūjiena	76	57.54 N	25.21 E
Rujm ar-Rashīd, Jabal ʌ	132	31.53 N	36.18 E
Rujm aṣ-Ṣakhrī	132	31.02 N	35.43 E
Rukan-shō ✦[2]	174m	26.06 N	127.32 E
Rukatunturi ʌ[2]	26	66.09 N	29.10 E
Ruki ≃	152	0.05 N	18.17 E
Rukni	126	23.33 N	86.33 E
Rukungiri	154	0.48 S	29.55 E
Rukwa □[4]	154	7.00 S	31.30 E
Rukwa, Lake ⊜	154	8.00 S	32.25 E
Rule	196	33.11 N	99.53 W
Rule Creek ≃	198	38.02 N	103.02 W
Ruleville	194	33.43 N	90.33 W
Rulle	52	52.20 N	8.04 E
Rully	58	46.52 N	4.45 E
Rulo	198	40.03 N	95.25 W
Rülzheim	56	49.09 N	8.16 E
Rum	61	47.08 N	16.51 E
Rum ≃	190	45.11 N	93.23 W
Ruma	38	45.00 N	19.49 E
Rumaat	164	5.49 S	132.48 E
Rumahtinggih	164	6.23 S	140.17 E
Rum'ancevo, S.S.S.R.	82	55.38 N	37.26 E
Rum'ancevo, S.S.S.R.	82	55.58 N	36.32 E
Rum'ancevo ◆[8]	83	48.21 N	38.06 E
Rumänien → Romania □[1]	38	46.00 N	25.30 E
Rumaysh	132	33.05 N	35.22 E
Rumbalara	162	25.20 S	134.29 E
Rumbek	140	6.48 N	29.41 E
Rumbeke	50	50.56 N	3.10 E
Rumberpon, Pulau I	164	1.50 S	134.15 E
Rumbling Bridge	46	56.10 N	3.35 W
Rumburk	54	50.57 N	14.32 E
Rum Cay I	238	23.40 N	74.53 W
Rumelange	56	49.28 N	6.02 E
Rumelifeneri	267b	41.14 N	29.06 E
Rumelihisarı ◆[8]	267b	41.05 N	29.03 E
Rumelihisarı ⊥	267b	41.05 N	29.02 E
Rumelikavağı ◆[8]	267b	41.11 N	29.04 E
Rumford	188	44.33 N	70.33 W
Rumford ≃	283	41.58 N	71.11 W
Rumia	30	54.35 N	18.25 E
Rumigny	50	49.48 N	4.16 E
Rumilly	62	45.52 N	5.57 E
R'uminskoje	82	56.31 N	38.47 E
Rum Jungle	164	13.01 S	131.00 E
R'umki	265a	59.47 N	30.02 E
Rumkiğ	130	39.00 N	39.18 E
Rümlang	58	47.27 N	8.32 E
Rummah, Wādī ar- V	128	26.12 N	44.04 E
Rummānah	142	31.01 N	32.40 E
Rummānah, Bi'r ar- ⊤[4]	142	31.00 N	32.40 E
Rummel	214	40.13 N	78.48 W
Rummelsburg → Miastko	30	54.01 N	17.00 E
Rummelsburg ◆[8]	264a	52.30 N	13.29 E
Rummenohl	263	51.17 N	7.32 E
Rumney	42	51.31 N	3.07 W
Rumoi	92a	43.56 N	141.39 E
Rumont	56	48.50 N	5.17 E
Rumphi	154	11.01 S	33.52 E
Rump Mountain ʌ	188	45.12 N	71.04 W
Rumson	208	40.22 N	73.59 W
Rumst	50	51.05 N	4.25 E
Rumula	164	16.35 S	145.20 E
Rumung I	174q	9.37 N	138.10 E
Rumuruti	154	0.16 N	36.32 E
Runan	100	33.01 N	114.22 E
Runanga	172	42.24 S	171.16 E
Runaway, Cape ›	172	37.32 S	177.59 E
Runazi	154	2.47 S	31.28 E
Runcorn ◆[8]	44	53.20 N	2.44 W
Rundeng	114	2.39 N	97.52 E
Rundēni	76	56.16 N	27.50 E
Rundu	156	17.52 S	19.43 E
Rundvik	26	63.32 N	19.26 E
Runere	154	3.06 S	33.16 E
Rūng, Kaôh I	110	10.44 N	103.14 E
Rungāni	120	26.38 N	65.43 E
Runge	222	28.52 N	97.42 W
Rungis	261	48.45 N	2.21 E
Rungis-Halles, Marché de ʋ	261	48.46 N	2.21 E
Rungsted	41	55.53 N	12.33 E
Rungus Point ›	116	13.43 N	123.58 E
Rungwa, Tan.	154	7.21 S	31.40 E
Rungwa, Tan.	154	6.57 S	33.31 E
Rungwa ≃	154	7.36 S	31.50 E
Rungwa Game Reserve ◆[4]	154	7.00 S	34.10 E
Rungwe	154	9.10 S	33.36 E
Runhällen	40	60.02 N	16.49 E
Runheji	100	32.30 N	116.05 E
Runkel	56	50.24 N	8.10 E
Runmarö I	40	59.17 N	18.46 E
Runn ⊜	40	60.33 N	15.40 E
Runnemede	285	39.51 N	75.04 W
Running Springs	228	34.12 N	117.07 W
Running Water Draw V	196	33.58 N	101.30 W
Runnymede □[8]	260	51.24 N	0.32 W
Runnymede ⊥	260	51.26 N	0.34 W
Rünthe	263	51.39 N	7.39 E
Runwell	260	51.37 N	0.32 E
Ruo ≃, Afr.	154	16.33 S	35.09 E
Ruo ≃, Zhg.	102	41.00 N	100.10 E
Ruo'ergai	102	33.16 N	102.55 E
Ruoheng	100	28.24 N	121.31 E
Ruokolahti	26	61.17 N	28.50 E
Ruoms	62	44.27 N	4.21 E
Ruoqiang	90	38.30 N	88.05 E
Ruoti	68	40.43 N	15.41 E
Ruovesi	26	61.59 N	24.05 E
Ruoxi	100	29.18 N	115.20 E
Rupanco	254	40.46 S	72.42 W
Rupanco, Lago ⊜	254	40.49 S	72.28 W
Rūpar	123	30.59 N	76.31 E
Rupari	168b	35.37 S	139.09 E
Rupat, Pulau I	114	1.50 N	101.35 E
Rupat, Selat ɰ	114	1.50 N	101.25 E
Rupdia	126	23.08 N	89.18 E
Rupea	38	46.02 N	25.13 E
Rupert, Id., U.S.	202	42.37 N	113.40 W
Rupert, Vt., U.S.	210	43.15 N	73.13 W
Rupert, W.V., U.S.	188	37.57 N	80.41 W
Rupert, Rivière de ≃	176	51.29 N	78.45 W
Rupert Creek ≃	166	20.53 S	142.23 E
Rupganj	126	23.48 N	90.31 E
Rūpnārāyan ≃	126	22.13 N	88.03 E
Ruponda	154	10.15 S	38.42 E
Ruppertenrod	56	50.37 N	9.05 E
Ruppiner See ⊜	54	52.48 N	12.50 E
Rupprechtseck ʌ	61	47.14 N	14.00 E
Rupt de Mad ≃	56	49.01 N	6.02 E
Rupt-sur-Moselle	58	47.56 N	6.40 E
Rupununi □[5]	246	3.00 N	59.00 W
Rupununi ≃	246	4.03 N	58.34 W
Rur (Roer) ≃	56	51.12 N	5.59 E
Rural Hall	192	36.14 N	80.17 W
Rural Retreat	192	36.53 N	81.16 W
Rural Ridge	279b	40.35 N	79.50 W
Rural Valley	214	40.48 N	79.18 W
Rurberg	56	50.37 N	6.22 E
Ruri-kei ♠	96	35.03 N	135.26 E
Rurrenabaque	248	14.28 S	67.34 W
Rurstausee ⊜[1]	56	50.36 N	6.22 E
Rurutu I	14	22.26 S	151.20 W
Rusambo	154	16.35 S	32.12 E
Rušan	120	37.58 N	71.30 E
Rusanov	78	50.29 N	31.09 E
Rusanovka	78	50.32 N	33.44 E
Rusape	154	18.32 S	32.07 E
Rusavkina-Popovščina	265b	55.42 N	38.04 E
Ruṣayriṣ, Khazzān ar- ⊜[1]	140	11.40 N	34.20 E
Ruschuk → Ruse	38	43.50 N	25.57 E
Ruscom ≃	214	42.18 N	82.38 W
Ruscom Station	214	42.13 N	82.39 W
Ruse, Blg.	38	43.50 N	25.57 E
Ruše, Jugo.	61	46.32 N	15.31 E
Rusera	124	25.45 N	86.02 E
Rush, Ire.	48	53.32 N	6.06 W
Rush, N.Y., U.S.	210	42.59 N	77.39 W
Rush, Pa., U.S.	210	41.47 N	76.03 W
Rush □[6]	218	39.37 N	85.27 W
Rush ≃, N.D., U.S.	198	47.00 N	96.54 W
Rush ≃, Wi., U.S.	190	44.34 N	92.19 W
Rushan (Xiacun)	98	36.54 N	121.29 E
Rush Center	198	38.27 N	99.18 W
Rush City	190	45.41 N	92.57 W
Rush Creek ≃, Co., U.S.	198	38.22 N	102.32 W
Rush Creek ≃, Ne., U.S.	198	41.27 N	102.32 W
Rush Creek ≃, N.Y., U.S.	284a	42.00 N	78.52 W
Rush Creek ≃, Oh., U.S.	188	39.38 N	82.33 W
Rush Creek ≃, Oh., U.S.	214	40.34 N	83.20 W
Rush Creek ≃, Ok., U.S.	196	34.42 N	97.10 W
Rushden	42	52.17 N	0.36 W
Rushford, Mn., U.S.	190	43.48 N	91.45 W
Rushford, N.Y., U.S.	210	42.23 N	78.15 W
Rush Hill	219	39.13 N	91.43 W
Rush Lake ⊜, On., Can.	190	47.48 N	82.12 W
Rush Lake ⊜, Wi., U.S.	190	43.56 N	88.49 W
Rushland	285	40.15 N	75.02 W
Rushmore	198	43.37 N	95.48 W
Rusholme ◆[8]	262	53.27 N	2.12 W
Rush Springs	196	34.46 N	97.57 W
Rushsylvania	216	40.27 N	83.40 W
Rushville, Il., U.S.	219	40.07 N	90.33 W
Rushville, In., U.S.	218	39.36 N	85.26 W
Rushville, Ne., U.S.	198	42.43 N	102.27 W
Rushville, N.Y., U.S.	210	42.45 N	77.13 W
Rusinga Island I	154	0.24 S	34.10 E
Rusizi (Ruzizi) ≃	154	3.16 S	29.14 E
Rusk	222	31.47 N	95.09 W
Rusk □[6]	222	32.10 N	94.50 W
Rusken ⊜	26	57.17 N	14.20 E
Ruskin, B.C., Can.	224	49.12 N	122.28 W
Ruskin, Fl., U.S.	220	27.43 N	82.26 W
Ruskington	44	53.02 N	0.23 W
Rusnė	76	55.18 N	21.22 E
Rušonu ezers ⊜	76	56.11 N	27.02 E
Rusovce	61	48.04 N	17.10 E
Russa	272b	22.29 N	88.21 E
Russas	250	4.56 S	37.58 W
Russbach ≃	264b	48.17 N	16.35 E
Russee	41	54.18 N	10.04 E
Russell, Mb., Can.	184	50.47 N	101.15 W
Russell, On., Can.	212	45.15 N	75.22 W
Russell, N.Z.	172	35.16 S	174.07 E
Russell, Ia., U.S.	190	40.58 N	93.11 W
Russell, Ks., U.S.	198	38.53 N	98.51 W
Russell, Ky., U.S.	188	38.31 N	82.41 W
Russell, Ma., U.S.	207	42.11 N	72.51 W
Russell, Mn., U.S.	198	44.19 N	95.57 W
Russell, Pa., U.S.	214	41.56 N	79.08 W
Russell, Cape ›	176	75.15 N	117.35 W
Russell, Mount ʌ	180	62.48 N	151.52 W
Russell Cave National Monument ♠	194	34.54 N	85.48 W
Russell Creek ≃	194	37.14 N	85.30 W
Russell Gardens	276	40.47 N	73.43 W
Russell Island I	176	73.55 N	98.25 W
Russell Islands II	175e	9.04 S	159.12 E
Russellkonda	120	19.56 N	84.35 E
Russell Lake ⊜	184	56.15 N	101.30 W
Russell Range ϰ	162	33.24 S	123.28 E
Russells Point	216	40.28 N	83.54 W
Russell Springs	194	37.03 N	85.05 W
Russellton	214	40.37 N	79.50 W
Russellville, Al., U.S.	194	34.30 N	87.43 W
Russellville, Ar., U.S.	194	35.16 N	93.08 W
Russellville, Ky., U.S.	194	36.50 N	86.53 W
Russellville, Mo., U.S.	194	38.30 N	92.26 W
Russellville, Oh., U.S.	218	38.51 N	83.47 W
Russellville, Or., U.S.	224	45.31 N	122.33 W
Rüsselsheim	56	50.00 N	8.25 E
Russi	66	44.22 N	12.02 E
Russia	216	40.14 N	84.24 W
Russian ≃	204	38.27 N	123.08 W
Russian Mission	180	61.47 N	161.19 W
Russian Soviet Federative Socialist Republic → Rossijskaja Sovetskaja Federativnaja Socialističeskaja Respublika □[3]	72	60.00 N	80.00 E
Russiaville	216	40.25 N	86.16 W
Russka	76	58.59 N	28.30 E
Russkaja ʋ[3]	9	74.46 S	136.52 W
Russkaja Bujlovka	78	50.22 N	40.03 E
Russkaja Gavan'	74	76.10 N	62.35 E
Russkaja Pol'ana	86	53.47 N	73.53 E
Russkaja Ṭalovka	80	49.59 N	49.05 E
Russkaja Žuravka	80	50.21 N	40.33 E
Russkij	89	43.03 N	131.50 E
Russkij, ostrov I	74	77.00 N	96.00 E
Russkij Aktaš	80	55.02 N	52.07 E
Russkij Brod	76	52.36 N	37.22 E
Russkij Kameškir	80	52.52 N	46.06 E
Russkij Turek	80	57.03 N	50.13 E
Russkij Vožoj	80	56.57 N	53.22 E
Russkij Zavorot, mys ›	24	68.58 N	54.34 E
Russkoje	83	47.45 N	38.56 E
Russkoje-Dobrino	80	54.22 N	52.28 E
Russko-Vysockoje	265a	59.42 N	29.56 E
Rust, B.R.D.	58	48.16 N	7.43 E
Rust, Öst.	61	47.48 N	16.41 E
Rustajskij	80	56.31 N	44.49 E
Rustam	123	34.21 N	72.17 E
Rustavi	84	41.33 N	45.02 E
Rustburg	192	37.16 N	79.06 W
Rustenburg	158	25.37 S	27.08 E
Rustfontein	158	30.28 S	29.17 E
Rustic Canyon V	280	34.04 N	118.31 W
Rustig	158	27.22 S	27.09 E
Rustington	42	50.48 N	0.31 W
Ruston, La., U.S.	194	32.31 N	92.38 W
Ruston, Wa., U.S.	224	47.17 N	122.30 W
Rusville	273d	26.10 S	28.18 E
Rutana	154	3.55 S	30.00 E
Rutčenkovo	83	47.57 N	37.44 E
Rute	34	37.19 N	4.22 W
Rütenbrock	52	52.50 N	7.10 E
Ruteng	115b	8.36 S	120.27 E
Rutenga	154	21.08 S	30.45 E
Rutersville	222	29.57 N	96.48 W
Rutgers University ʋ[2], N.J., U.S.	276	40.30 N	74.27 W
Rutgers University (Newark) ʋ[2], N.J., U.S.	276	40.44 N	74.10 W
Rutgers University (Camden) ʋ[2], N.J., U.S.	285	39.56 N	75.07 W
Ruth, Ms., U.S.	194	31.22 N	90.18 W
Ruth, Nv., U.S.	204	39.16 N	114.59 W
Rüthen	52	51.29 N	8.25 E
Rutherford, Ca., U.S.	226	38.28 N	122.25 W
Rutherford, N.J., U.S.	210	40.49 N	74.06 W
Rutherford, Tn., U.S.	194	36.07 N	88.59 W
Rutherfordton	192	35.22 N	81.57 W
Rutherglen, Scot., U.K.	46	55.50 N	4.12 W
Ruther Glen, Va., U.S.	208	37.56 N	77.27 W
Ruthin	44	53.07 N	3.18 W
Ruthton	198	44.10 N	96.06 W
Ruthven, On., Can.	214	42.03 N	82.40 W
Ruthven, Ia., U.S.	198	43.07 N	94.53 W
Rüti	58	47.16 N	8.51 E
Rutigliano	68	41.01 N	17.00 E
Rutino	68	40.18 N	15.04 E
Rutka ≃	80	56.22 N	46.38 E
Rutland, B.C., Can.	182	49.53 N	119.24 W
Rutland, Fl., U.S.	220	28.51 N	82.13 W
Rutland, Il., U.S.	216	40.59 N	89.03 W
Rutland, Ma., U.S.	207	42.22 N	71.56 W
Rutland, N.D., U.S.	198	46.03 N	97.30 W
Rutland, Vt., U.S.	188	43.36 N	72.58 W
Rutland □[6]	210	43.21 N	73.15 W
Rutland Island I	110	11.25 N	92.40 E
Rutland State Park ♠	207	42.23 N	72.01 W
Rutland Water ⊜[1]	42	52.39 N	0.38 W
Rutledge, Ga., U.S.	192	33.37 N	83.36 W
Rutledge, Pa., U.S.	285	39.54 N	75.20 W
Rutledge, Tn., U.S.	192	36.16 N	83.30 W
Rutshuru	154	1.11 S	29.27 E
Rüttenscheid ◆[8]	263	51.26 N	7.00 E
Rutter	190	46.06 N	80.40 W
Rutul	84	41.33 N	47.25 E
Ruukki	26	64.40 N	25.06 E
Ruurlo	52	52.05 N	6.26 E
Ruvo del Monte	68	40.51 N	15.32 E
Ruvo di Puglia	68	41.07 N	16.29 E
Ruvu	154	6.48 S	38.39 E
Ruvu ≃	154	6.23 S	38.52 E
Ruvubu (Rovubu) ≃	154	2.23 S	30.47 E
Ruvuma □[4]	154	11.00 S	36.00 E
Ruvuma (Rovuma) ≃	154	10.29 S	40.28 E
Ruwayān, Wādī ar- ±[7]	142	29.07 N	30.10 E
Ruwaybah ⊤[4]	140	15.39 N	28.45 E
Ruwayfī, Jabal ar- ʌ	132	31.12 N	36.00 E
Ruwenzori National Park ♠	154	0.15 S	30.00 E
Ruwenzori Range ϰ	154	0.23 N	29.54 E
Ruwer	56	49.47 N	6.43 E
Ruwer ≃	56	49.47 N	6.42 E
Ruya (Luia) ≃	154	16.34 S	33.12 E
Ruyang	100	34.10 N	112.26 E
Ruy Barbosa	255	12.18 S	40.27 W
Ruyigi	154	3.29 S	30.15 E
Ruyton-Eleven-Towns	42	52.48 N	2.54 W
Ruza	82	55.42 N	36.12 E
Ruza ≃	82	55.38 N	36.17 E
Ruzajevka, S.S.S.R.	80	54.04 N	44.57 E
Ruzajevka, S.S.S.R.	86	52.49 N	66.57 E
Ružany	76	52.52 N	24.53 E
Ružičnaja	78	49.24 N	26.58 E
Ružin	78	49.43 N	29.14 E
Ruzizi (Rusizi) ≃	154	3.16 S	29.14 E
Ružomberok	30	49.06 N	19.18 E
Ruzskoje vodochranilišče ⊜[1]	82	55.47 N	36.00 E
Ruzyně ⊠	54	50.06 N	14.17 E
Ruzzah, Jabal ʌ[2]	142	30.01 N	30.26 E
Rwamagana	154	1.57 S	30.34 E
Rwanda □[1], Afr.	138	2.00 S	30.00 E
Rwanda □[1], Afr.	154	2.00 S	30.00 E
Rwashamaire	154	0.49 S	30.08 E
Ry	41	56.05 N	9.46 E
Ryal Fold	262	53.41 N	2.30 W
Ryan	196	34.01 N	97.57 W
Ryan ≃	182	50.25 N	122.43 W
Ryan, Loch c	44	54.58 N	5.02 W
Ryan Peak ʌ	202	43.54 N	114.25 W
Ryans Creek ≃	169	36.43 S	146.12 E
Ryarsh	260	51.19 N	0.24 E
Ryazan' → R'azan'	80	54.38 N	39.44 E
Rybačij	76	55.09 N	20.51 E
Rybačij, poluostrov ›[1]	24	69.42 N	32.36 E
Rybačje, S.S.S.R.	85	42.26 N	76.12 E
Rybačje, S.S.S.R.	86	46.27 N	81.32 E
Rybackaja ◆[8]	265a	60.00 N	30.30 E
Rybackoje ◆[8]	265a	59.50 N	30.30 E
Rybakovka	78	46.37 N	31.20 E
Rybinsk → Andropov	76	58.03 N	38.52 E
Rybinsker Stausee → Rybinskoje vodochranilišče ⊜[1]	76	58.30 N	38.25 E
Rybinskije Budy	78	51.13 N	35.57 E
Rybinskoje	86	55.47 N	94.47 E
Rybinskoje vodochranilišče ⊜[1]	76	58.30 N	38.25 E
Rybkino	80	54.15 N	43.46 E
Rybnaja Sloboda	80	55.28 N	50.09 E
Rybnica	78	47.45 N	29.01 E
Rybnik	30	50.06 N	18.32 E
Rybnoje, S.S.S.R.	76	54.44 N	39.30 E
Rybnoje, S.S.S.R.	86	58.08 N	94.30 E
Rybnovsk	89	53.12 N	141.50 E
Ryburn ≃	262	53.43 N	1.54 W
Rybuška	80	51.17 N	45.26 E
Rychnov nad Kněžnou	30	50.10 N	16.17 E
Rychwał	30	52.05 N	18.09 E
Ryčkovo	86	58.09 N	61.43 E
Rycroft	182	55.45 N	118.43 W
Ryd	26	56.28 N	14.41 E
Rydaholm	26	56.59 N	14.16 E
Rydal, Austl.	170	33.29 S	150.02 E
Rydal, Pa., U.S.	285	40.06 N	75.06 W
Rydalmere	274a	33.49 S	151.02 E
Rydbo	40	59.28 N	18.11 E
Ryde, Austl.	170	33.49 S	151.06 E
Ryde, Eng., U.K.	42	50.44 N	1.10 W
Ryder	198	47.55 N	101.40 W
Ryder's Hill ʌ[2]	42	50.31 N	3.53 W
Ryderwood	224	46.22 N	123.02 W
Rydsgård	41	55.28 N	13.35 E
Rydzyna	30	51.48 N	16.40 E
Rye, Austl.	169	38.23 S	144.49 E
Rye, Eng., U.K.	42	50.57 N	0.44 E
Rye, N.Y., U.S.	210	40.58 N	73.41 W
Rye, Tx., U.S.	222	30.27 N	94.46 W
Rye ≃	44	54.10 N	0.45 W
Ryegate	202	46.17 N	109.15 W
Rye Hills-Rye Brook	276	41.00 N	73.41 W
Rye Lake ⊜	276	41.04 N	73.43 W
Ryeosu → Yŏsu	98	34.46 N	127.44 E
Rye Patch Reservoir ⊜[1]	204	40.38 N	118.18 W
Ryer Island I	282	38.05 N	122.01 W
Ryes	32	49.19 N	0.37 W
Ryfoss	26	61.09 N	8.49 E
Ryfylke ◆[1]	26	59.30 N	5.30 E
Rygge	26	59.23 N	10.43 E
Rygnestad	26	59.16 N	7.29 E
Ryhope	44	54.52 N	1.21 W
Rykaartspos	158	26.32 S	26.39 E
Ryker Lake ⊜	276	41.03 N	74.33 W
Rykerts	182	49.00 N	116.35 W
Ryki	30	51.39 N	21.56 E
Rykonec	76	59.33 N	36.34 E
Ryley	182	53.17 N	112.26 W
Ryloviči	76	52.31 N	32.04 E
Ryl'sk	78	51.36 N	34.43 E
Rylstone	170	32.48 S	149.58 E
Rymanów	30	49.34 N	21.53 E
Rýmařov	30	49.56 N	17.16 E
Ryn	30	53.56 N	21.33 E
Rynfield	273d	26.09 S	28.20 E
Rynok	80	45.39 N	47.34 E
Ryn-Peski ◆[2]	80	48.24 N	49.00 E
Ryō	270	34.44 N	135.55 E
Ryōhaku-sanchi ϰ	94	36.09 N	136.45 E
Ryojun → Lüshun	98	38.48 N	121.16 E
Ryōkami	94	36.00 N	138.58 E
Ryōke	268	35.58 N	139.33 E
Ryōnan	96	33.15 N	133.55 E
Ryōtsu	92	38.05 N	138.26 E
Rypin	30	53.05 N	19.25 E
Ryškany	78	47.58 N	27.32 E
Ryslinge	41	55.15 N	10.33 E
Rysy ʌ	30	49.12 N	20.04 E
Ryton	44	54.59 N	1.46 W
Ryton ≃	44	53.25 N	1.00 W
Ryton-on-Dunsmore	42	52.22 N	1.26 W
Ryūga-do ±[5]	96	33.39 N	133.45 E
Ryūgasaki	94	35.54 N	140.11 E
Ryūjin	96	33.53 N	135.29 E
Ryukyu Islands → Nansei-shotō II	90	26.30 N	128.00 E
Ryukyu Trench ✦[1]	12	24.45 N	128.00 E
Ryūmon-dake ʌ	270	34.26 N	135.53 E
Ryūō, Nihon	94	35.04 N	136.07 E
Ryūō, Nihon	94	35.39 N	138.30 E
Ryūsen	270	34.28 N	135.37 E
Ryūyō	94	34.40 N	137.48 E
Ržaksa	80	52.09 N	42.02 E
Ržanica	76	53.26 N	33.55 E
Ržava	78	51.14 N	36.43 E
Rzepin	30	52.22 N	14.50 E
Rzeszów	30	50.03 N	22.00 E
Rzeszów □[4]	30	50.00 N	22.00 E
Ržev	76	56.16 N	34.20 E
Ržiščov	78	49.58 N	31.03 E
Ržovka ◆[8]	265a	59.58 N	30.30 E

S

Name / Name	Page / Seite	Lat.°′ / Breite°′	Long.°′ / Länge°′ E = Ost
Sa	110	18.34 N	100.45 E
Sa ≃	105	40.22 N	117.58 E
Saa	152	4.22 N	11.27 E
Saʿad	132	31.28 N	34.32 E
Saʿādatābād	128	30.06 N	53.08 E
Sääksjärvi ⊜	26	61.24 N	22.24 E
Saal	54	54.19 N	12.29 E
Saalach ≃	64	47.51 N	13.00 E
Saal an der Donau	60	48.54 N	11.56 E
Saal an der Saale	56	50.19 N	10.21 E
Saalbach	64	47.23 N	12.38 E
Saalburg	54	50.30 N	11.43 E
Saaldorf	54	50.27 N	11.41 E
Saale ≃	54	51.57 N	11.55 E
Saaler Bodden c	54	54.20 N	12.28 E
Saales	58	48.21 N	7.07 E
Saaletalsperre ◆[6]	54	50.30 N	11.35 E
Saalfeld	54	50.39 N	11.22 E
Saalfelden	64	47.25 N	12.51 E
Šaamar	88	50.08 N	106.10 E
Saâne ≃, Fr.	50	49.54 N	0.56 E
Saane ≃, Schw.	58	46.59 N	7.16 E
Saanen	58	46.29 N	7.16 E
Saanenmöser	58	46.31 N	7.18 E
Saanich Inlet c	224	48.38 N	123.30 W
Saar → Saarland □[3]	56	49.20 N	7.00 E
Saar (Sarre) ≃	56	49.42 N	6.34 E
Saarbrücken	56	49.14 N	6.59 E
Saarburg	56	49.36 N	6.33 E
Sääre	76	57.56 N	22.02 E
Saarelouis → Saarlouis	56	49.21 N	6.45 E
Saaremaa I	76	58.25 N	22.30 E
Saarijärvi	26	62.43 N	25.16 E
Saarland □[3]	56	49.20 N	7.00 E
Saarlautern → Saarlouis	56	49.21 N	6.45 E
Saarlouis	56	49.21 N	6.45 E
Saarmund	264a	52.19 N	13.07 E
Saarn ◆[8]	263	51.24 N	6.53 E
Saarnberg ◆[8]	263	51.25 N	6.53 E
Saas Almagell	58	46.07 N	7.58 E
Saas Fee	58	46.07 N	7.55 E
Saas Grund	58	46.08 N	7.56 E
Saastal V	58	46.10 N	7.56 E
Saatly	84	39.56 N	48.23 E
Saavedra	252	37.45 S	62.22 W
Saavedra ◆[8]	288	34.33 S	58.28 W
Sab, Tônlé ⊜	110	13.00 N	104.00 E
Saba I	238	17.38 N	63.10 W
Saba ≃, Nihon	96	34.02 N	131.30 E
Saba ≃, S.S.S.R.	76	59.08 N	29.00 E
Saba Bank ✦[2]	238	17.30 N	63.30 W
Šabac	38	44.45 N	19.42 E
Sabadell	34	41.33 N	2.06 E
Sabae	94	35.57 N	136.11 E
Sabʿah	142	30.15 N	32.33 E
Sabah □[3]	112	5.20 N	117.10 E
Sabajevo	80	53.59 N	45.43 E
Sabak, Cape ›	181a	52.20 N	173.45 E
Sabak Bernam	114	3.46 N	100.59 E
Sabal	112	0.59 S	123.14 E
Sabalān, Kūhhā-ye ʌ	128	38.15 N	47.49 E
Sabalgarh	124	26.15 N	77.24 E
Sabaluka Game Reserve ◆[4]	140	16.18 N	32.40 E
Sabana	240m	18.20 N	65.44 W
Sabana, Archipiélago de II	240p	23.00 N	80.00 W
Sabana-Camagüey, Archipiélago de II	240p	22.30 N	79.00 W
Sabana de la Mar	238	19.04 N	69.23 W
Sabana de Mendoza	246	9.26 N	70.46 W
Sabanagrande, Hond.	236	13.50 N	87.15 W
Sabana Grande, P.R.	240m	18.05 N	66.58 W
Sabanalamar, Ensenada c	240p	21.36 N	78.44 W
Sabanalarga	246	10.38 N	74.55 W
Sabana Llana	240m	18.02 N	66.15 W
Sabancuy	232	18.58 N	91.11 W
Sabaneta, Rep. Dom.	238	19.30 N	71.21 W
Sabaneta, Ven.	246	8.46 N	69.56 W
Sabaneta, Puntan ›	174n	15.17 N	145.49 E
Sābang, India	126	22.11 N	87.36 E
Sabang (Dampelas), Indon.	112	0.11 N	119.51 E
Sabang, Indon.	114	5.55 N	95.19 E
Sabanilla	232	25.08 N	101.44 W
Šabanovo	82	55.38 N	38.43 E
Şabanözü	130	40.29 N	33.18 E
Sabará	255	19.54 S	43.48 W
Sabarei	154	4.20 N	36.55 E
Sābari ≃	122	17.34 N	81.15 E
Sābarmati ≃	120	22.18 N	72.22 E
Sabasṭīyah (Samaria)	132	32.17 N	35.12 E
Sabʿatayn, Ramlat as- ±[8]	144	15.30 N	46.20 E
Sabathu	123	30.59 N	76.59 E
Sabatini, Monti ϰ	66	42.10 N	12.15 E
Sabato ≃	66	41.08 N	14.45 E
Sabaudia	66	41.18 N	13.01 E
Sabaudia, Lago di c	66	41.16 N	13.02 E
Sabaúna	256	23.29 S	46.05 W
Saba Wanak	144	10.33 N	44.08 E
Sabaya	248	19.01 S	68.23 W
Ṣabāyā, Jabal I	144	18.35 N	41.03 E
Sabažo	84	42.14 N	41.48 E
Sabbioneta	64	45.00 N	10.39 E
Sabe	272c	19.11 N	73.02 E
Šabel'kovka	83	48.45 N	37.29 E
Šabel'sk	83	46.51 N	38.29 E
Sāberī, Hāmūn-e ⊜	128	31.30 N	61.20 E
Sabetha	198	39.54 N	95.48 W
Sabhā, Lībiyā	146	27.03 N	14.26 E
Ṣabḥā, Urd.	132	32.20 N	36.30 E
Sābhār	126	23.51 N	90.15 E
Sabi (Save) ≃, Afr.	156	21.00 S	35.02 E
Sabi ≃, Nihon	94	36.48 N	140.04 E
Sabicy	76	58.50 N	29.18 E
Sabidana, Jabal ʌ	140	18.04 N	36.50 E
Sabie	156	25.10 S	30.48 E
Sábiè ≃	156	25.19 S	32.18 E
Sabile	76	57.03 N	22.35 E
Sabillasville	208	39.42 N	77.27 W
Sabina	218	39.29 N	83.38 W
Sabina □[9]	36	42.15 N	12.42 E
Sabinal	196	29.19 N	99.27 W
Sabinal ≃	196	29.06 N	99.27 W
Sabinal, Península de ›[1]	240p	21.40 N	77.18 W
Sabiñánigo	34	42.31 N	0.22 W
Sabinas	232	27.51 N	101.07 W
Sabinas ≃, Méx.	232	27.37 N	100.42 W
Sabinas ≃, Méx.	232	26.51 N	99.34 W
Sabinas ≃, Méx.	234	22.59 N	98.58 W
Sabinas Hidalgo	232	26.30 N	100.10 W
Sabine ≃	178	30.00 N	93.45 W
Sabine, Mount ʌ, Ant.	9	71.55 S	169.33 E
Sabine, Mount ʌ, Austl.	169	38.38 S	143.44 E
Sabine, South Fork ≃	222	32.52 N	96.10 W
Sabine Bay c	176	75.35 N	109.30 W
Sabine Lake ⊜	194	29.50 N	93.50 W
Sabine Pass c	194	29.44 N	93.52 W
Sabine Peninsula ›[1]	176	76.20 N	109.30 W
Sabini, Monti ϰ	66	42.13 N	12.50 E
Sabinópolis	255	18.40 S	43.06 W
Sabinov	30	49.06 N	21.06 E
Sabinsville	210	41.52 N	77.31 W
Sabir, Jabal ʌ	144	13.25 N	44.06 E
Sabirabad	84	40.01 N	48.29 E
Šabla	38	43.32 N	28.32 E
Sabl'a, gora ʌ	24	64.48 N	58.50 E
Sablayan	116	12.50 N	120.46 E
Sable, Anse au c	275a	45.21 N	73.56 W
Sable, Anse de c	241o	16.07 N	61.34 W
Sable, Cape ›	186	43.25 N	65.35 W
Sable, Cape ›[1]	220	25.12 N	81.05 W
Sable, Île de I	160	19.15 S	159.56 E
Sable, Rivière du ≃	176	55.30 N	68.21 W
Sable Island I	186	43.55 N	59.50 W
Sables, Lac aux ⊜	206	46.53 N	72.22 W
Sables, River aux ≃	190	46.13 N	82.04 W
Sablé-sur-Sarthe	32	47.50 N	0.20 W
Sablinskoje	84	44.31 N	43.14 E
Sablūkah, Ash-Shallāl as- (Sixth Cataract) ⌊	140	16.20 N	32.42 E
Šablykino	76	52.51 N	35.12 E
Sabo, Centraf.	152	7.50 N	17.49 E
Šabo, S.S.S.R.	78	46.08 N	30.23 E
Saboeiro	250	6.32 S	39.54 W
Sabogal ≃	236	10.55 N	84.43 W
Sāboli ◆[8]	272a	28.43 N	77.18 E
Sabonkafi	150	14.38 N	8.45 E
Sabor ≃	34	41.10 N	7.07 W
Sabou	150	12.04 N	2.14 W
Sabourin, Lac ⊜	190	47.58 N	77.41 W
Sabra, Tanjung ›	164	2.17 S	132.19 E
Ṣabrātah	146	32.47 N	12.29 E
Sabres	32	44.09 N	0.44 W
Sabrevois	206	45.12 N	73.14 W
Sabrina Coast ±[2]	9	67.00 S	119.30 E
Sabuda, Pulau I	164	2.38 S	131.36 E
Sabugal	34	40.21 N	7.05 W
Sabugo	266c	38.49 N	9.18 W
Sabuka	273b	4.27 S	15.10 E
Sabula	190	42.04 N	90.10 W
Sabunči	84	40.26 N	49.56 E
Sabuncu	130	39.33 N	30.12 E
Saburovo	265b	55.53 N	37.16 E
Saburovo ◆[8]	265b	55.38 N	37.42 E
Ṣabyā	144	17.09 N	42.37 E
Sabyin	110	19.06 N	94.11 E
Sabyndy	86	50.53 N	70.33 E
Sabzevār	128	36.13 N	57.42 E
Sac ≃	194	38.01 N	93.43 W
Sacaba	248	17.23 S	66.02 W
Sacaca	248	18.05 S	66.26 W
Sacacomie, Lac ⊜	206	46.31 N	73.14 W
Sacagawea ≃	202	47.27 N	107.58 W
Sacajawea Peak ʌ	202	45.15 N	117.17 W
Sacanche	248	7.05 S	76.44 W
Sacandaga ≃	210	43.19 N	73.50 W
Sacandaga, West Branch ≃	210	43.22 N	74.17 W
Sacandica	152	5.58 S	15.56 E
Sacaola	152	12.57 S	22.25 E
Sacaton	200	33.04 N	111.44 W
Sacavém	266c	38.47 N	9.06 W
Sačchere	84	42.21 N	43.23 E
Sac City	198	42.25 N	94.59 W
Sacco ≃	66	41.31 N	13.32 E
Sacedón	34	40.29 N	2.43 W
Săcele	38	45.37 N	25.42 E
Šacha ≃	82	56.45 N	39.10 E
Sachalin □[4]	89	50.00 N	143.00 E
Sachalin, ostrov (Sakhalin) I	89	51.00 N	143.00 E
Sachalinskij zaliv c	89	53.45 N	141.30 E
Šachand	85	40.54 N	71.28 E
Sachayoj	252	26.41 S	61.50 W
Šachbuz	84	39.25 N	45.34 E
Šachdagskij chrebet ϰ	84	40.24 N	45.35 E
Saché	50	47.14 N	0.33 E
Šache ≃	84	43.47 N	39.27 E
Sachicapa	152	10.21 S	19.59 E
Sachigo ≃	176	55.06 N	88.58 W
Sachigo Lake ⊜	184	53.49 N	92.08 W
Sachimbo	152	9.14 S	20.16 E
Šachnovščina	78	49.08 N	35.53 E
Šachovskaja	76	56.02 N	35.29 E
Sachrang	64	47.41 N	12.15 E
Šachrichan	85	40.44 N	72.03 E
Šachrinau	85	38.34 N	68.20 E
Šachrisabz	72	39.03 N	66.50 E
Šachristan	85	39.47 N	68.49 E
Šachristan, pereval)(	85	39.33 N	68.33 E
Šachrovka	80	58.34 N	52.12 E
Sachse	222	32.59 N	96.36 W
Sachseln	58	46.52 N	8.15 E
Sachsen □[9]	30	52.45 N	9.30 E
Sachsenbrunn	54	50.27 N	10.56 E
Sachsenburg	64	46.50 N	13.21 E
Sachsenhagen	52	52.24 N	9.16 E
Sachsenhausen, B.R.D.	56	51.15 N	9.00 E
Sachsenhausen, D.D.R.	54	52.47 N	13.14 E
Sachs Harbour	176	72.00 N	125.00 W
Sächsische Schweiz ◆[1]	54	50.55 N	14.10 E
Šachterskij	180	64.42 N	177.40 E
Šachtinsk	86	49.40 N	72.37 E
Šachtnoje	83	47.57 N	38.17 E
Šacht'orsk, S.S.S.R.	83	48.03 N	38.28 E
Šacht'orsk, S.S.S.R.	89	49.11 N	142.07 E
Šacht'orskij ◆[8]	83	48.09 N	39.08 E
Šachty	83	47.42 N	40.13 E
Šachunja	80	57.40 N	46.37 E
Sachy	56	49.40 N	5.08 E
Sacile	64	45.57 N	12.30 E
Sacır (Sājūr) ≃	130	36.40 N	38.05 E
Šack, S.S.S.R.	76	53.25 N	27.41 E
Šack, S.S.S.R.	78	51.31 N	23.57 E
Šack, S.S.S.R.	80	54.01 N	41.43 E
Sackets Harbor	212	43.56 N	76.07 W
Sackville	186	45.54 N	64.22 W
Saclay	261	48.44 N	2.10 E
Saclay, Étang de ⊜	261	48.45 N	2.10 E
Saco, Me., U.S.	188	43.30 N	70.26 W
Saco, Mt., U.S.	202	48.27 N	107.20 W
Saco ≃	188	43.27 N	70.22 W
Saco Bay c	188	43.30 N	70.15 W
Sacol Island I	116	6.58 N	122.13 E
Sacotes	266c	38.48 N	9.20 W
Sacra, Isola I	267a	41.45 N	12.15 E
Sacra Família do Tinguá	256	22.29 S	43.36 W
Sacramento, Bra.	255	19.53 S	47.27 W
Sacramento, Ca., U.S.	226	38.34 N	121.29 W
Sacramento □[6]	226	38.35 N	121.30 W
Sacramento ≃, Ca., U.S.	204	38.03 N	121.56 W
Sacramento ≃, N.M., U.S.	200	32.16 N	105.31 W
Sacramento, Pampa del ≚	248	8.00 S	75.50 W
Sacramento Metropolitan Airport ⊠	226	38.42 N	121.37 W
Sacramento Mountains ϰ	200	32.45 N	105.30 W
Sacramento River Deep Water Ship Channel ≅	226	38.15 N	121.40 W
Sacramento South	226	38.32 N	121.26 W
Sacramento Valley V	204	39.15 N	122.00 W
Sacramento Wash V	200	34.43 N	114.28 W
Sacre ≃	248	12.56 S	58.18 W
Sacré-Cœur ʋ[1]	261	48.53 N	2.21 E
Sacred Heart	198	44.47 N	95.21 W
Sacriston	44	54.49 N	1.37 W
Sacro, Monte ʌ	68	40.13 N	15.20 E
Sacro Monte ʋ[1]	62	45.49 N	8.15 E
Sacrow ◆[8]	264a	52.26 N	13.06 E
Sacrower See ⊜	264a	52.27 N	13.06 E
Săcueni	38	47.21 N	22.06 E
Sacul	222	31.50 N	94.56 W
Sacupana	246	8.35 N	61.39 W
Sacuriuiná ≃	248	12.52 S	57.22 W
Sada, Esp.	34	43.21 N	8.15 W
Sada, Nihon	96	35.15 N	132.43 E
Sádaba	34	42.17 N	1.16 W
Sadābād, India	124	27.27 N	78.03 E
Saʿdābād, Īrān	128	29.23 N	51.07 E
Ṣadad	130	34.18 N	36.56 E
Ṣaʿdah	144	16.52 N	43.37 E
Sadaik Taung ʌ	110	15.09 N	98.12 E
Sadali	71	39.49 N	9.16 E
Sada-misaki ›	96	33.20 N	132.01 E
Sada-misaki-hantō ›[1]	96	33.26 N	132.13 E
Sadamitsu	96	34.02 N	134.04 E
Sadane ≃	115a	6.01 S	106.37 E
Sadang ≃	112	3.43 S	119.27 E
Sadanga	116	17.09 N	121.02 E
Sadani	154	6.03 S	38.47 E
Sadao	110	6.38 N	100.26 E
Sadarpur, Bngl.	126	23.28 N	90.02 E
Sādarpur, India	272a	28.33 N	77.21 E
Sadčikovka	86	53.01 N	63.27 E
Sadda	120	33.42 N	70.20 E
Saddle ≃	276	40.52 N	74.07 W
Saddleback ʌ	44	54.38 N	3.03 W
Saddle Brook	276	40.54 N	74.06 W
Saddlebunch Keys II	220	24.37 N	81.37 W
Saddle Lake Indian Reserve ◆[4]	182	54.00 N	111.40 W
Saddle Mountain ʌ, Co., U.S.	200	38.50 N	105.28 W
Saddle Mountain ʌ, Or., U.S.	224	45.58 N	123.41 W
Saddle Mountains ϰ	202	46.50 N	119.55 W
Saddle Mountain State Park ♠	224	45.58 N	123.41 W
Saddle Peak ʌ	110	13.09 N	93.01 E
Saddle River	276	40.54 N	74.05 W
Saddle Rock	276	40.48 N	73.45 W
Saddleworth, Austl.	168b	34.05 S	138.47 E
Saddleworth, Eng., U.K.	262	53.33 N	1.59 W
Saddleworth Moor ◆[3]	262	53.33 N	1.57 W
Sa-dec	110	10.18 N	105.46 E
Sadelkow	54	53.36 N	13.26 E
Sādhaura	124	30.23 N	77.13 E
Sādhuhāti	126	23.34 N	89.01 E
Sadieville	218	38.23 N	84.32 W
Sadiola	150	13.53 N	11.42 W
Sādiqābad	120	28.18 N	70.08 E
Sadiya	120	27.50 N	95.40 E
Saʿdīyah, Wādī V	144	20.35 N	39.38 E
Saʿdīyāt, Ra's as- ›	132	33.41 N	35.25 E
Sadler Lake ⊜	184	55.17 N	103.45 W
Sado I	92	38.00 N	138.25 E
Sado ≃	34	38.29 N	8.55 W
Sado-kaikyō ɰ	92	37.50 N	138.40 E
Sadon	84	42.51 N	44.00 E
Sadovoje, S.S.S.R.	80	46.56 N	44.23 E
Sadovoje, S.S.S.R.	80	47.46 N	44.30 E
Sadovoje Pervoje	78	51.33 N	40.29 E
Sadowara	92	32.02 N	131.26 E
Sādri	120	25.11 N	73.26 E
Šadrina	89	51.33 N	130.22 E
Šadrino	86	55.52 N	91.06 E
Šadrinsk	86	56.05 N	63.38 E
Sadsburyville	208	39.59 N	75.53 W
Sadulgarh	123	29.35 N	74.19 E
Sadulpur	123	28.38 N	75.24 E
Sädvaluspen	24	66.24 N	16.51 E
Sæby, Dan.	26	57.20 N	10.32 E
Sæby, Dan.	41	55.33 N	11.19 E
Saegertown	214	41.43 N	80.09 W
Sae Islands II	164	0.45 S	145.15 E
Saeki, Nihon	96	34.22 N	132.11 E
Saeki, Nihon	96	34.51 N	134.06 E
Saeki → Saiki, Nihon	96	32.57 N	131.54 E
Saengil-to I	98	34.19 N	126.59 E
Saerbeck	52	52.10 N	7.38 E
Saerluojiahu ⊜	120	33.55 N	86.55 E
Særslev, Dan.	41	55.31 N	10.11 E
Særslev, Dan.	41	55.43 N	11.23 E
Saeul	56	49.44 N	5.59 E
Ṣafā, Tulul aṣ- ʌ[1]	132	33.02 N	37.12 E
Safad → Zefat	132	32.58 N	35.30 E
Safājah, Jazīrat I	140	26.45 N	33.59 E
Safakulevo	86	54.59 N	62.33 E
Ṣafānīyah	142	28.49 N	30.48 E
Ṣafarābād	128	38.59 N	47.27 E
Šafárikovo	30	48.27 N	20.20 E
Safdar Jang Airport ⊠	272a	28.37 N	77.13 E
Safdar Jang's Tomb ⊥	272a	28.36 N	77.13 E
Safed Koh Range ϰ	123	33.58 N	70.25 E
Safe Harbor Dam ◆[6]	208	39.59 N	76.28 W
Safenbach ≃	61	47.06 N	16.05 E
Safety Bay	168a	32.18 S	115.43 E
Safety Harbor	220	27.59 N	82.41 W
Säffle	26	59.08 N	12.56 E
Safford	200	32.50 N	109.42 W
Saffron Walden	42	52.01 N	0.15 E
Safi	148	32.20 N	9.17 W
Safi □[4]	148	32.05 N	9.00 W
Safia	164	9.35 S	148.40 E
Ṣafīābād	128	36.45 N	57.58 E
Safīd ≃, Afg.	120	36.44 N	65.38 E
Safīd ≃, Īrān	128	37.26 N	49.55 E
Safīdābeh	128	30.56 N	60.35 E

Symbols in the index entries represent the broad categories identified in the key at the right. Symbols with superior numbers (ϰ[1]) identify subcategories (see complete key on page *I · 1).*

Kartensymbole in dem Registerverzeichnis stellen die rechts in Schlüssel erklärten Kategorien dar. Symbole mit hochgestellten Ziffern (ϰ[1]) bezeichnen Unterabteilungen einer Kategorie (vgl. vollständiger Schlüssel auf Seite *I · 1).*

Los símbolos incluídos en el texto del índice representan las grandes categorias identificadas con la clave a la derecha. Los símbolos con numeros en su parte superior (ϰ[1]) identifican las subcategorías (véase la clave completa en la página *I · 1).*

Les symboles de l'index représentent les catégories indiquées dans la légende à droite. Les symboles suivis d'un indice (ϰ[1]) représentent des sous-catégories (voir légende complète à la page *I · 1).*

Os símbolos incluídos no texto do índice representam as grandes categorias identificadas com a chave à direita. Os símbolos com números em sua parte superior (ϰ[1]) identificam as subcategorias (veja-se a chave completa à página *I · 1).*

ʌ	Mountain	Berg	Montaña	Montagne	Montanha
ϰ	Mountains	Berge	Montañas	Montagnes	Montanhas
)(	Pass	Pass	Paso	Col	Passo
V	Valley, Canyon	Tal, Cañon	Valle, Cañón	Vallée, Canyon	Vale, Canhão
≚	Plain	Ebene	Llano	Plaine	Planície
›	Cape	Kap	Cabo	Cap	Cabo
I	Island	Insel	Isla	Île	Ilha
II	Islands	Inseln	Islas	Îles	Ilhas
±	Other Topographic Features	Andere Topographische Objekte	Otros Elementos Topográficos	Autres données topographiques	Outros acidentes topográficos

ESPAÑOL / FRANÇAIS / PORTUGUÊS

Nombre / Nom / Nome	Página / Page / Página	Lat.°′	Long.°′ W = Oeste / W = Ouest / W = Oeste
Safīd Kūh, Selseleh-ye ʎ	**128**	34.30 N	63.30 E
Safidon	**124**	29.25 N	76.40 E
Safiental ∨	**58**	46.40 N	9.18 E
Safioune, Sebkhet ≡	**148**	32.16 N	5.27 E
Safipur	**126**	23.01 N	90.22 E
Safonovo, S.S.S.R.	**24**	65.42 N	47.39 E
Safonovo, S.S.S.R.	**76**	55.06 N	33.15 E
Safonovo, S.S.S.R.	**82**	55.33 N	38.17 E
Safraköy	**267b**	41.00 N	28.47 E
Safranbolu	**130**	41.15 N	32.45 E
Şaft al-ʿInab	**142**	30.49 N	30.41 E
Şaft al-Khammār	**142**	28.02 N	30.42 E
Şaft al-Laban	**273c**	30.02 N	31.10 E
Şaft al-Mulūk	**142**	30.49 N	30.41 E
Şaft Rāshīn	**142**	28.58 N	30.55 E
Şaft Turāb	**142**	30.54 N	31.07 E
Şafwān	**128**	30.07 N	47.43 E
Saga, Nihon	**92**	33.15 N	130.18 E
Saga, Nihon	**96**	33.05 N	133.06 E
Saga, S.S.S.R.	**86**	50.23 N	64.15 E
Saga, S.S.S.R.	**86**	49.25 N	55.17 E
Saga, Zhg.	**120**	29.30 N	85.22 E
Saga □ 5	**96**	33.21 N	130.28 E
Sagaba	**152**	11.17 S	23.07 E
Sagae	**92**	38.22 N	140.17 E
Sagaing	**110**	21.52 N	95.59 E
Sagaing □ 8	**110**	24.00 N	95.00 E
Sagak, Cape ›	**180**	52.48 N	169.08 W
Şagalaherang	**115a**	6.40 S	107.39 E
Šagalakasa	**80**	46.54 N	50.43 E
Sagami ≃	**94**	35.19 N	139.22 E
Sagamihara	**94**	35.34 N	139.23 E
Sagamihara-daichi ʎ 1	**268**	35.27 N	139.27 E
Sagamiko	**94**	35.37 N	139.12 E
Sagami-ko ⊜	**94**	35.35 N	139.16 E
Sagami-nada c	**94**	35.00 N	139.30 E
Sagami-wan c	**94**	35.15 N	139.25 E
Sagamore, Ma., U.S.	**207**	41.46 N	70.31 W
Sagamore, Pa., U.S.	**214**	40.46 N	79.13 W
Sagamore Beach	**207**	41.47 N	70.31 W
Sagamore Hill National Historic Site ⊥	**276**	40.53 N	73.30 W
Sagamore Hills	**279a**	41.02 N	81.26 W
Sagan → Żagań	**30**	51.37 N	15.19 E
Šagan ≃, S.S.S.R.	**86**	50.37 N	79.15 E
Sagån ≃, Sve.	**40**	59.35 N	16.54 E
Saganaga Lake ⊜	**190**	48.14 N	90.52 W
Saganashkee Slough ≃	**278**	41.41 N	87.53 W
Saganash Lake ⊜	**190**	49.04 N	82.35 W
Saganoseki	**96**	33.15 N	131.53 E
Şaganthit Kyun I	**110**	11.56 N	98.29 E
Šagany, ozero ⊜	**78**	45.43 N	29.53 E
Sagaon	**272c**	19.12 N	73.06 E
Sāgar, India	**122**	14.10 N	75.02 E
Sāgar, India	**124**	23.50 N	78.43 E
Sagara	**94**	34.41 N	138.12 E
Sagaranten	**115a**	7.13 S	106.52 E
Sagard	**54**	54.31 N	13.33 E
Sāgardīghi	**126**	24.17 N	88.06 E
Sagaredžo	**84**	41.44 N	45.20 E
Sāgar Island I	**126**	21.43 N	88.06 E
Sāgar Plateau ʎ 1	**124**	23.30 N	78.30 E
Sagavanirktok ≃	**180**	70.20 N	148.00 W
Sage, Mount ʌ	**240m**	18.25 N	64.39 W
Sage Creek ≃, N.A.	**202**	48.58 N	110.06 W
Sage Creek ≃, U.S.	**202**	44.50 N	108.26 W
Sage Creek ≃, Mt., U.S.	**202**	47.16 N	109.43 W
Sage Creek ≃, Mt., U.S.	**202**	48.20 N	110.03 W
Sagemace Bay c	**184**	51.49 N	100.03 W
Sagerton	**196**	33.05 N	99.58 W
Saggaubach ≃	**61**	46.43 N	15.24 E
Sag Harbor	**207**	40.59 N	72.17 W
Şaghbīn	**132**	33.37 N	35.42 E
Şaghīr, Al-Baḥr aṣ- ≊	**142**	31.09 N	31.56 E
Sagil	**86**	50.20 N	91.40 E
Saginaw, Mi., U.S.	**190**	43.25 N	83.56 W
Saginaw, Tx., U.S.	**222**	32.52 N	97.22 W
Saginaw ≃	**190**	43.39 N	83.51 W
Saginaw Bay c	**190**	43.50 N	83.40 W
Sagiz, S.S.S.R.	**80**	47.31 N	53.16 E
Sagiz, S.S.S.R.	**86**	48.12 N	54.56 E
Sagiz ≃	**86**	47.32 N	53.20 E
Sagleipie	**150**	7.00 N	8.52 W
Şaglek Bay c	**176**	58.35 N	63.00 W
Şaglyteniz, ozero ⊜	**86**	54.08 N	69.52 E
Šagonar	**86**	51.32 N	92.48 E
Sagrado	**64**	45.52 N	13.29 E
Sagres	**34**	37.00 N	8.56 W
Sag Sag	**164**	5.35 S	148.20 E
Sagsaj	**86**	48.54 N	89.37 E
Sagsajn ≃	**102**	44.50 N	96.26 E
Sagu, Indon.	**112**	8.15 S	123.13 E
Şagu, Rom.	**38**	46.03 N	21.17 E
Saguache	**200**	38.05 N	106.05 W
Saguache Creek ≃	**200**	37.52 N	105.51 W
Sagua de Tánamo	**240p**	20.35 N	75.14 W
Sagua la Chica ≃	**240p**	22.45 N	79.39 W
Sagua la Grande	**240p**	22.49 N	80.05 W
Sagua la Grande ≃	**240p**	22.56 N	80.01 W
Saguaro National Monument ♠	**200**	32.12 N	110.38 W
Saguenay ≃	**176**	48.08 N	69.44 W
Saguna	**272b**	22.59 N	88.29 E
Sagunay Lake	**216**	41.43 N	86.34 W
Sagunovka	**78**	49.17 N	32.23 E
Sagunto	**34**	39.41 N	0.16 W
Saguny	**78**	50.36 N	39.43 E
Sagutjevo	**76**	52.28 N	33.28 E
Sāgwāra	**120**	23.41 N	74.01 E
Sagy	**261**	49.03 N	1.57 E
Sagyndyk, mys ›	**84**	44.02 N	50.52 E
Sah	**150**	15.38 N	4.03 W
Saḥāb	**132**	31.53 N	36.00 E
Sahaba	**140**	18.55 N	30.28 E
Sahagún, Col.	**246**	8.57 N	75.27 W
Sahagún, Esp.	**34**	42.22 N	5.02 W
Saḥam	**132**	32.42 N	35.47 E
Saḥam al-Jawlān	**132**	32.46 N	35.56 E
Sahana Ambodipont	**157b**	14.37 S	50.11 E
Sahand, Kūh-e ʌ	**128**	37.44 N	46.27 E
Sahara ◆ 2	**10**	26.00 N	13.00 E
Sahāranpur	**124**	29.58 N	77.33 E
Sahārānpur □ 5	**124**	30.00 N	77.35 E
Sahara Occidental → Western Sahara □ 2	**148**	24.30 N	13.00 W
Sahara Occidentale → Western Sahara □ 2	**148**	24.30 N	13.00 W
Saharsa	**124**	25.53 N	86.36 E
Sahasinaka	**157b**	21.49 S	47.49 E
Sahasrail	**126**	23.19 N	89.43 E
Sahaswān	**124**	28.05 N	78.45 E
Sahel □ 5	**150**	14.30 N	0.30 W
Sahel, Canal du ≊	**150**	13.44 N	6.05 W
Sahel, Oued ≃	**34**	36.26 N	4.33 E
Sāhibabad	**272a**	28.40 N	77.22 E
Sahibābad ◆ 8	**272a**	28.45 N	77.05 E
Sāhibganj	**124**	25.15 N	87.39 E
Şahin	**130**	41.01 N	26.50 E
Šāhīwāl, Pāk.	**123**	30.40 N	73.06 E
Sāhiwāl, Pāk.	**123**	31.58 N	72.20 E
Sahlenburg	**52**	53.52 N	8.38 E
Şahneh	**128**	34.29 N	47.41 E
Şaḥrā', Bi'r ⍑ 4	**140**	22.52 N	28.37 E
Şaḥrajat al-Kubrā wa Kafr Jirjis Yūsuf	**142**	30.38 N	31.17 E
Sahtlam	**224**	48.48 N	123.54 W
Sahuaripa	**232**	29.03 N	109.14 W
Sahuarita	**200**	31.57 N	110.58 W
Sahuayo	**234**	20.04 N	102.43 W
Sahul Shelf ✢ 4	**14**	12.30 S	125.00 E
Şahwat al-Qamḥ	**132**	32.36 N	36.23 E
Šahy	**30**	48.05 N	18.57 E
Saï	**150**	13.50 N	5.00 W
Sai ≃, India	**124**	25.39 N	82.47 E
Sai ≃, Nihon	**94**	36.36 N	136.35 E
Sai ≃, Nihon	**94**	36.37 N	138.14 E
Saibai Island I	**164**	9.24 S	142.40 E
Sai Buri	**110**	6.42 N	101.37 E
Sai Buri ≃	**110**	6.43 N	101.39 E
Saïda	**148**	34.50 N	0.09 E
Saïda □ 5	**148**	33.00 N	0.30 W
Saidābād, Bngl.	**126**	24.18 N	89.43 E
Saʿīdābād, Īrān	**267d**	35.40 N	51.11 E
Saidaiji	**96**	34.39 N	134.02 E
Saïdia	**148**	35.04 N	2.15 W
Saʿidiyeh	**128**	36.26 N	48.48 E
Saido	**268**	35.52 N	139.41 E
Saidor	**164**	5.35 S	146.30 E
Saidpur, Bngl.	**124**	25.47 N	88.54 E
Saidpur, India	**124**	25.33 N	83.11 E
Saidu	**123**	34.45 N	72.21 E
Saigawa	**96**	33.39 N	130.57 E
Saignelégier	**58**	47.15 N	7.00 E
Saignon	**62**	43.52 N	5.26 E
Saigō	**92**	36.12 N	133.20 E
Sai-gon → Thanh-pho Ho Chi Minh	**269c**	10.45 N	106.40 E
Sai-gon ≃	**269c**	10.45 N	106.45 E
Saihaku	**96**	35.20 N	133.20 E
Saihan Toroi	**102**	41.41 N	100.26 E
Saijō, Nihon	**96**	33.55 N	133.11 E
Saijō, Nihon	**96**	34.56 N	133.07 E
Saijō ≃	**96**	34.48 N	132.51 E
Saikai-kokuritsu-kōen ♠	**92**	33.12 N	129.22 E
Sai Keng	**271d**	22.26 N	114.16 E
Saiki	**96**	32.57 N	131.54 E
Saiki-wan c	**96**	33.00 N	131.58 E
Sai Kung	**271d**	22.23 N	114.15 E
Saileati	**85**	38.57 N	74.45 E
Sailkupa	**126**	23.41 N	89.15 E
Saillans	**62**	44.42 N	5.11 E
Sailly	**261**	49.02 N	1.48 E
Sailmouille, Ruisseau ≃	**261**	48.37 N	2.17 E
Sailor Creek ≃	**202**	42.56 N	115.29 W
Şail-sous-Couzan	**62**	45.44 N	3.57 E
Šaim	**86**	60.21 N	64.14 E
Saima	**98**	41.00 N	124.14 E
Saimaa ⊜	**26**	61.15 N	28.15 E
Saimaa Canal ≊	**26**	61.05 N	28.18 E
Saimbeyli	**130**	38.00 N	36.06 E
Saín Alto	**234**	23.35 N	103.15 W
Saindak	**128**	29.17 N	61.34 E
Şā'īn Dezh	**128**	36.40 N	46.33 E
Sainghin-en-Weppes	**50**	50.33 N	2.54 E
Sainjang	**98**	39.15 N	125.51 E
Sainō-ha'iji ⊥	**96**	35.29 N	133.39 E
Sains-du-Nord	**50**	50.06 N	4.00 E
Sains-en-Gohelle	**50**	50.27 N	2.41 E
Sains-Richaumont	**50**	49.49 N	3.42 E
Saint Abb's Head ›	**46**	55.54 N	2.09 W
Sainte-Adèle	**206**	45.57 N	74.07 W
Sainte-Adresse	**50**	49.30 N	0.05 E
Saint-Adrien	**206**	45.49 N	71.43 W
Saint-Affrique	**32**	43.57 N	2.53 E
Saint-Agapit	**206**	46.34 N	71.27 W
Saint Agatha	**212**	43.26 N	80.36 W
Sainte-Agathe, Mb., Can.	**184**	49.34 N	97.10 W
Sainte-Agathe, Fr.	**62**	45.49 N	3.37 E
Sainte-Agathe [-de-Lotbinière]	**206**	46.23 N	71.24 W
Sainte-Agathe-des-Monts	**206**	46.03 N	74.17 W
Sainte-Agnès, Fr.	**62**	43.48 N	7.28 E
Saint Agnes, Eng., U.K.	**42**	50.18 N	5.13 W
Saint Agnes I	**42a**	49.54 N	6.20 W
Saint-Agrève	**62**	45.01 N	4.24 E
Saint-Aignan	**50**	47.16 N	1.23 E
Saint-Aimé (Massueville)	**206**	45.55 N	72.56 W
Saint Albans, Austl.	**169**	37.44 S	144.48 E
Saint Albans, Austl.	**170**	33.17 S	150.59 E
Saint Alban's, Nf., Can.	**186**	47.52 N	55.51 W
Saint Albans, Eng., U.K.	**42**	51.46 N	0.21 W
Saint Albans, Mo., U.S.	**219**	38.35 N	90.46 W
Saint Albans, Vt., U.S.	**188**	44.48 N	73.05 W
Saint Albans, W.V., U.S.	**188**	38.23 N	81.50 W
Saint Albans □ 8	**260**	51.45 N	0.20 W
Saint Albans ◆ 8	**276**	40.42 N	73.46 W
Saint Albans, Cape ›	**168b**	35.49 S	138.07 E
Saint Albans Cathedral ʋ 1	**260**	51.45 N	0.20 W
Saint Albert, Ab., Can.	**182**	53.38 N	113.38 W
Saint-Albert, P.Q., Can.	**206**	46.00 N	72.05 W
Saint Aldhelm's Head ›	**42**	50.34 N	2.04 W
Saint-Alexandre-de-Kamouraska	**186**	47.41 N	69.38 W
Saint-Alexis-des-Monts	**206**	46.28 N	73.08 W
Saint-Amable	**275a**	45.39 N	73.18 W
Saint-Amand	**56**	48.49 N	4.36 E
Saint-Amand-en-Puisaye	**50**	47.31 N	3.04 E
Saint-Amand-les-Eaux	**50**	50.26 N	3.26 E
Saint-Amand-Longpré	**50**	47.41 N	1.01 E
Saint-Amand-Montrond	**32**	46.44 N	2.30 E
Saint-Amant-Roche-Savine	**62**	45.34 N	3.38 E
Saint-Amarin	**58**	47.53 N	7.01 E
Saint-Ambroix	**62**	44.15 N	4.11 E
Sainte-Amélie	**184**	50.59 N	99.21 W
Saint-Amour	**58**	46.26 N	5.21 E
Saint-André	**157c**	20.57 S	55.39 E
Saint-André, Cap ›	**157b**	16.11 S	44.27 E
Saint-André, Ruisseau ≃	**275a**	45.22 N	73.29 W
Saint-André-Avellin	**206**	45.43 N	75.03 W
Saint-André-de-l'Eure	**50**	48.54 N	1.17 E
Saint-André-de-Valborgne	**62**	44.09 N	3.41 E
St.-André-Est	**206**	45.34 N	74.20 W
Saint-André-les-Alpes	**62**	43.58 N	6.30 E
Saint-André-les-Vergers	**50**	48.17 N	4.03 E
Saint Andrew	**241g**	13.15 N	59.33 W
Saint Andrew, Mount ʌ	**241h**	13.11 N	61.13 W
Saint Andrew Lakes ⊜	**212**	44.36 N	76.40 W
Saint Andrews, N.B., Can.	**186**	45.05 N	67.03 W
Saint Andrews, Scot., U.K.	**46**	56.20 N	2.48 W
Saint Andrews, S.C., U.S.	**192**	32.46 N	79.59 W
Saint Andrews Bay c	**46**	56.22 N	2.50 W
Saint Andrew's Cathedral ʋ 1	**271c**	1.18 N	103.51 E
Saint Andrews Channel ɰ	**186**	46.03 N	60.38 W
Saint Ann	**219**	38.43 N	90.22 W
Sainte-Anne, Guad.	**241o**	16.14 N	61.23 W
Saint Anne, Guernsey	**43b**	49.42 N	2.12 W
Sainte-Anne, Mart.	**240e**	14.26 N	60.53 W
Saint Anne, Il., U.S.	**216**	41.01 N	87.42 W
Sainte-Anne ≃	**206**	46.33 N	72.12 W
Saint Anne, Cathedral of ʋ 1	**273b**	4.18 S	15.19 E
Sainte Anne, Lac ⊜, Ab., Can.	**182**	53.43 N	114.27 W
Sainte-Anne, Lac ⊜, P.Q., Can.	**186**	50.05 N	67.50 W
Sainte-Anne-de-Beaupré	**186**	47.02 N	70.56 W
Sainte-Anne-de-Bellevue	**275a**	45.24 N	73.57 W
Sainte-Anne-de-la-Pérade	**206**	46.35 N	72.12 W
Sainte-Anne-de-Madawaska	**186**	47.15 N	68.02 W
Sainte-Anne-des-Chênes	**184**	49.40 N	96.40 W
Sainte-Anne-des-Monts	**186**	49.08 N	66.30 W
Sainte-Anne-des-Plaines	**206**	46.46 N	73.48 W
Saint Anne of the Congo ʋ 1	**273b**	4.16 S	15.17 E
Saint Anne's	**44**	53.45 N	3.02 W
Saint Ann's Bay	**241q**	18.26 N	77.08 W
Saint Anns Bay c	**186**	46.20 N	60.30 W
Saint Ann's Head ›	**42**	51.41 N	5.10 W
Saint-Anselme	**186**	46.37 N	70.58 W
Saint Ansgar	**190**	43.22 N	92.55 W
Saint-Anthème	**62**	45.31 N	3.55 E
Saint Anthony, N.B., Can.	**186**	46.22 N	64.45 W
Saint Anthony, Nf., Can.	**186**	51.22 N	55.35 W
Saint Anthony, Id., U.S.	**202**	43.57 N	111.40 W
Saint-Antoine, P.Q., Can.	**206**	45.46 N	73.59 W
Saint-Antoine, Fr.	**62**	45.10 N	5.13 E
Saint-Antonin	**32**	44.09 N	1.45 E
Saint-Apollinaire (Francoeur)	**206**	46.37 N	71.31 W
Saint Arnaud	**166**	36.37 S	143.15 E
Saint-Arnoult, Forêt de ♠	**261**	48.35 N	1.55 E
Saint-Arnoult-en-Yvelines	**50**	48.34 N	1.56 E
Saint Arvans	**42**	51.40 N	2.41 W
Saint Asaph	**44**	53.16 N	3.26 W
Saint-Astier	**32**	45.09 N	0.32 E
Saint Athan	**42**	51.24 N	3.25 W
Saint-Auban	**62**	43.51 N	6.44 E
Saint-Aubert, Mont ʌ 2	**50**	50.39 N	3.24 E
Saint Aubert Island I	**219**	38.40 N	91.52 W
Saint-Aubin, Fr.	**50**	49.53 N	0.53 E
Saint-Aubin, Fr.	**58**	47.02 N	5.20 E
Saint Aubin, Jersey	**43b**	49.11 N	2.10 W
Saint-Aubin, Schw.	**58**	46.54 N	6.47 E
Saint-Aubin-d'Aubigné	**32**	48.15 N	1.36 W
Saint-Aubin-lès-Elbeuf	**50**	49.18 N	1.01 E
Saint-Aubin-sur-Aire	**58**	48.42 N	5.27 E
Saint-Augustin	**157b**	23.33 S	43.46 E
Saint-Augustin ≃	**176**	51.14 N	58.41 W
Saint-Augustin-Deux-Montagnes	**275a**	45.38 N	73.59 W
Saint Augustine	**192**	29.53 N	81.18 W
Saint-Augustin Nord-Ouest ≃	**186**	51.16 N	58.42 W
Saint-Augustin-Saguenay	**186**	51.14 N	58.39 W
Saint-Aulaye	**32**	45.12 N	0.08 E
Saint Austell	**42**	50.20 N	4.48 W
Saint-Avertin	**50**	47.22 N	0.44 E
Saint-Avold	**56**	49.06 N	6.42 E
Saint-Ay	**50**	47.51 N	1.45 E
Saint-Aygulf	**62**	43.23 N	6.44 E
Saint Barbe	**186**	51.12 N	56.46 W
Saint Barnabas Chapel ʋ 1	**174c**	29.02 S	167.55 E
Saint-Barthélemy I	**238**	17.54 N	62.50 W
Saint-Basile	**186**	47.21 N	68.14 W
Saint-Basile-de-Portneuf	**206**	46.45 N	71.49 W
Saint-Basile-le-Grand	**206**	45.32 N	73.17 W
Saint Bathans, Mount ʌ	**172**	44.44 S	169.46 E
Sainte-Baume, Chaîne de la ʎ	**62**	43.20 N	5.45 E
Saint-Béat	**32**	42.55 N	0.42 E
Saint Bees	**44**	54.30 N	3.37 W
Saint Bees Head ›	**44**	54.32 N	3.38 W
Saint Benedict	**214**	40.38 N	78.44 W
Saint-Benoît, Fr.	**261**	48.40 N	1.55 E
Saint-Benoît, Réu.	**157c**	21.02 S	55.43 E
Saint-Benoît-du-Sault	**32**	46.27 N	1.23 E
Saint-Benoît-en-Woëvre	**56**	48.59 N	5.47 E
Saint Bernard	**218**	39.10 N	84.29 W
Saint-Bernard, Île I	**275a**	45.23 N	73.45 W
Saint-Bernard-de-Dorchester	**206**	46.30 N	71.08 W
Saint-Béron	**62**	45.30 N	5.43 E
Saint-Blaise, P.Q., Can.	**206**	45.13 N	73.17 W
Saint-Blaise, Schw.	**58**	47.01 N	6.59 E
Saint-Blaise-la-Roche	**58**	48.24 N	7.10 E
Saint Blaize, Cape ›	**158**	34.11 S	22.10 E
Saint Blazey	**42**	50.22 N	4.43 W
Saint-Blin	**58**	48.16 N	5.25 E
Saint-Bonaventure, P.Q., Can.	**206**	45.58 N	72.41 W
Saint Bonaventure, N.Y., U.S.	**210**	42.05 N	78.28 W
Saint-Boniface-de-Shawinigan	**206**	46.30 N	72.49 W
Saint-Bonnet	**62**	44.41 N	6.05 E
Saint-Bonnet-de-Joux	**58**	46.29 N	4.27 E
Saint-Bonnet-le-Château	**62**	45.25 N	4.04 E
Saint-Bonnet-le-Froid	**62**	45.09 N	4.27 E
Saint Brendan's	**186**	48.52 N	53.40 W
Saint-Brice-sous-Forêt	**261**	49.00 N	2.21 E
Saint Bride, Mount ʌ	**182**	51.30 N	115.57 W
Saint Bride's	**186**	46.55 N	54.10 W
Saint Brides Bay c	**42**	51.48 N	5.15 W
Saint Bride's Major	**42**	51.28 N	3.38 W
Saint-Brieuc	**32**	48.31 N	2.47 W
Saint-Brieux	**184**	52.38 N	104.52 W
Saint-Broing-Les-Moines, Fr.	**58**	47.41 N	4.50 E
Saint-Broing-les-Moines, Fr.	**58**	48.32 N	6.36 E
Saint-Bruno	**206**	45.32 N	73.21 W
Saint-Bruno, Mont ʌ 2	**275a**	45.33 N	73.19 W
Saint-Calais	**50**	47.55 N	0.45 E
Saint-Calixte-de-Kilkenny	**206**	45.57 N	73.51 W
Saint-Cannat	**62**	43.37 N	5.18 E
Saint-Casimir	**206**	46.40 N	72.08 W
Saint-Cassien, Lac de ⊜ 1	**62**	43.35 N	6.48 E
Saint Catharines	**212**	43.10 N	79.15 W
Saint Catharines Airport ⊠	**284a**	43.11 N	79.10 W
Saint Catherine	**220**	28.37 N	82.08 W
Saint Catherine, Monastery of → Qiddīsah Kātrīnā, Dayr al- ʋ 1	**140**	28.29 N	34.01 E
Saint Catherine, Mount ʌ	**241k**	12.10 N	61.40 W
Sainte-Catherine-de-Fierbois	**50**	47.09 N	0.39 E
Saint Catherines Island I	**192**	31.38 N	81.10 W
Saint Catherine's Point ›	**42**	50.34 N	1.15 W
Saint-Célestin (Annaville)	**206**	46.13 N	72.26 W
Saint-Céré	**32**	44.52 N	1.53 E
Saint-Cergue	**58**	46.27 N	6.09 E
Saint-Césaire	**206**	45.25 N	73.00 W
Saint-Cézaire-sur-Siagne	**62**	43.39 N	6.48 E
Saint-Chamas	**62**	43.33 N	5.02 E
Saint-Chamond	**62**	45.28 N	4.30 E
Saint-Chaptes	**62**	43.58 N	4.17 E
Saint Charles, Ar., U.S.	**194**	34.22 N	91.08 W
Saint Charles, Id., U.S.	**202**	42.06 N	111.23 W
Saint Charles, Il., U.S.	**216**	41.54 N	88.18 W
Saint Charles, Md., U.S.	**208**	38.36 N	76.56 W
Saint Charles, Mi., U.S.	**190**	43.17 N	84.08 W
Saint Charles, Mn., U.S.	**190**	43.58 N	92.03 W
Saint Charles, Mo., U.S.	**219**	38.47 N	90.28 W
Saint Charles □ 6	**219**	38.47 N	90.43 W
Saint-Charles ≃	**275a**	45.40 N	73.27 W
Saint-Charles, Lac ⊜	**206**	46.55 N	71.23 W
Saint-Charles-de-Drummond	**206**	45.54 N	72.28 W
Saint Charles Mesa	**198**	38.15 N	104.32 W
Saint-Charles-sur-Richelieu	**206**	45.41 N	73.11 W
Saint-Chef	**62**	45.38 N	5.22 E
Saint-Chély-d'Apcher	**32**	44.48 N	3.17 E
Saint-Chéron	**261**	48.33 N	2.07 E
Saint-Christophe-en-Bazelle	**50**	47.11 N	1.43 E
Saint-Christophe-Nevis → Saint Christopher-Nevis □ 1	**238**	17.20 N	62.45 W
Saint Christopher (Saint Kitts) I	**238**	17.20 N	62.45 W
Saint Christopher-Nevis □ 1, N.A.	**230**	17.20 N	62.45 W
Saint Christopher-Nevis □ 1, N.A.	**238**	17.20 N	62.45 W
Saint-Chrysostome	**206**	45.06 N	73.46 W
Saint-Ciers-sur-Gironde	**32**	45.18 N	0.37 W
Saint Clair, Mi., U.S.	**214**	42.48 N	82.29 W
Saint Clair, Mo., U.S.	**219**	38.20 N	90.58 W
Saint Clair, Pa., U.S.	**208**	40.43 N	76.11 W
Saint Clair, Pa., U.S.	**279b**	40.16 N	79.33 W
Saint Clair □ 6, Il., U.S.	**219**	38.31 N	90.00 W
Saint Clair □ 6, Mi., U.S.	**214**	42.50 N	82.42 W
Saint Clair ≃	**214**	42.37 N	82.31 W
Saint Clair, Lake ⊜	**214**	42.25 N	82.41 W
Saint Clair Beach	**281**	42.19 N	82.51 W
Saint Clair Flats	**214**	42.32 N	82.37 W
Saint Clair Flats ≡	**281**	42.35 N	82.36 W
Saint Clair Flats Canal ≊	**214**	42.20 N	82.58 W
Saint Clair Flats State Wildlife Area ◆ 4	**281**	42.36 N	82.40 W
Saint Clair Haven	**214**	42.34 N	82.47 W
Saint Clair Shores	**214**	42.29 N	82.53 W
Saint-Clair-sur-Epte	**50**	49.12 N	1.41 E
Saint Clairsville, Oh., U.S.	**214**	40.04 N	80.54 W
Saint Clairsville, Pa., U.S.	**214**	40.09 N	78.31 W
Saint Clair Tunnel ◆ 5	**214**	42.57 N	82.25 W
Saint-Claud	**32**	45.53 N	0.23 E
Saint-Claude, Mb., Can.	**184**	49.40 N	98.22 W
Saint-Claude, Fr.	**58**	46.23 N	5.52 E
Saint-Claude, Guad.	**241o**	16.02 N	61.42 W
Saint-Claude, Ruisseau ≃	**275a**	45.25 N	73.28 W
Saint Clears	**42**	51.50 N	4.30 W
Saint Clements	**212**	43.31 N	80.39 W
Saint Clements Bay c	**208**	38.17 N	76.42 W
Sainte-Clothilde	**206**	45.59 N	72.14 W
Sainte-Clotilde-de-Châteauguay	**206**	45.10 N	73.41 W
Saint-Cloud, Fr.	**50**	48.50 N	2.11 E
Saint Cloud, Fl., U.S.	**220**	28.14 N	81.16 W
Saint Cloud, Mn., U.S.	**190**	45.33 N	94.09 W
Saint-Cloud, Parc de ♠	**261**	48.50 N	2.13 E
Saint-Colomban-des-Villards	**62**	45.18 N	6.14 E
Sainte-Colombe	**58**	47.52 N	4.32 E
Saint Columb Major	**42**	50.26 N	5.03 W
Saint Combs	**46**	57.39 N	1.54 W
Saint-Constant	**206**	45.22 N	73.37 W
Saint-Cosme-en-Vairais	**50**	48.16 N	0.28 E
Sainte-Croix, P.Q., Can.	**206**	46.38 N	71.44 W
Sainte-Croix, Schw.	**58**	46.49 N	6.31 E
Saint Croix I	**241n**	17.45 N	64.45 W
Saint Croix ≃, N.A.	**186**	45.10 N	67.10 W
Saint Croix ≃, U.S.	**190**	44.45 N	92.49 W
Sainte-Croix-aux-Mines	**58**	48.16 N	7.13 E
Saint Croix Falls	**190**	45.24 N	92.38 W
Saint Croix Island I	**158**	33.48 S	25.45 E
Saint Croix Island National Monument ♠	**188**	45.08 N	67.08 W
Saint Croix National Scenic Riverway ♠	**190**	46.00 N	92.25 W
Saint Croix State Park ♠	**190**	46.00 N	92.40 W
Sainte-Croix-Vallée-Francaise	**62**	44.11 N	3.44 E
Saint-Cuthbert	**206**	46.09 N	73.14 W
Saint-Cyprien	**32**	44.52 N	1.02 E
Saint-Cyrille-de-Wendover	**206**	45.56 N	72.26 W
Saint-Cyr-L'École	**50**	48.48 N	2.04 E
Saint-Cyr-l'École, Aérodrome de ⊠	**261**	48.49 N	2.04 E
Saint Cyr Range ʎ	**180**	61.10 N	131.10 W
Sainte-Cyr-sous-Dourdan	**261**	48.34 N	2.02 E
Saint-Cyr-sur-Loire	**50**	47.24 N	0.40 E
Saint-Cyr-sur-Mer	**62**	43.11 N	5.43 E
Saint-Dalmas-de-Tende	**62**	44.03 N	7.35 E
Saint-Damien-de-Brandon	**206**	46.20 N	73.29 W
Saint David, Az., U.S.	**200**	31.54 N	110.12 W
Saint David, Il., U.S.	**190**	40.29 N	90.02 W
Saint David's, Nf., Can.	**186**	48.12 N	58.52 W
Saint Davids, On., Can.	**284a**	43.10 N	79.06 W
Saint David's, Wales, U.K.	**42**	51.54 N	5.16 W
Saint Davids, Pa., U.S.	**285**	40.02 N	75.22 W
Saint David's Cathedral ʋ 1	**42**	51.54 N	5.16 W
Saint David's Head ›	**42**	51.55 N	5.19 W
Saint David's Island I	**240a**	32.22 N	64.39 W
Saint Day	**42**	50.14 N	5.11 W
Saint-Denis, Fr.	**50**	48.56 N	2.22 E
Saint-Denis, Réu.	**157c**	20.52 S	55.28 E
Saint-Denis, Basilique ʋ 1	**261**	48.56 N	2.22 E
Saint-Denis-de-l'Hôtel	**50**	47.52 N	2.07 E
Saint-Denis-en-Bugey	**58**	45.57 N	5.20 E
Saint-Denis-Rivière-Richelieu	**206**	45.47 N	73.09 W
Saint Dennis	**42**	50.23 N	4.53 W
Saint-Didier-en-Velay	**62**	45.18 N	4.17 E
Saint-Didier-les-Bains	**62**	44.00 N	5.07 E
Saint-Dié	**58**	48.17 N	6.57 E
Saint-Disdier	**62**	44.44 N	5.54 E
Saint-Dizier	**58**	48.38 N	4.57 E
Saint Dogmaels	**42**	52.05 N	4.40 W
Saint-Donat-de-Montcalm	**206**	46.19 N	74.13 W
Saint-Donat-sur-l'Herbasse	**62**	45.07 N	5.00 E
Sainte-Dorothée ◆ 8	**275a**	45.32 N	73.49 W
Saint-Dyé-sur-Loire	**50**	47.39 N	1.29 E
Sainte → Saint			
Saint-Édouard-de-Maskinongé	**206**	46.20 N	73.09 W
Saint Edward	**198**	41.34 N	97.52 W
Saint-Égrève	**62**	45.14 N	5.41 E
Saint Eleanor's	**186**	46.25 N	63.49 W
Saint Elias, Cape ›	**180**	59.52 N	144.30 W
Saint Elias, Mount ʌ	**180**	60.18 N	140.55 W
Saint Elias Mountains ʎ	**180**	60.30 N	139.30 W
Saint-Élie	**250**	4.50 N	53.17 W
Saint Elmo	**219**	39.01 N	88.50 W
Saint-Éloi	**186**	48.02 N	69.14 W
Saint-Émile-de-Montcalm	**206**	46.06 N	74.00 W
Saint-Émile-de-Québec	**206**	46.52 N	71.20 W
Saint-Émile-de-Suffolk	**206**	45.56 N	74.55 W
Sainte-Enimie	**32**	44.22 N	3.26 E
Saint-Épain	**50**	47.08 N	0.32 E
Saintes, Bel.	**50**	50.42 N	4.10 E
Saintes, Fr.	**32**	45.45 N	0.38 W
Saintes, Îles des II	**241o**	15.52 N	61.37 W
Saint-Esprit ≃	**206**	45.52 N	73.27 W
Saint-Étienne	**62**	45.26 N	4.24 E
Saint-Étienne-de-Lugdarès	**62**	44.39 N	3.57 E
Saint-Étienne-de-Saint-Geoirs	**62**	45.20 N	5.21 E
Saint-Étienne-des-Grès	**206**	46.26 N	72.46 W
Saint-Étienne-de-Tinée	**62**	44.15 N	6.55 E
Saint-Étienne-du-Rouvray	**50**	49.23 N	1.06 E
Saint-Étienne-en-Dévoluy	**62**	44.42 N	5.56 E
Saint-Étienne-le-Laus	**62**	44.30 N	6.10 E
Saint-Étienne-les-Orgues	**62**	44.03 N	5.47 E
Saint-Étienne-lès-Remiremont	**58**	48.02 N	6.37 E
Saint-Eugène	**206**	45.30 N	74.28 W
Saint-Eustache	**206**	45.34 N	73.54 W
Saint-Evroult-Notre-Dame-du-Bois	**50**	48.48 N	0.28 E
Saint-Fabien	**186**	48.18 N	68.52 W
Saint Faith's	**158**	30.30 S	30.12 E
Saint-Fargeau	**50**	47.38 N	3.04 E
Saint-Fargeau-Ponthierry	**261**	48.33 N	2.32 E
Saint-Félicien, P.Q., Can.	**176**	48.39 N	72.26 W
Saint-Félicien, Fr.	**62**	45.05 N	4.38 E
Sainte-Félicité	**186**	48.54 N	67.20 W
Saint-Félix	**62**	45.48 N	5.58 E
Saint-Félix-de-Kingsey	**206**	45.48 N	72.12 W
Saint-Félix-de-Valois	**206**	46.10 N	73.26 W
Saint-Ferdinand (Bernierville)	**206**	46.06 N	71.34 W
Saintfield	**48**	54.28 N	5.50 W
Saint Fillans	**46**	56.23 N	4.07 W
Saint-Firmin	**62**	44.47 N	6.02 E
Saint-Firmin-sur-Loire	**50**	47.37 N	2.44 E
Saint-Flavien	**206**	46.31 N	71.36 W
Saint-Florent	**36**	42.41 N	9.18 E
Saint-Florentin	**50**	48.00 N	3.44 E
Saint-Florent-sur-Cher	**32**	46.59 N	2.15 E
Saint-Floris, Parc National ♠	**146**	9.40 N	21.35 E
Saint-Flour	**32**	45.02 N	3.05 E
Saint-Fons	**62**	45.42 N	4.52 E
Saint-Fortunat	**206**	45.58 N	71.36 W
Sainte-Foy	**206**	46.47 N	71.17 W
Sainte-Foy-la-Grande	**32**	44.50 N	0.13 E
Sainte-Foy-l'Argentière	**62**	45.42 N	4.28 E
Sainte-Foy-lès-Lyon	**62**	45.44 N	4.48 E
Sainte-Foy-Tarentaise	**62**	45.35 N	6.53 E
Saint Francis, Ks., U.S.	**198**	39.46 N	101.47 W
Saint Francis, S.D., U.S.	**198**	43.08 N	100.54 W
Saint Francis, Wi., U.S.	**216**	42.58 N	87.52 W
Saint Francis ≃, N.A.	**186**	47.10 N	68.57 W
Saint Francis ≃, U.S.	**194**	34.38 N	90.35 W
Saint Francis, Cape ›, Nf., Can.	**186**	47.50 N	52.47 W
Saint Francis, Cape ›, S. Afr.	**158**	34.14 S	24.49 E
Saint Francis, Lake ⊜	**206**	45.08 N	74.25 W
Saint Francis Bay c	**158**	34.35 S	25.10 E
Saint Francisville	**194**	30.46 N	91.22 W
Saint-François	**241o**	16.15 N	61.17 W
Saint-François ≃	**206**	46.07 N	72.55 W
Saint-François, Lac ⊜	**206**	45.55 N	71.10 W
Saint-François de Boundji	**152**	1.03 S	15.22 E
Saint-François-de-Laval ◆ 8	**275a**	45.40 N	73.34 W
Saint-François-du-Lac	**206**	46.04 N	72.50 W
Saint Francois Mountains ʎ 2	**194**	37.30 N	90.35 W
Saint-François-sur-Bugeon	**62**	45.24 N	6.21 E
Saint-Front	**62**	44.59 N	4.08 E
Saint-Gabriel	**206**	46.17 N	73.23 W
Saint-Gabriel-de-Gaspé	**186**	48.31 N	64.32 W
Saint-Gabriel-de-Rimouski	**186**	48.25 N	68.10 W
Saint-Gall → Sankt Gallen	**58**	47.25 N	9.23 E
Saint-Galmier	**62**	45.35 N	4.19 E
Sainte-Gauburge-Sainte-Colombe	**50**	48.42 N	0.26 E
Saint-Gaudens	**32**	43.07 N	0.44 E
Saint-Gaudens National Historic Site ⊥	**188**	43.29 N	72.19 W
Saint-Gaultier	**32**	46.38 N	1.25 E
Saint-Gély-du-Fesc	**62**	43.42 N	3.48 E
Saint-Genest-Lerpt	**62**	45.27 N	4.20 E
Saint-Genest-Malifaux	**62**	45.20 N	4.25 E
Sainte-Geneviève, P.Q., Can.	**275a**	45.29 N	73.52 W
Sainte Genevieve, Mo., U.S.	**194**	37.59 N	90.03 W
Sainte-Geneviève-de-Batiscan	**206**	46.32 N	72.20 W
Sainte-Geneviève-des-Bois	**50**	48.38 N	2.20 E
Saint-Gengoux-le-National	**58**	46.37 N	4.39 E
Saint-Genis-de-Saintonge	**32**	45.29 N	0.34 W
Saint-Genis-Laval	**62**	45.41 N	4.48 E
Saint-Genis-Pouilly	**58**	46.15 N	6.01 E
Saint-Genix-sur-Guiers	**62**	45.36 N	5.38 E
Saint-Geoire-en-Valdaine	**62**	45.27 N	5.38 E
Saint George, Austl.	**166**	28.02 S	148.35 E
Saint George, Ber.	**240a**	32.22 N	64.40 W
Saint George, N.B., Can.	**186**	45.08 N	66.49 W
Saint George, On., Can.	**212**	43.15 N	80.15 W
Saint George, Pa., U.S.	**214**	41.15 N	79.47 W
Saint George, S.C., U.S.	**192**	33.11 N	80.34 W
Saint George, Ut., U.S.	**200**	37.06 N	113.34 W
Saint George ◆ 8	**276**	40.39 N	74.05 W
Saint George, Cape ›, Nf., Can.	**186**	48.27 N	59.15 W
Saint George, Cape ›, Pap. N. Gui.	**164**	4.52 S	152.52 E
Saint George, Cape ›, Fl., U.S.	**192**	29.35 N	85.04 W
Saint George, Point ›	**204**	41.47 N	124.15 W
Saint George Island, Ak., U.S.	**180**	56.36 N	169.32 W
Saint George Island, Md., U.S.	**208**	38.07 N	76.29 W
Saint George Island I, Ak., U.S.	**180**	56.35 N	169.35 W
Saint George Island I, Fl., U.S.	**192**	29.39 N	84.55 W
Saint George's, Nf., Can.	**186**	48.26 N	58.29 W
Saint-Georges, P.Q., Can.	**188**	46.07 N	70.40 W
Saint-Georges, P.Q., Can.	**206**	46.37 N	72.40 W
Saint-Georges, Fr.	**58**	48.40 N	6.56 E
Saint George's, Gren.	**241k**	12.03 N	61.45 W
Saint-Georges, Guy. fr.	**250**	3.54 N	51.48 W
Saint Georges, De., U.S.	**208**	39.33 N	75.39 W
Saint Georges Basin c	**170**	35.07 S	150.36 E
Saint George's Bay c, Nf., Can.	**186**	48.20 N	59.00 W
Saint Georges Bay c, N.S., Can.	**186**	45.50 N	61.45 W
Saint George's Channel ɰ, Europe	**28**	52.00 N	6.00 W
Saint George's Channel ɰ, Pap. N. Gui.	**164**	4.30 S	152.30 E
Saint-Georges-de-Reneins	**58**	46.04 N	4.43 E
Saint-Georges-de-Windsor	**206**	45.42 N	71.50 W
Saint-Georges-en-Couzan	**62**	45.42 N	3.56 E
Saint Georges Head ›	**170**	35.12 S	150.42 E
Saint George's Island I	**240a**	32.22 N	64.40 W
Saint George Sound ɰ	**192**	29.47 N	84.42 W
Saint-Gérard, Bel.	**56**	50.21 N	4.45 E
Saint-Gérard, P.Q., Can.	**206**	45.46 N	71.25 W
Saint-Germain	**32**	48.54 N	2.05 E
Saint-Germain ≃	**206**	45.55 N	72.30 W
Saint-Germain, Forêt de ♠	**261**	48.55 N	2.05 E
Saint-Germain-de-Calberte	**62**	44.13 N	3.48 E
Saint-Germain-de-Grantham	**206**	45.50 N	72.34 W
Saint-Germain-de-Joux	**58**	46.11 N	5.44 E
Saint-Germain-des-Champs	**50**	47.25 N	3.55 E
Saint-Germain-du-Bois	**58**	46.45 N	5.15 E
Saint-Germain-du-Plain	**58**	46.42 N	4.58 E
Saint-Germain-en-Laye	**50**	48.54 N	2.05 E
Saint-Germain-en-Laye, Château de ⊥	**261**	48.54 N	2.06 E
Saint-Germain-Laval	**62**	45.50 N	4.01 E
Saint-Germain-Laxis	**261**	48.35 N	2.43 E
Saint-Germain-Lembron	**32**	45.28 N	3.14 E
Saint-Germain-lès-Arlay	**58**	46.46 N	5.34 E
Saint-Germain-lès-Corbeil	**261**	48.37 N	2.29 E
Saint-Germain-l'Herm	**32**	45.28 N	3.33 E
Saint-Germain-sur-Morin	**261**	48.53 N	2.51 E
Saint Germans	**42**	50.24 N	4.18 W
Saint-Germer-de-Fly	**50**	49.27 N	1.47 E
Saint-Gervais-d'Auvergne	**32**	46.02 N	2.49 E
Saint-Gervais-les-Bains	**62**	45.54 N	6.43 E
Saint-Gervasy	**62**	43.53 N	4.29 E
Saint-Géry	**32**	44.29 N	1.35 E
Saint-Gilles, Bel.	**50**	50.49 N	4.20 E
Saint-Gilles, P.Q., Can.	**206**	46.31 N	71.22 W
Saint-Gilles, Fr.	**62**	43.41 N	4.26 E
Saint-Gilles-Croix-de-Vie	**32**	46.42 N	1.57 W
Saint-Gingolph	**58**	46.24 N	6.52 E
Saint-Girons	**32**	42.59 N	1.09 E
Saint-Gobain	**50**	49.36 N	3.23 E
Saint Gotthard Pass → San Gottardo, Passo del)(	**58**	46.33 N	8.34 E
Saint Govan's Head ›	**42**	51.36 N	4.55 W
Saint-Gratien	**261**	48.58 N	2.17 E
Saint-Grégoire (Larochelle)	**206**	46.16 N	72.30 W
Saint Gregory, Mount ʌ	**186**	49.19 N	58.13 W
Saint-Guénolé	**32**	47.49 N	4.20 W
Saint-Guillaume-d'Upton	**206**	45.53 N	72.46 W
Saint-Héand	**62**	45.31 N	4.22 E
Saint Helena	**226**	38.30 N	122.28 W
Saint Helena □ 2	**10**	15.57 S	5.42 W
Saint Helena, Mount ʌ	**226**	38.40 N	122.38 W
Saint Helena Sound ɰ	**192**	32.27 N	80.25 W
Sainte-Hélène, Île I	**275a**	45.31 N	73.32 W
Sainte-Hélène-de-Bagot	**206**	45.44 N	72.44 W
Saint Helens, Austl.	**166**	41.20 S	148.15 E
Saint Helens, Eng., U.K.	**42**	50.42 N	1.06 W
Saint Helens, Eng., U.K.	**44**	53.28 N	2.44 W
Saint Helens, Or., U.S.	**224**	45.51 N	122.48 W
Saint Helens □ 8	**262**	53.28 N	2.45 W
Saint Helens, Mount ʌ 1	**224**	46.12 N	122.11 W
Saint Helens Canal ≊	**262**	53.27 N	2.42 W
Saint Helier	**43b**	49.12 N	2.37 W
Saint Henry	**216**	40.25 N	84.38 W
Sainte-Hermine	**32**	46.33 N	1.04 W
Sainthia	**126**	23.57 N	87.40 E
Saint-Hilaire-du-Harcouët	**32**	48.35 N	1.06 W
Saint-Hilarion	**261**	48.37 N	1.44 E
Saint-Hippolyte, Fr.	**58**	47.19 N	6.49 E
Saint-Hippolyte, Fr.	**62**	43.38 N	4.45 E
Saint-Hippolyte-de-Kilkenny	**206**	45.56 N	74.01 W
Saint-Hippolyte-du-Fort	**62**	43.58 N	3.51 E
Saint-Honorat, Mont ʌ	**62**	44.05 N	6.46 E
Saint-Hubert, Bel.	**56**	50.01 N	5.23 E

	English	Deutsch	Español	Français	Português
≃	River	Fluss	Río	Rivière	Rio
≊	Canal	Kanal	Canal	Canal	Canal
ʟ	Waterfall, Rapids	Wasserfall, Stromschnellen	Cascada, Rápidos	Chute d'eau, Rapides	Cascata, Rápidos
ɰ	Strait	Meeresstrasse	Estrecho	Détroit	Estreito
c	Bay, Gulf	Bucht, Golf	Bahía, Golfo	Baie, Golfe	Baía, Golfo
⊜	Lake, Lakes	See, Seen	Lago, Lagos	Lac, Lacs	Lago, Lagos
≡	Swamp	Sumpf	Pantano	Marais	Pântano
⊓	Ice Features, Glacier	Eis- und Gletscherformen	Accidentes Glaciales	Formes glaciaires	Acidentes glaciares
⍑	Other Hydrographic Features	Andere Hydrographische Objekte	Otros Elementos Hidrográficos	Autres données hydrographiques	Outros acidentes hidrográficos
✢	Submarine Features	Untermeerische Objekte	Accidentes Submarinos	Formes de relief sous-marin	Acidentes submarinos
□	Political Unit	Politische Einheit	Unidad Politica	Entité politique	Unidade política
ʋ	Cultural Institution	Kulturelle Institution	Institución Cultural	Institution culturelle	Instituição cultural
⊥	Historical Site	Historische Stätte	Sitio Histórico	Site historique	Sitio histórico
♠	Recreational Site	Erholungs- und Ferienort	Sitio de Recreo	Centre de loisirs	Area de Lazer
⊠	Airport	Flughafen	Aeropuerto	Aéroport	Aeroporto
■	Military Installation	Militäranlage	Instalación Militar	Installation militaire	Instalação militar
◆	Miscellaneous	Verschiedenes	Misceláneo	Divers	Diversos

ENGLISH — Name · Page · Lat.°′ · Long.°′ | **DEUTSCH** — Name · Seite · Breite°′ · Länge°′ E = Ost

Name	Page	Lat.°′	Long.°′
Saint-Hubert, P.Q., Can.	206	45.30 N	73.25 W
Saint-Hubert, Étang de ⊜	261	48.43 N	1.51 E
Saint-Hubert-le-Roi	261	48.43 N	1.52 E
Saint-Hugues	206	45.48 N	72.52 W
Saint-Hyacinthe	206	45.37 N	72.57 W
Saint-Hyacinthe □[6]	206	45.40 N	73.05 W
Saint-Ignace, N.B., Can.	186	46.42 N	65.05 W
Saint Ignace, Mi., U.S.	190	45.52 N	84.43 W
Saint Ignace Island I	190	48.48 N	87.55 W
Saint Ignatius, Guy.	246	3.20 N	59.47 W
Saint Ignatius, Mt., U.S.	202	47.19 N	114.05 W
Saint-Imier	58	47.09 N	7.00 E
Saint-Imier, Vallon de V	58	47.10 N	7.00 E
Saint-Isidore	186	47.33 N	65.03 W
Saint-Isidore-d'Auckland	206	45.16 N	71.31 W
Saint-Isidore-de-Laprairie	275a	45.18 N	73.41 W
Saint Ives, Austl.	274a	33.44 S	151.10 E
Saint Ives, Eng., U.K.	32	50.12 N	5.29 W
Saint Ives, Eng., U.K.	42	52.20 N	0.05 W
Saint Ives Bay c	42	50.14 N	5.28 W
Saint Jacob	219	38.43 N	89.46 W
Saint Jacobs	212	43.32 N	80.33 W
Saint-Jacques	206	45.57 N	73.34 W
Saint-Jacques ≃	275a	45.26 N	73.29 W
Saint James, Il., U.S.	219	38.57 N	88.51 W
Saint James, Mi., U.S.	190	45.45 N	85.30 W
Saint James, Mn., U.S.	198	43.58 N	94.37 W
Saint James, Mo., U.S.	194	37.59 N	91.36 W
Saint James, N.Y., U.S.	210	40.52 N	73.09 W
Saint James, Cape ≻	182	51.56 N	131.01 W
Saint James City	220	26.29 N	82.04 W
Saint James Islands II	240m	18.19 N	64.50 W
Saint James Palace ✤	260	51.30 N	0.08 W
Saint-Janvier	275a	45.43 N	73.56 W
Saint-Jean □[6]	206	45.15 N	73.20 W
Saint-Jean ≃, P.Q., Can.	186	48.46 N	64.26 W
Saint-Jean ≃, P.Q., Can.	186	50.17 N	64.20 W
Saint-Jean, Île I	275a	45.41 N	73.39 W
Saint-Jean, Lac ⊜	176	48.35 N	72.05 W
Saint-Jean, Rapides de ⌊	275a	45.19 N	73.15 W
Saint-Jean Airport ⊠	275a	45.18 N	73.17 W
Saint-Jean-aux-Bois	50	49.21 N	2.55 E
Saint-Jean-Baptiste	184	49.16 N	97.21 W
Saint-Jean-Baptiste-de-Rouville	206	45.31 N	73.07 W
Saint-Jean-Cap-Ferrat	62	43.41 N	7.20 E
Saint-Jean-d'Angély	32	45.57 N	0.31 W
Saint-Jean-d'Assé	50	48.09 N	0.07 E
Saint-Jean-de-Bournay	62	45.29 N	5.08 E
Saint-Jean-de-Braye	50	47.54 N	1.58 E
Saint-Jean-de-la-Ruelle	50	47.55 N	1.52 E
Saint-Jean-de-Losne	58	47.06 N	5.15 E
Saint-Jean-de-Luz	32	43.23 N	1.40 W
Saint-Jean-de-Maurienne	62	45.17 N	6.21 E
Saint-Jean-de-Monts	32	46.48 N	2.03 W
Saint-Jean-des-Piles	206	46.41 N	72.45 W
Saint-Jean-du-Gard	62	44.06 N	3.53 E
Saint-Jean-en-Royans	62	45.01 N	5.18 E
Saint-Jean-Pied-de-Port	32	43.10 N	1.14 W
Saint-Jean-Port-Joli	186	47.13 N	70.16 W
Saint-Jean-Soleymieux	62	45.30 N	4.02 E
Saint-Jean-sur-Richelieu	206	45.19 N	73.16 W
Saint-Jeoire	58	46.09 N	6.28 E
Saint-Jérôme	206	45.47 N	74.00 W
Saint Jo	196	33.41 N	97.31 W
Saint Joachim	214	42.16 N	82.38 W
Saint Joe	216	41.18 N	84.54 W
Saint Joe ≃	202	47.21 N	116.42 W
Saint John, N.B., Can.	186	45.16 N	66.03 W
Saint John, Jersey	43b	49.15 N	2.08 W
Saint John, In., U.S.	216	41.27 N	87.28 W
Saint John, Ks., U.S.	198	38.00 N	98.45 W
Saint John, N.D., U.S.	198	48.56 N	99.42 W
Saint John, Wa., U.S.	202	47.05 N	117.34 W
Saint John I	240m	18.20 N	64.45 W
Saint John ≃, Liber.	150	6.40 N	9.10 W
Saint John ≃, N.A.	186	45.15 N	66.04 W
Saint John, Cape ≻	186	50.00 N	55.32 W
Saint John, Lake ⊜, Nf., Can.	186	48.23 N	54.41 W
Saint John, Lake ⊜, On., Can.	212	44.41 N	79.20 W
Saint John Bay c	186	50.54 N	57.08 W
Saint John Island I	186	50.49 N	57.14 W
Saint Johns, Antig.	240c	17.06 N	61.51 W
Saint John's, Nf., Can.	186	47.34 N	52.43 W
Saint Johns → Saint-Jean-sur-Richelieu	206	45.19 N	73.16 W
Saint John's, I. of Man	44	54.13 N	4.38 W
Saint Johns, Az., U.S.	200	34.30 N	109.21 W
Saint Johns, Mi., U.S.	216	43.00 N	84.33 W
Saint Johns, Mo., U.S.	219	38.42 N	90.20 W
Saint Johns, Oh., U.S.	216	40.33 N	84.05 W
Saint Johns ≃, Ca., U.S.	226	36.25 N	119.25 W
Saint Johns ≃, Fl., U.S.	192	30.24 N	81.24 W
Saint Johnsburg	210	43.05 N	78.53 W
Saint Johnsbury	188	44.25 N	72.00 W
Saint Johns Creek ≃	219	38.34 N	91.01 W
Saint John's Jerusalem ⊥	260	51.25 N	0.14 E
Saint Johns Marsh ≋	220	27.45 N	80.40 W
Saint John's Point ≻	44	54.13 N	5.40 W
Saint John's University ✤[2]	276	40.43 N	73.48 W
Saint Johnsville	210	42.59 N	74.41 W
Saint Joseph, N.B., Can.	186	45.59 N	64.34 W
Saint Joseph, Dom.	240d	15.26 N	61.26 W
Saint-Joseph, Mart.	240e	14.40 N	61.03 W
Saint-Joseph, N. Cal.	175f	20.27 S	166.36 E
Saint-Joseph, Réu.	157c	21.22 S	55.36 E
Saint Joseph, Il., U.S.	194	40.06 N	88.02 W
Saint Joseph, La., U.S.	194	31.55 N	91.14 W
Saint Joseph, Mi., U.S.	216	42.05 N	86.29 W
Saint Joseph, Mn., U.S.	190	45.33 N	94.19 W
Saint Joseph, Mo., U.S.	194	39.46 N	94.50 W
Saint Joseph, Tn., U.S.	194	35.02 N	87.30 W
Saint Joseph □[6], In., U.S.	216	41.41 N	86.15 W
Saint Joseph □[6], Mi., U.S.	216	41.55 N	85.31 W
Saint Joseph ≃, U.S.	216	42.07 N	86.29 W
Saint Joseph ≃, U.S.	216	41.05 N	85.08 W
Saint Joseph, East Branch ≃	216	41.39 N	84.34 W
Saint-Joseph, Île I	275a	45.41 N	73.42 W
Saint-Joseph, Lac ⊜	206	46.54 N	71.38 W
Saint Joseph, Lake ⊜	176	51.05 N	90.35 W
Saint Joseph, West Branch ≃	216	41.39 N	84.34 W
Saint Joseph Bay c	192	29.47 N	85.21 W
Saint Joseph Channel ʊ	190	46.19 N	84.04 W
Saint-Joseph-d'Alma → Alma	186	48.33 N	71.39 W
Saint-Joseph-de-Beauce	186	46.18 N	70.53 W
Saint-Joseph-de-Mékinac	206	46.55 N	72.42 W
Saint-Joseph-de-Sorel	206	46.02 N	73.07 W
Saint-Joseph-du-Lac	275a	45.32 N	74.00 W
Saint Joseph Island I	190	46.13 N	83.57 W
Saint Joseph's University ✤[2]	285	40.00 N	75.14 W
Saint-Jouin-Bruneval	50	49.39 N	0.10 E
Saint-Jovite	206	46.07 N	74.36 W
Sainte-Julie	206	45.35 N	73.19 W
Saint-Julien	58	46.23 N	5.27 E
Saint-Julien-Chapteuil	62	45.02 N	4.04 E
Saint-Julien-du-Sault	50	48.02 N	3.18 E
Saint-Julien-du-Verdon	62	43.55 N	6.32 E
Saint-Julien-en-Beauchêne	62	44.37 N	5.42 E
Saint-Julien-en-Born	32	44.04 N	1.14 W
Saint-Julien-en-Genevois	58	46.08 N	6.05 E
Saint-Julien-en-Jarez	62	45.28 N	4.31 E
Saint-Julien-les-Villas	50	48.16 N	4.06 E
Saint-Julien-Molin-Molette	62	45.19 N	4.37 E
Sainte-Julienne	206	45.58 N	73.43 W
Saint-Junien	32	45.53 N	0.54 E
Saint Just, P.R.	240m	18.23 N	66.00 W
Saint Just, Eng., U.K.	42	50.07 N	5.42 W
Saint-Just-en-Chaussée	50	49.30 N	2.26 E
Saint-Just-en-Chevalet	32	45.55 N	3.50 E
Saint-Justin	206	46.15 N	73.05 W
Saint-Just-Malmont	62	45.20 N	4.19 E
Saint-Just-sur-Loire	62	45.29 N	4.16 E
Saint Keverne	42	50.03 N	5.06 W
Saint Kilda, Austl.	168b	34.44 S	138.32 E
Saint Kilda, Austl.	169	37.52 S	144.59 E
Saint Kilda, N.Z.	172	45.54 S	170.30 E
Saint Kilda I	28	57.49 N	8.36 W
Saint Kitts → Saint Christopher I	238	17.20 N	62.45 W
Saint-Lambert, P.Q., Can.	206	45.30 N	73.30 W
Saint-Lambert, Fr.	261	48.44 N	2.01 E
Saint Landry	194	30.50 N	92.15 W
Saint-Laurent, Mb., Can.	184	50.24 N	97.56 W
Saint-Laurent, P.Q., Can.	206	45.30 N	73.40 W
Saint-Laurent, Fr.	58	48.09 N	6.27 E
Saint-Laurent → Saint Lawrence ≃	176	49.30 N	67.00 W
Saint-Laurent-Blangy	50	50.18 N	2.48 E
Saint-Laurent-de-Chamousset	62	45.44 N	4.28 E
Saint-Laurent-du-Maroni	250	5.30 N	54.02 W
Saint-Laurent du Maroni □[8]	250	4.00 N	53.30 W
Saint-Laurent-du-Pont	62	45.23 N	5.44 E
Saint-Laurent-du-Var	62	43.40 N	7.11 E
Saint-Laurent-en-Caux	50	49.45 N	0.53 E
Saint-Laurent-en-Grandvaux	58	46.35 N	5.57 E
Saint-Laurent-et-Benon	32	45.09 N	0.49 W
Saint-Laurent-les-Bains	62	44.37 N	3.58 E
Saint-Laurent-sur-Saône	58	46.18 N	4.50 E
Saint Lawrence, Austl.	166	22.21 S	149.31 E
Saint Lawrence, Nf., Can.	186	46.55 N	55.24 W
Saint Lawrence □[6]	212	44.30 N	75.27 W
Saint Lawrence ≃	176	49.30 N	67.00 W
Saint Lawrence, Cape ≻	186	47.03 N	60.37 W
Saint Lawrence, Gulf of c	186	48.00 N	62.00 W
Saint Lawrence, Lake ⊜	206	44.56 N	75.04 W
Saint Lawrence Island I	180	63.30 N	170.30 W
Saint Lawrence Islands National Park ♠	212	44.18 N	76.08 W
Saint-Lawrence Seaway ≊	275a	45.43 N	73.25 W
Saint-Lazare	184	50.26 N	101.16 W
Saint-Lazare ◆[5]	261	48.53 N	2.20 E
Saint-Léandre	186	48.44 N	67.36 W
Saint-Léger-en-Yvelines	261	48.43 N	1.46 E
Saint-Léger-sur-Dheune	58	46.51 N	4.38 E
Saint Leo	220	28.20 N	82.15 W
Saint Leon	218	39.17 N	84.57 W
Saint-Léonard, N.B., Can.	186	47.10 N	67.56 W
Saint-Léonard, P.Q., Can.	206	45.35 N	73.35 W
Saint Leonard, Md., U.S.	208	38.28 N	76.30 W
Saint-Léonard-d'Aston	206	46.06 N	72.22 W
Saint-Léonard-de-Noblat	32	45.50 N	1.29 E
Saint Leonards, Eng., U.K.	42	50.51 N	0.34 E
Saint Leonards, Eng., U.K.	42	50.49 N	1.51 W
Saint-Leu-d'Esserent	50	49.13 N	2.25 E
Saint-Leu-la-Forêt	50	49.01 N	2.15 E
Saint-Liboire	206	45.39 N	72.46 W
Saint-Lô	32	49.07 N	1.05 W
Saint-Louis, Sk., Can.	184	52.56 N	105.49 W
Saint-Louis, Fr.	58	47.35 N	7.34 E
Saint-Louis, Guad.	241o	15.57 N	61.19 W
Saint-Louis, Réu.	157c	21.16 S	55.25 E
Saint-Louis, Sén.	150	16.02 N	16.30 W
Saint Louis, Mi., U.S.	190	43.24 N	84.36 W
Saint Louis, Mo., U.S.	219	38.37 N	90.11 W
Saint Louis, Tx., U.S.	222	32.18 N	95.20 W
Saint Louis □[6]	219	38.39 N	90.25 W
Saint-Louis ≃, P.Q., Can.	275a	45.19 N	73.53 W
Saint Louis ≃, U.S.	190	46.45 N	92.06 W
Saint-Louis, Baie de c	241o	15.57 N	61.20 W
Saint-Louis, Lac ⊜	206	45.24 N	73.48 W
Saint-Louis, Pointe ≻	275a	45.19 N	73.53 W
Saint Louis Crossing	218	39.19 N	85.51 W
Saint-Louis-de-Champlain	206	46.25 N	72.36 W
Saint-Louis-de-Kent	186	46.44 N	64.58 W
Saint Louis Park	190	44.56 N	93.20 W
Saint Louisville	214	40.10 N	82.25 W
Saint-Loup-sur-Aujon	58	47.53 N	5.05 E
Saint-Loup-sur-Semouse	58	47.53 N	6.16 E
Saint-Luc, P.Q., Can.	206	45.22 N	73.18 W
Saint-Luc, Schw.	58	46.13 N	7.36 E
Sainte-Luce	240e	14.28 N	60.56 W
Saint Lucia □[1], N.A.	230	13.53 N	60.58 W
Saint Lucia □[1], N.A.	241f	13.53 N	60.58 W
Saint Lucia, Cape ≻	158	28.25 S	32.25 E
Saint Lucia, Lake ⊜	158	28.05 S	32.26 E
Saint Lucia Channel ʊ	238	14.09 N	60.57 W
Saint Lucia Estuary	158	28.22 S	32.25 E
Saint Lucia Game Reserve ◆[4]	158	28.10 S	32.28 E
Sainte-Lucie, Fr.	36	41.42 N	9.22 E
Saint Lucie, Fl., U.S.	220	27.29 N	80.20 W
Saint Lucie □[6]	220	27.23 N	80.26 W
Saint Lucie Canal ≊	220	27.10 N	80.15 W
Saint Lucie Inlet c	220	27.10 N	80.10 W
Saint Lucie Lock ◆[5]	220	27.07 N	80.17 W
Saint-Lucien	261	48.39 N	1.38 E
Saint-Lupicin	58	46.24 N	5.47 E
Sainte-Magnance	50	47.27 N	4.04 E
Saint Magnus Bay c	46a	60.24 N	1.34 W
Saint Magnus Cathedral ✤[1]	46	58.58 N	2.57 W
Saint-Malo, P.Q., Can.	206	45.12 N	71.30 W
Saint-Malo, Fr.	32	48.39 N	2.01 W
Saint-Malo, Golfe de c	32	48.45 N	2.00 W
Saint-Mamert-du-Gard	62	43.53 N	4.12 E
Saint-Mammès	50	48.23 N	2.49 E
Saint-Mandé	261	48.50 N	2.25 E
Saint-Mandrier-sur-Mer	62	43.04 N	5.56 E
Saint-Marc	238	19.07 N	72.42 W
Saint-Marc, Canal de ʊ	238	18.50 N	72.45 W
Saint-Marc-des-Carrières	206	46.41 N	72.03 W
Saint-Marcel	58	46.47 N	4.54 E
Saint-Marcellin	62	45.09 N	5.19 E
Saint-Marcelline-de-Kildare	206	46.07 N	73.36 W
Saint-Marc-sur-Richelieu	275a	45.41 N	73.12 W
Saint-Mard	261	49.02 N	2.42 E
Saint Margaret Bay c	186	51.01 N	56.58 W
Saint Margaret's at Cliffe	42	51.09 N	1.24 E
Saint Margarets Bay c	186	44.35 N	64.00 W
Saint Margaret's Hope	46	58.49 N	2.57 W
Sainte-Marguerite ≃	176	50.09 N	66.36 W
Sainte-Marguerite, Baie c	186	50.06 N	66.36 W
Sainte-Marguerite-sur-Mer	50	49.55 N	0.57 E
Sainte-Marie	240e	14.47 N	61.00 W
Sainte-Marie, Cap ≻	157b	25.36 S	45.08 E
Sainte-Marie-aux-Mines (Markirch)	58	48.15 N	7.11 E
Saint Maries	202	47.18 N	116.33 W
Saint Maries ≃	202	47.19 N	116.33 W
Saint-Marin → San Marino □[1]	66	43.56 N	12.25 E
Saint Marks, S. Afr.	158	32.01 S	27.22 E
Saint Marks, Fl., U.S.	192	30.09 N	84.12 W
Saint Marks ≃	192	30.08 N	84.12 W
Sainte-Marthe-de-Gaspé	186	49.12 N	66.10 W
Sainte-Marthe-sur-le-Lac	275a	45.32 N	73.56 W
Saint-Martin (Sint Maarten) I	238	18.04 N	63.04 W
Saint-Martin, Cap ≻	240e	14.52 N	61.13 W
Saint Martin, Lake ⊜	184	51.37 N	98.29 W
Saint-Martin-Boulogne	50	50.43 N	1.38 E
Saint-Martin-d'Ardèche	62	44.18 N	4.35 E
Saint-Martin-d'Auxigny	50	47.12 N	2.25 E
Saint-Martin-de-Belleville	62	45.23 N	6.30 E
Saint-Martin-de-Bossenay	50	48.26 N	3.41 E
Saint-Martin-de-Bréthencourt	261	48.31 N	1.56 E
Saint-Martin-de-Crau	62	43.38 N	4.49 E
Saint-Martin-de-Londres	62	43.47 N	3.44 E
Saint-Martin-de-Nigelles	261	48.37 N	1.37 E
Saint-Martin-d'Entraunes	62	44.08 N	6.46 E
Saint-Martin-des-Champs	261	48.53 N	1.43 E
Saint-Martin-de-Valamas	62	44.56 N	4.22 E
Saint-Martin-d'Hères	62	45.10 N	5.46 E
Saint-Martin-du-Puy	50	47.20 N	3.52 E
Saint-Martin-du-Tertre	261	49.06 N	2.21 E
Saint-Martin-du-Var	62	43.49 N	7.12 E
Sainte-Martine	206	45.15 N	73.48 W
Saint-Martin-en-Bresse	58	46.49 N	5.04 E
Saint-Martin-la-Garenne	261	49.02 N	1.41 E
Saint-Martin-la-Plaine	62	45.32 N	4.36 E
Saint Martins, N.B., Can.	186	45.21 N	65.32 W
Saint Martin's, Eng., U.K.	42	52.55 N	2.59 W
Saint Martin's I	42a	49.58 N	6.20 W
Saint Martins Keys II	220	28.47 N	82.44 W
Saint-Martin-Vésubie	62	44.04 N	7.15 E
Saint Martinville	194	30.07 N	91.49 W
Saint Mary	194	37.52 N	89.58 W
Saint Mary ≃, B.C., Can.	182	49.37 N	115.38 W
Saint Mary ≃, N.A.	182	49.37 N	112.52 W
Saint Mary, Cape ≻	150	13.28 N	16.40 W
Saint Mary, Mount ∧	164	8.10 S	147.00 E
Saint Mary Bourne	42	51.16 N	1.24 W
Saint Mary Cray ◆[8]	260	51.23 N	0.07 E
Saint Mary Lake ⊜	202	48.40 N	113.30 W
Saint Marylebone ◆[8]	260	51.31 N	0.10 W
Saint Mary of the Lake Seminary ✤[2]	278	42.17 N	88.00 W
Saint Mary Peak ∧	166	31.30 S	138.33 E
Saint Mary Reservoir ⊜[1]	182	49.19 N	113.12 W
Saint Marys, Austl.	166	41.35 S	148.10 E
Saint Marys, Austl.	170	33.47 S	150.47 E
Saint Mary's, Nf., Can.	186	46.55 N	53.34 W
Saint Mary's, On., Can.	212	43.16 N	81.08 W
Saint Marys, Ak., U.S.	180	62.04 N	163.10 W
Saint Marys, Ga., U.S.	192	30.43 N	81.32 W
Saint Marys, Ks., U.S.	198	39.11 N	96.04 W
Saint Marys, Oh., U.S.	216	40.32 N	84.23 W
Saint Marys, Pa., U.S.	214	41.25 N	78.33 W
Saint Marys, W.V., U.S.	188	39.23 N	81.12 W
Saint Marys □[6]	208	38.17 N	76.38 W
Saint Mary's I	42a	49.55 N	6.18 W
Saint Marys ≃, N.S., Can.	186	45.02 N	61.54 W
Saint Marys ≃, N.A.	190	45.58 N	83.54 W
Saint Marys ≃, U.S.	192	30.43 N	81.27 W
Saint Marys ≃, U.S.	216	41.05 N	85.08 W
Saint Marys ≃, Md., U.S.	208	38.06 N	76.26 W
Saint Mary's, Cape ≻, Nf., Can.	186	46.49 N	54.12 W
Saint Marys, Cape ≻, N.S., Can.	186	44.05 N	66.13 W
Saint Marys, North Prong ≃	192	30.22 N	82.06 W
Saint Marys, South Prong ≃	192	30.22 N	82.06 W
Saint Mary's Bay	42	51.00 N	0.58 E
Saint Mary's Bay c, Nf., Can.	186	46.50 N	53.47 W
Saint Marys Bay c, N.S., Can.	186	44.25 N	66.10 W
Saint Marys City	208	38.11 N	76.26 W
Saint Mary's Hoo	260	51.28 N	0.36 E
Saint Marys Lake ⊜	278	42.17 N	87.59 W
Saint Mary's Marshes ≋	260	51.28 N	0.35 E
Saint-Mathieu	32	45.42 N	0.46 E
Saint-Mathieu, Pointe de ≻	32	48.20 N	4.46 W
Saint-Mathieu-de-Laprairie	275a	45.19 N	73.31 W
Saint Matthew Island I	180	60.30 N	172.45 W
Saint Matthews, Ky., U.S.	218	38.15 N	85.39 W
Saint Matthews, S.C., U.S.	192	33.39 N	80.46 W
Saint Matthias Group II	164	1.30 S	149.40 E
Saint-Maur-des-Fossés	50	48.48 N	2.30 E
Sainte-Maure-de-Touraine	32	47.07 N	0.37 E
Saint-Maurice, Fr.	261	48.49 N	2.25 E
Saint-Maurice, Schw.	58	46.13 N	7.00 E
Saint-Maurice □[6]	206	46.35 N	73.00 W
Saint-Maurice ≃	176	46.21 N	72.31 W
Saint-Maurice, Parc de ♠	206	46.52 N	73.10 W
Saint-Maurice-en-Montagne	58	46.34 N	5.50 E
Saint-Maurice-Montcouronne	261	48.35 N	2.07 E
Saint Mawes	42	50.09 N	5.01 W
Saint Mawgan	42	50.28 N	4.58 W
Saint-Max	58	48.42 N	6.13 E
Sainte-Maxime	62	43.18 N	6.38 E
Saint-Maximin-la-Sainte-Baume	62	43.27 N	5.52 E
Saint-Méen-le-Grand	32	48.11 N	2.12 W
Saint Meinrad	194	38.10 N	86.48 W
Sainte-Menehould	56	49.05 N	4.54 E
Saint-Menges	56	49.44 N	4.56 E
Sainte-Mère-Église	32	49.25 N	1.19 W
Saint Merryn	42	50.31 N	4.58 W
Saint-Méry	261	48.35 N	2.50 E
Sainte-Mesme	261	48.32 N	1.58 E
Saint-Mesmes	261	48.59 N	2.42 E
Saint Michael, Ak., U.S.	180	63.29 N	162.02 W
Saint Michael, Pa., U.S.	214	40.20 N	78.46 W
Saint Michaels	208	38.47 N	76.13 W
Saint-Michel, Fr.	50	49.55 N	4.08 E
Saint-Michel, Fr.	62	45.13 N	6.28 E
Saint-Michel ◆[8]	275a	45.35 N	73.35 W
Saint-Michel-de-Napierville	206	45.14 N	73.34 W
Saint-Michel-des-Saints	206	46.41 N	73.55 W
Saint-Michel-sur-Meurthe	58	48.19 N	6.54 E
Saint-Michel-sur-Orge	261	48.38 N	2.18 E
Saint-Mihiel	56	48.54 N	5.33 E
Saint Monance	46	56.12 N	2.46 W
Sainte-Monique-des-Deux-Montagnes	275a	45.40 N	74.00 W
Sainte-Montaine	50	47.29 N	2.19 E
Saint-Moritz → Sankt Moritz	58	46.30 N	9.50 E
Saint-Narcisse	206	46.34 N	72.28 W
Saint-Nazaire	32	47.17 N	2.12 W
Saint-Nazaire-en-Royans	62	45.04 N	5.15 E
Saint-Nazaire-le-Désert	62	44.34 N	5.17 E
Saint Nazianz	190	44.00 N	87.55 W
Saint Neots	42	52.14 N	0.17 W
Saint-Nicéphore	206	45.50 N	72.25 W
Saint-Nicolas → Sint-Niklaas, Bel.	50	51.10 N	4.08 E
Saint-Nicolas, Bel.	56	50.38 N	5.32 E
Saint-Nicolas, P.Q., Can.	206	46.42 N	71.24 W
Saint-Nicolas-aux-Bois	50	49.36 N	3.25 E
Saint-Nicolas-d'Aliermont	50	49.53 N	1.13 E
Saint-Nizier-du-Moucherotte	62	45.10 N	5.38 E
Saint-Nom-la-Bretèche	261	48.51 N	2.01 E
Saint Nora Lake ⊜	212	45.08 N	78.49 W
Saint-Norbert-d'Arthabaska	206	46.07 N	71.50 W
Sainte-Odile ✤[1]	58	48.26 N	7.24 E
Saint-Omer	50	50.45 N	2.15 E
Saintonge □[9]	32	45.30 N	0.30 W
Saint-Ouen, Fr.	50	50.02 N	2.03 E
Saint-Ouen, Fr.	261	48.54 N	2.20 E
Saint-Ouen-l'Aumône	50	49.03 N	2.06 E
Saint-Pacôme	186	47.24 N	69.57 W
Saint-Pamphile	186	46.58 N	69.47 W
Saint Pancras ◆[8]	260	51.32 N	0.07 W
Saint Pancras Station ◆[5]	260	51.32 N	0.08 W
Saint Paris	218	40.07 N	83.57 W
Saint-Pascal	186	47.32 N	69.49 W
Saint-Paterne	50	48.24 N	0.07 E
Saint-Pathus	261	49.04 N	2.48 E
Saint-Patrice, Lac ⊜	190	46.22 N	77.20 W
Saint Paul, Ab., Can.	182	53.59 N	111.17 W
Saint-Paul, Fr.	62	43.42 N	7.07 E
Saint-Paul, Fr.	62	44.31 N	6.45 E
Saint-Paul, Réu.	157c	21.00 S	55.16 E
Saint Paul, In., U.S.	218	39.25 N	85.28 W
Saint Paul, Ks., U.S.	198	37.31 N	95.10 W
Saint Paul, Mn., U.S.	190	44.57 N	93.05 W
Saint Paul, Ne., U.S.	198	41.13 N	98.27 W
Saint Paul, Or., U.S.	224	45.12 N	122.58 W
Saint Paul, Va., U.S.	192	36.54 N	82.18 W
Saint-Paul ≃, Can.	176	51.26 N	57.40 W
Saint Paul ≃, Liber.	150	6.23 N	10.48 W
Saint Paul, Cape ≻	150	5.49 N	0.57 E
Saint-Paul, Île I	6	38.43 S	77.29 E
Saint-Paul, Lac ⊜	206	46.18 N	72.29 W
Saint Paul Bay c	116	10.14 N	118.54 E
Saint-Paul-de-Chester (Chesterville)	206	45.57 N	71.49 W
Saint-Paul-en-Jarez	62	45.29 N	4.35 E
Saint-Paul-et-Valmalle	62	43.38 N	3.40 E
Saint-Paulien	62	45.08 N	3.49 E
Saint-Paulin	206	46.25 N	73.01 W
Saint Paul Island	180	57.07 N	170.17 W
Saint Paul Island I, N.S., Can.	186	47.15 N	60.10 W
Saint Paul Island I, Ak., U.S.	180	57.10 N	170.15 W
Saint Pauls	192	34.48 N	78.58 W
Saint Paul's Cathedral ✤[1]	260	51.31 N	0.06 W
Saint Paul's Cray ◆[8]	260	51.24 N	0.07 E
Saint Pauls Inlet c	186	49.50 N	57.45 W
Saint Paul's Point ≻	174e	25.04 S	130.05 W
Saint-Paul-Trois-Châteaux	62	44.21 N	4.46 E
Saint-Péravy-la-Colombe	50	48.00 N	1.42 E
Saint-Péray	62	44.57 N	4.50 E
Saint-Père	50	47.28 N	3.46 E
Saint Peter, Il., U.S.	219	38.52 N	88.51 W
Saint Peter, Mn., U.S.	190	44.19 N	93.57 W
Saint Peter, Lake ⊜	212	45.18 N	78.02 W
Saint Peter Island I	162	32.17 S	133.35 E
Saint Peter Port	43b	49.27 N	2.32 W
Saint Peters, N.S., Can.	186	45.40 N	60.52 W
Saint Peters, Mo., U.S.	219	38.48 N	90.37 W
Saint Peters, Pa., U.S.	285	40.11 N	75.44 W
Saint Peters Bay	186	46.25 N	62.35 W
Saint Petersburg → Leningrad, S.S.S.R.	76	59.55 N	30.15 E
Saint Petersburg, Fl., U.S.	220	27.46 N	82.40 W
Saint Petersburg, Pa., U.S.	214	41.10 N	79.37 W
Saint Petersburg Beach	220	27.43 N	82.44 W
Saint Peter's College ✤[2]	276	40.44 N	74.05 W
Saint-Philippe-d'Argenteuil	206	45.37 N	74.25 W
Saint-Philippe-de-Laprairie	275a	45.21 N	73.28 W
Saint-Pie	206	45.30 N	72.54 W
Saint-Pierre, P.Q., Can.	275a	45.27 N	73.39 W
Saint-Pierre, Fr.	62	45.40 N	3.45 E
Saint-Pierre, It.	62	45.42 N	7.14 E
Saint-Pierre, Mart.	240e	14.45 N	61.11 W
Saint-Pierre, Réu.	157c	21.19 S	55.29 E
Saint-Pierre, St. P./M.	186	46.47 N	56.11 W
Saint-Pierre I	186	46.47 N	56.11 W
Saint-Pierre ≃	275a	45.23 N	73.34 W
Saint-Pierre, Lac ⊜, P.Q., Can.	186	50.08 N	68.26 W
Saint-Pierre, Lac ⊜, P.Q., Can.	206	46.12 N	72.52 W
Saint-Pierre, Rade de ⚓[3]	240e	14.44 N	61.11 W
Saint Pierre and Miquelon (Saint-Pierre-et-Miquelon) □[2], N.A.	176	46.55 N	56.20 W
Saint Pierre and Miquelon (Saint-Pierre-et-Miquelon) □[2], N.A.	186	46.55 N	56.20 W
Saint-Pierre-d'Albigny	62	45.34 N	6.09 E
Saint-Pierre-de-Bœuf	62	45.22 N	4.45 E
Saint-Pierre-de-Broughton	206	46.15 N	71.12 W
Saint-Pierre-de-Chartreuse	62	45.20 N	5.49 E
Saint-Pierre-des-Corps	50	47.23 N	0.44 E
Saint-Pierre-de-Vacquière	62	43.52 N	4.13 E
Saint-Pierre-du-Vauvray	50	49.14 N	1.13 E
Saint-Pierre-Église	32	49.40 N	1.24 W
Saint-Pierre-en-Port	50	49.48 N	0.29 E
Saint-Pierre-et-Miquelon → Saint Pierre and Miquelon □[2]	186	46.55 N	56.20 W
Saint Pierre Island I	138	9.19 S	50.43 E
Saint Pierre-Jolys	184	49.26 N	96.59 W
Saint Pierre-le-Moûtier	32	46.48 N	3.07 E
Saint-Pierre-lès-Elbeuf	50	49.16 N	1.03 E
Saint-Pierre-sur-Dives	28	49.01 N	0.02 W
Saint-Pierreville	62	44.49 N	4.29 E
Saint-Point, Lac de ⊜	58	46.49 N	6.19 E
Saint-Pol-de-Léon	32	48.41 N	3.59 W
Saint-Pol-sur-Mer	50	51.02 N	2.21 E
Saint-Pol-sur-Ternoise	50	50.23 N	2.20 E
Saint-Polycarpe	206	45.18 N	74.18 W
Saint-Pons	32	43.29 N	2.46 E
Saint-Pourçain-sur-Sioule	32	46.19 N	3.17 E
Saint-Prex	58	46.29 N	6.28 E
Saint-Priest	62	45.42 N	4.57 E
Saint-Priest-en-Jarez	62	45.28 N	4.22 E
Saint-Prix	261	49.01 N	2.16 E
Saint-Prosper-de-Dorchester	188	46.13 N	70.29 W
Saint-Quentin, N.B., Can.	186	47.30 N	67.23 W
Saint-Quentin, Fr.	50	49.51 N	3.17 E
Saint-Quentin, Canal de ≊	50	49.36 N	3.11 E
Saint-Quentin, Étang de ⊜	261	48.47 N	2.01 E
Saint-Rambert-d'Albon	62	45.17 N	4.49 E
Saint-Rambert-en-Bugey	58	45.57 N	5.26 E
Saint-Rambert-sur-Loire	62	45.30 N	4.15 E
Saint-Raphaël	62	43.25 N	6.46 E
Saint-Raymond	206	46.54 N	71.50 W
Saint-Rédempter-de-Lévis	206	46.42 N	71.17 W
Saint Regis	202	47.17 N	115.06 W
Saint-Régis ≃, P.Q., Can.	275a	45.24 N	73.34 W
Saint Regis ≃, N.A.	188	45.00 N	74.39 W
Saint Regis ≃, Mt., U.S.	202	47.18 N	115.05 W
Saint Regis, West Branch ≃	188	44.47 N	74.46 W
Saint Regis Falls	188	44.40 N	74.32 W
Saint Regis Indian Reservation ◆[4]	206	44.58 N	74.39 W
Saint-Rémi	206	45.16 N	73.37 W
Saint-Rémi-d'Amherst	206	46.01 N	74.46 W
Saint-Rémy (lès-Chevreuse), Fr.	50	48.42 N	2.05 E
Saint-Rémy, Fr.	58	46.46 N	4.50 E
Saint Remy, N.Y., U.S.	210	41.54 N	74.01 W
Saint-Rémy-de-Provence	62	43.47 N	4.50 E
Saint-Rémy-en-Bouzemont	58	48.38 N	4.39 E
Saint-Rémy-lès-Chevreuse	261	48.42 N	2.05 E
Saint-Rémy-l'Honoré	261	48.45 N	1.53 E
Saint-Rémy-sur-Avre	50	48.46 N	1.15 E
Saint-Renan	32	48.26 N	4.37 W
Saint-Révérien	50	47.13 N	3.30 E
Saint-Rhémy	62	45.50 N	7.11 E
Saint-Riquier	50	50.08 N	1.57 E
Saint Robert	194	37.50 N	92.09 W
Saint-Roch-de-l'Achigan	206	45.51 N	73.36 W
Saint-Romain-de-Colbosc	50	49.32 N	0.22 E
Saint-Romain-le-Puy	62	45.33 N	4.07 E
Saint-Romans	62	45.07 N	5.19 E
Saint-Romuald	206	46.45 N	71.14 W
Sainte-Rosalie	206	45.38 N	72.54 W
Sainte-Rose	241o	16.20 N	61.42 W
Sainte-Rose ◆[8]	275a	45.36 N	73.47 W
Sainte-Rose-du-Lac	184	51.03 N	99.32 W
Saintry-sur-Seine	261	48.36 N	2.30 E
Saint-Saëns	50	49.40 N	1.17 E
Saint Sampson	43b	49.29 N	2.31 W
Saint-Saturnin-d'Apt	62	43.56 N	5.23 E
Saint-Sauveur, Fr.	50	47.37 N	3.12 E
Saint-Sauveur, Fr.	58	47.48 N	6.23 E
Saint-Sauveur-des-Monts	206	45.52 N	74.10 W
Saint-Sauveur-sur-Tinée	62	44.05 N	7.06 E
Saint-Savin	32	46.34 N	0.52 E
Sainte-Savine	50	48.18 N	4.03 E
Saint-Savinien	32	45.53 N	0.41 W
Saint Saviour	43b	49.11 N	2.06 W
Saint Sebastian Bay c	158	34.25 S	21.00 E
Saint-Sébastien	206	45.07 N	73.09 W
Saint-Sébastien, Cap ≻	157b	12.26 S	48.44 E
Saint-Seine-l'Abbaye	58	47.26 N	4.47 E
Saint Séverin	56	50.32 N	5.25 E
Saint Shotts	186	46.38 N	53.35 W
Sainte-Sigolène	62	45.14 N	4.15 E
Saint-Siméon	186	47.50 N	69.53 W
Saint-Simon	50	49.45 N	3.10 E
Saint Simons Island	192	31.09 N	81.22 W
Saint Simons Island I	192	31.14 N	81.21 W
Saint-Sixte ≃	206	45.39 N	75.08 W
Saintes-Maries, Golfe des c	62	43.25 N	4.31 E
Saintes-Maries-de-la-Mer	62	43.27 N	4.26 E
Sainte-Sophie-de-Mégantic	206	46.09 N	71.42 W
Saint-Soupplets	261	49.02 N	2.48 E
Saint Stanislas Bay c	174o	1.53 N	157.30 W
Saint-Stanislas-de-Kosta	206	45.11 N	74.08 W
Saint Stephen, N.B., Can.	186	45.12 N	67.17 W
Saint Stephen, S.C., U.S.	192	33.24 N	79.55 W
Saint-Sulpice-de-Favières	261	48.33 N	2.11 E
Saint-Sulpice-les-Feuilles	32	46.19 N	1.22 E
Sainte-Suzanne	58	47.30 N	6.46 E
Saint-Sylvestre	206	46.22 N	71.14 W
Saint-Symphorien, Fr.	32	44.26 N	0.30 W
Saint-Symphorien, Fr.	261	48.31 N	1.46 E
Saint-Symphorien-d'Ozon	62	45.38 N	4.52 E
Saint-Symphorien-sur-Coise	62	45.38 N	4.27 E
Sainte-Thècle	206	46.49 N	72.31 W
Saint-Théodore-d'Acton	206	45.41 N	72.35 W
Sainte-Thérèse	206	45.38 N	73.51 W
Sainte-Thérèse, Île I, P.Q., Can.	275a	45.41 N	73.28 W
Sainte-Thérèse, Île I, P.Q., Can.	275a	45.22 N	73.15 W
Saint-Thibault-des-Vignes	261	48.52 N	2.41 E
Saint Thomas, On., Can.	212	42.47 N	81.12 W
Saint Thomas, Mo., U.S.	219	38.22 N	92.13 W
Saint Thomas, N.D., U.S.	198	48.37 N	97.26 W
Saint Thomas → Charlotte Amalie, Vir. Is., U.S.	240m	18.21 N	64.56 W
Saint Thomas I	240m	18.21 N	64.55 W
Saint-Timothée	206	45.18 N	74.02 W
Saint-Tite	206	46.44 N	72.34 W
Saint-Tite-des-Caps	186	47.08 N	70.47 W
Saint Tome et Principauté → Sao Tome and Principe □[1]	152	1.00 N	7.00 E
Saint-Trivier-de-Courtes	58	46.28 N	5.05 E
Saint-Trivier-sur-Moignans	58	46.04 N	4.54 E
Saint-Tropez	62	43.16 N	6.38 E
Saint Tudy	42	50.33 N	4.43 W
Sainte-Tulle	62	43.47 N	5.46 E
Saint-Ubald	206	46.45 N	72.16 W
Saint-Urbain-de-Charlevoix	186	47.33 N	70.32 W
Saint-Ursanne	58	47.22 N	7.10 E
Saint-Uze	62	45.11 N	4.52 E
Saint-Valérien	50	48.11 N	3.06 E
Saint-Valéry-en-Caux	50	49.52 N	0.44 E
Saint-Valéry-sur-Somme	50	50.11 N	1.38 E
Saint-Vallier, Fr.	58	46.38 N	4.22 E
Saint-Vallier, Fr.	62	45.10 N	4.49 E
Saint-Vallier-de-Thiey	62	43.42 N	6.51 E
Saint-Varent	32	46.53 N	0.14 W
Saint-Venant	50	50.37 N	2.33 E
Saint-Véran	62	44.42 N	6.52 E
Sainte-Victoire, Montagne ∧	62	43.32 N	5.39 E
Saint-Victoret	62	43.25 N	5.14 E
Saint Vincent	198	48.58 N	97.13 W
Saint Vincent I	241h	13.15 N	61.12 W
Saint-Vincent, Baie de c	175f	22.00 S	166.05 E
Saint-Vincent, Cap ≻	157b	21.57 S	43.16 E
Saint Vincent, Cape ≻	166	43.18 S	145.50 E
Saint Vincent, Cape → São Vicente, Cabo de ≻	34	37.01 N	9.00 W
Saint Vincent, Gulf c	168b	35.00 S	138.05 E
Saint Vincent and the Grenadines □[1], N.A.	230	13.15 N	61.12 W
Saint Vincent and the Grenadines □[1], N.A.	241h	13.15 N	61.12 W
Saint-Vincent-de-Paul ◆[8]	275a	45.37 N	73.39 W
Saint-Vincent-de-Tyrosse	32	43.40 N	1.18 W
Saint Vincent Passage ʊ	238	13.30 N	61.00 W
Saint Vincent's	186	46.48 N	53.38 W
Saint-Vit	58	47.11 N	5.49 E
Saint-Vith	56	50.17 N	6.08 E
Saint-Vivien-de-Médoc	32	45.26 N	1.02 W
Saint-Vrain	261	48.33 N	2.20 E
Saint Walburg	184	53.39 N	109.12 W
Saint-Wandrille-Rançon	50	49.32 N	0.46 E
Saint-Wenceslas ≃	206	46.18 N	72.23 W
Saint Williams	212	42.40 N	80.25 W
Saint-Witz	261	49.05 N	2.34 E
Saint-Yrieix-la-Perche	32	45.31 N	1.12 E
Saint-Yvon	186	49.10 N	64.48 W
Saint-Zacharie	62	43.23 N	5.43 E
Saint-Zénon	206	46.33 N	73.49 W
Saipan I	174n	15.12 N	145.45 E
Saipan Channel ʊ	174n	15.05 N	145.41 E
Saipan International Airport ⊠	174n	15.07 N	145.43 E
Saiqi	100	27.00 N	119.43 E
Sairecábur, Cerro ∧	248	22.43 S	67.54 W
Saishu-to → Cheju-do I	90	33.20 N	126.30 E
Saita	96	34.08 N	133.49 E
Saita ≃	96	34.08 N	133.38 E
Saitama □[5]	94	36.00 N	139.30 E
Saitama University ✤[2]	268	35.52 N	139.36 E
Saito	92	32.06 N	131.24 E
Saitula	120	36.21 N	78.02 E

Symbols in the index entries represent the broad categories identified in the key at the right. Symbols with superior numbers (⋀[1]) identify subcategories (see complete key on page *I · 1).*

Kartensymbole in dem Registerverzeichnis stellen die rechts in Schlüssel erklärten Kategorien dar. Symbole mit hochgestellten Ziffern (⋀[1]) bezeichnen Unterabteilungen einer Kategorie (vgl. vollständiger Schlüssel auf Seite *I · 1).*

Los símbolos incluídos en el texto del índice representan las grandes categorias identificadas con la clave a la derecha. Los símbolos con numeros en su parte superior (⋀[1]) identifican las subcategorías (véase la clave completa en la página *I · 1).*

Les symboles de l'index représentent les catégories indiquées dans la légende à droite. Les symboles suivis d'un indice (⋀[1]) représentent des sous-catégories (voir légende complète à la page *I · 1).*

Os símbolos incluídos no texto do índice representam as grandes categorias identificadas com a chave à direita. Os símbolos com números em sua parte superior (⋀[1]) identificam as subcategorias (veja-se a chave completa à página *I · 1).*

∧ Mountain	Berg	Montaña	Montagne	Montanha
⋀ Mountains	Berge	Montañas	Montagnes	Montanhas
)(Pass	Pass	Paso	Col	Passo
V Valley, Canyon	Tal, Cañon	Valle, Cañón	Vallée, Canyon	Vale, Canhão
≚ Plain	Ebene	Llano	Plaine	Planície
≻ Cape	Kap	Cabo	Cap	Cabo
I Island	Insel	Isla	Île	Ilha
II Islands	Inseln	Islas	Îles	Ilhas
⊥ Other Topographic Features	Andere Topographische Objekte	Otros Elementos Topográficos	Autres données topographiques	Outros acidentes topográficos

Saiwai ◆8 268 35.33 N 139.41 E
Saiwa Swamp National Park ♦ 154 1.06 N 35.12 E
Saiyidān ◆8 272a 28.40 N 77.05 E
Sai Yok 110 14.07 N 99.08 E
Sajak 86 47.02 N 77.22 E
Sajam 164 0.53 S 132.41 E
Sajama 248 18.07 S 69.00 W
Sajama, Nevado ⋀ 248 18.06 S 68.54 W
Sajan → Sayan Mountains ⋀ 88 52.45 N 96.00 E
Sajanogorsk 86 53.08 N 91.29 E
Sajano-Šušenskoje vodochranilišče ⊜1 88 52.20 N 92.25 E
Sajantuj 88 51.44 N 107.30 E
Sajasan 84 43.03 N 46.17 E
Sajat 128 38.47 N 63.53 E
Sajchan 88 48.40 N 102.39 E
Sajchandulaan 102 44.40 N 109.01 E
Sajchan-Ovoo 102 45.27 N 103.54 E
Sajchin 80 48.50 N 46.47 E
Şajen 115a 7.40 S 112.31 E
Sajgino 80 57.46 N 46.51 E
Sajia 120 28.55 N 88.05 E
Sajid I 144 16.52 N 41.50 E
Sajmak' 120 37.27 N 74.44 E
Sajnšand 102 44.52 N 110.09 E
Sajó ≃ 30 47.56 N 21.08 E
Sajószentpéter 30 48.13 N 20.44 E
Sajram 85 42.18 N 69.45 E
Sajukino 80 52.47 N 41.59 E
Sājūr (Sacır) ≃ 130 36.40 N 38.05 E
Sak ≃ 158 30.02 S 20.40 E
Saka, Kenya 154 0.09 S 39.20 E
Saka, Nihon 96 34.20 N 132.31 E
Sakado 94 35.57 N 139.24 E
Sakae, Nihon 94 35.50 N 140.15 E
Sakae, Nihon 94 36.58 N 138.35 E
Sa Kaeo 110 13.49 N 102.04 E
Sakahogi 94 35.26 N 136.59 E
Sakai, Nihon 94 36.10 N 136.14 E
Sakai, Nihon 94 36.06 N 139.15 E
Sakai, Nihon 94 36.06 N 139.48 E
Sakai, Nihon 96 34.35 N 135.28 E
Sakai, Nihon 268 35.25 N 139.22 E
Sakai ≃ 94 35.18 N 139.29 E
Sakaide 96 34.19 N 133.52 E
Sakaigawa 94 35.35 N 138.37 E
Sakaiminato 96 35.33 N 133.15 E
Sakākah 128 29.59 N 40.06 E
Sakakawea, Lake ⊜1 198 47.50 N 102.20 W
Sakaki 94 36.28 N 138.11 E
Sakakita 94 36.25 N 138.01 E
Sakala, Pulau I 112 6.54 S 116.15 E
Sakami ≃ 176 53.40 N 76.40 W
Sakami, Lac ⊜ 176 53.15 N 76.45 W
Sakania 154 12.45 S 28.34 E
Sakar 128 38.56 N 63.45 E
Sakar ⋌ 38 41.59 N 26.16 E
Sakaraha 157b 22.55 S 44.32 E
Sakar-Čaga 128 37.38 N 61.40 E
Sakar Island I 164 5.25 S 148.05 E
Sakarya □4 130 40.45 N 30.35 E
Sakarya ≃ 130 41.07 N 30.39 E
Sakashita 94 35.34 N 137.32 E
Sakassou 150 7.27 N 5.18 W
Sakata 92 38.55 N 139.50 E
Sakauchi 94 35.36 N 136.25 E
Sakawa 96 33.30 N 133.17 E
Sakawa ≃ 94 35.15 N 139.11 E
Sakchu 98 40.23 N 125.01 E
Sakesar 123 32.33 N 71.56 E
Sakété 150 6.43 N 2.40 E
Sakhā 142 31.05 N 30.57 E
Sakhalin → Sachalin, ostrov I 89 51.00 N 143.00 E
Sākhar 120 32.57 N 65.32 E
Sakhi Sarwar 120 29.59 N 70.18 E
Sakhnīn 132 32.52 N 35.17 E
Sakhrīyāt, Jabal aş- ⋀ 132 31.01 N 36.21 E
Sakhtsar 128 36.53 N 50.41 E
Saki 78 45.09 N 33.35 E
Sāki ◆8 272c 19.06 N 72.53 E
Sakiai 76 54.57 N 23.03 E
Sākib 132 32.17 N 35.49 E
Sakiet Sidi Youssef 36 36.13 N 8.22 E
Sakijang Bendera, Pulau I 271c 1.13 N 103.51 E
Sakijang Pelepah, Pulau I 271c 1.13 N 103.52 E
Sakishima-shotō II 175d 24.46 N 124.00 E
Sakito 92 33.02 N 129.32 E
Sakkara → Saqqārah 142 29.51 N 31.13 E
Sakleshpur 122 12.58 N 75.47 E
Sakmara ≃ 86 51.46 N 55.01 E
Sako 270 34.53 N 135.47 E
Sakoli 120 21.05 N 79.59 E
Sakon Nakhon 110 17.10 N 104.09 E
Sakonnet 207 41.28 N 71.12 W
Sakonnet Point ⋟ 207 41.27 N 71.12 W
Sakoyra 150 14.17 N 1.24 E
Sakra, Pulau I 271c 1.16 N 103.42 E
Sakrand 120 26.08 N 68.16 E
Sakri 120 20.59 N 74.19 E
Sakrivier 158 30.54 S 20.28 E
Sakrow-Paretzer Kanal ≖ 264a 52.28 N 12.55 E
Saks 194 33.42 N 85.52 W
Saksagan' ≃ 78 47.53 N 33.18 E
Saksauldala ◆2 86 44.30 N 73.00 E
Sakskøbing 41 54.48 N 11.39 E
Sakti 124 22.02 N 82.58 E
Saku, Nihon 94 36.09 N 138.30 E
Saku, Nihon 94 36.13 N 138.29 E
Sakuba 154 19.00 S 32.10 E
Sakugi 96 34.52 N 132.43 E
Sakuma 94 35.05 N 137.48 E
Sakuma-dam ◆6 94 35.05 N 137.47 E
Sakuma-ko ⊜1 94 35.08 N 137.47 E
Sakura 94 35.43 N 140.14 E
Sakura ≃ 94 36.05 N 140.14 E
Sakurae 96 34.57 N 132.26 E
Sakurai 96 34.30 N 135.51 E
Sakura-tōge ⋊ 270 34.36 N 135.53 E
Saku-shima I 94 34.43 N 137.03 E
Sakutō 96 35.01 N 134.14 E
Sakwaso Lake ⊜ 184 53.01 N 91.55 W
Sakylä 26 61.02 N 22.20 E
Sakyō ◆8 270 35.02 N 135.48 E
Sal I 150a 16.45 N 22.55 W
Sal ≃ 80 47.31 N 40.45 E
Sal, Cay I 238 23.42 N 80.24 W
Sal, Ponta do ⋟ 266c 38.41 N 9.22 W
Sal, Punta ⋟ 236 15.55 N 87.37 W
Šal'a, Česko. 30 48.09 N 17.52 E
Sal'a, S.S.S.R. 86 57.15 N 58.43 E
Sala, Sve. 40 59.55 N 16.36 E
Sala, Ouadi V 146 17.00 N 20.53 E
Sala Baganza 64 44.43 N 10.14 E
Salabangka, Kepulauan II 112 3.02 S 122.25 E
Salaberry, Île de I 206 45.17 N 74.07 W
Salaberry-de-Valleyfield 206 45.15 N 74.08 W
Salaca ≃ 76 57.45 N 24.21 E
Salacgrīva 76 57.45 N 24.21 E
Sala Consilina 68 40.24 N 15.36 E
Salada, Laguna ⊜, Arg. 258 35.17 S 59.24 W
Salada, Laguna ⊜, Méx. 232 32.20 N 115.40 W
Saladas 252 28.15 S 58.38 W
Saladillo 252 35.38 S 59.46 W
Saladillo ≃ 252 29.05 S 63.25 W
Saladillo, Arroyo ≃ 258 35.33 S 59.04 W
Saladillo de Rodríguez, Arroyo ≃ 258 35.29 S 59.01 W
Saladillo Dulce, Arroyo ≃ 252 31.25 S 60.33 W
Salado, Arg. 252 28.18 S 67.15 W
Salado, Tx., U.S. 222 30.57 N 97.32 W
Salado ≃, Arg. 252 38.05 S 65.48 W
Salado ≃, Arg. 252 31.42 S 60.44 W
Salado ≃, Arg. 252 35.44 S 57.21 W
Salado ≃, Arg. 252 29.13 S 66.34 W
Salado ≃, Cuba 240p 20.36 N 76.56 W
Salado ≃, Méx. 232 26.52 N 99.19 W
Salado ≃, Méx. 234 18.44 N 103.36 W
Salado, Arroyo ≃, Arg. 254 41.37 S 65.02 W
Salado, Arroyo ≃, Arg. 254 40.35 S 66.33 W
Salado, Arroyo ≃, Méx. 232 24.25 N 111.34 W
Salado, Río ≃ 200 34.16 N 106.52 W
Salado Creek ≃, Tx., U.S. 196 29.14 N 98.25 W
Salado Creek ≃, Tx., U.S. 222 30.59 N 97.25 W
Salaga 150 8.33 N 0.31 W
Salagle 144 1.50 N 42.17 E
Salah 132 32.38 N 36.46 E
Şalāḥ ad-Dīn □4 128 34.15 N 43.55 E
Salahin 144 2.57 N 46.26 E
Sala'ilua 175a 13.41 S 172.34 W
Salair 86 54.13 N 85.47 E
Salairskij kr'až ⋀ 86 54.15 N 85.30 E
Sālaj □6 38 47.15 N 23.00 E
Salak 114 2.34 N 98.20 E
Salak, Gunung ⋀ 115a 6.42 S 106.44 E
Šalakuša 76 55.35 N 26.08 E
Salakas 24 62.15 N 40.17 E
Salal 146 14.51 N 17.13 E
Salamá, Chile 252 30.41 S 71.32 W
Salama, Liber. 150 6.40 N 10.05 W
Salālah, Süd. 140 21.19 N 36.13 E
Salālah, 'Umān 118 17.00 N 54.06 E
Salamá, Guat. 236 15.06 N 90.16 W
Salamá, Hond. 236 14.50 N 86.36 W
Salaman 115a 7.35 S 110.08 E
Salamanca, Chile 252 31.47 S 70.58 W
Salamanca, Esp. 34 40.58 N 5.39 W
Salamanca, Méx. 234 20.34 N 101.12 W
Salamanca, Perú 248 15.31 S 72.50 W
Salamanca, Perú 286d 12.05 S 77.00 W
Salamanca, N.Y., U.S. 210 42.09 N 78.42 W
Salamanga 158 26.28 S 32.39 E
Salamat □5 146 11.00 N 20.30 E
Salamat, Bahr ≃ 146 9.27 N 18.06 E
Salāmbek 120 28.18 N 65.09 E
Salamina 246 5.25 N 75.29 W
Salamínos, Órmos ⊂ 267c 37.56 N 23.27 E
Salamis 38 37.59 N 23.28 E
Salamís I 38 37.54 N 23.26 E
Salamis ⊥ 130 35.10 N 33.54 E
Salām Khān 120 31.47 N 66.45 E
Salamonia 216 40.23 N 84.52 W
Salamonie ≃ 216 40.50 N 85.43 W
Salamonie Lake ⊜1 216 40.46 N 85.37 W
Salāmūn 142 31.04 N 31.28 E
Salanda 130 38.50 N 34.32 E
Salandra 68 40.31 N 16.19 E
Salani 175a 14.00 S 171.33 W
Salantai 76 56.04 N 21.32 E
Salaparuta 70 37.47 N 13.00 E
Salaqui 246 7.18 N 77.33 W
Salaquí ≃ 246 7.27 N 77.07 W
Salāqūs 142 28.44 N 30.50 E
Salar 85 41.21 N 69.22 E
Salara 64 44.59 N 11.25 E
Salard 38 47.13 N 22.03 E
Salarjovo 265b 55.37 N 37.26 E
Salas 248 6.16 S 79.37 W
Salas de los Infantes 34 42.01 N 3.17 W
Salat ≃ 32 43.10 N 0.58 E
Salatiga 115a 7.19 S 110.30 E
Salaus 80 55.59 N 52.53 E
Salavat, S.S.S.R. 86 53.21 N 55.55 E
Salavat, Tür. 130 41.53 N 34.55 E
Salavaux 58 46.55 N 7.02 E
Salaverry 248 8.14 S 78.58 W
Salavina 252 28.48 S 63.25 W
Salawati I 164 1.07 S 130.52 E
Salawe 154 3.19 S 32.52 E
Salay 116 8.52 N 124.47 E
Salāya 120 22.19 N 69.35 E
Sala y Gómez, Isla I 18 26.28 S 105.28 W
Sala y Gómez Ridge ◆3 18 25.00 S 98.00 W
Salazgor' 88 54.07 N 43.09 E
Salba 88 53.14 N 92.36 E
Sālbani 126 22.38 N 87.20 E
Salbertrand 62 45.04 N 6.53 E
Salbohed 40 59.55 N 16.19 E
Salbosjön ⊜ 40 59.50 N 14.54 E
Şalbris 50 47.26 N 2.03 E
Salbuzdag, gora ⋀ 84 41.19 N 47.48 E
Salcajá 236 14.53 N 91.27 W
Salcantay, Nevado ⋀ 248 13.20 S 72.33 W
Salcedo, Pil. 116 11.09 N 125.40 E
Salcedo, Rep. Dom. 238 19.23 N 70.25 W
Salcha ≃ 180 64.29 N 147.00 W
Salching 60 48.49 N 12.34 E
Şalcia 38 43.57 N 24.56 E
Šalčininkai 76 54.18 N 25.23 E
Salcombe 42 50.13 N 3.47 W
Salda ≃ 86 58.48 N 61.20 E
Salda Gölü ⊜ 130 37.33 N 29.42 E
Saldaj 86 51.56 N 78.48 E
Saldaña 34 42.31 N 4.44 W
Saldaña ≃ 246 4.01 N 74.52 W
Saldanha 158 33.00 S 17.56 E
Saldanhabaai ⊂ 158 33.04 S 18.00 E
Saldanha Bay ⊂ 80 56.52 N 44.46 E
Saldez 252 38.12 S 61.47 W
Saldungaray 76 56.40 N 22.30 E
Saldus 166 38.06 S 147.04 E
Sale, Austl. 62 44.59 N 8.48 E
Sale, It. 148 34.04 N 6.50 W
Salé, Magreb 44 53.26 N 2.19 W
Sale, Eng., U.K. 108 3.55 N 126.40 E
Salebabu, Pulau I 74 66.33 N 66.40 E
Salechard 194 35.22 N 85.06 W
Sale Creek 241o 16.17 N 61.33 W
Salée, Rivière ⊻ 115b 8.34 S 117.57 E
Saleh, Teluk ⊂ 175a 13.44 S 172.10 W
Salelologa 124 11.39 N 78.10 E
Salem, B.R.D. 58 47.46 N 9.16 E
Salem, Ön., Can. 212 43.42 N 80.27 W
Salem, India 122 11.39 N 78.10 E
Salem, S. Afr. 158 33.28 S 26.29 E
Salem, Sve. 40 59.13 N 17.44 E
Salem, Ar., U.S. 194 36.22 N 91.49 W
Salem, Ct., U.S. 218 38.37 N 88.56 W
Salem, Il., U.S. 216 38.03 N 86.55 W
Salem, In., U.S. 218 38.60 N 86.55 W
Salem, Ia., U.S. 190 40.51 N 91.37 W
Salem, Ky., U.S. 194 37.15 N 88.14 W
Salem, Ma., U.S. 207 42.31 N 70.53 W
Salem, Mi., U.S. 281 42.24 N 83.34 W
Salem, Mo., U.S. 194 37.38 N 91.32 W
Salem, N.H., U.S. 207 42.47 N 71.12 W
Salem, N.J., U.S. 208 39.34 N 75.28 W
Salem, N.Y., U.S. 210 43.10 N 73.19 W
Salem, Oh., U.S. 214 40.54 N 80.51 W
Salem, Or., U.S. 224 44.56 N 123.02 W
Salem, S.D., U.S. 198 43.43 N 97.23 W
Salem, Ut., U.S. 200 40.03 N 111.40 W
Salem, Va., U.S. 192 37.17 N 80.03 W
Salem, W.V., U.S. 188 39.16 N 80.33 W
Salem, Wi., U.S. 216 42.33 N 88.06 W
Salem □6 208 39.34 N 75.20 W
Salem ≃ 208 39.34 N 75.28 W
Salem Airfield ⊠ 281 42.25 N 83.34 W
Salem Marasino 64 45.43 N 10.06 E
Salem Depot 285 42.47 N 71.12 W
Salem Harbor ⊂ 283 42.31 N 70.53 W
Salem Heights 224 44.54 N 123.02 W
Salemi 70 37.49 N 12.48 E
Salem Maritime National Historic Site ⊥ 207 42.31 N 70.53 W
Salem State College ⊻2 283 42.30 N 70.54 W
Salem Upland ⋀1 194 37.25 N 91.30 W
Salen, Sve. 26 61.10 N 13.16 E
Salen, Scot., U.K. 46 56.43 N 5.47 W
Salen, Scot., U.K. 46 56.31 N 5.57 W
Salentina, Penisola ⋟1 68 40.25 N 18.00 E
Salentine, Murge ◆1 68 40.02 N 18.13 E
Salento 68 40.15 N 15.13 E
Salernes 62 43.33 N 6.14 E
Salerno 68 40.41 N 14.47 E
Salerno □4 68 40.27 N 15.16 E
Salerno, Golfo di ⊂ 68 40.32 N 14.42 E
Salers 32 45.08 N 2.30 E
Salesbury 262 53.47 N 2.30 W
Salesópolis 256 23.32 S 45.51 W
Salève, Mont ⋀ 58 46.07 N 6.10 E
Salford 44 53.28 N 2.18 W
Salford □8 262 53.28 N 2.23 W
Salfords 260 51.12 N 0.10 W
Salgačova 24 62.19 N 39.35 E
Salgado 250 11.02 S 37.28 W
Salgan 80 55.14 N 45.30 E
Salgar 246 5.58 N 75.59 W
Salgija 86 47.35 N 70.36 E
Salgir ≃ 78 45.38 N 35.01 E
Salgótarján 30 48.07 N 19.48 E
Salgueiro 250 8.04 S 39.06 W
Salher ⋀ 122 20.43 N 73.56 E
Sali, Alg. 148 26.58 N 0.01 W
Šali, Jugo. 36 43.56 N 15.10 E
Šali, S.S.S.R. 80 55.41 N 49.40 E
Šali, S.S.S.R. 84 43.08 N 45.54 E
Sali ≃ 252 27.33 S 64.57 W
Salice Salentino 68 40.23 N 17.58 E
Salice Terme 62 44.55 N 9.01 E
Salici, Monte ⋀ 70 37.44 N 14.38 E
Salida, Ca., U.S. 226 37.42 N 121.05 W
Salida, Co., U.S. 200 38.32 N 105.59 W
Salies-de-Béarn 32 43.29 N 0.55 W
Salif 144 15.18 N 42.40 E
Salignac-Eyvignes 32 44.59 N 1.19 E
Salihli 130 38.29 N 28.09 E
Şalikha 126 23.18 N 89.22 E
Salikovo 82 55.30 N 36.13 E
Salim 140 12.52 N 28.40 E
Salima 154 13.47 S 34.26 E
Salimah, Wāhat ⊤4 140 21.22 N 29.19 E
Salimani 157a 11.47 S 43.17 E
Salimbatu 112 2.57 N 117.21 E
Salimi 152 9.24 S 23.35 E
Salin 110 20.35 N 94.39 E
Salina, Ks., U.S. 198 38.50 N 97.36 W
Salina, Ok., U.S. 196 36.17 N 95.09 W
Salina, Pa., U.S. 214 40.31 N 79.30 W
Salina, Ut., U.S. 200 38.57 N 111.51 W
Salina, Canale di ≖ 70 38.32 N 14.54 E
Salina, Isola I 70 38.34 N 14.50 E
Salina Cruz 234 16.10 N 95.12 W
Salina Point ⋟ 238 22.13 N 74.18 W
Salinas, Bra. 255 16.10 S 42.17 W
Salinas, Ec. 246 2.13 S 80.58 W
Salinas, P.R. 240m 17.59 N 66.18 W
Salinas, Ca., U.S. 226 36.40 N 121.39 W
Salinas ≃, Bra. 255 16.37 S 42.18 W
Salinas ≃, N.A. 236 16.28 N 90.33 W
Salinas ≃, Ca., U.S. 226 36.45 N 121.48 W
Salinas, Cabo de ⋟ 34 39.16 N 3.03 E
Salinas, Pampa de las ≅ 252 31.58 S 66.42 W
Salinas, Ponta das ⋟ 152 12.50 S 12.56 E
Salinas, Sierra de ⋀ 226 36.18 N 121.20 W
Salinas de Garci Mendoza 248 19.38 S 67.43 W
Salinas de Hidalgo 234 22.38 N 101.43 W
Salinas del Rey 196 27.38 N 102.24 W
Salinas Municipal Airport ⊠ 226 36.40 N 121.40 W
Salinas National Monument ♦ 200 34.05 N 106.14 W
Salinas Valley V 226 36.15 N 121.15 W
Salinas Victoria 196 25.53 N 100.19 W
Salin-de-Giraud 62 43.25 N 4.44 E
Salindres 62 44.10 N 4.10 E
Saline, La., U.S. 194 32.09 N 92.58 W
Saline, Mi., U.S. 216 42.10 N 83.46 W
Saline ≃, Ar., U.S. 194 33.44 N 93.58 W
Saline ≃, Ar., U.S. 194 33.10 N 92.08 W
Saline ≃, Il., U.S. 194 37.35 N 88.08 W
Saline ≃, Ks., U.S. 198 38.51 N 97.30 W
Saline ≃, Mi., U.S. 216 41.59 N 83.37 W
Saline, North Fork ≃ 194 37.44 N 88.19 W
Saline Bayou ≃ 194 31.45 N 92.58 W
Saline di Volterra 66 43.22 N 10.49 E
Saline Lake ⊜1 194 31.55 N 92.55 W
Salines, Point ⋟ 241k 12.00 N 61.48 W
Salines, Pointe des ⋟ 240e 14.24 N 60.53 W
Salineville 214 40.37 N 80.51 W
Salingyi 110 21.58 N 95.03 E
Şalinopolis 250 0.37 S 47.20 W
Salinskoje 86 55.43 N 93.46 E
Salins-les-Bains 58 46.57 N 5.53 E
Salins-les-Thermes 62 45.28 N 6.32 E
Salipazan 130 40.54 N 31.58 E
Salipolo 112 3.45 S 119.23 E
Salisbury, Austl. 168b 34.46 S 138.38 E
Salisbury, Dom. 240d 15.26 N 61.27 W
Salisbury, Eng., U.K. 42 51.05 N 1.48 W
Salisbury, Ct., U.S. 207 41.59 N 73.25 W
Salisbury, Md., U.S. 208 38.21 N 75.35 W
Salisbury, Ma., U.S. 207 42.50 N 70.51 W
Salisbury, Mo., U.S. 194 39.25 N 92.48 W
Salisbury, N.C., U.S. 192 35.40 N 80.28 W
Salisbury, Pa., U.S. 188 39.45 N 79.04 W
Salisbury → Harare 154 17.50 S 31.03 E
Salisbury Cathedral ⊻1 42 51.05 N 1.48 W
Salisbury Center 210 43.09 N 74.47 W
Salisbury Hall ⊥ 260 51.43 N 0.16 W
Salisbury Island I, Austl. 162 34.21 S 123.32 E
Salisbury Island I, N.T., Can. 176 63.30 N 77.00 W
Salisbury Mills 210 41.26 N 74.08 W
Salisbury Plain ≃ 42 51.12 N 1.55 W
Salisbury Plain ≃ 283 42.02 N 71.02 W
Salish Mountains ⋀ 202 48.15 N 114.45 W
Salito ≃ 70 37.29 N 13.46 E
Salitpa 194 31.37 N 88.01 W
Salitre ≃ 250 9.29 S 40.39 W
Salix 214 40.18 N 78.46 W
Şaljany 84 39.34 N 48.59 E
Şalkar, S.S.S.R. 80 48.03 N 46.53 E
Şalkar, S.S.S.R. 80 50.32 N 51.20 E
Şalkar, ozero ⊜ 80 50.33 N 51.12 E
Salkar-Jega-Kara, ozero ⊜ 86 50.45 N 60.54 E
Salkehatchie ≃ 192 32.37 N 80.53 W
Salkhad 132 32.29 N 36.43 E
Salkhia 272b 22.35 N 88.21 E
Salkum 224 46.31 N 122.37 W
Salladasburg 210 41.17 N 77.14 W
Sallagriffon 62 43.52 N 6.53 E
Sallanches 58 45.56 N 6.38 E
Salland ◆1 52 52.22 N 6.20 E
Salles-Curan 32 44.11 N 2.47 E
Salles-sous-Bois 62 44.28 N 4.56 E
Sallgast 54 51.35 N 13.51 E
Salling ◆1 26 56.40 N 9.00 E
Salliquelo 252 36.45 S 62.56 W
Sallisaw 196 35.27 N 94.47 W
Sallisaw Creek ≃ 196 35.28 N 94.52 W
Salluit 176 62.14 N 75.38 W
Sallūm 140 19.23 N 37.06 E
Sallūm, Khalīj as- ⊂ 146 31.41 N 25.16 E
Sallūyo, Nevado ⋀ 248 14.38 S 69.23 W
Sallyāna 124 28.22 N 82.12 E
Salm ≃, Bel. 56 50.22 N 5.52 E
Salm ≃, B.R.D. 56 49.51 N 6.51 E
Salmanli 130 40.55 N 30.18 E
Salmās 128 38.11 N 44.47 E
Salmchâteau 56 50.16 N 5.55 E
Salme 76 58.10 N 22.15 E
Salmi 24 61.22 N 31.53 E
Salmo 182 49.12 N 117.17 W
Salmon, Id., U.S. 202 45.10 N 113.53 W
Salmon ≃, B.C., Can. 182 54.05 N 122.34 W
Salmon ≃, N.B., Can. 186 46.06 N 65.56 W
Salmon ≃, On., Can. 212 44.11 N 77.15 W
Salmon ≃, N.A. 188 45.02 N 74.31 W
Salmon ≃, Ct., U.S. 207 41.29 N 72.29 W
Salmon ≃, Id., U.S. 202 45.51 N 116.46 W
Salmon ≃, N.Y., U.S. 212 43.35 N 76.12 W
Salmon ≃, Or., U.S. 224 45.03 N 124.00 W
Salmon ≃, Or., U.S. 224 45.22 N 122.02 W
Salmon, East Fork ≃ 202 44.16 N 114.19 W
Salmon, Middle Fork ≃ 202 45.18 N 114.36 W
Salmon, North Branch ≃ 212 43.32 N 75.48 W
Salmon, South Fork ≃ 202 45.23 N 115.31 W
Salmon Arm 182 50.42 N 119.16 W
Salmon-Bay 186 51.26 N 57.36 W
Salmon Creek ≃, N.Y., U.S. 210 43.16 N 77.02 W
Salmon Creek ≃, N.Y., U.S. 210 43.19 N 77.43 W
Salmon Creek ≃, Wa., U.S. 224 46.26 N 122.52 W
Salmon Creek ≃, Wa., U.S. 224 45.44 N 122.45 W
Salmon Falls Creek ≃ 202 42.43 N 114.51 W
Salmon Falls Creek Reservoir ⊜1 202 42.08 N 114.45 W
Salmon Gums 162 32.59 S 121.38 E
Salmon Lake ⊜ 212 44.49 N 78.28 W
Salmon Mountain ⋀ 188 45.14 N 71.08 W
Salmon Mountains ⋀ 204 41.00 N 123.00 W
Salmon Peak ⋀ 196 29.28 N 100.10 W
Salmon Point ⋟ 212 43.52 N 77.14 W
Salmon River Mountains ⋀ 202 44.45 N 115.30 W
Salmon River Reservoir ⊜1 212 43.32 N 75.52 W
Salmon Valley 182 54.05 N 122.41 W
Salmyš ≃ 86 52.01 N 55.21 E
Sal'nica 78 49.44 N 28.02 E
Salo, Centraf. 152 3.12 N 16.07 E
Salò, It. 64 45.36 N 10.31 E
Salo, Suomi 26 60.23 N 23.08 E
Salobel'ak 80 57.07 N 48.05 E
Salobra ≃ 248 20.12 S 56.29 W
Salomatino 80 50.01 N 44.50 E
Salome 200 33.46 N 113.36 W
Salomon, Cap ⋟ 240e 14.30 N 61.06 W
Salomon, Îles → Solomon Islands □1 175e 8.00 S 159.00 E
Salomón, Islas → Solomon Islands □1 175e 8.00 S 159.00 E
Salomone, Monte ⋀ 267a 41.47 N 12.44 E
Salomon-Inseln → Solomon Islands □1 175e 8.00 S 159.00 E
Salon ≃ 58 47.32 N 5.41 E
Salona 210 41.05 N 77.28 W
Salon-de-Provence 62 43.38 N 5.06 E
Salonga ≃ 152 0.10 S 19.50 E
Salonga, Parc National de la ♦ 152 1.45 S 21.20 E
Salonika → Thessaloníki 38 40.38 N 22.56 E
Salonta 38 46.48 N 21.40 E
Salor ≃ 34 39.39 N 7.03 W
Salorno (Salurn) 64 46.14 N 11.13 E
Saloslovo 265b 55.42 N 37.09 E
Şaloum ≃ 150 13.50 N 16.45 W
Salovka ≃ 265b 55.47 N 38.12 E
Salpausselkä ⋀ 26 61.00 N 26.30 E
Salqīn 130 36.08 N 36.27 E
Sal Rei 150a 16.11 N 22.55 W
Salsacate 252 31.19 S 65.05 W
Salsette Island I 272c 19.10 N 72.53 E
Salsilgo, Qawz ≐8 140 10.49 N 22.54 E
Salsipuedes, Canal de ≖ 232 28.37 N 113.00 W
Salsipuedes, Punta ⋟, C.R. 236 8.28 N 83.37 W
Salsipuedes, Punta ⋟, Méx. 232 32.05 N 116.53 W
Sal'sk 84 46.28 N 41.33 E
Sal'skij 24 61.48 N 35.58 E
Sal'sko-Manyčskaja gr'ada ⋀ 80 46.40 N 42.30 E
Salso ≃ 70 37.06 N 13.57 E
Salsomaggiore Terme 64 44.49 N 9.59 E
Salt ≃, U.S. 202 43.08 N 111.02 W
Salt ≃, Az., U.S. 200 33.23 N 112.18 W
Salt ≃, Ky., U.S. 194 38.00 N 85.57 W
Salt ≃, Mi., U.S. 281 42.39 N 82.47 W
Salt ≃, Mo., U.S. 219 39.28 N 91.23 W
Salt, Elk Fork ≃ 219 39.28 N 91.53 W
Salt, Middle Fork ≃ 219 39.28 N 91.49 W
Salt, North Fork ≃ 219 39.30 N 91.47 W
Salt, South Fork ≃ 219 39.28 N 91.49 W
Salta 252 24.47 S 65.25 W
Salta □4 252 25.00 S 64.30 W
Saltaim, ozero ⊜ 86 56.10 N 71.45 E
Saltair 224 48.57 N 123.46 W
Saltaire 276 40.39 N 73.12 W
Saltanovka 76 52.47 N 34.17 E
Saltara 66 43.45 N 12.54 E
Salt Ash, Austl. 170 32.47 S 151.55 E
Saltash, Eng., U.K. 42 50.24 N 4.12 W
Salt Basin ⊜ 196 31.50 N 105.00 W
Saltburn-by-the-Sea 44 54.35 N 0.58 W
Salt Cay I 240b 21.20 N 71.08 W
Saltcoats, Sk., Can. 184 51.03 N 102.12 W
Saltcoats, Scot., U.K. 46 55.38 N 4.47 W
Salt Creek ≃, On., Can. 275b 43.48 N 79.42 W
Salt Creek ≃, Ca., U.S. 204 36.15 N 116.49 W
Salt Creek ≃, Il., U.S. 194 40.08 N 89.50 W
Salt Creek ≃, Il., U.S. 278 41.49 N 87.50 W
Salt Creek ≃, In., U.S. 216 41.37 N 87.09 W
Salt Creek ≃, In., U.S. 218 39.27 N 85.09 W
Salt Creek ≃, In., U.S. 218 38.50 N 86.32 W
Salt Creek ≃, Ks., U.S. 198 39.06 N 97.44 W
Salt Creek ≃, N.M., U.S. 196 33.35 N 104.23 W
Salt Creek ≃, Oh., U.S. 218 39.30 N 96.43 W
Salt Creek ≃, Or., U.S. 202 43.43 N 122.26 W
Salt Creek ≃, Or., U.S. 224 45.09 N 123.13 W
Salt Creek ≃, Wy., U.S. 202 43.41 N 106.20 W
Salt Creek, Middle Fork ≃ 218 39.04 N 86.15 W
Salt Creek, North Fork ≃, In., U.S. 216 40.13 N 88.50 W
Salt Creek, North Fork ≃, In., U.S. 218 39.08 N 86.21 W
Salt Creek, West Branch ≃ 278 42.02 N 88.01 W
Salt Creek South Fork ≃ 218 39.02 N 86.16 W
Salt Draw V 196 31.19 N 103.28 W
Saltee Islands II 48 52.07 N 6.36 W
Salten 26 67.04 N 15.25 E
Saltfjellet Nasjonalpark ♦ 24 66.40 N 14.40 E
Saltford 42 51.24 N 2.27 W
Salt Fork Lake ⊜1 214 41.07 N 81.30 W
Salt Fork State Park ♦ 214 40.06 N 81.29 W
Saltholm I 41 55.38 N 12.46 E
Saltillo, Méx. 232 25.25 N 101.00 W
Saltillo, Ms., U.S. 194 34.22 N 88.40 W
Saltillo, Pa., U.S. 214 40.13 N 78.01 W
Saltillo, Tn., U.S. 194 35.22 N 88.12 W
Saltillo, Tx., U.S. 222 33.11 N 95.20 W
Salt Island I 240m 18.23 N 64.31 W
Salt Lake 158 29.16 S 24.00 E
Salt Lake ⊜ 196 34.03 N 103.05 W
Salt Lake City 200 40.45 N 111.53 W
Salto, Arg. 252 34.17 S 60.15 W
Salto, Bra. 255 23.12 S 47.17 W
Salto, Ur. 252 31.23 S 57.58 W
Salto ≃ 66 42.23 N 12.54 E
Salto, Lago del ⊜ 66 42.15 N 13.02 E
Salto da Divisa 255 16.00 S 39.57 W
Salto de las Rosas 252 34.43 S 68.14 W
Salto del Fraile ⋟ 286d 12.11 S 77.03 W
Salto Grande 255 22.54 S 49.59 W
Salton City 204 33.19 N 115.59 W
Salton Sea ⊜ 204 33.19 N 115.50 W
Salton Sea State Recreation Area ♦ 204 33.29 N 115.53 W
Saltonstall, Lake ⊜ 283 42.47 N 71.04 W
Saltora 126 23.32 N 86.56 E
Saltoro Kangri I ⋀ 123 35.24 N 76.51 E
Saltos del Guaira 252 24.03 S 54.17 W
Salt Pan Creek ⊂ 274a 33.59 S 151.02 E
Saltpeter Creek ⊂ 284b 39.20 N 76.22 W
Salt Point 210 41.44 N 73.42 W
Saltpond 150 5.12 N 1.04 W
Salt Range ⋀ 123 32.40 N 72.35 E
Salt River Indian Reservation ◆4 200 33.31 N 111.48 W
Saltsburg 214 40.29 N 79.27 W
Saltsjöbaden 40 59.17 N 18.18 E
Salt Slough ≃ 226 37.18 N 120.54 W
Saltspring Island I 224 48.47 N 123.30 W
Salt Springs Reservoir ⊜1 226 38.30 N 120.11 W
Saltville 192 36.52 N 81.45 W
Salt Wells Creek ≃ 200 41.39 N 108.59 W
Saltykovka, S.S.S.R. 80 52.07 N 44.05 E
Saltykovka, S.S.S.R. 265b 55.46 N 37.55 E
Saluda, S.C., U.S. 192 34.00 N 81.46 W
Saluda, Va., U.S. 208 37.36 N 76.35 W
Saluda ≃ 192 34.00 N 81.04 W
Saludecio 66 43.52 N 12.40 E
Saluen → Salween ≃ 12 16.31 N 97.37 E
Salue Timpuas, Selat ⊻ 112 1.55 S 124.00 E
Salug 116 8.07 N 122.47 E
Saluggia 62 45.14 N 8.00 E
Salumbar 120 24.08 N 74.03 E
Salunga 208 40.06 N 76.26 W
Saluping Island I 116 6.20 N 122.02 E
Salūq 'Afiq 130 36.36 N 39.07 E
Salūr 122 18.32 N 83.13 E
Saluzm → Salorno 64 46.14 N 11.13 E
Salussola 62 45.27 N 8.07 E
Salutáris 256 22.10 S 43.17 W
Saluzzo 62 44.39 N 7.29 E
Salvación, Bahía ⊂ 254 50.55 S 75.05 W
Salvado, Mount ⋀ 162 25.15 S 121.01 E
Salvador, Bra. 255 12.59 S 38.31 W
Salvador, Pil. 116 7.54 N 123.50 E
Salvador, Ca., U.S. 226 38.20 N 122.18 W
Salvador, El → El Salvador □1 236 13.50 N 88.55 W
Salvador, Lake ⊜ 194 29.45 N 90.15 W
Salvador Island I 116 15.31 N 119.55 E
Salvador María 258 35.18 S 59.10 W
Salvador Mazza 252 22.04 S 63.43 W
Salvage 186 48.41 N 53.38 W
Salvail ≃ 206 45.49 N 72.58 W
Salvaleón de Higüey 238 18.37 N 68.42 W
Salvaterra 250 0.46 S 48.31 W
Salvaterra de Magos 34 39.01 N 8.48 W
Salvatierra 234 20.13 N 100.53 W
Salve 68 39.51 N 18.17 E
Salve ≃ 32 44.41 N 1.16 E
Salwā, Bahr as- ⊂ 128 25.30 N 50.40 E
Salwā Bahrī 140 24.44 N 32.56 E
Salween ≃ 12 16.31 N 97.37 E
Salyer 204 40.53 N 123.35 W
Salyersville 192 37.45 N 83.04 W
Şalygino 78 51.34 N 34.06 E
Salza ≃, D.D.R. 54 51.23 N 11.50 E
Salza ≃, Öst. 61 47.40 N 14.43 E
Salzach ≃ 30 48.12 N 12.56 E
Salza Irpina 68 40.55 N 14.53 E
Salzbergen 52 52.19 N 7.20 E
Salzböde ≃ 56 50.40 N 8.42 E
Salzbrunn 156 24.23 S 18.00 E
Salzburg 64 47.48 N 13.02 E
Salzburg □3 64 47.25 N 13.15 E
Salzgitter 54 52.10 N 10.25 E
Salzgitter-Bad ◆8 52 52.04 N 10.23 E
Salzgitter-Barum ◆8 52 52.07 N 10.25 E
Salzgitter-Immendorf ◆8 52 52.09 N 10.26 E
Salzgitter-Lebenstedt ◆8 52 52.09 N 10.20 E
Salzgitter-Thiede ◆8 52 52.11 N 10.29 E
Salzgitter-Watenstedt ◆8 52 52.06 N 10.22 E
Salzhaff ⊂ 54 54.06 N 11.36 E
Salzhausen 52 53.13 N 10.09 E
Salzhemmendorf 52 52.04 N 9.35 E
Salzkammergut ◆1 64 47.45 N 13.30 E
Salzkotten 54 51.40 N 8.36 E
Salzmünde 54 51.31 N 11.49 E
Salzwedel 54 52.51 N 11.09 E
Sam, Gabon 152 0.58 N 11.16 E
Sam, India 120 26.50 N 70.31 E
Samā 132 32.28 N 36.14 E
Samā ≃ 248 18.10 S 70.40 W
Sam A. Baker State Park ♦ 194 37.16 N 90.34 W
Samacá 246 5.29 N 73.29 W
Samacimbo 152 13.33 S 16.59 E
Sama [de Langreo] 34 43.18 N 5.41 W
Samādiōn 142 30.20 N 30.57 E
Samagaltaj 88 50.36 N 95.03 E
Samaguri 124 26.12 N 92.51 E
Samāika ◆8 272a 28.32 N 77.05 E
Samaipata 248 18.09 S 63.52 W
Samal (Peñaplata) 116 7.05 N 125.42 E
Samalá ≃ 236 14.11 N 91.47 W
Samalanga 114 5.13 N 96.22 E
Samalayuca 200 31.21 N 106.28 W
Samaldy-Saj 85 41.12 N 72.11 E
Samales Group II 116 6.00 N 121.45 E
Samalga Pass ⊻ 180 52.48 N 169.25 W
Samal Island I 116 7.03 N 125.44 E
Samālkot 122 17.03 N 82.11 E
Samālūt 142 28.18 N 30.42 E
Samambaia ≃ 255 22.45 S 53.21 W
Samana 124 30.09 N 76.12 E
Samaná, Bahía de ⊂ 238 19.10 N 69.25 W
Samaná, Cabo ⋟ 238 19.18 N 69.09 W
Samana Cay I 238 23.06 N 73.42 W
Samandağı 130 36.07 N 35.56 E
Samandıra 130 40.59 N 29.13 E
Samandıra ≃ 267b 41.00 N 29.15 E
Samangān □4 120 36.15 N 67.40 E
Samangwa 152 4.24 S 24.10 E
Samani 92a 42.07 N 142.56 E
Samaniego 246 1.20 N 77.35 W
Samannūd 142 30.58 N 31.15 E
Samar I 116 12.00 N 125.00 E
Samar □4 116 11.50 N 125.00 E
Samara → Kujbyšev 80 53.12 N 50.09 E
Samara ≃, S.S.S.R. 78 48.27 N 35.07 E
Samara ≃, S.S.S.R. 80 53.10 N 50.04 E
Samarai 164 10.37 S 150.40 E
Samaria 62 45.38 N 8.47 E
Samarate 62 45.38 N 8.47 E
Samaria 89 47.15 N 138.46 E
Samaria, Id., U.S. 202 42.07 N 112.20 W
Samaria, Mi., U.S. 216 41.48 N 83.35 W
Samaria (As-Sāmirah) □9 132 32.15 N 35.10 E
Samarinda 112 0.30 S 117.09 E
Samaria, Mount ⋀ 169 36.52 S 146.03 E
Samariapo 246 5.15 N 67.48 W
Samarinda 112 0.30 S 117.09 E
Samarka 89 44.44 N 134.13 E
Samarkand 85 39.40 N 66.48 E
Samarkand □4 85 40.00 N 67.00 E
Samarrā' 128 34.12 N 43.52 E
Samar Sea ⊤2 116 12.15 N 124.15 E
Samarskoje, S.S.S.R. 83 46.56 N 39.41 E
Samarskoje, S.S.S.R. 86 52.02 N 58.10 E
Samarskoje, S.S.S.R. 86 49.00 N 83.23 E
Šamary 86 57.21 N 58.14 E
Samasata 123 29.21 N 71.33 E
Samassi 71 39.29 N 8.54 E
Samastipur 124 25.51 N 85.47 E
Samatlar 130 41.14 N 33.07 E
Samatya ◆8 267b 41.00 N 28.56 E
Samawāri 120 28.34 N 66.46 E
Samba, Centraf. 152 6.49 N 21.12 E
Sāmba, India 123 32.34 N 75.07 E
Samba, Zaïre 152 0.14 N 21.19 E
Samba, Zaïre 154 4.38 S 26.22 E
Samba Caju 152 8.46 S 15.24 E
Sambaetiba 256 22.41 S 42.48 W
Sambaiba 250 7.08 S 45.21 W
Sambalpur 120 21.27 N 83.58 E
Sambalpur □5 124 22.00 N 84.20 E
Sambar, Tanjung ⋟ 112 2.59 S 110.19 E
Sambas 112 1.20 N 109.15 E
Sambava 157b 14.16 S 50.10 E
Sambawizi 154 18.21 S 26.16 E
Sambayat 130 37.41 N 38.03 E
Sambāza 120 31.49 N 69.20 E
Sambek, S.S.S.R. 83 47.20 N 39.01 E
Sambek, S.S.S.R. 83 47.45 N 39.48 E
Sambek ≃ 83 47.16 N 39.01 E
Sambesi → Zambezi ≃ 138 18.55 S 36.04 E
Sambhal 124 28.35 N 78.33 E
Sāmbhar 124 26.55 N 75.12 E
Sāmbhar Lake ⊜ 120 26.58 N 75.05 E
Sambia → Zambia □1 154 14.30 S 27.30 E
Sambiase 68 38.58 N 16.17 E
Sambit, Pulau I 112 1.46 N 119.03 E
Sambito ≃ 250 5.40 S 42.10 W
Sambo 152 12.57 S 16.05 E
Samboan 116 9.32 N 123.18 E
Samboja 112 1.02 S 117.02 E
Sambolabbo 152 7.05 N 11.59 E
Sambor, Kam. 110 12.46 N 105.58 E
Sambor, S.S.S.R. 78 49.32 N 23.11 E
Samborombón ≃ 252 35.43 S 57.20 W
Samborombón, Bahía ⊂ 252 36.00 S 57.12 W
Samborondón 246 1.57 S 79.44 W
Sambre ≃ 32 50.28 N 4.52 E
Sambre à l'Oise, Canal de la ≖ 50 49.39 N 3.20 E
Sambreville 56 50.26 N 4.37 E
Sambriāl 123 32.28 N 74.21 E
Sambú ≃ 246 8.05 N 78.18 W
Sambuca di Sicilia 70 37.39 N 13.07 E
Sambuca Pistoiese 66 44.06 N 11.00 E
Sambughetti, Monte ⋀ 70 37.50 N 14.22 E
Sambungo 152 8.39 S 20.43 E
Sambusu 156 17.50 S 19.20 E
Samch'ŏk 98 37.27 N 129.10 E
Sam Chom, Khao ⋀ 110 8.07 N 99.26 E
Şamch'ŏnp'o 98 34.57 N 128.03 E
Samchor 84 40.50 N 46.02 E
Samdari 120 25.49 N 72.35 E
Samdžir, gora ⋀ 88 52.32 N 93.53 E
Same 154 4.04 S 37.44 E
Same ≃ 94 36.54 N 140.49 E
Samedan 58 46.33 N 9.52 E
Samegawa 94 37.02 N 140.31 E
Sāmen 94 34.12 N 48.42 E
Samene, Oued V 148 26.49 N 7.08 E
Samer 50 50.38 N 1.45 E
Sameru Dando ⋀ 124 27.02 N 90.20 E
Samet' 80 57.49 N 40.44 E
Samford 171a 27.23 S 152.53 E
Samfya 154 11.21 S 29.32 E
Samho 98 35.25 N 128.05 E
Samho 98 39.56 N 127.53 E
Saminka ≃ 265b 55.45 N 37.17 E
Samiria ≃ 246 4.42 S 74.13 W
Samish 224 48.35 N 122.28 W
Samish ≃ 224 48.38 N 122.29 W
Samish Bay ⊂ 224 48.36 N 122.28 W
Samish Lake ⊜ 224 48.39 N 122.24 W
Samj 132 32.27 N 36.30 E
Samka 110 20.09 N 96.57 E
Samlesbury 262 53.46 N 2.38 W
Samlesbury Aerodrome ⊠ 262 53.47 N 2.34 W
Samlesbury Bottoms 262 53.45 N 2.34 W
Samlesbury Higher Hall ⊥ 262 53.45 N 2.34 W
Şamlı 130 39.48 N 27.51 E
Sammamish, Lake ⊜ 224 47.36 N 122.06 W
Sammichele di Bari 68 40.53 N 16.57 E
Samnangjin 98 35.23 N 128.50 E
Samnaun 58 46.56 N 10.22 E
Samnaungruppe ⋀ 58 47.00 N 10.25 E
Sam Ngao 110 17.15 N 99.01 E
Samnū 146 27.17 N 14.53 E
Samnye 98 35.55 N 127.05 E
Samo 164 3.58 S 152.51 E
Samoa → American Samoa □2 175a 14.20 S 170.00 W
Samoa americane → American Samoa □2 175a 14.20 S 170.00 W
Samoa Basin ◆1 14 16.00 S 166.00 W
Samoa i Sisifo → Western Samoa □1 175a 13.55 S 172.00 W
Samoa Islands II 175a 14.00 S 171.00 W
Samoa Alto 252 30.25 S 70.58 W
Samoa Occidental → Western Samoa □1 175a 13.55 S 172.00 W
Samoa Occidentales → Western Samoa □1 175a 13.55 S 172.00 W
Samobor 36 45.48 N 15.43 E
Samoded 24 63.38 N 40.29 E
Samoëns 58 46.05 N 6.44 E
Samofalovka 80 48.57 N 44.13 E
Samoilovka 80 51.12 N 43.43 E
Samojlovka 64 38.42 N 23.33 E
Samokov 38 42.20 N 23.33 E
Samolaco 58 46.15 N 9.24 E
Samora ≃ 266c 38.50 N 8.57 W
Samos 38 37.45 N 27.00 E
Sámos I 38 37.48 N 26.44 E
Samosdelka 80 46.02 N 47.53 E
Samoset 220 27.28 N 82.34 W
Samosir, Pulau I 114 2.35 N 98.50 E
Samotevići 76 53.13 N 31.50 E
Samothrace → Samothráki I 38 40.30 N 25.32 E
Samothráki 38 40.28 N 25.31 E
Samothráki I 38 40.30 N 25.32 E
Şamouco 266c 38.43 N 8.59 W
Samovo 76 54.12 N 31.22 E
Samovol'no-Ivanovka 80 52.13 N 50.53 E
S'amozero 24 61.54 N 33.18 E
Sampacho 252 33.23 S 64.43 W
Sampaga 112 2.19 S 119.07 E
Sampaio Correia 256 22.52 S 42.36 W
Sampang 115a 7.12 S 113.15 E
Sampanahan 112 2.38 S 116.11 E
Sampara ≃ 112 3.49 S 122.28 E
Sampawams Creek ≃ 276 40.41 N 73.19 W
Sam Pervyj 86 45.28 N 56.06 E
Sampeyre 62 44.34 N 7.11 E
Sampierdarena 62 44.25 N 8.55 E
Sampieri 70 36.43 N 14.44 E
Sampit 112 2.32 S 112.57 E
Sampit ≃ 112 2.44 S 112.54 E
Sampit, Teluk ⊂ 112 3.05 S 113.03 E
Sampolawa 112 5.36 S 122.43 E
Sampson 279b 40.10 N 79.53 W

≃ River	Fluss	Río	Rivière	Rio	
≖ Canal	Kanal	Canal	Canal	Canal	
⌊ Waterfall, Rapids	Wasserfall, Stromschnellen	Cascada, Rápidos	Chute d'eau, Rapides	Cascata, Rápidos	
⊻ Strait	Meeresstrasse	Estrecho	Détroit	Estreito	
⊂ Bay, Gulf	Bucht, Golf	Bahía, Golfo	Baie, Golfe	Baía, Golfo	
⊜ Lake, Lakes	See, Seen	Lago, Lagos	Lac, Lacs	Lago, Lagos	
≅ Swamp	Sumpf	Pantano	Marais	Pântano	
⊠ Ice Features, Glacier	Eis- und Gletscherformen	Accidentes Glaciales	Formes glaciaires	Acidentes glaciares	
⊤ Other Hydrographic Features	Andere Hydrographische Objekte	Otros Elementos Hidrográficos	Autres données hydrographiques	Outros acidentes hidrográficos	
◆ Submarine Features	Untermeerische Objekte	Accidentes Submarinos	Formes de relief sous-marin	Acidentes submarinos	
□ Political Unit	Politische Einheit	Unidad Política	Entité politique	Unidade política	
⊻ Cultural Institution	Kulturelle Institution	Institución Cultural	Institution culturelle	Instituição cultural	
⊥ Historical Site	Historische Stätte	Sitio Histórico	Site historique	Sítio histórico	
♦ Recreational Site	Erholungs- und Ferienort	Sitio de Recreo	Centre de loisirs	Área de Lazer	
⊠ Airport	Flughafen	Aeropuerto	Aéroport	Aeroporto	
■ Military Installation	Militäranlage	Instalación Militar	Installation militaire	Instalação militar	
◆ Miscellaneous	Verschiedenes	Misceláneo	Divers	Diversos	

Sampson State Park
♦ 210 42.44 N 76.55 W
Sampués 246 9.11 N 75.23 W
Sampur 80 52.19 N 41.37 E
Sampwe 154 9.20 S 27.26 E
Şamrah 130 37.30 N 40.30 E
Šamrajevka 78 49.46 N 29.49 E
Samrāla 123 30.51 N 76.11 E
Sam Rayburn
Reservoir ⊜¹ 194 31.27 N 94.37 W
Samre 144 13.07 N 39.10 E
Samreboi 150 5.36 N 2.34 W
Samro, ozero ⊜ 76 58.57 N 28.49 E
Samrong, Khlong ≃ 269a 13.39 N 100.34 E
Sams 232 29.46 N 115.42 W
Samsat 130 37.30 N 38.31 E
Samsø I 41 55.52 N 10.37 E
Samsø Bælt ⊔ 41 55.48 N 10.47 E
Samson, Al., U.S. 194 31.06 N 86.02 W
Sam-son, Viet. 110 19.44 N 105.54 E
Samson I 42a 49.56 N 6.22 W
Samson Indian
Reserve ♦⁴ 182 52.48 N 113.10 W
Samsonovka 85 42.44 N 70.32 E
Samsonville 210 41.53 N 74.18 W
Sams Point ⋏ 210 41.40 N 74.22 W
Samsu 98 41.19 N 127.59 E
Samsun 130 41.17 N 36.20 E
Samsun □⁴ 130 41.15 N 36.00 E
Samsun Limani ⊂ 130 41.18 N 36.21 E
Samtens 54 54.21 N 13.17 E
Samthar 124 25.51 N 78.55 E
Samtown 194 31.16 N 92.26 W
Samtredia 84 42.10 N 42.20 E
Samu 112 2.01 S 115.57 E
Samūdragarh 126 23.21 N 88.20 E
Samuel, Mount ⋏ 162 19.41 S 134.09 E
Samuel P. Taylor
State Park ♦ 226 38.01 N 122.44 W
Samugheo 71 39.57 N 8.56 E
Samuhú 252 27.31 S 60.24 W
Samui, Ko I 110 9.30 N 100.00 E
Samukawa 94 35.22 N 139.23 E
Samundri 123 31.04 N 72.58 E
Samur ≃ 84 41.53 N 48.32 E
Samur-Apšeronskij
kanal ≅ 84 41.38 N 48.25 E
Samus' 86 56.46 N 84.44 E
Samusele 152 10.06 S 24.05 E
Samutlu 130 39.44 N 32.22 E
Samut Prakan 110 13.36 N 100.36 E
Samut Sakhon 110 13.32 N 100.17 E
Samut Songkhram 110 13.24 N 100.00 E
Samuyishankou ✕ 124 29.55 N 84.46 E
S'amža 76 60.01 N 41.02 E
San 150 13.18 N 4.54 W
San ≃, Asia 110 13.32 N 105.58 E
San ≃, Europe 30 50.44 N 21.50 E
San ≃, Zhg. 100 33.02 N 119.21 E
Saña, Perú 248 6.55 S 79.35 W
San 'ā', Yaman 144 15.23 N 44.12 E
Sana ≃, Jugo. 36 45.03 N 16.23 E
San'a ≃, S.S.S.R. 82 54.41 N 35.55 E
Sanaag □⁴ 144 10.30 N 47.45 E
Sanaba 150 12.25 N 3.49 W
Sanaba ≃ 150 15.06 N 10.55 W
Sanabū 142 27.30 N 30.47 E
Sanada 94 36.27 N 138.20 E
Sanaduva 252 27.57 S 51.48 W
Sanae ♦³ 9 70.30 S 2.30 W
Sanafe 142 30.47 N 31.21 E
Sanāfīr I 128 27.55 N 34.40 E
Sanaga ≃ 152 3.35 N 9.38 E
Sanage-yama ⋏ 94 35.12 N 137.10 E
Sanagōchi 96 33.59 N 134.28 E
San Agustín, Arg. 252 38.01 S 58.21 W
San Agustín, Arg. 252 31.59 S 64.23 W
San Agustín, Col. 246 1.53 N 76.16 W
San Agustín, Méx. 200 31.31 N 106.15 W
San Agustín, Perú 286d 12.02 S 77.07 W
San Agustin, Pil. 116 16.30 N 121.45 E
San Agustin, Pil. 116 12.25 N 120.59 E
San Agustin, Cape › 116 6.16 N 126.11 E
San Agustin, Plains
of ≍ 200 33.50 N 108.00 W
San Agustín
Atenango 234 17.38 N 97.59 W
San Agustín de Valle
Fértil 252 30.38 S 67.27 W
San Agustín Loxicha 234 16.01 N 96.38 W
San Agustín Oapan 234 17.58 N 99.27 W
San Agustín
Tlaxiaca 234 20.07 N 98.53 W
Sanak Islands II 180 54.25 N 162.35 W
San Alberto 196 27.30 N 101.20 W
San Alejo 236 13.26 N 87.58 W
Sān al-Ḥajar, Birkat
⊜ 142 31.03 N 31.54 E
Sān al-Ḥajar al-
Qibliyah 142 30.58 N 31.52 E
Sanalona, Presa ⊜¹ 232 24.53 N 107.00 W
San Ambrosio, Isla I 244 26.21 S 79.52 W
Sanam Chai, Khlong
≅ 269a 13.38 N 100.27 E
Sanana 112 2.04 S 125.58 E
Sanana, Pulau I 112 2.12 S 125.55 E
Sanand 120 22.59 N 72.23 E
Sanandaj 128 35.19 N 47.00 E
Sanandita 248 21.40 S 63.35 W
San Andreas 226 38.11 N 120.40 W
San Andreas Lake ⊜ 282 37.36 N 122.26 W
San Andreas Rift
Zone V 282 37.25 N 122.15 W
San Andrés, Col. 236 12.35 N 81.42 W
San Andrés, Col. 246 6.49 N 72.52 W
San Andrés, Méx. 232 27.14 N 114.14 W
San Andres, Pan. 236 8.36 N 82.44 W
San Andrés, Cerro ⋏ 234 19.48 N 100.36 W
San Andrés, Isla de I 236 12.32 N 81.42 W
San Andrés, Laguna
de ⊂ 234 22.40 N 97.52 W
San Andrés
Cohamiata 234 22.12 N 104.03 W
San Andrés de Giles 258 34.27 S 59.27 W
San Andrés de la
Barca 266d 41.27 N 1.59 E
San Andres
Mountains ⋏ 200 32.55 N 106.45 W
San Andres Point › 116 13.34 N 121.52 E
San Andrés
Sajcabajá 236 15.13 N 90.55 W
San Andrés
Tototepec ♦⁸ 286a 19.15 N 99.10 W
San Andrés Tuxtla 234 18.27 N 95.13 W
San Andrés y
Providencia □⁸ 238 12.30 N 81.45 W
San Angel
→ Villa Obregón
♦⁸ 286a 19.21 N 99.12 W
San Angelo 196 31.27 N 100.26 W
San Anselmo 226 37.58 N 122.33 W
San Antero 246 9.23 N 75.46 W
San Antonio, Arg. 252 24.22 S 65.20 W
San Antonio, Arg. 252 28.56 S 65.06 W
San Antonio, Belize 236 16.15 N 89.02 W
San Antonio, Chile 252 27.53 S 70.03 W
San Antonio, Chile 252 33.35 S 71.38 W
San Antonio, Col. 246 3.55 N 75.28 W
San Antonio, C.R. 236 10.12 N 85.26 W
San Antonio, Perú 248 6.22 S 76.21 W
San Antonio, Pil. 116 12.25 N 124.17 E
San Antonio, Pil. 116 14.57 N 120.05 E
San Antonio, P.R. 240m 18.30 N 67.07 W
San Antonio, T.T.P.I. 174n 15.08 N 145.43 E
San Antonio, Fl.,
U.S. 220 28.20 N 82.16 W
San Antonio, N.M.,
U.S. 200 35.06 N 106.22 W
San Antonio, Tx.,
U.S. 196 29.25 N 98.29 W
San Antonio, Ur. 252 31.22 S 57.48 W
San Antonio, Ur. 258 34.27 S 56.05 W
San Antonio, Ven. 286b 22.55 N 82.29 W
San Antonio □⁷ 246 45.28 N 9.19 E
San Antonio ≃, Méx. 196 29.13 N 103.47 W
San Antonio ≃, Méx. 232 31.00 N 116.15 W
San Antonio ≃, Méx. 234 18.14 N 101.52 W
San Antonio ≃, Ca.,
U.S. 226 35.52 N 120.48 W
San Antonio ≃, Tx.,
U.S. 196 28.30 N 96.50 W
San Antonio ≃¹ 288 34.24 S 58.31 W
San Antonio, Cabo
›, Arg. 252 36.40 S 56.42 W
San Antonio, Cabo
›, Cuba 240p 21.52 N 84.57 W
San Antonio, Lake
⊜¹ 226 35.55 N 121.00 W
San Antonio, Mount
⋏ 228 34.17 N 117.39 W
San Antonio, Punta
› 232 29.46 N 115.42 W
San Antonio, Rio ≃ 200 37.11 N 105.55 W
San Antonio Abad 34 38.58 N 1.18 E
San Antonio Bay ⊂,
Pil. 116 8.38 N 117.35 E
San Antonio Bay ⊂,
Tx., U.S. 196 28.20 N 96.45 W
San Antonio Canyon
V 280 34.12 N 117.40 W
San Antonio Creek ≃ 226 38.09 N 122.33 W
San Antonio Dam
♦⁶ 280 34.09 N 117.41 W
San Antonio de
Areco 258 34.15 S 59.28 W
San Antonio de
Bravo 232 30.10 N 104.42 W
San Antonio de
Galipán 286c 10.33 N 66.53 W
San Antonio de las
Alazanas 232 25.16 N 100.36 W
San Antonio del
Golfo 246 10.27 N 63.50 W
San Antonio de los
Baños 240p 22.53 N 82.30 W
San Antonio de los
Cobres 252 24.11 S 66.21 W
San Antonio del
Táchira 246 7.50 N 72.27 W
San Antonio de
Padua, Arg. 258 34.40 S 58.42 W
San Antônio de
Pádua, Bra. 255 21.32 S 42.11 W
San Antonio de
Padua, Méx. 234 22.35 N 104.30 W
San Antonio de
Padua, Mission ✝¹ 226 36.01 N 121.15 W
San Antonio de
Tamanaco 246 9.41 N 66.03 W
San Antonio
Eloxochitlán 234 18.11 N 96.52 W
San Antonio Heights 228 34.10 N 117.40 W
San Antonio
Mountain ⋏ 200 36.52 N 106.02 W
San Antonio Nogalar 234 23.04 N 98.22 W
San Antonio Oeste 254 40.44 S 64.56 W
San Antonio
Reservoir ⊜¹ 226 37.35 N 121.50 W
San Antonio
Suchitepéquez 236 14.32 N 91.25 W
San Antonio
Tecómitl ♦⁸ 286a 19.13 N 98.59 W
San Antonio Ticino 266b 45.35 N 8.46 E
San Antonio
Zomeyucan 286a 19.27 N 99.16 W
San'anzhuling 120 28.33 N 93.00 E
San Ardo 226 36.01 N 120.54 W
Sanaroa Island I 164 9.35 S 151.00 E
Sanary-sur-Mer 62 43.07 N 5.48 E
Sanatoga 285 40.15 N 75.36 W
Sanatoga Creek ≃ 285 40.14 N 75.36 W
Sanatorium 194 31.53 N 89.46 W
San Augustine 194 31.31 N 94.06 W
San Augustin Pass
✕ 200 32.26 N 106.34 W
Sanaur 124 30.18 N 76.27 E
Sanāw 144 17.50 N 51.00 E
Sanāwad 120 22.11 N 76.04 E
Sanāwān 123 30.18 N 71.04 E
Sanbao, Zhg. 102 26.55 N 106.09 E
Sanbao, Zhg. 105 40.20 N 116.02 E
Sanbaoyingzi 104 41.34 N 120.56 E
San Bartolomé
Ayautla 234 18.02 N 96.40 W
San Bartolomé de la
Cuadra 266d 41.26 N 2.02 E
San Bartolomeo in
Galdo 68 41.24 N 15.01 E
San Bartolo Morelos 234 19.41 N 99.29 W
San Basilio 71 39.32 N 9.11 E
San Baudilio de
Llobregat 34 41.21 N 2.03 E
San Benedetto, Alpe
di ⋏ 66 43.53 N 11.43 E
San Benedetto del
Tronto 66 42.57 N 13.53 E
San Benedetto in
Alpe 66 43.59 N 11.41 E
San Benedetto Po 64 45.02 N 10.55 E
San Benedicto, Isla I 232 19.18 N 110.49 W
San Benigno
Canavese 62 45.13 N 7.46 E
San Benito, Bol. 248 17.31 S 65.55 W
San Benito, Guat. 232 16.55 N 89.54 W
San Benito, Perú 248 7.26 S 78.56 W
San Benito, Tx.,
U.S. 196 26.07 N 97.37 W
San Benito □⁶ 226 36.51 N 121.24 W
San Benito ≃ 226 36.53 N 121.34 W
San Benito Mountain
⋏ 226 36.22 N 120.38 W
San Bernard ≃ 222 28.52 N 95.27 W
San Bernardino,
Schw. 58 46.28 N 9.12 E
San Bernardino, Ca.,
U.S. 228 34.07 N 117.18 W
San Bernardino □⁶ 228 34.40 N 117.17 W
San Bernardino,
Passo del ✕ 58 46.30 N 9.11 E
San Bernardino
Mountains ⋏ 204 34.10 N 116.45 W
San Bernardino
National Forest ♦ 280 34.12 N 117.38 W
San Bernardino
Strait ⊔ 116 12.32 N 124.10 E
San Bernardo, Arg. 252 27.17 S 60.42 W
San Bernardo, Chile 252 33.36 S 70.43 W
San Bernardo, Méx. 232 25.59 N 105.33 W
San Bernardo, Canal
≅ 286e 33.36 S 70.41 W
San Bernardo, Isla I 236 11.32 N 85.06 W
San Bernardo, Islas
de II 236 9.45 N 75.50 W
San Bernardo del
Viento 246 9.21 N 75.57 W
Sanbe-yama ⋏ 96 35.08 N 132.37 E
San Biagio 66 44.35 N 11.52 E
San Biagio di
Callalta 64 45.41 N 12.22 E
San Biagio Platani 70 37.31 N 13.32 E
San Biagio
Saracinisco 66 41.37 N 13.55 E
San Blas, Méx. 232 26.05 N 108.46 W
San Blas, Méx. 234 21.31 N 105.16 W
San Blas, Cape › 192 29.40 N 85.22 W
San Blas, Cordillera
de ⋏ 246 9.18 N 79.00 W
San Blas, Golfo de ⊂ 246 9.30 N 79.00 W
San Blas Atempa 234 16.16 N 95.10 W
San Blas de los
Sauces 252 28.24 S 67.05 W
San Bonifacio 64 45.24 N 11.16 E
San Borja 248 14.49 S 66.51 W
Sanborn, Ia., U.S. 198 43.10 N 95.39 W
Sanborn, Mn., U.S. 198 44.12 N 95.07 W
Sanborn, N.Y., U.S. 210 43.08 N 78.53 W
Sanborn, N.D., U.S. 198 46.56 N 98.13 W
San Bovio 266b 45.28 N 9.19 E
San Bruno 226 37.37 N 122.24 W
San Bruno, Point › 282 37.39 N 122.22 W
San Bruno Mountain
⋏ 282 37.42 N 122.25 W
Sanbu 94 35.39 N 140.23 E
San Buena Ventura,
Bol. 248 14.28 S 67.35 W
San Buenaventura,
Méx. 232 27.05 N 101.32 W
San Buenaventura
→ Ventura, Ca.,
U.S. 228 34.17 N 119.18 W
San Buono 66 41.59 N 14.34 E
San Calogero 68 38.34 N 16.01 E
San Calogero,
Monte ⋏ 70 37.57 N 13.44 E
San Candido
(Innichen) 64 46.44 N 12.17 E
Sancang 100 32.45 N 120.43 E
San Carlo 58 46.25 N 8.32 E
San Carlos, Arg. 252 27.45 S 55.54 W
San Carlos, Arg. 252 33.46 S 69.02 W
San Carlos, Arg. 252 25.56 S 65.56 W
San Carlos, Chile 252 36.25 S 71.58 W
San Carlos, Chile 286e 33.36 S 70.35 W
San Carlos, Méx. 232 29.01 N 100.51 W
San Carlos, Méx. 232 24.35 N 98.56 W
San Carlos, Nic. 236 11.07 N 84.47 W
San Carlos, Pan. 236 8.29 N 79.57 W
San Carlos, Para. 252 22.16 S 57.18 W
San Carlos, Pil. 116 10.30 N 123.25 E
San Carlos, Pil. 116 15.55 N 120.20 E
San Carlos, Az.,
U.S. 200 33.20 N 110.27 W
San Carlos, Ca.,
U.S. 226 37.29 N 122.15 W
San Carlos, Ur. 252 34.48 S 54.55 W
San Carlos, Ven. 246 9.40 N 68.36 W
San Carlos ≃, C.R. 236 10.47 N 84.12 W
San Carlos ≃, Az.,
U.S. 200 33.16 N 110.27 W
San Carlos ≃, Ven. 246 9.07 N 68.25 W
San Carlos, Canal ≅ 286e 33.25 S 70.38 W
San Carlos, Riacho ≃ 252 22.51 S 57.51 W
San Carlos Airport ⊠ 282 37.31 N 122.15 W
San Carlos Bay ⊂ 220 26.28 N 82.03 W
San Carlos
Borromeo, Mission
✝¹ 226 36.34 N 121.55 W
San Carlos Centro 252 31.44 S 61.06 W
San Carlos de
Bariloche 254 41.09 S 71.18 W
San Carlos de
Bolívar 252 36.15 S 61.06 W
San Carlos de
Chena 286e 33.35 S 70.44 W
San Carlos de
Guaroa 246 3.44 N 73.14 W
San Carlos de la
Rápita 34 40.37 N 0.36 E
San Carlos del Zulia 246 9.01 N 71.55 W
San Carlos de Río
Negro 246 1.55 N 67.04 W
San Carlos Indian
Reservation ♦⁴ 200 33.23 N 110.09 W
San Carlos
Reservoir ⊜¹ 200 33.13 N 110.24 W
San Carpoforo
Creek ≃ 226 35.47 N 121.19 W
San Casciano dei
Bagni 66 42.52 N 11.53 E
San Casciano in Val
di Pesa 66 43.39 N 11.11 E
San Cataldo, It. 68 40.23 N 18.17 E
San Cataldo, It. 70 37.29 N 13.59 E
San Cayetano 252 38.20 S 59.37 W
Sancergues 50 47.09 N 2.55 E
Sancerre 50 47.20 N 2.51 E
Sancerrois, Collines
du ⋏² 50 47.25 N 2.45 E
San Cesario di
Lecce 68 40.18 N 18.10 E
San Cesario sul
Panaro 64 44.34 N 11.02 E
Sancey-le-Grand 58 47.18 N 6.35 E
Sancha, Zhg. 105 40.27 N 116.26 E
Sancha, Zhg. 106 31.35 N 121.34 E
Sancha ≃ 102 26.55 N 106.06 E
Sanchaba 107 30.19 N 104.14 E
Sanchahe 89 44.59 N 126.04 E
Sanchakou 105 39.47 N 117.19 E
Sanchang 106 31.54 N 121.15 E
Sanchazi 104 41.07 N 124.15 E
Sanchazicun 104 42.03 N 123.59 E
Sanchenglong 89 44.02 N 120.58 E
Sánchez 238 19.14 N 69.36 W
Sanchez Creek ≃ 222 32.36 N 97.50 W
Sánchez Magallanes 234 18.18 N 93.52 W
Sānchi 124 23.29 N 77.44 E
Sanchih 100 25.16 N 121.30 E
San Chirico Raparo 68 40.11 N 16.05 E
Sanch'ŏng 98 35.26 N 127.54 E
Sanchung 269d 25.04 N 121.30 E
Sanch'ungch'iao 269d 25.12 N 121.35 E
San Cipirello 70 37.58 N 13.10 E
San Cipriano
Picentino 68 40.43 N 14.52 E
San Ciro de Acosta 234 21.38 N 99.49 W
San Clemente, Esp. 34 39.24 N 2.26 W
San Clemente, Ca.,
U.S. 228 33.25 N 117.36 W
San Clemente,
Arroyo de ≃ 266d 41.20 N 2.00 E
San Clemente a
Casauria ✝¹ 66 42.14 N 13.55 E
San Clemente de
Llobregat 266d 41.20 N 2.00 E
San Clemente Island
I 228 32.54 N 118.29 W
Sancoins 32 46.50 N 2.55 E
San Colombano al
Lambro 62 45.11 N 9.29 E
San Cono 70 37.17 N 14.22 E
Sanco Point › 116 8.15 N 126.27 E
San Cosme 252 27.22 S 58.31 W
San Cosme Xalostoc 234 19.24 N 98.03 W
San Cosmo
Albanese 68 39.35 N 16.25 E
San Costantino
Albanese 68 40.02 N 16.18 E
San Cristóbal, Arg. 252 30.19 S 61.14 W
San Cristóbal, Cuba 240p 22.43 N 83.03 W
San Cristóbal, Méx. 234 16.45 N 92.38 W
San Cristóbal, Ven. 246 7.46 N 72.14 W
San Cristóbal I 175e 10.36 S 161.45 E
San Cristóbal ≃ 286e 33.25 S 70.37 W
San Cristóbal ≃ 234 18.02 N 96.12 W
San Cristóbal, Bahía
de ⊂ 232 27.23 N 114.38 W
San Cristóbal, Cerro
⋏, Chile 286e 33.25 S 70.39 W
San Cristóbal, Cerro
⋏, Perú 286d 12.02 S 77.01 W
San Cristóbal, Isla I 246a 0.50 S 89.26 W
San Cristóbal
→ Saint
Christopher-Nevis
□¹ 238 17.20 N 62.45 W
San Cristóbal,
Volcán ⋏¹ 236 12.42 N 87.01 W
San Cristóbal de la
Barranca 234 21.03 N 103.26 W
San Cristóbal de la
Laguna 148 28.29 N 16.19 W
San Cristóbal de las
Casas 234 16.45 N 92.38 W
San Cristobal
Totonicapán 236 14.55 N 91.26 W
San Cristobal
Trench ♦¹ 14 11.15 S 162.45 E
San Cristóbal
Verapaz 236 15.23 N 90.24 W
San Cristobal Wash
V 200 32.47 N 113.44 W
San Croce, Monte ⋏ 66 41.17 N 13.58 E
Sancti-Spíritus 240p 21.56 N 79.27 W
Sancti-Spíritus □⁴ 240p 22.00 N 79.20 W
San Cugat, Riera de
≃ 266d 41.29 N 2.11 E
San Cugat del Vallés 266d 41.28 N 2.05 E
Sančursk 80 56.57 N 47.15 E
Sancy, Puy de ⋏ 32 45.32 N 2.49 E
Sand, B.R.D. 56 48.32 N 7.55 E
Sand, Nor. 26 59.29 N 6.15 E
Sand ≃, Ab., Can. 184 54.22 N 111.05 W
Sand ≃, S. Afr. 156 22.25 S 30.05 E
Sand ≃, S. Afr. 158 28.05 S 26.25 E
Sanda, Nihon 96 34.53 N 135.14 E
Sanda, Nihon 268 35.28 N 139.21 E
Sandafā al-Fa'r 142 28.32 N 30.40 E
Sandai 112 1.15 S 110.31 E
Sanda Island I 44 55.18 N 5.34 W
Sandakan 112 5.50 N 118.07 E
Sandakan,
Pelabuhan ⊂ 116 5.45 N 118.05 E
Sandal, Baie du ⊂ 175f 20.50 S 167.05 E
Sandal, Baie du ⊂ 175i 20.50 S 167.05 E
San Damián 248 12.02 S 76.24 W
San Damiano d'Asti 62 44.50 N 8.04 E
San Damiano Macra 62 44.29 N 7.16 E
Sāndān 110 12.42 N 106.01 E
Sandan, Chāh ⊤⁴ 128 28.59 N 63.27 E
Sandane 26 61.46 N 6.13 E
San Daniele del Friuli 64 46.09 N 13.00 E
Sandan-kyō ♦ 96 34.38 N 132.13 E
Sandanski 38 41.34 N 23.17 E
Sandaogang 89 46.08 N 130.05 E
Sandaogou, Zhg. 104 41.39 N 121.45 E
Sandaogou, Zhg. 105 39.33 N 115.27 E
Sandaohe 86 44.21 N 85.37 E
Sandaoliangzi 104 41.20 N 122.07 E
Sandaolingzi 104 40.58 N 124.08 E
Sandaozhen 89 47.25 N 126.25 E
Sandaré 150 14.42 N 10.18 W
Sandarigo 26 57.43 N 12.47 E
Sandarne 26 61.16 N 17.10 E
Sand Arroyo V 196 37.29 N 101.29 W
Sandata 80 46.16 N 41.46 E
Sandau 54 52.47 N 12.02 E
Sanday I 46 59.15 N 2.35 W
Sanday Sound ⊂ 46 59.11 N 2.31 W
Sandbach 44 53.09 N 2.22 W
Sandbank 46 55.59 N 4.58 W
Sandbanks
Provincial Park ♦ 212 43.55 N 77.17 W
Sandbochum 263 51.40 N 7.41 E
Sand City 226 36.37 N 121.51 W
Sand Coulee 202 47.23 N 111.10 W
Sand Coulee Creek ≃ 202 47.27 N 111.18 W
Sand Creek ≃, U.S. 200 41.13 N 105.43 W
Sand Creek ≃, In.,
U.S. 218 39.03 N 85.51 W
Sand Creek ≃, Ks.,
U.S. 198 37.26 N 98.12 W
Sand Creek ≃, Mn.,
U.S. 190 45.56 N 92.39 W
Sand Creek ≃, Mt.,
U.S. 202 47.18 N 106.45 W
Sand Creek ≃, S.D.,
U.S. 198 44.02 N 98.05 W
Sand Creek ≃, Wy.,
U.S. 200 43.27 N 105.26 W
Sand Creek ≃, Wy.,
U.S. 200 41.02 N 107.52 W
Sand Creek ≃, Wy.,
U.S. 202 44.16 N 107.55 W
Sand Cut 220 26.56 N 80.35 W
Sande, B.R.D. 52 51.45 N 8.39 E
Sande, B.R.D. 52 53.30 N 8.01 E
Sandefjord 26 59.08 N 10.14 E
San Demetrio
Corone 68 39.34 N 16.22 E
San Demetrio
ne'Vestini 66 42.17 N 13.34 E
Sanders, Az., U.S. 200 35.12 N 109.19 W
Sanders, Ky., U.S. 218 38.39 N 84.56 W
Sandersdorf, B.R.D. 60 48.54 N 11.37 E
Sandersdorf, D.D.R. 54 51.37 N 12.15 E
Sandersleben 54 51.40 N 11.34 E
Sanderson 196 30.08 N 102.23 W
Sanderstead ♦⁸ 260 51.20 N 0.05 W
Sanderston 168b 34.46 S 139.13 E
Sandersville, Ga.,
U.S. 192 32.58 N 82.48 W
Sandersville, Ms.,
U.S. 194 31.47 N 89.01 W
Sandeshkhali 126 22.22 N 88.53 E
Sandesneben 52 53.41 N 10.30 E
Sandfly Lake ⊜ 184 55.45 N 106.05 W
Sand Fork 188 38.54 N 80.45 W
Sandgate, Austl. 171a 27.20 S 153.05 E
Sandgate, Eng.,
U.K. 42 51.05 N 1.08 E
Sandhammaren › 26 55.23 N 14.12 E
Sandhamn 40 59.17 N 18.55 E
Sandhead 44 54.48 N 4.58 W
Sandheuwel 158 31.46 S 20.48 E
Sandhill, On., Can. 275b 43.50 N 79.49 W
Sand Hill, Ma., U.S. 207 42.13 N 70.44 W
Sand Hill ⋏² 210 42.31 N 77.37 W
Sand Hill ≃ 198 47.36 N 96.52 W
Sand Hills ⋏² 198 42.00 N 101.00 W
Sandhornøy I 24 67.05 N 14.10 E
Sandhurst 52 51.21 N 0.48 W
Sandhurst 42 51.19 N 0.48 W
Sāndi 124 27.18 N 79.57 E
Sandia 248 14.17 S 69.26 W
Sandia Crest ⋏ 200 35.13 N 106.27 W
Sandia Indian
Reservation ♦⁴ 200 35.15 N 106.30 W
Sandian 100 30.56 N 114.48 E
San Diego, Ca., U.S. 228 32.42 N 117.09 W
San Diego, Tx., U.S. 196 27.45 N 98.14 W
San Diego □⁶ 228 33.00 N 117.05 W
San Diego ≃, Cuba 240p 22.20 N 83.16 W
San Diego ≃, Ca.,
U.S. 204 32.46 N 117.13 W
San Diego, Cabo › 254 54.38 S 65.07 W
San Diego Aqueduct
≅¹ 228 32.55 N 116.55 W
San Diego Bay ⊂ 228 32.37 N 117.07 W
San Diego Creek ≃ 228 33.38 N 117.51 W
San Diego de Alcala,
Mission ✝¹ 228 32.48 N 117.06 W
San Diego de la
Unión 234 21.28 N 100.52 W
San Diego Naval
Training Center ■ 228 32.44 N 117.13 W
San Dieguito ≃ 228 32.58 N 117.16 W
Sandies Creek ≃ 222 29.06 N 97.20 W
Sandikli 130 38.28 N 30.17 E
Sandila 124 27.05 N 80.31 E
Sandilands 168b 34.31 S 137.46 E
Sandilands Village 240b 25.02 N 77.18 W
San Dimas 228 34.06 N 117.48 W
San Dimas Canyon
V 280 34.10 N 117.46 W
San Dimas Reservoir
⊜¹ 280 34.09 N 117.43 W
San Dionisio, Nic. 236 12.45 N 85.51 W
San Dionisio, Pil. 116 11.16 N 123.06 E
Sand Island I, Mid.
Is. 174g 28.12 N 177.23 W
Sand Island I, Hi.,
U.S. 229c 21.18 N 157.53 W
Sand Islet I 174g 28.16 N 177.23 W
Sandiway 262 53.14 N 2.36 W
Sand Key I 220 27.53 N 82.51 W
Sandkrug 54 53.52 N 13.52 E
Sandl 61 48.33 N 14.38 E
Sand Lake 210 42.38 N 73.32 W
Sand Lake ⊜, On.,
Can. 184 50.05 N 94.39 W
Sand Lake ⊜, On.,
Can. 212 44.34 N 76.15 W
Sand Lake ⊜, On.,
Can. 212 44.56 N 77.02 W
Sandling ⋏ 64 47.39 N 13.43 E
Sandnes 26 58.51 N 5.44 E
Sandness 46a 60.17 N 1.38 W
Sandoa 152 9.41 S 22.52 E
Sandogora 80 58.12 N 40.59 E
Sandomierz 30 50.41 N 21.45 E
San Domingo Creek
≃ 226 38.07 N 120.40 W
San Domino, Isola I 66 42.07 N 15.29 E
Sandon 260 51.43 N 0.32 E
Sandoná 246 1.17 N 77.28 W
San Donaci 68 40.27 N 17.55 E
San Donà di Piave 64 45.38 N 12.34 E
San Donato di Lecce 68 40.15 N 18.10 E
San Donato di Ninea 68 39.42 N 16.03 E
San Donato
Milanese 62 45.24 N 9.16 E
San Donato Val di
Comino 66 41.42 N 13.49 E
Sandongo 152 15.30 S 21.28 E
San Dorligo della
Valle 64 45.36 N 13.51 E
Sandouping 102 30.48 N 110.49 E
Sandoval 219 38.36 N 89.06 W
Sandovalina 255 22.27 S 51.44 W
Sandover ≃ 162 21.43 S 136.32 E
Sandovo 76 58.28 N 36.25 E
Sandoway 110 18.28 N 94.22 E
Sandown 42 50.39 N 1.09 W
Sandown Park
Racecourse ♦,
Austl. 274b 37.57 S 145.10 E
Sandown Park Race
Course ♦, Eng.,
U.K. 260 51.22 N 0.22 W
Sand Point, Ak.,
U.S. 180 55.20 N 160.30 W
Sandpoint, Id., U.S. 202 48.16 N 116.33 W
Sandrancourt 261 49.02 N 1.39 E
Sandray I 46 56.53 N 7.30 W
Sandridge, Eng.,
U.K. 260 51.47 N 0.18 W
Sand Ridge, N.Y.,
U.S. 210 43.15 N 76.14 W
Sandrigo 64 45.39 N 11.36 E
Sandringham, Austl. 166 24.05 S 139.04 E
Sandringham, Austl. 169 37.57 S 145.00 E
Sandringham, Eng.,
U.K. 42 52.50 N 0.30 E
Sandringham ♦⁸ 273d 26.09 S 28.07 E
Sandringham House
⊥ 42 52.50 N 0.30 E
Sand River Valley 158 28.28 S 29.33 E
Šandrovka 78 48.57 N 35.46 E
Sands Key I 220 25.30 N 80.11 W
Sandslån 26 63.01 N 17.47 E
Sandspit 182 53.14 N 131.50 W
Sands Point 276 40.51 N 73.43 W
Sands Point › 276 40.52 N 73.44 W
Sand Springs, Ok.,
U.S. 196 36.08 N 96.06 W
Sand Springs, Tx.,
U.S. 196 32.15 N 101.22 W
Sandspruit 158 27.18 S 29.48 E
Sandspruit ≃ 273d 26.07 S 28.04 E
Sandstedt 52 53.21 N 8.31 E
Sandston 208 37.31 N 77.18 W
Sandstone, Austl. 162 27.59 S 119.17 E
Sandstone, Mn.,
U.S. 190 46.07 N 92.52 W
Sandstone Creek ≃ 216 42.23 N 84.33 W
Sandu, Zhg. 100 29.46 N 120.12 E
Sandu, Zhg. 100 26.02 N 113.19 E
Sandu, Zhg. 100 29.12 N 114.40 E
Sandu, Zhg. 102 25.59 N 107.52 E
Sanduan 104 41.10 N 121.27 E
Sandu Ao ⊂ 100 26.35 N 119.50 E
Sandugan Point › 116 9.18 N 123.36 E
Sandumba 152 13.45 S 17.29 E
Sandun, Zhg. 106 30.19 N 120.05 E
Sandun, Zhg. 106 31.52 N 121.50 E
Sandun, Zhg. 106 32.19 N 121.27 E
Sanduo 100 32.49 N 119.42 E
Sandusky, In., U.S. 218 39.25 N 85.29 W
Sandusky, Mi., U.S. 190 43.25 N 82.49 W
Sandusky, N.Y.,
U.S. 210 42.30 N 78.23 W
Sandusky, Oh., U.S. 214 41.26 N 82.42 W
Sandusky □⁶ 214 41.21 N 83.07 W
Sandusky ≃ 214 41.27 N 83.00 W
Sandusky Bay ⊂ 214 41.27 N 82.52 W
Sand uul ⋏ 102 43.27 N 104.04 E
Sandvig 26 55.17 N 14.47 E
Sandvika 26 59.54 N 10.31 E
Sandviken 40 60.37 N 16.46 E
Sandweiler 56 49.37 N 6.13 E
Sandwich, Eng.,
U.K. 42 51.17 N 1.20 E
Sandwich, Il., U.S. 216 41.38 N 88.37 W
Sandwich, Ma., U.S. 207 41.45 N 70.29 W
Sandwich Bay ⊂,
Nf., Can. 176 53.35 N 57.15 W
Sandwich Bay ⊂,
Namibia 156 23.22 S 14.30 E
Sandwich del Sur,
Islas
→ South
Sandwich Islands
II 18 57.45 S 26.30 W
Sandwick, B.C.,
Can. 182 49.42 N 124.59 W
Sandwick, Scot.,
U.K. 46a 60.00 N 1.15 W
Sand Wick ⊂ 46 60.42 N 0.52 W
Sandwip I 124 22.29 N 91.26 E
Sandwīp Channel ⊔ 124 22.30 N 91.35 E
Sandwīp Island I 124 22.30 N 91.25 E
Sandy, Eng., U.K. 42 52.08 N 0.18 W
Sandy, Or., U.S. 224 45.23 N 122.15 W
Sandy, Pa., U.S. 214 41.07 N 78.47 W
Sandy, Ut., U.S. 200 40.35 N 111.53 W
Sandy ≃, Me., U.S. 188 44.45 N 69.52 W
Sandy ≃, Or., U.S. 224 45.34 N 122.24 W
Sandy ≃, Va., U.S. 192 36.35 N 79.25 W
Sandy Bay ⊂, Nic. 236 14.28 N 83.16 W
Sandy Bay ⊂, Ma.,
U.S. 283 42.40 N 70.37 W
Sandy Bay Indian
Reserve ♦⁴ 184 50.33 N 98.40 W
Sandy Bay Mountain
⋏ 188 45.47 N 70.25 W
Sandy Beach 210 43.04 N 78.55 W
Sandy Branch ≃ 284c 39.03 N 77.16 W
Sandy Cape ›,
Austl. 166 41.25 S 144.45 E
Sandy Cape ›,
Austl. 166 24.42 S 153.17 E
Sandy Creek 212 43.38 N 76.05 W
Sandy Creek ≃, U.S. 196 34.25 N 99.35 W
Sandy Creek ≃, U.S. 196 36.50 N 98.10 W
Sandy Creek ≃, Il.,
U.S. 219 39.34 N 90.35 W
Sandy Creek ≃, N.Y.,
U.S. 212 43.20 N 77.55 W
Sandy Creek ≃, N.Y.,
U.S. 212 43.44 N 76.15 W
Sandy Creek ≃, N.C.,
U.S. 192 36.08 N 78.02 W
Sandy Creek ≃, Oh.,
U.S. 214 40.38 N 81.26 W
Sandy Creek ≃, Pa.,
U.S. 214 41.18 N 79.51 W
Sandy Creek ≃, Tx.,
U.S. 196 30.34 N 98.42 W
Sandy Creek ≃, Tx.,
U.S. 222 29.02 N 96.33 W
Sandy Creek, East
Branch ≃ 210 43.17 N 78.03 W
Sandy Creek, North
Branch ≃ 212 43.51 N 75.58 W
Sandy Creek, West
Branch ≃ 210 43.17 N 78.03 W
Sandy Desert ♦² 128 28.40 N 62.30 E
Sandy Hook, Ct.,
U.S. 207 41.25 N 73.16 W
Sandy Hook, Ky.,
U.S. 192 38.05 N 83.07 W
Sandy Hook, Ms.,
U.S. 194 31.02 N 89.48 W
Sandy Hook ›² 208 40.27 N 74.00 W
Sandy Hook Bay ⊂ 276 40.26 N 74.03 W
Sandykači 128 36.33 N 62.34 E
Sandy Key I 220 25.02 N 81.01 W
Sandy Lake 214 41.20 N 80.04 W
Sandy Lake ⊜, Nf.,
Can. 186 49.16 N 57.00 W
Sandy Lake ⊜, On.,
Can. 184 53.02 N 93.00 W
Sandy Lake ⊜, On.,
Can. 212 44.33 N 78.24 W
Sandy Lick Creek ≃ 214 41.09 N 79.05 W
Sandy Point 238 17.22 N 62.50 W
Sandy Point ›, Austl. 168b 34.16 S 138.09 E
Sandy Point ›, Trin. 241r 11.09 N 60.50 W
Sandy Point ›, R.I.,
U.S. 207 41.14 N 71.35 W
Sandy Pond ⊜ 283 42.26 N 71.19 W
Sandy Ridge 214 40.49 N 78.14 W
Sandy Springs 192 33.55 N 84.22 W
Sandyville, Md., U.S. 208 39.31 N 76.55 W
Sandyville, Oh., U.S. 214 40.38 N 81.23 W
Sandžak ♦¹ 38 43.10 N 19.30 E
San Eladio 258 34.46 S 59.11 W
San Elizario 200 31.35 N 106.16 W
San Emigdio Creek ≃ 228 35.02 N 119.11 W
San Emilio 116 17.14 N 120.37 E
Sanen ≃ 115a 8.23 S 113.37 E
San Enrique 252 35.47 S 60.22 W
San Estanislao, Col. 246 10.24 N 75.09 W
San Estanislao,
Para. 252 24.39 S 56.26 W
San Esteban 236 15.17 N 85.52 W
San Esteban, Bahía
⊂ 232 25.38 N 109.14 W
San Esteban, Isla I 232 28.42 N 112.36 W
San Esteban de
Gormaz 34 41.35 N 3.12 W
San Fabian 116 16.05 N 120.25 E
San Fausto de
Campcentellas 266d 41.31 N 2.14 E
San Fele 68 40.49 N 15.32 E
San Felice (Sankt
Felix) 64 46.30 N 11.08 E
San Felice Circeo 66 41.14 N 13.05 E
San Felice sul
Panaro 64 44.50 N 11.08 E
San Felipe, Chile 252 32.45 S 70.44 W
San Felipe, Col. 246 1.55 N 67.06 W
San Felipe, Méx. 232 31.00 N 114.52 W
San Felipe, Méx. 234 21.29 N 101.13 W
San Felipe, Pil. 116 15.04 N 120.04 E
San Felipe, Tx., U.S. 222 29.48 N 96.06 W
San Felipe, Ven. 246 10.20 N 68.44 W
San Felipe, Castillo
de ⊥ 236 15.39 N 89.01 W
San Felipe, Cayos
de II 240p 21.58 N 83.30 W
San Felipe Aztatán 234 22.23 N 105.24 W
San Felipe Creek ≃ 204 33.09 N 115.46 W
San Felipe de Puerto
Plata 238 19.48 N 70.41 W
San Felipe de
Vichayal 248 4.52 S 81.05 W
San Felipe Indian
Reservation ♦⁴ 200 35.26 N 106.26 W
San Felipe Nuevo
Mercurio 232 24.22 N 102.06 W
San Felipe Pueblo 200 35.27 N 106.28 W
San Feliu de Guixols 34 41.47 N 3.02 E
San Feliu de
Llobregat 266d 41.23 N 2.03 E
San Félix ≃ 236 8.10 N 81.51 W
San Félix, Isla I 244 26.17 S 80.05 W
San Ferdinando di
Puglia 68 41.18 N 16.04 E
San Fermín 196 26.20 N 104.49 W
San Fermin, Punta › 232 30.25 N 114.40 W
San Fernando, Arg. 258 34.26 S 58.34 W
San Fernando, Chile 252 34.35 S 71.00 W
San Fernando, Esp. 34 36.28 N 6.12 W
San Fernando, Méx. 196 28.32 N 100.54 W
San Fernando, Méx. 200 31.16 N 110.36 W
San Fernando, Méx. 232 24.50 N 98.10 W
San Fernando, Méx. 234 16.52 N 93.13 W
San Fernando, Pil. 116 16.37 N 120.19 E
San Fernando, Pil. 116 12.30 N 123.46 E
San Fernando, Pil. 116 15.01 N 120.41 E
San Fernando, Trin. 241r 10.17 N 61.28 W
San Fernando, Ca.,
U.S. 228 34.16 N 118.26 W
San Fernando □⁵ 288 34.28 S 58.34 W
San Fernando ≃ 232 24.55 N 97.40 W
San Fernando,
Aeródromo ⊠ 288 34.27 S 58.35 W
San Fernando
Airport ⊠ 280 34.17 N 118.25 W
San Fernando Creek
≃ 196 27.28 N 97.46 W
San Fernando de
Apure 246 7.54 N 67.28 W
San Fernando de
Atabapo 246 4.03 N 67.42 W
San Fernando de
Henares 266a 40.26 N 3.32 W
San Fernando del
Valle de
Catamarca 252 28.28 S 65.47 W
San Fernando
Mission ✝¹ 280 34.16 N 118.28 W
San Fernando Point
› 116 16.38 N 120.17 E
San Fernando Valley
V 280 34.13 N 118.27 W
San Fili 68 39.20 N 16.09 E
San Filip del Mela 70 38.10 N 15.17 E
Sånfjället ⋏ 26 62.17 N 13.32 E
Sånfjällets
Nationalpark ♦ 26 62.20 N 13.40 E
San Floriano 64 46.02 N 12.18 E
Sanford, Co., U.S. 200 37.15 N 105.54 W
Sanford, Fl., U.S. 220 28.48 N 81.16 W
Sanford, Me., U.S. 188 43.26 N 70.46 W
Sanford, Mi., U.S. 190 43.40 N 84.22 W
Sanford, N.C., U.S. 192 35.28 N 79.10 W
Sanford, Tx., U.S. 196 35.42 N 101.32 W
Sanford ≃ 162 27.22 S 115.53 E
Sanford, Mount ⋏ 180 62.13 N 144.09 W
San Francesco,
Convento ✝¹, It. 66 42.28 N 12.45 E
San Francesco,
Convento ✝¹, It. 267a 42.03 N 12.46 E
San Francisco, Arg. 252 31.26 S 62.05 W
San Francisco, Col. 246 1.11 N 76.53 W
San Francisco, C.R. 236 9.49 N 85.15 W
San Francisco, Pan. 236 8.15 N 80.58 W
San Francisco, Pil. 116 8.30 N 125.56 E
San Francisco, Pil. 116 10.04 N 125.09 E
San Francisco, Ca.,
U.S. 226 37.46 N 122.25 W
San Francisco □⁶ 282 37.46 N 122.25 W
San Francisco □⁶ 226 37.45 N 122.22 W
San Francisco ≃,
Arg. 252 23.16 S 64.03 W
San Francisco
→ São Francisco
≃, Bra. 242 10.30 S 36.24 W
San Francisco ≃,
U.S. 200 32.59 N 109.22 W
San Francisco,
Arroyo ≃ 288 34.43 S 58.19 W
San Francisco, La
Cadena ⋏ 240m 18.19 N 67.10 W
San Francisco, Paso
de ✕ 252 26.53 S 68.19 W
San Francisco,
University of ✝² 282 37.46 N 122.26 W
San Francisco Bay ⊂ 226 37.43 N 122.17 W
San Francisco Creek
≃ 196 29.53 N 102.19 W
San Francisco
Culhuacán ♦⁸ 286a 19.20 N 99.08 W
San Francisco de
Arriba 232 26.15 N 102.50 W
San Francisco de
Borja 232 27.53 N 106.41 W
San Francisco de
Horizonte 196 25.56 N 103.26 W
San Francisco de la
Paz 236 14.55 N 86.14 W
San Francisco del
Camicero 236 12.30 N 86.18 W
San Francisco del
Chañar 252 29.47 S 63.56 W
San Francisco del
Mar 234 16.14 N 94.39 W

Symbols in the index entries represent the broad categories identified in the key at the right. Symbols with superior numbers (⋏¹) identify subcategories (see complete key on page *I · 1*).

Kartensymbole in dem Registerverzeichnis stellen die rechts in Schlüssel erklärten Kategorien dar. Symbole mit hochgestellten Ziffern (⋏¹) bezeichnen Unterabteilungen einer Kategorie (vgl. vollständiger Schlüssel auf Seite *I · 1*).

Los símbolos incluidos en el texto del índice representan las grandes categorías identificadas con la clave a la derecha. Los símbolos con numeros en su parte superior (⋏¹) identifican las subcategorías (véase la clave completa en la página *I · 1*).

Les symboles de l'index représentent les catégories indiquées dans la légende à droite. Les symboles suivis d'un indice (⋏¹) représentent des sous-catégories (voir légende complète à la page *I · 1*).

Os símbolos incluídos no texto do índice representam as grandes categorias identificadas com a chave à direita. Os símbolos com números em sua parte superior (⋏¹) identificam as subcategorias (veja-se a chave completa à página *I · 1*).

⋏ Mountain	Berg	Montaña	Montagne	Montanha
⋏ Mountains	Berge	Montañas	Montagnes	Montanhas
✕ Pass	Pass	Paso	Col	Passo
V Valley, Canyon	Tal, Cañon	Valle, Cañón	Vallée, Canyon	Vale, Canhão
≍ Plain	Ebene	Llano	Plaine	Planície
› Cape	Kap	Cabo	Cap	Cabo
I Island	Insel	Isla	Île	Ilha
II Islands	Inseln	Islas	Îles	Ilhas
⊥ Other Topographic Features	Andere Topographische Objekte	Otros Elementos Topográficos	Autres données topographiques	Outros acidentes topográficos

ESPAÑOL

Nombre	Página	Lat.°′	Long.°′ W = Oeste
San Francisco del Monte de Oro	252	32.36 S	66.08 W
San Francisco del Oro	232	26.52 N	105.51 W
San Francisco del Rincón	234	21.01 N	101.51 W
San Francisco de Macorís	238	19.18 N	70.15 W
San Francisco de Mostazal	252	33.59 S	70.43 W
San Francisco el Grande, Iglesia de ʋ [1]	266a	40.25 N	3.43 W
San Francisco Gotera	236	13.42 N	88.06 W
San Francisco International Airport ⊠	226	37.37 N	122.23 W
San Francisco Ixhuatán	234	16.22 N	94.29 W
San Francisco Maritime State Historical Park ♠	282	37.48 N	122.27 W
San Francisco-Oakland Bay Bridge ◆ [5]	282	37.48 N	122.22 W
San Francisco State Fish and Game Refuge ◆ [4]	282	37.35 N	122.25 W
San Francisco State University ʋ [2]	282	37.43 N	122.28 W
San Francisco Tlalcilalcalpa	234	19.18 N	99.46 W
San Francisco Zoological Gardens ♠	282	37.44 N	122.30 W
San Francisquito Creek ≃	282	37.28 N	122.07 W
San Franco, Cerro ∧	236	15.25 N	87.18 W
San Fratello	70	38.01 N	14.36 E
San Fratello ≃	70	38.02 N	14.34 E
Sanga, Ang.	152	11.07 S	15.22 E
Sanga, Burkina	150	11.10 N	0.10 E
Sanga, Mali	150	14.28 N	3.19 W
Sanga, Zaïre	154	7.02 S	28.21 E
San Gabriel, Ec.	246	0.36 N	77.49 W
San Gabriel, Ca., U.S.	228	34.05 N	118.06 W
San Gabriel ≃, Ca., U.S.	280	33.45 N	118.07 W
San Gabriel ≃, Tx., U.S.	222	30.46 N	97.01 W
San Gabriel, Isla I	258	34.28 S	57.54 W
San Gabriel, North Fork ≃, Ca., U.S.	280	34.15 N	117.52 W
San Gabriel, North Fork ≃, Tx., U.S.	196	30.38 N	97.41 W
San Gabriel, South Fork ≃	196	30.38 N	97.41 W
San Gabriel Arcangel, Mission ʋ [1]	280	34.06 N	118.06 W
San Gabriel Chilac	234	18.19 N	97.21 W
San Gabriel Dam ◆ [6]	280	34.13 N	117.52 W
San Gabriel Mountains ⋏	228	34.20 N	118.00 W
San Gabriel Peak ∧	280	34.15 N	118.06 W
San Gabriel Reservoir ⊜ [1]	228	34.13 N	117.51 W
Sangačal, mys ›	84	40.07 N	49.30 E
San Galgano, Abbazia di ʋ [1]	66	43.10 N	11.10 E
San Gallán, Isla I	248	13.51 S	76.28 W
Sangaly	24	61.08 N	43.19 E
Sangamankanda Point ›	122	7.01 N	81.52 E
Sangamner	122	19.34 N	74.13 E
Sangamon □ [6]	219	39.47 N	89.40 W
Sangamon ≃	194	40.07 N	90.20 W
Sangamon, South Fork ≃	219	39.48 N	89.32 W
Sanga Puitã	255	22.40 S	55.36 W
Sangar	74	63.55 N	127.31 E
Sangāreddipet	122	17.38 N	78.07 E
Sangar Sarāy	120	34.24 N	70.38 E
Sangasanga-dalam	112	0.40 S	117.14 E
Sanga Sanga Island I	116	5.04 N	119.47 E
Sangat	123	30.05 N	74.50 E
Sangatte	50	50.56 N	1.45 E
San Gavino Monreale	71	39.33 N	8.47 E
Sangay, Volcán ∧ [1]	246	2.00 S	78.20 W
Sang Bast	128	35.59 N	59.46 E
Sangbé	152	6.03 N	12.28 E
Sangchris Lake ⊜ [1]	219	39.35 N	89.30 W
Sangchris Lake State Park ♠	219	39.38 N	89.28 W
Sangchungshih	100	25.04 N	121.29 E
Sangeang, Pulau I	115b	8.12 S	119.04 E
Sang-e Māsheh	120	33.08 N	67.27 E
San Gemini	66	42.37 N	12.33 E
San Genesio Atesino	64	46.32 N	11.20 E
Sangenjaya ◆ [8]	268	35.38 N	139.40 E
Sanger, Ca., U.S.	226	36.42 N	119.33 W
Sanger, Tx., U.S.	196	33.21 N	97.10 W
Sangerhausen	54	51.28 N	11.17 E
San Germán, Cuba	240p	20.36 N	76.08 W
San Germán, P.R.	240m	18.05 N	67.03 W
San Germano Vercellese	62	45.21 N	8.15 E
San Geronimo	226	38.01 N	122.39 W
San Gerónimo, Arroyo ≃	258	33.57 S	56.05 W
Sangerville	188	45.09 N	69.21 W
Sanggan ≃	90	40.21 N	115.21 E
Sanggar, Teluk c	115b	8.20 S	118.18 E
Sanggau	112	0.08 N	110.36 E
Sangge-ri ◆ [8]	271b	37.41 N	127.05 E
Sanggi	112	5.27 S	104.30 E
Sanggin Dalai	102	38.11 N	105.17 E
Sanggona	112	3.52 S	121.46 E
Sangha □ [5], Centraf.	152	3.35 N	16.20 E
Sangha □ [5], Congo	152	1.00 N	15.30 E
Sangha ≃	152	1.13 S	16.49 E
Sanghar	120	26.02 N	68.57 E
San Giacomo (Sankt Jakob in Pfitsch)	64	46.57 N	11.36 E
San Giacomo Filippo	58	46.20 N	9.21 E
Sangihe, Kepulauan II	112	3.00 N	125.30 E
Sangihe, Pulau I	112	3.35 N	125.32 E
Sangijn dalaj nuur ⊜	88	49.17 N	99.00 E
San Gil	246	6.33 N	73.08 W
Sangilen, chrebet ⋏	88	50.18 N	96.30 E
San Gimignano	66	43.28 N	11.02 E
San Ginês de Vilasar	266d	41.31 N	2.22 E
San Ginesio	66	43.06 N	13.19 E
San Gion	58	46.38 N	8.50 E
San Giorgio	68	40.51 N	14.23 E
San Giorgio Canavese	62	45.20 N	7.48 E
San Giorgio della Richinvelda	64	46.03 N	12.52 E
San Giorgio del Sannio	68	41.04 N	14.51 E
San Giorgio di Lomellina	62	45.10 N	8.47 E
San Giorgio di Nogaro	64	45.50 N	13.13 E
San Giorgio di Piano	64	44.39 N	11.22 E
San Giorgio Ionico	68	40.27 N	17.23 E
San Giorgio la Molara	68	41.16 N	14.55 E
San Giorgio Lucano	68	40.07 N	16.23 E
San Giorgio Monferrato	62	45.07 N	8.23 E
San Giorgio Morgeto	68	38.23 N	16.06 E
San Giorgio Piacentino	62	44.57 N	9.44 E
San Giorgio su Legnano	266b	45.34 N	8.55 E
San Giovanni (Sankt Johann)	64	46.38 N	11.44 E

FRANÇAIS

Nom	Page	Lat.°′	Long.°′ W = Ouest
San Giovanni al Timavo (Sankt Johann in Ahrn)	64	46.58 N	11.57 E
San Giovanni a Piro	68	40.03 N	15.27 E
San Giovanni-Bianco	58	45.52 N	9.39 E
San Giovanni d'Asso	66	43.09 N	11.35 E
San Giovanni Gemini	70	37.38 N	13.39 E
San Giovanni Ilarione	64	45.30 N	11.15 E
San Giovanni in Croce	64	45.05 N	10.22 E
San Giovanni in Fiore	68	39.15 N	16.42 E
San Giovanni in Laterano ʋ [1]	267a	41.53 N	12.30 E
San Giovanni in Persiceto	64	44.38 N	11.11 E
San Giovanni la Punta	70	37.35 N	15.07 E
San Giovanni Lupatoto	64	45.23 N	11.03 E
San Giovanni Rotondo	68	41.42 N	15.44 E
San Giovanni Suergiu	71	39.07 N	8.31 E
San Giovanni Valdarno	66	43.34 N	11.32 E
San Giuliano, Lago di ⊜	68	40.37 N	16.30 E
San Giuliano Milanese	266b	45.24 N	9.17 E
San Giuliano Terme	66	43.46 N	10.26 E
San Giuseppe, It.	62	44.22 N	8.18 E
San Giuseppe, It.	70	37.58 N	13.11 E
San Giuseppe Vesuviano	68	40.50 N	14.30 E
San Giustino	66	43.33 N	12.10 E
San Giusto, Aeroporto di ⊠	66	43.11 N	10.21 E
San Giusto Canavese	62	45.19 N	7.49 E
Sangju	98	36.26 N	128.09 E
Sangkapura	115a	5.52 S	112.40 E
Sângkê ≃	110	13.13 N	103.41 E
Sangkhai	110	14.39 N	103.52 E
Sangkhla	110	15.07 N	98.28 E
Sangkulirang	112	0.59 N	117.58 E
Sāngla	123	31.43 N	73.23 E
Sangley Point ›	269f	14.30 N	120.55 E
Sangley Point Naval Base ■	269f	14.30 N	120.54 E
Sāngli	122	16.52 N	74.34 E
Sanglin	100	27.54 N	114.46 E
Sangluoshu	98	37.31 N	117.43 E
Sangmélima	152	2.56 N	11.59 E
Sangnyŏng-ni	98	38.14 N	126.54 E
Sango	270	34.36 N	135.42 E
San Godenzo	66	43.55 N	11.37 E
Sāngola	122	17.26 N	75.12 E
Sangolquí	246	0.19 S	78.27 W
San Gorgonio Mountain ∧	204	34.06 N	116.50 W
San Gottardo, Passo del)(	58	46.33 N	8.34 E
Sangou	98	41.02 N	118.11 E
Sangre de Cristo Mountains ⋏	200	37.30 N	105.15 W
San Gregorio, Arg.	252	34.19 S	62.02 W
San Gregorio, It.	66	42.19 N	13.29 E
San Gregorio, Ca., U.S.	226	37.19 N	122.23 W
San Gregorio, Ur.	252	32.37 S	55.40 W
San Gregorio, Ur.	258	33.57 S	56.45 W
San Gregorio, Arroyo ≃	258	33.59 S	56.50 W
San Gregorio Atlapulco ◆ [8]	286a	19.15 N	99.03 W
San Gregorio Creek ≃	282	37.19 N	122.25 W
San Gregorio Magno	68	40.39 N	15.24 E
San Gregorio State Beach ♠	282	37.19 N	122.24 W
Sangre Grande	241r	10.35 N	61.07 W
Sangro ≃	66	42.14 N	14.32 E
Sangrūr	123	30.14 N	75.50 E
Sangrūr □ [5]	123	30.16 N	75.52 E
Sangshuyuan	86	42.23 N	88.30 E
Sangsues, Lac aux ⊜	190	46.29 N	77.57 W
Sangtuda	85	38.04 N	69.04 E
Sanguandian	100	31.19 N	118.05 E
Sanguang	106	31.47 N	121.16 E
Sanguanmiao	100	32.25 N	114.04 E
Sanguanyingzi	104	41.39 N	120.44 E
Sangudo	182	53.53 N	114.54 W
Sangue, Rio do ≃	248	11.01 S	58.39 W
Sangüesa	34	42.35 N	1.17 W
Sanguinetto	64	45.11 N	11.09 E
Sanguliu	104	40.45 N	124.14 E
Sāngurli	272c	18.56 N	73.07 E
Sangutane ≃	156	24.07 S	33.47 E
Sangvor, S.S.S.R.	85	38.47 N	71.12 E
Sangvor, S.S.S.R.	85	38.53 N	71.06 E
Sangwa	154	5.30 S	26.00 E
Sangya	120	30.52 N	91.40 E
Sangyuanbao	105	40.15 N	115.32 E
Sangyuanbu	106	31.37 N	118.53 E
Sangyuanzhen	107	30.30 N	103.26 E
Sangzhi	102	29.18 N	110.02 E
Sangzidian	98	36.46 N	116.55 E
Sanharó	250	8.21 S	36.34 W
Sanhe, Zhg.	100	24.24 N	116.34 E
Sanhe, Zhg.	105	39.59 N	117.04 E
Sanhechang, Zhg.	102	31.22 N	106.48 E
Sanhechang, Zhg.	107	30.04 N	105.01 E
Sanhecun	98	42.28 N	129.39 E
Sanheji	100	32.42 N	117.55 E
Sanhekou	106	31.50 N	120.08 E
Sanhetun	104	42.38 N	123.38 E
Sanhezhan	89	52.34 N	126.02 E
Sanhezhen	100	31.30 N	117.14 E
Sanhezhuang	105	40.04 N	116.18 E
San Hipólito, Punta ›	232	26.59 N	113.59 W
Sanhsient'ai I	100	23.08 N	121.25 E
Sanhsing	100	24.40 N	121.39 E
Sanhu	100	27.55 N	115.24 E
Sanhui, Zhg.	107	30.06 N	106.36 E
Sanhui, Zhg.	107	29.57 N	105.53 E
Sanhūr	142	29.25 N	30.46 E
Sanhūr al-Madīnah	142	31.07 N	30.44 E
Sani	100	24.25 N	120.46 E
Sanibel	220	26.26 N	82.01 W
Sanibel Island I	220	26.27 N	82.06 W
San Ignacio, Arg.	252	27.16 S	55.32 W
San Ignacio, Bol.	248	14.53 S	65.36 W
San Ignacio, Bol.	248	16.23 S	60.59 W
San Ignacio, C.R.	236	9.48 N	84.09 W
San Ignacio, Hond.	236	14.38 N	87.02 W
San Ignacio, Méx.	232	27.27 N	112.51 W
San Ignacio, Méx.	234	23.12 N	100.12 W
San Ignacio, Méx.	234	23.55 N	106.25 W
San Ignacio, Para.	252	26.52 S	57.03 W
San Ignacio, Isla de I	232	25.25 N	108.54 W
San Ignacio, Laguna ⊜	232	26.54 N	113.13 W
San Ildefonso, Cape ›	116	16.02 N	121.59 E
San Ildefonso, Cerro ∧	236	15.31 N	88.17 W
San Ildefonso Indian Reservation ◆ [4]	200	35.53 N	106.08 W
San Ildefonso o La Granja	34	40.54 N	4.00 W
San Ildefonso Peninsula › [1]	116	16.10 N	122.05 E
San'in-kaigan-kokuritsu-kōen ♠	96	35.38 N	134.38 E
Sanino	265a	59.50 N	29.54 E
Sani Pass)(	158	29.34 S	29.19 E
San Isidro, Arg.	252	28.27 S	65.44 W
San Isidro, Arg.	258	34.27 S	58.30 W
San Isidro, C.R.	236	9.22 N	83.42 W
San Isidro, Méx.	200	31.31 N	106.18 W
San Isidro, Méx.	234	21.55 N	100.15 W
San Isidro, Nic.	236	12.56 N	86.12 W
San Isidro, Perú	286d	12.07 S	77.03 W
San Isidro, Pil.	116	11.24 N	124.21 E

PORTUGUÊS

Nome	Página	Lat.°′	Long.°′ W = Oeste
San Isidro, Tx., U.S.	196	26.42 N	98.27 W
San Isidro □ [5]	288	34.29 S	58.33 W
San Isidro el Real, Catedral de ʋ [1]	266a	40.25 N	3.42 W
Sanitaria Springs	210	42.09 N	75.46 W
Sanitatas	156	18.11 S	12.47 E
Sanitz	54	54.04 N	12.22 E
San Jacinto, Col.	246	9.50 N	75.08 W
San Jacinto, Méx.	196	25.29 N	103.44 W
San Jacinto, Pil.	116	12.34 N	123.44 E
San Jacinto, Ca., U.S.	228	33.47 N	116.57 W
San Jacinto □ [6]	222	30.35 N	95.10 W
San Jacinto ≃, Ca., U.S.	228	33.43 N	117.16 W
San Jacinto ≃, Tx., U.S.	222	29.46 N	95.05 W
San Jacinto, East Fork ≃	222	30.05 N	95.09 W
San Jacinto, West Fork ≃	222	30.02 N	95.15 W
San Jacinto Monument ⊥	222	29.45 N	95.01 W
San Jacinto Peak ∧	204	33.49 N	116.41 W
San Jacinto Valley V	228	33.50 N	117.05 W
Sanjahā	142	30.50 N	31.38 E
San Javier, Arg.	252	27.53 S	55.08 W
San Javier, Arg.	252	30.35 S	59.57 W
San Javier, Bol.	248	14.34 S	64.42 W
San Javier, Bol.	248	16.20 S	62.38 W
San Javier, Méx.	196	26.16 N	99.27 W
San Javier, Ur.	252	32.41 S	58.08 W
San Javier ≃	252	31.30 S	60.20 W
San Javier de Loncomilla	252	35.35 S	71.45 W
Sanjāwi	120	30.17 N	68.21 E
Sanje	154	0.46 S	31.30 E
San Jerónimo	236	15.03 N	90.12 W
San Jerónimo de Juárez	234	17.08 N	100.28 W
San Jerónimo Norte	252	31.33 S	61.05 W
Sanjiadian, Zhg.	105	39.22 N	115.58 E
Sanjiadian, Zhg.	105	40.09 N	116.36 E
Sanjiadian, Zhg.	105	39.58 N	116.06 E
Sanjiang, Zhg.	102	25.42 N	109.23 E
Sanjiang, Zhg.	107	29.33 N	104.03 E
Sanjiangzhen	107	30.31 N	103.48 E
Sanjiaocheng	102	36.47 N	104.40 E
Sanjiaopao	104	41.22 N	122.17 E
Sanjiaoshancun	104	40.42 N	122.49 E
Sanjiazhen	107	30.17 N	105.32 E
Sanjiazi, Zhg.	104	41.53 N	121.42 E
Sanjiazi, Zhg.	104	40.42 N	123.16 E
Sanjiazi, Zhg.	104	40.54 N	121.59 E
Sanjiazi, Zhg.	104	42.33 N	121.38 E
Sanjiazi, Zhg.	104	42.02 N	122.20 E
Sanjiaziyingzi	104	41.52 N	120.49 E
Sanjie, Zhg.	100	32.35 N	118.08 E
Sanjie, Zhg.	102	25.01 N	101.02 E
Sanjō	92	37.37 N	138.57 E
San Joaquín, Bol.	248	13.04 S	64.49 W
San Joaquín, Para.	252	24.57 S	56.07 W
San Joaquin, Pil.	116	10.35 N	122.08 E
San Joaquin, Ca., U.S.	226	36.36 N	120.11 W
San Joaquin □ [6]	226	37.57 N	121.17 W
San Joaquín ≃, Bol.	248	13.08 S	63.41 W
San Joaquin ≃, Ca., U.S.	226	38.03 N	121.50 W
San Joaquin, Middle Fork ≃	226	37.32 N	119.11 W
San Joaquin, North Fork ≃	226	37.32 N	119.11 W
San Joaquin, South Fork ≃	226	37.26 N	119.14 W
San Joaquin Valley V	204	36.50 N	120.10 W
San Jon	196	35.06 N	103.19 W
San Jorge, Arg.	252	31.54 S	61.52 W
San Jorge, El Sal.	236	13.25 N	88.21 W
San Jorge, Nic.	236	11.27 N	85.48 W
San Jorge ≃	246	9.07 N	74.44 W
San Jorge, Bahía de c	232	31.12 N	113.15 W
San Jorge, Cabo ›	254	45.47 S	67.21 W
San Jorge, Canal de → Saint George's Channel ᵿ	28	52.00 N	6.00 W
San Jorge, Golfo c	254	46.00 S	67.00 W
San Jorge, Golfo de c	34	40.53 N	1.00 E
San Jorge Island I	175e	8.27 S	159.35 E
San José, Arg.	252	27.46 S	55.47 W
San José, Bol.	248	14.13 S	68.05 W
San José, C.R.	236	9.56 N	84.05 W
San José, Ec.	246	1.42 S	79.01 W
San José, Hond.	236	14.54 N	88.44 W
San José, Méx.	196	28.16 N	100.15 W
San José, Méx.	232	27.32 N	110.09 W
San José, Para.	252	25.33 S	56.45 W
San Jose, Pil.	116	10.45 N	121.56 E
San Jose, Pil.	116	15.48 N	121.00 E
San Jose, Pil.	116	12.27 N	121.03 E
San Jose, T.T.P.I.	174n	15.09 N	145.43 E
San Jose, Ca., U.S.	226	37.20 N	121.53 W
San Jose, Ca., U.S.	282	37.20 N	121.53 W
San Jose, Il., U.S.	194	40.18 N	89.36 W
San Jose, N.M., U.S.	200	35.23 N	105.28 W
San José, Ven.	286c	10.34 N	66.57 W
San José □ [4]	236	9.40 N	84.00 W
San José □ [5]	258	34.15 S	56.45 W
San José □ [7]	286b	22.57 N	82.14 W
San Jose ≃, B.C., Can.	182	52.14 N	122.15 W
San José ≃, Ur.	258	34.38 S	56.29 W
San Jose, Arroyo ≃	282	38.03 N	122.30 W
San José, Golfo c	254	42.20 S	64.18 W
San José, Isla I, Méx.	232	25.00 N	110.38 W
San José, Isla I, Pan.	246	8.15 N	79.07 W
San José, Laguna c	240m	18.25 N	66.01 W
San Jose, Mission ʋ [1]	282	37.32 N	121.55 W
San Jose, Rio ≃	200	34.52 N	107.01 W
San José Ayuquila	234	17.58 N	97.57 W
San Jose Creek ≃	280	34.01 N	118.03 W
San José de Achuapa	236	13.03 N	86.35 W
San José de Aura	196	27.34 N	101.23 W
San Jose de Buan	116	12.02 N	125.01 E
San José de Chiquitos	248	17.51 S	60.47 W
San José de Feliciano	252	30.23 S	58.45 W
San José de Galipán	286c	10.35 N	66.54 W
San José de Galipán, Quebrada ≃	286c	10.37 N	66.54 W
San José de Gauribe	246	9.52 N	65.48 W
San José de Gracia	234	20.40 N	102.35 W
San José de Guanipa	246	8.54 N	64.09 W
San José de Jáchal	252	30.14 S	68.45 W
San José de la Esquina	252	33.06 S	61.42 W
San José de la Parilla	234	23.44 N	104.07 W
San José de la Popa	196	26.10 N	100.47 W
San José de las Flores	234	17.20 N	95.24 W
San José de las Lajas	240p	22.58 N	82.09 W
San José del Cabo	232	23.03 N	109.41 W
San José del Guaviare	246	2.35 N	72.38 W
San José de Llanetes	234	22.55 N	103.16 W
San José de los Molinos	248	13.57 S	75.41 W
San José de Lourdes	234	23.18 N	103.01 W
San José de Mayo	258	34.20 S	56.42 W
San José de Ocoa	238	18.33 N	70.30 W

Nome	Página	Lat.°′	Long.°′
San José de Ocuné	246	4.15 N	70.20 W
San José de Raíces	232	24.35 N	100.14 W
San José de Sisa	248	6.37 S	76.39 W
San José de Tiznados	246	9.23 N	67.33 W
San Jose Hills ⋏ [2]	280	34.04 N	117.49 W
San Jose Island I	196	28.10 N	96.45 W
San José Iturbide	234	21.00 N	100.23 W
San Jose Municipal Airport ⊠	226	37.22 N	121.56 W
San Jose State University ʋ [2]	282	37.20 N	121.53 W
San Juan, Arg.	252	31.32 S	68.31 W
San Juan, Guat.	236	15.52 N	88.53 W
San Juan, Méx.	196	29.34 N	104.36 W
San Juan, Méx.	232	27.47 N	103.57 W
San Juan, Perú	248	15.21 S	75.10 W
San Juan, Pil.	116	13.50 N	121.24 E
San Juan, Pil.	116	16.40 N	120.20 E
San Juan, Pil.	116	8.25 N	126.20 E
San Juan, P.R.	240m	18.28 N	66.07 W
San Juan □ [4]	252	31.00 S	69.00 W
San Juan □ [6]	224	48.34 N	122.59 W
San Juan ≃, Arg.	252	32.17 S	67.22 W
San Juan ≃, B.C., Can.	224	48.34 N	124.24 W
San Juan ≃, Col.	246	4.03 N	77.27 W
San Juan ≃, Méx.	232	26.22 N	98.51 W
San Juan ≃, N.A.	236	10.56 N	83.42 W
San Juan ≃, Perú	248	13.27 S	76.11 W
San Juan ≃, Pil.	269f	14.35 N	121.01 E
San Juan ≃, S.A.	246	1.11 N	78.33 W
San Juan ≃, U.S.	200	37.18 N	110.28 W
San Juan ≃, Ur.	258	34.17 S	57.58 W
San Juan ≃, Ven.	246	10.14 N	62.38 W
San Juan, Bahía de c	240m	18.27 N	66.07 W
San Juan, Cabezas de ›	240m	18.23 N	65.37 W
San Juan, Cabo ›, Arg.	254	54.44 S	63.44 W
San Juan, Cabo ›, Gui. Ecu.	152	1.08 N	9.23 E
San Juan, Embalse de ⊜ [1]	34	40.30 N	4.15 W
San Juan, Pasaje de ᵿ	240m	18.24 N	65.37 W
San Juan, Pico ∧	240p	21.59 N	80.09 W
San Juan, Port c	224	48.34 N	124.27 W
San Juan, Punta ›	174z	27.03 S	109.22 W
San Juan Basin ≚ [1]	200	36.15 N	108.20 W
San Juan Bautista, Esp.	34	39.05 N	1.30 E
San Juan Bautista, Méx.	196	26.58 N	101.24 W
San Juan Bautista, Para.	252	26.38 S	57.10 W
San Juan Bautista, Ca., U.S.	226	36.51 N	121.32 W
San Juan Bautista Cuicatlán	234	17.48 N	96.58 W
San Juan Bautista State Historical Park ♠	226	36.51 N	121.31 W
San Juan Capistrano	228	33.30 N	117.39 W
San Juan Capistrano Mission ʋ [1]	228	33.31 N	117.40 W
San Juan Colorado	234	16.32 N	97.55 W
San Juan Cotzal	236	15.26 N	91.01 W
San Juan Creek ≃, Ca., U.S.	226	35.40 N	120.22 W
San Juan Creek ≃, Ca., U.S.	228	33.28 N	117.41 W
San Juan de Abajo	234	20.48 N	105.13 W
San Juan de Aragón, Bosque ♠	286a	19.28 N	99.04 W
San Juan de Aragón, Zoológico de ♠	286a	19.28 N	99.05 W
San Juan de Colón	246	8.02 N	72.16 W
San Juan de Dios	286c	10.35 N	66.55 W
San Juan de Guadalupe	232	24.38 N	102.44 W
San Juan [de la Maguana]	238	18.48 N	71.14 W
San Juan de la Vega	234	20.38 N	100.46 W
San Juan del César	246	10.46 N	73.01 W
San Juan de Lima, Punta ›	234	18.36 N	103.42 W
San Juan de Limay	236	13.10 N	86.37 W
San Juan del Monte	269f	14.36 N	121.02 E
San Juan del Norte	236	10.55 N	83.42 W
San Juan del Oro ≃	248	21.02 S	65.19 W
San Juan de los Cayos	246	11.10 N	68.25 W
San Juan de los Lagos	234	21.15 N	102.18 W
San Juan de los Lagos ≃	234	21.18 N	102.33 W
San Juan de los Morros	246	9.55 N	67.21 W
San Juan del Piray	248	20.27 S	64.09 W
San Juan del Río, Méx.	232	24.47 N	104.27 W
San Juan del Río, Méx.	234	20.23 N	100.00 W
San Juan del Río ≃	234	20.40 N	99.30 W
San Juan del Salado	234	23.18 N	101.56 W
San Juan del Sur	236	11.15 N	85.52 W
San Juan de Micay ≃	246	3.05 N	77.32 W
San Juan de Payara	246	7.39 N	67.36 W
San Juan de Pirque	286e	33.38 S	70.30 W
San Juan de Sabinas	196	27.55 N	101.18 W
San Juan Despí	266d	41.22 N	2.04 E
San Juan de Vilasar	266d	41.30 N	2.24 E
San Juan Evangelista	234	17.54 N	95.08 W
San Juanico, Isla I	234	21.43 N	106.38 W
San Juanillo	236	10.02 N	85.44 W
San Juan Indian Reservation ◆ [4]	200	36.03 N	106.04 W
San Juan Island I	224	48.32 N	123.05 W
San Juan Island National Historical Park ♠	224	48.28 N	123.00 W
San Juan Islands II	224	48.36 N	122.50 W
San Juan Ixcaquixtla	234	18.27 N	97.49 W
San Juan Ixtayopan ◆ [8]	286a	19.14 N	99.00 W
San Juan Lachao	234	16.14 N	97.09 W
San Juan Mazatlán	234	17.02 N	95.25 W
San Juan Mountains ⋏	200	37.35 N	107.10 W
San Juan Naval Station ■	240m	18.28 N	66.06 W
San Juan Nepomuceno, Col.	246	9.57 N	75.05 W
San Juan Nepomuceno, Para.	252	26.06 S	55.58 W
San Juan Peyotán	234	22.24 N	104.21 W
San Juan Quiahije	234	16.17 N	97.20 W
San Juan Sacatepéquez	236	14.43 N	90.39 W
San Juan Sayultepec	234	17.27 N	97.17 W
San Juan y Martínez	240p	22.16 N	83.50 W
San Judas	234	23.15 N	100.52 W
San Julián, Arg.	254	49.18 S	67.43 W
San Julián, Méx.	234	21.01 N	102.10 W
San Julian, Pil.	116	11.45 N	125.27 E
San Julian, Quebrada ≃	286c	10.37 N	66.51 W
San Justo, Arg.	252	30.47 S	60.35 W
San Justo, Arg.	258	34.40 S	58.33 W
San Justo, Aeródromo ⊠	288	34.44 S	58.36 W
San Justo Desvern	266d	41.23 N	2.05 E
Sankanbiaiwa ∧	150	8.56 N	10.48 W
Sankaranayinārkovil	122	9.10 N	77.33 E
Sankarani ≃	150	12.01 N	8.19 W
Sankarpur	272b	22.51 N	88.27 E
Sānkdaha	126	22.46 N	89.10 E
Sankeng	100	23.36 N	112.48 E
Sankertown	214	40.28 N	78.35 W

Nome	Página	Lat.°′	Long.°′
Sankeshu	104	42.38 N	122.25 E
Sankeshwar	122	16.16 N	74.29 E
Sankey Brook ≃	262	53.22 N	2.38 W
Sankh ≃	124	22.15 N	84.48 E
Sankheda	120	22.10 N	73.35 E
Sankosh ≃	124	26.48 N	89.56 E
Sānkra	120	21.18 N	82.39 E
Sānkrāil	272b	22.34 N	88.14 E
Sankt Aegyd am Neuwalde	61	47.52 N	15.35 E
Sankt Andrä	61	46.46 N	14.49 E
Sankt Andrä vor dem Hagenthale	264b	48.19 N	16.13 E
Sankt Andreasberg	54	51.43 N	10.31 E
Sankt Anton am Arlberg	58	47.08 N	10.16 E
Sankt Antönien	58	46.58 N	9.49 E
Sankt Augustin	56	50.40 N	7.16 E
Sankt Bartholomä ʋ [1]	64	47.32 N	12.58 E
Sankt Blasien	58	47.46 N	8.07 E
Sankt Christopher-Nevis → Saint Christopher-Nevis □ [1]	238	17.20 N	62.45 W
Sankt Egidien	54	50.47 N	12.36 E
Sankt Florian ʋ [1]	61	48.12 N	14.23 E
Sankt Gallen, Öst.	61	47.41 N	14.37 E
Sankt Gallen, Schw.	58	47.25 N	9.23 E
Sankt Gallen □ [3]	58	47.10 N	9.08 E
Sankt Gallenkirch	58	47.01 N	9.59 E
Sankt Georgen, B.R.D.	58	48.07 N	8.20 E
Sankt Georgen, B.R.D.	58	47.59 N	7.47 E
Sankt Georgen, Öst.	61	46.43 N	14.55 E
Sankt Georgen im Attergau	64	47.56 N	13.29 E
Sankt Gertraud → Santa Gertrude	64	46.29 N	10.53 E
Sankt Gertrud ◆ [8]	54	53.52 N	10.47 E
Sankt Gilgen	64	47.46 N	13.22 E
Sankt Goar	56	50.09 N	7.43 E
Sankt Goarshausen	56	50.09 N	7.44 E
Sankt Helena → Saint Helena □ [2]	8	15.57 S	5.42 W
Sankt Hubert	56	51.23 N	6.26 E
Sankt Ingbert	56	49.17 N	7.06 E
Sankt Jakob → San Giacomo	64	46.57 N	11.36 E
Sankt Jakob im Lesachtal	64	46.41 N	12.56 E
Sankt Jakob im Rosental	61	46.33 N	14.03 E
Sankt Jakob in Defereggen	64	46.55 N	12.20 E
Sankt Johann → San Giovanni	64	46.38 N	11.44 E
Sankt Johann am Tauern	61	47.22 N	14.29 E
Sankt Johann im Pongau	64	47.21 N	13.12 E
Sankt Johann im Walde	64	46.54 N	12.37 E
Sankt Johann in Tirol	64	47.31 N	12.26 E
Sankt Kanzian	61	46.37 N	14.34 E
Sankt Leonhard → San Leonardo	64	46.49 N	11.15 E
Sankt Leonhard Am Forst	61	48.09 N	15.17 E
Sankt Leonhard im Pitztal	58	47.04 N	10.51 E
Sankt Lorenz ◆ [8]	52	53.51 N	10.40 E
Sankt Lorenz → Saint Lawrence ≃	176	49.30 N	67.00 W
Sankt Lorenzen → San Lorenzo di Sebato	64	46.47 N	11.54 E
Sankt Lorenzen im Lesachtal	64	46.42 N	12.47 E
Sankt Lorenz-Golf → Saint Lawrence, Gulf of c	186	48.00 N	62.00 W
Sankt Lorenz-Insel → Saint Lawrence Island I	180	63.30 N	170.30 W
Sankt Mang	58	47.44 N	10.21 E
Sankt Margarethen an der Raab	61	47.03 N	15.45 E
Sankt Märgen	58	48.00 N	8.05 E
Sankt Margrethen	58	47.27 N	9.36 E
Sankt Martin	64	47.28 N	13.23 E
Sankt Martin an der Raab	61	46.55 N	16.08 E
Sankt Martin in Gsies → San Martino in Casies	64	46.49 N	12.14 E
Sankt Mauritz	52	51.57 N	7.39 E
Sankt Michael im Lungau	64	47.06 N	13.38 E
Sankt Michael in Obersteiermark	61	47.20 N	15.01 E
Sankt Michel → Mikkeli	26	61.41 N	27.15 E
Sankt Moritz	58	46.30 N	9.50 E
Sankt Niklaus → San Nicolò d'Ultimo, It.	64	46.30 N	10.55 E
Sankt Niklaus, Schw.	58	46.11 N	7.48 E
Sankt Oswald	60	48.54 N	13.25 E
Sankt Paul im Lavanttal	61	46.42 N	14.52 E
Sankt Peter, B.R.D.	30	54.18 N	8.38 E
Sankt Peter, B.R.D.	58	48.01 N	8.01 E
Sankt Peter ʋ [1]	263	51.37 N	7.12 E
Sankt Peter am Kammersberg	61	47.11 N	14.11 E
Sankt Peter am Ottersbach	61	46.48 N	15.45 E
Sankt Peter in der Au	61	48.03 N	14.37 E
Sankt Pölten	61	48.12 N	15.37 E
Sankt-Quirinus-Dom ʋ [1]	263	51.12 N	6.42 E
Sankt Stefan an der Gail	64	46.37 N	13.31 E
Sankt Stefan im Rosental	61	46.54 N	15.42 E
Sankt Ulrich → Ortisei	64	46.34 N	11.40 E
Sankt Valentin	61	48.10 N	14.32 E
Sankt Veit an der Glan	61	46.46 N	14.21 E
Sankt Veit an der Gölsen	61	48.03 N	15.40 E
Sankt Veit im Pongau	64	47.20 N	13.09 E
Sankt-Viktors-Dom ʋ [1]	263	51.40 N	6.27 E
Sankt Vincent → Saint Vincent and the Grenadines □ [1]	241h	13.15 N	61.12 W
Sankt Wallburg → Santa Valburga	64	46.33 N	11.00 E
Sankt Wendel	56	49.28 N	7.10 E
Sankt-Willibrodi-Dom ʋ [1]	263	51.40 N	6.37 E
Sankt Wolfgang im Salzkammergut	64	47.44 N	13.27 E
Sankuru ≃	152	4.17 S	20.25 E
San Lázaro	252	22.10 S	57.55 W
San Lázaro, Cabo ›	232	24.48 N	112.19 W
San Lazaro Race Track ♠	269f	14.37 N	120.59 E
San Lazzaro di Savena	64	44.28 N	11.25 E
San Leandro	226	37.43 N	122.09 W
San Leandro Creek ≃	282	37.45 N	122.12 W
San Leo	66	43.54 N	12.21 E

Nome	Página	Lat.°′	Long.°′
San Leon	222	29.29 N	94.55 W
San Leonardo (Sankt Leonhard), It.	64	46.49 N	11.15 E
San Leonardo, Méx.	196	27.28 N	104.55 W
San Leonardo ≃	70	37.59 N	13.41 E
San Leone	70	37.16 N	13.35 E
Sanlicheng	100	31.48 N	114.12 E
Sanlidian	100	30.48 N	118.15 E
Sanlifan	100	30.51 N	115.15 E
Sanlintang	106	31.08 N	121.29 E
Sanlipu	106	31.46 N	119.03 E
Sanliuji	100	32.08 N	116.19 E
San Lope	246	6.12 N	71.56 W
San Lorenzo, Arg.	252	28.08 S	58.46 W
San Lorenzo, Arg.	252	32.45 S	60.44 W
San Lorenzo, Bol.	248	21.26 S	64.47 W
San Lorenzo, Ec.	246	1.17 N	78.50 W
San Lorenzo, Hond.	236	13.25 N	87.27 W
San Lorenzo, It.	68	38.01 N	15.50 E
San Lorenzo, Méx.	196	25.37 N	97.35 W
San Lorenzo, Méx.	232	25.32 N	102.11 W
San Lorenzo, Nic.	236	12.23 N	85.40 W
San Lorenzo, P.R.	240m	18.11 N	65.58 W
San Lorenzo, Ca., U.S.	226	37.40 N	122.07 W
San Lorenzo, Ven.	246	9.47 N	71.04 W
San Lorenzo ≃, Méx.	232	24.15 N	107.24 W
San Lorenzo ≃, Méx.	286a	19.28 N	99.16 W
San Lorenzo → Saint Lawrence ≃, N.A.	176	49.30 N	67.00 W
San Lorenzo ≃, Ca., U.S.	226	36.58 N	122.01 W
San Lorenzo, Bahía c	236	13.19 N	87.30 W
San Lorenzo, Cabo ›	246	1.04 S	80.56 W
San Lorenzo, Cerro ∧	254	47.37 S	72.19 W
San Lorenzo, Golfo del → Saint Lawrence, Gulf of c	186	48.00 N	62.00 W
San Lorenzo, Isla I, Méx.	232	28.38 N	112.51 W
San Lorenzo, Isla I, Perú	248	12.05 S	77.15 W
San Lorenzo Bellizzi	68	39.53 N	16.20 E
San Lorenzo Creek ≃, Ca., U.S.	226	36.12 N	120.38 W
San Lorenzo Creek ≃, Ca., U.S.	282	37.39 N	122.09 W
San Lorenzo de El Escorial	34	40.35 N	4.09 W
San Lorenzo de la Parrilla	34	39.51 N	2.22 W
San Lorenzo del Vallo	68	39.40 N	16.18 E
San Lorenzo di Sebato (Sankt Lorenzen)	64	46.47 N	11.54 E
San Lorenzo in Campo	66	43.36 N	12.56 E
San Lorenzo Nuovo	66	42.41 N	11.54 E
San Lorenzo Tenoxtitlan ⊥	234	17.44 N	94.45 W
San Lorenzo Tezonco ◆ [8]	286a	19.18 N	99.04 W
San Luca	68	38.09 N	16.04 E
Sanlúcar de Barrameda	34	36.47 N	6.21 W
Sanlúcar la Mayor	34	37.23 N	6.12 W
San Lucas, Bol.	248	20.06 S	65.07 W
San Lucas, Ec.	246	3.45 S	79.15 W
San Lucas, Méx.	232	24.13 N	103.04 W
San Lucas, Méx.	232	22.53 N	109.54 W
San Lucas, Ca., U.S.	226	36.08 N	121.01 W
San Lucas, Cabo ›	232	22.52 N	109.53 W
San Lucas, Serranía de ⋏	246	8.00 N	74.20 W
San Luis, Arg.	252	33.18 S	66.21 W
San Luis, Cuba	240p	20.12 N	75.51 W
San Luis, Cuba	240p	22.17 N	83.46 W
San Luis, Guat.	236	16.14 N	89.27 W
San Luis, Az., U.S.	200	32.04 N	111.57 W
San Luis, Co., U.S.	200	37.12 N	105.25 W
San Luis, Ven.	246	11.07 N	69.42 W
San Luis □ [4]	252	34.00 S	66.00 W
San Luis ◆ [8]	286b	23.05 N	82.20 W
San Luis, Arroyo ≃	258	34.10 S	57.44 W
San Luis, Laguna ⊜	248	13.45 S	64.00 W
San Luis, Sierra de ⋏	252	32.40 S	65.50 W
San Luis Acatlán	234	16.48 N	98.45 W
San Luis Creek ≃	200	37.42 N	105.44 W
San Luis de la Loma	234	17.18 N	100.55 W
San Luis de la Paz	234	21.18 N	100.31 W
San Luis del Cordero	232	25.26 N	104.18 W
San Luis del Palmar	252	27.31 S	58.34 W
San Luis Gonzaga	232	24.55 N	111.16 W
San Luis Gonzaga, Bahía c	232	29.48 N	114.22 W
San Luis Jilotepeque	236	14.39 N	89.44 W
San Luis Obispo	226	35.16 N	120.39 W
San Luis Obispo □ [6]	226	35.30 N	120.30 W
San Luis Pass c	222	29.05 N	95.08 W
San Luis Peak ∧	200	37.59 N	106.56 W
San Luis Potosí	234	22.09 N	100.59 W
San Luis Potosí □ [3]	234	22.30 N	100.30 W
San Luis Reservoir ⊜ [1]	226	37.07 N	121.05 W
San Luis Rey	228	33.14 N	117.20 W
San Luis Rey ≃	204	33.12 N	117.24 W
San Luis Rey, Mission ʋ [1]	228	33.14 N	117.20 W
San Luis Río Colorado	232	32.29 N	114.48 W
San Luis Soyatlán	234	20.12 N	103.18 W
San Luis State Recreation Area ♠	226	37.04 N	121.05 W
San Luis Valley V	200	37.25 N	106.00 W
Sanluri	71	39.34 N	8.54 E
San Macario	266b	45.36 N	8.47 E
Sanmaiden	270	34.34 N	135.51 E
San Mamete	58	46.02 N	9.04 E
San Mango d'aquino	68	39.03 N	16.11 E
San Manuel, Arg.	252	37.47 S	58.50 W
San Manuel, Méx.	234	17.37 N	93.24 W
San Manuel, Pil.	116	16.04 N	120.40 E
San Manuel, Az., U.S.	200	32.35 N	110.37 W
San Marcelino, El Sal.	236	13.22 N	89.03 W
San Marcelino, Pil.	116	14.58 N	120.09 E
San Marcello Pistoiese	66	44.03 N	10.47 E
San Marcial, Punta ›	232	25.30 N	111.01 W
San Marco, Chile	286e	33.37 S	70.38 W
San Marco, Esp.	34	43.13 N	8.17 W
San Marco, Capo ›, It.	70	37.30 N	13.01 E
San Marco, Capo ›, It.	71	39.51 N	8.26 E
San Marco Argentano	68	39.33 N	16.07 E
San Marco dei Cavoti	68	41.18 N	14.53 E
San Marco in Lamis	68	41.43 N	15.38 E
San Marco la Catola	68	41.31 N	15.00 E
San Marcos, Chile	252	30.56 S	71.03 W
San Marcos, Col.	246	8.39 N	75.08 W
San Marcos, C.R.	236	9.40 N	84.01 W
San Marcos, El Sal.	236	13.39 N	89.11 W
San Marcos, Guat.	236	14.58 N	91.48 W
San Marcos, Hond.	236	14.24 N	88.56 W
San Marcos, Hond.	236	15.17 N	88.23 W
San Marcos, Méx.	234	16.48 N	99.21 W
San Marcos, Méx.	234	20.02 N	99.20 W
San Marcos, Méx.	234	20.47 N	104.11 W
San Marcos, Ca., U.S.	228	33.08 N	117.09 W
San Marcos, Tx., U.S.	196	29.52 N	97.56 W

≃ River	Fluss	Río	Rivière	Rio
≍ Canal	Kanal	Canal	Canal	Canal
∟ Waterfall, Rapids	Wasserfall, Stromschnellen	Cascada, Rápidos	Chute d'eau, Rapides	Cascata, Rápidos
ᵿ Strait	Meeresstrasse	Estrecho	Détroit	Estreito
c Bay, Gulf	Bucht, Golf	Bahía, Golfo	Baie, Golfe	Baía, Golfo
⊜ Lake, Lakes	See, Seen	Lago, Lagos	Lac, Lacs	Lago, Lagos
≡ Swamp	Sumpf	Pantano	Marais	Pântano
⋇ Ice Features, Glacier	Eis- und Gletscherformen	Accidentes Glaciales	Formes glaciaires	Acidentes glaciares
⫪ Other Hydrographic Features	Andere Hydrographische Objekte	Otros Elementos Hidrográficos	Autres données hydrographiques	Outros acidentes hidrográficos

✥ Submarine Features	Untermeerische Objekte	Accidentes Submarinos	Formes de relief sous-marin	Acidentes submarinos
□ Political Unit	Politische Einheit	Unidad Politica	Entité politique	Unidade política
ʋ Cultural Institution	Kulturelle Institution	Institución Cultural	Institution culturelle	Instituição cultural
⊥ Historical Site	Historische Stätte	Sitio Histórico	Site historique	Sitio histórico
♠ Recreational Site	Erholungs- und Ferienort	Sitio de Recreo	Centre de loisirs	Area de Lazer
⊠ Airport	Flughafen	Aeropuerto	Aéroport	Aeroporto
■ Military Installation	Militäranlage	Instalación Militar	Installation militaire	Instalação militar
◆ Miscellaneous	Verschiedenes	Misceláneo	Divers	Diversos

San Marcos □5 236 15.00 N 91.55 W
San Marcos ≃, Méx. 234 20.17 N 97.32 W
San Marcos ≃, Tx., U.S. 196 29.29 N 97.28 W
San Marcos, Estadio de ♦ 286d 12.04 S 77.05 W
San Marcos, Isla I 232 27.13 N 112.06 W
San Marcos, Laguna de ⊜ 234 20.17 N 103.33 W
San Marcos, Universidad de ᵛ2 286d 12.03 S 77.05 W
San Marcos Arteaga 234 17.45 N 97.58 W
San Marcos de Colón 236 13.26 N 86.48 W
San Marino, S. Mar. 66 43.55 N 12.28 E
San Marino, Ca., U.S. 280 34.07 N 118.06 W
San Marino □1, Europe 22 43.56 N 12.25 E
San Marino □1, Europe 66 43.56 N 12.25 E
San Martín, Arg. 252 29.14 S 65.46 W
San Martín, Arg. 252 33.04 S 68.28 W
San Martín → General San Martín, Arg. 258 34.34 S 58.32 W
San Martín, Col. 246 3.42 N 73.42 W
San Martin, Ca., U.S. 226 37.05 N 121.37 W
San Martín, Ur. 258 33.45 S 57.37 W
San Martín □5 248 7.00 S 76.50 W
San Martín ≃ 248 13.08 S 63.43 W
San Martín ᵛ3 9 68.07 S 67.08 W
San Martín, Arroyo ≃ 258 33.49 S 57.44 W
San Martín, Cerro ∧1 234 18.19 N 94.48 W
San Martín, Cuchilla ⋏2 258 33.45 S 57.54 W
San Martín, Lago (Lago O'Higgins) ⊜ 254 49.00 S 72.40 W
San Martín, Volcán ∧1 234 18.33 N 95.12 W
San Martín de Bolaños 234 21.29 N 103.58 W
San Martín [de las Pirámides] 234 19.42 N 98.50 W
San Martín de las Vacas 196 25.30 N 101.20 W
San Martín de los Andes 254 40.10 S 71.21 W
San Martín de Valdeiglesias 34 40.21 N 4.24 W
San Martin Hidalgo 234 20.27 N 103.57 W
San Martino, It. 62 45.27 N 8.47 E
San Martino (Sankt Martin), It. 64 46.47 N 11.13 E
San Martino, It. 64 45.25 N 10.35 E
San Martino Buon Albergo 64 45.25 N 11.05 E
San Martino d'agri 68 40.14 N 16.04 E
San Martino di Castrozza 64 46.16 N 11.48 E
San Martino di Lupari 64 45.39 N 11.51 E
San Martino in Badia (Saint Martin) 64 46.41 N 11.52 E
San Martino in Casies (Sankt Martin in Gsies) 64 46.49 N 12.14 E
San Martino in Rio 64 44.44 N 10.48 E
San Martino Valle Caudina 68 41.01 N 14.39 E
San Martín Peras 234 17.19 N 98.15 W
San Marzano di San Giuseppe 68 40.27 N 17.30 E
San Marzano sul Sarno 66 40.46 N 14.35 E
San Mateo, Esp. 34 40.28 N 0.11 E
San Mateo, Méx. 234 22.59 N 103.30 W
San Mateo, Pil. 269f 14.42 N 121.07 E
San Mateo, Ca., U.S. 226 37.33 N 122.19 W
San Mateo, Fl., U.S. 192 29.36 N 81.35 W
San Mateo, N.M., U.S. 200 35.19 N 107.38 W
San Mateo, Ven. 246 9.45 N 64.33 W
San Mateo □6 226 37.25 N 122.20 W
San Mateo ≃ 286a 19.30 N 99.17 W
San Mateo Atenco 234 19.16 N 99.32 W
San Mateo Bridge ◆5 282 37.36 N 122.13 W
San Mateo Canyon V 228 33.23 N 117.36 W
San Mateo Creek ≃ 282 37.34 N 122.18 W
San Mateo del Mar 234 16.12 N 95.00 W
San Mateo Ixtatán 236 15.50 N 91.29 W
San Mateo Memorial Park ♦ 282 37.17 N 122.18 W
San Mateo Point ≻ 228 33.23 N 117.36 W
San Mateo Tecoloapan 286a 19.34 N 99.14 W
San Matías 248 16.22 S 58.24 W
San Matías, Golfo c 254 41.30 S 64.15 W
San Mauro Castelverde 70 37.55 N 14.11 E
San Mauro Forte 68 40.29 N 16.15 E
San Mauro la Bruca 68 40.07 N 15.17 E
San Mauro Marchesato 68 39.06 N 16.56 E
San Mauro Torinese 62 45.06 N 7.46 E
San Medi, Arroyo de ≃ 266d 41.28 N 2.06 E
Sanmen 100 29.06 N 121.24 E
San Menaio 68 41.56 N 15.58 E
Sanmen Wan c 100 29.08 N 121.44 E
Sanmenxia (Shanxian) 102 34.45 N 111.05 E
San Michele, Sacra di ᵛ1 62 45.11 N 7.21 E
San Michele all'Adige 64 46.12 N 11.08 E
San Michele al Tagliamento 64 45.46 N 12.59 E
San Michele di Ganzaria 70 37.17 N 14.26 E
San Michele Mondovì 62 44.23 N 7.54 E
San Michele Salentino 68 40.38 N 17.37 E
San Miguel, Arg. 252 28.00 S 57.36 W
San Miguel → General Sarmiento, Arg. 258 34.33 S 58.43 W
San Miguel, Bol. 248 16.42 S 61.01 W
San Miguel, Chile 286e 33.30 S 70.40 W
San Miguel, Ec. 246 1.44 S 79.01 W
San Miguel, El Sal. 236 13.29 N 88.11 W
San Miguel, Esp. 148 28.05 N 16.37 W
San Miguel, Méx. 234 23.23 N 98.10 W
San Miguel, Pan. 246 8.27 N 78.56 W
San Miguel, Perú 248 13.01 S 73.58 W
San Miguel, Perú 286d 12.06 S 77.07 W
San Miguel, Pil. 116 15.09 N 120.59 E
San Miguel, Ca., U.S. 226 35.45 N 120.41 W
San Miguel ≃, Bol. 248 13.52 S 63.56 W
San Miguel ≃, Méx. 232 29.16 N 110.53 W
San Miguel ≃, Méx. 234 18.16 N 100.40 W
San Miguel (Cuilco) ≃, N.A. 236 15.56 N 92.10 W
San Miguel ≃, S.A. 248 19.15 S 59.20 W
San Miguel ≃, Co., U.S. 200 38.23 N 108.48 W
San Miguel, Cerro ⋏2 248 19.19 S 60.36 W
San Miguel, Golfo de c 246 8.22 N 78.17 W
San Miguel, Volcán de ∧1 236 13.26 N 88.16 W
San Miguel Arcángel, Mission ᵛ1 226 35.44 N 120.42 W
San Miguel Bay c 116 13.50 N 123.10 E
San Miguel Canoa 234 19.09 N 98.05 W
San Miguel Chimalapa 234 16.43 N 94.41 W
San Miguel Creek ≃ 196 28.30 N 98.25 W
San Miguel de Allende 234 20.55 N 100.45 W
San Miguel de Cruces 232 24.25 N 105.51 W
San Miguel del Monte 258 35.27 S 58.48 W
San Miguel del Padrón ◆8 286b 23.05 N 82.19 W
San Miguel de Pallaques 248 7.00 S 78.51 W
San Miguel de Salcedo 246 1.02 S 78.34 W
San Miguel de Tucumán 252 26.49 S 65.13 W
San Miguel el Alto 234 21.01 N 102.21 W
San Miguel Island I, Pil. 116 13.23 N 123.48 E
San Miguel Island I, Ca., U.S. 204 34.02 N 120.22 W
San Miguel Islands II 116 7.45 N 118.28 E
San Miguelito 236 11.24 N 84.54 W
San Miguel Ixtahuacán 236 15.15 N 91.45 W
San Miguel Mountain ∧ 228 32.42 N 116.56 W
San Miguel Octopan 234 20.34 N 100.44 W
San Miguel [o San Graciano] 232 29.10 N 101.28 W
San Miguel Talea de Castro 234 17.22 N 96.15 W
San Miguel Tenango 234 16.16 N 95.36 W
San Miguel Totolapan 234 18.08 N 100.23 W
Sanming 100 26.14 N 117.36 E
San Miniato 66 43.41 N 10.51 E
San Murezzan → Sankt Moritz 58 46.30 N 9.50 E
Sannahed 40 59.06 N 15.09 E
Sannan 96 35.04 N 135.02 E
Sannār 140 13.33 N 33.38 E
San Narciso, Pil. 116 13.34 N 122.34 E
San Narciso, Pil. 116 15.01 N 120.05 E
Sannazzaro de'Burgondi 62 45.06 N 8.54 E
Sannicandro di Bari 68 41.00 N 16.48 E
Sannicandro Garganico 68 41.50 N 15.34 E
Sannicola 68 40.05 N 18.04 E
San Nicola, Isola I 66 42.07 N 15.30 E
San Nicola, Monte ∧ 68 38.35 N 16.24 E
San Nicola Arcella 68 39.51 N 15.48 E
San Nicola da Crissa 68 38.40 N 16.17 E
San Nicolás, Esp. 148 27.59 N 15.46 W
San Nicolás, Hond. 236 15.00 N 88.42 W
San Nicolás, Méx. 234 16.26 N 98.32 W
San Nicolás, Méx. 234 19.05 N 101.07 W
San Nicolás, Perú 248 15.13 S 75.12 W
San Nicolas, Pil. 116 18.09 N 120.38 E
San Nicolas, Pil. 116 16.04 N 120.46 E
San Nicolás ≃ 234 19.40 N 105.14 W
San Nicolás de Bari 240p 22.47 N 81.55 W
San Nicolás de los Arroyos 252 33.20 S 60.13 W
San Nicolás de los Garzas 196 25.45 N 100.18 W
San Nicolas Island I 204 33.15 N 119.31 W
San Nicolò di Comelico 64 46.35 N 12.31 E
San Nicolò d'Ultimo (Sankt Nikolaus) 64 46.30 N 10.55 E
San Nicolò Ferrarese 64 44.42 N 11.42 E
San Nicolò Gerrei 71 39.30 N 9.18 E
Sannieshof 158 26.30 S 25.47 E
Sannikova, proliv)(74 74.30 N 140.00 E
Sannīn, Jabal ∧ 132 33.57 N 35.52 E
Sannio, Monti del ⋏ 66 41.30 N 14.45 E
Sanniquellie 150 7.22 N 8.43 W
Sannohe 92 40.22 N 141.15 E
Sannois 261 48.58 N 2.15 E
Sannūr, Wādī V 142 28.58 N 31.03 E
Sano 94 36.19 N 139.35 E
Sañogasta 252 29.18 S 67.36 W
Sanok 30 49.34 N 22.13 E
Sânon ≃ 58 48.38 N 6.20 E
San Onofre 246 9.44 N 75.32 W
San Onofre Mountain ∧ 228 33.22 N 117.30 W
San Pablo, Chile 254 40.24 S 73.01 W
San Pablo, Col. 246 1.40 N 77.00 W
San Pablo, Pil. 116 14.04 N 121.19 E
San Pablo, Pil. 116 7.40 N 123.27 E
San Pablo, Ca., U.S. 226 37.57 N 122.20 W
San Pablo ≃, Bol. 248 14.52 S 63.40 W
San Pablo ≃, Pan. 236 7.51 N 81.10 W
San Pablo, Point ≻ 282 37.58 N 122.26 W
San Pablo, Punta ≻ 232 27.14 N 114.29 W
San Pablo Autopan 234 19.21 N 99.40 W
San Pablo Balleza 232 26.57 N 106.21 W
San Pablo Bay c 226 38.06 N 122.22 W
San Pablo Creek ≃ 282 37.58 N 122.30 W
San Pablo de Tiquina 248 16.13 S 68.52 W
San Pablo Huitzo 234 17.15 N 96.52 W
San Pablo Huixtepec 234 16.50 N 96.46 W
San Pablo Ostotepec ◆8 286a 19.11 N 99.04 W
San Pablo Reservoir ⊜1 282 37.56 N 122.15 W
San Pablo Ridge ∧ 282 37.55 N 122.15 W
San Pablo Strait)(282 37.58 N 122.26 W
San Pablo Villa de Mitla 234 16.55 N 96.24 W
Sanpada 272c 19.04 N 73.01 E
San Pancrazio Salentino 68 40.25 N 17.50 E
San Paolo 64 46.29 N 11.15 E
San Paolo di Civitate 68 41.44 N 15.15 E
San Pascual 116 13.08 N 122.59 E
San Pasqual Indian Reservation ◆4 228 33.12 N 116.58 W
San Pedrillo, Punta ≻ 236 8.39 N 83.45 W
San Pedro, Arg. 252 33.40 S 59.40 W
San Pedro, Arg. 252 24.14 S 64.52 W
San Pedro, Arg. 252 27.57 S 65.10 W
San Pedro, Bol. 248 14.20 S 64.50 W
San Pedro, Chile 252 21.57 S 68.34 W
San Pedro, Chile 254 33.54 S 71.28 W
San Pedro, Chile 286e 33.33 S 70.44 W
San Pedro, Col. 246 9.24 N 75.04 W
San Pedro, C.R. 236 9.56 N 84.03 W
San Pedro, C. Iv. 150 4.44 N 6.37 W
San Pedro, Para. 252 24.07 S 56.59 W
San Pedro, Tx., U.S. 196 27.47 N 97.40 W
San Pedro, Ur. 258 34.21 S 57.51 W
San Pedro, Ven. 246 8.50 N 71.58 W
San Pedro □5 252 24.15 S 56.30 W
San Pedro ◆8, Cuba 286b 23.03 N 82.27 W
San Pedro ◆8, Ca., U.S. 280 33.44 N 118.18 W
San Pedro ≃, Cuba 240p 21.09 N 78.30 W
San Pedro ≃, Méx. 234 21.45 N 105.30 W
San Pedro ≃, N.A. 200 32.59 N 110.47 W
San Pedro ≃, N.A. 232 17.45 N 91.25 W
San Pedro ≃, Ven. 286c 10.35 N 66.48 W
San Pedro, Arroyo ≃ 258 34.21 S 57.56 W
San Pedro, Point ≻, Ca., U.S. 282 37.59 N 122.27 W
San Pedro, Point ≻, Ca., U.S. 282 37.35 N 122.31 W
San Pedro, Punta ≻ 252 25.30 S 70.38 W
San Pedro, Volcán ∧1 252 21.53 S 68.25 W
San Pedro Apóstol 234 16.44 N 96.44 W
San Pedro Ayampuc 236 14.47 N 90.27 W
San Pedro Bay c, Pil. 116 11.11 N 125.05 E
San Pedro Bay c, Ca., U.S. 228 33.45 N 118.11 W
San Pedro Breakwater ◆5 280 33.42 N 118.16 W
San Pedro Carchá 236 15.29 N 90.16 W
San Pedro Channel)(228 33.35 N 118.25 W
San Pedro Creek ≃, Ca., U.S. 282 37.36 N 122.30 W
San Pedro Creek ≃, Tx., U.S. 222 31.34 N 95.14 W
San Pedro de Arriba 258 34.18 S 57.47 W
San Pedro de Atacama 252 22.55 S 68.13 W
San Pedro de Buena Vista 248 18.13 S 65.59 W
San Pedro de la Cueva 232 29.18 N 109.44 W
San Pedro de las Colonias 232 25.45 N 102.59 W
San Pedro del Gallo 232 25.33 N 104.18 W
San Pedro de Lloc 248 7.26 S 79.31 W
San Pedro del Norte 236 13.04 N 84.33 W
San Pedro del Paraná 252 26.46 S 56.15 W
San Pedro de Macorís 238 18.27 N 69.18 W
San Pedro de Premiá 266d 41.31 N 2.21 E
San Pedro El Alto 234 16.01 N 96.28 W
San Pedro Huamelula 234 16.02 N 95.40 W
San Pedro Jicayán 234 16.25 N 97.59 W
San Pedro Juchatengo 234 16.21 N 97.06 W
San Pedro Mártir ◆8 286a 19.16 N 99.10 W
San Pedro Mártir, Sierra ⋏ 232 30.45 N 115.13 W
San Pedro Mixtepec 234 16.00 N 97.07 W
San Pedro Peaks ⋏ 200 36.07 N 106.49 W
San Pedro Piedra Gorda 234 22.27 N 102.21 W
San Pedro Pinula 236 14.40 N 89.51 W
San Pedro Sacatepéquez 236 14.58 N 91.46 W
San Pedro Sula 236 15.27 N 88.02 W
San Pedro Tapanatepec 234 16.21 N 94.12 W
San Pedro Xalostoc 286a 19.32 N 99.05 W
San Pedro y Miquelón → Saint Pierre and Miquelon □2 186 46.55 N 56.20 W
San Pelayo 246 8.58 N 75.51 W
San Pellegrino 62 45.50 N 9.40 E
San Piero a Grado 66 43.41 N 10.21 E
San Piero in Bagno 66 43.51 N 11.58 E
San Pierre 216 41.12 N 86.53 W
San Pietro (Sankt Peter) 64 47.01 N 12.03 E
San Pietro, Isola di I 71 39.08 N 8.17 E
San Pietro a Maida 68 38.50 N 16.20 E
San Pietro di Cadore 64 46.34 N 12.35 E
San Pietro in Casale 64 44.42 N 11.24 E
San Pietro in Gu 64 45.37 N 11.40 E
San Pietro in Guarano 68 39.20 N 16.19 E
San Pietro in Palazzi 66 43.20 N 10.30 E
San Pietro in Vaticano ᵛ1 267a 41.54 N 12.28 E
San Pietro Vara 62 44.20 N 9.35 E
San Pietro Vernotico 68 40.29 N 18.00 E
San Pitch ≃ 200 39.03 N 111.51 W
Sanpoil ≃ 202 47.53 N 118.41 W
San Policarpio 116 12.11 N 125.30 E
San Polo d'Enza 64 44.38 N 10.26 E
Sanpu 98 34.09 N 117.10 E
Sanqiao 106 30.35 N 119.58 E
San Quentin 282 37.56 N 122.29 W
San Quentin State Prison ♦ 282 37.56 N 122.28 W
Sanquhar 44 55.22 N 3.56 W
San Quintin 116 16.00 N 120.50 E
San Quintín, Bahía de c 232 30.22 N 115.55 W
San Quintín, Cabo ≻ 232 30.21 N 116.00 W
San Quintín, Ventisquero ⊓ 254 46.52 S 74.05 W
San Quirico de Tarrasa 266d 41.32 N 2.05 E
San Quirico d'Orcia 66 43.03 N 11.36 E
Sanqutan 100 27.17 N 115.04 E
Sanquzhen 107 29.39 N 105.37 E
San Rafael, Arg. 252 34.36 S 68.20 W
San Rafael, Chile 252 35.19 S 71.32 W
San Rafael, Méx. 232 25.01 N 100.33 W
San Rafael, Méx. 232 28.34 N 111.42 W
San Rafael, Méx. 234 20.12 N 96.51 W
San Rafael, Ca., U.S. 226 37.58 N 122.31 W
San Rafael, N.M., U.S. 200 35.06 N 107.52 W
San Rafael, Ven. 246 10.58 N 71.44 W
San Rafael ≃, Bol. 248 18.38 S 58.55 W
San Rafael ≃, Ut., U.S. 200 38.47 N 110.07 W
San Rafael Bay c 282 37.58 N 122.28 W
San Rafael de Arriba 232 31.05 N 116.05 W
San Rafael de las Tortillas 196 26.49 N 99.32 W
San Rafael del Norte 236 13.12 N 86.06 W
San Rafael del Sur 236 11.51 N 86.27 W
San Rafael Desert ◆2 200 38.40 N 110.30 W
San Rafael Hills ⋏2 280 34.10 N 118.12 W
San Rafael Mountains ⋏ 204 34.45 N 119.50 W
San Rafael Oriente 236 13.23 N 88.21 W
San Rafael Swell ⋏1 200 38.40 N 110.45 W
San Ramón, Arg. 252 27.42 S 64.17 W
San Ramón, Bol. 248 13.17 S 64.43 W
San Ramón, C.R. 236 10.06 N 84.28 W
San Ramón, Hond. 236 14.41 N 84.43 W
San Ramón, Perú 248 11.08 S 75.20 W
San Ramon, Pil. 116 13.16 N 124.05 E
San Ramon, Ca., U.S. 282 37.47 N 121.59 W
San Ramón, Ur. 252 34.18 S 55.58 W
San Ramón, Bahía c 232 30.45 N 116.03 W
San Ramon Creek ≃ 282 37.54 N 122.03 W
San Ramón de la Nueva Orán 252 23.08 S 64.20 W
San Ramon Valley V 282 37.46 N 121.58 W
Sanrao 100 23.59 N 116.50 E
San-rei ∧ 96 33.50 N 133.59 E
San Remigio 116 11.05 N 123.56 E
San Remo, Austl. 169 38.31 S 145.22 E
San Remo, It. 62 43.49 N 7.46 E
San Remo, N.Y., U.S. 210 40.52 N 73.13 W
San Roberto 68 38.18 N 15.44 E
San Rodrigo ≃ 196 28.54 N 100.37 W
San Román ≃ 236 16.21 N 90.22 W
San Román, Cabo ≻ 246 12.12 N 70.00 W
San Roque, Arg. 252 28.34 S 58.43 W
San Roque, Arg. 252 30.17 S 68.41 W
San Roque, Esp. 34 36.13 N 5.24 W
San Roque, Pil. 269f 14.29 N 120.54 E
San Roque, T.T.P.I. 174n 15.15 N 145.47 E
San Roque, Cabo → São Roque, Cabo de ≻ 250 5.29 S 35.16 W
San Rosendo 252 37.16 S 72.43 W
San Rufo 68 40.26 N 15.28 E
San Saba 196 31.11 N 98.43 W
San Saba ≃ 196 31.15 N 98.36 W
San Saep, Khlong ≃ 269a 13.45 N 100.36 E
San Salvador, Arg. 252 29.16 S 57.31 W
San Salvador, Arg. 252 31.37 S 58.30 W
San Salvador, El Sal. 236 13.42 N 89.12 W
San Salvador (Watling Island) I 238 24.02 N 74.28 W
San Salvador ≃ 258 33.37 S 58.06 W
San Salvador, Cuchilla de ⋏2 258 33.56 S 57.45 W
San Salvador, Isla I 246a 0.14 S 90.45 W
San Salvador, Volcán de ∧1 236 13.44 N 89.17 W
San Salvador de Jujuy 252 24.11 S 65.18 W
San Salvador el Seco 234 19.08 N 97.39 W
San Salvatore, Monte ∧ 70 37.50 N 14.03 E
San Salvatore Monferrato 62 44.59 N 8.34 E
San Salvatore Telesino 68 41.14 N 14.30 E
San Salvo 66 42.03 N 14.44 E
Sansanné-Mango 150 10.21 N 0.28 E
Sans Bois Creek ≃ 196 35.20 N 94.50 W
San Sebastián, El Sal. 236 13.44 N 88.50 W
San Sebastián, Esp. 34 43.19 N 1.59 W
San Sebastián, Guat. 236 14.34 N 91.39 W
San Sebastián, Hond. 236 14.24 N 88.42 W
San Sebastián, Méx. 234 21.26 N 102.21 W
San Sebastián, Méx. 234 20.47 N 104.51 W
San Sebastián, Méx. 234 22.10 N 104.19 W
San Sebastián, P.R. 240m 18.20 N 66.59 W
San Sebastián, Bahía c 254 53.12 S 68.20 W
San Sebastián de la Gomera 148 28.06 N 17.06 W
San Sebastián de los Reyes 266a 40.33 N 3.38 W
San Sebastián de Yalí 236 13.18 N 86.11 W
San Sebastiano 64 45.38 N 10.16 E
San Sebastiano Curone 62 44.47 N 9.04 E
San Secondo Parmense 64 44.55 N 10.14 E
Sansepolcro 66 43.34 N 12.08 E
San Severino Lucano 68 40.01 N 16.08 E
San Severino Marche 66 43.13 N 13.10 E
San Severo 68 41.41 N 15.23 E
Sansha 100 26.58 N 120.12 E
Sanshengchang 89 44.51 N 120.21 E
Sanshierzhan 89 53.16 N 121.49 E
Sanshijia, Zhg. 98 41.44 N 119.15 E
Sanshijia, Zhg. 98 41.05 N 119.03 E
Sanshilibao 98 39.15 N 121.48 E
Sanshiling 106 30.51 N 119.29 E
Sanshisanzhan 89 53.10 N 121.27 E
Sanshui 100 23.11 N 112.53 E
San Sigismondo (Sankt Sigmund) 64 46.49 N 11.46 E
San Simeon 226 35.39 N 121.11 W
San Simón, Méx. 204 30.30 N 115.58 W
San Simon, Az., U.S. 200 32.16 N 109.13 W
San Simón ≃, Bol. 248 13.13 S 63.31 W
San Simon ≃, Az., U.S. 200 32.50 N 109.39 W
San Simon Wash V 200 31.45 N 112.25 W
San Siro ◆8 266b 45.29 N 9.07 E
Sanski Most 36 44.46 N 16.40 E
Sanso 150 11.43 N 6.51 W
San Solano 252 31.29 S 65.55 W
Sansom Park Village 222 32.48 N 97.24 W
Sanson 172 40.13 S 175.25 E
San Sosti 68 39.40 N 16.02 E
San Sperate 71 39.21 N 9.00 E
Sans Souci ♦ 274a 33.59 S 151.08 E
Sans-Souci ⊥ 238 19.37 N 72.12 W
Sanssouci, Schloss ᵛ 54 52.24 N 13.02 E
San Stefano Ticino 266b 45.29 N 8.55 E
Santa, Perú 248 8.59 S 78.36 W
Santa, Pil. 116 17.29 N 120.26 E
Santa ≃ 248 8.58 S 78.39 W
Santa, Isla de I 248 9.02 S 78.40 W
Santa Adélia 255 21.16 S 48.48 W
Santa Albertina 255 20.02 S 50.44 W
Santa Amalia 34 39.01 N 6.01 W
Santa Ana, Arg. 252 27.22 S 55.34 W
Santa Ana, Bol. 248 13.45 S 65.35 W
Santa Ana, Bol. 248 15.31 S 67.30 W
Santa Ana, Bol. 248 18.43 S 58.44 W
Santa Ana, Col. 246 9.19 N 74.35 W
Santa Ana, Ec. 246 1.13 S 80.23 W
Santa Ana, El Sal. 236 13.59 N 89.34 W
Santa Ana, Méx. 232 24.04 N 100.30 W
Santa Ana, Méx. 232 30.33 N 111.07 W
Santa Ana, Méx. 234 19.19 N 98.11 W
Santa Ana, Ca., U.S. 228 33.44 N 117.52 W
Santa Ana, Ven. 246 9.19 N 64.39 W
Santa Ana ≃ 228 33.38 N 117.57 W
Santa Ana, Volcán de ∧1 236 13.50 N 89.38 W
Santa Ana Canyon V 280 33.53 N 117.43 W
Santa Ana de Chena 286e 33.34 S 70.47 W
Santa Ana Heights 228 33.39 N 117.54 W
Santa Ana Indian Reservation ◆4 200 35.28 N 106.37 W
Santa Ana Island I 175e 10.50 S 162.28 E
Santa Ana Maya 234 20.00 N 101.01 W
Santa Ana Mountains ⋏ 228 33.45 N 117.35 W
Santa Ana Pacueco 234 20.22 N 102.00 W
Santa Ana Race Track ♦ 269f 14.35 N 121.01 E
Santa Ana Tlacotenco ◆8 286a 19.10 N 98.59 W
Santa Anita 234 20.33 N 103.27 W
Santa Anita Canyon V 280 34.12 N 118.01 W
Santa Anita Park ♦ 280 34.08 N 118.03 W
Santa Anna 196 31.44 N 99.19 W
Santa Apolonia 196 25.38 N 97.59 W
Santa Bábara 255 11.57 S 38.58 W
Santa Bárbara, Chile 252 37.40 S 72.01 W
Santa Bárbara, Col. 246 5.53 N 75.35 W
Santa Bárbara, Hond. 236 14.53 N 88.14 W
Santa Bárbara, Méx. 232 26.48 N 105.49 W
Santa Bárbara, Méx. 234 18.52 N 101.07 W
Santa Barbara, Ca., U.S. 204 34.25 N 119.42 W
Santa Bárbara, Ven. 246 3.57 N 67.06 W
Santa Bárbara, Ven. 246 7.47 N 71.10 W
Santa Bárbara □5 236 15.10 N 88.20 W
Santa Barbara □6 228 33.28 N 119.02 W
Santa Bárbara ≃ 248 16.58 S 61.39 W
Santa Bárbara, Morro de ∧ 287a 22.57 S 43.28 W
Santa Bárbara, Ribeirão ≃ 256 22.00 S 45.43 W
Santa Bárbara, Túnel ◆5 287a 22.56 S 43.12 W
Santa Barbara Channel)(204 34.15 N 119.55 W
Santa Bárbara de Samaná 238 19.13 N 69.19 W
Santa Bárbara do Monte Verde 256 21.58 S 43.42 W
Santa Bárbara do Sul 252 28.22 S 53.15 W
Santa Barbara Island I 228 33.28 N 119.02 W
Santa Branca 256 23.24 S 45.53 W
Santa Branca, Reprêsa ⊜1 256 23.20 S 45.50 W
Santaca 158 26.36 S 32.32 E
Santa Catalina, Arg. 252 21.57 S 66.04 W
Santa Catalina, Pan. 236 8.47 N 81.20 W
Santa Catalina, Pil. 116 9.20 N 122.51 E
Santa Catalina, Ur. 258 33.49 S 57.29 W
Santa Catalina, Arroyo ≃ 288 34.46 S 58.27 W
Santa Catalina, Gulf of c 228 33.20 N 117.45 W
Santa Catalina, Isla I 232 25.40 N 110.47 W
Santa Catalina, Laguna ⊜ 288 34.46 S 58.27 W
Santa Catalina de Armara 34 43.02 N 8.49 W
Santa Catalina Island I 228 33.23 N 118.24 W
Santa Catarina, Méx. 204 31.37 N 115.48 W
Santa Catarina, Méx. 232 25.41 N 100.28 W
Santa Catarina, Méx. 234 19.18 N 101.10 W
Santa Catarina □3 252 27.00 S 50.00 W
Santa Catarina, Ilha de I 252 27.36 S 48.30 W
Santa Catarina Yosonotú 234 16.59 N 97.39 W
Santa Caterina di Pittinuri 71 40.06 N 8.30 E
Santa Caterina Valfurva 64 46.25 N 10.29 E
Santa Caterina Villarmosa 70 37.35 N 14.02 E
Santa Cecília 252 26.56 S 50.27 W
Santa Cesarea Terme 68 40.02 N 18.29 E
Santa Clara, Arg. 252 29.33 S 68.31 W
Santa Clara, Col. 246 2.43 S 69.43 W
Santa Clara, Cuba 240p 22.24 N 79.58 W
Santa Clara, Méx. 232 29.17 N 107.01 W
Santa Clara, Méx. 234 19.41 N 102.30 W
Santa Clara, Ca., U.S. 226 37.20 N 121.56 W
Santa Clara, Ut., U.S. 200 37.07 N 113.39 W
Santa Clara □6 226 37.20 N 121.53 W
Santa Clara ≃, Ca., U.S. 228 34.14 N 119.16 W
Santa Clara ≃, Ut., U.S. 200 37.05 N 113.36 W
Santa Clara, Bahía de c 240p 23.05 N 80.30 W
Santa Clara, University of ᵛ2 282 37.21 N 121.56 W
Santa Clara Coatitla 286a 19.34 N 99.04 W
Santa Clara de Olimar 252 32.55 S 54.58 W
Santa Clara Indian Reservation ◆4 200 35.59 N 106.10 W
Santa Clara Valley V 226 37.10 N 121.40 W
Santa Clarita 286d 12.00 S 77.01 W
Santa Clotilde 246 2.34 S 73.44 W
Santa Coloma de Cervelló 266d 41.22 N 2.01 E
Santa Coloma de Farnés 34 41.52 N 2.40 E
Santa Coloma de Gramanet 266d 41.27 N 2.13 E
Santa Comba Dão 34 40.24 N 8.08 W
Santa Cristina 64 46.34 N 11.43 E
Santa Cristina d'aspromonte 68 38.15 N 15.58 E
Santa Croce 64 46.05 N 12.18 E
Santa Croce, Capo ≻ 70 37.14 N 15.15 E
Santa Croce, Lago di ⊜ 64 46.10 N 12.20 E
Santa Croce Camerina 70 36.50 N 14.31 E
Santa Croce del Sannio 68 41.23 N 14.43 E
Santa Croce di Magliano 66 41.42 N 14.59 E
Santa Croce Sull'Arno 66 43.42 N 10.47 E
Santa Cruz, Bol. 248 17.48 S 63.10 W
Santa Cruz, Bra. 250 6.13 S 36.01 W
Santa Cruz, Bra. 255 19.56 S 40.09 W
Santa Cruz, Chile 252 34.38 S 71.22 W
Santa Cruz, C.R. 236 10.16 N 85.36 W
Santa Cruz, Méx. 200 31.14 N 110.35 W
Santa Cruz, Méx. 234 23.05 N 97.50 W
Santa Cruz, Perú 248 6.37 S 78.57 W
Santa Cruz, Pil. 116 6.50 N 125.25 E
Santa Cruz, Pil. 116 14.17 N 121.25 E
Santa Cruz, Pil. 116 13.29 N 122.02 E
Santa Cruz, Pil. 116 13.04 N 120.43 E
Santa Cruz, Pil. 116 15.46 N 119.55 E
Santa Cruz (Tubajon), Pil. 116 10.19 N 125.33 E
Santa Cruz, Ca., U.S. 226 36.58 N 122.01 W
Santa Cruz, Ven. 246 8.25 N 71.39 W
Santa Cruz, Ven. 286c 10.26 N 67.01 W
Santa Cruz □4 254 49.00 S 70.00 W
Santa Cruz □5 248 17.30 S 61.30 W
Santa Cruz □6 226 36.58 N 122.01 W
Santa Cruz ◆8, Bra. 256 22.56 S 43.41 W
Santa Cruz ◆8, India 272c 19.05 N 72.50 E
Santa Cruz ≃, Arg. 254 50.08 S 68.20 W
Santa Cruz ≃, Cuba 286b 23.04 N 82.29 W
Santa Cruz ≃, N.A. 200 32.42 N 111.33 W
Santa Cruz, Ilha I 287a 22.52 S 43.07 W
Santa Cruz, Isla I 246a 0.38 S 90.23 W
Santa Cruz, Sierra de ⋏ 236 15.40 N 89.15 W
Santa Cruz Basin ◆1 14 12.00 S 163.00 E
Santa Cruz Cabrália 255 16.17 S 39.02 W
Santa Cruz da Graciosa 148a 39.05 N 28.01 W
Santa Cruz das Flores 148a 39.27 N 31.07 W
Santa Cruz da Vitória 255 14.57 S 39.48 W
Santa Cruz de el Seibo 238 18.46 N 69.02 W
Santa Cruz de Goiás 255 17.19 S 48.30 W
Santa Cruz de Juventino Rosas 234 20.39 N 101.00 W
Santa Cruz de la Palma 148 28.41 N 17.45 W
Santa Cruz de la Zarza 34 39.58 N 3.10 W
Santa Cruz del Norte 240p 23.09 N 81.55 W
Santa Cruz del Quiché 236 15.02 N 91.08 W
Santa Cruz del Sur 240p 20.43 N 78.00 W
Santa Cruz de Mudela 34 38.38 N 3.28 W
Santa Cruz de Tenerife 148 28.27 N 16.14 W
Santa Cruz de Tenerife □4 148 28.15 N 17.00 W
Santa Cruz do Capibaribe 250 7.57 S 36.12 W
Santa Cruz do Piauí 250 7.09 S 41.48 W
Santa Cruz do Prata 256 21.12 S 46.45 W
Santa Cruz do Rio Abaixo 256 23.18 S 45.24 W
Santa Cruz do Rio Pardo 255 22.55 S 49.37 W
Santa Cruz do Sul 252 29.43 S 52.26 W
Santa Cruz International Airport ⊠ 272c 19.05 N 72.52 E
Santa Cruz Island I 204 34.01 N 119.45 W
Santa Cruz Islands II 14 11.00 S 166.15 E
Santa Cruz Meyehualco ◆8 286a 19.20 N 99.03 W
Santa Cruz Mountains ⋏ 226 37.15 N 122.00 W
Santa Cruz Point ≻ 116 15.44 N 119.52 E
Santa Cruz Tacache Mina 234 17.51 N 98.07 W
Santadi 71 39.05 N 8.43 E
Santa Domenica Talao 68 39.49 N 15.51 E
Santa Domenica Vittoria 70 37.55 N 14.58 E
Santa Eduviges 286e 33.33 S 70.39 W
Santa Elena, Arg. 252 30.57 S 59.48 W
Santa Elena, Ec. 246 2.14 S 80.51 W
Santa Elena, El Sal. 236 13.22 N 88.25 W
Santa Elena, Méx. 196 27.59 N 103.56 W
Santa Elena, Méx. 232 27.28 N 102.33 W
Santa Elena, Méx. 234 18.39 N 101.34 W
Santa Elena ≃ 248 15.42 S 67.13 W
Santa Elena, Bahía de c 246 2.06 S 80.53 W
Santa Elena, Golfo de c 236 10.59 N 85.50 W
Santa Elena, Punta ≻, C.R. 236 10.54 N 85.57 W
Santa Elena, Punta ≻, Ec. 246 2.11 S 81.00 W
Santa Elena del Gomero 286e 33.29 S 70.46 W
Santa Elena de Uairén 246 4.37 N 61.08 W
Santa Elisabetta 70 37.26 N 13.33 E
Santa Emilia 286e 33.23 S 70.39 W
Santa Eufemia 34 38.36 N 4.54 W
Santa Eugenia 34 42.33 N 9.00 W
Santa Eulalia, Esp. 34 40.34 N 1.19 W
Santa Eulalia, Guat. 236 15.45 N 91.29 W
Santa Eulalia del Río 34 38.59 N 1.31 E
Santa Fe, Arg. 252 31.38 S 60.42 W
Santa Fé, Bra. 255 15.40 S 51.16 W
Santa Fé, Bra. 255 23.01 S 51.48 W
Santa Fé, Cuba 240p 21.45 N 82.45 W
Santa Fe, Esp. 34 37.11 N 3.43 W
Santa Fé, Hond. 236 15.55 N 86.05 W
Santa Fé, Pan. 236 8.31 N 81.05 W
Santa Fe, Pil. 116 11.09 N 123.47 E
Santa Fe, Pil. 116 16.10 N 120.57 E
Santa Fe, Pil. 116 12.10 N 122.00 E
Santa Fe, Mo., U.S. 219 39.22 N 91.49 W
Santa Fe, N.M., U.S. 200 35.41 N 105.56 W
Santa Fe □4 252 31.00 S 61.00 W
Santa Fé ◆8 286b 23.05 N 82.31 W
Santa Fe ≃, Fl., U.S. 192 29.53 N 82.53 W
Santa Fe ≃, N.M., U.S. 200 35.36 N 106.20 W
Santa Fé, Aeropuerto ⊠ 286b 23.04 N 82.28 W
Santa Fe, Isla I 246a 0.49 S 90.04 W
Santa Fé, Ribeirão ≃ 287b 23.24 S 46.48 W
Santa Fe Baldy ∧ 200 35.50 N 105.46 W
Santa Fe Dam ◆6 280 34.07 N 117.58 W
Santa Fé do Sul 255 20.13 S 50.56 W
Santa Fe Flood Control Basin ⊜1 280 34.07 N 117.58 W
Santa Fe Springs 280 33.56 N 118.04 W
Santa Filomena 250 9.07 S 45.56 W
Santa Fiora 66 42.50 N 11.35 E
Santa Flavia 70 38.05 N 13.31 E
Sant'Agata Bolognese 64 44.40 N 11.08 E
Sant'Agata de'Goti 68 41.05 N 14.30 E
Sant'Agata del Bianco 68 38.05 N 16.05 E
Sant'Agata di Militello 70 38.04 N 14.38 E
Sant'Agata di Puglia 68 41.09 N 15.23 E
Sant'Agata Feltria 66 43.52 N 12.12 E
Sant'Agata sul Santerno 66 44.26 N 11.51 E
Santa Gertrude (Sankt Gertraud) 64 46.29 N 10.53 E
Santa Gertrudis 196 26.09 N 98.44 W
Santa Giusta, Stagno di ⊜ 71 39.52 N 8.35 E
Sant'Agostino 64 44.48 N 11.23 E
Sāntāhār 124 24.48 N 88.59 E
Santa Helena 250 2.14 S 45.18 W
Santa Helena de Goiás 255 17.43 S 50.35 W
Santai, Zhg. 85 39.14 N 77.42 E
Santai, Zhg. 86 44.35 N 81.18 E
Santai, Zhg. 102 31.10 N 105.02 E
Santai, Zhg. 104 41.48 N 121.53 E
Santai, Zhg. 104 41.56 N 123.11 E
Santai, Zhg. 105 38.58 N 115.49 E
Santa Inês 255 13.17 S 39.48 W
Santa Inés, Bahía c 232 26.59 N 111.59 W
Santa Inés, Isla I 254 53.45 S 72.45 W
Santa Inés Ahuatempan 234 18.25 N 98.01 W
Santa Inés Zacatelco 234 19.13 N 98.14 W
Santa Iria de Azóia 266c 38.51 N 9.05 W
Santa Isabel, Arg. 252 36.15 S 66.56 W
Santa Isabel, Arg. 252 33.54 S 61.42 W
Santa Isabel, Bra. 256 23.19 S 46.14 W
Santa Isabel, Ec. 246 3.21 S 79.19 W
Santa Isabel → Malabo, Gui. Ecu. 152 3.45 N 8.47 E
Santa Isabel, P.R. 240m 17.58 N 66.24 W
Santa Isabel I 175e 8.00 S 159.00 E
Santa Isabel ≃ 236 15.59 N 90.00 W
Santa Isabel, Pico de ∧ 152 3.35 N 8.46 E
Santa Isabel Creek ≃ 196 27.39 N 99.38 W
Santa Isabel de las Lajas 240p 22.25 N 80.18 W
Santa Isabel de Sihuas 248 16.20 S 72.06 W
Santa Isabel do Araguaia 250 6.07 S 48.19 W
Santa Isabel do Rio Prêto 256 22.14 S 44.05 W
Santaizi 104 41.21 N 121.36 E
Santa Josefa 116 8.02 N 125.57 E
Santa Julia 286e 33.30 S 70.38 W
Santa Juliana 255 19.19 S 47.32 W
Sant'Alberto 66 44.32 N 12.09 E
Santa Leopoldina 255 20.05 S 40.32 W
Sant'Alfio 70 37.44 N 15.08 E
Santāl Parganas □5 124 24.30 N 87.20 E
Sāntalpur 120 23.45 N 71.10 E
Santa Luce 66 43.28 N 10.34 E
Santa Lucía, Arg. 252 28.59 S 59.06 W
Santa Lucía, Arg. 252 31.32 S 68.29 W
Santa Lucía, Cuba 240p 22.40 N 83.58 W
Santa Lucía, Cuba 240p 20.59 N 77.25 W
Santa Lucía, Cuba 240p 21.02 N 76.00 W
Santa Lucia, It. 64 46.28 N 10.21 E
Santa Lucía, Ur. 258 34.27 S 56.24 W
Santa Lucía, Ven. 246 8.07 N 69.46 W
Santa Lucía → Saint Lucia □1 241f 13.53 N 60.58 W
Santa Lucía ≃ 258 34.48 S 56.22 W
Santa Lucia, Cabo → Saint Lucia, Cape ≻ 158 28.25 S 32.25 E
Santa Lucía, Cuchilla ⋏2 258 34.09 S 56.11 W
Santa Lucía Chico ≃ 258 34.21 S 56.20 W
Santa Lucía Cotzumalguapa 236 14.20 N 91.01 W
Santa Lucia Creek ≃ 226 36.13 N 121.30 W
Santa Lucia del Mela 70 38.09 N 15.17 E
Santa Lucia di Piave 64 45.51 N 12.17 E
Santa Lucia Range ⋏ 226 36.00 N 121.20 W
Santa Lugarda, Punta ≻ 232 26.44 N 109.48 W
Santa Luísa de Baixo 256 22.46 S 45.49 W
Santaluz 250 11.15 S 39.22 W
Santa Luzia, Bra. 250 6.53 S 36.56 W
Santa Luzia, Port. 34 37.44 N 8.24 W
Santa Luzia I 150a 16.46 N 24.45 W
Santa Magdalena 252 34.30 S 63.56 W
Santa Magdalena, Isla I 232 24.55 N 112.15 W
Santa-Manza, Golfu di c 71 41.37 N 9.22 E
Santa Margarita 226 35.23 N 120.36 W
Santa Margarita ≃ 228 33.14 N 117.25 W
Santa Margarita, Isla de I 232 24.27 N 111.50 W
Santa Margarita Lake ⊜1 226 35.20 N 120.28 W
Santa Margarita Mountains ⋏ 228 33.30 N 117.25 W
Santa Margherita di Belice 70 37.41 N 13.01 E
Santa Margherita Ligure 62 44.20 N 9.12 E
Santa María, Arg. 252 26.41 S 66.02 W
Santa Maria, Bra. 252 29.41 S 53.48 W
Santa Maria, C.V. 150a 16.36 N 22.54 W
Santa María, C.R. 236 9.39 N 83.57 W
Santa María, Méx. 196 28.02 N 101.38 W

Symbols in the index entries represent the broad categories identified in the key at the right. Symbols with superior numbers (⋏1) identify subcategories (see complete key on page I · 1).

Kartensymbole in dem Registerverzeichnis stellen die rechts in Schlüssel erklärten Kategorien dar. Symbole mit hochgestellten Ziffern (⋏1) bezeichnen Unterabteilungen einer Kategorie (vgl. vollständiger Schlüssel auf Seite I · 1).

Los símbolos incluídos en el texto del índice representan las grandes categorías identificadas con la clave a la derecha. Los símbolos con numeros en su parte superior (⋏1) identifican las subcategorías (véase la clave completa en la página I · 1).

Les symboles de l'index représentent les catégories indiquées dans la légende à droite. Les symboles suivis d'un indice (⋏1) représentent des sous-catégories (voir légende complète à la page I · 1).

Os símbolos incluídos no texto do índice representam as grandes categorias identificadas com a chave à direita. Os símbolos com números em sua parte superior (⋏1) identificam as subcategorias (veja-se a chave completa na página I · 1).

∧ Mountain	Berg	Montaña	Montagne	Montanha
⋏ Mountains	Berge	Montañas	Montagnes	Montanhas
)(Pass	Pass	Paso	Col	Passo
V Valley, Canyon	Tal, Cañon	Valle, Cañón	Vallée, Canyon	Vale, Canhão
≃ Plain	Ebene	Llano	Plaine	Planície
≻ Cape	Kap	Cabo	Cap	Cabo
I Island	Insel	Isla	Île	Ilha
II Islands	Inseln	Islas	Îles	Ilhas
± Other Topographic Features	Andere Topographische Objekte	Otros Elementos Topográficos	Autres données topographiques	Outros acidentes topográficos

ESPAÑOL — Nombre | Página | Lat.°′ | Long.°′ W = Oeste

FRANÇAIS — Nom | Page | Lat.°′ | Long.°′ W = Ouest

PORTUGUÊS — Nome | Página | Lat.°′ | Long.°′ W = Oeste

Symbol	English	Deutsch	Español	Français	Português
≐	River	Fluss	Río	Rivière	Rio
≡	Canal	Kanal	Canal	Canal	Canal
⌞	Waterfall, Rapids	Wasserfall, Stromschnellen	Cascada, Rápidos	Chute d'eau, Rapides	Cascata, Rápidos
⋓	Strait	Meeresstrasse	Estrecho	Détroit	Estreito
⊂	Bay, Gulf	Bucht, Golf	Bahía, Golfo	Baie, Golfe	Baía, Golfo
⊚	Lake, Lakes	See, Seen	Lago, Lagos	Lac, Lacs	Lago, Lagos
⩸	Swamp	Sumpf	Pantano	Marais	Pântano
⍓	Ice Features, Glacier	Eis- und Gletscherformen	Accidentes Glaciales	Formes glaciaires	Acidentes glaciares
⫧	Other Hydrographic Features	Andere Hydrographische Objekte	Otros Elementos Hidrográficos	Autres données hydrographiques	Outros acidentes hidrográficos
✢	Submarine Features	Untermeerische Objekte	Accidentes Submarinos	Formes de relief sous-marin	Acidentes submarinos
□	Political Unit	Politische Einheit	Unidad Politica	Entité politique	Unidade política
ᵾ	Cultural Institution	Kulturelle Institution	Institución Cultural	Institution culturelle	Instituição cultural
⊥	Historical Site	Historische Stätte	Sitio Histórico	Site historique	Sitio histórico
♠	Recreational Site	Erholungs- und Ferienort	Sitio de Recreo	Centre de loisirs	Area de Lazer
⊠	Airport	Flughafen	Aeropuerto	Aéroport	Aeroporto
■	Military Installation	Militäranlage	Instalación Militar	Installation militaire	Instalação militar
◆	Miscellaneous	Verschiedenes	Misceláneo	Divers	Diversos

Name	Page	Lat.°′	Long.°′
São José dos Campos, Bra.	**256**	22.10 S	45.06 W
São José dos Campos, Bra.	**256**	23.11 S	45.53 W
São José dos Lopes	**256**	21.48 S	43.53 W
São José dos Pinhais	**252**	25.31 S	49.13 W
São José do Turvo	**256**	22.21 S	43.59 W
São Julião da Barra	**266c**	38.40 N	9.21 W
São Julião do Tojal	**266c**	38.51 N	9.08 W
São Leopoldo	**252**	29.46 S	51.09 W
São Lourenço	**256**	22.07 S	45.03 W
São Lourenço ≐	**248**	17.53 S	57.27 W
São Lourenço, Pantanal de ≋	**248**	17.30 S	56.30 W
São Lourenço da Serra	**256**	23.52 S	46.57 W
São Lourenço d'Oeste	**252**	26.24 S	52.46 W
São Lourenço do Ipixuna	**250**	4.28 S	44.54 W
São Lourenço do Sul	**252**	31.22 S	51.58 W
São Luís	**250**	2.31 S	44.16 W
São Luís de Montes Belos	**255**	16.32 S	50.20 W
São Luís do Curu	**250**	3.40 S	39.14 W
São Luís Do Paraitinga	**256**	23.14 S	45.20 W
São Luís do Quitunde	**250**	9.20 S	35.33 W
São Luís do Tocantins	**255**	14.17 S	47.59 W
São Luís Gonzaga	**252**	28.24 S	54.58 W
São Mamede	**250**	6.56 S	37.06 W
São Manuel	**255**	22.44 S	48.34 W
São Manuel ≐	**242**	7.21 S	58.03 W
São Marcos ≐	**255**	18.15 S	47.37 W
São Mateus, Bra.	**255**	18.44 S	39.51 W
São Mateus, Bra.	**256**	22.49 S	43.23 W
São Mateus, Port.	**148a**	38.26 N	28.27 W
São Mateus ≐	**255**	13.48 S	46.54 W
São Mateus, Braço Norte ≐	**255**	18.37 S	40.05 W
São Mateus, Braço Sul ≐	**255**	18.37 S	40.05 W
São Mateus de Minas	**256**	22.42 S	46.03 W
São Mateus do Sul	**252**	25.52 S	50.23 W
São Miguel	**250**	6.13 S	38.30 W
São Miguel I	**148a**	37.47 N	25.30 W
São Miguel ≐	**255**	16.26 S	41.00 W
São Miguel do Anta	**255**	20.42 S	42.43 W
São Miguel do Araguaia	**255**	13.19 S	50.13 W
São Miguel d'Oeste	**252**	26.45 S	53.34 W
São Miguel do Guamá	**250**	1.37 S	47.27 W
São Miguel dos Campos	**250**	9.47 S	36.05 W
São Miguel dos Macacos	**250**	1.11 S	50.28 W
São Miguel do Tapuio	**250**	5.30 S	41.20 W
São Miguel Paulista(Baquiriru) ◆[8]	**256**	23.30 S	46.26 W
Saona, Isla I	**238**	18.09 N	68.40 W
Saonara	**64**	45.22 N	11.59 E
Saône ≐	**58**	45.44 N	4.50 E
Saône-et-Loire □[5]	**32**	46.42 N	4.45 E
Saonek	**164**	0.28 S	130.47 E
Saoner	**120**	21.23 N	78.54 E
São Nicolau I	**150a**	16.35 N	24.15 W
São Nicolau ≐	**250**	5.45 S	42.02 W
São Paulo, Bra.	**256**	23.32 S	46.37 W
São Paulo, Bra.	**287b**	23.32 S	46.37 W
São Paulo □[3]	**255**	22.00 S	49.00 W
São Paulo □[7]	**287b**	23.33 S	46.38 W
São Paulo, Ribeirão de ≐	**256**	22.16 S	46.37 W
São Paulo de Olivença	**246**	3.27 S	68.48 W
São Paulo do Potengi	**250**	5.55 S	35.45 W
São Pedro, Bra.	**255**	19.53 S	51.55 W
São Pedro, Bra.	**256**	22.12 S	46.46 W
São Pedro ≐	**255**	16.30 S	41.17 W
São Pedro de Viseu	**250**	2.33 S	49.33 W
São Pedro do Estoril	**266c**	38.42 N	9.22 W
São Pedro do Ivaí	**255**	23.51 S	51.51 W
São Pedro do Piauí	**250**	5.56 S	42.43 W
São Pedro do Sul, Bra.	**252**	29.37 S	54.10 W
São Pedro do Sul, Port.	**34**	40.45 N	8.04 W
São Rafael	**250**	5.47 S	36.55 W
São Raimundo das Mangabeiras	**250**	7.01 S	45.29 W
São Raimundo de Codó	**250**	4.21 S	43.37 W
São Raimundo Nonato	**250**	9.01 S	42.42 W
Saorge	**62**	43.59 N	7.33 E
Saori	**94**	35.11 N	136.44 E
São Romão	**255**	16.22 S	45.04 W
São Roque	**256**	23.32 S	47.08 W
São Roque, Cabo de ≻	**250**	5.29 S	35.16 W
São Roque da Fartura	**256**	21.51 S	46.45 W
São Roque do Paraguaçu	**255**	12.51 S	38.51 W
São Salvador → Salvador	**255**	12.59 S	38.31 W
São Sebastião	**256**	23.48 S	45.25 W
São Sebastião, Canal de ʯ	**256**	23.48 S	45.23 W
São Sebastião, Ilha de I	**256**	23.50 S	45.18 W
São Sebastião, Pico de ∧	**256**	23.52 S	45.23 W
São Sebastião, Ponta ≻	**156**	22.07 S	35.30 E
São Sebastião da Bela Vista	**256**	22.10 S	45.45 W
São Sebastião da Boa Vista	**250**	1.42 S	49.31 W
São Sebastião da Grama	**256**	21.43 S	46.49 W
São Sebastião da Vitória	**256**	21.14 S	44.25 W
São Sebastião do Barreado	**256**	22.04 S	43.38 W
São Sebastião do Maranhão	**255**	18.05 S	42.35 W
São Sebastião do Paraíso	**255**	20.55 S	47.00 W
São Sebastião do Rio Claro	**255**	15.45 S	51.30 W
São Sebastião do Rio Verde	**256**	22.13 S	44.58 W
São Sebastião dos Peitudos	**256**	22.19 S	46.29 W
São Sebastião dos Robertos	**256**	22.13 S	46.32 W
São Sebastião do Umbuzeiro	**250**	8.09 S	37.01 W
São Sepé	**252**	30.10 S	53.34 W
São Simão, Bra.	**255**	18.56 S	50.30 W
São Simão, Bra.	**255**	21.30 S	47.33 W
São Simão ≐	**248**	12.40 S	63.04 W
São Tiago	**255**	20.55 S	44.30 W
São Timóteo	**255**	13.51 S	42.11 W
São Tomé, Bra.	**250**	5.58 S	36.04 W
São Tomé, S. Tom./P.	**152**	0.20 N	6.44 E
São Tomé I	**152**	0.12 N	6.39 E
São Tomé ≐	**250**	8.10 S	58.13 W
São Tomé, Cabo de ≻	**255**	21.59 S	40.59 W
São Tomé, Pico de ∧	**152**	0.16 N	6.33 E
São Tomé, Ribeirão ≐	**256**	21.26 S	46.02 W
Sao Tome and Principe □[1], Afr.	**138**	1.00 N	7.00 E
Sao Tome and Principe □[1], Afr.	**152**	1.00 N	7.00 E
São Tomé das Letras	**256**	21.43 S	44.59 W
Saou	**62**	44.39 N	5.04 E
Saoura, Oued V	**148**	29.00 N	0.55 W
São Valério ≐	**250**	11.20 S	48.28 W
São Vicente, Bra.	**250**	6.13 S	36.41 W
São Vicente, Bra.	**256**	23.58 S	46.23 W
São Vicente I	**150a**	16.50 N	25.00 W
São Vicente, Cabo de ≻	**34**	37.01 N	9.00 W
São Vicente, Ribeirão ≐	**256**	21.59 S	45.40 W
São Vicente de Minas	**256**	21.42 S	44.27 W
São Vicente Ferrer, Bra.	**250**	2.53 S	44.52 W
São Vicente Ferrer, Bra.	**250**	7.35 S	35.30 W
Sápai	**38**	41.02 N	25.41 E
Sapallanga	**248**	12.09 S	75.11 W
Sapanca	**130**	40.41 N	30.16 E
Sapang Baho ≐	**269f**	14.33 N	121.06 E
Sapao	**116**	10.01 N	126.02 E
Sapão ≐	**250**	11.01 S	45.32 W
Saparua, Pulau I	**164**	3.34 S	128.40 E
Sapatgrām	**124**	26.20 N	90.08 E
Sapé, Bra.	**250**	7.06 S	35.13 W
Sapé, Bra.	**256**	22.16 S	46.34 W
Sape, Indon.	**115b**	8.34 S	118.59 E
Sapé ≐	**287a**	22.52 S	43.02 W
Sape, Selat ʯ	**115b**	8.39 S	119.18 E
Sapeaçu	**255**	12.44 S	39.13 W
Sapele	**150**	5.54 N	5.41 E
Sapello ≐	**200**	35.47 N	104.59 W
Sapelo Island I	**192**	31.28 N	81.15 W
Saperkino	**80**	54.05 N	51.38 E
Şaphane	**130**	39.01 N	29.14 E
Šapian Bay ⊂	**116**	11.33 N	122.37 E
Sapindji	**152**	9.39 S	23.12 E
Şapitwa ∧	**154**	15.57 S	35.36 E
Šapki	**76**	59.36 N	31.14 E
Šapkina ≐	**24**	66.44 N	52.25 E
Šapkino	**80**	51.42 N	42.24 E
Šapkovo, S.S.S.R.	**76**	55.47 N	33.20 E
Sapkovo, S.S.S.R.	**82**	54.34 N	39.10 E
Sapodilla Cays I	**236**	16.08 N	88.15 W
Saponara	**70**	38.11 N	15.26 E
Saponé	**150**	12.03 N	1.36 W
Sap'o-ri	**98**	40.49 N	129.31 E
Sap'ornaja	**265a**	59.46 N	30.41 E
Saporoschje → Zaporožje	**78**	47.50 N	35.10 E
Saposoa	**248**	6.56 S	76.48 W
Sapou	**175c**	7.18 N	151.53 E
Sapožok	**80**	53.56 N	40.41 E
Sappa Creek ≐	**198**	40.07 N	99.38 W
Sappa Creek, Middle Fork ≐	**198**	39.40 N	100.53 W
Sappa Creek, North Fork ≐	**198**	39.47 N	100.35 W
Sappa Creek, South Fork ≐	**198**	39.47 N	100.35 W
Sappada	**64**	46.34 N	12.41 E
Sapphire Mountains ⋏	**202**	46.20 N	113.45 W
Sappho	**224**	48.04 N	124.16 W
Sappington	**219**	38.32 N	90.22 W
Sapporo	**92a**	43.03 N	141.21 E
Şapri	**68**	40.04 N	15.38 E
Šapša	**76**	60.34 N	34.01 E
Sap Songkhla, Thale ⊂	**110**	7.13 N	100.30 E
Šapsugskaja	**78**	44.45 N	38.05 E
Sapta-ri	**271b**	37.43 N	126.44 E
Sapt Kosi ≐	**124**	26.31 N	86.58 E
Sapu	**152**	12.29 S	19.26 E
Sapucaí	**256**	22.19 S	46.42 W
Sapucaí ≐	**256**	21.33 S	45.40 W
Sapucaia	**256**	22.00 S	42.54 W
Sapucaí-Mirim	**256**	22.44 S	45.45 W
Sapucaí-Mirim ≐	**256**	22.12 S	45.53 W
Sapudi, Pulau I	**115a**	7.06 S	114.20 E
Sapulpa	**196**	35.59 N	96.06 W
Sapulu	**115a**	6.54 S	112.57 E
Sapuran	**115a**	7.28 S	109.58 E
Sapwe	**154**	10.57 S	28.10 E
Sāq, Jabal ∧[2]	**128**	26.17 N	43.16 E
Sāqiat al-ʿAbd	**140**	20.48 N	30.19 E
Sāqiyat Makkī	**142**	30.00 N	31.13 E
Şaqqārah	**142**	29.51 N	31.13 E
Şaqqārah (Step Pyramid) ⊥	**142**	29.52 N	31.13 E
Saqqez	**128**	36.14 N	46.16 E
Saquarema	**256**	22.56 S	42.30 W
Saquarema, Lagoa de ⊂	**256**	22.55 S	42.33 W
Saquena	**248**	4.40 S	73.31 W
Saquish Neck ≻[1]	**283**	42.00 N	70.37 W
Saquisilí	**246**	0.51 S	78.40 W
Sāra, Bngl.	**126**	24.07 N	89.02 E
Sara, Burkina	**150**	11.43 N	3.50 W
Sara, Pil.	**116**	11.16 N	123.01 E
Sara, S.S.S.R.	**80**	54.38 N	46.46 E
Sarāb	**128**	37.56 N	47.32 E
Sarabia	**234**	20.31 N	101.05 W
Sarabia ≐	**234**	17.11 N	94.56 W
Sarābiyūm	**142**	30.23 N	32.17 E
Sara Buri	**110**	14.32 N	100.55 E
Saracena	**68**	39.46 N	16.09 E
Saraceno, Monte ∧	**66**	41.27 N	14.44 E
Saracura ≐	**255**	12.18 S	40.07 W
Saracuruna ≐	**287a**	22.41 S	43.13 W
Saraféré	**150**	15.50 N	3.42 W
Saragosa	**196**	31.01 N	103.39 W
Saragossa → Zaragoza	**34**	41.38 N	0.53 W
Saraguay ◆[8]	**275a**	45.31 N	73.45 W
Saraguro	**246**	3.36 S	79.13 W
Sarai	**80**	53.44 N	41.00 E
Saraikela	**124**	22.43 N	85.57 E
Sarāi Naurang	**123**	32.50 N	70.47 E
Saraipali	**120**	21.20 N	83.00 E
Säräisniemi	**26**	64.27 N	26.47 E
Sarajas de Madrid ◆[8]	**266a**	40.28 N	3.35 W
Sarajčik	**80**	47.30 N	51.43 E
Sarajevo	**38**	43.52 N	18.25 E
Saraj-Gir	**80**	53.36 N	53.24 E
Saraji	**166**	22.21 S	148.18 E
Sarajskij	**80**	47.19 N	40.45 E
Sarakhs	**128**	36.32 N	61.11 E
Saraktaš	**86**	51.50 N	56.22 E
Sarala	**86**	54.52 N	89.14 E
Şaraland	**194**	30.49 N	88.04 W
Šaraldaj	**88**	51.01 N	107.38 E
Saralžinskaja	**80**	49.12 N	48.55 E
Saramacca □[5]	**250**	4.45 N	56.00 W
Saramacca ≐	**250**	5.51 N	55.53 W
Saramaguacán ≐	**240p**	21.30 N	77.17 W
Şaran, Fr.	**50**	47.57 N	1.53 E
Šaran, S.S.S.R.	**80**	54.49 N	54.00 E
Saran', S.S.S.R.	**86**	49.46 N	72.52 E
Saran □[5]	**124**	26.00 N	84.30 E
Saran, Gunung ∧	**112**	0.25 S	111.18 E
Saranac	**216**	42.55 N	85.12 W
Saranac ≐	**188**	44.42 N	73.27 W
Saranac Lake	**188**	44.19 N	74.07 W
Saranakan, gora ∧	**88**	52.35 N	113.50 E
Şaranap	**226**	37.53 N	122.06 W
Šaranbaš-Kn'azevo	**80**	54.58 N	54.09 E
Saranda	**154**	5.43 S	34.59 E
Sarandapótamos ≐	**267c**	38.26 N	23.54 E
Sarandë	**38**	39.52 N	20.00 E
Sarandi	**252**	27.56 S	52.55 W
Sarandí ◆[8]	**258**	34.40 S	58.21 W
Sarandí del Yi	**252**	33.21 S	55.38 W
Sarandí Grande	**258**	33.44 S	56.20 W
Şarandira	**256**	21.50 S	43.11 W
Šaranga	**80**	57.11 N	46.34 E
Sarangani Bay ⊂	**116**	5.57 N	125.11 E
Sarangani Island I	**116**	5.27 N	125.28 E
Sarangani Islands II	**116**	5.25 N	125.26 E
Sarangani Strait ʯ	**116**	5.31 N	125.23 E
Sārangarh	**120**	21.36 N	83.05 E
Sārangpur	**124**	23.34 N	76.28 E
Sārankhola	**126**	22.18 N	89.47 E
Saranley	**144**	2.22 N	42.17 E
Saranpaul'	**24**	64.14 N	60.53 E
Saransk	**80**	54.11 N	45.11 E
Sarantina, Valle V	**64**	46.35 N	11.25 E
Sara Peak ∧	**150**	9.41 N	9.17 E
Saraphi	**110**	18.43 N	99.03 E
Sarapiquí ≐	**236**	10.43 N	83.56 W
Şarapó ≐	**287a**	22.46 S	43.37 W
Šarapovo, S.S.S.R.	**80**	55.17 N	44.42 E
Šarapovo, S.S.S.R.	**82**	55.11 N	37.16 E
Sarapuí ≐	**287a**	22.46 S	43.24 W
Sarapuí, Canal ≍	**287a**	22.44 S	43.16 W
Sarapul	**80**	56.28 N	53.48 E
Sarapul'skaja vozvyšennost' ⋏[1]	**80**	56.15 N	53.30 E
Sarapul'skoje	**89**	48.52 N	135.59 E
Sarāqib	**130**	35.52 N	36.48 E
Sarare	**246**	9.47 N	69.10 W
Sarar Plain ≚	**144**	9.25 N	46.17 E
Sará-Sará	**256**	23.40 S	47.05 W
Sara Sara, Nevado ∧	**248**	15.19 S	73.27 W
Sarasota	**220**	27.20 N	82.31 W
Sarasota □[6]	**220**	27.10 N	82.21 W
Sarasota Bay ⊂	**220**	27.23 N	82.39 W
Sarasota-Bradenton Airport ⊠	**220**	27.24 N	82.33 W
Sarasota Springs	**220**	27.17 N	82.28 W
Saraswati ≐	**272b**	22.59 N	88.22 E
Sarata	**78**	46.02 N	29.38 E
Sarath	**126**	24.14 N	86.50 E
Saratoga, Austl.	**170**	33.28 S	151.21 E
Saratoga, Ca., U.S.	**226**	37.15 N	122.01 W
Saratoga, In., U.S.	**216**	40.14 N	84.55 W
Saratoga, Tx., U.S.	**222**	30.17 N	94.31 W
Saratoga, Wy., U.S.	**200**	41.27 N	106.48 W
Saratoga □[6]	**210**	43.00 N	73.51 W
Saratoga Battlefield Monument ⊥	**210**	43.05 N	75.36 W
Saratoga Creek ≐	**282**	37.25 N	121.58 W
Saratoga Lake ⊜	**210**	43.01 N	73.39 W
Saratoga National Historical Park ♠	**210**	43.00 N	73.38 W
Saratoga Passage ʯ	**224**	48.10 N	122.30 W
Saratoga Spa State Park ♠	**210**	43.03 N	73.50 W
Şaratoga Springs	**210**	43.04 N	73.47 W
Šara-Togot	**88**	53.01 N	106.43 E
Saratok	**112**	1.44 N	111.20 E
Saratov	**80**	51.34 N	46.02 E
Saratov □[4]	**76**	52.00 N	42.40 E
Saratovka	**86**	51.12 N	54.54 E
Saratovskoje vodochranilišče ⊜[1]	**80**	52.45 N	48.30 E
Saraurcu ∧	**246**	0.06 S	77.55 W
Sarāvān, Īrān	**128**	27.15 N	62.40 E
Saravan, Lao	**110**	15.43 N	106.25 E
Sarawak □[3]	**112**	2.30 N	113.30 E
Saray	**130**	41.26 N	27.55 E
Saraya, Guinée	**150**	10.46 N	10.24 W
Saraya, Sén.	**150**	12.50 N	11.45 W
Sarayakpınar	**130**	41.46 N	26.29 E
Sarāyān	**128**	33.51 N	58.31 E
Saraycık	**130**	40.57 N	35.08 E
Sarayevo → Sarajevo	**38**	43.52 N	18.25 E
Sarayköy	**130**	37.55 N	28.58 E
Sarayönü	**130**	38.17 N	32.25 E
Sarbaj	**80**	53.39 N	51.34 E
Sarbāz	**128**	26.39 N	61.15 E
Sarbinowo	**54**	52.40 N	14.40 E
Sárbogárd	**30**	46.53 N	18.38 E
Sarca ≐	**64**	45.52 N	10.52 E
Sarce ≐	**50**	48.09 N	4.18 E
Sarcee Indian Reserve ◆[4]	**182**	50.58 N	114.06 W
Sarcelle, Passe de la ʯ	**175f**	22.29 S	167.12 E
Sarcelles	**50**	49.00 N	2.23 E
Sarche di Calavino	**64**	46.03 N	10.57 E
Sarcidano ◆[1], It.	**36**	39.55 N	9.05 E
Şarcidano ◆[1], It.	**71**	39.49 N	9.10 E
Šarčino	**86**	53.09 N	81.45 E
Sarclet	**46**	58.22 N	3.07 W
Sarcoxie	**194**	37.04 N	94.06 W
Sārda (Kāli) ≐	**124**	27.22 N	81.23 E
Sard āb)(	**123**	36.40 N	71.32 E
Sārda Canal ≍	**124**	28.59 N	80.07 E
Sardagna	**64**	46.03 N	11.06 E
Sardah	**124**	24.18 N	88.44 E
Sardanyola	**266d**	41.30 N	2.09 E
Sardaq	**128**	34.48 N	58.07 E
Sardara	**71**	39.37 N	8.49 E
Sardār Chāh	**128**	27.58 N	64.50 E
Sardārpur	**120**	22.39 N	74.59 E
Sardārshahr	**120**	28.26 N	74.29 E
Sar Dasht, Īrān	**128**	36.09 N	45.28 E
Sar Dasht, Īrān	**128**	32.32 N	48.52 E
Sardegna □[4]	**71**	40.00 N	9.00 E
Sardegna (Sardinia) I	**71**	40.00 N	9.00 E
Sardhana	**124**	29.09 N	77.37 E
Sardiha	**126**	22.22 N	87.09 E
Sardina	**246**	2.02 N	67.07 W
Sardinal	**236**	10.31 N	85.39 W
Sardinata	**246**	8.05 N	72.48 W
Sardinia, N.Y., U.S.	**210**	42.32 N	78.31 W
Sardinia, Oh., U.S.	**218**	39.00 N	83.48 W
Sardinia → Sardegna I	**71**	40.00 N	9.00 E
Sardinien → Sardegna I	**71**	40.00 N	9.00 E
Sardis, B.C., Can.	**224**	49.08 N	121.57 W
Sardis, Al., U.S.	**194**	32.17 N	86.59 W
Sardis, Ga., U.S.	**192**	32.58 N	81.45 W
Sardis, Ky., U.S.	**218**	38.31 N	83.57 W
Sardis, Ms., U.S.	**194**	34.26 N	89.55 W
Sardis, Pa., U.S.	**279b**	40.29 N	79.42 W
Sardis, Tn., U.S.	**194**	35.27 N	88.18 W
Sardis Lake ⊜[1]	**194**	34.27 N	89.43 W
Şardona, Piz ∧	**58**	46.55 N	9.15 E
Šardonem'	**24**	63.56 N	44.37 E
Sareks Nationalpark ♠	**24**	67.15 N	17.30 E
Sarektjåkkå ∧	**24**	67.25 N	17.46 E
Sārenga, India	**126**	22.46 N	87.02 E
Sārenga, India	**272b**	22.31 N	88.13 E
Sarentino (Sarnthein)	**64**	46.38 N	11.21 E
Sar-e Pol	**120**	36.14 N	65.55 E
Sar-e Pol-e Žahāb	**128**	34.28 N	45.52 E
Sarepta	**194**	32.53 N	93.26 W
Sarezzo	**64**	45.39 N	10.12 E
Sargans	**58**	47.03 N	9.26 E
Sargatskoje	**86**	55.37 N	73.30 E
Sargé-lès-le-Mans	**50**	48.02 N	0.14 E
Sargent, Ga., U.S.	**192**	33.25 N	84.52 W
Sargent, Ne., U.S.	**198**	41.38 N	99.22 W
Sargent Creek ≐	**226**	35.57 N	120.52 W
Şargodha	**123**	32.05 N	72.40 E
Šargol'džin	**88**	52.21 N	114.42 E
Sargorod	**78**	48.44 N	28.05 E
Sargou ≐	**85**	43.25 N	73.50 E
Şargul', ozero ⊜	**86**	54.35 N	78.51 E
Šargun	**85**	38.37 N	67.53 E
Sarh	**146**	9.09 N	18.23 E
Sarhli, Djebel ∧	**34**	36.06 N	0.40 E
Sārī	**128**	36.34 N	53.04 E
Saría I	**38**	35.50 N	27.15 E
Saribi, Tanjung ≻	**164**	1.36 S	135.25 E
Sarıbuğday	**130**	40.35 N	35.35 E
Sáric	**232**	31.08 N	111.23 W
Saricumbe	**152**	12.12 S	19.46 E
Sarigan I	**108**	16.42 N	145.47 E
Sarıgazi	**267b**	41.01 N	29.12 E
Sarıgöl	**130**	38.14 N	28.43 E
Sarıkamış	**130**	40.20 N	42.35 E
Sarıkaya	**130**	38.47 N	32.15 E
Sarikei	**112**	2.07 N	111.31 E
Sarıköy	**130**	40.12 N	27.36 E
Sarilhos Grandes	**266c**	38.41 N	8.58 W
Sarilhos Pequenos	**266c**	38.41 N	8.59 W
Sarim	**154**	0.23 S	40.58 E
Şārim, Kabd aş- ◆[1]	**130**	34.34 N	39.33 E
Sarimbun, Pulau I	**271c**	1.26 N	103.41 E
Sarina	**166**	21.26 S	149.13 E
Sarine ≐	**58**	46.54 N	7.14 E
Sariñena	**34**	41.48 N	0.10 W
Sarıoğlan, Tür.	**130**	39.05 N	35.59 E
Sarıoğlan, Tür.	**130**	37.12 N	32.33 E
Saripul'	**85**	38.26 N	70.08 E
Sarīr	**146**	27.36 N	22.32 E
Sarısu	**84**	39.01 N	42.55 E
Sarita	**196**	27.13 N	97.47 W
Sariwŏn	**98**	38.31 N	125.44 E
Sarıyar Gölü ⊜[1]	**130**	40.02 N	31.40 E
Şarıyer	**130**	41.10 N	29.03 E
Šarja	**80**	58.24 N	45.30 E
Sarju (Babai) ≐	**124**	27.42 N	81.16 E
Sark I	**43b**	49.26 N	2.21 W
Sark ≐	**44**	54.58 N	3.04 W
Şarkad	**30**	46.44 N	21.23 E
Šarkan	**80**	57.18 N	53.53 E
Şarkand	**86**	45.26 N	79.54 E
Şarkîkaraağaç	**130**	38.04 N	31.23 E
Şarkışla	**130**	39.21 N	36.26 E
Šarkovščina	**76**	55.22 N	27.28 E
Şarköy	**130**	40.37 N	27.06 E
Şarlat-la-Canéda	**32**	44.53 N	1.13 E
Šarlauk	**128**	38.13 N	55.38 E
Şarles	**198**	48.56 N	98.59 W
Šarlyk	**86**	52.55 N	54.35 E
Sarmakovo	**84**	43.43 N	43.12 E
Sarmanovo	**80**	55.15 N	52.36 E
Sărmaşu	**38**	46.46 N	24.11 E
Sarmatskaja ≐	**83**	47.20 N	38.48 E
Sármellék	**30**	46.44 N	17.10 E
Sarmi	**164**	1.51 S	138.44 E
Sarmiento	**254**	45.36 S	69.05 W
Sarmiento ≐	**288**	34.25 S	58.35 W
Sarmiento, Cerro ∧	**254**	54.27 S	70.50 W
Sarmiento, Lago ⊜	**254**	51.04 S	72.45 W
Särna	**26**	61.41 N	13.08 E
Sarna, ozero ⊜	**80**	48.24 N	44.38 E
Sarnano	**66**	43.02 N	13.18 E
Sārnāth ⊥	**124**	25.24 N	83.01 E
Sarnen	**58**	46.54 N	8.15 E
Sârnena ⋏	**38**	42.35 N	25.10 E
Sarner See ⊜	**58**	46.52 N	8.13 E
Sarnia	**214**	42.58 N	82.23 W
Sarnico	**64**	45.40 N	9.57 E
Sarno	**68**	40.49 N	14.37 E
Sarnow	**54**	53.45 N	13.37 E
Sarnowa	**30**	51.38 N	16.54 E
Sarnthein → Sarentino	**64**	46.38 N	11.21 E
Šarnutovskij	**80**	47.40 N	43.46 E
Sarny	**78**	51.21 N	26.36 E
Şaroako	**112**	2.31 S	121.22 E
Šaroargun ≐	**84**	43.02 N	45.44 E
Sarolangun	**112**	2.18 S	102.42 E
Saroma-ko ⊜	**92a**	44.08 N	143.50 E
Saron	**158**	33.11 S	19.01 E
Saronikós Kólpos ⊂	**38**	37.54 N	23.12 E
Saronno	**62**	45.38 N	9.02 E
Saros Körfezi ⊂	**130**	40.30 N	26.20 E
Şárospatak	**30**	48.19 N	21.34 E
Šarovka	**78**	50.01 N	35.27 E
Sarpa	**80**	47.07 N	45.29 E
Şarpa, ozero ⊜	**80**	47.18 N	45.20 E
Šarpajevka	**78**	48.34 N	40.59 E
Sar Passage ʯ	**175b**	7.12 N	134.23 E
Şarpinskije ozera ⊜	**80**	47.30 N	45.00 E
Šar Planina ⋏	**38**	42.05 N	20.50 E
Sarpsborg	**26**	59.17 N	11.07 E
Sarpy Creek ≐	**202**	46.15 N	107.09 W
Sárrabus ◆[1]	**71**	39.23 N	9.21 E
Sarralbe	**56**	49.00 N	7.01 E
Sarras	**62**	45.11 N	4.48 E
Sarrath, Oued V	**36**	35.59 N	8.23 E
Sarratt	**260**	51.41 N	0.29 W
Sarre	**62**	45.43 N	7.15 E
Sarre (Saar) ≐	**56**	49.42 N	6.34 E
Sarre Blanche ≐	**56**	48.41 N	7.01 E
Sarrebourg	**58**	48.44 N	7.03 E
Sarrebruck → Saarbrücken	**56**	49.14 N	6.59 E
Sarreguemines	**56**	49.06 N	7.03 E
Sarre Rouge ≐	**56**	48.41 N	7.01 E
Sarre-Union	**56**	48.56 N	7.05 E
Sarria	**34**	42.47 N	7.24 W
Sarriá ◆[8]	**266d**	41.24 N	2.08 E
Sarro	**150**	13.43 N	5.15 W
Sarroch	**71**	39.04 N	9.00 E
Sars	**86**	56.33 N	57.07 E
Sarsfield	**212**	45.27 N	75.21 W
Sarsina	**66**	43.55 N	12.08 E
Sarsol	**272c**	19.02 N	73.01 E
Sarstedt	**52**	52.14 N	9.51 E
Sarstein ∧	**64**	47.36 N	13.41 E
Sarstoon ≐	**236**	15.53 N	88.55 W
Sarsuna	**272b**	22.28 N	88.18 E
Sart	**56**	50.31 N	5.56 E
Sartang ≐	**74**	67.44 N	133.12 E
Sarteano	**66**	42.59 N	11.52 E
Sartell	**190**	45.37 N	94.12 W
Sartène	**36**	41.36 N	8.59 E
Sarthe □[5]	**32**	48.00 N	0.05 E
Sarthe ≐	**32**	47.30 N	0.32 W
Sartičala	**84**	41.43 N	45.10 E
Sartilly	**32**	48.45 N	1.27 W
Sartirana Lomellina	**62**	45.07 N	8.39 E
Sartlan, ozero ⊜	**86**	55.00 N	78.35 E
Sartol'gen	**80**	48.57 N	47.03 E
Sartrouville	**261**	48.57 N	2.10 E
Saru	**85**	42.20 N	77.55 E
Sarufutsu	**92a**	45.16 N	142.12 E
Saruhanlı	**130**	38.44 N	27.34 E
Şarūr	**128**	23.22 N	58.07 E
Šar Us ≐	**88**	47.08 N	97.38 E
Saru-shima I	**268**	35.17 N	139.42 E
Sarvadyk	**80**	46.07 N	44.07 E
Sárvár	**30**	47.15 N	16.57 E
Sarver	**214**	40.44 N	79.45 W
Sarvestān	**128**	29.16 N	53.13 E
Sárvíz ≐	**30**	46.24 N	18.41 E
Saryagač	**85**	41.27 N	69.10 E
Saryassija	**85**	38.25 N	67.57 E
Sarybarak	**85**	43.24 N	71.30 E
Sarybasat	**86**	46.38 N	60.27 E
Sarybulak, S.S.S.R.	**85**	40.54 N	73.49 E
Sarybulak, S.S.S.R.	**86**	49.27 N	76.27 E
Saryč, mys ≻	**78**	44.23 N	33.45 E
Sarychosor	**85**	38.32 N	69.49 E
Sarydala	**85**	41.11 N	70.27 E
Saryg-Sep	**88**	51.30 N	95.36 E
Sary-Išikotrau ◆[2]	**86**	45.30 N	76.00 E
Sarykoby	**85**	43.44 N	72.35 E
Sarykol'skij chrebet ⋏	**120**	38.00 N	74.30 E
Sarykomej	**86**	45.12 N	74.11 E
Sarykopa, ozero ⊜	**86**	50.22 N	64.08 E
Sarymogol	**85**	39.55 N	72.47 E
Sarymoin, ozero ⊜	**86**	51.36 N	64.30 E
Şaryozek	**86**	44.22 N	77.59 E
Šarypovo	**86**	55.33 N	89.12 E
Saryšagan	**86**	46.07 N	73.38 E
Sarysu	**86**	48.23 N	69.59 E
Sarysu ≐	**86**	45.12 N	66.36 E
Sary-Taš	**85**	39.44 N	73.15 E
Sarytau	**86**	49.54 N	76.41 E
Saryžaz	**72**	42.55 N	79.38 E
Sarzana	**64**	44.07 N	9.58 E
Sarzanello, Fortezza di ⊥	**64**	44.08 N	9.58 E
Sarzeau	**32**	47.32 N	2.46 W
S'as' ≐	**76**	60.09 N	32.30 E
Saʿsaʿ, Sūrīy.	**132**	33.17 N	36.02 E
Sasa, Yis.	**132**	33.02 N	35.24 E
Sasabe	**200**	31.27 N	111.31 W
Sasabe ≐	**200**	30.41 N	111.56 W
Sasabeneh	**144**	7.55 N	43.39 E
Sasaga-mine ∧	**96**	33.49 N	133.17 E
Sasaginnigak Lake ⊜	**184**	51.36 N	95.40 W
Sasago-tunnel ◆[5]	**94**	35.38 N	138.47 E
Sasaguri	**96**	33.37 N	130.32 E
Sasak	**110**	0.01 S	99.42 E
Sasakwa	**196**	34.56 N	96.31 W
Sasamungga	**175e**	7.02 S	156.47 E
Sasao	**270**	34.57 N	135.20 E
Sasar, Tanjung ≻	**115b**	9.17 S	119.56 E
Sasarām	**124**	24.57 N	84.02 E
Sasayama	**96**	35.04 N	135.13 E
Sasa-yama ∧	**96**	33.03 N	132.40 E
Sasbach	**58**	48.08 N	7.37 E
Sasco Brook ≐	**276**	41.07 N	73.18 W
Sásd	**30**	46.15 N	18.06 E
Sasebo	**92**	33.10 N	129.43 E
Sasebo Naval Base ■	**92**	33.09 N	129.45 E
Saseenos	**224**	48.24 N	123.40 W
Saseginaga, Lac ⊜	**190**	47.06 N	78.35 W
Sashalom ◆[8]	**264c**	47.31 N	19.11 E
Sas-hegy ∧[2]	**264c**	47.23 N	19.18 E
Sashiki	**174m**	26.10 N	127.47 E
Sashima	**94**	36.08 N	139.51 E
Saskatchewan □[4], Can.	**176**	54.00 N	105.00 W
Saskatchewan □[4], Can.	**184**	54.00 N	105.00 W
Saskatchewan ≐	**184**	53.12 N	99.16 W
Saskatoon	**184**	52.07 N	106.38 W
Saskylach	**74**	71.55 N	114.01 E
Saslaya, Cerro ∧	**238**	13.45 N	85.03 W
Sasmik, Cape ≻	**180**	51.36 N	177.55 W
Sāsni	**124**	27.43 N	78.05 E
Sasolburg	**158**	26.48 S	27.45 E
Sason Dağları ⋏	**130**	38.15 N	41.32 E
Sasovo	**80**	54.21 N	41.54 E
Saspamco	**196**	29.14 N	98.18 W
Saspul Gompa	**123**	34.15 N	77.09 E
Sassafras, Austl.	**274b**	37.52 S	145.21 E
Sassafras, Ky., U.S.	**192**	37.14 N	83.06 W
Sassafras ≐	**208**	39.23 N	76.02 W
Sassafras Mountain ∧	**192**	35.03 N	82.48 W
Sassafras Neck ≻[1]	**208**	39.25 N	75.55 W
Sassandra	**150**	4.58 N	6.05 W
Sassandra □[5]	**150**	5.00 N	6.40 W
Sassandra ≐	**150**	4.58 N	6.05 W
Sassano	**68**	40.20 N	15.33 E
Sassari	**71**	40.44 N	8.33 E
Sassari □[4]	**71**	40.40 N	9.00 E
Sassbach ≐	**61**	46.43 N	15.48 E
Sasse ≐	**62**	44.15 N	5.55 E
Sassello	**62**	44.29 N	8.30 E
Sassenage	**62**	45.12 N	5.40 E
Sassenberg	**52**	51.59 N	8.02 E
Sassenheim	**52**	52.13 N	4.31 E
Sassnitz	**54**	54.31 N	13.38 E
Sassocorvaro	**66**	43.47 N	12.30 E
Sasso di Castalda	**68**	40.30 N	15.40 E
Sassoferrato	**66**	43.26 N	12.51 E
Sasso Marconi	**64**	44.24 N	11.15 E
S'as'stroj	**76**	60.08 N	32.34 E
Sassuolo	**64**	44.33 N	10.47 E
Sastobe	**85**	42.34 N	70.00 E
Sastown	**150**	4.40 N	8.26 W
Sastre	**252**	31.45 S	61.50 W
Sas van Gent	**52**	51.14 N	3.47 E
Sasyk, ozero ⊜	**78**	45.12 N	33.31 E
Sasykkol', ozero ⊜	**86**	46.35 N	81.00 E
Şasykoli	**80**	47.33 N	47.00 E
Šat ≐	**82**	54.08 N	37.47 E
Satadougou	**150**	12.21 N	10.07 W
Satah Mountain ∧	**182**	52.29 N	124.41 W
Şatakunta ◆[1]	**26**	61.30 N	23.00 E
Šatalovka	**78**	51.09 N	38.16 E
Šatalovo	**76**	54.20 N	32.27 E
Sata-misaki ≻	**92**	30.59 N	130.40 E
Satāna	**122**	20.35 N	74.12 E
Satanov	**78**	49.15 N	26.16 E
Satanta	**198**	37.26 N	100.59 W
Sátão	**34**	40.44 N	7.44 W
Sātāra	**122**	17.41 N	73.59 E
Satarar Uskamp	**156**	24.29 S	31.47 E
Sataua	**175a**	13.28 S	172.40 W
Sātbāria, Bngl.	**126**	23.52 N	89.26 E
Sātbāria, India	**272b**	22.25 N	88.33 E
Satellite Beach	**220**	28.10 N	80.35 W
Satellite Channel ʯ	**224**	48.43 N	123.30 W
Satema	**152**	4.18 N	21.42 E
Satengar, Pulau I	**112**	7.31 S	117.17 E
Säter	**40**	60.21 N	15.45 E
Sātgāchia	**126**	23.16 N	88.08 E
Sātghara	**272b**	22.44 N	88.21 E
Saticoy	**228**	34.17 N	119.09 W
Satilla ≐	**192**	30.59 N	81.28 W
Satilpa Creek ≐	**194**	31.39 N	88.05 W
Satin	**222**	31.21 N	97.02 W
Satipo	**248**	11.16 S	74.37 W
Satırlar	**130**	37.30 N	29.46 E
Sátiro Dias	**250**	11.36 S	38.36 W
Satis	**80**	55.02 N	43.48 E
Satīt (Tekeze) ≐	**140**	14.20 N	35.50 E
Satka	**86**	55.03 N	59.01 E
Satkānia	**120**	22.04 N	92.03 E
Şātkhira	**124**	22.43 N	89.06 E
Šatki	**80**	55.11 N	44.08 E
Satla Bīl ≋	**126**	22.54 N	90.04 E
Satluj → Sutlej ≐	**120**	29.23 N	71.02 E
Satna	**124**	24.35 N	80.50 E
Satna □[5]	**124**	24.30 N	80.50 E
Sato, Cañada de ≐	**288**	34.35 S	58.38 W
Satomi	**94**	36.43 N	140.30 E
Şátoraljaújhely	**30**	48.24 N	21.39 E
Šatov	**61**	48.48 N	16.01 E
Šatovo	**82**	54.56 N	37.14 E
Satow	**54**	53.59 N	11.51 E
Sātpura Range ⋏	**122**	22.00 N	78.00 E
Sätrabrunn	**40**	59.51 N	16.27 E
Şatriano di Lucania	**68**	40.33 N	15.33 E
Šatrovo	**86**	56.31 N	64.38 E
Satrup	**41**	54.41 N	9.35 E
Satsop ≐	**224**	47.03 N	123.30 W
Satsop, Middle Fork ≐	**224**	47.05 N	123.30 W
Satsop, West Fork ≐	**224**	47.02 N	123.32 W
Satsuma	**194**	30.51 N	88.03 W
Satsuma-hantō ≻[1]	**92**	31.25 N	130.25 E
Satsunan-shotō II	**93b**	29.00 N	130.00 E
Sattahip	**110**	12.40 N	100.54 E
Sattānkulam	**122**	8.27 N	77.56 E
Satte	**94**	36.04 N	139.43 E
Sattel	**58**	47.05 N	8.42 E
Sattenapalle	**122**	16.24 N	80.11 E
Satthwa	**110**	17.46 N	94.30 E
Sattledt	**61**	48.04 N	14.03 E
Satui	**112**	3.47 S	115.27 E
Sātuli	**272b**	22.33 N	88.34 E
Satu Mare	**38**	47.48 N	22.53 E
Satu Mare □[6]	**38**	47.40 N	23.00 E
Şatun	**110**	6.37 N	100.04 E
Šatura	**80**	55.34 N	39.32 E
Saturna	**224**	48.43 N	123.11 W
Saturna Island I	**224**	48.47 N	123.08 W
Şaturnino M. Laspiur	**252**	31.42 S	62.29 W
Šaturtorf	**76**	55.34 N	39.26 E
Satus Creek ≐	**202**	46.16 N	120.07 W
Satus Peak ∧	**224**	46.15 N	120.45 W
Satyamangalam	**122**	11.31 N	77.15 E
Satzkorn	**264a**	52.29 N	12.59 E
Sau ≐	**269c**	10.46 N	106.48 E
Sauble ≐	**212**	44.40 N	81.17 W
Sauce, Arg.	**252**	30.05 S	58.46 W
Sauce, Perú	**248**	6.44 S	76.10 W
Sauce, Ur.	**258**	34.39 S	56.04 W
Sauce, Arroyo del ≐, Arg.	**288**	34.41 S	58.50 W
Sauce, Arroyo del ≐, Ur.	**258**	34.26 S	57.28 W
Sauce Chico ≐	**252**	38.47 S	62.18 W
Sauce Corto, Arroyo ≐	**252**	36.55 S	61.48 W
Sauce Grande ≐	**252**	38.59 S	61.07 W
Saucier	**194**	30.38 N	89.08 W
Saucillo	**232**	28.01 N	105.17 W
Sauda	**26**	59.39 N	6.20 E
Saudade	**256**	21.56 S	43.03 W
Sauđárkrókur	**24a**	65.46 N	19.41 W
Saúde	**250**	10.56 S	40.24 W
Saúde ◆[8]	**287b**	23.37 S	46.37 W
Saudi Arabia (Al-ʿArabīyah as-Saʿūdīyah) □[1]	**118**	25.00 N	45.00 E

Name	Seite	Breite°′	Länge°′ E = Ost
Saudi-Arabien → Saudi Arabia □[1]	**118**	25.00 N	45.00 E
Saudron	**58**	48.30 N	5.20 E
Sauer (Sûre) ≐, Europe	**56**	49.44 N	6.31 E
Sauer ≐, Europe	**56**	48.55 N	8.10 E
Sauerkohl-Berge ⋏[2]	**264a**	52.20 N	13.45 E
Sauerlach	**64**	47.58 N	11.38 E
Sauerland ◆[1]	**52**	51.10 N	8.00 E
Sauêruiná ≐	**248**	12.00 S	58.43 W
Sauêuiná ≐	**248**	12.24 S	58.40 W
Saug ≐	**116**	7.27 N	125.44 E
Saugatuck, Ct., U.S.	**276**	41.08 N	73.23 W
Saugatuck, Mi., U.S.	**216**	42.39 N	86.12 W
Saugatuck ≐	**276**	41.07 N	73.22 W
Saugatuck Reservoir ⊜[1]	**207**	41.16 N	73.22 W
Saugeen ≐	**190**	44.30 N	81.22 W
Saugeen Indian Reserve ◆[4]	**212**	44.33 N	81.18 W
Saugerties	**210**	42.04 N	73.57 W
Saughall	**262**	53.13 N	2.58 W
Saugor → Sāgar	**124**	23.50 N	78.43 E
Saugor □[5]	**124**	24.00 N	78.50 E
Saugstad, Mount ∧	**182**	52.15 N	126.31 W
Saugus, Ca., U.S.	**228**	34.24 N	118.32 W
Saugus, Ma., U.S.	**207**	42.27 N	71.00 W
Saugus ≐	**283**	42.28 N	70.58 W
Saugus Iron Works National Historical Site ⊥	**283**	42.28 N	71.01 W
Sauh, Tanjong ≻	**114**	3.46 N	100.49 E
Saujil	**252**	28.11 S	66.14 W
Saujon	**32**	45.40 N	0.56 W
Sauk ≐, Mn., U.S.	**198**	45.36 N	94.10 W
Sauk ≐, Wa., U.S.	**224**	48.30 N	121.37 W
Sauk Centre	**198**	45.44 N	94.57 W
Sauk City	**190**	43.16 N	89.43 W
Sauk Rapids	**190**	45.35 N	94.09 W
Sauksaj ≐	**85**	39.11 N	72.15 E
Sauk Village	**216**	41.29 N	87.34 W
Saukville	**190**	43.22 N	87.56 W
Saül	**250**	3.37 N	53.12 W
Şaulape ⋏	**61**	46.55 N	14.40 E
Šaul'der	**85**	42.47 N	68.24 E
Sauldre ≐	**50**	47.16 N	1.30 E
Sauldre, Canal de la ≍	**50**	47.36 N	2.06 E
Saulgau	**58**	48.01 N	9.30 E
Saulgrub	**64**	47.40 N	11.01 E
Saulheim	**56**	49.51 N	8.09 E
Saulieu	**50**	47.16 N	4.14 E
Saulkrasti	**76**	57.17 N	24.25 E
Saulnot	**58**	47.34 N	6.38 E
Sault-au-Mouton	**186**	48.33 N	69.15 W
Sault au Récollet ◆[8]	**275a**	45.34 N	73.39 W
Sault aux Cochons, Rivière du ≐	**186**	48.44 N	69.04 W
Sault-de-Vaucluse	**62**	44.05 N	5.25 E
Saulteaux ≐	**182**	55.16 N	114.25 W
Saulteaux Indian Reserve ◆[4]	**184**	53.08 N	108.18 W
Sault-lès-Rethel	**50**	49.30 N	4.22 E
Sault Sainte Marie, On., Can.	**190**	46.31 N	84.20 W
Sault Sainte Marie, Mi., U.S.	**190**	46.29 N	84.20 W
Saulx ≐, Fr.	**56**	48.45 N	4.35 E
Saulx ≐, Fr.	**261**	48.41 N	2.19 E
Saulx-de-Vesoul	**58**	47.42 N	6.17 E
Saulx-les-Chartreux	**261**	48.42 N	2.16 E
Saulxures-sur-Moselotte	**58**	47.57 N	6.46 E
Şaum'ani	**84**	41.21 N	44.46 E
Šaum'anovsk	**84**	40.26 N	46.34 E
Saumarez Reef ✢[2]	**166**	21.50 S	153.40 E
Saumlaki	**164**	7.57 S	131.19 E
Saumon, Rivière au ≐	**206**	45.41 N	71.27 W
Saumons, Rivíere aux ≐	**186**	49.25 N	62.15 W
Saumur	**32**	47.16 N	0.05 W
Saundatti	**122**	15.47 N	75.07 E
Saundersfoot	**42**	51.43 N	4.43 W
Saunders Island I, Falk. Is.	**9**	57.47 S	26.27 W
Saunders Island I, Falk. Is.	**254**	51.20 S	60.10 W
Saunders Point ∧[2]	**162**	27.52 S	125.38 E
Saunderstown	**207**	41.30 N	71.25 W
Saunemin	**216**	40.54 N	88.24 W
Saupite	**152**	13.54 S	17.43 E
Sauquoit	**210**	43.00 N	75.16 W
Sauquoit Creek ≐	**210**	43.08 N	75.16 W
Saura	**84**	44.14 N	50.50 E
Sauran	**85**	43.29 N	67.50 E
Saurimo	**152**	9.39 S	20.24 E
Saur-Mogila ⊥	**83**	47.56 N	38.46 E
Sausalito	**226**	37.51 N	122.29 W
Sausar	**120**	21.39 N	78.47 E
Sauškin	**80**	49.30 N	43.32 E
Sausset-les-Pins	**62**	43.20 N	5.07 E
Saussy	**58**	47.28 N	4.57 E
Sausu	**112**	1.00 S	120.30 E
Saútar	**152**	11.06 S	18.27 E
Sauteurs	**241k**	12.14 N	61.38 W
Sauteurs Bay ⊂	**241k**	12.14 N	61.38 W
Sauvas	**62**	44.19 N	4.09 E
Sauve	**62**	43.56 N	3.57 E
Sauveterre	**62**	44.02 N	4.48 E
Sauveterre-de-Béarn	**34**	43.24 N	0.56 W
Sauveterre-de-Guyenne	**32**	44.42 N	0.05 W
Sauvie Island I	**224**	45.41 N	122.49 W
Sauvo	**26**	60.21 N	22.42 E
Sauwald ◆[3]	**60**	48.28 N	13.40 E
Sauzal	**200**	31.37 N	106.18 W
Sauze di Cesana	**62**	44.56 N	6.51 E
Sauze d'Oulx	**62**	45.02 N	6.52 E
Sava, It.	**68**	40.24 N	17.34 E
S'ava, S.S.S.R.	**80**	58.01 N	46.22 E
Sava ≐	**38**	44.50 N	20.26 E
Sävaån ≐	**40**	59.45 N	17.24 E
Savage, Md., U.S.	**208**	39.08 N	76.49 W
Savage, Mt., U.S.	**198**	47.27 N	104.20 W
Savai'i I	**175a**	13.35 S	172.25 W
Savala ≐	**80**	51.03 N	41.30 E
Savalen ⊜	**26**	62.15 N	10.29 E
Savalou	**150**	7.56 N	1.58 E
Savana Island I	**240m**	18.20 N	65.05 W
Savana Passage ʯ	**240m**	18.21 N	65.04 W
Savane ≐	**186**	51.08 N	71.26 W
Savanna, Il., U.S.	**190**	42.05 N	90.09 W
Savanna, Ok., U.S.	**196**	34.49 N	95.50 W
Savannah, Ga., U.S.	**192**	32.05 N	81.06 W
Savannah, Mo., U.S.	**194**	39.56 N	94.49 W
Savannah, N.Y., U.S.	**210**	43.04 N	76.45 W
Savannah, Oh., U.S.	**214**	40.57 N	82.21 W
Savannah, Tn., U.S.	**194**	35.13 N	88.14 W
Savannah ≐	**192**	32.02 N	80.53 W
Savannah River Plant ◆[3]	**192**	33.15 N	81.40 W
Savannah Sound	**192**	25.06 N	76.09 W
Savannakhét	**110**	16.33 N	104.45 E
Savanna-la-Mar	**241q**	18.13 N	78.08 W
Savanna Portage State Park ♠	**190**	46.51 N	93.10 W
Sāvantvādi	**122**	15.54 N	73.49 E
Savanūr	**122**	14.58 N	75.21 E
Sävar	**26**	63.54 N	20.34 E
Savara ≐	**62**	45.42 N	7.12 E
Savasse ≐	**62**	45.03 N	5.02 E
Savaştepe	**130**	39.22 N	27.40 E
Savcılıbüyükoba	**130**	39.14 N	33.41 E
Savé	**150**	8.02 N	2.29 E
Save (Sabi) ≐, Afr.	**156**	21.00 S	35.02 E
Save ≐, Fr.	**32**	43.47 N	1.17 E
Sāveh	**128**	35.01 N	50.20 E
Savelli	**68**	39.19 N	16.47 E
Savelugu	**150**	9.37 N	0.49 W
Savenay	**32**	47.22 N	1.57 W
Săveni	**38**	47.57 N	26.52 E
Saverdun	**32**	43.14 N	1.35 E

Symbols in the index entries represent the broad categories identified in the key at the right. Symbols with superior numbers (⋏[1]) identify subcategories (see complete key on page *I · 1).*

Kartensymbole in dem Registerverzeichnis stellen die rechts in Schlüssel erklärten Kategorien dar. Symbole mit hochgestellten Ziffern (⋏[1]) bezeichnen Unterabteilungen einer Kategorie (vgl. vollständiger Schlüssel auf Seite *I · 1).*

Los símbolos incluídos en el texto del índice representan las grandes categorias identificadas con la clave a la derecha. Los símbolos con numeros en su parte superior (⋏[1]) identifican las subcategorías (véase la clave completa en la página *I · 1).*

Les symboles de l'index représentent les catégories indiquées dans la légende à droite. Les symboles suivis d'un indice (⋏[1]) représentent des sous-catégories (voir légende complète à la page *I · 1).*

Os símbolos incluídos no texto do índice representam as grandes categorias identificadas com a chave à direita. Os símbolos com números em sua parte superior (⋏[1]) identificam as subcategorias (veja-se a chave completa à página *I · 1).*

∧ Mountain	Berg	Montaña	Montagne	Montanha
⋏ Mountains	Berge	Montañas	Montagnes	Montanhas
)(Pass	Pass	Paso	Col	Passo
V Valley, Canyon	Tal, Cañon	Valle, Cañón	Vallée, Canyon	Vale, Canhão
≚ Plain	Ebene	Llano	Plaine	Planície
≻ Cape	Kap	Cabo	Cap	Cabo
I Island	Insel	Isla	Île	Ilha
II Islands	Inseln	Islas	Îles	Ilhas
⊥ Other Topographic Features	Andere Topographische Objekte	Otros Elementos Topográficos	Autres données topographiques	Outros acidentes topográficos

ESPAÑOL — Nombre | Página | Lat.°′ | Long.°′ W = Oeste
FRANÇAIS — Nom | Page | Lat.°′ | Long.°′ W = Ouest
PORTUGUÊS — Nome | Página | Lat.°′ | Long.°′ W = Oeste

Savernake Forest ◆3 42 51.24 N 1.38 W
Saverne 56 48.44 N 7.22 E
Savery Creek ≃ 200 41.01 N 107.27 W
Saviči, S.S.S.R. 76 52.25 N 29.03 E
Saviči, S.S.S.R. 78 51.37 N 30.17 E
Savick Brook ≃ 262 53.49 N 2.37 W
Savièse 58 46.16 N 7.20 E
Savigliano 62 44.38 N 7.40 E
Savignano Irpino 68 41.14 N 15.11 E
Savignano sul Panaro 64 44.29 N 11.02 E
Savignano sul Rubicone 66 44.05 N 12.24 E
Savignone 62 44.34 N 8.58 E
Savigny-lès-Beaune 58 47.04 N 4.49 E
Savigny-le-Temple 261 48.35 N 2.35 E
Savigny-sur-Braye 50 47.53 N 0.49 E
Savigny-sur-Orge 50 48.40 N 2.21 E
Savill Gardens ♦ 260 51.27 N 0.36 E
Savincy 78 49.24 N 37.04 E
Savines 62 44.32 N 6.24 E
Savinjske Alpe ⋏ 61 46.23 N 14.35 E
Savinka, S.S.S.R. 80 50.06 N 47.06 E
Savinka, S.S.S.R. 82 54.27 N 38.52 E
Savino 80 56.35 N 41.13 E
Savino-Borisovskaja 24 62.38 N 44.34 E
Savinsk 89 52.10 N 140.23 E
Savinskij 24 62.58 N 40.08 E
Savio 66 44.18 N 12.18 E
Savio ≃ 66 44.19 N 12.20 E
Saviore dell'Adamello 64 46.05 N 10.24 E
Săvîrșin 38 46.01 N 22.14 E
Šavitaipale 26 61.12 N 27.42 E
Šavnik 38 42.57 N 19.05 E
Savognin 58 46.36 N 9.36 E
Savoie ▫5 32 45.30 N 6.25 E
Savo Island I 175e 9.08 S 159.49 E
Savolaks ◆1 26 62.00 N 28.00 E
Sav'olovo 82 56.52 N 37.22 E
Sav'olovo Station ◆5 265b 55.48 N 37.35 E
Savona, B.C., Can. 182 50.45 N 120.50 W
Savona, It. 62 44.17 N 8.30 E
Savona, N.Y., U.S. 210 42.17 N 77.13 W
Savona ▫4 62 44.18 N 8.16 E
Savonlinna 26 61.52 N 28.53 E
Savonnières 50 47.21 N 0.33 E
Savonranta 26 62.11 N 29.12 E
Savoonga 180 63.42 N 170.27 W
Savory Creek ≃ 162 23.22 S 122.37 E
Savoureuse ≃ 58 47.31 N 6.51 E
Savoy 196 33.34 N 96.21 W
Savran' 78 48.09 N 30.04 E
Savruši 80 55.02 N 50.40 E
Sävsjö 26 57.25 N 14.40 E
S'avta 24 67.08 N 61.45 E
Savu Basin ✢1 14 9.15 S 123.15 E
Savudrija 64 45.30 N 13.30 E
Savur 130 37.33 N 40.53 E
Savusavu 175g 16.16 S 179.21 E
Savusavu Bay c 175g 16.45 S 179.15 E
Savu Sea → Sawu, Laut ⊤2 112 9.40 S 122.00 E
Savuto ≃ 68 39.02 N 16.06 E
Savvatejevka 88 52.20 N 103.39 E
Savvino, S.S.S.R. 82 55.43 N 36.48 E
Savvino, S.S.S.R. 82 56.33 N 37.47 E
Savvo-Borz'a 88 50.46 N 118.18 E
Ṣawāb, Wādī aṣ- V 130 34.36 N 40.25 E
Sawah 112 2.23 N 115.14 E
Sawahlunto 112 0.40 S 100.47 E
Sawai 164 2.58 S 129.09 E
Sawai, Teluk c 164 2.52 S 129.12 E
Sawai Mādhopur 124 25.59 N 76.22 E
Sawai Madhopur ▫5 124 26.15 N 74.45 E
Sawākin 140 19.07 N 37.20 E
Sawal, Gunung ∧ 115a 7.12 S 108.16 E
Sawan, Indon. 115b 8.08 S 115.11 E
Sawan, Mya. 110 24.30 N 96.19 E
Sawang 114 0.45 N 103.21 E
Sawankhalok 110 17.19 N 99.50 E
Sawara 94 35.53 N 140.30 E
Sawata 92 38.00 N 138.16 E
Sawatch Range ⋏ 200 39.10 N 106.25 W
Sawbridgeworth 42 51.50 N 0.09 E
Sawdā', Jabal as- ⋏2 146 28.40 N 15.30 E
Sawdā', Qurnat as- ∧ 130 34.18 N 36.07 E
Sawdirī 140 14.25 N 29.05 E
Sawel Mountain ∧ 48 54.49 N 7.02 W
Sawhāj 140 26.33 N 31.42 E
Sawi 110 10.14 N 99.07 E
Sawin, Lac ⊜ 206 46.32 N 73.54 W
Sawknah 146 29.04 N 15.47 E
Ṣawl 142 29.21 N 31.14 E
Sawla 150 9.17 N 2.25 W
Saw Log Creek ≃ 198 38.07 N 99.42 W
Saw Mill ≃ 276 40.56 N 73.53 W
Sawmill Brook ≃, Ma., U.S. 283 42.34 N 70.46 W
Sawmill Brook ≃, N.J., U.S. 276 40.28 N 74.26 W
Sawmill Creek ≃, N.J., U.S. 276 40.46 N 74.05 W
Sawmill Creek ≃, Pa., U.S. 279b 40.10 N 79.58 W
Sawmill Pond Brook ≃ 276 41.10 N 74.23 W
Sawmill Run ≃ 285 40.07 N 75.21 W
Sawmills 154 19.31 S 28.02 E
Sawqarah, Dawḥat c 118 18.35 N 57.15 E
Sawston 42 52.07 N 0.10 E
Sawtayr ⊤4 140 17.03 N 30.24 E
Sawtooth National Recreation Area ♦ 202 44.00 N 114.55 W
Sawtry 42 52.27 N 0.17 W
Sawu, Laut (Savu Sea) ⊤2 112 9.40 S 122.00 E
Sawu, Pulau I 112 10.30 S 121.54 E
Sawyer, Mi., U.S. 216 41.53 N 86.35 W
Sawyer, N.D., U.S. 198 48.05 N 101.03 W
Sawyers Hill ∧2 186 47.11 N 53.52 W
Sawyers Valley 168a 31.54 S 116.13 E
Sawyerville, P.Q., Can. 206 45.20 N 71.34 W
Sawyerville, Il., U.S. 219 39.05 N 89.48 W
Sawyerwood 214 41.02 N 81.27 W
Saxby ≃ 166 18.25 S 140.53 E
Saxdalen 40 60.09 N 14.57 E
Saxen ⊜ 40 59.46 N 14.25 E
Saxike 120 30.44 N 86.22 E
Saxilby 44 53.17 N 0.40 W
Saxis 208 37.55 N 75.43 W
Saxmundham 42 52.13 N 1.29 E
Saxon, Schw. 58 46.09 N 7.11 E
Saxon, Wi., U.S. 190 46.29 N 90.24 W
Saxonburg 214 40.45 N 79.49 W
Saxon Woods Park ♦ 276 40.59 N 73.45 W
Saxony → Sachsen ▫9 30 52.45 N 9.30 E
Saxton 214 40.12 N 78.14 W
Say 150 13.07 N 2.21 E
Sāy, Jazīrat I 140 20.42 N 30.20 E
Saya de Malha Bank ✢4 12 10.30 S 61.30 E
Sayama, Nihon 94 35.51 N 139.24 E
Sayama, Nihon 270 34.31 N 135.34 E
Sayama-kyūryō ⋏2 268 35.47 N 139.24 E
Sayán 248 11.08 S 77.12 W
Sayan Mountains (Sajany) ⋏ 88 52.45 N 96.00 E
Sayansk 88 54.02 N 102.06 E
Sayaxché 232 16.31 N 90.10 W
Saybrook, Il., U.S. 216 40.25 N 88.31 W
Saybrook, Oh., U.S. 214 41.50 N 80.51 W
Saybrook Manor 207 41.17 N 72.23 W
Sayda, D.D.R. 54 50.43 N 13.25 E
Ṣaydā (Sidon), Lubnān 132 33.33 N 35.22 E
Ṣaydnāyā 132 33.42 N 36.22 E
Sayghān 120 35.11 N 67.42 E
Sayḥūt 144 15.12 N 51.14 E
Sayil ⊥ 232 20.16 N 89.42 W
Saylah 142 29.21 N 30.58 E
Saylorsburg 210 40.54 N 75.19 W
Saylorville Lake ⊜1 190 41.48 N 93.46 W
Säynätsalo 26 62.08 N 25.46 E
Sayō 96 35.00 N 134.22 E
Ṣayqal, Baḥr ⊜ 132 33.40 N 37.06 E
Sayram Hu ⊜ 86 44.36 N 81.13 E
Sayre, Ok., U.S. 196 35.17 N 99.38 W
Sayre, Pa., U.S. 210 41.58 N 76.30 W
Sayreville 208 40.27 N 74.21 W
Sayula, Méx. 232 29.22 N 111.33 W
Sayula, Méx. 234 19.52 N 103.37 W
Sayula, Laguna de ⊜ 234 20.03 N 103.31 W
Sayula de Alemán 234 17.52 N 94.57 W
Sayville 210 40.44 N 73.04 W
Sayward 182 50.22 N 125.55 W
Saywūn 144 15.56 N 48.47 E
Saza 92 33.14 N 129.39 E
Sazanit I 38 40.30 N 19.16 E
Sazdy, S.S.S.R. 80 46.57 N 49.19 E
Sazdy, S.S.S.R. 86 47.22 N 61.48 E
Saze 62 43.56 N 4.41 E
Sažino 86 56.20 N 58.11 E
Sazlijka ≃ 38 42.02 N 25.52 E
Şazonovo 76 59.04 N 35.14 E
Šazud 120 37.43 N 72.11 E
Sazykul', ozero ⊜ 86 55.22 N 67.34 E
Sba 148 28.13 N 0.08 W
Sbeïtla 148 35.14 N 9.08 E
Sbiba 36 35.33 N 9.05 E
Scaddan 162 33.27 S 121.43 E
Scaër 32 48.02 N 3.42 W
Scafati 68 40.45 N 14.31 E
Scafell Pikes ∧ 44 54.27 N 3.12 W
Scaggsville 208 39.09 N 76.54 W
Scajaquada Creek ≃ 284a 42.56 N 78.53 W
Scala, Teatro alla ʊ 266b 45.28 N 9.11 E
Scala Coeli 68 39.27 N 16.53 E
Scalasaig 46 56.04 N 6.11 W
Scalby 44 54.18 N 0.27 W
Scalea 68 39.49 N 15.48 E
Scaletta Zanclea 70 38.03 N 15.28 E
Scalloway 46a 60.08 N 1.18 W
Scalpay I, Scot., U.K. 46 57.17 N 5.59 W
Scalpay I, Scot., U.K. 46 57.52 N 6.40 W
Scalp Level 214 40.14 N 78.50 W
Scalp Mountain ∧2 44 55.04 N 7.24 W
Scammon 198 37.16 N 94.49 W
Scammon Bay 180 61.53 N 165.38 W
Scammon Bay c 180 61.53 N 165.54 W
Scammonden Water ⊜1 262 53.38 N 1.56 W
Scampton 44 53.18 N 0.34 W
Scandale 68 39.07 N 16.57 E
Scandia 198 39.47 N 97.47 W
Scandiano 64 44.36 N 10.43 E
Scandicci 66 43.45 N 11.11 E
Scanlon 190 46.42 N 92.25 W
Scanno 66 41.54 N 13.53 E
Scansano 66 42.41 N 11.20 E
Scantic ≃ 207 41.52 N 72.38 W
Scapa 182 51.52 N 111.59 W
Scapa Flow c 46 58.55 N 3.06 W
Scapegoat Mountain ∧ 202 47.19 N 112.50 W
Ščapino 74 55.19 N 159.25 E
Ščapov 80 51.01 N 51.11 E
Ščapovo 82 55.09 N 38.11 E
Scappoose 224 45.45 N 122.52 W
Ščara ≃ 76 53.27 N 24.45 E
Scaramia, Capo › 70 36.47 N 14.29 E
Scarba I 46 56.11 N 5.43 W
Scarborough, Austl. 168a 31.54 S 115.45 E
Scarborough, On., Can. 212 43.47 N 79.15 W
Scarborough, Trin. 241r 11.11 N 60.44 W
Scarborough, Eng., U.K. 44 54.17 N 0.24 W
Scarborough Centre ◆9 275b 43.47 N 79.16 W
Scarborough Point › 171a 27.12 S 153.07 E
Scarborough Shoal I1 116 15.08 N 117.46 E
Scardroy 46 57.31 N 4.59 W
Scargill 172 42.56 S 172.57 E
Scarinish 46 56.29 N 6.48 W
Scarisbrick 262 53.37 N 2.56 W
Scărișoara 38 44.00 N 24.35 E
Scarlino 66 42.54 N 10.51 E
Scarp I 46 58.02 N 7.08 W
Scarpe ≃ 50 50.30 N 3.27 E
Scarperia 66 44.00 N 11.21 E
Scarper Peak ∧ 282 37.32 N 122.26 W
Scarriff 48 52.55 N 8.31 W
Scarsdale, Austl. 169 37.40 S 143.40 E
Scarsdale, N.Y., U.S. 210 40.59 N 73.49 W
Scartaglin 48 52.10 N 9.26 W
Scarth Hill 262 53.33 N 2.52 W
Sčastje 83 48.44 N 39.14 E
Scatarie Island I 186 46.00 N 59.44 W
Scatter Creek ≃ 224 46.48 N 123.06 W
Scauri, It. 66 41.15 N 13.42 E
Scauri, It. 70 36.45 N 11.58 E
Scavaig, Loch c 46 57.09 N 6.10 W
Scawfell Island I 166 20.52 S 149.36 E
Sceale Bay 162 33.01 S 134.12 E
Sceaux 50 48.47 N 2.17 E
Sceaux, Château de ⊥ 261 48.46 N 2.18 E
Ščedrin 76 52.53 N 29.33 E
Ščedrovka 83 49.30 N 40.17 E
Ščeglovo 265a 60.02 N 30.46 E
Ščeljajur 24 65.21 N 53.21 E
Ščelkan ≃ 80 50.47 N 43.33 E
Ščelkovo 76 55.55 N 38.00 E
Ščemilovo 265b 55.48 N 38.05 E
Scena 64 46.41 N 11.12 E
Scenery Hill 214 40.05 N 80.04 W
Sceptre 184 50.51 N 109.15 W
Ščerbakovo, S.S.S.R. 74 65.15 N 160.30 E
Ščerbakovo, S.S.S.R. 86 56.01 N 73.29 E
Ščerbakty 86 52.29 N 78.09 E
Ščerbinka 82 55.31 N 37.35 E
Ščerbinovka 83 48.26 N 37.50 E
Scerni 66 42.07 N 14.34 E
Scey-sur-Saône-et-Saint-Albin 58 47.40 N 5.58 E
Schaale ≃ 54 53.21 N 10.49 E
Schaalsee ⊜ 54 53.35 N 10.57 E
Schaan 58 47.10 N 9.31 E
Schabs → Sciaves 64 46.46 N 11.40 E
Schachendorf 61 47.16 N 16.26 E
Schaefferstown 208 40.17 N 76.17 W
Schaephuysen 263 51.26 N 6.29 E
Schaerbeek 50 50.51 N 4.23 E
Schafberg ∧ 64 47.47 N 13.27 E
Schäferberg ∧2 264a 52.25 N 13.08 E
Schaffhausen 58 47.42 N 8.38 E
Schaffhausen ▫3 58 47.40 N 8.35 E
Schafstädt 54 51.23 N 11.46 E
Schäftlarn 64 47.59 N 11.28 E
Schagen 52 52.46 N 4.47 E
Schaghticoke 210 42.54 N 73.35 W
Schalchen 60 48.07 N 13.10 E
Schale 52 52.26 N 7.37 E
Schalkau 54 50.24 N 11.00 E
Schalke ◆8 263 51.31 N 7.05 E
Schälker Heide ◆3 263 51.24 N 7.36 E
Schalksmühle 56 51.14 N 7.31 E
Schaller 198 42.30 N 95.18 W
Schanck, Cape › 169 38.30 S 144.53 E
S-Chanf 58 46.36 N 9.59 E
Schanfigg V 58 46.51 N 9.38 E
Schanghai → Shanghai 106 31.14 N 121.28 E
Schangnau 58 46.50 N 7.52 E
Schapbach 58 48.22 N 8.17 E
Schapen 52 52.24 N 7.33 E
Schaprode 54 54.31 N 13.10 E
Scharbeutz 54 54.03 N 10.44 E
Schardenberg 60 48.32 N 13.30 E
Schardenberg ∧2 263 51.27 N 6.28 E
Schärding 60 48.27 N 13.26 E
Scharhörn I 52 53.57 N 8.25 E
Schari → Chari ≃ 146 12.58 N 14.31 E
Scharl 263 51.06 N 7.40 E
Scharmützelsee ⊜ 54 52.15 N 14.03 E
Scharnhorst ◆8 263 51.32 N 7.32 E
Scharnitz 64 47.23 N 11.17 E
Scharnitzer Klause)(64 47.24 N 11.16 E
Scharrel 52 53.04 N 7.42 E
Scharzfeld 52 51.37 N 10.22 E
Schässburg → Sighișoara 38 46.13 N 24.48 E
Schauinsland ∧ 58 47.55 N 7.54 E
Schaumburg 216 42.02 N 88.05 W
Schaut 84 43.43 N 42.32 E
Schebeli → Shabeelle ≃ 144 0.12 S 42.45 E
Scheessel 52 53.10 N 9.29 E
Schefferville 176 54.48 N 66.50 W
Scheggia 66 43.24 N 12.40 E
Scheggino 66 42.43 N 12.50 E
Scheibbs 61 48.00 N 15.10 E
Scheiblingstein 264b 48.16 N 16.13 E
Scheidegg 58 47.35 N 9.51 E
Scheifling 61 47.09 N 14.24 E
Scheinfeld 56 49.40 N 10.27 E
Schelde (Escaut) ≃ 50 51.22 N 4.15 E
Schelklingen 58 48.22 N 9.44 E
Schell Creek Range ⋏ 204 39.10 N 114.40 W
Schellenberg ∧ 60 48.18 N 13.03 E
Schellsburg 214 40.03 N 78.39 W
Schelsen ◆8 263 51.09 N 6.31 E
Schenectady 210 42.48 N 73.56 W
Schenectady ▫6 210 42.47 N 73.53 W
Schenefeld 52 53.36 N 9.49 E
Schenevus 210 42.32 N 74.49 W
Schenevus Creek ≃ 210 42.29 N 74.59 W
Schenkendorf 264a 52.16 N 13.35 E
Schenkenhorst 264a 52.20 N 13.12 E
Schenklengsfeld 56 50.49 N 9.50 E
Schenley 214 40.41 N 79.40 W
Schenley Park ♦ 279b 40.26 N 79.56 W
Schepsdorf-Lohne 52 52.30 N 7.16 E
Schererville 216 41.30 N 87.27 W
Scherfede 52 51.32 N 9.02 E
Scherlebeck 263 51.37 N 7.08 E
Schermbeck 52 51.41 N 6.52 E
Schermerhorn 52 52.36 N 4.52 E
Schermützelsee ⊜ 54 52.34 N 14.04 E
Scherpenheuve 56 50.59 N 4.59 E
Scherpenzeel 52 52.05 N 5.30 E
Schertz 196 29.33 N 98.16 W
Schesch, Erg → Chech, Erg ◆2 148 25.00 N 2.15 W
Schesslitz 60 49.59 N 11.01 E
Schevelinge-Stausee ⊜1 263 51.08 N 7.26 E
Scheveningen ◆8 52 52.06 N 4.18 E
Schichallion ∧ 46 56.40 N 4.06 W
Schiedam 52 51.55 N 4.24 E
Schieder 52 51.55 N 9.09 E
Schiefbahn 56 51.14 N 6.31 E
Schierke 54 51.46 N 10.40 E
Schierling 60 48.50 N 12.08 E
Schiermonnikoog 52 53.24 N 6.10 E
Schiermonnikoog I 52 53.28 N 6.15 E
Schiers 58 46.59 N 9.41 E
Schiessen 58 48.18 N 10.14 E
Schiffdorf 52 53.32 N 8.39 E
Schiffenensee ⊜ 58 46.50 N 7.10 E
Schifferstadt 56 49.23 N 8.22 E
Schiffshebewerk ◆5 263 51.37 N 7.19 E
Schihkiatschwang → Shijiazhuang 98 38.03 N 114.28 E
Schijndel 52 51.37 N 5.25 E
Schikoku → Shikoku I 92 33.45 N 133.30 E
Schildau 54 51.27 N 12.56 E
Schilde 56 51.14 N 4.34 E
Schilde ≃ 54 53.26 N 10.53 E
Schildow 54 52.38 N 13.23 E
Schildwolde 52 53.14 N 6.49 E
Schiller Park 216 41.57 N 87.52 W
Schillingsfürst 56 49.17 N 10.15 E
Schillingstedt 54 51.14 N 11.11 E
Schilpario 64 46.01 N 10.09 E
Schiltach 58 48.17 N 8.20 E
Schiltigheim 58 48.36 N 7.45 E
Schimborn 56 50.03 N 9.11 E
Schimmert 56 50.55 N 5.50 E
Schinveld 56 50.57 N 5.59 E
Schinznach Bad 58 47.27 N 8.10 E
Schio 64 45.43 N 11.21 E
Schipbeek ≃ 52 52.14 N 6.09 E
Schiphol, Luchthaven ⊠ 52 52.17 N 4.40 E
Schipkau 54 51.31 N 13.53 E
Schippenbeil → Sępopol 30 54.15 N 21.00 E
Schirgiswalde 54 51.05 N 14.27 E
Schirmeck 58 48.29 N 7.13 E
Schirnding 54 50.05 N 12.13 E
Schisuoka → Shizuoka 94 34.58 N 138.23 E
Schivelbein → Świdwin 30 53.47 N 15.47 E
Schjetman Reef ✢2 14 15.10 N 178.40 W
Schkeuditz 54 51.24 N 12.13 E
Schkoder-See → Scutari, Lake ⊜ 38 42.12 N 19.18 E
Schkölen 54 51.02 N 11.49 E
Schkopau 54 51.23 N 11.59 E
Schladen 54 52.01 N 10.32 E
Schladming 64 47.23 N 13.41 E
Schlanders → Silandro 64 46.38 N 10.46 E
Schlangen 52 51.49 N 8.50 E
Schlangenbad 56 50.05 N 8.05 E
Schlänitz-See ⊜ 264a 52.27 N 12.57 E
Schlanstedt 54 52.00 N 11.02 E
Schlater 194 33.38 N 90.20 W
Schlegel Lake ⊜ 276 40.59 N 74.03 W
Schlei c 41 54.36 N 9.51 E
Schleiden 56 50.31 N 6.28 E
Schleife 54 51.32 N 14.32 E
Schleinitz Range ⋏ 164 3.10 S 151.40 E
Schleithal 56 48.59 N 8.02 E
Schleitheim 58 47.45 N 8.29 E
Schleiz 54 50.34 N 11.49 E
Schlema 54 50.40 N 12.40 E
Schlepzig 54 52.01 N 13.53 E
Schlesien → Silesia ▫9 30 51.00 N 16.45 E
Schlesischer (Ost) Bahnhof ◆5 264a 52.30 N 13.26 E
Schleswig, B.R.D. 41 54.31 N 9.33 E
Schleswig, Ia., U.S. 198 42.09 N 95.26 W
Schleswig-Holstein ▫3 30 54.20 N 9.40 E
Schlettau 54 50.33 N 12.56 E
Schlettstadt → Sélestat 58 48.16 N 7.27 E
Schleusingen 54 50.31 N 10.45 E
Schlichtingsheim → Szlichtyngowa 30 51.43 N 16.15 E
Schlicke ∧ 58 47.31 N 10.37 E
Schlieben 54 51.43 N 13.23 E
Schliengen 58 47.46 N 7.35 E
Schlieren 58 47.24 N 8.27 E
Schliersee 64 47.44 N 11.51 E
Schlitz 56 50.40 N 9.33 E
Schlochau → Człuchów 30 53.41 N 17.21 E
Schloppe → Człopa 30 53.06 N 16.08 E
Schloss Holte 52 51.52 N 8.35 E
Schloss Neuhaus 52 51.44 N 8.43 E
Schlossvippach 54 51.06 N 11.08 E
Schloss Zeil 64 47.52 N 10.00 E
Schlotheim 54 51.14 N 10.39 E
Schluchsee 58 47.49 N 8.10 E
Schluchsee ⊜ 58 47.49 N 8.10 E
Schlucht, Col de la)(58 48.04 N 7.02 E
Schlüchtern 56 50.20 N 9.31 E
Schluderns → Sluderno 64 46.40 N 10.35 E
Schlüsselburg 52 52.29 N 9.04 E
Schlüsselfeld 56 49.45 N 10.37 E
Schlutup ◆8 54 53.53 N 10.48 E
Schmachtendorf ◆8 263 51.32 N 6.49 E
Schmalfeld 52 53.52 N 9.58 E
Schmalkalden 54 50.43 N 10.26 E
Schmallenberg 56 51.09 N 8.17 E
Schmalnau 56 50.27 N 9.47 E
Schmannewitz 54 51.24 N 12.58 E
Schmarsau 54 52.54 N 11.21 E
Schmelz 56 49.27 N 6.51 E
Schmida ≃ 61 48.21 N 16.09 E
Schmidmühlen 60 49.16 N 11.56 E
Schmidt 56 50.39 N 6.25 E
Schmidtsdrif 158 28.41 S 24.02 E
Schmiedeberg 54 50.50 N 13.40 E
Schmiedefeld 54 50.37 N 10.49 E
Schmilka 54 50.53 N 14.14 E
Schmöckwitz ◆8 264a 52.23 N 13.39 E
Schmölln 54 50.53 N 12.20 E
Schmutter ≃ 58 48.42 N 10.46 E
Schnabelwaid 60 49.49 N 11.35 E
Schnackenburg 54 53.02 N 11.32 E
Schnait 56 48.47 N 9.23 E
Schnaitsee 60 48.04 N 12.22 E
Schnaittach 60 49.31 N 11.19 E
Schnaittenbach 60 49.33 N 12.01 E
Schnakenbek 52 53.23 N 10.30 E
Schnecksville 208 40.41 N 75.36 W
Schneealpe ⋏ 61 47.41 N 15.36 E
Schneeberg 54 50.36 N 12.38 E
Schneeberg ∧, B.R.D. 54 50.03 N 11.51 E
Schneeberg ∧, Öst. 61 47.47 N 15.47 E
Schneidemühl → Piła 30 53.10 N 16.44 E
Schneider 216 41.11 N 87.26 W
Schneifel ⋏1 56 50.15 N 6.25 E
Schneverdingen 52 53.07 N 9.47 E
Schney 56 50.10 N 11.04 E
Schober Gruppe ⋏ 64 46.55 N 12.42 E
Schobüll 41 54.30 N 9.00 E
Schöckl ∧ 61 47.11 N 15.28 E
Schodn'a 82 55.57 N 37.18 E
Schodn'a ≃ 265b 55.50 N 37.25 E
Schoenbrunn Village State Memorial ⊥ 214 40.27 N 81.24 W
Schofield 190 44.54 N 89.36 W
Schofield Barracks ■ 229c 21.30 N 158.04 W
Schofields 274a 33.42 S 150.52 E
Schöftland 58 47.18 N 8.03 E
Schoharie 210 42.39 N 74.18 W
Schoharie ▫6 210 42.40 N 74.19 W
Schoharie Creek ≃ 210 42.57 N 74.18 W
Schoharie Reservoir ⊜1 210 42.22 N 74.26 W
Scholen 52 52.44 N 8.46 E
Scholes 44 53.49 N 1.25 W
Schollene 54 52.41 N 12.13 E
Schöllenen V 58 46.40 N 8.35 E
Schöller 263 51.14 N 7.01 E
Schöllkrippen 56 50.05 N 9.14 E
Schöllnach 60 48.45 N 13.11 E
Scholls 224 45.24 N 122.55 W
Scholven ◆8 263 51.36 N 7.01 E
Schömberg, B.R.D. 56 48.47 N 8.38 E
Schömberg, B.R.D. 58 48.13 N 8.46 E
Schomberg, On., Can. 212 44.00 N 79.41 W
Schonach 58 48.08 N 8.11 E
Schönaich 56 48.39 N 9.03 E
Schönau, B.R.D. 56 49.26 N 8.49 E
Schönau, B.R.D. 58 47.47 N 7.53 E
Schönau, B.R.D. 64 47.37 N 12.59 E
Schönau → Świerzawa 30 51.01 N 15.54 E
Schönbeck 54 53.34 N 13.34 E
Schönberg, B.R.D. 54 54.23 N 10.22 E
Schönberg, B.R.D. 60 48.50 N 13.20 E
Schönberg, D.D.R. 54 50.11 N 12.19 E
Schönberg, D.D.R. 54 53.50 N 11.38 E
Schönberg, D.D.R. 54 50.31 N 11.57 E
Schönberger Strand 54 54.25 N 10.24 E
Schönberg im Stubaital 64 47.11 N 11.25 E
Schönbrunn 54 50.32 N 10.53 E
Schönbrunn, Schloss ʊ 264b 48.11 N 16.19 E
Schönbrunner Schlosspark ♦ 264b 48.11 N 16.19 E
Schondra ≃ 56 50.07 N 9.44 E
Schönebeck, D.D.R. 54 53.03 N 12.13 E
Schönebeck, D.D.R. 54 52.01 N 11.44 E
Schönebeck ◆8 263 51.28 N 6.56 E
Schöneberg ◆8 264a 52.29 N 13.21 E
Schöneck, B.R.D. 56 50.13 N 8.52 E
Schöneck, D.D.R. 54 50.23 N 12.20 E
Schönecken 56 50.09 N 6.27 E
Schönefeld 264a 52.23 N 13.30 E
Schöneiche 54 52.28 N 13.41 E
Schönenwerd 58 47.22 N 8.00 E
Schönerlinde 264a 52.39 N 13.27 E
Schönewalde 54 51.49 N 13.13 E
Schönfeld 264a 52.41 N 13.44 E
Schönfliess 264a 52.39 N 13.20 E
Schongau 58 47.49 N 10.54 E
Schönhagen, B.R.D. 41 54.38 N 10.01 E
Schönhagen, B.R.D. 52 51.41 N 9.33 E
Schönhausen, B.R.D. 263 51.37 N 7.38 E
Schönhausen, D.D.R. 54 52.35 N 12.02 E
Schönheide 54 50.30 N 12.31 E
Schönholthausen 56 51.11 N 8.00 E
Schöningen 54 52.08 N 10.58 E
Schönkirchen 54 54.20 N 10.15 E
Schönlanke → Trzcianka 30 53.03 N 16.28 E
Schönmünzach 56 48.36 N 8.22 E
Schonnebeck ◆8 263 51.29 N 7.04 E
Schönningstedt 52 53.32 N 10.15 E
Schönow 54 52.40 N 13.32 E
Schönsee 60 49.31 N 12.33 E
Schönthal 60 49.21 N 12.36 E
Schonungen 56 50.03 N 10.18 E
Schönwald, B.R.D. 54 50.12 N 12.05 E
Schönwald, B.R.D. 58 48.06 N 8.11 E
Schönwalde, B.R.D. 54 54.11 N 10.45 E
Schönwalde, D.D.R. 54 52.40 N 13.26 E
Schönwalde, D.D.R. 54 52.37 N 13.07 E
Schönwalde, Forst ◆3 264a 52.42 N 13.28 E
Schönwies 58 47.11 N 10.39 E
Schoodic Lake ⊜ 188 45.21 N 68.54 W
Schoolcraft 216 42.06 N 85.38 W
Schoolhouse Run ≃ 285 40.13 N 75.27 W
Schoombee 158 31.28 S 25.30 E
Schoondijke 52 51.21 N 3.32 E
Schoonebeek 52 52.29 N 6.52 E
Schoonhoven 52 51.56 N 4.51 E
Schoorl 52 52.42 N 4.41 E
Schopfheim 58 47.39 N 7.49 E
Schopfloch 56 49.07 N 10.18 E
Schopp 56 49.21 N 7.41 E
Schöppenstedt 54 52.08 N 10.46 E
Schöppingen 52 52.05 N 7.14 E
Schorfheide 54 52.56 N 13.43 E
Schorfheide ◆3 54 52.55 N 13.35 E
Schörfling 64 47.56 N 13.36 E
Schorndorf 56 48.48 N 9.31 E
Schortens 52 53.31 N 7.56 E
Schoten 50 51.15 N 4.30 E
Schötmar 52 52.04 N 8.45 E
Schotten 56 50.30 N 9.07 E
Schottland → Scotland ▫8 28 57.00 N 4.00 W
Schouten, Kepulauan II 164 0.55 S 135.55 E
Schouten Island I 166 42.19 S 148.17 E
Schouten Islands II 164 3.30 S 144.40 E
Schouwen I 52 51.43 N 3.50 E
Schrader Creek ≃ 210 41.43 N 76.30 W
Schrader Range ⋏ 164 5.05 S 144.15 E
Schramberg 58 48.13 N 8.23 E
Schram City 219 39.09 N 89.27 W
Schrankogel ∧ 64 47.02 N 11.06 E
Schraplau 54 51.26 N 11.40 E
Schreiber 190 48.48 N 87.15 W
Schrems 61 48.47 N 15.04 E
Schrick 61 48.30 N 16.37 E
Schriever 194 29.44 N 90.48 W
Schrobenhausen 60 48.33 N 11.17 E
Schröcken 58 47.15 N 10.05 E
Schroffenstein ∧ 158 27.11 S 18.42 E
Schroon ≃ 188 43.29 N 73.49 W
Schroon Lake ⊜ 188 43.47 N 73.46 W
Schrozberg 56 49.20 N 9.59 E
Schruns 58 47.04 N 9.55 E
Schulenburg, B.R.D. 52 52.12 N 9.47 E
Schulenburg, Tx., U.S. 222 29.40 N 96.54 W
Schuls → Scuol 58 46.48 N 10.18 E
Schultz Lake ⊜ 176 64.45 N 97.30 W
Schulzendorf 54 52.22 N 13.35 E
Schulzenhöhe 264a 52.29 N 13.47 E
Schumacher 190 48.28 N 81.18 W
Schüpfheim 58 46.57 N 8.01 E
Schüren ◆8 263 51.30 N 7.32 E
Schussen ≃ 58 47.37 N 9.32 E
Schussenried 58 48.00 N 9.40 E
Schüttenberg ∧2 61 48.05 N 16.44 E
Schutter ≃ 58 48.34 N 7.50 E
Schüttorf 52 52.19 N 7.13 E
Schützenbruch → Kalety 30 50.34 N 18.54 E
Schuyler, Ne., U.S. 198 41.26 N 97.03 W
Schuyler, Va., U.S. 192 37.47 N 78.41 W
Schuyler ▫6, Il., U.S. 219 40.07 N 90.34 W
Schuyler ▫6, N.Y., U.S. 210 42.23 N 76.52 W
Schuyler Lake 210 42.47 N 75.02 W
Schuylerville 210 43.06 N 73.34 W
Schuylkill ▫6 210 40.41 N 76.12 W
Schuylkill ≃ 208 39.53 N 75.12 W
Schuylkill Canal ≅ 285 40.14 N 75.42 W
Schuylkill Haven 208 40.37 N 76.10 W
Schwaan 54 53.56 N 12.06 E
Schwabach 60 49.20 N 11.01 E
Schwaben ▫5 58 48.15 N 10.30 E
Schwaben ▫9 30 48.10 N 9.25 E
Schwabing ◆8 60 48.10 N 11.34 E
Schwäbische Alb ⋏ 58 48.25 N 9.30 E
Schwäbisch Gmünd 56 48.48 N 9.47 E
Schwäbisch Hall 56 49.07 N 9.44 E
Schwabmünchen 58 48.11 N 10.45 E
Schwabstedt 41 54.23 N 9.11 E
Schwadorf 264b 48.04 N 16.35 E
Schwafheim 263 51.25 N 6.39 E
Schwagstorf 52 52.31 N 7.45 E
Schwaigern 56 49.08 N 9.03 E
Schwalenberg 52 51.52 N 9.11 E
Schwalm ≃ 56 51.10 N 9.25 E
Schwalmstadt 56 50.55 N 9.11 E
Schwalmtal 56 51.13 N 6.16 E
Schwanden 58 47.00 N 9.04 E
Schwandorf 60 49.20 N 12.08 E
Schwanebeck, D.D.R. 54 52.37 N 13.32 E
Schwanebeck, D.D.R. 54 51.58 N 11.07 E
Schwanenstadt 60 48.03 N 13.46 E
Schwanenwerder ◆8 264a 52.27 N 13.10 E
Schwaner, Pegunungan ⋏ 112 0.40 S 112.40 E
Schwanewede 52 53.14 N 8.35 E
Schwangau 58 47.35 N 10.44 E
Schwansen ◆1 41 54.35 N 9.50 E
Schwante 264a 52.44 N 13.05 E
Schwarme 52 52.54 N 9.01 E
Schwarmstedt 52 52.40 N 9.37 E
Schwartau ≃ 54 53.56 N 10.41 E
Schwarza, D.D.R. 54 50.38 N 10.32 E
Schwarza, D.D.R. 54 50.41 N 11.19 E
Schwarza ≃, D.D.R. 54 50.41 N 11.19 E
Schwarza ≃, Öst. 61 47.43 N 16.13 E
Schwarzach, B.R.D. 60 48.55 N 12.49 E
Schwarzach, Öst. 58 47.27 N 9.45 E
Schwarzach ≃ 60 49.36 N 12.08 E
Schwarzach im Pongau 64 47.19 N 13.09 E
Schwarzbach ≃, B.R.D. 56 49.16 N 7.18 E
Schwarzbach ≃, B.R.D. 263 51.19 N 6.44 E
Schwarzburg 54 50.38 N 11.12 E
Schwarze Elster ≃ 54 51.49 N 12.51 E
Schwarze Laber ≃ 60 49.00 N 12.03 E
Schwarzenbach am Wald 54 50.17 N 11.37 E
Schwarzenbach an der Saale 54 50.13 N 11.56 E
Schwarzenbek 52 53.30 N 10.29 E
Schwarzenberg, B.R.D. 263 51.24 N 6.42 E
Schwarzenberg, D.D.R. 54 50.32 N 12.47 E
Schwarzenberg Park ♦ 264b 48.14 N 16.15 E
Schwarzenborn 56 50.37 N 9.58 E
Schwarzenbruck 60 49.21 N 11.14 E
Schwarzenburg 58 46.49 N 7.21 E
Schwarzenfeld 60 49.23 N 12.08 E
Schwarze Pumpe 54 51.32 N 14.20 E
Schwarzer Berg ∧2 263 51.41 N 7.12 E
Schwarzer Mann ∧ 56 50.15 N 6.21 E
Schwarzer Regen ≃ 60 49.10 N 12.50 E
Schwarzes Meer → Black Sea ⊤2 22 43.00 N 35.00 E
Schwarzheide 54 51.29 N 13.51 E
Schwarzkogel ∧ 61 47.25 N 15.25 E
Schwarzrand ⋏ 156 25.37 S 16.50 E
Schwarzriegel ∧ 60 49.14 N 12.56 E
Schwarzsee 58 46.40 N 7.20 E
Schwarzwald (Black Forest) ⋏ 58 48.00 N 8.15 E
Schwarzwälder Hochwald ◆3 56 49.39 N 6.55 E
Schwatka Mountains ⋏ 180 67.25 N 157.00 W
Schwaz 64 47.20 N 11.42 E
Schwechat 264b 48.08 N 16.29 E
Schwechat ≃ 264b 48.08 N 16.34 E
Schweden → Sweden ▫1 24 62.00 N 15.00 E
Schwedeneck 41 54.27 N 10.05 E
Schwedt 54 53.03 N 14.17 E
Schweez 54 53.53 N 12.24 E
Schweflinghausen 263 51.16 N 7.25 E
Schwegenheim 56 49.16 N 8.20 E
Schwei 52 53.24 N 8.21 E
Schweich 56 49.49 N 6.45 E
Schweidnitz → Świdnica 30 50.51 N 16.29 E
Schweighausen 58 48.13 N 7.57 E
Schweighouse-sur-Moder 56 48.49 N 7.44 E
Schweinfurt 56 50.03 N 10.14 E
Schweinitz 54 51.48 N 13.01 E
Schweinrich 54 53.10 N 12.37 E
Schweiz → Switzerland ▫1 58 47.00 N 8.00 E
Schweizer Nationalpark ♦ 58 46.38 N 10.11 E
Schweizer-Reneke 158 27.11 S 25.18 E
Schwelm 56 51.17 N 7.17 E
Schwendi 58 48.10 N 9.58 E
Schwenke 263 51.11 N 7.26 E
Schwenksville 285 40.16 N 75.28 W
Schwepnitz 54 51.20 N 13.57 E
Schwerin 54 53.38 N 11.25 E
Schwerin ▫5 54 53.30 N 11.30 E
Schwerin ◆8 263 51.33 N 7.20 E
Schwerin an der Warthe → Skwierzyna 30 52.36 N 15.30 E
Schweriner See ⊜ 54 53.45 N 11.28 E
Schwertberg 61 48.16 N 14.35 E
Schwerte 56 51.26 N 7.34 E
Schwetzingen 56 49.23 N 8.34 E
Schweyen 56 49.10 N 7.24 E
Schwieberdingen 56 48.52 N 9.04 E
Schwiebus → Świebodzin 30 52.15 N 15.32 E
Schwielochsee ⊜ 54 52.03 N 14.12 E
Schwielowsee ⊜ 54 52.20 N 12.57 E
Schwitten 263 51.27 N 7.48 E
Schwyz 58 47.02 N 8.40 E
Schwyz ▫3 58 47.05 N 8.40 E
Sciacca 70 37.31 N 13.03 E
Sciara 70 37.55 N 13.45 E
Sciaves (Schabs) 64 46.46 N 11.40 E
Scicli 70 36.47 N 14.42 E
Scie ≃ 50 49.55 N 1.02 E
Science and Industry, Museum of ʊ 278 41.47 N 87.35 W
Sciez 58 46.20 N 6.23 E
Şcigliano 68 39.08 N 16.19 E
Ščigry 78 51.53 N 36.55 E
Scilla 68 38.15 N 15.44 E
Scilly, Isles of II 42a 49.55 N 6.20 W
Ścinawa 30 51.25 N 16.27 E
Scio, N.Y., U.S. 210 42.10 N 77.59 W
Scio, Oh., U.S. 214 40.23 N 81.05 W
Scio, Or., U.S. 202 44.42 N 122.50 W
Scionzier 58 46.03 N 6.34 E
Sciota 210 40.56 N 75.19 W
Scioto ▫6 218 38.48 N 83.01 W
Scioto ≃ 188 38.44 N 83.01 W
Scioto Brush Creek ≃ 218 38.50 N 83.01 W
Scipio, In., U.S. 218 39.05 N 85.43 W
Scipio, Ut., U.S. 200 39.14 N 112.06 W
Scipio Center 210 42.47 N 76.34 W
Şcippo Creek ≃ 218 39.31 N 82.59 W
Ščit ∧ 36 44.02 N 17.47 E
Ščitkoviči 76 53.13 N 27.59 E
Scituate 207 42.11 N 70.43 W
Scituate Reservoir ⊜1 207 41.47 N 71.36 W
Sclafani Bagni 70 37.49 N 13.51 E
Scobey 202 48.47 N 105.25 W
Scoffera, Passo della)(62 44.29 N 9.07 E
Scofield Reservoir ⊜1 200 39.47 N 111.09 W
Şcoglitti ◆8 70 36.53 N 14.26 E
Ščokino 76 54.01 N 37.31 E
Şcole 42 52.22 N 1.10 E
Ščolkovo 82 55.55 N 38.00 E
Scoltenna ≃ 64 44.15 N 10.50 E
Scolt Head › 42 52.58 N 0.42 E
Scone 166 32.03 S 150.52 E
Scooba 194 32.49 N 88.28 W
Scopello 62 45.46 N 8.06 E
Scordia 70 37.18 N 14.51 E
Scoresby 274b 37.54 S 145.14 E
Scorrano, It. 66 42.35 N 13.49 E
Şcorrano, It. 68 40.05 N 18.18 E
Ščors 78 51.49 N 31.59 E
Ščorsk 78 48.22 N 34.06 E
Scorzè 64 45.34 N 12.06 E
Scotch ≃ 206 45.27 N 74.59 W
Scotch Plains 210 40.39 N 74.23 W
Scotchtown 210 41.29 N 74.21 W
Scotia, Ne., U.S. 198 41.27 N 98.42 W
Scotia, N.Y., U.S. 210 42.49 N 73.57 W
Scotia Lake ⊜ 190 47.05 N 81.23 W
Scotia Ridge ✢3 18 54.00 S 50.00 W
Scotia Sea ⊤2 9 56.00 S 40.00 W
Scotland, On., Can. 212 43.01 N 80.22 W
Scotland, Pa., U.S. 208 39.58 N 77.35 W
Scotland, S.D., U.S. 198 43.08 N 97.43 W
Scotland, Tx., U.S. 196 33.40 N 98.28 W
Scotland ▫8 28 57.00 N 4.00 W
Scotland Neck 192 36.07 N 77.25 W
Scotland Run ≃ 285 39.39 N 75.03 W
Şcotlandville 194 30.31 N 91.10 W
Ščot'ovo 83 48.09 N 39.04 E
Scotrun 210 41.04 N 75.19 W
Scotsburn 186 45.39 N 62.51 W
Scotstown 206 45.32 N 71.17 W
Scott, Sk., Can. 184 52.23 N 108.50 W
Scott, Ms., U.S. 194 33.35 N 91.04 W
Scott, Oh., U.S. 216 40.59 N 84.35 W
Scott ▫6, Il., U.S. 219 39.38 N 90.27 W
Scott ▫6, In., U.S. 218 38.41 N 85.46 W
Scott ▫6, Ky., U.S. 218 38.18 N 84.35 W
Scott ≃ 204 41.48 N 123.02 W
Scott, Cape › 182 50.47 N 128.26 W
Scott, Mount ∧, Ok., U.S. 196 34.44 N 98.32 W
Scott, Mount ∧, Or., U.S. 202 42.56 N 122.01 W
Scott Air Force Base ■ 219 38.32 N 89.52 W
Scott Base ʊ3 9 77.50 S 166.25 E
Scottburgh 158 30.19 S 30.40 E
Scott City, Ks., U.S. 198 38.28 N 100.54 W
Scott City, Mo., U.S. 194 37.13 N 89.31 W
Scott Cove c 276 41.03 N 73.28 W
Scott Creek ≃ 226 37.02 N 122.13 W
Scottdale, Mi., U.S. 216 42.03 N 86.27 W
Scottdale, Pa., U.S. 214 40.06 N 79.35 W
Scotter 44 53.29 N 0.40 W
Scott Glacier ⊓, Ant. 9 66.15 S 100.05 E
Scott Glacier ⊓, Ant. 9 85.45 S 153.00 W
Scott Haven 279b 40.15 N 79.47 W
Scott Island I 212 44.36 N 76.20 W
Scott Islands II 182 50.48 N 128.40 W
Scott Lake 220 25.56 N 80.13 W
Scott Mountain ∧ 202 44.11 N 115.47 W
Scott Peak ∧ 202 44.21 N 112.50 W
Scott Reef ✢2 160 14.00 S 121.50 E
Scott Run ≃ 284c 38.58 N 77.12 W
Scotts 216 42.11 N 85.24 W
Scottsbluff 198 41.52 N 103.40 W
Scotts Bluff National Monument ♦ 198 41.49 N 103.41 W
Scottsboro 194 34.40 N 86.02 W
Scottsburg, In., U.S. 218 38.41 N 85.46 W
Scottsburg, N.Y., U.S. 210 42.40 N 77.43 W
Scottsdale, Austl. 166 41.10 S 147.31 E
Scottsdale, Az., U.S. 200 33.30 N 111.53 W
Scotts Flat Reservoir ⊜1 226 39.17 N 120.55 W
Scotts Head › 240d 15.13 N 61.23 W
Scotts Hill 194 35.31 N 88.15 W
Scotts Level Branch ≃ 284b 39.22 N 76.45 W
Scottsmoor 220 28.46 N 80.53 W
Scotts Valley 226 37.03 N 122.00 W
Scottsville, Ky., U.S. 194 36.45 N 86.11 W
Scottsville, N.Y., U.S. 210 43.01 N 77.44 W
Scott Township 279b 40.32 N 80.11 W
Scottville, Il., U.S. 219 39.29 N 90.06 W
Scottville, Mi., U.S. 190 43.57 N 86.16 W
Scour ≃ 44 55.13 N 3.46 W
Scourie 46 58.20 N 5.08 W
Scout Lake 184 49.22 N 106.00 W
Scranton, Ia., U.S. 198 42.01 N 94.32 W
Scranton, N.Y., U.S. 210 42.44 N 78.50 W
Scranton, N.D., U.S. 198 46.08 N 103.08 W
Scranton, Pa., U.S. 210 41.24 N 75.39 W
Scremerston 44 55.44 N 1.59 W
Screven 192 31.29 N 82.01 W
Screw ≃ 164 3.55 S 142.50 E
Scribner 198 41.40 N 96.39 W
Scridain, Loch c 46 56.21 N 6.07 W
Scripps Institution of Oceanography ʊ3 228 32.52 N 117.15 W
Scrivia ≃ 62 45.03 N 8.54 E
Scroggins 222 32.58 N 95.11 W
Scrooby 44 53.25 N 1.01 W
Şcrub Island I 240m 18.28 N 64.31 W
Ščučin 76 53.36 N 24.45 E
Ščučinsk 86 52.56 N 70.12 E

Symbol	English	Deutsch	Español	Français	Português
≃	River	Fluss	Río	Rivière	Rio
≅	Canal	Kanal	Canal	Canal	Canal
⌞	Waterfall, Rapids	Wasserfall, Stromschnellen	Cascada, Rápidos	Chute d'eau, Rapides	Cascata, Rápidos
)(	Strait	Meeresstrasse	Estrecho	Détroit	Estreito
c	Bay, Gulf	Bucht, Golf	Bahía, Golfo	Baie, Golfe	Baía, Golfo
⊜	Lake, Lakes	See, Seen	Lago, Lagos	Lac, Lacs	Lago, Lagos
≡	Swamp	Sumpf	Pantano	Marais	Pântano
⊓	Ice Features, Glacier	Eis- und Gletscherformen	Accidentes Glaciales	Formes glaciaires	Acidentes glaciares
⊤	Other Hydrographic Features	Andere Hydrographische Objekte	Otros Elementos Hidrográficos	Autres données hydrographiques	Outros acidentes hidrográficos
✢	Submarine Features	Untermeerische Objekte	Accidentes Submarinos	Formes de relief sous-marin	Acidentes submarinos
▫	Political Unit	Politische Einheit	Unidad Politica	Entité politique	Unidade política
ʊ	Cultural Institution	Kulturelle Institution	Institución Cultural	Institution culturelle	Institução cultural
⊥	Historical Site	Historische Stätte	Sitio Histórico	Site historique	Sitio histórico
♦	Recreational Site	Erholungs- und Ferienort	Sitio de Recreo	Centre de loisirs	Area de Lazer
⊠	Airport	Flughafen	Aeropuerto	Aéroport	Aeroporto
■	Military Installation	Militäranlage	Instalación Militar	Installation militaire	Instalação militar
◆	Miscellaneous	Verschiedenes	Misceláneo	Divers	Diversos

Symbols in the index entries represent the broad categories identified in the key at the right. Symbols with superior numbers (⋀[1]) identify subcategories (see complete key on page *I · 1).*

Kartensymbole in dem Registerverzeichnis stellen die rechts in Schlüssel erklärten Kategorien dar. Symbole mit hochgestellten Ziffern (⋀[1]) bezeichnen Unterabteilungen einer Kategorie (vgl. vollständiger Schlüssel auf Seite *I · 1).*

Los símbolos incluídos en el texto del índice representan las grandes categorias identificadas con la clave a la derecha. Los símbolos con numeros en su parte superior (⋀[1]) identifican las subcategorías (véase la clave completa en la página *I · 1).*

Les symboles de l'index représentent les catégories indiquées dans la légende à droite. Les symboles suivis d'un indice (⋀[1]) représentent des sous-catégories (voir légende complète à la page *I · 1).*

Os símbolos incluídos no texto do índice representam as grandes categorias identificadas com a chave à direita. Os símbolos com números em sua parte superior (⋀[1]) identificam as subcategorias (veja-se a chave completa à página *I · 1).*

English	Deutsch	Español	Français	Português
∧ Mountain	Berg	Montaña	Montagne	Montanha
⋀ Mountains	Berge	Montañas	Montagnes	Montanhas
)(Pass	Pass	Paso	Col	Passo
V Valley, Canyon	Tal, Cañon	Valle, Cañón	Vallée, Canyon	Vale, Canhão
≚ Plain	Ebene	Llano	Plaine	Planície
› Cape	Kap	Cabo	Cap	Cabo
I Island	Insel	Isla	Île	Ilha
II Islands	Inseln	Islas	Îles	Ilhas
⊥ Other Topographic Features	Andere Topographische Objekte	Otros Elementos Topográficos	Autres données topographiques	Outros acidentes topográficos

ESPAÑOL

Nombre	Página	Lat.°′	Long.°′ W = Oeste
Senica	30	48.41 N	17.22 E
Senigallia	66	43.43 N	13.13 E
Senirkent	130	38.07 N	30.33 E
Senise	68	40.09 N	16.18 E
Senj	36	44.59 N	14.54 E
Senja I	24	69.20 N	17.30 E
Senjitu	98	41.56 N	116.25 E
Senjō-san ʌ	96	35.26 N	133.36 E
Senkevičevka	78	50.32 N	25.02 E
Senkobo	154	17.38 S	25.58 E
Sen'kovo	83	49.31 N	37.43 E
Şenköy	130	36.05 N	36.05 E
Šenkursk	24	62.08 N	42.53 E
Senlac	184	52.29 N	109.41 W
Şenlikköy ◆[8]	267b	40.59 N	28.47 E
Senlis	50	49.12 N	2.35 E
Senlisse	261	48.41 N	1.59 E
Senmonorom	110	12.27 N	107.12 E
Senn, Ḍahr ou ≗[4]	150	18.30 N	11.00 W
Sennaja	78	45.15 N	37.01 E
Sennan	96	34.22 N	135.17 E
Senne(Zenne) ≃	50	51.04 N	4.26 E
Sennecey-le-Grand	58	46.39 N	4.52 E
Senne II → Sennestadt	52	51.59 N	8.37 E
Sennen	42	50.04 N	5.42 W
Sennestadt	52	51.59 N	8.37 E
Senneterre	190	48.23 N	77.15 W
Senneville	275a	45.27 N	73.57 W
Sennevoy-le-Bas	50	47.48 N	4.17 E
Senno	76	54.49 N	29.43 E
Sennoj, S.S.S.R.	80	52.11 N	46.57 E
Sennoj, S.S.S.R.	80	50.16 N	43.37 E
Sennokura-yama ʌ	94	36.49 N	138.50 E
Sennori	71	40.47 N	8.35 E
Sennwald	58	47.16 N	9.30 E
Sennybridge	42	51.57 N	3.34 W
Senoia	192	33.18 N	84.33 W
Senonches	50	48.33 N	1.02 E
Senones	58	48.24 N	6.59 E
Senorbì	71	39.32 N	9.08 E
Sénou	150	12.31 N	6.56 W
Sénouire ≃	62	45.16 N	3.25 E
Senqu → Orange ≃	156	28.41 S	16.28 E
Senqunyane ≃	158	30.03 S	28.10 E
Senriyama	270	34.47 N	135.30 E
Sens	50	48.12 N	3.17 E
Sensburg → Mrągowo	30	53.52 N	21.19 E
Sense ≃	58	46.54 N	7.14 E
Sensée ≃	50	50.16 N	3.06 E
Sensée, Canal de la ≊	50	50.14 N	3.17 E
Sensuntepeque	236	13.52 N	88.38 W
Şenta	38	45.56 N	20.04 E
Šentala	80	54.27 N	51.29 E
Sentani, Danau ⊜	164	2.36 S	140.34 E
Sentarum, Danau ⊜	112	0.51 N	112.06 E
Sentas	86	49.19 N	82.28 E
Sentelek	86	51.13 N	83.44 E
Şentery	154	5.22 S	25.45 E
Šentilj	61	46.41 N	15.40 E
Sentinel	196	35.09 N	99.10 W
Sentinel Butte ʌ	198	46.53 N	103.50 W
Sentinel Peak ʌ	182	54.54 N	121.57 W
Sentinel Range ⋀	9	78.10 S	85.30 W
Şentino ≃	66	43.24 N	12.59 E
Šentjur	36	46.13 N	15.24 E
Sentolo	115a	7.50 S	110.13 E
Sentosa I	271c	1.15 N	103.50 E
Sento Sé	250	9.40 S	41.18 W
Sentsū-zan ʌ	96	35.09 N	133.11 E
Senyavin Islands II	14	6.55 N	158.00 E
Senye	152	1.34 N	9.50 E
Senza	154	3.02 N	26.19 E
Senzaki-wan ⊂	96	34.24 N	131.15 E
Sen-zan ʌ	96	34.21 N	134.51 E
Senzig	54	52.17 N	13.39 E
Senzu-dake ʌ	270	34.57 N	135.52 E
Seo de Urgel	34	42.21 N	1.28 E
Seohāra	124	29.13 N	78.35 E
Seolag-san Kukrip Kongwŏn ♠	98	38.09 N	128.24 E
Seon	58	47.21 N	8.10 E
Seonāth ≃	122	21.44 N	82.28 E
Seoni	124	22.05 N	79.32 E
Seoni □[5]	124	22.30 N	79.40 E
Seoni Mālwa	124	22.27 N	77.28 E
Seorīnārāyan	120	21.44 N	82.35 E
Seoul → Sŏul	98	37.33 N	126.58 E
Seoul Bridge ◆[5]	271b	37.32 N	126.56 E
Seoul National University ʊ[2]	271b	37.28 N	126.57 E
Seoul Stadium ♠	271b	37.35 N	127.02 E
Seoul Station ◆[5]	271b	37.34 N	126.58 E
Sepahat	114	1.34 N	101.53 E
Sepang	114	2.42 N	101.45 E
Sepanjang, Pulau I	112	7.10 S	115.50 E
Separation Creek ≃	200	41.59 N	107.28 W
Separation Point ≻	172	40.47 S	173.00 E
Sepasu	112	0.43 N	117.35 E
Sepatini ≃	248	7.36 S	65.24 W
Sépeaux	50	47.57 N	3.14 E
Sepetiba ◆[8]	256	22.58 S	43.42 W
Şepetiba, Baía de ⊂	256	23.00 S	43.48 W
Šepetovka	78	50.11 N	27.04 E
Sepi	175e	8.33 S	159.50 E
Sepik ≃	164	3.51 S	144.34 E
Sepino	66	41.24 N	14.37 E
Sep'o	98	38.39 N	127.22 E
Sępólno Krajeńskie	30	53.28 N	17.32 E
Sépone → Muang Xépôn	110	16.41 N	106.14 E
Sepopa	156	18.13 S	22.13 E
Sępopol	30	54.15 N	21.00 E
Sepoti ≃	248	6.43 S	61.38 W
Sepotuba ≃	248	15.56 S	57.39 W
Seppenrade	52	51.46 N	7.23 E
Sepphoris → Ẕippori	132	32.45 N	35.17 E
Seppois-le-Bas	58	47.33 N	7.10 E
Septeuil	261	48.54 N	1.41 E
Sept Frères, Lac des ⊜	206	46.20 N	75.10 W
Sept-Îles (Seven Islands)	186	50.12 N	66.23 W
Septvaux	50	49.34 N	3.23 E
Sepulga ≃	194	31.11 N	86.46 W
Sepúlveda	34	41.18 N	3.45 W
Sepulveda ◆[8]	280	34.13 N	118.28 W
Sepulveda Dam ◆[6]	280	34.10 N	118.29 W
Sepulveda Flood Control Basin ≚[1]	228	34.11 N	118.29 W
Seputih ≃	112	4.40 S	105.51 E
Sepyč	80	58.11 N	54.08 E
Sequals	64	46.10 N	12.50 E
Sequatchie ≃	192	35.02 N	85.38 W
Sequeros	34	40.31 N	6.01 W
Sequillo ≃	34	41.45 N	5.30 W
Sequim	224	48.04 N	123.06 W
Sequim Bay ⊂	224	48.03 N	123.02 W
Sequoia National Park ♠	204	36.30 N	118.30 W
Sera	96	34.36 N	133.03 E
Şera, Pulau I	164	7.40 S	131.05 E
Šerabad	128	37.40 N	67.01 E
Serachs	128	36.32 N	61.13 E
Serafeddin Dağları ⋀	130	39.05 N	41.10 E
Şerafimovič	80	49.36 N	42.43 E
Šeragul	88	54.29 N	100.56 E
Seraidi	36	36.55 N	7.41 E
Seraing	56	50.36 N	5.29 E
Seraja ≃	82	56.15 N	38.45 E
Seram (Ceram) I	164	3.00 S	129.00 E
Seram, Laut (Ceram Sea) ⊤[2]	108	2.30 S	128.00 E
Serampore	126	22.45 N	88.21 E
Serang	115a	6.07 S	106.09 E
Serang ≃	115a	6.43 S	110.35 E
Serangoon	271c	1.22 N	103.54 E
Serangoon ≃	271c	1.24 N	103.56 E
Serangoon, Pulau I	271c	1.25 N	103.56 E
Serangoon Harbour ⊂	271c	1.23 N	103.57 E

FRANÇAIS

Nom	Page	Lat.°′	Long.°′ W = Ouest
Serapo	66	41.13 N	13.34 E
Serasan, Pulau I	112	2.30 N	109.03 E
Serasan, Selat ɯ	112	2.20 N	109.00 E
Seravalle Sesia	62	45.41 N	8.19 E
Seravezza	64	43.59 N	10.13 E
Seraya, Pulau I	271c	1.16 N	103.43 E
Serayevo → Sarajevo	38	43.52 N	18.25 E
Şerayu ≃	115a	7.41 S	109.06 E
Šerbakul'	86	54.38 N	72.24 E
Serbeulangit, Pegunungan ⋀	114	3.45 N	97.50 E
Serbia → Srbija □[3]	38	44.00 N	21.00 E
Serchio ≃	64	43.47 N	10.16 E
Serdar	130	37.08 N	36.27 E
Serdce-Kamen', mys ≻	180	66.57 N	171.40 W
Serdež	80	57.17 N	48.17 E
Serditoje	83	48.02 N	38.24 E
Serdo	144	11.58 N	41.18 E
Serdoba ≃	80	52.34 N	44.01 E
Serdobsk	80	52.28 N	44.13 E
Séré'ama, Mont ʌ	175f	13.47 S	167.29 E
Serebr'anka, S.S.S.R.	83	48.55 N	38.08 E
Serebr'anka, S.S.S.R.	86	57.13 N	70.42 E
Serebr'anka, S.S.S.R.	265b	55.45 N	37.55 E
Serebr'anka ≃	265b	55.47 N	37.42 E
Serebr'ansk	86	49.43 N	83.20 E
Serebr'anyj Bor ◆[8]	265b	55.48 N	37.25 E
Serebr'anyje Prudy	82	54.28 N	38.44 E
Serebrovo	88	55.24 N	97.52 E
Serechoviči	78	51.25 N	24.40 E
Sered'	30	48.17 N	17.44 E
Sereda, S.S.S.R.	76	55.54 N	35.31 E
Şereda, S.S.S.R.	80	58.00 N	40.27 E
Šeredar' ≃	82	55.56 N	39.04 E
Seredejskij	76	54.03 N	35.14 E
Seredići	76	53.35 N	35.51 E
Seredina-Buda	78	52.11 N	34.01 E
Serednikovo, S.S.S.R.	80	55.15 N	39.40 E
Serednikovo, S.S.S.R.	265b	55.56 N	37.14 E
Seredn'ovo	265b	55.35 N	37.18 E
Seredžius	76	55.05 N	23.25 E
Şereflikoçhisar	130	38.56 N	33.33 E
Şeregeš	86	52.57 N	88.02 E
Seregno	62	45.39 N	9.12 E
Serein ≃	50	47.55 N	3.31 E
Şeremban	114	2.43 N	101.56 E
Šeremetjevka	80	55.23 N	51.32 E
Šeremetjevo, Aeroport ⊠	82	55.59 N	37.24 E
Šeremetjevskij	82	55.59 N	37.30 E
Seremuk ≃	164	1.36 S	131.46 E
Serena	216	41.29 N	88.44 W
Seren del Grappa	64	45.59 N	11.51 E
Serengeti National Park ♠	154	2.20 S	34.50 E
Serengeti Plain ≚	154	2.50 S	35.00 E
Serengka	112	1.40 S	110.40 E
Serenje	154	13.15 S	30.14 E
Şereno	256	21.19 S	42.39 W
Šereševo	76	52.33 N	24.13 E
Seret ≃	78	48.38 N	25.52 E
Serfaus	58	47.02 N	10.36 E
Ser'ga	86	57.46 N	56.52 E
Sergač	80	55.32 N	45.28 E
Sergeant	214	41.38 N	78.45 W
Sergeant Bluff	198	42.24 N	96.21 W
Sergeja Kirova, ostrova II	74	77.12 N	89.30 E
Sergejeviči	76	53.30 N	27.45 E
Sergejevka, S.S.S.R.	83	48.40 N	37.22 E
Sergejevka, S.S.S.R.	86	53.51 N	67.25 E
Sergejevka, S.S.S.R.	86	51.39 N	68.13 E
Sergejevka, S.S.S.R.	89	44.22 N	131.39 E
Sergejevka, S.S.S.R.	89	43.21 N	133.22 E
Sergejevo	86	57.18 N	86.02 E
Sergen	38	41.42 N	27.42 E
Sergijevka	78	51.46 N	41.05 E
Sergijevskaja, S.S.S.R.	76	60.16 N	43.54 E
Sergijevskaja, S.S.S.R.	80	50.16 N	43.47 E
Sergijevskij	80	51.56 N	51.54 E
Sergili	85	41.13 N	69.14 E
Sergines	50	48.20 N	3.15 E
Sergino	72	62.30 N	65.38 E
Sergipe □[3]	250	10.30 S	37.30 W
Sergokala	84	42.27 N	47.40 E
Sergozero, ozero ⊜	24	66.47 N	36.42 E
Seria	112	4.39 N	114.23 E
Serian	112	1.10 N	110.34 E
Seriana, Valle V	64	45.55 N	9.55 E
Seriate	62	45.41 N	9.43 E
Seribu, Kepulauan II	115a	5.36 S	106.33 E
Seribudolok, Indon.	114	2.51 N	99.04 E
Seribudolok, Indon.	114	2.56 N	98.37 E
Sericho	154	1.05 N	39.05 E
Seridó ≃	250	6.12 S	37.10 W
Sérifontaine	50	49.21 N	1.46 E
Sérifos	38	37.09 N	24.31 E
Sérifos I	38	37.11 N	24.31 E
Sérignan-du-Comtat	62	44.11 N	4.51 E
Sérigny ≃	176	56.47 N	66.00 W
Serik	130	36.55 N	31.06 E
Seringa, Serra da ⋀[1]	250	7.00 S	50.40 W
Seringapatam	122	12.25 N	76.42 E
Serino	68	40.51 N	14.52 E
Serio ≃	62	45.16 N	9.45 E
Serir Dağı ʌ	130	39.39 N	42.41 E
Seritinga	256	21.54 S	44.30 W
Serjol	24	60.02 N	48.58 E
Serkhe, Cerro ʌ	248	17.22 S	69.22 W
Serkout, Djebel ʌ	148	23.30 N	6.48 E
Serkovo	82	54.28 N	38.46 E
Şerles ʌ	64	47.08 N	11.23 E
Šerlovaja Gora	88	50.34 N	116.15 E
Serm ◆[8]	263	51.21 N	6.42 E
Sermaise	261	48.32 N	2.05 E
Sermaises	50	48.18 N	2.12 E
Sermaize-les-Bains	56	48.47 N	4.55 E
Serman	80	53.34 N	46.22 E
Sermata, Kepulauan II	164	8.10 S	128.40 E
Sermide	64	45.00 N	11.18 E
Sermilik ⊂[2]	176	65.37 N	38.03 W
Sermizelles	50	47.32 N	3.48 E
Şermoneta	66	41.33 N	12.59 E
Šerna ≃	82	55.51 N	38.34 E
Sernambitiba	287a	22.41 S	42.59 W
Sernambitiba, Pontal de ≻	287a	23.02 S	43.27 W
Serniki	78	51.49 N	26.14 E
Sernovodsk	80	53.56 N	51.17 E
Sernur	80	56.56 N	49.09 E
Sernyy Zavod	128	39.59 N	58.50 E
Séro	150	14.48 N	11.04 W
Serodino	252	32.37 S	60.57 W
Ser'odka	76	58.10 N	28.12 E
Seroglazka	80	47.01 N	47.29 E
Ser'ogovo	24	62.20 N	50.36 E
Serooskerke	52	51.42 N	3.50 E
Seropédica	256	22.44 S	43.43 W
Serov	86	59.29 N	60.31 E
Serovo	85	40.27 N	71.12 E
Serowe	156	22.25 S	26.44 E
Ser'oža ≃	80	55.34 N	42.29 E
Serpa	34	37.56 N	7.36 W
Serpa, Ilha de I	246	3.07 S	58.19 W
Serpeddi, Punta ʌ	71	39.22 N	9.18 E
Serpejsk	76	54.20 N	34.59 E
Serpent, Rivière au ≃	186	49.33 N	71.14 W
Serpentine	168a	32.22 S	115.59 E
Serpentine ≃, Austl.	168a	32.33 S	115.46 E
Serpentine ≃, B.C., Can.	224	49.05 N	122.50 W
Serpentine Dam ◆[6]	168a	32.25 S	116.08 E
Serpentine Lakes ⊜	162	28.32 S	129.09 E
Serpent Mound State Memorial ⊥	218	39.02 N	83.26 W

PORTUGUÊS

Nome	Página	Lat.°′	Long.°′ W = Oeste
Serpents Mouth ɯ	241r	10.00 N	62.00 W
Serpis ≃	34	38.59 N	0.09 W
Serpnevoje	78	46.18 N	29.02 E
Serpuchov	82	54.55 N	37.25 E
Serpukhov → Serpuchov	82	54.55 N	37.25 E
Serqo → Sark I	43b	49.26 N	2.21 W
Serra	255	20.07 S	40.18 W
Serra, Monte ʌ	66	43.46 N	10.33 E
Serra Branca	250	7.29 S	36.40 W
Serracapriola	68	41.48 N	15.09 E
Serrada	64	45.53 N	11.09 E
Serra d'aiello	68	39.05 N	16.08 E
Serra de'Conti	66	43.33 N	13.02 E
Serra di Corvo, Lago di ⊜[1]	68	40.51 N	16.14 E
Serradifalco	70	37.27 N	13.53 E
Serra do Navio	250	0.59 N	52.03 W
Serra do Salitre	255	19.06 S	46.41 W
Serra dos Órgãos, Parque Nacional da ♠	256	22.26 S	43.02 W
Serra Grande	250	7.15 S	38.19 W
Sérrai	38	41.05 N	23.32 E
Serramanna	71	39.25 N	8.55 E
Serramazzoni	64	44.25 N	10.47 E
Serramonte Center ◆[9]	282	37.40 N	122.28 W
Serrana	255	21.14 S	47.36 W
Serrana Bank ✦[4]	236	14.23 N	80.12 W
Serra Negra	256	22.36 S	46.42 W
Serra Negra do Norte	250	6.40 S	37.24 W
Serrania	255	21.33 S	46.03 W
Serranilla Bank ✦[4]	236	15.50 N	79.50 W
Serrano, Isla I	254	48.30 S	74.45 W
Serranópolis	255	18.16 S	52.00 W
Serranos	256	21.51 S	44.30 W
Serra Preta	255	12.09 S	39.20 W
Serrara	68	40.42 N	13.54 E
Serraria, Bra.	250	6.49 S	35.38 W
Serraria, Bra.	256	22.01 S	43.12 W
Serra San Bruno	68	38.35 N	16.20 E
Serra San Quirico	66	43.27 N	13.01 E
Serrastretta	68	39.01 N	16.25 E
Serrat, Cap ≻	36	37.14 N	9.13 E
Serra Talhada	250	7.59 S	38.18 W
Serravalle, It.	66	43.57 N	12.30 E
Serravalle, It.	66	42.47 N	13.01 E
Serravalle all'Adige	64	45.49 N	11.01 E
Serravalle Scrivia	62	44.43 N	8.51 E
Serre	68	40.35 N	15.11 E
Serre ≃	50	49.41 N	3.23 E
Serrenti	71	39.29 N	8.58 E
Serre-Ponçon, Barrage de ◆[6]	62	44.33 N	6.30 E
Serre-Ponçon, Lac de ⊜[1]	62	44.30 N	6.17 E
Serres	62	44.26 N	5.43 E
Serrezuela	252	30.38 S	65.23 W
Serri	71	39.42 N	9.08 E
Serrières	62	45.19 N	4.45 E
Serrinha	250	11.39 S	39.00 W
Serriola, Bocca)(	66	43.31 N	12.21 E
Serris	261	48.51 N	2.47 E
Serrita	250	7.56 S	39.19 W
Sêrro	255	18.37 S	43.23 W
Serrote ≃	248	21.27 S	54.40 W
Şersale	68	39.01 N	16.44 E
Šerstin	76	52.39 N	31.03 E
Šerstobitovo	86	57.16 N	78.52 E
Sertã	34	39.48 N	8.06 W
Sertaneja	255	23.03 S	50.50 W
Sertânia	250	8.05 S	37.16 W
Sertãozinho	256	22.19 S	46.03 W
Sertig-Dörfli	58	46.44 N	9.51 E
Sertung, Pulau I	115a	6.06 S	105.24 E
Seru	144	7.50 N	40.28 E
Şerua, Pulau I	164	6.18 S	130.01 E
Šerubaj-Nura ≃	86	49.54 N	72.31 E
Serui	164	1.53 S	136.14 E
Seruini ≃	248	7.42 S	66.42 W
Serule	156	21.58 S	27.20 E
Serutu, Pulau I	112	1.42 S	108.45 E
Seruwai	114	4.21 N	98.10 E
Sérvia	38	40.11 N	22.00 E
Servi Burnu ≻	130	41.40 N	28.06 E
Servigliano	66	43.05 N	13.29 E
Servon	261	48.43 N	2.35 E
Servoz	58	45.56 N	6.46 E
Serwaru	112	8.10 S	127.42 E
Sêrxü	102	33.04 N	97.45 E
Seryševo	89	51.08 N	128.20 E
Şes, Munții ⋀	38	47.05 N	22.30 E
Šešan	180	66.46 N	171.26 W
Sesayap ≃	112	3.36 N	117.15 E
Sesayap-lama	112	3.36 N	117.03 E
Sešča	76	53.45 N	33.23 E
Sese Islands II	154	0.20 S	32.20 E
Seseke ≃	263	51.37 N	7.32 E
Sesfontein	156	19.07 S	13.39 E
Sesheke	152	17.28 S	24.18 E
Seshu	105	39.33 N	115.37 E
Sesia ≃	62	45.05 N	8.37 E
Sesia, Val V	62	45.47 N	8.05 E
Sesibu	112	4.02 N	116.33 E
Seskar, ostrov I	76	60.02 N	28.23 E
Şeskarö	26	65.44 N	23.44 E
Šešma ≃	80	55.27 N	51.05 E
Sesmarias ≃	256	22.28 S	44.27 W
Sesoko-jima I	174m	26.38 N	127.52 E
Sespe	228	34.23 N	118.58 W
Sespe Creek ≃	204	34.23 N	118.57 W
Sessa	152	13.56 S	20.38 E
Sessa Aurunca	68	41.14 N	13.56 E
Séssé	146	11.30 N	17.34 E
Sessenheim	56	48.48 N	7.59 E
Şesta Godano	62	44.17 N	9.40 E
Šestakovka	78	48.32 N	31.58 E
Şestakovo, S.S.S.R.	82	56.21 N	35.49 E
Šestakovo, S.S.S.R.	88	56.29 N	103.59 E
Şestao	34	43.18 N	3.00 W
Šestern'a	78	47.33 N	33.16 E
Sestino	66	43.42 N	12.18 E
Sesto (Sexten)	64	46.42 N	12.21 E
Sesto Calende	62	45.44 N	8.38 E
Sesto Fiorentino	66	43.50 N	11.12 E
Sestola	64	44.14 N	10.46 E
Sesto San Giovanni	62	45.32 N	9.14 E
Sestra ≃, S.S.S.R.	80	52.11 N	49.36 E
Sestra ≃, S.S.S.R.	82	56.43 N	37.14 E
Sestriere	62	44.57 N	6.53 E
Sestri Levante	62	44.16 N	9.24 E
Sestri Ponente	62	44.25 N	8.51 E
Sestroreck	76	60.06 N	29.58 E
Sestroreckij Razliv, ozero ⊜	265a	60.04 N	30.00 E
Şestu	71	39.18 N	9.05 E
Šešupe ≃	76	55.03 N	22.12 E
Šešurga	80	57.29 N	47.35 E
Šešuvis ≃	76	55.13 N	22.15 E
Şeta, Nihon	270	34.58 N	135.55 E
Šeta, S.S.S.R.	76	55.17 N	24.15 E
Seta ≃	270	34.56 N	135.54 E
Setagaya ◆[8]	268	35.39 N	139.40 E
Setail ≃	115a	8.30 S	114.21 E
Setaka	96	33.09 N	130.28 E
Setana	92a	42.26 N	139.51 E
Setapak	114	3.11 N	101.42 E
Setauket	210	40.57 N	73.07 W
Sète	62	43.24 N	3.41 E
Sete Barras	252	24.23 S	47.55 W
Sete Cidades, Parque Nacional de ♠	250	3.50 S	41.40 W
Sete de Setembro ≃	255	12.56 S	52.51 W
Sete Lagoas	255	19.27 S	44.14 W
Sete Pontes	256	22.51 S	43.05 W
Sete Quedas, Cachoeira das ⌊	250	9.27 S	56.41 W
Sete Quedas, Parque Nacional de ♠	252	24.02 S	54.12 W
Sete Quedas, Salto das ⌊	252	24.02 S	54.16 W
Sete Rios ◆[8]	266c	38.45 N	9.10 W
Setesdal V	26	59.25 N	7.25 E
Seth Ward	196	34.13 N	101.42 W
Seti ≃	124	28.58 N	81.06 E
Setlagodi	158	26.16 S	25.06 E
Seto, Nihon	94	35.14 N	137.06 E
Seto, Nihon	96	33.27 N	132.15 E
Seto, Nihon	96	34.44 N	134.02 E
Setoda	96	34.18 N	133.05 E
Seto-naikai ⊤[2]	96	34.20 N	133.30 E
Seto-naikai-kokuritsu-kōen ♠	96	34.15 N	133.28 E
Seton Hall University ʊ[2]	276	40.45 N	74.15 W
Seton Lake ⊜	182	50.45 N	122.05 W
Seton Portage	182	50.43 N	122.18 W
Seto-saki ≻	174m	26.51 N	128.18 E
Setouchi	93b	28.10 N	129.15 E
Seto-zaki ≻	96	33.40 N	135.20 E
Setraki	78	49.23 N	40.49 E
Setta ≃	64	44.22 N	11.14 E
Settat	148	33.04 N	7.37 W
Settat □[4]	148	33.05 N	7.30 W
Sette Bagni ≃	267a	42.00 N	12.31 E
Setté Cama	152	2.32 S	9.45 E
Settecamini ◆[8]	267a	41.56 N	12.37 E
Sette-Daban, chrebet ⋀	74	62.00 N	138.00 E
Settee Lake ⊜	184	57.03 N	96.55 W
Settepani, Monte ʌ	62	44.15 N	8.12 E
Settimo Milanese	266b	45.29 N	9.03 E
Settimo San Pietro	71	39.17 N	9.11 E
Settimo Torinese	62	45.09 N	7.46 E
Settimo Vittone	62	45.33 N	7.50 E
Settingiano	68	38.55 N	16.31 E
Setting Lake ⊜	184	55.00 N	98.38 W
Settle	44	54.04 N	2.16 W
Settlement Point ≻	169	38.25 S	145.25 E
Settlers	156	25.02 S	28.30 E
Settlers Cabin Regional Park ♠	279b	40.26 N	80.10 W
Settons, Lac des ⊜	50	41.11 N	4.04 E
Settsu	96	34.46 N	135.33 E
Setúbal	34	38.32 N	8.54 W
Setúbal □[5]	266c	38.37 N	9.00 W
Setúbal, Baía de ⊂	34	38.27 N	8.53 W
Setun' ≃	265b	55.44 N	37.33 E
Seui	71	39.50 N	9.19 E
Seúl → Sŏul	98	37.33 N	126.58 E
Seul, Lac ⊜	184	50.20 N	92.30 W
Seul Choix Point ≻	190	45.56 N	85.52 W
Seulimeum	114	5.22 N	95.35 E
Seulo	71	39.52 N	9.14 E
Seumanyam	114	3.45 N	96.38 E
Seurre	58	47.00 N	5.09 E
Seuzach	58	47.32 N	8.44 E
Sev ≃	76	52.24 N	34.10 E
Sevagram	122	20.45 N	78.30 E
Sevan	84	40.34 N	44.57 E
Sevan, ozero ⊜	84	40.20 N	45.20 E
Sévaré	150	14.32 N	4.06 W
Sevastopol'	78	44.36 N	33.32 E
Şevastopol'skij	86	53.08 N	65.44 E
Ševčenko	72	43.35 N	51.05 E
Ševčenkovo, S.S.S.R.	78	49.41 N	37.10 E
Ševčenkovo, S.S.S.R.	78	45.33 N	29.20 E
Ševčenkovo, S.S.S.R.	78	51.40 N	33.39 E
Ševčenkovo Vtoroje	78	47.29 N	36.08 E
Sevelen, B.R.D.	52	51.29 N	6.25 E
Şevelen, Schw.	58	47.07 N	9.29 E
Ševelevskaja	24	60.52 N	44.12 E
Ševelevskij Majdan	80	54.25 N	42.15 E
Seven ≃	44	54.11 N	0.52 W
Seven Caves ≗[5]	218	39.13 N	83.23 W
Seven Creeks ≃	169	36.43 S	145.34 E
Seven Harbors	216	42.40 N	83.34 W
Sevenhill	168b	33.53 S	138.38 E
Seven Hills, Austl.	274a	33.46 S	150.57 E
Seven Hills, Oh., U.S.	214	41.23 N	81.40 W
Seven Islands → Sept-Îles	186	50.12 N	66.23 W
Seven Kings ◆[8]	260	51.34 N	0.05 E
Seven Mile	218	39.28 N	84.33 W
Sevenmile Bridge ◆[5]	220	24.41 N	81.11 W
Sevenmile Creek ≃	218	39.28 N	84.33 W
Sevenoaks, Eng., U.K.	42	51.16 N	0.12 E
Seven Oaks, Tx., U.S.	222	30.51 N	94.51 W
Sevenoaks □[8]	260	51.18 N	0.10 E
Sevenoaks Weald	260	51.14 N	0.12 E
Seven Palm Lake ⊜	220	25.12 N	80.44 W
Seven Persons	184	49.52 N	110.54 W
Seven Sisters	42	51.46 N	3.43 W
Seven Sisters Peaks ⋀	182	54.58 N	128.10 W
Seventy Mile House	182	51.18 N	121.24 W
Seven Valleys	208	39.51 N	76.46 W
Sévérac-le-Château	32	44.19 N	3.04 E
Severance Center ◆[9]	279a	41.31 N	81.33 W
Sever'anskij les ♠	83	48.55 N	38.00 E
Severka ≃	82	55.10 N	38.45 E
Severn, S. Afr.	158	26.36 S	22.52 E
Severn, Md., U.S.	208	39.08 N	76.41 W
Severn, N.C., U.S.	208	36.30 N	77.11 W
Severn, Va., U.S.	208	37.17 N	76.24 W
Severn ≃, On., Can.	176	56.02 N	87.36 W
Severn ≃, On., Can.	212	44.52 N	79.41 W
Severn ≃, U.K.	42	51.35 N	2.40 W
Severn, Mouth of the ≃	42	51.25 N	3.00 W
Severnaja Dvina ≃	24	64.32 N	40.30 E
Severnaja Sos'va ≃	72	64.10 N	65.28 E
Severnaja Zeml'a II	74	79.30 N	98.00 E
Severna Park	208	39.04 N	76.32 W
Severn Bridge ◆[5]	42	51.39 N	2.42 W
Severn Lake ⊜	184	53.54 N	90.48 W
Severnoje, S.S.S.R.	80	58.02 N	41.26 E
Severnoje, S.S.S.R.	80	54.06 N	52.32 E
Severnoje, S.S.S.R.	83	48.04 N	38.44 E
Severnoje, S.S.S.R.	84	44.49 N	42.51 E
Severnoje, S.S.S.R.	86	56.21 N	78.23 E
Severn River ⊂, Md., U.S.	208	38.58 N	76.28 W
Severn River ⊂, Va., U.S.	208	37.19 N	76.25 W
Severn Tunnel ◆[5]	42	51.35 N	2.44 W
Severnyj, S.S.S.R.	24	67.38 N	64.06 E
Severnyj, S.S.S.R.	265b	55.56 N	37.33 E
Severnyje uvaly ⋀[2]	24	59.30 N	49.00 E
Severnyj Kommunar	80	58.23 N	54.02 E
Severnyj Prijut	84	43.16 N	41.51 E
Severnyj Ural ⋀	24	63.00 N	59.00 E
Severo-Bajkal'skoje nagorje ⋀[1]	88	57.00 N	111.00 E
Severočeský Kraj □[4]	30	50.30 N	14.00 E
Severodoneck	83	48.58 N	38.27 E
Severodvinsk	24	64.34 N	39.50 E
Severo-Dvinskij kanal ≊	76	59.45 N	38.22 E
Severo-Jenisejskij	74	60.22 N	93.01 E
Severo-Kazachstanskaja Oblast' □[4]	86	54.30 N	69.00 E
Severo-Kuril'sk	74	50.40 N	156.08 E
Severomoravský Kraj □[4]	30	49.45 N	17.50 E
Severomorsk	24	69.05 N	33.24 E
Severo-Mujskij chrebet ⋀	88	56.30 N	114.00 E
Severo-Osetinskaja Avtonomnaja Sovetskaja Socialističeskaja Respublika □[3]	84	43.00 N	44.15 E
Severo-Sibirskaja nizmennost' ≚	74	73.00 N	100.00 E
Severoural'sk	86	60.09 N	59.57 E
Severo-Zadonsk	82	54.02 N	38.24 E
Severskaja	78	44.51 N	38.42 E
Severskij Donec ≃	72	47.35 N	40.54 E
Severskij Donec-Donbass, kanal ≊	83	48.55 N	37.45 E
Severucha	86	58.28 N	63.25 E
Severy	198	37.37 N	96.13 W
Seveso	62	45.39 N	9.09 E
Şeveso ≃	266b	45.30 N	9.12 E
Ševětin	61	49.06 N	14.35 E
Sevettijärvi	24	69.26 N	28.38 E
Sevier ≃	200	39.04 N	113.06 W
Sevier, East Fork ≃	200	38.14 N	112.12 W
Sevier Bridge Reservoir ⊜[1]	200	39.21 N	111.57 W
Sevier Desert ◆[2]	200	39.25 N	112.50 W
Sevier Lake ⊜	200	38.55 N	113.09 W
Sevierville	192	35.52 N	83.33 W
Sevilla, Col.	246	4.16 N	75.57 W
Sevilla, Esp.	34	37.23 N	5.59 W
Sevilla, Isla I	236	8.14 N	82.24 W
Seville → Sevilla, Esp.	34	37.23 N	5.59 W
Seville, Fl., U.S.	192	29.19 N	81.29 W
Seville, Oh., U.S.	214	41.00 N	81.51 W
Sevir	130	39.12 N	38.13 E
Şevketiye	130	40.05 N	27.51 E
Ševli ≃	89	54.08 N	133.04 E
Sevlievo	38	43.01 N	25.06 E
Sevran	50	48.56 N	2.32 E
Sevrej	102	43.35 N	102.12 E
Sèvres	50	48.49 N	2.12 E
Sévrier	58	45.52 N	6.08 E
Şevsk	78	52.09 N	34.30 E
Ševykan	88	54.20 N	106.49 E
Sewa ≃	150	7.18 N	12.08 W
Sewanee	194	35.04 N	85.55 W
Seward, Ak., U.S.	180	60.06 N	149.26 W
Seward, Ne., U.S.	198	40.54 N	97.05 W
Seward, N.Y., U.S.	210	42.43 N	74.37 W
Seward, Pa., U.S.	214	40.25 N	79.01 W
Seward Glacier ⊓	180	60.22 N	140.15 W
Seward Peninsula ≻[1]	180	65.00 N	164.00 W
Sewaren	276	40.33 N	74.15 W
Sewekow	54	53.15 N	12.39 E
Sewell, Chile	252	34.05 S	70.23 W
Sewell, N.J., U.S.	208	39.45 N	75.08 W
Sewen	58	47.48 N	6.54 E
Sewernaja-Semlja → Severnaja Zeml'a II	74	79.30 N	98.00 E
Seweweekspoort	158	33.22 S	21.25 E
Sewickley	214	40.32 N	80.11 W
Sewickley Creek ≃	279b	40.14 N	79.47 W
Sewickley Heights	279b	40.33 N	80.09 W
Sewickley Hills	279b	40.34 N	80.08 W
Sewri ◆[8]	272c	19.00 N	72.51 E
Sewu, Pegunungan ⋀	115a	8.05 S	110.35 E
Sexcello	152	3.58 S	11.38 E
Sexsmith	182	55.21 N	118.47 W
Sexten → Sesto	64	46.42 N	12.21 E
Sexton	218	39.42 N	85.27 W
Sexton Island I	276	40.39 N	73.14 W
Seya ◆[8], Nihon	268	35.29 N	139.29 E
Seya ◆[8], Nihon	268	35.27 N	139.30 E
Seybaplaya	232	19.39 N	90.40 W
Seybaplaya, Punta ≻	232	19.39 N	90.42 W
Seybothenreuth	60	49.54 N	11.43 E
Seybouse, Oued ≃	148	36.54 N	7.47 E
Seychellen → Seychelles □[1]	138	4.35 S	55.40 E
Seychelles □[1]	138	4.35 S	55.40 E
Seychelles Bank ✦[4]	12	4.45 S	55.30 E
Seyches	32	44.33 N	0.18 E
Seyda	54	51.53 N	12.53 E
Şeydābād	128	34.51 N	50.36 E
Seydim	130	40.33 N	34.45 E
Seydişehir	130	37.25 N	31.51 E
Seyðisfjörður	24a	65.16 N	14.00 W
Seyfe Gölü ⊜	130	39.13 N	34.23 E
Seyhan ≃	130	36.43 N	34.53 E
Seyhan Gölü ⊜[1]	130	37.05 N	35.13 E
Seyitgazi	130	39.27 N	30.43 E
Seylac	144	11.21 N	43.29 E
Seymour, Austl.	169	37.02 S	145.08 E
Seymour, Ciskei	158	32.33 S	26.46 E
Seymour, Ct., U.S.	207	41.23 N	73.04 W
Seymour, In., U.S.	218	38.57 N	85.53 W
Seymour, Ia., U.S.	190	40.40 N	93.07 W
Seymour, Mo., U.S.	194	37.08 N	92.46 W
Seymour, Tx., U.S.	196	33.35 N	99.15 W
Seymour, Wi., U.S.	190	44.30 N	88.19 W
Seymour ≃	182	51.05 N	126.50 W
Seymour Inlet ⊂	182	51.03 N	127.10 W
Seymour Johnson Air Force Base ■	192	35.21 N	77.58 W
Seymour Range ⋀	224	48.40 N	124.00 W
Seymourville	194	30.27 N	91.29 W
Seyne	62	44.21 N	6.21 E
Seynod	58	45.53 N	6.05 E
Seyring	264b	48.20 N	16.29 E
Seyringer Graben ≊	264b	48.18 N	16.33 E
Seyssel	58	45.57 N	5.49 E
Şeytan ≃	267b	41.06 N	28.59 E
Šežana	36	45.42 N	13.52 E
Sézanne	50	48.43 N	3.43 E
Şezela	158	30.24 S	30.42 E
Šežim	24	62.07 N	58.21 E
Sezimbra	34	38.26 N	9.06 W
Sezimovo Ústí	30	49.23 N	14.42 E
Sezze	66	41.30 N	13.03 E
Sfax	148	34.44 N	10.46 E
Sfax □[8]	148	34.50 N	10.20 E
Sferracavallo ◆[8]	70	38.12 N	13.17 E
Sfîntu-Gheorghe	38	45.52 N	25.47 E
Sfîntu Gheorghe, Brațul ≃[1]	38	44.53 N	29.36 E
Sfîntu Gheorghe, Ostrovul I	38	45.07 N	29.22 E
Sfizef	148	35.14 N	0.15 W
Sforzesco, Castello ⊥	266b	45.28 N	9.11 E
's-Gravendeel	52	51.46 N	4.37 E
's-Gravenhage (The Hague)	52	52.06 N	4.18 E
's-Gravenzande	52	52.00 N	4.10 E
Sgritheall, Beinn ʌ	46	57.08 N	5.35 W
Sgurgola	66	41.40 N	13.09 E
Sha ≃, Zhg.	98	37.31 N	117.50 E
Sha ≃, Zhg.	100	26.35 N	118.02 E
Sha ≃, Zhg.	100	33.39 N	114.38 E
Sha ≃, Zhg.	104	41.21 N	123.07 E
Sha'alav, Har ʌ	132	30.04 N	35.06 E
Sha'alvim	132	31.52 N	34.59 E
Shaanxi (Shensi) □[4]	102	35.00 N	109.00 E
Sha'ar HaGolan	132	32.41 N	35.36 E
Sha'ar Menashe	132	32.27 N	35.01 E
Shab'ā	132	33.21 N	35.45 E
Shaba □[4]	154	8.00 S	27.00 E
Shābah	142	31.11 N	30.46 E
Shabakunk Creek ≃	285	40.15 N	74.43 W
Shabās al-Milḥ	142	31.12 N	30.39 E
Shabās ash-Shuhadā'	142	31.05 N	30.45 E
Shabās 'Umayr	142	31.06 N	30.48 E
Shabbona	216	41.46 N	88.52 W
Shabeellaha Dhexe □[4]	144	3.00 N	46.00 E
Shabeellaha Hoose □[4]	144	1.30 N	44.15 E
Shabeelle (Shebele) ≃	144	0.12 S	42.45 E
Shabestar	128	38.11 N	45.42 E
Shabomeka Lake ⊜	212	44.54 N	77.09 W
Shabotik ≃	190	48.50 N	85.34 W
Shabqadar	123	34.13 N	71.34 E
Shabrāmant	142	29.56 N	31.12 E
Shabshīr al-Ḥiṣṣah	142	30.52 N	31.04 E
Shabunda	154	2.42 S	27.20 E
Shabwah	144	15.22 N	47.01 E
Shache (Yarkand)	120	38.25 N	77.16 E
Shacheng	105	40.25 N	115.31 E
Shacheng Gang ⊂	100	27.10 N	120.24 E
Shackan Indian Reserve ◆[4]	182	50.17 N	121.12 W
Shackleton Glacier ⊓	9	84.35 S	176.15 W
Shackleton Ice Shelf ⊓	9	66.00 S	100.00 E
Shackleton Range ⋀	9	80.40 S	26.00 W
Shaddādī	130	36.02 N	40.45 E
Shādegān	128	30.40 N	48.38 E
Shade Gap	214	40.11 N	77.52 W
Shadehill Reservoir ⊜[1]	198	45.45 N	102.15 W
Shade Mountain ʌ	208	40.34 N	77.30 W
Shades Glen	210	41.11 N	75.42 W
Shadi	100	26.08 N	114.49 E
Shadian	98	35.30 N	114.26 E
Shading	102	31.20 N	94.40 E
Shadow Lake ⊜, On., Can.	212	44.43 N	78.48 W
Shadow Lake ⊜, Ma., U.S.	283	42.50 N	71.14 W
Shadow Lake ⊜, N.J., U.S.	276	40.21 N	74.06 W
Shado-Wood Village	214	40.35 N	79.12 W
Shadrinsk → Šadrinsk	86	56.05 N	63.38 E
Shadui	102	31.30 N	100.10 E
Shady Cove	202	42.04 N	122.36 W
Shady Grove, Fl., U.S.	192	30.17 N	83.37 W
Shady Grove, Tx., U.S.	222	32.48 N	97.01 W
Shady Hills	216	40.36 N	85.41 W
Shady Shores	222	33.10 N	97.02 W
Shadyside	188	39.58 N	80.45 W
Sha'f	132	32.38 N	36.51 E
Shafer, Lake ⊜	216	40.47 N	86.46 W
Shafer Butte ʌ	202	43.47 N	116.05 W
Shafir	132	31.42 N	34.44 E
Shaft	128	37.12 N	49.24 E
Shafter	226	35.30 N	119.16 W
Shaftesbury	42	51.01 N	2.12 W
Shafton	279b	40.20 N	79.42 W
Shaftsburg	216	42.48 N	84.18 W
Shaftsbury	210	43.00 N	73.11 W
Shafu	100	22.25 N	113.01 E
Shag ≃	172	45.29 S	170.49 E
Shagamu	150	6.51 N	3.39 E
Shageluk	180	62.36 N	159.32 W
Shag Rocks II[1]	244	53.33 S	42.02 W
Shaguotun	104	41.10 N	120.38 E
Shāhābād, India	122	17.08 N	76.56 E
Shāhābād, India	123	30.10 N	76.53 E
Shāhābād, India	124	27.39 N	79.57 E
Shāhābād, India	272c	19.01 N	73.02 E
Shāhābād, Īrān	128	37.32 N	56.54 E
Shāhābād, Īrān	267d	35.49 N	51.29 E
Shāhābād □[5]	124	25.10 N	84.00 E
Shāhāda	120	21.28 N	74.18 E
Shah Alam	114	3.04 N	101.33 E
Shahba	132	32.51 N	36.37 E
Shāhbandar	120	24.10 N	67.54 E
Shāhbāz Kalāt	128	26.42 N	63.58 E
Shāhbāzpur ɯ	124	22.05 N	90.50 E
Shahdād, Namakzār-e ≚	128	30.30 N	58.30 E
Shāhdādkot	120	27.51 N	67.54 E
Shāhdādpur	120	25.56 N	68.37 E
Shāhdara, India	272a	28.30 N	77.25 E
Shāhdara, Pāk.	123	31.38 N	74.18 E
Shāhdara ◆[8]	272a	28.40 N	77.18 E
Shahdol	124	23.20 N	81.21 E
Shahdol □[5]	124	23.30 N	81.10 E
Shahe, Zhg.	98	36.56 N	114.30 E
Shahe, Zhg.	98	34.44 N	118.58 E
Shahe, Zhg.	98	37.01 N	119.43 E
Shahe, Zhg.	102	22.06 N	109.43 E
Shahedian	100	33.01 N	113.44 E
Shaheji	100	32.26 N	118.14 E
Shahepu	104	41.08 N	121.01 E
Shaheyi	98	39.53 N	118.31 E
Shaheying	104	40.50 N	120.46 E
Shahezhan	98	35.49 N	116.23 E
Shahezhen	105	40.08 N	116.15 E
Shahezi	89	46.05 N	129.20 E
Shāhganj	124	26.03 N	82.41 E
Shāhgarh, India	120	27.07 N	69.54 E
Shāhgarh, India	124	24.19 N	79.08 E
Shaḥḥāt	146	32.49 N	21.52 E
Shāhī Kowt	123	34.16 N	70.34 E
Shāh-i-Mashhad	128	35.03 N	63.58 E
Shāhjahānpur	124	27.53 N	79.55 E
Shāhjahānpur □[5]	124	28.00 N	79.55 E
Shāh Jūy	120	32.31 N	67.25 E
Shāh Kot	123	31.34 N	73.29 E
Shah Mosque ʊ[1]	267d	35.40 N	51.25 E
Shāhpur, India	122	16.42 N	76.50 E
Shāhpur, Pāk.	120	28.43 N	68.25 E
Shāhpur, Pāk.	123	32.17 N	72.26 E
Shāhpura, India	120	27.23 N	75.58 E
Shāhpura, India	120	25.38 N	74.56 E
Shāhpura, India	124	23.11 N	80.42 E
Shāhpur Chākar	120	26.09 N	68.39 E
Shahrak	120	34.06 N	64.18 E
Shahr-e Bābak	128	30.07 N	55.09 E
Shahr-e Monjān	120	36.02 N	70.46 E
Shahr-e Ṣafā	128	31.50 N	66.22 E
Shahrestān	120	34.22 N	66.47 E
Shahr Kord	128	32.19 N	50.50 E
Shāhrūd ≃	128	37.17 N	48.43 E
Shahu	100	30.11 N	113.39 E
Shāhzādpur	126	24.10 N	89.36 E
Shā'ib al-Banāt, Jabal ʌ	140	26.59 N	33.29 E
Shaighālu	120	31.11 N	68.49 E
Shaikhpura	124	25.09 N	85.51 E
Shaikou	100	27.19 N	117.35 E
Sha'īrah, Jabal ʌ[2]	132	30.06 N	34.17 E
Sha'īrah, Jabal ash- ⋀	132	29.31 N	34.29 E
Shājāpur	124	23.26 N	76.16 E
Shājāpur □[5]	124	23.45 N	76.15 E
Shajian	100	24.46 N	117.38 E
Shajianzi	98	41.01 N	125.26 E
Shajiazhuang	106	32.13 N	120.53 E
Shajing	100	23.36 N	114.06 E
Shajingzi	102	37.42 N	105.09 E
Shakaga-dake ʌ	96	33.11 N	130.53 E
Shakaga-hana ≻	96	34.25 N	134.14 E
Shakaga-take-tunnel ◆[5]	96	33.27 N	130.52 E
Shakardarra	123	33.14 N	71.30 E
Shakargarh	123	32.16 N	75.10 E
Shakarpura	272a	28.46 N	77.21 E
Shakarpur Khās ◆[8]	272a	28.38 N	77.17 E
Shakaskraal	158	29.26 S	31.14 E
Shakawe	156	18.23 S	21.50 E
Shakeng	98	42.13 N	116.35 E
Shaker Heights	214	41.28 N	81.32 W
Shaker Heights Park ♠	279a	41.29 N	81.33 W
Shakespeare	212	43.22 N	80.49 W
Shākhen	128	33.22 N	59.32 E
Shakhty → Šachty	83	47.42 N	40.13 E
Shaki	150	8.39 N	3.25 E
Shākir, Jazīrat I	140	27.30 N	33.59 E
Shakopee	190	44.47 N	93.31 W
Shakotan-hantō ≻[1]	92a	43.20 N	140.30 E
Shakou	100	24.25 N	113.32 E
Shakshūk	142	29.28 N	30.42 E
Shaktoolik	180	64.20 N	161.09 W
Shakujii ◆[8]	268	35.45 N	139.37 E
Shakūrpur ◆[8]	272a	28.41 N	77.09 E
Shala, Lake ⊜	144	7.25 N	38.30 E
Shalalth	182	50.44 N	122.13 W
Shalatayn, Bi'r ⊤[4]	140	23.08 N	35.36 E
Shaleitian Dao I	98	39.03 N	118.44 E
Shaler Mountains ⋀	176	72.35 N	110.45 W
Shaleshanto	156	19.09 S	23.58 E
Shalford	260	51.09 N	0.34 W
Shālimah	142	31.14 N	30.52 E
Shalimar Railroad Station ◆[5]	272b	22.33 N	88.19 E
Shaling, Zhg.	104	41.09 N	122.22 E
Shaling, Zhg.	104	41.20 N	123.01 E
Shalingpu	104	41.47 N	123.11 E
Shalingzi	105	40.42 N	114.55 E
Shaliuhe, Zhg.	102	36.28 N	98.57 E
Shaliuhe, Zhg.	105	39.53 N	117.56 E

Symbol	English	Deutsch	Español	Français	Português
≃	River	Fluss	Río	Rivière	Rio
≊	Canal	Kanal	Canal	Canal	Canal
⌊	Waterfall, Rapids	Wasserfall, Stromschnellen	Cascada, Rápidos	Chute d'eau, Rapides	Cascata, Rápidos
ɯ	Strait	Meeresstrasse	Estrecho	Détroit	Estreito
⊂	Bay, Gulf	Bucht, Golf	Bahía, Golfo	Baie, Golfe	Baía, Golfo
⊜	Lake, Lakes	See, Seen	Lago, Lagos	Lac, Lacs	Lago, Lagos
≡	Swamp	Sumpf	Pantano	Marais	Pântano
⊓	Ice Features, Glacier	Eis- und Gletscherformen	Accidentes Glaciales	Formes glaciaires	Acidentes glaciares
⊤	Other Hydrographic Features	Andere Hydrographische Objekte	Otros Elementos Hidrográficos	Autres données hydrographiques	Outros acidentes hidrográficos
✦	Submarine Features	Untermeerische Objekte	Accidentes Submarinos	Formes de relief sous-marin	Acidentes submarinos
□	Political Unit	Politische Einheit	Unidad Politica	Entité politique	Unidade política
ʊ	Cultural Institution	Kulturelle Institution	Institución Cultural	Institution culturelle	Institução cultural
⊥	Historical Site	Historische Stätte	Sitio Histórico	Site historique	Sitio histórico
♠	Recreational Site	Erholungs- und Ferienort	Sitio de Recreo	Centre de loisirs	Area de Lazer
⊠	Airport	Flughafen	Aeropuerto	Aéroport	Aeroporto
■	Military Installation	Militäranlage	Instalación Militar	Installation militaire	Instalação militar
◆	Miscellaneous	Verschiedenes	Misceláneo	Divers	Diversos

Symbols in the index entries represent the broad categories identified in the key at the right. Symbols with superior numbers (∧[1]) identify subcategories (see complete key on page I · 1).

Kartensymbole in dem Registerverzeichnis stellen die rechts in Schlüssel erklärten Kategorien dar. Symbole mit hochgestellten Ziffern (∧[1]) bezeichnen Unterabteilungen einer Kategorie (vgl. vollständiger Schlüssel auf Seite I · 1).

Los símbolos incluidos en el texto del índice representan las grandes categorías identificadas con la clave a la derecha. Los símbolos con numeros en su parte superior (∧[1]) identifican las subcategorías (véase la clave completa en la página I · 1).

Les symboles de l'index représentent les catégories indiquées dans la légende à droite. Les symboles suivis d'un indice (∧[1]) représentent des sous-catégories (voir légende complète à la page I · 1).

Os símbolos incluídos no texto do índice representam as grandes categorias identificadas com a chave à direita. Os símbolos com números em sua parte superior (∧[1]) identificam as subcategorias (veja-se a chave completa à página I · 1).

∧ Mountain	Berg	Montaña	Montagne	Montanha
∧ Mountains	Berge	Montañas	Montagnes	Montanhas
⌘ Pass	Pass	Paso	Col	Passo
∨ Valley, Canyon	Tal, Cañon	Valle, Cañón	Vallée, Canyon	Vale, Canhão
≡ Plain	Ebene	Llano	Plaine	Planície
≻ Cape	Kap	Cabo	Cap	Cabo
I Island	Insel	Isla	Île	Ilha
II Islands	Inseln	Islas	Îles	Ilhas
✦ Other Topographic Features	Andere Topographische Objekte	Otros Elementos Topográficos	Autres données topographiques	Outros acidentes topográficos

ESPAÑOL · FRANÇAIS · PORTUGUÊS

Nombre / Nom / Nome	Página / Page	Lat.°′	Long.°′ W = Oeste / W = Ouest
Shika	94	37.01 N	136.47 E
Shikami-yama ∧	270	34.47 N	135.10 E
Shikano	96	35.28 N	134.04 E
Shikārpur, India	122	14.16 N	75.21 E
Shikārpur, India	124	28.17 N	78.01 E
Shikārpur, Pāk.	120	27.57 N	68.38 E
Shikatsu	94	35.14 N	136.53 E
Shikengkong ∧	100	24.56 N	113.00 E
Shikewusumiao	102	40.13 N	108.52 E
Shiki	94	35.50 N	139.35 E
Shikishima	94	35.41 N	138.32 E
Shikohābād	124	27.06 N	78.36 E
Shikoku I	92	33.45 N	133.30 E
Shikoku-sanchi ⋀	96	33.47 N	133.30 E
Shikoma	268	35.11 N	139.56 E
Shikotsu-ko ⊜	92a	42.45 N	141.20 E
Shikotsu-Tōya-kokuritsu-kōen ♦	92a	42.47 N	141.00 E
Shikuang	106	31.54 N	121.24 E
Shil	272c	19.09 N	73.03 E
Shilabo	144	6.05 N	44.48 E
Shilbottle	44	55.23 N	1.42 W
Shildon	44	54.38 N	1.39 W
Shiliangji	100	33.54 N	115.14 E
Shilibao	105	39.55 N	116.29 E
Shilihe	104	41.31 N	123.22 E
Shiling	106	30.26 N	119.35 E
Shilipeng	106	31.14 N	119.35 E
Shilipu, Zhg.	105	40.15 N	117.58 E
Shilipu, Zhg.	105	39.29 N	116.18 E
Shilipu, Zhg.	105	39.11 N	115.59 E
Shiliuban	100	24.08 N	117.33 E
Shillelagh	48	52.45 N	6.32 W
Shillingstone	42	50.54 N	2.14 W
Shillington	208	40.18 N	75.57 W
Shillong	120	25.34 N	91.53 E
Shilo, Canadian Forces Base ■	184	49.49 N	99.38 W
Shiloh, Il., U.S.	219	38.34 N	89.54 W
Shiloh, N.J., U.S.	208	39.27 N	75.17 W
Shiloh, Oh., U.S.	214	40.58 N	82.36 W
Shiloh, Oh., U.S.	218	39.49 N	84.13 W
Shiloh, Oh., U.S.	218	39.49 N	84.13 W
Shiloh, Pa., U.S.	208	39.59 N	76.49 W
Shiloh ⊥	132	32.03 N	35.17 E
Shiloh National Military Park ♦	194	35.06 N	88.21 W
Shilong, Zhg.	100	23.07 N	113.48 E
Shilong, Zhg.	102	23.54 N	109.40 E
Shilong, Zhg.	107	30.15 N	106.34 E
Shilou	100	22.58 N	113.29 E
Shima, Nihon	92	34.13 N	136.51 E
Shima, Nihon	270	34.59 N	135.20 E
Shima, Zhg.	100	24.27 N	117.49 E
Shima, Zhg.	107	29.38 N	105.50 E
Shimabara	92	32.47 N	130.22 E
Shimachang, Zhg.	107	28.59 N	105.55 E
Shimachang, Zhg.	107	29.03 N	105.36 E
Shimada, Nihon	94	34.49 N	138.11 E
Shimada, Nihon	268	35.59 N	139.25 E
Shimagahara	94	34.46 N	136.03 E
Shima-hantō ›[1]	94	34.26 N	136.33 E
Shimamiao	106	32.08 N	119.20 E
Shimamoto	96	34.53 N	135.40 E
Shimane □[5]	96	35.00 N	132.30 E
Shimane-hantō ›[1]	96	35.30 N	133.00 E
Shimantan	100	33.17 N	113.28 E
Shimanto ≐	96	32.56 N	133.00 E
Shimata ≐	96	33.57 N	131.55 E
Shimber Berris ∧	144	10.44 N	47.15 E
Shimei	106	32.14 N	120.10 E
Shimen, Zhg.	98	39.44 N	118.52 E
Shimen, Zhg.	102	29.28 N	111.17 E
Shimen, Zhg.	105	40.06 N	117.42 E
Shimen, Zhg.	106	30.37 N	120.26 E
Shimen, Zhg.	107	29.36 N	106.27 E
Shimen, Zhg.	107	29.09 N	106.02 E
Shimencun, Zhg.	106	31.21 N	119.34 E
Shimencun, Zhg.	106	30.23 N	119.41 E
Shimendong	100	28.16 N	120.07 E
Shimengou	104	40.40 N	123.43 E
Shimenjie	100	29.34 N	116.44 E
Shimenlou	100	28.58 N	114.51 E
Shimenying	105	39.54 N	116.05 E
Shimenzi	89	48.30 N	121.31 E
Shimian	102	29.18 N	102.22 E
Shimiaozi	104	40.39 N	123.31 E
Shimizu	92	35.01 N	138.29 E
Shimizu → Tosa-shimizu	92	32.46 N	132.57 E
Shimizu, Nihon	92a	43.01 N	142.53 E
Shimizu, Nihon	94	36.02 N	136.09 E
Shimizu, Nihon	94	35.01 N	138.29 E
Shimizu, Nihon	96	34.05 N	135.26 E
Shimizu-tunnel ◆[5]	94	36.52 N	138.55 E
Shimminato	94	36.47 N	137.04 E
Shimobe	94	35.27 N	138.29 E
Shimoda	94	34.40 N	138.57 E
Shimodate	94	36.18 N	139.59 E
Shimofusa	94	35.52 N	140.21 E
Shimofusa-daichi ⋀[1]	268	35.45 N	139.58 E
Shimofusa-kōkūkichi, Kaijō-jieitai- ■	94	35.50 N	140.05 E
Shimofusa Naval Air Base ■	268	35.48 N	140.01 E
Shimoga	122	13.55 N	75.34 E
Shimogawara	268	35.56 N	139.21 E
Shimogōri	268	35.21 N	140.03 E
Shimogyō ◆[8]	270	34.59 N	135.45 E
Shimohōya	268	35.45 N	139.34 E
Shimoichi	96	34.22 N	135.47 E
Shimoigusa ◆[8]	268	35.43 N	139.37 E
Shimoji	175d	24.45 N	125.16 E
Shimoji-jima I	175d	24.49 N	125.09 E
Shimojō	94	35.24 N	137.47 E
Shimokawa	92a	44.18 N	142.39 E
Shimokita-hantō ›[1]	92	41.15 N	141.00 E
Shimomatsu	270	34.27 N	135.23 E
Shimomizo	268	35.31 N	139.23 E
Shimoni	154	4.39 S	39.23 E
Shimoniikura	268	35.47 N	139.38 E
Shimonita	94	36.13 N	138.47 E
Shimonoseki	96	33.57 N	130.57 E
Shimookudomi	268	35.53 N	139.26 E
Shimoryūzu-zaki ›	96	33.30 N	133.34 E
Shimosakamoto	270	35.03 N	135.53 E
Shimosuwa	94	36.04 N	138.05 E
Shimotajiri	270	34.57 N	135.28 E
Shimotomi	268	35.50 N	139.29 E
Shimotsu	96	34.10 N	135.08 E
Shimotsuchidana	268	35.24 N	139.27 E
Shimotsui	96	34.26 N	133.47 E
Shimotsuma	94	36.11 N	139.58 E
Shimotsuruma	268	35.29 N	139.28 E
Shimoya	268	35.23 N	139.21 E
Shimoyama	94	35.02 N	137.19 E
Shimoyugi	268	35.38 N	139.23 E
Shimura ◆[8]	268	35.46 N	139.41 E
Shin, Loch ⊜	46	58.06 N	4.34 W
Shinagawa ◆[8]	268	35.37 N	139.45 E
Shinan	102	22.43 N	109.54 E
Shinano	94	36.48 N	138.13 E
Shinano ≐	92	37.56 N	139.03 E
Shinarā	142	28.47 N	30.46 E
Shināṣ	128	24.46 N	56.28 E
Shināwari	123	33.32 N	70.48 E
Shinbārī	273c	30.07 N	31.09 E
Shīndand	128	33.18 N	62.08 E
Shindenbaru-kichi, Kōkū-jieitai- ■	92	32.04 N	131.30 E
Shindo	268	35.21 N	139.21 E
Shiner	222	29.25 N	97.10 W
Shingbwiyang	110	26.41 N	96.13 E
Shingishū → Sinŭiju	98	40.05 N	124.24 E
Shinglehouse	214	41.57 N	78.11 W
Shingle Springs	226	38.40 N	120.56 W
Shingo	96	34.59 N	133.23 E
Shingū, Nihon	92	33.44 N	135.59 E
Shingū, Nihon	96	34.55 N	134.33 E
Shingū, Nihon	96	33.56 N	133.38 E
Shingwidzi	156	23.05 S	31.25 E
Shingwidzi (Singuédeze) ≐	156	23.53 S	32.17 E
Shinichi	96	34.33 N	133.16 E
Shining Tor ∧	262	53.16 N	2.01 W
Shinīrah	132	32.22 N	36.45 E
Shinji	96	35.24 N	132.54 E
Shinji-ko ⊜	96	35.27 N	132.58 E
Shinjō, Nihon	92	38.46 N	140.18 E
Shinjō, Nihon	270	34.30 N	135.44 E
Shinjuku ◆[8]	268	35.41 N	139.42 E
Shinkawa	94	35.09 N	136.50 E
Shīnkay	120	31.57 N	67.26 E
Shinkolobwe	154	11.02 S	26.35 E
Shinmachi	94	36.16 N	139.07 E
Shinminato ≐	270	34.38 N	135.09 E
Shinnārah, Minqār ⊥[4]	142	28.52 N	30.38 E
Shīn Naray	120	31.19 N	66.43 E
Shinnayō	96	34.04 N	131.47 E
Shinnecock Bay c	207	40.52 N	72.28 W
Shinnel Water ≐	44	55.13 N	3.49 W
Shinness	46	58.05 N	4.28 W
Shinnston	188	39.23 N	80.18 W
Shino-jima I	94	34.39 N	137.00 E
Shinsai-bashi ◆[8]	270	34.40 N	135.31 E
Shinshār	130	34.36 N	36.44 E
Shinshiro	94	34.54 N	137.30 E
Shinshū-shinmachi	94	36.34 N	138.01 E
Shintone	94	35.50 N	140.20 E
Shinyanga	154	3.40 S	33.26 E
Shinyanga □[4]	154	3.45 S	33.00 E
Shin-yōdo ≐[1]	270	34.41 N	135.26 E
Shio	94	36.52 N	136.48 E
Shiobara	94	36.58 N	139.49 E
Shiocton	190	44.26 N	88.34 W
Shiogama	92	38.19 N	141.01 E
Shiojiri	94	36.06 N	137.58 E
Shiojiri-tōge)(	94	36.05 N	138.02 E
Shiomi-dake ∧	94	35.34 N	138.12 E
Shionoe	96	34.10 N	134.05 E
Shiono-misaki ›	92	33.26 N	135.45 E
Shioya	94	36.46 N	139.51 E
Shioya ◆[8]	270	34.38 N	135.06 E
Shioya-zaki ›, Nihon	92	33.26 N	135.45 E
Shioya-zaki ›, Nihon	94	36.59 N	140.59 E
Shiozawa	94	37.02 N	138.51 E
Shipai, Zhg.	100	23.08 N	113.21 E
Shipai, Zhg.	106	31.30 N	120.55 E
Shipanpu	107	30.28 N	104.23 E
Shipantuo	107	30.25 N	106.13 E
Ship Bottom	208	39.38 N	74.10 W
Shipbourne	260	51.15 N	0.17 E
Ship Cove	186	47.06 N	54.05 W
Shipdham	42	52.37 N	0.53 E
Shiping, Zhg.	102	28.20 N	107.42 E
Shiping, Zhg.	102	23.47 N	102.30 E
Ship Island I	194	30.13 N	88.55 W
Shipley	44	53.50 N	1.47 W
Shipman, Il., U.S.	219	39.07 N	90.03 W
Shipman, Va., U.S.	192	37.43 N	78.50 W
Shippan Point ›	276	41.01 N	73.32 W
Shippegan	186	47.45 N	64.42 W
Shippensburg	208	40.03 N	77.31 W
Shippenville	214	41.15 N	79.28 W
Shippingport	214	40.38 N	80.25 W
Shippō	94	35.10 N	136.48 E
Shiprock	200	36.47 N	108.41 W
Ship Rock ∧	200	36.42 N	108.50 W
Shipshaw ≐	186	48.27 N	71.12 W
Shipshewana	216	41.40 N	85.34 W
Shipston-on-Stour	42	52.04 N	1.37 W
Shipton-under-Wychwood	42	51.51 N	1.35 W
Shipu, Zhg.	100	29.13 N	121.55 E
Shipu, Zhg.	106	31.15 N	121.03 E
Shiqi → Zhongshan	100	22.31 N	113.22 E
Shiqian	102	27.31 N	108.20 E
Shiqiao, Zhg.	100	33.12 N	112.36 E
Shiqiao, Zhg.	100	26.58 N	114.23 E
Shiqiao, Zhg.	106	30.30 N	119.11 E
Shiqiao, Zhg.	107	30.25 N	104.31 E
Shiqiaopu	107	30.05 N	105.23 E
Shiqiaozi	104	41.27 N	123.43 E
Shiqma ≐	132	31.36 N	34.30 E
Shiquan, Zhg.	102	33.03 N	108.17 E
Shiquan, Zhg.	106	30.30 N	120.48 E
Shirahama, Nihon	94	34.54 N	139.54 E
Shirahama, Nihon	96	33.40 N	135.20 E
Shirahata-yama ∧	96	34.54 N	134.23 E
Shiraitono-taki ⌊	94	35.18 N	138.38 E
Shirakami-misaki ›	92a	41.24 N	140.12 E
Shirakawa, Nihon	94	37.07 N	140.13 E
Shirakawa, Nihon	94	35.35 N	137.12 E
Shirakawa, Nihon	94	36.16 N	136.54 E
Shirakawa-no-seki-ato ⊥	94	37.03 N	140.15 E
Shirakawa-tōge ∧[2]	270	34.42 N	135.07 E
Shirako	94	35.26 N	140.23 E
Shirākol	126	22.18 N	88.16 E
Shirakura-yama ∧	94	35.00 N	137.46 E
Shirama-yama ∧	96	34.01 N	135.23 E
Shiramine	94	36.10 N	136.37 E
Shirane	94	35.38 N	138.28 E
Shirane-san ∧, Nihon	94	36.38 N	138.32 E
Shirane-san ∧, Nihon	94	36.48 N	139.22 E
Shirane-san (Kita-dake) ∧, Nihon	94	35.40 N	138.15 E
Shiranuka	92a	42.57 N	144.05 E
Shiraoi	92a	42.33 N	141.21 E
Shiraoka	94	36.01 N	139.40 E
Shiraone	272c	19.03 N	73.01 E
Shirasawa	94	36.40 N	139.08 E
Shirase Glacier ⊓	9	70.10 S	38.35 E
Shirati	154	1.08 S	33.59 E
Shīrāz	128	29.36 N	52.32 E
Shirbīn	142	31.11 N	31.32 E
Shirdley Hill	262	53.36 N	2.58 W
Shire (Chire) ≐	154	17.42 S	35.19 E
Shirebrook	44	53.12 N	1.13 W
Shiremanstown	208	40.13 N	76.57 W
Shiretoko-hantō ›[1]	92a	44.00 N	145.00 E
Shiretoko-kokuritsu-kōen ♦	92a	44.08 N	145.10 E
Shiretoko-misaki ›	92a	44.14 N	145.17 E
Shīrīn ≐	120	36.49 N	65.01 E
Shīr Kūh ∧	128	31.37 N	54.04 E
Shirland	216	42.27 N	89.12 W
Shirley, B.C., Can.	224	48.23 N	123.54 W
Shirley, Il., U.S.	216	40.24 N	89.04 W
Shirley, In., U.S.	218	39.53 N	85.34 W
Shirley, Ma., U.S.	207	42.32 N	71.39 W
Shirley Plantation ⊥	208	37.21 N	77.15 W
Shirleysburg	214	40.18 N	77.53 W
Shīr Manṣūr, Jabal ⋀	132	33.41 N	36.02 E
Shiro	222	30.37 N	95.53 W
Shiroi	94	35.48 N	140.04 E
Shiroishi	92	38.00 N	140.37 E
Shirokawa	96	33.23 N	132.46 E
Shirone	92	37.46 N	139.01 E
Shirotori, Nihon	94	35.53 N	136.52 E
Shirotori, Nihon	96	34.15 N	134.20 E
Shirouma-dake ∧	94	36.45 N	137.46 E
Shiroyama	94	35.35 N	139.19 E
Shiro-yama ∧	270	34.38 N	135.53 E
Shirpur	120	21.21 N	74.53 E
Shirrell Heath	42	50.55 N	1.12 W
Shirshābah	142	30.47 N	31.10 E
Shīrvān	128	37.24 N	57.55 E
Shisaka-jima I	96	34.07 N	133.11 E
Shisanling	105	40.19 N	116.16 E
Shi San Ling (Ming Tombs) ⊥	105	40.19 N	116.13 E
Shisanzhan	89	51.21 N	125.43 E
Shisha Hai ⊜	271a	39.57 N	116.22 E
Shishaldin Volcano ∧[1]	180	54.45 N	163.57 W
Shishan	104	41.16 N	121.30 E
Shishi	100	24.48 N	118.38 E
Shishikui	96	33.34 N	134.18 E
Shishi Shan ∧	100	24.44 N	117.54 E
Shishmaref	180	66.14 N	166.09 W
Shishmaref Inlet c	180	66.07 N	165.50 W
Shishou	102	29.43 N	112.19 E
Shisht al-An'ām	142	30.52 N	30.44 E
Shisiazhan	89	51.36 N	125.42 E
Shisixian	104	40.53 N	122.59 E
Shisler Point ›	284a	42.52 N	79.08 W
Shisui	94	35.43 N	140.16 E
Shitai	100	30.13 N	117.27 E
Shitan, Zhg.	100	27.44 N	112.42 E
Shitan, Zhg.	100	23.10 N	113.47 E
Shitang, Zhg.	100	28.16 N	121.36 E
Shitang, Zhg.	102	25.38 N	110.50 E
Shitangwan	106	31.40 N	120.13 E
Shitara	94	35.05 N	137.35 E
Shithāthah	128	32.33 N	43.29 E
Shiting, Zhg.	100	27.36 N	113.16 E
Shiting, Zhg.	105	39.31 N	115.41 E
Shitoufangzi	89	48.38 N	126.08 E
Shitougouzi	89	49.19 N	125.55 E
Shitoumiao	102	41.41 N	106.50 E
Shitoumiaozi	104	41.38 N	121.26 E
Shitoushan	105	40.27 N	116.13 E
Shitoushuangmiao	98	41.28 N	118.55 E
Shituan	107	30.09 N	105.01 E
Shitunwei	104	41.07 N	121.31 E
Shiva, Horvot (Subeita) ⊥	132	30.53 N	34.38 E
Shively	218	38.12 N	85.49 W
Shivering, Mount ∧	170	34.08 S	150.02 E
Shivpuri	124	25.26 N	77.39 E
Shivpuri □[5]	124	25.20 N	77.40 E
Shivwits Plateau ⋀[1]	200	36.15 N	113.40 W
Shiwaku-shotō II	96	34.20 N	133.45 E
Shiwan, Zhg.	100	27.17 N	112.57 E
Shiwan, Zhg.	100	28.12 N	113.49 E
Shiwan, Zhg.	100	23.01 N	113.04 E
Shiwan, Zhg.	102	37.35 N	109.01 E
Shiwenchang	104	41.43 N	123.54 E
Shiwu	89	43.48 N	124.13 E
Shixi, Zhg.	100	28.16 N	117.45 E
Shixi, Zhg.	100	28.16 N	115.36 E
Shixia	105	40.20 N	114.59 E
Shixian	89	43.05 N	129.47 E
Shixiancun	106	31.12 N	120.29 E
Shixiechang	107	29.51 N	106.41 E
Shixing	100	24.58 N	114.03 E
Shixun	100	24.44 N	118.11 E
Shiyachang	107	30.27 N	106.31 E
Shiyan, Zhg.	102	32.38 N	110.44 E
Shiyan, Zhg.	107	30.22 N	104.27 E
Shiyangchang, Zhg.	107	29.56 N	105.37 E
Shiyangchang, Zhg.	107	30.42 N	105.57 E
Shiyanqiao	107	29.19 N	105.22 E
Shiyiwei	106	31.59 N	120.43 E
Shiyizhan	89	51.13 N	125.52 E
Shiyu	107	29.46 N	106.06 E
Shizhangzi	98	40.24 N	119.48 E
Shizheng	100	24.32 N	115.50 E
Shizhenjie	100	28.51 N	116.56 E
Shizhong, Zhg.	100	24.57 N	117.06 E
Shizhong, Zhg.	106	30.44 N	120.16 E
Shizhongtan	107	30.26 N	104.35 E
Shizhu, Zhg.	100	28.48 N	120.06 E
Shizhu, Zhg.	102	29.56 N	108.09 E
Shizhuang	106	32.08 N	120.31 E
Shizhuangzi, Zhg.	104	42.24 N	122.53 E
Shizhuangzi, Zhg.	105	40.38 N	116.59 E
Shizhuzi	104	41.18 N	121.35 E
Shizichang	107	29.32 N	106.14 E
Shizigu	105	39.23 N	118.08 E
Shizikou	100	24.12 N	113.38 E
Shizilin	106	31.26 N	121.25 E
Shizipo	105	40.21 N	115.07 E
Shizipu	106	30.59 N	119.07 E
Shizuchi-kokutei-kōen ♦	96	33.45 N	133.08 E
Shizugawa	92	38.40 N	141.27 E
Shizui, Zhg.	89	43.08 N	126.06 E
Shizui, Zhg.	98	38.52 N	113.42 E
Shizuma ≐	96	35.12 N	132.28 E
Shizunai	92a	42.20 N	142.22 E
Shizuoka	94	34.58 N	138.23 E
Shizuoka □[5]	94	35.00 N	138.00 E
Shkodër	38	42.05 N	19.30 E
Shkumbin ≐	38	41.01 N	19.26 E
Shō ≐	94	36.47 N	137.04 E
Shoal ≐	194	30.41 N	86.39 W
Shoal Cape ›	162	33.53 S	121.07 E
Shoal Creek ≐, U.S.	194	34.50 N	87.33 W
Shoal Creek ≐, U.S.	194	37.05 N	94.42 W
Shoal Creek ≐, U.S.	194	40.28 N	92.42 W
Shoal Creek ≐, Il., U.S.	219	38.28 N	89.35 W
Shoal Creek ≐, Mo., U.S.	194	39.44 N	93.32 W
Shoal Creek, East Fork ≐	219	38.51 N	89.30 W
Shoal Creek, Middle Fork ≐	219	39.05 N	89.33 W
Shoal Creek, West Fork ≐	219	39.05 N	89.33 W
Shoal Harbour	186	48.11 N	53.59 W
Shoalhaven ≐	170	34.52 S	150.44 E
Shoalhaven Bight c[3]	170	34.52 S	150.47 E
Shoal Lake	184	50.26 N	100.34 W
Shoal Lake ⊜	184	49.32 N	95.00 W
Shoal Point ›	276	41.08 N	73.15 W
Shoals	194	38.39 N	86.47 W
Shoals, Bay of c	168b	35.37 S	137.37 E
Shoalwater Bay c	166	22.02 S	150.25 E
Shōbara	96	34.51 N	133.01 E
Shōboku	96	35.06 N	134.07 E
Shobonier	219	38.52 N	89.05 W
Shōbu	94	36.04 N	139.36 E
Shōdai	270	34.51 N	135.42 E
Shōdo-shima I	96	34.30 N	134.17 E
Shoeburyness	42	51.32 N	0.48 E
Shoe Cove	186	49.55 N	55.33 W
Shoemakersville	208	40.30 N	75.58 W
Shōgawa	94	36.34 N	136.59 E
Shogunle	273a	6.35 N	3.21 E
Shohola	210	41.28 N	74.55 W
Shohola Creek ≐	210	41.28 N	74.55 W
Shokambetsu-dake ∧	92a	43.43 N	141.31 E
Shokan	210	41.58 N	74.13 W
Shōkawa	94	36.02 N	136.57 E
Sholāpur	122	17.41 N	75.55 E
Sholinghur	122	13.07 N	79.25 E
Shomera	132	33.05 N	35.17 E
Shomolu	273a	6.32 N	3.23 E
Shōmyō-no-taki ⌊	94	36.35 N	137.24 E
Shona, Eilean I	46	56.47 N	5.52 W
Shōnai	96	33.11 N	131.26 E
Shōnai ≐	94	35.04 N	136.50 E
Shōnan	268	35.50 N	140.02 E
Shongum	276	40.50 N	74.33 W
Shongum Lake ⊜	276	40.51 N	74.32 W
Shongwe	158	27.24 S	32.25 E
Shōō	96	35.02 N	134.08 E
Shooters Hill	170	33.54 S	149.52 E
Shooters Island I	276	40.39 N	74.10 W
Shopiere	216	42.34 N	88.57 W
Shoranūr	122	10.46 N	76.17 E
Shorāpur	122	16.31 N	76.45 E
Shoreacres, B.C., Can.	182	49.26 N	117.32 W
Shore Acres, Ca., U.S.	226	38.02 N	121.58 W
Shore Acres, Ma., U.S.	207	42.12 N	70.44 W
Shore Acres, N.J., U.S.	208	40.01 N	74.06 W
Shoreacres, Tx., U.S.	222	29.37 N	95.01 W
Shoreditch ◆[8]	260	51.32 N	0.05 W
Shoreham, Eng., U.K.	260	51.20 N	0.11 E
Shoreham, Mi., U.S.	216	42.03 N	86.30 W
Shoreham-by-Sea	42	50.49 N	0.16 W
Shorewood, Il., U.S.	216	41.32 N	88.12 W
Shorewood, Wi., U.S.	216	43.05 N	87.53 W
Shorewood Hills	216	43.04 N	89.26 W
Shorkot	123	30.50 N	72.04 E
Shorkot Road	123	30.47 N	72.15 E
Shorne	260	51.25 N	0.26 E
Short Acres	226	36.21 N	119.38 W
Short Beach	207	41.15 N	72.50 W
Short Creek	214	40.11 N	80.55 W
Shortland Islands II	175e	6.55 S	155.53 E
Short Mountain ∧	192	36.23 N	83.10 W
Shortsville	210	42.57 N	77.13 W
Shoshone	202	42.56 N	114.24 W
Shoshone ≐	202	44.52 N	108.11 W
Shoshone, North Fork ≐	202	44.29 N	109.18 W
Shoshone, South Fork ≐	202	44.27 N	109.14 W
Shoshone Basin ⊻[1]	202	43.05 N	108.05 W
Shoshone Lake ⊜	202	44.22 N	110.43 W
Shoshone Mountains ⋀	204	39.00 N	117.30 W
Shoshone Peak ∧	204	36.56 N	116.16 W
Shoshone Range ⋀	204	40.20 N	116.50 W
Shoshong	156	22.59 S	26.30 E
Shoshoni	200	43.14 N	108.06 W
Shostka → Šostka	78	51.52 N	33.30 E
Shotley Gate	42	51.58 N	1.15 E
Shotton	262	53.12 N	3.02 W
Shotton Colliery	44	54.44 N	1.20 W
Shotts	46	55.49 N	3.48 W
Shotwick	262	53.14 N	2.59 W
Shou'anzhen	107	30.16 N	103.37 E
Shouchang	100	29.22 N	119.13 E
Shoufeng	100	23.52 N	121.30 E
Shouguang	98	36.53 N	118.42 E
Shouning	100	27.27 N	119.30 E
Shournagh ≐	48	51.53 N	8.35 W
Shoushan	104	41.12 N	123.03 E
Shouwangfen	105	40.35 N	117.48 E
Shouxian	100	32.35 N	116.47 E
Shouyang	102	37.59 N	113.09 E
Shōwa, Nihon	94	36.37 N	139.04 E
Shōwa, Nihon	96	34.43 N	133.39 E
Showell	208	38.23 N	75.12 W
Show Low	200	34.15 N	110.01 W
Shqipëri → Albania □[1]	38	41.00 N	20.00 E
Shreve	214	40.40 N	82.01 W
Shreveport	194	32.30 N	93.44 W
Shrevewood	284c	38.53 N	77.13 W
Shrewsbury, Eng., U.K.	42	52.43 N	2.45 W
Shrewsbury, Ma., U.S.	207	42.17 N	71.42 W
Shrewsbury, N.J., U.S.	208	40.19 N	74.03 W
Shrewsbury, Pa., U.S.	208	39.46 N	76.40 W
Shrewsbury River c	276	40.21 N	74.00 W
Shrewton	42	51.12 N	1.55 W
Shri Lakshmi Narayan Temple ♮[1]	272a	28.38 N	77.12 E
Shriner Mountain ∧	210	40.56 N	77.20 W
Shrivenham	42	51.36 N	1.39 W
Shropshire □[6]	42	52.40 N	2.40 W
Shropshire Union Canal ≅	262	53.17 N	2.53 W
Shrub Oak	210	41.20 N	73.49 W
Shrule	48	53.30 N	9.08 W
Shu ≐	98	34.07 N	118.30 E
Shuajingsi	102	32.00 N	103.05 E
Shuanfeng Shan ∧	107	29.26 N	105.47 E
Shuang ≐	269d	25.00 N	121.31 E
Shuangbai	102	24.54 N	101.32 E
Shuangcheng	89	45.21 N	126.17 E
Shuangchengzi	105	40.11 N	118.03 E
Shuangdian	100	32.23 N	120.51 E
Shuangdun	106	32.13 N	121.08 E
Shuangfeng, Zhg.	102	27.24 N	112.05 E
Shuangfeng, Zhg.	106	31.31 N	121.01 E
Shuangfeng, Zhg.	106	31.31 N	121.02 E
Shuangfeng Shan ∧	100	24.28 N	114.43 E
Shuangfengyi	107	29.27 N	105.09 E
Shuangfu	105	39.48 N	117.44 E
Shuangfuchang, Zhg.	107	29.41 N	103.31 E
Shuangfuchang, Zhg.	107	30.08 N	103.32 E
Shuanggang, Zhg.	89	45.07 N	122.59 E
Shuanggang, Zhg.	100	28.11 N	117.30 E
Shuanggetun	89	48.58 N	129.57 E
Shuanggou, Zhg.	98	34.03 N	117.37 E
Shuanggou, Zhg.	100	32.12 N	112.21 E
Shuanggou, Zhg.	100	33.16 N	118.10 E
Shuanggufen	107	29.38 N	104.11 E
Shuanghe, Zhg.	100	31.33 N	116.46 E
Shuanghe, Zhg.	100	31.41 N	112.46 E
Shuanghe, Zhg.	107	29.40 N	104.48 E
Shuanghe, Zhg.	107	30.07 N	105.10 E
Shuanghe, Zhg.	107	30.15 N	104.44 E
Shuanghechang, Zhg.	107	28.51 N	104.51 E
Shuanghechang, Zhg.	107	29.25 N	106.17 E
Shuanghechang, Zhg.	107	29.12 N	105.43 E
Shuanghechang, Zhg.	107	29.18 N	105.36 E
Shuang-hsi	269d	25.01 N	121.39 E
Shuangji ≐	100	34.05 N	114.24 E
Shuangjiang, Zhg.	100	26.48 N	116.28 E
Shuangjiang, Zhg.	102	23.37 N	99.41 E
Shuangjiang, Zhg.	107	30.13 N	105.45 E
Shuangjiangqiao	102	25.19 N	98.51 E
Shuangjianji	100	33.12 N	116.40 E
Shuangjingzi	104	42.28 N	123.42 E
Shuangkou	105	39.15 N	117.02 E
Shuangliao	89	43.31 N	123.30 E
Shuanglin	106	30.47 N	120.19 E
Shuanglingzi, Zhg.	104	40.54 N	124.10 E
Shuanglingzi, Zhg.	104	40.50 N	123.06 E
Shuangliu	107	30.34 N	103.55 E
Shuangliushu	100	31.56 N	115.12 E
Shuanglongtai	104	40.56 N	122.39 E
Shuangmiao, Zhg.	100	28.24 N	120.45 E
Shuangmiao, Zhg.	100	32.09 N	116.52 E
Shuangmiaozi, Zhg.	104	42.25 N	122.17 E
Shuangmiaozi, Zhg.	104	42.02 N	121.52 E
Shuangpai	110	25.57 N	111.32 E
Shuangpaishi	106	31.24 N	118.59 E
Shuangqiao, Zhg.	100	32.29 N	116.41 E
Shuangqiao, Zhg.	105	39.54 N	116.37 E
Shuangqiao, Zhg.	106	30.59 N	118.47 E
Shuangshanzi	98	40.21 N	119.08 E
Shuangshipu	107	29.14 N	104.42 E
Shuangshiqiao, Zhg.	107	29.22 N	105.51 E
Shuangshiqiao, Zhg.	107	29.23 N	104.29 E
Shuangshu	105	39.34 N	117.01 E
Shuangshutai	89	43.50 N	121.15 E
Shuangtaizi, Zhg.	104	41.34 N	121.12 E
Shuangtaizi, Zhg.	104	42.21 N	124.10 E
Shuangtaizi, Zhg.	104	42.25 N	123.11 E
Shuangtaizi, Zhg.	104	41.00 N	122.34 E
Shuangtaizi, Zhg.	104	41.11 N	121.14 E
Shuangtaizi ≐	104	40.59 N	121.51 E
Shuangtaizihe Kou ≐[1]	104	40.55 N	121.50 E
Shuangtang, Zhg.	100	28.01 N	116.44 E
Shuangtang, Zhg.	105	39.03 N	116.17 E
Shuangtang, Zhg.	105	38.53 N	116.54 E
Shuangtangdian	106	30.59 N	118.51 E
Shuangtuo	105	39.14 N	117.20 E
Shuangtuozhen	105	39.29 N	118.23 E
Shuangxi, Zhg.	100	27.01 N	119.03 E
Shuangxi, Zhg.	106	30.24 N	119.50 E
Shuangyang	89	43.32 N	125.42 E
Shuangyangdian	104	41.07 N	121.16 E
Shuangyaocun	105	38.55 N	117.03 E
Shuangyashan	89	46.37 N	131.22 E
Shu'ayb, Wādī ᐯ	132	31.54 N	35.38 E
Shu'ayt, Wādī ᐯ	144	17.30 N	52.00 E
Shubenacadie ≐	186	45.20 N	63.30 W
Shublik Mountains ⋀	180	69.31 N	145.40 W
Shubrā al-Khaymah	142	30.06 N	31.15 E
Shubrā Bābil	142	30.54 N	31.11 E
Shubrā Khalfūn	142	30.29 N	31.05 E
Shubrā Khīt	142	31.02 N	30.43 E
Shubuta	194	31.51 N	88.41 W
Shucheng	100	31.27 N	116.57 E
Shueib Dam ◆[6]	132	31.54 N	35.39 E
Shufu	85	39.27 N	75.52 E
Shufuka Shan ∧	89	50.28 N	123.10 E
Shugudali	89	52.47 N	124.02 E
Shuheyingzi	104	42.18 N	122.16 E
Shuhezhen	106	31.35 N	121.35 E
Shūhō	96	34.13 N	131.18 E
Shuhong	100	28.39 N	120.09 E
Shuibatang	102	28.39 N	107.03 E
Shuibei, Zhg.	100	28.04 N	115.01 E
Shuibei, Zhg.	106	31.40 N	119.39 E
Shuichaoyang	100	26.22 N	117.57 E
Shuicheng	102	26.41 N	104.50 E
Shuidao	98	37.10 N	121.33 E
Shuidiangou	89	47.43 N	122.40 E
Shuidong, Zhg.	106	31.23 N	119.37 E
Shuidong, Zhg.	106	30.47 N	118.57 E
Shuidongjie	106	31.07 N	119.33 E
Shuiduixia	106	30.17 N	118.50 E
Shuihai	100	33.02 N	120.26 E
Shuihouling	100	30.43 N	116.26 E
Shuiji	100	27.26 N	118.20 E
Shuijiahuangdi	104	42.14 N	123.28 E
Shuijian	105	40.09 N	115.58 E
Shuijing	102	26.10 N	99.09 E
Shuijingtang	102	28.50 N	108.11 E
Shuikou, Zhg.	100	26.59 N	117.41 E
Shuikou, Zhg.	100	26.22 N	118.44 E
Shuikou, Zhg.	100	24.00 N	115.55 E
Shuikou, Zhg.	100	26.18 N	113.46 E
Shuikou, Zhg.	102	25.54 N	109.06 E
Shuikou, Zhg.	107	29.29 N	103.42 E
Shuikouchang	107	29.33 N	103.40 E
Shuikouguan	102	22.30 N	106.34 E
Shuikoushan	102	26.30 N	112.30 E
Shuikouxu	100	25.09 N	114.28 E
Shuiliandong	98	42.12 N	125.09 E
Shuimenzi	98	39.36 N	122.19 E
Shuimingqiao	106	31.03 N	119.09 E
Shuimoqipan	85	39.51 N	76.42 E
Shuiquan'gou	104	41.58 N	121.50 E
Shuiquanzi, Zhg.	104	42.15 N	121.32 E
Shuiquanzi, Zhg.	104	40.53 N	121.05 E
Shuitangzi	102	29.18 N	101.10 E
Shuiting	100	29.10 N	119.14 E
Shuitou, Zhg.	100	24.43 N	118.25 E
Shuitou, Zhg.	100	23.53 N	113.37 E
Shuitou, Zhg.	100	27.38 N	120.16 E
Shuitouwei	100	26.06 N	115.28 E
Shuituzhen	107	29.47 N	106.31 E
Shuiyang	106	31.14 N	118.47 E
Shuiyang ≐	106	31.14 N	118.48 E
Shuiye	98	36.08 N	114.07 E
Shuizhai	98	36.54 N	117.24 E
Shuizhuyang	100	26.59 N	119.13 E
Shujāābād	123	29.53 N	71.18 E
Shujālpur	124	23.24 N	76.43 E
Shujiawazi	104	42.20 N	121.57 E
Shuksan, Mount ∧	224	48.50 N	121.36 W
Shulan	89	44.27 N	126.57 E
Shulaps Peak ∧	182	50.57 N	122.31 W
Shule	85	39.23 N	76.06 E
Shule ≐	102	40.50 N	94.10 E
Shullsburg	190	42.34 N	90.13 W
Shulu (Xinji)	98	37.54 N	115.13 E
Shumagin Islands II	180	55.07 N	159.45 W
Shumatuscacant ≐	283	42.03 N	70.51 W
Shumen → Šumen	38	43.16 N	26.55 E
Shūnah, Wādī ash- ᐯ	142	29.38 N	32.13 E
Shun'an	100	30.57 N	117.57 E
Shūnat Nimrīn	132	31.54 N	35.37 E
Shunayn, Sabkhat ⊜	146	30.30 N	21.00 E
Shunchang	100	26.50 N	117.48 E
Shunde	100	22.50 N	113.14 E
Shundian	100	34.15 N	113.20 E
Shundianqiao	106	31.24 N	120.41 E
Shunge	102	37.25 N	95.27 E
Shungnak	180	66.53 N	157.02 W
Shunhechang	107	29.57 N	104.42 E
Shunlongchang	107	30.04 N	103.27 E
Shunshanpu	104	42.08 N	122.21 E
Shuntianhu	100	24.08 N	114.48 E
Shunyi	105	40.08 N	116.38 E
Shuoduzong	102	30.48 N	95.47 E
Shuojiaji	100	33.42 N	119.44 E
Shuping	107	29.19 N	104.43 E
Shupīyan	123	33.43 N	74.50 E
Shuqayyiqah, Nafūd ⊥[8]	128	25.45 N	43.55 E
Shuqualak	194	32.58 N	88.34 W
Shūr ≐, Īrān	128	30.57 N	57.42 E
Shūr ≐, Īrān	128	34.38 N	51.46 E
Shūrāb, Īrān	128	33.43 N	56.29 E
Shūrāb, Īrān	128	28.09 N	60.18 E
Shūrāb ≐	128	32.40 N	54.50 E
Shuraytah, Ra's ›	128	26.24 N	56.22 E
Shurhabil Ben Hasna Dam ◆[6]	132	32.32 N	35.36 E
Shuri	174m	26.13 N	127.43 E
Shurkhua	110	22.15 N	93.38 E
Shurugwi	154	19.40 S	30.00 E
Shūsf	128	31.48 N	60.01 E
Shūsh	128	32.11 N	48.15 E
Shushan	210	43.05 N	73.21 W
Shushan Hu ⊜	98	35.36 N	116.27 E
Shūshtar	128	32.03 N	48.51 E
Shuswap ≐	182	50.50 N	119.00 W
Shuswap Lake ⊜	182	50.57 N	119.15 W
Shuṭab	142	27.08 N	31.14 E
Shutendōji-yama ∧	96	33.06 N	130.54 E
Shuteye Peak ∧	226	37.21 N	119.25 W
Shutlingsloe ∧	262	53.13 N	2.02 W
Shūtō	96	34.05 N	132.05 E
Shuwak	140	14.23 N	35.52 E
Shuwaykah	132	32.20 N	35.02 E
Shuwaysh, Rujm ash- ∧	132	32.30 N	36.27 E
Shuya	174m	26.40 N	128.06 E
Shuya → Šuja	24	61.55 N	34.12 E
Shuyak Island I	180	58.35 N	152.30 W
Shuyang	98	34.08 N	118.47 E
Shuyūkh al-Fawqanī	130	36.46 N	38.03 E
Shuzenji	94	34.58 N	138.56 E
Shwangliao → Liaoyuan	89	42.54 N	125.07 E
Shwebo	110	22.34 N	95.42 E
Shwegun	110	17.09 N	97.39 E
Shwegyin	110	17.55 N	96.53 E
Shweli (Longchuan) ≐	102	23.56 N	96.17 E
Shwenyaung	110	20.46 N	96.57 E
Shyamdih	126	23.47 N	86.56 E
Shyok	120	34.11 N	78.08 E
Shyok ≐	120	35.13 N	75.53 E
Si ≐	98	35.11 N	116.42 E
Sia	164	6.49 S	134.19 E
Siabu	114	1.01 N	99.29 E
Siachen Glacier ⊓	123	35.30 N	77.00 E
Siagne ≐	62	43.32 N	6.57 E
Siāhān Range ⋀	120	27.25 N	64.30 E
Siak ≐	114	1.13 N	102.09 E
Siak-kecil ≐	114	1.16 N	102.08 E
Siaksriinderapura	114	0.46 N	102.04 E
Sialang	114	1.31 N	99.27 E
Sialejevskaja P'atina	80	53.49 N	44.32 E
Siālghuni	126	22.33 N	90.27 E
Siālkot	123	32.30 N	74.31 E
Sialsūk	120	23.24 N	92.45 E
Siam → Thailand □[1]	110	15.00 N	100.00 E
Siam, Gulf of → Thailand, Gulf of c	110	10.00 N	101.00 E
Siamanna	71	39.55 N	8.46 E
Sian → Xi'an, Zhg.	102	34.15 N	108.52 E
Si'an, Zhg.	106	30.54 N	119.39 E
Siangtan → Xiangtan	100	27.51 N	112.54 E
Sianhala	150	10.03 N	6.51 W
Sianów	30	54.15 N	16.16 E
Siantan, Pulau I	112	3.10 N	106.15 E
Sianzhuang	100	33.05 N	119.13 E
Siapa ≐	246	2.07 N	66.28 W
Siargao Island I	116	9.53 N	126.02 E
Siari	123	34.56 N	76.44 E
Siasconset	207	41.15 N	69.58 W
Siasi	116	5.33 N	120.49 E
Siasi Island I	116	5.33 N	120.51 E
Šiaškotan, ostrov I	74	48.49 N	154.06 E
Siátista	38	40.16 N	21.33 E
Siaton	116	9.04 N	123.02 E
Siaton ≐	116	9.02 N	123.02 E
Siaton Point ›	116	9.03 N	123.01 E
Siau, Pulau I	112	2.42 N	125.24 E
Siaugues-Saint-Romain	62	45.06 N	3.38 E
Šiauliai	76	55.56 N	23.19 E
Siazan'	84	41.05 N	49.06 E
Sibago Island I	116	6.45 N	122.24 E
Sibā'ī, Jabal as- ∧	140	25.43 N	34.09 E
Sibaj	86	52.42 N	58.39 E
Sibālay	126	23.50 N	89.47 E
Sibalom	116	10.47 N	122.01 E
Sibanicú	240p	21.14 N	77.31 W
Sibao	100	25.55 N	116.42 E
Sibari, Piana di ⊻	68	39.45 N	16.25 E
Sibasa	156	22.53 S	30.33 E
Sibati	86	47.12 N	88.15 E
Sibayi ⊜	158	27.20 S	32.40 E
Sibay Island I	116	11.51 N	121.29 E
Sibbald	184	51.23 N	110.09 W
Sibbald Point Provincial Park ♦	212	44.19 N	79.19 W
Šibbe	85	39.53 N	72.05 E
Sibbo	26	60.22 N	25.16 E
Şibchar	126	23.21 N	90.09 E
Šibenik	36	43.44 N	15.54 E
Siberia → Sibir' ◆[1]	74	65.00 N	110.00 E
Siberia Occidental, Llanura de → Zapadno-Sibirskaja ravnina ⊻	72	60.00 N	75.00 E
Sibérie Occidental, Dépression de la → Zapadno-Sibirskaja ravnina ⊻	72	60.00 N	75.00 E
Siberut, Pulau I	108	1.20 S	98.55 E
Sibi	120	29.33 N	67.53 E
Sibiči	89	46.04 N	135.22 E
Sibigo	114	2.51 N	95.55 E
Sibillini, Monti ⋀	66	42.54 N	13.13 E
Sibir' (Siberia) ◆[1]	74	65.00 N	110.00 E
Sibir'akova, ostrov I	74	72.50 N	79.00 E
Sibircevo	89	44.12 N	132.26 E
Sibiti	152	3.41 S	13.21 E
Sibiti ≐	154	3.49 S	34.46 E
Sibiu	38	45.48 N	24.09 E
Sibiu □[6]	38	46.00 N	24.15 E
Sible Hedingham	42	51.58 N	0.35 E
Sibley, Il., U.S.	216	40.35 N	88.23 W
Sibley, Ia., U.S.	198	43.23 N	95.45 W
Sibley, La., U.S.	194	32.33 N	93.18 W
Sibley, Ms., U.S.	194	31.22 N	91.23 W
Sibley Peninsula ›[1]	190	48.25 N	88.45 W
Sibley Provincial Park ♦	190	48.25 N	88.49 W
Siboa	112	0.30 N	120.02 E
Sibochi	107	28.50 N	104.32 E
Sibolga	114	1.45 N	98.48 E
Sibolga, Teluk c	114	1.38 N	98.45 E
Siborang	114	1.08 N	99.26 E
Siborongborong	114	2.13 N	98.59 E
Sibpur, Bngl.	124	24.02 N	90.44 E
Sibpur, India	272b	22.24 N	88.33 E
Sibpur, India	272b	22.34 N	88.19 E
Sibsa ≐[1]	126	22.01 N	89.30 E
Sibsāgar	120	26.59 N	94.39 E
Sibu	112	2.18 N	111.49 E
Sibu, Pulau I	114	2.13 N	104.04 E
Sibuatan, Gunung ∧	114	2.56 N	98.24 E
Sibuguey ≐	116	7.38 N	122.48 E
Sibuguey Bay c	116	7.30 N	122.40 E
Sibuko, Teluk c	112	4.00 N	118.26 E
Sibut	152	5.44 N	19.05 E
Sibuti	112	4.03 N	113.48 E
Sibutu Island I	112	4.46 N	119.29 E
Sibutu Passage ꭒ	116	4.50 N	119.35 E
Sibuyan Island I	116	12.25 N	122.34 E
Sibuyan Sea ⫪[2]	116	12.50 N	122.40 E
Siby	150	12.23 N	8.20 W
Sibyŏn	98	38.19 N	126.41 E
Sicamous	182	50.50 N	119.00 W
Sicapoo, Mount ∧	116	18.01 N	120.56 E
Sicasica	248	17.22 S	67.45 W
Siccus ≐	166	31.26 S	139.30 E
Şichakou	98	41.39 N	116.26 E
Šichany	80	52.07 N	47.13 E
Sichifulo ≐	154	17.26 S	25.02 E
Si Chon	110	9.00 N	99.54 E
Sichote-Alin' ⋀	89	48.00 N	138.00 E
Sichote-Alinskij zapovednik ♦	89	45.15 N	136.15 E
Šichtovo	76	55.43 N	32.18 E
Sichuan (Szechwan) □[4]	102	31.00 N	105.00 E
Sichuan Pendi ⊻[1]	102	30.00 N	105.00 E
Sichuanzhai	102	23.02 N	101.44 E
Sicié, Cap ›	62	43.03 N	5.51 E
Sicignano degli Alburni	68	40.34 N	15.18 E
Sicilia □[4]	36	37.30 N	14.00 E
Sicilia (Sicily) I	70	37.30 N	14.00 E
Sicilia, Isla de → Sicilia I	70	37.30 N	14.00 E
Sicily → Sicilia I	70	37.30 N	14.00 E
Sicily, Strait of ꭒ	36	37.20 N	11.20 E
Sicily Island	194	31.50 N	91.39 W
Sickingmühle	263	51.42 N	7.07 E
Sicklerville	208	39.43 N	74.58 W
Sicogon Island I	116	11.27 N	123.16 E
Sico Tinto ≐	236	15.58 N	84.58 W
Sicuani	248	14.16 S	71.13 W
Siculiana	70	37.20 N	13.25 E
Şicun	106	31.55 N	119.18 E
Šid	38	45.08 N	19.13 E
Sīdah, Qārat ∧[2]	142	30.16 N	29.58 E
Sidamo □[4]	144	5.00 N	39.00 E
Sidao	271a	39.51 N	116.26 E
Sidaohe	105	40.24 N	117.17 E
Sidareja	115a	7.29 S	108.47 E
Sidas	112	0.24 N	109.46 E
Sidcup ◆[8]	260	51.25 N	0.06 E
Siddeburen	52	53.25 N	6.52 E
Siddinghausen	263	51.32 N	7.48 E
Siddington	262	53.14 N	2.14 W
Siddipet	122	18.06 N	78.51 E
Sideia Island I	164	10.35 S	150.50 E
Sidel'kino	80	54.32 N	51.08 E
Sidenreng	112	4.03 S	119.38 E
Sidéradougou	150	10.40 N	4.15 W
Siderno	68	38.16 N	16.18 E
Şiderópolis	252	28.35 S	49.26 W
Šiderty ≐, S.S.S.R.	80	50.10 N	52.20 E
Šiderty ≐, S.S.S.R.	86	52.32 N	74.50 E
Sidhauli	124	27.17 N	80.50 E
Sídheros, Ákra ›	38	35.19 N	26.19 E
Sidhi	124	24.25 N	81.53 E
Sidhi □[5]	124	24.10 N	82.10 E
Sidhirókastron	38	41.14 N	23.22 E
Sidhpur	120	23.55 N	72.23 E
Sīdī 'Abd ar-Raḥmān	140	30.58 N	29.44 E
Sidi Aïch	34	36.37 N	4.42 E
Sidi Aïssa	148	35.53 N	3.48 E
Sidi Akacha	34	36.28 N	1.18 E
Sidi Ali	34	36.06 N	0.25 E
Sidi Ali, Oued ᐯ	148	34.07 N	2.05 W
Sidi Ali Ben Nasrallah	36	35.15 N	9.50 E
Sīdī Barrānī	140	31.36 N	25.55 E
Sidi bel Abbès	148	35.13 N	0.10 W
Sidi Bel Abbes □[5]	148	35.00 N	1.00 W
Sidi Bennour	148	32.30 N	8.30 W
Sidi Bou Zid	148	35.02 N	9.30 E
Sidi Bou Zid □[8]	148	35.00 N	9.15 E
Sidi Daoud	36	37.00 N	10.55 E
Sidi el Hani, Sebkhet ⊜	36	35.33 N	10.25 E
Sīdī Ghāzī	142	31.12 N	31.03 E
Sīdī Ḥunaysh	140	31.10 N	27.37 E
Sidi Ifni	148	29.24 N	10.12 W

≐	River	Fluss	Río	Rivière	Rio
≅	Canal	Kanal	Canal	Canal	Canal
⌊	Waterfall, Rapids	Wasserfall, Stromschnellen	Cascada, Rápidos	Chute d'eau, Rapides	Cascata, Rápidos
ꭒ	Strait	Meeresstrasse	Estrecho	Détroit	Estreito
c	Bay, Gulf	Bucht, Golf	Bahía, Golfo	Baie, Golfe	Baía, Golfo
⊜	Lake, Lakes	See, Seen	Lago, Lagos	Lac, Lacs	Lago, Lagos
⩨	Swamp	Sumpf	Pantano	Marais	Pântano
⊓	Ice Features, Glacier	Eis- und Gletscherformen	Accidentes Glaciales	Formes glaciaires	Acidentes glaciares
⫪	Other Hydrographic Features	Andere Hydrographische Objekte	Otros Elementos Hidrográficos	Autres données hydrographiques	Outros acidentes hidrográficos
✦	Submarine Features	Untermeerische Objekte	Accidentes Submarinos	Formes de relief sous-marin	Acidentes submarinos
□	Political Unit	Politische Einheit	Unidad Política	Entité politique	Unidade política
♮	Cultural Institution	Kulturelle Institution	Institución Cultural	Institution culturelle	Institução cultural
⊥	Historical Site	Historische Stätte	Sitio Histórico	Site historique	Sitio histórico
♦	Recreational Site	Erholungs- und Ferienort	Sitio de Recreo	Centre de loisirs	Area de Lazer
⊠	Airport	Flughafen	Aeropuerto	Aéroport	Aeroporto
■	Military Installation	Militäranlage	Instalación Militar	Installation militaire	Instalação militar
◆	Miscellaneous	Verschiedenes	Misceláneo	Divers	Diversos

Symbols in the index entries represent the broad categories identified in the key at the right. Symbols with superior numbers (∧1) identify subcategories (see complete key on page I · 1).

Kartensymbole in dem Registerverzeichnis stellen die rechts in Schlüssel erklärten Kategorien dar. Symbole mit hochgestellten Ziffern (∧1) bezeichnen Unterabteilungen einer Kategorie (vgl. vollständiger Schlüssel auf Seite I · 1).

Los símbolos incluidos en el texto del índice representan las grandes categorías identificadas con la clave a la derecha. Los símbolos con números en su parte superior (∧1) identifican las subcategorías (véase la clave completa en la página I · 1).

Les symboles de l'index représentent les catégories indiquées dans la légende à droite. Les symboles suivis d'un indice (∧1) représentent des sous-catégories (voir légende complète à la page I · 1).

Os símbolos incluídos no texto do índice representam as grandes categorias identificadas com a chave à direita. Os símbolos com números em sua parte superior (∧1) identificam as subcategorias (veja-se a chave completa à página I · 1).

∧ Mountain	Berg	Montaña	Montagne	Montanha
∧ Mountains	Berge	Montañas	Montagnes	Montanhas
)(Pass	Pass	Paso	Col	Passo
V Valley, Canyon	Tal, Cañon	Valle, Cañón	Vallée, Canyon	Vale, Canhão
≃ Plain	Ebene	Llano	Plaine	Planície
> Cape	Kap	Cabo	Cap	Cabo
I Island	Insel	Isla	Île	Ilha
II Islands	Inseln	Islas	Îles	Ilhas
⊥ Other Topographic Features	Andere Topographische Objekte	Otros Elementos Topográficos	Autres données topographiques	Outros acidentes topográficos

≃	River	Fluss	Río	Rivière	Rio
≌	Canal	Kanal	Canal	Canal	Canal
∟	Waterfall, Rapids	Wasserfall, Stromschnellen	Cascada, Rápidos	Chute d'eau, Rapides	Cascata, Rápidos
ɰ	Strait	Meeresstrasse	Estrecho	Détroit	Estreito
c	Bay, Gulf	Bucht, Golf	Bahía, Golfo	Baie, Golfe	Baía, Golfo
⊜	Lake, Lakes	See, Seen	Lago, Lagos	Lac, Lacs	Lago, Lagos
⊞	Swamp	Sumpf	Pantano	Marais	Pântano
⊓	Ice Features, Glacier	Eis- und Gletscherformen	Accidentes Glaciales	Formes glaciaires	Acidentes glaciares
⫪	Other Hydrographic Features	Andere Hydrographische Objekte	Otros Elementos Hidrográficos	Autres données hydrographiques	Outros acidentes hidrográficos

⊸	Submarine Features	Untermeerische Objekte	Accidentes Submarinos	Formes de relief sous-marin	Acidentes submarinos
□	Political Unit	Politische Einheit	Unidad Política	Entité politique	Unidade política
ɤ	Cultural Institution	Kulturelle Institution	Institución Cultural	Institution culturelle	Instituição cultural
⊥	Historical Site	Historische Stätte	Sitio Histórico	Site historique	Sitio histórico
♠	Recreational Site	Erholungs- und Ferienort	Sitio de Recreo	Centre de loisirs	Area de Lazer
⊠	Airport	Flughafen	Aeropuerto	Aéroport	Aeroporto
■	Military Installation	Militäranlage	Instalación Militar	Installation militaire	Instalação militar
◆	Miscellaneous	Verschiedenes	Misceláneo	Divers	Diversos

Name (ENGLISH) / Name (DEUTSCH)	Page / Seite	Lat.°′ / Breite°′	Long.°′ / Länge°′ (E = Ost)
Smith Island I, Wa., U.S.	224	48.19 N	122.50 W
Smith Island II	208	38.01 N	76.02 W
Smithland	194	37.08 N	88.24 W
Smithmill	214	40.46 N	78.25 W
Smith Mountain ∧	280	34.17 N	117.52 W
Smith Mountain Lake ⊜[1]	192	37.10 N	79.40 W
Smith Peak ∧	202	48.50 N	116.39 W
Smith Peninsula >[1]	9	74.25 S	61.15 W
Smith Point	222	29.27 N	94.45 W
Smith Point >, N.S., Can.	186	45.51 N	63.25 W
Smith Point >, Tx., U.S.	222	29.32 N	94.46 W
Smith Point >, Va., U.S.	208	37.53 N	76.14 W
Smithport	214	40.50 N	78.52 W
Smith River	204	41.55 N	124.08 W
Smiths	194	32.32 N	85.05 W
Smithsburg	208	39.39 N	77.34 W
Smiths Creek	214	42.55 N	82.36 W
Smiths Falls	212	44.54 N	76.01 W
Smiths Fork ≃	202	41.23 N	110.12 W
Smiths Grove	194	37.03 N	86.12 W
Smiths Mills	276	41.01 N	74.22 W
Smith Sound ⊔	182	51.18 N	127.48 W
Smithton, Austl.	166	40.51 S	145.07 E
Smithton, Il., U.S.	219	38.24 N	89.59 W
Smithton, Mo., U.S.	194	38.40 N	93.05 W
Smithton, Pa., U.S.	279b	40.09 N	79.44 W
Smithtown	210	40.52 N	73.13 W
Smithtown Bay ⊂	276	40.57 N	73.12 W
Smith Valley	218	39.36 N	86.12 W
Smithville, On., Can.	212	43.06 N	79.33 W
Smithville, Ga., U.S.	192	31.54 N	84.15 W
Smithville, In., U.S.	218	39.04 N	86.30 W
Smithville, Ms., U.S.	194	34.04 N	88.23 W
Smithville, Mo., U.S.	194	39.23 N	94.34 W
Smithville, N.J., U.S.	208	39.59 N	74.44 W
Smithville, N.J., U.S.	285	39.29 N	74.27 W
Smithville, Oh., U.S.	214	40.51 N	81.51 W
Smithville, Tn., U.S.	194	35.57 N	85.48 W
Smithville, Tx., U.S.	222	30.00 N	97.09 W
Smithville Flats	210	42.24 N	75.49 W
Smithville Lake ⊜[1]	194	39.25 N	94.30 W
Smögen	26	58.21 N	11.13 E
Smoke Creek ≃, Mt., U.S.	198	48.18 N	104.41 W
Smoke Creek ≃, N.Y., U.S.	284a	42.49 N	78.52 W
Smoke Creek, South Branch ≃	284a	42.49 N	78.49 W
Smoke Creek Desert ◆[2]	204	40.30 N	119.40 W
Smoke Lake ⊜	212	45.32 N	78.41 W
Smokeless	214	40.24 N	76.02 W
Smokerun	214	40.48 N	78.26 W
Smoketown	208	40.02 N	76.12 W
Smokey, Cape >	186	46.38 N	60.21 W
Smokey Dome ∧	202	43.29 N	114.56 W
Smoky ≃	182	56.10 N	117.21 W
Smoky Bay	162	32.22 S	133.56 E
Smoky Cape >	166	30.56 S	153.05 E
Smoky Hill ≃	198	39.03 N	96.48 W
Smoky Hill, North Fork ≃	198	38.55 N	101.17 W
Smoky Lake	182	54.07 N	112.28 W
Smøla I	24	63.24 N	8.00 E
Smol'anica	76	52.42 N	24.38 E
Smol'aninovo	89	43.19 N	132.28 E
Smol'any	76	54.36 N	30.04 E
Smolensk	76	54.47 N	32.03 E
Smolenskaja vozvyšennost' ⋏[1]	76	54.30 N	33.00 E
Smolenskoje	86	52.20 N	85.05 E
Smoleviči	76	54.02 N	28.05 E
Smólikas ∧	38	40.06 N	20.52 E
Smoljan	38	41.35 N	24.41 E
Smolny ʋ	265a	59.57 N	30.24 E
Smolovka	76	55.33 N	30.13 E
Smoot	200	42.37 N	110.54 W
Smoothstone ≃	184	55.20 N	106.39 W
Smoothstone Lake ⊜	184	54.40 N	106.50 W
Smorgon'	76	54.29 N	26.24 E
Smorodovka	76	57.08 N	29.52 E
Smotrič	78	48.56 N	26.34 E
Smotrič ≃	78	48.34 N	26.38 E
Smuškovoje	80	47.20 N	45.55 E
Smyčka	82	56.04 N	35.56 E
Smygehamn	41	55.21 N	13.22 E
Smygehuk >	41	55.21 N	13.23 E
Smyley, Cape >	9	72.26 S	78.10 W
Smyrna → İzmir	130	38.25 N	27.09 E
Smyrna, De., U.S.	208	39.17 N	75.36 W
Smyrna, Ga., U.S.	192	33.53 N	84.30 W
Smyrna, N.Y., U.S.	210	42.41 N	75.34 W
Smyrna, Tn., U.S.	194	35.58 N	86.31 W
Smyrna ≃	208	39.22 N	75.31 W
Smyšl'ajevka	80	53.15 N	50.22 E
Smyth, Canal ⊔	254	52.15 S	73.40 W
Smythe, Mount ∧	176	57.54 N	124.53 W
Smythe Park ♦	275b	43.41 N	79.30 W
Smythesdale	169	37.38 S	143.41 E
Sn'adin	78	52.04 N	28.19 E
Snæfell ∧, Ísland	24a	64.48 N	15.32 W
Snaefell ∧, I. of Man	44	54.16 N	4.27 W
Snæfellness >[1]	24a	64.50 N	23.00 W
Snag	180	62.24 N	140.22 W
Snaght, Slieve ∧	44	55.12 N	7.20 W
Snagost'	78	51.21 N	34.54 E
Snahapish ≃	224	47.38 N	124.11 W
Snaith	44	53.41 N	1.02 W
Sn'ajevo	80	52.34 N	46.11 E
Snake ≃, Yk., Can.	180	65.58 N	134.10 W
Snake ≃, U.S.	202	46.12 N	119.02 W
Snake ≃, Ca., U.S.	226	39.07 N	121.43 W
Snake ≃, Mn., U.S.	190	45.49 N	92.46 W
Snake ≃, Mn., U.S.	198	48.26 N	97.07 W
Snake ≃, Ne., U.S.	198	42.47 N	100.48 W
Snake Bight ⊂[3]	220	25.10 N	80.50 W
Snake Brook ≃	283	42.18 N	71.22 W
Snake Creek ≃, Mt., U.S.	202	48.32 N	108.53 W
Snake Creek ≃, Ne., U.S.	198	42.01 N	102.45 W
Snake Creek ≃, S.D., U.S.	198	44.58 N	98.29 W
Snake Creek, South Fork ≃	198	45.02 N	98.36 W
Snake Creek Canal ≋	220	25.57 N	80.11 W
Snake Indian ≃	182	53.11 N	118.00 W
Snake Range ⋏	204	39.00 N	114.15 W
Snake Rapids ∟	212	45.14 N	77.20 W
Snake River Plain ≚	202	43.00 N	113.00 W
Snake Valley	169	37.37 S	143.35 E
Snake Valley ∨	204	39.20 N	113.55 W
Snaptun	41	55.49 N	10.04 E
Snares Islands II	9	48.00 S	166.30 E
Snasahögarna ∧	26	63.13 N	12.21 E
Sn'atyn	78	48.28 N	25.34 E
Snay Pôl	110	11.40 N	105.13 E
Sneads	192	30.42 N	84.55 W
Snedsted	26	56.54 N	8.32 E
Sneedville	192	36.31 N	83.13 W
Sneek	52	53.02 N	5.40 E
Sneekermeer ⊜	52	53.02 N	5.45 E
Snee-osh-Beach	224	48.24 N	122.33 W
Sneeuberg ∧	158	32.25 S	19.12 E
Sneeuberg ⋏	158	31.46 S	24.20 E
Snekkersten	41	56.00 N	12.36 E
Snelgrove	275b	43.44 N	79.49 W
Snelling	204	37.31 N	120.26 W
Snettisham	42	52.53 N	0.30 E
Snežnaja ≃	88	51.28 N	104.38 E
Snežnik ∧	36	45.35 N	14.27 E
Snežnoje	83	48.01 N	38.46 E
Śniardwy, Jezioro ⊜	30	53.46 N	21.44 E
Snicarte	219	40.07 N	90.14 W
Snicarte Island I	219	40.08 N	90.12 W
Snigir'ovka	78	47.06 N	32.47 E
Snina	30	48.59 N	22.07 E
Snipe Keys II	220	24.40 N	81.38 W
Snipe Lake ⊜	182	55.07 N	116.46 W
Snizort, Loch ⊂	46	57.34 N	6.28 W
Snøde	41	55.05 N	10.55 E
Snodland	42	51.20 N	0.27 E
Snoghøj	41	55.31 N	9.43 E
Snøhetta ∧	26	62.20 N	9.17 E
Snohomish	224	47.54 N	122.05 W
Snohomish □[6]	224	48.02 N	121.41 W
Snohomish ≃	224	48.01 N	122.13 W
Snønipa ⛿	26	61.42 N	6.41 E
Snook	222	30.29 N	96.28 W
Snoqualmie	224	47.31 N	121.49 W
Snoqualmie ≃	224	47.50 N	122.03 W
Snoqualmie, Middle Fork ≃	224	47.31 N	121.46 W
Snoqualmie, North Fork ≃	224	47.31 N	121.46 W
Snoqualmie, South Fork ≃	224	47.31 N	121.46 W
Snoqualmie Falls	224	47.32 N	121.49 W
Snoqualmie Mountain ∧	224	47.27 N	121.25 W
Snoqualmie Pass)(	224	47.25 N	121.25 W
Snøtinden ∧	24	66.38 N	14.00 E
Snov	76	53.13 N	26.24 E
Snov ≃	78	51.45 N	31.45 E
Snover	190	43.27 N	82.58 W
Snowbird Lake ⊜	176	60.41 N	103.00 W
Snow Canyon State Park ♦	200	37.11 N	113.42 W
Snow Creek ≃	224	47.59 N	122.53 W
Snowden, Sk., Can.	184	53.30 N	104.41 W
Snowden, Pa., U.S.	279b	40.16 N	79.58 W
Snowden Oaks	284c	39.04 N	76.52 W
Snowdenville	285	40.11 N	75.36 W
Snowdon ∧	44	53.04 N	4.05 W
Snowdonia National Park ♦	28	53.00 N	3.57 W
Snowdoun	194	32.14 N	86.17 W
Snowdrift	176	62.23 N	110.47 W
Snowflake	200	34.30 N	110.04 W
Snow Hill, Md., U.S.	208	38.10 N	75.23 W
Snow Hill, N.C., U.S.	192	35.27 N	77.40 W
Snowking Mountain ∧	224	48.24 N	121.17 W
Snow Lake	184	54.53 N	100.02 W
Snow Lakes ⊜	224	47.29 N	120.45 W
Snowmass Mountain ∧	200	39.07 N	107.04 W
Snow Mountain ∧	226	39.23 N	122.45 W
Snow Peak ∧	202	48.35 N	118.29 W
Snows Brook ≃	283	42.47 N	71.06 W
Snow Shoe	214	41.02 N	77.57 W
Snowshoe Butte ∧	224	47.13 N	121.22 W
Snowshoe Peak ∧	202	48.13 N	115.41 W
Snowtown	166	33.47 S	138.13 E
Snow Water Lake ⊜	204	41.07 N	115.00 W
Snowy ≃	166	37.48 S	148.32 E
Snowy Mountain ∧	188	43.42 N	74.23 W
Snowy Mountains ⋏	166	36.30 S	148.20 E
Snowyside Peak ∧	202	43.57 N	114.58 W
Snubba Range ⋏	171b	35.40 S	148.10 E
Snuŏl	110	12.04 N	106.26 E
Snyder, Ok., U.S.	196	34.39 N	98.57 W
Snyder, Tx., U.S.	196	32.43 N	100.55 W
Snyder □[6]	210	40.47 N	77.03 W
Snydertown	210	40.53 N	76.40 W
Soacha	246	4.35 N	74.13 W
Soahany	157b	18.42 S	44.13 E
Soaker, Mount ∧	172	45.23 S	167.15 E
Soalala	157b	16.06 S	45.20 E
Soalara	157b	23.36 S	43.44 E
Soaloka	157b	18.32 S	45.15 E
Sŏam	98	38.01 N	126.43 E
Soamanonga	157b	23.52 S	44.47 E
Soān ≃	123	33.01 N	71.44 E
Soan-do I	98	34.09 N	126.39 E
Soanierana Ivongo	157b	16.55 S	49.35 E
Soanindrariny	157b	19.54 S	47.14 E
Soap Creek ≃	190	40.55 N	92.14 W
Soap Lake	202	47.23 N	119.29 W
Soasiu → Tidore	108	0.40 N	127.26 E
Soatá	246	6.20 N	72.41 W
Soavina	157b	20.23 S	46.56 E
Soavinandriana	157b	19.09 S	46.45 E
Soay I	46	57.08 N	6.14 W
Soazza	58	46.22 N	9.13 E
Sob ≃	78	48.42 N	29.17 E
Sobaek-sanmaek ⋏	98	36.00 N	128.00 E
Sobat ≃	140	9.22 N	31.33 E
Sobernheim	56	49.47 N	7.38 E
Soběšice	60	49.12 N	13.41 E
Soběslav	30	49.15 N	14.44 E
Sobger ≃	164	3.44 S	140.20 E
Sobič	78	51.52 N	33.14 E
Sobinka	80	55.59 N	40.01 E
Soboba Indian Reservation ◆[4]	228	33.47 N	116.54 W
Soboko	140	6.49 N	24.50 E
Sobolekovo	80	55.39 N	51.53 E
Sobolev	80	51.56 N	51.43 E
Sobolevka	78	48.36 N	29.30 E
Sobolevo	82	55.31 N	38.43 E
Sobolino	88	53.23 N	119.42 E
Sobótka	30	50.55 N	16.45 E
Sobradinho	252	29.24 S	53.03 W
Sobrado	34	41.02 N	8.16 W
Sobral	250	3.42 S	40.21 W
Sobrance	30	48.45 N	22.11 E
Sobrante Ridge ∧	282	37.58 N	122.15 W
Sobrarbe ◆[1]	34	42.22 N	0.10 E
Sobue	94	35.15 N	136.43 E
Søby	41	54.56 N	10.16 E
Soča	64	46.20 N	13.39 E
Soča (Isonzo) ≃	64	45.47 N	13.32 E
Socaire	252	23.36 S	67.51 W
Socamirim	256	23.37 S	47.12 W
Socchieve	64	46.25 N	12.52 E
Soc-giang	110	22.54 N	106.01 E
Socgorodok	78	50.11 N	38.09 E
Soch	85	39.57 N	71.08 E
Soch ≃	85	40.20 N	71.02 E
Sochaczew	30	52.14 N	20.14 E
Sochaux	58	47.31 N	6.50 E
Soch'e → Shache	120	38.25 N	77.16 E
Sochi → Soči	84	43.35 N	39.45 E
Sŏch'ŏn	98	36.05 N	126.41 E
Sochondo	88	51.49 N	112.32 E
Sochondo, gora ∧	88	49.44 N	111.05 E
Soch'ŏng-do I	98	37.46 N	124.45 E
Sochor, gora ∧	88	51.18 N	105.15 E
Soči	84	43.35 N	39.45 E
Social Circle	192	33.39 N	83.43 W
Social Security Administration ʋ	284b	39.19 N	76.44 W
Sociedade Hípica Paulista ♦	287b	23.36 S	46.41 W
Société, Îles de la (Society Islands) II	14	17.00 S	150.00 W
Society Hill	192	34.30 N	79.51 W
Society Islands → Société, Îles de la II	14	17.00 S	150.00 W
Society Ridge ⊕[3]	14	17.00 S	151.00 W
Soco ≃	238	18.27 N	69.12 W
Socoltenango	232	16.13 N	92.15 W
Socompa, Paso)(	252	24.27 S	68.18 W
Soconusco, Sierra de → Madre, Sierra ⋏	236	15.20 N	92.20 W
Socorro, Bra.	256	22.36 S	46.32 W
Socorro, Col.	246	6.29 N	73.16 W
Socorro, Pil.	116	9.37 N	125.58 E
Socorro, N.M., U.S.	200	34.03 N	106.53 W
Socorro, Tx., U.S.	200	31.39 N	106.18 W
Socorro ◆[8]	287b	23.39 S	46.42 W
Socorro, Isla I	232	18.45 N	110.58 W
Sócota	248	6.18 S	78.44 W
Socotora, Isla → Suquṭrā I	118	12.30 N	54.00 E
Socotra → Suquṭrā I	118	12.30 N	54.00 E
Socuéllamos	34	39.17 N	2.48 W
Soda Creek	182	52.21 N	122.18 W
Soda Creek ≃	226	38.48 N	122.29 W
Soda Lake ⊜, Ca., U.S.	204	35.08 N	116.04 W
Soda Lake ⊜, Ca., U.S.	226	35.15 N	119.53 W
Sodankylä	24	67.29 N	26.32 E
Soda Springs	202	42.39 N	111.36 W
Soddy-Daisy	194	35.16 N	85.10 W
Sodegaura	94	35.26 N	139.57 E
Söderälgen ⊜	40	59.43 N	14.35 E
Söderåsen ⋏[2]	41	56.04 N	13.05 E
Söderbärke	40	60.05 N	15.33 E
Söderby-Karl	40	59.53 N	18.41 E
Söderfors	40	60.23 N	17.14 E
Söderhamn	26	61.18 N	17.03 E
Söderköping	26	58.29 N	16.18 E
Södermanland □[9]	41	59.12 N	16.49 E
Södermanlands Län □[6]	40	59.15 N	16.40 E
Södernmanland □[9]	40	59.12 N	16.49 E
Söderslätt □[9]	41	55.29 N	13.15 E
Södertälje	40	59.12 N	17.37 E
Södertörn >[1]	40	59.05 N	18.00 E
Sodhra	123	32.28 N	74.11 E
Sodingen ◆[8]	263	51.32 N	7.15 E
Sodium	158	30.11 S	23.09 E
Sodo	144	6.52 N	37.47 E
Sodom → Sedom ⊥	132	31.04 N	35.23 E
Sodpur	272b	22.39 N	88.23 E
Södra Åby	41	55.23 N	13.18 E
Södra Björkfjärden ⊂	40	59.18 N	17.32 E
Södra Hörken ⊜	40	60.02 N	15.02 E
Södra Kvarken ⊔	26	60.15 N	19.05 E
Södra Råda	40	59.01 N	14.10 E
Södra Sandby	41	55.43 N	13.20 E
Södra Vi	26	57.45 N	15.48 E
Sodražica	36	45.46 N	14.38 E
Sodus	210	43.14 N	77.03 W
Sodus Bay ⊂	210	43.15 N	76.58 W
Sodus Creek ≃	210	43.13 N	76.56 W
Sodus Point	210	43.16 N	76.59 W
Sŏdu-su ≃	98	42.05 N	129.00 E
Sodwalls	170	33.31 S	149.59 E
Sodwana Bay National Park ♦	158	27.30 S	32.39 E
Soe	112	9.52 S	124.17 E
Soeda	96	33.34 N	130.52 E
Soekmekaar	156	23.28 S	29.58 E
Soela väin ⊔	76	58.40 N	22.35 E
Soerabaja → Surabaya	115a	7.15 S	112.45 E
Soest, B.R.D.	52	51.34 N	8.07 E
Soest, Ned.	52	52.09 N	5.18 E
Soestdijk	52	52.11 N	5.18 E
Soestdijk, Paleis ʋ	52	52.12 N	5.15 E
Soeste ≃	52	53.10 N	7.44 E
Soesterberg	52	52.07 N	5.17 E
Soeurs, Île des I	275a	45.28 N	73.33 W
Sofádhes	38	39.20 N	22.06 E
Sofala	170	33.05 S	149.42 E
Sofala □[5]	156	19.00 S	35.00 E
Sofia → Sofija	38	42.41 N	23.19 E
Sofia ≃	157b	15.27 S	47.23 E
Sofiero	41	56.05 N	12.39 E
Sofija (Sofia)	38	42.41 N	23.19 E
Sofijevka, S.S.S.R.	78	46.33 N	34.03 E
Sofijevka, S.S.S.R.	78	48.04 N	33.52 E
Sofijevskij	83	48.12 N	38.52 E
Sofijsk, S.S.S.R.	89	51.34 N	139.52 E
Sofijsk, S.S.S.R.	89	52.15 N	133.58 E
Sofjanga	24	65.52 N	31.15 E
Sofje-Kondratjevka	83	48.18 N	38.12 E
Sofjino	82	55.30 N	38.11 E
Sofrino	82	56.09 N	37.56 E
Sofronovo	76	59.48 N	36.54 E
Sogakofe	150	6.00 N	0.36 E
Sogamoso	246	5.43 N	72.56 W
Sogamoso ≃	246	7.13 N	73.56 W
Soğanlı	267b	40.55 N	29.12 E
Soğanlı Dağları ⋏	130	40.30 N	40.30 E
Soğanlı Geçidi)(	130	40.33 N	40.16 E
Sogcho → Sokch'o	98	38.12 N	128.36 E
Sogda	89	50.24 N	132.12 E
Sögel	52	52.50 N	7.31 E
Sogliano al Rubicone	66	44.00 N	12.18 E
Sognafjorden ⊂[2]	26	61.06 N	5.10 E
Søgne	26	58.05 N	7.49 E
Sogne Fjord → Sognafjorden ⊂[2]	26	61.06 N	5.10 E
Sogn og Fjordane □[6]	26	61.30 N	6.50 E
Sogod, Pil.	116	10.45 N	124.00 E
Sogod, Pil.	116	10.23 N	124.59 E
Sogod Bay ⊂	116	10.15 N	125.02 E
Sogo Nur ⊜	102	42.18 N	101.08 E
Sogoža ≃	76	58.28 N	39.06 E
Sogri-san Kukrip Kongwŏn ♦	98	36.33 N	127.52 E
Söğüt	130	40.00 N	30.11 E
Söğütalan	130	40.03 N	28.34 E
Söğüt Gölü ⊜	130	37.03 N	29.53 E
Söğütlü	130	40.54 N	30.29 E
Sohāg → Sawhāj	140	26.33 N	31.42 E
Sohāgpur, India	124	23.19 N	81.21 E
Sohāgpur, India	124	22.42 N	78.12 E
Soham	42	52.20 N	0.20 E
Sohano	175e	5.27 S	154.40 E
Soharkha	272a	28.35 N	77.24 E
Sohebele Game Reserve ◆[4]	156	24.27 S	31.27 E
Soheit-Tinlot	56	50.29 N	5.22 E
Sohland	54	51.02 N	14.25 E
Söhlde	52	52.11 N	10.14 E
Sohna	124	28.15 N	77.04 E
Sŏhŭng	98	38.27 N	126.10 E
Sŏhwa-ri	98	38.15 N	128.13 E
Soignes, Forêt de ◆[3]	56	50.47 N	4.25 E
Soignies (Zinnik)	50	50.35 N	4.04 E
Soignolles-en-Brie	261	48.39 N	2.42 E
Soin	150	12.47 N	3.49 W
Soindres	261	48.57 N	1.40 E
Soini	26	62.52 N	24.13 E
Sointula	182	50.38 N	127.01 W
Soisalo ∧	26	62.40 N	28.10 E
Soissons	50	49.22 N	3.20 E
Soisy-sous-Montmorency	261	48.59 N	2.18 E
Soisy-sur-Seine	261	48.39 N	2.27 E
Sōja	96	34.40 N	133.45 E
Sojana	24	65.48 N	43.20 E
Sojat	120	25.55 N	73.40 E
Šojda	24	61.11 N	37.40 E
Sojiji Temple ʋ[1]	268	35.31 N	139.41 E
Sojitra	120	22.33 N	72.43 E
Šojna	24	67.52 N	44.08 E
Sŏjosŏn-man ⊂	98	39.20 N	124.50 E
Sojoton Point >	116	9.58 N	122.27 E
Sojuz Sovetskich Socialističeskich Respublik → Union of Soviet Socialist Republics □[1]	148	60.00 N	80.00 E
Sok ≃	80	53.24 N	50.08 E
Sōka, Nihon	94	35.49 N	139.48 E
Soka, Taehan	271b	37.30 N	126.48 E
Sokal'	78	50.29 N	24.17 E
Šokal'skogo, proliv ⊔	74	79.00 N	100.25 E
Sokch'o	98	38.12 N	128.36 E
Söke	130	37.45 N	27.24 E
Sokehs Passage ⊔	174r	7.01 N	158.11 E
Sokele	154	9.55 S	24.36 E
Sokhós	38	40.49 N	23.21 E
Sokir'any	78	48.27 N	27.25 E
Sokirincy	78	50.42 N	32.46 E
Sokna	26	60.14 N	9.54 E
Sokodé	150	8.59 N	1.08 E
Sokol, S.S.S.R.	74	72.24 N	126.48 E
Sokol, S.S.S.R.	76	59.28 N	40.10 E
Sokol, S.S.S.R.	89	47.14 N	142.45 E
Sokol ∧	60	49.03 N	13.31 E
Sokólka, Pol.	30	53.25 N	23.31 E
Sokolka, S.S.S.R.	80	55.34 N	51.30 E
Sokol'niki ◆[8]	265b	55.48 N	37.41 E
Sokol'niki, park ♦	265b	55.48 N	37.41 E
Sokol'nikovo	82	55.21 N	35.49 E
Sokolo	150	14.44 N	6.08 W
Sokologornoje	78	46.29 N	34.58 E
Sokolov	54	50.09 N	12.40 E
Sokolova-Gora	78	50.19 N	28.36 E
Sokolova Pustyn'	82	54.51 N	38.03 E
Sokolovka	86	55.06 N	69.12 E
Sokolovo, S.S.S.R.	24	65.21 N	56.57 E
Sokolovo, S.S.S.R.	76	52.55 N	34.39 E
Sokolovo, S.S.S.R.	80	52.49 N	42.26 E
Sokolovo, S.S.S.R.	82	56.02 N	36.55 E
Sokolovo, S.S.S.R.	86	52.33 N	84.46 E
Sokolovo-Kundr'učenskij	83	47.50 N	39.57 E
Sokołów	30	50.14 N	22.07 E
Sokołów Podlaski	30	52.25 N	22.15 E
Sokol'skoje	80	57.08 N	43.13 E
Sokone	150	13.53 N	16.22 W
Sokoto	150	13.04 N	5.16 E
Sokoto □[3]	150	12.05 N	5.30 E
Sokoto ≃	150	11.20 N	4.10 E
Šokpar	85	43.49 N	74.21 E
Sŏkp'o-ri	98	37.46 N	125.27 E
Sokrutovka	80	47.54 N	46.33 E
Šokša	76	58.24 N	42.27 E
Soksa-ri	98	40.40 N	127.17 E
Sokskije jary ⋏[2]	80	54.10 N	51.30 E
Sŏk-to I	98	38.40 N	125.00 E
Sokuluk	85	42.52 N	74.18 E
Sokur, S.S.S.R.	80	52.01 N	45.48 E
Sokur, S.S.S.R.	86	55.13 N	83.13 E
Sol', Česko.	30	48.56 N	21.36 E
Sol', S.S.S.R.	83	48.43 N	38.02 E
Sol, Costa del ±[2]	34	36.30 N	4.30 W
Sol, Rio do ≃	248	6.45 S	67.05 W
Sola, Nor.	26	58.53 N	5.36 E
Sola, Vanuatu	175f	13.53 S	167.33 E
Sola, Zaïre	154	5.09 S	27.06 E
Soła ≃	30	50.04 N	19.13 E
Solacolu	38	44.23 N	26.34 E
Sola de Vega	234	16.31 N	96.59 W
Solai	154	0.02 N	36.09 E
Šolaksaj	86	51.45 N	64.48 E
Solana	220	26.56 N	82.01 W
Solana Beach	228	32.59 N	117.16 W
Solander, Cape >	274a	34.01 S	151.14 E
Solander Island I	172	46.34 S	166.53 E
Solânea	250	6.45 S	35.39 W
Solangāri	272b	22.36 N	88.27 E
Sol'anka ≃	80	50.10 N	51.20 E
Solano	116	16.31 N	121.11 E
Solano □[6]	226	38.15 N	121.52 W
Solar, Morro ∧[2]	286d	12.11 S	77.02 W
Solarino	70	37.06 N	15.07 E
Solaro	266b	45.37 N	9.05 E
Solaro, Monte ∧	68	40.33 N	14.13 E
Solberg	26	63.47 N	17.38 E
Solbiate Arno	62	45.42 N	8.48 E
Solbiate Olona	266b	45.39 N	8.53 E
Solca, Arg.	252	30.46 S	66.28 W
Solca, Rom.	38	47.42 N	25.50 E
Solčava	61	46.25 N	14.41 E
Sol'cy	76	58.08 N	30.20 E
Soldados, Cerro ∧	246	2.54 S	79.10 W
Soldatskaja	84	43.48 N	43.49 E
Soldatskoje	85	40.52 N	68.56 E
Soldatsko-Stepnoje	80	49.32 N	45.30 E
Sölde ◆[8]	263	51.31 N	7.35 E
Sol de Julio	252	29.33 S	63.27 W
Sölden	64	46.58 N	11.00 E
Sölderholz ◆[8]	263	51.29 N	7.35 E
Soldier Creek ≃	198	39.04 N	95.39 W
Soldier Field ♦	278	41.52 N	87.37 W
Soldier Key I	220	25.35 N	80.10 W
Soldier Point >	240c	17.02 N	61.41 W
Soldier Pond	186	47.09 N	68.34 W
Soldiers Grove	190	43.23 N	90.46 W
Soldin → Myślibórz	30	52.55 N	14.52 E
Soldotna	180	60.29 N	151.04 W
Sole, Val di ∨	64	46.20 N	10.45 E
Solebury	208	40.23 N	75.02 W
Solec Kujawski	30	53.06 N	18.14 E
Soledad, Col.	246	10.55 N	74.46 W
Soledad, Ca., U.S.	226	36.25 N	121.19 W
Soledad, Ven.	246	8.10 N	63.34 W
Soledad, Cerro ∧	196	26.29 N	103.23 W
Soledad de Doblado	234	19.03 N	96.25 W
Soledad Díez Gutiérrez	234	22.12 N	100.57 W
Soledade	252	28.50 S	52.30 W
Soledade de Minas	256	22.04 S	45.03 W
Soledad Pass)(	228	34.30 N	118.07 W
Soleduck ≃	224	47.55 N	124.35 W
Solemar	256	24.05 S	46.36 W
Solen	198	46.23 N	100.47 W
Solenoje	80	46.14 N	42.32 E
Solentiname, Archipiélago de II	236	11.10 N	85.00 W
Solenzara	36	41.51 N	9.23 E
Solenzo	150	12.11 N	4.05 W
Solero	62	44.55 N	8.30 E
Solers	261	48.40 N	2.43 E
Solesmes	50	50.11 N	3.30 E
Soleure → Solothurn	58	47.13 N	7.32 E
Solferino	64	45.23 N	10.34 E
Solginskij	24	61.05 N	41.19 E
Solgne	56	48.58 N	6.18 E
Solgonskij kr'až ∧	86	55.30 N	91.00 E
Solheim, Nor.	26	60.53 N	5.27 E
Solheim, S. Afr.	273d	26.11 S	28.10 E
Soliera	64	44.45 N	10.55 E
Soligalič	76	59.05 N	42.17 E
Solignac-sur-Loire	62	44.58 N	3.53 E
Soligny-la-Trappe	50	48.37 N	0.32 E
Soligorsk	76	52.48 N	27.32 E
Solihull	42	52.25 N	1.45 W
Solikamsk	86	59.39 N	56.47 E
Solila	157b	21.25 S	46.37 E
Sol'-Ileck	86	51.10 N	54.59 E
Soliman	148	36.42 N	10.30 E
Solimões → Amazon ≃	242	0.10 S	49.00 W
Solin ≃	50	48.02 N	2.43 E
Solingen	56	51.10 N	7.05 E
Solís, Arg.	258	34.18 S	59.20 W
Solís, Ur.	252	34.36 S	55.29 W
Solís, Presa ⊜[1]	234	20.05 N	100.36 W
Soliseño	196	26.01 N	97.48 W
Söll	64	47.30 N	12.11 E
Šollar	84	41.40 N	48.38 E
Sollas	46	57.39 N	7.21 W
Sollefteå	26	63.10 N	17.16 E
Sollenau	61	47.53 N	16.15 E
Sollentuna	40	59.28 N	17.54 E
Sóller	34	39.46 N	2.42 E
Søllerød	41	55.49 N	12.31 E
Sollerön I	26	60.55 N	14.37 E
Søllested	41	54.49 N	11.17 E
Solliès-Pont	62	43.11 N	6.03 E
Solling ⋏	52	51.45 N	9.35 E
Söllingen	54	52.05 N	10.55 E
Solln ◆[8]	60	48.05 N	11.31 E
Sollom	262	53.40 N	2.50 W
Sollstedt	54	51.25 N	10.31 E
Solms	56	50.32 N	8.24 E
Søln ∧	26	61.55 N	11.30 E
Solna	40	59.22 N	18.01 E
Solncedar	78	44.34 N	38.01 E
Solncevo	265b	55.39 N	37.24 E
Solnečnogorsk	82	56.11 N	36.59 E
Solnhofen	56	48.53 N	10.59 E
Solo → Surakarta	115a	7.35 S	110.50 E
Solo ≃	115a	6.47 S	112.33 E
Šolochovskij	80	48.18 N	41.03 E
Solodča	80	49.39 N	44.17 E
Solodniki	80	48.25 N	45.16 E
Solofra	68	40.50 N	14.51 E
Sologne ◆[1]	50	47.50 N	2.00 E
Šologoncy	74	66.13 N	114.14 E
Solok	112	0.48 S	100.39 E
Sololá, Guat.	236	14.46 N	91.11 W
Solola, Som.	144	0.07 N	41.31 E
Sololá □[5]	236	14.40 N	91.15 W
Solomennikova	86	58.20 N	89.02 E
Solomennoje	24	61.51 N	34.19 E
Solomon, Az., U.S.	200	32.48 N	109.37 W
Solomon, Ks., U.S.	198	38.55 N	97.22 W
Solomon ≃	198	38.54 N	97.22 W
Solomon, North Fork ≃	198	39.29 N	98.26 W
Solomon, South Fork ≃	198	39.29 N	98.26 W
Solomon Basin ⊕[1]	14	7.00 S	152.00 E
Solomon Islands □[1], Oc.	14	8.00 S	159.00 E
Solomon Islands □[1], Oc.	175e	8.00 S	159.00 E
Solomon Islands II	14	8.00 S	159.00 E
Solomons	208	38.20 N	76.28 W
Solomon Sea ⊤[2]	14	8.00 S	155.00 E
Solon, India	123	30.55 N	77.07 E
Solon, Ia., U.S.	190	41.48 N	91.29 W
Solon, Me., U.S.	188	44.56 N	69.51 W
Solon, Oh., U.S.	214	41.23 N	81.26 W
Solon, Zhg.	89	46.36 N	121.13 E
Solonešnoje	86	51.40 N	84.21 E
Solonka	80	50.13 N	41.28 E
Sol'onoje, S.S.S.R.	78	48.13 N	34.52 E
Sol'onoje, S.S.S.R.	83	49.18 N	37.39 E
Sol'onoje, S.S.S.R.	84	44.03 N	40.53 E
Sol'onoje, ozero ⊜	86	55.20 N	70.05 E
Sol'onoje Ozero	78	45.53 N	34.27 E
Sol'onoje Zajmišče	80	47.56 N	46.07 E
Solonópole	250	5.44 S	39.01 W
Solon Springs	190	46.21 N	91.49 W
Solopaca	68	41.11 N	14.33 E
Solor, Kepulauan II	112	8.25 S	123.30 E
Solor, Pulau I	112	8.27 S	123.05 E
Solotča	80	54.48 N	39.51 E
Solothurn	58	47.13 N	7.32 E
Solothurn □[3]	58	47.25 N	7.35 E
Solotobe	86	44.38 N	66.05 E
Solotvin	78	48.42 N	24.25 E
Solotvina	78	47.57 N	23.52 E
Soloveckije ostrova II	24	65.07 N	35.53 E
Solovjovka	76	60.46 N	30.09 E
Solovjovsk, S.S.S.R.	88	49.55 N	115.42 E
Solovjovsk, S.S.S.R.	89	54.14 N	124.26 E
Solre-le-Château	50	50.10 N	4.05 E
Solre-sur-Sambre	50	50.18 N	4.08 E
Solsona	34	41.59 N	1.31 E
Solt	30	46.48 N	19.00 E
Šolta, Otok I	36	43.23 N	16.15 E
Soltānābād	128	36.23 N	58.02 E
Soltau	52	52.59 N	9.49 E
Solton	86	52.50 N	86.28 E
Solunto ⊥	70	38.06 N	13.32 E
Solus, Mount ∧	168a	32.28 S	116.13 E
Solutré-Pouilly	58	46.18 N	4.43 E
Solva	42	51.52 N	5.11 W
Solva ≃	42	51.52 N	5.17 W
Solvang	204	34.36 N	120.08 W
Solvarbo	40	60.24 N	15.40 E
Solvay	210	43.03 N	76.12 W
Sölvesborg	26	56.03 N	14.33 E
Sol'vyčegodsk	24	61.21 N	46.52 E
Solway Firth ⊂[1]	44	54.50 N	3.35 W
Solwezi	154	12.11 S	26.25 E
Soly	76	54.31 N	26.11 E
Solymár	264c	47.36 N	18.56 E
Solza	24	64.33 N	39.29 E
Sōma, Nihon	92	37.48 N	140.57 E
Soma, Tür.	130	39.10 N	27.36 E
Somabula	154	19.41 S	29.41 E
Sōmahara-chūtonchi, Rikujō-jieitai- ■	94	36.23 N	138.58 E
Somain	50	50.22 N	3.17 E
Somalia (Somaliya) □[1], Afr.	136	6.00 N	48.00 E
Somalia (Somaliya) □[1], Afr.	144	6.00 N	48.00 E
Somali Basin ⊕[1]	12	0.00	52.00 E
Somalie → Somalia □[1]	144	6.00 N	48.00 E
Somaliland → Somalia □[1]	144	6.00 N	48.00 E
Somali Republic → Somalia □[1]	144	6.00 N	48.00 E
Somaliya → Somalia □[1]	144	6.00 N	48.00 E
Somalomo	152	3.23 N	12.44 E
Sŏman	98	41.20 N	128.54 E
Somanga	154	8.24 S	39.17 E
Sombernon	58	47.18 N	4.42 E
Sombo	152	8.42 S	20.57 E
Sombor	38	45.46 N	19.07 E
Sombra	214	42.43 N	82.29 W
Sombrerete	234	23.38 N	103.39 W
Sombreretillo	196	26.19 N	99.58 W
Sombrero I	238	18.36 N	63.26 W
Sombrero Channel ⊔	110	7.41 N	93.35 E
Sombrio	252	29.07 S	49.40 W
Sombrio, Lagoa do ⊂	252	29.12 S	49.42 W
Şomcuta-Mare	38	47.31 N	23.29 E
Somenos	224	48.49 N	123.44 W
Somercotes	44	53.04 N	1.22 W
Somerdale, N.J., U.S.	208	39.50 N	75.01 W
Somerdale, Oh., U.S.	214	40.34 N	81.22 W
Someren	52	51.24 N	5.44 E
Somero	26	60.37 N	23.32 E
Sõmerpalu	76	57.51 N	26.48 E
Somers, Ct., U.S.	207	41.59 N	72.26 W
Somers, Mt., U.S.	202	48.04 N	114.13 W
Somers, Wi., U.S.	216	42.38 N	87.54 W
Somersby	170	33.25 S	151.17 E
Somerset, Mb., Can.	184	49.24 N	98.39 W
Somerset, Co., U.S.	200	38.55 N	107.28 W
Somerset, Ky., U.S.	192	37.05 N	84.36 W
Somerset, Md., U.S.	284c	38.58 N	77.05 W
Somerset, Ma., U.S.	207	41.46 N	71.07 W
Somerset, N.J., U.S.	208	40.44 N	74.34 W
Somerset, Oh., U.S.	188	39.48 N	82.17 W
Somerset, Pa., U.S.	188	40.00 N	79.04 W
Somerset, Tx., U.S.	196	29.13 N	98.40 W
Somerset, Wi., U.S.	190	45.07 N	92.40 W
Somerset □[6], Eng., U.K.	42	51.08 N	3.00 W
Somerset □[6], Md., U.S.	208	38.12 N	75.41 W
Somerset □[6], N.J., U.S.	208	40.34 N	74.37 W
Somerset □[6], Pa., U.S.	214	40.09 N	79.00 W
Somerset Airport ⊠	276	40.37 N	74.40 W
Somerset Center	216	42.03 N	84.25 W
Somerset East	158	32.42 S	25.35 E
Somerset Hills Airport ⊠	276	40.41 N	74.32 W
Somerset Island I, Ber.	240a	32.17 N	64.52 W
Somerset Island I, N.T., Can.	176	73.15 N	93.30 W
Somerset Reservoir ⊜[1]	171a	27.03 S	152.35 E
Somerset West	158	34.08 S	18.50 E
Somersham	42	52.23 N	0.01 E
Somers Point	208	39.19 N	74.35 W
Somersworth	188	43.15 N	70.51 W
Somerton, Eng., U.K.	42	51.03 N	2.44 W
Somerton, Az., U.S.	200	32.35 N	114.42 W
Somerton ◆[8]	285	40.06 N	75.01 W
Somerton Creek ≃	208	36.32 N	76.55 W
Somervell □[6]	222	32.15 N	97.45 W
Somerville, Austl.	169	38.13 S	145.10 E
Somerville, Ma., U.S.	207	42.23 N	71.06 W
Somerville, N.J., U.S.	210	40.34 N	74.36 W
Somerville, Oh., U.S.	218	39.33 N	84.38 W
Somerville, Tn., U.S.	194	35.14 N	89.21 W
Somerville, Tx., U.S.	222	30.20 N	96.31 W
Somerville Lake ⊜[1]	222	30.18 N	96.40 W
Someș (Szamos) ≃	38	48.07 N	22.22 E
Someșu Cald ≃	38	46.44 N	23.22 E
Someșu Mare ≃	38	47.12 N	24.12 E
Someșu Mic ≃	38	47.09 N	23.55 E
Someșu Rece ≃	38	46.44 N	23.22 E
Somino	76	59.21 N	34.52 E
Somis	228	34.16 N	119.00 W
Sŏmjin-gang ≃	98	34.58 N	127.46 E
Somma, It.	66	42.40 N	12.44 E
Somma, It.	266b	45.41 N	8.42 E
Sommacampagna	64	45.24 N	10.50 E
Somma Lombardo	62	45.41 N	8.42 E
Sommariva	166	26.24 S	146.36 E
Sommariva del Bosco	62	44.46 N	7.47 E
Sommatino	70	37.20 N	13.59 E
Somme □[5]	50	49.55 N	2.30 E
Somme ≃, Fr.	50	49.01 N	4.12 E
Somme ≃, Fr.	50	50.11 N	1.39 E
Somme, Baie de la ⊂	50	50.14 N	1.33 E
Somme, Canal de la ≋	50	49.55 N	2.43 E
Sommedieue	56	49.05 N	5.28 E
Sommelsdijk	52	51.45 N	4.09 E
Sommen ⊜	26	58.01 N	15.15 E
Sommepy-Tahure	56	49.15 N	4.33 E
Sommerberg	263	51.27 N	7.32 E
Sömmerda	54	51.10 N	11.07 E
Sommerfeld → Lubsko	30	51.46 N	14.59 E
Sommersdorf	54	53.17 N	14.11 E
Sommersted	41	55.19 N	9.19 E
Sommesous	50	48.44 N	4.12 E
Somme Woods ♦	278	42.09 N	87.49 W
Somnitel'nyj	89	52.12 N	139.04 E
Somo ≃	190	45.29 N	89.48 W
Somogy □[6]	30	46.25 N	17.35 E
Somonauk	216	41.38 N	88.40 W
Somonauk Creek ≃	216	41.32 N	88.41 W
Somosierra, Puerto de)(	34	41.09 N	3.35 W
Somosomo	175g	16.46 S	179.58 W
Somosomo Strait ⊔	175g	16.47 S	179.58 E
Somotillo	236	13.02 N	86.55 W
Somoto	236	13.28 N	86.35 W
Somovo, S.S.S.R.	76	52.53 N	34.58 E
Somovo, S.S.S.R.	78	51.44 N	39.23 E
Sompeta	122	18.56 N	84.36 E
Somplago	64	46.21 N	13.04 E
Sompolno	30	52.24 N	18.31 E
Somport, Puerto de)(	34	42.48 N	0.31 W
Sompuis	50	48.41 N	4.23 E
Somuncurá, Meseta de ⋏[1]	254	41.30 S	67.15 W
Şomvix	58	46.44 N	8.56 E
Šomyškol'	86	46.30 N	59.53 E
Son, Ned.	52	51.31 N	5.30 E
Son, Nor.	26	59.31 N	10.42 E
Son ≃	124	25.42 N	84.52 E
Soná	236	8.01 N	81.19 W
Sona-Bata	152	4.54 S	15.09 E
Sonādugi	126	22.47 N	90.40 E
Sonaguera	236	15.38 N	86.20 W
Sonahula	124	25.05 N	87.09 E
Sonāmarg	123	34.18 N	75.18 E
Sonāmukhi	126	23.18 N	87.25 E
Sonāmura	120	23.29 N	91.17 E
Sonāpur	126	23.42 N	89.30 E
Sonar	164	2.33 S	133.00 E
Sonār ≃	124	24.24 N	79.56 E
Sonari	272c	18.52 N	72.59 E
Sonārpur	272b	22.26 N	88.25 E
Sonātikri	272b	22.57 N	88.20 E
Sonceboz	58	47.11 N	7.11 E
Sonchamp	261	48.35 N	1.53 E
Sŏnch'ŏn	98	39.48 N	124.55 E
Soncino	62	45.24 N	9.52 E
Sondags ≃, S. Afr.	158	28.43 S	30.16 E
Sondags ≃, S. Afr.	158	33.44 S	25.51 E
Sondalo	64	46.20 N	10.19 E
Sønderå ≃	41	54.53 N	8.59 E
Sønderborg	41	54.55 N	9.47 E
Sønderby	41	55.47 N	10.01 E
Sønder Felding	41	55.57 N	8.47 E
Sønderhav	41	54.51 N	9.30 E
Sønderjylland □[6]	41	55.10 N	9.15 E
Sønder Nærå	41	55.18 N	10.30 E
Sønder Omme	41	55.50 N	8.54 E
Sondershausen	54	51.22 N	10.52 E
Søndersø	41	55.29 N	10.16 E
Sondi	114	2.58 N	98.52 E
Søndre Strømfjord	176	66.59 N	50.40 W
Søndre Strømfjord ⊂[2]	176	66.30 N	52.15 W
Sondrio	64	46.10 N	9.52 E
Sondrio □[4]	58	46.10 N	10.03 E
Sonduga	76	60.08 N	41.55 E
Sone ≃	126	21.34 N	86.54 E
Sonepur	120	20.50 N	83.55 E
Sonestown	210	41.21 N	76.33 W
Song, Malay.	112	2.01 N	112.33 E
Song, Nig.	146	9.50 N	12.38 E
Song, Thai	110	18.28 N	100.11 E
Song ≃	100	27.02 N	118.18 E
Song'ao	100	29.36 N	121.41 E
Songbahutun	104	41.28 N	121.11 E
Songbu	100	31.05 N	114.48 E
Sŏngbyŏn-ni	98	38.03 N	125.18 E
Song-cau	110	13.27 N	109.13 E
Sŏng-ch'ŏn-gang ≃	98	39.48 N	127.35 E
Songcun	106	30.26 N	119.43 E
Songe	26	58.41 N	9.00 E
Songea	154	10.41 S	35.39 E
Songeons	50	49.33 N	1.52 E
Songgaizhen	107	29.03 N	105.54 E
Songgang	100	22.49 N	113.51 E
Songgato ≃	164	3.26 S	140.22 E
Songhe	100	31.10 N	113.20 E
Songhua ≃	89	47.44 N	132.32 E
Songhuahu ⊜	89	43.20 N	127.07 E
Songhuajiang	89	44.46 N	125.54 E
Songhwa	98	38.21 N	125.08 E
Songino	88	48.54 N	95.54 E
Sŏngjang-ni	98	41.02 N	126.50 E
Songjiachang	107	28.47 N	104.55 E
Songjiang	106	31.01 N	121.14 E
Songjiangzhen	98	42.12 N	126.56 E
Songjiapu	107	29.38 N	104.44 E
Songjiaying	105	40.38 N	115.14 E
Sŏngjin → Kimch'aek	98	40.41 N	129.12 E
Songjŏng	98	35.10 N	126.46 E
Sŏngju	98	35.55 N	128.16 E
Songkan	102	28.27 N	106.50 E
Songkhla	110	7.12 N	100.36 E
Songkou, Zhg.	100	25.48 N	118.36 E
Songkou, Zhg.	100	24.32 N	116.24 E
Songlinba	100	24.00 N	115.59 E
Songlindian	105	39.25 N	115.54 E
Songling	89	48.02 N	121.12 E
Song Ling ⋏, Zhg.	98	41.10 N	120.09 E
Song Ling ⋏, Zhg.	104	41.30 N	120.30 E
Songlukelujia	120	29.15 N	84.49 E
Songmen	100	28.19 N	121.34 E
Songming	102	25.24 N	102.59 E
Sŏngmo-do I	98	37.42 N	126.18 E
Sŏngnae-ri	98	39.28 N	126.59 E
Sŏngnam	98	37.26 N	127.08 E
Sŏng-ni	98	39.38 N	127.06 E
Songnim	98	38.44 N	125.38 E
Songo	152	7.22 S	14.51 E
Songololo	152	5.42 S	14.02 E
Songot ∧	154	3.59 N	34.28 E
Songpan	102	32.40 N	103.24 E
Song Phi Nong	110	14.13 N	100.03 E
Sŏngsa-ri	271b	37.38 N	126.52 E
Songshancun	104	41.02 N	121.09 E
Songshu	98	39.50 N	122.06 E
Songshugou	105	41.02 N	117.49 E
Songtangmiao	106	31.08 N	119.16 E
Songtao	102	28.06 N	109.05 E

Symbols in the index entries represent the broad categories identified in the key at the right. Symbols with superior numbers (⋏[1]) identify subcategories (see complete key on page *I · 1)*.

Kartensymbole in dem Registerverzeichnis stellen die rechts in Schlüssel erklärten Kategorien dar. Symbole mit hochgestellten Ziffern (⋏[1]) bezeichnen Unterabteilungen einer Kategorie (vgl. vollständiger Schlüssel auf Seite *I · 1)*.

Los símbolos incluídos en el texto del índice representan las grandes categorias identificadas con la clave a la derecha. Los símbolos con numeros en su parte superior (⋏[1]) identifican las subcategorías (véase la clave completa en la página *I · 1)*.

Les symboles de l'index représentent les catégories indiquées dans la légende à droite. Les symboles suivis d'un indice (⋏[1]) représentent des sous-catégories (voir légende complète à la page *I · 1)*.

Os símbolos incluídos no texto do índice representam as grandes categorias identificadas com a chave à direita. Os símbolos com números em sua parte superior (⋏[1]) identificam as subcategorias (veja-se a chave completa à página *I · 1)*.

	English	Deutsch	Español	Français	Português
∧	Mountain	Berg	Montaña	Montagne	Montanha
⋏	Mountains	Berge	Montañas	Montagnes	Montanhas
)(	Pass	Pass	Paso	Col	Passo
∨	Valley, Canyon	Tal, Cañon	Valle, Cañón	Vallée, Canyon	Vale, Canhão
≚	Plain	Ebene	Llano	Plaine	Planície
>	Cape	Kap	Cabo	Cap	Cabo
I	Island	Insel	Isla	Île	Ilha
II	Islands	Inseln	Islas	Îles	Ilhas
±	Other Topographic Features	Andere Topographische Objekte	Otros Elementos Topográficos	Autres données topographiques	Outros acidentes topográficos

ESPAÑOL — Nombre / Página / Lat.°′ / Long.°′ W = Oeste
FRANÇAIS — Nom / Page / Lat.°′ / Long.°′ W = Ouest
PORTUGUÊS — Nome / Página / Lat.°′ / Long.°′ W = Oeste

Nombre	Página	Lat.°′	Long.°′ W = Oeste
Songtun	98	39.54 N	123.56 E
Songuj	24	68.47 N	33.00 E
Songu-ri	98	37.49 N	127.09 E
Songwe, Zaïre	154	3.24 S	26.16 E
Songwe, Zaïre	154	12.25 S	29.40 E
Songwe ≃	154	9.43 S	33.56 E
Songxi, Zhg.	100	26.16 N	116.59 E
Songxi, Zhg.	100	27.33 N	118.46 E
Songxia, Zhg.	100	25.44 N	119.36 E
Songxia, Zhg.	100	30.07 N	120.51 E
Songxian	102	34.10 N	112.05 E
Songyan	98	37.13 N	113.43 E
Songyin	106	30.54 N	121.13 E
Songyin ≃	100	28.18 N	119.44 E
Songzhangzi	98	41.13 N	119.08 E
Songzhuang	106	32.06 N	121.17 E
Son-ha	110	15.03 N	108.34 E
Son-hoa	110	13.02 N	108.58 E
Soni, Ehi ∧	146	20.49 N	17.23 E
Sonico	64	46.10 N	10.21 E
Sonid Youqi	102	42.44 N	112.40 E
Sonid Zuoqi	102	43.58 N	113.59 E
Soninho ≃	250	10.13 S	46.56 W
Sonīpat	124	28.59 N	77.01 E
Sonkach	124	22.59 N	76.21 E
Sonk'ol', ozero ⊜	85	41.50 N	75.08 E
Sonkovo	76	57.47 N	37.09 E
Son-la	110	21.19 N	103.54 E
Sonmiāni	120	25.26 N	66.36 E
Sonmiāni Bay c	120	25.15 N	66.30 E
Sonnberg ∧	264b	48.20 N	16.15 E
Sonneberg	54	50.22 N	11.10 E
Sonnefeld	56	50.13 N	11.08 E
Sonnen	60	48.41 N	13.43 E
Sonnenberg ∧[2]	61	47.52 N	16.28 E
Sonnewalde	54	51.42 N	13.38 E
Sonning Common	42	51.31 N	0.59 W
Sonningdale	184	52.24 N	107.40 W
Sonnino	66	41.25 N	13.14 E
Sonntagberg	61	47.59 N	14.45 E
Sono	270	34.48 N	135.55 E
Sono, Rio do ≃, Bra.	250	8.58 S	48.11 W
Sono, Rio do ≃, Bra.	255	17.02 S	45.32 W
Sonobe	96	35.06 N	135.28 E
Sonogno	58	46.21 N	8.47 E
Sonoita	232	31.51 N	112.50 W
Sonoita Creek ≃	200	31.30 N	110.58 W
Sonoma	226	38.17 N	122.27 W
Sonoma □[6]	226	38.26 N	122.35 W
Sonoma Creek ≃	226	38.10 N	122.24 W
Sonoma Mountains ⋏	226	38.17 N	122.35 W
Sonoma Peak ∧	204	40.52 N	117.36 W
Sonoma State Historical Park ♠	226	38.18 N	122.28 W
Sononder	158	29.43 S	21.51 E
Sonop	158	25.39 S	27.42 E
Sonora, Ca., U.S.	226	37.59 N	120.22 W
Sonora, Tx., U.S.	196	30.34 N	100.38 W
Sonora □[3]	232	29.20 N	110.40 W
Sonora ≃	232	28.48 N	111.33 W
Sonoran Desert ◆[2]	16	30.00 N	113.00 W
Sonora Pass)(	226	38.19 N	119.37 W
Sonostrov	24	66.09 N	34.10 E
Sonoyta ≃	200	31.16 N	113.26 W
Sonpār Hills ⋏[2]	124	24.20 N	82.15 E
Sonqor	128	34.47 N	47.36 E
Sŏnsan	98	36.16 N	128.17 E
Sonsbeck	52	51.37 N	6.22 E
Sonseca	34	39.42 N	3.57 W
Sonskyn	158	30.47 S	26.28 E
Sonsón	246	5.42 N	75.18 W
Sonsonate	236	13.43 N	89.44 W
Sonsorol Islands II	108	5.20 N	132.13 E
Sonstorp	40	58.45 N	15.36 E
Sonstraal	158	27.07 S	22.28 E
Sontag	194	31.39 N	90.12 W
Son-tay	110	21.08 N	105.30 E
Sonthofen	58	47.31 N	10.17 E
Sontra	56	51.04 N	9.56 E
Sonwān	124	27.40 N	81.45 E
Sonyea	210	42.41 N	77.50 W
Soo → Sault Sainte Marie	190	46.29 N	84.20 W
Soochow → Suzhou	106	31.18 N	120.37 E
Sooke	224	48.23 N	123.43 W
Sooke ≃	224	48.23 N	123.42 W
Sooke Basin c	224	48.23 N	123.40 W
Sooke Lake ⊜	224	48.33 N	123.42 W
Sooner Lake ⊜[1]	196	36.26 N	97.02 W
Soonwald ⋏	56	49.55 N	7.40 E
Sooyaac	144	0.03 N	42.17 E
Sopachuy	248	19.29 S	64.31 W
Sopa Sopa Head ›	164	1.58 S	146.35 E
Sopchoppy	192	30.03 N	84.29 W
Soperton	192	32.22 N	82.35 W
Sopetrán	246	6.30 N	75.46 W
Sop Hao	110	20.33 N	104.27 E
Sophia	192	37.42 N	81.15 W
Sopki	76	57.06 N	30.55 E
Sopockin	76	53.50 N	23.39 E
Sopot	30	54.28 N	18.34 E
Sop Pong	110	22.04 N	102.03 E
Sop Prap	110	17.53 N	99.20 E
Soprabolzano	64	46.32 N	11.24 E
Sopron	61	47.41 N	16.36 E
Sopronhorpács	61	47.29 N	16.44 E
Sopronkövesd	61	47.33 N	16.45 E
Soptykol'	86	51.16 N	75.45 E
Sopur	123	34.18 N	74.28 E
Sŏp'yŏng-ni	98	35.01 N	127.24 E
Soquel	226	36.59 N	121.57 W
Soquel Creek ≃	226	36.58 N	121.57 W
Sor, Ribeira de ≃	34	39.00 N	8.17 W
Sora	66	41.43 N	13.37 E
Sorada	122	19.45 N	84.26 E
Sorae-san ∧	271b	37.27 N	126.47 E
Soraga	64	46.22 N	11.39 E
Soragna	64	44.56 N	10.07 E
Söråker	26	62.31 N	17.30 E
Sorano	66	42.41 N	11.43 E
Sorapani	84	42.05 N	43.05 E
Soras	248	14.07 S	73.37 W
Sorata	248	15.47 S	68.40 W
Soratte, Monte ∧	66	42.15 N	12.30 E
Sorau → Żary	30	51.38 N	15.09 E
Soraya	248	14.10 S	73.19 W
Sorbas	34	37.07 N	2.07 W
Sorbas, gora ∧	86	47.25 N	84.12 E
Sörberge	26	62.31 N	17.22 E
Sorbhog	120	26.30 N	90.52 E
Sorbie	44	54.48 N	4.26 W
Sorbo ≃	85	38.45 N	69.20 E
Sorbolo	64	44.51 N	10.28 E
Sorbonne ♥[2]	261	48.51 N	2.21 E
Sorcier, Lac au ⊜	206	46.42 N	73.24 W
Sordevolo	62	45.34 N	7.59 E
Sordo ≃	234	16.30 N	97.31 W
Sore	32	44.20 N	0.35 W
Sorel	206	46.02 N	73.07 W
Sorell	166	42.47 S	147.33 E
Sorell, Cape ›	166	42.12 S	145.10 E
Sorel Point ›	43b	49.16 N	2.10 W
Sörenberg	58	46.50 N	8.03 E
Sorento	219	39.00 N	89.34 W
Soreq ≃	132	31.56 N	34.42 E
Soresina	64	45.17 N	9.51 E
Sörfjärden c	40	59.24 N	16.50 E
Sørfjorden c[2]	26	60.24 N	6.40 E
Sørfold	24	67.28 N	15.22 E
Sörforsa	26	61.40 N	17.00 E
Sorge ≃	41	54.21 N	9.25 E
Sorgono	71	40.01 N	9.06 E
Sorgues	62	44.00 N	4.52 E
Sorgun	130	39.49 N	35.11 E
Sori	62	44.22 N	9.06 E
Soria	34	41.46 N	2.28 W
Soriano	252	33.24 S	58.19 W
Soriano □[5]	258	33.45 S	57.45 W
Soriano Calabro	68	38.36 N	16.14 E
Soriano nel Cimino	66	42.25 N	12.14 E
Sorico	58	46.10 N	9.22 E
Sorido	164	1.09 S	136.03 E
Sori-do I	98	34.26 N	127.48 E
Sørli	26	64.15 N	13.45 E
Sormonne ≃	56	49.46 N	4.40 E
Sorn	46	55.30 N	4.18 W
Sorne ≃	58	47.22 N	7.22 E
Sorø, Dan.	41	55.26 N	11.34 E
Soro, India	120	21.17 N	86.40 E
Soro, Monte ∧	70	37.56 N	14.42 E
Sorocaba	255	23.29 S	47.27 W
Sorocá-Buçu ≃	256	23.38 S	47.13 W
Soročinka	80	47.30 N	51.44 E
Soročinsk	80	52.26 N	53.10 E
Soročkino	86	57.02 N	68.52 E
Soroco	240m	18.22 N	65.38 W
Sorok	88	52.20 N	100.12 E
Sorok ≃	61	47.07 N	16.50 E
Soroki	78	48.09 N	28.17 E
Sorokino, S.S.S.R.	86	53.45 N	84.58 E
Sorokino, S.S.S.R.	86	54.13 N	91.31 E
Sorokošiči	78	51.12 N	30.35 E
Soroksár ◆[8]	264c	47.24 N	19.07 E
Soroksári-Duna ≃[1]	264c	47.19 N	19.02 E
Sorol I[1]	108	8.08 N	140.23 E
Soron	124	27.53 N	78.45 E
Sorong	164	0.53 S	131.15 E
Sororó ≃	250	5.24 S	49.07 W
Sorot' ≃	76	57.04 N	28.50 E
Soroti	154	1.43 N	33.37 E
Sorovskije	86	59.53 N	71.34 E
Sørøya I	24	70.36 N	22.46 E
Sorpestausee ⊜[1]	56	51.20 N	7.56 E
Sorraia ≃	34	38.56 N	8.53 W
Sorrento, Austl.	169	38.20 S	144.45 E
Sorrento, It.	68	40.37 N	14.22 E
Sorrento, Fl., U.S.	220	28.48 N	81.33 W
Sorrento, La., U.S.	194	30.11 N	90.51 W
Sorris Sorris	156	20.57 S	14.50 E
Sør Rondane Mountains ⋏	9	72.00 S	25.00 E
Sorsakoski	26	62.27 N	27.39 E
Sorsatunturi ∧	24	67.24 N	29.38 E
Sorsele	24	65.30 N	17.30 E
Sorsk	86	54.01 N	90.12 E
Sorso	71	40.48 N	8.34 E
Sorsogon	116	12.58 N	124.00 E
Sorsogon □[4]	116	12.50 N	123.55 E
Sorsogon Bay c	116	12.55 N	123.55 E
Sörstafors	40	59.35 N	16.13 E
Sorsu	85	40.17 N	70.48 E
Sort	34	42.24 N	1.08 E
Sortandy	86	51.42 N	71.00 E
Sortat	46	58.33 N	3.13 W
Sortavala	24	61.42 N	30.41 E
Sortino	70	37.09 N	15.02 E
Sortland	24	68.40 N	15.20 E
Sør-Trøndelag □[6]	26	63.00 N	10.40 E
Sorūbī	120	34.36 N	69.43 E
Sorunda	40	59.01 N	17.48 E
Sörup	41	54.43 N	9.40 E
Sõrve neem ›	76	57.54 N	22.03 E
Sörvik	40	60.11 N	15.09 E
Sorviži	80	57.52 N	48.32 E
Sosa, D.D.R.	54	50.30 N	12.39 E
Sosa, Taehan	271b	37.29 N	126.47 E
Soša ≃	82	56.31 N	36.05 E
Sŏsan	98	36.47 N	126.26 E
Sösdala	41	56.02 N	13.40 E
Sos del Rey Católico	34	42.30 N	1.13 W
Sosedka	80	53.15 N	42.40 E
Sosedno	76	58.14 N	28.42 E
Sosenka ≃, S.S.S.R.	265b	55.35 N	37.23 E
Sosenka ≃, S.S.S.R.	265b	55.47 N	37.42 E
Sosenki	82	55.34 N	37.26 E
Sösetalsperre ◆[6]	52	51.44 N	10.20 E
Soshigaya ◆[8]	268	35.39 N	139.36 E
Sösjöfjällen ⋏	26	63.53 N	13.15 E
Soška	24	62.42 N	50.40 E
Soskovo	76	52.45 N	35.23 E
Sosna ≃	76	52.42 N	38.55 E
Sosneado, Cerro ∧	252	34.45 S	69.59 W
Sosnica	78	51.32 N	32.28 E
Sosnicy	76	57.38 N	30.25 E
Sosnogorsk	24	63.37 N	53.51 E
Sosnovaja Maza	80	52.30 N	47.53 E
Sosnovaja Pol'ana ◆[8]	265a	59.50 N	30.09 E
Sosnovec	24	64.26 N	34.27 E
Sosnovica	76	60.21 N	40.50 E
Sosnovka, S.S.S.R.	24	66.30 N	40.32 E
Sosnovka, S.S.S.R.	80	56.13 N	47.13 E
Sosnovka, S.S.S.R.	80	57.48 N	51.43 E
Sosnovka, S.S.S.R.	80	56.17 N	51.17 E
Sosnovka, S.S.S.R.	80	53.14 N	41.22 E
Sosnovka, S.S.S.R.	80	57.16 N	53.31 E
Sosnovka, S.S.S.R.	80	54.06 N	46.38 E
Sosnovka, S.S.S.R.	80	52.26 N	43.29 E
Sosnovka, S.S.S.R.	82	54.31 N	38.08 E
Sosnovka, S.S.S.R.	82	54.54 N	38.41 E
Sosnovka, S.S.S.R.	85	42.40 N	73.55 E
Sosnovka, S.S.S.R.	86	59.10 N	81.18 E
Sosnovka, S.S.S.R.	86	51.26 N	79.28 E
Sosnovka, S.S.S.R.	88	54.09 N	109.35 E
Sosnovo, S.S.S.R.	76	60.33 N	30.15 E
Sosnovo, S.S.S.R.	80	56.42 N	54.35 E
Sosnovoborsk	80	53.18 N	46.16 E
Sosnovoje	78	50.49 N	27.00 E
Sosnovo-Oz'orskoje	88	52.31 N	111.30 E
Sosnovskij	86	54.36 N	73.10 E
Sosnovskoje	80	55.48 N	43.10 E
Sosnovyj Bor, S.S.S.R.	76	59.55 N	29.07 E
Sosnovyj Bor, S.S.S.R.	76	52.32 N	29.36 E
Sosnovyj Bor, S.S.S.R.	86	57.07 N	55.03 E
Sosnovyj Solonec	80	53.17 N	49.33 E
Sosnowiec	30	50.18 N	19.08 E
Soso	194	31.45 N	89.16 W
Sosok	112	0.17 N	110.14 E
Sospel	62	43.53 N	7.27 E
Sospirolo	64	46.09 N	12.04 E
Sossusvlei ⊜	156	24.40 S	15.23 E
Šoštanj	61	46.23 N	15.03 E
Šostka	78	51.52 N	33.30 E
Sŏsura	98	42.16 N	130.37 E
Sos'va, S.S.S.R.	72	63.40 N	62.06 E
Sos'va, S.S.S.R.	86	59.10 N	61.50 E
Sos'va ≃	86	59.32 N	62.20 E
Sosyka ≃	78	46.35 N	39.05 E
Sot' ≃	80	58.00 N	40.39 E
Sota ≃	150	11.52 N	3.24 E
Sotério ≃	248	11.36 S	65.10 W
Sotik	154	0.41 S	35.21 E
Sotkamo	26	64.08 N	28.25 E
Sotnicyno	80	54.17 N	41.49 E
Soto de Aldovea	266a	40.26 N	3.27 W
Soto de Pajares	266a	40.17 N	3.32 W
Soto la Marina	234	23.46 N	98.13 W
Soto la Marina ≃	234	23.45 N	97.45 W
Sotomayor	248	19.18 S	65.03 W
Sotonera, Embalse de la ⊜[1]	34	42.05 N	0.48 W
Sotouboua	150	8.34 N	0.59 E
Sotta, Fr.	71	41.32 N	9.12 E
Sotta, Fr.	71	41.32 N	9.12 E
Sottens	58	46.39 N	6.44 E
Sottern ⊜	40	59.02 N	15.29 E
Sotteville	50	49.25 N	1.06 E
Sottile, Punta ›	70a	35.30 N	12.38 E
Sottomarina	64	45.13 N	12.17 E
Sottrum	52	53.06 N	9.14 E
Sottrup	41	54.57 N	9.43 E
Sottunga I	26	60.08 N	20.40 E
Souain-Perthes-lès-Hurlus	56	49.11 N	4.32 E
Souanké	152	2.05 N	14.03 E
Soubakaniédougou	150	10.28 N	5.01 W
Soubré	150	5.47 N	6.36 W
Soubré □[5]	150	5.50 N	6.40 W
Soudan	166	20.05 S	137.00 E
Soudan → Sudan □[1]	140	15.00 N	30.00 E
Soude ≃	50	48.52 N	4.10 E
Soudersburg	208	40.01 N	76.09 W
Souderton	208	40.18 N	75.19 W
Souesmes	50	47.27 N	2.10 E
Soufflay	152	2.01 N	14.54 E
Soufflenheim	56	48.50 N	7.58 E
Soufflot, Lac ⊜	190	47.24 N	78.31 W
Souflíon	38	41.12 N	26.18 E
Soufrière	241f	13.52 N	61.04 W
Soufrière ∧, Guad.	241o	16.03 N	61.40 W
Soufrière ∧, St. Vin.	241h	13.20 N	61.11 W
Soufrière Bay c, Dom.	240d	15.14 N	61.22 W
Soufrière Bay c, St. Luc.	241f	13.51 N	61.04 W
Sougahatchee Creek ≃	194	32.38 N	85.50 W
Sougne-Remouchamps	56	50.29 N	5.40 E
Souguer	148	35.12 N	1.30 E
Souhegan ≃	188	42.51 N	71.29 W
Souillac	32	44.54 N	1.29 E
Souilly	56	49.01 N	5.17 E
Souk-El-Arba-Des-Beni-Hassan	34	35.16 N	5.20 W
Souk-Khemis-Du-Sahel	34	35.17 N	6.05 W
Souk Larbat Gharb	148	34.43 N	6.01 W
Sŏul (Seoul), Taehan	98	37.33 N	126.58 E
Sŏul (Seoul), Taehan	271b	37.33 N	126.58 E
Sŏul □[4]	98	37.34 N	127.00 E
Soulac-sur-Mer	32	45.31 N	1.07 W
Soulaines-Dhuys	58	48.22 N	4.44 E
Soulanges □[6]	206	45.20 N	74.15 W
Soulanges, Canal de ≅	275a	45.20 N	73.58 W
Soulougou	150	13.01 N	0.23 E
Soulsbyville	226	37.59 N	120.16 W
Soultzeren	58	48.04 N	7.06 E
Soultz-Haut-Rhin	58	47.53 N	7.14 E
Soultzmatt	58	47.58 N	7.14 E
Soultz-sous-Forêts	56	48.56 N	7.53 E
Soummam, Oued ≃	34	36.45 N	5.04 E
Sound Beach	210	40.57 N	72.58 W
Sounding Creek ≃	184	52.06 N	110.28 W
Sounding Lake ⊜	184	52.08 N	110.29 W
Sound View Park ♠	276	40.49 N	73.52 W
Soúnion, Ákra ›	38	37.39 N	24.02 E
Soup Harbour c	212	43.51 N	77.11 W
Souppes-sur-Loing	50	48.11 N	2.44 E
Souq Ahras	148	36.23 N	8.00 E
Sources, Mont aux ∧	158	28.46 S	28.52 E
Soure, Bra.	250	0.44 S	48.31 W
Soure, Port.	34	40.03 N	8.38 W
Sour el Ghozlane	148	36.10 N	3.45 E
Souris, Mb., Can.	184	49.38 N	100.15 W
Souris, P.E., Can.	186	46.21 N	62.15 W
Souris ≃	198	49.39 N	99.34 W
Sourlake	194	30.09 N	94.25 W
Sourland Mountain ∧[2]	208	40.29 N	74.43 W
Sourou ≃	150	12.45 N	3.25 W
Souroukaha	150	8.13 N	5.08 W
Souš	54	50.32 N	13.34 E
Sous, Oued V	148	30.27 N	9.31 W
Sousa	250	6.45 S	38.14 W
Sousânia	255	16.11 S	49.05 W
Sousas	256	22.52 S	46.59 W
Sousel	34	38.57 N	7.40 W
Sous-le-Vent, Îles → Leeward Islands II	238	17.00 N	63.00 W
Sousse	148	35.49 N	10.38 E
Sousse □[8]	148	35.40 N	10.30 E
Sout ≃, S. Afr.	158	28.56 S	20.40 E
Sout ≃, S. Afr.	158	31.35 S	18.24 E
Sout ≃, S. Afr.	158	33.03 S	23.28 E
South ≃, Ia., U.S.	190	41.29 N	93.20 W
South ≃, Ma., U.S.	283	42.10 N	70.43 W
South ≃, Mo., U.S.	219	39.52 N	91.26 W
South ≃, N.J., U.S.	208	40.29 N	74.23 W
South ≃, N.C., U.S.	192	34.20 N	78.03 W
South ≃, Va., U.S.	192	37.46 N	79.23 W
South ≃, Va., U.S.	208	38.02 N	77.23 W
South Acton	207	42.27 N	71.27 W
South Africa (Suid-Afrika) □[1], Afr.	138	30.00 S	26.00 E
South Africa (Suid-Afrika) □[1], Afr.	156	30.00 S	26.00 E
Southall ◆[8]	260	51.31 N	0.23 W
South Alligator ≃	164	12.15 S	132.24 E
Southam	42	52.15 N	1.23 W
South Amboy	208	40.28 N	74.17 W
South America ⊥[1]	4	15.00 S	60.00 W
South America ⊥[1]	18	15.00 S	60.00 W
South Amherst, Ma., U.S.	207	42.20 N	72.30 W
South Amherst, Oh., U.S.	214	41.22 N	82.14 W
Southampton, N.S., Can.	186	45.35 N	64.15 W
Southampton, On., Can.	212	44.29 N	81.23 W
Southampton, Eng., U.K.	42	50.55 N	1.25 W
Southampton, Ma., U.S.	207	42.13 N	72.43 W
Southampton, N.Y., U.S.	207	40.53 N	72.23 W
Southampton, Pa., U.S.	285	40.10 N	75.02 W
Southampton □[6]	208	36.42 N	77.05 W
Southampton (Eastleigh) Airport ⊠	42	50.57 N	1.21 W
Southampton, Cape ›	176	62.09 N	83.40 W
Southampton Island I	176	64.20 N	84.40 W
South Andaman I	110	11.45 N	92.45 E
South Anna ≃	192	37.48 N	77.25 W
South Apopka	220	28.39 N	81.31 W
Southard	208	40.08 N	74.14 W
Southards Pond ⊜	276	40.43 N	73.20 W
South Ashburnham	207	42.36 N	71.56 W
South Aulatsivik Island I	176	56.45 N	61.30 W
South Australia □[3]	162	30.00 S	135.00 E
South Australian Basin ✣[1]	14	38.00 S	126.00 E
Southaven	194	34.59 N	90.02 W
South Bald Mountain ∧	200	40.45 N	105.41 W
South Baldy ∧	200	33.59 N	107.11 W
South Banda Basin ✣[1]	14	6.30 S	127.30 E
Southbank	182	54.02 N	125.46 W
South Barre	207	42.23 N	72.05 W
South Barrington	278	42.06 N	88.07 W
South Barrule ∧[2]	44	54.12 N	4.40 W
South Barwon	169	38.17 S	144.30 E
South Bass Island I	214	41.39 N	82.49 W
South Bay	220	26.39 N	80.42 W
South Bay c, Mb., Can.	184	56.43 N	99.00 W
South Bay c, N.T., Can.	176	63.58 N	83.30 W
South Bay c, On., Can.	190	45.38 N	81.50 W
South Bay c, On., Can.	212	43.55 N	77.03 W
South Bay c, On., Can.	212	44.52 N	79.47 W
South Bay c, Fl., U.S.	220	26.42 N	80.45 W
South Bay c, Va., U.S.	208	37.14 N	75.52 W
South Bay c, Wa., U.S.	224	46.53 N	124.04 W
South Baymouth	190	45.33 N	82.01 W
South Beach ♠	276	40.35 N	74.05 W
South Beacon Mountain ∧	210	41.29 N	73.57 W
South Bedias Creek ≃	222	30.54 N	95.42 W
South Bellingham	207	42.03 N	71.28 W
South Belmar	208	40.10 N	74.02 W
South Beloit	216	42.29 N	89.02 W
South Bend, In., U.S.	216	41.41 N	86.15 W
South Bend, Wa., U.S.	224	46.40 N	123.48 W
South Benfleet	42	51.33 N	0.34 E
South Bentinck Arm c	182	52.15 N	126.50 W
South Bethlehem	214	41.00 N	79.20 W
South Bihar Plains ≚	124	25.15 N	84.30 E
South Bloomfield	218	39.43 N	82.59 W
Southborough, Eng., U.K.	42	51.10 N	0.15 E
Southborough, Ma., U.S.	207	42.18 N	71.31 W
South Bosque ≃	222	31.29 N	97.16 W
South Boston	192	36.41 N	78.54 W
South Boston ◆[8]	283	42.20 N	71.03 W
South Bound Brook	276	40.33 N	74.32 W
South Bradenton	220	27.27 N	82.35 W
South Branch, Nf., Can.	186	47.55 N	59.02 W
South Branch, N.J., U.S.	276	40.33 N	74.42 W
South Brent	42	50.25 N	3.50 W
Southbridge, N.Z.	172	43.49 S	172.15 E
Southbridge, Ma., U.S.	207	42.04 N	72.02 W
South Britain	207	41.28 N	73.15 W
Southbrook, Austl.	171a	27.41 S	151.43 E
Southbrook, N.Z.	172	43.20 S	172.36 E
South Brook ≃	285	39.52 N	75.44 W
South Brookfield	186	44.23 N	64.58 W
South Brooklyn ◆[8]	276	40.41 N	73.59 W
South Bruny I	166	43.23 S	147.17 E
South Buganda □[5]	154	0.30 S	31.35 E
South Burlington	188	44.28 N	73.10 W
Southbury	207	41.28 N	73.12 W
South Butler	210	43.08 N	76.46 W
South Byfield	283	42.44 N	70.54 W
South Byron	210	43.03 N	78.04 W
South Cairo	210	42.17 N	73.57 W
South Canaan	210	41.30 N	75.25 W
South Cape ›	175g	17.01 S	179.55 E
South Carolina □[3], U.S.	178	34.00 N	81.00 W
South Carolina □[3], U.S.	192	34.00 N	81.00 W
South Carver	207	41.50 N	70.44 W
South Castor ≃	212	45.15 N	75.23 W
South Cave	44	53.46 N	0.35 W
South Cerney	42	51.40 N	1.56 W
South Chagrin Reservation ♠	279a	41.25 N	81.25 W
South Channel Ʉ, Pil.	116	14.20 N	120.37 E
South Channel Ʉ, Mi., U.S.	190	45.38 N	84.32 W
South Channel ≃[1]	281	42.32 N	82.40 W
South Chaplin	207	41.46 N	72.07 W
South Charleston, Oh., U.S.	218	39.49 N	83.38 W
South Charleston, W.V., U.S.	188	38.22 N	81.41 W
South Chatham	207	41.40 N	70.01 W
South Chelmsford	283	42.34 N	71.23 W
South Chicago ◆[8]	278	41.44 N	87.33 W
South China Basin ✣[1]	12	15.00 N	115.00 E
South China Sea ⍑[2]	108	10.00 N	113.00 E
South Cle Elum	224	47.11 N	120.56 W
South Coast Botanic Garden ♠	280	33.47 N	118.21 W
South Coatesville	208	39.58 N	75.49 W
South Coffeyville	196	36.59 N	95.37 W
South Concho ≃	196	31.21 N	100.28 W
South Corinth	210	43.12 N	73.51 W
South Corning	210	42.07 N	77.02 W
South Cotabato □[4]	116	6.15 N	125.00 E
South Creek ≃	170	33.36 S	150.50 E
South Crest	273d	26.15 S	28.07 E
South Dakota □[3], U.S.	178	44.15 N	100.00 W
South Dakota □[3], U.S.	198	44.15 N	100.00 W
South Dandalup ≃	168a	32.35 S	115.53 E
South Dandalup Dam ◆[6]	168a	32.38 S	116.04 E
South Darenth	260	51.24 N	0.15 E
South Dartmouth	207	41.35 N	70.56 W
South Dayton	210	42.21 N	79.03 W
South Deerfield	207	42.28 N	72.36 W
South Dennis, Ma., U.S.	207	41.41 N	70.09 W
South Dennis, N.J., U.S.	208	39.10 N	74.49 W
South Dorset	210	43.13 N	73.04 W
South Dorset Downs ⋏[1]	42	50.40 N	2.25 W
South Dos Palos	226	36.57 N	120.39 W
South Downs ⋏[1]	42	50.55 N	0.25 W
South Dum-Dum	126	22.37 N	88.25 E
South Duxbury	207	42.01 N	70.41 W
South East □[5]	156	25.00 S	25.45 E
Southeast Asia Treaty Organization Headquarters ♥	269a	13.45 N	100.31 E
South East Cape ›, Austl.	166	43.39 S	146.50 E
Southeast Cape ›, Ak., U.S.	180	62.55 N	169.42 W
Southeast Indian Ridge ✣[3]	6	50.00 S	110.00 E
South East Mountain ∧	241k	12.05 N	61.40 W
South Easton	207	42.02 N	71.04 W
Southeast Pacific Basin ✣[1]	6	60.00 S	115.00 W
South East Point ›	174o	1.40 N	157.10 W
South Egg Harbor	208	39.31 N	74.39 W
South Egremont	207	42.09 N	73.25 W
South Elgin	216	41.59 N	88.17 W
South Elkhorn Creek ≃	218	38.13 N	84.48 W
South El Monte	280	34.03 N	118.02 W
Southend	44	55.20 N	5.38 W
Southend Municipal Airport ⊠	42	51.34 N	0.41 E
Southend-on-Sea	42	51.33 N	0.43 E
Southend-on-Sea □[8]	260	51.33 N	0.41 E
Southend Pier ◆[5]	260	51.31 N	0.44 E
South English ≃	190	41.30 N	91.56 W
Southern □[4], Malawi	154	15.30 S	35.00 E
Southern □[4], S.L.	150	8.00 N	12.15 W
Southern □[4], Zam.	154	16.30 S	27.00 E
Southern □[5], Bots.	156	24.45 S	24.00 E
Southern □[5], Ug.	154	0.30 S	30.30 E
Southern Alps ⋏	172	43.30 S	170.30 E
Southern California, University of ♥[2]	280	34.02 N	118.17 W
Southern Cook Islands II	14	20.00 S	159.00 W
Southern Cross	162	31.13 S	119.19 E
Southern Ghāts ⋏	122	9.30 N	77.00 E
Southern Highlands □[5]	164	6.00 S	143.30 E
Southern Indian Lake ⊜	176	57.10 N	98.40 W
Southern Leyte □[4]	116	10.50 N	124.55 E
Southern Lueti ≃	152	16.14 S	23.13 E
Southern Pines	192	35.10 N	79.23 W
Southern Ute Indian Reservation ◆[4]	200	37.05 N	107.45 W
Southern View	219	39.46 N	89.39 W
Southern Yemen → Yemen, People's Democratic Republic of □[1]	144	15.00 N	48.00 E
Southery	42	52.32 N	0.23 E
South Esk ≃, Austl.	166	41.25 S	147.08 E
South Esk ≃, Scot., U.K.	46	56.42 N	2.32 W
South Esk ≃, Scot., U.K.	46	55.53 N	3.04 W
Southesk Tablelands ⋏[1]	162	20.50 S	126.40 E
South Essex	207	42.38 N	70.46 W
South Euclid	214	41.31 N	81.31 W
Southey	184	50.56 N	104.30 W
South Fabius ≃	219	39.54 N	91.30 W
South Fallsburg	210	41.42 N	74.37 W
South Farmbridge	260	51.38 N	0.41 E
South Farmingdale	276	40.43 N	73.26 W
Southfield, Ma., U.S.	207	42.06 N	73.14 W
Southfield, Mi., U.S.	216	42.28 N	83.13 W
Southfields	210	41.15 N	74.11 W
South Fiji Basin ✣[1]	14	26.00 S	175.00 E
Southfleet	260	51.25 N	0.19 E
South Floral Park	276	40.43 N	73.42 W
South Foreland ›	42	51.09 N	1.23 E
South Fork, Co., U.S.	200	37.40 N	106.38 W
South Fork, Pa., U.S.	214	40.22 N	78.47 W
South Fort George	182	53.54 N	122.45 W
South Forty Foot Drain ≅	42	52.56 N	0.15 W
South Fox Island I	190	45.25 N	85.50 W
South Fulton	194	36.30 N	88.52 W
South Gate, Ca., U.S.	228	33.57 N	118.12 W
Southgate, Fl., U.S.	220	27.18 N	82.32 W
Southgate, Mi., U.S.	216	42.12 N	83.11 W
Southgate, Wa., U.S.	224	47.10 N	122.30 W
Southgate ◆[8]	260	51.38 N	0.08 W
Southgate U.S.A. ◆[9]	279a	41.25 N	81.32 W
South Georgia I	244	54.15 S	36.45 W
South Gibson	210	41.44 N	75.38 W
South Glamorgan □[6]	42	51.30 N	3.25 W
South Glastonbury	207	41.40 N	72.35 W
South Glens Falls	210	43.17 N	73.38 W
South Grafton	207	42.11 N	71.42 W
South Grand ≃	194	38.18 N	93.28 W
South Grand Island Bridge ◆[5]	284a	43.00 N	78.56 W
South Green	260	51.37 N	0.26 E
South Greensburg	214	40.17 N	79.33 W
South Hackensack	276	40.51 N	74.02 W
South Hadley, Ma., U.S.	188	42.15 N	72.34 W
South Hadley, Ma., U.S.	207	42.15 N	72.34 W
South Hadley Falls	207	42.13 N	72.36 W
South Hamilton	207	42.36 N	70.52 W
South Hams ≚	42	50.22 N	3.50 W
South Hanningfield	260	51.39 N	0.31 E
South Hanover	283	42.05 N	70.51 W
South Harbor c	269f	14.33 N	120.58 E
South Hartford	210	43.21 N	73.25 W
South Harwich	207	41.40 N	70.02 W
South Hātia Island I	124	22.19 N	91.07 E
South Haven, In., U.S.	216	41.32 N	87.08 W
South Haven, Ks., U.S.	198	37.03 N	97.24 W
South Haven, Mi., U.S.	216	42.24 N	86.16 W
South Hayling	42	50.47 N	0.59 W
South Head ›	274a	33.50 S	151.17 E
South Heart ≃	182	55.34 N	116.11 W
South Heights	279b	40.35 N	80.14 W
South Hempstead	276	40.41 N	73.37 W
South Henderson	192	36.17 N	78.25 W
South Henik Lake ⊜	176	61.30 N	97.30 W
South Hero	188	44.38 N	73.18 W
South Hetton	44	54.48 N	1.24 W
South Hill, N.Y., U.S.	210	42.25 N	76.33 W
South Hill, Va., U.S.	192	36.43 N	78.07 W
South Hills ◆[8]	273d	26.15 S	28.05 E
South Hills Village ◆[9]	279b	40.21 N	80.03 W
South Hingham	207	42.11 N	70.52 W
South Hogan Creek ≃	218	39.03 N	84.54 W
South Holland	216	41.36 N	87.36 W
South Holston Lake ⊜[1]	192	36.35 N	82.00 W
South Honcut Creek ≃	226	39.19 N	121.35 W
South Honshu Ridge ✣[3]	14	24.00 N	142.00 E
South Hopkinton	207	41.24 N	71.45 W
South Horr	154	2.06 N	36.55 E
South Houston	222	29.39 N	95.14 W
South Huntington	276	40.49 N	73.23 W
South Indian Basin ✣[1]	6	60.00 S	120.00 E
South Indian Lake	184	56.46 N	98.57 W
Southington, Ct., U.S.	207	41.35 N	72.52 W
Southington, Oh., U.S.	214	41.19 N	80.57 W
South International Falls	190	48.35 N	93.23 W
South Ionia	216	42.57 N	85.04 W
South Island I, India	122	10.03 N	72.17 E
South Island I, Kenya	154	2.38 N	36.36 E
South Island I, N.Z.	172	43.00 S	171.00 E
South Island I, T.T.P.I.	175c	6.59 N	151.59 E
South Islet I	116	8.44 N	119.49 E
South Jacksonville	219	39.42 N	90.13 W
South Kemptville Creek ≃	212	44.54 N	75.41 W
South Kenosha	216	42.32 N	87.50 W
South Kensington Museums ♥	260	51.30 N	0.11 W
South Kent	207	41.40 N	73.28 W
South Kirkby	44	53.34 N	1.20 W
South Konkan Hills ⋏[2]	122	17.00 N	73.30 E
South Korea → Korea, South □[1]	98	36.30 N	128.00 E
South Ladder Creek ≃	198	38.41 N	101.34 W
South Laguna	228	33.30 N	117.45 W
Southlake	222	32.57 N	97.09 W
South Lake ⊜, On., Can.	212	44.26 N	76.13 W
South Lake ⊜, Fl., U.S.	220	28.37 N	80.52 W
South Lake Tahoe	226	38.56 N	119.58 W
South Lancaster	207	42.26 N	71.41 W
Southland, Ky., U.S.	218	38.01 N	84.31 W
Southland, Mi., U.S.	216	42.13 N	84.24 W
Southland, Tx., U.S.	196	33.22 N	101.33 W
Southland ◆[9]	282	37.39 N	122.06 W
South Laurel	284c	39.05 N	76.52 W
Southlawn, Il., U.S.	219	39.45 N	89.37 W
South Lawn, Md., U.S.	284c	38.48 N	76.59 W
South Layhill	284c	39.04 N	77.03 W
South Lebanon	218	39.22 N	84.12 W
South Lee	207	42.16 N	73.16 W
South Lima	210	42.51 N	77.41 W
South Line Island I	276	40.37 N	73.30 W
South Llano ≃	196	30.30 N	99.46 W
South Lockport	284a	43.09 N	78.42 W
South Lorain	279a	41.27 N	82.08 W
South Loup ≃	198	41.04 N	98.40 W
South Luangwa National Park ♠	154	12.50 S	31.45 E
South Luconia Shoals ✣[2]	112	5.00 N	112.42 E
South Lynnfield	283	42.31 N	71.00 W
South Lyon	216	42.27 N	83.39 W
South Macmillan ≃	180	63.03 N	133.18 W
South Magnetic Pole ◆	9	65.53 S	139.28 E
South Malosmadulu Atoll I[1]	122	5.10 N	72.58 E
South Manitou Island I	190	45.01 N	86.07 W
South Marsh Island I	208	38.06 N	76.02 W
South Medford	202	42.18 N	122.50 W
South Media	285	39.54 N	75.23 W
South Melbourne	274b	37.50 S	144.57 E
South Merrimack	207	42.48 N	71.33 W
South Miami	220	25.42 N	80.17 W
South Miami Heights	220	25.35 N	80.22 W
South Middleboro	207	41.49 N	70.49 W
South Milford	216	41.31 N	85.16 W
South Mills	192	36.26 N	76.19 W
South Milwaukee	216	42.54 N	87.51 W
South Mimms	260	51.42 N	0.14 W
Southminster	42	51.40 N	0.50 E
South Modesto	226	37.38 N	120.58 W
South Mokelumne ≃	226	38.08 N	121.35 W
South Molton	42	51.01 N	3.50 W
South Monroe	216	41.54 N	83.25 W
Southmont	214	40.18 N	78.56 W
South Montrose	210	41.48 N	75.53 W
South Moose Lake ⊜	184	53.46 N	100.08 W
South Mountain	208	39.51 N	77.29 W
South Mountain ∧, U.S.	208	39.40 N	77.30 W
South Mountain ∧, Id., U.S.	202	42.44 N	116.54 W
South Mountain Reservation ♠	276	40.45 N	74.18 W
South Mount Vernon	214	40.23 N	82.23 W
South Nahanni ≃	176	61.03 N	123.20 W
South Naknek	180	58.43 N	157.00 W
South Nation ≃	188	45.34 N	75.06 W
South Negril Point ›	241q	18.15 N	78.22 W
South New Berlin	210	42.31 N	75.23 W
South New Castle	214	40.58 N	80.21 W
South New River Canal ≅	220	26.04 N	80.12 W
South Norfolk → Chesapeake	208	36.43 N	76.15 W
South Normanton	44	53.06 N	1.20 W
South Norwalk Reservoir ⊜[1]	276	41.11 N	73.27 W
South Norwood ◆[8]	260	51.24 N	0.04 W
South Nutfield	260	51.14 N	0.08 W
South Nyack	276	41.04 N	73.55 W
South Ockendon	42	51.32 N	0.18 E
South Ogden	200	41.11 N	111.58 W
Southold	207	41.03 N	72.25 W
South Onondaga	210	42.56 N	76.13 W
South Orange	276	40.47 N	74.15 W
South Orkney Islands II	9	60.35 S	45.30 W
South Oroville	226	39.30 N	121.33 W
South Otselic	210	42.38 N	75.46 W
Southowram	262	53.43 N	1.50 W
South Oxhey	260	51.38 N	0.23 W
South Oyster Bay c	276	40.38 N	73.28 W
South Palo Duro Creek ≃	196	36.06 N	101.29 W
South Para ≃	168b	34.36 S	138.45 E
South Para Reservoir ⊜[1]	168b	34.42 S	138.52 E
South Paris	188	44.13 N	70.30 W
South Park	216	41.44 N	88.18 W
South Park ♠, N.Y., U.S.	284a	42.50 N	78.50 W
South Park ♠, Pa., U.S.	279b	40.19 N	80.01 W
South Pasadena, Ca., U.S.	280	34.06 N	118.08 W
South Pasadena, Fl., U.S.	220	27.46 N	82.43 W
South Pass)(	200	42.22 N	108.55 W
South Pass Ʉ	175c	7.14 N	151.48 E
South Passage Ʉ, Austl.	171a	27.22 S	153.26 E
South Passage Ʉ, Oh., U.S.	214	41.35 N	82.45 W
South Patrick Shores	220	28.12 N	80.35 W
South Pekin	190	40.29 N	89.39 W
South Pender	224	48.45 N	123.14 W
South Pender Island I	224	48.45 N	123.10 W
South Perth	168a	31.59 S	115.52 E
South Petherton	42	50.58 N	2.49 W
South Philadelphia ◆[8]	285	39.56 N	75.10 W
South Philipsburg	214	40.53 N	78.13 W
South Pittsburg	194	35.00 N	85.42 W
South Plainfield	210	40.34 N	74.24 W
South Platte ≃	178	41.07 N	100.42 W
South Platte, North Fork ≃	200	39.25 N	105.10 W
South Point ›, Austl.	166	39.00 S	146.20 E
South Point ›, Ba.	238	22.50 N	74.52 W
South Point ›, Barb.	241g	13.02 N	59.31 W
South Point ›, Pil.	116	10.24 N	122.30 E
South Pole ◆	9	90.00 S	0.00
South Porcupine	190	48.28 N	81.13 W
Southport, Austl.	171a	27.58 S	153.25 E
Southport, Eng., U.K.	44	53.39 N	3.01 W
Southport, Ct., U.S.	207	41.08 N	73.17 W
Southport, Fl., U.S.	194	30.17 N	85.38 W
Southport, In., U.S.	218	39.39 N	86.07 W
Southport, N.Y., U.S.	210	42.03 N	76.49 W
Southport, N.C., U.S.	192	33.55 N	78.01 W
South Portland	188	43.38 N	70.14 W
South Portsmouth	218	38.43 N	83.00 W
South Pottstown	208	40.14 N	75.39 W
South Prairie Creek ≃	224	47.08 N	122.10 W
South Raisin ≃	206	45.08 N	74.35 W
South Range	190	47.04 N	88.38 W
South Renovo	214	41.19 N	77.44 W
South Reservoir ⊜[1]	283	42.27 N	71.07 W
South Ribble □[8]	262	53.45 N	2.42 W
South River, On., Can.	190	45.50 N	79.23 W
South River, N.J., U.S.	208	40.26 N	74.23 W
South River c	208	38.57 N	76.29 W
South Rockwood	216	42.04 N	83.16 W
South Ronaldsay I	46	58.46 N	2.58 W
South Roxana	219	38.50 N	90.04 W
South Royalston	207	42.37 N	72.08 W
South Rukuru ≃	154	10.46 S	34.14 E
South Russell	214	41.25 N	81.21 W
South Salmara	124	25.55 N	90.01 E
South Sand Bluff ›	158	31.19 S	30.01 E
South Sandwich Islands II	18	57.45 S	26.30 W
South Sandwich Trench ✣[1]	18	56.30 S	25.00 W
South Sandy Creek ≃	212	43.43 N	76.12 W
South San Francisco	226	37.39 N	122.24 W
South San Gabriel	280	34.03 N	118.05 W
South San Jose Hills	280	34.01 N	117.55 W
South San Ramon Creek ≃	282	37.42 N	121.55 W
South Santiam ≃	202	44.41 N	123.00 W
South Saskatchewan ≃	184	53.15 N	105.05 W
South Saugeen ≃	212	44.08 N	81.02 W
South Seaville	208	39.10 N	74.45 W
South Setauket	210	40.54 N	73.06 W
South Shafter	226	35.28 N	119.17 W
South Shetland Islands II	9	62.00 S	58.00 W
South Shields	44	55.00 N	1.25 W
South Shore	218	38.43 N	82.59 W
South Shore ◆[8]	278	41.46 N	87.35 W
South Shore Mall ◆[9]	276	40.44 N	73.15 W
South Shore Plaza ◆[9]	283	42.13 N	71.01 W
Southside	174h	2.49 S	171.43 W
South Side ◆[8]	279b	40.26 N	79.58 W
Southside Place	222	29.42 N	95.26 W
South Sioux City	198	42.28 N	96.24 W
South Skunk ≃	190	41.15 N	92.02 W
South Slocan	182	49.28 N	117.32 W
South Solon	218	39.44 N	83.36 W
South Sound Ʉ	48	53.02 N	9.28 W
South Spicer Island I	176	68.06 N	79.13 W
South Standard	219	39.21 N	89.47 W
South Station ◆[5]	283	42.21 N	71.04 W

	English	Deutsch	Español	Français	Português
≃	River	Fluss	Río	Rivière	Rio
≅	Canal	Kanal	Canal	Canal	Canal
ᒪ	Waterfall, Rapids	Wasserfall, Stromschnellen	Cascada, Rápidos	Chute d'eau, Rapides	Cascata, Rápidos
Ʉ	Strait	Meeresstrasse	Estrecho	Détroit	Estreito
c	Bay, Gulf	Bucht, Golf	Bahía, Golfo	Baie, Golfe	Baía, Golfo
⊜	Lake, Lakes	See, Seen	Lago, Lagos	Lac, Lacs	Lago, Lagos
≡	Swamp	Sumpf	Pantano	Marais	Pântano
⊓	Ice Features, Glacier	Eis- und Gletscherformen	Accidentes Glaciales	Formes glaciaires	Acidentes glaciares
⍑	Other Hydrographic Features	Andere Hydrographische Objekte	Otros Elementos Hidrográficos	Autres données hydrographiques	Outros acidentes hidrográficos

	English	Deutsch	Español	Français	Português
✣	Submarine Features	Untermeerische Objekte	Accidentes Submarinos	Formes de relief sous-marin	Acidentes submarinos
□	Political Unit	Politische Einheit	Unidad Politica	Entité politique	Unidade política
♥	Cultural Institution	Kulturelle Institution	Institución Cultural	Institution culturelle	Institução cultural
⊥	Historical Site	Historische Stätte	Sitio Histórico	Site historique	Sitio histórico
♠	Recreational Site	Erholungs- und Ferienort	Sitio de Recreo	Centre de loisirs	Area de Lazer
⊠	Airport	Flughafen	Aeropuerto	Aéroport	Aeroporto
■	Military Installation	Militäranlage	Instalación Militar	Installation militaire	Instalação militar
◆	Miscellaneous	Verschiedenes	Misceláneo	Divers	Diversos

ENGLISH / DEUTSCH

Name / Name	Page / Seite	Lat.°′ / Breite°′	Long.°′ / Länge°′ E = Ost
South Sterling	210	41.17 N	75.21 W
South Stickney	278	41.45 N	87.46 W
South Stony Brook	276	40.53 N	73.07 W
South Stradbroke Island I	171a	27.51 S	153.25 E
South Streator	216	40.39 N	88.23 W
South Suburban → Behāla	126	22.31 N	88.19 E
South Sulphur ≃	196	33.23 N	95.18 W
South Sunday Creek ≃	202	46.27 N	105.54 W
South Superior	200	41.45 N	108.57 W
South Swansea	207	41.43 N	71.12 W
South Sydney	274a	33.55 S	151.13 E
South Taranaki Bight ⊂[3]	172	39.40 S	174.10 E
South Tasman Rise ✦[3]	6	49.00 S	148.00 E
South Temple	208	40.24 N	75.55 W
South Thompson ≃	182	50.41 N	120.21 W
South Toms River	208	39.56 N	74.12 W
South Torrington	198	42.02 N	104.10 W
South Towanda	210	41.45 N	76.27 W
South Tucson	200	32.11 N	110.58 W
South Turkeyfoot Creek ≃	216	41.25 N	83.58 W
South Turlock	226	37.29 N	120.51 W
South Twillingate Island I	186	49.37 N	54.47 W
South Tyne ≃	44	54.59 N	2.08 W
South Ubian	116	5.11 N	120.30 E
South Uist I	46	57.15 N	7.21 W
South Umpqua ≃	202	43.20 N	123.25 W
South Valley	210	42.42 N	74.43 W
South Valley Hills ⋏[2]	285	40.00 N	75.40 W
South Valley Stream	276	40.38 N	73.44 W
South Venice	220	27.03 N	82.25 W
South Ventana Cone ∧	204	36.17 N	121.38 W
South Vestal	210	42.01 N	76.00 W
South Vietnam → Vietnam □[1]	108	16.00 N	108.00 E
Southview	214	40.20 N	80.16 W
Southview Apartments	284c	38.50 N	77.00 W
South Vijayapuri	122	16.49 N	79.33 E
South Wabasca Lake ⊜	182	55.54 N	113.45 W
South Wales	210	42.43 N	78.35 W
South Walpole	283	42.06 N	71.15 W
Southwark ◆[8]	42	51.30 N	0.06 W
South Warren Reservoir ⊜[1]	168b	34.43 S	138.55 E
Southwater	42	51.01 N	0.21 W
South Waverly	210	41.59 N	76.32 W
South Weald	260	51.37 N	0.16 E
Southwell	44	53.05 N	0.58 W
South Wellfleet	207	41.55 N	69.59 W
South Wellington	224	49.06 N	123.53 W
Southwest	214	40.12 N	79.32 W
South West Bay ⊂	240b	25.00 N	77.32 W
Southwest Branch ≃	284c	38.53 N	76.48 W
South Westbury	276	40.45 N	73.35 W
South West Cape >, Austl.	166	43.34 S	146.02 E
Southwest Cape >, N.Z.	172	47.17 S	167.28 E
Southwest Cape >, Ak., U.S.	180	63.18 N	171.27 W
Southwest Cape >, Vir. Is., U.S.	241n	17.41 N	64.54 W
Southwest Channel ɥ	220	27.34 N	82.45 W
South West City	194	36.30 N	94.36 W
South Westerlo	210	42.27 N	74.02 W
Southwest Greensburg	214	40.17 N	79.33 W
Southwest Harbor	188	44.16 N	68.19 W
Southwest Indian Ridge ✦[3]	6	30.00 S	60.00 E
Southwest Miramichi ≃	186	46.58 N	65.35 W
Southwest Museum ❦	280	34.06 N	118.13 W
Southwest National Park ♠	166	43.15 S	146.15 E
Southwest Pacific Basin ✦[1]	6	40.00 S	150.00 W
Southwest Point >, Ba.	238	25.51 N	77.13 W
South West Point >, Kiribati	174o	1.52 N	157.33 W
Southwest Point >, Pap. N. Gui.	164	2.14 S	146.34 E
Southwest Road ɥ	240m	18.20 N	65.00 W
South Weymouth	283	42.10 N	70.57 W
South Weymouth Naval Air Station ■	207	42.09 N	70.57 W
South Whitley	216	41.05 N	85.37 W
South Whittier	280	33.57 N	118.02 W
South Wichita ≃	196	33.43 N	99.29 W
Southwick, Eng., U.K.	42	50.50 N	0.13 W
Southwick, Ma., U.S.	207	42.03 N	72.46 W
South Williamson	192	37.40 N	82.17 W
South Williamsport	210	41.13 N	76.59 W
South Wilmington	216	41.10 N	88.16 W
South Windham	188	43.44 N	70.25 W
South Windsor	207	41.49 N	72.37 W
Southwold	42	52.20 N	1.40 E
Southwood	210	42.59 N	76.08 W
Southwood Acres	207	41.59 N	72.32 W
South Woodham Ferrers	42	51.39 N	0.37 E
South Woodslee	214	42.14 N	82.43 W
South Woodstock	207	41.56 N	71.57 W
Southworth	224	47.31 N	122.30 W
South Yadkin ≃	192	35.45 N	80.27 W
South Yamhill ≃	224	45.13 N	123.08 W
South Yarmouth	207	41.40 N	70.11 W
South Yorkshire □[6]	44	53.30 N	1.15 W
South Yuba ≃	226	39.17 N	121.12 W
South Zeal	42	50.44 N	3.54 W
Soutpan	158	28.43 S	26.04 E
Soutpansberg ⋏	156	22.55 S	29.30 E
Souttouf, Adrar ⋏	148	22.15 N	15.40 W
Souvigny	32	46.32 N	3.11 E
Souzy-la-Briche	261	48.32 N	2.09 E
Sovata	38	46.35 N	25.04 E
Soverato	68	38.41 N	16.33 E
Sovere	64	45.49 N	10.01 E
Sovereign Hill Historical Park ⊥	169	37.37 S	143.51 E
Sovereign Mountain ∧	180	62.08 N	148.36 W
Soveria Mannelli	68	39.05 N	16.22 E
Sövestad	41	55.30 N	13.47 E
Sovetabad	85	40.48 N	72.58 E
Sovetašen, S.S.S.R.	84	39.50 N	45.03 E
Sovetašen, S.S.S.R.	84	40.06 N	44.33 E
Sovetka	83	47.30 N	39.15 E
Sovetsk, S.S.S.R.	76	53.56 N	37.39 E
Sovetsk, S.S.S.R.	76	55.05 N	21.53 E
Sovetsk, S.S.S.R.	80	57.37 N	48.58 E
Sovetskaja, S.S.S.R.	80	49.00 N	42.07 E
Sovetskaja, S.S.S.R.	84	44.46 N	41.11 E
Sovetskaja, S.S.S.R.	84	44.02 N	44.03 E
Sovetskaja Gavan'	89	48.58 N	140.18 E
Sovetskich Oficerov, pik ∧	85	38.26 N	73.18 E
Sovetskij, S.S.S.R.	76	60.32 N	28.41 E
Sovetskij, S.S.S.R.	78	45.20 N	34.56 E
Sovetskij, S.S.S.R.	80	56.46 N	48.32 E
Sovetskij, S.S.S.R.	85	40.11 N	71.19 E
Sovetskij, S.S.S.R.	85	38.02 N	69.35 E
Sovetskij, S.S.S.R.	86	51.04 N	56.29 E
Sovetskoje, S.S.S.R.	78	50.21 N	39.01 E
Sovetskoje, S.S.S.R.	80	51.27 N	46.44 E
Sovetskoje, S.S.S.R.	80	47.18 N	44.31 E
Sovetskoje, S.S.S.R.	84	43.19 N	43.36 E
Sovetskoje, S.S.S.R.	84	42.52 N	45.41 E
Şovetskoje, S.S.S.R.	85	42.17 N	70.15 E
Sovgenovskij	78	45.02 N	40.14 E
Sovicille	66	43.17 N	11.13 E
Sovico	266b	45.39 N	9.16 E
Soviet Union → Union of Soviet Socialist Republics □[1]	72	60.00 N	80.00 E
Søvik	26	62.33 N	6.18 E
Søvind	41	55.54 N	10.01 E
Sovpolje	24	65.18 N	43.55 E
Sow ≃	42	52.48 N	2.00 W
Sowa Pan ≚	156	20.45 S	26.00 E
Sowek	164	0.49 S	135.30 E
Sowerby, Eng., U.K.	44	54.13 N	1.21 W
Sowerby, Eng., U.K.	262	53.42 N	1.56 W
Sowerby Bridge	44	53.43 N	1.54 W
Soweto	158	26.14 S	27.54 E
Sowjetisches Ehrenmal ⊥	264a	52.29 N	13.28 E
Sowjetunion → Union of Soviet Socialist Republics □[1]	72	60.00 N	80.00 E
Soy	56	50.17 N	5.31 E
Sōya-kaikyō → La Perouse Strait ɥ	89	45.45 N	142.00 E
Sōya-misaki >	92a	45.31 N	141.56 E
Soyang-chŏsuji ⊜[1]	98	37.56 N	127.53 E
Soyapango	236	13.42 N	89.09 W
Soyers Lake ⊜	212	45.02 N	78.37 W
Soyet	124	24.12 N	76.10 E
Soyland Moor ◆[3]	262	53.40 N	2.02 W
Soyo	152	6.07 S	12.18 E
Soyons	62	44.53 N	4.51 E
Sož ≃, S.S.S.R.	78	51.57 N	30.48 E
Soz' ≃, S.S.S.R.	82	56.48 N	36.44 E
Şozimskij	24	59.44 N	52.16 E
Šožma	24	61.56 N	40.15 E
Sozopol	38	42.25 N	27.42 E
Sozzago	266b	45.24 N	8.43 E
Spa	56	50.30 N	5.52 E
Space Needle ❦	224	47.38 N	122.23 W
Space Obelisk ⊥	265b	55.49 N	37.38 E
Spadafora	70	38.13 N	15.22 E
Spada Lake ⊜[1]	224	47.57 N	121.40 W
Spaden	52	53.34 N	8.38 E
Spahl	56	50.39 N	9.55 E
Spaichingen	58	48.04 N	8.44 E
Spain (España) □[1], Europe	22	40.00 N	4.00 W
Spain (España) □[1], Europe	34	40.00 N	4.00 W
Spakenburg	52	52.15 N	5.23 E
Spalato → Split	36	43.31 N	16.27 E
Spalding, Austl.	166	33.30 S	138.37 E
Spalding, Sk., Can.	184	52.20 N	104.30 W
Spalding, Eng., U.K.	42	52.47 N	0.10 W
Spalding, Mo., U.S.	219	39.38 N	91.32 W
Spalding, Ne., U.S.	198	41.41 N	98.21 W
Spalt	56	49.10 N	10.55 E
Spam Island I	174h	2.48 S	171.43 W
Spanaway	224	47.06 N	122.26 W
Spandau ◆[8]	54	52.33 N	13.12 E
Spandau, Berliner Forst ◆[3]	264a	52.35 N	13.11 E
Spang	41	54.56 N	9.50 E
Spangenberg	56	51.07 N	9.40 E
Spangler	214	40.38 N	78.46 W
Spaniard's Bay	186	47.37 N	53.17 W
Spanien → Spain □[1]	34	40.00 N	4.00 W
Spanish	190	46.12 N	82.21 W
Spanish ≃	190	46.11 N	82.19 W
Spanish Camp	222	29.23 N	96.10 W
Spanish Fork	200	40.06 N	111.39 W
Spanish Lake	219	38.47 N	90.12 W
Spanish North Africa □[2], Afr.	34	35.53 N	5.19 W
Spanish North Africa □[2], Afr.	134	35.53 N	5.19 W
Spanish Peak ∧	202	44.24 N	119.46 W
Spanish Point >	240a	32.18 N	64.48 W
Spanish Sahara → Western Sahara □[2]	134	24.30 N	13.00 W
Spanish Town	241q	17.59 N	76.57 W
Spannberg	61	48.27 N	16.44 E
Sparagio, Monte ∧	70	38.03 N	12.46 E
Sparbach	264b	48.04 N	16.11 E
Spargi, Isola I	71	41.14 N	9.21 E
Sparkford	42	51.02 N	2.34 W
Sparkill	276	41.02 N	73.56 W
Sparkle Lake	210	41.18 N	73.47 W
Sparkman	194	33.55 N	92.50 W
Sparks, Ga., U.S.	192	31.10 N	83.26 W
Sparks, Nv., U.S.	226	39.32 N	119.45 W
Sparland	190	41.02 N	89.26 W
Sparlingville	214	42.58 N	82.30 W
Sparneck	54	50.09 N	11.50 E
Sparreholm	40	59.04 N	16.49 E
Sparrow Bush	210	41.23 N	74.43 W
Sparrow Lake ⊜	212	44.49 N	79.24 W
Sparrowpit	262	53.19 N	1.52 W
Sparrows Point	208	39.13 N	76.28 W
Sparrows Point >	284b	39.12 N	76.30 W
Sparta, On., Can.	212	42.42 N	81.05 W
Sparta → Spárti, Ellás	38	37.05 N	22.27 E
Sparta, Ga., U.S.	192	33.16 N	82.58 W
Sparta, Il., U.S.	194	38.07 N	89.42 W
Sparta, Ky., U.S.	218	38.40 N	84.54 W
Sparta, Mi., U.S.	190	43.09 N	85.42 W
Sparta, N.J., U.S.	210	41.02 N	74.38 W
Sparta, N.C., U.S.	192	36.30 N	81.07 W
Sparta, Oh., U.S.	214	40.24 N	82.42 W
Sparta, Tn., U.S.	194	35.55 N	85.27 W
Sparta, Wi., U.S.	190	43.56 N	90.48 W
Sparta Brook ≃	276	41.08 N	73.52 W
Spartak Garden ♠	265a	59.51 N	30.30 E
Sparta Lake	210	41.03 N	74.34 W
Spartanburg, In., U.S.	218	40.03 N	84.51 W
Spartanburg, S.C., U.S.	192	34.56 N	81.55 W
Spartansburg	214	41.49 N	79.41 W
Spartel, Cap >	34	35.48 N	5.56 W
Spárti (Sparta)	38	37.05 N	22.27 E
Spartivento, Capo >, It.	68	37.55 N	16.04 E
Spartivento, Capo >, It.	71	38.53 N	8.50 E
Spas-Demensk	76	54.25 N	34.01 E
Spas-Klepiki	80	55.08 N	40.13 E
Spass	82	55.55 N	35.55 E
Spassk-Dal'nij	89	44.37 N	132.48 E
Spasskij	86	53.42 N	59.12 E
Spasskij Zavod	86	49.32 N	73.17 E
Spasskoje, S.S.S.R.	76	53.06 N	36.24 E
Spasskoje, S.S.S.R.	80	55.52 N	45.42 E
Spasskoje, S.S.S.R.	82	54.05 N	38.28 E
Spassk-R'azanskij	80	54.24 N	40.23 E
Spas-Zaulok	82	56.29 N	36.34 E
Spáta	267c	38.00 N	21.31 E
Spátha, Ákra >	38	35.42 N	23.44 E
Spaulding	219	39.52 N	89.32 W
Spaulding, Lake ⊜[1]	226	39.20 N	120.37 W
Speaks	222	29.15 N	96.42 W
Spean, Glen V	46	56.53 N	4.45 W
Spean Bridge	46	56.53 N	4.54 W
Spear, Cape >	186	47.32 N	52.32 W
Spearfish	198	44.29 N	103.51 W
Spearman	196	36.11 N	101.11 W
Spearsville	218	39.21 N	86.11 W
Spearville	198	37.51 N	99.45 W
Spearwood	168a	32.07 S	115.47 E
Speas Artemidos (Rock Tombs) ⊥	142	27.54 N	30.52 E
Specchia	68	39.57 N	18.18 E
Spechtsbrunn	54	50.30 N	11.14 E
Speckhorn ◆[8]	263	51.39 N	7.11 E
Spectacle Island I	283	42.19 N	70.59 W
Spectrum ♠	285	39.54 N	75.10 W
Spectrum Range ⋏	180	57.30 N	130.40 W
Spednic Lake ⊜	186	45.36 N	67.35 W
Speed	218	38.24 N	85.45 W
Speed ≃	212	43.23 N	80.22 W
Speedway	218	39.48 N	86.16 W
Speicher	58	47.24 N	9.27 E
Speichersee ⊜	60	48.13 N	11.45 E
Speightstown	241g	13.15 N	59.39 W
Speigletown	210	42.48 N	73.38 W
Speikkogel ∧	61	47.14 N	15.03 E
Speinshart	60	49.47 N	11.49 E
Speising ◆[8]	264b	48.10 N	16.17 E
Speke ◆[8]	262	53.21 N	2.51 W
Speke Gulf ⊂	154	2.20 S	33.15 E
Speke Hall ⊥	262	53.20 N	2.52 W
Speldorf ◆[8]	263	51.25 N	6.52 E
Spellen	263	51.37 N	6.37 E
Spello	66	42.59 N	12.40 E
Spelthorne □[8]	260	51.25 N	0.28 W
Spelve, Loch ⊂	46	56.22 N	5.46 W
Spenard	180	61.11 N	149.55 W
Spence Bay	176	69.32 N	93.31 W
Spencer, In., U.S.	194	39.17 N	86.45 W
Spencer, Ia., U.S.	198	43.08 N	95.08 W
Spencer, Ma., U.S.	207	42.14 N	71.59 W
Spencer, Ne., U.S.	198	42.52 N	98.42 W
Spencer, N.Y., U.S.	210	42.12 N	76.29 W
Spencer, N.C., U.S.	192	35.41 N	80.26 W
Spencer, Oh., U.S.	214	41.06 N	82.07 W
Spencer, S.D., U.S.	198	43.43 N	97.35 W
Spencer, Tn., U.S.	194	35.44 N	85.28 W
Spencer, W.V., U.S.	188	38.48 N	81.21 W
Spencer, Wi., U.S.	190	44.45 N	90.17 W
Spencer, Cape >, Austl.	166	35.18 S	136.53 E
Spencer, Cape >, N.B., Can.	186	45.12 N	65.55 W
Spencer, Cape >, Ak., U.S.	180	58.14 N	136.40 W
Spencer, Mount ∧	224	49.03 N	124.38 W
Spencer, Point >	180	65.18 N	166.50 W
Spencer Brook ≃	283	42.28 N	71.22 W
Spencer Creek ≃, On., Can.	212	43.17 N	79.54 W
Spencer Creek ≃, Mo., U.S.	219	39.33 N	91.20 W
Spencer Field ⊠	281	42.31 N	83.33 W
Spencer Gulf ⊂	166	34.00 S	137.00 E
Spencer Lake ⊜	224	47.16 N	122.57 W
Spencerport	210	43.11 N	77.48 W
Spencertown	210	42.20 N	73.33 W
Spencerville, On., Can.	212	44.51 N	75.33 W
Spencerville, In., U.S.	216	41.16 N	84.55 W
Spencerville, Md., U.S.	208	39.06 N	76.58 W
Spencerville, Oh., U.S.	216	40.42 N	84.21 W
Spences Bridge	182	50.25 N	121.21 W
Spenge	52	52.08 N	8.28 E
Spennymoor	44	54.42 N	1.35 W
Spenser Mountains ⋏	172	42.15 S	172.30 E
Sperenberg	54	52.08 N	13.22 E
Sperillen ⊜	26	60.28 N	10.03 E
Sperling	224	49.08 N	122.33 W
Sperlinga	70	37.46 N	14.21 E
Sperlonga	66	41.15 N	13.26 E
Spermaceti Cove ⊂	276	40.26 N	73.59 W
Sperone, Capo >	71	38.57 N	8.25 E
Sperrin Mountains ⋏	48	54.50 N	7.05 W
Sperry Creek ≃	279a	41.29 N	81.53 W
Sperry Rand Corporation ❦[3]	276	40.45 N	73.42 W
Sperryville	188	38.39 N	78.13 W
Spessart ◆[1]	56	50.10 N	9.20 E
Spesutie Island I	208	39.27 N	76.05 W
Spétsai I	38	37.16 N	23.08 E
Spevakovka	83	49.03 N	38.54 E
Spexard	52	51.52 N	8.24 E
Spey ≃	46	57.40 N	3.06 W
Spey Bay ⊂	46	57.41 N	3.00 W
Speyer	56	49.19 N	8.26 E
Speyerbach ≃	56	49.19 N	8.27 E
Speyside	241r	11.18 N	60.32 W
Spezia → La Spezia	62	44.07 N	9.50 E
Spezzano Albanese	68	39.40 N	16.19 E
Spezzano della Sila	68	39.18 N	16.20 E
Sphinx → Abū al-Hawl ⊥	142	29.59 N	31.08 E
Spiazzo	64	46.07 N	10.40 E
Spiceland	218	39.50 N	85.26 W
Spicer	198	45.13 N	94.56 W
Spicer Creek ≃	284a	43.02 N	78.53 W
Spicer Meadow Reservoir ⊜[1]	226	38.23 N	119.59 W
Spicheren	56	49.12 N	6.58 E
Spickard	194	40.14 N	93.35 W
Spicket ≃	283	42.42 N	71.09 W
Spieka	52	53.45 N	8.35 E
Spiekeroog I	52	53.46 N	7.42 E
Spiess Seamount ✦[3]	8	54.40 S	0.15 E
Spiez	58	46.41 N	7.39 E
Şpijkenisse	52	51.21 N	4.20 E
Špikov	78	48.46 N	28.35 E
Spilamberto	64	44.32 N	11.01 E
Spilimbergo	64	46.07 N	12.54 E
Spilinga	68	38.37 N	15.54 E
Spillersboda	40	59.42 N	18.51 E
Spillimacheen ≃	182	50.55 N	116.20 W
Spillville	190	43.12 N	91.57 W
Spilsby	44	53.11 N	0.06 E
Spinazzola	68	40.58 N	16.06 E
Spīn Būldak	120	31.01 N	66.24 E
Spincourt	56	49.20 N	5.40 E
Spindale	192	35.21 N	81.55 W
Spindoli	66	43.12 N	12.54 E
Spinea-Orgnano	64	45.29 N	12.10 E
Spinetta Marengo	62	44.53 N	8.41 E
Spinnerstown	208	40.26 N	75.26 W
Spinoso	68	40.16 N	15.58 E
Spires → Speyer	56	49.19 N	8.26 E
Spirit Lake, Id., U.S.	202	47.57 N	116.52 W
Spirit Lake, Ia., U.S.	198	43.25 N	95.06 W
Spirit Lake ⊜	224	46.16 N	122.08 W
Spirit River	182	55.47 N	118.50 W
Spiritwood	184	53.22 N	107.31 W
Spiro	194	35.14 N	94.37 W
Spirovo	76	57.26 N	34.59 E
Spišská Nová Ves	30	48.57 N	20.34 E
Spitak	84	40.51 N	44.16 E
Spital am Pyhrn	61	47.39 N	14.20 E
Spithead >	42	50.45 N	1.05 W
Spit Point >	162	20.02 S	119.00 E
Spitsbergen I	12	78.45 N	16.00 E
Spitsbergen Bank ✦[4]	12	76.00 N	23.00 E
Spittal an der Drau	64	46.48 N	13.30 E
Spittal of Glenshee	46	56.48 N	3.28 W
Spitz	61	48.22 N	15.25 E
Spitzbergen und Jan Mayen → Svalbard □[2]	12	78.00 N	20.00 E
Spitzer-Berg ∧[2]	264a	52.38 N	13.35 E
Spixworth	42	52.40 N	1.20 E
Spjelkavik	26	62.28 N	6.23 E
Splavnucha	80	51.05 N	45.22 E
Splendora	222	30.14 N	95.10 W
Split	36	43.31 N	16.27 E
Split, Cape >	186	45.20 N	64.30 W
Split Lake ⊜	184	56.08 N	96.15 W
Splitrock Reservoir ⊜[1]	276	40.58 N	74.27 W
Spluga, Passo della (Splügenpass))(	58	46.30 N	9.20 E
Splügen	58	46.33 N	9.20 E
Splügenpass (Passo della Spluga))(	58	46.30 N	9.20 E
Spodsbjerg	41	54.56 N	10.50 E
Spofford	196	29.11 N	100.25 W
Spoģi	76	56.05 N	26.44 E
Spokane	202	47.39 N	117.25 W
Spokane ≃	202	47.54 N	118.20 W
Spokane, Mount ∧	202	47.55 N	117.07 W
Spokane Indian Reservation ◆[4]	202	47.55 N	118.00 W
Spokojnaja	84	44.15 N	41.25 E
Špola	78	49.01 N	31.24 E
Spoleto	66	42.44 N	12.44 E
Spoltore	66	42.27 N	14.08 E
Spondigna	64	46.38 N	10.37 E
Spondon	42	52.54 N	1.25 W
Sponds Hill ∧[2]	262	53.19 N	2.03 W
Spóng	110	13.27 N	105.34 E
Spoon ≃	194	40.18 N	90.04 W
Spooner	190	45.49 N	91.53 W
Spořice	54	50.26 N	13.25 E
Spornitz	54	53.24 N	11.43 E
Spornoje	74	62.20 N	151.03 E
Sporovo	76	52.25 N	25.20 E
Spørring	41	56.18 N	10.09 E
Sportforum ♠	264a	52.33 N	13.29 E
Sport Hill	207	41.14 N	73.16 W
Sporting Hill	208	40.09 N	76.26 W
Sportsman's Park Race Track ♠	278	41.50 N	87.46 W
Spotorno	62	44.14 N	8.25 E
Spot Pond ⊜	283	42.27 N	71.06 W
Spotswood, Austl.	274b	37.50 S	144.53 E
Spotswood, N.J., U.S.	208	40.23 N	74.23 W
Spotsylvania	208	38.12 N	77.35 W
Spotsylvania □[6]	208	38.15 N	77.30 W
Spotsylvania Court House Battlefield ⊥	208	38.15 N	77.35 W
Sprague, Mb., Can.	184	49.02 N	95.38 W
Sprague, Wa., U.S.	202	47.18 N	117.58 W
Sprague ≃	202	42.34 N	121.51 W
Sprague, North Fork ≃	202	42.26 N	121.07 W
Sprague, South Fork ≃	202	42.26 N	121.07 W
Spragueville	207	41.53 N	71.32 W
Sprain Ridge Park ♠	276	40.59 N	73.51 W
Sprankle Mills	214	41.00 N	79.07 W
Spratly Island I	108	8.38 N	111.55 E
Spratt Point >	212	44.36 N	80.01 W
Spray	202	44.50 N	119.47 W
Spray Lakes Reservoir ⊜[1]	182	50.55 N	115.20 W
Spreča ≃	38	44.45 N	18.06 E
Spreckels	226	36.36 N	121.34 W
Spreckelsville	229a	20.53 N	156.24 W
Spree ≃	54	52.32 N	13.13 E
Spreenhagen	54	52.20 N	13.52 E
Spreeufontein	158	33.22 S	20.45 E
Spreewald ◆[1]	54	51.50 N	14.05 E
Spremberg	54	51.34 N	14.22 E
Sprendlingen	56	49.51 N	7.59 E
Spresiano	64	45.46 N	12.16 E
Spring	222	30.04 N	95.25 W
Spring ≃, U.S.	194	36.52 N	94.44 W
Spring ≃, Ar., U.S.	194	36.08 N	91.05 W
Spring, North Fork ≃	194	37.18 N	94.21 W
Spring, South Fork ≃	194	36.19 N	91.30 W
Spring Arbor	216	42.12 N	84.33 W
Spring Bay ⊂	200	41.40 N	112.50 W
Springbok	156	29.43 S	17.55 E
Springboro, Oh., U.S.	218	39.33 N	84.14 W
Springboro, Pa., U.S.	214	41.48 N	80.22 W
Spring Branch ≃	284b	39.26 N	76.35 W
Springbrook, On., Can.	275b	43.39 N	79.47 W
Springbrook, Md., U.S.	284c	39.03 N	77.00 W
Spring Brook, N.Y., U.S.	210	42.49 N	78.40 W
Spring Brook ≃	278	41.58 N	87.59 W
Springbrook Forest	284c	39.03 N	77.01 W
Springbrook National Park ♠	171a	28.15 S	153.18 E
Springburn	172	43.40 S	171.28 E
Spring City, Pa., U.S.	208	40.10 N	75.32 W
Spring City, Tn., U.S.	192	35.41 N	84.51 W
Spring City, Ut,. U.S.	200	39.28 N	111.29 W
Spring Coulee V	198	48.31 N	100.54 W
Spring Creek, N.Z.	172	41.28 S	173.58 E
Spring Creek, Pa., U.S.	214	41.53 N	79.32 W
Spring Creek ≃, Austl.	166	24.12 S	140.58 E
Spring Creek ≃, U.S.	198	40.30 N	101.21 W
Spring Creek ≃, Ga., U.S.	192	30.54 N	84.45 W
Spring Creek ≃, Il., U.S.	216	40.49 N	87.50 W
Spring Creek ≃, Il., U.S.	219	39.52 N	89.37 W
Spring Creek ≃, Il., U.S.	278	41.32 N	88.04 W
Spring Creek ≃, Mo., U.S.	219	38.21 N	91.10 W
Spring Creek ≃, Nv., U.S.	204	39.55 N	117.50 W
Spring Creek ≃, N.D., U.S.	198	47.15 N	101.48 W
Spring Creek ≃, Pa., U.S.	214	40.56 N	77.47 W
Spring Creek ≃, Pa., U.S.	214	41.24 N	78.57 W
Spring Creek ≃, S.D., U.S.	198	43.52 N	102.42 W
Spring Creek ≃, S.D., U.S.	198	45.54 N	100.18 W
Spring Creek ≃, Tx., U.S.	222	30.02 N	95.16 W
Springdale, Nf., Can.	186	49.30 N	56.04 W
Springdale, Ar., U.S.	194	36.11 N	94.07 W
Springdale, Oh., U.S.	218	39.17 N	84.28 W
Springdale, Pa., U.S.	214	40.32 N	79.47 W
Springdale, S.C., U.S.	192	33.57 N	81.06 W
Springdale, Ut,. U.S.	200	37.11 N	112.59 W
Springdale, Wa., U.S.	202	48.03 N	117.44 W
Spring Dale, W.V., U.S.	192	37.52 N	80.48 W
Springe	52	52.12 N	9.32 E
Springer	196	36.21 N	104.35 W
Springers Brook ≃	285	39.44 N	74.41 W
Springerville	200	34.08 N	109.17 W
Springfield, N.S., Can.	186	44.38 N	64.52 W
Springfield, On., Can.	212	42.50 N	80.56 W
Springfield, N.Z.	172	43.20 S	171.55 E
Springfield, S. Afr.	158	29.02 S	22.53 E
Springfield, Co., U.S.	198	37.24 N	102.36 W
Springfield, Fl., U.S.	194	30.09 N	85.36 W
Springfield, Ga., U.S.	192	32.22 N	81.18 W
Springfield, Il., U.S.	219	39.48 N	89.38 W
Springfield, Ky., U.S.	194	37.41 N	85.13 W
Springfield, Ma., U.S.	207	42.06 N	72.35 W
Springfield, Mi., U.S.	216	42.19 N	85.14 W
Springfield, Mn., U.S.	198	44.14 N	94.58 W
Springfield, Mo., U.S.	194	37.12 N	93.17 W
Springfield, N.J., U.S.	276	40.43 N	74.18 W
Springfield, Oh., U.S.	218	39.55 N	83.48 W
Springfield, Or., U.S.	202	44.02 N	123.01 W
Springfield, Pa., U.S.	285	39.55 N	75.19 W
Springfield, S.C., U.S.	192	33.29 N	81.16 W
Springfield, S.D., U.S.	198	42.51 N	97.53 W
Springfield, Tn., U.S.	194	36.30 N	86.53 W
Springfield, Vt., U.S.	188	43.17 N	72.28 W
Springfield, Va., U.S.	284c	38.45 N	77.13 W
Springfield, Lake ⊜[1]	219	39.44 N	89.36 W
Springfield Center	210	42.50 N	74.53 W
Springfield Estates	284c	38.47 N	77.11 W
Springfield Lake ⊜	285	40.11 N	75.00 W
Springfield Lake ⊜[1]	222	31.36 N	96.33 W
Springfield Mall ◆[9]	284c	38.46 N	77.11 W
Springfield Plateau ⋏[1]	194	37.10 N	93.30 W
Springfontein	158	30.19 S	25.36 E
Spring Garden	246	6.59 N	58.31 W
Spring Garden Brook ≃	276	40.46 N	74.23 W
Spring Garden Township	208	39.57 N	76.44 W
Spring Glen, N.Y., U.S.	210	41.40 N	74.26 W
Spring Glen, Pa., U.S.	208	40.38 N	76.37 W
Spring Glen, Ut,. U.S.	200	39.39 N	110.51 W
Spring Green	190	43.10 N	90.04 W
Spring Grove, Il., U.S.	216	42.26 N	88.13 W
Spring Grove, Mn., U.S.	190	43.33 N	91.38 W
Spring Grove, Pa., U.S.	208	39.52 N	76.51 W
Springhill, N.S., Can.	186	45.39 N	64.03 W
Spring Hill, Ca., U.S.	226	39.15 N	121.03 W
Spring Hill, Fl., U.S.	220	28.33 N	82.27 W
Springhill, La., U.S.	194	33.00 N	93.28 W
Spring Hill, Pa., U.S.	214	40.23 N	78.40 W
Spring Hill, Tn., U.S.	194	35.45 N	86.55 W
Spring Hill, Tx., U.S.	222	32.34 N	94.48 W
Springhills	216	40.16 N	83.22 W
Spring Hope	192	35.56 N	78.06 W
Springhouse, B.C., Can.	182	51.55 N	122.07 W
Spring House, Pa., U.S.	285	40.11 N	75.14 W
Spring Lake, Mi., U.S.	216	43.04 N	86.11 W
Spring Lake, N.J., U.S.	208	40.09 N	74.01 W
Spring Lake, N.C., U.S.	192	35.10 N	78.58 W
Spring Lake ⊜, Mi., U.S.	216	43.06 N	86.11 W
Spring Lake ⊜, N.J., U.S.	276	40.35 N	74.25 W
Spring Lake Heights	208	40.09 N	74.01 W
Spring Mill, Oh., U.S.	214	40.54 N	82.36 W
Spring Mill, Pa., U.S.	285	40.04 N	75.17 W
Spring Mill Reservoir ⊜[1]	262	53.39 N	2.13 W
Spring Mills	210	40.51 N	77.34 W
Spring Mill State Park ♠	218	38.43 N	86.25 W
Spring Mount	208	40.17 N	75.28 W
Spring Mountains ⋏	204	36.10 N	115.40 W
Spring Pond ⊜	283	42.30 N	70.57 W
Springport, In., U.S.	218	40.03 N	85.24 W
Springport, Mi., U.S.	216	42.22 N	84.41 W
Spring Run	214	40.09 N	83.47 W
Springs	158	26.13 S	28.25 E
Springs □[5]	273d	26.14 S	28.30 E
Springs Aerodrome ⊠	273d	26.15 S	28.24 E
Springside	285	40.04 N	74.51 W
Springs Junction	172	42.19 S	172.11 E
Springsure	166	24.07 S	148.05 E
Springton	168b	34.43 S	139.05 E
Springtown	222	32.58 N	97.41 W
Springvale, Austl.	162	17.48 S	127.41 E
Springvale, Austl.	166	23.33 S	140.42 E
Springvale, Austl.	169	37.57 S	145.09 E
Springvale, Me., U.S.	188	43.28 N	70.47 W
Springvale South	274b	37.58 S	145.09 E
Spring Valley, Ca., U.S.	228	32.44 N	116.59 W
Spring Valley, Il., U.S.	190	41.19 N	89.11 W
Spring Valley, Mn., U.S.	190	43.41 N	92.23 W
Spring Valley, N.Y., U.S.	210	41.06 N	74.02 W
Spring Valley, Oh., U.S.	218	39.36 N	84.00 W
Spring Valley, Tx., U.S.	222	29.47 N	95.31 W
Spring Valley, Wi., U.S.	190	44.50 N	92.14 W
Spring Valley V	204	39.15 N	114.25 W
Spring Valley Creek ≃	204	39.20 N	114.25 W
Springview	198	42.49 N	99.44 W
Springville, Al., U.S.	194	33.46 N	86.28 W
Springville, Ca., U.S.	204	36.08 N	118.49 W
Springville, Ia., U.S.	190	42.03 N	91.26 W
Springville, N.J., U.S.	285	39.56 N	74.52 W
Springville, N.Y., U.S.	210	42.30 N	78.40 W
Springville, Pa., U.S.	210	41.42 N	75.55 W
Springville, Ut,. U.S.	200	40.09 N	111.36 W
Springwater	210	42.38 N	77.35 W
Springwood	170	33.42 S	150.33 E
Sprint ≃	44	54.22 N	2.45 W
Sprite Creek ≃	210	43.08 N	74.44 W
Sproat Lake ⊜	182	49.16 N	125.03 W
Sprockhövel	56	51.22 N	7.15 E
Sprogels Run ≃	285	40.14 N	75.37 W
Sprogø I	41	55.20 N	10.58 E
Sprottau → Szprotawa	30	51.34 N	15.33 E
Sprötze	52	53.18 N	9.49 E
Sproul	214	40.16 N	78.28 W
Sprout Brook ≃	276	40.54 N	74.05 W
Spruce ≃	184	53.15 N	105.43 W
Spruce Brook	186	48.45 N	58.11 W
Spruce Creek	214	40.37 N	78.08 W
Spruce Creek ≃	210	43.07 N	74.46 W
Spruce Grove	182	53.32 N	113.55 W
Spruce Knob ∧	188	38.42 N	79.32 W
Spruce Knob-Seneca Rocks National Recreation Area ♠	188	38.50 N	79.20 W
Spruce Lake	184	53.32 N	109.05 W
Spruce Mountain ∧, Az., U.S.	200	34.28 N	112.24 W
Spruce Mountain ∧, Nv., U.S.	204	40.33 N	114.49 W
Spruce Pine, Al., U.S.	194	34.23 N	87.43 W
Spruce Pine, N.C., U.S.	192	35.54 N	82.03 W
Spruce Run Reservoir ⊜[1]	210	40.40 N	74.57 W
Spruce Run State Park ♠	210	40.40 N	74.56 W
Spruce Woods Provincial Park ♠	184	49.42 N	99.05 W
Spry	208	39.55 N	76.41 W
Spry Lake ⊜	212	44.44 N	81.15 W
Spulico, Capo >	68	39.58 N	16.39 E
Spur	196	33.28 N	100.51 W
Spurfield	182	55.13 N	114.16 W
Spurger	194	30.42 N	94.11 W
Spurn Head >	44	53.34 N	0.07 E
Spurr, Mount ∧	180	61.18 N	152.15 W
Sputendorf	264a	52.20 N	13.13 E
Spuzzum	182	49.41 N	121.25 W
Spy Hill	184	50.36 N	101.41 W
Spy Pond ⊜	283	42.24 N	71.09 W
Squally Channel ɥ	182	53.10 N	129.15 W
Squamish	182	49.42 N	123.09 W
Squamish ≃	182	49.45 N	123.09 W
Squam Lake ⊜	188	43.45 N	71.32 W
Square Butte Creek ≃	198	46.55 N	100.55 W
Square Lake ⊜	186	47.03 N	68.20 W
Squatec	186	47.53 N	68.43 W
Squaw Cap Mountain ∧	186	47.53 N	66.53 W
Squaw Creek ≃, Id., U.S.	202	43.51 N	116.22 W
Squaw Creek ≃, Il., U.S.	278	42.21 N	88.07 W
Squaw Creek ≃, Or., U.S.	202	44.27 N	121.20 W
Squaw Creek Lake ⊜[1]	222	32.19 N	97.47 W
Squaw Harbor	180	55.11 N	160.30 W
Squaw Hill ∧	200	41.48 N	105.02 W
Squaw Island I	284a	42.56 N	78.54 W
Squaw Peak ∧, Ca., U.S.	226	39.11 N	120.16 W
Squaw Peak ∧, Mt., U.S.	202	47.10 N	114.21 W
Squaw Rapids	184	53.41 N	103.20 W
Squaw Rapids Dam ◆[6]	184	53.40 N	103.25 W
Squaw Run ≃	279b	40.29 N	79.52 W
Squaw Valley State Recreation Area ♠	226	39.12 N	120.15 W
Squibnocket Point >	207	41.18 N	70.47 W
Squilax	182	50.52 N	119.35 W
Squillace	68	38.47 N	16.31 E
Squillace, Golfo di ⊂	68	38.50 N	16.50 E
Squinzano	68	40.26 N	18.03 E
Squire	192	37.14 N	81.36 W
Squires, Mount ∧	162	26.12 S	127.28 E
Squirrel ≃	180	66.57 N	160.27 W
Squirrel Hill ◆[8]	279b	40.26 N	79.55 W
Squirrel Hill Tunnel ◆[5]	279b	40.26 N	79.55 W
Squirrel's Heath ◆[8]	260	51.35 N	0.13 E
Şragen	115a	7.26 S	111.02 E
Šramkovka	78	50.10 N	32.05 E
Srbija (Serbia) □[3]	38	44.00 N	21.00 E
Srbija □[9]	38	43.00 N	21.00 E
Srbobran	38	45.33 N	19.48 E
Srê Âmběl	110	11.07 N	103.46 E
Sredinnyj chrebet ⋏	74	56.00 N	158.00 E
Sredna Gora ⋏	38	42.30 N	25.00 E
Sredn'aja Achtuba	80	48.43 N	44.52 E
Sredn'aja Mokla ≃	88	55.01 N	119.37 E
Sredn'aja Nanaki, gora ∧	89	52.26 N	132.50 E
Sredn'aja Ol'okma	88	55.26 N	120.33 E
Srednegorje	76	60.34 N	29.25 E
Sredneje Kujto, ozero ⊜	24	65.08 N	31.15 E
Srednekolymsk	74	67.27 N	153.41 E
Srednerusskaja vozvyšennost' ⋏[1]	72	52.00 N	38.00 E
Srednesibirskoje ploskogorje ⋏[1]	74	65.00 N	105.00 E
Srednij Ikorec	78	51.05 N	39.45 E
Srednij Kalar	88	55.51 N	117.24 E
Srednij Ural ⋏	86	58.00 N	59.00 E
Srednij Urgal	89	51.09 N	132.59 E
Srednij Vas'ugan	86	59.16 N	78.15 E
Srednyj	83	48.09 N	39.50 E
Srê Khtŭm	110	12.10 N	106.52 E
Śrem	30	52.08 N	17.01 E
Srê Moăt	110	13.18 N	107.10 E
Sremska Mitrovica	38	44.58 N	19.37 E
Sremski Karlovci	38	45.12 N	19.57 E
Srêng ≃	110	13.21 N	103.27 E
Srêpŏk ≃	110	13.33 N	106.16 E
Sretensk	88	52.15 N	117.43 E
Sretenskoje	88	56.28 N	96.25 E
Srīdharpur	126	23.04 N	89.25 E
Sri Dūngargarh	120	28.05 N	74.00 E
Sri Gangānagar	123	29.55 N	73.53 E
Sri Hargobindpur	123	31.41 N	75.39 E
Srīkākulam	122	18.18 N	83.54 E
Sri Karanpur	123	29.50 N	73.27 E
Sri Lanka □[1], Asia	118	7.00 N	81.00 E
Sri Lanka □[1], Asia	122	7.00 N	81.00 E
Sri Lanka I	122	7.00 N	81.00 E
Sri Mohangarh	120	27.17 N	71.14 E
Srīnagar, Bngl.	126	23.32 N	90.18 E
Srīnagar, India	123	34.05 N	74.49 E
Srīnagar, India	124	30.13 N	78.47 E
Srīnagar Airport ⊠	123	34.00 N	74.52 E
Srīpur, Bngl.	126	24.12 N	90.29 E
Srīpur, Bngl.	126	23.36 N	89.24 E
Srīrampur, India	122	19.34 N	74.34 E
Srirāmpur, India	272b	22.49 N	88.29 E
Srīrangam	122	10.52 N	78.41 E
Sri Thep ⊥	110	16.25 N	101.04 E
Srīvardhan	122	18.02 N	73.01 E
Şrīvilliputtūr	122	9.31 N	77.38 E
Środa Śląska	30	51.10 N	16.36 E
Środa Wielkopolski	30	52.14 N	17.17 E
Srpska Crnja	38	45.43 N	20.42 E
Ssangmun-ni ◆[8]	271b	37.39 N	127.02 E
Ssuchunghsi	100	22.06 N	120.44 E
Ssup'ing → Siping	89	43.12 N	124.20 E
St. → Saint			
Staaken ◆[8]	264a	52.32 N	13.08 E
Staaken, Flugplatz ⊠	264a	52.32 N	13.06 E
Staaten ≃	164	16.24 S	141.17 E
Staaten River National Park ♠	164	16.40 S	143.00 E
Staatsburg	210	41.50 N	73.55 W
Staatz	61	48.40 N	16.29 E
Stabbursdalen Nasjonalpark ♠	24	70.06 N	24.30 E
Staberhuk >	54	54.24 N	11.19 E
Stabroek	50	51.20 N	4.22 E
Stachanov	83	48.34 N	38.40 E
Stachy	60	49.06 N	13.40 E
Stack, Loch ⊜	46	58.20 N	4.55 W
Stackpole Head >	42	51.37 N	4.54 W
Stack Skerry I[2]	46	59.01 N	4.31 W
Stacksteads	262	53.41 N	2.13 W
Stacyville	190	43.26 N	92.46 W
Stad-Delden	52	52.16 N	6.42 E
Stade	52	53.36 N	9.28 E
Staden, Bel.	50	50.59 N	3.01 E
Staden, B.R.D.	56	50.20 N	8.54 E
Städjan ∧	26	61.55 N	12.52 E
Stadl an der Mur	61	47.05 N	13.58 E
Stadlandet >[1]	26	62.07 N	5.18 E
Stadlau ◆[8]	264b	48.14 N	16.28 E
Stadl-Paura	64	48.05 N	13.53 E
Stadskanaal	52	53.00 N	6.55 E
Stadtallendorf	56	50.50 N	9.01 E
Stadtbergen	58	48.22 N	10.50 E
Stadt Haag	30	48.07 N	14.34 E
Stadthagen	52	52.19 N	9.13 E
Stadtilm	54	50.47 N	11.05 E
Städtische Rahmede	263	51.17 N	7.40 E
Stadtkyll	56	50.21 N	6.32 E
Stadtlauringen	56	50.11 N	10.22 E
Stadtlengsfeld	56	50.47 N	10.07 E
Stadtlohn	52	51.59 N	6.55 E
Stadtoldendorf	52	51.53 N	9.37 E
Stadtprozelten	56	49.47 N	9.25 E
Stadtroda	54	50.51 N	11.44 E
Stadtsteinach	54	50.09 N	11.30 E
Stadt Wehlen	54	50.58 N	14.02 E
Stadum	41	54.44 N	9.03 E
Stäfa	58	47.15 N	8.44 E
Staffa I	46	56.25 N	6.20 W
Staffanstorp	41	55.38 N	13.13 E
Staffelberg ∧	56	50.06 N	11.02 E
Staffelde	264a	52.44 N	13.00 E
Staffelsee ⊜	64	47.42 N	11.10 E
Staffelstein	56	50.06 N	11.00 E
Staffin	46	57.37 N	6.12 W
Staffora ≃	62	45.04 N	9.01 E
Stafford, Eng., U.K.	42	52.48 N	2.07 W
Stafford, Ct., U.S.	207	41.59 N	72.17 W
Stafford, Ks., U.S.	198	37.57 N	98.36 W
Stafford, N.Y., U.S.	210	42.59 N	78.04 W
Stafford, Tx., U.S.	222	29.37 N	95.34 W
Stafford, Va., U.S.	208	38.25 N	77.24 W
Stafford □[6]	208	38.25 N	77.30 W
Staffordshire □[6]	28	52.50 N	2.00 W
Stafford Springs	207	41.57 N	72.18 W
Staffordsville	188	37.49 N	82.50 W
Staffordville	207	41.59 N	72.15 W
Stagen	112	3.18 S	116.10 E
Stag Pond ⊜	276	40.59 N	74.42 W
Stahl-Berg ∧[2]	264a	52.21 N	13.46 E
Stahlbrode	54	54.14 N	13.17 E
Stahle	52	51.50 N	9.25 E
Stahnsdorf	54	52.23 N	13.13 E
Stahringen	58	47.47 N	8.58 E
Staicele	76	57.50 N	24.45 E

Symbols in the index entries represent the broad categories identified in the key at the right. Symbols with superior numbers (⋏[1]) identify subcategories (see complete key on page *I · 1).*

Kartensymbole in dem Registerverzeichnis stellen die rechts in Schlüssel erklärten Kategorien dar. Symbole mit hochgestellten Ziffern (⋏[1]) bezeichnen Unterabteilungen einer Kategorie (vgl. vollständiger Schlüssel auf Seite *I · 1).*

Los símbolos incluídos en el texto del índice representan las grandes categorias identificadas con la clave a la derecha. Los símbolos con numeros en su parte superior (⋏[1]) identifican las subcategorías (véase la clave completa en la página *I · 1).*

Les symboles de l'index représentent les catégories indiquées dans la légende à droite. Les symboles suivis d'un indice (⋏[1]) représentent des sous-catégories (voir légende complète à la page *I · 1).*

Os símbolos incluídos no texto do índice representam as grandes categorias identificadas com a chave à direita. Os símbolos com números em sua parte superior (⋏[1]) identificam as subcategorias (veja-se a chave completa à página *I · 1).*

∧ Mountain	Berg	Montaña	Montagne	Montanha
⋏ Mountains	Berge	Montañas	Montagnes	Montanhas
)(Pass	Pass	Paso	Col	Passo
V Valley, Canyon	Tal, Cañon	Valle, Cañón	Vallée, Canyon	Vale, Canhão
≚ Plain	Ebene	Llano	Plaine	Planície
> Cape	Kap	Cabo	Cap	Cabo
I Island	Insel	Isla	Île	Ilha
II Islands	Inseln	Islas	Îles	Ilhas
≐ Other Topographic Features	Andere Topographische Objekte	Otros Elementos Topográficos	Autres données topographiques	Outros acidentes topográficos

ESPAÑOL — Nombre · Página · Lat.°′ · Long.°′ W = Oeste
FRANÇAIS — Nom · Page · Lat.°′ · Long.°′ W = Ouest
PORTUGUÊS — Nome · Página · Lat.°′ · Long.°′ W = Oeste

Nombre / Nom / Nome	Página / Page	Lat.°′	Long.°′
Staines	42	51.26 N	0.31 W
Staines Reservoirs ⊜[1]	260	51.27 N	0.30 W
Stainforth	44	53.36 N	1.01 W
Staining	44	53.49 N	2.59 W
Stainland	262	53.40 N	1.53 W
Stainmore Forest ➔[3]	44	54.30 N	2.10 W
Stains	261	48.57 N	2.23 E
Stainz	61	46.54 N	15.16 E
Stairtown	222	29.43 N	97.44 W
Stajki	78	50.05 N	30.54 E
Staked Plain → Estacado, Llano ≚	196	33.30 N	102.40 W
Stäket	40	59.28 N	17.48 E
Stakroge	41	55.53 N	8.51 E
Stalać	38	43.40 N	21.25 E
Stalbridge	42	50.58 N	2.23 W
Stalden	58	46.14 N	7.52 E
Stalettì	68	38.46 N	16.32 E
Stalham	42	52.47 N	1.31 E
Stalheim	26	60.50 N	6.40 E
Stalhofen	61	47.05 N	15.16 E
Stalin → Varna, Blg.	38	43.13 N	27.55 E
Stalin → Brașov, Rom.	38	45.39 N	25.37 E
Stalin (Kuçovë), Shq.	38	40.48 N	19.54 E
Stalinabad → Dušanbe	85	38.35 N	68.48 E
Stalingrad → Volgograd	80	48.44 N	44.25 E
Stalino → Doneck	83	48.00 N	37.48 E
Stalinogorsk → Novomoskovsk	82	54.05 N	38.13 E
Stalinogród → Katowice	30	50.16 N	19.00 E
Stalinsk → Novokuzneck	86	53.45 N	87.06 E
Stallarholmen	40	59.22 N	17.12 E
Ställberg	40	59.59 N	14.55 E
Ställdalen	40	59.56 N	14.56 E
Stallwang	60	49.03 N	12.40 E
Stalowa Wola	30	50.35 N	22.02 E
Stalybridge, Eng., U.K.	44	53.29 N	2.03 W
Stalybridge, Eng., U.K.	262	53.29 N	2.04 W
Stambaugh	190	46.04 N	88.37 W
Stamford, Austl.	166	21.16 S	143.49 E
Stamford, Eng., U.K.	42	52.39 N	0.29 W
Stamford, Ct., U.S.	207	41.03 N	73.32 W
Stamford, N.Y., U.S.	210	42.24 N	74.36 W
Stamford, Tx., U.S.	196	32.56 N	99.48 W
Stamford, Vt., U.S.	207	42.45 N	73.04 W
Stamford, Lake ⊜[1]	196	33.05 N	99.35 W
Stamford Bridge	44	53.59 N	0.55 W
Stamford Brige Stadium ♠	260	51.29 N	0.11 W
Stamford Harbor ⊂	276	41.02 N	73.32 W
Stamford Museum ♁	276	41.07 N	73.33 W
Stammbach	54	50.09 N	11.41 E
Stammersdorf ➔[8]	264b	48.18 N	16.25 E
Stammham	60	48.15 N	12.53 E
Stammheim, B.R.D.	56	48.41 N	8.46 E
Stammheim, Schw.	58	47.38 N	8.47 E
Stampede Reservoir ⊜[1]	226	39.29 N	120.07 W
Stamping Ground	218	38.16 N	84.41 W
Stampriet	156	24.20 S	18.28 E
Stamps	194	33.21 N	93.29 W
Stams	64	47.16 N	10.59 E
Stanaford	188	37.48 N	81.09 W
Stanardsville	188	38.17 N	78.26 W
Stanberry	194	40.13 N	94.32 W
Stanborough	260	51.47 N	0.13 W
Stancija-Gorčakovo	85	40.25 N	71.45 E
Stancionno-Ojašinskij	86	55.28 N	83.53 E
Standard, Ab., Can.	182	51.07 N	112.59 W
Standard, Ak., U.S.	180	64.47 N	148.32 W
Standard, Ca., U.S.	226	37.59 N	120.20 W
Standard, Pa., U.S.	214	40.10 N	79.32 W
Standard Oil Company Refinery ♁[3]	282	37.57 N	122.24 W
Standard Shaft	279b	40.10 N	79.32 W
Standedge Canal Tunnel ➔[5]	262	53.34 N	2.00 W
Standedge Railway Tunnel ➔[5]	262	53.34 N	2.00 W
Standerton	158	26.58 S	29.07 E
Standiford Field ⊠	218	38.11 N	85.44 W
Standing Rock Indian Reservation ➔[4]	198	45.50 N	101.10 W
Standing Stone Creek ≃	214	40.30 N	78.00 W
Standing Stones ⊥	46	58.12 N	6.48 W
Standish, Eng., U.K.	44	53.36 N	2.41 W
Standish, Mi., U.S.	190	43.58 N	83.57 W
Standish Monument ⊥	283	42.01 N	70.41 W
Standon	42	51.53 N	0.02 E
Stanfield, Az., U.S.	200	32.52 N	111.57 W
Stanfield, Or., U.S.	202	45.46 N	119.12 W
Stanford, S. Afr.	158	34.26 S	19.29 E
Stanford, Ca., U.S.	226	37.25 N	122.08 W
Stanford, Ky., U.S.	192	37.31 N	84.39 W
Stanford, Mt., U.S.	202	47.09 N	110.13 W
Stanford Center ➔[9]	282	37.27 N	122.10 W
Stanford Heights	210	42.46 N	73.53 W
Stanford le Hope	42	51.31 N	0.26 E
Stanford Linear Accelerator ♁[3]	282	37.25 N	122.12 W
Stanford Rivers	260	51.41 N	0.13 E
Stanford University ♁[2]	282	37.26 N	122.10 W
Stanfordville	210	41.52 N	73.43 W
Stånga	26	57.17 N	18.28 E
Stångån ≃	26	58.27 N	15.37 E
Stångby	41	55.46 N	13.10 E
Stange	26	60.43 N	11.11 E
Stanger	158	29.27 S	31.14 E
Stanghella	64	45.08 N	11.45 E
Stanhope, Eng., U.K.	44	54.45 N	2.01 W
Stanhope, Ia., U.S.	190	42.17 N	93.47 W
Stanhope, N.J., U.S.	210	40.54 N	74.42 W
Staničnо-Luganskoje	83	48.39 N	39.30 E
Stanislaus □[6]	226	37.39 N	121.00 W
Stanislaus ≃	226	37.40 N	121.14 W
Stanislaus, Clark Fork ≃	226	38.22 N	119.52 W
Stanislaus, Middle Fork ≃	226	38.09 N	120.21 W
Stanislaus, North Fork ≃	226	38.09 N	120.21 W
Stanislaus, South Fork ≃	226	38.04 N	120.25 W
Stanislav, S.S.S.R.	78	46.34 N	32.09 E
Stanislav → Ivano-Frankovsk, S.S.S.R.	78	48.55 N	24.43 E
Stanislavčik	78	48.58 N	28.07 E
Stanisławów → Ivano-Frankovsk	78	48.55 N	24.43 E
Stanke Dimitrov	38	42.16 N	23.07 E
Staňkov	60	49.34 N	13.04 E
Stanley, Austl.	166	40.46 S	145.18 E
Stanley, N.B., Can.	186	46.17 N	66.44 W
Stanley, Falk. Is.	254	51.42 S	57.51 W
Stanley, H.K.	271d	22.13 N	114.12 E
Stanley, Eng., U.K.	44	54.52 N	1.42 W
Stanley, Scot., U.K.	46	56.28 N	3.27 W
Stanley, N.Y., U.S.	210	42.49 N	77.06 W
Stanley, N.C., U.S.	192	35.21 N	81.05 W
Stanley, N.D., U.S.	198	48.19 N	102.23 W
Stanley, Va., U.S.	188	38.34 N	78.30 W
Stanley, Wi., U.S.	190	44.57 N	90.56 W
Stanley ≃	171a	27.09 S	152.32 E
Stanley, Mont ∧[2]	273b	4.19 S	15.15 E
Stanley Bay ⊂	271d	22.12 N	114.12 E
Stanley Falls ⌞	154	0.30 N	25.12 E
Stanley Mills	275b	43.46 N	79.44 W
Stanley Mound ∧	271d	22.14 N	114.12 E
Stanley Park ♠, B.C., Can.	224	49.19 N	123.09 W
Stanley Park ♠, Eng., U.K.	262	53.26 N	2.57 W
Stanley Park ♠, Eng., U.K.	262	53.49 N	3.02 W
Stanley Reservoir ⊜[1]	122	11.54 N	77.50 E
Stanleyville → Kisangani	154	0.30 N	25.12 E
Stanlow	44	53.17 N	2.52 W
Stanmore ➔[8]	260	51.37 N	0.19 W
Stannards	210	42.05 N	77.55 W
Stann Creek	232	16.58 N	88.13 W
Stannington	44	55.06 N	1.40 W
Stanovoj chrebet ⋏	74	56.20 N	126.00 E
Stanovoje nagorje (Stanovoy Mountains) ⋏	88	56.00 N	114.00 E
Stanovoj Kolodez'	76	52.51 N	36.16 E
Stanovoy Mountains → Stanovoje nagorje ⋏	88	56.00 N	114.00 E
Stans	58	46.57 N	8.22 E
Stansbury	168b	34.55 S	137.47 E
Stansmore Range ⋏	162	21.23 S	128.33 E
Stansstad	58	46.59 N	8.20 E
Stanstead	206	45.01 N	72.05 W
Stanstead □[6]	206	45.10 N	72.00 W
Stanstead Abbots	42	51.47 N	0.01 E
Stansted	260	51.20 N	0.18 E
Stansted Mountfitchet	42	51.54 N	0.12 E
Stanthorpe	166	28.39 S	151.57 E
Stanton, Eng., U.K.	42	52.19 N	0.53 E
Stanton, Ca., U.S.	228	33.48 N	117.59 W
Stanton, De., U.S.	208	39.43 N	75.37 W
Stanton, Ia., U.S.	198	41.05 N	95.11 W
Stanton, Ky., U.S.	192	37.50 N	83.51 W
Stanton, Mi., U.S.	190	43.17 N	85.04 W
Stanton, Mo., U.S.	219	38.16 N	91.06 W
Stanton, Ne., U.S.	198	41.57 N	97.13 W
Stanton, N.D., U.S.	198	47.19 N	101.22 W
Stanton, Tn., U.S.	194	35.27 N	89.24 W
Stanton, Tx., U.S.	196	32.07 N	101.47 W
Stantonsburg	192	35.36 N	77.49 W
Stanwell	260	51.27 N	0.29 W
Stanwell Moor	260	51.28 N	0.30 W
Stanwood	224	48.14 N	122.22 W
Stanwood Gardens	285	40.07 N	74.57 W
Stanwyck Estates	285	39.42 N	75.33 W
Stanzach	58	47.23 N	10.34 E
Stanz im Mürztal	61	47.28 N	15.30 E
Stapelburg	54	51.53 N	10.40 E
Stapelfeld	52	53.36 N	10.13 E
Staphorst	52	52.37 N	6.12 E
Stapleford	42	52.56 N	1.16 W
Stapleford Abbotts	260	51.38 N	0.10 E
Stapleford Aerodrome ⊠	260	51.39 N	0.08 E
Stapleford Tawney	260	51.40 N	0.11 E
Staplehurst	42	51.10 N	0.33 E
Staples	198	46.21 N	94.47 W
Stapleton, Al., U.S.	194	30.44 N	87.47 W
Stapleton, Ne., U.S.	198	41.28 N	100.30 W
Stąporków	30	51.09 N	20.34 E
Star', S.S.S.R.	76	53.37 N	34.09 E
Star, Ms., U.S.	194	32.05 N	90.02 W
Star, N.C., U.S.	192	35.24 N	79.47 W
Stará Boleslav	54	50.12 N	14.42 E
Starachowice	30	51.03 N	21.04 E
Stara Fužina	64	46.17 N	13.54 E
Staraja	265a	59.55 N	30.38 E
Staraja Belica, S.S.S.R.	76	54.42 N	29.38 E
Staraja Belica, S.S.S.R.	78	51.59 N	35.13 E
Staraja Belogorka	80	52.05 N	53.17 E
Staraja Derevn'a ➔[8]	265a	59.59 N	30.15 E
Staraja Duginka	82	54.20 N	38.45 E
Staraja Kriuša	78	50.12 N	41.09 E
Staraja Kulatka	80	52.43 N	47.37 E
Staraja Kupavna	82	55.48 N	38.10 E
Staraja Majačka	78	46.30 N	33.11 E
Staraja Majna	80	54.36 N	48.57 E
Staraja Poltavka	80	50.28 N	46.28 E
Staraja Porubežka	80	52.03 N	49.11 E
Staraja Račejka	80	53.22 N	48.03 E
Staraja Rudn'a	76	52.50 N	30.17 E
Staraja Russa	76	58.00 N	31.23 E
Staraja Ruza	82	55.39 N	36.20 E
Staraja Sachča	80	54.25 N	49.58 E
Staraja Sin'ava	78	49.36 N	27.37 E
Staraja Sitn'a	82	54.56 N	38.09 E
Staraja Terizmorga	80	54.16 N	44.32 E
Staraja Toropa	76	56.17 N	31.40 E
Staraja Ušica	78	48.35 N	27.07 E
Staraja Veduga	78	51.48 N	38.31 E
Staraja Vičuga	80	57.16 N	41.53 E
Staraja Vyževka	78	51.27 N	24.24 E
Staranzano	64	45.49 N	13.30 E
Stara Pazova	38	44.59 N	20.10 E
Stara Planina (Balkan Mountains) ⋏	38	42.45 N	25.00 E
Stará Role	54	50.14 N	12.47 E
Starav, Ben ∧	46	56.32 N	5.03 W
Stará Voda	60	50.00 N	12.36 E
Stara Zagora	38	42.25 N	25.38 E
Starbejevo	265b	55.55 N	37.28 E
Starbrick	214	41.50 N	79.12 W
Starbuck, Mb., Can.	184	49.46 N	97.36 W
Starbuck, Mn., U.S.	198	45.36 N	95.31 W
Starbuck, Wa., U.S.	202	46.31 N	118.07 W
Starbuck I	14	5.37 S	155.53 W
Starčenkovo	78	47.17 N	36.59 E
Star City, Sk., Can.	184	52.53 N	104.21 W
Star City, Ar., U.S.	194	33.56 N	91.50 W
Star City, In., U.S.	216	40.58 N	86.33 W
Starcross	42	50.38 N	3.27 W
Stare Czarnowo	54	53.16 N	14.45 E
Staré Sedliště	60	49.45 N	12.42 E
Starford	214	40.42 N	78.58 W
Stargard Szczeciński (Stargard in Pommern)	30	53.20 N	15.02 E
Stargo	200	33.04 N	109.21 W
Star Harbour ⊂	175e	10.47 S	162.18 E
Stari Bar	38	42.06 N	19.08 E
Starica, S.S.S.R.	76	56.30 N	34.56 E
Starica, S.S.S.R.	76	59.04 N	29.30 E
Starica, S.S.S.R.	80	48.13 N	45.56 E
Stari Grad	36	43.11 N	16.36 E
Starij R'ad	76	58.05 N	34.54 E
Starina	76	59.37 N	44.42 E
Stari Vlah ➔[1]	38	43.35 N	20.15 E
Star Junction	214	40.04 N	79.46 W
Stark □[6]	214	40.48 N	81.22 W
Starke	192	29.56 N	82.06 W
Starke □[6]	216	41.18 N	86.37 W
Starkey	210	42.32 N	76.56 W
Starkville	194	33.27 N	88.49 W
Star Lake	224	47.22 N	122.18 W
Star Mountains ⋏	164	5.05 S	141.05 E
Starnberg	60	48.00 N	11.20 E
Starnberger See ⊜	64	47.55 N	11.18 E
Starnikovo	82	55.22 N	38.24 E
Staroalejskoje	86	51.00 N	82.01 E
Starobačaty	86	54.14 N	86.07 E
Starobaltačevo	86	56.01 N	55.56 E
Starobel'sk	83	49.16 N	38.56 E
Starobeševo	83	47.44 N	38.03 E
Starobin	76	52.44 N	27.28 E
Staročerkasskaja	83	47.15 N	40.03 E
Starocuruchajtuj	88	50.12 N	119.15 E
Staroderev'ankovskaja	78	46.08 N	38.58 E
Starodub	76	52.35 N	32.46 E
Starod'umejevo	80	55.16 N	54.22 E
Starogan'kino	80	53.55 N	52.15 E
Starogard Gdański	30	53.59 N	18.33 E
Staroignatjevka	83	47.32 N	37.47 E
Staroje	76	59.16 N	40.40 E
Staroje Bajsarovo	80	55.31 N	53.54 E
Staroje Drožžanoje	80	54.44 N	47.34 E
Staroje Ibrajkino	80	54.52 N	51.02 E
Staroje Jaškino	80	52.49 N	52.57 E
Staroje Jermakovo	80	54.04 N	51.59 E
Staroje Oleničevo	80	45.34 N	47.11 E
Staroje Rachino	76	58.08 N	32.39 E
Staroje Šajgovo	80	54.18 N	44.26 E
Staroje Šajmurzino	80	54.45 N	47.58 E
Staroje Selo	76	55.14 N	29.54 E
Staroje Sindrovo	80	54.25 N	44.06 E
Staroje Slavkino	80	52.34 N	45.08 E
Staroje Ustje	80	53.28 N	41.51 E
Starojurjevo	80	53.21 N	40.42 E
Starokazačje	78	46.21 N	29.59 E
Starokonstantinov	78	49.46 N	27.13 E
Starokuručevo	80	55.09 N	54.04 E
Starolaspa	83	47.34 N	37.59 E
Staroleuškovskaja	78	45.59 N	39.44 E
Staromichajlovka	83	47.58 N	37.36 E
Starominskaja	78	46.31 N	39.04 E
Staromlinovka	78	47.42 N	36.49 E
Staromušta	80	55.49 N	54.14 E
Staronikolajevo	82	55.37 N	36.16 E
Staro-Podgorodneje	82	54.46 N	38.57 E
Staropokrovka	85	42.50 N	75.18 E
Staroščerbinovskaja	78	46.37 N	38.40 E
Staroseslavino	80	53.12 N	40.25 E
Starošešminsk	80	55.22 N	51.15 E
Starosiedle	54	51.50 N	14.50 E
Starosoldatskoje	86	56.12 N	72.37 E
Starosubchangulovo	86	53.06 N	57.26 E
Starotimoškino	24	53.43 N	47.32 E
Starotitarovskaja	78	45.14 N	37.09 E
Staroutkinsk	86	57.14 N	59.20 E
Staroverovka	78	49.33 N	35.42 E
Starožilovo	80	54.14 N	39.55 E
Starožil'sk	80	56.34 N	47.17 E
Star Peak ∧	204	40.32 N	118.10 W
Starr	214	41.32 N	79.22 W
Starrucca	210	41.54 N	75.28 W
Start Bay ⊂	42	50.17 N	3.36 W
Start Point ›	42	50.13 N	3.38 W
Startup	224	47.52 N	121.44 W
Starvation Reservoir ⊜[1]	200	40.15 N	110.30 W
Starved Rock State Park ♠	216	41.19 N	88.58 W
Staryj Ajbesi	80	54.57 N	47.03 E
Staryj-Ajdar	83	48.43 N	39.11 E
Staryj Bagr'až	80	54.54 N	51.39 E
Staryj Bir'uz'ak	84	44.47 N	46.54 E
Staryj Bol'ševik	265b	55.57 N	37.47 E
Staryj Čartorijsk	78	51.15 N	25.54 E
Staryj Čhop'or	80	51.30 N	42.58 E
Staryj Čindant	88	50.33 N	115.33 E
Staryje Burasy	80	52.16 N	46.09 E
Staryje Dorogi	76	53.02 N	28.16 E
Staryje Maty	80	55.14 N	53.55 E
Staryje Popel'uchi	78	48.18 N	28.55 E
Staryje Senžary	78	49.25 N	34.27 E
Staryje Turdaki	80	53.55 N	45.29 E
Staryje Z'atcy	80	57.21 N	52.39 E
Staryj Kazangal	80	50.15 N	47.39 E
Staryj Kistruss	80	54.28 N	40.34 E
Staryj Krym, S.S.S.R.	78	45.03 N	35.05 E
Staryj Krym, S.S.S.R.	83	47.10 N	37.30 E
Staryj Lesken	84	43.20 N	43.55 E
Staryj Medved'	76	58.18 N	30.30 E
Staryj Merčik	78	49.58 N	35.46 E
Staryj Oskol	78	51.19 N	37.51 E
Staryj Sambor	78	49.27 N	22.59 E
Staryj Terek ≃	84	44.00 N	47.24 E
Staryj Tukšum	80	53.42 N	48.33 E
Starý Plzenec	60	49.42 N	13.28 E
Stary Sącz	30	49.34 N	20.38 E
Stassfurt	54	51.51 N	11.34 E
Staszów	30	50.34 N	21.20 E
State Center	190	42.01 N	93.09 W
State College	214	40.47 N	77.51 W
State Fair Grounds ♠	284b	39.27 N	76.38 W
Stateline, Ca., U.S.	226	38.57 N	119.57 W
State Line, Ms., U.S.	194	31.26 N	88.28 W
Stateline, Nv., U.S.	204	38.58 N	119.56 W
Staten Island I	276	40.35 N	74.09 W
Staten Island Mall ➔[9]	276	40.35 N	74.10 W
Statenville	192	30.42 N	83.01 W
State Park Place	219	38.40 N	90.03 W
State Road	192	36.19 N	80.52 W
Statesboro	192	32.26 N	81.47 W
Statesville	192	35.46 N	80.53 W
Stateville Correctional Center ♁	278	41.35 N	88.06 W
Station Peak	162	21.10 S	118.11 E
Statte	68	40.34 N	17.12 E
Statue of Liberty National Monument ♠	210	40.41 N	74.03 W
Staubbachfall ⌞	58	46.35 N	7.55 E
Staufen	58	47.53 N	7.44 E
Staufenberg	56	50.40 N	8.43 E
Staughton Vale	169	37.51 S	144.17 E
Staunton, Il., U.S.	219	39.00 N	89.47 W
Staunton, Va., U.S.	188	38.08 N	79.04 W
Staunton → Roanoke ≃	192	35.56 N	76.43 W
Stavanger	26	58.58 N	5.45 E
Stave ≃	224	49.10 N	122.26 W
Stave Lake ⊜	182	49.15 N	122.21 W
Staveley	44	53.16 N	1.20 W
Stavelot	56	50.23 N	5.56 E
Stavely, Ab., Can.	182	50.10 N	113.38 W
Stavely, Eng., U.K.	44	54.22 N	2.49 W
Staveren	52	52.53 N	5.22 E
Stavern	26	59.00 N	10.02 E
Stavišče	78	49.23 N	30.12 E
Stavnoje	78	48.59 N	22.40 E
Stavropol', S.S.S.R.	72	45.02 N	41.59 E
Stavropol → Toljatti, S.S.S.R.	80	53.31 N	49.26 E
Stavropol' □[8]	84	44.38 N	43.30 E
Stavrovo	80	56.08 N	40.00 E
Stavsnäs	40	59.17 N	18.41 E
Stawell	166	37.04 S	142.46 E
Stawell ≃	166	20.38 S	142.55 E
Stawiski	30	53.23 N	22.09 E
Stawiszyn	30	51.55 N	18.07 E
Staxigoe	46	58.28 N	3.04 W
Stayner	212	44.25 N	80.05 W
Stayton	202	44.48 N	122.47 W
Stazzema	64	43.59 N	10.19 E
Ste. → Saint			
Steamboat	226	39.22 N	119.44 W
Steamboat Creek ≃	226	39.31 N	119.42 W
Steamboat Mountain ∧	200	41.58 N	108.58 W
Steamboat Slough ≃	226	38.11 N	121.40 W
Steamboat Springs	200	40.29 N	106.49 W
Steamburg	210	42.07 N	78.54 W
Stearns	192	36.41 N	84.28 W
Stearns Pond ⊜	283	42.37 N	71.04 W
Stębark	30	53.30 N	20.08 E
Stebbins	180	63.32 N	162.18 W
Stebl'ov	78	49.24 N	31.06 E
Stechow	54	52.38 N	12.28 E
Steckborn	58	47.40 N	8.55 E
Stederdorf	52	52.21 N	10.15 E
Stedten	54	51.26 N	11.41 E
Stedum	52	53.18 N	6.41 E
Steeg	58	47.14 N	10.17 E
Steel ≃	190	48.46 N	86.54 W
Steel City	210	40.38 N	75.20 W
Steele, Mo., U.S.	194	36.05 N	89.49 W
Steele, N.D., U.S.	198	46.51 N	99.54 W
Steele ➔[8]	263	51.27 N	7.05 E
Steele, Mount ∧	200	41.50 N	107.00 W
Steele Creek ≃, Tx., U.S.	222	31.13 N	96.19 W
Steele Creek ≃, Tx., U.S.	222	32.01 N	97.28 W
Steeles Corners	275b	43.48 N	79.25 W
Steeleville	194	38.00 N	89.39 W
Steelhead	224	49.13 N	122.19 W
Steel's Drift	158	27.21 S	29.30 E
Steels Point ›	174c	29.02 S	168.00 E
Steels Run ≃	279b	40.25 N	79.38 W
Steelton, N.Y., U.S.	284a	42.47 N	78.49 W
Steelton, Pa., U.S.	208	40.14 N	76.50 W
Steelville	194	37.58 N	91.21 W
Steenbergen	52	51.35 N	4.19 E
Steenburg Lake ⊜	212	44.50 N	77.41 W
Steenderen	52	52.04 N	6.11 E
Steenkool	164	2.07 S	133.32 E
Steens Mountain ⋏	202	42.35 N	118.40 W
Steenvoorde	50	50.48 N	2.35 E
Steenwijk	52	52.47 N	6.08 E
Steepbank ≃	184	57.01 N	111.28 W
Steephill Lake ⊜	184	55.58 N	103.08 W
Steep Holm I	42	51.21 N	3.07 W
Steeping ≃	44	53.06 N	0.18 E
Steeple Claydon	42	51.56 N	0.59 W
Steep Point ›	162	26.08 S	113.08 E
Steep Rock	184	51.26 N	98.48 W
Stefanie, Lake (Chew Bahir) ⊜	144	4.40 N	36.50 E
Stefansson Island I	176	73.20 N	105.45 W
Ștefan Vodă	38	44.19 N	27.19 E
Steffisburg	58	46.47 N	7.39 E
Steg	58	47.21 N	8.56 E
Stegalovka	76	52.24 N	38.19 E
Stege	41	54.59 N	12.18 E
Stegeborg	26	58.26 N	16.35 E
Stege Bugt ⊂	41	55.01 N	12.50 E
Stegelitz	54	53.08 N	13.51 E
Steger	216	41.28 N	87.38 W
Stegersbach	61	47.10 N	16.10 E
Steglitz ➔[8]	264a	52.28 N	13.19 E
Stehag	41	55.54 N	13.23 E
Stehekin	224	48.18 N	120.39 W
Stehekin ≃	224	48.21 N	120.40 W
Steiermark □[3]	30	47.10 N	15.10 E
Steigerwald ⋏	56	49.40 N	10.20 E
Steigra	54	51.18 N	11.39 E
Steilacoom	224	47.10 N	122.36 W
Steimbke	52	52.40 N	9.22 E
Stein, B.R.D.	60	49.25 N	11.01 E
Stein, Ned.	56	50.57 N	5.46 E
Stein, Schw.	58	47.33 N	7.58 E
Steina	54	51.12 N	14.01 E
Steinach, B.R.D.	58	48.18 N	8.04 E
Steinach, D.D.R.	54	50.25 N	11.10 E
Steinach, Öst.	64	47.05 N	11.28 E
Steinach ≃	56	50.11 N	11.12 E
Steinamanger → Szombathely	61	47.14 N	16.38 E
Stein am Rhein	58	47.40 N	8.51 E
Steinau	56	50.23 N	9.27 E
Steinau → Ścinawa	30	51.25 N	16.27 E
Steinbach, B.R.D.	56	48.43 N	8.10 E
Steinbach, Mb., Can.	184	49.32 N	96.41 W
Steinbach-Hallenberg	54	50.42 N	10.34 E
Steinberg ∧[2]	263	51.05 N	7.27 E
Steinberger Slough ≃	282	37.33 N	122.13 W
Steinbourg	56	48.46 N	7.25 E
Steindorf	61	46.42 N	14.01 E
Steinen	58	47.38 N	7.44 E
Steinernes Meer ⋏	64	47.30 N	12.58 E
Steinfeld, B.R.D.	52	52.35 N	8.12 E
Steinfeld, D.D.R.	54	50.22 N	10.44 E
Steinfeld, Öst.	64	46.45 N	13.15 E
Steinfort	56	49.40 N	5.55 E
Steinforth	263	51.09 N	6.32 E
Steinfurt	52	52.09 N	7.21 E
Steingaden	58	47.42 N	10.51 E
Steinhagen, B.R.D.	52	52.00 N	8.24 E
Steinhagen, D.D.R.	54	54.13 N	12.59 E
Steinhatchee ≃	192	29.40 N	83.24 W
Steinhausen	156	21.49 S	18.20 E
Steinhausen ♁[1]	58	48.01 N	9.41 E
Steinheid	54	50.28 N	11.04 E
Steinheim, B.R.D.	52	51.52 N	9.05 E
Steinheim, B.R.D.	56	48.58 N	9.16 E
Steinheim, B.R.D.	58	48.01 N	10.09 E
Steinhöfel	54	52.24 N	14.10 E
Steinhöring	60	48.05 N	12.02 E
Steinhude	52	52.27 N	9.21 E
Steinhuder Meer ⊜	52	52.28 N	9.19 E
Steinkjer	26	64.01 N	11.30 E
Steinkopf	156	29.18 S	17.43 E
Steinloge	52	52.54 N	8.19 E
Stein-Neukirch	56	50.41 N	8.03 E
Steinpass)(	64	47.39 N	12.45 E
Steinsdorf	54	52.02 N	14.40 E
Steinshamn	26	62.47 N	6.29 E
Steinstücken ➔[8]	264a	52.23 N	13.08 E
Steinwiesen	54	50.17 N	11.28 E
Stekene	50	51.12 N	4.02 E
Stekl'anka	76	59.08 N	41.37 E
Steklino	76	56.51 N	32.10 E
Steksovo	80	55.17 N	43.25 E
Stella, It.	62	44.24 N	8.30 E
Stella, S. Afr.	158	26.38 S	24.48 E
Stella, Ne., U.S.	198	40.13 N	95.46 W
Stella Niagara	210	43.12 N	79.02 W
Stella-Plage	50	50.29 N	1.35 E
Stellaquo Indian Reserve ➔[4]	182	54.03 N	124.55 W
Stellarton	186	45.34 N	62.40 W
Stelle	52	53.23 N	10.06 E
Stellenbosch	158	33.58 S	18.50 E
Steller, Mount ∧	180	60.30 N	143.02 W
Stelvio, Parco Nazionale dello ♠	58	46.30 N	10.40 E
Stelvio, Passo dello)(	58	46.32 N	10.27 E
Stemwede	52	52.25 N	8.27 E
Stenay	56	49.29 N	5.11 E
Stendal	54	52.36 N	11.51 E
Stende	76	57.09 N	22.33 E
Stenden	263	51.25 N	6.27 E
Stenhammars slott ⊥	40	59.03 N	16.31 E
Stenhousemuir	46	56.02 N	3.48 W
Stenico	64	46.03 N	10.51 E
Stenlille	41	55.32 N	11.36 E
Stenløse	41	55.46 N	12.12 E
Stenness, Loch of ⊜	46	59.00 N	3.15 W
Stenón	267c	37.58 N	22.20 E
Stenón Návstathmou ⊔	267c	37.58 N	23.33 E
Stensätra	40	60.36 N	16.44 E
Stensele	24	65.05 N	17.09 E
Stenstorp	26	58.16 N	13.43 E
Stenstrup	41	55.07 N	10.31 E
Stentrop	263	51.30 N	7.49 E
Stenungsund	26	58.05 N	11.49 E
Stepan'	78	51.10 N	26.18 E
Stepanakert	84	39.49 N	46.44 E
Stepanavan	84	41.00 N	44.23 E
Stepancevo, S.S.S.R.	80	56.08 N	41.42 E
Stepancevo, S.S.S.R.	82	56.22 N	36.10 E
Stepancy	78	49.42 N	31.18 E
Stepano-Krynka	83	47.55 N	38.21 E
Stepanovka, S.S.S.R.	78	50.58 N	34.37 E
Stepanovka, S.S.S.R.	80	52.04 N	53.02 E
Stepanovka, S.S.S.R.	86	57.13 N	67.26 E
Stepanovo	82	55.43 N	38.28 E
Stepanovskoje	265b	55.47 N	37.10 E
Stepan Razin	84	40.24 N	49.59 E
Stepanščino	82	55.15 N	38.30 E
Stepenitz ≃	54	53.48 N	11.10 E
Stephans-Dom ♁[1]	264b	48.12 N	16.23 E
Stephanskirchen	64	47.51 N	12.11 E
Stephen	198	48.27 N	96.52 W
Stephen A. Forbes State Park ♠	219	38.44 N	88.46 W
Stephen F. Austin State Historic Park ♠	222	29.48 N	96.05 W
Stephens	194	33.24 N	93.04 W
Stephens, Cape ›	172	40.42 S	173.57 E
Stephens, Port ⊂	166	32.45 S	152.05 E
Stephens City	188	39.05 N	78.13 W
Stephens Creek	166	31.50 S	141.30 E
Stephens Island I	182	54.10 N	130.45 W
Stephens Knob ∧[2]	192	36.37 N	84.20 W
Stephens Lake ⊜[1]	184	56.26 N	95.07 W
Stephens Mills	210	42.23 N	77.38 W
Stephenson	190	45.24 N	87.36 W
Stephenson, Lake ⊜	222	29.35 N	94.40 W
Stephenson, Mount ∧	9	69.49 S	69.43 W
Stephens Passage ⊔	180	57.50 N	133.50 W
Stephentown	210	42.33 N	73.23 W
Stephentown Center	210	42.34 N	73.25 W
Stephenville, Nf., Can.	186	48.33 N	58.35 W
Stephenville, Tx., U.S.	196	32.13 N	98.12 W
Stephenville Crossing	186	48.30 N	58.26 W
Stepn'ak	86	52.50 N	70.50 E
Stepney ➔[8]	260	51.31 N	0.02 W
Stepnica	54	53.40 N	14.36 E
Stepnoj	80	48.56 N	45.36 E
Stepnoje, S.S.S.R.	80	51.24 N	46.52 E
Stepnoje, S.S.S.R.	84	44.17 N	44.36 E
Step Pyramid → Saqqārah ⊥	142	29.52 N	31.14 E
Steps Point ›	174u	14.22 S	170.45 W
Steptoe Valley V	204	39.25 N	114.45 W
Stepurino	76	56.24 N	35.16 E
Sterdyń	30	52.35 N	22.18 E
Sterkaar	158	31.05 S	23.42 E
Sterkrade ➔[8]	263	51.31 N	6.51 E
Sterkspruit	158	30.32 S	27.22 E
Sterkstroom	158	31.32 S	26.32 E
Sterlibaševo	86	53.28 N	55.15 E
Sterling, S. Afr.	158	31.16 S	21.28 E
Sterling, Ak., U.S.	180	60.32 N	150.48 W
Sterling, Co., U.S.	198	40.37 N	103.12 W
Sterling, Ct., U.S.	207	41.42 N	71.49 W
Sterling, Il., U.S.	190	41.47 N	89.41 W
Sterling, Ks., U.S.	198	38.12 N	98.12 W
Sterling, Ma., U.S.	207	42.26 N	71.45 W
Sterling, Mi., U.S.	190	44.02 N	84.01 W
Sterling, Ne., U.S.	198	40.27 N	96.22 W
Sterling, N.Y., U.S.	210	43.20 N	76.39 W
Sterling, Oh., U.S.	214	40.58 N	81.51 W
Sterling, Ok., U.S.	196	34.45 N	98.10 W
Sterling, Va., U.S.	208	39.00 N	77.25 W
Sterling City	196	31.50 N	100.59 W
Sterling Creek ≃	210	43.20 N	76.42 W
Sterling Forest Lake ⊜	276	41.10 N	74.16 W
Sterling Heights	214	42.34 N	83.01 W
Sterling Junction	207	42.24 N	71.46 W
Sterling Park	282	37.41 N	122.26 W
Sterling Run	214	41.25 N	78.12 W
Sterlington	194	32.41 N	92.05 W
Sterlitamak	86	53.37 N	55.58 E
Sternberg	54	53.43 N	11.49 E
Sternberg in der Neumark → Torzym	30	52.20 N	15.04 E
Šternberk	30	49.44 N	17.18 E
Șternstein ∧	61	48.34 N	14.16 E
Šterovka	83	48.19 N	38.57 E
Sterup	41	54.44 N	9.44 E
Sterzing → Vipiteno	64	46.54 N	11.26 E
Stęszew	30	52.18 N	16.42 E
Štětí	54	50.25 N	14.23 E
Stetson Pond ⊜	283	42.02 N	70.50 W
Stetten am kalten Markt	58	48.07 N	9.04 E
Stettin → Szczecin	30	53.24 N	14.32 E
Stettler	182	52.19 N	112.43 W
Steuben □[6], In., U.S.	216	41.38 N	85.00 W
Steuben □[6], N.Y., U.S.	210	42.20 N	77.19 W
Steubenville	214	40.22 N	80.38 W
Stevenage	42	51.55 N	0.14 W
Stevens, N.J., U.S.	285	40.05 N	74.49 W
Stevens, Pa., U.S.	208	40.13 N	76.09 W
Stevens, Lake ⊜	224	48.01 N	122.05 W
Stevens, Mount ∧	172	40.48 S	172.27 E
Stevens Creek ≃, Ca., U.S.	282	37.26 N	122.05 W
Stevens Creek ≃, S.C., U.S.	192	33.34 N	82.03 W
Stevens Creek Park ♠	282	37.17 N	122.04 W
Stevens Creek Reservoir ⊜[1]	282	37.17 N	122.05 W
Stevens Institute of Technology ♁[2]	276	40.44 N	74.02 W
Stevenson, Al., U.S.	194	34.52 N	85.50 W
Stevenson, Md., U.S.	284b	39.25 N	76.43 W
Stevenson, Wa., U.S.	224	45.42 N	121.53 W
Stevenson Creek ≃	162	27.06 S	135.33 E
Stevenson Entrance ⊔	180	58.45 N	152.20 W
Stevenson Lake ⊜	184	53.56 N	96.09 W
Stevens Pass)(	224	47.45 N	121.04 W
Stevens Peak ∧	202	47.27 N	115.46 W
Stevens Point	190	44.31 N	89.34 W
Stevenston	46	55.39 N	4.45 W
Stevens Village	180	66.00 N	149.05 W
Stevensville, On., Can.	284a	42.57 N	79.04 W
Stevensville, Md., U.S.	208	38.58 N	76.18 W
Stevensville, Mi., U.S.	216	42.00 N	86.31 W
Stevensville, Mt., U.S.	202	46.30 N	114.05 W
Stevensville, Pa., U.S.	210	41.46 N	76.11 W
Stevinson	226	37.20 N	120.51 W
Stevns Klint ⩡[4]	41	55.18 N	12.27 E
Steward	216	41.51 N	89.01 W
Stewardson	219	39.15 N	88.37 W
Stewart, B.C., Can.	182	55.56 N	129.59 W
Stewart, Mn., U.S.	190	44.43 N	94.29 W
Stewart ≃	180	63.18 N	139.25 W
Stewart, Cape ›	164	11.57 S	134.45 E
Stewart, Isla I	254	54.52 S	71.12 W
Stewart, Mount ∧	166	20.12 S	145.29 E
Stewart Island I	172	47.00 S	167.50 E
Stewart Islands II	175e	8.25 S	162.52 E
Stewart Lake ⊜	219	40.09 N	90.16 W
Stewart Manor	276	40.43 N	73.41 W
Stewarton	46	55.41 N	4.31 W
Stewartstown, N. Ire., U.K.	48	54.35 N	6.41 W
Stewartstown, Pa., U.S.	208	39.45 N	76.35 W
Stewartsville, Mo., U.S.	194	39.45 N	94.29 W
Stewartsville, N.J., U.S.	208	40.41 N	75.06 W
Stewartsville, Pa., U.S.	279b	40.21 N	79.46 W
Stewart Valley	184	50.36 N	107.50 W
Stewartville	190	43.51 N	92.29 W
Stewiacke	186	45.08 N	63.21 W
Steyerberg	52	52.34 N	9.01 E
Steyning	42	50.53 N	0.20 W
Steynsburg	158	31.15 S	25.49 E
Steynsrus	158	27.58 S	27.33 E
Steyr	61	48.03 N	14.25 E
Steyr ≃	61	48.02 N	14.25 E
Steyregg	61	48.17 N	14.22 E
Steytlerville	158	33.21 S	24.21 E
Stežki	80	53.06 N	41.13 E
Stezzano	62	45.38 N	9.39 E
Sthal	126	24.12 N	89.44 E
Știa	66	43.48 N	11.42 E
Štiavnické vrchy ⋏	30	48.40 N	18.45 E
Stickle Pond ⊜	276	40.59 N	74.25 W
Stickney, Il., U.S.	216	41.49 N	87.46 W
Stickney, S.D., U.S.	198	43.35 N	98.26 W
Stidsvig	41	56.12 N	13.08 E
Stiefingbach ≃	61	46.47 N	15.35 E
Stiege	54	51.40 N	10.53 E
Stiene	76	57.26 N	24.34 E
Stienitzfliess ≃	264a	52.33 N	13.43 E
Stienitz-See ⊜	264a	52.30 N	13.49 E
Stiens	52	53.15 N	5.45 E
Stiepel ➔[8]	263	51.25 N	7.15 E
Stif	148	36.09 N	5.26 E
Stif □[5]	148	36.15 N	5.10 E
Stiftskirche ♁[1]	263	51.23 N	7.00 E
Stige	41	55.26 N	10.25 E
Stigler	196	35.15 N	95.07 W
Stigliano	68	40.24 N	16.14 E
Stigtomta	40	58.48 N	16.47 E
Stikine ≃	180	56.40 N	132.30 W
Stikine Ranges ⋏	180	58.45 N	130.00 W
Stiklestad	26	63.48 N	11.33 E
Stilbaai	158	34.24 S	21.26 E
Stiles	210	40.40 N	75.30 W
Stiles Pond ⊜	283	42.41 N	71.02 W
Stilesville	210	42.05 N	75.24 W
Stilfontein	158	26.50 S	26.50 E
Stilís	38	38.55 N	22.36 E
Still	148	34.20 N	5.51 E
Stillaguamish ≃	224	48.11 N	122.22 W
Stillaguamish, North Fork ≃	224	48.11 N	122.07 W
Stillaguamish, South Fork ≃	224	48.11 N	122.07 W
Stillhouse Hollow Lake ⊜[1]	222	31.00 N	97.35 W
Stilling	41	56.04 N	10.00 E
Stillman Valley	216	42.07 N	89.11 W
Stillmore	192	32.26 N	82.12 W
Still Pond	208	39.19 N	76.02 W
Still Run ≃	285	39.49 N	75.18 W
Stillwater, B.C., Can.	182	49.46 N	124.18 W
Stillwater, Mn., U.S.	190	45.03 N	92.48 W
Stillwater, N.J., U.S.	210	41.02 N	74.52 W
Stillwater, N.Y., U.S.	210	42.56 N	73.39 W
Stillwater, Oh., U.S.	214	40.20 N	81.18 W
Stillwater, Ok., U.S.	196	36.06 N	97.03 W
Stillwater, Pa., U.S.	210	41.09 N	76.22 W
Stillwater ≃, Mt., U.S.	202	45.38 N	109.17 W
Stillwater ≃, Oh., U.S.	218	39.47 N	84.12 W
Stillwater Creek ≃	214	40.25 N	81.22 W
Stillwater Range ⋏	204	39.50 N	118.15 W
Stillwell, Il., U.S.	219	40.13 N	91.11 W
Stillwell, Ok., U.S.	194	35.49 N	94.38 W
Stilo	68	38.29 N	16.28 E
Stilo, Punta ›	68	38.28 N	16.36 E
Stimberg ∧[2]	263	51.40 N	7.15 E
Stimigliano	66	42.18 N	12.34 E
Stimson, Mount ∧	202	48.31 N	113.36 W
Stinchar ≃	44	55.06 N	5.00 W
Stinear Nunataks ⋏	9	69.42 S	64.40 E
Stine Canal ≊	226	35.15 N	119.08 W
Stine Mountain ∧	202	45.44 N	113.07 W
Stingray Point ›	208	37.33 N	76.18 W
Stînisoara, Munții ⋏	38	47.10 N	26.00 E
Stinking Water Creek ≃	198	40.22 N	101.07 W
Stinnett	196	35.49 N	101.26 W
Stintino	71	40.56 N	8.13 E
Știntonville	273d	26.14 S	28.13 E
Štip	38	41.44 N	22.12 E
Stiperstones ∧	42	52.35 N	2.56 W
Stiring-Wendel	56	49.12 N	6.56 E
Stírka ∧	60	49.24 N	13.34 E
Stirling, Austl.	162	21.44 S	133.45 E
Stirling, Austl.	168a	31.54 S	115.47 E
Stirling, Austl.	168b	35.00 S	138.43 E
Stirling, Ab., Can.	182	49.30 N	112.31 W
Stirling, On., Can.	212	44.18 N	77.33 W
Stirling, Scot., U.K.	46	56.07 N	3.57 W
Stirling, N.J., U.S.	210	40.40 N	74.29 W
Stirling, Mount ∧	162	31.50 S	117.38 E
Stirling Castle ⊥	46	56.07 N	3.57 W
Stirling City	204	39.54 N	121.31 W
Stirling Range ⋏	162	34.23 S	117.50 E
Stirling Range National Park ♠	162	34.22 S	118.00 E
Stirling Reservoir ⊜[1]	168a	33.08 S	116.03 E
Stirrat	192	37.43 N	82.00 W
Știssing Mountain ∧	210	41.57 N	73.42 W
Štitary	61	48.56 N	15.51 E
Stittsville	212	45.15 N	75.55 W
Stittville	210	43.13 N	75.17 W
Stjärnhov	40	59.05 N	17.00 E
Stjärnsund, Sve.	40	60.26 N	16.12 E
Stjärnsund, Sve.	40	58.51 N	14.55 E
Stjernøya I	24	70.18 N	22.45 E
Stjørdalshalsen	26	63.28 N	10.56 E
Stöberhai ∧	54	51.39 N	10.34 E
Stobi ⊥	38	41.34 N	21.58 E
Stochod ≃	78	51.52 N	25.38 E
Stock	260	51.40 N	0.27 E
Stock, Étang du ⊜	56	48.45 N	6.55 E
Stockach	58	47.51 N	9.00 E
Stöckalp	58	46.48 N	8.17 E
Stockamöllan	41	55.57 N	13.22 E
Stockbridge, Eng., U.K.	42	51.07 N	1.29 W
Stockbridge, Ga., U.S.	192	33.32 N	84.14 W
Stockbridge, Ma., U.S.	207	42.17 N	73.19 W
Stockbridge, Mi., U.S.	216	42.27 N	84.10 W
Stockbridge Bowl ⊜	207	42.20 N	73.19 W
Stockbridge Indian Reservation ➔[4]	190	44.52 N	88.53 W
Stockbury	260	51.20 N	0.39 E
Stockby	40	59.20 N	17.41 E
Stockdale, Oh., U.S.	218	38.57 N	82.51 W
Stockdale, Tx., U.S.	196	29.14 N	97.57 W
Stockelsdorf	52	53.54 N	10.38 E
Stöcken	54	53.00 N	10.40 E
Stockerau	61	48.23 N	16.13 E
Stockertown	208	40.45 N	75.15 W
Stockett	202	47.21 N	111.09 W
Stockheim	56	50.19 N	9.01 E
Stöckheim bei Braunschweig	52	52.12 N	10.31 E
Stockholm, Sve.	40	59.20 N	18.03 E
Stockholm, Me., U.S.	186	47.02 N	68.08 W
Stockholm, N.J., U.S.	210	41.05 N	74.31 W
Stockholm, Lake ⊜	276	41.04 N	74.32 W
Stockholms Län □[6]	40	59.30 N	18.20 E
Stock Island	220	24.34 N	81.45 W
Stockland	216	40.37 N	87.36 W
Stockport, Eng., U.K.	44	53.25 N	2.10 W
Stockport, N.Y., U.S.	210	42.19 N	73.45 W
Stockport □[8]	262	53.23 N	2.08 W
Stocksbridge	44	53.27 N	1.34 W
Stockstadt	56	49.48 N	8.28 E
Stocksund	40	59.23 N	18.04 E
Stockton, Austl.	170	32.55 S	151.47 E
Stockton, Al., U.S.	194	30.59 N	87.51 W
Stockton, Ca., U.S.	226	37.57 N	121.17 W
Stockton, Il., U.S.	190	42.20 N	90.00 W
Stockton, Ks., U.S.	198	39.26 N	99.15 W
Stockton, Md., U.S.	208	38.03 N	75.24 W
Stockton, Mo., U.S.	194	37.41 N	93.47 W
Stockton, N.J., U.S.	208	40.24 N	74.58 W
Stockton, N.Y., U.S.	214	42.19 N	79.22 W
Stockton, Ut., U.S.	200	40.27 N	112.21 W
Stockton Heath, Eng., U.K.	44	53.22 N	2.34 W
Stockton Heath, Eng., U.K.	262	53.22 N	2.35 W
Stockton Metropolitan Airport ⊠	226	37.54 N	121.15 W
Stockton-on-Tees	44	54.34 N	1.19 W
Stockton Plateau ⋏[1]	196	30.30 N	102.30 W
Stockton Reservoir ⊜[1]	194	37.40 N	93.45 W
Stockton Springs	188	44.29 N	68.51 W

≃ River	Fluss	Río	Rivière	Rio
≊ Canal	Kanal	Canal	Canal	Canal
⌞ Waterfall, Rapids	Wasserfall, Stromschnellen	Cascada, Rápidos	Chute d'eau, Rapides	Cascata, Rápidos
⊔ Strait	Meeresstrasse	Estrecho	Détroit	Estreito
⊂ Bay, Gulf	Bucht, Golf	Bahía, Golfo	Baie, Golfe	Baía, Golfo
⊜ Lake, Lakes	See, Seen	Lago, Lagos	Lac, Lacs	Lago, Lagos
≡ Swamp	Sumpf	Pantano	Marais	Pântano
⊓ Ice Features, Glacier	Eis- und Gletscherformen	Accidentes Glaciales	Formes glaciaires	Acidentes glaciares
⊤ Other Hydrographic Features	Andere Hydrographische Objekte	Otros Elementos Hidrográficos	Autres données hydrographiques	Outros acidentes hidrográficos

✧ Submarine Features	Untermeerische Objekte	Accidentes Submarinos	Formes de relief sous-marin	Acidentes submarinos
□ Political Unit	Politische Einheit	Unidad Politica	Entité politique	Unidade política
♁ Cultural Institution	Kulturelle Institution	Institución Cultural	Institution culturelle	Institução cultural
⊥ Historical Site	Historische Stätte	Sitio Histórico	Site historique	Sitio histórico
♠ Recreational Site	Erholungs- und Ferienort	Sitio de Recreo	Centre de loisirs	Area de Lazer
⊠ Airport	Flughafen	Aeropuerto	Aéroport	Aeroporto
■ Military Installation	Militäranlage	Instalación Militar	Installation militaire	Instalação militar
➔ Miscellaneous	Verschiedenes	Misceláneo	Divers	Diversos

ENGLISH / DEUTSCH

Symbols in the index entries represent the broad categories identified in the key at the right. Symbols with superior numbers (⋀[1]) identify subcategories (see complete key on page *I · 1).*

Kartensymbole in dem Registerverzeichnis stellen die rechts in Schlüssel erklärten Kategorien dar. Symbole mit hochgestellten Ziffern (⋀[1]) bezeichnen Unterabteilungen einer Kategorie (vgl. vollständiger Schlüssel auf Seite *I · 1).*

Los símbolos incluídos en el texto del índice representan las grandes categorias identificadas con la clave a la derecha. Los símbolos con numeros en su parte superior (⋀[1]) identifican las subcategorías (véase la clave completa en la página *I · 1).*

Les symboles de l'index représentent les catégories indiquées dans la légende à droite. Les symboles suivis d'un indice (⋀[1]) représentent des sous-catégories (voir légende complète à la page *I · 1).*

Os símbolos incluídos no texto do índice representam as grandes categorias identificadas com a chave à direita. Os símbolos com números em sua parte superior (⋀[1]) identificam as subcategorias (veja-se a chave completa à página *I · 1).*

∧ Mountain	Berg	Montaña	Montagne	Montanha
⋀ Mountains	Berge	Montañas	Montagnes	Montanhas
)(Pass	Pass	Paso	Col	Passo
V Valley, Canyon	Tal, Cañon	Valle, Cañón	Vallée, Canyon	Vale, Canhão
≚ Plain	Ebene	Llano	Plaine	Planície
≻ Cape	Kap	Cabo	Cap	Cabo
I Island	Insel	Isla	Île	Ilha
II Islands	Inseln	Islas	Îles	Ilhas
⊥ Other Topographic Features	Andere Topographische Objekte	Otros Elementos Topográficos	Autres données topographiques	Outros acidentes topográficos

ESPAÑOL — Nombre | Página | Lat.°′ | Long.°′ W = Oeste

FRANÇAIS — Nom | Page | Lat.°′ | Long.°′ W = Ouest

PORTUGUÊS — Nome | Página | Lat.°′ | Long.°′ W = Oeste

Nombre	Página	Lat.°′	Long.°′ W = Oeste
Sud-Ouest, Pointe du ›	186	49.23 N	63.36 W
Sudovaja Višn'a	78	49.49 N	23.22 E
Südradde ≃	52	52.41 N	7.34 E
Süd-Sandwich-Inseln → South Sandwich Islands II	18	57.45 S	26.30 W
Süd-Shetland-Inseln → South Shetland Islands II	9	62.00 S	58.00 W
Sudūd	142	30.25 N	30.54 E
Südwest-Kap → South West Cape ›	166	43.34 S	146.02 E
Sudweyhe	52	52.59 N	8.53 E
Sudža	78	51.12 N	35.16 E
Sue	96	33.35 N	130.30 E
Sue ≃	140	7.41 N	28.03 E
Sueca	34	39.12 N	0.19 W
Suecia → Sweden □[1]	24	62.00 N	15.00 E
Sue Creek c	284b	39.17 N	76.24 W
Suedberg	208	40.32 N	76.28 W
Suède → Sweden □[1]	24	62.00 N	15.00 E
Suemez Island I	182	55.17 N	133.21 W
Suèvres	50	47.40 N	1.28 E
Suez → As-Suways	142	29.58 N	32.33 E
Suez, Gulf of → Suways, Khalīj as- c	140	29.00 N	32.50 E
Suez Canal → Suways, Qanāt as- ≍	142	29.55 N	32.33 E
Sūf	132	32.19 N	35.50 E
Ṣufaynah	128	23.09 N	40.32 E
Suffern	210	41.06 N	74.09 W
Suffern Park	276	41.07 N	74.07 W
Suffield, Ab., Can.	184	50.12 N	111.10 W
Suffield, Ct., U.S.	207	41.58 N	72.39 W
Suffield, Oh., U.S.	214	41.01 N	81.21 W
Suffield, Canadian Forces Base ■	184	50.15 N	111.10 W
Suffolk	208	36.43 N	76.35 W
Suffolk □[6], Eng., U.K.	42	52.10 N	1.00 E
Suffolk □[6], Ma., U.S.	207	42.21 N	71.04 W
Suffolk □[6], N.Y., U.S.	210	40.55 N	72.40 W
Suffolk, Ruisseau ≃	206	45.48 N	74.59 W
Suffolk Downs Race Track ♠	283	42.23 N	71.00 W
Ṣūfīān	128	38.17 N	45.59 E
Sufi-Kurgan	85	40.02 N	73.30 E
Sufu → Kashi	85	39.29 N	75.59 E
Suga-jima I	94	34.29 N	136.53 E
Sugana, Val V	64	46.00 N	11.40 E
Sugandha	272b	22.54 N	88.20 E
Sugandy	85	43.27 N	74.38 E
Sugano	268	35.44 N	139.56 E
Sugar ≃, U.S.	190	42.26 N	89.12 W
Sugar ≃, N.H., U.S.	188	43.24 N	72.24 W
Sugar ≃, N.Y., U.S.	212	43.31 N	75.19 W
Sugar City	202	43.52 N	111.44 W
Sugarcreek, Oh., U.S.	214	40.30 N	81.39 W
Sugarcreek, Pa., U.S.	214	41.25 N	79.52 W
Sugar Creek ≃, U.S.	216	40.47 N	87.45 W
Sugar Creek ≃, Il., U.S.	194	40.09 N	89.38 W
Sugar Creek ≃, Il., U.S.	219	38.28 N	89.37 W
Sugar Creek ≃, Il., U.S.	219	39.48 N	89.32 W
Sugar Creek ≃, In., U.S.	194	39.51 N	87.21 W
Sugar Creek ≃, In., U.S.	218	39.21 N	86.00 W
Sugar Creek ≃, Mi., U.S.	281	42.06 N	83.36 W
Sugar Creek ≃, N.Y., U.S.	210	42.38 N	77.09 W
Sugar Creek ≃, Oh., U.S.	214	40.31 N	81.28 W
Sugar Creek ≃, Oh., U.S.	216	40.57 N	84.11 W
Sugar Creek ≃, Oh., U.S.	218	39.27 N	83.25 W
Sugar Creek ≃, Ok., U.S.	196	35.05 N	98.10 W
Sugar Creek ≃, Pa., U.S.	210	41.47 N	76.27 W
Sugar Creek ≃, Wi., U.S.	216	42.43 N	88.19 W
Sugar Grove, Il., U.S.	216	41.45 N	88.27 W
Sugargrove, Pa., U.S.	214	41.59 N	79.21 W
Sugar Grove, Va., U.S.	192	36.46 N	81.24 W
Sugar Hill	192	34.06 N	84.02 W
Sugar Island I, On., Can.	212	44.26 N	77.17 W
Sugar Island I, Mi., U.S.	190	46.25 N	84.12 W
Sugar Land	222	29.37 N	95.38 W
Sugar Loaf	210	41.19 N	74.17 W
Sugar Loaf → Pão de Açúcar ∧	287a	22.57 S	43.09 W
Sugarloaf ∧[2]	214	41.24 N	81.06 W
Sugarloaf Hill ∧[2]	274b	37.58 S	145.19 E
Sugarloaf Key I	220	24.40 N	81.32 W
Sugarloaf Mountain ∧, Ky., U.S.	218	38.13 N	83.32 W
Sugarloaf Mountain ∧, Me., U.S.	188	45.01 N	70.22 W
Sugar Loaf Mountain ∧, Md., U.S.	208	39.16 N	77.23 W
Sugar Loaf Mountain ∧, Ok., U.S.	194	35.02 N	94.28 W
Sugarloaf Mountain ∧[2]	220	28.39 N	81.44 W
Sugarloaf Peak ∧	280	34.14 N	117.38 W
Sugarloaf Point ›, Austl.	166	32.26 S	152.33 E
Sugar Loaf Point ›, On., Can.	284a	42.52 N	79.17 W
Sugarloaf Ridge State Park ♠	226	38.26 N	122.29 W
Sugar Notch	210	41.11 N	75.55 W
Sugar Pine Point State Park ♠	226	39.03 N	120.07 W
Sugartown	285	40.00 N	75.31 W
Sugauli Bazar	124	26.46 N	84.44 E
Sugbai Passage ʊ	116	5.22 N	120.33 E
Sugbay	116	7.31 N	123.19 E
Sugbuhan Point ›	116	10.04 N	126.04 E
Suggi Lake ⊜	184	54.22 N	102.47 W
Suginami ◆[8]	268	35.42 N	139.38 E
Sugita ◆[8]	268	35.23 N	139.38 E
Sugito	94	36.02 N	139.44 E
Şugla Gölü ⊜	130	37.20 N	32.02 E
Šugnou	85	38.35 N	70.20 E
Sugod	116	12.03 N	124.09 E
Sugoj ≃	74	64.15 N	154.29 E
Šugonovo	82	54.41 N	36.41 E
Šugozero	76	59.55 N	34.12 E
Šugurovo, S.S.S.R.	80	53.25 N	46.29 E
Šugurovo, S.S.S.R.	80	54.31 N	52.06 E
Sugut ≃	112	6.26 N	117.43 E
Suguta ≃	154	2.03 N	36.33 E
Suguti	154	1.44 S	33.39 E
Suhai Hu ⊜	102	38.50 N	94.00 E
Suhaitu	102	44.50 N	93.39 E
Sūhānak	267d	35.48 N	51.32 E
Ṣuḥār	128	24.22 N	56.45 E
Suheli Par I[1]	122	10.03 N	72.17 E
Suhl	54	50.37 N	10.41 E
Suhl □[5]	54	50.40 N	10.30 E
Suhlendorf	54	52.55 N	10.46 E
Suhopolje	36	45.48 N	17.30 E
Suhr	58	47.22 N	8.05 E
Suhr ≃	58	47.25 N	8.04 E
Suhum	150	6.05 N	0.27 W
Şuhut	130	38.32 N	30.33 E
Šūi	120	28.37 N	69.19 E
Suia-Miçu ≃	250	11.13 S	53.15 W
Suianzhan	89	53.07 N	125.20 E
Suiattle ≃	224	48.20 N	121.33 W
Suichang	100	28.34 N	119.14 E
Suichuan	100	26.26 N	114.32 E
Suichuan ≃	100	26.30 N	114.45 E
Suid Afrika → South Africa □[1]	156	30.00 S	26.00 E
Suide	102	37.32 N	110.12 E
Suiding	86	44.03 N	80.49 E
Suido-suigenchi ⊜[1]	270	34.54 N	135.17 E
Suidvaal	158	26.52 S	29.47 E
Suifenhe	89	44.24 N	131.10 E
Suifu, Nihon	94	36.37 N	140.29 E
Suifu → Yibin, Zhg.	107	28.47 N	104.38 E
Suigō-kokutei-kōen ♠	94	36.05 N	140.20 E
Suigō-Tsukuba-kokutei-kōen ♠	94	36.00 N	140.20 E
Suihua	89	46.37 N	127.00 E
Suijiang	102	28.31 N	104.07 E
Suileng	89	47.18 N	127.10 E
Suining, Zhg.	100	33.54 N	117.56 E
Suining, Zhg.	102	26.21 N	110.00 E
Suining, Zhg.	107	30.31 N	105.34 E
Suipacha	252	34.45 S	59.41 W
Suiping	100	33.10 N	113.57 E
Suippe ≃	50	49.25 N	3.57 E
Suippes	56	49.08 N	4.32 E
Suir ≃	48	52.15 N	7.00 W
Suisse → Switzerland □[1]	58	47.00 N	8.00 E
Suisun Bay c	226	38.06 N	122.00 W
Suisun City	226	38.14 N	122.02 W
Suisun Creek ≃	226	38.12 N	122.06 W
Suita	96	34.45 N	135.32 E
Suitland	284c	38.50 N	76.55 W
Suixi, Zhg.	100	33.56 N	116.46 E
Suixi, Zhg.	102	21.25 N	110.15 E
Suixian, Zhg.	98	34.26 N	115.05 E
Suixian, Zhg.	100	31.42 N	113.20 E
Suiyang, Zhg.	89	44.26 N	130.53 E
Suiyang, Zhg.	102	27.56 N	107.18 E
Suiyangdian	100	32.04 N	112.55 E
Suiza → Switzerland □[1]	58	47.00 N	8.00 E
Suize ≃	58	48.08 N	5.08 E
Suizhong	98	40.20 N	120.19 E
Šuja, S.S.S.R.	24	61.55 N	34.12 E
Šuja, S.S.S.R.	80	56.50 N	41.23 E
Šuja ≃, S.S.S.R.	24	61.54 N	34.15 E
Šuja ≃, S.S.S.R.	80	57.56 N	43.15 E
Sujānagar	126	23.57 N	89.25 E
Sūjāngarh	120	27.42 N	74.28 E
Sujāwal	120	24.36 N	68.05 E
Suji	107	29.35 N	103.37 E
Sujiabu	100	31.38 N	116.22 E
Sujiaqiao	105	39.24 N	116.10 E
Sujiatun	104	41.40 N	123.22 E
Sujiawan	107	29.48 N	104.57 E
Sujiawu	105	39.17 N	115.55 E
Sujiazui	100	33.40 N	119.29 E
Šujskoje	76	59.22 N	40.59 E
Sujutkina Kosa, mys ›	84	44.13 N	47.15 E
Sukabihanawa	112	9.30 S	124.57 E
Sukabumi	115a	6.55 S	106.56 E
Sukadana, Indon.	112	1.15 S	109.57 E
Sukadana, Indon.	115a	5.05 S	105.33 E
Sukadana, Teluk c	112	1.24 S	109.50 E
Sukagawa	92	37.17 N	140.23 E
Sukamandi	115a	6.20 S	107.39 E
Sukamara	112	2.43 S	111.11 E
Sukanegara	115a	7.06 S	107.07 E
Sukapura	115a	7.52 S	113.03 E
Sukaraja, Indon.	112	2.21 S	110.37 E
Sukaraja, Indon.	115a	7.27 S	108.12 E
Sukaraja, Indon.	115a	7.27 S	109.17 E
Sukarno, Pegunungan → Jaya, Puncak ∧	164	4.05 S	137.11 E
Sukau	112	5.32 N	118.17 E
Sukchar	272b	22.42 N	88.22 E
Sukch'ŏn	98	39.24 N	125.38 E
Sukematsu	270	34.31 N	135.26 E
Sukeva	26	63.52 N	27.26 E
Sukhnah, ʻAyn ⍑[4]	142	29.35 N	32.15 E
Sukhothai	110	17.01 N	99.49 E
Sukhumi → Suchumi	84	43.01 N	41.02 E
Sukkertoppen	176	65.25 N	52.53 W
Sukkozero	24	63.11 N	32.18 E
Sukkur	120	27.42 N	68.52 E
Sukkwan Island I	182	55.05 N	132.45 W
Suklāra	126	23.11 N	86.21 E
Sukmanovka	78	51.47 N	41.34 E
Sukodadi	115a	7.06 S	112.19 E
Sukoharjo	115a	7.41 S	110.50 E
Sukovo	82	54.54 N	38.19 E
Sukroml'a	76	56.53 N	34.44 E
Sukses	156	21.01 S	16.52 E
Suksun	86	57.07 N	57.24 E
Sukumo	92	32.56 N	132.44 E
Sukun, Pulau I	115b	8.07 S	122.08 E
Sukunka ≃	182	55.37 N	121.37 W
Sul, Baía do c	252	27.40 S	48.35 W
Sul, Canal do ʊ	250	0.10 S	49.30 W
Sula I	26	61.08 N	4.55 E
Sula ≃, S.S.S.R.	24	67.16 N	52.07 E
Sula ≃, S.S.S.R.	78	49.40 N	32.41 E
Sula, Kepulauan II	112	1.52 S	125.22 E
Sulaco ≃	236	14.58 N	87.45 W
Sulaimān Khel	123	33.41 N	71.01 E
Sulaimān Range ⋏	120	30.30 N	70.10 E
Sulak, S.S.S.R.	80	51.52 N	48.21 E
Sulak, S.S.S.R.	84	43.16 N	47.32 E
Sulak ≃	84	43.20 N	47.34 E
Sulakyurt	130	40.10 N	33.44 E
Sulang	115a	6.48 S	111.23 E
Sulat	116	11.49 N	125.27 E
Sulauan Point ›	116	8.37 N	124.29 E
Sulawesi (Celebes) I	112	2.00 S	121.00 E
Sulawesi Selatan □[4]	112	3.30 S	120.00 E
Sulawesi Tengah □[4]	112	1.00 N	123.00 E
Sulawesi Tenggara □[4]	112	4.00 S	122.00 E
Sulawesi Utara □[4]	112	0.30 N	124.00 E
Sulaymān, Birak (Solomon's Pools) ⊥	132	31.41 N	35.10 E
Sulby	44	54.18 N	4.29 W
Sulcis ◆[1]	71	39.04 N	8.41 E
Sūldeh	128	36.34 N	52.01 E
Sulechów	30	52.06 N	15.37 E
Sulęcin	30	52.26 N	15.08 E
Suleja	86	55.09 N	58.50 E
Sulejów	30	51.22 N	19.53 E
Sulejówek	30	52.14 N	21.17 E
Sülemaniye Camii ♁[1]	267b	41.00 N	28.57 E
Sulen, Mount ∧	164	3.25 S	142.15 E
Sule Skerry I[2]	46	59.05 N	4.26 W
Süleymanlı	130	37.54 N	36.50 E
Sülfeld	52	53.48 N	10.14 E
Ṣūlgan	267d	35.49 N	51.15 E
Šul'ginka	83	49.08 N	38.56 E
Šulğino, S.S.S.R.	82	55.50 N	35.55 E
Šul'gino, S.S.S.R.	82	54.33 N	37.35 E
Sulia	154	1.32 S	26.33 E
Suliki	112	0.06 S	100.27 E
Sulima	150	6.58 N	11.35 W
Sulin	83	48.54 N	40.07 E
Sulina	38	45.09 N	29.40 E
Sulina, Braţul ≃[1]	38	45.09 N	29.41 E
Sulincheer	102	42.41 N	109.20 E
Sulingen	52	52.41 N	8.47 E
Sulinskij	83	47.52 N	40.06 E
Sulitelma ∧	24	67.08 N	16.24 E
Sulkava	26	61.47 N	28.23 E
Sullana	248	4.53 S	80.41 W
Sullane ≃	48	51.53 N	8.56 W
Sulligent	194	33.54 N	88.08 W
Sullivan, Il., U.S.	194	39.35 N	88.36 W
Sullivan, In., U.S.	194	39.06 N	87.24 W
Sullivan, Mo., U.S.	219	38.12 N	91.09 W
Sullivan, Oh., U.S.	214	41.02 N	82.13 W
Sullivan, Wi., U.S.	216	43.00 N	88.35 W
Sullivan □[6], N.Y., U.S.	210	41.39 N	74.42 W
Sullivan □[6], Pa., U.S.	210	41.25 N	76.29 W
Sullivan Canyon V	280	34.03 N	118.30 W
Sullivan Creek ≃	226	37.53 N	120.25 W
Sullivan Lake ⊜	182	52.00 N	112.00 W
Sullivan Stadium ♠	283	42.05 N	71.16 W
Sullivanville	210	42.14 N	76.46 W
Sully-sur-Loire	50	47.46 N	2.22 E
Sulm ≃	61	46.45 N	15.34 E
Sulmona	66	42.03 N	13.55 E
Sulot' ≃	82	56.41 N	38.01 E
Sulphur, Yk., Can.	180	63.47 N	138.53 W
Sulphur, In., U.S.	218	38.14 N	86.28 W
Sulphur, Ky., U.S.	218	38.29 N	85.16 W
Sulphur, La., U.S.	194	30.14 N	93.22 W
Sulphur, Ok., U.S.	196	34.30 N	96.58 W
Sulphur ≃, Ab., Can.	182	53.50 N	119.10 W
Sulphur ≃, U.S.	194	33.07 N	93.52 W
Sulphur Creek ≃	198	44.46 N	102.25 W
Sulphur Draw V	196	33.12 N	102.17 W
Sulphur Springs, In., U.S.	218	40.00 N	85.26 W
Sulphur Springs, Oh., U.S.	214	40.52 N	82.52 W
Sulphur Springs, Tx., U.S.	222	33.08 N	95.36 W
Sulphur Springs Draw V	196	32.12 N	101.36 W
Sulphur Springs Valley V	200	31.50 N	109.50 W
Sulsul	144	5.06 N	44.55 E
Sultan	224	47.51 N	121.48 W
Sultan ≃	224	47.52 N	121.49 W
Sultana	226	36.33 N	119.20 W
Sultanahmet Camii ♁[1]	267b	41.00 N	28.58 E
Sultan Alonto, Lake ⊜	116	7.53 N	124.15 E
Sultana Point ›	168b	35.08 S	137.45 E
Sulṭanatābād	267d	35.46 N	51.28 E
Sultançiftlikköy	267b	41.02 N	29.11 E
Sultandağı	130	38.32 N	31.14 E
Sultandağı ∧	130	38.58 N	27.26 E
Sultanhanı	130	38.15 N	33.33 E
Sultanhisar	130	37.53 N	28.10 E
Sultan Kudarat □[4]	116	6.20 N	124.20 E
Sultan Mosque ♁[1]	271c	1.18 N	103.52 E
Sultānpur, India	123	31.13 N	75.11 E
Sultānpur, India	124	26.16 N	82.04 E
Sultānpur □[5]	124	26.20 N	82.00 E
Sultānpur Dabās ◆[8]	272a	28.46 N	77.03 E
Sultan sa Barongis	116	6.46 N	124.38 E
Sultan-Saly	83	47.21 N	39.35 E
Sulu	164	5.25 S	151.00 E
Sulu □[4]	116	6.00 N	121.00 E
Suluan Island I	116	10.46 N	125.57 E
Sulu Archipelago II	116	6.00 N	121.00 E
Sulu Basin ✣[1]	12	8.00 N	121.30 E
Suluchi ⊜	124	30.12 N	86.20 E
Sülüklü	130	39.05 N	30.58 E
Sul'ukta	85	39.56 N	69.34 E
Sululta	144	9.10 N	38.48 E
Sulunṭah	146	32.36 N	21.43 E
Suluova (Suluca)	130	40.47 N	35.42 E
Sulūq	146	31.39 N	20.15 E
Sūlūru	122	13.42 N	80.01 E
Sulusaj	85	38.50 N	67.05 E
Sulusaray	130	40.00 N	36.06 E
Sulu Sea ⍑[2]	116	8.00 N	120.00 E
Suly	86	53.45 N	66.30 E
Sulz	58	48.18 N	7.51 E
Sulz am Neckar	58	48.21 N	8.37 E
Sulzano	64	45.41 N	10.05 E
Sulzbach	56	49.18 N	7.07 E
Sulzbach ≃	60	48.36 N	13.02 E
Sulzbach am Kocher	56	48.58 N	9.50 E
Sulzbach-Rosenberg	60	49.30 N	11.45 E
Sulzberger Bay c	9	77.00 S	152.00 W
Sulzbrunn	58	47.41 N	10.20 E
Sulzburg	58	47.50 N	7.42 E
Sülze	52	52.46 N	10.02 E
Šum, S.S.S.R.	76	59.52 N	31.46 E
Šum, S.S.S.R.	88	54.51 N	95.18 E
Suma ◆[8]	270	34.39 N	135.08 E
Šum'ači	76	53.52 N	32.25 E
Šumadija ◆[1]	38	44.10 N	20.50 E
Sumalata	112	0.59 N	122.30 E
Sumallo ≃	224	49.14 N	121.05 W
Sumampa	252	29.22 S	63.28 W
Šumanaj	86	42.37 N	59.08 E
Sumangat, Tanjong ›	116	6.35 N	117.33 E
Sumano-ura ♠	96	34.38 N	135.08 E
Sūmār	128	33.52 N	45.39 E
Sumarokovo	82	55.46 N	35.55 E
Sumas	202	49.00 N	122.15 W
Sumas ≃	224	49.09 N	122.12 W
Sumatera (Sumatra) I	108	0.05 S	102.00 E
Sumatera Barat □[4]	112	0.30 S	100.30 E
Sumatera Selatan □[4]	112	3.00 S	104.00 E
Sumatera Utara □[4]	114	2.20 N	99.00 E
Sum'atino	82	55.00 N	36.21 E
Sumatou	107	30.28 N	104.03 E
Sumatra → Sumatera I	108	0.05 S	102.00 E
Sumaúma	248	7.50 S	60.02 W
Sumava Resorts	216	41.10 N	87.26 W
Sumayḥ	140	12.43 N	30.50 E
Sumba I	115b	10.00 S	120.00 E
Sumba, Île I	152	1.44 S	19.32 E
Sumba, Selat ʊ	115b	9.05 S	120.00 E
Sumbar ≃	128	38.00 N	55.17 E
Sumbawa I	115b	8.40 S	118.00 E
Sumbawa Besar	115b	8.30 S	117.26 E
Sumbawanga	154	7.58 S	31.37 E
Sumbay	248	15.58 S	71.23 W
Sumbe	152	11.13 S	13.50 E
Sümber	90	46.21 N	108.20 E
Sumbilla	34	43.10 N	1.40 W
Sumbing, Gunung ∧	115a	7.23 S	110.04 E
Sumbu National Park ♠	154	8.50 S	30.25 E
Sumburgh Head ›	46a	59.53 N	1.20 W
Sumburgh Roost ʊ	46	59.49 N	1.19 W
Šumbut	80	55.33 N	50.41 E
Sumbuya	150	7.39 N	11.58 W
Sumdo	120	35.01 N	78.41 E
Sumé	250	7.39 S	36.55 W
Sumedang	115a	6.52 S	107.55 E
Sümeg	30	46.59 N	17.17 E
Šumek	86	48.42 N	85.32 E
Šumen	38	43.16 N	26.55 E
Sumène	62	43.59 N	3.43 E
Sumenep	115a	7.01 S	113.52 E
Šumerl'a	80	55.30 N	46.26 E
Sumgait	84	40.36 N	49.38 E
Sumgait ≃	84	40.37 N	49.37 E
Šumicha	86	55.14 N	63.19 E
Sumida ◆[8]	268	35.42 N	139.48 E
Sumida ≃	268	35.40 N	139.47 E
Sumidouro	256	22.03 S	42.41 W
Sumilao	116	8.18 N	124.57 E
Šumilino	76	55.18 N	29.37 E
Šumilinskaja	80	49.58 N	41.26 E
Suminoe ◆[8]	270	34.36 N	135.28 E
Sumisu-jima I	90	31.27 N	140.03 E
Sumiswald	58	47.02 N	7.45 E
Sumiyoshi ◆[8]	270	34.36 N	135.31 E
Sumki	86	55.03 N	65.44 E
Sumkino	86	58.09 N	68.21 E
Sumlog ≃	116	6.53 N	126.02 E
Summer Bridge	44	54.03 N	1.41 W
Summerdale	208	40.18 N	76.56 W
Summerfield, Fl., U.S.	220	29.00 N	82.02 W
Summerfield, Mo., U.S.	219	38.17 N	91.49 W
Summerfield, N.C., U.S.	192	36.12 N	79.54 W
Summerford, Nf., Can.	186	49.29 N	54.47 W
Summerford, Oh., U.S.	218	39.55 N	83.29 W
Summerhill, Ire.	48	53.29 N	6.44 W
Summerhill, Pa., U.S.	214	40.22 N	78.46 W
Summer Island I	190	45.34 N	86.39 W
Summer Isles II	46	58.02 N	5.28 W
Summer Lake ⊜	202	42.50 N	120.45 W
Summerland	182	49.36 N	119.41 W
Summerland Reserve ◆[4]	169	38.31 S	145.10 E
Sümmern	56	51.25 N	7.43 E
Summer Palace ♁	265a	59.53 N	29.55 E
Summerseat	262	53.38 N	2.19 W
Summerside	186	46.24 N	63.47 W
Summersville, Mo., U.S.	194	37.10 N	91.39 W
Summersville, W.V., U.S.	188	38.16 N	80.51 W
Summerton	192	33.36 N	80.21 W
Summertown	194	35.26 N	87.18 W
Summerville, On., Can.	275b	43.37 N	79.34 W
Summerville, Ga., U.S.	192	34.28 N	85.20 W
Summerville, Pa., U.S.	214	41.06 N	79.11 W
Summerville, S.C., U.S.	192	33.00 N	80.11 W
Summit, Eng., U.K.	262	53.40 N	2.05 W
Summit, Ak., U.S.	180	63.20 N	149.08 W
Summit, Ca., U.S.	228	34.20 N	117.25 W
Summit, Il., U.S.	216	41.47 N	87.48 W
Summit, Ms., U.S.	194	31.17 N	90.28 W
Summit, N.J., U.S.	210	40.44 N	74.21 W
Summit, N.Y., U.S.	210	42.35 N	74.35 W
Summit, S.D., U.S.	198	45.18 N	97.02 W
Summit, Wa., U.S.	224	47.10 N	122.21 W
Summit □[6]	214	41.05 N	81.31 W
Summit Creek ≃	224	46.00 N	121.10 W
Summit Farms	284b	39.19 N	76.32 W
Summit Hill	210	40.49 N	75.52 W
Summit Lake	182	54.17 N	122.38 W
Summit Lake ⊜	224	47.04 N	123.07 W
Summit Mountain ∧	204	39.23 N	116.28 W
Summit Park	276	41.09 N	74.03 W
Summit Park Mall ◆[9]	284a	43.05 N	78.56 W
Summit Peak ∧	200	37.21 N	106.42 W
Summit Rock ∧	172	45.25 S	170.04 E
Summit Station	208	40.34 N	76.12 W
Summitville, In., U.S.	216	40.20 N	85.38 W
Summitville, N.Y., U.S.	210	41.37 N	74.27 W
Summitville, Oh., U.S.	214	40.41 N	80.53 W
Summt	264a	52.41 N	13.22 E
Summter See ⊜	264a	52.42 N	13.23 E
Šumná	61	48.56 N	15.52 E
Sumnal	120	35.45 N	78.40 E
Sumner, Ia., U.S.	190	42.50 N	92.05 W
Sumner, Ms., U.S.	194	33.58 N	90.22 W
Sumner, Wa., U.S.	224	47.12 N	122.14 W
Sumner, Lake ⊜	172	42.42 S	172.13 E
Sumner, Lake ⊜[1]	196	34.38 N	104.25 W
Sumner Lake State Park ♠	196	34.38 N	104.24 W
Sumner Strait ʊ	180	56.15 N	133.45 W
Sumoto	96	34.21 N	134.54 E
Sumpangbinangae	112	4.24 S	119.36 E
Šumperk	30	49.58 N	16.58 E
Sumpiuh	115a	7.37 S	109.21 E
Sumprabum	110	26.33 N	97.34 E
Sumpter	281	42.10 N	83.29 W
Sumrall	194	31.25 N	89.32 W
Sumsar	85	41.18 N	71.19 E
Š'umsi	80	57.07 N	51.37 E
Šumskij	88	54.48 N	99.09 E
Šumskij Posad	24	64.15 N	35.25 E
Šumskoje	78	50.07 N	26.07 E
Šumšu, ostrov I	74	50.45 N	156.20 E
Sumter	192	33.55 N	80.20 W
Sumter □[6]	220	28.38 N	82.08 W
Sumusṭā al-Waqf	142	28.55 N	30.51 E
Sumy	78	50.55 N	34.45 E
Sumy □[4]	76	52.10 N	33.40 E
Sumzom	102	29.45 N	96.10 E
S'un' ≃, S.S.S.R.	80	55.44 N	54.16 E
Sun ≃, Mt., U.S.	202	47.30 N	111.19 W
Sun ≃, Zhg.	107	29.13 N	106.21 E
Suna, Kenya	154	1.05 S	34.26 E
Suna, S.S.S.R.	80	57.51 N	50.05 E
Suna ≃	24	62.08 N	34.12 E
Sunagawa	92a	43.29 N	141.55 E
Sun al-Heteimi ⍑[4]	132	31.05 N	34.00 E
Sunʻ al-Menīʻi ⍑[4]	132	31.07 N	34.12 E
Sunām	123	30.08 N	75.48 E
Sunāmganj	120	25.04 N	91.24 E
Sunami	94	35.25 N	136.40 E
Sunan	98	39.13 N	125.41 E
Sunapee Lake ⊜	188	43.23 N	72.03 W
Sunart, Loch ⊜	46	56.41 N	5.43 W
Sunashinden	268	35.53 N	139.30 E
Sunaysilah ⊜	128	35.35 N	41.53 E
Sunbāṭ	142	30.48 N	31.12 E
Sunbright	192	36.14 N	84.40 W
Sunburst	202	48.52 N	111.54 W
Sunbury, Austl.	169	37.35 S	144.44 E
Sunbury, Eng., U.K.	260	51.25 N	0.26 W
Sunbury, N.C., U.S.	192	36.26 N	76.36 W
Sunbury, Oh., U.S.	214	40.14 N	82.51 W
Sunbury, Pa., U.S.	210	40.51 N	76.47 W
Sunchales	252	30.56 S	61.34 W
Sunch'ang	98	35.23 N	127.07 E
Sunchild Indian Reserve ◆[4]	182	52.43 N	115.24 W
Sünching	60	48.53 N	12.21 E
Suncho Corral	252	27.56 S	63.27 W
Sunch'ŏn, C.M.I.K.	98	39.26 N	125.54 E
Sunch'ŏn, Taehan	98	34.57 N	127.28 E
Sun City, Az., U.S.	200	33.35 N	112.16 W
Sun City, Ca., U.S.	228	33.42 N	117.11 W
Sun City, Fl., U.S.	220	27.40 N	82.28 W
Sun City Center	220	27.43 N	82.21 W
Suncook	188	43.07 N	71.27 W
Suncook ≃	188	43.08 N	71.28 W
Sunda, Selat (Sunda Strait) ʊ	112	6.00 S	105.45 E
Sundance	198	44.24 N	104.22 W
Sundar	112	4.54 N	115.12 E
Sundar ∧	124	28.26 N	84.20 E
Sundarbans ◆[1]	126	22.00 N	89.00 E
Sundargarh	124	22.07 N	84.02 E
Sundargarh □[5]	124	22.18 N	84.30 E
Sundarnagar	123	31.32 N	76.53 E
Sunda Shelf ✣[4]	14	5.00 N	107.00 E
Sunda Strait → Sunda, Selat ʊ	112	6.00 S	105.45 E
Sunday Creek ≃	169	37.02 S	145.05 E
Sundby, Dan.	41	54.42 N	11.48 E
Sundby, Sve.	40	59.23 N	17.03 E
Sundbyberg	40	59.22 N	17.58 E
Sundbyholm	40	59.27 N	16.37 E
Sundbyholms slott ⊥	40	59.27 N	16.37 E
Sunde	26	59.50 N	5.43 E
Sunderland, On., Can.	212	44.16 N	79.04 W
Sunderland, Eng., U.K.	44	54.55 N	1.23 W
Sunderland, Ma., U.S.	207	42.28 N	72.34 W
Sunderland, Vt., U.S.	210	43.06 N	73.06 W
Sundern	56	51.20 N	8.00 E
Sünderup	41	54.46 N	9.27 E
Sundhausen	54	50.56 N	10.40 E
Sundhouse	58	48.15 N	7.36 E
Sundi-Lutete	152	4.34 S	14.14 E
Sundown, Austl.	162	26.14 S	133.12 E
Sundown, N.Y., U.S.	210	41.53 N	74.28 W
Sundown, Tx., U.S.	196	33.27 N	102.29 W
Sundra	273d	26.11 S	28.33 E
Sundre	182	51.48 N	114.38 W
Sundridge, On., Can.	190	45.46 N	79.24 W
Sundridge, Eng., U.K.	260	51.17 N	0.18 E
Sunds	41	56.12 N	9.01 E
Sundsbruk	26	62.27 N	17.22 E
Sundsvall	26	62.23 N	17.18 E
Sundwig	263	51.23 N	7.47 E
Suneori	268	35.56 N	139.24 E
Sunfield	216	42.45 N	84.59 W
Sunfish Creek ≃	218	39.01 N	83.03 W
Sunflower	194	33.32 N	90.32 W
Sunflower, Mount ∧	198	39.04 N	102.01 W
Sungaianyar	112	2.55 S	116.18 E
Sungaiapit	114	1.09 N	102.10 E
Sungaibamban	114	3.26 N	99.09 E
Sungaibatu	112	0.48 N	110.45 E
Sungai Bayor	114	5.15 N	100.47 E
Sungaibuntu	112	6.03 S	107.24 E
Sungaidareh	112	0.58 S	101.30 E
Sungaigerong	112	2.59 S	104.52 E
Sungaiguntung	112	0.18 N	103.37 E
Sungaikakap	112	0.04 S	109.10 E
Sungai Kolok	114	6.02 N	101.58 E
Sungailangsat	112	0.52 S	101.18 E
Sungai Lembing	114	3.55 N	103.02 E
Sungailiat	112	1.51 S	106.08 E
Sungailimau	112	0.31 S	100.03 E
Sungaimanasip	114	1.49 N	100.54 E
Sungainipah	114	0.57 N	98.57 E
Sungaipakning	114	1.20 N	102.09 E
Sungaipenuh	112	2.05 S	101.23 E
Sungaipenyu	112	0.16 N	109.04 E
Sungai Petani	114	5.39 N	100.30 E
Sungaipinang	112	0.48 S	114.04 E
Sungairampah	114	3.29 N	99.09 E
Sungairotan, Indon.	112	1.39 S	102.51 E
Sungairotan, Indon.	112	3.06 S	104.18 E
Sungaisalak	112	0.27 S	102.59 E
Sungaiselan	112	2.24 S	105.59 E
Sungai Siput	114	4.49 N	101.04 E
Sungaitampang	114	2.20 N	100.07 E
Sungaitiram	112	0.47 S	117.12 E
Šungaj	80	48.32 N	46.46 E
Sungari → Songhua ≃	89	47.44 N	132.32 E
Sungchiang → Songjiang	106	31.01 N	121.14 E
Sungezhuang	105	40.15 N	116.39 E
Sungguminasa	112	5.12 S	119.27 E
Sungi ≃	115b	8.38 S	115.06 E
Sungi Point ›	116	10.55 N	125.50 E
Sungkai	114	4.00 N	101.19 E
Sung Kong I	271d	22.11 N	114.17 E
Sung Noen	110	14.54 N	101.50 E
Sungsang	112	2.22 S	104.56 E
Sungshan Domestic Airport ⊠	269d	25.04 N	121.33 E
Sungurlu	130	40.10 N	34.23 E
Sunhezhen	105	40.03 N	116.31 E
Suni	71	40.17 N	8.33 E
Suning	98	38.25 N	115.50 E
Sunjiabu	106	30.55 N	118.54 E
Sunjiadizi	104	42.09 N	124.09 E
Sunjiagou	104	40.45 N	120.39 E
Sunjiajiang	105	40.10 N	115.32 E
Sunjiakanzi	104	40.42 N	123.02 E
Sunjiawan	104	41.59 N	121.42 E
Sunjiazhai	106	30.55 N	121.52 E
Sunjikāy	140	12.20 N	29.46 E
Sunkar, gora ∧	86	44.15 N	73.50 E
Sunken Meadow State Park ♠	207	40.54 N	73.16 W
Sun Kosi ≃	124	26.55 N	87.09 E
Sunland ◆[8]	280	34.16 N	118.19 W
Sunland Park	200	32.15 N	106.45 W
Sunlight Creek ≃	202	44.47 N	109.23 W
Sunlongwan	104	41.19 N	122.57 E
Sunman	218	39.14 N	85.05 W
Sunnansjö	40	60.13 N	14.57 E
Sunndalsøra	26	62.40 N	8.33 E
Sunne	26	59.50 N	13.09 E
Sunnemo	40	59.53 N	13.43 E
Sunnersta	40	59.48 N	17.39 E
Sunnī, Khawr V	140	7.09 N	28.41 E
Sunningdale	260	51.24 N	0.38 W
Sunninghill	42	51.25 N	0.40 W
Sunnybrae	186	45.24 N	62.30 W
Sunny Corner	170	33.23 S	149.53 E
Sunny Crest	278	41.33 N	87.42 W
Sunnydale	224	47.28 N	122.20 W
Sunnyland	220	27.17 N	82.29 W
Sunnylvsfjorden c[2]	26	62.17 N	7.01 E
Sunnymead	228	33.56 N	117.14 W
Sunnynook	182	51.17 N	111.40 W
Sunnyridge	273d	26.10 S	28.11 E
Sunnyside, Nf., Can.	186	47.51 N	53.55 W
Sunnyside, Ca., U.S.	226	32.40 N	117.01 W
Sunny Side, Tx., U.S.	222	29.54 N	96.04 W
Sunnyside, Ut., U.S.	200	39.33 N	110.23 W
Sunnyside, Wa., U.S.	202	46.19 N	120.00 W
Sunnyside ⊥	276	41.03 N	73.52 W
Sunnyslope, Ab., Can.	182	51.40 N	113.32 W
Sunnyslope, Wa., U.S.	224	47.30 N	122.44 W
Sunnyvale, Ca., U.S.	226	37.22 N	122.02 W
Sunnyvale, Tx., U.S.	222	32.48 N	96.33 W
Sunol	282	37.36 N	121.53 W
Sunol Ridge ∧	282	37.38 N	121.56 W
Sun Prairie	216	43.11 N	89.12 W
Sunray	196	36.01 N	101.49 W
Sunrise, Ky., U.S.	218	38.33 N	84.14 W
Sunrise, Tx., U.S.	222	31.17 N	96.53 W
Sunrise, Wy., U.S.	200	42.19 N	104.42 W
Sunrise Heights	216	42.18 N	85.09 W
Sunrise Mall ◆[9]	276	40.41 N	73.26 W
Sunrise Manor	204	36.08 N	115.04 W
Sunrise Peak ∧	224	46.20 N	121.46 W
Sun River Terrace	216	41.06 N	87.45 W
Sunset, La., U.S.	194	30.24 N	92.04 W
Sunset, Tx., U.S.	196	33.27 N	97.46 W
Sunset ◆[8]	282	37.45 N	122.30 W
Sunset Bay	214	42.11 N	79.24 W
Sunset Beach, Ca., U.S.	280	33.43 N	118.04 W
Sunset Beach, Hi., U.S.	229c	21.40 N	158.02 W
Sunset Country ◆[1]	166	35.00 S	141.30 E
Sunset Crater National Monument ♠	200	35.18 N	111.21 W
Sunset Heights	196	31.53 N	102.22 W
Sunset Hill	276	40.26 N	74.35 W
Sunset Hills	279b	40.35 N	80.15 W
Sunset Peak ∧	280	34.13 N	117.42 W
Sunset Prairie	182	55.50 N	120.48 W
Sunset Trailer Park	278	42.06 N	87.48 W
Sunset Valley	214	40.18 N	79.44 W
Sunshine, Austl.	169	37.47 S	144.50 E
Sunshine, Ak., U.S.	180	62.10 N	150.04 W
Sunshine Island I	271d	22.16 N	114.03 E
Sunshine Point ›	281	42.36 N	82.47 W
Sunshine Skyway Bridge ◆[5]	220	27.37 N	82.39 W
Suntai ≃	146	8.05 N	10.04 E
Suntar	74	62.10 N	117.40 E
Suntar-Chajata, chrebet ⋏	74	62.00 N	143.00 E
Suntaug Lake ⊜	283	42.32 N	71.00 W
Süntel ⋏	52	52.12 N	9.25 E
Sun Temple ♁[1]	273c	29.55 N	31.11 E
Sunter ◆[8]	269e	6.09 S	106.50 E
Sunter, Kali ≍	269e	6.07 S	106.50 E
Sunti ≃	272b	22.37 N	88.34 E
Suntrana	180	63.51 N	148.51 W
Suntsar	128	25.31 N	62.00 E
Suntu	144	8.06 N	36.57 E
Sun Valley, Id., U.S.	202	43.41 N	114.21 W
Sun Valley, Nv., U.S.	226	39.34 N	119.47 W
Sun Valley ◆[8]	280	34.14 N	118.21 W
SunValley Center ◆[9]	282	37.58 N	122.03 W
Sun Village	228	34.35 N	118.03 W
Sunwapta ≃	182	52.32 N	117.41 W
Sunwi-do I	98	37.44 N	125.15 E
Sunwu	89	49.27 N	127.20 E
Sunwui → Jiangmen	100	22.35 N	113.05 E
Sunyani	150	7.20 N	2.20 W
Sunying	98	34.30 N	114.21 E
Sunža ≃	84	43.26 N	46.08 E
Sunženskij chrebet ⋏	84	43.21 N	45.00 E
Sun Zhong Shan Ling (Tomb of Sun Yat Sen) ⊥	106	32.10 N	118.56 E
Suojarvi	24	62.05 N	32.21 E
Suolahti	26	62.34 N	25.52 E
Suomenlahti → Finland, Gulf of c	26	60.00 N	27.00 E
Suomenselkä ∧	26	63.59 N	27.00 E
Suomi → Finland □[1]	24	64.00 N	26.00 E
Suomussalmi	26	64.53 N	29.05 E
Suō-nada ⍑[2]	96	33.50 N	131.30 E
Suonenjoki	26	62.37 N	27.08 E
Suonne ⊜	26	61.40 N	26.30 E
Suordach	74	66.43 N	132.04 E
Suoshu	106	31.57 N	119.00 E
Suoxian	120	31.50 N	93.45 E
Supamo ≃	246	6.48 N	61.50 W
Supaul	124	26.07 N	86.36 E
Supe	144	8.37 N	35.38 E
Superbe ≃	50	48.35 N	3.53 E
Superga, Basilica di ♁[1]	62	45.05 N	7.46 E
Superior, Az., U.S.	200	33.17 N	111.05 W
Superior, Mt., U.S.	202	47.11 N	114.53 W
Superior, Ne., U.S.	198	40.01 N	98.04 W
Superior, Wi., U.S.	190	46.43 N	92.06 W
Superior, Laguna c	234	16.20 N	94.55 W
Superior, Lake ⊜	190	48.00 N	88.00 W
Superior Lake ⊜	228	35.15 N	117.02 W
Superior Valley V	228	35.16 N	117.00 W
Supersano	68	40.01 N	18.14 E
Supetar	36	43.23 N	16.33 E
Suphan Buri	110	14.28 N	100.07 E
Suphan Buri ≃	110	13.29 N	100.17 E
Süphan Dağı ∧	84	38.54 N	42.48 E
Supino	66	41.37 N	13.14 E
Sūpkhār	124	22.12 N	80.56 E
Supoj ≃	78	49.38 N	31.48 E
Suponevo	76	53.12 N	34.18 E
Supoqiao	107	30.40 N	103.59 E
Süpplingen	54	52.14 N	10.54 E
Supraśl	30	53.13 N	23.20 E
Supraśl ≃	30	53.04 N	22.56 E
Sup'ung	98	40.27 N	124.57 E
Sup'ung-chŏsuji ⊜[1]	98	40.30 N	125.05 E
Supur	126	23.01 N	86.52 E
Suputinskij zapovednik ♠	89	43.40 N	132.20 E
Sūq-ʻAbs	144	15.59 N	43.04 E
Sūq ash-Shuyūkh	128	30.53 N	46.28 E
Suqʻat al-Jamal	140	12.48 N	27.42 E
Suqian	100	33.59 N	118.18 E
Suqiao, Zhg.	100	34.08 N	113.47 E
Suqiao, Zhg.	105	39.03 N	116.29 E
Sūq Suwayq	128	24.23 N	38.27 E
Suquamish	224	47.43 N	122.33 W
Suquṭrā (Socotra) I	118	12.30 N	54.00 E
Ṣūr (Tyre), Lubnān	132	33.16 N	35.11 E
Ṣūr, ʻUmān	118	22.35 N	59.31 E
Sur, Cabo ›	174z	27.12 S	109.26 W
Sur, Point ›	226	36.18 N	121.54 W
Sur, Punta ›	252	36.52 S	56.40 W
Sura	80	53.53 N	45.45 E
Sura ◆[8]	272b	22.33 N	88.25 E
Sura ≃	80	56.06 N	46.00 E
Sura, Cape ›	144	11.10 N	47.30 E
Ṣūrāb, Pāk.	120	28.29 N	66.16 E
Šurab, S.S.S.R.	85	40.03 N	70.33 E
Surabaya	115a	7.15 S	112.45 E
S'urachi, Nuraghe ⊥	71	40.01 N	8.33 E
Ṣurad	142	30.59 N	30.54 E
Surag-san ∧	271b	37.42 N	127.04 E
Surahammar	40	59.43 N	16.13 E
Sūrak	128	25.43 N	58.48 E
Surakarta	115a	7.35 S	110.50 E
Suramana	112	0.50 S	119.33 E
Surami	84	42.01 N	43.34 E
Ṣūrān, Īrān	128	27.18 N	62.04 E
Šuran, S.S.S.R.	80	55.22 N	49.50 E
Ṣūrān, Sūrīy.	130	36.34 N	37.13 E
Ṣūrān, Sūrīy.	130	35.17 N	36.45 E
Suran ≃	58	46.02 N	5.19 E
Šurany	30	48.06 N	18.14 E
Surar	144	7.27 N	40.57 E
Surat, Austl.	166	27.09 S	149.04 E
Surat, India	120	21.10 N	72.50 E
Sūratgarh	123	29.19 N	73.54 E
Surat Thani (Ban Don)	110	9.08 N	99.19 E
Surava	80	52.57 N	41.18 E
Suraż, Pol.	30	52.58 N	22.58 E
Suraž, S.S.S.R.	76	53.01 N	32.24 E
Suraž, S.S.S.R.	76	55.25 N	30.44 E
Surbiton ◆[8]	260	51.24 N	0.18 W
Surbo	68	40.24 N	18.08 E
Surbourg	56	48.55 N	7.51 E
Surchan	80	46.39 N	49.38 E
Surchandarja ≃	85	37.58 N	67.50 E
Surchandarjinskaja Oblast' □[4]	85	38.00 N	67.30 E
Surchdara	85	38.37 N	69.55 E
Surchob ≃	85	38.53 N	70.03 E
Šurči	85	37.59 N	67.47 E
Surco	286d	12.09 S	77.01 W
Surco ≃	286d	12.13 S	77.03 W
Surdulica	38	42.41 N	22.10 E
Sûre (Sauer) ≃	56	49.44 N	6.31 E
Šureksor, ozero ⊜	86	52.16 N	75.50 E
Surendorf	41	54.28 N	10.04 E
Surendranagar	120	22.42 N	71.41 E
Suresnes	261	48.52 N	2.14 E
Suretka	236	9.34 N	82.56 W
Surf City	208	39.39 N	74.09 W
Surfers Paradise	171a	28.00 S	153.26 E
Surfside, Fl., U.S.	220	25.52 N	80.07 W
Surfside, Tx., U.S.	222	28.57 N	95.17 W
Surgères	32	46.07 N	0.45 W
Surgidero	240p	22.41 N	82.18 W
Surgijn ≃	88	47.20 N	95.50 E
Surgoinsville	192	36.28 N	82.51 W
Sürgü	130	38.01 N	37.59 E
Sürgücü	130	37.35 N	40.44 E
Surguja □[5]	124	23.15 N	83.00 E
Surgut	74	61.14 N	73.20 E
Surhuisterveen	52	53.10 N	6.10 E
Sūri (Bīrbhūm), India	126	23.55 N	87.32 E
Suri, Pap. N. Gui.	164	7.10 S	143.55 E
Suria	272b	22.51 N	88.33 E
Suriāpet	122	17.09 N	79.37 E
Suribachi-yama ∧[2]	174f	24.45 N	141.17 E
Suribao ≃	116	11.33 N	125.28 E
Surigao	116	9.45 N	125.30 E
Surigao del Norte □[4]	116	9.35 N	125.36 E
Surigao del Sur □[4]	116	9.00 N	126.00 E
Surigao Strait ʊ	116	10.15 N	125.23 E
Surikova	86	56.59 N	91.31 E
Surin	110	14.53 N	103.29 E
Surinam → Suriname □[1]	250	4.00 N	56.00 W
Suriname □[5]	250	5.30 N	55.00 W
Suriname □[1], S.A.	242	4.00 N	56.00 W
Suriname □[1], S.A.	250	4.00 N	56.00 W
Šurinda	88	55.13 N	113.23 E
Suring	190	44.59 N	88.22 W
Surkh Hisār	267d	35.43 N	51.33 E
S'urkum	89	50.08 N	140.31 E
S'urkum, mys ›	89	50.05 N	140.41 E
Šurma	80	56.58 N	50.21 E
Sūrmaq	128	31.03 N	52.48 E
Surmelin ≃	50	49.04 N	3.13 E
Surnadalsøra	26	62.59 N	8.39 E
Surodadi	115a	6.53 S	109.15 E
Surovaticha	80	55.45 N	43.56 E
Surovikino	80	48.36 N	42.51 E
Surovo	88	55.37 N	105.36 E

Symbol	English	Deutsch	Español	Français	Português
≃	River	Fluss	Río	Rivière	Rio
≍	Canal	Kanal	Canal	Canal	Canal
⌞	Waterfall, Rapids	Wasserfall, Stromschnellen	Cascada, Rápidos	Chute d'eau, Rapides	Cascata, Rápidos
ʊ	Strait	Meeresstrasse	Estrecho	Détroit	Estreito
c	Bay, Gulf	Bucht, Golf	Bahía, Golfo	Baie, Golfe	Baía, Golfo
⊜	Lake, Lakes	See, Seen	Lago, Lagos	Lac, Lacs	Lago, Lagos
⊞	Swamp	Sumpf	Pantano	Marais	Pântano
❄	Ice Features, Glacier	Eis- und Gletscherformen	Accidentes Glaciales	Formes glaciaires	Acidentes glaciares
⍑	Other Hydrographic Features	Andere Hydrographische Objekte	Otros Elementos Hidrográficos	Autres données hydrographiques	Outros acidentes hidrográficos

Symbol	English	Deutsch	Español	Français	Português
✣	Submarine Features	Untermeerische Objekte	Accidentes Submarinos	Formes de relief sous-marin	Acidentes submarinos
□	Political Unit	Politische Einheit	Unidad Politica	Entité politique	Unidade política
♁	Cultural Institution	Kulturelle Institution	Institución Cultural	Institution culturelle	Instituição cultural
⊥	Historical Site	Historische Stätte	Sitio Histórico	Site historique	Sitio histórico
♠	Recreational Site	Erholungs- und Ferienort	Sitio de Recreo	Centre de loisirs	Area de Lazer
⊠	Airport	Flughafen	Aeropuerto	Aéroport	Aeroporto
■	Military Installation	Militäranlage	Instalación Militar	Installation militaire	Instalação militar
◆	Miscellaneous	Verschiedenes	Misceláneo	Divers	Diversos

ENGLISH: Name · Page · Lat.°′ · Long.°′ — DEUTSCH: Name · Seite · Breite°′ · Länge°′ E = Ost

Surprise 200 33.37 N 112.19 W
Surprise, Lake ⊜ 222 29.33 N 94.41 W
Surprise Valley V 204 41.35 N 120.05 W
Surquillo 286d 12.07 S 77.02 W
Surrency 192 31.43 N 82.11 W
Surrey 198 48.14 N 101.07 W
Surrey □6 42 51.10 N 0.20 W
Surrey, University of ♦2 260 51.14 N 0.36 W
Surrey Heath □8 260 51.23 N 0.35 W
Surry 208 37.08 N 76.50 W
Surry □6 208 37.10 N 76.50 W
Sursee 58 47.10 N 8.06 E
Sursés V 58 46.34 N 9.38 E
Sursk 80 53.04 N 45.42 E
Surskij Majdan 80 55.01 N 46.32 E
Surskoje 80 54.30 N 46.44 E
Surt 146 31.12 N 16.35 E
Surt, Khalīj (Gulf of Sidra) c 146 31.30 N 18.00 E
Surtainville 28 49.25 N 1.50 W
Surtanāhu 120 26.22 N 70.00 E
Surte 26 57.49 N 12.01 E
Surtsey I 24a 63.16 N 20.32 W
Suru 164 6.50 S 144.45 E
Surubim ≐ 250 11.15 S 48.27 W
Surubiú ≐ 250 3.58 S 48.52 W
Sürüç 130 36.58 N 38.24 E
Suruga-wan c 94 34.51 N 138.33 E
Surui 256 22.40 S 43.07 W
Surui ≐ 287a 22.42 S 43.07 W
Surulangun 112 2.37 S 102.45 E
Suru-Lere ◆8 273a 6.31 N 3.22 E
Surumu ≐ 246 3.22 N 60.19 W
Surveyor Creek ≐ 198 40.20 N 102.38 W
Surveyor Point › 168b 34.47 S 137.51 E
Survilliers 261 49.06 N 2.33 E
Surwold 52 53.00 N 7.30 E
Sury-le-Comtal 62 45.32 N 4.10 E
Šuryškary 74 65.54 N 65.22 E
Susa, It. 62 45.08 N 7.03 E
Susa, Nihon 96 34.37 N 131.36 E
Susā ≐ 41 55.11 N 11.46 E
Susa, Valle di V 62 45.09 N 7.10 E
Sūsah 146 32.54 N 21.58 E
Susak, Otok I 36 44.31 N 14.18 E
Susaki 96 33.22 N 133.17 E
Susami 96 33.33 N 135.30 E
Susamyr 85 42.09 N 73.58 E
Susamyr ≐ 85 42.08 N 74.03 E
Susamyrtau, chrebet ⋏ 85 42.08 N 73.15 E
Susan 208 37.25 N 76.19 W
Susan ≐ 204 40.19 N 120.17 W
Susan, Port c 224 48.10 N 122.25 W
Susana Knolls 228 34.16 N 118.41 W
Susanino, S.S.S.R. 76 59.30 N 30.22 E
Susanino, S.S.S.R. 80 58.09 N 41.36 E
Susanino, S.S.S.R. 89 52.47 N 140.06 E
Susanville 204 40.24 N 120.39 W
Šušary, S.S.S.R. 265a 59.46 N 30.21 E
Šušary, S.S.S.R. 265a 59.48 N 30.23 E
Susch 58 46.46 N 10.04 E
Susegana 64 45.51 N 12.15 E
Suşehri 130 40.11 N 38.06 E
Süsel 54 54.04 N 10.43 E
Šušenskoje 86 53.19 N 91.58 E
Sušice 60 49.14 N 13.32 E
Susitna 180 61.33 N 150.31 W
Susitna ≐ 180 61.16 N 150.30 W
Susleny 78 47.25 N 28.59 E
Suslonger 80 56.18 N 48.13 E
Susn'aki Pervoje 86 57.53 N 88.47 E
Susobana ≐ 94 36.37 N 138.11 E
Susoh 114 3.43 N 96.50 E
Susong 100 30.09 N 116.06 E
Susono 94 35.09 N 138.54 E
Suspiro del Moro, Puerto x 34 37.04 N 3.39 W
Susquehanna 210 41.56 N 75.36 W
Susquehanna □6 210 41.50 N 75.50 W
Susquehanna ≐ 188 39.33 N 76.05 W
Susquehanna, West Branch ≐ 210 40.53 N 76.47 W
Susquehanna State Park ♦ 208 39.36 N 76.09 W
Susques 252 23.25 S 66.29 W
Sussa ≐ 152 7.22 S 17.05 E
Süssen 56 48.41 N 9.45 E
Süssenbrunn ◆8 264b 48.17 N 16.30 E
Süsser See ⊜ 54 51.30 N 11.40 E
Sussex, N.B., Can. 186 45.43 N 65.31 W
Sussex, N.J., U.S. 210 41.12 N 74.36 W
Sussex, Va., U.S. 208 36.54 N 77.16 W
Sussex, Wi., U.S. 216 43.08 N 88.13 W
Sussex □6, De., U.S. 208 38.42 N 75.23 W
Sussex □6, N.J., U.S. 210 41.08 N 74.41 W
Sussex □6, Va., U.S. 208 36.50 N 77.15 W
Sussex, East □6 42 50.55 N 0.15 E
Sussex, Vale of V 42 50.57 N 0.17 W
Sussex Inlet 170 35.11 S 150.36 E
Sussey 50 47.13 N 4.22 E
Sustenhorn ∧ 58 46.42 N 8.28 E
Susten Pass x 58 46.44 N 8.27 E
Susteren 52 51.04 N 5.51 E
Šustikovo 82 55.17 N 35.59 E
Susu 174m 26.47 N 128.19 E
Susubona 175e 8.18 S 159.27 E
Susui 112 4.56 N 116.41 E
Susuman 74 62.47 N 148.10 E
Susurluk 130 39.54 N 28.10 E
Susuzmüsellim 130 41.06 N 27.03 E
Sušvė ≐ 76 55.10 N 23.49 E
Susz 30 53.44 N 19.20 E
Sutāhāta 126 22.08 N 88.07 E
Sutak 123 33.12 N 77.28 E
Sutama 94 35.47 N 138.25 E
Sut-Chol' 86 51.24 N 91.17 E
Sütçüler 130 37.30 N 30.59 E
Sutera 70 37.31 N 13.44 E
Sutersville 214 40.14 N 79.48 W
Suthat, Wat ♦1 269a 13.45 N 100.30 E
Sutherland, Austl. 170 34.02 S 151.04 E
Sutherland, S. Afr. 158 32.24 S 20.40 E
Sutherland, Ia., U.S. 198 42.58 N 95.29 W
Sutherland, Ne., U.S. 198 41.09 N 101.07 W
Sutherland ≐ 182 54.29 N 125.05 W
Sutherland, Lake ⊜ 224 48.05 N 123.42 W
Sutherlands 168b 34.10 S 139.13 E
Sutherlin 202 43.23 N 123.18 W
Sutihāna 272a 28.31 N 77.26 E
Sutlej (Satluj) (Langchuhe) ≐ 120 29.23 N 71.02 E
Sutri 66 42.14 N 12.13 E
Sutrio 64 46.31 N 12.59 E
Sutschou → Xuzhou, Zhg. 98 34.16 N 117.11 E
Sutschou → Suzhou, Zhg. 106 31.18 N 120.37 E
Sutter 226 39.10 N 121.45 W
Sutter □6 226 39.08 N 121.37 W
Sutter Buttes ∧ 226 39.12 N 121.50 W
Sutter Bypass ≐ 226 38.47 N 121.38 W
Sutter Creek 226 38.23 N 120.48 W
Sutter Creek ≐ 226 38.22 N 120.59 W
Sutton, Austl. 171b 35.10 S 149.15 E
Sutton, P.Q., Can. 206 45.06 N 72.37 W
Sutton, Eng., U.K. 42 52.23 N 0.07 E
Sutton, Eng., U.K. 260 51.12 N 0.26 W
Sutton, Ak., U.S. 180 61.43 N 148.53 W
Sutton, Ma., U.S. 207 42.09 N 71.45 W
Sutton, Ne., U.S. 198 40.36 N 97.51 W
Sutton, W.V., U.S. 188 38.39 N 80.42 W
Sutton ◆8 42 51.22 N 0.12 W
Sutton, Monts ⋏ 206 45.05 N 72.30 W
Sutton-at-Hone 260 51.25 N 0.14 E
Sutton Bridge 42 52.46 N 0.12 E
Sutton Coldfield 42 52.34 N 1.48 W
Sutton Courtenay 42 51.39 N 1.17 W
Sutton Forest 170 34.35 S 150.19 E
Sutton in Ashfield 44 53.08 N 1.15 W
Sutton Lake ⊜1 188 38.40 N 80.40 W
Sutton Lane Ends 262 53.14 N 2.06 W
Sutton Leach 262 53.26 N 2.42 W
Sutton on Sea 44 53.19 N 0.17 E
Sutton on Trent 44 53.10 N 0.49 W
Sutton Park 276 40.49 N 74.42 W
Sutton Place ⊥ 260 51.16 N 0.33 W
Suttons Bay 190 44.58 N 85.39 W
Sutton Scotney 42 51.10 N 1.21 W
Sutton Valence 42 51.12 N 0.36 E
Sutton Veny 42 51.11 N 2.08 W
Sutton Weaver 262 53.18 N 2.41 W
Sutton West 212 44.18 N 79.22 W
Suttor ≐ 166 21.25 S 147.45 E
Suttrop 56 51.27 N 8.22 E
Suttsu 92a 42.48 N 140.14 E
Sutwik Island I 180 56.34 N 157.05 W
Suunduk ≐ 86 51.46 N 58.46 E
Suurberge ⋏ 158 33.18 S 25.32 E
Suurbraak 158 34.00 S 20.39 E
Suure-Jaani 76 58.33 N 25.28 E
Suur Pakri I 76 59.20 N 23.55 E
Suva 175g 18.08 S 178.25 E
Suvainiškis 76 56.10 N 25.17 E
Suvalovo Oz'orki ◆8 265a 60.02 N 30.18 E
Suva Planina ⋏ 38 43.10 N 22.10 E
Suvari 130 37.32 N 37.18 E
Suvasvesi ⊜ 26 62.39 N 28.12 E
Suvel'an 84 40.30 N 50.09 E
Suvereto 66 43.05 N 10.40 E
Suvo 88 53.39 N 110.00 E
Suvorka 88 56.33 N 103.24 E
Suvorov 82 54.07 N 36.30 E
Suvorovo, S.S.S.R. 78 45.34 N 28.59 E
Suvorovo, S.S.S.R. 82 56.07 N 35.54 E
Suwa, Ityo. 144 14.17 N 41.06 E
Suwa, Nihon 94 36.02 N 138.08 E
Suwa-ko ⊜ 94 36.05 N 138.05 E
Suwałki 30 54.07 N 22.56 E
Suwałki □4 30 54.10 N 22.15 E
Suwannaphum 110 15.33 N 103.47 E
Suwannee ≐ 192 29.18 N 83.09 W
Suwannee Lake ⊜ 184 56.08 N 100.10 W
Suwanose-jima I 93b 29.38 N 129.43 E
Suwanose-suidō ⊔ 93b 29.32 N 129.40 E
Suwarrow I1 14 13.15 S 163.05 W
Suwaydah 130 35.46 N 39.38 E
Suwayliḥ 132 32.02 N 35.50 E
Suways, Khalīj as- (Gulf of Suez) c 140 29.00 N 32.50 E
Suways, Qanāt as- (Suez Canal) ≅ 142 29.55 N 32.33 E
Suwŏn 98 37.17 N 127.01 E
Suwon-dong 98 41.54 N 129.43 E
Suxi 100 29.25 N 120.07 E
Suxian 100 33.38 N 116.58 E
Suya 150 9.28 N 3.11 E
Suykbulak 86 49.48 N 80.50 E
Suyo 246 4.30 S 80.00 W
Suzak 85 44.07 N 68.28 E
Suzaka 94 36.39 N 138.19 E
Suzano 256 23.32 S 46.20 W
Suzano □7 287b 23.35 S 46.18 W
Suzdal' 80 56.25 N 40.26 E
Suze ≐ 58 47.08 N 7.14 E
Suze-la-Rousse 62 44.17 N 4.51 E
Suzhi 98 42.11 N 113.42 E
Suzhou (Soochow) 106 31.18 N 120.37 E
Suzhuang 105 40.04 N 116.44 E
Suzi ≐ 98 41.55 N 124.17 E
Suzigou 98 40.25 N 123.25 E
S'uzikozero 24 61.48 N 37.20 E
Suz'omka 76 52.19 N 34.05 E
Suzu 92 37.25 N 137.17 E
Suzuka 94 34.51 N 136.35 E
Suzuka ≐ 94 34.54 N 136.39 E
Suzuka-kokutei-kōen ♦ 94 35.00 N 136.25 E
Suzuka-sammyaku ⋏ 94 35.00 N 136.25 E
Suzuki 268 35.43 N 139.31 E
S'uz'um 80 58.02 N 47.32 E
Suzu-misaki › 92 37.31 N 137.21 E
Suzun 86 53.47 N 82.19 E
Suzzara 64 45.00 N 10.45 E
Sværdborg 41 55.05 N 11.54 E
Sval'ava 78 48.33 N 22.59 E
Svalbard □2 12 78.00 N 20.00 E
Svalöv 41 55.55 N 13.06 E
Svaneholm 41 55.30 N 13.28 E
Svaneke 26 55.08 N 15.09 E
Svanetskij chrebet ⋏ 84 42.55 N 42.42 E
Svängsta 26 56.16 N 14.46 E
Svanninge 41 55.07 N 10.15 E
Svanskog 26 59.11 N 12.33 E
Svapa ≐ 76 51.44 N 34.56 E
Svappavaara 24 67.39 N 21.04 E
Švarcevskij 82 54.06 N 37.59 E
Svärdsjö 26 60.45 N 15.55 E
Švaricha 80 57.33 N 49.37 E
Svartå 40 59.18 N 14.31 E
Svartälven ≐ 40 59.19 N 14.35 E
Svartån ≐ 40 59.37 N 16.33 E
Svarte 41 55.25 N 13.43 E
Svartenhuk ›1 176 71.55 N 55.00 W
Svärtinge 40 58.39 N 16.00 E
Svartisen ⊓ 24 66.38 N 14.00 E
Svartlöga I 40 59.34 N 19.03 E
Svartsjölandet I 40 59.22 N 17.41 E
Svataj 74 67.57 N 151.54 E
Svatava 54 50.11 N 12.35 E
Svatava ≐ 54 50.32 N 12.07 E
Sv'atica ≐ 80 58.22 N 51.43 E
Sv'atogorskaja 83 49.04 N 37.32 E
Sv'atoj Nos, mys ›, S.S.S.R. 24 68.10 N 39.45 E
Sv'atoj Nos, mys ›, S.S.S.R. 74 72.52 N 140.42 E
Sv'atoj Nos, poluostrov ›1 88 53.40 N 108.50 E
Sv'atoslavka 80 51.20 N 43.26 E
Svatovo 83 49.23 N 38.13 E
Svay Chék 110 13.48 N 102.58 E
Svay Riěng 110 11.05 N 105.48 E
Sveafallen ⊾ 40 59.10 N 14.22 E
Svebølle 41 55.38 N 11.20 E
Sveča 80 58.16 N 47.32 E
Svedala 41 55.30 N 13.14 E
Svėdasai 76 55.41 N 25.22 E
Sveg 26 62.02 N 14.21 E
Švėkšna 76 55.31 N 21.37 E
Svelgen 26 61.47 N 5.15 E
Svelvik 26 59.37 N 10.24 E
Švenčionėliai 76 55.10 N 26.00 E
Švenčionys 76 55.07 N 26.10 E
Svendborg 41 55.03 N 10.37 E
Svenljunga 26 57.30 N 13.07 E
Svennevad 40 59.01 N 15.22 E
Svensen 224 46.10 N 123.39 W
Svenstorp 41 55.46 N 13.15 E
Svenstrup 26 56.59 N 9.52 E
Šventoji 76 56.02 N 21.05 E
Šventoji ≐ 76 55.06 N 24.22 E
Sverbejevo 89 53.36 N 123.15 E
Sverdlovo, S.S.S.R. 76 55.36 N 28.35 E
Sverdlovo, S.S.S.R. 82 56.38 N 36.37 E
Sverdlovsk, S.S.S.R. 83 48.05 N 39.40 E
Sverdlovsk, S.S.S.R. 86 56.51 N 60.36 E
Sverdrup, ostrov I 74 74.35 N 79.30 E
Sverige → Sweden □1 24 62.00 N 15.00 E
Sverkestaån ≐ 40 59.28 N 15.28 E
Svermov 54 50.09 N 14.05 E
Svessa 78 51.57 N 33.54 E
Sveti Arhandjel Mihajlo ♦1 38 42.07 N 21.28 E
Sveti Jovan Bigorski ♦1 38 41.38 N 20.37 E
Svetilovići 76 52.48 N 31.19 E
Sveti Nikole 38 41.52 N 21.58 E
Sveti Petar u Šumi 64 45.11 N 13.52 E
Svetlaja 89 46.33 N 138.18 E
Světlá nad Sázavou 30 49.40 N 15.25 E
Svetlanovo 83 48.42 N 38.28 E
Svetlogorsk, S.S.S.R. 76 54.57 N 20.10 E
Svetlogorsk, S.S.S.R. 76 52.38 N 29.42 E
Svetlograd 72 45.20 N 42.40 E
Svetloje 80 57.03 N 53.38 E
Svetlovodsk 78 49.04 N 33.15 E
Svetlyj, S.S.S.R. 76 54.41 N 20.08 E
Svetlyj, S.S.S.R. 86 50.47 N 60.53 E
Svetlyj, S.S.S.R. 88 58.26 N 115.55 E
Svetlyj Jar 80 48.29 N 44.46 E
Svetogorsk 24 61.07 N 28.51 E
Svetozarevo 38 43.58 N 21.16 E
Svežen'kaja 80 54.01 N 42.26 E
Svidník 30 49.18 N 21.35 E
Švihov 60 49.29 N 13.17 E
Svijaga ≐ 80 55.47 N 48.40 E
Svilajnac 38 44.14 N 21.13 E
Svilengrad 38 41.46 N 26.12 E
Svindal 26 58.30 N 7.28 E
Svinecea ∧ 38 44.48 N 22.09 E
Svinesund 26 59.06 N 11.16 E
Svinninge 41 55.43 N 11.28 E
Svir' 76 54.51 N 26.24 E
Svir' ≐ 76 60.30 N 32.48 E
Svirica 76 60.29 N 32.51 E
Svirsk 88 53.04 N 103.21 E
Svir'stroj 76 60.48 N 33.43 E
Sviščovka 80 52.51 N 43.44 E
Svisloč', S.S.S.R. 76 53.02 N 24.06 E
Svisloč', S.S.S.R. 76 53.26 N 28.59 E
Svisloč' ≐ 76 53.26 N 28.59 E
Svištov 38 43.37 N 25.20 E
Svit 30 49.03 N 20.12 E
Svitávka 30 49.30 N 16.37 E
Svitavy 30 49.45 N 16.27 E
Svitino 82 54.54 N 35.49 E
Svoboda, S.S.S.R. 78 51.58 N 36.17 E
Svoboda, S.S.S.R. 78 47.12 N 40.39 E
Svobodnaja 89 46.48 N 143.23 E
Svobodnoje 83 47.32 N 37.34 E
Svobodnyj, S.S.S.R. 80 52.20 N 46.22 E
Svobodnyj, S.S.S.R. 89 51.24 N 128.08 E
Svobodnyj Port 78 46.20 N 31.51 E
Svoge 38 42.58 N 23.21 E
Svojna 82 54.09 N 36.39 E
Svol'na ≐ 76 55.43 N 28.02 E
Svolvær 24 68.14 N 14.34 E
Svor 54 50.47 N 14.36 E
Svorkmo 26 63.10 N 9.45 E
Svratka ≐ 61 49.11 N 16.38 E
Svržno 60 49.35 N 12.46 E
Svullrya 26 60.25 N 12.24 E
Swābi 123 34.07 N 72.28 E
Swadlincote 42 52.47 N 1.33 W
Swaffham 42 52.39 N 0.41 E
Swain 210 42.29 N 77.51 W
Swain Reefs ✦2 166 21.40 S 152.15 E
Swainsboro 192 32.35 N 82.20 W
Swains Island I1 14 11.03 S 171.05 W
Swakop ≐ 156 22.38 S 14.36 E
Swakopmund 156 22.41 S 14.34 E
Swakopmund □5 156 23.00 S 15.00 E
Swale □8 260 51.21 N 0.41 E
Swale ≐ 44 54.06 N 1.20 W
Swale Canyon V 224 45.49 N 121.05 W
Swale Creek ≐ 224 45.49 N 121.05 W
Swaledale V 44 54.25 N 1.47 W
Swallowfield 218 38.21 N 84.51 W
Swalmen 52 51.15 N 6.02 E
Swamp City 222 32.29 N 94.56 W
Swampscott 207 42.28 N 70.55 W
Swan 222 32.26 N 95.22 W
Swan ≐, Austl. 168a 32.03 S 115.45 E
Swan ≐, Can. 184 52.30 N 100.47 W
Swan ≐, Ab., Can. 182 55.31 N 115.17 W
Swan ≐, Mn., U.S. 190 47.01 N 93.16 W
Swan ≐, Mt., U.S. 202 48.04 N 114.05 W
Swan Acres 279b 40.33 N 80.02 W
Swanage 42 50.37 N 1.58 W
Swan Bay c 169 38.14 S 144.40 E
Swan Creek ≐, Austl. 171a 28.08 S 152.13 E
Swan Creek ≐, Mi., U.S. 216 41.58 N 85.19 W
Swan Creek ≐, Mi., U.S. 216 41.58 N 83.17 W
Swan Creek ≐, Oh., U.S. 216 41.39 N 83.32 W
Swan Creek ≐, S.D., U.S. 198 45.19 N 100.15 W
Swan Creek, North Branch ≐ 281 42.06 N 83.23 W
Swan Creek Point › 281 42.40 N 82.39 W
Swanee → Suwannee ≐ 192 29.18 N 83.09 W
Swan Hill 166 35.21 S 143.34 E
Swan Hills 182 54.43 N 115.24 W
Swan Hills ⋏2 182 54.48 N 115.52 W
Swanington 216 40.35 N 87.17 W
Swan Island I 169 38.15 S 144.41 E
Swan Islands → Santanilla, Islas II 238 17.25 N 83.55 W
Swank Creek ≐ 224 47.07 N 120.45 W
Swan Lake, Mb., Can. 184 49.24 N 98.46 W
Swan Lake, Mt., U.S. 202 47.55 N 113.50 W
Swan Lake, N.Y., U.S. 210 41.45 N 74.48 W
Swan Lake ⊜, Mb., Can. 184 52.30 N 100.45 W
Swan Lake ⊜, On., Can. 184 54.17 N 91.12 W
Swan Lake ⊜, Il., U.S. 219 38.57 N 90.33 W
Swan Lake ⊜, Mn., U.S. 190 44.19 N 94.15 W
Swanland 44 53.44 N 0.29 W
Swanley 42 51.24 N 0.12 E
Swanlinbar 48 54.10 N 7.42 W
Swannanoa 192 35.36 N 82.23 W
Swannanoa, Lake ⊜ 276 41.01 N 74.31 W
Swan Peak ∧ 202 47.43 N 113.38 W
Swanquarter 192 35.24 N 76.20 W
Swan Range ⋏ 202 47.50 N 113.40 W
Swan River 184 52.06 N 101.16 W
Swansboro 192 34.41 N 77.07 W
Swanscombe 260 51.27 N 0.19 E
Swansea, Austl. 166 42.08 S 148.04 E
Swansea, Austl. 170 33.05 S 151.38 E
Swansea, Wales, U.K. 42 51.38 N 3.57 W
Swansea, Il., U.S. 219 38.32 N 89.59 W
Swansea, Ma., U.S. 207 41.44 N 71.11 W
Swansea, S.C., U.S. 192 33.44 N 81.05 W
Swansea ◆8 275b 43.38 N 79.28 W
Swansea Bay c 42 51.35 N 3.52 W
Swans Island I 188 44.10 N 68.25 W
Swanson Lake ⊜1 198 40.09 N 101.06 W
Swanton, Oh., U.S. 216 41.35 N 83.53 W
Swanton, Vt., U.S. 206 44.55 N 73.07 W
Swanville 190 45.54 N 94.38 W
Swanzey Center 207 42.49 N 72.10 W
Swartberg 158 30.15 S 29.23 E
Swarthmore 208 39.54 N 75.21 W
Swarthmore College ♦2 285 39.54 N 75.21 W
Swart-Kei ≐ 158 32.09 S 27.24 E
Swart-Mfolozi ≐ 158 28.22 S 31.58 E
Swartplaas 158 26.08 S 26.57 E
Swartruggens 156 25.40 S 26.42 E
Swartruggens ⋏ 158 33.02 S 19.35 E
Swartswood Lake 210 41.04 N 74.51 W
Swartswood State Park ♦ 210 41.05 N 74.50 W
Swartz Creek 216 42.57 N 83.49 W
Swarupkāti 126 22.45 N 90.06 E
Swarupnagar 126 22.49 N 88.52 E
Swarzędz 30 52.26 N 17.05 E
Swasey Peak ∧ 200 39.23 N 113.19 W
Swasey Wash V 200 39.15 N 112.53 W
Swasiland → Swaziland □1 158 26.30 S 31.30 E
Swāt ≐ 123 34.20 N 71.34 E
Swatara Creek ≐ 208 40.11 N 76.44 W
Swa-Tenda 152 7.09 S 17.07 E
Swatow → Shantou 100 23.23 N 116.41 E
Swauger Creek ≐ 226 38.16 N 119.16 W
Swauk Pass x 224 47.21 N 120.40 W
Sway 42 50.47 N 1.37 W
Swayzee 216 40.30 N 85.49 W
Swaziland □1, Afr. 138 26.30 S 31.30 E
Swaziland □1, Afr. 158 26.30 S 31.30 E
Swea City 190 43.23 N 94.19 W
Swede Hill 279b 40.17 N 79.34 W
Swedeland 285 40.05 N 75.20 W
Sweden (Sverige) □1, Europe 22 62.00 N 15.00 E
Sweden (Sverige) □1, Europe 24 62.00 N 15.00 E
Sweden Valley 214 41.45 N 77.56 W
Swede Run ≐ 285 40.02 N 74.58 W
Swedesboro 208 39.44 N 75.18 W
Swedesburg 285 40.06 N 75.20 W
Swedish Knoll ∧ 200 39.16 N 111.26 W
Swedru 150 5.32 N 0.43 W
Sween, Loch c 46 55.59 N 5.39 W
Sweeney Plan 279b 40.11 N 79.48 W
Sweeny 222 29.02 N 95.41 W
Sweeny Park ♦ 284a 43.02 N 78.52 W
Sweet Briar 192 37.33 N 79.04 W
Sweetgrass 182 49.00 N 111.57 W
Sweet Grass Creek ≐ 202 45.47 N 109.47 W
Sweetgrass Hills ⋏2 202 48.55 N 111.30 W
Sweet Grass Indian Reserve ◆4 184 52.44 N 108.45 W
Sweetheart Abbey ♦1 44 54.59 N 3.38 W
Sweet Home, Or., U.S. 202 44.23 N 122.44 W
Sweet Home, Tx., U.S. 222 29.21 N 97.04 W
Sweetsers 216 40.34 N 85.46 W
Sweet Springs 194 38.57 N 93.24 W
Sweet Valley 210 41.17 N 76.09 W
Sweetwater, Fl., U.S. 220 25.46 N 80.21 W
Sweet Water, Il., U.S. 219 40.03 N 89.42 W
Sweetwater, Tn., U.S. 192 35.36 N 84.27 W
Sweetwater, Tx., U.S. 196 32.28 N 100.24 W
Sweetwater ≐ 202 42.31 N 107.02 W
Sweetwater Creek 220 27.59 N 82.33 W
Sweetwater Creek ≐, Tx., U.S. 196 35.18 N 99.57 W
Sweetwater Creek ≐, Tx., U.S. 196 32.40 N 100.06 W
Sweetwater Mountains ⋏ 226 38.30 N 119.17 W
Swellendam 158 34.02 S 20.26 E
Swepsonville 192 36.01 N 79.21 W
Swerdlowsk → Sverdlovsk 86 56.51 N 60.36 E
Świdnica (Schweidnitz) 30 50.51 N 16.29 E
Świdnik 30 51.14 N 22.41 E
Świdwin 30 53.47 N 15.47 E
Świebodzice 30 50.52 N 16.19 E
Świebodzin 30 52.15 N 15.32 E
Świecie 30 53.25 N 18.28 E
Świerzawa 30 51.01 N 15.54 E
Świerzno 54 53.57 N 14.59 E
Świeta 54 53.35 N 14.36 E
Świętokrzyskie, Góry ⋏ 30 50.55 N 21.00 E
Świętokrzyski Park Narodowy ♦ 30 50.55 N 21.00 E
Swift ≐, Eng., U.K. 42 52.23 N 1.16 W
Swift ≐, Ak., U.S. 180 61.53 N 156.18 W
Swift ≐, Ma., U.S. 207 42.12 N 72.22 W
Swift Creek ≐, Al., U.S. 194 32.25 N 86.38 W
Swift Creek ≐, N.C., U.S. 192 35.12 N 77.05 W
Swift Creek ≐, N.C., U.S. 192 35.57 N 77.35 W
Swift Creek ≐, Va., U.S. 208 37.17 N 77.15 W
Swift Current 184 50.17 N 107.50 W
Swift Current Creek ≐ 184 50.40 N 107.44 W
Swifton 194 35.49 N 91.07 W
Swift Reservoir ⊜1 224 46.04 N 122.05 W
Swiftwater 210 41.06 N 75.20 W
Swilly ≐ 48 54.57 N 7.42 W
Swilly, Lough c 48 55.10 N 7.38 W
Swimming ≐ 276 40.21 N 74.05 W
Swimming River Reservoir ⊜1 276 40.19 N 74.07 W
Świna ≐1 54 53.55 N 14.17 E
Swinburne, Cape › 176 71.14 N 98.34 W
Swinden Reservoirs ⊜1 262 53.48 N 2.10 W
Swindle Island I 182 52.32 N 128.35 W
Swindon 42 51.34 N 1.47 W
Swinemünde → Świnoujście 30 53.53 N 14.14 E
Swineshead 42 52.56 N 0.09 W
Swinford 48 53.57 N 8.57 W
Swinging Bridge Reservoir ⊜1 210 41.37 N 74.48 W
Swinomish Indian Reservation ◆4 224 48.25 N 122.33 W
Świnoujście (Swinemünde) 30 53.53 N 14.14 E
Swinton, Eng., U.K. 44 53.28 N 1.20 W
Swinton, Eng., U.K. 262 53.31 N 2.20 W
Swinton, Scot., U.K. 46 55.43 N 2.15 W
Swissvale 279b 40.25 N 79.52 W
Swisttal 56 50.41 N 6.55 E
Switzerland □6 218 38.45 N 85.04 W
Switzerland □1, Europe 22 47.00 N 8.00 E
Switzerland □1, Europe 58 47.00 N 8.00 E
Swona I 46 58.45 N 3.03 W
Swordfish Seamount ✦3 14 18.25 N 158.25 W
Swords 48 53.28 N 6.13 W
Swords Range ⋏ 166 21.57 S 141.32 E
Swormville 284a 43.02 N 78.42 W
Sworton Heath 262 53.21 N 2.28 W
Swoyerville 210 41.18 N 75.52 W
Syalach 74 66.12 N 124.00 E
Syam 58 46.42 N 5.57 E
Syāmnagar 126 22.11 N 89.07 E
Syāmpur, India 126 22.18 N 88.02 E
Syāmpur, India 272b 22.29 N 88.13 E
Sybille Creek ≐ 198 42.07 N 105.02 W
Syburg ◆8 263 51.25 N 7.29 E
Sycamore, Ga., U.S. 192 31.40 N 83.38 W
Sycamore, Il., U.S. 216 41.59 N 88.41 W
Sycamore, Oh., U.S. 214 40.56 N 83.10 W
Sycamore Creek ≐, Az., U.S. 200 33.38 N 111.40 W
Sycamore Creek ≐, Mi., U.S. 216 42.43 N 84.32 W
Sycamore Creek ≐, Oh., U.S. 214 40.59 N 83.12 W
Sycamore Creek ≐, Tx., U.S. 229 29.14 N 100.48 W
Sycamore Gardens 285 39.42 N 75.42 W
Sycamore Island I 279b 40.29 N 79.52 W
Sycamore Slough ≐ 226 38.48 N 121.44 W
Sycan ≐ 202 42.27 N 121.15 W
Sycaway 210 42.44 N 73.39 W
Syčova 86 57.35 N 69.20 E
Syčovka 76 55.50 N 34.17 E
Syców 30 51.19 N 17.43 E
Sydenham, Austl. 274b 37.42 S 144.46 E
Sydenham, On., Can. 212 44.25 N 76.36 W
Sydenham ◆8, S. Afr. 273d 26.09 S 28.06 E
Sydenham ◆8, Eng., U.K. 260 51.26 N 0.03 W
Sydenham ≐, On., Can. 190 42.33 N 82.25 W
Sydenham ≐, On., Can. 212 44.35 N 80.57 W
Sydenham Lake ⊜ 212 44.25 N 76.35 W
Sydenham West 274b 37.41 S 144.39 E
Sydney, Austl. 170 33.52 S 151.13 E
Sydney, Austl. 274a 33.52 S 151.13 E
Sydney, N.S., Can. 186 46.09 N 60.11 W
Sydney, Fl., U.S. 220 27.58 N 82.12 W
Sydney, University of ♦2 274a 33.53 S 151.11 E
Sydney Bay c, On., Can. 212 44.54 N 81.05 W
Sydney Bay c, Norf. I. 174c 29.04 S 167.57 E
Sydney Bay Bluff ≐4 212 44.54 N 81.07 W
Sydney Harbour Bridge ◆5 170 33.52 S 151.12 E
Sydney Lake ⊜ 184 50.40 N 94.24 W
Sydney Mines 186 46.14 N 60.14 W
Sydney Point › 174d 0.53 S 169.36 E
Syferbult 158 26.00 S 27.20 E
Sygan 279b 40.21 N 80.08 W
Syke 52 52.54 N 8.49 E
Sykesville, Md., U.S. 208 39.22 N 76.58 W
Sykesville, Pa., U.S. 214 41.03 N 78.49 W
Sykkylven 26 62.24 N 6.35 E
Syktyvkar 24 61.40 N 50.46 E
Sylacauga 194 33.10 N 86.15 W
Sylarna ∧ 26 63.02 N 12.13 E
Sylhet 120 24.54 N 91.52 E
Syloga 24 63.50 N 43.39 E
Sylsjön ⊜ 26 62.56 N 12.11 E
Sylt I 30 54.54 N 8.20 E
Sylva 192 35.22 N 83.13 W
Sylva ≐ 86 57.39 N 56.54 E
Sylvan 224 45.30 N 122.41 W
Sylvan Beach 210 43.11 N 75.43 W
Sylvan Glen 285 40.11 N 75.42 W
Sylvan Grove 198 39.00 N 98.23 W
Sylvan Hills 194 34.50 N 92.13 W
Sylvania, Austl. 274a 34.01 S 151.07 E
Sylvania, Ga., U.S. 192 32.45 N 81.38 W
Sylvania, Oh., U.S. 214 41.43 N 83.42 W
Sylvania, Pa., U.S. 210 41.48 N 76.51 W
Sylvania Heights 274a 34.02 S 151.06 E
Sylvan Lake, Ab., Can. 182 52.19 N 114.05 W
Sylvan Lake, Il., U.S. 278 42.15 N 88.03 W
Sylvan Lake, Mi., U.S. 281 42.37 N 83.20 W
Sylvan Lake ⊜, Ab., Can. 182 52.21 N 114.10 W
Sylvan Lake ⊜, In., U.S. 216 41.29 N 85.20 W
Sylvan Lake ⊜, Mi., U.S. 281 42.37 N 83.20 W
Sylvan Pass x 202 44.28 N 110.08 W
Sylvan Shores 220 28.49 N 81.41 W
Sylvensteinsee ⊜1 64 47.34 N 11.32 E
Sylvester, Ga., U.S. 192 31.31 N 83.50 W
Sylvester, Tx., U.S. 196 32.43 N 100.15 W
Sylvester, Mount ∧2 186 48.11 N 55.04 W
Sylvia 198 37.57 N 98.24 W
Sym 74 60.20 N 88.23 E
Symmes Creek ≐ 188 38.26 N 82.27 W
Sym'a 76 65.22 N 57.42 E
Syndal 274b 37.53 S 145.09 E
Synkovo 82 55.21 N 37.38 E
Synnyr, chrebet ⋏ 88 56.50 N 111.10 E
Syntul 80 55.00 N 41.18 E
Synžereja 78 47.38 N 28.09 E
Syon House ⊥ 260 51.29 N 0.19 W
Syosset 210 40.49 N 73.30 W
Syowa ♦3 9 69.00 S 39.35 E
Syracuse → Siracusa, It. 70 37.04 N 15.18 E
Syracuse, In., U.S. 216 41.25 N 85.45 W
Syracuse, Ks., U.S. 198 37.58 N 101.45 W
Syracuse, Ne., U.S. 198 40.39 N 96.11 W
Syracuse, N.Y., U.S. 210 43.02 N 76.08 W
Syracuse Hancock International Airport ⊠, N.Y., U.S. 210 43.07 N 76.07 W
Syracuse Hancock International Airport ⊠, N.Y., U.S. 212 43.07 N 76.07 W
Syrčan 80 57.22 N 50.15 E
Syrdarja 85 40.52 N 68.38 E
Syrdarja (Syr Darya) ≐ 72 46.03 N 61.00 E
Syrdarjinskaja Oblast' □4 85 40.40 N 68.45 E
Syr-Darya → Syrdarja ≐ 72 46.03 N 61.00 E
Syre 46 58.22 N 4.14 W
Syre ≐ 56 49.35 N 6.08 E
Syria (As-Sūrīyah) □1, Asia 118 35.00 N 38.00 E
Syria (As-Sūrīyah) □1, Asia 128 35.00 N 38.00 E
Syriam 110 16.46 N 96.15 E
Syrian Desert → Shām, Bādiyat ash- ◆2 128 32.00 N 40.00 E
Syrie → Syria □1 128 35.00 N 38.00 E
Syrien → Syria □1 128 35.00 N 38.00 E
Syrskij 76 52.34 N 39.29 E
Sysert' 86 56.29 N 60.49 E
Sysmä 26 61.30 N 25.41 E
Sysola ≐ 24 61.42 N 50.53 E
Sysslebäck 26 60.44 N 12.52 E
Syston 42 52.42 N 1.04 W
Systyg-Chem 88 52.40 N 95.30 E
Syt'kovo 76 56.31 N 34.01 E
Sytykanskij, porog ⊾ 88 57.49 N 118.33 E
Syukunoshō 270 34.50 N 135.32 E
Syväjärvi ⊜ 26 63.16 N 28.06 E
Syzran' 80 53.09 N 48.27 E
Syzran' ≐ 80 53.04 N 48.26 E
Szabadka → Subotica 38 46.06 N 19.39 E
Szabolcs-Szatmár □6 30 48.00 N 22.10 E
Szada 264c 47.38 N 19.19 E
Szamocin 30 53.02 N 17.08 E
Szamos (Someș) ≐ 38 48.07 N 22.20 E
Szamotuły 30 52.37 N 16.35 E
Szarvas 30 46.52 N 20.34 E
Szatmárnémeti → Satu Mare 38 47.48 N 22.53 E
Százhalombatta 264c 47.18 N 18.56 E
Szczawnica 30 49.26 N 20.30 E
Szczecin (Stettin) 30 53.24 N 14.32 E
Szczecin □4 30 53.45 N 15.00 E
Szczecinek (Neustettin) 30 53.43 N 16.42 E
Szczeciński, Zalew (Oderhaff) c 54 53.46 N 14.14 E
Szczekociny 30 50.38 N 19.50 E
Szczuczyn 30 53.34 N 22.18 E
Szczytno 30 53.34 N 21.00 E
Szechwan → Sichuan □4 102 31.00 N 105.00 E
Szechwan Basin → Sichuan Pendi ⊏1 102 30.00 N 105.00 E
Szécsény 30 48.06 N 19.31 E
Szeged 30 46.15 N 20.09 E
Szeghalom 30 47.01 N 21.11 E
Székesfehérvár 30 47.12 N 18.25 E
Szekszárd 30 46.21 N 18.42 E
Szemenyecsörnye 61 46.30 N 16.37 E
Szentendre 30 47.40 N 19.05 E
Szentendrei-Duna ≐ 264c 47.39 N 19.04 E
Szentendrei-sziget I 264c 47.39 N 19.07 E
Szentes 30 46.39 N 20.16 E
Szentgotthárd 61 46.57 N 16.17 E
Szentpéterfa 61 47.06 N 16.29 E
Szeping → Siping 89 43.12 N 124.20 E
Szépművészeti Múzeum ♦ 264c 47.31 N 19.05 E
Szerencs 30 48.09 N 21.13 E
Szigethalom 264c 47.20 N 19.00 E
Szigetszentmiklós 264c 47.21 N 19.03 E
Szilas (Palotai)-patak ≐ 264c 47.36 N 19.06 E
Szlichtyngowa 30 51.43 N 16.15 E
Szob 30 47.50 N 18.52 E
Szolnok 30 47.10 N 20.12 E
Szolnok □6 30 47.12 N 20.11 E
Szombathely 61 47.14 N 16.38 E
Szprotawa 30 51.34 N 15.33 E
Sztum 30 53.56 N 19.01 E
Szubin 30 53.00 N 17.44 E
Szydłowiec 30 51.14 N 20.51 E
Szypliszki 30 54.15 N 23.05 E

T

Ta ≐ 94 36.17 N 139.54 E
Taacyn ≐ 102 45.09 N 101.27 E
Taal, Lake ⊜ 116 13.55 N 121.00 E
Taalintehdas → Dalsbruk 26 60.02 N 22.31 E
Taan ≐ 100 24.24 N 120.36 E
Taancan Point › 116 10.00 N 125.01 E
Taavetti 26 60.55 N 27.34 E
Tabacal 252 23.16 S 64.15 W
Tabacal, Quebrada ≐ 286c 10.31 N 67.02 W
Tabaco 116 13.23 N 123.44 E
Tabacundo 246 0.03 N 78.12 W
Tabai ≐ 164 3.01 S 135.52 E
Tabalosos 248 6.21 S 76.41 W
Tabanan 115b 8.32 S 115.08 E
Tabango 116 11.19 N 124.22 E
Tabankulu 158 30.58 S 29.19 E
Tabaqah 130 35.52 N 38.34 E
Tábara 34 41.49 N 5.57 W
Tabar Island I 164 2.55 S 152.05 E
Tabar Islands II 164 2.50 S 152.00 E
Tabarka 148 36.57 N 8.45 E
Tabarz 54 50.52 N 10.31 E
Ṭabas, Īrān 128 33.36 N 56.54 E
Ṭabas, Īrān 128 32.48 N 60.14 E
Tabasará ≐ 236 8.00 N 81.39 W
Tabasco 232 32.35 N 114.55 W
Tabasco □3 232 18.15 N 93.00 W
Tabat 86 52.57 N 90.43 E
Tabatinga ≐ 255 17.24 S 43.18 W
Tabayama 94 35.47 N 138.55 E
Tabayin 110 22.42 N 95.19 E
Tabb 208 37.08 N 76.29 W
Tabei 98 39.44 N 122.29 E
Tabelbala 148 29.23 N 3.15 W
Tabelbala, Kahal ≐8 148 28.30 N 2.00 W
Taber 182 49.47 N 112.08 W
Taberg, Sve. 26 57.41 N 14.05 E
Taberg, Sve. 40 59.50 N 14.08 E
Taberg, N.Y., U.S. 210 43.18 N 75.37 W
Tabernacle 285 39.50 N 74.42 W
Tabernes de Valldigna 34 39.04 N 0.16 W
Tabi 152 8.10 S 13.18 E
Tabiang 174d 0.52 S 169.35 E
Tabiano Terme 64 44.48 N 10.21 E
Tabira 250 7.35 S 37.33 W
Tabiteuea 174t 1.25 N 173.07 E
Tabiteuea I1 14 1.20 S 174.50 E
Tabla 150 13.46 N 3.01 E
Tabla, Cerro de la ∧ 240m 18.03 N 66.08 W
Tablada 288 34.42 S 58.32 W
Tablas, Cabo › 252 31.51 S 71.34 W
Tablas Island I 116 12.24 N 122.02 E
Tablas Plateau ⋏1 116 9.43 N 122.43 E
Tablas Strait ⊔ 116 12.40 N 121.48 E
Tablat 34 36.24 N 3.19 E
Table Bay c 158 33.53 S 18.27 E
Table Cape › 172 39.06 S 178.00 E
Tableland 162 17.17 S 127.00 E
Table Mountain ∧, Nf., Can. 186 47.43 N 59.13 W
Table Mountain ∧, S. Afr. 158 33.57 S 18.25 E
Table Mountain ∧, Az., U.S. 200 32.49 N 110.31 W
Table Rock 198 40.10 N 96.05 W
Table Rock Lake ⊜1 194 36.35 N 93.30 W
Tabletop ∧, Austl. 162 22.32 S 123.55 E
Table Top ∧, Az., U.S. 200 32.46 N 112.07 W
Tabletop Mountain ∧ 171b 35.58 S 148.30 E
Tabley Mere ⊜ 262 53.17 N 2.25 W
Tabligbo 150 6.35 N 1.30 E
Tablones 240m 18.15 N 65.45 W
Taboan ≐ 116 17.57 N 122.11 E
Taboão, Ribeirão do ≐ 287b 23.40 S 46.28 W
Taboão da Serra 256 23.38 S 46.46 W
Taboco ≐ 248 19.53 S 55.58 W
Taboga 236 8.48 N 79.33 W
Tabogon 116 10.57 N 124.02 E
Tábor, Česko. 30 49.25 N 14.41 E
Tabor, S.S.S.R. 74 71.16 N 150.12 E
Tabor, Ia., U.S. 198 40.53 N 95.40 W
Tabor, N.J., U.S. 276 40.52 N 74.29 W
Tabor, S.D., U.S. 198 42.56 N 97.39 W
Tabor, Mount → Tavor, Har ∧ 132 32.41 N 35.23 E
Tabora 154 5.01 S 32.48 E
Tabora □4 154 5.15 S 32.45 E
Tabor City 192 34.08 N 78.52 W
Tabory 86 58.31 N 64.33 E
Tabou 150 4.25 N 7.21 W
Tabrīz 128 38.05 N 46.18 E
Tábua, Riacho da ≐ 250 9.12 S 44.25 W
Tabuaço 34 41.07 N 7.34 W
Tabuaeran I1 14 3.52 N 159.20 W
Tabuão 256 21.59 S 44.02 W
Tábuas 256 22.12 S 43.37 W
Tabu-dong 98 36.03 N 128.31 E
Tabuelan 116 10.49 N 123.52 E
Tabūk, Ar. Su. 128 28.23 N 36.35 E
Tabuk, Pil. 116 17.24 N 121.25 E
Tabuleiro 256 21.22 S 43.15 W
Tabuleiro do Norte 250 5.15 S 38.07 W
Tabuny 86 52.46 N 78.45 E
Tabuse 96 33.57 N 132.03 E
Tabuyung 114 0.51 N 99.00 E
Tabwémasana, Mont ∧ 175f 15.20 S 166.44 E
Täby 40 59.30 N 18.03 E
Tacagua, Quebrada ≐ 286c 10.37 N 67.02 W
Tacámbaro ≐ 234 18.29 N 101.07 W
Tacámbaro de Codallos 234 19.14 N 101.28 W
Tacaná 236 15.14 N 92.05 W
Tacaná, Volcán ∧1 236 15.08 N 92.06 W
Tacañitas 252 28.38 S 62.36 W
Tacaratu 250 9.06 S 38.10 W
Taceno 58 46.02 N 9.21 E
T'ačev 78 48.02 N 23.34 E
Taché, Lac ⊜ 176 64.00 N 120.00 W
Tacheng 86 46.45 N 82.57 E
Tacherting 60 48.05 N 12.34 E
Tachia 100 24.21 N 120.37 E
Tachia ≐ 100 24.20 N 120.33 E
Tachiaochang Airport ⊠ 107 32.01 N 118.47 E
Tachiataš 72 42.22 N 59.35 E
Tachibana, Nihon 96 33.11 N 130.36 E
Tachibana, Nihon 96 33.54 N 132.17 E
Tachichilte, Isla de I 232 24.59 N 108.04 W
Tachie ≐ 182 54.40 N 124.50 W
Tachikawa 94 35.42 N 139.25 E
Tachikawa Air Base ■ 268 35.43 N 139.25 E
Tachinger See ⊜ 60 47.58 N 12.45 E
Táchira □3 246 7.50 N 72.05 W
Tachoshui 100 24.20 N 121.44 E
Tachov 60 49.48 N 12.38 E
Tachta, S.S.S.R. 80 45.54 N 42.07 E
Tachta, S.S.S.R. 89 53.08 N 139.53 E
Tachta-Bazar 128 35.57 N 62.50 E
Tachtabrod 86 52.38 N 67.34 E
Tachtakupyr 86 43.02 N 60.17 E
Tachtamygda 89 54.06 N 123.34 E

Symbols in the index entries represent the broad categories identified in the key at the right. Symbols with superior numbers (⋏1) identify subcategories (see complete key on page I · 1).

Kartensymbole in dem Registerverzeichnis stellen die rechts in Schlüssel erklärten Kategorien dar. Symbole mit hochgestellten Ziffern (⋏1) bezeichnen Unterabteilungen einer Kategorie (vgl. vollständiger Schlüssel auf Seite I · 1).

Los símbolos incluídos en el texto del índice representan las grandes categorías identificadas con la clave a la derecha. Los símbolos con numeros en su parte superior (⋏1) identifican las subcategorías (véase la clave completa en la página I · 1).

Les symboles de l'index représentent les catégories indiquées dans la légende à droite. Les symboles suivis d'un indice (⋏1) représentent des sous-catégories (voir légende complète à la page I · 1).

Os símbolos incluídos no texto do índice representam as grandes categorias identificadas com a chave à direita. Os símbolos com números em sua parte superior (⋏1) identificam as subcategorias (veja-se a chave completa à página I · 1).

∧ Mountain	Berg	Montaña	Montagne	Montanha
⋏ Mountains	Berge	Montañas	Montagnes	Montanhas
x Pass	Pass	Paso	Col	Passo
V Valley, Canyon	Tal, Cañon	Valle, Cañón	Vallée, Canyon	Vale, Canhão
= Plain	Ebene	Llano	Plaine	Planície
› Cape	Kap	Cabo	Cap	Cabo
I Island	Insel	Isla	Île	Ilha
II Islands	Inseln	Islas	Îles	Ilhas
≐ Other Topographic Features	Andere Topographische Objekte	Otros Elementos Topográficos	Autres données topographiques	Outros acidentes topográficos

ESPAÑOL

Nombre	Página	Lat. °′	Long. °′ W = Oeste
Tacima	250	6.30 S	35.39 W
Tacina ≃	68	38.56 N	16.53 E
Tacinskij	80	48.13 N	41.17 E
Taciuã, Lago ≃	246	4.29 S	60.35 W
Tacloban	116	11.15 N	125.00 E
Taclobo	116	12.20 N	122.34 E
Tacna, Perú	248	18.01 S	70.15 W
Tacna, Az., U.S.	200	32.41 N	113.57 W
Tacna □[5]	248	17.40 S	70.20 W
Tacoignières	261	48.50 N	1.40 E
Tacoma	224	47.15 N	122.26 W
Tacoma Narrows Bridge ◆[5]	224	47.16 N	122.33 W
Taconic	207	42.02 N	73.24 W
Taconic Range ⋏	210	42.30 N	73.20 W
Taconic State Park ♠	210	42.05 N	73.34 W
Tacony ◆[8]	285	40.02 N	75.03 W
Tacony Creek ≃	285	40.01 N	75.06 W
Tacony Creek Park ♠	285	40.02 N	75.07 W
Tacony Palmyra Bridge ◆[5]	285	40.01 N	75.02 W
Taco Pozo	252	25.37 S	63.17 W
Tacotalpa	234	17.36 N	92.49 W
Tacotalpa ≃	234	17.50 N	92.52 W
Tacuarembó	252	31.44 S	55.59 W
Tacuarembó ≃	252	32.25 S	55.29 W
Tacuarí ≃	252	32.46 S	53.18 W
Tacuatí	252	23.27 S	56.35 W
Tacuba ◆[8]	286a	19.28 N	99.12 W
Tacubaya	232	28.20 N	104.34 W
Tacubaya ◆[8]	286a	19.25 N	99.12 W
Tacurong	116	6.42 N	124.42 E
Tacurú, Laguna ⊜	258	34.58 S	58.25 W
Tacutu (Takutu) ≃	246	3.01 N	60.29 W
Tadain	270	34.52 N	135.24 E
Tadami	92	37.21 N	139.19 E
Tadaoka	270	34.29 N	135.24 E
Tadasuni	71	40.06 N	8.53 E
Tadcaster	44	53.53 N	1.16 W
Tademaït, Plateau du ⋏[1]	148	28.30 N	2.00 E
Tadenac Lake ⊜	212	45.03 N	79.56 W
Tādepallegūdem	122	16.50 N	81.30 E
Tadía, Ciénaga de ⊜	246	6.48 N	76.49 W
Tadine	175f	21.33 S	167.52 E
Tadio, Lagune ⊂	150	5.11 N	5.15 W
Tadjemout	148	25.37 N	3.48 E
Tadjenanet	34	36.08 N	5.59 E
Tadjeraout, Oued V	148	21.17 N	1.19 E
Tadjoura	144	11.47 N	42.54 E
Tadjoura, Golfe de ⊂	144	11.42 N	43.00 E
Tadley	42	51.21 N	1.08 W
Tado	94	35.08 N	136.38 E
Tadok	114	3.58 N	96.19 E
Tadotsu	96	34.16 N	133.45 E
Tadoule Lake ⊜	176	58.36 N	98.20 W
Tadoussac	186	48.09 N	69.43 W
Tādpatri	122	14.55 N	78.01 E
Taduno	112	1.55 S	123.05 E
Tadworth	42	51.17 N	0.14 W
Tadžikabad	85	39.07 N	70.50 E
Tadžikskaja Sovetskaja Socialističeskaja Respublika □[3]	72	39.00 N	71.00 E
T'aean	98	36.46 N	126.16 E
T'aebaek-san ∧	98	37.06 N	128.55 E
T'aebaek-sanmaek ⋏	98	37.40 N	128.50 E
Taebu-do I	98	37.15 N	126.35 E
Taech'ŏn	98	36.22 N	126.34 E
Taech'ŏng-do I	98	37.49 N	124.43 E
Taedong	98	39.05 N	125.31 E
Taedong-gang ≃	98	38.42 N	125.15 E
Taegu	98	35.52 N	128.35 E
Taegu □[4]	98	35.50 N	128.35 E
Taegwan	98	40.13 N	125.12 E
Taehan-Min'guk → Korea, South □[1]	98	36.30 N	128.00 E
Taehŭksan-do I	98	34.40 N	125.25 E
Taehŭng	98	40.06 N	126.56 E
Taehwajŏn	271b	37.36 N	126.52 E
T'aein	98	35.40 N	126.55 E
Taejin	98	36.34 N	129.24 E
Taejŏn	98	36.20 N	127.26 E
Taejujŏm	98	38.24 N	127.58 E
T'aemo-san ∧	271b	37.27 N	127.04 E
Taeng ≃	110	19.06 N	98.57 E
Taer	102	34.09 N	98.50 E
Ta'erwan	100	31.49 N	113.25 E
Taeryanghwa	98	41.14 N	129.42 E
Tafahi I	14	15.51 S	173.43 W
Tafahnā al-'Azab	142	30.36 N	31.15 E
Tafalla	34	42.31 N	1.40 W
Tafanlieh	100	21.58 N	120.46 E
Ṭafas	132	32.44 N	36.04 E
Tafāsīkh, Ghurd at- ≛[8]	142	29.43 N	29.45 E
Tafassasset, Oued (Oued Tafassâsset) V	148	20.56 N	10.12 E
Tafassâsset, Ténéré du ◆[2]	146	21.00 N	11.00 E
Tafea □[8]	175f	19.30 S	169.00 E
Tafelbaai → Table Bay ⊂	158	33.53 S	18.27 E
Tafermaar	164	6.51 S	134.06 E
Taff ≃	42	51.27 N	3.09 W
Tafiré	150	9.04 N	5.10 W
Tafí Viejo	252	26.44 S	65.16 W
Taflan	130	41.25 N	36.09 E
Tafna, Oued ≃	34	35.17 N	1.30 W
Tafo	150	6.13 N	0.22 W
Tafraoute	148	29.40 N	8.58 W
Taft, Īrān	128	31.45 N	54.14 E
Taft, Pil.	116	11.54 N	125.25 E
Taft, Ca., U.S.	204	35.08 N	119.27 W
Taft, Fl., U.S.	220	28.23 N	81.24 W
Taft, Ok., U.S.	196	35.45 N	95.32 W
Taft, Tx., U.S.	196	27.58 N	97.23 W
Taftān, Kūh-e ∧	128	28.36 N	61.06 E
Tafton	210	41.25 N	75.11 W
Taga, Nihon	94	35.13 N	136.17 E
Taga, Nihon	270	34.49 N	135.49 E
Taga, W. Sam.	175a	13.46 S	172.28 W
Tagabukid	116	7.00 N	126.21 E
Taga Dzong	124	27.04 N	89.53 E
Tagagawik ≃	180	66.30 N	159.00 W
Tagaj	80	54.18 N	47.39 E
Tagajō	92	38.20 N	141.00 E
Tagan	86	54.57 N	77.18 E
Tagana-an	116	9.42 N	125.35 E
Taganrog	83	47.12 N	38.56 E
Taganrogskij zaliv ⊂	78	47.00 N	38.23 E
Tagant □[4]	150	18.20 N	11.30 W
Tagânt ◆[1]	150	18.00 N	12.00 W
Tagapula Island I	116	12.04 N	124.12 E
Tågarp	41	55.56 N	12.57 E
Tagauayan Island I	116	10.58 N	121.13 E
Tagawa	96	33.38 N	130.49 E
Tagaytay	116	14.06 N	120.56 E
Tagbara	152	5.56 N	21.09 E
Tagdempt → Tihert	148	35.28 N	1.21 E
Tage	164	6.20 S	143.20 E
Tageren Canal ≊	174q	9.33 N	138.09 E
Taggia	62	43.52 N	7.51 E
Taghit	148	30.55 N	2.02 W
Taghkanic Creek ≃	210	42.13 N	73.45 W
Taghmon	48	52.18 N	6.39 W
Tagig	269f	14.32 N	121.04 E
Tagig ≃	269f	14.31 N	121.05 E
Tagilaran	116	9.39 N	123.51 E
T'aginka	78	46.47 N	33.04 E
Tagish Lake ⊜	180	59.45 N	134.15 W
Tagliacozzo	66	42.04 N	13.14 E
Tagliamento ≃	64	45.38 N	13.06 E
Tagliata, Monte della ∧	64	44.34 N	9.48 E
Taglio di Po	64	45.00 N	12.12 E
Tagna	88	53.36 N	101.54 E
Tagna ≃	88	53.38 N	101.53 E
Tago	116	9.02 N	126.13 E
Tago ≃	116	9.01 N	126.14 E
Tagoloan	116	8.32 N	124.45 E

FRANÇAIS

Nom	Page	Lat. °′	Long. °′ W = Ouest
Tagolo Point ›	116	8.44 N	123.23 E
Tagon Harbour ⊂	162	33.53 S	123.00 E
Tagounit	148	29.58 N	5.36 W
Tagourâret ⍑[4]	150	17.45 N	7.43 W
Tagow Bāy	120	35.42 N	66.03 E
Tagrina, Oued V	148	21.00 N	6.16 E
Taguatinga	255	12.25 S	46.26 W
Tagubanhan Island I	116	11.08 N	123.07 E
Tagudin	116	16.56 N	120.27 E
Taguedoufat V	150	14.50 N	7.42 E
Taguke	120	32.07 N	84.35 E
Tagul ≃	88	55.35 N	97.45 E
Tagula Island I	160	11.30 S	153.30 E
Tagum	116	7.28 N	125.48 E
T'agun	86	53.56 N	85.38 E
Tagun Bay ⊂	116	13.55 N	123.46 E
Tagus (Tejo) (Tajo) ≃	34	38.40 N	9.24 W
T'agyŏng-ni	98	38.04 N	126.03 E
Tah, Sebkha ⊜	148	27.45 N	12.42 W
Taha	89	47.33 N	124.14 E
Tahaa I	14	16.38 S	151.30 W
Tahakopa	172	46.31 S	169.23 E
Tahala	148	34.04 N	4.20 W
Tahan, Gunong ∧	114	4.38 N	102.14 E
Tahanaoute	148	31.24 N	7.54 W
Tahāneh-ye Ney Basteh	128	32.59 N	60.53 E
Tahara	94	34.40 N	137.16 E
Tahart	148	22.51 N	5.12 E
Tahat ∧	148	23.18 N	5.47 E
Taheke	172	35.27 S	173.39 E
Ṭāherī	128	27.42 N	52.21 E
Tahgong, Puntan ›	174n	15.06 N	145.39 E
Tahifet	148	22.58 N	5.55 E
Tahir	130	38.47 N	38.17 E
Tahir geçidi)(	130	39.54 N	42.22 E
Tahiryuak Lake ⊜	176	70.56 N	112.20 W
Tahiti I	174s	17.37 S	149.27 W
Tahkuna neem ›	76	59.07 N	22.36 E
Tahlequah	196	35.54 N	94.58 W
Ṭahmā wa Minshāt 'Abd as-Sayyid	142	29.38 N	31.14 E
Tahmoor	170	34.13 S	150.36 E
Tahneta Pass)(	180	61.53 N	147.20 W
Tahoe, Lake ⊜	226	39.07 N	120.03 W
Tahoe City	226	39.10 N	120.08 W
Tahoe Lake ⊜	176	70.15 N	108.45 W
Tahoe Paradise	226	38.52 N	120.01 W
Tahoe Valley	226	38.55 N	120.00 W
Tahoka	196	33.10 N	101.47 W
Taholah	224	47.20 N	124.17 W
Tahoua	150	14.54 N	5.16 E
Tahoua □[5]	150	16.00 N	5.00 E
Tahquamenon ≃	190	46.34 N	85.02 W
Tahquamenon Falls State Park ♠	190	46.29 N	85.05 W
Tahsi	100	24.57 N	121.53 E
Tahsis	182	49.55 N	126.39 W
Ṭahṭā	140	26.46 N	31.30 E
Tahtaköprü	130	39.57 N	29.39 E
Tahtsa Lake ⊜	182	53.42 N	127.26 W
Tahtsa Peak ∧	182	53.33 N	127.47 W
Tahu	100	24.26 N	120.52 E
Tahuamanú ≃	248	11.06 S	67.36 W
Tahuata I	174y	9.57 S	139.05 W
Tahulandang, Pulau I	112	2.20 N	125.25 E
Tahuna	112	3.37 N	125.29 E
Tahuofang ⊜[1]	104	41.55 N	124.07 E
Tahuya ≃	224	47.23 N	123.03 W
Ṭahwāy	142	30.22 N	30.52 E
Taḥwīṭat an-Nahr	132	33.52 N	35.31 E
Taï, C. Iv.	150	5.52 N	7.27 W
Tai, It.	64	46.25 N	12.20 E
Tai, Nihon	270	34.31 N	135.26 E
Tai ◆[8]	270	34.45 N	135.00 E
Taiaçupeba	256	23.40 S	46.11 W
Tai'an, Zhg.	98	36.12 N	117.07 E
Tai'an, Zhg.	104	41.23 N	122.27 E
Tai'an, Zhg.	107	30.05 N	105.47 E
Tai'angang	106	31.43 N	121.40 E
Taiarapu, Presqu'île de ›[1]	174s	17.47 S	149.14 W
Taibai	102	34.00 N	107.18 E
Taibai Shan ∧, Zhg.	98	39.19 N	114.11 E
Taibai Shan ∧, Zhg.	102	33.54 N	107.46 E
Taibilla, Sierra de ⋏	34	38.10 N	2.10 W
Taibon Agordino	64	46.18 N	12.00 E
Taibus Qi (Baochang)	98	41.56 N	115.22 E
Taicang	106	31.26 N	121.07 E
T'aichou → Taizhou	100	32.30 N	119.58 E
Taichu → T'aichung	100	24.09 N	120.41 E
T'aichung	100	24.09 N	120.41 E
Taicunzhen	106	31.27 N	119.03 E
Taiden → Taejŏn	98	36.20 N	127.26 E
Taiei	94	35.49 N	140.25 E
Taieri ≃	172	46.03 S	170.11 E
Taif → Aṭ-Ṭā'if	144	21.16 N	40.24 E
Taigu	102	37.28 N	112.30 E
Tai Hang	271d	22.17 N	114.11 E
Taihang Shan ⋏	102	38.00 N	114.00 E
Taihape	172	39.40 S	175.48 E
Taihe, Zhg.	100	33.11 N	115.36 E
Taihe, Zhg.	100	26.49 N	114.55 E
Taihe, Zhg.	107	30.10 N	105.56 E
Taihezhen, Zhg.	89	44.47 N	123.29 E
Taihezhen, Zhg.	107	30.07 N	103.50 E
Taihezhen, Zhg.	107	30.06 N	106.03 E
Taihezhen ⊥	110	25.41 N	100.07 E
Taiho	174m	26.39 N	128.07 E
Taihoku → T'aipei	100	25.03 N	121.30 E
T'aihsi	100	23.42 N	120.11 E
T'aihsien → Taizhou	100	32.30 N	119.58 E
Taihu	100	30.26 N	116.16 E
Tai Hu ⊜	106	31.15 N	120.10 E
Taijiang	102	26.32 N	108.22 E
Taijimiao	98	40.55 N	113.46 E
Taijinai'erhu ⊜	120	37.15 N	93.20 E
Taijüan → Taiyuan	102	37.55 N	112.30 E
Taikang	98	34.04 N	114.50 E
Taikkyi	110	17.19 N	95.58 E
Taikou	102	31.53 N	111.07 E
Taiko-yama ∧	96	35.46 N	135.12 E
Taikyu → Taegu	98	35.52 N	128.35 E
Tailai	89	46.23 N	123.27 E
Tai Lam Chung	271d	22.22 N	114.01 E
Tai Lam Chung Reservoir ⊜[1]	271d	22.23 N	114.01 E
Tailem Bend	166	35.16 S	139.27 E
Tailfingen	58	48.15 N	9.01 E
Tai Long, H.K.	271d	22.25 N	114.22 E
Tai Long, H.K.	271d	22.13 N	113.59 E
Tai Long Bay ⊂	271d	22.24 N	114.24 E
Taima, Nihon	96	34.30 N	135.42 E
T'aima, T'aiwan	100	22.37 N	120.59 E
Taimba	74	60.18 N	98.58 E
Taimei	100	23.19 N	114.29 E
Tai Mong Tsai	271d	22.24 N	114.18 E
Tai Mo Shan ∧	271d	22.25 N	114.07 E
Taimyr-Halbinsel → Tajmyr, poluostrov ›[1]	74	76.00 N	104.00 E
Tain	46	57.48 N	4.04 W
Tainaka	270	34.36 N	135.37 E
T'ainan	100	23.00 N	120.12 E
T'ainanhsien	100	23.18 N	120.19 E
Taínaron, Ákra ›	38	36.22 N	22.30 E
Taining	100	26.54 N	117.09 E
Tain-l'Hermitage	62	45.04 N	4.51 E
Tai O, H.K.	100	22.15 N	113.51 E
Taio, It.	64	46.20 N	11.04 E
Taiobeiras	255	15.49 S	42.14 W
Tai Pang Wan ⊂	100	22.30 N	114.24 E
Taipas	255	12.15 S	47.09 W
T'aipei, T'aiwan	100	25.03 N	121.30 E
T'aipei, T'aiwan	269d	25.03 N	121.30 E
T'aipei □[6]	269d	25.00 N	121.40 E
Taipei Bridge ◆[5]	269d	25.04 N	121.30 E

PORTUGUÊS

Nome	Página	Lat. °′	Long. °′ W = Oeste
T'aipeihsien	100	25.00 N	121.27 E
Taipei Institute of Technology ⊻[2]	269d	25.02 N	121.32 E
Taipei New Park ♠	269d	25.03 N	121.31 E
T'aipei Shih □[7]	269d	25.05 N	121.33 E
Taiping, Malay.	114	4.51 N	100.44 E
Taiping, Zhg.	100	30.18 N	118.12 E
Taiping, Zhg.	100	22.49 N	113.41 E
Taiping, Zhg.	102	22.40 N	107.05 E
Taiping, Zhg.	107	30.24 N	103.37 E
Taipingchang, Zhg.	102	27.25 N	103.04 E
Taipingchang, Zhg.	107	29.33 N	103.33 E
Taipingchang, Zhg.	107	29.53 N	106.04 E
Taipingchang, Zhg.	107	29.55 N	103.49 E
Taipingchang, Zhg.	107	30.10 N	106.21 E
Taipingchang, Zhg.	107	30.39 N	105.54 E
Taipingchang, Zhg.	107	30.25 N	103.46 E
Taipingchuan, Zhg.	89	44.23 N	123.11 E
Taipingchuan, Zhg.	98	42.36 N	127.20 E
Taipingdian	102	32.08 N	111.45 E
Taipingkou	100	29.50 N	113.35 E
Taipingling	89	43.26 N	128.09 E
Taipingshan, Zhg.	98	40.34 N	122.25 E
Taipingshan, Zhg.	104	41.36 N	123.41 E
Taipingshao	98	40.54 N	125.08 E
Taipingsi	107	29.24 N	103.34 E
Taipingxigou	104	42.36 N	121.13 E
Taipingzhai	104	42.14 N	124.07 E
Taipingzhen, Zhg.	89	46.44 N	130.44 E
Taipingzhen, Zhg.	102	35.42 N	107.37 E
Taipingzhen, Zhg.	107	29.24 N	105.47 E
Taipingzhen, Zhg.	107	30.26 N	104.12 E
Taipingzhuang, Zhg.	104	42.38 N	123.45 E
Taipingzhuang, Zhg.	105	40.03 N	116.24 E
Taipingzhuang, Zhg.	105	40.08 N	117.36 E
Tai Po Hoi ⊂	271d	22.26 N	114.12 E
Tai Po Tsai	271d	22.21 N	114.15 E
Taipu	250	5.37 S	35.36 W
Taira, Nihon	94	36.26 N	136.57 E
Taira → Iwaki, Nihon	94	37.03 N	140.55 E
Tairetá	256	22.36 S	43.42 W
Tairiqiao	106	30.59 N	121.33 E
Tais	112	4.06 S	102.34 E
Taisen-zan ∧	96	33.06 N	131.17 E
Taisha → Izumo, Nihon	96	35.22 N	132.46 E
Taisha, Nihon	96	35.24 N	132.40 E
Taishaku-kyō ♠	96	34.53 N	133.13 E
Taishaku-zan ∧, Nihon	94	36.58 N	139.28 E
Taishaku-zan ∧, Nihon	270	34.47 N	135.07 E
Taishan, Zhg.	98	39.01 N	113.36 E
Taishan, Zhg.	102	22.16 N	112.44 E
Taishanchang	107	30.32 N	106.42 E
Taishi, Nihon	96	34.50 N	134.33 E
Taishi, Nihon	270	34.31 N	135.39 E
Taishō	96	33.12 N	132.58 E
Taishō ◆[8]	270	34.38 N	135.27 E
Tai Shui Hang	271d	22.25 N	14.13 E
Taishun	100	27.33 N	119.43 E
Tai Tam Bay ⊂	271d	22.13 N	114.13 E
Taitao, Península de ›[1]	254	46.30 S	74.25 W
Taitapu	172	43.40 S	172.33 E
Taitō ◆[8]	268	35.43 N	139.47 E
Tai Tong	271d	22.25 N	114.01 E
Taitouying	98	40.02 N	119.12 E
Taitō-zaki ›	94	35.18 N	140.25 E
T'aitung	100	22.45 N	121.09 E
Taivalkoski	26	65.34 N	28.15 E
Tai Wan	271d	22.10 N	114.15 E
Taiwan (T'aiwan) □[1], Asia	90	23.30 N	121.00 E
Taiwan (T'aiwan) □[1], Asia	100	23.30 N	121.00 E
T'aiwan I	100	23.30 N	121.00 E
Taiwan Strait ⋓	100	24.00 N	119.00 E
Tai Wan Tau	271d	22.18 N	114.17 E
Taixi	100	24.42 N	116.56 E
Taixian	100	32.31 N	120.09 E
Taixing	106	32.11 N	120.01 E
Taixizhen	106	31.03 N	119.49 E
Taiyang	100	30.12 N	119.19 E
Taiyanggong	271a	39.58 N	116.25 E
Taïyetos Óros ⋏	38	37.16 N	22.12 E
Taiyuan	102	37.55 N	112.30 E
Taizhao	120	30.01 N	93.08 E
Taizhou	100	32.30 N	119.58 E
Taizhou Liedao II	100	28.30 N	121.53 E
Taizi ≃	98	41.00 N	122.26 E
Ta'izz	144	13.38 N	44.04 E
Tāj al-'Izz	142	30.57 N	31.35 E
Tajarḥī	146	24.21 N	14.28 E
Tajbola	24	68.26 N	33.19 E
Tajdakovo	82	54.29 N	37.32 E
Tajerouine	36	35.54 N	8.34 E
Tajetteret, Oued V	148	21.20 N	7.22 E
Tajga	86	56.04 N	85.37 E
Tajgonos, mys ›	74	60.35 N	160.08 E
Tajgonos, poluostrov ›[1]	74	61.20 N	161.00 E
Tajik Soviet Socialist Republic → Tadžikskaja Sovetskaja Socialističeskaja Respublika □[3]	72	39.00 N	71.00 E
Tajima	94	37.12 N	139.46 E
Tajimi	94	35.19 N	137.08 E
Tajique	200	34.45 N	106.17 W
Tajiri	270	34.24 N	135.18 E
Tajitos	232	30.58 N	112.18 W
Tajlakdžegen	86	43.54 N	60.29 E
Tajlakovy	86	59.20 N	74.04 E
Tajmura ≃	72	63.46 N	98.01 E
Tajmyr, ozero ⊜	74	74.30 N	102.30 E
Tajmyr, poluostrov ›[1]	74	76.00 N	104.00 E
Tajna	88	56.27 N	95.30 E
Tajninka	265b	55.54 N	37.45 E
Tajo → Tagus ≃	34	38.40 N	9.24 W
Tajožnyj, S.S.S.R.	86	56.09 N	94.29 E
Tajožnyj, S.S.S.R.	88	56.13 N	94.55 E
Tajpur, India	124	29.10 N	78.29 E
Tajpur, India	124	25.51 N	85.41 E
Tājpur, India	272b	22.44 N	88.16 E
Tajpur Khurd ◆[8]	272a	28.35 N	77.03 E
Tajrīsh	128	35.48 N	51.25 E
Tajšet	88	55.57 N	98.00 E
Tajsojgan	80	48.19 N	53.29 E
Tajturka	88	52.51 N	103.28 E
Tajumulco, Volcán ∧[1]	236	15.02 N	91.55 W
Tajuña ≃	34	40.07 N	3.35 W
Tājūrā', Lībiyā	146	32.53 N	13.21 E
Tajura, S.S.S.R.	88	57.00 N	106.35 E
Tajura ≃	88	57.00 N	106.35 E
Tajžina	86	53.38 N	87.28 E
Tak	110	16.52 N	99.08 E
Takāb	128	36.24 N	47.07 E
Takabanare-jima I	174m	26.22 N	127.59 E
Takabara	150	11.50 N	11.30 W
Takachiho	92	32.42 N	131.18 E
Takachu	156	22.37 S	21.58 E
Takada → Bungo-takada	96	33.33 N	131.27 E
Takada → Yamato-takada	96	34.31 N	135.45 E
Takagi	268	35.56 N	139.35 E
Takahagi	94	36.43 N	140.43 E
Takahama, Nihon	94	34.55 N	136.59 E
Takahama, Nihon	94	37.00 N	136.46 E
Takahama, Nihon	96	35.29 N	135.33 E
Takahara ≃	94	36.28 N	137.15 E
Takahashi	96	34.47 N	133.37 E
Takahashi ≃	96	34.31 N	133.42 E
Takahe, Mount ∧	9	76.16 S	112.14 W
Takaido ◆[8]	268	35.40 N	139.37 E
Takaishi	96	34.32 N	135.26 E
Takaka	172	40.51 S	172.48 E
Takakkaw Falls ∟	182	51.30 N	116.28 W
Takalaou	146	10.07 N	19.48 E
Takalar	112	5.28 S	119.24 E

Takamatsu, Nihon	94	36.46 N	136.43 E
Takamatsu, Nihon	96	34.20 N	134.03 E
Takami-shima I	96	34.19 N	133.41 E
Takamiya	96	34.47 N	132.44 E
Takami-yama ∧	94	34.25 N	136.05 E
Takamori	94	35.33 N	137.53 E
Takanabe	92	32.08 N	131.30 E
Takanawa-hantō ›[1]	96	33.58 N	132.56 E
Takanawa-san ∧	96	33.56 N	132.51 E
Takane, Nihon	94	36.02 N	137.29 E
Takane, Nihon	94	35.50 N	138.25 E
Takanezawa	94	36.37 N	139.59 E
Takano	96	35.02 N	132.55 E
Takanosu	92	40.13 N	140.22 E
Takao → Kaohsiung	100	22.38 N	120.17 E
Takaoka	94	36.45 N	137.01 E
Takao-kokutei-kōen ♠	94	35.38 N	139.15 E
Takao-san ∧, Nihon	94	35.38 N	139.15 E
Takao-san ∧, Nihon	270	34.49 N	135.51 E
Takapau	172	40.02 S	176.21 E
Takapuna	172	36.47 S	174.47 E
Takara-jima I	93b	29.09 N	129.13 E
Takarazuka	270	34.49 N	135.21 E
Takasago	96	34.45 N	134.48 E
Takasaki	94	36.20 N	139.01 E
Takase	96	34.10 N	133.45 E
Takase ≃	94	36.28 N	137.52 E
Takashima, Nihon	92	32.39 N	129.45 E
Takashima, Nihon	94	35.18 N	136.01 E
Taka-shima I	96	34.50 N	131.50 E
Takashippu	174m	26.24 N	127.44 E
Takasu	94	35.57 N	136.53 E
Takata → Rikuzen-takata	92	39.01 N	141.38 E
Takata → Joetsu	94	37.06 N	138.15 E
Takata	96	33.06 N	130.28 E
Takatō	94	35.50 N	138.04 E
Takatomi	94	35.29 N	136.47 E
Takatori	96	34.27 N	135.48 E
Takatori-yama ∧	96	33.18 N	130.43 E
Takatori-yama ∧[2]	268	35.18 N	139.37 E
Takatsu ≃	96	34.42 N	131.49 E
Takatsuki, Nihon	94	35.28 N	136.14 E
Takatsuki, Nihon	96	34.51 N	135.37 E
Takaungu	154	3.41 S	39.51 E
Ta-kaw	110	21.36 N	98.56 E
Takayama, Nihon	94	36.08 N	137.15 E
Takayama, Nihon	94	36.37 N	138.57 E
Takayama, Nihon	94	36.40 N	138.21 E
Takayama, Nihon	270	34.45 N	135.44 E
Takayanagi, Nihon	94	37.13 N	138.38 E
Takayanagi, Nihon	268	35.25 N	139.57 E
Tak Bai	114	6.16 N	102.03 E
Takčijan	85	38.32 N	68.03 E
Takebe	96	34.52 N	133.54 E
Takefu	94	35.54 N	136.10 E
Takehara	96	34.21 N	132.55 E
Takela	120	37.54 N	76.44 E
Takeli	85	40.30 N	69.25 E
Takenake	120	34.11 N	81.20 E
Takeno ≃	96	35.45 N	135.06 E
Takenotsuka ◆[8]	268	35.48 N	139.48 E
Takeo	92	33.12 N	130.01 E
Takeoka	268	35.12 N	139.51 E
Tåkern ⊜	26	58.21 N	14.48 E
Takeshi	94	36.17 N	138.14 E
Take-shima I	93b	30.49 N	130.26 E
Take-shima (Tok-to) II	92	37.17 N	131.53 E
Tākestān	128	36.04 N	49.43 E
Taketa	96	32.58 N	131.24 E
Taketoyo	94	34.51 N	136.55 E
Takêv	110	10.59 N	104.47 E
Take-yama ∧[2]	268	35.13 N	139.39 E
Takhādīd ⍑[4]	128	29.59 N	44.30 E
Takhār □[4]	120	36.30 N	69.30 E
Takhatpur	124	22.09 N	81.52 E
Ta Khli	110	15.15 N	100.21 E
Ta-khoa	110	21.13 N	104.18 E
Takht-e Jamshīd ⊥	128	29.57 N	52.52 E
Takht-i-Bhāi	123	34.17 N	71.56 E
Tāki, India	126	22.36 N	88.55 E
Taki, Nihon	94	34.30 N	136.33 E
Taki, Nihon	96	35.16 N	132.38 E
Taki, Pap. N. Gui.	175e	6.29 S	155.50 E
Takijuk Lake ⊜	176	66.15 N	113.05 W
Takikawa	92a	43.33 N	141.54 E
Takingeun	114	4.38 N	96.50 E
Takino	96	34.56 N	134.58 E
Takipur	126	24.19 N	87.58 E
Takitimu Mountains ⋏	172	45.41 S	167.53 E
Takla Lake ⊜	182	55.25 N	125.53 W
Takla Landing	182	55.29 N	125.58 W
Takla Makan → Taklimakan Shamo ◆[2]	90	39.00 N	83.00 E
Taklimakan Shamo ◆[2]	90	39.00 N	83.00 E
Tako	94	35.44 N	140.28 E
Takob	85	38.50 N	68.57 E
Tako-bana ›	96	35.36 N	133.06 E
Takolekaju, Pegunungan ⋏	112	2.00 S	121.00 E
Takoma Park	284c	38.58 N	77.00 W
Takoradi → Sekondi-Takoradi	150	4.59 N	1.43 W
Takotna	180	62.56 N	156.04 W
Takow → Kaohsiung	100	22.38 N	120.17 E
Takpochao, Okso ∧	174n	15.11 N	145.45 E
Takrouna	36	36.09 N	10.20 E
Taksino	82	56.19 N	36.10 E
Takslesluk Lake ⊜	180	61.04 N	162.55 W
Taksony	264c	47.20 N	19.04 E
Taku	92	33.17 N	130.08 E
Taku ≃	180	58.26 N	133.59 W
Takuan, Mount ∧	175e	6.27 S	155.36 E
Takua Pa	110	8.53 N	98.21 E
Taku Glacier ⍓	180	58.35 N	134.10 W
Takum	150	7.17 N	9.59 E
Takuma	96	34.13 N	133.40 E
Takundi	152	4.45 S	16.34 E
Takutea I	14	19.49 S	158.18 W
Takut Tangug Bay ⊂	116	6.33 N	122.15 E
Takutu (Tacutu) ≃	246	3.01 N	60.29 W
Takysie Lake	182	53.54 N	125.53 W
Tāl	123	34.55 N	72.13 E
Tala, Bngl.	126	22.46 N	89.16 E
Tāla, India	124	23.43 N	81.02 E
Tala, Méx.	234	20.40 N	103.42 W
Talā, Miṣr	142	30.41 N	30.56 E
Tala, Ur.	252	34.21 S	55.46 W
Tala, Arroyo del ≃	258	33.37 S	56.34 W
Talacogon	116	8.28 N	125.46 E
Talaga	112	2.11 S	125.53 E
Talagang	123	32.55 N	72.25 E
Talagante	252	33.40 S	70.56 W
Talagou	104	41.37 N	120.32 E
Talaimannar	122	9.05 N	79.44 E
Talāja	120	21.21 N	72.03 E
Talak ◆[1]	150	18.20 N	6.00 E
Talakag	116	8.16 N	124.37 E
Talakan	89	49.38 N	133.18 E
Talakovka	83	47.10 N	37.43 E
Tālāla	120	21.02 N	70.32 E
Talalajevka	78	50.51 N	33.08 E
Talamanca, Cordillera de ⋏	236	9.30 N	83.40 W
Talamba	123	30.32 N	72.14 E
Talamone	66	42.33 N	11.08 E
Talana, It.	71	40.02 N	9.30 E
Talana, S. Afr.	158	28.10 S	30.15 E
Talandža	89	49.27 N	131.35 E
Talang, Gunung ∧	112	1.11 S	100.43 E
Talangbatu	112	4.06 S	105.29 E
Talangbetutu	112	2.53 S	104.41 E
Talangpadang	112	5.21 S	104.11 E
Talangrimbo	112	3.29 S	105.25 E
Talant	58	47.19 N	5.00 E
Talap	80	48.26 N	48.03 E
Talara	246	4.34 S	81.17 W

Talarrubias	34	39.02 N	5.14 W
Talas	85	42.32 N	72.14 E
Talas ≃	85	44.02 N	69.37 E
Talasea	164	5.20 S	150.05 E
Talasskij-Alatau, chrebet ⋏	85	42.10 N	72.00 E
Talatakoh, Pulau I	112	0.22 S	122.05 E
Tal'at al-Jamā'ah, Rujm ∧	132	30.23 N	35.30 E
Talata Mafara	150	12.35 N	6.04 E
Talaud, Kepulauan II	108	4.20 N	126.50 E
Talavera	116	15.35 N	120.55 E
Talavera de la Reina	34	39.57 N	4.50 W
Talawanta	166	18.38 S	140.16 E
Talawdī	140	10.38 N	30.23 E
Talayan	116	6.55 N	124.24 E
Tālbāndh	126	22.03 N	86.20 E
Talbingo	171b	35.34 S	148.18 E
Talbingo Reservoir ⊜[1]	171b	35.43 S	148.20 E
Talbot	169	37.11 S	143.43 E
Talbot ≃	212	44.28 N	79.10 W
Talbot, Cape ›	164	13.48 S	126.43 E
Talbot Brook	168a	32.01 S	116.40 E
Talbot Brook ≃	168a	32.10 S	116.49 E
Talbot Islands II	164	9.15 S	142.08 E
Talbot Lake ⊜, Mb., Can.	184	54.00 N	99.55 W
Talbot Lake ⊜, On., Can.	212	44.42 N	78.51 W
Talbotton	192	32.40 N	84.32 W
Talbotville Royal	214	42.48 N	81.15 W
Talbragar ≃	166	32.12 S	148.37 E
Talca	252	35.26 S	71.40 W
Talcahuano	252	36.43 S	73.07 W
Tālcher	120	20.57 N	85.13 E
Talco	196	33.21 N	95.06 W
Talcottville	207	41.49 N	72.30 W
Talcy, Château de ⊥	50	47.46 N	1.27 E
Taldan	89	53.40 N	124.48 E
Tāldāngra	126	23.02 N	87.06 E
Taldom	82	56.44 N	37.32 E
Taldyapan, S.S.S.R.	80	48.07 N	47.08 E
Taldyapan, S.S.S.R.	80	49.46 N	50.14 E
Taldyk, pereval)(	85	39.47 N	73.11 E
Taldykuduk	80	50.09 N	49.33 E
Taldy-Kurgan	86	45.00 N	78.23 E
Taldy-Kurgan Oblast' □[4]	85	44.00 N	78.00 E
Tale	150	9.26 N	1.07 W
Taleex	144	9.09 N	48.26 E
Tal-e Khosravī	128	30.37 N	51.35 E
Talence	32	44.49 N	0.35 W
Talent	202	42.14 N	122.47 W
Taley	152	6.40 N	16.23 E
Talgar	85	43.18 N	77.18 E
Talgar, pik ∧	85	43.05 N	77.20 E
Talgarreg	42	52.08 N	4.18 W
Talgarth	42	52.00 N	3.15 W
Ṭalḥ, 'Ilw aṭ- ∧[2]	142	28.30 N	29.38 E
Talhār	120	24.53 N	68.49 E
Tali, Pointe de ›	241o	15.56 N	61.12 W
Talia, Austl.	162	33.19 S	134.54 E
Talia, Méx.	196	25.44 N	102.26 W
Taliabu, Pulau I	112	1.48 S	124.48 E
Talian Dao I	98	39.03 N	122.52 E
Talibon	116	10.09 N	124.19 E
Talibong, Ko I	110	7.15 N	99.23 E
Talica, S.S.S.R.	76	58.44 N	41.34 E
Talica, S.S.S.R.	80	58.01 N	51.30 E
Talica, S.S.S.R.	86	57.00 N	63.43 E
Talickij Čamlyk	80	52.02 N	40.32 E
Talien → Lüda	98	38.53 N	121.35 E
Talihina	196	34.45 N	95.02 W
Tālīkota	122	16.29 N	76.19 E
Talikud Island I	116	6.56 N	125.42 E
Talim Island I	116	14.21 N	121.14 E
Talimuashili	85	39.08 N	77.03 E
Taling Chan	269a	13.46 N	100.27 E
Taliouine	148	30.36 N	7.49 W
Taliparamba	122	12.03 N	75.21 E
Tali Post	140	5.54 N	30.47 E
Talisay, Pil.	116	14.08 N	122.55 E
Talisay, Pil.	116	10.44 N	122.58 E
Talisayan	116	9.00 N	124.55 E
Talisei, Pulau I	112	1.51 N	125.05 E
Talish-Mikeyli	84	39.23 N	48.22 E
Talish Mountains (Kūhhā-ye Ṭavālesh ⋏	128	38.42 N	48.18 E
Talisker	46	57.17 N	6.27 W
Taliwang	115b	8.44 S	116.52 E
Tal'ka	76	53.22 N	28.21 E
Talkeetna	180	62.20 N	150.07 W
Talkeetna Mountains ⋏	180	62.10 N	148.15 W
Ṭalkhā	142	31.03 N	31.22 E
Talkheh ≃	128	37.40 N	45.46 E
Tālkot	124	29.37 N	81.19 E
Talladale	46	57.42 N	5.29 W
Talladega	194	33.26 N	86.06 W
Tall 'Afar	128	36.22 N	42.27 E
Tallaght	48	53.26 N	6.21 W
Tal Lah, India	126	22.19 N	87.18 E
Tallah, Miṣr	142	28.05 N	30.44 E
Tallahaga Creek ≃	194	32.55 N	88.58 W
Tallahala Creek ≃	194	31.12 N	89.05 W
Tallahassee	192	30.26 N	84.16 W
Tallahatchie ≃	194	33.33 N	90.10 W
Tall al-Abyaḍ	130	36.41 N	38.57 E
Tall al-'Amārnah (Akhetatem) ⊥	142	27.38 N	30.54 E
Tall al-Maskhūtah (Succotah) ⊥	142	30.33 N	32.07 E
Tallanalla	168a	33.06 S	116.07 E
Tallangatta	166	36.13 S	147.15 E
Tallangatta Creek ≃	171b	36.15 S	147.13 E
Tallapoosa	194	33.44 N	85.17 W
Tallapoosa ≃	194	32.30 N	86.16 W
Tallard	62	44.28 N	6.03 E
Talla Reservoir ⊜[1]	46	55.29 N	3.24 W
Tallarook, Mount ∧	169	37.22 S	145.19 E
Tall ar-Ratābah (Pithom) ⊥	142	30.32 N	32.06 E
Tall ar-Rub' (Mendes) ⊥	142	30.58 N	31.31 E
Tallassee	194	32.32 N	85.53 W
Tall as-Sulṭān ⊥	132	31.52 N	35.27 E
Tall Banī 'Umrān	142	27.40 N	30.54 E
Tall Basṭah (Bubastis) ⊥	142	30.34 N	31.31 E
Tällberg	26	60.49 N	15.00 E
Tall Bīsah	130	34.50 N	36.44 E
Talleyville	208	39.48 N	75.32 W
Tallinn	76	59.25 N	24.45 E
Tall Kalakh	130	34.40 N	36.15 E
Tall Kayf	128	36.29 N	43.08 E
Tall Kūshik	130	36.48 N	42.04 E
Tallmadge	214	41.06 N	81.27 W
Tallman	276	41.07 N	74.06 W
Tallman Mountain State Park ♠	276	41.01 N	73.54 W
Talloires	62	45.51 N	6.13 E
Tallong	170	34.44 S	150.05 E
Tallow	48	52.05 N	8.00 W
Tall Rāk	142	30.54 N	31.43 E
Tall Rif'at	130	36.28 N	37.06 E
Tall Salḥab	130	35.15 N	36.22 E
Tall Tamir	130	36.39 N	40.22 E
Tallula	219	39.56 N	89.56 W
Tallulah	194	32.24 N	91.11 W
Tally	80	53.08 N	53.04 E
Tally Ho	274b	37.52 S	145.09 E
Tālma	126	23.29 N	89.54 E
Talmage, Ca., U.S.	204	39.08 N	123.10 W
Talmage, Ne., U.S.	198	40.31 N	96.01 W
Talmage, Pa., U.S.	208	40.07 N	76.13 W
Talmalmo	171b	35.56 S	147.30 E
Talmas	50	50.02 N	2.20 E
Talmazy	78	46.38 N	29.40 E
Tal'menka	86	53.51 N	83.35 E
Talmine	46	58.31 N	4.26 W
Talmont	32	46.28 N	1.37 W
Tal'niki	88	52.47 N	102.24 E
Tal'noje	78	48.53 N	30.42 E

Talo ∧	144	10.44 N	37.55 E
Taloda	120	21.34 N	74.13 E
Talofofo	174p	13.21 N	144.45 E
Talofofo Bay ⊂	174p	13.20 N	144.46 E
Taloga	196	36.02 N	98.57 W
Taloje	88	55.24 N	95.40 E
Taloje Budrukh	272c	19.05 N	73.05 E
Talok	112	1.03 N	118.48 E
Talon, Lake ⊜	190	46.18 N	79.05 W
Talonan, Tano ›	115b	9.07 S	117.02 E
Tāloqān	120	36.44 N	69.33 E
Taloro ≃	71	40.08 N	8.58 E
Talovaja	78	51.06 N	40.44 E
Talovka, S.S.S.R.	80	49.58 N	45.01 E
Talovka, S.S.S.R.	80	50.25 N	47.35 E
Talovka, S.S.S.R.	84	44.14 N	46.36 E
Talovka, S.S.S.R.	86	51.27 N	81.54 E
Talovka, S.S.S.R.	86	57.10 N	93.09 E
Talovoje	83	48.18 N	39.40 E
Talpa	196	31.47 N	99.43 W
Talpa de Allende	234	20.23 N	104.51 W
Talquin, Lake ⊜[1]	192	30.26 N	84.33 W
Tālsa	272b	22.49 N	88.33 E
Talsarnau	42	52.54 N	4.03 W
Talsi	76	57.15 N	22.36 E
Talšik	86	53.42 N	71.53 E
Taltal	252	25.24 S	70.29 W
Taltapin Lake ⊜	182	54.19 N	125.20 W
Taltson ≃	176	61.23 N	112.45 W
Talu	112	0.14 N	99.59 E
Taludaa	112	0.20 N	123.28 E
Taluk	112	0.32 S	101.35 E
Talumphuk, Laem ›	110	8.30 N	100.10 E
Taluti, Teluk ⊂	164	3.21 S	129.45 E
Talvik'ul'a	24	68.45 N	29.19 E
Talwandi Bhāi	123	30.51 N	74.56 E
Talwood	166	28.30 S	149.30 E
Taly	78	49.51 N	40.04 E
Ṭalyā	142	30.16 N	31.00 E
Talybont	42	52.29 N	3.59 W
Tama, Arg.	252	30.31 S	66.32 W
Tama, Nihon	94	35.37 N	139.27 E
Tama, Ia., U.S.	190	41.58 N	92.34 W
Tama ≃	94	35.32 N	139.47 E
Tama Cemetery ◆	268	35.41 N	139.31 E
Tamacuarí, Pico ∧	246	1.15 N	64.45 W
Tamadjert	148	25.36 N	7.20 E
Tamagawa, Nihon	94	37.12 N	140.24 E
Tamagawa, Nihon	96	34.01 N	132.56 E
Tamagawa ◆[8]	268	35.37 N	139.39 E
Tamagawa-josui ≃	268	35.42 N	139.35 E
Tamakautonga	174v	19.05 S	169.55 W
Tamaki	94	34.29 N	136.38 E
Tama-kyūryō ⋏[2]	268	35.35 N	139.30 E
Tamala, Austl.	162	26.42 S	113.45 E
Tamala, S.S.S.R.	80	52.33 N	43.16 E
Tamalameque	246	8.52 N	73.49 W
Ṭamalāy	142	30.30 N	30.51 E
Tamale	150	9.25 N	0.50 W
Tamalea	112	2.29 S	119.19 E
Tamalpais, Mount ∧	226	37.56 N	122.35 W
Tamalpais Valley	226	37.53 N	122.32 W
Tamamura	94	36.18 N	139.07 E
Taman, Indon.	115a	7.25 S	112.41 E
Taman', S.S.S.R.	78	45.13 N	36.43 E
Tamana	92	32.55 N	130.33 E
Tamana I	14	2.29 S	175.59 E
Tamaná, Cerro ∧	246	5.02 N	76.17 W
Tamana, Mount ∧[2]	241r	10.28 N	61.12 W
Tamanaco ≃	246	9.25 N	65.23 W
Tamanan	115a	8.01 S	113.49 E
Tamanar	148	31.00 N	9.35 W
Tamandaré	250	8.45 S	35.06 W
Tamandourirt, Oued V	150	19.39 N	2.04 W
Tamanduatei ≃	287b	23.36 S	46.35 W
Tamanhint	146	27.13 N	14.36 E
Tamani	150	13.20 N	6.50 W
Tamaniquá	246	2.38 S	65.44 W
Taman Negara ♠	114	4.43 N	102.23 E
Tamano	96	34.30 N	133.56 E
Tamanskij zaliv ⊂	78	45.18 N	36.45 E
Tamanthi	110	25.19 N	95.18 E
Tamanusi	112	1.48 S	121.18 E
Tamapatz	234	21.35 N	99.09 W
Tamaqua	208	40.47 N	75.58 W
Tamaquari, Ilha I	246	0.28 S	64.55 W
Tamar ≃, Austl.	166	41.04 S	146.47 E
Tamar ≃, Eng., U.K.	42	50.22 N	4.10 W
Támara	246	5.50 N	72.10 W
Tamarac ≃	198	48.29 N	97.07 W
Tamarack Lake ⊜[1]	214	41.35 N	80.05 W
Tamarite de Litera	34	41.52 N	0.26 E
Tamaroa	194	38.08 N	89.14 W
Tamarome	164	2.54 S	133.38 E
Tamarugal, Pampa del ≃	248	21.00 S	69.25 W
Tamashima	96	34.32 N	133.40 E
Tamási	30	46.38 N	18.18 E
Tamaské	150	14.49 N	5.39 E
Tamatsukuri	94	36.06 N	140.25 E
Tamaulipas □[3]	232	24.00 N	98.45 W
Tamaya ≃	248	8.31 S	74.13 W
Tamayu	96	35.25 N	133.01 E
Tama Zoological Park ♠	268	35.39 N	139.24 E
Tamazula	232	24.57 N	106.57 W
Tamazula de Gordiano	234	19.38 N	103.15 W
Tamazulapan [del Progreso]	234	17.41 N	97.34 W
Tamazunchale	234	21.16 N	98.47 W
Tamba	96	35.09 N	135.25 E
Tambach-Dietharz	54	50.48 N	10.36 E
Tambacounda	150	13.47 N	13.40 W
Tamba Dabatou	150	11.48 N	10.40 W
Tambak	115a	5.45 S	112.37 E
Tambakboyo	115a	6.48 S	111.50 E
Tamba-kōchi ⋏	270	34.58 N	135.25 E
Tamba-kōchi ⋏[1], Nihon	92	35.20 N	135.30 E
Tambakrejo	115a	7.16 S	111.36 E
Tambalan	112	3.08 N	115.34 E
Tambangsawah	112	3.02 S	102.11 E
Tambara, Moç.	154	16.45 S	34.15 E
Tambara, Nihon	96	33.54 N	133.04 E
Tāmbaram	122	12.55 N	80.07 E
Tambaú ≃	256	21.34 S	47.05 W
Tambault, Île à I	275a	45.20 N	73.51 W
També	250	7.25 S	35.06 W
Tambea	112	4.12 S	121.36 E
Tambej	74	71.30 N	71.50 E
Tambelan, Kepulauan II	112	1.00 N	107.30 E
Tambelan Besar, Pulau I	112	0.58 N	107.34 E
Tambellup	162	34.02 S	117.39 E
Tamberías	252	31.28 S	69.25 W
Tambisan, Pulau I	116	5.27 N	119.10 E
Tambler	116	6.03 N	125.09 E
Tambo, Austl.	166	24.53 S	146.15 E
Tambo, Perú	248	12.56 S	74.01 W
Tambo ≃, Austl.	166	37.51 S	147.48 E
Tambo ≃, Perú	248	17.10 S	71.51 W
Tambo ≃, Perú	248	10.43 S	73.45 W
Tamboara	255	23.09 S	52.33 W
Tambo Grande	248	4.56 S	80.21 W
Tambohorano	157b	17.30 S	43.58 E
Tamboli	112	3.57 S	121.20 E
Tambolongang, Pulau I	112	6.36 S	120.24 E
Tambopata ≃	248	12.36 S	69.11 W
Tambor	236	9.43 N	85.01 W
Tambora, Gunung ∧	115b	8.14 S	117.55 E
Tamboril	250	4.50 S	40.20 W
Tamborine	171a	27.53 S	153.08 E
Tamborine Mountain ∧[2]	171a	27.55 S	153.10 E
Tamboritha, Mount ∧	166	37.28 S	146.41 E
Tambov	80	52.43 N	41.25 E
Tambov □[4]	78	51.45 N	41.20 E
Tambovka, S.S.S.R.	80	47.18 N	47.23 E
Tambovka, S.S.S.R.	89	50.06 N	128.04 E
Tambo Yacu ≃	246	2.31 S	73.40 W
Tambre ≃	34	42.49 N	8.53 W

≃ River	Fluss	Río	Rivière	Rio
≊ Canal	Kanal	Canal	Canal	Canal
∟ Waterfall, Rapids	Wasserfall, Stromschnellen	Cascada, Rápidos	Chute d'eau, Rapides	Cascata, Rápidos
⋓ Strait	Meeresstrasse	Estrecho	Détroit	Estreito
⊂ Bay, Gulf	Bucht, Golf	Bahía, Golfo	Baie, Golfe	Baía, Golfo
⊜ Lake, Lakes	See, Seen	Lago, Lagos	Lac, Lacs	Lago, Lagos
☷ Swamp	Sumpf	Pantano	Marais	Pântano
⍓ Ice Features, Glacier	Eis- und Gletscherformen	Accidentes Glaciales	Formes glaciaires	Acidentes glaciares
⍑ Other Hydrographic Features	Andere Hydrographische Objekte	Otros Elementos Hidrográficos	Autres données hydrographiques	Outros acidentes hidrográficos

✦ Submarine Features	Untermeerische Objekte	Accidentes Submarinos	Formes de relief sous-marin	Acidentes submarinos
□ Political Unit	Politische Einheit	Unidad Politica	Entité politique	Unidade política
⊻ Cultural Institution	Kulturelle Institution	Institución Cultural	Institution culturelle	Instituição cultural
⊥ Historical Site	Historische Stätte	Sitio Histórico	Site historique	Sitio histórico
♠ Recreational Site	Erholungs- und Ferienort	Sitio de Recreo	Centre de loisirs	Area de Lazer
⊠ Airport	Flughafen	Aeropuerto	Aéroport	Aeroporto
■ Military Installation	Militäranlage	Instalación Militar	Installation militaire	Instalação militar
◆ Miscellaneous	Verschiedenes	Misceláneo	Divers	Diversos

ENGLISH — DEUTSCH

Symbols in the index entries represent the broad categories identified in the key at the right. Symbols with superior numbers (⋏[1]) identify subcategories (see complete key on page *I · 1).*

Kartensymbole in dem Registerverzeichnis stellen die rechts in Schlüssel erklärten Kategorien dar. Symbole mit hochgestellten Ziffern (⋏[1]) bezeichnen Unterabteilungen einer Kategorie (vgl. vollständiger Schlüssel auf Seite *I · 1).*

Los símbolos incluídos en el texto del índice representan las grandes categorias identificadas con la clave a la derecha. Los símbolos con numeros en su parte superior (⋏[1]) identifican las subcategorías (véase la clave completa en la página *I · 1).*

Les symboles de l'index représentent les catégories indiquées dans la légende à droite. Les symboles suivis d'un indice (⋏[1]) représentent des sous-catégories (voir légende complète à la page *I · 1).*

Os símbolos incluídos no texto do índice representam as grandes categorias identificadas com a chave à direita. Os símbolos com números em sua parte superior (⋏[1]) identificam as subcategorias (veja-se a chave completa à página *I · 1).*

English	Deutsch	Español	Français	Português
∧ Mountain	Berg	Montaña	Montagne	Montanha
⋏ Mountains	Berge	Montañas	Montagnes	Montanhas
)(Pass	Pass	Paso	Col	Passo
V Valley, Canyon	Tal, Cañon	Valle, Cañón	Vallée, Canyon	Vale, Canhão
≚ Plain	Ebene	Llano	Plaine	Planície
› Cape	Kap	Cabo	Cap	Cabo
I Island	Insel	Isla	Île	Ilha
II Islands	Inseln	Islas	Îles	Ilhas
± Other Topographic Features	Andere Topographische Objekte	Otros Elementos Topográficos	Autres données topographiques	Outros acidentes topográficos

ESPAÑOL: Nombre · Página · Lat.°′ · Long.°′ W = Oeste
FRANÇAIS: Nom · Page · Lat.°′ · Long.°′ W = Ouest
PORTUGUÊS: Nome · Página · Lat.°′ · Long.°′ W = Oeste

Nombre / Nom / Nome	Página / Page	Lat.°′	Long.°′
Tashi Gang Dzong	120	27.19 N	91.34 E
Tashikuergan	120	37.49 N	75.14 E
Tashimalike	85	39.06 N	75.41 E
Tashiyi	100	29.43 N	112.48 E
Ṭashk, Daryācheh-ye ⊜	128	29.45 N	53.35 E
Tashkent → Taškent	85	41.20 N	69.18 E
Tāshkurghān → Kholm	120	36.42 N	67.41 E
Tashuik'u	269d	25.13 N	121.30 E
Tasikmalaya	115a	7.20 S	108.12 E
Tasīl	132	32.50 N	35.58 E
Tåsinge I	41	55.00 N	10.36 E
Taširovo	82	55.25 N	36.39 E
Tasitan	85	39.17 N	76.07 E
Tåsjö	26	64.13 N	15.54 E
Tåsjön ⊜	26	64.15 N	15.47 E
Taskajevo	86	55.06 N	78.36 E
Taškent	85	41.20 N	69.18 E
Taškent □[4]	85	41.00 N	69.30 E
Taškepri	128	36.18 N	62.38 E
Taşkesen	130	39.43 N	41.29 E
Taskesken	86	47.15 N	80.44 E
Taşköprü	130	41.30 N	34.14 E
Taskul	164	2.35 S	150.25 E
Taš-Kumyr	85	41.21 N	72.14 E
Taškyja	85	40.16 N	74.19 E
Tašla	80	51.47 N	52.46 E
Tasman, Mount ʌ	172	43.34 S	170.09 E
Tasman Basin ✢[1]	6	43.00 S	158.00 E
Tasman Bay c	172	41.00 S	173.20 E
Tasmania □[3]	166	43.00 S	147.00 E
Tasmania I	166	42.00 S	147.00 E
Tasmanien → Tasmania I	166	42.00 S	147.00 E
Tasman Mountains ⋏	172	41.07 S	172.33 E
Tasman Peninsula ≻[1]	166	43.05 S	147.50 E
Tasman Sea ⫪[2]	14	40.00 S	163.00 E
T'asmin ≏	78	49.05 N	32.48 E
Tăşnad	38	47.29 N	22.35 E
Tasoba	80	49.47 N	49.52 E
Taşova	130	40.46 N	36.20 E
Tasrār Sharīf	123	33.52 N	74.46 E
Taşrumi	84	38.48 N	44.04 E
Tassajara Creek ≏	282	37.41 N	121.53 W
Tassara	150	16.48 N	5.39 E
Tassdorf	264a	52.30 N	13.47 E
Tassialouc, Lac ⊜	176	59.03 N	74.00 W
Tassin-la-Demi-Lune	62	45.46 N	4.47 E
Tasso Lake ⊜	212	45.27 N	78.56 W
Tassu, Serra di lu ʌ	71	41.01 N	9.08 E
Taštagol	86	52.47 N	87.53 E
Tastiota	232	28.22 N	111.23 W
Tåstrup	41	55.39 N	12.19 E
Taštyp	86	52.48 N	89.54 E
Tasucu	130	36.19 N	33.53 E
Tasutkol'skoje vodochranilišče ⊜[1]	85	43.22 N	74.00 E
Tata, Magreb	148	29.44 N	7.56 W
Tata, Magy.	30	47.39 N	18.18 E
Tata □[4]	148	29.40 N	7.45 W
T'at'a, vulkan ʌ[1]	92a	44.21 N	146.15 E
Tataa, Pointe ≻	174s	17.34 S	149.37 W
Tatabánya	30	47.34 N	18.26 E
Tatahuicapan	234	18.14 N	94.45 W
Tatal	80	47.17 N	46.16 E
Tatalin ≏	102	37.30 N	95.28 E
Tatamy	208	40.44 N	75.15 W
Tataouine	148	32.56 N	10.27 E
Tata Raphael, Camp ■	273b	4.18 S	15.17 E
Tatarbunary	78	45.49 N	29.36 E
Tatarinka	76	55.58 N	33.54 E
Tatarino	78	50.36 N	39.07 E
Tatarinovo, S.S.S.R.	82	55.13 N	37.56 E
Tatarinovo, S.S.S.R.	82	56.34 N	38.25 E
Tatarischer Sund → Tatarskij proliv Ա	89	50.00 N	141.15 E
Tatarka, S.S.S.R.	76	53.16 N	28.48 E
Tatarka, S.S.S.R.	86	53.58 N	75.05 E
Tatarlar	130	41.46 N	26.55 E
Tatarovo ◆[8]	265b	55.46 N	37.26 E
Tātārpur ◆[8]	272a	28.39 N	77.07 E
Tatarsk	86	55.13 N	75.58 E
Tatarskaja Avtonomnaja Sovetskaja Socialističeskaja Respublika □[3]	80	55.00 N	51.00 E
Tatarskij Kandyz	80	54.07 N	53.07 E
Tatarskij proliv (Tatar Strait) Ա	89	50.00 N	141.15 E
Tatarskij Sajman	80	53.18 N	47.07 E
Tatarskoje-Maklakovo	80	55.48 N	45.34 E
Tatar Strait → Tatarskij proliv Ա	89	50.00 N	141.15 E
Tatau ≏	112	3.07 N	112.49 E
Tatau Island I	164	2.50 S	152.00 E
Tataurovo, S.S.S.R.	76	58.44 N	43.20 E
Tataurovo, S.S.S.R.	80	57.48 N	49.34 E
Tataurovo, S.S.S.R.	88	51.37 N	112.56 E
Tate	192	34.25 N	84.22 W
Tate ≏	166	17.22 S	143.44 E
Tatebayashi	94	36.15 N	139.32 E
Tate Gallery ʋ	260	51.29 N	0.08 W
Tateishi-misaki ≻	94	35.46 N	136.01 E
Tateiwa	94	37.05 N	139.32 E
Tateiwa-chosuichi ⊜[1]	96	34.33 N	132.10 E
Tatelang	120	38.28 N	85.35 E
Tateshina	94	36.16 N	138.19 E
Tateyama, Nihon	94	34.59 N	139.52 E
Tateyama, Nihon	94	36.40 N	137.19 E
Tate-yama ʌ	94	36.35 N	137.37 E
Tathlina Lake ⊜	176	60.32 N	117.32 W
Tathlīth, Wādī V	144	20.44 N	44.17 E
Tathong Point ≻	271d	22.14 N	114.17 E
Tathra	166	36.44 S	149.59 E
Tatikawa → Tachikawa	94	35.42 N	139.25 E
Tatiščevo, S.S.S.R.	80	51.40 N	45.35 E
Tatiščevo, S.S.S.R.	82	56.24 N	37.31 E
Tatitlek	180	60.52 N	146.41 W
Tatla Lake	182	51.55 N	124.36 W
Tatla Lake ⊜	182	52.00 N	124.25 W
Tatlayoko Lake	182	51.39 N	124.24 W
Tatlayoko Lake ⊜	182	51.30 N	124.25 W
Tatlow, Mount ʌ	182	51.23 N	123.52 W
Tatnam, Cape ≻	176	57.16 N	91.00 W
Tatomi	94	35.36 N	138.31 E
Tatoosh Island I	224	48.24 N	124.44 W
Tatos Dağları ⋏	130	40.44 N	41.00 E
Tatranský národní park ♠	30	49.10 N	20.05 E
Tatrzański Park Narodowy ♠	30	49.15 N	20.00 E
Tatsfield	260	51.18 N	0.02 E
Tatsuno, Nihon	94	35.59 N	137.59 E
Tatsuno, Nihon	96	34.52 N	134.33 E
Tatsunokuchi	94	36.27 N	136.35 E
Tatsuruhama	94	37.04 N	136.53 E
Tatsuyama	94	34.58 N	137.49 E
Tatta	120	24.45 N	67.55 E
Tattenhall	44	53.06 N	2.46 W
Tatton Hall ⊥	262	53.20 N	2.23 W
Tatton Mere ⊜	262	53.19 N	2.22 W
Tatton Park ♠	262	53.20 N	2.22 W
Tatty	85	43.12 N	73.19 E
Tatu ≏	100	24.12 N	120.29 E
Tatuapé ◆[8]	287b	23.32 S	46.34 W
Tatuk Lake ⊜	182	53.32 N	124.15 W
Tatum, N.M., U.S.	196	33.15 N	103.19 W
Tatum, Tx., U.S.	222	32.19 N	94.31 W
Tat'ung → Datong	102	40.05 N	113.18 E
Tat'un Shan ʌ	269d	25.11 N	121.31 E
Tatvan	130	38.30 N	42.16 E
Tatzuli ≏	100	24.08 N	121.39 E
Tau, Am. Sam.	174w	14.14 S	169.32 W
Tau, Nor.	26	59.04 N	5.54 E
Tau, S.S.S.R.	80	49.40 N	47.17 E
Tau I	174w	14.15 S	169.30 W
Tauá	250	6.01 S	40.26 W
Taualap Pass Ա	175c	7.28 N	151.36 E
Tauari	250	1.07 S	47.04 W
Taubaté	256	23.02 S	45.33 W
Tauber ≏	56	49.46 N	9.31 E
Tauberbischofsheim	56	49.37 N	9.40 E
Taucha	54	51.23 N	12.30 E
Taučik	72	44.21 N	51.19 E
Tauern-Tunnel ◆[5]	64	47.05 N	13.05 E
Täuffelen	58	47.04 N	7.12 E
Taufkirchen	60	48.21 N	12.08 E
Taufstein ʌ	56	50.31 N	9.14 E
Taughannock Creek ≏	210	42.33 N	76.36 W
Taughannock Falls State Park ♠	210	42.32 N	76.35 W
Tauini ≏	246	0.30 N	58.22 W
Taujskaja guba c	74	59.20 N	150.20 E
Taukum ◆[2]	86	44.50 N	75.30 E
Taulabé	236	14.38 N	87.59 W
Taulihawa	124	27.32 N	83.03 E
Taulov	41	55.33 N	9.37 E
Taumarunui	172	38.52 S	175.17 E
Taumaturgo	248	8.57 S	72.48 W
Taum Sauk Mountain ʌ	194	37.34 N	90.44 W
Taunay	248	20.18 S	56.05 W
Taunay, Cascatinha ⌞	287a	22.57 S	43.17 W
Taung	158	27.33 S	24.47 E
Taungbon	110	15.25 N	97.50 E
Taungdwingyi	110	20.01 N	95.33 E
Taunggon	110	23.38 N	96.32 E
Taunggyi	110	20.47 N	97.02 E
Taungnyo Range ⋏	110	15.38 N	97.56 E
Taungup	110	18.51 N	94.14 E
Taungup Pass)(	110	18.40 N	94.45 E
Taunsa	123	30.42 N	70.39 E
Taunton, Eng., U.K.	42	51.01 N	3.06 W
Taunton, Ma., U.S.	207	41.54 N	71.05 W
Taunton, N.Y., U.S.	210	43.01 N	76.13 W
Taunton ≏	207	41.42 N	71.10 W
Taunton, Vale of V	42	51.02 N	3.08 W
Taunton Lake ⊜	285	39.51 N	74.51 W
Taunton Lakes	285	39.51 N	74.51 W
Taunus ⋏	56	50.10 N	8.15 E
Taunusstein	56	50.08 N	8.08 E
Taupiri	172	37.37 S	175.11 E
Tauplitz	61	47.33 N	14.00 E
Taupo	172	38.41 S	176.05 E
Taupo, Lake ⊜	172	38.49 S	175.55 E
Tauragė	76	55.15 N	22.17 E
Taurak	86	51.35 N	85.01 E
Tauranga	172	37.42 S	176.10 E
Taurasi	68	41.00 N	14.57 E
Taureau, Réservoir ⊜[1]	206	46.46 N	73.50 W
Tauri ≏	164	8.08 S	146.06 E
Taurianova	68	38.21 N	16.01 E
Tauripampa	248	12.35 S	76.07 W
Taurisano	68	39.57 N	18.13 E
Taurisma	248	15.10 S	72.51 W
Tauroa Point ≻	172	35.10 S	173.04 E
Taurovo	86	59.36 N	73.18 E
Taurus Mountains → Toros Dağları ⋏	130	37.00 N	33.00 E
Tauste	34	41.55 N	1.15 W
Tautira	174s	17.44 S	149.09 W
Tauu Islands II	14	4.45 S	157.00 E
Tauxigny	50	47.13 N	0.50 E
Tauz	84	41.00 N	45.38 E
Tavaí	252	26.07 S	55.32 W
Tavajvaam ≏	180	64.56 N	177.30 E
Tavajza	89	45.12 N	136.44 E
Ṭavālesh, Kūhhā-ye → Talish Mountains ⋏	128	38.42 N	48.18 E
Tavanasa	58	46.45 N	9.04 E
Tavannes	58	47.13 N	7.12 E
Tavant	50	47.07 N	0.23 E
Tavares, Bra.	250	7.38 S	37.54 W
Tavares, Fl., U.S.	220	28.48 N	81.43 W
Tavares, Ilha dos I	287a	22.49 S	43.06 W
Tavarnelle Val di Pesa	66	43.33 N	11.10 E
Tavas	130	37.34 N	29.04 E
Tavastehus → Hämeenlinna	26	61.00 N	24.27 E
Tavaux	58	47.02 N	5.24 E
Tavda	86	58.03 N	65.15 E
Tavda ≏	72	57.47 N	67.16 E
Tave ≏	62	44.07 N	4.42 E
Tavera ≏	64	46.29 N	11.21 E
Taverham	42	52.41 N	1.12 E
Taverna	68	39.01 N	16.35 E
Tavern Creek ≏	194	38.19 N	92.18 W
Tavernelle, It.	64	44.18 N	10.04 E
Tavernelle, It.	66	43.00 N	12.09 E
Tavernes	62	43.36 N	6.01 E
Tavernier	220	25.00 N	80.30 W
Tavernole sul Mella	64	45.45 N	10.14 E
Taverny	50	49.02 N	2.13 E
Taveta, Kenya	154	3.24 S	37.41 E
Taveta, Tan.	154	9.01 S	35.37 E
Taveuni I	175g	16.51 S	179.58 W
Taviano	68	39.59 N	18.05 E
Tavil'dara	85	38.43 N	70.28 E
Tavira	34	37.07 N	7.39 W
Tavistock, On., Can.	212	43.19 N	80.50 W
Tavistock, Eng., U.K.	42	50.33 N	4.08 W
Tavn-Gašun	80	46.01 N	45.55 E
Tavolara, Isola I	71	40.54 N	9.42 E
Tavoliere ◆[1]	68	41.35 N	15.25 E
Tavolžan	86	52.44 N	77.27 E
Tavor, Har (Mount Tabor) ʌ	132	32.41 N	35.23 E
Távora ≏	34	41.09 N	7.35 W
Tavoy	110	14.05 N	98.12 E
Tavoy Point ≻	110	13.32 N	98.10 E
Tavričanka	89	43.22 N	131.52 E
Tavričeskoje	86	54.35 N	73.38 E
Tavry	265a	59.55 N	30.42 E
Tavsalayihüseyan	130	38.38 N	40.32 E
Tavşanlı	130	39.33 N	29.30 E
Tavsi	130	37.56 N	38.39 E
Tavua	175g	17.27 S	177.51 E
Tavy ≏	42	50.16 N	4.10 W
Taw ≏	42	51.04 N	4.11 W
Tawa	172	41.10 S	174.51 E
Tawa ≏	124	22.48 N	77.48 E
Tawaeli	112	0.43 S	119.51 E
Tawakoni, Lake ⊜[1]	222	32.55 N	96.00 W
Tawar, Laut ⊜	114	4.38 N	96.54 E
Tawara	270	34.27 N	135.57 E
Tawarada	268	35.19 N	140.04 E
Tawaramoto	96	34.33 N	135.48 E
Tawas City	190	44.16 N	83.30 W
Tawau	112	4.15 N	117.54 E
Tawd ≏	262	53.36 N	2.48 W
Tawe ≏	42	51.37 N	3.55 W
Tāwi ≏	123	32.40 N	74.41 E
Ṭawīlah, Juzur II	140	27.35 N	33.46 E
Tawitawi □[4]	116	5.20 N	120.00 E
Tawitawi Group II	116	5.10 N	120.15 E
Tawitawi Island I	116	5.10 N	120.00 E
Ṭawkar	140	18.26 N	37.44 E
Tawu	100	22.22 N	120.54 E
Ṭāwūq	128	35.08 N	44.27 E
Tāwurghā'	146	32.02 N	15.09 E
Ṭawwah Banī Ibrāhīm	142	28.05 N	30.41 E
Taxco de Alarcón	234	18.33 N	99.36 W
Taxenbach	64	47.17 N	12.58 E
Taxi	89	49.26 N	126.08 E
Taxila	123	33.44 N	72.49 E
Taxisco	236	14.04 N	90.28 W
Taxusi	102	32.58 N	98.10 E
Tay ≏, On., Can.	212	44.53 N	76.07 W
Tay ≏, Yk., Can.	180	62.34 N	134.22 W
Tay ≏, Scot., U.K.	46	56.22 N	3.21 W
Tay, Firth of c[1]	46	56.26 N	3.00 W
Tay, Lake ⊜	162	32.55 S	120.48 E
Tay, Loch ⊜	46	56.31 N	4.10 W
Tayabamba	248	8.17 S	77.18 W
Tayabas	116	14.01 N	121.35 E
Tayabas Bay c	116	13.45 N	121.45 E
Tayan	112	0.02 S	110.07 E
Tayandu, Kepulauan II	164	5.30 S	132.15 E
Tayayi	105	39.25 N	115.03 E
Tayeegle	144	4.02 N	44.31 E
Taylor, B.C., Can.	182	56.10 N	120.41 W
Taylor, Az., U.S.	200	34.27 N	110.05 W
Taylor, Ar., U.S.	194	33.06 N	93.27 W
Taylor, Mi., U.S.	216	42.14 N	83.16 W
Taylor, Mo., U.S.	219	39.56 N	91.32 W
Taylor, Ne., U.S.	198	41.46 N	99.22 W
Taylor, Pa., U.S.	210	41.23 N	75.42 W
Taylor, Tx., U.S.	222	30.34 N	97.24 W
Taylor ≏	200	38.40 N	106.51 W
Taylor, Mount ʌ, N.Z.	172	43.30 S	171.19 E
Taylor, Mount ʌ, N.M., U.S.	200	35.14 N	107.37 W
Taylor Creek ≏, On., Can.	275b	43.42 N	79.20 W
Taylor Creek ≏, Il., U.S.	219	39.13 N	90.18 W
Taylor Lake Village	222	29.36 N	95.03 W
Taylor Mountain ʌ	202	44.53 N	114.13 W
Taylor Mountains ⋏	180	60.50 N	157.20 W
Taylor Run ≏	285	39.57 N	75.39 W
Taylors	192	34.55 N	82.17 W
Taylors Bush Park ♠	275b	43.42 N	79.19 W
Taylors Island	208	38.28 N	76.17 W
Taylor Springs	219	39.08 N	89.30 W
Taylors Run ≏	279b	40.11 N	79.57 W
Taylorstown	214	40.10 N	80.23 W
Taylorsville, In., U.S.	218	39.17 N	85.57 W
Taylorsville, Ky., U.S.	194	38.01 N	85.20 W
Taylorsville, Ms., U.S.	194	31.49 N	89.25 W
Taylorsville, N.C., U.S.	192	35.55 N	81.10 W
Taylorsville Dam ◆[6]	218	39.53 N	84.10 W
Taylortown, N.J., U.S.	276	40.56 N	74.24 W
Taylortown, Oh., U.S.	214	40.28 N	80.40 W
Taylortown Reservoir ⊜[1]	276	40.58 N	74.22 W
Taylorville	219	39.32 N	89.17 W
Taylorville, Lake ⊜[1]	219	39.30 N	89.15 W
Taymā'	128	27.38 N	38.29 E
Taymouth	186	46.11 N	66.37 W
Taymyr Peninsula → Tajmyr, poluostrov ≻[1]	74	76.00 N	104.00 E
Tay-ninh	110	11.18 N	106.06 E
Taynuilf	46	56.25 N	5.14 W
Tayoltita	232	24.05 N	105.56 W
Tayport	46	57.27 N	2.53 W
Táyros	267c	37.58 N	23.42 E
Tayside □[4]	46	56.30 N	3.30 W
Taytay, Pil.	116	10.49 N	119.31 E
Taytay, Pil.	116	14.34 N	121.08 E
Taytay Bay c	116	10.55 N	119.35 E
Tayu	115a	6.32 S	111.02 E
Tayüan, T'aiwan	100	25.04 N	121.11 E
Tayuan, Zhg.	89	51.27 N	124.16 E
Tayug	116	16.02 N	120.45 E
Tayyārah	140	13.12 N	30.47 E
Ṭayyebāt	128	34.44 N	60.45 E
Taz ≏	72	67.32 N	78.40 E
Taza	148	34.16 N	4.01 W
Taza □[4]	148	34.05 N	3.45 W
Tazawa-ko ⊜	92	39.43 N	140.40 E
Tazenakht	148	30.35 N	7.12 W
Tazewell, Tn., U.S.	192	36.27 N	83.34 W
Tazewell, Va., U.S.	192	37.06 N	81.31 W
Tazhuang	105	39.55 N	117.13 E
Tazicheng	89	46.35 N	123.06 E
Tazigou ≏	104	41.44 N	121.30 E
Tazin ≏	176	60.26 N	110.45 W
Tazin Lake ⊜	176	59.47 N	109.03 W
T'ažinskij	86	56.07 N	88.31 E
Tāzirbū ⫪[4]	146	25.45 N	21.00 E
Tazishan	107	29.28 N	104.14 E
Tazlina	180	62.04 N	145.25 W
Tazlina Lake ⊜	180	61.50 N	146.30 W
Tazoult-Lambese	34	35.29 N	6.15 E
Tazovskaja guba c	74	69.05 N	76.00 E
Tazovskij	74	67.28 N	78.42 E
Tazovskij poluostrov ≻[1]	72	68.35 N	76.00 E
Tazrouk	148	23.25 N	6.16 E
Tazumal ⊥	236	13.59 N	89.41 W
Tāzumuddin	126	22.29 N	90.53 E
Tazungdām	102	28.02 N	97.35 E
Tbessa	148	35.28 N	8.09 E
Tbessa □[5]	148	35.10 N	8.00 E
Tbilisi	84	41.43 N	44.49 E
Tbilisskaja	78	45.23 N	40.12 E
Tchad → Chad □[1]	146	15.00 N	19.00 E
Tchad, Lac (Lake Chad) ⊜	146	13.20 N	14.00 E
Tchaguine Golo	146	10.03 N	16.19 E
Tchamba	150	9.02 N	1.25 E
Tch'ang-Cha → Changsha	100	28.12 N	112.58 E
Tchaourou	150	8.53 N	2.36 E
Tchécoslovaquie → Czechoslovakia □[1]	30	49.30 N	17.00 E
Tchefuncta ≏	194	30.22 N	90.10 W
Tchékapika	152	1.17 S	16.11 E
Tcheliabinsk → Čel'abinsk	86	55.10 N	61.24 E
Tcheng-Tcheou → Zhengzhou	102	34.48 N	113.39 E
Tchentlo Lake ⊜	182	55.11 N	125.00 W
Tchériba	150	12.16 N	3.05 W
Tchesinkut Lake ⊜	182	54.05 N	125.40 W
Tchetti	150	7.50 N	1.40 E
Tchibanga	152	2.51 S	11.02 E
Tchigaï, Plateau du ⋏[1]	146	21.30 N	14.50 E
Tchikala-Tcholohanga	152	12.38 S	16.03 E
Tchin-Tabáradene	150	15.58 N	5.50 E
Tchitondi	152	4.33 S	12.08 E
Tcholliré	146	8.24 N	14.10 E
Tchong-K'ing → Chongqing	107	29.34 N	106.35 E
Tchořovice	60	49.27 N	13.48 E
Tchula	194	33.10 N	90.13 W
T.C. Steele State Memorial ⊥	218	39.08 N	86.20 W
Tczew	30	54.06 N	18.47 E
Té ≏	110	12.27 N	106.02 E
Te, Kinh ≊	269c	10.45 N	106.42 E
Tea ≏	246	0.30 S	65.09 W
Teaca	38	46.55 N	24.31 E
Teacapán	234	22.33 N	105.45 W
Tea Creek ≏	284a	43.02 N	79.06 W
Teaehoa, Pointe ≻	174y	9.51 S	139.01 W
Teague	222	31.37 N	96.17 W
Teahupoo	174s	17.51 S	149.13 W
Te Anau	172	45.25 S	167.43 E
Te Anau, Lake ⊜	172	45.12 S	167.48 E
Teanaway ≏	224	47.10 N	120.50 W
Teanaway, Middle Fork ≏	224	47.15 N	120.53 W
Teanaway, North Fork ≏	224	47.22 N	120.53 W
Teaneck	210	40.53 N	74.00 W
Teangue	46	57.07 N	5.50 W
Teano	68	41.15 N	14.04 E
Teapa	234	17.33 N	92.57 W
Teapa ≏	234	17.58 N	92.54 W
Te Araroa	172	37.38 S	178.22 E
Tearinibai	174t	1.35 N	172.58 E
Te Aroha	172	37.33 S	175.43 E
Teaticket	207	41.33 N	70.35 W
Tea Tree	162	22.11 S	133.17 E
Teatree Gully	168b	34.49 S	138.44 E
Te Atukura ʌ	174k	21.14 S	159.45 W
Te Awamutu	172	38.01 S	175.19 E
Teba, Esp.	34	36.58 N	4.56 W
Teba, Indon.	164	1.29 S	137.54 E
Tebakang	112	1.06 N	110.30 E
Tebas	256	21.35 S	42.44 W
Tebay	44	54.26 N	2.35 W
Tebbetts	219	38.37 N	91.57 W
Teberda	84	43.28 N	41.45 E
Teberdinskij zapovednik ♠	84	43.20 N	41.45 E
Tebes	286d	12.07 S	77.00 W
Tebicuary ≏	252	26.36 S	58.16 W
Tebicuary-Mí ≏	252	26.26 S	56.51 W
Tebingbulan	112	3.03 S	103.44 E
Tebingtinggi, Indon.	112	0.36 N	101.36 E
Tebingtinggi, Indon.	112	3.36 S	103.05 E
Tebingtinggi, Indon.	114	3.20 N	99.09 E
Tebingtinggi, Pulau I	114	0.54 N	102.45 E
Tébourba	36	36.49 N	9.51 E
Téboursouk	148	36.28 N	9.15 E
Téboursouk, Monts de ⋏	36	36.30 N	9.10 E
Tebra ≏	76	56.51 N	21.12 E
Tebstrup	41	55.59 N	9.53 E
Tebulosmta, gora ʌ	84	42.33 N	45.19 E
Tebza ≏	80	58.23 N	41.19 E
Tecalitlán	234	19.26 N	103.15 W
Tecamachalco	234	18.53 N	97.44 W
Tecate	232	32.34 N	116.38 W
Tech ≏	32	42.36 N	3.03 E
Teche, Bayou ≏	194	29.43 N	91.13 W
Techendorf	64	46.43 N	13.17 E
Techiman	150	7.35 N	1.56 W
Techimentia	150	7.11 N	2.02 W
Techirghiol	38	44.03 N	28.36 E
Techlé	148	21.35 N	14.58 W
Techny	278	42.07 N	87.49 W
Techou → Dezhou	98	37.27 N	116.18 E
Techtin	76	53.51 N	29.44 E
Tecka	254	43.29 S	70.48 W
Tecka ≏	254	42.37 S	70.25 W
Tecklenburg	52	52.13 N	7.48 E
Teckomatorp	41	55.52 N	13.05 E
Tecolote Creek ≏	200	35.22 N	105.15 W
Tecolotlán	234	20.13 N	104.03 W
Tecolutla ≏	234	20.29 N	97.00 W
Tecomán	234	18.55 N	103.53 W
Tecomate, Laguna c	234	16.35 N	99.25 W
Tecomaxtlahuaca	234	17.21 N	98.02 W
Tecominoacán	234	17.53 N	93.37 W
Tecopa	204	35.50 N	116.13 W
Tecozautla	234	20.32 N	99.38 W
Tecpan de Galeana	234	17.15 N	100.41 W
Tecpán Guatemala	236	14.46 N	91.00 W
Tecpatán	234	17.08 N	93.18 W
Tecuala	234	22.23 N	105.27 W
Tecuamburro, Volcán ʌ[1]	236	14.09 N	90.24 W
Tecuantepec ≏	234	20.16 N	97.27 W
Tecuci	38	45.50 N	27.26 E
Tecumseh, On., Can.	214	42.19 N	82.54 W
Tecumseh, Mi., U.S.	216	42.00 N	83.56 W
Tecumseh, Ne., U.S.	198	40.22 N	96.11 W
Tecumseh, Ok., U.S.	196	35.15 N	96.56 W
Ted Ceidaar Dabole	144	4.24 N	43.55 E
Teddington ◆[8]	260	51.25 N	0.20 W
Tédji	146	11.46 N	21.19 E
Tedori ≏	94	36.29 N	136.28 E
Tedrow	216	41.37 N	84.13 W
Tedžen	128	37.23 N	60.31 E
Tedžen (Harīrūd) ≏	128	37.24 N	60.38 E
Tedženstroj	128	36.55 N	60.53 E
Teec Nos Pos	200	36.56 N	109.42 W
Teeli	86	51.07 N	90.14 E
Teels Marsh ≡	204	38.12 N	118.21 W
Teen ⊜	40	59.07 N	14.40 E
Teerijärvi → Terjärv	26	63.32 N	23.30 E
Tees ≏	44	54.34 N	1.16 W
Tees Bay c	44	54.39 N	1.07 W
Teesdale V	44	54.38 N	2.07 W
Teesside → Middlesbrough	44	54.35 N	1.14 W
Teesside (Saint George) Airport ⊠	44	54.31 N	1.25 W
Teeswater	212	44.00 N	81.17 W
Teeswater ≏	212	44.18 N	81.17 W
Tefé	246	3.22 S	64.42 W
Tefé ≏	242	3.35 S	64.47 W
Tefé, Lago de ⊜	246	3.27 S	64.47 W
Tefen	130	41.19 N	32.08 E
Tefenni	130	37.18 N	29.47 E
Tefft	216	41.12 N	86.58 W
Tefle	150	5.59 N	0.35 E
Tegal	115a	6.52 S	109.08 E
Tegalombo	115a	8.04 S	111.17 E
Tégama ◆[1]	150	15.50 N	8.12 E
Tega-numa ⊜	268	35.51 N	140.04 E
Tegel ◆[8]	264a	52.35 N	13.17 E
Tegel, Berliner Forst ♠	264a	52.37 N	13.16 E
Tegelen	52	51.21 N	6.09 E
Tegeler See ⊜	264a	52.35 N	13.15 E
Tegernsee	64	47.43 N	11.45 E
Tegernsee ⊜	64	47.42 N	11.45 E
Teggiano	68	40.23 N	15.32 E
Teghra	124	25.29 N	85.57 E
Tegid, Llyn ⊜	42	52.53 N	3.36 W
Tegina	150	10.05 N	6.14 E
Tegineneng	112	5.12 S	105.10 E
Tegistyk	85	44.02 N	68.22 E
Teglio	64	46.10 N	10.04 E
Tégua I	175f	13.15 S	166.37 E
Tegualda	254	41.02 S	73.26 W
Tegucigalpa	236	14.06 N	87.13 W
Tegul'det	86	57.19 N	88.10 E
Tehachapi	228	35.07 N	118.26 W
Tehachapi Creek ≏	228	35.17 N	118.38 W
Tehachapi Mountains ⋏	228	35.00 N	118.40 W
Tehachapi Pass)(	228	35.06 N	118.18 W
Tehamiyam	140	18.20 N	36.32 E
Te Hapua	172	34.31 S	172.54 E
Tehar ◆[8]	272a	28.38 N	77.07 E
Te Haroto	172	39.08 S	176.36 E
Tehata	126	23.43 N	88.32 E
Tehek Lake ⊜	176	64.55 N	95.38 W
Teheran → Tehrān	128	35.40 N	51.26 E
Téhini	150	9.36 N	3.40 W
Tehoohaivei, Cap ≻	174y	9.49 S	138.54 W
Te Hope O Te Keho, Cap ≻	174y	10.02 S	139.06 W
Tehoru	164	3.23 S	129.30 E
Tehrān, Īrān	128	35.40 N	51.26 E
Tehrān, Īrān	267d	35.40 N	51.26 E
Tehrān, University of ʋ[2]	267d	35.42 N	51.24 E
Tehrān Pars ◆[8]	267d	35.44 N	51.32 E
Tehri	124	30.23 N	78.29 E
Tehri Garhwāl □[5]	124	30.30 N	78.30 E
Tehrthum	124	27.07 N	87.32 E
Tehuacán	234	18.27 N	97.23 W
Tehuacana	222	31.44 N	96.33 W
Tehuacana Creek ≏, Tx., U.S.	222	31.31 N	97.02 W
Tehuacana Creek ≏, Tx., U.S.	222	31.50 N	95.59 W
Tehuantepec, Méx.	234	18.41 N	103.17 W
Tehuantepec, Méx.	234	16.20 N	95.14 W
Tehuantepec ≏	234	16.10 N	95.07 W
Tehuantepec, Golfo de c	234	16.00 N	94.50 W
Tehuantepec, Istmo de ⊥[3]	234	17.00 N	95.00 W
Tehuantepec Ridge ✢[3]	16	13.30 N	98.00 W
Tehuelches	254	46.56 S	67.27 W
Tehuipango	234	18.31 N	97.04 W
Tehuitzingo	234	18.21 N	98.17 W
Teichl ≏	61	47.46 N	14.10 E
Teichröda	54	50.45 N	11.18 E
Teichwolframsdorf	54	50.43 N	12.14 E
Teide, Parque Nacional del ♠	148	28.15 N	16.30 W
Teide, Pico de ʌ	148	28.16 N	16.38 W
Teifi ≏	42	52.07 N	4.42 W
Teifiside ◆[1]	42	52.02 N	4.22 W
Teiga Plateau ⋏[1]	140	15.38 N	25.40 E
Teign ≏	42	50.33 N	3.29 W
Teignmouth	42	50.33 N	3.30 W
Teise ≏	260	51.13 N	0.25 E
Teisendorf	64	47.51 N	12.49 E
Teisnach	60	49.02 N	13.00 E
Teita	234	17.05 N	97.25 W
Teith ≏	46	56.08 N	3.59 W
Teitipac	234	16.54 N	96.34 W
Teixeira	250	7.13 S	37.15 W
Teixeira Pinto	150	12.10 N	13.55 W
Teixeiras	255	20.39 S	42.51 W
Teixeira Soares	252	25.22 S	50.27 W
Tejakula	115b	8.08 S	115.20 E
Tejamén	232	24.48 N	105.07 W
Tejkovo	80	56.52 N	40.34 E
Tejo → Tagus ≏	34	38.40 N	9.24 W
Tejon Creek ≏	228	35.08 N	118.53 W
Tejon Pass)(	228	34.48 N	118.52 W
Tejupan, Punta ≻	234	18.20 N	103.32 W
Tejupilco de Hidalgo	234	18.54 N	100.09 W
Te Kaha	172	37.44 S	177.41 E
Tekai ≏	114	4.14 N	102.23 E
Tékakwitha, Île I	275a	45.25 N	73.42 W
Tekam ≏	114	3.52 N	102.27 E
Tekamah	198	41.46 N	96.13 W
Te Kao	172	34.39 S	172.57 E
Tekapo, Lake ⊜	172	43.53 S	170.31 E
Te Karaka	172	38.28 S	177.52 E
Tekāri	124	24.56 N	84.50 E
Te Kauwhata	172	37.24 S	175.09 E
Tekax de Álvaro Obregón	232	20.12 N	89.17 W
Teke	130	41.04 N	29.39 E
Teke, ozero ⊜	86	53.48 N	73.00 E
Teke Burnu ≻, Tür.	130	38.05 N	26.36 E
Teke Burnu ≻, Tür.	130	40.02 N	26.10 E
Tekeli	86	44.48 N	78.57 E
Tekes	86	43.10 N	81.43 E
Tekes ≏	86	43.36 N	82.32 E
Tekeze (Satīt) ≏	140	14.20 N	35.50 E
Tekirdağ	130	40.59 N	27.31 E
Tekirdağ □[4]	130	41.00 N	27.30 E
Tekkali	122	18.37 N	84.14 E
Tekke	130	40.43 N	36.12 E
Tekkiraz	130	40.59 N	37.08 E
Tekman	130	39.38 N	41.31 E
Tekoa	202	47.13 N	117.04 W
Tekong, Pulau I	271c	1.24 N	104.03 E
Tekong Kechil, Pulau I	271c	1.25 N	104.01 E
Tekonsha	216	42.05 N	84.59 W
Te Kopuru	172	36.02 S	173.56 E
Tekouiat, Oued V	148	22.25 N	2.35 E
Tékro ⫪[4]	146	19.30 N	20.58 E
Tekstil'ščiki	82	55.57 N	37.49 E
Tekstil'ščiki ◆[8]	265b	55.42 N	37.44 E
Teku	112	0.46 S	123.26 E
Te Kuiti	172	38.20 S	175.10 E
Tekukor, Pulau I	271c	1.14 N	103.50 E
Tel ≏	122	20.50 N	83.54 E
Tela, Hond.	236	15.44 N	87.27 W
Tela, India	272a	28.44 N	77.20 E
Tela, Bahía de c	236	15.48 N	87.30 W
Teladuomu	120	29.38 N	84.13 E
Telaga	116	6.51 N	117.03 E
Telaga, Teluk c	114	2.10 N	98.00 E
Telaga-kulon	115a	6.58 S	108.18 E
Télagh	148	34.47 N	0.34 W
Telaopengshashan ʌ	120	30.33 N	86.25 E
Tel Ashqelon ⊥	132	31.39 N	34.32 E
Telavåg	26	60.16 N	4.49 E
Telavi	84	41.55 N	45.28 E
Tel Aviv □[5]	132	32.05 N	34.48 E
Tel Aviv-Yafo	132	32.03 N	34.46 E
Telč	30	49.11 N	15.27 E
Tel'čje	76	53.21 N	36.20 E
Telde	148	28.00 N	15.25 W
Tele ≏, Afr.	158	30.26 S	27.33 E
Tele ≏, Zaïre	152	2.48 N	23.54 E
Telechany	76	52.31 N	25.51 E
Teleckoje, ozero ⊜	86	51.35 N	87.40 E
Telefomin	164	5.10 S	141.35 E
Telegapulang	112	2.55 S	112.25 E
Telegino	80	52.55 N	44.34 E
Telegrafo, Pizzo ʌ	70	37.37 N	13.10 E
Telegraph Canyon V	280	33.55 N	117.45 W
Telegraph Cove	182	50.33 N	126.50 W
Telegraph Creek	180	57.55 N	131.10 W
Telemark □[6]	26	59.30 N	8.40 E
Telemba	88	52.43 N	113.16 E
Telembí ≏	246	1.50 N	78.16 W
Telén	252	36.16 S	65.30 W
Telen ≏	112	0.26 S	116.42 E
Telenešty	78	47.30 N	28.22 E
Teleño ʌ	34	42.21 N	6.23 W
Teleorman □[6]	38	44.00 N	25.15 E
Teleorman ≏	38	43.52 N	25.26 E
Téléphone, Île du I	273b	4.20 S	15.12 E
Telerig	38	43.51 N	27.40 E
Telertheba, Djebel ʌ	148	24.10 N	6.51 E
Telescope Peak ʌ	204	36.10 N	117.05 W
Telescope Point ≻	241k	12.08 N	61.36 W
Telese	68	41.13 N	14.32 E
Telesterion ⊥	267c	38.02 N	23.32 E
Telferner	222	28.51 N	96.53 W
Telfes	64	47.10 N	11.22 E
Telford, Eng., U.K.	42	52.40 N	2.28 W
Telford, Pa., U.S.	208	40.19 N	75.19 W
Telfs	64	47.18 N	11.04 E
Telgte	52	51.59 N	7.47 E
Telica ≏	236	14.43 N	86.08 W
Telica, Volcán ʌ[1]	236	12.36 N	86.50 W
Telida	180	63.23 N	153.16 W
Telikovka	80	52.35 N	48.17 E
Télimélé	150	10.54 N	13.02 W
Telixtlahuaca	234	17.18 N	96.54 W
Telizi	265a	59.42 N	29.59 E
Teljo, Jabal ʌ	140	14.42 N	25.56 E
Telkwa	182	54.42 N	127.03 W
Telkwa ≏	182	54.41 N	127.02 W
Tel Lakhish ⊥	132	31.34 N	34.51 E
Tellaro ≏	70	36.50 N	15.06 E
Tell City	194	37.57 N	86.46 W
Teller	180	65.16 N	166.22 W
Tellicherry	122	11.45 N	75.32 E
Tellico ≏	192	35.36 N	84.13 W
Tellico Plains	192	35.21 N	84.17 W
Tellier	254	47.39 S	66.03 W
Tellier, Lac ⊜	206	46.23 N	74.00 W
Tello	246	3.04 N	75.08 W
Telluride	200	37.56 N	107.48 W
Tel'ma	88	52.43 N	103.41 E
Tel'mana	83	48.30 N	39.18 E
Tel'manovo	83	47.24 N	38.02 E
Tel Megiddo ⊥	132	32.35 N	35.11 E
Telmen	88	48.38 N	97.37 E
Telmen nuur ⊜	88	48.50 N	97.18 E
Tel Mond	132	32.15 N	34.56 E
Tel'novskij	89	49.22 N	142.05 E
Teloekbetoeng → Telukbetung	115a	5.27 S	105.16 E
Telogia Creek ≏	192	30.16 N	84.44 W
Telok Anson	114	4.02 N	101.01 E
Telok Datok	114	2.49 N	101.31 E
Teloloapan	234	18.21 N	99.51 W
Telpaneca	236	13.32 N	86.17 W
Telsen	254	42.24 S	66.57 W
Telsen, Arroyo ≏	254	42.51 S	66.48 W
Telšiai	76	55.59 N	22.15 E
Telti	71	40.52 N	9.21 E
Teltow	54	52.23 N	13.16 E
Teltow ◆[1]	264a	52.18 N	13.25 E
Teltower Hochfläche ⋏[1]	264a	52.22 N	13.20 E
Teltowkanal ≊	264a	52.26 N	13.35 E
Telukbatang	112	1.00 S	109.46 E
Telukbayur, Indon.	112	2.09 N	117.24 E
Telukbayur, Indon.	112	1.00 S	100.22 E
Telukbetung	115a	5.27 S	105.16 E
Telukbrombang	114	2.03 N	100.52 E
Telukbutun	112	4.13 N	108.12 E
Telukdalem	114	0.34 N	97.49 E
Teluklanjut	112	0.09 N	103.29 E
Teluklecah	114	1.51 N	101.44 E
Telukmerbau	114	2.04 N	100.38 E
Telukpambang	114	1.28 N	102.28 E
Teluk Punggur, Ujung ≻	112	3.53 S	102.17 E
Teluksamak	114	0.52 N	103.03 E
Telumengtangshan ʌ	120	30.33 N	86.27 E
Teluša	76	53.03 N	29.31 E
Tem'	88	55.21 N	100.44 E
Tema	150	5.38 N	0.01 E
Temae	174s	17.29 S	149.46 W
Temagami, Lake ⊜	190	47.00 N	80.05 W
Temaju, Pulau I	112	0.29 N	108.52 E
Temalacacingo	234	17.52 N	98.41 W
Te Manga ʌ	174k	21.13 S	159.45 W
Temangan Baharu	114	5.42 N	102.09 E
Temangga	112	0.27 N	111.21 E
Temanggung	115a	7.18 S	110.10 E
Temascal, Méx.	234	23.24 N	104.14 W
Temascal, Méx.	234	18.15 N	96.20 W
Temascaltepec ≏	234	18.47 N	100.41 W
Tem'asovo	86	52.59 N	58.06 E
Temastián	234	21.53 N	103.28 W
Tematagi I[1]	14	21.41 S	140.40 W
Temax	232	21.09 N	88.56 W
Tembe	154	0.16 S	28.14 E
Tembe ≏	158	26.03 S	32.26 E
Tembeling	114	4.04 N	102.19 E
Tembeling ≏	114	4.04 N	102.20 E
Tembenči ≏	74	64.36 N	99.58 E
Tembesi ≏	112	1.43 S	103.06 E
Tembilahan	112	0.19 S	103.09 E
Tembisa	158	25.58 S	28.14 E
Temblador	246	8.59 N	62.44 W
Tembleque	34	39.42 N	3.30 W
Temblor Range ⋏	226	35.20 N	119.55 W
Tembo Aluma	152	7.42 S	17.17 E
Tembuè	154	14.52 S	32.58 E
Tembuland □[9]	158	31.30 S	27.40 E
Teme ≏	42	52.09 N	2.18 W
Temecula	228	33.29 N	117.08 W
Temecula Creek ≏	228	33.28 N	117.08 W
Temengor	114	5.19 N	101.22 E
Temerin	38	45.24 N	19.53 E
Temerloh	114	3.27 N	102.25 E
Temescal Canyon V	280	34.04 N	118.32 W
Temescal Wash V	228	33.40 N	117.20 W
Temesvár → Timișoara	38	45.45 N	21.13 E
Temiang, Pulau I	112	0.19 N	104.23 E
Teminabuan	164	1.26 S	132.01 E
Temir	86	49.08 N	57.06 E
Temir ≏	86	48.31 N	57.27 E
Temirgojevskaja	78	45.07 N	40.16 E
Temirlanovka	85	42.36 N	69.17 E
Temirtau, S.S.S.R.	86	53.08 N	87.28 E
Temirtau, S.S.S.R.	86	50.05 N	72.56 E
Témiscamie, Lac ⊜	186	51.11 N	72.12 W
Témiscaming	190	46.43 N	79.06 W
Témiscouata, Lac ⊜	186	47.41 N	68.47 W
Temixco	234	18.50 N	99.14 W
Temnik ≏	88	51.00 N	106.18 E
Temnikov	80	54.38 N	43.12 E
Temnikovo	265b	55.43 N	38.01 E
Temo ≏	71	40.21 N	8.47 E
Temoaya	234	19.28 N	99.35 W
Temora	166	34.26 S	147.32 E
Temósachic	232	28.57 N	107.51 W
Tempe	200	33.24 N	111.54 W
Tempe, Danau ⊜	112	4.06 S	119.57 E
Tempelburg → Czaplinek	30	53.34 N	16.14 E
Tempelfelde	264a	52.43 N	13.43 E
Tempelhof ◆[8]	264a	52.28 N	13.23 E
Temperance	216	41.46 N	83.34 W
Temperanceville	208	37.53 N	75.32 W
Temperley ◆[8]	258	34.47 S	58.24 W
Tempest, Mount ʌ[2]	171a	27.10 S	153.26 E
Tempilang	112	2.07 S	105.40 E
Tempino	112	1.44 S	103.29 E
Tempio di Clitunno ⊥	66	42.48 N	12.45 E
Tempio Pausania	71	40.54 N	9.06 E
Tempisque ≏	236	10.12 N	85.14 W
Temple, Ok., U.S.	196	34.16 N	98.14 W
Temple, Pa., U.S.	208	40.24 N	75.55 W
Temple, Tx., U.S.	222	31.05 N	97.20 W
Temple City	228	34.06 N	118.03 W
Templecombe	42	51.00 N	2.25 W
Temple Ewell	42	51.09 N	1.16 E
Temple Hills Park	284c	38.48 N	76.57 W
Templemore	48	52.48 N	7.50 W
Templers	168b	34.28 S	138.45 E
Temple Sowerby	44	54.39 N	2.35 W
Templestowe	169	37.45 S	145.07 E
Temple Terrace	220	28.02 N	82.23 W
Templeton, Austl.	166	18.26 S	142.28 E
Templeton, P.Q., Can.	212	45.29 N	75.36 W
Templeton, Ca., U.S.	226	35.33 N	120.42 W
Templeton, In., U.S.	216	40.31 N	87.12 W
Templeton, Ma., U.S.	207	42.33 N	72.04 W
Templeton, Pa., U.S.	214	40.55 N	79.27 W
Templeton ≏	166	21.14 S	138.13 E
Temple University ʋ[2]	285	39.59 N	75.09 W
Templeuve, Bel.	50	50.38 N	3.16 E
Templeuve, Fr.	50	50.32 N	3.10 E
Templi, Valle dei ⊥	70	37.17 N	13.35 E
Templin	54	53.07 N	13.30 E
Templiner See ⊜	264a	52.22 N	13.01 E
Templo Island I	116	13.09 N	122.52 E
Tempoal	234	21.31 N	98.23 W
Tempoal ≏	234	21.47 N	98.27 W
Tempy	82	56.38 N	37.18 E
Temr'uk	78	45.17 N	37.23 E
Temr'ukskij zaliv c	78	45.24 N	37.20 E
Temse	50	51.08 N	4.13 E
Temù	64	46.15 N	10.28 E
Temuco	252	38.44 S	72.36 W
Temuka	172	44.15 S	171.17 E
Temwen I	174r	6.52 N	158.19 E
Tena	246	0.59 S	77.49 W
Tenabo	232	20.03 N	90.14 W
Tenacatita, Bahía c	234	19.17 N	104.50 W
Tenafly	210	40.55 N	73.57 W
Tenaha	194	31.57 N	94.15 W
Tenakee Springs	180	57.47 N	135.13 W
Tenakill Brook ≏	276	40.59 N	73.58 W
Tena Kourou ʌ[2]	150	10.45 N	5.25 W
Tenāli	122	16.15 N	80.35 E
Tenamaxtlán	234	20.13 N	104.10 W
Tenancingo [de Degollado]	234	18.58 N	99.36 W
Tenango del Valle	234	19.07 N	99.33 W
Tenantongo, Presa ⊜[1]	286a	19.28 N	99.16 W
Tenasillahe Island I	224	46.14 N	123.27 W
Tenasserim	110	12.05 N	99.01 E
Tenasserim □[8]	110	12.00 N	99.00 E
Tenay	58	45.55 N	5.30 E
Tenaya Creek ≏	226	37.44 N	119.35 W
Tenbury Wells	42	52.19 N	2.35 W
Tenby	42	51.41 N	4.43 W
Tence	62	45.07 N	4.17 E
Tench Island I	164	1.40 S	150.40 E
Tencin	62	45.19 N	5.58 E
Tenda, Colle di (Col de Tende))(	62	44.09 N	7.34 E
Tendaho	144	11.48 N	40.52 E
Tendai-san ʌ	270	34.55 N	135.28 E
Tende	62	44.05 N	7.36 E
Tende, Col de (Colle di Tenda))(	62	44.09 N	7.34 E
Tende, Tunnel de ◆[5]	62	44.09 N	7.34 E
Ten Degree Channel Ա	110	10.00 N	93.00 E
Tendeka	158	27.44 S	30.54 E
Tendō	92	38.21 N	140.22 E
Tendrara	148	33.04 N	1.59 W
Tendrovskaja kosa ≻[2]	78	46.12 N	31.50 E
Tendrovskij zaliv c	78	46.15 N	31.55 E

	English	Deutsch	Español	Français	Português
≏	River	Fluss	Río	Rivière	Rio
≊	Canal	Kanal	Canal	Canal	Canal
⌞	Waterfall, Rapids	Wasserfall, Stromschnellen	Cascada, Rápidos	Chute d'eau, Rapides	Cascata, Rápidos
Ա	Strait	Meeresstrasse	Estrecho	Détroit	Estreito
c	Bay, Gulf	Bucht, Golf	Bahía, Golfo	Baie, Golfe	Baía, Golfo
⊜	Lake, Lakes	See, Seen	Lago, Lagos	Lac, Lacs	Lago, Lagos
≡	Swamp	Sumpf	Pantano	Marais	Pântano
⊓	Ice Features, Glacier	Eis- und Gletscherformen	Accidentes Glaciales	Formes glaciaires	Acidentes glaciares
⫪	Other Hydrographic Features	Andere Hydrographische Objekte	Otros Elementos Hidrográficos	Autres données hydrographiques	Outros acidentes hidrográficos
✢	Submarine Features	Untermeerische Objekte	Accidentes Submarinos	Formes de relief sous-marin	Acidentes submarinos
□	Political Unit	Politische Einheit	Unidad Politica	Entité politique	Unidade política
ʋ	Cultural Institution	Kulturelle Institution	Institución Cultural	Institution culturelle	Instituição cultural
⊥	Historical Site	Historische Stätte	Sitio Histórico	Site historique	Sitio histórico
♠	Recreational Site	Erholungs- und Ferienort	Sitio de Recreo	Centre de loisirs	Area de Lazer
⊠	Airport	Flughafen	Aeropuerto	Aéroport	Aeroporto
■	Military Installation	Militäranlage	Instalación Militar	Installation militaire	Instalação militar
◆	Miscellaneous	Verschiedenes	Misceláneo	Divers	Diversos

ENGLISH — Name, Page, Lat.°′, Long.°′
DEUTSCH — Name, Seite, Breite°′, Länge°′ E = Ost

Tendürek Dağı ∧ 84 39.22 N 43.52 E
Ténenkou 150 14.28 N 4.55 W
Tenente Marques ≃ 248 11.10 S 59.56 W
Tenente Portela 252 27.22 S 53.45 W
Tenentes 256 22.48 S 46.20 W
Ténéré ◆[2] 146 19.00 N 10.30 E
Ténéré, Erg du ⊥[8] 146 17.35 N 10.55 E
Tenerife I 148 28.19 N 16.34 W
Ténès 148 36.31 N 1.14 E
Ténès, Cap > 34 36.33 N 1.21 E
Tenexpa 234 17.11 N 100.43 W
Tenextepango 234 18.43 N 98.57 W
Teng ≃ 110 19.52 N 97.45 E
Tengah, Kepulauan II 112 7.30 S 117.30 E
Tengah Airfield ⊠ 271c 1.23 N 103.42 E
Teng'aopu 104 41.05 N 122.49 E
Tengchong 102 25.04 N 98.29 E
Tengen 58 47.49 N 8.40 E
Tenggarong 112 0.24 S 116.58 E
Tengger Shamo ◆[2] 102 38.00 N 104.40 E
Tenggol, Pulau I 114 4.48 N 103.38 E
Tenghilan 112 6.14 N 116.19 E
Tengi ≃ 114 3.24 N 101.10 E
Tengiz, ozero ⊜ 86 50.24 N 68.57 E
Tengjiabao 100 31.10 N 115.29 E
Tengqiao 110 18.22 N 109.46 E
Tengra 272b 22.48 N 88.32 E
Tengréla 150 10.29 N 6.24 W
Tengréla □[5] 150 10.30 N 7.30 W
Tengtian 100 27.38 N 115.40 E
Tengtiaohe (Na) ≃ 110 22.05 N 103.09 E
Ten'guševo 80 54.46 N 42.44 E
Tengxian, Zhg. 98 35.08 N 117.10 E
Tengxian, Zhg. 102 23.21 N 110.53 E
Teniente Rodolfo Marsh ⊠[3] 9 62.12 S 58.54 W
Tenigerbad 58 46.42 N 8.57 E
Tenino 224 46.51 N 122.51 W
Tenis, ozero ⊜ 86 56.09 N 71.56 E
Teniya-zaki > 174m 26.33 N 128.09 E
Teniz, ozero ⊜ 86 54.08 N 64.34 E
Tenjin ≃ 96 35.30 N 133.53 E
Tenjo, Mount ∧[2] 174p 13.25 N 144.42 E
Tenkāsi 122 8.58 N 77.18 E
Tenke, Zaïre 154 10.35 S 26.07 E
Tenke, Zaïre 154 11.26 S 26.45 E
Tenkeli 74 70.01 N 140.58 E
Tenkergynpil'gyn, laguna ⊂ 180 68.30 N 178.00 W
Ten'ki 80 55.26 N 49.00 E
Tenkiller Ferry Lake ⊜[1] 196 35.43 N 95.00 W
Tenkodogo 150 11.47 N 0.22 W
Tenmile ≃, Ma., U.S. 283 41.58 N 71.20 W
Tenmile ≃, N.Y., U.S. 210 41.40 N 73.31 W
Ten Mile Creek ≃, On., Can. 284a 43.07 N 79.11 W
Ten Mile Creek ≃, Ky., U.S. 218 38.43 N 84.46 W
Tenmile Creek ≃, Oh., U.S. 216 41.42 N 83.33 W
Tenmile Creek ≃, Pa., U.S. 188 40.08 N 80.22 W
Tenmile Creek ≃, Tx., U.S. 222 32.34 N 96.34 W
Ten Mile Lake ⊜ 186 51.06 N 56.41 W
Tenmile Run ≃ 276 40.27 N 74.35 W
Tenmile Wash V 200 32.52 N 113.28 W
Tenmoku-san ∧ 94 35.52 N 139.03 E
Tenna ≃ 66 43.14 N 13.47 E
Tennant Creek 162 19.40 S 134.10 E
Tennenbronn 58 48.11 N 8.20 E
Tennengau ◆[1] 64 47.40 N 13.15 E
Tennen-Gebirge ∧ 64 47.30 N 13.15 E
Tennent 208 40.16 N 74.20 W
Tennent Pond ⊜ 276 40.26 N 74.20 W
Tennessee □[3] 178 35.50 N 85.30 W
Tennessee ≃ 178 37.04 N 88.33 W
Tennessee Colony 222 31.50 N 95.50 W
Tenneville 56 50.06 N 5.32 E
Tennille 192 32.56 N 82.48 W
Tenno 64 45.55 N 10.49 E
Tennōji ◆[8] 270 34.39 N 135.31 E
Teno 252 34.52 S 71.11 W
Tenom 112 5.08 N 115.57 E
Ténos, Pointe > 240e 14.48 N 61.00 W
Tenosique de Pino Suárez 232 17.29 N 91.26 W
Tenri 96 34.36 N 135.51 E
Tenryū, Nihon 94 35.16 N 137.51 E
Tenryū, Nihon 94 34.52 N 137.49 E
Tenryū ≃ 94 34.39 N 137.47 E
Tensas ≃ 194 31.38 N 91.49 W
Tensed 202 47.09 N 116.55 W
Tensift, Oued ≃ 148 32.02 N 9.22 W
Ten Sleep 202 44.02 N 107.27 W
Tensta 40 60.02 N 17.40 E
Tente 263 51.07 N 7.11 E
Tente ◆[8] 263 51.18 N 7.14 E
Tenteksor ⊞ 80 47.18 N 53.24 E
Tentena 112 1.47 S 120.39 E
Tenterden 42 51.05 N 0.42 E
Tenterfield 166 29.03 S 152.01 E
Tent Hill 171a 27.36 S 152.14 E
Ten Thousand Islands II 220 25.50 N 81.33 W
Tentolomatinan, Gunung ∧ 112 0.56 N 121.48 E
Tentugal 250 1.19 S 46.59 W
Tentulia 272b 22.50 N 88.28 E
Teocaltiche 234 21.26 N 102.35 W
Teocelo 234 19.23 N 96.58 W
Teocuitatlán de Corona 234 20.07 N 103.24 W
Teocuitlapa 234 17.22 N 98.58 W
Teodelina 252 34.11 S 61.32 W
Teófilo Cunha 287a 22.39 S 43.34 W
Teófilo Otoni 255 17.51 S 41.30 W
Teofipol' 78 49.50 N 26.25 E
Teohotepapa, Pointe > 174y 9.46 S 138.48 W
Teohotupa, Pointe > 174y 9.46 S 138.50 W
Teo Lakes ⊜ 184 51.30 N 109.21 W
Teolo 64 45.21 N 11.40 E
Teomabal Island I 116 6.20 N 120.51 E
Teor 64 45.51 N 13.03 E
Teora 68 40.51 N 15.15 E
Teotihuacán ⊥ 234 19.44 N 98.50 W
Teotitlán del Camino 234 18.08 N 97.05 W
Teotitlán del Valle 234 17.02 N 96.30 W
Tepa, Ghana 150 7.00 N 2.10 W
Tepa, Indon. 164 7.52 S 129.31 E
Tepalcatepec 234 19.11 N 102.51 W
Tepalcatepec ≃ 234 18.50 N 102.05 W
Tepalcatepec, Arroyo ≃ 234 17.25 N 100.40 W
Tepalcingo 234 18.36 N 98.51 W
Tepa Point > 174v 19.07 S 169.56 W
Tepatepec 234 20.14 N 99.05 W
Tnnnnnnnán [de Morelos] 234 20.49 N 102.44 W
Tepatlaxco [de Hidalgo] 234 19.04 N 97.58 W
Tepe 130 37.48 N 40.47 E
Tepeaca 234 18.58 N 97.54 W
Tepeapulco 234 19.47 N 98.33 W
Tepechitlán 234 21.40 N 103.20 W
Tepecoacuilco [de Trujano] 234 18.18 N 99.29 W
Tepecoacuilo ≃ 234 17.59 N 99.47 W
Tepeguaje, Méx. 196 25.40 N 99.50 W
Tepeguaje, Méx. 234 23.30 N 97.50 W
Tepehuanes 232 25.21 N 105.44 W
Tepehuanes, Río los ≃ 232 25.10 N 105.25 W
Tepeji del Río 232 19.54 N 99.21 W
Tepelenë 38 40.18 N 20.01 E
Tepelmeme [de Morelos] 234 17.51 N 97.21 W
Tepelská vrchovina ∧[1] 60 50.00 N 13.00 E
Tepepan ◆[8] 286a 19.16 N 99.08 W
Tepetixtla 234 17.13 N 100.08 W
Tepetlixpa 234 19.02 N 98.49 W
Tepi 144 7.10 N 35.23 E
Tepic 234 21.30 N 104.54 W
Tepko 168b 34.58 S 139.11 E
Teplá 60 49.59 N 12.52 E
Teplá ≃ 54 50.14 N 12.52 E
Teplice 54 50.39 N 13.48 E
Teplik 78 48.40 N 29.44 E
Teplitz → Teplice 54 50.39 N 13.48 E
Teplooz'orsk 89 49.00 N 131.48 E
Teplovka 80 51.33 N 51.33 E
Teplovo 80 55.25 N 42.56 E
Tepoca, Bahía de ⊂ 232 30.15 N 112.50 W
Te Pohue 172 39.15 S 176.41 E
Tepopa, Cabo > 232 29.22 N 112.27 W
Teposcolula 234 17.31 N 97.29 W
Te Puia 172 38.04 S 178.18 E
Te Puke 172 37.47 S 176.20 E
Tepuxtepec, Presa ⊜[1] 234 20.02 N 100.13 W
Tepuzhuacán 234 20.53 N 104.33 W
Tequepa, Bahía de ⊂ 234 17.17 N 101.05 W
Tequila 234 20.54 N 103.47 W
Tequisquiac 234 19.55 N 99.09 W
Tequisquita Slough ≃ 226 36.58 N 121.27 W
Tequma 132 31.27 N 34.35 E
Ter ≃, Esp. 34 42.01 N 3.12 E
Ter ≃, Ityo. 144 7.20 N 42.11 E
Ter ≃, Eng., U.K. 42 51.50 N 0.36 E
Téra 150 14.01 N 0.45 E
Tera ≃ 34 41.54 N 5.44 W
Teradomari 92 37.38 N 138.46 E
Terai 94 36.26 N 136.30 E
Teraina I 14 4.43 N 160.24 W
Ter'ajevo 82 56.11 N 36.07 E
Terakhāda 126 22.56 N 89.40 E
Teralba 170 32.58 S 151.37 E
Teramo 66 42.39 N 13.42 E
Teramo □[6] 66 42.39 N 13.41 E
Terampa 112 3.14 N 106.14 E
Terán 234 16.45 N 93.10 W
Terang 169 38.14 S 142.55 E
Teranum 114 3.44 N 101.49 E
Ter Apel 52 52.53 N 7.04 E
Terarama 164 8.00 S 141.50 E
Teras 114 3.45 N 101.49 E
Teratak 112 0.46 S 110.32 E
Terborg 52 51.55 N 6.21 E
Terbuny 76 52.08 N 38.17 E
Tercan 130 39.47 N 40.24 E
Terceira I 148a 38.43 N 24.13 W
Tercero ≃ 252 32.55 S 62.19 W
Tercero de Febrero, Parque ◆ 288 34.34 S 58.25 W
Terdal 122 16.30 N 75.03 E
Terdoppio, Torrente ≃ 266b 45.30 N 8.37 E
Terebovl'a 78 49.18 N 25.43 E
Terebuš 82 54.16 N 38.09 E
Terebuinec 76 59.01 N 33.39 E
Terechovka 78 52.13 N 31.27 E
Terechovo 82 55.50 N 35.45 E
Te Rehunga 172 40.13 S 176.01 E
Tereida 140 10.35 N 31.17 E
Terek, S.S.S.R. 84 43.29 N 44.08 E
Terek, S.S.S.R. 85 40.01 N 73.33 E
Terek ≃ 84 43.44 N 46.33 E
Terekli-Mekteb 84 44.10 N 45.53 E
Terek-Saj 85 41.32 N 71.09 E
Terektinskij chrebet ∧ 86 50.30 N 86.00 E
Terekty 80 48.34 N 49.02 E
Terence Bay 186 44.28 N 63.43 W
Teren'ga 80 53.42 N 48.24 E
Terengganu □[3] 114 5.00 N 103.00 E
Terengganu ≃ 114 5.17 N 103.05 E
Terenino 76 54.31 N 33.35 E
Terenkuduk 80 48.24 N 47.11 E
Terenni ⊥ 150 16.30 N 9.35 W
Terenos 255 20.26 S 54.50 W
Terensaj 86 51.36 N 59.31 E
Terenuzek 86 45.05 N 64.59 E
Teresina 250 5.05 S 42.49 W
Tereška ≃ 80 51.48 N 46.26 E
Teresópolis 256 22.26 S 42.59 W
Terespol 30 52.05 N 23.36 E
Teresva 78 48.01 N 23.42 E
Terevaka, Cerro ∧ 174z 27.05 S 109.23 W
Terezín 54 50.31 N 14.08 E
Tergauči 85 41.11 N 71.30 E
Tergnier 50 49.39 N 3.18 E
Tergun Daba Shan ∧ 102 38.25 N 95.55 E
Terhorne 52 53.02 N 5.46 E
Teriang 114 3.14 N 102.25 E
Teriang ≃ 114 3.19 N 102.31 E
Teribe ≃ 236 9.22 N 82.32 W
Terib'orka 24 69.08 N 35.08 E
Terihi I 174y 10.02 S 138.49 W
Teripa ≃ 114 3.53 N 96.23 E
Teritjan (Teerijärvi) 26 63.32 N 23.31 E
Terkos Gölü ⊜ 130 41.20 N 28.35 E
Terlago 64 46.06 N 11.02 E
Terlano 64 46.32 N 11.15 E
Terlingua 196 29.19 N 103.37 W
Terlingua Creek ≃ 196 29.10 N 103.36 W
Terlizzi 68 41.08 N 16.32 E
Termas de Río Hondo 252 27.29 S 64.52 W
Terme 130 41.12 N 36.59 E
Terme del Brennero (Brennerbad) 64 46.58 N 11.29 E
Terme di Stigliano 66 42.09 N 12.01 E
Terme di Suio 68 41.18 N 13.51 E
Terme di Valdieri 62 44.12 N 7.16 E
Termeno (Tramin) 64 46.20 N 11.14 E
Termez 72 37.14 N 67.16 E
Termignon 62 45.17 N 6.49 E
Terminal 258 34.09 S 57.31 W
Terminal Island I 280 33.45 N 118.15 W
Terminal Island Coast Guard Base ■ 280 33.43 N 118.17 W
Termini Imerese 70 37.59 N 13.42 E
Termini Imerese, Golfo di ⊂ 70 38.01 N 13.45 E
Terminillo, Monte ∧ 66 42.28 N 13.00 E
Términos, Laguna de ⊂ 232 18.37 N 91.33 W
Termit, Massif de ∧ 146 16.15 N 11.17 E
Termoli 66 42.00 N 15.00 E
Termonde → Dendermonde 50 51.02 N 4.07 E
Termsdorf 264a 52.16 N 13.48 E
Tern ≃ 42 52.47 N 2.32 W
Ternate, Indon. 108 0.48 N 127.24 E
Ternate, Pil. 116 14.17 N 120.43 E
Ternberg 61 47.58 N 14.22 E
Terney 89 45.03 N 136.37 E
Terneuzen 52 51.20 N 3.50 E
Terni 66 42.34 N 12.37 E
Terni □[4] 66 42.41 N 12.19 E
Ternitz 61 47.44 N 16.03 E
Ternoise ≃ 50 50.23 N 2.01 E
Ternopol' 78 49.34 N 25.36 E
Ternovatoje 78 47.50 N 36.09 E
Ternovka, S.S.S.R. 78 51.40 N 41.37 E
Ternovka, S.S.S.R. 78 47.02 N 32.01 E
Ternovka, S.S.S.R. 78 48.32 N 29.58 E
Ternovka, S.S.S.R. 78 47.56 N 35.06 E
Ternovka, S.S.S.R. 80 51.53 N 46.32 E
Ternovoje 80 51.03 N 43.43 E
Ternovskaja 78 45.53 N 40.24 E
Terolak 114 3.53 N 101.23 E
Terong 114 4.43 N 100.44 E
Terontola 64 43.13 N 12.02 E
Terpe 54 51.32 N 14.19 E
Terpenija, mys > 89 48.39 N 144.44 E
Terpenija, zaliv ⊂ 89 49.00 N 143.30 E
Terra Alta 188 39.26 N 79.32 W
Terra Bella 204 35.58 N 119.03 W
Terra Boa 255 23.45 S 52.27 W
Terrace 182 54.31 N 128.35 W
Terrace Bay 190 48.47 N 87.06 W
Terracina 66 41.17 N 13.15 E
Terra del Sole 66 44.11 N 11.57 E
Terral 196 33.53 N 97.56 W
Terralba 71 39.43 N 8.39 E
Terra Linda 226 38.01 N 122.32 W
Terranova → Newfoundland □[4] 176 52.00 N 56.00 W
Terra Nova Bay ⊂ 9 74.45 S 164.30 E
Terranova da Sibari 68 39.39 N 16.20 E
Terranova di Pollino 68 39.59 N 16.18 E
Terranova di Sicilia → Gela 70 37.04 N 14.15 E
Terra Nova Lake ⊜ 186 48.30 N 54.20 W
Terra Nova National Park ◆ 186 48.37 N 53.56 W
Terranuova Bracciolini 66 43.33 N 11.35 E
Terra Rica 255 22.43 S 52.38 W
Terrarossa, Foce di)(64 44.12 N 10.26 E
Terra Roxa d'Oeste 252 24.08 S 53.59 W
Terras, Pinhal do ◆[3] 266c 38.39 N 9.02 W
Terra Santa 250 2.06 S 56.29 W
Terrasini 70 38.09 N 13.05 E
Terrasse-Vaudreuil 206 45.24 N 73.59 W
Terrasson-la-Villedieu 32 45.08 N 1.18 E
Terravecchia 68 39.29 N 16.58 E
Terrebonne 206 45.42 N 73.38 W
Terrebonne □[6] 206 46.00 N 74.10 W
Terrebonne Bay ⊂ 194 29.09 N 90.35 W
Terre Ceia 220 27.35 N 82.35 W
Terre-de-Bas 241o 15.51 N 61.39 W
Terre-de-Bas I 241o 15.52 N 61.38 W
Terre de Feu → Tierra del Fuego, Isla Grande de I 254 54.00 S 69.00 W
Terre-de-Haut 241o 15.58 N 61.35 W
Terre-de-Haut I 241o 15.52 N 61.35 W
Terre des Hommes ◆ 275a 45.31 N 73.32 W
Terre Haute 194 39.28 N 87.24 W
Terre Hill 208 40.09 N 76.03 W
Terrell 222 32.44 N 96.16 W
Terrell, Lake ⊜ 224 48.52 N 122.41 W
Terrell Hills 196 29.28 N 98.27 W
Terrenceville 186 47.40 N 54.44 W
Terre-Neuve → Newfoundland □[4] 176 52.00 N 56.00 W
Terre Noire Creek ≃ 194 33.49 N 92.55 W
Terre Rouge Creek ≃ 194 33.49 N 93.11 W
Terres australes et antarctiques françaises → French Southern and Antarctic Territories □[2] 6 49.30 S 69.30 E
Terrey Hills 170 33.41 S 151.14 E
Terrigal 170 33.27 S 151.27 E
Terrington Saint Clement 42 52.45 N 0.18 E
Territoires du Nord-Ouest → Northwest Territories □[4] 176 70.00 N 100.00 W
Territorio Británico de la Antártica → British Antarctic Territory □[2] 9 60.00 S 45.00 W
Territorio Británico del Océano Índico → British Indian Ocean Territory □[2] 12 7.00 S 72.00 E
Territorios del Noroeste → Northwest Territories □[4] 176 70.00 N 100.00 W
Terror Point > 182 53.10 N 129.56 W
Terrugem 266c 38.51 N 9.20 W
Terry, Ms., U.S. 194 32.05 N 90.17 W
Terry, Mt., U.S. 198 46.47 N 105.18 W
Terry Peak ∧ 198 44.19 N 103.50 W
Terryville, Ct., U.S. 207 41.40 N 73.00 W
Terryville, N.Y., U.S. 210 40.54 N 73.03 W
Tersa, S.S.S.R. 80 51.55 N 44.43 E
Tersa, S.S.S.R. 80 50.53 N 43.48 E
Tersa ≃ 80 50.46 N 44.40 E
Tersakkan ≃ 86 51.15 N 67.10 E
Terschelling I 52 53.24 N 5.20 E
Tersiva, Punta ∧ 62 45.37 N 7.28 E
Terskej-Alatau, chrebet ∧ 85 41.55 N 77.00 E
Terskij chrebet ∧ 84 43.32 N 45.00 E
Terslev 41 55.22 N 11.59 E
Tersløse 41 55.31 N 11.30 E
Tertenia 71 39.42 N 9.34 E
Terter ≃ 84 40.35 N 47.22 E
Teru 123 36.11 N 72.45 E
Teruel, Col. 246 2.44 N 75.33 W
Teruel, Esp. 34 40.21 N 1.06 W
Terujak 114 4.23 N 97.31 E
Terutao, Ko I 114 6.35 N 99.40 E
Tervakoski 26 60.48 N 24.37 E
Tervel 38 43.45 N 27.24 E
Tervola 26 66.05 N 24.48 E
Tervuren 56 50.49 N 4.31 E
Terwagne 56 50.27 N 5.20 E
Terwolde 52 52.16 N 6.06 E
Terzaghi Dam ◆[6] 182 50.49 N 122.12 W
Terzigno 68 40.48 N 14.29 E
Teržola 84 42.12 N 42.59 E
Tes 88 50.27 N 93.30 E
Tešá, Magy. 30 48.02 N 18.51 E
Teša, S.S.S.R. 80 55.30 N 42.50 E
Tesalia 246 2.29 N 75.44 W
Tešanj 38 44.37 N 18.00 E
Tes-Chem (Tesijn) ≃ 88 50.28 N 93.04 E
Teschen → Český Těšín 30 49.45 N 18.37 E
Teschendorf 54 52.51 N 13.10 E
Tescott 198 39.00 N 97.52 W
Tesdrero, Cerro ∧ 234 22.47 N 103.04 W
Tesenev 144 15.07 N 36.41 E
Tesero 64 46.17 N 11.31 E
Teshekpuk Lake ⊜ 180 70.35 N 153.30 W
Teshikaga 92a 43.29 N 144.28 E
Te-shima I, Nihon 96 34.29 N 134.05 E
Te-shima I, Nihon 96 34.24 N 133.40 E
Teshio 92a 44.53 N 141.44 E
Teshio ≃ 92a 44.53 N 141.44 E
Teshio-sanchi ∧ 92a 44.15 N 142.05 E
Tešig 88 49.56 N 102.44 E
Tesijn (Tes-Chem) ≃ 88 50.28 N 93.04 E
Tesimo (Tisens) 64 46.34 N 11.10 E
Teslić 38 44.37 N 17.51 E
Teslin 180 60.09 N 132.45 W
Teslin ≃ 180 61.34 N 134.54 W
Teslin Lake ⊜ 180 60.15 N 132.57 W
Tesouras ≃ 255 14.36 S 50.51 W
Tesouro 255 16.04 S 53.34 W
Tesovo 82 55.34 N 36.05 E
Tesperhude 52 53.24 N 10.24 E
Tessa, Oued ≃ 36 36.34 N 8.54 E
Tessa-Ararai, Oued V 148 26.18 N 1.58 E
Tessala, Djebel ∧ 34 35.17 N 0.48 W
Tessala, Monts du ∧ 34 35.25 N 0.45 W
Tessalit 150 20.12 N 1.00 E
Tessancourt-sur-Aubette 261 49.02 N 1.55 E
Tessaoua 150 13.45 N 7.59 E
Tessei ≃ 96 34.56 N 133.20 E
Tessenderlo 56 51.04 N 5.05 E
Tesserete 58 46.04 N 8.58 E
Tessin 54 54.01 N 12.28 E
Tessin → Ticino □[3] 58 46.20 N 8.45 E
Tessy-sur-Vire 32 48.58 N 1.04 W
Test ≃ 42 50.55 N 1.29 W
Testa, Capo > 71 41.14 N 9.08 E
Teştik 130 40.08 N 38.45 E
Teston, On., Can. 275b 43.52 N 79.32 W
Teston, Eng., U.K. 260 51.15 N 0.26 E
Testour 36 36.33 N 9.27 E
Tesuque 200 35.45 N 105.55 W
Têt ≃ 32 42.44 N 3.02 E
Tetachuck Lake ⊜ 182 53.20 N 125.50 W
Tetagouche ≃ 186 47.38 N 65.41 W
Tetas, Punta > 252 23.31 S 70.38 W
Tetbury 42 51.39 N 2.10 W
Tete 154 16.13 S 33.35 E
Tete □[5] 154 15.15 S 32.40 E
Tété ≃ 146 9.12 N 20.29 E
Tête-à-la-Baleine 186 50.41 N 59.20 W
Tête du Parmelan ∧ 58 45.57 N 6.14 E
Tête-Jaune-Cache 182 52.57 N 119.26 W
Te Teko 172 38.02 S 176.48 E
Tetepare Island I 175e 8.43 S 157.33 E
Tetépisca, Lac ⊜ 186 51.00 N 69.25 W
Teterboro 276 40.52 N 74.03 W
Teterboro Airport ⊠ 276 40.51 N 74.04 W
Teterchen 56 49.14 N 6.34 E
Tetere ≃ 88 59.30 N 105.00 E
Teterev ≃ 78 51.01 N 30.05 E
Teterow 54 53.46 N 12.34 E
Teteven 38 42.55 N 24.16 E
Tetiaroa I[1] 14 17.05 S 149.32 W
Tetica de Bacares ∧ 34 37.15 N 2.25 W
Tetijev 78 49.23 N 29.41 E
Tetla 234 19.26 N 98.06 W
Tetlin 180 63.08 N 142.31 W
Tetlin Lake ⊜ 180 63.05 N 142.45 W
Teton 202 43.53 N 111.40 W
Teton ≃, Id., U.S. 202 43.54 N 111.51 W
Teton ≃, Mt., U.S. 202 47.56 N 110.31 W
Tetonia 202 43.49 N 111.09 W
Teton Range ∧ 202 43.45 N 110.50 W
Tétouan 148 35.34 N 5.23 W
Tétouan □[4] 148 35.30 N 5.30 W
Tetovo 38 42.01 N 20.58 E
Tétreauville ◆[8] 275a 45.36 N 73.32 W
Tetri-Ckaro 84 41.34 N 44.28 E
Tetschen → Děčín 54 50.48 N 14.13 E
Tetsuta 96 34.56 N 133.28 E
Tettau 54 50.28 N 11.15 E
Tettenhall 42 52.36 N 2.09 W
Tettens 52 53.38 N 7.53 E
Tettnang 58 47.40 N 9.35 E
Tetuán → Tétouan 148 35.34 N 5.23 W
Tetufera, Mont ∧ 174s 17.40 S 149.26 W
Tetulbāria 126 21.58 N 90.03 E
Tetulia ≃[1] 126 22.15 N 90.37 E
Teturi 154 1.04 N 29.08 E
Tet'uši 80 54.57 N 48.50 E
Tet'uškoje 80 54.18 N 48.03 E
Teublitz 60 49.13 N 12.05 E
Teuchern 54 51.07 N 12.01 E
Teuco ≃ 252 25.38 S 60.12 W
Teufelshöhle ⊥[5] 60 49.45 N 11.25 E
Teufels-Insel → Diable, Île du I 250 5.17 N 52.35 W
Teufelsmoor ◆[3] 52 53.15 N 8.50 E
Teufen 58 47.23 N 9.23 E
Teufenbach 61 47.08 N 14.21 E
Teulada 71 38.58 N 8.46 E
Teulada, Capo > 71 38.52 N 8.38 E
Teúl de González Ortega 234 21.28 N 103.29 W
Teulon 184 50.23 N 97.16 W
Teun, Pulau I 164 6.59 S 129.08 E
Teunom ≃ 114 4.26 N 95.48 E
Teunz 60 49.29 N 12.23 E
Teupitz 54 52.08 N 13.36 E
Teuplitz → Tuplice 30 51.41 N 14.50 E
Teureubangan Cut 114 3.12 N 97.18 E
Teuri-tō I 92a 44.25 N 141.19 E
Teuschnitz 54 50.24 N 11.23 E
Teutleben 54 50.57 N 10.33 E
Teutli, Cerro del ∧ 286a 19.14 N 99.01 W
Teutoburger Wald ◆[3] 52 52.10 N 8.15 E
Teutopolis 194 39.07 N 88.28 W
Teutschenthal 54 51.27 N 11.46 E
Teuva 26 62.29 N 21.44 E
Tevere ≃ 66 41.44 N 12.14 E
Teverya (Tiberias) 132 32.47 N 35.32 E
Teviot ≃ 44 55.36 N 2.26 W
Teviot Brook ≃ 171a 27.51 S 152.57 E
Teviotdale V 44 55.25 N 2.50 W
Teviothead 44 55.21 N 2.56 W
Tevli 76 52.20 N 24.15 E
Tevriz 86 57.34 N 72.24 E
Te Waewae Bay ⊂ 172 46.15 S 167.30 E
Tewah 112 1.05 S 113.42 E
Te Whaiti 172 38.35 S 176.47 E
Tewkesbury 42 51.59 N 2.09 W
Tewksbury 207 42.36 N 71.14 W
Tew-Mac Airport ⊠ 283 42.36 N 71.12 W
Tewo 102 34.02 N 103.05 E
Texada Island I 182 49.40 N 124.24 W
Texana, Lake ⊜[1] 222 28.58 N 96.32 W
Texarkana, Ar., U.S. 194 33.26 N 94.02 W
Texarkana, Tx., U.S. 194 33.25 N 94.02 W
Texas, Austl. 166 28.51 S 151.11 E
Texas, Oh., U.S. 216 41.26 N 83.57 W
Texas □[3], U.S. 178 31.30 N 99.00 W
Texas □[3], U.S. 196 31.30 N 99.00 W
Texas City 222 29.23 N 94.54 W
Texcaltitlán 234 18.54 N 99.55 W
Texcoco □[7] 286a 19.28 N 99.01 W
Texcoco, Lago de ⊜ 234 19.30 N 99.00 W
Texcoco [de Mora] 234 19.31 N 98.53 W
Texel I 52 53.05 N 4.45 E
Texhoma 196 36.30 N 101.46 W
Texico 196 34.23 N 103.03 W
Texistepec 234 17.53 N 94.47 W
Texline 196 36.23 N 103.01 W
Texoma, Lake ⊜[1] 196 33.55 N 96.37 W
Teyá 266d 41.30 N 2.19 E
Teyateyaneng 158 29.07 S 27.34 E
Teyéa ⊥ 38 37.29 N 22.24 E
Teylān 120 35.32 N 64.47 E
Teynham 42 51.20 N 0.50 E
Teyvareh 120 33.21 N 64.25 E
Teza ≃ 80 56.32 N 41.53 E
Teziutlán 234 19.49 N 97.21 W
Težler, gora ∧ 84 40.42 N 44.37 E
Tezoatlán [de Segura y Luna] 234 17.42 N 97.49 W
Tezpur 120 26.37 N 92.48 E
Tezzeron Lake ⊜ 182 54.41 N 124.25 W
Tha ≃ 110 20.07 N 100.35 E
Tha-anne ≃ 176 60.31 N 94.37 W
Thabana-Ntlenyana ∧ 158 29.28 S 29.16 E
Thaba Nchu 158 29.17 S 26.52 E
Thabankulu ∧ 158 27.30 S 30.20 E
Thaba-Putsoa Range ∧ 158 29.45 S 27.55 E
Thabaung 110 17.02 N 94.48 E
Thabawleikkyi 110 12.01 N 99.12 E
Thabazimbi 158 24.41 S 27.21 E
Thabor, Mont ∧ 62 45.07 N 6.34 E
Thabyu 110 15.36 N 98.29 E
Thach-by 110 14.40 N 109.04 E
Thacher Island I 207 42.38 N 70.35 W
Thādiq 128 25.18 N 45.52 E
Thagyettaw 110 13.45 N 98.09 E
Thai-binh 110 20.27 N 106.20 E
Thailand (Prathet Thai) □[1], Asia 108 15.00 N 100.00 E
Thailand (Prathet Thai) □[1], Asia 110 15.00 N 100.00 E
Thailand, Gulf of ⊂ 110 10.00 N 101.00 E
Thailande → Thailand □[1] 110 15.00 N 100.00 E
Thailandia → Thailand □[1] 110 15.00 N 100.00 E
Thai Nguyen 110 21.36 N 105.50 E
Thai-nguyen 110 21.36 N 105.50 E
Thak 120 30.32 N 70.13 E
Thakhek → Muang Khammouan 110 17.24 N 104.48 E
Thākurdwāra 124 29.12 N 78.51 E
Thākurdwāri 272b 22.34 N 88.28 E
Thākurgaon 124 26.02 N 88.28 E
Thākurpukur 272b 22.28 N 88.19 E
Thākurvādi 272c 18.54 N 73.04 E
Thal, D.D.R. 54 50.55 N 10.23 E
Thal, Pāk. 123 33.22 N 70.33 E
Tha'l, Jabal ∧ 140 14.13 N 24.14 E
Thala 36 35.35 N 8.40 E
Thalang 110 8.01 N 98.19 E
Thal-Assling 64 46.47 N 12.38 E
Thalāthah 142 30.35 N 32.20 E
Thal Desert ◆[2] 123 31.30 N 71.40 E
Thale 54 51.45 N 11.02 E
Thalfang 56 49.45 N 6.59 E
Thalgau 64 47.50 N 13.15 E
Thalheim 54 50.42 N 12.51 E
Thalheim bei Wels 61 48.09 N 14.02 E
Tha Li 110 17.37 N 101.25 E
Thalia 196 33.59 N 99.32 W
Thālith, Ash-Shallāl ath- (Third Cataract) ᒐ 140 19.49 N 30.19 E
Thalitter 56 51.13 N 8.53 E
Thalkirch 58 46.38 N 9.16 E
Thallon 166 28.38 S 148.52 E
Thallwitz 54 51.26 N 12.40 E
Thalmah, Marsā ⊂ 142 29.03 N 32.38 E
Thalmässing 60 49.05 N 11.13 E
Thalwil 58 47.17 N 8.34 E
Thamar, Jabal ∧ 144 13.53 N 45.30 E
Thame 42 51.45 N 0.59 W
Thames 172 37.08 S 175.33 E
Thames ≃, On., Can. 190 42.19 N 82.27 W
Thames ≃, Eng., U.K. 42 51.28 N 0.43 E
Thames ≃, Ct., U.S. 207 41.18 N 72.05 W
Thames, Firth of ⊂ 172 37.00 S 175.25 E
Thames Barrier ◆[5] 260 51.29 N 0.03 E
Thames Ditton 260 51.23 N 0.21 W
Thames Estuary ⊂[1] 260 51.30 N 0.40 W
Thamesford 212 43.04 N 81.00 W
Thames Haven 260 51.30 N 0.31 E
Thamesville 214 42.33 N 81.59 W
Thamīt, Wādī V 146 31.15 N 16.06 E
Thammasat, University of ⊠[2] 269a 13.45 N 100.30 E
Thamūd, Bi'r ⊤[4] 144 17.15 N 49.54 E
Thāna, India 122 19.12 N 72.58 E
Thāna, Pāk. 128 28.55 N 63.45 E
Thāna □[5] 272c 19.12 N 73.05 E
Thāna Creek ⊂ 272c 19.00 N 72.57 E
Thāna Ghāzi 124 27.25 N 76.19 E
Thāna Kasba 124 25.13 N 77.20 E
Thanbyuzayat 110 15.58 N 97.44 E
Thandaung 110 19.04 N 96.41 E
Thānedārwāla 123 32.36 N 71.07 E
Thānesar 124 29.59 N 76.49 E
Thanet, Isle of I 42 51.22 N 1.20 E
Thanet Lake ⊜ 212 44.47 N 77.46 W
Thang-binh 110 15.44 N 108.22 E
Thangoo 162 18.10 S 122.22 E
Thangool 166 24.29 S 150.35 E
Thanh-hoa 110 19.48 N 105.46 E
Thanh-my-tay 269c 10.49 N 106.46 E
Thanh-pho Ho Chi Minh (Sai-gon), Viet. 110 10.45 N 106.40 E
Thanh-pho Ho Chi Minh (Sai-gon), Viet. 269c 10.45 N 106.40 E
Thanjāvūr 122 10.48 N 79.09 E
Thānkot 124 27.41 N 85.11 E
Thann 58 47.49 N 7.05 E
Thannhausen 58 48.17 N 10.28 E
Thāno Bula Khān 120 25.22 N 67.50 E
Than-uyen 110 22.00 N 103.54 E
Thaoge ≃ 156 20.27 S 22.36 E
Thaon-les-Vosges 58 48.15 N 6.25 E
Tha Pla 110 17.48 N 100.32 E
Thap Than ≃ 110 15.21 N 104.06 E
Tharabwin West 110 12.17 N 99.03 E
Tharād 120 24.24 N 71.38 E
Tharandt 54 50.59 N 13.35 E
't Harde 52 52.25 N 5.53 E
Thar Desert (Great Indian Desert) ◆[2] 120 27.00 N 71.00 E
Thargomindah 166 28.00 S 143.49 E
Thāri Pātan ∧ 124 28.58 N 82.04 E
Thar Nhom 140 7.26 N 30.29 E
Tharptown 210 40.48 N 76.34 W
Tharr, Wüste → Thar Desert ◆[2] 120 27.00 N 71.00 E
Tharrawaddy 110 17.39 N 95.48 E
Tharrawaw 110 17.41 N 95.28 E
Tharros ⊥ 71 39.52 N 8.26 E
Tharsuinn, Beinn ∧ 46 57.47 N 4.21 W
Tharthār, Wādī ath- V 128 33.59 N 43.12 E
Tharwa 171b 35.31 S 149.04 E
Tha Sala 110 8.40 N 99.56 E
Thásos 38 40.47 N 24.42 E
Thásos I 38 40.41 N 24.47 E
Thásos ⊥ 38 40.46 N 24.33 E
Tha Tako 110 15.38 N 100.29 E
Thatcham 42 51.25 N 1.15 W
Thatch Cay I 240m 18.22 N 64.52 W
Thatcher 200 32.50 N 109.45 W
Thatch Island I 276 40.38 N 73.23 W
That-khe 110 22.16 N 106.28 E
Thaton 110 16.55 N 97.22 E
That Phanom 110 16.57 N 104.44 E
Thatto Heath 262 53.26 N 2.45 W
Tha Tum 110 15.19 N 103.41 E
Thau, Bassin de ⊂ 32 43.23 N 3.36 E
Thaungdut 110 24.26 N 94.42 E
Thaungyin ≃ 110 17.50 N 97.42 E
Tha Uthen 110 17.34 N 104.36 E
Thawville 216 40.41 N 88.07 W
Thaxted 42 51.57 N 0.20 E
Thaya (Dyje) ≃ 61 48.37 N 16.56 E
Thayawthadangyi Kyun I 110 12.20 N 98.00 E
Thayer, Il., U.S. 219 39.32 N 89.46 W
Thayer, In., U.S. 216 41.10 N 87.20 W
Thayer, Ks., U.S. 198 37.29 N 95.28 W
Thayer, Mo., U.S. 194 36.31 N 91.32 W
Thayetchaung 110 13.52 N 98.16 E
Thayetmyo 110 19.19 N 95.11 E
Thayngen 58 47.45 N 8.42 E
Thazi 110 20.51 N 96.05 E
The Aldermen Islands II 172 36.58 S 176.05 E
Theale 42 51.27 N 1.04 W
Thealka 192 37.49 N 82.47 W
The Basin 274b 37.51 S 145.19 E
Thebes → Thívai 38 38.21 N 23.19 E
Thebes 194 37.13 N 89.28 W
Thebes ⊥ 140 25.42 N 32.37 E
The Bight 238 24.19 N 75.24 W
The Birket ≃ 262 53.24 N 3.01 W
The Bluffs ⊥[4] 210 43.22 N 76.40 W
The Bourne ≃ 260 51.22 N 0.29 W
The Calvados Chain II 164 11.10 S 152.40 E
The Capital ⊠ 284c 38.53 N 77.00 W
The Cheviot ∧ 44 55.28 N 2.09 W
The Citadel ⊥ 273c 30.02 N 31.15 E
The Cloisters ⊠ 276 40.52 N 73.56 W
The Colony 222 33.05 N 96.52 W
The Coorong ⊂ 168b 35.40 S 139.15 E
The Coteau ∧[2] 184 51.10 N 107.30 W
The Curragh ◆ 48 53.10 N 6.52 W
The Dalles 224 45.35 N 121.10 W
The Dalles Dam ◆[6] 224 45.37 N 121.08 W
The Deeps ⊂ 46a 60.09 N 1.23 W
Thedford 198 41.58 N 100.34 W
Thedinghausen 52 52.58 N 9.01 E
The Dome of the Rock (Mosque of Omar) ⊠[1] 132 31.47 N 35.13 E
The Downs ⊤[3] 42 51.13 N 1.27 E
Theebine 166 25.57 S 152.33 E
The English Companys Islands II 164 11.50 S 136.32 E
The Entrance 170 33.21 S 151.30 E
Theessen 54 52.14 N 12.02 E
The Everglades ⊞ 220 26.00 N 80.40 W
The Father ∧ 164 5.03 S 151.20 E
The Fens ⊞ 42 52.38 N 0.02 E
The Fiery Range ∧ 171b 35.30 S 148.40 E
The Fishing Lakes ⊜ 184 50.45 N 103.51 W
The Flash ⊜ 262 53.29 N 2.33 W
The Flat Tops ∧ 200 40.00 N 107.10 W
The Forest of Nisene Marks State Park ◆ 226 37.03 N 121.53 W
The Glenkens ◆[1] 44 55.10 N 4.15 W
Thégon 110 18.39 N 95.25 E
The Granites 162 20.35 S 130.21 E
The Granites ∧ 162 20.35 S 130.20 E
The Graves II 283 42.22 N 70.52 W
The Grove 222 31.16 N 97.32 W
The Hague → 's-Gravenhage 52 52.06 N 4.18 E
The Heads > 202 42.44 N 124.31 W
The Hermitage ⊠ 265a 59.56 N 30.20 E
The Home Park ◆ 260 51.28 N 0.36 W
The Hunters Hills ∧[2] 172 44.30 S 170.50 E
Theinkun 110 11.53 N 99.09 E
The Isles Lagoon ⊂ 174o 1.50 N 157.23 W
Theiss → Tisa ≃ 38 45.15 N 20.17 E
Theissen 54 51.05 N 12.06 E
The Key Indian Reserve ◆[4] 184 51.45 N 102.08 W
The Lake Fleet Islands II 212 44.18 N 76.07 W
The Lakes National Park ◆ 166 38.05 S 147.40 E
Thelon ≃ 176 64.16 N 96.05 W
The Long Mynd ∧ 42 52.35 N 2.48 W
The Lower Hope ≃[1] 260 51.28 N 0.28 E
Thelwall 262 53.23 N 2.32 W
The Lynd 166 18.56 S 144.30 E
Them 41 56.06 N 9.33 E
The Machars □[8] 44 54.50 N 4.30 W
The Machars ◆[1] 44 55.20 N 4.33 W
The Mall in Columbia ◆[9] 284b 39.13 N 76.52 W
Themar 54 50.30 N 10.37 E
The Meadows Race Track ◆ 279b 40.13 N 80.12 W
The Mere ⊜ 262 53.20 N 2.24 W
Théméricourt 261 49.05 N 1.54 E
The Minch ⊔ 46 58.10 N 5.50 W
The Moors ◆[1] 44 54.56 N 4.40 W
The Mumbles 42 51.34 N 4.00 W
Then 123 32.26 N 75.44 E
The Narrows ⊔ 276 40.37 N 74.03 W
The Navy Islands II 212 44.21 N 76.03 W
The Naze > 42 51.53 N 1.16 E
The Needles > 42 50.39 N 1.34 W
Thénezay 32 46.43 N 0.02 W
Thenia 148 36.43 N 3.34 E
Theniet el Hadd 148 35.47 N 2.01 E
The Oa ◆[1] 46 55.37 N 6.16 W
The Oaks, Austl. 170 34.04 S 150.34 E
The Oaks, Ca., U.S. 226 39.13 N 121.05 W
Theodore, Austl. 166 24.57 S 150.05 E
Theodore, Sk., Can. 184 51.25 N 102.54 W
Theodore, Al., U.S. 194 30.32 N 88.10 W
Theodore Francis Green Airport ⊠ 207 41.44 N 71.26 W
Theodore Roosevelt Inaugural National Historical Site ⊥ 284a 42.54 N 78.52 W
Theodore Roosevelt Island I 284c 38.54 N 77.03 W
Theodore Roosevelt Lake ⊜[1] 200 33.42 N 111.07 W
Theodore Roosevelt National Park (South Unit) ◆, N.D., U.S. 198 46.55 N 103.26 W
Theodore Roosevelt National Park (North Unit) ◆, N.D., U.S. 198 47.34 N 103.24 W
Theodor-Heuss-Brücke ◆[5] 263 51.15 N 6.45 E
Theog 123 31.07 N 77.21 E
Theológos 38 40.39 N 24.41 E
The Orchards 284b 39.18 N 76.50 W
Théoule-sur-Mer 62 43.31 N 6.57 E
The Oval ⊥ 260 51.29 N 0.07 W
The Pages II 168b 35.47 S 138.17 E
The Paps ∧ 48 52.00 N 9.17 W
The Pas 184 53.50 N 101.15 W
The Peak ∧ 192 36.24 N 81.39 W
Thepha 110 6.52 N 100.58 E
The Pilot ∧ 166 36.45 S 148.13 E
The Pinnacle ∧[2] 219 39.22 N 90.55 W
Thérain ≃ 50 49.15 N 2.27 E
The Rajah ∧ 182 53.15 N 118.31 W
The Rand → Witwatersrant ◆[1] 158 26.00 S 27.00 E
The Range 154 19.00 S 31.04 E
Theresa 212 44.12 N 75.47 W
Theresa Creek ≃ 166 23.26 S 148.09 E
Theresa Park 274a 34.01 S 150.39 E
Theresienstadt → Terezín 54 50.31 N 14.08 E
The Rhins >[1] 44 54.50 N 5.00 W
The Rip ⊂ 169 38.17 S 144.37 E
The Riverstone Wildlife Refuge ◆[4] 274a 33.42 S 150.51 E
Thermaïkós Kólpos ⊂ 38 40.23 N 22.47 E
Thermalito 226 39.31 N 121.36 W
Thermopílai ⊥ 38 38.48 N 22.33 E
Thermopolis 200 43.38 N 108.12 W
Thermopylae → Thermopílai ⊥ 38 38.48 N 22.33 E
The Road ⊂ 42a 49.56 N 6.20 W
The Rock 166 35.16 S 147.07 E
The Rockies ∧ 224 46.39 N 122.22 W
Theron Mountains ∧ 9 79.05 S 28.15 W
The Rope ⊥[4] 174e 25.04 S 130.05 W
Thérouanne 50 50.38 N 2.15 E
The Savannahs ⊜ 220 27.19 N 80.17 W
Theseion ⊥ 267c 37.58 N 23.43 E
Thesiger Bay ⊂ 176 71.30 N 124.05 W
The Sisters ∧[2] 162 26.17 S 126.40 E
The Slot → New Georgia Sound ⊔ 175e 8.00 S 158.10 E
The Sluice ⊔ 262 53.41 N 2.57 W
The Sny ≃ 219 39.16 N 90.44 W
The Solent ⊔ 42 50.46 N 1.20 W
The Sound ⊔, Austl. 274a 33.49 S 151.17 E
The Sound (Øresund) ⊔, Europe 41 55.50 N 12.40 E
The Springs 207 40.52 N 72.32 W
Thesprotikón 38 39.15 N 20.47 E
Thessalía □[9] 38 39.30 N 22.00 E
Thessalon 190 46.15 N 83.34 W
Thessaloníki (Salonika) 38 40.38 N 22.56 E
Thessalonique → Thessaloníki 38 40.38 N 22.56 E
The Storr ∧ 46 57.31 N 6.12 W
The Swale ⊔ 42 51.22 N 0.56 E
Thet ≃ 42 52.27 N 0.33 E
The Tauride Palace ⊠ 265a 59.57 N 30.23 E
The Terraces ⊥[4] 162 28.40 S 121.32 E
Thetford 42 52.25 N 0.45 E
Thetford-Mines 206 46.05 N 71.18 W
The Thorofare ⊔ 208 37.15 N 75.54 W
The Thumbs ∧ 172 43.35 S 170.44 E
Thetis Island 224 49.59 N 123.40 W
Thetis Island I 224 49.00 N 123.41 W
The Twelve Pins ∧ 48 53.31 N 9.50 W
The Twins ∧ 172 41.14 S 172.39 E
Theunissen 158 28.30 S 26.41 E
Theux 56 50.32 N 5.49 E
The Valley 238 18.13 N 63.04 W
Thevenard 162 32.09 S 133.38 E
Thevenard Island I 162 21.27 S 115.00 E

Symbols in the index entries represent the broad categories identified in the key at the right. Symbols with superior numbers (∧[1]) identify subcategories (see complete key on page I · 1).

Kartensymbole in dem Registerverzeichnis stellen die rechts in Schlüssel erklärten Kategorien dar. Symbole mit hochgestellten Ziffern (∧[1]) bezeichnen Unterabteilungen einer Kategorie (vgl. vollständiger Schlüssel auf Seite I · 1).

Los símbolos incluidos en el texto del índice representan las grandes categorías identificadas con la clave a la derecha. Los símbolos con numeros en su parte superior (∧[1]) identifican las subcategorías (véase la clave completa en la página I · 1).

Les symboles de l'index représentent les catégories indiquées dans la légende à droite. Les symboles suivis d'un indice (∧[1]) représentent des sous-catégories (voir légende complète à la page I · 1).

Os símbolos incluídos no texto do índice representam as grandes categorias identificadas com a chave à direita. Os símbolos com números em sua parte superior (∧[1]) identificam as subcategorias (veja-se a chave completa à página I · 1).

∧ Mountain	Berg	Montaña	Montagne	Montanha
∧ Mountains	Berge	Montañas	Montagnes	Montanhas
)(Pass	Pass	Paso	Col	Passo
V Valley, Canyon	Tal, Cañon	Valle, Cañón	Vallée, Canyon	Vale, Canhão
≃ Plain	Ebene	Llano	Plaine	Planície
> Cape	Kap	Cabo	Cap	Cabo
I Island	Insel	Isla	Île	Ilha
II Islands	Inseln	Islas	Îles	Ilhas
⊥ Other Topographic Features	Andere Topographische Objekte	Otros Elementos Topográficos	Autres données topographiques	Outros acidentes topográficos

ESPAÑOL

Nombre	Página	Lat.°′	Long.°′ W = Oeste
The Wash ⊂	42	52.55 N	0.15 E
The Weald ◆[1]	42	51.05 N	0.05 E
The Whirlpool ≃	284a	43.07 N	79.04 W
The Winehead ∧	210	40.58 N	77.28 W
The Woodlands	222	30.09 N	95.27 W
The Wrekin ∧[2]	42	52.41 N	2.34 W
Theydon Bois	260	51.40 N	0.06 E
Theys	62	45.18 N	6.00 E
Thiais	261	48.46 N	2.23 E
Thiant	50	50.18 N	3.27 E
Thiaucourt-Regniéville	56	48.57 N	5.52 E
Thibaudeau	184	57.05 N	94.08 W
Thiberville	50	49.08 N	0.27 E
Thibodaux	194	29.47 N	90.49 W
Thicket	222	30.24 N	94.38 W
Thicket Portage	184	55.19 N	97.42 W
Thiéblemont-Farémont	58	48.41 N	4.44 E
Thief ≃	198	48.08 N	96.10 W
Thief Lake ⊜	198	48.30 N	95.55 W
Thief River Falls	198	48.07 N	96.10 W
Thiéle ≃	58	47.03 N	7.05 E
Thiel Mountains ⋏	9	85.15 S	91.00 W
Thielsen, Mount ∧	202	43.09 N	122.04 W
Thiendorf	54	51.17 N	13.44 E
Thiene	64	45.42 N	11.29 E
Thiensville	216	43.14 N	87.58 W
Thier	263	51.05 N	7.22 E
Thiérache, Collines de la ⋏[2]	50	49.50 N	3.50 E
Thierhaupten	56	48.34 N	10.54 E
Thiers	62	45.51 N	3.34 E
Thiersheim	54	50.04 N	12.07 E
Thierville-sur-Meuse	56	49.10 N	5.21 E
Thiès	150	14.48 N	16.56 W
Thiès □[4]	150	14.45 N	16.50 W
Thiesi	71	40.31 N	8.43 E
Thiessow	54	54.16 N	13.43 E
Thieux	261	49.01 N	2.40 E
Thieveley Pike ∧[2]	262	53.45 N	2.12 W
Thika	154	1.03 S	37.05 E
Thikombia Island I	175g	15.44 S	179.55 W
Thilay	56	49.52 N	4.49 E
Thilenius, Cape ›	164	1.35 S	149.57 E
Thimbu	124	27.28 N	89.39 E
Thines	62	44.29 N	4.03 E
Thingvallavatn ⊜	24a	64.12 N	21.10 W
Thingvellir	24a	64.17 N	21.07 W
Thio	175f	21.37 S	166.14 E
Thionville	56	49.22 N	6.10 E
Thiou	150	13.48 N	2.40 W
Thíra	38	36.25 N	25.26 E
Thíra I	38	36.24 N	25.29 E
Third ≃	276	40.49 N	74.08 W
Third Cataract → Thālith, Ash-Shallāl ath- ∟	140	19.49 N	30.19 E
Third Cliff ⫠[4]	283	42.11 N	70.43 W
Third Creek ≃, Mo., U.S.	219	38.26 N	91.40 W
Third Creek ≃, N.C., U.S.	192	35.47 N	80.31 W
Third Han-gang Bridge ◆[5]	271b	37.32 N	127.00 E
Third Herring Brook ≃	283	42.07 N	70.48 W
Third Lake ⊜	206	45.14 N	71.12 W
Third Street Station ◆[5]	282	37.46 N	122.23 W
Thirlmere	170	34.12 S	150.34 E
Thirlmere ⊜	44	54.33 N	3.04 W
Thiron	50	48.19 N	0.59 E
Thironne ≃	50	48.17 N	1.15 E
Thirroul	170	34.19 S	150.56 E
Thirsk	44	54.14 N	1.20 W
Thirtieth Street Station ◆[5]	285	39.57 N	75.11 W
Thirtymile Creek ≃	198	46.22 N	102.03 W
Thirtymile Point ›	210	43.22 N	78.29 W
Thisted	26	56.57 N	8.42 E
Thistilfjörður ⊂	24a	66.20 N	15.25 W
Thistledown Race Track ♠	279a	41.26 N	81.32 W
Thistle Island I	166	35.00 S	136.09 E
Thistletown ◆[8]	275b	43.44 N	79.33 W
Thithia Island I	175g	17.45 S	179.18 W
Thívai (Thebes)	38	38.21 N	23.19 E
Thiverval-Grignon	261	48.51 N	1.55 E
Thiviers	32	45.25 N	0.56 E
Thizy	32	46.02 N	4.19 E
Thjórsá ≃	24a	63.47 N	20.48 W
Thlewiaza ≃	176	60.28 N	94.45 W
Thoa ≃	176	60.30 N	109.47 W
Tho-chu, Dao II	110	9.20 N	103.28 E
Thoen	110	17.36 N	99.12 E
Thohoyandou	156	23.00 S	30.29 E
Thoi-binh	110	9.21 N	105.05 E
Thoirette	58	46.16 N	5.32 E
Thoiry	261	48.52 N	1.48 E
Thoissey	58	46.10 N	4.48 E
Tholen	52	51.32 N	4.12 E
Tholen I	52	51.35 N	4.05 E
Tholey	56	49.29 N	7.02 E
Thollon	58	46.23 N	6.43 E
Thomas, Ok., U.S.	196	35.44 N	98.44 W
Thomas, Pa., U.S.	279b	40.15 N	80.06 W
Thomas, Wa., U.S.	224	47.21 N	122.13 W
Thomas, W.V., U.S.	188	39.08 N	79.29 W
Thomasboro	216	40.15 N	88.11 W
Thomas Creek ≃	202	44.40 N	122.56 W
Thomas Hill Reservoir ⊜[1]	194	39.40 N	92.40 W
Thomas J. O'Brien Lock and Dam ◆[5]	278	41.39 N	87.35 W
Thomas Lake ⊜	184	57.00 N	96.43 W
Thomas Mountains ⋏	9	75.32 S	70.57 W
Thomas Point ›	208	38.54 N	76.28 W
Thomaston, Al., U.S.	194	32.15 N	87.37 W
Thomaston, Ct., U.S.	207	41.40 N	73.04 W
Thomaston, Ga., U.S.	192	32.53 N	84.19 W
Thomaston, Me., U.S.	188	44.04 N	69.10 W
Thomaston, N.Y., U.S.	276	40.47 N	73.43 W
Thomaston, Tx., U.S.	222	29.00 N	97.09 W
Thomastown, Austl.	274b	37.41 S	145.01 E
Thomastown, Ire.	48	52.31 N	7.08 W
Thomasville, Al., U.S.	194	31.54 N	87.44 W
Thomasville, Ga., U.S.	192	30.50 N	83.58 W
Thomasville, N.C., U.S.	192	35.52 N	80.04 W
Thomasville, Pa., U.S.	208	39.56 N	76.51 W
Thomes Creek ≃	204	39.59 N	122.06 W
Thom Lake ⊜	184	55.24 N	96.08 W
Thomlinson, Mount ∧	182	55.33 N	127.29 W
Thompson, Mb., Can.	184	55.45 N	97.45 W
Thompson, Ct., U.S.	207	41.57 N	71.51 W
Thompson, Ia., U.S.	190	43.22 N	93.46 W
Thompson, Mo., U.S.	219	39.11 N	91.59 W
Thompson, N.D., U.S.	198	47.46 N	97.06 W
Thompson, Oh., U.S.	214	41.41 N	81.03 W
Thompson, Pa., U.S.	210	41.52 N	75.31 W
Thompson ≃, B.C., Can.	182	50.15 N	121.33 W
Thompson ≃, U.S.	194	39.45 N	93.36 W
Thompson Creek ≃, U.S.	198	45.04 N	104.25 W
Thompson Creek ≃, Ms., U.S.	194	31.10 N	88.54 W
Thompson Falls	202	47.35 N	115.20 W
Thompson Island I	283	42.23 N	71.01 W
Thompson Pass)(	180	61.08 N	145.45 W

FRANÇAIS

Nom	Page	Lat.°′	Long.°′ W = Ouest
Thompson Peak ∧	204	41.00 N	123.03 W
Thompson Place	224	47.03 N	122.45 W
Thompson Ridge	210	41.34 N	74.20 W
Thompson Run ≃	279b	40.24 N	79.50 W
Thompsons	222	29.30 N	95.36 W
Thompsons Creek ≃	284a	43.03 N	79.08 W
Thompson Sound ʯ	172	45.09 S	166.57 E
Thompsontown	208	40.33 N	77.14 W
Thompsonville	190	44.31 N	85.56 W
Thomsen ≃	176	74.08 N	119.35 W
Thomson, Ga., U.S.	192	33.28 N	82.30 W
Thomson, Il., U.S.	190	41.58 N	90.06 W
Thomson, N.Y., U.S.	210	43.07 N	73.35 W
Thomson ≃, Austl.	166	25.11 S	142.53 E
Thomson ≃, Austl.	169	37.58 S	146.32 E
Thomson Lake ⊜[1]	184	49.45 N	106.35 W
Thon ≃	50	49.53 N	3.55 E
Thon Buri	110	13.43 N	100.29 E
Thônes	62	45.53 N	6.20 E
Thong	260	51.24 N	0.24 E
Thong Hoe	271c	1.25 N	103.42 E
Thong Pha Phum	110	14.44 N	98.38 E
Thong-tay-hoi	269c	10.50 N	106.39 E
Thongwa	110	16.46 N	96.32 E
Thon-lac-nghiep	110	11.20 N	108.54 E
Thonnance-lès-Joinville	58	48.27 N	5.10 E
Thonon-les-Bains	58	46.22 N	6.29 E
Thonotosassa	220	28.03 N	82.18 W
Thonze	110	17.38 N	95.47 E
Thorah Island I	212	44.27 N	79.14 W
Thorame-Haute	62	44.06 N	6.33 E
Thorburn	186	45.34 N	62.33 W
Thoreau	200	35.24 N	108.13 W
Thorembais-les-Béguines	56	50.40 N	4.49 E
Thorenc	62	43.48 N	6.49 E
Thorens-Glières	58	45.59 N	6.15 E
Thorez → Torez	83	48.01 N	38.37 E
Thorhild	182	54.10 N	113.07 W
Thorial	140	8.40 N	29.56 E
Thorigny-sur-Marne	261	48.53 N	2.42 E
Thorigny-sur-Oreuse	50	48.17 N	3.24 E
Thórisvatn ⊜	24a	64.50 N	19.26 W
Thörl	61	47.31 N	15.13 E
Thorlákshöfn	24a	63.53 N	21.18 W
Thormanby	44	54.10 N	1.14 W
Thorn, Ned.	52	51.10 N	5.50 E
Thorn → Toruń, Pol.	30	53.02 N	18.35 E
Thornaby-on-Tees	44	54.34 N	1.18 W
Thornapple ≃, Mi., U.S.	216	42.56 N	85.28 W
Thornapple ≃, Wi., U.S.	190	45.28 N	91.16 W
Thornapple Lake ⊜	216	42.37 N	85.11 W
Thornburg	279b	40.26 N	80.05 W
Thornbury, Austl.	274b	37.45 S	145.00 E
Thornbury, On., Can.	212	44.34 N	80.26 W
Thornbury, N.Z.	172	46.17 S	168.06 E
Thornbury, Eng., U.K.	42	51.37 N	2.32 W
Thorn Creek ≃	278	41.36 N	87.35 W
Thorndale, On., Can.	212	43.06 N	81.08 W
Thorndale, Tx., U.S.	222	30.36 N	97.12 W
Thorndike	207	42.11 N	72.20 W
Thorndon	42	52.17 N	1.08 E
Thorne	44	53.37 N	0.58 W
Thorne ≃	184	54.56 N	90.35 W
Thorne Bay	182	55.44 N	132.32 W
Thorney	42	52.37 N	0.07 W
Thorngumbald	44	53.43 N	0.10 W
Thornhill, On., Can.	275b	43.48 N	79.25 W
Thornhill, S. Afr.	273d	26.07 S	28.09 E
Thornhill, Scot., U.K.	44	55.15 N	3.46 W
Thornhurst	210	41.11 N	75.35 W
Thornleigh	274a	33.44 S	151.05 E
Thornton, Austl.	171a	27.49 S	152.23 E
Thornton, Eng., U.K.	44	53.53 N	3.02 W
Thornton, Eng., U.K.	262	53.30 N	3.00 W
Thornton, Eng., U.K.	262	53.47 N	1.51 W
Thornton, Scot., U.K.	46	56.10 N	3.09 W
Thornton, Ar., U.S.	194	33.46 N	92.29 W
Thornton, Ca., U.S.	226	38.14 N	121.25 W
Thornton, Co., U.S.	200	39.52 N	104.58 W
Thornton, Il., U.S.	278	41.35 N	87.37 W
Thornton, Pa., U.S.	285	39.54 N	75.32 W
Thornton, Tx., U.S.	222	31.24 N	96.34 W
Thornton Beach ♠	282	37.42 N	122.30 W
Thornton Dale	44	54.14 N	0.43 W
Thornton Hough	262	53.19 N	3.03 W
Thornton-le-Moors	262	53.16 N	2.50 W
Thorntonville	196	31.34 N	102.55 W
Thornwood	210	41.07 N	73.46 W
Thornwood Common	260	51.43 N	0.08 E
Thorny Mountain ∧[2]	194	37.06 N	91.10 W
Thorofare	285	39.50 N	75.11 W
Thorold	212	43.07 N	79.12 W
Thorold South	284a	43.06 N	79.12 W
Thoronet, Abbaye du ▼[1]	62	43.28 N	6.16 E
Thorp, Wa., U.S.	224	47.04 N	120.40 W
Thorp, Wi., U.S.	190	44.57 N	90.47 W
Thorpe	260	51.24 N	0.32 W
Thorpe-le-Soken	42	51.52 N	1.10 E
Thorp Spring	222	32.28 N	97.49 W
Thorsby, Ab., Can.	182	53.14 N	114.03 W
Thorsby, Al., U.S.	194	32.54 N	86.42 W
Thorshavn → Tórshavn	22	62.01 N	6.46 W
Thórshöfn	24a	66.13 N	15.17 W
Thorsø	41	56.18 N	9.48 E
Thorsteinson Lake ⊜	184	57.15 N	97.30 W
Thorton Moor Reservoir ⊜[1]	262	53.47 N	1.55 W
Thot-not	110	10.16 N	105.32 E
Thouars	32	46.59 N	0.13 W
Thouin, Cape ›	162	20.20 S	118.12 E
Thoune → Thun	58	46.45 N	7.37 E
Thourotte	50	49.29 N	2.53 E
Thousand Islands II	212	44.15 N	76.12 W
Thousand Islands International Bridge ◆[5]	212	44.20 N	75.58 W
Thousand Lake Mountain ∧	200	38.25 N	111.29 W
Thousand Oaks	228	34.10 N	118.50 W
Thousand Ships Bay ⊂	175e	8.25 S	159.40 E
Thousand Springs Creek ≃	200	41.17 N	113.51 W
Thowa ≃	154	1.33 S	40.03 E
Thowgla Creek ≃	171b	36.10 S	147.57 E
Thrace □[9]	38	41.20 N	26.45 E
Thrakikón Pélagos ⊤[2]	38	40.15 N	24.28 E
Thrall	222	30.35 N	97.18 W
Thrapston	42	52.24 N	0.32 W
Thrasher Lake ⊜	212	44.55 N	78.58 W
Thread Creek ≃	216	43.01 N	83.42 W
Thredbo Village	171b	36.29 S	148.19 E
Three Bridges	208	40.31 N	74.47 W
Three Brothers ∧	224	47.23 N	120.45 W
Three Brothers Mountain ∧	224	49.10 N	120.46 W
Three Creek ≃	208	36.47 N	77.10 W
Three Fathoms Cove ⊂	271d	22.26 N	114.17 E
Three Fingered Jack ∧	202	44.29 N	121.50 W
Three Fingers ∧	224	48.10 N	121.41 W
Three Fools Creek ≃	224	48.53 N	120.57 W
Three Forks	202	45.53 N	111.33 W
Three Hills	182	51.42 N	113.16 W
Three Hummock Island I	166	40.26 S	144.55 E
Three Kings Islands II	172	34.10 S	172.05 E
Three Lakes	190	45.47 N	89.09 W
Three M Airport ⊠	285	40.08 N	74.51 W
Three Mile Bay	212	44.04 N	76.11 W
Three Mile Plains	186	44.58 N	64.07 W

PORTUGUÊS

Nome	Página	Lat.°′	Long.°′ W = Oeste
Three Oaks	216	41.47 N	86.36 W
Three Pagodas Pass)(	110	15.18 N	98.23 E
Threepoint Lake ⊜	184	55.41 N	98.56 W
Three Points, Cape ›	150	4.45 N	2.06 W
Three Rivers, Austl.	162	25.07 S	119.09 E
Three Rivers → Trois-Rivières, P.Q., Can.	206	46.21 N	72.33 W
Three Rivers, Ma., U.S.	207	42.10 N	72.21 W
Three Rivers, Mi., U.S.	216	41.56 N	85.37 W
Three Rivers, Tx., U.S.	196	28.27 N	98.10 W
Three Rivers □[8]	260	51.40 N	0.27 W
Three Sisters	158	31.54 S	23.06 E
Three Sisters ∧	202	44.10 N	121.46 W
Three Sisters Islands II	175e	10.10 S	161.57 E
Three Springs, Austl.	162	29.32 S	115.45 E
Three Springs, Pa., U.S.	214	40.12 N	77.59 W
Threlkeld	44	54.38 N	3.03 W
Throat ≃	184	51.48 N	93.30 W
Throckley	44	54.59 N	1.45 W
Throckmorton	196	33.10 N	99.10 W
Throgs Neck ◆[8]	276	40.49 N	73.49 W
Throgs Neck Bridge ◆[5]	276	40.48 N	73.48 W
Throgs Point ›	276	40.48 N	73.48 W
Throop	210	41.27 N	75.36 W
Throssel, Lake ⊜	162	27.27 S	124.16 E
Throssel Range ⋏	162	22.03 S	121.43 E
Thrushel ≃	42	50.39 N	4.15 W
Thruway Mall ◆[9]	284a	42.55 N	78.46 W
Thuan-chau	110	21.26 N	103.41 E
Thu-duc	269c	10.51 N	106.45 E
Thueyts	62	44.41 N	4.13 E
Thuilley-aux-Groseilles	58	48.34 N	5.58 E
Thuin	50	50.20 N	4.17 E
Thul	120	28.14 N	68.46 E
Thulaythiwāt, Tilāl ath- ∧	132	30.58 N	36.40 E
Thulba ≃	56	50.11 N	9.52 E
Thule	16	76.34 N	68.47 W
Thum	54	50.40 N	12.57 E
Thumb Peak ∧	116	9.48 N	118.36 E
Thumby	41	54.35 N	9.54 E
Thun	58	46.45 N	7.37 E
Thun Chang	110	19.25 N	100.53 E
Thunder Bay	190	48.23 N	89.15 W
Thunder Bay ⊂, On., Can.	190	48.24 N	89.00 W
Thunder Bay ⊂, On., Can.	212	44.48 N	80.03 W
Thunder Bay ⊂, Mi., U.S.	190	45.00 N	83.22 W
Thunder Bay ≃	190	45.04 N	83.25 W
Thunder Bay, North Branch ≃	190	45.08 N	83.35 W
Thunderbird, Lake ⊜[1]	196	35.15 N	97.20 W
Thunderbolt	192	32.02 N	81.03 W
Thunder Butte ∧	198	45.19 N	101.53 W
Thunder Butte Creek ≃	198	45.13 N	101.42 W
Thunder Creek ≃, Sk., Can.	184	50.23 N	105.32 W
Thunder Creek ≃, Wa., U.S.	224	48.40 N	121.05 W
Thunder Hills ⋏[2]	184	54.30 N	106.00 W
Thunder Mountain ∧[2]	216	42.16 N	86.20 W
Thundersley	260	51.34 N	0.35 E
Thunersee ⊜	58	46.40 N	7.45 E
Thüngen	56	49.56 N	9.51 E
Thung Song	110	8.09 N	99.41 E
Thung Wa	110	7.06 N	99.46 E
Thur ≃, Fr.	58	48.05 N	7.23 E
Thur ≃, Schw.	58	47.36 N	8.35 E
Thurcroft	44	53.24 N	1.16 W
Thurgau □[3]	58	47.35 N	9.00 E
Thurgovie → Thurgau □[3]	58	47.35 N	9.00 E
Thüringen	58	47.12 N	9.45 E
Thüringen □[9]	54	51.00 N	11.00 E
Thüringer Wald ⋏	30	50.40 N	10.50 E
Thürkow	54	53.50 N	12.33 E
Thurles	48	52.41 N	7.49 W
Thurmont	208	39.37 N	77.24 W
Thurn, Pass)(	64	47.19 N	12.24 E
Thurnau	60	50.01 N	11.23 E
Thurnham	260	51.17 N	0.36 E
Thurnscoe	44	53.31 N	1.19 W
Thurnwald Range ⋏	164	4.45 S	141.15 E
Thurø	41	55.03 N	10.40 E
Thurrock □[8]	260	51.30 N	0.21 E
Thursby	44	54.51 N	3.03 W
Thursday Island	164	10.35 S	142.13 E
Thurso, P.Q., Can.	206	45.36 N	75.15 W
Thurso, Scot., U.K.	46	58.35 N	3.32 W
Thurso ≃	46	58.36 N	3.30 W
Thurstaston	262	53.21 N	3.08 W
Thurston	42	52.15 N	0.49 E
Thurston □[6]	224	46.59 N	122.42 W
Thurston Island I	9	72.20 S	99.00 W
Thusis	58	46.42 N	9.26 E
Thwaites Ice Tongue ⊓	9	74.45 S	106.30 W
Thy ◆[1]	26	57.00 N	8.30 E
Thyborøn	26	56.42 N	8.13 E
Thylungra	166	26.04 S	143.28 E
Thyolo	154	16.10 S	35.10 E
Thyregod	41	55.54 N	9.16 E
Thysville → Mbanza-Ngungu	152	5.15 S	14.52 E
Tiadiaye	150	14.25 N	16.42 W
Tiahuanacu	248	16.33 S	68.42 W
Tía Juana	246	10.16 N	71.22 W
Tian ≃	105	40.42 N	116.33 E
Tiana, Esp.	266d	44.29 N	2.16 E
Tiana, It.	71	40.04 N	9.08 E
Tian'anmen Square ⊥	271a	39.55 N	116.23 E
Tianbao	100	24.36 N	117.35 E
Tianchang	100	32.41 N	119.01 E
Tiancunpu	105	39.06 N	115.41 E
Tiandeng	102	23.09 N	107.10 E
Tiandong	102	23.36 N	107.08 E
Tian'e	102	25.01 N	107.20 E
Tianeti	84	42.07 N	44.59 E
Tianfanjie	100	29.20 N	116.50 E
Tiangang, Zhg.	89	43.24 N	125.54 E
Tiangang, Zhg.	89	43.55 N	127.00 E
Tiangongsi	105	39.14 N	115.53 E
Tianguá	250	3.44 S	40.59 W
Tianhe	100	27.01 N	114.30 E
Tianhekou	100	32.08 N	113.25 E
Tianhelong	89	43.56 N	120.39 E
Tianhuang	98	35.29 N	117.18 E
Tianjara Mountain ∧	170	35.11 S	150.18 E
Tianjia, Zhg.	104	41.07 N	122.03 E
Tianjia, Zhg.	107	29.40 N	105.08 E
Tianjiaba	102	32.08 N	110.03 E
Tianjiatun	104	41.39 N	123.44 E
Tianjiawopu	104	42.28 N	122.38 E
Tianjiazhen	100	29.56 N	115.26 E
Tianjin (Tientsin)	105	39.08 N	117.12 E
Tianjing	106	31.27 N	120.46 E
Tianjin Shi (Tientsin Shih) □[7]	98	39.30 N	117.15 E
Tianjun	102	37.25 N	98.58 E
Tiankai	105	39.38 N	115.51 E
Tiankoura	150	10.46 N	3.16 W
Tiankoye	150	12.35 N	12.40 W
Tianlin, Zhg.	102	24.14 N	106.03 E
Tianlin, Zhg.	107	29.49 N	105.19 E
Tian Ling ∧	89	44.22 N	129.52 E
Tianmashan	106	31.04 N	121.08 E
Tianmen	100	30.39 N	113.06 E
Tianmu Shan ⋏	100	30.25 N	119.30 E
Tianpu	106	31.56 N	121.07 E
Tianqiaochang	104	40.52 N	121.02 E
Tianqiaoling	89	43.26 N	129.38 E
Tianquan	102	30.10 N	102.48 E
Tian Shan → Tien Shan ⋏	90	42.00 N	80.00 E
Tianshenggang	106	32.03 N	120.45 E
Tianshifu	98	41.17 N	124.21 E
Tianshui	102	34.30 N	105.58 E
Tianshuijing, Zhg.	102	40.17 N	95.21 E
Tianshuijing, Zhg.	104	41.19 N	121.48 E
Tianshuituo	105	39.20 N	118.12 E
Tianshuizhan	104	41.00 N	123.34 E
Tiantai	100	29.09 N	121.02 E
Tiantang	102	22.32 N	111.55 E
Tiantou, Zhg.	100	28.48 N	120.39 E
Tiantou, Zhg.	100	26.19 N	115.57 E
Tianwangsi	106	31.45 N	119.12 E
Tianxin, Zhg.	100	27.53 N	113.06 E
Tianxin, Zhg.	100	28.11 N	114.35 E
Tianxin, Zhg.	102	27.21 N	111.00 E
Tianxingqiao	106	32.05 N	119.57 E
Tianxiyang	100	26.31 N	118.33 E
Tianyang	102	23.51 N	106.34 E
Tianyangping	107	29.11 N	105.16 E
Tianyar	115b	8.12 S	115.30 E
Tianzhen	98	40.28 N	114.06 E
Tianzhongying	100	33.13 N	115.22 E
Tianzhu, Zhg.	102	37.14 N	102.59 E
Tianzhu, Zhg.	102	26.50 N	109.00 E
Tianzhuang, Zhg.	100	25.43 N	113.40 E
Tianzhuang, Zhg.	105	39.25 N	117.54 E
Tianzhuangtai	104	40.50 N	122.08 E
Tiao ≃	106	30.56 N	120.11 E
Tiaodengchang	107	30.47 N	106.22 E
Tiarel	174s	17.32 S	149.20 W
Tiarno	64	45.53 N	10.40 E
Tiaro	166	25.44 S	152.35 E
Tiassalé	150	5.54 N	4.50 W
Tiati ∧	154	1.19 N	35.56 E
Ti'avea	175a	13.57 S	171.24 W
Tiawichi Creek ≃	222	32.19 N	94.44 W
Tiba → Chiba	94	35.36 N	140.07 E
Tibagi	252	24.30 S	50.24 W
Tibaji ≃	252	22.47 S	51.01 W
Tibari	154	5.01 N	31.43 E
Tibasti, Sarīr ◆[2]	146	24.00 N	17.00 E
Tibati	152	6.27 N	12.38 E
Tibbermore	46	56.22 N	3.32 W
Tibbie	194	31.21 N	88.14 W
Tibe	144	9.03 N	37.08 E
Tibel'ti	88	51.46 N	103.11 E
Tiber → Tevere ≃	66	41.44 N	12.14 E
Tiberias → Teverya	132	32.47 N	35.32 E
Tiberias, Lake → Kinneret, Yam ⊜	132	32.48 N	35.35 E
Tiberina, Val ∨	66	43.31 N	12.10 E
Tibesti ⋏	146	21.30 N	17.30 E
Tibet → Xizang Zizhiqu □[4]	90	32.00 N	88.00 E
Tibet, Lake ⊜	220	28.27 N	81.31 W
Tibet, Plateau of → Qing Zang Gaoyuan ⋏[1]	12	33.00 N	92.00 E
Tibiao	116	11.17 N	122.02 E
Tibiao Point ›	116	11.18 N	122.02 E
Tibidabo ∧	266d	41.25 N	2.07 E
Tibiri, Niger	150	13.06 N	4.00 E
Tibiri, Niger	150	13.34 N	7.04 E
Tibiriçá ≃	255	21.43 S	50.15 W
Tibirke	41	56.03 N	12.07 E
Tiblawan	116	6.29 N	126.06 E
Tiblemont, Lac ⊜	190	48.14 N	77.18 W
Ţibleş, Munţii ⋏	38	47.38 N	24.05 E
Ţibnah	132	32.59 N	36.13 E
Tibnīn	132	33.12 N	35.25 E
Tibro	26	58.26 N	14.10 E
Tiburon	226	37.52 N	122.27 W
Tiburón, Cabo ›	246	8.42 N	77.24 W
Tiburón, Isla I	232	29.00 N	112.23 W
Tiburon Peninsula ›[1]	282	37.53 N	122.28 W
Ticao Island I	116	12.31 N	123.42 E
Ticao Pass ʯ	116	12.38 N	123.47 E
Tice	220	26.40 N	81.48 W
Tice Creek ≃	282	37.53 N	122.03 W
Ticehurst	42	51.03 N	0.25 E
Tichigan	216	42.50 N	88.12 W
Tichigan Lake ⊜	216	42.49 N	88.13 W
Tîchît	150	18.28 N	9.30 W
Tîchît, Ḍahr ⫠[4]	150	18.30 N	9.25 W
Tichmenevo, S.S.S.R.	76	58.00 N	38.36 E
Tichmenevo, S.S.S.R.	89	49.12 N	142.54 E
Ticho	144	7.50 N	39.32 E
Tichon	24	59.23 N	46.38 E
Tichonova Pustyn'	82	54.38 N	36.09 E
Tichonoviči	78	51.56 N	32.09 E
Tichonovka	88	53.13 N	104.13 E
Tichookeanskij	89	43.00 N	132.24 E
Tichoreck	78	45.51 N	40.09 E
Tichtozero	24	65.35 N	30.27 E
Tichvin	76	59.39 N	33.31 E
Tichvinskaja gr'ada ∧	76	59.30 N	34.30 E
Ticino □[3]	58	46.20 N	8.45 E
Ticino ≃	36	45.09 N	9.14 E
Tickfaw	194	30.34 N	90.28 W
Tickfaw ≃	194	30.20 N	90.28 W
Tickhill	44	53.26 N	1.06 W
Ticomán ◆[8]	286a	19.31 N	99.08 W
Ticonderoga	188	43.50 N	73.25 W
Ticul	232	20.24 N	89.32 W
Tīdah	142	31.15 N	30.50 E
Tidaholm	26	58.11 N	13.57 E
Tidan ≃	40	58.42 N	13.58 E
Tiddim	110	23.23 N	93.39 E
Tide Lake ⊜	184	50.33 N	111.20 W
Tideswell	44	53.16 N	1.46 W
Tidewater	208	37.51 N	76.42 W
Tidewater ◆[1]	208	37.45 N	77.00 W
Tidikelt ≡	148	26.54 N	1.20 E
Tidioute	214	41.41 N	79.24 W
Tidirhine, Jebel ∧	148	34.50 N	4.30 W
Tidjidit, Erg ◆[2]	148	23.30 N	1.00 E
Tidjikja	150	18.33 N	11.25 W
Tidö	40	59.30 N	16.28 E
Tidone ≃	62	45.04 N	9.32 E
Tidore	108	0.40 N	127.26 E
Tiébissou	150	7.10 N	5.13 W
Tiechang, Zhg.	98	41.44 N	126.11 E
Tiechang, Zhg.	100	24.10 N	115.30 E
Tiechang, Zhg.	102	26.34 N	103.58 E
Tiechang, Zhg.	105	40.04 N	118.12 E
Tiechangpu	107	29.29 N	104.20 E
Tiefenbach	60	49.26 N	12.35 E
Tiefenbroich	263	51.18 N	6.49 E
Tiefencastel	58	46.40 N	9.35 E
Tiefensee	54	52.41 N	13.50 E
Tiefo	107	29.45 N	104.33 E
Tiegenhof → Nowy Dwór Gdański	30	54.13 N	19.06 E
T'iehling → Tieling	104	42.18 N	123.49 E
Tiekou	98	37.16 N	121.13 E
Tiel	52	51.54 N	5.25 E
Tieli	89	46.59 N	128.02 E
Tielinanmuhu ⊜	120	31.05 N	85.35 E
Tieling	104	42.18 N	123.49 E
Tielt	50	51.00 N	3.19 E
Tielutou	100	27.49 N	115.48 E
Tiémé	150	9.33 N	7.19 W
T'iencHing → Tianjin	105	39.08 N	117.12 E
T'ienchung	100	23.52 N	120.35 E
Tienen	56	50.48 N	4.57 E
Tiengen	58	47.38 N	8.16 E
Tiénigboué	150	8.11 N	5.43 W
Tienko	150	10.14 N	7.29 W
Tien Shan ⋏	90	42.00 N	80.00 E
T'ienshui → Tianshui	102	34.30 N	105.58 E
Tientsin → Tianjin	105	39.08 N	117.12 E
Tien-yen	110	21.20 N	107.24 E
Tiepido ≃	64	44.30 N	10.59 E
Tie Plant	194	33.44 N	89.47 W
Tierga	34	41.37 N	1.36 W
Tiergarten ◆[8]	264a	52.31 N	13.21 E
Tiergarten ♠	264a	52.31 N	13.21 E
Tieroko, Tarso ∧	146	20.45 N	17.52 E
Tierp	40	60.20 N	17.30 E
Tierpark ♠	264a	52.30 N	13.32 E
Tierra Amarilla, Chile	252	27.29 S	70.17 W
Tierra Amarilla, N.M., U.S.	200	36.42 N	106.32 W
Tierra Blanca, Méx.	196	27.12 N	104.53 W
Tierra Blanca, Méx.	234	18.25 N	96.20 W
Tierra Blanca ≃	234	21.02 N	99.50 W
Tierra Blanca Creek ≃	196	34.58 N	101.55 W
Tierra Buena	226	39.09 N	121.40 W
Tierra Colorada, Méx.	234	17.10 N	99.35 W
Tierra Colorada, Méx.	234	17.56 N	92.39 W
Tierra Colorada, Bajo de la ≡[1]	254	42.52 S	66.48 W
Tierra de Campos ◆[1]	34	42.10 N	4.50 W
Tierra del Fuego □[8]	254	54.00 S	67.00 W
Tierra del Fuego, Isla Grande de I	254	54.00 S	69.00 W
Tierra del Fuego, Parque Nacional ♠	254	54.39 S	68.30 W
Tierra del Norte → Severnaja Zeml'a II	74	79.30 N	98.00 E
Tierralta	246	8.11 N	76.04 W
Tierra Nueva	234	17.47 N	93.28 W
Tierra Redonda Mountain ∧	226	35.47 N	120.59 W
Tierras Australes y Antárticas Francesas → French Southern and Antarctic Territories □[2]	6	49.30 S	69.30 E
Tierras Coloradas	234	22.24 N	104.35 W
Tieshan	100	30.14 N	114.52 E
Tieshanguan	100	23.30 N	113.54 E
Tietar ≃	34	39.50 N	6.01 W
Tietê	255	23.07 S	47.43 W
Tietê ≃	255	20.40 S	51.35 W
Tiéti	175f	20.57 S	165.19 E
Tieton	224	46.42 N	120.45 W
Tieton ≃	224	46.45 N	120.45 W
Tieton, South Fork ≃	224	46.38 N	121.08 W
Tietzow	264a	52.43 N	12.56 E
Tif	148	27.00 N	1.37 E
Tiffany Mountain ∧	202	48.40 N	119.56 W
Tiffin	214	41.07 N	83.11 W
Tiffin ≃	216	41.17 N	84.23 W
Tiflis → Tbilisi	84	41.43 N	44.49 E
Tifton	192	31.27 N	83.30 W
Tiftona	192	35.05 N	85.10 W
Tiga, Île I	175f	21.07 S	167.49 E
Tiga, Pulau I	112	5.43 N	115.39 E
Tigalda Island I	180	54.05 N	165.05 W
Tigapuluh, Pegunungan ⋏	112	1.05 S	102.30 E
Tigard	224	45.25 N	122.46 W
Tigasaki → Chigasaki	94	35.19 N	139.24 E
Tigbauan	116	10.41 N	122.22 E
Tigeaux	261	48.50 N	2.54 E
Tiger Lake ⊜	220	27.53 N	81.22 W
Tiger Stadium ♠	281	42.20 N	83.04 W
Tigery	261	48.38 N	2.31 E
Tighennif	148	35.20 N	0.21 E
Tighvein ∧[2]	46	55.30 N	5.10 W
Tigil'	74	57.48 N	158.40 E
Tiglid	148	28.31 N	10.15 W
Tiglione ≃	62	44.48 N	8.27 E
Tignale	64	45.44 N	10.44 E
Tignall	192	33.52 N	82.44 W
Tignère	152	7.22 N	12.39 E
Tignes	62	45.30 N	6.55 E
Tignish	186	46.57 N	64.02 W
Tignousti, Jebel ∧	148	31.31 N	6.44 W
Tigoda ≃	76	59.22 N	31.54 E
Tigray □[4]	144	13.40 N	40.00 E
Tigre	258	34.25 S	58.34 W
Tigre □[5]	288	34.24 S	58.37 W
Tigre ∧	234	19.53 N	102.59 W
Tigre ≃, Arg.	288	34.25 S	58.35 W
Tigre → Tigris ≃, Asia	128	31.00 N	47.25 E
Tigre ≃, Méx.	234	22.43 N	97.51 W
Tigre ≃, Perú	246	4.26 S	74.05 W
Tigre ≃, Ven.	246	9.20 N	62.30 W
Tigre, Cerro ∧	236	8.31 N	83.28 W
Tigre, Isla del I	258	34.47 S	56.23 W
Tigre, Punta del ›	258	34.46 S	56.33 W
Tigres, Baía dos ⊂	152	16.38 S	11.46 E
Tigris (Dicle) (Dijlah) ≃	128	31.00 N	47.25 E
Tiguabos	240p	20.14 N	75.21 W
Tiguentourine	148	27.50 N	9.18 E
Tiguesmat ⋏[2]	148	24.54 N	8.14 W
Tigy	50	47.48 N	2.12 E
Tigyaing	110	23.46 N	96.08 E
Tigzert, Oued ∨	148	28.20 N	9.35 W
Tigzirt	34	36.54 N	4.08 E
Tīh, Jabal at- ⋏[1]	140	29.30 N	34.00 E
Tihany ⊥	30	46.54 N	17.53 E
Tihert	148	35.28 N	1.21 E
Tihert □[5]	148	35.00 N	1.45 E
Ţihnāwī, Wādī aţ- ∨	142	28.11 N	30.46 E
Tihua → Ürümqi	86	43.48 N	87.35 E
Tihuatlán	234	20.43 N	97.32 W
Tijamuchi ≃	248	14.10 S	64.58 W
Tijesno	36	43.48 N	15.39 E
Tījī	146	32.01 N	11.22 E
Tijuana	232	32.32 N	117.01 W
Tijuana ≃	204	32.33 N	117.07 W
Tijuca ◆[8]	287a	22.56 S	43.14 W
Tijuca, Barra da ʯ	287a	23.01 S	43.18 W
Tijuca, Floresta da ♠	287a	22.56 S	43.17 W
Tijuca, Lagoa da ⊂	287a	22.59 S	43.20 W
Tijuca, Pico da ∧	287a	22.56 S	43.17 W
Tijucas	252	27.14 S	48.38 W
Tijucas do Sul	252	25.55 S	49.12 W
Tijuco ≃	255	18.40 S	50.05 W
Tijuco Prêto	256	22.56 S	46.40 W
Tikal ⊥	232	17.20 N	89.39 W
Tīkamgarh	124	24.44 N	78.50 E
Tīkamgarh □[5]	124	25.00 N	79.00 E
Tikaré	150	13.17 N	1.43 W
Tikchik Lakes ⊜	180	60.07 N	158.35 W
Tikei, Île I	14	14.58 S	144.32 W
Tikhand ◆[8]	272a	28.31 N	77.17 E
Tikhoretsk → Tichoreck	78	45.51 N	40.09 E
Tikitiki	172	37.48 S	178.24 E
Tiko	152	4.05 N	9.22 E
Tikokino	172	39.49 S	176.27 E
Tikrīt	128	34.36 N	43.42 E
Tikša	24	64.07 N	32.27 E
Tikšeozero, ozero ⊜	24	66.16 N	31.53 E
Tiksi	74	71.36 N	128.48 E
Tiku	112	0.24 S	99.56 E
Til	130	38.44 N	41.49 E
Tila ≃	124	29.08 N	81.35 E
Tiladummati Atoll I[1]	122	6.50 N	73.05 E
Tilamuta	112	0.30 N	122.20 E
Tilape ≃	234	18.06 N	94.31 W
Tilarán	236	10.28 N	84.59 W
Tilbalakan, Laguna ⊂	236	15.30 N	84.17 W
Tilbānah	142	30.59 N	31.27 E
Tilburg	52	51.34 N	5.05 E
Tilbury, On., Can.	214	42.16 N	82.26 W
Tilbury, Eng., U.K.	42	51.28 N	0.23 E
Tilcara	252	23.34 S	65.22 W
Tilcha	166	29.36 S	140.54 E
Til-Châtel	58	47.31 N	5.10 E
Tilden, Il., U.S.	219	38.12 N	89.40 W
Tilden, Ne., U.S.	198	42.02 N	97.50 W
Tilden, Tx., U.S.	196	28.28 N	98.33 W
Tilden Lake ⊜	226	38.07 N	119.36 W
Tilden Woods	284c	39.03 N	77.09 W
Tilemsès	150	15.37 N	4.44 E
Tilemsi, Vallée du ∨	150	16.15 N	0.02 E
Tilff	56	50.34 N	5.35 E
Tilghman Island I	208	38.42 N	76.20 W
Tilhar	124	27.59 N	79.44 E
Tilia, Oued ∨	148	27.27 N	0.01 W
Tiligul ≃	78	47.04 N	30.57 E
Tiligulo-Berezanka	78	46.52 N	31.24 E
Tiligul'skij liman ⊜	78	46.48 N	31.08 E
Tiliktino	82	56.06 N	36.36 E
Tilimsen	148	34.52 N	1.15 W
Tilimsen □[5]	148	35.00 N	2.00 W
Tilin	110	21.42 N	94.04 E
Tilisarao	252	32.44 S	65.18 W
Till ≃, Eng., U.K.	44	53.16 N	0.37 W
Till ≃, Eng., U.K.	44	55.41 N	2.12 W
Tillaberi	150	14.13 N	1.27 E
Tillamook	202	45.27 N	123.50 W
Tillamook □[6]	224	45.25 N	123.39 W
Tillamook ≃	224	45.28 N	123.53 W
Tillamook Bay ⊂	224	45.30 N	123.53 W
Tillamook Head ›	224	45.57 N	124.00 W
Tillanchāng Dwīp I	110	8.30 N	93.37 E
Tillberga	40	59.41 N	16.37 E
Tille ≃	58	47.07 N	5.21 E
Tillery, Lake ⊜[1]	192	35.17 N	80.05 W
Tilley	182	50.27 N	111.39 W
Tilli	126	23.57 N	89.57 E
Tillia	150	16.08 N	4.47 E
Tillicoultry	46	56.09 N	3.45 W
Tillicum	224	47.08 N	122.33 W
Tillières-sur-Avre	50	48.46 N	1.04 E
Tilling Bourne ≃	260	51.13 N	0.34 W
Tillmans Corner	194	30.43 N	88.05 W
Tillson	210	41.49 N	74.04 W
Tillsonburg	212	42.51 N	80.44 W
Tillyfourie	46	57.11 N	2.35 W
Tilogne	150	15.58 N	13.36 W
Tilomar	112	9.21 S	125.08 E
Tílos I	38	36.25 N	27.25 E
Tilpa	166	30.57 S	144.24 E
Tilrhemt	148	33.10 N	3.21 E
Tilsit → Sovetsk	76	55.05 N	21.53 E
Tilt ≃	46	56.46 N	3.50 W
Tilton, Il., U.S.	194	40.05 N	87.38 W
Tilton, Ky., U.S.	218	38.22 N	83.45 W
Tilton, N.H., U.S.	188	43.26 N	71.35 W
Tilton ≃	224	46.33 N	122.33 W
Tiltonsville	214	40.10 N	80.41 W
Tilzapotla	234	18.29 N	99.16 W
Tim	78	51.37 N	37.07 E
Tim ≃	76	52.15 N	37.22 E
Timā	140	26.54 N	31.26 E
Timah, Bukit ∧[2]	271c	1.21 N	103.47 E
Timahoe	44	53.20 N	6.49 W
Timaná	246	1.58 N	75.56 W
Timane ≃	248	20.34 S	59.15 W
Timanskij kr'až ∧	24	65.00 N	51.00 E
Timar	84	38.49 N	43.27 E
Timaricha	80	57.33 N	44.47 E
Timarni Muafi	124	22.22 N	77.22 E
Timaru	172	44.24 S	171.15 E
Timaševo, S.S.S.R.	80	53.21 N	51.12 E
Timaševo, S.S.S.R.	82	55.08 N	36.29 E
Timaševsk	78	45.37 N	38.57 E
Timau, It.	64	46.35 N	13.00 E
Timau, Kenya	154	0.05 N	37.14 E
Timavo San Giovanni	64	45.48 N	13.37 E
Timay al-Amdīd	142	30.57 N	31.32 E
Timbákion	38	35.04 N	24.46 E
Timbalier Bay ⊂	194	29.10 N	90.20 W
Timbaúba	250	7.31 S	35.19 W
Timbedgha	150	16.15 N	8.10 W
Timber	224	45.43 N	123.17 W
Timber Creek ≃	198	44.49 N	98.17 W
Timber Lake, Il., U.S.	278	42.14 N	88.07 W
Timberlake, Oh., U.S.	214	41.41 N	81.25 W
Timber Lake, S.D., U.S.	198	45.26 N	101.04 W
Timber Run ≃	284b	39.27 N	76.52 W
Timber Trails	278	41.52 N	87.57 W
Timberview	284b	39.13 N	76.45 W
Timbío	246	2.20 N	76.40 W
Timbira ≃	287a	22.41 S	43.13 W
Timbiras	250	4.15 S	43.57 W
Timblin	214	40.58 N	79.12 W
Timbó, Bra.	252	26.50 S	49.18 W
Timbo, Guinée	150	10.38 N	11.50 W
Timbo, Liber.	150	5.37 N	9.43 W
Timbó ≃	287a	22.52 S	43.16 W
Timboon	169	38.29 S	142.59 E
Timbuctoo	285	40.00 N	74.49 W
Timbuktu → Tombouctou	150	16.46 N	3.01 W
Timbun Mata, Pulau I	112	4.39 N	118.28 E
Timel'ga	86	58.53 N	76.42 E
Timelkam	60	48.00 N	13.36 E
Times Square ♠	276	40.45 N	74.00 W
Timétrine	150	19.27 N	0.26 W
Timétrine ⋏	150	19.20 N	0.42 W
Timeu Creek ≃	182	54.28 N	114.27 W
Timewell	219	40.00 N	90.52 W
Timgad ⊥	148	35.29 N	6.28 E
Timilpan	234	19.52 N	99.45 W
Timimoun	148	29.14 N	0.16 E
Timimoun, Sebkha de ⊜	148	29.00 N	0.05 E
Timinar	140	19.02 N	30.29 E
Timi Ouli, Ehi ∧	146	21.08 N	16.31 E
Timir'azevo	76	55.05 N	21.37 E
Timir'azevskij	86	56.29 N	84.54 E
Timirevo	82	55.08 N	39.10 E
Timirist, Râs ›	150	19.23 N	16.32 W
Timiș □[6]	38	45.40 N	21.20 E
Timiș (Tamiš) ≃	38	44.51 N	20.39 E
Timiskaming, Lake ⊜	190	47.10 N	79.25 W
Timișoara	38	45.45 N	21.13 E
Timkoviči	76	53.03 N	27.00 E
Timkovo	82	55.56 N	38.37 E
Timmendorfer Strand	54	54.00 N	10.46 E
Timmernabben	26	56.58 N	16.26 E
Timmins	190	48.28 N	81.20 W
Timmonsville	192	34.08 N	79.56 W
Timms Hill ∧[2]	190	45.27 N	90.11 W
Timok ≃	38	44.13 N	22.40 E
Timon	250	5.06 S	42.49 W
Timonovo	82	56.13 N	37.02 E
Timor I	112	9.00 S	125.00 E
Timor Sea ⊤[2]	14	11.00 S	128.00 E
Timor Timur □[4]	112	8.35 S	126.00 E
Timor Trough ✣[1]	14	9.50 S	126.00 E
Timošino, S.S.S.R.	76	60.05 N	36.10 E
Timošino, S.S.S.R.	80	57.50 N	44.25 E
Timotes	246	8.59 N	70.44 W
Timothy Lake ⊜[1]	224	45.07 N	121.47 W
Timoudi	148	29.19 N	1.09 W
Timousserarène ≃	150	16.21 N	8.07 E
Timpanogos Cave National Monument ♠	200	40.18 N	111.52 W
Timpas Creek ≃	198	38.02 N	103.38 W
Timpaus, Pulau I	112	1.51 S	124.01 E
Timperley	262	53.24 N	2.19 W
Timpia ≃	248	11.35 S	72.58 W
Timpson	194	31.54 N	94.23 W
Timpton ≃	74	58.43 N	127.12 E
Timsāh, Buḥayrat at- (Lake Timsah) ⊜	142	30.34 N	32.17 E
Timsah, Lake → Timsāh, Buḥayrat at- ⊜	142	30.34 N	32.17 E
Timšer	24	62.06 N	54.40 E
Tims Ford Lake ⊜[1]	194	35.15 N	86.10 W

≃	River	Fluss	Río	Rivière	Rio
≊	Canal	Kanal	Canal	Canal	Canal
∟	Waterfall, Rapids	Wasserfall, Stromschnellen	Cascada, Rápidos	Chute d'eau, Rapides	Cascata, Rápidos
ʯ	Strait	Meeresstrasse	Estrecho	Détroit	Estreito
⊂	Bay, Gulf	Bucht, Golf	Bahía, Golfo	Baie, Golfe	Baía, Golfo
⊜	Lake, Lakes	See, Seen	Lago, Lagos	Lac, Lacs	Lago, Lagos
≡	Swamp	Sumpf	Pantano	Marais	Pântano
⊓	Ice Features, Glacier	Eis- und Gletscherformen	Accidentes Glaciales	Formes glaciaires	Acidentes glaciares
⊤	Other Hydrographic Features	Andere Hydrographische Objekte	Otros Elementos Hidrográficos	Autres données hydrographiques	Outros acidentes hidrográficos

✣	Submarine Features	Untermeerische Objekte	Accidentes Submarinos	Formes de relief sous-marin	Acidentes submarinos
□	Political Unit	Politische Einheit	Unidad Politica	Entité politique	Unidade política
▼	Cultural Institution	Kulturelle Institution	Institución Cultural	Institution culturelle	Instituição cultural
⊥	Historical Site	Historische Stätte	Sitio Histórico	Site historique	Sitio histórico
♠	Recreational Site	Erholungs- und Ferienort	Sitio de Recreo	Centre de loisirs	Area de Lazer
⊠	Airport	Flughafen	Aeropuerto	Aéroport	Aeroporto
■	Military Installation	Militäranlage	Instalación Militar	Installation militaire	Instalação militar
◆	Miscellaneous	Verschiedenes	Misceláneo	Divers	Diversos

Timun	114	0.50 N	103.22 E
Timur	85	42.50 N	68.26 E
Tīn, Ra's at- ›	146	32.37 N	23.08 E
Tina ≏	158	31.18 S	29.14 E
Tinaca Point ›	116	5.33 N	125.20 E
Tinaco	246	9.42 N	68.26 W
Tinaga Island I	116	14.28 N	122.56 E
Ţīnah, Khalīj aţ- ⊂	140	31.08 N	32.40 E
Tinahely	48	52.48 N	6.28 W
Tinaja, Punta ›	248	16.14 S	73.39 W
Tinajas, Cerro de las ∧	232	29.57 N	112.12 W
Tinalmud	116	13.36 N	122.53 E
Tinambac	116	13.49 N	123.19 E
Tinambung	112	3.31 S	119.01 E
Ti-n-Amzi V	150	18.20 N	4.32 E
Tinapagee	166	29.28 S	144.23 E
Tinaquillo	246	9.55 N	68.18 W
Tindari, Capo ›	70	38.10 N	15.03 E
Tinderry Peak ∧	171b	35.42 S	149.16 E
Tindila	150	10.16 N	8.15 W
Tindis	126	21.35 N	86.44 E
Tindivanam	122	12.15 N	79.39 E
Tindouf	148	27.50 N	8.04 W
Tindouf, Hamada de ◆[1]	148	27.30 N	9.00 W
Tindouf, Sebkha de ≚	148	27.45 N	7.15 W
Tineba, Pegunungan ⩚	112	1.40 S	120.25 E
Tinée ≏	62	43.55 N	7.11 E
Tineg ≏	116	17.38 N	120.37 E
Tineo	34	43.20 N	6.25 W
Ting ≏	100	24.24 N	116.35 E
Tinga ∧	146	9.21 N	23.38 E
Tingambato	234	19.30 N	101.52 W
Tinggi, Pulau I	114	2.18 N	104.07 E
Tingha	166	29.57 S	151.13 E
Tinghert, Ḥamādat (Plateau du Tinghert) ⩚[1]	148	29.00 N	9.00 E
Tinghert, Plateau du (Ḥamādat Tinghert) ⩚[1]	148	29.00 N	9.00 E
Tinghsien → Dingxian	98	38.32 N	114.59 E
Tingka, Bukit ∧	116	5.20 N	117.06 E
Ting Kau	271d	22.22 N	114.05 E
Tingkawk Sakan	110	26.04 N	96.44 E
Tingkou	98	36.34 N	119.46 E
Tinglev	41	54.56 N	9.15 E
Tinglin	106	30.53 N	121.17 E
Tingliuhe	98	39.34 N	118.49 E
Tingloy	116	13.40 N	120.52 E
Tingmerkpuk Mountain ∧	180	68.34 N	162.28 W
Tingo de Saposoa	248	7.07 S	76.38 W
Tingo María	248	9.09 S	75.56 W
Tingqian	100	30.10 N	115.54 E
Tingsiqiao	100	29.50 N	114.12 E
Tingsryd	26	56.32 N	14.59 E
Tingstäde	26	57.44 N	18.36 E
Tingsted	41	54.49 N	11.56 E
Tinguá	256	22.36 S	43.26 W
Tingüindín	234	19.45 N	102.29 W
Tinguipaya	248	19.11 S	65.51 W
Tingvoll	26	62.54 N	8.12 E
Tingvollfjorden ⊂[2]	26	62.50 N	8.11 E
Tingwick	206	45.50 N	71.58 W
Tingwon Group II	164	2.35 S	149.45 E
Tingzitou	106	30.12 N	119.46 E
Tinharé, Ilha de I	255	13.30 S	38.58 W
Tinh-bien	110	10.36 N	104.57 E
Tinian	174n	14.58 N	145.38 E
Tinian I	174n	15.00 N	145.38 E
Tinian Harbor ⊂	174n	14.57 N	145.36 E
Tinié	150	14.20 N	1.28 W
Tiniguiban	116	11.22 N	119.30 E
Tinitian	116	10.04 N	119.12 E
Tinjar ≏	112	4.04 N	114.18 E
Tinjil, Pulau I	115a	6.58 S	105.47 E
Tinker Air Force Base ■	196	35.25 N	97.24 W
Tinkers Creek ≏, Md., U.S.	284c	38.46 N	76.57 W
Tinkers Creek ≏, Oh., U.S.	214	41.22 N	81.37 W
Tinkertown	283	42.01 N	70.44 W
Tinkisso ≏	150	11.21 N	9.10 W
Tinley Creek ≏	278	41.39 N	87.45 W
Tinley Creek Woods ♠	278	41.39 N	87.47 W
Tinley Park	216	41.34 N	87.47 W
Tinniswood, Mount ∧	182	50.19 N	123.50 W
Tinnoset	26	59.43 N	9.02 E
Tinnsjø ⊜	26	59.54 N	8.55 E
Tinogasta	252	28.04 S	67.34 W
Tinompo	112	2.09 S	121.17 E
Tínos	38	37.32 N	25.10 E
Tínos I	38	37.38 N	25.10 E
Tin Rerhoh, Tassili ⩚	150	19.40 N	4.00 E
Tinrhir	148	31.28 N	5.30 W
Tin Sam	271d	22.22 N	114.11 E
Tinskoj	88	56.10 N	96.55 E
Tinsley	194	32.43 N	90.27 W
Tinsukia	120	27.30 N	95.22 E
Tintagel, B.C., Can.	182	54.12 N	125.35 W
Tintagel, Eng., U.K.	42	50.40 N	4.45 W
Tintagel Head ›	42	50.41 N	4.46 W
Tintaldra	171b	36.03 S	147.56 E
Tintas, Rio das ≏	287a	22.52 S	43.28 W
Tinte, Cerro ∧	248	22.40 S	67.02 W
Tintern Abbey ʋ[1]	42	51.41 N	2.40 W
Tintern Parva	42	51.42 N	2.40 W
Tintigny	56	49.41 N	5.31 E
Tintina	252	27.02 S	62.43 W
Tintinara	166	35.54 S	140.03 E
Tintioulé	150	10.13 N	9.12 W
Tinto ∧	46	55.36 N	3.39 W
Tinto ≏	34	37.12 N	6.55 W
Ti-n-Toumma ◆[1]	146	16.04 N	12.40 E
Tintwistle	262	53.28 N	1.58 W
Tinui	172	40.53 S	176.04 E
Tinwald	172	43.55 S	171.43 E
Ti-n-Zaouatene	150	19.55 N	2.52 E
Tio	144	14.42 N	40.58 E
Tioga, Il., U.S.	219	40.13 N	91.21 W
Tioga, N.D., U.S.	198	48.23 N	102.56 W
Tioga, Pa., U.S.	210	41.55 N	77.08 W
Tioga □[6], N.Y., U.S.	210	42.06 N	76.16 W
Tioga □[6], Pa., U.S.	210	41.45 N	77.17 W
Tioga ◆[8]	285	40.00 N	75.10 W
Tioga ≏	210	42.09 N	77.05 W
Tioga Center	210	42.04 N	76.21 W
Tioga Pass)(	226	37.54 N	119.16 W
Tioga Terrace	210	42.03 N	76.07 W
Tiojala	24	61.10 N	23.52 E
Tioman, Pulau I	114	2.48 N	104.10 E
Tiona	214	41.45 N	79.03 W
Tione di Trento	64	46.02 N	10.43 E
Tionesta	214	41.30 N	79.27 W
Tionesta Creek ≏	214	41.28 N	79.22 W
Tionesta Lake ⊜[1]	214	41.28 N	79.28 W
Tioor, Pulau I	164	4.45 S	131.45 E
Tior	140	6.23 N	31.11 E
Tioro	112	4.41 S	122.36 E
Tioro, Selat ⋓	112	4.40 S	122.20 E
Tioroniaradougou	150	9.21 N	5.38 W
Tioughnioga ≏	210	42.14 N	75.51 W
Tioughnioga, East Branch ≏	210	42.36 N	76.10 W
Tipac, Monte ∧[2]	250	3.34 N	51.20 W
Tipasa	34	36.35 N	2.27 E
Tipitapa	236	12.12 N	86.06 W
Tipp City	218	39.57 N	84.10 W
Tippecanoe, In., U.S.	216	41.12 N	86.06 W
Tippecanoe, Oh., U.S.	214	40.16 N	81.17 W
Tippecanoe □[6]	216	40.25 N	86.53 W
Tippecanoe ≏	216	40.31 N	86.47 W
Tippecanoe, Lake ⊜	216	41.20 N	85.46 W
Tippecanoe Battlefield State Memorial ⊥	216	40.31 N	86.52 W
Tippecanoe River State Park ♠	216	41.07 N	86.36 W
Tipperary, Austl.	164	13.44 S	131.02 E
Tipperary, Ire.	48	52.29 N	8.10 W
Tipperary □[6]	48	52.40 N	8.20 W
Tipton, Eng., U.K.	42	52.32 N	2.05 W
Tipton, Ca., U.S.	226	36.03 N	119.18 W
Tipton, In., U.S.	216	40.16 N	86.02 W
Tipton, Ia., U.S.	190	41.46 N	91.07 W
Tipton, Mi., U.S.	216	42.01 N	84.04 W
Tipton, Mo., U.S.	194	38.39 N	92.46 W
Tipton, Ok., U.S.	196	34.30 N	99.08 W
Tipton, Pa., U.S.	214	40.38 N	78.18 W
Tipton □[6]	216	40.17 N	86.02 W
Tipton, Mount ∧	200	35.32 N	114.12 W
Tiptonville	194	36.22 N	89.28 W
Tip Top Mountain ∧	190	48.16 N	85.59 W
Tiptree	42	51.49 N	0.45 E
Tiptūr	122	13.16 N	76.29 E
Tiputini ≏	246	0.47 S	75.32 W
Tiquicheo	234	18.53 N	100.44 W
Tiquisate	236	14.17 N	91.22 W
Tiracambu, Serra do ⩚[1]	250	3.15 S	46.30 W
Tira Chapéu, Morro ∧	256	22.45 S	44.39 W
Tiradentes	255	21.07 S	44.11 W
Tiradero	232	17.47 N	91.10 W
Tīrah, Baḩr ≊	142	31.03 N	31.15 E
Tīrān, Jazīrat I	128	27.56 N	34.34 E
Tīrān, Maḑīq ⋓	140	27.58 N	34.28 E
Tiran, Strait of → Tīrān, Maḑīq ⋓	140	27.58 N	34.28 E
Tirana → Tiranë	38	41.20 N	19.50 E
Tiranë	38	41.20 N	19.50 E
Tirano	64	46.13 N	10.10 E
Tiraque	248	17.37 S	65.04 W
Tiraspol'	78	46.51 N	29.38 E
Tirat Karmel	132	32.46 N	34.58 E
Tirat Ẕevi	132	32.25 N	35.32 E
Tirau	172	37.59 S	175.45 E
Tire	130	38.04 N	27.45 E
Tirebolu	130	41.00 N	38.48 E
Tiree I	46	56.31 N	6.49 W
Tire Hill	214	40.16 N	78.55 W
Tires (Tiers), It.	64	46.28 N	11.31 E
Tires, Port.	266c	38.43 N	9.21 W
Tires ◆[1]	148	23.30 N	13.10 W
Tîrgovişte	38	44.56 N	25.27 E
Tîrgu Bujor	38	45.52 N	27.54 E
Tîrgu-Cărbuneşti	38	44.58 N	23.31 E
Tîrgu-Frumos	38	47.13 N	27.00 E
Tîrgu-Jiu	38	45.02 N	23.17 E
Tîrgu-Lăpuş	38	47.27 N	23.52 E
Tîrgu Mureş	38	46.33 N	24.33 E
Tîrgu-Neamţ	38	47.12 N	26.22 E
Tîrgu-Ocna	38	46.15 N	26.37 E
Tîrgu-Secuiesc	38	46.00 N	26.08 E
Tîrgusor	38	44.28 N	28.25 E
Tirhahart, Oued V	148	23.45 N	3.10 E
Tiria, Monte ∧	71	40.23 N	9.16 E
Tirich Mīr ∧	123	36.15 N	71.50 E
Tirilye	130	40.23 N	28.47 E
Tirins ⊥	38	37.36 N	22.48 E
Tirio	164	8.25 S	143.00 E
Tiriro	150	10.27 N	8.39 W
Tiris Zemmour □[4]	148	24.10 N	9.30 W
Tirl'anskij	86	54.14 N	58.35 E
Tirna ≏	122	18.04 N	76.57 E
Tîrnava Mare ≏	38	46.09 N	23.42 E
Tîrnava Mică ≏	38	46.11 N	23.55 E
Tîrnăveni	38	46.20 N	24.17 E
Tírnavos	38	39.45 N	22.17 E
Tirnovo → Veliko Târnovo	38	43.04 N	25.39 E
Tiro	214	40.54 N	82.46 W
Tirodi	120	21.41 N	79.42 E
Tirol □[3]	64	47.15 N	11.20 E
Tiroler Ache (Grossache(≏	60	47.51 N	12.30 E
Tirolo (Tirol)	64	46.42 N	11.10 E
Tiros	255	19.00 S	45.58 W
Tiroungoulou	146	9.34 N	22.09 E
Tīr Pol	128	34.36 N	61.15 E
Tirrenia	66	43.38 N	10.17 E
Tirreno, Mare → Tyrrhenian Sea ⊤[2]	36	40.00 N	12.00 E
Tirry ≏	46	58.02 N	4.26 W
Tirsā, Mişr	142	29.25 N	30.49 E
Tirsā, Mişr	273c	29.58 N	31.12 E
Tirschenreuth	60	49.53 N	12.21 E
Tirschtiegel → Trzciel	30	52.23 N	15.52 E
Tirso ≏	71	39.53 N	8.32 E
Tirsted	41	54.44 N	11.21 E
Tirstrup	41	56.18 N	10.42 E
Tirstrup Lufthavn ⊠	41	56.20 N	10.37 E
Tīrthahalli	122	13.42 N	75.14 E
Tirua Point ›	172	38.23 S	174.38 E
Tiruchchirāppalli	122	10.49 N	78.41 E
Tiruchendūr	122	8.29 N	78.07 E
Tiruchengodu	122	11.23 N	77.56 E
Tirukkalukkunram	122	12.37 N	80.04 E
Tirukkoyilūr	122	11.57 N	79.12 E
Tiruliai	76	55.47 N	23.22 E
Tirumangalam	122	9.50 N	77.59 E
Tirunelveli	122	8.44 N	77.42 E
Tirupati	122	13.39 N	79.25 E
Tirupparangunram	122	9.53 N	78.05 E
Tiruppattūr, India	122	12.30 N	78.34 E
Tiruppattūr, India	122	10.08 N	78.37 E
Tiruppur	122	11.06 N	77.21 E
Tirūr	122	10.54 N	75.55 E
Tiruttani	122	13.11 N	79.38 E
Tirutturaippūndi	122	10.32 N	79.39 E
Tiruvalla	122	9.23 N	76.34 E
Tiruvallūr	122	13.09 N	79.55 E
Tiruvālūr	122	10.46 N	79.39 E
Tiruvannāmalai	122	12.13 N	79.04 E
Tiruvettipuram	122	12.40 N	79.33 E
Tiruvottiyūr	122	13.09 N	80.18 E
Tiruvur	122	17.06 N	80.38 E
Tisa (Tisza) ≏	38	45.15 N	20.17 E
Tis'ah	142	30.02 N	32.35 E
Tisaiyanvilai	122	8.20 N	77.53 E
Tisaren ⊜	40	59.00 N	15.08 E
Tisbury	42	51.04 N	2.03 W
Tisdale	184	52.51 N	104.04 W
Tishomingo, Ms., U.S.	194	34.38 N	88.13 W
Tishomingo, Ok., U.S.	196	34.14 N	96.40 W
Tisisat Falls ∟	144	11.29 N	37.35 E
Ţīsīyah	132	32.24 N	36.27 E
Tisjön ⊜	26	60.55 N	12.58 E
Tiskilwa	190	41.17 N	89.30 W
Tiskino	86	58.05 N	83.10 E
Tiškovka	78	48.29 N	30.56 E
Tiškovo, S.S.S.R.	80	46.02 N	48.36 E
Tiškovo, S.S.S.R.	82	56.05 N	37.44 E
Tisma	236	12.05 N	86.01 W
Tisnaren ⊜	40	58.57 N	15.57 E
Tišnevo	82	55.10 N	36.17 E
Tišnov	30	49.21 N	16.25 E
Tisovec	30	48.43 N	19.57 E
Tissa	146	7.26 N	10.16 E
Tissemsilt	148	35.35 N	1.50 E
Tissø ⊜	41	55.35 N	11.18 E
Tīsta ≏	124	25.23 N	89.43 E
Tisul'	86	55.45 N	88.19 E
Tisvildeleje	41	56.03 N	12.05 E
Tisza (Tisa) ≏	38	45.15 N	20.17 E
Tiszaföldvár	30	46.59 N	20.15 E
Tiszafüred	30	47.37 N	20.46 E
Tiszavasvári	30	47.58 N	21.22 E
Tit	148	23.00 N	5.10 E
Titaf	148	27.26 N	0.13 W
Titāgarh	126	22.45 N	88.22 E
Titano, Monte ∧	66	43.55 N	12.28 E
Titao	150	13.46 N	2.04 W
Tit-Ary	74	71.58 N	127.01 E
Titel	38	45.12 N	20.18 E
Tithwal	123	34.24 N	73.47 E
Titicaca, Lago ⊜	248	15.50 S	69.20 W
Titicus	207	41.18 N	73.30 W
Titi Karangan	114	5.31 N	100.37 E
Titikaveka	174k	21.15 S	159.45 W
Titisee-Neustadt	58	47.54 N	8.13 E
Titlagarh	122	20.18 N	83.09 E
Titlis ∧	58	46.47 N	8.25 E
Tito	68	40.35 N	15.40 E
Titograd	38	42.26 N	19.14 E
Titonka	190	43.14 N	94.02 W
Titou	100	29.52 N	112.42 E
Titova Korenica	36	44.45 N	15.43 E
Titovka	83	48.59 N	39.44 E
Titovo, S.S.S.R.	80	53.17 N	43.41 E
Titovo, S.S.S.R.	82	54.19 N	36.56 E
Titovo, S.S.S.R.	82	55.35 N	39.07 E
Titovo Užice	38	43.51 N	19.51 E
Titovo Velenje	61	46.22 N	15.07 E
Titov Veles	38	41.41 N	21.48 E
Titov vrh ∧	38	42.00 N	20.51 E
Titran	26	63.40 N	8.18 E
Tittabawassee ≏	190	43.23 N	83.59 W
Titteri ⩚	34	36.00 N	3.30 E
Titterstone Clee Hill ∧[2]	42	52.23 N	2.35 W
Titting	60	49.00 N	11.13 E
Tittling	60	48.44 N	13.23 E
Tittmoning	60	48.04 N	12.46 E
Titu	38	44.41 N	25.32 E
Titule	154	3.17 N	25.32 E
Titus □[6]	222	33.05 N	94.58 W
Titusville, Fl., U.S.	220	28.36 N	80.48 W
Titusville, N.J., U.S.	208	40.18 N	74.52 W
Titusville, Pa., U.S.	214	41.37 N	79.40 W
Titz	56	51.01 N	6.25 E
Tiu Chung Chau I	271d	22.20 N	114.19 E
Tiumpan Head ›	46	58.16 N	6.09 W
Tiuni	120	30.57 N	77.51 E
Tiva ≏	154	2.20 S	38.48 E
Tivaouane	150	14.57 N	16.49 W
Tiveden ⩚[2]	40	58.45 N	14.40 E
Tiverton, Eng., U.K.	42	50.55 N	3.29 W
Tiverton, R.I., U.S.	207	41.37 N	71.12 W
Tivoli, Gren.	241k	12.10 N	61.37 W
Tivoli, It.	66	41.58 N	12.48 E
Tivoli, N.Y., U.S.	210	42.03 N	73.54 W
Tivoli, Tx., U.S.	196	28.27 N	96.53 W
Tivoli ♠	41	55.40 N	12.34 E
Ţiwāl, Wādī V	146	10.22 N	22.43 E
Tiwi, Pil.	116	13.27 N	123.41 E
Ţīwī, 'Umān	128	22.49 N	59.16 E
Tiwuronto	115b	8.48 S	120.09 E
Tixtla [de Guerrero]	234	17.35 N	99.26 W
Tiyās	130	34.33 N	37.40 E
Tiyo, Pegunungan ⩚	164	4.00 S	135.30 E
Tizapán ◆[8]	286a	19.20 N	99.13 W
Tizapán el Alto	234	20.10 N	103.04 W
Tizatlán ⊥	234	19.21 N	98.15 W
Tizayuca	234	19.50 N	98.59 W
Tizimín	232	21.10 N	88.10 W
Tizi-Ouzou	148	36.48 N	4.02 E
Tizi Ouzou □[5]	148	36.40 N	4.10 E
Tizmant ash-Sharqīyah	142	29.03 N	31.03 E
Tiznados ≏	246	8.16 N	67.47 W
Tiznit	148	29.43 N	9.44 W
Tiznit □[4]	148	29.40 N	9.45 W
Tizoc	196	25.41 N	101.59 W
Tjällmo	40	58.43 N	15.21 E
Tjeukemeer ⊜	52	52.54 N	5.50 E
Tjilatjap → Cilacap	115a	7.44 S	109.00 E
Tjirebon → Cirebon	115a	6.44 S	108.34 E
Tjolotjo	154	19.47 S	27.46 E
Tjøme I	26	59.07 N	10.24 E
Tjörn I	26	58.00 N	11.38 E
Tjörnarp	41	56.00 N	13.37 E
Tkibuli	84	42.21 N	42.59 E
Tkvarčeli	84	42.51 N	41.41 E
Tlachichuca	234	19.06 N	97.25 W
Tlacoapa	234	17.09 N	98.52 W
Tlacolula [de Matamoros]	234	16.57 N	96.29 W
Tlacotalpan	234	18.37 N	95.40 W
Tlacotepec	234	17.46 N	99.59 W
Tlacuitapa	234	21.14 N	102.12 W
Tláhuac □[7]	286a	19.17 N	99.00 W
Tláhuac ◆[8]	286a	19.16 N	99.00 W
Tlahualilo de Zaragoza	232	26.07 N	103.27 W
Tlahuelilpa de Ocampo	234	20.08 N	99.14 W
Tlahuitoltepec	234	17.04 N	95.59 W
Tlajomulco de Zúñiga	234	20.28 N	103.27 W
Tlalchapa	234	18.24 N	100.28 W
Tlalcozotitlán	234	17.54 N	99.15 W
Tlalixtac de Cabrera	234	17.04 N	96.39 W
Tlalixtaquilla	234	17.21 N	98.28 W
Tlalnepantla	286a	19.33 N	99.12 W
Tlalnepantla □[7]	286a	19.32 N	99.12 W
Tlalnepantla ≏	286a	19.31 N	99.16 W
Tláloc, Cerro ∧	234	19.25 N	98.42 W
Tlalpan □[7]	286a	19.13 N	99.12 W
Tlalpan ◆[8]	286a	19.17 N	99.10 W
Tlalpujahua	234	19.48 N	100.10 W
Tlaltenango de Sánchez Román	234	21.47 N	103.19 W
Tlaltenco ◆[8]	286a	19.17 N	99.01 W
Tl'ančetamak	80	55.28 N	52.37 E
Tlapa	234	17.33 N	98.33 W
Tlapacoyan	234	19.58 N	97.13 W
Tlapaneco ≏	234	18.05 N	98.48 W
Tlapehuala	234	18.13 N	100.31 W
Tlapeng	156	23.15 S	21.49 E
Tlaquepaque	234	20.39 N	103.19 W
Tl'arata	84	42.07 N	46.22 E
Tlatlauqui	234	19.51 N	97.29 W
Tlaxcala □[3]	234	19.25 N	98.10 W
Tlaxcala [de Xicoténcatl]	234	19.19 N	98.14 W
Tlaxcoapan	234	20.05 N	99.13 W
Tlaxco [de Morelos]	234	19.37 N	98.07 W
Tlaxiaco	234	17.16 N	97.41 W
Tlaxmalac	234	18.21 N	99.25 W
Tlazazalca	234	19.58 N	102.04 W
Tletat ed Douair	34	35.59 N	2.55 E
Tlētē Ouāte Gharbī, Jabal ∧	130	35.20 N	39.13 E
Tlevak Strait ⋓	182	55.03 N	132.58 W
Tlhakgameng	158	26.27 S	24.21 E
Tloch	84	42.38 N	46.28 E
Tlučiná	60	49.44 N	13.14 E
Tlumač	78	48.52 N	25.01 E
Tłuszcz	30	52.26 N	21.26 E
Tmassah	146	26.22 N	15.47 E
Tmīsān	146	27.32 N	13.19 E
Tnâot ≏	110	11.29 N	104.57 E
Tnekvejem ≏	180	65.50 N	177.31 E
Toa ≏	240p	20.23 N	74.32 W
Toa, Cuchilias de ⩚	240p	20.27 N	74.58 W
Toa Alta	240m	18.23 N	66.15 W
Toa Baja	240m	18.27 N	66.15 W
Toabré ≏	236	8.56 N	80.33 W
Toaca ∧	38	46.59 N	25.57 E
Toachi ≏	246	0.08 N	79.18 W
Toahayaná	232	26.08 N	107.44 W
Toamasina	157b	18.10 S	49.23 E
Toamasina □[4]	157b	18.00 S	48.40 E
Toandonggu	98	40.33 N	127.35 E
Toandos Peninsula ›[1]	224	47.43 N	122.47 W
Toano, It.	64	44.23 N	10.34 E
Toano, Va., U.S.	208	37.22 N	76.48 W
Toano Draw V	204	41.27 N	114.35 W
Toano Range ⩚	204	40.50 N	114.20 W
Toast	192	36.30 N	80.37 W
Toay	252	36.40 S	64.21 W
Toba, Mali	150	11.52 N	7.28 W
Toba, Nihon	94	34.29 N	136.51 E
Toba, Zhg.	102	31.18 N	97.40 E
Toba ≏	182	50.30 N	124.15 W
Toba, Danau ⊜	114	2.35 N	98.50 E
Tobacco ≏	190	43.49 N	84.24 W
Tobacco Plains Indian Reserve ◆[4]	182	49.04 N	115.06 W
Tobacco Root Mountains ⩚	202	45.35 N	112.00 W
Tobago I	241r	11.15 N	60.40 W
Toba Inlet ⊂	182	50.20 N	124.50 W
Toba Kākar Range ⩚	120	31.15 N	68.00 E
Tobalai, Pulau I	164	1.37 S	128.20 E
Tobarra	34	38.35 N	1.41 W
Tobas	252	28.08 S	62.42 W
Tobašino	80	56.56 N	47.40 E
Toba Tek Singh	123	30.58 N	72.29 E
Tobe	96	33.44 N	132.47 E
Tobejuba, Isla I	246	9.20 N	60.52 W
Tobekuduk	86	49.50 N	54.15 E
Tobelo	108	1.44 N	128.01 E
Tobelombang	112	0.57 S	122.00 E
Tobercurry	48	54.03 N	8.43 W
Tobermorey	166	22.15 S	138.00 E
Tobermory, Austl.	166	27.17 S	143.41 E
Tobermory, On., Can.	190	45.15 N	81.40 W
Tobermory, Scot., U.K.	46	56.37 N	6.05 W
Toberonochy	46	56.13 N	5.38 W
Tōbetsu	92a	43.13 N	141.31 E
Tobi I	108	3.00 N	131.10 E
Tobias	198	40.25 N	97.20 W
Tobias Barreto	250	11.11 S	38.01 W
Tobiishi-bana ›	174f	24.45 N	141.17 E
Tobin, Mount ∧	204	40.22 N	117.32 W
Tobin Lake ⊜, Austl.	162	21.45 S	125.49 E
Tobin Lake ⊜, Sk., Can.	184	53.40 N	103.35 W
Tobique ≏	186	46.46 N	67.42 W
Tobi-shima I	92	39.12 N	139.34 E
Toblach → Dobbiaco	64	46.44 N	12.14 E
Tobo, Indon.	164	3.34 S	130.11 E
Tobo, Sve.	40	60.16 N	17.39 E
Toboali	112	3.00 S	106.30 E
Tobol	86	52.40 N	62.39 E
Tobol ≏	86	58.10 N	68.12 E
Toboli	112	0.43 S	120.05 E
Tobol'sk	86	58.12 N	68.16 E
Tobong-san ∧	271b	37.42 N	127.01 E
Tobor	150	12.39 N	16.16 W
Toboso	116	10.43 N	123.31 E
Tobré	150	10.12 N	2.08 E
Tobruk → Ţubruq	146	32.05 N	23.59 E
Tobseda	24	68.36 N	52.14 E
Tōbu	94	36.21 N	138.20 E
Toburdanovo	80	55.22 N	47.38 E
Toby, Mount ∧	207	42.29 N	72.32 W
Tobyhanna	210	41.10 N	75.25 W
Tobyhanna Creek ≏	210	41.07 N	75.39 W
Tobyhanna State Park ♠	210	41.13 N	75.25 W
Tobyš ≏	24	65.30 N	51.00 E
Tocaima	246	4.28 N	74.38 W
Tocantínia	250	9.33 S	48.22 W
Tocantinópolis	250	6.20 S	47.25 W
Tocantins ≏, Bra.	242	1.45 S	49.10 W
Tocantins ≏, Bra.	250	5.21 S	55.58 W
Tocantins, Parque Nacional do ♠	255	13.42 S	47.37 W
Tocantinzinho ≏	255	13.57 S	48.20 W
Toccoa	192	34.34 N	83.19 W
Toccoa (Ocoee) ≏	192	35.12 N	84.40 W
Toce ≏	58	45.56 N	8.29 E
Tochcha Lake ⊜	182	54.56 N	125.54 W
Tochigi	94	36.23 N	139.44 E
Tochigi □[5]	94	36.45 N	139.45 E
Tochimilco	234	18.54 N	98.34 W
Tochio	92	37.28 N	139.00 E
Tochoj	88	50.30 N	105.00 E
Tochta	24	62.14 N	48.48 E
Tochtamyš	120	37.50 N	74.39 E
Tockholes	262	53.42 N	2.31 W
Tockoje	80	52.32 N	52.45 E
Töcksfors	26	59.30 N	11.50 E
Točnik	60	49.27 N	13.19 E
Toco, Chile	252	22.05 S	69.35 W
Toco, Trin.	241r	10.50 N	60.57 W
Tocoa	236	15.41 N	86.03 W
Tócome ≏	286c	10.29 N	66.49 W
Toconao	252	23.11 S	68.01 W
Tocopilla	252	22.05 S	70.12 W
Tocos do Mogi	256	22.22 S	46.06 W
Tocumwal	166	35.49 S	145.34 E
Tocuyo ≏	246	11.03 N	68.23 W
Tocuyo de la Costa	246	11.02 N	68.23 W
Toda	94	35.48 N	139.41 E
Toda Bhīm	124	26.55 N	76.49 E
Todaiji Temple ʋ[1]	270	34.42 N	135.51 E
Todang-ni	271b	37.37 N	126.50 E
Toda Rai Singh	120	26.01 N	75.29 E
Todd	214	40.16 N	78.04 W
Todd ≏	162	24.52 S	135.48 E
Todd Estates	285	39.40 N	75.43 W
Toddington	42	51.57 N	0.32 W
Todd Point ›	284b	39.15 N	76.27 W
Toddville, Md., U.S.	208	38.17 N	76.04 W
Toddville, N.Y., U.S.	210	41.17 N	73.53 W
Todeli	112	1.40 S	124.29 E
Todenyang	154	4.32 N	35.56 E
Todi	66	42.47 N	12.24 E
Tödi ∧	58	46.49 N	8.56 E
Todmorden, Austl.	162	27.08 S	134.48 E
Todmorden, Eng., U.K.	44	53.43 N	2.05 W
Todoga-saki ›	92	39.33 N	142.05 E
Todoromi	270	34.53 N	135.28 E
Todos Santos, Bol.	248	16.48 S	65.08 W
Todos Santos, Méx.	232	23.27 N	110.13 W
Todos Santos, Bahía ⊂	232	31.48 N	116.42 W
Todro	154	3.21 N	30.14 E
Todtenhausen	52	52.20 N	8.56 E
Todtmoos	58	47.44 N	8.00 E
Todtmoos Au	58	47.42 N	7.58 E
Todtnau	58	47.50 N	7.56 E
Toe Head ›	46	57.50 N	7.08 W
Tōei	94	35.04 N	137.41 E
T'oejo	98	39.54 N	127.46 E
Toéssé	150	11.50 N	1.16 W
Toetoes Bay ⊂	172	46.38 S	168.43 E
Tofield	182	53.22 N	112.40 W
Tofino	182	49.09 N	125.54 W
Töfsingdalens Nationalpark ♠	26	62.09 N	12.30 E
Tofte	26	59.33 N	10.34 E
Toften ⊜	40	59.03 N	14.36 E
Tofterup	41	55.39 N	8.50 E
Toftlund	41	55.11 N	9.04 E
Toga	94	36.27 N	137.02 E
Toga I	175f	13.26 S	166.42 E
Togakushi	94	36.44 N	138.05 E
Togakushi-yama ∧	94	36.46 N	138.04 E
Toganas	80	50.49 N	52.02 E
Tōgane	94	35.33 N	140.22 E
Togauchi	96	34.34 N	132.13 E
Togdheer □[4]	144	9.00 N	46.00 E
Toggenburg V	58	47.15 N	9.10 E
Togho	152	6.01 N	17.26 E
Togi	94	37.08 N	136.44 E
Togiak	180	59.04 N	160.24 W
Togiak Bay ⊂	180	59.00 N	160.30 W
Togian, Kepulauan II	112	0.20 S	122.00 E
Togian, Pulau I	112	0.22 S	121.56 E
Töging am Inn	60	48.15 N	12.35 E
Togliatti → Toljatti	80	53.31 N	49.26 E
Togni	140	18.04 N	35.13 E
Tōgō, Nihon	94	35.05 N	137.03 E
Tōgō, Nihon	96	35.28 N	133.53 E
Togo □[1], Afr.	134	8.00 N	1.10 E
Togo □[1], Afr.	150	8.00 N	1.10 E
Togochale	144	9.33 N	43.18 E
Tōgō-ike ⊜	96	35.28 N	133.54 E
Togoron	116	12.35 N	123.37 E
Tögrög, Mong.	102	45.46 N	94.48 E
Tögrög, Mong.	102	45.32 N	102.59 E
Togtoh	102	40.22 N	111.11 E

ENGLISH

Name	Page	Lat.°′	Long.°′
Togučin	86	55.16 N	84.23 E
Togur	86	58.24 N	82.49 E
Togura	94	36.29 N	138.09 E
Toguzak ≏	86	54.06 N	62.50 E
Toguzbulak	85	42.06 N	76.44 E
Togwotee Pass)(	202	43.45 N	110.04 W
Tŏgyu-san ∧	98	35.46 N	127.40 E
Tŏgyu-san Kukrip Kongwŏn ♠	98	35.52 N	127.45 E
Togyz	86	47.34 N	60.33 E
Tōhaku	96	35.30 N	133.40 E
Tohakum Peak ∧	204	40.11 N	119.27 W
Tohāna	124	29.42 N	75.54 E
Tohiea, Mont ∧	174s	17.33 S	149.49 W
Tohma ≏	130	38.31 N	38.25 E
Toholampi	26	63.46 N	24.15 E
Tohopekaliga, Lake ⊜	220	28.12 N	81.23 W
Tohor, Tanjong ›	114	1.51 N	102.42 E
T'ohyŏn-ni	98	39.53 N	124.52 E
Toi, Nihon	94	34.54 N	138.47 E
Toi, Niue	174v	18.57 S	169.51 W
Toijala	26	61.10 N	23.52 E
Toili	112	1.27 S	122.24 E
Toi-misaki ›	92	31.20 N	131.22 E
Tōin	94	35.05 N	136.35 E
Toinya	140	6.17 N	29.44 E
Toi Šar	120	31.06 N	69.54 E
Toiyabe Range ⩚	204	39.10 N	117.10 W
Tojg	128	32.04 N	61.48 E
To-jima I	96	33.12 N	132.22 E
Tojo, Indon.	112	1.17 S	121.11 E
Tōjō, Nihon	96	34.53 N	133.16 E
Tōjō, Nihon	270	34.55 N	135.04 E
Tojtepa	85	41.03 N	69.22 E
Tōju-in ʋ[1]	94	35.19 N	136.04 E
Tok	180	63.19 N	142.59 W
Tok ≏	80	52.46 N	52.22 E
Tokaanu	172	38.58 S	175.46 E
Tokachi ≏	92a	42.44 N	143.42 E
Tokachi-dake ∧	92a	43.25 N	142.41 E
Tokachi-heiya ≚	92a	43.00 N	143.30 E
Tōkagi	268	35.42 N	139.56 E
Tokai, Malay.	114	6.01 N	100.24 E
Tōkai, Nihon	94	36.27 N	140.34 E
Tōkai, Nihon	94	35.00 N	136.53 E
Tokaj ≏	78	51.18 N	41.04 E
Tokala	112	1.47 S	121.43 E
Tōkamachi	94	37.08 N	138.46 E
Tokanui	172	46.34 S	168.56 E
Tokara-kaikyō ⋓	93b	30.10 N	130.10 E
Tokara-rettō II	93b	29.36 N	129.43 E
Tokarevka	86	50.08 N	73.12 E
Tokar Game Reserve ◆[4]	140	18.15 N	37.45 E
Tokaris	130	37.45 N	38.50 E
Tokar'ovka	80	51.59 N	41.09 E
Tokar'ovo, S.S.S.R.	76	55.17 N	35.04 E
Tokar'ovo, S.S.S.R.	265b	55.38 N	37.55 E
Tokashiki-jima I	93b	26.11 N	127.21 E
Tokat	130	40.19 N	36.34 E
Tokat □[4]	130	40.25 N	36.30 E
Tŏkchŏk-kundo II	98	37.14 N	126.07 E
Tŏkch'ŏn	98	39.46 N	126.19 E
Tokeland	224	46.42 N	123.58 W
Tokelau □[2]	14	9.00 S	171.45 W
Tokelau-Inseln → Tokelau □[2]	14	9.00 S	171.45 W
Tokelau Islands II	4	9.00 S	171.45 W
Tokeneke Brook ≏	276	41.03 N	73.28 W
Tŏkhŭng-ni	98	40.02 N	127.08 E
Toki	94	35.21 N	137.11 E
Toki ≏	94	35.12 N	136.52 E
Tokio → Tōkyō	94	35.42 N	139.46 E
Toki Point ›	174a	19.19 N	166.35 E
Tokiwadaira	268	35.48 N	139.57 E
Tokko	74	59.59 N	119.52 E
Tokko ≏	88	58.42 N	119.50 E
Toklar	130	38.26 N	36.01 E
Toklat ≏	180	64.27 N	150.17 W
Tokma	88	58.13 N	105.42 E
Tokmak, S.S.S.R.	78	47.15 N	35.43 E
Tokmak, S.S.S.R.	85	42.55 N	75.18 E
Toko	172	39.20 S	174.24 E
Tököl	264c	47.19 N	18.58 E
Tokolimbu	112	2.48 S	121.34 E
Tokomaru	172	40.28 S	175.30 E
Tokomaru Bay	172	38.08 S	178.18 E
Tokoname	94	34.53 N	136.51 E
Toko Range ⩚	166	23.05 S	138.20 E
Tokoro ≏	92a	44.07 N	144.05 E
Tokoroa	172	38.14 S	175.52 E
Tokorozawa	94	35.47 N	139.28 E
Tokovskoje	78	47.38 N	33.59 E
Tokrau ≏	86	46.48 N	75.24 E
Toksook Bay	180	60.32 N	165.06 W
Toksovo	76	60.09 N	30.31 E
Tok-to (Take-shima) II	92	37.17 N	131.53 E
Toktogul	85	41.50 N	72.50 E
Toktogul'skoje vodochranilišče ⊜[1]	85	41.50 N	72.55 E
Toku Island I	14	18.10 S	174.11 W
Tokuji	96	34.11 N	131.40 E
Tokul Creek ≏	224	47.35 N	121.50 W
Tokung	112	0.18 S	114.28 E
Tokuno-shima I	93b	27.45 N	128.58 E
Tokur	89	53.10 N	132.53 E
Tokura	270	34.58 N	135.18 E
Tokura-tōge)(	96	35.17 N	134.31 E
Tokusaga-mine ∧	96	34.26 N	131.41 E
Tokushima	96	34.04 N	134.34 E
Tokushima □[5]	96	33.45 N	134.00 E
Tokuyama, Nihon	94	35.42 N	136.29 E
Tokuyama, Nihon	96	34.03 N	131.49 E
Tokwe ≏	154	21.09 S	31.30 E
Tōkyō, Nihon	94	35.42 N	139.46 E
Tōkyō, Nihon	268	35.42 N	139.46 E
Tōkyō □[5]	94	35.45 N	139.30 E
Tokyo Bay → Tōkyō-wan ⊂	94	35.25 N	139.47 E
Tōkyō-daigaku-uchūkūkan-kenkyūsho ʋ[3]	92	31.17 N	131.05 E
Tokyo Disneyland ♠	268	35.37 N	139.53 E
Tōkyō-kō ⊂	268	35.37 N	139.47 E
Tōkyō-kokusai-kūkō ⊠	94	35.45 N	140.21 E
Tokyo Station ◆[5]	268	35.41 N	139.46 E
Tokyo Tower ʋ	268	35.39 N	139.45 E
Tokyo University ʋ[2]	268	35.42 N	139.46 E
Tokyo University of Education ʋ[2]	268	35.43 N	139.44 E
Tōkyō-wan (Tokyo Bay) ⊂	94	35.25 N	139.47 E
Tokzār	120	35.52 N	66.26 E
Tol I	175c	7.22 N	151.37 E
Tolaga Bay	172	38.22 S	178.18 E
Tolala	112	2.56 S	121.06 E
Tolang	114	1.56 N	99.26 E
Tolbert	52	53.10 N	6.21 E
Tolbo Nuur	86	48.25 N	90.17 E
Tolbuchino	80	57.51 N	40.03 E
Tolbuhin	38	43.34 N	27.50 E
Tolderol Point ›	168b	35.22 S	139.10 E
Tolé, Pan.	236	8.14 N	81.41 W
Tole, S.S.S.R.	85	42.40 N	70.08 E
Toledo, Bol.	248	18.10 S	67.25 W
Toledo, Bra.	252	24.44 S	53.45 W
Toledo, Bra.	256	22.44 S	46.23 W
Toledo, Col.	246	7.19 N	72.28 W
Toledo, Esp.	34	39.52 N	4.01 W
Toledo, Pil.	116	10.23 N	123.38 E
Toledo, Il., U.S.	194	39.16 N	88.14 W
Toledo, Ia., U.S.	190	41.59 N	92.34 W
Toledo, Oh., U.S.	214	41.39 N	83.33 W
Toledo, Or., U.S.	202	44.37 N	123.56 W
Toledo, Wa., U.S.	224	46.26 N	122.50 W
Toledo, Ur.	258	34.45 S	56.05 W
Toledo □[5]	236	16.20 N	88.55 W
Toledo, Montes de ⩚	34	39.33 N	4.20 W
Toledo Bend Reservoir ⊜[1]	194	31.30 N	93.45 W
Toledo Express Airport ⊠	216	41.35 N	83.49 W

DEUTSCH

Name	Seite	Breite°′	Länge°′ E = Ost
Tolentino	66	43.12 N	13.17 E
Tolfa	66	42.09 N	11.56 E
Tolfa, Monti della ⩚	66	42.08 N	11.54 E
Tolga, Alg.	148	34.46 N	5.22 E
Tolga, Nor.	26	62.25 N	11.00 E
Toli	86	45.57 N	83.37 E
Toliara	157b	23.21 S	43.40 E
Toliara □[4]	157b	24.00 S	45.00 E
Tolima □[5]	246	3.45 N	75.15 W
Tolima, Nevado del ∧	246	4.40 N	75.19 W
Tolimán, Méx.	234	19.36 N	103.55 W
Tolimán, Méx.	234	20.55 N	99.56 W
Tolitoli	112	1.02 N	120.49 E
Toljatti (Togliatti)	80	53.31 N	49.26 E
Tol'ka	74	64.02 N	81.55 E
Tolkmicko	30	54.20 N	19.31 E
Tolland	207	41.52 N	72.22 W
Tolland □[6]	207	41.52 N	72.22 W
Tollarp	26	55.56 N	13.59 E
Tollense ≏	54	53.54 N	13.02 E
Tollensesee ⊜	54	53.30 N	13.11 E
Tollesboro	218	38.33 N	83.34 W
Tollesbury	42	51.46 N	0.50 E
Tolleson	200	33.27 N	112.15 W
Tollhouse	226	37.01 N	119.23 W
Tolloche	252	25.30 S	63.32 W
Tølløse	41	55.37 N	11.45 E
Tollygunge ◆[8]	272b	22.30 N	88.21 E
Tolmači	76	57.26 N	35.41 E
Tolmačovo	76	58.52 N	29.55 E
Tolmezzo	64	46.24 N	13.01 E
Tolmin	36	46.11 N	13.44 E
Tolna	30	46.26 N	18.46 E
Tolna □[6]	30	46.30 N	18.35 E
Tolo	152	2.56 S	18.34 E
Tolo, Teluk ⊂	112	2.00 S	122.30 E
Toloa, Houma ›	174w	21.17 S	175.08 W
Tolob	46a	59.53 N	1.19 W
Toločin	76	54.25 N	29.42 E
Tolokiwa Island I	164	5.20 S	147.40 E
Tolomo	89	50.03 N	137.45 E
Tolong Bay ⊂	116	9.20 N	122.49 E
Tolongoina	157b	21.33 S	47.31 E
Tolono	194	39.59 N	88.15 W
Tolosa	34	43.08 N	2.04 W
Tolosa, Aeródromo ⊠	288	34.53 S	57.58 W
Tolovana ≏	180	64.51 N	149.45 W
Tolpuddle	42	50.45 N	2.18 W
Tolsan-do I	98	34.38 N	127.45 E
Tol'skij Majdan	80	54.57 N	44.39 E
Tolsta Head ›	46	58.20 N	6.10 W
Tolstoj, mys ›	74	59.10 N	155.12 E
Tolstoje	78	48.50 N	25.44 E
Tolstopal'cevo	265b	55.38 N	37.13 E
Tolt, North Fork ≏	224	47.42 N	121.49 W
Toltén	254	39.13 S	73.14 W
Tolten ≏	254	39.15 S	73.14 W
Tolti	123	35.02 N	76.06 E
Toltry ⩚[1]	78	49.00 N	26.10 E
Tolt-Seattle Water Supply Reservoir ⊜[1]	224	47.42 N	121.39 W
Tolú	246	9.31 N	75.35 W
Toluca	216	41.00 N	89.08 W
Toluca, Nevado de ∧[1]	234	19.08 N	99.44 W
Toluca [de Lerdo]	234	19.17 N	99.40 W
Tolvajarvi	24	62.17 N	31.27 E
Tolvdalselva ≏	26	58.10 N	8.00 E
Tolve	68	40.42 N	16.01 E
Tolwa	140	6.38 N	32.37 E
Tolworth ◆[8]	260	51.23 N	0.17 W
Tolyatti → Toljatti	80	53.31 N	49.26 E
Tolybaj	86	50.31 N	62.19 E
Tom' ≏, S.S.S.R.	86	56.50 N	84.27 E
Tom' ≏, S.S.S.R.	89	51.00 N	127.54 E
Toma	150	12.46 N	2.53 W
Tomah	190	43.58 N	90.30 W
Tomahawk	190	45.28 N	89.43 W
Tomakomai	92a	42.38 N	141.36 E
Tomakovka	78	47.48 N	34.44 E
Tomani	112	4.50 N	115.55 E
Tomanivi ∧	175g	17.37 S	178.01 E
Tomar, Port.	34	39.36 N	8.25 W
Tomar, S.S.S.R.	86	46.24 N	75.03 E
Tomari	89	47.47 N	142.03 E
Tomarovka	78	50.41 N	36.14 E
Tomarza	130	38.27 N	35.49 E
Tomás Barrón (Eucaliptus)	248	17.35 S	67.31 W
Tomasboda ∧[2]	40	59.24 N	14.58 E
Tomás Gomensoro	252	30.26 S	57.26 W
Tomašgorod	78	51.19 N	27.02 E
Tomasine ≏	190	46.40 N	76.16 W
Tomás Jofré	258	34.43 S	59.19 W
Tomášov	61	48.09 N	17.16 E
Tomašpol'	78	48.33 N	28.31 E
Tomaszów Lubelski	30	50.28 N	23.25 E
Tomaszów Mazowiecki	30	51.32 N	20.01 E
Tomatin	46	57.20 N	3.59 W
Tomatlán	234	19.56 N	105.15 W
Tomatlán ≏	234	19.50 N	105.23 W
Tomave	248	20.06 S	66.35 W
Tomazina	255	23.46 S	49.58 W
Tomba di Nerone ◆[8]	267a	41.57 N	12.27 E
Tombadonkéa	150	11.00 N	14.23 W
Tombador, Serra do ⩚[1]	248	12.00 S	57.40 W
Tomball	222	30.06 N	95.37 W
Tombe	140	5.49 N	31.41 E
Tombigbee ≏	194	31.04 N	87.58 W
Tombo, Punta ›	254	44.03 S	65.11 W
Tombôco	152	6.48 S	13.18 E
Tombolo	64	45.38 N	11.50 E
Tombos	255	20.55 S	42.02 W
Tombouctou (Timbuktu)	150	16.46 N	3.01 W
Tombouctou □[4]	150	18.20 N	3.50 W
Tombs of the Caliphs ⊥	273c	30.03 N	31.17 E
Tombstone	200	31.42 N	110.04 W
Tombstone Mountain ∧	180	64.25 N	138.30 W
Tombua	152	15.49 S	11.53 E
Tom Burke	156	23.05 S	28.00 E
Tomdoun	46	57.04 N	5.03 W
Tomé	252	36.37 S	72.57 W
Tomea, Pulau I	112	5.45 S	123.56 E
Tomé-Açu	250	2.25 S	48.09 W
Tomek	130	38.02 N	32.41 E
Tomelilla	26	55.33 N	13.57 E
Tomelloso	34	39.10 N	3.01 W
Tomerong	170	35.04 S	150.35 E
Tomhannock Reservoir ⊜[1]	210	42.51 N	73.33 W
Tomi ≏	152	5.07 N	19.19 E
Tomich	46	57.18 N	4.48 W
Tomichi Creek ≏	200	38.31 N	106.58 W
Tomifobia ≏	206	45.11 N	72.02 W
Tomiko Lake ⊜	190	46.32 N	79.49 W
Tomilino	265b	55.39 N	37.57 E
Tomini	112	0.30 N	120.32 E
Tomini, Teluk ⊂	112	0.20 S	121.00 E
Tominian	150	13.17 N	4.35 W
Tomintoul	46	57.14 N	3.22 W
Tomio ≏	270	34.35 N	135.44 E
Tomioka	94	36.15 N	138.54 E
Tomisato	94	35.44 N	140.19 E
Tomiura	94	35.03 N	139.50 E
Tomiyama, Nihon	94	35.11 N	137.48 E
Tomiyama, Nihon	94	35.05 N	139.51 E
Tomizawa	94	35.14 N	138.29 E
T'omkino	76	55.05 N	35.01 E
Tomkins Cove	210	41.15 N	73.59 W
Tomkinson Ranges ⩚	162	26.11 S	129.05 E
Tomkinsville	208	38.19 N	76.53 W
Tomlinson Run State Park ♠	214	40.33 N	80.34 W
Tommerup Stationsby	41	55.19 N	10.13 E
Tommot	74	58.58 N	126.19 E

Symbols in the index entries represent the broad categories identified in the key at the right. Symbols with superior numbers (⩚[1]) identify subcategories (see complete key on page *I · 1).*

Kartensymbole in dem Registerverzeichnis stellen die rechts in Schlüssel erklärten Kategorien dar. Symbole mit hochgestellten Ziffern (⩚[1]) bezeichnen Unterabteilungen einer Kategorie (vgl. vollständiger Schlüssel auf Seite *I · 1).*

Los símbolos incluídos en el texto del índice representan las grandes categorias identificadas con la clave a la derecha. Los símbolos con numeros en su parte superior (⩚[1]) identifican las subcategorías (véase la clave completa en la página *I · 1).*

Les symboles de l'index représentent les catégories indiquées dans la légende à droite. Les symboles suivis d'un indice (⩚[1]) représentent des sous-catégories (voir légende complète à la page *I · 1).*

Os símbolos incluídos no texto do índice representam as grandes categorias identificadas com a chave à direita. Os símbolos com números em sua parte superior (⩚[1]) identificam as subcategorias (veja-se a chave completa à página *I · 1).*

∧	Mountain	Berg	Montaña	Montagne	Montanha
⩚	Mountains	Berge	Montañas	Montagnes	Montanhas
)(	Pass	Pass	Paso	Col	Passo
V	Valley, Canyon	Tal, Cañon	Valle, Cañón	Vallée, Canyon	Vale, Canhão
≚	Plain	Ebene	Llano	Plaine	Planície
›	Cape	Kap	Cabo	Cap	Cabo
I	Island	Insel	Isla	Île	Ilha
II	Islands	Inseln	Islas	Îles	Ilhas
≐	Other Topographic Features	Andere Topographische Objekte	Otros Elementos Topográficos	Autres données topographiques	Outros acidentes topográficos

Symbol	English	Deutsch	Español	Français	Português
≃	River	Fluss	Río	Rivière	Rio
≊	Canal	Kanal	Canal	Canal	Canal
↳	Waterfall, Rapids	Wasserfall, Stromschnellen	Cascada, Rápidos	Chute d'eau, Rapides	Cascata, Rápidos
⊻	Strait	Meeresstrasse	Estrecho	Détroit	Estreito
⊂	Bay, Gulf	Bucht, Golf	Bahía, Golfo	Baie, Golfe	Baía, Golfo
⊜	Lake, Lakes	See, Seen	Lago, Lagos	Lac, Lacs	Lago, Lagos
⩸	Swamp	Sumpf	Pantano	Marais	Pântano
⊓	Ice Features, Glacier	Eis- und Gletscherformen	Accidentes Glaciales	Formes glaciaires	Acidentes glaciares
⊤	Other Hydrographic Features	Andere Hydrographische Objekte	Otros Elementos Hidrográficos	Autres données hydrographiques	Outros acidentes hidrográficos
✢	Submarine Features	Untermeerische Objekte	Accidentes Submarinos	Formes de relief sous-marin	Acidentes submarinos
□	Political Unit	Politische Einheit	Unidad Politica	Entité politique	Unidade política
♁	Cultural Institution	Kulturelle Institution	Institución Cultural	Institution culturelle	Instituição cultural
⊥	Historical Site	Historische Stätte	Sitio Histórico	Site historique	Sitio histórico
♠	Recreational Site	Erholungs- und Ferienort	Sitio de Recreo	Centre de loisirs	Area de Lazer
⊠	Airport	Flughafen	Aeropuerto	Aéroport	Aeroporto
■	Military Installation	Militäranlage	Instalación Militar	Installation militaire	Instalação militar
◆	Miscellaneous	Verschiedenes	Misceláneo	Divers	Diversos

Tragwein 61 48.20 N 14.37 E
Traição, Córrego ≃ 287b 23.36 S 46.41 W
Traid 34 40.40 N 1.49 W
Traiguén 252 38.15 S 72.41 W
Traiguén, Isla I 254 45.35 S 73.42 W
Trail 182 49.06 N 117.42 W
Trail Creek 216 41.41 N 86.51 W
Trailer Estates 220 27.24 N 82.34 W
Trail Ridge ∧ 192 30.35 N 82.05 W
Traînel 50 48.25 N 3.27 E
Trainer 285 39.50 N 75.25 W
Traipu 250 9.58 S 37.01 W
Traíra (Taraira) ≃ 246 1.04 S 69.26 W
Trairão ≃ 250 7.20 S 51.14 W
Trairas ≃ 255 14.07 S 48.31 W
Trairi 250 3.17 S 39.15 W
Traisen 61 48.02 N 15.37 E
Traisen ≃ 61 48.22 N 15.46 E
Traiskirchen 61 48.01 N 16.18 E
Traismauer 61 48.21 N 15.44 E
Traîtres, Baie des c 174y 9.50 S 139.02 W
Trajouce 266c 38.44 N 9.20 W
Trakai 76 54.38 N 24.56 E
Trakt 24 62.44 N 51.11 E
Träkvista 40 59.16 N 17.47 E
Tralee 48 52.16 N 9.42 W
Tralee Bay c 48 52.15 N 9.59 W
Trá Lí
→ Tralee 48 52.16 N 9.42 W
Tramatza 71 40.00 N 8.39 E
Tramayes 58 46.18 N 4.36 E
Tramelan 58 47.13 N 7.06 E
Tramin
→ Termeno 64 46.20 N 11.14 E
Trammel 192 37.00 N 82.17 W
Trammel Creek ≃ 194 36.52 N 86.23 W
Tramonti di sopra 64 46.18 N 12.47 E
Tramore 48 52.10 N 7.10 W
Tramperos Creek (Punta de Agua Creek) ≃ 196 35.32 N 102.27 W
Tramping Lake ⊜ 184 52.08 N 108.49 W
Tramutola 68 40.19 N 15.47 E
Trân 38 42.50 N 22.39 E
Tranås 26 58.03 N 14.59 E
Trancão ≃ 266c 38.48 N 9.06 W
Trancas 252 26.13 S 65.17 W
Trancoso, Méx. 234 22.44 N 102.22 W
Trancoso, Port. 34 40.47 N 7.21 W
Trand 123 34.38 N 72.59 E
Tranderup 41 54.52 N 10.22 E
Tranebjerg 41 55.50 N 10.36 E
Tranekær 41 55.00 N 10.51 E
Tranemo 26 57.29 N 13.21 E
Tranent 46 55.57 N 2.58 W
Tranental 158 27.09 S 19.33 E
Trang 110 7.33 N 99.36 E
Trangahy 157b 19.07 S 44.43 E
Trangan, Pulau I 164 6.35 S 134.20 E
Trangie 166 32.02 S 147.59 E
Tran Grande ≃ 116 6.43 N 124.01 E
Trängslet 26 61.25 N 13.40 E
Trani 68 41.17 N 16.26 E
Tranmere 262 53.23 N 3.01 W
Trannon ≃ 42 52.31 N 3.25 W
Tranoroa 157b 24.42 S 45.04 E
Tranquebar 122 11.02 N 79.51 E
Tranqueira ≃ 250 7.15 S 42.12 W
Tranqueras 252 31.12 S 55.45 W
Tranquility 218 38.58 N 83.32 W
Tranquilla 236 8.30 N 80.14 W
Tranquillity 226 36.38 N 120.15 W
Trans-en-Provence 62 43.30 N 6.29 E
Transfer 214 41.20 N 80.26 W
Transit Airport ≋ 284a 43.06 N 78.44 W
Transkei □1, Afr. 138 31.20 S 29.00 E
Transkei □1, Afr. 158 31.20 S 29.00 E
Transquaking ≃ 208 38.22 N 76.00 W
Transsylvanische Alpen
→ Carpaţii Meridionali ∧ 38 45.30 N 24.15 E
Transtrand 26 61.05 N 13.19 E
Transtrandsfjällen ∧ 26 61.17 N 13.00 E
Transvaal □4 156 25.00 S 29.00 E
Transylvania □9 38 46.30 N 24.00 E
Transylvanian Alps
→ Carpaţii Meridionali ∧ 38 45.30 N 24.15 E
Tranters Creek ≃ 192 35.33 N 77.05 W
Traona 58 46.09 N 9.31 E
Trapalcó, Salinas de ≚ 254 39.45 S 66.45 W
Trapani 70 38.01 N 12.31 E
Trapani □4 70 37.50 N 12.40 E
Traphole Brook ≃ 283 42.10 N 71.11 W
Trappe, Md., U.S. 208 38.39 N 76.03 W
Trappe, Pa., U.S. 208 40.12 N 75.29 W
Trappenkamp 54 54.03 N 10.16 E
Trapper Peak ∧ 202 45.54 N 114.18 W
Trappes 50 48.47 N 2.00 E
Trappeto 70 38.04 N 13.03 E
Trapuá ≃ 287b 23.36 S 46.17 W
Traralgon 169 38.12 S 146.32 E
Traralgon Creek ≃ 169 38.10 S 146.31 E
Traras, Monts des ∧ 34 35.10 N 1.40 W
Trarza □4 150 17.45 N 15.45 W
Trârza ◆1 150 18.00 N 15.00 W
Trasacco 66 41.57 N 13.32 E
Trasadingen 58 47.40 N 8.26 E
Trăscău, Munţii ∧ 38 46.23 N 23.33 E
Trasimeno, Lago ⊜ 66 43.08 N 12.06 E
Trask ≃ 224 45.28 N 123.53 W
Träslövsläge 26 57.04 N 12.16 E
Trasna 82 54.45 N 38.42 E
Tras-os-Montes □9 34 41.30 N 7.15 W
Trassem 56 49.34 N 6.31 E
Trăstenik 38 43.31 N 24.28 E
Trat 110 12.14 N 102.30 E
Tratalias 71 39.06 N 8.34 E
Tratzberg, Schloss ⊥ 64 47.23 N 11.44 E
Trauchgau 58 47.38 N 10.49 E
Traun 61 48.13 N 14.14 E
Traun ≃, B.R.D. 60 48.00 N 12.32 E
Traun ≃, Öst. 30 48.16 N 14.22 E
Traunkirchen 64 47.50 N 13.47 E
Traunreut 64 47.56 N 12.35 E
Traunsee ⊜ 64 47.51 N 13.48 E
Traunstein, B.R.D. 64 47.52 N 12.38 E
Traunstein, Öst. 61 48.26 N 15.07 E
Traunstein ∧ 64 47.52 N 13.50 E
Trautenstein 54 51.41 N 10.43 E
Travagliato 64 45.31 N 10.05 E
Trave ≃ 54 53.54 N 10.50 E
Travedona 62 45.48 N 8.40 E
Travellers Lake ⊜ 166 33.18 S 142.00 E
Travemünde ◆8 54 53.57 N 10.52 E
Traver 226 36.27 N 119.29 W
Travers, Mount ∧ 172 42.01 S 172.44 E
Travers, Val de V 58 46.57 N 6.38 E
Traverse, Lake ⊜ 198 45.43 N 96.40 W
Traverse Bay c 184 50.40 N 96.25 W
Traverse City 190 44.45 N 85.37 W
Traversella 62 45.30 N 7.45 E
Traverse Peak ∧ 180 65.10 N 159.12 W
Traversetolo 64 44.38 N 10.23 E
Travers Reservoir ⊜1 182 50.14 N 112.51 W
Travesía ⊥ 236 15.20 N 87.53 W
Travis 222 31.08 N 97.00 W
Travis □6 222 30.18 N 97.40 W
Travis, Lake ⊜1 196 30.27 N 98.00 W
Travis Air Force Base ■ 226 38.16 N 121.55 W
Travnik 36 44.14 N 17.40 E
Trawalla 169 37.26 S 143.29 E
Trawbreaga Bay c 48 55.17 N 7.18 W
Trawick 222 31.46 N 94.45 W
Trawsfynydd 42 52.54 N 3.55 W
Trayning 162 31.07 S 117.48 E
Trazegnies 50 50.28 N 4.19 E
Trbovlje 36 46.10 N 15.03 E
Treadwell 210 42.21 N 75.03 W
Treales 262 53.47 N 2.51 W
Treasure Island 220 27.46 N 82.46 W
Treasure Island I 226 37.48 N 122.22 W
Treasure Island Naval Station ■ 282 37.49 N 122.22 W
Trebatsch 54 52.05 N 14.09 E
Trebbia ≃ 62 45.04 N 9.41 E
Trebbin 54 52.13 N 13.13 E
Třebechovice pod Orebem 30 50.12 N 16.00 E
Trebel 54 52.59 N 11.20 E
Trebel ≃ 54 53.55 N 13.01 E
Trebelsee ⊜ 54 52.28 N 12.47 E
Třebenice 54 50.29 N 14.00 E
Trebgast 60 50.04 N 11.33 E
Třebíč 30 49.13 N 15.53 E
Trebinje 38 42.43 N 18.20 E
Trebisacce 68 39.52 N 16.32 E
Trebišov 30 48.40 N 21.47 E
Trebitz 54 51.45 N 12.44 E
Trebizond
→ Trabzon 130 41.00 N 39.43 E
Trebjerg ∧2 41 55.10 N 10.14 E
Třebkov 60 49.22 N 14.04 E
Treble Mountain ∧ 182 55.50 N 129.51 W
Treblinka 30 52.39 N 22.03 E
Trebnitz
→ Trzebnica 30 51.19 N 17.03 E
Třeboň 61 49.00 N 14.47 E
Třebouň ∧ 60 50.01 N 12.59 E
Trebsen 54 51.17 N 12.45 E
Trebur 56 49.56 N 8.25 E
Trecastagni 70 37.37 N 15.05 E
Trecate 62 45.26 N 8.44 E
Trecchina 68 40.02 N 15.46 E
Trece Martires 116 14.16 N 120.50 E
Trecenta 64 45.02 N 11.28 E
Tred Avon River ≃ 208 38.42 N 76.08 W
Tredegar 42 51.47 N 3.16 W
Tredici Archi, Ponte ◆5 66 41.32 N 14.57 E
Treene ≃ 41 54.22 N 9.05 E
Trees Mills 279b 40.23 N 80.13 W
Treffen 64 46.40 N 13.52 E
Treffort 58 46.16 N 5.22 E
Treffurt 56 51.08 N 10.14 E
Trèfle, Lac du ⊜ 200 46.36 N 83.50 W
Tregaron 42 52.13 N 3.55 W
Tregnago 64 45.31 N 11.10 E
Tregosse Islets II 166 17.41 S 150.43 E
Tregubovo 76 58.59 N 31.33 E
Tréguier 32 48.47 N 3.14 W
Treharris 42 51.41 N 3.16 W
Treherne 184 49.38 N 98.41 W
Trehörningsjö 26 63.42 N 18.48 E
Treia, B.R.D. 41 54.30 N 9.17 E
Treia, It. 66 43.19 N 13.19 E
Treig, Loch ⊜1 46 56.50 N 4.44 W
Treinta y Tres 252 33.14 S 54.23 W
Treis 56 50.10 N 7.17 E
Trekkopje 156 22.18 S 14.53 E
Trélazé 32 47.27 N 0.28 W
Trelde Næs ≻ 41 55.37 N 9.52 E
Trelew 254 43.15 S 65.18 W
Trelleborg 41 55.22 N 13.10 E
Treloar 219 38.39 N 91.10 W
Tremadog 42 52.56 N 4.09 W
Tremadog Bay c 42 52.52 N 4.15 W
Tremblant, Lac ⊜ 206 46.15 N 74.38 W
Tremblant, Mont ∧ 206 46.16 N 74.35 W
Tremblay, Hippodrome du ◆ 261 48.50 N 2.29 E
Tremblay-lès-Gonesse 261 48.59 N 2.34 E
Trembleur Lake ⊜ 182 54.51 N 125.07 W
Tremedal 255 14.58 S 41.24 W
Tremembé 256 22.58 S 45.33 W
Tremezzo 58 45.59 N 9.15 E
Tremino 88 56.42 N 98.04 E
Tremiti, Isole II 66 42.07 N 15.30 E
Tremo, La)(124 27.44 N 89.12 E
Tremont, Il., U.S. 190 40.31 N 89.29 W
Tremont, In., U.S. 216 41.39 N 87.02 W
Tremont, Pa., U.S. 208 40.37 N 76.23 W
Tremont ◆8 276 40.51 N 73.55 W
Tremont City 218 40.00 N 83.50 W
Tremonton 200 41.42 N 112.09 W
Třemošna 60 49.49 N 13.20 E
Třemošná ∧ 60 49.52 N 13.32 E
Tremp 34 42.10 N 0.54 E
Trempealeau 190 44.00 N 91.26 W
Trempealeau ≃ 190 44.02 N 91.32 W
Tremsbüttel 52 53.44 N 10.18 E
Trena 144 10.45 N 40.38 E
Trenčín 30 48.54 N 18.04 E
Trendelburg 52 51.34 N 9.25 E
Trenel 252 35.42 S 64.08 W
Treng 110 12.49 N 102.54 E
Trenggalek 115a 8.03 S 111.43 E
Trenque Lauquen 252 35.58 S 62.42 W
Trent, D.D.R. 54 54.31 N 13.15 E
Trent
→ Trento, It. 64 46.04 N 11.08 E
Trent ≃, On., Can. 212 44.06 N 77.34 W
Trent ≃, Eng., U.K. 28 53.42 N 0.41 W
Trent ≃, Eng., U.K. 44 53.42 N 0.41 W
Trent ≃, N.C., U.S. 192 35.05 N 77.02 W
Trent, Vale of V 42 52.44 N 1.50 W
Trent and Mersey Canal ≃ 262 53.19 N 2.39 W
Trente et un Milles, Lac des ⊜ 188 46.12 N 75.49 W
Trentham 169 37.23 S 144.19 E
Trentino-Alto Adige □4 64 46.30 N 11.20 E
Trento 64 46.04 N 11.08 E
Trento □4 64 46.08 N 11.07 E
Trentola-Ducenta 68 40.59 N 14.10 E
Trenton, N.S., Can. 186 45.37 N 62.38 W
Trenton, On., Can. 212 44.06 N 77.35 W
Trenton, Fl., U.S. 192 29.36 N 82.49 W
Trenton, Ga., U.S. 192 34.52 N 85.30 W
Trenton, Il., U.S. 219 38.36 N 89.40 W
Trenton, Ky., U.S. 194 36.43 N 87.15 W
Trenton, Mi., U.S. 216 42.08 N 83.10 W
Trenton, Mo., U.S. 194 40.04 N 93.36 W
Trenton, Ne., U.S. 198 40.10 N 101.00 W
Trenton, N.J., U.S. 208 40.13 N 74.44 W
Trenton, N.C., U.S. 192 35.04 N 77.21 W
Trenton, Oh., U.S. 218 39.29 N 84.27 W
Trenton, Tn., U.S. 194 35.58 N 88.56 W
Trenton, Tx., U.S. 196 33.26 N 96.20 W
Trenton Canadian Forces Base ■ 190 44.07 N 77.33 W
Trenton Channel ≃1 281 42.06 N 83.11 W
Trentwood 202 47.42 N 117.13 W
Trepalade 64 45.34 N 12.24 E
Trepassey 186 46.44 N 53.22 W
Trepassey Bay c 186 46.37 N 53.20 W
Treptow ◆8 54 52.29 N 13.29 E
Treptow an der Rega
→ Trzebiatów 30 54.04 N 15.14 E
Trepuzzi 68 40.24 N 18.05 E
Trequanda 66 43.11 N 11.40 E
Tresa ≃ 58 46.00 N 8.43 E
Tres Algarrobos 252 35.12 S 62.46 W
Tres Arboles 252 32.24 S 56.43 W
Tres Arroyos 252 38.23 S 60.17 W
Tres Cerros 254 48.13 S 67.33 W
Treščevo 82 54.11 N 37.55 E
Tresckow 210 40.54 N 75.58 W
Tresco I 42a 49.57 N 6.20 W
Três Corações 256 21.42 S 45.16 W
Trescore Balneario 62 45.42 N 9.50 E
Três Coroas 252 29.32 S 50.48 W
Tres de Febrero
→ Caseros 288 34.36 S 58.33 W
Tres de Febrero □5 288 34.36 S 58.35 W
Tres de Maio 252 27.47 S 54.14 W
Tresenda 64 46.10 N 10.05 E
Tres Esquinas 246 0.43 N 75.16 W
Três Fronteiras 255 20.13 S 50.55 W
Treshnish Isles II 46 56.30 N 6.24 W
Treshnish Point ≻ 46 56.33 N 6.21 W
Tre Signori, Picco dei (Dreiherrnspitze) ∧ 64 47.04 N 12.15 E
Três Ilhas 256 22.04 S 43.09 W
Tresinaro ≃ 64 44.39 N 10.47 E
Tres Isletas 252 26.21 S 60.26 W
Treskino 80 52.40 N 44.40 E
Três Lagoas 255 20.48 S 51.43 W
Tres Lagos 254 49.37 S 71.30 W
Três Marias, Represa ⊜1 255 18.12 S 45.15 W
Tres Montes, Golfo c 254 46.54 S 75.00 W
Tres Montes, Península ≻1 254 46.50 S 75.30 W
Tres Montosas ∧ 200 34.06 N 107.28 W
Tresnuraghes 71 40.15 N 8.31 E
Tres Palacios ≃ 196 28.45 N 96.09 W
Três Passos 252 27.27 S 53.56 W
Tres Picos 234 15.52 N 93.32 W
Tres Picos, Cerro ∧, Arg. 252 38.09 S 61.57 W
Tres Picos, Cerro ∧, Méx. 234 16.36 N 94.13 W
Tres Pinos 226 36.48 N 121.19 W
Tres Pinos Creek ≃ 226 36.47 N 121.21 W
Três Pontas 256 21.22 S 45.31 W
Três Pontas, Cabo das ≻ 152 10.23 S 13.32 E
Tres Puntas, Cabo ≻ 254 47.06 S 65.53 W
Três Ranchos 255 18.22 S 47.47 W
Tres Reyes Islands II 116 13.14 N 121.51 E
Tres Ríos, Bra. 256 22.07 S 43.12 W
Tres Ríos, C.R. 236 9.54 N 83.58 W
Tressancourt 261 48.55 N 2.00 E
Třešť 30 49.18 N 15.30 E
Tresta 46 60.14 N 1.21 W
Tres Valles 234 18.15 N 96.08 W
Tres Zapotes ⊥ 234 18.28 N 95.24 W
Tret'akovskaja Galereja v 265b 55.45 N 37.37 E
Tretet 114 4.40 N 96.51 E
Trets 62 43.27 N 5.41 E
Tretten 26 61.19 N 10.19 E
Treuburg
→ Olecko 30 54.03 N 22.30 E
Treuchtlingen 56 48.57 N 10.54 E
Treuen 54 50.32 N 12.18 E
Treuenbrietzen 54 52.06 N 12.52 E
Treuhandgebiet Pazifische Inseln
→ Trust Territory of the Pacific Islands □2 14 10.00 N 155.00 E
Trevelín 254 43.04 S 71.28 W
Trèves
→ Trier 56 49.45 N 6.38 E
Trevi 66 42.52 N 12.45 E
Treviglio 62 45.31 N 9.35 E
Trevignano Romano 66 42.09 N 12.15 E
Treviño 34 42.44 N 2.45 W
Treviso 64 45.40 N 12.15 E
Treviso □4 64 45.50 N 12.13 E
Trevor 216 42.30 N 88.07 W
Trevorton 208 40.46 N 76.40 W
Trevose 208 40.08 N 74.58 W
Trevose Head ≻ 42 50.33 N 5.01 W
Trevose Heights 285 40.09 N 74.59 W
Trévoux 58 45.56 N 4.46 E
Trexlertown 208 40.33 N 75.36 W
Treze Quedas ↘ 250 0.07 N 56.55 W
Trezevant 194 36.00 N 88.37 W
Trezzano 266b 45.25 N 9.04 E
Trezzo sull'Adda 62 45.36 N 9.31 E
Trgovište 38 42.21 N 22.05 E
Trhomné 60 49.55 N 13.05 E
Trhové Sviny 61 48.51 N 14.38 E
Triabunna 166 42.30 S 147.55 E
Triadelphia Reservoir ⊜1 208 39.13 N 77.01 W
Trialeti 84 41.33 N 44.07 E
Trialetskij chrebet ∧ 84 41.45 N 43.50 E
Triana 66 42.47 N 11.33 E
Triánda 38 36.24 N 28.10 E
Triangle, Eng., U.K. 262 53.42 N 1.56 W
Triangle, Va., U.S. 208 38.32 N 77.20 W
Triangle Lake 210 42.32 N 74.13 W
Triangul'atorov, pik ∧ 88 53.45 N 97.00 E
Triángulos, Arrecifes ◆2 232 20.57 N 92.16 W
Triaucourt-en-Argonne 56 48.59 N 5.04 E
Tribeni 126 22.59 N 88.24 E
Triberg 58 48.08 N 8.13 E
Tribes Hill 210 42.57 N 74.17 W
Tribobó 287a 22.52 S 43.01 W
Triborough Bridge ◆5 276 40.47 N 73.55 W
Tri Brata, gorog ∟ 86 57.25 N 95.39 E
Tribsees 54 54.05 N 12.45 E
Tribugá, Golfo de c 246 5.45 N 77.20 W
Tribune, Sk., Can. 184 49.15 N 103.50 W
Tribune, Ks., U.S. 198 38.28 N 101.45 W
Tribune Channel ⩍ 182 50.50 N 126.06 W
Tribuswinkel 264b 48.00 N 16.16 E
Tricao Malal 252 37.03 S 70.19 W
Tricarico 68 40.37 N 16.09 E
Tricase 68 39.56 N 18.22 E
Tricesimo 64 46.10 N 13.13 E
Trichardt 158 26.28 S 29.13 E
Trichiana 64 46.05 N 12.07 E
Trichinopoly
→ Tiruchchirāppalli 122 10.49 N 78.41 E
Trichūr 122 10.31 N 76.13 E
Tri Cities 222 32.09 N 95.56 W
Tricot 50 49.34 N 2.35 E
Tri County Supply Canal ≃ 198 40.49 N 100.06 W
Trida 166 33.01 S 145.01 E
Trident Peak ∧ 204 41.54 N 118.25 W
Triduby 78 48.06 N 30.24 E
Trieben 61 47.29 N 14.30 E
Triebes 54 50.41 N 12.01 E
Triel-sur-Seine 261 48.59 N 2.00 E
Trient
→ Trento 64 46.04 N 11.08 E
Triepkendorf 54 53.17 N 13.20 E
Trier 56 49.45 N 6.38 E
Trier □5 56 49.50 N 6.50 E
Triesen 64 47.06 N 9.31 E
Trieste (Triest) 64 45.40 N 13.46 E
Trieste □4 64 45.40 N 13.46 E
Trieste, Gulf of c 64 45.40 N 13.35 E
Triesting ≃ 264b 48.05 N 16.24 E
Trieux ≃ 32 48.50 N 3.06 W
Triftern 60 48.24 N 13.00 E
Trigal 248 18.17 S 64.08 W
Triggiano 68 41.04 N 16.55 E
Triglav ∧ 64 46.23 N 13.50 E
Triglitz 54 53.12 N 12.05 E
Trignano, Pizzo ∧ 66 42.36 N 13.30 E
Trigno ≃ 66 42.04 N 14.48 E
Trigueros 34 37.23 N 6.50 W
Trikala 38 39.34 N 21.46 E
Trikhonis, Límni ⊜ 38 38.34 N 21.28 E
Trikomon 130 35.17 N 33.53 E
Trikora, Puncak (Wilhelmina Peak) ∧ 164 4.15 S 138.45 E
Tri-Lakes 216 41.14 N 85.26 W
Trilbardou 261 48.57 N 2.48 E
Trilby 220 28.27 N 82.11 W
Trilesy 78 49.59 N 29.50 E
Trillick 48 54.27 N 7.30 W
Trillo 50 48.57 N 2.57 E
Trim 48 53.34 N 6.47 W
Triman 120 29.38 N 69.05 E
Trimbach 58 47.22 N 7.54 E
Trimble □6 218 38.37 N 85.20 W
Trim Creek ≃ 216 41.10 N 87.38 W
Trimdon 44 54.42 N 1.25 W
Trimley 42 51.59 N 1.19 E
Trimont 198 43.45 N 94.42 W
Trimonte 256 21.43 S 42.35 W
Trimpley 42 52.24 N 2.16 W
Trin 58 46.50 N 9.22 E
Trinchera Creek ≃ 200 37.19 N 105.45 W
Trincheras, Méx. 196 25.37 N 101.55 W
Trincheras, Méx. 232 30.24 N 111.32 W
Trincomalee 122 8.34 N 81.14 E
Trincomali Channel ⩍ 224 48.02 N 123.30 W
Trindade 255 16.40 S 49.30 W
Trindade I 244 20.31 S 29.19 W
Třinec 30 49.41 N 18.40 E
Tring 42 51.48 N 0.40 W
Trinidad, Bol. 248 14.47 S 64.47 W
Trinidad, Col. 246 5.25 N 71.40 W
Trinidad, Cuba 240p 21.48 N 79.59 W
Trinidad, Hond. 236 14.57 N 88.45 W
Trinidad, Co., U.S. 198 37.10 N 104.30 W
Trinidad, Tx., U.S. 222 32.08 N 96.05 W
Trinidad, Ur. 252 33.32 S 56.54 W
Trinidad I 241r 10.30 N 61.15 W
Trinidad, Golfo c 254 49.55 S 75.25 W
Trinidad, Isla I 252 39.08 S 61.58 W
Trinidad, Río la ≃ 234 17.49 N 95.09 W
Trinidad and Tobago □1, N.A. 230 11.00 N 61.00 W
Trinidad and Tobago □1, N.A. 241r 11.00 N 61.00 W
Trinità 62 44.30 N 7.45 E
Trinità, Lago della ⊜ 70 37.43 N 12.46 E
Trinità d'agultu 71 40.59 N 8.54 E
Trinitapoli 68 41.21 N 16.05 E
Trinitaria 232 16.07 N 92.03 W
Trinité, Havre de la c 240e 14.44 N 60.58 W
Trinity, Nf., Can. 186 48.59 N 53.55 W
Trinity, Tx., U.S. 222 30.56 N 95.22 W
Trinity □6 222 31.07 N 95.10 W
Trinity ≃, Ca., U.S. 204 41.11 N 123.42 W
Trinity ≃, Tx., U.S. 222 29.47 N 94.42 W
Trinity, Clear Fork ≃ 196 32.46 N 97.21 W
Trinity, East Fork ≃ 222 32.30 N 96.30 W
Trinity, Elm Fork ≃ 222 32.47 N 96.54 W
Trinity, South Fork ≃ 204 40.54 N 123.35 W
Trinity, West Fork ≃ 196 32.48 N 96.51 W
Trinity Bay c, Nf., Can. 186 48.00 N 53.40 W
Trinity Bay c, Tx., U.S. 222 29.40 N 94.45 W
Trinity Islands II 180 56.33 N 154.25 W
Trinity Mountain ∧ 202 43.36 N 115.26 W
Trinity Mountains ∧ 204 41.00 N 122.30 W
Trinity Park ◆ 275b 43.39 N 79.25 W
Trinity Peak ∧ 204 40.14 N 118.45 W
Trinity Site ⊥ 200 33.41 N 106.28 W
Trinkat Island I 110 8.05 N 93.30 E
Trinkitat 140 18.41 N 37.43 E
Trino 62 45.12 N 8.18 E
Trins 64 47.05 N 11.25 E
Trinway 214 40.08 N 82.00 W
Triolet 157c 20.03 S 57.32 E
Triolo ≃ 66 41.40 N 15.34 E
Trion 192 34.32 N 85.18 W
Trionto ≃ 68 39.37 N 16.45 E
Trionto, Capo ≻ 68 39.37 N 16.45 E
Triora 62 43.59 N 7.46 E
Tripi 70 38.03 N 15.06 E
Triplett Creek ≃ 218 38.10 N 83.27 W
Triplett Creek, North Fork ≃ 218 38.10 N 83.31 W
Tripoli
→ Tarābulus, Libiyā 146 32.54 N 13.11 E
Tripoli
→ Tarābulus, Lubnān 130 34.26 N 35.51 E
Tripoli 190 42.48 N 92.15 W
Trípolis 38 37.31 N 22.21 E
Tripolis
→ Tarābulus 146 32.54 N 13.11 E
Tripolitania
→ Tarābulus □9 146 31.00 N 15.00 E
Tripolje 78 50.07 N 30.46 E
Triponzo 66 42.50 N 12.56 E
Tripp 198 43.13 N 97.57 W
Trips Subdivision 281 42.34 N 83.25 W
Triptis 54 50.44 N 11.52 E
Tripura □3 120 24.00 N 92.00 E
Triquet, Lac ⊜ 186 50.42 N 59.47 W
Trisanna ≃ 58 47.07 N 10.30 E
Tristan da Cunha Group II 10 37.15 S 12.30 W
Tristan Island I 10 37.05 S 12.17 W
Tristán Suárez 258 34.53 S 58.34 W
Tristao, Îles II 150 10.53 N 14.58 W
Tristate Village 278 41.44 N 87.57 W
Triste 34 42.23 N 0.43 W
Triste, Golfo c 246 10.40 N 68.10 W
Trisūli ≃ 124 27.49 N 84.47 E
Tri-ton 110 10.25 N 105.00 E
Tritriva 157b 22.46 S 46.07 E
Trittau 52 53.37 N 10.25 E
Trittenheim 56 49.49 N 6.54 E
Triuggio 266b 45.40 N 9.16 E
Triumph 194 29.20 N 89.28 W
Triunfo 250 7.50 S 38.07 W
Triunfo, Igarapé ≃ 250 6.22 S 52.25 W
Triunfo de Madero 234 16.52 N 93.48 W
Trivandrum 122 8.29 N 76.55 E
Trivento 66 41.47 N 14.33 E
Trivero 62 45.40 N 8.10 E
Trivigno 68 40.35 N 15.59 E
Trkmanka ≃ 61 48.47 N 16.50 E
Trnava 30 48.23 N 17.35 E
Trnovo
→ Veliko Târnovo 38 43.04 N 25.39 E
Trobriand Island I 164 8.35 S 151.05 E
Trobriand Islands II 164 8.35 S 151.05 E
Tr'ochgolovyj Golec, gora ∧ 88 53.22 N 107.03 E
Tr'ochizbenka 83 48.45 N 38.58 E
Tr'ochsv'atskoje 82 56.29 N 37.03 E
Trochtelfingen 58 48.18 N 9.14 E
Trochu 182 51.50 N 113.13 W
Troense 41 55.02 N 10.39 E
Trofa, Arroyo de ≃ 266a 40.30 N 3.45 W
Trofaich 61 47.25 N 15.00 E
Trofarello 62 44.59 N 7.44 E
Trögd ≻1 40 59.31 N 17.15 E
Trogen 58 47.24 N 9.28 E
Trogir 36 43.31 N 16.15 E
Troglav ∧ 36 43.57 N 16.36 E
Tröglitz 54 51.04 N 12.11 E
Troia 68 41.22 N 15.18 E
Troica 76 54.24 N 40.14 E
Troice-Lykovo ◆8 265b 55.47 N 37.24 E
Troick, S.S.S.R. 86 54.06 N 61.35 E
Troick, S.S.S.R. 88 57.25 N 94.50 E
Troickaja 78 45.08 N 38.07 E
Troickij, S.S.S.R. 80 50.14 N 43.03 E
Troickij, S.S.S.R. 80 50.14 N 43.05 E
Troickij, S.S.S.R. 86 50.41 N 54.38 E
Troickij, S.S.S.R. 86 57.03 N 63.43 E
Troickij, S.S.S.R. 88 54.36 N 113.09 E
Troickije Rosl'ai 80 53.21 N 41.24 E
Troickij Sungur 80 53.17 N 47.37 E
Troickij Zavod 88 53.27 N 102.09 E
Troicko-Charcyzsk 83 47.58 N 38.16 E
Troickoje, S.S.S.R. 78 51.17 N 41.28 E
Troickoje, S.S.S.R. 78 49.55 N 38.19 E
Troickoje, S.S.S.R. 78 47.38 N 30.19 E
Troickoje, S.S.S.R. 80 46.26 N 44.15 E
Troickoje, S.S.S.R. 80 53.22 N 48.23 E
Troickoje, S.S.S.R. 80 53.06 N 52.32 E
Troickoje, S.S.S.R. 80 53.23 N 52.48 E
Troickoje, S.S.S.R. 82 55.23 N 37.25 E
Troickoje, S.S.S.R. 82 54.52 N 37.07 E
Troickoje, S.S.S.R. 83 47.22 N 38.53 E
Troickoje, S.S.S.R. 83 48.32 N 38.23 E
Troickoje, S.S.S.R. 86 52.58 N 84.40 E
Troickoje, S.S.S.R. 86 52.19 N 56.23 E
Troickoje, S.S.S.R. 86 59.07 N 58.25 E
Troickoje, S.S.S.R. 89 49.27 N 136.36 E
Troicko-Pečorsk 24 62.44 N 56.06 E
Troina 70 37.47 N 14.36 E
Troina ≃ 70 37.49 N 14.46 E
Troisdorf 56 50.49 N 7.08 E
Trois Fourches, Cap des ≻ 148 35.26 N 2.58 W
Trois-Îlets 240e 14.32 N 61.02 W
Trois-Pistoles 186 48.07 N 69.10 W
Trois Pitons, Morne ∧ 240d 15.22 N 61.20 W

ENGLISH

Name	Page	Lat.°′	Long.°′

Trois Ponts 56 50.22 N 5.52 E
Trois-Rivières, P.Q., Can. 206 46.21 N 72.33 W
Trois-Rivières, Guad. 241o 15.59 N 61.39 W
Trois-Rivières-Ouest 206 46.19 N 72.35 W
Troisvierges 56 50.08 N 6.00 E
Trojan 38 42.51 N 24.43 E
Trojanov 78 50.07 N 28.31 E
Trojanova Tabla ⊥ 38 44.37 N 22.20 E
Trojanovka 78 51.20 N 25.17 E
Trojanski prohod)(38 42.47 N 24.37 E
Trojebratskij 86 54.28 N 66.01 E
Trojekurovo, S.S.S.R. 76 53.00 N 38.58 E
Trojekurovo, S.S.S.R. 76 53.25 N 39.43 E
Troldhede 41 55.59 N 8.45 E
Trolleholm 41 55.54 N 13.15 E
Trollhättan 26 58.16 N 12.18 E
Trollheimen ∧ 26 62.51 N 9.05 E
Trombay ◆8 272c 19.02 N 72.57 E
Trombetas ≃ 250 1.55 S 55.35 W
Trombudo Central 252 27.18 S 49.47 W
Tromelin, Île I 138 15.52 S 54.25 E
Tromello 62 45.12 N 8.52 E
Tromper Wiek c 54 54.37 N 13.24 E
Trompia, Val V 64 45.44 N 10.12 E
Trompsburg 158 30.01 S 25.46 E
Troms □6 24 69.15 N 19.40 E
Tromsø 24 69.40 N 18.58 E
Trona 204 35.45 N 117.22 W
Tronador, Monte ∧ 254 41.10 S 71.54 W
Trondheim 26 63.25 N 10.25 E
Trondheimsfjorden c2 26 63.39 N 10.49 E
Trondheimsleia ⩍ 26 63.30 N 9.00 E
Tronto ≃ 66 42.54 N 13.55 E
Tronville-en-Barrois 56 48.43 N 5.17 E
Tronzano Vercellese 62 45.21 N 8.10 E
Troo 50 47.47 N 0.47 E
Troödos 130 34.55 N 32.53 E
Trooilapspan 158 28.40 S 21.25 E
Troon, Eng., U.K. 42 50.12 N 5.16 W
Troon, Scot., U.K. 46 55.32 N 4.40 W
Trooper 285 40.09 N 75.24 W
Troparevo 82 55.23 N 35.54 E
Tropar'ovo ◆8 265b 55.39 N 37.29 E
Tropas, Rio das ≃ 250 6.07 S 57.28 W
Tropea 68 38.41 N 15.54 E
Trophy Mountain ∧ 182 51.47 N 119.48 W
Tropic 200 37.37 N 112.04 W
Tropojë 38 42.24 N 20.10 E
Troppau
→ Opava 30 49.56 N 17.54 E
Trosa 40 58.54 N 17.33 E
Troškovo 80 57.19 N 46.05 E
Troškūnai 76 55.36 N 24.51 E
Trosna 76 52.26 N 35.46 E
Trossingen 58 48.04 N 8.38 E
Trostan ∧ 48 55.03 N 6.09 W
Trost'anec, S.S.S.R. 78 50.28 N 34.59 E
Trost'anec, S.S.S.R. 78 48.31 N 29.12 E
Tröstau 60 50.01 N 11.57 E
Trostberg 60 48.01 N 12.32 E
Trostenskoje, ozero ⊜ 82 55.52 N 36.29 E
Trotha ◆8 54 51.31 N 11.58 E
Trottiscliffe 260 51.19 N 0.21 E
Trotuş ≃ 38 46.03 N 27.14 E
Trotwood 218 39.47 N 84.18 W
Troublesome Creek ≃ 219 39.54 N 91.37 W
Troubridge Point ≻ 168b 35.11 S 137.41 E
Trou-du-Nord 238 19.38 N 72.01 W
Troumasse c 241f 13.49 N 60.54 W
Troup 222 32.08 N 95.07 W
Troup Head ≻ 46 57.41 N 2.18 W
Troupsburg 210 42.03 N 77.33 W
Trout 194 31.41 N 92.10 W
Trout ≃, N.T., Can. 176 61.19 N 119.51 W
Trout ≃, N.A. 206 45.05 N 74.10 W
Trout Brook ≃, Ma., U.S. 283 42.16 N 71.18 W
Trout Brook ≃, Ma., U.S. 283 42.39 N 71.16 W
Trout Creek, Mi., U.S. 190 46.28 N 89.00 W
Trout Creek, Mt., U.S. 182 47.50 N 115.35 W
Trout Creek, N.Y., U.S. 210 42.12 N 75.17 W
Trout Creek ≃, Az., U.S. 200 34.56 N 113.36 W
Trout Creek ≃, Or., U.S. 202 44.48 N 121.03 W
Trout Creek ≃, Or., U.S. 202 42.23 N 118.36 W
Trout Creek ≃, Pa., U.S. 285 40.07 N 75.24 W
Trout Creek ≃, Wa., U.S. 224 46.02 N 121.12 W
Trout Creek Pass)(200 38.54 N 105.58 W
Troutdale 224 45.32 N 122.23 W
Trout Lake 224 45.59 N 121.31 W
Trout Lake ⊜, B.C., Can. 182 50.35 N 117.26 W
Trout Lake ⊜, N.T., Can. 176 60.35 N 121.10 W
Trout Lake ⊜, On., Can. 184 51.13 N 93.20 W
Trout Lake ⊜, On., Can. 190 46.18 N 79.20 W
Trout Lake ⊜, On., Can. 190 46.13 N 80.35 W
Trout Lake Creek ≃ 224 46.00 N 121.30 W
Trout Peak ∧ 202 44.36 N 109.32 W
Trout River 186 49.29 N 58.08 W
Trout Run 210 41.23 N 77.03 W
Troutville, Pa., U.S. 214 41.02 N 78.47 W
Troutville, Va., U.S. 192 37.25 N 79.52 W
Trouville-sur-Mer 50 49.22 N 0.05 E
Trowbridge 42 51.20 N 2.13 W
Troxelville 210 40.48 N 77.12 W
Troy, Al., U.S. 194 31.48 N 85.58 W
Troy, Id., U.S. 202 46.44 N 116.46 W
Troy, Il., U.S. 219 38.43 N 89.52 W
Troy, In., U.S. 194 37.59 N 86.47 W
Troy, Ks., U.S. 198 39.46 N 95.05 W
Troy, Mi., U.S. 214 42.34 N 83.09 W
Troy, Mo., U.S. 219 38.58 N 90.58 W
Troy, Mt., U.S. 202 48.27 N 115.53 W
Troy, N.H., U.S. 207 42.49 N 72.10 W
Troy, N.Y., U.S. 210 42.43 N 73.41 W
Troy, N.C., U.S. 192 35.21 N 79.53 W
Troy, Oh., U.S. 218 40.02 N 84.12 W
Troy, Pa., U.S. 210 41.47 N 76.47 W
Troy, Tn., U.S. 194 36.20 N 89.09 W
Troy, Tx., U.S. 222 31.12 N 97.18 W
Troy ⊥ 130 39.57 N 26.15 E
Troy Brook ≃ 276 40.50 N 74.22 W
Troyes 50 48.18 N 4.05 E
Troy Grove 216 41.28 N 89.05 W
Troy Hills 210 40.51 N 74.23 W
Troy Lake ⊜ 204 34.49 N 116.33 W
Troy Meadows ≡ 276 40.50 N 74.22 W
Troy Peak ∧ 204 38.19 N 115.30 W
Trpanj 36 43.00 N 17.17 E
Trst
→ Trieste 64 45.40 N 13.46 E
Trstená 30 49.22 N 19.37 E
Trstenik 38 43.37 N 21.00 E
Truax 184 49.55 N 104.58 W
Trubč'ovsk 76 52.37 N 33.44 E
Trubetčino 76 52.53 N 39.33 E
Trubino, S.S.S.R. 82 54.58 N 36.42 E
Trubino, S.S.S.R. 82 55.59 N 38.08 E
Trub'ož ≃ 82 56.44 N 38.51 E
Truc-giang 110 10.14 N 106.23 E
Truchas 200 36.02 N 105.48 W
Truchas Peak ∧ 200 35.58 N 105.39 W
Truchtersheim 58 48.40 N 7.36 E
Trucial States
→ United Arab Emirates □1 128 24.00 N 54.00 E
Truckee 226 39.19 N 120.10 W
Truckee ≃ 204 39.51 N 119.24 W

DEUTSCH

Name	Seite	Breite°′	Länge°′ E = Ost

Trucksville 210 41.18 N 75.56 W
Trud 76 57.37 N 33.58 E
Trudfront 80 45.56 N 47.41 E
Trudnovo 86 56.39 N 91.30 E
Trudovaja 83 48.21 N 38.04 E
Trudovoj 80 51.42 N 52.43 E
Trues Creek ≃ 276 40.41 N 73.17 W
Truganina 274b 37.49 S 144.43 E
Truim ≃ 46 57.02 N 4.10 W
Truite, Lac à la ⊜ 190 47.16 N 78.17 W
Trujillo, Col. 246 4.10 N 76.19 W
Trujillo, Esp. 34 39.28 N 5.53 W
Trujillo, Hond. 236 15.55 N 86.00 W
Trujillo, Perú 248 8.07 S 79.02 W
Trujillo, Ven. 246 9.22 N 70.26 W
Trujillo □3 246 9.25 N 70.30 W
Trujillo Alto 240m 18.22 N 66.01 W
Trujillo Creek ≃ 196 35.28 N 102.52 W
Truk Islands II 175c 7.25 N 151.47 E
Truk Lagoon c 175c 7.25 N 151.45 E
Trull Brook ≃ 283 42.39 N 71.15 W
Truman 198 43.49 N 94.26 W
Trumann 194 35.40 N 90.30 W
Trumansburg 210 42.32 N 76.39 W
Trumbauersville 208 40.25 N 75.23 W
Trumbull 207 41.14 N 73.12 W
Trumbull □6 214 41.14 N 80.52 W
Trumbull, Mount ∧ 200 36.25 N 113.10 W
Trumon 114 2.49 N 97.38 E
Trun, Fr. 50 48.51 N 0.02 E
Trun, Schw. 58 46.45 N 8.58 E
Trundle 166 32.55 S 147.43 E
Trung-luong 110 13.57 N 109.15 E
Trunovskoje 80 45.29 N 42.08 E
Truro, Austl. 168b 34.25 S 139.07 E
Truro, N.S., Can. 186 45.22 N 63.16 W
Truro, Eng., U.K. 42 50.16 N 5.03 W
Truro, Ma., U.S. 207 41.59 N 70.03 W
Trusan ≃ 112 4.58 N 115.11 E
Truscott 196 33.45 N 99.49 W
Trušeny 78 47.04 N 28.41 E
Truşeşti 38 47.46 N 27.01 E
Trusetal 54 50.47 N 10.25 E
Truskavec 78 49.16 N 23.33 E
Truslejka 80 53.54 N 46.24 E
Trus Madi, Gunong ∧ 112 5.33 N 116.31 E
Trust Territory of the Pacific Islands □2 14 10.00 N 155.00 E
Truth or Consequences (Hot Springs) 200 33.07 N 107.15 W
Trutnov 30 50.34 N 15.55 E
Truxall 279b 40.33 N 79.33 W
Truxton, Mo., U.S. 219 39.00 N 91.14 W
Truxton, N.Y., U.S. 210 42.43 N 76.02 W
Truxton Wash V 200 35.38 N 114.04 W
Truyère ≃ 32 44.39 N 2.34 E
Trwyn Cilan ≻ 42 52.46 N 4.30 W
Tryon, Ne., U.S. 198 41.33 N 100.57 W
Tryon, N.C., U.S. 192 35.12 N 82.14 W
Tryonville 214 41.42 N 79.47 W
Trysil 26 61.19 N 12.16 E
Trysilelva (Klarälven) ≃ 26 59.23 N 13.32 E
Tryškiai 76 56.04 N 22.35 E
Tryweryn ≃ 42 52.24 N 3.35 W
Trzcianka 30 53.03 N 16.28 E
Trzciel 30 52.23 N 15.52 E
Trzcińsko-Zdrój 30 52.58 N 14.35 E
Trzebiatów 30 54.04 N 15.14 E
Trzebiel 54 51.37 N 14.50 E
Trzebież 30 53.42 N 14.31 E
Trzebinia 30 50.10 N 19.18 E
Trzebnica 30 51.19 N 17.03 E
Trzemeszno 30 52.35 N 17.50 E
Trzęsacz 54 54.05 N 14.58 E
Tržič 61 46.22 N 14.19 E
Tsacha Lake ⊜ 182 53.05 N 124.40 W
Tsala Apopka Lake ⊜ 220 28.52 N 82.20 W
Tsamkong
→ Zhanjiang 102 21.16 N 110.28 E
Tsandi 156 17.42 S 14.50 E
Tsangano 154 15.08 S 34.32 E
Ts'anghsien
→ Cangzhou 98 38.19 N 116.51 E
T'sangwu
→ Wuzhou 102 23.30 N 111.27 E
Ts'aot'un 100 23.59 N 120.41 E
Tsarabaria 157b 13.46 S 49.58 E
Tsaramandroso 157b 16.22 S 47.02 E
Tsaratanana 157b 16.47 S 47.39 E
Tsaratanana, Massif du ∧ 157b 14.00 S 49.00 E
Tsaraxaibis 158 27.25 S 19.22 E
Tsaritsyn
→ Volgograd 80 48.44 N 44.25 E
Tsau 156 20.12 S 22.22 E
Tsaukaib 156 26.37 S 15.31 E
Tsavo 154 2.59 S 38.28 E
Tsavo East National Park ◆ 154 2.11 S 38.25 E
Tsavo West National Park ◆ 154 2.55 S 37.55 E
Tsawwassen 224 49.01 N 123.06 W
Tsaydaychuz Peak ∧ 182 53.02 N 126.35 W
Tsayta Lake ⊜ 182 55.25 N 125.30 W
Tschad
→ Chad □1 146 15.00 N 19.00 E
Tschad-See
→ Chad, Lake ⊜ 146 13.20 N 14.00 E
Tschagguns 58 47.05 N 9.54 E
Tschamut 58 46.40 N 8.42 E
Tschangscha
→ Changsha 100 28.12 N 112.58 E
Tschangtschun
→ Changchun 89 43.53 N 125.19 E
Tschechoslowakei
→ Czechoslovakia □1 30 49.30 N 17.00 E
Tscheljuskin, Kap
→ Čel'uskin, mys ≻ 74 77.45 N 104.20 E
Tschengtu
→ Chengdu 107 30.39 N 104.04 E
Tschenstochau
→ Częstochowa 30 50.49 N 19.06 E
Tschernitz 54 51.35 N 14.37 E
Tscheschkaja-Bucht
→ Češskaja guba c 24 67.30 N 46.30 E
Tschida, Lake ⊜1 198 46.36 N 101.54 W
Tschingtau
→ Qingdao 98 36.06 N 120.19 E
Tschittagong
→ Chittagong 120 22.20 N 91.50 E
Tschuktschen-Meer
→ Chukchi Sea ⩇2 16 69.00 N 171.00 W
Tschungking
→ Chongqing 107 29.34 N 106.35 E
Tsekanyani 156 19.52 S 26.39 E
Tsembeyi 158 31.36 S 27.03 E
Ts'engwen ≃ 100 23.03 N 120.03 E
Tsenke ≃ 273b 4.24 S 15.26 E
Tses 156 25.58 S 18.08 E
Tsethang
→ Zedang 120 29.16 N 91.46 E
Tsévié 150 6.25 N 1.13 E
Tshabong 156 26.03 S 22.29 E
Tshabuta 152 7.47 S 23.16 E
Tshane 156 24.05 S 21.54 E
Tshaneni 158 26.00 S 31.47 E
Tshangalele, Lac ⊜ 154 10.55 S 27.03 E
Tshangu ≃ 273b 4.25 S 15.23 E
Tshela 152 4.59 S 12.56 E
Tshesebe 156 21.51 S 27.35 E
Tshibeke 154 2.44 S 28.36 E
Tshibinda 154 2.19 S 28.45 E
Tshibomba 152 9.02 S 22.34 E
Tshidilamolomo 156 25.50 S 24.41 E
Tshikapa 152 6.25 S 20.48 E
Tshilenge 152 6.15 S 23.46 E
Tshimbulu 152 6.29 S 22.51 E
Tshindjamba 152 10.54 S 22.41 E

Symbols in the index entries represent the broad categories identified in the key at the right. Symbols with superior numbers (∧1) identify subcategories (see complete key on page *I* · *1*).

Kartensymbole in dem Registerverzeichnis stellen die rechts in Schlüssel erklärten Kategorien dar. Symbole mit hochgestellten Ziffern (∧1) bezeichnen Unterabteilungen einer Kategorie (vgl. vollständiger Schlüssel auf Seite *I* · *1*).

Los símbolos incluidos en el texto del índice representan las grandes categorías identificadas con la clave a la derecha. Los símbolos con numeros en su parte superior (∧1) identifican las subcategorías (véase la clave completa en la página *I* · *1*).

Les symboles de l'index représentent les catégories indiquées dans la légende à droite. Les symboles suivis d'un indice (∧1) représentent des sous-catégories (voir légende complète à la page *I* · *1*).

Os símbolos incluídos no texto do índice representam as grandes categorias identificadas com a chave à direita. Os símbolos com números em sua parte superior (∧1) identificam as subcategorias (veja-se a chave completa à página *I* · *1*).

∧ Mountain	Berg	Montaña	Montagne	Montanha
∧ Mountains	Berge	Montañas	Montagnes	Montanhas
)(Pass	Pass	Paso	Col	Passo
V Valley, Canyon	Tal, Cañon	Valle, Cañón	Vallée, Canyon	Vale, Canhão
≚ Plain	Ebene	Llano	Plaine	Planície
≻ Cape	Kap	Cabo	Cap	Cabo
I Island	Insel	Isla	Île	Ilha
II Islands	Inseln	Islas	Îles	Ilhas
⊥ Other Topographic Features	Andere Topographische Objekte	Otros Elementos Topográficos	Autres données topographiques	Outros acidentes topográficos

ESPAÑOL

Nombre	Página	Lat.°′	Long.°′ W = Oeste
Tshinota	152	7.01 S	20.57 E
Tshinsenda	154	12.18 S	27.58 E
Tshisuku	152	6.26 S	19.55 E
Tshitadi	152	6.45 S	21.45 E
Tshoa	152	5.34 S	12.41 E
Tshofa	154	5.14 S	25.15 E
Tshopo ≃	154	0.33 N	25.07 E
Tshuapa ≃	152	0.14 S	20.42 E
Tshukudu	156	22.30 S	23.22 E
Tshumbiri	152	2.39 S	16.14 E
Tshwaane	156	22.29 S	22.03 E
Tsiafajavona ∧	157b	19.21 S	47.15 E
Tsianaloka	157b	18.08 S	44.50 E
Tsiémé ≃	273b	4.15 S	15.18 E
Tsiga	152	1.32 S	10.11 E
Tsihombe	157b	25.18 S	45.29 E
Tsilmamo	144	6.01 N	35.17 E
Tsimanampetsotsa, Lac ⊚	157b	24.08 S	43.46 E
Tsimilofo	157b	24.59 S	45.10 E
Tsimpsean Indian Reserve ◆[4]	182	54.30 N	130.22 W
Tsinan → Jinan	98	36.40 N	116.57 E
Tsineng	158	27.06 S	23.04 E
Tsinghai → Qinghai □[4]	90	36.00 N	96.00 E
Tsingkiang → Qingjiang	100	33.35 N	119.02 E
Tsingtao → Qingdao	98	36.06 N	120.19 E
Tsing Yi I	271d	22.21 N	114.05 E
Tsingyuan → Baoding	105	38.52 N	115.29 E
Tsinh-ho	110	22.22 N	103.14 E
Tsining → Jining	98	35.25 N	116.36 E
Tsinjoarivo	157b	19.37 S	47.40 E
Tsinjomitondraka	157b	15.36 S	47.08 E
Tsinling Shan → Qin Ling ʎ	102	34.00 N	108.00 E
Tsintsabis	156	18.45 S	17.51 E
Tsiribihina ≃	157b	19.42 S	44.31 E
Tsiroanomandidy	157b	18.46 S	46.02 E
Tsitondroina	157b	21.19 S	46.00 E
Tsitsihar → Qiqihar	89	47.19 N	123.55 E
Tsitsikama Forest and Coastal National Park ♠	158	33.57 S	23.53 E
Tsitsutl Peak ∧	182	52.44 N	125.47 W
Tsivory	157b	24.04 S	46.05 E
Tskhinvali → Cchinvali	84	42.13 N	43.56 E
Tsna → Cna ≃	80	54.32 N	42.05 E
Tsobis	156	19.27 S	17.30 E
Tsolo	158	31.18 S	28.37 E
Tsomo	158	32.00 S	27.42 E
Tsomo ≃	158	32.25 S	27.50 E
Tsowkêy	123	34.41 N	70.56 E
Tsoying	100	22.41 N	120.17 E
Tsu	94	34.43 N	136.31 E
Tsubakuro-dake ∧	94	36.24 N	137.42 E
Tsubame	92	37.39 N	138.56 E
Tsubata	94	36.40 N	136.44 E
Tsuboro-suigenchi ⊚[1]	270	34.24 N	135.54 E
Tsuchiura	94	36.05 N	140.12 E
Tsuchiyama	94	34.56 N	136.17 E
Tsuda, Nihon	96	34.17 N	134.15 E
Tsuda, Nihon	270	34.49 N	135.43 E
Tsuen Wan (Quanwan)	271d	22.22 N	114.07 E
Tsugaru-hantō ›[1]	92	41.00 N	140.30 E
Tsugaru-heiya ≚	92	40.49 N	140.27 E
Tsugaru-kaikyō ʮ	92a	41.35 N	141.00 E
Tsuge	94	34.37 N	135.57 E
Tsugu	94	35.10 N	137.37 E
Tsuha	174m	26.14 N	127.47 E
Tsuiki	96	33.40 N	131.03 E
Tsujidō	268	35.20 N	139.27 E
Tsukahara	268	35.18 N	139.58 E
Tsukechi	94	35.38 N	137.26 E
Tsuken-jima I	174m	26.15 N	127.57 E
Tsukigase	94	34.42 N	136.02 E
Tsukinowa-kofun ⊥	96	34.55 N	134.11 E
Tsukiyono	94	36.41 N	138.59 E
Tsukuba	94	36.13 N	140.06 E
Tsukuba-san ∧	94	36.13 N	140.06 E
Tsukude	94	34.59 N	137.25 E
Tsukui	94	35.35 N	139.16 E
Tsukumi	96	33.04 N	131.52 E
Tsukumono ◆[8]	270	34.50 N	135.11 E
Tsukushi-heiya ≚	96	33.20 N	130.30 E
Tsukushi-sanchi ʎ	92	33.30 N	130.30 E
Tsumagoi	94	36.31 N	138.32 E
Tsumeb	156	19.13 S	17.42 E
Tsumeb □[5]	156	19.00 S	17.30 E
Tsumeki-zaki ›	94	34.39 N	138.59 E
Tsumis Park	156	23.43 S	17.28 E
Tsumkwe	156	19.41 S	20.30 E
Tsuna	96	34.26 N	134.54 E
Tsunan	94	37.01 N	138.39 E
Tsunashima ◆[8]	268	35.32 N	139.38 E
Tsunekami-misaki ›	94	35.38 N	135.49 E
Tsuni → Zunyi	102	27.39 N	106.57 E
Tsuno-shima I	96	34.21 N	130.51 E
Tsuru	94	35.33 N	138.55 E
Tsuruga	94	35.39 N	136.04 E
Tsurugaoka-hachimangu Shrine ʊ[1]	268	35.19 N	139.33 E
Tsurugashima	268	35.56 N	139.24 E
Tsuruga-wan ⊂	94	35.45 N	136.04 E
Tsurugi	94	36.27 N	136.38 E
Tsurugi-dake ∧	94	36.37 N	137.37 E
Tsurugi-san ∧	96	33.51 N	134.06 E
Tsurugi-san-kokutei-kōen ♠	96	33.50 N	134.06 E
Tsuruhara	270	34.26 N	135.20 E
Tsuruma	268	35.51 N	139.33 E
Tsurumi ◆[8]	268	35.30 N	139.41 E
Tsurumi ≃	94	35.29 N	139.41 E
Tsurumi-dake ∧	96	33.17 N	131.26 E
Tsuruoka	92	38.44 N	139.50 E
Tsushima, Nihon	94	35.10 N	136.43 E
Tsushima, Nihon	96	33.05 N	132.30 E
Tsushima II	92	34.30 N	129.22 E
Tsushima-kaikyō (Eastern Channel) ʮ	92	34.00 N	129.00 E
Tsuwano	96	34.28 N	131.46 E
Tsuyama	96	35.03 N	134.00 E
Tsuyazaki	96	33.47 N	130.28 E
Tu → Tsu	94	34.43 N	136.31 E
Tua	152	3.38 S	16.36 E
Tua ≃	34	41.13 N	7.26 W
Tua, Tanjung ›	112	5.54 S	105.44 E
Tua-chua	110	21.55 N	103.21 E
Tuakau	172	37.16 S	174.57 E
Tual	164	5.40 S	132.45 E
Tualatin	224	45.23 N	122.45 W
Tualatin ≃	224	45.20 N	122.39 W
Tuam	48	53.31 N	8.50 W
Tuamarina	172	41.26 S	173.57 E
Tuamotu, Îles (Tuamotu Archipelago) II	14	19.00 S	142.00 W
Tuamotu Ridge ✦[3]	14	17.00 S	145.00 W
Tuan, Tanjong ›	114	2.23 N	101.52 E
Tuanan	112	2.07 S	114.24 E
Tuanfeng	100	30.38 N	114.51 E
Tuan-giao	110	21.35 N	103.25 E
Tuangku, Pulau I	114	2.10 N	97.18 E
Tuanlin	98	39.35 N	119.15 E
Tuannian	107	29.55 N	106.03 E
Tuanpi	100	30.44 N	115.13 E
Tuanshan	98	40.02 N	123.34 E
Tuanwang	98	36.45 N	120.38 E
Tuanxi	102	27.28 N	107.08 E
Tuapa	174v	18.57 S	169.54 W
Tuapeka Mouth	172	46.01 S	169.31 E
Tuapse	84	44.07 N	39.05 E

FRANÇAIS

Nom	Page	Lat.°′	Long.°′ W = Ouest
Tuaran	112	6.11 N	116.14 E
Tuas	114	1.19 N	103.38 E
Tuasivi	175a	13.40 S	172.07 W
Tuasivi, Cape ›	175a	13.40 S	172.07 W
Tuatapere	172	46.08 S	167.41 E
Tuath, Loch ʮ	46	56.30 N	6.12 W
Tuba	88	57.24 N	102.48 E
Tuba ≃	86	53.57 N	91.31 E
Tubac	200	31.36 N	111.02 W
Tuba City	200	36.08 N	111.14 W
T'ub'ak-Čekurča	80	56.05 N	49.56 E
Tubalan Head ›	116	6.30 N	125.35 E
Tuban	115a	6.54 S	112.03 E
Tubarão	252	28.30 S	49.01 W
Ṭūbās	132	32.19 N	35.22 E
Tubau	112	3.08 N	113.42 E
Tubbataha Reefs ✦[2]	116	8.51 N	119.56 E
Tubbergen	52	52.25 N	6.46 E
Tubbs Island I	282	38.08 N	122.26 W
Ṭubhār	142	29.19 N	30.42 E
Tubig ≃	116	11.54 N	125.25 E
Tubigan Island I	116	6.26 N	120.47 E
Tubingantan Point ›	116	5.54 N	120.55 E
Tübingen	58	48.31 N	9.02 E
Tübingen □[5]	58	48.10 N	9.30 E
Tubinskij	86	52.53 N	58.13 E
Tubize	50	50.41 N	4.12 E
T'ub-Karagan, mys ›	84	44.39 N	50.18 E
T'ub-Karagan, poluostrov ›[1]	84	44.30 N	50.30 E
Tubli	116	13.56 N	124.09 E
Tubod	116	8.03 N	123.48 E
Tubre	64	46.39 N	10.27 E
Ṭubruq (Tobruk)	146	32.05 N	23.59 E
Tuburan, Pil.	116	10.44 N	123.49 W
Tuburan, Pil.	116	6.39 N	122.16 E
Tubutama	200	30.53 N	111.29 W
Tucacas	246	10.48 N	68.19 W
Tucacas, Punta ›	246	10.50 N	68.14 W
Tucalota Creek ≃	228	33.32 N	117.10 W
Tucannon ≃	202	46.33 N	118.11 W
Tucano	250	10.58 S	38.48 W
Tucavaca ≃	248	18.37 S	58.59 W
T'uch'ang	100	24.35 N	121.29 E
Tucheim	54	52.17 N	12.11 E
Tüchen	54	53.04 N	12.05 E
T'uch'eng, T'aiwan	269d	24.59 N	121.26 E
Tucheng, Zhg.	98	38.53 N	121.15 E
Tucheng, Zhg.	102	28.12 N	105.58 E
Tuchengzi, Zhg.	98	41.20 N	116.29 E
Tuchengzi, Zhg.	98	40.29 N	124.24 E
Tuchengzi, Zhg.	104	42.27 N	122.44 E
Tuchengzicun	104	41.52 N	120.41 E
Tuchengziwuhao	98	40.56 N	113.58 E
Tuchlovice	54	50.06 N	14.00 E
Tuchola	30	53.35 N	17.50 E
Tuchów	30	49.54 N	21.03 E
T'uchtet	86	56.32 N	89.19 E
Tuckahoe, N.J., U.S.	208	39.17 N	74.45 W
Tuckahoe, N.Y., U.S.	276	40.57 N	73.49 W
Tuckahoe ≃	208	39.17 N	74.39 W
Tuckahoe Creek ≃	208	38.49 N	75.53 W
Tuckanarra	162	27.07 S	118.05 E
Tucker Heights	210	42.55 N	73.55 W
Tuckerman	194	35.43 N	91.11 W
Tuckernuck Island I	207	41.18 N	70.15 W
Tuckerton, N.J., U.S.	208	39.36 N	74.20 W
Tuckerton, Pa., U.S.	208	40.25 N	75.57 W
Tuckfield, Mount ∧	162	18.44 S	124.54 E
Tučkovo	82	55.36 N	36.28 E
Tucson	200	32.13 N	110.55 W
Tucumã, Paraná ≃[1]	246	3.58 S	66.26 W
Tucumán → San Miguel de Tucumán	252	26.49 S	65.13 W
Tucumán □[4]	252	27.00 S	65.30 W
Tucumcari	196	35.10 N	103.43 W
Tucumcari Mountain ∧	196	35.08 N	103.42 W
Tucunduva	252	27.39 S	54.27 W
Tucunuco	252	30.36 S	68.38 W
Tucuparé, Cachoeira do ∟	250	5.20 S	55.50 W
Tucupido	246	9.17 N	65.47 W
Tucupita	246	9.04 N	62.03 W
Tucuruí	250	3.42 S	49.27 W
Tucuruvi ◆[8]	287b	23.28 S	46.35 W
Tuczna	30	51.54 N	23.26 E
Tud ≃	42	52.38 N	1.15 E
Tudameda	112	10.52 S	122.55 E
Tudcum	252	30.14 S	69.15 W
Tude Å ≃	41	55.23 N	11.13 E
Tudela, Esp.	34	42.05 N	1.36 W
Tudela, Pil.	116	8.15 N	123.50 E
Tudela de Duero	34	41.35 N	4.35 W
Tudian	106	30.35 N	120.37 E
Tudichang	107	30.06 N	103.56 E
Tuditang	100	30.12 N	114.18 E
Tudmur (Palmyra)	130	34.33 N	38.17 E
Tudu	76	59.11 N	26.51 E
Tudweiliog	42	52.54 N	4.35 W
Tuela ≃	34	41.30 N	7.12 W
Tuen Mun	271d	22.24 N	113.58 E
Tuenno	64	46.20 N	11.01 E
Tueré ≃	250	2.48 S	50.59 W
Tuergate	85	40.28 N	75.21 E
Tufānganj	124	26.19 N	89.40 E
Tuffé	50	48.07 N	0.31 E
Tufi	164	9.05 S	149.20 E
Tufo	68	41.00 N	14.47 E
Tufts University ʊ[2]	283	42.24 N	71.07 W
Tufu Point ›	174w	14.13 S	169.32 W
Tug	130	38.27 N	42.16 E
Tugaske	184	50.53 N	106.16 W
Tugela	158	29.09 S	31.29 E
Tugela ≃	158	29.14 S	31.30 E
Tugela Falls ∟	158	28.45 S	28.58 E
Tugela Ferry	158	28.44 S	30.27 E
Tug Fork ≃	192	38.06 N	82.36 W
Tuggerah Lake ⊂	170	33.18 S	151.30 E
Tughlakābād ◆[8]	272a	28.31 N	77.16 E
Tugidak Island I	180	56.30 N	154.36 W
Tuglie	68	40.04 N	18.05 E
Tugnug Point ›	116	11.21 N	125.38 E
Tugolesskij Bor	80	55.33 N	39.49 E
Tugolukovo	80	51.56 N	41.40 E
Tugubun Point ›	116	7.00 N	126.27 E
Tuguegarao	116	17.37 N	121.44 E
Tugulym	86	57.04 N	64.39 E
Tugun	171a	28.09 S	153.30 E
Tugur	89	53.48 N	136.48 E
Tugur ≃	89	53.48 N	136.44 E
Tugúrio	256	21.15 S	43.35 W
Tugurskij poluostrov ›[1]	89	54.00 N	137.24 E
Tuguša	88	55.57 N	96.26 E
Tugutuj	88	52.40 N	104.50 E
Tuhai ≃	98	37.55 N	118.05 E
Tuhepu	104	40.54 N	122.49 E
Tuht	130	40.46 N	33.47 E
Tuhuangba	102	31.40 N	108.21 E
Tuibo	89	44.01 N	127.47 E
Tuichi ≃	248	14.36 S	67.35 W
Tuim	86	54.20 N	89.55 E
Tuineje	148	28.19 N	14.03 W
Tuirc, Beinn an ∧[2]	46	55.34 N	5.34 W
Tuitán	234	21.08 N	103.48 W
Tuitui	256	22.47 S	46.42 W
Tuj ≃	86	57.33 N	72.31 E
T'ujabuguz	85	40.58 N	69.15 E
Tujemojnak	86	49.20 N	62.55 E
Tuji-ri	98	41.31 N	127.12 E
Tujmazy	80	54.36 N	53.42 E
Tüjn Gol ≃	102	45.04 N	100.46 E
Tujunga ◆[8]	280	34.15 N	118.17 W
Tujunga Valley V	280	34.17 N	118.20 W
Tujunga Wash V	280	34.09 N	118.24 W
Tukaj	86	55.24 N	90.49 E
T'ukalinsk	86	55.52 N	72.12 E
Tukan	86	53.50 N	57.26 E
Tukan ≃	86	60.02 N	71.36 E
Tukangbesi, Kepulauan II	112	5.40 S	123.50 E

PORTUGUÊS

Nome	Página	Lat.°′	Long.°′ W = Oeste
Tukayyid	128	29.47 N	45.36 E
Ṭūkh, Miṣr	142	30.21 N	31.12 E
Ṭūkh, Miṣr	142	27.41 N	30.49 E
Ṭūkh al-Aqlām	142	30.52 N	31.26 E
Ṭūkh al-Khayl	142	28.06 N	30.40 E
Tukituki ≃	172	39.36 S	176.57 E
Tuk Méas	110	10.40 N	104.34 E
Tukolon'	88	55.24 N	107.42 E
Tukosméra, Mont ∧	175f	19.35 S	169.22 E
Tukpo	154	4.25 N	25.52 E
Tūkrah	146	32.32 N	20.34 E
Tuktoyaktuk	180	69.27 N	133.02 W
Tuktoyaktuk Peninsula ›[1]	180	69.45 N	131.20 W
Tukuj-Mekteb	84	44.20 N	45.11 E
Tukums	76	57.00 N	23.10 E
Tukuran	116	7.51 N	123.35 E
Tukuringra, chrebet ʎ	89	54.20 N	126.20 E
Tukuyu	154	9.15 S	33.39 E
T'uk'u Yüeh ∧	269d	25.02 N	121.38 E
Tukwila	224	47.28 N	122.15 W
Tula, Am. Sam.	174u	14.15 S	170.34 W
Tula, It.	71	40.44 N	8.59 E
Tula, Méx.	234	23.00 N	99.43 W
Tula, Nig.	146	9.50 N	11.28 E
Tula, S.S.S.R.	82	54.12 N	37.37 E
Tula □[4]	82	54.23 N	37.47 E
Tula ≃, Kenya	154	0.50 S	39.51 E
Tula ≃, Méx.	234	20.40 N	99.30 W
Tula ⊥	234	20.06 N	99.19 W
Tula de Allende	234	20.03 N	99.21 W
Tulaghi	175e	9.06 S	160.09 E
Tulai Nanshan ʎ	102	38.44 N	98.20 E
Tūlāk	128	33.58 N	63.44 E
Tulalip Indian Reservation ◆[4]	224	48.06 N	122.15 W
Tulancingo	234	20.05 N	98.22 W
Tulangbawang ≃	112	4.24 S	105.52 E
Tulaodian	104	41.13 N	121.27 E
T'ul'apsy	86	57.28 N	89.38 E
Tulare, Ca., U.S.	226	36.12 N	119.20 W
Tulare, S.D., U.S.	198	44.44 N	98.30 W
Tulare □[6]	226	36.20 N	119.18 W
Tulare Canal ≊	226	36.08 N	119.25 W
Tulare Lake Bed ⊚	226	36.03 N	119.49 W
Tulare Lake Canal ≊	226	36.04 N	119.39 W
Tularosa	200	33.04 N	106.01 W
Tularosa ≃	200	33.41 N	108.46 W
Tularosa Valley ≚[1]	200	32.45 N	106.10 W
Tulbagh	158	33.17 S	19.09 E
Tulbing	264b	48.16 N	16.09 E
Tulbinger Kogel ∧	264b	48.17 N	16.09 E
Tulcán	246	0.48 N	77.43 W
Tulcea	38	45.11 N	28.48 E
Tulcea □[6]	38	45.00 N	29.00 E
Tul'čin	78	48.39 N	28.52 E
Tulcingo de Valle	234	18.03 N	98.26 W
Tule ≃, Nic.	236	11.20 N	84.52 W
Tule ≃, Ca., U.S.	226	36.03 N	119.50 W
Tule, North Branch ≃	226	36.06 N	119.22 W
Tule, South Branch ≃	226	36.05 N	119.29 W
Tule Canal ≊	226	38.37 N	121.35 W
Tule Creek ≃	196	34.40 N	101.14 W
T'ulek	85	41.56 N	75.41 E
Tulelake	204	41.57 N	121.29 W
Tule Lake Sump ⊚[1]	204	41.54 N	121.32 W
Tulemalu Lake ⊚	176	62.58 N	99.25 W
T'ulenij, mys ›	84	40.12 N	50.22 E
T'ulenij, ostrov I	84	44.28 N	47.30 E
Tule River Indian Reservation ◆[4]	204	36.02 N	118.42 W
Tulette	62	44.17 N	4.56 E
Tule Valley V	200	39.20 N	113.25 W
T'ul'gan	86	52.22 N	56.12 E
Tul'goviči	78	51.47 N	29.38 E
Tuli	154	21.59 S	29.15 E
Tuli ≃	154	21.48 S	29.04 E
Tulia	196	34.32 N	101.45 W
Tuliahan ≃	269f	14.41 N	120.58 E
Tulica ≃	82	54.12 N	37.37 E
Tulik Volcano ∧[1]	180	53.22 N	168.03 W
Tulillo	234	22.30 N	104.05 W
Tuling	100	25.11 N	118.50 E
Tuliszków	30	52.05 N	18.17 E
Ṭūlkarm	132	32.19 N	35.02 E
T'ul'kino	86	59.49 N	56.30 E
T'ul'kubas	85	42.28 N	70.02 E
Tulla	48	52.52 N	8.45 W
Tullahoma	194	35.21 N	86.12 W
Tullamarine	274b	37.41 S	144.52 E
Tullamarine Airport ⊠	169	37.40 S	144.50 E
Tullamarine International Airport ⊠	274b	37.40 S	144.50 E
Tullamore, Austl.	166	32.38 S	147.34 E
Tullamore, On., Can.	275b	43.47 N	79.46 W
Tullamore, Ire.	48	53.16 N	7.30 W
Tullaroop Creek ≃	169	36.53 S	143.53 E
Tullaroop Reservoir ⊚[1]	169	37.07 S	143.52 E
Tull Bay ⊂	208	36.30 N	76.04 W
Tulle	32	45.16 N	1.46 E
Tullgarn	40	58.57 N	17.35 E
Tullibigeal	166	33.25 S	146.44 E
Tullinge	40	59.12 N	17.53 E
Tullins	62	45.18 N	5.29 E
Tulln	61	48.20 N	16.03 E
Tullner Feld ◆[1]	264b	48.19 N	16.10 E
Tulloch Reservoir ⊚[1]	226	37.53 N	120.35 W
Tullock Creek ≃	202	46.08 N	107.27 W
Tullos	194	31.49 N	92.19 W
Tullow	48	52.48 N	6.44 W
Tullus	140	11.03 N	24.33 E
Tully, Austl.	166	17.56 S	145.56 E
Tully, N.Y., U.S.	210	42.47 N	76.06 W
Tully Dam ◆[6]	207	42.39 N	72.11 W
Tullytown	208	40.09 N	74.49 W
Ṭulmaythah	146	32.43 N	20.57 E
Tuloma ≃	24	68.52 N	32.49 E
Tulpfontein	158	32.44 S	19.43 E
Tulsa	196	36.09 N	95.59 W
Tulsequah	176	58.35 N	133.35 W
Tulsī Lake ⊚	272c	19.11 N	72.55 E
Tulsk	48	53.47 N	8.16 W
Tul'skij	84	44.31 N	40.10 E
Tulstrup	41	56.07 N	9.46 E
Tultepec	234	19.41 N	99.08 W
Tultitlán □[7]	286a	19.39 N	99.09 W
Tultitlán de Mariano Escobedo	286a	19.39 N	99.09 W
Tuluá	246	4.06 N	76.11 W
Tuluksak	180	61.06 N	160.58 W
Tulum	232	20.13 N	87.28 W
Tulum ⊥	232	20.12 N	87.26 W
Tulumaya (Lavalle)	252	32.43 S	68.35 W
Tulumayo ≃	248	11.10 S	75.16 W
Tulun	88	54.35 N	100.33 E
Tulungagung	115a	8.04 S	111.54 E
Tulungselapan	112	3.15 S	105.19 E
Tuluran Island I	116	10.59 N	119.17 E
Tulu Welel ∧	144	8.53 N	34.47 E
Tulyehualco ◆[8]	286a	19.15 N	99.01 W
Tum	164	3.38 S	130.23 E
Tuma	80	55.09 N	40.34 E
Tuma ≃	236	13.03 N	84.44 W
Tumacacori National Monument ♠	200	31.25 N	111.01 W
Tumaco	246	1.49 N	78.46 W
Tumaco, Ensenada de ⊂	246	1.55 N	78.45 W
Tumak	80	46.14 N	48.31 E
Tumalykol'	86	48.21 N	60.03 E
Tuman'an	84	41.00 N	44.40 E
Tuman-gang (Tumen) ≃	98	42.18 N	130.41 E
Tumannaja, gora ∧	180	66.33 N	179.43 E
Tumanovo	76	55.25 N	34.39 E
Tumanšet ≃	88	55.53 N	97.30 E
Tumanskij	180	63.58 N	178.12 E
Tumany	74	60.56 N	155.56 E
Tumarbong	116	10.23 N	119.27 E
T'um'ati → Sklad	74	71.55 N	123.33 E
Tumatumari	246	5.22 N	59.00 W
Tumauini	116	17.17 N	121.49 E

Tumba	40	59.12 N	17.49 E
Tumba, Lac ⊚	152	0.48 S	18.03 E
Tumbarumba	171b	35.47 S	148.01 E
Tumbarumba Creek ≃	171b	35.58 S	148.03 E
Tumbaya	252	23.51 S	65.28 W
Tumbes	246	3.34 S	80.28 W
Tumbes □[4]	246	3.50 N	80.30 W
Tumbes (Puyango) ≃	246	3.30 S	80.27 W
Tumbes, Punta ›	252	36.37 S	73.07 W
Tumbiscatio de Ruiz	234	18.31 N	102.21 W
Tumble Mountain ∧	202	45.19 N	110.02 W
Tumbler Ridge	182	55.07 N	120.55 W
Tumblong	171b	35.09 S	148.00 E
Tumbotino	80	55.59 N	43.02 E
Tumbur	154	4.20 N	31.34 E
Tumby Bay	166	34.22 S	136.06 E
Tumča ≃	24	66.36 N	30.48 E
Tŭmch'on-ni ◆[8]	271b	37.34 N	126.51 E
T'umen', S.S.S.R.	86	57.09 N	65.32 E
Tumen, Zhg.	98	42.58 N	129.49 E
Tumen (Tuman-gang) ≃	98	42.18 N	130.41 E
T'umen'-Aryk	86	44.02 N	67.01 E
T'umencevo	86	53.20 N	81.31 E
T'umenec, porog ∟	88	56.38 N	99.00 E
Tumenpu	107	29.49 N	103.39 E
T'umenskaja Oblast' □[4]	24	65.00 N	62.00 E
Tumenskoje	82	55.00 N	38.32 E
Tumenzi	102	37.43 N	103.09 E
Tumeremo	246	7.18 N	61.30 W
Tumiritinga	255	18.58 S	41.38 W
Tumkūr	122	13.21 N	77.05 E
Tummel ≃	46	56.38 N	3.40 W
Tumnin ≃	89	49.18 N	140.22 E
Tumon Bay ⊂	174p	13.31 N	144.48 E
Tumos ≃	156	22.55 S	14.37 E
Tumoteqi	102	40.52 N	111.28 E
Tumpang	115a	8.00 S	112.46 E
Tumpat	114	6.12 N	102.10 E
Tumsar	120	21.23 N	79.44 E
Tumtum	182	47.53 N	117.40 W
Tumu, Ghana	150	10.52 N	1.59 W
Tumu, Zhg.	105	40.23 N	115.36 E
Tumuc-Humac Mountains ʎ	250	2.20 N	55.00 W
Tumupasa	248	14.09 S	67.55 W
Tumut	171b	35.18 S	148.13 E
Tumut ≃	171b	35.07 S	148.13 E
Tumut Pond Reservoir ⊚[1]	171b	35.59 S	148.25 E
Tumutuk	80	55.02 N	53.19 E
Tumwater	224	47.00 N	122.54 W
Tun ≃	110	17.25 N	98.42 E
Tuña ≃	246	1.30 N	73.55 W
Tuna Canyon V	280	34.03 N	118.36 W
Tunago Lake ⊚	180	66.18 N	125.50 W
Tuna-Hästberg	40	60.20 N	15.11 E
Tunapuna	241r	10.38 N	61.23 W
Tunari, Cerro ∧	248	17.18 S	66.22 W
Tunas Creek ≃	196	31.01 N	102.11 W
Tunas de Zaza	240p	21.38 N	79.33 W
Tūnat al-Jabal, Miṣr	142	27.46 N	30.44 E
Tūnat al-Jabal, Miṣr	142	28.13 N	30.43 E
Tunaydah	140	25.31 N	29.21 E
Tunçbilek	130	39.37 N	29.29 E
Tunceli	130	39.07 N	39.32 E
Tunceli □[4]	130	39.10 N	39.30 E
Tunchang	110	19.28 N	110.08 E
T'unch'i → Tunxi	100	29.44 N	118.18 E
Tunda, Pulau I	115a	5.49 S	106.16 E
Tundazi ∧	154	17.33 S	28.05 E
Tündern	52	52.04 N	9.22 E
Tūndla	124	27.12 N	78.17 E
Tundubai ⫪[4]	140	18.31 N	28.33 E
Tunduru	154	11.07 S	37.21 E
Tundyk ≃	86	51.04 N	77.24 E
Tundža ≃	38	41.40 N	26.34 E
Tune	41	55.36 N	12.11 E
Tunesien → Tunisia □[1]	148	34.00 N	9.00 E
T'unež, S.S.S.R.	82	54.37 N	38.29 E
Túnez → Tunis, Tun.	148	36.48 N	10.11 E
Túnez → Tunisia □[1]	148	34.00 N	9.00 E
T'ung ≃	74	63.46 N	121.35 E
Tunga	150	8.00 N	9.19 E
Tunga ≃	122	14.00 N	75.41 E
Tungabhadra ≃	122	15.57 N	78.15 E
Tungabhadra Reservoir ⊚[1]	122	15.16 N	76.21 E
Tungaru	140	10.14 N	30.42 E
Tungauan Bay ⊂	116	7.28 N	122.21 E
Tungchi University ʊ[2]	269b	31.18 N	121.29 E
Tungchi Yü I	100	23.15 N	119.40 E
T'ungchou → Tongxian	105	39.55 N	116.39 E
T'ungch'uan → Tongchuan	102	35.01 N	109.01 E
Tungch'üan Tao I	100	25.58 N	119.58 E
Tungelsta	40	59.06 N	18.02 E
Tung Hai → East China Sea ⫪[2]	90	30.00 N	126.00 E
Tungho	100	22.58 N	121.18 E
T'unghsien → Tongxian	105	39.55 N	116.39 E
T'unghua → Tonghua	98	41.41 N	125.55 E
Tunghwa → Tonghua	98	41.41 N	125.55 E
Tungi	126	23.53 N	90.24 E
Tungir ≃	88	55.24 N	120.32 E
Tungirskij chrebet ʎ	88	54.40 N	119.40 E
Tungkal ≃	112	0.48 S	103.29 E
Tungkang	100	22.28 N	120.26 E
Tungkillo	168b	34.49 S	139.04 E
Tungku	112	5.01 N	118.53 E
Tungla	236	13.18 N	84.26 W
T'ungliao → Tongliao	89	43.39 N	122.14 E
Tung Lung Island I	271d	22.15 N	114.17 E
Tung O	271d	22.12 N	114.08 E
Tungokočen	88	53.33 N	115.36 E
Tungsha Tao (Pratas Island) I	90	20.42 N	116.43 E
Tungshih	100	24.15 N	120.49 E
Tungsten	180	61.57 N	128.16 W
Tungsunga, Jabal ∧	140	11.29 N	23.21 E
Tungting Tao I	100	24.10 N	118.14 E
Tungurahua □[4]	246	1.15 S	78.35 W
Tunguska Crater ≜[6]	72	60.05 N	100.55 E
Tungyin Tao I	100	26.22 N	120.30 E
Tuni	122	17.21 N	82.33 E
Tunia ≃	246	1.13 N	72.44 W
Tunica	194	34.41 N	90.22 W
Tunis	148	36.48 N	10.11 E
Tunis □[8]	148	36.50 N	10.15 E
Tūnis → Tunisia □[1]	148	34.00 N	9.00 E
Tunis, Golfe de ⊂	36	37.00 N	10.30 E
Tunis et Banlieue □[8]	36	36.48 N	10.10 E
Tunisia (Tunisie) □[1], Afr.	134	34.00 N	9.00 E
Tunisia (Tunisie) □[1], Afr.	148	34.00 N	9.00 E
Tunisie → Tunisia □[1]	148	34.00 N	9.00 E
Tunis Sud □[8]	148	36.30 N	10.00 E
Tunitas Creek ≃	282	37.21 N	122.24 W
Tunja	246	5.31 N	73.22 W
Tunjang	114	6.16 N	100.21 E
Tunka	88	51.45 N	102.32 E
Tunkás	232	20.54 N	88.45 W
Tunkhannock	210	41.32 N	75.56 W
Tunkhannock Creek ≃	210	41.32 N	75.57 W
Tunkhannock Creek, East Branch ≃	210	41.38 N	75.43 W
Tunliu	102	36.19 N	112.54 E
Tunnel	210	42.13 N	75.44 W
Tunnel Hill, Ga., U.S.	192	34.50 N	85.02 W

Tunnelhill, Pa., U.S.	214	40.29 N	78.33 W
Tunnelton, In., U.S.	218	38.46 N	86.21 W
Tunnelton, W.V., U.S.	188	39.23 N	79.44 W
Tunnsjøen ⊚	24	64.43 N	13.24 E
Tunø I	41	55.57 N	10.26 E
Tuntenhausen	64	47.56 N	12.01 E
Tuntum	250	5.14 S	44.39 W
Tuntutuliak	180	60.22 N	162.38 W
Tununak	180	60.35 N	165.16 W
Tunungayualok Island I	176	56.05 N	61.05 W
Tunuyán	252	33.34 S	69.01 W
Tunuyán ≃	252	34.03 S	66.45 W
Tunxi	100	29.44 N	118.18 E
Tuo ≃, Zhg.	100	33.16 N	117.45 E
Tuo ≃, Zhg.	102	28.57 N	105.27 E
Tuobalage	120	31.37 N	88.10 E
Tuobuja	74	62.00 N	122.02 E
Tuocheng	100	24.05 N	115.13 E
Tuoe Shan ∧	102	24.20 N	103.32 E
Tuoheji	100	33.26 N	117.26 E
Tuoj-Chaja	74	62.32 N	111.18 E
Tuoji Dao I	98	38.09 N	120.14 E
Tuokedingling	120	32.45 N	84.55 E
Tuokusidawanling ∧	120	37.14 N	85.47 E
Tuoli	105	39.46 N	116.01 E
Tuolumne	226	37.57 N	120.14 W
Tuolumne □[6]	226	37.59 N	120.23 W
Tuolumne ≃	226	37.36 N	121.10 W
Tuolumne, Lyell Fork ≃	226	37.53 N	119.23 W
Tuolumne, North Fork ≃	226	37.54 N	120.15 W
Tuolumne, South Fork ≃	226	37.50 N	120.03 W
Tuolunduo	89	50.35 N	120.05 E
Tuowu	102	28.58 N	102.13 E
T'up	85	42.44 N	78.22 E
Tupã	255	21.56 S	50.30 W
Tupaciguara	255	18.35 S	48.42 W
Tupa Creek ≃	170	33.05 S	150.37 E
Tupana ≃	246	4.25 S	60.05 W
Tupanciretã	252	29.05 S	53.51 W
Tuparro ≃	246	5.13 N	67.50 W
Tupelo, Ms., U.S.	194	34.15 N	88.42 W
Tupelo, Ok., U.S.	196	34.36 N	96.25 W
Tupelo National Battlefield ⊥	194	34.13 N	88.44 W
Tupi	116	6.19 N	124.57 E
Tupičov	78	51.46 N	31.26 E
Tupik	88	54.26 N	119.57 E
Tupilac	116	7.40 N	122.30 E
Tupinambarana, Ilha I	246	3.00 S	58.00 W
Tupi Paulista	255	21.24 S	51.34 W
Tupiraçaba	255	14.29 S	48.34 W
Tupirama	250	8.58 S	48.12 W
Tupiza	248	21.27 S	65.43 W
Tuplice	30	51.41 N	14.50 E
Tupman	226	35.17 N	119.21 W
Tupper	182	55.31 N	120.02 W
Tupper Lake	188	44.13 N	74.29 W
Tupperville	214	42.36 N	82.16 W
Tupuai, Île I	14	23.18 S	149.30 W
Tupungato	252	33.22 S	69.08 W
Tupungato, Cerro ∧	252	33.22 S	69.47 W
Tupuseleia	164	9.33 S	147.18 E
Tuqiao, Zhg.	106	31.56 N	119.03 E
Tuqiao, Zhg.	106	31.39 N	120.24 E
Tuqiao, Zhg.	107	30.24 N	105.28 E
Tuqiaozhen	107	30.32 N	104.50 E
Tuquan	89	45.26 N	121.50 E
Túquerres	246	1.05 N	77.37 W
Tuquiaochang	107	29.47 N	106.01 E
Tura, India	124	25.31 N	90.13 E
Ṭurā, Miṣr	142	29.56 N	31.16 E
Tura, S.S.S.R.	74	64.17 N	100.15 E
Tura ≃, S.S.S.R.	86	57.12 N	66.56 E
Tura ≃, S.S.S.R.	88	51.36 N	114.09 E
Turabah	144	21.13 N	41.39 E
Turabah ⫪[4]	128	28.15 N	42.55 E
Turābah, ʿAyn at- ⫪[4]	132	31.36 N	35.25 E
Turāg ≃	126	23.45 N	90.21 E
Turaiyūr	122	11.10 N	78.37 E
Turakina	172	40.02 S	175.13 E
Turakina ≃	172	40.04 S	175.08 E
Turama ≃	164	6.50 S	143.05 E
Turambhe	272c	19.04 N	73.01 E
Turan, S.S.S.R.	88	51.38 N	101.40 E
Turan, S.S.S.R.	88	52.08 N	93.55 E
Turangi	172	39.00 S	175.49 E
Turano ≃	66	42.26 N	12.47 E
Turanskaja nizmennost' ≚	86	44.30 N	63.00 E
Turate	266b	45.39 N	9.00 E
Tur'at Ghunaym	142	31.16 N	31.29 E
Turbaco	246	10.20 N	75.25 W
Turbacz ∧	30	49.33 N	20.08 E
Turbat	128	25.59 N	63.04 E
Turbenthal	58	47.27 N	8.51 E
Turbigo	62	45.32 N	8.44 E
Turbio ≃	234	20.19 N	101.37 W
Turbo	246	8.06 N	76.43 W
Turbotville	210	41.06 N	76.46 W
Turbov	78	49.21 N	28.44 E
Turčasovo	24	63.06 N	39.12 E
Turchi, Balata dei ›	70	36.43 N	12.02 E
Turčiansky Svätý Martin → Martin	30	49.05 N	18.55 E
Turckheim	58	48.05 N	7.17 E
Turda	38	46.34 N	23.47 E
Turdej	76	53.22 N	38.01 E
Turee Creek	162	23.37 S	118.39 E
Turee Creek ≃	162	23.35 S	117.25 E
Turek	30	52.02 N	18.30 E
Turen	115a	8.10 S	112.41 E
Turenki	26	60.55 N	24.38 E
Turfan → Turpan	86	42.56 N	89.10 E
Turfan Depression → Turpan Pendi ≜[7]	86	42.40 N	89.10 E
Turffontein ◆[8]	273d	26.15 S	28.02 E
Turffontein Race Course ♠	273d	26.14 S	28.03 E
Turgaj, S.S.S.R.	86	49.38 N	63.28 E
Turgaj, S.S.S.R.	86	51.46 N	72.44 E
Turgaj ≃	86	48.01 N	62.45 E
Turgajskaja ložbina V	86	51.00 N	64.30 E
Turgajskaja Oblast' □[4]	86	50.00 N	65.20 E
Turgajskoje plato ʎ[1]	86	51.00 N	64.00 E
Türgen, Mong.	86	50.04 N	91.36 E
Turgen', S.S.S.R.	85	43.24 N	77.36 E
Turgen' ≃	85	43.50 N	77.38 E
Turgenevka	88	53.02 N	105.41 E
Turgenevo	80	54.50 N	46.19 E
Turginovo	82	56.30 N	36.00 E
Turgojak	86	55.10 N	60.07 E
Turgoš	76	59.18 N	35.10 E
Tŭrgovishte → Târgovište	38	43.15 N	26.34 E
Turgut	130	38.37 N	31.49 E
Turgutlu	130	38.30 N	27.43 E
Turgwi ≃	154	20.28 S	32.18 E
Turhal	130	40.24 N	36.06 E
Turi, It.	68	40.55 N	17.01 E
Türi, S.S.S.R.	76	58.48 N	25.26 E
Turia ≃	34	39.27 N	0.19 W
Turiaçu	250	1.41 S	45.21 W
Turiaçu ≃	250	1.36 S	45.19 W
Turiančajskij zapovednik ♠	84	40.40 N	47.35 E
Turij Rog	89	45.14 N	131.58 E
Turijsk	78	51.07 N	24.31 E
Turilovka	83	49.06 N	40.13 E
Turimetta Head ›	274a	33.42 S	151.19 E
Turimiquire, Cerro ∧	246	10.07 N	63.53 W
Turin, Ab., Can.	182	49.58 N	112.31 W
Turin → Torino, It.	62	45.03 N	7.40 E
Turin, N.Y., U.S.	212	43.38 N	75.25 W

Turinge	40	59.12 N	17.27 E
Turinsk	86	58.03 N	63.42 E
Turinskaja Sloboda	86	57.37 N	64.25 E
Turja ≃	78	51.48 N	24.52 E
Turka, S.S.S.R.	78	49.10 N	23.02 E
Turka, S.S.S.R.	88	52.57 N	108.13 E
Turka ≃	88	52.56 N	108.13 E
Turkana, Lake → Rudolf, Lake ⊚	144	3.30 N	36.05 E
Türkei → Turkey □[1]	22	39.00 N	35.00 E
Türkeli Adası I	130	40.30 N	27.30 E
Turkestan	85	43.18 N	68.15 E
Turkestanskij chrebet ʎ	85	39.35 N	69.15 E
Turkestanskij kanal ≊	85	42.44 N	69.00 E
Túrkeve	30	47.06 N	20.45 E
Turkey	196	34.23 N	100.53 W
Turkey □[1], Asia	22	39.00 N	35.00 E
Turkey □[1], Asia	130	39.00 N	35.00 E
Turkey ≃	190	42.43 N	91.01 W
Turkey Branch ≃	284c	38.52 N	76.48 W
Turkey City	214	41.11 N	79.37 W
Turkey Creek	164	17.02 S	128.12 E
Turkey Creek ≃, On., Can.	281	42.14 N	83.06 W
Turkey Creek ≃, U.S.	198	39.58 N	96.02 W
Turkey Creek ≃, In., U.S.	278	41.31 N	87.18 W
Turkey Creek ≃, Ia., U.S.	198	41.20 N	95.05 W
Turkey Creek ≃, Ks., U.S.	198	38.53 N	97.11 W
Turkey Creek ≃, Ne., U.S.	198	40.23 N	96.53 W
Turkey Creek ≃, Ok., U.S.	196	35.58 N	97.56 W
Turkey Creek ≃, Tx., U.S.	222	30.39 N	97.05 W
Turkey Island I	284c	38.58 N	77.12 W
Turkey Point ›, On., Can.	212	42.40 N	80.21 W
Turkey Point ›, Fl., U.S.	220	25.26 N	80.19 W
Turkey Point Provincial Park ♠	212	42.40 N	80.22 W
Turkey Run State Park ♠	194	39.54 N	87.13 W
Turkeytown	279b	40.12 N	79.44 W
Türkheim	58	48.03 N	10.38 E
Turki	80	51.59 N	43.16 E
Türkiye → Turkey □[1]	22	39.00 N	35.00 E
Turkmān Deh	267d	35.40 N	51.36 E
Turkmen-Kala	128	37.26 N	62.20 E
Turkmenskaja Sovetskaja Socialističeskaja Respublika □[3]	72	40.00 N	60.00 E
Turkmen Soviet Socialist Republic → Turkmenskaja Sovetskaja Socialističeskaja Respublika □[3]	72	40.00 N	60.00 E
Turk Mine	154	19.45 S	28.50 E
Turkoğlu	130	37.31 N	36.49 E
Turks and Caicos Islands □[2], N.A.	230	21.45 N	71.35 W
Turks and Caicos Islands □[2], N.A.	238	21.45 N	71.35 W
Turks Island Passage ʮ	238	21.25 N	71.19 W
Turks Islands II	238	21.24 N	71.07 W
Turks-und Caicos-Inseln → Turks and Caicos Islands □[2]	238	21.45 N	71.35 W
Turku (Åbo)	26	60.27 N	22.17 E
Turkwel ≃	154	3.06 N	36.06 E
Turlan	85	43.36 N	69.03 E
Turley	196	36.14 N	95.58 W
Turlock	226	37.29 N	120.50 W
Turlock Lake ⊚[1]	226	42.17 N	73.21 W
Turmalina	255	17.17 S	42.45 W
Turmantas	76	55.42 N	26.27 E
Turmerito, Quebrada ≃	286c	10.26 N	66.55 W
Turnagain ≃	180	59.06 N	127.35 W
Turnagain, Cape ›	172	40.29 S	176.37 E
Turnagain Arm ⊂	180	61.00 N	150.00 W
Turnagain Island I	164	9.34 S	142.18 E
Turna nad Bodvou	30	48.37 N	20.53 E
Turnau	61	47.33 N	15.20 E
Turnbull, Mount ∧	200	33.04 N	110.16 W
Turnbull, Mount ∧[2]	162	21.03 S	131.57 E
Turneffe Islands II	232	17.22 N	87.51 W
Turner, Austl.	162	17.50 S	128.17 E
Turner, Mt., U.S.	202	48.50 N	108.24 W
Turner, Or., U.S.	202	44.50 N	122.57 W
Turner ≃	162	20.21 S	118.25 E
Turner Field ⊠	285	40.13 N	75.13 W
Turners Falls	207	42.36 N	72.33 W
Turners Peninsula ›[1]	150	7.22 N	12.22 W
Turnersville, N.J., U.S.	285	39.46 N	75.03 W
Turnersville, Tx., U.S.	222	31.37 N	97.44 W
Turner Valley	182	50.40 N	114.17 W
Turnhout	52	51.19 N	4.57 E
Türnitz	61	47.57 N	15.30 E
Turnor Lake ⊚	184	56.32 N	108.38 W
Turnov	30	50.35 N	15.10 E
Tŭrnovo → Veliko Târnovo	38	43.04 N	25.39 E
Turnpike Lake ⊚	283	42.01 N	71.19 W
Turnu-Măgurele	38	43.45 N	24.53 E
Turnu Roșu, Pasul)(	38	45.33 N	24.16 E
Turnu-Severin → Drobeta-Turnu-Severin	38	44.38 N	22.39 E
Turobin	30	50.50 N	22.45 E
Turočak	86	52.16 N	87.08 E
Turon	198	37.48 N	98.25 W
Turon ≃	170	33.03 S	149.43 E
Turopin	78	51.00 N	24.27 E
Turopolje ≚	36	45.40 N	16.05 E
Tuross ≃	171b	36.09 S	149.39 E
Turov	78	52.04 N	27.44 E
Turovo	82	54.52 N	37.49 E
Turpan	86	42.56 N	89.10 E
Turpan Pendi (Turfan Depression) ≜[7]	86	42.40 N	89.10 E
Turques et Caicos, Îles → Turks and Caicos Islands □[2]	238	21.45 N	71.35 W
Turquía → Turkey □[1]	22	39.00 N	35.00 E
Turquie → Turkey □[1]	22	39.00 N	35.00 E
Turquino, Pico ∧	240p	19.59 N	76.50 W
Turrach	64	46.57 N	13.52 E
Turramurra	274a	33.44 S	151.08 E
Turrell	194	35.22 N	90.15 W
Turret Peak ∧	200	34.15 N	111.53 W
Turriaco	64	45.49 N	13.26 E
Turrialba	236	9.54 N	83.41 W
Turrialba, Volcán ∧[1]	236	10.02 N	83.46 W
Turriers	62	44.24 N	6.10 E
Turriff	46	57.32 N	2.28 W
Turritano ◆[1]	71	40.45 N	8.35 E
Turrubares, Cerro ∧	236	9.47 N	84.28 W
Tursi	68	40.15 N	16.28 E
Tursunzade	85	38.32 N	68.13 E
Turtas ≃	86	59.06 N	68.52 E
Turtipār	124	26.10 N	83.54 E
Turtle ≃, Mb., Can.	184	51.07 N	99.39 W
Turtle ≃, On., Can.	184	48.51 N	92.45 W
Turtle, North Branch ≃	198	47.57 N	97.35 W
Turtle Creek, N.B., Can.	186	45.58 N	64.53 W

Symbol	English	Deutsch	Español	Français	Português
≃	River	Fluss	Río	Rivière	Rio
≊	Canal	Kanal	Canal	Canal	Canal
∟	Waterfall, Rapids	Wasserfall, Stromschnellen	Cascada, Rápidos	Chute d'eau, Rapides	Cascata, Rápidos
ʮ	Strait	Meeresstrasse	Estrecho	Détroit	Estreito
⊂	Bay, Gulf	Bucht, Golf	Bahía, Golfo	Baie, Golfe	Baía, Golfo
⊚	Lake, Lakes	See, Seen	Lago, Lagos	Lac, Lacs	Lago, Lagos
⩩	Swamp	Sumpf	Pantano	Marais	Pântano
⍓	Ice Features, Glacier	Eis- und Gletscherformen	Accidentes Glaciales	Formes glaciaires	Acidentes glaciares
⫪	Other Hydrographic Features	Andere Hydrographische Objekte	Otros Elementos Hidrográficos	Autres données hydrographiques	Outros acidentes hidrográficos
✦	Submarine Features	Untermeerische Objekte	Accidentes Submarinos	Formes de relief sous-marin	Acidentes submarinos
□	Political Unit	Politische Einheit	Unidad Politica	Entité politique	Unidade política
ʊ	Cultural Institution	Kulturelle Institution	Institución Cultural	Institution culturelle	Institução cultural
⊥	Historical Site	Historische Stätte	Sitio Histórico	Site historique	Sitio histórico
♠	Recreational Site	Erholungs- und Ferienort	Sitio de Recreo	Centre de loisirs	Area de Lazer
⊠	Airport	Flughafen	Aeropuerto	Aéroport	Aeroporto
■	Military Installation	Militäranlage	Instalación Militar	Installation militaire	Instalação militar
◆	Miscellaneous	Verschiedenes	Misceláneo	Divers	Diversos

Turtle Creek, Pa., U.S. **214** 40.24 N 79.49 W
Turtle Creek ≐, Pa., U.S. **279b** 40.23 N 79.51 W
Turtle Creek ≐, S.D., U.S. **198** 44.55 N 98.29 W
Turtle Creek ≐, Wi., U.S. **216** 42.29 N 89.03 W
Turtle-Flambeau Flowage ⊜[1] **190** 46.05 N 90.11 W
Turtleford **184** 53.23 N 108.56 W
Turtle Harbor Channel ⊻ **220** 25.15 N 80.18 W
Turtle Islands II **150** 7.37 N 13.02 W
Turtle Lake, N.D., U.S. **198** 47.31 N 100.53 W
Turtle Lake, Wi., U.S. **190** 45.23 N 92.08 W
Turtle Lake ⊜ **184** 53.35 N 108.40 W
Turtle Mountain ∧[2] **184** 49.00 N 100.15 W
Turtle Mountain Indian Reservation ◆[4] **198** 48.51 N 99.45 W
Turtle Mountain Provincial Park ♦ **184** 49.03 N 100.15 W
Turtmann **58** 46.18 N 7.41 E
Turton and Entwistle Reservoir ⊜[1] **262** 53.39 N 2.25 W
Turton Bottoms **262** 53.38 N 2.24 W
Turton Moor ◆[3] **262** 53.40 N 2.29 W
Turton Tower ⊍ **262** 53.38 N 2.25 W
Turu ≐ **74** 64.38 N 100.00 E
Turua **172** 37.14 S 175.34 E
Turuchan ≐ **74** 65.56 N 87.42 E
Turuchansk **74** 65.49 N 87.59 E
Turuntajevo, S.S.S.R. **86** 56.38 N 85.59 E
Turuntajevo, S.S.S.R. **88** 52.12 N 107.37 E
Turusele ∧ **71** 40.09 N 9.34 E
Türüşmek **130** 39.03 N 39.32 E
Turvânia **255** 16.39 S 50.09 W
Turvo **252** 28.56 S 49.41 W
Turvo ≐, Bra. **255** 17.46 S 50.12 W
Turvo ≐, Bra. **255** 19.56 S 49.55 W
Turvo ≐, Bra. **256** 22.04 S 45.42 W
Turvo ≐, Bra. **256** 22.29 S 44.15 W
Turvo ≐, Bra. **256** 21.32 S 44.26 W
Turvo Grande ≐ **256** 21.42 S 44.22 W
Turvo Pequeno ≐ **256** 21.42 S 44.22 W
Turyu-san ∧ **98** 41.10 N 128.47 E
Turzovka **30** 49.25 N 18.39 E
Tusa **70** 37.59 N 14.14 E
Tusa ≐ **70** 38.01 N 14.16 E
Tusas, Rio ≐ **200** 36.23 N 106.03 W
Tuscaloosa **194** 33.12 N 87.34 W
Tuscaloosa, Lake ⊜[1] **194** 33.20 N 87.35 W
Tuscania **66** 42.25 N 11.52 E
Tuscarawas **214** 40.24 N 81.25 W
Tuscarawas □[6] **214** 40.30 N 81.27 W
Tuscarawas ≐ **214** 40.17 N 81.52 W
Tuscarora, N.Y., U.S. **210** 42.38 N 77.52 W
Tuscarora, Pa., U.S. **208** 40.46 N 76.02 W
Tuscarora Creek ≐, N.Y., U.S. **210** 42.07 N 77.14 W
Tuscarora Creek ≐, Pa., U.S. **208** 40.32 N 77.23 W
Tuscarora Creek, North Branch ≐ **210** 42.05 N 77.18 W
Tuscarora Indian Reservation ◆[4] **210** 43.09 N 78.57 W
Tuscarora Mountain ∧ **188** 40.10 N 77.45 W
Tuscarora Mountains ⋏ **204** 41.00 N 116.20 W
Tuscarora State Park ♦ **208** 40.48 N 76.01 W
Tuscarora Tunnel ◆[5] **214** 40.05 N 77.50 W
Tuscola, Il., U.S. **194** 39.47 N 88.16 W
Tuscola, Tx., U.S. **196** 32.12 N 99.48 W
Tuscolo ⊥ **267a** 41.48 N 12.42 E
Tuscumbia, Al., U.S. **194** 34.43 N 87.42 W
Tuscumbia, Mo., U.S. **194** 38.13 N 92.27 W
Tuse **41** 55.43 N 11.37 E
Tushan **98** 34.14 N 117.51 E
Tušino ◆[8] **265b** 55.50 N 37.26 E
Tuskegee **194** 32.25 N 85.41 W
Tusker Rock II[1] **42** 51.27 N 3.40 W
Tussey Mountain ∧ **214** 40.25 N 78.07 W
Tüssling **60** 48.13 N 12.36 E
Tustin **228** 33.44 N 117.49 W
Tustin Marine Corps Air Station (Helicopter) ■ **280** 33.43 N 117.50 W
Tustumena Lake ⊜ **180** 60.12 N 150.50 W
Tuszyn **30** 51.37 N 19.34 E
Tut **130** 37.48 N 37.55 E
Tuta **152** 14.37 S 20.45 E
Tutaekuri ≐ **172** 39.30 S 176.54 E
Tutaizi **104** 41.01 N 122.38 E
Tutajev **80** 57.53 N 39.32 E
Tutak **84** 39.32 N 42.46 E
Tutang **100** 29.21 N 116.24 E
Tutbury **42** 52.51 N 1.41 W
Tuthills Creek ≐ **276** 40.45 N 73.02 W
Tuticorin **122** 8.47 N 78.08 E
Tutin **38** 42.59 N 20.20 E
Tutkaul **85** 38.18 N 69.17 E
T'ut'kovo **82** 54.37 N 38.32 E
Tutóia **250** 2.45 S 42.16 W
Tutoko, Mount ∧ **172** 44.36 S 168.00 E
Tutong **112** 4.50 N 114.40 E
Tutova ≐ **38** 46.06 N 27.32 E
Tutrakan **38** 44.03 N 26.37 E
Tuttle, N.D., U.S. **198** 47.08 N 99.59 W
Tuttle, Ok., U.S. **196** 35.17 N 97.48 W
Tuttle Creek Lake ⊜[1] **198** 39.22 N 96.40 W
Tuttlingen **58** 47.59 N 8.49 E
Tutuala, Indon. **112** 8.24 S 127.15 E
Tutuban Station ◆[5] **269f** 14.37 N 120.58 E
Tutu Bay c **116** 5.55 N 121.12 E
Tutubu **154** 5.30 S 32.41 E
Tutuila I **174u** 14.18 S 170.42 W
Tuṭūn **142** 29.09 N 30.46 E
Tutupaca, Volcán ∧[1] **248** 17.01 S 70.22 W
Tutura **88** 54.46 N 105.15 E
Tututalak Mountain ∧ **180** 67.46 N 161.10 W
Tututepec **234** 16.09 N 97.38 W
Tutwiler **194** 34.00 N 90.25 W
Tutzing **64** 47.54 N 11.17 E
Tuul ≐ **90** 48.57 N 104.48 E
Tuupovaara **26** 62.29 N 30.36 E
Tuurun-Poorin lääni □[4] **26** 61.20 N 22.30 E
Tuusniemi **26** 62.49 N 28.30 E
Tuutapu, Cerro ∧ **174z** 27.08 S 109.24 W
T'uva-Guba **24** 69.08 N 33.32 E
Tuvalu □[1] **14** 8.00 S 178.00 E
Tuvinskaja Avtonomnaja Sovetskaja Socialističeskaja Respublika □[3] **88** 53.00 N 96.00 E
Tuvutha Island I **175g** 17.40 S 178.48 W
Tuwang **107** 29.06 N 105.48 E
Ṭuwayq, Jabal ⋏ **118** 23.00 N 46.00 E
Tuxedo Park, De., U.S. **285** 39.43 N 75.37 W
Tuxedo Park, N.Y., U.S. **210** 41.11 N 74.11 W
Tuxer Hauptkamm ∧ **64** 47.10 N 11.45 E
Tuxer Vorberge ⋏ **64** 47.10 N 11.45 E
Tuxford, Sk., Can. **184** 50.35 N 105.35 W
Tuxford, Eng., U.K. **44** 53.13 N 0.53 W
Tuxiaqiao **100** 28.47 N 121.29 E
Tuxpan, Méx. **234** 19.33 N 103.24 W
Tuxpan, Méx. **234** 21.37 N 104.07 W
Tuxpan, Méx. **234** 19.34 N 100.28 W
Tuxpan, Méx. **234** 21.57 N 105.18 W
Tuxpan ≐ **234** 20.59 N 97.18 W
Tuxpan de Rodríguez Cano **234** 20.57 N 97.24 W
Tuxsun **86** 42.47 N 88.38 E
Tuxtepec **234** 18.06 N 96.07 W
Tuxtla Chico **232** 14.57 N 92.10 W
Tuxtla Gutiérrez **234** 16.45 N 93.07 W
Túy **34** 42.03 N 8.38 W
Tuy ≐ **246** 10.24 N 65.59 W
Tuy-an **110** 13.17 N 109.16 E
Tuyen-hoa **110** 17.50 N 106.10 E
Tuyen-quang **110** 21.49 N 105.13 E
Tuy-hoa **110** 13.05 N 109.18 E
Tūysarkān **128** 34.33 N 48.27 E
Tuyün → Duyun **102** 26.12 N 107.31 E
Ṭuyūr, Burj aṭ- ∧[2] **140** 20.55 N 27.55 E
Tuža **80** 57.37 N 47.57 E
Tuzamapan **234** 19.24 N 96.51 W
T'uzašu, pereval)(**85** 42.21 N 73.48 E
T'uzbel' **85** 40.34 N 73.21 E
Tuzdykol', ozero ⊜ **80** 49.36 N 52.20 E
Tuz Gölü ⊜ **130** 38.45 N 33.25 E
Tuzigoot National Monument ♦ **200** 34.49 N 112.01 W
Ṭūz Khurmātū **128** 34.53 N 44.38 E
Tuzla, Jugo. **38** 44.32 N 18.41 E
Tuzla, Tür. **130** 36.42 N 35.05 E
Tuzla ≐ **84** 39.43 N 40.18 E
Tuzla Gölü ⊜ **130** 39.02 N 35.50 E
Tuzlov ≐ **83** 47.23 N 40.08 E
Tuzluca **84** 40.03 N 43.40 E
Tuzlukçu **130** 38.28 N 31.38 E
Tuzly **78** 45.52 N 30.05 E
Tvârdica, Blg. **38** 43.42 N 25.52 E
Tvardica, S.S.S.R. **78** 46.09 N 28.58 E
Tvedestrand **26** 58.37 N 8.55 E
Tveitsund **26** 59.01 N 8.32 E
Tver → Kalinin **82** 56.52 N 35.55 E
Tverca ≐ **76** 56.52 N 35.55 E
Twain Harte **226** 38.02 N 120.14 W
Twann **58** 47.06 N 7.10 E
Twante **110** 16.43 N 95.56 E
Twardogóra **30** 51.22 N 17.28 E
Tweed **212** 44.29 N 77.19 W
Tweed ≐ **44** 55.46 N 2.00 W
Tweeddale V **46** 55.37 N 2.55 W
Tweede Exloërmond **52** 52.55 N 6.58 E
Tweed Heads **171a** 28.10 S 153.31 E
Tweedmouth **44** 55.45 N 2.01 W
Tweedsmuir Provincial Park ♦ **182** 52.55 N 126.05 W
Tweedy Mountain ∧ **202** 45.29 N 112.58 W
Tweeling **158** 27.38 S 28.31 E
Twee Rivieren **158** 26.27 S 20.37 E
Tweespruit **158** 29.11 S 27.01 E
Twello **52** 52.14 N 6.06 E
Twelve Mile **216** 40.52 N 86.13 W
Twelve Mile Creek ≐, On., Can. **212** 43.11 N 79.16 W
Twelvemile Creek ≐, N.Y., U.S. **210** 43.18 N 78.51 W
Twelvemile Island I **279b** 40.32 N 79.51 W
Twelve Mile Lake ⊜, On., Can. **212** 45.02 N 78.43 W
Twelve Mile Lake ⊜, Sk., Can. **184** 49.29 N 106.14 W
Tweng **64** 47.11 N 13.36 E
Twente ◆[1] **52** 52.17 N 6.40 E
Twentekanaal ≍ **52** 52.15 N 6.40 E
Twentieth Century Fox Studios ⊍[3] **280** 34.03 N 118.25 W
Twentyfive Mile Wash V **200** 37.33 N 111.07 W
Twenty-Four-Parganas □[5] **126** 22.15 N 88.30 E
Twenty Mile Creek ≐ **212** 43.10 N 79.22 W
Twentynine Palms **204** 34.08 N 116.03 W
Twentynine Palms Marine Corps Center ■ **204** 34.25 N 116.10 W
Tweya **152** 0.54 S 19.05 E
Twickenham ◆[8] **260** 51.27 N 0.20 W
Twilight Cove c **162** 32.16 S 126.03 E
Twilight Park **210** 42.11 N 74.05 W
Twillingate **186** 49.39 N 54.46 W
Twin Beach **216** 42.34 N 83.24 W
Twinberg **61** 46.55 N 14.50 E
Twin Bridge Farm **285** 39.57 N 75.33 W
Twin Bridges **202** 45.32 N 112.19 W
Twin Butte Creek ≐ **198** 38.46 N 100.56 W
Twin Buttes ∧ **202** 44.20 N 122.15 W
Twin Buttes Reservoir ⊜[1] **196** 31.20 N 100.35 W
Twin City **192** 32.34 N 82.09 W
Twin Creek ≐ **218** 39.33 N 84.21 W
Twin Falls **202** 42.33 N 114.27 W
Twin Heads ⋏ **162** 20.13 S 126.30 E
Twin Hills **180** 59.23 N 159.58 W
Twin Lakes, Ca., U.S. **226** 36.58 N 122.00 W
Twin Lakes, Ga., U.S. **192** 30.42 N 83.12 W
Twin Lakes, In., U.S. **216** 41.19 N 86.23 W
Twin Lakes, Mi., U.S. **216** 42.02 N 86.04 W
Twin Lakes, Oh., U.S. **214** 41.11 N 81.21 W
Twin Lakes, Pa., U.S. **210** 41.24 N 74.54 W
Twin Lakes, Wi., U.S. **216** 42.31 N 88.14 W
Twin Lakes ⊜, Ca., U.S. **226** 38.09 N 119.21 W
Twin Lakes ⊜, Ct., U.S. **207** 42.02 N 73.26 W
Twin Lakes ⊜, Wa., U.S. **224** 47.55 N 120.51 W
Twin Oaks, Il., U.S. **278** 42.03 N 87.50 W
Twin Oaks, Pa., U.S. **208** 39.51 N 75.26 W
Twin Peak Islands II **162** 34.00 S 122.50 E
Twin Peaks **228** 34.12 N 117.12 W
Twin Peaks ⋏, Ca., U.S. **282** 37.45 N 122.27 W
Twin Peaks ⋏, Id., U.S. **202** 44.35 N 114.29 W
Twin Rocks, Or., U.S. **224** 45.36 N 123.57 W
Twin Rocks, Pa., U.S. **214** 40.29 N 78.51 W
Twinsburg **214** 41.18 N 81.26 W
Twin Valley **198** 47.15 N 96.15 W
Twisp **202** 48.21 N 120.07 W
Twiss Green **262** 53.27 N 2.32 W
Twist **52** 52.38 N 7.03 E
Twiste ≐ **52** 51.29 N 9.09 E
Twistringen **52** 52.48 N 8.38 E
Twitchell Reservoir ⊜[1] **204** 35.00 N 120.19 W
Twitya ≐ **180** 64.10 N 128.12 W
Two, Channel ⊻ **220** 24.50 N 80.45 W
Two Butte Creek ≐ **198** 38.02 N 102.08 W
Twofold Bay c **166** 37.06 S 149.55 E
Two Harbors **190** 47.01 N 91.40 W
Two Hills **182** 53.43 N 111.45 W
Two Lakes ⊜ **224** 46.22 N 121.27 W
Two Medicine ≐ **202** 48.29 N 112.14 W
Two Mile Creek ≐, On., Can. **284a** 43.16 N 79.06 W
Twomile Creek ≐, N.Y., U.S. **284a** 43.01 N 78.55 W
Twong **140** 8.18 N 28.20 E
Two Penny Run ≐ **285** 39.41 N 75.26 W
Two River Lake ⊜ **184** 53.52 N 91.27 W
Two Rivers **190** 44.09 N 87.34 W
Two Rivers Reservoir ⊜[1] **196** 33.17 N 104.45 W
Two Thumb Range ⋏ **172** 43.45 S 170.43 E
Two Wells **168b** 34.36 S 138.30 E
Twrch ≐, Wales, U.K. **42** 52.42 N 3.29 W
Twrch ≐, Wales, U.K. **42** 51.46 N 3.46 W
Twyford, Eng., U.K. **42** 51.29 N 0.53 W
Twyford, Eng., U.K. **42** 51.01 N 1.19 W
Twymyn ≐ **42** 52.38 N 3.44 W
Tyabb **169** 38.16 S 145.11 E
Tybee Island **192** 32.01 N 80.51 W
Tybju **24** 60.37 N 50.20 E
Tychy **30** 50.09 N 18.59 E
Tyczyn **30** 49.58 N 22.02 E
Tydal **26** 63.04 N 11.34 E
Tye **196** 32.27 N 99.52 W
Tyende Creek ≐ **200** 36.50 N 109.43 W
Tyendinaga Indian Reserve ◆[4] **212** 44.11 N 77.07 W
Tyers ≐ **169** 38.10 S 145.26 E
Tyfors **40** 60.09 N 14.12 E
Tygarts Creek ≐ **218** 38.43 N 82.57 W
Tygda **89** 53.07 N 126.20 E
Tygda ≐ **89** 52.35 N 127.55 E
Tygelsjö **41** 55.31 N 13.00 E
Tygh Valley **224** 45.14 N 121.10 W
Tyin ⊜ **26** 61.17 N 8.13 E
Tyja ≐ **88** 55.36 N 109.20 E
Tylden **158** 32.07 S 27.05 E
Tyldesley **44** 53.31 N 2.28 W
Tyler, Mn., U.S. **198** 44.16 N 96.08 W
Tyler, Pa., U.S. **214** 41.14 N 78.32 W
Tyler, Tx., U.S. **222** 32.21 N 95.18 W
Tyler □[6] **222** 30.47 N 94.32 W
Tyler, Lake ⊜[1] **222** 32.13 N 95.10 W
Tyler East, Lake ⊜[1] **222** 32.15 N 95.10 W
Tyler Park **284c** 38.52 N 77.12 W
Tylersburg **214** 41.23 N 79.19 W
Tyler State Park ♦, Pa., U.S. **208** 40.14 N 74.59 W
Tyler State Park ♦, Tx., U.S. **222** 32.29 N 95.14 W
Tylersville **210** 41.00 N 77.25 W
Tylerton **208** 37.58 N 76.01 W
Tylertown **194** 31.06 N 90.08 W
Tylla **40** 60.28 N 15.33 E
Tylösand **26** 56.39 N 12.44 E
Tylöskog ⋏[2] **40** 58.45 N 15.20 E
Tylovaj **80** 57.30 N 53.47 E
Tym ≐, S.S.S.R. **74** 59.25 N 80.04 E
Tym' ≐, S.S.S.R. **89** 51.51 N 143.10 E
Tymna, laguna c **180** 64.00 N 178.30 E
Tymochtee Creek ≐ **214** 40.57 N 83.16 W
Tymovskoje **89** 50.51 N 142.39 E
Tymsk **86** 59.24 N 80.18 E
Tynagh **48** 53.09 N 8.22 W
Tyndall **198** 42.59 N 97.51 W
Tyndall Air Force Base ■ **194** 30.04 N 85.35 W
Tyndaris ⊥ **70** 38.09 N 15.03 E
Tyndinskij **74** 55.10 N 124.43 E
Tyndrum **46** 56.27 N 4.44 W
Tyne ≐, Eng., U.K. **44** 55.01 N 1.26 W
Tyne ≐, Scot., U.K. **44** 56.01 N 2.37 W
Tyne and Wear □[6] **44** 54.55 N 1.35 W
Tynemouth **44** 55.01 N 1.24 W
Tyner **216** 41.24 N 86.24 W
Tyngsboro **283** 42.40 N 71.25 W
Tyngsjö **40** 60.18 N 13.53 E
Tynica **78** 51.08 N 32.54 E
Týn nad Vltavou **30** 49.14 N 14.26 E
Tynnelsö **40** 59.25 N 17.06 E
Tynset **26** 62.17 N 10.47 E
Tyonek **180** 61.02 N 151.17 W
Typta **88** 54.35 N 104.31 E
Tyr **89** 52.57 N 139.48 E
Tyre → Ṣūr **132** 33.16 N 35.11 E
Tyre **214** 40.26 N 80.16 W
Tyresö **40** 59.14 N 18.18 E
Tyret' **88** 53.41 N 102.19 E
Tyrgetuj **88** 51.27 N 113.46 E
Tyrifjorden ⊜ **26** 60.02 N 10.08 E
Tyringe **41** 56.10 N 13.35 E
Tyringham **207** 42.14 N 73.12 W
Tyrka **88** 54.30 N 107.09 E
Tyrma **89** 50.03 N 132.12 E
Tyrma ≐ **89** 50.29 N 131.18 E
Tyrnovo **78** 48.10 N 27.40 E
Tyrnyauz **84** 43.23 N 42.56 E
Tyrone, Ky., U.S. **218** 38.01 N 84.50 W
Tyrone, N.Y., U.S. **210** 42.25 N 77.03 W
Tyrone, Ok., U.S. **196** 36.57 N 101.03 W
Tyrone, Pa., U.S. **214** 40.40 N 78.14 W
Tyrone Lake ⊜ **281** 42.42 N 83.43 W
Tyrrell, Lake ⊜ **166** 35.21 S 142.50 E
Tyrrellspass **48** 53.23 N 7.22 W
Tyrrhenian Sea (Mare Tirreno) ⊤[2] **36** 40.00 N 12.00 E
Tyrrhenisches Meer → Tyrrhenian Sea ⊤[2] **36** 40.00 N 12.00 E
Tysmenica **78** 48.54 N 24.49 E
Tysnesøy I **26** 60.00 N 5.35 E
Tysons Corner **284c** 38.55 N 77.14 W
Tysons Corner Center ◆[9] **284c** 38.55 N 77.13 W
Tysons Green **284c** 38.55 N 77.15 W
Tysse **26** 60.22 N 5.45 E
Tyssedal **26** 60.07 N 6.34 E
Tysslingen ⊜ **40** 59.19 N 15.02 E
Tystberga **40** 58.52 N 17.15 E
Tystrup Sø ⊜ **41** 55.22 N 11.35 E
Tytherington **262** 53.17 N 2.08 W
Tytuvėnai **76** 55.36 N 23.12 E
Ty Ty **192** 31.28 N 83.38 W
Tyumen' → T'umen' **86** 57.09 N 65.32 E
Tyvrov **78** 49.01 N 28.30 E
Tywa ≐ **54** 53.13 N 14.29 E
Tywardreath **42** 50.22 N 4.41 W
Tywi ≐ **42** 51.46 N 4.22 W
Tywyn **42** 52.35 N 4.05 W
Tzanconeja ≐ **232** 16.35 N 91.35 W
Tzaneen **156** 23.50 S 30.09 E
Tzekung → Zigong **107** 29.24 N 104.47 E
Tzeliutsing → Zigong **107** 29.24 N 104.47 E
Tzimol **236** 16.16 N 92.16 W
Tzintzuntzan ⊥ **234** 19.38 N 101.34 W
Tzucacab **232** 20.04 N 89.03 W
Tzukung → Zigong **107** 29.24 N 104.47 E
Tzupo → Boshan, Zhg. **98** 36.29 N 117.50 E
Tzupo → Zibo, Zhg. **98** 36.47 N 118.01 E

U

Uaboe **174b** 0.31 S 166.55 E
Uac, Mount ∧ **116** 12.12 N 123.40 E
Uaçá ≐ **250** 4.13 N 51.32 W
Uagadugu → Ouagadougou **150** 12.22 N 1.31 W
Uamba **152** 7.12 S 16.25 E
Uamba (Wamba) ≐, Afr. **152** 3.56 S 17.12 E
Uamba ≐, Ang. **152** 7.58 S 17.09 E
Uampochane **158** 26.23 S 32.41 E
Uaoa Bay c **229a** 20.56 N 156.16 W
Uaran → Ouarâne ◆[1] **134** 21.00 N 10.30 W
Uato-Lari **112** 8.45 S 126.34 E
Uatumã ≐ **246** 2.26 S 57.37 W
Uauá **250** 9.50 S 39.28 W
Uaupés (Vaupés) ≐ **246** 0.02 N 67.16 W
Uaxactún ⊥ **232** 17.24 N 89.39 W
Ubá **255** 21.07 S 42.56 W
Uba ≐ **86** 50.15 N 81.41 E
Übach-Palenberg **56** 50.55 N 6.07 E
Ubagan ≐ **86** 54.24 N 64.45 E
Ubai **164** 5.40 S 150.40 E
Ubaidullāhganj **124** 22.59 N 77.36 E
Ubaíra **255** 13.16 S 39.39 W
Ubaitaba **255** 14.18 S 39.20 W
Ubajara **250** 3.51 S 40.56 W
Ubajara, Parque Nacional de ♦ **250** 3.47 S 40.56 W
Ubangi (Oubangui) ≐ **152** 0.30 S 17.42 E
Ubatã **255** 14.12 S 39.31 W
Ubaté **246** 5.19 N 73.49 W
Ubatuba **256** 23.26 S 45.04 W
Ubatuba, Baía de c **256** 23.27 S 45.02 W
Ubauro **120** 28.10 N 69.44 E
Ubay **116** 10.03 N 124.28 E
Ubaye **62** 44.28 N 6.22 E
Ubaye ≐ **62** 44.28 N 6.18 E
Ubayyiḍ, Wādī al- V **128** 32.34 N 43.48 E
Ubby **41** 55.37 N 11.13 E
Ube **96** 33.56 N 131.15 E
Ubed' ≐ **78** 51.27 N 32.29 E
Úbeda **34** 38.01 N 3.22 W
Uberaba **255** 19.45 S 47.55 W
Uberaba ≐ **255** 20.07 S 48.31 W
Uberaba, Lagoa ⊜ **248** 17.30 S 57.45 W
Überackern **60** 48.11 N 12.52 E
Über dem Wind, Inseln → Leeward Islands II **238** 17.00 N 63.00 W
Uberlândia **255** 18.56 S 48.18 W
Überlingen **58** 47.46 N 9.10 E
Überlinger See c **58** 47.45 N 9.09 E
Übersee **64** 47.49 N 12.28 E
Ubiaja **150** 6.38 N 6.21 E
Ubili **154** 1.07 S 26.55 E
Ubin, Pulau I **271c** 1.24 N 103.58 E
Ubinskoje **86** 55.19 N 79.41 E
Ubinskoje, ozero ⊜ **86** 55.30 N 80.05 E
Ubl'a **30** 48.55 N 22.23 E
Ubly **190** 43.42 N 82.55 W
Uboldo **266b** 45.37 N 9.00 E
Ubombo **158** 27.33 S 32.00 E
Ubondo **154** 0.52 S 25.37 E
Ubon Ratchathani **110** 15.14 N 104.54 E
Úborsko **60** 49.20 N 13.09 E
Ubort' ≐ **78** 52.06 N 28.28 E
Ubrique **34** 36.41 N 5.27 W
Ubudiah, Masjid ⊍[1] **114** 4.46 N 100.56 E
Ubundu (Ponthierville) **154** 0.21 S 25.29 E
Ubur-Tochtor **88** 50.06 N 113.37 E
Uča ≐, S.S.S.R. **82** 56.02 N 37.37 E
Uča ≐, S.S.S.R. **265b** 55.56 N 37.57 E
Ucacha **252** 33.02 S 63.31 W
Uč-Adži **128** 38.05 N 62.48 E
Učaly **86** 54.19 N 59.27 E
Učami **74** 63.50 N 96.29 E
Učaral **86** 46.10 N 80.56 E
Ucayali □[4] **248** 9.00 S 74.00 W
Ucayali ≐ **242** 4.30 S 73.27 W
Uccellina, Monti dell' ⋏ **66** 42.38 N 11.05 E
Uccle **50** 50.48 N 4.19 E
Uch **123** 29.14 N 71.03 E
Uchab **156** 19.47 S 17.42 E
Uchāna **124** 29.28 N 76.10 E
Uchaud **62** 43.45 N 4.16 E
Uchee Creek ≐ **192** 32.18 N 84.57 W
Uchihara **94** 36.22 N 140.21 E
Uchihata **270** 34.25 N 135.27 E
Uchiko **96** 33.33 N 132.39 E
Uchi Lake **184** 51.05 N 92.35 W
Uchinada **94** 36.39 N 136.39 E
Uchinomi **96** 34.30 N 134.20 E
Uchinoura **92** 31.16 N 131.05 E
Uchiumi **96** 33.01 N 132.30 E
Uchiura-wan c **92a** 42.20 N 140.40 E
Uchiza **248** 8.29 S 76.23 W
Uchoa **255** 20.56 S 49.13 W
Ucholovo **80** 53.47 N 40.29 E
Uchra ≐ **80** 58.20 N 39.00 E
Uchta, S.S.S.R. **24** 61.12 N 38.32 E
Uchta, S.S.S.R. **24** 63.33 N 53.38 E
Uchte **52** 52.30 N 8.54 E
Uchte ≐ **54** 52.46 N 11.45 E
Uchtoma **76** 60.10 N 38.02 E
Uchtspringe **54** 52.32 N 11.36 E
Učinskij Rybоučastok **86** 60.02 N 65.10 E
Učinskoje vodochranilišče ⊜[1] **82** 56.02 N 37.45 E
Uckange **56** 49.18 N 6.09 E
Ückendorf ◆[8] **263** 51.30 N 7.07 E
Uckermark □[9] **54** 53.10 N 13.35 E
Uckfield **42** 50.58 N 0.06 E
Üçköşe **130** 40.13 N 41.00 E
Uckro **54** 51.51 N 13.37 E
Učkupr'uk **85** 40.33 N 71.04 E
Učkurgan **85** 41.07 N 72.05 E
Ucluelet **182** 48.57 N 125.33 W
Ucon **202** 43.35 N 111.57 W
Ucria **70** 38.03 N 14.53 E
Učterek **85** 41.45 N 73.12 E
Úcua ≐ **152** 8.35 S 13.40 E
Učujevskij Majdan **80** 54.33 N 44.30 E
Učur ≐ **74** 58.48 N 130.35 E
Uda ≐, S.S.S.R. **88** 56.05 N 99.34 E
Uda ≐, S.S.S.R. **88** 51.47 N 107.33 E
Uda ≐, S.S.S.R. **89** 54.42 N 135.14 E
Udaipur **120** 24.35 N 73.41 E
Udaj ≐ **78** 50.05 N 33.07 E
Udala **126** 21.35 N 86.34 E
Udalguri **120** 26.46 N 92.08 E
Udall **198** 37.23 N 97.06 W
Udamalpet **122** 10.35 N 77.15 E
Udankudi **122** 8.26 N 78.01 E
Udaquiola **252** 36.34 S 58.31 W
Udarnyj **89** 49.07 N 142.09 E
Udaypur **124** 26.56 N 86.31 E
Udbina **36** 44.32 N 15.46 E
Udby **41** 55.05 N 11.57 E
Uddeholm **40** 60.01 N 13.37 E
Uddel **52** 52.15 N 5.46 E
Uddevalla **26** 58.21 N 11.55 E
Uddingston **46** 55.50 N 4.06 W
Uddjaur ⊜ **24** 65.55 N 17.49 E
Udel'naja **82** 55.38 N 38.03 E
Udel'naja ◆[8] **265a** 60.01 N 30.19 E
Uden **52** 51.40 N 5.36 E
Udenhout **52** 51.37 N 5.08 E
Uder **56** 51.22 N 10.05 E
Üdersdorf **56** 50.09 N 6.49 E
Udgīr **122** 18.23 N 77.07 E
Udhampur **123** 32.56 N 75.08 E
Udhruḥ **132** 30.20 N 35.36 E
Udi **150** 6.19 N 7.25 E
Udimskij **24** 61.09 N 45.52 E
Udine **64** 46.03 N 13.14 E
Udine □[4] **64** 46.10 N 13.00 E
Udipi **122** 13.21 N 74.45 E
Udjung-kulon, Menandjung >[1] **112** 6.45 S 105.20 E
Udmurtskaja Avtonomnaja Sovetskaja Socialističeskaja Respublika □[3] **80** 57.00 N 53.00 E
Udokan, chrebet ⋏ **88** 56.20 N 118.10 E
Udoml'a **76** 57.52 N 35.01 E
Udone-jima I **94** 34.28 N 139.18 E
Udono **92** 33.44 N 136.01 E
Udon Thani **110** 17.26 N 102.46 E
Udor, Mount ∧ **162** 23.30 S 131.01 E
Udot I **175c** 7.23 N 151.43 E
Udskaja guba c **89** 54.50 N 135.45 E
Udskoje **89** 54.32 N 134.26 E
Udubo **146** 11.57 N 10.38 E
Udy **78** 50.24 N 36.03 E
Udyl', ozero ⊜ **89** 52.06 N 139.48 E
Udža **74** 71.14 N 117.10 E
Udžary **84** 40.31 N 47.39 E
Uebigau **54** 51.35 N 13.18 E
Uebonti **112** 0.55 S 121.38 E
Uebonti, Teluk c **112** 0.50 S 121.45 E
Uecker ≐ **54** 53.45 N 14.04 E
Ueckeritz **54** 54.00 N 14.02 E
Ueckermünde **54** 53.44 N 14.03 E
Ueckermünder Heide ◆[3] **54** 53.40 N 14.10 E
Ueda **94** 36.24 N 138.16 E
Uedem **52** 51.40 N 6.16 E
Uedesheim ◆[8] **263** 51.10 N 6.48 E
Uegō **268** 35.13 N 139.56 E
Ueharu **175d** 24.25 N 123.46 E
Uehlfeld **56** 49.40 N 10.43 E
Uele ≐ **136** 4.09 N 22.26 E
Uelen **180** 66.10 N 169.48 W

ENGLISH Name	Page	Lat.°′	Long.°′

Uel'kal' **180** 65.32 N 179.17 W
Uelsen **52** 52.30 N 6.53 E
Uelzen, B.R.D. **52** 52.58 N 10.33 E
Uelzen, B.R.D. **263** 51.33 N 7.44 E
Ueno, Nihon **94** 36.05 N 138.47 E
Ueno, Nihon **94** 34.45 N 136.08 E
Ueno, Nihon **270** 34.53 N 135.14 E
Uenohara **94** 35.37 N 139.07 E
Ueno Park ♦ **268** 35.43 N 139.46 E
Uenoshiba **270** 34.33 N 135.28 E
Uerdingen ◆[8] **263** 51.21 N 6.39 E
Uere ≐ **154** 3.42 N 25.24 E
Uetersen **52** 53.41 N 9.39 E
Uettingen **56** 49.48 N 9.43 E
Uetz **264a** 52.28 N 12.56 E
Uetze **52** 52.28 N 10.11 E
Ufa **86** 54.44 N 55.56 E
Ufa ≐ **86** 54.40 N 56.00 E
Ufala, Punta > **70** 38.22 N 14.59 E
Uffculme **42** 50.54 N 3.20 W
Uffenheim **56** 49.32 N 10.14 E
Ufita ≐ **68** 41.09 N 14.56 E
Ufra **128** 40.00 N 53.02 E
Uft'uga ≐ **76** 59.46 N 39.21 E
Ugab ≐ **156** 21.08 S 13.40 E
Ugak Bay c **180** 57.25 N 152.45 W
Ugāle **76** 57.16 N 22.02 E
Ugalla ≐ **154** 5.08 S 30.42 E
Ugamskij chrebet ⋏ **85** 42.00 N 70.20 E
Uganda □[1] **154** 1.00 N 32.00 E
Uganik Island I **180** 57.53 N 153.28 W
Ugârčin **38** 43.06 N 24.25 E
Ugarit ⊥ **130** 35.35 N 35.45 E
Ugashik **180** 57.32 N 157.25 W
Ugashik Bay c **180** 57.34 N 157.38 W
Ugatkyn ≐ **180** 68.24 N 171.30 E
Ugento **68** 39.56 N 18.10 E
Ugep **150** 5.48 N 8.05 E
Ugerløse **41** 55.35 N 11.40 E
Uggiano la Chiesa **68** 40.06 N 18.27 E
Ughaybish **140** 10.52 N 31.05 E
Ughelli **150** 5.29 N 5.59 E
Ugie **158** 31.10 S 28.13 E
Ugie ≐ **46** 57.30 N 1.47 W
Ugíjar **34** 36.57 N 3.03 W
Ugine **62** 45.45 N 6.25 E
Uglegorsk, S.S.S.R. **83** 48.19 N 38.17 E
Uglegorsk, S.S.S.R. **89** 49.02 N 142.03 E
Uglekamensk **89** 43.13 N 133.11 E
Uglezavodsk **89** 47.21 N 142.38 E
Uglič **76** 57.32 N 38.19 E
Ugljan, Otok I **36** 44.05 N 15.10 E
Uglovaja **80** 57.01 N 52.57 E
Uglovka **76** 58.14 N 33.31 E
Uglovoje **89** 43.20 N 132.06 E
Uglovskoje **86** 51.23 N 80.12 E
Ugly-Zavod **78** 52.11 N 32.53 E
Ugnev **78** 50.23 N 23.44 E
Ugodiči **80** 57.10 N 39.30 E
Ugodskij Zavod **82** 55.02 N 36.45 E
Ugol'naja, buchta c **180** 63.00 N 179.20 E
Ugolnyy **180** 62.58 N 179.17 E
Ugoma ∧ **154** 4.00 S 28.45 E
Ugovizza **64** 46.31 N 13.29 E
Ugra **76** 54.47 N 34.17 E
Ugra ≐ **82** 54.30 N 36.07 E
Ugrojedy **78** 50.52 N 35.17 E
Ugr'umovo **82** 55.09 N 37.40 E
Ugtaal Cajdam **88** 48.17 N 105.25 E
Uguj **86** 56.02 N 76.03 E
Ug'ut **85** 41.24 N 74.50 E
Ugyak, Cape > **180** 58.17 N 154.04 W
Uh (Už) ≐ **30** 48.34 N 22.00 E
Uha-dong **98** 40.41 N 125.38 E
Uḥayjibah, Jabal al- ∧ **132** 30.11 N 34.33 E
Uherčice **61** 48.55 N 15.38 E
Uherské Hradiště **30** 49.05 N 17.28 E
Uherský Brod **30** 49.02 N 17.39 E
Uhingen **56** 48.42 N 9.35 E
Úhlava ≐ **60** 49.43 N 13.23 E
Uhlenhorst **156** 23.45 S 17.55 E
Ühlingen **58** 47.43 N 8.19 E
Uhlman Lake ⊜ **184** 56.40 N 98.23 W
Uhlstädt **54** 50.44 N 11.28 E
Uhrichsville **214** 40.23 N 81.20 W
Uhyst, D.D.R. **54** 51.11 N 14.13 E
Uhyst, D.D.R. **54** 51.24 N 14.30 E
Uiche **152** 12.03 S 21.02 E
Ui-do I **98** 34.37 N 125.51 E
Uig **46** 57.35 N 6.22 W
Uíge **152** 7.37 S 15.03 E
Uíge □[5] **152** 7.00 S 15.30 E
Ŭijŏngbu **98** 37.44 N 127.03 E
Ŭiju **98** 40.12 N 124.32 E
Uil **86** 49.05 N 54.40 E
Uil ≐ **80** 48.36 N 52.30 E
Uilpata, gora ∧ **84** 42.48 N 43.48 E
Uimaharju **26** 62.55 N 30.15 E
Uiñaimarca, Lago ⊜ **248** 16.20 S 68.50 W
Uinebona ≐ **246** 5.04 N 63.01 W
Uinskoje **86** 56.53 N 56.35 E
Uinta ≐ **200** 40.14 N 109.51 W
Uintah and Ouray Indian Reservation ◆[4] **200** 40.20 N 110.20 W
Uinta Mountains ⋏ **200** 40.45 N 110.05 W
Uiraúna **250** 6.31 S 38.25 W
Uis **156** 21.08 S 14.49 E
Ŭisŏng **98** 36.22 N 128.41 E
Uitenhage **158** 33.40 S 25.28 E
Uitgeest **52** 52.32 N 4.43 E
Uithoorn **52** 52.14 N 4.50 E
Uithuizen **52** 53.24 N 6.40 E
Uithuizermeeden **52** 53.24 N 6.42 E
Uitspanning **158** 26.46 S 29.56 E
Uj ≐, S.S.S.R. **86** 54.17 N 64.58 E
Uj ≐, S.S.S.R. **86** 57.06 N 74.12 E
Ujae I[1] **14** 9.05 N 165.40 E
Ujaly **86** 44.37 N 60.57 E
Ujandina ≐ **74** 68.23 N 145.50 E
Ujar **86** 55.48 N 94.20 E
Ujarrás ⊥ **236** 9.51 N 83.50 W
Ujedinenija, ostrov I **72** 77.28 N 82.28 E
Ujelang I[1] **14** 9.49 N 160.55 E
Ujemskij **24** 64.29 N 40.50 E
Újezd, Česko. **54** 50.03 N 14.44 E
Újezd, Česko. **60** 49.26 N 13.27 E
Újezd u Brna **61** 49.06 N 16.45 E
Újfehértó **30** 47.48 N 21.40 E
Ujgursaj **85** 40.53 N 71.03 E
Ujhāni **124** 28.01 N 79.01 E
Uji **96** 34.53 N 135.48 E
Uji ≐ **96** 34.53 N 135.42 E
Uji-guntō II **92** 31.11 N 129.27 E
Ujiie **94** 36.41 N 139.58 E
Ujiji **154** 4.55 S 29.41 E
Uji-tawara **96** 34.51 N 135.52 E
Uji-yamada → Ise **94** 34.29 N 136.42 E
Ujjain **120** 23.11 N 75.46 E
Újkér **61** 47.28 N 16.49 E
ʿUjmān **128** 25.25 N 55.27 E
Ujongtankayji **114** 3.32 N 97.13 E
Újpest ◆[8] **264c** 47.34 N 19.06 E
Ujście **30** 53.04 N 16.43 E
Ujskoje **86** 54.22 N 60.00 E
Ujum **85** 38.22 N 70.51 E
Ujung **112** 7.04 S 120.46 E
Ujungbatu **114** 0.43 N 100.31 E
Ujungberung **115a** 6.55 S 107.42 E
Ujunggading **110** 0.16 N 99.33 E
Ujunggenteng **115a** 7.22 S 106.24 E
Ujunglamuru **112** 4.40 S 119.58 E
Ujung Pandang (Makasar) **112** 5.07 S 119.24 E
Újvidék → Novi Sad **38** 45.15 N 19.50 E
Uk **88** 55.04 N 98.52 E
Uka, Nihon **174m** 26.48 N 128.14 E
Uka, S.S.S.R. **74** 57.50 N 162.06 E
Ukamas **158** 28.02 S 19.45 E
Ukara Island I **154** 1.50 S 33.03 E
ʿUkāsh, Wādī V **128** 34.18 N 40.42 E
Ukerewe Island I **154** 2.03 S 33.00 E
Ukhayḍir, Wādī V **132** 30.55 N 37.01 E

DEUTSCH Name	Seite	Breite°′	Länge°′ E = Ost

Ukhra **126** 23.39 N 87.14 E
Ukhrul **120** 25.07 N 94.22 E
Ukhta → Uchta **24** 63.33 N 53.38 E
Ukiah, Ca., U.S. **204** 39.09 N 123.12 W
Ukiah, Or., U.S. **202** 45.08 N 118.55 W
Ukibaru-jima I **174m** 26.18 N 128.00 E
Ukiha **96** 33.19 N 130.47 E
Uki Ni Masi Island I **175e** 10.15 S 161.45 E
Ukmergė **76** 55.15 N 24.45 E
Ukolnoi Island I **180** 55.14 N 161.34 W
Ukraine → Ukrainskaja Sovetskaja Socialističeskaja Respublika □[3] **78** 49.00 N 32.00 E
Ukrainka **86** 54.39 N 71.20 E
Ukrainsk **83** 48.06 N 37.18 E
Ukrainskaja Sovetskaja Socialističeskaja Respublika □[3] **78** 49.00 N 32.00 E
Ukrina ≐ **36** 45.05 N 17.56 E
Uks'anskoje **86** 55.57 N 63.01 E
Uktuz **86** 55.38 N 68.30 E
Uktym **24** 62.38 N 48.52 E
Uku **152** 11.24 S 14.15 E
Ukui **112** 0.09 S 102.11 E
Ukurejskij **88** 52.24 N 116.49 E
Ukuti **154** 3.39 N 33.32 E
Ukyō ◆[8] **270** 35.03 N 135.42 E
Ukyr **88** 49.28 N 108.52 E
Ula, India **272b** 22.43 N 88.33 E
Ula, Tür. **130** 37.05 N 28.26 E
Ula ≐ **86** 54.40 N 56.00 E
Ulaanbaatar **88** 47.55 N 106.53 E
Ulaanbaatar □[8] **88** 47.55 N 106.53 E
Ulaanbadrach **102** 44.07 N 110.11 E
Ulaan Chus **86** 49.02 N 89.23 E
Ulaangom **86** 49.58 N 92.02 E
Ulaan nuur ⊜ **102** 44.30 N 103.35 E
Ulaan Tajga ⋏ **88** 50.45 N 98.30 E
ʿUlab, Ṭaraq al- ⋏[2] **130** 33.55 N 38.18 E
Ula-Chuduk **80** 47.39 N 45.34 E
Ulak Island I **181a** 51.22 N 179.00 W
Ulakmedan **114** 2.43 N 99.38 E
Ulamba **152** 9.07 S 23.40 E
Ulamona **164** 5.00 S 151.15 E
Ulan **102** 36.59 N 98.26 E
Ulan Bator → Ulaanbaatar **88** 47.55 N 106.53 E
Ulanbel' **86** 44.48 N 71.10 E
Ulan Buh Shamo ◆[2] **102** 40.00 N 106.30 E
Ulan-Burgasy, chrebet ⋏ **88** 52.45 N 109.00 E
Ulan-Erge **80** 46.19 N 44.53 E
Ulang ≐ **236** 14.27 N 83.14 W
Ulanhot → Horqin Youyi Qianqi **89** 46.05 N 122.05 E
Ulānia **126** 22.12 N 90.29 E
Ulanov **78** 49.42 N 28.08 E
Ulanovo **78** 51.46 N 34.18 E
Ulanovskij **82** 54.04 N 37.51 E
Ulanów **30** 50.30 N 22.16 E
Ulansuhai Nur ⊜ **102** 40.56 N 108.49 E
Ulan-Ude **88** 51.50 N 107.37 E
Ulan-Ušotej **88** 50.45 N 105.29 E
Ulāpāra **126** 24.19 N 89.34 E
Ulaş **130** 39.27 N 37.03 E
Ul'ašovo **24** 65.27 N 56.57 E
Ulatis Creek ≐ **226** 38.18 N 121.00 W
Ul'atuj **88** 51.09 N 116.14 E
Ulawa Island I **175e** 9.46 S 161.57 E
Ulaya **154** 7.04 S 36.54 E
Ułazów **30** 50.17 N 23.00 E
Ul'ba **86** 50.16 N 83.22 E
Ul'banskij zaliv c **89** 53.45 N 137.50 E
Ulchin **98** 36.59 N 129.23 E
Ul'chun-Partija **88** 49.56 N 112.46 E
Ulcinj **38** 41.55 N 19.11 E
Ulco **158** 28.21 S 24.15 E
Ulcombe **260** 51.12 N 0.39 E
Ulcumayo **248** 11.01 S 75.55 W
Uldum **41** 55.51 N 9.36 E
Uldz ≐ **88** 49.56 N 115.31 E
Uleåborg → Oulu **26** 65.01 N 25.28 E
Ulefoss **26** 59.17 N 9.16 E
Ulen **198** 47.04 N 96.15 W
Ulety **88** 51.22 N 112.29 E
Ulfborg **26** 56.16 N 8.20 E
Ulft **52** 51.54 N 6.23 E
Ulgajsyn **86** 49.38 N 60.17 E
Ulgueira **266c** 38.47 N 9.28 W
Ulhās ≐ **272c** 19.13 N 73.01 E
Ulhāsnagar **122** 19.13 N 73.07 E
Uliast **86** 48.57 N 91.17 E
Uliastaj (Džavchlant) **88** 47.45 N 96.49 E
Úlice **60** 49.45 N 13.09 E
Ulindi ≐ **154** 1.40 S 25.52 E
Ulingan **164** 4.30 S 145.25 E
Ulithi I[1] **108** 9.58 N 139.40 E
Ulja **74** 58.51 N 141.50 E
Uljanino **82** 55.21 N 38.26 E
Uljanovka, S.S.S.R. **76** 59.38 N 30.46 E
Uljanovka, S.S.S.R. **78** 48.20 N 30.13 E
Uljanovka, S.S.S.R. **78** 50.58 N 34.18 E
Uljanovo, S.S.S.R. **76** 53.43 N 35.32 E
Uljanovo, S.S.S.R. **85** 40.07 N 68.30 E
Uljanovsk **80** 54.20 N 48.24 E
Uljanovskoje, S.S.S.R. **86** 50.02 N 73.42 E
Uljanovskoje, S.S.S.R. **89** 46.17 N 142.13 E
Ul'kajak ≐ **86** 48.54 N 62.00 E
Ul'kan **88** 57.14 N 107.19 E
Ul'kan ≐ **88** 55.53 N 107.45 E
Ul'ken-Karoj, ozero ⊜ **86** 54.00 N 71.58 E
Ulla **76** 55.14 N 29.15 E
Ulla ≐, Esp. **34** 42.39 N 8.44 W
Ulla ≐, S.S.S.R. **76** 55.14 N 29.14 E
Ulladulla **170** 35.21 S 150.29 E
Ullapool **46** 57.54 N 5.10 W
Ullastrell **266d** 41.31 N 1.58 E
Üllendahl ◆[8] **263** 51.19 N 7.18 E
Ullerslev **41** 55.22 N 10.40 E
Ullervad **40** 58.40 N 13.52 E
Ullin **194** 37.17 N 89.11 W
Üllő **264c** 47.23 N 19.21 E
Ullswater ⊜ **44** 54.34 N 2.54 W
Ullučaj ≐ **84** 42.18 N 48.08 E
Ullún **252** 31.28 S 68.42 W
Ullŭng-do I **92** 37.29 N 130.52 E
Ullvettern ⊜ **40** 59.27 N 14.16 E
Ullvi **40** 59.42 N 16.37 E
Ulm, B.R.D. **58** 48.24 N 10.00 E
Ulm, Mt., U.S. **202** 47.25 N 111.30 W
Ulma **38** 47.53 N 25.18 E
Ul'ma ≐ **89** 51.54 N 129.18 E
Ulmarra **166** 29.37 S 153.02 E
Ulmen **56** 50.13 N 6.59 E
Ulmeni **38** 45.04 N 26.39 E
Ulmer, Mount ∧ **9** 77.35 S 86.09 W
Ulmeu-Meisereich **56** 50.13 N 6.58 E
Ulongué **154** 14.37 S 34.19 E
Ulpur **126** 23.04 N 89.50 E
Ulricehamn **26** 57.47 N 13.25 E
Ulrichskirchen **61** 48.24 N 16.29 E
Ulrichstein **56** 50.34 N 9.11 E
Ulrum **52** 53.22 N 6.20 E
Ulsan **98** 35.34 N 129.19 E
Ulsta **46** 60.30 N 1.09 W
Ulsteinvik **26** 62.20 N 5.53 E
Ulster **210** 41.51 N 76.30 W
Ulster □[6] **210** 41.56 N 74.00 W
Ulster □[9] **48** 54.35 N 7.00 W
Ulster ≐ **56** 50.51 N 9.59 E
Ulster Canal ≍ **48** 54.08 N 7.22 W
Ultimo, Val D' V **64** 46.35 N 11.00 E
Ultraoriental, Cordillera (Serra do Divisor) ⋏ **248** 8.20 S 73.30 W
Ulu, Indon. **112** 2.45 N 125.24 E

Symbols in the index entries represent the broad categories identified in the key at the right. Symbols with superior numbers (⋏[1]) identify subcategories (see complete key on page *I · 1).*

Kartensymbole in dem Registerverzeichnis stellen die rechts in Schlüssel erklärten Kategorien dar. Symbole mit hochgestellten Ziffern (⋏[1]) bezeichnen Unterabteilungen einer Kategorie (vgl. vollständiger Schlüssel auf Seite *I · 1).*

Los símbolos incluídos en el texto del índice representan las grandes categorias identificadas con la clave a la derecha. Los símbolos con numeros en su parte superior (⋏[1]) identifican las subcategorías (véase la clave completa en la página *I · 1).*

Les symboles de l'index représentent les catégories indiquées dans la légende à droite. Les symboles suivis d'un indice (⋏[1]) représentent des sous-catégories (voir légende complète à la page *I · 1).*

Os símbolos incluídos no texto do índice representam as grandes categorias identificadas com a chave à direita. Os símbolos com números em sua parte superior (⋏[1]) identificam as subcategorias (veja-se a chave completa à página *I · 1).*

∧ Mountain	Berg	Montaña	Montagne	Montanha
⋏ Mountains	Berge	Montañas	Montagnes	Montanhas
)(Pass	Pass	Paso	Col	Passo
V Valley, Canyon	Tal, Cañon	Valle, Cañón	Vallée, Canyon	Vale, Canhão
≚ Plain	Ebene	Llano	Plaine	Planície
> Cape	Kap	Cabo	Cap	Cabo
I Island	Insel	Isla	Île	Ilha
II Islands	Inseln	Islas	Îles	Ilhas
⊥ Other Topographic Features	Andere Topographische Objekte	Otros Elementos Topográficos	Autres données topographiques	Outros acidentes topográficos

ESPAÑOL Nombre / FRANÇAIS Nom / PORTUGUÊS Nome	Página / Page	Lat. °′	Long. °′ W = Oeste / Ouest
Ulu, S.S.S.R.	74	60.19 N	127.24 E
Ulu, Sūd.	140	10.43 N	33.29 E
Ulúa ≃	236	15.53 N	87.44 W
Ulubāria	126	22.28 N	88.06 E
Ulubat Gölü ⊜	130	40.10 N	28.35 E
Ulubey	130	38.25 N	29.18 E
Uluborlu	130	38.05 N	30.28 E
Ulu Dağ ∧	130	40.04 N	29.13 E
Uludāngar	272b	22.51 N	88.31 E
Ulugan Bay ⊂	116	10.07 N	118.47 E
Ulugqat	85	39.48 N	74.21 E
Uluinggalau ∧	175g	16.54 S	179.59 E
Ulujul ≃	86	57.46 N	85.30 E
Ulukışla	130	37.33 N	34.30 E
Ulul I	14	8.35 N	149.40 E
Ulu Laho, Bukit ∧	114	5.43 N	101.27 E
Ulunchan	88	54.51 N	111.02 E
Ulundi	158	28.17 S	31.26 E
Ulunga	89	46.31 N	136.56 E
Ulungur ≃	86	46.59 N	87.27 E
Ulungur Hu ⊜	86	47.15 N	87.20 E
Ulurijskij Golec, gora ∧	88	50.12 N	111.45 E
Uluru National Park ♠	162	25.20 S	131.00 E
Ulus	130	41.35 N	32.39 E
Ulusara	126	24.16 N	90.36 E
Ulut ≃	116	12.00 N	125.27 E
Ulutau	86	48.39 N	67.01 E
Ulutau, gora ∧	86	48.39 N	66.56 E
Ulutau, gory ⋏	86	49.00 N	67.00 E
Ulu Tiram	114	1.36 N	103.49 E
Ulu Yam	114	3.27 N	101.38 E
Ulva	272c	18.59 N	73.02 E
Ulva I	46	56.29 N	6.14 W
Ulvenhout	52	51.34 N	4.48 E
Ulverston	44	54.12 N	3.06 W
Ulverstone	166	41.09 S	146.10 E
Ulvöarna II	26	63.01 N	18.40 E
Ulvshale › [1]	41	55.02 N	12.16 E
Ulvshyttan	40	60.18 N	15.22 E
Ulvsund ʉ	41	54.59 N	12.11 E
Ulyanovsk → Uljanovsk	80	54.20 N	48.24 E
Ulysses, Ks., U.S.	198	37.34 N	101.21 W
Ulysses, Ne., U.S.	198	41.04 N	97.12 W
Ulysses, Pa., U.S.	214	41.54 N	77.46 W
Uly-Žilanšik ≃	86	48.51 N	63.47 E
Ulzë	38	41.41 N	19.54 E
Uma	89	52.36 N	120.37 E
Umag	64	45.25 N	13.32 E
Umaji	96	33.33 N	134.03 E
Umal'tinskij	89	51.56 N	133.36 E
Umán, Méx.	232	20.53 N	89.45 W
Uman', S.S.S.R.	78	48.44 N	30.14 E
ʿUmān → Oman □ [1]	118	22.00 N	58.00 E
Uman I	175c	7.18 N	151.53 E
Umanak	176	70.40 N	52.07 W
Umanak Fjord ⊂ [2]	176	70.55 N	53.00 W
Umancevo	80	47.44 N	44.16 E
Umaralla ≃	171b	36.10 S	149.20 E
Umari	250	6.38 S	38.42 W
ʿUmarī, Qāʿal- ⊜	132	31.42 N	36.57 E
Umaria, India	124	23.32 N	80.50 E
Umaria, India	124	23.48 N	80.56 E
Umarizal	250	5.59 S	37.49 W
Umarkot	120	25.22 N	69.44 E
Umatac	174p	13.18 N	144.39 E
Umatilla, Fl., U.S.	220	28.55 N	81.39 W
Umatilla, Or., U.S.	202	45.55 N	119.20 W
Umatilla ≃	202	45.55 N	119.20 W
Umatilla, Lake ⊜ [1]	202	45.44 N	120.35 W
Umatilla Indian Reservation ⬅ [4]	202	45.41 N	118.31 W
Umayan ≃	116	8.13 N	125.50 E
Umaze	270	34.57 N	135.03 E
Umba	24	66.41 N	34.15 E
Umbagog Lake ⊜	188	44.45 N	71.05 W
Umbai	114	2.10 N	102.20 E
Umbargaon	122	20.12 N	72.45 E
Umbaúba	250	11.22 S	37.39 W
Umbelasha ≃	140	9.51 N	24.50 E
Umbertide	66	43.18 N	12.20 E
Umbogintwini	158	30.00 S	30.58 E
Umboi Island I	164	5.36 S	148.00 E
Umbrail, Pass (Giogo di Santa Maria))(	64	46.34 N	10.25 E
Umbria □ [4]	66	43.00 N	12.30 E
Umbriatico	68	39.21 N	16.55 E
Umbroli	272c	19.11 N	73.06 E
Umbukul	164	2.30 S	150.00 E
Umbuzeiro	250	7.41 S	35.40 W
Umbuzero, ozero ⊜	24	67.43 N	34.25 E
Ume ≃	154	16.40 S	28.26 E
Umeå	26	63.50 N	20.15 E
Umeälven ≃	24	63.47 N	20.16 E
Umedani	270	34.44 N	135.51 E
Umedpur	126	22.31 N	89.59 E
Umfolozi Game Reserve ⬅ [4]	158	28.19 S	31.50 E
Umfors	24	65.56 N	15.00 E
Umfreville Lake ⊜	184	50.18 N	94.45 W
Umfuli ≃	154	17.30 S	29.23 E
Umgungundhlovu ⊥	158	28.27 S	31.28 E
Umguza	154	19.25 S	27.51 E
Umhausen	64	47.08 N	10.56 E
Umhlanga Rocks	158	29.43 S	31.06 E
Umi	96	33.34 N	130.30 E
Umingan	116	15.56 N	120.50 E
Umkomaas	158	30.15 S	30.42 E
Umm ad-Daraj, Jabal ∧	132	32.19 N	35.48 E
Umm ʿAjārim ⩦ [8]	142	30.50 N	32.49 E
Umm al-Abīd	146	27.31 N	15.02 E
Umm al-ʿArāʾis, Wādī V	146	26.26 N	13.55 E
Umm al-Arānib	146	26.08 N	14.45 E
Umm al-Birak	128	23.25 N	39.13 E
Umm al-Ḥawāyā, Jabal ∧	142	28.41 N	31.06 E
Umm al-Jimāl, Khirbat ⊥	132	32.20 N	36.22 E
Umm al-Khashab	144	17.21 N	42.32 E
Umm al-Qaywayn	128	25.35 N	55.34 E
Umm al-Qiṭṭayn	132	32.19 N	36.38 E
Umm al-Quṣūr	142	27.23 N	30.54 E
Ummanz	54	54.28 N	13.10 E
Umm Artah, Wādī V	142	28.41 N	32.37 E
Umm as-Saʿd ⊥	132	33.16 N	36.47 E
Umm Badr	140	14.14 N	27.57 E
Umm Balad, Wādī V	142	27.40 N	32.39 E
Umm Bayyūʿd	140	12.05 N	31.40 E
Umm Bel	140	13.32 N	28.04 E
Umm Boim	140	11.43 N	25.57 E
Umm Dabbī	140	14.37 N	30.23 E
Umm Dam	140	13.45 N	30.59 E
Umm Dhibbān, Sūd.	140	14.14 N	29.37 E
Umm Dhibbān, Sūd.	140	15.26 N	32.51 E
Umm Digulgulaya	140	10.29 N	24.57 E
Umm Dīnār	142	30.12 N	31.04 E
Umm Durmān (Omdurman)	140	15.38 N	32.30 E
Umm el Faḥm	132	32.31 N	35.09 E
Ummeln	52	51.58 N	8.27 E
Ummendorf	54	52.09 N	11.11 E
Umm Habwah, Jabal ∧ [2]	142	27.23 N	31.29 E
Umm Ḥamāṭ	132	31.02 N	35.46 E
Umm Jamālah	140	11.27 N	28.12 E
Umm Kaddādah	140	13.36 N	26.42 E
Umm Khunān	273c	29.55 N	31.15 E
Umm Khushayb, Wādī V	142	30.24 N	32.43 E
Umm Kuwaykah	140	13.00 N	32.17 E
Umm Lajj	128	25.04 N	37.13 E
Umm Marahik, Jabal ∧ [2]	140	13.40 N	26.53 E
Umm Mirdi	140	18.59 N	33.32 E
Umm Mitmān ⩦ [8]	142	30.41 N	32.30 E
Umm Qantur	140	14.17 N	31.22 E
Umm Qurayn	140	9.58 N	28.55 E
Umm Quṣayr	132	31.40 N	35.53 E
Umm Raqm, Jabal ∧	142	30.14 N	31.52 E
Umm Rīshah, Birkat ⊜	142	30.21 N	30.22 E
Umm Rumaylah ⊤ [4]	140	16.55 N	31.40 E
Umm Ruwābah	140	12.54 N	31.13 E
Umm Saggāt, Wādī V	140	15.15 N	23.12 E
Umm Saysabān, Jabal ∧	132	29.45 N	35.10 E
Umm Sayyālah	140	14.25 N	31.10 E
Umm Shalīl	140	10.51 N	23.42 E
Umm Shanqah	140	13.14 N	27.14 E
Umm Shuṭūr	140	7.17 N	33.14 E
Umm Sidr, Wādī V	142	27.54 N	32.33 E
Umm Sughra ⊤ [4]	140	15.03 N	27.12 E
Umm ʿUmayd, Raʾs ∧	142	27.50 N	32.19 E
Umm ʿUmayyid, Biʾr ⊤ [4]	142	27.53 N	32.30 E
Umm ʿUmayyid, Wādī V	142	27.37 N	32.41 E
Umm Urūmah I	128	25.46 N	36.32 E
Umm Walad	132	32.39 N	36.26 E
Umm Zaytah, Jabal ∧ [2]	142	29.49 N	32.16 E
Umnak	180	53.17 N	168.20 W
Umnak Island I	180	53.25 N	168.10 W
Umnak Pass ʉ	180	53.20 N	167.45 W
Umnäs	24	65.24 N	16.10 E
Umniati	154	18.39 S	29.49 E
Umniati ≃	154	17.30 S	29.23 E
Um'ot, S.S.S.R.	80	54.08 N	42.42 E
Um'ot, S.S.S.R.	80	52.31 N	42.58 E
Umpferstedt	54	50.59 N	11.25 E
Umpqua ≃	202	43.42 N	124.03 W
Umpulo	152	12.38 S	17.42 E
ʿUmrān	144	15.50 N	43.56 E
ʿUmrānī, Wādī al- V	142	27.37 N	30.53 E
Umraniye, Tür.	130	38.37 N	30.48 E
Umraniye, Tür.	267b	41.01 N	29.05 E
Umrer	122	20.51 N	79.20 E
Umreth	120	22.42 N	73.07 E
Umsini, Gunung ∧	164	1.22 S	133.45 E
Ŭmsŏng	98	36.56 N	127.41 E
Umstead State Park ♠	192	35.52 N	78.47 W
Umtanum Creek ≃	224	46.52 N	120.35 W
Umtata	158	31.35 S	28.47 E
Umtentweni	158	30.42 S	30.28 E
Umuahia	150	5.33 N	7.29 E
Umuarama	255	23.45 S	53.20 W
Umurlu	130	37.50 N	27.58 E
Umzimkulu	158	30.16 S	29.56 E
Umzingwani ≃	154	22.12 S	29.56 E
Umzinto	158	30.22 S	30.33 E
Una, Bra.	255	15.18 S	39.04 W
Una, India	120	20.49 N	71.02 E
Una, India	123	31.29 N	76.17 E
Una ≃	36	45.16 N	16.55 E
Una, Mount ∧	172	42.13 S	172.35 E
Una, Ribeirão ≃	287b	23.31 S	46.18 W
Unac ≃	36	44.30 N	16.09 E
Uña de Gato	196	25.58 N	99.41 W
Unadilla, Ga., U.S.	192	32.15 N	83.44 W
Unadilla, N.Y., U.S.	210	42.19 N	75.18 W
Unadilla ≃	210	42.20 N	75.25 W
Unaí	255	16.23 S	46.53 W
Unakami	94	35.46 N	140.45 E
Unalakleet	180	63.53 N	160.47 W
Unalaska	180	53.52 N	166.32 W
Unalaska Island I	180	53.45 N	166.45 W
Unanderra	170	34.27 S	150.52 E
Unango	154	12.50 S	35.20 E
Únanov	61	48.54 N	16.04 E
Unao	124	25.35 N	78.36 E
Unare ≃	246	10.03 N	65.14 W
Unauna, Pulau I	112	0.10 S	121.35 E
Unayyir, Ḥarrat al- ⩦ [9]	128	25.20 N	37.45 E
ʿUnayzah	128	26.06 N	43.56 E
ʿUnayzah, Jabal ∧	132	30.30 N	35.47 E
Unazuki	94	36.49 N	137.35 E
Uncasville	207	41.26 N	72.06 W
Unchahra	124	24.23 N	80.47 E
Ŭnch'ŏn	98	38.34 N	125.26 E
Uncia	248	18.27 S	66.37 W
Uncompahgre ≃	200	38.45 N	108.06 W
Uncompahgre Peak ∧	200	38.04 N	107.28 W
Uncompahgre Plateau ⋏ [1]	200	38.30 N	108.25 W
Uncukul'	84	42.42 N	46.48 E
Unda	88	51.42 N	116.56 E
Unda ≃	88	51.25 N	116.05 E
Unden ⊜	40	58.47 N	14.26 E
Undenäs	40	58.39 N	14.25 E
Underberg	158	29.50 S	29.22 E
Under River	260	51.15 N	0.14 E
Undersåker	26	63.20 N	13.23 E
Underwood, In., U.S.	218	38.36 N	85.46 W
Underwood, N.D., U.S.	198	47.27 N	101.08 W
Underwood, Wa., U.S.	224	45.43 N	121.31 W
Undløse	41	55.36 N	11.35 E
Undory	80	54.37 N	48.25 E
Undu, Tanjung ›	115b	10.05 S	120.51 E
Undu Point ›	175g	16.08 S	179.57 W
Undva nina ›	76	58.32 N	21.55 E
Unea Island I	164	4.55 S	149.10 E
Uneča	76	52.50 N	32.40 E
Uneča ≃	76	52.50 N	31.56 E
Uneiuxi ≃	246	0.37 S	65.34 W
Úněšov	60	49.53 N	13.09 E
Unga Island I	180	55.15 N	160.45 W
Ungama Bay ⊂	154	2.45 S	40.20 E
Ungaran	115a	7.07 S	110.24 E
Ungarie	166	33.38 S	146.58 E
Ungarn → Hungary □ [1]	30	47.00 N	20.00 E
Ungava, Péninsule d' › [1]	176	60.00 N	74.00 W
Ungava Bay ⊂	176	59.30 N	67.30 W
Ungch'ŏn	98	35.07 N	128.44 E
Ungeny	78	47.12 N	27.48 E
Unggi	98	42.20 N	130.24 E
Ungurkuj	88	50.27 N	106.58 E
Ungvár → Užgorod	78	48.37 N	22.18 E
Unhos	266c	38.50 N	9.07 W
Unhošt'	54	50.04 N	14.08 E
Uni	80	57.46 N	51.30 E
União	250	4.35 S	42.52 W
União da Vitória	252	26.13 S	51.05 W
União dos Palmares	250	9.10 S	36.02 W
Unica	24	62.38 N	34.38 E
Unicoi	192	36.11 N	82.20 W
Unicorn Branch ≃	208	39.15 N	75.52 W
Unidad Santa Fe ⬅ [8]	286a	19.23 N	99.15 W
Uniejów	30	51.58 N	18.49 E
Unieux	62	45.24 N	4.16 E
Unije, Otok I	36	44.38 N	14.15 E
Unimak Island I	180	54.50 N	164.00 W
Unimak Pass ʉ	180	54.35 N	164.43 W
Unini ≃	246	1.41 S	61.31 W
Unión, Arg.	252	35.09 S	65.57 W
Union, On., Can.	212	42.42 N	81.12 W
Unión, Para.	252	24.48 S	56.33 W
Union, Il., U.S.	216	42.14 N	88.33 W
Union, Ia., U.S.	190	42.14 N	93.03 W
Union, Ky., U.S.	218	38.56 N	84.40 W
Union, La., U.S.	194	30.06 N	90.54 W
Union, Ms., U.S.	194	32.34 N	89.07 W
Union, Mo., U.S.	219	38.26 N	91.00 W
Union, N.J., U.S.	210	40.41 N	74.15 W
Union, Oh., U.S.	218	39.53 N	84.18 W
Union, Or., U.S.	202	45.12 N	117.51 W
Union, S.C., U.S.	192	34.42 N	81.37 W
Union, Wa., U.S.	224	47.21 N	123.06 W
Union, W.V., U.S.	192	37.35 N	80.32 W
Union □ [6], In., U.S.	218	39.38 N	84.56 W
Union □ [6], N.J., U.S.	208	40.40 N	74.11 W
Union □ [6], Oh., U.S.	214	40.18 N	83.19 W
Union □ [6], Pa., U.S.	210	40.58 N	76.54 W
Unión ⬅ [8]	258	34.53 S	56.08 W
Union Bay	182	49.35 N	124.53 W
Union Beach	208	40.26 N	74.10 W
Union Bridge	208	39.34 N	77.10 W
Union Center	210	42.09 N	76.04 W
Union City, Ca., U.S.	226	37.35 N	122.04 W
Union City, Ga., U.S.	192	33.35 N	84.32 W
Union City, In., U.S.	194	40.07 N	85.05 W
Union City, Mi., U.S.	216	42.04 N	85.09 W
Union City, N.J., U.S.	276	40.46 N	74.01 W
Union City, Oh., U.S.	216	40.11 N	84.48 W
Union City, Pa., U.S.	214	41.53 N	79.50 W
Union City, Tn., U.S.	194	36.25 N	89.03 W
Union City Dam ⬅ [6]	214	41.55 N	79.54 W
Uniondale, S. Afr.	158	33.40 S	23.08 E
Uniondale, In., U.S.	216	40.50 N	85.15 W
Uniondale, N.Y., U.S.	276	40.42 N	73.35 W
Union Dale, Pa., U.S.	210	41.43 N	75.30 W
Unión de Repúblicas Socialistas Soviéticas → Union of Soviet Socialist Republics □ [1]	72	60.00 N	80.00 E
Unión de Reyes	240p	22.48 N	81.32 W
Unión de San Antonio	234	21.06 N	101.58 W
Union des Émirats Arabes → United Arab Emirates □ [1]	128	24.00 N	54.00 E
Union des Républiques socialistes soviétiques → Union of Soviet Socialist Republics □ [1]	72	60.00 N	80.00 E
Unión de Tula	234	19.58 N	104.16 W
Union Flat Creek ≃	202	46.50 N	117.59 W
Union Gap	202	46.33 N	120.28 W
Union Grove, Tx., U.S.	222	32.34 N	94.55 W
Union Grove, Wi., U.S.	216	42.41 N	88.03 W
Unión Hidalgo	234	16.28 N	94.50 W
Union Hill	210	43.13 N	77.23 W
Union Lake	216	42.36 N	83.26 W
Union Lake ⊜, Mi., U.S.	216	42.03 N	85.11 W
Union Lake ⊜, Mi., U.S.	281	42.37 N	83.26 W
Union Lake ⊜, N.J., U.S.	208	39.25 N	75.03 W
Union Mills	216	41.29 N	86.46 W
Union of Soviet Socialist Republics □ [1], Europe	72	60.00 N	80.00 E
Union of Soviet Socialist Republics □ [1], Europe	74	60.00 N	100.00 E
Union Park	220	28.30 N	81.15 W
Union Pier	216	41.49 N	86.41 W
Union Point	192	33.36 N	83.04 W
Unionport, In., U.S.	218	40.07 N	85.06 W
Unionport, Oh., U.S.	214	40.21 N	80.51 W
Union Seamount ✢ [3]	16	49.35 N	132.45 W
Union Springs, Al., U.S.	194	32.08 N	85.42 W
Union Springs, N.Y., U.S.	210	42.50 N	76.41 W
Union Station ⬅ [5], On., Can.	275b	43.39 N	79.23 W
Union Station ⬅ [5], Ca., U.S.	280	34.04 N	118.14 W
Union Station ⬅ [5], D.C., U.S.	284c	38.54 N	77.00 W
Union Station ⬅ [5], Il., U.S.	278	41.53 N	87.38 W
Uniontown, Al., U.S.	194	32.26 N	87.30 W
Uniontown, Ky., U.S.	194	37.46 N	87.55 W
Uniontown, Md., U.S.	208	39.35 N	77.06 W
Uniontown, Oh., U.S.	214	40.58 N	81.24 W
Uniontown, Pa., U.S.	188	39.54 N	79.44 W
Union Valley Reservoir ⊜ [1]	226	38.50 N	120.26 W
Union Village	207	41.59 N	71.32 W
Unionville, On., Can.	275b	43.52 N	79.18 W
Unionville, Ct., U.S.	207	41.45 N	72.53 W
Unionville, In., U.S.	218	39.14 N	86.25 W
Unionville, Mi., U.S.	190	43.39 N	83.27 W
Unionville, Mo., U.S.	194	40.28 N	93.00 W
Unionville, N.J., U.S.	285	40.01 N	74.46 W
Unionville, N.Y., U.S.	210	41.18 N	74.34 W
Unionville, Oh., U.S.	214	41.47 N	81.00 W
Unionville, Pa., U.S.	285	39.54 N	75.44 W
Unionville Center	214	40.08 N	83.21 W
Uniopolis	216	40.36 N	84.05 W
Unipouheos Indian Reserve ⬅ [4]	184	53.52 N	110.21 W
Unisan	116	13.51 N	121.59 E
United	214	40.13 N	79.29 W
United Arab Emirates □ [1], Asia	118	24.00 N	54.00 E
United Arab Emirates □ [1], Asia	128	24.00 N	54.00 E
United Arab Republic → Egypt □ [1]	140	27.00 N	30.00 E
United Kingdom □ [1], Europe	22	54.00 N	2.00 W
United Kingdom □ [1], Europe	28	54.00 N	2.00 W
United Kingdom Sovereign Base Area ■	130	35.00 N	33.45 E
United Nations Headquarters ᵾ	276	40.45 N	73.58 W
United States □ [1]	178	38.00 N	97.00 W
United States Air Force Academy ■	200	39.00 N	104.55 W
United States Coast Guard Academy ■	207	41.22 N	72.06 W
United States Merchant Marine Academy ᵾ [2]	276	40.48 N	73.46 W
United States Military Academy ■	210	41.23 N	73.58 W
United States Naval Academy ■	208	38.59 N	76.30 W
United States Steel Corporation (Lorain Plant) ᵾ [3], Oh., U.S.	279a	41.27 N	82.07 W
United States Steel Corporation ᵾ [3], Pa., U.S.	279b	40.20 N	79.54 W
United States Steel Corporation ᵾ [3], Pa., U.S.	279b	40.25 N	79.54 W
United States Steel Corporation Fairless Works ᵾ [3]	285	40.09 N	74.45 W
Unity	184	52.27 N	109.10 W
Unity Reservoir ⊜ [1]	279b	40.17 N	79.30 W
Universal City	196	29.32 N	98.17 W
Universal City ᵾ [3]	280	34.09 N	118.21 W
Universal Mall ⬅ [9]	281	42.30 N	83.05 W
Università Degli Studi ᵾ [2]	266b	45.28 N	9.14 E
University	194	34.21 N	89.32 W
University City	219	38.39 N	90.19 W
University Gardens	276	40.46 N	73.43 W
University Heights, Ca., U.S.	226	37.26 N	122.12 W
University Heights, Oh., U.S.	279a	41.29 N	81.32 W
University Park, Il., U.S.	216	41.36 N	87.39 W
University Park, Md., U.S.	284c	38.58 N	76.57 W
University Park, N.M., U.S.	200	32.06 N	106.39 W
University Park, Tx., U.S.	222	32.52 N	96.47 W
University Place	224	47.14 N	122.32 W
University View	218	40.00 N	83.03 W
Unjha	120	23.48 N	72.24 E
Unkel	56	50.35 N	7.13 E
Unken	64	47.39 N	12.43 E
Unkurda	86	55.48 N	59.24 E
Unley	168b	34.57 S	138.35 E
Unna	52	51.32 N	7.41 E
Unna □ [8]	263	51.34 N	7.42 E
ʿUnnāb, Jabal al- ∧	132	29.57 N	36.55 E
ʿUnnāb, Wādī al- V	132	30.11 N	36.39 E
Unnão	124	26.32 N	80.30 E
Unnão □ [5]	124	26.30 N	80.30 E
Uno, Canal Numero ≡	252	36.17 S	57.08 W
Uno, Ilha I	150	11.12 N	16.15 W
Unoke	94	36.43 N	136.42 E
Ŭnp'a	98	38.26 N	125.45 E
Unpenji-san ∧	96	34.02 N	133.44 E
Unqua Point ›	276	40.39 N	73.26 W
Unquillo	252	31.14 S	64.19 W
Ŭnsan	98	39.25 N	126.01 E
Unseburg	54	51.56 N	11.30 E
Unserfrau → Madonna	64	46.43 N	10.52 E
Unsleben	56	50.22 N	10.15 E
Unst I	46a	60.45 N	0.53 W
Unstrut ≃	54	51.10 N	11.48 E
Un't	88	49.07 N	102.50 E
Unten	174m	26.41 N	128.00 E
Unterägeri	58	47.08 N	8.35 E
Unterbach, B.R.D.	263	51.12 N	6.54 E
Unterbäch, Schw.	58	46.17 N	7.48 E
Unter dem Wind, Inseln → Windward Islands II	238	13.00 N	61.00 W
Unterelchingen	58	48.27 N	10.07 E
Unterföhring	60	48.12 N	11.38 E
Unterfranken □ [5]	56	50.10 N	10.00 E
Untergermaringen	58	47.56 N	10.40 E
Unterglottertal	58	48.03 N	7.56 E
Untergriesbach	60	48.35 N	13.40 E
Untergröningen	56	48.55 N	9.53 E
Untergrüne	263	51.22 N	7.39 E
Unterhaching	60	48.04 N	11.38 E
Unterhausen	58	48.26 N	9.16 E
Unterinntal V	64	47.24 N	11.47 E
Unterjettenberg	64	47.41 N	12.49 E
Unterlaa ⬅ [8]	264b	48.08 N	16.25 E
Unterlüss	52	52.50 N	10.17 E
Untermauerbach	264b	48.14 N	16.12 E
Untermünkheim	56	49.09 N	9.44 E
Untermünstertal	58	47.51 N	7.46 E
Unteröwisheim	56	49.08 N	8.40 E
Unterrath ⬅ [8]	263	51.16 N	6.47 E
Unterschächen	58	46.52 N	8.47 E
Unterschwaningen	56	49.04 N	10.37 E
Unterseen	58	46.41 N	7.51 E
Untertauern	64	47.18 N	13.30 E
Unterterzen	58	47.07 N	9.15 E
Unterthingau	58	47.46 N	10.31 E
Unterueckersee ⊜	54	53.17 N	13.51 E
Unteruhldingen	58	47.43 N	9.14 E
Unterwasser	58	47.12 N	9.19 E
Unterweissbach	54	50.37 N	11.10 E
Unterwellenborn	54	50.39 N	11.26 E
Unterwössen	64	47.44 N	12.27 E
Unterzeiring	61	47.15 N	14.31 E
Untraverket	40	60.25 N	17.18 E
Ünye	130	41.08 N	37.17 E
Unža	80	58.01 N	44.01 E
Unža ≃	80	57.20 N	43.08 E
Unzen-Amakusa-kokuritsu-kōen ♠	92	32.45 N	130.17 E
Unzen-dake ∧	92	32.45 N	130.17 E
Unže-Pavinskaja	86	58.53 N	64.02 E
Uojan	88	56.07 N	111.38 E
Uono ≃	94	37.15 N	138.53 E
Uo-shima I	96	34.11 N	133.19 E
Uozu	94	36.48 N	137.24 E
Upa ≃	76	54.02 N	36.15 E
Upala	236	10.47 N	85.02 W
Upanema	250	5.38 S	37.15 W
Upano ≃	246	2.45 S	78.12 W
Upardāng Garhi	124	27.46 N	84.34 E
Upata	246	8.01 N	62.24 W
Upatoi Creek ≃	192	32.22 N	84.58 W
Upavon	42	51.18 N	1.49 W
Ŭpchŏ-ri	98	37.53 N	125.09 E
Upchurch	260	51.23 N	0.39 E
Upemba, Lac ⊜	154	8.36 S	26.26 E
Upemba, Parc National de l' ♠	154	9.10 S	26.35 E
Upernavik	176	72.47 N	56.10 W
Upgant-Schott	52	53.30 N	7.16 E
Uphal	140	6.58 N	34.16 E
Upham	198	48.34 N	100.43 W
Up Holland	262	53.33 N	2.44 W
Uphusen	52	53.01 N	8.58 E
Upi	116	6.57 N	124.09 E
Upía ≃	246	4.18 N	72.45 W
Upington	158	28.25 S	21.15 E
Upire ≃	246	11.27 N	68.58 W
Upland, Ca., U.S.	228	34.05 N	117.38 W
Upland, In., U.S.	216	40.28 N	85.29 W
Upland, Ne., U.S.	198	40.19 N	98.54 W
Upland, Pa., U.S.	285	39.51 N	75.23 W
Upleta	120	21.44 N	70.17 E
Upnuk Lake ⊜	180	60.21 N	158.58 W
Upolu I	175a	13.55 S	171.45 W
Upolu Point ›	229d	20.16 N	155.51 W
Uporovo	86	56.18 N	66.17 E
Upper □ [4]	150	10.30 N	1.30 W
Upper Arlington	218	40.00 N	83.03 W
Upper Arrow Lake ⊜	182	50.30 N	117.55 W
Upper Artichoke Reservoir ⊜ [1]	283	42.48 N	70.57 W
Upper Bay ⊂	276	40.41 N	74.03 W
Upper Beaconsfield	274b	38.01 S	145.25 E
Upper Berkshire Valley	276	40.56 N	74.35 W
Upper Beverley Lake ⊜	212	44.37 N	76.05 W
Upper Black Eddy	210	40.35 N	75.07 W
Upper Blackville	186	46.39 N	65.52 W
Upper Brookville	276	40.51 N	73.34 W
Upper Canada Village ⊥	206	44.57 N	75.03 W
Upper Castlereagh	274a	33.43 S	150.40 E
Upperco	208	39.33 N	76.50 W
Upper Coliban Reservoir ⊜ [1]	169	37.18 S	144.23 E
Upper Crystal Springs Reservoir ⊜ [1]	282	37.30 N	122.20 W
Upper Darby	208	39.55 N	75.16 W
Upper des Lacs Lake ⊜ [1]	198	48.50 N	102.07 W
Upper Egypt → Aṣ-Ṣaʿīd □ [9]	140	26.00 N	32.00 E
Upper End	262	53.17 N	1.52 W
Upper Erskine Lake ⊜	276	41.06 N	74.15 W
Upper Fairmount	208	38.06 N	75.47 W
Upper Falls	284b	39.26 N	76.24 W
Upper Ferntree Gully	274b	37.54 S	145.19 E
Upper Fraser	182	54.07 N	121.56 W
Upper Ganga Canal ≡	124	29.57 N	78.12 E
Upper Gap ʉ	212	44.06 N	76.50 W
Upper Goose Lake ⊜	184	51.44 N	92.44 W
Upper Greenwood Lake	276	41.10 N	74.22 W
Upper Greenwood Lake ⊜	276	41.11 N	74.23 W
Upper Hat Creek	182	50.38 N	121.35 W
Upper Humber ≃	186	49.10 N	57.28 W
Upper Hutt	172	41.08 S	175.04 E
Upper Iowa ≃	190	43.29 N	91.14 W
Upper Island Cove	186	47.39 N	53.12 W
Upper Keechi Creek ≃	222	31.23 N	95.42 W
Upper Klamath Lake ⊜	202	42.23 N	122.55 W
Upper Lake	204	39.10 N	122.54 W
Upper Lake ⊜	204	41.44 N	120.08 W
Upper Lehigh	210	41.02 N	75.55 W
Upper Liard	180	60.02 N	128.55 W
Upper Machodoc Creek ≃	208	38.18 N	77.02 W
Upper Manitou Lake ⊜	184	49.24 N	92.48 W
Upper Marlboro	208	38.48 N	76.45 W
Upper Matecumbe Key I	220	24.55 N	80.39 W
Upper Moutere	172	41.16 S	173.00 E
Upper Musquodoboit	186	45.08 N	62.57 W
Upper Mystic Lake ⊜	283	42.27 N	71.09 W
Upper Nyack	210	41.07 N	73.55 W
Upper Red Lake ⊜	198	48.10 N	94.40 W
Upper Rideau Lake ⊜	212	44.41 N	76.20 W
Upper River Rouge ≃	281	42.23 N	83.16 W
Upper Saddle River	276	41.03 N	74.05 W
Upper Saint Clair	279b	40.21 N	80.05 W
Upper Sandusky	214	40.49 N	83.16 W
Upper San Leandro Reservoir ⊜ [1]	226	37.47 N	122.07 W
Upper Sheila	186	47.28 N	64.56 W
Upper Straits Lake ⊜	281	42.35 N	83.24 W
Upper Sumas	224	49.01 N	122.12 W
Upper Takaka	172	41.02 S	172.50 E
Upper Tean	42	52.57 N	1.58 W
Upper Tooting ⬅ [8]	260	51.26 N	0.10 W
Upper Ugashik Lake ⊜	180	57.40 N	156.43 W
Upper Volta → Burkina Faso □ [1]	150	13.00 N	1.30 W
Upper Windigo Lake ⊜	184	52.30 N	91.35 W
Upper Yarra Reservoir ⊜ [1]	169	37.41 S	145.56 E
Upper Yosemite Fall ∟	226	37.45 N	119.36 W
Uppingham	42	52.35 N	0.43 W
Uppland □ [9]	40	59.59 N	17.48 E
Upplanda	40	60.14 N	17.44 E
Upplands Väsby	40	59.31 N	17.54 E
Uppsala	40	59.52 N	17.38 E
Uppsala Län □ [6]	40	60.00 N	17.45 E
Upright, Cape ›	180	60.17 N	172.15 W
Upsala → Uppsala	40	59.52 N	17.38 E
Upshi	120	33.50 N	77.49 E
Upshur □ [6]	222	32.45 N	94.55 W
Upstart, Cape ›	166	19.42 S	147.45 E
Upton, P.Q., Can.	206	45.39 N	72.41 W
Upton, Eng., U.K.	44	53.37 N	1.17 W
Upton, Eng., U.K.	260	51.30 N	0.35 W
Upton, Eng., U.K.	262	53.13 N	2.52 W
Upton, Eng., U.K.	262	53.23 N	3.06 W
Upton, Ky., U.S.	194	37.27 N	85.53 W
Upton, Ma., U.S.	207	42.10 N	71.36 W
Upton, Wy., U.S.	198	44.05 N	104.37 W
Upton Hill ∧ [2]	169	36.52 S	145.27 E
Upton upon Severn	42	52.04 N	2.13 W
Uptown ⬅ [8]	278	41.58 N	87.40 W
Upwell	42	52.36 N	0.12 E
Upwey	274b	37.54 S	145.20 E
Uquía, Cerro ∧	246	4.22 N	63.46 W
Ur ⊥	128	30.57 N	46.09 E
Urabá, Golfo de ⊂	246	8.25 N	76.53 W
Urachi	84	42.21 N	47.36 E
Uracoa	246	9.00 N	62.21 W
Urad	54	52.15 N	14.45 E
Uradome-kaigan ♠	96	35.35 N	134.21 E
Urad Zhonghou Lianheqi	102	41.42 N	108.49 E
Uraga	268	35.15 N	139.43 E
Uraga-kō ⊂	268	35.14 N	139.44 E
Uraga-suidō ʉ	94	35.13 N	139.45 E
Uragawara	94	37.09 N	138.26 E
Urahoro	92a	42.48 N	143.39 E
Uraj	86	60.08 N	64.48 E
Urakan	88	58.38 N	106.01 E
Urakawa	92a	42.09 N	142.47 E
Ural ≃	72	47.00 N	51.48 E
Uralla	166	30.39 S	151.30 E
Ural Mountains → Ural'skije gory ⋏	72	60.00 N	60.00 E
Uralo-Kl'uči	88	56.03 N	97.28 E
Uralovo	78	52.11 N	33.34 E
Ural'sk	80	51.14 N	51.22 E
Ural'skij	80	51.36 N	51.40 E
Ural'skije gory (Ural Mountains) ⋏	72	60.00 N	60.00 E
Urambo	154	5.04 S	32.03 E
Uran	272c	18.52 N	72.56 E
Urana	166	35.20 S	146.16 E
Urandangi	166	21.36 S	138.18 E
Urandi	255	14.46 S	42.38 W
Urangan	166	25.18 S	152.54 E
Urania, Austl.	168b	34.31 S	137.36 E
Urania, La., U.S.	194	31.51 N	92.17 W
Uranium City	176	59.34 N	108.36 W
Uranquinty	171b	35.12 S	147.15 E
Urarey	162	27.26 S	122.18 E
Urariá, Paraná ≃ [1]	246	3.03 S	57.43 W
Uraricaá ≃	246	3.20 N	61.56 W
Uraricoera	246	3.27 N	60.59 W
Uraricoera ≃	246	3.02 N	60.30 W
Uras	71	39.42 N	8.42 E
Urasaki	174m	26.40 N	127.53 E
Urasoe	174m	26.15 N	127.43 E
Ura-T'ube	85	39.55 N	68.59 E
Uravakonda	122	14.57 N	77.16 E
Uravan	200	38.22 N	108.44 W
Urawa	94	35.51 N	139.39 E
Urayasu	94	35.39 N	139.54 E
ʿUrayfan Nāqah, Jabal ∧	132	30.22 N	34.27 E
ʿUrayyiḍah, Biʾr ⊤ [4]	142	29.00 N	31.58 E
Urazmetovo	86	53.49 N	55.25 E
Urazovka	80	55.24 N	45.38 E
Urazovo	78	50.07 N	38.04 E
Urbach	56	50.53 N	7.05 E
Urban	224	48.38 N	122.40 W
Urbana, Ar., U.S.	194	33.09 N	92.26 W
Urbana, Il., U.S.	194	40.06 N	88.12 W
Urbana, In., U.S.	216	40.53 N	85.47 W
Urbana, Mo., U.S.	194	37.50 N	93.10 W
Urbana, Oh., U.S.	218	40.06 N	83.45 W
Urbancrest	218	39.53 N	83.05 W
Urbandale, Ia., U.S.	190	41.37 N	93.42 W
Urbandale, Mi., U.S.	216	44.09 N	85.11 W
Urbania	66	43.40 N	12.31 E
Urbanización La Pineda	266d	41.16 N	2.00 E
Urbanna	208	37.38 N	76.34 W
Urbano Santos	250	3.12 S	43.23 W
Urbe	62	44.29 N	8.36 E
Urbe, Aeroporto dell' ⊠	267a	41.57 N	12.30 E
Urbiña, Peña ∧	34	43.01 N	5.57 W
Urbino	66	43.43 N	12.38 E
Urbisaglia	66	43.12 N	13.23 E
Urcos	248	13.42 S	71.38 W
Urda	80	48.47 N	47.26 E
Urdaneta	116	15.59 N	120.34 E
Urdenbach ⬅ [8]	263	51.09 N	6.53 E
Urdinarrain	252	32.41 S	58.53 W
Urdoma	24	61.47 N	48.32 E
Urdžar	86	47.05 N	81.38 E
Uré	246	7.46 N	75.31 W
Ure ≃, Fr.	50	48.45 N	0.11 E
Ure ≃, Eng., U.K.	44	54.01 N	1.12 W
Urečje	76	52.57 N	27.54 E
Ūrein	142	30.58 N	30.42 E
Ureki	84	41.59 N	41.46 E
Ureliki	180	64.23 N	173.15 W
Uren'	80	57.28 N	45.49 E
Uren ⊜	40	58.59 N	16.44 E
Urén ≃	236	9.33 N	82.55 W
Ureña	246	7.55 N	72.28 W
Urenui	172	39.00 S	174.23 E
Uréparapara I	175f	13.32 S	167.20 E
Ures	232	29.26 N	110.24 W
Ureshino, Nihon	92	33.06 N	129.59 E
Ureshino, Nihon	94	34.37 N	136.29 E
Ureterp	52	53.05 N	6.10 E
Urewera National Park ♠	172	38.40 S	177.00 E
Urfa	130	37.08 N	38.46 E
Urfa □ [4]	130	37.20 N	39.15 E
Urft ≃	56	50.35 N	6.30 E
Urga → Ulaanbaatar	88	47.55 N	106.53 E
Urga	86	43.35 N	58.30 E
Urgamal	88	48.29 N	94.20 E
Urgenč	72	41.33 N	60.38 E
Urgnano	62	45.35 N	9.41 E
Urgučenskij Golec, gora ∧	88	53.30 N	118.08 E
Ürgüp	130	38.38 N	34.56 E
Urgut	85	39.23 N	67.15 E
Urho	86	46.48 N	89.45 E
Uri, India	123	34.05 N	74.02 E
Uri, It.	71	40.38 N	8.29 E
Uri □ [3]	58	46.50 N	8.40 E
Uriah	194	31.18 N	87.30 W
Uriangato	234	20.09 N	101.11 W
Uribante ≃	246	7.18 N	70.44 W
Uribe	246	3.13 N	74.24 W
Uribelarrea	258	35.09 S	58.54 W
Uribia	246	11.43 N	72.16 W
Urich	194	38.27 N	94.00 W
Urick ⬅ [8]	265a	59.50 N	30.11 E
Urickij	86	53.19 N	65.34 E
Urickoje	78	52.02 N	38.11 E
Urie ≃	46	57.19 N	2.30 W
Urimba	152	10.56 S	16.32 E
Urión, Canal ≃ [1]	288	34.24 S	58.31 W
Urique	232	27.13 N	107.55 W
Urique ≃	232	26.29 N	107.58 W
Uri-Rotstock ∧	58	46.52 N	8.33 E
Urituyacu ≃	246	4.45 S	75.28 W
Uriuana ≃	250	2.47 S	50.29 W
Urizura	94	36.30 N	140.27 E
Urjala	26	61.05 N	23.32 E
Urk	52	52.39 N	5.36 E
Urkan ≃	89	53.27 N	126.56 E
Urkarach	84	42.11 N	47.38 E
Urla	130	38.18 N	26.46 E
Urlaţi	38	44.59 N	26.14 E
Urlingford	48	52.42 N	7.35 W
Urlins	240c	17.02 N	61.52 W
Urluk	88	50.03 N	107.55 E
Urma	126	23.10 N	86.15 E
Urman, S.S.S.R.	86	54.52 N	56.52 E
ʿUrmān, Sūrīy.	132	32.30 N	36.45 E
Urmar Tanda	123	31.42 N	75.38 E
Urmary	80	55.42 N	47.57 E
Ürmeli	130	40.55 N	37.32 E
Urmetan	85	39.27 N	68.17 E
Urmi ≃	89	48.44 N	134.16 E
Urmia → Orūmīyeh	128	37.33 N	45.04 E
Urmia, Lake → Orūmīyeh, Daryācheh-ye ⊜	128	37.40 N	45.30 E
Urmston	44	53.27 N	2.21 W
Urnäsch	58	47.19 N	9.17 E
Urnersee ⊜	58	46.55 N	8.37 E
Üröm	264c	47.36 N	19.01 E
Uromi	150	6.44 N	6.18 E
Uroševac	38	42.22 N	21.09 E
Uroyán, Montañas de ⋏	240m	18.14 N	67.02 W
Urožajnoje, S.S.S.R.	84	43.42 N	44.13 E
Urožajnoje, S.S.S.R.	84	44.47 N	44.55 E
Urquhart, Glen V	46	57.20 N	4.35 W
Urrao	246	6.20 N	76.11 W
Urr Water ≃	44	54.53 N	3.49 W
Ursa	219	40.04 N	91.22 W
Uršel'skij	80	55.41 N	40.13 E
Ursensollen	60	49.24 N	11.46 E
Ursk	86	54.27 N	85.24 E
Urspring	56	48.33 N	9.53 E
Urtazym	86	52.12 N	58.50 E
Uru ≃	255	15.24 S	49.36 W
Uruaçu	255	14.30 S	49.10 W
Uruana	255	15.30 S	49.41 W
Uruapan	204	31.38 N	116.15 W
Uruapan [del Progreso]	234	19.25 N	102.04 W
Uruará ≃	250	2.06 S	53.38 W
Urubamba	248	13.18 S	72.07 W
Urubamba ≃	248	10.44 S	73.45 W
Urubaxi ≃	246	0.31 S	64.50 W
Urubu ≃	246	2.55 S	58.25 W
Urubu, Cachoeira do ∟	255	12.52 S	48.13 W
Urubu Grande ≃	250	10.51 S	49.47 W
Uruburetama	250	3.38 S	39.30 W
Urucará	250	2.32 S	57.45 W
Uruch ≃	84	43.28 N	44.06 E
Urucu ≃	246	4.11 S	63.36 W
Uruçuca	255	14.35 S	39.16 W
Uruçuí	250	7.14 S	44.33 W
Uruçuí, Serra da ⋏ [2]	250	9.00 S	44.45 W
Urucuia ≃	255	16.08 S	45.05 W
Uruçuí-Prêto ≃	250	7.20 S	44.38 W
Urucurituba	250	2.41 S	57.40 W
Urugi	94	35.16 N	137.42 E
Uruguaiana	252	29.45 S	57.05 W
Uruguay □ [1], S.A.	244	33.00 S	56.00 W
Uruguay □ [1], S.A.	252	33.00 S	56.00 W
Uruguay (Uruguai) ≃	252	34.12 S	58.18 W
Urugudejevskij Golec, gora ∧	88	51.25 N	102.09 E
Urul'ga	88	51.45 N	114.47 E
Urul'unguj ≃	88	50.24 N	119.08 E
Ur'um, ozero ⊜	86	54.33 N	78.30 E
Urumchi → Ürümqi	90	43.48 N	87.35 E
Ur'umkan ≃	88	52.35 N	120.08 E
Ürümqi	90	43.48 N	87.35 E
Urundel	252	23.33 S	64.25 W
Ur'ung-Chaja	74	72.48 N	113.23 E
Urun-Islāmpur	122	17.03 N	74.16 E
Uruoca	250	3.20 S	40.32 W
Urup	84	43.52 N	41.09 E
Urup ≃	84	44.49 N	41.10 E
Urup, gora ∧	84	43.38 N	40.58 E
Urup, ostrov I	74	46.00 N	150.00 E
Urupá ≃	248	10.54 S	61.57 W
Urupadi ≃	250	3.51 S	57.21 W
Urupês	255	21.13 S	49.17 W
Ur'upino	88	52.46 N	120.00 E
Ur'upinsk	80	50.47 N	41.59 E
Ururicaia, Ilha I	250	1.30 S	52.05 W
Uruša	89	54.03 N	122.54 E
Urus-Martan	84	43.08 N	45.32 E
Urusovo	82	54.15 N	38.26 E
Urussanga	252	28.31 S	49.19 W
Urussu	80	54.36 N	53.24 E
Urutaí	255	17.28 S	48.12 W
Urutaí, Ilha I	250	1.07 S	51.17 W
Urutaú	252	25.42 S	63.04 W
Uruti	172	38.57 S	174.32 E
Uruwira	154	6.27 S	31.21 E
Uryl'	86	49.15 N	86.20 E
Uryū-yama ∧	270	35.03 N	135.48 E
Uryv	78	51.07 N	39.10 E
Urzajbaš	80	54.43 N	54.23 E
Urziceni	38	44.43 N	26.38 E
Ürzig	56	49.59 N	7.01 E
Urzulei	71	40.06 N	9.30 E
Uržum	80	57.08 N	50.00 E
Us	261	49.06 N	1.58 E
Us ≃	86	52.07 N	92.15 E
Usa, Nihon	96	33.31 N	131.22 E
Usa, S.S.S.R.	86	54.03 N	88.45 E
Usa ≃, S.S.S.R.	24	65.57 N	56.55 E
Uša ≃, S.S.S.R.	76	54.00 N	28.55 E
Ušač' ≃	76	55.32 N	28.30 E
Ušači	76	55.11 N	28.37 E
Usada Island I	116	6.08 N	120.33 E
Usadel	54	53.26 N	13.11 E
Uşak	130	38.41 N	29.25 E
Uşak □ [4]	130	38.35 N	29.20 E
Ušaki	76	59.29 N	30.59 E

English	Deutsch	Español	Français	Português
≃ River	Fluss	Río	Rivière	Rio
≡ Canal	Kanal	Canal	Canal	Canal
∟ Waterfall, Rapids	Wasserfall, Stromschnellen	Cascada, Rápidos	Chute d'eau, Rapides	Cascata, Rápidos
ʉ Strait	Meeresstrasse	Estrecho	Détroit	Estreito
⊂ Bay, Gulf	Bucht, Golf	Bahía, Golfo	Baie, Golfe	Baía, Golfo
⊜ Lake, Lakes	See, Seen	Lago, Lagos	Lac, Lacs	Lago, Lagos
≣ Swamp	Sumpf	Pantano	Marais	Pântano
⊓ Ice Features, Glacier	Eis- und Gletscherformen	Accidentes Glaciales	Formes glaciaires	Acidentes glaciares
⊤ Other Hydrographic Features	Andere Hydrographische Objekte	Otros Elementos Hidrográficos	Autres données hydrographiques	Outros acidentes hidrográficos

English	Deutsch	Español	Français	Português
✢ Submarine Features	Untermeerische Objekte	Accidentes Submarinos	Formes de relief sous-marin	Acidentes submarinos
□ Political Unit	Politische Einheit	Unidad Politica	Entité politique	Unidade política
ᵾ Cultural Institution	Kulturelle Institution	Institución Cultural	Institution culturelle	Institução cultural
⊥ Historical Site	Historische Stätte	Sitio Histórico	Site historique	Sitio histórico
♠ Recreational Site	Erholungs- und Ferienort	Sitio de Recreo	Centre de loisirs	Area de Lazer
⊠ Airport	Flughafen	Aeropuerto	Aéroport	Aeroporto
■ Military Installation	Militäranlage	Instalación Militar	Installation militaire	Instalação militar
⬅ Miscellaneous	Verschiedenes	Misceláneo	Divers	Diversos

Usakos 156 22.01 S 15.32 E
Ušakovka 83 48.48 N 39.48 E
Ušakovo, S.S.S.R. 86 56.22 N 75.41 E
Ušakovo, S.S.S.R. 89 51.55 N 126.34 E
Usambara
Mountains ∧ 154 4.45 S 38.30 E
Usangu Flats ≐ 154 8.30 S 34.15 E
Usanovy 86 59.28 N 73.24 E
Ušaral 85 43.54 N 70.42 E
Usarp Mountains ∧ 9 71.10 S 160.00 E
Ušava 60 49.46 N 12.40 E
Usaymir, Wādī al- V 273c 30.04 N 31.25 E
Ušba, gora ∧ 84 43.08 N 42.40 E
Ušbas ≐ 85 43.55 N 69.39 E
Usborne, Mount ∧ 254 51.41 S 58.50 W
Ušče 38 43.28 N 20.37 E
Uščerpje 76 52.43 N 31.53 E
Uscio 62 44.25 N 9.10 E
Usedom 54 53.52 N 13.55 E
Usedom (Uznam) I 54 54.00 N 14.00 E
Useldange 56 49.47 N 5.59 E
Usellus 71 39.48 N 8.51 E
Usen' ≐ 80 54.44 N 53.38 E
'Usfān 144 21.55 N 39.21 E
Ushaa 152 14.55 S 23.18 E
Ushashi 154 2.00 S 33.57 E
'Ushayrah 144 21.46 N 40.38 E
Ushetu 154 4.10 S 32.16 E
Ushibuka 92 32.11 N 130.01 E
Ushiku 94 35.58 N 140.08 E
Ushimado 96 34.37 N 134.10 E
Ushuaia 254 54.48 S 68.18 W
Usibelli 180 63.51 N 148.47 W
Ušica ≐ 78 48.35 N 27.08 E
Usingen 56 50.20 N 8.32 E
Usini 71 40.40 N 8.32 E
Usinsk 24 65.58 N 56.39 E
Usisya 154 11.09 S 34.11 E
Usk, B.C., Can. 182 54.38 N 128.25 W
Usk, Wales, U.K. 42 51.43 N 2.54 W
Usk, Wa., U.S. 202 48.18 N 117.16 W
Usk ≐ 42 51.36 N 2.58 W
Üškanij kr'až ∧ 180 65.15 N 178.35 E
Uskedal 26 59.56 N 5.52 E
Usken ⊜ 40 59.39 N 15.01 E
Uskovo 265b 55.56 N 37.19 E
Üsküb
→ Skopje 38 41.59 N 21.26 E
Üsküdar 130 41.01 N 29.01 E
Uskumuruköy 267b 41.12 N 29.01 E
Uslar 52 51.39 N 9.38 E
Üslava ≐ 60 49.45 N 13.24 E
Usmajac 234 19.52 N 103.34 W
Usman', S.S.S.R. 76 52.02 N 39.44 E
Usman', S.S.S.R. 89 51.29 N 134.00 E
Usmanka 80 56.47 N 101.24 E
Usmānpur ✦[8] 272a 28.41 N 77.15 E
Usmas ezers ⊜ 76 57.11 N 22.10 E
Usmat 85 39.44 N 67.40 E
Usmate Velate 62 45.39 N 9.21 E
Ušmunskij Golec,
gora ∧ 89 51.40 N 118.35 E
Usmyn' 76 55.52 N 31.09 E
Ušna ≐ 80 55.43 N 42.12 E
Usoke 154 5.06 S 32.20 E
Usolje, S.S.S.R. 80 53.23 N 49.05 E
Usolje, S.S.S.R. 82 56.49 N 38.40 E
Usolje, S.S.S.R. 86 59.25 N 56.41 E
Usolje-Sibirskoje 88 52.47 N 103.38 E
Usolka ≐ 86 57.47 N 94.35 E
Uson 116 12.13 N 123.47 E
Usoro 150 5.34 N 6.13 E
Usovo 265b 55.44 N 37.13 E
Uspallata 252 32.35 S 69.20 W
Uspanapa ≐ 234 17.58 N 94.29 W
Uspenka, S.S.S.R. 80 50.38 N 41.28 E
Uspenka, S.S.S.R. 83 47.43 N 38.42 E
Uspenka, S.S.S.R. 83 48.23 N 39.10 E
Uspenka, S.S.S.R. 86 52.54 N 77.25 E
Uspenovka 80 51.16 N 53.36 E
Uspenskij 86 48.42 N 72.40 E
Uspenskoje 82 55.43 N 37.04 E
Usri ≐ 126 24.03 N 86.23 E
Ussaj 86 43.50 N 58.53 E
Ussassai 71 39.49 N 9.23 E
Usseglio 62 45.14 N 7.13 E
Ussel 32 45.33 N 2.18 E
Ussel 56 48.44 N 11.04 E
Usshers Creek ≐ 284a 43.03 N 79.02 W
Usson-en-Forez 62 45.23 N 3.56 E
Ussure 154 4.39 S 34.23 E
Ussuri (Wusuli) ≐ 89 48.27 N 135.04 E
Ussurijsk 89 43.48 N 131.59 E
Üst 123 36.56 N 72.53 E
Usta 80 57.26 N 45.40 E
Usta ≐ 80 56.53 N 45.28 E
Ust'-Ajsk 86 56.07 N 57.40 E
Ustaoset 26 60.30 N 8.04 E
Ustaritz 32 43.24 N 1.27 W
Ust'-Bagar'ak 86 56.08 N 61.52 E
Ust'-Barguzin 88 53.27 N 108.59 E
Ust'-Belaja 74 65.30 N 173.20 E
Ust'-Bol'šereck 74 52.48 N 156.14 E
Ust'-B'ur' 86 53.49 N 90.15 E
Ust'-Buzulukskaja 80 50.12 N 42.10 E
Ust'-Bystr'anskaja 80 47.49 N 41.03 E
Ust'-Čaja 86 58.17 N 82.38 E
Ust'-Čaryšskaja
Pristan' 86 52.24 N 83.39 E
Ust'-Čaun 74 68.47 N 170.30 E
Ust'-Choperskaja 80 49.36 N 42.24 E
Ust'-Čil'ma 24 65.27 N 52.06 E
Ust'-Čižapka 86 59.02 N 79.37 E
Ust'-Čorna 78 48.18 N 23.56 E
Ust'-Čornaja 88 52.57 N 119.02 E
Ust'-Dolyssy 76 56.09 N 29.39 E
Ust'-Doneckij 80 47.39 N 40.52 E
Ust'-Džegutinskaja 84 44.05 N 41.58 E
Uštěk 54 50.36 N 14.20 E
Ust'-Elegest 88 51.32 N 94.05 E
Uster 58 47.21 N 8.43 E
Ust'-Gr'aznucha 80 50.28 N 45.26 E
Ustica 70 38.42 N 13.11 E
Ustica, Isola di I 70 38.42 N 13.11 E
Ust'-Il'a 88 50.25 N 113.41 E
Ust'-Ilga 88 55.00 N 105.02 E
Ust'-Ilimsk 88 58.00 N 102.39 E
Ust'-Ilimskoje
vodochranilišče ⊜[1] 88 57.00 N 102.15 E
Ustilug 78 50.51 N 24.09 E
Ust'-Ilyč 24 62.32 N 56.41 E
Ústí nad Labem 54 50.40 N 14.02 E
Ústí nad Orlicí 30 49.58 N 16.24 E
Ustinov 80 56.51 N 53.14 E
Ustinovka, S.S.S.R. 78 47.57 N 32.32 E
Ustinovka, S.S.S.R. 83 48.49 N 38.34 E
Ust'-Išim 86 57.44 N 71.10 E
Ust'-Izes 86 55.56 N 76.56 E
Ust'-Ižora 265a 59.48 N 30.36 E
Ustja ≐ 24 61.30 N 42.36 E
Ust'-Javron'ga 24 63.25 N 44.21 E
Ustje, S.S.S.R. 76 60.49 N 32.49 E
Ustje, S.S.S.R. 76 59.38 N 39.43 E
Ustje, S.S.S.R. 80 57.47 N 39.47 E
Ustje, S.S.S.R. 82 55.16 N 36.20 E
Ustje, S.S.S.R. 86 57.46 N 94.42 E
Ustje-Kirovskoje 76 58.45 N 35.55 E
Ustka 30 54.35 N 16.50 E
Ust'-K'achta 88 50.32 N 106.16 E
Ust'-Kajtym 86 57.23 N 95.28 E
Ust'-Kalmanka 86 52.07 N 83.19 E
Ust'-Kamčatsk 74 56.15 N 162.30 E
Ust'-Kamenogorsk 86 49.58 N 82.38 E
Ust'-Kan, S.S.S.R. 86 50.57 N 84.45 E
Ust'-Kan, S.S.S.R. 86 56.31 N 93.48 E
Ust'-Karenga 88 54.26 N 116.30 E
Ust'-Karsk 88 52.43 N 118.48 E
Ust'-Katav 86 54.56 N 58.10 E
Ust'-Kemčug 86 57.13 N 90.30 E
Ust'-Kil'mez' 80 56.57 N 50.30 E
Ust'-Kišert' 86 57.22 N 57.15 E
Ust'-Koksa 86 50.18 N 85.36 E
Ust'-Kujda 74 70.01 N 135.36 E
Ust'-Kulom 24 61.42 N 53.40 E
Ust'-Kurd'um 80 51.39 N 46.12 E
Ust'-Kurenga 86 57.27 N 75.34 E
Ust'-Kut 88 56.46 N 105.40 E
Ust'-Labinsk 78 45.13 N 39.42 E
Ust'-Lubija 88 52.36 N 120.16 E
Ust'-Luga 76 59.40 N 28.15 E
Ust'-Lyža 24 65.44 N 56.36 E
Ust'-Maja 74 60.25 N 134.32 E
Ust'-Manja 72 62.11 N 60.20 E
Ust'-Naryk 86 54.20 N 87.25 E
Ust'-Nemda 80 57.03 N 50.22 E
Ust'-Nera 74 64.34 N 143.12 E
Ust'-Niman 89 51.28 N 132.42 E
Ust'-Ničža 88 56.34 N 121.37 E
Uštobe 86 45.16 N 78.00 E
Ust'-Omčug 74 61.09 N 149.38 E
Ust'-Ordynskij 88 52.48 N 104.45 E
Ust'-Ordynskij
Bur'atskij
Nacional'nyj Okrug
□[8] 88 53.30 N 104.00 E
Ust'-Oz'ornaja 88 50.42 N 117.06 E
Ust'-Oz'ornoje 86 58.54 N 87.48 E
Ust'-Paden'ga 24 61.53 N 42.36 E
Ust'-Pečengskoje 76 59.47 N 42.37 E
Ust'-Pinega 24 64.11 N 41.56 E
Ust'-Pit 86 58.59 N 91.44 E
Ust'-Pogožje 80 49.28 N 44.38 E
Ustreka 76 58.38 N 34.33 E
Ust'-Reki 24 62.12 N 46.45 E
Ustroń 30 49.43 N 18.49 E
Ustrzyki Dolne 30 49.26 N 22.37 E
Ust'-Šara 76 60.13 N 33.57 E
Ust'-Ščerbedino 80 51.53 N 42.52 E
Ust'-Šlav'anka ✦[8] 265a 59.50 N 30.32 E
Ust'-Šonoša 24 61.10 N 41.18 E
Ust'-Šumy 86 54.48 N 80.26 E
Ust'-Tara 86 56.41 N 74.39 E
Ust'-Tarka 86 55.34 N 75.42 E
Ust'-Tašino 89 51.07 N 129.35 E
Ust'-Tygda 89 52.35 N 127.53 E
Ust'-Tym 86 59.26 N 80.08 E
Ust'-Tyrma 89 50.29 N 131.18 E
Ust'uckoje 76 58.32 N 35.20 E
Ust'-Uda 88 54.10 N 103.03 E
Üstükran 130 39.16 N 41.17 E
Ust'-Ulagan 86 50.38 N 87.58 E
Ust'-Umal'ta 89 51.39 N 133.18 E
Ust'-Undurga 89 53.07 N 118.04 E
Ust'-Unja 24 61.48 N 57.48 E
Ustupo Yantupo 246 9.27 N 78.34 W
Ust'-Urgal 89 51.09 N 132.33 E
Ust'urt, plato ∧[1] 72 43.00 N 56.00 E
Ust'-Us 86 52.07 N 92.17 E
Ust'-Usa 24 65.59 N 56.54 E
Ust'-Uza 80 52.58 N 45.17 E
Ust'užna 76 58.51 N 36.26 E
Ust'-Vichoreva 88 56.17 N 101.24 E
Ust'-Voja 24 64.27 N 57.40 E
Ust'-Vyjskaja 24 62.57 N 46.41 E
Ust'-Vym' 24 62.14 N 50.24 E
Ust'-Žaza 88 53.10 N 111.40 E
Ust'-Žuja 88 58.48 N 118.12 E
Usu 86 44.27 N 84.37 E
Usuchčaj 84 41.25 N 47.53 E
Usuda 94 36.12 N 138.29 E
Usugli 88 52.39 N 115.16 E
Usui 96 33.34 N 130.42 E
Usuki 96 33.08 N 131.49 E
Usuki-wan ⊂ 96 33.10 N 131.52 E
Usulután 236 13.21 N 88.27 W
Usumacinta ≐ 232 18.24 N 92.38 W
Usumbura
→ Bujumbura 154 3.23 S 29.22 E
Ušumun 89 52.49 N 126.27 E
Ušur 80 57.47 N 52.58 E
Usuyŏng 98 34.35 N 126.18 E
Usu-zan ∧ 92a 42.32 N 140.51 E
Usv'aty 76 55.45 N 30.45 E
Uta 71 39.17 N 8.57 E
Utah □[3], U.S. 178 39.30 N 111.30 W
Utah □[3], U.S. 200 39.30 N 111.30 W
Utah Lake ⊜ 200 40.13 N 111.49 W
Utajärvi 26 64.45 N 26.23 E
Utamba 154 1.06 S 26.50 E
Utamboni ≐ 152 1.00 N 9.48 E
Utan 115b 8.24 S 117.07 E
Utano 94 34.28 N 135.59 E
Utapi 156 17.31 S 15.08 E
Utashinai 92a 43.31 N 142.03 E
Utata 88 50.51 N 102.45 E
'Utaybah, Buhayrat
al- ⊜ 132 33.31 N 36.37 E
Ute 198 42.03 N 95.42 W
Ute Creek ≐ 196 35.21 N 103.50 W
Utegi 154 1.20 S 34.35 E
Utelle 62 43.55 N 7.15 E
Utembo ≐ 152 17.06 S 22.01 E
Ute Mountain Indian
Reservation ✦[4] 200 37.10 N 108.35 W
Utena 76 55.30 N 25.36 E
Utengule 154 8.57 S 35.50 E
Ute Reservoir ⊜[1] 196 35.21 N 103.31 W
Üterský potok ≐ 60 49.48 N 13.06 E
Utersum 30 54.43 N 8.24 E
Utete 154 7.59 S 38.47 E
Utevka 80 52.57 N 50.58 E
Utfort 263 51.28 N 6.38 E
Uthai Thani 110 15.22 N 100.03 E
Uthal 120 25.48 N 66.37 E
U Thong 110 14.22 N 99.54 E
Uthumphon Phisai 110 15.05 N 104.08 E
Utiariti 248 13.02 S 58.17 W
Utica, Il., U.S. 216 41.20 N 89.00 W
Utica, In., U.S. 218 38.20 N 85.39 W
Utica, Ks., U.S. 198 38.38 N 100.10 W
Utica, Mi., U.S. 214 42.37 N 83.02 W
Utica, Ms., U.S. 194 32.06 N 90.37 W
Utica, Ne., U.S. 198 40.54 N 97.21 W
Utica, N.Y., U.S. 210 43.06 N 75.13 W
Utica, Oh., U.S. 214 40.14 N 82.27 W
Utica, Pa., U.S. 214 41.26 N 79.58 W
Utica
→ Utique ⫫ 36 37.03 N 10.03 E
Utiel 34 39.34 N 1.12 W
Utikoomak Lake
Indian Reserve
✦[4] 182 55.57 N 115.30 W
Utikuma Lake ⊜ 182 55.50 N 115.25 W
Utila 236 16.06 N 86.54 W
Utila, Isla de I 236 16.06 N 86.56 W
Utinga 287b 23.38 S 46.32 W
Utinga ≐ 255 12.34 S 41.20 W
Utique 36 37.03 N 10.03 E
Utique ⫫ 36 37.03 N 10.03 E
Utirik I[1] 14 11.15 N 169.48 E
Utlängan I 26 56.01 N 15.47 E
Utl'ukskij liman ⊂[1] 78 46.15 N 35.12 E
Ut'ma 86 57.35 N 71.45 E
Utmānzai 123 34.11 N 71.46 E
Utö I 40 58.56 N 18.16 E
Utokota 156 17.50 S 20.22 E
Utonde 152 1.56 N 9.49 E
Utopia, Austl. 162 22.14 S 134.33 E
Utopia, Tx., U.S. 196 29.37 N 99.32 W
Utorgoš 76 58.17 N 30.15 E
Utraula 124 27.19 N 82.25 E
Utrecht, Ned. 52 52.05 N 5.08 E
Utrecht, S. Afr. 158 27.38 S 30.20 E
Utrecht □[4] 52 52.05 N 5.10 E
Utrera 34 37.11 N 5.47 W
Utrik I[1] 14 11.15 N 169.48 E
Utsaladdy 224 48.15 N 122.30 W
Utsira 26 59.18 N 4.54 E
Utsjoki 24 69.53 N 27.00 E
Utsumi 96 34.21 N 133.17 E
Utsunomiya 94 36.33 N 139.52 E
Utta 80 46.20 N 46.00 E
Uttamapālaiyam 122 9.48 N 77.20 E
Uttaradit 110 17.38 N 100.06 E
Uttarkāshi 120 30.44 N 78.27 E
Uttarpara-Kotrung 272b 22.40 N 88.21 E
Uttar Pradesh □[3] 120 27.00 N 80.00 E
Uttendorf, Öst. 60 48.09 N 13.07 E
Uttendorf, Öst. 64 47.17 N 12.34 E
Uttenweiler 58 48.09 N 9.36 E
Ütterlingsen 263 51.15 N 7.45 E
Utting 60 48.02 N 11.05 E
Uttlesford □[8] 260 51.47 N 0.19 E
Uttoxeter 42 52.54 N 1.51 W
Utu 154 1.45 S 27.54 E
Utuado 240m 18.16 N 66.42 W
Utukok ≐ 180 70.04 N 162.18 W
Utulei 174u 14.17 S 170.40 W
Utunomiya
→ Utsunomiya 94 36.33 N 139.52 E
Utupua I 14 11.16 S 166.29 E
Utva ≐ 80 51.28 N 52.40 E
Utzenstorf 58 47.08 N 7.33 E
Uudenmaan lääni □[4] 26 60.30 N 25.00 E
Uulu 76 58.17 N 24.35 E
Üür ≐ 88 50.18 N 101.54 E
Uusikaarlepyy
(Nykarleby) 26 63.32 N 22.32 E
Uusikaupunki
(Nystad) 26 60.48 N 21.25 E
Uusimaa ✦[1] 26 60.30 N 25.00 E
Uvá, Bra. 255 15.53 S 50.25 W
Uva, S.S.S.R. 80 56.59 N 52.13 E
Uva ≐ 246 3.57 N 68.24 W
Uvalda 192 33.41 N 83.25 W
Uvalde 196 29.12 N 99.47 W
Úvaly 54 50.03 N 14.47 E
Uvân ≐ 40 60.01 N 13.37 E
Uvaroviči 76 52.36 N 30.44 E
Uvarovka 76 55.32 N 35.37 E
Uvarovo 80 51.59 N 42.15 E
Uvas Creek ≐ 226 36.58 N 121.33 W
Uvas Reservoir ⊜[1] 226 37.05 N 121.42 W
Uvat 86 59.09 N 68.54 E
'Uvda, Biq'at V 132 29.57 N 34.57 E
Uvdal 26 60.16 N 8.44 E
Uvel'skij 86 54.26 N 61.22 E
Uvernet 62 44.22 N 6.38 E
Uvero, Punta ≻ 241s 11.21 N 68.41 W
Uvinza 154 5.06 S 30.22 E
Uvira 154 3.24 S 29.08 E
Uvod' ≐ 80 56.26 N 41.26 E
Uvongo Beach 158 30.51 S 30.23 E
Uvs □[4] 86 50.00 N 92.00 E
Uvs nuur ⊜ 74 50.20 N 92.45 E
Uvworé ≻ 175f 18.47 S 169.16 E
Uwa 96 33.20 N 132.30 E
Uwajima 96 33.13 N 132.34 E
Uwak 114 4.23 N 97.07 E
Uwa-kai ⊤[2] 96 33.15 N 132.15 E
'Uwaybid, Jabal ∧ 142 30.06 N 32.09 E
Uwayl 140 8.46 N 27.24 E
'Uwaynāt 130 35.43 N 36.05 E
'Uwaynāt, Jabal al-
∧ 140 21.54 N 24.58 E
'Uwayrid, Ḥarrat al-
⫫[9] 128 27.00 N 37.30 E
Uwchland 285 40.05 N 75.42 W
Uwi, Pulau I 112 1.05 N 107.24 E
Uxbridge, On., Can. 212 44.06 N 79.07 W
Uxbridge, Ma., U.S. 207 42.04 N 71.37 W
Uxbridge ✦[8] 260 51.33 N 0.29 W
Uxin Qi 102 38.29 N 108.48 E
Uxmal 232 20.22 N 89.46 W
Uxmal ⫫ 232 20.22 N 89.46 W
Uyak Bay ⊂ 180 57.36 N 153.57 W
Uyama 270 34.50 N 135.41 E
U-yin 110 22.53 N 95.13 E
Uyo 150 5.03 N 7.56 E
Uyu ≐ 110 24.51 N 94.57 E
Uyuni 248 20.28 S 66.50 W
Uyuni, Salar de ≐ 248 20.20 S 67.42 W
Už (Uh) ≐, Europe 30 48.34 N 22.00 E
Už ≐, S.S.S.R. 78 51.15 N 30.12 E
Uza ≐, S.S.S.R. 76 57.48 N 29.31 E
Uza ≐, S.S.S.R. 80 53.02 N 45.18 E
Užanicha 86 54.41 N 81.02 E
Uzas 86 57.04 N 76.55 E
Užava 76 57.14 N 21.27 E
Uzbekskaja
Sovetskaja
Socialističeskaja
Respublika □[3] 72 41.00 N 64.00 E
Uzbek Soviet
Socialist Republic
→ Uzbekskaja
Sovetskaja
Socialističeskaja
Respublika □[3] 72 41.00 N 64.00 E
Uzda 76 53.27 N 27.13 E
Uzel 32 48.17 N 2.50 W
Uzerche 32 45.26 N 1.34 E
Uzès 62 44.01 N 4.25 E
Uzgen 85 40.46 N 73.18 E
Užgorod 78 48.37 N 22.18 E
Užice
→ Titovo Užice 38 43.51 N 19.51 E
Uzin 78 49.50 N 30.24 E
Uzkij Lug 88 50.42 N 108.01 E
Uzkoje ✦[8] 265b 55.37 N 37.32 E
Uzlovaja 76 53.59 N 38.10 E
Uzmorje 80 51.15 N 45.55 E
Uznach 58 47.14 N 9.00 E
Uznam (Usedom) I 54 54.00 N 14.00 E
Uzola ≐ 80 56.32 N 43.38 E
Uzon ≐ 80 53.38 N 49.43 E
Uz'ukovo 80 53.38 N 49.43 E
Üzümlü, Tür. 130 37.32 N 31.37 E
Üzümlü, Tür. 130 36.44 N 29.14 E
Uzun 85 38.22 N 68.03 E
Uzun Ada I 130 38.28 N 26.42 E
Uzunagač, S.S.S.R. 85 43.13 N 76.20 E
Uzunagač, S.S.S.R. 85 43.36 N 76.19 E
Uzunagač, S.S.S.R. 86 56.28 N 67.18 E
Uzunbulak 86 46.00 N 83.06 E
Uzunca ✦ 267b 40.58 N 28.50 E
Uzunköprü 130 41.16 N 26.41 E
Uzunkuduk 85 40.33 N 67.11 E
Uzunkuyu 130 38.17 N 26.33 E
Uzunovo 82 54.32 N 38.40 E
Užur 86 55.20 N 89.50 E
Užventis 76 55.47 N 22.39 E

V

Vä 40 55.59 N 14.05 E
Vaajakoski 26 62.16 N 25.54 E
Vääksy 26 61.11 N 25.33 E
Vaal ≐ 158 29.04 S 23.38 E
Vaala 26 64.26 N 26.48 E
Vaaldam ⊜[1] 158 26.55 S 28.12 E
Vaalhartsdam ⊜[1] 158 28.06 S 24.55 E
Vaalkop ∧ 158 31.21 S 26.31 E
Vaals 56 50.46 N 6.01 E
Vaalwater 156 24.20 S 28.03 E
Vaanta (Vanda) 26 60.16 N 25.03 E
Vaasa (Vasa) 26 63.06 N 21.36 E
Vaasan lääni □[4] 26 63.00 N 23.00 E
Vaassen 52 52.17 N 5.58 E
Vabalninkas 76 55.58 N 24.45 E
Vabkent 85 40.02 N 64.30 E
Vác 30 47.47 N 19.08 E
Vača 80 55.48 N 42.46 E
Vaca, Mount ∧ 226 38.24 N 122.06 W
Vacacaí ≐ 252 29.55 S 53.06 W
Vaca Key I 220 24.42 N 81.05 W
Vacaria 252 28.30 S 50.56 W
Vacaria ≐, Bra. 255 19.50 S 42.45 W
Vacaria ≐, Bra. 255 21.55 S 53.59 W
Vacas, Arroyo de las
≐ 258 34.00 S 58.18 W
Vacaville 226 38.21 N 121.59 W
Vacceo 64 46.02 N 13.25 E
Vacca, Kaap ≻ 241s 12.21 N 68.49 W ...
Vaccarès, Étang de
⊂ 62 43.32 N 4.34 E
Vach ≐ 74 60.45 N 76.45 E
Vacha 56 50.50 N 10.01 E
Vache, Île à I 238 18.05 N 73.38 W
Vaches, Île aux I 275a 45.41 N 73.30 W
Vaches, Rivière aux
≐ 206 46.02 N 72.46 W
Vachrušev 89 48.59 N 142.58 E
Vachrušev 83 48.10 N 38.46 E
Vachš ≐ 72 37.06 N 68.18 E
Vachšskij chrebet ∧ 85 38.35 N 69.45 E
Vachtan 80 57.58 N 46.42 E
Vačī 84 42.05 N 47.13 E
Vacía Talega, Punta
≻ 240m 18.27 N 65.54 W
Vacoas 157c 20.18 S 57.29 E
Vad, S.S.S.R. 80 55.32 N 44.12 E
Vad, Sve. 40 60.02 N 15.39 E
Vad ≐ 80 54.33 N 42.37 E
Väddö I 40 60.00 N 18.50 E
Vådeni 38 45.22 N 27.56 E
Vader 224 46.24 N 122.57 W
Vadheim 26 61.13 N 5.49 E
Vādi 272c 18.58 N 73.06 E
Vadino 76 55.16 N 33.16 E
Vadinsk 80 53.43 N 43.04 E
Vadnagar 120 23.47 N 72.38 E
Vado de Cedillos 200 31.05 N 105.50 W
Vado de Piedra 196 29.50 N 104.40 W
Vado Hondo 200 31.09 N 111.22 W
Vado Ligure 62 44.17 N 8.27 E
Vadret, Piz ∧ 58 46.41 N 9.57 E
Vadsbro 40 58.58 N 16.36 E
Vadsø 24 70.05 N 29.46 E
Vadstena 26 58.27 N 14.54 E
Vaduz 58 47.09 N 9.31 E
Vadvetjåkko
Nationalpark ✦ 24 68.35 N 18.20 E
Væggerløse 41 54.42 N 11.56 E
Værøy I 24 67.40 N 12.39 E
Vaga ≐ 24 62.48 N 42.56 E
Vagaj 86 57.56 N 69.01 E
Vagaj ≐ 86 57.59 N 69.01 E
Vågåmo 26 61.53 N 9.06 E
Vaganski Vrh ∧ 36 44.22 N 15.31 E
Vaggeryd 26 57.30 N 14.07 E
Vaghena Island I 175e 7.26 S 157.46 E
Vaglia 66 43.54 N 11.17 E
Vaglio Basilicata 68 40.40 N 15.55 E
Vagney 58 48.01 N 6.43 E
Vagnhärad 40 58.55 N 17.30 E
Vagues 258 34.19 S 59.26 W
Våh ≐ 30 47.55 N 18.00 E
Vahsel Bay ⊂ 9 77.48 S 34.39 W
Vaiano 66 43.58 N 11.07 E
Vaich, Loch ⊜ 44 57.43 N 4.46 W
Vaiden 194 33.19 N 89.44 W
Vaigai ≐ 122 9.21 N 79.00 E
Vaigat ∪ 176 70.11 N 53.00 W
Vaihingen an der
Enz 56 48.56 N 8.58 E
Vaijāpur 122 19.55 N 74.44 E
Vaikam 122 9.46 N 76.24 E
Väike-Maarja 76 59.08 N 26.15 E
Väike Pakri I 76 59.20 N 24.00 E
Vail, Co., U.S. 200 39.38 N 106.22 W
Vail, Ia., U.S. 198 42.03 N 95.11 W
Vaila I 46a 60.12 N 1.37 W
Vailala ≐ 164 7.55 S 145.25 E
Vaileka 175g 17.23 S 178.09 E
Vail Lake ⊜[1] 228 33.29 N 116.58 W
Vailly-sur-Aisne 50 49.25 N 3.31 E
Vailly-sur-Sauldre 50 47.27 N 2.39 E
Vail Mills 210 43.03 N 74.13 W
Vailoatai 174u 14.22 S 170.47 W
Vail Point ≻ 212 44.43 N 80.45 W
Vails Gate 210 41.27 N 74.04 W
Vaimali 175f 16.34 S 168.11 E
Vainode 76 56.26 N 21.50 E
Vaiont, Lago di ⊜ 64 46.21 N 12.21 E
Vaippār ≐ 122 9.01 N 78.17 E
Vair ≐ 58 48.27 N 5.42 E
Vairano Scalo 68 41.20 N 14.08 E
Vairao 174s 17.47 S 149.17 W
Vaires-sur-Marne 261 48.52 N 2.39 E
Vaison-la-Romaine 62 44.14 N 5.04 E
Vaitahu 174y 9.56 S 139.06 W
Vaîte 58 47.35 N 5.44 E
Vaitogi 174u 14.21 S 170.44 W
Vaitown 150 6.52 N 10.52 W
Vaitupu I 14 7.28 S 178.41 E
Vaja ≐ 80 57.27 N 46.00 E
Vajgač 72 70.25 N 58.46 E
Vajgač, ostrov I 72 70.00 N 59.30 E
Vakaga □[5] 146 10.00 N 22.30 E
Vakaga ≐ 146 9.48 N 21.32 E
Väkeaikoski 26 61.16 N 24.02 E
Väkhān ✦[1] 120 37.00 N 73.00 E
Vaklan 272c 19.07 N 73.06 E
Vaksdal 26 60.29 N 5.44 E
Vala ≐ 80 56.59 N 51.16 E
Valaam 24 61.23 N 30.57 E
Valaam, ostrov I 26 61.22 N 30.57 E
Vålådalen 26 63.10 N 12.57 E
Valadeces 196 26.14 N 98.40 W
Valadim 154 12.22 S 36.10 E
Valais (Wallis) □[3] 58 46.10 N 7.30 E
Valaisannes, Alpes ∧ 58 46.00 N 7.30 E
Val-Alain 206 46.24 N 71.45 W
Valamaz 80 57.32 N 52.05 E
Valandovo 38 41.19 N 22.34 E
Valangin 58 47.01 N 6.54 E
Valap 272c 19.03 N 73.08 E
Valare, Baie ⊂ 174q 17.21 S 151.27 W
Valašské Klobouky 30 49.08 N 18.01 E
Valašské Meziříčí 30 49.28 N 17.58 E
Valatie 210 42.24 N 73.40 W
Val-Bélair 272c 19.02 N 73.07 E
Valbella 206 46.51 N 71.26 W
Vålberg 58 46.45 N 9.33 E
Valbert 26 59.24 N 13.12 E
Valbo 56 51.07 N 7.44 E
Valbondione 40 60.40 N 17.04 E
Valbonnais 64 46.02 N 10.00 E
Valcanuta ✦[8] 62 44.54 N 5.54 E
Vålcedräm 267a 41.53 N 12.25 E
Valcheta 38 43.42 N 23.27 E
Valcheta, Arroyo ≐ 254 40.42 S 66.09 W
Valchetta ≐ 254 40.35 S 66.03 W
Valchiusella 267a 41.59 N 12.29 E
Valcivières 62 45.32 N 7.42 E
Valcourt 62 45.35 N 3.48 E
Valdagno 206 45.29 N 72.18 W
Valdahon 64 45.39 N 11.18 E
Valdai Hills 58 47.09 N 6.21 E
→ Valdajskaja
vozvyšennost' ∧[2] 24 57.00 N 33.30 E
Valdaj, S.S.S.R. 24 63.26 N 35.30 E
Valdaj, S.S.S.R. 76 57.59 N 33.14 E
Valdajskaja
vozvyšennost' ∧[2] 24 57.00 N 33.30 E
Valdarno V 66 43.45 N 11.24 E
Valdavia ≐ 34 42.24 N 4.16 W
Val-David 206 46.01 N 74.12 W
Valdebeba, Arroyo
de ≐ 266a 41.23 N 2.10 E
Valdeblore 62 44.04 N 7.12 E
Val-de-Cães 250 1.23 S 48.29 W
Valdecañas,
Embalse de ⊜[1] 34 39.45 N 5.30 W
Valdelândia 255 15.11 S 50.02 W
Val-de-Marne □[5] 261 48.47 N 2.29 E
Valdemärpils 76 57.22 N 22.35 E
Valdemarsvik 26 58.12 N 16.36 E
Valdepeñas 34 38.46 N 3.23 W
Valderaduey ≐ 34 41.31 N 5.42 W
Valderas 34 42.05 N 5.27 W
Valderice 70 38.03 N 12.38 E
Valderrobres 34 40.53 N 0.09 E
Valders 190 44.03 N 87.53 W
Valdés, Península ≻[1] 254 42.30 S 64.00 W
Val-des-Bois 188 45.54 N 75.35 W
Valdese 192 35.44 N 81.33 W
Valdes Island I 224 49.04 N 123.38 W
Valdez, Ec. 246 1.15 N 79.00 W
Valdez, Ak., U.S. 180 61.07 N 146.16 W
Valdieri 62 44.17 N 7.24 E
Val-d'Isère 62 45.27 N 6.59 E
Valdivia, Chile 254 39.48 S 73.14 W
Valdivia, Col. 246 7.11 N 75.27 W
Valdobbiadene 64 45.54 N 12.00 E
Valdoie 58 47.40 N 6.51 E
Val-d'Oise □[5] 261 49.10 N 2.10 E
Val-d'Or 190 48.07 N 77.47 W
Valdorf 52 52.09 N 8.51 E
Valdosta 192 30.49 N 83.16 W
Valdoviño 34 43.36 N 8.08 W
Valdres V 26 60.55 N 9.10 E
Valdurna (Durnholz) 64 46.44 N 11.26 E
Vale, Guernsey 43b 49.29 N 2.31 W
Vale, Or., U.S. 202 43.58 N 117.14 W
Valea lui Mihai 38 47.31 N 22.09 E
Vale de Lobos 266c 38.49 N 9.17 W
Valeene 218 38.26 N 86.24 W
Valeggio sul Mincio 64 45.21 N 10.44 E
Valehouse Reservoir
⊜[1] 262 53.29 N 1.57 W
Valemount 182 52.50 N 119.15 W
Valença, Bra. 255 13.22 S 39.05 W
Valença, Bra. 256 22.15 S 43.43 W
Valença, Port. 34 42.02 N 8.38 W
Valença do Piauí 250 6.24 S 41.45 W
Valençay 50 47.09 N 1.34 E
Valence
→ Valencia, Esp. 34 39.28 N 0.22 W
Valence, Fr. 62 44.56 N 4.54 E
Valencia, Esp. 34 39.28 N 0.22 W
Valencia, Hond. 236 14.47 N 85.18 W
Valencia, Pil. 116 7.57 N 125.03 E
Valencia, Ca., U.S. 228 34.26 N 118.36 W
Valencia, Pa., U.S. 214 40.40 N 79.59 W
Valencia, Ven. 246 10.11 N 68.00 W
Valencia □[4] 34 39.30 N 0.45 W
Valencia, Golfo de ⊂ 34 39.50 N 0.30 E
Valencia, Lago de ⊜ 246 10.15 N 67.45 W
Valencia, Quebrada ≐ 286c 10.30 N 66.46 W
Valencia de
Alcántata 34 39.25 N 7.14 W
Valencia de Don
Juan 34 42.18 N 5.31 W
Valencia Island I 48 51.52 N 10.20 W
Valenciennes 50 50.21 N 3.32 E
Văleni-de-Munte 38 45.12 N 26.03 E
Valensole 62 43.50 N 5.59 E
Valentano 66 42.34 N 11.49 E
Valente 250 11.34 S 39.27 W
Valentigney 58 47.28 N 6.50 E
Valentin 89 43.08 N 134.17 E
Valentín Alsina ✦[8] 288 34.40 S 58.25 W
Valentine, Ne., U.S. 198 42.52 N 100.33 W
Valentine, Tx., U.S. 196 30.34 N 104.29 W
Valentine Mountain
∧ 224 48.32 N 123.56 W
Valentinovka 265b 55.55 N 37.56 E
Valenton 261 48.45 N 2.28 E
Valenza 62 45.01 N 8.38 E
Valenzano 68 41.02 N 16.53 E
Valenzuela 269f 14.42 N 120.58 E
Våler 26 60.40 N 11.50 E
Valera 246 9.19 N 70.37 W
Valérien, Mont ∧[2] 261 48.53 N 2.13 E
Vale Royal □[8] 262 53.17 N 2.37 W
Valets, Lac ⊜ 190 48.32 N 76.30 W
Valette, La
→ Valletta 36 35.54 N 14.31 E
Valfabbrica 66 43.09 N 12.36 E
Valflaunès 62 43.48 N 3.52 E
Valfurva 64 46.27 N 10.25 E
Valfurva V 64 46.26 N 10.26 E
Valga 76 57.47 N 26.02 E
Valge ≐ 76 59.35 N 25.42 E
Valgorge 62 44.35 N 4.07 E
Valgrisanche 62 45.38 N 7.04 E
Valguarnera
Caropepe 70 37.30 N 14.23 E
Valhalla, S. Afr. 158 25.49 S 28.08 E
Valhalla, N.Y., U.S. 210 41.04 N 73.46 W
Valhalla, Lake ⊜ 276 40.56 N 74.22 W
Valhelle, Peninsula
≻[1] 236 9.05 N 81.51 W
Valiente, Punta ≻ 236 9.11 N 81.55 W
Valier, Il., U.S. 194 38.01 N 89.03 W
Valier, Mt., U.S. 202 48.18 N 112.14 W
Valier, Pa., U.S. 214 40.55 N 79.03 W
Valili ≐ 175g 16.39 S 179.10 E
Valinda 280 34.02 N 117.56 W
Valinhos 256 22.57 S 47.01 W
Valir 130 38.48 N 40.41 E
Valjevo 38 44.16 N 19.53 E
Valka 76 57.46 N 26.00 E
Valkeakoski 26 61.16 N 24.02 E
Valkenburg 56 50.52 N 5.50 E
Valkenswaard 52 51.21 N 5.28 E
Valki, S.S.S.R. 78 49.50 N 35.37 E
V'alki, S.S.S.R. 82 55.39 N 38.05 E
Valkininkas 76 54.21 N 24.50 E
Valla 40 59.02 N 16.23 E
Vallabhbhai Patel
Stadium ✦ 272c 18.59 N 72.49 E
Valladares 196 26.53 N 100.37 W
Valladolid, Ec. 246 4.33 S 79.08 W
Valladolid, Esp. 34 41.39 N 4.43 W
Valladolid, Méx. 232 20.41 N 88.12 W
Vallage ✦[1] 58 48.24 N 5.00 E
Vallåkra 41 55.58 N 12.52 E
Vallarsa 64 45.47 N 11.07 E
Vallata 68 41.02 N 15.15 E
Vallauris 62 43.35 N 7.03 E
Vallco Fashion Park
✦[9] 282 37.19 N 122.01 W
Valldal 26 62.20 N 7.21 E
Vall de Uxó 34 39.49 N 0.14 W
Valldoreix 266d 41.28 N 2.04 E
Valle, Esp. 34 43.14 N 4.18 W
Valle, It. 64 46.04 N 10.25 E
Valle, S.S.S.R. 76 56.30 N 24.44 E
Valle □[5] 236 13.30 N 87.35 W
Valle, Arroyo ≐ 226 37.39 N 121.54 W
Vallecas ✦[8] 266a 40.23 N 3.37 W
Valle Castellana 66 42.44 N 13.30 E
Vallecillo 196 26.40 N 99.58 W
Vallecito 226 38.07 N 120.27 W
Vallecitos 200 36.05 N 106.20 W
Vallecitos Creek ≐ 282 37.36 N 121.53 W
Vallecorsa 66 41.27 N 13.24 E
Valle Crucis Abby ✦[1] 42 52.59 N 3.12 W
Valle d'Aosta □[4] 62 45.45 N 7.25 E
Valle de Bravo 234 19.11 N 100.08 W
Valle de Guadalupe 234 21.00 N 102.37 W
Valle de Guanape 246 9.54 N 65.41 W
Valle de Juárez 234 19.53 N 102.51 W
Valle de la Pascua 246 9.13 N 66.00 W
Valle del Cauca □[5] 246 3.45 N 76.30 W
Valle de Olivos 232 27.12 N 106.17 W
Valle de San José 234 23.20 N 98.24 W
Valle de Santiago 234 20.23 N 101.12 W
Valle de Zaragoza 232 27.28 N 105.49 W
Valle di Cadore 64 46.24 N 12.20 E
Valle di Sotto 64 45.25 N 10.21 E
Valledolmo 70 37.45 N 13.50 E
Valledupar 246 10.29 N 73.15 W
Valle Edén 252 31.50 S 56.09 W
Vallefiorita 68 38.46 N 16.27 E
Vallegrande 248 18.29 S 64.06 W
Valle Hermoso, Arg. 252 31.07 S 64.29 W
Valle Hermoso, Méx. 196 25.39 N 97.49 W
Vallehermoso, Pil. 116 10.20 N 123.19 E
Vallejo 226 38.06 N 122.15 W
Valle Lomellina 62 45.09 N 8.40 E
Vallelunga
Pratameno 70 37.41 N 13.50 E
Valle Mosso 62 45.38 N 8.08 E
Vällen ⊜ 40 60.03 N 18.20 E
Vallenar 252 28.35 S 70.46 W
Vallendar 56 50.24 N 7.37 E
Vallensbæk 41 55.38 N 12.22 E
Vallentuna 40 59.32 N 18.05 E
Valleplera 66 41.55 N 13.14 E
Valleraugue 62 44.05 N 3.38 E
Valle Redondo 204 32.31 N 116.46 W
Vallermosa 71 39.22 N 8.48 E
Vallerotonda 66 41.33 N 13.55 E
Valleroy 56 49.12 N 5.55 E
Valles
→ Ciudad de
Valles 234 21.59 N 99.01 W
Valles Caldera ⫫[6] 200 35.52 N 106.33 W
Vallet 32 47.10 N 1.16 W
Valletta 36 35.54 N 14.31 E
Valley, Al., U.S. 194 32.49 N 85.10 W
Valley, Ne., U.S. 198 41.18 N 96.20 W
Valley, Wa., U.S. 182 48.10 N 117.43 W
Valley ≐ 184 51.21 N 99.55 W
Valley Bend 188 38.46 N 79.56 W
Valley Center, Ca.,
U.S. 228 33.13 N 117.02 W
Valley Center, Ks.,
U.S. 198 37.50 N 97.22 W
Valley City, N.D.,
U.S. 198 46.55 N 97.59 W
Valley City, Oh.,
U.S. 214 41.14 N 81.56 W
Valley Cottage 210 41.07 N 73.57 W
Valley Creek ≐, Pa.,
U.S. 285 40.06 N 75.28 W
Valley Creek ≐, Pa.,
U.S. 285 39.58 N 75.40 W
Valley Creek ≐, Tx.,
U.S. 196 31.43 N 100.02 W
Valleydale 280 34.06 N 117.56 W
Valley Falls, Ks.,
U.S. 198 39.20 N 95.27 W
Valley Falls, N.Y.,
U.S. 210 42.54 N 73.34 W
Valley Falls, R.I.,
U.S. 207 41.54 N 71.23 W
Valley Farms 200 32.59 N 111.26 W
Valleyfield 186 49.08 N 53.37 W
Valley Forge 285 40.05 N 75.28 W
Valley Forge Estates 285 40.05 N 75.26 W
Valley Forge
National Historical
Park ✦ 208 40.06 N 75.27 W
Valley Grove 214 40.05 N 80.34 W
Valley Head, Al.,
U.S. 194 34.34 N 85.36 W
Valley Head, W.V.,
U.S. 188 38.32 N 80.02 W
Valley Home 226 37.50 N 120.55 W
Valley Mede 284b 39.17 N 76.50 W
Valley Mills 222 31.39 N 97.28 W
Valley of Desolation
National
Monument ✦ 158 32.17 S 24.30 E
Valley of Fire State
Park ✦ 204 36.26 N 114.30 W
Valley of the Kings ⫫ 140 25.45 N 32.37 E
Valley Park 219 38.32 N 90.29 W
Valley Plaza ✦[9] 280 34.11 N 118.24 W
Valley Springs, Ca.,
U.S. 226 38.12 N 120.50 W
Valley Springs, S.D.,
U.S. 198 43.34 N 96.28 W
Valley Station 194 38.06 N 85.52 W
Valley Stream 210 40.39 N 73.42 W
Valley Stream ≐ 276 40.39 N 73.45 W
Valley Stream State
Park ✦ 276 40.41 N 73.42 W
Valleyview, Ab.,
Can. 182 55.04 N 117.17 W
Valley View, Il., U.S. 216 41.50 N 88.03 W
Valley View, Oh.,
U.S. 279a 41.23 N 81.37 W
Valley View, Pa.,
U.S. 210 40.38 N 76.32 W
Valley View, Tx.,
U.S. 196 33.29 N 97.10 W
Valley View Park 228 34.13 N 117.20 W
Vallgrund I 26 63.12 N 21.14 E
Valliant 196 34.00 N 95.05 W
Valli del Pasubio 64 45.41 N 11.15 E
Vallières 58 45.54 N 5.56 E
Vallimanca, Arroyo ≐ 252 35.40 S 60.02 W
Vallo 58 45.38 N 10.23 E
Vallirana 266d 41.23 N 1.56 E
Vallo 41 55.24 N 12.15 E
Vallo della Lucania 68 40.14 N 15.17 E
Valloire 62 45.10 N 6.26 E
Vallombrosa 64 43.44 N 11.32 E
Vallonia 218 38.50 N 86.05 W
Vallon-Pont-d'Arc 62 44.24 N 4.24 E
Vallorbe 58 46.43 N 6.22 E
Vallorcine 58 46.02 N 6.56 E
Vallouise 62 44.51 N 6.29 E
Vallromanas 266d 41.32 N 2.18 E
Valls 34 41.17 N 1.15 E
Valluga ∧ 58 47.09 N 10.12 E
Vallvidrera ✦[8] 266d 41.25 N 2.07 E
Vallvidrera, Riera de
≐ 266d 41.25 N 2.01 E
Val-Marie 184 49.14 N 107.44 W
Valmaseda 34 43.12 N 3.12 W
Valmeyer 219 38.17 N 90.18 W
Valmiera 76 57.33 N 25.24 E
Valmondois 261 49.06 N 2.12 E
Valmont 50 49.44 N 0.31 E
Valmontone 66 41.46 N 12.57 E
Valmy 56 49.05 N 4.46 E
Valognes 32 49.31 N 1.28 W
Valois 210 42.32 N 76.53 W
Valois, Baie de ⊂ 275a 45.26 N 73.47 W
Valok 78 45.47 N 34.57 E
Valona
→ Vlorë 38 40.27 N 19.30 E
Valongo 34 41.11 N 8.30 W
Valoria la Buena 34 41.48 N 4.32 W
Valparai 122 10.22 N 76.58 E
Valparaíso, Bra. 255 21.13 S 50.51 W
Valparaíso, Chile 252 33.02 S 71.38 W
Valparaíso, Méx. 234 22.46 N 103.34 W
Valparaiso, Fl., U.S. 194 30.29 N 86.29 W
Valparaiso, In., U.S. 216 41.28 N 87.03 W
Valparaiso, Ne., U.S. 198 41.04 N 96.49 W
Valparaíso □[4] 252 32.45 S 71.20 W
Valparaíso □[4] 234 22.33 N 103.39 W
Valpelline V 62 45.50 N 7.25 E
Valpolicella ✦[1] 64 45.25 N 10.52 E
Valpovo 38 45.39 N 18.26 E
Valprato Soana 62 45.31 N 7.33 E
Valréas 62 44.23 N 4.59 E
Valrico 220 27.57 N 82.16 W
Val Roveto V 66 41.52 N 13.30 E
Vals ≐ 158 27.23 S 26.30 E
Vals, Tanjung ≻ 164 8.26 S 137.38 E
Val-Saint-Michel 206 46.52 N 71.27 W
Valsbaai ⊂ 158 34.12 S 18.40 E
Valsequillo, Presa
⊜[1] 234 18.55 N 98.10 W
Valserine ≐ 58 46.05 N 5.50 E
Valserrhein ≐ 58 46.32 N 9.10 E
Valsertal V 58 46.37 N 9.10 E
Valsetz 202 44.50 N 123.39 W
Valsinni 68 40.10 N 16.26 E
Valsjöbyn 26 64.04 N 14.08 E
Valskog 40 59.27 N 15.57 E
Vals-les-Bains 62 44.40 N 4.22 E
Vals Platz 58 46.37 N 9.11 E
Vals-Près-le-Puy 62 45.01 N 3.52 E
Valstagna 64 45.51 N 11.39 E
Val-Suzon 58 47.25 N 4.54 E
Valtellina V 64 46.11 N 9.55 E
Valthermond 52 52.53 N 6.59 E
Valtice 60 48.44 N 16.45 E
Valtierrilla 234 20.32 N 101.08 W
Valtimo 26 63.40 N 28.48 E
Valtorta 58 45.59 N 9.32 E
Valtournanche 62 45.53 N 7.37 E
Valujec 76 52.46 N 33.23 E
Valujevka 80 46.44 N 43.43 E
Valujevo 265b 55.35 N 37.21 E
Valujki 78 50.13 N 38.08 E
Valvasone 64 45.59 N 12.52 E
Valverde 148 27.48 N 17.55 W
Valverde del Camino 34 37.34 N 6.45 W
Val Verde Park 228 34.27 N 118.40 W
Valyermo 228 34.26 N 117.50 W
Vamba ≐ 152 7.27 S 14.17 E
Vamdrup 41 55.25 N 9.17 E
Våmhus 26 61.08 N 14.28 E
Vamizi, Ilha I 154 11.02 S 40.40 E
Vammala 26 61.20 N 22.54 E
Vamori Wash V 200 31.57 N 112.21 W
Vamsadhāra ≐ 122 18.21 N 84.08 E
Van, Tür. 128 38.28 N 43.20 E
Van, Pa., U.S. 214 41.19 N 79.40 W
Van, Tx., U.S. 222 32.31 N 95.38 W
Van □[4] 84 39.00 N 43.45 E
Vanajanselkä ⊜ 26 61.09 N 24.15 E
Vanak 267d 35.45 N 51.23 E

Symbols in the index entries represent the broad categories identified in the key at the right. Symbols with superior numbers (∧[1]) identify subcategories (see complete key on page I · 1).

Kartensymbole in dem Registerverzeichnis stellen die rechts in Schlüssel erklärten Kategorien dar. Symbole mit hochgestellten Ziffern (∧[1]) bezeichnen Unterabteilungen einer Kategorie (vgl. vollständiger Schlüssel auf Seite I · 1).

Los símbolos incluidos en el texto del índice representan las grandes categorías identificadas con la clave a la derecha. Los símbolos con números en su parte superior (∧[1]) identifican las subcategorías (véase la clave completa en la página I · 1).

Les symboles de l'index représentent les catégories indiquées dans la légende à droite. Les symboles suivis d'un indice (∧[1]) représentent des sous-catégories (voir légende complète à la page I · 1).

Os símbolos incluídos no texto do índice representam as grandes categorias identificadas com a chave à direita. Os símbolos com números em sua parte superior (∧[1]) identificam as subcategorias (veja-se a chave completa à página I · 1).

∧ Mountain	Berg	Montaña	Montagne	Montanha
∧ Mountains	Berge	Montañas	Montagnes	Montanhas
≍ Pass	Pass	Paso	Col	Passo
V Valley, Canyon	Tal, Cañon	Valle, Cañón	Vallée, Canyon	Vale, Canhão
≐ Plain	Ebene	Llano	Plaine	Planície
≻ Cape	Kap	Cabo	Cap	Cabo
I Island	Insel	Isla	Île	Ilha
II Islands	Inseln	Islas	Îles	Ilhas
⫫ Other Topographic Features	Andere Topographische Objekte	Otros Elementos Topográficos	Autres données topographiques	Outros acidentes topográficos

Symbol	English	Deutsch	Español	Français	Português
≃	River	Fluss	Río	Rivière	Rio
≊	Canal	Kanal	Canal	Canal	Canal
∟	Waterfall, Rapids	Wasserfall, Stromschnellen	Cascada, Rápidos	Chute d'eau, Rapides	Cascata, Rápidos
⊻	Strait	Meeresstrasse	Estrecho	Détroit	Estreito
⊂	Bay, Gulf	Bucht, Golf	Bahía, Golfo	Baie, Golfe	Baía, Golfo
⊜	Lake, Lakes	See, Seen	Lago, Lagos	Lac, Lacs	Lago, Lagos
☷	Swamp	Sumpf	Pantano	Marais	Pântano
⛉	Ice Features, Glacier	Eis- und Gletscherformen	Accidentes Glaciales	Formes glaciaires	Acidentes glaciares
⊤	Other Hydrographic Features	Andere Hydrographische Objekte	Otros Elementos Hidrográficos	Autres données hydrographiques	Outros acidentes hidrográficos
✣	Submarine Features	Untermeerische Objekte	Accidentes Submarinos	Formes de relief sous-marin	Acidentes submarinos
□	Political Unit	Politische Einheit	Unidad Politica	Entité politique	Unidade política
♥	Cultural Institution	Kulturelle Institution	Institución Cultural	Institution culturelle	Instituição cultural
⊥	Historical Site	Historische Stätte	Sitio Histórico	Site historique	Sitio histórico
♠	Recreational Site	Erholungs- und Ferienort	Sitio de Recreo	Centre de loisirs	Area de Lazer
⊠	Airport	Flughafen	Aeropuerto	Aéroport	Aeroporto
■	Military Installation	Militäranlage	Instalación Militar	Installation militaire	Instalação militar
◆	Miscellaneous	Verschiedenes	Misceláneo	Divers	Diversos

ENGLISH — Name, Page, Lat.°′, Long.°′ / DEUTSCH — Name, Seite, Breite°′, Länge°′ E = Ost

Name	Page	Lat.°′	Long.°′
Verchn'aja Balkarija	84	43.06 N	43.24 E
Verchn'aja Buzinovka	80	49.04 N	43.12 E
Verchn'aja Čebula	86	56.02 N	87.36 E
Verchn'aja Chava	78	51.50 N	39.56 E
Verchn'aja Chila	88	52.06 N	115.54 E
Verchn'aja Chortica	78	47.51 N	35.01 E
Verchn'aja Čuginka	83	48.55 N	39.39 E
Verchn'aja Dobrinka	80	50.46 N	45.03 E
Verchn'aja Gniluša	78	50.16 N	40.23 E
Verchn'aja Grajvoronka	78	51.41 N	37.46 E
Verchn'aja Inta	24	66.00 N	60.20 E
Verchn'aja Maza	80	52.58 N	47.56 E
Verchn'aja Orl'anka	80	53.44 N	51.04 E
Verchn'aja Pyšma	86	56.55 N	60.37 E
Verchn'aja Salda	86	58.02 N	60.33 E
Verchn'aja Serebr'akovka	80	47.21 N	42.14 E
Verchn'aja Sin'ačicha	86	57.59 N	61.40 E
Verchn'aja Sysert'	86	56.26 N	60.46 E
Verchn'aja Tajmyra ≃	74	74.15 N	99.48 E
Verchn'aja Tarka	86	56.37 N	77.30 E
Verchnaja Tereška	80	52.54 N	47.24 E
Verchn'aja Tišanka	78	51.19 N	40.32 E
Verchn'aja Tojma	24	62.13 N	45.00 E
Verchn'aja Troica	76	57.15 N	37.08 E
Verchn'aja Tura	86	58.22 N	59.49 E
Verchn'aja Zaimka	88	55.51 N	110.09 E
Verchn'aja Zima	88	53.48 N	101.47 E
Verchneaks'onovskij	80	48.21 N	42.38 E
Verchneangarskij chrebet ⋏	88	56.20 N	111.30 E
Verchne-Anikin	83	48.09 N	39.59 E
Verchnebakanskij	78	44.52 N	37.39 E
Verchneber'ozovskij	86	50.17 N	82.13 E
Verchnebuzanskij	80	46.38 N	48.02 E
Verchnecaricynskij	80	48.23 N	43.57 E
Verchnedneprovsk	78	48.39 N	34.21 E
Verchnedneprovskij	76	54.59 N	33.21 E
Verchneduvannyj	78	48.20 N	39.48 E
Verchnedvinsk	76	55.47 N	27.56 E
Verchneimbatskoje	74	63.11 N	87.58 E
Verchnejarkejevo	80	55.27 N	54.19 E
Verchneje	78	48.53 N	38.28 E
Verchneje ◆[8]	83	48.53 N	38.28 E
Verchneje Šachlovo	82	55.02 N	37.15 E
Verchneje Sinevidnoje	78	49.06 N	23.34 E
Verchnekarabachskij kanal ≋	84	39.44 N	47.57 E
Verchnemakejevka	78	49.10 N	41.03 E
Verchnesadovoje	78	44.42 N	33.42 E
Verchnesjezžeje	80	52.44 N	51.15 E
Verchnespasskoje	80	52.39 N	41.47 E
Verchne-T'oploje	83	48.51 N	39.26 E
Verchnetulomskij	24	68.38 N	31.45 E
Verchneural'sk	86	53.53 N	59.13 E
Verchneusinskoje	86	52.14 N	93.01 E
Verchnevil'ujsk	74	63.27 N	120.18 E
Verchnevolynskoje	85	40.43 N	68.51 E
Verchnij Amyl	88	53.08 N	94.30 E
Verchnij Avz'an	86	53.32 N	57.33 E
Verchnij Balyklej	80	49.34 N	45.10 E
Verchnij Baskunčak	80	48.14 N	46.44 E
Verchnij Byk	78	50.43 N	41.14 E
Verchnije Dvoriki	82	56.28 N	38.22 E
Verchnije Kigi	86	55.25 N	58.37 E
Verchnije Korobki	80	50.19 N	44.38 E
Verchnije Lipki	80	49.38 N	43.51 E
Verchnije Tatyšly	86	56.17 N	55.52 E
Verchnij Ikorec	78	51.11 N	39.46 E
Verchnij Karačan	80	51.24 N	41.46 E
Verchnij Krasnyj Pereval	89	46.33 N	134.37 E
Verchnij Kužebar	86	53.22 N	93.15 E
Verchnij Landech	80	56.51 N	42.36 E
Verchnij Leb'ažinskij	80	46.45 N	47.50 E
Verchnij Lomov	80	53.28 N	43.34 E
Verchnij Lomovec	76	52.13 N	38.37 E
Verchnij Mamon	78	50.10 N	40.23 E
Verchnij Most	76	57.31 N	28.50 E
Verchnij Nejvinskij	86	57.17 N	60.09 E
Verchnij Petr'ak	86	57.29 N	77.30 E
Verchnij Rogačik	78	47.14 N	34.21 E
Verchnij Šergol'džin	88	50.12 N	108.20 E
Verchnij Tagil	86	57.22 N	59.56 E
Verchnij Takermen'	80	55.39 N	52.43 E
Verchnij Trojanov Val (Upper Trajan's Wall) ⊥	78	46.35 N	29.00 E
Verchnij Ufalej	86	56.04 N	60.14 E
Verchnij Ul'chun	88	49.34 N	112.32 E
Verchnij Uslon	80	55.47 N	48.57 E
Verchnij Zub, gora ∧	86	53.45 N	89.15 E
Verchnyje Nikul'asy	76	60.25 N	30.45 E
Verchnyj Jenisej (Ulug-Chem) ≃	88	51.47 N	92.00 E
Verchnyj Nagol'čik	83	48.05 N	39.06 E
Verchojansk	74	67.35 N	133.27 E
Verchojanskij chrebet ⋏	74	67.00 N	129.00 E
Vercholensk	88	54.06 N	105.35 E
Verchopuja	24	61.34 N	41.31 E
Verchošižemje	80	58.01 N	49.07 E
Verchososna	78	50.44 N	38.14 E
Verchoturje	86	58.52 N	60.48 E
Verchoturovo	86	58.22 N	95.21 E
Verchovažje	24	60.45 N	42.00 E
Verchovcevo	78	48.29 N	34.14 E
Verchovina	78	48.09 N	24.47 E
Verchovino	76	59.33 N	43.19 E
Verchovje	76	52.49 N	37.14 E
Verchovl'an'	82	55.03 N	38.21 E
Verchozim	80	52.56 N	46.23 E
Verchubinka	86	50.29 N	82.26 E
Verclause	62	44.23 N	5.26 E
Vercors ◆[1]	62	44.57 N	5.25 E
Verdalsøra	26	63.48 N	11.29 E
Verde ≃, Bra.	248	11.54 S	55.48 W
Verde ≃, Bra.	248	13.33 S	58.01 W
Verde ≃, Bra.	250	10.11 S	42.24 W
Verde ≃, Bra.	255	15.07 S	48.40 W
Verde ≃, Bra.	255	17.05 S	46.05 W
Verde ≃, Bra.	255	18.01 S	50.14 W
Verde ≃, Bra.	255	19.11 S	50.44 W
Verde ≃, Bra.	255	19.55 S	49.45 W
Verde ≃, Bra.	255	21.12 S	51.53 W
Verde ≃, Bra.	256	21.34 S	45.31 W
Verde ≃, Bra.	256	21.38 S	47.03 W
Verde ≃, Méx.	234	21.37 N	99.15 W
Verde ≃, Méx.	234	20.42 N	103.14 W
Verde ≃, Para.	252	23.09 S	57.37 W
Verde ≃, S.A.	248	13.59 S	60.24 W
Verde ≃, Az., U.S.	200	33.33 N	111.40 W
Verde, Arroyo ≃, Arg.	254	41.56 S	65.03 W
Verde, Arroyo ≃, Bol.	248	11.25 S	66.20 W
Verde, Costa ∸[2]	71	39.34 N	8.28 E
Verde Grande ≃	255	14.35 S	43.53 W
Verde Island I	116	13.33 N	121.05 E
Verde Island Passage ⋓	116	13.34 N	120.51 E
Verdello	62	45.36 N	9.37 E
Verden, B.R.D.	52	52.55 N	9.13 E
Verden, Ok., U.S.	196	35.05 N	98.05 W
Verde Pequeno ≃	255	14.48 S	43.31 W
Verdesela, Pinhal da ♠	266c	38.37 N	9.08 W
Verdi	226	39.31 N	119.59 W
Verdigre	198	42.35 N	98.02 W
Verdigre Creek ≃	198	42.42 N	98.03 W
Verdigris ≃	196	35.48 N	95.19 W
Verdinho ≃	255	17.29 S	50.27 W
Verdon	198	40.08 N	95.42 W
Verdon ≃	62	43.43 N	5.46 E
Verdon, Canal du ≋	62	43.43 N	5.57 E
Verdoy	210	42.46 N	73.48 W
Verduga	76	58.46 N	29.12 E
Verdugo Mountains ⋏	280	34.13 N	118.18 W
Verdun, P.Q., Can.	206	45.27 N	73.34 W
Verdun, Fr.	32	43.52 N	1.14 E
Verdun-sur-le-Doubs	58	46.54 N	5.01 E
Verdun-sur-Meuse	56	49.10 N	5.23 E
Verdura ≃	70	37.28 N	13.12 E
Vereb'jo	76	58.41 N	32.42 E
Vereeniging	158	26.38 S	27.57 E
Veregin	184	51.35 N	102.05 W
Vereinigte Arabische Emirate → United Arab Emirates □[1]	128	24.00 N	54.00 E
Vereinigte Königreich → United Kingdom □[1]	28	54.00 N	2.00 W
Vereinigte Staaten → United States □[1]	178	38.00 N	97.00 W
Vereja, S.S.S.R.	82	55.46 N	39.06 E
Vereja, S.S.S.R.	82	55.21 N	36.11 E
Vereja, S.S.S.R.	265b	55.37 N	38.02 E
Veremejki	76	53.46 N	31.15 E
Vereščagino, S.S.S.R.	74	64.14 N	87.37 E
Vereščagino, S.S.S.R.	80	58.05 N	54.40 E
Veresegyház	264c	47.39 N	19.17 E
Veresoč'	78	51.19 N	31.46 E
Veretje	82	54.08 N	36.17 E
Véretz	50	47.22 N	0.48 E
Verga	285	39.52 N	75.10 W
Verga, Cap ≻	150	10.12 N	14.27 W
Vergara, Esp.	34	43.07 N	2.25 W
Vergara, Ur.	252	32.56 S	53.57 W
Vergato	64	44.17 N	11.07 E
Vergel	196	25.39 N	103.32 W
Vergeletto	58	46.14 N	8.36 E
Vergemont Creek ≃	166	24.12 S	143.17 E
Vergennes	188	44.10 N	73.15 W
Verghereto	66	43.47 N	12.00 E
Vergiate	62	45.43 N	8.42 E
Vergons	62	43.55 N	6.35 E
Vergt	32	45.02 N	0.43 E
Vergulevka	83	48.24 N	38.32 E
Verigino	82	56.42 N	38.08 E
Verín	34	41.56 N	7.26 W
Veringenstadt	58	48.11 N	9.12 E
Verin Talin	84	40.23 N	43.53 E
Veriora	76	58.00 N	27.21 E
Veríssimo	255	19.42 S	48.18 W
Verkeerdevlei	158	28.48 S	26.48 E
Verkhneudinsk → Ulan-Ude	88	51.50 N	107.37 E
Verkhniy Ufaley → Verchnij Ufalej	86	56.04 N	60.14 E
Verkhnyaya Salda → Verchn'aja Salda	86	58.02 N	60.33 E
Verkhoyansk → Verchojansk	74	67.35 N	133.27 E
Verkykerskop	158	27.54 S	29.17 E
Verl (Senne I)	52	51.53 N	8.31 E
Vermaaklikheid	158	34.19 S	21.01 E
Vermaas	158	26.30 S	25.59 E
Vermand	50	49.52 N	3.09 E
Vermejo ≃	196	36.30 N	104.33 W
Vermelho ≃, Bra.	250	9.16 S	47.23 W
Vermelho ≃, Bra.	250	7.44 S	47.17 W
Vermelho ≃, Bra.	250	5.33 S	49.14 W
Vermelho ≃, Bra.	255	14.54 S	51.06 W
Vermenton	50	47.40 N	3.44 E
Vermette Lake ⊜	184	55.40 N	109.05 W
Vermezzo	266b	45.24 N	8.59 E
Vermiglio	64	46.18 N	10.42 E
Vermilion, Ab., Can.	182	53.22 N	110.51 W
Vermilion, Oh., U.S.	214	41.25 N	82.21 W
Vermilion □[6]	216	40.08 N	87.37 W
Vermilion ≃, Ab., Can.	184	53.44 N	110.18 W
Vermilion ≃, On., Can.	190	46.16 N	81.41 W
Vermilion ≃, Il., U.S.	216	41.19 N	89.04 W
Vermilion ≃, La., U.S.	194	29.46 N	92.09 W
Vermilion ≃, Mn., U.S.	190	48.16 N	92.30 W
Vermilion ≃, Oh., U.S.	214	41.26 N	82.22 W
Vermilion, Middle Fork ≃	216	40.12 N	87.45 W
Vermilion, North Fork ≃, Il., U.S.	216	40.49 N	88.30 W
Vermilion, North Fork ≃, Il., U.S.	216	40.13 N	87.39 W
Vermilion, South Fork ≃	216	40.49 N	88.30 W
Vermilion Bay	184	49.51 N	93.24 W
Vermilion Bay ⊂	194	29.40 N	92.00 W
Vermilion Lake ⊜, On., Can.	184	50.03 N	92.13 W
Vermilion Lake ⊜, Mn., U.S.	190	47.53 N	92.25 W
Vermilion Pass)(	182	51.14 N	116.03 W
Vermillion	198	42.46 N	96.55 W
Vermillion ≃	198	42.44 N	96.53 W
Vermillion, East Fork ≃	198	43.44 N	97.03 W
Vermillion, West Fork ≃	198	43.44 N	97.03 W
Vermillion Bluffs ∸[4]	200	40.50 N	108.30 W
Vermillion Creek ≃, U.S.	200	40.46 N	108.53 W
Vermillion Creek ≃, Ks., U.S.	198	39.12 N	96.13 W
Vermont, Austl.	274b	37.50 S	145.12 E
Vermont, Il., U.S.	194	40.17 N	90.25 W
Vermont □[3], U.S.	178	43.50 N	72.45 W
Vermont □[3], U.S.	188	43.50 N	72.45 W
Vermontville	216	42.37 N	85.01 W
Vernà, Pizzo di ∧	70	38.01 N	15.15 E
Vernaison	62	45.39 N	4.49 E
Vernal	200	40.27 N	109.31 W
Vernalis	226	37.37 N	121.17 W
Vernante	62	44.15 N	7.32 E
Vernayaz	58	46.08 N	7.02 E
Vernazza	62	44.08 N	9.41 E
Verndale	198	46.24 N	95.01 W
Verne	52	51.41 N	8.34 E
Verner	190	46.25 N	80.07 W
Verneuil	32	48.44 N	0.56 E
Verneuil-L'Étang	261	48.39 N	2.50 E
Verneuil-sur-Avre	50	48.44 N	0.56 E
Verneuil-sur-Seine	50	48.59 N	1.59 E
Verneukpan	158	30.00 S	21.00 E
Verneukpan ≚	158	30.00 S	21.10 E
Vernier	58	46.13 N	6.06 E
Verninge	41	55.18 N	10.13 E
Vernio	66	44.03 N	11.09 E
Vernole	68	40.17 N	18.18 E
Vernon, B.C., Can.	182	50.16 N	119.16 W
Vernon, On., Can.	212	45.10 N	75.28 W
Vernon, Fr.	50	49.05 N	1.29 E
Vernon, Al., U.S.	194	33.45 N	88.06 W
Vernon, Ca., U.S.	280	34.01 N	118.13 W
Vernon, Ct., U.S.	207	41.49 N	72.28 W
Vernon, Fl., U.S.	194	30.37 N	85.42 W
Vernon, Il., U.S.	219	38.48 N	89.05 W
Vernon, In., U.S.	218	38.59 N	85.36 W
Vernon, Mi., U.S.	216	42.56 N	84.02 W
Vernon, N.J., U.S.	210	41.11 N	74.29 W
Vernon, N.Y., U.S.	210	43.05 N	75.32 W
Vernon, Oh., U.S.	214	41.23 N	80.34 W
Vernon, Tx., U.S.	196	34.09 N	99.15 W
Vernon, Ut,. U.S.	200	40.05 N	112.25 W
Vernon, Lake ⊜	212	45.20 N	79.17 W
Vernon Dam ◆[6]	207	42.46 N	72.31 W
Vernon Hills	278	42.13 N	87.58 W
Vernonia	224	45.51 N	123.11 W
Vernon Lake ⊜[1]	194	31.15 N	93.25 W
Vernon River	186	46.12 N	62.50 W
Vernouillet	261	48.58 N	1.59 E
Vernoux-en-Vivarais	62	44.54 N	4.39 E
Verny	56	49.01 N	6.12 E
Vero ≃	34	42.00 N	0.10 E
Vero Beach	220	27.38 N	80.23 W
Véroia	38	40.31 N	22.12 E
Verolanuova	64	45.19 N	10.04 E
Verolavecchia	64	45.19 N	10.03 E
Veroli	66	41.41 N	13.25 E
Verona, On., Can.	212	44.29 N	76.42 W
Verona, It.	64	45.27 N	11.00 E
Verona, Ky., U.S.	218	38.49 N	84.39 W
Verona, Ms., U.S.	194	34.11 N	88.43 W
Verona, N.J., U.S.	276	40.49 N	74.14 W
Verona, N.Y., U.S.	210	43.08 N	75.34 W
Verona, Oh., U.S.	218	39.54 N	84.29 W
Verona, Pa., U.S.	279b	40.30 N	79.50 W
Verona, Wi., U.S.	216	42.59 N	89.31 W
Verona □[4]	64	45.25 N	11.02 E
Verona Beach	210	43.12 N	75.44 W
Verona Beach State Park ♠	210	43.14 N	75.44 W
Verona Park	216	42.21 N	85.09 W
Verónica	258	35.22 S	57.20 W
Verperluda, ostrov I	265a	59.59 N	30.01 E
Verplanck	210	41.15 N	73.58 W
Verran	166	33.51 S	136.18 E
Verrazano-Narrows Bridge ◆[5]	210	40.36 N	74.03 W
Verrès	62	45.40 N	7.42 E
Verrettes	238	19.03 N	72.28 W
Verrey-sous-Salmaise	58	47.26 N	4.40 E
Verrières, Bois de ♠	261	48.45 N	2.15 E
Verrières-le-Buisson	261	48.45 N	2.16 E
Versa ≃	62	44.54 N	8.16 E
Versailles, Fr.	50	48.48 N	2.08 E
Versailles, Il., U.S.	194	39.53 N	90.39 W
Versailles, In., U.S.	218	39.04 N	85.15 W
Versailles, Ky., U.S.	218	38.03 N	84.43 W
Versailles, Mo., U.S.	194	38.25 N	92.50 W
Versailles, N.Y., U.S.	210	42.31 N	78.59 W
Versailles, Oh., U.S.	216	40.13 N	84.29 W
Versailles, Pa., U.S.	279b	40.21 N	79.51 W
Versailles ◆[8]	288	34.38 S	58.31 W
Versailles, Château de ⊥	261	48.48 N	2.07 E
Versailles, Parc de ♠	261	48.49 N	2.06 E
Versailles State Park ♠	218	39.04 N	85.13 W
Verse ≃	263	51.15 N	7.46 E
Versec → Vršac	38	45.07 N	21.18 E
Versestausee ⊜[1]	263	51.11 N	7.41 E
Versien	158	27.05 S	27.52 E
Veršina Tei	86	53.20 N	89.36 E
Veršino-Darasunskij	88	52.20 N	115.32 E
Veršino-Šachtaminskij	88	51.21 N	117.50 E
Versmold	52	52.02 N	8.09 E
Versoix	58	46.16 N	6.10 E
Ver-sur-Launette	261	49.06 N	2.41 E
Vert	261	48.57 N	1.41 E
Vert, Cap ≻	150	14.43 N	17.30 W
Vert'ačij	80	48.57 N	43.53 E
Verte, Île I, P.Q., Can.	186	48.02 N	69.26 W
Verte, Île I, P.Q., Can.	275a	45.34 N	73.30 W
Vertedero	240m	18.05 N	66.15 W
Verteillac	32	45.21 N	0.22 E
Vertentes	250	7.54 S	35.59 W
Vertientes	240p	21.16 N	78.09 W
Vertijevka	78	51.10 N	31.51 E
Vertkovo	82	56.07 N	36.25 E
Vert-le-Grand	261	48.34 N	2.22 E
Vert-le-Petit	261	48.33 N	2.22 E
Vertlinskoje	82	56.14 N	36.58 E
Vertou	32	47.10 N	1.29 W
Vertova	62	45.48 N	9.50 E
Vert-Saint-Denis	261	48.34 N	2.37 E
Vertus	50	48.54 N	4.00 E
Verucchio	66	43.59 N	12.25 E
Verulam	158	29.45 S	31.02 E
Verulamium ⊥	260	51.45 N	0.22 W
Verviers	56	50.35 N	5.52 E
Vervins	50	49.50 N	3.54 E
Verwall Gruppe ⋏	58	47.02 N	10.10 E
Verwood	42	50.53 N	1.52 W
Veryan	42	50.13 N	4.54 W
Verzasca ≃	58	46.09 N	8.52 E
Verzegnis	64	46.25 N	12.59 E
Verzenay	50	49.10 N	4.09 E
Verzino	68	39.19 N	16.51 E
Verzuolo	62	44.36 N	7.29 E
Verzy	50	49.09 N	4.10 E
Vesanto	26	62.56 N	26.25 E
Vesava ◆[8]	272c	19.08 N	72.48 E
Vescovato, Fr.	36	42.30 N	9.26 E
Vescovato, It.	64	45.10 N	10.10 E
Vescovo di Squillace, Roccelletta del ⊥	68	38.48 N	16.35 E
Vesdre ≃	56	50.37 N	5.37 E
Veseja	76	53.04 N	27.41 E
Veselí nad Lužnicí	30	49.11 N	14.43 E
Veselí nad Moravou	30	48.58 N	17.22 E
Veselinovo	78	47.21 N	31.14 E
Veselovskoje	86	54.00 N	78.43 E
Veselovskoje vodochranilišče ⊜[1]	80	47.00 N	41.18 E
Vésenaz	58	46.14 N	6.12 E
Vešenskaja	80	49.38 N	41.43 E
Vesgre ≃	50	48.48 N	1.36 E
Vesijärvi ⊜	26	61.06 N	25.32 E
Vesjegonsk	76	58.40 N	37.16 E
Veškajma, S.S.S.R.	80	54.03 N	47.08 E
Veškajma, S.S.S.R.	80	54.04 N	47.02 E
Veški	265b	55.56 N	37.37 E
Vesle ≃	50	49.23 N	3.38 E
Vešn'aki ◆[8]	265b	55.44 N	37.49 E
Ves'olaja Gora	83	48.43 N	39.16 E
Ves'olaja Rošča	86	53.47 N	76.22 E
Vesole, Monte ∧	68	40.24 N	15.10 E
Ves'oloje, S.S.S.R.	78	47.01 N	34.55 E
Ves'oloje, S.S.S.R.	80	50.17 N	45.15 E
Ves'oloje, S.S.S.R.	83	47.10 N	38.45 E
Ves'oloje, S.S.S.R.	85	43.19 N	77.06 E
Ves'olo-Voznesenka	83	47.09 N	38.20 E
Ves'olyj, S.S.S.R.	80	47.06 N	40.45 E
Ves'olyj, S.S.S.R.	83	47.20 N	39.18 E
Ves'olyje Terny	78	48.07 N	33.32 E
Ves'olyj Jar, S.S.S.R.	86	51.18 N	81.07 E
Ves'olyj Jar, S.S.S.R.	89	43.57 N	135.28 E
Ves'olyj Podol, S.S.S.R.	78	49.36 N	33.16 E
Ves'olyj Podol, S.S.S.R.	86	53.31 N	65.54 E
Ves'olyj Pos'olok ◆[8]	265a	59.54 N	30.28 E
Vesoul	58	47.38 N	6.10 E
Vespasiano	255	19.40 S	43.55 W
Vespolate	62	45.21 N	8.40 E
Vesta	236	9.43 N	83.03 W
Vest-Agder □[6]	26	58.30 N	7.10 E
Vestal	210	42.05 N	76.03 W
Vestal Center	210	42.02 N	76.01 W
Vestavia Hills	194	33.26 N	86.46 W
Vestbygd	26	58.06 N	6.35 E
Vesterålen II	24	68.45 N	15.00 E
Vester Egede	41	55.16 N	11.59 E
Vesterø Havn	26	57.18 N	10.56 E
Vester Skerninge	41	55.03 N	10.28 E
Vester Sottrup	41	54.57 N	9.43 E
Vestfjorden ⊂[2]	24	68.08 N	15.00 E
Vestfold □[6]	26	59.15 N	10.10 E
Vestmannaeyjar	24a	63.26 N	20.12 W
Vestone	64	45.42 N	10.24 E
Vestreno	58	46.06 N	9.18 E
Vestsjælland □[6]	41	55.35 N	11.30 E
Vestvågøya I	24	68.15 N	13.50 E
Vésubie ≃	62	43.52 N	7.12 E
Vesubio → Vesuvio ∧[1]	68	40.49 N	14.26 E
Vesuv → Vesuvio ∧[1]	68	40.49 N	14.26 E
Vesuvio (Vesuvius) ∧[1]	68	40.49 N	14.26 E
Vesuvius → Vesuvio ∧[1]	68	40.49 N	14.26 E
Vesuvius Bay	224	48.53 N	123.35 W
Veszprém	30	47.06 N	17.55 E
Veszprém □[6]	30	46.50 N	17.30 E
Vésztő	30	46.55 N	21.16 E
Vet ≃	158	27.40 S	25.40 E
Vetapālem	122	15.47 N	80.19 E
Vetčin	76	52.27 N	28.10 E
Veterans Stadium ♠	285	39.54 N	75.10 W
Vétheuil	50	49.04 N	1.42 E
Vetju	24	62.57 N	50.44 E
Vetka	76	52.33 N	31.10 E
Vetlanda	26	57.26 N	15.04 E
Vetl'anka	80	52.52 N	51.09 E
Vetluga	80	57.51 N	45.47 E
Vetluga ≃	80	56.18 N	46.24 E
Vetlužskij, S.S.S.R.	80	57.11 N	45.07 E
Vetlužskij, S.S.S.R.	80	58.23 N	45.26 E
Vetoškino	80	57.18 N	49.44 E
Vetovo	38	43.42 N	26.16 E
Vetralla	66	42.19 N	12.03 E
Vetren	38	42.16 N	24.03 E
Vetrino	76	55.25 N	28.28 E
Vetriolo	64	46.02 N	11.18 E
Vetrișoaia	38	46.26 N	28.13 E
Větřni	61	48.46 N	14.17 E
Vetschau	54	51.47 N	14.04 E
Vettaikkāranpudūr	122	10.34 N	76.56 E
Vettisfossen ∟	26	61.22 N	7.55 E
Vetto	64	44.29 N	10.20 E
Vettore, Monte ∧	66	42.49 N	13.16 E
Vetulonia	66	42.51 N	10.58 E
Veules-les-Roses	50	49.52 N	0.48 E
Veulettes-sur-Mer	50	49.51 N	0.36 E
Veurne (Furnes)	50	51.04 N	2.40 E
Vevay	218	38.44 N	85.04 W
Vevelstad	24	65.43 N	12.30 E
Veveno, Khawr V	140	6.40 N	32.58 E
Vevey	58	46.28 N	6.51 E
Vex	58	46.13 N	7.24 E
Veyle ≃	58	46.18 N	4.50 E
Veynes	62	44.32 N	5.49 E
Veyrier	62	45.53 N	6.10 E
Vézelay	50	47.28 N	3.44 E
Vézelise	58	48.29 N	6.05 E
Vézénobres	62	44.03 N	4.09 E
Vézère ≃	32	44.53 N	0.53 E
Vezirköprü	130	41.09 N	35.28 E
Vezouze ≃	58	48.35 N	6.29 E
Vezza d'Oglio	64	46.14 N	10.24 E
Vezzana, Cima della ∧	64	46.17 N	11.50 E
Vezzano	64	46.05 N	11.00 E
Vezzano Ligure	64	44.09 N	9.52 E
Viacha	248	16.39 S	68.18 W
Viadana	64	44.56 N	10.31 E
Viadutos	252	27.34 S	52.01 W
Viai Island I	164	3.20 S	144.25 E
Viale	252	31.53 S	60.01 W
Vialonga	266c	38.52 N	9.05 W
Via Mala V	58	46.40 N	9.26 E
Viamão	252	30.05 S	51.02 W
Viamonte	252	33.44 S	63.06 W
Vian	196	35.29 N	94.58 W
Viana	250	3.13 S	45.00 W
Viana, Ilha do I	287a	22.52 S	43.08 W
Viana del Bollo	34	42.11 N	7.06 W
Viana do Alentejo	34	38.20 N	8.00 W
Viana do Castelo	34	41.42 N	8.50 W
Vianden	56	49.57 N	6.11 E
Vianen	52	52.00 N	5.05 E
Viangchan (Vientiane)	110	17.58 N	102.36 E
Viangphoukha	110	20.41 N	101.04 E
Viar ≃	34	37.36 N	5.50 W
Viareggio	64	43.52 N	10.14 E
Viarmes	50	49.08 N	2.22 E
Viatka → Kirov	80	58.38 N	49.42 E
Viaur ≃	32	44.08 N	2.23 E
Vibank	184	50.20 N	103.55 W
Víboras, Arroyo de las ≃	258	33.57 S	58.21 W
Viborg, Dan.	26	56.26 N	9.24 E
Viborg → Vyborg, S.S.S.R.	76	60.42 N	28.45 E
Viborg, S.D., U.S.	198	43.10 N	97.04 W
Viborg □[6]	41	56.18 N	9.27 E
Vibo Valentia	68	38.40 N	16.06 E
Vibraye	50	48.03 N	0.44 E
Viburnum	194	37.42 N	91.08 W
Viby	41	55.33 N	12.02 E
Viby ◆[8]	41	56.07 N	10.10 E
Vic, Étang de ⊂	62	43.29 N	3.50 E
Vicálvaro ◆[8]	266a	40.24 N	3.36 W
Vicarello	66	42.10 N	12.12 E
Vicari	70	37.49 N	13.34 E
Vicchio	66	43.56 N	11.28 E
Vicco	192	37.12 N	83.03 W
Vic-en-Bigorre	32	43.23 N	0.03 E
Vicência	250	7.40 S	35.20 W
Vicente, Point ≻	280	33.44 N	118.25 W
Vicente Casares	258	34.57 S	58.38 W
Vicente de Carvalho	256	23.56 S	46.19 W
Vicente Guerrero, Méx.	232	30.45 N	116.00 W
Vicente Guerrero, Méx.	234	18.24 N	92.53 W
Vicente Guerrero, Méx.	234	19.08 N	98.10 W
Vicente López	258	34.32 S	58.28 W
Vicente López □[5]	288	34.32 S	58.30 W
Vicente Noble	238	18.23 N	71.11 W
Vicenza	64	45.33 N	11.33 E
Vicenza □[4]	64	45.40 N	11.27 E
Viceroy	184	49.27 N	105.22 W
Vich	34	41.56 N	2.15 E
Vichada □[5]	246	5.00 N	69.30 W
Vichada ≃	246	4.55 N	67.50 W
Vichadero	252	31.48 S	54.43 W
Vichigasta	252	29.29 S	67.31 W
Vichoreva ≃	88	56.47 N	101.22 E
Vichorevka	88	56.12 N	101.09 E
Vichra ≃	76	54.01 N	31.52 E
Vichuga → Vičuga	80	57.13 N	41.56 E
Vichuquén	252	34.53 S	72.00 W
Vichy	32	46.08 N	3.26 E
Vici	196	36.08 N	99.17 W
Vickery	214	41.23 N	82.56 W
Vicksburg, Mi., U.S.	216	42.07 N	85.31 W
Vicksburg, Ms., U.S.	194	32.21 N	90.52 W
Vicksburg, Pa., U.S.	210	40.56 N	76.59 W
Vicksburg National Military Park ♠	194	32.24 N	90.52 W
Vico	36	42.10 N	8.48 E
Vico, Lago di ⊜	66	42.19 N	12.10 E
Vico Canavese	62	45.30 N	7.47 E
Vico del Gargano	68	41.54 N	15.57 E
Vico Equense	68	40.40 N	14.25 E
Vicoforte	62	44.21 N	7.54 E
Vicopisano	66	43.42 N	10.35 E
Viçosa, Bra.	250	9.24 S	36.14 W
Viçosa, Bra.	255	20.45 S	42.53 W
Viçosa do Ceará	250	3.34 S	41.05 W
Vicosoprano	58	46.22 N	9.37 E
Vicovaro	66	42.01 N	12.54 E
Vicq	261	48.49 N	1.50 E
Vic-Sur-Aisne	50	49.24 N	3.07 E
Vic-sur-Cère	32	44.59 N	2.37 E
Vic-sur-Seille	56	48.47 N	6.32 E
Victor, Ca., U.S.	226	38.08 N	121.12 W
Victor, Id., U.S.	202	43.36 N	111.06 W
Victor, Ia., U.S.	190	41.43 N	92.17 W
Victor, Mt., U.S.	202	46.25 N	114.08 W
Victor, N.Y., U.S.	210	42.58 N	77.24 W
Victor, Lac ⊜	186	50.35 N	61.50 W
Victorbur	52	53.29 N	7.20 E
Victor Harbor	168b	35.34 S	138.37 E
Victoria, Arg.	252	32.37 S	60.10 W
Victoria → Vitória, Bra.	255	20.19 S	40.21 W
Victoria, Cam.	152	4.01 N	9.12 E
Victoria, B.C., Can.	224	48.25 N	123.22 W
Victoria, P.E., Can.	186	46.13 N	63.29 W
Victoria, Chile	252	38.13 S	72.20 W
Victoria, Gren.	241k	12.12 N	61.42 W
Victoria, Guinée	150	10.50 N	14.33 W
Victoria (Xianggang), H.K.	271d	22.17 N	114.09 E
Victoria, Malay.	112	5.17 N	115.15 E
Victoria → Ciudad Victoria, Méx.	234	23.44 N	99.08 W
Victoria, Pil.	116	15.35 N	120.41 E
Victoria, Pil.	116	13.12 N	121.15 E
Victoria, Rom.	38	45.45 N	24.41 E
Victoria, Sey.	138	4.38 S	55.27 E
Victoria, Ks., U.S.	198	38.51 N	99.08 W
Victoria, Tx., U.S.	196	28.48 N	97.00 W
Victoria, Va., U.S.	192	36.59 N	78.13 W
Victoria □[3]	166	38.00 S	145.00 E
Victoria □[4]	154	20.54 S	31.21 E
Victoria □[6], On., Can.	212	44.35 N	78.50 W
Victoria □[6], Tx., U.S.	222	28.55 N	97.00 W
Victoria ◆[8]	288	34.28 S	58.31 W
Victoria ≃, Austl.	160	15.12 S	129.43 E
Victoria ≃, Nf., Can.	186	48.45 N	56.40 W
Victoria, Isla I	254	45.18 S	73.58 W
Victoria, Lake ⊜, Afr.	154	1.00 S	33.00 E
Victoria, Lake ⊜, Austl.	166	34.00 S	141.16 E
Victoria, Mount ∧, Mya.	110	21.14 N	93.55 E
Victoria, Mount ∧, Pap. N. Gui.	164	8.55 S	147.35 E
Victoria, Pont ◆[5]	275a	45.29 N	73.32 W
Victoria and Albert Museum ʊ	272c	18.59 N	72.50 E
Victoria Beach	184	50.43 N	96.33 W
Victoria Beach ∸[2]	273a	6.25 N	3.25 E
Victoria de Durango → Durango	234	24.02 N	104.40 W
Victoria de las Tunas	240p	20.58 N	76.57 W
Victoria Falls	154	17.56 S	25.50 E
Victoria Falls ∟	154	17.55 S	25.51 E
Victoria Falls National Park ♠	154	17.55 S	25.40 E
Victoria Gardens ♠	272c	18.59 N	72.50 E
Victoria Harbour	212	44.45 N	79.46 W
Victoria International Airport ⊠	224	48.39 N	123.26 W
Victoria Island I, N.T., Can.	176	71.00 N	110.00 W
Victoria Island I, Nig.	273a	6.26 N	3.26 E
Victoria Lake ⊜	273d	26.14 S	28.09 E
Victoria Lake ⊜[1]	186	48.18 N	57.30 W
Victoria Land ◆[1]	9	75.00 S	163.00 E
Victoria Lawn Tennis Association Courts ♠	274b	37.51 S	145.02 E
Victoria Memorial ⊥	272b	22.33 N	88.21 E
Victoria Memorial Hall ʊ	271c	1.17 N	103.51 E
Victoria Nile ≃	154	2.14 N	31.26 E
Victoria Park	168a	31.58 S	115.55 E
Victoria Park ♠, H.K.	271d	22.17 N	114.11 E
Victoria Park ♠, Eng., U.K.	262	53.23 N	2.34 W
Victoria Peak ∧, Belize	232	16.48 N	88.37 W
Victoria Peak ∧, B.C., Can.	182	50.03 N	126.06 W
Victoria Peak ∧, H.K.	271d	22.17 N	114.08 E
Victoria Peaks ⋏	116	9.22 N	118.20 E
Victoria Point	171a	27.35 S	153.18 E
Victoria Range ⋏, N.Z.	172	42.09 S	172.08 E
Victoria Range ⋏, Pil.	116	9.32 N	118.23 E
Victoria River Downs	164	16.24 S	131.00 E
Victorias	116	10.54 N	123.05 E
Victoria State Car Club Race Circuit ♠	274b	37.45 S	145.11 E
Victoria Station ◆[5], Eng., U.K.	260	51.29 N	0.09 W
Victoria Station ◆[5], Eng., U.K.	262	53.29 N	2.15 W
Victoria Strait ⋓	176	69.15 N	100.30 W
Victoria Terminus ◆[5]	272c	18.57 N	72.50 E
Victoria University of Manchester ʊ[2]	262	53.28 N	2.14 W
Victoriaville	206	46.03 N	71.57 W
Victoria West	158	31.25 S	23.04 E
Victorica	252	36.13 S	65.27 W
Victorino	246	2.48 N	67.50 W
Victorino de la Plaza	252	36.36 S	62.40 W
Victor Manuel Bueno	232	24.20 N	98.58 W
Victorville	228	34.32 N	117.17 W
Victory, Mount ∧	164	9.10 S	149.05 E
Victory Gardens	276	40.52 N	74.32 W
Victory Heights	214	41.22 N	79.46 W
Victory Hills	279b	40.11 N	79.53 W
Victory Mills	210	43.05 N	73.36 W
Victory Monument ⊥	269a	13.46 N	100.33 E
Vičuga	80	57.13 N	41.56 E
Vicuña	252	30.02 S	70.44 W
Vicuña Mackenna	252	33.54 S	64.23 W
Vidal, Kaap ≻	158	28.09 S	32.33 E
Vidalia, Ga., U.S.	192	32.13 N	82.24 W
Vidalia, La., U.S.	194	31.33 N	91.25 W
Vidal Ramos	252	27.23 S	49.22 W
Vidauban	62	43.26 N	6.26 E
Videbæk	26	56.05 N	8.38 E
Videira	252	27.00 S	51.08 W
Videle	38	44.16 N	25.31 E
Vidigueira	34	38.13 N	7.48 W
Vidim, Česko.	54	50.28 N	14.31 E
Vidim, S.S.S.R.	88	56.29 N	103.09 E
Vidin	38	43.59 N	22.52 E
Vidisha	124	23.32 N	77.49 E
Vidlica	24	61.10 N	32.21 E
Vidnoje	82	55.34 N	37.41 E
Vidogošči	82	56.42 N	36.23 E
Vidor	194	30.07 N	94.00 W
Vidos ≃	267b	40.58 N	28.53 E
Vidöstern ⊜	26	57.04 N	14.01 E
Vidourle ≃	62	43.32 N	4.08 E
Vidra, Rom.	38	44.16 N	26.11 E
Vidra, Rom.	38	45.55 N	26.54 E
Vidsel	24	65.51 N	20.24 E
Vidzeme □[9]	76	57.10 N	25.30 E
Vidzy	76	55.24 N	26.38 E
Vie ≃	50	49.05 N	0.04 E
Viecht	60	48.30 N	12.04 E
Viechtach	60	49.05 N	12.53 E
Viedma	254	40.48 S	63.00 W
Viedma, Lago ⊜	254	49.35 S	72.35 W
Viehberg ∧	61	48.33 N	14.37 E
Viehhausen	60	48.59 N	11.58 E
Vieil Armand ♠	58	47.52 N	7.10 E
Vieillard, Lac du ⊜	190	47.23 N	78.02 W
Vieille Case	240d	15.36 N	61.24 W
Vieira do Minho	34	41.39 N	8.09 W
Viejo ≃	236	12.28 N	86.21 W
Viejo, Cerro ∧	246	4.49 S	79.27 W
Viekšniai	76	56.16 N	22.31 E
Vielank	54	53.15 N	11.08 E
Viella	34	42.42 N	0.48 E
Vielle-Eglise-en-Yvelines	261	48.40 N	1.53 E
Vielsalm	56	50.17 N	5.55 E
Viels-Maisons	50	48.54 N	3.24 E
Viena → Vienne ≃	32	47.13 N	0.05 E
Vienenburg	54	51.57 N	10.34 E
Vienna, On., Can.	212	42.41 N	80.48 W
Vienna → Wien, Öst.	61	48.13 N	16.20 E
Vienna, Ga., U.S.	192	32.05 N	83.47 W
Vienna, Il., U.S.	194	37.25 N	88.54 W
Vienna, In., U.S.	218	38.39 N	85.46 W
Vienna, Md., U.S.	208	38.29 N	75.49 W
Vienna, Mo., U.S.	194	38.11 N	91.56 W
Vienna, N.J., U.S.	210	40.52 N	74.53 W
Vienna, Oh., U.S.	214	41.14 N	80.40 W
Vienna, S.D., U.S.	198	44.42 N	97.30 W
Vienna, Va., U.S.	208	38.29 N	75.49 W
Vienna, Va., U.S.	208	38.54 N	77.15 W
Vienna, W.V., U.S.	188	39.19 N	81.32 W
Vienne, Fr.	62	45.31 N	4.52 E
Vienne → Wien, Öst.	61	48.13 N	16.20 E
Vienne □[5]	32	46.35 N	0.30 E
Vienne ≃	32	47.13 N	0.05 E
Vienne-en-Arthies	261	49.04 N	1.44 E
Vienne-le-Château	56	49.11 N	4.53 E
Vientiane → Viangchan	110	17.58 N	102.36 E
Vientos, Paso de los → Windward Passage ⋓	238	20.00 N	73.50 W
Vieques	240m	18.09 N	65.27 W
Vieques, Isla de I	240m	18.08 N	65.25 W
Vieques, Pasaje de ⋓	240m	18.11 N	65.37 W
Vieques, Sonda de ⋓	240m	18.15 N	65.23 W
Vière ≃	56	48.46 N	4.41 E
Viereck	54	53.32 N	14.02 E
Vieremä	26	63.45 N	27.01 E
Vierfontein	158	27.03 S	26.46 E
Vierhouten	52	52.20 N	5.50 E
Vieringhausen ◆[8]	263	51.11 N	7.10 E
Vierlande ◆[1]	52	53.26 N	10.14 E
Viernau	54	50.40 N	10.32 E
Viernheim	56	49.32 N	8.34 E
Vierraden	54	53.06 N	14.17 E
Viersen	56	51.15 N	6.23 E
Vierumäki	26	61.06 N	25.57 E
Vierwaldstättersee ⊜	58	47.00 N	8.28 E
Vierzehnheiligen ʊ[1]	56	50.08 N	11.02 E
Vierzon	50	47.13 N	2.05 E
Viesca	232	25.21 N	102.48 W
Viesecke	54	53.01 N	12.01 E
Vieselbach	54	51.00 N	11.08 E
Viesīte	76	56.21 N	25.33 E
Vieste	68	41.53 N	16.10 E
Vietgest	54	53.45 N	12.20 E
Vietnam □[1], Asia	108	16.00 N	108.00 E
Vietnam □[1], Asia	110	16.00 N	108.00 E
Vietnam Veterans Memorial ⊥	284c	38.53 N	77.03 W
Vietri di Potenza	68	40.36 N	15.30 E
Vietri sul Mare	68	40.40 N	14.44 E
Viet-tri	110	21.18 N	105.26 E
Vietz → Witnica	30	52.40 N	14.55 E
Vieux-Condé	50	50.27 N	3.34 E
Vieux-Ferette	58	47.30 N	7.18 E
Vieux-Fort, P.Q., Can.	186	51.26 N	57.49 W
Vieux-Fort, Guad.	241o	15.57 N	61.43 W
Vieux Fort, St. Luc.	241f	13.44 N	60.57 W
Vieux-Fort, Pointe du ≻	241o	15.57 N	61.43 W
Vieux Fort Bay ⊂	241f	13.44 N	60.58 W
Vieux-Habitants	241o	16.04 N	61.46 W
Vieux-Thann	58	47.48 N	7.08 E
Vievis	76	54.46 N	24.48 E
View Park	280	34.00 N	118.20 W
Vieytes	258	35.16 S	57.35 W
Vif	62	45.03 N	5.40 E
Vig	41	55.51 N	11.36 E
Viga ≃	76	59.14 N	43.41 E
Vigala	76	58.43 N	24.22 E
Vigan	116	17.34 N	120.23 E
Vigarano Mainarda	64	44.50 N	11.30 E
Vigatto	64	44.43 N	10.20 E
Vigeland	26	58.05 N	7.18 E
Vigentino ◆[8]	266b	45.25 N	9.11 E
Vigersted	41	55.29 N	11.54 E
Vigese, Monte ∧	64	44.12 N	11.06 E
Vigésima Quinta de Abril, Ponte ◆[5]	266c	38.41 N	9.11 W
Vigevano	62	45.19 N	8.51 E
Viggianello	68	39.58 N	16.05 E
Viggiano	68	40.20 N	15.54 E
Viggiù	62	45.52 N	8.54 E
Vigia	250	0.48 S	48.08 W
Vigie Airport ⊠	241f	14.01 N	60.59 W
Vignacourt	50	50.01 N	2.12 E
Vignale	62	45.01 N	8.24 E
Vignanello	66	42.23 N	12.17 E
Vigneulles-lès-Hattonchâtel	56	48.59 N	5.43 E
Vigneux-sur-Seine	261	48.42 N	2.25 E
Vignola	64	44.29 N	11.00 E
Vignory	58	48.17 N	5.06 E
Vignot	56	48.46 N	5.36 E
Vigny	261	49.05 N	1.56 E
Vigo	34	42.14 N	8.43 W
Vigo, Ría de ⊂[1]	34	42.15 N	8.45 W
Vigodarzere	64	45.27 N	11.53 E
Vigo di Fassa	64	46.25 N	11.40 E
Vigolzone	62	44.55 N	9.40 E
Vigone	62	44.51 N	7.30 E
Vigonovo	64	45.23 N	12.00 E
Vigo-Rendena	64	46.05 N	10.43 E
Vigrestad	26	58.34 N	5.42 E
Viguzzolo	62	44.54 N	8.55 E
Vigy	56	49.12 N	6.18 E
Vihanti	26	64.29 N	25.00 E
Vihāri	123	30.02 N	72.21 E
Vihiers	32	47.09 N	0.32 W
Vihowa	123	31.08 N	70.30 E
Vihti	26	60.25 N	24.20 E
Viiala	26	61.13 N	23.47 E
Viinijärvi	26	62.39 N	29.14 E
Viinijärvi ⊜	26	62.44 N	29.17 E
Viipuri → Vyborg	76	60.42 N	28.45 E
Viitasaari	26	63.04 N	25.52 E
Viivikonna	76	59.19 N	27.42 E
Vijāpur	120	23.34 N	72.45 E
Vijayapuri	118	16.52 N	79.35 E
Vijayawāda	122	16.31 N	80.37 E
Vijosë (Aóös) ≃	38	40.37 N	19.20 E
Vik	40	59.44 N	17.28 E
Vik ⊥	40	59.44 N	17.27 E
Vika	40	60.31 N	15.42 E
Vikajärvi	24	66.37 N	26.12 E
Vikārābad	122	17.20 N	77.54 E
Vikbolandet ≻[1]	40	58.32 N	16.40 E
Viken	41	56.09 N	12.34 E
Viken ⊜	26	58.39 N	14.20 E
Vikern ⊜	40	59.30 N	14.55 E
Vikersund	26	59.59 N	10.02 E
Vikhroli ◆[8]	272c	19.07 N	72.56 E
Viking	182	53.06 N	111.46 W
Viking Village	218	39.05 N	84.18 W
Vikmanshyttan	40	60.17 N	15.49 E
Vikna	24	64.57 N	10.58 E
Vikna I	22	64.57 N	10.58 E
Vikramasingapuram	122	8.43 N	77.24 E
Viksøyri	26	61.05 N	6.35 E
Viktor	24	66.09 N	58.07 E
Viktorovka	86	52.51 N	62.32 E
Viktring	61	46.35 N	14.16 E
Vikulovo	86	56.49 N	70.37 E
Vil'a	80	55.15 N	42.13 E
Vila Alferes Chamusca	156	24.29 S	33.00 E
Vila Augusta	287b	23.28 S	46.32 W
Vila Boacaya ◆[8]	287b	23.29 S	46.44 W
Vila Brasil	248	22.22 S	54.34 W
Vila Caldas Xavier	154	15.59 S	34.12 E
Vila da Maganja	154	17.18 S	37.30 E
Vila da Ribeira Brava	150a	16.37 N	24.18 W
Viladecaballs	266d	41.33 N	1.58 E
Viladecáns	266d	41.19 N	2.00 E
Vila de Manica	156	18.56 S	32.53 E
Vila de Rei	34	39.40 N	8.09 W
Vila do Bispo	34	37.05 N	8.55 W
Vila do Conde	34	41.21 N	8.45 W
Vila do Porto	148a	36.56 N	25.09 W
Vila Flor	34	41.18 N	7.09 W
Vila Fontes	156	17.50 S	35.21 E
Vila Formosa ◆[8]	287b	23.34 S	46.33 W
Vilafranca del Penedés	34	41.21 N	1.42 E
Vila Franca de Xira	34	38.57 N	8.59 W
Vila Galvão	287b	23.27 S	46.33 W
Vila Gamito	154	14.12 S	33.00 E
Vila Gomes da Costa	156	24.19 S	33.38 E
Vila Gouveia	156	18.03 S	33.11 E
Vila Guilherme ◆[8]	287b	23.30 S	46.36 W
Vilaine ≃	32	47.30 N	2.27 W

Symbols in the index entries represent the broad categories identified in the key at the right. Symbols with superior numbers (⋏[1]) identify subcategories (see complete key on page *I · 1).*

Kartensymbole in dem Registerverzeichnis stellen die rechts in Schlüssel erklärten Kategorien dar. Symbole mit hochgestellten Ziffern (⋏[1]) bezeichnen Unterabteilungen einer Kategorie (vgl. vollständiger Schlüssel auf Seite *I · 1).*

Los símbolos incluídos en el texto del índice representan las grandes categorias identificadas con la clave a la derecha. Los símbolos con numeros en su parte superior (⋏[1]) identifican las subcategorías (véase la clave completa en la página *I · 1).*

Les symboles de l'index représentent les catégories indiquées dans la légende à droite. Les symboles suivis d'un indice (⋏[1]) représentent des sous-catégories (voir légende complète à la page *I · 1).*

Os símbolos incluídos no texto do índice representam as grandes categorias identificadas com a chave à direita. Os símbolos com números em sua parte superior (⋏[1]) identificam as subcategorias (veja-se a chave completa à página *I · 1).*

	English	Deutsch	Español	Français	Português
∧	Mountain	Berg	Montaña	Montagne	Montanha
⋏	Mountains	Berge	Montañas	Montagnes	Montanhas
)(	Pass	Pass	Paso	Col	Passo
V	Valley, Canyon	Tal, Cañon	Valle, Cañón	Vallée, Canyon	Vale, Canhão
≚	Plain	Ebene	Llano	Plaine	Planície
≻	Cape	Kap	Cabo	Cap	Cabo
I	Island	Insel	Isla	Île	Ilha
II	Islands	Inseln	Islas	Îles	Ilhas
∸	Other Topographic Features	Andere Topographische Objekte	Otros Elementos Topográficos	Autres données topographiques	Outros acidentes topográficos

ESPAÑOL — Nombre | Página | Lat.°′ | Long.°′ W = Oeste
FRANÇAIS — Nom | Page | Lat.°′ | Long.°′ W = Ouest
PORTUGUÊS — Nome | Página | Lat.°′ | Long.°′ W = Oeste

Vila Isabel ◆8 **287a** 22.55 S 43.15 W
Vila Jaguára ◆8 **287b** 23.31 S 46.45 W
Vilaka **76** 57.11 N 27.41 E
Vila Luísa **156** 25.44 S 32.40 E
Vilama, Laguna de ⊜ **252** 22.36 S 66.55 W
Vila Machado **156** 19.18 S 34.11 E
Vila Madalena ◆8 **287b** 23.33 S 46.42 W
Vila Maria ◆8 **287b** 23.31 S 46.34 W
Vila Mariana ◆8 **287b** 23.35 S 46.38 W
Vila Matilde ◆8 **287b** 23.32 S 46.31 W
Vila Muriqui **256** 22.56 S 43.57 W
Vilanculos **156** 22.01 S 35.19 E
Viļāni **76** 56.33 N 26.57 E
Vila Nova ≐ **250** 0.04 S 51.13 W
Vila Nova de Famalicão **34** 41.25 N 8.32 W
Vila Nova de Foz Côa **34** 41.05 N 7.12 W
Vila Nova de Gaia **34** 41.08 N 8.37 W
Vilanova de la Roca **266d** 41.33 N 2.17 E
Vila Novo de Ourém **34** 39.39 N 8.35 W
Vila Paiva de Andrada **156** 18.44 S 34.03 E
Vila Progresso **287a** 22.55 S 43.03 W
Vila Prudente ◆8 **287b** 23.35 S 46.33 W
Vila Real **34** 41.18 N 7.45 W
Vila Real de Santo António **34** 37.12 N 7.25 W
Vilar Formoso **34** 40.37 N 6.50 W
Vila Rica **246** 3.40 S 61.02 W
Vilarinho do Monte **250** 1.37 S 52.01 W
Vila Salazar **112** 8.27 S 126.27 E
Vila Vasco da Gama **154** 14.54 S 32.14 E
Vila Velha, Bra. **250** 3.13 N 51.13 W
Vila Velha, Bra. **255** 20.20 S 40.17 W
Vila Velha de Ródão **34** 39.38 N 7.40 W
Vila Verde, Port. **34** 41.39 N 8.26 W
Vila Verde, Port. **266c** 38.50 N 9.22 W
Vila Viçosa **34** 38.47 N 8.13 W
Vil'ča **78** 51.22 N 29.24 E
Vîlcea □6 **38** 45.19 N 24.00 E
Vildbjerg **41** 56.12 N 8.46 E
Vilejka **76** 54.30 N 26.53 E
Vilelas **252** 27.57 S 62.38 W
Vilenki **82** 54.16 N 38.55 E
Vil'gort, S.S.S.R. **24** 61.35 N 50.40 E
Vil'gort, S.S.S.R. **24** 60.34 N 56.24 E
Vilhelmina **26** 64.37 N 16.39 E
Vilhena **248** 12.43 S 60.07 W
Vilija ≐ **76** 54.54 N 25.35 E
Viljandi **76** 58.22 N 25.36 E
Viljoensdrif **158** 26.44 S 27.55 E
Viljoenshof **158** 34.40 S 19.42 E
Viljoenskroon **158** 27.12 S 27.00 E
Viljoenspos **158** 27.35 S 30.30 E
Vilkaviškis **76** 54.39 N 23.02 E
Vil'kickogo, ostrov I, S.S.S.R. **72** 73.29 N 75.50 E
Vil'kickogo, ostrov I, S.S.S.R. **74** 75.44 N 152.20 E
Vil'kickogo, proliv ꭒ **74** 77.55 N 103.00 E
Vilkija **76** 55.03 N 23.35 E
Vilkovo **78** 45.25 N 29.35 E
Villa Abecia **248** 21.00 S 65.23 W
Villa Aberastain **252** 31.39 S 68.35 W
Villa Acuña → Ciudad Acuña **232** 29.18 N 100.55 W
Villa Adelina ◆8 **288** 34.31 S 58.32 W
Villa Adriana ⊥ **66** 41.56 N 12.45 E
Villa Ahumada **232** 30.37 N 106.31 W
Villa Alberdi **252** 27.35 S 65.37 W
Villa Alejandrina **258** 33.46 S 58.21 W
Villa Alemana **252** 33.03 S 71.23 W
Villa Allende **252** 31.18 S 64.18 W
Villa Alta **234** 17.21 N 96.09 W
Villa Ana **252** 28.29 S 59.37 W
Villa Ángela **252** 27.35 S 60.43 W
Villa Atamisqui **252** 28.29 S 63.48 W
Villa Atuel **252** 34.50 S 67.54 W
Villaba **116** 11.13 N 124.23 E
Villa Ballester ◆8 **258** 34.32 S 58.33 W
Villabassa (Niederdorf) **64** 46.44 N 12.10 E
Villabate **70** 38.04 N 13.26 E
Villabé **261** 48.35 N 2.27 E
Villa Bella **248** 10.23 S 65.24 W
Villa Berthet **252** 27.17 S 60.25 W
Villablino **34** 42.56 N 6.19 W
Villa Borghese ʋ **267a** 41.55 N 12.29 E
Villa Bosch ◆8 **288** 34.35 S 58.34 W
Villa Bruzual **246** 9.20 N 69.06 W
Villa Bustos **252** 29.17 S 67.02 W
Villa Cañás, Arg. **252** 34.00 S 61.36 W
Villacañas, Esp. **34** 39.38 N 3.20 W
Villa Carlos Paz **252** 31.24 S 64.31 W
Villacarriedo **34** 43.14 N 3.48 W
Villacarrillo **34** 38.07 N 3.05 W
Villa Castelli, Arg. **252** 29.00 S 68.11 W
Villa Castelli, It. **68** 40.35 N 17.28 E
Villacastín **34** 40.47 N 4.25 W
Villach **64** 46.36 N 13.50 E
Villacidro **71** 39.27 N 8.44 E
Villa Ciudadela ◆8 **258** 34.38 S 58.34 W
Villa Clara □4 **240p** 22.30 N 80.00 W
Villa Colón **234** 20.48 N 100.03 W
Villa Concepción del Tío **252** 31.19 S 62.50 W
Villa Constitución **252** 33.14 S 60.20 W
Villa Corona **234** 20.25 N 103.41 W
Villa Cortese **266b** 45.34 N 8.53 E
Villacoublay, Aérodrome de ⊠ **261** 48.45 N 2.10 E
Villa Creek ≐ **226** 35.27 N 120.58 W
Villa Cuauhtémoc, Méx. **234** 19.24 N 99.34 W
Villa Cuauhtémoc, Méx. **234** 22.11 N 97.50 W
Villada **34** 42.15 N 4.58 W
Villa de Apaseo el Alto **234** 20.27 N 100.37 W
Villa de Arriaga **234** 21.54 N 101.23 W
Villadeati **62** 45.04 N 8.10 E
Villa de Comaltitlán **236** 15.13 N 92.35 W
Villa de Cos **234** 23.17 N 102.21 W
Villa de Cura **246** 10.02 N 67.29 W
Villa de Guadalupe **234** 23.22 N 100.46 W
Villa del Carmen **252** 32.57 S 65.03 W
Villa Delgado **236** 13.43 N 89.10 W
Villa del Pueblito **234** 20.32 N 100.27 W
Villa del Río **34** 37.59 N 4.17 W
Villa del Rosario, Arg. **252** 31.35 S 63.32 W
Villa del Rosario, Arg. **252** 30.47 S 57.55 W
Villa de María **252** 29.54 S 63.43 W
Villa de Mayo **258** 34.30 S 58.41 W
Villa de Méndez **232** 25.07 N 98.34 W
Villa de Nova Sintra **150a** 14.52 N 24.43 W
Villa de Reyes **234** 21.48 N 100.56 W
Villa de San Antonio **236** 14.16 N 87.36 W
Villa de San Francisco **236** 14.10 N 86.58 W
Villa de Soto **252** 30.51 S 64.59 W
Villa d'Este ⊥ **267a** 41.57 N 12.48 E
Villa Devoto ◆8 **288** 34.36 S 58.31 W
Villa Diamante ◆8 **288** 34.41 S 58.26 W
Villa di Chiavenna **58** 46.20 N 9.29 E
Villa Diego, Arg. **252** 33.01 S 60.37 W
Villadiego, Esp. **34** 42.31 N 4.00 W
Villa Dolores **252** 31.56 S 65.12 W
Villa Domínico ◆8 **258** 34.41 S 58.19 W
Villadose **64** 45.04 N 11.53 E
Villadossola **58** 46.04 N 8.16 E
Villa El Alto **252** 28.18 S 65.22 W
Villa el Carmen **236** 11.59 N 86.31 W
Villa Elisa **252** 32.10 S 58.24 W
Villa Elisa ◆8 **258** 34.50 S 58.05 W
Villa Escalante **234** 19.24 N 101.39 W
Villa Eufronio Viscarra **248** 17.59 S 65.36 W
Villa Flores **234** 16.14 N 93.14 W
Villa Florida **252** 26.23 S 57.09 W
Villafranca d'Asti **62** 44.55 N 8.02 E
Villafranca del Bierzo **34** 42.36 N 6.48 W
Villafranca de los Barros **34** 38.34 N 6.20 W
Villafranca di Verona **64** 45.21 N 10.50 E
Villafranca in Lunigiana **64** 44.17 N 9.57 E
Villafranca Piemonte **62** 44.47 N 7.33 E
Villafranca Sicula **70** 37.35 N 13.17 E
Villafranca Tirrena **70** 38.14 N 15.26 E
Villafrati **70** 37.54 N 13.29 E
Villa Frontera **232** 26.56 N 101.27 W
Villagarcía, Esp. **34** 42.36 N 8.45 W
Villa García, Méx. **234** 22.10 N 101.57 W
Village **196** 35.33 N 97.33 W
Village Creek ≐ **194** 35.28 N 91.19 W
Village Green **285** 39.52 N 75.26 W
Villa General Roca **252** 32.39 S 66.28 W
Village of Drummond Hill **285** 39.43 N 75.42 W
Village of the Branch **276** 40.51 N 73.11 W
Villa Giambruno **288** 34.48 S 58.13 W
Villa González **234** 22.50 N 98.27 W
Villa González Ortega **234** 22.30 N 101.55 W
Villagrán, Méx. **232** 24.29 N 99.29 W
Villagrán, Méx. **234** 20.31 N 100.59 W
Villagrande Strisaili **71** 39.58 N 9.30 E
Villa Grazia **70** 38.09 N 13.10 E
Villagrazia ◆8 **70** 38.05 N 13.20 E
Villa Grove **194** 39.51 N 88.09 W
Villaguay **252** 31.51 S 59.01 W
Villa Guerrero, Méx. **234** 21.59 N 103.36 W
Villa Guerrero, Méx. **234** 18.52 N 99.39 W
Villa Guillermina **252** 28.14 S 59.28 W
Villa Hayes **252** 25.06 S 57.34 W
Villahermosa **234** 17.59 N 92.55 W
Villa Hernandarias **252** 31.13 S 59.59 W
Villa Hidalgo, Méx. **204** 30.59 N 116.10 W
Villa Hidalgo, Méx. **234** 21.40 N 102.36 W
Villa Hidalgo, Méx. **234** 21.44 N 105.15 W
Villa Huidobro **252** 34.50 S 64.35 W
Villaines-la-Juhel **32** 48.21 N 0.17 W
Villa Iris **252** 38.10 S 63.15 W
Villa Jiménez **234** 19.55 N 101.35 W
Villa José L. Suárez ◆8 **288** 34.32 S 58.35 W
Villajoyosa **34** 38.30 N 0.14 W
Villa Juárez, Méx. **232** 27.10 N 109.50 W
Villa Juárez, Méx. **234** 22.20 N 100.17 W
Villa Krause **252** 31.34 S 68.32 W
Villa La Angostura **254** 40.47 S 71.40 W
Villalago **66** 41.56 N 13.50 E
Villa La Paz **252** 33.27 S 67.38 W
Villa Larca **252** 32.37 S 64.59 W
Villa Larroque **252** 33.02 S 59.01 W
Villalba, Esp. **34** 43.18 N 7.41 W
Villalba, It. **70** 37.39 N 13.50 E
Villalba, P.R. **240m** 18.08 N 66.30 W
Villa Lia **258** 34.07 S 59.26 W
Villalon **116** 11.31 N 124.22 E
Villalon ◆8 **286b** 23.03 N 82.26 W
Villalón de Campos **34** 42.06 N 5.02 W
Villalonga **254** 39.53 S 62.35 W
Villa López **232** 27.00 N 105.02 W
Villalpando **34** 41.52 N 5.24 W
Villa Lugano ◆8 **288** 34.41 S 58.28 W
Villalvernia **62** 44.49 N 8.51 E
Villa Lynch ◆8 **288** 34.36 S 58.31 W
Villa Madero, Arg. **288** 34.42 S 58.30 W
Villa Madero, Méx. **234** 19.24 N 101.16 W
Villa Mainero **232** 24.32 N 99.38 W
Villamar **71** 39.37 N 8.59 E
Villa María, Arg. **252** 32.25 S 63.15 W
Villa Maria, Pa., U.S. **214** 41.05 N 80.30 W
Villa María Grande **252** 31.39 S 59.54 W
Villa Martín, Bol. **248** 20.46 S 67.47 W
Villamartín, Esp. **34** 36.52 N 5.38 W
Villamarzana **64** 45.01 N 11.41 E
Villamassargia **71** 39.16 N 8.38 E
Villa Matoque **252** 25.49 S 63.49 W
Villa Mazán **252** 28.40 S 66.34 W
Villa Media Agua **252** 31.59 S 68.25 W
Villa Mercedes **252** 30.07 S 68.42 W
Villamil **246a** 0.56 S 91.01 W
Villa Minozzo **64** 44.22 N 10.28 E
Villa Montes **248** 21.15 S 63.30 W
Villa Morelos **234** 20.00 N 101.25 W
Villandraut **32** 44.28 N 0.23 W
Villa Nova, Md., U.S. **284b** 39.21 N 76.44 W
Villa Nova, Oh., U.S. **216** 40.33 N 84.26 W
Villanova, Pa., U.S. **208** 40.02 N 75.20 W
Villanova d'Asti **62** 44.57 N 7.56 E
Villanova Mondovì **62** 44.21 N 7.45 E
Villanova Monferrato **62** 45.11 N 8.28 E
Villanova Monteleone **71** 40.30 N 8.28 E
Villanova sull'Arda **64** 45.01 N 10.00 E
Villanova Tulo **71** 39.47 N 9.13 E
Villanova University ʋ2 **285** 40.02 N 75.21 W
Villa Nueva, Arg. **252** 32.26 S 63.15 W
Villa Nueva, Arg. **252** 32.54 S 68.47 W
Villanueva, Col. **246** 10.37 N 72.59 W
Villa Nueva, Guat. **236** 14.31 N 90.35 W
Villanueva, Hond. **236** 15.17 N 88.00 W
Villanueva, Méx. **234** 22.21 N 102.53 W
Villanueva, Nic. **236** 12.58 N 86.49 W
Villanueva, N.M., U.S. **200** 35.16 N 105.21 W
Villanueva de Córdoba **34** 38.20 N 4.37 W
Villanueva de la Serana **34** 38.58 N 5.48 W
Villanueva de la Sierra **34** 40.12 N 6.24 W
Villanueva de los Infantes **34** 38.44 N 2.59 W
Villanueva del Río y Minas **34** 37.39 N 5.42 W
Villanueva y Geltrú **34** 41.14 N 1.44 E
Villa Numancia **288** 34.55 S 58.24 W
Villa Obregón **234** 21.07 N 102.42 W
Villa Obregón ◆8 **286a** 19.21 N 99.12 W
Villa Ocampo **252** 28.28 S 59.22 W
Villa Ojo de Agua **252** 29.31 S 63.42 W
Villa Oliva **252** 26.01 S 57.53 W
Villa Opicina **64** 45.40 N 13.49 E
Villa Orestes Pereyra **232** 26.31 N 105.40 W
Villa Ottone (Uttenheim) **64** 46.52 N 11.57 E
Villa Park, Ca., U.S. **228** 33.48 N 117.48 W
Villa Park, Il., U.S. **278** 41.53 N 87.59 W
Villa Park Dam ◆6 **280** 33.48 N 117.46 W
Villa Pérez **240m** 18.12 N 66.47 W
Villapiana **68** 39.51 N 16.28 E
Villapiana Lido **68** 39.48 N 16.29 E
Villapinzón **246** 5.13 N 73.36 W
Villa Potenza **66** 43.19 N 13.25 E
Villaputzu **71** 39.26 N 9.34 E
Villa Quinteros **252** 27.14 S 65.33 W
Villa Quintilio Varo ⊥ **267a** 41.58 N 12.47 E
Villa Ramírez **252** 32.11 S 60.12 W
Villarcayo **34** 42.56 N 3.34 W
Villar-d'Arène **62** 45.02 N 6.20 E
Villard-Bonnot **62** 45.14 N 5.53 E
Villard-de-Lans **62** 45.04 N 5.33 E
Villardefrades **34** 41.43 N 5.15 W
Villar del Arzobispo **34** 39.44 N 0.49 W
Villareal **116** 11.34 N 124.56 E
Villa Real ◆8 **288** 34.37 S 58.31 W
Villa Regina **252** 39.06 S 67.04 W
Villa Reynolds **252** 33.43 S 65.23 W
Villa Rica **192** 33.43 N 84.55 W
Villa Rivero **248** 17.37 S 65.48 W
Villaroche **261** 48.37 N 2.39 E
Villa Romana del Casale ⊥ **70** 37.22 N 14.20 E
Villa Rosa, Arg. **258** 34.25 S 58.52 W
Villarosa, It. **70** 37.35 N 14.10 E
Villar Pellice **62** 44.48 N 7.09 E
Villar Perosa **62** 44.56 N 7.15 E
Villarreal **34** 39.56 N 0.06 W
Villarreales **196** 26.07 N 100.20 W
Villarrica, Chile **254** 39.16 S 72.13 W
Villarrica, Col. **246** 3.58 N 74.37 W
Villarrica, Para. **252** 25.45 S 56.26 W
Villarrica, Lago ⊜ **254** 39.15 S 72.06 W
Villarrobledo **34** 39.16 N 2.36 W
Villarrubia de los Ojos **34** 39.13 N 3.36 W
Villars, Arg. **258** 34.50 S 58.56 W
Villars, Schw. **58** 46.18 N 7.04 E
Villars-Colmars **62** 44.10 N 6.36 E
Villars-en-Azois **58** 48.04 N 4.45 E
Villars-les-Dombes **58** 46.00 N 5.01 E
Villars-sur-Var **62** 43.56 N 7.06 E
Villa Ruiz **258** 34.25 S 59.15 W
Villas **208** 39.01 N 74.56 W
Villa Sáenz Peña ◆8 **288** 34.36 S 58.31 W
Villa San Andrés ◆8 **288** 34.33 S 58.32 W
Villa Sandino **236** 12.03 N 84.59 W
Villa San Giovanni **68** 38.13 N 15.38 E
Villa San José **252** 32.12 S 58.13 W
Villa San Martín **252** 28.18 S 64.12 W
Villasanta **62** 45.37 N 9.18 E
Villa Santa, Montaña ∧ **236** 14.12 N 86.27 W
Villa Santa Maria **66** 41.57 N 14.21 E
Villa Santina **64** 46.24 N 12.55 E
Villa Santos Lugares ◆8 **288** 34.36 S 58.32 W
Villasayas **34** 41.21 N 2.37 W
Villa Serrano **248** 19.06 S 64.22 W
Villasimius **71** 39.08 N 9.31 E
Villasis **116** 15.54 N 120.35 E
Villasor **71** 39.23 N 8.56 E
Villa Tunari **248** 16.55 S 65.25 W
Villa Turdera ◆8 **288** 34.48 S 58.25 W
Villa Unión, Arg. **252** 29.18 S 68.12 W
Villa Unión, Arg. **252** 29.24 S 62.47 W
Villa Unión, Méx. **232** 28.15 N 100.43 W
Villa Unión, Méx. **234** 23.58 N 104.02 W
Villa Unión, Méx. **234** 23.12 N 106.14 W
Villa Vaca Guzmán **248** 19.54 S 63.48 W
Villa Valeria **252** 34.20 S 64.55 W
Villa Vallelonga **66** 41.52 N 13.37 E
Villa Vázquez **238** 19.45 N 71.27 W
Villaverde ◆8 **266a** 40.21 N 3.42 W
Villaverla **64** 45.39 N 11.29 E
Villa Verona **226** 39.28 N 121.33 W
Villavicencio **246** 4.09 N 73.37 W
Villa Vicente Guerrero **234** 23.45 N 103.59 W
Villaviciosa **34** 43.29 N 5.26 W
Villaviciosa de Córdoba **34** 38.05 N 5.01 W
Villa Victoria **234** 18.47 N 103.24 W
Villa Vomano **66** 42.37 N 13.46 E
Villazón **248** 22.06 S 65.36 W
Villa Zorraquín **252** 31.19 S 58.02 W
Villé **58** 48.20 N 7.18 E
Villebon, Lac ⊜ **190** 47.58 N 77.17 W
Villebon-sur-Yvette **261** 48.42 N 2.15 E
Villeconin **261** 48.31 N 2.08 E
Villecresnes **261** 48.43 N 2.32 E
Villecroze **62** 43.35 N 6.16 E
Ville-d'Avray **261** 48.50 N 2.11 E
Ville-de-Laval → Laval **206** 45.35 N 73.45 W
Villedieu **32** 48.50 N 1.13 W
Ville-en-Tardenois **50** 49.11 N 3.48 E
Villefort **62** 44.26 N 3.56 E
Villefranche **58** 45.59 N 4.43 E
Villefranche-de-Rouergue **32** 44.21 N 2.02 E
Villefranche-Sur-Cher **50** 47.18 N 1.46 E
Villefranche-sur-Mer **62** 43.42 N 7.19 E
Villejuif **50** 48.48 N 2.22 E
Villejust **261** 48.41 N 2.14 E
Ville-Marie **190** 47.19 N 79.26 W
Villemaur-sur-Vanne **50** 48.15 N 3.44 E
Villemeux-sur-Eure **50** 48.40 N 1.28 E
Villemoisson-sur-Orge **261** 48.40 N 2.19 E
Villemomble **261** 48.53 N 2.31 E
Villena **34** 38.38 N 0.51 W
Villenauxe-la-Grande **50** 48.35 N 3.33 E
Villeneuve, It. **62** 45.42 N 7.14 E
Villeneuve, Schw. **58** 46.24 N 6.55 E
Villeneuve-d'Ascq **50** 50.37 N 3.10 E
Villeneuve-d'Aveyron **32** 44.26 N 2.02 E
Villeneuve-de-Berg **62** 44.33 N 4.30 E
Villeneuve-la-Garenne **261** 48.56 N 2.20 E
Villeneuve-la-Guyard **50** 48.20 N 3.04 E
Villeneuve-l'Archevêque **50** 48.14 N 3.33 E
Villeneuve-le-Comte **261** 48.49 N 2.50 E
Villeneuve-le-Roi **50** 48.44 N 2.25 E
Villeneuve-lès-Avignon **62** 43.58 N 4.48 E
Villeneuve-lès-Maguelonne **62** 43.32 N 3.52 E
Villeneuve-Saint-Denis **261** 48.49 N 2.48 E
Villeneuve-Saint-Georges **50** 48.44 N 2.27 E
Villeneuve-sous-Dammartin **261** 49.02 N 2.39 E
Villeneuve-sur-Lot **32** 44.25 N 0.42 E
Villeneuve-sur-Yonne **50** 48.05 N 3.18 E
Villennes-sur-Seine **261** 48.56 N 2.00 E
Villenoy **50** 48.57 N 2.52 E
Villeny **50** 47.37 N 1.45 E
Villeparisis **50** 48.56 N 2.37 E
Villepinte **261** 48.58 N 2.32 E
Ville Platte **194** 30.41 N 92.16 W
Villepreux **261** 48.50 N 2.01 E
Villequier **50** 49.31 N 0.40 E
Villeron **261** 49.03 N 2.33 E
Villeroy **50** 48.59 N 2.47 E
Villers-Bocage, Fr. **32** 49.05 N 0.39 W
Villers-Bocage, Fr. **50** 49.59 N 2.20 E
Villers-Bretonneux **50** 49.52 N 2.31 E
Villers-Carbonnel **50** 49.52 N 2.54 E
Villers-Cotterêts **50** 49.15 N 3.05 E
Villers-Devant-Orval **56** 49.37 N 5.19 E
Villers-en-Arthies **261** 49.05 N 1.44 E
Villersexel **58** 47.33 N 6.26 E
Villers-Farlay **58** 47.00 N 5.45 E
Villers-la-Ville **50** 50.35 N 4.32 E
Villers-le-Lac **58** 47.04 N 6.40 E
Villers-lès-Nancy **58** 48.40 N 6.09 E
Villers-lès-Pots **58** 47.13 N 5.21 E
Villers-Outréaux **50** 50.02 N 3.18 E
Villers-Saint-Paul **50** 49.17 N 2.29 E
Villers-Semeuse **56** 49.44 N 4.45 E
Villerupt **56** 49.28 N 5.56 E
Villerville **50** 49.24 N 0.08 E
Ville-Saint-Georges → Saint-Georges **188** 46.07 N 70.40 W
Villes-sur-Auzon **62** 44.03 N 5.14 E
Ville-sur-Tourbe **56** 49.11 N 4.47 E
Villeta **246** 5.01 N 74.28 W
Villetta Barrea **66** 41.47 N 13.56 E
Villeurbanne **62** 45.46 N 4.53 E
Villevaudé **261** 48.55 N 2.39 E
Villeziers **261** 48.40 N 2.10 E
Villiers **158** 27.03 S 28.35 E
Villiers-Adam **261** 49.04 N 2.14 E
Villiersdorp **158** 34.00 S 19.19 E
Villiers-le-Bâcle **261** 48.44 N 2.08 E
Villiers-le-Bel **261** 49.00 N 2.23 E
Villiers-le-Sec **261** 49.04 N 2.23 E
Villiers-Saint-Frédéric **261** 48.49 N 1.54 E
Villiers-Saint-Georges **50** 48.39 N 3.25 E
Villiers-sur-Marne **261** 48.50 N 2.33 E
Villiers-sur-Morin **261** 48.52 N 2.53 E
Villigst **263** 51.26 N 7.35 E
Villingen-Schwenningen **30** 48.04 N 8.28 E
Villisca **198** 40.55 N 94.58 W
Villmanstrand → Lappeenranta **26** 61.04 N 28.11 E
Villmergen **58** 47.21 N 8.15 E
Villorba **64** 45.44 N 12.14 E
Villoresi, Canale ≚ **62** 45.33 N 9.31 E
Villotta **64** 45.52 N 12.45 E
Villupuram **122** 11.56 N 79.29 E
Vilm I **54** 54.19 N 13.32 E
Vilmnitz **54** 54.21 N 13.31 E
Vilna, Ab., Can. **182** 54.07 N 111.55 W
Vilna → Vilnius, S.S.S.R. **76** 54.41 N 25.19 E
Vilnius **76** 54.41 N 25.19 E
Vilosnes-sur-Meuse **56** 49.20 N 5.14 E
Vilppula **26** 62.01 N 24.31 E
Vils **58** 47.33 N 10.38 E
Vils ≐, B.R.D. **60** 48.37 N 13.11 E
Vils ≐, B.R.D. **60** 49.09 N 11.58 E
Vils ≐, Europe **58** 47.33 N 10.40 E
Vilsandi saar I **76** 58.23 N 21.52 E
Vilsbiburg **60** 48.27 N 12.12 E
Vilseck **60** 49.37 N 11.48 E
Vilsheim **60** 48.27 N 12.07 E
Vilshofen **60** 48.39 N 13.12 E
Vil'uj ≐ **74** 64.24 N 126.26 E
Vil'ujsk **74** 63.45 N 121.35 E
Vil'ujskoje vodochranilišče ⊜1 **74** 62.30 N 111.00 E
Vil'va **86** 58.37 N 56.52 E
Vilvoorde **50** 50.56 N 4.26 E
Vimercate **62** 45.37 N 9.22 E
Vimianzo **34** 43.07 N 9.02 W
Vimmerby **26** 57.40 N 15.51 E
Vimodrone **266b** 45.31 N 9.17 E
Vimoutiers **50** 48.55 N 0.12 E
Vimpeli **26** 63.09 N 23.48 E
Vimperk **60** 49.03 N 13.47 E
Vimy **50** 50.22 N 2.49 E
Vina **204** 39.55 N 122.03 W
Vina ≐ **146** 7.45 N 15.36 E
Viñac **248** 12.56 S 75.47 W
Viña del Mar **252** 33.02 S 71.34 W
Vinadi **58** 46.55 N 10.29 E
Vinadio **62** 44.18 N 7.10 E
Viñales **240p** 22.37 N 83.43 W
Vinalhaven **188** 44.02 N 68.49 W
Vinalhaven Island I **188** 44.05 N 68.52 W
Vinantes **261** 49.01 N 2.44 E
Vina Roni, Mount ∧ **175e** 8.10 S 157.28 E
Vinaroz **34** 40.28 N 0.29 E
Vinay **62** 45.13 N 5.24 E
Vinazco ≐ **234** 20.56 N 97.44 W
Vincennes, Fr. **50** 48.51 N 2.26 E
Vincennes, In., U.S. **194** 38.40 N 87.31 W
Vincennes, Bois de ♠ **261** 48.50 N 2.25 E
Vincennes, Château de ⊥ **261** 48.51 N 2.26 E
Vincennes, Étang de ⊜ **261** 48.47 N 2.45 E
Vincennes Bay ᑕ **9** 66.30 S 109.30 E
Vincent **194** 33.22 N 86.22 W
Vincent, Point ≻ **174c** 29.00 S 167.55 E
Vincentown **208** 39.56 N 74.44 W
Vinces **246** 1.32 S 79.45 W
Vinces ≐ **246** 1.39 S 79.47 W
Vinchiaturo **66** 41.29 N 14.35 E
Vinchina **252** 28.46 S 68.10 W
Vinchos **248** 13.16 S 74.21 W
Vinci **66** 43.47 N 10.55 E
Vinco **214** 40.25 N 78.52 W
Vindeby **41** 55.03 N 10.38 E
Vindelälven ≐ **24** 63.54 N 19.52 E
Vindeln **26** 64.12 N 19.44 E
Vinden, Mount ∧ **162** 27.01 S 115.38 E
Vinderslev **41** 56.15 N 9.26 E
Vinderup **26** 56.29 N 8.47 E
Vindhya Range ⩘ **120** 23.00 N 77.00 E
Vinding **41** 55.41 N 9.35 E
Vindinge **41** 55.19 N 10.45 E
Vine Brook ≐ **283** 42.27 N 71.13 W
Vinegar Hill ∧ **202** 44.43 N 118.34 W
Vine Grove **194** 37.48 N 85.58 W
Vine Hill **282** 38.00 N 122.06 W
Vineland, Mi., U.S. **216** 42.03 N 86.30 W
Vineland, N.J., U.S. **208** 39.29 N 75.01 W
Vinemont **194** 34.14 N 86.51 W
Vine Valley **210** 42.43 N 77.20 W
Vineyard Canyon V **226** 35.46 N 120.41 W
Vineyard Haven **207** 41.27 N 70.36 W
Vineyard Lake ⊜ **216** 42.05 N 84.13 W
Vineyard Sound ꭒ **207** 41.25 N 70.46 W
Vingåker **40** 59.02 N 15.52 E
Vingeanne ≐ **58** 47.21 N 5.29 E
Ving Ngün **110** 22.37 N 99.16 E
Vinh **110** 18.40 N 105.40 E
Vinhais **34** 41.50 N 7.00 W
Vinhas, Ribeira das ≐ **266c** 38.42 N 9.25 W
Vinh Cam-ranh ᑕ **110** 11.53 N 109.10 E
Vinh Cay-duong ᑕ **110** 10.10 N 104.45 E
Vinh-chau **110** 9.19 N 105.59 E
Vinhedo **256** 23.01 S 46.59 W
Vinh-linh **110** 17.04 N 107.02 E
Vinh-loc **269c** 10.49 N 106.34 E
Vinh-long **110** 10.15 N 105.58 E
Vinh Rach-gia ᑕ **110** 10.00 N 105.00 E
Vinh-tuy, Viet. **110** 9.37 N 105.22 E
Vinh-tuy, Viet. **110** 17.24 N 106.36 E
Vinica **36** 45.28 N 15.15 E
Vinita **196** 36.38 N 95.09 W
Vînju Mare **38** 44.26 N 22.52 E
Vinkekuil **158** 32.42 S 20.27 E
Vinkeveen **52** 52.13 N 4.54 E
Vinkovci **38** 45.17 N 18.49 E
Vin'kovcy **78** 49.02 N 27.14 E
Vinnhorst **52** 52.25 N 9.43 E
Vinnica **78** 49.14 N 28.29 E
Vinnica □4 **38** 48.30 N 28.30 E
Vinniki **78** 49.48 N 24.08 E
Vinnitsa → Vinnica **78** 49.14 N 28.29 E
Vinnum **263** 51.41 N 7.24 E
Vinogradov **78** 48.09 N 23.02 E
Vinogradovo, S.S.S.R. **82** 55.25 N 38.32 E
Vinogradovo, S.S.S.R. **82** 55.57 N 37.32 E
Vinogrobol' **78** 51.51 N 36.26 E
Vinön I **40** 59.12 N 15.43 E
Vinon-sur-Verdon **62** 43.43 N 5.48 E
Vinovo **62** 44.57 N 7.38 E
Vinslöv **26** 56.06 N 13.55 E
Vinson Massif ∧ **9** 78.35 S 85.25 W
Vinstra **26** 61.36 N 9.45 E
Vintilă Vodă **38** 45.28 N 26.44 E
Vinton, Ia., U.S. **190** 42.10 N 92.01 W
Vinton, La., U.S. **194** 30.11 N 93.34 W
Vinton, Va., U.S. **192** 37.16 N 79.53 W
Vintondale **214** 40.28 N 78.55 W
Vintrosa **40** 59.15 N 14.57 E
Viñuelas, Arroyo de ≐ **266a** 40.33 N 3.33 W
Viny **76** 58.22 N 32.13 E
Vinzelberg **54** 52.33 N 11.40 E
Vinzili **86** 56.58 N 65.46 E
Viola, Il., U.S. **190** 41.12 N 90.35 W
Viola, N.Y., U.S. **276** 41.08 N 74.05 W
Viola, Wi., U.S. **190** 43.30 N 90.40 W
Viola, Val V **64** 46.27 N 10.15 E
Violín, Isla I **236** 8.51 N 83.39 W
Viols-le-Fort **62** 43.45 N 3.42 E
Viosne ≐ **261** 49.03 N 2.06 E
Vipava **36** 45.51 N 13.58 E
Vipava ≐ **64** 45.54 N 13.33 E
Vipiteno (Sterzing) **64** 46.54 N 11.26 E
Vipos **252** 26.29 S 65.22 W
Vipperow **54** 53.19 N 12.41 E
Viqueque **112** 8.52 S 126.22 E
Vir, Otok I **36** 44.18 N 15.04 E
Vira **58** 46.08 N 8.51 E
Virac, Pil. **116** 13.35 N 124.15 E
Virac, Pil. **116** 16.22 N 120.39 E
Viracopos, Aeroporto de ⊠ **256** 23.00 S 47.08 W
Virac Point ≻ **116** 13.31 N 124.13 E
Viradouro **255** 20.53 S 48.18 W
Virago Sound ꭒ **182** 54.00 N 132.36 W
Viramgām **120** 23.07 N 72.02 E
Virandozero **24** 64.05 N 35.58 E
Viranşehir, Tür. **130** 39.00 N 36.39 E
Viranşehir, Tür. **130** 37.13 N 39.45 E
Vīrarājendrapet **122** 12.12 N 75.48 E
Virbalis **76** 54.38 N 22.49 E
Virden, Mb., Can. **184** 49.51 N 100.55 W
Virden, Il., U.S. **219** 39.30 N 89.46 W
Virden, N.M., U.S. **200** 32.41 N 109.00 W
Vire **32** 48.50 N 0.53 W
Vire ≐ **32** 49.20 N 1.07 W
Virelles **50** 50.04 N 4.20 E
Virelles, Étang de ⊜ **50** 50.04 N 4.21 E
Vireux-Molhain **56** 50.05 N 4.43 E
Vîrfurile **38** 46.19 N 22.31 E
Virgem da Lapa **255** 16.49 S 42.21 W
Virgen **64** 47.00 N 12.27 E
Vírgen del San Cristóbal ʋ1 **286e** 33.26 S 70.39 W
Vírgenes, Cabo ≻ **254** 52.22 S 68.20 W
Vírgenes, Islas → British Virgin Islands □2, N.A. **240m** 18.30 N 64.30 W
Vírgenes, Islas → Virgin Islands □2, N.A. **240m** 18.20 N 64.50 W
Virgen Tal V **64** 47.00 N 12.25 E
Virgil, On., Can. **284a** 43.13 N 79.08 W
Virgil, Ks., U.S. **198** 37.58 N 96.00 W
Virgil, N.Y., U.S. **210** 42.31 N 76.12 W
Virgilina **192** 36.33 N 78.52 W
Virgilio **64** 45.07 N 10.47 E
Virgin ≐ **200** 36.31 N 114.20 W
Virgin, North Fork ≐ **200** 37.10 N 113.01 W
Virginal-Samme **50** 50.38 N 4.12 E
Virgin Gorda I **240m** 18.30 N 64.24 W
Virgin Gorda Peak ∧ **240m** 18.30 N 64.24 W
Virginia, Austl. **168b** 34.40 S 138.34 E
Virgínia, Bra. **256** 22.20 S 45.06 W
Virginia, Ire. **48** 53.49 N 7.04 W
Virginia, S. Afr. **158** 28.12 S 26.49 E
Virginia, Il., U.S. **219** 39.57 N 90.12 W
Virginia, Mn., U.S. **190** 47.31 N 92.32 W
Virginia □3 **178** 37.30 N 78.45 W
Virginia Beach **208** 36.51 N 75.58 W
Virginia City, Mt., U.S. **202** 45.17 N 111.56 W
Virginia City, Nv., U.S. **226** 39.18 N 119.38 W
Virginia Creek ≐ **226** 38.13 N 119.14 W
Virginia Falls ᒪ **180** 61.38 N 125.42 W
Virginia Gardens **220** 25.49 N 80.17 W
Virginia Hills **208** 38.47 N 77.06 W
Virginia Key I **220** 25.44 N 80.09 W
Virginia Peak ∧ **204** 39.45 N 119.28 W
Virginia Ranch Reservoir ⊜1 **226** 39.20 N 121.19 W
Virginia Range ⩘ **226** 39.18 N 119.30 W
Virginiatown **190** 48.08 N 79.35 W
Virginia Water **260** 51.24 N 0.34 W
Virginie occidentale → West Virginia □3 **188** 38.45 N 80.30 W
Virgin Islands □2, N.A. **230** 18.20 N 64.50 W
Virgin Islands □2, N.A. **240m** 18.20 N 64.50 W
Virgin Islands II **240m** 18.00 N 64.40 W
Virgin Islands National Park ♠ **240m** 18.20 N 64.45 W
Virginópolis **255** 18.45 S 42.45 W
Virgin Passage ᑕ1 **240m** 18.20 N 65.10 W
Virginville **208** 40.31 N 75.52 W
Virgolândia **255** 18.27 S 42.18 W
Virieu **62** 45.29 N 5.28 E
Virieu-le-Grand **62** 45.51 N 5.39 E
Virihaure ⊜ **24** 67.20 N 16.35 E
Virje **36** 46.04 N 16.59 E
Virkie **46** 59.53 N 1.18 W
Virkkala **26** 60.12 N 24.01 E
Virklund **41** 56.07 N 9.34 E
Virneburg **56** 50.20 N 7.04 E
Virôchey **110** 13.59 N 106.49 E
Viroflay **50** 48.48 N 2.10 E
Viroin ≐ **56** 50.05 N 4.43 E
Virojoki **26** 60.35 N 27.42 E
Víron **267c** 37.57 N 23.45 E
Vironvay **50** 49.12 N 1.13 E
Viroqua **190** 43.33 N 90.53 W
Virovitica **36** 45.50 N 17.23 E
Virpazar **38** 42.15 N 19.05 E
Virrat **26** 62.14 N 23.47 E
Virsbo **40** 59.52 N 16.02 E
Virserum **26** 57.19 N 15.35 E
Virtaniemi **24** 68.53 N 28.27 E
Virton **56** 49.34 N 5.32 E
Vîrtopu **38** 44.12 N 23.21 E
Virtsu **76** 58.34 N 23.31 E
Virú **248** 8.25 S 78.45 W
Virudunagar **122** 9.36 N 77.58 E
Viru-Jaagupi **76** 59.15 N 26.28 E
Virulento **196** 28.52 N 104.21 W
Virunga, Parc National de ♠ **154** 1.00 S 29.15 E
Virungu **154** 7.04 S 29.46 E
Viru-Nigula **76** 59.27 N 26.41 E
Virvyčia ≐ **76** 56.13 N 22.34 E
Viry-Châtillon **50** 48.40 N 2.23 E
Vis **36** 43.03 N 16.12 E
Vis ≐, Fr. **62** 43.56 N 3.42 E
Vis (Fish) ≐, Namibia **156** 28.07 S 17.45 E
Vis ≐, S. Afr. **158** 30.53 S 20.23 E
Vis, Otok I **36** 43.02 N 16.11 E
Visale **175e** 9.15 S 159.42 E
Visalia **226** 36.19 N 119.17 W
Visalia Airport ⊠ **226** 36.19 N 119.23 W
Visayan Sea ⫧2 **116** 11.35 N 123.51 E
Visbek **52** 52.48 N 8.19 E
Visby **26** 57.38 N 18.18 E
Viscaya, Bahía de → Biscay, Bay of ᑕ **32** 44.00 N 4.00 W
Viscount **184** 51.57 N 105.39 W
Viscount Melville Sound ꭒ **176** 74.10 N 108.00 W
Visé **56** 50.44 N 5.42 E
Višegrad **38** 43.47 N 19.17 E
Vis-en-Artois **50** 50.15 N 2.56 E
Višera ≐ **76** 58.34 N 31.24 E
Viserba **66** 44.05 N 12.32 E
Viseu, Bra. **250** 1.12 S 46.07 W
Viseu, Port. **34** 40.39 N 7.55 W
Vişeu ≐ **38** 47.55 N 24.09 E
Vişeu de Sus **38** 47.44 N 24.22 E
Vishākhapatnam **122** 17.42 N 83.18 E
Vishoek **158** 34.08 S 18.26 E
Visim **86** 57.39 N 59.30 E
Visingsö I **26** 58.03 N 14.20 E
Visitation, Île de la I **275a** 45.35 N 73.40 W
Viskafors **26** 57.38 N 12.50 E
Viskan ≐ **26** 57.14 N 12.12 E
Viškil' **80** 58.05 N 48.19 E
Viskinge **41** 55.40 N 11.16 E
Visl'ajevo **82** 54.25 N 36.43 E
Vislanda **26** 56.47 N 14.27 E
Vislinskij zaliv ᑕ **30** 54.27 N 19.40 E
Vismen ⊜ **40** 59.17 N 14.17 E
Visnagar **120** 23.42 N 72.33 E
Višn'aki **265b** 55.47 N 37.54 E
Višn'akovo **82** 55.45 N 38.10 E
Višnevčik **78** 49.02 N 26.28 E
Visnevo **76** 54.08 N 26.14 E
Višnevoje, S.S.S.R. **78** 48.27 N 33.56 E
Višnevoje, S.S.S.R. **80** 52.38 N 43.26 E
Višňové **61** 48.59 N 16.09 E
Višn'ovec **78** 49.54 N 25.45 E
Višn'ovka, S.S.S.R. **78** 46.20 N 28.26 E
Višn'ovka, S.S.S.R. **86** 50.49 N 72.12 E
Viso, Monte ∧ **62** 44.40 N 7.07 E
Visoki Dečani, Manastir ʋ1 **38** 42.30 N 20.31 E
Visoko **38** 43.59 N 18.11 E
Visokoi Island I **18** 56.42 S 27.12 W
Visp **58** 46.18 N 7.53 E
Vispa ≐ **58** 46.18 N 7.52 E
Visrivier **158** 31.55 S 25.25 E
Vissefjärda **26** 56.32 N 15.35 E
Visselhövede **52** 52.59 N 9.35 E
Vissenbjerg **41** 55.23 N 10.08 E
Visso **66** 42.56 N 13.05 E
Vissoie **58** 46.13 N 7.36 E
Vista, Ca., U.S. **228** 33.12 N 117.14 W
Vista, N.Y., U.S. **210** 41.12 N 73.31 W
Vista Alegre, Arg. **252** 38.45 S 68.11 W
Vista Alegre, Bra. **256** 21.27 S 42.35 W
Vista Alegre, Chile **286e** 33.30 S 70.43 W
Vista Alegre, Perú **286d** 12.09 S 77.00 W
Vista Flores **252** 33.38 S 69.09 W
Vista Hermosa, Méx. **234** 19.38 N 103.22 W
Vista Hermosa, Méx. **234** 20.16 N 102.29 W
Vista La Mesa **228** 32.35 N 117.01 W
Vista Park **228** 35.21 N 118.55 W
Vistina **76** 59.47 N 28.29 E
Vistre ≐ **62** 43.40 N 4.15 E
Vistula → Wisła ≐ **30** 54.22 N 18.55 E
Visun' ≐ **78** 47.07 N 32.53 E
Vit ≐ **38** 43.41 N 24.45 E
Vita, Mb., Can. **184** 49.08 N 96.34 W
Vita, It. **70** 37.52 N 12.49 E
Vita ≐ **246** 6.11 N 67.31 W
Vitacura **286e** 33.24 S 70.36 W
Vitali **116** 7.22 N 122.18 E
Vitanje **36** 46.23 N 15.18 E
Vitarte **248** 12.02 S 76.56 W
Vit'azevka **78** 48.01 N 31.53 E
Vite **122** 17.17 N 74.33 E
Vitebsk **76** 55.12 N 30.11 E
Vitebsk Station ◆5 **265a** 59.55 N 30.21 E
Vitel, Laguna ⊜ **258** 35.32 S 58.07 W
Viterbo **66** 42.25 N 12.06 E
Viterbo □4 **66** 42.25 N 12.05 E
Vitiaz Strait ꭒ **164** 5.50 S 147.20 E
Vitichi **248** 20.13 S 65.29 W
Vitigudino **34** 41.01 N 6.26 W
Viti Levu I **175g** 18.00 S 178.00 E
Vitim **74** 59.28 N 112.34 E
Vitim ≐ **74** 59.26 N 112.34 E
Vitimskij **88** 58.14 N 113.18 E
Vitimskoje ploskogorje ⩘1 **88** 54.00 N 113.30 E
Vitinia ◆8 **267a** 41.47 N 12.24 E
Vitis **61** 48.45 N 15.10 E
Vítkov **30** 49.46 N 17.45 E
Vito **175e** 6.02 S 155.24 E
Vítor **248** 16.26 S 71.49 W
Vitor ≐ **248** 16.37 S 72.19 W
Vitória, Bra. **250** 2.54 S 52.01 W
Vitória, Bra. **255** 20.19 S 40.21 W
Vitoria, Esp. **34** 42.51 N 2.40 W
Vitória, Ilha da I **256** 23.45 S 45.01 W
Vitória da Conquista **255** 14.51 S 40.51 W
Vitória de Santo Antão **250** 8.07 S 35.18 W
Vitória do Mearim **250** 3.28 S 44.53 W
Vitorino Freire **250** 4.04 S 45.10 W
Vitravo ≐ **68** 39.11 N 17.05 E
Vitré **28** 48.08 N 1.12 W
Vitrey-sur-Mance **58** 47.49 N 5.45 E
Vitry-aux-Loges **50** 47.56 N 2.16 E
Vitry-en-Artois **50** 50.20 N 2.59 E
Vitry-la-Ville **50** 48.50 N 4.28 E
Vitry-le-François **56** 48.44 N 4.35 E
Vitry [-sur-Seine] **50** 48.48 N 2.24 E
Vitshumbi **154** 0.41 S 29.23 E
Vittangi **24** 67.41 N 21.36 E
Vitte **54** 54.34 N 13.06 E
Vitteaux **58** 47.24 N 4.32 E
Vittel **58** 48.12 N 5.57 E
Vittinge **40** 59.54 N 17.04 E
Vittoria, On., Can. **212** 42.46 N 80.19 W
Vittoria, It. **70** 36.57 N 14.32 E
Vittorio Veneto **64** 45.59 N 12.18 E
Vittsjö **26** 56.20 N 13.40 E
Vitulano **68** 41.10 N 14.38 E
Vitznau **58** 47.01 N 8.29 E
Viù **62** 45.14 N 7.22 E
Vivarais □9 **62** 44.40 N 4.30 E
Vivarais, Monts du ⩘ **62** 44.55 N 4.15 E
Viver **34** 39.55 N 0.36 W
Vivero **34** 43.40 N 7.35 W
Viverols **62** 45.26 N 3.53 E
Viverone, Lago di ⊜ **62** 45.25 N 8.02 E
Vivi ≐ **74** 63.52 N 97.50 E
Vivian **194** 32.52 N 93.59 W
Viviers **62** 44.29 N 4.41 E
Viviers-du-Lac **62** 45.39 N 5.54 E
Vivione, Passo del)(**64** 46.02 N 10.12 E
Vivonne **32** 46.26 N 0.16 E
Vivoratá **252** 37.40 S 57.39 W
Vivorillo, Cayos II **236** 15.50 N 83.18 W
Vivsta **26** 62.29 N 17.19 E
Viwa I **175g** 17.08 S 176.54 E
Vizagapatam → Vishākhapatnam **122** 17.42 N 83.18 E
Vizcaíno, Desierto de ◆2 **232** 27.40 N 114.40 W
Vizcaíno, Isla I **258** 33.47 S 59.15 W
Vizcaya □4 **34** 43.20 N 2.45 W
Vize **130** 41.34 N 27.45 E
Vize, ostrov I **72** 79.30 N 77.00 E
Vizianagaram **122** 18.07 N 83.25 E
Vizille **62** 45.05 N 5.46 E
Vižinada **36** 45.20 N 13.46 E
Vizinga **24** 61.05 N 50.04 E
Vižnica **78** 48.15 N 25.12 E
Vizzini **70** 37.10 N 14.53 E
Vizzola **266b** 45.38 N 8.42 E
Vjulka ≐ **82** 56.53 N 37.57 E
Vjunka ≐ **265b** 55.42 N 38.01 E
Vjuny **86** 55.31 N 82.55 E
Vlaanderen → Flanders □9 **50** 51.00 N 3.00 E
Vlaardingen **52** 51.54 N 4.21 E
Vlachovo Březí **60** 49.05 N 13.57 E
Vladař ∧ **54** 50.05 N 13.14 E
Vlădeasa ∧ **38** 46.45 N 22.48 E
Vlădeni **38** 47.25 N 27.20 E
Vladičin Han **38** 42.42 N 22.04 E
Vladikavkaz → Ordžonikidze **84** 43.03 N 44.40 E
Vladimir **80** 56.10 N 40.25 E
Vladimir □4 **82** 56.15 N 39.00 E
Vladimirec **78** 51.25 N 26.08 E
Vladimirovka, S.S.S.R. **78** 47.32 N 32.55 E
Vladimirovka, S.S.S.R. **80** 50.51 N 51.08 E
Vladimirovka, S.S.S.R. **83** 47.44 N 37.23 E
Vladimirovka, S.S.S.R. **86** 53.28 N 64.02 E
Vladimirskij Tupik **76** 55.42 N 33.18 E
Vladimirskoje **80** 56.49 N 45.07 E
Vladimir-Volynskij **78** 50.51 N 24.20 E
Vladivostok **89** 43.10 N 131.56 E
Vladyčnoje **76** 58.49 N 39.29 E
Vladykino ◆8 **265b** 55.52 N 37.36 E
Vlasenica **38** 44.11 N 18.56 E
Vlašim **30** 49.42 N 14.54 E
Vlaskovo **82** 56.11 N 36.31 E
Vlasotince **38** 42.58 N 22.08 E
Vlasovo, S.S.S.R. **74** 70.48 N 135.00 E
Vlasovo, S.S.S.R. **82** 56.38 N 38.14 E
Vlazoviči **76** 53.01 N 32.18 E
Vledder **52** 52.52 N 6.12 E
Vleesbaai ᑕ **158** 34.16 S 21.57 E
Vleikolk **158** 29.43 S 20.50 E
Vleuten **52** 52.05 N 5.02 E
Vlieland I **52** 53.15 N 5.00 E
Vlijmen **52** 51.42 N 5.15 E
Vlissingen (Flushing) **52** 51.26 N 3.35 E
Vlodrop **52** 51.08 N 6.05 E
Vloesberg → Flobecq **50** 50.44 N 3.44 E
Vlonë → Vlorë **38** 40.27 N 19.30 E
Vlorë **38** 40.27 N 19.30 E
Vlorës, Gji i ᑕ **38** 40.25 N 19.25 E
Vlotho **52** 52.10 N 8.51 E
Vltava ≐ **30** 50.21 N 14.30 E
Vluyn **52** 51.26 N 6.32 E
Vnukovo **82** 55.38 N 37.16 E
Vnukovo Airport ⊠ **265b** 55.37 N 37.17 E
Voca **196** 31.01 N 99.11 W
Vochrinka **82** 55.24 N 38.18 E
Vochtoga **76** 58.47 N 41.07 E
Počin **36** 45.37 N 17.32 E
Vöckla ≐ **64** 48.00 N 13.36 E

	English	Deutsch	Español	Français	Português
≐	River	Fluss	Río	Rivière	Rio
≚	Canal	Kanal	Canal	Canal	Canal
ᒪ	Waterfall, Rapids	Wasserfall, Stromschnellen	Cascada, Rápidos	Chute d'eau, Rapides	Cascata, Rápidos
ꭒ	Strait	Meeresstrasse	Estrecho	Détroit	Estreito
ᑕ	Bay, Gulf	Bucht, Golf	Bahía, Golfo	Baie, Golfe	Baía, Golfo
⊜	Lake, Lakes	See, Seen	Lago, Lagos	Lac, Lacs	Lago, Lagos
≡	Swamp	Sumpf	Pantano	Marais	Pântano
⩍	Ice Features, Glacier	Eis- und Gletscherformen	Accidentes Glaciales	Formes glaciaires	Acidentes glaciares
⫧	Other Hydrographic Features	Andere Hydrographische Objekte	Otros Elementos Hidrográficos	Autres données hydrographiques	Outros acidentes hidrográficos
✢	Submarine Features	Untermeerische Objekte	Accidentes Submarinos	Formes de relief sous-marin	Acidentes submarinos
□	Political Unit	Politische Einheit	Unidad Politica	Entité politique	Unidade política
ʋ	Cultural Institution	Kulturelle Institution	Institución Cultural	Institution culturelle	Institução cultural
⊥	Historical Site	Historische Stätte	Sitio Histórico	Site historique	Sitio histórico
♠	Recreational Site	Erholungs- und Ferienort	Sitio de Recreo	Centre de loisirs	Area de Lazer
⊠	Airport	Flughafen	Aeropuerto	Aéroport	Aeroporto
■	Military Installation	Militäranlage	Instalación Militar	Installation militaire	Instalação militar
◆	Miscellaneous	Verschiedenes	Misceláneo	Divers	Diversos

ENGLISH Name	Page	Lat.°′	Long.°′

W

DEUTSCH Name	Seite	Breite°′	Länge°′ E = Ost

Symbols in the index entries represent the broad categories identified in the key at the right. Symbols with superior numbers (⋏[1]) identify subcategories (see complete key on page *I · 1*).

Kartensymbole in dem Registerverzeichnis stellen die rechts in Schlüssel erklärten Kategorien dar. Symbole mit hochgestellten Ziffern (⋏[1]) bezeichnen Unterabteilungen einer Kategorie (vgl. vollständiger Schlüssel auf Seite *I · 1*).

Los símbolos incluídos en el texto del índice representan las grandes categorias identificadas con la clave a la derecha. Los símbolos con numeros en su parte superior (⋏[1]) identifican las subcategorías (véase la clave completa en la página *I · 1*).

Les symboles de l'index représentent les catégories indiquées dans la légende à droite. Les symboles suivis d'un indice (⋏[1]) représentent des sous-catégories (voir légende complète à la page *I · 1*).

Os símbolos incluídos no texto do índice representam as grandes categorias identificadas com a chave à direita. Os símbolos com números em sua parte superior (⋏[1]) identificam as subcategorias (veja-se a chave completa à página *I · 1*).

English	Deutsch	Español	Français	Português
∧ Mountain	Berg	Montaña	Montagne	Montanha
⋏ Mountains	Berge	Montañas	Montagnes	Montanhas
)(Pass	Pass	Paso	Col	Passo
V Valley, Canyon	Tal, Cañon	Valle, Cañón	Vallée, Canyon	Vale, Canhão
≃ Plain	Ebene	Llano	Plaine	Planície
≻ Cape	Kap	Cabo	Cap	Cabo
I Island	Insel	Isla	Île	Ilha
II Islands	Inseln	Islas	Îles	Ilhas
⊥ Other Topographic Features	Andere Topographische Objekte	Otros Elementos Topográficos	Autres données topographiques	Outros acidentes topográficos

ESPAÑOL — Nombre | Página | Lat.°′ | Long.°′ W = Oeste
FRANÇAIS — Nom | Page | Lat.°′ | Long.°′ W = Ouest
PORTUGUÊS — Nome | Página | Lat.°′ | Long.°′ W = Oeste

Wailo 144 9.25 N 48.55 E
Wailua 229b 22.03 N 159.20 W
Wailua River State Park ♦ 229b 22.02 N 159.21 W
Wailuku 229a 20.53 N 156.30 W
Waimahaka 172 46.31 S 168.49 E
Waimakariri ≃ 172 43.24 S 172.42 E
Waimamaku 172 35.33 S 173.29 E
Waimana 172 38.09 S 177.05 E
Waimana ≃ 172 38.04 S 177.00 E
Waimanalo 229c 21.21 N 157.43 W
Waimangaroa 172 41.43 S 171.46 E
Waimangura 115b 9.30 S 119.14 E
Waimarama 172 39.48 S 176.59 E
Waimate 172 44.44 S 171.02 E
Waimea, Hi., U.S. 229c 21.57 N 159.40 W
Waimea, Hi., U.S. 229d 21.38 N 158.03 W
Waimea Canyon V 229b 22.04 N 159.39 W
Waimea Canyon State Park ♦ 229b 22.04 N 159.40 W
Waimes 56 50.25 N 6.07 E
Wainfleet All Saints 44 53.07 N 0.14 E
Wainganga ≃ 122 18.50 N 79.55 E
Waingapu 115b 9.39 S 120.16 E
Waini ≃ 246 8.24 N 59.51 W
Wainscott 260 51.25 N 0.31 E
Wainstalls 262 53.45 N 1.56 W
Wainuiomata 172 41.16 S 174.57 E
Wainunu Bay c 175g 16.55 S 178.53 E
Wainwright, Ab., Can. 182 52.49 N 110.52 W
Wainwright, Ak., U.S. 180 70.38 N 160.01 W
Wainwright, Oh., U.S. 214 40.25 N 81.25 W
Waiohau 172 38.14 S 176.51 E
Waiotira 172 35.56 S 174.12 E
Waiouru 172 39.29 S 175.40 E
Waipa ≃ 172 37.41 S 175.09 E
Waipahi 172 46.07 S 169.15 E
Waipahu 229c 21.23 N 158.00 W
Waipaoa 172 38.32 S 177.54 E
Waipara 172 43.04 S 172.45 E
Waipara ≃ 172 43.09 S 172.48 E
Waipawa 172 39.56 S 176.36 E
Waipiata 172 45.11 S 170.10 E
Waipio Acres 229c 21.28 N 158.00 W
Waipio Bay c 229a 20.55 N 156.13 W
Waipiro 172 38.01 S 178.20 E
Waipu 172 35.59 S 174.27 E
Waipukurau 172 40.00 S 176.34 E
Wairakei 172 38.38 S 176.06 E
Wairarapa, Lake ⊜ 172 41.13 S 175.15 E
Wairau ≃ 172 41.30 S 174.04 E
Wairau Valley 172 41.34 S 173.32 E
Wairio 172 46.00 S 168.02 E
Wairoa 172 39.02 S 177.25 E
Wairoa ≃ 172 39.04 S 177.26 E
Waisanzao 106 30.57 N 121.52 E
Waischenfeld 60 49.51 N 11.21 E
Waïsisi 175f 19.30 S 169.22 E
Waitahanui 172 38.47 S 176.05 E
Waitahuna 172 45.59 S 169.46 E
Waitakaruru 172 37.15 S 175.23 E
Waitaki ≃ 172 44.57 S 171.09 E
Waitara, Austl. 274a 33.43 S 151.07 E
Waitara, N.Z. 172 39.00 S 174.13 E
Waitara ≃ 172 38.59 S 174.14 E
Waitarere 172 40.33 S 175.12 E
Waita Reservoir ⊜[1] 229b 21.55 N 159.27 W
Waitati 172 45.45 S 170.34 E
Waita-zan ∧ 96 33.08 N 131.10 E
Waite Hill 214 41.37 N 81.22 W
Waitemata 172 36.56 S 174.42 E
Waite Park 190 45.33 N 94.13 W
Waitoa 172 37.37 S 175.38 E
Waitotara 172 39.48 S 174.44 E
Waitotara ≃ 172 39.51 S 174.41 E
Waitpinga 168b 35.37 S 138.29 E
Waitsburg 202 46.16 N 118.09 W
Waitzen → Vác 30 47.47 N 19.08 E
Waiuku 172 37.15 S 174.45 E
Waiuta 172 42.18 S 171.49 E
Waiwera South 172 46.13 S 169.30 E
Waiwo 164 0.56 S 131.03 E
Waiya 164 3.13 S 128.55 E
Waizenkirchen 60 48.20 N 13.52 E
Wajiki 96 33.51 N 134.30 E
Wajima 92 37.24 N 136.54 E
Wajir 154 1.45 N 40.04 E
Waka, Ityo. 144 7.07 N 37.26 E
Waka, Tx., U.S. 196 36.17 N 101.03 W
Waka, Zaïre 152 1.01 N 20.13 E
Wakajabi 164 5.38 S 134.24 E
Wakakusa 94 35.36 N 138.29 E
Wakakusa-yama ∧[2] 270 34.42 N 135.52 E
Wakamatsu → Aizu-wakamatsu 92 37.30 N 139.56 E
Wakami ≃ 190 47.43 N 82.22 W
Wakami Lake ⊜ 190 47.29 N 82.51 W
Wakamiya 96 33.44 N 130.37 E
Wakano-ura ♦ 96 34.11 N 135.11 E
Wakarusa 216 41.32 N 86.03 W
Wakarusa ≃ 198 38.57 N 95.05 W
Wakasa 96 35.20 N 134.24 E
Wakasa-wan c 92 35.45 N 135.40 E
Wakasa-wan-kokutei-kōen ♦ 96 35.35 N 135.30 E
Wakatipu, Lake ⊜ 172 45.05 S 168.34 E
Wakatomika Creek ≃ 214 40.07 N 82.00 W
Wakato-ōhashi ✦[5] 96 33.54 N 130.49 E
Wakaw 184 52.39 N 105.44 W
Wakaw Lake ⊜ 184 52.40 N 105.35 W
Wakayama 96 34.13 N 135.11 E
Wakayama □[5] 96 34.00 N 135.20 E
Wakayanagi 92 38.46 N 141.08 E
Wake, Nihon 96 34.48 N 134.08 E
Wake, Zaïre 152 0.48 S 20.10 E
WaKeeney 198 39.01 N 99.53 W
Wakefield, N.Z. 172 41.24 S 173.03 E
Wakefield, Eng., U.K. 44 53.42 N 1.29 W
Wakefield, Ks., U.S. 198 39.12 N 97.00 W
Wakefield, Ma., U.S. 207 42.30 N 71.04 W
Wakefield, Ne., U.S. 198 42.16 N 96.51 W
Wakefield, Oh., U.S. 218 38.59 N 83.01 W
Wakefield, R.I., U.S. 207 41.26 N 71.30 W
Wakefield, Va., U.S. 192 36.58 N 76.59 W
Wakefield ≃ 168b 34.10 S 138.10 E
Wakefield Forest 284c 38.50 N 77.14 W
Wake Forest 192 35.58 N 78.30 W
Wake Island □[2], Oc. 14 19.17 N 166.36 E
Wake Island □[2], Oc. 174a 19.17 N 166.36 E
Wake Island I[1] 174a 19.18 N 166.38 E
Wake Island Air Force Base ■ 174a 19.17 N 166.37 E
Wake Lagoon c 174a 19.18 N 166.36 E
Wakema 110 16.36 N 95.11 E
Wakeman 214 41.15 N 82.23 W
Wakeman ≃ 182 51.00 N 126.30 W
Wakenda Creek ≃ 194 39.19 N 93.16 W
Wake Village 194 33.26 N 94.07 W
Wakhān → Vākhān ✦[1] 120 37.00 N 73.00 E
Waki 96 34.04 N 134.09 E
Wakis 164 6.13 S 150.17 E
Wakita 196 36.53 N 97.55 W
Wakkanai 92a 45.25 N 141.40 E
Wakkerstroom 158 27.24 S 30.10 E
Wakō 268 35.47 N 139.37 E
Wakomata Lake ⊜ 190 46.34 N 83.22 W
Wakonassin ≃ 190 46.28 N 81.51 W
Wakonda 198 43.00 N 97.06 W
Wakre 164 0.19 S 131.09 E
Waku 164 6.05 S 149.05 E
Waku Kundo 152 11.25 S 15.07 E
Wakunai 175e 5.52 S 155.13 E
Wakusimi ≃ 190 49.08 N 82.17 W
Wala ≃ 154 5.46 S 32.04 E
Wālājāpet 122 12.56 N 79.23 E
Walamba 154 13.29 S 28.45 E
Walamo 234 23.07 N 106.15 W
Walanae ≃ 112 4.08 S 119.58 E
Walang 102 28.33 N 100.54 E
Wal Athiang 140 7.42 N 29.40 E
Walawe ≃ 122 6.06 N 81.01 E
Walbeck 52 51.30 N 6.15 E
Walberswick 42 52.19 N 1.39 E
Walbran Creek ≃ 224 48.34 N 124.40 W
Walbridge 214 41.35 N 83.29 W
Wałbrzych (Waldenburg) 30 50.46 N 16.17 E
Walburg 222 30.44 N 97.35 W
Walbury Hill ∧[2] 42 51.21 N 1.30 W
Walcha 166 30.59 S 151.36 E
Walchensee ⊜ 64 47.36 N 11.20 E
Walcheren I 52 51.33 N 3.35 E
Walcheren, Kanaal door ≅ 50 51.26 N 3.35 E
Walchsee 64 47.39 N 12.19 E
Walcott, B.C., Can. 182 54.31 N 126.51 W
Walcott, Ia., U.S. 190 41.35 N 90.46 W
Walcott, N.D., U.S. 198 46.32 N 96.56 W
Walcott, Lake ⊜[1] 202 42.40 N 113.23 W
Walcourt 50 50.15 N 4.25 E
Wałcz 30 53.17 N 16.28 E
Wald 58 47.17 N 8.55 E
Wald ✦[8] 263 51.11 N 7.03 E
Waldai → Valdajskaja vozvyšennost' ⋀[2] 24 57.00 N 33.30 E
Waldaist ≃ 61 48.19 N 14.34 E
Wald am Schoberpass 61 47.27 N 14.40 E
Waldbauer ✦[8] 263 51.18 N 7.28 E
Waldbillig 56 49.47 N 6.18 E
Waldböckelheim 56 49.49 N 7.43 E
Waldbröl 56 50.53 N 7.37 E
Waldbronn 56 48.56 N 8.29 E
Waldburg 58 47.45 N 9.43 E
Waldeck, B.R.D. 56 51.12 N 9.04 E
Waldeck, B.R.D. 60 49.52 N 11.57 E
Walden, Co., U.S. 200 40.43 N 106.16 W
Walden, N.Y., U.S. 210 41.33 N 74.11 W
Walden, Lake ⊜ 281 42.39 N 83.46 W
Waldenbuch 56 48.38 N 9.07 E
Waldenburg, B.R.D. 56 49.11 N 9.38 E
Waldenburg, D.D.R. 54 50.52 N 12.36 E
Waldenburg → Wałbrzych, Pol. 30 50.46 N 16.17 E
Waldenburg, Schw. 58 47.23 N 7.45 E
Walden Pond ⊜, Ma., U.S. 283 42.26 N 71.20 W
Walden Pond ⊜, Ma., U.S. 283 42.28 N 71.00 W
Walden Ridge ∧ 194 35.30 N 85.15 W
Waldershof 60 49.59 N 12.04 E
Walderslade 260 51.21 N 0.32 E
Waldfischbach 56 49.17 N 7.40 E
Waldheim, Sk., Can. 184 52.37 N 106.38 W
Waldheim, D.D.R. 54 51.04 N 13.01 E
Waldighoffen 58 47.33 N 7.19 E
Wald im Pinzgau 64 47.15 N 12.14 E
Waldkappel 56 51.08 N 9.52 E
Waldkirch 58 48.05 N 7.57 E
Waldkirchen 60 48.44 N 13.37 E
Waldkirchen am Wesen 60 48.26 N 13.49 E
Waldkraiburg 60 48.12 N 12.28 E
Waldmohr 56 49.23 N 7.20 E
Waldmünchen 60 49.23 N 12.43 E
Waldnaab ≃ 60 49.36 N 12.08 E
Waldo, B.C., Can. 182 49.13 N 115.13 W
Waldo, Ar., U.S. 194 33.21 N 93.17 W
Waldo, Oh., U.S. 214 40.27 N 83.04 W
Waldoboro 188 44.05 N 69.22 W
Waldo Lake ⊜ 283 42.07 N 71.03 W
Waldo Lake ⊜[1] 202 43.44 N 122.03 W
Waldon ≃ 42 50.22 N 4.14 W
Waldorf 208 38.37 N 76.56 W
Waldport 202 44.25 N 124.04 W
Waldron, Sk., Can. 184 50.51 N 102.30 W
Waldron, Ar., U.S. 194 34.53 N 94.05 W
Waldron, In., U.S. 218 39.27 N 85.40 W
Waldron, Mi., U.S. 216 41.43 N 84.25 W
Waldron Island I 224 48.43 N 123.02 W
Waldsassen 60 50.00 N 12.18 E
Waldshut 58 47.37 N 8.13 E
Waldstatt 58 47.21 N 9.17 E
Waldthurn 60 49.40 N 12.20 E
Waldviertel ✦[1] 61 48.40 N 15.40 E
Waldwick 276 41.00 N 74.07 W
Walea, Selat ꓘ 112 0.40 S 122.00 E
Walembele 150 10.30 N 1.58 W
Walensee ⊜ 58 47.07 N 9.12 E
Walenstadt 58 47.07 N 9.19 E
Wales, Ak., U.S. 180 65.36 N 168.05 W
Wales, Ma., U.S. 207 42.04 N 72.13 W
Wales, Wi., U.S. 216 43.00 N 88.23 W
Wales □[8] 28 52.30 N 3.30 W
Wales Center 210 42.46 N 78.32 W
Wales Island I, B.C., Can. 182 54.45 N 130.30 W
Wales Island I, N.T., Can. 176 68.00 N 86.43 W
Walewale 150 10.21 N 0.48 W
Walgett 166 30.01 S 148.07 E
Walgreen Coast ⊥[2] 9 75.15 S 105.00 W
Walhachin 182 50.45 N 120.59 W
Walhalla, N.D., U.S. 198 48.55 N 97.55 W
Walhalla, S.C., U.S. 192 34.45 N 83.03 W
Walhalla ⊥ 60 49.03 N 12.14 E
Walheim 56 50.42 N 6.10 E
Walhonding 214 40.22 N 82.09 W
Walhonding ≃ 214 40.18 N 81.53 W
Wali 105 39.42 N 118.20 E
Walia 164 3.47 S 138.32 E
Walikale 154 1.25 S 28.03 E
Walincourt 50 50.04 N 3.20 E
Walis Island I 164 3.15 S 143.20 E
Walkaway 162 28.57 S 114.48 E
Walkden 44 53.32 N 2.24 W
Walkenried 54 51.35 N 10.37 E
Walker, Ia., U.S. 190 42.17 N 91.46 W
Walker, Mi., U.S. 216 43.00 N 85.46 W
Walker, Mn., U.S. 190 47.06 N 94.35 W
Walker, N.Y., U.S. 210 43.18 N 77.52 W
Walker □[6] 222 30.42 N 95.35 W
Walker ≃ 204 38.54 N 118.47 W
Walker, Lac ⊜ 186 50.16 N 67.09 W
Walker, Mount ∧[2] 171a 27.48 S 152.34 E
Walker Basin Creek ≃ 228 35.20 N 118.47 W
Walker Bay c 158 34.30 S 19.20 E
Walker Creek ≃, Az., U.S. 200 36.58 N 109.42 W
Walker Creek ≃, Ma., U.S. 283 42.38 N 70.44 W
Walker Creek ≃, Wy., U.S. 198 43.09 N 104.52 W
Walker Lake ⊜, Mb., Can. 184 54.42 N 96.57 W
Walker Lake ⊜, Ak., U.S. 180 67.10 N 154.26 W
Walker Lake ⊜, Nv., U.S. 204 38.44 N 118.43 W
Walker Lake ⊜[1] 210 40.48 N 77.11 W
Walker Point ≻ 158 34.05 S 22.57 E
Walker River Indian Reservation ✦[4] 204 39.00 N 118.40 W
Walkers Mill 279b 40.24 N 80.08 W
Walkersville 208 39.29 N 77.21 W
Walkerton, On., Can. 212 44.07 N 81.09 W
Walkerton, In., U.S. 216 41.28 N 86.28 W
Walkerton, Va., U.S. 208 37.43 N 77.01 W
Walkertown 192 36.10 N 80.09 W
Walker Valley 210 41.38 N 74.23 W
Walkerville 202 46.02 N 112.32 W
Walk Mill 262 53.46 N 2.12 W
Wall, Pa., U.S. 279b 40.24 N 79.47 W
Wall, S.D., U.S. 198 43.59 N 102.14 W
Wallace, Ca., U.S. 226 38.12 N 120.59 W
Wallace, Id., U.S. 202 47.28 N 115.55 W
Wallace, Ne., U.S. 198 40.50 N 101.09 W
Wallace, N.Y., U.S. 210 42.26 N 77.28 W
Wallace, N.C., U.S. 192 34.44 N 77.59 W
Wallaceburg 214 42.36 N 82.23 W
Wallace Lake ⊜ 279a 41.22 N 81.52 W
Wallaceton 214 40.57 N 78.17 W
Wallacetown 214 42.38 N 81.28 W
Wallach 263 51.35 N 6.34 E
Wallachia □[9] 38 44.00 N 25.00 E
Wallacia 170 33.52 S 150.39 E
Wallal Downs 162 19.47 S 120.40 E
Wallam Creek ≃ 166 28.40 S 147.20 E
Wallangarra 166 28.56 S 151.56 E
Wallaroo 168b 33.56 S 137.38 E
Wallaroo Mines 168b 33.57 S 137.41 E
Wallasey 44 53.26 N 3.03 W
Wallau 56 50.56 N 8.28 E
Walla Walla 202 46.03 N 118.20 W
Walldorf, B.R.D. 56 49.18 N 8.38 E
Walldorf, D.D.R. 54 50.36 N 10.23 E
Walldürn 56 49.35 N 9.22 E
Walled Lake 216 42.32 N 83.28 W
Walled Lake ⊜ 281 42.31 N 83.29 W
Wallen 216 41.09 N 85.09 W
Wallend 260 51.27 N 0.42 E
Wallenfels 54 50.16 N 11.28 E
Wallenhorst 52 52.21 N 8.01 E
Wallenpaupack, Lake ⊜ 210 41.25 N 75.12 W
Waller 222 30.04 N 95.56 W
Waller □[6] 222 30.00 N 96.00 W
Wallerawang 170 33.25 S 150.04 E
Wallern im Burgenland 61 47.43 N 16.56 E
Wallers 50 50.22 N 3.24 E
Wallersdorf 60 48.44 N 12.45 E
Wallersee ⊜ 64 47.55 N 13.11 E
Wallerstein 56 48.53 N 10.28 E
Wallgau 64 47.31 N 11.16 E
Wallgrove 274a 33.47 S 150.51 E
Wallhead Airport ⊠ 279a 41.21 N 82.09 W
Wallibou 241h 13.19 N 61.15 W
Wallingford, Eng., U.K. 42 51.37 N 1.08 W
Wallingford, Ct., U.S. 207 41.27 N 72.49 W
Wallingford, Pa., U.S. 285 39.54 N 75.22 W
Wallingford, Vt., U.S. 188 43.28 N 72.58 W
Wallington 276 40.51 N 74.06 W
Wallington ✦[8] 260 51.21 N 0.09 W
Wallis 222 29.37 N 96.03 W
Wallis → Valais □[3] 58 46.10 N 7.30 E
Wallis, Îles II 14 13.18 S 176.10 W
Wallis and Futuna □[2] 14 14.00 S 177.00 W
Wallisellen 58 47.25 N 8.36 E
Wallisville 222 29.50 N 94.44 W
Wallisville Lake ⊜[1] 222 29.50 N 94.45 W
Wallkill 210 41.36 N 74.11 W
Wallkill ≃, U.S. 210 41.51 N 74.03 W
Wallkill ≃, U.S. 276 41.11 N 74.35 W
Wallkill, Wildcat Branch ≃ 276 41.07 N 74.36 W
Wall Lake, Ia., U.S. 198 42.16 N 95.05 W
Wall Lake, Mi., U.S. 216 42.31 N 85.24 W
Wall Lake ⊜ 216 42.31 N 85.23 W
Wallmer Bridge 262 53.43 N 2.48 W
Wallmerod 56 50.29 N 7.56 E
Wallops Island I 208 37.52 N 75.27 W
Wallowa 202 45.34 N 117.31 W
Wallowa ≃ 202 45.43 N 117.47 W
Wallowa Mountains ⋀ 202 45.10 N 117.30 W
Walls, Scot., U.K. 46a 60.14 N 1.35 W
Walls, Ms., U.S. 194 34.57 N 90.09 W
Wallsbüll 41 54.47 N 9.14 E
Wallsend, Austl. 170 32.55 S 151.40 E
Wallsend, Eng., U.K. 44 55.00 N 1.31 W
Wallstawe 54 52.47 N 11.01 E
Wall Town Drainage Ditch ≅ 216 40.26 N 88.10 W
Wallula, Lake ⊜[1] 202 46.00 N 119.00 W
Walmer, S. Afr. 158 33.59 S 25.36 E
Walmer, Eng., U.K. 42 51.13 N 1.24 E
Walmersley 262 53.37 N 2.18 W
Walney, Isle of I 44 54.07 N 3.15 W
Walnut, Ca., U.S. 228 34.01 N 117.51 W
Walnut, Il., U.S. 190 41.33 N 89.35 W
Walnut, Ia., U.S. 198 41.28 N 95.13 W
Walnut, Ks., U.S. 198 37.36 N 95.04 W
Walnut, Ms., U.S. 194 34.56 N 88.53 W
Walnut, N.C., U.S. 192 35.50 N 82.44 W
Walnut ≃ 198 37.03 N 97.00 W
Walnut Canyon National Monument ♦ 200 35.10 N 111.31 W
Walnut Canyon Reservoir ⊜[1] 280 33.50 N 117.45 W
Walnut Cove 192 36.17 N 80.08 W
Walnut Creek, Ca., U.S. 226 37.54 N 122.03 W
Walnut Creek, Oh., U.S. 214 40.33 N 81.43 W
Walnut Creek ≃, Ca., U.S. 280 34.03 N 118.01 W
Walnut Creek ≃, Ca., U.S. 282 37.54 N 122.03 W
Walnut Creek ≃, Ks., U.S. 198 38.21 N 98.41 W
Walnut Creek ≃, Oh., U.S. 188 39.41 N 82.59 W
Walnut Creek ≃, Tx., U.S. 222 32.38 N 97.00 W
Walnut Creek, Middle Fork ≃ 198 38.32 N 100.08 W
Walnut Creek, South Fork ≃ 198 38.25 N 99.53 W
Walnut Grove, B.C., Can. 224 49.11 N 122.39 W
Walnut Grove, Ca., U.S. 226 38.15 N 121.31 W
Walnut Grove, Mn., U.S. 198 44.13 N 95.28 W
Walnut Grove, Ms., U.S. 194 32.35 N 89.27 W
Walnut Heights 282 37.53 N 122.08 W
Walnut Hill 219 38.29 N 89.03 W
Walnut Lake 281 42.33 N 83.19 W
Walnut Lake ⊜ 281 42.33 N 83.20 W
Walnut Park 280 33.58 N 118.13 W
Walnutport 208 40.45 N 75.35 W
Walnut Ridge 194 36.04 N 90.57 W
Walnut Springs 222 32.03 N 97.45 W
Walpert Ridge ∧ 282 37.38 N 122.00 W
Walpeup 166 35.08 S 142.02 E
Walpole, Austl. 162 34.57 S 116.44 E
Walpole, Ma., U.S. 207 42.08 N 71.15 W
Walpole, N.H., U.S. 188 43.04 N 72.25 W
Walpole Island I 214 42.34 N 82.30 W
Walpole Island Indian Reserve ✦[4] 214 42.32 N 82.37 W
Walpole Saint Peter 42 52.42 N 0.15 E
Walsall 42 52.35 N 1.58 W
Walschleben 54 51.04 N 10.56 E
Walsden 262 53.42 N 2.06 W
Walsenburg 200 37.37 N 104.46 W
Walsh, Austl. 164 16.39 S 143.54 E
Walsh, Ab., Can. 184 49.57 N 110.03 W
Walsh, Co., U.S. 198 37.23 N 102.16 W
Walsh, Ky., U.S. 218 38.41 N 82.58 W
Walsh ≃ 164 16.31 S 143.42 E
Walshaw Dean Reservoirs ⊜[1] 262 53.48 N 2.03 W
Walshville 219 39.04 N 89.37 W
Walsingham 212 42.41 N 80.32 W
Walsoorden 52 51.23 N 4.02 E
Walsrode 52 52.52 N 9.35 E
Walston 214 40.58 N 79.01 W
Walsum 52 51.32 N 6.41 E
Walt Disney World ♦ 220 28.26 N 81.35 W
Waltenhofen 64 47.40 N 10.17 E
Walterboro 192 32.54 N 80.40 W
Walter F. George Lake ⊜[1] 192 31.49 N 85.08 W
Walter Reed Army Medical Center ⊌ 284c 38.58 N 77.02 W
Walters 196 34.21 N 98.18 W
Waltersdorf, D.D.R. 54 50.52 N 14.38 E
Waltersdorf, D.D.R. 264a 52.22 N 13.35 E
Waltershausen 54 50.53 N 10.33 E
Waltershofen 58 47.46 N 9.55 E
Waltersville 194 32.22 N 90.52 W
Walthall 194 33.36 N 89.16 W
Waltham, Eng., U.K. 44 53.31 N 0.06 W
Waltham, Ma., U.S. 207 42.22 N 71.14 W
Waltham Abbey 42 51.42 N 0.01 E
Waltham Forest ✦[8] 42 51.35 N 0.01 W
Waltham on the Wolds 42 52.49 N 0.49 W
Walthamstow ✦[8] 260 51.35 N 0.01 W
Walthill 198 42.08 N 96.29 W
Walton, N.S., Can. 186 45.14 N 64.00 W
Walton, Eng., U.K. 42 51.24 N 0.25 W
Walton, Eng., U.K. 42 51.58 N 1.21 E
Walton, Fl., U.S. 220 27.17 N 80.15 W
Walton, In., U.S. 216 40.39 N 86.14 W
Walton, Ky., U.S. 218 38.52 N 84.36 W
Walton, N.Y., U.S. 210 42.10 N 75.07 W
Walton Hills 214 41.22 N 81.32 W
Walton-le-Dale 44 53.45 N 2.39 W
Walton on the Hill 260 51.17 N 0.15 W
Walton on the Naze 42 51.51 N 1.16 E
Walton Run ≃ 285 40.05 N 74.59 W
Waltonville 219 38.13 N 89.02 W
Waltrop 52 51.37 N 7.23 E
Walt Whitman Bridge ✦[5] 285 39.54 N 75.08 W
Walt Whitman Homes 285 39.52 N 75.11 W
Walt Whitman House State Historic Site ⊥ 276 40.49 N 73.25 W
Walt Whitman Mall ✦[9] 276 40.50 N 73.25 W
Waltz 216 42.06 N 83.23 W
Walupt Lake ⊜ 224 46.25 N 121.28 W
Walvisbaai (Walvis Bay) 156 22.59 S 14.31 E
Walvisbaai c 156 22.57 S 14.30 E
Walvis Bay → Walvisbaai 156 22.59 S 14.31 E
Walvis Bay □[8] 156 22.59 S 14.31 E
Walvis Ridge ✢[3] 10 28.00 S 3.00 E
Walwa 171b 35.58 S 147.45 E
Walwen 262 53.14 N 3.15 W
Walworth, N.Y., U.S. 210 43.08 N 77.17 W
Walworth, Wi., U.S. 216 42.31 N 88.35 W
Walworth □[6] 216 42.41 N 88.32 W
Walyunga National Park ♦ 168a 31.41 S 116.06 E
Walyungup, Lake ⊜ 168a 32.21 S 115.47 E
Walze 263 51.16 N 7.31 E
Walzin, Château de ⊥ 56 50.13 N 4.55 E
Wama 152 12.14 S 15.33 E
Wamac 219 38.31 N 89.08 W
Wamba, Kenya 154 0.59 N 37.19 E
Wamba, Nig. 150 8.58 N 8.36 E
Wamba, Zaïre 154 2.09 N 28.00 E
Wamba (Uamba) ≃ 152 3.56 S 17.12 E
Wambel ✦[8] 263 51.32 N 7.32 E
Wamego 198 39.12 N 96.18 W
Wamel 52 51.53 N 5.28 E
Wamesit 283 42.37 N 71.15 W
Wami ≃ 154 6.08 S 38.49 E
Wamiao 100 30.49 N 113.02 E
Wamic 224 45.13 N 121.16 W
Wamma ≃ 164 3.23 S 135.13 E
Wamme ≃ 56 50.10 N 5.16 E
Wamplers Lake ⊜ 216 42.05 N 84.09 W
Wampool ≃ 44 54.54 N 3.14 W
Wampsville 210 43.04 N 75.42 W
Wampú ≃ 236 14.59 N 85.03 W
Wampum 214 40.53 N 80.20 W
Wampus ≃ 276 41.07 N 73.43 W
Wampus Lake Reservoir ⊜[1] 276 41.09 N 73.43 W
Wamsasi 112 3.33 S 126.10 E
Wamsutter 200 41.40 N 107.58 W
Wamuran 171a 27.02 S 152.52 E
Wanaaring 166 29.42 S 144.09 E
Wanaka 172 44.42 S 169.09 E
Wanaka, Lake ⊜ 172 44.30 S 169.08 E
Wanakah 210 42.45 N 78.54 W
Wanamassa 208 40.14 N 74.02 W
Wanamie 210 41.10 N 76.02 W
Wanamingo 190 44.18 N 92.47 W
Wan'an, Zhg. 100 26.56 N 117.22 E
Wan'an, Zhg. 100 26.30 N 114.49 E
Wan'an ≃ 100 25.20 N 117.21 E
Wan'anchang 107 30.39 N 104.25 E
Wanapiri 164 4.33 S 135.59 E
Wanapitei ≃ 190 46.02 N 80.51 W
Wanapitei Lake ⊜ 190 46.45 N 80.45 W
Wanapum Lake ⊜[1] 202 47.00 N 120.00 W
Wanaque 210 41.02 N 74.17 W
Wanaque ≃ 276 40.58 N 74.17 W
Wanaque Reservoir ⊜[1] 210 41.05 N 74.17 W
Wanatah 216 41.25 N 86.53 W
Wanau 164 1.22 S 132.42 E
Wanbaoshan 89 44.12 N 125.11 E
Wanbi 166 34.46 S 140.19 E
Wanblee 198 43.34 N 101.40 W
Wanborough 42 51.33 N 1.42 W
Wanchangchang 107 29.43 N 104.19 E
Wanchese 192 35.50 N 75.38 W
Wanda 158 29.36 S 24.28 E
Wandai 164 3.41 S 136.41 E
Wandana 162 32.04 S 133.49 E
Wandawega 216 42.45 N 88.40 W
Wande 98 36.21 N 116.56 E
Wanderer 154 19.37 S 29.59 E
Wandering 168a 32.40 S 116.40 E
Wandering ≃ 182 55.05 N 112.30 W
Wanderup 41 54.41 N 9.20 E
Wandhofen 263 51.26 N 7.33 E
Wandingzhen 102 24.10 N 98.04 E
Wandlitz 54 52.45 N 13.26 E
Wandlitzer See ⊜ 264a 52.46 N 13.27 E
Wando 98 34.18 N 126.47 E
Wan-do I 98 34.21 N 126.42 E
Wandoan 166 26.08 S 149.57 E
Wandsbek ✦[8] 52 53.34 N 10.04 E
Wandsworth ✦[8] 42 51.27 N 0.11 W
Waneta Lake ⊜ 210 42.27 N 77.06 W
Wanette 196 34.57 N 97.01 W
Wanfang 104 41.57 N 122.52 E
Wanfoxia 102 40.04 N 95.55 E
Wanfried 56 51.10 N 10.10 E
Wanfu ≃ 98 35.10 N 116.35 E
Wang ≃ 110 17.08 N 99.02 E
Wanga 154 2.58 N 29.13 E
Wangal 164 6.10 S 134.12 E
Wanganderry, Mount ∧ 170 34.20 S 150.15 E
Wanganui 172 39.56 S 175.03 E
Wanganui ≃ 172 39.56 S 175.00 E
Wang'anzhen 105 39.19 N 114.54 E
Wangaratta 166 36.22 S 146.20 E
Wangary 166 34.33 S 135.29 E
Wangbaotaicun 104 41.10 N 123.18 E
Wangbenying 105 40.28 N 116.06 E
Wangbintun 104 41.58 N 123.43 E
Wangchang, Zhg. 107 28.52 N 105.55 E
Wangchang, Zhg. 107 29.05 N 104.40 E
Wangchangtuizigou 104 41.14 N 120.32 E
Wangcheng 100 28.23 N 112.48 E
Wang Chin 110 17.53 N 99.37 E
Wangcun 98 36.41 N 117.41 E
Wangcunkou 100 28.22 N 118.59 E
Wangdalong 102 29.25 N 99.03 E
Wangdian 106 30.37 N 120.44 E
Wangdu 98 38.43 N 115.09 E
Wangdu Phodrang 124 27.29 N 89.54 E
Wange 154 2.00 S 40.55 E
Wangels 54 54.16 N 10.45 E
Wangen an der Aare 58 47.14 N 7.39 E
Wangenbourg 58 48.37 N 7.19 E
Wangen im Allgäu 58 47.41 N 9.50 E
Wangerin → Węgorzyno 30 53.32 N 15.33 E
Wangerooge 52 53.48 N 7.54 E
Wangerooge I 52 53.46 N 7.55 E
Wangersen 52 53.22 N 9.25 E
Wangfu 104 42.05 N 121.29 E
Wanggameti, Gunung ∧ 115b 10.07 S 120.14 E
Wanggangpu 104 41.38 N 123.09 E
Wanggao 102 24.38 N 111.30 E
Wanggezhuang 105 40.00 N 117.52 E
Wanggil-li 271b 37.36 N 126.39 E
Wanggoutun 104 41.40 N 121.53 E
Wanghai 98 40.26 N 120.30 E
Wanghai Shan ∧ 104 41.37 N 121.41 E
Wanghechenggou 104 41.52 N 121.13 E
Wang Hin, Khlong ≅ 269a 13.48 N 100.35 E
Wanghu 98 39.47 N 113.54 E
Wanghuzhuang 105 38.50 N 117.05 E
Wāngi 58 47.30 N 8.57 E
Wangingsha 100 22.44 N 113.33 E
Wangi Wangi 170 33.04 S 151.35 E
Wangiwangi, Pulau I 112 5.20 S 123.35 E
Wangji, Zhg. 100 33.52 N 118.44 E
Wangji, Zhg. 100 34.00 N 117.46 E
Wangjia, Zhg. 106 31.59 N 121.13 E
Wangjia, Zhg. 106 32.07 N 120.59 E
Wangjiadian, Zhg. 100 31.26 N 113.58 E
Wangjiadian, Zhg. 105 40.03 N 117.29 E
Wangjiagou 104 42.33 N 123.16 E
Wangjiajing, Zhg. 98 37.49 N 115.23 E
Wangjiajing, Zhg. 98 39.56 N 122.11 E
Wangjiang 100 30.09 N 116.41 E
Wangjiangjing 106 30.53 N 120.43 E
Wang Jian Mu (Tomb of Wang Jian) ⊥ 107 30.38 N 104.04 E
Wangjiaputun 104 40.39 N 122.50 E
Wangjiapuzi, Zhg. 104 40.41 N 122.24 E
Wangjiapuzi, Zhg. 104 41.05 N 123.34 E
Wangjiaqiao 106 30.50 N 119.18 E
Wangjiashan 105 40.19 N 114.45 E
Wangjiashao 102 23.57 N 102.18 E
Wangjiatai 105 39.17 N 117.29 E
Wangjiaying, Zhg. 105 40.36 N 116.34 E
Wangjiaying, Zhg. 105 39.06 N 115.59 E
Wangjiazhai 106 31.21 N 121.37 E
Wangjiazui 106 31.16 N 120.18 E
Wangkantou 100 29.12 N 120.09 E
Wangkou 105 38.56 N 116.44 E
Wangkui 89 46.50 N 126.30 E
Wanglanzhuang 105 39.26 N 118.01 E
Wangling 100 27.13 N 113.26 E
Wangliu 100 32.25 N 115.40 E
Wangmiao 100 26.50 N 112.52 E
Wangmulazi 104 41.42 N 124.02 E
Wang Noi 110 14.13 N 100.44 E
Wangong 89 49.10 N 118.53 E
Wangpan Shan II 106 30.30 N 121.15 E
Wangpan Yang c 100 30.30 N 121.46 E
Wangpingchang 107 29.17 N 105.45 E
Wangqing 89 43.20 N 129.48 E
Wangqingmen 98 41.42 N 125.23 E
Wangqingtuo 105 39.11 N 116.53 E
Wangqinzhuang 105 39.15 N 117.05 E
Wangqucun 106 31.22 N 120.19 E
Wangs 58 47.02 N 9.26 E
Wang Saphung 110 17.18 N 101.46 E
Wangshanhutun 104 42.03 N 122.37 E
Wangshi 100 33.11 N 116.04 E
Wangsi 98 38.00 N 116.55 E
Wangsim-ni ✦[8] 271b 37.36 N 127.03 E
Wangsiying 107 30.34 N 103.29 E
Wangtai, Zhg. 98 36.05 N 119.59 E
Wangtai, Zhg. 100 26.39 N 117.57 E
Wangtan 100 29.45 N 120.40 E
Wang Thong 110 16.50 N 100.26 E
Wangtian 100 25.59 N 116.04 E
Wangting 106 31.26 N 120.26 E
Wangtongshitai 104 42.05 N 123.11 E
Wangtuan, Zhg. 98 37.32 N 116.08 E
Wangtuan, Zhg. 98 37.17 N 122.04 E
Wangtuanji 100 33.12 N 116.21 E
Wangu 107 30.19 N 106.05 E
Wanguzhen 107 29.41 N 105.57 E
Wangwenzhuang 105 38.53 N 117.15 E
Wangxiangshang 106 31.29 N 120.15 E
Wangxiangtai 105 40.02 N 115.09 E
Wangxiuqiao 106 31.38 N 121.03 E
Wangyangzhen 107 29.44 N 104.14 E
Wangyedian 98 41.36 N 118.17 E
Wangyefu 98 41.50 N 118.23 E
Wangyehmiao → Horqin Youyi Qianqi 89 46.05 N 122.05 E
Wangyiguantun 104 42.36 N 123.19 E
Wangzhai 98 34.09 N 116.47 E
Wangzhimawo 105 39.39 N 117.40 E
Wangzhong 98 35.08 N 116.58 E
Wangzhuang 100 33.07 N 117.29 E
Wangzhuangbu 98 39.27 N 113.56 E
Wangzhuangji 98 34.09 N 118.23 E
Wangzhuangzi 105 39.17 N 118.14 E
Wanham 182 55.44 N 118.24 W
Wanhedian 100 32.16 N 113.16 E
Wanheimerort ✦[8] 263 51.24 N 6.46 E
Wanhsien → Wanxian 102 30.52 N 108.22 E
Wanhuyu 102 38.24 N 110.40 E
Wani 122 20.04 N 78.57 E
Wani, Gunung ∧ 112 4.29 S 123.01 E
Wani, Laguna c 236 14.45 N 83.20 W
Wanie-Rukula 154 0.15 N 25.32 E
Wanigela 164 9.22 S 149.10 E
Wanipigow ≃ 184 51.11 N 96.18 W
Wanjiabu 100 28.51 N 115.39 E
Wanjiaqiao 106 30.25 N 119.07 E
Wanjiatun 98 40.03 N 119.51 E
Wanjindian 100 32.50 N 114.46 E
Wānkāner 120 22.37 N 70.56 E
Wankendorf 54 54.07 N 10.13 E
Wankum 56 51.24 N 6.20 E
Wanle Weyne 144 2.37 N 44.54 E
Wanli, T'aiwan 269d 25.11 N 121.41 E
Wanli, Zhg. 106 31.06 N 120.16 E
Wanna 52 53.44 N 8.46 E
Wanna Lakes ⊜ 162 28.30 S 128.27 E
Wān Namton 110 22.03 N 99.33 E
Wanne-Eickel 52 51.32 N 7.09 E
Wanneroo 168a 31.45 S 115.48 E
Wannery Creek ≃ 162 22.47 S 115.43 E
Wannian 100 28.42 N 117.03 E
Wanning 110 18.53 N 110.26 E
Wannsee ✦[8] 264a 52.25 N 13.09 E
Wanon Niwat 110 17.38 N 103.46 E
Wanouchi 94 35.17 N 136.38 E
Wānow 120 32.38 N 65.54 E
Wanparti 122 16.22 N 78.04 E
Wanquan 98 40.52 N 114.45 E
Wansdorf 264a 52.38 N 13.05 E
Wan-See → Van Gölü ⊜ 128 38.33 N 42.46 E
Wansen → Wiązów 30 50.49 N 17.11 E
Wanshan 107 30.23 N 106.06 E
Wanshouchang 107 29.26 N 105.55 E
Wanstead 172 40.08 S 176.32 E
Wanstead ✦[8] 260 51.34 N 0.02 E
Wantage 42 51.36 N 1.25 W
Wantagh 210 40.41 N 73.30 W
Wantan 102 30.03 N 110.18 E
Wantirna 274b 37.51 S 145.14 E
Wantirna South 274b 37.52 S 145.14 E
Wanxian, Zhg. 102 30.52 N 108.22 E
Wanxian, Zhg. 105 38.50 N 115.09 E
Wanyuan 102 32.04 N 108.02 E
Wanzai 100 28.06 N 114.27 E
Wanzarīk 146 27.31 N 13.29 E
Wanzhuang 105 39.34 N 116.36 E
Wanzleben 54 52.03 N 11.26 E
Wapack Range ⋀ 207 42.48 N 71.52 W
Wapakoneta 216 40.34 N 84.11 W
Wapanucka 196 34.22 N 96.25 W
Wapato 202 46.26 N 120.25 W
Wapawekka Hills ⋀[2] 184 54.45 N 104.20 W
Wapawekka Lake ⊜ 184 54.55 N 104.40 W
Wapella, Sk., Can. 184 50.15 N 102.00 W
Wapella, Il., U.S. 219 40.13 N 88.58 W
Wapello 190 41.10 N 91.11 W
Wapenamanda 164 5.35 S 143.55 E
Wapesi Lake ⊜ 184 50.34 N 92.21 W
Wāpi 122 20.22 N 72.54 E
Wapinda 152 3.41 N 22.48 E
Wapinitia Pass)(224 45.14 N 121.42 W
Wapisu Lake ⊜ 184 55.47 N 99.11 W
Wapiti ≃ 182 55.08 N 118.18 W
Wapizagonke, Lac ⊜ 206 46.43 N 73.02 W
Waples 222 32.29 N 97.43 W
Wapoga ≃ 164 2.42 S 136.06 E
Wappapello, Lake ⊜[1] 194 36.58 N 90.20 W
Wapping 207 41.50 N 72.33 W
Wappinger Creek ≃ 210 41.35 N 73.57 W
Wappingers Falls 210 41.35 N 73.54 W
Wapsipinicon ≃ 190 41.44 N 90.20 W
Waptus Lake ⊜ 224 47.30 N 121.10 W
Wapus ≃ 190 47.11 N 76.06 W
Wapus Lake ⊜ 184 56.27 N 102.12 W
Waqf aṣ-Ṣiwwān, Jibāl ⋀ 132 31.04 N 36.53 E
Wāqid 142 30.42 N 30.44 E
Waqqāṣ 132 32.33 N 35.36 E
War 192 37.18 N 81.41 W
Wara 94 35.45 N 137.05 E
Warabi 94 35.49 N 139.41 E
Wārāh 120 27.27 N 67.48 E
Warakaraket I 164 2.15 S 130.36 E
Waramaug, Lake ⊜ 207 41.42 N 73.22 W
Warangal 122 18.00 N 79.35 E
Wararisbari, Tanjung ≻ 164 1.05 S 136.23 E
Wārāseoni 120 21.45 N 80.02 E
Waratah, Austl. 166 41.27 S 145.32 E
Waratah, Austl. 170 32.54 S 151.44 E
Waratah Bay c 166 38.51 S 146.04 E
Warboys 42 52.24 N 0.04 W
Warbreccan 166 24.18 S 142.51 E
Warburg 52 51.29 N 9.08 E
Warburton, Austl. 169 37.46 S 145.41 E
Warburton, Pāk. 123 31.33 N 73.50 E
Warburton, Eng., U.K. 262 53.24 N 2.27 W
Warburton Aboriginal Reserve ✦[4] 162 26.20 S 127.00 E
Warburton Bay c 176 63.50 N 111.30 W
Warburton Creek ≃ 166 27.55 S 137.28 E
Warburton Range ⋀ 162 26.09 S 126.38 E
Warcha 123 32.25 N 71.59 E
Ward, Īrān 267d 35.48 N 51.10 E
Ward, N.Z. 172 41.50 S 174.08 E
Ward, Pa., U.S. 285 39.53 N 75.31 W
Ward ≃ 166 26.32 S 146.06 E
Ward, Mount ∧, Ant. 9 71.55 S 66.00 W
Ward, Mount ∧, N.Z. 172 43.52 S 169.50 E
Warda 222 30.03 N 96.55 W
Wardcliff 216 42.43 N 84.28 W
Ward Cove 182 55.24 N 131.44 W
Warden, S. Afr. 158 27.56 S 29.00 E
Warden, Wa., U.S. 202 46.58 N 119.02 W
Wardenburg 52 53.04 N 8.11 E
Warden Head ≻ 170 35.22 S 150.30 E
Warder 54 53.59 N 10.22 E
Wardersee ⊜ 54 53.58 N 10.26 E
Wardha 122 20.45 N 78.37 E
Wardha ≃ 122 19.38 N 79.48 E
Ward Hill ∧[2], Scot., U.K. 46 58.54 N 3.20 W
Ward Hill ∧[2], Scot., U.K. 46 58.57 N 3.09 W
Ward Hunt, Cape ≻ 164 8.05 S 149.55 E
Ward Hunt Strait ꓘ 164 9.25 S 149.55 E
Wardle 44 53.39 N 2.08 W
Wardlow 182 50.54 N 111.33 W
Ward Mountain ∧ 202 46.10 N 114.17 W
Wardner 182 49.25 N 115.26 W
Wardour, Vale of V 42 51.05 N 2.00 W
Wards Chapel 284b 39.24 N 76.52 W
Wards Island I 276 40.47 N 73.56 W
Ward's Stone ∧ 44 54.02 N 2.38 W
Wardsville, On., Can. 214 42.39 N 81.45 W
Wardsville, Mo., U.S. 219 38.29 N 92.10 W
Wardswell Draw V 196 32.39 N 102.35 W
Wardt 52 51.41 N 6.25 E
Wardūj ≃ 123 37.01 N 70.47 E
Ware, Eng., U.K. 42 51.49 N 0.02 W
Ware, Ma., U.S. 207 42.15 N 72.14 W
Ware ≃ 207 42.11 N 72.22 W
War Eagle Creek ≃ 194 36.14 N 94.00 W
Waregem 50 50.53 N 3.25 E
Wareham, Eng., U.K. 42 50.41 N 2.07 W
Wareham, Ma., U.S. 207 41.45 N 70.43 W
Warehouse Point 207 41.55 N 72.37 W
Waremme 56 50.41 N 5.15 E
Waren, D.D.R. 54 53.31 N 12.40 E
Waren, Indon. 164 2.16 S 136.20 E
Warenda 166 22.37 S 140.32 E
Warendorf 52 51.57 N 7.59 E
Ware River c 208 37.23 N 76.27 W
Ware Shoals 192 34.23 N 82.14 W
Waretown 208 39.47 N 74.11 W
Warffum 52 53.23 N 6.34 E
Warfusée-Abancourt 50 49.52 N 2.35 E
Warga 52 53.08 N 5.51 E
Wargalo 144 6.17 N 47.31 E
Wargla 148 31.59 N 5.25 E
Wargla □[5] 148 29.00 N 8.00 E
Warialda 166 29.32 S 150.34 E
Wariap 164 1.34 S 134.11 E
Warilau 164 5.24 S 134.30 E
Warilau, Pulau I 164 5.23 S 134.33 E
Warin 54 53.48 N 11.42 E
Warinanco Park ♦ 276 40.39 N 74.14 W
Warin Chamrap 110 15.12 N 104.53 E
Waring Mountains ⋀ 180 66.50 N 159.00 W
Wāris Alīganj 124 25.01 N 85.38 E
Warka 30 51.47 N 21.10 E
Warkopi 164 1.08 S 134.07 E
Warks Burn ≃ 44 55.03 N 2.08 W
Warkworth, On., Can. 212 44.12 N 77.53 W
Warkworth, N.Z. 172 36.24 S 174.40 E
Warkworth, Eng., U.K. 44 55.21 N 1.36 W
Warland, Eng., U.K. 262 53.41 N 2.05 W
Warland, Mt., U.S. 182 48.30 N 115.17 W
Warland Reservoir ⊜[1] 262 53.41 N 2.04 W
Warley → Smethwick 42 52.30 N 1.58 W
Warley Moor Reservoir ⊜[1] 262 53.47 N 1.57 W
Warlingham 42 51.19 N 0.04 W
Warlington 42 51.39 N 1.01 W
Warman 184 52.20 N 106.34 W
Warmandi 164 0.22 S 132.39 E
Warmbad, Namibia 156 28.29 S 18.41 E
Warmbad, S. Afr. 156 24.55 S 28.15 E
Warm Baths → Warmbad 156 24.55 S 28.15 E
Warm Beach 224 48.10 N 122.21 W
War Memorial Cross ⊥ 169 37.20 S 144.36 E
Warmenhuizen 52 52.43 N 4.44 E
Warmensteinach 60 49.59 N 11.47 E
Warmeriville 50 49.21 N 4.13 E
Warmington 42 52.08 N 1.24 W
Warminster, Eng., U.K. 42 51.13 N 2.12 W
Warminster, Pa., U.S. 208 40.12 N 75.06 W
Warminster Naval Air Development Center ■ 285 40.12 N 75.09 W
Warm Springs, Ga., U.S. 192 32.53 N 84.40 W
Warm Springs, Mt., U.S. 202 46.11 N 112.48 W
Warm Springs, Or., U.S. 202 44.45 N 121.15 W
Warm Springs, Va., U.S. 192 38.02 N 79.47 W
Warm Springs ≃ 202 44.52 N 121.04 W
Warm Springs Indian Reservation ✦[4] 224 45.00 N 121.25 W
Warm Springs Reservoir ⊜[1] 202 43.37 N 118.14 W

Symbol	English	Deutsch	Español	Français	Português
≃	River	Fluss	Río	Rivière	Rio
≅	Canal	Kanal	Canal	Canal	Canal
ᒪ	Waterfall, Rapids	Wasserfall, Stromschnellen	Cascada, Rápidos	Chute d'eau, Rapides	Cascata, Rápidos
ꓘ	Strait	Meeresstrasse	Estrecho	Détroit	Estreito
c	Bay, Gulf	Bucht, Golf	Bahía, Golfo	Baie, Golfe	Baía, Golfo
⊜	Lake, Lakes	See, Seen	Lago, Lagos	Lac, Lacs	Lago, Lagos
≡	Swamp	Sumpf	Pantano	Marais	Pântano
⊓	Ice Features, Glacier	Eis- und Gletscherformen	Accidentes Glaciales	Formes glaciaires	Acidentes glaciares
⫧	Other Hydrographic Features	Andere Hydrographische Objekte	Otros Elementos Hidrográficos	Autres données hydrographiques	Outros acidentes hidrográficos
✢	Submarine Features	Untermeerische Objekte	Accidentes Submarinos	Formes de relief sous-marin	Acidentes submarinos
□	Political Unit	Politische Einheit	Unidad Política	Entité politique	Unidade política
⊌	Cultural Institution	Kulturelle Institution	Institución Cultural	Institution culturelle	Instituição cultural
⊥	Historical Site	Historische Stätte	Sitio Histórico	Site historique	Sitio histórico
♦	Recreational Site	Erholungs- und Ferienort	Sitio de Recreo	Centre de loisirs	Area de Lazer
⊠	Airport	Flughafen	Aeropuerto	Aéroport	Aeroporto
■	Military Installation	Militäranlage	Instalación Militar	Installation militaire	Instalação militar
✦	Miscellaneous	Verschiedenes	Misceláneo	Divers	Diversos

Warnbro Sound ʊ 168a 32.20 S 115.40 E
Warnemünde ◆ [8] 54 54.10 N 12.04 E
Warner, Ab., Can. 182 49.17 N 112.12 W
Warner, N.H., U.S. 188 43.16 N 71.49 W
Warner, Ok., U.S. 196 35.29 N 95.18 W
Warner Lakes ⊜ 202 42.25 N 119.50 W
Warner Mountains ⋏ 204 41.40 N 120.20 W
Warner Peak ∧ 202 42.27 N 119.44 W
Warner Ranch 228 33.56 N 117.13 W
Warner Robins 192 32.37 N 83.36 W
Warners 210 43.05 N 76.20 W
Warners Pond ⊜ 283 42.28 N 71.24 W
Warnerville 210 42.34 N 74.30 W
Warnes, Arg. 252 34.55 S 60.31 W
Warnes, Bol. 248 17.30 S 63.10 W
Warnes Brook ≃ 276 40.25 N 74.18 W
Warneton 50 50.45 N 2.57 E
Warngau 64 47.50 N 11.41 E
Warnicken → Primorje 76 54.57 N 20.02 E
Warnkenhagen 54 54.00 N 11.04 E
Warnow ≃ 54 54.06 N 12.09 E
Warns 52 52.52 N 5.25 E
Warnsveld 52 52.08 N 6.13 E
Waroona 168a 32.50 S 115.55 E
Warpath ≃ 184 52.21 N 98.26 W
Warra 166 26.56 S 150.55 E
Warrabri Aboriginal Reserve ◆ [4] 162 21.00 S 134.20 E
Warracknabeal 166 36.15 S 142.24 E
Warr Acres 196 35.31 N 97.37 W
Warragamba Dam ◆ [6] 170 33.54 S 150.36 E
Warragul 169 38.10 S 145.56 E
Warrandyte 274b 37.45 S 145.13 E
Warrandyte South 274b 37.46 S 145.14 E
Warrāq al-ʿArab 273c 30.06 N 31.12 E
Warrāq al-Ḥaḍar, Jazīrat I 273c 30.07 N 31.13 E
Warrāq al-Hadar wa Ambūtbah wa Mīt an-Naṣārā 273c 30.06 N 31.13 E
Warrawagine 162 20.51 S 120.42 E
Warrawee 274a 33.44 S 151.07 E
Warrawong 170 34.29 S 150.53 E
Warrego ≃ 166 30.24 S 145.21 E
Warrego Range ⋏ 166 25.00 S 146.30 E
Warren, Austl. 166 31.42 S 147.50 E
Warren, Eng., U.K. 262 53.14 N 2.10 W
Warren, Ar., U.S. 194 33.36 N 92.03 W
Warren, Il., U.S. 190 42.29 N 89.59 W
Warren, In., U.S. 216 40.40 N 85.25 W
Warren, Ma., U.S. 207 42.12 N 72.11 W
Warren, Mi., U.S. 216 42.28 N 83.01 W
Warren, Mn., U.S. 198 48.11 N 96.46 W
Warren, Mo., U.S. 219 39.47 N 91.45 W
Warren, N.J., U.S. 276 40.37 N 74.30 W
Warren, Oh., U.S. 214 41.14 N 80.49 W
Warren, Or., U.S. 224 45.49 N 122.50 W
Warren, Pa., U.S. 214 41.50 N 79.08 W
Warren, R.I., U.S. 207 41.43 N 71.16 W
Warren □ [6], In., U.S. 216 40.21 N 87.17 W
Warren □ [6], Mo., U.S. 219 38.45 N 91.09 W
Warren □ [6], N.J., U.S. 210 40.49 N 75.05 W
Warren □ [6], N.Y., U.S. 210 43.26 N 73.43 W
Warren □ [6], Oh., U.S. 218 39.26 N 84.13 W
Warren □ [6], Pa., U.S. 214 41.51 N 79.08 W
Warren ≃ 162 34.35 S 115.50 E
Warren City 222 32.33 N 94.54 W
Warrendale 214 40.39 N 80.04 W
Warren Dunes State Park ♦ 216 41.56 N 86.36 W
Warren H. Manning State Park ♦ 283 42.34 N 71.18 W
Warren Park 218 39.46 N 86.03 W
Warren Peaks ⋏ 198 44.29 N 104.28 W
Warrenpoint 48 54.06 N 6.15 W
Warren Point > 180 69.44 N 132.30 W
Warrens 190 44.07 N 90.29 W
Warrensburg, Il., U.S. 219 39.56 N 89.04 W
Warrensburg, Mo., U.S. 194 38.45 N 93.44 W
Warrensburg, N.Y., U.S. 188 43.29 N 73.46 W
Warrensville 210 41.19 N 76.57 W
Warrensville Heights 214 41.26 N 81.32 W
Warrenton, S. Afr. 158 28.09 S 24.47 E
Warrenton, Ga., U.S. 192 33.24 N 82.39 W
Warrenton, Mo., U.S. 219 38.48 N 91.08 W
Warrenton, N.C., U.S. 192 36.23 N 78.09 W
Warrenton, Or., U.S. 224 46.09 N 123.55 W
Warrenton, Tx., U.S. 222 30.01 N 96.44 W
Warrenton, Va., U.S. 188 38.42 N 77.47 W
Warrenville 216 41.49 N 88.10 W
Warrenzin 54 53.54 N 12.57 E
Warri 150 5.31 N 5.45 E
Warriedar Hill ∧ [2] 162 29.06 S 117.06 E
Warriewood 274a 33.42 S 151.18 E
Warrill Creek ≃ 171a 27.39 S 152.44 E
Warrina 166 28.12 S 135.50 E
Warringah War Memorial ⊥ 274a 33.46 S 151.15 E
Warrington, N.Z. 172 45.43 S 170.35 E
Warrington, Eng., U.K. 44 53.24 N 2.37 W
Warrington, Fl., U.S. 194 30.23 N 87.16 W
Warrington, Pa., U.S. 285 40.15 N 75.08 W
Warrington □ [8] 262 53.24 N 2.33 W
Warrington Airport ⊠ 285 40.16 N 75.09 W
Warrior 194 33.48 N 86.48 W
Warrior Creek ≃ 192 31.15 N 83.34 W
Warrior Reefs ✦ [2] 164 9.35 S 143.10 E
Warriors Mark 214 40.42 N 78.08 W
Warrnambool 166 38.23 S 142.29 E
Warroad 198 48.54 N 95.18 W
Warrumbungle National Park ♦ 166 31.20 S 149.00 E
Warsak 123 34.10 N 71.25 E
Warsaw → Warszawa, Pol. 30 52.15 N 21.00 E
Warsaw, Il., U.S. 190 40.21 N 91.26 W
Warsaw, In., U.S. 216 41.14 N 85.51 W
Warsaw, Ky., U.S. 218 38.47 N 84.54 W
Warsaw, Mo., U.S. 194 38.14 N 93.22 W
Warsaw, N.Y., U.S. 210 42.44 N 78.07 W
Warsaw, N.C., U.S. 192 34.59 N 78.05 W
Warsaw, Oh., U.S. 214 40.20 N 82.00 W
Warsaw, Va., U.S. 208 37.57 N 76.45 W
Warsaw Station ◆ [5] 265a 59.54 N 30.19 E
Warschau → Warszawa 30 52.15 N 21.00 E
Warscheneck ∧ 61 47.39 N 14.14 E
Warshiikh 144 2.18 N 45.48 E
Warsop 44 53.13 N 1.09 W
Warspite 182 54.06 N 112.37 W
Warstein 56 51.26 N 8.21 E
Warszawa (Warsaw) 30 52.15 N 21.00 E
Warszawa □ [4] 30 52.15 N 21.00 E
Warta 30 51.42 N 18.38 E
Warta ≃ 30 52.35 N 14.39 E
Wartburg, S. Afr. 158 29.25 S 30.35 E
Wartburg, Tn., U.S. 192 36.06 N 84.35 W
Wartburg ⊥ 54 50.58 N 10.18 E
Wartenberg 60 48.24 N 11.59 E
Wartenberg ◆ [8] 264a 52.34 N 13.31 E
Warth 58 47.15 N 10.11 E
Warthan Creek ≃ 226 36.08 N 120.20 W
Warthe → Warta ≃ 30 52.35 N 14.39 E
Wartin 54 53.15 N 14.09 E
Warton, Eng., U.K. 44 54.09 N 2.47 W
Warton, Eng., U.K. 262 53.45 N 2.54 W
Warton Aerodrome ⊠ 262 53.45 N 2.54 W
Wartrace 194 35.31 N 86.20 W
Wartsberg ∧ [2] 263 51.25 N 6.29 E
Waru 164 3.24 S 130.40 E
Warud 120 21.28 N 78.16 E
Warunta, Laguna ⊜ 236 15.22 N 84.09 W
Waruta ≃ 164 3.18 S 140.08 E
Warwick, Austl. 171a 28.13 S 152.02 E
Warwick, P.Q., Can. 206 45.56 N 71.59 W
Warwick, Eng., U.K. 42 52.17 N 1.34 W
Warwick, Md., U.S. 208 39.25 N 75.46 W
Warwick, N.Y., U.S. 210 41.15 N 74.21 W
Warwick, R.I., U.S. 207 41.41 N 71.22 W
Warwick ≃ 208 37.05 N 76.33 W
Warwick Castle ⊥ 42 52.17 N 1.34 W
Warwick Channel ʊ 164 13.51 S 136.16 E
Warwick Farm Racecourse and Motor Race Track ♦ 274a 33.55 S 150.57 E
Warwickshire □ [6] 42 52.13 N 1.37 W
Warza 54 51.00 N 10.41 E
Wasaga Beach 212 44.31 N 80.01 W
Wasagu 150 11.25 N 5.49 E
Wasatch Mountain State Park ♦ 200 40.33 N 111.31 W
Wasatch Plateau ⋏ [1] 200 39.20 N 111.30 W
Wasatch Range ⋏ 200 40.40 N 111.35 W
Wasāwewāla 123 30.28 N 73.40 E
Wasbank 158 28.24 S 30.05 E
Wasbister 46 59.10 N 3.07 W
Wascana Creek ≃ 184 50.39 N 104.55 W
Wäschenbeuren 56 48.46 N 9.41 E
Wasco, Ca., U.S. 226 35.35 N 119.20 W
Wasco, Or., U.S. 224 45.35 N 120.41 W
Wasco □ [6] 224 45.10 N 121.12 W
Wase 150 9.06 N 9.59 E
Wase ≃ 146 8.27 N 10.06 E
Waseca 190 44.04 N 93.30 W
Waseda University † [2] 268 35.42 N 139.43 E
Wasekamio Lake ⊜ 184 56.45 N 108.45 W
Wasen 58 47.03 N 7.48 E
Wasfanārd 267d 35.39 N 51.21 E
Washademoak Lake ⊜ 186 45.48 N 65.58 W
Washago 212 44.45 N 79.20 W
Washburn, Il., U.S. 190 40.55 N 89.17 W
Washburn, Me., U.S. 186 46.47 N 68.09 W
Washburn, N.D., U.S. 198 47.17 N 101.01 W
Washburn, Wi., U.S. 190 46.40 N 90.53 W
Washburn, Mount ∧ 202 44.48 N 110.25 W
Washburn Lake ⊜ 176 70.03 N 106.50 W
Washdyke 172 44.21 S 171.14 E
Washicoutai 186 50.17 N 60.42 W
Washiga-take ∧ 94 35.56 N 136.58 E
Wāshim 122 20.06 N 77.09 E
Washimiya 94 36.06 N 139.40 E
Washington, Eng., U.K. 44 54.55 N 1.30 W
Washington, Ca., U.S. 226 39.22 N 120.48 W
Washington, Ct., U.S. 207 41.37 N 73.18 W
Washington, D.C., U.S. 208 38.53 N 77.02 W
Washington, D.C., U.S. 284c 38.53 N 77.02 W
Washington, Ga., U.S. 192 33.44 N 82.44 W
Washington, Il., U.S. 190 40.42 N 89.24 W
Washington, In., U.S. 194 38.39 N 87.10 W
Washington, Ia., U.S. 190 41.17 N 91.41 W
Washington, Ks., U.S. 198 39.49 N 97.03 W
Washington, Ky., U.S. 218 38.36 N 83.48 W
Washington, La., U.S. 194 30.36 N 92.03 W
Washington, Mi., U.S. 214 42.44 N 83.02 W
Washington, Mo., U.S. 219 38.33 N 91.01 W
Washington, N.J., U.S. 210 40.45 N 74.58 W
Washington, N.C., U.S. 192 35.31 N 77.01 W
Washington, Pa., U.S. 214 40.10 N 80.14 W
Washington, Tx., U.S. 222 30.20 N 96.10 W
Washington, Ut,. U.S. 200 37.07 N 113.30 W
Washington, Va., U.S. 188 38.42 N 78.09 W
Washington □ [6], Il., U.S. 219 38.21 N 89.23 W
Washington □ [6], In., U.S. 218 38.36 N 86.06 W
Washington □ [6], N.Y., U.S. 210 43.15 N 73.27 W
Washington □ [6], Or., U.S. 224 45.33 N 123.07 W
Washington □ [6], Pa., U.S. 214 40.10 N 80.15 W
Washington □ [6], R.I., U.S. 207 41.28 N 71.35 W
Washington □ [6], Tx., U.S. 222 30.15 N 96.20 W
Washington □ [6], Wi., U.S. 216 43.14 N 88.15 W
Washington □ [3], U.S. 178 47.30 N 120.30 W
Washington □ [3], U.S. 202 47.30 N 120.30 W
Washington, Lake ⊜, Fl., U.S. 220 28.07 N 80.45 W
Washington, Lake ⊜, Wa., U.S. 224 47.37 N 122.15 W
Washington, Mount ∧ 188 44.15 N 71.15 W
Washington Court House 218 39.32 N 83.26 W
Washington Crossing 208 40.17 N 74.52 W
Washington Crossing State Historic Site ⊥ 208 40.17 N 74.53 W
Washington Depot 207 41.38 N 73.18 W
Washington Heights ◆ [8] 276 40.52 N 73.56 W
Washington Island 190 45.23 N 86.55 W
Washington Island I 190 45.23 N 86.55 W
Washington Memorial Chapel † [1] 285 40.06 N 75.26 W
Washington Mills 210 43.03 N 75.16 W
Washington Monument ♦ 284c 38.53 N 77.03 W
Washington Monument State Park ♦ 208 39.30 N 77.38 W
Washington National Airport ⊠ 208 38.51 N 77.02 W
Washington-on-The-Brazos State Historic Park ♦ 222 30.20 N 96.09 W
Washington Park 219 38.38 N 90.05 W
Washington Park ♦, Il., U.S. 278 41.48 N 87.37 W
Washington Park ♦, Oh., U.S. 279a 41.27 N 81.40 W
Washington Pass)(224 48.32 N 120.39 W
Washington Place 218 39.47 N 86.01 W
Washington Rock State Park ♦ 276 40.37 N 74.28 W
Washington's Headquarters ⊥ 285 40.06 N 75.28 W
Washington Terrace 200 41.10 N 111.58 W
Washington Township 276 40.54 N 74.00 W
Washington Valley 276 40.48 N 74.32 W
Washington Valley Reservoir ⊜ [1] 276 40.36 N 74.34 W
Washingtonville, N.Y., U.S. 210 41.26 N 74.10 W
Washingtonville, Oh., U.S. 214 40.54 N 80.46 W
Washingtonville, Pa., U.S. 210 41.03 N 76.40 W
Washita ≃ 196 34.12 N 96.50 W
Washoe □ [6] 226 39.22 N 119.43 W
Washoe Lake ⊜ 226 39.16 N 119.48 W
Washougal 224 45.34 N 122.21 W
Washougal ≃ 224 45.35 N 122.23 W
Washow Bay ⊂ 184 51.22 N 96.47 W
Washtenaw □ [6] 216 42.15 N 83.50 W
Washtucna 202 46.45 N 118.18 W
Wāshuk 128 27.44 N 64.48 E
Washurn ≃ 44 53.54 N 1.39 W
Wasian 164 1.54 S 133.17 E
Wasilków 30 53.12 N 23.12 E
Wasilla 180 61.35 N 149.26 W
Wasior 164 2.43 S 134.30 E
Wāsiṭ □ [4] 128 32.45 N 45.25 E
Waskada 184 49.06 N 100.46 W
Waskahigan ≃ 182 54.45 N 117.12 W
Waskaiowaka Lake ⊜ 184 56.30 N 96.20 W
Waskatenau 182 54.07 N 112.47 W
Waskesiu Lake ⊜ 184 53.56 N 106.10 W
Waskom 194 32.29 N 94.04 W
Wąsosz 30 51.34 N 16.42 E
Waspam 236 14.44 N 83.58 W
Waspuk ≃ 236 14.38 N 84.26 W
Wasquehal 50 50.40 N 3.09 E
Wassaic 210 41.48 N 73.35 W
Wasselonne 58 48.38 N 7.27 E
Wassen 58 46.42 N 8.36 E
Wassenaar 52 52.07 N 4.24 E
Wassenberg 56 51.06 N 6.08 E
Wasseralfingen 56 48.52 N 10.06 E
Wasserbillig 56 49.44 N 6.30 E
Wasserburg am Inn 60 48.04 N 12.13 E
Wasserkuppe ∧ 56 50.30 N 9.56 E
Wasserkurl 263 51.33 N 7.38 E
Wasserleben 54 51.55 N 10.44 E
Wassertrüdingen 56 49.02 N 10.35 E
Wassigny 50 50.01 N 3.36 E
Wass Lake ⊜ 184 53.40 N 95.25 W
Wassmannsdorf 264a 52.22 N 13.28 E
Wassou 150 10.02 N 13.39 W
Wassy 58 48.30 N 4.57 E
Wast Water ⊜ 44 54.26 N 3.18 W
Wasu 164 6.00 S 147.15 E
Wasum 164 6.05 S 149.20 E
Wasungen 54 50.40 N 10.22 E
Watabeag Lake ⊜ 190 48.14 N 80.32 W
Watampone (Bone) 112 4.32 S 120.20 E
Watamu Marine National Park ♦ 154 3.23 S 40.00 E
Waṭan, Wādī al- V 142 30.26 N 31.49 E
Watansoppeng 112 4.21 S 119.53 E
Watapi Lake ⊜ 184 55.18 N 109.35 W
Watarai 94 34.26 N 136.37 E
Watarase ≃ 94 36.13 N 139.42 E
Wataru I 122 5.43 N 73.23 E
Watatic, Mount ∧ 207 42.42 N 71.53 W
Watauga 222 32.51 N 97.15 W
Watchet 42 51.12 N 3.20 W
Watch Hill 207 41.18 N 71.51 W
Watchung 276 40.38 N 74.27 W
Watchung Reservation ♦ 276 40.41 N 74.23 W
Water 262 53.44 N 2.14 W
Waterbeach 42 52.16 N 0.11 E
Waterberg 156 20.28 S 17.13 E
Waterberge ⋏ 156 24.30 S 28.00 E
Waterbury, Ct., U.S. 207 41.33 N 73.02 W
Waterbury, Vt., U.S. 188 44.20 N 72.45 W
Waterdale 158 30.40 S 24.02 E
Wateree ≃ 192 33.45 N 80.37 W
Wateree Lake ⊜ [1] 192 34.25 N 80.50 W
Waterend, Eng., U.K. 260 51.47 N 0.30 W
Water End, Eng., U.K. 262 53.41 N 2.15 W
Waterfall 214 40.08 N 78.04 W
Waterfall Gully Reserve ♦ 168b 34.58 S 138.40 E
Waterford, On., Can. 212 42.56 N 80.17 W
Waterford (Port Láirge), Ire. 48 52.15 N 7.06 W
Waterford, S. Afr. 158 33.05 S 25.00 E
Waterford, Ca., U.S. 226 37.38 N 120.46 W
Waterford, Ct., U.S. 207 41.20 N 72.09 W
Waterford, In., U.S. 216 41.40 N 86.50 W
Waterford, Mi., U.S. 216 42.42 N 83.24 W
Waterford, N.Y., U.S. 210 42.47 N 73.40 W
Waterford, Pa., U.S. 214 41.56 N 79.59 W
Waterford, Wi., U.S. 216 42.45 N 88.12 W
Waterford □ [6] 48 52.10 N 7.40 W
Waterford Harbour ⊂ 48 52.10 N 6.55 W
Waterford Mills 216 41.33 N 85.50 W
Waterford Works 208 39.43 N 74.50 W
Watergate Bay ⊂ 42 50.27 N 5.05 W
Watergrasshill 48 52.01 N 8.21 W
Watergrove Reservoir ⊜ [1] 262 53.39 N 2.08 W
Waterhen ≃ 184 54.38 N 107.47 W
Waterhen Lake ⊜, Mb., Can. 184 52.06 N 99.34 W
Waterhen Lake ⊜, Sk., Can. 184 54.28 N 108.25 W
Waterhouse Range ⋏ 162 24.01 S 133.25 E
Wateringbury 260 51.15 N 0.25 E
Wateringen 52 52.02 N 4.16 E
Water Island 276 40.41 N 73.02 W
Waterkloof 158 30.19 S 25.18 E
Waterloo, Austl. 164 16.38 S 129.18 E
Waterloo, Austl. 168a 33.20 S 115.47 E
Waterloo, Austl. 168b 33.59 S 138.53 E
Waterloo, Bel. 50 50.43 N 4.23 E
Waterloo, On., Can. 212 43.28 N 80.31 W
Waterloo, P.Q., Can. 206 45.21 N 72.31 W
Waterloo, S.L. 150 8.20 N 13.04 W
Waterloo, Eng., U.K. 44 53.28 N 3.02 W
Waterloo, Al., U.S. 194 34.55 N 88.03 W
Waterloo, Il., U.S. 219 38.20 N 90.08 W
Waterloo, In., U.S. 216 41.25 N 85.01 W
Waterloo, Ia., U.S. 190 42.29 N 92.20 W
Waterloo, N.Y., U.S. 210 42.54 N 76.51 W
Waterloo, Wi., U.S. 216 43.11 N 88.59 W
Waterloo □ [6] 212 43.30 N 80.30 W
Waterloo State Recreation Area ♦ 216 42.22 N 84.20 W
Waterloo Station ◆ [5] 260 51.30 N 0.07 W
Waterlooville 42 50.53 N 1.02 W
Waterman, Il., U.S. 216 41.46 N 88.46 W
Waterman, Wa., U.S. 224 47.34 N 122.35 W
Waterman Mountain ∧ 228 34.20 N 117.56 W
Waterman Wash V 200 33.21 N 112.31 W
Water Mill 207 40.55 N 72.21 W
Waterport 210 43.20 N 78.16 W
Waterport Pond ⊜ [1] 212 43.19 N 78.16 W
Waterproof 194 31.48 N 91.23 W
Waterside 214 40.11 N 78.23 W
Waterside Park 276 40.56 N 73.20 W
Watersmeet 190 46.16 N 89.10 W
Waterton ≃ 182 49.32 N 113.16 W
Waterton-Glacier International Peace Park ♦ 202 48.47 N 113.45 W
Waterton Lakes National Park ♦ 182 49.05 N 113.50 W
Watertown, Ct., U.S. 207 41.36 N 73.07 W
Watertown, Ma., U.S. 207 42.22 N 71.11 W
Watertown, N.Y., U.S. 212 43.58 N 75.54 W
Watertown, S.D., U.S. 198 44.53 N 97.06 W
Watertown, Wi., U.S. 216 43.11 N 88.43 W
Waterval-Boven 156 25.40 S 30.20 E
Watervale 168b 33.57 S 138.38 E
Water Valley, Ms., U.S. 194 34.09 N 89.37 W
Water Valley, N.Y., U.S. 284a 42.42 N 78.51 W
Water View 208 37.43 N 76.36 W
Waterville, N.S., Can. 186 45.03 N 64.41 W
Waterville, P.Q., Can. 206 45.16 N 71.54 W
Waterville, Ire. 48 51.49 N 10.13 W
Waterville, Ks., U.S. 198 39.41 N 96.44 W
Waterville, Me., U.S. 188 44.33 N 69.37 W
Waterville, Ma., U.S. 207 42.40 N 72.04 W
Waterville, Mn., U.S. 190 44.13 N 93.34 W
Waterville, N.Y., U.S. 210 42.55 N 75.22 W
Waterville, Oh., U.S. 216 41.30 N 83.43 W
Waterville, Pa., U.S. 210 41.19 N 77.22 W
Waterville, Wa., U.S. 202 47.38 N 120.04 W
Watervliet, Mi., U.S. 216 42.11 N 86.15 W
Watervliet, N.Y., U.S. 210 42.43 N 73.42 W
Watervliet Reservoir ⊜ [1] 210 42.43 N 73.58 W
Wates, Indon. 114 1.00 N 100.16 E
Wates, Indon. 115a 7.55 S 112.07 E
Wates, Indon. 115a 7.51 S 110.10 E
Watford, On., Can. 214 42.57 N 81.53 W
Watford, Eng., U.K. 42 51.40 N 0.25 W
Watford □ [8] 260 51.40 N 0.25 W
Watford City 198 47.48 N 103.16 W
Waʿth 140 8.10 N 32.07 E
Wathaman ≃ 184 57.16 N 102.52 W
Wathaman Lake ⊜ 184 56.55 N 103.43 W
Wathena 198 39.45 N 94.56 W
Watheroo 162 30.17 S 116.04 E
Wathlingen 52 52.32 N 10.09 E
Wath upon Dearne 44 53.29 N 1.20 W
Wati 120 28.02 N 96.59 E
Watino 182 55.43 N 117.37 W
Watkins Glen 210 42.22 N 76.52 W
Watkins Glen International Raceway ♦ 210 42.20 N 76.55 W
Watkins Glen State Park ♦ 210 42.22 N 76.55 W
Watkins Island I 284c 39.02 N 77.17 W
Watkins Lake ⊜ 281 42.40 N 83.22 W
Watkinsville 192 33.51 N 83.24 W
Watlaar 164 5.28 S 133.07 E
Watling Island → San Salvador I 238 24.02 N 74.28 W
Watlington 42 51.37 N 1.00 W
Watoga State Park ♦ 188 38.07 N 80.05 W
Watonga 196 35.50 N 98.24 W
Watonwan ≃ 198 44.04 N 94.07 W
Watopeka ≃ 206 45.34 N 72.00 W
Watou 50 50.51 N 2.37 E
Wat Phai Tan, Khlong ≋ 269a 13.48 N 100.33 E
Watrous, Sk., Can. 184 51.40 N 105.28 W
Watrous, N.M., U.S. 200 35.47 N 104.58 W
Watsa 154 3.03 N 29.32 E
Watseka 216 40.46 N 87.44 W
Watsi Kengo 152 0.48 S 20.33 E
Watson, Austl. 162 30.29 S 131.31 E
Watson, Sk., Can. 184 52.07 N 104.31 W
Watson, In., U.S. 218 38.22 N 85.41 W
Watsonia 274b 37.43 S 145.05 E
Watson Lake 180 60.07 N 128.48 W
Watsons Bay 274a 33.51 S 151.17 E
Watsons Creek 274b 37.40 S 145.13 E
Watsons Creek ≃ 274b 37.43 S 145.16 E
Watsontown 210 41.05 N 76.51 W
Watsonville 226 36.54 N 121.45 W
Watt 222 31.39 N 96.51 W
Watten 50 50.50 N 2.13 E
Watten, Loch ⊜ 46 58.29 N 3.19 W
Wattens 64 47.17 N 11.36 E
Wattenscheid 56 51.29 N 7.08 E
Wattenwil 58 46.46 N 7.30 E
Wattignies 50 50.35 N 3.03 E
Wattiwarriganna ≃ 162 28.57 S 136.10 E
Wattle Flat 170 33.08 S 149.41 E
Wattle Glen 274b 37.40 S 145.11 E
Wattle Park ♦ 274b 37.50 S 145.07 E
Watt Mountain ∧ 240d 15.19 N 61.19 W
Watton 42 52.35 N 0.48 E
Wattrelos 50 50.42 N 3.13 E
Watts ◆ [8] 280 33.56 N 118.15 W
Watts Bar Lake ⊜ [1] 192 35.48 N 84.39 W
Watts Branch ≃ 284c 39.03 N 77.15 W
Wattsburg 214 42.00 N 79.49 W
Watts Island I 208 37.48 N 75.53 W
Watts Mills 192 34.31 N 82.02 W
Wattville 273d 26.13 S 28.18 E
Wattwil 58 47.18 N 9.06 E
Watu 152 3.18 S 20.03 E
Watubela, Kepulauan II 164 4.35 S 131.40 E
Watudirang 115b 8.40 S 122.34 E
Watukancoa 112 1.36 S 121.48 E
Wat Wat 164 4.29 S 152.21 E
Watzekopf ∧ 58 46.59 N 10.48 E
Watzmann ∧ 64 47.33 N 12.55 E
Wau 164 7.20 S 146.45 E
Waubach 56 50.55 N 6.03 E
Waubaushene 212 44.45 N 79.42 W
Waubaushene Channel ʊ 212 44.46 N 79.45 W
Waubay 198 45.19 N 97.18 W
Waubay Lake ⊜ 198 45.25 N 97.25 W
Waubesa, Lake ⊜ 216 43.01 N 89.20 W
Waubra 169 37.21 S 143.39 E
Waubuno Creek ≃ 212 42.58 N 81.08 W
Wauchope, Austl. 162 20.36 S 134.15 E
Wauchope, Austl. 166 31.27 S 152.44 E
Wauchula 220 27.32 N 81.48 W
Wauconda, Il., U.S. 216 42.15 N 88.08 W
Wauconda, Wa., U.S. 182 48.43 N 119.00 W
Wauconda, Wa., U.S. 202 48.43 N 119.00 W
Waugh 184 49.40 N 95.13 W
Waugh Mountain ∧ 202 45.29 N 114.47 W
Waukara, Gunung ∧ 112 1.15 S 119.42 E
Waukaringa 166 32.18 S 139.26 E
Waukarlycarly, Lake ⊜ 162 21.25 S 121.50 E
Waukegan 216 42.21 N 87.50 W
Waukena 226 36.08 N 119.31 W
Waukesha 216 43.00 N 88.13 W
Waukesha □ [6] 216 43.02 N 88.20 W
Waukomis 196 36.16 N 97.53 W
Waukon 190 43.16 N 91.28 W
Waulsort 56 50.13 N 4.52 E
Wauna 224 47.22 N 122.38 W
Waunakee 216 43.11 N 89.27 W
Wauneta 198 40.25 N 101.22 W
Waupaca 190 44.21 N 89.05 W
Waupecan Creek ≃ 216 41.20 N 88.28 W
Waupoos Island I 212 43.59 N 76.58 W
Waupun 190 43.38 N 88.43 W
Wauregan 207 41.44 N 71.54 W
Waurika 196 34.10 N 97.59 W
Waurika Lake ⊜ [1] 196 34.15 N 98.05 W
Wausa 198 42.29 N 97.32 W
Wausau 190 44.57 N 89.37 W
Wausaukee 190 45.22 N 87.57 W
Wauseon 216 41.32 N 84.08 W
Waushakum Pond ⊜ 283 42.16 N 71.26 W
Wautoma 190 44.04 N 89.17 W
Wauwa 154 3.27 N 27.21 E
Wauwatosa 216 43.02 N 88.00 W
Wauzeka 190 43.05 N 90.52 W
Wave Hill 162 17.29 S 130.57 E
Waveland, Ma., U.S. 283 42.17 N 70.53 W
Waveland, Ms., U.S. 194 30.17 N 89.22 W
Waveney ≃ 42 52.28 N 1.45 E
Waver ≃ 44 54.52 N 3.17 W
Waverley, Austl. 169 37.53 S 145.10 E
Waverley, Austl. 274a 33.54 S 151.16 E
Waverley, N.Z. 172 39.46 S 174.38 E
Waverley, S. Afr. 158 31.58 S 26.28 E
Waverley, Ma., U.S. 283 42.23 N 71.11 W
Waverley ◆ [8] 273d 26.08 S 28.04 E
Waverly, Al., U.S. 194 32.44 N 85.35 W
Waverly, Fl., U.S. 220 27.59 N 81.37 W
Waverly, Il., U.S. 219 39.35 N 89.57 W
Waverly, Ia., U.S. 190 42.43 N 92.28 W
Waverly, Ks., U.S. 198 38.23 N 95.36 W
Waverly, Mi., U.S. 216 42.44 N 84.33 W
Waverly, Mn., U.S. 190 45.04 N 93.57 W
Waverly, Mo., U.S. 194 39.12 N 93.31 W
Waverly, Ne., U.S. 198 40.55 N 96.31 W
Waverly, N.Y., U.S. 210 42.00 N 76.31 W
Waverly, Oh., U.S. 218 39.07 N 82.59 W
Waverly, Pa., U.S. 210 41.32 N 75.42 W
Waverly, Tn., U.S. 194 36.05 N 87.47 W
Waverly, Va., U.S. 208 37.02 N 77.05 W
Waverly Hall 192 32.41 N 84.44 W
Wavre 56 50.43 N 4.37 E
Wavrin 50 50.34 N 2.55 E
Wāw 140 7.42 N 28.00 E
Wāw ≃ 140 7.03 N 27.13 E
Wawa, On., Can. 190 47.59 N 84.47 W
Wawa, Nig. 150 9.55 N 4.25 E
Wawa, Sūd. 140 20.26 N 30.21 E
Wawa ≃ 236 13.53 N 83.28 W
Wawaka 216 41.27 N 85.28 W
Wāw al-Kabīr 146 25.20 N 16.43 E
Wawanesa 184 49.36 N 99.41 W
Wawarsing 210 41.46 N 74.21 W
Wawasee, Lake ⊜ 216 41.24 N 85.41 W
Wawayanda State Park ♦ 276 41.11 N 74.26 W
Wawiag ≃ 190 48.25 N 91.07 W
Wawoi ≃ 164 8.01 S 143.33 E
Waworada, Teluk ⊂ 115b 8.44 S 118.51 E
Wawota 184 49.55 N 102.00 W
Waxahachie 222 32.23 N 96.50 W
Waxahachie, Lake ⊜ [1] 222 32.20 N 96.49 W
Waxhaw 192 34.55 N 80.44 W
Waxuecun 106 31.07 N 121.38 E
Waxweiler 56 50.05 N 6.22 E
Way, Lake ⊜ 162 26.48 S 120.18 E
Waya I 175g 17.18 S 177.08 E
Wayabula 108 2.17 N 128.12 E
Wayaopu 106 30.33 N 118.53 E
Waycross 192 31.12 N 82.21 W
Wayi 154 5.11 N 30.10 E
Wayland, Ia., U.S. 190 41.08 N 91.39 W
Wayland, Ky., U.S. 192 37.26 N 82.48 W
Wayland, Ma., U.S. 283 42.21 N 71.21 W
Wayland, Mi., U.S. 216 42.40 N 85.38 W
Wayland, N.Y., U.S. 210 42.34 N 77.35 W
Wayland, Oh., U.S. 214 41.10 N 81.04 W
Waylyn 192 32.51 N 79.59 W
Waymansville 218 39.04 N 86.03 W
Waymart 210 41.34 N 75.24 W
Wayne, Ab., Can. 182 51.23 N 112.39 W
Wayne, Mi., U.S. 216 42.16 N 83.23 W
Wayne, Ne., U.S. 198 42.13 N 97.01 W
Wayne, N.J., U.S. 210 40.55 N 74.16 W
Wayne, N.Y., U.S. 210 42.28 N 77.06 W
Wayne, Oh., U.S. 214 41.18 N 83.28 W
Wayne, Ok., U.S. 196 34.55 N 97.18 W
Wayne, Pa., U.S. 208 40.02 N 75.23 W
Wayne, W.V., U.S. 188 38.13 N 82.26 W
Wayne □ [6], Il., U.S. 219 38.25 N 88.40 W
Wayne □ [6], In., U.S. 218 39.50 N 84.54 W
Wayne □ [6], Mi., U.S. 216 42.14 N 83.12 W
Wayne □ [6], N.Y., U.S. 210 43.04 N 77.00 W
Wayne □ [6], Oh., U.S. 214 40.48 N 81.56 W
Wayne □ [6], Pa., U.S. 210 41.34 N 75.16 W
Wayne City 194 38.20 N 88.35 W
Wayne Lakes 218 40.01 N 84.39 W
Waynesboro, Ga., U.S. 192 33.05 N 82.00 W
Waynesboro, Ms., U.S. 194 31.40 N 88.38 W
Waynesboro, Pa., U.S. 208 39.45 N 77.34 W
Waynesboro, Tn., U.S. 194 35.19 N 87.45 W
Waynesboro, Va., U.S. 192 38.04 N 78.53 W
Waynesburg, Oh., U.S. 214 40.40 N 81.15 W
Waynesburg, Pa., U.S. 188 39.53 N 80.10 W
Waynesfield 216 40.36 N 83.59 W
Wayne State University † [2] 281 42.21 N 83.04 W
Waynesville, Il., U.S. 194 40.15 N 89.08 W
Waynesville, Mo., U.S. 194 37.49 N 92.12 W
Waynesville, N.C., U.S. 192 35.29 N 82.59 W
Waynesville, Oh., U.S. 218 39.32 N 84.05 W
Waynoka 196 36.34 N 98.52 W
Waynoka, Lake ⊜ [1] 218 38.55 N 83.47 W
Wayoh Reservoir ⊜ [1] 262 53.39 N 2.24 W
Waza 146 11.25 N 14.34 E
Waza, Parc National de ♦ 146 11.20 N 13.40 E
Wazay 120 33.22 N 69.26 E
Waziers 50 50.23 N 3.07 E
Wāzin 146 31.57 N 10.40 E
Wazīrābād 123 32.27 N 74.07 E
Wazīrābād ◆ [8] 272a 28.43 N 77.14 E
Wāzirpur ◆ [8] 272a 28.41 N 77.10 E
Wazuka 96 34.47 N 135.55 E
Wazuka ≃ 270 34.45 N 135.53 E
Wda ≃ 30 53.25 N 18.29 E
We, Pulau I 114 5.51 N 95.18 E
Wea Creek ≃ 216 40.24 N 86.57 W
Weagamow Lake ⊜ 184 52.53 N 91.22 W
Weald Park ♦ 260 51.38 N 0.14 E
Wealdstone ◆ [8] 260 51.36 N 0.20 W
Weam 164 8.40 S 141.08 E
Wear ≃ 44 54.55 N 1.22 W
Wearhead 44 54.45 N 2.13 W
Wearyan ≃ 164 15.57 S 136.51 E
Weatherford, Ok., U.S. 196 35.31 N 98.42 W
Weatherford, Tx., U.S. 222 32.45 N 97.47 W
Weatherford, Lake ⊜ [1] 222 32.47 N 97.41 W
Weatherly 210 40.56 N 75.50 W
Weatogue 207 41.51 N 72.49 W
Weaubleau 194 37.53 N 93.32 W
Weaver, Al., U.S. 194 33.45 N 85.48 W
Weaver, Tx., U.S. 222 33.10 N 95.25 W
Weaver ≃ 44 53.19 N 2.44 W
Weaver ≋ 262 53.19 N 2.45 W
Weaverham 44 53.16 N 2.35 W
Weaver Lake ⊜ 184 52.45 N 96.35 W
Weavertown 279b 40.16 N 80.11 W
Weaverville, Ca., U.S. 204 40.43 N 122.56 W
Weaverville, N.C., U.S. 192 35.41 N 82.33 W
Webau 54 51.10 N 12.04 E
Webb, Sk., Can. 184 50.11 N 108.12 W
Webb, Ms., U.S. 194 33.56 N 90.20 W
Webb Brook ≃ 283 42.32 N 71.14 W
Webb City 194 37.08 N 94.27 W
Webber Lake ⊜ 184 54.28 N 94.00 W
Webberville 216 42.40 N 84.10 W
Webbwood 190 46.16 N 81.53 W
Weber ≃ 200 41.13 N 112.16 W
Weber, Mount ∧ 182 55.32 N 128.31 W
Weber City 192 36.37 N 82.33 W
Weber Creek ≃ 226 38.46 N 121.00 W
Weber Hill 219 38.27 N 90.34 W
Weberi Bekera 144 9.39 N 39.03 E
Webster, Ab., Can. 182 55.26 N 118.42 W
Webster, Fl., U.S. 220 28.36 N 82.03 W
Webster, In., U.S. 218 39.54 N 84.57 W
Webster, Ma., U.S. 207 42.03 N 71.52 W
Webster, N.Y., U.S. 210 43.12 N 77.25 W
Webster, Pa., U.S. 214 40.11 N 79.50 W
Webster, S.D., U.S. 198 45.19 N 97.31 W
Webster, Wi., U.S. 190 45.52 N 92.22 W
Webster City 190 42.28 N 93.48 W
Webster Crossing 210 42.40 N 77.38 W
Webster Groves 219 38.35 N 90.21 W
Webster Lake ⊜ 216 41.19 N 85.41 W
Websters Corners, B.C., Can. 224 49.13 N 122.30 W
Websters Corners, N.Y., U.S. 284a 41.47 N 78.45 W
Webster Springs 188 38.28 N 80.24 W
Weches 222 31.33 N 95.14 W
Wechmar 54 50.53 N 10.47 E
Wechselburg 54 51.00 N 12.47 E
Weda 108 0.21 N 127.52 E
Wedau ◆ [8] 263 51.24 N 6.48 E
Wedau, Sportpark ♦ 263 51.25 N 6.47 E
Weddell Island I 254 51.55 S 61.00 W
Weddell Sea ‡ [2] 9 72.00 S 45.00 W
Wedderburn 166 36.25 S 143.37 E
Wedding ◆ [8] 264a 52.33 N 13.22 E
Weddinghofen 263 51.36 N 7.37 E
Wedel 52 53.35 N 9.41 E
Wedemark 52 52.33 N 9.44 E
Wedge Mountain ∧ 182 50.10 N 122.50 W
Wedgeport 186 43.44 N 65.59 W
Wedgewood 219 38.47 N 90.17 W
Wedmore 42 51.14 N 2.49 W
Wedowee 194 33.18 N 85.29 W
Wedron 216 41.26 N 88.46 W
Weduar, Tanjung > 164 6.00 S 132.50 E
Wedweil 140 9.00 N 27.12 E
Wedza 154 18.35 S 31.35 E
Weebo 162 28.01 S 121.03 E
Weed 204 41.25 N 122.23 W
Weed Heights 226 38.59 N 119.12 W
Weedon 206 45.42 N 71.28 W
Weedon Beck 42 52.14 N 1.05 W
Weedon Island I 220 27.51 N 82.36 W
Weed Patch 228 35.19 N 118.55 W
Weed Patch Hill ∧ [2] 218 39.10 N 86.13 W
Weedsport 210 43.02 N 76.33 W
Weedville 214 41.17 N 78.30 W
Weehawken 276 40.46 N 74.01 W
Weeim, Pulau I 164 1.29 S 130.14 E
Wee Jasper 171b 35.09 S 148.41 E
Weekapaug 207 41.20 N 71.45 W
Weeki Wachee Spring ♦ 220 28.32 N 82.35 W
Weeki Wachee Swamp ≋ 220 28.31 N 82.37 W
Weeks Point > 276 40.53 N 73.39 W
Weekstown 208 39.35 N 74.36 W
Weelde 56 51.25 N 5.00 E
Weeley 42 51.51 N 1.07 E
Weel Shimbirro 144 2.23 N 44.16 E
Weems 208 37.39 N 76.26 W
Weende 52 51.33 N 9.55 E
Weenen 158 28.57 S 30.03 E
Weener 52 53.10 N 7.21 E
Weeney Bay ⊂ 274a 34.01 S 151.10 E
Weeping Water 198 40.52 N 96.08 W
Weequahic Lake ⊜ 276 40.42 N 74.12 W
Weert 52 51.15 N 5.43 E
Weesatche 222 28.51 N 97.27 W
Weesby 41 54.50 N 9.08 E
Weesow 264a 52.39 N 13.43 E
Weesp 52 52.17 N 5.02 E
Weetfeld 263 51.38 N 7.49 E
Weethalle 166 33.53 S 146.38 E
Weeting 42 52.27 N 0.37 E
Weeton 262 53.48 N 2.56 W
Wee Waa 166 30.14 S 149.26 E
Weeze 52 51.37 N 6.12 E
Wefensleben 54 52.11 N 11.09 E
Weferlingen 54 52.19 N 11.02 E
Wegberg 56 51.08 N 6.16 E
Wegdraai 158 28.50 S 21.52 E
Wegeleben 54 51.53 N 11.10 E
Wegendorf 264a 52.36 N 13.45 E
Wegenstedt 54 52.23 N 11.11 E
Wegeringhausen 56 51.02 N 7.45 E
Weggis 58 47.02 N 8.26 E
Węgliniec 30 51.17 N 15.13 E
Węgorzewo 30 54.14 N 21.44 E
Węgorzyno 30 53.32 N 15.33 E
Węgrów 30 52.25 N 22.01 E
Wegscheid 60 48.36 N 13.48 E
Wehdel 52 53.30 N 8.48 E
Wehebach Stausee ⊜ [1] 56 50.45 N 6.20 E
Wehingen 58 48.08 N 8.47 E
Wehofen ◆ [8] 263 51.32 N 6.46 E
Wehr 58 47.37 N 7.54 E
Wehringhausen ◆ [8] 263 51.21 N 7.27 E
Wehrsdorf 54 51.03 N 14.22 E
Wei ≃, Zhg. 98 37.05 N 119.28 E
Wei ≃, Zhg. 98 36.51 N 115.43 E
Wei ≃, Zhg. 102 34.30 N 110.20 E
Weichang (Zhuizishan) 98 42.00 N 117.32 E
Weichsel → Wisła ≃ 30 54.22 N 18.55 E
Weichselboden 61 47.40 N 15.10 E
Weichuan 98 34.17 N 113.58 E
Weicun 106 31.59 N 119.55 E
Weida 54 50.45 N 12.04 E
Weida ≃ 54 50.47 N 12.06 E
Weiden am See 61 47.55 N 16.52 E
Weidenberg 60 49.57 N 11.43 E
Weiden in der Oberpfalz 60 49.41 N 12.10 E
Weidenstetten 56 48.33 N 9.59 E
Weiding 60 49.16 N 12.46 E
Weidling 264b 48.17 N 16.19 E
Weidlingau ◆ [8] 264b 48.13 N 16.13 E
Weidlingbach 264b 48.16 N 16.15 E
Weidlinger Bach ≃ 264b 48.18 N 16.20 E
Weifang 98 36.42 N 119.04 E
Weigelstown 208 39.59 N 76.49 W
Weihai 98 37.28 N 122.07 E
Weihaiwei → Weihai 98 37.28 N 122.07 E
Weihmichl 60 48.36 N 12.03 E
Weihnachtsinsel → Christmas Island □ [2] 112 10.30 S 105.40 E
Weijiagou 105 40.28 N 115.08 E
Weijiatang 106 31.25 N 118.55 E
Weijiazhuang 105 39.37 N 116.22 E
Weijiazui 100 30.29 N 117.20 E
Weijingtang 106 31.27 N 120.39 E
Weikersheim 56 49.29 N 9.54 E
Weil ≃ 56 50.28 N 8.16 E
Weil am Rhein 58 47.37 N 7.38 E
Weilburg 56 50.29 N 8.15 E
Weil der Stadt 56 48.45 N 8.52 E
Weiler 58 47.36 N 9.55 E
Weilerbach 56 49.29 N 7.37 E
Weilerswist 56 50.45 N 6.50 E
Weilheim 64 47.50 N 11.08 E
Weilheim an der Teck 56 48.37 N 9.32 E
Weilmoringle 166 29.15 S 146.51 E
Weilmünster 56 50.26 N 8.22 E
Weimar, B.R.D. 56 51.22 N 9.23 E
Weimar, D.D.R. 54 50.59 N 11.19 E
Weimar, Ca., U.S. 226 39.02 N 120.58 W
Weimar, Tx., U.S. 222 29.42 N 96.46 W
Weinan 102 34.29 N 109.29 E
Weinböhla 54 51.10 N 13.34 E
Weinel Cross Roads 279b 40.37 N 79.37 W
Weiner 194 35.37 N 90.53 W
Weinfelden 58 47.34 N 9.06 E
Weingarten, B.R.D. 56 49.05 N 8.31 E
Weingarten, B.R.D. 58 47.48 N 9.38 E
Weinheim 56 49.33 N 8.39 E
Weining, Zhg. 102 26.43 N 104.18 E
Weining, Zhg. 104 41.21 N 123.49 E
Weinsberg 56 49.10 N 9.17 E
Weinsberger Wald ◆ [3] 61 48.30 N 14.50 E
Weinviertel ◆ [1] 61 48.38 N 16.25 E
Weipa 164 12.41 S 141.52 E
Weippe 202 46.22 N 115.56 W
Weir, India 124 27.01 N 77.11 E
Weir, Ks., U.S. 198 37.18 N 94.46 W
Weir, Ms., U.S. 194 33.16 N 89.17 W
Weir ≃, Austl. 166 28.50 S 149.06 E
Weir ≃, Mb., Can. 184 56.54 N 93.21 W
Weir ≃, Ma., U.S. 283 42.16 N 70.53 W
Weir, Lake ⊜ 220 29.00 N 81.57 W
Weir River 184 56.49 N 94.04 W
Weirsdale 220 28.58 N 81.55 W
Weirton 214 40.25 N 80.35 W
Weisberg → Monguelfo 64 46.45 N 12.06 E
Weisburd 252 27.18 S 62.36 W
Weisburg 218 39.13 N 85.03 W

Symbols in the index entries represent the broad categories identified in the key at the right. Symbols with superior numbers (⋏ [1]) identify subcategories (see complete key on page *I · 1).*

Kartensymbole in dem Registerverzeichnis stellen die rechts in Schlüssel erklärten Kategorien dar. Symbole mit hochgestellten Ziffern (⋏ [1]) bezeichnen Unterabteilungen einer Kategorie (vgl. vollständiger Schlüssel auf Seite *I · 1).*

Los símbolos incluídos en el texto del índice representan las grandes categorias identificadas con la clave a la derecha. Los símbolos con numeros en su parte superior (⋏ [1]) identifican las subcategorías (véase la clave completa en la página *I · 1).*

Les symboles de l'index représentent les catégories indiquées dans la légende à droite. Les symboles suivis d'un indice (⋏ [1]) représentent des sous-catégories (voir légende complète à la page *I · 1).*

Os símbolos incluídos no texto do índice representam as grandes categorias identificadas com a chave à direita. Os símbolos com números em sua parte superior (⋏ [1]) identificam as subcategorias (veja-se a chave completa à página *I · 1).*

	English	Deutsch	Español	Français	Português
∧	Mountain	Berg	Montaña	Montagne	Montanha
⋏	Mountains	Berge	Montañas	Montagnes	Montanhas
)(	Pass	Pass	Paso	Col	Passo
V	Valley, Canyon	Tal, Cañon	Valle, Cañón	Vallée, Canyon	Vale, Canhão
≚	Plain	Ebene	Llano	Plaine	Planície
>	Cape	Kap	Cabo	Cap	Cabo
I	Island	Insel	Isla	Île	Ilha
II	Islands	Inseln	Islas	Îles	Ilhas
⊥	Other Topographic Features	Andere Topographische Objekte	Otros Elementos Topográficos	Autres données topographiques	Outros acidentes topográficos

ESPAÑOL · FRANÇAIS · PORTUGUÊS

Nombre / Nom / Nome	Página / Page	Lat. °′	Long. °′ W = Oeste / W = Ouest
Weischlitz	54	50.26 N	12.02 E
Weisendorf	56	49.37 N	10.49 E
Weiser	202	44.15 N	116.58 W
Weiser ≃	202	44.15 N	116.59 W
Weishan (Xiazhen), Zhg.	98	34.52 N	117.09 E
Weishan, Zhg.	100	29.41 N	120.48 E
Weishan, Zhg.	100	29.20 N	120.25 E
Weishan, Zhg.	102	25.15 N	100.20 E
Weishancheng	100	32.34 N	113.24 E
Weishanhe	104	40.47 N	123.31 E
Weishan Hu ◎	98	34.40 N	117.15 E
Weishanzhuang	105	39.40 N	116.25 E
Weishi	98	34.25 N	114.11 E
Weismain	54	50.05 N	11.14 E
Weisner Mountain ∧	194	34.02 N	85.40 W
Weissach	56	48.50 N	8.55 E
Weissbriach	64	46.41 N	13.15 E
Weisse Elster ≃	54	51.26 N	11.57 E
Weissenbach	264b	48.05 N	16.13 E
Weissenbach am Lech	58	47.26 N	10.39 E
Weissenberg	54	51.11 N	14.40 E
Weissenborn	54	50.52 N	13.25 E
Weissenbrunn	54	50.12 N	11.20 E
Weissenburg	58	46.39 N	7.28 E
Weissenburg in Bayern	56	49.01 N	10.58 E
Weissenfels	54	51.12 N	11.58 E
Weissenhorn	58	48.18 N	10.09 E
Weissensee	54	51.11 N	11.04 E
Weissensee ◈[8]	264a	52.33 N	13.27 E
Weissensee ◎	64	46.42 N	13.22 E
Weissenstadt	54	50.06 N	11.53 E
Weissenstein, B.R.D.	56	48.42 N	9.53 E
Weissenstein, Öst.	64	46.41 N	13.44 E
Weissenstein ∧	58	47.15 N	7.31 E
Weissenstein Tunnel ◈[5]	58	47.12 N	7.23 E
Weissenthurm	56	50.24 N	7.27 E
Weisser Main ≃	54	50.04 N	11.24 E
Weisser Nil → White Nile ≃	140	15.38 N	32.31 E
Weisser See → Beloje, ozero ◎	76	60.11 N	37.37 E
Weisser Stein ∧	56	50.23 N	6.20 E
Weisses Meer → Beloje more ∓[2]	24	65.30 N	38.00 E
Weisse Spitze ∧	64	46.52 N	12.21 E
Weissfluh ∧	58	46.50 N	9.48 E
Weisshorn ∧	58	46.06 N	7.42 E
Weissig	54	51.05 N	13.52 E
Weisskugel (Palla Bianca) ∧	64	46.48 N	10.44 E
Weiss Lake ◎[1]	192	34.15 N	85.35 W
Weissmeer-Ostsee Kanal → Belomorsko-Baltijskij kanal ≊	24	62.48 N	34.48 E
Weissport	210	40.50 N	75.42 W
Weisstannen	58	46.59 N	9.21 E
Weisswasser	54	51.30 N	14.38 E
Weisweiler	56	50.50 N	6.19 E
Weitang	105	40.24 N	117.24 E
Weitang ≃	104	42.19 N	122.18 E
Weitendorf	54	53.54 N	12.16 E
Weitensfeld	61	46.51 N	14.11 E
Weiterstadt	56	49.54 N	8.35 E
Weitian	100	27.43 N	118.46 E
Weitin	54	53.34 N	13.12 E
Weiting	106	31.22 N	120.47 E
Weitmar ◈[8]	263	51.27 N	7.12 E
Weitnau	58	47.38 N	10.07 E
Weitou	100	24.34 N	118.34 E
Weitra	61	48.42 N	14.54 E
Weituo	107	30.03 N	106.08 E
Weitzgrund	54	52.11 N	12.32 E
Weiwan	98	36.43 N	115.54 E
Weixdorf	54	51.09 N	13.48 E
Weixi, Zhg.	102	27.14 N	99.12 E
Weixi, Zhg.	107	30.12 N	106.39 E
Weixian, Zhg.	98	36.57 N	115.15 E
Weixian, Zhg.	98	36.22 N	114.56 E
Weixian (Hanting), Zhg.	98	36.52 N	119.07 E
Weixin	102	27.48 N	105.06 E
Weiyuan	107	29.33 N	104.39 E
Weiyuan ≃	102	22.50 N	100.20 E
Weiyuankou	100	30.09 N	115.15 E
Weiyuanpu	98	42.39 N	124.16 E
Weiz	61	47.13 N	15.37 E
Weizhen	98	37.17 N	114.44 E
Weizhou Dao I	102	21.03 N	109.04 E
Weizhou Wan c	100	24.34 N	118.30 E
Weizhuang	105	39.02 N	115.20 E
Weizi	98	40.04 N	123.10 E
Weizigou, Zhg.	104	42.25 N	122.47 E
Weizigou, Zhg.	104	41.05 N	120.38 E
Weizigou, Zhg.	104	42.05 N	120.34 E
Weizigoumen	98	41.58 N	116.49 E
Weiziyu	98	41.29 N	124.31 E
Wejherowo	30	54.37 N	18.15 E
Wekiva ≃	220	28.52 N	81.23 W
Wekiwa Springs State Park ♠	220	28.43 N	81.27 W
Wekoewa Punt ›	241s	12.14 N	68.24 W
Wekusko Lake ◎	184	54.45 N	99.50 W
Welaka	192	29.28 N	81.40 W
Welbourn Hill	162	27.21 S	134.06 E
Welch, Ok., U.S.	196	36.52 N	95.05 W
Welch, Tx., U.S.	196	32.56 N	102.08 W
Welch, W.V., U.S.	192	37.25 N	81.35 W
Welch Creek ≃	282	37.32 N	121.51 W
Welches	224	45.19 N	121.57 W
Welch Peak ∧	224	49.10 N	121.36 W
Welcome, On., Can.	212	43.58 N	78.21 W
Welcome, Mn., U.S.	198	43.40 N	94.37 W
Welcome, S.C., U.S.	192	34.49 N	82.26 W
Welcome Lake ◎	212	45.25 N	78.25 W
Welcome Monument ⊥	269e	6.11 S	106.49 E
Welden	58	48.27 N	10.40 E
Weldiya	144	11.50 N	39.41 E
Weldon, Sk., Can.	184	53.00 N	105.08 W
Weldon, Il., U.S.	219	40.07 N	88.45 W
Weldon, N.C., U.S.	192	36.25 N	77.35 W
Weldon, Tx., U.S.	222	31.01 N	95.34 W
Weldon ≃	194	40.06 N	93.38 W
Weldona	198	40.20 N	103.58 W
Weldon Brook ≃	276	40.58 N	74.35 W
Weleetka	196	35.20 N	96.08 W
Welega □[4]	144	9.40 N	35.50 E
Weleri	115a	6.58 S	110.04 E
Welfare Island I	276	40.45 N	73.57 W
Welgedag	273d	26.12 S	28.30 E
Welhamgreen	260	51.44 N	0.13 W
Welheim ◈[8]	263	51.32 N	6.59 E
Weligama	122	5.58 N	80.25 E
Welikaja → Velikaja ≃	76	57.48 N	28.20 E
Welkenraedt	56	50.40 N	5.59 E
Welker Seamount ✧[3]	16	55.07 N	140.20 W
Welkite	144	8.15 N	37.50 E
Welkom	158	27.59 S	26.45 E
Well	52	51.34 N	6.06 E
Welland	212	42.59 N	79.15 W
Welland ≃, On., Can.	212	43.04 N	79.03 W
Welland ≃, Eng., U.K.	42	52.53 N	0.02 E
Welland Canal ≊	212	43.03 N	79.13 W
Welland Junction	284a	42.57 N	79.14 W
Wellard	168a	32.19 S	115.50 E
Wellaune	54	51.34 N	12.33 E
Wellborn, Fl., U.S.	192	30.13 N	82.49 W
Wellborn, Tx., U.S.	222	30.32 N	96.18 W
Wellerode	56	51.14 N	9.34 E
Wellers Bay c	212	44.00 N	77.34 W
Wellers Creek ≃	278	42.03 N	87.53 W
Wellesbourne	42	52.12 N	1.35 W
Welles Harbor c	174g	28.12 N	177.26 W
Wellesley, On., Can.	212	43.28 N	80.45 W
Wellesley, Ma., U.S.	207	42.17 N	71.17 W
Wellesley ≃	168a	33.17 S	115.44 E
Wellesley College ⊍[2]	283	42.18 N	71.19 W
Wellesley Hills	283	42.19 N	71.17 W
Wellesley Island I	212	44.19 N	75.58 W
Wellesley Islands II	164	16.42 S	139.30 E
Wellesley Island State Park ♠	212	44.19 N	76.01 W
Wellesley Lake ◎	180	62.30 N	139.50 W
Wellfleet	207	41.56 N	70.02 W
Well Hill	260	51.21 N	0.09 E
Wellin	56	50.05 N	5.07 E
Welling ◈[8]	260	51.28 N	0.07 E
Wellingborough	42	52.19 N	0.42 W
Wellinghofen ◈[8]	263	51.28 N	7.29 E
Wellington, Austl.	166	32.33 S	148.57 E
Wellington, B.C., Can.	224	49.13 N	124.01 W
Wellington, On., Can.	212	43.57 N	77.21 W
Wellington, N.Z.	172	41.18 S	174.47 E
Wellington, S. Afr.	158	33.38 S	18.57 E
Wellington, Eng., U.K.	42	52.43 N	2.31 W
Wellington, Eng., U.K.	42	50.59 N	3.14 W
Wellington, Co., U.S.	200	40.42 N	105.00 W
Wellington, Il., U.S.	216	40.32 N	87.41 W
Wellington, Ks., U.S.	198	37.15 N	97.22 W
Wellington, Mo., U.S.	194	39.08 N	93.58 W
Wellington, Nv., U.S.	226	38.45 N	119.22 W
Wellington, Oh., U.S.	214	41.10 N	82.13 W
Wellington, Tx., U.S.	196	34.51 N	100.12 W
Wellington, Ut,. U.S.	200	39.32 N	110.44 W
Wellington □[6]	212	43.50 N	80.30 W
Wellington, Isla I	254	49.20 S	74.40 W
Wellington Bay c, N.T., Can.	176	69.30 N	106.30 W
Wellington Bay c, On., Can.	212	43.56 N	77.21 W
Wellington Channel ⊔	176	75.00 N	93.00 W
Wellington Point	171a	27.29 S	153.15 E
Wellington Reservoir ◎[1]	168a	33.24 S	116.01 E
Wellington Station	186	46.27 N	64.00 W
Wellman, Ia., U.S.	190	41.27 N	91.50 W
Wellman, Tx., U.S.	196	33.03 N	102.26 W
Wells, B.C., Can.	182	53.06 N	121.34 W
Wells, Eng., U.K.	42	51.13 N	2.39 W
Wells, Mi., U.S.	190	45.47 N	87.04 W
Wells, Mn., U.S.	190	43.44 N	93.43 W
Wells, Nv., U.S.	204	41.06 N	114.57 W
Wells, N.Y., U.S.	210	43.24 N	74.17 W
Wells, Tx., U.S.	222	31.29 N	94.56 W
Wells □[6]	216	40.44 N	85.11 W
Wells, Lake ◎	162	26.43 S	123.10 E
Wells, Mount ∧	168a	32.42 S	116.20 E
Wells, Mount ∧[2]	162	17.26 S	127.14 E
Wellsboro	210	41.44 N	77.18 W
Wells Bridge	210	42.22 N	75.15 W
Wellsburg, Ia., U.S.	190	42.27 N	92.56 W
Wellsburg, N.Y., U.S.	210	42.00 N	76.43 W
Wellsburg, W.V., U.S.	214	40.16 N	80.36 W
Wells Cathedral ⊍[1]	42	51.13 N	2.39 W
Wellsford	172	36.17 S	174.31 E
Wells Gray Provincial Park ♠	182	52.20 N	120.00 W
Wells Lake ◎	184	57.15 N	101.00 W
Wells-next-the-Sea	42	52.58 N	0.51 E
Wells Point ›	284b	39.17 N	76.23 W
Wells State Park ♠	207	42.09 N	72.05 W
Wells Tannery	214	40.05 N	78.10 W
Wellston, Oh., U.S.	188	39.07 N	82.31 W
Wellston, Ok., U.S.	196	35.41 N	97.03 W
Wellsville, Ks., U.S.	198	38.43 N	95.04 W
Wellsville, Mo., U.S.	219	39.04 N	91.34 W
Wellsville, N.Y., U.S.	210	42.07 N	77.56 W
Wellsville, Oh., U.S.	214	40.36 N	80.38 W
Wellsville, Pa., U.S.	208	40.03 N	76.56 W
Wellsville, Ut,. U.S.	200	41.38 N	111.55 W
Wellton	200	32.40 N	114.08 W
Welmel ≃	144	5.38 N	40.47 E
Welmen	263	51.39 N	6.41 E
Welney	42	52.31 N	0.15 E
Welo □[4]	144	11.50 N	40.20 E
Welper	263	51.25 N	7.12 E
Wels	61	48.10 N	14.02 E
Welschbillig	56	49.51 N	6.34 E
Welse ≃	54	53.10 N	14.18 E
Welsford	186	45.27 N	66.20 W
Welsh	194	30.14 N	92.49 W
Welshpool, Austl.	169	38.39 S	146.26 E
Welshpool, Wales, U.K.	42	52.40 N	3.09 W
Welsickendorf	54	51.54 N	13.08 E
Welsleben	54	52.00 N	11.38 E
Weltenburg	60	48.54 N	11.50 E
Welver	52	51.38 N	7.57 E
Welverdiend	158	26.23 S	27.16 E
Welwitschia	156	20.21 S	14.57 E
Welwyn Garden City	42	51.50 N	0.13 W
Welwyn Hatfield □[8]	260	51.47 N	0.12 W
Welzheim	56	48.53 N	9.38 E
Welzow	54	51.34 N	14.10 E
Wem	42	52.51 N	2.44 W
Wema	152	0.26 S	21.38 E
Wembere ≃	154	4.10 S	34.11 E
Wembley	182	55.09 N	119.08 W
Wembley ◈[8]	260	51.33 N	0.18 W
Wembley Stadium ♠, S. Afr.	273d	26.14 S	28.03 E
Wembley Stadium ♠, Eng., U.K.	260	51.33 N	0.17 W
Wembury	42	50.19 N	4.05 W
Wemding	56	48.52 N	10.43 E
Wemeldinge	52	51.31 N	4.00 E
Wemme	224	45.20 N	121.57 W
Wemperhardt	56	50.09 N	6.05 E
Wen ≃, Zhg.	98	35.28 N	118.32 E
Wen ≃, Zhg.	98	36.38 N	119.22 E
Wen'an	105	38.52 N	116.28 E
Wen'an Wa ≡	105	38.54 N	116.37 E
Wenas Creek ≃	224	46.42 N	120.35 W
Wenatchee	202	47.25 N	120.18 W
Wenatchee ≃	202	47.27 N	120.19 W
Wenatchee, Lake ◎	224	47.49 N	120.47 W
Wenatchee Mountains ⋏	202	47.20 N	120.45 W
Wenchang	110	19.41 N	110.48 E
Wencheng	100	27.50 N	120.05 E
Wenchi	150	7.42 N	2.07 W
Wenchow → Wenzhou	100	28.01 N	120.39 E
Wendaohezi	104	41.46 N	124.09 E
Wendel	279b	40.18 N	79.41 W
Wendell, Id., U.S.	202	42.46 N	114.42 W
Wendell, N.C., U.S.	192	35.46 N	78.22 W
Wendelsheim	56	49.46 N	7.59 E
Wendelstein	60	49.21 N	11.08 E
Wendelstein ∧	64	47.42 N	12.00 E
Wendelville	284a	43.04 N	78.47 W
Wenden, B.R.D.	52	52.19 N	10.30 E
Wenden, B.R.D.	56	50.57 N	7.51 E
Wenden, Az., U.S.	200	33.49 N	113.32 W
Wendeng	98	37.12 N	122.04 E
Wendesi	164	2.25 S	134.13 E
Wendilou	104	41.13 N	121.08 E
Wendisch Rietz	54	52.13 N	14.01 E
Wendish Baggendorf	54	54.04 N	12.56 E
Wendji	152	0.04 S	18.10 E
Wendland ◈[1]	54	53.00 N	11.10 E
Wendo	144	6.38 N	38.27 E
Wendover, Eng., U.K.	42	51.46 N	0.46 W
Wendover, Ut,. U.S.	200	40.44 N	114.02 W
Wenduine	50	51.18 N	3.05 E
Wenebegon ≃	190	46.53 N	83.12 W
Wenebegon Lake ◎	190	47.24 N	83.08 W
Wenfang	100	28.02 N	117.19 E
Weng	60	48.40 N	12.23 E
Weng ≃	100	24.10 N	113.24 E
Weng'an	102	26.53 N	107.22 E
Wengbo	120	31.23 N	86.40 E
Wengcheng	100	24.23 N	113.51 E
Wengdang	124	28.50 N	90.03 E
Wenge	152	0.03 N	24.01 E
Wengen, B.R.D.	58	47.41 N	10.09 E
Wengen, Schw.	58	46.36 N	7.56 E
Wengern	263	51.24 N	7.21 E
Wengjiabu	106	30.23 N	120.21 E
Wengong	107	30.11 N	104.09 E
Wenguantun	104	41.53 N	123.30 E
Wengyang	100	28.03 N	120.58 E
Wengyuan	100	24.21 N	114.08 E
Wenham	207	42.36 N	70.53 W
Wenham Lake ◎	283	42.35 N	70.53 W
Wenham Swamp ≡	283	42.37 N	70.55 W
Wenheng	100	25.42 N	116.45 E
Wenigzell	61	47.26 N	15.47 E
Wenjiachang	107	30.41 N	103.55 E
Wenjiang	107	30.42 N	103.49 E
Wenjiangban	100	26.01 N	117.51 E
Wenjiazhen	100	28.20 N	116.05 E
Wenling	100	28.22 N	121.20 E
Wenlock	164	13.06 S	142.58 E
Wenlock ≃	164	12.02 S	141.55 E
Wenlock Edge ⫠[4]	42	52.30 N	2.40 W
Wenlong	100	24.48 N	114.54 E
Wenmingsi	100	25.33 N	113.20 E
Wennigsen	52	52.16 N	9.34 E
Wenning ≃	44	54.07 N	2.39 W
Wennington ◈[8]	260	51.30 N	0.13 E
Wenniu	102	24.18 N	104.31 E
Wenns	58	47.10 N	10.44 E
Wenona, Il., U.S.	216	41.03 N	89.03 W
Wenona, Md., U.S.	208	38.08 N	75.57 W
Wenonah	208	39.47 N	75.08 W
Wenquan, Zhg.	86	44.59 N	81.04 E
Wenquan, Zhg.	100	23.37 N	113.43 E
Wenquansi	104	41.20 N	124.04 E
Wenshan	102	23.30 N	104.20 E
Wenshang	98	35.44 N	116.29 E
Wenshui, Zhg.	102	28.28 N	106.30 E
Wenshui, Zhg.	102	37.28 N	112.01 E
Wensickendorf	264a	52.45 N	13.23 E
Wensleydale V	44	54.19 N	2.00 W
Wensum ≃	42	52.37 N	1.19 E
Went ≃	44	53.39 N	0.59 W
Wentorf	52	53.30 N	10.15 E
Wentworth, Austl.	166	34.07 S	141.55 E
Wentworth, N.C., U.S.	192	36.24 N	79.46 W
Wentworth, S.D., U.S.	198	43.59 N	96.57 W
Wentworth Falls	170	33.43 S	150.22 E
Wentworth Park	273d	26.07 S	27.48 E
Wentworthville	274a	33.48 S	150.58 E
Wentzville	219	38.48 N	90.51 W
Wenxi	102	35.26 N	111.11 E
Wenxian	102	32.58 N	104.46 E
Wenxingchang	107	29.52 N	106.29 E
Wenyu ≃	105	39.56 N	116.40 E
Wenzenbach	60	49.05 N	12.12 E
Wenzhou	100	28.01 N	120.39 E
Wenzhu	100	27.01 N	113.58 E
Wenzhuangzicun	104	42.16 N	123.51 E
Weobley	42	52.09 N	2.51 W
Weohyakapka, Lake ◎	220	27.49 N	81.25 W
Wepener	158	29.46 S	27.00 E
Wépion	56	50.25 N	4.52 E
Weppersdorf	61	47.35 N	16.26 E
Wequetequock	207	41.21 N	71.52 W
Wera ≃	115b	8.20 S	120.43 E
Werbellin	54	52.53 N	13.41 E
Werbellinsee ◎	54	52.54 N	13.40 E
Werben	54	52.52 N	11.58 E
Werbomont	56	50.23 N	5.41 E
Werchojansker Gebirge → Verchojanskij chrebet ⋏	74	67.00 N	129.00 E
Werda	156	25.15 S	23.16 E
Werdau	54	50.44 N	12.22 E
Werden ◈[8]	263	51.23 N	7.00 E
Werder, D.D.R.	54	52.23 N	12.56 E
Werder, Ityo.	144	6.58 N	45.20 E
Werder ◈[1]	54	53.40 N	13.25 E
Werdohl	56	51.15 N	7.45 E
Were Ilu	144	10.37 N	39.28 E
Werfen	64	47.28 N	13.11 E
Weri	164	3.12 S	132.38 E
Werkel	56	51.09 N	9.18 E
Werkendam	52	51.49 N	4.53 E
Werl	52	51.33 N	7.54 E
Werlaburgdorf	54	52.04 N	10.31 E
Werl-Aspe	52	52.04 N	8.43 E
Werleshausen	56	51.19 N	9.54 E
Werlte	52	52.51 N	7.41 E
Wermelskirchen	56	51.08 N	7.13 E
Wermsdorf	54	51.17 N	12.56 E
Wern ≃	56	50.02 N	9.44 E
Wernadinga	166	18.07 S	139.58 E
Wernberg, B.R.D.	60	49.32 N	12.10 E
Wernberg, Öst.	64	46.37 N	13.56 E
Werne	52	51.40 N	7.38 E
Werne ◈[8]	263	51.29 N	7.18 E
Werneck, Bra.	256	22.13 S	43.19 W
Werneck, B.R.D.	56	49.59 N	10.05 E
Werneuchen	54	52.38 N	13.44 E
Wernigerode	54	51.50 N	10.47 E
Wernitz	264a	52.34 N	12.55 E
Wernsdorf	264a	52.22 N	13.43 E
Wernsdorfer See ◎	264a	52.23 N	13.42 E
Wernshausen	54	50.43 N	10.21 E
Wernstein	60	48.30 N	13.28 E
Werra ≃	30	51.26 N	9.39 E
Werribee	169	37.54 S	144.40 E
Werribee ≃	169	37.59 S	144.41 E
Werribee Gorge State Park ♠	169	37.40 S	144.21 E
Werribee South	169	37.56 S	144.42 E
Werries	52	51.41 N	7.53 E
Werrimull	166	34.24 S	141.26 E
Werrington	274a	33.45 S	150.46 E
Werris Creek	166	31.21 S	150.39 E
Werschweiler	56	49.27 N	7.13 E
Wersten ◈[8]	263	51.11 N	6.49 E
Wertach	58	47.36 N	10.25 E
Wertach ≃	58	48.24 N	10.53 E
Wertheim	56	49.46 N	9.31 E
Werther, B.R.D.	52	52.04 N	8.24 E
Werther, D.D.R.	54	51.29 N	10.46 E
Wertingen	56	48.34 N	10.41 E
Wervershoof	52	52.44 N	5.09 E
Wervik	50	50.47 N	3.02 E
Wervin	262	53.15 N	2.52 W
Werwaru	164	8.13 S	128.11 E
Weschnitz ≃	56	49.43 N	8.24 E
Weseke	52	51.54 N	6.51 E
Wesel	52	51.40 N	6.38 E
Wesel-Datteln-Kanal ≊	263	51.38 N	6.36 E
Wesenberg	54	53.17 N	12.58 E
Wesendahl	264a	52.36 N	13.49 E
Wesendorf	52	52.35 N	10.31 E
Weser ≃	52	53.32 N	8.34 E
Weser-Elbe-Kanal (Mittellandkanal) ≊	54	52.16 N	11.41 E
Weser-Ems □[6]	52	52.45 N	8.00 E
Wesergebirge ⋏	52	52.15 N	9.10 E
Wesham	262	53.48 N	2.53 W
Wesickaman Creek ≃	285	39.44 N	74.43 W
Wesiri	112	7.35 S	126.38 E
Weskan	198	38.52 N	101.57 W
Weslaco	196	26.09 N	97.59 W
Weslemkoon Lake ◎	212	45.02 N	77.25 W
Wesley, Dom.	240d	15.34 N	61.19 W
Wesley, Ia., U.S.	190	43.05 N	93.59 W
Wesleyville, Nf., Can.	186	49.09 N	53.34 W
Wesleyville, Pa., U.S.	214	42.08 N	80.00 W
Wessel, Cape ›	164	10.59 S	136.46 E
Wesseling	56	50.49 N	6.58 E
Wessel Islands II	164	11.30 S	136.25 E
Wesselsbron	158	27.50 S	25.23 E
Wesselsvlei	158	27.23 S	23.47 E
Wessington	198	44.27 N	98.41 W
Wessington Springs	198	44.04 N	98.34 W
Wessobrunn	64	47.52 N	11.01 E
Wesson	194	31.42 N	90.23 W
Wessum	52	52.05 N	6.58 E
West, Ms., U.S.	194	33.11 N	89.46 W
West, Tx., U.S.	222	31.48 N	97.05 W
West ≃, N.Y., U.S.	210	42.41 N	77.22 W
West ≃, Vt., U.S.	188	42.52 N	72.33 W
West Abington	207	42.05 N	70.58 W
Westacres	216	42.35 N	83.26 W
West Acton	207	42.28 N	71.28 W
West Alexander	214	40.06 N	80.31 W
West Alexandria	218	39.44 N	84.31 W
Westall, Point ›	162	32.55 S	134.04 E
West Allen ≃	44	54.55 N	2.19 W
West Allis	216	43.01 N	88.00 W
Westalton	219	38.51 N	90.13 W
West Amityville	276	40.41 N	73.26 W
West Andover	207	42.39 N	71.09 W
West Athens	280	33.55 N	118.18 W
West Atlantic City	208	39.23 N	74.28 W
West Babylon	210	40.43 N	73.21 W
Westbahnhof ◈[5]	264b	48.11 N	16.20 E
West Baines ≃	164	15.36 S	129.58 E
West Bangor	210	40.52 N	75.14 W
Westbank	182	49.50 N	119.38 W
West Barnstable	207	41.42 N	70.22 W
West Barrington	207	41.44 N	71.20 W
West Bay, N.S., Can.	186	45.43 N	61.10 W
Westbay, Fl., U.S.	194	30.17 N	85.52 W
West Bay c, Fl., U.S.	194	30.16 N	85.47 W
West Bay c, Tx., U.S.	222	29.15 N	94.57 W
West Bay Shore	276	40.42 N	73.16 W
West Belmar	208	40.10 N	74.02 W
West Bend, Ia., U.S.	198	42.57 N	94.26 W
West Bend, Wi., U.S.	190	43.25 N	88.11 W
West Bengal □[3]	124	24.00 N	88.00 E
West Bergholt	42	51.55 N	0.51 E
West-Berlin → Berlin (West), B.R.D.	54	52.30 N	13.20 E
West Berlin, N.J., U.S.	208	39.48 N	74.56 W
West-Berlin □[3]	264a	52.30 N	13.15 E
West Bernard Creek ≃	222	29.23 N	95.58 W
Westbevern	52	52.01 N	7.47 E
West Bhāgīrath Plain ≚	126	23.30 N	88.00 E
West Bijou Creek ≃	198	39.51 N	104.08 W
West Billerica	283	42.33 N	71.19 W
West Blocton	194	33.07 N	87.07 W
West Bloomfield	210	42.54 N	77.32 W
West Bolivar	214	40.23 N	79.10 W
Westborough	207	42.16 N	71.37 W
Westbourne	184	50.09 N	98.35 W
West Bow Creek ≃	198	42.46 N	97.08 W
West Boxford	283	42.42 N	71.04 W
West Boylston	207	42.22 N	71.47 W
West Bradenton	220	27.30 N	82.37 W
West Branch, Ia., U.S.	190	41.40 N	91.20 W
West Branch, Mi., U.S.	190	44.16 N	84.14 W
West Branch Reservoir ◎[1]	210	41.25 N	73.42 W
West Branch State Park ♠	214	41.07 N	81.05 W
Westbridge	182	49.10 N	118.59 W
West Bridgewater	207	42.01 N	71.00 W
West Bridgford	42	52.56 N	1.08 W
West Bristol	285	40.06 N	74.53 W
West Bromwich	42	52.31 N	1.56 W
Westbrook, Austl.	171a	27.36 S	151.52 E
Westbrook, On., Can.	212	44.16 N	76.38 W
Westbrook, Ct., U.S.	207	41.17 N	72.26 W
Westbrook, Me., U.S.	188	43.40 N	70.22 W
Westbrook, Mn., U.S.	198	44.02 N	95.26 W
Westbrook, Tx., U.S.	196	32.21 N	101.01 W
West Brook ≃	276	41.04 N	74.18 W
West Brookfield	207	42.14 N	72.08 W
Westbrookville	210	41.30 N	74.34 W
West Burlington, Ia., U.S.	190	40.49 N	91.09 W
West Burlington, N.Y., U.S.	210	42.42 N	75.11 W
West Burra I	46a	60.05 N	1.21 W
Westbury, Eng., U.K.	42	52.41 N	2.57 W
Westbury, Eng., U.K.	42	51.16 N	2.11 W
Westbury, N.Y., U.S.	276	40.45 N	73.35 W
Westbury-on-Severn	42	51.50 N	2.24 W
West Butte ∧	202	48.57 N	111.32 W
Westby, Austl.	171b	35.30 S	147.25 E
Westby, Mt., U.S.	198	48.52 N	104.03 W
Westby, Wi., U.S.	190	43.39 N	90.51 W
West Cache Creek ≃	196	34.13 N	98.23 W
West Caicos I	238	21.39 N	72.28 W
West Calder	46	55.52 N	3.35 W
West Caldwell	276	40.50 N	74.18 W
West Cameron	208	40.45 N	76.41 W
West Camp	210	42.07 N	73.56 W
West Canada Creek ≃	188	43.01 N	74.58 W
West Cape ›	172	45.54 S	166.26 E
West Cape Howe ›	162	35.08 S	117.36 E
West Cape May	208	38.56 N	74.56 W
West Carlisle	196	33.35 N	101.56 W
West Caroline Basin ✧[1]	14	4.00 N	138.00 E
West Carrollton	218	39.40 N	84.15 W
West Carson	280	33.57 N	118.23 W
West Carthage	212	43.58 N	75.36 W
West Catfish Creek ≃	212	42.46 N	81.04 W
West Channel ≃[1]	180	68.51 N	136.10 W
West Chelmsford	283	42.37 N	71.23 W
Westchester, Il., U.S.	216	41.51 N	87.52 W
West Chester, Pa., U.S.	208	39.57 N	75.36 W
Westchester, Va., U.S.	284c	38.51 N	77.16 W
Westchester □[6]	210	41.02 N	73.46 W
Westchester ◈[8], Ca., U.S.	280	33.55 N	118.25 W
Westchester ◈[8], N.Y., U.S.	276	40.51 N	73.52 W
West Chester Airport ⊠	285	39.59 N	75.35 W
Westchester County Airport ⊠	207	41.04 N	73.43 W
Westchester Creek ≃	276	40.48 N	73.51 W
Westchester Estates	284c	38.47 N	76.55 W
Westchester Station	186	45.37 N	63.40 W
West Chester University of Pennsylvania ⊍[2]	285	39.57 N	75.36 W
West Chicago	216	41.53 N	88.12 W
West Clandon	260	51.15 N	0.30 W
West Clarksville	210	42.08 N	78.15 W
West Clear Creek ≃	200	34.34 N	111.51 W
West Cleddau ≃	42	51.46 N	4.54 W
Westcliffe	200	38.08 N	105.27 W
Westcliffe ◈[8]	273d	26.11 S	28.02 E
Westcliff-on-Sea	260	51.32 N	0.41 E
West College Corner	218	39.34 N	84.48 W
West Collingswood Heights	285	39.59 N	75.07 W
West Columbia, S.C., U.S.	192	33.59 N	81.04 W
West Columbia, Tx., U.S.	222	29.08 N	95.38 W
West Concord, Ma., U.S.	207	42.27 N	71.23 W
West Concord, Mn., U.S.	190	44.09 N	92.53 W
West Conshohocken	285	40.04 N	75.19 W
West Cote Blanche Bay c	194	29.40 N	91.45 W
Westcott	260	51.13 N	0.22 W
Westcott Cove c	276	41.02 N	73.30 W
West Covina	228	34.04 N	117.56 W
West Creek	208	39.38 N	74.18 W
West Creek ≃, In., U.S.	216	41.12 N	87.30 W
West Creek ≃, Pa., U.S.	214	41.30 N	78.15 W
Westdale, Ma., U.S.	283	42.01 N	70.59 W
Westdale, N.Y., U.S.	210	43.23 N	75.49 W
West Danby	210	42.19 N	76.32 W
West Davenport	210	42.27 N	74.58 W
West Deane Park ♠	275b	43.40 N	79.34 W
West Decatur	214	40.56 N	78.17 W
West Delaware Aqueduct ≊[1]	210	41.52 N	74.31 W
West Demerara-Essequibo Coast □[5]	246	7.00 N	58.40 W
Westdene ◈[8]	273d	26.11 S	27.59 E
West Dennis	207	41.39 N	70.10 W
West Derby ◈[8]	262	53.26 N	2.54 W
West Derry	214	40.20 N	79.20 W
West Des Moines	190	41.34 N	93.42 W
West Dinājpur □[5]	124	25.30 N	88.20 E
West Ditch ≊	276	40.56 N	74.19 W
West Dolores ≃	200	37.35 N	108.21 W
West Drayton ◈[8]	260	51.30 N	0.29 W
West Duffins Creek ≃	212	43.51 N	79.04 W
West Duxbury	283	42.03 N	70.47 W
West Easton	210	40.41 N	75.14 W
West Eaton	210	42.51 N	75.39 W
Westecunk Creek ≃	208	39.37 N	74.16 W
West Edmeston	210	42.46 N	75.17 W
West Edmondale	284b	39.18 N	76.43 W
West Elizabeth	279b	40.17 N	79.54 W
West Elk Mountains ⋏	200	38.40 N	107.15 W
West Elk Peak ∧	200	38.43 N	107.13 W
West Elkton	218	39.35 N	84.33 W
West Ellicott	214	42.05 N	79.16 W
West Elmira	210	42.04 N	76.50 W
West End, Ba.	238	26.41 N	78.58 W
West End, Eng., U.K.	260	51.44 N	0.04 W
West End, Eng., U.K.	260	51.20 N	0.38 W
West End, Ar., U.S.	194	34.13 N	92.03 W
West End, Il., U.S.	216	42.17 N	89.09 W
West End, N.Y., U.S.	210	42.28 N	75.05 W
West End, N.C., U.S.	192	35.14 N	79.34 W
West End ◈[8], Eng., U.K.	260	51.32 N	0.24 W
West End ◈[8], Pa., U.S.	279b	40.27 N	80.02 W
Westende, Bel.	50	51.10 N	2.46 E
Westende, B.R.D.	263	51.25 N	7.24 E
Westendorf	64	47.26 N	12.13 E
Westenfeld ◈[8]	263	51.28 N	7.09 E
Westenholz	52	51.45 N	8.28 E
Westenschouwen	52	51.41 N	3.42 E
Westerbauer ◈[8]	263	51.20 N	7.23 E
Westerblokker	52	52.39 N	5.08 E
Westerbönen	263	51.36 N	7.46 E
Westerbork	52	52.51 N	6.37 E
Westerburg	56	50.33 N	7.58 E
Westercelle	52	52.36 N	10.05 E
Westerdale	46	58.27 N	3.30 W
Westeregeln	54	51.57 N	11.23 E
Westerham	42	51.16 N	0.05 E
Westerhausen	54	51.48 N	11.03 E
Westerholt	52	51.36 N	7.05 E
Westerholz ◈[3]	263	51.32 N	7.28 E
Westerich □[9]	56	49.15 N	7.20 E
Westerkappeln	52	52.18 N	7.52 E
Westerland	30	54.54 N	8.18 E
Westerlo, Bel.	56	51.05 N	4.55 E
Westerlo, N.Y., U.S.	210	42.31 N	74.03 W
Westerly	207	41.22 N	71.49 W
Western	198	40.23 N	97.11 W
Western □[4], Ghana	150	5.30 N	2.30 W
Western □[4], Kenya	154	0.30 N	34.35 E
Western □[4], Sol.Is.	175e	8.00 S	157.00 E
Western □[4], Zam.	152	16.00 S	24.00 E
Western □[5], Pap. N. Gui.	164	7.00 S	142.00 E
Western □[5], Ug.	154	1.00 N	31.00 E
Western ≃	166	22.22 S	142.25 E
Western Area □[4]	150	8.20 N	13.00 W
Western Australia □[3]	160	25.00 S	122.00 E
Western Branch ≃	284c	38.55 N	76.48 W
Western Canal ≊	226	39.28 N	121.35 W
Western Channel ⊔	98	34.40 N	129.00 E
Western Cove c	168b	35.43 S	137.38 E
Western Desert → Gharbīyah, Aṣ-Ṣaḥrā' al- ◈[2]	140	27.00 N	27.00 E
Western Division □[5]	175g	18.00 S	177.30 E
Western Ghāts ⋏	122	14.00 N	75.00 E
Western Highlands □[5]	164	5.30 S	143.30 E
Western Isles □[4]	46	57.40 N	7.00 W
Westernport	188	39.29 N	79.02 W
Western Port c	169	38.22 N	145.20 E
Western Sahara □[2], Afr.	134	24.30 N	13.00 W
Western Sahara □[2], Afr.	148	24.30 N	13.00 W
Western Samoa □[1], Oc.	14	13.55 S	172.00 W
Western Samoa □[1], Oc.	175a	13.55 S	172.00 W
Western Sayans → Zapadnyj Sajan ⋏	74	53.00 N	94.00 E
Western Shore	186	44.32 N	64.19 W
Western Springs	278	41.48 N	87.54 W
Westernville	210	43.18 N	75.23 W
Westerschelde c[1]	52	51.25 N	3.45 E
Westerstede	52	53.15 N	7.55 E
Westervelt	219	39.29 N	88.52 W
Westerville	214	40.07 N	82.55 W
Westerwald ⋏	56	50.40 N	7.55 E
West European Basin ✧[1]	10	47.00 N	15.00 W
West Exeter	210	42.48 N	75.09 W
West Fairview	208	40.16 N	76.54 W
Westfalen □[9]	52	51.50 N	7.30 E
Westfalenhalle ⊍	263	51.30 N	7.27 E
Westfalenpark ♠	263	51.30 N	7.28 E
West Falkland I	254	51.50 S	60.00 W
West Falls	210	42.42 N	78.41 W
West Falmouth	207	41.36 N	70.38 W
West Fargo	198	46.52 N	96.54 W
West Farleigh	260	51.15 N	0.27 E
West Farmington	214	41.23 N	80.58 W
Westfield, Eng., U.K.	42	50.55 N	0.35 E
Westfield, Il., U.S.	194	39.27 N	88.01 W
Westfield, In., U.S.	218	40.02 N	86.07 W
Westfield, Ma., U.S.	207	42.07 N	72.45 W
Westfield, N.J., U.S.	210	40.39 N	74.20 W
Westfield, N.Y., U.S.	214	42.19 N	79.34 W
Westfield, Pa., U.S.	210	41.55 N	77.32 W
Westfield, Tx., U.S.	222	30.01 N	95.24 W
Westfield, Wi., U.S.	190	43.53 N	89.29 W
Westfield ≃	207	42.05 N	72.35 W
Westfield, Middle Branch ≃	207	42.16 N	72.52 W
Westfield, West Branch ≃	207	42.13 N	72.52 W
Westfield Center	214	41.01 N	81.55 W
West Fiord c[2]	176	76.02 N	90.00 W
Westford, Ma., U.S.	283	42.34 N	71.26 W
Westford, N.Y., U.S.	210	42.39 N	74.48 W
West Fork	194	35.55 N	94.11 W
West Foxboro	283	42.05 N	71.17 W
West Frankfort	194	37.53 N	88.55 W
West Friesland ◈[1]	52	52.45 N	4.50 E
West Frisian Islands → Waddeneilanden II	52	53.26 N	5.30 E
West Fulton	210	42.34 N	74.28 W
Westgate, Austl.	166	26.35 S	146.12 E
Westgate, Mi., U.S.	216	43.03 N	85.42 W
Westgate on Sea	42	51.23 N	1.21 E
West Genesee Terrace	210	43.03 N	76.16 W
West Germany → Germany, Federal Republic of □[1]	30	51.00 N	9.00 E
West-Ghats → Western Ghāts ⋏	122	14.00 N	75.00 E
West Gilgo Beach	276	40.37 N	73.25 W
West Glacier	202	48.29 N	113.58 W
West Glamorgan □[6]	42	51.35 N	3.35 W
West Glens Falls	210	43.18 N	73.43 W
West Glenville	210	42.56 N	74.04 W
West Goshen	207	41.49 N	73.15 W
West Granby	207	41.57 N	72.50 W
West Grand Lake ◎	188	45.15 N	67.50 W
West Groton	207	42.36 N	71.37 W
West Grove	208	39.49 N	75.49 W
Westham	208	37.35 N	77.32 W
West Ham ◈[8]	260	51.31 N	0.01 E
West Hamburg	208	40.33 N	76.00 W
West Ham Football Club ♠	260	51.32 N	0.02 E
Westham Island I	224	49.05 N	123.10 W
West Hamlin	188	38.17 N	82.11 W
Westhampton, N.Y., U.S.	207	40.49 N	72.39 W
Westhampton, Va., U.S.	284c	38.54 N	77.11 W
West Hanningfield	260	51.40 N	0.30 E
West Hanover	283	42.07 N	70.53 W
West Harbor c	276	40.54 N	73.32 W
West Harbour	172	45.51 S	170.35 E
West Harrison	218	39.15 N	84.49 W
West Hartford	207	41.45 N	72.44 W
West Hartland	207	42.00 N	72.58 W
Westhausen	56	48.53 N	10.11 E
Westhaven, Ca., U.S.	204	41.03 N	124.06 W
West Haven, Ct., U.S.	207	41.16 N	72.57 W
Westhaven, Il., U.S.	278	41.35 N	87.51 W
West Haverstraw	210	41.12 N	73.59 W
West Hazleton	210	40.57 N	75.59 W
Westhead	262	53.34 N	2.51 W
West Hebron	210	43.14 N	73.22 W
West Heidelberg	274b	37.45 S	145.02 E
Westheim	56	49.03 N	9.44 E
West Helena	194	34.33 N	90.38 W
Westhemmerde	263	51.33 N	7.47 E
West Hempstead	276	40.42 N	73.39 W
West Henrietta	210	43.02 N	77.40 W
West Hickory	214	41.34 N	79.25 W
Westhill	46	57.09 N	2.17 W
West Hill ◈[8]	275b	43.46 N	79.11 W
Westhofen	263	51.25 N	7.31 E
Westhoff	222	29.12 N	97.28 W
Westhoffen	58	48.36 N	7.26 E
West Hollywood, Ca., U.S.	228	34.05 N	118.21 W
West Hollywood, Fl., U.S.	220	26.01 N	80.10 W
Westholme	224	49.52 N	123.42 W
West Homestead	279b	40.24 N	79.55 W
Westhope, N.D., U.S.	198	48.54 N	101.01 W
Westhope, Oh., U.S.	216	41.18 N	83.57 W
West Horndon	260	51.34 N	0.21 E
West Horsley	260	51.16 N	0.27 W
Westhoughton	262	53.33 N	2.32 W
West Hoxton	274a	33.55 S	150.49 E
West Humber ≃	212	43.44 N	79.33 W
West Humble	260	51.15 N	0.20 W
West Huntington	276	40.42 N	73.18 W
West Hurley	210	42.00 N	74.06 W
Westhuyzen	158	27.30 S	25.27 E
West Hyde	260	51.37 N	0.30 W
West Ice Shelf ⊓	9	67.00 S	85.00 E
Westick	263	51.35 N	7.38 E
Westig	263	51.22 N	7.45 E
West Indies II	230	19.00 N	70.00 W
Westindische Inseln → West Indies II	230	19.00 N	70.00 W
West Irian → Irian Jaya □[4]	164	5.00 S	138.00 E
West Island I, Austl.	164	15.36 S	136.34 E
West Island I, Ma., U.S.	207	41.36 N	70.50 W
West Islip	210	40.42 N	73.18 W
West Jan Mayen Ridge ✧[3]	10	71.00 N	13.00 W
West Jefferson, N.C., U.S.	192	36.24 N	81.29 W
West Jefferson, Oh., U.S.	218	39.56 N	83.16 W
West Jordan	200	40.36 N	111.56 W
Westkapelle, Bel.	50	51.19 N	3.18 E
Westkapelle, Ned.	52	51.32 N	3.27 E
West Keansburg	276	40.27 N	74.09 W
West Kettle ≃	182	49.07 N	119.00 W
West Kilbride	46	55.42 N	4.51 W
West Kill	210	42.13 N	74.31 W
West Kingsdown	42	51.21 N	0.17 E
West Kingston	207	41.28 N	71.33 W
West Kirby	44	53.22 N	3.10 W
Westkirchen	52	51.53 N	8.02 E
West Kittanning	214	40.49 N	79.32 W
West Lafayette, In., U.S.	216	40.25 N	86.54 W
West Lafayette, Oh., U.S.	214	40.16 N	81.45 W
Westlake, La., U.S.	194	30.15 N	93.15 W
Westlake, Oh., U.S.	214	41.27 N	81.55 W
Westlake, Tx., U.S.	222	32.59 N	97.12 W
West Lake ◎, On., Can.	212	43.56 N	77.17 W
West Lake ◎, Fl., U.S.	220	25.12 N	80.49 W
West Lake ◎, N.J., U.S.	276	40.58 N	74.22 W
West Lamma Channel ⊔	271d	22.13 N	114.04 E
West Lancashire □[8]	262	53.35 N	2.50 W
Westland, Mi., U.S.	216	42.19 N	83.24 W
Westland, Pa., U.S.	214	40.17 N	80.16 W
Westland Center ◈[9]	281	42.20 N	83.23 W
Westland National Park ♠	172	43.30 S	170.10 E
Westlands	207	42.37 N	71.20 W
West Lanham Hills	284c	38.57 N	76.53 W
West Laramie	200	41.18 N	105.37 W
West Lawn	284c	38.52 N	77.11 W
West Lebanon, In., U.S.	216	40.16 N	87.23 W
West Lebanon, Pa., U.S.	214	40.35 N	79.22 W
West Leechburg	214	40.37 N	79.37 W
Westleigh, S. Afr.	158	27.31 S	27.21 E
Westleigh, Eng., U.K.	262	53.30 N	2.31 W
West Leipsic	216	41.07 N	84.00 W
Westley	226	37.33 N	121.12 W
West Leyden	212	43.28 N	75.28 W
West Liberty, Ia., U.S.	190	41.34 N	91.15 W
West Liberty, Ky., U.S.	192	37.55 N	83.15 W
West Liberty, Oh., U.S.	216	40.15 N	83.45 W
West Liberty, Pa., U.S.	214	41.00 N	80.03 W
West Liberty, W.V., U.S.	214	40.10 N	80.35 W
West Liberty ◈[8]	279b	40.24 N	80.01 W
Westliche Sahara → Western Sahara □[2]	148	24.30 N	13.00 W
Westliche Sierra Madre → Madre Occidental, Sierra ⋏	232	25.00 N	105.00 W
Westline	214	41.47 N	78.46 W
West Linn	224	45.21 N	122.36 W

Symbol	English	Deutsch	Español	Français	Português
≃	River	Fluss	Río	Rivière	Rio
≊	Canal	Kanal	Canal	Canal	Canal
⌊	Waterfall, Rapids	Wasserfall, Stromschnellen	Cascada, Rápidos	Chute d'eau, Rapides	Cascata, Rápidos
⊔	Strait	Meeresstrasse	Estrecho	Détroit	Estreito
c	Bay, Gulf	Bucht, Golf	Bahía, Golfo	Baie, Golfe	Baía, Golfo
◎	Lake, Lakes	See, Seen	Lago, Lagos	Lac, Lacs	Lago, Lagos
≡	Swamp	Sumpf	Pantano	Marais	Pântano
⊓	Ice Features, Glacier	Eis- und Gletscherformen	Accidentes Glaciales	Formes glaciaires	Acidentes glaciares
∓	Other Hydrographic Features	Andere Hydrographische Objekte	Otros Elementos Hidrográficos	Autres données hydrographiques	Outros acidentes hidrográficos
✧	Submarine Features	Untermeerische Objekte	Accidentes Submarinos	Formes de relief sous-marin	Acidentes submarinos
□	Political Unit	Politische Einheit	Unidad Politica	Entité politique	Unidade política
⊍	Cultural Institution	Kulturelle Institution	Institución Cultural	Institution culturelle	Instituição cultural
⊥	Historical Site	Historische Stätte	Sitio Histórico	Site historique	Sitio histórico
♠	Recreational Site	Erholungs- und Ferienort	Sitio de Recreo	Centre de loisirs	Area de Lazer
⊠	Airport	Flughafen	Aeropuerto	Aéroport	Aeroporto
■	Military Installation	Militäranlage	Instalación Militar	Installation militaire	Instalação militar
◈	Miscellaneous	Verschiedenes	Misceláneo	Divers	Diversos

Name	Page	Lat.°′	Long.°′
West Linton	46	55.46 N	3.22 W
West Little Owyhee ≃	202	42.28 N	117.15 W
West Loch Roag c	46	58.13 N	6.53 W
West Loch Tarbert c, Scot., U.K.	46	57.55 N	6.54 W
West Loch Tarbert c, Scot., U.K.	46	55.48 N	5.32 W
Westlock	182	54.09 N	113.52 W
West Looe	42	50.21 N	4.28 W
West Lorne	214	42.36 N	81.36 W
West Los Angeles ◆[8]	280	34.03 N	118.28 W
West Lulworth	42	50.38 N	2.15 W
West Lunga ≃	154	13.06 S	24.39 E
West Lunga National Park ♠	154	12.55 S	25.10 E
West Malling	42	51.18 N	0.25 E
West Malling Aerodrome ⊠	260	51.16 N	0.24 E
West Manayunk	285	40.01 N	75.14 W
West Manchester	218	39.54 N	84.37 W
West Mansfield, Ma., U.S.	207	41.59 N	71.14 W
West Mansfield, Oh., U.S.	216	40.24 N	83.32 W
West Mariana Basin ✢[1]	14	15.00 N	137.00 E
West Mayfield	214	40.47 N	80.20 W
West Meadowview	216	41.08 N	87.52 W
Westmeath □[6]	48	53.30 N	7.30 W
West Medway	207	42.08 N	71.25 W
West Melbourne	220	28.04 N	80.39 W
West Memphis	194	35.08 N	90.11 W
West Meon	42	51.01 N	1.05 W
Westmere	210	42.41 N	73.52 W
West Mersea	42	51.47 N	0.55 E
West Miami	220	25.45 N	80.17 W
West Middlesex	214	41.10 N	80.27 W
West Middletown	214	40.15 N	80.25 W
West Midlands □[6]	42	52.30 N	2.00 W
West Mifflin	214	40.22 N	79.52 W
West Milford	210	41.07 N	74.22 W
West Millbury	207	42.11 N	71.48 W
West Mill Creek ≃	222	29.55 N	96.17 W
West Milton, Oh., U.S.	218	39.57 N	84.19 W
West Milton, Pa., U.S.	210	41.01 N	76.52 W
West Milwaukee	216	43.00 N	87.58 W
West Mineola	222	32.41 N	95.31 W
Westminster, Ca., U.S.	228	33.45 N	118.02 W
Westminster, Co., U.S.	200	39.50 N	105.02 W
Westminster, Md., U.S.	208	39.34 N	76.59 W
Westminster, Ma., U.S.	207	42.32 N	71.54 W
Westminster, Oh., U.S.	216	40.42 N	83.58 W
Westminster, S.C., U.S.	192	34.39 N	83.05 W
Westminster Abbey ʋ[1]	260	51.30 N	0.07 W
Westminster Mall ◆[9]	280	33.45 N	118.01 W
West Modesto	226	37.37 N	121.02 W
West Monroe	194	32.31 N	92.08 W
Westmont, Ca., U.S.	280	33.56 N	118.18 W
Westmont, Il., U.S.	278	41.47 N	87.58 W
Westmont, N.J., U.S.	285	39.54 N	75.02 W
Westmont, Pa., U.S.	214	40.18 N	78.57 W
West Monterey	214	41.03 N	79.39 W
West Montreal ≃	190	47.56 N	80.39 W
West Moors	42	50.49 N	1.55 W
Westmoreland, Ks., U.S.	198	39.23 N	96.24 W
Westmoreland, N.Y., U.S.	210	43.07 N	75.24 W
Westmoreland, Tn., U.S.	194	36.33 N	86.14 W
Westmoreland, Va., U.S.	208	38.04 N	76.34 W
Westmoreland □[6], Pa., U.S.	214	40.18 N	79.33 W
Westmoreland □[6], Va., U.S.	208	38.10 N	76.50 W
Westmoreland City	214	40.20 N	79.41 W
Westmoreland State Park ♠	208	38.09 N	76.50 W
Westmorland	204	33.02 N	115.37 W
Westmount	206	45.29 N	73.36 W
West Mountain ∧	188	43.51 N	74.43 W
West Mud Creek ≃	222	32.07 N	95.10 W
West Mustang Creek ≃	222	29.04 N	96.26 W
West Nab ∧	262	53.35 N	1.53 W
West Nanticoke	210	40.13 N	76.01 W
West New Britain □[5]	164	5.45 S	149.30 E
West Newbury	207	42.48 N	70.59 W
West Newton, Ma., U.S.	283	42.21 N	71.14 W
West Newton, Pa., U.S.	214	40.12 N	79.46 W
West New York	276	40.47 N	74.00 W
West Nicholson	154	21.06 S	29.25 E
West Nishnabotna ≃	198	40.39 N	95.37 W
West Nodaway ≃	194	40.38 N	95.01 W
West Norriton	208	40.08 N	75.22 W
West Norwood ◆[8]	260	51.26 N	0.06 W
West Novaya Zemlya Trough ✢[1]	10	73.30 N	50.00 E
West Nueces ≃	196	29.16 N	99.56 W
West Nyack	210	41.06 N	73.58 W
West Okaw ≃	219	39.32 N	88.42 W
Weston, Austl.	170	32.49 S	151.28 E
Weston, Malay.	112	5.13 N	115.36 E
Weston, Eng., U.K.	262	53.19 N	2.44 W
Weston, Co., U.S.	200	37.07 N	104.50 W
Weston, Ct., U.S.	207	41.12 N	73.22 W
Weston, Id., U.S.	202	42.02 N	111.58 W
Weston, Ma., U.S.	207	42.22 N	71.18 W
Weston, Mi., U.S.	216	41.46 N	84.06 W
Weston, Mo., U.S.	194	39.24 N	94.54 W
Weston, Ne., U.S.	198	41.11 N	96.44 W
Weston, Oh., U.S.	216	41.20 N	83.47 W
Weston, Or., U.S.	202	45.48 N	118.25 W
Weston, Pa., U.S.	210	40.57 N	76.09 W
Weston, W.V., U.S.	188	39.02 N	80.28 W
Weston □[8]	275b	43.43 N	79.31 W
Westonaria	273d	26.19 S	27.39 E
West Oneonta	210	42.28 N	75.07 W
Westönnen	52	51.33 N	7.58 E
Weston Reservoir ⊜[1]	283	42.21 N	71.18 W
Westons Mill Pond ⊜	276	40.28 N	74.25 W
Westons Mills	210	42.04 N	78.23 W
Weston-Super-Mare	42	51.21 N	2.59 W
Weston upon Trent	42	52.45 N	2.02 W
West Orange, N.J., U.S.	276	40.47 N	74.14 W
West Orange, Tx., U.S.	194	30.05 N	93.46 W
Westover, Md., U.S.	208	38.07 N	75.42 W
Westover, Pa., U.S.	214	40.45 N	78.40 W
Westover, Tn., U.S.	194	35.36 N	88.52 W
Westover, W.V., U.S.	188	39.38 N	79.58 W
Westover Air Force Base ■	207	42.12 N	72.33 W
Westoverledingen	52	53.10 N	7.28 E
Westowne	284b	39.17 N	76.43 W
West Palm Beach	220	26.42 N	80.03 W
West Palm Beach Canal ≅	220	26.38 N	80.03 W
West Paris	188	44.19 N	70.34 W
West Park	210	41.48 N	73.58 W
West Paterson	276	40.53 N	74.11 W
West Pawlet	210	43.21 N	73.15 W
West Peckham	260	51.15 N	0.22 E
West Pensacola	194	30.25 N	87.16 W
Westphalia, Ks., U.S.	198	38.10 N	95.29 W
Westphalia, Mi., U.S.	216	42.55 N	84.47 W
Westphalia, Mo., U.S.	219	38.26 N	91.59 W
West Pittsburg, Ca., U.S.	226	38.01 N	121.56 W
West Pittsburg, Pa., U.S.	214	40.55 N	80.21 W
West Pittston	210	41.19 N	75.47 W
West Plains	194	36.43 N	91.51 W
West Point, Ca., U.S.	226	38.23 N	120.31 W
West Point, Ga., U.S.	192	32.52 N	85.11 W
Westpoint, In., U.S.	216	40.21 N	87.03 W
West Point, Ia., U.S.	190	40.43 N	91.27 W
West Point, Ky., U.S.	194	37.59 N	85.56 W
West Point, Ms., U.S.	194	33.36 N	88.39 W
West Point, Ne., U.S.	198	41.50 N	96.42 W
West Point, N.Y., U.S.	210	41.23 N	73.57 W
West Point, Oh., U.S.	214	40.43 N	80.42 W
West Point, Pa., U.S.	285	40.12 N	75.18 W
West Point, Va., U.S.	208	37.31 N	76.47 W
West Point ∧	180	64.57 N	144.40 W
West Point ≻	186	46.37 N	64.25 W
West Point Lake ⊜[1]	192	33.00 N	85.10 W
West Pond ⊜	276	40.53 N	73.38 W
Westport, Nf., Can.	186	49.47 N	56.38 W
Westport, N.S., Can.	186	44.16 N	66.21 W
Westport, On., Can.	212	44.41 N	76.26 W
Westport, Ire.	48	53.48 N	9.32 W
Westport, N.Z.	172	41.45 S	171.36 E
Westport, Ct., U.S.	207	41.08 N	73.21 W
Westport, In., U.S.	218	39.10 N	85.34 W
Westport, Ky., U.S.	218	38.28 N	85.28 W
Westport, Ma., U.S.	207	41.37 N	71.04 W
Westport, Or., U.S.	224	46.07 N	123.22 W
Westport, Pa., U.S.	214	41.18 N	77.51 W
Westport, Wa., U.S.	224	46.53 N	124.06 W
West Portland	224	45.25 N	122.45 W
West Portland Park	224	45.21 N	122.37 W
Westport Point	207	41.31 N	71.04 W
West Portsmouth	218	38.45 N	83.01 W
West Prairie ≃	182	55.30 N	116.31 W
West Puente Valley	280	34.04 N	117.59 W
West Pullman ◆[8]	278	41.41 N	87.39 W
Westpunt ≻	241s	12.37 N	70.03 W
West Pymble	274a	33.46 S	151.08 E
West Quoddy Head ≻	188	44.49 N	66.57 W
West Rand	273d	26.07 S	27.45 E
Westray I	46	59.18 N	3.00 W
Westray Firth ʯ	46	59.12 N	2.55 W
West Redding	207	41.19 N	73.26 W
Westrem	50	50.58 N	3.52 E
West Richfield	214	41.14 N	81.39 W
West Richland	202	46.18 N	119.20 W
West River c	208	38.52 N	76.31 W
West Road ≃	182	53.19 N	122.52 W
West Rosebud Creek ≃	202	45.29 N	109.27 W
West Roxbury ◆[8]	283	42.17 N	71.09 W
West Rupert	210	43.14 N	73.14 W
West Rutland	188	43.35 N	73.02 W
West Ryde	274a	33.48 S	151.05 E
West Sacramento	226	38.34 N	121.31 W
West Saint Marys ≃	186	45.15 N	62.04 W
West Saint Modeste	186	51.36 N	56.42 W
West Salem, Il., U.S.	194	38.31 N	88.00 W
West Salem, Oh., U.S.	214	40.58 N	82.06 W
West Salem, Wi., U.S.	190	43.53 N	91.04 W
West Salt Creek ≃	200	39.13 N	108.54 W
Westsamoa → Western Samoa □[1]	175a	13.55 S	172.00 W
West Sand Lake	210	42.39 N	73.37 W
West Saugerties	210	42.07 N	74.03 W
West Sayville	276	40.43 N	73.05 W
West Sayville County Park ♠	276	40.43 N	73.06 W
West Scenic Park	220	27.55 N	81.39 W
West Scotia Basin ✢[1]	18	57.00 S	53.00 W
West Seneca	210	42.50 N	78.45 W
West Sepik □[5]	164	4.00 S	141.30 E
West Shoal Lake ⊜	184	50.20 N	97.41 W
West Siberian Plain → Zapadno-Sibirskaja ravnina ≚	72	60.00 N	75.00 E
Westsibirisches Flachland → Zapadno-Sibirskaja ravnina ≚	72	60.00 N	75.00 E
West Side Canal ≅	226	35.19 N	119.23 W
West Side Tennis Club ♠	276	40.43 N	73.51 W
West Simsbury	207	41.52 N	72.51 W
West Sister Island I	166	39.42 S	147.55 E
West Slope	224	45.29 N	122.45 W
West Spanish Peak ∧	200	37.23 N	104.59 W
West Springfield, Ma., U.S.	207	42.06 N	72.37 W
West Springfield, Pa., U.S.	214	41.57 N	80.29 W
West Springfield, Va., U.S.	208	38.46 N	77.13 W
West Stewartstown	206	44.59 N	71.31 W
West Stockbridge	207	42.20 N	73.22 W
West Stony Creek ≃	210	43.15 N	74.13 W
West Suffield	207	41.59 N	72.41 W
West Sunbury	214	41.00 N	79.54 W
West Sussex □[6]	42	50.55 N	0.35 W
West Swanzey	207	42.52 N	72.20 W
West Terre Haute	194	39.27 N	87.27 W
West-Terschelling	52	53.21 N	5.13 E
West Thompson Lake ⊜[1]	207	41.57 N	71.54 W
West Thurrock	260	51.29 N	0.16 E
West Tiana	207	40.52 N	72.33 W
West Tilbury	260	51.29 N	0.24 E
West Tisbury	207	41.22 N	70.40 W
West Toodyay	168a	31.33 S	116.27 E
West Torrens	168b	34.56 S	138.32 E
Westtown, N.Y., U.S.	210	41.20 N	74.32 W
Westtown, Pa., U.S.	285	39.56 N	75.33 W
West Townsend	207	42.40 N	71.44 W
West Turffontein ◆[8]	273d	26.16 S	28.02 E
West Union, Ia., U.S.	190	42.57 N	91.48 W
West Union, Oh., U.S.	218	38.47 N	83.32 W
West Union, W.V., U.S.	188	39.17 N	80.46 W
West Union Creek ≃	282	37.25 N	122.16 W
West Unity	216	41.35 N	84.26 W
West University Place	222	29.43 N	95.26 W
West Upton	207	42.10 N	71.37 W
Westvale	210	43.02 N	76.13 W
West Valley, Mt., U.S.	202	46.08 N	113.01 W
West Valley, N.Y., U.S.	210	42.24 N	78.37 W
West Valley City	200	40.42 N	111.57 W
West Vancouver	182	49.22 N	123.12 W
West View	214	40.31 N	80.02 W
West View Amusement Park ♠	279b	40.31 N	80.02 W
Westview Heights	207	41.33 N	73.05 W
Westville, N.S., Can.	186	45.34 N	62.43 W
Westville, In., U.S.	216	41.32 N	86.54 W
Westville, N.H., U.S.	207	42.49 N	71.07 W
Westville, N.J., U.S.	285	39.52 N	75.07 W
Westville, Oh., U.S.	218	40.07 N	83.51 W
Westville, Ok., U.S.	194	35.59 N	94.34 W
Westville, Pa., U.S.	214	41.13 N	78.50 W
Westville Center	206	44.57 N	74.24 W
Westville Grove	285	39.51 N	75.07 W
Westville Lake ⊜[1]	207	42.05 N	72.05 W
Westville Oaks	285	39.51 N	75.08 W
West Virginia □[3], U.S.	178	38.45 N	80.30 W
West Virginia □[3], U.S.	188	38.45 N	80.30 W
West-Vlaanderen □[4]	50	51.00 N	3.00 E
West Walker ≃	226	38.53 N	119.10 W
West Wallsend	170	32.54 S	151.35 E
Westward Ho!	42	51.02 N	4.15 W
West Wareham	207	41.47 N	70.45 W
West Warren	207	42.12 N	72.14 W
West Warwick	207	41.42 N	71.31 W
West Water ≃	46	56.47 N	2.38 W
West Webster	210	43.12 N	77.29 W
Westwego	194	29.54 N	90.08 W
West Wellow	42	50.58 N	1.35 W
West Whittier	280	33.59 N	118.03 W
West Wickham ◆[8]	260	51.22 N	0.01 W
West Willington	207	41.52 N	72.18 W
West Willow	216	42.14 N	83.34 W
West Windsor	210	42.06 N	74.46 W
West Winfield, N.Y., U.S.	210	42.53 N	75.11 W
West Winfield, Pa., U.S.	214	40.48 N	79.42 W
Westwold	182	50.28 N	119.45 W
Westwood, Ca., U.S.	204	40.18 N	121.00 W
Westwood, In., U.S.	218	39.55 N	85.25 W
Westwood, Ma., U.S.	207	42.12 N	71.14 W
Westwood, Mi., U.S.	216	42.18 N	85.38 W
Westwood, N.J., U.S.	210	40.59 N	74.01 W
Westwood, Pa., U.S.	214	40.18 N	78.56 W
Westwood ◆[8]	280	34.04 N	118.27 W
Westwood Lakes	220	25.44 N	80.22 W
Westworth Village	222	32.45 N	97.25 W
West Wyalong	166	33.55 S	147.13 E
West Wycombe	42	51.39 N	0.49 W
West Yarmouth	207	41.39 N	70.14 W
West Yegua Creek ≃	222	30.20 N	96.52 W
West Yellow Creek ≃	194	39.38 N	93.04 W
West Yellowstone	202	44.39 N	111.06 W
West York	208	39.57 N	76.45 W
West Yorkshire □[6]	44	53.45 N	1.40 W
Wetan, Pulau I	164	7.54 S	129.32 E
Wetar, Pulau I	112	7.48 S	126.18 E
Wetar, Selat ʯ	112	8.20 S	126.30 E
Wetaskiwin	182	52.58 N	113.22 W
Wete	154	5.04 S	39.43 E
Wethau	54	51.08 N	11.52 E
Wetherby	44	53.56 N	1.23 W
Wetherill Park	274a	33.51 S	150.54 E
Wethersfield	207	41.43 N	72.40 W
Wethmar	263	51.37 N	7.33 E
Wetiko Hills ⋏[2]	184	54.30 N	92.20 W
Wetluga → Vetluga ≃	80	56.18 N	46.24 E
Wetmore	198	39.38 N	95.48 W
Wet Mountains ⋏	200	38.00 N	105.10 W
Weto	152	7.57 N	7.50 E
Wetten	52	51.34 N	6.17 E
Wetter, B.R.D.	56	50.54 N	8.43 E
Wetter, B.R.D.	56	51.23 N	7.23 E
Wetter ≃	56	50.18 N	8.49 E
Wetterau □[9]	56	50.15 N	8.50 E
Wetteren	50	51.00 N	3.53 E
Wetterhorn ∧	58	46.39 N	8.08 E
Wetterstein Gebirge ⋏	64	47.25 N	11.05 E
Wettigan	110	18.57 N	95.21 E
Wettin	54	51.35 N	11.48 E
Wettingen	58	47.28 N	8.19 E
Wettringen	52	52.12 N	7.19 E
Wetumka	196	35.14 N	96.14 W
Wetumpka	194	32.32 N	86.12 W
Wetwang	44	54.01 N	0.34 W
Wetzikon	58	47.19 N	8.47 E
Wetzlar	56	50.33 N	8.29 E
Wetzstein ∧[2]	54	50.27 N	11.27 E
Wevelgem	50	50.48 N	3.10 E
Wevelinghoven	56	51.06 N	6.37 E
Wewahitchka	192	30.06 N	85.12 W
Wewak	164	3.35 S	143.40 E
Wewelsfleth	52	53.50 N	9.24 E
Wewer	52	51.41 N	8.42 E
Wewoka	196	35.09 N	96.29 W
Wexford, Ire.	48	52.20 N	6.27 W
Wexford, Pa., U.S.	214	40.38 N	80.03 W
Wexford □[6]	48	52.20 N	6.40 W
Wexford ◆[8]	275b	43.45 N	79.18 W
Wexford Harbour c	48	52.20 N	6.55 W
Wey ≃	42	51.23 N	0.28 W
Weyakwin Lake ⊜	184	54.30 N	106.00 W
Weyanoke	284c	38.48 N	77.09 W
Weyarn	64	47.51 N	11.48 E
Weyauwega	190	44.19 N	88.56 W
Weybridge	42	51.23 N	0.28 W
Weyburn	184	49.41 N	103.52 W
Weyer ◆[8]	263	51.10 N	7.01 E
Weyer Markt	61	47.52 N	14.41 E
Weyersheim	56	48.43 N	7.48 E
Weyhausen	52	52.47 N	10.23 E
Weyhe	52	52.59 N	8.52 E
Weymouth, N.S., Can.	186	44.25 N	66.00 W
Weymouth, Eng., U.K.	42	50.36 N	2.28 W
Weymouth, Ma., U.S.	207	42.13 N	70.56 W
Weymouth, N.J., U.S.	208	39.30 N	74.46 W
Weymouth, Cape ≻	164	12.37 S	143.27 E
Weymouth Back ≃	283	42.15 N	70.55 W
Weymouth Fore ≃	283	42.16 N	70.56 W
Weymouth Great Pond ⊜	283	42.12 N	71.02 W
Wezemaal	56	50.57 N	4.46 E
Wezep	52	52.27 N	6.00 E
Whakatane	172	37.58 S	177.00 E
Whakatane ≃	172	37.57 S	177.00 E
Whalan	274a	33.45 S	150.49 E
Whale Creek ≃	276	40.27 N	74.13 W
Whales, Bay of c	9	78.30 S	164.20 W
Whaley Bridge	44	53.20 N	1.59 W
Whaley Lake	210	41.33 N	73.40 W
Whaleysville	208	38.23 N	75.18 W
Whaleyville	208	36.37 N	76.41 W
Whalley	44	53.50 N	2.24 W
Whalom	207	42.34 N	71.44 W
Whalsay I	46a	60.20 N	0.59 W
Whangaehu ≃	172	40.03 S	175.06 E
Whangamata	172	37.12 S	175.52 E
Whangamomona	172	39.09 S	174.44 E
Whangara	172	38.34 S	178.13 E
Whangarei	172	35.43 S	174.19 E
Whangaruru Harbour c	172	35.22 S	174.21 E
Whaplode	42	52.48 N	0.02 W
Wharfe ≃	44	53.51 N	1.07 W
Wharfedale ∨	44	54.01 N	1.56 W
Wharles	262	53.49 N	2.50 W
Wharton, N.J., U.S.	210	40.53 N	74.34 W
Wharton, Oh., U.S.	214	40.52 N	83.21 W
Wharton, Tx., U.S.	222	29.18 N	96.06 W
Wharton, W.V., U.S.	188	37.54 N	81.40 W
Wharton □[6]	222	29.17 N	96.13 W
Wharton Basin ✢[1]	12	21.00 S	100.00 E
Wharton Lake ⊜	176	64.00 N	99.55 W
Wharton State Forest ♠	285	39.45 N	74.40 W
Whataroa	172	43.17 S	170.25 E
Whatatutu	172	38.23 S	177.50 E
What Cheer	190	41.24 N	92.21 W
Whatcom □[6]	224	48.48 N	121.59 W
Whatcom, Lake ⊜	224	48.43 N	122.20 W
Whately	207	42.26 N	72.38 W
Whatley	194	31.39 N	87.42 W
Whatshan Lake ⊜	182	50.00 N	118.03 W
Whauphill	44	54.49 N	4.29 W
Wheao ≃	172	38.34 S	176.39 E
Wheatfield	216	40.33 N	87.06 W
Wheathampstead	42	51.49 N	0.17 W
Wheatland, Ca., U.S.	226	39.00 N	121.25 W
Wheatland, Ia., U.S.	190	41.49 N	90.50 W
Wheatland, Pa., U.S.	214	41.12 N	80.28 W
Wheatland, Wy., U.S.	200	42.03 N	104.57 W
Wheatland Hills	208	40.02 N	76.21 W
Wheatland Reservoir ⊜[1]	200	41.52 N	105.36 W
Wheatley, On., Can.	214	42.06 N	82.27 W
Wheatley, Eng., U.K.	44	51.44 N	1.08 W
Wheatley, Ar., U.S.	194	34.54 N	91.06 W
Wheatley Hill	44	54.45 N	1.23 W
Wheaton, Il., U.S.	216	41.51 N	88.06 W
Wheaton, Md., U.S.	208	39.02 N	77.03 W
Wheaton, Mn., U.S.	198	45.48 N	96.29 W
Wheaton Plaza ◆[9]	284c	39.02 N	77.03 W
Wheaton Regional Park ♠	284c	39.03 N	77.02 W
Wheat Ridge	200	39.45 N	105.04 W
Wheelbarrow Peak ∧	204	37.27 N	116.05 W
Wheeler, In., U.S.	216	41.30 N	87.10 W
Wheeler, Ms., U.S.	194	34.34 N	88.36 W
Wheeler, Tx., U.S.	196	35.26 N	100.16 W
Wheeler ≃, P.Q., Can.	176	57.02 N	67.13 W
Wheeler ≃, Sk., Can.	184	57.20 N	105.30 W
Wheeler Air Force Base ■	229c	21.29 N	158.03 W
Wheeler Dam ◆[6]	283	42.48 N	71.12 W
Wheeler Island I	282	38.05 N	121.56 W
Wheeler Lake ⊜[1]	194	34.40 N	87.05 W
Wheeler Peak ∧, Ca., U.S.	226	38.25 N	119.17 W
Wheeler Peak ∧, Nv., U.S.	204	38.59 N	114.19 W
Wheeler Peak ∧, N.M., U.S.	200	36.34 N	105.25 W
Wheeler Ridge	228	35.06 N	119.01 W
Wheelersburg	218	38.43 N	82.51 W
Wheelers Hill	274b	37.55 S	145.11 E
Wheeling, Il., U.S.	216	42.08 N	87.55 W
Wheeling, W.V., U.S.	214	40.03 N	80.43 W
Wheeling Creek ≃	214	40.03 N	80.41 W
Wheelock	222	30.54 N	96.24 W
Wheelock ≃	44	53.12 N	2.26 W
Wheelton	262	53.41 N	2.36 W
Wheelwright, Arg.	252	33.47 S	61.13 W
Wheelwright, Ky., U.S.	192	37.19 N	82.43 W
Wheelwright Park ♠	283	42.15 N	70.49 W
Wheeny Creek ≃	170	33.26 S	150.50 E
Whela Creek ≃	162	26.17 S	116.50 E
Whelan, Mount ∧[2]	166	23.25 S	138.54 E
Whelpleyhill	260	51.44 N	0.33 W
Whernside ∧	44	54.14 N	2.23 W
Whetstone Creek ≃	214	40.23 N	83.03 W
Whetstone Gulf State Park ♠	212	43.44 N	75.27 W
Whickham	44	54.56 N	1.41 W
Whidbey Island I	224	48.15 N	122.40 W
Whidbey Island Naval Air Station ■	224	48.17 N	122.37 W
Whidbey Islands II	162	34.45 S	135.04 E
Whiddon Down	42	50.43 N	3.51 W
Whigham	192	30.52 N	84.19 W
Whigville	207	41.43 N	72.56 W
Whim Creek	162	20.50 S	117.50 E
Whinham, Mount ∧	162	26.04 S	130.15 E
Whippany	210	40.49 N	74.25 W
Whippany ≃	276	40.51 N	74.21 W
Whirl Creek ≃	212	43.28 N	81.12 W
Whirlwind Reefs ✢[2]	164	4.42 S	148.16 E
Whiskey Peak ∧	200	42.18 N	107.35 W
Whiskeytown-Shasta-Trinity National Recreation Area ♠	204	40.45 N	122.15 W
Whisky Chitto Creek ≃	194	30.31 N	92.55 W
Whiston	262	53.25 N	2.50 W
Whitacres	207	41.48 N	72.39 W
Whitaker	279b	40.24 N	79.53 W
Whitakers	192	36.06 N	77.42 W
Whitbourne	186	47.25 N	53.32 W
Whitburn, Eng., U.K.	44	54.57 N	1.22 W
Whitburn, Scot., U.K.	46	55.52 N	3.42 W
Whitby, On., Can.	212	43.52 N	78.56 W
Whitby, Eng., U.K.	44	54.29 N	0.37 W
Whitby, Eng., U.K.	262	53.17 N	2.54 W
Whitby Abbey ʋ[1]	44	54.28 N	0.38 W
Whitchurch, Eng., U.K.	42	51.53 N	0.51 W
Whitchurch, Eng., U.K.	42	51.14 N	1.20 W
Whitchurch, Eng., U.K.	42	51.52 N	2.39 W
Whitchurch, Eng., U.K.	42	52.58 N	2.41 W
Whitchurch-Stouffville	212	43.58 N	79.15 W
Whitcombe, Mount ∧	172	43.13 S	170.55 E
White, Ga., U.S.	192	34.16 N	84.44 W
White, S.D., U.S.	198	44.26 N	96.38 W
White □[6]	216	40.45 N	86.46 W
White ≃, B.C., Can.	182	50.23 N	115.35 W
White ≃, On., Can.	190	48.33 N	86.16 W
White ≃, N.A.	180	63.11 N	139.36 W
White ≃, U.S.	194	33.53 N	91.03 W
White ≃, U.S.	198	43.45 N	99.30 W
White ≃, U.S.	200	40.04 N	109.41 W
White ≃, Az., U.S.	200	33.44 N	110.13 W
White ≃, In., U.S.	194	38.25 N	87.44 W
White ≃, Mi., U.S.	190	43.25 N	86.21 W
White ≃, Nv., U.S.	204	37.42 N	115.10 W
White ≃, Or., U.S.	224	45.14 N	121.04 W
White ≃, Tx., U.S.	196	33.14 N	100.56 W
White ≃, Vt., U.S.	188	43.37 N	72.20 W
White ≃, Wa., U.S.	224	47.12 N	122.15 W
White ≃, Wa., U.S.	224	47.50 N	120.49 W
White ≃, Wi., U.S.	190	46.36 N	90.42 W
White ≃, Wi., U.S.	216	42.41 N	88.17 W
White, East Fork ≃, Az., U.S.	200	33.47 N	110.00 W
White, East Fork ≃, In., U.S.	194	38.33 N	87.14 W
White, Lake ⊜	162	21.05 S	129.00 E
White, Lake ⊜[1]	218	39.07 N	83.02 W
White, North Fork ≃, Az., U.S.	200	33.47 N	110.00 W
White, North Fork ≃, Co., U.S.	200	39.58 N	107.38 W
White, South Fork ≃	200	39.58 N	107.38 W
White, West Fork ≃	224	47.07 N	121.37 W
White Bay c	186	50.00 N	56.30 W
White Bear Indian Reserve ◆[4]	184	49.45 N	102.15 W
White Bear Lake	190	45.03 N	93.00 W
Whitebear Lake ⊜	184	51.05 N	108.05 W
White Bluff	194	36.06 N	87.13 W
White Breast Creek ≃	190	41.24 N	93.02 W
White Butte ∧	198	46.23 N	103.19 W
Whitecap Lake ⊜	184	56.54 N	95.14 W
White Cap Mountain ∧	188	45.35 N	69.13 W
White Castle	194	30.10 N	91.08 W
White Center	224	47.31 N	122.21 W
White Chuck ≃	224	48.11 N	121.27 W
White City, Fl., U.S.	220	29.53 N	85.13 W
White City, Ks., U.S.	198	38.47 N	96.44 W
White City Stadium ♠	260	51.31 N	0.14 W
White Clay Creek ≃, U.S.	198	43.12 N	102.48 W
White Clay Creek ≃, U.S.	285	39.42 N	75.37 W
White Cliffs, Austl.	162	28.26 S	122.57 E
White Cliffs, Austl.	166	30.51 S	143.05 E
White Cloud	190	43.33 N	85.46 W
White Cloud Island I	212	44.50 N	80.58 W
Whitecoomb ∧, N.Z.	172	45.36 S	169.05 E
White Coomb ∧, Scot., U.K.	44	55.26 N	3.20 W
Whitecourt	182	54.09 N	115.41 W
White Creek	210	42.58 N	73.18 W
White Creek ≃, In., U.S.	218	38.58 N	86.01 W
White Creek ≃, Wa., U.S.	224	46.01 N	121.08 W
White Deer, Pa., U.S.	210	41.05 N	76.52 W
White Deer, Tx., U.S.	196	35.26 N	101.10 W
White Deer Creek ≃	210	41.05 N	76.53 W
White Earth ≃	198	48.09 N	102.42 W
White Earth Indian Reservation ◆[4]	198	47.18 N	95.50 W
White Esk ≃	44	55.12 N	3.10 W
Whiteface	196	33.36 N	102.37 W
Whiteface ≃	190	46.58 N	92.48 W
Whiteface Mountain ∧	188	44.22 N	73.54 W
Whitefield, Eng., U.K.	44	53.33 N	2.18 W
Whitefield, Eng., U.K.	262	53.33 N	2.18 W
Whitefield, N.H., U.S.	188	44.22 N	71.36 W
Whitefish	202	48.24 N	114.20 W
Whitefish ≃	190	45.55 N	86.57 W
Whitefish Bay	216	43.06 N	87.54 W
Whitefish Bay c, On., Can.	184	49.26 N	94.14 W
Whitefish Bay c, N.A.	190	46.40 N	84.50 W
Whitefish Lake ⊜, Ab., Can.	182	54.22 N	111.55 W
Whitefish Lake ⊜, Mb., Can.	184	55.34 N	93.13 W
Whitefish Lake ⊜, N.T., Can.	176	62.41 N	106.48 W
Whitefish Lake ⊜, On., Can.	190	48.03 N	84.29 W
Whitefish Lake ⊜, On., Can.	212	45.18 N	79.47 W
Whitefish Lake ⊜, On., Can.	212	44.31 N	76.14 W
Whitefish Lake ⊜, Ak., U.S.	180	61.21 N	160.00 W
Whitefish Lake ⊜, Mt., U.S.	202	48.27 N	114.22 W
White Fish Lake Indian Reserve ◆[4]	182	54.20 N	111.45 W
Whitefish Point	190	46.45 N	84.59 W
Whitefish Point ≻	190	46.45 N	85.00 W
Whitefish Range ⋏	202	48.40 N	114.26 W
Whiteford	208	39.42 N	76.20 W
Whiteford Point ≻	42	51.38 N	4.14 W
White Fox	184	53.27 N	104.05 W
White Fox ≃	184	53.32 N	104.00 W
Whitegate	48	51.50 N	8.14 W
White Gull Creek ≃	184	53.44 N	104.20 W
Whitehall (Paulstown), Ire.	48	52.41 N	7.01 W
Whitehall, Scot., U.K.	46	59.07 N	2.37 W
White Hall, Ar., U.S.	194	34.16 N	92.05 W
White Hall, Il., U.S.	219	39.26 N	90.24 W
White Hall, Md., U.S.	208	39.37 N	76.37 W
Whitehall, Mi., U.S.	190	43.24 N	86.20 W
Whitehall, Mt., U.S.	202	45.52 N	112.05 W
Whitehall, N.Y., U.S.	188	43.33 N	73.24 W
Whitehall, Oh., U.S.	218	39.58 N	82.53 W
White Hall, Pa., U.S.	210	40.22 N	79.59 W
Whitehall, Pa., U.S.	214	40.21 N	79.59 W
Whitehall, Wi., U.S.	190	44.22 N	91.18 W
Whitehaven, Eng., U.K.	44	54.33 N	3.35 W
White Haven, Pa., U.S.	210	41.03 N	75.46 W
Whitehead	48	54.46 N	5.43 W
White Holme Reservoir ⊜[1]	262	53.41 N	2.02 W
Whitehorse, Yk., Can.	180	60.43 N	135.03 W
White Horse, N.J., U.S.	208	40.11 N	74.42 W
White Horse, Vale of ∨	42	51.37 N	1.37 W
Whitehorse Hill ∧[2]	42	51.34 N	1.34 W
Whitehouse, Scot., U.K.	46	57.13 N	2.37 W
Whitehouse, N.J., U.S.	210	40.37 N	74.46 W
Whitehouse, Oh., U.S.	216	41.31 N	83.48 W
White House, Tn., U.S.	194	36.35 N	86.49 W
Whitehouse, Tx., U.S.	222	32.13 N	95.14 W
White House ʋ	284c	38.54 N	77.02 W
White House Station	210	40.36 N	74.46 W
White Island I, Ant.	9	66.44 S	48.35 E
White Island I, N.T., Can.	176	65.50 N	84.50 W
White Island I, N.Z.	172	37.31 S	177.11 E
White Lake, Mi., U.S.	281	42.41 N	83.33 W
White Lake, N.Y., U.S.	210	41.40 N	74.50 W
White Lake, S.D., U.S.	198	43.43 N	98.42 W
White Lake, Wi., U.S.	190	45.09 N	88.45 W
White Lake ⊜, On., Can.	190	48.48 N	85.36 W
White Lake ⊜, On., Can.	212	44.47 N	76.45 W
White Lake ⊜, On., Can.	212	45.18 N	76.31 W
White Lake ⊜, On., Can.	212	44.27 N	77.03 W
White Lake ⊜, La., U.S.	194	29.45 N	92.30 W
White Lake ⊜, Mi., U.S.	281	42.40 N	83.34 W
Whiteland	218	39.33 N	86.05 W
Whitelaw	182	56.07 N	118.04 W
Whiteley Village	260	51.21 N	0.26 W
White Lick Creek ≃	218	39.30 N	86.23 W
White Lick Creek, East Fork ≃	218	39.35 N	86.22 W
White Lick Creek, West Fork ≃	218	39.38 N	86.23 W
Whiteman Air Force Base ■	194	38.44 N	93.34 W
Whiteman Airpark ⊠	280	34.15 N	118.25 W
Whiteman Range ⋏	164	5.50 S	149.55 E
Whitemans Creek ≃	212	43.10 N	80.21 W
Whitemark	166	40.07 S	148.01 E
White Marsh	284b	39.23 N	76.26 W
Whitemarsh Run ≃	284b	39.22 N	76.25 W
White Meadow Lake	210	40.55 N	74.31 W
White Meadow Lake ⊜	276	40.55 N	74.31 W
White Mills	210	41.32 N	75.12 W
White Mountain	180	64.41 N	163.24 W
White Mountain Peak ∧	204	37.38 N	118.15 W
White Mountains ⋏, U.S.	204	37.30 N	118.15 W
White Mountains ⋏, Az., U.S.	200	33.45 N	109.40 W
White Mountains ⋏, N.H., U.S.	188	44.10 N	71.35 W
Whitemouth	184	49.57 N	95.59 W
Whitemouth ≃	184	50.07 N	96.02 W
Whitemouth Lake ⊜	184	49.14 N	95.40 W
Whitemud ≃	184	50.15 N	98.37 W
Whiten Head ≻	46	58.34 N	4.36 W
White Nile (Al-Baḥr al-Abyaḍ) ≃	140	15.38 N	32.31 E
White Nile Dam → Jabal al-Awliyā', Khazzān ◆[6]	140	15.14 N	32.29 E
White Oak, Md., U.S.	284c	39.02 N	77.00 W
White Oak, Pa., U.S.	279b	40.20 N	79.48 W
White Oak, Tx., U.S.	222	32.32 N	94.52 W
White Oak ≃	192	34.40 N	77.07 W
White Oak Creek ≃, Oh., U.S.	218	38.47 N	83.57 W
White Oak Creek ≃, Tx., U.S.	194	33.16 N	94.39 W
White Oak Creek, East Fork ≃	218	39.00 N	83.53 W
White Oak Creek, North Fork ≃	218	39.00 N	83.53 W
White Oak Lake ⊜[1]	194	33.40 N	93.10 W
White Oak Regional Park ♠	279a	40.21 N	79.47 W
White Pass)(, N.A.	180	59.38 N	135.05 W
White Pass)(, Wa., U.S.	224	46.38 N	121.24 W
White Pigeon	216	41.47 N	85.38 W
White Pine, Mi., U.S.	190	46.45 N	89.35 W
Whitepine, Mt., U.S.	182	47.45 N	115.29 W
White Pine, Tn., U.S.	192	36.06 N	83.17 W
White Pines, Ca., U.S.	226	38.18 N	120.21 W
White Pines, Il., U.S.	278	41.57 N	87.57 W
White Plains, Md., U.S.	208	38.35 N	76.56 W
White Plains, N.Y., U.S.	210	41.02 N	73.45 W
White Plains, N.C., U.S.	192	36.26 N	80.38 W
White Pond ⊜	283	42.26 N	71.23 W
White River, On., Can.	190	48.35 N	85.15 W
Whiteriver, Az., U.S.	200	33.50 N	109.57 W
White River, S.D., U.S.	198	43.34 N	100.44 W
White River Junction	188	43.38 N	72.19 W
White Rock	224	49.02 N	122.49 W
White Rock Creek ≃, Ks., U.S.	198	39.55 N	97.51 W
White Rock Creek ≃, Tx., U.S.	222	30.54 N	95.16 W
White Rock Creek ≃, Tx., U.S.	222	32.43 N	96.44 W
White Rock Lake ⊜[1]	222	32.50 N	96.44 W
White Rocks ∧	192	36.40 N	83.27 W
Whiterocks ≃	200	40.26 N	109.55 W
White Roding	260	51.48 N	0.16 E
White Russia → Belorusskaja Sovetskaja Socialističeskaja Respublika □[3]	76	53.50 N	28.00 E
Whitesail Lake ⊜	182	53.30 N	127.00 W
White Salmon	224	45.43 N	121.29 W
White Salmon ≃	224	45.43 N	121.31 W
Whitesand ≃	184	51.34 N	101.55 W
White Sands Beach	207	41.18 N	72.09 W
White Sands Missile Range ■	200	32.23 N	106.28 W
White Sands National Monument ♠	200	32.46 N	106.20 W
Whitesboro, N.J., U.S.	208	39.02 N	74.51 W
Whitesboro, N.Y., U.S.	210	43.07 N	75.17 W
Whitesboro, Tx., U.S.	196	33.39 N	96.54 W
Whitesburg	192	37.07 N	82.49 W
White Sea → Beloje more ⊤[2]	24	65.30 N	38.00 E
White Settlement	222	32.45 N	97.27 W
Whiteshell Provincial Park ♠	184	50.00 N	95.25 W
Whiteside	219	39.11 N	91.01 W
Whiteside, Canal ʯ	254	53.55 S	70.15 W
White's Landing	214	41.25 N	82.54 W
White Springs	192	30.19 N	82.45 W
White Stone	208	37.38 N	76.23 W
Whitestone ◆[8]	276	40.47 N	73.49 W
White Stone Lake ⊜	184	56.25 N	97.31 W
Whitestown	218	39.59 N	86.20 W
White Sulphur Springs, Mt., U.S.	202	46.32 N	110.54 W
White Sulphur Springs, N.Y., U.S.	210	41.48 N	74.50 W
White Sulphur Springs, W.V., U.S.	192	37.47 N	80.17 W
Whites Valley	210	41.42 N	75.22 W
Whitesville, Ky., U.S.	194	37.40 N	86.52 W
Whitesville, N.Y., U.S.	210	42.02 N	77.45 W
Whitesville, W.V., U.S.	188	37.58 N	81.31 W
White Swan	224	46.22 N	120.43 W
Whiteswan Lakes ⊜	184	54.05 N	105.10 W
Whitevale	212	43.53 N	79.09 W
White Valley	214	40.25 N	79.36 W
Whiteville, N.C., U.S.	192	34.20 N	78.42 W
Whiteville, Tn., U.S.	194	35.19 N	89.08 W
White Volta (Volta Blanche) ≃	150	9.10 N	1.15 W
Whitewater, Ks., U.S.	198	37.57 N	97.08 W
Whitewater, Mt., U.S.	202	48.45 N	107.37 W
Whitewater, Wi., U.S.	216	42.50 N	88.43 W
Whitewater ≃, U.S.	218	39.10 N	84.47 W
Whitewater ≃, Ca., U.S.	204	33.30 N	116.03 W
Whitewater ≃, Mo., U.S.	194	37.01 N	89.43 W
Whitewater, Dry Fork ≃	218	39.11 N	84.47 W
Whitewater, East Fork ≃	218	39.24 N	85.01 W
Whitewater, Greens Fork ≃	218	39.45 N	85.07 W
Whitewater, Nolands Fork ≃	218	39.41 N	85.07 W
Whitewater Baldy ∧	200	33.20 N	108.39 W
Whitewater Bay c	220	25.16 N	81.00 W
Whitewater Creek ≃, N.A.	202	48.30 N	107.11 W
Whitewater Creek ≃, Ga., U.S.	192	32.21 N	84.03 W
Whitewater Creek ≃, Wi., U.S.	216	42.52 N	88.45 W
Whitewater Lake ⊜, Mb., Can.	184	49.15 N	100.20 W
Whitewater Lake ⊜, Wi., U.S.	216	42.47 N	88.42 W
Whitewater State Park ♠	218	39.36 N	84.58 W
White Woman Creek ≃	198	38.25 N	100.54 W
Whitewood, Austl.	166	21.28 S	143.36 E
Whitewood, Sk., Can.	184	50.20 N	102.15 W
Whitewood, S.D., U.S.	198	44.27 N	103.38 W
Whitewood, Lake ⊜	198	44.20 N	97.18 W
Whitewright	196	33.30 N	96.23 W
Whitfield	42	51.09 N	1.18 E
Whithorn, Jam.	241q	18.15 N	78.02 W
Whithorn, Scot., U.K.	44	54.44 N	4.25 W
Whitianga	172	36.50 S	175.42 E
Whiting, In., U.S.	216	41.40 N	87.29 W
Whiting, Ia., U.S.	198	42.07 N	96.08 W
Whiting, Ks., U.S.	198	39.35 N	95.36 W
Whiting, N.J., U.S.	208	39.57 N	74.22 W
Whiting, Wi., U.S.	190	44.29 N	89.33 W
Whiting Bay	44	55.29 N	5.06 W
Whiting Field Naval Air Station ■	194	30.43 N	87.02 W
Whitingham	207	42.47 N	72.53 W
Whitinsville	207	42.06 N	71.40 W
Whitland	42	51.50 N	4.37 W
Whitley □[6]	216	41.10 N	85.29 W

Symbols in the index entries represent the broad categories identified in the key at the right. Symbols with superior numbers (⋏[1]) identify subcategories (see complete key on page *I · 1*).

Kartensymbole in dem Registerverzeichnis stellen die rechts in Schlüssel erklärten Kategorien dar. Symbole mit hochgestellten Ziffern (⋏[1]) bezeichnen Unterabteilungen einer Kategorie (vgl. vollständiger Schlüssel auf Seite *I · 1*).

Los símbolos incluídos en el texto del índice representan las grandes categorias identificadas con la clave a la derecha. Los símbolos con numeros en su parte superior (⋏[1]) identifican las subcategorías (véase la clave completa en la página *I · 1*).

Les symboles de l'index représentent les catégories indiquées dans la légende à droite. Les symboles suivis d'un indice (⋏[1]) représentent des sous-catégories (voir légende complète à la page *I · 1*).

Os símbolos incluídos no texto do índice representam as grandes categorias identificadas com a chave à direita. Os símbolos com números em sua parte superior (⋏[1]) identificam as subcategorias (veja-se a chave completa à página *I · 1*).

∧ Mountain	Berg	Montaña	Montagne	Montanha
⋏ Mountains	Berge	Montañas	Montagnes	Montanhas
)(Pass	Pass	Paso	Col	Passo
∨ Valley, Canyon	Tal, Cañon	Valle, Cañón	Vallée, Canyon	Vale, Canhão
≚ Plain	Ebene	Llano	Plaine	Planície
≻ Cape	Kap	Cabo	Cap	Cabo
I Island	Insel	Isla	Île	Ilha
II Islands	Inseln	Islas	Îles	Ilhas
≗ Other Topographic Features	Andere Topographische Objekte	Otros Elementos Topográficos	Autres données topographiques	Outros acidentes topográficos

ESPAÑOL — Nombre / Página / Lat.°′ / Long.°′ W = Oeste

Whitley Bay 44 55.03 N 1.25 W
Whitley City 192 36.43 N 84.28 W
Whitley Row 260 51.15 N 0.09 E
Whitman 207 42.04 N 70.56 W
Whitman Mission National Historic Site ⊥ 202 46.01 N 118.30 W
Whitmans Pond ◎ 283 42.12 N 70.57 W
Whitman Square 208 39.45 N 75.03 W
Whitmire 192 34.30 N 81.36 W
Whitmore Lake 216 42.25 N 83.46 W
Whitmore Lake ◎ 281 42.26 N 83.45 W
Whitmore Mountains ⋏ 9 82.35 S 104.30 W
Whitmore Village 229c 21.30 N 158.01 W
Whitner Heights 226 36.37 N 119.32 W
Whitney, On., Can. 212 45.30 N 78.14 W
Whitney, Pa., U.S. 214 40.15 N 79.24 W
Whitney, Tx., U.S. 222 31.57 N 97.19 W
Whitney, Lake ◎[1] 222 31.55 N 97.23 W
Whitney, Mount ∧ 204 36.35 N 118.18 W
Whitney Point 210 42.19 N 75.58 W
Whitney Point Lake ◎[1] 210 42.25 N 75.55 W
Whitney Woods Reservation ♦ 283 42.13 N 70.51 W
Whitstable 42 51.22 N 1.02 E
Whitsunday Island I 166 20.17 S 148.59 E
Whitsunday Islands National Park ♦ 166 20.20 S 149.00 E
Whittaker 216 42.08 N 83.36 W
Whittemore, Ia., U.S. 198 43.03 N 94.25 W
Whittemore, Mi., U.S. 190 44.14 N 83.48 W
Whittier, Ak., U.S. 180 60.47 N 148.42 W
Whittier, Ca., U.S. 228 33.58 N 118.01 W
Whittier, N.C., U.S. 192 35.26 N 83.22 W
Whittier Narrows Dam ✦[6] 280 34.01 N 118.04 W
Whittier Narrows Flood Control Basin ◎[1] 280 34.02 N 118.04 W
Whittingham 44 55.24 N 1.54 W
Whittington 42 52.52 N 3.00 W
Whittle, Cap › 186 50.11 N 60.08 W
Whittle Hill ∧[2] 262 53.40 N 2.16 W
Whittle-le-Woods 262 53.41 N 2.38 W
Whittlesea, Austl. 169 37.31 S 145.07 E
Whittlesea, Ciskei 158 32.10 S 26.50 E
Whittlesey 42 52.34 N 0.08 W
Whittlesey, Mount ∧[2] 190 46.18 N 90.37 W
Whitwell 194 35.12 N 85.31 W
Whitwick 42 52.44 N 1.21 W
Whitworth 44 53.40 N 2.10 W
Whitworth Peak ∧ 224 49.05 N 121.13 W
Wholdaia Lake ◎ 176 60.43 N 104.10 W
Whonock 224 49.11 N 122.28 W
W. Howard Frankland Bridge ✦[5] 220 27.56 N 82.35 W
Whyalla 166 33.02 S 137.35 E
Whycocomagh 186 45.59 N 61.07 W
Whymper, Mount ∧ 224 48.57 N 124.10 W
Wiang Pa Pao 110 19.22 N 99.30 E
Wiang Phan 110 20.26 N 99.53 E
Wiarton 212 44.45 N 81.09 W
Wiasi 150 10.21 N 1.20 W
Wiau Lake ◎ 182 55.23 N 111.18 W
Wiawso 150 6.12 N 2.29 W
Wiay I 46 57.23 N 7.13 W
Wiązów 30 50.49 N 17.11 E
Wibaux 198 46.59 N 104.11 W
Wiblingen ✦[8] 58 48.21 N 9.58 E
Wichian Buri 110 15.39 N 101.07 E
Wichita 198 37.41 N 97.20 W
Wichita ≃ 196 34.07 N 98.10 W
Wichita Falls 196 33.54 N 98.29 W
Wichita Mountains ⋏ 196 34.45 N 98.40 W
Wichlinghofen ✦[8] 263 51.27 N 7.30 E
Wick 46 58.26 N 3.06 W
Wick ≃ 46 58.27 N 3.05 W
Wickatunk 276 40.21 N 74.14 W
Wickede 52 51.29 N 7.52 E
Wickede ✦[8] 263 51.32 N 7.37 E
Wickenburg 200 33.58 N 112.43 W
Wickepin 162 32.46 S 117.30 E
Wicker Memorial Park ♦ 278 41.34 N 87.28 W
Wickett 196 31.34 N 102.59 W
Wickford 42 51.38 N 0.31 E
Wickham, P.Q., Can. 206 45.45 N 72.30 W
Wickham, Eng., U.K. 42 50.54 N 1.10 W
Wickham ≃ 164 16.22 S 131.06 E
Wickham, Cape › 166 39.36 S 143.57 E
Wickham Bishops 260 51.47 N 0.40 E
Wickham Market 42 52.09 N 1.22 E
Wickiup Reservoir ◎[1] 202 43.40 N 121.43 W
Wickliffe, Ky., U.S. 194 36.58 N 89.05 W
Wickliffe, Oh., U.S. 214 41.06 N 80.43 W
Wickliffe, Oh., U.S. 214 41.36 N 81.27 W
Wicklow 48 52.59 N 6.03 W
Wicklow □[6] 48 53.00 N 6.30 W
Wicklow Head › 48 52.58 N 6.00 W
Wicklow Mountains ⋏ 48 53.02 N 6.24 W
Wickrath 56 51.07 N 6.24 E
Wicksteed Lake ◎ 190 46.46 N 79.40 W
Wicomico 208 37.17 N 76.31 W
Wicomico □[6] 208 38.22 N 75.36 W
Wicomico ≃ 208 38.13 N 75.55 W
Wicomico Church 208 37.49 N 76.23 W
Wiconisco 208 40.34 N 76.41 W
Wiconisco Creek ≃ 208 40.32 N 76.58 W
Wid ≃ 262 51.45 N 0.27 E
Widas ≃ 115a 7.30 S 112.08 E
Widden Brook ≃ 170 32.32 S 150.22 E
Widdern 56 49.19 N 9.25 E
Widdert ✦[8] 263 51.08 N 7.04 E
Widdop Reservoir ◎[1] 262 53.48 N 2.06 W
Widdrington Station 44 55.15 N 1.36 W
Wide Bay c, Pap. N. Gui. 164 5.05 S 152.05 E
Wide Bay c, Ak., U.S. 180 57.20 N 156.25 W
Widecombe in the Moor 42 50.35 N 3.48 W
Widemouth Bay 42 50.47 N 4.32 W
Widen 188 38.27 N 80.51 W
Widener College ʋ[2] 285 39.52 N 75.21 W
Wide Open 44 55.03 N 1.38 W
Widerøe, Mount ∧ 9 72.08 S 23.30 E
Wide Ruin Wash V 200 35.13 N 109.52 W
Widford 260 51.43 N 0.27 E
Widgeegoara Creek ≃ 166 27.30 S 145.55 E
Widgiemooltha 162 31.30 S 121.34 E
Widnes 44 53.22 N 2.44 W
Wi-do I 98 35.36 N 126.17 E
Widodaren 115a 7.25 S 111.14 E
Widuchowa 54 53.10 N 14.25 E
Wiebelskirchen 56 49.22 N 7.11 E
Więcbork 30 53.22 N 17.30 E
Wieck 54 54.06 N 13.26 E
Wied ≃ 56 50.26 N 7.27 E
Wieda 54 51.38 N 10.34 E
Wiederitzsch 54 51.24 N 12.22 E
Wiedlisbach 58 47.15 N 7.39 E
Wiefelstede 52 53.15 N 8.07 E
Wiehe 54 51.16 N 11.25 E
Wiehengebirge ⋏ 52 52.20 N 8.40 E
Wiehengebirge, Naturpark ♦ 52 52.20 N 8.20 E
Wiehl 56 50.57 N 7.31 E
Wiek 54 54.37 N 13.17 E
Wieleń 30 52.54 N 16.10 E
Wielichowo 30 52.08 N 16.21 E
Wieliczka 30 49.59 N 20.04 E
Wielkopolska ✦[1] 30 51.50 N 17.20 E
Wielkopolski Park Narodowy ♦ 30 52.15 N 16.50 E
Wieluń 30 51.14 N 18.34 E
Wiemelhausen ✦[8] 263 51.28 N 7.13 E
Wien (Vienna), Öst. 61 48.13 N 16.20 E

FRANÇAIS — Nom / Page / Lat.°′ / Long.°′ W = Ouest

Wien (Vienna), Öst. 264b 48.13 N 16.20 E
Wien □[3] 264b 48.12 N 16.22 E
Wien ≃ 264b 48.13 N 16.23 E
Wien, Universität ʋ[2] 264b 48.13 N 16.22 E
Wiener Berg ⋏[2] 264b 48.10 N 16.22 E
Wienerherberg 264b 48.03 N 16.33 E
Wiener Neudorf 61 48.05 N 16.19 E
Wiener Neustadt 61 47.49 N 16.15 E
Wiener Neustädter Kanal ≍ 61 48.05 N 16.22 E
Wienerwald ⋏ 61 48.10 N 16.00 E
Wienhagen ∧[2] 263 51.08 N 7.33 E
Wienhausen 52 52.35 N 10.11 E
Wien-Schwechat, Flughafen ⊠ 264b 48.07 N 16.33 E
Wiepke 54 52.36 N 11.20 E
Wieprz ≃ 30 51.34 N 21.49 E
Wieprza ≃ 30 54.26 N 16.22 E
Wieprz-Krzna, Kanał ≍ 30 51.56 N 22.56 E
Wiera ≃ 56 50.55 N 9.10 E
Wierden 52 52.22 N 6.35 E
Wieren 54 52.53 N 10.39 E
Wiergate 194 31.00 N 93.42 W
Wieringermeer ✦[1] 52 52.45 N 5.00 E
Wieringerwerf 52 52.51 N 5.02 E
Wieruszów 30 51.18 N 18.08 E
Wierzyca ≃ 30 53.51 N 18.50 E
Wies 61 46.43 N 15.16 E
Wies ʋ[1] 58 47.40 N 10.53 E
Wiesa 54 50.36 N 13.01 E
Wiesau 60 49.55 N 12.11 E
Wiesbaden 56 50.05 N 8.14 E
Wiesbaden □[5] 56 50.20 N 8.20 E
Wiescheid ✦[8] 263 51.08 N 6.59 E
Wiescherhöfen 263 51.39 N 7.46 E
Wiese ≃ 58 47.35 N 7.35 E
Wiesede 52 53.27 N 7.46 E
Wieselburg 61 48.08 N 15.09 E
Wiesen 58 46.43 N 9.43 E
Wiesenburg 54 52.07 N 12.26 E
Wiesenfeld 56 51.16 N 10.06 E
Wiesensteig 56 48.34 N 9.37 E
Wiesent ≃ 60 49.42 N 11.05 E
Wiesentheid 56 49.47 N 10.20 E
Wieseth ≃ 56 49.10 N 10.39 E
Wiesloch 56 49.17 N 8.42 E
Wiesmoor 52 53.25 N 7.43 E
Wieting 61 46.52 N 14.32 E
Wietmarschen 52 52.31 N 7.07 E
Wietze 52 52.39 N 9.50 E
Wietzen 52 52.43 N 9.04 E
Wigan 44 53.33 N 2.38 W
Wigan □[8] 262 53.32 N 2.35 W
Wiggensbach 58 47.44 N 10.14 E
Wigger ≃ 58 47.18 N 7.53 E
Wiggington 260 51.47 N 0.38 W
Wiggins, Co., U.S. 198 40.13 N 104.04 W
Wiggins, Ms., U.S. 194 30.51 N 89.08 W
Wiggins Fork ≃ 202 43.27 N 109.28 W
Wigglesworth 44 54.01 N 2.17 W
Wight, Isle of I 42 50.40 N 1.20 W
Wigmore, Eng., U.K. 42 52.19 N 2.51 W
Wigmore, Eng., U.K. 260 51.21 N 0.35 E
Wignehies 50 50.01 N 4.00 E
Wigston 42 52.36 N 1.05 W
Wigton 44 54.49 N 3.09 W
Wigtown 44 54.52 N 4.26 W
Wigtown Bay c 44 54.46 N 4.15 W
Wijchen 52 51.48 N 5.43 E
Wijhe 52 52.24 N 6.07 E
Wijk aan Zee 52 52.29 N 4.35 E
Wijk bij Duurstede 52 51.58 N 5.20 E
Wil 58 47.27 N 9.03 E
Wilbarger Creek ≃ 222 30.11 N 97.23 W
Wilber 198 40.28 N 96.57 W
Wilberforce, Austl. 170 33.33 S 150.50 E
Wilberforce, Oh., U.S. 218 39.42 N 83.52 W
Wilberforce Falls ∟ 176 67.07 N 108.47 W
Wilbraham 207 42.07 N 72.25 W
Wilbur 202 47.45 N 118.42 W
Wilburton 196 34.55 N 95.18 W
Wilcannia 166 31.34 S 143.23 E
Wilcock, Península ›[1] 254 50.40 S 74.00 W
Wilcox, Sk., Can. 184 50.07 N 104.44 W
Wilcox, Ne., U.S. 198 40.21 N 99.10 W
Wilcox, Pa., U.S. 214 41.34 N 78.41 W
Wilcox, Tx., U.S. 222 30.27 N 96.22 W
Wilcox, Mount ∧ 207 42.13 N 73.16 W
Wildalpen 61 47.39 N 14.59 E
Wildau 54 52.19 N 13.38 E
Wildbad im Schwarzwald 56 48.45 N 8.32 E
Wildberg, B.R.D. 56 48.37 N 8.44 E
Wildberg, D.D.R. 54 52.52 N 12.37 E
Wildboarclough 262 53.13 N 2.02 W
Wildcat Canyon Regional Park ♦ 282 37.56 N 122.17 W
Wildcat Creek ≃, Ca., U.S. 282 37.57 N 122.23 W
Wildcat Creek ≃, In., U.S. 216 40.28 N 86.52 W
Wildcat Creek, Middle Fork ≃ 216 40.25 N 86.46 W
Wildcat Creek, South Fork ≃ 216 40.26 N 86.48 W
Wildcat Hill ∧[2] 184 53.17 N 102.30 W
Wild Coast ±[2] 158 32.30 S 28.45 E
Wilde ✦[8] 288 34.42 S 58.20 W
Wildegg 58 47.25 N 8.11 E
Wildeman ≃ 164 5.33 S 139.13 E
Wildemann 52 51.49 N 10.17 E
Wildenbruch 264a 52.17 N 13.04 E
Wildenfels 54 50.40 N 12.35 E
Wildenstein 58 47.59 N 6.58 E
Wildenthal 54 50.27 N 12.37 E
Wilder 202 43.40 N 116.54 W
Wilderness 158 34.00 S 22.36 E
Wilderness of Judaea (Midbar Yehuda) ✦[2] 132 31.30 N 35.18 E
Wilderness State Park ♦ 190 45.42 N 84.57 W
Wildersville 194 35.46 N 88.21 W
Wildervank 52 53.04 N 6.51 E
Wildeshausen 52 52.54 N 8.26 E
Wildfield 212 43.49 N 79.44 W
Wildflecken 56 50.23 N 9.54 E
Wildfontein 158 31.04 S 24.50 E
Wildhaus 58 47.12 N 9.22 E
Wildhay ≃ 182 54.02 N 117.20 W
Wildhorn ∧ 58 46.21 N 7.22 E
Wildhorse Creek ≃, U.S. 198 40.36 N 102.00 W
Wildhorse Creek ≃, Ok., U.S. 196 34.32 N 97.10 W
Wild Horse Creek ≃, Wy., U.S. 198 44.39 N 106.08 W
Wild Horse Draw V 196 31.11 N 104.50 W
Wild Horse Hill ∧[2] 168a 33.12 S 116.40 E
Wild Horse Lake ◎ 202 48.58 N 110.00 W
Wildnest Lake ◎ 184 55.00 N 102.20 W
Wildon 61 46.53 N 15.31 E
Wild Rice ≃, Mn., U.S. 198 47.20 N 96.50 W
Wild Rice ≃, N.D., U.S. 198 46.45 N 96.47 W
Wild Rice, South Branch ≃ 198 47.12 N 96.38 W
Wildrose, N.D., U.S. 198 48.37 N 103.11 W
Wild Rose, Wi., U.S. 190 44.10 N 89.14 W
Wildseeloder ∧ 64 47.26 N 12.32 E
Wildspitze ∧ 58 46.53 N 10.52 E
Wildstrubel ∧ 58 46.24 N 7.32 E
Wildwood, Ab., Can. 182 53.37 N 115.14 W
Wildwood, Fl., U.S. 220 28.51 N 82.02 W
Wildwood, Il., U.S. 216 42.21 N 88.00 W
Wildwood, N.J., U.S. 208 38.59 N 74.48 W
Wildwood, Pa., U.S. 214 40.36 N 79.58 W
Wildwood, Lake ◎ 276 41.09 N 74.32 W
Wild Wood Beach 284b 39.15 N 76.25 W
Wildwood Canyon Park ♦ 280 34.13 N 118.17 W
Wildwood Crest 208 38.58 N 74.50 W

PORTUGUÊS — Nome / Página / Lat.°′ / Long.°′ W = Oeste

Wiley 224 46.33 N 120.39 W
Wilfersdorf 61 48.35 N 16.38 E
Wilge ≃, S. Afr. 158 25.34 S 29.10 E
Wilge ≃, S. Afr. 158 27.03 S 28.20 E
Wilgena 162 30.46 S 134.44 E
Wilgespruit ≃ 273d 26.07 S 27.52 E
Wilhelm, Lake ◎[1] 214 41.23 N 80.08 W
Wilhelm, Mount ∧ 164 5.45 S 145.05 E
Wilhelmina Gebergte ⋏ 250 3.45 N 56.30 W
Wilhelminakanaal ≍ 52 51.47 N 4.51 E
Wilhelminaoord 52 52.53 N 6.10 E
Wilhelmina Peak → Trikora, Puncak ∧ 164 4.15 S 138.45 E
Wilhelm-Pieck-Stadt Guben 54 51.57 N 14.43 E
Wilhelmsburg 61 48.06 N 15.36 E
Wilhelmsburg ✦[8] 52 53.30 N 10.00 E
Wilhelmshaven 52 53.31 N 8.08 E
Wilhelmshöhe, Schloss ⊥ 56 51.21 N 9.22 E
Wilhelmshorst 54 52.19 N 13.03 E
Wilhelmstadt ✦[8] 264a 52.31 N 13.11 E
Wilhelmstal 156 21.54 S 16.19 E
Wilhelmstein, Schloss ⊥ 52 52.28 N 9.18 E
Wilis, Gunung ∧ 115a 7.48 S 111.45 E
Wilkau-Hasslau 54 50.40 N 12.31 E
Wilkerson Pass)(200 39.02 N 105.32 W
Wilkes-Barre 210 41.14 N 75.52 W
Wilkes-Barre Scranton Airport ⊠ 210 41.20 N 75.45 W
Wilkesboro 192 36.08 N 81.09 W
Wilkes Island I 174a 19.18 N 166.34 E
Wilkes Land ✦[1] 9 69.00 S 120.00 E
Wilkeson 224 47.06 N 122.02 W
Wilket Creek ≃ 275b 43.43 N 79.21 W
Wilket Creek Park ♦ 275b 43.43 N 79.21 W
Wilkhaven 46 57.52 N 3.45 W
Wilkie 184 52.25 N 108.43 W
Wilkinsburg 214 40.26 N 79.51 W
Wilkinson 218 39.53 N 85.36 W
Wilkinson Lakes ◎ 162 29.40 S 132.39 E
Wilkins Sound ɥ 9 70.15 S 73.00 W
Wilkins Township 279b 40.25 N 79.50 W
Will □[6] 216 41.32 N 88.05 W
Will, Mount ∧ 180 57.31 N 128.46 W
Willacoochee 192 31.20 N 83.02 W
Willamette ≃ 202 45.39 N 122.46 W
Willamette, Middle Fork ≃ 202 44.01 N 123.01 W
Willamette, North Fork ≃ 202 43.46 N 122.32 W
Willamina 224 45.04 N 123.29 W
Willamina Creek ≃ 224 45.05 N 123.28 W
Willandra Billabong Creek ≃ 166 33.08 S 144.06 E
Willapa 224 46.40 N 123.39 W
Willapa ≃ 224 46.42 N 123.50 W
Willapa Bay c 224 46.37 N 124.00 W
Willard, Mo., U.S. 194 37.18 N 93.25 W
Willard, N.M., U.S. 200 34.35 N 106.01 W
Willard, N.Y., U.S. 210 42.40 N 76.52 W
Willard, Oh., U.S. 214 41.03 N 82.44 W
Willard, Ut,. U.S. 200 41.24 N 112.02 W
Willard, Wa., U.S. 224 45.48 N 121.38 W
Willards 208 38.23 N 75.20 W
Willaston, Austl. 168b 34.36 S 138.45 E
Willaston, Eng., U.K. 262 53.18 N 3.00 W
Willaumez Peninsula ›[1] 164 5.05 S 150.05 E
Willcox 200 32.15 N 109.49 W
Willcox Playa ◎ 200 32.08 N 109.51 W
Willebadessen 52 51.37 N 9.02 E
Willebroek 50 51.04 N 4.22 E
Willem Pretorius Game Reserve ✦[4] 158 28.16 S 27.13 E
Willemsoord 52 52.49 N 6.05 E
Willemstad, Ned. 52 51.42 N 4.26 E
Willemstad, Ned. Ant. 241s 12.06 N 68.56 W
Willenhall 42 52.36 N 2.02 W
Willerburn Acres 284c 39.03 N 77.10 W
Willeroo 164 15.17 S 131.35 E
Willer-sur-Thur 58 47.51 N 7.05 E
Willerswalde 54 54.07 N 13.08 E
Willesden ✦[8] 260 51.33 N 0.14 W
Willet 210 42.28 N 75.55 W
Willett Pond ◎ 283 42.11 N 71.14 W
Willey Creek ≃ 279a 41.25 N 81.25 W
William, Lac ◎ 206 46.07 N 71.34 W
William, Mount ∧, Austl. 166 37.17 S 142.36 E
William, Mount ∧, Austl. 169 37.13 S 144.47 E
William, Mount ∧[2] 168a 32.57 S 116.07 E
William "Bill" Dannelly Reservoir ◎[1] 194 32.10 N 87.10 W
William Boyce Regional Park ♦ 279b 40.28 N 79.45 W
William Creek 166 28.55 S 136.21 E
William Girling Reservoir ◎[1] 260 51.37 N 0.02 W
William H. Harsha Lake ◎[1] 218 39.02 N 84.07 W
William Lake ◎ 184 53.50 N 99.25 W
William Patterson College ʋ[2] 276 40.56 N 74.12 W
William P. Gleason Park ♦ 278 41.33 N 87.21 W
William Preston Lane Jr. Memorial Bridge ✦[5] 208 39.00 N 76.28 W
Williams, Austl. 168a 33.01 S 116.52 E
Williams, Az., U.S. 200 35.14 N 112.11 W
Williams, Ca., U.S. 226 39.09 N 122.08 W
Williams, Ia., U.S. 190 42.29 N 93.32 W
Williams, Mn., U.S. 198 48.46 N 94.57 W
Williams □[6] 216 41.35 N 84.33 W
Williams ≃, Austl. 166 20.04 S 141.08 E
Williams ≃, Austl. 168a 32.59 S 116.24 E
Williams ≃, Austl. 170 32.45 S 151.45 E
Williams, Cape › 9 70.29 S 164.05 E
Williams Air Force Base ■ 200 33.18 N 111.40 W
Williams Bay 216 42.34 N 88.32 W
Williamsburg, On., Can. 212 44.58 N 75.15 W
Williamsburg, In., U.S. 218 39.57 N 84.59 W
Williamsburg, Ia., U.S. 190 41.39 N 92.00 W
Williamsburg, Ky., U.S. 192 36.44 N 84.09 W
Williamsburg, Ma., U.S. 207 42.23 N 72.43 W
Williamsburg, Mo., U.S. 219 38.55 N 91.42 W
Williamsburg, Oh., U.S. 218 39.03 N 84.03 W
Williamsburg, Pa., U.S. 214 40.27 N 78.12 W
Williamsburg, Va., U.S. 208 37.16 N 76.42 W
Williamsburg ✦[8] 276 40.42 N 73.57 W
Williamsburg Bridge ✦[5] 276 40.43 N 73.58 W
Williams Center 216 41.26 N 84.36 W
Williams Creek ≃, Austl. 274a 33.57 S 150.58 E
Williams Creek ≃, In., U.S. 218 39.36 N 85.09 W
Williamsdale 171b 35.35 S 149.09 E
Williamsfield, Jam. 241q 17.56 N 77.46 W
Williamsfield, Oh., U.S. 214 41.32 N 80.32 W
Williams Fork ≃ 200 40.26 N 107.39 W
Williams Lake 182 52.08 N 122.09 W
Williams Lake Indian Reserve ✦[4] 182 52.07 N 122.00 W
Williams Mountain ∧[2] 194 34.15 N 94.33 W

Williamson, N.Y., U.S. 210 43.13 N 77.11 W
Williamson, W.V., U.S. 192 37.40 N 82.16 W
Williamson □[6] 222 30.40 N 97.32 W
Williamson ≃ 202 42.28 N 121.57 W
Williamson Head › 9 69.09 S 157.49 E
Williamsport, Nf., Can. 186 50.32 N 56.19 W
Williamsport, In., U.S. 216 40.17 N 87.17 W
Williamsport, Oh., U.S. 214 39.35 N 83.07 W
Williamsport, Pa., U.S. 210 41.14 N 77.00 W
Williamston, Mi., U.S. 216 42.41 N 84.16 W
Williamston, N.C., U.S. 192 35.51 N 77.03 W
Williamston, S.C., U.S. 192 34.37 N 82.28 W
Williamstown, Austl. 168b 34.40 S 138.53 E
Williamstown, Austl. 169 37.52 S 144.54 E
Williamstown, On., Can. 206 45.08 N 74.35 W
Williamstown, Ky., U.S. 218 38.38 N 84.33 W
Williamstown, Ma., U.S. 207 42.42 N 73.12 W
Williamstown, N.J., U.S. 208 39.41 N 74.59 W
Williamstown, N.Y., U.S. 212 43.26 N 75.54 W
Williamstown, Pa., U.S. 208 40.34 N 76.37 W
Williamstown, Vt., U.S. 188 44.07 N 72.32 W
Williamstown, W.V., U.S. 188 39.24 N 81.27 W
Williamstown Junction 285 39.45 N 74.56 W
Williamstown Lake ◎[1] 218 38.41 N 84.32 W
Williamsville, Il., U.S. 219 39.57 N 89.32 W
Williamsville, N.Y., U.S. 210 42.57 N 78.44 W
Williamtown 170 32.49 S 151.50 E
Willich 56 51.16 N 6.33 E
Willikies 240c 17.05 N 61.42 W
Willimantic 207 41.42 N 72.12 W
Willimantic ≃ 207 41.43 N 72.12 W
Willingale 260 51.44 N 0.19 E
Willingboro 208 40.01 N 74.52 W
Willingdon, Ab., Can. 182 53.50 N 112.08 W
Willingdon, Eng., U.K. 42 50.47 N 0.15 E
Willingdon, Mount ∧ 182 51.45 N 116.15 W
Willingen 56 51.17 N 8.37 E
Willingham 42 52.19 N 0.04 E
Willington, Eng., U.K. 42 52.50 N 1.33 W
Willington, Eng., U.K. 44 54.43 N 1.41 W
Willis, Mi., U.S. 216 42.09 N 83.33 W
Willis, Tx., U.S. 222 30.25 N 95.28 W
Willis ≃ 192 37.41 N 78.07 W
Willisau 58 47.07 N 8.00 E
Willis Group II 164 16.18 S 150.00 E
Willis Island I 186 48.48 N 53.42 W
Williston, S. Afr. 158 31.20 S 20.53 E
Williston, Fl., U.S. 192 29.23 N 82.26 W
Williston, N.D., U.S. 198 48.08 N 103.38 W
Williston, Oh., U.S. 214 41.36 N 83.20 W
Williston, S.C., U.S. 192 33.24 N 81.25 W
Williston Lake ◎[1] 176 55.40 N 123.40 W
Williston Park 276 40.45 N 73.38 W
Willisville 194 37.59 N 89.35 W
Willis Wharf 208 37.30 N 75.48 W
Williton 42 51.10 N 3.20 W
Willits 204 39.24 N 123.21 W
Willmar 198 45.07 N 95.02 W
Willmersdorf 264a 52.40 N 13.41 E
Willmore Wilderness Provincial Park ♦ 182 53.45 N 119.00 W
Willoughby, Austl. 170 33.48 S 151.12 E
Willoughby, Oh., U.S. 214 41.38 N 81.25 W
Willoughby, Cape › 166 35.51 S 138.07 E
Willoughby Bay c 240c 17.02 N 61.44 W
Willoughby Hills 214 41.35 N 81.25 W
Willow, Ak., U.S. 180 61.45 N 150.03 W
Willow, Mi., U.S. 216 42.07 N 83.24 W
Willow, N.Y., U.S. 210 42.05 N 74.14 W
Willow ≃, Ab., Can. 182 55.58 N 113.55 W
Willow ≃, B.C., Can. 182 54.03 N 122.21 W
Willow ≃, Mn., U.S. 190 46.40 N 93.35 W
Willow ≃, Wi., U.S. 190 44.59 N 92.46 W
Willowbrook, Sk., Can. 184 51.13 N 102.47 W
Willow Brook, Ca., U.S. 280 33.54 N 118.13 W
Willowbrook, Il., U.S. 278 41.46 N 87.56 W
Willowbrook, Md., U.S. 284c 39.02 N 77.11 W
Willow Brook ≃, On., Can. 212 43.53 N 80.16 W
Willow Brook ≃, Eng., U.K. 42 52.32 N 0.24 W
Willow Brook ≃, N.J., U.S. 276 40.20 N 74.10 W
Willowbrook Mall ✦[9] 276 40.53 N 74.15 W
Willowbrook Park ♦ 276 40.36 N 74.09 W
Willow Bunch 184 49.24 N 105.37 W
Willow Bunch Lake ◎ 184 49.27 N 105.28 W
Willow City 198 48.36 N 100.17 W
Willow Creek, Ca., U.S. 204 40.56 N 123.38 W
Willow Creek, Mt., U.S. 202 45.49 N 111.38 W
Willow Creek ≃, Ab., Can. 182 49.46 N 113.21 W
Willow Creek ≃, On., Can. 212 44.25 N 79.53 W
Willow Creek ≃, Ca., U.S. 226 37.09 N 119.27 W
Willow Creek ≃, Ca., U.S. 226 39.22 N 122.05 W
Willow Creek ≃, Il., U.S. 216 41.42 N 89.10 W
Willow Creek ≃, In., U.S. 216 41.15 N 85.08 W
Willow Creek ≃, Mi., U.S. 281 42.20 N 83.25 W
Willow Creek ≃, Mt., U.S. 202 48.10 N 111.11 W
Willow Creek ≃, Mt., U.S. 202 48.09 N 106.38 W
Willow Creek ≃, Mt., U.S. 202 46.28 N 108.28 W
Willow Creek ≃, Nv., U.S. 204 38.10 N 116.35 W
Willow Creek ≃, N.D., U.S. 198 48.34 N 100.27 W
Willow Creek ≃, Oh., U.S. 279a 41.20 N 82.03 W
Willow Creek ≃, Or., U.S. 202 45.48 N 120.01 W
Willow Creek ≃, Or., U.S. 202 44.00 N 117.13 W
Willow Creek ≃, Ut,. U.S. 200 40.02 N 109.45 W
Willow Creek, North Fork ≃ 226 37.13 N 119.30 W
Willow Creek, South Fork ≃ 226 39.32 N 122.10 W
Willowdale ✦[8] 275b 43.47 N 79.26 W
Willowdale State Forest ♦ 283 42.40 N 70.54 W
Willowdene 273d 26.18 S 29.57 E
Willowemac 210 41.55 N 74.41 W
Willowemoc Creek ≃ 210 41.53 N 74.48 W
Willow Glen ✦[8] 282 37.18 N 121.53 W
Willow Grove 208 40.08 N 75.06 W

Willow Grove Naval Air Station ■ 208 40.12 N 75.08 W
Willow Grove Park ♦ 285 40.08 N 75.08 W
Willow Hill 214 40.06 N 77.48 W
Willowick 214 41.37 N 81.28 W
Willow Lake 198 44.37 N 97.38 W
Willow Lake ◎, N.T., Can. 176 62.11 N 119.10 W
Willow Lake ◎, N.Y., U.S. 276 40.43 N 73.50 W
Willowlake ≃ 176 62.52 N 123.08 W
Willow Metropolitan Park ♦ 281 42.08 N 83.22 W
Willowmore 158 33.17 S 23.29 E
Willow Park 222 32.45 N 97.39 W
Willowra 162 21.15 S 132.35 E
Willow Reservoir ◎[1] 190 45.45 N 89.50 W
Willow Ridge Estates 284a 43.01 N 78.49 W
Willow River 182 54.04 N 122.28 W
Willow Run, De., U.S. 285 39.44 N 75.37 W
Willow Run, Mi., U.S. 216 42.14 N 83.35 W
Willow Run, Va., U.S. 284c 38.49 N 77.10 W
Willow Run Airport ⊠ 281 42.14 N 83.32 W
Willows 226 39.31 N 122.11 W
Willow Springs, Ca., U.S. 228 34.53 N 118.18 W
Willow Springs, Il., U.S. 278 41.44 N 87.51 W
Willow Springs, Mo., U.S. 194 36.59 N 91.58 W
Willow Springs, Pa., U.S. 279b 40.19 N 79.44 W
Willow Street 208 39.59 N 76.17 W
Willowvale 158 32.16 S 28.30 E
Willow Woods 284c 38.50 N 77.16 W
Will Rogers Beach State Park ♦ 280 34.01 N 118.30 W
Will Rogers State Park ♦ 280 34.03 N 118.31 W
Willroth 56 50.34 N 7.31 E
Wills Creek ≃, Austl. 166 22.43 S 140.02 E
Wills Creek ≃, Oh., U.S. 188 40.09 N 81.55 W
Wills Creek Lake ◎[1] 214 40.08 N 81.45 W
Willseyville 210 42.17 N 76.23 W
Willshire 216 40.45 N 84.48 W
Wills Point 222 32.43 N 96.01 W
Willston 284c 38.52 N 77.09 W
Willunga 168b 35.17 S 138.33 E
Wilmar 194 33.37 N 91.55 W
Wilmer, Al., U.S. 194 30.49 N 88.21 W
Wilmer, Pa., U.S. 285 40.07 N 75.32 W
Wilmer, Tx., U.S. 222 32.35 N 96.41 W
Wilmerding 279b 40.23 N 79.48 W
Wilmersdorf ✦[8] 264a 52.30 N 13.19 E
Wilmette 216 42.04 N 87.43 W
Wilmington, Austl. 166 32.39 S 138.07 E
Wilmington, Eng., U.K. 260 51.26 N 0.12 E
Wilmington, De., U.S. 208 39.44 N 75.32 W
Wilmington, Il., U.S. 216 41.18 N 88.08 W
Wilmington, Ma., U.S. 207 42.32 N 71.10 W
Wilmington, N.C., U.S. 192 34.13 N 77.56 W
Wilmington, Oh., U.S. 218 39.26 N 83.49 W
Wilmington, Vt., U.S. 188 42.52 N 72.52 W
Wilmington ✦[8] 280 33.47 N 118.16 W
Wilmington Manor 285 39.41 N 75.35 W
Wilmington Manor Gardens 285 39.40 N 75.34 W
Wilmore, Ky., U.S. 192 37.51 N 84.39 W
Wilmore, Pa., U.S. 214 40.23 N 78.43 W
Wilmot, Ar., U.S. 194 33.03 N 91.34 W
Wilmot, Oh., U.S. 214 40.39 N 81.38 W
Wilmot, S.D., U.S. 198 45.24 N 96.51 W
Wilmot, Wi., U.S. 216 42.31 N 88.11 W
Wilmot Woods ♦ 278 42.18 N 87.56 W
Wilmslow 44 53.20 N 2.15 W
Wilna → Vilnius 76 54.41 N 25.19 E
Wilnecote 42 52.36 N 1.40 W
Wilnsdorf 56 50.49 N 8.09 E
Wilpen 214 40.17 N 79.12 W
Wilpshire 262 53.47 N 2.28 W
Wilsall 202 45.59 N 110.39 W
Wilsdruff 54 51.05 N 13.32 E
Wilseder Berg ∧[2] 52 53.10 N 9.56 E
Wilseyville 226 38.23 N 120.31 W
Wilshamstead 42 52.05 N 0.27 W
Wilson, Austl. 166 32.00 S 138.22 E
Wilson, Ar., U.S. 194 35.34 N 90.02 W
Wilson, Ct., U.S. 207 41.48 N 72.38 W
Wilson, Il., U.S. 278 42.21 N 87.54 W
Wilson, Ks., U.S. 198 38.49 N 98.28 W
Wilson, La., U.S. 194 30.55 N 91.06 W
Wilson, N.Y., U.S. 210 43.18 N 78.49 W
Wilson, N.C., U.S. 192 35.43 N 77.54 W
Wilson, Ok., U.S. 196 34.09 N 97.25 W
Wilson, Pa., U.S. 208 40.41 N 75.14 W
Wilson, Tx., U.S. 196 33.19 N 101.44 W
Wilson ≃, Austl. 164 16.47 S 128.17 E
Wilson ≃, Austl. 166 27.38 S 141.24 E
Wilson ≃, Or., U.S. 224 45.28 N 123.53 W
Wilson, Cape › 176 66.59 N 81.28 W
Wilson, Mount ∧, Az., U.S. 200 35.59 N 114.37 W
Wilson, Mount ∧, Ca., U.S. 280 34.13 N 118.04 W
Wilson, Mount ∧, Co., U.S. 200 37.51 N 107.59 W
Wilson, Mount ∧, Nv., U.S. 204 38.15 N 114.23 W
Wilson, Mount ∧, Or., U.S. 224 45.04 N 121.39 W
Wilson, Mount ∧[2] 162 20.14 S 127.39 E
Wilson, Point ›, Austl. 169 38.05 S 144.30 E
Wilson, Point ›, Wa., U.S. 224 48.08 N 122.45 W
Wilson Cliffs ±[4] 162 22.03 S 127.09 E
Wilson Creek ≃, Tx., U.S. 222 33.07 N 96.35 W
Wilson Creek ≃, Wa., U.S. 202 47.25 N 119.07 W
Wilson Lake ◎[1], Al., U.S. 194 34.49 N 87.30 W
Wilson Lake ◎[1], Ks., U.S. 198 38.57 N 98.40 W
Wilson Range ⋏ 162 28.50 S 124.25 E
Wilson Run ≃, De., U.S. 285 39.48 N 75.35 W
Wilson Run ≃, Pa., U.S. 279b 40.13 N 79.37 W
Wilsons Beach 186 44.56 N 66.56 W
Wilson's Creek National Battlefield ♦ 194 37.06 N 93.27 W
Wilsons Promontory › 166 38.55 S 146.20 E
Wilsons Promontory National Park ♦ 166 39.00 S 146.25 E
Wilsonville, Il., U.S. 219 39.04 N 89.51 W
Wilsonville, Ne., U.S. 198 40.06 N 100.06 W
Wilsonville, Or., U.S. 224 45.18 N 122.46 W
Wilster 52 53.55 N 9.22 E
Wilthen 54 51.06 N 14.24 E
Wilton, Eng., U.K. 42 51.05 N 1.52 W
Wilton, Ct., U.S. 207 41.11 N 73.26 W
Wilton, Me., U.S. 188 44.35 N 70.13 W
Wilton, N.H., U.S. 207 42.50 N 71.44 W
Wilton, N.Y., U.S. 210 43.11 N 73.45 W
Wilton, N.D., U.S. 198 47.09 N 100.46 W
Wilton, Wi., U.S. 190 43.48 N 90.31 W
Wilton ≃ 164 14.45 S 134.33 E
Wilton Creek ≃ 212 44.12 N 76.56 W
Wilton Farm Acres 284b 39.18 N 76.50 W
Wilton Manors 220 26.09 N 80.08 W
Wiltshire □[6] 42 51.15 N 1.50 W
Wiltz 56 49.48 N 5.55 E

Wiluna 162 26.36 S 120.13 E
Wimapedi ≃ 184 55.27 N 99.07 W
Wimauma 220 27.42 N 82.17 W
Wimberley 196 30.00 N 98.06 W
Wimbledon 198 47.10 N 98.27 W
Wimbledon ✦[8] 260 51.25 N 0.12 W
Wimbledon Common ♦ 260 51.26 N 0.14 W
Wimborne Minster 42 50.48 N 1.59 W
Wimereux 50 50.46 N 1.37 E
Wimmelburg 54 51.31 N 11.30 E
Wimmenau 56 48.55 N 7.25 E
Wimmera ≃ 169 36.55 S 142.56 E
Wimmis 58 46.41 N 7.38 E
Winagami Lake ◎ 182 55.38 N 116.45 W
Winam c 154 0.15 S 34.35 E
Winamac 216 41.03 N 86.36 W
Winburg 158 28.37 S 27.00 E
Winburne 214 40.57 N 78.08 W
Wincanton 42 51.04 N 2.25 W
Wincham 262 53.16 N 2.29 W
Winchcombe 42 51.57 N 1.58 W
Winchelsea, Austl. 169 38.15 S 143.59 E
Winchelsea, Eng., U.K. 42 50.55 N 0.42 E
Winchendon 207 42.41 N 72.02 W
Winchester, On., Can. 212 45.06 N 75.21 W
Winchester, N.Z. 172 44.12 S 171.17 E
Winchester, Eng., U.K. 42 51.04 N 1.19 W
Winchester, Ca., U.S. 228 33.42 N 117.05 W
Winchester, Id., U.S. 202 46.14 N 116.37 W
Winchester, Il., U.S. 219 39.37 N 90.27 W
Winchester, In., U.S. 218 40.10 N 84.58 W
Winchester, Ky., U.S. 192 37.59 N 84.10 W
Winchester, Ma., U.S. 283 42.27 N 71.08 W
Winchester, N.H., U.S. 207 42.46 N 72.23 W
Winchester, Oh., U.S. 218 38.56 N 83.39 W
Winchester, Tn., U.S. 194 35.11 N 86.06 W
Winchester, Tx., U.S. 222 30.01 N 97.01 W
Winchester, Va., U.S. 188 39.11 N 78.10 W
Winchester Cathedral ʋ[1] 42 51.04 N 1.19 W
Winchmore Hill 260 51.39 N 0.39 W
Winchmore Hill ✦[8] 260 51.38 N 0.06 W
Wind ≃, Yk., Can. 180 65.49 N 135.18 W
Wind ≃, Wa., U.S. 224 45.43 N 121.47 W
Wind ≃, Wy., U.S. 202 43.35 N 108.13 W
Windang 170 34.32 S 150.53 E
Windau → Ventspils 76 57.24 N 21.36 E
Windber 214 40.14 N 78.50 W
Wind Cave National Park ♦ 198 43.32 N 103.25 W
Windeck 56 50.48 N 7.37 E
Winder 192 33.59 N 83.43 W
Winder, Lake ◎ 220 28.15 N 80.51 W
Windera 166 26.03 S 151.50 E
Windermere, B.C., Can. 182 50.30 N 115.58 W
Windermere, Eng., U.K. 44 54.23 N 2.54 W
Windermere, Fl., U.S. 220 28.30 N 81.32 W
Windermere ◎ 44 54.22 N 2.56 W
Windermere Lake ◎ 190 47.56 N 83.47 W
Winder Village 285 40.06 N 74.52 W
Windfall, Ab., Can. 182 54.11 N 116.15 W
Windfall, In., U.S. 216 40.21 N 85.57 W
Windgap 210 40.51 N 75.18 W
Windham, Ct., U.S. 207 41.41 N 72.09 W
Windham, N.H., U.S. 283 42.48 N 71.18 W
Windham, N.Y., U.S. 210 42.19 N 74.15 W
Windham, Oh., U.S. 214 41.14 N 81.02 W
Windham □[6], Ct., U.S. 207 41.55 N 71.55 W
Windham □[6], Vt., U.S. 207 42.50 N 72.43 W
Windham Manor 284c 39.04 N 77.00 W
Windhoek 156 22.34 S 17.06 E
Windhoek □[5] 156 22.30 S 17.00 E
Windigo ≃ 184 53.22 N 91.48 W
Windigo Lake ◎ 184 52.35 N 91.32 W
Windisch 58 47.29 N 8.13 E
Windischeschenbach 60 49.48 N 12.09 E
Windischgarsten 61 47.44 N 14.20 E
Wind Lake 216 42.49 N 88.09 W
Wind Lake ◎ 216 42.50 N 88.09 W
Windlass Run ≃ 284b 39.24 N 76.24 W
Windleite ∧ 54 51.22 N 10.56 E
Windlesham 260 51.22 N 0.40 W
Windley Key I 220 24.57 N 80.35 W
Windmill Point ›, On., Can. 284a 42.52 N 79.01 W
Windmill Point ›, Mi., U.S. 281 42.22 N 82.55 W
Windmill Point ›, Va., U.S. 208 37.37 N 76.17 W
Windom, Mn., U.S. 198 43.51 N 95.07 W
Windom, N.Y., U.S. 210 42.47 N 78.48 W
Windom Peak ∧ 200 37.37 N 107.35 W
Windorah 166 25.26 S 142.39 E
Windorf, B.R.D. 60 48.37 N 13.13 E
Windorf, Öst. 61 48.27 N 14.02 E
Window Rock 200 35.40 N 109.03 W
Wind Point 216 42.47 N 87.45 W
Wind River Indian Reservation ✦[4] 202 43.26 N 109.00 W
Wind River Peak ∧ 200 42.42 N 109.07 W
Wind River Range ⋏ 200 43.05 N 109.25 W
Windrush ≃ 42 51.42 N 1.25 W
Windsbach 56 49.14 N 10.50 E
Windsor, Austl. 168b 34.25 S 138.20 E
Windsor, Austl. 170 33.37 S 150.49 E
Windsor, Nf., Can. 186 48.57 N 55.40 W
Windsor, N.S., Can. 186 44.59 N 64.08 W
Windsor, On., Can. 214 42.18 N 83.01 W
Windsor, On., Can. 281 42.18 N 83.01 W
Windsor, P.Q., Can. 206 45.34 N 72.00 W
Windsor, Eng., U.K. 42 51.29 N 0.38 W
Windsor, Ca., U.S. 204 38.33 N 122.49 W
Windsor, Co., U.S. 200 40.28 N 104.54 W
Windsor, Ct., U.S. 207 41.51 N 72.38 W
Windsor, Il., U.S. 194 39.26 N 88.35 W
Windsor, In., U.S. 218 40.09 N 85.12 W
Windsor, Mo., U.S. 194 38.31 N 93.31 W
Windsor, N.J., U.S. 208 40.15 N 74.35 W
Windsor, N.Y., U.S. 210 42.05 N 76.39 W
Windsor, N.C., U.S. 192 35.59 N 76.56 W
Windsor, Oh., U.S. 214 41.32 N 80.56 W
Windsor, Pa., U.S. 208 39.54 N 76.35 W
Windsor, Vt., U.S. 188 43.29 N 72.23 W
Windsor, Va., U.S. 208 36.48 N 76.44 W
Windsor, Wi., U.S. 216 43.13 N 89.20 W
Windsor, Gare ✦[5] 275a 45.30 N 73.34 W
Windsor, University of ʋ[2] 281 42.18 N 83.04 W
Windsor Airport ⊠ 214 42.17 N 82.58 W
Windsor and Maidenhead □[8] 260 51.28 N 0.37 W
Windsor Castle ⊥ 42 51.29 N 0.36 W
Windsor Forest 192 31.58 N 81.07 W
Windsor Forest ✦[3] 42 51.27 N 0.43 W
Windsor Great Park ♦ 260 51.27 N 0.37 W
Windsor Heights 214 40.12 N 80.40 W
Windsor Hills 280 33.59 N 118.21 W
Windsor Locks 207 41.55 N 72.37 W
Windsor Race Course ♦ 260 51.29 N 0.39 W
Windsor Raceway ♦ 281 42.15 N 83.05 W
Windsor Terrace 284b 39.19 N 76.43 W
Windsorton 158 28.16 S 24.44 E
Windsorville 207 41.53 N 72.32 W
Windthorst 196 33.34 N 98.26 W
Windward Islands II 238 13.00 N 61.00 W

Symbol	English	Deutsch	Español	Français	Português
≃	River	Fluss	Río	Rivière	Rio
≍	Canal	Kanal	Canal	Canal	Canal
∟	Waterfall, Rapids	Wasserfall, Stromschnellen	Cascada, Rápidos	Chute d'eau, Rapides	Cascata, Rápidos
ɥ	Strait	Meeresstrasse	Estrecho	Détroit	Estreito
c	Bay, Gulf	Bucht, Golf	Bahía, Golfo	Baie, Golfe	Baía, Golfo
◎	Lake, Lakes	See, Seen	Lago, Lagos	Lac, Lacs	Lago, Lagos
≋	Swamp	Sumpf	Pantano	Marais	Pântano
⌘	Ice Features, Glacier	Eis- und Gletscherformen	Accidentes Glaciales	Formes glaciaires	Acidentes glaciares
≈	Other Hydrographic Features	Andere Hydrographische Objekte	Otros Elementos Hidrográficos	Autres données hydrographiques	Outros acidentes hidrográficos
✢	Submarine Features	Untermeerische Objekte	Accidentes Submarinos	Formes de relief sous-marin	Acidentes submarinos
□	Political Unit	Politische Einheit	Unidad Política	Entité politique	Unidade política
ʋ	Cultural Institution	Kulturelle Institution	Institución Cultural	Institution culturelle	Instituição cultural
⊥	Historical Site	Historische Stätte	Sitio Histórico	Site historique	Sítio histórico
♦	Recreational Site	Erholungs- und Ferienort	Sitio de Recreo	Centre de loisirs	Área de Lazer
⊠	Airport	Flughafen	Aeropuerto	Aéroport	Aeroporto
■	Military Installation	Militäranlage	Instalación Militar	Installation militaire	Instalação militar
✦	Miscellaneous	Verschiedenes	Misceláneo	Divers	Diversos

ENGLISH / DEUTSCH

Symbols in the index entries represent the broad categories identified in the key at the right. Symbols with superior numbers (⋏[1]) identify subcategories (see complete key on page *I · 1).*

Kartensymbole in dem Registerverzeichnis stellen die rechts in Schlüssel erklärten Kategorien dar. Symbole mit hochgestellten Ziffern (⋏[1]) bezeichnen Unterabteilungen einer Kategorie (vgl. vollständiger Schlüssel auf Seite *I · 1).*

Los símbolos incluídos en el texto del índice representan las grandes categorias identificadas con la clave a la derecha. Los símbolos con numeros en su parte superior (⋏[1]) identifican las subcategorías (véase la clave completa en la página *I · 1).*

Les symboles de l'index représentent les catégories indiquées dans la légende à droite. Les symboles suivis d'un indice (⋏[1]) représentent des sous-catégories (voir légende complète à la page *I · 1).*

Os símbolos incluídos no texto do índice representam as grandes categorias identificadas com a chave à direita. Os símbolos com números em sua parte superior (⋏[1]) identificam as subcategorias (veja-se a chave completa à página *I · 1).*

English	Deutsch	Español	Français	Português
∧ Mountain	Berg	Montaña	Montagne	Montanha
⋏ Mountains	Berge	Montañas	Montagnes	Montanhas
)(Pass	Pass	Paso	Col	Passo
V Valley, Canyon	Tal, Cañon	Valle, Cañón	Vallée, Canyon	Vale, Canhão
≚ Plain	Ebene	Llano	Plaine	Planície
≻ Cape	Kap	Cabo	Cap	Cabo
I Island	Insel	Isla	Île	Ilha
II Islands	Inseln	Islas	Îles	Ilhas
⊥ Other Topographic Features	Andere Topographische Objekte	Otros Elementos Topográficos	Autres données topographiques	Outros acidentes topográficos

ESPAÑOL · FRANÇAIS · PORTUGUÊS

Nombre / Nom / Nome	Página / Page	Lat.°′	Long.°′ W = Oeste / W = Ouest
Worcester □6, Md., U.S.	208	38.11 N	75.24 W
Worcester □6, Ma., U.S.	207	42.16 N	71.48 W
Worcester Municipal Airport ⊠	207	42.16 N	71.52 W
Worden, Il., U.S.	219	38.55 N	89.50 W
Worden, Mt., U.S.	202	45.57 N	108.09 W
Worden Pond ⊜	207	41.26 N	71.35 W
Wördern	61	48.20 N	16.13 E
Wörgl	64	47.29 N	12.04 E
Workai, Pulau I	164	6.40 S	134.40 E
Work Channel ʉ	182	54.30 N	130.15 W
Workers' Stadium ♠	271a	39.55 N	116.27 E
Workington	44	54.39 N	3.35 W
Worksop	44	53.18 N	1.07 W
Workum	52	52.57 N	5.26 E
Worland	202	44.01 N	107.57 W
World End Pond ⊜	283	42.45 N	71.12 W
Worli ◆8	272c	19.01 N	72.50 E
Wörlitz	54	51.50 N	12.25 E
Wormditt → Orneta	30	54.08 N	20.08 E
Wormerveer	52	52.28 N	4.46 E
Wormhoudt	50	50.53 N	2.28 E
Wormit	46	56.25 N	2.59 W
Wormley	260	51.44 N	0.01 W
Worms	56	49.38 N	8.22 E
Worms Head ≻	42	51.34 N	4.20 W
Wormshill	260	51.17 N	0.42 E
Wörnitz ≃	56	48.42 N	10.45 E
Woronesch → Voronež	78	51.40 N	39.10 E
Woronoco	207	42.09 N	72.49 W
Woronora	274a	34.01 S	151.03 E
Woronora ≃	274a	34.00 S	151.04 E
Woronora Reservoir ⊜1	170	34.08 S	150.56 E
Worplesdon	260	51.16 N	0.37 W
Worpswede	52	53.13 N	8.56 E
Wörrstadt	56	49.50 N	8.07 E
Wörsbach ≃	56	50.22 N	8.09 E
Worsbrough	44	53.31 N	1.29 W
Worsley	262	53.30 N	2.23 W
Worsthorne	262	53.47 N	2.11 W
Wörth, B.R.D.	56	49.48 N	9.09 E
Worth, B.R.D.	263	51.13 N	7.39 E
Worth, Il., U.S.	216	41.41 N	87.47 W
Worth, Lake ⊜1	222	32.48 N	97.28 W
Wortham	222	31.47 N	96.27 W
Wörth am Rhein	56	49.03 N	8.16 E
Wörth an der Donau	60	49.00 N	12.25 E
Wörth an der Isar	60	48.37 N	12.24 E
Worthen	42	52.38 N	3.00 W
Wörther See ⊜	61	46.37 N	14.10 E
Worthing	42	50.48 N	0.23 W
Worthington, In., U.S.	194	39.07 N	86.58 W
Worthington, Md., U.S.	284b	39.14 N	76.47 W
Worthington, Mn., U.S.	198	43.37 N	95.35 W
Worthington, N.Y., U.S.	276	41.02 N	73.50 W
Worthington, Oh., U.S.	214	40.05 N	83.01 W
Worthington, Pa., U.S.	214	40.50 N	79.37 W
Worthington Peak ∧	204	37.55 N	115.37 W
Wörthsee ⊜	60	48.03 N	11.10 E
Worthville, Ky., U.S.	218	38.36 N	85.04 W
Worthville, Pa., U.S.	214	41.02 N	79.08 W
Worton	208	39.16 N	76.05 W
Wŏrun-dong	98	39.36 N	125.20 E
Wosimi	164	2.54 S	134.31 E
Wostok → Vostok ⛉3	9	78.30 S	106.50 E
Wosu	112	2.21 S	121.50 E
Wotap, Pulau I	164	7.21 S	131.16 E
Wotho I1	14	10.06 N	165.59 E
Wotje I1	14	9.27 N	170.02 E
Wotton, P.Q., Can.	206	45.44 N	71.48 W
Wotton, Eng., U.K.	260	51.13 N	0.23 W
Wotton-under-Edge	42	51.39 N	2.21 W
Wotu	112	2.35 S	120.48 E
Woudenberg	52	52.05 N	5.25 E
Woudrichem	52	51.49 N	5.00 E
Woudsend	52	52.56 N	5.36 E
Wouldham	260	51.21 N	0.28 E
Wounded Knee	198	43.08 N	102.21 W
Wounded Knee Creek ≃	198	43.26 N	102.32 W
Wounta	236	13.33 N	83.32 W
Wounta, Laguna de ⊂	236	13.38 N	83.34 W
Wour	146	21.21 N	15.57 E
Wouri ≃	152	4.06 N	9.43 E
Woutchaba	152	5.13 N	13.05 E
Wouw	52	51.32 N	4.24 E
Wowan	166	23.55 S	150.12 E
Wowoni, Pulau I	112	4.08 S	123.06 E
Woyla ≃	114	4.18 N	95.56 E
Woy Woy	170	33.30 S	151.20 E
Woźniki	30	50.36 N	19.03 E
Wragby	44	53.18 N	0.19 W
Wrangel Island → Vrangel'a, ostrov I	74	71.00 N	179.30 W
Wrangell	180	56.28 N	132.23 W
Wrangell, Cape ≻	181a	52.50 N	172.26 E
Wrangell, Mount ∧	180	62.00 N	144.06 W
Wrangell Island I	180	56.15 N	132.10 W
Wrangell Mountains ⋏	180	62.00 N	143.00 W
Wrangell-Saint Elias National Park ♠	180	61.00 N	142.00 W
Wrath, Cape ≻	46	58.37 N	5.01 W
Wray	198	40.04 N	102.13 W
Wraysbury	260	51.27 N	0.33 W
Wrea Green	262	53.46 N	2.55 W
Wreck Bay ⊂	170	35.11 S	150.40 E
Wreck Island I	208	37.16 N	75.48 W
Wreck Reef ✢2	166	22.13 S	155.17 E
Wrecks, Bay of ⊂	174o	1.52 N	157.17 W
Wredenhagen	54	53.17 N	12.31 E
Wremen	52	53.39 N	8.30 E
Wren	216	40.48 N	84.46 W
Wrens	192	33.12 N	82.23 W
Wrentham, Ab., Can.	182	49.32 N	112.10 W
Wrentham, Eng., U.K.	42	52.23 N	1.40 E
Wrentham, Ma., U.S.	207	42.04 N	71.19 W
Wrentham State Forest ♠	283	42.02 N	71.20 W
Wrexham	44	53.03 N	3.00 W
Wriezen	54	52.43 N	14.08 E
Wright	278	41.31 N	87.21 W
Wright, Mount ∧, Austl.	166	31.12 S	142.26 E
Wright, Mount ∧, Mt., U.S.	202	47.58 N	112.49 W
Wright Brothers National Memorial ⊥	192	35.55 N	75.50 W
Wright City, Mo., U.S.	219	38.49 N	91.01 W
Wright City, Ok., U.S.	194	34.03 N	95.00 W
Wright City, Tx., U.S.	222	32.12 N	94.59 W
Wrightington Bar	262	53.37 N	2.42 W
Wright Patman Lake ⊜1	194	33.16 N	94.14 W
Wright-Patterson Air Force Base ■	218	39.49 N	84.03 W
Wright Peak ∧	204	38.59 N	122.46 W
Wrights	219	39.23 N	90.18 W
Wrightsboro	222	29.22 N	97.34 W
Wrights Corners	210	43.13 N	78.46 W
Wrightson, Mount ∧	200	31.42 N	110.50 W
Wrightstown, N.J., U.S.	208	40.02 N	74.37 W
Wrightstown, Pa., U.S.	208	40.17 N	74.58 W
Wrightstown, Wi., U.S.	190	44.19 N	88.09 W
Wrightsville, Ga., U.S.	192	32.43 N	82.43 W
Wrightsville, Pa., U.S.	214	40.01 N	76.31 W
Wrightsville Beach	192	34.12 N	77.47 W
Wrightwood	228	34.21 N	117.37 W
Wrigley, N.T., Can.	180	63.16 N	123.37 W
Wrigley, Tn., U.S.	194	35.54 N	87.20 W
Wrigley Field ♠	278	41.57 N	87.39 W
Wrigley Gulf ⊂	9	74.00 S	129.00 W
Writtle	42	51.44 N	0.26 E
Wrocław (Breslau)	30	51.06 N	17.00 E
Wrocław □4	30	51.15 N	17.00 E
Wrong Lake ⊜	184	52.38 N	96.10 W
Wronki	30	52.43 N	16.23 E
Wrotham	42	51.19 N	0.19 E
Wrotham Heath	260	51.18 N	0.21 E
Wrottesley, Cape ≻	176	74.33 N	121.32 W
Wroughton	42	51.31 N	1.46 W
Wroxham	42	52.42 N	1.24 E
Wroxton	184	51.14 N	101.53 W
Września	30	52.20 N	17.34 E
Wschowa	30	51.48 N	16.19 E
Wu ≃, Zhg.	98	34.25 N	117.55 E
Wu ≃, Zhg.	100	28.57 N	116.39 E
Wu ≃, Zhg.	100	24.48 N	113.35 E
Wu ≃, Zhg.	102	29.43 N	107.24 E
Wu ≃, Zhg.	102	27.03 N	109.53 E
Wu ≃, Zhg.	102	27.12 N	109.48 E
Wu'an	98	36.40 N	114.12 E
Wubaozhen	107	29.14 N	104.29 E
Wubin	162	30.06 S	116.38 E
Wubu	102	37.33 N	110.39 E
Wuchagou	89	46.46 N	120.16 E
Wuchang, Zhg.	89	44.54 N	127.08 E
Wuchang → Wuhan, Zhg.	100	30.36 N	114.17 E
Wuchang Hu ⊜	100	30.17 N	116.47 E
Wucheng, Zhg.	98	37.09 N	115.53 E
Wucheng (Jiucheng), Zhg.	98	37.13 N	116.02 E
Wucheng, Zhg.	100	33.28 N	113.44 E
Wucheng, Zhg.	100	29.10 N	115.59 E
Wucheng, Zhg.	100	29.36 N	118.10 E
Wuch'i	100	24.16 N	120.31 E
Wuchin → Changzhou	106	31.47 N	119.57 E
Wuch'iu Yü I	100	25.00 N	119.27 E
Wuchow → Wuzhou	102	23.30 N	111.27 E
Wuchuan, Zhg.	102	21.25 N	110.40 E
Wuchuan, Zhg.	102	28.25 N	107.56 E
Wuchuan, Zhg.	102	41.05 N	111.23 E
Wuchung → Wuzhong	102	37.57 N	106.10 E
Wucun	105	38.57 N	115.19 E
Wuda	102	39.30 N	106.40 E
Wudao	98	39.28 N	121.28 E
Wudaogou, Zhg.	98	41.43 N	127.05 E
Wudaogou, Zhg.	98	42.08 N	125.51 E
Wudaolianggou	104	40.59 N	120.35 E
Wudi	98	37.44 N	117.35 E
Wudian, Zhg.	100	31.57 N	112.46 E
Wudian, Zhg.	100	32.42 N	117.18 E
Wuding	102	25.32 N	102.23 E
Wuding ≃	102	37.05 N	110.20 E
Wudinna	166	33.03 S	135.28 E
Wudu, Zhg.	100	28.23 N	118.14 E
Wudu, Zhg.	100	27.37 N	119.00 E
Wudu, Zhg.	102	33.24 N	104.50 E
Wuduhe	102	31.03 N	111.03 E
Wuerqihan	89	49.37 N	121.45 E
Wufeng	102	30.11 N	110.33 E
Wufeng Shan I	106	31.07 N	120.16 E
Wufengxi	107	30.37 N	104.29 E
Wufu	100	30.06 N	120.58 E
Wugang	102	26.44 N	110.38 E
Wugong	102	34.20 N	108.04 E
Wugong Shan ∧	100	27.35 N	114.18 E
Wugong Shan ⋏	100	27.21 N	113.50 E
Wugouying	100	33.28 N	114.08 E
Wugunuoer	89	49.10 N	119.19 E
Wuhai	102	39.39 N	106.41 E
Wuhan	100	30.36 N	114.17 E
Wuhe, Zhg.	100	33.10 N	117.54 E
Wuhe, Zhg.	100	24.26 N	115.25 E
Wuhle ≃	264a	52.29 N	13.34 E
Wuhsi → Wuxi	106	31.35 N	120.18 E
Wuhsing → Huzhou	106	30.52 N	120.06 E
Wuhu, Zhg.	100	31.21 N	118.22 E
Wuhu, Zhg.	100	31.11 N	118.35 E
Wuhua	100	23.57 N	115.48 E
Wuhuanchi	104	42.20 N	121.51 E
Wuhuang	107	29.58 N	104.46 E
Wuhudongmiao	102	38.19 N	107.20 E
Wuji, Zhg.	98	34.12 N	119.02 E
Wuji, Zhg.	98	38.13 N	114.57 E
Wujia ≃	102	41.10 N	108.45 E
Wujiabeigou	104	40.57 N	123.50 E
Wujiang, Zhg.	100	31.52 N	118.28 E
Wujiang, Zhg.	100	27.14 N	115.15 E
Wujiang, Zhg.	106	31.10 N	120.38 E
Wujiangdu	102	27.16 N	106.48 E
Wujianpu	107	29.10 N	105.50 E
Wujiapai	105	39.32 N	117.18 E
Wujiapu	105	38.52 N	117.07 E
Wujiazhen	107	29.38 N	105.24 E
Wujiazhuang, Zhg.	105	40.35 N	115.20 E
Wujiazhuang, Zhg.	106	32.18 N	120.10 E
Wujiazi, Zhg.	89	46.27 N	123.34 E
Wujiazi, Zhg.	104	42.13 N	122.08 E
Wujiazi, Zhg.	104	42.30 N	121.10 E
Wujing	100	25.16 N	114.36 E
Wukang	106	30.33 N	119.58 E
Wukari	150	7.51 N	9.47 E
Wukeshu, Zhg.	89	46.02 N	123.45 E
Wukeshu, Zhg.	89	44.48 N	126.08 E
Wulai	100	24.52 N	121.33 E
Wulajia	89	48.23 N	129.58 E
Wulanheduojia	102	42.40 N	113.20 E
Wulanhutong	98	41.44 N	114.49 E
Wulanmuluhne ≃	120	34.15 N	93.11 E
Wulanmutou	104	42.23 N	121.21 E
Wulanwusu, Zhg.	86	44.20 N	85.50 E
Wulanwusu, Zhg.	102	41.39 N	107.48 E
Wular Lake ⊜	123	34.20 N	74.33 E
Wulasitai, Zhg.	89	43.15 N	121.27 E
Wulasitai, Zhg.	89	43.28 N	122.44 E
Wulateqianqi	102	40.39 N	109.05 E
Wulaxi	102	28.38 N	101.40 E
Wuleidao Wan ⊂	98	36.55 N	122.00 E
Wulfen	52	51.43 N	7.00 E
Wülfrath	56	51.17 N	7.02 E
Wulfsen	52	53.18 N	10.08 E
Wulfsode	52	53.04 N	10.13 E
Wulften	52	51.40 N	10.10 E
Wulian (Hongning)	98	35.47 N	119.15 E
Wulian Feng ⋏	102	28.03 N	103.57 E
Wuliangdian	104	41.52 N	122.16 E
Wuliang Shan ⋏	102	24.30 N	100.45 E
Wuliaru, Pulau I	164	7.27 S	131.04 E
Wulichuan	102	33.49 N	111.08 E
Wulie ≃	105	40.54 N	117.55 E
Wuling	98	35.53 N	114.36 E
Wuling Shan ∧	105	40.36 N	117.29 E
Wulitaizi	104	41.28 N	123.21 E
Wulizhuang	100	33.49 N	118.57 E
Wulka ≃	61	47.52 N	16.40 E
Wüllen	52	52.04 N	6.58 E
Wullwye Creek ≃	171b	36.30 S	148.49 E
Wulong, Zhg.	102	29.20 N	107.43 E
Wulong, Zhg.	104	41.39 N	124.13 E
Wulong ≃	98	36.35 N	120.56 E
Wulongbei	98	40.21 N	124.16 E
Wulsdorf ◆8	52	53.30 N	8.35 E
Wultschau	61	48.42 N	14.50 E
Wulu ≃	85	39.38 N	74.38 E
Wuluhan	115a	8.21 S	113.33 E
Wuluhayingzi	104	42.20 N	121.34 E
Wulumuch'i → Ürümqi	90	43.48 N	87.35 E
Wulumuqi → Ürümqi	90	43.48 N	87.35 E
Wuluo	102	26.09 N	108.15 E
Wulur	164	7.09 S	128.39 E
Wulu Station ◆5	271a	39.56 N	116.16 E
Wum	152	6.23 N	10.04 E
Wumang Dao I	98	39.14 N	123.03 E
Wumiaoxiang	107	30.23 N	104.17 E
Wuming	102	23.10 N	108.18 E
Wümme ≃	52	53.10 N	8.44 E
Wunamu	86	46.06 N	85.44 E
Wundowie	168a	31.46 S	116.22 E
Wundwin	110	21.05 N	96.02 E
Wuneba	154	4.50 N	30.20 E
Wungong ≃	168a	32.06 S	115.59 E
Wuning	100	29.17 N	115.06 E
Wünnenberg	52	51.31 N	8.42 E
Wunnummin Lake ⊜	176	52.55 N	89.10 W
Wun Rog	140	9.00 N	28.21 E
Wünschendorf	54	50.48 N	12.05 E
Wünsdorf	54	52.10 N	13.28 E
Wunsiedel	60	50.02 N	12.01 E
Wunstorf	52	52.25 N	9.26 E
Wuntho	110	23.54 N	95.41 E
Wunuer	89	48.53 N	121.15 E
Wupaowan	107	29.50 N	103.59 E
Wupatki National Monument ♠	200	35.24 N	111.14 W
Wuping	100	25.08 N	116.06 E
Wupper ≃	263	51.05 N	7.00 E
Wuppertal, B.R.D.	56	51.16 N	7.11 E
Wuppertal, B.R.D.	263	51.16 N	7.11 E
Wuppertal, S. Afr.	158	32.15 S	19.15 E
Wuqi, Zhg.	100	27.10 N	120.23 E
Wuqi, Zhg.	102	37.08 N	108.10 E
Wuqia	85	39.42 N	75.13 E
Wuqiang (Xiaofan)	98	38.03 N	115.58 E
Wuqing (Yangcun)	105	39.23 N	117.04 E
Wuraming	168a	32.48 S	116.16 E
Wurarga	162	28.25 S	116.17 E
Würenlingen	58	47.32 N	8.16 E
Wurgwitz	54	51.01 N	13.37 E
Wurm ≃, B.R.D.	56	51.08 N	6.10 E
Würm ≃, B.R.D.	56	48.53 N	8.42 E
Würm ≃, B.R.D.	60	48.10 N	11.28 E
Wurmannsquick	60	48.21 N	12.47 E
Wurmberg ∧	54	51.45 N	10.37 E
Wurno	150	13.17 N	5.24 E
Wurong	164	6.07 S	140.47 E
Würselen	56	50.49 N	6.08 E
Wurtsboro	210	41.35 N	74.29 W
Wurtsboro Hills	210	41.36 N	74.30 W
Wurtsmith Air Force Base ■	190	44.27 N	83.23 W
Wuruf	164	6.43 S	146.25 E
Wuryantoro	115a	7.54 S	110.51 E
Wurzbach	54	50.28 N	11.32 E
Würzburg	56	49.48 N	9.56 E
Wurzen	54	51.22 N	12.44 E
Wusanga	152	3.22 S	22.50 E
Wusha	100	30.39 N	117.18 E
Wushan, Zhg.	100	32.04 N	117.03 E
Wushan, Zhg.	102	34.38 N	105.04 E
Wushan, Zhg.	102	31.05 N	109.48 E
Wushan, Zhg.	106	31.44 N	118.58 E
Wusheng, Zhg.	100	29.56 N	119.25 E
Wusheng, Zhg.	107	30.21 N	106.17 E
Wushengchang	107	29.00 N	103.43 E
Wushenqi	102	38.58 N	109.01 E
Wushi, Zhg.	102	22.11 N	110.11 E
Wushi, Zhg.	106	31.44 N	120.59 E
Wushishi	150	9.46 N	6.07 E
Wushu	100	26.20 N	114.56 E
Wusi	175f	15.22 S	166.36 E
Wusih → Wuxi	106	31.35 N	120.18 E
Wuskwatim Lake ⊜	184	55.32 N	98.32 W
Wusong	106	31.23 N	121.29 E
Wusong ≃	106	31.15 N	121.29 E
Wust	54	52.33 N	12.07 E
Wüsten	52	52.06 N	8.47 E
Wüstensachsen	56	50.30 N	10.00 E
Wusterhausen	54	52.54 N	12.28 E
Wusterhusen	54	54.07 N	13.37 E
Wustermark	54	52.33 N	12.56 E
Wüstermarke	54	51.49 N	13.36 E
Wusterwitz	54	52.22 N	12.18 E
Wüsting	52	53.07 N	8.20 E
Wustrow, B.R.D.	54	52.55 N	11.07 E
Wustrow, D.D.R.	54	54.05 N	11.34 E
Wustrow ≻1	54	54.05 N	11.34 E
Wusuli (Ussuri) ≃	89	48.27 N	135.04 E
Wusuo	100	25.02 N	116.02 E
Wuta	106	31.31 N	120.39 E
Wutach ≃	58	47.37 N	8.15 E
Wutai, Zhg.	85	39.28 N	78.09 E
Wutai, Zhg.	86	44.36 N	82.06 E
Wutai, Zhg.	98	41.18 N	113.59 E
Wutai, Zhg.	102	38.44 N	113.17 E
Wutai Shan ∧	98	39.04 N	113.35 E
Wutai Shan ⋏	98	39.13 N	113.45 E
Wutaizi	104	42.27 N	123.17 E
Wutan	102	28.29 N	111.40 E
Wutanchang	107	29.15 N	106.04 E
Wutang	106	31.31 N	119.10 E
Wutangdun	106	30.38 N	120.08 E
Wutangjie	100	29.59 N	122.22 E
Wuteve, Mount ∧	150	8.09 N	9.56 W
Wutianzhen	100	30.23 N	117.12 E
Wutong	102	25.18 N	110.01 E
Wutonghaolai	89	42.55 N	120.15 E
Wutongqiao	107	29.26 N	103.51 E
Wutongwozi	102	42.27 N	95.17 E
Wutsin → Changzhou	106	31.47 N	119.57 E
Wutun	100	27.51 N	118.04 E
Wut'ungch'iao → Wutongqiao	107	29.26 N	103.51 E
Wutungkiao → Wutongqiao	107	29.26 N	103.51 E
Wutuohuo	102	40.51 N	101.48 E
Wuustwezel	50	51.23 N	4.36 E
Wuvulu Island I	164	1.45 S	142.50 E
Wuwei, Zhg.	100	31.18 N	117.54 E
Wuwei (Liangzhou), Zhg.	102	37.58 N	102.49 E
Wuxi, Zhg.	102	31.25 N	109.34 E
Wuxi (Wuhsi), Zhg.	106	31.35 N	120.18 E
Wuxi, Zhg.	106	31.20 N	118.39 E
Wuxi ≃	100	29.00 N	118.56 E
Wuxiang	102	36.51 N	113.00 E
Wuxingchang	106	31.13 N	119.23 E
Wuxuan	102	23.36 N	109.42 E
Wuyang, Zhg.	100	33.26 N	113.34 E
Wuyang, Zhg.	100	25.41 N	115.55 E
Wuyang, Zhg.	102	26.41 N	110.20 E
Wuyi, Zhg.	98	37.49 N	115.54 E
Wuyi, Zhg.	100	32.13 N	118.26 E
Wuyi, Zhg.	100	28.54 N	119.48 E
Wuying	89	48.05 N	129.15 E
Wuyi Shan ⋏	90	27.52 N	117.40 E
Wuyuan, Zhg.	100	29.15 N	117.49 E
Wuyuan, Zhg.	102	41.06 N	108.29 E
Wuyun	89	49.16 N	129.37 E
Wuyunqiao	100	26.02 N	114.52 E
Wuyur ≃	89	47.00 N	124.10 E
Wuzaizi	104	42.28 N	123.57 E
Wuzhai	102	38.58 N	111.55 E
Wuzhan	89	45.51 N	126.17 E
Wuzhen	106	30.46 N	120.29 E
Wuzhi Shan ∧, Zhg.	105	40.29 N	118.00 E
Wuzhishan ∧, Zhg.	110	18.57 N	109.43 E
Wuzhong	102	37.57 N	106.10 E
Wuzhou (Wuchow)	102	23.30 N	111.27 E
Wuzong	106	32.14 N	121.03 E
Wyaaba Creek ≃	164	16.27 S	141.35 E
Wyaconda	194	40.23 N	91.55 W
Wyaconda ≃	194	40.04 N	91.30 W
Wyalkatchem	162	31.10 S	117.22 E
Wyalusing	210	41.40 N	76.15 W
Wyalusing Creek ≃	210	41.40 N	76.16 W
Wyandanch	276	40.45 N	73.21 W
Wyandot	214	40.44 N	83.08 W
Wyandot □6	214	40.50 N	83.17 W
Wyandotte	216	42.12 N	83.09 W
Wyandotte Cave ⩝5	218	38.14 N	86.18 W
Wyandotte National Wildlife Refuge ◆4	281	42.14 N	83.08 W
Wyandra	166	27.15 S	145.59 E
Wyangala Reservoir ⊜1	166	33.58 S	148.55 E
Wyano	214	40.12 N	79.42 W
Wyatt, In., U.S.	216	41.31 N	86.10 W
Wyatt, Mo., U.S.	194	36.54 N	89.13 W
Wycheproof	166	36.05 S	143.14 E
Wychwood	273d	26.12 S	28.08 E
Wyckoff	210	41.00 N	74.10 W
Wydgee	162	28.51 S	117.49 E
Wydgelee	158	34.23 S	20.26 E
Wy-Dit-Joli-Village	261	49.06 N	1.50 E
Wye	42	51.11 N	0.56 E
Wye ≃, On., Can.	212	44.44 N	79.52 W
Wye ≃, U.K.	42	51.37 N	2.39 W
Wye ≃, Eng., U.K.	44	53.12 N	1.37 W
Wyee	170	33.11 S	151.29 E
Wye Lake ⊜	212	44.43 N	79.52 W
Wyemandoo ∧	162	28.31 S	118.32 E
Wyeville	190	44.01 N	90.23 W
Wyhl	58	48.09 N	7.39 E
Wyhra ≃	54	51.09 N	12.27 E
Wyk	30	54.42 N	8.34 E
Wyke Regis	42	50.36 N	2.29 W
Wykoff	190	43.42 N	92.16 W
Wylandville	279b	40.12 N	80.08 W
Wyleswood Lake ⊜	279a	41.20 N	81.55 W
Wylie, Pa., U.S.	279b	40.27 N	79.59 W
Wylie, Tx., U.S.	222	33.01 N	96.32 W
Wylie, Lake ⊜1	192	35.07 N	81.02 W
Wylye ≃	42	51.04 N	1.52 W
Wymah	171b	36.02 S	147.17 E
Wymark	184	50.07 N	107.44 W
Wymeswold	42	52.47 N	1.06 W
Wymondham	42	52.34 N	1.07 E
Wymore	198	40.07 N	96.39 W
Wynantskill	210	42.42 N	73.39 W
Wynberg	158	34.02 S	18.28 E
Wynbring	162	30.33 S	133.32 E
Wyncote	285	40.05 N	75.08 W
Wyndham, Austl.	164	15.28 S	128.06 E
Wyndham, N.Z.	172	46.20 S	168.51 E
Wyndmere	198	46.16 N	97.07 W
Wyndmoor	285	40.04 N	75.11 W
Wynigen	58	47.06 N	7.40 E
Wynndel	182	49.11 N	116.33 W
Wynne	194	35.13 N	90.47 W
Wynnewood, Ok., U.S.	196	34.38 N	97.09 W
Wynnewood, Pa., U.S.	285	40.00 N	75.16 W
Wynniatt Bay ⊂	176	72.55 N	110.30 W
Wynnum	171a	27.27 S	153.10 E
Wynona	196	36.32 N	96.19 W
Wynoochee ≃	224	46.58 N	123.35 W
Wynoochee Lake ⊜1	224	47.25 N	123.35 W
Wynot	198	42.44 N	97.10 W
Wynyard, Austl.	166	40.59 S	145.41 E
Wynyard, Sk., Can.	184	51.47 N	104.10 W
Wyocena	190	43.29 N	89.18 W
Wyodak	198	44.17 N	105.22 W
Wyola Lake ⊜	162	29.08 S	130.17 E
Wyoming, On., Can.	190	42.57 N	82.07 W
Wyoming, De., U.S.	208	39.07 N	75.33 W
Wyoming, Il., U.S.	190	41.03 N	89.46 W
Wyoming, Ia., U.S.	190	42.03 N	91.00 W
Wyoming, Mi., U.S.	216	42.54 N	85.42 W
Wyoming, N.Y., U.S.	210	42.49 N	78.05 W
Wyoming, Oh., U.S.	218	39.13 N	84.27 W
Wyoming, Pa., U.S.	210	41.18 N	75.50 W
Wyoming, R.I., U.S.	207	41.30 N	71.42 W
Wyoming □6, N.Y., U.S.	210	42.44 N	78.08 W
Wyoming □6, Pa., U.S.	210	41.32 N	75.57 W
Wyoming □3	178	43.00 N	107.30 W
Wyoming Peak ∧	200	42.36 N	110.37 W
Wyomissing	208	40.19 N	75.57 W
Wyong	170	33.17 S	151.25 E
Wyong Creek ≃	170	33.18 S	151.28 E
Wyperfield National Park ♠	166	35.30 S	142.00 E
Wyre ≃	44	53.55 N	3.00 W
Wyreema	171a	27.39 S	151.52 E
Wyre Forest ◆3	42	52.23 N	2.23 W
Wyrzysk	30	53.10 N	17.15 E
Wyśmierzyce	30	51.38 N	20.49 E
Wysoka	30	53.11 N	17.05 E
Wysokie Mazowieckie	30	52.56 N	22.32 E
Wysox	210	41.46 N	76.24 W
Wyszków	30	52.36 N	21.28 E
Wyszogród	30	52.23 N	20.11 E
Wythenshawe ◆8	262	53.24 N	2.17 W
Wythenshawe Hall ⊥	262	53.24 N	2.17 W
Wytheville	192	36.56 N	81.05 W
Wytschegda → Vyčegda ≃	24	61.18 N	46.36 E
Wyvis, Ben ∧	46	57.42 N	4.35 W
X			
Xaafuun	144	10.25 N	51.16 E
Xabregas ◆8	266c	38.44 N	9.07 W
Xá-Cassau	152	9.02 S	20.14 E
Xaclbal ≃	236	16.06 N	90.58 W
Xadani	234	15.56 N	96.04 W
Xai-Xai	156	25.02 S	33.34 E
Xalin	144	9.06 N	48.37 E
Xalpatláhuac	234	17.01 N	99.18 W
Xaltianguis	234	17.04 N	99.50 W
Xambioá	250	6.25 S	48.40 W
Xambrê ≃	255	24.02 S	53.59 W
Xam Nua	110	20.25 N	104.02 E
Xa-muong-man	110	10.58 N	108.01 E
Xá-Muteba	152	9.34 S	17.50 E
Xangongo	152	16.43 S	15.01 E
Xanten	52	51.39 N	6.26 E
Xánthi	38	41.08 N	24.53 E
Xanxerê	252	26.53 S	52.23 W
Xapecó ≃	252	27.06 S	53.01 W
Xapuri	248	10.39 S	68.31 W
Xapuri ≃	248	10.39 S	68.30 W
Xarardheere	144	4.39 N	47.51 E
Xar Moron ≃, Zhg.	90	43.25 N	121.41 E
Xar Moron ≃, Zhg.	102	43.02 N	111.20 E
Xarrama ≃	34	38.14 N	8.20 W
Xau, Lake ≡	156	21.15 S	24.38 E
Xauen → Chaouen	148	35.10 N	5.16 W
Xavantes ≃	250	10.40 S	50.41 W
Xavantina	255	21.15 S	52.48 W
Xa-vo-dat	110	11.09 N	107.31 E
Xaxim	252	26.56 S	52.31 W
X-Can	232	20.50 N	87.43 W
Xenia, Il., U.S.	219	38.38 N	88.38 W
Xenia, Oh., U.S.	218	39.41 N	83.55 W
Xénô	110	16.35 N	104.50 E
Xercavins, Arroyo de ≃	266d	41.30 N	2.02 E
Xerém	256	22.33 S	43.18 W
Xeres → Jerez de la Frontera	34	36.41 N	6.08 W
Xertigny	58	48.03 N	6.24 E
Xhumo	156	21.07 S	24.42 E
Xi ≃, Zhg.	100	25.14 N	118.03 E
Xi ≃, Zhg.	100	30.21 N	115.06 E
Xi ≃, Zhg.	100	24.34 N	117.30 E
Xi ≃, Zhg.	102	42.20 N	100.20 E
Xi ≃, Zhg.	102	22.25 N	113.23 E
Xi ≃, Zhg.	104	41.15 N	123.32 E
Xi ≃, Zhg.	104	41.30 N	121.26 E
Xi ≃, Zhg.	107	30.26 N	103.48 E
Xiaang	106	30.45 N	120.07 E
Xiaba	100	24.54 N	116.06 E
Xiabai, Zhg.	106	31.12 N	119.50 E
Xiabai, Zhg.	106	30.29 N	120.00 E
Xiabanghu	100	30.31 N	112.38 E
Xiabian	104	40.51 N	120.30 E
Xiabuji	100	28.19 N	116.20 E
Xiacang	105	39.47 N	117.24 E
Xiache	100	24.40 N	115.08 E
Xiachengzi	89	44.41 N	130.27 E
Xiachuan Dao I	102	21.40 N	112.37 E
Xiacun	105	40.21 N	116.14 E
Xiadao	100	26.34 N	118.16 E
Xiadian, Zhg.	98	37.06 N	120.19 E
Xiadian, Zhg.	100	31.26 N	114.17 E
Xiadian, Zhg.	105	39.57 N	116.55 E
Xiadianjie	100	25.13 N	118.27 E
Xiafeidi	98	42.18 N	124.21 E
Xiafu, Zhg.	100	25.01 N	113.41 E
Xiafu, Zhg.	100	23.52 N	115.45 E
Xiagaixin	102	22.36 N	99.59 E
Xiagang	106	31.55 N	120.13 E
Xiagezhuang	98	36.41 N	120.25 E
Xiaguan, Zhg.	98	39.07 N	114.09 E
Xiaguan, Zhg.	102	25.34 N	100.14 E
Xiaguan, Zhg.	106	32.06 N	118.44 E
Xiaguanjunchang	104	41.28 N	121.40 E
Xiaguanpi	100	24.04 N	117.06 E
Xiagucheng	102	36.47 N	102.53 E
Xiagucun	106	30.56 N	119.09 E
Xiahada	104	41.58 N	124.08 E
Xiahailangzhai	104	41.35 N	123.46 E
Xiahe	102	35.18 N	102.30 E
Xiahuangjintun	104	41.57 N	123.48 E
Xiahuayuan	105	40.29 N	115.17 E
Xiajiabaozi	98	42.16 N	124.37 E
Xiajialou	104	42.25 N	123.39 E
Xiajiang	100	27.32 N	115.08 E
Xiajiangdun	106	31.14 N	120.24 E
Xiajiangwu	106	30.29 N	119.00 E
Xiajiayuan	106	32.13 N	120.38 E
Xiajiezi	102	27.28 N	101.35 E
Xiajin	98	36.55 N	115.57 E
Xiakou	100	28.28 N	118.31 E
Xialianggang	105	39.14 N	115.07 E
Xialufang	102	31.11 N	103.38 E
Xiamaguan	102	37.14 N	106.28 E
Xiamen (Amoy)	100	24.28 N	118.07 E
Xiamen Gang ⊂	100	24.19 N	118.10 E
Xiamianzhen	107	30.08 N	106.32 E
Xiamin'ansutai	104	41.54 N	120.53 E
Xiamocun	106	31.09 N	119.22 E
Xi'an (Sian)	102	34.15 N	108.52 E
Xian ≃	107	29.22 N	104.44 E
Xianchenggu	98	36.53 N	115.17 E
Xiandu	100	25.04 N	117.44 E
Xianfeng, Zhg.	100	25.42 N	117.53 E
Xianfeng, Zhg.	102	29.41 N	109.02 E
Xiang ≃, Zhg.	100	25.35 N	115.49 E
Xiang ≃, Zhg.	102	29.00 N	112.56 E
Xiang'an	100	31.12 N	117.46 E
Xiangcheng, Zhg.	100	33.28 N	114.53 E
Xiangcheng, Zhg.	100	33.53 N	113.29 E
Xiangcheng, Zhg.	102	28.59 N	99.45 E
Xiangcheng, Zhg.	106	31.29 N	120.44 E
Xiangfan	102	32.03 N	112.01 E
Xiangfuguan	100	28.30 N	115.26 E
Xiangfusi	107	30.06 N	104.24 E
Xianggang → Victoria	271d	22.17 N	114.09 E
Xianggongshi	100	28.25 N	113.32 E
Xianggongzhuang	105	39.48 N	118.19 E
Xianghe	105	39.46 N	116.59 E
Xiangheguan	100	33.08 N	113.26 E
Xianghuazhen	106	31.31 N	121.43 E
Xiangjia, Zhg.	106	31.20 N	120.31 E
Xiangjia, Zhg.	106	31.19 N	120.23 E
Xiangjiachang	107	30.08 N	104.18 E
Xiangkhoang	110	19.20 N	103.22 E
Xiangkhoang, Plateau de ⋏1	110	19.30 N	103.10 E
Xiangning	102	36.01 N	110.45 E
Xiangride	102	36.02 N	98.08 E
Xiangshan, Zhg.	100	29.28 N	121.51 E
Xiangshan, Zhg.	105	39.59 N	116.12 E
Xiangshan Gang ⊂	100	29.38 N	121.48 E
Xiangshizhen	107	29.17 N	105.09 E
Xiangshui, Zhg.	100	23.15 N	114.10 E
Xiangshui, Zhg.	100	34.12 N	119.34 E
Xiangtan	100	27.51 N	112.54 E
Xiangtang	100	28.26 N	115.58 E
Xiangxiang	102	27.43 N	112.27 E
Xiangyang	105	39.13 N	115.25 E
Xiangyangkou	105	40.06 N	115.47 E
Xiangyin	100	28.40 N	112.53 E
Xiangyuan	102	36.32 N	113.00 E
Xiangyun	102	25.30 N	100.30 E
Xiangzhenpu	100	30.52 N	117.21 E
Xiangzhou, Zhg.	98	36.12 N	119.24 E
Xiangzhou, Zhg.	102	23.55 N	109.49 E
Xiangzhu	100	29.02 N	120.04 E
Xianinggang	100	28.20 N	112.56 E
Xianjiang	100	27.48 N	120.30 E
Xianju	100	28.51 N	120.44 E
Xianning	100	29.53 N	114.17 E
Xiannongtan Stadium ♠	271a	39.52 N	116.23 E
Xiannübu	100	25.36 N	114.40 E
Xianru	89	43.11 N	128.02 E
Xianshichang	107	28.43 N	105.44 E
Xianshui ≃	102	30.05 N	110.59 E
Xianshuigu	105	38.59 N	117.23 E
Xiantan, Zhg.	107	29.21 N	104.53 E
Xiantan, Zhg.	107	28.50 N	106.12 E
Xiantang	100	23.48 N	114.46 E
Xianxia Ling ⋏	100	28.30 N	118.46 E
Xianxian	98	38.13 N	116.06 E
Xianyang, Zhg.	100	28.02 N	118.30 E
Xianyang, Zhg.	102	34.22 N	108.42 E
Xianyou	100	25.23 N	118.40 E
Xianzhong	100	28.36 N	113.48 E
Xiao ≃	100	28.11 N	120.14 E
Xiao'an ≃	107	29.59 N	106.13 E
Xiao'ao	100	26.14 N	119.39 E
Xiaoazhang	102	23.42 N	104.58 E
Xiaobangniulu	104	41.34 N	122.46 E
Xiaobeigou	104	41.55 N	120.46 E
Xiaobeihe, Zhg.	104	42.39 N	123.58 E
Xiaobeihe, Zhg.	104	41.22 N	122.50 E
Xiaocaohu	86	43.06 N	88.30 E
Xiaochangshan Dao I	98	39.12 N	122.41 E
Xiaocheng	100	26.20 N	119.47 E
Xiaochengdu	106	30.59 N	120.04 E
Xiaochengzi, Zhg.	89	46.33 N	122.54 E
Xiaochengzi, Zhg.	89	42.56 N	123.12 E
Xiaochi	100	30.33 N	116.23 E
Xiaochikou	100	29.46 N	115.59 E
Xiaodanyang	106	31.38 N	118.43 E
Xiaodong	102	22.14 N	108.39 E
Xiao'ergou	89	49.12 N	123.42 E
Xiaofangshen	104	42.13 N	123.54 E
Xiaofanshan	105	40.16 N	115.19 E
Xiaofen	106	31.45 N	119.39 E
Xiaofeng	106	30.36 N	119.32 E
Xiaogan	100	30.55 N	113.54 E
Xiaogangkou	100	28.14 N	115.50 E
Xiaogaojiatun	104	41.02 N	121.59 E
Xiaogencaigangzi	104	41.48 N	122.42 E
Xiaogu	107	29.08 N	104.01 E
Xiaoguai	86	45.13 N	85.02 E
Xiaogushan	98	39.49 N	123.12 E
Xiaohaizhen	106	31.58 N	120.59 E
Xiaohaladaokou	98	42.37 N	119.32 E
Xiaohan	98	35.48 N	114.52 E
Xiaohe	106	32.01 N	119.52 E
Xiaohei Shan ∧	102	24.42 N	98.55 E
Xiaohekou	102	33.19 N	107.25 E
Xiaoheyan	98	42.26 N	119.38 E
Xiaoheying	102	32.37 N	104.23 E
Xiao Hinggan Ling (Lesser Khingan Range) ⋏	89	48.45 N	127.00 E
Xiaohongmen	271a	39.49 N	116.26 E
Xiaohu	100	27.20 N	118.14 E
Xiaohuying	98	41.09 N	117.13 E
Xiaoji, Zhg.	98	36.45 N	121.01 E
Xiaoji, Zhg.	100	27.08 N	113.15 E
Xiaoji, Zhg.	100	32.38 N	119.48 E
Xiaojiachang	107	30.18 N	106.28 E
Xiaojiagang	100	31.06 N	113.55 E
Xiaojialing	100	29.35 N	116.32 E
Xiaojiang	100	25.08 N	114.59 E
Xiaojianji	100	33.23 N	116.29 E
Xiaojiawu	105	39.36 N	116.36 E
Xiaojiayingzi	98	40.17 N	118.47 E
Xiaojieling	100	31.36 N	115.09 E
Xiaojin	102	31.00 N	102.21 E
Xiaojingfang	105	39.22 N	116.34 E
Xiaojiu	89	45.15 N	127.47 E
Xiaokaoshantun	104	42.10 N	123.53 E
Xiaokuli	89	50.18 N	120.20 E
Xiaokunshan	106	31.02 N	121.07 E
Xiaolan	100	22.41 N	113.14 E
Xiaoliangshan	104	42.05 N	122.32 E
Xiaoling, Zhg.	89	45.20 N	127.18 E
Xiaoling, Zhg.	104	42.18 N	123.23 E
Xiaoling ≃	104	41.06 N	121.07 E
Xiaolingzi	104	41.07 N	123.19 E
Xiaolinzhuang	104	41.36 N	124.01 E
Xiaolipu	98	36.24 N	116.35 E
Xiaolongtan	102	23.51 N	103.10 E
Xiaoluan ≃	98	41.36 N	117.05 E
Xiaolüzhuang	106	31.57 N	119.25 E
Xiaomei	100	27.50 N	118.58 E
Xiaomei Guan)(	100	25.17 N	114.17 E
Xiaomiaozi	98	41.24 N	114.25 E
Xiaonanhai	107	29.23 N	106.27 E
Xiaopikou	98	35.47 N	115.53 E
Xiaopingyang	102	23.22 N	109.13 E
Xiao Qaidam He ⊜	102	37.30 N	95.12 E
Xiaoqiao	100	26.57 N	118.30 E
Xiaoqiaotou	106	30.43 N	119.27 E
Xiaoqing ≃	98	37.17 N	118.52 E
Xiaoqingchuizi	104	42.30 N	123.39 E
Xiaoquandong	102	41.14 N	95.26 E
Xiaosanjiazi	104	42.34 N	123.23 E
Xiaosha ≃	104	41.13 N	122.45 E
Xiaoshakou	100	29.58 N	113.16 E
Xiaoshan	106	30.10 N	120.15 E
Xiaoshangqiao	100	33.43 N	113.58 E
Xiaoshi	100	27.27 N	116.49 E
Xiaoshixiang	100	30.36 N	116.38 E
Xiaoshu	106	30.48 N	119.46 E
Xiaoshun	100	29.11 N	119.51 E
Xiaosigou	98	40.53 N	118.33 E
Xiaosijia	104	42.24 N	120.46 E
Xiaotang	98	41.38 N	119.33 E
Xiaotanghe	98	42.04 N	127.10 E
Xiaotao	100	25.46 N	117.08 E
Xiaotazi	104	42.17 N	123.08 E
Xiaotian	100	31.12 N	116.33 E
Xiaotianji	100	32.45 N	115.36 E
Xiaotun	104	42.24 N	123.44 E
Xiaotunzicun	104	41.14 N	123.20 E
Xiaowa	104	41.03 N	122.04 E
Xiaowan	100	26.53 N	116.36 E
Xiaowangmiao	100	29.41 N	121.21 E
Xiaowutai Shan ∧	105	39.51 N	115.09 E
Xiaowutai Shan ⋏	105	39.50 N	115.00 E
Xiaoxi	100	25.48 N	115.21 E
Xiaoxi ≃	106	32.15 N	120.24 E
Xiaoxian	98	34.11 N	116.56 E
Xiaoxincheng	105	39.24 N	115.11 E
Xiaoxintian	271a	39.58 N	116.22 E
Xiaoxizhen	106	30.51 N	119.50 E
Xiaoyangjiadian	104	42.23 N	122.24 E
Xiaoyangqi	89	50.48 N	124.12 E
Xiaoyantai	104	41.26 N	123.10 E
Xiaoyaozhen	100	33.46 N	114.16 E
Xiaoyi	102	37.10 N	111.46 E
Xiaoying, Zhg.	98	37.18 N	118.04 E
Xiaoying, Zhg.	105	40.12 N	116.33 E
Xiaoyingcun	105	39.28 N	116.41 E
Xiaoyuan	107	30.00 N	104.56 E
Xiaozhan	105	38.55 N	117.25 E
Xiaozhang ≃	105	39.47 N	117.22 E
Xiaozhongdian	102	27.40 N	99.46 E
Xiaozhuang	104	41.30 N	121.27 E
Xiaozhujiawan	106	31.24 N	121.01 E
Xiapu, Zhg.	100	26.52 N	120.01 E
Xiapu, Zhg.	100	27.49 N	114.26 E
Xiaqialafangzi	104	41.48 N	121.44 E
Xiaqi Dao I	100	29.42 N	122.15 E
Xiaqiubao	98	37.01 N	119.54 E
Xiasantumen	105	38.50 N	114.48 E
Xiashe	106	30.33 N	120.11 E
Xiashesi	100	27.46 N	112.57 E
Xiashi → Haining	106	30.32 N	120.41 E
Xiashu	106	32.11 N	119.10 E
Xiashuerfowei	89	50.23 N	120.47 E
Xiashuiquan	104	41.52 N	123.38 E
Xiataizi	105	40.37 N	117.45 E
Xiatang, Zhg.	100	33.45 N	112.39 E
Xiatang, Zhg.	106	31.29 N	118.41 E
Xiatangtian	106	30.55 N	120.12 E
Xiataohuatu	104	41.42 N	120.36 E
Xiawa	98	42.39 N	120.35 E
Xiawajiang	106	30.59 N	121.51 E
Xiawaziyu	104	41.15 N	123.38 E
Xiaxi	106	31.43 N	119.45 E
Xiaxian	102	35.11 N	111.15 E
Xiaxiangcheng	102	28.42 N	99.59 E
Xiaxikou	100	26.15 N	118.59 E
Xiaxinhe	106	31.40 N	119.31 E
Xiayang, Zhg.	100	28.48 N	119.41 E
Xiayang, Zhg.	100	26.46 N	117.59 E
Xiayang, Zhg.	100	24.39 N	116.52 E
Xiayi	98	34.14 N	116.06 E
Xiaying, Zhg.	98	37.03 N	119.25 E
Xiaying, Zhg.	105	40.10 N	117.25 E
Xiayunling	105	39.43 N	115.44 E
Xiazhang	98	36.08 N	116.57 E
Xiazhen	100	28.39 N	118.21 E
Xiazhuang, Zhg.	98	35.28 N	118.43 E
Xiazhuang, Zhg.	100	27.22 N	119.01 E
Xiazhuang, Zhg.	105	39.54 N	117.01 E
Xiazhuang, Zhg.	105	39.38 N	115.26 E
Xiazikou	105	39.01 N	115.25 E
Xiban	107	30.32 N	106.12 E
Xibaqianmou	104	40.59 N	121.35 E
Xibeiyingzi	104	41.55 N	121.38 E
Xibo ≃	98	42.17 N	118.57 E
Xibu	100	31.46 N	118.17 E
Xicang	106	31.34 N	120.29 E
Xichang, Zhg.	102	27.58 N	102.13 E
Xichang, Zhg.	104	42.15 N	124.12 E
Xicheng	89	48.10 N	125.29 E
Xichong	102	31.00 N	105.52 E
Xicicun	105	39.29 N	116.08 E
Xico	234	19.25 N	97.00 W
Xicoténcatl	234	23.00 N	98.56 W
Xicotepec de Juárez	234	20.17 N	97.57 W
Xicun	100	27.46 N	114.14 E
Xidachuan	98	41.46 N	127.34 E
Xidapo	89	43.12 N	130.02 E
Xidaying	105	39.41 N	116.14 E
Xidian	100	29.32 N	121.26 E
Xiditou	105	39.16 N	117.23 E
Xidongting Shan ∧	106	31.07 N	120.16 E
Xié ≃	246	0.54 N	67.11 W
Xiecun	105	39.00 N	115.31 E
Xiedian	100	33.27 N	113.28 E
Xiefang	100	26.12 N	116.41 E
Xiegeer	120	28.38 N	87.04 E
Xieji	98	34.32 N	115.29 E
Xiejia	98	42.24 N	125.42 E
Xiejiagangzi	104	41.55 N	122.20 E
Xiejiapu	106	31.15 N	119.09 E
Xiejunmiao	107	30.15 N	103.40 E
Xielipuke	120	31.30 N	82.45 E
Xiemachang	107	29.46 N	106.22 E
Xiemata Shan ∧	89	50.28 N	120.47 E
Xiepu	100	30.02 N	121.37 E
Xieqiao, Zhg.	106	32.03 N	120.22 E
Xieqiao, Zhg.	106	30.29 N	120.34 E
Xietang	106	31.18 N	120.44 E
Xiexi	106	31.54 N	118.54 E
Xiexinggou	104	41.51 N	121.05 E
Xifei ≃	100	32.38 N	116.39 E
Xifeng, Zhg.	98	42.43 N	124.40 E
Xifeng, Zhg.	102	27.02 N	106.30 E
Xifengkou	105	40.24 N	118.19 E
Xifocun	104	41.26 N	122.33 E
Xigangzi	89	49.58 N	127.20 E
Xigaolizhuangzi	104	41.40 N	122.55 E
Xigaotan	98	38.18 N	116.13 E
Xigaotun	98	40.27 N	122.36 E
Xigazê	120	29.17 N	88.53 E
Xiguanjiatun	104	42.35 N	123.10 E
Xiguanyingzi	104	41.50 N	120.37 E

≃ River	Fluss	Río	Rivière	Rio	✢ Submarine Features	Untermeerische Objekte	Accidentes Submarinos	Formes de relief sous-marin	Acidentes submarinos
≍ Canal	Kanal	Canal	Canal	Canal	□ Political Unit	Politische Einheit	Unidad Politica	Entité politique	Unidade política
ʟ Waterfall, Rapids	Wasserfall, Stromschnellen	Cascada, Rápidos	Chute d'eau, Rapides	Cascata, Rápidos	⛉ Cultural Institution	Kulturelle Institution	Institución Cultural	Institution culturelle	Instituição cultural
ʉ Strait	Meeresstrasse	Estrecho	Détroit	Estreito	⊥ Historical Site	Historische Stätte	Sitio Histórico	Site historique	Sitio histórico
⊂ Bay, Gulf	Bucht, Golf	Bahía, Golfo	Baie, Golfe	Baía, Golfo	♠ Recreational Site	Erholungs- und Ferienort	Sitio de Recreo	Centre de loisirs	Area de Lazer
⊜ Lake, Lakes	See, Seen	Lago, Lagos	Lac, Lacs	Lago, Lagos	⊠ Airport	Flughafen	Aeropuerto	Aéroport	Aeroporto
≡ Swamp	Sumpf	Pantano	Marais	Pântano	■ Military Installation	Militäranlage	Instalación Militar	Installation militaire	Instalação militar
⊓ Ice Features, Glacier	Eis- und Gletscherformen	Accidentes Glaciales	Formes glaciaires	Acidentes glaciares	◆ Miscellaneous	Verschiedenes	Misceláneo	Divers	Diversos
⊤ Other Hydrographic Features	Andere Hydrographische Objekte	Otros Elementos Hidrográficos	Autres données hydrographiques	Outros acidentes hidrográficos					

Name	Page	Lat.°′	Long.°′
Xihaikou	**104**	40.50 N	121.05 E
Xihan ≃	**102**	33.30 N	106.02 E
Xihe, Zhg.	**100**	31.01 N	118.28 E
Xihe, Zhg.	**100**	31.41 N	113.27 E
Xihe, Zhg.	**102**	34.01 N	105.17 E
Xiheying	**105**	39.53 N	114.42 E
Xihezhuang	**105**	39.20 N	118.02 E
Xi Hu ⊜	**106**	30.15 N	120.08 E
Xihua	**100**	33.47 N	114.31 E
Xihuangcang	**106**	31.43 N	121.40 E
Xihuanzidong	**104**	41.31 N	122.28 E
Xihuashan, Zhg.	**100**	25.28 N	114.20 E
Xihuashan, Zhg.	**105**	40.07 N	116.54 E
Xihuishan	**104**	41.41 N	122.38 E
Xiis	**144**	10.53 N	46.54 E
Xiji, Zhg.	**102**	35.58 N	105.44 E
Xiji, Zhg.	**105**	39.49 N	116.52 E
Xijialong	**102**	23.31 N	103.51 E
Xijiang	**100**	25.50 N	115.49 E
Xijianshanzi	**104**	40.47 N	120.48 E
Xi Jiao Airfield ⊠	**271a**	39.58 N	116.15 E
Xijiapuzitun	**104**	41.26 N	123.50 E
Xikou, Zhg.	**89**	46.40 N	120.40 E
Xikou, Zhg.	**100**	28.52 N	119.11 E
Xikou, Zhg.	**100**	25.26 N	118.45 E
Xikou, Zhg.	**100**	29.14 N	114.24 E
Xikou, Zhg.	**100**	29.44 N	118.02 E
Xikou, Zhg.	**100**	29.11 N	114.23 E
Xikou, Zhg.	**106**	30.40 N	118.41 E
Xikouxu	**100**	25.24 N	117.03 E
Xikouzi	**89**	53.06 N	120.40 E
Xilai	**107**	30.20 N	103.29 E
Xilaiqiao	**106**	32.03 N	119.54 E
Xilaizhen	**106**	32.07 N	120.25 E
Xilin	**120**	28.33 N	87.48 E
Xi Ling (Western Tombs) ⊥	**105**	39.24 N	115.18 E
Xilintuo	**120**	30.08 N	88.04 E
Xilitla	**234**	21.20 N	98.58 W
Xiliuhe	**105**	38.58 N	116.32 E
Xiliushuyingzi	**104**	42.25 N	121.54 E
Xilókastron	**38**	38.05 N	22.38 E
Xiluga ≃	**98**	42.21 N	118.38 E
Xiluncun	**89**	47.08 N	126.26 E
Ximagou	**105**	40.16 N	117.50 E
Ximakou	**100**	30.33 N	113.47 E
Ximalatu	**89**	47.00 N	122.01 E
Ximalin	**98**	40.48 N	114.29 E
Ximiao	**102**	41.09 N	100.17 E
Ximucheng	**104**	40.42 N	122.54 E
Xin ≃	**100**	28.37 N	116.40 E
Xin'an, Zhg.	**89**	43.46 N	125.40 E
Xinan, Zhg.	**100**	25.26 N	117.35 E
Xin'an, Zhg.	**100**	26.44 N	116.13 E
Xin'an, Zhg.	**100**	23.02 N	114.56 E
Xin'an, Zhg.	**105**	39.09 N	116.38 E
Xin'an, Zhg.	**106**	31.47 N	120.09 E
Xin'an, Zhg.	**106**	31.30 N	120.22 E
Xin'an ≃	**100**	29.33 N	118.58 E
Xin'andian	**100**	32.37 N	114.03 E
Xin'andu	**100**	30.52 N	116.53 E
Xin'anji	**100**	33.22 N	115.13 E
Xin'anjiang Shuiku ⊜[1]	**100**	29.27 N	119.06 E
Xin'anpu	**104**	42.39 N	123.27 E
Xin'anqiao	**106**	32.16 N	121.07 E
Xin'ansuo	**102**	23.16 N	103.27 E
Xin'anzhen, Zhg.	**89**	44.06 N	123.46 E
Xin'anzhen, Zhg.	**105**	39.45 N	117.32 E
Xi'nanzhuang	**105**	40.48 N	118.23 E
Xinavane	**156**	25.02 S	32.47 E
Xinba, Zhg.	**98**	34.27 N	119.09 E
Xinba, Zhg.	**100**	30.24 N	116.52 E
Xinba, Zhg.	**106**	32.08 N	120.39 E
Xinba, Zhg.	**106**	32.16 N	119.45 E
Xinbao'an	**105**	40.27 N	115.24 E
Xin Barag Youqi (Altan Emel)	**88**	48.41 N	116.53 E
Xin Barag Zuoqi (Amgalang)	**88**	48.14 N	118.18 E
Xinbin, Zhg.	**98**	41.42 N	125.02 E
Xinbin, Zhg.	**106**	30.56 N	121.04 E
Xinbo	**98**	42.19 N	117.44 E
Xincai	**100**	32.44 N	114.59 E
Xincang, Zhg.	**106**	30.25 N	120.42 E
Xincang, Zhg.	**106**	30.44 N	121.11 E
Xinchang, Zhg.	**100**	29.30 N	120.53 E
Xinchang, Zhg.	**102**	28.03 N	103.46 E
Xinchang, Zhg.	**102**	25.10 N	104.18 E
Xinchang, Zhg.	**106**	31.42 N	121.46 E
Xinchang, Zhg.	**106**	31.02 N	121.38 E
Xinchang, Zhg.	**107**	30.29 N	106.21 E
Xinchang, Zhg.	**107**	30.16 N	104.29 E
Xinchang, Zhg.	**107**	29.20 N	104.15 E
Xinchang, Zhg.	**107**	29.38 N	104.33 E
Xinchangzi	**107**	29.40 N	103.46 E
Xincheng, Zhg.	**100**	25.34 N	114.36 E
Xincheng, Zhg.	**102**	24.09 N	108.46 E
Xincheng, Zhg.	**105**	38.59 N	117.33 E
Xincheng (Gaobeidian), Zhg.	**105**	39.20 N	115.51 E
Xincheng, Zhg.	**106**	30.48 N	120.36 E
Xincheng, Zhg.	**106**	32.17 N	119.14 E
Xinchengzi	**104**	42.03 N	123.30 E
Xinchepaizi	**86**	44.55 N	84.30 E
Xincunji	**100**	32.53 N	115.31 E
Xindai	**106**	30.49 N	121.05 E
Xindi	**104**	42.21 N	120.31 E
Xindian, Zhg.	**89**	45.55 N	127.50 E
Xindian, Zhg.	**98**	37.07 N	114.49 E
Xindian, Zhg.	**98**	37.29 N	118.28 E
Xindian, Zhg.	**100**	33.07 N	112.38 E
Xindian, Zhg.	**100**	31.33 N	115.16 E
Xindian, Zhg.	**100**	33.38 N	113.51 E
Xindian, Zhg.	**100**	29.40 N	113.40 E
Xindian, Zhg.	**105**	40.11 N	116.11 E
Xindian, Zhg.	**105**	40.47 N	116.49 E
Xindian, Zhg.	**105**	39.10 N	116.27 E
Xindian, Zhg.	**107**	29.19 N	105.40 E
Xindianbu	**100**	32.24 N	116.22 E
Xindianzi, Zhg.	**105**	40.04 N	118.01 E
Xindianzi, Zhg.	**107**	28.49 N	103.35 E
Xindianzi, Zhg.	**107**	29.03 N	103.46 E
Xindianzi, Zhg.	**107**	29.52 N	106.06 E
Xindianzi, Zhg.	**107**	29.46 N	105.11 E
Xindianzi, Zhg.	**107**	29.43 N	104.01 E
Xindu	**102**	23.59 N	111.46 E
Xinfatuncun	**104**	41.13 N	122.28 E
Xinfeng, Zhg.	**100**	25.24 N	114.56 E
Xinfeng, Zhg.	**100**	27.26 N	116.40 E
Xinfeng, Zhg.	**100**	33.19 N	120.30 E
Xinfeng, Zhg.	**100**	24.04 N	114.12 E
Xinfeng, Zhg.	**100**	24.05 N	116.53 E
Xinfeng, Zhg.	**106**	31.09 N	118.40 E
Xinfeng, Zhg.	**106**	32.05 N	119.34 E
Xinfeng, Zhg.	**106**	30.43 N	120.55 E
Xinfeng ≃	**100**	23.42 N	114.42 E
Xinfeng Shuiku ⊜[1]	**100**	23.52 N	114.30 E
Xing'an, Zhg.	**89**	48.49 N	121.45 E
Xing'an, Zhg.	**102**	25.37 N	110.31 E
Xin'gang, Zhg.	**106**	31.56 N	120.57 E
Xingang, Zhg.	**106**	32.03 N	120.25 E
Xing'antun	**89**	51.31 N	120.08 E
Xingcheng	**104**	40.37 N	120.43 E
Xingguo	**100**	26.21 N	115.19 E
Xinghai	**102**	35.31 N	99.36 E
Xinghe	**98**	40.48 N	113.58 E
Xinghua	**100**	32.57 N	119.50 E
Xinghua Wan ⊂	**100**	25.20 N	119.20 E
Xingjing	**102**	29.43 N	102.59 E
Xingkai Hu (ozero Chanka) ⊜	**89**	45.00 N	132.24 E
Xingliu	**100**	33.04 N	115.41 E
Xinglong, Zhg.	**100**	32.05 N	112.51 E
Xinglong, Zhg.	**102**	35.38 N	106.08 E
Xinglong, Zhg.	**105**	40.26 N	117.34 E
Xinglong, Zhg.	**107**	30.36 N	106.20 E
Xinglong, Zhg.	**107**	30.20 N	106.07 E
Xinglongchang, Zhg.	**107**	30.25 N	104.06 E
Xinglongchang, Zhg.	**107**	29.34 N	106.09 E
Xinglongchang, Zhg.	**107**	29.54 N	105.26 E
Xinglongcun	**89**	49.50 N	125.12 E
Xinglongdian, Zhg.	**104**	42.16 N	124.00 E
Xinglongdian, Zhg.	**104**	41.59 N	123.03 E
Xinglonggou, Zhg.	**104**	41.46 N	120.38 E
Xinglonggou, Zhg.	**104**	40.45 N	123.08 E
Xinglongpao	**89**	46.27 N	125.47 E
Xinglongtai	**104**	42.30 N	123.48 E
Xingning	**100**	24.09 N	115.45 E
Xingou, Zhg.	**100**	30.41 N	113.57 E
Xingou, Zhg.	**100**	30.08 N	112.56 E
Xingren	**102**	25.27 N	105.13 E
Xingrenbu	**102**	37.06 N	105.12 E
Xingshanbao	**89**	45.30 N	125.45 E
Xingtai	**98**	37.04 N	114.29 E
Xingtan	**100**	22.46 N	113.07 E
Xingtang	**98**	38.26 N	114.33 E
Xingtian	**100**	27.30 N	118.02 E
Xingu ≃	**242**	1.30 S	51.53 W
Xinguan	**100**	33.38 N	118.05 E
Xingwenping	**102**	29.24 N	103.23 E
Xingxian	**102**	38.36 N	111.15 E
Xingxing	**106**	30.39 N	121.09 E
Xingyi, Zhg.	**98**	38.18 N	115.01 E
Xingyi, Zhg.	**102**	25.06 N	104.58 E
Xingzhuangzi	**105**	40.34 N	115.00 E
Xingzi	**100**	29.28 N	116.01 E
Xinhe, Zhg.	**98**	37.32 N	115.14 E
Xinhe, Zhg.	**100**	28.30 N	121.27 E
Xinhe, Zhg.	**105**	39.03 N	117.37 E
Xinhe, Zhg.	**106**	31.59 N	121.21 E
Xinhekou	**89**	48.22 N	130.45 E
Xinheng	**100**	23.38 N	116.18 E
Xinhezhen	**106**	31.35 N	121.31 E
Xinhezhuang	**106**	31.10 N	118.46 E
Xinhua	**102**	27.37 N	111.02 E
Xinhuai ≃	**100**	34.23 N	120.05 E
Xinhuang	**106**	30.37 N	120.55 E
Xinhui	**100**	22.32 N	113.02 E
Xining (Sining)	**102**	36.38 N	101.55 E
Xiniu, Zhg.	**100**	24.10 N	113.07 E
Xiniu, Zhg.	**106**	31.25 N	120.07 E
Xiniuguchengzi	**104**	41.01 N	122.24 E
Xinji, Zhg.	**98**	35.19 N	115.36 E
Xinji, Zhg.	**100**	33.24 N	114.44 E
Xinji, Zhg.	**105**	39.52 N	117.10 E
Xinji, Zhg.	**105**	40.04 N	118.21 E
Xinjiaji	**98**	36.56 N	116.59 E
Xinjian, Zhg.	**100**	28.46 N	120.02 E
Xinjian, Zhg.	**100**	28.34 N	115.47 E
Xinjian, Zhg.	**106**	31.33 N	119.39 E
Xinjiang, Zhg.	**100**	24.29 N	113.52 E
Xinjiang, Zhg.	**102**	35.40 N	111.11 E
Xinjiang, Zhg.	**106**	32.05 N	120.40 E
Xinjianglang	**106**	30.58 N	120.54 E
Xinjiang Uygur Zizhiqu (Sinkiang) □[4]	**90**	40.00 N	85.00 E
Xinjiapu	**105**	40.32 N	115.57 E
Xinjiazhuang	**105**	40.31 N	114.58 E
Xinjie	**102**	26.48 N	101.15 E
Xinjieji	**89**	52.08 N	126.24 E
Xinjin (Pulandian), Zhg.	**98**	39.24 N	121.58 E
Xinjin, Zhg.	**107**	30.25 N	103.49 E
Xinjingzi	**86**	42.13 N	87.36 E
Xinjuntun	**105**	39.39 N	117.57 E
Xinkai ≃	**89**	43.37 N	123.36 E
Xinkaigang	**106**	31.55 N	120.56 E
Xinkengdong	**100**	26.09 N	113.46 E
Xinle (Dongchangshou)	**98**	38.24 N	114.47 E
Xinli	**89**	44.41 N	126.45 E
Xinlitun, Zhg.	**89**	43.34 N	125.18 E
Xinlitun, Zhg.	**104**	42.00 N	122.09 E
Xinlitun, Zhg.	**104**	42.15 N	122.51 E
Xinlizhuang	**105**	39.17 N	116.10 E
Xinmin	**104**	42.00 N	122.48 E
Xinmintun	**104**	41.39 N	123.02 E
Xinning	**102**	26.19 N	110.45 E
Xinping	**102**	24.06 N	101.58 E
Xinpu	**100**	24.31 N	116.08 E
Xinqianhu	**98**	37.59 N	118.15 E
Xinqiao, Zhg.	**106**	31.32 N	119.04 E
Xinqiao, Zhg.	**106**	31.04 N	121.18 E
Xinqiao, Zhg.	**107**	29.32 N	106.28 E
Xinqiao, Zhg.	**107**	30.10 N	103.50 E
Xinqiao, Zhg.	**107**	30.33 N	105.33 E
Xinqiaotou	**106**	31.00 N	119.24 E
Xinqiaozhen	**107**	29.36 N	103.39 E
Xinqiu	**98**	41.53 N	119.41 E
Xinqizhou	**100**	28.56 N	115.50 E
Xinqu	**86**	44.57 N	85.15 E
Xinquan	**100**	25.23 N	116.38 E
Xinsanyu	**106**	31.58 N	120.07 E
Xinshao	**102**	27.11 N	111.20 E
Xinshengzhen	**107**	29.29 N	104.39 E
Xinshi, Zhg.	**106**	30.37 N	120.19 E
Xinshi, Zhg.	**106**	32.04 N	120.02 E
Xinshizhen, Zhg.	**102**	28.39 N	104.02 E
Xinshizhen, Zhg.	**107**	30.20 N	104.35 E
Xinshu ≃	**98**	34.41 N	119.12 E
Xintai	**98**	35.54 N	117.44 E
Xintaimen	**98**	40.50 N	120.23 E
Xintaizi, Zhg.	**104**	41.06 N	122.42 E
Xintaizi, Zhg.	**104**	42.07 N	123.36 E
Xintang, Zhg.	**100**	23.08 N	113.36 E
Xintang, Zhg.	**102**	30.13 N	109.30 E
Xintang, Zhg.	**106**	31.02 N	119.59 E
Xintangcun	**106**	31.53 N	119.31 E
Xintanpu	**100**	29.43 N	114.54 E
Xintian	**102**	25.53 N	112.05 E
Xintun	**104**	42.11 N	123.45 E
Xinvi	**105**	40.04 N	118.21 E
Xinwei	**100**	25.21 N	115.48 E
Xinwen (Suncun)	**98**	35.53 N	117.40 E
Xinxian, Zhg.	**100**	31.38 N	114.51 E
Xinxian, Zhg.	**102**	38.25 N	112.48 E
Xinxiang	**98**	35.20 N	113.51 E
Xinxim ≃	**250**	7.57 S	53.20 W
Xinxing, Zhg.	**89**	43.16 N	129.48 E
Xinxing, Zhg.	**100**	22.40 N	112.52 E
Xinxing, Zhg.	**102**	19.57 N	109.32 E
Xinxu, Zhg.	**100**	22.52 N	114.20 E
Xinxu, Zhg.	**100**	24.57 N	117.34 E
Xinyang	**100**	32.08 N	114.04 E
Xinyao	**100**	27.39 N	118.52 E
Xinye	**100**	32.33 N	112.21 E
Xinyi (Xin'anzhen), Zhg.	**98**	34.22 N	118.21 E
Xinyi (Dongzhen), Zhg.	**102**	22.13 N	110.50 E
Xinyi ≃	**100**	34.29 N	119.49 E
Xinying	**102**	36.03 N	105.35 E
Xinyu	**100**	27.49 N	114.57 E
Xinyuan	**86**	43.08 N	82.31 E
Xinzao	**100**	23.02 N	113.26 E
Xinzha	**102**	23.41 N	101.09 E
Xinzhai, Zhg.	**98**	39.24 N	118.46 E
Xinzhai, Zhg.	**98**	36.24 N	118.37 E
Xinzhai, Zhg.	**102**	24.33 N	99.08 E
Xinzhan	**100**	33.33 N	114.50 E
Xinzhang	**105**	39.05 N	116.46 E
Xinzhangzi	**105**	40.45 N	117.50 E
Xinzhao	**102**	39.32 N	107.52 E
Xinzhazhen	**106**	31.50 N	119.52 E
Xinzhen, Zhg.	**98**	35.37 N	114.03 E
Xinzhen, Zhg.	**105**	39.01 N	116.22 E
Xinzhen, Zhg.	**106**	31.24 N	121.24 E
Xinzheng	**100**	34.25 N	113.43 E
Xinzhou, Zhg.	**100**	30.50 N	114.47 E
Xinzhou, Zhg.	**102**	19.48 N	109.18 E
Xinzhuang, Zhg.	**98**	35.05 N	117.56 E
Xinzhuang, Zhg.	**271a**	39.56 N	116.31 E
Xinzhuangtou	**105**	39.25 N	115.45 E
Xinzhuangzi, Zhg.	**104**	41.05 N	121.23 E
Xinzhuangzi, Zhg.	**105**	40.14 N	116.59 E
Xinzhuangzi, Zhg.	**105**	40.32 N	115.10 E
Xinzhuangzi, Zhg.	**105**	38.52 N	117.21 E
Xinzhuangzi, Zhg.	**105**	39.20 N	118.25 E
Xiongdi Yu II	**100**	23.33 N	117.40 E
Xiongjiachang	**102**	26.31 N	105.39 E
Xiongxian	**105**	38.59 N	116.05 E
Xiongyuecheng	**98**	40.10 N	122.08 E
Xipamanu ≃	**248**	10.43 S	67.50 W
Xiping, Zhg.	**100**	28.27 N	119.29 E
Xiping, Zhg.	**100**	33.23 N	114.02 E
Xiping'anhe	**104**	40.47 N	122.01 E
Xiqia	**106**	31.03 N	119.37 E
Xiqilichiquan	**89**	49.59 N	119.27 E
Xiqin	**100**	26.33 N	118.06 E
Xiqing Shan ⋏	**102**	35.30 N	101.30 E
Xique-Xique	**250**	10.50 S	42.44 W
Xiriri, Lago ⊜	**250**	1.37 S	55.56 W
Xiruá ≃	**248**	6.03 S	67.50 W
Xisanshilipu	**100**	32.40 N	117.31 E
Xisantai	**98**	39.38 N	121.37 E
Xishan, Zhg.	**100**	28.34 N	115.37 E
Xishan, Zhg.	**105**	39.38 N	118.10 E
Xishanqiao	**106**	31.57 N	118.43 E
Xishanxicun	**105**	40.01 N	116.50 E
Xisha Qundao (Paracel Islands) II	**108**	16.30 N	112.15 E
Xishijiazi	**104**	41.46 N	120.55 E
Xishiqiao	**106**	31.53 N	120.06 E
Xishu	**98**	36.41 N	113.49 E
Xishui	**100**	30.27 N	115.13 E
Xishuiyu	**105**	40.25 N	116.16 E
Xisuhupu	**104**	41.41 N	123.14 E
Xitai	**98**	40.37 N	120.12 E
Xitan	**100**	23.47 N	117.08 E
Xitang	**106**	30.57 N	120.53 E
Xitangqiao, Zhg.	**106**	31.49 N	120.38 E
Xitangqiao, Zhg.	**106**	30.37 N	121.01 E
Xitaoyuan	**104**	40.57 N	122.11 E
Xiti	**120**	33.27 N	82.48 E
Xitianmu Shan ∧	**106**	30.21 N	119.25 E
Xitiao ≃	**106**	30.57 N	120.10 E
Xiting	**106**	32.07 N	121.00 E
Xitole	**150**	11.43 N	14.50 W
Xituan	**105**	39.29 N	115.47 E
Xiu ≃	**100**	29.13 N	115.56 E
Xiujiangpu	**104**	41.17 N	123.02 E
Xiuning	**100**	29.47 N	118.10 E
Xiushan	**102**	28.29 N	108.52 E
Xiushui	**100**	29.04 N	114.33 E
Xiushui ≃	**104**	42.03 N	122.58 E
Xiushuihe	**104**	42.22 N	123.01 E
Xiuyan	**98**	40.17 N	123.18 E
Xiwei	**100**	25.22 N	117.46 E
Xiweizigou	**104**	42.01 N	121.59 E
Xiwenquan	**107**	29.42 N	106.07 E
Xiwu	**100**	29.40 N	121.30 E
Xiwukou	**106**	30.24 N	118.54 E
Xixi	**100**	26.45 N	118.42 E
Xixia	**102**	33.22 N	111.28 E
Xixian, Zhg.	**100**	32.21 N	114.44 E
Xixian, Zhg.	**102**	36.43 N	110.52 E
Xixiang	**102**	32.48 N	107.55 E
Xixiangyang	**105**	39.33 N	116.02 E
Xixiaojie	**104**	40.42 N	122.12 E
Xixiashu	**106**	31.57 N	119.49 E
Xixing	**106**	30.11 N	120.13 E
Xiyang, Zhg.	**98**	37.37 N	113.42 E
Xiyang, Zhg.	**100**	25.50 N	117.25 E
Xiyang, Zhg.	**106**	31.49 N	120.43 E
Xiyang, Zhg.	**106**	31.52 N	119.23 E
Xiyang Dao I	**100**	26.32 N	120.04 E
Xiyangji	**100**	33.25 N	116.22 E
Xiyangjiao	**106**	31.43 N	120.23 E
Xiyangshugou	**104**	40.41 N	122.44 E
Xiyangzhuang	**106**	31.50 N	119.22 E
Xiyingzi	**104**	41.55 N	122.34 E
Xiyou	**98**	37.24 N	119.56 E
Xiyushi	**106**	30.36 N	119.26 E
Xizang Zizhiqu (Tibet) □[4]	**90**	32.00 N	88.00 E
Xizhi ≃	**100**	23.04 N	114.31 E
Xizhimen Station ◆[5]	**271a**	39.56 N	116.21 E
Xizhong Dao I	**98**	39.26 N	121.17 E
Xizhou	**100**	29.29 N	121.39 E
Xizi	**98**	41.48 N	119.16 E
Xkalak	**232**	18.16 N	87.50 W
Xlukehu ⊜	**120**	31.42 N	89.30 E
Xochapa	**234**	17.39 N	95.46 W
Xochimilco □[7]	**286a**	19.14 N	99.05 W
Xochimilco ◆[8]	**286a**	19.16 N	99.06 W
Xochimilco, Lago de ⊜	**286a**	19.16 N	99.06 W
Xochipala	**234**	17.48 N	99.39 W
Xochistlahuaca	**234**	16.47 N	98.15 W
Xochitlán	**234**	19.59 N	97.36 W
Xom-binh-phuoc	**269c**	10.40 N	106.47 E
Xom-long-moc	**110**	18.51 N	105.01 E
Xom-xoai-minh	**269c**	10.42 N	106.50 E
Xoxocotla	**234**	18.41 N	99.15 W
Xu ≃	**100**	28.17 N	116.05 E
Xuancheng	**106**	30.58 N	118.45 E
Xuan'en	**102**	30.00 N	109.20 E
Xuanfeng	**100**	27.42 N	114.08 E
Xuang ≃	**110**	19.58 N	102.15 E
Xuanhan	**102**	31.24 N	107.43 E
Xuanhua	**105**	40.37 N	115.03 E
Xuanhuadian	**100**	31.42 N	114.29 E
Xuanhui ≃	**98**	38.07 N	117.45 E
Xuanjiabao	**106**	32.17 N	120.01 E
Xuanjiangying	**98**	41.25 N	116.45 E
Xuan-loc	**110**	10.56 N	107.14 E
Xuantan	**107**	29.12 N	105.34 E
Xuan-thoi-thuong	**269c**	10.52 N	106.34 E
Xuanwei	**102**	26.07 N	104.05 E
Xuanzhuang	**105**	39.29 N	118.07 E
Xubu	**98**	40.02 N	113.43 E
Xuchang, Zhg.	**100**	34.03 N	113.49 E
Xuchang, Zhg.	**107**	29.06 N	104.31 E
Xucheng	**98**	35.56 N	116.27 E
Xucun	**106**	30.27 N	120.22 E
Xudazhuang	**100**	33.44 N	117.53 E
Xuddun	**144**	9.09 N	47.28 E
Xuddur	**144**	4.07 N	43.54 E
Xueao	**100**	29.27 N	121.30 E
Xueba	**120**	29.58 N	93.48 E
Xuebu	**106**	31.43 N	119.22 E
Xuecheng	**98**	34.50 N	117.16 E
Xuedian, Zhg.	**100**	34.04 N	113.04 E
Xuedian, Zhg.	**100**	34.30 N	113.44 E
Xuefanggou	**104**	41.57 N	121.01 E
Xuefeng	**100**	33.21 N	118.22 E
Xuehu	**98**	34.08 N	116.27 E
Xueshan Zhang ∧	**100**	24.24 N	113.37 E
Xueshuiwen	**89**	49.10 N	129.45 E
Xuetangpuzi	**104**	40.38 N	123.53 E
Xueyanqiao	**106**	31.30 N	120.06 E
Xuezhen	**106**	31.35 N	118.38 E
Xuguanzhen	**106**	31.23 N	120.30 E
Xuguichenxiaodian	**106**	32.07 N	121.20 E
Xuguit Qi (Yakeshi)	**89**	49.17 N	120.41 E
Xuji	**100**	31.50 N	116.22 E
Xujiabu	**100**	29.27 N	116.18 E
Xujiadong	**100**	25.54 N	113.02 E
Xujiadu	**100**	28.18 N	114.44 E
Xujiagou	**104**	42.17 N	124.04 E
Xujiapuzi	**104**	40.44 N	123.18 E
Xujiatou	**106**	31.19 N	119.25 E
Xujiazhai, Zhg.	**106**	31.11 N	121.46 E
Xujiazhai, Zhg.	**269b**	31.23 N	121.17 E
Xuliying	**105**	39.28 N	116.02 E
Xun ≃, Zhg.	**89**	49.27 N	128.55 E
Xun ≃, Zhg.	**102**	23.28 N	111.18 E
Xunhe	**89**	49.18 N	128.04 E
Xunhua	**102**	35.49 N	102.26 E
Xunjiansi	**105**	40.50 N	116.04 E
Xunke	**89**	49.35 N	128.25 E
Xunle	**102**	25.17 N	108.12 E
Xunmukou	**98**	34.03 N	114.42 E
Xunshansuo	**98**	37.10 N	122.29 E
Xunwu	**100**	24.58 N	115.38 E
Xunwu ≃	**100**	24.28 N	115.26 E
Xunxian	**98**	35.43 N	114.31 E
Xupu, Zhg.	**102**	27.44 N	110.24 E
Xupu, Zhg.	**106**	31.45 N	120.54 E
Xushe	**106**	31.24 N	119.39 E
Xushi	**106**	31.40 N	120.57 E
Xushui	**105**	39.02 N	115.39 E
Xutian	**98**	34.10 N	114.03 E
Xuwan	**100**	27.55 N	116.31 E
Xuwen	**102**	20.21 N	110.11 E
Xuxiandai	**106**	30.40 N	120.47 E
Xuxiang	**106**	31.33 N	120.13 E
Xuyen-moc	**110**	10.34 N	107.25 E
Xuyi	**100**	33.01 N	118.29 E
Xuyong	**102**	28.10 N	105.24 E
Xuzhou (Süchow)	**98**	34.16 N	117.11 E
Xuzhuang	**106**	31.09 N	120.32 E
Y			
Yaak	**182**	48.50 N	115.42 W
Yaan	**102**	30.03 N	103.02 E
Yaapeet	**166**	35.46 S	142.03 E
Yaaq-Baraawe	**144**	1.57 N	43.11 E
Ya'aqov Housman, Sede-Te'ufa ⊠	**132**	29.33 N	34.59 E
Yaba ◆[8]	**273a**	6.30 N	3.23 E
Yaba College of Technology ⊍[2]	**273a**	6.32 N	3.23 E
Ya'bad	**132**	32.27 N	35.10 E
Yabakei	**96**	33.27 N	131.07 E
Yabassi	**152**	4.28 N	9.58 E
Yabe	**96**	33.09 N	130.49 E
Yabe ≃	**96**	33.06 N	130.26 E
Yabelo	**144**	4.54 N	38.05 E
Yablis	**236**	14.10 N	83.49 W
Yablonovy Range → Jablonovyj chrebet ⋏	**88**	53.30 N	115.00 E
Yabrīn ⩶[4]	**128**	23.17 N	48.58 E
Yabrūd	**130**	33.58 N	36.40 E
Yabu, Nihon	**96**	35.22 N	134.47 E
Yabu, Nihon	**174m**	26.36 N	127.57 E
Yabucoa	**240m**	18.03 N	65.53 W
Yabuki	**94**	37.12 N	140.19 E
Yabuli	**89**	44.55 N	128.35 E
Yacambu, Parque Nacional ♠	**246**	9.40 N	69.42 W
Yacaré Norte, Riacho ≃	**252**	22.43 S	58.14 W
Yachengzhen	**110**	18.25 N	109.11 E
Yachi ≃	**102**	27.18 N	107.15 E
Yachimata	**94**	35.39 N	140.19 E
Yachiyo, Nihon	**94**	35.43 N	140.07 E
Yachiyo, Nihon	**94**	36.10 N	139.53 E
Yaciretá, Isla I	**252**	27.25 S	56.30 W
Yaco	**248**	17.09 S	67.24 W
Yaco (Iaco) ≃	**248**	9.03 S	68.34 W
Yacolt	**224**	45.51 N	122.24 W
Yacuiba	**248**	22.02 S	63.45 W
Yacuma ≃	**248**	13.38 S	65.23 W
Yada ≃	**96**	35.38 N	134.37 E
Yādgīr	**122**	16.46 N	77.08 E
Yadkin ≃	**192**	35.23 N	80.03 W
Yadkinville	**192**	36.08 N	80.39 W
Yad Mordekhay	**132**	31.35 N	34.34 E
Yadong	**124**	27.29 N	88.55 E
Yādūdah	**132**	32.40 N	36.04 E
Yaenengu	**152**	2.28 N	23.15 E
Yaeyama-rettō II	**175d**	24.20 N	124.00 E
Yāfā	**132**	32.41 N	35.17 E
Yafran	**146**	32.04 N	12.31 E
Yaftābād	**267d**	35.39 N	51.19 E
Yafuquan	**85**	39.12 N	76.09 E
Yagachi-shima I	**174m**	26.40 N	128.01 E
Yağcılar	**130**	39.25 N	28.23 E
Yageg	**144**	3.16 N	44.00 E
Yagi	**96**	35.04 N	135.32 E
Yagishiri-tō I	**92a**	44.26 N	141.25 E
Yağlıca Dağı ∧	**84**	40.18 N	43.18 E
Yago	**234**	21.50 N	105.04 W
Yagonde	**152**	0.02 N	22.41 E
Yagoona	**274a**	33.55 S	151.02 E
Yagoua	**146**	10.20 N	15.14 E
Yaguachi	**246**	2.07 S	79.41 W
Yaguachi ≃	**246**	2.02 S	79.44 W
Yaguajay	**240p**	22.19 N	79.14 W
Yaguala ≃	**236**	15.25 N	86.40 W
Yaguará	**246**	2.40 N	75.31 W
Yaguaraparo	**246**	10.34 N	62.49 W
Yaguarí	**252**	31.31 S	54.58 W
Yaguarón (Jaguarão) ≃	**252**	32.39 S	53.12 W
Yaguas ≃	**246**	2.45 S	70.04 W
Yaguhu ⊜	**120**	28.40 N	91.45 E
Yagur	**132**	32.44 N	35.04 E
Yahagi ≃	**94**	34.50 N	136.59 E
Yahagong	**102**	28.24 N	99.11 E
Yahara ≃	**190**	42.48 N	89.07 W
Yahata → Kitakyūshū	**96**	33.53 N	130.50 E
Yahe, Zhg.	**89**	45.24 N	130.24 E
Yahe, Zhg.	**106**	31.44 N	119.52 E
Yaheladazeshan ∧	**120**	35.12 N	95.20 E
Yahila	**152**	0.13 N	24.28 E
Yahk	**182**	49.05 N	116.05 W
Yahmūm al-Asmar, Jabal ∧	**142**	29.56 N	31.38 E
Yaho	**268**	35.41 N	139.27 E
Yahōga-take ∧	**96**	33.04 N	130.50 E
Yahongqiao	**105**	39.45 N	117.51 E
Yahualica	**234**	21.08 N	102.51 W
Yahuma	**152**	1.05 N	23.13 E
Yahyalı	**130**	38.07 N	35.22 E
Yai ≃	**114**	5.02 N	101.47 E
Yai, Khao ∧, Asia	**110**	12.27 N	99.26 E
Yai, Khao ∧, Thai	**110**	15.25 N	99.20 E
Yainax Butte ∧	**202**	42.20 N	121.16 W
Yaita, Nihon	**94**	36.48 N	139.56 E
Yaita, Nihon	**268**	35.57 N	140.03 E
Yaitopya → Ethiopia □[1]	**144**	9.00 N	39.00 E
Yaizu	**94**	34.52 N	138.20 E
Yajiang	**102**	30.02 N	101.05 E
Yaka	**130**	41.15 N	34.01 E
Yakacık	**267b**	40.55 N	29.13 E
Yakage	**96**	34.37 N	133.35 E
Yakak, Cape ›	**180**	51.38 N	177.00 W
Yakapınar	**130**	37.00 N	35.36 E
Yakarta → Jakarta	**115a**	6.10 S	106.48 E
Yakchāl	**128**	31.47 N	64.41 E
Yake-dake ∧	**94**	36.14 N	137.35 E
Yakehu ⊜	**120**	34.55 N	87.20 E
Yake-yama ∧	**94**	36.55 N	138.03 E
Yakhchāl	**120**	31.47 N	64.41 E
Yakima	**202**	46.36 N	120.30 W
Yakima □[6]	**224**	46.34 N	121.03 W
Yakima ≃	**202**	46.15 N	119.02 W
Yakima Firing Center ■	**202**	46.44 N	120.10 W
Yakima Indian Reservation ◆[4]	**224**	46.16 N	121.03 W
Yakkan ≃	**96**	33.34 N	131.22 E
Yakmach	**128**	28.45 N	63.51 E
Yako	**150**	12.58 N	2.16 W
Yakō ◆[8]	**268**	35.32 N	139.41 E
Yakobi Island I	**180**	58.00 N	136.30 W
Yakoma	**152**	4.05 N	22.27 E
Yakou	**100**	24.46 N	118.46 E
Yakuendai	**268**	35.43 N	140.03 E
Yakuluku	**154**	4.20 N	28.48 E
Yakumo	**92a**	42.15 N	140.16 E
Yakuno	**96**	35.19 N	135.00 E
Yakushi-dake ∧	**94**	36.28 N	137.33 E
Yakushi-ji ⊍[1]	**94**	36.25 N	139.53 E
Yaku-shima I	**93b**	30.20 N	130.30 E
Yakutat	**180**	59.33 N	139.44 W
Yakutat Bay ⊂	**180**	59.40 N	140.00 W
Yakutat Seamount ⊹[3]	**16**	35.15 N	48.00 W
Yakutsk → Jakutsk	**74**	62.00 N	129.40 E
Yala, Ghana	**150**	10.07 N	1.52 W
Yala, Thai	**110**	6.33 N	101.18 E
Yalaha	**220**	28.44 N	81.48 W
Yalahán, Laguna de ⊂	**232**	21.30 N	87.15 W
Yalakdereköy	**130**	40.36 N	29.33 E
Yalata	**162**	31.29 S	131.52 E
Yalata Aboriginal Reserve ◆[4]	**162**	31.30 S	131.45 E
Yalca, Laguna ⊜	**258**	35.34 S	57.55 W
Yalding	**260**	51.13 N	0.26 E
Yale, B.C., Can.	**182**	49.34 N	121.26 W
Yale, Mi., U.S.	**190**	43.07 N	82.47 W
Yale, Ok., U.S.	**196**	36.06 N	96.41 W
Yale, Va., U.S.	**208**	36.50 N	77.17 W
Yale, Lake ⊜	**220**	28.54 N	81.45 W
Yale, Mount ∧	**200**	38.51 N	106.18 W
Yale Lake ⊜[1]	**224**	46.00 N	122.12 W
Yalgar ≃	**162**	26.09 S	117.57 E
Yalgoo	**162**	28.20 S	116.41 E
Yalgorup National Park ♠	**168a**	32.55 S	115.41 E
Yali	**152**	0.04 N	21.03 E
Yaliji	**98**	36.06 N	114.56 E
Yalikamba	**152**	1.17 S	22.30 E
Yalinga	**152**	6.31 N	23.15 E
Yalisere	**152**	0.11 N	22.33 E
Yalleroi	**166**	24.04 S	145.45 E
Yallourn	**169**	38.11 S	146.21 E
Yallourn North	**169**	38.09 S	146.22 E
Yalnızçam Dağları ⋏	**84**	41.10 N	42.25 E
Yalnızçam Geçidi)(	**130**	41.03 N	42.20 E
Yalobusha ≃	**194**	33.33 N	90.10 W
Yaloká	**152**	5.19 N	17.05 E
Yalong ≃	**102**	26.37 N	101.48 E
Yalova	**130**	40.39 N	29.15 E
Yalta → Jalta	**78**	44.30 N	34.10 E
Yalu	**89**	48.34 N	122.09 E
Yalu (Amnok-kang) ≃, Asia	**98**	39.55 N	124.22 E
Yalu ≃, Zhg.	**89**	46.56 N	123.30 E
Yalufi	**152**	0.45 N	24.26 E
Yaluzangbujiang → Brahmaputra ≃	**120**	24.02 N	90.59 E
Yalvaç	**130**	38.17 N	31.11 E
Yalwal Creek ≃	**170**	34.50 S	150.23 E
Yamachiche	**206**	46.16 N	72.50 W
Yamachiche ≃	**206**	46.16 N	72.48 W
Yamada, Nihon	**92**	39.28 N	141.57 E
Yamada, Nihon	**94**	35.49 N	140.36 E
Yamada, Nihon	**94**	36.34 N	137.05 E
Yamada, Nihon	**96**	33.33 N	130.47 E
Yamada → Tosa-yamada	**96**	33.36 N	133.41 E
Yamada, Nihon	**174m**	26.26 N	127.47 E
Yamada, Nihon	**270**	34.31 N	135.39 E
Yamada, Nihon	**270**	34.48 N	135.32 E
Yamada ≃	**270**	34.47 N	135.04 E
Yamaga, Nihon	**96**	33.01 N	130.41 E
Yamaga, Nihon	**96**	33.27 N	131.30 E
Yamagata, Nihon	**92**	38.15 N	140.20 E
Yamagata, Nihon	**94**	36.38 N	140.24 E
Yamagata, Nihon	**94**	36.10 N	137.52 E
Yamagawa	**92**	31.12 N	130.39 E
Yamaguchi, Nihon	**94**	35.33 N	137.33 E
Yamaguchi, Nihon	**96**	34.10 N	131.29 E
Yamaguchi, Nihon	**270**	34.50 N	135.15 E
Yamaguchi □[5]	**96**	34.20 N	131.30 E
Yamaguchi-chosuichi ⊜[1]	**268**	35.46 N	139.25 E
Yama-Hita-Hiko-san-kokutei-kōen ♠	**96**	33.25 N	131.02 E
Yamakawa	**96**	34.04 N	134.15 E
Yamakita	**94**	35.21 N	139.05 E
Yamakuni	**96**	33.24 N	131.02 E
Yamakuni ≃	**96**	33.37 N	131.12 E
Yamām, Jabal al- ∧	**132**	30.02 N	35.28 E
Yamamoto, Nihon	**96**	34.07 N	133.44 E
Yamamoto, Nihon	**270**	34.38 N	135.38 E
Yamanaka	**94**	36.15 N	136.22 E
Yamanakako	**94**	35.24 N	138.52 E
Yamanaka-ko ⊜	**94**	35.25 N	138.52 E
Yamanashi	**94**	35.40 N	138.40 E
Yamanashi □[5]	**94**	35.30 N	138.30 E
Yamanouchi	**94**	36.44 N	138.25 E
Yamasaki	**96**	35.00 N	134.33 E
Yamashina ◆[8]	**270**	34.58 N	135.49 E
Yamashiro, Nihon	**94**	34.45 N	135.49 E
Yamashiro, Nihon	**96**	33.57 N	133.45 E
Yamaska (Saint-Michel)	**206**	46.00 N	72.55 W
Yamaska □[6]	**206**	46.00 N	72.45 W
Yamaska ≃	**206**	46.06 N	72.56 W
Yamaska, Mont ∧[2]	**206**	45.27 N	72.52 W
Yamaska Nord ≃	**206**	45.17 N	72.51 W
Yamaska Sud-Est ≃	**206**	45.17 N	72.55 W
Yamate	**270**	34.30 N	135.27 E
Yamatengwumulu	**102**	38.38 N	97.05 E
Yamato, Nihon	**94**	35.48 N	136.54 E
Yamato, Nihon	**94**	35.29 N	139.29 E
Yamato, Nihon	**94**	37.10 N	138.56 E
Yamato, Nihon	**96**	33.08 N	130.26 E
Yamato ≃	**96**	34.36 N	135.26 E
Yamato-Aogaki-kokutei-kōen ♠	**94**	34.40 N	135.50 E
Yamato-kōriyama	**96**	34.38 N	135.47 E
Yamato-takada	**96**	34.31 N	135.45 E
Yamatsuri	**94**	36.52 N	140.25 E
Yamazaki	**268**	35.56 N	139.54 E
Yamba	**166**	29.26 S	153.22 E
Yambata	**152**	2.26 N	21.58 E
Yambéring	**150**	11.49 N	12.21 W
Yambio	**154**	4.34 N	28.23 E
Yambol → Jambol	**38**	42.29 N	26.30 E
Yambou Head ›	**241h**	13.09 N	61.09 W
Yamboyo	**152**	0.40 N	22.18 E
Yambrasbamba	**248**	5.45 S	77.54 W
Yambuya	**154**	1.16 N	24.33 E
Yamdena, Pulau I	**164**	7.36 S	131.25 E
Yame	**96**	33.28 N	130.34 E
Ya Men ⊂	**100**	22.09 N	113.05 E
Yamenkou	**105**	39.53 N	116.12 E
Yamenying	**89**	43.25 N	122.19 E
Yamethin	**110**	20.26 N	96.09 E
Yamhill	**224**	45.21 N	123.11 W
Yamhill □[6]	**224**	45.15 N	123.20 W
Yamhill ≃	**224**	45.14 N	123.00 W
Yamia	**150**	13.24 N	10.18 E
Y'Ami Island I	**108**	21.07 N	121.57 E
Yamizo-san ∧	**94**	36.56 N	140.17 E
Yamma Yamma, Lake ⊜	**166**	26.20 S	141.25 E
Yamoussoukro	**150**	6.49 N	5.17 W
Yampa	**200**	40.09 N	106.54 W
Yampa ≃	**200**	40.32 N	108.59 W
Yampa Plateau ⋏[1]	**200**	40.25 N	109.00 W
Yamparáez	**248**	19.10 S	65.10 W
Yampi Sound	**160**	15.15 S	123.30 E
Yamsay Mountain ∧	**202**	42.56 N	121.22 W
Yamu	**102**	43.48 N	94.48 E
Yamuna ≃	**120**	25.25 N	81.50 E
Yamuna Bridge ◆[5]	**272a**	28.40 N	77.14 E
Yamunānagar	**124**	30.07 N	77.18 E
Yan	**114**	5.48 N	100.22 E
Yan ≃, S. Lan.	**122**	8.55 N	81.01 E
Yan ≃, Zhg.	**102**	36.24 N	110.28 E
Yanac	**166**	36.08 S	141.26 E
Yanacachi	**248**	16.23 S	67.43 W
Yanadani	**96**	33.32 N	133.01 E
Yanagawa	**96**	33.10 N	130.24 E
Yanagi	**270**	34.25 N	135.56 E
Yanagimoto	**270**	34.34 N	135.51 E
Yanahara	**96**	34.55 N	134.05 E
Yanaha-shima I	**174m**	26.54 N	127.56 E
Yanahuara	**248**	16.24 S	71.33 W
Yanai	**96**	33.58 N	132.07 E
Yanaka	**268**	35.24 N	140.01 E
Yanam	**122**	16.44 N	82.13 E
Yan'an	**102**	36.36 N	109.28 E
Yanaoca	**248**	14.13 S	71.26 W
Yanbian	**102**	26.55 N	101.30 E
Yanbu', Ar. Su.	**128**	24.05 N	38.03 E
Yanbu, Zhg.	**100**	23.05 N	113.10 E
Yanbutou	**100**	29.52 N	115.04 E
Yanceyville	**192**	36.24 N	79.20 W
Yanchang	**102**	36.31 N	110.08 E
Yancheng, Zhg.	**100**	33.36 N	113.57 E
Yancheng, Zhg.	**100**	33.24 N	120.09 E
Yanchep	**168a**	31.33 S	115.41 E
Yanchep National Park ♠	**168a**	31.32 S	115.40 E
Yanchi, Zhg.	**102**	37.52 N	107.22 E
Yanchi, Zhg.	**105**	40.02 N	115.53 E
Yanchuan	**102**	36.56 N	110.05 E
Yanco	**166**	34.36 S	146.25 E
Yanco Creek ≃	**166**	35.16 S	145.07 E
Yanda Creek ≃	**166**	30.28 S	145.45 E
Yandal	**162**	27.33 S	121.07 E
Yandama Creek ≃	**166**	30.00 S	140.10 E
Yandé, Île I	**175f**	20.03 S	163.49 E
Yandev	**150**	7.20 N	9.01 E
Yandina	**175e**	9.07 S	159.13 E
Yandja	**152**	1.41 S	17.43 E
Yandongi	**152**	2.51 N	22.16 E
Yandoon	**110**	17.02 N	95.39 E
Yandua Island I	**175g**	16.49 S	178.18 E
Yandun	**102**	42.20 N	94.09 E
Yanfeng	**102**	25.53 N	101.01 E
Yanfolila	**150**	11.11 N	8.09 W
Yang ≃, Thai	**110**	15.44 N	104.00 E
Yang ≃, Zhg.	**105**	40.24 N	115.20 E
Yanga	**234**	18.50 N	96.48 W
Yangambi	**154**	0.47 N	24.28 E
Yangan, Austl.	**171a**	28.12 S	152.13 E
Yang'an, Zhg.	**98**	37.38 N	117.09 E
Yan'gang	**100**	26.02 N	116.22 E
Yangarakata	**154**	3.01 N	30.28 E
Yangasa Levu I	**175g**	18.57 S	178.26 W
Yangbajing	**120**	30.06 N	90.33 E
Yangce	**100**	32.58 N	113.14 E
Yangcha	**98**	41.11 N	126.15 E
Yangchang	**107**	30.22 N	103.42 E
Yangcheng, Zhg.	**102**	35.29 N	112.25 E
Yangcheng, Zhg.	**106**	31.24 N	120.47 E
Yangcheng Hu ⊜	**106**	31.26 N	120.47 E
Yangchiang → Yangjiang	**102**	21.51 N	111.56 E
Yangch'ŏn ◆[8]	**271b**	37.34 N	126.51 E
Yangchow → Yangzhou	**100**	32.24 N	119.26 E
Yangchu	**98**	37.11 N	120.47 E
Yangch'üan → Yangquan	**98**	37.52 N	113.36 E
Yangchun	**102**	22.10 N	111.46 E
Yangcun, Zhg.	**100**	28.07 N	117.40 E
Yangcun, Zhg.	**100**	23.26 N	114.30 E
Yangcun, Zhg.	**105**	39.09 N	115.50 E
Yangcunqiao	**100**	29.36 N	119.28 E
Yangdachengzi	**89**	43.59 N	124.25 E
Yangdalinzi	**98**	42.38 N	125.07 E
Yangdang	**100**	32.23 N	112.39 E
Yangdian	**106**	31.08 N	119.45 E
Yang'erzhuang	**98**	38.18 N	117.30 E
Yangfang	**105**	40.07 N	116.07 E
Yangfangpu	**105**	40.48 N	115.01 E
Yangfengang	**105**	39.07 N	116.52 E
Yangfenzhen	**106**	30.28 N	120.03 E
Yanggang Do □[4]	**98**	41.15 N	128.00 E
Yangganzhen	**106**	31.00 N	119.15 E
Yanggao	**98**	40.25 N	113.44 E
Yanggezhuang	**105**	40.09 N	116.48 E
Yanggong-ni	**271b**	37.39 N	126.37 E
Yanggu, Taehan	**98**	38.06 N	127.59 E
Yanggu, Zhg.	**98**	34.44 N	114.48 E
Yanggu, Zhg.	**98**	36.08 N	115.48 E
Yangguanpu	**100**	32.13 N	115.31 E
Yanghang	**106**	31.22 N	121.26 E
Yanghe	**100**	33.47 N	118.23 E
Yanghexi	**102**	29.39 N	108.40 E
Yanghu	**100**	32.34 N	116.30 E
Yanghua	**107**	30.11 N	104.45 E
Yanghua ≃	**107**	30.09 N	104.42 E
Yangi-Yul' → Jangijul'	**85**	41.07 N	69.03 E
Yangji, Zhg.	**98**	36.44 N	113.56 E
Yangji, Zhg.	**98**	34.25 N	116.06 E
Yangji, Zhg.	**100**	34.19 N	119.28 E
Yangjia, Zhg.	**98**	34.19 N	119.28 E
Yangjia, Zhg.	**106**	30.41 N	120.15 E
Yangjiachang, Zhg.	**107**	29.23 N	104.21 E
Yangjiachang, Zhg.	**107**	29.45 N	105.21 E
Yangjiafeng	**100**	30.49 N	112.47 E
Yangjiagou	**105**	39.18 N	117.54 E
Yangjiajie	**107**	30.18 N	104.39 E
Yangjian	**106**	31.39 N	120.33 E
Yangjiang	**102**	21.51 N	111.56 E
Yangjiaogou	**98**	37.16 N	118.50 E
Yangjiaqiao, Zhg.	**100**	27.44 N	112.46 E
Yangjiaqiao, Zhg.	**106**	31.53 N	121.42 E
Yangjiaqiao, Zhg.	**106**	32.02 N	121.26 E
Yangjiatao	**105**	39.49 N	117.51 E
Yangjiawopu	**104**	42.21 N	122.57 E
Yangjiazeng	**105**	40.12 N	117.04 E
Yangjiazhangzi	**104**	40.48 N	120.33 E
Yangjie	**102**	24.49 N	100.22 E
Yangjishi	**100**	26.39 N	113.14 E
Yangkou	**100**	26.47 N	117.51 E
Yangkoushi	**100**	28.39 N	118.53 E
Yanglinjie	**100**	29.07 N	113.27 E
Yangliupu, Zhg.	**100**	30.52 N	118.37 E
Yangliupu, Zhg.	**107**	30.09 N	104.03 E
Yangliuqing	**105**	39.08 N	117.01 E
Yangloudong	**100**	29.31 N	113.44 E
Yanglousi	**100**	29.30 N	113.38 E
Yangluo	**100**	30.41 N	114.34 E
Yangluomayu	**104**	40.47 N	122.54 E
Yangmachang	**107**	30.39 N	103.45 E
Yangma Dao I	**98**	37.28 N	121.37 E
Yangmahe	**107**	30.29 N	104.31 E
Yangmeisi	**100**	25.42 N	114.30 E
Yangmiao, Zhg.	**98**	34.11 N	114.53 E
Yangmiao, Zhg.	**106**	30.51 N	120.49 E
Yangmingshan ◆[8]	**269d**	25.09 N	121.33 E
Yangming Shan ∧	**102**	26.03 N	111.56 E
Yangmugou, Zhg.	**98**	40.36 N	124.28 E
Yangmugou, Zhg.	**104**	41.11 N	123.50 E
Yangmulin	**105**	40.06 N	115.12 E
Yangon → Rangoon	**110**	16.47 N	96.10 E
Yangor	**174b**	0.31 S	166.54 E
Yangpingguan	**102**	32.51 N	106.09 E
Yangpu	**100**	27.14 N	119.08 E
Yangp'yŏng	**98**	37.30 N	127.29 E
Yangp'yŏng-ni	**98**	40.53 N	127.58 E
Yangqi	**106**	31.23 N	119.57 E
Yangquan	**98**	37.52 N	113.36 E
Yangriwan	**102**	31.37 N	110.49 E
Yangsan	**98**	35.21 N	129.03 E
Yangshan, Zhg.	**98**	41.13 N	120.24 E
Yangshan, Zhg.	**98**	35.13 N	116.13 E
Yangshan, Zhg.	**102**	24.28 N	112.38 E
Yangshigangzi	**104**	41.42 N	122.59 E
Yangshitun	**104**	42.06 N	123.44 E
Yangshu	**106**	31.39 N	120.08 E
Yangshugemen	**105**	40.55 N	118.18 E
Yangshugou-donggou	**104**	41.43 N	120.41 E
Yangshuling	**98**	41.02 N	118.47 E
Yangshuo	**102**	24.45 N	110.24 E
Yangtan	**106**	30.42 N	119.11 E
Yangtian Zhang ∧	**100**	24.37 N	115.38 E
Yangting	**98**	37.24 N	122.07 E
Yangtou	**100**	23.26 N	115.24 E
Yangtze → Chang ≃	**90**	31.48 N	121.10 E
Yanguan	**106**	30.26 N	120.32 E
Yangwan, Zhg.	**100**	28.22 N	116.46 E
Yangwan, Zhg.	**106**	31.03 N	120.22 E
Yangxi, Zhg.	**100**	30.11 N	118.39 E
Yangxi, Zhg.	**100**	27.18 N	114.10 E
Yangxian	**102**	33.03 N	107.47 E
Yangxiang, Zhg.	**106**	31.29 N	119.35 E
Yangxiang, Zhg.	**106**	31.12 N	121.01 E
Yangxiangtun	**104**	40.58 N	122.48 E
Yangxiaodian	**100**	31.46 N	116.45 E
Yangximu ≃	**104**	42.04 N	123.00 E
Yangxin, Zhg.	**98**	37.39 N	117.34 E
Yangxin, Zhg.	**100**	29.51 N	115.12 E
Yangxiudian	**271a**	39.44 N	116.32 E
Yangyang	**98**	38.04 N	128.36 E
Yangyuan (Xicheng)	**98**	40.01 N	114.10 E
Yangze	**100**	26.57 N	118.23 E
Yangzhong	**106**	32.16 N	119.49 E
Yangzhou	**100**	32.24 N	119.26 E
Yangzhuang	**100**	33.36 N	118.58 E
Yangzhujuanzi	**104**	41.38 N	122.46 E
Yangzhuoyonghu ⊜	**120**	28.58 N	90.44 E
Yangzi	**100**	31.19 N	112.36 E
Yangzishao	**98**	42.28 N	126.09 E
Yanhaiyingzi	**104**	41.52 N	123.05 E
Yanhe, Zhg.	**100**	31.16 N	115.07 E
Yanhe, Zhg.	**102**	28.37 N	108.35 E
Yanhecheng	**105**	40.04 N	115.43 E
Yanheying	**98**	40.02 N	119.03 E
Yanhui	**98**	37.54 N	113.51 E
Yanina → Ioánnina	**38**	39.40 N	20.50 E
Yanji, Zhg.	**98**	34.41 N	115.27 E
Yanji, Zhg.	**98**	42.57 N	129.32 E

Symbols in the index entries represent the broad categories identified in the key at the right. Symbols with superior numbers (⋏[1]) identify subcategories (see complete key on page *I · 1)*.

Kartensymbole in dem Registerverzeichnis stellen die rechts in Schlüssel erklärten Kategorien dar. Symbole mit hochgestellten Ziffern (⋏[1]) bezeichnen Unterabteilungen einer Kategorie (vgl. vollständiger Schlüssel auf Seite *I · 1)*.

Los símbolos incluídos en el texto del índice representan las grandes categorias identificadas con la clave a la derecha. Los símbolos con numeros en su parte superior (⋏[1]) identifican las subcategorías (véase la clave completa en la página *I · 1)*.

Les symboles de l'index représentent les catégories indiquées dans la légende à droite. Les symboles suivis d'un indice (⋏[1]) représentent des sous-catégories (voir légende complète à la page *I · 1)*.

Os símbolos incluídos no texto do índice representam as grandes categorias identificadas com a chave à direita. Os símbolos com números em sua parte superior (⋏[1]) identificam as subcategorias (veja-se a chave completa à página *I · 1)*.

ENGLISH	DEUTSCH	ESPAÑOL	FRANÇAIS	PORTUGUÊS
∧ Mountain	Berg	Montaña	Montagne	Montanha
⋏ Mountains	Berge	Montañas	Montagnes	Montanhas
)(Pass	Pass	Paso	Col	Passo
V Valley, Canyon	Tal, Cañon	Valle, Cañón	Vallée, Canyon	Vale, Canhão
≚ Plain	Ebene	Llano	Plaine	Planície
› Cape	Kap	Cabo	Cap	Cabo
I Island	Insel	Isla	Île	Ilha
II Islands	Inseln	Islas	Îles	Ilhas
⊥ Other Topographic Features	Andere Topographische Objekte	Otros Elementos Topográficos	Autres données topographiques	Outros acidentes topográficos

ESPAÑOL · FRANÇAIS · PORTUGUÊS

Nombre / Nom / Nome	Página / Page	Lat.°′	Long.°′ W = Oeste / Ouest
Yanji (Longjing), Zhg.	98	42.47 N	129.26 E
Yanji, Zhg.	98	34.17 N	115.39 E
Yanjia	104	40.57 N	121.41 E
Yanjiabao	106	32.19 N	120.07 E
Yanjiadian	98	39.48 N	121.49 E
Yanjiahe	100	31.48 N	114.50 E
Yanjiajie	104	41.02 N	121.32 E
Yanjiao	105	39.56 N	116.48 E
Yanjiapu	105	39.52 N	118.00 E
Yanjiatuozi	104	42.27 N	123.47 E
Yanjiawopeng	104	40.59 N	121.17 E
Yanjin	98	35.11 N	114.11 E
Yanjing, Zhg.	102	29.00 N	98.34 E
Yanjing, Zhg.	107	29.56 N	106.21 E
Yankalilla	168b	35.28 S	138.21 E
Yankalilla Bay ⊂	168b	35.28 S	138.15 E
Yankari Game Reserve ◆[4]	146	9.45 N	10.30 E
Yankdŏk	98	39.14 N	126.41 E
Yankee Lake	210	41.35 N	74.33 W
Yankee Springs State Recreation Area ♠	216	42.38 N	85.30 W
Yankee Stadium ♠	276	40.50 N	73.56 W
Yankeetown	220	29.01 N	82.42 W
Yan Kit	271c	1.22 N	103.58 E
Yankton	198	42.52 N	97.23 W
Yankton Indian Reservation ◆[4]	198	43.10 N	98.22 W
Yanling, Zhg.	98	34.07 N	114.11 E
Yanling, Zhg.	106	31.54 N	119.30 E
Yanliumiao	100	32.01 N	116.52 E
Yanmeimeizi	105	39.42 N	115.03 E
Yanna	166	26.56 S	146.03 E
Yannarie ≃	162	22.28 S	114.48 E
Yanqi	90	42.00 N	86.15 E
Yanqian, Zhg.	100	24.54 N	116.14 E
Yanqian, Zhg.	100	26.15 N	117.28 E
Yanqianhu	104	42.16 N	123.12 E
Yanqiao	106	31.41 N	120.17 E
Yanqidoumen	106	31.17 N	118.42 E
Yanqing	105	40.28 N	115.58 E
Yanque	248	15.39 S	71.39 W
Yanrey	162	22.31 S	114.48 E
Yanshan, Zhg.	98	38.05 N	117.13 E
Yanshan, Zhg.	100	28.18 N	117.41 E
Yanshan, Zhg.	102	23.41 N	104.21 E
Yan Shan ⋏	105	40.20 N	117.40 E
Yanshankou	105	39.59 N	117.42 E
Yanshi	100	25.17 N	117.10 E
Yanshi ≃	100	25.20 N	117.17 E
Yanshou	89	45.28 N	128.20 E
Yansi	100	29.48 N	118.20 E
Yanṭā	132	33.36 N	35.57 E
Yantabulla	166	29.21 S	145.00 E
Yantai (Chefoo), Zhg.	98	37.33 N	121.20 E
Yantai, Zhg.	105	39.47 N	116.38 E
Yantan, Zhg.	100	28.28 N	120.44 E
Yantan, Zhg.	100	28.55 N	120.11 E
Yantan, Zhg.	107	29.17 N	104.52 E
Yantian, Zhg.	100	26.53 N	119.53 E
Yantian, Zhg.	100	27.21 N	114.22 E
Yantic ≃	207	41.31 N	72.05 W
Yantietang ≊	106	31.49 N	120.46 E
Yanting	102	31.19 N	105.23 E
Yantis	222	32.56 N	95.35 W
Yantongshan, Zhg.	89	43.17 N	126.00 E
Yantongshan, Zhg.	105	40.42 N	115.06 E
Yanwangshan	104	41.36 N	123.57 E
Yanweigang	98	34.30 N	119.48 E
Yanxi	100	24.46 N	117.47 E
Yanxia	100	29.34 N	114.50 E
Yanxidu	100	26.51 N	114.58 E
Yanxing	102	25.23 N	101.42 E
Yan Yean Reservoir ⊜[1]	169	37.33 S	145.08 E
Yanyegongsi	106	32.02 N	121.41 E
Yanyuan	102	27.29 N	101.32 E
Yanzhou	98	35.33 N	116.50 E
Yanziji	106	32.09 N	118.49 E
Yanzijiao	102	23.38 N	100.12 E
Yanzikou	102	27.31 N	105.21 E
Yao, Centraf.	152	5.19 N	19.36 E
Yao, Nihon	96	34.37 N	135.36 E
Yao, Tchad	146	12.51 N	17.34 E
Yao Airport ⊠	270	34.36 N	135.36 E
Yao'an	102	25.32 N	101.12 E
Yaoba	107	28.45 N	105.39 E
Yaocun, Zhg.	98	36.12 N	113.50 E
Yaocun, Zhg.	98	35.41 N	116.57 E
Yaocun, Zhg.	105	39.09 N	115.32 E
Yaodafangshen	104	42.27 N	122.59 E
Yaoerwan	105	40.49 N	115.27 E
Yaogongbu	100	29.51 N	120.18 E
Yaohongcaopao	104	40.55 N	122.26 E
Yaohuamen	106	32.08 N	118.52 E
Yaohuangdi	104	41.32 N	122.48 E
Yaojiaji	100	31.14 N	114.22 E
Yaojiaqiao	106	32.10 N	119.46 E
Yaojiatun	104	41.18 N	121.57 E
Yaojiawopeng	104	41.47 N	122.25 E
Yaojie	102	36.26 N	102.59 E
Yaoling	100	24.49 N	113.58 E
Yaolugou	98	40.34 N	119.24 E
Yaoluzi	104	41.26 N	121.34 E
Yaopi	100	26.52 N	113.38 E
Yaopu	100	32.14 N	118.20 E
Yaoqianhutun	104	41.32 N	123.36 E
Yaoshizhen	107	30.11 N	105.30 E
Yaotou	100	26.38 N	114.48 E
Yaotsu	94	35.28 N	137.09 E
Yaotun, Zhg.	89	49.28 N	127.30 E
Yaotun, Zhg.	104	40.59 N	122.18 E
Yaotutun	104	42.06 N	123.29 E
Yaoundé	152	3.52 N	11.31 E
Yaowan	98	34.12 N	118.03 E
Yaowangmiao	98	40.47 N	120.10 E
Yaoxian	102	34.56 N	108.53 E
Yaoya ≃	236	13.28 N	84.14 W
Yao Yai, Ko I	110	8.00 N	98.35 E
Yaozhan	89	52.53 N	125.13 E
Yap I	174q	9.31 N	138.06 E
Yapacaní	248	16.45 S	64.18 W
Yapacani ≃	248	16.00 S	64.25 W
Yapakopra	164	4.24 S	135.05 E
Yapehe	152	0.13 S	24.27 E
Yapei (Tamale Port)	150	9.10 N	1.10 W
Yapen, Pulau I	164	1.45 S	136.15 E
Yapen, Selat ʯ	164	1.30 S	136.10 E
Yapero	164	4.59 S	137.11 E
Yapeyú	252	29.28 S	56.49 W
Yaphank	207	40.50 N	72.56 W
Yappar ≃	166	18.22 S	141.16 E
Yap Trench ✦[1]	14	8.30 N	138.00 E
Yaqian	100	26.38 N	114.30 E
Ya'qūb	140	12.29 N	25.11 E
Yaque del Norte ≃	238	19.51 N	71.41 W
Yaqui	232	27.19 N	110.01 W
Yaqui ≃	232	27.37 N	110.39 W
Yaquina ≃	202	44.37 N	124.04 W
Yara	240p	20.16 N	76.57 W
Yaracuy □[3]	246	10.20 N	69.10 W
Yaraka	166	24.53 S	144.04 E
Yaratuar	164	2.58 S	134.40 E
Yarbasan	130	38.59 N	28.49 E
Yarcombe	42	50.52 N	3.05 W
Yardea	166	32.23 S	135.32 E
Yardley	208	40.14 N	74.50 W
Yardville	208	40.10 N	74.39 W
Yare ≃	42	52.35 N	1.44 E
Yarí ≃	246	0.23 S	72.16 W
Yariga-take ∧	94	36.20 N	137.39 E
Yārik	123	32.06 N	70.47 E
Yarīm	144	14.29 N	44.21 E
Yaring	110	6.52 N	101.22 E
Yaritagua	246	10.05 N	69.08 W
Yarkand → Shache	120	38.25 N	77.16 E
Yarkand → Yarkant ≃	90	40.28 N	80.52 E
Yarkant (Yarkand) ≃	90	40.28 N	80.52 E
Yarker	212	44.23 N	76.46 W
Yarkhūn ≃	123	36.17 N	72.30 E
Yarlarweelor	162	25.35 S	117.59 E
Yarle Lakes ⊜	162	30.15 S	131.27 E
Yarloop	168a	32.57 S	115.54 E
Yarma	130	37.49 N	32.54 E
Yarmouth, N.S., Can.	186	43.50 N	66.07 W
Yarmouth, Eng., U.K.	42	50.42 N	1.29 W
Yarmouth → Great Yarmouth, Eng., U.K.	42	52.37 N	1.44 E
Yarmouth, Me., U.S.	188	43.48 N	70.11 W
Yarmouth, Ma., U.S.	207	41.42 N	70.13 W
Yarmu	164	4.18 S	142.17 E
Yarmūk, Nahr al- ≃	132	32.38 N	35.34 E
Yaroupi ≃	250	2.47 N	52.28 W
Yarra ≃	169	37.51 S	144.54 E
Yarra Bend National Park ♠	274b	37.48 S	145.01 E
Yarra Glen	169	37.40 S	145.23 E
Yarragon	169	38.12 S	146.04 E
Yarra Junction	169	37.47 S	145.37 E
Yarraloola	162	21.34 S	115.52 E
Yarram	166	38.33 S	146.41 E
Yarraman	171a	26.50 S	151.59 E
Yarrangobilly	171b	35.39 S	148.28 E
Yarrangobilly ≃	171b	35.48 N	148.23 E
Yarrangobilly Caves ◆[5]	171b	35.44 S	148.29 E
Yarraville	274b	37.49 S	144.53 E
Yarrawonga	166	36.01 S	146.00 E
Yarra Yarra Lakes ⊜	162	29.40 S	115.47 E
Yarrow, B.C., Can.	224	49.05 N	122.02 W
Yarrow, Scot., U.K.	46	55.32 N	3.01 W
Yarrow ≃	262	53.40 N	2.49 W
Yarrowee ≃	169	38.07 S	144.04 E
Yarrow Point	224	47.39 N	122.13 W
Yarrow Reservoir ⊜[1]	262	53.38 N	2.34 W
Yarrow Water ≃	44	55.34 N	2.51 W
Yarty ≃	42	50.47 N	3.01 W
Yarumal	246	6.58 N	75.24 W
Yarvicoya, Cerro ∧	248	20.07 S	69.00 W
Yasa	152	3.42 S	21.24 E
Yasaka, Nihon	96	35.39 N	135.07 E
Yasaka, Nihon	96	34.46 N	132.04 E
Yasa-Lokwa	152	5.15 S	19.24 E
Yasato	94	36.14 N	140.12 E
Yasawa I	175g	16.47 S	177.31 E
Yasawa Group II	175g	17.00 S	177.23 E
Yasendu	152	0.27 N	24.20 E
Yashanjie	106	30.51 N	119.03 E
Yashbum	144	14.19 N	46.56 E
Yashi	150	12.23 N	7.54 E
Yashikera	150	9.46 N	3.28 E
Ya-shima I	96	33.44 N	132.09 E
Yashima ♠	96	34.23 N	134.08 E
Yashio	268	35.49 N	139.51 E
Yashiro	96	34.55 N	134.58 E
Yashiro-jima I	96	33.55 N	132.15 E
Yāsīn	123	33.57 N	72.30 E
Yasku	146	12.20 N	12.30 E
Yasothon	110	15.45 N	104.08 E
Yass	166	34.50 S	148.55 E
Yassy → Iași	38	47.10 N	27.35 E
Yasu, Nihon	94	35.03 N	136.01 E
Yasu, Nihon	96	33.32 N	133.45 E
Yasuda	96	33.26 N	133.59 E
Yasugi	96	35.26 N	133.15 E
Yāsūj	128	30.42 N	51.06 E
Yasun Burnu ›	130	41.09 N	37.41 E
Yasuni ≃	246	0.56 S	75.23 W
Yasuoka	94	35.22 N	137.50 E
Yasuura	96	34.17 N	132.45 E
Yasuzuka	94	37.08 N	138.28 E
Yata	248	13.20 S	66.35 W
Yata ≃, Bol.	248	10.29 S	65.26 W
Yata ≃, Centraf.	146	10.23 N	22.45 E
Yatabe	94	36.02 N	140.04 E
Yatağan	130	37.20 N	28.09 E
Yatakala	150	14.48 N	0.22 E
Yata-Ngaya, Réserve de Faune de la ◆[4]	146	9.15 N	23.30 W
Yāṭar	132	33.09 N	35.20 E
Yatate-yama ∧	92	34.10 N	129.10 E
Yaté	175f	22.09 S	166.57 E
Yates □[6]	210	42.40 N	77.03 W
Yatesboro	214	40.48 N	79.20 W
Yates Center	198	37.52 N	95.43 W
Yates City	190	40.46 N	90.00 W
Yathata Island I	175g	17.15 S	179.32 W
Yathkyed Lake ⊜	176	62.41 N	98.00 W
Yating	102	25.03 N	106.05 E
Yatomi	94	35.06 N	136.43 E
Yatsuga-take ∧	94	35.59 N	138.23 E
Yatsuga-take-chūshin-kōgen-kokutei-kōen ♠	94	36.03 N	138.20 E
Yatsuka	96	35.17 N	133.42 E
Yatsuo	94	36.34 N	137.08 E
Yatsushiro	92	32.30 N	130.36 E
Yatsushiro-kai ⊂	92	32.20 N	130.25 E
Yaṭṭah	132	31.27 N	35.05 E
Yatta Plateau ⋏[1]	154	2.00 S	38.00 E
Yatton	42	51.24 N	2.49 W
Yatua ≃	246	1.43 N	66.30 W
Yatusiro → Yatsushiro	92	32.30 N	130.36 E
Yauca	248	15.40 S	74.32 W
Yauca ≃	248	15.41 S	74.31 W
Yauco	240m	18.02 N	66.51 W
Yauco ≃	240m	17.59 N	66.48 W
Yauco, Embalse de ⊜[1]	240m	18.07 N	66.50 W
Yauli	248	11.41 S	76.06 W
Yaundé → Yaoundé	152	3.52 N	11.31 E
Yaupi	246	2.59 S	77.50 W
Yautepec	234	18.53 N	99.04 W
Yau Tong	271d	22.18 N	114.13 E
Yauyos	248	12.24 S	75.57 W
Yāval	120	21.10 N	75.42 E
Yavarí (Javari) ≃	242	4.21 S	70.02 W
Yavarí Mirim ≃	246	4.31 S	71.44 W
Yavaros	232	26.42 N	109.31 W
Yavatmāl	122	20.24 N	78.08 E
Yaven Yaven Creek ≃	171b	35.06 S	147.46 E
Yavero ≃	248	12.06 S	72.57 W
Yavi	130	39.48 N	36.13 E
Yaví, Cerro ∧	246	5.32 N	65.59 W
Yavita	246	2.55 N	67.26 W
Yaviza	246	8.11 N	77.41 W
Yavne	132	31.53 N	34.45 E
Yaw ≃	110	20.55 N	94.49 E
Yawahara	268	35.59 N	140.01 E
Yawata, Nihon	96	34.52 N	135.42 E
Yawata → Kitakyūshū, Nihon	96	33.53 N	130.50 E
Yawata, Nihon	268	35.32 N	140.08 E
Yawatahama	96	33.27 N	132.24 E
Yaxchilan ⊥	232	16.54 N	90.58 W
Yaxi	102	27.32 N	106.45 E
Yaxian	110	18.20 N	109.30 E
Yaxierhu ⊜	120	34.59 N	81.35 E
Yaxigang	106	31.23 N	119.10 E
Yaxley	42	52.31 N	0.16 W
Yayama	152	1.16 S	23.07 E
Yaylak	130	37.23 N	38.20 E
Yayouta	150	8.11 N	8.30 W
Yayuan	98	41.47 N	126.11 E
Yazd	128	31.53 N	54.25 E
Yazd □[4]	128	32.00 N	54.30 E
Yazi	98	37.04 N	121.17 E
Yazichangcun	104	41.16 N	122.26 E
Yazıhan	130	38.36 N	38.11 E
Yazmān	123	29.08 N	71.45 E
Yazoo ≃	194	32.22 N	91.00 W
Yazoo City	194	32.51 N	90.24 W
Ybbs ≃	61	48.10 N	15.06 E
Ybbs an der Donau	61	48.11 N	15.05 E
Ybbsitz	61	47.56 N	14.53 E
Ybor City	220	27.57 N	82.27 W
Ybycuí	252	26.01 S	57.03 W
Yding Skovhøj ∧[2]	41	56.00 N	9.48 E
Ydstebøhavn	26	59.08 N	5.15 E
Ydžid Parma ⋏	24	63.06 N	58.15 E
Ye	110	15.15 N	97.51 E
Yea	169	37.13 S	145.26 E
Yea ≃	169	37.11 S	145.23 E
Yeading ◆[8]	260	51.32 N	0.24 W
Yeadon, Eng., U.K.	44	53.52 N	1.41 W
Yeadon, Pa., U.S.	285	39.56 N	75.15 W
Yeagertown	208	40.38 N	77.34 W
Yealm ≃	42	50.18 N	4.03 W
Yealmpton	42	50.21 N	3.59 W
Yebawgyi	110	18.40 N	94.35 E
Yebbi-Bou	146	20.58 N	18.04 E
Yébigué, Enneri V	146	22.04 N	17.49 E
Yèbles	261	48.38 N	2.46 E
Yebyu	110	14.15 N	98.12 E
Yecapixtla	234	18.53 N	98.52 W
Yecheng	120	37.54 N	77.25 E
Yech'ŏn	98	36.40 N	128.26 E
Yecla	34	38.37 N	1.07 W
Yécora	232	28.20 N	108.58 W
Yedashe	110	19.09 N	96.21 E
Yedikule ◆[8]	267b	40.59 N	28.55 E
Yedikule Suriarı ⊥	267b	40.59 N	28.55 E
Yédinga, Ouadi V	146	15.46 N	20.05 E
Yedseram ≃	146	12.30 N	14.05 E
Yeed	144	4.33 N	43.02 E
Yeeda	162	17.36 S	123.39 E
Yeelanna	166	34.09 S	135.45 E
Yeelirrie	162	27.17 S	120.06 E
Yeernuozhahu ⊜	120	32.30 N	89.30 E
Yegor'yevsk → Jegorjevsk	82	55.23 N	39.02 E
Yegros	252	26.24 S	56.25 W
Yegua Creek ≃	222	30.23 N	96.18 W
Yeguas, Río de las ≃	34	37.22 N	4.45 W
Yehliu	269d	25.12 N	121.41 E
Yehliu Chia ›	269d	25.13 N	121.42 E
Yehud	132	32.02 N	34.53 E
Yei	154	4.05 N	30.40 E
Yei ≃	140	6.15 N	30.13 E
Yeji, Ghana	150	8.13 N	0.39 W
Yeji, Zhg.	100	31.52 N	115.55 E
Yekaterinburg → Sverdlovsk	86	56.51 N	60.36 E
Yekaterinodar → Krasnodar	78	45.02 N	39.00 E
Yekaterinoslav → Dnepropetrovsk	78	48.27 N	34.59 E
Yekokora ≃	152	1.20 N	20.21 E
Yekumbo	152	1.02 S	23.27 E
Ye Kyun I	110	18.37 N	93.47 E
Yelarbon	166	28.34 S	150.45 E
Yele	150	8.25 N	11.50 W
Yelets → Jelec	76	52.37 N	38.30 E
Yélimané	150	15.08 N	10.34 W
Yell I	46a	60.36 N	1.06 W
Yellandu	122	17.36 N	80.20 E
Yellow ≃, U.S.	194	30.33 N	87.00 W
Yellow ≃, In., U.S.	216	41.16 N	86.50 W
Yellow ≃, Ia., U.S.	190	43.05 N	91.11 W
Yellow ≃, Wi., U.S.	190	44.58 N	91.18 W
Yellow ≃, Wi., U.S.	190	43.59 N	90.03 W
Yellow ≃, Wi., U.S.	190	46.01 N	92.22 W
Yellow → Huang ≃	90	37.32 N	118.19 E
Yellow Breeches Creek ≃	208	40.13 N	76.51 W
Yellow Creek ≃, U.S.	194	33.34 N	88.20 W
Yellow Creek ≃, Co., U.S.	200	40.10 N	108.24 W
Yellow Creek ≃, Oh., U.S.	214	40.34 N	80.40 W
Yellow Creek ≃, Tn., U.S.	194	36.26 N	87.34 W
Yellow Creek, North Fork ≃	214	40.33 N	80.42 W
Yellow Creek State Park ♠	214	40.35 N	79.02 W
Yellowdine	162	31.18 S	119.39 E
Yellow Grass	184	49.49 N	104.08 W
Yellowhead Pass)(	182	52.53 N	118.28 W
Yellow House Draw V	196	33.35 N	101.50 W
Yellowknife	176	62.27 N	114.21 W
Yellowknife ≃	176	62.31 N	114.19 W
Yellow Lake ⊜	212	44.20 N	75.36 W
Yellow Medicine ≃	198	44.44 N	95.25 W
Yellow Mountain ∧	166	32.30 S	146.51 E
Yellow Sea ⊤[2]	90	36.00 N	123.00 E
Yellow Springs	218	39.48 N	83.53 W
Yellowstone ≃	178	47.58 N	103.59 W
Yellowstone, Clarks Fork ≃	202	45.39 N	108.43 W
Yellowstone Falls ∟	202	44.43 N	110.30 W
Yellowstone Lake ⊜	202	44.25 N	110.22 W
Yellowstone National Park	202	44.59 N	110.42 W
Yellowstone National Park ♠	202	44.30 N	110.35 W
Yellowtail Dam ◆[6]	202	45.12 N	107.57 W
Yell Sound ʯ	46a	60.32 N	1.15 W
Yellville	194	36.13 N	92.41 W
Yelm	224	46.56 N	122.36 W
Yelma	162	26.30 S	121.40 E
Yelusuhu ⊜	120	35.11 N	92.15 E
Yelvertoft	166	20.13 S	138.53 E
Yelverton	42	50.30 N	4.05 W
Yelwa	150	10.51 N	4.46 E
Yema ≃	102	41.25 N	95.10 E
Yemadu	86	43.36 N	81.50 E
Yemagong	124	29.28 N	89.06 E
Yemaotai	104	42.20 N	122.53 E
Yemassee	192	32.41 N	80.51 W
Yematan	102	34.40 N	98.16 E
Yemen (Al-Yaman) □[1], Asia	118	15.00 N	44.00 E
Yemen (Al-Yaman) □[1], Asia	144	15.00 N	44.00 E
Yemen, People's Democratic Republic of □[1], Asia	118	15.00 N	48.00 E
Yemen, People's Democratic Republic of □[1], Asia	144	15.00 N	48.00 E
Yemen, República Popular Democrática del → Yemen, People's Democratic Republic of □[1]	144	15.00 N	48.00 E
Yémen, République démocratique populaire du → Yemen, People's Democratic Republic of □[1]	144	15.00 N	48.00 E
Yen	152	2.27 N	12.41 E
Yenagoa	150	4.55 N	6.19 E
Yenakiyevo → Jenakijevo	83	48.14 N	38.13 E
Yenangyaung	110	20.28 N	94.52 E
Yenanma	110	19.46 N	94.48 E
Yen-bai	110	21.42 N	104.52 E
Yen-chau	110	21.03 N	104.18 E
Yench'eng → Yancheng	100	33.24 N	120.09 E
Yenchi → Yanji	98	42.57 N	129.32 E
Yenda	166	34.15 S	146.11 E
Yende Millimou	150	8.53 N	10.11 W
Yendéré	150	10.12 N	4.58 W
Yendi	150	9.26 N	0.01 W
Ye-ngan	110	21.09 N	96.27 E
Yenge ≃	152	0.55 S	20.40 E
Yengema	150	8.43 N	11.10 W
Yengisar	85	38.57 N	76.03 E
Yengo	152	0.22 N	15.29 E
Yengo, Mount ∧	170	32.59 S	150.51 E
Yéni	150	13.26 N	2.59 E
Yeniçağa	130	40.46 N	32.02 E
Yenice, Tür.	130	39.45 N	28.55 E
Yenice, Tür.	130	39.55 N	27.18 E
Yenice, Tür.	130	36.59 N	35.03 E
Yenice ≃	130	37.36 N	35.35 E
Yenicekale	130	37.37 N	36.37 E
Yeniceoba	130	38.53 N	32.48 E
Yenifoça	130	38.44 N	26.51 E
Yenikapı ◆[8]	267b	41.00 N	28.57 E
Yeniköy, Tür.	130	37.04 N	30.36 E
Yeniköy, Tür.	130	39.46 N	28.00 E
Yeniköy ◆[8]	267b	41.07 N	29.04 E
Yenimehmetli	130	39.26 N	32.10 E
Yenipazar, Tür.	130	37.48 N	28.12 E
Yenipazar, Tür.	130	40.11 N	30.31 E
Yenişehir	130	40.16 N	29.39 E
Yenisey → Jenisej ≃	72	71.50 N	82.40 E
Yennadon	224	49.14 N	122.34 W
Yenne	62	45.42 N	5.46 E
Yennora	274a	33.52 S	150.58 E
Yenshuichen	100	23.20 N	120.16 E
Yentna ≃	180	61.34 N	150.28 W
Yeo ≃	42	51.02 N	2.49 W
Yeola	122	20.02 N	74.29 E
Yeo Lake ⊜	162	28.04 S	124.23 E
Yeoman	216	40.40 N	86.43 W
Yeoval	166	32.45 S	148.40 E
Yeovil	42	50.57 N	2.39 W
Yeoville ◆[8]	273d	26.12 S	28.04 E
Yepachic	232	28.26 N	108.23 W
Yeppoon	166	23.08 S	150.45 E
Yerba Buena, Montaña ∧	236	14.05 N	87.26 W
Yerba Buena Island I	282	37.48 N	122.22 W
Yères ≃	50	50.02 N	1.19 E
Yerevan → Jerevan	84	40.11 N	44.30 E
Yerilla	162	29.28 S	121.49 E
Yering	274b	37.41 S	145.23 E
Yerington	226	38.59 N	119.09 W
Yerington Indian Reservation ◆[4]	226	39.05 N	119.12 W
Yerkes	285	40.10 N	75.27 W
Yerkes Astronomical Observatory ♥[3]	216	42.34 N	88.34 W
Yerkesik	130	37.07 N	28.17 E
Yerköy	130	39.38 N	34.29 E
Yermasóyia	130	34.43 N	33.05 E
Yermenonville	261	48.33 N	1.37 E
Yermo	204	34.54 N	116.49 W
Yeroḥam	132	31.00 N	34.55 E
Yerolimín	38	36.28 N	22.24 E
Yèrre ≃	50	48.01 N	1.16 E
Yerres	50	48.43 N	2.30 E
Yerres ≃	50	48.43 N	2.27 E
Yerseke	52	51.29 N	4.02 E
Yerupaja, Nevado ∧	248	10.16 S	76.54 W
Yerushalayim (Al-Quds) (Jerusalem)	132	31.46 N	35.14 E
Yerushalayim □[5]	132	31.45 N	35.00 E
Yerville	50	49.40 N	0.54 E
Yesa, Embalse de ⊜[1]	34	42.36 N	1.09 W
Yesan	98	36.41 N	126.50 E
Yeshenpu	104	40.51 N	122.32 E
Yeshiva University ♥[2]	276	40.51 N	73.55 W
Yeshvi	272c	18.55 N	73.03 E
Yeşil ≃	130	41.24 N	36.35 E
Yeşilhisar	130	38.21 N	35.06 E
Yeşilkent	130	36.59 N	36.10 E
Yeşilköy	130	40.57 N	28.49 E
Yeşilköy Burnu ›	267b	40.57 N	28.50 E
Yeşilyurt	130	38.18 N	38.15 E
Yeso	196	34.26 N	104.36 W
Yeso Creek ≃	196	34.13 N	104.15 W
Yesŏng-gang ≃	98	37.53 N	126.24 E
Yessentuki → Jessentuki	84	44.03 N	42.51 E
Yeste	34	38.22 N	2.18 W
Yes Tor ∧	42	50.42 N	4.00 W
Yesud HaMa'ala	132	33.03 N	35.36 E
Yetholme	170	33.27 S	149.49 E
Yetman	166	28.54 S	150.46 E
Yetminster	42	50.53 N	2.33 W
Yetsou I	152	2.08 S	10.42 E
Yettem	226	36.29 N	119.16 W
Yetti	164	3.00 S	140.53 E
Yetti ◆[1]	148	26.10 N	7.50 W
Ye-u	110	22.46 N	95.26 E
Yeu, Île d' I	32	46.42 N	2.20 W
Yevpatoriya → Jevpatorija	78	45.12 N	33.22 E
Yexian, Zhg.	98	37.13 N	119.54 E
Yexian, Zhg.	100	33.37 N	113.20 E
Yexie	106	30.56 N	121.19 E
Yextla ≃	234	18.00 N	100.06 W
Yeysk → Jejsk	78	46.42 N	38.16 E
Yeyuan	98	36.22 N	118.27 E
Yeywa	110	21.41 N	96.24 E
Yezd → Yazd	128	31.53 N	54.25 E
Yeze Hu ⊜	106	31.08 N	120.40 E
Yezhuang	105	39.10 N	116.18 E
Yezhuhe	105	40.53 N	118.13 E
Ygatimí	252	24.05 S	55.30 W
Ygnacio Canal ≊	282	37.55 N	122.03 W
Yguazú ≃	252	25.20 S	55.00 W
Yhú	252	24.59 S	55.59 W
Yi	98	42.08 N	118.48 E
Yi ≃, Ur.	252	33.07 S	57.08 W
Yi ≃, Zhg.	98	34.07 N	118.15 E
Yi ≃, Zhg.	100	34.10 N	112.10 E
Yi ≃, Zhg.	105	39.14 N	115.46 E
Yi'an	89	47.55 N	125.20 E
Yiannitsá	38	40.48 N	22.25 E
Yibao	106	30.25 N	119.53 E
Yibin (Ipin)	107	28.47 N	104.38 E
Yibutan	107	28.54 N	104.40 E
Yicanghe	100	32.47 N	120.43 E
Yichang (Ichang)	102	30.42 N	111.17 E
Yicheng, Zhg.	98	36.48 N	114.17 E
Yicheng, Zhg.	98	34.46 N	117.37 E
Yicheng, Zhg.	102	31.43 N	112.07 E
Yichexun	102	26.50 N	103.28 E
Yichuan, Zhg.	100	34.26 N	112.24 E
Yichuan, Zhg.	102	36.04 N	110.06 E
Yichun, Zhg.	90	47.42 N	128.55 E
Yichun, Zhg.	100	27.50 N	114.23 E
Yicun	105	38.57 N	115.37 E
Yidan	89	43.24 N	125.25 E
Yidie	102	37.08 N	110.30 E
Yidu, Zhg.	98	36.41 N	118.28 E
Yidu, Zhg.	102	30.22 N	111.22 E
Yidun	102	29.56 N	99.22 E
Yiewsley ◆[8]	260	51.31 N	0.28 W
Yifag	144	12.02 N	37.44 E
Yifeng, Zhg.	100	33.19 N	113.47 E
Yifeng, Zhg.	100	28.26 N	114.46 E
Yigaolou	106	30.56 N	120.20 E
Yiğitaliler	130	39.52 N	26.37 E
Yigou	98	35.51 N	114.20 E
Yiguqihu ⊜	120	31.05 N	86.55 E
Yihe	100	23.50 N	114.53 E
Yihechang	107	30.23 N	106.24 E
Yi He Yuan (Summer Palace) ♥	105	40.00 N	116.16 E
Yihezhuang, Zhg.	98	37.53 N	118.23 E
Yihezhuang, Zhg.	104	41.15 N	122.57 E
Yihuang	100	27.34 N	116.10 E
Yihuang ≃	100	28.05 N	116.18 E
Yijiangzhen	100	30.55 N	118.28 E
Yijiawan	100	27.58 N	113.01 E
Yijiazi	104	42.29 N	122.41 E
Yijingpu	105	40.08 N	117.47 E
Yijinqiao	100	30.54 N	117.12 E
Yijitathu ⊜	120	35.00 N	87.00 E
Yijun	102	35.24 N	109.00 E
Yikengaolu	102	42.17 N	98.19 E
Yikou	100	26.45 N	117.00 E
Yilaha	89	48.50 N	125.10 E
Yilan	89	46.19 N	129.34 E
Yilaxi	89	43.47 N	126.08 E
Yıldızdağı ∧	130	40.08 N	36.56 E
Yıldızeli	130	39.52 N	36.38 E
Yilehuli Shan ⋏	89	51.20 N	124.30 E
Yili	107	30.45 N	105.58 E
Yiliang, Zhg.	102	24.58 N	103.07 E
Yiliang, Zhg.	102	27.35 N	104.01 E
Yiliekede	89	48.51 N	121.37 E
Yilin	100	33.36 N	119.37 E
Yiling	100	32.30 N	119.46 E
Yiliping	120	37.55 N	93.30 E
Yilliminning	162	32.54 S	117.22 E
Yilong, Zhg.	89	47.28 N	125.23 E
Yilong, Zhg.	102	31.34 N	106.19 E
Yilong, Zhg.	102	25.20 N	103.14 E
Yimachi	104	42.11 N	122.15 E
Yimatu	104	41.55 N	121.25 E
Yimen, Zhg.	100	33.39 N	116.02 E
Yimen, Zhg.	102	24.43 N	102.10 E
Yimuhe	89	52.45 N	120.07 E
Yin ≃, Mya.	110	20.04 N	95.01 E
Yin ≃, Zhg.	98	42.19 N	118.37 E
Yinan (Jiehu)	98	35.37 N	118.30 E
Yinbaing	110	17.25 N	97.46 E
Yinchuan	102	38.30 N	106.18 E
Yindarlgooda, Lake ⊜	162	30.45 S	121.55 E
Yindi	154	1.35 N	27.40 E
Yinfang	105	39.07 N	114.52 E
Ying ≃	100	32.30 N	116.32 E
Yingcheng	100	30.57 N	113.32 E
Yingchengzi, Zhg.	89	44.08 N	125.56 E
Yingchengzi, Zhg.	98	38.58 N	121.23 E
Yingchengzi, Zhg.	104	41.50 N	124.04 E
Yingchengzi, Zhg.	104	42.22 N	124.14 E
Yingde	100	24.12 N	113.24 E
Yingen	102	41.09 N	104.45 E
Yingfang	105	40.14 N	116.17 E
Yinggehai	110	18.31 N	108.44 E
Yinggen	110	19.04 N	109.48 E
Yinghe	100	32.16 N	116.31 E
Yingjin ≃	98	42.20 N	119.19 E
Yingkoshih ≃	269d	25.06 N	121.43 E
Yingkou, Zhg.	104	40.40 N	122.14 E
Yingkou (Dashiqiao), Zhg.	104	40.38 N	122.30 E
Yingpan, Zhg.	102	25.48 N	106.18 E
Yingpan, Zhg.	102	24.44 N	99.38 E
Yingpanjie	102	25.27 N	98.24 E
Yingqiao	100	33.58 N	113.39 E
Yingshan, Zhg.	100	30.45 N	115.39 E
Yingshan, Zhg.	100	31.38 N	113.50 E
Yingshan, Zhg.	102	31.08 N	106.31 E
Yingshang	100	32.38 N	116.15 E
Yingshouyingzi, Zhg.	105	40.33 N	117.38 E
Yingshouyingzi, Zhg.	105	40.49 N	117.55 E
Yingtan	100	28.14 N	117.00 E
Yingtaogou	104	42.08 N	121.57 E
Yingtaoyuan	104	41.10 N	123.05 E
Yingtian	100	28.50 N	112.56 E
Yingxiangjie	107	29.24 N	105.11 E
Yingxianpu	104	41.20 N	121.31 E
Yining (Kuldja)	86	43.54 N	81.21 E
Yinjiadai	106	32.03 N	120.07 E
Yinjiang	102	28.02 N	108.28 E
Yinjiawopeng	104	42.34 N	121.01 E
Yinkanie	166	34.20 S	140.19 E
Yinkeng	100	26.14 N	115.34 E
Yinliu	105	39.59 N	117.23 E
Yinmabin	110	22.05 N	94.54 E
Yinmahe	89	44.07 N	125.44 E
Yinmatu ≃	98	40.57 N	117.43 E
Yinnietharra	162	24.39 S	116.11 E
Yinnyein	110	16.48 N	97.23 E
Yinong	102	30.19 N	101.01 E
Yinping	98	34.15 N	118.39 E
Yinqiaotou	106	31.52 N	119.13 E
Yin Shan ⋏	102	41.48 N	109.00 E
Yinshanzhen	107	29.41 N	104.58 E
Yinwogou	98	41.55 N	117.55 E
Yinxian	100	29.50 N	121.38 E
Yinxiang	106	31.55 N	118.49 E
Yinxianji	100	32.07 N	116.32 E
Yinyangjie	104	42.16 N	121.23 E
Yinyuan	102	23.26 N	101.54 E
Yinzhan'ao	100	23.33 N	113.07 E
Yio Chu Kang	271c	1.23 N	103.51 E
Yi'ong	102	30.17 N	94.51 E
Yi Pak	271d	22.19 N	114.00 E
Yipinchang	107	29.17 N	106.34 E
Yipinglang	102	25.11 N	101.51 E
Yiqian	100	26.34 N	116.11 E
Yirba Muda	144	6.12 N	38.42 E
Yirga Alem	144	6.52 N	38.22 E
Yirkā	132	32.57 N	35.13 E
Yirol	140	6.33 N	30.30 E
Yirrkala Mission	164	12.14 S	136.56 E
Yirshi	89	47.20 N	119.45 E
Yirwa	140	7.47 N	27.15 E
Yisaduo	102	28.50 N	96.44 E
Yishan, Zhg.	100	27.32 N	120.32 E
Yishan, Zhg.	102	24.40 N	108.35 E
Yishui	98	35.50 N	118.41 E
Yisikan	89	49.09 N	124.47 E
Yisra'el → Israel □[1]	132	31.30 N	35.00 E
Yisuhe	100	27.46 N	112.54 E
Yitajing	102	42.32 N	94.12 E
Yitang, Zhg.	98	35.10 N	118.16 E
Yitang, Zhg.	100	31.06 N	113.42 E
Yíthion	38	36.45 N	22.34 E
Yiting	100	29.15 N	119.57 E
Yitong	89	43.20 N	125.17 E
Yitong ≃	98	42.40 N	125.58 E
Yitulihe	89	50.38 N	121.34 E
Yiwu, Zhg.	100	29.18 N	120.04 E
Yiwu, Zhg.	102	43.15 N	94.45 E
Yiwu, Zhg.	102	22.00 N	101.28 E
Yiwulü Shan ⋏	104	41.42 N	121.42 E
Yixi	100	23.45 N	116.38 E
Yixian, Zhg.	100	29.55 N	117.56 E
Yixian, Zhg.	104	41.32 N	121.15 E
Yixian, Zhg.	105	39.21 N	115.29 E
Yixiken	89	52.57 N	125.40 E
Yixing	106	31.22 N	119.50 E
Yixingbu	105	39.12 N	117.12 E
Yixingchang	107	30.37 N	106.38 E
Yixu	100	26.02 N	119.16 E
Yixun ≃	98	41.16 N	117.35 E
Yiyang, Zhg.	100	28.23 N	117.25 E
Yiyang, Zhg.	102	28.36 N	112.20 E
Yiyang, Zhg.	102	34.30 N	112.10 E
Yiyuan (Nanma)	98	36.11 N	118.08 E
Yiyuankou	98	40.10 N	119.35 E
Yizhang	100	25.26 N	112.56 E
Yizheng	106	32.16 N	119.12 E
Yizikong	102	25.38 N	104.28 E
Yizre'el	132	32.33 N	35.20 E
Yizre'el, 'Emeq ≚	132	32.36 N	35.14 E
Ylakiai	76	56.17 N	21.51 E
Yläne	26	60.53 N	22.55 E
Ylihärmä	26	63.09 N	22.47 E
Ylikitka ⊜	26	66.08 N	28.30 E
Ylimarkku → Övermark	26	62.38 N	21.30 E
Ylistaro	26	62.57 N	22.31 E
Ylivieska	26	64.05 N	24.33 E
Ylöjärvi	26	61.33 N	23.36 E
Ymeray	261	48.31 N	1.42 E
Ymir	182	49.17 N	117.13 W
Yndin	24	61.24 N	55.10 E
Yngaren ⊜	40	58.52 N	16.35 E
Yngen ⊜	40	59.44 N	14.18 E
Yngern ⊜	40	59.09 N	17.22 E
Yntaly	86	48.58 N	70.55 E
Ynykčanskij	74	60.15 N	137.43 E
Yoakum	222	29.17 N	97.09 W
Yobi, Indon.	164	1.43 S	138.04 E
Yobi, Indon.	164	1.42 S	136.27 E
Yockanookany ≃	194	32.40 N	89.40 W
Yoco	246	10.36 N	62.24 W
Yocona ≃	194	34.11 N	90.11 W
Yōda	268	35.24 N	139.25 E
Yoder	216	40.55 N	85.10 W
Yodo ≃	96	34.41 N	135.25 E
Yodoe	96	35.28 N	133.26 E
Yodogawa ◆[8]	270	34.42 N	135.28 E
Yoe	208	39.55 N	76.39 W
Yōga ◆[8]	268	35.38 N	139.38 E
Yogo	94	35.33 N	136.12 E
Yog Point ›	116	14.06 N	124.12 E
Yogyakarta	115a	7.48 S	110.22 E
Yogyakarta □[4]	115a	7.45 S	110.30 E
Yoho National Park ♠	182	51.26 N	116.30 W
Yoichi	92a	43.12 N	140.41 E
Yojoa, Lago de ⊜	236	14.50 N	88.00 W
Yŏju	98	37.18 N	127.37 E
Yōka	96	35.24 N	134.46 E
Yokadouma	152	3.31 N	15.03 E
Yōkaichi	94	35.06 N	136.12 E
Yōkaichiba	94	35.42 N	140.33 E
Yokamba	152	0.01 N	22.17 E
Yokana	152	0.45 N	22.53 E
Yokawa	96	34.52 N	135.06 E
Yokchi-do I	98	34.38 N	128.15 E
Yokkaichi, Nihon	94	34.58 N	136.37 E
Yokkaichi, Nihon	96	33.32 N	131.20 E
Yoko	152	2.36 S	20.06 E
Yokoate-jima I	93b	28.48 N	129.00 E
Yokohama, Nihon	94	35.27 N	139.39 E
Yokohama, Nihon	268	35.27 N	139.39 E
Yokohama-kō ⊂	268	35.27 N	139.39 E
Yokohama National University ♥[2]	268	35.25 N	139.36 E
Yokohama Park Baseball Ground ♠	268	35.26 N	139.39 E
Yokolo	152	0.36 S	23.04 E
Yokonuma	268	35.58 N	139.27 E
Yokoshiba	94	35.40 N	140.28 E
Yokosuka	94	35.18 N	139.40 E
Yokosuka District Naval Headquarters ■	268	35.17 N	139.39 E
Yokosuka-kō ⊂	268	35.18 N	139.39 E
Yokosuka Naval Base ■	94	35.18 N	139.41 E
Yokota, Nihon	96	35.10 N	133.06 E
Yokota, Nihon	268	35.23 N	140.01 E
Yokota, Nihon	270	34.40 N	135.55 E
Yokota Air Base ■	268	35.45 N	139.21 E
Yokote	92	39.18 N	140.34 E
Yola	146	9.12 N	12.29 E
Yolaina, Serranías de ⋏	236	11.40 N	84.20 W
Yolo	226	38.44 N	121.48 W
Yolo □[6]	226	38.41 N	121.46 W
Yolo ≃	273b	4.19 S	15.20 E
Yolo Bypass ≃	226	38.25 N	121.40 W
Yolombó, Col.	246	6.36 N	75.01 W
Yolombo, Zaïre	152	1.32 S	23.15 E
Yolonga	152	1.36 S	23.12 E
Yom ≃	110	15.52 N	100.16 E
Yombi	152	1.26 S	10.37 E
Yomou	150	7.34 N	9.16 W
Yona	174p	13.25 N	144.47 E
Yonabaru	174m	26.12 N	127.45 E
Yonago	96	35.26 N	133.20 E
Yonaguni	175d	24.27 N	122.57 E
Yonaguni-shima I	175d	24.27 N	123.00 E
Yonaha-dake ∧[2]	174m	26.43 N	128.13 E
Yŏnan	98	37.55 N	126.10 E
Yoncalla	202	43.35 N	123.16 W
Yŏnch'on ◆[8]	271b	37.38 N	127.04 E
Yoneshiro ≃	92	40.13 N	140.01 E
Yonezawa	92	37.55 N	140.07 E
Yŏngam	98	34.48 N	126.40 E
Yongamp'o	98	39.55 N	124.24 E
Yŏngan, C.M.I.K.	98	41.15 N	129.30 E
Yong'an, Zhg.	100	25.58 N	117.22 E
Yongan, Zhg.	107	30.44 N	106.16 E
Yong'an, Zhg.	107	29.13 N	104.46 E
Yong'an ≃	100	28.52 N	121.04 E
Yonganbao	98	40.15 N	119.52 E
Yong'anchang	107	30.24 N	103.58 E
Yong'anshi	100	28.13 N	113.19 E
Yŏngbyŏn	98	39.49 N	125.48 E
Yongchang, Zhg.	100	29.13 N	119.20 E
Yongchang, Zhg.	102	38.17 N	101.59 E
Yongchangzhen	106	31.42 N	121.44 E
Yongcheng	100	33.58 N	116.21 E
Yongch'ŏn, C.M.I.K.	98	39.59 N	124.28 E
Yŏngch'ŏn, Taehan	98	38.07 N	127.05 E
Yŏngch'ŏn, Taehan	98	35.58 N	128.56 E
Yongch'ŏn-dong	98	41.18 N	129.40 E
Yongchuan	107	29.21 N	105.54 E
Yongchun	100	25.21 N	118.21 E
Yongdeng	102	36.48 N	103.14 E
Yongdian	98	40.34 N	124.48 E
Yongding	100	24.46 N	116.43 E
Yongding ≃, Zhg.	100	24.42 N	116.34 E
Yongding ≃, Zhg.	105	39.20 N	117.04 E
Yongdingmen Station ◆[5]	271a	39.52 N	116.23 E
Yŏngdŏk	98	36.26 N	129.23 E
Yŏngdong	98	36.10 N	127.48 E
Yŏngdŭngp'o ◆[8]	271b	37.32 N	126.54 E
Yongfeng, Zhg.	100	29.44 N	116.49 E
Yongfeng, Zhg.	100	27.19 N	115.24 E
Yongfengchang	107	30.33 N	105.05 E
Yongfu	100	25.05 N	117.20 E
Yonggang	98	38.52 N	125.21 E
Yonggangonch'ŏn	98	38.53 N	125.14 E
Yonggi	98	36.24 N	128.24 E
Yongguzhai	98	34.05 N	116.50 E
Yonghe	100	28.18 N	113.51 E
Yongheshi	100	28.18 N	113.51 E
Yonghŭng	98	39.32 N	127.13 E
Yŏnghŭng-do I	98	37.16 N	126.28 E
Yŏnghŭng-man ⊂	98	39.15 N	127.30 E
Yongi	89	43.40 N	126.30 E
Yŏngil-man ⊂	98	36.02 N	129.26 E
Yongji	102	34.51 N	110.29 E
Yongjia, Zhg.	100	28.11 N	120.42 E
Yongjia, Zhg.	107	29.34 N	106.01 E
Yŏngjong-do I	98	37.30 N	126.31 E
Yŏngju	98	36.50 N	128.37 E
Yongkang, Zhg.	100	32.32 N	117.24 E
Yongkang, Zhg.	100	28.53 N	120.02 E
Yongkou	100	26.16 N	118.19 E
Yongle, Zhg.	89	45.45 N	125.12 E
Yongle, Zhg.	105	39.32 N	115.59 E
Yongle ≃	100	26.54 N	113.12 E
Yongledian	105	39.43 N	116.46 E
Yonglong	106	31.34 N	121.48 E
Yonglonghe	100	30.46 N	112.48 E
Yŏngmi-dong	98	39.40 N	125.31 E
Yongnian (Linmingguan)	98	36.47 N	114.30 E
Yongnianchang	107	29.08 N	104.51 E
Yongning, Zhg.	100	24.43 N	118.42 E
Yongning, Zhg.	102	22.42 N	108.50 E
Yongning, Zhg.	102	27.47 N	100.38 E
Yongning, Zhg.	102	38.20 N	106.17 E
Yongningcheng	105	40.34 N	116.11 E
Yongningjian	98	39.56 N	121.48 E
Yong Peng	114	2.01 N	103.04 E
Yongping, Zhg.	100	28.12 N	117.45 E
Yongping, Zhg.	102	25.28 N	99.33 E
Yongqing, Zhg.	105	39.19 N	116.29 E
Yongqing, Zhg.	107	30.00 N	105.27 E
Yongquan	100	28.46 N	121.19 E
Yongren	102	26.08 N	101.40 E
Yŏngsan-gang ≃	98	34.54 N	126.32 E
Yongsan-ni	98	38.52 N	125.56 E
Yŏngsanp'o	98	34.58 N	126.44 E
Yongshan	102	28.15 N	103.24 E
Yongshanqiao	100	29.06 N	117.17 E
Yongsheng	102	26.42 N	100.43 E
Yongshou	102	34.43 N	108.05 E
Yongshun	102	28.57 N	109.41 E
Yongshunchang	107	30.06 N	105.26 E
Yongtai	100	25.54 N	118.58 E
Yŏngwŏl	98	37.12 N	128.28 E
Yŏngwŏn	98	39.49 N	126.32 E
Yongwŏn-ni	98	40.41 N	128.42 E
Yongxin, Zhg.	100	26.56 N	114.18 E
Yongxin, Zhg.	107	28.59 N	106.32 E
Yongxing, Zhg.	98	40.11 N	123.52 E
Yongxing, Zhg.	100	26.08 N	113.06 E
Yongxing, Zhg.	102	39.08 N	110.31 E
Yongxing, Zhg.	106	31.56 N	120.55 E
Yongxing, Zhg.	107	30.13 N	105.06 E

Symbol	English	Deutsch	Español	Français	Português
≃	River	Fluss	Río	Rivière	Rio
≊	Canal	Kanal	Canal	Canal	Canal
∟	Waterfall, Rapids	Wasserfall, Stromschnellen	Cascada, Rápidos	Chute d'eau, Rapides	Cascata, Rápidos
ʯ	Strait	Meeresstrasse	Estrecho	Détroit	Estreito
⊂	Bay, Gulf	Bucht, Golf	Bahía, Golfo	Baie, Golfe	Baía, Golfo
⊜	Lake, Lakes	See, Seen	Lago, Lagos	Lac, Lacs	Lago, Lagos
≚	Swamp	Sumpf	Pantano	Marais	Pântano
⊓	Ice Features, Glacier	Eis- und Gletscherformen	Accidentes Glaciales	Formes glaciaires	Acidentes glaciares
⊤	Other Hydrographic Features	Andere Hydrographische Objekte	Otros Elementos Hidrográficos	Autres données hydrographiques	Outros acidentes hidrográficos
✦	Submarine Features	Untermeerische Objekte	Accidentes Submarinos	Formes de relief sous-marin	Acidentes submarinos
□	Political Unit	Politische Einheit	Unidad Politica	Entité politique	Unidade política
♥	Cultural Institution	Kulturelle Institution	Institución Cultural	Institution culturelle	Instituição cultural
⊥	Historical Site	Historische Stätte	Sitio Histórico	Site historique	Sitio histórico
♠	Recreational Site	Erholungs- und Ferienort	Sitio de Recreo	Centre de loisirs	Area de Lazer
⊠	Airport	Flughafen	Aeropuerto	Aéroport	Aeroporto
■	Military Installation	Militäranlage	Instalación Militar	Installation militaire	Instalação militar
◆	Miscellaneous	Verschiedenes	Misceláneo	Divers	Diversos

Z

ENGLISH

DEUTSCH

Symbols in the index entries represent the broad categories identified in the key at the right. Symbols with superior numbers (⩘[1]) identify subcategories (see complete key on page *I · 1).*

Kartensymbole in dem Registerverzeichnis stellen die rechts in Schlüssel erklärten Kategorien dar. Symbole mit hochgestellten Ziffern (⩘[1]) bezeichnen Unterabteilungen einer Kategorie (vgl. vollständiger Schlüssel auf Seite *I · 1).*

Los símbolos incluídos en el texto del índice representan las grandes categorias identificadas con la clave a la derecha. Los símbolos con numeros en su parte superior (⩘[1]) identifican las subcategorías (véase la clave completa en la página *I · 1).*

Les symboles de l'index représentent les catégories indiquées dans la légende à droite. Les symboles suivis d'un indice (⩘[1]) représentent des sous-catégories (voir légende complète à la page *I · 1).*

Os símbolos incluídos no texto do índice representam as grandes categorias identificadas com a chave à direita. Os símbolos com números em sua parte superior (⩘[1]) identificam as subcategorias (veja-se a chave completa à página *I · 1).*

∧ Mountain	Berg	Montaña	Montagne	Montanha
⩘ Mountains	Berge	Montañas	Montagnes	Montanhas
)(Pass	Pass	Paso	Col	Passo
V Valley, Canyon	Tal, Cañon	Valle, Cañón	Vallée, Canyon	Vale, Canhão
≚ Plain	Ebene	Llano	Plaine	Planície
≻ Cape	Kap	Cabo	Cap	Cabo
I Island	Insel	Isla	Île	Ilha
II Islands	Inseln	Islas	Îles	Ilhas
⊥ Other Topographic Features	Andere Topographische Objekte	Otros Elementos Topográficos	Autres données topographiques	Outros acidentes topográficos

	English	Deutsch	Español	Français	Português
≃	River	Fluss	Río	Rivière	Rio
≊	Canal	Kanal	Canal	Canal	Canal
⌊	Waterfall, Rapids	Wasserfall, Stromschnellen	Cascada, Rápidos	Chute d'eau, Rapides	Cascata, Rápidos
⋓	Strait	Meeresstrasse	Estrecho	Détroit	Estreito
c	Bay, Gulf	Bucht, Golf	Bahía, Golfo	Baie, Golfe	Baía, Golfo
◎	Lake, Lakes	See, Seen	Lago, Lagos	Lac, Lacs	Lago, Lagos
≕	Swamp	Sumpf	Pantano	Marais	Pântano
⍓	Ice Features, Glacier	Eis- und Gletscherformen	Accidentes Glaciales	Formes glaciaires	Acidentes glaciares
⊤	Other Hydrographic Features	Andere Hydrographische Objekte	Otros Elementos Hidrográficos	Autres données hydrographiques	Outros acidentes hidrográficos
✣	Submarine Features	Untermeerische Objekte	Accidentes Submarinos	Formes de relief sous-marin	Acidentes submarinos
□	Political Unit	Politische Einheit	Unidad Politica	Entité politique	Unidade política
⛫	Cultural Institution	Kulturelle Institution	Institución Cultural	Institution culturelle	Instituição cultural
⊥	Historical Site	Historische Stätte	Sitio Histórico	Site historique	Sitio histórico
♠	Recreational Site	Erholungs- und Ferienort	Sitio de Recreo	Centre de loisirs	Area de Lazer
⊠	Airport	Flughafen	Aeropuerto	Aéroport	Aeroporto
■	Military Installation	Militäranlage	Instalación Militar	Installation militaire	Instalação militar
◆	Miscellaneous	Verschiedenes	Misceláneo	Divers	Diversos

ENGLISH

Name	Page	Lat.°′	Long.°′
Žigalovo	88	54.48 N	105.08 E
Zigana Dağları ⌃	130	40.37 N	39.30 E
Žigansk	74	66.45 N	123.20 E
Zigazinskij	86	53.50 N	57.20 E
Zigong (Tzukung)	107	29.24 N	104.47 E
Ziguéy	146	14.43 N	15.47 E
Zigui	102	31.00 N	110.31 E
Ziguinchor	150	12.35 N	16.16 W
Žigulevsk	80	53.25 N	49.27 E
Žiguli	80	53.22 N	49.19 E
Žiguli ⌃	80	53.20 N	49.40 E
Zigutaicun	104	42.01 N	121.16 E
Zihedian	98	36.48 N	118.22 E
Zihuatanejo	234	17.38 N	101.33 W
Zihukou, Zhg.	100	28.44 N	112.33 E
Zihukou, Zhg.	100	28.55 N	118.08 E
Ziiyang	102	32.31 N	108.48 E
Zijančurino	86	51.33 N	56.55 E
Žijenkum	85	42.50 N	69.00 E
Zijiao	98	37.21 N	117.25 E
Zijin	100	23.40 N	115.11 E
Zijingguan	105	39.23 N	115.12 E
Zijin Shan ∧ [2]	106	32.04 N	118.51 E
Zikejevo	76	53.44 N	34.52 E
Zikhron Ya'aqov	132	32.34 N	34.57 E
Zikoufang	100	26.22 N	117.24 E
Zilair	86	52.14 N	57.30 E
Žilaja Kosa	80	46.49 N	53.12 E
Žilaja Tambica	24	62.32 N	36.09 E
Zile	130	40.18 N	35.54 E
Zili	102	26.50 N	100.27 E
Žilina	30	49.14 N	18.46 E
Žilino	76	54.54 N	21.56 E
Zillah, Lībiyā	146	28.33 N	17.35 E
Zillah, Wa., U.S.	202	46.24 N	120.15 W
Ziller ≐	64	47.24 N	11.50 E
Zillertal V	64	47.20 N	11.50 E
Zillertaler Alpen (Alpi Aurine) ⌃	64	47.00 N	11.55 E
Zillis	58	46.38 N	9.27 E
Zillisheim	58	47.41 N	7.16 E
Zilly	54	51.56 N	10.49 E
Zilme	144	16.25 N	43.49 E
Žiloj, ostrov I	84	40.19 N	50.36 E
Žiloj Bor	76	59.06 N	34.37 E
Žil'ovo	82	54.59 N	38.02 E
Ziltendorf	54	52.12 N	14.37 E
Zilupe	76	56.23 N	28.07 E
Zilwaukee	190	43.28 N	83.55 W
Zima	88	53.55 N	102.04 E
Zima ≐	88	53.52 N	102.02 E
Žima, gora ∧	88	53.18 N	107.38 E
Zimapán	234	20.45 N	99.21 W
Zimatlán de Alvarez	234	16.52 N	96.47 W
Zimba	154	17.19 S	26.13 E
Zimbabwe □ [1], Afr.	138	20.00 S	30.00 E
Zimbabwe □ [1], Afr.	154	20.00 S	30.00 E
Zimbor	38	47.00 N	23.16 E
Zimella	64	45.20 N	11.22 E
Zimi	150	7.19 N	11.18 W
Zimljansker-Stausee → Ciml'anskoje vodochranilišče ⊜ [1]	80	48.00 N	43.00 E
Zimmara, Monte ∧	70	37.45 N	14.16 E
Zimn'ackij	80	49.44 N	42.53 E
Zimnicea	38	43.39 N	25.21 E
Zimogorje	83	48.35 N	38.56 E
Zimonino	76	53.47 N	31.52 E
Zimovniki	80	47.08 N	42.28 E
Zimovskoje	86	57.31 N	86.52 E
Zin, Naḥal V	132	30.57 N	35.19 E
Zinacatepec	234	18.20 N	97.15 W
Zinal	58	46.08 N	7.38 E
Zinapécuaro [de Figueroa]	234	19.52 N	100.49 W
Zinave, Parque Nacional de ♠	156	21.35 S	33.35 E
Zinder	150	13.48 N	8.59 E
Zinder □ [5]	146	15.00 N	10.30 E
Zinga	152	3.43 N	18.35 E
Zinga Mulike	154	9.09 S	38.44 E
Zingaro, Passo dello)(	70	37.43 N	14.50 E
Zingst	54	54.26 N	12.41 E
Zingst ≻ [1]	54	54.25 N	12.50 E
Zingwanda	140	7.10 N	27.56 E
Ziniaré	150	12.35 N	1.18 W
Žiniške ≐	85	43.14 N	78.30 E
Zinkgruvan	40	58.49 N	15.05 E
Zin'kov	78	49.04 N	27.04 E
Zinnik → Soignies	50	50.35 N	4.04 E
Zinnowitz	54	54.04 N	13.55 E
Zinswiller	56	48.55 N	7.35 E
Zion, Il., U.S.	216	42.26 N	87.49 W
Zion, Md., U.S.	208	39.40 N	75.57 W
Zionhill	208	40.29 N	75.24 W
Zion National Park ♠	200	37.10 N	113.00 W
Zionsville	218	39.57 N	86.15 W
Zionz Lake ⊜	184	51.25 N	91.52 W
Zipaquirá	246	5.02 N	74.00 W
Žipkovšino	88	51.52 N	112.59 E
Zippori	132	32.45 N	35.17 E
Zipsendorf	54	51.02 N	12.16 E
Ziqlāb, Wādī V	132	32.30 N	35.34 E
Zir	130	39.59 N	33.21 E
Zira	123	30.58 N	74.59 E
Zirahuén, Laguna ⊜	234	19.27 N	101.44 W
Žir'akovo	86	57.53 N	65.37 E
Zirándaro	234	18.27 N	100.59 W
Zirāpur	124	24.01 N	76.22 E
Žir'atino	76	53.15 N	33.44 E
Zirbitzkogel ∧	61	47.04 N	14.34 E
Zirchow	54	53.53 N	14.08 E
Zirgan	86	53.14 N	55.55 E
Žirje, Otok I	36	43.40 N	15.39 E
Zirl	64	47.17 N	11.14 E
Zirndorf	56	49.26 N	10.58 E
Žirnov	80	48.13 N	41.06 E
Žirnovsk	80	51.00 N	44.46 E
Ziro	120	27.38 N	93.42 E
Žiroškino	82	55.22 N	38.03 E
Žirovnice	30	49.15 N	15.11 E
Zishan	100	25.57 N	115.35 E
Zistersdorf	61	48.32 N	16.45 E
Zisterzienserabtei ⛪ [1]	56	49.01 N	8.47 E
Zisuntang	106	30.38 N	118.42 E
Zitácuaro	234	19.24 N	100.22 W
Zitácuaro ≐	234	18.51 N	100.44 W
Zitadelle ⊥	264a	52.33 N	13.13 E
Žiteli	24	65.04 N	47.26 E
Žitenice	54	50.35 N	14.08 E
Žitjevo	76	59.54 N	41.06 E
Žitkoviči	78	52.14 N	27.54 E
Žitkovo	76	60.42 N	29.20 E
Žitkur	80	48.57 N	46.17 E
Zitlala	234	17.38 N	99.05 W
Zitlaltepec	234	19.12 N	97.54 W
Žitnoje	80	45.49 N	47.41 E
Žitomir	78	50.16 N	28.40 E
Zitong	102	31.43 N	105.10 E
Zittau	54	50.54 N	14.47 E
Zitundo	156	26.45 S	32.50 E
Zıvarık	130	38.19 N	32.53 E
Zivint	130	37.13 N	30.18 E
Ziwa Magharibi □ [4]	154	2.00 S	31.30 E
Ziway, Lake ⊜	144	8.00 N	38.50 E
Ziwuji	100	32.55 N	115.58 E
Zixi, Zhg.	100	27.42 N	117.02 E
Zixi, Zhg.	100	28.01 N	117.46 E
Zixing	100	26.00 N	113.23 E
Ziya ≐	105	39.09 N	117.10 E
Ziyang	107	30.07 N	104.39 E
Ziyuan	102	26.01 N	110.31 E
Ziyun	102	25.43 N	106.05 E
Ziz, Oued V	148	30.39 N	4.26 W
Žizdra	76	53.45 N	34.44 E
Žizdra ≐	82	54.14 N	36.12 E
Zizers	58	46.56 N	9.34 E
Zizhong	107	29.48 N	104.50 E
Zizhou	102	37.37 N	109.41 E
Žižica	76	56.17 N	31.21 E
Žižickoje, ozero ⊜	76	56.14 N	31.15 E
Žižma ≐	76	53.54 N	25.36 E
Zlarin	36	43.42 N	15.50 E
Zlatá Koruna ⛪ [1]	61	48.52 N	14.22 E
Zlatar	36	46.06 N	16.05 E
Zlaté Moravce	30	48.25 N	18.24 E
Zlatica	38	42.43 N	24.08 E
Zlatograd	38	41.23 N	25.06 E
Zlatoust	86	55.10 N	59.40 E
Zlatoustovsk	89	52.58 N	133.38 E
Zlín → Gottwaldov	30	49.13 N	17.41 E
Zlīṭan	146	32.28 N	14.34 E
Žlobin	76	52.54 N	30.03 E
Złocieniec	30	53.33 N	16.01 E
Złoczew	30	51.25 N	18.36 E
Zlonice	54	50.15 N	14.07 E
Złotoryja	30	51.08 N	15.55 E
Złotów	30	53.22 N	17.02 E
Žlutice	54	50.03 N	13.10 E
Zlydnev	80	48.46 N	45.48 E
Zlynka, S.S.S.R.	76	52.25 N	31.44 E
Zlynka, S.S.S.R.	78	48.28 N	31.32 E
Zmeinogorsk	86	51.10 N	82.13 E
Zmeinyj, ostrov I	78	45.15 N	30.12 E
Žmerinka	78	49.02 N	28.06 E
Żmigród	30	51.29 N	16.55 E
Žminj	36	45.09 N	13.55 E
Zmi'ovka	76	52.40 N	36.23 E
Zna → Cna ≐	80	54.32 N	42.05 E
Znaim → Znojmo	61	48.52 N	16.02 E
Znamenka, S.S.S.R.	76	54.54 N	34.34 E
Znamenka, S.S.S.R.	78	48.43 N	32.40 E
Znamenka, S.S.S.R.	80	52.24 N	41.26 E
Znamenka, S.S.S.R.	83	48.51 N	37.22 E
Znamenka, S.S.S.R.	86	53.10 N	79.30 E
Znamenka, S.S.S.R.	86	53.32 N	91.54 E
Znamenka, S.S.S.R.	86	50.05 N	79.32 E
Znamenka, S.S.S.R.	88	54.42 N	104.50 E
Znamenka Vtoraja	78	48.43 N	32.35 E
Znamensk	76	54.37 N	21.13 E
Znamenskoje, S.S.S.R.	76	53.17 N	35.41 E
Znamenskoje, S.S.S.R.	80	53.19 N	42.57 E
Znamenskoje, S.S.S.R.	86	57.08 N	73.55 E
Znamenskoje, S.S.S.R.	265b	55.45 N	37.09 E
Żnin	30	52.52 N	17.43 E
Znob'-Novgorodskoje	78	52.16 N	33.36 E
Znojmo	61	48.52 N	16.02 E
Zoagli	62	44.20 N	9.16 E
Zoar	158	33.30 S	21.28 E
Zoar Village State Memorial ⊥	214	40.36 N	81.27 W
Zoarville	214	40.35 N	81.24 W
Zobia	154	2.58 N	25.56 E
Zöblitz	54	50.39 N	13.14 E
Zóbuè	154	15.38 S	34.26 E
Zocca	64	44.21 N	10.59 E
Žochova, ostrov I	74	76.04 N	152.40 E
Zod	84	40.12 N	45.52 E
Zódhia	130	35.10 N	33.00 E
Žodino	76	54.06 N	28.21 E
Žodiški	76	54.38 N	26.26 E
Zoétélé	152	3.15 N	11.53 E
Zoetermeer	52	52.03 N	4.30 E
Zofingen	58	47.18 N	7.57 E
Zogang	102	29.55 N	97.44 E
Zogno	62	45.48 N	9.40 E
Zográfos	267c	37.59 N	23.46 E
Zohar	132	31.36 N	34.42 E
Zohreh ≐	128	30.04 N	49.34 E
Zok	130	38.02 N	41.33 E
Zola Predosa	64	44.29 N	11.12 E
Zolder	56	51.01 N	5.18 E
Zoldo Alto	64	46.22 N	12.06 E
Zolfo Springs	220	27.29 N	81.47 W
Zolka ≐	84	44.17 N	43.51 E
Żółkiewka	30	50.55 N	22.51 E
Zollhaus	56	50.17 N	8.04 E
Zollikofen	58	47.00 N	7.28 E
Zollikon	58	47.20 N	8.35 E
Zolling	60	48.27 N	11.46 E
Zol'noje	80	53.27 N	49.48 E
Zoločov, S.S.S.R.	78	50.17 N	35.59 E
Zoločov, S.S.S.R.	78	49.47 N	24.52 E
Zolotaja Gora	89	54.16 N	126.36 E
Zolotaja Lipa ≐	78	48.59 N	25.04 E
Zolotari	80	49.46 N	46.21 E
Zolotar'ovka	80	53.04 N	45.20 E
Zolotkovo	80	55.32 N	41.06 E
Zolotniki	78	49.17 N	25.23 E
Zolotoje, S.S.S.R.	80	50.51 N	45.53 E
Zolotoje, S.S.S.R.	83	48.41 N	38.31 E
Zolotoj Kolodec	83	48.32 N	37.15 E
Zolotoj Potok	78	48.54 N	25.20 E
Zolotonoša	78	49.40 N	32.02 E
Zolotucha	80	47.49 N	46.44 E
Zolotuchino	78	52.05 N	36.23 E
Žoltoje, S.S.S.R.	78	47.47 N	33.50 E
Žoltoje, S.S.S.R.	78	48.30 N	33.31 E
Ž'oltoje, S.S.S.R.	83	48.39 N	39.07 E
Žoltyje Vody	78	48.21 N	33.31 E
Žolymbet	86	51.45 N	71.44 E
Zomba	154	15.23 S	35.18 E
Zomergem	50	51.07 N	3.33 E
Zone Point ≻	42	50.08 N	5.00 W
Zongchang	107	28.52 N	104.36 E
Zongjiaxiang	269b	31.12 N	121.22 E
Zongo	152	4.21 N	18.36 E
Zonguldak	130	41.27 N	31.49 E
Zonguldak □ [4]	130	41.30 N	32.15 E
Zongwe	154	5.05 S	27.55 E
Zongyang	100	30.42 N	117.12 E
Zonhoven	56	50.59 N	5.21 E
Zonnebeke	50	50.52 N	2.59 E
Zons	56	51.07 N	6.50 E
Zontehuitz, Cerro ∧	232	16.50 N	92.38 W
Zonza	36	41.45 N	9.10 E
Zoo, Bahnhof ◆ [5]	264a	52.30 N	13.20 E
Zooafskolk	158	29.56 S	20.24 E
Zoom ≐	52	51.30 N	4.14 E
Zoppot → Sopot	30	54.28 N	18.34 E
Zopten am Berge → Sobótka	30	50.55 N	16.45 E
Zopui	120	23.39 N	92.14 E
Zörbig	54	51.37 N	12.07 E
Zorge	54	51.38 N	10.38 E
Zorge ≐	54	51.27 N	10.54 E
Zorgo	150	12.15 N	0.36 W
Zorgongo	150	12.16 N	0.48 W
Zorinsk	83	48.25 N	38.34 E
Zorita	34	39.17 N	5.42 W
Zorkul', Ozero ⊜	120	37.27 N	73.40 E
Zorn ≐	56	48.45 N	7.55 E
Zorneding	60	48.05 N	11.49 E
Zornica	38	42.23 N	26.56 E
Zorra, Arroyo de la ≐	196	29.31 N	101.13 W
Zorritos	246	3.40 S	80.40 W
Zorzor	150	7.46 N	9.28 W
Zöschen	54	51.21 N	12.07 E
Zossen	54	52.13 N	13.27 E
Zoti	84	41.53 N	42.28 E
Zottegem	50	50.52 N	3.48 E
Zou □ [5]	150	8.00 N	2.15 E
Zou ≐	150	6.28 N	2.25 E
Zouan-Hounien	150	6.55 N	8.13 W
Zouar	146	20.27 N	16.32 E
Zouérat	148	22.42 N	12.30 W
Zoug → Zug	58	47.10 N	8.31 E
Zoulabot	152	3.17 N	14.02 E
Zoumagang	107	29.28 N	106.18 E
Zoumayi	98	39.07 N	114.34 E
Zouping	98	36.53 N	117.42 E
Zourma	150	11.22 N	0.49 W
Zousfana, Oued V	148	30.29 N	2.17 W
Zoutelande	52	51.30 N	3.30 E
Zoutkamp	52	53.20 N	6.18 E
Zouxian	98	35.24 N	117.00 E
Žovka	76	58.26 N	28.52 E
Žovnino	78	49.23 N	32.41 E
Žovten', S.S.S.R.	78	49.03 N	24.45 E
Žovten', S.S.S.R.	78	47.14 N	30.20 E
Žovtnevoje, S.S.S.R.	78	46.52 N	32.02 E
Žovtnevoje, S.S.S.R.	78	49.39 N	34.09 E
Žovtnevoje, S.S.S.R.	78	50.57 N	34.22 E
Žovtnevoje, S.S.S.R.	78	51.15 N	28.07 E
Zozaya, Picacho de ∧	232	27.10 N	102.34 W
Zozov	78	49.19 N	29.01 E
Zrenjanin	38	45.23 N	20.24 E
Zriba	36	36.20 N	10.16 E
Zrmanja ≐	36	44.15 N	15.32 E
Zruč nad Sázavou	30	49.45 N	15.07 E
Zscherndorf	54	51.36 N	12.15 E
Zschieren ◆ [8]	54	51.00 N	13.52 E
Zschopau	54	50.44 N	13.04 E
Zschopau ≐	54	51.08 N	13.03 E
Zschorlau	54	50.34 N	12.38 E
Zschornewitz	54	51.43 N	12.25 E
Zschortau	54	51.28 N	12.21 E
Žuanbalyk	86	45.04 N	61.51 E
Žuantobe	86	44.45 N	68.54 E
Zuarungu	150	10.47 N	0.48 W
Zuata ≐	246	7.52 N	65.22 W
Zubaydīyah, Jabal az- ∧	132	33.48 N	37.02 E
Zubayr, Jazā'ir az- II	144	15.05 N	42.05 E
Zubayr, Wādī V	142	27.27 N	32.41 E
Zubcov	76	56.10 N	34.34 E
Zubkoviči	78	51.02 N	27.41 E
Zubova Pol'ana	80	54.04 N	42.51 E
Zubovka	80	54.16 N	51.06 E
Zubovo, S.S.S.R.	76	54.33 N	35.29 E
Zubovo, S.S.S.R.	76	60.19 N	36.57 E
Zubovo, S.S.S.R.	80	56.52 N	44.08 E
Zuccarello	62	44.07 N	8.07 E
Zuccone, Monte ∧	62	44.26 N	9.37 E
Zuchwil	58	47.12 N	7.33 E
Zuckerhütl ∧	64	46.58 N	11.09 E
Zudañez	248	19.06 S	64.44 W
Zudar	54	54.15 N	13.20 E
Z'udev, ostrov I	80	45.35 N	47.58 E
Zuel	64	46.31 N	12.08 E
Zuénoula	150	7.26 N	6.03 W
Zuénoula □ [5]	150	7.25 N	6.00 W
Zuera	34	41.52 N	0.47 W
Zufaytat Mashtūl	142	30.20 N	31.21 E
Zug	58	47.10 N	8.31 E
Zug □ [3]	58	47.00 N	8.30 E
Zugdeli	88	55.03 N	111.10 E
Zugdidi	84	42.30 N	41.53 E
Zugersee ⊜	58	47.08 N	8.30 E
Zug Island I	281	42.17 N	83.07 W
Zugló ◆ [8]	264c	47.31 N	19.08 E
Zugres	83	48.01 N	38.15 E
Zugspitze ∧	64	47.25 N	10.59 E
Zugurma Game Reserve ◆ [4]	150	9.55 N	5.00 E
Zühlsdorf	264a	52.44 N	13.24 E
Zui	76	57.06 N	31.37 E
Zuid-Beijerland	52	51.45 N	4.22 E
Zuid-Beveland I	52	51.25 N	3.45 E
Zuidbroek	52	53.10 N	6.52 E
Zuidelijk Flevoland ◆ [1]	52	52.22 N	5.20 E
Zuiderzee → IJsselmeer ≆ [2]	52	52.45 N	5.25 E
Zuidholland □ [4]	52	52.00 N	4.30 E
Zuidhorn	52	53.14 N	6.24 E
Zuidlaren	52	53.05 N	6.41 E
Zuid-Willemsvaart ≍	52	51.12 N	5.52 E
Zuidwolde	52	53.15 N	6.35 E
Žuja	78	45.03 N	34.20 E
Žuja ≐	88	58.45 N	118.11 E
Zújar ≐	34	39.01 N	5.47 W
Zújar, Embalse del ⊜ [1]	34	38.50 N	5.20 W
Zujevka, S.S.S.R.	80	58.25 N	51.10 E
Zujevka, S.S.S.R.	83	48.04 N	38.15 E
Z'ukajka	80	58.12 N	54.43 E
Žukopa	76	56.33 N	32.42 E
Žukopa ≐	76	56.54 N	32.46 E
Žukovka, S.S.S.R.	76	53.32 N	33.44 E
Žukovka, S.S.S.R.	86	56.05 N	91.42 E
Žukovka, S.S.S.R.	265b	55.44 N	37.15 E
Žukovskaja	80	47.37 N	42.28 E
Žukovskij	82	55.35 N	38.08 E
Žukovskoje	80	46.05 N	41.21 E
Żukowo	30	54.21 N	18.22 E
Zula	144	15.11 N	39.41 E
Zula ≐	234	20.21 N	102.46 W
Žulanka	86	54.22 N	80.36 E
Zulayl, Wādī az- V	132	32.09 N	36.03 E
Žuldyz	80	49.16 N	49.30 E
Žulebino	265b	55.42 N	37.51 E
Zuli ≐	102	36.35 N	104.35 E
Zulia □ [3]	246	10.00 N	72.10 W
Zulia ∧	154	4.07 N	33.58 E
Zulia ≐	246	9.04 N	72.18 W
Züllichau → Sulechów	30	52.06 N	15.37 E
Zülpich	56	50.41 N	6.39 E
Züls → Biała	30	50.23 N	17.40 E
Zulueta	240p	22.22 N	79.34 W
Zululand □ [9]	158	28.10 S	32.00 E
Z'ul'z'a	88	52.33 N	116.13 E
Žumala	80	50.29 N	49.47 E
Zumar, Tur'at az- ≍	273c	29.58 N	31.15 E
Zumarraga	116	11.38 N	124.50 E
Zumate, Cerro ∧	234	20.10 N	98.40 W
Zumba	246	4.52 S	79.09 W
Zumbo	154	15.36 S	30.25 E
Zumbro ≐	190	44.18 N	91.56 W
Zumbro, North Fork ≐	190	44.15 N	92.29 W
Zumbro, South Fork ≐	190	44.15 N	92.29 W
Zumbrota	190	44.17 N	92.40 W
Zumpango	234	19.48 N	99.06 W
Zumpango, Lago de ⊜	234	19.46 N	99.09 W
Zumpango del Río	234	17.39 N	99.30 W
Zundert	52	51.28 N	4.40 E
Zundi	152	10.28 S	16.48 E
Zune	156	18.59 S	35.18 E
Zungeru	150	9.48 N	6.09 E
Zungri	68	38.39 N	15.59 E
Zungur	150	9.58 N	9.47 E
Zungwini	158	27.34 S	30.53 E
Zunhua	105	40.12 N	117.58 E
Zuni, N.M., U.S.	200	35.04 N	108.51 W
Zuni, Va., U.S.	208	36.51 N	76.49 W
Zuni ≐	200	34.39 N	109.40 W
Zuni Indian Reservation ◆ [4]	200	35.15 N	108.20 W
Zunsuzhi	102	44.40 N	112.50 E
Zunyi	102	27.39 N	106.57 E
Zuo ≐	102	22.50 N	108.06 E
Zuo'an	100	26.10 N	114.16 E
Zuodeng	102	23.27 N	106.57 E
Zuogezhuang	105	39.01 N	116.37 E
Zuomaozigou	104	42.12 N	120.41 E
Zuomuchedonghu ⊜	120	28.25 N	88.15 E
Zuoquan	102	37.03 N	113.30 E
Zuosuo	102	27.45 N	100.54 E
Zuotema	120	35.50 N	80.45 E
Zuowei	105	40.41 N	114.43 E
Zuoxiunulemiao	88	48.08 N	115.38 E
Zuoyun	102	40.02 N	112.54 E
Zuoz	58	46.36 N	9.58 E
Županja	38	45.04 N	18.42 E
Zūq Mīkhā'īl	132	33.58 N	35.37 E
Žura, S.S.S.R.	78	47.31 N	29.04 E
Zura, S.S.S.R.	80	57.37 N	53.26 E
Zūrābād	128	38.49 N	44.35 E
Žuraviči, S.S.S.R.	76	53.15 N	30.33 E
Žuraviči, S.S.S.R.	78	50.59 N	25.43 E
Žuravl'ovka, S.S.S.R.	83	48.13 N	38.58 E
Žuravl'ovka, S.S.S.R.	86	51.57 N	69.56 E
Zurayghiṭ	128	26.29 N	40.33 E
Žurban	89	54.12 N	127.56 E
Zurich, On., Can.	190	43.26 N	81.37 W
Zurich, Ned.	52	53.06 N	5.23 E

DEUTSCH

Name	Seite	Breite°′	Länge°′ E = Ost
Zürich, Schw.	58	47.23 N	8.32 E
Zürich □ [3]	58	47.25 N	8.40 E
Zürich, Flughafen ⊠	58	47.27 N	8.33 E
Zurich, Lake ⊜	278	42.12 N	88.06 W
Zürichsee ⊜	58	47.13 N	8.45 E
Zurigo → Zürich	58	47.23 N	8.32 E
Zurmi	150	12.46 N	6.48 E
Żuromin	30	53.04 N	19.55 E
Zurq, Al-Qārāt az- ∧ [2]	142	29.00 N	29.55 E
Zürs	58	47.10 N	10.10 E
Zuru	150	11.27 N	5.12 E
Zurzach	58	47.35 N	8.18 E
Zuša ≐	76	53.27 N	36.23 E
Zusam ≐	56	48.42 N	10.45 E
Žusandala ◆ [2]	86	44.20 N	75.00 E
Zushi	94	35.18 N	139.35 E
Zusmarshausen	58	48.24 N	10.35 E
Züssow	54	53.59 N	13.32 E
Žut, Otok I	36	43.52 N	15.19 E
Zutiua ≐	250	3.43 S	45.29 W
Žutovo Vtoroje	80	47.49 N	43.51 E
Zutphen	52	52.08 N	6.12 E
Zützen	54	51.57 N	13.38 E
Zuwārah	146	32.56 N	12.06 E
Zuwayzā	132	31.42 N	35.55 E
Z'uzel'skij	86	56.29 N	60.07 E
Žužemberk	36	45.50 N	14.56 E
Z'uzino	265b	55.40 N	38.07 E
Z'uzino ◆ [8]	265b	55.39 N	37.35 E
Žuzymdyk	85	43.05 N	69.08 E
Zv'agino	265b	55.59 N	37.48 E
Zvannoje	78	51.23 N	34.33 E
Zvenigorod	82	55.44 N	36.51 E
Zvenigorodka	78	49.04 N	30.57 E
Zvenigovo	80	55.58 N	48.02 E
Zverevo	83	48.01 N	40.07 E
Zverinogolovskoje	86	54.28 N	64.50 E
Zvezdec	38	42.07 N	27.25 E
Zvezdnyj	88	56.49 N	106.27 E
Zvíkovec	60	49.56 N	13.42 E
Zvishavane	154	20.20 S	30.02 E
Zvolen	30	48.35 N	19.08 E
Zvon ∧	60	49.33 N	12.39 E
Zvornik	38	44.23 N	19.06 E
Zwaag	52	52.40 N	5.05 E
Zwaagwesteinde	52	53.15 N	6.04 E
Zwadība	152	3.04 N	14.02 E
Zwanenburg	52	52.23 N	4.45 E
Zwartemeer	52	52.43 N	7.03 E
Zwarte Meer ⊜	52	52.37 N	5.57 E
Zwartsluis	52	52.37 N	6.04 E
Zweckel ◆ [8]	263	51.36 N	6.59 E
Zwedru	150	6.04 N	8.08 W
Zweibrücken	56	49.15 N	7.21 E
Zweifall	56	50.43 N	6.15 E
Zweisimmen	58	46.33 N	7.22 E
Zweite Wiener Hochquellenleitung ≍ [1]	61	48.10 N	16.14 E
Zwenkau	54	51.13 N	12.19 E
Zwentendorf	61	48.21 N	15.55 E
Zwesten	56	51.03 N	9.10 E
Zwettl	61	48.37 N	15.10 E
Zwevegem	50	50.48 N	3.20 E
Zwevezele	50	51.02 N	3.12 E
Zwickau	54	50.44 N	12.29 E
Zwickauer Mulde ≐	54	51.10 N	12.48 E
Zwiefalten	58	48.14 N	9.28 E
Zwiefaltendorf	58	48.13 N	9.31 E
Zwierzyniec	30	50.37 N	22.58 E
Zwiesel	60	49.01 N	13.14 E
Zwieselstein	64	46.56 N	11.02 E
Zwijndrecht	52	51.49 N	4.39 E
Zwillbrock	52	52.04 N	6.42 E
Zwingenberg, B.R.D.	56	49.43 N	8.37 E
Zwingenberg, B.R.D.	56	49.25 N	9.02 E
Zwischenahner Meer ⊜	52	53.12 N	8.01 E
Zwochau	54	51.28 N	12.16 E
Zwoleń	30	51.22 N	21.35 E
Zwölfaxing	264b	48.06 N	16.28 E
Zwolle, Ned.	52	52.30 N	6.05 E
Zwolle, La., U.S.	194	31.37 N	93.38 W
Zwönitz	54	50.38 N	12.49 E
Zwota	54	50.21 N	12.25 E
Żychlin	30	52.15 N	19.39 E
Zymoetz ≐	182	54.33 N	128.26 W
Zyr'anka	74	65.45 N	150.51 E
Zyr'anovsk	86	49.43 N	84.20 E
Zyr'anovskij	86	57.46 N	61.42 E
Zyr'anskoje	86	56.50 N	86.38 E
Żyrardów	30	52.04 N	20.25 E
Zyryanovsk → Zyr'anovsk	86	49.43 N	84.20 E
Żyrzyn	30	51.30 N	22.07 E
Żywiec	30	49.41 N	19.12 E